DICTIONARY OF INTERNATIONAL BIOGRAPHY

A BIOGRAPHICAL RECORD OF CONTEMPORARY ACHIEVEMENT

VOLUME ELEVEN
1975

PART II
K–Z

Hon. General Editor:
ERNEST KAY

With
A Memoir of
**HER MAJESTY JULIANA,
QUEEN OF THE NETHERLANDS**

MELROSE PRESS LIMITED
CAMBRIDGE AND LONDON, ENGLAND

I.S.B.N. 0 900332 32 8

Library of Congress Catalog Card Number: 64-1109

I.B.M. Computer Typesetting by Print Origination, Liverpool.
Printed and bound by the Cambridge University Press,
Cambridge, England

Dedicated to

Her Majesty

JULIANA,

QUEEN OF

THE NETHERLANDS

FOREWORD BY THE HON. GENERAL EDITOR

With the publication of this new Volume XI, the "Dictionary of International Biography" again becomes a two-part set and will remain so for the foreseeable future. D.I.B. X was published in four parts to commemorate the tenth anniversary and included an index of approaching a hundred thousand entrants whose biographies were published in D.I.B. I to X. Volume XI, which contains more than fifteen thousand biographies, has taken fifteen months to produce. Work on Volume XII, 1976 Edition, had begun before the present Volume had gone to press.

Librarians in many countries have commented appreciatively on Volume X index and it is now our intention to update and enlarge the index every five years.

Unfortunately, Volume X was somewhat late in publication, partly because of its massive size and partly because of the three-day working week in British industry which lasted for three months and which was caused by the serious energy crisis. Biographees had only just received their copies when the death occurred of His Excellency, M. Georges Pompidou, President of the Republic of France, to whom Volume X was dedicated. It will be recalled that each Edition is dedicated to a Head of State and contains a memoir on the life and work of the Head of State concerned, together with a frontispiece portrait. Of the ten Kings and Presidents to whom D.I.B. has been dedicated over the years, nine are still in office.

*   *   *

An important decision taken by my colleagues and myself during the past year to arrange a Convention in July, 1975, has been communicated to our biographees who have received invitations to attend. The Convention will be held at the Waldorf-Astoria Hotel, New York City, and, at the time of writing this Foreword, it appears as though it will be highly successful, with several hundred men and women from many parts of the world taking part.

The Convention, organized by the International Biographical Centre, of Cambridge, England, will be attended by biographees of other works published at the Centre in addition to D.I.B.: these include "The World Who's Who of Women", "Men of Achievement", "The International Who's Who in Poetry", "International Who's Who in Art and Antiques", "World Who's Who of Musicians" and "World Who's Who of Authors".

*   *   *

In Cambridge we have strengthened our links with the University: this Edition of D.I.B. is printed and bound by the Cambridge University Press who will also be working closely with us on other titles.

D.I.B. researchers in many parts of the world have been particularly active during the past year in sending to me the names and addresses of men and women who qualify for biographical inclusion. Many hundreds of biographees have also made recommendations: their interest is much appreciated.

With recommendations coming from so many people in so many countries, it has been found impossible to avoid a certain amount of duplication and some of our biographees have received two or in some cases even more questionnaires. I apologize for the inconvenience that has been caused but I would add that receipt of duplicate questionnaires means that the recipient has been recommended by an *additional* source or sources.

I will repeat what I wrote in my last Foreword: the criterion for inclusion is "contemporary achievement" whether that achievement be at international, national, regional or even local level. Many D.I.B. biographees do not appear (as yet) in a national "Who's Who".

It cannot be too strongly stressed that there is no charge or fee of any kind for inclusion and no obligation to purchase.

Finally, let me state that great care has been taken in extracting information from questionnaires and accompanying documents which biographees have sent to me. Even so, it is possible that a few errors have crept in: if so, my apologies in advance.

International Biographical Centre,
Cambridge, CB2 3QP,
England.

August 1974.

A Memoir of

HER MAJESTY JULIANA,
QUEEN OF THE NETHERLANDS

Her Majesty Queen Juliana Louise Emma Mary Wilhelmina, Queen of the Netherlands, Princess of Orange-Nassau, Duchess of Mecklenburg, was born at The Hague on 30th April 1909, the only child of Queen Wilhelmina and her consort, Prince Henry of Mecklenburg. She was educated privately, then at the University of Leiden.

It was not until 1931, when she was 22 years old, that she performed her first major task in public life by becoming honorary chairman of the National Committee for Public Assistance which had been formed during the grave economic depression to supplement government measures by private enterprise. The Committee was outstandingly successful and was responsible for alleviating the suffering and distress of tens of thousands of unemployed and underemployed citizens who were living well below the poverty line.

Juliana took an active interest in this work and enlisted the financial support of many industrialists in Amsterdam, Rotterdam, The Hague, Eindhoven and other Dutch cities. Her initiation to public work gave her a penetrating knowledge of leadership and this was duly recognized in 1934 when, by unanimous consent, she became Chairman of The Netherlands Red Cross in succession to her father.

On 7th January 1937 she was married at The Hague to Prince Bernhard Leopold Frederik Everhard Julius Coert Karel Godfried Pieter, Prince of Lippe-Biesterfeld, who on the same day was created Prince of the Netherlands by Royal decree. The first of their four daughters, the Crown Princess Beatrix Wilhelmina Armgard, was born at Soestdijk Palace on 31st January 1938, followed by Princess Irene Emma Elisabeth at Soestdijk on 5th August 1939; Princess Margriet Francisca at Ottawa, Canada, on 19th January 1943; and Princess Maria Christina at Soestdijk on 18th February 1947. As will be related later in this memoir, three of the four Princesses caused public protests in later years and demonstrations which at one time appeared to be threatening the Crown.

Early in World War II, in May 1940, the German Wehrmacht invaded The Netherlands and the Dutch Royal family took refuge in

England. Prince Bernhard remained in England as Commander-in-Chief of the Dutch Forces in exile and Princess Juliana took her two daughters, Beatrix and Irene, to Canada. They set up home in Ottawa and stayed there until the end of the war. It was during these five years that Juliana established what was to become a close personal friendship with Mrs. Eleanor Roosevelt, wife of the then President of the United States, Franklin D. Roosevelt. She also made several visits to the United States, Surinam and the Dutch West Indies.

Meanwhile, the Wehrmacht and the Luftwaffe were devastating The Netherlands. Indeed, within days of the departure of the Royal family, the centre of Rotterdam had been destroyed by air bombardment: in four hours the city was ablaze and some 25,000 homes had been destroyed. The Dutch Commander surrendered and the Germans moved into Amsterdam, then quickly occupied the rest of the country. The five-day war in The Netherlands ended when Hitler appointed Seyss-Inquart as German Commissioner for the occupied country. The resistance by the Dutch people was magnificent and many Dutchmen were executed by the Germans.

For more than four years little authentic news came out of Holland although it was known that the Dutch were suffering greater privations than anyone else in Europe and that their standard of living had fallen to near-starvation level. Then, on 17th September 1944, the British-American Airborne Division landed near Nijmegen and Arnhem with the aim of cutting off the Rhine crossings from Holland to Germany. The invasion failed and, after suffering crippling casualties, the Airbourne Division had to retreat across the Lower Rhine.

It was not until April 1945 that the Allies succeeded in liberating Holland. The Commanders were appalled at what the Dutch people had suffered through shortage of food and other essentials.

*   *   *

Upon the expulsion of the Germans the Royal family returned to Holland in the summer of 1945 and immediate plans were made for the reconstruction of the battered country. Alongside material reconstruction the Dutch Government pursued a crash programme of social welfare and Princess Juliana again became the head of the organization established to give help to hundreds of thousands of Dutch people who were in dire financial difficulties

Twice during the illness of the aging Queen Wilhelmina—in 1947 and 1948—Juliana acted as Regent and there was little surprise when, on 4th September 1948, Wilhelmina abdicated in favour of her daughter. Two days later, Juliana was sworn in and inaugurated (without crowning) as Queen of The Netherlands at the Niewe Kerk, Amsterdam. Her accession was a glittering occasion in post-war Europe, with guests attending from all parts of the world. Among them was Britain's Princess Margaret who, at 18, was making her first visit to Europe. Queen Juliana, in her speech at the ceremony, made two significant statements:

"We must not flinch from sacrifice. If necessary, we must be ready to throw ballast overboard."

"I wish to say with emphasis that to a Queen her duties as a mother are as important as they are to any other Dutch woman."

She has kept her word on both counts. Much ceremony and protocol were abolished and she brought up her children as "ordinarily" as possible. The Princesses were educated first at an "advanced" school but this experiment proved to be unsuccessful and they were transferred to a local high school. Princess Beatrix matriculated at Leiden, her mother's old University, and Princess Irene gained a Diploma in Spanish from the University of Utrecht. The Princesses were encouraged to take part in sports and other leisure activities, including cycling, and at one time the bicycles of the Royal family became household words. Although the few remaining Royal ceremonies continued to take place at the palace on the Dam in Amsterdam, the Queen and her family took permanent residence at the country palace at Soestdijk, near Baarn. Soestdijk is an attractive semi-circular white building set among a background of enormous trees. One part of the palace is furnished in Dutch traditional style with much marble and paintings and is used for official occasions; the other is modern and comfortable and is occupied by the family.

*   *   *

The reign of Queen Juliana has been a momentous one, beginning during reconstruction after war devastation and continuing through the independence of the Dutch Empire, the worst floods Holland has ever experienced, the union of Holland, Belgium and Luxembourg, and dramatic family problems.

On 27th December 1949 the Queen signed the transfer of sovereignty of the Dutch East Indies to the new Republic of Indonesia. Five years later she assented to a new Statute of the Realm under which the colonial status of Surinam and the Dutch Antilles was abolished and became autonomous parts of the

Kingdom of The Netherlands.

So fast was the domestic reconstruction that Holland became the first nation, in 1953, to renounce American aid.

The terrible floods of 31st January and 1st February 1953 resulted in the deaths of nearly two thousand people and in damage estimated at fifteen billion Guilders. After the floods the Delta Act was passed by the Dutch Parliament and, under this, works were begun in the south-west of the country to protect the nation from hurricanes, and the rivers of South Holland and Zeeland were dammed on the seaboard. During the floods the Queen, characteristically, helped with the rest of the Dutch people "wearing her gumboots".

During the decade of 1950 to 1960 The Netherlands played a large part in creating the Benelux Union and also became a member of the North Atlantic Treaty Organization, the Western Union, and the European Coal and Steel Community. Holland was also one of the original six nations in the European Economic Community, with Belgium, Luxembourg, France, Italy and West Germany. The Community was extended to nine in 1972 with the addition of the United Kingdom, Ireland and Denmark.

Queen Juliana celebrated her silver wedding in 1962 when many guests from abroad journeyed to Holland, including the Shahanshah of Iran, King Baudouin of Belgium, King Olav of Norway, and the Duchess of Kent. In 1966 her income was increased by the Dutch Parliament to more than five million Guilders a year, making her the wealthiest monarch in the world. The House of Orange has always been extremely rich with real estate and other interests in the United States as well as in other countries.

On 4th September 1973 Juliana celebrated twenty-five years as Queen of the Netherlands but, by contrast to her silver wedding, this was a national rather than an international event.

*   *   *

Queen Juliana succeeded her greatly-loved mother in her mother's lifetime and this, of course, created problems for her. Although Holland is a constitutional monarchy, the monarch has remarkable personal powers—far wider than, for instance, in Britain. She is not, by any means, a rubber stamp and she often asserts her authority. Yet, in spite of her personal popularity and the high regard for the House of Orange, many protests, Governmental and public, were voiced against some of her actions, beginning very early in her reign. Her youngest daughter, Princess Christina, was born almost blind and Juliana, in her endeavours as a mother, sought the advice of a "faith healer" and other "quacks". The "faith healer" became a constant visitor to Soestdijk Palace and developed a close personal relationship with the Queen. Christina's eyesight did not improve but members of Parliament, and even some Ministers, objected strongly to the Queen's medical advisers.

But there was worse to come for the Queen of the Netherlands. In 1964 her second daughter, Princess Irene, became a Roman Catholic and married Prince Carel Hugo de Bourbon Parma, the Carlist claimant to the Spanish throne. Although she later renounced her right to succession to the Dutch throne, the Dutch Protestants (the majority of the nation) rose in anger.

There was much worse to come. In 1965 the Crown Princess Beatrix, heir to the Dutch throne, became engaged to a German diplomat, Claus George Willem Otto Frederik Geert von Amsberg. Dutch resistance fighters took great exception to this engagement (after suffering harrowing experiences at the hands of the Germans during the occupation of The Netherlands) but the Dutch Parliament finally ratified the engagement and Beatrix and Claus were married in Amsterdam on 10th March 1966.

Throughout the bitter controversy regarding the marriages of Irene and Beatrix the attitude of the Queen and Prince Bernhard was that they should marry whom they wished. They did—and the Queen now has nine grandchildren.

*   *   *

The Queen, often reported to be the richest woman in the world, still centres her life around Soestdijk Palace. She argues with and advises her Ministers and is well accustomed to crises in a country which finds it difficult to maintain a stable government. As recently as 1972 she admitted that, in the whole world, The Netherlands was the worst-hit nation regarding inflation which has risen dramatically over the past several years until now it is the highest in Europe.

Over the years Queen Juliana has mellowed. Many of her prejudices have disappeared and she is now once more at the head of the affairs of her Government. Princess Christina is still almost blind but this is accepted by the Queen and it is extremely doubtful if she will ever again resort to unconventional medical care.

Queen Juliana, Queen of the Netherlands, must by now be the most popular Monarch in the world. She is a woman of the people. She is trusted by the people and by successive Governments, all of which have been coalitions. Her acceptance is shown in many ways for it has been said at the highest possible level: "If The Netherlands were to become a Republic, Juliana would be the first President."

Numbering of the reference books mentioned in D.I.B.

TABLE OF ABBREVIATIONS

The following abbreviations are normally used in the compilation of biographical sketches

Acad.—Academic, Academy
Acct.—Accountant
Acctcy.—Accountancy
Acctng.—Accounting
Addl.—Additional
Admin.—Administration
Admnstr.—Administrator
Adv.—Advance, Advanced, Advancement
Advsr.—Advisor
Advsry.—Advisory
Advt.—Advertising, Advertisement
Agcy.—Agency
Agric.—Agriculture
Agricl.—Agricultural
Agt.—Agent
Ala.—Alabama
Alta.—Alberta
Am.—America, American
Anthol.—Anthology
Anthropol.—Anthropology
Appt.—Appointment
Apt.—Apartment
Arbtr.—Arbitrator, Arbitration
Arch. Architecture
Archaeol.—Archaeology
Archt.—Architect
Archtl.—Architectural
Ariz.—Arizona
Ark.—Arkansas
Assn.—Association
Assoc.—Associate
Asst.—Assistant
Astron.—Astromony
Athl.—Athletic(s)
Attng.—Attending
Atty.—Attorney
Aus.—Australia, Australian

B.—born
B.A.—Bachelor of Arts
B.Agric.—Bachelor of Agriculture
Bapt.—Baptist
Balt.—Baltimore
B.Arch.—Bachelor of Architecture
B.B.A.—Bachelor of Business Administration
B.B.C.—British Broadcasting Corporation
B.C.—British Columbia
B.C.E.—Bachelor of Civil Engineering
B.C.L.—Bachelor of Civil Law
Bd.—Board
B.D.—Bachelor of Divinity
B.E.—Bachelor of Education
B.E.E.—Bachelor of Electrical Engineering
B.E.M.—British Empire Medal
B.F.A.—Bachelor of Fine Arts
B.H.S.—Bachelor of Household Science
Bio.—Biology
Biog.—Biography, Biographical
Biol.—Biological
B.J.—Bachelor of Journalism
Bldg.—Building

B.L.S.—Bachelor of Library Science
Blvd.—Boulevard
Bot.—Botany
Br.—Branch
B.S.—Bachelor of Science
B.Sc.—Bachelor of Science
B.S.T.—Bachelor of Sacred Theology
B.Th.—Bachelor of Theology
Bur.—Bureau
Bus.—Business

Calif.—California
Capt.—Captain
Cath.—Catholic
Cert.—Certificate, Certified
Ch.—Church
Chap.—Chaplain
Chapt.—Chapter
Ch.B.—Bachelor of Surgery
Chem.—Chemistry, Chemical
Chgo.—Chicago
Chmbr. of Comm.—Chamber of Commerce
Chmn.—Chairman
Cinn.—Cincinnati
Cit.—Citation
Clin.—Clinic, Clinical
Cmdr.—Commander
C.O.—Commanding Officer
Co.—Company
Col.—Colonel
Coll.—College
Colo.—Colorado
Comm.—Committee
Commn.—Commission
Commng.—Commissioning
Commnr.—Commissioner
Commun.—Community
Comp.—Comparative
Conf.—Conference
Cong.—Congress
Congl.—Congregational
Conn.—Connecticut
Cons.—Consultant, Consulting
Conserv.—Conservation
Contbn.—Contribution
Contbng.—Contributing
Contbr.—Contributor
Conven.—Convention
Coop.—Cooperative
Coord.—Coordinator, Coordinating
Corp.—Corporation
Corres.—Correspondent, Corresponding
Coun.—Council
Cres.—Crescent
Ct.—Court
Ctr.—Centre
Ctrl.—Central
Cty.—County
Curric.—Curriculum

D.Agric.—Doctor of Agriculture
D.C.—District of Columbia
D.C.L.—Doctor of Civil Law

D.D.—Doctor of Divinity
D.D.S.—Doctor of Dental Surgery
Del.—Delaware
Deleg.—Delegate
Democ.—Democratic
Dept.—Department
Dev.—Development
D.F.C.—Distinguished Flying Cross
D.I.H.—Doctor of Industrial Hygiene
Dip.—Diploma
Dipl.—Diplomate
Dir.—Director
Dist.—District
Disting.—Distinguished
Div.—Division
Divl.—Divisional
D. Litt.—Doctor of Literature
D.M.D.—Doctor of Medical Dentistry
D.M.S.—Doctor of Medical Science
Doct.—Doctorate
D.P.H.—Doctor of Public Health, Doctor of Public Hygiene
D.P.M.—Doctor of Pediatric Medicine
Dpty.—Deputy
Dr.—Doctor, Drive
D.Sc.—Doctor of Science
D.S.C.—Distinguished Flying Cross, Doctor of Surgical Chiropody
D.S.T.—Doctor of Sacred Theology
D.V.M.—Doctor of Veterinary Medicine
D.V.S.—Doctor of Veterinary Science

E.—East
Econ.—Economic, Economics
Ed.—Editor
Ed.B.—Bachelor of Education
Ed.D.—Doctor of Education
Edit.—Edition
Editl.—Editorial
Ed.M.—Master of Education
Educ.—Education
Elec.—Electric, Electrical
Electn.—Electrician
Elem.—Elementary
Ency.—Encyclopaedia
Endocr.—Endocrinology
Engl.—English
Engr.—Engineer
Engrng.—Engineering
Episc.—Episcopal
Estab.—Established, Establishment
Exec.—Executive
Exhib.—Exhibition
Ext.—Extention

Fac.—Faculty
F.B.I.—Federal Bureau of Investigation

Fed.—Federal
Fedn.—Federation
Fla.—Florida
Fndg.—Founding
Fndr.—Founder
For.—Foreign
Fr.—Father
Frat.—Fraternity
F.R.C.P.—Fellow, Royal College
    of Physicians, England
F.R.C.S.—Fellow, Royal College
    of Surgeons, England
F.R.S.—Fellow of the Royal
    Society, England
Ft.—Fort

Ga.—Georgia
Gall.—Gallery
Gastroent.—Gastroenterology
G.B.—Great Britain
Gen.—General
Geog.—Geography
Gdn.—Garden
Gov.—Governor
Govng.—Governing
Govt.—Government
Grad.—Graduate
Grp.—Group
Gt.—Great
Gtr.—Greater
Gyn.—Gynaecology,Gynaecological
Hd.—Head
H.H.D.—Doctor of Humanities
Hist.—History
Histn.—Historian
Hlth.—Health
Hon.—Honour, Honorary
Hosp.—Hospital
H.Q.—Headquarters
H.S.—High School
Hwy.—Highway

I.F.E.E.—Institute of Electrical
    and Electronics Engineers
Ill.—Illinois
incl.—include, including
Ind.—Indiana, Industry
Indl. Industrial
Indpls.—Indianapolis
Info.—Information
Ins.—Insurance
Insp.—Inspector
Inst.—Institute
Instn.—Institution
Instr.—Instructor
Instrn.—Instruction
Int.—International

J.B.—Jurum Baccalaureus
J.D.—Doctor of Jurisprudence
Jr.—Junior
Jrnl.—Journal
Jrnlsm.—Journalism
J.S.D.—Doctor of Juristic Science
Jt.—Joint

Kan.—Kansas
Kt.—Knight
Ky.—Kentucky

La.—Louisiana
L.A.—Los Angeles
Lab.—Labour, Laboratory

Lang.—Language
Ldr.—Leader
Lectr.—Lecturer
Legl.—Legislative
L.H.D.—Doctor of Humane
    Letters
L.I.—Long Island
Lib.—Library
Libn.—Librarian
Lit.—Literature
Litt.B.—Bachelor of Letters
Litt.D.—Doctor of Letters
LL.B.—Bachelor of Laws
LL.D.—Doctor of Laws
LL.M.—Master of Laws
Lt.—Lieutenant
Luth.—Lutheran

M.A.—Master of Arts
M.Agric.—Master of Agriculture
Mag.—Magazines
Maj.—Major
Man.—Manitoba
M.Arch.—Master of Architecture
Mass.—Massachusetts
Math.—Mathematical
Mathn.—Mathematician
Maths.—Mathematics
Mats.—Materials
M.B.—Bachelor of Medicine
M.B.A.—Master of Business
    Administration
Mbr.—Member
Mbrship.—Membership
M.C.E.—Master of Civil Engineering
Md.—Maryland
M.D.—Doctor of Medicine
M.Div.—Master of Divintiy
Me.—Maine
M.E.—Mechanical Engineer
Mech.—Mechanics, Mechanical
M.Ed.—Master of Education
Med.—Medicine
M.E.E.—Master of Electrical
    Engineering
Mem.—Memorial
Met.—Metropolitan
Meth.—Methodist
M.F.A.—Master of Fine Arts
Mfg.—Manufacturing
Mfr.—Manufactuer
Mgmt.—Management
Mgr.—Manager
Mich. Michigan
Mil.—Military
Min.—Minister, Ministry
Minl.—Ministerial
Minn.—Minnesota
Miss.—Mississippi
M.L.—Master of Laws
M.Litt.—Master of Literature
M.L.S.—Master of Library
    Science
M.M.E.—Master of Mechanical
    Engineering
Mo.—Missouri
Mod.—Modern
Mont.—Montana
M.P.—Member of Parliament
M.P.H.—Master of Public Health
Mpls.—Minneapolis
M.S.—Master of Science
M.Sc.—Master of Science

Msgr.—Monseigneur
M.S.T.—Master of Sacred Theology
M.S.W.—Master of Social Work
Mt.—Mount
Mtg.—Meeting
Mtn.—Mountain
Mus.—Museum
Mus.B.—Bachelor of Music
Mus.D.—Doctor of Music
Mus.M.—Master of Music

N.—North
Nat.—National
N.A.T.O.—North Atlantic Treaty
    Organization
N.B.—New Brunswick
N.C.—North Carolina
N.D.—North Dakota
Neb.—Nebraska
Nev.—Nevada
Nfld.—Newfoundland
N.H.—New Hampshire
N.J.—New Jersey
N.M.—New Mexico
N.S.—Nova Scotia
N.S.W.—New South Wales
num.—numerous
N.Y.—New York
N.Y.C.—New York City
N.Z.—New Zealand

Observ.—Observatory
Obst.—Obstetrics
Obstrn.—Obstetrician
Off.—Office, Officer
O.F.M.—Order of Friars Minor
    (Franciscan)
Okla.—Oklahoma
Ont.—Ontario
Op.—Operation
O.P.—Order of Preachers
    (Dominican)
Orch.—Orchestra
Ore.—Oregon
Org.—Organization
Orgl.—Organizational
Orgr.—Organizer
Orth.—Orthodox

Pa.—Pennsylvania
Pathol.—Pathology
P.E.—Physical Education
P.E.N.—Poets, Playwrights,
    Editors, Essayists and Novelists
Pharm.D.—Doctor of Pharmacy
Pharm.M.—Master of Pharmacy
Ph.B.—Bachelor of Philosophy
Ph.D.—Doctor of Philosophy
Phila.—Philadelphia
Philol.—Philology
Philos.—Philosophy
Photog.—Photography
Phys.—Physics, Physical
Physiol.—Physiology
Physn.—Physician
Pitts.—Pittsburgh
Pk.—Park
Pkwy.—Parkway
Pl.—Place
Pol.—Politics
Poly.—Polytechnic
Posn.—Position
Postgrad.—Postgraduate

R.—Public Relations
ac.—Practice
ep.—Preparatory
es.—President
esby.—Presbyterian
n.—Principal
od.—Production
of.—Professor
ofn.—Profession
og.—Programme
oj.—Project
ych.—Psychiatry, Psychiatrist
ychol.—Psychology, Pyschological
   —Point
T.A.—Parent Teacher
   Association
nr.—Partner
b.—Public
blr.—Publisher
bls.—Publications
te.—Private
Q.—Province of Quebec

A.F.—Royal Air Force
r.—Reader
f.—Reference
g.—Region, Regional
hab.—Rehabilitation
lig.—Religion
ls.—Relations
p.—Representative
pub.—Republic, Republican
s.—Residence, Resident
td.—Retired
ev.—Reverend
I.—Rhode Island
N.—Registered Nurse
sch.—Research
schr.—Researcher
te.—Route

—South
sk.—Saskatchewan
C.—South Carolina
.D.—Doctor of Science
hl.—School
hlrship.—Scholarship
hol.—Scholar, Scholastic
ci.—Science
D.—South Dakota

S.E.A.T.O.—Southeast Asia
   Treaty Organization
Sec.—Secretary
Sect.—Section
Sem.—Seminary
Serv.—Service
Sev.—Several
S.F.—San Francisco
Sgt.—Sergeant
S.H.A.E.F.—Supreme Headquarters,
   Allied Expeditionary Forces
S.H.A.P.E.—Supreme Headquarters,
   Allied Powers in Europe
S.J.—Society of Jesus (Jesuit)
S.J.D.—Doctor of Juristic Science
Soc.—Society
Sociol.—Sociology, Sociological
Sr.—Senior
St.—Saint, Street
Statn.—Statistician
Stats.—Statistics
S.T.B.—Bachelor of Sacred Theology
S.T.D.—Doctor of Sacred Theology
S.T.M.—Master of Sacred Theology
Stn.—Station
Supt.—Superintendent
Supvsr.—Supervisor
Symph.—Symphony

Tas.—Tasmania
Tchr.—Teacher
Tech.—Technical
Techn.—Technician
Technol.—Technology
Tel.—Telephone
Tenn.—Tennessee
Terr.—Terrace
Tex.—Texas
Th.D.—Doctor of Theology
Theol.—Theology, Theological
Th.M.—Master of Theology
thru'—through
Treas.—Treasurer
Trng.—Training
T.V.—Television
T.V.A.—Tennessee Valley
   Authority
Twp.—Township
Ty.—Territory

U.A.R.—United Arab Republic
U.K.—United Kingdom
U.N.—United Nations
Un.—United
U.N.E.S.C.O.—United Nations
   Educational, Scientific and
   Cultural Organization
U.N.I.C.E.F.—United Nations
   International Children's
   Emergency Fund
Unit.—Unitarian
Univ.—University
U.S.—United States
U.S.A.—United States of America
U.S.A.A.F.—United States Army
   Air Force
U.S.A.F.—United States Air Force
U.S.N.—United States Navy
U.S.N.R.—United States Naval
   Reserve
U.S.S.R.—Union of Soviet
   Socialist Rebublics

Va.—Virginia
Vet.—Veterinary, Veterinarian
V.I.—Virgin Islands
Vic.—Victoria
Vis.—Visiting
Voc.—Vocational
Vol.—Volunteer, Voluntary
V.P.—Vice President
Vt.—Vermont

W.—West
Wash.—Washington
W.H.O.—World Health
   Organization
Wis.—Wisconsin
Wkr.—Worker
W.Va.—West Virginia
Wyo.—Wyoming

Y.M.C.A.—Young Men's Christian
   Association
yr.—year
Y.W.C.A.—Young Women's
   Christian Association

Zool.—Zoology, Zoological

DICTIONARY

OF

INTERNATIONAL BIOGRAPHY

KÄÄRIÄINEN, Erkki, b. 30 Oct. 1909. Geodesist. Educ: M.Sc., 1934; Ph.D., 1953; Prof., 1964. Appts: Leveller, Geodetic Inst., Helsinki, Finland, 1936-60; Jr. State Geodesist, ibid., 1960-64; Sr. State Geodesist, 1964-. Mbrships: Nordisk Geodetic Commn; Finnish Geographical Soc; Astronomical Soc. Ursa; Universala Esperanto Assn; Lions Club. Publs. incl: Adjustments of the Northern Bloc in Unified European Levelling Networks, 1960; The Second Levelling of Finland in 1935-55, 1963; Astronomical Determinations of Latitude & Longitude in 1954-60, 1970. Hons: Cross Of Liberty; Knight 1st Class, Order of the White Rose; War Mem. Medals & recognition of official merits. Address: Geodetic Inst., Pasilankatu 43, 00240 Helsinki 24, Finland. 43, 90, 134.

KAATZ, Lawrence Earl, b. 5 Mar. 1935. Architect. Educ: Univ. of Tex., Arlington; 1953-55; B.A., Tulane Univ., La., 1960; Appts: (w. following Archts.) L.M. Gernsbacher, Ft. Worth, Tex., 1954; Nolan Norman Holan, New Orleans, La., 1958; Grogan & Scoggins, Irving, Tex., 1965; Kirk & Voich, Ft. Worth, 1967; Harwood K. Smith & Ptnrs., Dallas, Tex., 1968-72; Architectonics, 1972-. Mbrships: Dallas Chapt., Am. Inst. of Archts.; Dallas Chapt., Construction Specifications Inst. Address: P.O. Box 5324, Arlington, TX 76011, U.S.A. 7.

KABDEBO, Thomas George, b. 5 Feb. 1934. Librarian. Educ: Eötvös Univ., Budapest, Hungary; Univ. Coll., Cardiff, U.K. Appts: Temp. Asst. Libn., Univ. Coll., Cardiff, 1960-61; Asst. Libn., Univ. Coll., London, 1962-69; Univ. Libn., Univ. of Guyana, 1969-72; Polytech. Libn., City of London Polytech., 1973-74. Mbrships: PEN; World Poetry Soc.; A.P.T.; Lib. Assn. Publs: Geman Hungaria, 1962; Fortified Princecriptions on Poetry, 1964; Erettsègi (novel), 1970; Twohearted (poems), 1973; Magyar odisszeuszok (short stories), 1974; Ed., Attila József-Poems, 1966, A Tribute to Gyula Illyès, 1968 & Gyula Illyès-Selected Poems, 1969. Address: 61 Gowan Ave., London SW6, U.K.

KÄBIN, Ilo, b. 18 Feb. 1921. Doctor of Medicine. Educ: studied Med., Tartu (Dorpat) Univ., 1940-43; studied Med., Uppsala Univ., Sweden, 1945-50; studied Surg., U.S.A., 1956, 1958. Appts. incl: Battalion Dr., volunteer in Finnish Army, Karelian Peninsula, 1943-44; • Acting Chief Surg., Hosp., Landskrona, Sweden, 1956-69; Gen. Surg. & Pvte. Prac.,

Landskrona, Sweden, 1960-. Mbrships: Swedish Med. Soc., Stockholm; S.Swedish Medico-Hist. Soc., Lund, Sweden; Baltic Soc., Munich, German Fed. Repub.; former Estonians' Rep., Sweden. Publs. incl: Maal Ja Merel, 1972, Swedish edit., Till Lands Och Till Sjoss, 1974; num. contbns. on Surg., Internal Med. & Med. Hist. in profl. jrnls. Hons: Finnish Continuation War Commemorative Medal; Cross of Eastern Karelia, Finland, 1944. Address: Sundgatan 6, S 261 61 Landskrona, Sweden. 43.

KABRAJI, Fredoon (Jehangir), b. 1897. Poet; Journalist. Educ: London Univ. Appts: Reporter, Feature Writer, Sub-ed., var. Indian nationalist newspapers, Bombay, 1926-30; Publicity Mgr., var. orgs., India, 1930-35; Free-lance Journalist, contbng. to Time & Tide, Pol. Quarterly, Manchester Guardian, New Statesman, etc., U.K., 1935-. Past Mbrships: Royal Soc. of Lit., London; P.E.N. (Engl. Ctr.), London. Poetry Publs: A Minor Georgian's Swan Song, 1944; The Cold Flame, 1956; contbn. to anthol., This Strange Adventure. Contbr., poems, English Review, Spectator, London Mercury, Atlantic Monthly. Address: 48 Huntingdon Rd., London, N2 9DU, U.K. 3, 30, 139.

KABUYE, Christine Sophie, b. 21 Nov. 1938. Taxonomic Botanist. Educ: B.Sc., Makerere Univ. Coll., 1964. Appts: Botanist, E. African Herbarium, E. African Agric. & Forestry Rsch. Org., Nairobi, Kenya, 1964-71; Botanist i/c, 1971-. Mbrships: Association pour l'Etude Taxonomique de la Flore d'Afrique Tropicale; Int. Assn. Plant Taxonomy. Contbr., reports & articles, profl. jrnls. Address: E. African Herbarium, P.O. Box 45166, Nairobi, Kenya.

KAEGI, Walter Emil, Jr., b. 8 Nov. 1937. Professor of History. Educ: A.B., Haverford Coll., 1959; A.M., Harvard, 1960; Ph.D., 1965. Appts. incl: Asst. Prof., Byzantine & Roman Hist., Univ. of Chgo., 1965-69; Assoc. Prof., ibid, 1969-74; Prof., 1974-; Fellow, Inst. for Rsch. in the Humanities, Univ. of Wis., 1967-68; Mbr., Schl. of Hist. Studies, Inst. for Adv. Study, Princeton, N.J., 1970-71. Mbrships. incl: Am. Hist. Assn.; Medeaeval Acad.; Am. Soc. Ch. Hist.; Am. Philol. Assn.; Phe Beta Kappa. Publs: Byzantium & the Decline of Rome, 1968, 70; Byzantine Military Unrest 471-843; num. articles. Hons. incl: Travel Grant, Am. Coun. of Learned Socs. to Athens, Greece, 1970; Grant, Am. Rsch. Inst.

in Turkey, 1973. Address: 5305 S. Greenwood Ave., Chgo., IL 60615, U.S.A. 8, 13.

KAFE, Joseph Kofi Thompson, b. 20 Jan. 1933. Librarian. Educ: B.A., Univ. Coll. of Ghana, 1960; Schl. of Libnship. & Archives, Univ. Coll., London Univ., U.K., 1961-62. Appts. incl: Trainee, Jr. Asst. Libn., 1960-62; Asst. Libn., 1962-1972; Acting Libn., 1972-. Mbrships: Ghana. Lib. Assn.; British Lib. Assn. Publs. incl: Balme Library Theses, Vols. 1-3, 1969-71, (annotated list of Theses accessioned in Balme Lib., Univ. of Ghana); Ghana, (annotated Bibliog. of Acad. Theses, 1920-70, in Commonwealth, Repub. of Ireland & U.S.A.). Address: Univ. of Ghana, Balme Lib., P.O. Box 24, Legon, Accra, Ghana.

KĀĞITÇI, Mehmed Ali, b. 20 Aug. 1899. Chemist. Educ: Dip., Chem. Engrng., Univ. of Istanbul, Turkey, 1922; Certs., Mineralogy, Gen. Maths., & Biol. & Med. Chem.; Adv. Tech. Schl., Hannover, Germany; French Schl. of Paper-Making, Univ. of Grenoble; Dip., Paper Engr. E.F.P.E.F.P., ibid, 1927. Appts. incl: Prof., Gen. Chem., Turkish Naval Acad. & of Indl. & Biol. Chem., Chem. Inst., Istanbul; Dir., Fndr., Izmit Paper Mfg.; Advsr., Paper Ind.; Dir., Fndr., Lab. of Scientific Rsch. in Ceramics, Kutahya, 1941; Dir., Municipal Lab., Istanbul; Dir., Inst. of Hygiene, Instanbul; Prof., Tech. Univ. Mbrships: incl: Fndg. Mbr., Turkish Chem. Soc.; Fndg. Mbr., Int. Soc. for Fat Rsch. Publs. incl: Cellulose et Papier, 1928; PH, force d'acidité et d'alcalinité, 1931; Historique de la paperterie, 1936; Guide alimentaire, 1949; Redressement économique et les ressources nationales, 1952; Beitrag zur Türkischen Papiergeschichte, 1963; Papiers marbrés turcs, 1969. Recip., var. hons. Holds sev. patents. Address: Heybeliada, Istanbul, Turkey. 43.

KAHLER, Woodland, pseudonym of the Marquis of Saint Innocent, b. 6 Feb. 1895. Writer. Educ: Phillips Acad., Andover, Mass., 1914; B.A., Yale Univ., 1918; Sorbonne Univ., Paris, France, 1923-24. Publs: Early to Bed; Smart Setback; False Front; Giant Dwarf; Portrait in Laughter; Cravings of Desire; Essays, poems etc. Mbrships: Life, Sons of Am. Revolution; Pres., World Org. of Culture, Paris; Pres., Coun. for World Govt., The Hague, Netherlands; Pres., Int. Vegetarian Union, U.K.; Rep., UNESCO; Assn. for Protection of Animals in India; Friends of Buddhism; Cercle de l'Union & Cercle Interallié, France. Hons: Kt., Order of Merit, France; Kt., St. John the Bapt., Spain; Hon. Degree, Int. Pythagorean Philos Soc.; Hon. Dip., Vie et Action, France. Address: 208 Australian Ave., Palm Beach, FL 33480, U.S.A. 2, 22, 43, 91.

KAHLERT, Fern DuComb. Pharmacist (ret.'d); Genealogist; Lecturer. Educ: St. Louis Coll. of Pharm., 1930. Appts: Evening Supvsr., Pharm., Barnes Hosp., St. Louis, Mo., 1951-57; Chief Pharmacist, Mem. Hosp., Belleville, Ill., 1957-63; Evening Supvsr., Pharm., Deaconess Hosp., St. Louis, Mo., 1968-70. Mbrships: Nat. League Am. Pen Women; DAR (Benjamin Mills Chap., Greenville, Ill.); Pa., Ill., Ga., Nat. Genealogical Socs. Contbr. to genealogical jrnls. Address: Town View Apts., Carlyle, IL 62231, U.S.A.

KAHN, (Lord), b. 10 Aug. 1905. Professor of Economics. Educ: Kings Coll., Cambridge Univ., U.K., 1924-. Appts. incl: Fellow, Kings Coll., Cambridge Univ., U.K., 1930-; Lectr. in Econs., Cambridge Univ., 1933-51; Hd. Bursar, Kings Coll., Cambridge Univ., 1935-46; Lectr. in Econs., Kings Coll., 1937-51; 1st Bursar, Kings Coll., 1946-51; Prof. of Econs., Univ. of Cambridge, 1951-72; Prof. Emeritus, ibid, 1972-. Mbrships: Royal Automobile Club. Publs: various articles & essays on Employment & Growth. Hons. incl: C.B.E., 1946; Fellowship, British Acad.; Life Peerage, 1965. Address: Kings Coll., Cambridge.CB2 1ST, U.K. 1.

KAHN, Louis Isadore, b. 20 Feb. 1901. University Professor. Educ: B. Archt., Univ. of Pa., 1924. Appts. incl: Cons. Archt., U.S. Housing Authority, 1937; Chief Critic of Archtl. Design, Yale Univ., 1947; Res. Archt., Am. Acad. in Rome, 1950-51; Prof. of Archt., Yale Univ., 1948-57; Albert Bemis Prof., Schl. of Archt. & Planning, MIT, 1956; Prof. of Archt., Univ. of Pa., 1957; Paul Philippe Cret Chair in Archt., Univ. of Pa., 1966; Paul Philippe Cret Prof. Emeritus, ibid, 1971. Exhibs: Paintings & drawings made during travels, Pa. Acad. of Fine Arts, 1929-30; Archt. in Govt. Housing, Mus. of Mod. Art, N.Y., 1930; Single Building Exhib., Richards Med. Towers, ibid, 1963; 'The Work of Louis I. Kahn', La Jolla Mus. of Art, 1965; One-man retrospective exhib., Mus. of Mod. Art, N.Y., 1966. Commns. incl: New Engrng. Campus, Tel-Aviv Univ.; Palazzo dei Congressi, Venice, Italy; Franklin D. Roosevelt Meml., N.Y. Mbr. of var. civic commns. & Fellow of int. insts. Recip., 9 hon. degrees & num. awards inclng: Royal Gold Medal for Archt., Royal Inst. of Brit. Archts., U.K., 1972; Gold Medal, Nat. Inst. Arts & Letters, N.Y., 1973. Address: 1501 Walnut St., Philadelphia 2, PA, U.S.A.

KAHN, Ralph H., b. 17 Aug. 1920. Art Gallery Director. Educ: in Europe & U.S.A. German emigrant to U.S.A. & U.S. Citizen since 1943. Appts. incl: U.S. Govt. employee for over 20 yrs.; Dir., Contemporary Art Gall., Dallas, 1964-, planning & supvsing. art exhibs. Personal Art Collect. incls. work by Braque, Chagall, Klee, Miro, Picasso & pre-Columbian & primitive pieces. Lectures throughout S. Western States of Am. on subjects related to contemporary art & broadcast on ABC TV network in 1973. Mbrships: V.P., Terra Linda Art Assn., Calif.; Pres., Tex. Fine Arts Assn., Dallas Chapt.; Am. Soc. of Appraisers. Address: Contemporary Gall., 2800 Routh St., Dallas, TX 75201, U.S.A. 37.

KAHN, Samuel, b. 16 June 1897. Psychiatrist; Author. Educ: B.S., Emory Univ., 1920; M.D., 1921; A.M., N.Y. Univ., 1923; Ph.D., 1932; Intern, Metropolitan Hosp., N.Y.C., 1921-22; Res., City Hosp., 1922-23. Appts. incl: Lectr., N.Y. Univ., 1925-27; Psych., Sing Sing, 1929-31; Clin. Prof., Neurol. & Psych., Georgetown & Geo. Wash. Univs.; Chief Psych., Gallinger Hosp., 1929-31; Assoc. Prof., L.I. Univ., 1945-54; Now Adjunct Prof., Psych.; Pvte. Prac., Psychoanalysis; Clin. Psych., Mt. Sinai, N.Y. Postgrad. Hosps.; Fellow, Royal Soc. of Hlth. Mbrships. incl: num. med., psychol., sociol. & anthropol. socs., Mason (Shriner); Rotarian. Publs. incl: How to Study, 1939; Master Your Mind, 1951; Public Speaking, 1952; Inferiorities & Superiorites, 1954; Effective Studying and Learning, 1973; Essays on Longevity, 1974; Why We Laugh, 1974. Author of many other publs. in field. Address: 410 Albany Post Rd., Croton-on-Hudson, NY 10520, U.S.A. 6.

KAHN, Sanders A., b. 20 Jan. 1910. Real Estate Consultant; Professor; Writer. Educ: B.B.A., CCNY, 1947; M.B.A., CCNY, 1947; M.B.A., 1949, Ph.D., 1962, N.Y. Univ. Appts: Adams & Co., 1939-41; Dwight-Helmsley Corp., V.P., Walter Oertly Assocs., Inc., 1948-49; Asst. Prof., Real Estate, Univ. of Fla., 1949-51; Mgr., Real Estate Planning Div., Port of N.Y. Authority, 1952-54; Adjunct Prof. & Supvsr. of Real Estate Educ., CUNY, 1952-; Pres., Sanders A. Kahn Assocs., Inc. & Transportation Realty Dev. Co., 1954-. Mbrships. incl: Dir., Citizens Housing & Planning Coun. of N.Y.; Fellow, Past Pres., Gtr. N.Y. Chapt., Past N.Y. State Dir., Am. Soc. of Appraisers; Fellow, Inc. Soc. of Valuers & Auctioneers, U.K.; Past Nat. Dir., other offs., Am. Right of Way Assn. Publs: Real Estate Appraisal & Investment (co-author), 1963; Fundamentals of Right of Way Acquisition. Essays on (co-author), 1972; Contbr. to profl. jrnls. Address: Sanders A. Kahn Assocs., Inc., 535 Fifth Ave., N.Y., NY 10017, U.S.A. 2, 6.

KAHN, Theodore Charles, b. 13 Oct. 1912. Hominologist; Psychologist; Educator. Educ: B.A., Yale Univ., 1935; M.A. (counseling), Columbia Univ., 1940; Ph.D., Univ. of Southern Calif., 1950; M.A. (clin. psych.), Mills Coll., 1952; Doktor Rerum Naturalium, Johannes Gutenburg Univ., Mainz, German Fed. Repub., 1960. Appts. incl: Chief Psychol., USAF, 1950-65; Lectr., Wittenberg Univ., Univ. of Md., 1954-56, & San Antonio City Coll., 1960-65; Prof. & Hd., Dept. of Behavioural Sci., Southern Colo. State Coll., 1965-. Mbrships. incl: Fellow, Fndr. & 1st Pres., Int. Soc. for Study of Symbols; Fellow, Am. Psychol. Assn. & AAAS. Publs: The Kahn Test of Symbol Arrangement; The Kahn Intelligence Tests; The Kahn Aphasia Tests; (books) Psychological Techniques in Diagnosis & Evaluation; Contemporary Methods in Psychology & Counselling (sr. author); An Introduction to Hominology—The Study of the Whole Man; Contemporary Methods in Clinical Psychology & Counseling (co-author), 1973; Articles in profl. jrnls. Recip. sev. hons. Address: c/o Dept. of Behavioral Sci., Southern Colo. State Coll., Pueblo, CO 81001, U.S.A. 2, 9, 14.

KAHRE, Clifford George, b. 19 Jan. 1924. Teacher; Bookkeeper. Educ: A.A., Centralia Township. Jr. Coll., Ill., 1957; B.A., McKendree Coll., Labanon, Ill., 1957; H.H.D., London Inst. for Applied Rsch., 1973. Appts: Tchr., Clinton Co., Ill., 1945-48; Assessor, Lake Township, Clinton Co., 1946-50; Bookkeeper, Barger Trucking co., Hoffman, Ill., 1949-; Prin. & Coach, N. Wamac Schl., Centralia, Ill., 1950-53; Supt. & Tchr., Ashley Community Consolidated Schl., Ashley, Ill., 1955-71. Mbrships. incl: Deleg., Cleveland Conven., NEA, 1958; Ill. Elementary Schl. Prins. Assn.; Nat. Elementary Schl. Prins. Assn; Ill. Prins. Assn.; Ill. State Hist. Soc.; Hon. Life Mbr., Ashley Pub. Schl. PTA; Pres., Wash. Co. Assn. for Mental Hlth., 1968; Fndr. Mbr., U.S. Capitol Hist. Soc., Nat. Hist. Soc. & U.S. Numismatic Assn.; etc. Hons. incl: Hon. Doct. of Rhymes, Rhyme Univ., Eden, N.Y., 1959; num. hons. & awards from Ashley Community Consolidated Schl., 1959-71. Address: 1303 Case St., Centralia, IL 62801, U.S.A. 120.

KAILIS, Michael George, b. 14 Feb. 1929. Company Governing Director. Educ: Univ. of W.A., Nedlands, Australia. Appts: Estab. Fishing & Seafood Processing complex, W.A., S.A., & Groote Eylandt, N.T., also Shipbuilding, W.A., 1960; Cons., Trade, Fishing, & Mining, Indonesia, Singapore, & Japan; Govng. Dir., M.G. Kailis (1962) Pty. Ltd.; Govng. Dir., M.G. Kailis Gulf Fisheries Pty. Ltd.; Govng. Dir., M.G. Kailis Exports Pty. Ltd.; P.T. Kailis Aru Marine Products; Western Marine Serv. Co. Mbrships. incl: Trustee, Muscular Dystrophy Assn.; Tattersall's Club; W.A. Club. Recognized as pioneer of the mod. shrimp ind. in Exmouth Gulf by Govt. of W.A.

Address: P.O. Box 745, Fremantle, W.A., Australia 6160. 23.

KAIN, Richard Morgan, b. 19 Dec. 1908. University Professor; Scholar. Educ: A.B., Swarthmore Coll., 1930; M.A., Univ. of Chgo., 1931; Ph.D., ibid, 1934. Appts. incl: Augustana Coll., SD, 1933-34; Ohio Wesleyan Univ., 1934-40; Univ. of Louisville, 1940-, Chmn., Div. of Humanities, ibid, 1963-69; Vis. Prof., N. Western Univ., 1948, Harvard Univ., 1950, Univs. of Colo., Mass. & N.Y. & Univ. of Wash; Fulbright Prof., Venice, Italy, 1961-62; Univ. Coll., Dublin, Repub. of Ireland, 1972. Mbrships: Phi Beta Kappa; MLA; Mod. Human Rsch. Assn.; AAUP; Am. Comm. Irish Studies. Publs. incl: Fabulous Voyager: James Joyce's Ulysses; Co-author, Joyce, the Man, the Work, the Reputation; Dublin in the Age of W.B. Yeats & James Joyce; The Workshop of Daedalus. Address: Univ. of Louisville, Louisville, KY 40208, U.S.A. 2, 3, 7, 13, 15, 30, 125.

KAINA, (Rev.) William H., b. 27 Nov. 1932. Pastor, Congregational Church. Educ: B.A., Yankton Coll., S.D., 1955, B.Th., 1956; B.D., Oberlin Grad. Schl., 1963. Appts: Pastor, E. Maui Congl. Chs., 1956-60; Student pastor, Sullivan Ch., Oberlin, Ohio, 1961-63; Pastor, Lihue Union Ch., Kauai, 1963-69, Pearl Harbor Mem. Com. Ch., 1969-71; Coord., Hawaiian Coun., Christian Chs. of Hawaii Conf., 1971-. Mbrships. incl: State Coun. of Hawaiian Congl. Chs., (Pres., 1971); Kauai Econ. Dev. Adv. Commn.; Am. Red Cross; Pearl Harbor Rotary Club; Kauai Evangelical Assn. (Chap.); Kauai YMCA (Dir. 1966-69); Kamehameha Schls. Assn., Pres. P.T.A., 1958-59, Dir., 1965. Co-publr., A New Hawaiian Hymnal, 1972. Address: 2103 Nuuanu Ave., Honolulu, HI 96817, U.S.A.

KAISER, George, b. 27 Nov. 1911. Farmer & Rancher. Appts: Pres., Baldwin Co. Farm Bur., 1958-; Dir., S. Baldwin Hosp., 1954-. Pres., 1956-62, S. Baldwin Bank, 1958-, S.W. Ala. Pecan Assn., 1961-, Baldwin Co. Cattlemens Assn., 1963-67, Ala. Pesticide Inst., 1966-69, Ala. Farm Bur. Fedn., 1971-. Mbrships: S. Baldwin Chmbr. of Comm. (Past Pres. & Dir.); Foley Rotary Club (Pres., 1965-66); Roman Cath. Ch.; Foley Laymans Club, Sec. & Treas.; Trustee St. Benedict Sch., 1964-68. Recip. of disting. serv. awards, S. Baldwin Hosp., 1958, Ala. Agric., 1971. Address: Rt. 2 Box 23, Foley, AL, U.S.A. 7, 125.

KAISER, Katherine Elizabeth, b. 15 May 1915. Teacher. Educ: B.S., Bob Jones Univ., 1954; M.A., Tchrs. Coll., Columbia Univ., 1955; Fellowship, African Studies, Northwestern Univ., 1967; other postgrad. studies, U.S.A. & Kenya. Appts: Tchr., Schenectady Pub. Schls., N.Y., 1956-60; Tchr., Columbia Univ. Engl. Lang. Team (sponsored by Agcy. for Int. Dev.), Kabul, Afghanistan, 1960-62; Cons. & Resource Tchr. in Inter-Cultural Rels., Schenectady City Schls., 1963-68; Tchr., ibid, 1968-. Mbrships. incl: Nat. & State Fedn. Bus. & Profl. Women's Clubs Inc. (Pres. Schenectady Br. 1970-72 & holder of num. other offs.); AAUW (var. offs.); U.N. Assn.; Advsry. Bd., Refreshing Spring Child Day Care Ctr.; First Presby. Ch., Schenectady; N.Y. State United Tchrs.; NEA. Publs: Series on Asia, Schenectady Gazette, 1960-62. Hons: Gen. Elec. Co. Patent Award, 1948. Address: 110 Union St., Apt. 8, Schenectady, NY 12305, U.S.A. 130.

KAJAS, Seppo Veli, b. 15 Jan. 1929. Physician. Educ: Lic. med., Univ. of Turku,

Finland, 1954, Radiolst., 1957, Dr. Med. & Surg., 1967. Appts: Asst. Physn., Univ. Hosp., Turku, 1955-58; Chief Physn., Dist. Hosp., Rauma, 1958-. Mbrships: Finnish Assn. of Radiol; Lions Club. Author of profl. dissertation, 1967. Address: Dist. Hosp., 26130 Rauma 13, Finland.

KAKAR, Sudhir, b. 25 July 1938. Psychologist. Educ: B. Engrng., Gujrat Univ., Pakistan, 1958; D. Kfm., Univ. of Mannheim, Germany, 1964; Ph.D., Univ. of Vienna, Austria, 1968; Training at Sigmund Freud Inst., Frankfurt, Germany, 1972-. Appts: Lectr., Harvard Univ.; Rsch. Fellow, Harvard Bus. Schl., ibid; Prof. Organisational Behaviour, Indian Inst. of Mgmt., Ahmedabad; Vis. Prof., Sigmund Freud Inst., Frankfurt, Germany. Mbrships: Indian Psychological Assn.; Grp. for Applied Psychoanalysis. Publs: Frederick Taylor: a Study in Personality & Innovation, 1970; Conflict & Choice, 1970; Co-Ed., Understanding Organisational Behavior, 1971; Personality & Authority in Work, 1974; Co-Ed., Psychodynamik der Unternehmensführing, 1974; The Inner World: Childhood & Society in India (in preparation). Hons: Award for Young Writers, Karolyi Fndn., 1972. Address: 1 Tilak Marg, JAIPUR, India. 30.

KALEEM, James Samuel, b. 10 Mar. 1908. Educationist. Educ: London Inst. of Educ., U.K. Appts: Tchr., sev. schls., Ghana, 1927-48; Sr. Housemaster, Govt. Trng. Coll., Tamale, 1949-54; Acting Prin., Pusiga Tchr. Trng. Coll., 1955-57; Tutor, Vernacular Lang., Govt. Secondary Schl., Tamale, 1958-59; Sr. Educ. Off., 1960; Regional Educ. Off.-Prin. Educ. Off., 1961-69. Mbrships: Chmn., Bur. of Ghana Langs.; Ghana Lib. Bd.; Ghana Nat. Arts Coun.; Past Chmn., Ctr. for Civic Educ.; Ghana Red Cross Soc.; Past Chmn., Tamale Municipal Coun. Publs: Sev. primers, story books, & verses, for teaching Dagbani lang. in primary & middle schls. Hons: Cert. & Badge for meritorious serv. in Min. of Educ., 1946; Grand Medal of Ghana for meritorious serv., 1969. Address: c/o Ministry of Education, P.O. Box 101, Tamale, Ghana. 135.

KALEJAIYE, (Chief) Alaba, b. 25 Oct. 1917. Secretary & Trade Unionist. Educ: Mich. State Univ., U.S.A.; Oxford Univ., U.K. Appts: Clerk, United African Co. Ltd., Lagos, Nigeria; Sec. Gen., Nigeria Civil Serv. Union, 1952-. Mbrships: Corp. of Nigeria Bd. Mgmt.; Nat. Labour Advsry. Coun., Nigeria; Fed. Staff Housing Bd.; Lagos Juvenile Employment Comm.; Lagos Manpower Comm.; Gen. Sec., Ososa United Soc., Lagos; Gen. Sec. Odogbolu Golden Club, Lagos; Soc. Sec., Young Christian Fellowship, King's Ch., Enu-Owa, Lagos. Mbr., Order of the Niger. Address: 7 Salami Saibu St., Palm Grove, Ikorodu Rd., P.O. Box 840, Lagos, Nigeria. 135.

KALES, Robert Gray, b. 14 Mar. 1904. Industrialist. Educ: Dip., Philips Exeter Acad., 1919-23; B.S.C.E., MIT, 1928; M.B.A., Harvard Grad. Schl. of Bus. Admin., 1933. Appts. incl: Pres. & Dir., Jefferson Terminal Warehouse, 1934-, Kales Realty Co., 1935-, Kales Kramer Invest. Co., 1935-, Midwest Underwriters, Inc., Detroit, Mich., 1938-, Indl. Resources, Inc., 1950-70; Chmn. of Bd., Whitehead & Kales Co., Mich., 1934-, Automotive Bin Serv. Co., Mich., 1968-, Automotive Bin Serv. Co., Inc., N.Y. & Ohio, 1967-; V.P. & Dir., Basin Oil Co., Mich., 1947-. Mbrships. incl: Acad. of Pol. & Soc. Sci.; Am. Inst. of Mgmt.; Sigma Chi; Active mbr. of patriotic orgs. Hons: Order of the Croix de Guerre, France, 1959; Order of Lafayette,

1965. Address: 87 Cloverly Rd., Grosse Pointe Farms, MI 48236, U.S.A. 8, 12, 16.

KALES, Shirley M. (Mrs. Robert G. Kales), b. 18 Feb. 1927. Personnel Consultant; Program Director. Appts: Mbr., Advt. & Publicity Staff, Bielfield Agcy., Detroit, 1955-59; Mbr., Advt. & Sales Dept., Mich. Bell Telephone Co., 1959-60; Mbr., Sales Promotion & Advt. Staff, Mich. Consolidated Gas Co., 1960-61; Dir., Automotive Bin Serv. Co., Inc., 1968-71; Personnel Dir., Kales Kramer Investment Co., 1967-. Mbrships. incl: Detroit Review Club; Detroit Women's Coun., Navy League of U.S.; Fine Arts Soc., Detroit; Women's City Club, Detroit. Address: 87 Cloverly Rd., Grosse Pointe Farms, MI 48236, U.S.A.

KALLAND, Earl Stanley, b. 26 June 1910. Educator; Clergyman. Educ: Th.B., Bible Inst. of L.A., 1936; Th.B., Gordon Coll. of Theol. & Missions, Boston, 1937; B.D., Gordon Divinity Schl., ibid, 1940; Th.D., ibid, 1942. Appts: Pastor, Rock Hill Bapt. Ch., Boston, 1936-42, First Ch., Sayre, Pa., 1942-44, Calvary Bapt. Ch., Burbank, Calif., 1944-45; Prof. Biblical Lit. & Exegesis, L.A. Theol. Sem., 1944-45, Old Testament & Hebrew, Calif. Bapt. Theol. Sem., L.A., 1945-46, Western Bapt. Theol. Sem., Portland, Ore., 1946-55; Dean, ibid, 1946-47; Pres., ibid, 1947-55; Dean, Conservative Bapt. Theol. Sem., Denver, Colo., 1956-73; Prof., Old Testament Dept., ibid, 1956-. Mbrships: Comm. Bible Translation (New Int. Version), 1965-; Am. Schls. Oriental Rsch., Evang. Theol. Soc. (Treas., 1960-63); Bd. Concern, Inc., 1962-65; Soc. Biblical Lit. & Exegesis; Nat. (Chmn. Sem. Div. Educ. Comm., 1959-62, V.P.-Chmn., Educ. Comm., 1960-65, Exec. Comm. Commn. Higher Educ., 1966-, Bd. Admin., 1962-70), Colo. (Bd. Dirs., 1960-62), Denver (Pres., 1958-59, 1st V.P., 1960-62) Assn. Evangelicals; Assn. Higher Educ.; NEA; Colo. Temperance Fedn. (Bd., 1958-62); Int. Ocean. Fndn.; Nat. Wild Life Fedn.; Smithsonian Instn.; Ams. United; Phi Alpha Chi. Author of var. articles on relig. subjects in sev. encys., word books & periodicals. Recip. of D.D., Denver Conservative Bapt. Sem., 1954. Address: Conservative Baptist Theol. Seminary, P.O. Box 10,000, Univ. Park Stn., Denver, CO 80210, U.S.A. 2.

KALLENBACH, Hans, b. 24 Dec. 1907. Academy Director. Educ: Univs. of Frankfurt & Giessen, Germany, 1926-30; Dr.phil., 1930. Tchr., schls., 1930-36; Univ. Lectr., German Lang. & Lit., Dir., Tchr. Trng. Coll., 1936-45; Co-fndr. & Dir., Evangelical Acad., Hessen & Nassau, 1945-72. Mbrships: Bd. of Dirs., Evangelische Studiengemeinschaft, Heidelberg; Bd. of Trustees, Evangelische Zentralstelle für Weltanschauungsfragen, Stuttgart; Ch. Ldrship.; Bd. of Dirs., Arbeitsgemeinschaft Friedhof und Denkmal, Kassel. Publs. incl: Aufgabe und Struktur der Gemeinde heute, 1969; Solidarität mit der Welt, 1969; Akademie im Wandel, 1970; Die Bedrohung des Menschen, 1971; Das Oberrheintal—Umweltschutz und Lebensraum, 1972. Recip., D.theol., Univ. of Mainz, 1970. Address: Saalburgstrasse 52, 6382 Friedrichsdorf 1, German Fed. Repub. 43.

KÄLLENIUS, Sten Ivar Rune, b. 20 Jan. 1912. Managing Director. Educ: LL.B., Univ. of Lund, Sweden; Ct. Prac., 1937-40. Appts: Off. of Pub. Prosecutor, 1940-42; Bldg. Sect., Royal Swedish Fortifications Admin., 1943-46; Sec. Gen., Assoc. Gen. Contractors & House Builders of Sweden, 1946; Mng. Dir., ibid, 1955-; Mbr., var. govt. commns.; Mbr., Lower House, Swedish Riksdag, 1959-64. Mbr.,

Sällskapet. Publs: Byggnadsjuridik, 1958; Entreprenadjuridik, 1960; Byggnadsjuridik 2, 1965. Hons: Cmdr., Royal Order of Vasa; Order of White Rose, Finland; Gold Medal of Merit, Nat. Swedish Home Guard; Medal, Royal Patriotic Soc. Address: Box 27029, S-102 51 Stockholm, Sweden. 43.

KALPALA, Osmo (Yrjö Teuvo Pentti), b. 9 July 1925. Company President & Managing Director. Educ: Economic Studies, Commercial Coll., Helsinki, Finland. Appts: Pres., Oy Fagent Ab/Kalapalinna Oy, 1950-71; Pres., Radiotukku Oy, 1952-70; Pres., Sinipiste Oy, 1958-69; Pres., Osmo Kalpala Oy, 1971-. Mbrships. incl: Ch. Coun., Helsinki-Lauttasaari, 1963-; Lions Club, ibid; Pres., ibid, 1964-65; Lions Int.; Chmn., Dist. Govs. Coun., Multiple Dist. 107/Finland, ibid, 1969-70; Dir., Leo Club Sect., ibid, 1972-74; Coun., Lauttasaari Säättiö Fndn. & Chmn. of Bd., Lauttasaari-Seura, 1968-71; Sports Drivers Assn. of Finland; Charter Pres., ibid, 1963-67, 1968-70, 1972-73; Finnish Ski Assn. Publs. incl: Slalom Sport Handbook, 1966; articles on skiing & motor racing. Hons. incl: III. Cup Winner, Lions Int., 1969; Presl. Medal, ibid, 1970; Silver Plaque, Sport Drivers' Assn., 1963; Gold Plaque, ibid, 1970; num. awards for skiing & rally driving. Address: Hakolahdentie 33, SF-00200, Helsinki 20, Finland.

KALTOVICH, Edith Rusconi, b. 13 Dec. 1925. Professor; Writer; Translator. Educ: M.A., Mt. Holyoke Coll., Mass.; Trenton State Coll., N.J.; N.Y. Univ. Appts. incl: Engl. Tchr., DeMaria Coll., 1948-52; Lang. Asst., Mt. Holyoke Coll., 1954-56; Chmn., Spanish Dept., Westover Schl., 1956-58; Substitute Tchr., Florence Twp & Burlington Schls., 1958-67; Agt., lit. & art from Argentina & U.S.A., 1967-; Tchr., Adult Ed., Florence Mem. H.S., 1969-; Bilingual Tchr., Ulysses S. Wiggins Schl., Camden, N.J., 1971-72, & Carroll Robbins Schl., Trenton, N.J., 1972-. Mbr. & Off., acad. & profl. orgs. Publs: Romances to the Argentina Children (translation); Collect Telegrams—Poems of Urgency (translation). Num. contbns., translations & original poems & articles, var. anthols., mags., newspapers. Recip., acad. & profl. awards. Address: 129 Kinsmans Rd., Florence, NJ 08518, U.S.A. 57.

KALUSIN, Carlos, b. 15 Sept. 1908. Industrialist. Educ: H.S. & Postgrad. Appts: Gen. Mgr. & Fndr., Kalusin Importing Co. (KICO); Fndr., Talectro Ltd. & Hidromac Ltd. Mbrships: 33rd Degree Mason; Fndr. & 1st Pres., B'nai Brith Lodge; Fndr. & frequent Pres., Jewish Community; Country Club; Exec. Club; Club Barranquilla. Recip. sev. distinctions & hon. mention from Israeli Govt. Address: P.O. Box 295, Barranquilla, Colombia.

KALYANVALA, Zerina, b. 25 Jan. 1939. Advertising & Public Relations Executive. Educ: B.A., Calcutta Univ., India. Appts: Sr. Account Exec., Grant Advt. Int. Inc., 1964-67; Advt. & P.R. Mgr., Shalimar Paints Ltd., 1967-; Mbr., Advsry. Coun., Commercial Serv., All India Radio. Mbrships: Exec. Coun., Indian Soc. of Advertisers; Exec. Coun., Calcutta Chapt., P.R. Soc. of India; Governing Comm., Calcutta Schl. of Music; Tollygunge Club, Calcutta; Advt. Club, ibid; Advt., Prog. & Entertainment Comm., Calcutta Polo Club; Women's Voluntary Serv. Publs: Articles on advt. & the paint ind. Lecturer on Interior Decorating. Hons: Cert. for Best Radio Voice, Calcutta Univ., 1957. Address: Shalimar Paints Ltd., P.O. Box No. 2472, Calcutta 700001, India.

KAMALI, Sabih Ahmad, b. 1 July 1927. Teacher. Educ: M.A., LL.B., 1947, Aligarh Muslim Univ., India; M.A., Islamic Studies, 1955, Ph.D., 1959, McGill Univ., Canada. Appts: Tchr., Engl., Aligarh Muslim Univ., 1948, var. Indian colls., 1948-53; Rsch. Fellow, Inst. of Islamic Studies, McGill Univ., 1953-59; Tchr., Arabic or Islamic Studies, Calcutta Univ., 1961, Aligarh Muslim Univ., 1962-63; Univ. of Ghana, Legon, 1963-; Univ. of Abadan, Nigeria, 1967, Harvard Univ., U.S.A., 1969-70. Mbrships: Mbr., Sec. or Pres., Islamic socs. in Canada, U.S.A., Nigeria, Ghana, India; Am. Histl. Assn.; Sec., Indian Students Assn., McGill Univ.; W. African Exam. Coun. Publs: Translator, al-Ghazali's Tahafut al-Falasifah, 1958; Types of Islamic Thought, 1965; Articles in profl. jrnls., U.S.A., India, Pakistan, Nigeria, Ghana. Address: Dept. for Study of Religions, Univ. of Ghana, Legon, Accra, Ghana, W. Africa. 135.

KAMAR, Astrid Elaine Wennermark, b. 29 Nov. 1934. Toy Manufacturing Company Executive Vice President. Educ: Sawyer's Bus. Schl., 1952-53. Appts: Secretarial position, Stn. KTTV, Hollywood, Calif., 1955-56; For. Serv. of State Dept., Wash. & Kingston, Jamaica, 1956-57; Co-Fndr., Kamar, Inc., mfg. stuffed toys, Gardena, Calif., 1958; Exec. V.P., ibid, 1958-; Dir., Kamar Int., Kamar Int. S.A., Love Things & Kamar, Inc., Universal Motor Cars, Wennermark Investments, Moon Imports, Sun Imports; Co-Fndr., Jolimar, Briquedese Brindes Ltd., Lisbon, Portugal, 1972. Mbrships: Chmn., Fndr., L.A. Chapt., Valley Orthopedic Hosp. Comm., 1969-72; Bd. of Dirs., Valley Orthopedic Clin. Creator of world's first Flying Toy Showroom w. her custom-decorated D-18, 9-passenger Beechcraft tri-gear aircraft. Recip., Int. Woman of the Yr. Award, 1971. Address: 1757 Paseo del Mar, Palos Verdes Estates, CA 90274, U.S.A. 5, 138.

KAMBLY, Arnold H., Doctor of Medicine, Psychiatry. Educ: A.B., Univ. of Mich.; M.A., ibid; M.S. in Neuroanatomy; Specialty Bds. in Neurol., 1950; Am. Specialty Bds. in Psych., 1951. Appts: Mbr. of Fac., Univ. of Mich. Schl. of Med., 1952; Pvte. Prac. in Psych., 1952-; Med. Dir., The Univ. Ctr., Mich.; Med. Dir., Midwest Inst. for Individual & Grp. Treatment. Mbrships: AMA; Am. Psych. Assn.; Orthopsych. Assn.; Am. Group Psychotherapy Assn.; Int. Transactional Analysis Assn.; Tchng. Mbr., ibid, 1973; Detroit Yacht Club. Author of The ABC's of PAC: An Introduction to Transactional Analysis & of papers on adolescent psych. having to do w. acad. underachievement. Address: 1075 Country Club Rd., Ann Arbor, MI 48105, U.S.A.

KAMI, Michael John, b. 28 Dec. 1922. Management Consultant; Lecturer. Educ: B.S., MIT, Boston, Mass., 1948; Hon. L.H.D., Starr King Schl. for Min., Berkeley, Calif., 1969. M.B.A., Fla. Atlantic Univ., Boca Raton, Fla., 1970; Ed.D., ibid, 1974. Appts. incl: Corporate Dir., Long-Range Planning, Int. Bus. Machines Corp., N.Y., 1950-64; V.P. Corporate Planning, Xerox Corp., Rochester, N.Y., 1964-67; Pres., Corporate Planning, Inc., Mgmt. Cons., Lighthouse Pt., Fla., 1967-. Mbrships: Tau Beta Pi; N. Am. Soc. for Corporate Planning, Inc.; U.S. Power Squadron, Pompano Beach, Fla. Publs: Corporate Management in Crisis: Why The Mighty Fail (co-author), 1974; num. articles in Mgmt. books & jrnls. Hons: United Fund of Northern Westchester Achievement Award, 1962. Address: 2456 N.E. 26th St., Lighthouse Pt., FL 33064, U.S.A.

KAMINSKY, Alice R. Professor of English. Educ: B.A., Wash. Sq. Coll. of Arts & Sci., N.Y.

Univ., U.S.A., 1946; M.A., N.Y. Univ., 1947; Ph.D., ibid, 1952. Appts: Grad. Asst., N.Y. Univ., 1947-49; Instr., Engl., Hunter Coll., CUNY, 1952-53; Instr., Engl., Cornell Univ., Ithaca, N.Y., 1954-57 & 1959-63; Instr., Logic, Broome Community Coll., SUNY, 1958-59; Asst. Prof., Engl., State Univ. Coll., Cortland, N.Y., 1963-64; Assoc. Prof., ibid, 1964-68; Prof., 1968-74. Mbrship: MLA. Publs: George Henry Lewes as Critic, 1968; Logic: A Philosophical Introduction (w. J. Kaminsky), 1974; Ed., Literary Criticism of George Henry Lewes, 1964; Essays in profl. jrnls. & book. Address: English Dept., State University College at Cortland, Cortland, NY 13045, U.S.A.

KAMISH, Phillip, b. 17 Aug. 1925. Colonel, Dental Services, U.S. Air Force. Educ: Northwestern Univ., Chgo., Ill.; Schl. of Scis., & Schl. of Dentistry, Loyola Univ., Chgo.; Schl. of Dentistry, Loma Linda Univ., Calif.; Armed Forces Inst. of Pathol., Wash. D.C.; U.S. Army Inst. of Dental Rsch., Wash. D.C.; Wilford Hall USAF Hosp., San Antonio, Tex.; Letterman Army Hosp., San Francisco, Calif. Appts. incl: Chief, Examination & Treatment Planning Sect.; Chief, Oral Diagnosis; Asst. Base Dental Surg.; Cons. in Gen. Dentistry; Currently, Col. & Wing/Base Dental Surg., Offutt Air Force Base, Neb. Mbrships. incl: Fellow, Int. Coll. of Dentists, 1971; Fellow, Acad. of Gen. Dentistry, 1968; Am. Acad. of Oral Pathol.; Air Force Sect.; Am. Dental Assn.; Fellow, Royal Soc. for Hlth.; Alpha Sigma Nu. Contbr. of dental articles to newspapers & mil. base publs. Hons. incl: USAF Commendation Medal, Va., 1965; USAF Commendation Medal, Calif., 1968. Address: Dental Services (SGD), Ehrling Bergquist USAF Regional Hospital, Strategic Air Command, Offutt Air Force Base, NB 68113, U.S.A. 6.

KAMM, Dorinda Jan, b. 17 Oct. 1952. Author. Grand-d. of local poet, Raymond B. Snediker. Free-lance Novelist & Lectr. Mbr: Nat. Honor Soc. of Am. Publs: Cliff's Head (novel), 1971, reprinted Germany 1973; Devil's Doorstep (novel), 1972. Address: 82 New Hyde Park Rd., Franklin Sq., NY 11010, U.S.A. 30.

KAMM, Jacob O., b. 29 Nov. 1918. Economist. Educ: A.B., Baldwin-Wallace Coll., 1940; M.A., Brown Univ., 1942; Ph.D., Ohio State Univ., 1948. Appts. incl: Assoc. Prof. of Econs., Baldwin-Wallace Coll., 1946-48; Prof. of Econs. & Dir., Schl. of Commerce, ibid, 1948-53; V.P.-Chmn. & Chief Exec. Off., Cleveland Quarries Co., 1953-; Finance & Treas.-Pres., Am. Ship Bldg. Co., 1967-; Dir., ibid, Baldwin Corp., Cardinal Fed. Savings & Loan Assn., Cleveland Quarries Co., Fairmont Foods Co., A.W. Fenton Co. Inc., Nordson Corp., Oatey Co. & United Screw & Bolt Co. Mbrships. incl: Pres. & Chmn., Exec. Comm., 1960-61, Exec. Comm., 1959-61, Ind. Assn. of N. Ctrl. Ohio; Trustee, 1968-, Exec. Comm., 1970-, Ohio Mfrs. Assn.; Hon. Mbr., Mental Hlth. Comm., 1964-69; Brown Univ. Club, N.Y.C.; Union Club, Cleveland, Ohio; Am. Fin. Assn.; Am. Econs. Assn.; Royal Econ. Soc.; AAUP; Beta Gamma Sigma; Delta Mu Delta. Publs. incl: Decentralization of Securities Exchanges, 1942; Introduction to Modern Economics (co-author), 1950; Essays in Finance (co-author), 1953; Economics of Investment, 1951; Making Profits in the Stock Market, 1952 (rev. 1959, 61 & 66); Investor's Handbook, 1954; contbr. An Economist's View column to The Plain Dealer, 1964-68, num. articles to fin. jrnls. Contbng. Ed., Webster's New World Dictionary of the Am. Lang. Hons. incl: LL.D., Baldwin-Wallace Coll., 1963, Erskine Coll., 1971; Wisdom Award of Hon.,

1970. Address: Route 1, Huron, OH 44839, U.S.A. 2, 12, 13, 14, 16, 28, 30, 123, 128, 130.

KAMM, Josephine Mary (Mrs.). Author. Admnstve. & journalistic appts., Min. of Info., 1939-46. Mbrships: Past Exec. Comm., Engl. Ctr., Int. PEN; Past Nat. Coun. & Exec. Gomm., Nat. Book League; Dpty.-Chmn., Comm. of Mgmt., Fawcett Lib. Publs. incl: How Different From Us; Daughter of the Desert; Hope Deferred; Rapiers & Battleaxes; Indicative Past; 20 books for young people inclng: The Story of Mrs. Pankhurst; The Story of Fanny Burney; A New Look at the Old Testament; The Hebrew People. Recip. of Isaac Siegel Mem. Juvenile Award for "Return to Freedom", 1963. Address: 39/67 Elm Park Gardens, London, SW10 9QE, U.K.

KAMPMANN, (Olfert) Viggo (Fischer), b. 21 July 1910. Politician. Educ: Grad., Pol. Econ., Univ. of Copenhagen, Denmark. Appts. incl: Nat. Bur. of Stats., 1933-44; Asst. Hd., Govt. Comm. on Employment, 1944-46; Hd., Govt. Econ. Secretariat, 1947-50; Pres., Mortgage Bank of Denmark, 1950-53; Prime Min. & Chancellor of Denmark, 1950, 1953-60 & 1960-62. Mbrships. incl: Nat. Life Ins. Co., (Bd., 1950-53, Pres., 1962-); K.A.B. building Soc., (Vice Pres. 1963). Publs: En route, 1960; The Socialist Society, 1967; Economic democracy, 1970; My former Life, 1971; The population explosion, 1972; Power and Dispower, 1973; Six social-democratic prime ministers, written by the seventh, 1973; contbr. to num. profl. jrnls. Hons: Tourist medal, 1961, Hans Knudsen medal, 1969. Address: Vejbo, St. Thorøie, 4640, Fakse, Denmark. 12, 128.

KANAGARATNAM, Sinnappu, b. 4 Sept. 1916. Corporate Executive. Educ: B.A., Ceylon Univ., 1940. Appts: Audit Asst., Turquand, Young & Co., Chartered Accts., 1947; Sec./Acct., Lewis Brown & Co. Ltd., 1947-54; Sr. Acct., Gal Oya Dev. Bd., 1954-56; Sec./Acct., Dev. Finance Corp. of Ceylon, 1956, Asst. Gen. Mgr. (Admin.), 1967, Gen. Mgr., Dir., & Chief Exec., 1972-. Address: Development Finance Corporation of Ceylon, P.O. Box 1397, Colombo 7, Sri Lanka, Ceylon.

KANDALLA, Fuad Abdul-Karim, b. 5 Oct. 1905. Cardiologist; Physician; Surgeon. Educ: M.D., Am. Univ. of Beirut, Lebanon, 1937; French State Bd. Exam. Licence, 1937; London Univ. State Bd. Exam. Dip., U.K., 1938; Appts. incl: Pvte. Clin. Work, 1938-72; Fndr. & Owner, Special Lib., Containing about 4000 vols. & num. med. jrnls.; w. Fertility Clin., London, 1938; Ven. Diseases, St. Thomas Hosp., 1938; Cardiovascular Diseases, Mass. Gen. Hosp., Harvard Univ., U.S.A., 1947-48. Fellow, Royal Soc. Trop. Med. & Hygiene, U.K., 1937; Royal Soc. Med., 1961. Mbrships. incl: VI World Congress Cardiol., London, 1970; 8th European Congress Ballistocardiol., Yugoslavia, 1971; F.I.B.A. Author of num. reports & papers presented to int. & nat. sci. Congresses. Broadcaster, Baghdad Broadcasting Stn. Address: P.O. Box 982 Beirut, Lebanon. 107.

KANDELL, Alice Susan, b. 6 Nov. 1938. Clinical Psychologist; Professional Photographer; Author. Educ: B.A., Sarah Lawrence Coll., Bronxville, N.Y., U.S.A., 1960; Ph.D. in Psychol., Harvard Univ., 1967. Appts: Rsch. Psychologist, Jewish Bd. of Guardians, 1963-66; Clin. Psychologist & Asst. in Psychiatry (Psychol.), Schl. of Med., Mt. Sinai Hosp., N.Y., 1968-71. Publs: Sikkim: The Hidden Kingdom, 1971; Mountaintop Kingdom: Sikkim (w. C. Salisbury), 1971.

Address: 11 E. 68th St., N.Y., NY 10021, U.S.A.

KANE, (Hon.) Edward William Scott, b. 29 Apr. 1899. Judge. Educ: B.A., Univ. of Alta., Canada, 1920; LL.B., ibid, 1922. Appts: Served as Cadet, R.A.F., WW I; Called to Bar of Alta., 1922; Justice, Appellate Div., Supreme Ct. of Alta, 1961-; Ex-officio Mbr., Trial Div., ibid, 1961-; Mbrships. incl: Advsry. Bd., Salvation Army, Edmonton, Alta.; Edmonton Gen. Hosp.; Chmn., Alta. Rhodes Schol. Selection Comm.; Edmonton Bar Assn.; Pres., ibid, 1935-36; Law Soc. of Alta.; Sec,-Treas. & Solicitor, ibid, 1938-52; Bencher, ibid, 1954-61; V.P., ibid, 1959-61; Dependents Advsry Bd., Edmonton, WW II; Past-mbr., Bd. of Stewards, Robertson United Ch., Edmonton; The Edmonton Club; Dir., Mayfair Golf & Country Club. Address: 11603 Edinboro Rd., Edmonton, Alta., Canada.

KANE, Hugh Carlton, b. 2 Sept. 1917. Psychologist; Educator. Educ: B.A., Adrian Coll., Mich., U.S.A., 1942; M.S., Univ. of Southern Calif., L.A., 1953; Ph.D., Laurence Univ., Sarasota, Fla., 1972. Appts. incl: Neuro-Psychiatric Staff, USN, WWII; Pub. Schl. Tchr., Elem. & Special Educ., 1949-68; Assoc. Prof., Educ., & Supvsr., Prac. Tchrs., Mansfield State Coll., Pa., 1968-70; Lectr., Psychol., Ext. Div., Univ. Coll. of Oswego, N.Y., 1971-72; Assoc. Psychologist, Reception Ctr., N.Y. State Dept. of Mental Hygiene, Elmira, N.Y., 1970-. Mbrships: NEA; N.Y. State Tchrs. Assn. of Tchrs. of Handicapped; Pa. Coun. for Exceptional Children; Pa. State Educ. Assn. Contbr., num. poems in mags. & newspapers. Recip., 32-degree Mason, 1970. Address: RD# 2, Gillett, PA 16925, U.S.A.

KANE, Michael M., b. 10 Mar. 1922. International Consultant Architect-Planner. Educ: Bachelor of Interior Design, Univ. of Mich., 1943, B. of Arch., ibid, 1949; postgrad., Western Reserve Univ., 1946, Case Inst. Technol., 1946, '60, La Sorbonne, Ecole du Louvre, Scola Cantorum, Paris, France, 1960-61. Appts. incl: Prin., Michael M. Kane & Assocs., archts., Cleveland & Lorain, Ohio, Buena Pk., Calif., 1950-62; Arch. Advsr. Cons., AID Dept. of State, 1962-63; Regional Archt., Ctrl. Am. & Panama, Am. Inst. Free Labor Dev., 1964-68; Dev. Advsr. to Pres., Queensborough Community Coll., CUNY, 1968-71; Prin., Michael M. Kane, AIA, Christiansted, St. Croix, V.I., 1972-. Mbr., var. profl. orgs. Contbr., articles, profl. jrns. Recip., var. awards. Address: 348 King St., Christiansted, St. Crois, VI 00820, U.S.A. 2.

KANE, Philip Francis, b. 1 Dec. 1920. Chemist. Educ: B.Sc., London Univ., 1948. Appts: Techn., Standard Telephones & Cables Ltd., London, U.K., 1938-48; Rsch. Chemist, Laporte Chems. Ltd., Luton, U.K., 1948-52; Chief Analyst, ibid, 1952-57; Lab. Supvsr., Chemagro Corp., Kan. City, Mo., U.S.A. 1957-59; Lab. Dir., Tex. Instruments Inc., Dallas, Tex., 1959-. Mbrships: Chem. Soc., London; Fellow, Royal Inst. of Chem.; Past Pres., N. Tex. Sect., Chmn., Nat. meeting 1972, Soc. for Applied Spectroscopy; Past Chmn., Dallas Soc. of Analytical Chemists. Publs: Characterization of Semiconductor Materials (co-author), 1970; Characterization of Solid Surfaces (co-ed), 1974. Contbr. to var. sci. jrnls. & publs. Recip., Award, Dallas Soc. of Analytical Chemists, 1967. Address: Tex. Instruments Inc., P.O. Box 5936, M.S. 147, Dallas, TX 75222, U.S.A. 7, 14, 125.

KANE, (Rev.) Thomas Aquinas, b. 30 Nov. 1940. Psychologist; Clergyman. Educ: B.A., St.

Edward's Univ., Austin, Tex., 1962; M.A., Spanish, Nat. Univ. of Mexico, 1964; M.A., Psychol., Rutgers Univ., New Brunswick, N.J., 1966; M.A., Educ., St. Bonaventure Univ., Olean, N.Y., 1968; S.T.M., Boston Univ., Mass., 1970; Ph.D., Psychol., Univ. of Birmingham, U.K., 1973. Appts: Ordained Roman Cath. priest, 1969; Educator, Parochial Schls., N.Y.C.; Therapist, N.Y. State Div. of Youth, 1967-69; Therapist, The Ledges Schl. for Exceptional Children, 1967-71; Psychologist, Boston State Hosp., 1969-70; Pastor, St. Mary's Ch., Uxbridge, Mass., 1970-71; Fndr., Clin. Dir., Cons. Ctr. for Clergy & Religious, 1971-; Therapist, Elliot House Probation Hostel, Birmingham, U.K., 1972-73; Fndr., Exec. Dir., House of Affirmation, Int. Therapeutic Ctr. for Clergy & Religious, Whitinsville. Mass., 1973; Cons., Vatican, 1972-73. Mbrships: Am. & British Psychol. Assns.; Am. Assn. Mental Deficiency; var. profl. orgs. Publs: Existential Influences in Psychopathology of the Religious Professional, 1972; The Medical Theological Dialogue, 1973; Identity & Social Change, 1973; contbr. to num. theol., educl., & psychol. jrnls. Hons: Outstanding Young Ldr., Worcester, Mass., 1972; Wall St. Jrnl. Fellow, 1964. Address: House of Affirmation, Int. Therapeutic Ctr. for Clergy & Religious, 120 Hill St., Whitinsville, MA 01588, U.S.A. 6.

KANFER, Irma (pen-name, Irène Kanfer). Writer. Educ: var. univs., Warsaw, Geneva, Paris; B.A. Appts: Jrnlst.; Lit. & Art Critic; Translater, books & articles; Poet & Short-Story Writer. Poetry Collects. & other publs. incl: Les Deux accords; Sur la Voie Luctée; le Sablier Endormi; Poland (A study, for French Info. Off.); Le Luth Brisé (1st French anthol. of Ghetto poems, translations from Polish & Yiddish), 2 edits.; Ombre du Soleil; Contes du Milieu de la Nuit (Stories). Hons: 2nd Prize, Decouverte-Poesie, 1962; Prix Guillaume Apollineire, 1966; Prize, Decouverte-Prose, 1972. Address: 35 Ave. Gabriel Péri, 94300 Vincennes, France. 55.

KANGWAMU, Frederick J.I., b. 24 Dec. 1931. School Teacher; Business Executive. Educ: Secondary Standards, Kitabi Sem.; Tchr., St. George's T.T.C., Ibanda, & Kyambogo Nat. T.T.C. Appts: Hd., var. primary schls., Ankole Dist., 1952-56; Hd., Ibanda Secondary Schl. 1958-60; M.P., 1961-64; Hd., var. schls., 1964-73; Mng. Dir., Mugisha Trading Co. (U) Ltd., 1973-. Mbrships: Treas., Ankole Br., Uganda Tchrs. Assn.; Treas., Ankole Culture Comm.; Mbr., Bd. of Govs., var. secondary schls & tchr. trng. colls. Address: P.O. Box 37, Mbarara, Uganda, E. Africa. 89.

KANIGOWSKI, Walter W., b. 7 Oct. 1924. Aquatic Director. Educ: B.A., La Salle Coll.; M.A., Villanova Univ. Appts. incl: Owner, Kanigowski Schl. of Swimming, Riverside, N.J.; Water Safety Chmn., Burlington Chapt., ARC, 1947-; Dir. & Fndg. Mbr., 1972 Schls., Del. Valley Safety Servs. Inst.; Dean, Water Safety Sect., DUSP 11; Instr., Trnr., ARC; Fa. Mbr., Am. Red Cross Nat. Aquatic Schls.; Chmn., Annual Workshop, N.J. Schl. Bds. Assn., 1972; Dir., Del. Valley Safety Progs. Inst., 1972, 1973, 1974. Mbrships: Pres., Bd. of Educ., Riverside, 3 yrs.; Bd. of Dirs., Educ. Improvement Ctr. N.J.; Co-Chmn., Annual Workshop, Mbr., Finance Comm. & Special Educ. Comm., N.J. Schl. Bds. Assn.; Burlington Schl. Bds. Assn.; Commodore Longfellow Soc.; Riverside Post 146, Am. Legion; Chmn., Burlington Co. Chapt., Am. Red Cross, 1970, 1971, 1972, 1973. Hons: Nat. Red Cross Safety Servs. Medal, 1974. Address: 116 Monroe St., Riverside, NJ 08075, U.S.A. 129, 130, 139.

KANISTRAS, Photios, b. 14 Nov. 1900. General Inspector of Education. Educ: Univ. of Athens, Greece. Appts: Prof., 1924-43; Dir. of Gymnasium, 1943-51; General Insp. of Educ., 1951-. Mbrships: Union of Greek Philologists; Sci. Soc.; Soc. of Friends of Letters. Author of notes & translation of Horace's "Carmina". Recip. of mil. medal. Address: Alkamenous Street 158, Athens, Greece, TT220.

KANTABUTRA, Bundhit, b. 23 Oct. 1916. Actuary & Statistician. Educ: B.S.B.A., Far Eastern Univ., Manila, 1937; M.S., Univ. of the Philippines, 1938; M.B.A., Univ. of Chicago, Ill., 1940; var.grad. courses. Appts: Dir., Ctrl. Statistical Servs., 1960-63; Dir.Gen., Nat. Stat.Servs., 1964-70; Chmn. & Prof. of Stats., Stats.Dept., Chulalongkorn Univ., 1955-70; Cons.Actuary & Statn. (pvte.pract.) 1970-. Mbrships: Fellow, Am.Statl.Assn.; Hon., Life Ins.Assn. of Thailand; Int.Stat Inst., The Hague, Netherlands; V.P., Bangkok Mus. Grp., 1967-70; Pres. Thai Statl. Assn., 1974-76. Publs: Thai Life Tables, 1947; The Economic & National Income of Thailand, 1957; Life Insurance in Thailand, 1972. Recip., Prim Min. Pibun Songgram Disting. Serv. Award, 1953. Address: Kantabutra & Kantabutra, Sibunruang Bldg. No. 2, 1/7 Convent Rd., Bangkok Metropolis, Thailand.

KANTSO, Jens, b. 26 July 1935. Painter. Educ: Studies in Oslo, Norway; Stockholm, Sweden; Zurich, Switzerland; Paris, France. Exhibs: Début, Copenhagen, Denmark, 1961; Copenhagen, 1964, 1966, 1968, 1970; Den Permanente, ibid, 1972, 1973; Århus, Denmark, 1963, 1966, 1968; Silkeborg, Denmark, 1971, 1972, 1973; Esbjerg, Denmark, 1971, 1972; Athens, Greece, 1964; Gothenburg, Sweden, 1966; Florence, Italy, 1970; Husquarna, Sweden, 1973; 15th & 16th Internationale, N.Y.C., U.S.A., 1972 & 1973. Represented in Danish Min. of Culture, The Carlsberg Fndn. & in Art Collections in Denmark, Sweden, Germany, Greece, U.S.A. & Canada. Wall painting 100 metres square, Slagelse, Denmark, 1970. Schlrship., The Tuborg Fndn. Address: Garvergårdsvej 27, 4200 Slagelse, Denmark.

KANWAR, Mahfooz A. Teacher. Educ: B.A., M.A., Univ. of Punjab, Lahore; M.A., Univ. of Waterloo, Ont., Univ. of Alta., Univ. of Tex., El Paso. Appts. incl: Asst. to Prof., Conrad Grebel Coll., Univ. of Waterloo, 1968-69; Instr., Mt. Royal Coll., Calgary, Alta., 1969-. Mbrships. incl: Am. Sociological Assn.; Canadian Assn. Sociol. & Anthropol.; Pakistan Sociological Assn.; Int. Fedn. of Insts. for Soc. & Socio-Religious Rsch. Publs. incl: Sociology of Family: An Interdisciplinary Approach (ed.), 1971; Sociology of Criminal Behavior (ed.), 1972; Sociology of Religion: Changing Conceptions in the Structure of Islam, 1973. Num. monographs, papers, articles in field. Recip. of Ont. Grad. Fellowship, 1967-69. Address: Dept. of Sociology, Mt. Royal Coll., Lincoln Park Campus, Calgary, Alta., T3E 6K6, Canada.

KAPACINSKAS, Joseph, b. 20 Oct. 1907. Engineer. Educ: Grad., Allied Inst. of Technol., Chgo., Ill., 1960; Dip., Bachelor of Tool Engrng. Appts: w. City Kaunas Transit Authority, Lithuania, 1929-30; Electn., Nat. Railroad, ibid, 1939-44; w. Nat. Railroad, Treuchtlingen, Germany, 1944-45; Instr. in Motor Dr. Course & Chief Electn., UN Relief & Rehab. Admin., Weissenburg, ibid, 1946-47; Electn., C.B. & Q.R.R., now Burlington Northern Inc., U.S.A., 1951-72. Mbrships. incl: Chgo. Sect., Lithuanian Engrs. & Archts. Assn.;

Sec., Chgo. Sect., Lithuanian Jrnlst. Assn.; AAAS, 1961-68; Am. Soc. of Tool & Mfg. Engrs., 1959-68. Publs: Siaubingos Dienos—Horrifying Days, 1965; Išeivio Dalia—Emigrant's Fate, 1974. Contbr., Lithuanian papers. Address: 6811 S. Maplewood Ave., Chgo., IL 60629, U.S.A.

KAPELINSKI, Franciszek Jozef, b. 24 Dec. 1914. Linguist, University Senior Lecturer. Educ: Liceum T. Chalubinskiego, Radom & Univ. of Warsaw, Poland; Mag.Pr., Warsaw, 1936; Cert. de Dr. Français, Paris, France, Dipl. d'ét.fr., Bordeaux-Toulouse-Pau, France. Appts. incl: Diplomatic Serv., Poland; War Serv., Polish Army, 1939-45; Tchr. & Hdmaster., Polish Sec. Schl.; Insp., Engl. Lang. Tchng.; Lectr., U.K., 1958; Lectr., Engl., Nigerian Coll. of Arts, Sci. & Technol., Zaria, Nigeria, 1958-62; Lectr., Engl., Ahmadu Bello Univ., ibid, 1962-64, Lectr., French, 1964, Sr. Lectr., 1965, Acting Hd., Dept. of Langs., 1965-69. Mbrships. incl: Asst. Sec., Fed. Int. des Langues et Lits. Mod.; Soc. de Linguistique Romane; Assn. Int. des Études Françaises; Assn. Int. de Lit. Comparée; Int. Assn. of Tchrs. of Engl. as a For. Lang.; Histl. Soc. of Nigeria; Assn. of Polish Univ. Profs. & Lectrs. Abroad. Publs. incl: Observations on Phonetic Interference in Learning English and French in Nigeria; Teaching English at Short Intensive Courses; Sev. books in French & Polish. Hons. incl: Chevalier des Palmes Académiques, 1970; Defence & War Medals, 1939-45. Address: Ahmadu Bello Univ., Zaria, Nigeria. 135.

KAPFER, Miriam Bierbaum, b. 8 May 1935. Educator; Educational Researcher. Educ: B.Mus.Ed., Drake Univ., U.S.A., 1956; M.Mus.Ed., Univ. of Kan., 1958; Postgrad. study, Univ. of Aberdeen, U.K.; Ph.D., Ohio State Univ., 1964. Appts: Instr., Tchr., var. colls., Schls., Neb., Kan., Ohio, 1958-64; Tchr., Music & Engl., Libn. & Rsch. Specialist, Clark Co. Schl. Dist., Las Vegas, Nev., 1964-70; Curric. & Publs. Specialist, Ctr. to Improve Learning & Instrn., Univ. of Utah, 1970-73; Co-Dir., Life-Involvement Model Proj., Bur. of Educl. Rsch., ibid, 1973-. Mbrships. incl: Past Pres., Omega Chapt. Mu Phi Epsilon; Alpha Lambda Delta; Pi Kappa Lambda; Pi Lambda Theta; Past State V.P., var. other offs., Nev. Music Educators Assn. & Mbr., State Certification Bd., 2 yrs.; Life, Music Educators Nat. Conf.; Am. Educl. Rsch. Assn.; Luth. Ch.-Mo. Synod. Publs. incl: Behavioral Objectives in Curriculum Development, 1971; Learning Packages in American Education, 1972. Also Ed., Nevada Notes, Educl. Rsch. Reports, & contbr. to num. jrnls. Recip. sev. awards & schlrships. Address: 4344 Pin Oak St., Salt Lake City, UT 84117, U.S.A. 5, 30. 138.

KAPFER, Philip Gordon, b. 4 July 1936. Educator; Educational Researcher. Educ: B.A., Univ. of Northern Iowa, 1958; M.A., ibid, 1959; Postgrad. study, Southwestern Coll., 1960-61; Ph.D., Ohio State Univ., 1964; Postgrad. study, Univ. of Nev., Las Vegas, 1968-70. Appts. incl: Tchng. Asst., Chem., Ohio State Univ., Columbus, 1961-64; Chem. & Physics Tchr., H.S. Curric. & Rsch. Cons., Elem. Schl. Rsch. & Dissemination Specialist, E.S.E.A. Title III Proj. Dir., Clark Co. Schl. Dist., Las Vegas, Nev., 1964-70; Assoc. Prof., Assoc. Dir. & Dir., Life-Involvement Model Proj., Bur. of Educl. Rsch., Univ. of Utah, 1970-; Cons. to over 100 univs., pub. schl. dists. & state-wide & regional projs., 1966-. Mbrships: Assn. for Supvsn. & Curric. Dev.; Am. Educl. Rsch. Assn.; Phi Delta Kappa; Life mbr., Nat. Sci. Tchrs. Assn.; Life mbr., NEA; Mo. Synod, Luth. Ch. Author of publs. in field. Recip. of hons. Address: 4344 Pin Oak St., Salt Lake City, UT 84117, U.S.A. 30, 117.

KAPLAN, David Joseph, b. 9 July 1909. Company Chairman. Educ: Omaha Pub. Schls. Bd. Chmn., Fndr., Blue Star Foods, Inc., 1935-. Mbrships: Nat. Poultry Hall of Fame; Gen. Chmn., Fund Raising Campaign, Mercy Hosp., Council Bluffs; Lay Bd. Mbr., Omaha Archdiocese Educ. Fund Dr.; Chmn. & Originator of Bd. of Trustees, Mercy Hosp.; Chmn. of Bd., Des Moines Diocese Fund Dr.; Pres., Christian Home, Council Bluffs, 1971; Bd. Trustees, City of Hope; Chmn., Advsry. Bd., St. Albert Cath. H.S., 1971; Coun., Boy Scouts of Am.; Wisdom Hall of Fame; Div. Dir., Equestrian Order of the Holy Sepulchre; Past Lay Bd., St. Joseph Hosp.; Past Bd., St. Mary's Coll.; Past Bd. Dirs., St. Jospeh Orphanage, Wyo.; Council Bluffs Chmbr. of Comm.; Kts. of Columbus; Past Pres., Council Bluffs Co. Club; Elks. Hons. incl: Kt. of Holy Sepulchre, 1951; Kt. Cmdr. in Equestrian Order of Holy Sepulchre, 1952; Kt. w. Stars & Grand Cross, ibid, 1955; Coronet Medal, St. Edward's Univ., Austin, Tex.; Am. Award, Council Bluffs B'Nai B'rith Lodge, 1967; City of Hope Humanitarian Award, 1970; Pvte. Audience w. H.H. Pope Paul VI, 1972; J.G. Lemen Humanitarian Award for dedicated serv. to children, 1966-72. Address: Christian Home of Council Bluffs, IA 51501, U.S.A. 8, 16, 120, 130, 131.

KAPLAN, Frederick Israel. Historian. Educ: B.A., Univ. of Calif., Berkeley, 1942; M.A., ibid, 1947; Ph.D., 1957. Appts: Exchange Schlr., Moscow Univ., U.S.S.R., 1960-61; Travelling Rsch. Fellow, Rsch. Prog. on Hist. of CPSU, Columbia Univ.; Instr., Asst. Prof.-Prof. of Hist., Mich. State Univ. Mbrships: Am. Histl. Assn.; Am. Assn. for Advancement of Slavic Studies; Assn. for Asian Studies; Popular Culture Assn. Author, Bolshevik Ideology & the Ethics of Soviet Labor, 1968. Contbr., articles, histl. subjects, var. publs., inclng. Am. Slavic & E. European Review. Address: Department of Humanities, Michigan State University, E. Lansing, MI 48823, U.S.A. 13, 30.

KAPLAN, Judith Helene Letich, b. 20 July 1938. Administrator; Executive. Educ: B.A., Hunter Coll., 1960. Appts: Pres., Tipex Inc., Holliswood, N.Y., 1965-; Life Underwriter, N.Y. Life Ins., 1964-69; Registered Rep., Scheinman Hochstin & Trotta, N.Y., Brokerage Firm, 1969-70; V.P., Alpha Capital Corp., N.Y., Financial Holding Co., 1970-73; Pres. & Chairperson, Utopia Recreation Corp., N.Y.C., Pre-schls. & day camp, 1971-. Mbrships: Coord., Image Comm., Nat. Org. for Women, N.Y.; Legislative Chairperson, AAUW, Queens, N.Y.; Nat. Women's Pol. Caucauses; Trustee, Kaplan Charitable Fndn., N.Y., 1970-73. Author of articles in Majority Report, N.Y.C. Hon: Women's Ldrs. Round Table, 1966. Address: 86-55 Santiago St., Holliswood, NY 11423, U.S.A. 5, 138.

KAPLAN, Mortimer, b. 15 Mar. 1913. Consulting Economist; Actuary. Educ: B.A., Harvard Coll., Mass., 1936; M.A., Columbia Univ., 1937; U.S. Naval Postgrad. Schl., Monterey, Calif., 1965; Appts. incl: Actuarial Expert Witness, U.S. Congressional Comms.; Advsr., Off. of Sci. & Technol., Exec. Off. of Pres., U.S.; Cons. Economist & Actuary, 1969-; Economist & Actuary, U.S. Off. Price Admin., 1942-43, Fed. Housing Admin., 1947-50; Assoc. Chief Actuary, ibid, 1950-61, Chief Actuary, 1961-69. Mbrships. incl: Fellow, Conf. of Actuaries in Pub. Prac.; Lambda Alpha. Publs. incl: Ed., Essays in the Theory of Risk & Insurance, 1968; Contbr. to Earthquake

Hazard Reduction; num. profl. articles. Recip., num. hons. inclng. Superior Sustained Performance Award, Fed. Housing Admin., 1955. Address: 472 Chestnut St., Springfield, MA 01107, U.S.A. 6, 7, 14.

KAPLAN, Samuel I., b. 15 Aug. 1909. Oral & Maxillofacial Surgeon. Educ: B.S., Univ. of Pitts., 1933; D.D.S., Dental Schl., ibid, 1933; Postgrad., Yale, 1946; Grad. Study Soc., Histol. & Pathol., 1948. Appts: Chief, Dental Dept., Mt. Sinai Hosp., 1947-72; Cons., Oral Surg., Middlesex Hosp., 1947-; Sec., Med. Staff, Mt. Sinai Hosp., 1954, 1957, 1958; Supvsng. Oral Surg., Intern Prog., Fones Schl. of Hygiene, 1962-. Mbrships. incl: Sec., Hartford Chapt., Alpha Omega, 1946; Pres., Conn. Soc. of Oral Surgs., 1948; Hartford Dental Soc.; Conn. State Dental Soc.; Am. Dental Soc.; Am. Soc. of Oral Surgs.; Int. Soc. of Oral Surgs.; Am. Soc. for Advancement of Gen. Anesthesia in Dentistry; Am. Dental Soc. of Anesthesiol.; Am. Jewish Congress. Author of 4 articles in med. jrnls. Recip., Alpha Omega Recognition Award, 1972. Address: 100 Constitution Plaza, Hartford, CT 06103, U.S.A.

KAPNOVKÁYAS, Christos, b. 21 Nov. 1901. Professor. Educ: Univ. of Athens; Univ. of Berlin, Germany; Ph.D., Univ. of Leipzig. ibid, 1930. Appts: Tchr., Trapantzion Gymnasion, Siatista, 1924-26; Lectr., Univ. of Athens, 1931-37; Extraordinarius Prof. of Latin Studies, ibid, 1937-39; Ordinarius Prof., 1939-. Mbrships: Kritiker Collaborator, Deutsche Literaturzeitung; Sci. Soc. Athens; Soc. Byzantinische Studies. Author of num. publs. Address: Siatista, Kosánis, Macedonia, Greece.

KAPP, Dorothy (Mrs. Louis Kapp), b. 14 Aug. 1910. Organist; Pianist; Music Teacher. Educ: Grad., Sherwood Music Schl., Chgo.; special courses, music theory, vocal tchng., playing & tchng. ch. music., Univ. of Evansville, Ind. Appts: Pianist & Organist, radio progs., 25 yrs.; Ch. Organist & Choir Dir.; Music Contests Judge, Ind. State Coll., Evansville, 1968-. Tchr. of dancing; Tchr., organ, piano, & singing, Va., Fla., Ind., Ky., 1929-; Dir., World's Largest Organ Concert, 1966, 1967. Mbrships. incl: Organizer & Pres., Lincoln Trail Organ Club, Tell City, Ind., 1967; Pres., Coterie Club, 2 yrs.; V.P., Nat. Fedn. of Music Clubs, Dist. 8; Organ & Piano Tchrs. Assn.; Am. Coll. of Musicians. Hons. incl: 2 Organ Schlrships; Cert. of Merit, youth & ch. work in music. Address: 819 Reuben St., Tell City, IN 47586, U.S.A.

KAPPELER, Franz, b. 7 Apr. 1898. Ambassador. Educ: studies in law & pol econ., Zurich, Geneva, Berne. Appts: Tribunal practice, Aurich & Horgan; Fed. Pol. Dept., Berne, 1926; Counsellor, Swiss Legation, Berlin, Germany, 1936; Chief of Finance Sect. Pol. Dept., mbr. of financial & econ. commns. & deleg. at num. int. negotiations, 1944; Min. to Lebanon, Syria, Iraq, 1950; Min. to Jordan, 1951; Min. to S. Africa, 1956; Ambassador, ibid, 1960; Ambassador to Madagascar, 1961. Chmn., Solidaritätsfonds der Auslandschweiz, 1966-73. Address: Gartenstrasse 14, CH 3074 Muri/Be, Switzerland.

KARAFYLLAKIS, Antonios Leonedas, b. 17 Apr. 1908. Painter; Sculptor. Educ: Grad., Schl. of Fine Art, Nat. Tech. Univ. of Athens, Greece, 1934. Appts: Prof. of Art, & Dir., Fine Arts, Rhodes, 1945-50; Pvte. Prac. as Artist, 1950-; Owner, El Greco Art Gall. & Art Schl., Wash. D.C., U.S.A., 1960-. Mbrships: Royal Art Soc., Australia; Am. Art Soc.; Am. Art League; Wash. Landscape Club. Paintings incl: Perth View, Calgoolie Pub. Mus., Australia; The Three Hundred Spartans, Nat. Picture Gall. &

Alexander Soutzo's Mus., Athens; Portraits of A. Diacos, Mayor of Rhodes, Admiral Ioanidis, Gov. of Dodecanese, & Patriarch Timotheos, Jerusalem. Recip., num. prizes for paintings at exhibs. in Greece & sev. cities in U.S.A. Address: El Greco Art Gallery, 1717 Connecticut Ave., N.W., Washington, DC 20009, U.S.A. 105, 133.

KARAILA (previously Gustafson), Erkki Hugo K., b. 29 June 1913. Chief Physician. Educ: M.D., 1943. Appts: Rural Physn., Finland, 1945-50; Sanatorial Physn., ibid, 1950-65; Chief Physn., ibid, 1965-. Mbrships: Finnish Med. Fedn.; Duodecim Med. Soc.; Rotary Club of Hyvinkää. Publs. incl: On the Possibility of Staining the Tubercle Bacillus Using Surface-active Agents; On the Risk of Infection in a Sanatorium for Pulmonary Tuberculosis; On the Combined Effect of Certain Surface-active Agents & Antibiotics. Hons: Liberty Cross 4, 1940; Liberty Cross 4 w. Oak leaves, 1941; Med. Capt., 1962. Address: 05250 Kiljava, Finland. 43.

KARAS, Mieczyslaw, b. 10 Feb. 1924. University Professor. Educ: Grad. in Polish & Slavonic linguistics, Jegellonian Univ., Cracow, Poland. Appts: Hd., Polish Philol. Dept., Jagellonian Univ.; Vice-Chancellor, ibid, 1972-; Hd., works on Atlas & Dictionary of Polish Dialects, 1957-. Mbrships: Int. Comm. on Onomastic Sci.; Int. Comm. of Slavists. Publs: Polish Dialects of Orave, 1965; Place Names of the Type Podgora, Zalas, 1965; Toponymie des iles elaphiques (sur l'Adriatique), 1968; Mary Atlas Swar Polsluch, tom 1-13, 1957-70. Recip., Polish State Prize, 1972. Address: Kochanowskiego 11 15, Cracow, Poland.

KARATZENIS, Christos, b. 28 Mar. 1900. Major General. Educ: Grad. Maths., Athens Univ., Greece; D.S., Univ. of Sorbonne, Paris, France. Appts: 2nd Lt. Artillery-Major Gen., Greek Army, 1920-52; Retired from Army, 1953; Prof. Higher Maths., Schl. of Evelpides & Polytech. Schl. of Engrs., Athens, 1933-39; Town-Major, Garrisons Jerusalem & Cairo, 1942-44; Dir. var. Brs. & Sects., Gen. Staff Greek Army & Gen. Staff Nat. Defence, & Sec. Gen. War, Supreme Coun. of Greece, 1945-52; Mbr., Greek Delegation, Paris Peace Conf., 1946; Dir. Gen. Prime Min.'s Pol. Bur., 1953-55. Mbrships. incl: Lit. Assn. Parnassos. Publs. incl: Eléments de Géométrie Analytique; Eléments de Calcul Différentiel & Intégral; Eléments de Mécanique Appliquée. Hons. incl: Num. Orders of Chivalry, Greece, France, Belgium, Netherlands, Yugoslavia, Italy, German Fed. Repub.; Medal of Vatican, 1953; Recip. num. Mil. Hons. Address: 12 Aigheos St. 12, Athens (201), Greece.

KARCHER, Henri, b. 26 Oct. 1908. Surgeon. Educ: Fac. of Med., Paris, France. Appts: Physn., Surg., Paris, 1939-; Volunteered for Infantry, 1940; Joined Free French Forces of Gen. de Gaulle, 1940; took part in 13 mil. campaigns; Hd., Detachment which took the German gov. of Paris prisoner, 1944; Retd. from mil. as Col.; Deleg. to Nat. Assembly from Paris, 1958-62, Moselle, 1962-67; Gen. Councillor, Sarrebourg, 1962-67; V.P., Nat. Assembly, 1962-64; Expert, Paris Cts. Mbrships: French Soc. of Bone & Orthopedic Surg.; Bd. of Dirs., Assn. of Free French; Admin. Coun., Maison de la Chasse et de la Nature (House of Hunting & Nature). Hons. incl: Grand Prix du Disque for 'la capitulation du général von Choltitz', 1951; Cmdr., Legion of Hon.; Cross of the Liberation; Cross of 1939-45 War; Medal of the Resistance; Cross of Voluntary Combattant in the Resistance;

Colonial Medal, etc. Address: 6 Ave. du Colonel Bonnet, 75016, Paris, France. 43, 91.

KARGLEDER, Charles Leonard, b. 19 July 1939. Educator. Educ: A.B., Univ. of S.D., 1960; M.A., Univ. of Ala., 1962; Ph.D., ibid, 1968. Appts: Grad. Asst., Univ. of Ala., 1962-63; Instr., Spring Hill Coll., Mobile, Ala., 1963-65, Asst. Prof., 1968-71, Assoc. Prof., 1971-, currently, Chmn., Dept. of Langs. Mbrships: AAUP; Am. Translators & S. Atlantic Mod. Langs. Assns.; Acad. Pol. Sci.; Am. Tchrs. of Spanish & Portuguese; Am. Coun. Tchng. For. Langs.; S. Eastern Coun. Latin Am. Studies. Translator, Muchas Gracias, Adios, by Jorge Guillen, Motley mag., 1965. Recip., Nat. Defense Educ. Act Fellowship, 1960-63. Address: Dept. of Languages, Spring Hill College, Mobile, AL 36608, U.S.A. 125, 131.

KARIV, Benjamin Zeev, b. 3 Aug. 1920. Managing Director of National Water Company. Educ: B.Sc. Econ., Jerusalem Univ., Israel; var. courses in mgmt. & econ. Appts: Mgmt. positions in Kibutz, 1939-47; var. positions in Mekoroth Water Co.; Mbr. of Bd., ibid, 1957; Dpty. Mng. Dir., 1960-; Mng. Dir., 1967-. Mbrships. incl: Bd. of newspaper Davar & of Tahal; Former mbr. of Bd., Israeli Football Assn.; Ctrl. Comm., Israeli Labour Party. Author of papers submitted to Int. Congresses: The Israeli Water Network & its Economics; The Economy of Water. Hons: Independence Award, 1948; Sinai Award, 1956; Award for Service in Six-day War, 1967. Address: 27 Havradim St., Ganejehuda, Israel.

KARK, Robert M., b. 29 Aug. 1911. Physician; Educator. Educ: B.A., Univ. of Cape Town, S. Africa, 1931; MRCS, LPCP, Guy's Hosp. Med. Schl., Univ. of London, U.K., 1935; MRCP, 1937; DCH, 1935; FRCP, 1953. Appts. incl: Rsch. Fellow, Thorndike Mem. Lab. & Asst. Med., Boston City Hosp. U.S.A., 1938-41; Rsch. Fellow, Harvard Fatigue Lab., 1946; Asst. Dir., Med. Nutrition Lab., Chgo., 1947-50; Vis. Prof. & Acting Hd., Dept. of Med., Meharry Med. Coll., Nashville, Tenn., 1949-50; Prof., Med., Univ. of Ill., 1950-; Prof., Med., Rush Med. Coll., 1970-. Mbrships. incl: Gov., Northern Ill., Am. Coll. Physns.; Hon. Life, Am. Med. Soc. Vienna, 1965; Food & Nutrition Bd., Nat. Rsch. Coun.; Past Pres., Am. Assn. for Study of Liver Diseases; Cons., VA; Am. Soc. for Clin. Investigation. Contbr. to med. publs. Recip., var. hons. Address: 1753 W. Congress Parkway, Chicago, IL 60612, U.S.A.

KARNER, Franz Hans Maria, b. 2 Apr. 1904. Banker. Appts: Det Transatlantiske Kompagniet A/S, Copenhagen, 1920-21; Allg. Oest. Boden-Credit-Anstallt, Vienna, 1922-26; Maduro's Bank, Curacao, 1926-29; Mgr., E. Moreno Brandao, ibid, 1930-31; Mng. Dir., Aruba Trading Co., 1931-42; Hd., Crisis Bur., Neth. Ant. Govt., WWII; Ptnr., Edwards, Henriquez & Co., Curacao, 1945-. Mbrships: Rotary Club; Chmn., Bd. Trustees, Law Schl. of the Netherlands, Antilles, Fndn. Clin. Higher Educ., Fndn. Preservation of Monuments, etc. Hons: Off., Order of Orange Nassau, 1954; Grosses Ehrenzeichen Repub. Oesterreich, 1955; Zilveren Anjer, 1968; Hon. Consul Gen. of Austria, 1946. Address: P.O. Box 353, Curacao, Netherlands Antilles.

KARNIOL, Hilda Hutterer (Mrs. Frank Karniol), b. 28 Apr. 1910. Artist; Educator. Educ: Acad. for Women, Vienna, Austria, 1926-30. Appts: Instr. in Fine Arts, Susquehanna Univ., Selinsgrove, Pa., 1959-; Lectr.; Artist-in-Residence, Fed. Gov. Cultural

Enrichment Prog. for Clearfield, Clinton, Ctr. & Lycoming Cos., Pa., 1967; Art Advsr., Bicentennial Comm., Sunbury, Pa. Mbrships. incl: Nat. Forum of Profl. Artists; Société d'Honneur Française; Pi Delta Phi; Sigma Alpha Iota. Over 100 solo exhibs., inclng. Susquehanna Univ., 1952-; Adha Artzt Gall., N.Y.C., 1960; Univ. of Minn., St. Paul, 1969; Purdue Univ., W. Lafayette, Ind., 1973. Permanent collects: Delaware Art Ctr., Wilmington; U.S. Govt., Dept. Hlth., Welfare & Educ. Recip., 1st Prize in Portraiture, Berwick Art Ctr., Pa. Address: 960 Race St., Sunbury, PA 17801, U.S.A. 5, 6.

KARP, Peter Simon, b. 9 Dec. 1932. Research Institute Executive. Educ: B.A., Hobart Coll., 1954; M.F.A., Columbia Univ., 1957. Appts: Rsch. Assoc., Bur. of Advt., Am. Newspaper Publishers Assn., N.Y.C., 1956-57; Dir., Media & Rsch., Smith, Hagel & Knudsen, Inc., N.Y.C., 1958-60; Exec. V.P., Bennett-Chaikin Rsch., Inc., N.Y.C., 1961-66; Pres., MMRA Marketing & Opinion Rsch., Inc., N.Y.C., 1966-; Mng. Dir., Concept Testing Inst., Dir., Bus. Sci. Inst. & Dir., Children's Marketing Workshop, N.Y.C., 1968-; Rsch. Proj. Dir., Wm. Scranton Gubernatorial Campaign, 1964, & Kenneth Keating Senate Campaign, 1966. Mbrships. incl: Fund Raising Bd., Vanderbilt YMCA; Am. Marketing Assn.; Special Libs. Assn.; Boy Scouts of Am. Contbr. to marketing jrnls. Recip. of hons. Address: 4 Radcliff Dr., Upper Nyack, NY 10960, U.S.A.

KARRICH, Hans-Joachim, b. 2 Mar. 1930. Managing Director of Breweries. Educ: Grad., Univs. of Freiburg & Heidelberg, Germany; Dip. in Econs., 1953. Appts: Mgr., Königsbacher Biervertrieb, Trier, 1961-; Mng. Dir., Königsbacher Brauerei A.G., Koblenz, 1965-; Mgr., Brauhaus Fried. Winter, & Richmodis-Bräu, Cologne, 1967-; Mgr., Brauerei Zum Walfisch, Aachen, 1969-; Mgr., Brauerei A. Bonnet & Cie., Meisenheim, 1969-; Mgr., Bad Emser Getränkevertriebs, Bad Ems, 1971-; Chmn., Hirschbrauerei A.G., Dusseldorf, 1972-. Mbrships: Bd. of Dirs., Brauerbund Hessen-Mittelrhein, 1967-; Advsry. Bd., Frankfurter-Allianz-Versicherungs A.G., 1968-; Chmbr. of Comm., 1968-; Bundersverband der Deutschen Industrie, 1968-; Comm., Deutscher Brauerbund, 1971-; Publs: Sev. articles in newspapers & mags. Address: Neustadt 5, 54 Koblenz, German Federal Repub. 43, 92.

KARSH, Yousuf, b. 23 Dec. 1908. Photographer. Appts: Vis. Prof. of Photography, Schl. of Fine Arts, Ohio Univ., Athens; Vis. Prof. of Fine Arts, Emerson Coll., Boston, Mass.; Photographic Advsr., EXPO '67, Japan. Rep. in perm. collections incl: Mus. Mod. Art & Metro. Mus. Art N.Y.C.; Art Inst. of Chgo.; Nat. Portrait Gall., London, U.K.; St. Louis Art Mus., Rochester, N.Y. Mbrships: incl: Trustee, Photographic Arts & Scis. Fndn.; Hon. Fellow, Royal photographic Soc. of Gt. Brit. Publs. incl: In Search of Greatness, 1962; Faces of our Time, 1971. Hons. incl: LL.D., Queen's Univ., Kingston, Ont., Carleton Univ., Ottawa; Canada Coun. Medal, 1965; Medal of Serv., Order of Canada, 1968. Address: 130 Sparks St., Ottawa, Canada.

KARSTEDT, Peter, b. 26 Mar. 1909. Librarian. Educ: Doct. in Law; studies in libnship. Appts:' Prussian Acad. of Scis., 1935-40; Libn., Stadtbibliothek, Lübeck, Germany, 1934 & Chief Libn., 1945-71. Mbr., Soc. of German Libns. Publs: Soziologie der Bibliothek, 2nd. edit., 1965; Ethik more juridico, 1956; Livlandische Historien 1556-61,

(Ed.) 1953; contbr. to profl. publs. Address: Fritz-Reuter-Str. 1, 24 Lübeck 1, German Fed. Repub. 43. 92.

KARYOTAKIS, Theodore, b. 21 July 1903. Composer. Educ: Studied with D. Mitropoulos & M. Varvoglis. Mbrships: Gen. Sec., Union of Greek Composers; Gen. Sec., Greek Nat. Comm., Int. Music Coun.; Coun., State Orch. of Athens, Greece; Artistic Comm., Nat. Theatre (Opera). Published compositions incl: Petite Symph. for String Orch.; Divertimento for Orch.; Symph. in One Movement; Rhapsody for Violin & Orch.; Trio for Clarinet, Viola & Piano; 2 Violin Sonatas; Sonatina for Solo Cello; Sonatina for Viola & Piano; String Quartet, with Voice; Song of Songs, Oratorio; Num. songs with piano accompaniment. Recip., King George of Greece Decoration. Address: Ipirou 33, Athens, Greece.

KASE, Judith Baker, b. 13 Dec. 1932. College Professor of Theatre Arts. Educ: B.A., Univ. of Del., 1955; M.A., Case Western Reserve Univ., 1956. Appts. incl: Agnes Scott Coll., Decatur, Ga., 1956-57; Univ. of Tenn., Knoxville, Tenn., 1957-58; Univ. of Md. in Germany, 1959-60; Univ. of N.H., Durham, N.H., 1961-69; Dir., Theatre Resources for Youth, Somersworth, N.H., 1965-69; Univ. of S. Fla., Tampa, Fla., 1969-. Mbrships: Exec. Comm., U.S. Ctr. of Assites; Am. Theatre Assn., Chmn., Standards Comm.; Children's Theatre Assn.; Speech Communication Assn.; AAUP; United Fac. of Fla.; Southeastern Theatre Assn. Publs. incl: contbn. in Give Them Roots & Wings (Eds., D. Schwartz & D. Aldrich), 1972; contbn. in The Recreation Program Guide (Ed., J. Kujoth), 1972; 3 stories & lesson analyses in Stories For Creative Acting by C. Robert Kase, 1961; num. articles in profl. jrnls. Dir. of many plays for University of S. Fla. inclng. touring prods. Hons: Recognition Citation, Children's Theatre Assn., recd. at Nat. Conven., 1971. Address: Theatre Dept., Univ. of S. Fla., Tampa, FL 33612, U.S.A. 125.

KASER, David, b. 12 Mar. 1924. Librarian. Educ: A.B., Houghton Coll., 1949; M.A., Univ. of Notre Dame, 1950; A.M.L.S. & Ph.D., Univ. of Mich., 1956. Appts: Asst. Dir., Wash. Univ. Libs., 1956-60; Dir., Jt. Univ. Libs. (Vanderbilt Univ.), 1960-68, Cornell Univ. Libs., 1968-73; Prof., Grad. Lib. Schl., Ind. Univ., 1973-. Mbrships: Assn. of Coll. & Rsch. Libs. (Pres., 1968-69); Tenn. Lib. Assn. (Pres., 1968-69); Am. Antiquarian Soc.; Bibliographical Soc. of Am.; Phi Beta Kappa; Grolier Club. Publs: Messrs. Carey & Lea of Philadelphia, 1957; Cost Book of Carey & Lea, 1963; Joseph Charless, 1963; Books in America's Past, 1966; Library Development in 8 Asian Countries, 1969; Book Pirating in Taiwan, 1969; College & Research Libraries, 1962-69 (Ed.) Recip. of Guggenheim Fellowship, 1967. Address: Grad. Lib. Schl., Ind. Univ., Bloomington IN 47401, U.S.A. 2, 13, 30.

KASLIWAL, Rajmal, b. 20 Nov. 1906. Physician. Educ: M.B.B.S., Lucknow, 1929; D.T.M. & H. (U.K.), 1931; M.D., Lucknow, 1934. Appts. incl: Dir. of Med. Servs., Jaipur, India, 1948-51, Dir. of Med. & Hlth. Servs., Fajasthan State, 1949-51; Prof. & Hd., Dept. of Med., SMS Med. Coll., 1951-66; Princ., SMS Med. Coll., Jaipur, 1949-51, '55-66; Emeritus Prof., Med., ibid, 1967-; Emeritus Med. Sci., I.C.M.R., 1972-. Mbrships. incl: Fellow, Royal Coll. Physns., London, U.K., Indian Acad. Med. Scis., Indian Nat. Sci. Acad., Am. Coll. Chest Physns. Contbr. of articles to profl. jrnls. Hons. incl: Gold Medal, Assn. Physns., India, 1970; Tammara Patra, 1972. Address: S.M.S. Med. Coll., Jaipur 4, Rajasthan, India.

KASONGO, Harrison Peter, b. 27 June 1934. Businessman. Appts. incl: Ndola City Councillor, Zambia, 1963-74; Constituency Sec., United Nat. Indepedence Pty., 1970; Chmn., Zambia Coun. for the Handicapped, Copper Belt & N. Area Bd. Mbrships: Insakwe/Mitanda Admission & Review Comm.; Ndola Theatre Club; Copperbelt Probation Sub-Comm.; Ndola Urban Local Coun. of Educ.; Local Govt. Assn. of Zambia; Ndola P.T.A; Ndola Nutrition Grp. Address: P.O. Box 1336, Ndola, Zambia. 135.

KASPERSON, Roger E., b. 29 Mar. 1938. College Professor & Administrator. Educ: B.A., Clark Univ., 1959; M.A., Univ. of Chgo., 1962; Ph.D., ibid, 1966. Appts: Instr., Dept. of Geol. & Geography, Univ. of Conn., 1964-66; Asst. Prof., Dept. of Geography & James Madison Coll., Mich. State Univ., 1966-68; Cons., Ctr. for Educl. Rsch., Univ. of Puerto Rico, 1969-71; Dean of Coll. & Assoc. Prof. Govt. & Geography, Clark Univ., Worcester, Mass., 1971-. Mbrships: Am. Pol. Sci. Assn.; Am. Acad. Pol. & Soc. Scis.; Assn. Am. Geographers; Am. Geographical Soc. Publs: The Structure of Political Geography (co-ed.), 1969; Geography in an Urban Age: Political Geography, 1970. Profl. papers. Address: Clark University, 750 Main St., Worcester, MA 01610, U.S.A.

KÅSS, Erik, b. 22 Feb. 1923. Physician. Educ: M.D., Univ. of Oslo, Norway, 1955. Appts. incl: w. Cons., Defence Med. Corps., 1954-69; Hd., Physn., Oslo Sanitetsforening Rheumatism Hosp., 1962; Prof., Rheumatol., Univ. of Oslo, 1966; WHO Expert, Rheumatol., 1966. Mbrships: incl: Chmn., Norwegian Rheumatol. Soc.; Chmn. & Ldr., Rsch. Coun., Norwegian Rheum. Assn.; Chmn., Licentiate Comm., Med. Fac., 1967. Author of approx. 75 sci. publs. Hons: UN Emergency Forces Medal for Serv. of Peace, 1958; Kt., 1st Class, Royal Norwegian Order of St. Olav, 1973. Address: Oslo Sanitetsforenings Revmatismesykehus, Akersbakken 27, Oslo 1, Norway. 134.

KASTEEL, (His Excellency Dr.) Petrus Albertus, b. 4 Nov. 1901. Diplomat. Educ: Doct. Pol. & Soc. Scis., Cath. Univ., Louvain, Belgium. Appts: Ed.-in-Chief, sev. major Dutch newspapers until 1940. Gov.-Gen., Netherlands Antilles, W. Indies, 1942-48; Her Netherlands Majesty's Ambassador to Chile, Ireland, Israel & Missions to other countries; Currently, Her Netherlands Majesty's Amb. Extraordinary & Plenipotentiary. Mbr., Order of the Holy Sepulchre. Author of num. publs. Hons: Kt. Order Netherlands Lion; Kt. Grand Cross of sev. Orders (St. Gregory the Great, etc.); Kt. Cmdr. Légion d'Honneur. Address: Via della Conciliazione 44, I-00193, Rome, Italy. 34.

KATAJAINEN, Veikko Antero Tapio, b. 3 Feb. 1914. Administrator. Educ: Law degree, Univ. of Helsinki, Finland, 1945; Atty. at Law, 1948. Appts. incl: Hd., Div. (Secretariat), Soc. Ins. Instn., 1959; Dept. Hd., ibid, 1961-; Acting Dir., SII, 1961-62; Dpty. Bd. Mbr., 1960-65, 69-71; Exper, Chmn. or Sec., sev. Coun. of State Comms.; Mbr., Espoo City Wage Bd., 1957-65; Vice Chmn., ibid, 1959-65. Mbrships. incl: Bd. & Rep., Fndn. for Support of Musical Art in Finland, 1957-; Bd. Chmn., Kaultakähkän Kiipulasäätiö Fndn., 1962-72; Bd., 1972-; Sec. for Soc. Affairs, Finnish Municipal Assn., 1969-. Author of sev. articles in periodicals. Hons. incl: Cross of Liberty, 3rd & 4th class; Medal of Hon., Winter War, 1939-40; Medal of Hon., 1941-44; Cross, 1st class, Order of the White Rose. Address: Pilvettärenpolku 1, 02100 Tapiola, Finland. 43.

KATAVISTO, Martti V.S., b. 27 Mar. 1919. Physician. Educ: M.D., 1947; Specialist in Ophthalmol., 1951; D.M.S., 1964. Appts: Asst. Physn., Helsinki Gen. Hosp., 1948-51; Ophthalmologist, Central Mil. Hosp., Helsinki, 1951-53; Chief Physn., Ophthalmol. Dept., N. Karelia Central Hosp., Joensuu, 1953-. Hd. of Hosp., 1963-73. Mbrships: Finnish Ophthalmological Soc.; Sec., ibid, 1951-52, Chmn., 1962-63; Assn. Finnish Ophthalmologists; Chmn., ibid, 1972; Med. Assn. N. Karelia; Chmn., ibid, 1959; Rotary Club of Joensuu; Pres., ibid, 1969-70. Papers & articles, profl. publs. Recip., Cross of Liberty, 1942, w. Oak Leaves, 1944. Address: Nepenmäenkatu 1.C.10, 80210 Joensuu 21, Finland. 43, 90.

KATEN, Thomas Ellis, Associate Professor of Philosophy. Educ: B.S., Temple Univ., 1954; A.M., Univ. of Pa., 1958; postgrad. studies New Schl. of Soc. Rsch., & N.Y. Univ. Appts. incl: Instr., Univ. of Del., 1960-63; Asst. Prof., Monmouth Coll., 1963-65; Asst. Prof.-Assoc. Prof., Community Coll. of Phila., 1965-. Mbrships. incl: Fund for Animals, Inc.; Animal Protection Inst. of Am.; New England Anti-Vivisection Soc.; Am. Civil Liberties; Am. Philosophical Assn. Publs: Doing Philosophy, 1973; Series articles, Watchman Waketh but in Vain, in Midlothian Times, 1967. Address: 7612 Lexington Ave., Phila., PA 19152, U.S.A. 6.

KATER, (Sir) Gregory (Blaxland), b. 15 May 1912. Chartered Electrical Engineer; Grazier. Educ: M.A., Univ. of Cambridge. Appts: Chmn., Commercial Banking Co. of Sydney, Ltd.; Chmn., Elec. Equipment of Australia, Ltd.; Chmn., Mercantile & Gen. Reins. Co. of Australia, Ltd.; Chmn., Oil Search, Ltd.; Chmn., Permanent Trustee Co., Ltd.; Dir., C.S.R. Co., Ltd.; Dir., H.E. Kater & Son Pty., Ltd. (Egelabra Stud); Dir., Metal Manufactures, Ltd.; Dir., Vickers Australia, Ltd.; Dir., W.R. Carpenter Holdings, Ltd. Mbrships. incl: Fellow, Instn. of Elec. Engrs.; Fellow, Australian Inst. of Engrs.; Dir., N.S.W. Soc. for Crippled Children; Australian Club, Sydney; Jr. Carlton Club, London, U.K.; Liveryman, Worshipful Co. of Broderers, London. Hon: Kt. Bach., 1974. Address: 56 Pitt St., Sydney, N.S.W., Australia 2000. 12, 16. 23.

KATES, George William, b. 17 Oct. 1922. Lawyer. Educ: LL.B., Univ. of Fla., Gainesville, U.S.A., 1949; J.D., ibid. Appts: USAF, 1940-45; Municipal Judge, El Portal, Fla., 1950-54; Ptnr., Kates, Ress, Gomez & Rosenberg, Attys.-at-Law, N. Miami, Fla., 1954-69; Pres. & Dir., Bahamas Developers Ltd., Miami, 1964-66; Bd. Chmn., Second Nat. Bank of N. Miami, 1966-68; Pres. & Dir., The Grand Bahama Dev. Co. Ltd. & Grp. Cos., 1966-. Mbrships: Dir., Crime Commn. of Gtr. Miami; Past Lt. Gov., Kiwanis Int.; Boy Scouts of Am.; Chi Phi; Phi Delta Phi. Address: P.O. Box F.2666, Freeport, Grand Bahama, Bahamas. 16.

KATO, Ken, b. 16 Sept. 1914. Ophthalmologist. Educ: M.A., Keio Univ., Tokyo, Japan, 1938; D.Med.Sci., ibid, 1951. Appts: w. Keio Univ., Tokyo, 1938-63; Med. Off., Japanese Army, 1938-47; Instr. of Ophthalmol., Keio Univ., 1951-56; Assoc. Prof., ibid, 1956-63; Prof., Nihon Univ., Tokyo, 1963-; Dir., Ophthalmol. Dept., Surugadai-Hosp., ibid, 1963-; Vice-Dir., ibid, 1970-; Vis. Prof., Univ. of Pa., U.S.A., 1972; Chmn., Dept. Ophthalmol., Nihon Univ., 1973-. Mbrships: Mng. Dir., Japanese Ophthalmological Soc., 1973-; Bd. of Councillors, Japan Diabetic Soc., Japan Coll.

Angiol. & Japan Soc. Psychosomatic Med.; Alumni Assn., Dept. Ophthalmol., Univ. of Pa., U.S.A., 1962-. Author of monographs & num. ophthalmological articles & essays. Hons: Order of the Sacred Treasure (Zuihosho), 1942, Order of the Rising Sun (Kyokujitsu-sho), 1940, in recognition of servs. as med. off., WWII. Address: 3-10-17 Yagisawa, Hoya-shi, Tokyo, Japan (Area 188).

KATO, Mutsumi, b. 20 Mar. 1911. Commissioner of the National Personnel Authority of Japan. Educ: Grad., Tokyo Inst. of Technol., 1934; Doct., 1953. Appts: Prof., Tokyo Inst. of Technol., 1954-71; Dir. of Rsch., Lab. of Engrng. Materials, 1968-69; Pres., Tokyo Inst. of Technol., 1969-73; Commnr., Nat. Personnel Auth. Mbrships: Pres., Bldg. Coun. (Nat. Bur. of Construction), 1971-74, Nat. Univs. Assn., 1973, Japanese Inst. of Arch. & Bldg. Engrng., 1971-72, Japanese Concrete Inst., 1972-74; Chmn., Rsch. Comm. for New Univs., Nat. Bur. of Educ., 1973-74; Univ. Chartering Coun., ibid, 1969-74. Publs: Transmission of Stress between Concrete & its Reinforcement (thesis), 1953. Recip. Thesis Prize, Japanese Inst. of Arch. & Bldg. Engrng., 1953. Address: 1-15-5 Himonya Meguro-ku, Tokyo, Japan.

KATO, Sadatake, b. 5 May 1907. Chemist; Business Executive. Educ: Grad., Fac. Pharmaceutical Scis., Univ. of Tokyo, Japan, 1932; Ph.D., Kyoto Univ., Japan, 1944. Appts. incl: Chem. Engr., Toyoseiyaku K.K., 1932-41; Assoc. Prof., Fac. of Pharmaceutical Scis., Kyoto Univ., 1941-47; Dir., Rsch. & Dev., Dainippon Pharmaceutical Co. Ltd., 1947-62; Exec. Mgng. Dir., Dainabot Radioisotope Lab., Ltd., 1962-67; Lectr., Kyushu Univ., 1966-74; Vis. Prof., Kitasato Univ., 1968-74; Pres., Dainabot Radioisotope Lab., Ltd., 1968-. Mbrships: Off., World Fed. Nuclear Med. & Biol.; Am. Chem. Soc. Nuclear Med.; Trustee, Radiation Soc. of Japan; Japan Soc. Nuclear Med. Contbr. to Sci. jrnls. Address: 1-17-24, Midorigaoka, Megro-ku, Tokyo 152, Japan.

KATSELIS, Pelos, b. 3 July 1908. Theatre Director; Professor of Dramatic Art; Writer. Educ: Fac. of Law, Athens; Profl. Drama Schls., Greece & Germany. Appts: Mgr. & Dir., Charriot of Thespis, Athens, 1938-41; Dir., Nat. Theatre, Athens, 1941-46; Dir., Nat. Lyrical Theatre, Athens, 1946-56; Fndr. & Dir., Dramatic Schl. of Athens, 1956-; Mgr. & Dir., Personal Grps., Greece, 1956-62; Fndr., Nature Theatre, Greece, 1961-65; Cultural Advsr. & Dir., Festivals of Nat. Tourist Org. of Greece, 1965-67. Mbrships: Soc. Greek Writers; Pres., Union of Prods., Conductors, Choreographers, Scenery & Lighting Designers. Publs: Shakespeare's Characters, 1942; On the Theatre, 1947. Essays & dramatic criticism, newspapers & mags., 1933-67. Address: Megalou Alexandrou St. 38, Nea Smirni, Athens, Greece. 43.

KATSUKI, Shibanosuke, b. 30 June 1907. Medical College President. Educ: Grad., Kyushu Univ. Schl. of Med., Japan, 1930; Asst., Med. Clin., Göttingen, Germany, 1936. Appts: Asst. Prof., Kyushu Univ., 1941-; Prof., Dept. of Internal Med., Kumamoto Univ. Med. Schl., 1950-; Prof., Dept. of Internal Med., Kyushu Univ. Schl. of Med., 1956-; Prof. Emeritus, Kyushu Univ., 1971; Pres., Med. Coll. of Miyazaki, 1974-. Mbrships: Corres. mbr., Am. Neurological Assn.; Hon. mbr., Am. Acad. of Neurol.; Hon. mbr., Deutsche Gesellschaft für Neurologie; O'seas mbr., Royal Soc. of Med. Author of Hisayama Study, follow up study of stroke & hypertension over 10 yrs. Address:

Hirao 3-Chome 26-14, Chuoku, Fukuoka City, Japan.

KATZ, Hilda, b. 2 June 1909. Oil & Watercolor Painter; Graphic Artist. Educ: Nat. Acad. of Design; New Schl. of Soc. Rsch., 1940-41. Mbrships: Am. Graphic Artists; Conn. Acad. Fine Arts; Print Club, Albany; Boston Printmakers; Wash. Printmakers; Am. Color Print Soc.; Phila. Water Color Club; Audubon Artists; Nat. Assn. Women Artists; Artists Equity, N.Y.; Life, Hall of Fame; Hunterdon Art Ctr.; Life Fellow, Metropol. Mus. of Art; Advsry., Marquis Biographical Lib. Soc., etc. Special collections of artist's work only (L. & M. Katz Mem. Collections): U.S. Nat. Mus., 18 works, 1965; Univ. of Me. Art Mus., 16 works, 1965; Lib. of Congress, 37 works, 1965; Metropol. Mus. of Art, 29 works, 1965; Nat. Collection Fine Arts, 10 works, 1966; Nat. Gall. of Art, 3 works, 1966; Nat. Air & Space Mus., 4 works, 1970; Nat. Collection Fine Arts, 19 Original Print blocks, 1971; Lib. of Congress, 15 original print blocks, 1971; N.Y. Pub. Lib., 6 prints, 2 original print blocks, 1971; U.S. Nat. Mus., 13 prints, 13 original print blocks, 1972. Represented in permanent mus. Collections inclng: Balt. Mus. of Art; Syracuse Univ.; Univs. of Me. & Minn.; Calif. State Lib.; Fogg Mus.; Franklin D. Roosevelt Collection; Newark Pub. Lib.; museums in Israel. Invitation one-man shows incl: Calif. State Lib., 1953; Miami Beach Art Ctr., Fla., 1958; Old State Capitol Mus., La. Exhibs. incl: Soc. Am. Graphic Artists; Nat. Acad. of Design; Congress for Jewish Culture; Springfield Art Mus.; Pa. Acad. Fine Arts; La. Art Commn.; Brooklyn Mus. Int. exhibs. incl: Int. Women's Clubs, U.K.; Italian Fedn. Women in Art; Venice Biennial, Italy; also exhibs. in France, Israel, Japan, etc. Hons. incl: Plaque of Honor, Hall of Fame, 1966; Award Plaque, Community Ldrs. of Am., 1969-72; Cert. of Merit, Marquis Biographical Lib. Soc., 1969; Daughter of Mark Twain, 1970; Art awards incl: Audubon Artists, 1944; Graphic Grp. Prize, 1950; Peoria Art Ctr., 1950; Soc. Miniature Painters, Gravers, Sculptors, Best Landscape, 1959; sev. purchase awards. Address: 915 West End Ave., Apt. 5D, N.Y., NY 10025, U.S.A. 2, 5, 6, 34, 37, 55, 57, 64, 68, 105, 128, 129, 130, 132, 133, 138.

KATZ, Irving Isaac, b. 31 Mar. 1907. Synagogue Administrator. Educ: City Yeshiva, Riga, Russia; Spencerian Bus. Coll., U.S.A.; Western Reserve Univ. & Law Schl., Cleveland, Ohio. Appts. incl: Ordained Rabbi; former Educator-Admnstr., Oheb Zedek Congregation, Cleveland, Ohio, & Anshe Emeth Temple, Youngstown, Ohio; Exec. Sec., Temple Beth El, Detroit, Mich., 1939-; Fndr. & 1st Pres., Coun. of Synagogue Exec. Dirs. of Metropol. Detroit; Mbr., Culture Commn., Jewish Community Coun. of Metropol. Detroit. Mbr., num. community orgs. Publs. incl: Successful Synagogue Administration; Beth El Story—With a History of the Jews in Michigan Before 1850. Co-Ed., Mich. Jewish Hist. Mag. Contbr., Ency. Judaica, var. newspapers & histl. jrnls. Recip., var. citations & awards. Address: 16159 Oxley Rd., Apt. 203, Southfield, MI 48075, U.S.A. 8, 30, 55.

KATZ, J. Lawrence, b. 18 Dec. 1927. Professor; Director, Lab. for Crystallographic Biophysics. Educ: B.S., 1950, M.S., 1951, Ph.D., 1957, Polytech. Inst. of Brooklyn, U.S.A. Appts: Tchng. Fellow in Phys., P.T. Instr., Instr. & Sr. Rsch. Fellow in Math., Polytech., Inst. of Brooklyn, N.Y.; Hd., X-Ray Lab., Curtis-Wright, Woodridge, N.J., 1956; Fac. Mbr., Rensselaerm Polytech. Inst., Troy, N.Y., 1956-; Nat. Sci. Fndn. Fellowship; Rsch. Asst., Crystallography, Univ. Coll., London,

U.K., 1959-60; Rsch. Asst., Physico-Chem. Measurement Lab., Knolls Atomic Power Lab., Schenectady, N.Y., 1967; Vis. Prof., Biomed. Engrng. & Oral Biol., Schls. of Engrng. & Med., Univ. of Miami, Fla., 1969-70; Vis. Prof., Biophys. & Biomed. Engrng., Gifu Coll. of Dentistry., Gifu, Japan, 1972. Mbrships. incl: Am. Crystallog, Assn.; Am. Phys. Soc.; Int. Assn. for Dental Rsch.; Prof. Comm., Orthopaedic Rsch. Soc., 1973-; Engrng. in Biol. & Med. Trng. Comm. of Nat. Inst. of Hlth., 1968-71. Address: Dept. of Phys., Rensselaer Polytech. Inst., Troy, NY 12181, U.S.A. 2, 6, 130.

KATZ, Milton, b. 29 Nov. 1907. Lawyer; Diplomat. Educ: A.B., Harvard Univ., 1927; LL.B., ibid, 1931. Appts. incl: Prof. of Law & Burn Prof. of Admin. Law, Harvard Univ., 1946-50 Dir. of Int. Legal Studies & Henry L. Stimson Prof. of Law, ibid, 1954-; Ambassador & Chief in Europe of Marshall Plan, 1950-51; Assoc. Dir., Ford Fndn., 1951-54; Mbr., Herter Comm. on For. Affairs Personnel, 1961-63, & many other govt. comms.; Cons., Asst. Sec. for Educ. of HEW, 1966. Mbr. many orgs. & fndns. inclng: Chmn. of Bd., Carnegie Endowment for Int. Peace; Trustee, World Peace Fndn. & Int. Legal Ctr.; Pres., Citizens Rsch. Fndn. Publs: 5 books inclng: The Things That are Caesar's, 1966; The Relevance of International Adjudication, 1968; contbr. books & periodicals. Hons: Legion of Merit, 1945; Commendation Ribbon, 1945. Address: c/o Harvard Law School, Cambridge MA 02138, U.S.A. 1, 2, 3, 6, 9, 12, 13, 15, 34, 43, 55.

KATZ, Phyllis A. (Mrs.), b. 9 Apr. 1938. University Professor. Educ: A.B., Syracuse Univ., 1957; Ph.D., Yale Univ., 1961. Appts. incl: Instr., Psychol., Queens Coll., 1962-63; Asst. Prof., Psychol., N.Y. Univ., 1963-67; Assoc. Prof., ibid, 1967-69; Assoc. Prof., CUNY, 1969-72; Prof. Hd., Edicl. Psychol. Doctoral Prog., ibid, 1972-73; Prof., 1973-. Fellow, Am. Psychol. Assn. Mbrships. incl: Eastern Psychol. Assn.; Soc. for Rsch. in Child Dev.; AAUP; AAAS; Sigma Xi. Author of many publs. in field; Ed., profl. jrnls. Hons. incl: Grant, Nat. Inst. for Child Hlth. & Dev., 1966-68; Grant, NICHD, 1968-72; Grant, Off. of Child Dev., 1972-75. Address: CUNY, Grad. Ctr., 33 W. 42nd St., N.Y., NY 10036, U.S.A. 5, 6, 14, 132, 138, 141.

KATZEN, Harry Milton, b. 20 June 1900. Rabbi. Educ: Grad., Odessa Univ.,. Russia, 1920; M.A., Columbia Univ., U.S.A., 1927; M.H.L., Jewish Theological Sem., 1928; Rabbi (summa cum laude), Dr. Hebrew Lit., Appts: Rabbi, Temple B'nai Brith, Somerville, Mass., 1928-29, Temple Beth El, Dorchester, 1929-35, Nathan Straus Jewish Ctr., Bronx, N.Y., 1935-40, Temple Beth El of Bensonhurst, Brooklyn, N.Y., 1940-; Chap., Montefiore Hosp., 1936-44, Jewish Hosp. of Brooklyn, 1946-, Cumberland Hosp., Brooklyn, 1948-; Civilian Chap., Ft. Hamilton, 1942-45. Mbrships: Brooklyn & N.Y. Bds. of Rabbis; Am. Acads., Jewish Rsch., Pol. Sci., Pol. & Soc. Sci.; B'nai Brith Zionist Org. of Am.; Alumni Assn. of Grad. Schls., Columbia Univ. Hons. incl: D.D., Jewish Theological Sem. of Am., 1966; var. sem. prizes. Address: 7110 21st Ave., Brooklyn, NY 11204, U.S.A.

KATZEN, Pell Lila (Mrs. Philip Katzen). Sculptor. Educ: Art Students League, N.Y.C.; Cooper Union, N.Y.C.; Hans Hofmann schl., N.Y.C. & Provincetown, Mass. Appts: Lectr., Balt Mus., Kalamazoo Art Ctr., Mich., Archtl. League, N.Y.C., Centro Venezolano, Caracas, Santa Barbara Mus., Calif., MIT, Coll. Art

Conf., Art Students League, State Univ. at Purchase, N.Y. & Cranbrook Acad., Mich. On permanent exhib: Max Hutchinson Ltd., N.Y.C.; Jacobs Ladder Gall., Wash. D.C. Sculpted: Light Floors, Archtl. League, N.Y.C., 1968; Universe as Environment, N.Y. Univ. & State Univ. at Purchase, N.Y., 1969; Lanterna Magika, Czech Theatre Facade, Expo 70, Osaka, Japan, 1970; Media Wall, C. & P. Telephone Co., Balt., 1972; Liquid Tunnel, Sao Paulo Exhib., Explorations, 1970; Slip-Edge Bis. Whitney Mus. Biennial, 1972. Mbrships: Archtl. League, N.Y.C.; Coll. Art Assn.; AAUP. Hons: Tiffany Fndn. Fellow, 1964; Archtl. League Grantee, 1968; Nat. Endowment Grantee, 1973. Address: 345 W. Broadway, New York, NY 10013, U.S.A. 5, 37.

KAUFFMAN, Robert Wallace, b. 22 Nov. 1931. Minister. Educ: A.B., Hillsdale Coll., Mich., U.S.A.; B.D., Grad. Schl. of Theol., Oberlin Coll., Ohio; Master of Divinity, Vanderbilt Univ., Nashville, Tenn. Appts: Pastor, First Congregational Ch., Genesee, Wis., 1956-63; Pastor, Union Congregational Ch., Waupun, Wis., 1963-68; Pastor, First Congregational Ch., Sandusky, Ohio, 1968-. Num. mbrships. incl: Chmn., S.W. Assn. Wis. United Ch. of Christ, 1965-68; V.P., Milwaukee Ministerial Assn., 1960-61; Pres. Sandusky Ministerial Assn., 1970-71; V.P., Mental Hlth. Bd., Erie Co., 1969-; Chmn., N.W. Ohio Dist. Rsch. & Planning Comm., 1970-; Deleg., Rotary Int., Lausanne, Switzerland, 1973; Kappa Sigma Kappa. Recip., First Prize in Co., First Prize in Congressional Dist., & Second Prize in State Bar Contest, for essay, The Advantages of an Independent Judiciary in the United States. Address: 2609 Merriweather Dr., Sandusky, OH 44870, U.S.A. 8.

KAUFMAN, Herbert E., b. 28 Sept. 1931. Physician; Professor of Ophthalmology. Educ: A.B., Princeton Univ., 1952; M.D., Harvard Med. Schl., 1956. Appts: Assoc. Prof. & Chief of Ophthalmol., Coll. of Med., Univ. of Fla., 1962-64, Prof., Dept. of Ophthalmol., 1964-70; Ophthalmol. & Pharmacol., 1970-; Chmn., Dept. of Ophthalmol, 1964-. Mbrships: Trustee, Assn. for Rsch. in Ophthalmol.; Dir., Eye Bank Assn. of the Ams.; Corneal Task Force; Nat. Eye Inst.; Contact Lens Assn. of Physns. (Dir., 1972). Publs: Jrnl. of Chemotherapy, 1967-, Investigative Ophthalmol., 1972- (Ed.); contbr. to num. profl. publs. Recip. of var. profl. awards. Address: Dept. of Ophthalmol., c-512 MSB, Univ. of Fla. Coll. of Med., Gainesville, FL 32610, U.S.A. 2, 7, 17.

KAUFMAN. William H.. b. 6 Jan. 1913. Physician. Educ: A.B., Johns Hopkins Univ., 1934; M.D., Duke Univ., 1937; M.S., Univ. of Va., 1947. Appts. incl: Res. Fellow in Dermatol., Univ. of Va. Med. Ctr., 1945-47; Assoc. Prof. of Dermatol., ibid., 1965-; Cons. Dermatologist at U.S. VA Hosp., & to var. community & regional hosps.; Pvte. practice as Dermatologist, Roanoke, Va., 1947-. Mbrships: Fellow, Am. Acad. of Dermatol., & Am. Coll. of Physicians; Edit. Bd., Va. Med. Monthly; Roanoke Acad. of Med., (past Pres); Va. Dermatological Soc., (past Pres); Med. Soc. of Va; AMA; Sigma Xi. Contbr. of articles to var. publs. Address: 127 McClanahan St., S.W., Roanoke, VA 24014, U.S.A. 7, 17.

KAUFMANN, Felix. Company President; Consultant to Governments, International Organizations & Industry. Educ: Gordonstoun Schl.; B.Sc. (Hons.), D.I.C., Indl. Chem., Univ. of London; British Inst. Mgmt. Appts. incl: Cons., WHO & others, 1952-56; Exec. V.P., Kerr Int. Inc., 1957-62; Pres., Kerr Italia, S.P.A., 1959-62; Dir., Futures Prog., Hudson

Inst., 1962-65; Mgr., Corporate Planning, Hoffman-LaRoche Inc., 1965-71; Pres., Science for Business Inc., 1963-. Mbrships: Am. Acad. Pol. & Soc. Sci.; AAAS; Am. Chem. Soc.; World Future Soc. Publs: World Government & the U.S. National Interest, 1965; Decisionmaking, Eastern & Western Style, 1970; The Strategic Decisionmakers, 1971; Forecasting, Analysis & Decisionmaking, 1971; Organizational Decisions, 1972; Hard & Soft Health Technology of the Future, 1973; Medicine in the Year 2000, 1974. Address: 203 W. 81, N.Y., NY 10024, U.S.A. 130.

KAUFMANN, Herbert Joseph, b. 6 June 1924. Pediatric Radiologist. Educ: Univs. of Basle & Geneva, Switzerland; Boston City Hosp., Boston Med. Ctr., Mass., 1953-58. Appts: Prof., Med. Fac., & Dir., Dept. of Radiol., Children's Hosp., Univ. of Basle, Switzerland, 1963-71; Prof. of Radiol., Med. Schl., Univ. of Pa., U.S.A., & Radiologist-in-Chief, Children's Hosp. of Phila., 1971-. Mbrships. incl: Corres. Mbr., Soc. Pediatric Radiol., 1961-73; European Soc. of Pediatric Radiol.; Fndr. & Pres., ibid, 1966-67; Hon. Mbr., Radiol. Soc. Brazil, Sociedade Gaucha de Radiologia, 1970-; Int. Skeletal Soc.; Steering Comm. Mbr., ibid, 1972; Phila. Roentgen Ray Soc., 1973; Swiss X-Ray Soc. Over 100 papers, topics in field. Fndr. & Ed.-in-Chief, Progress in Pediatric Radiology, 1964. Address: Children's Hospital of Philadelphia, 34th St., Philadelphia, PA 19104, U.S.A.

KAUFMANN, Walter, b. 1 July 1921. Professor. Educ: B.A., Williams Coll., 1941; M.A., Harvard Univ., 1942, Ph.D., 1947. Appts: Prof., Princeton Univ., 1947-; Prof., Philos., ibid, 1962-; Fulbright Prof., Heidelberg, Germany, 1955-56, Jerusalem, Israel, 1962-63; Vis. Prof., Columbia, Cornell, New Schl. for Soc. Rsch., Univs. of Mich. & Wash. & Purdue. Publs. incl: Nietzsche: Philosopher, Psychologist, Antichrist, 3rd edit., 1968; Critique of Religion & Philosophy, 2nd edit., 1972; From Shakespeare to Existentialism, rev. edit., 1960; The Faith of a Heretic, 1961; Cain & Other Poems, rev. edit., 1971; Hegel; Reinterpretation, Texts, & Commentary, 1965; Tragedy & Philosophy, 1968; Without Guilt & Justice: From Decidophobia & Autonomy, 1973; translator, num. books from German; Ed., Existentialism from Dostoevsky to Sartre, 1956, Philosophical Classics, rev. edit., 1968, Religion From Tolstoy to Camus, 1961, & Hegel's Political Philosophy, 1970. Hons: Phi Beta Kappa, 1941; Int. Leo Baeck Prize, 1961. Address: Dept. of Philos., Princeton Univ., Princeton, NJ 08540, U.S.A. 2, 13, 30, 43, 92, 128.

KAULA, Prithvi Nath, b. 15 Mar. 1924. Professor of Library Science. Educ: M.A., Punjab, India; B.Lib.Sc. (changed into M.Lib.Sc.), Delhi; Dip.Lib.Sc., Banaras Hindu Univ. Appts. incl: Libn., Min. of Labour, Govt. of India, 1951-58; Rdr. in Lib. Sci. (1st position in the country), Univ. of Delhi, 1958-60; Univ. Libn. & Hd., Dept. of Lib. Sci., Banaras Hindu Univ., 1960-67; UNESCO Expert, UNESCO Regional Ctr. for Western Hemisphere, 1967-68; Prof. & Hd., Dept. of Lib. Sci., also Univ. Libn., Banaras Hindu Univ., 1971; Prof. & Hd., Dept. of Lib. Sci., ibid, 1971-. Mbrships. incl: Fndr. & Gen. Sec., Delhi Lib. Assn., 1953-55; V.P., ibid, 1955-58; Gen. Sec., 1958-60; Fndr., Fedn. of Indian Lib. Assns., 1966; Fndr., Indian Assn. of Tchrs. of Lib. Sci., 1969; Gen. Sec., L.A.T.L.I.S., 1969-73; Pres., ibid, 1973-. Author of 34 publs., 300 tech. papers, over 250 book reviews & over 1000 notes & info. scores of lib. plans &

reports. Recip. of hons. Address: C 1, Banaras Hindu Univ., Varanasi-221005, India. 93.

KAULILI, Alvina Nye, b. 20 Oct. 1918. Music Educator & Director. Educ: Mus.B., New Engl. Conservatory of Music, Mass., 1942; M.A. in Music, Tchrs. Coll., Columbia Univ., N.Y., 1958; Specialist Dip. in Music, ibid, 1962. Appts: Music Tchr., Music Coord., Chmn. of Music Dept. in var. schls., Hawaii, 1942; Lectr., Maui Community Coll.; Dir., Honolulu Police Choral Grp., 1958-72; Music Dir., var. musicals, Honolulu Community Theatre & Chinese Civic Assn.; Dir. & Advsr. for Na Kini of Hawaii (youth grp.). Mbrships: State Pres., Delta Kappa Gamma Soc., 1973-75; Past Pres., Beta Chapt., ibid; Past Pres., Alpha Alpha Chapt., Epsilon Sigma Alpha; 3rd V.P., Hawaii Music Educators Assn.; Chmn., State Coun. on Hawaiian Heritage; State Fndn. Culture & Arts; Bd. Dirs., Hawaiian Music Fndn.; Sec., Aloha Week Hawaii, Inc.; Mu Phi Epsilon. Author & Composer, Lei of Friendship, for Delta Kappa Gamma Soc. Named Tchr. of Yr., 1955. Address: 317 Kaimuki Ave., Honolulu, HI 96816, U.S.A. 78.

KAUPER, Paul Gerhardt, b. 9 Nov. 1907. Legal Educator. Educ: A.B., Earlham Coll., 1929; J.D., Univ. of Mich., 1932. Appts: Asst. Prof., Law, Univ. of Mich. Law Schl., 1936-39; Assoc. Prof., ibid, 1939-46; Prof., 1946-65; Henry M. Butzel Prof. of Law, 1965-. Pres., Nat. Order of the Coif, 1965-67; Exec. Comm., 1968-70. Publs: Frontiers of Constitutional Liberty, 1957; Civil Liberties & the Constitution, 1962; Religion & the Constitution, 1964; Cases & Materials on Constitutional Law, 4th edit., 1972. Hons: Ross Essay Prize, Am. Bar Assn., 1951; Fac. Disting. Achievement Award, Univ. of Mich., 1959; Henry Russel Lectr., ibid, 1971; LL.D., Heidelberg Univ., 1970. Address: Legal Rsch. Bldg., Univ. of Mich., Ann Arbor, MI 48104, U.S.A. 2, 13, 128, 130.

KAUPPI, Raili Marjatta, b. 10 Apr. 1920. Professor of Philosophy. Educ: ph. cand., Univ. of Helsinki, Finland, 1949; ph. lic., ibid 1956; ph. dr., ibid, 1961. Appts. incl: Libn., Helsinki City Lib., 1942-63; Lectr. in Lib. Sci., Univ. of Tampere (formerly Schl. of Social Scis.), Finland, 1963-66; acting Prof. of Philos., ibid, 1966-69; Prof. of Philosophy, 1969-. Mbrships: Assn. of Symbolic Logic; Gottfried-Wilhelm-Leibniz-Gesellschaft; Societas Philosophica Fennica. Publs. incl: Uber die Leibnizsche Logik, 1960; Einführung in die Theorie der Begriffsseysteme, 1967. Address: University of Tampere Kalevantie 4, Tampere, Finland.

KAUPPILA, Veikko Aulis, b. 14 May 1937. Managing Director. Educ: Dip.Eng., 1965, M.Sc., 1967, Univ. of Helsinki. Appts: Structural Planner, Eino Viljo engrng. co., 1964-67; Tech. Mgr., 1967-69, Mng. Dir., 1970-, Assn. of the Concrete Ind. in Finland. Num. mbrships. incl: Off. Deleg., Bur. Int. of Béton Manufacturé; Pres., & Mbr., Bd. of Dirs., Bldg. Info. Inst.; Bd. of Dirs., Finnish Dept. Nordic Road Tech. Assn.; Bd. of Dirs., Finnish Concrete Assn.; Bd. of Dirs., State Tech. Rsch. Ctr., Concrete Lab.; Assn. of Finnish Civil Engrs.; Am. Concrete Inst. Ed., Finnish tech. jrnls. Hons: Mark of Hon. of Acad. Nation, 1969. Address: Lapinlahdenkatu 1 a A 8, SF-00180 Helsinki 18, Finland. 43.

KAUR, Jasbir, 26 Oct. 1935. Physician. Educ: M.B. B.S., Panjab Univ., India, 1960; D.C.H., London, U.K., 1965; Dip., Am. Bd. Pediatrics, 1966. Appts. incl: Res., Royal Childrens Hosp., Melbourne, Australia,

1968-69; Clin. Asst., Haematol. Rsch. Clin., ibid, 1969-71; Hon. Clin. Asst., 1971-72; Med. Officer, Maternal Infant & Pre-Schl. Welfare Div., Dept. of Hlth., Vic., 1971-72, 73-; Paediatrician, Rural Hlth. Rsch. Proj., Narangwal, Ludihiana, India, 1972-73; Hon. Clin. Asst., Paediatric Outpatient, Queen Victoria Hosp., Melbourne, Aust., 1973-. Fellowships: Am. Acad. Pediatrics; Aust. Mbr., Community Pediatric Sect., ibid. Mbrships: Aust. Med. Assn.; Vic. Med. Womens Assn.; Soropomist Club, Melbourne; Indian Acad. Pediatrics. Address: Dept. of Maternal & Child Hlth., 272-282 Queen St., Melbourne, Australia 3000.

KAUREL, Finn, b. 17 Dec. 1914. Principal. Educ: Sivilokonom, Norwegian H.S. of Econs. & Bus. Admin, 1940; Commercial Tchr's. Exam., ibid, 1941. Appts: Lector, Commercial Gym., Oslo, 1941-62; Prin., Commercial Gym. & Schl., Tønsberg, 1962-. Mbrships: Norwegian Assn. of Commerce Tchrs. (Chmn. 1946-53); Nordic Comm. for Commerce Educ. (Chmn. 1950-55, 1965-70). Author of var. textbooks on Bus. Econ., Acctcy. & Arithmetic. Address: Box 173, 3101 Tønsberg, Norway. 134.

KAUTZ, Lynford English, b. 5 Apr. 1915. Educational Administrator. Educ: Grad., W. Chester State Coll., Pa., 1936; Grad., Jourden Schl. of Publicity & Promotion, Phila., 1946; Grad., Am. TV Inst., Chgo., 1948. Appts. incl: Mid-West Dir., Nat. Fund for Med. Educ., 1951-54; Dir. of Dev. & PR, Northwestern Univ., 1954-62; V.P. for Dev., Boston Univ., 1962-67; Dir. of Resources, Fletcher Schl. of Law & Diplomacy, Tufts Univ., Boston, 1967-69; Dir., Off. of Instnl. Dev., Smithsonian Instn., Wash. D.C., 1969-. Mbrships: Economic Club, Chgo.; Chgo. Club; Algonquin Club, Boston; Longwood Cricket Club, Chestnut Hill, Mass.; Am. Coll. PR Soc.; Am. Alumni Assn.; Trustee, Arden Shore Assn., Lake Bluff, Ill. Publs: Articles on Isntnl. Advancement & Planning in profl. jrnls. Hons: Recip., Purple Heart, U.S. Army, WWII; Career Recognition Award, Nat. Assn. Dev. Offs., 1970. Address: 1002 Abbey Way, The Cloisters, Mclean, VA 22101, U.S.A. 2, 7.

KAVEY, Lillia (Mrs.), b. 19 July 1889. Banker; Broker. Educ: Banking, Finance, Corporate Law courses, Columbia Univ. & N.Y. Univ. Appts. Owner, pvte. bank, N.Y.C. Mbrships: Pres. Jewish Community Ctr.; Organizer, num. youth clubs, inclng. Carver Ctr., Don Bosco Ctr.; Jewish Theol. Sem. & Nat. Women's League, Mbr., 50 yrs., now Exec. Hon. Bd. Mbr.; Deleg. ibid, Nat. Peace Conf. Publs: Num. articles, Nat. Women's League jrnl., local newspapers. Hons: N.Y. Champion Basketball Gold Medal, 1905; Gold Medal, Jewish Community Ctr.; Num. hons. for civic activities, inclng. saving of 500 lives, concentration camps, WWII. Address: 48 Elmont Ave., Port Chester, NY 10573, U.S.A. 5, 6, 55, 76.

KAWAHARA, Fred Katsumi, b. 26 Feb. 1921. Chemist. Educ: B.S., Univ. of Tex., 1944; Ph.D., Univ. of Wis., 1948; Fellow, Univ. of Chgo., 1951-53. Appts: Chief, Organic Analyses Lab.; Analytical Quality Control Lab., Nat. Environmental Protection Agcy.; Sr. Rsch. Sci., Standard Oil Co., Ind.; currently Special Cons. & Grp. Ldr., Oil Analyses Lab. Mbrships: Fellow, Am. Inst. of Chemists; Int. Kiwanis; Am. Chem. Soc.; Sigma Xi; Phi Lambda Upsilon. Approx. 45 publs. & Patents. Address: 2530 Eight Mile Rd., Cinn., OH 45244, U.S.A. 8, 14, 16.

KAWAKITA, Nagamasa, b. 30 Apr. 1903. President, Towa Company, Ltd.; President, Foreign Film Importers and Distributors Association. Educ: Nat. Peking Univ., China, 1923. Appts. incl: Fndr. Pres., Towa Co. Ltd., Japan, 1928-; Pres., For. Film Importers & Distributors Assn., ibid, 1958-; Pres., Toho Int. Corp.1959-. Mbrships. incl: Tokyo Club; Bd. Mbr., Maison Franco-Japonaise. Works incl: Prod., many Chinese films in China; Prod. of co-prod. films with different countries; Introduced many for. films to Japan. Hons. incl: Order of Arts & Letters, France, 1959; Order of Commendatore, Italy, 1959; Medal of Merit w. Blue Ribbon, Japan, 1964; Legion d'Honour, France, 1968; Order of the Sacred Treasure, Japan, 1973. Address: 2-2 Yukinoshita Kamakura, Japan.

KAWAMURA, Rusty Tatsuo, b. 17 June 1924. General Contractor; U.S. Army Officer. Educ: Univ. of Hawaii, 1947-51; Command & Gen. Staff Coll., Ft. Leavenworth, Kan., 1961-66; U.S. Army War Coll., Carlisle Barracks, Pa., 1970-72. Appts: Mbr., U.S. Army Reserve, 1949-; Currently Lt. Col., HQ IX Corps (Augmentation); Gen. Contractor 1953-; Housing Bd. of Appeals, City & Co. of Honolulu, 1971-76. Mbrships: Dir., Chmbr. of Comm. of Hawaii, 1971-73; Sec., Honolulu Japanese Chmbr. of Comm., 1971-73; 2nd V.P., ibid, 1973-74; V.P., Moanalua HS Assn., 1973-74. Pres: Hawaii Builders Assn., 1960; Amfac Contractors Assn., 1961-; Oahu Contractors Assn., 1962; Moanalua Elem. Schl. PTA, 1966-67; Moanalua Gardens Community Assn., 1969-70; Dir., Moanalua Intermediate Schl. PTA, 1968-73; Dist. Chmn., Repubn. Party of Hawaii, 1961-62. Author of Should Academic Credit Be Given for ROTC (thesis), 1971. Address: 1236 Ala Amoamo St., Honolulu, HI 96819, U.S.A. 16, 78.

KAWIN, Bruce F., b. 6 Nov. 1945. Teacher; Poet. Educ: A.B., Columbia Univ., 1967; M.F.A., Cornell Univ., 1969; Ph.D., ibid, 1970; UCLA Film Schl. Appts. incl: Tchng. Fellow, Cornell Univ., 1967-70; Asst. Prof. English, Wells Coll., Aurora, N.Y., 1970-73; Lectr. English & Film, Univ. of Calif., Riverside, 1973-74; poetry readings in U.S. Univs. Poetry pamphlets: Breakwater, 1964; Slides, 1971. Books incl: Telling It Again & Again: Repetition in Literature & Film, 1972; 2 books in preparation; poems & articles in nat. jrnls; former Ed., Columbia Review. Hons: Acad. of Am. Poets Prize, Honorable Mention, 1969. Address: 467 W. 8th St., Claremont, CA 91711, U.S.A.

KAY, David Cyril, b. 5 Sept. 1932. Psychiatrist. Educ: B.S., Wheaton Coll., Ill., 1954; M.D., Schl. of Med., Univ. of Ill., 1958; Intern, Presby.-St. Luke's Hosp., Chgo., Ill., 1958-59; Res. Psych., Ill. State Psych. Inst., Chgo., 1962-64. Appts: Commnd. Off., Pub. Hlth. Serv., 1959-; Staff Physn., PHS Hosp., Ft. Worth, Tex., 1959-61; Staff Psych., Nat. Inst. of Mental Hlth., Clin. Rsch. Ctr., 1964-66 & Addiction Rsch. Ctr., Lexington, Ky., 1964-; Chief, Expmntl. Psych. Unit, 1966-69; Expmntl. Psych. Sect., 1969-, NIMH Addiction Rsch. Ctr.; Fellow, Mental Hlth. Career Dev. Prog. Mbrships. incl: Dipl., Am. Bd. of Psych. & Neurol.; Int. Brain Rsch. Org.; AMA; N.Y. Acad. of Sci.; AAAS; Am. Soc. of Pharmacol. & Expmntl. Therapeutics; Am. Psych. Assn.; Soc. for Neurosci. Author of articles in profl. publs. Address: NIMH Addiction Rsch. Ctr., P.O. Box 2000, Lexington, KY 40507, U.S.A. 14, 112.

KAY, Ernest, b. Darwen, Lancashire, U.K. Editor; Publisher; Author. Appts. incl: Hon. Gen. Ed. & Chmn. of Edit. Board, Dictionary of International Biography, 1967-, Mbr., Edit. & Advisory Board, 1960-67; Hon. Gen. Ed. of many other biog. ref. books; Pres., Melrose Press Ltd., Cambridge, U.K.; Chmn. & Mng. Dir., Kay Sons & Daughter Ltd., Publishers, London; Chmn., Kay Law & Mockridge Ltd., Publrs; previously Mng. Ed. daily newspapers in U.K., incl. The Evening News, London. Books incl: Isles of Flowers: The Story of the Isles of Scilly, 1956, '64, '67; Great Men, 1956, '60; Pragmatic Premier: An Intimate Portrait of Harold Wilson, 1967, '68; The Wit of Harold Wilson, 1967, '68. Hons: United Poets Laureate International Gold Medal, 1966; Emperor Haile Selassie I Gold Medal, 1971; Knight of Mark Twain, 1972; Silver Key to City of Las Vegas, 1972; Nom. by Repub. of Philippines for Nobel Peace Prize, 1973. Mbrships: Royal Society of Arts (Life Fellow), London; Accademia di Filologia Classica, Milan, Italy; Community of European Writers (Founder Mbr.), Rome, Italy; World Academy of Art and Science, New York City; National Arts Club, N.Y.C.; etc. Address: Orcheston, 11 Madingley Road, Cambridge CB3 0EG, U.K. 3, 11, 29, 30, 32, 43, 45, 48, 57, 128, 137.

KAY, Felix Ross, b. 16 Feb. 1927. Physician; Surgeon. Educ: B.S., Bacteriol., Univ. of Okla., 1951; M.D., 1959; B.S., Chem., Ctrl. State Univ. of Okla., 1955. Appts: Rsch. Asst., Organic Chem. Lab., E.I. DuPont de Nemours & Co., Wilmington, Del. & Okla. Ordinance Works, Chateau; Engr., USAF; AAF Tech. Trng. Cmd. Grad. & Instr., Med. Tech. Schl.; Chief Technol., Amarillo, Tex., AFB Hosp. & Boca Raton, Fla. AFB Hosp.; Fellow, Am. Acad. Family Physns.; Chief of Staff, Midwest City Mem. Hosp. Mbrships. incl: Okla. Co. Med. Soc., Okla. City; Deleg., Okla. City, Okla. State Med. Assn.; AMA; Southern Med. Assn.; Int. Coll. Surgs.; Phi Sigma; Lambda Tau; Alpha Chi. Author of med. articles. Hons. incl: Spec. Citation, Sacramento Chmbr. of Comm., Calif., 1970; Spec. Citation, Outstanding Serv., USAF, 1972. Address: 6520 E. Reno Ave., Med. Arts Bldg. of Midwest City, Midwest City, OK 73110, U.S.A. 125.

KAY, Lester Williams. Consultant Oral Surgeon & Reader in Oral Surgery. Educ: Guy's Hosp. & Dental Schls., Univ. of London. Appts: Reporter, 1937-41; Air Crew Navigator, RAF, 1941-46; Lectr., Oral Surg., Univ. of Durham, 1959-62; Sr. Lectr. & Cons. Oral Surg., Inst. of Dental Surg., Univ. of London, 1962-68; Asst. Ed., Ed., Brit. Jrnl. of Oral Surg., 1963-73; Cons. Oral Surg. & Rdr. in Oral Surg., Univ. of London, 1968-; Hd. of Admissions & Casualty Dept., Eastman Dental Hosp. Mbrships: BMA; Mbr., Rep. Bd., Brit. Dental Assn.; Comm. of Mgmt., Eastman Dental Hosp.; Coun. Mbr., Brit. Assn. of Oral Surgs.; Mbr., Exec. Sub-comm., Univ. Dental Tchrs. & Rsch. Wkrs. Grp.; Ctrl. Comm. for Hosp. Dental Serv. Num. publs. incl: The Impacted Wisdom Tooth, 1965, 2nd edit., 1969; Drugs in Dentistry, 1969, '72; An Outline of Oral Surgery, 2 vols., 1971. Address: Tympany, Beckenham Park Place, Beckenham, Kent, U.K. 3.

KAY, M. Jane, b. 31 Aug. 1925. Personnel Manager. Educ: B.S., Univ. of Detroit, Mich., 1948; M.A., Wayne State Univ., 1952; M.B.A., Univ. of Mich., 1963; Certified Admin. Mgr. (C.A.M.) Admin. Mgmt. Soc., 1971. Appts: incl: w. Detroit Edison Co., Mich. 1943- as Sr. Personnel Interviewer, 1950-60, Personnel Coord. for Women, 1960-65, Off. Employment Admnstr., 1965-70, Gen. Employment Admnstr., 1970-71, Dir., Personnel Servs., 1971-72, Mgr. Employee Rels. & Mbr. Mgmt. Coun., 1972-; Instr., Evening Coll. Bus. & Admin., Univ. of Detroit, 1963-; Instr. &

Seminar Ldr., num. other Mgmt. Courses, 1961-. Mbrships: Int. Assn. Personnel Women (Pres. 1969-70); Women's Economic Club (Pres. 1972-73); Alpha Sigma Lambda; Phi Gamma Nu (Nat. V.P. 1955-57); Gamma Pi Epsilon; Sigma Iota Epsilon; num. other civic & profl. orgs. Publs: Women in Management—Past, Present, Future (NAM Report), 1972; Contbr. to profl. jrnls. Hons. incl: Headliner Award, Women of Wayne State Univ., 1970. Address: 3495 Bishop Rd., Detroit, MI 48224, U.S.A. 5.

KAY, Richard Andrew, b. 15 November 1945. Publisher. Educ: Bootham Schl., York, U.K.; B.Sc. Econ. (Hons.), London School of Economics & Political Science, Univ. of London. Appts. incl: Edit. writer, Time & Tide magazine, London, 1966; Assistant, Dictionary of International Biography, 1967, Head of Mailing, 1968-70, Manager, 1970-, Dir., 1972-; Chmn., Eddison Press Ltd., Publishers; Dir., Kay Sons & Daughter Ltd., Publishers; formerly Leader & Pianist, Dr. K's Blues Band, touring U.K. and Europe. Address: 3 Westland Terrace, North Street, Cambridge, U.K.

KAYE, Geraldine, b. 14 Jan. 1925. Writer. Educ: B.Sc. (Econ.), London Univ., 1949. Mbrships: Soc. of Authors; Mbrship. Sec., W. Country Writer's Assn.; Chmn., Bristol Writer's Circle. Publs: Oh Essie, 1960; The Boy Who Wanted to Go Fishing, 1960; Kwasi Goes to Town, 1962; Kofi and the Eagle, 1963; Chik and the Bottle House, 1965; Tail of the Siamese Cat, 1965; The Raffle Pony, 1966; The Blue Rabbit, 1966; Kassim and the Sea Monkey, 1967; Koto and the Lagoon, 1968; Tawno, Gypsy Boy, 1968; Runaway Boy, 1971; Nowhere to Stop, 1972; Marie Alone, 1973. Address: 39 High Kingsdown, Bristol BS2 8EW, U.K. 3.

KAYE, Norman, b. 22 Sept. 1922. Realtor; Poet; Songwriter; Stock Broker; Insurance Broker. Educ: Attended Syracuse Univ. & Albion Coll.; A.L.D., Univ. of China, Hong Kong. Appts: Pres., MKT Music Publng. Co., Skip Music Publng. Co., & Norman Kaye Real Estate Co.; Past Pres., Western Empire Petroleum Co.; Realtor, Las Vegas. Mbrships. incl: Nat. Bd. Realtors; Nat. Assn. Real Estate Appraisers; Nat. Assn. Security Dealers; Pres., Nev. Poet Laureate Soc.; Bd. of Dirs., Nev. State Drug Abuse Coun. Publs. incl: (novel) The Death of Cock Robin, & the Events that led to it; (songs) The Shepherd of Love, Home of The Good Shepherd; The Song Of St. Jude, Home of St. Jude; Throw a Dime My Way, Nat. March of Dimes Theme Song; Have A Heart, Lend A Hand, Variety Clubs & Hosps.; Let's Love; Stay; I'm in Love, etc. Hons. incl: Poet Laureate, Nev.; num. ASCAP awards. Address: 4813 Paradise Rd., Las Vegas, NV 89109, U.S.A.

KAYMAKÇALAN, Şükrü, b. 12 June 1923. Medical Doctor. Educ: Med. Schl., Istanbul Univ., 1946; M.S., Schl. Postgrad. Studies, Univ. of Mich., Ann Arbor, U.S.A., 1954. Appts: Physn., Malaria Control Campaign, Anatolia, 1948-50; Asst. of Pharmacol., Refik Saydam Central Inst. Hygiene, Ankara, Turkey, 1950-52; Rockefeller Fndn. Fellow, Dept. Pharmacol., Univ. of Mich., Ann Arbor, U.S.A., 1952-54; Sr. Pharmacologist, Drug Control Div., Refik Saydam Central Inst. Hygiene, Ankara, Turkey, 1954-59; Chmn., Dept. Pharmacol., Eageen Univ. Med. Schl., 1959-61; Prof. & .Chmn., Dept. Pharmacol., Ankara Univ. Med. Schl., 1961-. Mbr., var. med. orgs., & Fndr. Mbr., Turkish Pharmacological Soc. Num. articles & 4 books, mainly on drug dependence. Address: Enis Behiç Koryürek Sok. 11/16, Çankaya—Ankara, Turkey.

KEARNS, William Michael, Jr., b. 26 June 1935. Investment Banker. Educ: A.B., Univ. of Maine, 1957; A.M., N.Y. Univ., 1960; Postgrad., ibid, 1960-64; Boston Coll. Law Schl., 1957-58. Appts: Chase Manhattan Bank, N.Y.C., 1958-59; Fac. Mbr., Fairleigh Dickinson Univ., N.J., 1958-68;; Security Analyst, Hayden, Stone Co., Inc., N.Y.C., 1960-62; Instructure Security Analysis, N.Y. Inst. of Finance, 1961-67; Assoc., Institutional Sales & Syndicate Dept., Kuhn, Loeb & Co., N.Y.C., 1962-64; Asst. V.P., ibid, 1964-66; V.P., ibid, 1966-68; Sales Mgr., ibid, 1968-70; Gen. Ptnr., ibid, 1970-; Adj. Prof., Grad. Schl. of Bus. Admin., N.Y. Univ., 1971-72. Mbrships. incl: Trustee, Morris Mus. of Arts & Scis.; Investment Assn., N.Y.; V.P., ibid, 1970; Securities Ind. Assn.; Exec. Comm., N.Y. Dist., ibid, 1970; Vice-Chmn., ibid, 1973; Chmn., ibid, 1974; Beta Theta Pi; Kappa Phi Kappa. Address: Dellwood Dr., Madison, NJ 07940, U.S.A. 2.

KEATING, Henry Reymond Fitzwalter, b. 31 Oct. 1926. Author. Educ: Trinity Coll., Dublin. Mbrships: Chmn., Crime Writers Assn., 1970-71; Detection Club. Publs: Death & the Visiting Firemen; Zen There Was Murder; A Rush on the Ultimate; The Dog It Was That Died; Death of a Fat God; The Perfect Murder; Is Skin-deep, Is Fatal; Inspector Ghote's Good Crusade; Inspector Ghote Caught in Meshes; Inspector Ghote Hunts the Peacock; Inspector Ghote Breaks An Egg; Inspector Ghote Goes By Train; The Strong Man; Inspector Ghote Trusts the Heart; Bats Fly Up for Inspector Ghote, 1974; The Underside, 1974. Recip., Crime Writers Assn. Golden Dagger, 1964. Address: 35 Northumberland Pl., London W2 5AS, U.K. 1.

KEATING, Maud Elizabeth, b. 21 Dec. 1903. Bank Executive. Educ: Grad., Pvte. Secs. Workshop. Appts: Pvte. Sec., White & Wycokoff Mfg. Co., Holyoke, 1928-57, Worthington Corp., 1947-52; Pvte. Sec. to Pres., Asst. Cashier, Exec. Sec. & Notary Pub., Holyoke Nat. Bank, 1952-. Mbrships: Holyoke Chapt., Nat. Secs. Assn. Int.; Pioneer Valley Chapt. Nat. Assn. of Bank Women Offs.; Holyoke Speakers Club; Friends of Holyoke Mus.; Exec. Secs. Seminar Grp., N.Y.C. Am. Soc. of Notaries of Wash., D.C.; Blessed Sacrament Ch. Women's Club; Nat. Coun. of Cath. Women. Drawings accepted for publ. Recip. of award, Nat. Secs. Assn. Int., Holyoke Chapt. Address: 14 Charles St., Holyoke, MA 01040, U.S.A. 5, 138.

KEDDIE, James Alfred Grant, b. 10 Nov. 1900. Physician. Educ: M.B., Ch.B., M.D., Univ. of St. Andrews; D.P.H., Cambridge Univ.; Dip. in Pub. Admin., London Schl. of Econs. Appts: Res. House Physn., Gen. Hosp., Birkenhead, Ruchill Fever Hosp., Glasgow, Royal Manchester Children's Hosp.; Dpty. Med. Off. of Hlth., Nuneaton; Med. Insp. of Aliens, Dover; Dpty. Med. Off. of Hlth., W. Bromwich; Med. Off. for Schl. Hlth., Dept. Hlth. for Scotland. Mbrships: British Med. Assn.; Soc. of Community Med. Papers & reports, Gov. publs. Med. articles, var. profl. jrnls. Address: 11 St. Ninian's Ter., Edinburgh 10, U.K. 3.

KEE, Robert, b. 15 Oct. 1919. Author; Broadcaster. Educ: M.A., Magdalen Coll., Oxford. Appts: Reporter, Picture Post, 1949-51; Picture Ed., W.H.O., 1953; Special Corres., Observer, 1956-57; Lit. Ed., Spectator, 1957; Special Corres., Sunday Times, 1957-58; B.B.C. TV, 1958-62; Independent TV, 1962-. Mbrships: A.C.T.T.; Soc. of Authors; Brooke's Club. Publs. incl: A Crowd is not Company, 1947; The Impossible Shore, 1949; A Sign of the Times, 1955; Refugee World, 1961; The Green Flag, 1972. Recip. Atlantic Award for Lit., 1946. Address: c/o Lloyds Bank Ltd., 112-114 Kensington High St., London W8, U.K.

KEEFE, Mildred Jones, b. 14 Aug. 1896. Educator (Retired); Writer. Educ: New England & Cinn. Conservatories of Music; Concert Artists in Voice & Piano; B.S., Educ., 1934, A.M., 1936, Boston Univ.; Special studies, Univ. of Cinn, & Syracuse Univ., N.Y.; Grad. study, Smith Coll., Mass.; Study tours in Europe. Appts. incl: Pianist, Tchr., Pvte. Studio, Boston, Mass., 1917-26; Educl. Dir., 1st Unitarian Ch., Cinn., Ohio, 1926-30; Musical Dir. & Asst. Prof. of Fine Arts in Relig., Boston Univ., 1934-40; Dir., Dramatic Art Dept., 1945-71, Dir. of Fine Arts Dept., 1952-71, Greenbrier Coll., Lewisburg, W. Va.; Now ret'd. Mbrships. incl: Smithsonian Assocs.; Pres., Women's Alliance, Unitarian Mem. Ch., Fairhaven, Mass.; Pres., Creative Arts Coun. of Fairhaven; Coll. Club, New Bedford, Mass.; Mattapoisett Woman's Club; AAUP; Nat. League Am. Pen Women, W. Va.; Intercontinental Biographical Assn., U.K.; Centro Studi e Scambi Int., Rome, Italy; Advsry., Marquis Biographical Lib. Assn.; AAUW (State Arts Chmn., 1953-55); Fndr. & Coord., Creative Arts Festival of W. Va., Inc., Charleston, 1955-68; Greenbrier Valley, 1969-72; Pi Gamma Mu; Pi Lambda Theta. Publs. incl: Poetry Anthol., Choric Interludes, 1942, 3rd. ed. '69; Poems, White Beauty, 1956; Poems in var. mags. Hons: Medal, Int. Who's Who in Community Serv., 1972; Awards & citations for achievement in the arts. Address: 10 Pearl St., Mattapoisett, MA 02739, U.S.A. 5, 6, 11, 22, 57, 128, 129, 132, 138.

KEEFFE, Jim, b. 20 Aug. 1919. Parliamentarian. Appts: State Govt. Employee; Trade Union Official; Org., Queensland Br. of the Australian Labour Party, (ALP), 1956-60; Sec., ibid, 1960-65; Nat. Pres., 1962-70; Elected to the Senate for Qld., 1964-70, '70-. Mbrships: Chmn., Senate Standing Comm. on Soc. Environment; Jt. House Comm.; Senate Select Comm. on Offshore Petroleum Resources, 1967-71; Coun. of the Australian Inst. of Aboriginal Studies; Jt. Standing Comm. on the Northern Territory; Australian Parly. Del., 3rd Int. Conf. on the Environment, Vienna, 1972; State Councillor & Nat. Del., Australian Legion of Ex-Servicemen & Women; Former Pres., Inst. of Int. Affairs Legion of Ex-Servicemen & Women; Former Pres., Inst. of Int. Affairs; Qld. Littoral Soc.; Aust. Wildlife Preservation Soc.; Amnesty Int.; Irish Assn.; Returned Servs. League; Cath. Readers & Writers Assn.; Fabian Soc. of Qld.; Aust. Observer, World Peace Coun.; sev. reform assns. Publs: sev. short stories; num. articles & pamphlets on social reform, Aboriginal affairs, etc. Address: P.O. Box 47, Townsville, Qld. Australia 4810.

KEELER, Clinton Clarence. Teacher; Writer. Educ: B.A., Okla. State Univ.; Ph.D. Univ. of Minn.; Grad. Study, Johns Hopkins Univ., Balt., Md. Appts: Lt. USNR, Active Duty Pacific, 1942-46; Instr., Okla. State Univ. & Univ. of Minn., 1946-52; Prof. of Engl. SUNY at Cortland, 1952-56; Prof. of Engl. Okla. State Univ., 1956-67; Hd., Dept. of Engl Lang. & Lit., ibid, 1968-; Ed., Cimarron Review, 1968-. Mbrships: Modern Poetry Soc., World Poetry Soc.; MLA; Am. Studies Assn. Nat. Coun. of Tchrs. of Engl. Contbr. of poems to literary jrnls.; Contbr. to profl. jrnls. Hons: Outstanding Serv. as Tchr., Okla. State Univ. 1964. Address: 4 Preston Pl., Stillwater, OK 74074, U.S.A. 2, 11, 13.

KEELEY, Elizabeth Ruth Said, b. 29 May 1900. Retired Toy Shop Manager. Appts: Sec. & Payroll Clerk, Payroll Dept., Corning Glass Works Off., 1918-30; Mgr., Toy Shop, A.W. Keeley's Sporting Goods Store, 1952-58. Mbrships. incl: Pres., Woman's Club, Corning, N.Y., 1969-70 & 1970-71; Club Publicity Chmn., ibid, 1969-71; Fedn. Fund Raising Proj., 1970-71; Registrations, N.Y. State Fedn. Conven., Corning, 1958; 1st V.P. & Prog. Chmn., 1973-74; Pres., Women of Christ Ch., 1951-53; Recording Sec., Ch. Women United, 1953-55; 10 yr. Cancer Survey, N.Y. State, 1962-72. Hons. incl: Cert. for Disting. Serv. to the Community & State, N.Y. Fedn. of Women's Clubs; Recommendation of Corning Woman's Club, name on Hon. Roll. of N.Y. State Fedn. of Women's Clubs, 1972. Address: 7 Pinewood Circle, Corning, NY 14830, U.S.A. 130.

KEELIN, John Edward, b. 8 Aug. 1928. Concert Pianist. Educ: B.Mus., James Millikin Conservatory of Music, 1951; Artist-Pupil, Elisabeth Kravis, Concert Pianist, Boston, Mass. Appts: Concert Pianist; Bass Baritone; Artist in Res., NYC; w. Ill. Wesleyan Schl. of Music. Mbr., Phi Mu Alpha, Beta Theta Chapt. Author, Eleven Tone Music. Address: 1704 East Adams St., Springfield, IL U.S.A. 126.

KEESING, Nancy Florence (Mrs. A.M. Hertzberg), b. 7 Sept. 1923. Writer. Educ: Dipl. Soc. Studies, Univ. of Sydney, Australia. Appts: Free-lance writer, ed., critic; Mbr., Lit. Bd., Australian Coun. for the Arts, Nat. Lit. Bd. of Review. Mbrships: Australian Soc. of Authors (mgmt. comm.; Ed., The Australian Author); V.P., N.S.W. Br., Engl. Assn.; P.E.N.; Royal Australian Histl. Soc.; Australian Jewish Histl. Soc. (comm. of mgmt.). Publd. Poetry: Imminent Summer, 1951; Three Men & Sydney, 1955; Showground Sketchbook, 1968. Children's Books: By Gravel & Gum, 1966; The Golden Dream, 1974. Criticism: Douglas Stewart, 1969; Elsie Carew, Australian Primitive Poet, 1965; Australian Post-War Novelists (edited w. notes & introduction), 1974. Ed., var anthols. Address: Australian Soc. Authors, 6th Floor, 252 George St., Sydney, N.S.W., Australia 2110. 55.

KEETON, Morris T., b. 1 Feb. 1917. College Administrator. Educ: B.A., Southern Meth. Univ., 1935; M.A., 1936; M.A., Harvard Univ., 1937; Ph.D., 1938. Appts: incl: Coll. Pastor, Antioch Coll., 1947-60; Asst. Prof., ibid, 1947; Assoc. Prof., 1949; Prof., Philos. & Relig., 1956; Assoc. Dean. of Fac., 1960; Dean, Fac., 1963; Acad. V.P., 1966; Provost, 1972. Mbrships. incl: Pres., Am. Assn. for Higher Educ., 1972-73; Am. Philos. Assn.; Am. Friends Serv. Comm. Publs. incl: Values Men Live By, 1960; Co-Auth., Ethics for Today, 5th edit., 1973; Struggle & Promise: A Future for Colleges, 1969; Models & Mavericks, 1971; Shared Authority on Campus, 1971. Address: 10989 Swanfield Rd., Columbia, MD 21044, U.S.A. 2, 8.

KEGAN, Elizabeth Hamer (Mrs. Lawrence Robert Kegan), b. 4 Jan. 1912. Assistant Librarian of Congress, Washington, D.C., U.S.A. Educ: B.A., Hist., Univ. of Tenn., 1933; Fellow, Hist., ibid, 1933-34; Grad. work, Hist. & Pol. Sci., Univ. of Tenn. & Am. Univ., Wash. D.C. Appts: Rsch. Asst., Ed., Admin. Asst. i/c., Survey of Fed. Archives in the States, 1936-40; Publs. Writer & P.R. positions. Nat. Archives & Records Serv., 1950-51; ibid; Info. & Publs. Off., 1951-60; Asst. Libn. for Pub. Affairs, 1960-63; Asst. Libn. of Congress, 1963-, Lib. of Congress. Mbrships: Hon. Fellow, Fndg., Coun., Soc. of Am. Archivists; Hon. Trustee, Gtr.

Wash. Educl. TV Assn., 1966; Mass. Histl. Soc., 1972-; Fellow, Mass. Histl. Soc. Lib.; Pres. Coun. for Grad. Schl. of Arts & Sci., N.Y. Univ., 1968-; ALA; Am. & Southern Histl. Assns.; D.C. Lib. Assn.; Int. Coun. on Archives; Manuscript Soc.; S.C. Histl. Soc.; Org. of Am. Histns.; Am. Assn. of State & Local Hist.; Nat. Trust for Hist. Preserv.; Friend of Folger, John Carter Brown, Duke Univ. & Schlesinger Libs.; Brit. Mus. Soc.; U.S. Comm. for Am. Lib. in Paris. Deleg. to following meetings: Int. Fedn. of Lib. Assns., The Hague, 1966, Copenhagen, 1969; White House Conf. on Int. Cooperation, 1965; Int. Congress on Archives, Florence, 1956, Brussels, 1964, Wash. D.C., 1966. Madrid, 1968, Moscow, 1972. Publs: Contbr. to Dictionary of American History & periodicals; Author, govt. publs. & brochures; Article, The Library of Congress & Enhanced Bibliographic Services to History, in Bibliography & the Historian, 1967; Ed., Inventory of Federal Archives in the States, Annual Report of the Archivist of the United States, 1944-50, Annual Report of Franklin D. Roosevelt Lib., 1944-50; Annual Report of the Librarian of Congress, 1951-62; World War II Surrender Documents. Recip., Phi Kappa Phi Schlrship. Address: Lib. of Congress, 10 1st St. S.E., Wash., D.C. 20540, U.S.A. 5, 6, 7, 15, 42, 132, 138.

KEHLER, Bernard Claud, b. 15 Nov. 1916. Dentist. Educ: D.D.S., Coll. of Dentistry, Emory Univ., 1939; F.A.C.D. Appts: Dentist-in-charge, Kiwanis Dental Clinic, W. Palm Beach, Fla., 1939-40; Prosthodontist (Major), USAF, 1942-46; Ed., Pinellas Co. News, 1957-59. Pvte. Prac., St. Petersburg, Fla., 1940-42. Past Pres: Pinellas Co. Dental Soc.; Exchange Club of St. Petersburg; W. Coast Dental Soc. Histn., Fla Dental Assn., 1960-66. Active off. & mbr., Christ Meth. Ch., 1952-. Hons: Fellow of Am. Coll. of Dentistry; Royal Soc. Hlth., London, England. Address: 285 8th St. N., St. Petersburg, FL 33701, U.S.A. 7.

KEHOE, Robert A., b. 18 Nov. 1893. Physician & Emeritus University Professor. Educ: Ohio State Univ., 1914-15; B.S., Univ. of Cinn., Ohio, 1918; M.D., ibid, 1920. Appts. incl: Asst. Prof.-Assoc. Prof., Physiol., Univ. of Cinn., 1921-39; Med. Dir., Ethyl Gasoline Corp., 1925-58; Fndr. & Dir., Kettering Lab. of Applied Physiol., Univ. of Cinn., 1924-65; Dir., Kettering Lab. Occupational Hlth., ibid, 1928-65; Prof. Emeritus Occupational Med., ibid, 1965-; Chief Med. Cons., Associated Octel Co. Ltd. Mbrships. incl: AMA; Ohio State Med. Assn.; Am. Acad. of Occupational Med.; Pres., ibid; Am. Industrial Hygiene Assn.; Pres., ibid; Am. Physiol. Soc.; Publs: The Occupational Lead Exposure of Men Engaged in Mixing Tetraethyl Lead (Ethyl Fluid) with Gasoline, 1936; The Harben Lectures of 1960, London, U.K. Contbr. of num. articles on lead poisoning to profl. jrnls. Address: The Kettering Lab., College of Medicine, Univ. of Cincinnati, 3223 Eden Ave., Cincinnati, OH 45219, U.S.A.

KEIL, (Günther Walter Gustav) Albert, b. 22 Sept. 1907. Industrialist; University Professor. Educ: Dr.phil.nat., Univ. of Freiburg im Breisgau, Germany, 1933. Appts: Asst., Kaiser Wilhelm Inst. for metal rsch., Stuttgart, 1934-36; Var. indl. appts., 1936-45; Asst., O.N.E.R.A., Paris, France, 1946-49; Indl. activity, 1949-63; Asst., Forschunginst. für Edelmetalle & Metallchemie, Schäbisch Gemünd, 1963-65; Industrialist, INOVAN-Stroebe KG & Prof., Elec. Engrng. Fac., Univ. of Karlsruhe, 1966-. Mbrships: Dir., sci. sect., Verband Deutscher Elektrotechniker; Deutsche Bunsegesellschaft; Deutsche Gessellschaft für Metallkunde; Deutsche Gesellschaft für Galvanotechnik; Inst. of

Metals; Am. Soc. for Metals. Publs: Werkstoffe für Elektrische Kontakte, 1960; Over 100 articles in sci. & tech. jrnls. Recip., Ragnar Holm Sci. Achievement Award, Holm Seminar, Chgo., III., U.S.A., 1973. Address: Goldschmiedeschulstr. 6, D-753 Pforzheim, German Fed. Repub. 43.

KEILBACH, Wilhelm, b. 10 Sept. 1908. University Professor. Educ: Dr.phil., Rome, Italy, 1931; Dr.theol., ibid, 1935. Appts: Ordained to Cath. priesthood, Rome, 1933; Inaugurated, Univ. of Zagreb, Jugoslavia, 1937; Extraordinary Prof., ibid, 1943-50; Full Prof. & Dean, Theol. Fac., 1950-54; Full Prof., Univ. of Vienna, Austria, 1955-56; Full Prof., Univ. of Munich, 1956-; Dean, Theol. Fac., ibid, 1960-61. Mbrships: 1st Chmn., Int. Soc. for Psychol. of Relig., 1969-; Acting Gen. Sec., Görres-Gesellschaft zur Pflege der Wissenschaft, 1967-; Acting Dir., Inst. der Görres-Gesellschaft für interdisziplinäre Forschung, 1965-. Publs: Die Problematik der Religionen, 1936; Wissen & Glauben, 1944; Einübung ins philosophische Denken, 1960; Religiöses Erleben, 1973; 2 books in Croatian lang.; Ed., Münchener Theologische Zeitschrift, 1956-, & Archiv für Religionspsychologie, 1960-. Hons. incl: Culture Prize, Baden-Württemberg, 1968; Dr.theol., Theol. Fac., Zagreb. Address: Hiltenspergerstr. 107/1, D-8 Munich 40, German Fed. Repub.

KEITH, K Wymand, (formerly Leonard Claude Bowen), b. 16 Nov. 1924. Author & Prison Reformist. Educ: Corres. Course, Creative Writing, Univ. of Ore. Appts: Shipyard Wkr., Richmond, Calif.; U.S. Army, 1943; Calif. Highway Patrolman & Asst. Mgr., Grocery Store, 1944-46; Served 15 yrs. of prison sentences totalling 25 yrs., in var. States inclng. Ark., Neb., Okla. & Ore., mainly for cheque frauds, 1946-65; Assoc. Ed., Eyeopener, prison publ., McAlester, Okla., 1957; Ed., Shadows, prison publ., Ore., 1963-64; Profl. Writer, 1965-. Mbrships: PTA, Agnew Elementary Schl., Santa Clara, Calif.; Pres., ibid, 1972; Am. Legion, Post 39, Gilbert, Ariz., 1973. Publs: Long Line Rider: the Story of Cummins Prison Farm, 1971; Life Jackets & Food, in Georgia Jrnl., Aug. 1973; Secret of Mendocino, Journey to Freedom (in preparation); articles in newspapers. Address: 2262 E. Broadway, Apt. B, Mesa, AZ 85204, U.S.A. 30.

KEITH, William Henry, b. 31 Oct. 1929. Writer; Public Relations & Marketing Executive. Educ: Univ. of Wis.; San Diego State Coll.; Special Courses, Columbia Univ. Appts. incl: Serv., USN; Free-lance Writer/Photographer, Pres., Willaim H. Keith & Assocs. Ops. Mgr., WHJB Cablevision; Admin. Asst. to Pres., WHJB Inc.; Int. P.R. Dir., Imperial Coun., AAONMS; Dir. P.R., Chgo Boys Clubs; Gen. Mgr., WCYC Radio; Dir., Ctr. for Communications Arts; Chgo Boys Clubs Educl. Corp.; V.P., Marketing & Communications, Dynamic Marketing Progs. Inc.; V.P., Letterpower Inst. Mbrships: Publicity Club. Chgo.; var. Comms., ibid; Associated Bus Writers of Am. P.R.S.A.; U.S. Coast Guard Aux. Writer-Dir., radio documentary, What Trees Do We Plant; Writer-Dir.-Prod., Men of the Red Fez num. other Radio, TV & Motion picture documentaries. Contbr., num. bus & trade publs. Ghost writer, num. articles. Hons. incl: Documentary of the Yr., PBA, 1965. Address: 2424 E. Oakton St., Arlington Heights IL 60601, U.S.A.

KELL, Winona Day, b. 24 Mar. 1901. Retired College Professor. Educ: A.B., Asbury Coll., Wilmore, Ky.; M.A., Univ. of Ky.,

Lexington; Additional grad. work, Univ. of Chgo. & Coll. of Idaho. Appts: Prof., Reinhardt Coll., Waleska, Ga.; Prof., Kingswood Coll., Ky.; Prof., Olivet Nazarene Coll., Kankakee, III.; Prof., Asbury Coll., Wilmore, Ky. Mbrships: AAUW; Pres., Chinese Am. Christian Assn., Chgo.; State Off., Ky. W.C.T.U.; Rep. from Asbury Coll. to Chgo. Workshop, N. Central Assn. of Liberal Arts. Address: 2306 Lowry, Plant City, FL 33566, U.S.A. 125.

KELLENBENZ, Hermann, b. 28 Aug. 1913. University Professor. Educ: Grad., Kiel Univ., Germany, 1938; Qualified as Lectr., Würzburg Univ., 1949; Rockefeller Fndn. Schlr., Harvard, U.S.A., & Ecole Pratique des Hautes Etudes, Paris, France, 1952-54. Appts: Prof., Econ. & Soc. Hist., Nürnberg, 1957, Cologne Univ., 1960, Nürnberg Univ., Erlangen, 1970; Dir., Fuggar Archives, 1970. Mbrships: Acad. of Sci., Göttingen; Karingl. Ac. Wetenschappen etc., Belgium; Det Kong. Danske Videnskabernes Selskal, Copenhagen, Denmark. Publs. incl: Neuve-Brésil, in l'histoire quantitative du Brésil de 1800 a 1930, 1973; Die Methoden der Wirtschaftshistoriker (co-author), 1972; Grundlagen des Studiums der Wirtschaftsgeschichte, 1973. Address: Findelgasse 7, 85 Nürnberg, German Fed. Repub.

KELLER, Douglas Doyle, b. 5 Apr. 1932. Dentist. Educ: La. State Univ., 1950-52; Northeast State Univ., 1952-53; Loyola Univ. of New Orleans, La., 1953-57. Mbrships. incl: Am. Assn. of Dental Examiners; Bd. of Dirs., Coun. of Dental Care Corp.; La. State Bd. of Dental Examiners; Int. Coll. of Dentistry; Am. Coll. of Dentistry; Dir., La. Dental Assn., 1960-70; V.P. 5th Dist. Dental Assn., 1961-62, Pres., 1964; Bd. of Dirs., Northeast Area Hlth. planning Coun., 1969-73; Pres., La. State Bd. of Dentistry, 1973. Am. Dental Assn.; Xi Phi. Address: 312 Durham, Bastrop, LA 71220, U.S.A.

KELLER, Margaret Gilmer (Mrs. George H. Keller III). Educator. Educ: A.B., Trinity Coll., Wash. D.C., U.S.A.; A.M., Columbia Univ., N.Y.C. Appts. incl: Acting Chmn., Hist. Dept., Trinity Coll., 1935-36; Steelton H.S., Pa., 1937-41; Teaneck H.S. N.J., 1941-42; Engl. Dept., Rutgers Univ., New Brunswick, N.J., 1946-; Chmn., For. Lang. Dept., Glen Rock H.S., N.J., 1956-. Num. Mbrships. incl: NEA; N.J. Educ. Assn.; Pa. Educ. Assn.; Am. Classical Assn.; Mod. Lang. Assn. of N.J.; AAUW; Rutgers Univ. Fac. Club; Dir., Nat. Bd., Trinity Coll. Alumnae Assn., 1960-63 & 1967-71, Nat. Pres., 1963-67; Women's Nat. Republican Club, N.Y.C.; Phi Chi Theta. Hons. incl: 5 Citations for Disting. Serv. to Rutgers Univ.; Robert Ax Award for Disting. Tchng., Glen Rock, 1971; Outstanding Secondary Educator of Am., U.S. Jaycees, 1973. Address: 200 Phelps Rd., Ridgewood, NJ 07450, U.S.A. 5, 6.

KELLETT, William Hiram Jr., b. 15 Oct. 1930. College Professor; Environmental Systems Designer. Educ: B.Arch., Tex. A. & M. Univ., 1960; M.Arch., ibid., 1967. Appts: Asst. Engr., Johnston & Davis Engrs., Victoria, Tex., 1954; Chief Designer, Hall Engrng. Co., Bryan, Tex., 1955-64; Asst. Prof. of Arch.-Prof. of Arch., Tex. A. & M. Univ., 1963-. Mbrships. incl: Am. Soc. Heating, Refrigerating & Air Conditioning Engrs.; Refrigerating Engrs. & Techns. Assn.; Am. Inst. Archts.; AAUP; Phi Theta Kappa; Tau Beta Pi; Tau Delta Sigma. Address: 1000 Esther Blvd., Bryan, TX 77801, U.S.A. 7.

KELLEY, Robert Lloyd, b. 2 June 1925. Professor of History. Educ: A.B., Univ. of

Calif., Santa Barbara, 1948; M.A., Stanford Univ., 1949; Ph.D., 1953. Appts. incl: Inst., Hist., Univ. of Calif., Santa Barbara, 1955-57; Asst. Prof., ibid, 1957-62; Asst. to Chancellor, 1960-62; Assoc. Prof., 1962-68; Prof., 1968-; Cons., Off. of Atty. Gen., State of Calif., 1963-73; Mbr., Commn. for Tchr. Preparation & Licensing, ibid, 1973-; Chmn., Univ. of Calif., Santa Barbara Acad. Senate, 1973-75. Mbrships: Am. Hist. Assn.; Org. of Am. Histns. Publs. incl: Co-Auth., The Stream of American History, 1965; The Tranatlantic Persuasion: The Liberal-Democratic Mind in the Age of Gladstone, 1969; The Sounds of Controversy: Crucial Arguments in the American Past, 1975; articles in profl. jrnls. Recip., Louis Knott Koontz Mem. Award, Pacific Coast Br., Am. Hist. Assn., 1965. Address: 2851 Vista Elevada, Santa Barbara, CA 93105, U.S.A. 9, 13, 30.

KELLOGG, Charles Flint, b. 28 Oct. 1909. Professor of History. Educ: A.B., Columbia Univ., 1931; M.A., Harvard Univ., 1933; Dip., Gen. Theological Sem. of Epsicl. Ch., 1936; Ph.D., Johns Hopkins Univ., 1963; Hon. L.H.D., 1960. Appts. incl: Curate, Ch. of the Mediator, N.Y.C., 1936-37; Rector, ibid, 1937-43; Rector, Ch. of St. Stephen & The Incarnation, Wash. DC, 1943-45; Instr.-Boyd Lee Spahr Prof. Am. Hist., Dickinson Coll., Carlisle, Pa., 1946-68; sev. admin. positions & mbr. num. Faculty Comms., ibid. Mbrships. incl: former Pres. & mbr. Exec. Comm. Bard-St. Stephen's Coll. Alumni Assn.; Exec. Comm., Assn. of Episcl. Colls.; AAUP; Org. of Am. Histns.; Pi Gamma Mu; Exec. Comm. Bd. & Recording Sec., Am. Assn. Tchrs. of Chinese Lang. & Culture. Publs. incl: NAACP: A History of the National Association for the Advancement of Colored People, Vol. 1, 1967, 1973 (Vol. II in preparation); contbns. to sev. books & encys.; book reviews & articles in profl. jrnls. Recip. num. acad. hons. Address: 100 Mooreland Ave., Carlisle, PA 17013, U.S.A. 6, 13, 139.

KELLOGG, Jack L., b. 7 Mar. 1933. Lawyer. Educ: A.B., Wabash Coll., Crawfordsville, Ind., 1955; J.D., N.Y. Univ. Schl. of Law, 1958. Appts. incl: Assoc., McCanliss & Early, N.Y.C., 1958-67; Ptnr., ibid, 1967-. Mbrships. incl: Admitted to N.Y. State Bar, 1959; Bar Assn., N.Y.C.; Pres., Wabash Coll. Alumni Assn., 1969-; Dir., Nat. Assn. of Wabash Men, 1969-71; The Bankers Club of Am.; Phi Kappa Psi; Tau Kappa Alpha. Hons. incl: Root Tilden Schol., N.Y. Univ. Schl. of Law, 1955-58; Clerk Moot Ct., ibid, 1958. Address: 140 Broadway, N.Y., NY 10005, U.S.A. 117.

KELLOGG-SMITH, Ogden, b. 21 Apr. 1920. Educator; Sculptor. Educ: A.B., St. John's Coll., Annapolis, Md., 1943; M.A., Putney Grad. Schl. of Tchr. Educ., Vt., 1962. Appts. incl: Yacht Broker & Dealer, Designer & Cons., Priwing Products Co., Balt., Md., 1947-61; Counsellor, Tchr., Asst. Hd., Gunston Schl., Centreville, Md., 1950-57; Founding Dir., Tchr., Key Schl., Annappolis, Md., 1958-62; Founding Hd., Tchr., Bay Country Schl., Arnold, Md., 1962-71; Fndr., Dir., Bay Country Inst., ibid, 1971-; Tchr. of Sculpture, Acad. of Arts., Easton, Md., 1973-. Mbrships. incl: Marine Technol. Soc.; The Acad. of the Arts; Chesapeake Bay Maritime Mus.; Ocean Soc.; Chesapeake Bay Fndn.; Corsica River Yacht Club; Int. Oceanographic Fndn. Contbr., Underseas Technology & Bio-Science mags. Recip., awards for sculpture, 1962, 1963, 1973. Address: Rt. 4, Box 6, Arnold, MD 21012, U.S.A. 6.

KELLSTADT, Charles H., b. 9 Oct. 1896. Chief Executive Officer. Educ. at Ohio State Univ. Num. appts. incl: Dir., Sears, Roebuck & Co., 1948-67, V.P., Southern Ty., Atlanta, Ga., 1950-57, Pres., Chgo., Ill., 1958-60, Chmn., ibid, 1960-62; Chmn., Bd. of Trustees, Savings & Profit Sharing Pension Fund of Sears, Roebuck & Co. Employees, Chgo., Ill., 1962-67; Chmn. & Chief Exec. Off., Gen. Dev. Corp., Miami, Fla., 1963-, Pres., 1965-70. Num. mbrships. incl: Advsry. Bd., Univ. of Miami Schl. of Bus.; Bd. of Advsrs., Cath. Charities; Vice-Chmn., Eisenhower Exchange Fellowships, Inc.; Past Vice-Chmn., Bd. of Govs. & Finance Comm., Am. Red Cross; Chmn., Nat. Conf. of Christians & Jews, 1959; Past Chmn., Radio Free Europe; Past Trustee, Univ. of Miami. Hons. incl: LL.D., Mundelein Coll., Chgo., 1959; D.C.S., Duquesne Univ., Pitts., Pa., 1960; LL.D., Rockhurst Coll., Kan. City, 1960; D.C.S., Suffolk Univ., Boston, Mass., 1961; LL.D., Loyola Univ., Chgo., 1962; Mbr., Cleveland Hall of Fame, 1940; Disting. Serv. Award, Press Club of Ohio, 1959; Citation of Appreciation, Dept. of Defense, 1971. Address: 1111 S. Bayshore Drive, Miami, FL 33131, U.S.A.

KELLY, Athol Herrick, b. 14 Aug. 1927. Trade Association Executive; Company Director. Educ: B.Comm., Univ. of Melbourne. Appts: Admin. Off., Australian P.O., 1950-57; Exec. Off., Univ. of N.S.W., 1957-59; Sec. /Registrar, Pharm. Soc. of Vic., 1959-64; Exec. V.P., Vic. Automobile Chmbr. of Comm., Melbourne, 1964-. Mbrships: Assoc., Australian Soc. of Accts.; Fellow, Chartered Inst. of Secs.; Assoc. Fellow, Australian Inst. of Mgmt.; J.P. Var. publs. on road safety. Hons: 1st Place Australia, final exam, Chartered Inst. of Secs. Address: Victorian Automobile Chamber of Commerce, 464 St. Kilda St., Melbourne, Vic., Australia 3004. 23.

KELLY, Baxter B., III, b. 23 Apr. 1943. Attorney. Educ: Wake Forest Univ., 1961-63; B.A., Univ. of S.C., 1966; J.D., Univ. of S.C. Schl. of Law, 1969. Law Prac., 1969-. Mbrships: Pres., E. Cooper Civic Coun.; Charleston Lawyers Club; Am. Bar Assn.; S.C. Bar Assn.; Charleston Co. Bar Assn.; Am. Judicature Soc.; Charleston Lodge, Elks; Past Pres., Optimist Club of E. Cooper; Life, Optimist Int., 1970. Hons: Outstanding Ldr., Optimist Club of E. Cooper, 1971-72; Optimist of the Yr., 1972-73. Address: 1058 Cottingham Dr., Mount Pleasant, SC 29464, U.S.A. 125.

KELLY, Edward, M. Jr., b. 3 Sept. 1923. Researcher; Writer. Educ: A.B. Hamilton Coll., 1948; LL.B., Univ. del Zulia, Venezuela, 1950; Grad. studies, Georgetown Univ., 1947-48, '61-62. Appts. incl: Gen. Mgr., TV Digest, Inc., 1961-67; Adminstve. Asst., Congressman Seymour Halpern, 1968-69; Cons., var. works, 1970-74. Mbrships: Am. Pol. Sci. Assn.; Delta Sigma Rho; Pi Delta Epsilon; Past 1st V.P., Int. Assn. TV Eds. Author of over publd. 1000 articles. Hons: Man of Yr., Jr. Chmbr. of Comm., 1952; U.S. Press Judge, Int. TV Festivals, Montreux, Switzerland, & Cannes, France. Address: 3000 Connecticut Ave. N.W., Suite 111, Washington DC 20008, U.S.A. 114, 125.

KELLY, (Rev. Msgr.) George Anthony, b. 17 Dec. 1918. Priest; Research Professor; Writer, Educ: M.A., Cath. Univ. of Am., Wash. D.C., 1943; Ph.D., ibid, 1946. Appts. incl: Dir., Family Life Bur., N.Y.C., 1955-65; Dir., Dept. of Educ., Cath. Archdiocese of N.Y., 1966-70; Pastor, St. John the Evangelist Ch., N.Y.C., 1970-; John A. Flynn Prof. in Contemporary Cath. Problems, St. John's Univ., Jamaica,

N.Y., 1970-. Mbrships. incl: AAUP; Am. Sociological Assn.; Am. Cath. Sociological Soc.; Assn. for the Sociol. of Relig.; Am. Cath. Histl. Soc. Publs. incl: Catholic Marriage Manual, 1958; Birth Control & Catholics, 1963; Your Child & Sex, 1964; The Christian Role in Today's Society, 1966; The Parish, 1973; Ed., Reflections on Contemporary Catholic Problems, 1971; Ed., Government Aid to Nonpublic Schools: Yes or No? , 1972. Hons: Domestic Prelate in the Cath. Ch., 1960; The Rev. Msgr. George A. Kelly Guidance Ctr., N.Y.C., 1973. Address: St. John's University, Grand Central & Utopia Parkways, Jamaica, NY 11439, U.S.A. 6.

KELLY, J. Norman, b. 14 Jan. 1907. Lieutenant-Colonel (Retired, AUS); Retired Director of Department of Military & Veterans Affairs in County of Los Angeles. Educ: Schl. of Govt., Univ. of Southern Calif.; L.A. City Coll.; Grad., Cmnd. & Gen. Staff Coll. Mbrships: Fndng. Dir., L.A. Chapt., Assn. U.S. Army; V.Chmn., Armed Forces Comm., L.A. Chmbr. of Comm., 7 yrs.; Nat. Advsry Coun. Americanism Educl. Le ague; Bd. Dirs., Sonoma Plaza Community Theatre; Past Pres. Am. Legion Luncheon Club (L.A.); Past Pres., Speechcrafters; Past Cmndr., L.A. Co. Post 810, Am. Legion & L.A. Post 1, Am. Veterans of WWI & II; Bicentennial '76 Comm. Recip. of hons. Address: Int. Blvd., Sonoma, CA 95476, U.S.A. 9, 59.

KELLY, John T., b. 6 Dec. 1933. Police Officer; Real Estate Broker. Educ: LL.B., LaSalle Univ., Phila., Pa., U.S.A., 1965; C.S.A., Adelphi Univ., Garden City, N.Y., 1972. Appts. incl: Serv. in N.Y.C. Police Dept., 1957-, successively as Patrolmsn; Telephone Technician; Accident Investigator; Detective, Narcotics Bur.; Sgt.; C.O. & Planning Off., 15 Detective Div., Narcotics Squad; First Neighborhood Police Chief, N.Y.C., 1970-; Salesman, Premium Realty, Brooklyn, N.Y., 1963; Broker & Pres., Brentwood Realty Corp., Brentwood, N.Y. Mbrships. incl: Holy Name Soc., N.Y. Police Dept.; Emerald Soc., ibid; Detective Endowment Assn.; Int. Narcotics Offs. Assn.; Pres., Brentwood Chmbr. of Comm., 1970-72; Columbia Soc. of Real Estate Appraisers. Hons. incl: Nat. Defense Medal; 25 Citations for Bravery, N.Y.C. Police Dept. Address: 151 Bridle Way, Oakdale, NY 11769, U.S.A. 6.

KELLY, Margaret McLaurin Ricaud (Mrs.), b. 22 Mar. 1910. Retired Teacher; Poet. Educ: A.B., Winthrop Coll., S.C., U.S.A.; Postgrad. study, Univ. of Fla., Gainesville; Duke Univ., Durham, N.C.; Univ. of Miami, Coral Gables, Fla.; Univ. of N.C., Chapel Hill; Univ. of S.C., Columbia, S.C.; St. Andrew Univ., N.C.; Coher Coll., S.C. Appts: Attendance Tchr., Marlboro Co., S.C.; Tchr. Rep., 13 Southern States; Physical Educ. Coach. Mbrships. incl: Colonial Dame of the XVII Century; Magna Carta Dames; French Huguenot Soc.; Geneal. Soc. of Torrance, Calif.; Most Noble Order of the Garter; Geneal. Soc. of London, U.K.; Life Saving Examiner, Red Cross. Contbr. to The State, S.C., The Charlotte Observer, N.C., News & Courier, S.C. & Marlboro Herald Advocate; Poems in New Voices in American Poetry, 1972, '73 & '74; Collect. of 32 verses in An Anthology of Verse, 1974. Address: 402 Fayetteville Ave., Bennetsville, SC 29512, U.S.A. 125, 128, 138.

KELLY, Mary Claire (Coleman), b. 15 Sept. 1916. Coal Company Executive. Educ: B.A., Beria Coll., Ky., 1962; M.S. of Lib. Sci., Univ. of Ky., 1967; M.S., ibid, Lexington, 1968. Appts: Pres., Greasy Creek Coal Co., 1946-50;

V.P.-Pres., Sutton By-Products Coal Corp., 1956-68; w. Ky. Dept. of Libs., 1965-68; Pres., Sutton-Coleman Coal Corp., 1968-; Proprietor, Claire's Book & Gift Shop, 1969-73. Mbrships: Past Pres., Pikeville Br., AAUW; Past Pres., Pike Co. Historical Soc.; Ky. Historical Soc.; Univ. of Ky.; Grad. Educ. Club. Ed., Sesquicentennial Issue of Pike Co. Hist. Compiled Date on Eastern Ky. Hons: Rsch. Assistantships, Coun. of Southern Mtns., Beria, Ky., 1959-60, & Ky. Rsch. Fndn., 1962-64 & 1972-73. Address: P.O. Box 7027, Lexington, KY 40502, U.S.A. 5, 7.

KELLY, Michael John, b. 9 July 1928. Industrialist. Educ: B.S., Mich. State Univ., 1949. Chmn. of Bd., Mfrs. Capital Corp., Chgo., Ill., Mfg. Consultants, Woodstock, Ill., Flex-Weld, Inc., Bartlett, Ill., Atlantic India Rubber Co., Chgo., Ill., Mogul Rubber Corp., Goshen, Ind., Chgo. Fittings Corp., Broadview, Ill., U.S. Flexible Metallic Tubing Co., San Fran., Calif., & Keflex Inc., L.A., Calif. Mbrships: Psi Upsilon; Econ. Club; Chgo. Club; Lake Geneva Country Club. Recip., Air Medal for serv. w. USAAF, 1943-46. Address: 9210 Country Club Rd., Woodstock, IL 60098, U.S.A.

KELLY, Ronald Arthur, b. 11 June 1929. Film Director and Writer. Educ: Univ. of B.C., Canada, 1947-53. Appts: TV Prod., Canadian Broadcasting Co., 1952-55; Wrote, directed & produced films in Mexico, Europe & Canada, 1955-59; Prod., films for BBC, 1960-62, CBC, 1962-70, & CTV, 1970-72. Mbrships: Alpha Delta Phi; Chmn., Coun. Canadian Film-Makers. Films: (writer, prod. & dir.) The Tearaways; The Thirties; The Open Grave; The Gift; The Last Man in the World; Waiting for Caroline; The Megantic Outlaw; Springhill; The Shield. Hons. incl: Canada Coun. Grant, 1959; Golden Palm, Cannes Film Festival, 1962; Wilderness Award for Best Canadian Film, 1964-66; Canada Medal, 1967; Gold Medal, N.Y. Film Festival, 1973. Address: 101 Chaplin Cres., Toronto, Ont., Canada. 88.

KELLY, Roselyn Kam (Mrs. J. Edmund Kelly), b. 8 Jan. 1896. Volunteer Social Worker-Executive; Housewife & Mother. Has been in voluntary soc. work for 59 yrs., 1913-72. Mbrships. (all are past offs.): Fndr., Chmn., Bishop's Comm. for Christian Home & Family, Cath. Diocese of Buffalo, N.Y., 1949-72, Volunteer Bur. of Cath. Charities, 12 yrs.; 1st Pres., Ladies of Charity; Finance Chmn. & V.P., N.Y. State Conf. on Soc. Work; Chmn., Women's Div., Cath. Charities, 4 yrs., Buffalo Soc. Serv. Exchange; Sec., Buffalo Chapt., Am. Red Cross, 15 yrs.; Chmn., Red Cross Women's Div. Fund Appeal, Home Nursing Comm. & Grey Ladies Unit at Sisters Hosp.; Chmn., Soc. Serv., Int. Fedn. Cath. Alumni. Hons. incl: Medal of Noble Cross for Ch. & Pontiff, awarded by Pope Pius XII, 1949; Benemerenti Medal, awarded by Pope Paul VI, 1964; L.H.D., D'Youville Coll., Buffalo, 1971. Address: Carriage House Apts., 6 Spring St., Williamsville, NY 14221, U.S.A. 49.

KELLY, Thomas, b. 25 Jan. 1909. University Professor. Educ: B.A., Manchester Univ., U.K., 1929; M.A., ibid, 1947; Ph.D., Liverpool Univ., 1957. Appts: Dir., Ext. Studies, Liverpool Univ., 1948-; Prof., Adult Educ., ibid, 1967-. Fellow, Royal Hist. Soc., 1957. Mbrships: Hon. Sec., Univ. Coun. for Adult Educ., 1961-68; Chmn., Nat. Inst. Adult Educ., 1969-. Publs: History of Adult Education in Great Britain, 1962, '70; Early Public Libraries, 1966. Author of other works in field of adult educ. Fellow, Birkbeck Coll.,

1971. Address: Liverpool Univ., U.K. 3, 128, 131.

KELSEY, (Rev.) Ridell Archibald, Jr., b. 10 May 1917. Clergyman. Educ: B.C.S., Drake Univ., Des Moines, Iowa; B.S.T., Boston Univ., Mass.; Willamette Univ., Salem, Ore. Appts. incl: Served as Pastor of Meth. Chs. in: S. Middlesboro & S. Carver, Mass., 1941-42; W. Salem & Summit, Ore., 1942-45; Mt. Morris, Ill., 1945-49; Evergreen Park, Ill., 1949-60; Sterling, Ill., 1960-63; Brookfield, Ill., 1963-; Former Mbr., N. Ill. Conf. Sec. Staff; Treas., Staff, Comm. on Conf. Rels.; Bd., Hosp. & Homes; Mbr., Bd. of Pensions; Radio Preacher, Stns. WEBH & WEAW; Guest appearance, TV Channel 26, etc. Mbrships. incl: Sec., Bd. of Pensions, N. Ill. Conf., United Meth. Ch. Bd.; West Cook Co. Heart Assn., 1968-; Gross Schl. PTA, Brookfield, 1967-; Chap., Brookfield Wing, Civil Air Patrol, 1963-; Mason, serving in many capacities, e.g. Past Grand Chap., Grand Lodge of Ill. of Ancient Free & Accepted Masons; AASR; Ill. Cmdr. in Chief, Oriental Consistory, Valley of Chgo., AASR, 1972-; Disciplined Order of Christ; Blvd. Chapt. No. 588, Order of Eastern Star; Unity Conclave No. 62, Order of True Kindred; York Rite Coll. No. 15; Ill. State & World Meth. Histl. Soc.; The Philalethes Soc.; Life Mbr., Oriental Consistory, 1971. Contbr. to mags. Recip. many hons. inclng. Cert. Meritorious Serv., Chgo. Heart Assn., 1971, Grand Chaplain of Grand Coun. of Royal & Select Mstr., Kt. York Cross of Honor, Hon. Legion of Honor, Order of DeMolay & Grand Cross of Color, Int. Order of Rainbow for Girls. Address: 9001 W. Lincoln Ave., Brookfield, IL 60513, U.S.A. 116, 120.

KELTON, John Tremain, b. 12 Mar. 1909. Lawyer. Educ: S.B., MIT, Cambridge, U.S.A., 1932; LL.B., Harvard Law Schl., 1935. Appts: Watson, Bristol, Johnson & Leavenworth, 1935-40 & 1946-49; U.S. Army, 1940-46; Watson, Johnson, Leavenworth & Blair, 1950-53; Watson, Leavenworth, Kelton & Taggart, 1954-. Mbrships: Bd. of Mgrs., Am. Patent Law Assn., 1964-67, Pres., 1973-74; Coun., Patent, Trademark & Copyright Sect., Am. Bar Assn., 1970-74; Assn. of the Bar of the City of N.Y.; Union League Club; Harvard Club; Chemists' Club. Address: 100 Park Ave., N.Y., NY 10017, U.S.A.

KEMAL, Yasar, b. 1923. Writer. Appts: Jrnlst., var. Turkish newspapers & publs., 1951-. Mbrships: Turkish Jrnlsts.' Union; Turkish Writers' Union (Pres.); Authors Guild, N.Y.C., U.S.A.; F.I.I., Zürich, Switzerland. Publs: Fifteen books, mainly novels but inclng. short stories, essays. etc., in Turkish. Books translated into Engl: Memed My Hawk, 1961; The Wind from the Plain, 1963; Anatolian Tales, 1968; They Burn the Thistles, 1973; Iron Earth, Copper Sky, 1974. Num. translations of works into other langs. Hons: Varlik Award, Best Turkish Novel of 1956; Ilhan Iskender Theatre Award, Ankara, 1956; First Prize, Int. Theatre Festival, Nancy, France, 1966. Address: P.K. 14, Basinköy, Istanbul, Turkey.

KEMBALL, Robin, b. 29 Oct. 1920. University Professor. Educ: Univ. of Freiburg, Germany, 1937-38; Sorbonne, Univ. of Paris, France, 1938-39; Clare Coll., Cambridge, U.K., 1939-40; Univ. of Basle, Switzerland, 1952-58. Appts: Inst. of E. European Studies, Univ. of Fribourg, Switzerland, 1964-69; Swiss Fed. Inst. Technol., Zurich, 1964-71; Lectr., Univ. of Lausanne, 1968-69; Chargé de cours, ibid, 1969-70, Asst. Prof., 1970-73, Prof., Russian Lang. & Lit., 1973-. Mbrships: Swiss Acad. Soc. of Slavists, 1971-; Pres., ibid, 1974-75. Publs: Alexander Blok—A Study in Rhythm & Metre,

1965; verse translations of var. Russian poets. Author, articles on Russian 19th Century authors. Address: Villa La Pensée, 1807 Blonay, Switzerland.

KEMBLE, James. Consultant Surgeon & Urologist. Educ: St. Andrew's Coll.; Univ. of Sydney, Australia; St. Bartholomew's Hosp., London; Ch.M; F.R.C.S. (Engl.); F.R.C.S. (Edinburgh). Appts: Cons. Surg. & Urologist, Battersea & Putney Hosp. Grp., W. London Hosp.; Lectr., Fac. of Med.; Ed., W. London Med. Jrnl. Mbrships: Fellow, Royal Soc. of Med.; Councillor, Osler Club; Soc. of Authors; BMA; Brit. Assn. of Urol. Surgs.; W. London Medico-Chirurgical Soc. Publs: Idols & Invalids; Hero-Dust; Surgery for Nurses; Napoleon Immortal, The Medical History & Private Life of Napoleon Bonaparte; St. Helena during Napoleon's Exile, Gorrquer's Diary. Contbr. to num. jrnls. & newspapers; Author, histl. monographs. Address: 24 Keswick Rd., London SW15 2JP, U.K. 3, 30, 43, 139.

KEMPER, Robert (Bob) Mitchell, Jr., b. 20 Mar. 1926. Cost Estimating Engineer. Educ: N.C. State Coll. of A. & E., Raleigh, U.S.A., 1943-44; Ohio State Univ., Columbus, 1944-45; B.S., Tenn. Univ., Knoxville, 1946-49. Appts: Construction Insp. w. Giffels & Valett, Inc., 1949-51; Corps Engrs., U.S. Army, 1951-53; Asst. Off. Engr. w. Ebasco Servs., Inc., 1953; Construction Engr., Nuclear Div., Union Carbide Corp., 1953-; Partner, Construction Co., Oak Ridge, Tenn., 1954-60; Instr., Engr. Schl., Fort Belvoir, Va.; Trng. & Technol. Schl., Oak Ridge, Tenn. Mbrships. incl: Constitution Chmn., Charter Mbr., Smokey Mountain Square Dance Callers & Round Dance Tchrs. Assn.; Past Chmn. & Sec.-Ed., Dixie Round Dance Coun.; Pres., Savoyards Opera Co.; Treas., Finance Chmn. & Past Chmn., Student Exchange Prog., UN Comm. of Oak Ridge; Past Exec. V.P., Sec. & Treas., Jaycees. Creative Works: Choreographed round dances; taught & served as panelist at sev. state, regional & nat. square dance convens. Address: 102 Case Lane, Oak Ridge, TN 37830, U.S.A. 7, 125.

KEMPSTER, George Alfred, b. 26 July 1908. Dentist. Educ: D.M.D., Tufts Univ., Medford, Mass., U.S.A., 1932; Postgrad., ibid, 1932-40, MIT, 1939, Columbia Univ., N.Y., 1946 & 1947. Appts: Gen. Dentist, Bridgewater, Mass., 1932-41; 1st Lt.-Major, U.S. Army Infantry, 1941-45; Chief Clinician & Periodontist, Kennedy Gen. Hosp., 1943-45; Pvte. Prac., Brockton, Mass., 1946-; Schl. Dentist, ibid, 1947-51; Clinician, Annual Meeting, Am. Dental Assn., San. Fran., Calif., 1972. Mbrships: Am. Dental Assn.; Mass. Dental Soc.; Tufts Dental Alumni Assn.; Retired Offs. Assn.; Psi Omega. Holder: sev. patents, copyrights, & trademarks, for dental charts, dental admin., & methods of home care of the teeth. Address: 608 River St., Norwell, MA 02061, U.S.A. 6.

KENDALL, Alice B. (Mrs. Kenneth K. Kendall, Jr.), b. 14 Apr. 1919. Artist; Poet; Editor. Educ: Vesper George Schl. of Art, Boston, Mass., 1941; Frazier Schl. of Painting, Provincetown, Mass., Summer, 1941. Appts. incl: Poetry Ed. & Critic, Writer's Rsch. Digest, 1969-70; Staff Writer, Feedback Jrnl., 1970-71; Ed., ibid, 1971-. Mbrships: Delphian Soc. 1965-, Seminar Bd. Chmn.; Writer's Workshop of Orange Co., 1968-70-, Pres., 1968-70, Treas., 1971-73; Calif. Fedn. of Chaparral Poets, 1971-; Poetry Soc. of Southern Calif., 1971-; Anaheim Art Assn., 1969-; Glass Mtn. Inn, Inc., 1969-; Centro Studi E Scambi Int., 1970-. Publs: num. conthns. in literary mags. & work appears in many anthols. inclng. A Study In

Crimson, Echoes Of Faith, Dance Of The Muse, Anthology of American Poetry, Book X & XI, Yearbook Of Modern Poetry, The Birth Of Day, Grains Of Sand, Outstanding Contemporary Poetry & International Who's Who In Poetry Anthology. Hons. incl: Poetry Prizes, Writers Workshop of Orange Co., 1967, 69, 70, 71, 72; Poetry Prize, SCAF Poets, 1969; Poetry Prize, Poetry Soc. of S. Calif., 1973. Address: 2105 W. Forest Ln., Anaheim, CA 92804, U.S.A. 5, 11.

KENDALL, Alice Rebecca. Writer; Artist. Educ: Dip. in Art, Edinburgh Coll. of Art, U.K. Appts: Co-Fndr., Sec. & Organiser, The Music Party (Ensemble for performing 18th & 19th century music on authentic instruments), 1971-; Ed., Fedn. of British Artists Quarterly, 1972-. Mbrships: Soc. of Women Artists (Hon. Treas. 1965, V.P. 1972-); Fellow Royal Zool. Soc. Scotland. Publs: Author & Illustrator, Funny Fishes; Contbr. to mags. Exhibs: w. Mother, Alice Kendall, Cooling Galls., 1948, 1956. Exhibitor at Paris Salon, France, Royal Acad., Royal Scottish Acad. Murals: British Coun., Min. of Labour. Portrait commissioned by Royal Soc. Edinburgh. Work reproduced num. mags. Music: 2 series of 5 recitals w. Music Party Ensemble, inclng. Radio recital; LPs in preparation. Address: 35 Beaufort Gdns., London SW3 1PW, U.K. 3, 19.

KENDALL, Carlton Waldo, (pen name, Odlaw Ladnek), b. 17 Aug. 1895. Author; Research Specialist; Executive. Educ: Univ. of Calif., Berkeley, 4 yrs.; studies & travel, London, Paris, Rome, Madrid, Geneva, Oxford, Cambridge, Princeton, Yale, Harvard, Johns Hopkins Univ. Appts. incl: Pacific Coast Corres., Fly, Aero & Hydro, & others, 1909-13; Pres., Bay City Aero Supply Co., 1910-12; Special Corres., League of Nations, Geneva, Switzerland, 1924; Sec.-Dir., Kendal Investment Co., 1927-29; Mgr.-Dir., Pacific Enameling & Mfg. Co., 1939-47; Rep., Tomorrow Mag., UN Conf. on Int. Org., S.F., 1945, Del. 5th Nat. Conf. of U.S. Nat. Comm. for UNESCO, S.F., 1957; Dir., Charles Nelson Co. (Consolidated Lumber), Wilmington, Calif., 1955-65. Mbrships: Authors League of Am., N.Y.C.; Am. Acad. of Pol. & Soc. Scis., Phila.; AAAS; Aahmes Shrine, 32 degree Mason, Oakland Scottish Rite. Publs: The Truth About Korea (used as ref. book, Wash. Disarmament Conf.), 1919; Magic Herbs, Cause of Insanity. Contbr. of poetry to anthologies, newspapers, & of num. articles to jrnls. & reviews etc. Address: 1410 Jackson St., Oakland, CA 94612, U.S.A. 59.

KENDALL, Donald McIntosh, b. 16 Mar. 1921. Manufacturing Executive. Educ: Western Ky. State Coll., Bowling Green, U.S.A. Appts: Pres., Pepsi-Cola Int.; Pres., Pepsi-Cola Co.; Pres., Pepsi Co., Inc.; Chmn., Pepsi Co., Inc. Mbrships: Chmn., Ctr. for Resources Recovery, Inc., 1970-; Chmn., Emergency Comm. for Am. Trade, 1969-; Bd. of Dirs., Boys Clubs of Am.; Bus. Coun. for Int. Understanding; Boy Scouts of Am.; Bus. Grp. for Latin Am.; Accion Int.; Chmn., U.S.-U.S.S.R. Comm. on Trade & Econs., 1973. Address: Pepsi Co., Inc., Purchase, NY 10577, U.S.A. 2.

KENDE, Jan S., b. 26 Mar. 1928. Conductor; Composer. Educ: Studied w. Kodaly (composition), B. Szabolcsi (hist. of music), L. Weiner (chmbr. music), Ferencsik (conducting), Franz Liszt Acad. of Music, Budapest, Hungary; Master's degree, composition, 1949; Studied w. Vaclav Talich (conducting), Jan Cikker (composition), Univ. of Performing Arts, Bratislava, Czechoslovakia; Master's degree, conducting, 1953. Appts.

Banska Hystrica, Czechoslovakia, 1959-62; Music Dir., Prin. Conductor, State Opera Kosice, & Prof., State Conservatory, 1962-68; Chmn., Music Dept., High Moving Schl., Wilton, N.H., U.S.A. & guest conductor, Juilliard Schl., N.Y., 1969-70. Mbrships: Czechoslovak Composers Union; Am. Symph. Orch. League. Compositions incl: Divertimento for string orch.; Symphonic Variations for symph. orch. Recip. of hons. Address: 66-01 Burns St., Rego Park, NY 11374, U.S.A.

KENDEL, Dorla Dean (Mrs. Robert L. Kendel), b. 16 Apr. 1930. Company Executive & Representative. Appts. incl: Tchr., Oil Painting, LaCrescenta, Calif., 1960-62; Rep., Air Conditioning Specialities Co., Inc., LaCrescenta, Calif., 1962-; Sec.-Treas., ibid, 1970-. Mbrships. incl: Am. Soc. Heating, Refrigerating & Air Conditioning Engrs.; active mbr. scouting, schl. & sport activities. Address: 2926 Foothill Blvd., La Crescenta, CA 91214, U.S.A. 5.

KENDERESSY, Louis K., b. 18 Sept. 1920. Writer. Educ: Grad., Acad. of Theatrical Art, Budapest, Hungary, 1944. Asst. Dir., Budapest Nat. Theater, 1944. Publs: (Play) The Woman's Crime, 1942, staged at Nat. Theater; (Novels) The Great Actress, 1943, Hungary; Fight for the Legacy, 1958, Marriage in Foursome, 1960, The Waiting Lady, 1962, Who is my real Husband, 1964, The New Manufacturer, 1966, U.S.A.; in English, The Simson's Hotel & He who accepted Jesus Christ (in preparation). Literary Vis. to Hungarian communities in Canada & U.S.A. & in Austria, France, Germany, Italy, Switzerland & U.K. Address: P.O. Box-811 Stn. "A", Toronto, Ont., M5W IG3, Canada.

KENDRICK, Virginia Catherine. Pianist; Composer. Educ: Univ. of Minn., 1928-33. Appts: Organist, 1st Ch. of Christ Scientist, Excelsior, Minn., 1962-72; Organ music cons., Schmitt Music Co., Mnpls., 1958-; Pianist, Andahazy Ballet Co., Mnpls., 1958-. Mbrships: Am. Guild of Organists; Nat. Fedn. Music Clubs; Sigma Kappa; Mu Phi Epsilon. Compositions: Wealth of Mine, 1941; Little Red Hen, 1955; Goody Two Shoes, 1956; From My Window, 1960; Green is the Willow, 1965; Little Miss Whuffit, 1962; White Sky, 1967; Music is Beauty, 1969; Tribute, 1970; Jade Summer, 1971; Before the World Was (Prov. 8), 1973. Address: 5800 Echo Rd., Shorewood, MN 55331, U.S.A. 5.

KENEC'HDU, Tanguy, b. 28 July 1914. Civil Servant, Retd.; Political Writer; Lecturer. Educ: Lic. és L., Sorbonne, Paris. Appts: Var. civil service appts. in Corps Prefectoral; Asst. Sec.-Gen., Western European Union, London, 1950-55; Chef de Cabinet to Min. of Agric., France, 1959-61; Sr. Lectr. on Brit. Affairs, Free Fac. of Paris. Publs: 1 book in French, num. articles in Le Monde, Perspectives, etc. Hons: Croix de Guerre, 1939-45; Officier des Palmes Academiques. Address: Párkizel, 35350 Saint-Coulomb, France. 91.

KENN, Charles William, b. 2 Jan. 1907. Retired Parole Officer; Authority on Hawaii. Educ: A.B., Univ. of Hawaii, 1931. Appts: Dir. of Hawaiian Activities, Rec. Commn., City & Co. of Honolulu, 1934-35; Parole Off., Bd. of Paroles & Pardons, Territory of Hawaii, 1934-45; Dept. of Parole & Home Placement, Juvenile, 1945-47; Vis. Sci., Anthropol. & Folklore, Univ. of Calif. L.A., 1948. Mbrships. incl: V.P.-Trustee, Hawaiian Lang. League, 1936; Var. offs., Republican Party; Charter, Nat. Hist. Soc. Publs. incl: Some Hawaiian Relationship Terms Re-examined, 1939; The

Kahuna & the Social Worker, 1935; Hawaiians of the Gold Rush (California), 1955; A Visit to the Gold Fields in 1858, 1965; Gunnen Mono (The 1st Japanese Immigration to Hawaii in 1868), 1968. Address: 827-A103 Kahuna Ln, Honolulu, HI 96814, U.S.A. 51, 68, 78.

KENNEALLY, Joseph Thomas, b. 31 July 1926. Company Chairman & Chief Executive Officer. Educ: B.A., Univ. of Minnesota, 1949; M.A., ibid, 1950. Appts. incl: Northern Trust Co., Chgo., 1952-54; Asst. to Sr. Partner, E.F. Hutton & Co., N.Y.C., 1954-57; V.P., F.W. Richmond & Co., N.Y.C., 1957-59; Exec. V.P., Houston Oil Field Materials Co. Inc., (now Int. Systems & Controls Corp.), 1959-60; Pres., ibid, 1960-62; Chmn. of Bd. & Chief Exec. Off., 1964-; Dir. of Adela Ltd., Lima, Peru Houston Citizens Bank & Trust Co., Texas & Petroleum Equipment Suppliers Assn.; Trustee, Univ. of St. Thomas, Houston. Mbrships: Metropolitan Club; Kansas City Club; River Oaks Country Club. Address: P.O. Box 2589, Houston, TX 77001, U.S.A. 2, 7.

KENNEDY, James R., b. 31 July 1911. Executive. Educ: Grad., Univ. of Wis., 1935. Appts: worked for Home Ins. Co., N.Y. & Puerto Rico, 1935-40; Peat, Marwick, Mitchell & Co., N.Y., 1940-44; Acct. in Plastics Div., Celanese Corp., Newark, N.J., 1944-47; V.P., Indl. Rels., ibid, N.Y., 1947-57; V.P., Financial, N.Y., 1957-60; Exec. V.P., N.Y., 1960-65; V.Chmn., N.Y., 1965-. Mbrships: The Sky Club, N.Y.C.; The Board Room, N.Y.; The Princeton Club, N.Y.; Essex Fells Co. Club, N.J. Address: Celanese Corp. 1211 Ave. of the Americas, N.Y., NY 10036, U.S.A.

KENNEDY, (Rev. Dr.) James William, b. 22 Aug. 1905. Clergyman. Educ: Tex. A & M Coll., 1923-24; Univ. of Colo., 1927-29; Northwestern Univ., 1929-32; A.B., Stephen F. Austin State Coll., 1934; S.T.M., Univ. of S., 1946. Appts. incl: Rector, Epiphany, Atlanta, Ga., 1937-39; All Saints, Richmond, Va., 1939-45, Christ Ch., Lexington, Ky., 1945-55, & Ch. of the Ascension, N.Y.C., 1955-64; Dir. & Ed., Forward Movt. Publs., Cinn., Ohio., 1964-. Num. Publs. incl: Parson's Sampler; Venture of Faith; A Lenten Query; He That Gathereth; Evanston Scrapbook; Holy Island; The Unknown Worshipper; Minister's Shoptalk. Address: 412 Sycamore St., Cinn., OH 45202, U.S.A. 1, 2, 118.

KENNEDY, Janice Madigan, b. 5 Apr. 1924. Assistant Professor of Textiles & Clothing. Educ: B.S., Mansfield State Tchrs. Coll., Pa., 1946; M.S., Cornell Univ., 1966; postgrad., Pa. State Univ., & Marywood Coll., Scranton, Pa. Appts: Tchr., Troy Area H.S., Pa., 1946-69; Asst. Prof., Mansfield State Coll., Pa., 1969-. Mbrships: Am. Assn. Coll. Profs. of Textiles & Clothing; AAUW; APSCUF/PAHE; PSEA; NEA; Kappa Delta Pi, MSTC, 1945; Kappa Omicron Phi; Conclave Mgr., Nat. Coun., ibid, 1963-72; Mu Chapt., Omicron Nu, 1965; Pi Lambda Theta, 1965; Am. & Pa. Home Econs. Assns.; Int. Fedn. Home Econs. Contbr., Am. Dyestuff Reporter, 1968. Hons: State Degree, Pa. Future Homemakers of Am., 1965; Cons. & Coord., N.Am. Projs., Coun. Int. Contact, London, U.K., 1966-. Address: R.D. 2., Box 184, Troy, PA 16947, U.S.A. 5, 6, 138.

KENNEDY, John de Navarre, b. 31 May 1888. Retired Judge; Author. Educ: B.A., Cambridge Univ., U.K., 1909. Appts: Judge, Co. Court, Peterborough, Ont., Canada, 1952-63; formerly lawyer w. firm Manning, Mortimer & Kennedy, Toronto, Ont., Canada; Ed., Chitty's Law Jrnl., 1963-. Mbrships: Canadian Soc. Painters in Watercolour; Sec.,

Canadian Lawn Tennis Assn., 1922-45; Pres., Canadian Fed. Humane Socs. Arts & Letters Club, Toronto; R.C.Y.C., ibid. Publs: In the Shadow of the Cheka; Crime in Reverse; The Rain of Death; The History of the Department of Munitions & Supply; Aids to Jury Charges, Criminal; co-author, Les Assises Criminelles. Exhibs of paintings incl: Royal Canadian Acad.; Canadian Soc. Painters in Water Colour; Ont. Soc. Artists; Nat. Call. of Canada. Address: 707 Weller St., Peterborough Ont., Canada. 88.

KENNEDY, Joseph J., Jr., b. 17 Nov. 1923. Music Educator; Violinist; Arranger/Composer. Educ: Carnegie Millon Univ.; B.S.Mus., Va. State Coll.; Mus.M., Duquesne Univ.; Va. Commonwealth Univ. Appts: Supvsr. of Music, Richmond, Va. Pub. Schls.; Res. Violinist. Richmond Symph. Orch., ibid; Staff Mbr., Afro-Am. Studies Dept., Va. Commonwealth Univ. Mbrships: Am. Fedn. Musicians; Music Educators Nat. Conf.; Arranger/Composer, Broadcast Music Incorp.; Rotary Club, Richmond, Va.; Phi Mu Alpha Sinfonia; Nat. Bd. Mbr., Am. Youth Symph. & Chorus, 1973. Compositions. incl: A Lazy Atmosphere; Serious Moods; Somewhat Eccentric; Tempo for Two; Surrealism; You Can Be Sure; The Fantastic Vehicle; Illusions Opticas; Dialogue for Flute, Cello & Piano; Suite for Trio & Orchestra; num. recorded arrangements & transcriptions. Address: Richmond Pub. Schls., 301 N. 9th St., Richmond, VA 23219, U.S.A.

KENNEDY, Kieran A., b. 14 July 1935. Economist. Educ: Dip. Pub. Admin., B.Comm., M.Econ.Sc., Univ. Coll., Dublin, Repub. of Ireland 1954-60; B.Phil., Nuffield Coll., Oxford, U.K., 1963; Ph.D., Harvard Univ., 1968. Appts. incl: Sr. Rsch. Off., Economic & Soc. Rsch. Inst., ibid, 1968-70; Economic Cons., Central Bank of Ireland, 1970-71; Dir., Economic & Soc. Rsch. Inst., Dublin, 1971-. Mbrships. incl: Am. Economic Assn.; Royal Irish Acad.; Coun. Mbr., Statistical & Soc. Inquiry Soc. of Ireland; Coun. Mbr., Irish Inst. Int. Affairs. Publs: Productivity & Industrial Growth: The Irish Experience, 1971. Contbr. to profl. jrnls. & publs. Hons. incl: Coyne Mem. Schlrship, 1960; Elected Student, Nuffield Coll., Oxford, 1961; Fellow, Harvard Univ., 1963. Address: Dir., Economic & Soc. Rsch Inst., 4 Burlington Road, Dublin 4, Ireland. 30.

KENNEY, Susan Gildersleeve, (Mrs. John A. Kenney), b. 1 June 1925. Investment Advisor. Educ: Antioch Coll., Yellow Springs, Ohio, 1943-47. Appts. incl: Editor, Oil Statistics Co., Babson Park, Mass., 1948-52; V.P., ibid, 1952-59; Independent Financial Cons., Spear & Staff Inc. & Oil Statistics Co., 1961-65; Pres. & Dir., Oil Statistics Co., 1967-73. Mbrships: N.Y. Soc. Security Analysts; Boston Soc. Security Analysts; Am. Petroleum Inst.; Independent Patroleum Assn. Profl. publs. incl: Oil Shale Today; Offshore Oil Industry: An Analysis. Hons: Kentucky Colonel. Address: 67 Fuller Brook Rd., Wellesley, MA 02181, U.S.A. 5, 6, 16, 57,132.

KENNY, Bettie Ilene Cruts (Bik), b. 5 June 1931. Author; Artist. Educ: B.A., Univ. of Wash., 1971. Appts: Ptnr., w. husband Donald K. Kenny, Bettie Kenny Diamund-Punt (Diamond-Point) Art-Glass Engraving Co., Seattle; Res. Artist, Mus. of Hist. & Ind., Seattle, 6 wks., 1973; Gen. Chmn., Artists Equity Seafair Art Show, Seattle, 1973; Docent, Tacoma Art Mus., 1973-74. Mbrships: Pres., Wash. State AEA, until 1976; Artists Equity Assn.; Pacific N.W. Arts Assn.; I.P.A. Painting Exhibs: Boeing Art Shows, 1958-60; Bellevue Arts & Crafts, 1958, '59; 1 Man Show, Boeing Co-Works, 1961; Artist in Action,

Bellevue Arts & Crafts, 1962; W. Seattle Hiyu Painting Exhibit, 1965; Frye Art Mus., 1968; N.B. of C., W. Seattle, 1969; State Capitol Mus., Olympia, 1973; Mus. of Hist. & Ind., Seattle, 1973; Solo Exhibg., Seattle, 1974. Diamund-Punt Art-Glass Engravings in pvte. collects: Pres. Nixon portrait on glass & Tricia Nixon & Edward Cox wedding commemorative, White House; Pres. J.F. Kennedy Mem. Glass Portrait, Smithsonian Instn.; Gov. Daniel J. Evans Portrait on glass, Gov's. Mansion, Olympia, Wash.; Pres. Lincoln, smiling mem. portrait, Corning Mus. of Glass, N.Y.; Lawrence Welk; Mus. of Hist. & Ind., Seattle. Hons. incl: 4 Merit Award, Boeing, 1958; Invitational Appearance on TV for Interview & demonstration of Diamund-Punt Technique, 1972; Letters of Commendation, Gov. Evans of Wash., & Lawrence Welk, 1972. Address: P.O. Box 1503, Seattle, WA 98103, U.S.A. 37, 57.

KENT, Ellen Louisa Margaret, b. 15 Apr. 1894. Certificated Teacher. Educ: Day Trng. Dept., Univ. of Bristol; Pvte. tuition in piano w. Ernest Read; Licentiate, Royal Acad. of Music. Appts. incl: Wesleyan Schl., Portland; Asst. to husband, Mochdre C.E. Schl., Montgomeryshire; Hd. Tchr., Schl., Sussex. Publs. (under name "Margaret") incl: The Twins at Hillside Farm; The Twins at the Seaside; Animals of the Farm (8 books); Stories for Language Training; Out-of-Doors Stories; Seaside Stories; Little Nature Stories; Favourite Crosswords for Children (2 books); Music incls: Musical Reading Games; Melody Making in the Infant School; Melody Making in the Junior School; Zoo Nonsense Songs; Toy Shop Songs. The Baby Moses (Play with Music); A Nativity Play; Music for Percussion Bands (Grade 1 & Grade 2). Address: Meon, 3 Alexander Way, Botley, Southampton, SO3 2ED, U.K. 3, 30, 137, 138.

KENT, Francis Lawrence, b. 4 Jan. 1908. Librarian. Educ: B.A., Corpus Christi Coll., Cambridge Univ., U.K., 1929; M.A., ibid, 1931; Univ. of Strasbourg, France, Summers 1928, 1929. Appts: Asst. Keeper, Printed Books, British Mus., London, 1931-46; Sub-Ed; Turkish News, BBC (seconded from British Mus.), 1944-45; Univ. Libn., Univ. of Bristol, 1946-50; Hd., UNESCO Lib., Paris, Franc, 1951-57; Univ. Libn., Am. Univ. of Beirut, Lebanon, 1957-73; Ford Fndn. Cons., Riyadh Univ. Lib. Dev. Proj., Saudi Arabia, 1970; Libn., Am. Coll. of Switzerland & Leysin Am. Schl., Switzerland, 1973-. Mbrships: Library Assn., U.K.; ASLIB (former Mbr. of Coun. & Chmn., Conf. Comm.); Assn. des Bibliohtécaires Francais, 1952-57; Lebanese Lib. Assn., 1961-73. Publs: Jt.-Compiler, British Mus. Subject Index, 1933-46; Jt.-Ed., World List of Scientific Periodicals, 1952; Contbr. to Ency. Britannica, other encys. & profl. jrnls. Address: American Coll. of Switzerland, 1854 Leysin, Switzerland. 43, 97.

KENT, Geoffrey, b. 30 Jan. 1914. Physician. Educ: M.D., Amsterdam, 1939; Ph.D., Northwestern Univ. Med. Schl., 1958. Appts: Chief Med. Asst. & Asst. Dir., Hematol., Clin. Investigations & Rsch., Manchester Royal Infirmary, U.K., 1939-44; Pathol., Royal Army Med. Corps., 1944-47; Sr. Registrar, Chase Farm Hosp., London,1947-50; Sr. Pathol. & Assoc. Dir., Dept. of Pathol., Cook Co. Hosp., Chgo., U.S.A., 1953-57; Chief, Pathol., W. Suburban Hosp., Oak Park, Ill., 1958-69; Chmn., Dept. of Pathol., Chgo Wesley Mem. Hosp., 1969-72; Prof., Pathol., Northwestern Univ. Med. Schl. Fellow, Coll. of Am. Pathols. Mbrships. incl: Am. Assn. of Pathols. & Bacteriols.; AMA; Am. Soc. for Exptl. Pathol., AAAS; Am. Soc. for Cell Biol.; Am. Assn. for

the Study of Liver Disease. Author of num. publs. in field. Address: Northwestern Mem. Hosp., Wesley Pavilion, Dept. of Pathol., 250 E. Superior St., Chicago, IL 60611, U.S.A.

KENT, Homer Austin, Jr., b. 13 Aug. 1926. Educator; Clergyman. Educ: B.A., Bob Jones Univ., 1947; B.D., Grace Theol. Sem., Winona Lake, Ind., 1950; Th.M., 1952; Th.D., 1956. Appts: Prof., N.T. & Greek, Grace Theol. Sem., 1951-; Dean, ibid, 1962-. Mbrships: Vice Chmn., Midwest Sect., Evangelical Theol. Soc., 1969-70; Chmn., 1970-71; Am. Assn. Higher Educ. Publs: The Pastoral Epistles, 1958; Ephesians: The Glory of the Church, 1971; Jerusalem to Rome, 1972; The Epsitle to the Hebrews, 1972; Light in the Darkness: Studies in the Gospel of John, 1974. Address: Grace Theological Sem., Winona Lake, IN 46590, U.S.A. 13, 15, 120. 139, 141.

KENT, Joel Gilbert, b. 13 Mar. 1933. Industrial Engineer; Government Official. Educ: B.S., Univ. of Miami, 1958; M.Graphoanalysis, Int. Graphoanalysis Soc., 1971. Appts: Planring Engr, Proposal Coordinator, Dynatronics Inc., Orlando, Fla., 1958-63; Sr. Engrng. Writer, RCA Serv. Co., Cocoa Beach, Fla., 1964; Apollo Data Mgr., Installation Data Mgr., John F. Kennedy Space Ctr., Fla., 1964-. Mbrships: Past Dir., Cocoa Beach Chapt., Am. Inst. Industrial Engrs.; V.P., Fla. Graphoanalysts; Fac., Congress & Inst., Int. Graphoanalysis Soc. Pioneered development of Apollo Data Mgmt. System & Installation Reports Mgmt. System for NASA, John F. Kennedy Space Ctr. Hons: Bunker Schlrship, 1969; Pres.'s Cert. Merit, Int. Graphoanalysis Soc., 1972. Address: 601 Robert Way, Satellite Beach, FL 32937, U.S.A. 7, 57.

KENT, Thomas Worrall, b. 3 Apr. 1922. Public Servant & Writer. Educ: M.A., Corpus Christi Coll., Oxford Univ., U.K., 1950. Appts: Edit. Writer, The Manchester Guardian, U.K., 1946-50; Asst. Ed., The Economist, London, 1950-54; Ed., The Winnipeg Free Press, Canada, 1954-59; V.P., Chemcell Ltd., Montreal, 1959-61; Policy Sec. to Rt. Hon. L.B. Pearson, Ldr. of Opposition & then Prime Min. of Canada, 1961-65; Dpty. Min., Manpower & Immigration, Govt. of Canada, 1966-68; Dpty. Min., Regional Economic Expansion, ibid, 1968-71; Pres. & Chief Exec. Off., Cape Breton Dev. Corp., N.S., 1971-; Bd., New Brunswick Multiplex Corp. N.S.; Bd. Sydney Steel Corp, N.S.; Mbrships: Coun. Mining Soc. of N.S.; Canadian Inst. of Pub. Admin. Publs: Social Policy for Canada, 1962; num. articles on pol. & economic subjects. Address: 1803 Cabot House, Sydney, Nova Scotia, Canada. 88.

KENYON, James William, b. 20 Feb. 1910. Publishing Executive; Author. Educ: Archbishop Temple's Schl., London. Appts: Pres., APER, 1958; Ed., Assns. Jrnl. News & Views, NFS News Mag., Higher Educ. Jrnl.; Ed., Blond's Ency. of Educ., 1969. Publs. incl: On My Right, 1940; Racing Wheels, 1941; Peter Trant: Cricketer Detective, 1944; Mystery at Brinsford, 1946; Lightweight Honours, 1947; The Fourth Arm, 1948; Traitor's Gold, 1952; The Girl Who Lost Her Curls, 1957; Easter Egg, 1960; Boxing History, 1962; Focus on Cars, 1963; Ann of Appleby's, 1964; Emergency Ward 10 Readers (Ed.), 1965. Contbr., mags. & jrnls., inclng. The Bookseller, Eagle, Leicester Mercury, British Books, Fire, Boxing News, Times Educl. Supplement, The Teacher. Address: 31 Stonehill Dr., Great Glen, Leicestershire, U.K.

KEPLINGER, Lorraine Joyce (Mrs. Richard A. Keplinger), b. 9 Apr. 1931. Musician;

Businesswoman. III. Wesleyan Univ. Music Schl., 1949; Tusc. Co. Br., Kent State Univ., New Philadelphia, Ohio, 1963-67. Appts: w. Structo Mfg. Co., Freeport, III., 1950; w. Burgess Battery Co., ibid, 1950-51; Gantt's Grocery, Lena, 1951-52; Self-employed, custom tailoring of clerical vestments, 1956-59; Owner, Operator, Gospel Book & Music Co., 1962-; Pvte. Instr., musical instruments. Performing musician. Mbrships: Unit Pres., Am. Legion Aux., 1961-67; Co. Pres., 1965-66; Unit. Treas., 1971-; Unit Pres., PTA, 1062-64; Coun. V.P., 1964-66; Coun. Pres., 1966-68; Personell Mgr., Tusc. Co. Philharmonic Orch., 1968-; Music Study Club, Dover, 1971-; Hon. Life, Ohio Congress PTA. Hons. incl: Past Pres. Pin, Am. Legion Aux., 1963; Past Pres. Pin, Co. Legion Aux., 1966; Past Pres. Pin., Unit, PTA, 1965; Past Pres. Pin, Coun., PTA, 1969. Address: 144 3rd St., S.W., New Philadelphia, OH 44663, U.S.A. 5, 138.

KEPPLER, Helen Thul (Mrs. John A. Keppler), b. 2 Oct. 1918. Industrial Executive. Appts. incl: Rep., Girl Scouts, U.S.A., 1957; Mbr., Woodland Schl. Bd. of Educ., Plainfield, 1957-58; Corp. Off., Nick Thul, Inc., 1941-, K-T Corp., N. Plainfield, 1957-, Thul Auto Parts, Inc., 1963-73, Thul Machine Works, 1963-. Mbrships: Plainfield Camera & Raritan Valley Country Clubs; Repub. party. Address: 10 Mtn. Trail, Warren, NJ 07060, U.S.A. 5.

KERBER, Roger, b. 11 July 1907. Professor; Writer. Educ: Ph.D., Vienna Univ., Austria. Appts: Tchr., Viennese secondary schls.; Prof., Inst. Français de Vienne; Headmaster, Theresianische Akad., Vienna; Rdr., Vienna Univ.; Prof., Diplomatische Akad., Vienna. Mbrships: Int. Fellowship, former scouts & guides, 1967-73; Chmn., World Coun., 1971-73. Publs: Grammatik der französ Sprache; Apprenons le franççais; Enrichissons notre vocabulaire; Französank praktisch und idiomatisch; J'apprends le français; Kennst du? Kannst du? ; 1, 2, 3—los! ; Hons: Off. d'Acad., 1949; Off. de l'Ordre des Palmes, 1959; Chev. de la Légion d'Honneur, 1964; Grosses Ehrenzeichen für Verdienste um die Repub. Oesterreich, 1972; Off. de l'Ordre Nat. du Mérite, 1973; Croix de Dieppe, 1973. Address: A-1030, Hintzerstr. 10, Vienna, Austria. 43.

KERDEL-VEGAS, Francisco, b. 3 Jan. 1928. Physician. Educ: Med. studies, Ctrl. Univ. of Venezuela, Caracas, 1945-51, Physn. & Surg. Degree, ibid, 1951; Internship, Hosp. Carlos J. Bello, Caracas, 1949-51; Clin. Fellow in Dermatol., Mass. Gen. Hosp. & Harvard Med. Schl., Boston, U.S.A., 1951-52; Res. Dermatol., N.Y. Univ. Postgrad. Med. Schl., 1952-54; M.S., N.Y. Univ., 1954; D.M.S., Ctrl. Univ. of Venezuela, 1966. Appts. incl: Asst. Prof. Dermatol., Med. Schl., Ctrl. Univ. of Venezuela, 1954-58; Assoc. Prof. Dermatol., ibid, 1958-61; Prof. Dermatol., ibid, 1961-; Vis. Sci., Dept. of Experimental Pathol., ARC Inst. of Animal Physiol., Cambridge, U.K., 1966-67; V. Rector, Univ. Simón Bolívar, Caracas, 1968-69. Mbrships. incl: Trinity Coll., Cambridge Univ., 1966-; Fellow, Nat. Acad. Med., Venezuela, 1969- & Acad. of Scis., Venezuela, 1971-; Hon., Affiliated & Corres. Mbr. num. profl. socs. Publs: 2 textbooks on Dermatol.; sev. monographs on Med. subjects; num. Sci. papers in European Med. jrnls. Hons. incl: Martin Vegas Prize for Rsch. work, Venezuelan Dermatological Soc., 1960, 1964; C.B.E., 1973. Address: Apartado 60391, Caracas 106, Venezuela. 136.

KEREN, Zvi, b. 9 May 1926. Drip Irrigation Engineer. Educ: Herzlia H.S., Tel Aviv, 1944; Infantry Offs. Schl., Israel Army, 1957; Water Engrng. Courses, Tel Aviv & Haifa, 1965-70. Appts: Treas., Kibbutz Hatzerim, 1952-53, 1956-57; Hd., Design & Engrng. Dept., Netafim Waterworks, Hatzerim Ltd., 1965-. Mbrships: Nat. Bd. Israel Boy & Girl Scouts Fedn., 1955-; Chief Scout Exec., Jewish Boy & Girl Scouts of Israel1959-60. Author, The Settlement of 11 New Settlements in the Negev., 1966. Var. pamphlets, drip irrigation, 1965-73. Hons: Independence War Award, 1949; Hagana Award, 1950; Service Award, 1950; Sinai Campaign Award, 1956; Aleh Award, 1958; Six Days War Award, 1967. Address: Kibbutz Hatzerim, M.P. Negev, 85305, Israel. 55.

KERLIN, (Mrs.) Geraldine Young, b. 4 Sept. 1919. Electric Utility Executive. Educ: Grad., Morris H.S. Appts: Mgr., Western Auto, 1939-49; Ins. Agt. w. Wingate Ins. Agcy., 1949-56; Owner, Young Ins. Agcy., 1956-50; V.P., Wellsboro Elec. Co., Pa., 1956-60; Pres., ibid, 1960-. Mbrships: Tioga Co. Planning Commn., 1970-; Bd. Dirs., Crow Fndn.; Bus. & Profl. Womens Club. Address: P.O. Box 112, Wellsboro, PA 16901, U.S.A. 5, 6, 132.

KERMODE, John Frank, b. 29 Nov. 1919. University Professor. Educ: Liverpool Univ. Appts: Lectr., King's Coll., Newcastle, 1947-49, Reading Univ., 1949-58; J.E. Taylor Prof., Manchester Univ., 1958-65; Winterstroke Prof., Bristol Univ., 1965-67; Lord Northcliffe Prof., Univ. Coll., London, 1967-74; King Edward VII Prof., Cambridge Univ., 1974-. Mbrships: Fellow, Brit. Acad.; Fellow, Royal Soc. of Lit. Publs: Arden edit. of The Tempest, 1954; Romantic Image, 1957; The Living Milton, 1960; Wallace Stevens, 1960; Puzzles & Epiphanies, 1962; The Sense of Ending, 1967; Continuities, 1968; Modern Essays, 1971; Oxford Anthology of English Literature (w. others), 1973. Address: King's Coll., Cambridge, U.K. 1, 2.

KERPER, Ruth Patterson. Securities Broker. Educ: B.A., Lake Erie Coll., Painesville, Ohio, 1937; Grad. study, Clarke & Loras Colls., Dubuque, Iowa; Computer Programming, Gen. Elec., Chgo., III.; Securities & Commodities, N.Y. Inst. of Finance, N.Y.C. Appts. incl: Registered Rep. (Acct. Exec.) for Bache & Co., Inc., Phoenix, Ariz., 1971-, & Dain, Kalman & Quail, Cubuque, Iowa; Tchr., Clarke Coll., Dubuque, Iowa, 5 yrs. Mbrships: Regent, Julien Dubuque Chapt., DAR, 1968-70; Iowa State Chmn., Music, ibid, 1970-71; Dubuque, Co. Dir. of Water Safety, Am. Red Cross, 4 yrs.; Bd. of Dirs., ibid, 8 yrs.; Dir., Investment Clubs, var. brs., AAUW; Bus. & Profl. Women; Kappa Alpha Sigma, 1937. Recip., 25 yr. award for var. servs. in water safety, Am. Red Cross. Address: 1929 E. Medlock Dr., Phoenix, AZ 85016, U.S.A. 130.

KERR, Adelaide. Writer; Journalist. Educ: Univ. of Kan., Lawrence, 1 yr.; State Univ. of Mont., Missoula, 2 yrs.; N.Y. Univ., N.Y.C., 2 yrs. Appts. incl: Edit. Staff, Associated Press, 25 yrs.; For. Corres. & Features Ed., AP Paris Bur., France, 5 yrs.; Special Assignment, AP London Bur., U.K., 3 months; Writer, AP Newsfeatures Serv., 17 yrs.; Fndr. & Ed., AP Woman's Page; Fndr. & Writer, column "These Women"; Specialized in features on UN & soc. problems. Mbrships: Author's Guild Inc.; Author's League of Am.; Overseas Press Club of Am., Inc., Bd. Govs., 2 yrs. Author, How to Pray & What to Pray For. Address: 130 E. 39th St., N.Y., NY 10016, U.S.A. 132, 138.

KERR, Ann Thomas, (Mrs. William E. Kerr), b. 3 June 1911. Teacher; Secretary; Homemaker. Appts: Tchr., Pitts. Acad., until 1939; Personal Sec. to Pres., J. & L. Steel

Corp., until 1944. Mbrships: V.P., Pitts. Opera & Pitts. Music Guild; Pres., Magee Hosp. Aux.; Dir., Civic Light Opera; Nat. Soc. Arts & Letters; 20th Century Club; Pitts. Symphony; Opera Workshop. Author 2 books on travel in Europe & Far East. Address: 927 Hulton Rd., Oakmont, PA 15139, U.S.A.

KERR, Clark, b. 17 May 1911. Professor; Academic Administrator. Educ: A.B., Swarthmore Coll., 1932; M.A., Stanford Univ., 1933; Ph.D., Econs., Univ. of Calif. at Berkeley, 1939. Appts: Asst., Assoc. Prof., Univ. of Wash., 1940-45; Assoc., Prof., Prof., Econs. & Indl. Rels., Schl. of Bus. Admin., Univ. of Calif., Berkeley, 1945-73; Prof. Emeritus, 1974; Chancellor, Univ. of Calif., Berkeley, 1952-58; Pres., Univ. of Calif., 1958-67; Chmn., Exec. Dir., Carnegie Commn. on Higher Educ., Berkeley, 1967-73; Chmn., Staff Dir., Carnegie Coun. on Policy Studies in Higher Educ., 1974-. Mbrships. incl: Int., Am., Western & Royal Economic Assns.; Charter Mbr., Nat. Acad. of Educ. Publs. incl: Unions, Management & the Public, 1948, 3rd edit., 1967; The Uses of the University, 1964, 5 edits. Recip., Hon. degrees from 26 univs. & colls. U.S.A., Scotland, Hong Kong, Chile, France; Alexander Meiklejohn Award, AAUP, 1964; Clark Keer Award, Univ. of Calif., Berkeley, 1968. Address: Carnegie Coun. on Policy Studies in Higher Education, 2150 Shattuck Ave., Berkeley, CA 94704, U.S.A. 2, 14, 59, 139, 141.

KERR, Frank John, b. 8 Jan. 1918. Astronomer. Educ: B.Sc., Univ. of Melbourne, Australia, 1938; M.Sc., ibid, 1940; M.A. Harvard Univ., U.S.A., 1951; D.Sc., Univ. Melbourne, 1962. Appts: Rsch. Schlr., Univ. Melbourne, 1939; Staff Mbr., CSIRO Radiophys. Lab., Sydney, 1940-68; Vis. Sci., Leiden Univ., 1957; Vis. Prof., Univ. of Tex., U.S.A., 1964, Univ. of Md., 1966-68; Prof., Univ. of Md., 1968-, Dir., Astronomy Prog., 1973-. Mbrships. incl: Int. Astronomical Union; V.P., Commn. 33, ibid, 1973-76, Org. Comm. Mbr., 3 commns. & 4 symposia; Councillor, Am. Astronomical Soc.; Astronomical Soc. of Australia. Var. papers, astronomical jrnls. Hons. incl: Ormsby Hamilton Prize, 1939; Fulbright Travel Grant, 1950-51; Leverhulme Fellowship, 1967; NSF Rsch. Grants, annually, 1967-74. Address: Astronomy Prog., University of Maryland, College Pk., MD 20742, U.S.A. 14, 23.

KERR, (Sir) Hamilton William, b. 1 Aug. 1903. Retired Member of Parliament. Educ: Balliol Coll., Oxford, U.K. Appts: M.P., Oldham, 1931-45, Cambridge City, 1950-66; Parliamentary Pvte. Sec., Rt. Hon. Alfred Duff Cooper, 1933-38; Parliamentary Sec., Min. of Hlth., 1945; Parliamentary Pvte. Sec., Rt. Hon. Harold Macmillan, 1963-66. Mbrships: Chancellor, Primrose League, 1963-65; Master of Patternmakers, 1966-67. Hons: Created Baronet, Birthday Hons., 1957; Chevalier, Legion of Hon., 1960; LL.D., Cambridge, 1972. Address: Mill House, Whittlesford, Cambridge, U.K. 1.

KERR, Rupert Harry Augustus, b. 10 Nov. 1907. Retired Government Officer. Appts: Govt. Off., Jamaica; Revenue Clerk, 1927-42; Asst. Collector, Taxes, 1942-44; Excise Insp., 1944-49; Collector, Taxes, 1949-53; Surveyor, Customs, 1953-55; Sr. Collector, Taxes, 1955; Area Insp., 1956-59; Chief Insp., Customs, 1959-60; Dpty. Collector Gen., 1960-63; Collector Gen., 1963. Mbrships: Nat. Geographic Soc.; Kingston Cricket Club; Masonic Dist., Grand Lodge of England P.D.G.W.; Justice of Peace, Parish of Kingston;

Spirit Licence Authority, ibid. Address: 29 Hope Blvd., Kingston 6, Jamaica, West Indies.

KERSCHBAUMER, Luisa, b. 22 Jan. 1893. M.D., Retired Physician & Surgeon in General Practice & Psychiatry; Poet; Artist. Appts. incl: Cleveland State Hosp.; St. Louis City Sanitarium; St. Louis Mental San.; St. Louis Schl. Phys.; Mitchell, San., Peoria, Ill.; Hastings State Hosp., Minn.; Overlook Gen. Hosp., N.J.; Youngstown Receiving Hosp.; Willard State Hosp., N.Y.; Now Ret'd. Life Fellow Am. Psych. Assn. Mbr., Mahoning Co. Med. Soc., Minn. Publs: Contbr., Jrnl. for Nervous & Mental Disease & Psychoanalysis Review; Poems in anthols. Cyclo-Flame; New Voices in American Poetry, 1972. Hons: Medal, Am. Psych. Assn. for meritorious contbns. to psych., 1969; Medals for painting, Am. Physns. Art. Assn., N.Y. Address: Willard State Hosp., Willard, NY 14588, U.S.A. 11, 112.

KERSEY, George Euclid, b. 3 Apr. 1927. Attorney-at-Law. Educ: B.S., Univ. of Colo., Boulder, U.S.A., 1952; Tripos Hons., Univ. of Cambridge, U.K., 1953; S.M., MIT, 1956; LL.B., Harvard Law Schl., 1959. Appts. incl: Patent Atty., Bell Telephone Labs., Inc., Murray Hill, N.J., 1959-66; Dike, Thompson & Bronstein, Attys.-at-Law, Boston, Mass., 1966-68; Patent Atty., Western Elec. Co., Inc., N.Y.C., 1968-72; Woodward, Kersey & Kojima, Attys.-at-Law, N.Y.C., 1972-73; Cons., Legal Aspects of Indl. Property, 1973-. Mbrships. incl: N.Y. State Bar, 1960; N.J. State Bar, 1963; Mass. State Bar, 1966; Bar of U.S. Supreme Ct., 1964; Am. Bar Assn.; N.Y. State Bar Assn.; N.Y. Patent Law Assn.; Sigma Xi; Tau Beta Pi; Sigma Tau; Sigma Pi Sigma; Eta Kappa Nu; Pi Mu Epsilon; Delta Sigma Rho. Author, Conversion of Numerical Information, 1963. Holder, 2 U.S. Patents on controlled circuits. Recip., Fndn. Fellowship, Rotary Int., 1952. Address: Allerton Rd., Annandale, NJ 08801, U.S.A. 6.

KERSHAW, Beulah F. (Mrs. Bryan I. Kershaw), b. 9 Jan. 1919. Song Writer; Poet; Music Teacher. Educ: Pvte. Music Study, 20 yrs. Appts: Mgr., Al Terry (Hickory Records), Al Terry, TV, Radio; Mgr., Lucky Le Roy, TV, Records; Mgr., Russell Eliot, TV, Radio, Nightclubs. Author, books of poems by Beulah, Vols. I & II. Records: If You Want a Broken Heart, I'll be Glad When I'm Free. A Woman in Love, The Stranger, Kennedy, I Walk in Beauty, There's Something About God. Recip. of Awards. Address: Rte. 1, Beulah Records, Crossville, IL 62827, U.S.A.

KERSHAW, John Hugh D'Allenger, b. 2 Aug. 1931. Author. Educ: London Univ., U.K. Appts: Tutor, Lit., Inst. S. Marcellina, London Br., Wkrs. Educ: Assn. & Extra-Mural Dept., London Univ.; Ed., ABC TV progs., Tempo & Callan; Prod., Armchair Theatre, Thames TV. Mbrships: Soc. of Authors; Writers Guild of G.B. Publs: The Present Stage, 1966; A Meeting in Casa, 1973; 25 TV plays, 1970-74; TV series, Rainbow, 1973-74; Lyrics, Fanfare the Orchestra; Libretto, Song Cycle, Corinea; Libretto, George & the Dragonfly. Address: c/o Felix de Wolfe & Assocs., 1 Roberts St., London, WC2N 6BH, U.K. 3, 11.

KESSELL, James Everett, b. 13 Oct. 1915. Artist. Educ: Coventry Coll. of Art, U.K. Appts: Profl. Artist & Art Tutor, Coventry Educ. Authorities, 1956-69; Fndr. & Prin., James Kessell Schl. of Art, 1969-. One man exhibs., Birmingham, 1967, 70. Exhibs. incl: Herbert Art Gall., Coventry, 1965; European Artists, N.Y., 1969; Northampton Art Gall., 1970; Coventry Cathedral, 1973. Fellow, Royal

Soc. Arts. Mbrships. incl: Royal Birmingham Soc. Artists; 'Coventry Art Guild. Commnd. works incl: Sir Henry Parkes Birthplace, Coventry Corp.; Coventry City F.C., Coventry Corp.; Portrait, Bishop of N.Y.; Portrait, Bishop of Coventry; Portrait, Bishop of Carlisle. Works in pvte. & pub. collects. throughout the world. Recip., Silver Medal & Dip., Accad. Int., Rome, 1970. Address: The Studios, Church Lane, Eastern Green, Coventry, CU5 7BX, U.K. 43, 105, 128, 133.

KESSLER, Horace Andrew, b. 17 Oct. 1908. Educator; Music Publisher; Songwriter. Educ: B.A., 1952, M.A., 1960, Univ. of Denver. Appts: Colo. State Hwy. Dept., Denver, 1936-42; Supvsr., war mats., U.S. War Dept., Ogden, Utah, 1942-43; USAAF, 1943-45; Tchr., elem. schls., La Junta, Colo., 1952-63; Elem. schl. prin., ibid, 1963-71; Retd., 1971; Owner, Mgr., Kessler Music, La Junta, 1955-. Num. mbrships. incl: Var. offs., PTA & Boy Scouts of Am.; Past Chmn., Colo. Assn. of Schl. Execs.; Life Mbr., Dept. of Elem. Schl. Prins., NEA; Var. comms., Colo. Educ. Assn.; Past Pres., La Junta Educ' Assn., & deleg., NEA & Colo. Educ. Assn. convs.; Nat. Ch. Music Fellowship. Songs incl: My Jesus Walks with Me; Dwell Thou in Me; I Turn My Eyes to Him; He Came; Colorado Moon. Hons: Sharpshooter, Marsken Medals, Good Conduct Medal, WWII. Address: 936 W. 5th St., Las Animas, CO 81054, U.S.A. 9, 22, 57, 60, 120, 126, 129, 131.

KESSLER, Shirley. Artist; Educator; Art Lecturer. Educ: N.Y. Univ., 1940; Art Students League, N.Y.C., 1941-44; Sam Brecher Studio, N.Y.C., 1940-42. Art Tchr., Adult Educ., Bd. of Educ., N.Y.C., 1946-. Mbrships. incl: Pres., Nat. Assn. of Women Artists, 1967-70; Permanent Advsry. Bd., ibid, 1971-; Chmn., Traveling U.S.A. Watercolor exhibts, 1961-65; Nat. Soc. of Painters in Casein & Acrylic; Bd. of Dirs., N.Y. Soc. of Women Artists, 1970-74; Am. Fedn. of Arts; Artists Equity Assn.; Hon. mbr., Soc. d'Encouragement au Progres, Paris, France, 1970-; Nat. Coun. of Jewish Women; Am. Jewish Congress. 43 one-man exhibitions in U.S.A. & Canada; Represented in juried group shows in Europe, S. Am., Mexico, Canada; Permanent collects. in U.S.A. Hons. incl: Medal of Hon., Nat. Assn. of Women Artists, 1970; Art Laureate, Rosette, Nat. Medal of Hon., Paris, France, 1970. Address: 185 E. 85th St., N.Y., NY, U.S.A.

KESSLER, Stuart Alan, b. 10 Feb. 1939. Architect. Educ: B.A., Univ. of Va., 1959; Postgrad. Studies, N.Y. Univ. Schl. of Law, 1959-60, Columbia Univ., 1961-64, Harvard Grad. Schl. of Design, 1970. Appts: Construction Supvsr., DeMatteis Org., N.Y.C., 1960-62; Designer & Supvsr., S.J. Kessler & Sons, Archts., Engrs. & Planners, N.Y.C., 1962-, Ptnr., 1972-; Pres., Claridge Co., Real Estate Developers, N.Y.C., 1964-; V.P., Kessler Assocs., Boston, Mass., 1969-. Mbrships: Am. Insts. of Archts. & Planners; Royal Inst. British Archts.; Boston & N.Y. Socs. of archts.; Urban Land Inst. Contbr., Apt. Construction News, Progressive Arch. Inventor, Phased Community Redevelopment. Hons. incl: City Club of N.Y. Award, 1965; Nat. Apt. Assn. Award, 1969. Address: S.A. Kessler & Sons, 598 Madison Ave., N.Y., NY 10022, U.S.A. 2, 6.

KETRON, (Rev.) Louis T., b. 18 Aug. 1935. United Methodist Minister. Educ: B.S., E. Tenn. State Univ., 1962; Postgrad. study, Emory Univ., Atlanta, Ga., 1962-65. Appts: Tchr., Rhea Co., Tenn., Schl. System, 1964-67. Pres., Optimist Club, Dayton, Tenn., 1966. Publs: Historical Maps: Bloomingdale-Arcadia,

Tenn., 1970; Hawkins County, Tenn., 1971; Knox County, Tenn., 1971. Address: Rte. 9, Kimberlin Heights Pike, Knoxville, TN 37920, U.S.A.

KETTUNEN, Pentti Olavi, b. 7 Jan. 1932. Professor of Materials Science. Educ: Dip. Engr., Inst. of Technol., Helsinki, Finland, 1958; Licentiate of Technol. (Ph.D.), ibid, 1963; Doctor of Technol., 1965. Appts. incl: Sr. Asst. in Phys. Metallurgy, Inst. of Technol., Helsinki, 1962-64; Engr. i/c, Lab. of Electron Microscopy, ibid, 1964-65; Rsch. Off., Outokumpu Oy, Helsinki, 1965-66; Rsch. Off., U.S. Atomic Energy Commn., Mats. Sci. Div., Argonne Nat. Lab., Argonne, Ill., U.S.A., 1966-69; Prof. of Mech. Metallurgy, then Mats. Sci., Tampere Univ. of Techno., Tampere, Finland, 1969-. Mbrships: Finnish Tech. Soc.; Finnish Soc. for Engrs. of Mining & Metallurgy; Coun. of Crystallography, Finnish Soc. of Physicists; Admin. Bd., Scandinavian Soc. of Electron Microscopy, 1964-65; Metallurgical Soc. of AIME. Publs: Approx. 60 papers on Phys. Metallurgy & Mats. Sci. Address: Lohitie 2 A 5, 02170 Haukilahti, Finland. 56, 134.

KEYFETZ, Carl Kivie, b. 12 Oct. 1907. Queen's Counsel. Educ: Oakwood Collegiate, 1927; Osgoode Hall, 1930. Appts: Adjutant, C.O., Legal Dept., then Air Force H.Q., RCAF Admin. Br., 1941-45; Q.C., 1951; Ptnr., law firm, Gordon, Keyfetz, Hall, Baker & Goodman, Toronto, Ont.; Legal Counsel, Canadian Hemophilia Soc., Gen. Wingate Br. of Royal Canadian Legion, Canadian Orthopaedic Shoe Mfrs.' Assn.; Dir., num. financial & commercial corps. Mbrships. incl: Hon. Pres., Sportsmen's Lodge, B'nai B'rith; Hon. V.P., Jewish Nat. Fund; Hon. Sec., Baycrest Ctr. Geriatric Care; Bd. Mbr., George Brown Coll. Applied Arts & Technol.; United Jewish Welfare Fund; Canadian Bar Assn.; Pi Lambda Phi. Hons: Man of Yr., Jewish Home for Aged, Toronto, 1966; Man of Month, Metropol Toronto. Address: Suite 1919, 390 Bay St., Toronto 1, Canada M5H 2Y2. 55, 88.

KEYNAN, Alexander, b. 18 Feb. 1921. Biologist. Educ: Ph.D., Hebrew Univ., Jerusalem, 1950; Post-Doctoral studies & rsch., Columbia Univ., Cold Spring Harbour, Pacific Grove, U.S.A., 1952-59. Appts: Scientific Dir., Israeli Inst. Biological Rsch., 1952-62; Vis. Prof. Bacteriol., Hebrew Univ. of Jerusalem, 1958-65, Chmn., Inst. Life Scis., 1967-71, V.P. & Chmn., Rsch. Authority, 1969-; Vis. Prof. Biol., Dept. Biological M.I.T., Cambridge, Mass., U.S.A., 1962-63; Miller Vis. Prof., Univ. of Ill., Urbana, 1965; Chmn., Nat. Coun. Rsch. & Dev., Prime Min.'s Off., Govt. of Israel, 1963-67. Mbrships. incl: Advsry. Coun. for Sci. Technol. for Dev. to Sec. Gen. of UN; European Molecular Biol. Org.; Israel Biochem. Soc.; Soc. Gen. Physiol. Num. sci. papers, int. sci. jrnls. Address: Hebrew University of Jerusalem, Jerusalem, Israel. 94.

KHACHATUROV, Tigran Sergejevich, b. 6 Oct. 1906. Economist. Educ: Grad., Dept. of Stats., Fac. of Soc. Scis., Moscow Univ., U.S.S.R., 1926. Appts. incl: Scientific worker, Ctrl. Statistical Bd., 1926-29 & Inst. of Transport Econs., 1929-33; Lectr., Econs. of Transportation, Inst. of Transportation Engrs., 1930-40; Prof., ibid, 1940-54; Corres. Mbr., Acad. of Scis., U.S.S.R., 1943-66; Dpty. Dir., Rsch. Inst. of Railway Transp., 1943-45; Dir., ibid, 1945-49; Dir., Inst. of Complex Transp. Problems, Acad. of Scis., 1955-59; Chief, Sector of Investments, Inst. of Econs., Acad. of Scis., 1959-66; Academician (Full Mbr., Acad. of Scis.), 1966; Chief, Econs. Dept., Acad., 1967-71; Ed.-in-Chief, Voprosy Economiki (monthly) (Problems of Econs.), 1966-; Prof., Fac. of Econs., Moscow Univ., 1971-. Mbrships: Acad. of Scis., U.S.S.R., 1966; Hon. Mbr., Acad. of Scis. of Hungary, 1970; Mbr., Exec. Comm., Int. Econ. Assn., 1968-; Scientific Coun. of Problems of Effectiveness of Investments, Acad. of Scis., Chmn., 1957-. Author of many books in profl. field translated into sev. langs. & num. articles in nat. & int. jrnls. Hons: 4 Orders of Red Banner of Labour, 1942, 1945, 1966, 1971; Order of Red Star, 1945; Sev. Medals, 1939, 1945, 1948. Address: Ulitsa Academika Petrovskogo, 3, Kw. 30, Moscow V-419, U.S.S.R.

KHADHIRI, Riadh Kit, b. 29 June 1932. Associate Professor of Business Administration. Educ: B.B.A., Univ. of Miss., 1957; M.S., ibid, 1958; D.B.A., Miss. State Univ., 1970. Appts. incl: Rsch. Assoc., Bur. Bus. & Economic Rsch., State Coll., Miss. State Univ., 1966-68; Assoc. Prof., Nicholls State Univ., Thibodaux, La., 1968-71; Assoc. Prof., Ctr. Bus. Admin., St. Edward's Univ., Austin, Tex., 1971-. Mbrships: Am. Economic Assn.; Southern Economic Assn.; Acad. Miss. Economists; Southwestern Soc. Sci. Assn.; AAUP; Acad. of Mgmt; Theta Chi Fraternity; Alpha Kappa Psi Fraternity; Omicron Delta Epsilon. Address: 9302 Heatherwood Dr., Austin, TX 78745, U.S.A. 7.

KHAN, Kanwar Habib, b. 12 Feb. 1938. University Teacher; Counseling Psychologist. Educ: B.A., Univ. of Punjab, Lahore, Pakistan, 1960. M.A. Educ., ibid, 1963; M.A. Pol. Sci., 1965; M.S., Univ. of Wis., U.S.A., 1971. Appts: Engl. tchr. & Prin., var. schls.; Asst. Dist. Insp. of Schls., 1963-68; Asst. Master, Westwoodside Ch. of England Schl., Doncaster, U.K., 1968-70; Assoc. Instr., Ind. Univ., 1971-74. Mbrships: Chmn., Soc. Evil Eradication Coun., Maharwali, Pakistan, 1960-63; Pres., Univ. of Wis. Chapt., Muslim Students' Assn., 1970-71; Am. Psychological Assn.; Am. Educl. Rsch. Assn.; Int. Soc. of Educl. Planners. Publs: Contbns. to profl. jrnls. Recip., Fellowship, Univ. of Punjab, 1962-63. Address: Dept. of Educational Psychology, Indiana University, Bloomington, IN 47401, U.S.A.

KHAN, Suhail Ashraf, b. 6 Oct. 1938. Petroleum Engineer (Operational Research). Educ: B.Sc., St. John's Coll., Agra. India, 1957; B.Sc. Petroleum Engrng., Indian Schl. of Mines, 1961; M.S., Stanford Univ., Calif., U.S.A., 1962; D.E., ibid, 1965. Appts: Rsch. Asst., Petroleum Engrng. Dept., Stanford Univ., 1962; Instr., Phys. Sci. Dept., ibid, 1963; Jr. Scientist, C.B. Assocs, Los Altos, Calif., 1964; Hd., Dept. of Reservoir Engrng., Venezuelan Petroleum Corp., 1965; Hd., Proj. Analysis (Systems) Dept., Directorate of Prod., ibid, 1966-. Mbrships: Soc. of Petroleum Engrs. (Pres., Western Venezuelan Sect. 1972); Sigma Xi; Venezuelan Soc. Geologist, Mineralogist & Petroleum Engrs. Contbr. to Profl. Jrnls. Hons. incl: Hancock Fund Fellowship, Stanford Univ., 1961-62; Petroleum Rsch. Fund Fellowship, Am. Chem. Soc., 1962-63; Petroleum Rsch. Grant, CONICIT (Nat. Rsch. Coun., Venezuela), 1972-74. Address: Edif. Acasa, Apt. 9A, Ave. El Milagro, Maracaibo, Venezuela. 136.

KHANBEGIAN, Jean M. Artist; Writer. Educ: Art Schl., N.Y.C.; The Schl. of Visual Art; Parsons Schl. of Design; Art Students League. Appts: w. ARTIST Mag., N.Y. Off., 1965-66; Full-time Artist w. gall. showing own works in summer; has had num. pvte. showings & travelling exhibs. apart from own gall.; specializes in Marine subjects. Publs: Painting Sea & Sky, 1967. Paintings used for mag.

covers: Readers Digest, Oct. 1973 of U.S. Edit. & June 1974; Yankee Magazine, scheduled to appear in 1975. Hons: 1st Prize for Dusk, 1963, 2nd Prize for Atlantic Winds, 1964, both from St. Lukes Art Guild, Whitestone, N.Y.; Hon. Mention, Armenian Students Cultural Soc., 1965. Address: RFD No. 1, Ellsworth, ME 04605, U.S.A.

KHAZANOFF, Amram, b. Nov. 1891 (d. 17 Aug. 1973). Agriculturist-Agronomist. Educ: Am. Coll., Beirut, Lebanon, 1910; B.S., Univ. of Calif., 1915; M.S., ibid, 1916. Appts: Asst., Agricl. Experimentation Ctr., Zikhron-Yaakov, Israel, 1911-13; Hd. Agriculturist, Palestine Jewish Colonization Assn., 1920-40; Vine & Citrus Grower, Gedera, 1940-73; Hd., local community, ibid, 1941-47. Author of num. articles in Engl. & Hebrew in field of agric. & agricl. rsch. Prin. contbns. in discovery of new almond & orange varieties, inclng. variety Khazanoff. Recip. of Prize for Agricl. Rsch., Vulcany Instn., Dept. of Agric., Univ. of Jerusalem. Address: c/o Mrs. Ester Khazanoff, Bilustr. 15, Gedera, Israel.

KHERDIAN, David, b. 17 Dec. 1931. Poet; Editor Educ: B.S., Univ. of Wis., 1960. Appts: Lit. Cons., Northwestern Univ., 1965; Poetry Judge, Vincent Price Awards in Creative Writing, Inst. of Am. Indian Arts, Santa Fe, N.M., 1968; Rare Book Cons., Fresno State Coll., 1968; Instr., ibid, 1969-70; Ed., Ararat Mag., 1970-71; Poet-in-the-Schls., State of N.H., 1971-72. Mbr., P.E.N. Publs: A Bibliography of William Saroyan: 1934-64, 1965; Six Poets of the San Francisco Renaissance: Portraits and Checklists, 1967; On the Death of My Father & other Poems, 1970; Down at the Santa Fe Depot: 20 Fresno Poets (co-ed.), 1970; Homage to Adana, 1970; Looking Over Hills, 1972; Visions of America: by the Poets of Our Time (ed.), 1973; A David Kherdian Sampler, 1974; The Nonny Poems, 1974; Ed., Settling America: The Ethnic Expression of 14 Contemporary Poets, 1974. Address: E. Chatham, NY 12060, U.S.A. 30.

KHOSLA, Ved Mitter, b. 13 Jan. 1926. Oral & Maxillo-facial Surgeon. Educ: Univ. of Cambridge, U.K., 1945; L.D.S.R.C.S., Univ. of Edinburgh & Royal Coll of Surgs., Edinburgh, U.K., 1950; F.D.R.C.S., ibid, 1958; L.D.S., Coll. of Dental Surgs., Saskatchewan, Canada, 1962; Intern, Oral Surg., Selly Oak Hosp., Birmingham, U.K., 1950; Res., Oral Surg., Nottingham Gen. Hosp., U.K., 1957-58; City Hosp., ibid, 1957-58; Utrecht Hosp., Holland, 1951. Appts. incl: Cons. Oral Surg., Govt. of Tanzania, Mwanza Hosp., 1959-62, Kerrobert Hosp., Saskatchewan, Canada; Asst. Prof., Oral Surg., Univ. of Calif., San Fran., 1967-, Div., Postdoctoral Studies in Oral Surg., 1968-; Chief, Oral Surg., San Fran. Gen. Hosp., 1968-; Planning Commn., ibid, 1968-; Oral Surg. Cons., San Quentin State Prison, 1968-; Lectr., V.A. Hosp., San Fran., 1970-, Univ. of Pacific, 1971-; Vis. Cons., Fresno Co. Hosp. Dental Clin., 1969. Fellow, ·Royal Coll. of Surgs., Edinburgh, Int. Assn. of Oral Surgs., AAAS, Royal Soc. of Hlth. Mbrships. incl: Am. Dental Assn.; Canadian Dental Assn.; N.Y. Acad. of Scis.; Am. Soc. of Oral Surgs. Contbr. of articles to profl. jrnls. Address: 410 N. San Mateo Dr., Suite B., San Mateo, CA 94401, U.S.A. 9, 120.

KHUNER, Alfred, b. 9 Sept. 1897. Civil Engineer. Educ: Degree in Civil Engrng., Tech. Univ., Vienna. Appts. incl: Surveyor i/c. Carpathian Mountains cable railway construction, for Seilbahn AG, Vienna; Structural Engr., Vienna, 1928-38, Singapore, 1½ yrs., & w. S.H. Nickell & Co., Melbourne,

Australia. Designing Engr., State Rivers & Water Supply Commn., Vic., Australia, over 18 yrs.; Sr. Lectr., Civil Engrng., Swinburne Tech. Coll., & Royal Melbourne Inst. of Technol.; Retirement, 1969. Mbrships. incl: Instn. of Engrs., Australia; Fed. Councillor & Br. Comm. Mbr., Assn. Profl. Engrs., Australia; Councillor, Retired State Employees Assn. of Vic.; Hon. Sec., Retired Off.'s Assn., State Rivers & Water Supply Commn., Vic. Profl. reports, State Rivers & Water Supply Commn., Vic. Address: Flat 1, 41 Milton St., Elwood, Vic., Australia, 3184. 55.

KIDDE, John Lyon, b. 5 June 1934. Executive. Educ: Columbia Law Schl., 1955-56; A.B., Engl., Princeton Univ., 1959. Appts: Indl. Rsch. Analyst, Federated Employers of San Francisco, 1956-57; Specialist Trng. Regtl. Corres. Clerk-Instr. in Mil. Law, Logistics Schl., U.S. Army, Fort Dix, N.J., 1957-58; Financial Dir., Walter Kidde S.A., Rio de Janeiro, Brazil, 1959-61; European Mgr., Walter Kidde & Co., Inc., Paris, France, 1962-66; Jt. Mng. Dir., ibid, Northolt, U.K. (as well as Corporate European Mgr.), 1966-67; Dir., Int. Ops., Walter Kidde & Co., Inc. (U.S.A.), 1967-68; V.P. & Dir., Int. Op., ibid, 1968-. Mbrships: Int. Advsry., Bd. of the N.J. Bank, N.A., 1971; Bd. of Trustees, Int. Coll. of Cayman Islands, B.W.I., 1972; Bd. Trustees, Nat. Coun. on Crime & Delinquency, 1973; Bd. Trustees, Pace Univ., N.Y.C., 1973, etc. Address: c/o Walter Kidde & Co., Inc., 9 Brighton Rd., Clifton, NJ 07012, U.S.A.

KIDWAI, Saied A., b. 23 Apr. 1926. Management & Public Affairs Consultant. Educ: B.A.; Dip. Jrnlsm. Appts: Publicity Off., Constitutional Reforms Dept., Hyderabad State Govt., 1944-47; Corres., McGraw Hill World News for Pakistan, 1948-49; P.R. Exec., Burmah Oil Grp. of Cos. in Pakistan, 1949-60, Gen. Mgr. (P.R.), 1970-73; Ed., PROGRESS, Burmah Oil Grp.'s Monthly Newspaper, 1953-73; Mgr., P.R., Burmah Oil & Gas Grp. of Cos. in Pakistan, 1960-70; Mng. Dir., S.A. Kidwai & Assocs., 1973-. Mbr., var. profl. orgs. Publs: Natural Gas in Pakistan, 1960; Search for Petroleum Resources in Pakistan. Documentary film, Oil in Pakistan. Hons: Middle Atlantic Assn. of Indl. Eds. Award, 1958; British Assn. of Indl. Eds. Merit Award, 1960. Address: Gandara House, D/8, KDA-1, Karachi-8, Pakistan. 16.

KIENBERGER, Alfred, b. 14 July 1907. Hotelier. Educ: Profl. Schl., Lausanne; Comm. Schl., Rolle. Appts: Mgr., Waldhaus Vulpera, 1928; Mgr., Luxor Hotel, Luxor, Egypt, winters, 1929-37; Mgr., Grand Hotel Hof Ragaz, summers, 1932-40; Mng. Dir., Altein Grand Hotel, Arosa, winters, 1937-38; Mng. Dir., Three Kings Hotel, Basel, 1941-73; Pres., Profl. Schl. & Tourist Assn., Basel, Verenahof Hotels & Thermal Baths, Baden, & Waldhaus Sils-Maria, Engadin; V.P., Hotels Quellenhof & Hof Ragaz, Bad-Ragaz, & Bellvue Palace Hotel, Berne; Dir., Grand Nat., Lucerne, Grand Hotel, Stockholm, & Hotel Merian am Rhein Basel. Mbrships: Hon. Mbr., Hotel Keepers Assn., Basel; Kiwanis; Skal; Swiss-Am. Soc.; Sec., Hotels de Grande Classe Int.; Pres., Publs. Comm., Int. Hotel Assn., Paris. Author, sev. publs. on Swiss & Int. hotel bus. Address: Hotel Merian am Rhein, Rheingasse. 2, CH 4058 Basel, Switzerland.

KIENITZ, Hermann, b. 4 May 1913. Chemist. Educ: Dr. rer. nat., Univ. of Breslau, 1938. Appts: Asst., Univ. & Tech. Acad., Breslau, 1939-44; Chmn., BASF AG, Physico-Analytical Lab., 1942-; Rsch. Staff, ibid, 1967-; Prof., Tech. Univ., Munich, 1969-.

Mbrships: Assn. of German Chems.; Chmn., Div. "Analytische Chemie", 1962-67, 71-76; Int. Union of Pure & Applied Chem; Chmn., Commn. of Physico-chem. Calibrations & Measurements, 1972-75; Bd. of Trustees & Sci. Advsry. Bd., Inst. for Spectrochem. & Applied Spectroscopy, Dortmund; Gen. Consultative Comm., Commn. of European Communities (Euratom), Brussels. Publs: Ed., Massenspektrometry, 1968, & sev. publs. on physico-analytical chem.; Contbr. to profl. publs. Address: WOH-Forschung B 1, BASF Aktiengesellschaft, D-6700, Ludwigshafen/Rhein, German Fed. Repub.

KIESEWETTER, Evelyn Cundiff (Mrs. Frank H. Kiesewetter), b. 16 Oct., 1908. Educator. Educ: Cinn. Conservatory of Music, 1931; A.B., Univ. of Ky., 1938; M.A., ibid, 1953; Postgrad. work, ibid. Appts: Tchr., Fayette Co. Bd. of Educ., Ky., 1930-; Counselor & Asst. Dir., Lexington Playgrounds Ky., & Girl's Camps, Ind., 1930-49; Tchr., Univ. of Ky., 1953-60; Educational Cons., Houghton-Mifflin Publrs., Boston, Mass., 1957-61; Tchr., Morehead State Univ., 1961; Educational Cons., Zaner-Bloser Co., Columbus, Ohio, summers 1962-69. Mbrships. incl: Am. Assn. for Supervision & Curriculum Dev.; Nat. Educ. Assn.; Blue Grass Trust for Historic Preservation; Henry Clay Mem. Fndn.; Ctrl. Ky. Concert & Lecture Assn.; Bd. Mbr., ibid; Nat. Audubon Soc.; Cinn. Opera Guild; Metropolitan Opera Guild; Phi Beta; Kappa Delta Pi; Alumni Assn., Univ. of Ky.; Episcopal Ch. Address: Merrick Pl., 3520 Milam Ln.-Apt. 409, Lexington, KY 40502, U.S.A. 5, 7, 15, 22, 57, 125, 132.

KIESEWETTER, Frank Howard, b. 27 Oct. 1909. Senior Design Engineer. Educ: Univ. of Cinn.; B.S., Univ. of Ky., 1935. Appts. incl: Mech. Cons. Engr., Warren & Ronald Cons. Engrs., Louisville, Ky., 1938-42; Mech. Cons. Engr., Design & Construction Camp Breckenridge, Allied Archt. Engrs., Morganfield, Ky., 1942; Staff Off., USAAF, 1942-46; Sr. Design Engr., Emery Inds., Inc., 1946-71. Mbrships. incl: Registered Profl. Engr., State of Ohio; Am. Soc. Heating & Refrigerating Engrs.; Alumni Assn., Univ. of Ky.; Henry Clay Mem. Fndn.; Blue Grass Trust for Historic Preservation; Ctrl. Ky. Concert & Lecture Assn.; Metropolitan Opera Guild; Nat. Audubon Soc.; Ky. Civil War Round Table; Masonic Lodge; Boy Scouts of Am.; var. Comms., ibid. Hons: DeMolay Legion of Honor; Plaque for work on behalf of Oak Hill Schls., Ky., from grateful community, 1960; Admiral, Commonwealth of Ky., 1970; Scouter's Award. Address: Merrick Pl., 3520 Milam Ln.-Apt. 409, Lexington, KY 40502, U.S.A. 7, 22, 125, 131.

KIESOW, Lutz A., b. 27 Jan. 1931. Biochemist. Educ: Univ. of Berlin; Med. Acad. of Dusseldorf, German Fed. Repub.; B.S., 1953; M.D., 1958. Appts: Res. Asst., Dept. of Physiological Chem., Univ. of Berlin, Germany, 1958-60; Hd., Lab. of Cell Physiol., Dept. of Physiological Chem., 1960-62; Int. Postdoctoral Rsch. Fellow, U.S. Dept. of HEW, NIH, Bethesda, Md., U.S.A. 1962; Res. Biochem., Bioenergetics Div., Naval Med. Rsch. Inst., Bethesda, 1963-64; Hd., Molecular Energetics Div., Bioenergetics Labs., 1964-70, Dir. of Experimental Med., 1970-. Mbrships: AAAS; Am. Soc. Biological Chem.; Am. Soc. Microbiol.; Undersea Med. Soc. Author, scientific boks & articles. Nomination by Sec. of U.S. Navy for Nat. Civil Serv. League Special Achievement Award, 1974. Address: Experimental Medicine, Naval Medical Research Inst., Bethesda, MD 20014, U.S.A. 57.

KIEV, (Rabbi) I. Edward, b. 21 Mar. 1905. Rabbi; Librarian. Educ: Columbia Univ., U.S.A.; M.H.L. Jewish Inst. Relig., 1927; Ordained in 1927; D.H.L., Hebrew Union Coll., Jewish Inst. Relig., 1956. Appts: Rsch. Asst., Jewish Inst. Relig., 1927-28; Asst. Libn., Hebrew bibliographer, ibid, 1928-43; Libn., Hebrew Union Coll., ibid, 1943-; Chap., Dept. Hosps., N.Y., 1928-; Sea View Hosp. Synagogue, 1930; Assoc. Rabbi, Cong. Habonim, 1963-73; Sec., Jewish Cultural Reconstruction, N.Y., 1949-51. Mbrships: Chmn., Israel Matz Fndn.; Trustee, Alexander Kohut Mem. Fndn.; Nissan Touroff Fndn.; Acad. Relig.; AAUP; Am. Acad. Jewish Rsch.; Am. Jewish Histl. Soc.; Am. Oriental Soc.; Israel Exploration Soc.; Israel Histl. Soc.; Mekize Nirdamim Soc.; Soc. Jewish Bibliophiles; N.Y. Bd. Rabbis; Ctrl. Conf. Am. Rabbis. Publs: Contbr. articles to mags. & annuals & Assoc. Ed., Jewish Book Annual, 1952-, Studies in Bibliography & Booklore, 1953-; Trans. Kafra Haggadah, 1949. Address: 40 W. 68th St., N.Y., NY 10023, U.S.A. 2, 55.

KIEWITT, Eva Lorene, b. 12 Aug. 1927. Educator; Librarian. Educ: B.S., Ball State Univ., Muncie, Ind., 1949; M.A., Ind. Univ., Bloomington, 1960; Ph.D., 1973. Appts. incl: Libn., E. Gary, Ind., 1958-60; Libn., Ulm, Germany, 1960-62; Libn., Bloomington, Ind., U.S.A., 1962-67; Univ. Libn., Schl. of Educ., Ind. Univ., 1967-73; Coll. Tchr.-Libn., Grad. Lib. Schl., ibid, 1973-. Mbrships. incl: ALA; Am. Soc. Info. Sci.; Am. Assn. Schl. Libns.; Assn. Am. Lib. Schls.; Beta Phi Mu; Delta Kappa Gamma; Pi Lambda Theta; Assn. of Educl. Communications & Technol.; Assn. of Coll. & Rsch. Libs.; Ind. Lib. Assn.; State Pres., Ind. Schl. Libns. Assn., 1968-69. Author of publs. in field. Address: 4100 Cambridge Dr., Bloomington, IN 47401, U.S.A.

KILBRACKEN, (Lord) John Raymond Godley, b. 17 Oct. 1920. Writer; Photographer; Farmer. Educ: Balliol Coll., Oxford, 1939-40, '46-47; B.A., M.A. (PPE), 1947. Appts: Serv. as Air Pilot, R.N.V.R., 1940-46; Lt. Cmdr., 1944; Commanded 835 & 714 Naval Air Squadrons; Staff Reporter, Daily Mirror & Sunday Express, 1947-51; Free-lance, 1951-. Mbrships. incl: Parly. Labour Party; Hon. Sec., Connacht Hereford Breeders' Assn.; Sponsor, Comm. for Freedom in Mozambique. Publs. incl: Even for an Hour (poems), 1940; Tell Me the Next One, 1950; The Master Forger, 1951; A Peer behind the Curtain, 1959; Shamrocks & Unicorns, 1962; Van Meegeren, 1967. TV documentaries: The Yemen, 1964; Morgan's Treasure, 1965; Kurdistan, 1966. Recip. of D.S.C., 1945. Address: Killegar, Cavan, Repub. of Ireland. 1.

KILCHRIST, Rubie Guidroz, b. 28 July 1917. Realtor. Educ: Schlrship. to Int. Corres. Schl., Scranton, Pa.; Gen. Bus., 1935-37; Grad., Realtors Inst. of La., G.R.I. Designation; Attended Seminars of Real Estate Inst. & Appraisal Seminars; Completed Real Estate Mgmt. Courses. Appts: Clerk, TBA Ins. Co., Lafayette, La., 1937-39; Acct., La. Pub. Utilities, ibid, 1941-43; Real Estate Salesman, Charlie Lett Real Estate, ibid, 1964-65; Realtor, Owner-Mgr., Rubie Kilchrist R.E., 1966-. Mbrships: V.P., Lafayette R.E. Bd., 1973 (Treas., 1972); Exec. Bd., Multiple Listing Serv., Lafayette Bd. Realtors, 1971-74; Nat. Assn. Realtors, Farm & Land Brokers St. of La & Lafayette Bds. Realtors, 1969; Chmbr. of Comm., Lafayette; Million Dollar Sales Club; Cath. Daughters of Am.; Ladies Altar Soc., St. John Cathedral; Mt. Carmel PTA (Pres., 1946-48); Better Bus. Bur. Hons: Merit Award for Achievement, Nat. Assn. Realtors, 1972, & Lafayette Bd. Realtors, 1973. Address: 1207

Lafayette St., Lafayette, LA 70501, U.S.A. 125.

KILGOUR, Ruth Edwards, b. 28 Apr. 1902. Educator. Owner of the greatest collection of traditional headgear in the world - collected over 25 yrs. from 52 countries. Publs. incl; A Pageant of Hats, publd. by McBridge, N.Y.C., 1958. Author of the section on the Hat in the Encyclopedia Americana, 1970, & took photos to illustrate this sect. Address: 66 Malden St., W. Boylston, MA 01583, U.S.A. 5, 6.

KILGOUR, Vernon Earl, b. 25 Nov. 1916. Author & Inventor. Appts. incl; Corporator & Trustee, Clinton Savings Bank, Mass.; Agt. & Bus. Mgr. Cheney Index to Knowledge, 1945-. Author of Clinton Boys & the Phantom Raider, 1943. Holds patent for adjustable spectacles. Address: 66 Malden St., W. Boylston, MA 01583, U.S.A. 6.

KILICHAN, Esat, b. 12 Nov. 1924. Surgeon. Educ: Univs. of Istanbul & Paris; Dr. med., for agrégé fac. of med. Appts: Doctor, 1947; Orthopaedic Surg., 1952; Asst. Prof., 1955; Dip., Fac. Med., Paris, France, 1961-62; Prof., 1965. Mbrships. incl: Turkish Socs. of Med., Surg., Orthopaedy, Traumatol., Physiotherapy, Sport Med; French Socs. of Orthopaedy & Traumatol., & Infantile Surg.; Turkish & French Leagues against Rheumatism; Int. Soc. Orthopaedic Surg. & Traumatol. Author of books in field & on history & philately. Address: Orthopaedic Clin., Gureba Hospital, Istanbul, Turkey. 43.

KILLIAN, Hans, b. 5 Aug. 1892. Professor of Surgery. Educ: Studied Med. in Munich & Freiburg; M.D., Freiburg, 1921; Med. lab. Asst., 1st Med. Clin., Munich; Asst., Robert Koch Inst. for Infectious Diseases, Berlin, 2½ yrs.; Voluntary Asst., Pharmacological Inst., Munich, 1 yr. Appts. incl: Served WWI; Hd. Physn. & Dept. Dir., mil. hosp., Freiburg, 1940; Bldr., reserve mil. hosp., Strassburg & Dir., Surg. Dept., ibid; Cons. Surg., 16th Army, 1941; Prof., Dept. of Surg., Univ. of Breslau, Hd. Surg., Breslau & Cons. Surg., Lower Silesia, 1943; Cons. Surg., Raum Halle & Hd. Physn., mil. hosp. for restorative surg., 1945; Dir. & Hd. Physn., gen. hosp., Baden-Baden, German Fed. Repub., 2½ yrs.; Independent Surg., Freiburg/Br. & Donauschingen, 1949-. Mbrships. incl: Co-Fndr., Int. Gesellschaft für Cardio-Anglochirurgle, Turin, 1951; Co-Fndr., Deutsche Gesellschaft für Anästhesiologie, 1952; Fndr., Deutscher Berufsverband der Chirugen, 1960; Corres. mbr., French & Am. Socs. for Anaesthesiol. Author of num. publs. in field. Recip. of hons. Address: Riedbergstrasse 24, 78 Freiburg i, Br., Günterstal, German Fed. Repub.

KILLINEN, Paulo Kullervo, b. 15 Mar. 1912. Naval Officer; Business Executive. Educ: Finnish Naval Acad., 1934; War Coll., 1948; Doct. in Pol. Sci., Helsinki Univ., 1956. Appts: Off., Finnish Navy, 1934-60; Tchr., War Coll., 1955-57; Mil. & Naval Attaché, London, 1958-60; Reader in Int. Pols., Helsinki Univ., 1958-68; Mng. Dir., Finnish News Agency STT-FNB, 1961-72; Dir., de Jersey Co. (Finland) Ltd., 1960-62, 1973-; Commodore, Finnish Navy, Retired. Mbrships: Past Pres., Naval Offs. Assn. & Pol. Sci. Assn.; Past V.P., Coun. for Psychol. Defense; Pres., Finnish Navy League; Coun. for Civil Defense; Past Pres., European News Agencies Grp. 39. Publs. incl: Demokratia ja totaalinen sota, 1956; Kansainvälinen politiikka I-II, 1958; Kansallinen etu ja kansainvälinen kehitys, 1967. Pääsihterrikelpa, 1973. Hons. incl: Finnish Freedom Cross 2., 3., w. oak leaf bar, 3. & 4.; German Iron Cross; Commdr. Swedish Sword Order; &c. Address: Maamonlahdentie 1 D 18, 00200 Helsinki 20, Finland. 90.

KILPATRICK, Patricia Baldwin (Mrs.), b. 19 May 1927. Educator. Educ: Ohio Wesleyan Univ., 1945-47; A.B., Flora Stone Mather Coll., 1947-49; M.A., Western Reserve Univ., 1949-51. Appts: Tchr., Am. Hist. & Phys. Educ., Lorain H.S., Ohio, 1951-52 & Hlth. & Phys. Educ., Lakewood, Ohio, 1962; Instr., Hlth. & Phys. Educ., Western Reserve Univ., 1962-65; Asst. Dean & Asst. Prof., Case Western Reserve Univ., 1965-71; Assoc. Dean, ibid, 1972-. Mbrships: Nat. & Ohio Assns. of Women Deans, Admins. & Counselors; Fndr., Northeastern Ohio Coll. Hlth. Educ.; Am. Assn. of Hlth. Phys. Educ. & Rec.; Dist. Pres., Kappa Alpha Theta; Bd. of Mgrs., Sec., Univ. Christian Movement. Contbr. to Encyclopaedia of Education, 1970 & report of Comm. on Status of Women, Case Western Reserve Univ., 1973. Address: c/o Baker Bldg., Western Reserve Coll., Case Western Reserve Univ., Cleveland, OH 44106, U.S.A. 5, 132.

KIM, Bong Chin, b. 5 Oct. 1916. Business Executive. Educ: B.A., Univ. of Japan, 1938. Appts: Mbr., Tax Reform Comm., Min. of Finance, Repub. of Korea, 1948-60; Ed. in Chief, HapDong News Agcy., 1954-57; Edit. Writer, HanKook Ilbo (daily newspaper), 1958-60; Mbr., Govt. Econ. Advsry. Coun., Repub. of Korea, 1960-61; Mng. Dir., Korea Teade Assn., 1960-63; V.P., Seoul KyungJe (daily econ. newspaper), 1963-65; Exec. Vice Chmn., Korea Chmbr. of Comm. & Int. Commercial Arbitration Comm. of Korea, 1966-69; Mbr., Unemployment Relief Comm., Min. of Hlth. & Soc. Affairs, 1968-71; Pres., Daihan Life Ins. Co., 1969-71; Pres., Kong Yong Chem. Co. & Daihan Plastic Co., 1971-73; Dir., Korea Chmbr. of Comm., 1969-; Chmn., Korea Flour Mills Indl. Assn., 1973-; Dir., Fedn. of Korean Inds., 1974-. Mbrships: Int. Rotary Club; Hang Yang Country Golf Club. Publs: Economics of Today, 1952; Economic Dialogue, 1953. Address: Korea Flour Mills Indl. Assn., 5 Yang Dong, Choong-Ku, Seoul, Korea.

KIM, Lyun Joon, b. 20 Feb. 1914. University Founder & President; Company Executive. Educ: A.B., Chosun Christian Coll., 1939. Appts: Fndr. & Pres., Hanyang Univ., 1939-73; Mbr., Bd. Dirs., Ewha Womans Univ., 1940; Fndr., Hanyang Attached Girls' Middle & H.S., 1960; Pres., Daihan Daily Newspaper, 1960-73; Publr., Union Christian Press, 1963; Chmn., Bd. Dirs., Hankuk Theological Coll., 1968; Owner, Korea Shipping Corp., 1968-; Fndr., Paiknam Tourist Co., 1969-; Fndr., Hanyang Univ., Hosp., 1972. Mbrships: Chmn., Korwan Fedn. Athletics, 1968; Dir., Policy Rsch. Inst. of Korea, 1964-; Chmn., Seoul Comm., Int. League for Rights of Man, 1966-; Korea Rep., World Univ. Serv., 1965; Vice-Chmn., Korea Comm., Int. Vocational Trng. Competition, 1966-73. Publs: 100 Lyrical Compositions, Vol. I, 1972, Vol. II, 1973, Vol. III, IV, V, 1974. Hons; Dr. of Laws, Yonsei Univ., 1961, Windsor Univ., Canada, 1972, Coll. of Chinese Culture, Repub. of China, 1973; Dr. of Lit., Southern Ill. Univ., U.S.A. 1973. Address: Hanyang Univ., Seoul, Korea.

KIM, Young H., b. 17 Oct. 1927. Orthodontist. Educ: D.D.S., Seoul Nat. Univ., Korea, 1949; M.S., Univ. of Rochester, N.Y., U.S.A., 1958; D.M.D., Tufts Univ., Mass., 1960. Appts: Instr. in Orthodontics, Forsyth Dental Ctr., & Harvard Schl. of Dental Med., 1960; Assoc. Prof., Schl. of Grad. Dentistry, Boston Univ., 1966; Clin. Prof., Coll. of Dentistry, Yonsei Univ., Seoul, Korea, 1971. Mbrships: Am. Dental Assn.; Am. Assn. of Orthodontists; Omicron Kappa Upsilon. Contbr. profl. jrnls. & publs. Address: 30 Colpitts Rd., Weston, MA 02193, U.S.A. 57.

KIMBALL, John Thomas, b. 5 Nov. 1910. Business Manager; Administrator; Utility Executive. Educ: B.S., Millsaps Coll., Jackson, Miss., 1934. Appts: Salesman, Sales Mgr., Personnel Mgr., Sales Promotion & Advt. Mgr., Ops. Mgr., Miss. Power & Light Co., 1934-45; Exec. Dir., Agricl. & Indl. Bd., State of Miss., 1945-46; V.P., Exec. V.P., Ariz. Pub. Serv. Co., 1946-54; V.P., Gen. Mgr., Bd. Mbr., Idaho Power Co., 1954-59; Exec. V.P. Bd. Mbr., Am. & For. Power Co., N.Y.C., 1959-63; Sr. V.P., Bd. Mbr., Elec. Bond & Share Co., N.Y.C., 1963-68; V.P., Exec. V.P., Pres., Grand Bahama Port Authority, Freeport, Bahamas, 1968-73; Retd., Elec. Bond & Share, 1968, & Port Authority, 1973; Cons. in Bahamas, New England Petroleum Co., N.Y.C. Mbrships: Electronics & Elec. Engrs. Inst.; Bankers Club, Miami, Fla.; E. Hill Club, Nassau; Hon. Mbr., Christ Ch. Meth., N.Y.C.; Past Mbr., Bd. of Trustees, ibid; Past Mbr., Metropol. Club, N.Y.C., Recess Club, Nat. Assn. of Mfrs. Tax Comm. Hons: Miss. Outstanding Young Man, 1945; Silver Beaver, Silver Antelope, Silver Buffalo, Boy Scouts of Am.; Outstanding Alumni, Millsaps Coll., Jackson, Miss.; Cited num. times for serv. to community & state. Address: Box F-1192, Freeport, Bahamas, 2.

KIMBER, David Miles, b. 15 Dec. 1931. Management Consultant. Educ: Hallebury & Imperial Servs. Coll., 1945-49; Air Trng. Schl., Syerston, 1950-51; Ashridge Coll., 1970. Appts: Commn. in Fleet Air Arm (Pilot), Air-Warfare & Flying Instr., 1950-58; Sales & Mktng. positions in petroleum ind., 1960-68; Divisional Dir., Int. Mgmt. Consultancy, 1969; Mng. Dir., Indl. Trainers Ltd., 1970; Assoc. Dir., Cargill Attwood Int., 1971; Assoc. Dir., U Grp. Dev. Ltd., 1972. Mbrships: European Fndn. Mgmt. Dev.; Am. Soc. Trng. & Dev.; Assn. Tchrs. of Mgmt.; British Inst. Mgmt.; Inst. of Mktng.; British Assn. Commercial & Indl. Educ.; Naval Club; Fleet Air Arm Assn.; Brevet Flying Club; Assn. Round Tables (ret'd). Author of articles in field. Presentations to Int. Confs. in Africa & Int. Trng. & Dev. Conf.; also to UNO, 1972-73, & UN High Commn. for Refugees. Address: Industrial Trainers Ltd., 11-12 The Green, London W5 5EA, U.K.

KIMBLE, Vesta Baker (Mrs.), b. 25 Dec. 1900. Independent Oil Operator; Poet; Musician. Educ: pvte. music tuition. Appts. incl: played in Frank Daugherty Orch.; Prof. over KFYO Radio, Breckenridge, Tex.; Accompanist to violinist H.R. DeRoeck. Publs. incl: 75-poem book printed & copywrited for gift purposes; contbr. poems to Anthol. of Am. Poetry, Visions in Verse, Ideals Mag., etc. Donor of num. poem cards to Sunday Schls. & Funeral Homes. Mbrships. incl: Poetry Soc. of Tex.; Annual Fellow, Intercontinental Biog. Assn.; V.P., Breckenridge Poetry Soc.; Official Poet, Stephens Co. Hosp. Aux. Address: 701 W. Hullum St., Breckenridge, TX 76024, U.S.A. 5, 11, 57, 125, 128, 132.

KIMMER, Wilton H., b. 24 Jan. 1910. Science Educator; Registered Pharmacist. Educ: Grad. in Pharmacy, Baylor Univ., Dallas, Tex., U.S.A. 1931; A.B., High Pt. Coll., N.C., 1933; M.Sc., Phila. Coll. of Pharmacy & Sci., Pa., 1937; Postgrad., Ripon Coll., Wis., 1969; St. Cloud State Coll., Minn., 1971. Appts: Chief Chem., Filter Products Div., Johnson & Johnson, New Brunswick, N.J., 1937-43; Dir.,

Co. Seat Savings & Loan Assn., 1945-70; Treas., ibid, 1963-70; Dir., Family Savings & Loan Assn., 1970-. Mbrships: N. Brunswick Bd. of Educ., 1951-58; Pres., 1957; Middlesex Co. Schl. Bds. Assn., 1951-58, Pres., 1954; New Brunswick Kiwanis Club, 1945-59, Pres., 1956; Masonic Fraternity, 1934-. Publs: Articles on dairy ind. in trade mags. Recip., 25 Yr. Cert. of Serv., N.J. Savings & Loan League, 1971. Address: 947 Hollywood St., North Brunswick, NJ 08902, U.S.A. 6, 130.

KIMPEL, Benjamin Franklin, b. 9 May 1905. Professor. Educ: B.A., Univ. of Wis., 1926; Ph.D., Yale Univ., 1932; Ordained, Am. Unitarian Assn. Appts: Prof., Philos. & Relig., Kan. Wesleyan Univ., 1933-37; Prof., Philos., Drew Univ., Madison, N.J., 1938-72; Emeritus Prof., ibid, 1972-. Mbrships: Beta Beta Beta; Kappa Pi; Pi Gamma Mu; Psi Chi; Phi Sigma Tau; Sigma Phi; Am. Philos. Assn.; AAUP. Publs. incl: Religious Faith, 1954; Moral Principles in the Bible, 1956; Language & Religion, 1957; Principles of Moral Philosophy, 1960; Kant's Critical Philosophy, 1964; Hegel's Philosophy of History, 1964; Nietzsche's Beyond Good & Evil, 1964; Schopenhauer's Philosophy, 1965; Philosophy of Zen Buddhism, 1966. Recip., sev. Fellowships. Address: West St., N. Bennington, VT 05257, U.S.A. 2, 6, 13.

KIMURA, Kazuo K., b. 16 Sept., 1920. Physician. Educ: B.S., Univ. of Wash., Seattle, 1942; M.Sc., Univ. of Nebraska, Lincoln, 1944; Ph.D., Univ. of Ill., Chicago, 1949; M.D., St. Louis Univ., Mo., 1953; Internship, Mass. Gen. Hosp., Boston, 1954-55; Asst. Res. in Pediatrics, ibid, 1955-56; Sr. Res. & Chief Res. in Pediatrics, Raymond Blank Mem. Hosp. for Children, Des Moines, Iowa, 1956-57. Appts. incl: Dir., Med. Rsch. Dept., ICI Am. Inc., Wilmington, Delaware; Asst. Staff in Pediatrics, Wilmington Gen. Hosp. & Cons. in Pediatrics, Delaware Hosp., Wilmington, 1964-67; Cons. in Pediatrics, Wilmington Med. Ctr., 1968-; VP & Sci. Dir., Hazleton Labs. Inc., Vienna, Va. 1973-. Mbrships. incl: AAAS, 1944- (Fellow, 1958-); Am. Med. Assn., 1960-; Fellow, Am. Coll. of Physns., 1968; Fellow, Am. Coll. of Clin. Pharmacol., 1972; Fellow, Royal Soc. of Med., London, 1973; Rho Chi Soc.; Pi Mu Chi; Sigma Xi. Contbr. of num. articles to var. profl. jrnls. Address: Hazleton Laboratories, Inc., 9200 Leesburg Turnpike, Vienna, VA 22180, U.S.A.

KINDS, Levander, b. 22 Mar. 1919. Clergyman; Educator. Educ: B.A., Western Reserve Univ., Cleveland; M.A., Grad. Schl., ibid, 1945; D.D., Leland Coll., 1953. Appts. incl: Prof., Philos., Leland Coll., Baker, La., 1945-47; Prof., Romance Langs., Tougaloo Coll., Miss., 1947-50; Prof., Soc. Sci. & Dept. Chmn., Pres., Natchez Jr. Coll., Miss., 1950-68; Dir., Community Crossroads stn. WNAT, ibid, 1953-57; Feature Ed., Natchez Times, 1953-62; Pastor, Mount Heroden Bapt. Ch., Vicksburg, Miss., 1960-; Asst. Prof., Soc. Sci., Alcorn State Univ., Lorman, Miss., 1968-. Mbrships: Am. Acad. of Pol. & Soc. Scis.; MLA; Warren Co. Bapt. Assn.; Southern Regional Hnrs. Coun. Author of poems, articles & conf. papers. Recip. Award as Fndr. & Dir., Comm. Ctr., 1958. Address: P.O. Box 597, Natchez, MS 39120, U.S.A. 7, 11, 15, 111, 125, 126, 129, 130.

KING, Cortney Ringgold (Mrs.). Educator. Educ: B.S., Elizabeth City State Univ., 1939; M.S., A & T State Univ., N.C., 1956. Appts: Tchr., Beaufort Co. Schls., 1939-47, Wash. Elem. Schl., 1947-62. Mbrships: Interracial meeting, (Chmn. 1945-52); Women's Christian Temperance Union (Pres. local chapt., 1949-58); Beaufort Co. Chapt. for retarded children (Vice Pres.) Recip., hons. from Wash., N.C. Minl. Alliance, 1958. Address: 401 W. 5th. St., Wash., NC 27889, U.S.A.

KING, Dan Madison, b. 7 Nov. 1914. Librarian; Associate Professor of Library Science. Educ: A.B., Hanover Coll., 1938; B.L.S., Syracuse Univ., 1940; & courses at var. other univs. Appts. incl: Dist. Supvsr., WPA Lib. Serv. Proj., Ind. State Lib., Indpls., Ind., 1940-42; Asst. Libn., i/c of Art Schl. Lib., Cooper Union for Advancement of Sci. & Art, N.Y.C., 1942-43; Libn-i/c., Cooper Union Libs., N.Y.C., 1943-46; chief, Ref. Dept., Grand Rapids Pub. Lib., Grand Rapids, Mich., 1946-48; Hd. Libn., Minn. State Histl. Soc., St. Paul, Minn., 1949-54; Hd. Libn., Ky. Wesleyan Coll. Lib., Owensboro, Ky., 1954-. Mbrships. incl: Comm. assignments, ALA; Nat. Chmn. Mus. Div., Special Libs. Assn., 1953-54; Ind. State Histl. Soc. Contbr. to: Lib. Jrnl.; Minn. Libs.; Ky. Lib. Assn. Bulletin. Address: Ky. Wesleyan Coll. Lib., 3000 Frederica St., Owensboro, KY, U.S.A. 7, 139.

KING, Henry L., b. 29 Apr. 1928. Lawyer. Educ: A.B., Columbia Univ., 1948; LL.B., Yale Univ., 1951. Appts: Joined Davis Polk & Wardwell law firm as Assoc., 1951; Ptnr., ibid, 1961-. Mbrships. incl: Pres., Alumni Fedn. of Columbia Univ., 1973-; Pres., Columbia Coll. Alumni Assn., 1966-68; Chmn., Columbia Coll. Fund, 1972-73; Trustee, Exec. Comm. Mbr., Nat. Lawyers' Comm. for Civil Rights Under Law; Dir., Treas., Berkshire Farm Ctr. & Serv. for Youth; Trustee, Lenox Schl., 1964-73; V.P.; Bd. of Govs., Hay Harbor Club, Fishers Island, N.Y. Recip., Columbia Alumni Medal for Conspicuous Serv., 1968. Address: 960 Park Ave., N.Y., NY 10028, U.S.A. 6, 32.

KING, Joseph Clement, b. 20 Aug. 1922. Physician; Internist. Educ: B.S., Tulane Univ., 1944; M.D., 1946. Appts: Instr., Zool., Tulane Univ., 1941-42; Attng. Physn., Louis A. Weiss Mem. Hosp., Chgo.; Assoc. in Med., Northwestern Univ. Med. Schl., 1954-66; Asst. Prof., Abraham Lincoln Schl. of Med., Univ. of Ill., 1973-. Fellowships: Am. Coll. Physns.; Am. Coll. Geriatrics; Royal Soc. Med.; Am. Coll. Gastroenterol.; Royal Soc. Hlth. Mbrships: Chgo. Soc. Internal Med.; Dipl., Am. Bd. Internal Med.; Am. Geriatrics Soc.; Am. Rheumatism Soc.; Chgo. Med. Soc.; AMA; Ill. Med. Soc.; Am., Chgo. Heart Assns.; AAAS; Bd. Dir., Tulane Med. Alumni Assn., 1970-73; Phi Beta Kappa; Alpha Omega Alpha. Contbr. to profl. publs. Address: 1500 Sheridan Rd., Apt. 6H, Wilmette, IL 60091, U.S.A. 8, 14, 17.

KING, Joseph Willet, b. 26 Aug. 1934. Child, Adolescent Psychiatrist. Educ: B.A., Southern Meth. Univ., U.S.A., 1956; M.D., Southwestern Med. Schl., Univ. of Tex., 1962; Extern, Timberlawn Psych. Hosp., Dallas, 1960-62; Intern, Baylor Univ. Med. Ctr., Dallas, 1962-63; Res., Timberlawn Psych. Hosp., 1963-64, Dallas VA Hosp., 1965, Tex. Fellowship, Dept. of Child Psych., Univ. of Tex., 1965-67, Hillside Psych. Hosp., 1967. Appts. (all in Tex.): Clin. Staff, Child Psych., Shady Brook Schl., Richardson, 1965-; Clin. Instr., Dept. of Child Psych., Southwestern Med. Schl., Univ. of Tex., 1967-; Attng. Staff (Jr. Active) Dallas Co. Hosp. Dist., 1967-; Assoc. Attng. Mbr., Child Psych., Children's Med. Ctr., Dallas, 1967-; Staff Mbr., Dir. of Adolescent Servs., Timberlawn Psych. Hosp., 1967-. Num. mbrships. incl: Fellow, Am. Psych. Assn.; Fellow, Am. Orthopsych. Assn.; Nat. V.P., Am. Soc. for Adolescent Psych.; AMA; Dipl., Am. Bd. of Psych. & Neurol.; Am.

Acad. for Child Psych.; Acad. of Relig. & Mental Hlth. Development of a Protreatment Group Process Among Hospitalized Adolescents (w. others), 1970; Contbr. to profl. jrnls; Address: 4645 Samuell Blvd., Dallas, TX 75228, U.S.A.

KING, Linderson Ethel, b. 17 June 1928. Social Worker. Educ: B.S., St. Paul's Coll., Lawrenceville, Va., 1956; M.S.W., N.Y. Univ. Grad. Schl. of Soc. Work, 1963. Appts: N.Y.C. Dept. of Soc. Servs., Soc. Investigator, 1958-63; Case Worker, 1963, Supvsr., 1963-, currently w. Bur. of Child Welfare Protective Servs. Mbrships: Nat. Assn. of Soc. Work; Acad. of Cert. Soc. Wkrs.; N.Y. State Cert. Soc. Wkrs.; St. Paul's Coll. Alumni Assn.; N.Y. Univ. Gen. & Grad. Schl. of Soc. Work; Delta Sigma Theta; Nat. Conf. on Soc. Work; Soc. Serv. Employees Union; N.A.A.C.P.; YWCA; Un Assn. of USA; Wall St. Choral Soc.; Episcopal Ch. Women of Trinity Parish; Nat. Coun. of Women of U.S., Inc.; Clinton Hill Tenant Assn. Hons. incl: Outstanding Alumnus, Brooklyn Chapt., Delta Sigma Theta, 1963. Address: 185 Clinton Ave., 2F, Brooklyn, NY 11205, U.S.A. 5, 6, 22, 132.

KING, Peter D(eWitt), b. 20 Feb. 1927. Psychiatrist; Psychoanalyst. Educ: B.A., Univ. of Chgo., Ill., U.S.A., 1950; B.S. & M.D., ibid, 1954; Res. in Psych., Warren State Hosp., 1955-58; USPHS Fellow, Child Psych., Reiss-Davis Clin., L.A., Calif., 1959-61. Appts. incl: Clin. Dir. & Dir. of Rsch., Madison, Ind., State Hosp., 1958-59; Asst. Prof. of Psych., Med. Ctr., & Staff Psych., Neuropsychiatric Inst., Med. Schl., Univ. Coll. of L.A., 1961-62; Asst. Clin. Prof. of Psych., ibid, 1962-67; Attng. Psych., L.A. Co. Gen. Hosp., 1962-; Assoc. Clin. Prof. of Psych., Schl. of Med. Univ. of Southern Calif., L.A., 1967-. Num. mbrships. incl: Pres., L.A. Grp. Psychotherapy Soc.; Fellow, Am. Psychiatric Assn.; Bd., Am. Assn. Publs: The Principle of Truth, 1960; Rsch. articles in profl. jrnls. Recip., Wisdom Award of Honor, 1969. Address: 5363 Balboa Blvd., Suite 240, Encino, CA 91316, U.S.A. 9, 17, 28, 74, 131.

KING, Peter Kenneth, b. 5 May 1922. University Lecturer. Educ: London Univ. Appts: Lectr., Fac. of Modern & Medieval Langs., Cambridge Univ., 1952-59; Lectr. in Dutch, ibid, 1959-. Mbrships: Fellow, St. Edmund's House, Cambridge; Maatschappy der Nederlandse Letterkunde. Publs: Dawn Poetry in the Netherlands, 1971; Multatuli, 1972; Word Index, J. van den Vondel, 'Bespiegelingen van Godt en Godtsdienst' & 'Lucifer', 1973. Address: St. Edmund's House, Cambridge Univ., Cambridge, U.K. 3.

KING, Ruby Thompson (Mrs. Seaborn L. King). Educator. Educ: A.B. & M.A.; Scarritt; Univ. of Ga.; Fla. State Univ. Appts. incl: Tchr., Engl., 12th Grade, Coffee H.S., Douglas, Ga.; Lowndes & Glynn Cos., Ga.; Charter Mbr., Sponsor, Tri-Hi-Y Int.; Int. Chmn., Convocation, ibid; Jurisdiction Off., Meth. W.S.C.S.; High Ch. Conf.; State News Reporter, Atlanta Jrnl.; Trustee, Thompson-King Fndn.; Bd: Mbr., Florence Crittenden Home; Apptd., White House Nat. Traffic Safety Coun.; Chmn., Coffee H.S. Fac. Welfare Comm.; Chmn., Fac. Fellowship Commn.; Mbr., Am. Security Coun. Mbrships: Ga. Assn. Engl. Tchrs.; Philharmonic Soc.; Jr. Womens Club; Wesleyan Guild; S. Ga. Hist. Soc.; Ga. Speech Assn.; Nat. Trust Hist. Preservation; Sponsor, State of Ga. Y.I.C.; active on many levels in Meth. Ch.; DAR; U.S.O.; Seaman's Bethel; Am. Security Coun.; United Daughters of the Confederacy; NEA; AAUW; Nat. Coun. Tchrs. of Engl.; Red Cross,

Polio, Heart Fund, Cancer & Red Feather Drives; ASPR; GAE; Albert Schweitzer Fellowship. Contbr. of poetry & prose to daily newspapers; poetry appears in 8 anthols. Hons. incl: Star Tchr. Award, Ga. State Chmbr. of Comm.; Named Citizen of Yr. by Mayor & City Coun.; Ga. Journalistic Award. Address: P.O. Box 428, Douglas, GA 31533, U.S.A. 5, 7, 11, 57, 68, 70, 128.

KING, Sol, b. 19 July 1909. Architect. Educ: B.S., Univ. of Mich., 1934. Appts. incl: Albert Kahn Assocs., Detroit, Mich., 1935; Proj. Archt., ibid, 1938; Assoc., ibid, 1948; Mbr., Bd. Dirs., ibid, 1955; V.P., ibid, 1955-58; Dir. of Arch., ibid, 1956; Pres., ibid, 1958-; Mbr., Pub. Advsry. Panel on Archtl. Servs., Gen. Servs. Admin., Fed. Govt. & Chmn., Sub-Comm., Archt.-Engr. Responsibilities toward Proj. Budget & Co-ordination of Design Contract Documents, 1967-69. Mbrships: Fellow, Am. Inst. of Archts. & holds off. in num. related Comms.; Bd. Dirs., V.P., Detroit Chapt., Am. Inst. of Archts.; V. Chmn., State Bd. of Registration for Archts., 1972; State Bd. of Registration for Profl. Engrs., 1972; Chmn., Archtl. & Engrng. firms, Nat. Comm. for Econ. Dev., 1973; mbr. num. Acad. & Civic orgs. Hons. incl: Univ. of Mich. Sesquicentennial Award, 1967; Gold Medal, Mich. Soc. of Archts., 1967; Honored by Newcomen Soc. in N. Am., 1970; Wisdom Award of Honor, Wisdom Hall of Fame, 1970. Address: 16500 N. Park Drive, Southfield, MI 48075, U.S.A. 2, 16, 55.

KING, Stella Lennox, (Mrs. Robert Glenton). Writer. Educ: Bournemouth Schl. for Girls; Southern Coll. of Art. Appts: Writer & Illustrator, Bournemouth Times Grp.; Staff Writer, London Evening Standard, Mirror Grp. & Sunday Express; Contbr. to Beaverbrook Newspapers, Times, etc. Mbr. of Gray's Inn. Publs: Once Upon a Time (w. Robert Glenton), 1960; Princess Marina, Her Life & Times, 1969; in preparation, biography of Yvonne Rudellat (no title as yet). Address: Morar Cottage, Ridge Ln., Watford, Herts., U.K. 3.

KINGHAM, Joshua Rowland, b. 24 Mar. 1899 (decd.). Merchant. Educ: B.A.Sc., Univ. of B.C., Canada, 1921; M.Sc., MIT, Cambridge, Mass., U.S.A., 1922. Appts: Served WWI & WWII; A.D.C. Lt. Gov. of B.C., 1937-50; Advsry. Comm., J. Kingham Co. Ltd., from 1950; Pres., ibid; Pres., Kingham-Gillespie Coal Co. Ltd. Mbrships: Union Club of B.C.; Victoria Golf Club; Victoria Rotary Club. Address of Mrs. Kingham: 3485 Upper Terrace, Victoria, B.C., Canada.

KING-HELE, Desmond George, b. 3 Nov. 1927. Scientist; Author. Educ: B.A.(Hons.), Trinity Coll., Cambridge, 1948. Appts: Scientific Off., Royal Aircraft Establishment, Farnborough, 1948-68, Dpty. Chief Scientific Off., 1968-. Mbrships: Fellow, Royal Soc., Royal Astronomical Soc.; Int. Acad. of Astronautics. Publs: Shelley: His Thought & Work, 1960, 2nd edit., 1971; Satellites & Scientific Research, 1962; Erasmus Darwin, 1963; Theory of Satellite Orbits in an Atmosphere, 1964; Observing Earth Satellites, 1966; Essential Writings of Erasmus Darwin, 1968; The End of the Twentieth Century?, 1970; Poems & Trixies, 1972. Hons. incl: Eddington Gold Medal, Royal Astronomical Soc., 1971; Lagrange Prize, Academie Royale de Belgique, 1972; Bakerian Lectr., Royal Soc., 1974. Address: 3 Tor Rd., Farnham, Surrey, U.K. 1.

KINGMAN, Dong, b. 31 Mar. 1911. Artist. Works represented in num. permanent collects.

inclng: Adelphi Univ., N.Y.; Am. Acad. Arts & Letters, ibid; Art Inst. of Chgo.; Brooklyn Mus. of Art, N.Y.; Boston Mus. of Art, Mass.; Dartmouth Coll., Hanover, N.H.; De Young Mus. of Art, San Fran.; Fort Wayne Art Inst., Ind.; Honolulu Acad. of Art, Hawaii; L.A. Co. Fair Assn., Calif.; Nat. Acad. of Design, N.Y.; Mus. of Mod. Art, ibid; Metropol. Mus. of Art, ibid; San Fran. Mus. of Art, Calif.; State Univ. Coll., N.Y.; Toledo Mus. of Art, Ohio; Time Mag. Collect., N.Y.; Wadsworth Atheneum, Hartford, Conn.; Univ. of Neb., Lincoln. Mbr., Am. Watercolor Soc. Co-author, City on the Golden Hill. Hons. incl: Guggenheim Fellowship, 1942, '43; Audubon Artists Medal of Hon., 1946, & Award, 1958; $500 Prize, Metropol. Mus. of Art, N.Y., 1952; Am. Watercolor Soc. Awards, 1956, '62, '64, '65, '67, Silver Award, 1960, & Lena Newcastle Mem. Award, 1972; Walter Bigg Mem. Award, Nat. Acad. of Design, 1971; The High Winds Medal, A.W.S. Annual Exhib., 1973. Address: c/o Hammer Galls., 51 E. 57th St., N.Y., NY 10022, U.S.A.

KINGSLAND, R., b. 19 Oct. 1916. Civil Servant. Appts. incl: Mgr., Kingsford-Smith Airport, Mascot, N.S.W., 1948-49; Dir., S. Australian Region, Dept. of Civil Aviation, 1950-51; Dir., Northern Territory Region, ibid, 1951-52; Chief Admin. Asst. to Chief of Air Staff, Royal Australian Air Force, 1952-53; Asst. Sec., Dept. of Air, Melbourne, 1954-58; 1st Asst. Sec., Dept. of Defence, 1958-63; Sec., Dept. of Interior, 1964-70. Mbrships. incl: Chmn., Canberra Schl. of Music Coun.; Trustee, Australian War Mem. & Canberra Theatre Ctr. Hons: Disting. Flying Cross, 1943; C.B.E. (Civil Div.), 1967. Address: P.O. Box 21 WODEN. A.C.T., Australia 2606. 23.

KINGS NORTON of Wotton Underwood, (The Lord), (Sir Harold Roxbee Cox), b. 6 June 1902. Engineer; Industrialist. Educ: Trainee, Austin Motor Co., 1918-22; B.Sc., 1st Class Hons., (Lon.) External Deg., 1922; Imperial Coll., 1922-24. Appts: Design Team on R.101, 1924-29; Airworthiness Dept., RAE, 1929-31; Chief Tech. Off., RAW, 1931; RAE, Farnborough, 1931-37; Chief Tech. Off., Air Registration Bd., 1938-39; Supt. of Sci. Rsch., RAE, 1939-40; Dpty. Dir., Sci. Rsch., & Dir., Special Projs., Min. of Fuel & Power, 1940-44; Chmn., Power Jets Ltd., 1944-46; Dir., Nat. Gas Turbine Estab., 1946-48; Chief Sci., Min. of Fuel & Power, 1948-54; Chmn., Coun. for Sci. & Indl. Rsch., 1961-65; Chmn., Coun. for Nat. Acad. Awards, 1964-71; Chmn., Air Registration Bd., 1965-72; Pres., Royal Inst. of G.B., 1970-; Chancellor, Cranfield Inst. of Technol., 1970-; Dir., var. cos., 1954-. Publs: Num. tech. papers. Num. hons. incl: R.38 Mem. Prize, 1928; Busk Mem. Prize, 1934; Wright Bros. Lectr., 1940; Medal of Freedom, Silver Palm, U.S.A., 1947; James Clayton Prize, 1952; Kt. Bach., 1953; Life Peer, 1965; Var. hon. degs., U.K. univs. Address: 3 Upper Harley St., London N.W.1, U.K. 1, 2, 34.

KINMONT, David Bruce, b. 14 Nov. 1932. Artist; Tutor in Fine Arts. Educ: Regional Coll. of Art, Manchester, U.K.; St. John's Coll., Cambridge Univ. Appts: Sr. Lectr. in Art, Endsleigh Coll. of Educ., Hull, 1960-66; Vis. Lectr., Ripon Hall, Oxford, 1964; Sr. Lectr. in Art, Sidney Webb Coll. of Educ., London, 1968-69; Staff Tutor Fine Arts, Univ. of Bristol, 1969-; Temporary Rsch., Geo. Wash. Univ., Wash. D.C., U.S.A., 1974. Major Paintings incl: Triptych, 1968; Becoming, 1971; Not Yet: No Longer, 1973; Tightrope, 1974; All Over, 1974. Solo Exhibs. incl: Ferens Art Gall., Hull, 1963; St. John's Coll., Cambridge, 1968; Van Dyke Gall., Univ. of

Bristol, 1971. Pub. Lectures incl: Bath Festival, 1970; Stroud Festival, 1971; G.H. Leonard Mem. Lecture, Univ. of Bristol, 1971; Univ. of Southampton, 1971. Address: The Lent House, Clevedon Rd., Flax Bourton, Bristol, U.K.

KINNAN, Marjorie Gearhart (Mrs. Joseph F. Kinnan), Guidance Counselor. Educ: A.B., Pittsburgh Univ., Pa., U.S.A.; M.A., S. Fla. Univ., Tampa; Specialist courses in schl. psych. Appts: Soc. Wkr., 1930's; Med. Soc. Wkr., 1958-60; Guid. Counselor, 1968-. Mbrships: Div. Pres., AAUW; Pres., Local Chapt., Am. Personnel & Guid. Assn.; Dir., Fla. Assn. Mental Hlth., 1967-73; Past Pres., Am. Legion Auxiliary; Delta Delta Delta; Alpha Delta Kappa. Contbr. articles to Elem. Guid. & Counseling Mag. Hons: Marge Kinnan Schlrship. estab. at Manatee Jr. Coll., Bradenton, Fla., 1968; Recip. bronze & gold medallions, Fla. Assn. Mental Hlth., volunteer work & servs. to Bd., 1970, '74; Awarded Bibles, 1st United Meth. Ch., Bradenton, for work w. children & youth, 1957, '68. Address: 3309 2nd Ave. W., Bradenton FL 33505, U.S.A. 125.

KINNEAR, Willis Hayes, b. 1 Jan. 1907. Editor & Director of Magazine. Educ: DePauw Univ., 1925-27: B.A.. Univ. of Mich., 1929. Appts: w. Manuscripts, Inc., Indpls.. Ind., 1929-31; Publix Theaters, Detroit, Mich., 1931-35; Fox West Coast Theaters, Hillman Shane Advt. Agcy., Fanchon & Marco, L.A., Calif., 1935-50; Mfr., L.A., 1950-53; Dir., Sci. of Mind Publs. & Ed., Sci. of Mind Mag., ibid, 1953-. Mbrships: Am. Acad. of Relig.; Acad. of Relig. & Mental Hlth.; Philos. of Sci. Assn.; Acad. of Parapsychol. & Med.; Assn. of Humanistic Psychol.; Beta Theta Pi. Publs. incl: 30-Day Mental Diet; The Creative Power of Mind (ed.); co-author: It Can Happen to You; A New Design For Living; The Magic Of The Mind; Practical Application of Science of Mind; Thoughts Are Things; It's Up To You (Revised & Edit.). Hon. Dr. of Humanities, Utd. Ch. of Relig. Sci., 1967. Address: 3251 W. Sixth St. L.A., CA 90020, U.S.A. 9, 14, 16, 111.

KINNEY, Abbott Ford, b. 11 Nov. 1909. Radio Executive; Historian; Writer. Educ: Ark. Coll., Batesville. Appts: Ed. & Publr., The Dermott News; Ptnr., Delta Drug. Co.; Pres. & Gen. Mgr., S.E. Ark. Broadcasters, Inc., 1951. Mbrships: Ark. Geol. & Conservation Commn., 1959-63; Miss. River Pkway. Commn., 1961-72; Ark. State Planning Commn., 1963-; Dermott City Planning Commn., 1961-; Ruth Veasey Educ. Fndn., 1962-; Co. Lib. Commn., 1963-; Co. Hosp. Commn., 1964-; St. Mary's Hosp. Bd.; Ark. Econ. Assn.; Edit. Advsry. Bd., Int. Broadcasters Soc.; Nat. Assn. Broadcasters; Ark. Broadcasters Assn.; Nat. Coun. Rep., Exec. Bd. Mbr., Past Pres. DeSoto Area Coun., Boy Scouts of Am.; Rotary Club; Am. Numismatics Assn.; Ark. Hist. Assn. Contbr. columns & articles to newspapers, jrnls., etc. Hons: Silver Beaver, 1951 & 30-yr. Vets. Award, 1970, both Boy Scouts of Am.; name given to Abbott Kinney Day, S.E. Ark., 1955; Citizenship award, Dermott Chmbr. of Comm, 1960; Outstanding Community Leader of Ark., 1969. Address: 202 S. Trotter St., Dermott, AR 71638, U.S.A. 7, 12, 16, 128, 130.

KINNEY, (Donald) Richard, b. 21 June 1923. Educator; Lecturer; Poet. Educ: B.A., Mt. Union Coll., Alliance, Ohio, 1954; L.H.D., ibid, 1966. Appts: Radio, TV & Platform in 15 countries; Guest Lectr., Harvard Univ., Univ. of Chile & Univ. of Paraguay; has given approx. 1000 luncheon or dinner talks; Exec. Dir., Hadley Schl. for the Blind, Winnetka, Ill. Mbrships: Pi Gamma Mu; Sigma Alpha Epsilon; Advsry. Comm., Ctr. for Deaf-Blind Youths &

Adults, HEW, Wash. D.C.; Am. Assn. of Wkrs. for the Blind; Winnetka Lions Club; Chmn., Advsry. Comm. on Servs. for the Deaf-Blind, World Coun. for the Welfare of the Blind; N. Shore Chess Club. Publs: Independent Living without Sight & Hearing; Flight of Arrows; Flutes beyond the Day; Encore; Harp of Silence; Blindness, 1968; Whispers to the Sky, 1974; contbr. articles, essays, short stories, poems & humor to var. periodicals. Hons: Citation of Meritorious Serv. to Lit.; Midland Author's Soc.; Hellen Keller Gold Medal for Lit. Excellence; Anne Sullivan Gold Medal; Dialogue Pub. Serv. Award, 1969; Ill. Handicapped Citizen of the Yr., 1970; Lions Amb. of Goodwill, 1971. Address: c/o The Hadley Schl. for the Blind, 700 Elm St., Winnetka, IL 60093, U.S.A. 2, 57.

KINS, Gloria Starr, b. 23 Feb. 1927. Publisher. Educ: N.Y. Univ., New Schl. for Soc. Rsch. Appts. incl: U.N. Corres., Embassy Life of Wash. D.C., 1957-66; Assoc. Prod., The Caspar Citron Show, WQXR, 1960-64; Asst. to Soc. Columnist of Jrnl. Am., 1964-66; Prod., Int. Affairs & Celebrities, Sandy Lesberg Prods., WOR, 1964-67; Soc. & Diplomatic Ed., Status Mag., Curtis Publng. Co., 1967-70; Hd. of Edit., N.Y. Off., Holiday & Saturday Post, 1970-72; N.Y. Ed., Boletin Diplomatico of Mexico, 1963-73; Assoc. Publr., Embassy Mag. of London, 1972-73; Wkly. Columnist, Metropolitan Voice of N.Y., 1970-73; Currently Hd. N.Y. Edit. Off., Tatler & Bystander Mag. of London in N.Y. Mbrships. incl: Bd. Dirs., Metropolitan Comm., UNICEF; Pan-Am. Soc.; Portuguese-Am. Soc.; Bd. Dirs., U.S. Comm. for Refugees, Inc.; sev. other soc. & cultural orgs. Hons. incl: Gran Maestre de la Orden National del Merito, Paraguay, 1963; sev. citations. Address: 131 E. 66th St., N.Y., NY 10021, U.S.A. 132.

KIPEL, Vitaut, b. 30 May 1927. Librarian; Geologist. Educ: Ph.D., Univ. Catholique de Louvain, Belgium; M.L.S., Rutgers Univ., U.S.A. Appts: Field Geologist, 1954-58; Libn., Bibliographic Coord., 1st Asst., Sci. & Tech. Div., N.Y. Pub. Lib., 1960-; Ed.-in-Chief, Heritage Review, Newark, N.J. Mbrships: Société Belge de Geologie; Geol. Soc. of Am. Author, sci. papers. Address: N.Y. Public Library, Science & Technical Div., 42nd St. & 5th Ave., N.Y., NY 10018, U.S.A.

KIRBY, E.J., b. 16 Aug. 1911. Solicitor. Educ: Dr. of Laws, Vienna, Austria, 1934; LL.B., Sydney, Australia, 1945. Appts: Solicitor, Supreme Ct. of N.S.W. & High Ct. of Australia, 1946; Notary Pub., 1953; Sr. Ptnr., E.J. Kirby & Co.; Comm. for Postgrad. Studies, Dept. of Law, Univ. of Sydney; Dir., 2 listed pub. cos. & 37 proprietary cos. Mbrships: Rotary Club; Australian Golf Club, Sydney; Am. Nat. Club, Sydney; Royal Automobile Club, Sydney. Hons: Golden Order of Merit of Austria, 1967; Kt. Cmdr. of St. Agatha, 1971; Kt., Sovereign & Mil. Order of Malta, 1972. Address: Law Soc. Bldg., 170 Phillip St., Sydney, N.S.W., Australia 2000. 23.

KIRBY, Kathleen Sarah Newcomb; b. 5 Apr. 1903. Teacher & Lecturer in Science. Educ: Univ. of London Tchrs. Dip., London Day Trng. Coll., U.K., 1926; M.Sc., London, 1928, A.K.C., 1925, King's Coll., London. Appts: on staff, W. Riding Emergency Trng. Colls., 1947-51; Bio. Tchr., Royal Schl. for Daughters of Army Offs., Bath, 1954-57; on staff, Hereford Trng. Coll, 1957-60; Prin. Lectr. in Sci., Swinton Day Trng. Coll., W. Riding, 1960-63. Mbrships: Full, Free Painters & Sculptors, London, 1972; Field Studies Coun. Publs: Nature Study for Schools, 1957; The Development of Chloroplasts in the Spores of Osmunda, in Jrnl. of Royal Microscopical Soc., vol. XLVIII, 1928. Address: 28 Gay St., Bath BA1 2PD, U.K.

KIRBY, (The Rev.) Money Alian, b. 8 Aug. 1914. Teacher; Minister. Educ: B.A., Music, Philander Smith Coll., Little Rock, Ark., U.S.A., 1950; Theol. study, etc. at Lane Coll. Ministerial Trng. Schls.; Southern State Coll., Magnolia, Ark.; Ark. Univ., Fayetteville; Southern Univ., Baton Rouge, La.; Ark. Univ., Pine Bluff. Appts. incl: Tchr., Ch. & Black Hist.; Chmn., Soc. Studies Dept., Walker H.S., 1968-74; Bd. mbr., Columbia Co. Educ. Assn., 1972-73; Pres., Walker Schl. Dist., 1973-74; Pres., Community Action Coun., Magnolia, Ark., 1969-74; Org. & Dir., Civic & Voters Assn., 1971-74. Mbrships: Magnolia Columbia Co. Civil League, 1971-74; Mason. Publs: Insight, prose, poetry & quotations, 1959; Arkansas-At-A-Glance, A Closer Look At Arkansas, Arkansas In Full View; Songs: Let-Us-Drink (for Communion servs.), 1961; Out-Yonder, 1961; I-Will-See-Peace, 1964 & num., as yet, unpubld. works. Hons. incl: Cert. of excellence for musical ability & performance, 1949; Scout Masters Award, 1971. Address: 513 S. Madison Ave., Magnolia, AR 71753, U.S.A. 125.

KIRCHMAYER, Martin, b. 1 Feb. 1923. Geologist; University Professor. Educ: Garden Archt. & Bus. Schl., Steyr, Upper Austria; Mil. Acad., Potsdam, Germany; Univ. of Vienna, Austria; Dr.phil.nat.habil. Appts: Infantry Off., WWII; Asst. Prof., Univ. of Vienna, Austria; Cons. for Engrng. Geol., Vienna; Rsch. Assoc., Tech. Univ., Clausthal-Zellerfeld, German Fed. Repub.; Rsch. Assoc., Prakla Co., Geophysics, Hanover; Assoc. Prof., Univ. of Heidelberg; Var. temporary working & rsch. & tchng. contracts. Mbrships: Live mbr., Mineralogical Soc. of Austria; Fellow, Geological Soc. of Am.; Live mbr., AAAS; Am. Nat. Assn. of Geol. Tchrs.; Life mbr., Geological Soc. of Sweden; Schlaraffia Haidelberga, Heidelberg. Author of about 70 publs. in sci. papers. Hons. incl: M. Neumayr Prize, Univ. of Vienna, 1956; Quincy Ward Boese Fellowship, Columbia Univ., N.Y., U.S.A., 1957. Address: 22 Michael-Gerber-Str., D 6903 Neckargemünd, Heidelberg, German Fed. Repub 43.

KIRIAKOPOULOS, George C., b. 3 June 1926. Dentist. Educ: A.A., Univ. of Paris, France, 1947; A.B., Brooklyn Coll., CUNY, U.S.A., 1950; D.D.S., Schl. of Dental & Oral Surg., Columbia Univ., N.Y., 1955; Cert. in Oral Surg., Lenox Hill Hosp., N.Y.C., 1955. Appts: Assoc. Dir., Dept. of Dentistry, St. Giles Hosp., Brooklyn., N.Y., 1955-60; Attending Oral Surg., Lenox Hill Hosp., N.Y.C., 1956-60; Assoc. Dir., Dept. of Oral Surg., ibid, 1960-64; Instr., Dept. of Pedodontics, Schl. of Dental & Oral Surg., Columbia Univ., 1956-72; Asst. Prof. of Dentistry, ibid, 1972-. Mbrships. incl: Am. Dental Assn.; N.Y. State Dental Soc.; Am. Assn. of Hosp. Dentists; Omicron Kappa Upsilon Fraternity of Coll. Profs.; Fellow, Royal Soc. of Hlth., London, U.K. Publs: Your Child's Teeth-The Layman's View, 1966; Who Wants to be a Dentist? , 1968. Recip., Medal of Meritorious Serv. award, Lenox Hill Hosp., N.Y., 1964. Address: 2205 MacKay Ave., Ft. Lee, NJ 07024, U.S.A. 6.

KIRK, Donald, b. 7 May 1938. Journalist. Educ: A.B., Princeton Univ., 1959; M.A., Univ. of Chgo., 1965; postgrad. studies, Fulbright Schol., Indian Schl. of Int. Studies, New Delhi, 1962-63; Ford Fndn. Fellow, Columbia Univ., 1964-65. Appts: Asia Corres., Washington Star, 1967-70; Far E. Corres., Chgo. Tribune, 1971-.

Mbrships. incl: Soc. of Mag. Writers, Inc.; Authors Guild of Am.; Overseas Press Club of Am. Author of Wider War: The Struggle for Cambodia, Thailand & Laos, 1971. Recip. 3 awards, Overseas Press Club, N.Y., 1967-73; Edward Scott Beck Award, 1972. Address: c/o Chgo. Tribune, Nikkei Bldg., 1-9-5 Otemachi, Chiyoda Ku, Tokyo 100, Japan. 30.

KIRK, Geoffrey Stephen, b. 3 Dec. 1921. University Teacher. Educ: Clare Coll., Cambridge, U.K. Appts: Fellow, Trinity Hall, Cambridge, 1948-70, 1974-; Lectr., then Rdr. in Greek, Cambridge Univ., 1949-63; Prof. of Classics, Yale Univ., U.S.A., 1964-70; Sather Prof. of Classical Lit., Berkeley, U.S.A., 1969; Prof. of Classics, Bristol Univ., U.K., 1971-73; Regius Prof. of Greek, Cambridge Univ., 1974-. Fellow, British Acad., 1959-, V.P., 1972-73. Publs: Heraclitus, the Cosmic Fragments, 1952; The Presocratic Philosophers (co-author), 1956; The Songs of Homer, 1962; Myth, 1970; The Nature of Greek Myths, 1974. Address: Trinity College, Cambridge, U.K. 1.

KIRK, John Esben, b. 8 Nov. 1905. Professor of Medicine. Educ: M.D., Univ. of Copenhagen, Denmark, 1929; Ph.D., ibid, 1936. Appts. incl: Res. Physn., Univ. Hosp. Copenhagen, 1936-39; Dir., City Hlth. Labs., ibid, 1936-39; Chief Med. Dept. Holstebro Co. Hosp., 1939-47; Dir., Rsch., Div. Gerontol., Wash. Univ. Schl. Med., U.S.A., 1947-1973; Asst. Prof., Med., Wash. Univ., 1947-50; Assoc. Prof., ibid, 1951-64; Prof., 1964-73; Emeritus Prof., 1973-. Mbrships. incl: Past Ed. & Treas., Gerontol. Soc.; Co-Fndr. & Past Pres., Am. Soc. Study of Premortal Condition; Am. Coll. Physns. Publs. incl: Hand Washing: Quantitative Studies on Skin Lipid Removal by Soaps and Detergents based on 1500 Experiments, 1966; Enzymes of the Arterial Wall, 1969; num. other books & papers. Recip. of hons. Address: 7320 Fernbrook Dr., St. Louis, MO 63123, U.S.A. 2, 8, 14, 15, 28, 43, 50, 54, 120.

KIRK, Virginia, b. 22 Dec. 1895. Clinical Psychologist. Appts. incl: Dir., Nursing, Emma Pendleton Bradley Home, Riverside, R.I., 1931-35; Rsch. Assoc., Williamson Co., Child Guidance Study, Franklin, Tenn., 1935-42; Instr., Clin. Psychol., Vanderbilt Univ. Schl of Med., 1943-47; Asst. Prof., 1947-53; Assoc. Clin. Prof., Clin. Psychol., Emeritus, 1960-; Pt.-time Pvte. Prac., Clin. Psychol., 1947-60, full-time, ibid, 1960-72; Currently, Cons. Clin. Psychologist, Specialized Ctr. of Rsch. in Newborn Lung Disorders, Vanderbilt Univ. Schl. of Med., Nashville. Author, Introduction to Psychology, 1935; num. other works. Address: 666 Timber Ln., Regency Pk., Nashville, TN 37215, U.S.A.

KIRKEGAARD, (Jens) Preben, b. 8 Jan. 1913. Rector. Educ: Final Exam., Danish Lib. Schl., 1936; Study Tours, UK, 1938 & Canada (UNESCO Schlrship.), 1949; Lib. Schls. in U.S.A., 1957. Appts: Asst. Libn., Aarhus, 1936-44; Chief Libn., Holstebro, 1945 & Vejle, 1946-55; Rector, Royal Schl. of Libnship., 1956-; UNESCO Advsr. on Lib. Educ., Greek Govt., 1962. Mbrships: Int. Advsry. Comm. on Documentation, Libs. & Archives, 1971-; Co-Ed., LIBRI, Int. Lib. Review, 1957-; Exec. Bd., Int. Fedn. of Lib. Assn., 1965-73; Danish Inst. for Info. About Denmark & Cultural Coop. w. Other Countries, 1973-; Danish Nat. Commn., UNESCO, 1958-; Lib. Coun., 1965-. Publs: Public Libraries in Denmark, 1948, Engl. Ed., 1950, Italian, 1955, German, 1956, French, 1960; Contbr. to var. profl. periodicals & monographs. Hons: Kt. of Dannebrog, 1968. Address: c/o The Royal School of Librarianship, 6 Birketinget, DK-2300 Copenhagen S., Denmark. 43.

KIRKMAN, William Patrick, b. 23 Oct. 1932. Secretary, Cambridge University Appointments Board. Educ: B.A., Oriel Coll., Oxford, U.K., 1955-; M.A., ibid, 1959; M.A., Cambridge Univ. Appts: Edit. Staff, Express & Star, Wolverhampton, 1955-57; The Times, 1957-64; Africa Corres., ibid, 1962-64; Asst. Sec., Oxford Univ. Appts. Comm., 1964-68; Sec., Cambridge Univ. Appts. Bd., 1968-. Mbrships: Fellow, Wolfson Coll., Cambridge; Chmn., Standing Conf. of Univ. Appts. Servs., 1971-73; Trustee, Sir Halley Stewart Trust; Fellow, Royal Commonwealth Soc. Author, Unscrambling An Empire, 1966. Contbr., BBC & var. jrnls. Recip., Heath Harrison Travelling Schlrship., 1954. Address: 19 High St., Willingham, Cambridge CB4 5ES, U.K. 1.

KIRKPATRICK, Nellie Grace Woll (Mrs. Ralph Wayne Kirkpatrick), b. 23 Mar. 1909. Teacher; Artist & Portraitist; Lecturer. Educ: B.Ed., Western Ill. Univ., Chgo. Acad. of Fine Arts; Art Inst. of Chgo.; Pvte. art studies. Appts. incl: Tchr., Slauson Jr. H.S., Ann Arbor, Mich.; Art Tchr., Kenosha Tech. Inst., 16 yrs.; Lectr., State Cosmetol. Inst., 2 summer sessions. One-man shows incl: The Mus., Kenosha; Veteran's Admin. Bldg., ibid; Chgo. Arts Grp. Nat. shows Smithsonian Instr. & Int. Platform Assn., Wash. D.C.; Salt Palace, Salt Lake City, Utah. Work in pvte. collects., sev. states of U.S.A. Contbr. to Wis. Anthol. of Poetry & Sunday Arts Grp. Anthols. Composer, song Your Dear Valentine, 1972. Mbrships. incl: Intercontinental Biographical Assn.; Art Chmn., Chgo. Br., Nat. League Am. Pen Women, 1973-74; Sec., Greater Kenosha Arts Coun., ibid; 3rd V.P. & Art Chmn., Chgo., Sunday Arts Grp., ibid; Kenosha Art Assn. & Symph. League. Creative Works; Prize-winning mural (from Chgo.'s Wabash Musical Mile contest) on stage of Performing Arts Ctr., Milwaukee, Wis., 1972; Designed commissioned mural for 5-state Northern Environmental Coun. & The Wilderness Soc., 1973. Hons. incl: State & nat. art prizes; Margaret Dingle Award, Best-in-the-Show, Chgo. Br., Nat. League Am. Pen Women, 1970; Woman of Yr., Municipal Art League, Chgo. Address: 2020 69th St., Kenosha, WI 53140, U.S.A. 57, 132.

KIRKUP, James, b. 23 Apr. 1929. Poet; Translator; Teacher. Educ: B.A., King's Coll., Durham Univ., U.K. Appts: Gregory Fellow, Poetry, Leeds Univ., 1950-52; Sr. Lectr., Engl. & Drama, Bath Acad. of Art, 1953-56; Various univ. posts, Sweden, Spain, France, Malaysia, U.S.A. & Japan, 1956-72. Fellow, Royal Soc. Lit., 1962. Mbrships: Soc. of Authors; Pres., Poets' Soc. Japan. Publs. incl: Many translations of Dürrenmatt, de Beauvoir, Valery, Ibsen, Supervielle, Japanese mod. poets, etc.; (Poetry) The Body Servant; A Bewick Bestiary; Japan Physical; (Travel) Streets of Asia; One Man's Russia; Filipinescas; (Autobiography) The Only Child; Sorrows, Passions & Alarms; (Novels) The Love of Others; Insect Summer. Hons: Atlantic Award, Rockefeller Fndn., 1950; Japan PEN Club Prize, 1964; Mabel Batchelder Award, 1967; Borestone Mtn. Poetry Awards, 1970,'71. Address: BM-Box 2780, London, WC1V 6XX, U.K. 11, 128, 131.

KIRSCH, Joachim, b. 24 Nov. 1907. Surgeon. Educ: Univ. of Leipzig, Germany; Univ. of Edinburgh, U.K.; Dr.med.dent., 1931; Dr.med., 1936. Appts. incl: Chief Physn., Hanover, 1944; Chief Surg., Schwarmstadt Emergency Hosp., 1945-59; Chief Surg. & Dir.,

Oststadt Krankenhaus, Hanover, 1959-73; Retd., 1973. Mbrships: Deutsche Gesellschaft für Chirurgie; Anglo-German Med. Soc.; Royal Soc. of Med., London, U.K.; Hon. mbr., Verband der Leitenden Krankenhausärzte, 1972. Author of num. articles in surg. & dental publs. Hons. incl: Iron Cross, Class I & II, WW II; Medal of hon., German Red Cross, 1959; Hon. Prof., Med. Univ., Hanover, 1957; Disting. Serv. Medal, Niedersächsischer Verdienstorden, 1973. Address: Lechwiesenstr. 49, 8923 Lechbruch, German Fed. Repub.

KIRWAN, Katharyn Grace (Mrs. Gerald Bourke Kirwan, Jr.), b. 1 Dec. 1913. Librarian; Merchant. Educ: Tex. Woman's Univ., Denton, 1932-33; B.A., B.S., ibid, 1935-37; Univ. of Puget Sound, Tacoma, Wash., 1933-34; Univ. of Wash., Seattle, 1941. Appts: Libn., Brady Sr. H.S., Tex., 1937-38 & McCamey Sr. H.S., Tex., 1938-43; w. U.S.N. active Reserve, 1943-46; Mgr., Milady's Frock Shop, Monroe, Wash., 1946-61; Owner, ibid, 1961-; City Councilwoman, City of Monroe, 1969-73; Mayor, ibid, 1974-. Mbrships: Delta Kappa Gamma; Commnr., Snohomish Co. Hosp. Dist. No. 1, 1970-; Chmbr. of Comm.; Mem. Chmn., Monroe Chapt., Am. Cancer Soc., 1961-; Snohomish Co. Police Servs. Action Coun., 1971; Monroe Pub. Lib. Bd.; AAUS; USN Inst.; Ret. Offs. Assn.; Naval Reserve Assn.; Snohomish Co. Pharmaceutical Aux. Address: Monroe Public Library, Corner of Hill & Blakely Sts., Monroe, WA 98272, U.S.A. 5, 138.

KISAKUREK, Nahit Turgut, b. 13 Feb. 1926. Civil Engineer. Educ: M.S., Fed. Tech. Inst. of Zurich, Switzerland. Appts: Static Engr., Nabolt Engrng., Basle, Switzerland, 1950-51; Reserve Off., Turkish Airforce Command, 1951-52; Site Engr., harbour facilities, Trabzon, Turkey, 1952-56; Chief Engr., & Dir., Verdi Grp. of Cos., Ankara, 1956-69; Ptnr. & Pres., Arzu Insaat ve Ticaret Ltd. Sti., Ankara, 1969-. Mbrships: Int. Assn. Bridge & Structural Engrng., Zurich; Civil Engrng. Assn., Ankara; Assn. for Bridge & Structural Engrng of Turkey; Sporting Club, Kavaklidere, Ankara. Address: Sah Riza Pehlevi Caddesi 55/3, Kavaklidere, Ankara, Turkey. 43.

KISH, Leslie, b. 27 July 1910. University Professor; Research Scientist. Educ: B.S., C.C.N.Y., 1939; M.A., Univ. of Mich., 1948, Ph.D., 1952. Appts: Statn., U.S. Bur. of Census, Dept. of Agric., 1940-42; Meteorologist, U.S.A.C., 1942-45; Survey Rsch. Ctr., Inst. for Soc. Rsch., Univ. of Mich., 1947-, Rsch. Sci., 1963-; Staff, Sociol. Dept., ibid, 1951-, Prof., 1960-. Mbrships: Am. Statsl. Assn. (V.P. 1973); Royal, Int. & Inter-Am. Statsl. Assns.; Am. Soc. Assn.; Pop. Assn. of Am.; Int. Union for Sci. Study of Population; Int. Assn. of Survey Stats. (Coun.). Publs: Survey Sampling, 1965; Sampling Error Program Package, 1972; contbr. to books & profl. publs. Address: Inst. for Soc. Rsch., Univ. of Mich., Ann Arbor, MI 48106, U.S.A. 2, 14, 128.

KISHNER, Mel A., b. 17 May 1915. Artist. Educ: B.S. in Art Educ., Milwaukee State Tchrs. Coll., 1938. Appts: Supvsng. Designer, WPA Art Prog., 1938; Art Tchr., Wis. Coll. of Music, 1938-39; Tchr., Milwaukee Pub. Schls., 1940; Artist, Milwaukee Jrnl. Co., 1940; Art Dir., Jrnl. Co., 1970-; Artist in Res. & Tchr., Experimental Art Educ. Prog., U.S. Dept. of Hlth. Educ. & Welfare, 1967-68; Artist in Res., Nicolet Coll., 1970-72. Mbrships: Pres., Exec. Bd., Wis. Painters & Sculptors; Chtr. Mbr., V.P., Exec. Bd., Illustrators & Designers of Milwaukee; Wis. Watercolor Soc.; Nat. Assn. of Realistic Artists; Milwaukee Press Club; Sigma

Delta Chi; Chmn., Bd. of Dirs., 1968, Milwaukee Jrnl. Unit Holders Coun.; Trustee & Pres., 1969-72, Univ. of Wis. Milwaukee Alumni Assn. Recip. of num. awards for paintings in Nat. Regional exhibs. Works in pub. & pvte. collections world wide. Address: The Milwaukee Jrnl. Co., 333 W. State St., WI 53201, U.S.A. 8.

KISHON, Ephraim, b. 23 Aug. 1924. Writer. Educ: studied Hist. of Art, Budapest Univ. Appts. incl: Writer, daily humour column, "Chad-Gadia", Maariv (Israeli newspaper) & translation appears in Jerusalem Post (English), Die Woche In Israel (German), Uk Kelet (Hungarian), Przeglad (Polish), etc. Author of books & plays in Hebrew, translated into many other langs. & contbr. to most periodicals & newspapers throughout world. Writer & Dir. of films. Books Publs. (in hardback, paperback & var. lang. edits.) incl: Look Back, Mrs. Lot; Noah's Ark, Tourist Class; Unfair To Goliath; Blow Softly In Jericho; The Seasick Whale; So Sorry We Won; Woe To The Victors. Comedy Plays (translated & performed throughout world) incl: The License; His Friend At Court; Black On White; Pull Out The Plug, The Water Is Boiling; Crooks All; How, Now Juliet! Radio Plays; The Blaumilch Canal; Ziggy & Habboobah; Backstage; The last Angry Kick. Films: Sallah Shabbati; Ervinka; The Big Dig (The Blaumilch Canal); The Policeman. Mbrships: Writer's Org.; Jrnlst.'s Org.; Pres., Israel Film Prod.'s Assn. Recip. many awards & hons. for lit. & film prods. inclng. Israeli Herzl Prize, Jabotinsky Recip. of awards. Address: 48 Hamitnadev St., Afeka 69690, Israel.

KISLING, Erik August, b. 17 June 1916. Dental Surgeon. Educ: Med. Scis., 1935-36; Dental Scis., 1936-39; Postgrad. study, Stockholm, 1945-46 & Ann Arbor, Mich., U.S.A., 1953-54; Specialist of Orthodontics, 1957; Dr. Odont., Copenhagen, 1966. Appts. incl: Asst. Prof. of Pedodontics, 1946, Assoc. Prof. of Pedodontics, 1952-65, Prof. of Pedodontics, Hd. of Dept., Royal Dental Coll., Copenhagen, Denmark, 1965-. Mbrships: Int. Assn. of Dentistry for Children, V.P., 1971-73, Pres., 1973, Danish Sect., Nordic Pedodontic Soc., Pres., 1964; Nordic Pedodontic Soc., Pres., 1962-64, 1969-71; Danish Assn. of Children's Dentistry; Hon. Mbr., S. Korean Assn. of Dentistry for Children, 1969 & Soc. Française de Pédodontie, 1973; Danish Orthodontic Soc.; European Orthodontic Soc.; Fedn. Dentaire Int.; Scandinavian Dental Assn.; Danish Dental Assn.; Danish-Icelandish Horse Club. Publs. incl: co-author, Nordic Text-book of Pedodontics, long series of scientific articles, 1970. Hons. incl: Fulbright Fellowship, 1953. Kt. of Dannebrog, 1969; Address: Royal Dental Coll., Copenhagen, Jagtvej 160, DK 2100 Copenhagen, Ø, Denmark.

KISOR, Hazel Theresa, b. 1 Apr. 1942. Educator. Educ: B.S., Jacksonville State Univ., Ala., U.S.A., 1964; B.A., ibid, 1965; M.S., 1969; Ph.D., Univ. of Ala., 1974. Appts: Tchr., Piedmont H.S. Ala., 1964-73; Tchr., Gadsden State Jr. Coll., Ala., 1971-74; Dir., Ext. Ctr., ibid, 1972-; Admin. Asst. to Supt., Piedmont City Schls., 1973-. Mbrships. incl: Pres., Piedmont Br., AAUW, 1971; V.P., Piedmont Tchrs. Assn., 1969-70, Pres., 1970-71; Treas., Dist. V, Ala. Educ. Assn., 1971-74; NEA; Ala. Fedn. of For. Lang. Tchrs.; Int. House Prog., Jacksonville State Univ.; 1st V.P., Piedmont Jaycettes; Supt., Youth Dept., First Meth. Ch.; Dist. Off., Women's Soc. of Christian Serv.; Pi Gamma Mu; Kappa Delta Epsilon; Kappa Delta Pi. Author, A Conceptual Model for a Professional Development Plan for a Small

School System (dissertation). Recip., Fellowship, R.J. Reynolds Tobacco Co., 1971. Address: Route 5, Box 175, Piedmont, AL 36272, U.S.A. 76, 125.

KISSINGER, Walter B., b. 21 June 1924. Business Executive. Educ: B.A., Princeton Univ., N.J., 1951; M.B.A., Harvard Bus. Schl., Cambridge, Mass., 1953. Appts: Asst. to V.P., Gen. Tire & Rubber Co., Akron, Ohio, 1953-56; Pres., Adv. Vacuum Prods. Co., Stamford, Conn., 1957-62; Exec. V.P. / Dir., Glass-Tite Inds., Providence, R.I., 1960-62; V.P. & Gen. Mgr., Harman-Kardon, Inc., Plainview, N.Y.; Asst. to Pres., Jerrold Corp., 1963-64; Exec. V.P. & Dir., Jervis Corp., Hicksville, N.Y., 1964-68; Pres. & Chief Exec. Off., Allen Group Inc., Melville, N.Y., 1969-; Chmn., ibid, 1972-. Mbrships: Princeton Club of N.Y.; Bay Club, Huntington, N.Y. Recip., Commendation Medal, 1945. Address: The Allen Group Inc., 534 Broad Hollow Rd., Melville, NY 11746, U.S.A. 2.

KITABATAKE, Takashi, b. 6 May 1928. Professor of Radiology. Educ: Grad., Schl. of Med., Hirosaki Univ., Japan, 1952. Appts: Asst. Prof. of Radiol., Nagoya City Univ. Hosp., 1963; Chief Radiologist, Aichi Cancer Ctr. Hosp., Nagoya, 1964; Prof. of Radiol., Niigata Univ. Hosp., 1967-. Mbrships: Japan Radiological Soc.; Japan Radiation Rsch. Soc.; Japanese Soc. of Nuclear Med.; Japan Soc. for Cancer Therapy; Japan Lung Cancer Soc. Publs: Radiation Hazards, 1968; Radiodiagnosis of Digestive Organs, 1971; Judgment of Radiation Injury, 1972; Num. papers on radiological rsch. Address: Dept. of Radiology, Niigata University School of Medicine, Niigata 951, Japan.

KITTLEMAN, Martha Adrienne Haywood (Mrs. Edmund Taylor Kittleman), b. 31 Dec. 1936. Interior Decorator. Educ: Univ. of N.C., Chapel Hill; Longwood Coll., Farmville, Va; Univ. of Miss. Appts. incl: Supvsr., Fedl. Serv. Campaign for N.C., 1957-58; Rep., Douglas Van Dorn Cards, 1966-71; Kindergarten & Sunday Schl. Tchr. Mbrships: Intercontinental Biog. Assn.; Patroness, Deb. Assembly, N.Y.; Dames of Magna Charta; Colonial Dames, XVII Century; Delta Delta Delta; DAR; United Daughters of the Confederacy; Philbrook Arts Mus. Address: 110 Fleetwood Place, Bartlesville, OK 74003, U.S.A. 5, 132, 138.

KITZINGER, Sheila, b. 29 Mar. 1929. Social Anthropologist; Writer; Childbirth Educator. Educ: Dipl., Soc. Anthropol., Oxford Univ., 1951; B.Litt., ibid, 1954. Appts. incl: Hon. Fellow, Soc. Anthropol., St. Mary's Hosp., London, U.K., 1973-; Prenatal Tchr. & Advsry. Panel Mbr., Nat. Childbirth Trust of Gt. Britain; Cons. Bd. Mbr., Int. Childbirth Educ. Assn. Mbr., Inst. of Hlth. Educ., Gt. Britain. Publs. incl: The Experience of Childbirth, 1962; Ed., Episiotomy—Physical & Emotional Aspects, 1972. Contbr. to med. & scientific books, & var. med. & hlth. jrnls. Hons: Hon. Mbrships., Equipo Medico de Estudios Psicofisices de Analgesia Obstetrica de Bogota, 1969; Joost de Blank Award, 1971-73. Address: Standlake Manor, Standlake, Nr. Witney, Oxfordshire, England.

KJELDAAS, Arnljot, b. 22 Jan. 1916. Composer & Organist. Educ: Organist Exam., 1940; Exam. as Prof. of singing, 1941; Studies in Piano w. Reimar Riefling, Organ w. Arild Sandvold, Composing w. Bjarne Brustad, Ludvig Irgens-Jensen & Jean Rivier, France, 1949; Orch. conducting w. Oivin Fjeldstad. Appts: Organist, Honefoss, Norway, 1942-44; Music Critic, Arbeider Bladet, Oslo, 1945-46;

Organist Rjukan, ibid, 1946-56; Choir & Orch. Conductor, Organist & Conductor, Ski, 1956-63; Currently Music Tchr., Ski Ungdomsskole. Mbr., Norwegian Composers Assn. Compositions incl: Romance for violin & orch.; Hymn "Op Huis Herrens Egen Rost"; Misericordia "Gry og Grid"; My Country Sings. Hons. incl: Prize, Composers' Competition, Norwegian Composers Assn., 1944; Travel schlrship., Tono, 1949. Address: Box 37, 1405 Langhus, Norway. 134.

KLAASSEN, Leo Hendrik, b. 21 June 1920. University Professor. Educ: Ph.D., Econs. Appts. incl: Rsch. Fellow, Netherlands, Econs. Inst., Rotterdam, 1945-51; Chief of Rsch., ibid, 1951-59; Dir., 1959-68; Pres., 1968-; Prof., Erasmus Univ., Rotterdam, 1959-. Fellow, Am. Geog. Soc. Mbrships. incl: Econometric Soc.; Regional Sci. Assn.; Demographic Assn., Neths. Publs. incl: Area Economic & Social Redevelopment, 1965; Selecting Industries for Location in Depressed Areas, 1967; Social Amenities in Area Economic Growth, 1968; Co-Auth., Economic Policy in the Netherlands, 1968; Ed. & Co-Auth., Regional Economics, 1972; Co-Auth., Migration Policy, 1972; The Impact of Changes in Society on the Demand for Passenger & Freight Transport, 1973; German Labour Market Policy, 1974. Recip., Medal of Hon., Univ. of Gdánsk, Poland. Address: Neths. Econ. Inst., 50 Burgemeester Oudlaan, Rotterdam 3016, Netherlands.

KLARMAN, Joseph L., b. 1909. Journalist. Educ: Tchrs. Sem. Appts: Fndr., Revisionist Movement (Jewish Zionist Movement), Poland; Ed., Jewish (Yiddish) newspaper "Unser Welt", Poland; Active during WWII in Constantinople, Turkey, in rescue ops. for European Jewry; Ldr., illegal aliyah in Balkan countries, 1944-48; Mbr., Political Comm., Lake Success, N.Y., U.S.A., prior to UNO partition decision of Palestine; Deleg., var. Zionist World Congresses & elected to Zionist Action. Comm.; World Chmn., Zionist Revisionist Movement. Mbrships: Exec., World Zionist Org.; Exec., Jewish Agcy.; World Chmn., Youth Aliyah (Immigration & Educ. Agcy. for Jewish Children); V.P., Fedn. Int. des Communautés d'enfants. Address: 45 Sderot Hen, Tel Aviv, Israel. 94.

KLASSEN, Robert Leonard, b. 10 Nov. 1935. Librarian; Planner; Educator. Educ: B.A., Calif. State Univ., Fresno, 1957; M.L.S., Univ. of Calif., Berkeley, 1959. Appts. incl: Asst. Supvsr., Calif. State Lib., Sacramento, 1962-68; Planning/Rsch. Prog. Off., Div. of Lib. Progs., U.S. Off. of Educ., Wash. D.C., 1968-71; Planning & Legislation Off., Bur. of Libs. & Learning Resources, U.S. Off. of Educ., 1971-73; Chief, Planning Staff, ibid, 1973-. Mbrships. incl: Bd. of Dirs., Special Libs. Assn., 1973-76; Chmn., Standards Comm., Ref. & Adult Servs., ALA, 1969-; Am. Soc. for Info. Sci.; Beta Phi Mu. Contbr. to jrnls. Recip. of hons. Address: 2423 N. Roosevelt St., Arlington, VA 22207, U.S.A. 7.

KLAUCK, James J., b. 22 Oct. 1930. Marketing Executive. Educ: B.A., Dickinson Coll., 1952; Postgrad. studies, N.Y. Univ., 1956-58. Appts. incl: Econ. Analyst, Esso Int., N.Y.C., 1954-63; Market Rsch. Specialist, C.P.C. Int., ibid, 1963-64; Mgr., Market Rsch., The Singer Co., ibid, 1965-67; Mgr., Market Rsch., Aluminium Assn., ibid, 1967-69; Dir. Marketing, Gen. Cable Corp., V.P., Gen. Cable Export Corp., V.P. Electrack (subsidiary of Gen. Cable), N.Y.C., 1969-73. Dir., Sales & Marketing, Scovill Mfg., Waterbury, Conn., 1973-; Commnr. of Recreation, Pelham, N.Y. Mbrships: Am. Mgmt. Assn.; Am. Marketing

Assn.; Copper Dev. Assn.; Aluminum Assn.; Nat. Elec. Mfrs. Assn.; Nat. Coun. Phys. Distribution Mgmt.; Copper Club; Shenorock Shore Club; Waterbury Club; N.Y. Athletic Club. Address: 525 Monterey Ave., Pelham Manor, NY 10803, U.S.A. 6.

KLECKER, Joe (Joseph) W. Ed., b. 21 May 1899. Honorary Bank Manager; ex-Delegate, General Management for Foreign Banks. Educ: Institut pour Journalistes de Belgique. Appts. incl: Credit Dept., Banque de Bruxelles; Hd., Secretariat, Banque Belge d'Afrique (affiliate); Mbr. of Mgmt., Banque de Bruxelles, Charleroi, then Ghent; For. Dept., ibid, WWII; Official mission to re-establish banking & commercial rels. in Europe & o'seas, after WWII; Hon. Mgr., Banque de Bruxelles, Brussels. Mbrships. incl: Soc. de l'Ordre de Léopold; Co-fndr. & dir., Belgo-German Chmbr. of Comm., Belgo-Polish Chmbr. of Comm., Soc. Belgo-Allemande; Dir., Belgo-Turkish, Belgo-Austrian Chmbrs. of Comm.; Belgian Por-Mozart Comm.; Centre d'Etudes Bancaires et Financières. Hons. incl: Grosses Verdienstkreuz, Germany, 1961; Décoration belge du Travail de Ière classe, 1965. Address: Avenue des Ortolans 89, B-1170 Brussels, Belgium. 43.

KLEEMAN, Robert H., b. 4 Feb. 1931. Dentist. Educ: B.S., L.I. Univ., 1952; D.D.S., Loyola Univ., 1956; Postgrad. in Oral Surg., N.Y. Univ., 1957. Appts: Attng. Dentist, Dept. of Oral Surg., Queens Gen. Hosp., 1958-63; Attng. Dentist, St. Agatha Home for Children, 1958-62; Guest Lectr., Special Radiation Procedure Course, Queens Gen. Hosp. Ctr., 1958-62; Corporate Exec., Beta Int. Inc.; Inter-Global Investments Ltd. Mbrships. incl: Anaphy, L.I. Univ.; Corres. Sec., ibid; Am. Dental Assn.; Am. Dental Soc. of Anesthesiol.; Int. Acad. of Orthodontics; Am. Soc. of Dentistry for Children. Works of art included in following exhibs: 3rd Annual Exhib., Women's Club, Eastchester, N.Y.; The Palette Studio, Yonkers, N.Y.; I. Miller Salon, Scarsdale, N.Y.; XIII Int. Dental Congress, Cologne, Germany. Hons: Third Prize, Art Exhib., XIII Int. Dental Congress, Cologne, 1963. Address: 6645 Broadway, Riverdale, NY 10471, U.S.A. 6.

KLEILER, Frank Munro, b. 17 Apr. 1914. U.S. Government Official. Educ: A.B., Antioch Coll., Yellow Springs, Ohio, 1938. Appts: Clerk to Bd. mbr., Nat. Mediation Bd., Wash. D.C., 1937-39; Asst. to Bd. mbr., Nat. Labor Rels. Bd., Wash., 1939-41; Field Examiner, ibid, 1941-44; Regional Dir., Pitts. Region, 1944-47; Exec. Sec., Wash. D.C., 1947-51 & 1953-60; Disputes Dir., Wage Stabilization Bd., Wash. D.C., 1951-53; Dpty. Commnr., Bureau of Labor-Mgmt. Reports, 1960-62; Dir., Off. of Welfare & Pension Plans, 1962-63; Dir., Off. of Labor-Mgmt. & Welfare-Pension Reports, 1963-70; Dpty. Asst. Sec., U.S. Dept. of Labor, 1970-. Mbrships: Acad. of Pol. Sci.; Industrial Rels. Rsch. Assn. Publs: Canadian Regulation of Pension Plans, 1970; European Regulation of Pension Plans, 1971. Hons: Sec. of Labor's Awards for Notable Career Serv., 1968 & Disting. Serv., 1964. Address: 9100 Warren St., Silver Springs, MD 20910, U.S.A. 2.

KLEIN, David Ballin, b. 15 Apr. 1897. Psychologist. Educ: A.B., CCNY; M.A., Ph.D., Columbia Univ. Appts: Prof. of Psychol., Univ. of Tex., 1923-47; Prof. of Psychol. & Dir., Psychol. Serv. Ctr., Univ. of Southern Calif., 1948-62; Prof. Emeritus, ibid, 1962-. Mbrships: Fellow, Am. Psychol. Assn., AAAS; Sigma Xi; Western Psychol. Assn.; Calif. State Psychol. Assn. Publs. incl: The Experimental Production of Dreams During Hypnosis; General Psychology; Abnormal Psychology; Mental

Hygiene—A Survey of Personality Disorders & Mental Health; A History of Scientific Psychology—Its Origins & Philosophic Backgrounds; "Dreams & Dreaming" in 1970 edit., Ency. Britannica. Address: 11901 Sunset Blvd., L.A., CA 90049, U.S.A. 2.

KLEIN, Martin John Herman, b. 26 Feb. 1937. Electronic Design Engineer. Educ: Assoc. of Sci. degree, Spring Garden Coll., Chestnut Hill, Pa., U.S.A., 1959; Sev. dips. for courses in bus. mgmt., tech. trng. in radio & TV, etc. Appts. incl: Electronic Techn., Comprehensive Designers, Inc., Phila., Pa., 1960-62; Electronic & Systems Evaluation Specialist, Vehicle Calibration, Gen. Elec. Co., Phila., 1964-70; Pvte. Prac. as Engrng. Cons., 1971-73; Electronic Design Engr., Andresen Indl. Instruments, Inc., Phila., 1974-; Pvte. tutor in Jr. & H.S. Maths. in many areas. Mbrships. incl: IEEE; Am. Soc. of Cert. Engrng. Techns.; Int. Brotherhood of Magicians; TV Serv. Assn. of Del. Valley; Del. Valley Bus. Assn. Recip. of num. commendations for profl. & soc. servs. Address: 1247 June Rd., Huntingdon Valley, PA 19006, U.S.A. 2, 6.

KLEIN, Richard M., b. 17 Mar. 1923. Botanist. Educ: A.Sc., Chgo. Jr. Coll., 1942; B.S., 1947; M.S., 1948, Ph.D.; 1951, Univ. of Chgo.; Grad. study, Univ. of Rochester & Marine Biol. Lab. Appts: Fellow, Nat. Inst. of Hlth., 1948-49; Fellow, Am. Cancer Soc., 1951-53; Assoc. Curator, Curator, N.Y. Botanical Garden, 1953-57; Caspary Curator, ibid, 1957-67; Prof., Bot., Univ. of Vt., 1967-. Mbrships: Coun. Mbr., Chmn., Comm. on Educ. & Developmental Sect., Mbr., Edit. Bd., Plant Sci. Bulletin, Botanical Soc. of Am.; Coun. Mbr., Photobiol. Soc. of Am.; Am. Scandinavian Socs. of Plant Physiol.; Corres. Mbr., Canadian Soc. of Plant Physiol.; Sigma Xi. Publs: Discovering Plants; Research Methods in Plant Science; Monographs, reviews & articles. Hons: Bausch & Lomb Sci. Medal, 1940; Conservation Educator for 1970. Address: Dept. of Botany, Univ. of Vermont, Burlington, VT 05401, U.S.A. 14.

KLEIN-ASTRACHAN, Olga, b. 17 Jan. 1917. Painter; Ceramic Artist. Educ: Acad. des Beaux Arts, Berlin, Germany; Grande Chaumière Paris, France. Exhibs. incl: Galerie Montmorency, Paris; Galerie le Peristyle, ibid; Galerie 88; Bastion St. André, Antibes, France; Palais Miramar, Cannes, ibid; Grimbels Salon Terres Latines, Pitts. U.S.A.; Galerie Spector, N.Y. Permanent exhibs: Galerie Katia Granoff, Paris; Mus. Ariana, Geneva, Switzerland. Works in many pvte. collections & owned by Min. of State of Cultural Affairs (France). Hons: Chevalier de l'Ordre Nat. du Mérite, Min. des Affaires Culturelles, Paris, 1972; Medaille de Bronze Artistes Francais; Prix des Arts Décoratif, Salon des Femmes Peintres & Sculpteurs. Address: 10 Ave. du Château, 92200 Neuilly S/Seine, France. 34, 132, 138.

KLEINMAN, Daniel J., b. 18 May 1915. Dentist. Educ: D.D.S., Schl. of Dentistry, Univ. of Mich., 1938; Var. courses, Univ. of Pa., 1950-55; Armed Forces Inst. of Pathol., Wash. D.C. Appts. incl: Pvte. prac., 1939-42, 1945-46; Chief of Dental Serv., VA, Outpatient Clin., N.Y., 1958-70; Acting Dir., ibid, 1970; Chief of Dental Serv., VA Hosp., Brooklyn, N.Y., 1970-; Clin. Asst. Prof., Dept. of Prosthodontics, Seton Hall Coll. of Med. & Dentistry, 1959-69; Clin. Assoc. Prof., Dept. of Prosthodontics, Coll. of Med. & Dentistry of N.J., 1969-; Fac. Mbr., Temperomandibular Jt. Clin. & Geriatrics Clin. Mbrships. incl: Cons., Coun. on Hosps., Am. Dental Assn., 1973-74; Mbr. of Coun. on Hosp. Dental Serv., N.J. Dental Assn., 1972-74;

AAUP; Nominating Comm., Am. Assn. of Hosp. Dentists, 1973; AAAS; Am. Acad. of Oral Pathol.; Post Treas., Am. Legion, 1966-71. Contbr. to jrnls. Address: VA Hosp., Brooklyn, NY 11209, U.S.A.

KLEINSCHMIDT, Anthony Andrew, b. 9 Nov. 1917. Library Administrator. Educ: B.A., Josephinum Coll., Worthington, Ohio, 1939; B.S., Rosary Coll., River Forest, Ill., 1946. Appts: Prof. of German, Josephinum Coll., Worthington, 1946-60, Dir. of Libs., 1946-. Prof. of Liturgy, Sem. Dept., 1960-71; Chap., Ohio State Schl. for Deaf, Columbus, 1954-60, Ohio State Schl. for Blind, 1954-. Mbrships: Cath. Lib. Assn.; Chmn., Sem. Sect., ibid, 1954-55, Chmn., Cataloging & Classification Sect., 1958-60; Am. & Ohio Lib. Assns.; Cath. Liturgical Conf.; Worthington Pub. Lib. Bd. Trustees, 1966-72, Chmn., 1967-58; Josephinum Alumni Assn.; Chap., Local Chapt., Cath. Alumni Club Int., 1972-. Articles, Cath. Lib. World, Pastoral Life. Address: Josephinum College, Worthington, OH 43085, U.S.A. 8, 15.

KLEMENTYNOVSKI, Zvi, b. 3 Aug. 1904. Advocate. Educ: Grad., Univ. Stefan Batory, Vilna, 1928; Magister Juris. Appts: Legal Advsr. to Ctrl. Fedn. Bldrs. & Contractors, Israel; Atty., World Zionist Movement, 1966-. Mbrships: Acad. Int. Lex. & Sci.; Exec., World Org. Jewish Jurists; Comm., Int. Affairs, Bar Assn., Israel; Ctrl. Comm., Independent Liberal Party, Israel; Dpty. Mayor, Tel Aviv Yaffo, 1966-73. Contbr. to "Builder & Contractor" jrnl. Address: 18 Mikve Israel St., Tel-Aviv, Israel.

KLEMM, Friedrich, b. 22 Jan. 1904. Retired Library Director; University Professor. Educ: Studied at Univ. of Dresden, Germany, 1925-30; State secondary schl. tchrs. exam., 1930; State exam. for sci. libn., 1932. Appts: Sci. Libn., Deutsches Museum, Munich, 1932-57; Lib. Dir., ibid, 1957-69; Promoted to Dr.rer,nat., Munich, 1948; Hon. Prof., Tech. Univ., Munich, 1959; Sci. collaborator, rsch. inst., Deutsches Mus. für die Geschichte der Naturwissenschaft & der Technik, 1963-. Mbrships: Deutsche Akad. der Naturforscher Leopoldina, Halle; Acad. Int. d'Histoire des Sciences, Paris, France; Corres. mbr., Soc. for the Hist. of Technol., Cleveland, Ohio, U.S.A.; Deutsche Gesellschaft für Geschichte der Med., Naturwissenschaft & Technik; Bereichs Technikgeschichte des Vereins Deutscher Ingenieure. Author of publs. in field. Recip. of hons. Address: Grünwalder Strasse 53, 8 Munich 90, German Fed. Repub.

KLEMM, Wilhelm Karl, b. 5 Jan. 1896. Professor. Educ: Dr.phil., Breslau Univ., Germany, 1923. Appts: Asst. to Prof., Tech. Univ., Hannover, Germany, 1923-33; Prof. Chem. & Dir. Inst. Inorg. Chem., Tech. Univ. Danzig, 1933-45; Kiel Univ., 1947-51; Muenster Univ., 1951-64. Mbrships: Pres., Int. Union Pure & Applied Chem., 1965-67; V.P., ICSU, 1966-68; Pres., Gesellschaft Deutscher Chemiker, 1952-53; Rektor, Münster Univ., 1957-58; Acads. Halle. Munich, Vienna, Göttingen, Düsseldorf. Publs: Magnetochemie, 1936; Morganische Chemie, 1971; Exp. Einführung in die Morganische Chemie (w. W. Fischer), 1971 & 200 publs. on phys. properties of molten salts; Magnetochemistry; Lanthanoids; Transition metals; Intermetallic compounds; Semimetals; Fluorides etc. Hons. incl: E.K. I & other WWI decorations; Grosser Bundesverdienstkreuz, FRG, 1966; Liebig Medal, 1951; Carl-Duisberg Plakelle, 1963; Moissan-Médaille, 1953; Lavoisier Médaille, 1965; Hon. mbr; Soc. Chim. de France; Ges. Deutscher Chemiker; Verein Oesterr. Chemiker;

Dr. h.c. Bordeaux, Dijon, Lille. Address: Theresiengrund 22, D44 Münster/Westf., German Fed. Repub. 43, 92.

KLEMPNER, Irving M., b. 28 Nov. 1924. University Professor. Educ: B.A., Brooklyn Coll., 1951; M.S., Columbia Univ., 1952; D.L.S., 1967. Appts. incl: Profl. Libn., Lib. of Congress, 1953-54, 56; Catalog Libn., Nat. Lib. of Med., 1955; Supvsry. Libn., Naval Intelligence Schl., 1956-57; Supvsry. Libn., Naval Applied Sci. Lab., 1957-68; Mgr., Info. Servs., United Nuclear Corp., 1958-67; Prof., Schl. of Lib. & Info. Sci., SUNY, Albany, 1967-. Mbrships. incl: Special Libs. Assn.; Assn. of Am. Lib. Schls.; ALA; Chmn., Upstate N.Y. Chapt., Am. Soc. for Info. Sci., 1973-. Author of many profl. publs. Recip., Cert. of Distinction, NATO Adv. Study Inst. in Info. Sci., Wales, 1973. Address: State Univ. of N.Y., Schl. of Lib. & Info. Sci., 1400 Washington Ave., Albany, NY 12222, U.S.A.

KLEPFISZ, Heszel, b. 1 Mar. 1910. Educator; Author; Rabbi. Educ: Rabbinical Sem., Warsaw; Ph.D., Un.iv. of Warsaw. Appts: Ed., Dos Judische Togblat, Warsaw, 1931-39, Echo Zydowskie, Warsaw, 1932-34 & Di Woch, Paris, 1939-40; Sr. Jewish Chaplain, Polish Forces on Western Front, 1940-49; Lectr., Hebrew Coll., Glasgow, Scotland, 1950-52 & Tchrs. Sem. & Coll. of Jewish Studies, Miami, U.S.A., 1958-60; Prin., Escuela Hebrea, San Jose, Costa Rica, 1953-58; Rector, Albert Einstein Inst., Panama, Repub. of Panama, 1961-; Rabbi, Ashkenazic Community, Panama, 1961-; Prof., Univ. of Panama, 1964-; Regent, ibid, 1968-69. Mbrships: Hon. Judeo-Christian Assn., San Jose, Costa Rica; Nat. Commns., UNESCO, 1968-. Educ. Reform, Min. of Educ., Panama, 1970- & Sci. & Technol., Min. of Educ., Panama, 1972-. Publs: Judisher antail in oifshtand fun 1831, 1934; Di Prager Shechita, 1935; Maimonides, 1936; Kobieta Zydowska, 1937; Un Año en el Instituto Alberto Einstein, 1962; Realidad y Visión, 1965; Baal Schen Tov, 1967; Rabi Menajem Zemba, 1968; Cultura Espiritual del Judaísmo Polaco, 1969; Diez Mensajes de Graduación, 1971. Hons: Polish, French & British War Medals; Medal of Liberation for Special Merits, City of Ghent, Belgium, 1944; Distinction for work as Regent, Univ. of Panama, 1968; Dipl. of Recognition, Min. of Educ., Panama, 1971; D.Litt., Univ. of Zurich. Address: c/o Inst. Alberto Einstein, Apartado 7085, Panama 5, Repub. of Panama. 55.

KLEPZIG, Helmut, b. 27 Mar. 1916. Physician. Educ: Studies at Frankfurt/Main, Bern, Heidelberg & Freiburg/Br., M.D., 39; Appts. incl: Dr. in Mil. Hosps., 1939-46; Medizinische Klinik, Univ. Freiburg/Br., 1946-58; Prof., Univ. of Frankfurt/Main; Co-Ed., Medizinische Klinik (jrnl.); Med. Supt., Klinik für Herz- & Gefässkrankheiten der KVB, Konigsteints., 1958-; Prof. Med., 1960-. Mbrships: Deutsche Gesellschaft für Kreislaufforschung; Deutsche Gessellschaft für Innere Medizin. Publs. incl: num. articles on cardiological problems. Address: Klinik der KVB, Sodener Str. 43, D 624 Konigstein/Ts.

KLIEN, Bertha Anne (Mrs. William F. Moncreiff), b. 16 May 1898. Physician. Educ: M.D., Univ. of Vienna, Austria, 1925. Appts: Intern, Allgemeines Krankenhaus, City of Vienna, 1925-26; Asst. Eye Clin., Univ. of Vienna, 1926-28; Asst. Prof., Ophthalmol., Rush Med. Coll., U.S.A., 1929-39; Assoc. Prof., ibid, 1939-46; Asst. Attng. Ophthalmol., Presby. Hosp., 1929-47; Assoc. Prof., Northwestern Univ., 1946-52; Attng. Ophthalmol., Wesley Mem. Hosp., 1946-52;

Assoc. Prof., Ophthalmol., Univ. of Chgo., 1954-59; Prof., ibid, 1959-65; Emeritus Prof., 1965-. Mbrships. incl: Verhoeff Soc. Ocular Pathol. (Charter Mbr.; Pres., 1964); Chgo. Ophthalmol. Soc. (Pres., 1964); AMA; Sigma Xi; Acad. Ophthalmol. & Otolar. Author of profl. publs. Hons. incl: Gold Medal, AMA, 1948; Silver Medal, Ill. State Sci. Exhibit Awards, 1947. Address: 2615 E. 76th St., Chgo., IL 60649, U.S.A.

KLIEN, Walter, b. 27 Nov. 1928. Pianist. Educ: Konservatorium, Graz, Austria; Acad. of Music, Vienna; Study of composition under Paul Hindemith, piano under A. Benedetti-Michelangeli. Concert Tours: Europe, Far East, S. Am., S. Africa, U.S.A. Solist, Music Festivals at Salzburg, Vienna, Edinburgh, Athens, Prague, Barcelona, Prades, Marlboro, Lucerne, Berlin. Soloist with leading orchs., inclng. Berlin, Vienna Philharmonic, New Philharmonia, London Symph. Orch., London Philharmonic, Phila. & Cleveland Symph. Orchs., Engl. Chamber Orch., etc. Recordings: 1st complete recording of Brahms solo piano works; Complete Mozart solo piano works, etc. Hons: Prizes, int. piano competitions, Bolzano, Paris, Vienna, 1951, '52, '53; Wiener Floetenuhr, record prize, best Mozart recording, 1969. Address: c/o Harold Holt Ltd., 122 Wigmore St., London W1, U.K. 4, 86.

KLIMOV, Alexis, b. 19 Apr. 1937. Writer; Professor. Educ: Licence, Philos. & Letters, Univ. of Liège, Belgium, 1960; Agrégé, ibid. Appts: Prof., Greek & Latin, 1961-64; Prof., Philos. & Lit., Ctr. of Univ. Studies, Trois-Rivières, P.Q., Canada, 1964-69; Dir. Inst. of Hist. of Religs., ibid, 1967-69; Prof., Dept. of Philos., Univ. of P.Q., Trois-Rivières, & Dir., Rsch. Grp. in Hist. of Religs. & Prehistoric Archaeol., 1969-; Vis. Prof., Dept. of Philos., Univ. of Montreal, 1972-74. Mbrships. incl: Fndr., Pres., Philos. Club, Trois-Rivières, 1965; Edit. Bd., Scis. religieuses/Studies in Relig., 1971-. Publs. incl: Nicolas Berdiaeff ou la Révolte contre l'objectivation, 1967; Dostoïevski ou la Connaissance périlleuse, 1971; Le "Philosophe Teutonique" ou l'Esprit d'Aventure.Suivi des Confessions de Jacob Boehme, 1973; contbr. to var. profl. publs. Recip., sev. hons. Address: 1051 Rue des Chênes, Trois-Rivières, P.Q. G8Y 2PT, Canada. 6.

KLINCKOWSTROM, Harald H.M.A., b. 20 June 1897, d. 28 Feb. 1973. Artist Painter. Baron (Friherre) introduced under No. 262, 1776, extinct in Sweden 28 Feb. 1973. Educ: Acad. of Art, Stockholm, Sweden; var. painting schls. Made sev. scientific visits to Iceland, Greenland & Aaroe Islands in youth. Mbrships: Club of Artists; Royal Sailing Assn.; Svenska Jägerförbundet i Stockholm, 1914; Stockholms Läns Kungl. Hushallnings Sällskap, 1940; Samfundet för Hembygdsvard Ekerö; Nat. Geog. Soc., Wash. D.C.; Hon., Gall. Mouffe, Paris, France, 1971. Exhibs: Konstnärshuset, Stockholm, 1916; Cia Cilli; Gummessons; Thurestams, etc.; many separate exhibs. in Ctrl. Sweden & in S. of Country, 1937-72; Biarritz, France, 1970; San Remo, Italy, 1970; Gall. Mouffe, Paris, 1971; The Breakers, Palm Beach, Fla., U.S.A. 1972. Work is represented at Mod. Mus., Stockholm & at Mus. of Art, Gothenburg. Hons. incl: Dip., Gall. Vallombreuse, Biarritz, 1970; Dip., Accademia Int. Tommaso Campanella, Rome, 1970; Dip. w. medal, Int. Art Exhib., San Remo, 1970. Address of the Barroness Blanka Klinckowström: Stafsund, 170 10 Ekerö, Sweden. 105, 133.

KLINGEN, Leonard Gerard, b. 29 June 1924. Economist. Educ: B.Comm., Univ.

N.S.W., Sydney, Australia; M.Ec., Sydney Univ.; Ph.D., Miami Univ., Fla., U.S.A., 1974. Appts: Netherlands & Brit. Army, WW II, 1945-47; Scheduling Off., w. Borg-Warner, Sydney, Australia, 1956-60; Statl. Off.-Supt. O.R., Qantas Airways, 1960-68; Mgr., O.R., Eastern Airlines, 1968-. Mbrships: Past Pres., James Cook Astron. Soc., Sydney; Ops. Rsch. Soc. of Am.; Am. Econ. Soc.; Am. Inst. Indl. Engrs.; Southern Cross Astron. Soc., Miami, Fla., U.S.A.; Mus. of Sci., ibid; AGIFORS; Am. Register Sci. & Tech. Personnel (Nat. Sci. Fndn.). Contbr. papers to sev. confs. in field, incl: Material Forecasting Studies, 1966; Control of cost by Ratio Analysis, 1967; Statistical Analysis of airline costs, 1970; Dynamic simulation solves problems in facilities planning and adds a new dimension to convential cost analysis, 1971. Address: 10945 SW 107 Ave., Miami, FL 33156, U.S.A. 125.

KLINGENSMITH, Don Joseph, b. 1 Apr. 1901. Radio Minister; New Testament Translator. Educ: A.B., John Fletcher Coll., 1928; M.A., Okla. State Univ., 1941; B.D., Garrett Sem., 1946; Ph.D., Fla. State Christian Coll., 1970. Appts. incl: Supt., Ponca (Indian) Meth. Mission, 1936-43; W. Wis., 1943-50; Speciality Sales, 1950-54; Pres., Mandan Window Co., 1954-58; Pres., Mandan Motors until 1965; Radio Min., 1965-. Mbrships. incl: Hon. Chief & Councilman, Ponca Indians, 1940; Chmn., Commn. on Indian Work, Okla. Coun. Chs., 1938-43; Gov.'s Commn. on Conservation, 1968-70; Pres., Mo. Valley Chapt., Isaac Walton League, 1968-70; Dist. Committeeman, Repub. Party, 1970-; Lions Int. Publs: Good News as Told By Luke, M.D.; Todays English New Testament, Vol. 1, Matthew, Mark, Luke-Acts. Hons. incl: D.D., 1968; Litt.D., 1969; Able Toastmaster, 1970. Address: Box 122, Mandan, N.D. 58554, U.S.A. 2, 22, 34, 57, 126, 128, 131.

KLINGENSMITH, Thelma Hyde (Mrs. Don J. Klingensmith), b. 23 May 1904. Educator. Educ: B.A., John Fletcher Coll., 1928; M.S. in Ed., Univ. of N.D., 1962; Okla. Univ., Garrett Sem. Appts: Tchr., Rural Schl., Almont, N.D., 1922-24; Exec. Sec., Young People's Gospel League, Chgo., 1928-30; Asst. Supt., Ponca Meth. Indian Mission, Okla., 1936-43; H.S. Engl.Tchr., Almont N.D., 1950-53; Supt. Schls., Morton Co., N.D., 1959-. Mbrships incl: Advsr., Morton Co. Lib. Bd., 1960-; ALA; NEA; N.D. Educ. Assn.; N.D. Lib. Assn.; Dir., N.D. Div., Am. Cancer Soc., 1958-72; Sec., ibid, 1960-66; Dir. & Treas., Action Comm. for Environ. Educ., 1968-; Legis. Rep., N.D. Co. Supt. Assn., 1963-66; N.D. & Am. Assn. Schl. Admnstrs.; N.D. & Am. Lib. Assns.; Sec.-Treas., Trustee Sect., NDLA, 1971-73; Chmn., Pub. Affairs Comm., Dist. VII, Zonta Club, 1968-70. Publs: Contbng. Ed., The Gospel Torch, 1928-30; Ed., Almont Jubilee Hist. Book, N.D., 1956; Ed., Morton Co. Tchr's. Bull., 1959-. Recip. of hons. Address: 206 Collins Ave., Mandan, ND 58554, U.S.A. 5, 8, 15, 22, 120, 132

KLINGER, Eric, b. 23 May 1933. Professor. Educ: A.B. Harvard Univ., 1954; Ph.D., Univ. of Chgo., 1960. Appts: Rsch. Assoc., Assn. of Am. Med. Colls., 1957-60; Clin. Psychol. Trainee, Vets. Admin., 1957-60; Instr., Univ. of Wis., Madison, 1960-62; Asst Prof. thro' Prof. Psychol. & Chmn., Div. of Soc. Scis., Univ. of Minn., Morris, 1962-. Appts: Am. Psychol. Assn.; AAAS; Sigma Xi; AAUP; Midwestern & Minn. Psychol. Assns.; Assn. for Psychophysiol. Study of Sleep. Publs: Structure & Functions of Fantasy, 1971; articles in psychol. jrnls. Recip. Horace T. Morse Standard Oil Award for contbn. to undergrad. educ., 1972. Address: c/o Div. of Social Sciences, Univ. of Minnesota, Morris, MN 56267, U.S.A. 14, 30,

KLINKHAMMER, Carl, b. 22 Jan. 1903. Catholic Priest. Educ: Univs. of Innsbruck & Bonn; Dr.phil., Bonn, 1926; Priesterseminar, Cologne. Appts: Ordained, Cologne, 1929; Tchr., Erzbischöfliches Gymnasium, Opladen, 1929; Chap. (Ruhr Chap.), St. Johann, Essen-Altenesse, 1931; Preventive arrest, imprisonment on remand, prison, 2 yrs., 1933; Underground work, WWII; Chap., Münsterkirche, Bonn, 1946; Priest, Bunkerkirche St. Sakrament, Düsseldorf, 1947-. Mbrships: Cath. Film Commn., Cologne; Erzbischöfliche Okumenische Bistunskommn., Cologne; Wilhelm-Böhler-Club, Bonn. Publs: Gespaltene Christenheit, darf das sein, 1960; Versöhnte Christenheit, 1961; Kirche auf dem Weg zur Einheit, 1964; Erneuerung oder Restauration? ; Lects. & journalistic work. Hons: Title of Ruhr Chap.; German Fed. Repub. medal of hon., 1st class. Address: Heerdterlandstr. 270, 4 Düsseldorf-Heerdt, German Fed. Repub. 43.

KLUGER-ALIAV, Ruth. Author. Educ: Univ. Degree in Law & Sociol. Appts: Dir., Press & P.R., Zim Navigation Co. Ltd., Israel, 1949-71; Currently Lectr. & Author. Mbrships. incl: Pres., Fedn. of Bus. & Profl. Women; Coun. mbr., Int. P.R. Assn.; Chmn., P.R. in Israel; Exec. mbr. & Hon. Treas., Chmn., Ethics Comm., Israel Advertisers Assn.; Pioneer Women & Working Mothers in Israel, over 35 yrs. Author of The Last Escape, the story of the launching of the illegal immigration movement to rescue Jews from Hitler Europe & bring them by "the secret ships" to Palestine, breaking the British blockade. Hons: Croix de la Lorraine, France, 1947; Legion of Hon., France; Aleh Award, Govt. of Israel, 1968; Decorated by Govt. of Liberia, Ivory Coast; Masada Award; Woman of the Yr. Award, Fend. of Jewish Women in Am., 1974. Address: 81 Bograshov St., Tel Aviv, Israel.

KNAPP, Elma Virginia Bonner (Mrs. Walter L. Knapp), b. 29 Aug. 1909. Librarian. Educ: Western Reserve Univ. (Cleveland Coll.); Fenn Coll.; John Huntington Polytechnic Inst. Appts. incl: Promotion & edit. work, Warren C. Platt (Publrs., Oil trade jrnls.), 1943-53; Writer, advt., Midwest Purchasing Agent mag., 1954; Writer, newspaper publicity, radio & TV commercials, Bonne Bell, Inc., 1955; Writer, campaign material for nat. sales contest, Babee-Tenda Corp., 1956-57; Hd., Adult Basic Educ. Class Loans, Cleveland Pub. Lib., compiling & revising, List Of Adult Basic Education Books By Subject & Grade Levels, which is used throughout U.S.A. & occasionally abroad. Mbrships: ALA; Ohio Lib. Assn.; Women's Advt. Club, Cleveland; Adult Educ. Coun. of Gtr. Cleveland; Coun. on Human Rels.; Friends of Cleveland Pub. Lib., Inc.; Cleveland Mus. of Art. Address: 28413 Wolf Rd., Bay Village, OH 44140, U.S.A. 5, 138.

KNAUBER, David Lawrence, b. 27 June 1936. Teacher. Educ: B.A., Univ. of Omaha, 1958; M.Div., McCormick Theological Sem., 1961; M.A., Univ. of Colo., 1970. Appts. incl: Asst. Pastor, 1st Presby. Ch., Durango, Colo., 1961-64; Pastor, Presby. Chs., Georgetown & Idaho Springs, Colo., 1964-68; Administrative Asst. to Prof. T. Fest, 1968-70; Instr. in Communication (Area Head—1973), Community Coll. of Denver, 1971-. Mbrships: Int. Soc. for Gen. Semantics; Int. Assn. of Communication; former mbr., Kiwanis Int.; Lions Int. & Rotary Int. Address: Community

Coll. of Denver, 1200 Broadway, Denver, CO 80203, U.S.A.

KNELSON, Nelda R., b. 16 June 1915. Mental Health Supervisor. Educ: Special trng., Dixon State Schl., Ill.; Sank Valley Coll., Dixon, Ill. Appts. as Real Estate Salesman & Mental Hlth. Supvsr. Mbrships: Lee Co. & State Histl. Soc.; Past Pres., Dixon Woman's Club; Bd. mbr., 13th Dist. Fedn. of Women's Clubs, 6 yrs.; Past Pres., Lee Co. Home Bur.; Past Noble Grand, Minnie Bill Rebekah Lodge; Deleg., Rebekah State Assembly; Civil Liberty Union; Treas., Dixon Community Players; Past active mbr., PTA; Past Counselor, 4H Camp; Ldr., Girl Scouts, over 20 yrs.; Club Scout, 10 yrs.; Sec., C.R.O.P.; Organizer, Dixon Writers Group (defunct). Publs: Out of the Inkwell, 1959; Out of the Fire, 1960; Out of the Mist, 1968; Reincarnation (song), 1973; It's So Lonely Out There (song), 1973. Address: 2016 W. First St., Dixon, IL 61021, U.S.A. 138.

KNEPPER, Alvin, b. 17 Dec. 1925. Educator; Administrator; Political Scientist; Author. Educ: A.B., Ursinus Coll., 1949; M.A., Ph.D., Grad. Schl. of Arts & Scis., N.Y. Univ. Appts. incl: Adv., City Charter Revision Commn., Ithaca, N.Y., 1968-69; Commnr., Human Rights Commn., Tompkins Co., N.Y., 1970; Vice Chmn., Mayor's Educ. Comm. (Higher & Secondary), Ithaca, N.Y., 1969; Cons. to Supt., Itaca Schl. Dist., ibid, 1968-70; Asst. to Pres., Tompkins-Cortland Community Coll., SUNY, Groton, 1968-70; Adminstrv. Cons. to Chmn., Tompkins Co. Bd. Reps., 1970-; num. other admin., tchng., lecturing & pol. appts. Mbrships. incl: Int. Am., N.Y. State, New Engl. pol. sci. assns.; AAUP; Am. Acad. Pol. & Soc. Sci.; Am. Hist. Assn. Author of num. books, pamphlets & articles in fields. Hons. incl: Purple Heart; num. grants & awards for profl. servs. Address: 100 Fairview Sq., Apt. 4F, Ithaca, NY 14850, U.S.A. 6, 13, 14, 15.

KNIGHT, Ernest L., b. 19 Mar. 1932. Professor of Biology. Educ: B.S., Ala. A. & M.; M.A., N.Y. Univ., 1959; Ph.D., ibid, 1963. Appts: Tchr. of Sci., Bd. of Educ., Evergreen, Ala.; Instr., Dept. of Sci. Educ., N.Y. Univ.; Lectr. in Phys. Sci., Fashion Inst. of Technol., N.Y.C.; Lectr., Brooklyn Coll., CUNY; Assoc. Prof. of Biol., Nassau Community Coll., SUNY; Asst. Prof. of Sci. Educ., City Coll. Mbrships: Life mbr., Nat. Sci. Tchrs. Assn.; Am. Inst. of Biological Sci.; AAAS; AAUP; Am. Mus. of Natural Hist.; Bd. of Trustees, Ala. A. & M. Univ. Fndn., 1970-73; Nat. Pres., Ala. A. & M. Univ. Alumni Assn., 1970-74. Contbr. to Sci. Educ. & Nassau Review. Hons: Hons. Schlr. Award, N.Y. Univ., 1966; Given testimonial dinner for Ch. & Community Servs., 1970. Address: 2075 2nd Ave., N.Y., NY 10029, U.S.A. 14, 125, 131.

KNIGHT, Frida Frances Emma (Mrs. B.C.J.G. Knight), b. 11 Nov. 1910. Writer. Educ: Hoch's Konservatorium, Frankfurt, German Fed. Repub, 1928-29; Royal Coll. of Music, London, U.K., 1929-32. Appts. incl: Organiser of Music & Drama, Manchester Univ. Settlement, U.K., 1933-35; Extra-mural Tutor, Music & Drama, Hull Univ. Coll., 1935-36; Organiser, Cultural activities, Spanish Relief Comm., 1936-39; Asst. Ed., Free French H.Q. Info., London, U.K., 1941-43; Tchng. posts, Reading Educ. Authority, 1956-70. Author of books, translations, articles in literary & pop. jrnls. & Broadcaster, BBC Radio Stns. 3 & 4. Books incl: Dawn Escape, 1942; The Strange Case Of Thomas Walker, 1956; University Rebel—The Life Of William Frend, 1970; Beethoven & The Age Of Revolution, 1973. Translations incl: The Mud Hut Dwellers, 1952;

Mitrea Cocor, 1953; The Lost Letter, 1956. Address: 28 Park Parade, Cambridge CB5 8AL, U.K. 3, 43.

KNIGHT, George Wilson, b. 19 Sept. 1897. Educ: B.A., St. Edmund Hall, Oxford Univ., 1923; M.A., ibid, 1931. Appts: Master, Dean Close Schl., Cheltenham, 1925-31; Chancellors' Prof. of Engl., Trinity Coll., Univ. of Toronto, Canada, 1931-40; Master, Stowe Schl., 1941-46; Reader, English Lit., Leeds Univ., 1946-55; Prof., Engl. Lit., ibid, 1955-62; Emeritus Prof., 1962-. Mbrships: Fellow, Royal Soc. of Lit. & Int. Soc. of Arts & Letters, Kreuzlingen, Switzerland; V.P., Spiritualist Assn. of Gt. Britain; Pres., Devonshire Assn., 1971; Engl. Assn. W. Country Writers' Assn. Publs: The Wheel of Fire; The Imperial Theme; The Crown of Life; Shakespearean Religion; The Mutual Flame; Shakespearian Production; The Shakespearian Tempest; The Starlit Dome; Neglected Powers; The Last of the Incas (drama); Gold-Dust (poetry); studies of Byron &, John Cowper Powys. Hons: Fellow, St. Edmund Hall, 1966; Litt.D., Univ. of Sheffield, 1967; D.Litt., Univ. of Exeter, 1968; C.B.E., 1968. Address: Caroline House, Streatham Rise, Exeter EX4 4PE, U.K. 1, 11, 34, 35. 129.

KNIGHT, Gilfred Norman, b. 12 Sept. 1891. Barrister-at-Law; Civil Servant; Indexer. Educ: M.A., Balliol Coll., Oxford Univ., 1918. Tancred Schol., Lincoln's Inn, called to Bar by Lincoln's Inn. Appts. incl: Serv. WWI to Staff, Judge Advocate-Gen., 1918-19; wounded 1915; Asst. Sec., W. India Comm., 1919-26, 1938-39; Sec., W. Indian & Atlantic Grp., Brit. Empire Exhib., 1923-24; Sec., Co. of London Territorial Army Assn., 1927; Guardian of Heir Apparent of Rampur, India, 1931-32; Civil Serv., 1940-56, Censorship, 1940-42, War Off., 1942-56. Mbrships. incl: Fndr., 1st Sec., 1957, Chmn., 1962, Pres., 1969-, Soc. of Indexers; Queen's Engl. Soc.; Civil Serv. Club; W. India Comm. Publs. incl: The Pocket History of Freemasonry, 1953, & The Freemason's Pocket Reference Book, 1955 (w. F.L. Pick); Training in Indexing, 1969; The Pocket Cyclopaedia of Freemasonry (w. F.L. Smyth), 1974; King, Queen & Knight: A Chess Anthology (w. W.F. Guy), 1974; Indexing, The Art of, 1974-75. Num. contbns. to periodicals. Hons: Wheatley Gold Medal for outstanding index of 1967. Address: Scio House, Portsmouth Rd., London SW15 3TD, U.K. 1.

KNIGHT, H. Ralph, b. 13 Jan. 1895, d. 22 May 1972. Author; Editor. Educ: Grad., Union Coll., Schenectady, N.Y., U.S.A., 1917; Pulitzer Schl. of Jrnlsm., Columbia Univ., N.Y.C., 1918. Appts: Ed., Glens Falls Post-Star, N.Y., 1923-44; Assoc. Ed., Saturday Evening Post, 1944-61. Mbr., Psi Upsilon. Publs: The Burr-Hamilton Duel, 1968; Learning to Talk to the Wrold Beyond: An Introduction to the Joy of Immortality, 1969; Num. short stories, articles, & humorous essays in Saturday Evening Post. Address: c/o Mrs. D.W. Knight, 456 Rockland Ave., Merion Station, PA., U.S.A. 30.

KNIGHT, Harold Murray, b. 13 Aug. 1919. Banker. Educ: Master of Commerce, Univ. of Melbourne, 1961. Appts: Commonwealth Bank of Aust., 1936-40, 1946-55; Statistics Div., Int. Monetary Fund, 1955-59; Asst. Chief, Statistics Dept., ibid, 1957-59; Reserve Bank of Aust., 1960-; Dpty. Gov. & Dpty. Chmn. of Bd., 1968-. Served w. Aust. Imperial Forces & Royal Aust. Navy, 1940-46. Publs: Introducción al Análisis Monetario, 1959; G.L. Wood Mem. Lecture, 1971. Recip., Disting. Serv. Cross. Address: 39 Hull Rd., Beecroft, N.S.W., Australia. 2000.

KNIGHT, Harry W., b. 20 Apr. 1909. Management Consultant; Investment Banker. Educ: A.B., Amherst Coll., Mass., 1931; Harvard Grad. Schl. of Bus. Admin., 1931-32; M.A., Northwestern Univ., Evanston, Ill., 1940. Appts. incl: V.P., Booz, Allen & Hamilton, N.Y.C., 1945-66; Chmn., Knight, Gladieux & Smith, N.Y.C., 1966-72; Pres., Hillsboro Assocs., N.Y.C., 1973-; Dir., Stott Capital Dev. Corp., Burlington Inds., Inc., INA Life Ins. Co. of N.Y., Waldorf Astoria Hotel, Foxboro Co., Shearson Funds & Agricon Int. Ltd. Mbrships. incl: Trustee, Comm. for Econ. Dev., Amherst Coll., Hampshire Coll. & Hudson Inst.; Gov., UN Assn.; Univ. Club of N.Y.; Delta Kappa Epsilon; For. Policy Assn. Recip., medal for eminent serv., Amherst Coll. Address: Hillsboro Assocs., Inc., 640 Fifth Ave., N.Y., NY 10019, U.S.A. 2.

KNIGHT, James Allen, b. 20 Oct. 1918. Professor of Psychiatry; University Administrator. Educ: A.B., Wofford Coll., 1941; B.D., Duke Univ., 1944; M.D., Vanderbilt Univ. Schl. of Med., 1952; M.P.H., Tulane Univ. Schl. of Med., 1962. Appts. incl: Chap., Lt. Sr. Grade, USN, 1944-46; Intern., Grady Mem. Hosp., 1952-53, Asst. Res., Duke Hosp., 1953-54, Res. in Psych., Tulane Univ. Serv. of Charity Hosp., 1955-58; Asst. Prof., Baylor Univ. Coll. of Med., 1958-61, Asst. Dean, 1960-61; Assoc. Prof., Schls. Med. & Pub. Hlth., Tulane Univ., 1961-63, Profl., Schls. Med., Pub. Hlth. & Tropical Med., 1964-, Assoc. Dean, Schl. of Med., 1964-. Mbr., var. profl. orgs. Publs. incl: Conscience & Guilt, 1969; Medical Student: Doctor in the Making, 1973. Active contbr., profl. jrnls. Address: School of Medicine, Tulane University, 1430 Tulane Ave., New Orleans, LA 70112, U.S.A. 2.

KNIGHT, Pauline Eleanor Tetrick (Mrs. Clarance A. Knight), b. 4 Oct. 1913. Nursing Educator. Educ: Nursing Dip., A.A., Huntington Mem. Hosp., Pasadena, Calif., 1948; B.S., Univ. of Wash., Seattle, 1951; M.A., Columbia Univ., 1959; Psych. Nursing, Univ. of Calif., San Fran., 1964-65. Appts: Charge Nurse, Huntington Mem. Hosp., Pasadena, Calif., 1948-49; Staff Nurse, P.H.N., King Co. Hlth. Dept., Seattle, Wash., 1951-58; Supvsr., P.H.N., Pierce Co. Hlth. Dept., Tacoma, 1959-61; San Mateo Co. Hlth. Dept., Calif., 1961-64; Asst. Prof., Chico, 1973-. Mbrships. incl: Am. Nurses Assn.; Calif. Nurses Assn.; Am. Pub. Hlth. Assn. Writer & contbr., courses in nursing. Recip., Continuing Educ. Grant, UCLA, 1970-72. Address: 10914 Wheeler Drive Rt. A, Lower Lake, CA 95457, U.S.A. 5, 9.

KNIPPA, Louis John, b. 24 Nov. 1912. Regional Production Manager. Educ: B.S., Univ. of Houston, Tex., 1951. Appts: Constrn. Supt., Brown & Root, Houston, 1933-50; Asst. V.P., Phillips Inds., Dayton, Ohio, 1964-65; Pres., Am. Roofing Mfg. Co., Miamisburg, 1965-68; Plant Mgr., Philip Carey Co., Cinn., 1950-64; V.P., Mfg., ibid, 1968; Regional Prod. Mgr., Celotex Corp., 1968-. Served, USNR, 1943-44. Address: 2020 W. Alexander Bell Road, Dayton, OH 45459, U.S.A. 16.

KNIZIA, Klaus Günther Friedrich Heinrich, b. 18 June 1927. Company Director. Educ: Dr.Ing., Tech. Univ., Karlsruhe, German Fed. Repub., 1959. Appts: Bd. of Dirs., Vereinigte Elektrizitätswerke Westfalen AG, Dortmund; Mng. Dir., Gemeinschaftswerk Hattingen GmbH, Hattingen; Mng. Dir., Hochtemperatur-Kernkraftwerk GmbH, Uentrop; Mng. Dir., Euroäische Gesellschaft zur Auswertung von Erfahrungen bei Planung, Bau & Betrieb von Hochtemperatur-reaktoren GmbH, Uentrop; Chmn., Bd. of Dirs., VGB

Techn. Vereinigung der Grosskraftwerksbetreiber e.V., Essen; Bd. of Dirs., Rheinisch-Westfalen Technischer Uberwachungsverein, Essen; Chmn., Bd. of Dirs., L. & C. Steinmüller GmbH & Steinmüller Verwaltungs-GmbH, Gummersbach. Mbrships: Tech. Advsry. Bd., Allianz Versicherungs-AG, Munich; Chmn. of Bd., Gesellschaft der Freunde, Univ. Dortmund; Comm. mbr., German Nat. Comm., World Energy Conf., Düsseldorf. Author, Die Thermodynamik des Dampfkraftprozesses, 1966. Address: Ostwall 51, 46 Dortmund, German Fed. Repub. 43, 92.

KNOBLOCH, Rudolf, b. 11 May 1905. Professor. Educ: M.U.Dr., Charles Univ., Prague, Czechoslovakia, 1928; D.Sc., 1960. Appts. incl: Asst., Dept. of Ophthalmol., Charles Univ., Prague, 1930-36; Hd., Dept. of Ophthalmol., Jihlava Dist. Hosp., 1936-38; Pizeň Dist. Hosp., 1938-42; '45-46; Deprived of position by Nazi authorities, 1942-45; Hd., Ophthalmic Dept., Med. Fac., Pizeň Br., Charles Univ., Prague, 1946. Pres., Czechoslovak Ophthalmol. Assn. Author of books & papers in field. Hons: Gold Badge, 15th Anniversary of Fndn. of Socialist Acad.; Medal in memory of Jan Hus, Charles Univ., 1965; Czechoslovak Mil. Medal, 1st Degree, 1947; Order of Work, 1966; Gold Mem. Medal, Charles Univ., 1971. Address: Moskevská tr. c. 4, Plzeň, CSSR.

KNOWLTON, William Allen, b. 19 June 1920. Lieutenant General, U.S. Army. Educ: B.A., U.S. Mil. Acad., West Point, 1943; M.A., Columbia Univ., 1957; Nat. War Coll., Wash. D.C., 1959-60. Appts: w. 87th Cavalry Recon. Squad., 7th Armored Div., Europe, WW II; Army Gen. Staff., 1947-49; SHAPE Staff, 1951-54; Assoc. Prof. of Soc. Scis., U.S. Mil. Acad., 1955-58; Army Attache, Tunisia, 1961-63; Staff Off & Asst. Div. Cmdr., Vietnam, 1966-68; Sec. of Army Staff, 1968-70; Supt. of U.S. Mil. Acad., 1970-74; Chief of Staff, U.S. European Cmnd., 1974-. Mbrships. incl: Coun. on For. Rels.; Am. Acad. of Pol. & Soc. Scis.; Acad. of Pol. Sci.; Assn. of U.S. Army; Airborne Assn.; Nat. Coun., Boy Scouts of Am.; Past Mbr., Exec. Coun., Soc. of Colonial Wars, etc. Contbr. to Ency. Americana, Reader's Digest & others. Hons: Recip. many mil. decorations inclng: DSM; Silver Star (2 OLC); DFC; Vietnamese Nat. Order 5th Class; Viet. Gallantry Cross w/Palm also Geo. Wash. Medal, Freedoms Fndn., 1957-58 & Hon. LL.D., Univ. of Akron, 1972. Address: Chief of Staff, U.S. European Cmnd., APO 09128, U.S. Army, U.S.A. 2, 6, 14.

KNOX, David Broughton, b. 26 Dec. 1916. Church of England Minister. Educ: B.A., Univ. of Sydney, N.S.W., Australia; A.L.C.D., Coll. of Divinity, St. John's Hall, London, U.K.; B.D., M.Th., Univ. of London; Univ. of Cambridge; D.Phil., Univ. of Oxford. Appts: Chap., R.N.V.R., 1943-47; Lectr., Moore Theol. Coll., Newton, N.S.W., Australia, 1947-50; Tutor, Wycliffe Hall, Oxford, U.K., 1951-53; Vice Prin., Moore Coll., Newton, Australia, 1954-58; Prin., ibid, 1959-. Publs: Doctrine of Faith in the Reign of King Henry VIII; The Thirty-Nine Articles; The Doctrine of the Lord's Supper in Early English Reformed Writings; Justification by Faith. Address: Moore Coll., Carillon Ave., Newtown, N.S.W., Australia 2042. 3, 23, 128.

KNOX, Nancy (Therese H.) b. 16 Apr. 1923. Business Executive; Marketing & Design Consultant. Educ: St. Xaners Acad., Providence, R.I., 1941; Regis Coll., Weston, Mass., 1941-42; Bryant Coll., Providence, 1942. Appts: Asst. Fashion Dir., I. Miller Shoes, N.Y.C., 1953-55; Ptnr., Clark Knox (o'seas)

Fashion Consultants, 1956-59; Co-Fndr., Sec. of Corp., Jags Unlimited Inc., 1959-63; Co-Fndr., Pres. of Corp., Renegades, 1963-73; w. Consulting European & Argentine firms for U.S.A. export, 1973-. Mbrships: Shoe Women's Exec. V.P., 1967-68; The Fashion Grp.; Mgmt. Comm., Garland Coll. Hons. incl: Coty Award, 1970; Creative Menswear Award, 1969; Caswell Massey Award, 1959. Address: 2 Beekman Pl., N.Y., NY 10022, U.S.A. 5, 132.

KNOX, Robert Buick, b. 10 Oct. 1918. Professor of Ecclesiastical History. Educ: M.A., B.D., Queen's Univ., Belfast; Presby. Coll. Belfast; B.A., Ph.D., London Univ. Appts: Presby. Min., Ballydown & Katesbridge Chs., Ireland, 1942-57; Prof., Ecclesiastical Hist., Theol. Coll., Aberystwyth, 1958-68; Prof., Westminster Coll., Cambridge Univ., 1968-. Mbrship: Ecclesiastical Hist. Soc. Publs: James Ussher, Archbishop of Armagh; Voices from the Past; Wales & 'Y Goleuad'. Address: Westminster Coll., Cambridge, U.K.

KNUDSEN, (Rev.) Carl, b. 6 Dec. 1897. Minister of Religion. educ: A.B., Mont. Wesleyan (now Rocky Mtn.) Coll., 1921; M.Div., Boston Univ. Schl. of Theol., 1924. Appts: served, WW I, II; Pastor, Ctrl. Square Congl. Ch., Bridgwater, Mass., 1927-31; Ch. of the Pilgrimage, Plymouth, Mass., 1931-46; Assoc. Prof. of Sociol., then Hd. of Dept., 1946-49; 1st full-time Chap., N.Y. State Hosps. (appointed by Gov. Harriman to Middletown State Hosp.), 1954-62. Mbrships. incl: Moderator, Pilgrim Assn. of Congl. Chs., 1934-62; Sec., Comm. to Establish Coun. of Soc. Action, Congl. Chs.; 1934; Chap., 4200 USN students, Harvard Univ., 1944-46; Chap. of Married Veterans of Columbia Univ. & families, 1946-49; Ctr. for Study of Democratic Instns., Santa Barbara, Calif.; Retd. Offs. Assn. Publs: Renewed by the Spirit, 1930; Num. articles in religious publs. Address: 1190 Amherst St., Buffalo, NY 14216, U.S.A.

KNUDSEN, Knud-Endre, b. 29 June 1921. Consulting Engineer. Educ: Civil Engr., Norwegian Inst. of Technol., Trondheim, Norway, 1946; Ph.D., Lehigh Univ., Bethlehem, Pa., U.S.A., 1949. Appts. incl: Mng. Dir., Norconsult, Ethiopia, 1956-59; Expert, NATO Int. Staff, Paris, France, 1959-61; Mng. Dir., Norconsult A.S., Oslo, Norway, 1961-69; Chmn., Bd. of Dirs., ibid, 1969-71; Pvte. Prac., Dr. K.E. Knudsen, Cons. Engr., 1969-; Mng. Dir., Saga Petroleum A/S & Co., Oslo, 1973-. Mbrships. incl: Norwegian Acad. of Tech. Scis.; Norwegian Assn. of Cons. Engrs.; Norwegian Soc. of Profl. Engrs.; Chmn., Rsch. Comm. for the Norwegian Continental Shelf, Norwegian Coun. for Sci. & Indl. Rsch., 1969-. Author of articles & papers in field. Recip., Royal Norwegian Order of St. Olav, Kt., 1st Class, 1970. Address: Maries vei 20, 1322 Høvik, Norway. 134.

KNYVETT, Alan Ferrers, b. 3 Feb. 1925. Medical Practitioner. Educ: M.B., B.S., Univ. of Qld., Australia, 1947. Appts. incl: Res. Med. Off., Royal Brisbane Hosp., 1947-48; Med. Registrar, ibid, 1949; Tchng. Registrar, Univ. of Qld., 1950-51; House Physn., Hammersmith Hosp. & Postgrad. Med. Schl., London, U.K., 1952; Med. Registrar, Hosp. for Tropical Diseases, London, 1953-54; Specialist Physn., Royal Brisbane Hosp., Australia, 1954-; Dpty. Gen. Med. Supt., ibid, 1954-67; Gen. Med. Supt., ibid, 1967-; Dpty. Chmn., Qld. Radium Inst.; Mbr. of Coun., Qld. Inst. of Med. Rsch.; Mbr., Fac. of Med., Univ. of Qld. Mbrships: Fellow, Royal Australasian Coll. of Physns.; Fellow, Australian Coll. of Med. Administrators, Exec. Comm. Mbr., Mbr. of

Coun., Mbr. of Bd. of Censors; Royal Coll. of Physns., London; Australian Med. Assn., Qld. Br. Coun.; Gastro-Enterological Soc. of Aust.; Gastro-Enterological Soc. of Qld., former Coun. Mbr., Sec. & Pres. Contbr. to profl. jrnls. Hons: D'Arcy Cowan Prize for rsch. in Thoracic Med., 1967. Address: Royal Brisbane Hosp., Brisbane Base Hosps. P.O., Qld., Australia 4029. 23.

KOARK, Hans Joachim, b. 4 Aug. 1921. University Professor; Geologist. Educ: Ph.D., Innsbruck, Austria, 1949; Phil. lic., Uppsala, Sweden, 1952. Appts: Rsch. Asst., Uppsala Univ., 1950-56; Lectr., ibid, 1956-63; Sr. Sci., Swedish Natural Sci. Rsch. Coun., 1963-71; Assoc. Prof., ibid, 1971-. Mbrships: Soc. de Géol. de Appliquée aux Gites Minéraux; Soc. of Econ. Geols.; Am. & London, U.K. Mineral. Socs.; Deutsche Mineral. Gesellschaft; Geol. Vereinigung; Gesellschaft für Geol. Wissenschaften der D.D.R.; Schweizerische Mineral.-Petrographische Gesellschaft; Geol. Föreningen (Stockholm); Geol. Säuskapet i Finland. Publs: Monograph Series on Mineral Deposits (Ed.); Mineralium Deposita (co-Ed.); contbr. to num. profl. publs. Address: Geol. Inst., Univ. of Uppsala, Box 555, S-751 22 Uppsala 1, Sweden. 43, 134.

KOCH, Carol Ann (Jackson), b. 25 Mar. 1938. Housewife. Educ: Chandler Schl. for Women; Var. Courses in Educ. for dyslexia & learning disabilities. Appts: Dept. Sec., Lincoln Lab., MIT & MITRE Corp.,–1960; Voluntary Wkr. w. learning disability children, Okaloosa Co. Schl. System, Fla; Initiated Head-Start Prog., ibid. Mbrships: League of Women Voters (Bd. Mbr. Chelmsford, Mass. 1964-66, Okaloosa Co. 1967-71, Pres., ibid 1970-71, 1st V.P. 1973]; Beta Sigma Phi (V.P. Delta Chapt. 1972-73); Boy Scouts of Am. (Scout Ldrs. Wife Cert., Den Mother 1971-72); Ldr., Girl Scouts of Am., 1972-73. Publs: Ecology Preservation for the State of Florida. Hons: Schl. Bd., Okaloosa Co., Fla.; Scouters Wife Award, 1971, 1972; Girl of Yr., Beta Sigma Phi, 1972-73. Address: 325 Yacht Club Drive, Fort Walton Beach, FL 32548, U.S.A. 76, 125.

KOCH, Helen L., b. 26 Aug. 1895. Psychologist. Educ: Ph.B., Univ. of Chgo., 1918; Ph.D., ibid. Appts: Instr.-Prof., Univ. of Tex., 1921-29; Assoc. Prof.-Prof., Univ. of Chgo., 1929-60; Lectr., Univ. of Southern Calif., summer, 1962; Lectr., Univs. of Frankfurt, Marburg & Würzburg, Germany. Fellow, Am. Psychol. Assn., 1923. Mbrships: Phi Beta Kappa; Sigma Xi; A Fndr., Delta Kappa Gamma. Publs: Seven Monographs & Papers, 1928-62; Twins & Twin Relations, 1966. Hons: G. Stanley Hall Award, Div. of Genetic Psychol., Am. Psychol. Assn., 1960; Int. Achievement Award, Delta Kappa Gamma, 1974. Address: 1130 S. Michigan Ave., Apt. 1501, Chgo., IL 60605, U.S.A.

KOCHANT, Helen Evelyne Hoffmann (Mrs. William Kochant), b. 31 Dec. 1929. Educator. Educ: B.S., Fordham Univ., 1951; M.S., ibid, 1956; M.A., Columbia Univ., 1960; Ed.D., Tchrs. Coll., ibid, 1968. Appts: Elementary Schl. Tchr., Villa Maria Acad., N.Y.C., 1951-55; N.Y. Pub. Schl. System, 1955-60; Instr., Educ., Tchrs. Coll., Columbia Univ., N.Y.C., 1961-63; Asst. Prof. Prof. of Elem. Educ., SUNY, New Paltz, N.Y., 1963-. Mbrships: incl: Nat. Coun. Tchrs. of Engl.; Int. Reading Assn.; Nat. Assn. Educ. of Young Children; ALA; N.Y. State Tchrs Assn.; Alpha Chapt., Delta Kappa Gamma; Pi Lambda Theta; Kappa Delta Pi. Co-author of The World of Language, book 2, 1970, Book E, 1973; Co-ed., Individualizing Learning. Author of bookreview of C. Georgiou's Children and Their Literature, 1970.

Address: P.O. Box 482, New Paltz, NY 12561, U.S.A. 5, 138, 141.

KOCHER, Friedrich W. A., b. 7 Sept., 1904. Painter; Collector; Restorer. Educ: Acad. of Karlsruhe, Germany. Appts: Free-lance Artist, Builder & designer of homes; Restorer of old master paintings for pvte. colls. Mbrships: life mbr., Reichsverband der bildende Kuenste, Germany; Calif. Art Club, U.S.A.; V.P., San Vernando Guild; Charter bd. mbr. & life mbr., Am. Inst. of Fine arts; Painters & Sculptors club of L.A. (Pres.); Pres., Am. Artist of the W., 1964-. Hons. incl: The Sovereign Order of Alfred the Great, The Alfredian Order, 1969; Chevalier Grand Cross, 1969; doct. of fine arts, 1969; doct. of humanities, 1969. Address: P.O. Box 19869, L.A., CA 90019, U.S.A.

KOCH-OLSEN, Ib, b. 19 Apr. 1914. Author. Educ: M.A., Copenhagen Univ., Denmark, 1938; Broadcasting & TV courses, 1942, 1957. Appts: Tchr., Roskilde H.S., 1938-42; Sec., Wkrs. Educl. Assn., 1942-43; Prog. Sec., Danish Broadcasting System, 1943-46; Mng. Dir., Dansk Kulturfilm, & Prod. i/c., Film Comm., Danish Govt., 1946-57; Dir., Roskilde H.S., 1957-62; Literary activities, 1962; Advsr., Cultural TV Sect., Danish Broadcasting System, 1969. Mbrships. incl: Past V.P. & Pres., Students' Assn.; Ctrl. Bd. & Gen. Coun., Nat. Soc. for Preservation of Natural Amenities, 1964; Fndr., Pres., Roskilde Art Gall., 1965; Pres., Dansk Kulturfilm, 1970. Publs. incl: Denmark's History of Civilization I-II, 1968; I flugst går tiden 1871 (Flight of the Time, From Paris Commune to the Danish International), 1971. Address: Sct. Ibsvej 11, 4000 Roskilde, Denmark. 134.

KOCK, (Lars Anders) Wolfram, b. 29 Aug. 1913. Assistant Professor of Medicine. Educ: Med. lic., 1941; Med. dr., 1952. Appts: House-surg., several hosps., Stockholm, Sweden, 1940-51; Asst. Prof., med. histl. rsch., Karolinska Inst., Stockholm, 1953-; Med.Dir., Swedish Philips Co., 1954-; Dir., Mus. of Med. Hist., Stockholm, 1955-; Sr. Med. Off., Defence Med. Admin. Serv., 1957-. Mbrships. incl: Hon. Sec., Soc. Int. d'Histoire de la médicine, 1964-70; Hon. Sec., Sect. for Med. Hist., Swedish Soc. for Med. Scis., 1947-; Corres. mbr., Int. Acad. of Hist. of Med. Publs. incl: Olof af Acrel, 1967; Svenska läkare som vitterlekare, 1970; Ed.-in-chief, Medicinhistorisk arsbok, 1953-, & Nordisk medicin-historisk arsbok, 1968-; About 200 papers in gen. med. Recip. of hons. Address: Mäster Samuelsgatan 4, 111 44 Stockholm, Sweden. 43, 133.

KOCKELMANS, Joseph John, b. 1 Dec. 1923. Professor of Philosophy; Author. Educ: Bacc., Lic., Ph.D., Inst. of Medieval Philosophy, Angelico, Rome, 1951; postdoctoral studies in Venlo, Leyden & Louvain, 1951-63. Appts. incl: Prof. of Philos., New Schl. for Soc. rsch., N.Y., 1964-65, Univ. of Pitts., 1965-68, Pa. State Univ., 1968-; Dir. Interdisciplinary Grad. Prog. in Humanities, ibid, 1972-. Mbrships. incl: Am. Philosophical Assn.; AAAS; AAUP. Num. publs. incl: Author of Edmund Husserl's Phenomenological Psychology, 1967, The World in Science & Philosophy, 1968; Ed. of Phenomenology & Natural Science (w. Th. Kisiel), 1970, On Heidegger & Language, 1972, Contemporary European Ethics, 1972; Co-ed., Man & World., int. philosophical jrnl, & Dutch Heidegger Lib. Recip. of Gold Medal, Teyler's Tweede Genootschap, Haarlem, 1958. Address: 903 Willard Cir., State Coll., Pa 16801, U.S.A. 2, 6.

KOCSIS-SZUCS, Ferenc, b. 8 Oct. 1930. College Professor. Educ: Dip., Agric. Tech., Budapest, Hungary, 1951; Dip., Innsbruck Tech., Innsbruck, Austria, 1957; M.S., Univ. of Bologna, Italy, 1960; Sc.D., ibid, 1961; Johns Hopkins Univ., Balt., Md., 1962; Ph.D. cand., Univ. of Pitts., U.S.A. Appts: Instr., Balt. Jr. Coll., Md., 1961-62; Asst. Prof., Georgetown Coll., Y., 1962-64 & State Coll., Slippery Rock, Pa., 1964-66; Vis. Rsch. Assoc., Univ. of Pitts., 1966-67; Prof. & Chmn., ibid, 1967-72; Prof., 1972-. Mbr. of many profl. orgs. inclng: Charter Mbr., Int. Assn. of Geochem. & Cosmochem. & Assn. of Mathematical Geol. Publs: Climatic Changes & Landscape Development in Moraine State Pk., Pa., 1972-; Pollution Problems & Abatement in the Slippery Rock Watershed, Pa., 1971; contbr. to profl. publs. Recip., Gold Medal, Acad. of Sci. of Rome, 1970 & other hons. Address: 318 Englewood Ave., New Castle, PA 16105, U.S.A. 14.

KODAMANOGLU, Mehmet Nuri, b. 16 Aug. 1923. Educator. Educ: Univ. of Istanbul & High Coll. of Educ., Istanbul, Turkey. Appts: Maths. Tchr., H.S., 1945-49; Insp. Gen., Min. of Educ., 1952-56; Mbr., Higher Coun. of Educ., ibid, 1956-60; Lectr., Gazi Inst. of Educ. & High Coll. of Educ., Ankara, 1960-61; Advsr., Turkish State Planning Org., 1962; Permanent Under-Sec., Min. of Educ., 1963-65; M.P., Dpty. for Yozgat & Nigde, Turkish Parliament, 1965-73; Min. of Energy & Natural Resources, 1972-73. Mbrships: Pres., Assn. of Grads. of High Colls. of Educ., Turkey; Inst. of Admin. Scis., Fac. of Pol. Scis., Ankara Univ. Publs: Translator, Principles of the New Education, 1954; Author, Education in Turkey, 1964; Turkish National Education & Its Financial Problems, 1964. Address: c/o Hilmi I. Kodaman, M.D., 225 Park Lane, Douglaston, NY 11363, U.S.A.

KOENIGSBERGER, Helmut Georg, b. 24 Oct. 1918. Historian. Educ: B.A., Gonville & Caius Coll., Cambridge, U.K., 1940; M.A., 1944; Ph.D., 1949. Appts. incl: Lectr., Econ. Hist., Queens Univ., Belfast, 1948-51; Sr. Lectr., Econ. Hist., Univ. of Manchester, 1951-60; Prof., Mod. Hist., Univ. of Nottingham, 1960-66; Prof., Early Mod. European Hist., Cornell Univ., U.S.A., 1966-73; Prof., Hist., Univ. of London, Kings Coll., U.K., 1973-. Fellow, Royal Hist. Soc. Mbrships. incl: Sec.-Gen., Int. Commn. for Hist. of Rep. & Parliamentary Instns.; Corres., Real Acad. de la Hist., Madrid. Publs. incl: The Pratice of Empire, 1951, 69; Estates & Revolutions, 1971; The Habsburgs & Europe 1516-1660, 1971; Ed. Luther: A Profile, 1973. Recip., Guggenheim Fellowship, 1971. Address: Dept. of Hist., Kings Coll., Strand, London, WC2R 2LS, U.K. 1.

KOESTLER, Arthur, b. 5 Sept. 1905. Author. Educ: Univ. of Vienna, Austria. Appts. incl; Special Corres., The Times, (London), Palestine, 1945; Special Corres., Manchester Guardian & New York Herald Tribune, 1948; Vis. Chubb Fellow, Yale Univ., New Haven, Conn, U.S.A., 1950; Fellow, Ctr. for Advanced Study in Behavioural Scis., Stanford Calif., 1964-65. Fellow, Royal Soc. Lit. Mbr., Inst. Patentees & Inventors, Publs. incl; The Act of Creation, 1964; The Ghost in the Machine, 1967; Drinkers of Infinity, 1968; Beyond Reductionism, (co—ed.), 1969; The Case of the Midwife Toad, 1971; The Roots of Conscience, 1972. Hons: Sonning Prize, Univ. of Copenhagen, Denmark, 1968; LL.D., Queen's Univ., Kingston, Ont., Canada, 1968. Address: c/o A.D.Peters, 10, Buckingham St., London W.C.2, U.K. 1, 2, 131.

KOH, Hesung Chun, b. 3 July 1929. Sociologist. Educ: B.S., Dickinson Coll., Carlisle, Pa., 1951; M.A., Boston Univ., 1953; Ph.D., ibid, 1959. Appts. incl: Asst. Harvard-Yenching Lib., 1952-57; Cataloger, Peabody Mus. Lib. of Arch. & Ethnol., Harvard Univ., 1957-59; Rsch. Assoc., Human Rels. Area Files, Yale Univ., 1961-; Vis. Lectr., Yale Law Schl., 1963-66; Dir. Info. Systems, Assn. for Asian Studies, 1969-71; currently Dir., Systems & Dev., & E. Asian Area Rsch., Assoc. Sec., Human Rels. Area Files, Inc., & Rsch. Assoc., Yale Univ. Mbr., Fellow & Off., var. acad. & profl. orgs. Many publs., sociol., comp. rsch. & info. systems. Recip., acad. fellowships, rsch. & study grants. Address: Human Rels. Area Files, 2054 Yale Stn., New Haven, CT 06515, U.S.A.

KOH, Kwang Lim, b. 20 Oct. 1920. Professor of Political Science. Educ: LL.B., Law Schl., Imperial Univ., Keijo (Seoul), Korea, 1945; M.A., Rutgers Univ., New Brunswick, N.J., 1950; Ph.D., ibid, 1953; LL.M., Harvard Law Schl., 1952; S.J.D., ibid, 1955; LL.B., Boston Coll. Law Schl., 1961. Appts. incl: Lectr., Boston Univ. Law Schl., 1953-60; Korean Envoy Extraordinary & Min. Plenipotentiary to UN & U.S.A., 1960; Korean Deleg. to UN Gen. Assembly, 1960-61; Lectr., Yale Law Schl., 1961-64; Assoc. Prof., Pol. Sci., Hofstra Univ., L.I., N.Y., 1962-66; Prof., Pol. Sci. & Dir., Ctr. for Area & Interdisciplinary Studies, Ctrl. Conn. State Coll., New Britain, 1966-. Mbrships. incl: Am. Soc. of Int. Law; Am. Pol. Sci. Assn.; Assn. for Asian Studies. Publs: Chinese Legal History, 1969; In Korean: British Government, 1970; French Government, 1971; American Review, I & II, 1972-73; papers & articles. Address: Ctr. for Area & Interdisciplinary Studies, Central Connecticut State Coll., New Britain, CT 06050, U.S.A. 6, 14.

KOHL, Karl P., b. 6 July 1896. University Professor. Educ: Univ. of Erlangen, Germany, 1918-21; State exam. in Maths. & Physics, 1921-22; Promoted to Dr., 1923; Inaugurated, for Physics, 1927. Appts: Pvte. Tutor, Physics, & Univ. Lectr., Erlangen, 1927-39; Sci. Cons., T.K.D., Nürnberg, Pintsch A.G. Berlin, 1929-38; Lab. Hd., P.T.R., Berlin, 1934-38; Sci. Cons., Tobis-Film A.G., 1939; Meteorologist, A.O.K. Berlin, 1939-44; Sci. Cons., Telefunken Berlin, 1945; Rsch., 1945-. Mbrships: German Phys. Assn., 1922-; Phys.-Med. Soc., Erlangen, 1922-; Advsr., Heinrich Hertz Assn., Berlin, 1931; German Assn. for Philos., 1950-; European Phys. Soc., 1971-. Author of Grundlagenforschung, I 1970, II 1970, III 1972, IV 1974, V 1974. Address: Herzogenauracher Str. 3, 8510 Fürth-Vach, German Fed. Repub. 43.

KOHLER, Hans Georg, b. 25 Apr. 1921. Judge; Author. Educ: Dip. in Law, Law Fac., Univ. of Vienna, Austria; Univ. of World's Commerce, Vienna; Univ. of Agric., Vienna. Appts: Prac. in Law Cts., Karlsruhe, German Fed. Repub., 1947-48; Official-in-Charge, Int. Pvte. Law, Dept. of Justice, Vienna, Austria, 1951-52, 1954; Publr., Schriftenreihe für internationales Recht, 1961-; Collaborator in Juris-Classeur de Droit Comparé, Paris, France. Publs: Erbschaften im Ausland, 1952, 2nd edit. 1962; Das internationale Erbrecht in Lehre, Gesetzgebung & Staatsvertrag, 1953; Internationales Privatrecht, 1959, 3rd edit. 1966; Internationales Kindschaftsrecht, 1964; Beglaubigungsverträge, 1973; Nachlass-Vormundschaft-Unterhalt (Multi- & bilaterale Abkommen), 1973; Ausländisches Testamentsrecht, 1974. Hons. Title of Professor, Fed. Pres. of Repub. of Austria,

1973. Address: Invalidenstrasse 13/46, 1030 Vienna III., Austria. 43.

KOHN, Walter, b. 8 Feb. 1909. Librarian. Educ: Law, Univ. of Berlin, Germany, 1928-31; Law, Univ. of Frankfurt am Main, 1931-33; M.S.L.S., Univ. of Southern Calif., L.A., U.S.A., 1955. Appts: Hd., Catalog Dept., Coalinga Dist. Lib., Calif., 1955-61; Ref. Libn., Stanislaus State Coll., 1961-62; Catalog Libn., Lib., Calif. State Univ., Chico, 1962-. Mbrships: Calif. Lib. Assn.; Calif. Lib. Week Comm., 1957; Calif. Tchrs. Assn.; 1st Hon. Life Mbr., Glendale Lapidary & Gem. Soc.; Golden Empire Gem. & Mineral Soc., Chico, Calif.; Fndng. Pres., Coalinga Rockhound Soc., 1955; Pres.'s Int. Rels. Comm. Chico State Coll., 1967. Contbr. of articles to Gems & Minerals Mag., Lapidary Jrnl. & Westways Mag. Author of newspaper articles, book reviews & translator of articles from German & French into Engl. Address: c/o Calif. State Univ. Library, Chico, CA 95926, U.S.A. 42.

KOHN, Zillah L. (Mrs. Sylvan H. Kohn), b. 2 Feb. 1897. Teacher; Magazine Editor. Educ: Grad., Rice Univ. (formerly Rice Inst.), 1917; Yale Coll. Appts. incl: Engl. Tchr., Ctrl. H.S., Houston, Tex., 1917-19; Registrar, Coll. Councillor, South East H.S., Houston, Tex., 1917-21; Ed., Mrs. G.I. (publ., Women's Org. of Jewish Welfare Bd. for Jewish families of soldiers serving overseas), 1945-51; Ed., Outlook, (nat. quarterly jrnl., Women's League for Conservative Judaism), 1958-70; Columnist, ibid, Idea Exchange, 1970-. Mbrships: V.P., PTA; Jewish Welfare Bd., Women's Org., Nat. Bd.; Women's League for Conservative Judaism, Exec., Nat., State & Local Bds., Br. V.P., Recording Sec., Corres. Sec. & Treas.; Jewish Book Coun. of Am.; Synagogue Sisterhood. Address: 259 Reynolds Ter. Apt. A6, Orange, NJ 07050, U.S.A. 5, 55.

KOHRS, El Dean Vere, b. 4 May 1934. Psychologist. Educ: B.A., Augustana Coll., 1955; M.A., Univ. of Mo. at Kan. City, 1958; Ph.D., N.Y. Univ., 1960. Appts. incl: Cons., Psychol., Lab. of Psychol. Studies Stevens Inst. of Technol., Hoboken, N.J., 1963-65; Counseling Admnstr., Kilmer Job Corps. Ctr., Edison, ibid, 1965-66; Dir., Children's Bur., Passaic, 1966-69; Psychol. & Mgr., Campbell Co. Off., Northern Wyo. Mental Hlth. Ctr., 1969-72; Clin. Dir., Ctrl. Wyo. Counseling Ctr., 1972-. Mbrships. Pres., Wyo Psychol. Assn.; Chmn., Wyo. Bd. of Psychol. Examiners; Am. & Rocky Mtn. Psychol. Assns.; Am. Personel & Guid. Assn.; AAAS. Nat. Vocational Guid. Assn.; Sigma Xi. Author of articles in profl. jrnls. inclg. Behavioral approaches to problem drinkers in a Rural Community, 1973; Social Consequences of Technological Change and Energy Development, 1973; Social Consequences of Boom Growth in Wyoming, 1974; & of Chapt. on "Lower Class Adolescents" in book of readings. Address: 5080 Yesness Ln., Casper, WY 82601, U.S.A. 15, 126.

KOIKE, Tsuneo, b. 7 Feb. 1901. Professional Engineer. Educ: B.S., Univ. of Hawaii, 1924. Appts: Funchino Surveying & Engrng., 1924-26; Hutchinson Sugar Co. Ltd., 1926-69; Co. of Hawaii, Dept. Pub. Works, 1969; Instr. in Civil engrng. (surveying), Univ. of Hawaii, Hilo Coll., 1969-71; Pvte. Profl. Prac. & Cons., 1969-. Mbrships. incl: Engrng. Assn. of Hawaii; Co. of Hawaii Bd. of Water Supply, 1955-69; Am. Water Works Assn.; Fellow, Am. Soc. Civil Engrs.; Nat. & Hawaii Socs. Profl. Engrs.; Am. Congress on Surveying & Mapping (Fellow); Pres., Naalchu Schl. PTA, 1932-33; Naalehu Boy Scouts (comm.,

1932-65); Pres., Naalehu Hongwanji Mission, 1934-35. Hons. incl: Merit Badge, Counselor Award, Boy Scouts of Am.; Award, State Buddhist Layman's Assn., 1969. Address: 39 Mauna Loa St., Hilo, HI 96720, U.S.A. 9, 16.

KOIVISTOINEN, Eino, b. 10 May 1907. Master Mariner (Sea-Captain), retired; Author. Educ: Commercial Schl.; Inst. of Navigation; 2nd Mate's Exam., 1932; Chief Mate's Exam., 1933; Mstr.'s Exam., 1938; Navy Reserve Offs., Schl., 1941. Appts. incl: Seaman, Finnish, Swedish & British ships, 1924-31; 1st Off., submarine mothership (Sr. Lt.), 1941-44; 3rd, 2nd & Chief Mate & Capt., Finnish ships, 1932-45; Insp. Soc. Servs. for Seamen, Bd. of Navigation, 1946-55; Hd. of Navigation Dist., Kotka, 1955-70. Author of 15 boks. Publs. incl: Herring Fishing Off The Coast Of Iceland, 1948; The Conqueror Of The South Sea, 1953; An Angel Without Wings, 1962; The Blue Sea & Other Stories, 1967; The Old Tramp, 1973; 2 plays, Silken Sails, 1960 & The Shadows, 1964; num. articles. Hons. incl: sev. WWII medals; Kt. White Rose of Finland, 1969. Address: Kuusisenkatu 1, 48100 Kotka 10, Finland. 43, 90, 134.

KOKINOPOULOS, Felix Eftychios, b. 15 Oct. 1908. Retired Professor. Educ: Grad., Civil Engrng., Nat. Tech. Univ., Athens, Greece, 1929; Postgrad., Tech. H.S., Munich, Germany, 1936-38; Dozent, Nat. Tech. Univ., Athens, 1944. Appts. incl: Asst. Prof. of Structural Analysis, Nat. Tech. Univ., Athens, 1944-56; Hd., Inst. of Testing Mats., ibid, 1956-58; Prof. of Structural Analysis & Hd., Inst. of Structural Analysis & Aseismic Rsch., 1958-73; Dean, Civil Engrng. Dept., 1962-65; Rector, 1967-69. Mbrships. incl: Tech. Chmbr. of Greece; Am. Soc. of Civil Engrs.; European Assn. for Earthquake Engrng.; Hd., Greek Mission to Germany, 1947-53. Publs. incl: Buckling of Thin Plates, 1944; The Secret of Light, 1955; Introduction to Atomic Physics, 1957; Elasticity Problems, & Photoelastic Investigations on Models, 1961-63; Structural Analysis, Vol. I, 1968; Num. contbns. to symposia & int. confs. Hons: Decoration awarded by King Paul, 1959; Decoration awarded by King Constantine, 1966. Address: Ferron St. 28, Athens (104), Greece. 43.

KOLET, Ezra, b. 6 Jan. 1914. Joint Secretary, Government of India (Retired). Appts: Employed in Govt. of India serv. for 34 yrs. as: Under-Sec., Min. of Finance; Dpty. Sec., ibid; 1st Treas. & Fndr. Mbr., Indian Govt. Ctrl. Soc. Welfare Bd.; Advsr., Finance Comms., Univs. of Delhi, Benares & Aligarh; Chmn., Gen. Ins. Assn. of India; Chief Controller of Chartering & Jt. Sec., Govt. of India. Mbrships: Fndr. & Pres., Jewish Welfare Assn., New Delhi; Fndr. & Past-Pres., Benevolent Fund for Low Paid Govt. Employees; Past-Pres., Govt. of India Ctrl. Secretariat Serv. Assn.; Bnei Brith Lodge, Bombay; Fndr. Mbr. & Sec., Delhi Symph. Orch. Publs: Love, the Basis of All Religions; Contbr. of Music Criticisms to Indian Press. Author, Brochures for Concerts of Delhi Symph. Orch. Hons: Govt. of India Arbitrator, 1973. Address: 74 Babar Rd., New Delhi, India. 55.

KOLIN, Sacha, b. 9 May 1911. Painter in Watercolor & Mixed Media; Sculptor. Educ: B.S., Realschule, Vienna, Austria, 1929; art studies, Wiener Kunstgewerbeschule & Acad. of Fine Arts, Vienna, 1930-32; pupil w. Naoum Aronson, stone carver, Paris, France, 1933-34. Solo exhibs. incl: Permanent Exhib. Decorative Arts & Crafts, Rockefeller Ctr., N.Y.C., 1937; Coeval Gall., 1955, Condon Reilly Gall., 1959, 1960, E. Hampton Gall., 1965; Everson Mus. of

Art, Syracuse, N.Y., 1973. Grp. Exhibs. incl: Smithsonian Instn., Wash. D.C.; Salon des Realtées Nouvelles, Paris, France; Contemporary Art Bldg., 1940 World's Fair, N.Y.C. Permanent Collects. incl: Fordham Univ. Art Collect., N.Y.C.; Nat. Collect. Find Arts, Wash. D.C.; Johnson Mus. of Cornell Univ. Address: 1651 2nd Ave., N.Y., NY 10028, U.S.A.

KOLLAR, Veronica Marie, b. 4 Jan. 1918. Teacher. Educ: B.S. in Ed., Calif. State Coll., Pa., 1946; M.Ed., Univ. of Pitts., Pa., 1948; Univ. of Ala., Tuscaloosa, 1962; Univ. of W.Va., Morgantown, 1964. Univ. of Md., College Park, 1968; Pa. State Univ., 1971; Nova Univ., Ft. Lauderdale, Fla., 1972. Appts: Elem. Tchr. & Prin., South Union Township, Uniontown, Pa., 1937-60; Tchr., South Union Jr. & Sr. H.S., ibid, 1960-62; Grade 5 Lab. Schl., Slippery Rock State Coll., 1962-63; T.V. Tchng., ibid, 1963-64, Supervision of Student Tchrs., 1964-. Mbrships. incl: Corres. Sec., Uniontown Coll. Club; Delta Kappa Gamma; Local Pres., Pa. State Educ. Assn.; State Treas., Assn. for Supervision & Curric. Dev.; Regional Sec. Treas., Assn. for Tchr. Educators. Address: Student Tchng. Dept., Slippery Rock State Coll., Slippery Rock, PA 16057, U.S.A. 5, 6, 22, 132.

KOLLBRUNNER, C.F., b. 15 May 1907. Consulting Engineer. Educ: Dip. Civil Engrng. Swiss Fed. Inst. of Technol., Zurich, 1931; D. Tech. Sci., ibid, 1934. Appts: Centre d'Etudes & de Recherches Géotechniques, Paris, France, 1936; Brunner U. Co., Zurich, Switzerland, 1937-43; Gen. Mgr., Conrad Zschokke Steel Constructions, Doettingen, ibid, 1943-68; Cons. Engr., Zollikon, ibid, 1969-. Mbrships. incl: Swiss Engrs. & Archts. Assn.; Int. Assn. for Bridge & Structural Engrng.; Rotary Club, Zurich; Hon. Mbr., Tech. Commn., Swiss Steel Construction Assn, 1966. Author of over 530 papers & books on Underground engrng., steel construction, stability, torsion, mil. engrng. Hons: Senator, Vienna, Austria, 1958; Doct. Tech. Sci., Lausanne Univ., 1967. Address: Witellikerstrasse 50, CH-8702, Zollikon, Switzerland.

KOLLER, Anne Hesse, b. 19 Aug. 1931. Marketing & Merchandising Executive. Educ: City Coll., N.Y.C., 1954-56; B.A., Hunter Coll., N.Y.C., 1970. Appts. incl: Asst. Merchandising Ed., Look Mag., N.Y.C., 1955-57; V.P., Roger Wade Prods. Inc., N.Y.C., 1957-59; Pres. & Exec. Prod., Rossmore Prod. & Selling Methods Inc., N.Y.C., 1959-69; Dir. of Advt. & Sales Promotion, GAF-Lenco Photo Products Corp., N.Y.C., 1969-71, Synchronex Corp., N.Y.C., 1971-72; Pres. & Ed.-in-Chief, Union Leisure Corp., N.Y.C., 1971-72; Pres. & Exec. Prod., A.H. Koller Assocs. Inc., N.Y.C., 1972-. Mbrships: County Comm., Repub. Party, Yonkers, N.Y., 1951-57; Sr. Girl Scout Ldr., Bronxville, N.Y., 1963-68. Writer & prod., var. films & live prods., bus. promotion. Address: 54 Rossmore Ave., Bronxville P.O., Yonkers, NY 10708, U.S.A.

KOLLMANN, Franz Friedrich Paul, b. 15 Oct. 1906. Professor. Educ: Dipl.-Ing., Dr.-Ing., Tech. Univ., Munich; Dr.-Ing., Tech. Univ., Berlin. Appts. incl: Prof. & Dir. of Mech. Technol. Dept., German Instn. for Forestry & for. products rsch., Eberswalde, 1934-45; Prof., Univ. of Hamburg, Dir., Fed. Inst. for Forestry & for. prod. rsch., Reinbek, 1949-54; Prof., Univ. of Munich, Dir., Inst. for Wood Rsch. & Wood Technol., Munich, 1954-72; Cons., FAO & German Govt. Mbrships: Royal Swedish Acad. Tech. Sci.; Finnish Acad. Tech. Sci.;

Italian Acad. Sci. of Forestry; Forest Prods. Rsch. Soc.; Int. Acad. Wood Sci.; Hon. Pres., Deutsche Gesellschaft fur Holzforschung; Hon. mbr., Osterreich Gesellschaft fur Holzforschung; Past Pres., Rotary Club, Munchen Mitte. Publs. incl: Holzspanwerkstoffe, 1966; Principles of Wood Science & Technology, Vol. 1, Solid Wood (with W.A. Cote), 1968. Hons. incl: Kt., Royal Swedish Cross, 1960; Gt. Cross of Fed. Order of Merit, 1970. Address: Isolde Kurzstrasse 24, D8 Munich 81, German Fed. Repub. 92.

KØLMARK, Henry Gunnar, b. 30 May 1914. Biochemist; Geneticist. Educ: Mag. scient., Univ. of Copenhagen, Denmark, 1950; Phil. dr., Univ. of Uppsala, Sweden, 1969. Appts. incl: Dept. of Genetics, Royal Agricl. Coll. of Denmark, 1948-49; Inst. of Genetics, Univ. of Copenhagen, 1950-52 & 1954-57; Osborn Botanical Lab., Yale Univ., U.S.A., 1952-54; Oak Ridge Nat. Lab., Biol. Div., U.S.A., 1957-60; Med. Rsch. Coun., Mutagenesis Rsch. Unit, Edinburgh Univ., U.K., 1961-63; Hartley Botanical Labs., Liverpool Univ., U.K., 1963-64; Inst. of Physiological Bot., Uppsala Univ., 1964-69; Dept. of Genetics & Plant Breeding, Royal Agricl. Coll. of Sweden, Uppsala, 1969-. Mbrships: Nordic Genetics Soc.; Swedish Microbiological Soc.; Societas Physiologiae Plantarum Scandinavica. Biochemical & Microbial gentics rsch. publd. in profl. jrnls. Address: Dept. of Genetics & Plant Breeding, Royal Agricultural Coll. of Sweden, S-750 07 Uppsala 7, Sweden. 134.

KOLODY, John Theodore, b. 19 June 1920. Hospital Administrator. Educ: B.S., Ind. Univ. of Pa., 1942; M.S., Columbia Univ., N.Y.C., 1947. Appts. incl: Lectr., Schl. of Hosp. Admin., St. Johns Univ. & Admin. Res., St. Barnabas Hosp., N.Y., 1946-47; Admin. Asst.-Asst. Dir.-Assoc. Dir., ibid; Currently, Exec. Dir., 1967-. Mbrships. incl: Am. Coll. Hosp. Admnstrs.; AAAS; Am. Pub. Hlth. Assn.; Am. Hosp. Assn.; Gerontol. Soc.; Sec.-Treas., Hosp. Adminstrs. Club, N.Y.; Coun. of Hosp. Admnstrs., N.Y.C.; Admin. Conf. Grp., N.Y.; Bronx Hosp. Admnstrs. Assn.; Bd. Dirs., Bronx Chapt., Nat. Multiple Sclerosis Soc.; Bd. Dirs., Bronx Chmbr. of Comm.; Bd. Dirs., Bronx & Nat. Chapts., Nat. Conf. Christians & Jews; Bronx Red Cross Serv. Chapt.; Bronx Soc. for Prevention of Cruelty to Children; Comm. on Govt. Rels., Hosp. Assn. of N.Y. State; Comm. of Govt. Rels., Gtr., N.Y. Hosp. Assn.; Profl. Servs. Comm., ibid; Long Term. Comm. Recip., 5 Battle Stars, Atlantic & Pacific Theatres, WWII. Address: St. Barnabas Hosp., 183rd St. & 3rd Ave., Bronx, NY 10457, U.S.A.

KONARZ-KONARZEWSKA, Irene, b. 11 Aug. 1931. Chemical Engineer; Artist. Educ: Acad. of Fine Arts, Warsaw, Poland, 1948-55; Fac. of Chem., 1952-56. Appts: Inst. of Chem., Warsaw. 1-Man Expositions: Saint Lô; Romorantin, France. Grp. Exhibs: Belgium; Denmark; Monaco; UNESCO; N.Y.; Japan. Mbr., Int. Arts Guild, Monte Carlo. Creative Works incl: Series of about 50 landscapes; Flowers, Portraits, & Folklore; Num. easel-paintings in oil, tempera, pencil; Ch. Polychromes. Recip., num. dips. & hons. Address: 7 Rue Murillo, Paris 8, France.

KONARZ-KONARZEWSKI, Stanislaw, b. 22 Jan. 1914. Artist; Painter; Sculptor; Historian. Educ: Acad. of Fine Arts, Munich, Germany & Cracovie, Poland. Appts: Prof., Inst. of Plastic Arts; Fine Arts Expert, Tribunals. 1-man Exhibs: Saint Lô, France, 1973; Tours, 1974. Grp. Exhibs: Poland; Belgium; Denmark; Monoco; Spain; France; U.S.A. Mbrships: Union of Polish Artists &

Painters; Int. Arts Guild, Monaco. Artistic works incl: (illuminated miniatures) Ben Aciba; Mère de la vie; Messie Franck; Prière; Beau Josephe; Rencontre; Prince Boleslav et les Juifs; Statue de Calisia; Kasimir le Grand et les Juifs; Marchands de Dantzig; Trouvaille de Moïse; (cycles) Martirologie de la Nation Polonaise; Martirologie des Juifs Polonais; Histoire de la Pologne. Hons. incl: 3 gold medals, Poland; 2 Grands Prix; var. dips. & hon. mentions. Address: 7 Rue Murillo, 75008 Paris, France.

KONDO, Yoji, b. 26 May 1933. Astrophysicist. Educ: B.A., Tokyo Univ. of For. Studies, 1958; M.S., Univ. of Pa., U.S.A., 1963; Ph.D., ibid, 1965. Appts. incl: Nat. Acad. of Scis.-Nat. Rsch. Coun. Rsch. Assoc., NASA Goddard Space Flight Ctr., 1965-68; Staff Astron., NASA Manned Spacecraft Ctr., 1968-69; Chief, Astrophys. Sect., ibid, 1969-; Adjunct Mbr., Grad. Fac. in Phys., Univ. of Houston, 1968-; Adjunct Assoc. Prof.-Prof., Phys. & Astron., Univ. of Okla., 1971-. Mbrships: Am. Astron. Soc.; Chmn., Comm. for Astron. Observations from Outside Earth's Atmosphere, Int. Astron. Union; Fellow, AAAS. Contbr. articles to profl. publs., inclng: On the Mass Determination of the Collapsed Objects in Close Binaries—Applications to Black-holes & Neutron Stars, Astrophys. Space Sci. Hons: Pawling Fellow & Harrison Schlr., Univ. of Pa., 1963-65. Address: c/o Astrophysics Sect., NASA Johnson Space Ctr., Houston, TX 77058, U.S.A. 7, 14.

KONDONASSIS, Alexander J., b. 8 Feb. 1928. Professor of Economics. Educ: A.B., DePauw Univ., Greencastle, Ind., U.S.A., 1952; M.A., Ind. Univ., Bloomington, 1953; Ph.D., ibid, 1961. Appts: Lectr., Ind. Univ., 1956-58; Asst. Prof., Univ. of Okla., Norman, 1958-62; Assoc. Prof., ibid, 1962-64; Prof., 1964-70; Chmn., Dept. of Econs., 1961-71; Fulbright Prof., Schl. of Econs. & Bus., Athens, Greece, 1965-66; David Ross Boyd Prof., Econs., Univ. of Okla., 1970-. Mbrships: Am. Econ. Assn.; Southern Econ. Assn.; Southwestern Soc. Sci. Assn.; AAUP; Lions Int.; Beta Gamma Sigma; Omicron Delta Epsilon. Publs: The EEC & Her Association with Israel, Spain, Turkey, & Greece, 1972; Mediterranean Europe & the EEC (co-author), 1974; Num. articles in econ. jrnls. & contbns. to bokks. Recip., Regents Award for Superior Tchng., Univ. of Okla., 1964. Address: 307 W. Brooks, Dept. of Economics, University of Oklahoma, Norman, OK 73069, U.S.A. 2, 7.

KONDRATYEV, Kirill, b. 14 June 1920. Professor of Physics. Educ: Grad. & Post-grad., Leningrad Univ., U.S.S.R.; Dr.Honoris Causa, Budapest Univ., 1969. Appts. incl: Scientific Rsch. worker & Lectr., Physics Dept., Leningrad Univ., 1946-; Hd., Chair of Atmospheric Phys., Dept. of Phys., ibid & collaborated as Chief, Dept. of Radiation Studies, Main Geophys. Observ., 1958-. Mbrships: Soviet Soc. of Astronomers & Geodesists; Soviet Soc. of Naturlaists; Hon. Mbr., Royal Meteorological Soc., U.K.; For. Hon. Mbr. Am. Acad. of Arts & Scis.; Deutsche Adademie der Naturforscher Leopoldina. Publs. incl: The Thermal Regime Of The Upper Atmospheric Layers, 1960; Meteorological Satellites, 1964; Actinometry, 1965; Radiation In The Atmosphere, 1969; Thermal Sounding Of The Atmosphere From Satellites, 1970; Space Methods For Terrestrial Studies, 1971; Satellite Climatology, 1971; Urban Settlements & Planetary Climate, 1972; Meteorology Of Mars, 1972; Investigation Of Natural Environment From Manned Orbital Stations (co-author & Ed.), 1972; Remote Sensing Of Minor Gaseous & Aerosol Components Of The Atmosphere From Space, 1974. Hons. incl: Gold Medal, World Meteorological Org., 1967; WMO Lecture & Monograph, 1971. Address: Leningrad Univ., Leningrad, U.S.S.R.

KONG, Jin Au, b. 27 Dec. 1942. College Professor. Educ: B.S., Taiwan Univ., 1962; M.S., Chiao Tung Univ., 1965; Ph.D., Syracuse Univ., 1968. Appts: Postdoctoral Rsch. Engr., Syracuse Univ., 1968-69; Vinton Hayes Postdoctoral Fellow of Engrng. & Asst. Prof. of Elec. Engrng., MIT, 1969-71; Asst. Prof. of Elec. Engrng., MIT, 1971-73; Assoc. Prof. of Elec. Engrng., ibid, 1973-. Mbrships: IEEE; Am. Phys. Soc.; Optical Soc. of Am.; Am. Geophys. Union; URSI; Phi Tau Phi; AAAS; AAUP; Sigma Xi; N.Y. Acad. of Sci. Technical publs. appear in sci. & engrng. jrnls. such as: Proceedings of IEEE; Jrnl. of Geophys. Rsch.; Jrnl. of Optical Soc. of Am.; Jrnl. of Acoustical Soc. of Am.; Jrnl. of Applied Physics, etc. Address: 36-357, MIT, Cambridge, MA 02139, U.S.A. 14, 130.

KONRICK, Vera Bishop (Mrs. Rudolph Joseph Konrick), b. 4 Mar. 1900. Poet & Artist. Author of Moon Flame (poems), 1953 & var. poems in newspapers, mags. & such anthols. as Eros, 1939, Conquerors of Tomorrow, 1947, This Shall Endure, 1955, With No Secret Meaning, 1957, To Each His Song, 1958, The Minds Create, 1961, Fire, Sleet & Candlelight, 1961, Flame Annual, 1964, 1965, Nat. Poetry Day Anthol., 1965, From Sea to Sea in Song, 1966, Best Broadcast Poetry, 1969, Moon Age Poets, 1970; Histl. articles in such Pen Women anthols. as Louisiana Leaders & Vignettes of Louisiana. Appts. incl: Treas., 1954-58, Histn., Archivist, 1958-, Nat. League of Pen Women, Crescent City; La. Chmn., Nat. Poetry Day Comm., 1956-63; Chmn., W. N.Y. Nat. Poetry Day, 1963-; Asst. Dir., World Poetry Day, 1966- (secured N.Y. State Poetry Day Proclamation from Gov., 1970-73); Life Mbr. & V.P., Avalon World Arts Acad., San Angelo, Tex. Mbr., Am. Poetry League, etc. Hons. incl: Silver Medal & Dip. of Merit, Centro Studie Scambi Int., Rome, Italy, 1968; Dr. of Lit. Leadership, the Philippines, 1968. Address: c/o Golden Atom Publs., P.O. Box 1101, Rochester, NY 14603, U.S.A. 5, 6.

KONUK, Erdoğan, b. 24 July 1926. Medical Doctor. Educ: Grad., Schl. of Med., Istanbul Univ., Turkey, 1951; Post-grad. study, specialist in ENT & cosmetic facial surg., Univ. of Paris, France. Appts: Chief Asst., Schl. of Med., Istanbul Univ., 1955-61; Asst. Prof., ibid, 1961-66; Hd. of own pvte. clin., 1966-; Attng. Surg., Nat. Theatre of Istanbul, 1966-. Mbrships: Turkish Med. Soc.; Turkish ENT Soc.; Turkish Plastic Surg. Soc.; Chief, Admin. Comm., Cagdas Tip Dergisi, mag. of hlth., Istanbul. Publs: Num. papers & booklets on Ear, Nose & Throat & Cosmetic Facial Surg. Address: Büyükdere Cad. 26/4, Mecidiyeköy, Istanbul, Turkey. 43.

KOONTS, J. Calvin, b. 19 Sept. 1924. College Professor. Educ: A.B., Catawba Coll., 1945; M.A. in Sociol., Geo. Peabody Coll., Nashville, Tenn., 1949; Ph.D., Educ., ibid, 1958; postdoctoral study in psychol., Harvard Univ., 1960. Appts. incl: Asst. to Dir. of Student Tchng., Geo. Peabody Coll., 1951-52; Prof. of Educ. & Psychol., Erskine Coll., S.C., 1949-51; Hd. of the Dept. of Educ., 1953-; Tchr. of Adult Educ., Abbeville Co. Community Ctr., 1955; Tchr. of the Univ. of S.C. Ext. courses, 1955-56. Mbrships. incl: Sec.-Treas., Salisbury, N.C. Unit of the N.C. Educ. Assn., 1946-47; Official Liaison Rep., S.C. to Am. Assn. of Colls. for Tchr. Educ.,

1964 (chosen by this body to conduct study tour of educl. insts. in Pakistan); Fndr., S.C. Assn. for Student Tchng.; Pres., ibdi, 1955-56; Fellow, Am. Acad. of Poets; Nat. Del. Assembly of Assn. of Tchr. Educators, rep. S.C. Publs: (song) I'm Living in a Dream, 1947; (coll. verse) Straws in the Wind, 1968; var. contbns. to anthols. Recip. var. hons. Address: Erskine Coll., Due West, SC, U.S.A. 7, 15, 84.

KOOT, Ton, b. 1 Mar. 1907. Adviser on Cultural History; Author; Lecturer. Educ: Govt. Official Courses; Rockefeller Fndn. Student. Appts. incl: Curator, Amsterdam Histl. Mus.; Gen. Sec., Rijksmus., Amsterdam, 1945-70; Gov., Muyden Castle, 1948-72; Advsr., Cultural Affairs, Min. of Culture & Dir., State Mus. Het Loo, Apeldoorn, 1970-72. Mbrships. incl: Pres., Cultural Soc. Circle, Muyden; Rotary Club, Amsterdam S.Soc. for Preservation of Netherlands Monuments; Bd., Amsterdam Dept., Fndn. Européene de la Culture. Publs. incl: B-P. de Chief, 1937; En nu—Nederland in!, 1948; Amsterdam as it is, 1948; The Spell of the Netherlands, 1952; Rijksmuseum, 1958; Dat was de Muden, 1966; Help! Ze verpesten ons Land, 1973; On the Canals of Amsterdam, 1973. Columnist, Dutch newspapers. Hons. incl: Off. d'Académie, France, 1954; Recip., Orders of Chivalry, Sweden, Netherlands, Belgiu& Norway, 1955-64; Recip., Jamboree Medal, Rembrandt Medal. Address: Muzenhof, Stadionweg 148, Amsterdam, Netherlands.

KÖPECZI, Béla, b. 16 Sept. 1921. Association Official. Appts. incl: Prof., Eötvös Larand Univ., Budapest, Hungary, 1966-; Vice Rector, ibid, 1967-70; Dpty. Sec. Gen., Hungarian Acad. of Scis., 1970-71; Gen. Sec., ibid, 1972-. Mbrships. incl: Presidium, Soc. for Dissemination of Knowledge; Pres., Lit. Comm. Publs. incl: Socialist Realism, 1970; Reform or Revolution, 1970; Idea History Literature, 1972; Revolté ou révolutionnaire? Sándor Petofi 1823-73, 1973. Hons. incl: Medal of Hungarian Peoples Repub., Bronze, 1952; Eminent Wkr. ofEduc., 1970; Bugarth Paul Medal, 1972. Address: Hungarian Acad. of Scis., 1051 Budapest, V. Roosevelt tér 9, Hungary.

KOPS, Bernard, b. 28 Nov. 1926. Writer. Educ: Elem. schl. until 13 yrs. old. Poetry Publs: Poems, 1955; Poems & Songs, 1958; An Anemone for Antigone, 1959; Erica I Want to Read You Something, 1967; For the Record, 1971. Novels: Awake for Mourning, 1958; Yes From No Man's Land, 1965; The Dissent of Dominic Shapiro, 1966; By the Waters of Whitechapel, 1969; The Passionate Past of Gloria Gaye, 1971; Settle Down Simon Katz, 1973; Partners, (in preparation). Play Publs: The Hamlet of Stepney Green, 1960; The Dream of Peter Mann, 1960; Four Plays, 1964; The Boy Who Wouldn't Play Jesus, 1965. Autobiography: The World Is a Wedding, 1963. Recip., Bursary for Drama, Arts Coun. of Gt. Britain, 1957. Address: Flat 1, 35 Canfield Gdns., London, N.W.6., U.K.

KÖRBLER, Juraj, b. 2 Oct. 1900. Physician; Oncologist. Educ: M.D., Med. Fac., Univ. of Freiburg im Breisgau, Germany, 1923; special studies, Lyon, Paris, Stockholm, Prague. Appts: Chief, Inst. Radium Therapy, Zagreb, Yugoslavia, 1931; Docent, Med. Fac., Univ. of Zagreb, 1936, Prof., 1943, Lectr. Med. Phys., 1943; Chief, Cancer Rsch. Div., Inst. Med. Rsch., Yugoslav Acad., Zagreb, 1953; Chief, Oncological Inst., Zagreb, 1954. Mbrships. incl: Croatian Cancer Soc.; Pres., ibid, 1940; Croatian Soc. Med. Hist. Pres., ibid, 1949; Soc. Scientific Thought: Pres., ibid, 1955. Publs.

incl: Maligni tumori, 1929; Rak, 1934, 2nd edit., 1973; Klinische Krebsprobleme, 1940; Iatrophysika, 1957; Der Spinnerinnenkreba, 1962; Gesischte der Krebskrankheit, 1973. Over 200 other publs. on cancer, sci. jrnls. Recip., Gold Medal for Cancer Rsch., Rome, 1968. Address: Gajeva 35, 41000 Zagreb, Yugoslavia. 50, 129, 131.

KORBONSKI, Stefan, b. 2 Mar. 1903. Lawyer. Educ: Magister of Law, Univ. of Poznan, Poland. Appts: Chmn., Polish Peasant Party, Bialystok Dist., 1939; Mbr., 1st Wartime Underground Govt. of Poland, 1940-41; Chief, Gen. Resistance of Poland, 1941-44; Sec. of Interior, Underground Govt., 1944; Acting Dpty. Prime Min., 1945; Mbr., Polish Parliament, 1947; Chmn., Assembly of Captive European Nations, var. yrs. 1958-74. Mbrships: Int. Pen Club in Exile; Am. Coun. of Polish Cultural Clubs; Polish Juridical Soc. in U.S.A.; Polish Home Army Soldiers Circle; Polish Underground Movement Study Trust; Polish Assn. of Former Pol. Prisoners; Polish Inst. of Arts & Scis. Publs. incl: Warsaw in Exile, 1966; Between the Hammer & the Anvil (in Polish), 1969; Author of articles in jrnls. Recip., Alfred Jurzykowski Fndn, Inc. Award in field of lit., 1973. Address: 2238 Decatur Pl. N.W. Apt. 1, Wash. DC 20008, U.S.A. 3, 30.

KORESHI, (His Excellency) Sami Ullah Mujahid, b. 6 Jan. 1926. Career Diplomat. Educ: B.A., Delhi Univ., India, 1944; M.A. (Philos.), ibid, 1946; M.A. (Int. Rels.), Fletcher Schl. Law & Diplomacy, Boston, Mass., U.S.A.; Ph.D., Ottawa Univ., Canada. Appts: Lectr. Islamia Coll., Julludur; Govt. Coll., Hyderabad, Sind, Pakistan; Magistrate, Multan; Joined For. Serv., 1949, serving in var. Pakistan missions abroad; Under-Sec., For. Min.; Dir.-Dir-Gen. ibid; High Commnr. to Nigeria, W. Africa & Ambassador to Niger, Dahomey & Cameroon, 1969-72; Ambassador to Lebanon & Cyprus, 1972-. Mbrships. incl: Sec., Muslim Students Assn., Delhi Province Chief Cmndr., All-India Muslim Students Nat. Guard; Jt. Sec., U.P. Muslim Students Assn.; Sec., Pakistan For. Serv. Assn. Lectured to Nigerian Inst. Int. Law on The Idealogy of Pakistan: A historical interpretation of Muslim Nationalism in the Sub-Continent, 1970. Address: 2699 Lyons St., Ras Beirut, Beirut, Lebanon.

KORINGER, Franz, b. 19 June 1921. Music School Director. Educ: Steiermärkisches Landeskonservatorium, Graz, Austria; Leaving exam., 1950; Holiday course, Darmstadt, 1963 & 1964. Appts: Lectr., Hist. of Music, Volkshochschule, Mannheim, Germany, 1950; Dir., Expositur Arnfel, Bezirksmusikschule, Leibnitz, Austria, 1951-55; Dir., Music Schl., Leibnitz, 1955-; Tchr., Landesmusikschule, Graz, 1968-; Choir-master, Steirischer Sängerbund & Leibnitz Choral Soc. 1846. Mbrships: Osterreichischer Komponistenbund; Gesellschaft der Autoren, Komponisten & Musikverleger; Die Künstlergilde; Arbeitsgemeinschaft der Musikerzieher Osterreichs. Composer of works for choir & orchestra & of chamber music. Recip. of hons. inclng. Austrian Medal of hon. for Art & Sci., 1972. Address: Im Mitterfeld 14, A-8430 Leibnitz, Austria. 43.

KORMONDY, Edward J., b. 10 June 1926. Educator. Educ: B.S., Biol., Tusculum Coll., 1950; M.S., 1951, Ph.D., Zool., 1955, Univ. of Mich. Appts: Instr., Zool., Univ. of Mich., 1955-57; Curator of Insects, Univ. of Mich. Mus. of Zool., 1956-57; Asst. Prof., Zool., 1957-63, Assoc. Prof., Biol., 1963-67, Oberlin Coll.; Acting Assoc. Dean., Coll. of Arts & Scis., ibid, 1966-67; Prof., Biol., 1967-69; Dir.,

Commn. on Undergrad. Educ. in Biol. Scis., & Dir., Off. of Biol. Educ., Am. Inst. of Biol. Scis., 1968-71; Fac. Mbr., Evergreen State Coll., Wash., 1971-; V.P. & Provost, ibid, 1973-. Mbrships: Exec. Comm., Nat. Assn. of Biol. Tchrs.; Ecol. Soc. of Am.; Am. Soc. of Limnol. & Oceanog.; Soc. of Sigma Xi; AAAS. Publs: Introduction to Genetics, A Program for Self-Instruction, 1964; Readings in Ecology, 1965; Concepts of Ecology, 1969, also Finnish, Spanish, Portuguese edits.; Co-ed., 3 books, contbr. to profl. jrnls. Hons: Nat. Insts. of Hlth. Post-doct. Fellowship, 1963-64. Address: Evergreen State Coll., Olympia, WA 98505, U.S.A. 2, 14.

KORN, David, b. 27 Apr. 1934. Professor. Educ: B.S., Georgetown Univ., 1958; M.S., ibid, 1960; Ph.D., 1964. Appts: Rsch. Assoc., Machine Transl., Georgetown Univ., 1957-63; Asst. Prof., Coll. of Wm. & Mary, Norfolk, Va., 1958-61; Prof. & Chmn., Dept. of German & Russian Studies, Chmn., Humanities Div., Howard Univ., 1961-; Dir., Lang. Labs., ibid, 1968; Assoc. Dir., Peace Corps Trng. Prog. for Guyana, 1966; Assoc. Res. Dir., Coun. for Int. Exchange, 1968; Sr. Cons. to Asst. Sec. of Educ., HEW, Sr. Assoc., Nat. Inst. of Educ., HEW, 1973-. Mbrships: Am. Assn. Tchrs. of Slavic & E. European Langs.; MLA; Gov., Mbr. Exec. Comm., V.P., Schl. of Langs. & Linguistics, Georgetown Univ. Alumni Assn., 1969-72; Bd. of Dirs., Jewish Soc. Serv. Agcy., 1969-74; Bd. of Dirs., on Exec. Comm., Jewish Community Coun. of Gtr. Wash., 1971-73. Contbr. num. publs. to field inclng: The GAT Machine Dictionary (co-author), 1959; The Russian Verb, 1966. Hons: sev. schlrships. & fellowships; Key to City of Norfolk, 1962. Address: c/o Dept. of German-Russian, Howard Univ., Washington, DC 20001, U.S.A. 2, 7, 15.

KÖRNER, Stephan, b. 26 Sept. 1913. Professor of Philosophy. Educ: jur.Dr., Charles' Univ., Prague, Czechoslovakia; Ph.D., Trinity Hall, Cambridge, U.K. Appts: Army Serv., 1936-39, 1943-46; Lectr. in Philos., Bristol Univ., 1946-52, Prof., 1952-, Dean, Fac. of Arts, 1965-66, Pro-Vice-Chancellor, 1968-71; Vis. Prof., var. unvis., U.S.A., 1957, '60, '64, '67; Prof., Yale Univ., U.S.A., 1970-. Mbrships. incl: Aristotelian Soc., 1967; Pres., Int. Union of Hist. & Philos. of Sci., 1969; Mind Assn., 1973. Publs. incl: Kant, 1955; Conceptual Thinking, 1955; Observation & Interpretation (Ed.), 1957; Experience & Theory, 1966; What is Philosophy? , 1969. Contbr., profl. jrnls. Recip., FBA, 1967. Address: Dept. of Philosophy, The University, Bristol BS8 1RJ, U.K. 1, 3.

KORNFELD, Phyllis L. Professor of Education. Educ: B.A., M.S., Brooklyn Coll., CUNY. Appts: Tchr., Elem. Grade Schl.; Reading Clinician, Psych. Clin.; Reading Supvsr., Schl. for Emotionally Disturbed; Prof. of Reading, Lang. Arts & Children's Lit., Co-Dir., Reading Clin., Yeshiva Univ., N.Y.C. Mbrships: Fellow, Am. Orthopsychiatric Assn., 1972; Phi Delta Kappa, 1972; Mensa; Am. Educl. Rsch. Assn.; Past Pres., V.P., & Sec., Manhattan Coun., Int. Reading Assn. Author, Aspects of Reading Instruction: Levels of Behavior, in Proceedings of Conf. on Oral Lang. Skills, N.Y.C. Bd. Educ., Bur. Speech Improvement, 1973. Address: 124 Laurel Rd., New City, NY 10956, U.S.A. 5.

KORTNER, Peter, b. 4 Dec. 1924. Writer. Educ: B.A., UCLA. Appts: Prod.-Writer, The Farmer's Daughter, ABC-TV; Prod-Writer, The Dupont Show w. June Allyson, CBS; Prod-Writer, Playhouse 90, CBS. Mbrships: Writers Guild of G.B.; British Film Inst.;

Grosvenor House Swimming Pool & Gymnasium. Publs: Jim for Sale, 1970; A Slightly Used Woman, 1973; (in preparation) Breakfast with a Stranger, 1975. Recip. Emmy Award from Am. TV for Playhouse 90, 1958, '59. Address: 156 Holland Rd., London W14 8BE, U.K. 3, 30.

KORTSCHAK, Hugo P., b. 4 Sept. 1911. Chemist. Educ: B.S., Yale Univ., 1933; Ph.D., Univ. of Zurich, Switz., 1936. Biochem., Experiment Stn. of Hawaiian Sugar Planters' Assn., 1936-. Mbrships: Am. Chem. Soc. (Sect. Chmn., 1945-46); Sigma Xi; AAAS; Am. Friends Serv. Comm.; Honolulu Symph. Orch. Contbr. of num. articles to sci. jrnls. Address: Hawaiian Sugar Planters' Assn., 1527 Keeaumoko St., Honolulu, HI 96822, U.S.A. 14, 78.

KOSCHORRECK, Walter, b. 16 Jan. 1915. University Library Director. Educ: Studied jurisprudence, Univ. of Königsberg, 1938-41; Dr.jur., Univ. of Jena, 1952. Appts: Lib. Asst., Univ. Lib., Jena, Deutsche Bücherei, Leipzig, 1948-50; Sci. Libn., Univ. Lib., Jena, 1951-52; Libn., Lib., Deutsches Institut für Rechtswissenschaft, 1952-53; Univ. Lib., Heidelberg, 1953-; Dir., ibid, 1965-. Publs. incl: Geschichte des Deutschen Leihverkehres, 1958; Die Heidelberger Bilderhandschrift des Sachsenspiegels (commentary), 1970; Co-ed. (w. Dr. Wilfried Werner), Facsimilia Heidelbergensia. Ausgewählte Handschriften der Universitätsbibliothek Heidelberg; Co-Ed., Heidelberger Jahrbücher, from Vol. 10 (1966); Articles in jrnls. Address: Universitätsbibliothek Heidelberg, Plöck 107-109, D-69 Heidelberg, German Fed. Repub. 92.

KOSKENNIEMI, Matti, b. 19 Dec. 1908. Professor Emeiruts. Educ: Ph.D., Univ. of Helsinki, Finland, 1936. Appts: Insp. of Schls., 1936-44; Prof. of Educ., Univ. of Jyväskylä, 1944-48; Prof. of Educ., Univ. of Helsinki, 1955-72. Mbrships: Finnish Acad. of Sci. & Letters; Finnish Soc. of Educl. Rsch.; Govng. Bd., CERI/OECD, 1971-73. Publs: Soziale Gebilde & Prozesse in der Schulklasse, 1936; The Substitute Teacher as Indicator, 1957; The Development of Young Elementary School Teachers, 1965; Elemente der Unterrichtstheorie, 1971. Hons: War Medals, 1939-40 & 1941-44; Cmdr., Finnish Order of the Lion; Kt., 4th Class, Freedom Cross of Finland. Address: Mariankatu 15a, SF-00170 Helsinki 17, Finland. 43, 90.

KOSKINEN, Aarne Antti, b. 7 April 1915. Professor. Educ: M.A., Univ. of Helsinki, 1946; Ph.D. ibid, 1953. Appts. incl: Hist. Tchr., Munkkiniemem Yhteiskoulu, 1952-; Rsch. Fellow, Acad. of Finland, 1962-; Prof. of Ethnology, Univ. of Helsinki, 1973-. Mbrships: Polynesian Soc.; Royal Anthropological Inst.; Société des Océanistes; Finnish Soc. for Comparative Religs.; Finnish Historical Soc. Publs: Missionary Influence as a Political Factor in the Pacific Islands, 1953; Ariki The First-Born, 1960; Linking of Symbols: Polynesian Patterns 1-2, 1063; Kite: Polynesian Insights into Knowledge, 1968; Place Name Types & Cultural Sequence in Polynesia, 1973. Address: Institute of Ethnology, Univ. of Helsinki, Loutsikatu 4 A 1, 00160 Helsinki 16, Finland. 90, 134.

KOSKINEN, Pauli Tapani, b. 16 Mar. 1921. Sculptor. Educ: Schl. of Arts & Crafts, Finland, 1944-47; Finnish Acad. of Art Schl., 1947-50; num. study tours, Europe & Russia, 1948-69. Appts: Tchr., Sculpture Grp., Kouvola Municipal Adult Educ. Coll., 1966-73, & Kuusankosen Municipal Wkrs.' Evening Schl.,

1968-73. Num. works in granite, bronze & other materials, 1948-. Mbrships. incl: Jyväskylä Arts Soc.; Kouvola Soc. of Arts. Hons: Keirkneri Grant, 1951; A Kordelin Fndn., 1952; Ctrl. F. Cultural Fndn. Grant, 1959; Finnish Cultural Fndn. Kymenlaakso Fndn., 1966; Jenny & Antti Wihuri Fndn., 1968; Kymi Co. Art Bd. Art Award, 1969; various mil. medals. Address: Tanelinkatu 12, 45140 Kouvola 14, Finland. 134.

KOSKY, Pat B., b. 16 Jan. 1936. Counselor. Educ: Assoc. B.S., Mount Ida Jr. Coll.; A.B., Anna Maria Coll.; Master's Degree, Boston Coll.; Postgrad. work, Assumption Coll., Johns Hopkins Univ. Appts: Dir. of Guidance, Grafton, 1962-64; Counselor & Student Activities Advsr., Catonsville Community Coll., Md., 1964-65; Counselor, Marlborough H.S., Mass., 1965-69; Counselor, Framingham North H.S., Mass., 1969-. Mbrships: Pres.-Elect., Mass. Personnel & Guidance Assn., 1974; Treas., Mass. Schl. Counselors Assn., 1973; Profl. Dev. Chmn. M.P.G.A. & M.S.C.A.; Nat. Voc. Guidance Assn; Am. Personnel & Guidance Assn.; Assn. for Counselor Educators;Mass. Tchrs.' Assn.; Framingham Tchrs.' Assn. Co-author, Scientific pulse. Address: 2 Maxdale Rd., Worcester, MA 01602, U.S.A. 2, 5, 6, 132.

KOSLER, Alois Maria, b. 3 Aug. 1901: Retired Grammar School Professor. Educ: Univs. of Munich, Freiburg/Breisgau, Berlin & Breslau, Germany; Dr.phil., Univ. of Breslau, 1928-29. Appts. Probationary tchr., Central & Upper Silesia; Asst. master, Beuthen, Upper Silesia; Lectr., Tchr. Trng. Coll., Beuthen, 1939; Asst. master, pvte. schl., 1953-66; Sr. Asst. master, 1957-; Title of Prof., 1966. Mbrships. incl: Eichendirff soc., 1932-; Wangener Kreis, Gesellschaft für Lit. & Kunst "Der Osten", 1950-; Ghmn., ibid, 1969-; Kulturwerk Schlesien e.V.; Künstlergilde, 1967-; Ostdeutscher Kulturrat, 1973-; Oberschlesische StudienLilfe, e.V. Publs. incl: Profil der Dichtung Oberschlesiens, 1956; Ed., Schlesische Liebesgeschichten, 1967; Der deutsche Beitrag Oberschlesiens zur Kultur, 1972; Num. essays. Hons. incl. Silver medal, Landsmannschaft der Oberschlesier, 1973. Address: Südl. Auffahrtsallee 62, D 8000 Munich 19, German Fed. Repub. 43.

KOSLOUSKY, Itzhok, b. 3 Dec. 1898. Retired Factory Worker; Editor. Appts: Tchr., Europe; Tchr., Jewish Schl., U.S.A., 1921; Factory Wkr., cutter on ladies' garments, until retirement; Ed., B'nai Yiddish Mag. Mbrships: Former mbr., B'nai B'rith; Workmen's Circle; Fndr., B'nai Yiddish Movement, 1967. Publs: Ed., Under the Cuban Heaven (in Yiddish), 1939; Our Credo (B'nai Yiddish Brochure), 1968. Recip., 2 citiations for activity, B'nai B'rith, 1968 & 1970. Address: 387 Grand St., N.Y., NY 10002, U.S.A.

KOSNETTER, Johann, b. 27 July 1902. Emeritus University Professor. Educ: Univ. of Vienna, Austria, 1921-25; Cath.-theol. fac., Bible Inst., Rome, Italy, 1931-34; Evangelical theol. fac., Univ. of Berlin, 1934; Dr. theol., 1930; Lic. bibl., 1934. Appts: Ordained as priest, 1925; Chap., then relig. tchr., schls., 1925-31; Univ. Lectr., New Testament, 1936; Extra-ordinary Prof., 1937; Prof., 1946; Dean, cath.-theol. fac., 1949-50, 1954-55, 1960-61. Mbrships: Vienna Cath. Acad.; Richard Wagner soc. Publs. incl: Nietzsche & das katholische Priesterbild, 2 edits. 1970, translated into French, 1971; Articles in Vienna Cath. Acad. yrbook., Festschrift für H. Peichl, Festschrift für Franz Loidl, 1971. Hons: Papal house prelate, 1965; Silver medal for servs. in Austria,

1973. Address: Gentzgasse 14, 1180 Vienna, Austria.

KOSOLAPOFF, Gennady Michael, b. 2 Sept. 1909. Chemist. Educ: B.S.Chem.Eng., Cooper Union, N.Y.C., 1932; M.S., Univ. of Mich., 1933; Sc.D., ibid, 1936. Appts: Libbey Owens Ford Glass Co., Toledo, Ohio, 1936-38; Monsanto Chem. Co., Dayton, Ohio, 1938-48; Auburn Univ. (formerly Ala. Polytech. Inst.), 1948-; Currently Prof. of Chem., ibid; Abstractor, Chemical Abstracts-former, 1940-; Sect. co-ed., ibid, 1965-. Mbrships: Chem. Soc., London; Former mbr., AAAS; Former councillor, Auburn Sect., Am. Chem. Soc. Publs: Organophosphorus Compounds, 1950; Organic Compounds of Phosphorus (multivol. set in process of gradual appearance), 1973-74; Articles in chem. jrnls. in U.S.A., U.K. & U.S.S.R. Hons: Cooper Union Postgrad. Fellowship, 1933-35; Univ. of Mich. Special Predoctoral Fellowship, 1935-36. Address: P.O. Box 830, Auburn, AL 36830, U.S.A. 2, 14, 16, 125.

KOSSOFF, David, b. 24 Nov. 1919. Actor; Author. Educ: Northern Polytech. Coll. of Arch. Appts: Furniture Designer, 1937-39; Aircraft Draughtsman, 1939-45; BBC Rep. Actor, 1945-51; Free-lance Actor & Author, 1951-; One-Man Show Performer, 1963-. Mbrships: FRSA. Publs: Bible Stories Retold, 1968; The Book of Witnesses, 1971; The Three Donkeys, 1972; The Voices of Masada, 1973. Recip. British Film Acad. Award, 1954. Address: 45 Roe Green Close, Hatfield, Herts., U.K. 1, 58.

KOSTELANETZ, Richard (Cory), b. 14 May 1940. Writer; Poet; Critic; Cultural Historian. Educ: A.B., Brown Univ., 1962; M.A., Columbia Univ., 1966; King's Coll., Univ. of London, U.K. Appts. incl: Co-Proprietor, Assembling Press, 1970-; Co-Fndr. & Ed., Assembling (annual publn.), 1970-; Contbng. Ed., Arts in Society, The Humanist & Lotta Poetica; Prog. Assoc., Thematic Studies, John Jay Coll. of Criminal Justice, CUNY, 1972-73. Mbrships: Phi Beta Kappa; Nat. Artworkers Community. Full-time, Writer, 1965- & author of poetry, prose, fiction & non-fiction & work included in num. anthols. & periodicals. Exhibd. visual poems & fictions as paintings & graphics in galls. & mus.' throughout world inclng. Int. Cyclopedia of Plans & Occurrences, Anderson Gall., Va. Commonwealth Univ., Richmond, 1973. Given Illuminated Demonstrations of poetry & fiction at univs. & pub. instns. inclng. R.I. Schl. of Design, N.Y. Univ. & SUNY. Publs. incl: The New American Arts (co-author & ed.), 1965; Music Of Today, 1967; The Theatre Of Mixed Means, 1968, 1971; Master Minds, 1969; Visual Language, 1970; In The Beginning, 1971; Accounting, 1972; The End Of Intelligent Writing, 1974; I Articulations/Short Fictions, 1974; Ed. w. introductions num. publns. Recip. sev. Schlrships. & Fellowships. inclng. Pulitzer Fellowship in Critical Writing, 1965 & Guggenheim Fellowship, 1967. Address: 90 Kosteianetz & Ritholz, 80 Pine St., 38th Fl., N.Y., NY 10003, U.S.A. 2, 6, 13, 30, 128.

KOSTEM, Celal Nizamettin, b. 8 Feb. 1939. Associate Professor of Civil Engineering. Educ: Dip. Engr., Civil & Structural Engrng., Istanbul Tech. Univ., Turkey, 1961; Ph.D., Univ. of Arizona, Tucson, U.S.A., 1966. Appts. incl: 1st Lt., Special Staff, Turkish Army, 1961-63; Cons., Structural Engrng., Turkey & U.S.A., 1961-; Postdoctoral Rsch. Assoc., Fritz Engrng. Lab., Lehigh Univ., Bethlehem, Pa., 1966-68; Dir., Fallout Shelter & Protective Construction Courses, U.S.A., 1967-; Asst., Prof.-Assoc.

Prof., Civil Engrng., Fritz Engrng. Lab., Lehigh Univ., 1968-; Chmn., Computer-Systems Grp., ibid, 1968-. Mbrships. incl: AAAS; Am. Concrete Inst.; Assn. for Computing Machinery; Am. Soc. Civil Engrs.; var. Comms., ibid; Int. Assn. of Bridge & Structural Engrng.; Sigma Xi. Author of Tech. Reports & contbr. to profl. jrnls. Hons: Fulbright Schol. & Fellow, 1963-64, 1964-65, 1965-66. Address: Fritz Engineering Laboratory, Lehigh University, Bethlehem, PA 18015, U.S.A.

KOSTEN, Andrew, b. 16 Apr. 1926. Psychoanalyst. Educ: B.S.E., Univ. of Mich., 1947; M.A., Rutgers Univ., N.B., N.J., 1950; Ph.D., Temole Univ., Phila., Pa., 1954; N.Y. Univ. & New Schl. for Soc. Rsch., N.Y.C., 1958-60; Cert., Am. Inst. for Relig. & Psych., 1965; Grad., Am. Inst. for Psychotherapy & Psychoanalsis, 1970. Appts: Fac. Guest Lectr., Fairleigh Dickinson Univ., 1955-; Pvte. Prac., 1960-; Socio-Med. Rsch., Cornell Univ. Med. Coll., N.Y.C., 1967-70; Fndr., Clinician, Central Park South Ctr. for Psychotherapy, 1970. Mbrships: AAUP; Soc. of Authors & Composers; Bd. of Govs., Art Students League, 1964-66; Am. Anthropol. Assn.; Am. Philos. Assn.; Am. Sociol. Assn. Publs: How You Can Conquer Loneliness: A Modern Guide to Affirmative Living, 1961; Christian Courage for Everyday Living, 1962. Ed. & Translr., Devotions & Prayers of Martin Luther, 1960. Ed., Matheson Devotional Classic, 1963. Hons: Scribners Award, 1949; Dist. Alumni Award, 1964. Address: 320 Van Buren Ave., Teaneck, NJ 07666, U.S.A. 6, 30, 130.

KOSTMAYER, John Houston, b. 15 June 1915. Financial Services Executive. Educ: Tulane Univ., 1932-34, 35-36; Univ. of the S., 1934-35. Appts: V.P. & Dir., 1st Investor Corp., N.Y.C., 1953-67; V.P. Grp. Exec., ITT-Financial Servs., N.Y.C., 1967-73; Chmn. & Pres., Waddell & Reed, Inc., 1973-; Pres., United Funds Inc., United Vanguard Funds, Inc., United Continental Income Fund, Inc. & United Continental Growth Funds, Inc., all 1973-; Chmn., United Investors Life Ins. Co., Kan. City Security Corp. & Rsch. Mgmt. Assocs. Inc., all 1973- Address: 4940 Summit Ave., Kansas City, MO 64112, U.S.A.

KOSTRZEWSKI, Jan Karol, b. 2 Dec. 1915. Physician. Educ: Dip., Med. Fac., Warsaw Univ., Poland, 1945; M.D., Jagiellonian Univ., 1948; M.P.H., Harvard Schl. of Pub. Hlth., U.S.A., 1958. Appts. incl: Underground army sanitary serv., Warsaw Uprising, & prisoner of War camp, 1944-45; Chief, typhus vaccine dept., State Inst. of Hygiene Prod. Lab., Cracow, 1945-51; Sr. Lectr., dept. communicable disease, Jagiellonian Univ., 1947-50; Sr. Lectr., Dept. edidemiol., Warsaw Med. Schl., 1951-53; Chief, epidemiological dept., State Inst. of Hygiene, Warsaw, 1951-; Assoc. Prof., epidemiol., 1954; Full prof., 1965; Vice Min. of Hlth. & Chief State Sanitary Insp., 1961-68; Min. of Hlth. & Soc. Welfare, 1968-72; Sec., Med. Sect., Polish Acad. of Scis., 1972-. Mbrships. incl: Corres. mbr., Polish Acad. of Scis.; V.P., World Hlth. Assembly, 1969; Exec. Bd., WHO, 1973-; Experts Panel, ibid. Author of 160 publs. on microbiol., epidemiol. & community med. Recip. of hons. Address: Nat. Inst. of Hygiene, Chocimska 24, 00 791 Warsaw, Poland.

KOTELLY, John Christopher, b. 28 Mar. 1938. Computer Scientist; Mathematician in Robotics. Educ: B.S., MIT, 1960; M.S., Northeastern Univ., 1973. Appts: Asst. to Prof. Norbert Wiener, MIT, 1959-60; Mathn., computer logics, Electronics Rsch. Lab., ibid, 1960-62; Rsch. in laser physics, Rsch. Lab.,

USAF, Bedford, Mass., 1962-64; Math. Logician, Robotics, Electronic Rsch. Lab., NASA, Cambridge, 1964-70; V.P., Treas., Cyberfacts, Inc., Sudbury, Mass., 1970-72; Sr. Mathn., Systems Analysist, USAF Rsch. Lab. Mbrships: Am. Math. Assn.; Maths. Assn. of Am.; Charles Sanders Pierce Philosophical Soc.; Sigma Xi. Author of articles & papers in field. Hons: Guest Lectr., Sloan Schl., MIT, 1968, Harvard Bus. Schl., 1969 & Bus. Schl., Univ. of Tex., Austin, 1969; NASA Fellowship, 1968-70. Address: 235 Gray St., Arlington, MA 02174, U.S.A.

KOTHARI, Rajni, b. 13 Aug. 1928. Researcher. Educ: B.Sc., Univ. of London, U.K. Appts: Sr. Lectr., Econs., Univ. of Baroda, India, 1958-60; Rdr., Pol. Sci., ibid, 1960-62; Dir., Ctr. for Study of Developing Socs., Delhi, India, 1963-. Mbrships: Sec., Acad. for Pol. & Soc. Rsch., Delhi, 1967-; Indian Coun. of Soc. Sci. Rsch., New Delhi, 1969-72; Bd., Int. Soc. Sci. Coun., Paris, 1970-; Chmn., Soc. Sci. Comm., Indian Agricl. Commn. Publs: Politics in India, 1970; Ed., Caste in Indian Politics, 1970; The Political Economy of Development, 1971; Footsteps Into The Future: A Third World Perspective, 1974; Ed., State & Nation Building in the Third World, 1974. Hon: Fellow, Ctr. for Adv. Study in Behavioral Scis., Calif., U.S.A., 1968-69. Address: Ctr. for Study of Developing Socs., 29 Rajpur Rd., Delhi-6, India. 30.

KOTHRIS, Emmanuel, b. Nov. 1904. Lawyers; former Deputy & Minister. Educ: Dip. en droit, Univ. of Athens, Greece. Appts: Staff, Min. of Justice, lawyer in Athens, Mbr. of Admin. Coun., Liberal party-1935; Dir., Bur. Pol. of Papandréou-Venizelos Govt., Cairo, Egypt, after 1944; Pres., Union Hellino-Tchécoslovaque & Union Parlementaire Héllino-Hongrois, V.P., l'Inst. Culturel Héllino-Am.; Min., Présidence du Govt., Prévoyance Sociale & of Commerce, 1965-66. Mbrships: Lawyers of Athens; Municipal Coun. of Athens; Athens Club; Gen. Sec., Liberal Club of Athens; Coun., Bar of Athens. Hons: Cmdr. du Phénix, Greece; l'Ordre de Grand Croix, Rumanian, Yugoslav & Egyptian govts. Address: lakinthos 24, Paychiko, Athens, Greece.

KOTIN, Albert, b. 7 Aug. 1907. Painter & Professor of Art. Educ: Studies Art w. var. Masters, Paris France & N.Y.C., 1924-32 & 1946-49. Appts. incl: Cartography Instr., Army Engr. Schl., Fort Belvoir, Va., 1943-46; Instr., CCNY, 1947-51; Instr., Engrng. Drawing, Polytechnic Inst. of Brooklyn, N.Y., 1952-61; Disting. Vis. Artist, Southern Ill. Univ., 1963; Artist-in-Res., Stout State Univ., Wis., 1964-66; Prof. of Art, L.I. Univ. Brooklyn Ctr., N.Y., 1966-; Cons. to Cultural Comm., Mexican Olympic Org., 1968. Work in permanent colls: Syracuse Mus. of Fine Art, N.Y.; Hampton Inst.; Kalamazoo Art Inst., Mich.; Brooklyn Pub. Lib.; Newark bd. of Educ., N.J.; L.I. Univ., N.Y. Solo Exhibs: Hacker Gall., N.Y.C., 1951; Grand Ctrl. Moderns, ibid, 1958; Tanager Gall., ibid, 1959; Byron Gall., 1964. Participant in num. grp. exhibs., 1947-73. Hons: Winner, Nat. Mural Competition, Arlington Post Off., N.J., 1937; Purchase Award, Longview Fund, 1962. Address: 42 E. 12th St., N.Y., NY 10003, U.S.A.

KOTOWICZ, Caroline S., b. 26 July 1918. Poet. Pub. & pvte. educ: Poetry Publs. & Anthols. incl: Golden Harvest Anthol.; The Soul & the Singer, 1970; Young Publications; Ideals; Quodermi Di Poesia; The Spring Anthol.; La Poésie Contemporaine; South Milu. Voice Jrnl.; Anthol. of Am. Poetry, Book V,

VI, VII, VIII, IX, X, XI; Int. Hall of Fame Poets Anthol.; Moon Age Poets Anthol.; Poetry of Our Times; Poems Out of Wis., Vol. III & IV; Nine Muses Anthol., Vols. I & II, & many others; Poetry Ed., Poets Corner, S. Milwaukee Voice Jrnl. Newspaper. Mbrships. incl: Am. Poetry Soc.; Wis. Fellowship of Poets; Fla. State Poetry Soc.; Ariz. State Poetry Soc.; Int. Poetry Soc.; Ill. State Poetry Soc.; United Poets Laureate Int.; League of Minn. Poets; Hon., Alpha Upsilon Chapt., Epsilon Sigma Alpha; Histl. Soc. of S. Milwaukee, Wis.; Arrowhead Grp.; World Poetry Soc. Hons. incl: World Poet Award for "Torn Out Page of Love"; Many 1st awards in Nat. Poetry Contests; Poet Laureate, Am. Poets Fellowship; "Inky Trails" Special Poet Laureate, Idaho, 1971; Cit. Award of Hon., UN Comm. Day, World Congress of Poets. Address: 215 Fairview Ave., S. Milwaukee, WI 53172, U.S.A. 69.

KÖTSCHAU, Karl, b. 19 Jan. 1892. Physician. Educ: Med. studies, Berlin, Freiburg & Kiel, Germany; State exam., Berlin, 1920; Grad., Königsberg, 1921; Intern, Med. Univ. Clin., Jena, 1923-27. Appts: Worked at Med. Clin. der Charite, Pharmacological Inst. & Radiol. Inst., Berlin, 1928; Dir., Internal Dept., Berlin-Reinickendorfer Hosp., 1933; Dir., Clin. & Polyclin. for Biol. Med., Univ. of Jena, 1934; Dir., Clin. 2 for Internal Med. & Nature Cure, Nürnberg, until 1945; Work in sanatoria. Publs: Vorsorge oder Fürsorge, 1954; Wandlungen in der Medizin, 1957; Medizin am Scheideweg, 1960; Frütherapie durch Herdausschaltung, 1974; Aufbau einer Biologischen Medizin, in Vol. 40, Wissensch. Forschungsberichte (w. Adolf Meyer-Abich), 1936. Address: Lindenweg 23, 8201 Schlossberg b. Rosenheim, German Fed. Repub.

KOTSCHNIG, Walter M., b. 9 Apr. 1901. Government Official, Writer. Educ: Univs. of Graz, Austria & Kiel, Germany, 1920-24; Dr. Pol. Sci., Inst. of World Econs., Kiel, 1924. Appts: 1st Asst., Inst. of World Econs., Kiel, 1924-25; Sec.-Gen., Int. Student Serv., Geneva, 1925-34; Dir., High Commn. for Refugees, League of Nations, Geneva, 1934-36; Prof. of Comp. Educ., Smith & Mt. Holyoke Colls., Mass., 1937-44; Chief., Div. of Int. Org. Affairs—Dpty. Asst. Sec. of State, US Dept. of State, 1944-71; US Depty. Rep., UN Econ. & Soc. Coun., 1946-71; US Deleg., UNESCO, ILO, FAO & UN Econ. Commns. in Europe, the Orient, Africa & Latin Am.; Drug Abuse Control Cons., UN, 1971-73. Mbrships: Trustee, Inst. of Int. Educ., N.Y.C., 1946-52; Coun. of For. Rels., N.Y.C. Publs: Ed., The University in a Changing World, 1932; Unemployment in the Learned Professions, 1937; Slaves Need No Leaders, 1943; Co-author, The United Nations & Promotion of the General Welfare, 1957; Co-author, The United Nations & Economic & Social Cooperation, 1957; Co-author, The Global Partnership, 1967. Hons: St. Seva Order, Yugoslavia, 1929; Offs. Cross, Civil Serv. Order, Bulgaria, 1929; Disting. Hon. Award, Dept. of State, 1971; Personal Rank of Min., conferred by Pres. Kennedy, 1961. Address: 3518 Bradley Lane, Chevy Chase, MD 20015, U.S.A. 2, 5, 128.

KOUMANTOS, George, b. 12 Feb. 1925. Barrister; Professor. Educ: Law Studies, Univ. of Athens, Greece; LL.D., Univ. of Hamburg, Germany. Appts: Barrister, 1955-; Asst. Prof., Law Fac., Univ. of Athens, 1960-; Special Advsr. to Min. of Educ., 1964-65; Legal Advsr., Greek Nat. Broadcasting Inst., 1964-67. Mbrships. incl: Int. Commn. Jurists; Assn. Littéraire & Artistique Int.; Int. Gesellschaft für Urheberrecht; Greek Inst. Int. & For. Law.

Publs: Erwerberhaftung bei Unternehmensverausserung. Rechtsvergleichende Studien zur Verdinglichung des Gläubigerrechts, 1955; The Subjective Good Faith. A Contribution to the Problems of Knowledge & Ignorance in the Field of Civil Law, 1958; Copyright Law, 1967; The University Education, 1970; Democratic State & Culture, 1972; A Civil Lawyer's Apology, 1972. Address: Fokionos Negri St. 2, Athens 803, Greece. 43.

KOUTSOURIS, Rennos, b. 9 Apr. 1907. Architect. Educ: Archl. Dipl., Tech. Univ., Dresden, Germany. Appts: Arch., Min. of Pub. Works; Pvte. Archl. Prac., Athens., Greece. Past Pres., Hellenic Assn. Dipl. Archts. Designer of num. pub. & pvte. bldgs. throughout Greece; also Geneva, Switzerland & Brussels, Belgium. Contbr. of articles to profl. jrnls. Hons. incl: Cross of the Cmdr. of Phoenix, Greece; Cmdr., Order of Leopold 11, Belgium; 1st Prize for Housing dev. of Nea Smirni, Athens, 1935; 1st & wnd Prize for Off. Bldg., Stadiou str. ctr. of Athens, 1968. Address: Kolonaki Sq. 18a, Athens T.T. 138, Greece. 43.

KOUYOUMZELIS, Theodore George, b. 1 Dec. 1906. Physicist. Educ: M.Chem., Univ. of Athens, 1928; Dr.Sc., ibid, 1932. Appts. incl: Fac., Univ. of Athens, 1926-58; Prof. extraordinary, 1949-58; Prof., Hd. of Phys. Lab., Tech. Univ. of Athens, 1958-72; Dean, Fac. of Chem. Engrng., 1961-69, Emeritus 1972; Prof., Royal Naval Acad., Piraeus, 1947-72; Sec.-Gen., Greek Atomic Energy Commn., 1954-60; V.P., ibid, 1972; Permanent Greek Rep., CERN, Geneva, 1955-; V.P., CERN, 1973. Mbrships: Greek Chem. Soc.; European & Greek Phys. Socs.; Greek & Am. Nuclear Socs.; Am. Phys. Soc. Publs: Nuclear Physics, 1947; Theoretical Electricity, 1948, 1969; Alternating Currents, 1948, 1958; Vibrations and Waves, 1948, 1969; Elements of Physics and Elementary Nuclear Particles, (w. S. Peristerakis), vols. 1-4, 1960-73. Contbr. to profl. jrnls. Recip. Cmdr., Order of the Phoenix, Order of St. Geo. Address: 23 Pindou str., Filothei-Athens, Greece. 34, 43, 50, 56.

KOVACH, Francis J., b. 19 July 1918. Professor of Philosophy. Appts. incl: Asst. Prof., Coll. St. Scholastica, Duluth, Minn., 1954-59; Asst. Prof., St. Benedicts Coll., Atchison, Kan., 1959-62; Grad. Asst. Prof., Villavona Univ., Pa., 1962-64; Skogsberg Assoc. Prof., Phils., Univ. of Okla., Norman, 1964-. Mbrships. incl: Am. Cath. Philos. Assn., Wash. D.C.; Am. Soc. Aesthetics, Cleveland, Ohio. Publs. incl: Die Aesthetik des Thomas von Aquin: eine genetische und systematische Analyse, 1961; Philosophy of Beauty, 1973.; num. articles in philos. jrnls. Address: Dept. of Philos., Univ. of Okla., Norman, OK 73069, U.S.A. 7, 13.

KOVACHEVICH, Elizabeth A., b. 14 Dec. 1936. Judge. Educ: A.A., St. Petersburg Jr. Coll., Fla., 1956; B.B.A., Univ. of Miami, 1958; J.D., Stetson Univ. Coll. of Law, 1961. Appts. incl: Admitted to prac., U.S., Dist. Ct., Middle & Southern Dists. & U.S. 5th Circuit Ct. of Appeals, 1961; Admitted to prac. before U.S. Supreme Ct., 1968; 1st Woman Circuit Judge, 6th Judicial Circuit in & for Pinellas & Pasco Cos., Fla., 1973-79; Mbr., Defense Advsry. Comm. on Women in the Serv., U.S. Dept. of Defense, 1973-75. Mbrships. incl: Am., Fla. & St. Petersburg Bar Assns.; Fla. Assn. of Women Lawyers; Pinellas Co. & Am. Trial Lawyers; Am. Judicature Soc.; Pres.'s Commn. on White House Fellows, 1973-; 20th Annual Nat. Security Forum, Air War Coll., Maxwell AFB, Ala., 1973. Prod. & Doord., TV prod., A Race to Judgement, 1967. Recip. of sev. awards inclng. Man of Yr. Award, Kts. of Columbus, 1972. Address: 2459 Woodlawn Cir. E., St. Petersburg, FL 33704, U.S.A. 5, 7, 16, 46, 57, 76, 132.

KOVACS, Helen von Magyary-Kossa, b. 27 Apr. 1912. Medical Librarian. Educ: Higher educl. instns. in U.K., Belgium, Austria & U.S.A. Appts: Personnel Dir. & Hosp. Admnstr., U.S. Mil. Installations, Germany, 1945-48; Periodiicals & Dental Libn., Univ. of Ala. Med. Ctr., Birmingham, U.S.A., 1948-53; Asst. Curator, Hd. Libn., N.Y. Univ. Coll. of Dentistry, 1954-57; Assoc. Libn., Med. Rsch. Lib. of Brooklyn, SUNY, Downstate Med. Ctr., Brooklyn, N.Y., 1957-61; Dir. of Libs., ibid, 1961-. Mbrships: Bd. of Dirs., Med. Lib. Assn., 1970-72; Comm. Chmn., ibid; Conven. Chmn., Waldorf-Astoria, 1971; N.Y. Regional Grp. Chmn., 1955-56; Special Libs. Assn.; Acad. Libs. of Brooklyn; Assn. of Am. Med. Colls.; Am. Assn. for the Hist. of Med.; Nat. Writers Club; ALA. Publs: A Medical Librarian? What's That?, forthcoming; 10 profl. articles on med. lib. subjects & rsch.; Ed. & Compiler of several local lib. publs. Address: 220 Reichelt Rd., New Milford, NJ 07646, U.S.A. 5, 6, 42.

KOVALEVSKY, Leonid. Structural Engineer. Educ: Tech. Fac., Univ. of Belgrade, Yugoslavia, 1942; Dr. Ing., Tech. Univ., Munich, Germany, 1950. Appts: Engr., Corbeth, Thinghir & Co., N.Y.C.; Sr. Engr., Konski Engrs. & Erdman Hooley & Co., Syracuse; Sr. Rsch. Spec. & Mbr., Tech. Staff, N. Am. Rockwell Corp., L.A. & Downey, Calif. Mbr., Am. Soc. Civil Engrs. Co-Author: Shell Analysis Manual, 1968; Land Land of Space Vehicles; Analysis of Shells, 1972; Discontinuity Stresses in Metallic Pressure Vessels, 1972; Interaction with Transportation & Handling Systems, 1972; num. tech. reports. Recip., Medal, Am. Hist., Am. Legion. Address: 1024 Via Nogales, Palos Verdes Estates, CA 90274, U.S.A. 9, 59, 128, 131.

KOVEL, Ralph Mallory, b. 20 Aug. 1920. Author; Syndicated Newspaper Columnist; Antiques Expert; Food Broker. Educ: Ohio State Univ. Appts. incl: Owner & Pres., Ralph M. Kovel & Assocs.; Syndicated Columnist, Know Your Antiques, 1955-; TV Series 'Know Your Antiques', syndicated on PBL (non-commercial TV). Publs. incl: (co-author w. Terry H. Kovel) Directory of American Silver, Pewter & Silver Plate, 1961; American Country Furniture, 1965; Know Your Antiques, 1967; The Complete Antiques Price List, 1968, 4th edit., 1971; The Official Bottle Price List, 1971; (w. T. Kovel) The Kovel Collector's Guide to Limited Editions, 1974. Hons: Outstanding Prog. Achievement, Nat. Acad. of TV Arts & Scis., (w. T. Kovel)., 1970-71; Annual Award, Nat. Antiques Show, 1974. Address: 22000 Shaker Blvd., Shaker Heights, OH 44122, U.S.A. 2, 8, 30, 131.

KOVEL, Terry H. (Mrs. Ralph M. Kovel), b. 27 Oct. 1928. Syndicated Newspaper Columnist; Antiques Expert. Publs. incl: (co-author w. Ralph M. Kovel) Syndicated Column, Know Your Antiques, 1955-; (books) Directory of American Silver, Pewter & Silver Plate, 1961; American Country Furniture, 1965; Know Your Antiques, 1967; The Complete Antique Price List, 1968, 4th edit., 1971; The Official Bottle Price List, 1971; (w. R. Kovel) The Kovel Collector's Guide to Limited Editions, 1974. Co-author w. husband of many mag. articles. Hons: (w. R. Kovel) Awards, Nat. Acad. TV Arts & Scis., & Nat. Antiques Show. Address: 22000 Shaker Blvd., Shaker Heights, OH 44122, U.S.A. 2, 5, 8, 30.

KOWALSKI, John J., b. 8 Oct. 1928. Teacher; Writer; Poet. Educ: A.B., Emerson Coll., Boston, Mass.; Ed.M., Worcester State Coll., Mass. H.S. Tchr., Lyman Hall H.S., Wallingford, Conn. Mbrships: Fndr., Acad. of Am. Poets; Fellow, Int. Poetry Soc. Contbr. to The Chgo. Tribune, English Jrnl., The Clearing House, Dion, The Denver Post, American Bard, Cyclo-Flame, Voices Int., Hartford Courant, Air Force Times, Broadway Laughs etc. Address: 118 Algonquin Dr., Wallingford, CT 06492, U.S.A. 11.

KOWEINDL, Karl, b. 21 Jan. 1910. Educator; Administraotr. Educ: Ph.D., Univ. of Vienna, 1934; Tchng. Dip., ibid, 1935. Appts: German & Engl. Tchr., Grammar & Secondary Tech. & Voc. Schls., 1935; Insp., Min. of Educ., 1953; Sektionsrat, ibid, 1957; Ministerialrat, 1963; Lectr., Univ. of Commerce, Vienna, 1960-; Dept. Hd., Min. of Educ., 1965. Publs: Deutsch für Wirtschaft und Technik, 5th edit., (co-author), 1973; Einführung in die Literatur des deutschen Sprachraumes von ihren Anfängen bis zur Gegenwart, mit besonderer Berücksichtigung des österreichischen Schrifttums, 3 vols., 5th edit., (co-quthor), 1973; Deutsche für gewerbliche und hauswirtschaftliche Frauenberufe, 4th edit., (co-author), 1973; Untersuchungen zur österreichischen Literatur des 20. Jahrhunderts, 5 vols., (ed.); Commercial Correspondence, 2nd edit., (co-author), 1966. Recip. Das grosse Ehrenzeichen für Verdienste, Austrian Repub., 1965. Address: Wattmanngasse 26, A-1130 Vienna, Austria. 43.

KOWPAK, Alberta Mary Falter, b. 4 May 1921. Executive Secretary; Business Manager. Educ: B. Comm.; Special courses. Appts: V.P., N.J. FloodS ales Assn.; V.P., Flood Drug Co.; Sec., Alumni Affairs, & Bookstore Mgr., Tiffin Univ., Ohio. Mbrships: Alpha Iota; Rosary Altar Soc.; Pres., St. Francis Aux., 1970-71; Ohio Assn. of Coll. Stores; Nat. Assn. of Coll. Stores; Eagles; Bus. & Profl. Women's Club; Altursa Int.; Am. Legion. Recip., all expenses paid trip to Portugal, Spain, Italy & France. Address: 23 Frost Parkway, Tiffin, OH 44883, U.S.A.

KOWTONIUK, Filimon D., b. 5 Sept. 1923. Professor. Educ: B.A., Kamianeč Pedagogical Inst., Ukraine, 1943; M.A., Inst. of Critical Langs., Windham Coll., Vt., U.S.A., 1963; Ph.D., Ukrainian Free Univ., Munich, Germany, 1970. Appts. incl: U.S. Info. Off., Voice of Am., 1949-50; Educl. Rehab. Ctr., N.Y.C., 1951-59; Rsch. & Dev. Ctr., Allied Chem. Co., Hopewell, Va., 1960-65; Prof., Va. State Coll., Petersburg, 1965-; Free-lance Cons. on E. European Hist. & Soviet & Communist Affairs. Mbrships. incl: AAUP; Univ. Profs. for Acad. Order Assn.; Acad. Int. Libre des Scis. & des Lettres; Am. Assn. of Tchrs. of German; Am. Assn. of Tchrs. of Slavic & E. European Langs. Publs: Goethe & East European Literatures, 1943; County Alexey Tolstoy as Writer, 1948; Critical Analysis of Marxism -Leninism, 1948; Lomonosow & Russian Literary Language, 1963; Ira Aldridge & Taras Shevchenko, 1968; Decembrists Revolt in Russia, 1970. Hons. incl: Cert. of Distinction, UNRRA, 1948; Hon. Mbrship., Alpha Mu Gamma, 1968; Liberty Award, Congress of Freedom, U.S.A., 1973. Address: 2110 Dolin St., Hopewell, VA 23860, U.S.A. 13.

KOZINA, Antun, b. 25 Dec. 1922. Archivist. Educ: at Tchrs. Trng. Schl. & Schl. for Archivists, Zagreb, Yugoslavia. Appts: Clerk 1946; Chief, Dist. of Krapina, 1949-50; Archivist, 1950-59; Fndr., Dir., Krapina i okolica Mus. & Mus. of Ljudevit Gaj, Krapina,

1966-. Mbrships: Mus. Soc. of Croatia; Fellow, Ethnol. Soc. of Yugoslavia; Alpinist Soc., Krapina. Publs: Contbr. to num. newspapers & mags., Yugoslavia, 1950-, inclng. Borba, Vjesnik, Slobodni dom. Author of books & monographs, inclng: Vidovčanski trvlist, 1947; Selo govori o svojoj proslosti, 1958; Krapina i okolica, 1960; Hrvatsko Zagorje u NOB, 1959; Hrvatsko Zagorje, 1964; Krapinski Vandrček, 1970. Currently corres., sev. mags. in Yugoslavia concerned with hist., museums & mountaineering. Hons: Orden zasluge za narod, 1946; 2 medals, City of Zagreb, 1965, '70; Medal, City of Krapina, 1972; sev. awards & diplomas, 1952-70. Address: P.P. 42, Bregovita 12/20, 41230 Krapina, Yugoslavia. 133.

KOZLIK, Theodore, Jr., b. 12 Nov. 1944. Educational Specialist; Director of Special Services. Educ: B.A., Glassboro State Coll., N.J., U.S.A., 1966; M.A., ibid, 1968; M.A., Newark State Coll., Union, N.J., 1972; M.A., Rutgers Univ., New Brunswick, N.J., 1974. Appts. incl: Learning Disability Specialist, Sayreville, N.J., 1969-70; Dir., Special Servs., Marlboro, N.J., 1970-71; Dir., Special Servs., Milltown, N.J., 1971-73; Dir., Special Servs., Spottswod Schls., N.J., 1973-; Cons. Learning Disability Tchr., Pvte. Prac., 1969-. Mbrships. incl: Fellow, Am. Assn. on Mental Deficiency; Exec., Assn. of Learning Disability Tchr. Consultants; Coun. of Admnstrs. & Supvsrs. of Special Educ.; Nat. Assn. of Pupil Personnel Admnstrs.; Coun. for Exceptional Children. Arranger, Hindemith Sonata for Clarinet & Piano, arranged for Clarinet & Orch., 1968. Address: Box 267G, RD1, Hgw. 516, Matawan; NJ 07747, U.S.A. 6.

KRACHER, Alfred, b. 2 Mar. 1911. University Professor. Educ: Lehramtsprüfung in Latin, 1936, in German, 1937, Ph.D., 1940, Univ. of Vienna. Appts: Tchr., grammar schl, Vienna, 1937-50; Univ. Asst., Univ. of Graz, 1950, Lectr., 1956, Extraord. Prof., 1961, Ord. Prof., 1963-; Dean of Fac., ibid, 1964-65; Vis. Prof., summers, Middlebury Coll., Vt., U.S.A., 1963, '67. Mbrships: Corres. Mbr., Jugoslavian Acad. of Sci. & Arts; Mbr., Austrian Rep., Int. Assn. for Germanic Studies; Pres., Johann-Joseph-Fux-Gesselschaft. Publs: Millstätter Genesis- und Physiologus— Handschrfit, 1967; Articles in jrnls. Address: University of Graz, German Dept., A-8010 Graz, Austria. 43, 86.

KRAEMER, Barbara A. (Sister Mary Immaculata, CSFN), b. 19 July 1932. Educator; Administrator. Educ: B.A., Holy Family Coll., Phila., 1958; M.A., Middlebury Coll., Vt., 1961; D.M.L., ibid, 1969; further studies in France & Italy. Appts. incl: Nazareth Acad. Grade Schl., 1953-54; Instr., Mod. Lang. Dept., Holy Family Coll., Phila., 1958-61; Alumnae Dir., Holy Family Coll., 1960-72; Asst. Prof., Mod. Lang. Dept., ibid, 1961-66; Residence Hall Moderator, Holy Family Coll., 1962-69; Assoc. Prof., Mod. Lang. Dept., ibid, 1966-71; Prof., ibid, 1971-; Acting Dean, Holy Family Coll., Spring Semester, 1971; Acad. Dean, ibid, 1972-. Mbrships. incl: Am. Assn. of Tchrs. of French, V.P., Phila. Chapt., 1967-69 & Pres., 1969-71; MLA, Phila., Exec. Coun. Mbr., 1964-65, 1969-71; Alpha Mu Gamma; Am. Conf. & Pa. Assn. of Acad. Deans; Eastern Assn. of Coll. Deans; Am. Assn. for Higher Educ.; Pa. MLA. Publs. incl: book reviews & articles; Ed., Alumnae Newspaper, Holy Family Coll., 1960-72. Hons. incl: Grad. Seminar Award, 1960. Address: Holy Family Coll., Grant & Frankford Aves., Phila., PA 19114, U.S.A. 130.

KRAFFT, Julia Clark. Executive. Educ: Ellis Bus. Coll., Elgin, Ill. Appts: Fndr.-Pres., Steven's Candy Kitchens & Affiliates, Chgo., Ill., sold 1957; Fndr.-Pres., Honey Bear Farms, Genoa City, Wis., sold 1966; Owner, Little Traveler, Geneva, Ill., sold 1963. Mbrships: Bus. & Profl. Women's Club, Chgo.; Women's Advt. Club, Chgo.; Zonta Club, Chgo.; Women's Athletic Club, Chgo.; Lake Geneva Garden Club, Ill.; Arts Club, Chgo.; Lyric Opera of Chgo.; Chmn., Chgo. Beautiful Comm.; Ill. Children's Home & Aid; Trustee, Carthage Coll., Racine, Wis.; Salvation Army Advsry. Bd.; Rancho Santa Fe Garden Club; Cuyamaca Club, San Diego; Engl. Speaking Union, San Diego. Hons: Citizen's Award, Veterans of For. Citation, Am. Legion; Award, Chgo. Police Dept.; Disting. Serv. Cert., AMVETS, 1954. Address: P.O. Box 228, Rancho Santa Fe, CA 92067, U.S.A.

KRAFT, Walter O., b. 19 July 1920. Business Executive; Corporate President. Educ: San Diego Army & Navy Acad., 4 yrs.; Univ. of S. Calif.; after call to active duty, var. U.S. Army Serv. Schls. Appts: Serv. WWII to Major w. 47th Infantry Regiment, 9th Div., in Africa, Sicily, France, Rhineland, Ardennes & Ctrl. Europe; Mgr., Men's Clothing Dept., 1946-54; V.P., Dept. Store Mgr., Perin Inc., 1955-58; Pres., O. Kraft & Son Inc., 1959-; Chmn., Kodiak Island Dev. Comm., 1961; Mbr., City Planning Commn., 1959-64; Pres., Kodiak Area Dev. Corp., 1962-63; Employment Commnr., State of Alaska, 1966-67; Vice Chmn. & Dir., Kodiak Island Hosp., 1967-68. Mbrships: Dir., Kodiak Rotary Club, 1959-60; Dir., Local Chmbr. of Comm., 1960-61; Mbr., U.S. Chmbr. of Comm., 1968-; Life, U.S. Navy League, 1971; Bd., Am. Security Coun., 1971; Nat. Bd. of Sponsors, Inst. for Am. Strategy, 1973; Univ. of S. Calif. Assocs., & Life, Fac. Ctr. Assoc., 1973; Wash. Athletic Club, Seattle; Seattle Univ. Century Club; The Racquet Club of Palm Springs; Charter mbr., Kodiak Elke Club. Hons: Combat Infantry Badge; Silver Star, Bronze Star w. Oak Leaf Cluster; Purple Heart w. Oak Leaf Cluster; Presidential Unit Citation w. Oak Leaf Cluster; Am. Theatre Medal; European African Middle Eastern Serv. Medal w. 6 bronze stars; Victory Medal; German Occupation Medal; Belgian Fourragere; 10-yr. Serv. Reserve Medal, 1956; Fellow, Presidents—Am. Inst. of Mgmt., 1973. Address: P.O. Box 1217, Kodiak, AK 99615, U.S.A. 9, 57.

KRAG, Erik, b. 13 Jan. 1902. Professor (Retd.). Educ: M.A., Univ. of Oslo, Norway, 1926; Ph.D., ibid, 1933; Russian Lang. & Lit., USSR, 1923-25, 1927-28; Czech Lang. & Lit., Prague, 1934-35; Polish Lang. & Lit., Warsaw, 1936. Appts: Rdr., Univ. of Oslo, Norway, 1938-46; Prof., Hist. of Lit., esp. Russian, 1946-70. Mbrships: Norwegian Acad. of Sci. & Letters, 1942-; Norwegian Acad. for Lang. & Lit.; Societas Johnsoniana; Hon. Mbr., Assn. of Scandinavian Slavists. Publs. incl: The Struggle against the West in Russian Intellectual Life, 1932; Leo Tolstoy: Youthful Works, War & Peace, 1937; Dostojevskiy, 1962; (dramatic works) A Little Man's Wedding, 1952; The Childless One, 1966; (translations) Gogol's Dead Souls, 1927; Tolstoy's War & Peace, 1930-31. Recip., Fridtjof Nansen's Award, 1938. Address: Universitetet i Oslo, Slavisk-Baltisk Institutt, Postboks 1028, Oslo 3, Norway. 43.

KRAKOWSKI, Adam J., b. 8 Nov. 1914. Psychiatrist. Educ: M.D., Jagiellonski Univ. Med. Schl., Cracow, Poland, 1939; Specialist in Psych., 1943; Qualified Psych., 1952. Appts. incl: Dir. & Child Guidance Psych., N.Y. State

Dept. of Mental Hygiene, 1958-69; Prof. of Psych., Dept. of Med. & Hlth. Educ., Plattsburgh State Univ. of Arts & Sci., N.Y.; Cons. in Psych., Plattsburgh Air Force Base Hosp. & Will Rogers Hosp., Saranac Lake, N.Y.; Chief & Dir., Psychosomatic Unit, Div. Psych. Liaison & Rsch., Champlain Valley Physns. Hosp. Med. Ctr., Plattsburgh, 1971-. Mbrships. incl: Fellow, Am. Psych. Assn., AMA, Am. Geriatrics Soc., Royal Soc. of Hlth., Acad. of Psychosomatic Med.; Pres., ibid, 1970. Publs: Contbng. Co-Ed., Child Psychiatry & the General Practitioner, 1962; num. articles in profl. jrnls. Hons. incl: Virtuti Militari, Polish Army, 1944; Presl. Citation for Community Work, N.Y. State Med. Soc., 1965; Fellow, Polish Psych. Assn. Address: Suite 103, 210 Cornelia St., Plattsburgh, NY 12901, U.S.A.

KRAKOWSKI, Meyer, b. 27 Dec. 1901. Educator. Educ: Univ. of Toronto, Canada, 1921-22; UCLA, 1922-24; A.B., Univ. of Calif., Berkeley, 1924-25; M.A., ibid, 1927; Summer sessions, Stanford Univ., 1933. Univ. of Mexico, 1941 & 1942, Univ. of Paris, France, 1945. Appts. incl: Pasadena City Coll., U.S.A., 1929; Instr. to Prof., For. Langs. Dept., L.A. City Coll., 1929-67; Summer sessions, UCLA, 1934, '35, '47. Mbrships. incl: AAUP; S.W. Conf. on Renaissance; Bd., Overseers Univ. of Judaism, L.A., 1954-58; Bd. Gov., Schl. of Educ., 1947-54; Chmn., Lib. Comm., 1953-56; I.O.B.B.; Delta Phi Alpha; Co-Fndr., Calif. Coun. of For. Lang. Tchrs., 1956; L.A. Co. Mus. of Art; Sierra Club; Philol. Assn. of the Pacific Coast; V.P., 1930-31, Pres., 1931-32, Fndr. Res. Coun., 1932, Modern Lang. Assn. of S. Calif.; Co-Fndr., 1931, & Nat. Pres., 1940-42, Alpha Mu Gamma; Fndr., Chmn., Nat. Comm. on Intercultural Rels., ibid, 1948-; Area committee, prof. prep., MLA, 1959-60; Life Fellow, Int. Inst. of Arts & Letters, 1961. Publs. incl: Aspects of Contemporary Civilization (ed.), 1956; Goethe & Our Times, in Mod. Lang. Forum, 1949. Hons: Pvte.-Capt., USAAC, 1942-46; Order of Merit, 1st Class, German Fed. Repub., 1967; Plaque for Disting. Serv. & Hon. Life Mbrship., MLA of S. Calif., 1966. Address: 1628 Lyman Pl., L.A., CA 90027, U.S.A. 9, 13, 15, 55, 59.

KRAMER, Nora (Mrs.). Author; Anthologist; Children's Book Reviewer; Lecturer; Consultant; Sculptor. Educ: Beaux Arts Inst., N.Y.C., 1920-21; Schl. of Mus. of Fine Arts, Boston, Mass., 1929-30; CCNY, 1939-43; Sculpture Workshops, New Schl. for Soc. Rsch., N.Y., 1970-. Appts. incl: Cons. (under name Eleanor Brent), The Little Bookshop, Macy's, N.Y.C., 1943-53; Creator & Dir., The Bookplan, 1944-; Ed.-in-Chief, The Bookwoman, 1954-56; Ed. Cons., Scholastic's Arrow Book Club, 1958-. Mbrships: Children's Book Comms., Child Study Assn. of Am., 1934-, Engl.-Speaking Union's Children's Books-Across-the-Sea, 1953-, & Nat. Conf. of Christians & Jews, 1947-; Women's Nat. Book Assn.; Authors Guild. Publs: Nora Kramer's Storybook for Threes & Fours, 1955; Nora Kramer's Storybook for Fives & Sixes, 1956; Coppercraft & Silver, Made at Home (w. husband), 1958, paperback ed., 1971; The Cozy Hour Storybook, 1960; The Arrow Book of Ghost Stories, 1960; The Grandma Moses Storybok, 1961; Tricky Tales, 1970; Princess Tales, 1971; The Ghostly Hand & Other Haunting Tales, 1972; Ed. &/or Abridged var. other books for children; Contbr. articles & book reviews to var. publs. Sculptures incl. portrait busts, figures in the round & var. works in terra cotta. Address: 46 Jane St., N.Y.C., NY 10014, U.S.A. 5, 6.

KRAMISH, Arnold, b. 6 June 1923. Diplomat; Physicist; Author. Educ: B.S., Univ. of Denver; A.M., Harvard Univ.; Doct., Univ. of Paris. Appts: Sr. Rschr., Rand Corp., 1951-68; Prof.-in-Res., Univ. of Calif., 1965-66; Vis. Prof., London Schl. of Econs., 1967; V.P., Inst. for the Future, 1968-70; Adjunct Prof. of Int. Studies, Univ. of Miami, 1969-; U.S. Sci. Liaison Attache, UNESCO, Paris, 1970-. Mbrships: Int. Inst. for Strategic Studies; AAAS; Fellow, Inst. for Strategic Studies, London. Publs: Atomic Energy for your Business; Atomic Energy in the Soviet Union; The Peaceful Atom in Foreign Policy; Die Zukunft der Nichtatomaren; etc. Contbr. to var. jrnls. Address: American Embassy, Avenue Gabriel, Paris 1, France. 2, 14, 30, 50, 56.

KRAMPER, (Rev.) James Peter, b. 11 Apr. 1912. Librarian; Catholic Priest. Educ: A.B., St. Louis Univ., 1936; Ph.L., ibid, 1938; M.A., 1942. Appts: joined Soc. of Jesus, 1931; Ordained Priest, RC Ch., 1944; Prof., Creighton Univ., 1953-; Dir. of Libs., ibid, 1954-. Mbrships: ALA; Am. Cath. Lib. Assn.; Assn. Higher Educ.; Nat. Microfilm Assn. Address: Creighton Univ., 2500 California St., Omaha, NB 68131, U.S.A. 2, 108.

KRAR, Stephen Frank, b. 20 July 1924. Teaching & Technical Author. Educ: Univ. of Toronto Tchr. Trng. Course, 1954-55. Appts: Elec. & Machine Shop Instr., Niagara Falls Collegiate & Vocl. Inst., 1955-56; Machine Shop Instr., John F. Ross Collegiate & Vocl. Inst., Guelph, Ont., 1956- 62; Tech. Dir., Trng.) Mbrships: Pres., Welland Curlin Club, 1973-74; Pres., Ont. Vocl. Educ. Assm., 1964; Chmn., Ont. Machine Shop Roundtable, 1959-60, etc. Publs: Technology of Machine Tools (also French edn.); Machine Shop Training, 1st & 2nd edns. (also Spanish edn.); Turning Technology; Grinding Technology; Transparency Books, 1,2,3,4. Address: 420 Fitch St., Welland, Ont., Canada L3C 4W8.

KRASNOW, (Dr.), Frances, (Mrs. Marcus Thau), b. 16 Oct. 1894. Consultant Biochemist; Educator; Administrator. Educ: B.S., Barnard Coll., Columbia Univ., 1917; A.M., Columbia Univ., 1917; Ph.D., ibid, 1922. Appts. incl: Tchng. & Rsch. Staff, Dept. of Biochem., Columbia Univ., 1918-32; Rsch. Fellow, Vanderbilt Clinic, Columbia Univ., 1918-19; Rhein & Levy Fund, 1920-28; Lehn & Fink Fund, 1925-26; Cons., N.Y. State Dept. of Labor, 1929; Dept. of Dermatol. & Syphilol., Post-grad Schl. & Hosp., 1928-40; Staff Mbr., Caries Rsch. C'wealth. Fund, 1930-32; Hd., Basic Sources & Asst. Dir., Schl. for Dental Hygienists, Guggenheim Dental Clinic, 1932-44; Dir., Rsch. Dept., ibid, 1944-52; Rsch. Dir., Universal Coatings Inc., N.J., 1952-; Rsch. Cons., N.Y., 1952-. Mbrships. incl: Phi Beta Kappa; Am. Chem. Soc.; Life, AAAS; Life, N.Y. Acad. of Med.; Life, AMA; Sigma Xi; Life, N.Y. Acad. of Scis.; V.P. & Pres., Int. Soc. for Dental Rsch., 1945-49; various positions, Alumni Assn., Tchrs. Inst.-Sem. Coll.; Area Chmn., Am. Red Cross, 1944; various positions, U.S. War Bond Drives; Hon., N.Y.C. & N.Y. State Dental Hygiene Assns. Publs. incl: Guide to Bacteriology, 1932; Bacteriology Laboratory Guide, 1941; My Autobiograph y, (in preparation); num. articles, books, papers etc. in profl. jrnls. Recip. of many hons. Address: 405 E. 72nd St., N.Y., NY 10021, U.S.A. 5, 6, 10, 14, 15, 25, 28, 55, 128.

KRAUCH, Velma Ann, b. 21 Sept. 1916. Free-lance Writer. Educ: Calif. State Univ., Northridge, U.S.A. Appts: Tchr., Nursery Schl.; Girl Friday to Suspense writers. Mbr., Assn. of

Women's Active Return to Educ. Author, Three Stacks & You're Out. Free-lance contbr. to newspapers & mags. Recip., Minerva Award, for achievement in writing Three Stacks & You're Out, Assn. of Women's Active Return to Educ., 1972. Address: 1716 Roscomare Rd., Los Angeles, CA 90024, U.S.A. 30.

KRAUSE, Lloyd Thomas, b. 23 Feb. 1920. Educator; Composer. Educ: Dip., USN Schl. of Music, 1939; B.A., San Diego State Coll., 1948; Profl. Tchng. Cert., Univ. of Hawaii, 1962; Grad. work, Music Composition, 1963. Appts. incl: Musician, USN, 1938-45; Tchr., 1948-62; Bandmaster, Royal Hawaiian Band, 1963-68; Arranger, Honolulu Symph. Orch., 1969-; Mgr., Honolulu Pops Orch., 1949-58; Special Arrangements for Royal Hawaiian Band & other musical grps. Mbrships: Bd., Kaimuki Christian Ch. Schl.; Elder & Dir., Kaimuki Ch.; Gen. Mgr., Civic Light Opera Assn., 1952-55; Life Mbr., Musicians' Assn. of Hawaii, 1974. Address: Honolulu Symph., Suite 303, 1000 Bishop St., Honolulu, HI 96813, U.S.A. 78.

KRAUT, Bojan, b. 12 Apr. 1908. Educator. Educ: Dipl.ing., Univ. of Zagreb, Yugoslavia, 1932. Appts: Engr., factory making carriages, machines & bridges, Slavonski Brod, 1937-46; Prof., Metal Technol., Fac. Mech. Engrng., Univ. of Ljubljana, 1946-; Prod. Dir., Litostroj, 1948-53; Counsellor, ibid, 1953-59; Dir., Inst. Mech. Engrng., 1960-70. Hon. Mbrships: Assn. Mech. & Elec. Engrs. & Techns. of Yugoslavia; Assn. Mech. Engrs. & Techns. of Slovenia. Publs: Manual for Mechanical Engineering, 1954, '56, '63, '64, '65, '67, '70, '73, '74; Ed., mech. jrnl. Strojniski vestnik, 1955-. Hons: Medal of merit for nation III, 1949; Medal of work w. gold wreath, 1965. Address: 3 Valvazorjeva, Ljubljana, Yugoslavia.

KRAUTKREMER, Franz, b. 22 Aug. 1927. President of the Schottel Group. Educ: Univ. of Cologne, Germany. Appts: Assoc., Schottel-Werft Josef Becker KG, Spay, 1952-; Dir., ibid, & Dir. & Pres., subsidiaries in Germany, Holland, U.K., Switzerland, U.S.A., Argentine, France & Singapore, 1967-. Mbrships: Lions Club, Koblenz; Bd., Kreisparkasse, ibid; Comm. of Credit, ibid. Publ: Innerbetriebliche Standortfragen in einem Werfbetrieb. Hons: Cross of Merit, Fed. Repub., 1971. Address: Mainzerstrasse 99, D 5401 Spay/Rhein, German Federal Repub. 43.

KREEL, Beverley M., b. 26 Apr. 1939. Financial Consultant; Poetess; Free-lance Writer. Educ: Ph.D., Univ. of Sask., 1973. Appts: Hd., Allan Bus. Univ., Sask., Canada, 1958-59; Bd. Dirs., Dale-ITI Inc., N.Y.C., 1972-; Green's Mag., Detroit, Mich. Mbrships. incl: Bd. of Community Rels., Flint Community Coun., 1969-72; Nat. Women's League, 1969-71; Major Poets Chapt., Am. Poetry Fellowship Soc. Ed. of Yearbook of Modern Poetry, & Outstanding Contemporary Poets. Contbr. to Voices Int., People, Christian Mother, Major Poets, The Bulletin. Address: 460 Thomas Ln., Grand Blanc, MI 48439, U.S.A. 57.

KREIELSHEIMER, Kurt Samuel, b. 22 May 1903. Associate Professor of Physics (retired). Educ: D.Ing., Tech. H.S., Darmstadt, Germany. Appts: Rsch. Fellow, Heinrich Hertz Inst., Berlin, & Chief German Radio Techn., Polar Yr. Expedition, 1932-34; Rsch. Fellow, Acad. Assistance Coun., London, U.K., 1934-35; Rsch. Physicist, Neon Signs (Australasia) Ltd., Sydney, Australia, 1935-39; Sr. Physicist, Dept. of Scientific & Indl. Rsch., Auckland, N.Z., 1939-45; Sr. Lectr., Radio Phys., Univ. of Auckland, 1945-52; Assoc. Prof., ibid, 1952-.

Mbrships: Fellow, Inst. of Phys.; Instn. of Elec. Engrs., London; Working Grp., Jt. Comm. on Atmospheric Elec., Int. Union of Geodesy & Geophys., 1967; Int. Commn. on Atmospheric Elec., Int. Assn. of Meteorol. & Atmospheric Elec., 1971. Author, 31 scientific papers in profl. jrnls. Address: 603 Sandringham Rd., Mt. Albert, Auckland 3, New Zealand. 38, 55.

KREIN, Catherine Mitchell, b. 7 Feb. 1940. Political Writer; Researcher; Producer. Educ: B.S., Fordham Univ.; M.S., Hunter Grad. Schl.; Currently in attendance for film cert., N.Y. Univ. Appts: Exec. Sec. to Fred Friendly, Pres. of CBS News; Administrative Asst., Writer, Rschr. to Walter Cronkite, CBS News; Writer, Rschr., CBS News Election Unit; Writer, Rschr., Producer, Special Events Unit, CBS News. Mbrships: Nat. Acad. of TV Arts & Scis.; Writers Guild of Am.; Am. Acad. of Pol. & Soc. Scis.; Ctr. for Study of Democratic Instns.; Ctr. for Study of the Presidency; Mus. of Modern Art. Author of bi-monthly CBS News Pol. Calendar & Report, 1972. Address: 151-31-88th St., Apt. 6L, Howard Beach, NY 11414, U.S.A. 132.

KREISEL, Henry, b. 5 June 1922. Professor of English; University Vice President. Educ: B.A., 1946, M.A., 1947, Univ. of Toronto; Ph.D., Univ. of London, 1954. Appts: Lectr., Asst., Assoc. Prof., Engl., Univ. of Alb., 1947-59; Prof., 1959, Hd., Dept. of Engl., 1961-67; Sr. Assoc. Dean of Grad. Studies, 1969-70; V.P. (Acad.), 1970-. Mbrships: Fellow, Royal Soc. of Arts; Past Pres., Assn. of Canadian Univ. Tchrs. of Engl.; Past Pres., Assn. of Acad. Staff of Univ. of Alb.; Past V.P., Edmonton Art Gall. Publs: The Rich Man, 1948; The Betrayal, 1964; Stories, articles in periodicals; TV, radio plays—The Betrayal, 1965; He Who Sells His Shadow. Hons: 10 major undergrad. schlrships., 1942-46; Reuben Wells Leonard Fellowship, Univ. of Toronto, 1946; Travelling Fellowship, Royal Soc. of Canada, 1953; Pres.' Medal, Univ. of Western Ont., 1960. Address: Univ. of Alberta, Edmonton, Alberta, Canada. 2, 9, 13, 55, 88.

KREKELER, Heinz L., b. 20 July 1906. Diplomatist. Educ: Ph.D., Univ. of Berlin, Germany, 1930; Also at Univs. of Freiburg, Munich & Göttingen. Appts: Chem. Engr., var. firms, 1930-47; Mbr., Lippe Diet, 1946, Diet of N. Rhine-Westphalia, 1947-50; Fed. Assembly, 1949; Ptnr. & firm Dir., Ellers-Schünemann Verlag (Publrs.), Bremen, 1948-; Consul-Gen., N.Y., U.S.A., 1950-51; Charge d'Affaires, German Fed. Repub., Wash. D.C., 1951-53; Ambassador, 1953-58; European Commnr., Euratom, 1958-64. Mbrships: Deutsche Gesellschaft für Auswärtige Politik; Akademischer Segler Verein, Munich; Max Planck Gesellschaft z. Förderung der Wissenschaften; Hon. mbr., Am. Chmbr. of Comm. in Germany. Publs: Die Diplomatie, 1965; Die Aussenpolitik, 1967. Hons: Grand Cross, 2nd Class, Order of Merit, German Fed. Repub., 1971; Grande Ufficiale dell'Ordine al Merito, 1959; Commendatore con Placca dell'Ordine S. Gregorio il Grande; Grand Off., Order of Leopold; LL.D., Xavier Univ. & Univ. of S.C., U.S.A. Address: Gut Lindemannshof, 4902, Bad Salzuflen 1, German Fed. Repub. 2, 12, 34.

KRENKEL, John H., b. 9 Apr. 1906. Educator; Historian. Educ: B.S., Univ. of Ill., U.S.A., 1933; M.A., Claremont Grad. Schl., Calif., 1935; Ph.D., Univ. of Ill., 1937. Tchng. appts. incl: Chgo. Tchrs. Coll., Ill., 1938-43; Valparaiso Univ., Ind., 1943-44; Western N.M. Univ., Silver City, 1944-45; Ft. Hays Kan. State Coll., 1945-46; Univ. of Okla., Norman,

1946-47; Ariz. State Univ., Tempe, 1947-. Mbrships. incl: Am. Histl. Assn.; Southern Histl. Assn.; Western Histl. Assn.; Phi Eta Sigma. Publs: Illinois Internal Improvements 1818-1848; Richard Yates, Civil War Governor; Richard Yates, the Younger, Illinois Governor & Congressman; Life & Times of Joseph Fish, Mormon Pioneer; 12 articles; 400 abstracts in Historical Abstracts. Recip., Disting. Serv. Award, Phi Eta Sigma, 1973. Address: 619 E. Erie Dr., Tempe, AZ 85282, U.S.A. 30, 51, 120, 128.

KRETZSCHMAR, Charles Paul, b. 11 Dec. 1924. University Professor. Educ: B.S., Univ. of Md., 1950; M.A., ibid, 1952. Appts. incl: Civilian Commodity-Ind. Analyst, Dept. of Army, Balt., 1953; Fac. Mbr., Univ. of Md. O'seas Prog., Germany, Morocco, Greece, Turkey, 1955-58; Assoc. Prof., Sociol., Monroe Community Coll., Rochester, N.Y., 1962-64; Vis. Prof., Ind. State Univ., Pa., summer 1960, UNB Main Campus, Fredericton, N.B., summer 1968, Dalhousie Univ., Halifax, N.S., summer 1969; Currently Asst. Prof., Dept. of Sociol. & Anthropol., Univ. of N.B., St. John. Mbrships: Canadian Sociol. & Anthropol. Assn.; Am. Sociol. Assn.; Assn. for Evolutionary Econs.; Am. Statl. Soc.; Am. Econ. Assn.; Canadian Assn. of Univ. Tchrs.; AAUP; Beta Gamma Sigma. Contbr. of articles to profl. jrnls. Address: Dept. of Sociol. & Anthropol., Univ. of N.B., St. John, N.B., Canada. 6, 130.

KREUGER, (Erik Johan) Ragnar, b. 4 Aug. 1897. Engineer. Educ: Grad., Inst. of Technol. & Acad. of Engrng., Streltiz, Germany, 1922. Appts: Post in Kreuger & Toll, 1923-24; Engr., Oy Yleinen Insinööritoimisto, Finland, 1924; Mng. Dir., ibid, 1925-54; Chmn., Bd. of Dirs., 1954-. Mbrships: Vice Chmn., Nordenskiöld Soc. Trustees; Bird Dog Sect., Finnish Kennel Club; Danish Pointer Club. Publs: Contbns. to ornithological mags.; Articles in tech. engrng. jrnls.; Articles in publs. of Danish Kennel Club & Finnish Kennel Club. Owned, & donated to Univ. of Helsinki, Finland, the second largest collection of bird's eggs in the world (70,000 eggs). Owns an animal & bird sanctuary. Hons: Cmdr. of Order of the Lion of Finland; 5 war medals; Counsellor of Ind., 1952; Ph.D., Univ. of Helsinki, 1973. Address: Kalastajatorpantie 10, 00330 Helsinki 33, Finland. 43, 90.

KRIARAS, Emmanuel, b. 28 Nov. 1906. Professor Emeritus. Educ: B.A., Univ. of Athens, Greece, 1929; D.Lit., ibid, 1938. Appts: Ed., Medieval Archives, Acad. of Athens, 1930-39; Dir., Medieval Archives, ibid, 1939; Rsch. Wkr., Nat. Ctr. of Sci. Rsch., Paris, France, 1946-48; Prof., Fac. of Letters, Univ. of Salonika, Greece, 1950-; Sec. Gen., Inst. of Neohellenic Studies, ibid, 1960-63; Pres., Ctr. for Byzantine Studies, 1966-67. Mbrships. incl: Acad. of Scis. & Arts, Palermo, Italy; Linguistic Soc. of Paris. Publs. incl: Etudes sur les Sources de l'Erotocritos, 1938; Romans Byzantins Chevaleresques, 1955; La Complainte de Constantinople, 1956, 2nd ed. 1965; Psichari, 1959; Dictionnaire de la Littérature Populaire Grecque Mediévale, 3 vols., 1969-73. Hons. incl: Cmdr.'s Cross, Order of the Phoenix, 1952; Legion of Honour, 1958; Cmdr.'s Cross, Order of George I of Greece, 1961; Cmdr., Order of Merit of the Repub. of Italy, 1964; Grand Cmdr., Order of the Phoenix, 1969. Address: 1, Rue Anghélaki, Thessalonica (353), Greece.

KRIEG, (Gustav Albert) Werner, b. 13 June 1908. Librarian. Educ: Studied Classical Philol., German Philol. & Philos., Univs. of Marburg & Halle, Germany, 1927-33; Dr.phil., 1934; State exam. for higher educ., 1934. Appts. incl: Univ. Lib., Halle, 1936; Prussian State Lib., Berlin, 1937; Univ. & town lib., Cologne, 1947; Dir., ibid, 1960-71; Dir., Libn. trng. inst., N. Rhine-Westphalia, 1960-73; Hon. Prof., books & lib. org., Univ. of Cologne, 1968. Mbrships: German libns. assn.; Bibliophiles assn., Cologne. Publs: Ed., Aus der Welt des Bibliothekars. Festschrift für Rudolf Juchhoff, & Arbeiten aus dem Bibliothekar-Lehrinstitut, 1961-63; Articles in lib. jrns. Hons: Order of merit, German Fed. Repub., 1968; Grand Order of merit, ibid, 1973; Recip. of Festschrift. Address: 21 Lindauer Str., D 5 Cologne 41, German Fed. Repub. 43, 92.

KRIEGER, Emil, b. 8 Sept. 1902. Sculptor; Designer. Educ: Wood carver's exam., Meisterschule, Kaiserslautern, 1917-20; Graphic & Ceramic studies, staatliche Kunstgewerbeschule, Munich, 1921-24; Master pupil w. Prof. Wackerle, Akademie der Bildenden Künste, Munich, 1924-31; Studied in Spain, France, Italy, Greece. Prof., Akademie der Bildenden Künste, Munich, 1946-. Mbr., Munich Sezession, 1928. Works incl: Kore, Schloss Koblenz, 1949; Jüngling mit Helm, Kaiserslautern; Mädchen mit Trauben; Langemarckdenkmal, Belgium; Richard Wagner Bust, Nat. theatre, Munich; 2 Reliefs, Winderstand & Ergebung, for Dietrich Bonhoeffer Gedächtniskirche, Kaiserslautern; Drawings in pvte., town & state collects. Hons. incl: Culture Prize, Rheinland-Pflaz, 1962; Seerosen Prize, Munich, 1965. Address: Hohenzollernstr. 16, 8 Munich 40, German Fed. Repub.

KRIGE, Eileen Claire Berenice (Eileen Jensen Krige), b. 12 Nov. 1904. Social Anthropologist. Educ: M.A., Univ. of the Witwatersrand, S. Africa, 1927; B.A., ibid, 1930; Attended Malinowski's Seminars, London Schl. of Econs., U.K., 1936; D.Litt., Rand, 1940. Appts: Lectr., Univ. of the Witwatersrand, 1935; Lectr., Sociol., Rhodes Univ., Grahamstown, 1942-44; Lectr., Soc. Anthropol., Univ. of Natal, 1948-53; Sr. Lectr., ibid, 1953-59; Prof., Soc. Anthropol. & Hd., Dept. of African Studies, 1960-70; Prof. Emeritus, 1970-; Dean, Fac. of Soc. Sci., 1962-64. Mbrships: Rsch. Fellow, Int. African Inst., 1936-39; Assn. of Soc. Anthropologists of Gt. Britain & the Commonwealth; Pres., Nat. Coun. of Women, Grahamstown, 1942-44. Publs. incl: The Social System of the Zulus, 1936, 4th impression, 1969; The Realm of a Realm Queen (w. J.D. Krige), 3rd impression, 1965; Articles in symposia & jrnls. Recip., Nat. Sci. Fndn. Fellowship, Univ. of Fla., U.S.A., 1970-71. Address: 185 Trematon Dr., Morningside, Durban, 4001, Natal, S. Africa.

KRIKKER, Margaret Ann (Mrs. Albert B. Karasz). Physician. Educ: B.A., SUNY, 1945; M.D., Albany Med. Coll., 1949. Appts: Intern, Ellis Hosp., Schenectady, 1949-50; Prac. of Med., Specializing in Family Med., Albany, N.Y., 1950-; Mbr. Staffs, Albany Med. Ctr. Hosps., Clin. Asst., Med., 1950-; Asst. in Med.-Assoc. in Med., Albany Med. Coll., 1951-; Assoc. Dispensary Physn., Clins., 1960-. Mbrships: Fellow, Am. Acad. Family Prac.; AMA; N.Y. State & Albany Co. Acad. of Family Prac.; N.Y. State & Albany Co. Med. Socs.; Ridgefield Tennis Assn.; Helderberg Ski Club. Address: 164 Colonial Ave., Albany, NY 12208, U.S.A. 5.

KRINER, James Irwin, b. 19 Feb. 1933. Business Executive: International Management Consultant. Educ: Dip., Electrophysics, Ind. Med. Schl., 1956; B.S., Physics, Butler Univ., 1958; Courses in maths., physics, bus. admin., acctng., marketing, etc. Appts: Rsch. Asst., Lectr., Ind. Univ. Med. Ctr., 1955-58; European Dir., Int. Dir., Int. V.P., Packard Instn. Int., Zurich & Downers Grove, Ill., 1958-69; Mgr. Dir., Hycel Europa B.V., Waterloo, Belgium, 1972-; Mgmt. Cons., European, Am. cos., 1973-. Mbrships: Sigma Xi; Rsch. Soc. of Am.; Am. Phys. Soc.; Am. Inst. of Physics; IEEE; Past Pres., KME; Chmbrs. of Comm., Belgium, Switzerland. Publs: Rsch. & dev. of instrumentation, treatment of epilepsy & nervous disorders; Num. papers in profl. jrnls.; Lectr. Hons: Var. medals & scholastic awards in Chem., Physics, Maths., 1949-58; Nat. Sci. Fndn. Award in Physics, 1958. Address: Ave. Bellevue 74, 1410 Waterloo, Belgium. 8.

KRINGELBACH, Jørgen, b. 8 June 1915. Physician & Pediatrician. Educ: Grad., 1942; Specialist, intern. med. 1950, pediatrics 1955. Appts: Asst. Physn., var. Hosps., Denmark, 1942-57; Chief Physn., Children's Dept., Ctrl. Hosp., Nykøbing Falster, Denmark, 1957-. Mbrships: Danish Boy Scouts Assn.; Dist. Commnr. & Mbr. of Leadership, ibid, 1952-67; Comm., ibid, 1968-; Int. Advsry. Comm., Scouting w. the Handicapped, Boy Scouts Assn., 1963-70. Publs: Num. papers, particularly on clin. pediatric subjects, in pediatric & med. jrnls. Hons: Honour Medal, Danish Boy Scouts Assn., 1953; Golden Order of Merit, ibid, 1955; Silver Wolf, ibid, 1968; Honour Medal, Save the Children, 1960. Address: Children's Dept., Central County Hosp., 4800—Nykøbing Falster, Denmark. 43.

KRIPPNER, Stanley. Institute Program Planning Coordinator. Educ: B.S., Univ. of Wis., Madison, 1954; M.A., Northwestern Univ., Evanston, Ill., 1957; Ph.D., ibid, 1961. Appts. incl: Dir., Child Study Ctr., Kent State Univ., Ohio, 1961-64; Dir., Dream Lab., Maimonides Med. Ctr., Brooklyn, N.Y., 1964-73; Sr. Rsch. Assoc., Div. of Parapsychol. & Psychophysics, ibid, 1973-; Dir. of Rsch., N.Y. Inst. for Child Dev., N.Y.C., 1968-; Dir. of Rsch., Churchill Schl., N.Y.C., 1972-; Prog. Planning Coord., Humanistic Psychol. Inst., San Fran., Calif., 1973-. Mbrships. incl: Hon. V.P., Albert Schweitzer Cultural Assn., Mexico City, Mexico; V.P., Western Hemisphere, Int. Psychotronic Rsch. Assn.; Pres., Assn. for Humanistic Psychol., 1974-75; Fellow, Am. Soc. of Clin. Hypnosis; Voting Mbr., Am. Soc. for Psychical Rsch.; Int. Psychotronic Rsch. Assn.; Int. Soc. for Gen. Semantics. Author or co-author of over 200 articles in var. psychological, psych. & educl. jrnls.; Co-author of Dream Telepathy, 1973. Recip. of hons. Address: 515 Howard Ave., Staten Island, NY 10301, U.S.A. 6, 14, 28, 57, 128, 141.

KRISHNA, Kanwal, b. 3 Jan. 1910. Painter. Educ: Engrng. Study, 1 yr.; Govt. Art Coll., Calcutta, India, 1933-39; Studied Graphics w. Stanlay William Hayter, Paris, 1953. Appts: Commissioned by Indian Govt. to paint life & landscape in Sikkim & Delai Lama Ceremony in Tibet, 1939; Commissioned to paint life & landscape in N.W.F.P. inclng. Khyber Chitral, Kafiristan & Afghanistan, 1945; Commissioned to paint Army Ops. in Kashmir Against Pakistan, 1948; Invited by Norwegian Govt. to paint life & landscape in Northern Norway & Islands of Spitsbergen. Mbrships: Fndr. Mbr., Delhi Silpi Chakra, New Delhi; Chmn., ibid, 3 yrs. Publd. in var. mags. & periodicals. Hons. incl: 1st Award, All India Exhib., 1954; Gold Medal for Water Colour, ibid, 1955; Silver Plaque, Int. Biannale, Sao Paulo, Brazil, 1963. Address: Mod. Schl., Barakhamba Rd., New Delhi-1, India. 133.

KRISZTINKOVICH, Maria (Mrs. J.E. Horvath), b. 22 Mar. 1918. Senior Library Assistant. Educ: Acad. of Commerce, Budapest. Appts: Sr. Lib. Asst., Univ. of B.C. Lib., Canada, 1961-. Mbrships: English Ceramic Circle; Keramikfreunde der Schweiz; Vereniging van Vriended der Nederlandse Ceramiek; Keramos Gesellschaft der Keramikfreunde; Vancouver Museums & Planetarium Assn.; San. Fran. Ceramic Circle. Publs: Faenze (no. 3) 1959; Medelingenblad, Vrienden van de Nederlandse Ceramiek (no. 14), 1959; A Doukhobor Bibliography, ref. publ., Univ. of B.C., 1968-72; French Revolutionary Pamphlets, ref. publ., Univ. of B.C., 1973; var. other contbns. to reviews. Address: 3837 Osler St., Vancouver 9, B.C., Canada.

KRIVINE, Jarvis David, b. 22 Feb. 1919. Journalist. Educ: B.A. (Hons.), Christ Church, Oxford, U.K., 1940. Appts: Serv., to Lt., Br. Army, 1941-46; ILO Corres., Israel, 1953-57; Dir., Tech. Assistance Bur., Prime Min.'s Off., 1957-58; Econ. Corres., Jerusalem Post, 1960-. Ed., Proceedings of 3rd Rehovoth Conf., Praeger, N.Y., U.S.A., 1967. Address: 27a He'Chalutz St., Jerusalem, Israel.

KRIVOY, William A., b. 2 Jan. 1928. Pharmacologist. Educ: B.S., Coll. Arts & Scis., Georgetown Univ., Wash. D.C., 1948; M.S., Schl. of Med., ibid, 1949; Ph.D., 1953. Appts: Pharmacologist, Chem. Corps Med. Labs., Army Chem. Ctr., Md., 1950-54; Postdoctoral Rsch. Fellow, U.S. Pub. Hlth. Serv., Dept. Pharmacol., Univ. of Pa., Phila., 1954-55, & Dept. Pharmacol., Univ. of Edinburgh, U.K., 1955-67; Instr., Dept. Pharmacol., Tulane Univ., New Orleans, La., U.S.A., 1957-59; Asst. Prof.-Assoc. Prof., Dept. Pharmacol., Baylor Univ., Houston, Tex., 1959-68; Pharmacologist, Addiction Rsch. Ctr., Nat. Inst. Mental Hlth., Lexington, Ky., 1968-. Mbrships. incl: Am. Soc. Clin. Pharmacol. & Therapeutics; Biophysical Soc.; N.Y. Acad. Scis.; Western Pharmacol. Soc. Papers, reports, articles, profl. jrnls. & publs. Address: NIDA-ARC., P.O. Box 2000, Lexington, KY 40507, U.S.A.

KROEPELIN, Hans Wolfram Dietrich, b. 28 Dec. 1901. Professor Emeritus. Educ: Univs. of Frieburg, Berlin & Tech. Univ., Berlin, Germany; Dr.phil., 1926; Erlangen Univ. 1930-35. Appts: Prof. of Gen. Chem., Univ. of Istanbul, 1935-37; Chemist, Schwarzheide BRABAG, 1938-45; Prof. & Dir., Inst. of Applied Chem., Erlangen Univ., 1945-46; Prof. & Dir., Inst. of Chem. Technol., Brunswick (Braunschweig) Tech. Univ., 1946-72; Emeritus, 1972-. Mbrships. incl: Dean, Natural Sci. & Philos. fac., Brunswick Tech. Univ. 1948-49; Rector, ibid, 1963-64; Prorector, 1965-66; Pres., Brunswick sci. soc., 1960-63; Pres., European assn. of organic chem., 1962-63; Corres. Mbr., Soc. Royale des Sciences de Liege, 1971. Author of publs. in field. Hons: Ehren-Ritter, 1960, & Rechts-Ritter, 1968, Order of St. John; Grosses Verdienstkreuz, Niedersächsischen Verdienstordens, 1973. Address: Hermann-Riegelstr. 12, D 33 Braunschweig, German Fed. Repub.

KROGSHEDE, Kristian, b. 12 Feb. 1893. Director of Sports Institute. Educ: Studies in var. schls. in Denmark, Finland, Germany & U.S.A. Appts: Prof., H.S. of Phys. Educ., Ollerup, 1920-37; Fndr. & Dir., Inst. Sup. de Sports, Gerlev, 1938-; Dir., Danish Women's Team to Olympics, Berlin, 1936; Dir., Danish Men's Team to Lingia of Stockholm & Students' Team in Belgium, 1939; Num. tours throughout Europe, 1946-54. Mbrships: Danish Socs. of Shooting, Gymnastics & Sport. Publs.

incl: Fri Idraet, Folkedans, Anstandsdanse og Menuetter. Competitor in Gymnastics & Athletics at Olympics, Antwerp, 1920, & Paris, 1924. Address: Frederiksborgvej 135, Roskilde, Denmark. 43.

KROHN, Ernst C., b. 23 Dec. 1888. Teacher & Bibliographer. Appts: Tchr. of Piano, 1909-53; Lectr., Hist. of Music, Washington Univ., St. Louis, Mo., 1934-50; Dir. of Music, St. Louis, 1953-63; Hon. Curator, Gaylord Music Lib., Washington Univ.; Asst. Ed., Shattinger Music Co. Mbrships: Musicians Guild of St. Louis; Pres., ibid; Medieval Acad. of Am.; Renaissance Soc.; Int. Music Soc.; Mo. Historical Soc. Publs: Century of Missouri Music, 1922; Missouri Music, 1971. Address: 428 E. Jackson Rd., St. Louis, MO 63114, U.S.A. 30.

KROHN, Hellmut, b. 29 Aug. 1897. Jurist. Educ: Dr.'s degree, int. law, Univ. of Hamburg, Germany. Appts: Mil. serv., 1915-19; Commercial man, Hamburg & Chile, 1920-27; Employee & Departmental Chief, Siemens A.G., Berlin, 1928-46; Mil. serv., WWII; Town Clerk, Celle, Lower Saxony, 1947; Advsry. activity, 1963-. Hon. Life mbr., Int. Union of Mayors, Stuttgart-Paris. Author of articles in Niemeyers Zeitschrift für internationales Recht & Zeitschrift für Politik. Hons: Iron Cross, Classes I & II, War decoration of Austria & Bulgaria, 1916; German Fed. Cross of Merit, Class I, & Cross of Merit, Red Cross, 1962. Address: Lueneburger Heerstrasse 10, Celle, German Fed. Repub.

KROMAN, Erik Jørgensen, b. 26 Feb. 1892. Archivist. Educ: Cand. mag., Copenhagen, 1925; Dr. Phil., ibid, 1947. Appts. incl: Ed., Editions of the old Country Laws of Denmark, 1925; Archivist, National Archives, 1930; Chief Archivist, ibid, 1956-62; Lectr., Palaeography, Copenhagen Univ., 1947-68. Mbrships: Det danske Sprog- og Litteraturelskab, 1928; Selskabet for Udgivelse af Kilder til dansk Historie, 1941; Kungl. samfundet für utgifvande af handskrifter rörande Skandinaviens historia, 1958. Author of num. publs. inclng: Marstal Sofarts Historie indtil 1925, 1928; Skriftens Historie i Danmark fra Reformationen til Nutiden, 1943; Middelalderlig Skrift, 1951; Ambrosius Stub og hans aeroske Forbindelser, 1967; Den danske Rigslovgivning indtil 1400, 1971. Hons: Knight, Order of Dannebrog, 1953. Address: Hesselvang 8, 2900 Hellerup, Denmark. 43, 134.

KROMPHARDT, Karl, b. 9 Nov. 1924. Editor. Educ: Dip., Univ. of Kiel, German Fed. Repub., 1954. Appts: Publisher's Rdr., Vieweg-Verlag, Braunschweig, 1955; Co-Fndr., Verlag Karl Heinrich Bock, Bad Honnef, Bonn/Rhine, 1965; Ed., "Physikalische Blätter" (Physik Verlag, Weinheim/Bergstrasse), Bonn/Rhine, 1973. Mbrships: Deutsche Physikalische Gesellschaft; Astronomische Gesellschaft; Verband Alter Wingolfiten; Reporter, Humboldt-Gesellschaft. Author, Vom Zukunftsauftrag der neuen Universität, 1963. Recip., Iron Cross, 2nd Class, 1944. Address: Schmidtbonnstr. 10, D-53 Bonn 1, German Fed. Repub. 43.

KRONACKER, (Baron) Paul Georges, b. 5 Nov. 1897. Belgian Minister of State; Industrialist. Educ: Univ. of Brussels. Appts. incl: Mbr., House of Reps., Belgium, 1946-68; Successively, Min. of Imports, Min. for Supplies, 1944-47; Spkr., House of Reps., 1958-61. Mbrships. incl: Govt. Comm. for Peaceful Atomic Energy Dev.; late Chmn., Int. Sugar Coun.; Chmn., Nat. Permanent Comm. for Agricl. Inds., Brussels; Hon. Chmn., Int.

Commn. for Agricl. Inds., Paris; Mbr., Control Comm., Ecole Nationale Superieure d'arch. et des arts Visuels. Author, Souvenirs de Paix et de Guerre, & several publs. on econ. & sci. matters. Hons. incl: Grand Croix de l'Ordre de la Couronne; Grand Officier de l'Ordre de Léopold, Croix de Guerre (Belgium), WWI & II; Off., Legion of Merit, U.S.A.; Cmdr., Légion d'Honneur, France. Address: St. Katelijnevest 54, B-2000 Antwerp, Belgium. 34, 43.

KRONOVET, Milton, b. 13 July 1904. Dealer in Autographs, Manuscripts & Historical Documents, Retired Dr. of Chiropractic. Educ: B.S., CCNY, 1928; Grad. Schl., Columbia Univ., 1928-29; Dr. of Chiropractic, N.Y. Schl. of Chiropractic, 1935; Licensed, Dr. of Chiropractic, N.Y. State & Vt. Appts: Pvte. prac., Chiropractic, 1935-67; Tchr., Basic Scis., Chiropractic Inst. of N.Y., 1936-67; Prof. & Chmn., Dept. of Orthopedics, ibid, 1955-67. Mbrships: Antiquarian Booksellers' Assn.; Manuscript Soc.; Universal Autograph Collectors' Club; Am. Philatelic Soc.; Soc. of Philatelic Americans; Kts. of Pythias. Publ: Fundamentals of Histology. Hons: Fellow, Int. Coll. of Chiropractic, 1946; Yrbook. Dedication, Chiropractic Inst. of N.Y., 1954; Alumni Assn. Award, ibid, 1964. Address: 881-C Balmoral Ct., Lakewod, NJ 08701, U.S.A. 6.

KROON, Sigurd, b. 10 Jan. 1915. Educator. Educ: B.A., 1935; Final Univ. Examination, 1945; Dissertation, 1948. Appts. incl: Asst. Prof., Univ. of Lund, Sweden, 1948-53; Prof., Tchrs. Coll., Lund, 1953-60, Malmö, 1960-71; Prin., Kristianstad's Tchrs. Coll., 1971-. Mbrships: Commission des statuts synodaux de la société de l'histoire de l'Eglise de France (Corresponding). Publs: Det svenska prästmötet under medeltiden, 1948; Ordinarium missae, 1953; Kyrkohistoria för gymnasiet, 1955; Löftet, offret & lagen. Fran biblisk forntid till kyrklig nutid, 1970. Hons: Off., Palmes académiques, France, 1954; Knight, Order of the North Star, 1971. Address: Stora Tomegatan 8, 223 51 Lund, Sweden. 134.

KRUEGER, Hilmar Carl, b. 19 Apr. 1904. Vice Provost for University Branches & Community & Technical Programs; Professor of History. Educ: B.A., Northwestern Coll., 1925; Ph.D (Hist.), Univ. of Wis., 1932. Appts. incl: Instr.-Asst. Prof.-Assoc. Prof. of Hist., Milwaukee Ctr., Univ. of Wis., 1929-40; Chmn., Dept. of Hist., ibid, 1935-40; Taft Asst. Prof.-Assoc. Prof.-Prof. of Medieval Hist., Univ. of Cinn., Ohio, 1940-61; Hd., Dept. of Hist., ibid, 1960-63; Fndr. & Dean of Univ. Coll., 1960-69, of Raymond Walers Coll., 1967-69, & of Tri-Co. Ctr., 1968-69, Univ. of Cinn; Vice-Provost for Univ. Brs. & Community & Tech. Progs., ibid, 1969-; Vis. Lectr. at sev. Italian Univs., 1949-57. Mbrships. incl: Am. Histl. Assn.; Medieval Acad. of Am.; Societa Ligure di Storia Patria, Genoa, Italy; Nat. Bd. of Dirs., Torch Int., Int. Pres., 1971-72; Omicron Delta Kappa. Publs. incl: Notai Liguri del sec. XII e XIII: Lanfranco (1202-1226) (w. R.L. Reynolds), 3 vols., 1951-53; Co-author, 3 other books on Italian hist; Num. articles & reviews in hist. & other jrnls. Hons. incl: Appreciation Cert., Cinn. Personnel Assn.; Commencement Speaker at num. H.S.'s. Address: University of Cincinnati, 201 Hanna Hall, Cincinnati, OH 45221, U.S.A.

KRUG, (Mrs.) Adele Jensen, b. 30 Mar. 1908. Educator. Educ: B.A., Gallaudet Coll., Wash. D.C.; M.S., Cath. Univ. of Am., Wash. D.C. Appts: Instr., R.I. Schl. for the Deaf, Providence, 1930-32; Instr., Gallaudet Coll., Wash. D.C., 1955-63, Asst. Prof., 1963-67,

Assoc. Prof., 1967-. Mbrships: AAUP; ALA; D.C. Lib. Assn.; Amos Kendall Soc.; Convention of Am. Instrs. of the Deaf; Nat. Assn. of the Deaf; Gallaudet Coll. Alumni Assn.; Phi Kappa Zeta; Nat. Sec.-Treas., ibid, 1936-47, Nat. Pres., 1954-60; PTA, D.C. Pub. Schls.; Pres., ibid, 1953-56; Women's Auxiliary, Nat.; Luth. Home. Contbr., Am. Annals of the Deaf. Address: Gallaudet College, Washington, DC 20002, U.S.A. 5, 6, 15, 42, 57, 132, 138.

KRUGER, Hardy, b. 12 Apr. 1928. Actor; Writer. Educ: Berlin H.S. Free-lance actor & writer. Mbr., Equity; Screen Actors Guild. Publs: Eine Farm in Afrika, 1970; Die Kinder von der Kastner-Farm, 1971; Wer Stehrend Stirbt, Lebt Länger, 1973. Hons: Grand Prix du Cinema Francais, 1961; Prix Femina, 1962; Best Actor of Yr., Yugoslavia, 1968. Address: 813 Starnberg am See, Max-Emanual-Str. 16, German Fed. Repub. 2, 92.

KRUSJNA, Karel Jindřich (pseudonym, John Danius), b. 28 Sept. 1913. Author. Educ: University of Bratislava, Czechoslovakia. Appts: w. Royal Lib., S., 1968-. Mbrships: Literární Klub, Stockholm. Publs: Three of Millions, 1966; Snowstorm, 1968; White Adventure, 1969; (as John Danius) K smrti odsouzený vypráví, 1971; Zavrazdení & Jménem Satana, 1972; Pan Dadácek má dovolenou, Jedenáctý obvod & Snehová boufe, 1973. Address: Erik Segersällsv. 15 1, 126 50 Hägersten, Sweden. 134.

KRUSKAMP, Janet, b. 10 Dec. 1934. Artist; Teacher; Juror. Educ: Chouinard Art Inst., L.A. Art works, in oil or egg tempera, are included in pub. & pvte. collections throughout the world inclng. Grand Gall., Inc., Seattle, Wash., Rosicrucian Egyptian Mus., San Jose, Calif, Triton Mus. of Art, Santa Clara, Calif. & CVAA & La Grange Coll. (La Grange Nat. Competition), La Grange, Ga. Participated in num. Grp. Exhibs. throughout world & has held many Solo Exhibs. Grp. Shows. incl: Am. Artists Profl. League Grand Nat., N.Y., 1972, '73 & '74; Springville Mus. of Art 50th Annual, Springville, Utah; M.H. DeYoung Mem. Mus. Soc. of Western Artists Annual, San Fran.; Prix de Paris, Galls. Raymond Duncan, Paris, France; Artistes U.S.A., Galls. Raymond Duncan, Paris & N.Y.; La Grange Nat. Art Competition, La Grange, Ga. Recent Solo Exhibs. incl: 2 major shows, Rosicrucian Egyptian Mus., San Jose, Calif.; Triton Mus. of Art, Santa Clara, Calif.; Charles & Emma Frye Art Mus., Seattle, Wash., 1974; Mus. of Southwest in Midland, Tex., 1974. Mbrships: Fellow, Am. Artists Profl. League, N.Y.; Soc. of Westen Artists, San Fran.; former Pres., Los Gatos Art Assn., 1969. Recip. num. awards & prizes inclng. 1st Grand Prize & "Andy" Trophy, 1973 Grand Galleria Nat. Art Competition, Seattle, Wash. Address: 1627 Hyde Drive, Los Gatos, CA 95030, U.S.A. 5, 37, 138.

KU, Yu Hsiu, b. 24 Dec. 1902. Electrical Engineer; Educator Educ: Grad., Tsing Hua Coll., Peking, China, 1923; S.B., MIT, U.S.A., 1925; S.M., ibid, 1926; Sc.D., 1928. Appts. incl: Dean Engrng., Tsing Hua Univ., 1932-37; Vice Min. of Educ., Rep. of China, 1938-44; Dean, Engrng., 1931-32, Pres., 1944-45, Ctrl. Univ.; Commnr. of Educ., Shanghai, 1945-47; Pres., Chengchi Univ., 1947-49; Vis. Prof., MIT, U.S.A., 1950-52; Prof., Univ. of Pa., 1952-71; Prof. Emeritus, ibid, 1972-. Fellow of IEEE, N.Y. & London. Mbrships. incl: Gen. Assembly, Int. Union Theoretical & Applied Mechs.; Past Pres., Chinese Inst. Elec. Engrs.; Acad. Sinica, U.S. Nat. Comm. on Theoretical & applied

Mechs. Publs. incl: Analysis & Control of Nonlinear Systems, 1958; Electric Energy Conversion, 1959; Transient Circuit Analysis, 1961; var. literary works, poems, inclng. Selected Poems, 2 vols., 1973. Collected Scientific Papers, 1971; Var. literary works, poems. Recip. of many hons. inclng: Hon. LL.D., Univ. Pa., Lamma Medal, IEEE, Gold Medal, Chinese Inst. E.E., 1972. Address: Moore Schl. of Elec. Engrng., Univ. of Pennsylvania, Philadelphia, PA 19174, U.S.A. 2, 12, 14, 26, 128.

KUBENA, John A., b. 17 Mar. 1900. County Clerk. Educ: Tex. A & M Univ., College Stn. Appts: Hd. Teller, Gulf State Bank, Houston, Tex., 1922-24; Owner, Kubena Chevrolet Co., Fayetteville, Tex., 1928-31; Co. Clerk, Fayette Co., La Grange, Tex., 1935-73. Mbrships: Life Mbr., Master Masons; Life Mbr., Shriner, Arabia Temple, Houston; Sec.-Treas., Fayette Co. Democratic Exec. Comm., 1928-34; Pres., Co. & Dist. Clerk's Assn., 1942-45; Pres., La Grange Lions Club, 1945; Supreme Lodge SPJST, Fraternal Ins.; Dir. & V.P., Temple, Tex., 1953-56 & 1962-73; Sec. & Treas., Fayette Co. Wildlife Coun., 1960-73; Dir., Sportsmen's Clubs of Tex., 1961-65; V.P., ibid, 1965-73. Hons. incl: Outstanding Co. Clerk in Tex., 1971; Life Mbrship. as Nat. Pigeon Judge & breeder of French Mtn. Pigeons, Nat. Pigeon Show, Houston, 1973. Address: 557 N. Monroe, La Grange, TX 78945, U.S.A.

KUBIAK, Teresa, b. 26 Dec. 1937. Opera Singer. Grad., magna cum laude, Music Acad., Lodz, Poland. Soloist in Lodz Opera Grand Theatre. Has appeared on most famous operatic stages in world, incl. N.Y., Chgo., Houston, San Fran., Miami, Covent Garden, London, Staatsoper, Vienna, Venice, Lisbon, Staatsoper, Munich, Prague & Leipzig; Undertaken prin. role in Tosca, Aida, Madame Butterfly, Queen of Spades, Manon Lescaut, Elektra, Lohengrin, Maskenbal, Fliegender, Holländer, Jenufa; Her Debut in U.S.A. was Goldmark's opera The Queen of Sheba at Carnegie Hall in 1970; then appeared in Euryanthe at N.Y. Philharmonic. Apart from operatic performances, she also takes part in symphonic concertos, singing oratorios, masses, incl. Britten's Requiem, Verdi's Requiem & Szymanowski's III Symphony. Has recorded La Calisto, Argo, Glagolitic Mass, The Queen of Sheba & Eurynthe. Recip. prizes at Katowice, 1960 & Lodz, 1961 & at Int. Competitions of Music at Helsinki, Finland, 2nd prize, 1962; Toulouse, France, bronze medal, 1963; Munich, Germany, 2nd prize, 1965; Moscow, Russia, Diploma, 1966. Address: Narutowicza 75E, 90-132 Lodz, Poland. 5.

KUBICZ, Józef, b. 26 Oct. 1906. Physician; Dermatologist. Educ: Ph.D., Jan Kazimierz Univ., Lvov, Poland, 1930; Med. Fac., ibid, 1936-39; Grad., Med. Inst., Lvov, 1941; M.D., Med. Schl., Wroclaw, 1950. Appts: Subs. Asst.-Demonstrator, Physiol. Chem., Jan Kazimierz Univ., Lvov, 1939-41; Bacteriol., Inst. Control Typhoid Fever, Lvov, 1941-43; Asst., Pediatric Clin., ibid, 1943-45; Sr. Asst.-Assoc. Prof., Dermatol. Clin., Wroclaw, 1946-54; Dir.-Extraordinary Prof., Clin. Skin Diseases, 1954-; Vice-Dean-Dean, Med. Fac., Wroclaw, 1956-60. Mbrships: Pres., Wroclaw Div., Polish Dermatol. Soc., 1961-; Past Pres., Wroclaw Div. Polish Physiolog. Soc.; Wroclaw Sci. Soc.; Polish Med. Soc.; Edit.-Bd. Przeglad Dermatol. Author 82 papers & 23 preliminary communications, incl. Acne uratica faciei cum keratosi folliculari uratica corporis, 1973; Eczema senile cum alopecia mucinosa, 1973; Haemangiomatosis centrofacialis et teleangiectasiae symmetricae corporis congenitae, 1973. Recip. Golden Cross Distinction, 1959. Address: Curie-Sklodowaskiej 48/8, 50-369 Wroclaw, Poland. 50, 131.

KUBLY, Herbert Oswald, b. 26 Apr. 1915. Author; Educator; Farmer. Educ: B.A., Univ. of Wis. Appts: Reporter, Pitts. Sun-Telegraph, 1937-42; N.Y. Herald Tribune, 1942-44; Music Critic, Time mag., 1945-47; Sec., Dramatists League of Am., 1947-49; Fulbright Lectr., Univ. of Milan, Italy, 1950; Assoc. Prof., Univ. of Ill., 1949-54; Writer, Holiday & Life mags., 1955-61; Vis. Lectr., Columbia Univ. & New Schl. for Soc. Rsch., 1962-64; Prof., San Fran. State Coll., 1964-68; Writer-in-Res. & Prof., Engl., Univ. of Wis. Owner, Operator, Wilhelm Tell Farm, New Glarus, Wis. Mbrships: Authors League of Am.; Dramatists Guild of Am.; Coun. for Wis. Writers. Publs. incl: Men to the Sea, 1944, Inherit the Wind, 1948 (plays); American in Italy (travel), 1955; Italy, 1961, Switzerland, 1964; At Large (essays), 1964; The Dutchess of Glover (novel), 1964; Contbr. to num. mags. Hons: Nat. Book Award, for American in Italy, 1956; 1st Award, Coun. for Wis. Writers, 1970. Address: Humanities Div., Univ. of Wis., Parkside, Kenosha, WI 53140, U.S.A. 1, 29.

KUBO, Ryogo, b. 15 Feb. 1920. Professor of Physics. Educ: B.D., Dept. of Phys., Univ. of Tokyo, 1941; Ph.D., ibid, 1949. Appts: Asst. Prof., Dept. of Phys., Univ. of Tokyo, 1948-54, Prof., Dept. Phys., Fac. of Sci., 1954-, Dean, Fac. of Sci., 1968-71; Vis. Prof., Univ. of Chgo., U.S.A., 1963, Univ. of Pa., 1963-64, SUNY at Stony Brook, 1972. Pres., Physical Soc. of Japan, 1964-65; V.P., Int. Union of Pure & Applied Phys., 1973-. Mbrships: Physical Soc. of Japan; Pres., ibid, 1964-65; V.P., Int. Union of Pure & Applied Phys., 1973-; Am. Physical Soc.; Hon. For. Mbr., Am. Acad. of Sci. & Arts. Publs. (co-author): Statistical Mechanics, 1965; Thermodynamics, 1968; Solid State Physics, 1969. Contbr., profl. publs. Hons. incl: Fujiwara Prize, 1970; Order of Culture, Japan, 1973. Address: Dept. of Physics, Faculty of Science, University of Tokyo, Bunkyoku, Tokyo 113, Japan.

KUBY, Thomas E. Public Relations & Educational Consultant. Educ: B.S., Schl. of Jrnlsm., Ohio Univ., 1955; 30 postgrad. courses/seminars, at 12 univs., since 1955. Appts: Supvsr., P.R./Advt., Diamond Shamrock Corp., Cleveland, Ohio, 1955-60, Creative Servs. & Publs., Brunswick Corp., Chgo., Ill., 1960-62; Sr. Writer, Ed., Grp. Ldr. Presentations, Martin Marietta Corp., Orlando, Fla., 1962-66; Dir. Communications, TRW Inc., Cleveland, 1966-73; Tom Kuby & Assoc., Chagrin Falls, Ohio, 1973-. Mbrships. incl: Treas., Gtr. Cleveland Chapt., P.R. Soc. Am.; Am. Soc. for Trng. & Dev.; Creative Educ. Fndn.; Adult Educ. Coun. Contbr., num. articles, mags., trade jrnls. Hons. incl: PRSA Golden Achievement Award; 4 Geo. Wash. Medals, Freedoms Fndn., 1958-61; 23 profl. awards. Address: 7236 Chagrin Rd., Chagrin Falls, OH 44022, U.S.A. 8, 24.

KUCZER, Michael John, b. 23 Oct. 1910. Artist. Educ: Winnipeg Schl. of Art, Man., 1925-27; Royal Coll. of Mus., London, U.K., 1929-34 (violin). Appts: dual career as Artist/Concert Violinist; Violinist w. Royal Philharmonic Orch., 1930's; Commercial Designer; Tool Maker & Insp. in aircraft firm, WWII; Mus. Tchr. Hons: Schlrships to Winnipeg Schl. of Art, 1925-27; Royal Schl. Schrlships, 2 yrs. to Royal Coll. of Mus., London, 1929 - extensions, 1931, 32, 33. Address: R.R.2, Stouffville, Ont., Canada L0H 1LO.

KUEHLER, Marilyn Kay, b. 19 Oct. 1945. Journalist; Free-lance Writer. Educ: St. Mary's Univ., San Antonio, Tex.; Incarnate Word Coll., ibid; B.J., Univ. of Tex., Austin, 1967. Appts: Reporter, Youth Ed., Abilene Reporter News, Abilene, Tex., 1967-69; City Hall Reporter, Women's Ed., Honolulu Advertiser, Honolulu, Hawaii, 1969-72; Biographer of Archbishop Robert E. Lucey (retd.), manuscript to be publd. in 1974, 1972-. Mbrships: Theta Sigma Phi; Honolulu Press Club; San Antonio Conservation Soc. Free-lance Articles: A Resident Looks at Hawaii, Doctors' Finances Mag., 1972; Tower Heroes, The Minn. Daily, 1966. Recip., Hon. Mention for Feature Writing, Tex. Assocd. Press Mng. Eds. Annual Contest, 1969. Address: 8710 Data Pt., No. 6912, San Antonio, TX 78229, U.S.A. 78.

KUEHN, Herman, b. 3 June 1932. Chemist. Educ: Dr.'s degree, Munich Univ., Germany, 1957. Appts: Hd., Lab., Doerner Inst., Munich, 1959-73; Swiss Inst. of Art Knowledge, Zurich, Switzerland, 1974-. Mbrships: Int. Inst. for Conservation; Int. Comm. of Museums. Publs: Pigmente in den Gemälden der Schack-Galerie, 1969; Erhaltung & Pflege von Kunstwerken & Antiquitäten mit Materialkunde & Einführung in Kunstlerische Techniken, Vol. I, 1974; Articles & rsch. reports on scientific examination of paintings & on mus. environment in ref. wks., ency. & profl. jrnls. Address: 8 Munich 70, Pfeuferstrasse 33/VI, German Federal Repub. 133.

KUESEL, Thomas Robert, b. 30 July 1926. Engineer. Educ: B.E., Yale Univ., 1946; M. Engrng., ibid, 1947. Appts: incl: Structural Engr., Proj. Engr. & Assoc., Parsons, Brinckerhoff, Quade & Douglas, N.Y.C., 1947-63; Proj. Mgr., San Fran. Off., ibid, 1967-68, Ptnr., Dir. & Sr. V.P., N.Y., 1968-; Asst. Mgr. of Engrng., Parsons, Brinckerhoff-Tudor-Bechtel, San Fran., 1963-67. Mbrships. incl: U.S. Nat. Comm. on Tunneling Technol., 1972-; Vice Chmn., Org. for Econ. Co-operation & Dev., Int. Tunneling Conf., Wash. D.C., 1970; Fellow, Am. Soc. of Civil Engrs. & Am. Cons. Engrs. Coun.; Int. Assn. for Bridge & Structural Engrng.; British Tunneling Soc.; Underground Construction Rsch. Coun., Yale Sci. & Engrng. Assn.; Tau Beta Pi, Sigma Xi. Publs. incl: Presented papers to num. confs. on excavations & tunneling; Design projs. incl. Newport Suspension Bridge, R.I., 1959-63; NORAD Combat Ops. Ctr., Colo. Springs, 1962, San Fran. Bay Area Rapid Transit System, 1963-68; Hampton Rds. Bridge-Tunnel, Va., 1969-74. Address: Parsons, Brinckerhoff, Quade & Douglas, 1 Penn Plaza, 250 W. 34th St., N.Y., NY 10001, U.S.A. 6, 26.

KUFELDT, George, b. 4 Nov. 1923. Professor; Minister. Educ: A.B., Anderson Coll., Ind., 1945; Th.B., ibid, 1946; B.D., Schl. of Theol., ibid, 1953. Appts: Pastor, Ch. of God, Homestead, Fla., 1948-50, Cassopolis, Mich., 1954-57, Lansdale, Pa., 1957-60; Asst. Prof., Schl. of Theol., Anderson Coll., 1961-66; Assoc. Prof. of Old Testament, ibid, 1966-. Mbrships: Soc. of Biblical Lit.; Nat. Assn. Profs. of Hebrew; Wesleyan Theol. Soc.; Soc. for Pentecostal studies; Am. Hellenic Educl. Progressive Assn.; Am. Histl. Soc. of Germans from Russia. Author, The Book of Proverbs, The Wesleyan Bible Commentary, Vol. 11, 1968. Address: 907 N. Nursery Rd., Anderson, IN 46012, U.S.A. 13.

KUHN, Anne Wicker (Mrs.), University Professor. Educ: Music Dip., Trinity Coll. of Music, London, U.K.; 2 Lang. Dips., Germany, 1951, '52; B.A., John Fletcher Coll., U.S.A.; M.A., Boston Univ.; Harvard Univ., 1942-45;

Germanic Langs., ibid, 1966-69; Certs., Goethe Inst., Munich, Germany, summers, 1966, '67, '69-71; Univ. of Munich, 1971; Columbia Univ., U.S.A.; Sanskrit & Marathi, Yeotmal, India, 1957-58; Doct. Candidate, Boston Univ., U.S.A., 1971-. Appts. incl: Libn., Harvard Univ., Andover-Harvard Theol. Lib., Harvard Coll.-Widener, 1939-44; Tchr., U.S. Armed Forces, Munich, Germany, 1951-53; Tchr., Union Biblical Sem., Yeotmal, India, 1957-58; Prof., Germany, Asbury Coll., 1961-65, 1971-; Relief & rehab. work among refugees & displaced persons, W. Germany, Jordan, Holland, Belgium, & France. Mbrships. incl: Soc. of Friends; AAUW; Ky. & Nat. Educ. Assns.; Comm. Chmn., Am. Assn. of Tchrs. of German; Daughters of the Am. Revolution; Pres., Delta Phi Alpha; V.P., Harvard Dames. Publs. incl: The Effect of Protestant Reformation upon music of the Church, 1942; The Influence of Paul Gerhardt on Wesleyan Hymnody, 1969. Contbr. to var. profl. jrnls. Hons. incl: Delta Phi Alpha Award, 1965-66; Thomas Mann Award, 1967; German Consular Award, 1967. Address: 406 Kenyon Ave., Wilmore, KY 40390, U.S.A. 5, 13, 15, 22, 125, 132, 138.

KÜHNLE, Günther Maximilian, b. 6 Oct. 1927. Business Executive. Educ: Dr.rer.pol., Univ. Appts: Chmn., Bd. of Dirs., Winschermann GmbH, Düsseldorf; Chmn., Advsry. Body, Geraldy & Raab Karcher GmbH, Saarbrücken, & Rhenania Saarbrücken; Advsr., Kohlbecher & Co. GmbH, Saarbrücken, & Notgemeinschaft Deutscher Steinkohlenbergbau GmbH, Essen; Bd., Saarlor, Saarbrücken-Strassburg, Rhespag, Ludwigshafen, & Manufrance N.V., Rotterdam; Pres., Saar-Pfalz-Kanal-Verein e.V., Saarbrücken. Address: Saarbergwerke Aktiengesellschaft, Trierer Str. 1, 66 Saarbrücken, German Fed. Repub.

KUKKÄMAKI, Tauno Johannes, b. 11 Oct. 1909. Geodesist. Educ: Ph.D., Turku Univ., Finland, 1933. Appts: State Geodesist, Finnish Geodetic Inst., 1935-55; Acting Dir., ibid, 1955-63; Dir., 1963-. Mbrships: 1st V.P., Int. Assn. of Geodesy; Finnish Acad. of Scis.; Finnish Acad. of Tech. Scis.; Soc. of Mil. Scis. Publs: Untersuchungen über die Endmasse aus geschmolzenem Quarz, 1933; Ohio Standard Baseline, 1969. Hons: Finnish Cross of Independence, 3rd class w. oak leaves, & 4th class; Cmdr., Lion of Finland. Address: Geodeettinen laitos, Pasilank. 43 A, SF-00240, Helsinki, Finland.

KULCSAR, Francis E., b. 8 Oct. 1901. Physician. Educ: M.D., Med. Schl. of Debrecen, Hungary, 1925; Intern, Univ. Hosps., ibid, 1925-26. Appts. incl: Asst. Prof., Univ. Hosp., Nervous & Mental Disturbance, Budapest, 1936-40; Assoc. Prof., Univ. of Budapest, 1940; Prof. & Chmn., Univ. Hosp., Nervous & Mental Disturbance, Szeged, 1940-44; Asst. Dir., Trng., N.C. Hosp. Bd. of Control., Raleigh, U.S.A., 1955-59; Clin. Dir., Portsmouth Receiving Hosp., Ohio, 1959-64. Mbrships: AMA; Am. Psych. Assn.; Am. Acad. Neurol.; Eastern Assn. EEG. Author of sci. publs. Address: P.O. Box 318 Portsmouth, OH 45662, U.S.A.

KULKA, Louise Therese, b. 26 May 1921. Librarian; News Service & Information Administrator. Educ: B.A. (summa cum laude), St. Mary's Coll., Notre Dame, Ind., 1942; M.A., Western Reserve Univ., 1956; M.L.S., Kent State Univ., 1973. Appts: Publicity Asst., Gtr. Cleveland Red Cross Chapt., 1946-48, Western Reserve Univ., 1949-52, Fenn Coll., 1953-55; Publicity Sec., Cleveland Coun. on World Affairs, 1952-53; Dir., News Serv., St. Mary's

Coll., 1955-56, Pub. Info., Fenn Coll., 1956-58, News Bur., Oberlin Coll., 1958-71, Acting Dir., P.R., 1970-71; Pt.-time Asst., Kent Free Lib., Ohio, 1972; Libn., Bus. Info. Dept., Cleveland Pub. Lib., 1972-. Past mbr. & off., var. welfare & civic orgs. Contbr., jrnls., mags. & newspapers. Recip., var. acad. prizes & awards. Address: 404 N. Leavitt Rd., Apt. C-3, Amherst, OH 44001, U.S.A. 15.

KULLBERG, (Gustav Adolf) Wilhelm, b. 30 Dec. 1909. Industrialist. Educ: Technical. Appts. incl: Fndr. & Mng. Dir., H. Kullberg Fabrikker, Halden, Norway. Address: H. Kullberg Fabrikker, P.O. Box 62, 1751 Halden, Norway. 43.

KULLMANN, Ortwin, b. 17 Aug. 1925. Industrialist. Educ: Pontificia Universitas Gregoriana, Rome, Italy; Univ. of Evansville, Ind., U.S.A.; Am. Inst. for For. Trade, Phoenix, Ariz.; Thunderbird Grad. Schl. of Int. Mgmt., Ariz.; B.A.; B. For. Trade; M.B.A.; Doct., Bus. Admin.; Ph.D. Appts: Dir., Thomas Josef Heimbach GmbH, Düren, German Fed. Repub., until 1961; Dir., Armstrong Kork GmbH, Münster, until 1963; Dir., J.J. Marx, Lambrecht, until 1965; Unlimited ptnr., Fritz Bracht K.G., Lüdenscheid, Chmn. of Bd., Bracht Group of Cos., & Pres., Temeter Iberica S.A., Badalona, Spain. Mbrships: Am. Marketing Assn.; Pres., Rotary Club, Lüdenscheid, 1973-74. Publs. incl: German Management Structures & Practices, 1972; Temeter in the United States Market, 1973. Recip. of hons. Address: Parkstrasse 143, 5880 Lüdenscheid, German Fed. Repub. 43.

KUMLER, Wilma Asbury, b. 20 Nov. 1946. University Consultant; Photographer. Educ: B.S., Eastern Ky. Univ., Richmond, Ky., 1968; M.S., Ohio State Univ., Columbus, Ohio, 1971. Appts: Yearbook Advsr., Wilmington H.S., Ohio, 1968-71; Home Econs. Tchr., ibid, 1968-71; Cons. & Photographer, Ohio State Univ., Columbus, 1971-72. Mbrships: Sigma Delta Epsilon; Omicron Nu; Alpha Phi Gamma; Young Republican's Club; Asst. Ed., Milestone (Eastern Ky. Univ.'s Yearbook), 1967-68; Collegiate Pentacle, 1967-68; Kappa Delta Pi, 1966-68; CWENS, 1965-66. Author of article Forecast, in Home Econs. Mag., 1969; Photographs publd. in 1968 & 1969 edits. of Hurricane's Eye, Wilmington H.S. Yearbook, Ohio. Hons: Mary King Burrier Schlrship. Award for Outstanding Jr. Home Econs. Major, Eastern Ky. Univ., Richmond, 1967; Sr. Citation for Student Publs., ibid, 1967. Address: 538 Terry Lane, Ft. Mitchell, KY 41017, U.S.A. 125, 130.

KUMM, William Howard, b. 2 June 1931. Engineering Manager. Educ: B.A., Amherst Coll., Amherst, Mass., 1952; Cert. of Bus. Admin., Johns Hopkins Univ., Balt., Md., 1959. Appts. incl: Supvsry. Engr., Westinghouse Surface Div., Balt., 1961-62; Supvsry. Engr., Systems Ops. Div., Balt., 1962-67; Mgr., Adv. Concept Engrng. Sect., Westinghouse Ocean Rsch. & Engrng. Ctr., Annapolis, Md., 1967-71; Ind. Interchange Exec., Nat. Oceanic & Atmospheric Admin., Dept. of Commerce, Wash., D.C., 1971-72; Staff Mbr., Nat. Advsry. Comm. on Oceans & Atmosphere, ibid, 1972; Mbr., Maritime Admin., Rsch. & Dev. Off., 1972; Cons., Space Satellite Tracking Ground Stns.; Participant, Nat. Acad. of Engrng. Marine Bd. Planning Effort for Future Ocean Survey & Exploration Techniques, 1972. Mbrships. incl: IEEE; Rural Area Dev. Bd., Carroll Co., N.H., 1964-65; State Chartered Citizens Advsry. Comm. on Educ., 1970-72; Marine Tech. Soc. Address: 511 Heavitree Lane, Severna Park, MD 21146, U.S.A.

KUNCEWICZ, Jerzy Karol, b. 31 July 1893. Lawyer; Scientist; Writer. Educ: Fac. of Sci., Liège Univ., Belgium; Studied Law, Warsaw Univ., Poland. Attorney-at-Law. Appts: Theoretician, Co-Fndr., Mbr. Exec. Bd., Polish Peasant Party, 1917-39; Mbr., Ctrl. Comm., Polish Independence Movement, 1918-20; Acting Chmn., Polish Nat. Coun., London, U.K., 1946-47; Co-Fndr., Peasant Int., 1946-56; Fndr. & Dir., Peasant Int. Agcy. & Bulletin. Mbr: Int. PEN Club, London Ctr. Publs: Przebudowa (Reconstruction); Na Nowych Drogach (The New Ways); Republika Globu (World Republic); Meeting With Tomorrow; Bialy Wróbel & other plays; Infinity & Reality. Address: c/o Witold Kuncewicz, Old Kennels, Flint Hill, VA 22627, U.S.A. 43.

KUNICKI-GOLDFINGER, Wladyslaw Jersy Henryk, b. 13 Feb. 1916. University Professor. Educ: Ph.M., Jagiellonian Univ., Krakow, 1938; Dr. Sci. Nat., M. Curie-Sklodowska Univ., Lublin, 1948; Habilitation, Microbiol., ibid, 1950. Appts: Pvte. Rsch. Asst., Dept. Soil Microbiol., Jagiellonian Univ., 1939; Polish Army, E., Mid-E., Africa & Italy, 1939-47; Lectr., Vet. Microbil. & Gen. Microbiol., M. Curie-Sklodowska Univ., 1947-50; Prof., Hd. Chair of Gen. Microbiol., ibid, 1950-55; Prof., Hd., Chair of Microbiol., Wroclaw Univ., 1956-61; Dir., Botan. Inst., ibid, 1957-61; Hd., Dept. Microbiol. Genetics, Inst. Immunol. Ther. Exp. Acad. Sci., Wroclaw, 1956-61; Prof. Ord., Hd., Chair of Microbiol., Warsaw Univ., 1961-70; Dir., Inst. Microbiol., ibid, 1970-72; Hd., Lab. Microbiol. Genetics, Dept. Genetics, Acad. of Sci., Warsaw, 1961-68; Vice-Dir., Inst. Biochem. Biophys., ibid, 1967-68; Vis. Prof., Univ. of Calif., Davis, U.S.A., 1970. Mbrships: Corres., Polish Acad. of Scis., 1965-; Fndr., on Gov. Bd. until 1970, Polish Microbiol. Soc.; Ed. Acta Microbiol. Polon., 1952-71; Polish Gentics Soc.; Gentics Soc. of Am. Publs: General Microbiology (in Polish), 1958; Life of Bacteria (in Polish), 1967, in 3rd ed.; Heritage & Future (in Polish), 1974; over 70 rsch. publs., most in Engl. on var. microbiol. problems. Hons: State Prize for Sci. Activity, 1955; Prize of Min. of Higher Educ., 1971 & 73. Address: c/o Inst. of Microbiol., Warsaw Univ., Nowy Swiat 67, 00-046 Warsaw, Poland.

KUNISHIO, Koichiro, b. 6 Sept. 1905. Business Executive; Administrator. Educ: Fac. of Law, Tokyo Univ., 1929. Appts: Chmn., Nitta Belting Co & Chiyoda Shoes Co.; Gov., Ibaragi Prefecture; Dir., Bd. of Econ. Stabilization & Pub. Corp. of Ind. Rehab.; Mbr., copyright Coun., Govt. Agcy. for Cultural Affairs. Mbrships: Pres., Japan Soc. of Rights of Authors & Composers; Tokyo Chmbr. of Comm. & Ind.; Japan Fedn. of the Employers Assn. Publs: The Aims of the Law Concerning the Intermediatory Business of Copyrights. Address: 24-20 Nakamachi 5 chome, Setagaya-ku, Tokyo 158, Japan.

KUNITZ, Stanley, b. 29 July 1905. Writer; Educator. Educ: B.A., Harvard Univ, 1926; M.A., ibid, 1927. Appts: Ed., Wilson Lib. Bulletin, 1928-42; Prof. of Lit., Bennington Coll., Vt., 1946-49; Lectr., New Schl. for Soc. Rsch., N.Y.C., 1950-58; Lectr., Columbia Univ., N.Y.C., 1963-66; Adjunct Prof., Schl. of the Arts, ibid, 1967-; Ed., Yale Series of Younger Poets, 1969-. Mbrships: Chmn., Dept. of Lit., Nat. Inst. of Arts & Letters; Chancellor, Acad. of Am. Poets; Exec. Bd., Am. PEN; Bd. of Dirs., Fine Arts Work Ctr., Provincetown, Mass.; Phi Beta Kappa. Publs. incl: Intellectual Things, 1930; Passport to the War, 1944; Selected Poems, 1958; The Testing-Tree, 1971; The Terrible Threshold, 1974; The Coat Without a Seam, 1974; Sev. translations from

Russian. Hons. incl: Harriet Monroe Award, 1958; Pulitzer Prize for Poetry, 1959; Litt.D., Clark Univ., Worcester, Mass., 1961; Fellowship Award, Acad. of Am. Poets, 1968; Fellowship, Yale Univ., 1969-; Cons. in Poetry, Lib. of Congress, 1974-. Address: 157 W. 12th St., N.Y., NY 10011, U.S.A. 2, 13, 34, 128.

KUNKEL, Otto A., b. 15 May 1912. Museum Director. Educ: trained as Baker & Histn: Master Baker; Mill Dir.; Dir., European Bread Mus., Judge, German Agricl. Assn. Mbrships: Study Group for Grain Rsch.; Hist. Soc., Göttingen; Homeland Union of Lower Saxony; Hon. mbr., various German Bakers' Guilds. Publs: Die Welt des Brotes in Kunst; num. articles in German daily press, in special lit. & in jrnl. of Study Group for Grain Rsch. Recip: 1st class Verdienstkreuz, 1972 & des Eberhard Paech Prize, 1974. Address: Europäisches Brotmuseum, 3403 Mollenfelde/Friedland, German Fed. Repub.

KUNTZ, Elmer Lee. Educational Administrator. Educ: B.S., Midwestern Univ. Wichita Falls, Tex., 1955; M.Ed., Tex. A & M Univ., 1964; Ph.D., Grad. Schl. of Educ., ibid, 1968. Appts. incl: U.S. Army, 2 yrs.; Supvsr. & Tchr., Voc. Educ. & Sci. Progs., Independent Schls., Munday, Tex., 1958-60, Breckenridge, 1960-63; Pt.-time Grad. Asst. to Dean, Grad. Coll., Tex. A & M Univ., 1963-66; Dir. of Admissions, Counseling & Financial Aids, Tex. State Tech. Inst., Waco, 1966-67, Dir., Sweetwater Campus, 1968; Dir., Rsch. & Dev., State Tech. Inst., Memphis, Tenn., 1969; Pres., Elko Community Coll., Nev., 1970-73; Registrar & Dir. of Rsch., Okla. Coll. of Liberal Arts, Chickasha, 1973-. Mbr., profl. orgs. Articles, voc. trng. & educ., var. publs. Recip., profl. awards. Address: 3127 S. 9th, Chickasha, OK 73018, U.S.A. 125.

KUPKA, Edmund Hans Paul, b. 27 July 1917. University Lecturer. Educ: Ph.D., Univ. of Graz, Austria, 1934; Lectr., ibid, 1950. Appts: Sci. Asst., Inst. of Bacteriol., Univ. of Graz, 1939; Sci. Asst., Zool. Inst., ibid, 1940-57; Sci. Asst., Zool. Inst., Univ. of Zurich, Switzerland, 1947-48; Dpty. Dir., UNESCO Middle East Sci. Cooperation Off., Cairo, Egypt, 1958-64; Hd., Dept. Med. Entomol., Inst. Pasteur de Tunis, Tunisia, 1966-68. Mbrships: Deutsche Zoologische Gesellschaft; Hammer Purgstall Gesellschaft. Author of over 30 sci. publs. in physiol., cell rsch. & parasitol. Hons: Gabriela Zuccari schlrship., Univ. of Padua, Italy, 1954; Theodor Körner Prize, 1956 & 1957. Address: Himmelreichweg 80, 8044, Graz, Austria. 43, 86.

KUPRIAN, Hermann Josef, b. 12 Apr. 1920. Professor. Educ: Univs. of Vienna, Innsbruck & Zurich. Appts: Prof., Landeck; Dir., Volkshochschule & Kulturreferat, Landeck; Prof., Innsbruck 1962-; Fndr., Castle entertainments, Landeck. Mbrships: Pres., Gesellschaft für Literatur & Kunst der Turmbund, Inssbruck; Ritterschaft von San Yuste, Spain; PEN Club, Austria; Die Kogge, Westphalia. Publs. incl: Dramatic works: Das kleine Schemenspiel; Das grosse Schemenspiel; Vor den Fenstern; Solferino; Lamasabathani; Poetry: Der blaue Spiegel; Abendländischer Melancholie; Traumtexte; Hymne vom Wissen. Hons: Dramatic Prize, Innsbruck, 1954; Prize, Youth Culture Week, Austria; Silver Rose lyrical prize, Salzburg, 1969. Address: Hunoldstr. 20/4, A 6020 Innsbruck, Austria.

KUPRIANOFF, Ria, b. 1 Jan. 1917. Artist. Educ: Akademie der bildenden Künste, Karlsruhe. Dir., Kindermalschule Ria Kuprianoff. Mbrships: Badischer Kunstverein;

Württ. Kunstverein; Gedok, Fedn. Int. des Arts. One-man shows: Int. Forum, Burg Liebenzell, 1968; Galerie Schumacher, Munich, 1968; Univ. of Karlsruhe, 1971; Galerie Altschwager, Hamburg, 1973; Goethe Gymnasium, Ettlingen, 1973. Group Exhibs: Badischer Kunstverein, Karlsruhe; Salon European, Nancy, etc. Address: Südl. Hildapromenade 12, 75 Karlsruhe 1, German Fed. Repub.

KUREPA, R. Duro, b. 16 Aug. 1907. University Professor. Educ: Dip., Philos. Fac., Univ. of Zagreb, Yugoslavia, 1931; Doct., Paris, France, 1935; Postgrad. studies, Warsaw, Poland, 1937, Princeton, N.J., U.S.A., 1959-60. Appts: Asst., Univ. of Zagreb, 1931-32; Secondary Schl., 1937-38; Lectr., Univ. of Zagreb, 1938-45; Full Prof., Univ. of Zagreb, 1946-65; Full Prof., Univ. of Belgrade, 1965-; Vis. Prof., Boulder, Colo., U.S.A., 1960; Dir., Math. Inst., Fac. of Sci., Zagreb, 1943-65, Belgrade, 1969-. Mbrships: Pres., Educ. Coun. of Serbia, 1968-72; V.P., Int. Comm., Math. Inst., 1952-62; Corres. mbr., Yugoslav Acad. of Sci., Zagreb, 1952-; Math. Socs., Yugoslavia, France, U.S.A.; Pres. of Union of Socs. of Mathns., Physicists & Astronomers of Yugoslavia, 1956-60; Pres., Interbalkans Comm., Math. Balkan Lib., Belgrade. Author of over 300 books & papers. Recip. of hon., Order of Work, 1965. Address: Laze Simića 9, Belgrade, Yugoslavia. 131.

KURFEHS, Harold C., Jr., b. 10 Dec. 1939. Advertising Director. Educ: B.S., St. Peter's Coll., Jersey City, N.J., 1962; M.B.A., Wharton Schl. of Finance & Commerce, Univ. of Pa., 1964. Appts: Prod. Mgr., Am. Brands, Inc., N.Y.C., 1958-62, 1964-66; Account Exec., Benton & Bowles, Inc., N.Y.C., 1966-68; Account Mgr., Wells, Rich, Greene, Inc., N.Y.C., 1968-69; V.P., Dir. of Marketing, Meta-Lang. Prods., Inc., N.Y.C., 1969-70; Sr. Account Exec., McCaffrey & McCall, Inc., N.Y.C., 1970-71; Advt. Mgr., Ethan Allen, Inc., Danbury, Conn., 1972; Dir. of Advt., ibid, 1973. Mbrships: Am. Marketing Assn.; Assn. of Nat. Advertisers; Wharton Grad. Club of N.Y.; Chmn., N.E. Leonia Civic Assn., N.J., 1971-72. Hons. incl: Oaklawn Fndn. Schol., N.Y., 1962; Pi Sigma Phi Award, Propeller Club of U.S., 1964. Address: 20 Strawberry Ridge Rd., Ridgefield, CT 06877, U.S.A. 6.

KUROKAWA, Noriaki Kisho, b. 8 Apr. 1934. Architect. Educ: Grad., Kyoto Univ., Japan, 1957; Postgrad., Arch., Tokyo Univ., 1957-62. Appts: Pres., Kisho N. Kurokawa Arch. & Assocs. & Urban Design Cons.; Dir., Inst. Soc. Engrng.; Advsr., Japan Nat. Railways, Min. of Pub. Welfare, Min. of Educ., & Japan Fndn. Mbrships: Archtl. Inst. of Japan; Japan Soc. Futurol.; City Planning Inst. of Japan. Publs. incl: Concrete Prefabricated House, 1960; Metabolism, 1960; Prefabricated House, 1963; Urban Design, 1964; Action Architecture, 1964; Death & Life of Great American Cities (translation), 1968; Homo Movens, 1969; Complete Work Series of Existing Architects of Japan, 1971, etc. Archt. works incl: Nitto Food Co., 1963; Ctrl. Lodge, Nat. Children's Land; Sakura City Hall, 1969; var. pavilions, Expo '70; Bank of Fukuoka, 1973. Recip., num. awards. Address: Aoyama Bldg., 11th floor, 1-2-3 Kita Aoyama, Minato-Ku, Tokyo, Japan.

KURTZ, Bernward Ulrich, b. 30 Oct. 1936. Architect. Educ: Kaiserslautern Schl. of Arch., 1954-57. Appts: Michael Gooss Archts., Neustadt/Wstr., W. Germany, 1957-61; Prin., Bernward U. Kurtz Eng., ibid, 1961-63; Design Archt., J.G.L. Poulson Archts., London, U.K., 1963-65; E.N. Turano Archts., N.Y.C., U.S.A.,

1965-66, Eggers & Higgins, Archts., ibid, 1966-70; Prin., The Eggers Ptnrship., Archts. & Planners, 1970-74; Ptnr., ibid, 1974-. Mbrships: Am. Inst. Archts.; Nat. Coun. Archl. Registration Bds.; N.Y. State Assn. Archts. Arch. incls: Am. Hoechst Corp. H.Q. Bldg.; BASF Wyandotte Corp. H.Q. Bldg.; Fairfield Univ. Sci. Ctr.; Ind. Univ. Nuclear Accelerator Bldg. Hons: New Good Neighbour Award, N.J. Bus. Mag., 1970, '71; Hon. Award, L.I. Assn. Commerce & Ind., 1972. Address: 333 E. 46th St., N.Y., NY 10017, U.S.A. 6, 130.

KURTZ, Paul, b. 21 Dec. 1925. Professor; Author. Educ: B.A., N.Y. Univ., 1948; M.A., Columbia Univ., 1949; Ph.D., ibid, 1952. Appts: Prof., Philos., SUNY, Buffalo; Ed., The Humanist Mag., U.S.A. Mbrships: Bd. Dirs., Am. Humanist Assn., Int. Humanist & Ethical Union (Utrecht), & Univ. Ctrs. for Rational Alternatives. Publs: Decision & the Condition of Man, 1965; Tolerance & Revolution (co-ed. w. S. Studanovic), 1971; Language & Human Nature, 1972; A Catholic/Humanist Dialogue (w. A. Dundeyne), 1972; The Humanist Alternative, 1973; Humanist Manifesto II, 1973; The Fullness of Life, 1974. Address: The Humanist, 923 Kensington Ave., Buffalo, NY 14215, U.S.A. 2, 13.

KURUBO, (Brigadier) George Tamunoiyowunam, b. 27 July 1934. Soldier; Diplomat. Educ: Govt. Coll., Umuahia, Nigeria; Royal Mil. Acad., Sandhurst, U.K.; Grad. var. inter. & Advcd. mil. cmnd. & staff Colls. Appts: Var. mil. staff & cmnd. posts; Hd., Nigerian Air Force, 1966-; Mbr. Fed. Nigerian Exec. Coun. & Supreme Mil. Coun., 1966-; Nigerian Ambassador to U.S.S.R., 1967-73. Mbr. sev. soc. & sporting clubs. Recip. Nigerian mil. & nat. medals. Address: Min. External Affairs, Lagos, Nigeria.

KURYŁOWICZ, Włodzimierz, b. 26 Sept. 1910. Physician; Professor of Microbiology. Educ: M.D., Lvov Univ., Poland, 1938. Appts: Asst. Prof.-Extraordinary Prof., Warsaw Univ.; Sr. Scientist, State Inst. of Hygiene, Cracow, 1945-47; Sr. Scientist, State Inst. of Hygiene, Warsaw, 1947-57; Vis. Scientist, Chinese Acad. of Scis., Peking, Shanghai, China, 1957-58; Sr. Scientist, Inst. of Tuberculosis, Poland, 1958-64; Gen. Dir., State Inst. of Hygiene, Warsaw, 1964-; Prof., ibid. Mbrships: Polish Acad. of Learning, 1950; Academia Nat. de Medicina, Brazil, 1961; Polish Acad. of Scis., 1964; Acad. of Med. Scis., U.S.S.R., 1966; Acad. Nat. de Med., France, 1969; German Acad. of Scis., 1971; Consultative Comm. on Med. Rsch., WHO, 1967-70; Hon. mbr., scis. socs. of U.S.S.R., Hungary, Italy, Egypt, Japan. Author of over 200 sci. papers dealing w. gen. & med. microbiol. Hons: State Prize, 2nd Class, 1950, 1st Class, 1968; Cmdr., Cross w. Star, Polish People's Repub., 1968; Cmdr., Cross w. Star, Finnish Lion, 1971. Address: State Inst. of Hygiene, 24 Chocimska, 00791 Warsaw, Poland.

KURZMAN, Paul A., b. 25 Nov. 1938. Social Work Educator & Administrator. Educ: A.B., Princeton Univ.; M.S., Columbia Univ.; Ph.D., N.Y. Univ. Appts. incl: Rsch. Fellow, Nat. Inst. of Mental Hlth., 1963-64; Mbr. Acad. of Cert. Soc. Workers, 1964-; Licensed as Cert. Soc. Worker, SUNY, 1966-. Pre-Doctl. Fellow, U.S. Pub. Hlth. Serv., 1967-70; Acting Exec. Dir., Lower Eastside Neighborhoods Assn. & Staff Dir., Two Bridges Neighborhood Coun., N.Y.C., 1967-70; Asst. Commnr. Youth Servs., Human Resources Admin., N.Y.C., 1970-72; Prog. Dir., Indl. Soc. Welfare Ctr., Columbia Univ. Schl. of Soc. Work & Adjunct Asst. Prof., Hunter Coll. Schl. of Soc. Work, CUNY, 1972-;

Soc. Welfare Cons., pub. & pvte. sectors. Mbrships. incl: V.P., N.Y.C. Chapt., Nat. Assn. of Soc. Workers; Co-Chmn., Bd. Dirs., Michael Schwerner Mem. Fund; Dir. serv. charitable orgs. Publs. incl: Harry Hopkins & The New Deal, 1974; Ed. & contbr. sev. books in field of Soc. Work; papers presented to profl. confs. & Insts. & num. articles in profl. jrnls. Hons. incl: Dr. Martin E. Dworkis Mem. Award, 1970 & Fndrs. Day Award, 1971, N.Y. Univ. Address: 75 Montgomery St., N.Y., NY 10002, U.S.A. 30.

KUSAMA, Yayoi, b. 22 Mar. 1941. Painter; Sculptress. Educ: Kyoto Municipal Schl. of Art, Japan; Art Students League, N.Y.C., U.S.A. One Man Exhibs. incl: Aggregation 1000 Boats, N.Y.C., 1963; Driving Image Show, 1964; Sex Food Obsession Show, The Hague, 1965; Phallus Garden Environment, Am., Europe, Japan, 1965; Floor Show & Endless Love Show, N.Y.C., 1966; Driving Image Show w. Macaroni Room, ·Milan, 1966; Fillmore E. Theatre Happening, 1968; Garden Nude Orgy Happening, Mus. of Mod. Art, N.Y., 1969; Fashion Show Nude Happening, Venice, 1970. Grp. Exhibs. incl: Brooklyn Mus., 1958; Städt Mus., Leverkusen, Germany, 1961; Pitts. Mus., U.S.A., 1961; Whitney Mus., 1962; City Mus., Amsterdam, 1962; Inst. Contemp. Art, 1964, 65; Mus. of Mod. Art, Stockholm, 1965; Met. Mus. Tokyo, 1965; Mus. of Mod. Art, N.Y.C., 1965; 33 Venice Biennial, 1966. Organized & presented happenings, N.Y.C. parks. Inventor, infinity mirror room. Address: Sanko Mansion, 1 Sanko-cho, Shinjuka-ku, Tokyo, Japan.

KUSHNER, David Zakeri, b. 22 Dec. 1935. Musicologist; Univeristy Professor. Educ: B.Mus., Boston Univ.; M.Mus., Coll.-Conservatory of Music, Univ. of Cinn.; Ph.D., Univ. of Mich. Appts: Studio Tchr., Piano & Theory, Ellenville, N.Y., 1961-64; Asst. Prof., Miss. State Coll. for Women, 1964-66; Assoc. Prof., Radford Coll., Va., 1966-68; Prof., ibid, 1968-69; Prof., Music., Doctoral Rsch. Fac. & Chmn., Musicol. Fac., Univ. of Fla. Mbrships. incl: Chmn., Bd. Dirs. & Fest. Chmn., Am. Liszt Soc.; Chmn., Southern Chapt., Am. Musicol. Soc.; Life, Music Tchrs. Nat. Assn.; Life, Phi Mu Alpha Sinfonia; Pres., Univ. of Fla. Chapt., Pi Kappa Lambda. Contbr. to music publs. Hons: Grants., Humanities Coun., Univ. of Fla., 1970; Univ. of Fla. Lib. Resources Grant, 1971; Univ. of Fla., Bur. of Rsch. Grant, 1972. Address: 2215 N.W. 21st Ave., Gainesville, FL 32601, U.S.A. 21.

KUSHNER, Lawrence Maurice, b. 20 Sept. 1924. Administrator; Physical Chemist. Educ: B.S., Queens Coll., Flushing, N.Y., U.S.A., 1945; A.M., Princeton Univ., N.J., 1947; Ph.D. ibid, 1949. Appts. incl: Phys. Chem., Nat. Bur. of Standards, Wash. D.C., 1948-56; Chief, Metal Phys. Sect., Metallurgy Div., ibid, 1956-61; Chief, Metallurgy Div., 1961-66; Dpty. Dir.-Dir., Inst. for Applied Technol., 1966-69; Dpty. Dir., Nat. Bur. of Standards, 1969-73; Commnr., Consumer Product Safety Commn., 1973-. Mbrships. incl: AAAS; Am. Phys. Soc.; Am. Chem. Soc.; Energy Comm., Gov.'s Sci. Advsry. Coun. to Gov. of Md.; Bd. of Mgrs., Wash. Acad. of Scis.; Fed. Profl. Assn; Am. Soc. for Testing & Materials; Bd. of Dirs., Sigma Xi. Author or co-author, 31 scientific papers. Hons. incl: Gold Medal Award, Dept. of Commerce, 1968; Meritorious Serv. Award, Am. Nat. Standards Inst., 1973. Address: 18700 Walkers Choice Rd., Gaithersburg, MD 20760, U.S.A. 2, 6, 14, 128.

KUSIN, Vladimir Victor, b. 2 Dec. 1929. Senior Editor; Editor. Educ: Commercial

Acad., Frýdek, Czechoslovakia; Schl. of Pol. & Economic Sci., Prague; Charles Univ., Prague. Appts: Univ. lectr., translator, profl. abstractor, journalist, in Czechoslovakia, 1953-68; Rsch. Fellow, Comenius Ctr., Univ. of Lancaster, U.K., 1969; Sr. Ed., Soviet & E. European Abstracts Series (ABSEES), Univ. of Glasgow, 1970-. Mbr., Exec. Comm., Nat. Assn. for Soviet & E. European Studies. Publs. incl: The Intellectual Origins of the Prague Spring, 1971; Political Grouping in the Czechoslovak Reform Movement, 1972; Translator into Czech, Bikini Beach, by G. Bocca, & Rosencrantz & Guildenstern Are Dead, by T. Stoppard. Address: Inst. of Soviet & E. European Studies, Univ. of Glasgow, 9 Southpark Terr., Glasgow W.2, U.K.

KUSNADI, b. 1 Apr. 1921. Artist; Critic. Educ: Algemeene Middelbaare Schl., Jogjakarta, 1940-42; Keimin Bunka Shidosho, Jakarta. Appts. incl: Co-fndr., Art Acad. of Indonesia, Jogjakarta, 1950; Lectr., ibid, 1950-66; Chief, Div. of Fine Art, Art Dept., Min. of Educ. & Culture, Jogjakarta, 1950-66 & Jakarta, 1967-; Ed.-in-Chief, Budaya mag., Jogjakarta, 1952-63; Curator, Nat. Art Gall., 1963 & Art Collect., Min. of Educ. & Culture, Jogjakarta, 1964-66 & Jakarta, 1967-; Chief Ed., Art mag., Jakarta, 1973-; Ed., Scis. & Arts prog., Radio Repub. of Indonesia, 1973-. Represented in permanent collects: Min. of Educ. & Culture & Art Coun., Jakarta. Dir. of films: Dances of Java & Bali, 1959; The Indonesian Batik, 1970; Wayang in Indonesia, 1972. Mbrships. incl: Fndr. Mbr., Int. Assn. of Plastic Art, Jogjakarta, 1959-65 & Bandung, 1966-; Indonesian Rep., Int. Confs., World Crafts Coun., 1968 & 69; Comm., Pertamina Exhib. of Art, Jakarta, 1971. Publs: pre-advsry. working paper on Indonesian art, 1957 & 58; contbr. articles on art to mags. & jrnls. Recip. Am. State Dept. Grant, 1963-64. Address: Jalan H. Agus Salim 60, Jakarta, Indonesia.

KÜTHE, Karlheinz, b. 8 Mar. 1908. Phytologist. Educ: Studied biol., geog. & geol., Univs. of Munich, Vienna, Berlin & Giessen; Sci. Tchrs. exam. & grad., biol., 1926; State exam., 1930. Appts: Inst. für Pflanzenkrankheiten, Landesberg/Warthe; Dir., Pflanzenschutzamt, Salzburg, 1939-; Officoal expert, Inst. für Kartoffelkäferbekämpfung (Leptinotarsa decemlineata), Biologische Bundesanstalt, 1951-52; Dir., Bezirksstelle für Pflanzenschutz, Giessen, 1953-; Sci. Asst., Inst. für Phytopathologie, Univ. of Giessen, 1973-. Mbrships: Landessprecher für Hessen, Deutsche Phytomedizinische Gesellschaft, 1962-72; Pres., Deutsche Unitarier, 1949-63; Local Dir., Hessen, ibid, currently; 2nd Chmn., Deutscher Volksbund für Geistesfreiheit, 1973-. Publs. incl: Author of num. publs. in field. Address: Rabenweg 36, D-6300 Giessen, German Fed. Repub.

KUTTNER, Bernard A., b. 13 Jan. 1934. Attorney. Educ: A.B., Dartmouth Coll., 1955; Univ. of Va. Law Schl., 1956; Jur.D., Seton Hall Univ. Law Schl., 1959. Appts: in pvte. prac., 1960-. Mbrships. incl: Chmn., Conflict of Interests Comm., N.J. Bar Assn.; V.P., Essex Co. Pk. Commn., 1973-74; Sect. on Judicial Admin., Am. Bar Assn.; Chmn., Trial & Appellate Litigation Comm., Essex. Co. Bar Assn.; Lions Club; Jaycees; Anti-Defamation League of N.J. Publs: Code of Ethics for Municipal Officials, 1966; Law as the Instrument of Social Change, 1974. Hons. incl: Outstanding Young Man of N.J., 1967. Address: 11 Commerce St., Newark, NJ 07102, U.S.A. 6, 55, 111.

KUZNIAR, Zofina, b. Austria. Artist. Educ: Studied Art w. pvte. tutor, Pierre Kuss; Oil Portraiture Class. Operates own bus., Zofina's Oil Portraiture Studio. Address: 2416 N. Harding Ave., Chicago, IL 60647, U.S.A. 105.

KVARVING, Johan Furuseth, b. 16 Sept. 1904. Norwegian Gymnasium Principal. Educ: Cand. Philol., 1930; Pedagogic Exam., 1931. Appts: Ldr., Steinkjer Rural Gymnasium, 1932; Mbr. City Coun., Steinkjer, 1945-51; Dpty. Mayor, Steinkjer, 1948-51; Juror, Frostating Ct. of Appeals, 1945-71; Prin., Steinkjer Pub. Rural Gymnasium, 1947-72. Prog. Coun., Trondheim Dept., Norwegian Broadcasting Corp. Mbrships: Dpty. Chmn., Nord-Trondelag Hist. Soc.; Dpty. Chmn., Nord-Innherad Mus. Soc.; Past Chmn., Nord-Trondelag Art Soc. Publs: Skolar og undervisning i Nord-Trondelag, 1954; Nord-Trøndelag i litteraturen, 1954. Recip. of Norwegian Royal Order of Merit. Address: Furuskogvegen 4, 7700 Steinkjer, Norway. 134.

KVENDBO, Bjarne Odvar, b. 21 Sept. 1921. Administration & Exploration General Manager. Educ: Bus. Coll., Norway; Sales & Advt. Cons. Course, Sweden; Swedish Nat. Econ. Course, Sweden; Bus. Mgmt., Am. Schl., U.S.A.; Administrative Procedure, McGill Univ., Montreal, Canada; Mining Mgmt., Mining Econs. & Human Rels. in Ind., Dept. of Engrng. & Applied Geophysics, ibid; Exec. Dev. Inst. Dip. Course, to be completed 1974; LL.B. student, La Salle Ext. Univ., Chgo., U.S.A., 1968-; Imperial Coll., London, U.K., 1971. Appts. incl: Sales Mgr., Gresvig Ltd., Canada, 1960-69; Gen. Mgr., Scandia Mining & Exploration Ltd., 1964-; Pres. & Dir., ibid, 1965-; Chmn., Scandiore Mining & Exploration Pty. Ltd., N.S.W., Australia, 1973-. Mbrships. incl: Canadian Mining & Metallurgy Inst.; Canadian Prospectors & Developers Assn.; Canadian Nuclear Assn.; Am. Mgmt. Assn.; Royal Canadian Legion. Recip., Norwegian war participant medal w. rosette. Address: 253 Florian, Rosemere, P.Q., Canada.

KVIFTE, G., b. 8 Feb. 1914. Professor of Physics & Meteorology. Educ: Cand. real, Univ. of Oslo, Norway, 1942; Dr. philos., ibid, 1953. Appts. incl: Res. Asst., Dept. of Phys., Univ. of Oslo, 1937-46; Asst. Prof., ibid, 1947-53; Assoc. Prof., Univ. of Bergen, 1953; Prof. of Phys. & Meteorol., Agricl. Univ. of Norway, 1954-; Rector (V. Chancellor), ibid, 1961-68; Chmn., Ctrl. Comm. for Norwegian Rsch., 1969-; V. Chmn., Norwegian Nat. Comm. for UNESCO, 1973-. Mbrships: Norwegian Acad. of Sci.; Int. Union of Geodesy & Geophys.; Norw. Geophysl. Assn.; Norw. Phys. Soc.; Am. Geophysl. Union; Norw. Polytech. Assn. Publs. incl: work on optical spectroscopy, cosmical geophys. (upper air phys.), agrometeorol. & entomol. (odonata). Address: Dept. of Phys. & Meteorol., Agricl. Univ. of Norway, 1432 AAS—NLH, Norway. 43.

KWON, E. Hyock, b. 13 July 1923. University Professor; College Dean. Educ: Grad., Coll. of Med., Seoul Nat. Univ., 1947; Grad., Postgrad. Course, ibid, 1951; M.P.H., Schl. of Pub. Hlth., Univ. of Minn., 1956; Dr. of Med. Sci., Seoul Nat. Univ., 1960. Appts: Asst. to Prof., Seoul Nat. Univ., 1947-48; Instr., ibid, 1948-50; Supt., Civil Affairs Hosp., IXth Corps, US Force in Korea, 1951-54; Asst. Prof.-Prof., Coll. of Med., Seoul Nat. Univ., 1956-; Dean, Coll. of Med., ibid, 1970-; Dir., Reproductive Med. & Population, 1972-. Mbrships: Korean Med. Assn.; Assn. of Korean Med. Colls.; Chmn., Med. Comm., Planned Parenthood Fedn., Korea; Comm. for the Org. of Rsch. & Evaluation, IPPF Ctrl. Med. Comm.;

World Acad. of Arts & Sci. Publs: Public Health; Communicable Disease Control; Population & Health; Population in Korea; Studies in Urban Population; contbr. approx. 100 articles to profl. jrnls., particularly studies of social & tech. aspects of contraception & population control. Hons: Medal of Freedom, USA, 1953; Citation, Pres. of the Repub. of Korea, 1963; Citation, Prime Min., ibid, 1967; Sam-il Cultural Award, 1968; Nat. Medal, Repub. of Korea, 1970. Address: Coll. of Med., Seoul Nat. Univ., 28, Yunkeun-Dong, Chongno-Gu, Seoul, Korea.

KWON, Tai-Hyung, b. 15 Sept. 1932. Professor of Physics. Educ: B.S., Univ. of Ga., Athens, Ga., 1963; M.S., ibid, 1965; Ph.D., ibid, 1967; Postdoctl. Rsch., Ga. Inst. of Technol., Atlanta, Ga., 1967-69. Appts. incl: Capt., Repub. of Korea Army, 1953-60; Grad. Tchng. & Rsch. Asst., Univ. of Ga., 1963-67; Postodctl. Rsch. Fellow, Ga. Inst. of Technol., 1967-69; Asst. Prof. Phys., Univ. of Montevallo, Ala., 1969-. Mbrships: Am. Phys. Soc.; Am. Assn. Phys. Tchrs.; Phi Beta Kappa; Phi Kappa Phi; Sigma Xi. Contbr. to profl. jrnls. Hons: Wheatley Phys. Award, 1963; Frederick Gardner Cottrell Grant, 1971. Address: 1877 Tall Timbers Drive, Birmingham, AL 35226, U.S.A. 7, 14, 125.

KY, Nguyen Trong, b. 10 Nov. 1928. Doctor of Medicine. Educ: Med. studies, Paris, France; Cert. of Engl. Proficiency, Cambridge Univ., U.K. Appts: Allergist, Allergy Ctr., Broussais Hosp.; Acupunctor, St. Antoine Hosp., Paris. Mbrships: French Soc. of Allergy; French Soc. of Immunol.; British Soc. of Allergy; European Acad. of Allergy; Cercle du Bois de Boulogne; Racing Club. Author of 35 publs. in allergol., on asthma, hay fever, ORL diseases, skin diseases, eye diseases, microbial diseases; Discoverer of a blood test for drug allergy. Hons: Laureat, Fac. of Med., Paris, 1956; Laureat, French Acad. of Med., 1957. Address: 57 Ave. de Segur, Paris 75007, France. 43.

KYLE, Elizabeth (Agnes M.R. Dunlop), Author. Publs. incl: approx. 50 books, Britain & Am. (also translations); (novels) The Tontone Bell, 1951; Conor Sands, 1952; Forgotten as a Dream, 1953; The Regent's Candlesticks, 1954; A Stillness in the Air, 1956; The Other Miss Evans, 1958; P Oh Say, Can You See? 1959; Return to the Alcazar, 1962; (children's books) Queen of Scots, 1957; Maid of Orleans, 1957; The Money Cat, 1958; The Eagle's Nest, 1961; Girl with a Lantern, 1961; Girl with an Easel, 1963; Girl with a Pen, 1964; Girl with a Song, 1964; Girl with a Destiny, 1965; The Boy who asked for More, 1966; Love is for the Living, 1966; High Season, 1968; Queen's Evidence, 1969; The Song of the Waterfall, 1969. Address: c/o Messrs. A.M. Heath, 35 Dover St., London WIX 4EB, U.K. 1, 131.

KYLIN, Anders (Olof), b. 25 July 1925. Professor. Educ: Fil.kand., Univ. of Lund, Sweden, 1945; Fil.mag., ibid 1947; Fil. lic., 1954; Fil.dr., 1960. Appts: Tchng. Asst. & Rsch. Schlor., Univ. of Lund, 1948-60; Lectr., Bio., Second. Schl., Umea, Sweden, 1960-61; Lectr., Plant Physiol., Univ. of Stockholm, 1961-67; Rsch. Lectr., ibid, 1967-73; Prof., Royal Veterinary & Agric. Univ. Copenhagen, Denmark, 1973-; sometime Guest Rsch. Wkr., U.S.A. & Netherlands. Mbrships: Ed.-in-chief, Physiologia Plantarum, Scandinavian Soc. for Plant Physiol., 1971-. Contbr. about 60 papers to sci. publs. Hons: Fulbright Schlrships., U.S. Govt., 1963-64 & 68-69; Zorn Schlrship., Sweden-Am. Fndn., 1963-64. Address: c/o Dept. of Plant Physiol. & Anatomy, Royal

Veterinary & Agricl. Univ., DK-1871 Copenhagen, Denmark.

KYONG, Sang Hyon, b. 24 July 1937. Engineer. Educ: Seoul Nat. Univ., Korea, 1956-58; B.S., Univ. of R.I., Kingston, U.S.A., 1961; Ph.D., MIT, Cambridge, U.S.A., 1965. Appts: Nuclear Engr., Argonne Nat. Lab., Ill., 1965-66; Mbr., Tech. Staff, Bell Telephone Labs., Holmdel, N.J., 1966-; Adjunct Asst. Prof. of Nuclear Engrng., N.Y. Univ., 1968-69. Mbrships: Am. Nuclear Soc.; IEEE; Coun., Korean Scis. & Engrs. Assn. of Am.; Korean Nuclear Soc.; Soc. for Indl. & Applied Maths.; Phi Kappa Phi; Sigma Xi; Tau Beta Pi. Publs: Contbns. to tech. jrnls. Address: 37A Ravine Drive, Matawan, NJ 07747, U.S.A. 6, 14.

KYOSTIO, O.K. b. 3 Dec. 1913. Professor. Educ: M.A., Ph.D. Appts: Tchr., 1935-46; Tchr. trng. insp., 1947-52; Rdr., Jyväskylä Univ., Finland, 1956-63; Prof. & Dean, Tchrs. Coll., Oulu Univ., 1964-. Publs. incl: Work tests as indicators of vocational fitness, 1966; A study of teacher role expectations, 1968; Attainment in coeducational and segregated schools, 1970; Education in Finland, 1971; The changing role of schooling in society, 1973; Reading in Finland (Comparative Reading), 1973. Recip. hons. Address: Kasarmintie 4, 90100 Oulu 10, Finland. 90.

KYRIAKIDES, Stelios, b. 4 May 1910. Public Power Corporation Employee. Appt: Cashier, Athens-Piraeus Electricity Co., Greece. Mbrships: Comm., Olympia Athletic Club, Cyprus, 1936-69, Amateur Athletic Assn., 1949-71; Philothey Athletic Club, 1956-73; Philothey Boy Scouts, 1950-58, Philothey Sports Ctr., 1971-74. Contbr. of articles on sport to var. mags. & sports papers. Hons. incl: Gold Medal, Order of the Phoenix, King Paul I of Greece, 1953; Copper Medal, City of Athens, Silver Medal City of Piraeus, Gold Medal, City of Patras, 1946; Copper Medal, Min. of Educ., 1939; Silver & Copper Medals, Amateur Athletic Assn., 1950, 1965; City of Boston, State of Mass. Medals, & Honorary Distinction Cup, Greek Olympic Assn., 1946; Boston Marathon 50th Anniversary Gold & Diamond Medal; Nat. Champion of Greece (over 50 times); Over 250 gold, silver & bronze medals & 80 cups from nat. & int. meetings. Address: 30, 28th October St., Philothey, Athens, Greece. 43.

KYRIAZIS, Christ W. Psychologist. Educ: B.A., Geo. Wash. Univ., Wash. D.C., 1948; M.A., ibid, 1949; Ph.D., ibid, 1963; Post-doctoral Course, Grad. Schl., U.S. Dept. of Agric. Appts. incl: Serv., USAAF, WW II; Univ. Teaching Fellow & Lectr. in Psychol., Geo. Wash. Univ., 1955-59; Clin. Psychologist, St. Elizabeth's Hosp., U.S. Dept. of Hlth., Educ. & Welfare, 1959-64; Scientist Admnstr., NIGMS, NIH, ibid, 1964-66; Psychologist Cons., Rev. Duniels Parochial Schl., D.C., 1964-66; Evaluation & Placement Off., Vista-OEO, Exec. Off.. of Pres, 1966-67; Dir. of Selection, ibid, 1967-72; Coord., Coop. Volunteer Progs., Action, 1972-73; Lectr., Psychol., Grad. Schl., U.S. Dept. of Agric., 1973-. Mbrships: Am. Psychological Assn.; D.C. Psychological Assn.; AAAS; Sigma Chi; Psi Chi. Author, var. Papers & Internal Reports; Conthr. to profl. jrnls. Hons: Chosen to give Psi-Chi Invited Address, Psi-Chi-Am. Psychological Assn. Conven., 1972. Address: 4000 Tunlaw Rd., N.W., Washington, DC 20007, U.S.A. 57.

KYTE, Elinor Diederich Clemons (Mrs.), b. 2 Nov. 1922. Professor of English. Educ: B.A., Miami Univ., Ohio, 1950; M.A., Univ. of Tex., Austin, 1957; Ph.D., ibid, 1961; Postgrad. work, Manchester Coll., Ind., 1953, Univ. of Mich., Ann Arbor, 1958. Appts: Served, USNR (WR), 1943-45; Grad. tchng. asst., Univ. of Tex., Austin, 1958-61; Prof., Northern Ariz. Univ., Flagstaff, 1961-; Dir., N.D.E.A. Inst. in E.S.O.L., N.A.U., 1968. Mbrships: Ariz. State Core Curric. Comm. for Adult Educ., 1968-70; Past Pres., Ariz. Bilingual Coun.; Linguistic Soc. of Am.; Nat.. Coun. of Tchrs. of Engl.; Tchrs. of Engl. To Spkrs. of other Langs.; Rocky Mt. MLA; Sigma Delta Pi; Phi Beta Kappa; Phi Kappa Phi. Author of monograph & 2 articles in jrnls. Recip., Bd. of Regents fellowship, Univ. of Tex., 1959. Address: Box 5598, Northern Ariz. Univ., Flagstaff, AZ 86001, U.S.A. 5.

L

LAASONEN, (Veikko) Pentti (Johannes), b. 14 Mar. 1916. University Rector. Educ: M.A., Helsinki Univ., Finland, 1937; Ph.D., ibid, 1944. Appts: Asst. in Maths., Helsinki Univ., 1939-43; Mathn., State Airplane Factory, Tampere, 1943-48; Prof., Strength of Mats., Helsinki Univ. of Technol., 1948-61; Vis. Prof. Maths., Univ. of Calif., U.S.A., 1956-58; Prof. Applied Maths., Helsinki Univ., Finland, 1961-62; Prof. Maths., Helsinki Univ. of Technol., 1962-; Rector, ibid, 1970-. Mbrships: Finnish Acad. of Scis. (Treas. 1961-); Gesellschaft für Angewandte Math. & Mechanik; Austrian Math. Soc.; Finnish Acad. Tech. Scis.; Finnish Soc. of Scis. Publs: Over 80 papers on math. & technological subjects. Hons: Finnish Freedom Cross, Class 4, 1942; Cmdr., Order of Finnish Lion, 1966; Order of Romanian Star, Class 4, 1971; Icelandic Hawk's Order, 1972. Address: Helsinki Univ. of Technology, 02150 Otaniemi, Finland.

LAATZ, Mary Jane, b. 27 Dec. 1916. Medical Librarian. Educ: A.B., Butler Univ., 1938; B.S.L.S., Western Reserve Univ., 1939. Appts: Libn., Ind. Univ. Ext. Div., Indianapolis, 1939-41; Cataloger, Ind. Univ. Schl. Med. Lib., 1941-51; Ref. Libn., 1951, '53-57; Acting Libn., 1951-53; Med. Libn. & Asst. Prof., Med. Lit., 1957-73; Med. Libn. & Assoc. Prof., 1973-. Mbrships: Chapt Pres., Special Libs. Assn., 1960-61; Chmn., Exec. Comm., Midwest Regional Med. Lib., 1968-69, '69-70; Med. Lib. Assn. (Chmn., Schlrship. Comm., 1973-74); Sec.-Treas., John Shaw Billings Hist. of Med. Soc., 1966-67; Bus. & Profl. Women's Club of Indianapolis; Symph. Soc.; Delta Gamma Jt. author of article in profl. bulletin. Address: Indiana Univ., Schl. of Medicine Lib., 1100 W. Michigan St., Indianapolis, IN 46202, U.S.A. 2, 8.

LABARGE, Margaret Wade, b. 18 July 1916. Historian/Writer. Educ: B.A., Radcliffe Coll., Harvard Univ.; B.Litt., St. Anne's, Oxford Univ., U.K. Sessional Lectr., Notre Dame Coll., Univ. of Ottawa, Canada & Carleton Univ. Mbr., Phi Beta Kappa, 1968. Publs: Simon de Montfort, 1962; A Baronial Household of the Thirteenth Century, 1965; Saint Louis, 1968; The Cultural Tradition of Canadian Women, a study for the Royal Commn. on the Status of Women, 1971; Court, Church & Castle, 1972. Address: 312-211 Wurtemburg St., Ottawa, Ont., K1N 8R4, Canada. 138.

LABBENS, Jean, b. 4 Nov. 1921. United Nations Official. Educ: Univs. of Lille, Lyon, Paris, Chgo.; Dr. Philos., Dr. Sociol. Appts: incl: Prof., Fac. of Philos., Lyon, France, 1951-63; UNESCO Expert in Higher Educ., 1963-68; Chief, UNESCO Mission, Brazil, 1968-71; Dept. of Soc. Scis., UNESCO, Paris, France, 1971-72; Res. Rep., UN Dev. Prog., Peru, 1972-. Mbrships: Pres., Int. Conf. on Sociol. of Relig., 1955-61; Assoc. (For.) Mbr., Am. Sociological Assn.; French Sociological Soc.; Soc. for Int. Dev. Publs. incl: Les 99 Autres, 1954; La Sociologie Religieuse, 1960; La Condition Sous Proletarienne, 1965; Le Quart Monde, 1969. Address: UN, Apartado 4480, Lima, Peru. 43, 91.

LABIDI, Abdelwahab, b. 22 Apr. 1929. Bank Preisdent. Educ: Coll. Sadiki, Tunisia, 1945-51; Inst. des Hautes Etudes, Tunis, 1952; Degree, Fac. of Law, Univ. of Paris, 1952-57. Appts: Asst. Insp., Credit Industriel et Commercial, Paris; Fondé de Pouvoirs, Bank of Tunisia, 1959-60; Dpty. Dir., Tunisian Nat. Agricl. Bank, 1960-64, Hd. of Loans Dept., 1960-62, Insp. Gen., 1962-64; Mgr., Soc. Tunisienne de Banque, 1964-69; Gen. Mgr., Nat. Dev. Bank of Repub. of Niger, 1964-; V.P., African Dev. Bank, 1969-; Interim Pres., ibid, 1970-; Pres., 1970-. Hons: Chevalier de l'Ordre de la République Tunisienne; Off. de l'Ordre Nat. de la République du Niger. Address: c/o African Dev. Bank, P.O. Box 1387, Abidjan, Ivory Coast.

LACAYO, Maria Perez-Alonso, b. 17 July 1912. Educator. Educ: M.Ed., Guadalupe Coll., Managua, Nicaragua, 1931; M.A., Fla. State Univ., Tallahassee, 1955; Ph.D., ibid, 1962. Appts: H.S. Tchr., Emma Willard Schl., Troy, N.Y., 1941-42; Kindergarten Tchr., Blessed Sacrament Schl., Tallahassee, 1954-58; Asst. Prof., Univ. Schl., Tallahassee, 1958-60; Lang. Supvsr., Lion Co. Pub. Schls., Fla., 1960-67; Co. Educl. TV Tchr., ibid, 1962-67; Hd., For. Lang. Dept., Tallahassee Community Coll., 1967-72. Mbrships. incl: MLA; Fla. Educl. TV; Fla. State Univ. Alumni Assn.; Chapt. Pres., Am. Assn. Tchrs. of Spanish & Portuguese, 1965-66; Nat. Assn. Educl. Broadcasters; AAUP; NEA; Phi Kappa Phi; Delta Kappa Gamma. Author of El Español es Facil, Level I, 1962, Level II, 1963, Level III, 1965. Address: 2211 High Rd., Tallahassee, FL 32303, U.S.A. 5, 7, 125, 132.

LACEY, Robert David Weston, b. 3 Jan. 1944. Journalist & Author. Educ: Selwyn Coll., Cambridge Univ., U.K., 1963-67; M.A. & Dip. of Educ., ibid. Appts: Writer, Illustrated London News, 1968; Asst. Ed., Sunday Times Colour Mag., 1969; Ed. of Sunday Times 'Look!' Pages, 1973. Comm. Mbr., Cambridge Union. Publs: Robert, Earl of Essex, An Elizabethan Icarus, 1971; Henry VIII, 1972; Sir Walter Ralegh, 1973; The Queens of the North Atlantic, an illustrated history of the great Cunard liners, 1973. Address: 68 Melbourne Grove, London SE22, U.K.

LACKEY, Guy Annadale, b. 23 July 1891. Educator. Educ: Austin Coll., Tex.; Univ. of Okla.; Univ. of Chgo. Appts. incl: Tchr. & Admnstr. Pub. Schls. in Okla.; Prof. & Hd. Depts. of Educ. & Psychol., Chicora Coll., Huron Coll., Okla. State Univ., Southwestern Coll., Kansas, & State Univ. System of N.Y. (Geneseo); Okla. State Univ., 1925-61, Emeritus. Mbrships: former Chapt. Pres., Phi Beta Kappa (Okla. Alpha), Phi Kappa Phi, Phi Delta Kappa, Kappa Delta Pi, Psi Chi, Pi Gamma Mu, Red Red Rose. Publs. incl: Geography of Oklahoma, 1940; Child Growth & Development Emphases in Teacher Education, 1944; num. articles & essays. Hons: Col. on Staff, Gov. Howard Edmondson, Okla., 1961. Address: 326 S. Stallard St., Stillwater, OK 74074, U.S.A. 7, 15, 22, 125, 126, 128, 130, 141.

LACKNER, Henriette (Mrs. Cecil Abraham), b. 27 Feb. 1922. Medical Doctor. Educ: M.B., Ch.B., Leeds Univ. Schl. Med., U.K., 1945; M.D., ibid, 1948; M.R.C.P., Royal Coll. Physns., London, 1948; Internships at Leeds Gen. Infirmary, 1946-48; Postgrad. Med. Schl., Hammersmith Hosp., London, 1948-49; Canadian Red Cross Mem. Hosp., Taplow, Bucks., 1949-54; Resdcy., Post-grad. Med. Schl., Hammersmith Hosp., London, 1954. Appts: Asst. Physn., Med. Outpatients, Groote Schuur Hosp., S. Africa, 1962; Physn. i/c Arthritis Clin., ibid, 1962; Jr. Lectr., Dept. Med., Capetown Univ., S. Africa, 1962; Rsch. Sci., Am. Nat. Red Cross, 1963; Clin. Asst. Vis. Physn., Bellevue Hosp., 1966-; Asst., Dept. Med., Univ. Hosp., 1966-; Instr., Clin. Pathol.-Asst. Prof., Med., N.Y. Med. Ctr.,

1965-. Mbrships: N.Y. Soc. for Study of Blood; Am. Soc. Hematol.; Coun. on Thrombosis, Am. Heart Assn. Co-Author num. papers to profl. jrnls. Hons: Hardwicke Prize in Med.; W. Riding Practitioners Prize for Med. Address: N.Y. Univ. Med. Ctr., Dept. Med., 550 1st Ave., N.Y., NY 10016, U.S.A.

LA CLAUSTRA, Vera B. (Derrick) (Mrs. Seraphin La Claustra). b. 11 Apr. 1903. Retd. Cosmetician; Author. Educ: Dip., Beauty Coll Operator, Beauty Salon, Oakland, Calif., 11 yrs. Mbrships. incl: Avalon World Arts Acad.; Centro Studi E Scambi Int.; Hon. mbr., Mark Twain Soc.; Poetry League; Am. Poetry League; World Poetry Soc. Intercontinental, India; Calif. Fed. Chaparral Poets; Ladies Aux., Vets. of For. Wars., Publs. incl: By the Cool Waters, 1953; The Purple Wheel, 1953; Gongs of Light, 1971; poems incld. in numerous anthols. & over 50 newspapers & jrnls. in Am., India & Italy. Hons. incl: 2 dips. of merit, Accad. Int. L. Da Vinci, Rome, 1962, '68; World Poetry Soc. Intercontinental Dip. of Merit, 1970; Citation of Merit for poem in Poet (India) World Poetry Soc.; 1970. Address: 400 Perkins St., Apt. 209 Oakland, CA 94610, U.S.A. 5, 11, 59, 128, 131.

LaCOUR, Leonard Francis, b. 28 July 1907. Cytologist. Appts: Sr. Experimental Off., John Innes Inst., 1948; Chief Experimental Off., ibid, 1956; Sr. Prin. Sci. Off., 1970; Ret., 1972. Hon. Prof., Schl. of Biol. Scis., Univ. of E. Anglia, Norwich, 1973. Mbrships: Genetical Soc.; FRS, 1970. Publs: The Handling of Chromosomes (w. C.D. Darlington). Hons: MBE, 1952; OBE, 1973. Address: c/o Schl. of Biol. Scis., Univ. of E. Anglia, Norwich NOR 88C, U.K. 1, 128.

LA CROIX, (Rev.) Francis A., b. 23 Sept. 1906. Clergyman. Educ: A.B., Baldwin-Wallace Coll., 1929; B.D., Oberlin Grad. Schl. Theol., 1932. Appts: Pastor, Pilgrim Ch., Elyria, Ohio; 1st Congl. Ch., N. Fairfield, Ohio, 1932-35; N. Congl. Ch., Columbus, Ohio, 1935-40; 1st Congl. Ch., Turentum, Pa., 1940-47; 1st Congl. Christian Ch., Maplewood, N.J., 1947-. Mbrships. incl: Nat. Soc., & Jrnlstic. Fraternities, Baldwin-Wallace Coll.; Lit. Soc., Baldwin-Wallace Coll.; Counsellor, Juvenile Ct., Columbus, Ohio; Bd. Dirs., Turentum Pub. Lib; Scribe & Chmn., Ch. Ext., Ch. & Min., NJUCC; Nat. Free-lance Photographers Assn. Author sev. pvtely. printed publs. Address: 29 Burnett Ave., Maplewood, NJ 07040, U.S.A. 6.

LACROIX, Jean-Paul, b. 22 Mar. 1914. Author; Journalist. Educ: Lic.ès Lettres. Appts: Prof.; Jrnlst, France Tireur, 1947-54, Cunard Enchaine, 1947-56, Paris-Presse, 1956-69; France-Soir, 1969-73. Mbrship: Acad. Rebalais. Publs: 8 books in French, 1947-67, The Innocent Gunman (Le Gangster aux Etoiles), 1954. Hons: Grand Prize for Humour, 1947; Alphonse-Allais Prize, 1957; Rabelais Prize, 1967. Address: 25 rue Saint-Denis, 92100 Boulogne-Billancourt, France.

LACY, Barbara (Mrs. Conway Gilcreast), b. 19 Jan. 1930. Librarian. Educ: B.A., Philander Smith Coll., 1959; Univ. of Ark., 1960; Cath. Univ. of Am.; D.C. Tchrs. Coll., 1973. Appts: Tchr.-Libn., St. Francis Co. Pub. Schls., 1950-65; Libn., Summer's Jr. High Schl., La Plata, Md., 1965-68; Libn., Draper Elem. Schl., Wash. D.C., 1968-. Mbrships: Hillside Civic Assn.; Election Judge, Prince Geo. Co., Med.; Republican Club; Roman Cath. Mbr., D.C. Assn. of Schl. Libns.; ALA. Address: 1206 Glacier Ave., Hillside, MD 20027, U.S.A.

LADD, Samuel Appleton, Jr., b. 17 Oct. 1906. Educator; College Administrator. Educ: B.S., Bowdoin Coll., Brunswick, Me. Appts: Account Exec., Dickie Raymond Advt. Agcy., 1933-37, Milton Bradley Co., Springfield Mass., 1937-40, J.L. Hammett, Cambridge Mass., 1940-44; Fac.-Dir. of Placement, Admin. Off. & Tennis Coach, Bowdoin Coll., Brunswick, Me., 1944-72. Mbrships. incl: Pres., Easter Coll. Placement Offs., 1950-51; Dir., Coll. Placement Coun., 1950-51; Advsry. Bd., Coll. Guidance Serv., 1951-69; U.S. Lawn Tennis Assn.; Dir., New England Tennis Assn.; USLTA Umpires Assn.; Pres., Bd., Community Hosp.; V.P. & Trustee, Regional Mem. Hosp., Brunswick, Me.; Town & Coll. Club, Brunswick, Me.; Cumberland Club, Portland, Me. Publs: Placement Procedures; Contbr. to jrnls. & profl. publs. Hons: Alumni Fund Award; Zeta Psi Serv. Award; Lambda Chapt. Award; var. tennis awards & prizes. Address: 7 Longfellow Ave., Brunswick, ME 64011, U.S.A. 6.

LADISA, Leonardo, b. 7 June 1911. Bank Director. Educ: Grad., Econs. & Commerce. Appts: Cons. & Dir., var. banking insts., inclng. the Savings Bank of Genoa & Imperia. Hons: Commendatore, w. Merit, of Italian Repub.; Commendatore of San Sepolcro Equestrian Order. Address: Cassa di Reiparmio di Genova e Imperia, Via Cassa di Risparmio 15, 16123 Genoa, Italy. 43.

LADJEVARDI, Ahmad, b. 6 May 1920. Business Executive. Educ: Bus. Schl., Tehran, Iran; Columbia Univ., U.S.A. Pres. & Bd. Mbr. & Chmn. of many cos. inclng: Arien Trading Co. Ltd.; Behshahr Ind. Co. Ltd.; Container Corp. of Iran; Iran Steel Bldg. Corp.; Paxan Corp. of Iran; Behshahr Ind. Grp., 1944-. Mbrships. incl: Nat. Comm. for Standardization of Food & Agric. Produce; Trustee, Danesh-Saraya Aly (Tchrs. Coll.); Stanford Rsch. Inst.; Int. Imedc Alumni Assn.; Bd., Pars Am. Club; Pres. Assn. Inc.; Iran Mgmt. Assn. Hons: Min. of Econ. Award for Ind. Fair, 1966-67; Min. of Econ. Award for Ind. Dev.; Min. of Educ. Award, 1st Degree. Address: 167 Farmanieh Ave., Dazashib, Tehran, Iran.

LAFFIN, John, b. 21 Sept. 1922. Author; Journalist; Military Historian; Lecturer. Educ: M.A., London, U.K.; D.Litt., Brantridge. Appts. incl: Chief Instr., Examiner, ICS, (Australia), Engl., Creative Writing & Jrnlism, 1951-56; Hd., Engl., Geog., Sociol. Dept., Mayfield Coll., U.K., 1958-69; Advsr., NATO, Tactics & Strategy, 1961-68; For. Corres., var. publs. Mbrships. incl: Dir., Britons for International Integrity, 1974. Royal Geog. Soc.; Royal Hist. Soc.; Royal United Serv. Instn. Author 72 books, inclng: Women in Battle; The Hunger to Come; New Geography, 1966-67, 1968-70, 1970-71; Anatomy of Captivity; Links of Leadership. Swifter Than Eagles; Surgeons in the Field; Americans in Battle; Letters From the Front 1914-18; The French Foreign Legion; Devil's Goad; Fadayeen: The Arab-Israeli Dilemma; The Arab Mind. Address: York House, Cusop Hay-on-Wye, Hereford, U.K. 3, 23.

LA FORTUNE, Knolly Stephen, b. 2 Jan. 1920. School Master. Educ: Govt. Tchrs. Coll., Trinidad, 1943-45; Goldsmith's Coll., Univ. of London, 1954-56; Univ. of London, 1959-72. Appts: Asst. Master, Secondary & Intermediate Schls., Trinidad, 1945-57; Hd. of Lib., St. Paul's Secondary Schl., Woolwich, London, 1968-69; Asst. Master in 13 Comprehensive Schls., Inner London Educ. Authority, 1958-, currently at Samuel Pepys Comprehensive Schl. Mbrships. incl: Soc. of Authors; Nat. Union Tchrs. Publs. incl: incld. in Moments of

Inspiration (anthol.); Commemoration Anthology, W.I. Fed., Trinidad. Trinidad Tchr. of the Yr. 1952, Trinidad & Tobago Press Assn. Address: 68 Arthurdon Rd., Brockley, London S.E.4., England. 3.

LAFUENTE, Hernandez Eusebio, b. 6 Sept. 1920. Civil Engineer. Educ: Studies in Madrid, & Navarra Univ., Barcelona, Spain. Appts: Engr., Barcelona Port, 1947-50; Mgr., Inimex (Morocco), 1951-60; Sub. Mgr., Fuerzas Elec. de Cataluna, 1961-68; Gen. Mgr., Co. Trasmediterranea, 1968-. Cons. to var. cos. Mbrships: Assn. of Hidalgos a Fuero de Espana; Exec. Pres. Amigos de Menorca; Vice Pres. Nautical Club, Mahon; Real Club de Polo, Barcelona. Lectr. on econ. & tech. subjects to univs. & cultural assns. Hons. incl: Cmdr., La Orden de Isabel la Catolica & del Santo Sepulcro, 1971; Kt., La Orden del Santo Sepulcro & de Cisneros, 1966 & 1972. Address: Compañia Trasmediterranea, Zurbano, 73, Madrid-3, Spain.

LAGERSPETZ, Kari Yrjö Henrik, b. 6 Sept. 1931. Professor of Zoophysiology. Educ: Cand. Phil., Univ. of Helsinki, 1954; Mag. Phil., ibid, 1955; Ph.D., Univ. of Turku, Finland, 1960. Appts: Instr., Dept. Zool., Univ. of Turku, 1952, 1956; Asst., ibid, 1955, 1956-62; Lectr., Zoophysiol., 1960-64; Rsch. Fellow, Finnish Nat. Sci. Coun., 1962-64; Prof., Zoophysiol., ibid, 1964-; Hd. of Dept. of Zool., Univ. of Turku, 1952, 1956; Asst., ibid, 1955, 1956-62; Lectr., Zoophysiol., 1960-64; Rsch. Fellow, Finnish Nat. Sci. Coun. 1962-64; Prof., Zoophysiol., ibid, 1964-; Hd. of Dept. of Zool., Univ. of Turku, 1973-. Mbrships: Pres., Turku Univ. Students Corp., 1969-72; Physiological Soc. Finland; Soc. for Comp. Physiol (U.K.). Publs: Teleological Explanations & Terms in Biology: A Study in Theoretical Biology, 1959; The Animal & the Machine, 1966. About 80 publs. on animal physiol. & theoretical biol. Co-Ed., Annales Zoologici Fennici, 1965-. Address: Vähä Hämeenkatu 7 C, SF-20500 Turku 50, Finland. 43.

LAGERSTROM, Ake Bertil Georg, b. 29 May 1916. Journalist; Author; Playwright. Educ: Upsala Univ., 1935-39. Appts: Ed., Enköpingsposten 1943-44; Sub-Ed., Filmjournalen, 1945-48; Reporter, FIB/Aktuellt, 1964-. Publs: Rag-dolls, 1943; Grass Widower, 1945; The Bewitched Ditch, 1946; Svartlöga, the Story of an Island, 1959; Ships from the Seven Seas, 1962; Also author 3 adventure novels, 3 children's books & num. short stories; Numl translations from Engl., French & German. Plays: The Musical Alley (12 pts. for radio), 1958; Nachspiel, 1963; The Glass Wall, 1967; Jericho, 1970; The Flamingo March, 1970. Address: Södra Kungsvägen 216 A, 181 62 Lidingö, Sweden.

LAGUNDOYE, Sulaiman Botsende, b. 13 Oct. 1935. Medical Practitioner; University Teacher; Radiologist. Educ: Nigerian Coll. of Arts, Sci. & Technol. (now Univ. of Ife), 1953-55; M.B.B.S. (Lond.), Univ. Coll. (now Univ. of Ibadan), 1953-55; M.B.B.S. (Lond.), Univ. Coll. (now Univ. of Ibadan), Ibadan, 1961; D.M.R.D., Univ. of Edinburgh, 1966. Appts: House Surg., Univ. Coll. Hosp., Ibadan, 1961, Adeoyo Hosp., Ibadan, 1962; Med. Off., Oyo Gen. Hosp., 1961; Rural Med. Off., Ughelli Rural Hlth. Ctr., 1962-63; Med. Off., Govt. Chest Clin., Ibadan, 1963-66; Sr. Med. Off. (Radiol.), Akure Gen. Hosp., 1966-67; Lectr.-Reader, Radiol., Univ. of Ibadan, 1967-; Hon. Cons. Radiol., Univ. Coll. Hosp., Ibadan, 1967. Mbrships: Fndn. Fellow, Nigerian Med. Coun. in Radiol., 1970; Sec., Nigerian Med. Coun. Examining Bd. in Radiol., 1973; Int.

Study Grp. for Rsch. in Cardiac Metabolism, 1971; Sec., Assn. of Radiols. of W. Africa, 1969-71; Treas., ibid, 1971-72; Patron, Ibadan Dist. Table Tennis Assn., 1969-72; Chmn., Ibadan Fedn. of Boys & Girls Clubs, 1971-73; Vice Chmn., Western State Table Tennis Assn., 1971-74; Bd. of Govs., St. Catherine Girls' Grammar Schl., OWO, 1970-74; Steering Comm., Med. Advsry. Comm., Univ. Coll. Hosp., 1974; Histl. Soc. of Nigeria. Contbr. articles to profl. jrnls. Address: 9, Ebrohime Rd., Univ. of Ibadan, Ibadan, Nigeria. 135.

LAHR, Eugène-Julien, b. 21 Apr. 1897. Retired Professor. Educ: Studied at Univs. of Luxemburg, Munich, Strasburg, 1918-22; Dr., natural scis., 1922; Pedagogy exam., 1925. Appts: Prof., chem., natural & geographic scis., Luxemburg, 1925, Esch-sur-Alzelle, 1926-37, Luxemburg Lycée, 1937-40, Luxemburg Athénée, 1945-58; Prof. emeritus, 1958-; Prisoner of war, German concentration camps, WWII; Dir., Luxemburg City's Meteorological Stn., 1946-72; Major of Luxemburg Army as nat. del. at SHAPE'S Meteorological Comm. for coordng. servs., & Nat. deleg., NATO's Meteorological Comms., 1946-62. Author of num. publs. in field. Recip. of hons. Address: 75 rue Ermesinde, Luxemburg. 43, 87.

LAIDLAW THOMSON, Edward, b. 18 May 1913. Consultant Physician. Educ: M.B., Ch.B., Edinburgh Univ., U.K., 1935; M.D., 1943; M.R.C.P., 1943; F.R.C.P., 1951. Appts. incl: Prin. Med. Off., State of Johore, Malaya, 1945-46; Chmn., Med. Advsry. Bd., Singapore, 1954-57, Brit. Med. Assn., ibid, 1954-56; Hon. Clin. Asst., Dept. of Cardiol., Middx. Hosp., London, U.K., 1959-63, W. London Hosp., 1963-67; Hon. Cons. Physn., Musician's Benevolent Soc. & Trinity Coll. of Music, 1964-68; Med. Dir., Med. Ctr., Lyford Cay, Nassau, Bahamas, 1968-. Mbrships: Fellow, Royal Soc. Med., Royal Soc. Tropical Med. & Hygiene; Hon. Mbr., Singapore Turf Club, Lyford Cay Club. Contbr. of articles to profl. jrnls. Address: Med. Ctr., Lyford Cay, P.O. Box N 7776, Nassau, Bahamas.

LAING, Robert Louis, b. 2 May 1932. Company Executive. Educ: B.S., Univ. of Mich., Ann Arbor, 1958. Appts. incl: Aerospace Systems Design Engr., Gen. Dynamics, Ft. Worth, Tex., 1958-62; Fndr., Cons., Vita-Spike Inds., Ft. Worth, 1959-62; Proprietor, Vita-Spike Tree Care, Mpls., 1967-; Electronic Rsch. Cons., Laing Dev. Co., Ft. Worth, 1962-70; Pres., Clean-Flo Labs., Inc., Mpls., 1970-. Patentee in Agricl. & Limnological Chem. & In Electronic field. Mbrships: Inst. of Elec. & Electronic Engrs.; Water Hyacinth Control Soc. Publs: A Non-Toxic Lake Management Program, Hyacinth Control Jrnl., Vol. 12, 1974. Hons: Award for Outstanding Servs. (Electronic contbns.), Fndn. for Advancement of Chiropractic Rsch., 1968. Address: 4328 Courtland Rd., Minnetonka, MN 55343, U.S.A. 7, 8, 16, 139.

LAIR, Nard, b. 7 June 1916. Physician. Educ: B.S., Tex. Tech. Univ., Lubbock, 1939. M.S., 1940; M.D., Univ. of Tenn., 1947. Appts. incl: Pvte. prac., Gen. Med. & Aerospace Med., 1951-; Staff, Baylor Univ. Hosp., Dallas, St. Paul Hosp. & NASA Infirmary, Nat. Aerospace Ctr., Houston; Med., Cons., FAA, 1954-; Med. Cons., FBI, 1958-; Med. Cons., CIA, 1958-. Med. Cons., NASA, 1962-. Fellowships: Fndg. Charter, Am. Acad. of Family Prac.; Am. Acad. Gen. Prac.; Royal Soc. Hlth., U.K. Mbrships. incl: Dallas Co. Med. Soc.; Tex. Med. Assn. Southern Med. Soc.; Tex. Geriatric Soc.; Air

Medics Assn.; Flying Physns. Assn.; Phi Beta Pi; Civil Aviation Med. Assn.; Am. Acad. Air Traffic Control. Address: 9331 E. Lake Highlands Dr., Dallas, TX 75218, U.S.A. 2.

LAIRD, Maxwell O'Neil, b. 2 Jan. 1903. Consulting Civil & Electrical Engineer; Geodetic Engineer. Educ: B.S.C.E., Purdue Univ., USA, 1925; B.S.E.E., N.Y. Univ., 1934; Phillips Univ.; Rutgers Univ. Appts: City Mgr., City of Eaton Rapids, Mich., 1925-29; Overseas Div., & Long Lines Engrng. Depts., Am. Tel. & Tel. Co., 1929-58; Defence Projs. Div., Western Electric Co., 1958-62; Methods Engr., Long Lines Engrng. Dept., A.T. & T. Co., 1962-68; Cons. Geodetic & Geophys. Engr., 1968-. Mbrships. incl: Hopewell Township Utilities Auth., 1955-; Fellow, Am. Soc. Civ. Engrs.; Am. Forestry Assn.; Canadian Inst. of Surveying; Nat. Acad. Scis. Author, Approx. 50 tech. papers. Citations & Certs. of Appreciation from: Govt. of Hungary, 1937; Danish Royal Navy, 1960; Texas Surveyors Assn., 1966; Am. Soc. Civ. Engrs., 1968; Canadian Inst. of Surveying., 1970. Address: 22 Dublin Rd., Pennington, NJ 08534, USA. 6, 26, 64.

LAKE, Allen Leonard, b. 17 Sept. 1924. Professor of Biology. Educ: Bachelor's degree, Edinboro State Coll., Pa.; Master's degree, Univ. of Buffalo, N.Y.; Advanced level, Univ. of Ky. Appts: Served WWII; Hd., Sci. Dept., Lees Jr. Coll., 1950-57; Assoc. Prof., Morehead State Univ., 1957-. Mbrships: AAAS; Ky. Acad. of Sci.; Chmn., Zool. Sect., ibid; Assn. of Southeastern Biologists; Int. Oceanographic Fndn.; Co. Chmn., Am. Red. Cross. Inventor of Lake Polychromatic Discs (microscope filters) & author of book, Lake Polychromatic Discs; Author of 9 papers to Ky. Acad. of Sci.; Illustrator, Modern Phys. Sci.; Permanent exhibitions, biological photos., Fenton T. West Mem. Mus., electron micrographs & photomicrographs, Lappin Hall, Morehead State Univ. Hon: Disting. Prof., Morehead State Univ., 1970. Address: Box 782, Morehead State Univ., Morehead, KY 40351 U.S.A. 28, 125.

LAKE, Richard Harrington. International Business Executive. Educ: B.S., M.A., Roosevelt Univ.; Grad. of: Army Command & Gen. Staff Coll.; Strategic Intelligence Schl.; Mil. Govt. Schl.; Mil. Police Schl.; Dept. of State For. Serv. Inst. Appts. incl: Free-lance Writer & For. Motion Picture Mktng. Cons., 1938-41; Army 2nd Lt. to Lt.-Col. commanding Infantry & Mil. Police Corps units, 1941-61; Fac. Mbr., Coll. of Bus. Admin., Roosevelt Univ., 1958-60; Kennedy Admin. Appointee under Sec. of Commerce, 1961; Alternate Delegate for Sec. of Commerce, 1st White House Food for Peace Conf., 1961; Exec. Sec., U.S. For-Trade Zones Bd., 1961-69; Dir., For.-Trade Zones Staff, 1961-69; Pres., Richard H. Lake Assn., 1970-; Cons., UN Indl. Dev. Org. Missions, Belize, British Honduras, 1973, Trinidad & Tobago, 1974. Mbrships. incl: Perm. Int. Assn. of Navigation Congresses; Nat. Assn. of Bus. Economists; Am. Assn. of Port Authorities; Soc. for Int. Dev.; Co. of Mil. Histns; Retired Offs. Assn.; Res. Offs. Assn.; Ill. Assn. of Chiefs of Police; Contbr. of num. articles in govt & pvte. publs. Recip. of var. mil. citations. Address: Richard H. Lake Assocs., Box 385, Annandale, VA 22003, U.S.A. 2, 7, 16.

LAKERNICK, Philip Stephen, b. 24 Jan. 1943. Hospital Administrator. Educ: Assoc. Sc., Univ. of New Haven, Conn. 1964, B.Sc., 1966; M. Hosp. Admin., Med. Coll. of Va., 1968; Res., Gen. Hosp. of Va. Beach, 1967, King's Daughters Children's Hosp., 1968. Appts: Asst. Admnstr., Mem. Gen. Hosp.,

Golden Clin. Med. Ctr., 1968-70, Assoc. Admnstr., 1971-; Asst. Prof., Hosp. Mgmt. Prog., Salem Coll., 1968-70; Lectr., Hosp. Mgmt., Davis & Elkins Coll., 1973. Mbrships. incl: Am. Hosp. Assn.; Am. Coll. Hosp. Admnstrs.; Deleg., Monongahela Valley Hosp. Conf. (Sec. 1973); Elkins Jaycees, 1968-71; Pres., Bd. of Dirs., United Fund of Randolph Co. (V.P., 1972-73); Pres., Hlth. Planning Authority of Region VII; Area Hlth. Educ. Ctr. Consortium (Bd. Mbr. & Chmn., 1973); Alpha Phi Omega (Sectl. Chmn., 1970-72); B.P.O.E. Lodge 1135. Recip. of profl. awards. Address: Rt. 1, Box 330-2, Elkins, WV, U.S.A. 117, 125.

LAKIN, Leonard, b. 9 July 1931. Educator. Educ: B.B.A. (cum laude), CCNY, 1953; J.D., Schl. of Law, N.Y. Univ. Appts. incl: Ptnr., Levinson & Cobb, Hawaii, 1958-60; Asst. Gen. Counsel, Walter E. Heller & Co. Inc., 1960-62; Assoc. Gen. Counsel, A.J. Armstrong Co. Inc., 1962-64; Sec., Gen. Counsel, Nat. Car Rental System Inc., 1964-65; Assoc. Prof. of Law, Bernard Baruch Coll., CUNY, 1967-; Radio Commentator & Host, Baruch Coll. Presents, Stn. WBMB; Cons., Bd. Examiners, Am. Inst. Certified Pub. Accts. Mbr. & Off., profl. orgs. Publs. (co-author): A Guide to Secured Transactions; CPA Business Law Examination Review; Cases & Materials in the Law of Business Contracts (rev. edit.). Co-ed., book, Multistate Bar Examination Review. Contbr., profl. jrnls. CCNY Goodwill Ambassador to Mexico, 1953. Address: Holly Pl., Briarcliff Manor, NY 10510, U.S.A. 55.

LAL, Brij Basi, b. 17 Feb. 1915. Professor of Mathematics; College Administrator. Educ: M.Sc., 1st Class, Allahabad Univ., 1941; D.Phil., ibid, 1943. Appts: Lectr., Allahabad Univ., 1943-44; Sr. Prof. Maths., B.R. Coll., Agra, 1944-45; Prof. & Hd. of Dept., Govt. Post-grad. Colls., U.P., 1954-71, Prin., 1971-73; Chmn., Bd. of Studies, Agra Univ., 1966-69, Acad. & Senate Coun. Mbr., 1966-71, Exec. Coun. Mbr., 1968-71, Dean, Fac. of Sci., 1968-71; Prin., M.B. Post-grad. Coll., Haldwani, U.P., 1973-. Author, books for Degree & Post-grad. standards. Papers, var. rsch. jrnls., theory of polytropes. Recip., S.A. Hill Mem. Rsch. Prize, 1943. Address: M.B. Postgraduate College, Haldwani (Nainital), U.P., India.

LALANCETTE, Jean-Marc, b. 21 Apr. 1934. Chemist; Administrator. Educ: B.Sc., Univ. of Montreal, P.Q., Canada, 1957; M.Sc., ibid, 1958; Ph.D., 1960. Appts. incl: Prof. of Chem., Univ. of Sherbrooke, P.Q., 1969-; Hd., Chem. Dept., ibid, 1960-67; Dean of Sci. Fac. 1967-72; V.P., Rsch., 1972-. Mbrships. incl: Chmn., local sect., Chem. Inst. of Canada, 1961-63; Mbr., Schlrships. Selection Comm., Nat. Rsch. Coun., Canada, 1966-67; Chmn., Canadian Assn. for the Adv. of Sci., 1970-71; Chmn., Comm. of Deans, Fac. of Scis. & Applied Scis., 1968-70; Chmn., Organic Chem. Sect., Chem. Inst. of Canada, 1969-72; Fellow, Chem. Inst. of Canada, 1969; Orientation Comm., Chem. Sect., Nat. Rsch. Coun. of Canada, 1969-71; Chmn., Regional Planning Rsch. Ctr., Univ. of Sherbrooke, P.Q., 1971-. Num. publs. in var. profl. jrnls. and the holder of 7 patents. Hons. incl: Medal, Gov. Gen. of Canada, 1954; Schlrship., Nat. Rsch. Coun. of Canada, 1957-60. Address: Univ. of Sherbrooke, Sherbrooke, P.Q., Canada.

LALIVE, d'Epinay Jean-Flavien, b. 1 May 1915. Lawyer. Appts. incl: Atty., Geneva, 1941-46; Sec. of Bd., then Sec.-Gen., Jt. Relief Comm., Int. Red Cross, Geneva, 1941-46; 1st Sec., Int. Ct. of Justice, The Hague, Netherlands, 1947-53; Gen. Counsel, UNRWA, Middle E., 1953-58; Sec.-Gen., Int. Comm. of

Jurists, Geneva, Switzerland, 1958-61; currently, Sr. Ptnr., Lalive & Budin, attys.-at-law, Geneva, Switzerland, & Chmn. of Bd., Fndn. Grand-Theatre (Opera); Hon. Consul for Thailand. Mbrships: Hon. Mbr., Int. Commn. Jurists; Am. & Swiss Socs. Int. Law; British Inst. Int. & Comp. Law; Int. Bar & Law Assns. Publs. incl: L'Immunité de juridiction des Etats et des Organizations internationales, 1953; sev. books, num. articles, int., comp., corp. & arbitration law. Hons: Cmdr., Order of Cedar, Lebanon, 1958; Bellot Prize, Geneva. Address: 20 rue Sénebier, CH 1211 Geneva 12, Switzerland. 103.

LALL, Durga, b. 19 Feb. 1906. Artist. Exhibited in U.K., France, India, New Zealand & Australia. One Man Shows incl: Gallery Appolonaire & Imperial Inst., London, U.K.; Raymond Duncan, Paris, France, Established London Art Gallery & Art Contact Group & mag. in London; emigrated to Australia, 1959; established Art Galls. in Sydney & exhibited w. The Contemporary Art Soc.; opened Mus. of Mod. Art, the Cultural Ctr. & The Studio Gall., Wellington, New Zealand; works in many pvte. collects. & film made of work for Ark. Univ. Lib. for Mod. Art. Address: P.O. Box K.631, Haymarket Post Office, Sydney, Australia.

LAMB, Fred Michael, b. 26 Sept. 1939. Wood Technologist. Educ: B.S., Pa. State Univ. Pk., 1961; M.S., ibid, 1962. Appts: 1st Lt., Ordnance Corps, U.S. Army, 1963-66; Rsch. Off., Forest Products Lab., Ottawa, Ont., Canada, 1965-66; Rsch. Wood Technologist, U.S. Forest Serv., Duluth, Minn., 1966-68; Asst. Prof., Div. Forestry & Wildlife Resources, Va. Polytech. Inst. & State Univ., Blacksburg, 1968-. Mbrships. incl: Chmn., Polution Contral & Abatement Comm., Forest Products Rsch. Soc.; Soc. Wood Sci. & Technol.; Am. Soc. Safety Engrs.; Xi Sigma Pi; Gamma Sigma Delta; Phi Epsilon Phi; Epsilon Sigma Phi. 25 tech. articles, wood technol., indl. noise control. Over 30 papers, wood technol., indl. noise & safety, var. nat. & regional tech. soc. meetings. Recip., Grad. Tchng. Assistantship, Pa. State Univ., 1961. Address: 15 Griggs St., Christiansburg, VA 24073, U.S.A.

LAMB, Lynton Harold, b. 15 Apr. 1907. Artist & Author. Educ: LCC (now GLC) Ctrl. Schl. of Arts & Crafts, UK. Appts: Designer, The Publisher, Oxford Univ. Press, UK, 1930-72; Free-lance Designer; Mbr., Staff, Slade Schl. of Fine Art, 1950-71; Lectr., Methods & Materials of Painting, Royal Coll. of Art, 1956-69; Gen. Ed., Oxford Paperbacks, Handbooks for Artists. Fellowships: Royal Soc. Arts; Soc. Ind. Artists (Pres., ibid, 1951-53). Mbrships. incl: London Grp.; Arts Coun. of Gt. Britain, 1951-54. Works incl: Archtl. decorations in various mediums for Orient Liners, 1935-50; Commemorative Binding for Coronation Bible, 1953; Designed £1, 10/-, 5/-, & 2/6 postage stamps for new reign, 1955; Purcell Mem., Royal Festival Hall, London, 1959. Publs. incl: Preparation for Painting, 1954; Drawing for Illustration, 1962; Materials & Methods of Painting, 1970. Contbr. to Chamber's Ency., Oxford Illustrated Old Testament & illustrator of approx. 100 books. Recip. of Int. Philatelic Art Soc. Award, 1960. Address: Rose Cottage, Sandon, Nr. Chelmsford, Essex, UK. 1, 3, 34, 128.

LAMB, Sybil Vashta, b. 14 Apr. 1906. Educator. Educ: B.A., Grinnell Coll., 1927; Cert., Pasadena Community Playhouse Schl. of Theatre, 1935; M.A., State Univ. of Iowa, 1952; Grad., Ind. State Tchrs. Coll. Appts: Instr., Dir., Drama & Speech Activities, Nashua H.S., Iowa, 1928-30; Boone H.S. & Jr. Coll.,

1930-45; Dubuque Sr. H.S., 1945-69; Dubuque Hempstead Sr. H.S., 1969-73; Speech Tchr., Area 1 Adult Educ. Br., Voc. Tech. Schl., 1968-; Retd., 1973. Mbrships incl: Trustee, Int. Thespian Soc., 1966-72; Int. Dir., 1968-70; Past Pres., Dubuque Lambda Chapt., Delta Kappa Gamma; Bus. & Profl. Womens Club; Am. Theatre Assn.; NEA; Iowa Educ. Assn.; Iowa Speech Tchrs.; AAUW; Speech Assn. Am. Contbr. to profl. publs. Hons. incl: Int. Thespian Soc. Plaque for disting. serv. as Int. Trustee, 1966-72; E. Iowa Int. Thespian Award for Serv., 1971. Address: 3700 Pennsylvania Ave., Apt. C28, Dubuque, IA 52001, U.S.A.

LAMB, (Rev.) Wayne Alexander, b. 6 Nov. 1905. Clergyman. Educ: A.B., Asbury Coll., Wilmore, Ky., 1930; B.D., Asbury Theological Sem., 1931; M.A., Vanderbilt Univ., Nashville, Tenn., 1932; Grad. Study, Yale Univ. Divinity Schl., 1936. Appts. incl: Pastor, First Meth. Ch., Greenfield, Tenn., 1932-36, Aldersgate Meth. Ch., Paducah, Ky., 1936-40, First Meth. Ch., McKenzie, Tenn., 1940-44, Hays Ave. Meth. Ch., Jackson, Tenn., 1944-48, Union Ave. Meth. Ch., Memphis, Tenn., 1948-59; Dist. Supt., Paducah Dist., Memphis Conf., Meth. Ch., 1959-64, Paris Dist., Memphis Conf. United Meth. Ch., 1969-73, & Memphis-Asbury Dist., 1973-. Mbrships. incl: Kiwanis Club, Rotary Club, Eta Sigma Phi, Scottish Rite. Articles publd. in The Christian Advocate, Tidings, The Herald, A Yr. of Evangelism. Hons. incl: D.D., Asbury Coll., 1946; Ky. Col., State of Ky., 1962. Address: 5460 Shady Grove Rd., Memphis, TN 38117, U.S.A. 7, 57, 116.

LAMBERG, Bror-Axel, b. 1 Mar. 1923. Professor; Physician. Educ: Cand. med., Helsinki Univ., Finland, 1946; Lic.med., 1949; Dr.med., 1953. Appts. incl: Asst. Physn., 4th Dept. Med., Univ. of Helsinki, 1952-55; Asst. Clin. Prof., 1st Dept. Med., ibid, 1959-62; Asst. Chief Physn., 1962-65; Assoc. Clin. Prof., 3rd Dept. of Med., 1965-70; Profl., 1971; Asst. Physn., Dept. of Med., Maria Hosp., 1955-59; Dir., Minerva Fndn. Inst. of Med. Rsch., 1959-71. Mbrships. incl: Nordisk Insulinfond Sci. Advsry. Panel, 1972-; Vice Chmn., Med. Rsch. Coun., Acad. of Finland, 1971-73; Finnish Soc. for Internal Med.; Ciba Fndn. Sci. Advsry. Bd., 1967; Hon., Swedish Soc. Endocrinol., 1972. Author, Kilpirauhasen taudit, 1968 & 200 other publs. Hons: Liberty Cross with Swords, 1944; Runeberg Award, 1954; Mellin Award, 1960; Duodecim Award 1964; Finska Läkaresällskapte Award, 1970 Address: Endocrine Rsch. Unit, Univ. of Helsinki, Minerva Fndn., P.O. Box 819, SF-00101 Helsinki 10, Finland. 43, 50, 90 134.

LAMBERT, Abbott Lawrence, b. 19 Mar 1919. Certified Public Accountant. Educ: B.A. Columbia Univ., 1940; M.S., Grad. Schl. Bus. ibid, 1946. Appts: Pub. Acct., Appel & Brach 1940-42; Capt., U.S. Army Finance Dept., & Instr., Off. Candidate Schl., 1942-46; Instr. Woolf W. Lambert & Co., 1946-48; Pres. Carthage Fabrics Corp., N.C., V.P., Chopak Mills Inc., N.Y.C., 1948-71; Cert. Pub. Acct. M.R. Weiser & Co., 1971-. Mbrships: N.Y. State Soc. Cert. Pub. Accts.; Am. Arbitration Assn Nat. Panel of Arbitrators; Bd. of Govs. & Sec. Fairview Country Club; Harmonie Club; City Athletic Club. Address: 1025 5th Ave., N.Y. NY 10028, U.S.A. 6.

LAMBERT, Donald Andrew, b. 10 Dec 1927. University Professor. Educ: B.S., Univ. o Minn., 1950; M.A. 1963; Ph.D. Cand.; Air Wa Coll. Air Univ., 1973-74. Appts: Prof., Univ. o Minn.; Serv. Army of U.S., 1945-47; USAF & USAFR, to Lt. Col., 1950-. Mbrships: Advsr.

BSA; PTA, Mpls. & Monticello. Recip., USAF
Outstanding Unit Award. Address: Rural Rte.
1, Box 93, Monticello, MN 55362, U.S.A. 130.

LAMBERT, Erika Matilda, Dental Surgeon;
Dentist. Educ: D.D.S., Univ. of Latvia, 1932;
D.M.D., Univ. of Tuebingen, Germany, 1947;
D.D.S., Univ. of Pitts., U.S.A., 1964. Appts:
Dentist-Intern, Hosp., Pitts.; Currently, Dentist,
Rimersburg Med. Ctr., 1966-. Mbrships: Am. &
Pa. Dental Assns.; Odontological Soc. of Pa.;
Pa. Dental Serv. Soc.; Upsilon Alpha Zeta.
Address: P.O. Box 309, Rimersburg, PA 16248,
U.S.A. 6.

LAMBERT, Gavin, b. 23 July 1924.
Novelist; Critic; Screenwriter. Educ: Magdalen
Coll., Oxford, U.K. Ed., Sight & Sound,
1950-55. Mbrships: Acad. of Motiin Picture
Arts & Scis.; Screenwriters' Guild. Publs:
Books: The Slide Area, 1959; Inside Daisy
Clover, 1963; Norman's Letter, 1966; A Case
for the Angels, 1968; The Goody People, 1971;
On Cukor, 1972; GWTW, 1973; Screenplays:
Sons & Lovers, 1960; The Roman Spring of
Mrs. Stone, 1961; Inside Daisy Clover, 1965;
Film: Another Sky, 1955. Recip., Thomas R.
Coward Mem. Award for Fiction (U.S.A.) for
Norman's Letter, 1966. Address: B.P. 368,
Tanger Prin., Tangier, Morocco. 30.

LAMBERT, Rene, b. 23 July 1930.
Professor of Gastroenterology. Appts: Dir.,
Rsch. Unit of Digestive Physiopathol., 1964;
Prof., Schl. of Med., Lyon, France. Mbrships:
Am. Gastroenterological Assn.; British Soc. of
Gastroenterol.; Soc. Nat. Francaise de
Gastroenterologie. Publs: Les aspects recents de
L'ulcère experimental, 1958; Surgery of the
digestive system in the rat, 1965; Papers on the
pathophysiol. of peptic ulcers & mucous
secretions, gastro intestinal hormones. Address:
Pavillon H., Hosp. Edouard Herriot, Lyon
69003, France.

LAMBO, Awonola Olufunmilola, b. 20 Oct.
1932. Research Parasitologist (Medical). Educ:
B.Sc., Univ. of Nigeria, Nsukka, 1961; M.Sc.,
London Schl. of Hygiene & Tropical Med.,
Univ. of London, U.K., 1972. Appts: Lab.
Asst., 1953-54; Sci. Master, 1955; Rsch.
Parasitologist (Med.), 1966-. Mbrships: Nigeria
Inst. Int. Affairs; Sci. Assn. of Nigeria; Soc. of
Hlth., Nigeria; UN Assn. of Nigeria; Fellow,
Royal Soc. of Tropical Med. & Hygiene, 1972.
Contbr., med. articles & papers, mags., jrnls., &
bulletins, inclng. Your Hlth. Mag., Jrnl. of
Nigerian Med. Assn., WHO bulletin. Hons. incl:
Fed. Nigerian Govt. Schlrship, 1964-66; WHO
Fellowship, 1967, 1971-72. Address: Federal
Malaria Research Institute, Yaba, Lagos State,
Nigeria. 135.

LAMBROUCOS, John, b. 13 Dec. 1913. Civil
Servant. Educ: Grad., Econs. & Commerce.
Appts: w. Min. of Finance, Athens, 1936-47;
Prof. of Econs., medium range schl., 1935-48;
w. Min. of Coordination, 1947; Dir., ibid, 1951;
Dir.-Gen., 1955-70; Sec.-Gen., 1956-63; Dir.
Gen.-Coord., 1970; Ret'd. as Councillor, ibid &
Min. of Nat. Econ., 1970-73. Currently, Sec.
Gen. Min. of Coordination & Progng.; V.P.,
Greek Refineries of Aspropyrgos,
Nestle-Hellas., Indl. Investment Co. Omega, etc.
Mbrships: Num. Bds., Socs., inclng. Econ. Dev.
Financing Org. (1955-61), Agricl. Bank
(1964-67), V.P., Ctr. for Econ. Rschs.
(1961-64). Publs: Articles in newspapers &
mags. Hons: Silver Cross, Order of George A,
1947; Cmdr., Order of Phoenix, 1957, Order of
George A, 1961; Grand Cmdr., Order of
Phoenix, 1967, Order of George A, 1970; Das
Grosse Verdienstkreuz Mit/Stern, 1960; Grande
Ufficiale dell'Ordine al Merito, 1962; Off.,

Légion d'Honneur, 1966; Medal of Disting.
Servs., 1970. Address: 102 A, Vassilissis Sofias,
Av., Athens (610), Greece. 43.

LAMBUR, Charles H., b. 30 Oct. 1910.
Corporation President. Educ: B.S.E.M., Schl.
Mines & Metallurgy, Mo. Univ., Rolla, U.S.A.
Appts: Corps Engrs., U.S. Army, Ft. Belvoir,
Va.; Kodokan, Japan; Mining Engr., Phila. Coal
& Iron Co., Pa.; Sahara Coal Co.; M.E. & Ed.,
Coal Age, McGraw Hill Publg. Co., N.Y.; Dir.,
Mines, Simpson Creek Collieries, N.Y. W. Va.,
Ill., Pa.; Pres. & Gen. Mgr., U.S. Coal Co., N.Y.
& W. Va.; Pres., Shahmoon Inds.; Pres., Tekera
Int.; Pres. & Chief Exec., Schneider Corp.,
N.Y.; Served WWII, Col Command Eng. XII
AFSC, 1940-45. Mbrships: Theta Kappa Phi;
Sports Chmn., N.Y. Athletic Club; Sports
Chmn., AAU of U.S.A.; U.S. Olympic Judo
Comm.; U.S.A. Nat. Judo Chmn., Maccabian
Games; AIME; Navy League, U.S. Bd. Dirs.,
Acapulco; Bd. Dirs., U.S. Judo Assn.; Bd. Dirs.,
SFII; Monte Carlo Golf Club; Shinnecock Hills
Golf Club. Publs: The Economics of the
Mineral Industries, 1959; Contbr. Chapt: Coal
Marketing & Trade & num. jrnl. articles. Recip.
many sports trophies. Address: 303 5th Ave.,
N.Y., NY 10016, U.S.A. 6, 16.

LAMEERE, William A. E. A., b. 30 June
1904. University Professor. Educ: A.M.,
Harvard Univ., 1929; Doct. Phil., Univ. of
Brussels, Belgium, 1932; Dip., Ecole Pratique
des Hautes Etudes, Paris, France, 1936. Appts.
incl: Mbr., Belgian Historic Inst., Rome, Italy,
1934-38; For. Mbr., French Schl., Athens,
Greece, 1938-40; Dir., Belgian Acad., Rome,
1954-59; Ordinary Prof., Fac. of Philos. &
Letters, Univ. of Brussels, 1948-. Mbrships.
incl: SEC, European Soc. of Culture, Venice;
Assn. of Belgian Writers in French Lang.; Int.
Assn. of Papyrologists; Ernest Renan Soc.,
Paris; Exec. Bur., Int. Assn. for Hist. of Religs.,
1955-65. Publs. incl: La tradition manuscrite de
la correspondance de Grégoire de Chypre
patriarche de Constantinople (1283-1289),
1937; Pages Romaines, 1939; Sur la tombe de
Franz Cumont, 1948; Aperçus de paléographie
homérique, 1960. Hons. incl: Chevalier, Order
of Leopold, 1947; Grand Off., Order of Crown
of Belgium, 1972. Address: 77 Blvd. Brand
Whitlock, 1200 Brussels, Belgium. 43. 87.

LAMIRANDE, Emilien, b. 22 May 1926.
Educator. Educ: B.A., Univ. of Ottawa,
Canada, 1949; L.Ph., 1950; M.A., 1941; L.Th.,
1955; D.Th., Leopold-Franzens Univ.,
Innsbruck, Austria, 1960; S.T.M., Union Theol.
Sem., N.Y., U.S.A., 1965. Appts: Lectr.-Assoc.
Prof., St. Paul Univ., Ottawa, Canada, 1954-64;
Prof., ibid, 1964-71; Dean, 1967-69; Prof.,
Univ. of Ottawa, 1970-; Chmn., Dept. Relig.
Studies, 1972-. Mbrships: V.P., Canadian Soc.
Theol.; Am. Acad. Relig. Publs. incl: Dieu chez
les hommes: La signification du Pavillon
chrétien, 1967; etudes sur l'Ecclésiologie de
saint Augustin, 1969; La situation
ecclésiologique des Donatisten chez saint
Augustin, 1972. Address: Dept. of Relig.
Studies, Univ. of Ottawa, 177 Waller St.,
Ottawa, Ont., K1N 6N5 Canada.

LAMISON, Mary Frances, b. 16 May 1916.
Extension Specialist in Home Management.
Educ: A.A., Eastern N.M. Univ., 1935; B.S.,
N.M. State Univ., 1940; M.A., Wash. State
Univ., 1950; Postgrad. study, Univs. of Alaska,
Minn. Appts: Tchr., Home Econs., N.M. &
Wash., 1940-58; State Supvsr., Voc. Home
Econs., State of Alaska, & Univ. of Alaska
Home Econs. Tchr. Trnr., 1958-61; Univ. of
Minn. Agric. Ext. Serv. Specialist. Mbrships:
Am., Minn. Home Econs. Assns.; Am. Coun. on
Consumer Interests; Epsilon Sigma Phi.

Address: Univ. of Minn., North Hall, Room 40, St. Paul, MN 55101, U.S.A. 5, 15.

LAMONT, Corliss, b. 28 Mar. 1902. Author; Educator; Organization Executive. Educ: A.B. Harvard, Univ., 1924; Ph.D., Columbia Univ., 1932. Appts; Instr., Philos., Columbia Coll., 1928-32; Instr. New Schl. Soc. Rsch., 1940-42; Lectr., Columbia Schl. Gen. Studies, 1947-59, Assoc., Columbia Univ., Sems, 1971-. Mbrships. incl: P.E.N., 1923; Phi Beta Kappa; Bd. Dirs., Am. Civil Liberties Union, 1932-54; P. Chmn., Nat. Coun. Am-Soviet Friendship, 1943-46; Pres., Bill of Rights Fund, 1954-66; Chmn., Nat. Emergency Civil Liberties Comm., 1965-; V.P., Exec. Bd.; Poetry Soc. Am. Publs. incl: The Illusion of Immortality, 1935; The Independent Mind, 1952; Soviet Civilization, 1952; Freedom is as Freedom Does, 1956; The Philosophy of Humanism, 1957; Freedom of Choice Affirmed, 1967; A Humanist Wedding Service, 1970; Lover's Credo, 1972; Voice in the Wilderness: Collected Essays, 1974; Ed., Man Answers Death; An. Anthol. of Poetry; Dialogue on John Dewey; Dialogue on Geo. Santayana; The Trial of Eliz. Gurley Flynn by the Am. Civil Liberties Union. The Thomas Lamonts in America; Remembering John Masefield. 1971; Address: 315 W. 106th St., N.Y., NY 10025, U.S.A. 2, 3, 6, 11, 13, 15, 34, 131.

LAMPIO, Teppo Sakari, b. 24 May 1921. Director. Educ: M.A., Univ. of Helsinki, Finland, 1950; Ph.D., 1965. Appts: Game Biol., Finnish Game Fndn., 1944-54; Dir., Finnish Hunters League, 1954-63; Dir., Hunters Ctrl. Org., 1962-72; Dir., Game & Fisheries Rsch. Inst., Game Rsch. Div., 1972-; Ed. in Chief, Metsästäjä & Jägaren, 1947-72. Mbrships. incl: Coord., Int. Waterfowl Rsch. Bur., Hunting Rationalization Div. & Rsch., 1969-; State Rep., Conseil Int. de la Chasse, 1969-; V.P., Migratory Game Bird Comm., 1973-. Publs. incl: Metsästys, 1967; Eräelämäm Arvot, 1967; Hunting in Finland, 1967; Hunters by Occupational Status in Finland, 1972. Hons. incl: Cross in Liberty, 4th class, 1941; w. oak leaves, 1944; Badge of Merit in Gold, Finnish Hunters League, 1956. Address: Game & Fisheries rsch. Inst., Game Rsch. Div., Unioninkatu 45 B 42, 00170 Helsinki 17, Finland. 43, 90, 134.

LANA, Italo, b. 25 Feb. 1921. Professor of Latin Literature. Educ: Grad., Classical Philol., Univ. of Turin, 1946. Appts: Asst. Prof., Latin Lit., Univ. of Turin, 1948-52, Univ. of Cagliari, 1952-53, Univ. of Pisa, 1953-56; Prof., Classical Philol., Univ. of Turin, 1956-61; Prof., Latin Lit., ibid, 1961-; Fndr., Dir., Rsch. Grp. in Classical Pol. Thought, ibid, 1964-. Mbrships: Acad. of Sci., Turin; Dir., Corpus Scriptorum Latinorum Paravianum. Publs: Antologia della Letteratura Latina, 3 vols., 1964-67; Studi sul pensiero politico-classico, 1973. Contbr. to var. jrnls. recip., 2 war crosses & distinction in War of Liberation, 1943-45. Address: Facoltà di Lettere e Filosofia, Istituto di Filologia Classica A. Rostagni, Via S. Ottavio 20, Turin, Italy.

LANCASTER, Leslie Eugene, b. 15 Jan. 1932. Mathematical Statistician. Educ: B.S., Univ. of Wash., Seattle, U.S.A., 1960; M.S., Univ. of Neb., 1965; Postgrad., Geo. Wash. Univ., Wash. D.C., 1966-. Appts: Reliability Engr., Aerojet-Gen. Corp., Azusa, Calif., 1961; Reliability Engr., Space-Gen. Corp., El Monte, Calif., 1963-64; Tchng. Asst., Computer Ctr., Univ. of Neb., 1961-63 & 1964-65; Programmer, Roland F. Beers, Inc., Alexandria, Va., 1965-66; Sr. Programmer & Analyst, Ctr. for Naval Analysis, Arlington, Va., 1966-68; Sr. Analyst, Wolf Rsch. & Dev. Corp., Riverdale,

Md., 1968-70; Sr. Analyst, Computer Sci. Corp., Silver Spring, Md., 1970-73; Cons., Braddock, Dunn & McDonald, Inc., 1973-. Mbrships: Inst. of Math. Stats.; Am. Statistical Assn. Publs: A Redundancy Study of a Finite System in the Theory of Reliability, 1965; Rsch. paper read at Jt. Conf. on Math. & Computer Aids to Design, 1969. Address: 5812 Lamont Drive, New Carrollton, MD 20784, U.S.A. 6.

LANCASTER, Martha Jean, b. 14 Jan. 1937. Nursing Instructor; University Professor. Educ: A.A., Reinhardt Jr. Coll., 1960; Dip., R.N., Baroness Erlanger Hosp. Schl. of Nursing, 1963; B.S.N., Emory Schl. of Nursing, 1965; M.N., ibid, 1966; postgrad. work, Memphis State Univ. Grad. Ctr. & Univ. of Tenn. Appts: Instr., Pediatric Nursing, Baroness Erlanger Hosp. Schl. of Nursing, Chattanooga, Tenn. 1964-65; Instr., Coll. of Nursing, Univ. of Tenn., 1966-72; Assoc. Prof. of Nursing, ibid, 1972-; Clin. Supvsr., Newborn Ctr., City of Memphis Hosps., 1972-. Mbrships: Am. Nurses Assn.; Nurses Assn. of Am. Coll. of Obstrns. & Gynecologists; Southern Perinatal Assn.; Comm. Mbr., Nursing Prac., Tenn. Nurses Assn.; Sigma Theta Tau Contbr., profl. publs. Address: 2786 Madison Ave., Apt. 8, Memphis, TN 38111, U.S.A. 125.

LANCEN, Serge, b. 5 Nov. 1922. Composer. Educ: Conservatoire National Supérieur de Musique, Paris; composition w. Tony Aubin, counterpoint & fugue w. Noël Gallon. Appt: Tchr., Université Musicale Internationale de Paris, 1972-. Orchl. Works incl: Concerto for Piano, 1947; Concerto for Harmonica, 1954; Manhattan Symphony, 1962; Concerto for Violin, 1966; Fantaisie Creole, 1967; Festival à Kerkrade, 1967; Fantaisie Concertante for oboe, 1970; Cap Kennedy, 1970; Symphonie de Paris, 1973. Chamber music & lyrical works incl: Printanieres, 1953; Zwiefache, 1956; Narcisse, 1957; Concert a Six, 1961; La Mauvaise Conscience, 1962; Concertos da Camera for flute & for string double bass, 1962. Ballets: Cadence, 1951; Les Prix, 1954. Var. other compositions, inclng. film music. Hons. incl: Prix de Rome, 1950; Harriet Cohen's Int. Music Award, 1960. Address: 65 Rue La Fontaine, 75016 Paris, France.

LANCIONE, Bernard Gabe, b. 3 Feb. 1939. Lawyer. Educ: Ohio Univ., Athens, Ohio, 1956-60; Franklin Law Schl., Capitol Univ., 1961-65. Appts. incl: Ohio Dept. of Highways, 1961-63; Atty. Gen.'s Off., Ohio, 1963-65; A.G. Lancione, Atty. at Law, Bellaire, Ohio, 1965-68; Lancione, Lancione & Lancione, Attys. at Law, Bellaire, Ohio, 1968-. Mbrships: Legal Advsr., Young Democrats Club of Am.; Ohio Democratic State Exec. Comm.; Am. Arbitration Assn.; Ohio Acad. of Trial Lawyers, Bd. Trustees, 1969-73; Am. Bar Assn.; Ohio State Bar Assn.; Am. Judicature Soc.; Dir., Farmers & Merchants Bank; Legal Counsel, Young Democrats of Ohio, 1966-68; Belmont Co. Asst. Prosecutor-Mbr.; Bellaire City Solicitor; Young Democratic Club of Ohio, Pres., 1970-72. Hons: Outstanding Young Men of Am., 1972; Award Merit of Trial Lawyers, 1972; Award of Merit, Young Democrats of Am., 1973. Address: Lancione, Lancione & Lancione, Attys. at Law, Profl. Complex, Bellaire, OH 43906, U.S.A. 8, 114, 130.

LAND, George Thomas Lock, Researcher; Author. Educ: Millsaps Coll., Jackson, Miss.; Univ. of Veracruz, Jalapa, Mexico. Appts: Dir. Gen., TV del Norte, Monterrey & Mexico, D.F., 1960-62; V.P., Roman Corp., St. Louis, U.S.A., 1962-64; Chmn., Transolve Inc., Cambridge,

Mass., 1964-67; Chief Exec., Chmn., Innotek Corp., N.Y.C., 1967-71; Chmn., Ptnr., Turtle Bay Inst., 1971-. Mbrships. incl: Nat. Action Comm. on Drug Educ., H.E.W.; N.Y. Acad. Scis.; AAAS; Soc. Gen. Systems Rsch.; Am. Soc. Cybernetics; Creative Educ. Fndn. Publs: Innovation Systems, 1967; Innovation Technology, 1968; Grow or Die—The Unifying Principle of Transformation, 1973. Address: 135 E. 50th St., New York, NY 10022, U.S.A. 2, 130.

LAND, Mary Elizabeth, b. Sept. 1908. Author. Educ: Gulf Park Coll., Miss., 1924-25; Grad., Cheyney-Trnet Schl. Poetry, Calif., 1937. Appts. incl: Ed., weekly syndicated column, Outdoors South, 1947-48; Staff Writer, Southern Outdoors Mag., 1959-61, W. Bank Guide, New Orleans, 1962-63; Commentator for own conservation, outdoor prog., Miss. Soundings, WGCM, Gulfport, Miss. Mbrships. incl: Past Prog. Chmn., Metairie Ridge Chapt., DAR; Pres., Miss., Nat. League Am. Pen Women; Nat. Fedn. Am. Press Women; Colonial Dames XVII Century; Co-Fndr., New Orleans Chapt., & Exec. Bd., Nat. Soc. Arts & Letters; Outdoor Writers Assn. Am.; Int. Womens Fishing Assn. Publs: Shadows of the Swamp (poetry), 1940; Mary Land's Louisiana Cookery, 1955; New Orleans Cuisine, 1969; Abode (poetry), 1972. Recip. of hons. Address: 1314 Williams Ave., Natchitoches, LA 71457, U.S.A. 7.

LANDAU, Edwin Maria, b. 20 Sept. 1904. Writer; Journalist; Scholar. Educ: Univs. of Heidelberg, Freiburg, Vienna, Kiel, & Breslau; Doctorate degree, 1927. Appts: Owner, Verlag die Runde, Publrs., Berlin, 1931-36; w. Benno Schwabe & Cie., Basle, Switzerland, 1936-38; freelance jrnlst., writer, translater & pvte. schol., Zurich, 1945-. Mbrships: Comm. Mbr., P.E.N.; Assn. de la Presse étrangère en Suisse; Past Comm. Mbr., ibid; Int. Schutzverband deutschprachiger Schriftsteller, Zurich; Past Pres., ibid; Soc. Paul Claudel, Paris; Soc. Claudel en Belgique; Paul Claudel Soc., N.Y. Ed., Works of Paul Claudel, 6 vols. Translator Claudel poetry, prose & plays, also Voltaire, Moliere, Racine. Created Chevalier de l'Ordre des arts et des lettres. Address: Gemeindestr. 21, CH-8032 Zurich, Switzerland. 43.

LANDAU, Sol, b. 21 June 1920. Rabbi; Educator; Writer. Educ: B.A., Brooklyn Coll.; M.A., N.Y. Univ.; Ph.D., Fla. State Univ.; Rabbi & M.H.L., Jewish Theological Sem. of Am. Appts. incl: Rabbi, Whitestone Hebrew Ctr., Whitestone, N.Y., 1952-56; Rabbi, Park Synagogue, Cleveland, Ohio, 1956-60; Rabbi, Beth Hillel, Wilmette, Ill., 1960-63; Rabbi, Park Synagogue, Cleveland, Ohio, 1963-65; Rabbi, Beth David Cong., Miami, Fla., 1965-. Mbrships: Pres., Dade Co. Mental Hlth. Assn.; Pres., S.E. Region, Rabbinical Assembly; Chmn., Dade Co. Youth Advsry. Bd.; TV Coordinator, The Still Small Voice, Miami, Fla.; AAUP; Adult Educ. Assn. of U.S.A. Publs: Christian-Jewish Relations, 1959; Length Of Our Days, 1961; Bridging Two Worlds, 1967. Hons: Homiletics Prize, Jewish Theological Sem., 1951; Jerusalem Liberation Award, Bards of Israel, 1967; City of Miami Recognition on 20th Ordination Yr., 1971; Co. Govt. Award for Youth Serv., 1972; Mental Hlth. Award on Presidency Completion, 1973. Address: 2625 SW 3rd Ave., Miami, FL 33129, U.S.A.

LANDAUER, James Dittman, b. 27 Dec. 1902. Real Estate Consultant. B.S., Dartmouth Coll., 1923; Harvard Law Schl., 1923-24. Appts. incl: Chmn. of Bd., James D. Landauer Assocs., Inc., N.Y.C., 1961-; Pres. & Dir., Grand Central Bldg., Inc., 1962-67; Dir., Oliver

Tyrone Corp., Pitts., Home Title Div., Chgo. Title Ins. Co., Erie Lackawanna Railway Co., Phoenix Assurance Co. of N.Y. & London Guarantee & Accident Co. of N.Y.; Trustee, E. River Savings Bank, N.Y.C.; Trustee, Chase Manhattan Mortgage & Realty Trust; Trustee & V.P., Mem. Hosp. & Sloan-Kettering Cancer Ctr., 1962-; Dir., N.Y.C. Pub. Dev. Corp., 1968-. Mbrships. incl: Pres., Real Estate Bd. of N.Y., Inc., 1963-65; Gov., ibid, 1963-67; Dir., Am. Soc. of Real Estate Counselors, 1961-63; Dir., Nat. Assn. of Real Estate Bds., 1960-66; Int. Real Estate Fedn. Address: 510 Park Ave., N.Y., NY 10022, U.S.A.

LANDER, Herbert Josef Theresia, b. 5 Mar. 1908. Film Producer; Director. Educ: Gymnasium; Univ. of Vienna, Austria; Dipl. rer. mere. Appts. incl: Prod. of documentary films; Specialized in prod. of instruction films; Expeditions. Mbrships. incl: Bd. of Film Prods. Recip. of num. nat. & int. awards. Address: Prinzregentenstr. 85, 1 Berlin 31, German Fed. Repub.

LANDERS, Newlin Jewel, b. 10 July, 1906. Businessman. Educ: Contractors Schl.; Personnel Mgmt. Appts: former Owner, Landers Machine Co., Bell Gardens & E., L.A., Calif.; former Co-owner, Selwyn-Landers Valve Co., L.A.; former Owner, Havasu Landing, Calif.; Owner, Navajo Tract, Apple Valley Fndr., Landers, Calif. Mbrships: Trustee Loyal Order of Moose, Landers, Calif.; Sheriff Rangers of Yucca Valley; Law Officers' Assn. of Am.; Sponsor, Little League Baseball, Yucca Valley; Donor of Land to Landers Fire Station & Women's Club; Hons: Businessman of the Week, KSST Am. Radio 1420, 1969; Hon. Mbr., Landers Volunteer Fire Dept.; Plaque for 13 years service w. Sheriff's Search & Rescue, 1972; Badge for Yucca Valley Dary. Sheriff Ranges for San Bernardino Co., 1972. Address: 905 Landers Lane, Landers, CA 92284, U.S.A. 22, 59, 120, 130.

LANDERS, Vernette (Mrs. Newlin J. Landers), b. 3 May 1912. School District Counselor; Writer. Educ: A.B., Univ. of Calif., L.A.; M.A., ibid; Ed.D. Appts: Tchr., Sec ondary Schls., Montebello, Calif., 22 yrs.; Prof., Long Beach City Coll., Calif., 1 yr.; Prof., L.A. State Coll., 1 yr.; Dean of Girls, 19 Palms H.S., Calif., 5 yrs.; Dist. Counselor, Morongo Unified Schl. Dist., 8 yrs.; Coord, Adult Educ., ibid; Clerk- i/c Landers Post Office, 1962-. Mbrships: Phi Beta Kappa; Pi Lambda Theta; Sigma Delta Pi; Pres., Montebello Bus. & Profl. Women's Club; Pres., Hablamos Toastmistress Club, Whittier; V.P., Landers Assn. Inc.; Bd. of Dirs., Desert Ears; Nat. Hist. Assn; Sec., Landers Volunteer Fire Dept.; Nat. Ret'd. Tchrs. Assn.; Postal Commemorative Soc.; Smithsonian Assocs.; Life, Hi-Desert Playhouse Guild and Mem. Hosp. Guild. Contbr. of profl. articles to educ. mags. & govt. publs. Recip. of var. hons. inclng: Creating Recognition Award, Int. Personnel Rsch., 1972. Address: 905 Landers Ln., Landers, CA 92284, U.S.A. 5, 22, 57, 59, 120, 126, 130.

LANDESMAN, Alter F., b. 5 Dec. 1895. Rabbi; Organization Executive. Educ: B.A., Western Reserve Univ., 1917; M.A., Tchrs. Coll., Columbia Univ., 1922; Ordination as Rabbi, Jewish Theological Sem., 1922. Appts. incl: Exec. Dir., Hebrew Educl. Soc. of Brooklyn, 1922-61, Dir. Emeritus, 1961-; Pres., Metropol. Assn. of Jewish Ctr. Wkrs., 1927-30; Chmn., Educ. Comm., United Synagogue of Am., 1929-45; Fndr., Brownsville Neighborhood & Welfare Coun., Pres., 1938-41; V.P., Jewish Book Coun. of Am.; Corres. Sec., Rabbinical Assembly of Am. Publs: Curriculum for Jewish Religious Schools, 1922; Brownsville, Birth, Development & Passing of a Jewish Community, 1971. Hons: Degrees of D.H.L., 1948, D.D., 1953; 1st Annual Award, Jt. Commn. Synagogue Rels., Fedn. Jewish Philanthropies, 1959. Address: 1608 E. 94th St., Brooklyn, NY 11236, U.S.A. 55.

LANDIS, Charles, b. 21 July 1917. Cabaret Executive. Educ: B.A., Univ. of Minn. Appts: Pres., Largo Inc., L.A., 1957-, Lanvan Artists Prods. Ltd., L.A., 1965-, Chas. Landis Enterprises, L.A., 1967-, Cal-Hyland Corp., Sacramento Calif., 1968-; Ptnr., Mission Rd. Enterprises, L.A., 1968-; Owner, Clan Record Co., Monterey Park, Calif., 1970-; Sec.-Treas., Roxy Theatre Corp., Hollywood, Calif., 1971-. Mbrships: Pres., Night Club Operators of Am., 1965-66. Recip. Hon. Mayorship, W. Hollywood, Calif., 1968, 69, 70 & 71. Address: 530 Chalette Dr., Beverly Hills, CA 90210, U.S.A. 9.

LANDMANN, Frederic H. (Fritz), b. 1 Apr. 1933. Marketing Executive. Educ: B.S., Wharton Schl. of Finance & Commerce, Univ. of Pa., 1955. Appts: Financial Analyst, 1st Camden Nat. Bank, N.J., 1955-60; Art Publr., Dir. of Mktng., Food Engrng. Mag., Chilton Co., Phila., Pa., 1960-68; Publr., Media/Scope Mag., N.Y.C., 1968-70; Exec. V.P., Dir., Co-Fndr., Markets Maxima, Princeton, N.J., 1970-72; Sr. V.P. & Dir., ITT/TDI, N.Y.C., 1972-. Mbrships: Nat. Assn. Mgrs. (mktng. comm.); Am. Soc. Mag. Eds.; Assn. Indl. Advts.; Broadcast Promotion Assn.; Int. Newspaper Promotion Assn.; Int. Oceanographic Soc.; Sigma—ITT; St. Anthony fraternity, Delta Psi; U.S. Armor Assn. Author of mag. articles. Hons: Gold Chevron, Standard Rate & Data Serv., 1968, '67. Address: 28 Terhune Rd., Princeton, NJ 08540, U.S.A. 16.

LANDOLT, Emil, b. 23 Sept. 1895. Former Mayor of Zurich, Switzerland. Educ: LL.D., Dip. of Solicitor, Univs. of Zurich & Berne. Appts: Dept. Sec., Finance Dept., Canton of Zurich, 1926-33; 1st Sec., Zurich Chmbr. of Comm., 1933-42; Pres., Supreme Ct., taxation, Canton of Zurich, 1934-51; Mbr., Town Coun., City of Zurich, 1942-49; Mayor, City of Zurich, 1949-66. Mbrships: incl: Past Pres., New Helvetic Soc., Zurich; Pres., Swiss Soc. of Pub. Utility; Pres., Swiss Conf. on Pub. Welfare; Pres., Fed. Comm., Swiss Nat. Mus.; Past Master, Zurich Guild of the Carpenters; Past Pres., Union of Swiss Cities. Author of publs. Hons: Mbr., 20 cultural, soc. & sport socs.; C.B.E.; Off. de la Legion d'Honneur. Address: Winkelwiese 10, CH-8001, Zurich, Switzerland.

LANDON, Alison, (Mrs. Donald O. Landon). Writer; Business Executive. Educ: Univ. of Wis., Eau Claire; postgrad. work, Univ. of Wis., Madison. Appts: incl: Ed. & Asst. to Publr., Profl. Press, Chgo., 1940-41; Writer & Asst. to 1st V.P., Fensholt Co., Chgo., 1942-45; Dir. of Advt. & Sales Promotion, Durallium Labs., Durallium Products Corp., & Ceramicast., Chgo., 1945-48; Owner & Operator, Alison Landon Advt., Chgo., 1948-51; Writer & Asst. to Pres., Warren Wells, Inc., N.Y.C., 1955-56; Sr. Copywriter.,, Cortez F. Enloe, Inc., N.Y.C., 1957-58; Fndr., Owner & Operator, Alison Landon Assocs., Warren, N.J., 1958-. Author, Your Good Health, 1957. Contbr., The Copywriter's Guide, 1958. Ghost writer, var. articles, monographs, books. Recip., profl. awards & commendations. Address: P.O. Box 4226, Warren, NJ 07060, U.S.A. 5, 6, 132.

LANDRAM, Christina Louella Oliver, b. 10 Dec. 1922. Librarian. Educ: B.A., Tex. Woman's Univ., 1945; B.S.L.S., ibid, 1946;

M.L.S., 1951. Appts: Cataloger, Lib. of Congress, Wash. D.C., 1946-48, U.S. Info. Ctr., Tokyo, Japan, 1948-50, Tex. Technological Univ., 1950-51, U.S. Dept. of Agric. Lib., Wash. D.C., 1953-54; Libn., Yokota AFB, Japan, 1954-55, St. Mary's Hosp., W. Palm Beach, Fla., 1957-59, Jacksonville H.S., Ark., 1959-61; Coord., Shelby Co. Libs., Memphis, Tenn., 1961-63; Hd., Catalog Dept., Ga. State Univ., Atlanta, Ga., 1963-; Cons., Re-org. of Catalog Dept., Tuskegee Inst., 1972. Mbrships: ALA; Southeastern Lib. Assn.; Chmn., Resources & Tech. Servs. Sect., Ga. Lib. Assn., 1969-71; Pres., Metro-Atlanta Lib. Assn., 1967-68. Author of 2 papers in libs. Address: 1802 Alderbrook Rd. N.E., Atlanta, GA 30345, U.S.A. 5, 138.

LANDRUM, Opal Virginia, b. 17 Nov. 1918. U.S. Government Official. Educ: A.B., Ala. Coll., Montevallo, 1935; M.A., Am. Univ., Wash. D.C., 1955; Ph.D., ibid, 1965. Appts: Tchr., Pub. Schls., Jefferson Co., Ala., 1935-42; Operations Off., Ordnance Dept., War Dept., Navajo Ordnance Depot, Flagstaff, Ariz., 1942-44, Anniston Ordnance Depot, Ala., 1944-46; Planning Off., Rsch. & Dev., Off. of the Quartermaster Gen., Dept. of Army, Wash. D.C., 1947-56; Heraldic Prog. Admnstr., ibid, 1956-60; Heraldic Prog. Mgr., Inst. of Heraldry, U.S. Army, Alexandria, Va., 1960-. Mbrships: AAAS; Am. Pol. Sci. Assn.; Co. Mil. Histns.; Confederate Mem. Lit. Soc.; Pi Sigma Alpha. Author, A Case Study, Heraldic Rr., Rsch. & Dev. Div. Off. of the Quartermaster General, Dept. of the Army, Dept. of Defense, 1955. Recip., Meritorious Civilian Serv. Award, Dept. of Army, 1969. Address: 1600 S. Eads St., Arlington, VA 22202, U.S.A. 5, 14.

LANDRUM, Roy E., b. 1 May 1941. Principal. Educ: A.B., B.S., Middle Tenn. State Univ., Murfreesboro. Appts: Prin., Palmer Elem. Schl., Tenn., Gassaway Elem. Schl., & (currently) Auburn H.S., Auburntown, Tenn.; Classroom Tchr., Grundy Co., Tenn. for 2 yrs. Mbrships: Pi Kappa Delta; Cannon Co. Educl. Assn.; NEA; Nat. Second. Prins. Assn.; Tenn. Educ. Assn. Hons: Forensics Award, 1962. Address: 1807 Kings Ct., Murfreesboro, TN 37130, U.S.A. 125.

LANDRY, Bernard E., b. 20 Aug. 1936. Labor Relations Administrative Manager. Educ: B.A., St. Michael's Coll.; Villanova Law Schl. Administrative Mgr., Labor Rels., N.Y.C. Off-Track Betting Corp., N.Y.C. Positions in Jaycees: Chmn., Jaycee Lake Park Proj. & Sec.-Treas., Greater Denville Area Jaycees, 1966; Pres., Greater Denville Area Jaycees, 1967; Transferred to N.Y.C. Jaycees, 1967; Dist. Pres., ibid, 1968; Pres., 1969; Chmn. of Bd., 1970; Chmn., Monte Carlo Night, & P.R. Chmn., Dist. One, Div. One, 1971; Dir. of Mbrship., 1972; Pres., N.Y. Senate, 1973. Jaycee Hons. incl: October Growth Award, Dist. One, Div. One, 1969; Community Involvement Award, Spark Plug, 1969; Chmn. of Bd. Plaque, Spark Plug, 1970; Ldrship. in Action Cert., 1970; Chmn. of Yr., Spark Plug, 1971. Address: 48-23, 42nd St., Apt. 6F, Sunnyside, NY 11104, U.S.A. 117, 130.

LANDTMAN, Christian, b. 23 May 1922. Managing Director. Educ: M.Sc., Helsinki Univ. of Technol., Finland, 1948. Appts. incl: Lectr., Helsinki Univ. of Technol., 1949-57; Workshop Engr., Oy Wärtsilä Ab, Helsinki Shipyard, 1954-56; Tech. Mgr. & Chief, Drawing Off., ibid, 1956-58; Tech. Mgr., ibid, 1958-61; Managing Dir., ibid, 1962-71; Managing Dir., Oy Wärtsilä Ab Shipyard Grp., 1971-. Mbrships. incl: Engrng. Soc. in Finland; Assn. of Finnish Metal & Engrng. Inds.; Finnish Metal Trades

Employees' Assn. Publs: Laivojen Koneistot, 1959; Maskintekniska synpunkter på diesel-elektrisk fartygsdrift, 1961; Technische Gesichtspunkte uber moderne grosse Eisbrecher, 1961; Finnish Icebreakers, 1969. Hons: Finnish Freedom Cross, 4th class w. sword, 1944; 1st Class, Order of the White Rose, 1964; Chevalier, Order of Vasa, Sweden, 1964; Commandeur, Ordre de Leopold II, Belgium, 1969; Cmdr., Lion of Finland, 1970. Address: Oy Wärtsilä Ab, Shipyard Group, Sörnäisten rantatie 11, 00530 Helsinki 53, Finland. 43, 90, 134.

LANE, Colon Terry, b. 13 Dec. 1927. Administrator, Special Education (Mentally Retarded). Educ: B.G.S. (Pol. Sci.), Univ. of Omaha, Neb., 1967; M.Ed., Clemson Univ., 1969; Ph.D. Candidate, Univ. of S.C. Appts: Serv. USAF, 1948-67; medically retired as Sr. Master Sgt., Personnel Supt., 1967; Mbr. of Staff, Whitten Village (residential Instn. for Mentally Retarded), S.C., 1968-, as Mgr. Sheltered Workshop & Dir. Sheltered Workshops & Pre-Voc. Trng. 1968-71, Prin., Schl. for Trainable Mentally Retarded 1971-72, Asst. Dir. of Educ., Trng. & Recreation 1972-. Mbrships: Coun. for Exceptional Children (Past Regional Pres.); Am. Assn. on Mental Deficiency; Coun. of Admnstrs. of Special Educ.; NEA; Coun. for Basic Educ. Publs: Major Contbr., Manual for Training of Paraprofessionals in Mental Retardation, 1969; Co-Author, paper for CEC Int. Convention, 1970. Hons: Commendation Ribbons, Meritorious Serv. 1958-63, 1963-67, USAF. Address: Whitten Village, Clinton, SC 29325, U.S.A. 125.

LANE, Constance Ethel Grambling, b. 6 Aug. 1946. College Music Teacher; Flautist. Educ: Mus.B., Centenary Coll., Shreveport, La., 1968; Mus.M., La. State Univ., Baton Rouge, 1970; currently Doctoral Candidate, ibid. Appts: Prin. Flute, Shreveport Symph., 1964-68, Ohio Symph., Lakeside, 1968, S.C. Philhamonic, 1974; Flutist, Baton Rouge Symph., 1968-71; Flute Instr., Univ. of S.C., 1970-. Mbrships: Pi Kappa Lambda; Phi Kappa Phi; Nat. Assn. Coll. Wind & Percussion Instrs.; Coll. Music Soc.; Music Educators Nat. Conf.; S.C. State Bd., Music Tchrs. Nat. Assn.; Phi Beta. Solo recitals, 1964-. Mbr., Univ. of S.C. Fac. Wood Wind Quintet, 1970-, Baroque Trio, Trio, 1974-. Address: 2014 Mary Hill Dr., Columbia, SC 29210, U.S.A.

LANE, George Bertram, b. 10 June 1943. College Music Teacher; Trombonist. Educ: B.Mus., N.Tex. State Univ., Denton; M.Sc., Kan. State Tchrs. Coll., Emporia; D. Mus. Arts Cand., Univ. of Tex., Austin; studied w. Leon Brown & Terry Cravens. Appts: Solo Recitalist, as appeared w. var. univ. bands & orchs., 1962-; Trombonist, Am. Wind Symph., 1963, Abilene (Tex.) Philharmonic, 1965-67, Austin Tex.) Symph., 1970-72, & Columbia (S.C.) Philharmonic, 1972-74; Tchr., Music Facs., Abilene Christian Coll., Tex., 1965-67, David Lipscomb Coll., Nashville, Tenn., 1970, Univ. of Tex., Austin, 1970-72 & Univ. of S.C., 1972-; Assoc. Ed., The Brass Press, Nashville, 1970-; Music Dir., Covenant Presby. Ch., Columbia, 1972-. Mbrships: Sec., Int. Trombone Assn.; Coll. Music Soc.; Phi Mu Alpha Sinfonia; Nat. Assn. of Coll. Wind & Percussion Instrs.; Music Tchrs. Nat. Assn.; Kappa Kappa Psi; Soc. for Commng. New Music, Music Educators' Nat. Conf. Publs: Concise Daily Routine for Trombone, 1970; Ed., Sonata a 3 by J.J. Fux (2 vols., Trombone, Cello & Continuo), 1974. Address: 2014 Mary Hill Dr., Columbia, SC 29210, U.S.A. 125.

LANE, Helen Murchison, b. 1 June 1924. Civic Worker. Educ: B.A., Sweet Briar Coll., 1946. Mbrships: Jr. League of Jacksonville, Fla. Inc., (Pres. 1959); Past-Pres., Acacia Garden Circle; Garden Ctr., Jacksonville; Colonial Dames; Adams Environmental Awards Comm., 1973-74; Mayor's Histl. & Cultural Conservation Comm., 1972-74; Chmn., Action Plan for the Arts, 1973; Arts Assembly, 1974-76; Symph. Bd., 1973-74; Bd. of Dirs., Bartram Schl., 1972-74; Sweet Briar Alumnae Assn. (Exec. Comm. 1970). Publs: The Best of Lucifer, 1969; Co-author, The Queen Victoria Cooks, 1971. Frequent Lectr. Restored a Victorian house. Address: 3790 Ortega Blvd., Jacksonville, FL 32210, U.S.A. 5, 7, 132.

LANE, (Sister), M. Claude, b. 7 Feb. 1915. Librarian & Archivist. Educ: B.A., Our Lady of Lake Coll., San Antonio, Tex., 1953; M.L.S., Univ. of Tex., 1961. Appts. incl: Tchr., choral Dir. & Libn., Dominican Sisters' Elem. & HS, Tex. & Calif., 1933-71; Prin., St. Mary's Elem. Schl., Orange, Tex., 1958-60; Archiv., Cath. Archives of Tex., Austin, 1960-61, '64-67, '71-; Lib. Cons., Diocese of Austin Educl. Off., 1964-69, '71-; Lib.-AV Coord., St. Pius H.S., Houston, 1967-71. Mbrships. incl: Coun., Soc. of S.W. Archives., 1972-74; Cath. Lib. Assn.; Nat. Advsry. Coun., ibid, 1965-71; Am. & Tex. Lib. Assns.; Soc. of Am. Archivs.; Ch. Archives Comm., ibid. Tex. State Histl. Assn.; Am. Cath. Histl. Assn.; Am. Assn. State & Local Hist. Publs: Catholic Archives of Texas: History & Preliminary Inventory, 1961; Catholic Archives of Texas (brochure); article in profl. jrnl. Address: Box 13327 Capitol Stn., Austin, TX 78711, U.S.A. 5, 132, 138.

LANE, Sylvia, b. 26 May 1916. Professor of Agricultural Economics. Educ: A.B. (Economics), Univ. of Calif., 1934; M.A. (Economics), ibid, 1936; Ph.D., Univ. of Southern Calif., 1957. Appts: Lectr.-Asst. Prof., Univ. of Southern Calif., 1947-60; Assoc. Prof. of Econs., San Diego State Coll., Calif., 1961; Assoc. Prof. of Finance, ibid, 1965; Assoc. Prof. & Finance Assoc. Dir., Ctr. for Econ. Educ., Calif. State Coll. at Fullerton, 1965-69; Chmn., Dept. of Finance, ibid, 1967-69; Prof. of Agricl. Econs., Univ. of Calif., Davis, 1969-. Mbrships: Pres.-Elect, Am. Econs. Assn.; Exec. Comm., Western Econs. Assn.; Am. Agricl. Econs. Assn.; Western Agricl. Assn.; Omicron Delta Epsilon. Publs: Personal Finance (w. E.B. Phillips), 1969; Reports on taxation; Contbns. to jrnls. Hons. incl: Ford Fellowship in Econs., Univ. of Calif., L.A., 1963; Ford Fellowship in Finance, Univ. of Chgo., Ill., 1965; Fellowship in Econs., ibid, 1968. Address: Dept. of Agricl. Econs., University of California, Davis, CA 95616, U.S.A. 5, 14.

LANG, Ernest Byron, b. 12 June 1911. Teacher. Educ: B.S., Jacksonville State Univ., Ala.; M.S., George Peabody Coll. for Tchrs., Nashville, Tenn.; N.D.E.A. Inst. in Educl. Media, Auburn Univ., Ala.; Summer Workshop for Tchrs. of Migrant Children, N.Y. St. Ctr. for Migrant Studies. Appts: Served WWII; Classroom Tchr., Dekalb Co. Schls., 22 yrs.; H.S. Prin., ibid, 15 yrs.; Title I Coord., 8 yrs.; Dir. of Educ. for Migrant Children, 7 yrs. Mbrships. incl: Pres., Dekalb Co. Tchrs. Assn.; NEA; Ala. Educ. Assn.; Nat. Assn. of Secondary Schl. Prins.; Int. Reading Assn.; Nat. Assn. of Migrant Educ.; Am. Legion; Veterans of For. Wars; Chmn., Sand Mtn. Water Authority; Exec. Comm., Dekalb Co. Hosp. Authority; Retired Sr. Volunteer Advsry. Comm. Address: Box 7, Ider, AL 35981, U.S.A. 130.

LANG, John Albert, Jr., b. 15 Nov. 1910. Educator; Government Official. Educ: A.B., Univ. of Neb., 1930; M.A., 1931. Appts. incl: Maj. Gen., USAFR; Congressional Asst. & Staff Cons., 1946-61; Admin. Asst. to Sec., USAF, 1961-71; V.P., E. Carolina Univ., 1971-72; Sec., N.C. Dept. of Mil. & Veterans Affairs, 1972-73; Vice Chancellor, E. Carolina Univ., 1973-. Mbrships. incl: Phi Beta Kappa; Pres., N.C. Soc. of Wash. D.C., 1951-53; Pres., Congressional Secs. Club, 1953-54; Pres., D.C. Dept., Reserve Officers Assn., 1955-56; Air Force Hist. Advsry. Comm., 1971-; Nat. Acad. Mgmt. Contbr. to var. publs. Hons. incl: Army Commendation Medal, 1945; Air Force Commendation Medal, 1956; Legion of Merit, USAF, 1962; Air Force Meritorious Serv. Award, 1969; Disting. Serv. Medal, USAF, 1972. Address: 114 King George Rd., Greenville, NC 27834, U.S.A. 2, 7.

LANG, Ludwig, b. 20 Apr. 1902. Retired Departmental Head. Educ: Tchr. trng. coll.; Dr.phil., Univ. of Vienna, Austria. Appts. as Tchr., Pedagogic Prof., Schl. Insp., Cabinet Coun., Fed. Min. of Educ., & Departmental Hd. Mbrships: Cath. Acad., Vienna; Psychol. Assn. Publs: Befehlen & Gehorchen, 1936; Landschule & ländliche Erziehung, 2nd edit, 1950; Landschulerneuerung, Landschulplan, 1950; Das Schulhaus der Gegenwart, 1951; Neue Wege zur Schülerkenntnis, 3rd edit, 1958; Erziehung in dieser Zeit, 1955; Lehrplan—Kommentare, 1964-; Pädagogische Probleme des Schulgesetzwerkes, 1962 (1965). Recip., Grand medal of hon. for servs. to Repub. of Austria. Address: Schönbrunnerstrasse 2/32, 1040 Vienna, Austria. 43, 86.

LANG, Margo Terzian (Mrs. J.M. Lang). Professional Artist in Watercolor/Oils, Landscapes-Portraits, Sculpture-Ceramics. Educ: Fresno State Univ., Calif., 1939-42; Stanford Univ., Palo Alto., Calif., 1948-50; Prado Mus., Madrid, Spain, 1957-59; Ariz. State Univ., Tempe, 1960-61; Special Workshops w. prominent artists Dong Kingman, Ed Whitney, Rex Brandt, etc. Appts: Lectr.; Dir. of Painting Workshops. Mbrships: Nat. Soc. of Arts & Letters (Nat. Bd. Mbr., 1971-72); Am. Artists Profl. League; Smithsonian Assoc., Nat. Mbr., Wash., D.C.; The Engl. Speaking Union; Ariz. Watercolor Assn.; Phoenix Art Mus.; Phoenix Symph. Assn. & Musical Theater Guild (Bd. Mbr. 1964-69); Goodwill Aux.; Friends of Mexican Art. Int. Competitions: Paintings selected for reproduction & publ. in N.Y. Life Ins. Calendars, 1969, '70, & in Am. Fine Art Series, 1971. Special Commns.: Sunrise Tomorrow for Glass & Garden Ch., Scottsdale, Ariz.; Arizona Scenes for Pepsi Cola Bldg., Phoenix, Ariz. Over 15 one-man shows in Mex., N.Y.C., Calif. & Ariz., 1965-; Over 50 paintings selected by U.S. Dept. of State to hang in U.S. Embassies worldwide; 7 paintings selected by Nat. Collect. of Fine Art Mus., Smithsonian Instn., Wash., D.C. for their permanent collect. Voice of America Radio interviews, beamed to E. Europe & Middle East. Recip. of Best of Show Award, 1970, '72, '73, & Silver Medal for Excellence, 1971, Int. Platform Assn., Wash., D.C. Address: The Marhaba Studio, 6127 Calle del Paisano, Scottsdale, AZ 85251, U.S.A. 5, 37, 57, 130.

LANG, William Rawson, b. 16 Feb. 1909. Educator. Educ: B.Sc., Univ. of Western Australia, 1931; B.A., ibid, 1934; M.Sc., 1939; D.Sc., 1961. Appts: Sci. Master, Wesley Coll., W.A., 1931-34; Sci. Lectr., Perth Tech. Coll., 1934-36; Rsch. Phys., Inst. of Agric., Univ. of W.A., 1937-38; Tutor in Phys., St. George's Coll., ibid, 1937; Off.-in-Chief, Sci.

Investigations, Gordon Inst. of Technol., Geelong, Vic., 1933-45; Fndn. Hd. of Textile Coll., ibid, 1945-69; Hd., Schl. of Applied Scis., 1969-74; Dpty. Prin., 1970-74. Mbrships. incl: Fellow, Australian Coll. Educ. (chmn., Vic. chapt., 1969-71); Fellow, Textile Inst., Manchester (hon. life mbr.); Fellow, Inst. Phys., Australian Inst. Phys. Publs. incl: Sheep & Wool in Australia, 1967, '72; co-author, The Televiewing Habits of Secondary School Children in Geelong, for Vic. chapt., Australian Coll. Educ., Aug. 1965. Hons: Warner Mem. Medal, Textile Inst., 1966; Serv. Medal, ibid, 1960. Address: 13 Humble St., Geelong East, Vic., Australia 3219.

LANGE, Frederick Emil, b. 24 May 1908. Patent Lawyer. Educ: A.B., Univ. of Neb., 1928; LL.B., M.P.L., Wash. Coll. of Law, 1932. Appts: Examiner, U.S. Patent Off., 1929-35; Patent Lawyer, Honeywell, Inc., 1935-63; Mgr., Mnpls. Patent Dept., ibid, 1954-63; Ptnr., Dorsey, Marquart, Windhorst, West & Hallady, 1965-73; Sole Prac., 1973-. Mbrships: Minn. Bar Assn.; Dist. of Columbia Bar Assn.; Hennedin Co. Bar Assn.; Am. Bar Assn.; Am. Patent Law Assn.; Pres., Minn. Patent Law Assn., 1954-55; Am. Judicature Soc.; Bd. of Trustees, 1st Unitarian Soc., 1970-71; Chmn., Minn. Br., World Federalists, 1958-60; Nat. Exec. Coun., ibid, 1958-64; Minn. Exec. Coun. Recip., Disting. Serv. Award, Univ. of Neb., 1968. Address: 1938 Midwest Plaza Bldg., 801 Nicollet Mall, Minneapolis, MN 55402, U.S.A. 16.

⁕LANGE, Victor, b. 13 July 1908. University Professor. Educ: Oxford Univ., U.K.; M.A. Toronto, Canada; Ph.D., Leipzig, Germany. Appts: Lectr., Univ. Coll., Toronto, Canada; Assoc. Prof., German Lit., Cornell Univ. U.S.A.; John N. Woodhull Prof., Mod. Langs. Princeton Univ.; Hon. Prof., Free Univ., Berlin Germany. Mbrships: Pres., Int. Assn. Germanic Studies; V.P., MLA; V.P., Am. Assn. Tchrs. of German; Chmn., Am. Coun. German Studies Dir., Nat. Carl Schurz Assn. Publs: Modern German Literature; Humanistic Scholarship in America; Goethe Essays; German Classicism Hons. incl: Cmdrs. Cross, German Order of Merit; Gold Medal, Goethe Inst.; Prize for Scholarship, German Acad. Address: 230 E Pyne Bldg., Princeton Univ., Princeton, N. 08540, U.S.A. 2, 13, 43, 92.

LANGENSKIÖLD, Anders (Fabian), b. May 1916. Physician; Professor. Educ: M.D. Univ. of Helsinki, 1943. Appts: Lectr., Gen surg., Univ. of Helsinki, 1951-63; Hd., Surg Dept., Helsinki Deaconess Hosp., 1955-56; Hd. Orthopaedic Hosp., Invalid Fndn., Helsinki 1956-68; Prof., Orthopaedics & Traumatol. Univ. of Helsinki, 1969-; Hd., Dept. of Orthopaedics & Traumatol., Helsinki Univ. Ctrl Hosp., 1969-. Mbrships: Corresp. Mbr., Brit Orthopaedic Assn.; Pres., Finnish Med. Soc. 1967, Finnish Orthopaedic Assn., 1963-67 Scandinavian Orthopaedic Assn., 1962-64 Chmn., Bd., Scandinavian Soc. for Rehabil. 1966-; Finnish Sci. Soc.; V.P., Int. Soc. fo Rehabil. of Disabled; Corresp. Mbr., Am Orthopaedic Assn.; Bd. Dirs., Oy Stockman Ab., 1960-; Bd. Admnstrs., Nordisk Foreningsbanken, 1972-; Chmn., Editl. Bd. Acta Orthopaedica Scandinavica, 1970- Contbr. of articles to profl. jrnls. Hons: Pou Guiladal Award, Scandinavian Orthopaedi Assn., 1962; E.J. Nystrom Award, Finnish Sc Soc., 1973. Address: Mellstensvägen 17. B. 16 SF-02170, Gäddvik, Finland. 43.

LANGENSKIÖLD, (Baron) Lars (Gusta Adolf), b. 11 Sept. 1913. Company Executive Educ: Grad. Engr., Inst. of Technol., Helsinki

Finland; Naval Archt., Chalmers, Gothenburg, Sweden. Appts. incl: Mbr. Bd. Dirs., Finland Steamship Co. Ltd., Helsinki, Finland, 1965-68; Mng. Dir., ibid, 1969-. Mbrships: V.P., Finnish Shipowners Assn.; Inst. of Marine Engrs.; Börsklubben. Hons: Kt., 1st Class, Lion of Finland, 1964; Cmdr., White Rose of Finland, 1973; C.B.E., 1974. Address: Finland Steamship Co. Ltd., Eteläranta 8, SF-00130, Helsinki 13, Finland. 43.

LANGER, Torben Wang, b. 7 June 1924. Librarian; Editor; Author. Educ: Cand. mag. (Romance langs.), Copenhagen Univ., Denmark, 1952. Appts: Asst. Libn., Royal Lib., Copenhagen, 1955-63; Dpty. Libn., Head of Periodicals Dept., ibid, 1963-; Ed. of jrnls., Naturens Verden, 1963-70, & Lepidoptera, 1965-70; Hd. of Ency. Dept. & Ed.-in-chief Lademanns Leksikon, Lademann Editors, 1968-. Mbrships: E. African Wildlife Soc; Var. entomolical & zoological socs. in Denmark, U.S.A., & Netherlands. Publs: Num. monographs on insect & other animal life, & on Africa; articles, radio & TV work. Hons: Mbr., Lepidopterological Soc., Copenhagen, 1958. Address: Gammel Køgevej 785B, 2660 Brøndbystrand, Denmark. 134.

LANGE-SEIDL, Annemarie. Professor. Educ: Univs. of Munich, Germany; Copenhagen, Denmark & Paris, France; Dr.phil. Mbrships: Pres., Florian-Seidl-Archiv; Accad. Int. di Pontzen, Naples, Italy; Hochschullehrerverband, Regensburger Schriftstellerkreis. Publs: Theoretical Papers—Zaubersänger und Spielmann, 1946; Experiment und Kunstwerk, 1948; Literaturstreit als Weg aum Erfolg, 1949; Mit dem eigenen Ich auf Du und Du. Uber Spiegelscheu und Reflexion, 1951; Publikationsmöglichkeiten der Wissenschaft, 1952; Das Nachkriegstheater, sein Publikum und sein Verständnis aus der modernen Sprachwissenschaft und Philosophie, 1972; Psycholinguistik, eine Einführung in offene Probleme, 1973; Signe du zéro, zéro de signe, 1974; Theorie nichtsprachlicher Zeichen, 1974. Address: Uttinger Strasse 10, D800 Munich 70, German Fed. Repub.

LANGFELDT, Steffen, b. 21 Dec. 1930. Architect; Interior Designer. Educ: Univ. of Southern Calif. Practising Archt. & Interior Designer in Scandinavian countries using design techniques based on his study of environmental psychol. w. special ref. to function of light. Formerly, Tchr., Norwegian Folks Univ. & engaged in field rsch. as Cons. on application of light. Lectures, broadcasts & writes num. articles & has devised a test prog. to determine influence of colour on hlth. Mbrships: Selskapet for Lyskultur; Assoc., La Comm.Int. de l'Eclairage; Assn. Int. Contre le Bruit; Norway-Am. Assn.; Norsk Farve Forum; Assoc., Norwegian Colour Coun. Address: Pernilles vei 3a, 1412 Sofiemyr, Oslo, Norway. 43.

LANGFORD, Charles Cecil, b. 6 Oct. 1917. Agriculturalist. Appts: United Fruit Co., St. Catherine Farms, Jamaica, 1937-42; Lands Dept., Min. of Agric. & Lands, 1942-60; Asst. Commnr. of Lands, ibid, 1960-61; Dpty. Commnr. of Lands, 1961; Commnr. of Lands, 1962-71; Mng. Dir., The Frome Monymusk Land Co. Ltd., 1971-. Mbrships: Commnr., Jamaica Racing Commn.; Underground Water Authority; Inst. of Dirs.; V.P., Jamaica Horse Assn.; All Jamaica Polo Assn.; Kingston Polo Club; Royal Jamaica Yacht Club; Kingston Cricket Club; Jamaica Club; Manchester Club; Liguanea Club. Address: P.O. Box 114, Kingston 5, Jamaica, W. Indies. 96, 109.

LANGHAM, Norma E. Educator. Educ: B;S., Ohio State Univ., U.S.A., 1942; B. Theatre Arts, Pasadena Playhouse Coll. Theatre Arts, 1944; M.A., Stanford, 1956; Postgrad. work, Summer Radio-TV Inst., 1960; Pasadena Inst. Radio, 1944-45. Appts: Tchr., Sci., Calif. H.S., 1942-43; Asst., Off. Pub. Info., Denison Univ., Granville, Ohio, 1955; Instr., Speech Dept., Westminster Coll., New Wilmington, Pa., 1957-58; Instr., Theatre Dept., Calif. State Coll., 1959; Asst. Prof., 1960-62; Assoc. Prof., 1962-; Co-Fndr., Dir., Children's Theatre, 1962-. Mbrships: AAUP; Am. Educl. Theatre Assn.; Internat. Children's Theatre Assn.; Children's Theatre Fndn.; Co-Fndr. & Past Pres., Calif. Br., AAUW; Alpha Psi Omega; Omicron Nu. Publs: Plays: Magic in the Sky, 1963; John Dough, 1968; Dutch Painting, 1968; Lect., The Science of the Art. Recip. Freedoms Fndn. Award, Play, John Dough, 1968. Address: Calif. State Coll., California, PA 15419, U.S.A. 5, 6, 13, 138.

LANGKILDE, H. O., b. 2 Apr. 1921. Landowner. Educ: B.Sc., Royal Veterinary & Agric. Coll. of Copenhagen, 1946. Appts: Farm bailiff, Kejrup, 1946-67 & Bramstrup, 1947-62; Owner, Bramstrup, 1952-. Mbrships. incl: Dairy of Odense, Bd. 1956-66, Vice-Chmn., 1964-66; Haglskadeforsikringsselskabet for De danske Østifter, Bd., 1957-73; Landbrugets Arbejdsgiverforening for Fyens Stift, Bd., 1962, Vice-Chmn., 1969-72; Andelsforeningernes Frugtexportudvalg, Chmn., 1959-63; Danske Frugtavleres Samvirke, Vice-Chmn., 1958-61; Den almindelige Brandforsikring for Landbygninger, Coun., 1959, Bd., 1960, Controlling Chmn., 1970; Andelsbogtrykkeriet i Odense & Fyens Stiftpatriotiske Selskab, Coun.; Damage & Life Ins., Danmark, Coun., 1971. Writer, magazine & newspaper articles. Address: Bramstrup, 5653 Nr. Lyndelse, Denmark.

LANGLEY, Abner James, b. 9 May 1910. Clergyman. Educ: B.Th., Gordon Coll., Boston, Mass., 1934; M.A., Boston Univ., Mass., 1935; B.D., Acadia Univ., Wolfville, N.S., Canada, 1936. Appts. incl: Min., Immanuel Bapt. Ch., Truro, N.S., 1936-40, Central Bapt. Ch., St. John, N.B., 1940-50, W. End Bapt. Ch., Halifax, N.S., 1950-56 & 1st Bapt. Ch., Moncton, N.B., 1956-68; Assoc. Prin., Acadia Divinity Coll., Wolfville, N.S., 1968-71; Prin., ibid, 1971-; Trustee, 1967; Dean of Theol., Acadia Univ., 1971-. Mbrships. incl: Chmn., Bd. of Dirs., Atlantic Bapt. Coll., 1957-60; Exec. Canadian O'seas Mission Bd., 1960-66; Vice Chmn., ibid, 1965-67; Chmn., 1967-70; V.P., Lords Day Alliance, Canada; Bd. mbr., Canadian Bible Soc., N.B.; Exec. Comm., Bapt. World Alliance, 1961-65; Deleg., Bapt. World Congresses, 1939-65; Canadian Rep., N. Am. Bapt. Fellowship Comm., 1966-70. Contbr. to jrnls. Recip., D.D., Acadia Univ., 1961. Address: 3 Sunset Terr., Wolfville, N.S., Canada. 6, 13, 131.

LANGLO, Kristian, b. 3 May 1894. Superintendent of schools. Educ: Tchrs. Coll.; Studied for. langs., Univs. of Oslo, Norway, Jena, Germany, & Berlin; Studied langs. & schl. systems, European countries & U.S.A. Appts. incl: Chmn., local coun. of broadcasting, 1946-62; Mayor of Alesund, Norway, 1948-49; Chmn., Bd. of Dirs., Tafjord Power Plant, 1950-63; Supt. of schls., Möre & Romsdal Co., 1953-64; Mbr. of Storting (Parliament, 1950-53 & 1961-64; Mbr. of Bd., Norwegian Interparliamentary group, Coun. of Europe, Strasbourg, 1950-53; Mbr., Norwegian delegation to UN, 1962-64; Mbr., Main Bd. of Dirs., Norwegian State Railways; Bd. of Dirs., Norwegian-Indian Proj., Kerala, India. Mbrship.

in many humanitarian, social & nat. & political orgs. Author of books in field, & of articles in newspapers & jrnls. Address: 6000 Alesund-Nörve, Norway. 43.

LANGSAM, Walter Consuelo, b. 2 Jan. 1906. President Emeritus; Distinguished Service Professor. Educ: B.S., CCNY, 1925; M.A., Columbia Univ., 1926; Ph.D., ibid, 1930. Appts: Instr. & Asst. Prof., Hist., Columbia Univ., 1927-35; Prof., Union Coll., 1938-45; Pres., Wagner Coll., N.Y., 1945-52, Gettysburg Coll., Pa., 1952-55, Univ. of Cinn., Ohio, 1955-71; Pres. Emeritus & Disting. Serv. Prof., Univ. of Cinn., 1971-. Mbrships. incl: Hon. Consul of Finland in Cinn.; Bd. of Consultants, Nat. War Coll., Wash. D.C.; Dir., Diamond Int. Corp.; Hon. Chmn., Am. Music Schlrship. Assn.; Mbr.-at-Large, Nat. Coun., Boy Scouts of Am. Publs. incl: Historic Documents of World War II, 1958; World History Since 1870, 1963; Where Freedom Exists, 1967; An Honor Conferred, A Title Awarded. A History of The Commercial Club of Cincinnati, 1880-1972, 1973. Hons. incl: Outstanding Civilian Serv. Medal, Dept. of the Army, 1968, w. Laurel Leaf Cluster, 1971, & 2nd Laurel Leaf Cluster, 1972; Silver Beaver Award, Boy Scouts of Am., 1973. Address: 621 Library, Univ. of Cinn., Cinn., OH 45221, U.S.A. 2, 8, 30, 34, 128, 129, 131.

LANSON, Lucienne Therese, b. 18 Mar. 1930. Physician; Obstetrician-Gynecologist. Educ: B.A., Univ. of Calif., Berkeley, 1951; M.D. (magna cum laude), Woman's Med. Coll. of Pa., Phila., 1960; Intern., St. Joseph's Hosp., Denver, Colo., 1960-61; Res., Gen. Surg., Woman's Med. Coll. of Pa., 1961-62, Ob. & Gyn., 1962-65. Appts. incl: 1st Lt., Woman's Med. Specialist Corps, U.S. Army, 1953-54; Pvte. Prac., Ob. & Gyn., San Francisco, Calif., 1965-67, 1969-; Instr., Ob. & Gyn., Woman's Med. Coll. of Pa., 1967-69; Mbrships: Dipl., Am. Bd. Ob. & Gyn., 1967; Fellow, Am. Coll. Obstetricians & Gynecologists, 1969; Life Mbr., Calif. Schlrship Fedn.; Am. & Calif. Med. Assns.; San Francisco Co. Med. Soc.; Alpha Omega Alpha. Recip., Am. Cancer Soc. Fellowship, 1963. Address: 418 Lansdale Ave, San Francisco, CA 94127, U.S.A. 5, 138.

LANTZSCH-NÖTZEL, Arno Martin, Artist. Educ: Art Acads. in Europe. Painting, portraits & graphic art included in pvte. & pub. collects. throughout Europe. & in num. Art Shows & One-Man Exhibs. Mbrships. incl: Artists' Union, Dusseldorf; Int. Art Guild, Monaco; Assn. Artisti, Napoli, Italy; Acad. Int. T.C., Rome, Italy. Recip. num. medals & Dips. in Monaco, San Marino & Italy, etc. Address: Ehrenstr. 10b, 4 Dusseldorf, German Fed. Repub. 43, 105, 133.

LANZANO, Ralph E., b. 26 Dec. 1926. Civil Engineer & Sanitary Engineer. Educ: B.C.E., N.Y. Univ., 1959; Profl. Engr., N.Y. State, 1966. Appts. incl: Jr. Civil Engr., N.Y.C. Dept. of Pub. Works, 1960-63; Asst. Civil Engr., ibid, 1963-68; Civil Engr., N.Y.C. Dept. of Water Resources, 1969-71; Sr. Sanitary Engr., Parsons, Brinckerhoff, Quade & Douglas, 1971-72; Civil Engr., N.Y.C. Dept. of Water Resources, 1972-. Mbrships. incl: Royal Soc. for Promotion of Hlth.; Am. Soc. for Testing & Mats.; N.Y. Acad. of Sci.; Am. Soc. Civil Engrs.; Am. Soc. Profl. Engrs.; N.Y. Soc. Profl. Engrs.; Am. Mgmt. Assn.; Am. Concrete Inst.; Am. Pub. Hlth. Assn.; Am. Inst. of Steel Construction; Soc. of Plastics Engrs.; Am. Water Works Assn.; Chi Epsilon. Donor of seats to Metropolitan Opera House, Lincoln Ctr., N.Y.C. & N.Y. Univ. Address: 17 Cottage Ct.,

Huntington Station, NY 11746, U.S.A. 6, 22, 57, 129, 130, 133, 139.

LAPSLEY, William Winston, b. 14 Jan. 1910. Retired Army Officer; Executive, Public Utility. Educ: B.S., U.S. Mil. Acad., 1935; M.S., Univ. of Calif., Berkeley, 1937; Grad., Engr. Schl., 1938, Armed Forces Staff Coll., 1947, Army War Coll., 1951. Appts. incl: Chief Engr., Supply & maintenance Br., HQ AFFE/8A Camp Zama, Japan, 1954-56; Cmdng. Off., U.S. Army Engr. Maintenance Ctr., Columbus, Ohio, 1956-58; Div. Engr., U.S. army Engr. Div., Ohio River, Cinn., 1958-60; Cmdng. Gen., 7th Logistical Command USARPAC, Korea, 1960-61; Div. Engr., U.S. Army Engr. Div., N. Pacific Portland, Ore., 1962-65; Cmdng. Off., U.S. Army Mobility Command, Warren, Mich., 1965-67; Prog. Mgr., For. Ops., Kaiser Jeep Corp., Taipei, Taiwan, 1967-68; Asst. V.P., Connsolidated Edison Co. of N.Y., Inc., 1969-73; Pres., ibid, 1973-. Mbrships. incl: Assn. U.S. Army; Soc. of Am. Mil. Engrs.; U.S. Comm. Large Dams.; Newcomen Soc., N. Am. Recip. of mil. hons. Address: 4 Irving Pl., N.Y., NY 10003, U.S.A. 2, 9.

LAQUEUR, Walter, b. 26 May 1921. Historian; Writer. Appts: Univ. Affiliations: Univ. of Chgo., U.S.A.; Johns Hopkins Univ; Univ. of Tel Aviv, Israel; Current Positions: Dir., Inst. of Contemporary Hist. & Wiener Lib., London, U.K.; Chmn., Rsch. Coun., Ctr. for Strategic & Int. Studies, Wash. D.C., U.S.A.; Ed., Jrnl. of Contemporary History. Mbrships: Int. Club, Wash. D.C.; var. learned socs. & edit. advsry. bds. Publs. incl: Communism & Nationalism in the Middle East, 1956; Young Germany, 1962; Russia & Germany, 1965; The Fate of the Revolution, 1967; The Road to War, 1968; The Struggle for the Middle East, 1969; Europe since Hitler, 1970; A History of Zionism, 1973; Out of the Ruins of Europe, 1973; Confrontation, 1974; Weimar, 1974. Hons: Rockefeller Fellowships, 1958, 1963; Disting. Writers Award, CSIS, Georgetown Univ., 1969; Guggenheim Fellowship, 1972; Annual Lit. Award, Jewish Chronicle, 1974. Address: 4 Devonshire St., London, W1, U.K. 1, 2.

LARABEE, Lottie B. College Consultant; Lecturer. Educ: M.A., Ph.D., N.Y. Univ., 1955; M.M., Am. Conservatory of Music, Chgo. Appts: Assoc. Dir., Ext., Univ. of S.D., Springfield; Acting Dept. Chmn., Tchr., Supvsr., Lock Haven State Coll., Pa.; Dir., Larabee Schl., Chgo.; Coll. Cons., Baldwin, N.Y. & Ft. Lauderdale, Fla.; Exec. Dir., Am. Assn. Independent Coll. & Univ.; Presidents; Ed., "The Coll. & Univ. Pres."; Asst. to Pres. & Prof. of Higher Educ., Acad. Asst. to Pres., V.P. for Acad. Affairs, Ft. Lauderdale Univ.; Lectr. thru' U.S.A. Mbrships: AAAS; Am. Assn. for Higher Educ.; Nat. Assñ. of Dirs. in U.S.; Kappa Delta Pi; Sigma Alpha Iota (Formerly Nat. Ed.); New England Historic Geneal. Soc. Publs. incl: Administrators Who Subvert Learning, Their Residence & Education; A Parent's Guide to Collegs & Universities; Financial & Professional Management for College Teachers. Recip., Disting. Serv. Plaque, Am. Assn. Independent Coll. & Univ. Presidents. Address: 1201 S.E. 2nd St., Ft. Lauderdale, FL 33301, U.S.A. 5, 7, 15, 22, 28, 57, 125, 130, 132, 138.

LARIMORE, Leon, b. 22 July 1911. Minister. Educ: A.B., Western Ky. Univ., 1949; B.D., Southern Bapt. Theol. Sem., 1952. Appts. incl: V.P., Ky. Bapt. Conven., 1965; Moderator, Long Run Assn. of Bapts., 1971-72; Pres., Exec. Bd., ibid, 1971-72; Mbr., State Bd. of Ky. Bapt. Conven., 1972-73, Admnstrve. Comm.,

Ky. Bapt. Conven., 1972-73; Vice Chmn., Admnstrve. Comm., Ky. Bapt. Conven., 1972-73. Mbrships: Ky. Col.; Pres., Horse Cave Rotary Club, 1956; Mason; Ky. Admiral. Hons: Disting. Serv. Award, Am. Cancer Soc., 1954, '56; D.D., Campbellsville Coll., 1960. Address: 1726 S. 3rd St., Louisville, KY 40208, U.S.A. 7.

LARKIN, Philip Arthur, b. 9 Aug. 1922. University Librarian. Educ: St. John's Coll., Oxford Univ. Appts: Libn., var. libs., 1943-55; Libn., Brynmor Jones Lib., Univ. of Hull, 1955-. Publs: The North Ship (poems), 1945; Jill (novel), 1946, 2nd edit., 1964; The Less Deceived (poems), 1955; The Whitsun Weddings (poems), 1964; All that Jazz (essays), 1970; Oxford Book of 20th Century English Verse (ed.), 1973; High Windows (poems), 1974. Hons: Queen's Gold Medal for Poetry & Arts Coun.'s Triennial Award for Poetry, 1965; Hon. D.Litt.-Belfast, 1969, Leicestershire, 1970, Warwickshire, 1973, St. Andrews, Sussex, 1974. Address: Brynmor Jones Lib., The University, Hull, Yorks., U.K.

LAROCQUE, Martial Louis, b. 25 July 1911. Magistrate. Educ: Licence, Law; Dip., Superior Studies in Pvte. Law. Appts. incl: Examining Magistrate, Auxerre, 1938-43; V.P., Auxerre Tribunal, 1933-44; Sec. Gen., Ct. of Appeals, 1944-46; Sub., Tribunal of the Seine, 1946-56; Prin. Examining Magistrate, ibid, 1956-59; Councillor, Paris Ct. of Appeal, 1959-66; Pres. of Chamber, ibid, 1966-70; Councillor, Cour de Cassation, highest ct. of appeal, 1970; Pres., Mbr., var. nat. commns. Mbr., Nat. Assn. of Resistance Veterans. Publs. incl: Judicial & Histl. publs.; (novels) Meurtre au Palais; Mort le Venin. Hons: Off., Legion of Hon., 1972; Medal of the Resistance, 1945; Medal for Mil. Valor, 1961; Order of Civil Merit, 1963, etc. Address: Villa Netty, 45 ter ave. de la Division Leclerc, 95170 Deuil-La-Barre, France. 43, 91.

LaROSE, Winifred Millicent Stranahan (Mrs. Howard A. LaRose). Civic Worker; Construction Company Executive; Motel Owner & Operator. Educ: Grad., Lake George Union Free School. Appts: Real Estate Saleswoman, Deininger-Leavitt, Inc., Lake George, N.Y., 1934-39; Sec.-Treas., Howard A. LaRose Constrn. Co., Inc., Glen Falls, N.Y., 1938-; Owner, Mocking Bird Hill resort, Lake George, 1954-; Dir., First Nat. Bank Lake George, 1964-66. Mbrships: Chmn., Warren Co. Heart Fund, 1965-72 (Treas., 1967-72, Warren Co. Rep. for Eastern N.Y., 1967-); Fund Raising Sec., Adirondack Hudson River Assn., 1966-; N.Y. State Legislative Forum, 1964- (Conservation Comm., 1970-; Chmn., ibid, 1973); Fund Raising Chmn., Warren Co. Vol. Comm. on Children & Community Servs., 1956-; Gov.'s Advsry. Coun. Study Commn. for Future Adirondacks, 1968-70; Warren o. Rep. N.Y. State Citizen's Info. Serv., 1970-72; Mbrship. Sec., Adirondack Conservancy Comm., 1971-; Women's Task Force, Empire State Coll., 1971-; Adirondack Regl. Vice-Chmn., N.Y. State Environmental Planning Lobby, 1972-; Advsry. Coun., State of N.Y. Dept. Environmental Conservation, 1974-;; Bd. Dirs., Warren Co. Hlth. Assn., 1954-58; Bd. Govs., SUNY at Albany Fndn.; Lake George Bus. & Profl. Women's Club (V.P., 1964-65, Civic Participation Chmn., 1969-70, Legislative Chmn., 1970-72); N.Y. Forest Owners Assn. (Dir., 1966-71); Adirondack Park Assn. (V.P., 1964-71, Dir., 1964-, Historic Sites Chmn., 1968-73); var. posts, Lake George & Rogers Island Hist. Assns.; Wilderness Soc.; Nat. Trust for Historic Preservation; The Sierra Club; Friends of the Earth; Cold River Chapt.,

Adirondack Mountain Club; Order Eastern Star. Hons: Plaque for Heart Assn. work, 1969, '72; Citation for Conservation Work, Adirondack Park Assn., 1969; Award, N.Y. State Conservation Coun., 1969; Community Award, 1968. Address: Mocking Bird Hill, Lake George, NY 12845, U.S.A. 5.

LARSEN, Bjørn, b. 3 Apr. 1922. Secretary General, Royal Norwegian Ministry for Consumer Affairs & Government Administration. Educ: Grad. in Econs., Univ. of Oslo, Norway, 1947. Appts: Dir., Econ. Dept., European Free Trade Assn., Geneva, Switzerland, 1961-62; Dir. Gen. for Medium & Long Term Planning, Min. of Finance, Oslo, 1963-71; Sec. Gen., Min. of Defence, 1971-72; Sec. Gen., Min. for Consumer Affairs & Govt. Admin., 1972-. Recip., Eisenhower Fellowship, 1969. Address: Forbruker-og Administrasjonsdepartementet, Oslo-Dep., Oslo 1, Norway.

LARSEN, E.R., b. 1 Apr. 1925. Headmaster. Educ: B.A., Univ. of B.C., Canada,' 1948; B.A., Oxford Univ., U.K., 1953; M.A., ibid. Appts: Housemaster, Shawnigan Lake Schl., 1948-50; Asst. Hdmaster., ibid, 1953-57; Exec. Asst. to Min. of Nat. Defence, Canada, 1957-58; Hdmaster., Shawnigan Lake Schl., 1958-67; Hdmaster., Appleby Coll., Oakville, Ont., 1968-. Mbrships. incl: Pres., Independent Schls. Assn. of B.C., 1962-64; Pres., Canadian Hdmasters. Assn., 1965-67 & 1972-73; Fndr. Mbr. of Bd. of Govs., Strathcona Lodge Schl., B.C., 1959; Fndr. Mbr. of Bd. of Govs., Cliffside Prep. Schl., B.C., 1959; Mbr., Canadian Field Hockey Team in World Tournament, France, 1963. Hons. incl: O.O.D.E. Schlrship. for B.C. to Oxford, 1952; Oxford Soc. Prize, 1952. Address: Appleby Coll., 530 Lakeshore West, Oakville, Ont., Canada. 88.

LARSEN, Karsten Arvid, b. 28 May 1904. Business Executive. Educ: Diplomé Ecole Supérieure de Commerce du Havre, Le Havre, France, 1925. Appts: Fish Dept., Osca;Larsen A/S., Aalesund, Norway, 1927-; Pres. of Bd., Gen. Mgr., ibid, 1946-; Pres., Chmbr. of Comm., Aalesund, 1949-52; Vice Consul for Finland, 1951-; Bd. Mbr., Norwegian Export Coun., 1961-; Consul for France, 1961-; Pres. of Bd., Ins. Co. TRYGD, Aslesund, 1967-; Chmn., Spanish-Norwegian Chmbr. of Comm., Oslo, 1968-; Pres., Assn, Norwegian Salt Fish & Dried Fish Exporters; Coun. Mbr., Norwegian Export Credit Inst.; Bd. Mbr., J.E. Devold A/S., Aalesund. Mbr. & Off., Rotary Int., Aalesund, & var. clubs. Hons. incl: Mbr. of Hon., Chmbr. of Comm., Aalesund, 1958; Vice-Mayor, City of Aalesund, 1960-65, Mayor, 1966-67; Finlands LEJON, 1967. Address: Oscar Larsen A/S., Post Box 10, Aalesund, Norway. 43.

LARSEN, Knud, b. 18 Jan. 1895. Librarian. Educ: Cand. Theol., Univ. of Copenhagen, Denmark, 1920; Exam. in librarianship, ibid, 1921. Appts: Libn., Copenhagen Schl. of Economics & Bus. Admin., 1922-62; Bibliographer, UNESCO lib., Paris, France, 1948-49; Lectr., Royal Schl. of Libnship., Copenhagen, 1957-63 & 1965-70; Dir., E. African Schl. of Libnship., Makerere Univ. Coll., Uganda, 1963-64; Dir. of UNESCO courses in libnship., Copenhagen, 1966, 1968 & 1970. Publs: Dansk Biblioteksfører, 1936; Boghandelens Bibliografi, 1943, 2nd edit. 1951; Biblioteksorientering, 1943, 2nd edit. 1954; National Bibliographical Services, 1953 (French & Spanish edits., 1955, Arabic edit., 1956, Japanese edit., 1957); Frederik Rostgaard og Bøgerne, 1970; Co-ed., Nicolai Stenonis Opera Theologica I-II, 1941-47. Mbrships: Comm. of

Danish Lib. Assn., 1957-62 & mbr. of its sects., 1934-62. Address: 99 Vangeledet, DK 2830 Virum, Denmark. 43.

LARSEN, Otto, b. 22 Apr. 1902. Librarian; Theologian. Educ: Grad. of Theology, Copenhagen, Denmark, 1926; Grad. of Lib. Schl., Copenhagen, 1936. Appts: Sec., Danish Union of Christian Students, 1926-28; Vicar of pastorate Øster Ulslev-Godsted, 1928-32; Asst. Libn., Lyngby, Denmark; Libn., State & Univ. Lib., Aarhus, 1938-71. Publs. incl: Gud blev Menneske (God was made Man), 1933; Det Moderne Gudsbegreb (The Modern Concept of God), 1950; Ordet, Tvivlen og Troen (The Word, the Doubt & the Belief), 1972; Ed., State & Univ. Lib. annual catalogue on selection of recent for. literature; contbns. to jrnls & newspapers. Hons: Knight, Order of Dannebrog, 1971. Address: Lønstrupvej 8, 8250 Egaa, Denmark. 43, 134.

LARSON, Golden Robert, b. 15 Jan. 1906. Banker. Educ: Univ. of Utah, 1924-28; J.D., Geo. Wash. Univ., 1939; Am. Inst. of Banking. Appts: Auditor, Utah State Nat. Bank, Salt Lake City, 1921-32; Sr. Review Examiner, FDIC, Wash. D.C., 1932-43; Treas., Motion Picture Soc. of Ams., Hollywood, Calif., 1943-48; V.P., United Calif. Bank, L.A., 1949-71; Corp. Cons., Dev. Systems Int., L.A.; Assoc., Kazanjian Bros. Inc., Beverly Hills, Calif. Mbrships. incl: V.P., Region, S. Calif. Bd. of Govs., Chapman Coll.; Nat. Committeeman, Jr. Democrats, 1931-34; Exec. Comm., Trust Div., Chmn., Income & Expense Comm., Trust Ops. Comm., Calif. Bankers Assn.; Bd. of Dirs., Van Nuys Community Hosp. Fndn.; Salt Lake Co. Treas., Democratic Party, 1931-32; L.A. Finance Comm., Girl Scouts of Am., 1949; Swedish Club of L.A., Inc.; Kappa Sigma; Delta Theta Phi. Address: 11945 Hartsook St., N. Hollywod, CA 91607, U.S.A.

LARSON, Jean (Mrs. H.F. Parks), b. 25 July 1930. Writer; Arabist. Educ: Trained in Ballet, age 10-; Tutored in var. langs. inclng. Greek & Latin; Winthrop. Coll., Rock Hill, S.C. Appts: Active in Am.-Arab Rels.; Toured Iowa delivering message from Gov. concerning Women in the Arts. Publs: Palace in Bagdad; The Silkspinners; Jack Lar; The Glass Mountain; Contbr. poetry & non-fiction to var. periodicals. Hons: Nominated for Wm. Allen White Award & Winner, ALA Notable Book of 1967, both for The Silkspinners; Winner, Lewis Carroll Shelf Award, 1973, for Jack Lar. Address: Box 98, Garwin, IA 50632, U.S.A. 5, 30, 138.

LARSON, Rachel Harris (Mrs. John W. Henry), b. 1 Aug. 1913. Research Biochemist. Educ: B.S., Appalachian State Tchrs. Coll., Boone, N.C., 1940; M.S., Georgetown Univ., Wash. D.C., 1949; Ph.D., ibid, 1958. Appts. incl: Tech. Asst. to Jr. Chemist, Insl. Hygiene Rsch. Lab., Nat. Insts. of Hlth., 1942-48; Asst. Chemist to Rsch. Chemist, Nat. Inst. of Dental Rsch., Nat. Insts. of Hlth., 1948-; Vis. Sci., Royal Dental Coll., Aarhus, Denmark, 1971-72; Chief, Preventive Methods Dev. Sect., Nat. Caries Prog., Nat. Insts. of Hlth., 1972-. Mbrships: Fellow, Am. Coll. of Dentists, 1965; Fellow, AAS, 1952; Int. Assn. for Dental Rsch., 1953; Am. Inst. of Nutrition, 1964; Sigma Delta Epsilon. Publs: Over 40 resch. papers, mostly as co-author, in profl. jrnls; contbr. chapts. to sev. sci. books. Address: National Institute of Dental Research, National Institutes of Health, Bethesda, MD 20014, U.S.A. 5, 14.

LARSSON, Carl Rune B., b. 6 Feb. 1923. Musical Director. Educ: Royal Swedish Acad.

of Music, 1940-46, 1950-52. Appts: Asst. Conductor & Pianist, Oscar Theatre, Stockholm, 1947-48, Royal Theatre, ibid, 1948-52; Conductor, Grand Theatre, Gothenburg, 1952-62; Chief Conductor, Gävle Symph. Orch., 1962-67; Dir. of Music, Univ. of Uppsala, 1967-. Mbrships: Theatrical & Musical Coun. of Sweden; Royal Acad. of Arts & Scis., Uppsala; rotary. Publs: Musical Co-operation: a Proposal about the Future Shape of Musical Life in Uppsala, 1973; A Proposal about a House of Music in Uppsala, 1973. Hons: The King's Award, 1956; Award for Meritorious Artistic Activity, Co. of Uppsala, 1973. Address: Kyrkogårdsgatan 4, 75235 Uppsala, Sweden. 43, 134.

LARSSON, Knut Georg Valdemar, b. 3 Sept. 1910. Author. Appts: Archive Wkr., Malmö Mus. Art Dept., 1960-. Mbr., Swedish Union of Authors. Publs: Ute blommar rosmarin, 1948; Röd lykta, 1950; Eldslägga, 1951; Av jord, 1959; Det röda och det bla, 1961; Efterdyning, 1969. Hons. incl: Rdrs. Circle Fund & Book Lottery, Sjöbergs Schlrship., 1960-70; Awards, Swedish Authors Fund, 1960-72; Malmö City Cultural Schlrship., 1964. Address: Edward Lindahlsgatan 14 c, 217 42 Malmö, Sweden. 134.

LARSSON, Lars-Erik, b. 18 May 1927. University Professor. Educ: Civ. ing., Chalmers Univ. of Technol., Gothenburg, Sweden, 1949; Tehn. lic., 1955; Tehn. dr., 1959. Appts. incl: w. Labs. du Bâtiment & des Travaux Publics, Paris, France, 1949-50; 1st Asst., Dept. of Water Bldg., Chalmers Univ. of Technol. Gothenburg, 1951-55; Dept. Structural Engrng., ibid, 1955-59; Prof., Bldg. Technol., 1966-; Cons. Engr., Hjalmar Granholm AB, 1959-66. Mbr. of profl. orgs. Author of publs. in field. Kt., Order of the North Star, 1970. Address: Chalmers Univ. of Technol., Fack, 40220 Gothenburg 5, Sweden. 134.

LARSSON, Maj Gudrun, b. 1 Jan. 1914. Author. Appts: Communal Councillor, 1942-45, 1950-62; Mbr. Co. Coun., 1942-45; Chmn., Schl. Bd., 1955-63; Mbr., Royal Commns. on Books, 1948-52, & Schls., 1957-61; Mbr., Ctrl. Cultural Coun. 1959-. Mbrships: Swedish Authors' Union (Bd., 1953-65); State Traffic Safety Bd., 1967-; Norden Assn. (Ctrl. Bd., 1969-). Publs: (poetry) Möte på perrong, 1963; Blågul akvarell, 1968; Nygammal stad (w. others), 1970; (prose lyrics & reportage)Finlandsresa, 1971; (book) Kvinnor i tidsspegel, 1971. Awards: Karin Collin Schlrship., 1968; Litteraturfrämjandets Stipendium, 1971. Address: Luttra, 521 00 Falköping, Sweden. 134.

LARUE, Ron D., b. 8 Sept. 1932. Advertising, Public Relations & Marketing Executive. Educ: Bus. Admin., N.D. State Schl. of Sci.; Arts & Sci., Univ. of Wash.; Burnley Schl. of Advt., Seattle, Wash.; Dale Carnegie Ldrship. Trng. (speaking & human rels.); sev. seminars. Appts: Tooling Engr., Boeing Airplane Co., 1955-57; Aerospace Designer, ibid, 1957; Art Dir., 1958; Audio/Visual Supvsr., 1959; Prod. Mgr., Advt., Weyerhaeuser Co., 1960-63; Promotion Mgr., ibid, New Products, 1964-66; Merchandising Mgr., 1966-72; Dir. of Advt. & P.R., Western Int. Hotels, 1972-. Mbrships: Seattle Advt. Fed.; Advt. Assn. of the West; Am. Advt. Fed.; Assn. of Nat. Advertisers; Soc. of Am. Travel Writers; Seattle Chmbr. of Comm.; Tacoma Elks Lodge; V. Chmn., P.R. Advisory Bd., Am. Hotel & Motel Assn.; Western Int. Hotels/United Air Lines Marketing Comm. Has exhibited & sold paintings in the Northwest U.S.A. Hons: Am. Bus. Press Award, Advt., 1969; Award of

Excellence Exhibits, Am. Inst. of Architects, 1968; Printing Inds. of Am. Award, Publs., 1970; First Prize, Consumer Advt., Hotel Sales Mgmt. Assn., 1973. Address: 1035 156th N.E., Bellevue, WA 98007, U.S.A.

LASBURY, Leah B. (Mrs. Clyde P. Lasbury), b. 11 Apr. 1915. Realtor; Painter. Educ: A.B., Rollins Coll., Winter Pk., Fla., 1936; B.S., Simmons Coll., Boston, Mass., 1937; study w. Syd Solomon, Sarasota, Fla., 1954-56. Appts: Exec. Trng. Squad & Asst. Buyer, G. Fox & Co., Hartford, Conn., 1937-40; Fndr. & currently Sec.-Treas., Lee Lasbury Inc., 1952-74; Dir., J.E. Bartlett & Sons, Inc., 1940-74. Mbrships. incl: Charter Mbr., New Coll. Advd. Pntrs. Grp., Sarasota, Fla.; Pres., Fla. Artist Grp., Inc., 1971-74; Charter Dir., A Solo Theatre Festival Assn., Sarasota (Ringling Mus.), 1963-74; Dir., Sarasota Co. T.B. Assn., 1970-74; Charter Dir., Sarasota Co. Lib. Advsry. Bd.; Dir., Sarasota Co. Histl. Soc., 1972-; Pres., Elsie Quirk Lib. 1974-; Nat. Assn. Women Artists; Past Pres., Englewood Chmbr. of Comm., 1965; Org., Charter Pres. & Dir., Englewood Bd. Realtors. Has held sev. one-man shows; Work represented in num. pvte. collects. Address: P.O. Box 777, Englewod, FL 33533, U.S.A. 5, 7, 15, 16, 57, 132, 138.

LASCARIS COMNENUS MICOLAW, (Prince) Juan Arcadio, (Imperial & Royal Highness), b. 1 Oct. 1926. Counsellor; Author. Educ: Univ. studies in Law, Sociol. & Hist. Mbr. of the Dynasty Láscaris Comnenus of Constantinople. Appt: Dir. of Review of Byzantine Studies, I.P.H.B.A.U. Publs: Funcion educadora del seguro escolar; Influencia educativo-social de la previsión en la pedagogia escolar; Los orfanotrofiosgriegos y su perduración en Byzancio; I.P.H.B.A.U. Motivos de su creación y sus fines; Los Cotos Escolares; Las Mutualidades Escolares. Address: c/Alonso Cano, Apartado 818, 66—Madrid 3, Spain.

LASLETT, William Lenox, b. 5 Oct. 1937. Architect. Educ: B.A., Fine Arts, Colgate Univ. Hamilton, N.Y., 1959; M.Arch., Yale Univ. New Haven, Conn., 1963. Ptnr., Basil G.F. Laslett, William L. Laslett, Archts.-Planners, Fayetteville, N.C., 1965-. Mbrships: N.C. Chapt., Am. Inst. Archts.; Sec., 1970-72; V.P., 1972-73, ibid; Dir., S. Atlantic Region, Am. Inst. Archts., 1973. Major works: U.S. Post Off. & Courthouse, Fayetteville, N.C. (Assoc. Archt., Arthur C. Jenkins); Pope Elem. Schl., Ft. Bragg, ibid; Sci. Bldg. & Acad. Bldg., Fayetteville State Univ.; Cape Fear H.S., Cumberland Co., N.C.; Salvation Army HQ, Fayetteville; Wallace O'Neal Day Schl., Southern Pine, N.C.; Hlth. & Soc. Servs. Bldg., Fayetteville. Address: 209 Fairway Dr., P.O. Box 3961, Fayetteville, NC 28305, U.S.A. 7.

LASSETTRE, Edwin N., b. 26 Oct. 1911. Physical Chemist; Professor. Educ: B.Sc., Mont. State Coll., 1933; Ph.D., Calif. Inst. of Technol. Appts: Fac. Mbr., Dept. of Chem., Ohio State Univ., 1937-62; Prof., ibid, 1949-62; Rsch. Sci., Grp. Ldr., Manhattan Proj., Columbia Univ., 1944, Union Carbide & Carbon Chems. Corp., 1945; Staff Fellow, Mellon Inst., 1962-67; Staff Fellow & Prof. of Chem. Phys., Carnegie-Mellon Univ., 1967-. Mbrships: Am. Chem. Soc.; Fellow, Am. Phys. Soc. Contbr. articles in sci. jrnls. Address: 224 E. Waldheim Rd., Pittsburgh, PA 15215, U.S.A. 2, 14, 50, 128.

LASSITER, Isaac Steele, b. 4 July 1941. Railroader; Poet. Educ: B.S., Campbell Coll., 1970. Appts. incl: Language Arts Tchr., Johnston Co. Schls., 1966-71; Maintenance of Way employee, Norfolk Southern Rwy. Co., 1971-. Mbrships: N.C. Poetry Soc.; Major Poets, PMA. Publs: The Owl's Nest Betrayal (Poetry), 1971; poems in anthols. & jrnls. Address: P.O. Box 552, Candor, NC 27229, U.S.A. 30, 57.

LASSITER, Roy Carroll, b. 2 Mar. 1935. Assistant Professor of Speech-Communication. Educ: B.S., Sul Ross State Univ., Alpine, Tex.; M.Ed., Univ. of Tex., Austin. Appts: Speech & Hearing Therapist, El Paso Pub. Schls., Tex., 1956-61; Res. Dir., Playhouse Theatre, El Paso, 1961-63; Asst. Prof. Speech-Communication, Sul Ross State Univ., 1963-. Mbrships: AAUP; Patron Mbr., Am. Civil Liberties Union; Patron Mbr., Southern Speech Assn; Regional Off., Tau Kappa Epsilon; Phi Delta Kappa; Alpha Chi; Alpha Psi Omega; Kappa Delta Pi; Sigma Tau Delta. Address: P.O. Box 62, Alpine, TX 79830, U.S.A.

LASSITER, Vernice (Vernice Lassiter Brown). Artist. Educ: w. Joseph Hirsch, Univ. of Ala.-August Trovoahe; w. Robert Brackman, Famous Artist Schl.; w. Valdi Maris, Art Students League. Appts: Tchr., children's classes; Lectr. & Demonstrator, has appeared on TV. Exhibs: Mobile Art Gall.; Mobile Pub. Lib.; Mobile Skyline Country Club; Mobile Womans Club; Battle House, Mobile; Ramada Inn; Albert Pick, Mobile; Grand Hotel, Fairhope; Palmer House, Chgo.; Montgomery Mus.; Birmingham Mus.; Sarasota Art Assn., Fla.; "Chatel Gall.", Georgetown; Edgewater Plaza Annual; 1870 Room Widemans, Meridian, Miss.; Gall. 21, Birmingham; W. Pt. Cown Art Gall.; "Old Orchard" Art Ctr., Chgo. Chosen to exhib. watercolors in Southeastern Annual Exhib., Atlanta, Ga., 1957, & in 26th & 27th Miniature Painters, Sculptors & Gravers Soc. of Wash. D.C. show, Smithsonian Inst., 1959. Mbrships: Mobile, Birmingham & Eastern Shore Art Assns. Hons. incl: Watercolor chosen to be presented to Mayor of Malagna Spain, Mobile Cultural Exchange Prog.; one of top 3 paintings in Sears Vincent Price Travelling Show; Reproduction of Jr. Miss Painting purchased by United Air Lines to present to each Jr. Miss, 1970; 1st, Watercolor, Eastern Art Assn. Juried Exhib., 1965; 1st Watercolor, Gold Plaque, Ala. State Fair, 1965; 1st, Mobile Art Assn. Annual Show, 1974. Address: 4951 Winslow Dr., Mobile, AL 36608, U.S.A. 5.

LASSMAN, Laurance Philip, b. 21 June 1913. Neurological Surgeon. Educ: Queen Mary Coll. & London Hosp. Med. Coll., Univ. of London; Qualified as Registered Med. Practitioner, London Hosp., 1937; MRCS (Engl.), LRCP (London), 1937; M.B., B.S. (London), 1938; FRCS (Engl.), 1948. Appts: Cons. Neurol. Surg., No. 1 Regional Hosp. Bd. & Royal Victoria Infirmary & Newcastle Univ. Hosps.; Surg. i/c, Dept. of Neurol. Surg., Regional Neurol. Ctr., Newcastle Gen. Hosp., Newcastle upon Tyne; Lectr., Paediatric Neurosurg., Univ. of Newcastle upon Tyne. Mbrships. incl: Bd. of Govs., Kenton Schl.; Soc. British Neurol. Surgs.; Fellow, V.P., Int. Coll. of Angiol.; Bd. of Trustees, Angiol. Rsch. Fndn.; Fellow, Royal Soc. of Med. Contbr. to profl. publs. inclng. Chapts. on Neurosurgery & Congenital Malformations of the Spine to Practice of Surgery, 1973. Address: 45, Clayton Rd., Newcastle upon Tyne NE1 4RQ, U.K.

LASSNER, Eric Joseph, b. 22 Oct. 1912. Opera & Concert Singer; Actor; Stage Manager; Art Historian. Educ: Univs. of Cracow, Prague & Vienna; Stage Dancing & Singing studies; Ph.D. Appts. incl: German & Polish Lang. Tchr., Berlitz Schl., Prague, Czechoslovakia, 1932-33; Solo Dancer w. Neves Deutsches Theater, Prague, 1933-39; Acting & Asst. Stage

Mng. Soloist, Hans Weidt "Le Ballet Dynamique" (dance grp.), Prague, 1936; Authorized Rep., Fed. Min. of Agric. for negotiations in Prague, 1945-47; Opera Singer Dip., Acad. Mozarteum, Salzburg, 1950 & performances in Austria included Theatres, Concerts, Oratories & Ch. music; Guest perfs. in Germany, Norway & Fndr., Theaterkjelleren in Oslo; Fndr., Hd., Stage Mgr. & Soloist, Wiener Kammeroper, 1953-54; Hd., Art Hist. Tours to European countries, N. Africa & Asia; active in Book-trade, 1954-60; Mgr. of Art Exhibs. & occasionally Art Critic & Cons.; Recitations of poetry of World Lit. & Famous Solloquies & Lectr. in Art Hist. & Soc. Hist. in many countries. Publs. incl: essays, short stories & translations of Slavic Lit. Hons. incl: Max Reinhardt Jubilaemsmedaille der Salzburger Festspiele, 1970. Address: Rainergasse 11, Palais Schönburg-Hartenstein, 1040 Vienna, Austria. 86.

LAST, Clifford Frank, b. 13 Dec. 1918. Sculptor. Educ: Royal Melbourne Inst. of Technol. Art Schl., Australia, 1947-49. Appts: Lt., Hampshire Regiment, British Army, 1944-46; Sr. Lectr., Mercer House Tchrs. Trng. Coll., Melbourne, 1955-62. Mbrships: Commonwealth Art Advsry. Bd., 1970-73; Acquisitions Bd., Nat. Gall., Canberra, 1973-; Coun., Victorian Sculptors Soc., 1948-52; Ctr. Five Sculpture Group, 1962-73. Sculptures in num. collections inclng. Nat. Art Collection, Canberra; Nat. Gall. of Vic.; Nat. Gall. of Malaya; Regional Galls. of sev. Australian cities; Australian Chancery, Wash. D.C., U.S.A.; Churches; Indl. firms, Melbourne & Sydney. One-man exhibs: Melbourne, Adelaide, Sydney. Survey exhibs: London, U.K., N.Z., Malaya, & Nat. Galls. in Australia. Hons. incl: Crouch Prize, 1965; Lions Club Sculpture Award, 1966; Capt. Cook Bicentenary Sculpture Prize, 1970. Address: 72 Osborne St., S. Yarra, Melbourne, Vic., Australia 3141. 23.

LATHAM, Freer Helen (Mrs. R.J. Latham), 4 July 1907. Teacher. Educ; Sydney Tchrs. Coll., 1926. Appts: Tchr., Dept. of Educ., N.S.W. Mbrships: Pres., World Fed. Meth. Women, 1961-66; Area Pres., Australian, ibid, 1956-61; Pres. Emeritus, 1966-; V.P. World Meth. Coun. 1961-66; Rep. of Meth. Women's Fed. to UN & Nat. Coun. of Women; Australasian Fed. of Meth. Women Exec., Life V.P., N.S.W. Meth. Women's Fed.; Pan Pacific S.E. Asian Assn. Recip., Key to City of Louisville, Ky., U.S.A., 1963., Ky. Colonel, 1963. Address: 1 Bampi Place, Castle Cove 2069, N.S.W., Australia. 116, 138.

LATHAM, Iris Anne, b. 14 Aug. 1925. Radio Broadcaster, Producer & Host; Writer. Appts: Writer, WTNS radio, Coshocton, Ohio, 1946-50; Continuity Dir., WGL radio, Ft. Wayne, Ind., 1951-54; Traffic Mgr., WHIZ radio, Zanesville, Ohio, 1954-57; Women's Dir., WANE radio, Ft. Wayne, Ind., 1957-64; Writer, prod. & host; interview prog., WGL radio, Ft. Wayne, 1964-. Mbrships: Treas., Zonta Int., Ft. Wayne, 1971-74; Ft. Wayne Press Club; Am. Women in Radio & TV. Chmn. of judges, City Coun. Internships, 1972; March of Dimes Bd., 1970-72; Advsr., Soc. League of Interested Women, 1969. Radio series incl: They Came To America; The Woman Alcoholic; Marriage Today; Europeans Today; Black Legacies. Hons. incl: Special Serv. Award, Allen Co. Cancer Soc., 1973; Personality of the Month, Sterling Mag. Publ., 1974. Address: 3610 Mulberry Rd., Ft. Wayne, IN 46804, U.S.A. 5, 138.

LATHAM, Jessie Johnson, b. 15 Feb. 1920. Elementary School Principal. Educ: B.A., Univ.

of Ala., 1941; M.A., ibid, 1949; further studies, Southern Meth. Univ., Nova Univ. Appts: Tchr., Ala. Schls., Wilcox Co., 1941-43, Ala. Co. Schls., Tuscaloosa, 1946-49, Pleasant Grove Independent Schl. Dist., 1952-54; 4th Grade Homeroom Tchr., Tex. Independent Schl. Dist., Dallas, 1954-57, Elem. Prin., 1957-. Mbrships: Dallas Tex. Schl. Admin. Assn., Principals' Advsry. Comm., 1973-; Sec., ibid, 1964-65; Life Mbr., Tex. State Tchrs. Assn.; NEA; Nat. Assn. Supvsn. Curriculum Dev.; Tex. Elem. Principals Supvsrs. Assn.; Assn. Childhood Educ.; Nat. Assn. Elem. Schl. Prins.; Delta Kappa Gamma; Pres., Epsilon Chapt., ibid, 1968-70; Dallas Mus. Fine Arts. Recip., var. awards. Address: 9949 Woodgrove, Dallas, TX 75218, U.S.A. 125.

LATHAM, Leslie Vivian, b. 7 June 1917. Company Director. Educ: Fellow, Australian Ins. Inst., 1946; Fellow, Australian Soc. Accts., 1957. Appts. incl: Executive w. AMP Soc., W.A. & Vic., 1951-62; Pres., Ins. Inst. of W.A., 1955; Gen. Mgr. & Dir., Underwriting & Ins. Ltd., 1962-73; Dir., Adriatic Grp. Cos., 1973-. Mbrships. incl: Stock Exchange Club; Naval & Mil. Club; Ivanhoe Historical Soc. Contbr. to Australian Ins. Jrnl. Address: 4 Charteris Dr., E. Ivanhoe, Vic., Australia 3079. 23, 128.

LATHAM, Linda Mae, b. 15 Feb. 1949. Teacher; Free-lance Journalist. Educ: B.S., Univ. of Southern Miss., Hattiesburg, 1971; M.S., ibid, 1973; further work, Miss. State Univ. Appts: P.R. work, E. Ctrl. Jr. Coll., 1970-72; Tchr., Sebastopol H.S., 1972-73; Tchr. & Publ. Advsr., Meridian Municipal Schls., 1973-. Mbrships: Phi Theta Kappa, 1967; Phi Pakka Phi; Lambda Iota Tau; Miss. & Nat. Press Women; Miss. Assn. Educl. Jrnlsts.; Miss. Educ. Assn.; P.R. Dir., Meridian Tchrs. Assn. Contbr., articles, Young America Speaks, Clarion-Ledger, Jackson Daily News, Educl. Adv. Hons. incl: E. Ctrl. Jr. Coll. Hall of Fame, 1969; Jr. Jrnlst. Merit Award, 1970. Address: P.O. Box 273, Decatur, MS 39327, U.S.A. 125.

LATHROP, Joyce Keen (Mrs. Mitchell Lee Lathrop), b. 25 Nov. 1939. Civic and Charitable Worker. Educ: Goucher Coll., Balt., Md.; B.A., Univ. of Southern Calif., 1961. Married Lt. Cmdr. Mitchell Lee Lathrop, 1959; three children. Mbrships. incl: Dir., L.A. Orphanage Guild Jrs., 1968-, V.P., 1973-; Dir., Assistance League of Glendale, Calif., 1967-70; Metropol. Opera Nat. Coun., N.Y.; Aux. of Hosp. of the Good Samaritan, L.A. Hons. incl: Volunteer Serv. Award, Huntington Mem. Hosp., Pasadena, Calif., 1967; Off. Companion, The Mil. & Hospitaller Order of St. Lazarus of Jerusalem, 1973. Address: 1375 Inverness Dr., Pasadena, CA 91103, U.S.A. 5, 20, 22, 70, 71, 72, 74, 75, 128.

LATHROP, Mitchell Lee, bl 15 Dec. 1937. Trial Lawyer; Naval Officer. Educ: B.Sc., U.S.N. Acad., Annapolis, Md., 1959; J.D., Univ. of Southern Calif. Law Schl., L.A., 1966. Appts. incl: Commnd. Off. on active serv., U.S.N., 1959-63; Dpty. Co. Counsel, L.A. Co., 1966-68; Lawyer, Brill, Hunt, DeBuys & Burby, L.A., 1968-70; Ptnr., Macdonald, Halsted & Laybourne, ibid, 1970-. Mbrships. incl: Western Regional Chmn. & Exec. Comm. Mbr., Metropolitan Opera Nat. Coun., 1971-; Pres., Opera Assocs. of the Music Ctr., L.A., 1970-72; Gov., Soc. of Colonial Wars, 1972; Sec., British United Servs. Club, 1974; Dir., Music Ctr. Opera Assn., L.A., 1971-; Gov., Order of the Fndrs. & Patriots of Am., 1969; Plantagenet Soc.; Vice Chancellor, Grand Priory of Am. of the Mil. & Hospitaller Order of St. Lazarus of Jerusalem. Author of num. articles of interest to the legal profn. Hons. incl: Trustee, Honnold

Lib. of the Claremont Colls., Calif. & The Thacher Schl., Ojai, Calif. Address: Sixth Floor, 1200 Wilshire Blvd., Los Angeles, CA 90017, U.S.A. 9, 20, 22, 70, 71, 72, 74, 75, 128.

LATIMER, Hugh A., b. 11 Apr. 1926. Utility Company Executive. Educ: Va. Polytech. Inst., U.S.A., 1944-45, 1946-48. Appts: Admin. Asst.-Staff Engr., Chesapeake & Potomac Telephoe Co., Va. (Richmond); Staff Engr., Chesapeake & Potomac Telephone Co. (Wash. D.C.); Plant Engr.-Equipment & Bldg. Engr., Chesapeake & Potomac Telephone Co., Va. (Richmond); Chief Engr.-V.P. & Gen. Mgr., Chesapeake & Potomac Telephone Co., W. Va. (Charleston); Asst. V.P., Am. Telephone & Telegraph Co. (N.Y.); V.P. & Treas., Ill. Bell Telephone Co. (Chgo.). Chmn., Bd., W. Va. Wesleyan Coll. & Hon. Mbr. Omicron Delta Kappa, Tau Beta Pi, Pi Delta Epsilon & Eta Kappa Nu. Address: Ill. Bell Telephone Co., 225 W. Randolph St., HQ 28A, Chgo., IL 60606, U.S.A.

LATOUR, George Emile, b. 14 Aug. 1936. Fraternity Executive. Educ: B.A., Univ. of R.I., 1960. Appts: Newspaper reporter, Providence Jrnl., Evening Bulletin, 1961-64; Owner & Pres., Lamplighter Liquors, 1964-67; Newspaper reporter, Pawtuxet Valley Daily Times, W. Warwick, R.I., 1967-69; Nat. Exec. Sec., Ed., Phi Mu Delta Fraternity Inc., Lancaster, Pa., 1969-; Ed., Triangle Mag., 1969-; Admnstr., Triangle Trust Fund, 1969-, Phi Mu Delta Fndn., 1969-. Mbrships: Big Brothers of R.I.; Big Brothers of Lancaster; Nu Eta Alumni Bd. Govs. (Sec. & V.P.), 1967-69; Phi Mu Delta; (life mbr.); Fraternity Execs. Assn.; Conestoga Country Club; Fraternity Schlrship. Offs. Assn.; Interfraternity Rsch. & Advsry. Coun. Recip., Nat. Editl. Award, Fleet Cadets of Am., 1968. Address: 97 Wellington Rd., Lancaster, PA 17603, U.S.A. 6.

LAUBACH, Roger Alvin, b. 3 July 1922. Food Services Executive. Educ: Dip. In Bus. Admin., Churchman Bus. Coll., Easton, Pa., 1941; B.S., Rider Coll., 1949; Certified Pub. Acct. Appts: Lybrand, Ross Bros. & Montgomery, Certified Pub. Accts., N.Y.C., 1949-60; Asst.-Treas., Coca-Cola Bottling Co., N.Y.C., 1960-63; Mgr., Audits & Systems, Atlantic Rsch. Corp., Alexandria, Va., 1964-65; Controller, Ely-Cruikshank Co., Inc. (formerly Horace S. Ely & Co.), N.Y.C., 1965-71; Asst. Treas., ibid, 1966-67; Treas., Dir., 1966-71; Dir., Phila. acctng. ctr. Ogden Foods, Inc., Phila., 1971; Treas., ibid, 1972. Mbrships. incl: Dir., N.Y. Fed. Savings & Loan Assn.; Real Estate Bd., N.Y., Inc.; Bd. dirs., Op. Eye-Opener; N.J. Br., Am. Inst. of Certified Pub. Accts. Address: Warren Glen Box 74A, Bloomsbury, NJ 08804, U.S.A. 6.

LAUCK, Marie Theresia. Lawyer; State Senator. Educ: B.A., St. Mary-of-the-Woods Coll.; M.A., Butler Univ.; J.D., Ind. Univ. Schl. of Law, Indpls. Div. Appts. incl: Probation Officer, Municipal Cts., Marion Co., 1935-48; Civilian Instr., Adjutant Gen.'s Schl., U.S. Army, 1951-55; Lawyer, 1955-; Admitted to prac. in U.S. Supreme Ct., 1955; Elected to House of Reps., Indiana Gen. Assembly, 1958; Elect. State Senator, 1964, re-elected, 1972; only woman in State of Ind. ever to have been elected both to House & to Senate of Ind. Gen. Assembly. Mbrships. incl: Ind. Deleg., Nat. Assn. Women Lawyers; Judicature Soc. & other local & State Bar Assns.; Org. Women Legislators; Chmn., Nat. Legion of Decency, 1934-; Pres., Ind. Assn. Women Lawyers. Contbr. to Cath., Schol. & Educ. Jrnls. Recip. of awards for servs. to community, inclng. by J.P. Assn., 1973 & Intergroup Coun. of Women,

Indpls., 1974. Address: 323 Peoples Bank Bldg., Indianapolis, IN 46204, U.S.A.

LAUDRUM, Alice, b. 29 June 1909. Retail Buyer. Educ: Art Major 2 yrs., Tex. Women's Univ. & Southern Meth. Univ. during Summers; Pvte. tuition, oil painting. Appts. incl: Responsible for buying & merchandising of all sportswear, lingerie & jr. wear, Nathan's Inc., 1938-. Mbrships: Chmn., Downtown Merchants & Special Coordinator of local City Art shows & retail fashion shows working w. Galveston Chmbr. of Comm., Tex.; Dir., Galveston Art League, Inc.; Tex. Assn. Retarded Children; Galveston Cultural Arts Coun. Oil paintings exhibd. in many shows inclng. Am. Bank Gall., 1968. Address: 1818 Church St. Apt. 1, Galveston, TX 77550, U.S.A. 5.

LAUGHLIN, Louis Gene, b. 20 Sept. 1937. Banker; Economist. Educ: B.A., Univ. of Calif., Santa Barbara, 1960; postgrad. work, Claremont Grad. Schl., 1966-70. Appts: Mgr., Wheeldex-L.A. Co., L.A., Calif., 1960-62; V.P., Warner/Walker & Assocs., Inc., ibid, 1962; Rep., A.C. Nielsen Co., Chgo., Ill., 1962-64; Cons., Spectra-Sound Corp., 1964-65; Rsch. Analyst, Security-1st Nat. Bank, L.A., 1964-67, Asst. Rsch. Mgr., 1967-68; Asst. V.P., Security Pacific Nat. Bank, ibid, 1968-72, V.P. & Mgr., Market Info. & Rsch. Div., 1972-. Mbrships. incl: Nat. Assn. Bus. Economists; Charter Mbr., Southern Calif. Chapt., ibid; Am. Econ. Assn.; Bank & Am. Marketing Assns.; Western Econ. Assn.; Am. Statistical Assn.; Sec., Econs., Town Hall of Calif., 1966. Address: 4782 Glen Albyn Dr., L.A., CA 90065, U.S.A.

LAUGHLIN, Myron Penn, b. 7 May 1893. Lawyer; Engineer. Educ: Registered Profl. Engr., 1916; E.E., Pratt Inst., 1917; Wharton Schl. Acctng. & Finance, Univ. of Pa., 1919; Mass. Inst. Technol., 1920; Mbr., Ga. Bar, 1927; Mbr., Fed. Bar, 1928. Appts: Engr., Electromech. Dev. Rsch. Corp., & Jefferson Phys. Lab., Harvard Univ., 1920; Stoker & Combustion Dev., Am. Engrng. Co., Phila., Pa., 1920-21; Patent Agt., N.Y., 1921-26; Patent Lawyer, Atlanta, Ga., 1927; Pres., Dir., Fla. Defense Inds. Inc., 1942-43; currently Patent Lawyer, St. Petersburg, Fla., & Owner, Laughlin Engrng. Mbrships: Order of Lafayette; Order of Masonry; Episcopalian. Author of Money From Ideas, 1950. Holder, 28 patents. mech. engrng. Recip., M. Penn L. Awards to law & engrng. students for rsch. Address: 1916, 7th St. N., St. Petersburg, FL 33704, U.S.A.

LAU-LAVIE, Naphtali, b. 23 June 1926. Journalist. Educ: Academic & Rabbinical. Appts: Journalist, Israeli press, 1952-56; Sr. Pol. & Mil. Corres., News Ed., Haaretz daily newspaper, 1956-70; Spokesman, Min. of Defence, Asst. to Min. for Press & Pub. Affairs, 1970-. Mbr., Journalists Assn. in Israel. Publs: Moshe Dayan, 1968; Piotrkow. Articles, pol. & soc. affairs, newspapers. Address: 15 Mate Aharon St., Ramat Gan, Israel. 94.

LAURENCE, A.E.B., b. 6 Jan. 1907. British Consuul; Industrial Managing Director. Appts. incl: Mgr., Laurence & Co., Ltd., 1946-; British Vice Consul—Consul, Cali, Colombia, S. Am., 1946-; Managing Dir., Molino Dagua, ibid, 1950-; Vice Dean—Dean, Consular Corps, 1957-67; Chmn., Bd. Govs., Colegio Colombo-Britanico, 1957-; Hon. Dean, Consular Corps, 1968-. Mbrships: Royal Automobile Club, London; Club Campestre, Cali; Club de Ejecutivos; Corporacion de Desarrollo Social; London Scottish Regiment Old Comrades Assn. Hons: Order of British Empire, 1963. Address: British Consulate, Apartado Aereo 1326, Cali, Colombia, S. Am.

LAURENCE, William Leonard, b. 7 Mar. 1888. Journalist. Educ: Harvard, 1912; Univ. of Besançon, France, 1919; Boston Univ. Law Schl., 1925; Hon. Sc.D., Boston Univ., 1946 & Stevens Inst. of Technol., 1951; Hon. D.H.L., Grinnell Coll., 1951 & Yeshiva Univ., 1957. Appts. incl: Reporter, N.Y. World, 1926-30; Sr. Sci. Reporter, N.Y. Times, 1930-56; Official U.S. Reporter, Atomic Bomb Proj., 1945; Exclusive Reporter, Atomic Bomb Mission over Japan, 1945; Sci. Ed., N.Y. Times, 1956-64. Mbrships. incl: Harvard Club, N.Y.C.; The Players; Overseas Press Club. of Am.; Nat. Press Club, Wash.; British-Am. Club, Majorca; Life Mbr., Nat. Assn. of Sci. Writers, Pres., 1939-40; Dramatists Guild, Authors League of Am.; PEN; Sigma Delta Chi; Fellow,AAAS. Publs: Dawn Over Zero, The Story Of The Atomic Bomb; The Hell Bomb; Men & Atoms. Hons. incl: Pulitzer Prize, 1937, 1946; George Westinghouse Disting. Sci. Writers Award, AAAS, 1946; Univ. of Mo. Medal for Disting. Serv. to Jrnlsm., 1947; Grady Gold Medal, Am. Chem. Soc., 1958. Address: Monsenor Palmer 28, Palma de Mallorca, Majorca, Spain.

LAURENTIN, René, b. 19 Oct. 1917. Priest; Professor; Journalist. Educ: Cath. Inst., Paris, France; Licencié ès-Lettres, ibid; Docteur ès-lettres, Sorbonne, 1952; Doct., Theol., Cath. Inst., 1953. Appts. incl: Served in WW II; Prof., Theol., Cath. Univ., Angers, 1953-; Cons., Commns. preparatory to Vatican II Coun., 1960; Expert, ibid, 1962-65, & Corres. of Coun., Figaro; Vis. Prof., Univs. in U.S., Canada, & Italy. Mbrships. incl: Int. Marist Acad., Rome; V.P., French Soc. for Marist Studies, 1962; Elector Mbr., Nat. Ctr. of Scientific Rsch. Publs. incl: num. works on Virgin Mary & Vatican II; Développement et Salut; Nouveaux Ministères et fin du clergé; Réorientation de l'Eglise après le Troisième Synode; Lourdes-Documents authentiques, 6 vols.; Vie de Bernadette, 2 vols.; contbr. to var. jrnls. Recip., num. hons. inclng. Marian Award, Cath. Univ., Dayton, Ohio, 1965; var. war medals. Address: Grand-Bourg, 91000 Evry, France. 91.

LAURIKAINEN, K.V., b. 6 Jan. 1916. Professor. Educ: Cand. of Philos., Univ. of Helsinki, 1940; Dr. Philos., ibid, 1950. Appts: Lectr., Math. Sci., Inst. of Technol., Turku, 1946-56; Assoc. Prof., Phys., ibid, 1956-60; Prof., Nuclear Physics, Univ. of Helsinki, 1960-; Hd., Dept. of Nuclear Phys., 1961-; Hd., Computing Bur., ibid, 1961-; Rector, N.-Karelian Summer Univ., 1966-69; Chmn., Finnish Comm. for Particle Phys./CERN Comm., 1967-. Mbrships: Vice-Chmn., then Chmn., Finnish Phys. Soc., 1959-62; Pörssiklubi, Helsinki; AAAS; etc. Contbr. to sci. publs. in field, also textbooks & semi-popular books in Finnish, inclng: Modernin fysiikan alkeita (Introduction to Modern Physics), 1961; Nykyfysiikan ongelmia (Problems in Modern Physics), 1967; Atomistiikan aatemaailma (Fundamental Ideas of Atomistics), 1973. Address: c/o Dept. of Nuclear Physics, Siltavuorenpenger 20, SF 00170 Helsinki 17, Finland. 43, 50, 90.

LAURILA, Simo Heikki, born 15 Jan. 1920. Professor of Geodesy. Educ: B.Sc., Inst. Technol., Finland, 1946; M.Sc., 1948; Ph.D., 1953. Appts: Rschr. & Lectr., Finnish Govt., 1948-55; Prof. & Rschr., Ohio State Univ., U.S.A., 1955-66; Chmn., Dept. Geoscis., Univ. of Hawaii, 1969-; UN Expert in Sri Lanka, 1972; Vis. Prof., Helsinki Tech. Univ., 1973. Mbrships: Am. Geophys. Union; N.Y. Acad. Scis.; AAAS; Sigma Xi; Am. Soc. Photogrammetry; Finnish, ibid. Author of two books & 53 other sci. publs. Recip., Fulbright

Sr. Lectrship. Award, 1973. Address: Dept. of Geosciences, Univ. of Hawaii, 2525 Correa Rd., Honolulu, HI 96822, U.S.A. 2, 14, 28, 50.

LAUTERBACH, Carl Julius, b. 21 Nov. 1906. Artist; Author; Archivist. Educ: Staatl. Kunstakademie, Düsseldorf, Germany, 1924-30; Studied in Paris, France, 1930-31. Fndr., "Archiv Lauterbach"—"Sammlung kulturpolitischer Dolumente"; Int. histl. press exhibitions; Collaborator, press, film ind. & TV. Mbrships: Das Junge Rheinland; Bd. of Dirs., Rheinische Sezession; Antinazi-Widerstandsgruppe Düsseldorfer Künstler, 1933-45. 1st group exhibition of paintings 1947. Publs: 6 Lithographien, 1932-33; Zeichungen—Carl Lauterbach (biographical forward by Dr. Anna Klapheck), 1948; Lebensweisheiten aus dem Bergischen (collector & illustrator), 1951; Postkarten-Album, 1960, French edit. 1961; Mit besten Grüssen, 1963. Hons:, Dürer Prize, Nürnberg, 1930; Bundesverdienstorden am Bande, German Fed. Repub., 1972. Address: Sittarderstr. 5, 4 Düsseldorf, German Fed. Repub. 43.

LAUTZENHEISER, Barbara J., b. 15 Nov. 1938. Actuary. Educ: B.A., Neb. Wesleyan Univ., 1960; Fellow, Soc. of Actuaries, 1969. Appts. incl: Actuarial Trainee, Bankers Life Nebraska, Lincoln, Neb., 1960-64; Programmer & Systems Analyst, ibid, 1964-65; Asst. Actuary, ibid, 1965-69; Assoc. Actuary, ibid, 1969-70; 2nd V.P. & Actuary, ibid, 1970-72; V.P. & Actuary, ibid, 1972-; Guest Speaker, sev. acad. instns. & at profl. soc. meetings. mbrships. incl: Phi Kappa Phi, 1960-; Pi Gamma Mu, 1960-; Am. Acad. of Actuaries; Neb. Actuaries Club, Bd. Mbr., 1969-70, 1971-74, Sec.-Treas., 1971-72, Pres., 1972-73, Chmn. Bd., 1973-74; Agcy. Rels. Comm., Lincoln Community Servs.; Corp. Financial Planning Comm., Life Off. Mgmt. Assn.; Comm. on Sex Equality, Am. Life Ins. Assn.; P.R. Comm., Soc. of Actuaries; Bd. Mbr., Lincoln Chmbr. of Comm. Contbr. to profl. jrnls. Hons. incl: Young Alumni Serv. Award, Neb. Wesleyan Univ., 1971. Address: Bankers Life Neb., P.O. Box 81889, Lincoln, NB, U.S.A. 5, 76, 138.

LAUX, Peter John, b. 7 Jan. 1922. Librarian. Educ: B.S., St. Norbert Coll., West de Pere, Wis., 1948; M.A., Marquette Univ., Milwaukee, 1949; M.S.L.S., Univ. of Wis., Madison, 1952. Appts: Libn. I, Milwaukee Pub. Lib., 1952-54; Libn. II, ibid, 1954; Assoc. Libn., Georgetown Univ., Wash. D.C., 1954-60; Dir. of Lib., Canisius Coll, Buffalo, N.Y., 1960-; Chmn., Bd. Trustees, Western N.Y. Lib. Resources Coun., 1974-. Publs: A Man's Home is his Hassle, 1969; Contbng. Ed., Column 'Professionaly Speaking' Cath. Lib. World, 1963-66. Contbr. to mags. & profl. jrnls. Address: 251 Parkside Ave., Buffalo, NY 14214, U.S.A. 2, 6, 30, 46, 108, 128.

LAVARÉLLO OBRENOVITSCH, (His Royal Highness) Marziano II Francesco Giuseppe Maria Pio, b. 17 Mar. 1921. Artist, writer, historiographer. Educ: Studies in Pol. Sci., Litt., Fine Arts, Ancient Hist., Mod. Hist. Appts: authority on Mod. glass-making art. Mbrships. incl: Fndr. of Int. Confederation of the Lineage of St. Constantine the Great; Sovereign Pres. of Royal Serbian Acad. of Sci., Litt. & Art; Hon. Rector of G. Galilei Univ.; Mbr. of High Coun. of Imperial Ottoman Byzantine Confederation and Traditionalist Int. Confederation; High Patron of Holy Serbian Orthodox Legitimist Autocton Consiliary Ch., of the Orthodox Belonissia, of Antioch, of the Indies, of Am. & of the Celts. Publs. incl: Antologia del Ritratto dei Reali di Serbia e

Romani Imperatori; Liriche; La flotta Lavarello. Contbr. to var. art exhibs. Hons: Grand Hereditary Master of the Nat. Serbian Equestrian Orders; Kt. of Supreme Order of Holy Spirit, (the Royal House of France); Grand Kt. of Mexican Eagle & Grand Cross of Imperial Mil. Orde;of Our Lady of Guadeloupe (the Imperial House of Mexico); Kt. of Order of the Glory, (Imperial House of Turkey); Gold medal of Int. Comm. for Unity & Universality of Culture of Univ. of Rome; Gold medal of Commune of Rome. Address: Via Piemonte 101, 00187, Rome, Italy. 43.

LAVERGNE, Julio Armando, Physician. Educ: A.B., Univ. of Pa., Phila., 1931; M.D., ibid, 1935, M.Sc., 1950. Appts. incl: Retd. Prof., Ob. & Gyn., Schl. of Med., Univ. of Panama; Fndg. Mbr., Past Pres., Panama Ob. & Gyn. Soc.; Fndg. Mbr., Pres., Family Planning Assn. of Panama; V.P., Regional Coun., Western Hemisphere Region, Int. Planned Parenthood Fedn. Mbr., Govng. Body, ibid; Gyn., Medicos Unidos, Panama. Mbrships. incl: Soc. Panamena de Obstetricia Y Ginecologia; Asociacion Medica Nacional de Panama; Med. Soc. of Isthmian Canal Zone; AMA. Author, num. articles in profl. publs. Address: P.O. Box 4425, Panama 5, Repub. of Panama.

LAVERY, Kenneth Reid, b. 29 Jan. 1930. Chartered Accountant. Educ: B.A., Univ. of Toronto; C.A.; R.I.A.; C.M.C. Appts: Ptnr.-Mng. Ptnr., P. S. Ross & Ptnrs., Mgmt. Cons.; Ptnr., Touche Ross & Co., Chartered Accts.; Pres., Brewers Assn. of Canada; Profl. career largely concerned w. num. seminars & confs. for univs., Fed. Govt., profl. assns., regarding mgmt. dev. & socio-econ. environment in Canada in 2000 A.D. Mbrships. incl: Inst. Chartered Accts. of Ont.; Soc. Industrial & Cost Accts. of Canada; Canadian Ops. Rsch. Soc.; Canadian Tax Fndn.; Inst. of Assn. Executives. Author of Selective Inventory Management; Contbr. sev. jrnls. on var. industrial & commercial subjects. Address: 122 Willingdon Rd., Rockcliffe Park, Ottawa, Ont., K1M 2G1, Canada.

LAVOIE, Léo, b. 18 Mar. 1913. Company Executive. Educ: St. Francois Xavier Coll., Riviere-du-Loup, P.Q., Canada; Adv. Mgmt. Prog., Harvard Univ., U.S.A. Appts. incl: Mgr., Provincial Bank, var. brs., P.Q., Canada, 1940-55; Asst. to Pres., ibid, 1955; Asst. Gen. Mgr., 1955; Gen. Mgr., 1957; Mbr., Bd. Dirs., 1960; V.P. & Gen. Mgr., 1966; Pres. & Chief Exec. Off., 1967. Dirships. incl: Canadair Ltd.; Alliance Compagnie Mutuelle d'assurance-vie; Canadian Reinsurance Co. Ltd.; Canadian Reassurance Co. Ltd.; Tele-Metropole Corp. Mbrships. incl: Mount-Royal Club; Club St. Denis; Cercle de la Place d'Armes Inc.; Canadian Club of Montreal. Recip., Doct. ès scis. commerciales, Univ. of Montreal, 1970. Address: 221 St. James St. W., Montreal, P.Q. H2Y 1M7, Canada.

LAVOIX, Rodolphe Louis, b. 5 Nov. 1902. Estate Agent. Educ: Fac. of Law, Caen, France; Bachelier, Capacitaire en droit. Appts: Commercial Agt., Ciments d'Origny-Sainte Benoite, 1925; Estate Agt., Cabourg, 1944-; Pres., 15th Regional Union, Fedn. of Estate Agts., 1956-; Admnstr., Nat. Fedn. of Estate Agts., 1956-. Mbrships. incl: Caen Chmbr. of Comm. & Ind., 1959-; Pres., Tourist Info. Bur., 1957-; Departmental Off. of Tourism, 1969-; Int. Advsr., Lions Club; V.P., Cabourg Riding Club; Treas., Cabourg Yacht Club; Bur., Departmental Fedn. of Hunters. Columnist, L'Echo des Plages, 2 yrs., Hons: Chevalier, Sporting & Touristic Merit; Mbr., Order of British Empire; Medal of Hon., Profl.

Syndicates; Chevalier, Agricl. Merit, 1974. Address: Le Logis, Cabourg 14390, France. 43, 91.

LAW, Douglas B., b. 14 Feb. 1918. Publisher; Barrister at Law. Educ: M.A., Cambridge Univ., U.K., 1943; Called to the Bar, Middle Temple, London, 1950. Appts. incl: Legal Adviser, Associated Iliffe Press Ltd., London, 1951-59; Dpty. Chmn. & Mng. Dir., Grampian Publishing Ltd., Glasgow, 1961-67; Chmn., Melrose Press Ltd., Cambridge. U.K., (publrs. of D.I.B., D.L.A.C.B., D.A.B., D.S.B., International Who's Who in Poetry, Int. Who's Who in Art & Antiques), 1970-. Address: Achateilasaig, Morar, Inverness-shire, U.K.

LAW, Thomas Hart, b. 6 July 1918. Lawyer. Educ: A.B., Univ. of Tex., 1939; J.D., ibid, 1942. Appts: Assoc., White, Taylor & Chandler, Austin, Tex., 1942; Lt., USNR, 1942-46; Assoc., Thompson, Walker, Smith & Shannon, Ft. Worth, Tex., 1946-50; Ptnr., Tilley, Hyder & Law, Ft. Worth, 1950-67, Stone, Tilley, Parker, Snakard, Law & Brown, Ft. Worth, 1967-71, Law, Snakard, Brown & Gambill, Ft. Worth, 1971-; Gen. Counsel, Gearhart-Owen Inds. Inc., Ft. Worth & Dénver Railway Co. Mbrships. incl: Phi Eta Sigma, 1936; Phi Beta Kappa, 1939; Pi Sigma Alpha, 1938; Delta Sigma Rho, 1940; Fellow, Tex. Bar Fndn., 1968, Am. Coll. of Probate Counsel, 1970, Am. Bar Fndn., 1971; Pres., Ft. Worth Area Chmbr. of Comm., Ft. Worth Crippled Children's Soc., Ft. Worth Rotary Club, Ft. Worth Exchange Club, State Jr. Bar of Tex. & Metropolitan Dinner Club; Chmn., Ft. Worth Civil Serv. Commn.; V.P., Tex. Philos. Soc. & Univ. of Tex. Law Schl. Assn.; V.P. & Trustee, Univ. of Tex. Fndn.; Trustee, Exec. Comm., Tarrant Co. United Fund & Community Servs.; Vice Chmn., Tarrant Co. Planning Commn.; Parliamentarian, Tarrant Co. Dem. Exec. Comm.; Exec. Bd., Longhorn Coun., Boy Scouts of Am. Recip. Ft. Worth's Outstanding Young Man, 1950. Address: Ft. Worth Nat. Bank Bldg., Ft. Worth, TX 76102, U.S.A. 2, 7, 113, 124.

LAWLER, Joseph Christopher, b. 3 May 1920. Engineering Executive. Educ: B.S. (cum laude), Northeastern Univ., 1943; M.S., Harvard Univ., 1947. Appts: Lt., Civil Engrng. Corps, USN, 1944-46; Proj. Engr., Camp Dresser & McKee Inc., Cons. Environmental Engrs., Boston, Mass., 1947-52, Ptnr., 1952-70, Pres., Chmn. of Bd., 1970-; Mbr., N. Reading Pub. Schl. Bldg. Comm., 1956-60, N. Reading Schl. Comm., 1960-61; Dir., Nat. Coun., Northeastern Univ., 1964-. Mbrships. incl: 1st V.P., Dir., Nat. Coun. Profl. Servs. Firms, 1972-74; Am. Water Works Assn.; Nat.Soc. Profl. Engrs.; Tau Beta Pi. Contbr., Handbook of Applied Hydraulics, 1969. Articles, profl. jrnsl. Hons. incl: New England Award, Tau Beta Pi, 1972; Election to Nat. Acad. of Engrng., 1973. Address: 16 Winter St., N. Reading, MA 02108, U.S.A. 6.

LAWLER, Lillian B., b. 30 June 1898. Professor of Classics. Educ: B.A., Univ. of Pittsburgh, Pa., U.S.A., 1919; M.A., Univ. of Iowa, Ames, 1921; Ph.D., ibid, 1925. Appts. incl: Asst. Prof., Classics, Univ. of Kan.,Lawrence, 1926-29; Instr., Classics, Hunter Coll., N.Y.C., 1929-30; Asst. Prof., ibid, 1930-43; Assoc. Prof., 1943-55; Prof., 1955-59; Prof. Emeritus, 1959-; Vis. Prof., Univ. of Iowa, 1961-67; Assoc. Ed., Auxilium Latinum, 1931-68; Ed., Classical Outlook, 1936-57. Mbrships. incl: Am. Philological Assn.; V.P., Am. Classical League; Past Pres., Classical Assn. of the Atlantic States; Phi Beta Kappa; Eta Sigma Phi; Pi Lambda Theta. Publs. incl: The

Latin Club, 1929, 10th edit. 1968; Adventures in Language, 1941; The Dance in Ancient Greece, 1964; Sev. Latin tchng. playlets; Num. contbns. to profl. jrnls. Recip., Prix de Rome Fellowship, 1925-26. Address: 1133 Howell St., Iowa City, IA 52240, U.S.A. 2, 13, 30, 51, 138.

LAWLIS, (Mrs.) Maggie Inez, b. 28 July, 1892. Civic Worker. Appts: Hd., John Brown Kitchen Dept., 1933; Tchr., 5th & 6th Grades, Sulphur Springs, Ark., 1943-44; House Mother, John Brown Mil. Acad., ibid, 4 mths.; Deleg. Nat. Conven., San Antonio, Tex., 1957. Mbrships. incl: United Method. Ch.; Pres., Woman's Soc. Christian Serv., 1942-43; Former Tchr., Ladies Bible Class; Pres., Woman's Christian Temperance Union. Hons: Life mbr., Woman's Soc. Christian Serv. & Ark. Woman's Christian Temperance Union. Address: 718 N. Mt. Olive, Silvan Springs, AR 72761, U.S.A. 125.

LAWLOR, John James, b. 5 Jan. 1918. Professor of English Language & Literature. Educ: B.A., Univ. of Oxford, 1939; D.Litt. ibid. Appts: Lectr., Engl., Brasenose & Trinity Colls., Univ. of Oxford, 1947-50; Univ. lectr. Engl. Lit., Univ. of Oxford, 1949-50; Prof., Engl. Lang. & Lit., & Hd. of Dept., Univ. of Keele, 1950-; Vis. Prof., Brandeis Univ., Waltham, Mass., U.S.A., 1966, Univ. of Hawaii, 1972, & Rhodes Univ., Grahamstown, S. Africa, 1973. Mbrships. incl: Sec.-Treas., Int. Assn. of Univ. Profs. of Engl.; Pres., N. Staffordshire Drama Assn.; V.P., The Navy League. Publs. incl: The Tragic Sense in Shakespeare, 1960; "Piers Plowman": An Essay in Criticism, 1962; To Nevill Coghill, from Friends (w. W.H. Auden), 1966; Chaucer, 1969; Ed., The New University, 1968. Recip., Fellowship, Soc. of Antiquaries; Fellowship, Folger Shakespeare Lib., Wash. D.C., U.S.A., 1962. Address: 14 Church Plantation, Keele, Staffordshire ST5 5AY, U.K. 1, 43, 128, 139.

LAWRENCE, Arlene White, b. 11 Nov. 1916. Minister. Educ: A.A., Belleview Coll., Westminster, Colo., 1936; Belleview Bible Sem.; B.A., Alma White Coll., Zarephath, N.J., 1941; M.A., Columbia Univ., N.Y.C., 1963. Appts. as: Min.; Music educator; Asst. Dir., WAWZ, Zarephath, N.J., WAKW, Cinn., Ohio, & KPOF, Denver, Colo.; Conductor of weekly Children's Bible Story Hour broadcasts over 3 stns.; Radio vocalist; Violinist; Choir Dir.; Tchr., music & speech. Mbrships: V.P., Pillar of Fire Ch. Soc. Inc.; V.P., Pillar of Fire, London, U.K.; Bd. of Trustees, Pillar of Fire, Cinn., Ohio, & Brooklyn, N.Y.; Friends of Alma White Coll. Assn.; Nat. Trust for Historic Preservation, Wash. D.C. Author of publs. in field. Address: Aux Route 3, Box 166, Belle Mead, NJ 08502, U.S.A. 5, 128.

LAWRENCE, George Andrew, b. 10 Nov. 1914. Corporation Executive. Educ: A.B., Cornell Univ., Ithaca, N.Y., 1936. Appts: Mgr.,N.Y. Br., Taylor Wine Co., Hammondsport, 1938-44; Asst. Winery Mgr., ibid, 1938-44, Sec., Treas., & Dir., 1955-64, Exec. V.P. & Dir., 1962-64, Pres., Chief Exec. Off. & Dir., 1964-. Mbrships: Nat. Coun., Am. Planning Assn.; Pres.'s Coun., Am. Inst. Mgmt.; Finger Lakes Wine Growers Assn.; Cornell Univ. Coun.; pres., Cornell Univ. Class of 1936; Trustee, & Vice Chmn., Alfred Univ.; Sigma Delta Chi; Kappa Delta Rho. Recip., Wisdom Soc. Award of Hon., 1973. Address: P.O. Box 306, Hammondsport, NY 14840, U.S.A. 2, 6, 16.

LAWRENCE, Gladys Wilkinson (Mrs. Paul William Lawrence), b. 30 May 1904. Civic

Worker. Educ: A.B., Unif. of Neb.; Grad. work, Smith Coll., Mass.; Ind. Univ.; Les Hirondelles, Geneva, Switzerland. Fndr. of: Nat. Charity League; Nat. Flower Guild; Los Floristas Headdress Ball, & num. others; The LawrencyCompany (Steel & Aluminium). Mbrships. incl: Asst. League of Southern Calif.; LA Country Club; Life, Soc. Serv. Aux.; Life, Charter, St. Anne's Guild; Life, Good Shepherd Guild; Life, Fndr., Pres., Nat. Charity League; Co-Fndr., Las Benevolas of Asst. League; Past Pres., Women's Breakfast Club, Fndr. & Pres. Emeritus. Nat. Flower Guild; Past Pres., Univ. of Neb. Alumni Assn.; Opera Guild, Southern Calif.; Southern Calif. Symph. Assn.; Fndr., Footlighters, etc. Recip. of num. hons. for civic activities, inclng. Kentucky Colonel; Admiral, Gt. Navy of Neb.; Int. Patroness of Debutante Balls, London, Rome, Vienna, Paris. Address: 10467 Sunset Blvd., Bel Air, Los Angeles, CA 90024, U.S.A.

LAWRENCE, Ruddick C., b. 5 Jan. 1912. Business Executive. Educ: B.A., Univ. of Wash., 1934. Appts. incl: N.Y. Mgr., Assoc. Advt. Mgr., Fortune Mag., N.Y.C., 1946-50; Dir., Sales Dev., TV Network, Dir.,, Promotion, Planning Dev., Radio & TV Networks, Nat. Broadcasting Co., ibid, 1950-53; V.P., N.Y. Stock Exchange, 1953-68; V.P., Continental Oil Co., Stamford, 1968-. Mbrships. incl: Chmn., Bd. of Trustees, Sarah Lawrence Coll., 1964-69; Bd. Mgrs., N.Y. Botanical Garden; Dir., Int. Film Fndn.; Dir., World Adventure Series; Trustee, Wall St. Ctr.; Vice Chmn., Gov. Invest-in-Am. Nat. Coun., Inc.; Exec. V.P., Dir., U.S.-Arab Chmbr. of Comm.; Phi Kappa Psi; Sigma Delta Chi. Recip., Star of Jordan, King Hussein of Jordan, 1973. Address: 3 Wellington Circle, Bronxville, NY 10703, U.S.A. 2, 6, 16, 128.

LAWRENCE, Teleté Zorayda (Lester), b. 5 Aug. 1910. Educator; Speech & Voice Pathologist. Educ: B.A., Univ. of Calif., Berkeley, 1932; M.A., Tex. Christian Univ., 1963; Pvte. voice study w. Edgar Schofield, N.Y.C., 1936-41; Studied drama w. Enrica Clay Dillon, N.Y.C., 1937-40. Appts: Mbr., Am. Lyric Theatre (Opera), N.Y.C., 1939-; Soloist, Central Presby. Ch., N.Y.C., 1937-41; Dept. of Speech Communication, Tex. Christian Univ., 1959-; Currently Assoc. Prof., Speech Pathol. & Univ. Speech Pathologist, Specialist & Cons. in Disorders of Voice & Related Therapeutic Procedures, Mbr., Grad. Fac. & Lectr. in Phoniatrics; Pvte. Prac. in Speech & Voice Pathol. Mbrships. incl: Pres. of Delta, Tex. Chapt., Phi Beta Kappa, 1973-74; Int. Assn. of Logopedics & Phoniatrics; Int. Soc. of Phonetic Scis.; Am. Speech & Hearing Assn.; Am. Dialect Soc.; Speech Communication Assn. of Am.; AAUP. Author of Handbook for Instructors of Voice & Diction, 1968, & of papers at 7 Congresses. Recip. of hons. Address: 3860 S. Hills Circle, Ft. Worth, TX 76109, U.S.A. 5, 7, 15, 125, 132, 138.

LAWRENCE, Thomas Fulton Coleman, b. 26 Nov. 1915. Civil Engineer. Educ: B.Sc., Univ. of Sydney, Australia, 1935; B.E., ibid, 1937. Appts. incl: Tech. Supt., Australian Nat. Airways, 1946/48; Prin. Sci. Off., Royal Aircraft Estab., U.K., 1948-53; Prin. Sci. Off., High Speed Aerodynamics Div., Supt., Systems Assessment Div., & Dpty. Dir., Trials, Weapons Rsch. Estab., Dept. of Supply, Australia, 1953-65; Chief Supt., Aeronautical Rsch. Labs., Dept. of Supply, 1965-67; Controller, Rsch. & Dev., Ctrl. Off., Dept. of Supply, 1967-68; Dpty. Sec., Rsch. & Engrng., ibid, 1968-. Mbrships. incl: Fellow, Instn. of Engrs., Australia; Fellow, Royal Aeronautical Soc.; Coun., Australian Nat. Univ. Publs: Articles in jrnls. Address: 44 Jacka Place, Campbell, A.C.T., Australia 2601. 23.

LAWRENCE, Trudys. Educator; Health Education Adviser to Governments. Educ: B.A., Whittier Coll., Calif.; M.S., Univ. of Southern Calif., L.A.; Ph.D., ibid. Appts: Missionary, India, 1940-47; Tchr., L.A. City & Co. Schls., 1950-56; Supvsr. of Hlth. Educ., L.A: City Schls., 1956-66; Schl. Hlth. Educ. Advsr., WHQ to Govts. of Philippines, 1966-68, Taiwan, 1967, Malaysia, 1967, Nigeria, 1968-72, Zambia, 1972; Lectr., Calif. State Univ., L.A., 1972-73. Mbrships: Southern Calif. Comm., WHO; Union Int. pour l'Educ. Sanitare; Am. Pub. Hlth. Assn.; Fellow, Am. Schl. Hlth. Assn.; Assn. for Supvsn. & Curric. Dev.; Pi Lambda Theta; Pres., Sigma Chapt., Univ. of Southern Calif. Publs. incl: Getting Along, Situation-Response Test for Grades 7, 8, 9 (a Standardized Test for Secondary Schools—illustrated); Articles in var. jrnls. inclng. Educl. Horizons, The Rsch. Quarterly, Int. Jrnl. of Hlth. Educ. Hons. incl: Special Achievement Award, Hlth. Educ. Assn. of the Philippines, Manila, 1968; Ldrship. Recognition Award, Southern Calif. Coun. of Pi Lambda Theta, L.A., Calif., 1973. Address: 5532 Poplar Blvd., L.A., CA 90032, U.S.A. 5, 15.

LAWSON, Robert Sutherland, b. 31 May 1908. Surgeon. Educ: M.B., Ormond Coll., Univ. of Melbourne, 1931; M.S., ibid, 1935; F.R.C.S. (U.K.), 1938; F.R.A.C.S., 1940. Appts: War S., Col. (R. of O.), RAAMC, Middle E. & Borneo, 1940-46; Hon. Surg., Alfred Hosp., Melbourne, 1946-; Lectr., Surg. Anatomy, Univ. of Melbourne, 1950-64. Mbrships: Coun. Mbr., Scotch Coll., Melbourne, 1959-; Royal Australasian Coll. Surgs.; Chmn., Vic. State Comm., ibid, 1962-64; Fellow, Australian Med. Assn.; Pres., Vic. Br. Coun., ibid, 1967. Articles var. med. jrnls. inclng. Australian & N.Z. Jrnl. of Surg., Med. Jrnl. of Australia. Hons: Hallett Prize, Royal Coll. Surgs. (U.K.), 1935; 5th Hamilton Russell Mem. Lectr., 1966; 9th Gordon-Taylor Mem. Lectr., 1973. Address: 21 John St., Kew, Vic., Australia 3101. 23.

LAWTON, William H., b. 1 Nov. 1937. Mathematician. Educ: A.A., Univ. of Calif., Berkeley, 1957; A.B., ibid, 1959; M.A., 1962; Ph.D., 1965. Appts: Math. Assoc., Eastman Kodak Co., Rochester, N.Y., 1962-63; Tchng. Asst., Univ. of Calif., Berkeley, 1963-64; Tchng. Assoc., ibid, 1964-65; Internal math. Cons., Grp. Leader, Math. Applications Grp., Eastman Kodak Co., 1965-; Adjunct Prof., Univ. of Rochester, 1965-67. Mbrships. incl: Am. Statl. Assn. (Assoc. Ed., Technometrics; sec.-treas., sect. on phys. & eng. scis.); Am. Soc. for Quality Control (nat. prog. chmn. for statl. & chem. subgrps., 1967, '68, '70); Inst. for math. stats.; Soc. for Indl. & Applied Math.; Sigma Xi (life mbr.). Author of prol. papers & contbr. to profl. book. Hons: Shewell Award, Chem. Div., Am. Soc. Quality Control, 1970; Wilcoxon Award Technometrics jrnl., 1971. Address: 91 Saddlehorn Dr., Rochester, NY 14626, U.S.A. 6, 14.

LAX, David, b. 16 May 1910. Artist. Educ: Cert., Fine Arts, Ethical Culture Schl., 1928; Archipenko Ecole des Beaux Arts, 1929; Nat. Acad., 1930; Apprentice, Atelier Victor Frisch, 1928-30. Appts: Art Dir., Glasscraft Corp., 1928-31, Mills Music Corp., 1932-42, Mills Artists, Inc., 1932-42, Laurel Press, 1942-50, & U.S. Army, 1942-45; Combat Artist, U.S. Army, 1942-45; Art Instr., VA, Curative Workshop, 1950-57; Guest Lectr., Art Prog., Bd. of Educ., N.Y., 1950-57; Chmn., Art Dept.; Dutchess Community Coll., SUNY, 1958-. Mbrships. incl: Grand Ctrl. Art Galls.; Assoc. Am. Artists; AAUP; NEA; Wash. Irving Gall. Art Exhibs. incl: Annual Fndrs. Shows, Grand Ctrl. Art Galls., 1938-65; Corcoran Mus.; British Mus.; Galérie Borghese, Paris; Carnegie Inst.; Pentagon War Art Collect., 1944-70; Assoc. Am. Artists; The New Schl.; Gall. of Mod. Art, N.Y.; Calif. State Colls. Collect.; Nat. Arts Club. Recip., var. hons. & awards for art work. Address: Box 94, Red Hook, NY 12571, U.S.A. 37.

LAX, Philip, b. 22 Apr. 1920. Interior Designer & Consultant. Educ: B.S., N.Y. Univ., 1940; Postgrad., 1941-42. Mbrships. incl: Profl. Mbr., Nat. Soc. Interior Designers; Bd. Trustees, 1958-61, 70-73; Am. Abritration Assn.; Mayor's Budget Comm., Meplewood, N.J., 1958-59; Gov's. Conf. on Educ., N.J., 1966; Chmn., United Jewish Appeal, Maplewood, 1966; Bd. Trustees, B'nai B'rith Fndn., Wash. D.C., 1967-74; Trustee, Henry Monsky Fndn., Wash. D.C., 1968-74; Trustee, Leo N. Levi Hosp., Hot Springs, Ark., 1968-71; Pres., B'nai B'rith Ctr., Rochester (Mayo Clin.), 1965-70; Currently, Hon. Pres.; Int. V.P., B'nai B'rith, 1968-71; Fndng. Mbr., N.Y. Univ. Club, 1956. Hons: Commendation, N.J. State Senate, 1967; B'nai B'rith Fndn. Award, 1968; B'nai B'rith Humanitarian Award, Pres's. Medal, 1969. Address: 35 Claremont Dr., Maplewood, NJ 07040, U.S.A. 6, 55.

LAYCOX, W. Jack, b. 11 Mar. 1924. Artist; Illustrator. Educ: Univ. of Calif., Berkeley; B.A., San Fran. State Univ., Calif. Appts: U.S. Govt. Tech. Illustrator, Atomic Energy Commn., 1943-46; Art Dir., Bacon Am. Corp., Muncie, Ind., 1946-59; Owner, Profl. Artist, Jack Laycox Galls., 1960-. Mbrships: Soc. of Western Artists; Pres., Soc. of Barbershop Quartet Singers of Am., 1973. Author, Dramatic Paintings From Familiar Scenes, 1972. Commns. incl: 13 paintings, Crown Zellerback Callendar, 1964; 12 paintings, Gen. Tire Int. Calendar, 1972, '73; 30 oils, Delta Air Lines; 10 oils, Thompson Aircraft Corp., 1966; 13 oils, Donald Art Co., Fine Arts Reproductions; num. watercolors, Mission-Regency Cards. Num. works in pvte. & pub. collects. Recip., num. hons. Address: P.O. Box 5054, Carmel, CA 93921, U.S.A.

LAYSON, Addison S., b. 10 Mar. 1939. Educ: Howard Coll.; Young Harris Coll.; Oglethorpe Univ. Appts: Employee Benefit Mgr., Dekalb Co. Municipality, Ga.; Asst. Personnel Mgr.,. Fulton Cotton Mills, Atlanta, Ga.; Personnel Mgr., Thomas Pride Carpets, Calhoun, Ga.; Mfg. Gen. Mgr., V.P., Ops., V.P., Indl. Rels., Venture Carpets, Calhoun. Mbrships: Bd. of Dirs., Gordon Co., Community Chest & Gordon Co. Red Cross. Address: Venture Carpets, P.O. Box 209, Calhoun, GA 30701, U.S.A. 125.

LAZAR, Allan William, b. 11 June 1931. Pathologist. Educ: B.S., Univ. of Scranton, Pa., 1953; M.D., Jefferson Med. Coll., Phila., 1957. Appts: Intern, Detroit Receiving Hosp., 1957-58; Res., Pathol., Univ. of Chgo. Hosps. & Clins., 1958-62; Chief Res., Pathol., ibid, 1961-62, Instr., 1961-62; Chief., Rsch. & Trng., Armed Forces Inst. of Pathol., Wash. D.C., 1962-63; Assoc., Pathol., Columbia Univ. Coll. Physns. & Surgs., 1964-66; Asst. Prof., Pathol., Fairleigh Dickinson Univ. Dental Schl., 1967-; Pres., Gyn Cytol. & Pathol. Assocs., 1964-. Mbrships: Fellow, Coll. Am. Pathologists; Int. Coll. Pathol.; AMA. Author, num. publs. in field. Num. paintings in pvte. collects. Hon: Sigma Xi, 1960. Address: 117 Ft. Lee Rd., Leonia, NJ 07605, U.S.A. 6, 46.

LAZARO LOZANO, Bonifacio. Painter. Educ: Schl. of Fine Arts, Lisbon, Portugal; San Fernando Schl. of Fine Arts, Madrid, Spain. Exhibs. incl: 10 exhibs., Nat. Soc. of Fine Arts, Lisbon, 1941-59; Salon Nacional, Madrid, 1941, 1962; Ateneo Gall., Barcelona, 1944; Macarron Gall., Madrid, 1944 & 56; Grife & Escoda Gall., Madrid, 1965 & 73; Buenos Aires, Argentina, 1943; Andre Weil Gall., Paris, 1953; Univ. of Leeds, U.K., 1957. Represented in permanent collects. inclng: Mus. of Contemporary Art, Lisbon; Gulbenkian Mus., Lisbon; Mus. of Lourenço Marques, Mozambique; Badajoz Mus., Spain; Home & For. Offs., Madrid; pvte. collects. in N. & S. Am. & in Europe. Mbrships: Fine Arts Soc., Lisbon; Fine Arts Circle, Madrid. Hons. incl: Conde de Cartagena Prize, Madrid, 1934; Silver Medal, Nat. Exhib., Madrid, 1943; Gold Medal, Nat. Exhib., Lisbon, 1949; Gold Medal, Arts Biennial, Madrid, 1963; Order of Christ, Portugal, 1946. Address: Avda. de los Toreros, 22, Madrid 28, Spain. 43.

LAZARON, Morris Samuel, b. 16 Apr. 1888. Rabbi; Author; Painter. Educ: M.A., Univ. of Cinn.; Ordained Rabbi, Hebrew Union Coll., Cinn.; Grad. work, Johns Hopkins Univ. Appts: Min., Wheeling, W. Va., 1914-15; Retd. Chap., U.S.A., one of 4 chaps. who officiated at Burial of Unknown Soldier, Arlington Cemetery, Va., 1921; Missions to U.K. under auspices of State Dept. & British For. Off., 1941, & Middle East, under Am. Friends of Middle East, 1952; Former Min., Balt. Hebrew Cong. Mbrships: Ctrl. Conf. Am. Rabbis; Am. Coun. for Judaism; Co-Fndr., U.S. Army Chaps. Assn. (now U.S. Mil. Chaps. Assn.); Blowing Rock, N.C., Co. Club; The Breakers Golf Club, Palm Beach, Fla. Publs: Common Ground; Olive Trees in Storm; Bridges, Not Walls; Religious Servies for Jewish Youth; Consolations of our Faith; Articles in The Atlantic Monthly, The Christian Century, The Churchman, etc. Hons: Gottheil Award for Serv. to Jewish Community, 1933; Litt.D., Rutgers Univ., 1942; Citation, U.S. Chaps. Assn. Address: 241 W. Indies Dr., Palm Beach, FL 33480, U.S.A. 2, 6, 130.

LAZEROWITZ, Morris, b. 22 Oct. 1907. Educator. Educ: Univ. of Neb., 1929-31; A.B., Univ. of Mich., 1933; Ph.D., 1936; Rackham Fellow, Harvard Univ., 1937-38. Appts: Fac. Mbr., Smith Coll., Northampton, Mass., 1938-; Prof., Philos., ibid, 1954-; Sophia & Austin Smith Prof., 1964-; Fulbright Prof., Bedford Coll., Univ. of London, U.K., 1951-52; Prof. Emeritus, Smith Coll., Northampton, Mass., 1973. Mbrships. incl: Am. Philos. Soc.; Aristotelian Soc.; AAUP; Royal Inst. Philos.; Nat. Coun., For. Policy Assn. Publs. incl: The Structure of Metaphysics, 1955; Studies in Metaphilosophy, 1964; Philosophy & Illusion, 1968; G.E. Moore. Essays in Retrospect, 1970; Psychoanalysis & Philosophy (co-author), 1970; Ludwig Wittgenstein, Philosophy & Language, 1972. Address: Smith Coll., Northampton, MA 01060, U.S.A. 2, 12, 128, 131.

LEAF, Robert Jay, b. 27 July 1944. Dentist. Educ: Cornell Univ., 1962-65; D.M.D., Harvard Schl. of Dental Med., 1969. Appts: Ptve. Prac. Dentistry, N.Y.C., 1969-; Pres., Universal Profl. Bldgs. Inc., ibid, & Cons. on Hlth. Ctrs., 1970-. Mbrships: Sigma Alpha Mu; Am. Dental Assn.; First Dist. Dental Soc.; N.Y. State Dental Soc.; Northeast Gnathological Soc.; Am. Preventive Dentistry Assn. Address: 2 East 54th St., N.Y., NY 10022, U.S.A. 6.

LEAL, H. Allan, b. 15 June 1917. Lawyer. Educ: B.A., McMaster Univ., Canada, 1940; Grad., Osgoode Hall Law Schl., 1948; LL.M., Law Schl., Harvard Univ., U.S.A., 1957. Called to Ont. Bar, Canada, 1948. Appts: Practised Law w. Erichsen-Brown & Leal, Toronto, 1948-50; Lectr., Osgoode Hall Law Schl., 1950-56; V.Dean, Prof., 1956-58; Dean, Prof., 1958-66; Mbr., Ont. Law Reform Commn. 1964-; Chmn., ibid, 1966-; Q.C., 1959. Mbrships. incl: Univ. Club, Toronto; Lawyers Club; Bd. of Dirs., 1969-, 2nd V.P., 1970, 1st V.P., 1971, Empire Club of Canada. Hons: LL.D., McMaster Univ., 1963; Schol. awards. Contbr. to law jrnls. Address: Ont. Law Reform Commn., 16th Floor, 18 King St. East, Toronto, Ont. M5C 1C5, Canada. 139.

LEANDER, Sigfrid, b. 25 Feb. 1893. Retired Educator; Author; Lecturer. Educ: Fil.kand., Univ. of Lund, Sweden, 1932. Appts: Army Off., 1917-26; Antiquarian, Province of Blekinge, 1933-44; Educl. Off., Staff of Defence, 1943-50; Mng. Dir., Stockholms arbetareinstitut, (Wkrs. Inst.), 1953-74. Hdmaster., Liberala studieforbundet, (Liberal Study Assn.), 1954-60. Publs. incl: Den ljusa stigen (novel), 1923; Folkbildning—vad är det? 1953; Under arbetareinstitutets tak, 1955; Hundra år i Blekinge, 1963; Ett hundraårigt boktryckeri, 1964; Från Anton Nyström till Vi som vet mest, 1965; Folk och bildning, Operation folkbildningsminnen, 1966; Sen eko, 1968; Utsikt över Karlskrona, 1970-71. Ed., Folkbildning och forskning, 1970; En folkbildares bibliografi, 1973. Recip., num. hons. inclng. Nordiska museets silvermedalj, 1973 & Sokrates-Priset, 1973. Address: Stortorget 14, 111 29 Stockholm, Sweden. 134.

LEARMONTH, William Glenn, b. 23 Oct. 1896. Lawyer; Banker. Educ: LL.B., Union Univ., 1921; Admitted N.Y. Bar, 1921. Appts: Learnmouth & Ratcliff, attys., Watertown, N.Y.; U.S. Commnr., N. Dist., N.Y., 1925-72. Past Pres., Dir., First Nat. Bank, Dexter, N.Y. Counsel, Watertown Housing Authority; V.P., Folts Home for Aged, Herkimer, N.Y. Mbrships: Am., N.Y. State, Jefferson Co. Bar. Assns.; Am. Legion; Life Mbr., Jefferson Co. Histl. Soc.; Nat. Coun. of Juvenile Ct. Judges, YMCA; Chmbr. of Comm.; Am. Judicature Soc.; U.S. Power Squadron; Past Pres., Rotary Club; Chancellor, Meth. Ch. Hons: First Citizen of Watertown, 1946. Address: 234 Michigan Ave., Watertown, NY 13601, U.S.A. 6.

LEASE, Richard Jay, b. 10 Dec. 1914. University Professor; Police Officer. Educ: Wittenberg Univ., 1932-33; B.A., Univ. of Ariz., 1937; M.A., ibid, 1961; var. further studies in police sci., psychol. at univs., insts., & profl. law enforcement schls. Appts. incl: Patrolman-Sgt., Tucson Police Dept., 1938-42; Off., USMC, 1942-46; Sgt.-Acting Capt., Tucson Police Dept., 1946-53; Investigator, Pima Co. Sheriff's Dept., 1953-56; Sci. Tchr., Tucson Pub. Schls. 1957-59; Lectr., Dept. of Police Admin., Ind. Univ., 1960-65; Prof., Dept. Police Sci., N.m. State Univ., 1965-. Mbrships. incl: Fellow & Past Sec., Gen. Sect., Am. Acad. of Forensic Scis.; Int. Assn. Forensic Scis.; Brit. & Canadian Acads. Forensic Scis.; Int. Assn. Chiefs of Police; NEA; AAAS; Mason; Sigma Chi; Past V.P., Southern N.M. Capt., Assn. of U.S. Army, Life mbr., Ariz. Rifle & Pistol Assn. & num. other profl. police or mil. orgs.; currently, Sr. Warden, Lodge of Perfection, Southern N.M. Scottish Rite Consistory. Publs: Alcohol & Road Traffic: Problems of Enforcement & Prosecution (w. Dr. Robert F. Borkenstein), 1963; As the Twig is Bent, 1969; var. articles in newspapers & jrnls. Ed., What's New, 1970-73. Recip. of var. hons. Address: 2145 Boise Dr.,

Las Cruces, NM 88001, U.S.A. 9, 14, 22, 120, 130, 139.

LEATHERWOOD, Ann Morrow (Mrs. Timothy M. Leatherwood), b. 25 May 1936. University Instructor. Educ: B.A., Univ. of Ala., 1958; M.A., 1964. Appts: Birmingham Co. Schl. System, 1958; Mobile Co. Schl. System, 1959-65; Engl. Instr., Univ. of S. Ala., Mobile, 1965-. Mbrships: Phi Beta Kappa; Treas., Pres., Delta Gamma, 1954; Delta Gamma Alumnae Assn., 1958; City Recommendations Chmn., V.P., Pres., ibid; MLA; S. Atlantic MLA; V.P., Alpha Lambda Delta, 1956; Delta Kappa Gamma; Treas., Univ. of S. Ala. Womens Club, 1973-74. Ala. Conservancy. Publs: Thaumaturgist's Prophecy; On Incompatibility. Address: Engl. Dept., Univ. of S. Ala., Mobile, AL 36688, U.S.A. 76, 125.

LEATON, Edward K., b. 2 Oct. 1928. Acturarial & Consulting Company Executive. Educ: B.S., M.E., Lehigh Univ., Pa.; M.B.A., Yale Univ. Appts: Grad. Instr Yale Univ., 1949-50; Trainee-Asst. Supt., Gen. Motors Corp., 1950-54; V.P., Dir. of Mfg., Rows Mfg. Co., 1954-57; Dir., Va. Fibre Corp.; Gen. Agt., Edward K. Leaton Agcy.; Cons., Lambert M. Huppeler Co. Inc., 1957-69, Exec. V.P., 1969-74, Pres. & Dir, 1974-; Pres. & Dir., Leaton & Huppeler Co. Inc., 1967-. Mbrships. incl: Am. Soc. of Pension Actuaries; Comm. of Nat. Cystic Fibrosis Fndn.; Leadership Comm., Community Fund; Am. Ord. Assn.; Chmn. of Bd., Life Underwriters Assn., N.Y.; Assn. Adv. Life Und.; Union League & Yale Clubs. Contbr. to num. profl. jrnls. & speaker to nat. & regional orgs. Address: Maplewood Drive, Darien, CT 06820, U.S.A. 2, 6.

LEAVITT, Joseph Stevenson, b. 11 Sept. 1905. Physician. Educ: B.S., Webster Univ., 1931; M.D., Univ. of Lausanne, Switzerland, 1936; Postgrad. Study, Tchng. Hosps., Paris, Vienna, Brussels, 1936-37. Appts: Pres., U.S. Drug & Chem. Corp., 1957; Past Trustee, Mass. Lying-in & Gen. Hosp., U.S.A.; Past Pres., Webster Manor Hosp., 1957-59; Dir., Surety Bank & Trust Co., Wakefield, 1960-72; Former Pres. & Chmn. of Bd., ibid. Mbrships: AMA; Mass. Med. Soc.; Israel Med. Soc.; Bd. of Trustees, YMCA, 1972-; Dir., Wakefield YMCA, 1949-72; Dir., Am. Red Cross, 1972-; Nat. Geograph. Soc.; Am. Jewish Congress; Brandeis Univ. Assn.; New Century Club; 32° Mason (Shriner); Elks; Kiwanis Int.; Nat. Chautauqua Soc.; Hon. Treas. & Past Pres., Temple Emmanuel of Wakefield; Donor w. wife of "Interfaith Me. to 4 Chapts.". Address: 8 Avon St., Wakefield, MA 01880, U.S.A. 6, 55, 128.

LeBATO, Loretta Ann Thibodeaux, b. 15 Aug. 1935. Associate Professor of Physical Education. Educ: B.S., McNeese State Univ., Lake Charles, La., 1956; M.Ed., ibid, 1963; M.S.Ed., 1965; Ph.D., Tex. Woman's Univ., 1970. Appts: St. Charles Acad., 1956-57; w. Calcusieu Parish Schl. Bd., Oak Pk. Jr. H.S., 1958, La Grange Jr. H.S., 1958-61, 1962-64, F.K. White Jr. H.S., 1964-66; Instr., McNeese State Univ., 1966-69, Asst. Prof., 1970-71, Assoc. Prof., 1971-. Mbrships. incl: Am. Assn. Hlth., Phys. Educ. & Recreation; Am. Schl. Hlth. Assn.; Am. Coll. of Sports Med.; Treas., La. Omicron Chapt., Alpha Delta Kappa. Papers & articles, profl. jrnls. Hon. selection for presentation of rsch. paper, Nat. Convention, Am. Assn. Hlth., Phys. Educ. & Recreation, Detroit, Mich., 1971. Address: 521 Orchard Dr., Lake Charles, LA 70601, U.S.A. 125.

LE BRETON, Constant Jules, b. 11 Mar. 1895. Artist. Expositions incl: Salon des Artistes Indépendants; Salon d'Automne; Salon des Tuileries; (pvte. exhibs.) Galerie Durand Ruel; Galerie Schmit, etc. Illustrator, var. books. Num. portraits inclng: Maréchal Pétain; Léon Binet; H. Mondoz; G. Portmann; Léon Jouhaux; Beatrice Bretty; Charles Dullin; Mrs. Davis Somerset; Maximilien Luce; Ingrid Bergmann, etc. Hons. incl: Chevalier, Legion of Hon.; Florence Blumenthal Prize; Fragonard Prize; Grand Prix, Ile de France. Address: 21 Rue Visconti, Paris 6, France.

Le CAIN, Errol John, b. 5 Mar. 1941. TV Commercial Designer; Book Illustrator. Educ: St. Joseph's Instn., Singapore. Appts: Designer & Animator Pearl & Dean, 1956-60, & Richard Williams Films Ltd., 1960-68; Free-lance artist, as book illustrator & designer & animator for TV Commercials, 1968-. Publs. incl: King Arthur's Sword; The Cabbage Princess; Sir Orfeo (by Anthea Davis), illustrator only; The Faber Book of Children's Songs, illustrator; Rhymes & Verses (by Walter De la mare), illustrator; The Rime of the Ancient Mariner, illustrator; The Lotus & the Grail (by R. Harris), illustrator. Work shown at Woodstock Gall., London, 1974. Address: 80 Grove Park Terr., London W4, U.K. 3.

LECKIE, H. Keith, b. 18 Apr. 1911. Agricultural Economist. Educ: Elem. Tchng. Cert., London Normal Schl., 1929; B.A., Univ. of Western Ont., 1937; B.A., ibid, 1938; M.A., Univ. of Toronto, 1948. Appts: Economist, Economics Div., Canada Dept. of Agric., Ottawa, 1938-45; Prof. of Agricultural Economics, Ont. Agricultural Coll., Guelph, 1945-50; Acting Hd. of Dept., ibid, 1949; Dir., Info. Servs., Meat Packers Coun. of Canada, 1951-54; Sec. Treas., ibid, 1954-60; Gen. Mgr., 1960-. Mbrships. incl: Pres., Canadian Agric. Economics Soc., 1953; V.P., Agricultural Inst. of Canada, 1968; Pres., Central Ont. Br., Ont. Inst. of Agrologists, 1964; Dir., Roayl Agric. Winter Fair, 1960-; Agricultural Rsch. Inst. of Ont. Author of num. publs. in field. Address: Meat Packers Coun. of Canada, 5233 Dundas St. W., Islington, Ont., Canada.

LECOCQ, René Gabriel, b. 27 June 1897. Retired Professor; Mayor. Educ: Tchng. Cert. & Dip., Adv. Engl. Studies, Fac. of Letters, Lille, France. Appts: Asst. Prof., Lycée d' Haubourdin, until 1932; Prof., Lycée de Tourcoing, until 1958; Elected Dpty., legislature, 1958; Mayor, Tourcoing, 1959-; Gen. Councillor, N. of France, 1964-; V.P., Lille Urban Community, 1968-; Mbr., Nat. Couns. of Slaughterhouses & Water. Mbrships: Financial Agcy. of Artois-Picardie Basin; Comm., Artois-Picardie Basin; Admin. Coun., Regional Comm. for Maladjusted Children & Adolescents. Hons. incl: Chevalier, Legion of Hon., 1968; Cmdr., Order of Acad. Palms, 1970; Silver Medal, Youth & Sports, 1971; Off., Nat. Order of Merit, 1973; Cross of Chevalier, Order of Leopold, 1969; var. war medals. Address: 353 Rue du Blanc Seau, 59200 Tourcoing, France.

LECOQUE, Al., b. 21 Mar. 1891. Artist; Sculptor; Writer. Educ: studied w. individual tutors, Prague & Zegreb; Acad. des Beaux Arts, Paris, France; studied w. painter, Emile Bernard in Paris & in the company of sev. notable painters & sculptors inclng. Renoir. Work included in pub. & pvte. collects. in Europe & U.S.A. Pvte. Collects. incl: Pres.' Eisenhower & Nixon, U.S.A. Pub. Collects. incl: Mus. of City of Prague; Mus. of Old Montmartre, Paris; Okla. Art Ctr., Okla City, U.S.A; Mus. of Mod. Art, Israel. Exhibd. in num. Grop. shows inclng. Biennales of Venice, 1926, 1928 & w. Emile Bernard, Frederick B. Anthon Gall., Beverly

Hills, 1963. One Man Exhibs. incl: Gall. Andre, Paris, 1925; Gall. Galic, Split, Yugoslavia, 1940; Nat. Gall. of Mod. Art, Rome Italy, 1949, 1950; Metcalf Gall. of Art, L.A., Calif., 1958; Lilienfeld Gall., N.Y., 1968; Continental Art Gall., San Fran., 1970; Univ. of Santa Clara, Calif., 1970. Publs: Renoir My Friend; Girl With A Wooden Leg; Capri, Unfinished Portrait; Tragique Weekend; Painter David. Hons. incl: 1st Prize, Archt. Turek, Prague, 1914; Gold Medal, Soc. des Arts, Scis., Lettres, Parris, 1966. Address: 8079 Selma Ave., L.A., CA 90046, U.S.A. 37, 59, 105.

LEDBETTER, Barbara A. Neal, b. 24 Nov. 1925. Teacher; Archivist; Writer. Educ: B.S., N. Tex. State Univ., 1947; M.E., W. Tex. State Univ., 1954. Appts: Tchr., Tex. Pub. Schls., 1947-; Archivist, Ft. Belknap Archives, Newcastle, Tex. Mbrships: Tex. State Tchrs. Assn.; Life Mbr., Tex. Ind. Arts Assn.; Ft. Belknap Soc.; Ft. Belknap Genealogical Assn.; Graham's Womans Club; Chapparal Dinner Club. Author, 16 books, 1961-. Weekly hist. features, Graham News, local hist. news features, Tex. Sunday newspapers. Contbr., mags., bulletins, brochures. Lectures & broadcasts. Address: Murray Route, Graham, TX 76046, U.S.A. 5, 125.

LEDERER, Katherine Gay, b. 19 Mar. 1932. Professor of English. Educ: B.A., Sam Houston State Univ., 1952; M.A., Univ. of Ark., 1958; Ph.D., ibid, 1967. Appts: Tchr., Houston Pub. Schls., 1953-56; Grad. Asst., Instr., Univ. of Ark., 1956-60; Prof., Engl., Southwest Mo. State Univ., 1960-. Mbrships: AAUP; MLA; Alpha Psi Omega; Bd. Mbr., Planned Parenthood; Springfield Little Theatre. Address: 614 S. Holland, Springfield, MO 65806, U.S.A. 5, 13, 120.

LEDOUX, André, b. 29 Nov. 1919. Professor. Educ: Facs. of Sci., Paris & Bordeaux, France; Agrégé, Natural Scis., 1945; Docteur ès Scis., 1949; Engr., ORSTOM, 1946. Appts: Researcher, Ivory Coast, 1946-50; Lectr., Fac. of Scis., Toulouse & Ecole Nat. Supérieure Agronomique, 1950-53; Prof., 1953-57; Prof., Chair of Applied Zool., 1957-; Dir., Nat. Inst. of Univ. Studies, Yaoundi, Cameroon & Fndr., Fed. Univ., 1961-63; Hon. Vice-Chancellor of the Univ., 1964. Mbrships: Soc. of Entomol., Zool., & Ecol., Pres., French Sect., Int. Union for Study of Social Insects; V.P., Fndr., Soc. for Protection of Nature in Midi-Pyrenees. Publs: La Biologie et le Comportement des Fourmis; l'Entomologie Forestière, Hons: Prize, Entomol. Soc. of France; Off., Nat. Order of Acad. Palms. Address: Clairval, Chemin de Pechbusque, 31400 Pouvourville, Toulouse, France. 43, 91.

LEE, (Sir) Desmond, b. 30 Aug. 1908. College Administrator; University Academic. Educ: Corpus Christi Coll., Cambridge, 1927-31. Appts: Fellow, Corpus Christi Coll., 1933-48, Tutor, 1935-48, Univ. Lectr. in Classics, 1935-48; Headmaster, Clifton Coll., 1948-54, Winchester Coll., 1954-68; Fellow, Wolfson Coll., 1968-73; Pres., Hughes Hall, Cambridge, 1974-. Mbr., Headmasters' Conf., 1948-68, Chmn., 1959-60, 1967. Publs: Zeno of Elea; Aristotle Meteorologica; Plato: Republic; Plato: Timaeus of Critias. Articles, var. periodicals. Hons: Charles Oldham Schol., Cambridge Univ., 1930; Kt. Bachelor, 1961; Litt.D., Nottingham Univ. Address: 8 Barton Close, Cambridge, CB3 9LQ, U.K. 1.

LEE, J. Murray, b. 25 Oct. 1904. Professor. Educ: A.B., Occidental Coll., 1926; A.M., Tchrs. Coll., Columbia Univ., 1928; Ph.D., ibid, 1934. Appts. incl: Dean, Schl. of Educ., Wash.

State Univ., 1941-54; Prof., ibid, 1954-56; Prof., Univ. of Miami, 1956-58; Chmn., Dept. of Elem. Educ., Southern III. Univ., 1958-68; Prof., ibid, 1968-73; Prof. Emeritus, 1973-. Mbrships: Phi Delta Kappa; Am. Educl. Rsch. Assn.; Assn. for Supvsn. & Curric. Dev.; Profs. of Curric. Publs: Lee Clark Reading Readiness Test, 1931, '63; The Child & His Curriculum, 1940, '50, '60; The Child & His Development, 1958; Foundations of Elementary Education, 1969; Elementary Education, 1967, '73. Address: 907 Taylor Dr., Carbondale, IL 62901, U.S.A. 2, 8, 15, 141.

LEE, (John) Robert Jr. b. 22 July, 1921. Physician; Pediatrician. Educ; A.B. Columbia Coll., N.Y.C., 1943; M.D., Cornell Univ., Med. Coll., 1946; Pediatric Res., N.Y. Med. Coll. 1954-56; Fellow, Pediatric Neurol. & Psych. ibid, 1956-57; Fellow, Pediatric Endocrinol. Johns Hopkins Hosp., Balt., Md., 1957-58. Appts. incl; Pysn.; Feight Surg., USN. 1949-54; Asst. Prof. Pediatrics, N.Y. Med. Coll. 1960-; Dir. Profl. Trng. & Assoc. Dir. Pediatrics, Ctr. for Mental Retardation, ibid, 1962-70; Pvte. Pediatric Prac., Flushing, N.Y., 1961-; Fed. Aviation Med. Examiner, 1965 w. Adolescent & Young Adult Drug Addiction Progs., Brooklyn & Queens, 1972-; Pediatric Cons. in CP, N.Y.C. Dept. Hlth., Bur. Child Hlth. & Handicapped Children, 1963-71; Hd. Start Cons., Am. Acad. Pediatrics, 1967-; Med. Dir. Assn. for Children's Retarded Mental Dev. 1970-; Bd. of Dirs., Jill Famm Fndn., N.Y.C., 1971-; Attng. Pediatrician, Flower 5th Ave, Hosp. & Metropol. Hosps., N.Y.C., 1961-. Schl. Hlth. Cons., N.Y.C. Dept. of Hlth., 1973-. Mbrships. incl: Fellow, Am. Acad. Pediatrics; Am. Coll. Physns., Am. Acad. Cerebral Palsy; Royal Soc. Med.; Dipl., Am. Bd. Pediatrics & Nat. Bd. Med. Examiners; AAAS; Am. Assn. on Mental Deficiency; Am. Soc. Human Genetics; N.Y. Acad. Scis.; Columbia Club; N.Y.C. Mil. Order of World Wars; Navy League. Author, Mental Retardation Inventory, for Assn. for Children w. Retarded Mental Dev., 1973, & publs. in field. Recip. N.Y. State Regents Schlrship., 1940-43. Address: 162-16, 35th Ave., Flushing, NY 11358, U.S.A. 2, 6, 17, 57.

LEE, Margaret H.Y., b. 23 Mar. 1940. Librarian. Educ: B.A., Taiwan Provincial Chung-Hsing Univ., China, 1961; M.L.S., George Peabody Coll. of Tchrs., Nashville, Tenn., 1964. Appts: Asst. Cataloger, Lincoln Mem. Lib., S.D. State Univ., Brookings, 1965-66; Ref. & Cataloging Libn., Ingham Co. Lib., Mason, Mich., 1966-70; Cataloger & Rdr.'s Advsr., Fresno Co. Free Lib., Fresno, Calif., 1971-. Mbr., China Inst. of Land Econs. & Land Reform, Taiwan, China. Feature articles, Central Daily News, Taiwan. Address: Fresno County Free Library, 2420 Mariposa, Fresno, CA, U.S.A.

LEE, Patsie Sinkey (Mrs. Earl E. Lee). Motion Picture Producer. Educ: Grad., Superior State Tchrs. Coll., 1925; Postgrad., Univ. of Minn., 1925-26, Univ. of Wash., 1931. Appts: Feature writer, rotogravure type releases, Seattle Times, 1931; Mag., rotogravure, non fiction releases through A.P., U.P.I., Acme, Pictorial Press of London, Seattle Times, Seattle Post Intelligence, Seattle Star, 1932-46; Prod., films, Wash. State Game Dept., Seattle, 1946-; Supvsr., P.R. Dept., ibid, 1949; Prod. films, for Warner Bros. Studio, Burbank, released in 1948 & 1949. Mbr., Nat. League of Am. Pen Women. Hons: Matrix Table Award 1946; Nat. League of Am. Pen Women Award, 1948. Address: Pinehurst Rd., Bend, OR 97701, U.S.A. 5, 9.

LEE, Polly Jae (pseudonym, Jae Gardiner Lee) (Mrs. Richard H. Lee), b. 26 Nov. 1929. Author; Lecturer; Poetess. Educ: B.S., Univ. of Hawaii; M.S., Philathea Coll., London, Ont., Canada. Appts. incl: Writer of tech. manuals, Ohio Wholesale Wine Dealers, Columbus, U.S.A., 1956-57, Annie Whittemyer Home (orphanage), Davenport, Iowa, 1960; Hd. of tech. processing, Grand Rapids Pub. Lib., Mich., 1960-61; Dir., Waterford Lib., ibid, 1962-65; Acquisition Libn., 1965-67, Dir. of E. Side Br., 1969-72, Asst. Ref. Libn., 1967-69, Pontiac Pub. Libs., Mich.; Has devoted time to writing, 1972-. Mbrships: incl: Offs., Multiple Sclerosis Soc.; ALA; Mich. Lib. Assn.; Soc. of Friends; Democrat; Women's Int. League for Peace & Freedom; Fellowship of Reconcilliation. Publs: Poems in Friends Jrnl., Child Life, etc.; Articles in var. lib. & profl. jrnls.; Short stories in Am. Hist. & Hist. Today; Books incl: Wine Growing in the United States, 1958; Manual for House Parents, 1960. Winner of awards. Address: 299 Auburn Ave., Pontiac, MI 48058, U.S.A. 30, 57, 130.

LEE, Rern, b. 19 Sept. 1938. Painter. Educ: Grad., Nanyang Acad. of Fine Arts, Singapore. Appts: worked w. father in his studio for sev. yrs; Singapore, England, France, Italy, Holland & Germany, 1967-72. Represented in permanent collects: Indonesian Pres. Palaces, Jakarta & Bogor; Nanyang Univ. Mus., Singapore. Mbrships. incl: Soc. of Chinese Artists in Indonesia; S.E. Asia Art Assn. Address: Jalan Gedong 11-A, Jakarta VI/16, Indonesia.

LEE, Ryang, b. 6 July 1915. Professor. Educ: Grad., Keijo Tech. Coll., 1937; Grad., Tokyo Inst. of Technol., 1941; Dr. Eng., Seoul Nat. Univ., 1962. Appts: Prof., Dept. of Mech. Engrng., Coll. of Engrng., Seoul Nat. Univ., 1946-; Dean, Coll. of Engrng., ibid, 1963-69; Chmn., Korean Soc. of Mech. Engrs., 1960-62; Mbr., Econ. & Sci. Advsry. Comm., R.O.K., 1968-; Trustee, Korea Advanced Inst. of Sci., 1971-. Mbrships: Korean Soc. Mech. Engrs.; Korea Sci. Club. Contbr. articles to profl. jrnls. Hons: Camellia Medal, R.O.K., 1972. Address: 5-9 Dongsung-dong, Seoul, Repub. of Korea.

LEE, Sylvan Burton, b. 5 Jan. 1916. Biochemist; Industrial Executive. Educ: B.S., Univ. of Wis., 1938; M.S., ibid, 1939, Ph.D., 1943. Appts. incl: Serv. to Lt., Jr. Grade, USNR, 1944-46; Hd. Streptomycin Plant, Merck & Co., Elkton, N.J., 1945-47, Supt. of Fermentation, Rahway, N.J., 1947-50; Dir., Supt., Mgr., var. depts., E.R. Squibb & Sons, New Brunswick, N.J., 1950-54; Asst. to Pres., E.R. Squibb & Sons Div., Olin Mathieson Chem. Corp., N.Y.C., & overseas assignments, . Am. & Europe, 1954-58; V.P., Dir. Ops., Sales & Hunter Co., Chgo., 1958-62, Divl. V.P. Gen. Mgr., 1962-65; Gen. Mgr., Fine Chems. Chem. Div. of Gen. Mills Inc., 1965-70, V.P. Biochems., Gen. Mills Chems. Inc., Mpls., 1970-. Mbr., Profl. orgs. Num. profl. publs. Indl. fermentations, antibiotics. Recip., Army Commendation Award. Address: General Mills Chemicals Inc., 4620 W. 77th St., Minneapolis, MN 55435, U.S.A. 8, 16.

LEE, Thomas Edward, b. 6 Apr. 1914. Archaeologist. Educ: B.A., Wayne Univ., 1944; Postgrad. study, Univ. of Toronto, Canada & Univ. of Chgo.; M.A., Anthropol., Univ. of Mich., 1949; Doctoral studies, ibid, 1949-50. Appts: Anthropologist, Nat. Mus. of Canada, Ottowa, 1950-59; Fndng. Dir., Anthropological Assn. of Canada, 1963-, & Ed., Anthropological Jrnl. of Canada; Fndng. Dir., Guild of Am. Prehistorians, 1964-; Vis. Prof., Ctr. for Nordic Studies, Laval Univ., P.Q.,

1966-. Mbrships: Fellow, Instuto Interamericano; Hon. Life Mbr., Order of Conquerors of the North; Hon. Life Mbr., Ont. Archaeol. Soc.; Fellow, Pa. Inst. of Anthropol. Over 100 archaeological publs. inclng: Archaeological Investigations of a longhouse, Pamiok Island, Ungava, 1970; Archaeological Findings, Gyrfalcon to Eider Islands, Ungava, 1970. Hons: King's Honour List, Mentioned in Despatches, Jan., 1946. Address: 1575 Forlan Drive, Ottawa, Ont. KC2 OR8, Canada. 6.

LEE, Ting Hui, b. 5 May 1931. Educator. Educ: M.A., Univ. of Singapore. Appts. incl: Pol. Sec., Min. of Culture, Singapore, 1959; Dpty. Dir., Pol. Study Ctr., ibid, 1964-71; Vis. Prof., Hist. Dept., Nanyang Univ., 1968-69; Dept. of Pol. Sci., Univ. of Western Ont., Canada, 1971-72; currently Sr. Rsch. Assoc., Inst. of S.E. Asian Studies, Singapore. Mbrships: Pres., Island Soc., Singapore, Singapore Assn. Writers; V.P., S.E. Asian Soc., Singapore; Councillor, China Soc., ibid; Pyramid Club. Publs. incl: Selected Poems; Philosophical Essays; Theoretical Observations of Political Practice in the Republic; Anthology of Chinese Literature in Malaysia & Singapore; Kuo Mojo' Interpretations of the Pre-Ts'In Philosophers. Recip., Pub. Serv. Star, Repub. of Singapore, 1969. Address: Inst. of S.E. Asian Studies, Univ. of Singapore, Singapore. 98.

LEE, William Arthur. Antiquarian Bookseller; Painter. Educ: St. Aloysius Coll., Glasgow, U.K. One-Man Exhib., Glasgow, 1968-69. Major Works, Oil & Water Colours. Mbrships: Coun., Univ. of Glasgow Bibliographical Soc.; Washing Green Soc., Glasgow; Antiquarian Booksellers' Assn. Author of Bibliographical Publs. Hons: Mil. decorations, 1946. Address: 90 St. Mary's St., Ely, Cambs., CB7 4HH, U.K. 133.

LEE OF ASHERIDGE, Jennie (Lady) b. 3 Nov. 1904. Writer; Lecturer. M.A. & LL.B., Edinburgh Univ. Appts: Tchr., 1928-29; Elected House of Commons, 1929-31 & 45-70; House of Lords, 1971-. Mbrships: Tribune Dir. until 1964; Nat. Exec., Labour Pty., until 1970; Anglo-Chinese Cultural Comm. Publs: Russia Our Ally; Tomorrow is A New Day (in U.S. called This Great Journey). Hons: Prizeman, Roman Law & Constitutional Hist., Edinburgh Univ., 1925; Privy Councellor, 1967; Hon. Deg., Open Univ., 1973. Address: 67 Chester Row, London SW1 U.K. 1.

LEECH, Clifford, b. 16 Jan. 1909. University Professor; Author. Educ: B.A., Queen Mary Coll., Univ. of London, 1930; M.A., ibid, 1932; Ph.D., 1935. Appts. incl: Lectr.-Sr. Lectr.-Prof., Univ. of Durham, U.K., 1936-63; Prin., St. Cuthbert's Soc., Durham, 1946-52; Dean, Fac. of Arts, Univ. of Durham, 1959-61; Prof., Univ. of Toronto, Canada, 1963-. Fellow, Royal Soc. of Canada, 1969. Publs. incl: Shakespeare's Tragedies & Other Studies, 1950; John Ford & the Drama of his Time, 1957; The John Fletcher Plays, 1962; Tragedy (The Critical Idiom), 1969; The Dramatist's Experience with other Essays in Literary Theory, 1970. Hons: Doct., Univ. of Clermont-Ferrand, 1962; D.Litt., Acadia Univ., Nova Scotia, Canada, 1969. Address: Dept. of English, Univ. Coll., Toronto, Canada. 1, 131.

LEEDY, Emily L. (Mrs. William N. Leedy), b. 24 Sept. 1921. Educator; Counselor. Educ: B.S., Rio Grande Coll.; M.Ed., Ohio Univ. Appts: Tchr., 1941-56; Counselor, 1956-60; Univ. Counselor, Prof. & Admnstr., 1960-69; Dir., Guidance, Cath. Latin Schl., Cleveland, Ohio, 1969-71; Dir., Womens Servs. Div., Ohio Bur. of Employment Servs., Columbus, 1971-.

Mbrships: Pres., Ohio Commn. on Status of Women, 1971-72; Womens Equity Action League; Womens City Club of Cleveland; Pres., Cleveland Coun. on Status of Women, 1970-72; Treas., Zonta Club of Berea, 1970-72; Delta Kappa Gamma; Phi Delta Gamma. Hons: Cleveland Woman of Achievement, 1969; Nike Award, Ohio Fed. of Bus. & Profl. Womens Clubs, 1973; Emily Leedy Schlrship named by Tau Chapt., Delta Kappa Gamma, 1974. Address: 580 Lindberg Blvd., Berea, OH 44017, U.S.A. 5, 8, 128, 130, 132, 138.

LEEF, Nimrod, b. 18 Nov. 1924. Engineer; Architect; Town Planner; Geologist; Geodesist. Educ: Hebrew Univ., Mtn. Scopus; Technion, Haifa. Appts: Dir., Photogrammetric Inst., Jerusalem, 1951-; Dir., The Photogrammetric & Engrng. Co. Ltd., 1968-; Chief Archt. & Town Planner, Min. of Jerusalem, 1964-65; Town Planner & Co-Author of master plan, The City of Rishon Lezion, 1958-68; Pvte. Cons., var. dev. projs. in Israel, 1968-74. Mbrships: Assn. of Engrs. & Archts. in Israel; Union of Archts., Israel; Union of Engrs., Israel; Am. Soc. of Photogrammetry; Registered Engr. & Archt.; Jerusalem Mgmt. Independent Liberal Party, Israel. Publs. incl: Master-Plan - Rishon Lezion City of 100,000 Inhabitants; Israel first Land Use 1:20,000 scale. Address: P.O. Box 7211, Jerusalem, Israel.

LEE LOY, (Mrs.) Marion Frances Kaleleonalani McGregor, b. 28 Nov. 1911. Educator. Educ: B.A., Univ. of Hawaii, 1933; 5th yr. Cert., ibid, 1934. Appts. incl: Tchr: Hilo Intermediate, 1937-42. '42-45; Hilo H.S., 1945-47, '50-51; Kaahumanu, 1952-53; Kapalama Schl., 1953-60; Farrington H.S., 1960-. Mbrships. incl: Pres., Hawaii State Classroom Tchrs.' Assn., 1961-63 & Oahu Classroom Tchrs.' Assn., 1959-60; Dir., Hawaii Educ. Assn., 1963-65; Trustee, Hawaii Educ. Assn., 1971-74; Pres., Oahu Educ. Assn., 1965-66 & Kamehameha Alumnae Assn., 1952-55; Pres., YWCA Fedn. 1964-65; State Pres., Chi State, Kappa Kappa Iota, 1968-70 & Delta Conclave, ibid, 1971-73; Gov.'s Commn. on Status of Women, 1964-66; Beta State Parliamentarian, Delta Kappa Gamma, 1971-73. Address: 1322 Kapalama Ave., Honolulu, HI 86817, U.S.A.

LEFF, Vera Miriam (Mrs.) Journalist. Educ: Dip. in Sociol. Free-lance writer, working in collaboration w. late husband, mainly on soc. med. Mbrships: Humanist Soc.; Chmn., original grp., campaign for nuclear disarmament. Publs. incl: Non-fiction: The Greatness of London; Scunthorpe-our town; Riverside Story (The History of the Borough of Bermondsey); The Story of Tower Hamlets; Fiction: The Struggle; The Wife of the Prisoner; books in collaboration w. Dr. S. Leff (sev. trans.); articles in jrnls. Address: 598 Finchley Rd., London, NW11 7RX, U.K. 3.

LEGAN, William E(verett), b. 28 Feb. 1902. Business Management & Training Consultant. Educ: B.S., SW Mo. State Coll., 1929; M.S., Wash. Univ., St. Louis, Mo., 1940. Appts: HS Tchr. & Prin., SW Mo. High Schls., 1923-29; Southwestern Bell Telephone, St. Louis, 1929-67; Cons., Top Mgmt. Seminar, Army Mgmt. Engrn. Trng. Admin., 1967-69; Trustee, Mo. Valley Coll., 1944-; Pres., ibid, 1970-72; Episcopal-Presby. Fndn. for Aging: Bd. Dirs., 1961-, V.P., 1961-70, & Pres. 1970-; Pres., Episc. Presby. Fndn. for the Ageing; Trustee, Mo. Valley Coll.; Presby. Elder. Mrbships. incl: Am. Econ. Assn.; Am. Acad. Pol. & Soc. Sci.; Wash. Univ. Alumni Club; Beta Gamma Sigma; Omicron Chi Epsilon. Hons: L.H.D., Mo. Valley

Coll., 1963. Address: 1179 Kirkham Rd., St Louis, MO 63122, U.S.A. 8, 16, 120, 128, 130.

LEGAULT, Maurice J., b. 31 May 1926 Company President. Educ: Bus. course, Forti Bus. Coll., Canada; Sr. George Williams Univ. M.MM.C., M.T.C., Univ. of Western Ont. Appts Mgr., Pure Spring Bottling Co., 1952-54; Sales Supvsr., La Brasserie Labatt Limitée, 1954 Montreal Sales Mgr., ibid, 1956; Territoria Sales Mgr., 1958; Sales Gen. Mgr., 1962; V.P. & Marketing Mgr., 1965; V.P. & Gen. Mgr., 1969 Pres. & Gen. Dir., 1971. Mbrships. incl Chevaliers de Colomb; Montreal Chmbr. o Comm.; Advt. & Sales Execs. Club of Montreal Sales & Marketing Execs. of Montreal; Clul Canadien; Dir., Grands Ballets Canadiens; Lif Dir., Notre-Dame Hosp. & Festival Int. d Musique; Exec. Comm., Palestre Nationale Canadian Cancer Soc.; Exec. mbr., Canadia Safety Coun.; Dir., Canadian Profl. Golfer Assn., Quebec. Address: 50 Labatt St., LaSalle Quebec, Canada.

LEGERE, Martin J., b. 17 Nov. 1916 Business Executive. Educ: St. Francis Xavie Univ., Antigonish, N.S., Canada; Fac. Soc. Scis. Laval Univ., Quebec. Appts. incl: Fieldman Coop. Movement, St. Francis Xavier Univ. 1938-40; Auditor, Credit Unions & Coops. N.B., 1940-46; Gen. Mgr., La Fedn. des Caisse Populaires Acadiennes, 1946-, La Soc d'Assurance des Caisses Populaires Acadiennes 1948-; V.P., Newspaper 'Evangeline', 1950-65 Pres., Caraquet Schl. Bd., 1960-65 Directorships incl: La Caisse Populaire d Caraquet, 1938-71; Maritime Provs. Bd. o Trade, 1954-62; La Soc. des Artisans; Caraque Hosp.; Le Conseil de Vie Française; Coop. Ins Servs., 1964-. Mbrships. incl: Treas., Children' Aid Soc., Gloucester Co., 1948-66; Pres., Cath Youth Assn., 1940-50; Sec., Caraquet Chmbr of Comm.; Pres., N.B. Indl. Finance Bd.; Ctr Comm., Int. Coop. Alliance, 1967-. Hons. incl Bene Merentis Medal, M.C.S., St. Joseph Univ. 1950; Dr. Admin. Scis., Mocton Univ., 1971 Address: C.P. 90, Caraquet, N.B., Canada, 3, 6 16, 57, 131.

LEGGETT, Douglas Malcolm Aufrère, b. 2 May 1912. University Administrator. Educ M.A., Trinity Coll., Cambridge, U.K., 193 Ph.D., 1939; D.Sc., London, 1960. Appts Lectr., Maths. Queen Mary Coll., London Univ 1937-39; Royal Aircraft Est., Farnborough Hants., 1939-45; Dpty. Sec., Royal Aeronau Soc., 1945-50; Rdr., Applied Maths., King Coll., London, 1950-60; Prin., Battersea Col of Technol., 1960-66; Vice-Chancellor, Univ. c Surrey. Fellowships: Royal Aeronaut. Soc Inst. of Maths. & Its. Applications. Contbr. t Sci. & tech. jrnls. Address: Univ. of Surrey Guildford, Surrey GU2 5XH, U.K. 43, 47.

LEGGETTE, Earl Charles, b. 3 July 1940 University Professor; Educationa Administrator. Educ: A.B., Rust Coll., Holl Springs, Miss., 1963; M.A.T., Miss. State Univ. 1969; Ed.D., Rutgers Univ., 1973. Appts Maths. & Sci. Tchr., Hunter H.S., Drew, Miss. 1962-65; Instr. & Coord., Maths. & Sci. Dept. Utica Jr. Coll., Miss., 1966-71; Assoc. Prof. o Educ., Assoc. Dir., Tchr. Corps, Jackson Stat Univ., Miss., 1973-. Mbrships. incl: AAUP Fndng. Mbr., Jackson Bike Assn.; Miss. Tchrs Assn.; NEA; Math. Assn. of Am.; Nat. Coun. o Tchrs. of Maths.; Phi Delta Kappa; Mu Sigma Phi Beta Sigma; Wash. Valley Hunting Club Pres., Utica Mens Club. Author, profl. papers Hons. incl: Tchr. of Yr. Award, 1965; Fore Fndn. Fellowship, 1967, '68. Address: 470 Village Dr., Jackson, MS 39206, U.S.A. 125.

LEGGITT, Dorothy, b. 19 Feb. 1903. Professor of Education; Secretary. Educ: T.D., Univ. of Ill., Charlston; Ph.D., Univ. of Chgo., Ill., 1930; M.A., ibid, 1933. Appts: Tchr., var. Ill. schls., 1920-35, 52-54; Critic Tchr., Northern Ill. State Univ., DeKalb, 1936-37; HS Tchr., Clayton, Mo., & Critic, Wash. Univ., St. Louis, 1937-52; Tchr. Specialist, Park Ridge, Ill., 1954-61; Reading Specialist, Joliet Jr. Coll. (Ill.), Skokie (Ill.) & Kenosha (Wis.), 1961-65; Study Skills Clinician, Jr. Coll., Palm Beach, Fla., 1965-73; Prof. & Lectr., summer sessions at num. colls. & univs.; has held summer positions as Sec. in Bus. inclng. Supvsr. of Typing Off., Union Carbide & Carbon Co., & Hd. of Women's Div., Zinser Personnel Serv. Mbrships: Int. Reading Assn.; Nat. Reading Conf; DAR; Pi Lambda Theta; Ill. Educ. Assn.; Century & Alumni Clubs, Univ. of Chgo.; Alumni Assn., Univ. of Ill. Publs: Study Skills, 1945; num. articles in jrnls. Hons: Walgreen Fndn. Award in Soc., Civic & Pol. Instns., 1944; Pi Lambda Theta Schlrships. Award; Citizenship Award, USO, St. Louis. Address: P.O. Box 1432, Chicago, IL 60690, U.S.A. 5, 125.

LEGNANI, Emilio, b. 3 Mar. 1918. Retired Naval Officer; Vice Chief Pilot, Genoa Harbour. Educ: Royal Naval Academy, Italy. Appts: Active serv., Italian Navy, retired in rank of Cmdr.; V.P., Radar Observer Schl., Genoa; Mbr., Merchant Marine Acad.; Counsellor, Italian Inst. of Navigation, Rome; Vice Chief Pilot, Genoa Harbour. Mbrships: Italian Maritime Capts.; Nat. Pres., ibid; Int. Fedn. Master Marine Assns., London, U.K.; V.P., ibid; Italian Yacht Club, Genoa; Golf Club of Rapallo, ibid; Navy Club, Rome; Navy Sailing Club, ibid. Publ: Paper on Radar Training for Merchant Marine Officers. Hons: Cross for Mil. Gallantry, 1941; Gold Medal, Mil. Gallantry, 1942; 3 Crosses for Mil. Merit; Kt., Crown of Italy; Off. Kt. of Italian Repub. Address: Via Assarotti 7, Genoa, Italy. 43, 95.

LEGRIS, Jacques Marie Albert René, b. 22 Feb. 1919. Journalist; Writer; Script-writer. Educ: Schl. of Pol. Scis., France; Fac. of Law & Letters, Paris. Appts: Dpty. Dir., Off. of French Radio-diffusion & TV, (ORTF), 1945; Dir., U.K. Sect., ibid, 1948, Responsible for Paris Tribune, 1960, Ed., Tribunals & Debates, 1962-68, Dir., Documentation Serv., 1969-. Mbrships. incl: Soc. of Men of Letters; Nat. Syndicate of Translators; Soc. of Dramatic Authors & Composers. Publs. incl: Toros, Aficion et Gastronomie; num. radio translations & adaptations. Serials for radio incl: Les Mystères de Paris; L'Affaire Lecoq. Films incl: Trente Ans d'Histoire; Jacques Copeau, seul maitre, 1917, 1918; Rhénanie 36; Yalta; Lénine par Lénine; Et Salambo? ; Flamenco, etc. Hons. incl: Prize, Festival of Monte Carlo, 1966; Special Mention, Festival of Cannes, 1970. Address: Télévision Française—O.R.T.F., Documentation Actualité Télévisée, 15 Rue Cognacq-Jay, 75007 Paris, France. 43, 91.

LEGUM, Colin, b. 2 Jan. 1919. Journalist. Appts: Pol. Corres., Daily & Sunday Express, Johannesburg, S. Africa, 1936-38; Ed., The Forward & The Mineworker, Johannesburg, 1939-44, The Labour Illustrated Bulletin, Johannesburg, 1944-49; Assoc. Staff Mbr., Tavistock Inst. of Human Rels., London, 1949-52; C'wlth. Corres. & Assoc. Ed., The Observer, London, 1949-; Ed., Africa Contemporary Record, 1968-, Pall Mall/Praeger Lib. of African Affairs, 1966-72. Mbrships: Africa Bur.; Africa Educ. Trust; Africa Publs. Trust; Gen. Sec., S. Africa Labour Party, 1945-48; Johannesburg City Coun., 1942-48. Publs: Attitude to Africa (w. others), 1951;

Must We Lose Africa? , 1954; Bandung, Cairo & Accra, 1958; Congo Disaster, 1960; Pan-Africanism, a Political Guide, 1962, 1965; Ed., Africa Handbook, 1963, 66 & 68; South Africa, Crisis for the West (w. Margaret Legum), 1964; Ed., Zambia—Independence & After, 1966; The Bitter Choice (w. Margaret Legum), 1968; The Africa Contemporary Record, annually 1969-74. Address: 15 Denbigh Gdns., Richmond, Surrey, U.K. 3, 30.

LEHESMAA, Esko Arvo Sakari, b. 14 Jan. 1933. Architect. Educ: Grad., Tech. Univ. of Helsinki, Finland, 1951; Dip., ibid, 1959. Appts: Free-lance jrnlst. & artist, 1953-60; Pvte. Prac. as architect, 1960-; Contbg. Ed., sev. int. publs., 1963-; Ed.-in-chief, Finnish Archtl. Review, 1971. Mbrships. incl: Union of Finnish Archts.; Finnish Archtl. Mus.; Comm., Finnish Yacht Racing Union, 1960-; Vice-Commodore, Finnish Yacht Club, 1970-. Designer: Approx. 50 bldgs. inclng. Marina, Finnish Yacht Club, Helsinki; Tech. Schl., Kajaani; Hlth. Ctr., Juuka; Dwelling houses; Indl. bldgs.; Supermarkets; also naval arch. & restorations of sailing & fishing vessels. Publs: Contbns. to Finnish & int. press, books, translations. Address: Pietarinkatu 20, SF-00140 Helsinki 14, Finland. 43.

LEHMAN, Maxwell. Public Administration Specialist. Educ: B.A., Rutgers Univ., U.S.A.; Master Pub. Admin., N.Y. Univ.; Postgrad. study, Harvard Univ. Appts: Ed., Civil Serv. Ldr., Govt. news columnist, N.Y. Post; Ed., Sci. Progress, Am. Spectator, 1940-55; Sec., Mayor's Cabinet, 1955-65; Chmn. & Mbr., num. Bds. & Comms.; Prof., Pub. Admin., N.Y. Univ., 1950-67; Exec. Dir., Metropol. Regional Coun., 1956-66; Dpty. City Adminstr., 1st Dpty. City Adminstr. & Acting City Administr., N.Y.C., 1955-66; Pub. Admin. Specialist, Ford Fndn., w. Tunisian Govt., 1966-68; Dir., Pub. Admin. Ctr., Long Island Univ., 1968-71; V.-Chmn. & Staff Dir., Task Force, Jurisdiction & Structure, State Study Commn., N.Y.C., 1971-72; Prof., Pol. & Managerial Communication, Grad. Schl. Human Communication, Fairfield Univ., Conn., 1971-; Dir., Special Studies, State Charter Revision Commn., N.Y.C., 1971-. Mbr. profl. & soc. orgs. Publs. incl: Concept of Multiple Functional Regios in the Tri-State Metropolitan Region, 1972; L'Organization et Methodes: Son But, Ses Moyens et Son Utilization, 1967. Address: 360 Ctrl. Pk. W., N.Y.C. NY 10025, U.S.A.

LEHMANN, Arno, b. 23 May 1901. Professor Emeritus, Educ: studied Theol., Theological Sem. & Univ., Leipzig, German Democratic Repub.; Dict., Karl Marx Univ., ibid, 1947. Appts. incl: Vicar, 1925-26; Lutheran Leipzig Mission, India, 1926-34; Pastor & Mission Sec., Dresden, German Democratic Repub., 1934-50; Prof., Martin Luther Univ., Wittenberg, 1950-66. Mbrships: Deutsche Gesellschaft für Missionswissenschaft; Int. Assn. of Mission Studies; Int. Assn. of Tamil Rsch. Publs. incl: Die Hymnen des Tayumanavar, 1935; Gottes Volk in veilen Ländern, 1955; Afroasiatische Christliche Kunst, 1966; over 800 other books & articles. Hons: Hon. Doct. of Theol., Friedrich Schiller Univ., German Democratic Repub., 1957; Hon. Doct. of Divinity, St. Louis, U.S.A., 1966. Address: Kirschbergweig 18, 402 Halle/S, German Democratic Repub. 2.

LEHMANN, Hermann, b. 8 July 1910. Professor of Clinical Biochemistry. Educ: Univs. of Freiburg, Frankfurt, Berlin, & Heidelberg, Germany; M.D., Univ. of Basle, Switzerland, 1934; Ph.D., Univ. of Cambridge,

U.K., 1938. Appts. incl: Beit Mem. Rsch. Fellow, Dept. of Biochem., Univ. of Cambridge, 1938-42; Med. Off., Royal Army Med. Corps, 1943-47; Colonial Med. Rsch. Off., Uganda, 1947-49; Pathologist, Pembury Hosp., 1949-51; Sr. Lectr.-Rdr., St. Bartholomew's Hosp., London, 1951-63; Prof., Clin. Biochem., Univ. of Cambridge, 1963-. Mbrships. incl: Fellow, Royal Soc.; F.R.C.P.; Fellow, Royal Coll. of Pathol.; Pres. Elect (1975), British Soc. of Haematol.; Dir., Abnormal Haemoglobins, Med. Rsch. Coun. Publs: Man's Haemoglobin (w. R.G. Huntsman), 1966, 2nd edit. 1974; Contbns. to med. & biochem. jrnls. Hons. incl: Darwin Prize, Univ. of Cambridge, 1938; Professorship, Univ. of Freiburg, 1966; M.D., Univ. of Frankfurt, 1972. Address: Dept. of Biochemistry, Addenbrooke's Hospital, Hills Rd., Cambridge CB2 2QR, U.K. 1.

LEHMANN, John Frederick, b. 2 June 1907. Author; Editor. Educ: B.A., Trinity Coll., Cambridge. Appts: Fndr. & Ed., New Writing & Penguin New Writing, 1936-50 & London Mag., 1954-61; Ptnr. & Gen. Mgr. w. Leonard & Virginia Woold, Hogarth Press, 1938-46; Fndr. & Mgng. Dir., John Lehmann Ltd. (Publrs.), 1946-52; Vis. Prof., Univ. of Tex. at Austin & State Univ. of Calif. at San Diego, 1970-72. Mbrships. incl: Pres., Alliance Française in Gt. Britain, 1955-63 & Royal Lit. Fund., 1966-. Publs. incl: The Age of the Dragon (poetry), 1951; Evil Was Abroad (novel), 1938; 2 vol. autobiog., 1955, 50 & 66, condensed & called In My Own Time for U.S., 1969; A Nest of Tigers, 1968; Holborn, 1970. Ed. many anthols., etc. Hons. incl: C.B.E., 1964; decorations from French & Greek govts. Address: 85 Cornwall Gardens, London SW7, U.K. 1, 3.

LEHMANN, Markus Hugo, b. 31 Mar. 1919. Musician; Teacher. Educ: Univ. of Salzburg, Austria; N. Western Music Acad., Detmold & Darmstadt-Kranischstein, Germany. Appts. incl: Organist & Choir-Conductor, Salzburg, 1948-50; Conductor at opera houses, Germany, 1953-62; Mus. Dir., Opera Grp., Staatliche Hochschule für Musik, Freiburg i. Br., 1963-. Compositions incl: Opera, Der Kleine Bahnhof, 1956, Die Wette, 1965, Der Prasident, 1970; Ballets, Danses en Blanc et Noir, 1952, L'enfer sur Terre, 1962; Vocal works; Mass in G major, 1937, Lied der Kentauren 1953; works for orch., solo instruments, choirs & organ; Lieder & chamber music. Address: Urach Strasse 39, D-7800 Freiburg i.Br., German Fed. Repub. 43, 92.

LEHMANN-HAUPT, Christopher Charles Herbert, b. 14 June 1934. Book Reviewer. Educ: B.A., Swarthmore Coll., Pa., U.S.A.; M.F.A., Yale Univ., New Haven, Conn. Appts: Book Ed., A.S. Barnes & Co., 1961-62; Book Ed., Holt, Rickert & Winston, 1962-63; Book Ed., Dial Press, 1963-65; Ed., N.Y. Times Book Review, 1965-69; Sr. Daily Book Reviewer, N.Y. Times, 1969-. Mbrships: Century Assn.; Riverdale Yacht Club. Address: c/o N.Y. Times, 229 W. 43rd St., N.Y., NY 10036, U.S.A. 6.

LEHNERT, Bo (Peter), b. 30 Mar. 1926. Professor of Plasma Physics & Fusion Research. Educ: Civilingenjör (M.S.), Royal Inst. of Technol., Stockholm, Sweden, 1950; Tekn.licentiat (Doct.), ibid, 1953; Tekn.doktor (Swedish Doct.), 1955. Appts: Rsch. Asst., Royal Inst. of Technol., Stockholm, 1950-55; Asst. Prof., ibid, 1955-63; Assoc. Prof. (Bitr. Prof.), Swedish Atomic Rsch. Coun., Stockholm, 1963-68; Full Prof., ibid, & Royal Inst. of Technol., 1968-. Mbrships: Int. Fusion Rsch. Coun., I.A.E.A., Vienna, Austria, 1970-;

Chmn., Plasma Physics Div., European Phys. Soc., Geneva, Switzerland, 1969-72; Vice Chmn., ibid, 1972-; Fellow, Inst. of Maths. & its Applications, U.K., 1973-; Swedish Soc. I.D.U.N., Stockholm, 1957-; Int. Astronomical Union, 1958; Swedish Acad. of Scis., 1974-. Author of 2 books, over 80 original papers & 8 reviews in field. Recip., Edlund Prize, Swedish Acad. of Scis., 1974-. Author of 2 books, over 80 original papers & 8 reviews in field. Recip., Edlund Prize, Swedish Acad. of Scis., 1962. Address: Dept. of Plasma Physics & Fusion Rsch., Royal Inst. of Technol., S-10044, Stockholm 70, Sweden. 43, 56, 134.

LEHNUS. Miria Lee, b. 18 Dec. 1939. Teacher; Administrator. Educ: B.A., N. Ctrl. Coll., Naperville, Ill., 1961; Grad. Work, Univ. of S. Fla., Tampa & Univ. of Tampa, Fla. Appts: Tchr., Schaumberg Dist., Cook Co., Ill., 1961-63; Tchr., St. Paul Evangelical United Brethren Schl., Tampa, Fla., 1963-64; Prin., ibid, 1964-68; Asst. Dir., Tampa United Meth. Ctrs., 1968-; Lectr. thru'out Fla. on behalf of Tampa United Meth. Ctrs. & Mission of the Ch. today. Mbrships: Fla. Comm. for Children & Youth; Southern Assn. of United Meth. Mission Schls.; Southeastern Jurisdiction Assn. for Deaconnesses & Home Missionaries, United Meth. Ch.; Regional Personnel Comm. for Bd. of Global Mins., ibid; Four a Forum of Fla.; var. choral grps. Address: 3305 Fifteenth St., Tampa, FL 33605, U.S.A. 76, 125.

LEHR, Milton W., b. 27 Oct. 1924. College Professor. Educ: B.A., Northwestern State Coll., Alva, Okla., 1949; M.Ed., Phillips Univ., 1952; Ed.D., Univ. of Okla.; Univ. of Minn., 1958. Appts: Tchr., Maths.; pub. schls., 1948-54, 55-56; Tchr., Northwestern State Coll., Okla., 1956-74; Dir., Tchr. Educ. & Chmn., Div. of Educ., ibid, 11 yrs.; Currently, Prof., Educ. Mbrships: Kappa Delta Pi; Alpha Psi Omega; Pres., Northwestern Okla. Maths. Tchrs.; Pres., Alumni Assn., Northwestern State Coll.; Chmn., Bd., NWSC Fndn.; Pres., Northwestern State Coll. Chapt., AAUP; Pres., Okla. Conf., AAUP; Phi Delta Kappa. Contbr. to educ. publs. Address: 1800 Locust Dr., Alva, OK 73717, U.S.A. 15, 125.

LEHRER, Thomas Andrew, b. 9 Apr. 1928. Songwriter; Teacher. Educ: B.A., Harvard Coll. 1946; Grad. work, ibid, 1946-48, '49-'53, '60-'65; M.A., 1947; Grad. work, Columbia Univ., 1948-49. Appts: Lectr., Educ., Harvard Grad. Schl. of Educ., 1963-65; Lectr., Psychol., Wellesley Coll., 1965; Lectr., Pol. Sci., MIT, 1962-71. Mbrships: Am. Math. Soc.; Inst. Math. Stats.; Am. Stat. Assn.; Am. Soc. of Composers, Authors & Publrs. Publs: The Tom Lehrer Song Book; Tom Lehrer's Second Song Book; also recordings. Address: 11 Sparks St., Cambridge, MA 02138, U.S.A. 1, 2, 128.

LEHRMAN, Hal, b. 7 Jan. 1911. Foreign Correspondent; Author; Lecturer. Educ: B.A., Cornell Univ., Coll. of Arts & Scis., Ithaca, N.Y., 1931; Cornell Grad. Schl. of Hist., 1931-33; Cert., Ecole des Chartes, Paris, France, 1934. Appts. incl: Num. assignment tours to Eastern Europe, N. Africa & the Middle East for N.Y. Times Mag., N.Y. Herald Tribune, The Nation Mag., London News Chronicle, London Statesman & Nation, Daily Express, Fortune Mag., Wall St. Jrnl. Commentary, Reporter Mag., NEA, N.Y. Post, Toronto Star, etc.; Exec. Ed., For. Newsfeatures, N.Y.C., 1959-. Mbrships. incl: Fndr. mbr., O'seas Press Club of Am., 1939; Var. terms as Gov. & V.P., & Pres., ibid, 1967-70; Coun. on For. Rels. Author of books, monographs & articles in jrnls. at home &

abroad. Recip. of hons. Address: 160 E. 48th St., N.Y., NY 10017, U.S.A. 55.

LEHRMANN, (Rabbi) Cuno (Charles Chanan), Professor. Educ: Tchrs. Coll., Wurzburg, Germany; Univs. of Wurzburg, Berlin & Lausanne; Licencié ès Lettres; Ph.D.; Rabbi. Appts: Lectr., Lausanne Univ., Switzerland, 1938-48; Chief Rabbi, Luxembourg, 1949-58; Chief Rabbi, W. Berlin, 1960-71; Greek Prof., Bar Flau Univ., Israel, 1958-60. Mbr., Pres., Currently Mentor, Bnai Brith Lodge, Berlin. Publs: L'élément juif dans la littérature française, 1960-61; The Jewish element in French Literature, 1970; Jewish influences in European Thought, 1974; Henrich Heine, 1957; La Communauté juive de Luxembourg, 1953; L'âme luxembourgeoise, 1963. Recip., Luxembourg Nat. Prize for Lit., 1959. Address: Sybelstrasse 19, 1 Berlin 12, German Fed. Repub. 43.

LEHTOLA, A. Olav, b. 9 Apr. 1938. Managing Director. Educ: Engr., shipbuilding, 1963. Appts: Engr., Wärtsilä Shipyard, Turku, Finland, 1963-65; Cons., H.B. Maynard, Gothenburg, Sweden, 1966-67; Cons., Rastor AB, Helsinki, Finland, 1967; Tech. Mgr., Lainatekstiili Oy, Hämeenlinna, 1967-70; Mng. Dir., Oy Scanconsult AB, Tampere, 1970-; Dir., Bd., Oy Scanlon AB, 1973-. Mbrships: Officer, Sr. Chmbr., Hämeenlinna, 1967-70; Pres., Finnish Fed. of Productivity, Tampere; Pres., Labour Hlth. Ctr., Hämeenlinna. Publs. incl: Universal Maintenance Standards & Universal Officer Standards, 1967; Graphical Analysis of Decisions, 1969. Recip., Prize, Unilever Ltd., 1969. Address: Tohlopinkatu 15 B, 33100 Tampere 10, Finland. 43, 134.

LEIBBRAND, Anne-Marie Margarete, b. 12 June 1913. University Professor. Educ: Study of med. & philos., Univs. of Breslau, Heidelberg, Rostock, Jena; State exam., 1937; Doct., 1939; Bavarian dist. med. off. exam., 1951; Rsch. in med. hist., Erlangen, then Munich, 1946-. Appts: Clin. Psych., Erlangen, German Fed. Repub., -1953; Inauguration, hist. of med., Univ. of Munich, 1962; Ed., "Med. Klinik", 1961-63; Prof., specializing in hist. of psychopathol., psychotherapy, hist. of sexol., hist. of dentistry, Univ. of Munich, 1970. Mbrships: Société de l'histoire de méd., Paris; Soc. Moreau de Tours, Paris. Publs. incl: Die Gestalt des Arztes bei Emile Zola, 1969; Foremen des Eros (w. W. Leibbrand), 2 vols., 1972. Contbr. to jrnls. Address: Nordendstr. 2, Munich 40, German Fed. Repub. 43, 92.

LEIBBRAND, Werner, b. 23 Jan. 1896. Professor of the History of Medicine & Psychiatrist. Educ: Dr. of Med., Univ. of Berlin, Germany, 1919. Appts: Clinical Dr. & Soc. Psych., Berlin, 1919-33; Dir. of Asylum & Hon. Prof. Med. Hist., Sem. for Med. Hist., Erlangen, 1945; Reader, Munich, 1953; Prof., 1958-69; Emeritus Prof. Mbrships: Lectr., Soc. Moreau de Tours, Soc. Médicopsychologique, Soc. de l'Histoire de Médecine, France; Acad. of Templers, Bologna, Italy; Soc. della Storia di Sanitá, Rome; Acad. of Hist. of Med., London, U.K.; Int. Soc. of Med. Hist. Publs. incl: Romantische Medizin, 1936; Das Gespräch über die Gesündheit, 1946; Spekulative Medizin der Romantik, 1954; Vinzenz von Paul; Der Wahnsinn (w. A. Leibbrand-Wetley). Contbr. to num. books & jrnls. Hons: Off., Ordre des Palmes Académiques de France, 1971. Address: Munich 40, Nordenstrasse 2, German Fed. Repub.

LEIBHOLZ, Gerhard, b. 15 Nov. 1901. Professor of Law. Educ: Dr. phil., Heidelberg Univ., 1921; Dr. jur utruisque, Berlin Univ.,

1924. Appts: Dist. Judge, 1926; Referent, Inst. of Pub. Law & Int. Law, 1926-29; Lectr., Constitutional Law & Pub. Law, 1928; Prof., Pub. Law & Pol. Sci., Greifswal, 1929-31, Univ. of Göttingen, 1931-35; Prof. Emeritus, ibid, 1936-58; Fellowship, World Coun. of Churches, Magdelan Coll., Oxford Univ., U.K., 1939-51; Prof., Göttingen Univ., 1958-72; Asst. Justice, Fed. Constitutional Ct., German Fed. Repub., 1951-71; Titular Prof., Coll. of Europe, 1953-. Mbr., num. nat. & int. orgs. Publs: Books in German; Engl. edits incl: Christianity, Politics & Power, 1942; Politics & Law, 1965. Hons: Grosses Verdienstkreuz mit Stern u. Schulterband. Address: Herzbergerlandstr. 57, 34 Gottingen, German Fed. Repub.

LEIBLER, Isi Joseph, b. 9 Oct. 1934. Company Director. Educ: B.A., Melbourne Univ., Australia, 1956. Mbrships: Pres., Vic. Jewish Bd. Dpts.; Sr. V.P., Exec. Coun. Australian Jewry. Publs: Soviet Jewry and Human Rights, 1965; The Case for Israel, 1972. Address: 116 Kooyong Rd., N. Caulfield, 3161, Vic., Australia. 23.

LEIFERMAN, Silvia Weiner (Mrs. Irwin H. Leiferman), Artist; Sculpturer; Civic Worker. Educ: Univ. of Chgo., 1960-61; Painting & Design studies in Chgo., Mexico, Rome, Madrid & Provincetown, Mass. Appts. incl: Silvia & Irwin Leiferman Fndn.; Pres., Active Accessories by Silvia, Chgo., 1964-. Exhibd. num. One-Man & Grp. Art shows & work included in many pub. & pvte. collections throughout world. One-Man Exhibs. incl: D'Arcy Galls., N.Y.C., 1964; Miami Mus. of Mod. Art, 1966, 1972; Contemporary Gall., Palm Beach, Fla., 1966; Hall Gall., Miami Beach (Perm. Exhib.), 1972. Grp. Exhibs. incl: Miami Mus. of Mod. Art, 1967; Int. Platform Assn., 1967; Hollywood Mus. of Art, 1968; Gall. 99, Miami, Fla., 1968; Barry Coll., 1968; Artists Equity at Crystal House, Miami Beach, 1968; Beau Art Gall., Lowe Mus., Univ. of Miami (Perm.). Mbrships. incl: Fndr., Mt. Sinai Hosp. of Gtr. Miami, Gtr. Technion Israel Inst. of Technol. for 1972, Ballet Soc. of Miami, Lowe's Mus. of Miami, Gtr. Art Ctr. of Miami & Philharmonic Soc. of Miami; Life Mbr., Bd. Mbr. & Trustee, Nathan Goldblatt Soc. for Cancer Rsch.; Life Mbr., Brandeis Univ., Art Inst. of Chgo., Miami Mus. of Mod. Art & Royal Soc. of Encouragement of Arts, Mgrs. & Commerce, London, U.K.; Life Fellow, Royal Soc. of Arts & Scis., London, U.K.; active mbr. num. cultural, religious & civic orgs. Recip. many civic & nat. awards inclng. Woman of Valor, State of Israel, 1963, Citation from Israel for creating & organizing Presentation Ball, 1965 & Awards & Citation from U.S. Govt. & Treasury Dept. Address: Ocean Pavillion, 5601 Collins Ave., Miami Beach, FL 33140, U.S.A. 2, 5, 7, 8, 55, 57, 94, 125, 130, 132, 133.

LEIGH, Aurelia Ilean, b. 28 July 1908. Elementary Schools Supervisor, Retd. Educ: B.S., Mary Washington Coll.; M.Ed., Univ. of Va. Appts. (all in Va.): Bus. Tchr., S. Norfolk H.S., 1931-38; Sec. to Supt. of Schls., 1938-43; Clerk, Schl. Bd., 1938-63; Asst. H.S. Prin., Acting Supt. of Schls. & Asst. to Supt. of Schls., 1943-52; Prin., Elem., Jr. & Sr. H.S., 1st Prin., Oscar Frommel Smith H.S., & Dir. of Instrn., S. Norfolk, 1952-63; Elem. Supvsr., Chesapeake, 1963-73. Mbrships: Past Va. State Publicity Chmn., Delta Kappa Gamma, & Past Pres., Gamma Chapt.; Past Pres., Dist. L, Va. Educ. Assn.; Life Mbr., NEA; Past Sec., Tidewater Regional Supvrs.; Past Mbr., DePaul Hosp. Educ. Bd.; Past Bd. of Dirs., Women's Div., Chmbr. of Comm.; Reading Assn.; Deacon, Elder, Sunday Schl. Supt., Gt. Bridge

Presby. Ch. Contbr. to jrnls.; Author pamphlets, booklets. Hons: Hon. Pres., S. Norfolk Sports Club, 1955; Outstanding Woman of Chesapeake, Women's Div., Chmbr. of Comm., 1972. Address: 240 Robert St., Chesapeake, VA 23320, U.S.Ä. 5, 7, 15, 125, 132, 138.

LEIGH, Stephen, b. 21 May 1931. Industrial Designer. Educ: Cooper Union for the Advencement of Sci. & Art. Appts: Designer, Robert Gruen Assocs., N.Y.C., 1951-55; Designer, Proj. Dir., Michael Saphier Assocs., ibid, 1955-59; Pres., Stephen Leigh & Assocs., 1959-; Interior Designer, Random House, Inc.; Art Dir., Grp. Mag., Jrnl. of Psychoanalysis in Grps.; Cons. Interior Designer, Real Estate Ind.; United Jewish Appeal; U.S. Pavilion & Venezuelan Pavilion, N.Y. World's Fair, 1963. Mbrships: Am. Inst. Interior Design; Real Estate Bd., N.Y. State; Cooper Union Alumni Assn.; Young Men's Real Estate Assn. Exhibs., sculptures & paintings, 1970-72; rep. in pvte. colls. Contbr. of articles to profl. jrnls. Recip., Am. Inst. Archts. Design Award, 1964, '65. Address: 4-1/2 E. 65th St., N.Y., NY 10021, U.S.A. 6.

LEIGHTON-MILLS, Horace Eugene, b. 23 Oct. 1906. Educator; Journalist; Author. Appts: Accounts Clerk, oil fields, 1919-31; Acct., Y.C.O. oilfields, 1931-33; Reporter, Feature Writer, Sub-ed., Trinidad Guardian, 1934-43; Censor, Spanish Imperial Censorship, 1943-45; Second. Schl. Tchr., 1946-59; Prin., Independence Coll., Tobago, 1959-74; Staff Corres., Express Newspaper, Tobago, 1973-. Mbrships: Dir. & Treas., Tobago Lions Club; PR & Welfare Off., Tobago Red Cross Soc.; Hon. Mbr., Chmnr. of Comm.; Royal Soc. of Lit.; Can. Author's Assn.; Alliance Française. Publs: Anthology of Poems & Three Act Plays, 1966; Second Anthology of Poems & 10 Short Stories, 1968; Then & Now (novel), 1973. Address: c/o Independence Coll., Roxborough, Tobago, W. Indies.

LEIJONHUFVUD, (Baron) Hans C., b. 6 Sept. 1941. Publisher; Public Relations Officer; Management Consultant. Educ: Ph.D. Appts. incl: Press & TV Jrnlst., Publr., Copywriter, Designer, Entertainer, 1958-62; Mng. Ed., Projekt, 1961-72; Dir. of P.R., Info. & Advt., KFAI AB, 1962-72; Art Advsr., KFAI AB & others, 1965-; Mgmt. Cons., org. & info. policies, corp. guides, design & art, 1968-. Mbrships. incl: Chmn. & Vice Chmn., Swedish Student's Union, Students' Press Union, 1958-60; Chmn., Societas Logicae-Philosophica, 1969-; Mbr. & Bd. Mbr., Swedish P.R. Assn., Int. Fedn. of Jrnlsts. Publs. incl: New Teenager Market, 1959; Kreuger, 1960; Modern Retailing in Sweden, 1966; Warehousing, 1967; Fenollosa, 1971; Wittgenstein, 1972; Kierkegaard, 1973. Address: Artilleri 22, S 11451 Stockholm OE, Sweden. 16, 24.

LEINO, Väinö Jalmari, b. 6 Mar. 1922. Mayor. Educ: Fac. of Law, Univ. of Helsinki, Finland, 1949. Appts: Occasional Asst., City Office, Tampere, 1945, 46; Legal Asst., City of Tampere, 1946-48; Asst. Lawyer, ibid, 1948-51; Lawyer, City of Lahti, 1951-57; Village Mgr., Riihimäki, 1957-59; Mayor, ibid, 1960-62; Mayor, Hämeenlinna, 1962-64; Mayor, Turku, 1964-. Mbrships. incl: Chmn., Finnish British Soc., Turku; Chmn., Gothenburg Soc., Turku, 1964-; Vice Chmn., Paasikivi Soc., 1965-; Admin., Chmbr. of Comm., Turku, 1965-; Bd. Commnrs., Univ. of Turku, 1966-. Hons: Puol PR K, 1966; Ruots VR K, 1968; SL K, 1969; UNK LR kmr, 1971; Isl HR K, 1972; TDR K, 1973. Address: Turun kaupunginkanslia, Kristiinankatu 1, SF 20100 Turku 10, Finland. 134.

LEIPONEN, Kauko (Olavi Antero), b. 14 Nov. 1911. Managing Director. Educ: Degree in Civil Engrng., Univ. of Technol., Helsinki, Finland. Appts. incl: Engr., Draining Assn., 1938-44; Vice-Chmn. of Bd., ibid, 1945-47; Ed.-in-Chief, mag. Talkootyö, 1942-45; Hd., Land Clearing Work, Dept. of Agric., 1944-45; Mng. Dir., Finnish Brick Ind. Assn., 1946-; Ed.-in-Chief, mag. TIILI, 1949-; Mng. Dir., Brick Ind. Employers' Assn., 1952-69; Vice Chmn. of Bd., Maanpuolustuslehden Kustannus Oy, 1957-62; Mbr. of Bd., ibid, 1968-70; Chmn., ibid, 1971-72. Mbrships: Finnish Ceramic Assn.; Bd. ibid, 1949-; Chmn. & Bd. Mbr., var. Fndns., 1953-63; var. tech. & civic orgs., 1933-. Publs: Num. articles in mags. & newspapers, 1936-; Chmn., Edit. Bds., var. books on Structural Engrng., 1944-. Hons: Liberty Cross V R3 & V R4 w. Swords; Engrng. Lt.-Col., 1967. Address: Mäensyrjä 3 B, 02160 Westend, Finland. 43.

LEISCHNER, Anton, b. 22 May 1908. Physician; Specialist in Psychiatry & Neurology. Educ: M.D., Univ. of Prague, Czechoslovakia, 1933. Appts: Hd. Physn., Psych. & Neurological Clin., Univ. of Prague, 1942; Hd. Physn., Clin for Brain Injuries, Bonn, Germany, 1953; Prof., Univ. of Bonn, 1957; Dir., Clin. for Lang. Disturbances, Bonn, 1969. Mbrships: Gesellschaft f. Hirntraumatologie & Klinische Hirnpathologie; Pres., ibid; German Soc. of Neurol.; German Electroencephalographic Soc.; German Soc. of Youth Psych. Publs: Co-Author, Klinische & sprachwissenschaftliche Untersuchungen zum Agrammatismus, 1952; Die Störungen der Schriftsprache: Agraphie & Alexie, 1957; Das Lebenschicksal hirnverletzter Jugendlicher & Kinder, 1962; The Agraphias, in Handbook of Clinical Neurology, Volume 4, 1969; Die Rehabilitation der Aphasie in den romanischen Ländern nebst Beiträgen zur Aphasieforschung, 1970; 53 articles in med. jrnls. Address: Rhein. Landesklinik für Sprachgestörte, Postfach 7229, 53 Bonn, German Federal Repub.

LEITHERER, Arthur Eugene, b. 2 July 1914. Milling Company Executive. Educ: Ph.B., DePaul Univ., Chgo., 1939; specialist studies, Coll. of Adv. Traffic, Chgo. Appts: Dept. of Transportation, Chgo. Cold Storage, 1933-38, Montgomery Ward, 1938-42; Corn Prods. Refining (now CPC Int.), 1942-52; Allied Mills Inc., Chgo, 1952-, currently V.P., Transportation. Mbrships: Pres., Nat. Indl. Traffic League; Shippers Advsry. Bd.; Past Gen. Chmn., ibid; Chgo. Traffic Club; Past Pres., ibid; Registered Practitioner, Interstate Commerce Comm.; Fndr. Mbr., Am. Soc. Traffic & Transportation; Nat. Assn. ICC Practitioners; Nat. Freight Traffic Assn.; Am. Feed Mfrs. Assn.; Past Chmn., Transport Exec. Comm. Address: 801 Inverness Rd., Lisle, IL 60532, U.S.A.

LEITZSEY, Barney Burr, b. 2 Aug. 1903. Public School Superintendent. Educ: A.B., Newberry Coll., S.C., 1925; M.A., Univ. of S.C., 1942. Appts. incl: Prin., Harlee Elem. Schl., & Florence Jr. H.S., 1942-54; Asst. Supt., Florence Pub. Schls. Dist. 1, 1954-67; Dir., Marion Mullins Voc. Schl., S.C., & Clerk Co. Bd. Educ., S.C., 1967-73. Pres. var. Educ. & Co. Assns. Mbrships. incl: S.C. Educ. Assn.; NEA; State Voc. Assn.; Nat. Voc. Assn. Mbr. num. other educ. assns & civic orgs. Hons. incl: Hon. Mbrships., Civil Air Patrol, 1968; voted Outstanding Voc. Person., Voc. Tchrs. of S.C., 1973. Address: P.O. Box 695, Marion, SC 29571, U.S.A.

LE LACHEUR, Rex A. de Putron, b. 5 Jan. 1910. Musician; Baritone; Composer; Choral

Director. Appts: Special Music Cons. to jt. Senate-H. of C. Comm. on Nat. & Royal Anthems, 1967; Dir. & Fndr., The Rex Le Lacheur Singers, 1956; Musical Advsr. to Festival of the Performing Arts, 1963; Baritone Soloist w. Centennial Choir. Mbrships. incl: Canadian Club; Ottawa Tennis Club. Compositions incl: Forever England, 1941; Ave Maria, 1942; All Suddenly the Wind, 1942; Chant de Samson, 1945; Centennial Hymn, 1967; Sonata da Chiesa for Carillon; She Walks in Beauty; Three Shakespaerian Trios, 1974; There is Sweet Music Here, 1974; Invocation and Benediction, 1974. Address: 2044 Woodglen Cres., Ottawa K1J 6G4, Canada. 88.

LE LIONNAIS, François, b. 3 Oct. 1901. Scientific Advisor. Educ: Mathn., Ingénieur chimiste, Univ. of Strasbourg, France. Appts. incl: Chief, Sci. Educ. Div., UNESCO; Sci. Comm., la Radiodiffusion TV francaise; Sci. Expert, Euratom, SEMEC project; BICETI Advsr., French Assn. for investigational & opl. rsch. (AFIRO). Mbrships. incl: l'Assn. des écrivains sci. de France (Hon. Pres.); Admin. Coun., Fr. Assn. Advancement Scis.; Cons. Comm., l'Acad. des Scis., Comm. de restauration des oeuvres d'Art; l'Acad. française; PEN Club of France; l'Assn. IDEE (Hon. Pres.). Publs: Les Grands Courants de la Pensée Mathematique; La Science au XXe siècle: La méthode dans des Sciences modernes; Le Temps; Dictionnaire des Sciences & l'Anthologie des Nombres Remarquables (in preparation). Hons: Cmdr., Légion d'honneur; Cmdr. de l'Ordre pour la Recherche et l'invention. Address: 23 route de la Reine, 92100 Boulogne-sur-Seine, France.

LEM, Richard Douglas, b. 24 Nov. 1933. Artist. Educ: B.A., Univ. of Calif. L.A.; M.A., Calif. State Univ.; Otis Art Inst.; Calif. Inst. Arts. Mbr., Univ. Calif. L.A. Alumni Assn. Recip. of L.A. Fine Arts Soc. & Art Guide Award for Painting, 1965. Address: 1861 Webster Ave., L.A., CA 90026, U.S.A. 37.

LEMBERG, Kai, b. 28 Nov. 1919. Director of Town Planning. Educ: cand. polit., Univ. of Copenhagen, Denmark, 1945. Appts: Econ. Advsr., Min. of Transport, 1955-56; Dir. of Gen. Planning, City of Copenhagen, 1968-; Mbr., Tech. Comm., Metropol. Regional Planning Bd., Gtr. Copenhagen, 1968-; Danish deleg., OECD Sector Grp of the Urban Environment, 1971-; Chmn., ibid, 1973-. Mbrships: Exec. Comm., Danish Town Planning Assn., 1952-70; Assn. Univ. Econs.; Assn. Town Planners. Publs. incl: Malsettingen ved en regionplanlegging, 1964; Planning in Greater Copenhagen, 1970; Pedestrian Streets & Other Motor Vehicle Traffic Restraints in Central Copenhagen, 1971, '73. Address: Copenhagen Gen. Planning Dept., Østergade 26, Copenhagen K. 1100, Denmark. 43.

LE MEHAUTE, Bernard, b. 29 Mar. 1927. Engineer. Educ: Lic. ès Scis., Univ. of Toulouse, France, 1951; Dip. Hydrodynamics, Univ. of Paris, 1953; D.Sc., Univ. of Grenoble, 1957. Appts. incl: Grp. Mgr., Neyrpic-Soreah, Grenoble, 1953-57; Vis. Prof., Ecole Polytech., Montreal, Canada, 1957-59; Rsch. Assoc.-Prof., Queen's Univ., Kingston, Ont., 1959-61; Dir. Geomarine Div., Nat. Engrng. Sci. Corp., Pasadena, U.S.A., 1961-67; V.P., Bd. of Dirs. & Off., Tetra Tech, Inc., 1967-; Cons., C.E.R.C., 1962, O.N.R., 1963, Atomic Energy Commn., 1964; Advsr., Nat. Oceanographic & Atmospheric Agcy., 1971. Mbrships. incl: Int. Assn. of Hydraulic Rsch.; Coun. on Wave Rsch.; Am. Soc. of Civil Engrs. Publs: Ocean Sciences, Physical Oceanography, 1964; An Introduction to Hydrodynamics & Water Waves, 1969;

Theory of Explosion-Generated Water Waves, 1971; Advances in HydroScience, Vol. 7. Address: 2159 Highland Vista Drive, Arcadia, CA 91006, U.S.A. 9, 14, 131.

LEMESLE, Robert, b. 26 Apr. 1894. Professor of Botany. Educ: Lic. ès scis., Rennes, France, 1921; Doct. en Méd., Paris, 1923; Doct. ès scis. naturelles, ibid, 1925. Appts: Asst. in Botany, Fac. des Scis., Poitiers, 1930, Dir. of Studies, 1941, Sr. Lectr., 1949; Actg. Prof., l'Ecole Prép. de Med. et Pharm., 1934, Prof., 1937; Prof., l'Ecole Nat. de Med. et Pharm., Poitiers, 1955-. Contbr. to Les Comptes Rendus de l'Acad. des Scis., Revue Générale de Botanique & num. other profl. publs., 1923-66. Hons. incl: Lauréat, Soc. Botanique de France, 1945, Acad. des Scis., 1945 & 1954; Comdr., Ordre des Palmes Académiques 1962; Chevalier, Légion d'Honneur, 1964; work mentioned in num. scientific publs. Address: 6 Rue du Moulin à Vent, 86000 Poitiers, France.

LEMOIGNE, Marcel (Alexandre Henri), b. 18 Nov. 1905. Civil Engineer. Educ: l'Ecole Polytechnique, promotion 1923; Ecole d'Officiens d'Artillerie de Fontainebleau, 1923, & d'Application des Manufactures de l'Etat, 1926-28. Appts: Ingr., Serv. d'Exploitation Indl. des Tabacs & des Allumettes, Paris & Le Mans, 1928-35, Dir., Lille, 1935, Ingr. en chef, ibid, 1938-39, Le Mans & Dir., Regional des Vertes, 1945-70. Mbrships. incl: Soc. des Ingrs. Civils de France, Pres., Le Mans Sect.; Délég. Gen., La Sarthe du Souvenirs Francais; Soc. Mycol. de la Sarthe, Pres.; Soc. d'entraide des membres de la Légion d'honneur, Vice Pres., la Sarthe, Pres., le Mans; Soc. Hist. et Archeol., La Sarthe, Vice Pres.; Soc. Littéraire du Maine, Vice Pres. Publs: Histoire du Tabac; Les Papes français; (poetry) Brest et ses alentours; contbr. to profl. publs. & to anthols. of poetry. Hons: Chevalier de la Légion d'Honneur, 1947, Off., 1956. Address: 10 place des Comtes du Maine, 72000 Le Mans, France. 43, 91.

LEMON, Henry Martyn, b. 23 Dec. 1915. Physician; Professor. Educ: S.B., Univ. Chgo., 1938; M.D., Harvard Med. Schl., 1940; Intern, Univ. of Chgo., Billings Hosp., 1940-41; Med. Res., Univ. of Chgo., 1941-42; Chief Med. Res., Boston Univ. Hosp., Mass., 1946-48; Rsch. Asst., Army Epidemiol. Bd., 1942-45. Appts: Asst. Prof.-Assoc. Prof., Med., Boston Univ. Schl. of Med., 1948-61; Hd., Cancer Trng., ibid; Dir., Eugene C. Eppley Inst. for Rsch. in Cancer & Prof. of Internal Med., Univ. of Neb., Omaha, 1961-68; Prof. of Internal Med., Hd., Div. of Oncol., ibid, 1968-. Mbrships: AMA; Neb. State Med. Assn.; Am. Coll. Physns.; Am. Assn. Cancer Rsch.; James Ewing Soc.; Am. Soc. for Clin. Oncol.; Ctrl. Soc. for Clin. Rsch.; N.Y. Acad. Sci. Author of num. profl. publs. Hons. incl: Univ. of Chgo. Med. Alumni Disting. Serv. Award, 1952; 1st Oak Leaf Cluster, U.S. Army, 1968. Address: Dept. Internal Med., Univ. of Neb. Med. Ctr., Omaha, NB 68105, U.S.A. 8, 14.

LEMTIS, Horst Guenther, b. 24 Aug. 1923. Professor of Obstetrics & Gynaecology. Educ: M.D., Univ. of Kiel, 1954; Intern, Univ. of Hamburg, & Gen. Hosp. of St. Georg, Hamburg, 1954-56; Scientific Asst. Dr., Univs. of Marburg/Lahn, Göttingen & Hamburg, 1956-63. Appts: Hd. Physn., 2nd Women's Clin. & Policlin., Free Univ. of Berlin, 1963-67; Univ. Lectr. of Ob. & Gyn., 1967-69; Prof. & Hd. of Team, Experimental Gynaecol., Women's Clin. & Policlin., Klinikum Steglitz, ibid, 1969-. Mbrships. incl: German Soc. Gyn.; Soc. of Ob. & Gyn.; German Soc. for Attending

Venerological Diseases. Author, some 70 publs., ob. & gyn., monographs, & contbns., handbooks. Recip., Disertation Prize, Fac. of Med., Univ. of Kiel, 1952. Address: Frauenklinik und Poliklinik im Klinikum Steglitz der Freien Universtät Berlin, 1 Berlin 45, Hindenburgdamm 30, Germany. 43, 92.

LENGYEL, Alfonz, b. 21 Oct. 1921. Professor. Educ: Law Degree, Law Schl., Hungary, 1948; B.A., M.A., San Jose State Univ., Calif., U.S.A.; Ph.D., Univ. of Paris, Sorbonne, France; Post-doctoral studies, Ecole de Louvre, Museol. & Mus. de l'Homme. Appts: Asst. Prof., San Jose State Univ., Calif., 1961-63; Prof., Univ. of Md., European Div., 1964-68; Prof., Wayne State Univ., Detroit, Mich., 1968-72; Prof. & Dir. of Art & Archaeol. Prog., Northern Ky. State Coll., Highland Hts. Ky., 1972-; Dir., Carthage Proj., U.S.A. (Tunisia), 1974-79. Mbrships. incl: Fndr. & Exec. Dir., Toscan-Am. Archaeol. Assn.; Archaeol. Inst. of Am. Publs. incl: Etruscology, 1973; Archaeological Manual, 1973; Handbook of Panonian Archaeology, forthcoming. Hons: Rockefeller Grant, 1957; Kress Fellowship, 1957 & 1968; French Govt. Grant, 1962, 1963; Kt., Order of St. John; Kt. of Malta; Kt., Mil. Order of Constantinian St. George; Kt. Templar, Order of S. Ladislavs of Hungary. Address: Northern Ky. State Coll., Highland Hts., KY 41076, U.S.A. 13.

LENGYEL, Cornel Adam, b. 1 Jan. 1915. Writer; Educator. Appts. incl: Mgr., Forty-Niner Theatre, Georgetown, Calif., 1946-49; Lectr., Engl. Lit., Sacramento State Coll., Calif., 1962-; Vis. Lectr., Writer-in-res., Hamline Univ., St. Paul, Minn., 1968-69; Guest Lectr., MIT, Cambridge, Mass., 1969; Transl. from Hungarian; Ed. Cons., HEW; Educl. Dir., Int. Ladies Garment Workers Union Local 22. Mbrships: Authors Guild; Poetry Soc. of Am.; Am. Hist. Soc.; AAUP. Publs: poetry—Thirty Pieces, 1933, First Psalms, 1950, Fifty Poems, 1965, Four Dozen Songs, 1970 & The Lookout's Letter, 1971; plays—The World's My Village, 1935, Jonas Fugitive, 1936, The Giants's Trap, 1938, The Atomic Clock Fantasy, 1951, prod. in The Hague, 1954, Eden, Inc., 1954, revised w. title Omega, 1963, Will of Startford, prod., 1964 & Three Plays, 1964; history—American Testament, the Story of a Promised Land, 1956, Four Days in July, 1958, (abridged paper ed., 1968), I, Benedict Arnold, The Anatomy of Treason, 1960, Presidents of the U.S.A., 1961, Ethan Allan & the Green Mountain Boys, 1961, & The Declaration of Independence, 1969; The Creative Self, Aspects of Man's Quest for Self-Knowledge & the Springs of Creativity, 1971; contbr. poems, articles, reviews, criticism, etc. to jrnls. Selected Poems recorded by Lib. of Congress, 1961. Recip. sev. awards inclng: Alice Fay di Castagnola Award for book-in-progress, Poetry Soc. of Am., 1971. Address: Adam's Acres West, El Dorado Nat. Forest, Georgetown CA 95634, U.S.A. 9, 30, 34.

LENK, John, b. 17 Dec. 1919. Lecturer; World Traveler. Educ: Baccalaureate in Humanities, Pilsen, Czechoslovakia; Dip. Int. Law, Acad. du Droit Int., Hague, Netherlands; other dips. Appts. incl: Gen. Mgr., Maunaloa Broadcasting Corp., Kona, Hawaii, U.S.A., 1964-66; Fndr., Ed. & Publr., Kona Torch, weekly, Kailua Kona, ibid, 1961-68; Lectr., Econ. Geog. & Current Events in Philos., Univ. of Hawaii, Hilo, 1970-71; Interdisciplinary Lectr., approx. 60 colls. & univs. in U.S.A. & abroad, 1968-; Lectr., Educl. TV Coll. Network; Held Global Studies Seminars for H.S. Tchrs.; Planning & escorting round the world as Lectr. of Washington State 'Classroom in the Sky', 1974; Has traveled extensively in about 90 countries; Composer of Performer Piano Mus.; Fluent in 7 langs. Mbrships: Bd. of Dirs., Rotary Int.; Publicity Chmn., Lions Int.; Arctic Cir. Club; Nat. Geog. Soc.; Big I. Press Club & Safety Coun.; Hawaii Visitors Bur. (Goodwill Ambassador on world lecture tour). Contbr., columns & edits. in own newspaper, Kona Torch, articles in var. Newspapers & mags., U.S.A. & Europe. Address: P.O. Box 1234, Kamuela, HI 96743, U.S.A. 78.

LENT, Constantin Paul van, b. 21 Sept. 1915. Publishing Company Executive. Educ: Dip., Mech. Engrng., Univ. of Mittweida, Germany, 1937; Postgrad., N.Y.U., 1939, Columbia, 1939, New Schl. for Soc. Rsch., U.S.A., 1950. Appts. incl: Rschr. in aviation, rockets & jets, space travel, 1932-; Pres., Pen-Ink Pub. Co., N.Y.C., 1942-; Corporate patents specification writer, engrng. cons., 1947-; Rsch. engr. or engrng. cons., DeJure, Inc., 1966-67, Nat. Design Co., 1966-72, Singer Co., 1969-71; Practising psychonetician, 1965-; Dean, Univ. for Space Sci. Engrng., N.Y.C., 1970-. Mbrships. incl: Past V.P., Am. Rocket Soc.; Fndr., Nat. Rocket & Jet Set; Int. Soc. of Aviation Writers; Fndr., Theozoeye Soc.; Fndr., Int. Congress True Democracy; Dir., Soc. for Econ. Advancement, 1970-72. Publs. incl: What to Invent—How to Invent, 1965; Escape from Russia, 1972. Contbr. to num. articles to mags. Paintings exhibited at Miami Art Mus., Miami Civic Ctr. Address: Room 514, 50 E. 42nd St., N.Y., NY 10017, U.S.A. 6.

LEONARD, Edwin Deane, b. 22 Apr. 1929. Lawyer. Educ: B.A., The Principia Coll., Elsah, Ill., 1950; LL.B., Harvard Univ. Law Schl., 1953; LL.M., Geo. Wash. Law Schl., Wash. D.C., 1956. Appts: Mil. Serv., 1st Lt., Judge Advocate Gen.'s Corps, U.S. Army, 1953-56; Employed Davis, Polk, Wardwell, Sunderland & Kiendl, & successor firm, 1956-; Mbr. of Firm, ibid, 1961-. Mbrships: Assn. of Bar of City of New York; Chmn., Corp. Law Comm., ibid, 1972-; Am. Bar Assn.; N.Y. State Bar Assn. Hons: Commendation Ribbon w. Medal Pendant, 1956. Address: 1148 Fifth Ave., N.Y., NY 10028, U.S.A. 6.

LEONARD, Gladys Jane (DeHart) (Mrs Raymond Leonard), b. 18 Dec. 1909. Homemaker. Educ: Meredith Coll., Raleigh, N.C.; Brenau Coll., Gainesville, Ga. Mbrships: DAR; U.D.C.; Warren Co. (Miss.) Histl. Soc.; Ky. Histl. Soc.; Brush & Palette Club, Brenau Coll.; OES, Asheville, N.C.; var. genealogical socs. Address: P.O. Drawer H.H., Bryson City, NC 28713, U.S.A. 22, 132.

LEONARD, Jackson Day, b. 2 Sept. 1915. Consulting Chemical Engineer. Educ: B.S., Pa State Univ., 1937; num. tech. grad. courses. Appts: Var. tech. posts, duPont, 10 yrs., Allied Chemical, 4 yrs., Merck, 1 yr.; Pres. & Fndr., Leonard Process Co. Inc., 1948-. Mbrships: Nat. Soc. Profl. Engrs.; Am. Inst. Chem. Engrs; Am. Chem. Soc.; Raritan Valley Soc. Profl. Engrs. Known world wide for dev. of Amine Technol.; Licensees incl. Chem. Cos. in U.S.A. & 16 for. countries. Holder, var. Patents in 16 countries. Contbr. to num. tech. publs. Address: 480 Park Ave., N.Y., NY 10022, U.S.A. 6, 26.

LEONARD, Julia Rebecca Kluttz (Mrs. Hugh Preston Leonard), b. 2 Mar. 1921. Primary School Teacher. Educ: A.B., Lenoir Rhyne Coll., Hickory, N.C., 1942; Catawba Coll., 1951; Univ. of Va. Ext. Appts: Primary Schl. Tchr., Pub. Schls., Danville, Va. Mbrships: DEA; VEA; Recording Sec., PTA; Hon. Life Mbr., ibid, 1963; Pres., Vesper Gdn. Club; Bus.

& Profl. Women's Club; Ladies' Benevolent Soc.; Luth. Ch. of Ascension; Past. Sec. & Hon. Life Mbr., LCW; Nat. Hon. Beta Club. Contbr. to Garden Club Cookbook, 1970. Hons: Medals for Integrity & Extracurricular Activity, 1938; 1st & 2nd Grade Reading Contest Winner; Hon. Mention Civitan Trophy, 1938. Address: 152 Dublin Ct., Danville, VA 24541, U.S.A. 125, 138.

LEONARD, Maurice, b. 27 July, 1939. Writer. Appts. incl: Asst. to Ed., Dictionary of Internat. Biog., 1963-67, Mbr. Ed. Sub-Comm., 1963-. Publs. incl: Messenger to the Masters, 1964; Enigmatic Mr. Gudjieff, 1965; Wickedest Man in the World, 1965; Contrib. to Bibliography of Monaco, Bibliog. of Iran; Contrib. to various jrnls. Voc. Cert. (Distinction), English Speaking Bd., 1967. Address: New Arts Theatre Club, Gt. Newport St., London W.1., England.

LEONARD, Raymond Wesley, b. 12 Dec. 1909. Civil Engineer (Retired). Educ: B.S., N.C. State Univ., Raleigh; M.P.H., Yale Univ., New Haven, Conn. Appts: w. U.S. Bur. of Pub. Roads, Gattinburg, Tenn.; N.C. State Hwy. Comm., Raleigh & N.C. State Bd. of Hlth., Bryson City; U.S.T.V.A. Chattanooga, U.S.G.S. Asheville, N.C., & Pitts., Pa.; U.S. Corps of Engrs., N.C. Dist., Wilmington, 1946-53; Miss. River Commn. & Lower Miss. Valley Div., Vicksburg, 1953-73. Mbrships. incl: Nat. Soc. Profl. Engrs.; Soc. Am. Mil. Engrs.; Am. Soc. Civil Engrs.; Charter Inter Am. Assn. of Sanitary Engrs.; N.C. Soc. Engrs.; Fellow, Royal Soc. of Hlth.; N.C. State & Yale Alumni Assns.; Fellow, Yale Univ., 1945; Tau Beta Pi & Phi Kappa Phi, N.C. State Univ., 1931; A.F. & A.M. Shrine, York Rite & Scottish Rite Masonic Bodies. Address: P.O. Drawer HH, Bryson City, NC 28713, U.S.A. 22, 26, 83, 125, 128.

LEONARD, William Norris, b. 13 Dec. 1912. Professor of Economics. Educ: A.B., Univ. of Va., 1936; M.A., Univ. of Tex., 1938; Ph.D., Columbia Univ., 1945. Appts: Instr. in Econs., Univ. of Conn., 1939-42; Transportation Off., War Prod. Bd., Wash.D.C., 1942-45; Coord. of Planning, Trans-World Airlines, Kan. City, Mo., 1945-46; Assoc. Prof., Rutgers Univ., New Brunswick, N.J., 1946-49; Prof. & Hd., Dept. of Econs., Pa. State Univ., 1949-53; Prof., Hofstra Univ., 1953-, Chmn. of Econs. Dept. & Soc. Scis. Div., 1953-59, Asst. Pres. of Univ., 1965-66. Mbr. & Off., profl. orgs. Publs. incl: Business Size, Market Power & Public Policy, 1969; articles, var. profl. jrnls. Hons. incl: Plaque for serv. as V.P., L.I. YMCA, 1969; Fulbright Lectr., Univ. of Haiti, 1974. Address: 55 Garden St., Garden City, NY 11530, U.S.A. 2, 12, 14, 51.

LEONARDY, Herberta Ann. Lawyer; Registered Parliamentarian. Educ: Ph.B., LL.B., J.D., John B. Stetson Univ., DeLand, Fla.; Additional study, Nat. Univ. of Colombia, Bogota. Appts. incl: Law Libn., Schl. of Law, Univ. of Miami, 1939-40; Instr. in Parliamentary Law, Evening Div., ibid, resigned to prac. parliamentary law; Serves 15 nat. & state orgs. as profl. parliamentarian; Instr., by tape recording, Nat. Assn. of Parliamentarians. Mbrships. incl: Educ. Chmn., Nat. Assn. of Parliamentarians, 1954-55; 1st V.P., ibid, 1957-59; Nat. Pres., 1959-61; Chmn., Testing Admnstrs., 1969-71; Chmn., Revision Comm. for "Questions & Answers", 1971; Former Pres., Fla. Unit of Registered Parliamentarians; DAR; Hon. mbr., Beta Sigma Phi; Phi Delta Delta. Publs. incl: Leonardy's Parliamentary Law Chart; An Elementary Course in Parliamentary Procedure; Compiler,

Parliamentary Law Kit. Recip. of hons. Address: 1809 Brickell Ave., Apt. 413, Miami, FL 33129, U.S.A. 5, 77, 128, 132.

LEONE, Edmund, b. 17 Aug. 1906. Banker. Educ: B.C.S., N.Y. Univ., 1928; LL.B., St. Lawrence Univ., 1931; LL.M. (cum laude), ibid, 1932. Appts. incl: Admission, N.Y. Bar, 1933; Credit Mgr., Capitol Nat. Bank, 1924-28; Jr. Credit Asst., Mfrs. Trust Co. (now Mfrs. Hanover Trust Co.), N.Y.C., 1928, var. exec. posts, 1928-55, Gen. Admin. Off., Mbr., Gen. Admin Bd., 1955-63, V.P. Admin., 1961-63, V.P., Sec., Mbr., Gen. Admin. Bd., 1963-71; w. U.S. Army, 1943-44; Pres., Dir., Chief Exec. Off., Union State Bank, Nannet, N.Y., 1972-; V.P., Dir., Gallatin Co.; V.P., Sec., Mfrs. Hanover Int. Finance Corp., Mfrs. Hanover Int. Banking Corp.; V.P., Mfrs. Hanover Corp. Mbrships. incl: Am. Soc. Corporate Secs.; Financial Execs. Inst.; Nat. Assn. Bank Auditors & Comptrollers; Beta Gamma Sigma. Address: 215-43 27th Ave., Bayside Gables, NY 11360, U.S.A. 6.

LEONHART, William Harold, b. 2 May 1906. Reinsurance Broker; Consultant. Educ: Balt. City Coll. Night Schl., 1921-26. Appts: Pres., Leonhart & Co., Inc., ins., reins., brokers, Balt., Md., 1943-; Chmn., Leonhart Assocs. Inc., Balt., 1970-; Cons., publicity & sales promotion. Mbrships: Civitan Club of Balt.; Pres., ibid, 1949-50; Civitan Int.; Chmn., Comm. for Mentally Retarded, ibid, 1951-52, Chmn., Int. Safety Comm., 1953; Frederick Acad. of the Visitation; Chmn., Advsry. Bd., ibid, 1965-; Boys Town Homes Md., Inc.; Pres., ibid, 1970-71; Exec. Comm., Balt. Chapt., ARC; Md. Chapt., SAR. Publr., The Fabulous Octogenarian. Address: 215 E. Church St., Frederick, MD 21701, U.S.A. 6, 16, 27.

LEON-SOH, (Mrs.) Felice Marjorie (also known as Che' Intan, in Malay meaning Madam Diamond), b. 30 Nov. 1922. Educationist; Playwright; Poet; Novelist; Author; Social Worker; Politician; Stateswoman; Business Executive. Educ: R.C. Covent & Tchrs. Trng. Coll., Singapore. Appts. incl: Coll. Lectr.; Schl. Prin.; M.P.; Fndr. & Chmn. Singapore Congress Party; Sec.-gen., New Singapore Liberal Socialist Party (after merging S'pore Congress Party w. old S'pore Liberal Socialist Party); Fndr. & Chmn., S'pore Canine Welfare Assn.; Fndr. & Chmn., Felicia Grp. of Cos. w. HQ at Nassau, Bahamas. Special achievement: Arranged 1st summit meeting between Pres. Soekarno of Indonesia & Premier Tengku Abdul Rahman of Malaysia, Tokyo, June 1965. Publs: Singapore Premier vs the Press; Nixon's Visit to Red China averts 3rd World War; Malaysian Transition; sev. plays, poems, novels. Address: Katong P.O. Box 77, Singapore 15, Repub. of Singapore. 98, 132.

LEON-SOTOMAYOR, Luis Angel, b. 2 Aug. 1931. Physician. Educ: B.S. & Med. Tech., Univ. of Puerto Rico, 1954; M.D., ibid, 1958. Appts. incl: Instr. in Med., Tulane Univ. & Dir., Alcoholic Rsch. Div., Charity Hosp., New Orleans, 1961-62; Instr., Med. Coll. of Ga., Augusta, 1963-65; Univ. of Tex. Med. Br., 1965-; Pvte. Prac., Galveston, Tex., 1965-; Chmn., Dept. of Med., Galveston Co. Hosp., Tex. City, 1965-68; Sec., Drs. Clin., Galveston, 1970-. Mbrships. incl: Sigma Xi; Alpha Omega Alpha; Royal Soc. of Med.; Royal Soc. of Hlth.; Dip., Am. Bd. of Internal Med.; Nat. Bd. of Med. Examinrs; Fellow, A.C.P.; Am. Coll. of Cardiol.; Am. Coll. of Chest Physns.; AMA; etc. Publs. Myxedema Coma, 1964; Cirrhosis of Liver and Hepatoma, 1966; Epidemic Diencephalomyelytis, 1969. Contbr. to profl. jrnls. Recip. Commendation for Outstanding

Achievement, U.S. Army, 1963-65. Address: 1501 Broadway, Galveston, TX 77550, U.S.A.

LEPEHNE, Renate, b. 3 Apr. 1931. Educator. Educ: B.S., Boston Univ.; M.Ed., Northeastern Univ. Appts. incl: Instrnl. Programmer, Bolt Beranek & Newman Inc., Cambridge, Mass., 1961-64; Cons., ind. concerns, schl. systems & publrs., 1964-; Officer of Instrn., Forsyth Dental Ctr. Schl. for Dental Hygienists, Boston, 1966-72; Fac. Mbr., Northeastern Univ., 1964-73; Dir., Div. of Programmed Learning, 1969-70; Dir., Off. for Instrnl. Design, Open Coll., Bunker Hill Community Coll., 1973-. Mbrships. incl: Am. Assn. for Higher Educ.; Educ. Rsch. Assn.; AAUP; Phi Delta Kappa; Soc. for Educl. Communication & Technol. Author of programmed learning texts, study courses & papers. Address: 650 Huntington Ave., Boston, MA 02115, U.S.A. 5, 138.

LEPORE, Michael J. b. 8 May 1910. Physician. Educ: B.S., N.Y. Univ., 1929; M.S., Univ. of Rochester, 1931; Rsch. Fellow in Physiol., Schl. of Med., ibid, 1930-31; Rsch. in Pathol., 1933; M.D., 1934; Intern, Duke Univ. Hosp., 1934-35; Rsch. Fellow, Schl. of Med., Yale Univ., 1935-36; Asst. Res. in Med., Duke Univ. Hosp., 1936-37. Appts. incl: Cons. in Gastroenterol., 1960-; Attending Physn. in Med. & Dir., Gastroenterol. in Med. & Surg., St. Vincent's Hosp. & Med. Ctr., N.Y., 1966-; Prof., Clin. Med. & Attending Physn., Univ. Hosp., N.Y. Univ. Schl. of Med., 1968-. Fellowships: Am. Coll. of Physns.; N.Y. Acad. of Med.; N.Y. Acad. of Scis. Mbrships. incl: Diplomate, Am. Bd. of Internal Med., 1943; AMA; Am. Gastroenterological Assn.; AAAS; Am. Therapeutic Soc. Contbr. to num. med. jrnls. Recip., Army Commendation Ribbon, Cmdng. Gen., Western Pacific Base Command, 1946. Address: 550 Park Ave., N.Y., NY 10021, U.S.A.

LEPORE, Ralph Frank, b. 2 Mar. 1913. Law Enforcement. Appts. incl: Clerk of Police Ct., Wheeling Police Dept., W.Va., 1936-41; Special Agent., Fed. Bureau of Investigation. Wash. D.C., 1941-48; Chief Dep. Sheriff, Ohio County, Wheeling, W.Va., 1949-53; Chmn., W.Va. Racing Commn., Chas., W.Va., 1953-57; V.P., Fidelifax of the Alleghencies-Pittsburgh, Pa. & Int. Rsch. Consultants Inc., Pittsburgh, Pa., 1957-60; Compliance Officer, U.S. Dept. of Labor, Cleveland, Ohio, 1961-64; V.P., Intelligence Service Inc., Cleveland, Ohio, 1965; Pres., 1967; V.P., American Land Reclamation & Resort Corp., Cleveland, Ohio & Mt. Savage, Md., 1968; Sheriff & Treas., Ohio Co., Wheeling, W.Va., 1969-72. Mbrships. incl: Pres., Amen Corner Pgh., Pa.; Variety Club, Tent No. 1, Pgh., Pa.; Dapper Dan, Pgh., Pa.; Am. Soc. of Ind. Security, Chicago, Ill.; Soc. of Former Spec. Agents of Fed. Bureau of Invest., N.Y.; Nat. Police Acad. Associates, Wash. D.C.; Nat. Sheriffs Assoc., Wash. D.C.; Int. Assoc. of Chief of Police, Wash. D.C.; numerous other police and sheriffs orgs. Address: 22 Hamilton Ave., Wheeling, WV 26003, U.S.A. 6, 114.

LEPPIK, Elmar Emil. Educator; Botanist; Plant Pathologist; Evolutionist. Educ: M.Bot., & Dr. Natural Scis., Tech. Univ. of Zurich, Switzerland. Appts: Prof., Augustan Coll., Sioux Falls, S.D., 1950-55; Prof., Univ. of Minn., 1955-57; Prof., Iowa State Univ. 1957-64; Rsch. Botanist, U.S.D.A., 1964-. Fellow, sev. sci. socs. Mbr. inclng. corres. & hon. many sci & cultural socs., U.S.A. & other countries. Author of many books, monographs in sev. langs. in various countries Author of 360 sci. jrnl. papers. Address: Plant Genetics &

Germplasm Inst., USDA, ARC-West, S.Bldg Rm. 326, Beltsville, MD 20705, U.S.A. 6, 8, 14 28, 50, 125.

LERCH, Pierre, b. 28 Aug. 1927 Physico-Chemist. Educ: Ingénieur-chimist EPUL; Dr. és scis. Appts: Chief phys., Ctr Anticancéreux Romand; Prof., Berne Univ. Switzerland; Dir., Inst. de Radiophys Appliquée; Ord. Prof., Ecole Polytech Fédérale; Dir., Inst. d'Electrochimie et d Radiochimie. Mbrships; Soc. Suisse de Phys. Soc. Suisse de Chimie; Soc. de Chimie Phys. Soc. Chimique de France; Comité de la Soc Suisse de Radiobiol.; Comité de l'Assn. suiss de l'énergie atomique. Author about 100 sci papers in field. Address: Inst. de Radiophys Appliquée, Av. César-Roux 29, Lausanne Switzerland.

LERHEIM, Magne, b. 14 Dec. 1929 Assistant University Director. Educ: Cand. jur. Univ. of Oslo, Norway; Dipl., Coll. of Europe Bruges, Belgium. Appts: Sec., Min. of Educ. Oslo, 1958-59; Sec. Gen., Nat. Comm. of Int Youth Cooperation & Nat. Comm. of Atlanti Assn., 1959-61; Hd. of Off., Univ. of Bergen 1961-63; Under Sec., Min. of Educ., Lyn Govt., 1963; Under Sec., Min. of Finance Borten Govt., 1965-67; Univ. Sec., Univ. o Bergen, 1967; Asst. Univ. Dir., ibid, 1968- Occasional Mbr. of Parliament, 1969-72 Mbrships: Chmn., Norwegian Student Assn. 1958; Chmn., Norwegian Young Liberals 1959-61; Exec. Comm., Liberal Party, 1964-72 New Liberal Party (pro-European), 1972-; Vic Chmn., ibid, 1972-73; Chmn., ibid, 1973- Publs: The Problem of Sovereignty in Relatio to Integration on a Super-National Level, 1958 Norsk Livsform & EEC, 1972; Kvifor Norge bö bli medlem av EEC, 1972. Address: Universit of Bergen, Muséplass 1, 5014—Bergen-Universitetet, Norway, 1934.

le RICHE, William Harding, b. 21 Mar 1916. Physician; University Professor. Educ B.S., Univ. of Witwatersrand, S. Africa, 1936 M.B., Ch.B., ibid, 1943; M.D., 1949; M.P.H. Harvard Univ., U.S.A., 1950; Fellow, Am. Col of Physns., 1972; F.R.C.P. (Canada), 1972 Appts. incl: Cons. in Epidemiol., Dept. of Nat Hlth. & Welfare, Ottawa, Canada, 1952-54 Rsch. Med. Off., Physns.' Servs. Inc., Toronto 1954-57; Staff, Dept. of Pub. Hlth., Schl. o Hygiene, Univ. of Toronto, 1957-; Prof. of Pub Hlth., ibid, 1959; Prof. & Hd., Dept. o Epidemiol. & Biometrics, 1962-; Assoc., Dep of Med., 1969; Staff, Sunnybrook Hosp. Toronto, 1969. Mbr., Inst. of Med. Scis., 1969 Author of publs. in field. Address: Schl. o Hygiene, Univ. of Toronto, Toronto 5, Ont. Canada. 14, 50, 88.

LERNER, Alan Jay, b. 31 Aug. 1918 Playwright & Lyricist. Educ: Harvard Univ Mbrships. incl: Songwriters Hall of Fame, 1971 Pres.'s Comm. for Nat. Cultural Ctr., Wash. D.C., 1962; Bd. of Govs., Nat. Hosp. for Speech Disorders. Broadway Musical Plays incl: (w Frederick Loewe) Brigadoon, 1947; Paint You Wagon, 1951; My Fair Lady, 1956; Camelot 1960; (w. Kurt Weill) Love Life, 1948; (w Burton Lane) On A Clear Day You Can Se Forever, 1965; (w. Andre Previn) Coco, 1969 Screen Plays incl: An American in Paris, 1951 Brigadoon, 1954; Gigi, 1958; My Fair Lady 1964; Camelot, 1968; Paint Your Wagon, 1969 On A Clear Day You Can See Forever, 1970 Hons. incl: (3 Acad. Awards) Best Screen Play An American in Paris, 1951; Best Screen Play & Best Song, Gigi, 1958. Address: 745 Fifth Ave. N.Y., N.Y. 10022, U.S.A. 128.

LERNER, Lawrence, b. 21 Sept. 1923. Executive, Interior Architecture. B.A., Brooklyn Coll., 1948. Appts: Designer, Michael Saphier Assocs., 1952; V.P., Exec. V.P., Pres., ibid, 1952-61; Pres., Saphier, Lerner, Schindler, Environetics, Inc., N.Y.C., 1961-72; Chmn. of Bd. & Pres., ibid, 1972-; Dir., Pilot Woodworking Co., Inc., 1968-; Vis. Prof., Schl. of Arch., Design & Planning, Ohio Univ. Mbrships: Young Pres.' Org.; World Bus. Coun.; Dean's Coun., Grad. Schl. of Mgmt., Univ. of Calif. at L.A.; Metropolitan Club, Chgo. Publs: Contract Design (co-author); Articles in profl. jrnls. Address: Saphier, Lerner, Schindler, Environetics, Inc., 600 Madison Ave., N.Y., NY 10022, U.S.A. 16.

LERNER, Max, b. 20 Dec. 1902. Journalist; Educator. Educ: A.B., Yale Univ., 1923; A.M. Wash. Univ., 1925; Ph.D., Brookings Grad. Schl. of Econs. & Govt., 1927. Appts: incl: Lectr., Nat. War Coll. & Ind. Coll. of The Armed Forces; Newspaper Columnist, N.Y. Post; currently, Prof., Am. Civilization & World Politics, Brandeis Univ. Publs. incl: America As A Civilization; The Age of Overkill; Ideas Are Weapons; The Unfinished Country; The Mind & Faith of Justice Holmes; Education & A Radical Humanism; Tocqueville & American Civilization. Address: c/o New York Post, 210 South St., New York, N.Y. 10002, U.S.A. 6.

LERNER, Mortimer Milton, b. 13 Apr. 1915. Attorney. Educ: A.B., CUNY, 1934; L.D., Columbia Law Schl., 1937. Appts. incl: Special Agt., Security & Intelligence Corps., U.S. Dept. Defense, 1942-43; Nat. Panel of Arbitrators, Am. Arbit. Assn., 1971-; Chmn., Pub. Rels. & Law Comms., Mr. Sword Fndn., 1969-; Co-Fndr. & V.Chmn., Bd. Trustees, Mus. of the Media, 1969-. Mbrships: The New Yorker Club, 1971-; Inst. for Cultural Rsch., London; Bd. Advsrs., Anthos Inst., Inc.; Aurion Inst., 1969-. Contbr. to law publs. Recip. acad. hon. Address: 60 East 42nd St., New York, NY 10017, U.S.A. 6.

LERNER, Nathan, b. 12 Oct. 1925. Lawyer. Educ: Dr., Law & Soc. Scis., Univ. of Buenos Aires, Argentina. Appts: Prac. lawyer, Buenos Aires, 1950-62; Hd., Latin-Am. Desk, World Jewish Congress, N.Y., U.S.A., 1963-66; Exec. Dir., World Jewish Congress, Israel Br., 1966-; P.T. Lectr., Tel-Aviv & Haifa Univs., 1971-. Mbrships: Treas., Israel Br., Int. Law Assn.; Israel Bar. Publs: The U.N. Convention on the Elimination of all Forms of Racial Discrimination, 1970; The Crime of Incitement to Group Hatred, 1965; Esquema del Derecho Israeli, 1963; En Defensa de los Derechos Humanos, 1958 & articles & essays in specialized publs. Address: P.O. Box 14177, Tel-Aviv, Israel. 55, 94.

LEROUX, Yves, b. 30 Apr. 1929. Journalist. Educ: Paris Fac. of Law. Appts. incl: Gen. Deleg., Jeunesses Musicales de France, Paris, 1954-63; Reporter & Ed., Economy, 1963-67; Ed., Connaissance des Hommes, 1965-; Mgr., Ed., l'Information Dentaire, 1967-; Fndr. & Ed., Le Journal de Biologie buccale, 1973-. Mbrships. incl: Fndr., Sec.-Gen., l'Association Culturelle Connaissance des Hommes, 1961; Pres., l'Assocation Parisienne des Amis de François Mauriac, 1973. Publs: La Bruyère de Septembre, 1971; Robert Lumblot, 1972; L'Escalier de la Nuit, 1973; Gabriel Fournier, 1973; Jean Commère, (in preparation); Paul Collomb, (in preparation). Pseudonyms, Yves Frontenac & Bertrand Duplessis. Hons: Laureate of the Acad.; Paul Harmottan Prize, Beaux Arts, 1973. Address: Imprimerie SIEP, 23 Rue de la Haute Bercelle, 7300—Avon, France.

LEROY, (Fr.) Pierre Jean Marie, S.J., b. 24 Aug. 1900. Priest. Educ: Nancy Univ.; Theol. schlrship., Univ. Coll., Dublin, Repub. of Ireland; D.Sc., Sorbonne, Paris, France. Appts: Asst. & Dir., Hoang-Ho Pei-Ho Mus., Tientsin, China; Dir., Geol. Inst., Pekin; Nat. Coun. for Sci. Rsch., Paris, France; Rsch. Assoc., Station Physiol., Coll. de France; Fellow, Chgo. Univ., Ill., U.S.A.; Dir., Laboratory, Gif sur Yvette, France. Publs: Pierre Teilhard de Chardin, tel que je l'ai connu; La carrière scientifique de P. Teilhard de Chardin (w. Louis Barjon); Dans le village des Sinanthropes: lettres inédites de P. Teilhard de Chardin et J. Gunnar Andersson & more than 250 sci. publs. on Biol. Hon: Chev., Légion d'Honneur. Address: 2 Rue de l'Ecole des Postes, 78000, Versailles, France, 43. 91.

LEROY-BEAULIEU, Henri (Marie), b. 22 Mar. 1910. Company Director. Educ: Ecole libre des Scis. Politiques, Fac. de Droit & Fac. des Scis., Paris, France; Licence en Droit; Barrister; Cert., Univ. of Paris. Appts: For. policy Corres., Jrnl. des Débats; Gen. Sec., Impex Co. Ltd. (Schneider-Creusot group); Fndr., Chmn. & Gen. Mgr., L'atome Industriel Co. Ltd., 1961; Hon. Chmn., ibid, 1968-; Conseiller du Commerce extérieur de la France, 1958-68; Bd. of Dirs., Syndicat des Producteurs Autonomes d' Electricité, 1974; Owner & Mgr., elec. co. Mbrships: Cercle de l'Union, Paris; Union Interalliée, Paris. Author of var. reports & articles on agric., econ. & for. policy. Hons: Winner of Moller Cup, Aéro-Club of France, 1937; Kt., Royal Order of Laos. Address: 43 Rue Saint Didier, 75116, Paris, France. 43, 91.

LEROY-BEAULIEU, Michel (Pierre Paul), b. 9 Feb. 1904. Diplomat (retd.). Educ: Ecole libre des Scis. Politiques, France; Fac. des Lettres, Paris; Balliol Coll., Oxford, U.K., 1922-24; Licence ès Lettres, Univ. of Paris; Bachelier en Droit. Appts. incl: Advsr., UN Commn. for Codification of Int. Law, 1947; Gen. Sec., Interministerial Commn. for Human Rights in France; Advsr. to prof. Réné Cassin & French Rep., UN Human Rights Commn.; Ambassador to Bolivia, 1960, on special leave, 1965, retd. 1969; Runs wife's estates in Costa Rica (sold 1969) & Morocco. Mbrships: Nouveau Cercle, Paris; Racing-Club de France, Paris. Publs: Le Prix de Munich; Var. reports & articles on for. policy during & after WW II. Hons: Croix de guerre, 1940; Off., Royal Order of Orange-Nassau, 1948; Kt., Legion of Hon., 1957. Address: 1 Rue Marietta Martin, 75016 Paris, France. 43, 91.

LEROY-BEAULIEU, Paul, b. 9 July 1902. Financial Administrator; Company Executive. Educ: Dip. de l'Ecole des Sciences Politiques, Sorbonne, Paris; Dip., Econs. & Pol. Sci., Balliol Coll., Oxford, U.K., 1922. Appts. incl: Inspr. of Finance, 1929; Financial Attache, French Embassy, Rome, Italy, 1935, Wash. D.C., U.S.A., 1937; Dir. For. Trade, Min. of Finance, Paris, France, 1940; Dir. of Supplies, French Comm. of Nat. Liberation under de Gaulle, Algiers, 1943; French Rep., Finance Directorate, Allied Control Coun., Berlin, Germany, 1945; Econ. & Financial Councillor, French Cmdr.-in-Chief, 1948, French Embassy, Bonn, 1949; Chmn., Financial & Econ. Bd., NATO, 1951; Financial Councillor, French Embassy, London, U.K., 1952-58; Inspr. Gen. of Finances, France, 1956. Dir., Channel Tunnel Study Grp., 1958; Chmn., Soc. Iron Ore Mines of Mauritania, 1958-72; Dir., S.A. Dunlop, France, & Channel Tunnel Investment Ltd., London, U.K. Mbr., soc. & sporting clubs. Hons. incl: Cmdr., Legion of Honour; Grand Off., Mauritanian Order of Merit. Address: 51 Blvd. Beauséjour XVI, Paris, France.

LESCOE, Francis Joseph, b. 17 May 1916. Educator; Clergyman. Educ: B.A., St. Mary's Univ., Balt., 1938; S.T.B., 1940; S.T.L., 1942; M.A., Univ. of Toronto, Canada, 1947; Ph.D., 1949. Ordained to Cath. Priesthood, 1942. Appts: Asst. Pastor, St. Thomas Apostle Ch., W. Hartford, 1942-46; Mbr. Fac., St. Joseph Coll., ibid, 1945-; Assoc. Prof., ibid, 1950-54; Prof., philos., 1954-; Chmn., philos. dept., 1954-70; Chmn. & Prof. of palaeography, McAuley Inst., 1969-. Mbrships: AAUP; Am. Cath. Philos. Assn.; Mediaeval Acad. of Am.; Trustee, Edward Reardon Trust, 1970-. Publs: Sancti Thomas Aquinatis Tractatus de Substantiis Separatis: Existentialism: With or Without God; Ed., McAuley Lecture series, 1953-. Address: 243 Steele Rd., W. Hartford, CT 06117, U.S.A. 6.

LESLIE, Sylvia Adina, b. 18 Mar. 1912. Home Economist. Educ: B.Sc. Appts: Village Instr., Social Dev. Commn., Jamaica, W.I., 1945-48; Dist. Off., ibid, 1948-53; 3F Off., 1953-55; Home Econ. Off., 1955-62; Specialist Off., Textiles & Clothing, 1962-69; Chief Home Econ. Off., 1969-; Trainer & Supvsr., Home Econ. Component, Peace Corps Volunteers, U.S.A. & Jamaica, 1970-73. Mbrships: Exec. Mbr., Jamaica Home Econ. Assn.; Nat. Consumers' League; Chmn., Credit Comm., Jamaica Welfare Credit Union; Am. Univ. Grads. Assn. Author, One Pot Meal Booklet, 1972. Address: 24 Charlton Dr., Ewarton, St. Catherine, Jamaica, W. Indies, 136.

LESPES, Henri, b. 7 Mar. 1909. Engineer; Writer. Educ: Nat. Schl. of Mines, Paris, France. Appts: Engr., var. enterprises, 1933-44; Mgmt. Cons., 1951-; Served in WW II; Dpty., Seine & Marne, 1945-51; Judge, High Constitutional Ct., 1951-56; Writer. Mbrships: Co-Fndr., Confédération Générale des Cadres (Gen. Cofedn. of Mgrs.); V.P., Gen. Assn. of French Veterans residing in Spain. Publs: incl: Corps à corps avec les Blindés; De l'usine au maquis; L'usine sans änse. Hons: War Cross, 1939-45; Off., Legion of Hon.; Cmdr., Order of Leopold, 1958; Cmdr., Order of Cisperos, 1969; Laureate, Acad. Française. Address: 'Els Pilons', Calle de Colon, Salou, Tarragona. Spain. 43, 91.

LESSER, Gilda, b. 5 June 1912. Microbiologist; Biological Chemist. Educ: B.S., N.Y. Univ., 1932; M.S., ibid, 1945. Appts: Rsch. Asst., Dept. Experimental Endocrinol. & Herpetol., Am. Mus. Natural Hist., N.Y.C., 1932-33; Asst. Bacteriol., Rschr. in Hematol., Brookdale Hosp., Brooklyn, 1933-36; Hd. Lab. & Microbiol., Bklyn. Cancer Inst., ibid, 1936-41; Microbiol., Fordham Hosp., N.Y., 1941-42; Chief Mucol., MacLean Labs., Bklyn., 1942-44; Rsch. Assoc., E.R. Squibbs & Co., New Brunswick, N.J., 1944-45; Biochem.-Microbiol., Allied Food Ind., Perth Amboy, ibid, 1945-51; Microbiol., C.F. Kirk Co., N.Y., 1951-52; Dir.-Cons., Bio-Indl. Rsch. Labs., Bklyn., 1952-. Mbrships: AAAS; Mu Chi Sigma; AAUW; IBS; Artist Mbr., Mus. Modern Art. Address: 385 E. 18th St., Brooklyn, NY 11226, U.S.A. 5.

LESTINA, Letitia. Educator. Educ: B.S., Univ. of Chgo., 1929; M.S., ibid, 1937; Postgrad., Newnham Coll., Cambridge, U.K., 1938-39. Appts: Assoc. Dir., Co-Fndr., Astro-Sci. Workshop, The Adler Planetarium w. Nat. Sci. Fndn., 1963-72; Fndr. & Organizer, Exec. Sec., The Ill. Sci. Lect. Assn. w. Nat. Sci. Fndn., The Christmas Lects., 1972. Mbrships: AAAS; Assn. of Am. Geographers; British Assn. of Univ. Women; AAUW. Address: 880 Lake Shore Dr., Chgo., IL 60611, U.S.A. 5, 34, 57, 128, 132.

LETULLE, Maurice, b. 16 Oct. 1929. Notary. Educ: Dr. of Law; Dr. of Judicial Sci.; Dir., Schl. of Pol. Sci. Appts. incl: Notary, Paris, 1957; Mbr., Advsry. Coun. for Commercial Legislation, 1965; Pres., F.N.A.P.L., 1973. Mbrships: Automobile Club de France; Club des Cent. Hons: Chevalier, Légion d'Honneur, 1971; Off., Mérite Nationale, 1973. Address: 12 Rue d'Anjou, Paris 8, 75 France.

LEUTGOEB, Rosalia Aloisia (Mrs. John Leutgoeb), b. 2 Apr. 1901. Professor Emeritus. Educ: B.S., Marquette Univ., 1935; M.S., ibid, 1936; Ph.D., 1938. Appts: Instr., St. Ambrose Coll., Iowa, 1940-42; Rsch. Chem., Red Star Yeast Co., Milwaukee, Wis., 1942-44 & U.S Govt. Labs., 1944-45; Assoc. Prof., Mundelein Coll., 1945-49; Rsch. Chem., Froedtert Grain & Malt, 1950-52; Prof. of Chem. & Chmn., Dept of Chem., Northland Coll., 1953-70; Mbrships Am. Chem. Soc.; AAAS; Midwest Assn Chems.; Tchrs. in Liberal Arts Colls.; Sigma Gamma Chi. Contbr. of sci. articles to profl jrnls. Recip. of Edward A. Urhig Award for Excellence in Tchng. Address: R1, Box 164 Ashland, WI 54806, U.S.A. 5, 8, 14, 15, 23, 51 128.

LEVALLEY, Guy Glenn, b. 21 Oct. 1942 Teacher; Theatrical Designer. Educ: B.A. Glassboro State Coll., N.J., U.S.A., 1964; M.A. Univ. of Iowa, 1967. Appts. incl: Asst. Tech Dir., N.Y. Shakespeare Festival Mobile Theatre 1967; Asst. Prof. of Theatre, Monticello Coll. 1967-68; Asst. Prof. of Theatre, Tech. Dir., & Theatre Designer, Prince George's Coll., 1968 Mbrships: Am. Theatre Assn.; U.S. Inst. of Theatre Technol.; NEA. Author, An Annotated Bibliography of Stage Lighting for Dance 1972. Designer, 2 scenes in Theatre U.S.A 1972. Hons: Scarlet Masque Award, 1962 Purple Masque Award, 1963; Medallion Award in Theatre, 1964; Best Lighting Design, D.C Play contest, 1970. Address: 9524 Hemlockhil Ave., College Pk., MD 20740, U.S.A. 6,, 125.

Le VAN, James Henry, b. 9 Jan. 1905 Environmental Engineer. Educ: C.E., Lehig Univ., Bethlehem, Pa., 1926; S.M., Harvar Univ., 1931. Appts: Off. i/c., Scioto Rive Investigation, 1937-38, Aedes Aegypti Contro Unit, 1938-40; Asst. Liaison Off., U.S. Arm 4th Serv. Cmd., 1941-43; Chief Sanitary Engr War Shipping Admin., 1944-45; Dist. Engr U.S. Pub. Hlth. Serv., 1948-51; Res. Engr Water Supply & Sewerage, Levittown, Pa 1952-55; Asst. Sanitary Engr., Lt. Jr. Grade, t Sanitary Engr. Dir., Capt., U.S. Pub. Hlth Serv., & Chief Sanitary Engr. Off., U.S. Coas Guard, 1958-69; retirement, 1969. Mbr., prof orgs. Author, Ship Sanitation. Var. publs., shi sanitation & yellow fever mosquito contro Recip., Coast Guard Commendation Meda 1969. Address: 3911 Parsons Rd., Chevy Chase MD 20015, U.S.A.

LEVANON, Eliyahu Yoshua, b. 5 Ma 1903. Rabbi; Author. Educ: Ordained Rabb Yeshivat Etz Haim; Tchrs. Dip., Tchr. Sem Jerusalem; Appts: Staff mbr., Min. of Religiou Affairs, 1948-; Cultural Off., Israel Defenc Forces. Mbr., masons. Publs: be Misholei h Moledet, 1934; Yalkut Hebron, 1937; Ish h Torah ve Hama'aseh, 1946; Sha'arei Krav 1944; Sihim Ka'arazim, 1949; ha Misdar Dom 1956; Amud Yerushalaim, 1963; Even h Bohan, 1963; Yizkor Diyerushalayim; be Rur Hamor ve Hamachpel; Tehelim (psalms), 196! Se'ehipim; Torah ou Shemot ha Parshi'o Hons: Medals of Israel, ot hahaganah, 1953, o ha Mishmar, 1958, ot Aleh, 1968. Addres Min. of Religious Affairs, Jerusalem, Israel. 5!

LEVAVY, Zvi, b. 1 Oct. 1910. Certified Public Accountant. Educ: B.C.S., N.Y. Univ., 1934. Appts: Sec., Palestine Trust Co., Tel Aviv, Palestine, 1934-36; Sec., Chief Acct., Palestine Brewery Richon Le Zion, 1936-38; Comptroller, Zionist Org. Am., 1940-43; formerly sr. ptnr., Popkin & Levavy accts.; currently prin. ptnr., Zvi Levavy & Co., C.P.A.'s. Mbrships: Pres., Perth Amboy Zionist Org., 1949-50; mbr. at large, Jewish Community Coun., Perth Amboy (Pres., 1963-66); Int. Coun. Jt. Distribution Comm., Int. Affairs Nat. Community Rels. Coun., 1968-73; V.P., Perth Amboy Bd. Educ., 1966-74, Perth Amboy Bd. Schl. Estimate, 1966-74; Middlesex Co. Coll.; Fndr., Pres., Morris J. & Betty Kaplun Fndn.; Trustee, Hillel Acad.; Am. Inst. C.P.A.'s; N.Y. & N.J. Socs. C.P.A.'s; Bd. Govs., Dropsie Univ., Am. Assn. Jewish Educ. Address: 21 E. 40th St., N.Y., NY 10016, U.S.A.

LEVENSON, Harold A., b. 2 May 1919. Insurance Executive; Theatrical Producer. Appts. incl: Agt., Occidental Life Ins. Co., Pasadena, 1950; Gen. Agt., Guaranty Union Life of Beverly Hills, Pasadena, 1950-58; Gen. Agt., United Life & Accident Ins. Co., 1958-; Pres., Harold Levenson Productions, Inc. Producer of many Successful stage productions clng. Born Yesterday, 1963; Abie's Irish Rose, 1964; Flame-out, 1968; There's A Girl in My Soup; & Tom Jones: Address: 7080 Hollywood Blvd., Suite 422, Hollywood, CA 90028, U.S.A. 9, 16, 59.

LEVENSON, Rasaline, b. 10 Sept. 1915. Political Science Teacher & Researcher. Educ: B.A., Univ. of Calif., Santa Barbara, 1952; M.A., Univ. of Calif., Berkeley, 1953; M.S., Univ. of Conn., 1962; Ph.D., ibid, 1971. Appts: Newspaper ed., W. L.A. Independent, L.A., Calif., 1938-42; Served, U.S. Army (W.A.C.), 1942-45; Rschr., Dept. of Army, Tokyo, Japan, 1946-48; Writer, U.S. Railroad Retirement Bd., Chgo., 1958; Tchr.-Rschr., Inst. of Pub. Serv., Univ. of Conn., 1958-72; Assoc. Prof., Calif. State Univ., Chico, 1972-. Mbrships: Am. Soc. for Pub. Admin.; Am. Pol. Sci. Assn.; Nat. Municipal League; USAFR. Publs. incl: The Legislative Role in Urban Affairs: A Bibliography, 1973; Women in Government & Politics: A Bibliography of American & Foreign Sources, 1973; The Big & the Small in Local Government: Connecticut & California Share Municipal Problems, Conn. Govt., 1973. Address: Dept. of Pol. Sci., Calif. State Univ., Chico, CA 95926, U.S.A. 5, 14.

LEVENSTEIN, Aaron, b. 11 Nov. 1910. Educator; Author. Educ: B.A., CCNY, 1930; J.D., N.Y. Law Schl., 1934. Appts: Law Prac., 1934-40; Directing Ed., Rsch. Inst. of Am., 1940-60; Prof. of Mgmt., Baruch Coll., CUNY, 1960-; Cons., City of Hope Med. Ctr., 1965-; Ed., Interaction-The Mgmt. Psychol. Letter, 1972-; Mbr., editl. bd., Freedom at Issue, 1970-; Dir. in W. Bengal, Bangladesh Refugee Prog., Int. Rescue Comm., 1971-. Mbrships: Bd. Dirs., Freedom House, League for Indl. Democracy; Exec. Comm., Jewish Labour Comm.; City Club of N.Y.; Indl. Rels. Rsch. Assn. Publs. incl: Labor Today & Tomorrow, 1945; Why People Work, 1962; They Chose Freedom, 1964; Freedom's Advocate (co-author), 1965; Use Your Head, 1965; Testimony for Man, 1967. Address: Baruch Coll., CUNY, 17 Lexington Ave., N.Y., NY 10010, U.S.A. 6.

LEVER, Chauncey Waldo, b. 11 Oct. 1925. Banker. Educ: B.S., Wofford Coll., Spartanburg, S.C.; Univ. of N.C. Appts. incl: Dir., Pub. Rels. Dept., Abney Mills & Irwin Mills, S.C., N.C. & Miss., 1954-57; V.P., S.C. Nat. Bank, 1957-62; Div. Dir. & Gen. Exec., S.C. State Dev. Bd., 1963-64; V.P., Fla. 1st Nat. Bank, Jacksonville, Fla., 1965-71; Dir., Fla. Nat. Bank of Jacksonville & at Lake Shore; Pres. & Dir., Fla. 1st Nat. Bank of Jacksonville; Pres. & Dir., Fla. Nat. Banks of Fla. Ltd., 1971-. Mbrships. incl: Assn. of Reserve City Bankers; Kappa Sigma; Pi Gamma Mu; Nat. Defense Comm., U.S. Chmbr. of Comm.; Pub. Rels. Soc. of Am.; Past Pres., Southern Assn. of Sci. & Ind.; Bd. of Assocs., Wofford Coll.; Chmn., Bd. of Trustees, Southside United Meth. Ch.; etc. Recip. Nat. Freedoms Fndn. Award, 1951-52. Address: Florida National Banks of Florida Inc., Florida First National Bank Bldg., P.O. Drawer 689, Jacksonville, FL 32217, U.S.A.

LEVERKUS, C. Erich, b. 15 Mar. 1925. Banker. Educ: Univs. of Bonn & Tübingen, Germany; Dipl. Volkswirt, 1955; Dr.rer.pol., 1957. Appts: Dir., chem. ind., 1957-70; Investment Officer, Iduna Ins. Grp., Hamburg, 1958-60; Ptnr., Wilhelm Rée Jr. Bank, Hamburg, 1961-, (J. Magnus & Co.-Whilhelm Rée Jr., 1972-); Fndr., Mng. Ptnr., Dr. Leverkus & Seohne. Mbrships: Coun., Vereinigte Evangelisch Lutherische Kirche Deutschlands; Chmbr. of Pub. Responsibility, Evangelischen Kirche in Deutschland; Dir., Alten Eichen Hosp. & Walther Blohm Stiftung; Dir., Deutsche Schutzvereinigung für Wertpapierbesetz, LV Hamburg & Schleswig-Holstein; Versammlung Eines Ehrbaren Kaufmanns zu Hamburg; Rotary Club; Corps Borussia zu Bonn; Corps Palatia zu Bonn. Publs. incl: Contbr., Festschrift für Rudolf Johns, 1965; Nordelbische Pastorenfamilien und ihre Nachkommen, 1973. Hons: Ehrenritter, Johanniterorden, 1951; Rechtsritter, 1966. Address: c/o J. Magnus & Co.-Wilhelm Rée Jr., Bank, Paulstr. 5, 2 Hamburg 1, German Fed. Repub. 43, 92.

LÉVESQUE, J. Adrien, b. 16 Sept. 1923. Agriculturist. Educ: B.A., Bathurst Univ., Canada, 1945; B.S.A., Laval Univ. (Ste. Anne de la Pocatière), 1949. Appts: Agricl. rep., Bathurst, N.B., 1949-50; Asst. Agricl. rep., Edmunston, N.B., 1950-59; Agricl. rep., Grand Falls, N.B., 1959-60; Elected to N.B. Legislature, gen. election, 1960; Min. of Agric. & Rural Dev., N.B., 1960-70; Ins. agt. & salesman, T.R.C., 1970-72; Appointed Nat. Farm Products Marketing Coun., 1972. Mbrships. incl: Agricl. Inst. of Canada; Grand Kt., Faithful Navigator, Kt. of Columbus; Sec., V.P., Richelieu Club; Poll Chmn., Min., Liberal Pty. Hons: Dr. of Soc. Sci., Bathurst, 1961; Medal of Agricl. Merit, Ste. Anne de la Pocatière, 1961; Centennial medal, 1967. Address: 559 Blair Rd., Ottawa, Ont., Canada, K1J 7M3.

LEVEY, Michael Vincent, b. 8 June 1927. Author; Art-Historian. Educ: B.A., Exeter Coll., Oxford Univ., U.K., 1951. Appts. incl: Asst. Keeper, Nat. Gall., London, U.K., 1951-66; Dpty. Keeper, ibid, 1966-68; Keeper, ibid, 1968-73; Dir., ibid, 1973-. Publs. incl: Painting In XVIIIth Century Venice, 1959; From Giotto to Cézanne, 1962; Dürer, 1964; Rococo to Revolution, 1966; Early Renaissance, 1967; A History of Western Art, 1968; The Life & Death of Mozart, 1971; Painting At Court, 1971; Art & Architecture In 18th Century France (co-author), 1973. Hons: MVO, 1965; Hawthornden Prize, 1968; Fellow, Exeter Coll., Oxford Univ., U.K., 1973. Address: 3/185 Old Brompton Rd., London SW5 OAN., U.K. 1.

LEVI, Anthony Herbert Tigar, b. 30 May 1929. University Teacher & Administrator. Educ: Advanced Maths., Manresa Coll., Roehampton, 1951-52; Philos., Munich, 1952-55; Mod. Langs., Oxford, 1955-58; Ph.D., Oxford Univ., 1963. Appts: Tutor, Mod. Langs., Campion Hall, Oxford, 1964-71; Lectr., Christ Ch., Oxford, 1966-71; Vis. Lectr., Univ. of Warwick, 1966-67, Rdr. in French, 1967-70, Personal Chair in French, 1970-71; Buchanan Prof. of French, Univ. of St. Andrews, 1971-. Publs: French Moralists, The Theory of the Passions, 1585-1649, 1964; Religion in Practice, 1966; Humanism in France at the end of the Middle Ages & in the early renaissance (Ed.), 1971; Erasmus: The Praise of Folly, 1971. Num. articles, papers, reviews, var. jrnls. Address: Dept. of French., Buchanan Building, Union St., St. Andrews, Fife, U.K.

LEVI, Edward Hirsch, b. 26 June 1911. Lawyer; University President. Educ: Ph.B., Univ. of Chgo., 1932; J.D., 1935; J.S.D., Yale Univ., 1938. Appts. incl: Asst. Prof., Law, Univ. of Chgo., 1936-40; Prof., ibid, 1945; Dean, Law Schl., 1962-68; Pres., 1968; Spec. Asst. to Atty. Gen., Wash. D.C., 1940-45. Fellow, Am. Acad. Arts & Scis. Mbrships. incl: Coun., Am. Law Inst.; Trustee, Russell Sage Fndn.; Trustee, Urban Inst.; Trustee, Int. Legal Ctr.; White House Task Force on Educ., 1966-67; Phi Beta Kappa; Pres's. Task Force on Priorities in Higher Educ., 1969-70. Publs. incl: Point of View, 1969; The Crisis in the Nature of Law, 1969; The Collective Morality of a Maturing Society, 1973; The Place of Professional Education in the Life of the University, 1971. Hons: Order of the Coif; Off., French Legion of Hon., 1973; num. hon. degrees. Address: 5801 Ellis Ave., Chicago, IL 60637, U.S.A. 1, 2, 8, 34, 128.

LEVI, Lennart, b. 20 May 1930. Physician. Appts. incl: Physn., State Rehab. Clin., Stockholm, Sweden, 1956-58; Rsch. Physn., Dept. of Med. Psych., Karolinska Hosp., Stockholm, 1959-; Dir., Lab. for Clin. Stress Rsch. & Med. Rsch. Grp., Swedish Army, 1959-; Dir., WHO Int. Rsch. and Training Ctr. on Psychosocial Factors and Hlth., 1973-; Med. Cons., Swedish AEG Concern, Stockholm, 1961-. Mbrships. incl: Swedish Med. Soc.; Am. Psychosomatic Soc.; Soc. for Psychophysiol. Rsch.; AAAS; WHO Expert Panel on Mental Hlth. Publs. incl: Korper, Seele & Krankheit, 1964; Stress: Sources, Management & Prevention, 1967; Stress: Introduzione alla medicina psicosomatica, 1968; From Sick-bed to Work-Table, 1966; The Stress of Everyday Work (co-author), 1967; Emotional Stress: Physiological & Psychological Reactions (Ed.), 1967; Society, Stress & Disease—The Psychosocial Environment & Psychosomatic Diseases, 1971; Stress and Distress in Response to Psychosocial Stimuli, 1972. Address: Lab. for Clinical Stress Research, Fack, 10401, Stockholm 60, Sweden. 30, 50.

LEVI, Michael M., b. 19 Feb. 1929. Physician. Educ: B.A., Yugoslavia, 1947; M.S., Univ. of Lausanne, Switzerland, 1953; M.D., Univ. of Geneva, 1957, Doct., 1958. Appts: Asst., Ob. & Gyn., Columbia Univ., 1965-67; Instr., ibid, 1967-68, Asst. Clin. Prof., 1968-73; Asst. Vis. Gyn., Francis Delafield Hosp., N.Y., 1965; Asst. Vis. Obstrn.-Gyn., Harlem Hosp., 1965-68, Assoc. Obstrn.-Gyn., 1968, Asst. Dir. Ob.-Gyn., 1970-72; Med. Dir., O.B.G.Y.N. Assocs., 1971-. Mbrships. incl: Fellow, Am. Coll. Ob. & Gyn. & Int. Coll. of Surg.; Dipl., Am. Bd. of Ob. & Gyn.; Publs. incl. more than 20 original publs. & 3 books. Hons. incl: Award for Scientific Thesis, WHO, 1958; Best Scientific Paper, Pan Am. Cancer Cytol. Cong.,

N.Y.C., 1967; Fndn. Prize Thesis, Am. Assn. of Obstrns. & Gyns., 1970. Address: 999 Third Ave., Brooklyn, NY 11232, U.S.A. 6, 17.

LEVI, Raphael, b. 14 Aug. 1922. Business Executive. Educ: Lycée Français, Alexandria, Egypt. Appts: Mgr., Ste. Admar, Paris, 1950; Mng. Dir., ODC France, Paris, 1953-57; joined Empain-Schneider Grp., 1958, currently Pres., Secopa S.A., Paris, Mng. Dir., Decofra, Paris, Dir., Ferex, Antwerp, Belgium, Afimex, London, U.K., Escompte Corp. of Am., N.Y.C. Address: 22 Rue d'Aguesseau, Paris 8, France. 43, 91.

LEVIN, Allen Jay, b. 27 May 1932. Attorney at Law. Educ: B.A., Univ. Coll., N.Y. Univ., 1954; J.D., Schl. of Law, Univ. of Miami, 1957; also Univ. of Bridgeport, Conn., & Schl. of Law, Boston Univ. Appts. incl: Legal Counsel, Port Charlotte Civic Assn., Fla., 1961-64, & 1967-; Legal Counsel, Charlotte Harbor Fire Control Dist., 1965-; Judge, Small Claims Ct., Charlotte Co., 1962-72; Judge, Municipal Ct., N. Port Charlotte, 1972-. Mbrships. incl: Am. Bar Assn.; Fla. Bar, Charlotte Co. Bar Assn; Am. Judicature Soc., Tau Epsilon Rho Legal Fraternity; Alpha Epsilon Pi Fraternity; Past Pres., Dir., Port Charlotte Jewish Community Grp. Address: 834 N.E. Beacon Dr., Port Charlotte, FL 33952, U.S.A. 7, 81, 117.

LEVIN, Alvin Irving, b. . 22 Dec. 1921. Educator. Educ: B.M., Univ. of Miami, Fla., 1941; M.A., Calif. State Univ., L.A., 1955; Ed.D., UCLA, 1968. Appts: Composer-Arranger for motion pictures, TV & theater, Allied Artists, Eagle-Lion Studios, 1945-65; Training & Supvsng. Tchr., L.A. Unified Schl. Dist., 1957-65; Adult Educ. Instr., ibid, 1962-63; Rsch. Specialist, Off. of the Supt., 1965-67; Asst. Prof., Educ. Rsch. Calif. State Univ., L.A., 1968-69; Asst. Prof. Elem. Educ., Calif. State Univ., Northridge, 1969-73; Pres. & Fndr., The Alvin Irving Levin Philanthropic Fndn., 1973. Mbrships: L.A. World Affairs Coun.; Phi Delta Kappa; Am. Statistica' Assn.; AAUP; Nat. Soc. for the Study of Educ.; Int. Coun. on Educ. for Tchng. Publs: Symposium: Values in Kaleidoscope, 1973; Happy Land, a Music-drama, 1971; My Ivory Tower, 1950; rsch. publs; educ. films video tape recordings. Recip. of Schlrship Awards, Univ. of Miami, Fla., 1938-41. Address: 12416 Magnolia Blvd., North Hollywood, CA 91607, U.S.A. 9, 30, 57, 75, 120, 139.

LEVIN, Nora, b. 20 Sept. 1916. Teacher, Writer. Educ: B.S., Temple Univ., Phila., Pa., 1938; B.S., Drexel Univ., Phila., Pa., 1941. Appts: Ref. Libn., Pub. Documents Dept., Free Lib. of Phila., 1941-43; Rsch. Libn., Time, Inc., 1943-44; Hd., Edit. Lib., Holiday Mag., 1945-47; Hist. Instr., Phila. Pub. High Schls. 1948, 1953-71; Hist. Instr., Gratz Coll., Phila. 1971-. Mbrships: Bd. of Dirs., Jewish Community Rels. Coun. of Phila.; Comm. of 1000 for Soviet Jewry; Authors' Guild. Publs: The Holocaust: The Destruction of European Jewry, 1933-45, 1968; Articles in jrnls. inclng. Nation, The Progressive, Common-weal, Midstream, Congress Bi-Weekly Reconstructionist, Jewish Frontier. Hons: Alternate Selection, Book-of-the Month Club 1968; De Voto Fellowship to Breadloaf Coll., Middlebury, Vt., 1969. Address: 1220 W. Chelten Ave., Phila., PA 19126, U.S.A. 5, 30.

LEVIN, Shaul, b. 31 Oct. 1905. Educator Diplomat. Educ: P.H.D., Mod. & Medieval Hist. & Geog., Berlin Univ., 1932. Appts. Appts. incl: Tchr., H.S., Tel Aviv, Israel, 1934-45

Hdmstr., Shalva H.S., Tel Aviv, Israel, 1945-48; Dir. of Educ. & Cultural Activities, Municipality of Nathania, 1948-53; Dir. of Educ., Cultural & Youth Activities, Municip. of Tel Aviv-Jaffo, 1953-69; Councillor for Cultural Affairs for Western Europe, Israel Embassy, Paris & Permanent Deleg., UNESCO, 1956-58; Ministre Conseiller (Culture & Info.) for S. Am., Israel Embassy, Rio de Janeiro, 1963-65; Israel Ambassador in Cameroun & Guinea Equatorial, 1969-71; Dir. Gen., Evening Univ., Tel Aviv, Israel, 1971-73. Mbrships. incl: Mbr. of Presidency, Nat. Coun. for Culture & Arts, Pres., Theatre Sect., 1954-69; Pres., Union of Dirs. of Educ., Israel, 1954-69; Pres., Exec. Comm., Noar Lenoar Org., Israel. Publs: plays & poetry in German & Hebrew; articles on educl. & pol. topics in Israeli jrnls. Hons. incl: Legion d'Honneur, Chevalier, 1959; Prizes for Educ., Nathania, 1953 & Tel Aviv, 1969; Pour e Merite (Cameroun) Cmdr., 1971. Address: Sd. Hachail 11, Yad Elyahu, Tel Aviv 67310, Israel. 94.

LEVIN, William Harold, b. 30 Sept. 1926. Educator; Librarian. Appts. incl: Tchr., Latin, Engl., French & Spanish, Taylor Allderdice H.S., 1955-61; Chmn., Dept. of For. Langs., 1961-62; Tchr., Latin, French & Engl., Schenley H.S., 1962-66; Lectr., Spanish & French, Point Pk. Coll., Pitts., Pa., 1962-68; Libn., Peabody H.S. (Pitts. Pub. Schls.) 1967-70, '71-; Libn., Bd. of Educ. Profl. Lib., 1970-71. Mbrships: Beta Phi Mu, Int. Honorary Lib. Sci. Fraternity; MLA of Pitts. (Corres. Sec., 1960-61; Pres., 1961-62); Am., Pa., Pitts. Fedns. of Tchrs.; Metropolitan Opera Guild. Publs: Spanish Lang. Section, Modern Language Methodology Manual, 1961. Address: 4625 Fifth Ave., Apt. 708, Pitts., PA 15213, U.S.A. 42, 131.

LEVIN, Zev, b. 30 Aug. 1927. Economist; Diplomatist. Educ: B.A., Econs., Univ. of Minn., Mpls., U.S.A.; M.A., Labor Econs., Univ. of Wis. Appts: Int. Dept., Gen. Fedn. of Labour n Israel, 1953-58; Spec. Rep. to Cyprus & Greece, Int. Confedn. of Free Trade Unions, 1958-59; Israeli Consul Gen., Cyprus, 1959-60; Israeli Ambassador, Cyprus, 1960-62; Mbr., Exec. Comm., & Dir., Int. Dept., Gen. Fedn. of Labour in Israel, 1962-66; Israeli Ambassador, Kenya, 1966-69; Dir. & Corporate Mgr., Maritimecor S.A., 1970-. Mbrship: Exec. Comm., Fedn. of Disabled War Veterans, Israel, Chmn., 1954-57. Publs: Articles on trade union & labour subjects. Address: Im Glockenacker 53, 8053 Zurich, Switzerland.

LEVINE, Abe Lewis (Al), b. 9 Nov. 1915. Detective; Investigator; Author; Composer; Songwriter. Educ: special courses in criminol., criminal investigation, Univ. of Denver & Denver F.B.I.; Denver Police Dept. Acad. Appts: Police Detective, Denver Police Dept., 1940-66; Investigator, Denver Dist. Atty.'s Off., 1966-73. Mbrships: ASCAP, N.Y.C.; Denver Police Protective Assn.; Denver Police Pension Assn.; Colo. Assn. Dist. Atty. Investigators; Metropol. Law Enforcement Assn.; Beth Joseph Congregation, Denver. Publd. Songs incl: Don't Say You're a Dream; Today is Your Birthday; Shadow of the Blues; I Ain't Gonna Worry No More; The Man Behind the Badge; Keep the Faith; I Love to eat Chili in Chile. Elected on 2 occasions to Denver Post (Newspaper) Hall of Fame, 1948. Address: 245 Fairfax, Denver, CO 80220, U.S.A. 55.

LEVINE, Herbert Jerome, b. 27 Dec. 1906. Surgeon. Appts. incl: Chief of Staff, 1953; Sec.-Treas., Hosp. Staff, 1957, & Chief of Med., 1961, St. Mary's Hosp., Centralia, Ill; Surg., Mo. Pacific Railroad. Fellowships: Royal Soc.

of Hlth. (London); Am. Acad. Family Physns.; U.S.A. Publs: I Knew Sister Kenny; Tributes & Random Thoughts; Contbr. of articles to profl. jrnls. Address: Centralia, IL, U.S.A. 8.

LEVINE, Lewis, b. 30 Oct. 1899. Civil Engineer (Structural Branch). Educ: C.E., M.C.E., Brooklyn Polytechnic Inst. Appts. incl: Civil Engr., Brazil, Venezuela, W. Indies, Greece, Turkey, Iraq & Burma, 1940-48; Structural Engr., Tippets, Abbet, McCarthy, Stratton, 1950-57; Chief Structural Engr., David Volkert & Assocs., Wash. D.C., 1957-. Mbrships: Fellow & Life Mbr., Assn. of Surveyors & Civil Engrs.; Mbr., Soc. Am. Mil. Engrs. Address: c/o David Volkert & Assocs., 4701 Sangamore Rd., Bethesda, MD 20016, U.S.A. 7.

LEVINSON, Boris M., b. 1 July 1907. Clinical Psychologist. Educ: B.S., CUNY, 1937; M.S., ibid, 1938; Ph.D., N.Y. Univ., 1947; Dipl. Clin. Psychol., 1957. Appts: Ptve. Prac., 1938-; Clin. Psych., Vets. Rehab. & Mental Hygiene Clins., Brooklyn Jewish Hosp., 1944-48; Asst. Prof., Ferkauf Grad. Schl. of Humanities & Soc. Scis., Yeshiva Univ., N.Y., 1951-53; Assoc. Prof., ibid, 1953-56; Prof., 1956-73; Dir., Psych. Ctr., 1956-63; Chief Psych., Jewish Mem. Hosp., N.Y.C., 1957-59; Adjunct Prof., John Jay Coll., CUNY, 1972-; Prof., Touro Coll., 1973-. Mbrships: Fellow, Am. Psychol. Assn.; Soc. for Personality Assessment; N.Y. Soc. Clin. Psychol.; N.Y. Acad. Sci.; N.Y. State & Eastern Psych. Assns.; Psi Chi; Phi Delta Kappa. Publs. incl: Pet-Oriented Child Psychotherapy, 1969; Pets & Human Development, 1972. Address: 86-35 Queens Blvd., Apt. 65, Elmhurst, NY 11373, U.S.A. 6, 15, 28, 50, 54, 55, 64.

LEVITAS, Elliott Harris, b. 26 Dec. 1930. Lawyer. Educ: A.B., Emory Univ., 1952; J.D., ibid, 1956; M.A., Univ. Coll., Oxford; postgrad., Schl. of Law, Univ. of Mich., 1954-55; Admitted to Bar to practice all Fed. & State Cts., Ga., and Supreme Ct. U.S., 1955. Appts: Ptnr., Arnall, Golden & Gregory, Atlanta, Ga., 1955-; Rep., Ga. House of Reps., 1965-; Chmn., Joint House-Senate Comm. on Housing, 1969, House Comm. Community Affairs, 1970- & Joint House-Senate Comm. on Metropolitan Rapid Transit, 1973-. Mbrships. incl: Ga. & Am. Bar Assns; Executive Bd., Southern Regional Anti-Defamation League; Trustee, Atlanta Jewish Community Ctr.; Phi Beta Kappa. Named as Ga. Speaker of the Yr., Emory Univ. Forensics Soc., 1970. Address: 1000 Fulton Fed. Bldg., Atlanta, GA 30303, U.S.A. 7.

LEVITCH, Harry Herman, b. 24 Dec. 1916. Diamond Specialist; Designer; Jeweler. Educ: LL.B., Coll. of Law, Southern Univ., & Memphis State Univ. Grad., Colored Stones, Diamond Grading & Evaluation, Gemological Inst. of Am. Appts: Legal Br., USAAF, WWII; Pres., Harry Levitch Jewelers, Inc. Mbrships: Pres. Elect, B'nai B'rith Dist., Grand Lodge Number 7; Exec. Comm. Mbr., Bd. Dirs., March of Dimes, & Memphis & Shelby Co. Music Commn.; Bd. Trustees, Leo N. Levi Nat. Arthritic Hosp., Hot Springs, Nat. Pk., Ark.; Retail Jewelers of Am.; Jewelers Vigilance Comm. Hons: B'nai B'rith Volunteer of Yr. Award for Community & Veterans Servs., 1967; Outstanding Contbn. Award, Nat. Fndn. March of Dimes, 1971. Address: 147 Union Ave., Memphis, TN 38103, U.S.A. 7, 125.

LEVITCH, Joel Allen. Writer & Film Producer. Educ: B.A., Yale Univ.; M.A., ibid. Appts: Writer, Columbia Broadcasting System; Pres. & Exec. Prod., Jason Films. Films incl:

Strat; Veronica; Weekend; Mike & Kathy; A Way to Life. TV Films: Daddy Can't Find My Socks; Petition to Deny. Solo special shows: Mus. of Modern Art, N.Y.C., 1969, 1972; Whitney Mus., 1972. Mbr: Writers Guild of Am. Publs: Co-Author, Contraband of War, 1970; Diary of Eddie Jacobson, Wash. Post Feature Story (Pub. Affairs Series). Hons: Blue Ribbon, Am. Film Festival, 1969; Special Jury Gold Medal, Atlanta Film Festival, Ga., 1969; Two Silver Hugos, Chgo. Int. Film Festival, 1970; 3 Gold Medals, Int. Film Festival, 1970; 3 Gold Medals, Int. Film & TV Festival, 1969-70; 4 Chris Awards, Columbus Film Festival, 1969-70; 3 Golden Eagle Awards, Cine, 1969, 1973; 1st Prize, Festival dei Popoli, Florence, Italy, 1970; Best of Category, San Fran. Film Festival, 1970; Teheran Film Festival, Iran, 1973. Address: 2621 Palisade Ave., Riverdale, NY 10463, U.S.A.

LEVITT, Alfred, b. 15 Aug. 1894. Artist. Educ: Columbia Univ.; Studied Art, Art Students· League, Hans Hofman, N.Y.C., Grande Chaumière, Paris, France. Appts: Serv., USNR, WWI; Fndr., Dir. & Tchr. of Painting & Drawing, Ecole Moderne de Provence, St. Rémy de Provence, France, 1949-50, 1959-62. Lectr. on Modern Art & Cave Art. Rsch. on Cave Art in France, Spain, Italy & U.K. Solo Exhibs: Babcock Galls., N.Y.C., 1945, 1946; Art Alliance, Phila., Pa., 1947. Grp. Exhibs. incl: Brooklyn Mus., N.Y., 1947, 1951, 1953, 1955, 1959; Whitney Mus. Am. Art, N.Y., 1949, 1953, 1955. Permanent Collects: Neveh-Sha'anan Mus., Haifa, Israel; num. pvte. collects., U.S.A. & Europe. Mbrships. incl: Archaeol. Inst. of Am.; Soc. Préhistorique de l'Ariège; France; Archaeol. Soc., Staten Island, N.Y.; Modern Artists of Cape Ann, Mass. (Coord. Chmn. 1947); Fellow, MacDowell Colony, Peterboro, N.H., 1956. Contbr. to. profl. jrnls. Address: 505 W. Broadway, N.Y., NY 10012, U.S.A. 37, 55.

LEVITT, Irving Francis, b. 3 July 1915. Industrialist. Educ: B.S., Univ. Mich., 1936. Appts. incl: Advt. Mgr., feature writer, Braddock Pa. Free Press, 1936-37; Advt. Mgr., Levitt Bros. Furniture Stores, 1936-38; Ptnr., Exec. Admnstr., Stores in Braddock, Vandergrift & New Kensington, Pa., 1938-; Exec. Asst., V.P., Levinson Steel Co., Pitts., 1942-44; Real estate indl. dev.; Treas., Lepar, Inc.; Pres., Chmn., Bd., Union Screw & Mfg. Co., Pitts., Investment Capitol Corp.; Pres., Kirwan Heights Land Co.; King Land Co. (Ind.), Blawnox Realty Co.; Chmn. Bd., Apollo Inds., Inc.; Chmn. Bd., Dir., Apollo Int. Corp.; Pres., Dir., Apollo-Peru, S.A., Oakland Investment Corp., Pitts.; V.P., Dir., Apollo Indl., Inc. Apollo Investment Co., Pitts.; Sr. V.P., Parker-Levitt Corp., Sarasota, Fla., Marble Island, Inc., Vt. Mbrships. incl: Trustee, Levitt Fndn.; Nat. Sales Execs. Club (bd. dirs.). Address: 22F Gateway Towers, Pittsburg, PA 15222, U.S.A. 6.

LEVITT, Norma U. Communal Leader. Educ: B.A., Wellesley Coll., 1937; Grad. Schl. of Econs., Univ. of Chgo., 1938-39; grad. work, Univ. of Calif. Appts. incl: Mbr., Advsry. Comm. on Family Life, Great Neck Bd. of Educ., N.Y., 1950-51; Dir., Schl. Jewish Studies, Temple Beth-El of Great Neck, 1955-; Off., Wellesley Class, 1957-63; V.P., Jewish Theatre for Children, 1960-; Vice Chmn., Bd. of Trustees, Union of Am. Hebrew Congregations. Mbr. & Off., num. Jewish instns. & orgs. Mbr., Phi Beta Kappa. Author: plays, stories, articles, poetry, & Jewish services. Hons. incl: Eleanor Roosevelt Award, Woman of the Yr., 1973; var. serv. awards. Address:

Jewish Braille Inst. of Am. Inc., 110 E. 30th St., N.Y., NY 10016, U.S.A. 5, 6, 55.

LEVY, George Aaron, b. 25 July 1933 Company President. Educ: B.S., Univ. of Fla. Gainsville, 1958. Appts. incl: Sports Corres. Tampa Tribune, 1956-58; Salesman & Sales Mgr., Fla. Sporting Goods, 1959-60; Fndr. & Pres., George A. Levy Inc., 1960-; Dir., Dale Mabry State Bank, 1973-; Chmn., Bd. Trustees Hillsborough Community Coll., 1971- Mbrships. incl: Dir. & Coach, Gtr. Tampa Swimming Assn., 1956-58; Fndr., ibid; V.P., Fla. West Coast Sports Assn., 1971-; Sigma Delta Chi; Tau Epsilon Phi; Pres., Tampa Sports Club, 1966-67; Dir., Gator Football Boosters Inc., 1973-; Chmn., Sports Comm., Gtr. Tampa Chmbr. of Comm.; V.P., Tampa Chapt., Nat Football Fndn.; Fndr., Tampa Sports Awards Banquet; Charter, Sword & Shield Club. Hons incl: Sportswriters & Broadcasters Award 1963; Pres's. Award, Gtr. Tampa Chmbr. of Comm., 1966; Pioneer Award for outstanding contbn. to sports & youth, City of Tampa 1971. Address: George A. Levy Inc., 2614 W Kennedy Blvd., Tampa, FL 33609, U.S.A. 81 117, 125.

LEVY, Harold, b. 1 Jan. 1917. Company Executive. Educ: B.S., N.Y. Univ., 1937 postgrad., 1938. Appts: Exec. Vice Pres. Flagstaff Foods, Perth Amboy, 1955-; Sr. Vice Pres. & Sec., Flagstaff Corp. H.Q., N.Y.C. 1969-; Dir., Dukeland Packing Co., Balt. & V-W Elmicke Assocs. Inc., Bronxville. Mbrships: Bd of Mgrs., Perth Amboy Savs. Instn.; Bd. o' adjustment, Perth Amboy, Chmn., 1966-; Bd of trustees, Rutgers Prep. Schl.; Kiwanian Club Address: 141 Water St., Perth Amboy, N. 08861, U.S.A.

LEVY, Robert A., b. 12 Oct. 1941 Investment Adviser. Educ: B.B.A., Am. Univ. 1963; M.B.A., ibid, 1964; Dr. Phil. in Bus Admin., ibid, 1966. Appts. incl: Cons., H Zinder & Assocs., Inc., Wash. D.C., 1961-64 Lectr. Financial Mgmt. (part-time), Am. Univ. 1964-66; Pres. & Chmn., Computer Direction Advsrs., Inc., Silver Spring, Md., 1966-; Mgng Ptnr., Alpha Securities, Silver Spring, Md. 1968-; invited Speaker & Lectr. to profl. orgs num. occasions. Mbrships. incl: Am. Mgmt Assn.; Am. Econ. Assn.; Am. Finance Assn. Bd. Dirs., Wash. Soc. of Investment Analysts Phi Kappa Phi; Omicron Delta Epsilon; Pres. Coun., Am. Inst. of Mgmt. 1st Pres. & Exec Comm. Mbr., Doctl. Assn., Schl. Bus. Admin. Am. Univ. Contbr. to profl. jrnls. & books Hons. incl: Wall Street Jrnl. Student Achievement Award; Am. Univ. Grad Fellowship in Acctng.; Graham & Dodd Jr Analysts Citation, Financial Analysts Fed. 1966; sev. Schlrships. Address: 8750 Georgia Ave., Silver Spring, MD 20910, U.S.A. 6, 125

LEVY, Samuel, b. 26 Apr. 1924. Architect Educ: B.S., Litt.B., Colegio Pedro II, Rio de Janeiro, 1943; Archt., Faculdade Nacional de Arquitetura, Universidade do Brazil, 1949 postgrad., Urban Planning Schl. of Arch. Columbia Univ., 1960. Appts. incl: Asst.-Job Capt.-Designer w. sev. cos., 1957-66; Proj Archt. & Mgr., Tippetts, Abbett, McCarthy Stratton, N.Y.C., 1966-70; Cons. Archt., N.Y. 1972; Asst. V.P., Mgr., Premises Design, 1s Nat. City Bank, N.Y.C., 1973-. Mbrships. incl Am. Inst. Archts.; Institutio de Arquitetos do Brazil; N.Y. State Soc. Archts. 2nd Prize Winner, Assoc. Archt. Competition for Senate Bldg., Brazil, 1955. Recip. of Travelling Fellowship, Faculdade Nacional de Arquitetura Univ. of Brazil, 1949. Address: 119-46 80th Rd., Kew Gnds., N.Y., NY 11415, U.S.A. 6.

LEVY, Walter James, b. 21 Mar. 1911. Economic Consultant. Educ: Univs. of Berlin, Freiburg, Munich, Hamburg, Heidelberg, Kiel. Appts. incl: Cons., Dept. of Defense, U.S.A., 1951-54; Cons., Int. Co-operation Admin., 1956-57; Cons., Dept. of State, Off. of Under Sec. & Asst. Secs., 1960-; Oil Advsr. to Special Emissary of Pres. Kennedy to Pres. of Indonesia, 1963; Cons. to European Economic Community, 1970. Mbrships: Advsry. Coun. to Schl. of Advanced Int. Studies, Johns Hopkins Univ.; Coun. on For. Rels. Author, num. reports & articles for jrnls. inclng. Foreign Affairs & the London Economist. Hons. incl: Decoration of Dato Setia Laila Jasa conferred by High Highness the Sultan of Brunei, 1968; Order of Taj, Iran, 1969; Honorary Companion in The Most Disting. Order of St. Michael & St. George, H.M. Queen Elizabeth II, 1973. Address: 30 Rockefeller Plaza, N.Y., NY 10020, U.S.A. 2, 6, 12, 14, 16, 34, 128.

LEWANDOWSKA, (Sister) Mary Theodosette, b. 10 Apr. 1905. Educator. Educ: B.A., Marywood Coll., Scranton, Pa., 1944; M.A., Villanova Univ., Pa., 1950; postgrad. studies, Fribourg Univ., Switzerland, 1950, Providence, Coll., R.I., U.S.A., 1955, Cath. Univ. of Am., 1958, Stanford Univ., Calif., 1967, Pitts. Univ., Pa., 1973. Appts: Tchr., var. high schls., until 1952; Prin., Sacred Heart of Mary Schl., Balt., Md., 1952-55, Nazareth Acad., Phila., Pa., 1955-59, 1963-72; Superior, Nazareth Hosp., Phila., 1972-. Mbrships. incl: V.P., Polish-Am. Histl. Assn.; Am. Histl. Assn.; Nat. Cath. Educ. Assn.; Nat. Assn. of Secondary Schl. Principals; Bd. of Trustees, & Chmn., Plant & Grounds Comm., Nazareth Hosp. Co-contbr., New Cath. Ency., 1967. Recip., Summer Prog. Schlrship., Georgetown Univ., 1965. Address: Nazareth Hospital, 2601 Holme Ave., Philadelphia, PA 19152, U.S.A. 5, 130, 138.

LEWIN, Keith Kerton, b. 19 Apr. 1931. Artist; Portrait Painter; Art Teacher. Educ: incl: Cert. Med. Art, Hunter Coll., CUNY; Fellowship, Art Students League of N.Y. Inst. of Fine & Applied Art; Cert. Respiratory Therapy Techns. Appts. Incl: Tutor, num. Art Classes, Jamaica; Tutor, Int. Free Art Workshop, N.Y., U.S.A., 1964; Fac. Mbr., Waltann Schl. of Creative Arts, Brooklyn, N.Y., 1966-67. Mbrships. incl: Fndr., Jamaica Arts Club; Int. Soc. for Educ. thru' Art, Switzerland; Int. Friends' Art Guild; Past-Pres., ibid; Fellow, Royal Soc. Arts, U.K.; Assoc., Royal Drawing Soc., U.K. Solo exhibs. incl: Jamaica Lib. Serv., 1961; UN Ctr., N.Y.C., 1964; Christ Ch. Meth. Art Gall., ibid, 1967; Bertrand Russell Centenary, Rotunda Gall., London, U.K. Participant, num. grp. exhibs; Works incld. in num. pvte. & pub. colls. in Europe, Am., & Canada. Hons. incl: Cert. of Honor, Int. Art Competition, Puerto Rico, 1952; Cert. for Outstanding Achievement, Arts & Cultural Affairs Comm., U.S.A.; num. schlrships. & fellowships. Address: 1865 52nd St., Brooklyn, NY 11204, U.S.A. 133.

LEWIN, Leonard C., b. 2 Oct. 1916. Writer. Educ: A.B., Harvard Univ., 1936. Publs: Report From Iron Mountain, U.S.A., 1967, '68, U.K., 1968, other countries, 1968-70; Triage, U.S.A., 1972, '73, U.K., 1972, France ("Le Tri"), 1972/73; A Treasury of American Political Humor, U.S.A., 1964, '68; Articles, satire, parody, criticism, 1963-. Address: 10 Water St., Stonington, CT 06378, U.S.A.

LEWIS, Alphonse, b. 9 Dec. 1937. College Administrator. Educ: B.S., Tougaloo Coll.; M.S., Ind. Univ.; Ph.D., Ohio State Univ. Appts. incl: Instr. & Assoc. Dir. Counseling Servs., Ky. State Coll., 1967-68; Rsch. Assoc., Coll. of Med., Ohio State Univ., 1968-70; Prof. & Dean of Continuing Educ., Fayetteville State Univ. & N.C. State Univ., 1970-71; Dean of Academic Affairs, Jarvis Christian Coll., Hawkins, Tex., 1971-. Mbrships. incl: Nat. Assn. Higher Educ.; Nat. Assn. Coll. & Univ. Admnstrs.; Nat. Assn. Student & Personnel Admnstrs.; Phi Delta Kappa; Beta Kappa Chi. Publs. incl: The Five Mode Study, 1968-69; The Use of the Computer in the Medical School Admission Process, 1969; The Role of the Black Professional in Planning Designing & Implementing Competency Based Programs on Black & White College Campuses (w. E.K. Adams), 1974; var. Rsch. Proposals. Hons. incl: Fellowship, Am. Coun. on Educ., 1972. Address: P.O. Drawer B, Hawkins, TX 75765, U.S.A. 46, 125.

LEWIS, Anthony, b. 27 Mar. 1927. Newspaper Columnist. Educ: B.A., Harvard Coll., 1948. Appts: Deskman, Sunday Dept., N.Y. Times, 1948-52; Reporter, Wash. Daily News, 1952-55; Legal Corres., Wash. Bur., N.Y. Times, 1955-64; Chief London Corres., ibid, 1964-72; Columnist, 1969-. Mbrships: Tavern Club, Boston; Garrick Club, London; Century Assn., N.Y. Publs: Gideon's Trumpet, 1964; Portrait of a Decade, 1964; num. articles in jrnls. & mags. Hons: Pulitzer Prize for Nat. Corres., 1955 & 64; Nieman Fellowship, 1956-57; LL.D., Rutgers & Adelphi Univs. Address: 84 State St., Boston, MA 02109, U.S.A. 1, 2.

LEWIS, (Sir) Anthony Carey, b. 2 Mar. 1915. Professor of Music; Musician. Educ: M.A., Mus.B., Peterhouse Coll., Cambridge Univ., U.K., 1935; Hon. Mus.D., Birmingham Univ., U.K.; Hon. R.A.M. Appts. incl: Music Staff, BBC, 1932-46; Peyton-Barber Prof. Music, Univ. of Birmingham, 1947-68; Dean, Fac. of Arts, ibid, 1961-64; Prin., Royal Acad. of Music, London, U.K., 1968-. Compositions incl: Horn Concerto; A Tribute of Praise, for Chorus. Conductor num. recordings Mbrships: former Chmn., Music Panel, Arts Coun. of Gt. Britain; former Pres., Royal Musical Assn.; former Chmn., Music Advsry. Comm., British Coun. Publs: Fndr. & Gen. Ed., Musica Britannica, 35 Vols. in progress; sev. Edits. musical works. Hons: C.B.E., 1967. Address: Royal Acad. of Music, Marylebone Rd., London NW1, U.K. 1, 4.

LEWIS, (Sir) George Stephen, b. 7 Dec. 1908. Architect. Educ: incl: Grad., Boston Archtl. Ctr. Schl., 1931 & Schl. of Arch., Harvard Univ., 1932; Rotch Travelling Fellow, 1933-35; Harvard Schl.; Grad., Cmd. & Gen. Staff Coll., 1956 & U.S. Army Engr. Schl., 1957; Grad., Ind. Coll. of the Armed Forces, 1963; MIT, Boston & Northeastern Univs. Appts. incl: Nat. Deleg., Am. Inst. Archts. Convention, 1946, 48, 50, 51, 57-63, 65-74; Nat. 'Legislative Minuteman', A.I.A., 1969-74; Tri-Regional Deleg., Construction Specifications Inst., 1967, 68, 69, 71; Mbr., Nat. Advsry. Comm. of Guidelines Prog. for Construction Mats., 1970-71, 72; Rep., Nat. A-E Pub. Affairs Conf., Wash. D.C., 1972-74. Mbrships. incl: Nat. V.P. & Dir., Order of Lafayette, 1959-74; Pres. & Nat. Deleg., Reserve Offs. Assn. Chapt. 4, 1960-61; Investigation for Awards Comm., 1970-71; Nominating Comm. & Army Coun. 1974. Pres. & Dir., Roslindale Bd. of Trade, 1948, 49, 50; Chmn., Comm. of Mbrship. Listing. Mil. Order of WWs, 1958-59; Disting. Serv. Award Comm., 1969-70; Exec. Comm., 1973-74. Contbr. to newspapers & profl. jrnls. Hons. incl: Kt. (Royal) France S.M.O.T.J., 1961; Grant Kt., 1962; Grand Silver Medal, City of Paris, France,

1962; Hall of Fame, Wisdom Soc., Calif., 1970; Award, Outstanding Serv. & Sustained High Quality Performance, Navy Dept., 1968. Address: 1376 Commonwealth Ave., Boston, MA 02134, U.S.A. 2, 16, 22, 131.

LEWIS, Hywel David, b. 21 May 1910. University Professor. Educ: Univ. Coll., Bangor, U.K.; Jesus Coll., Oxford Univ.; B.A., 1932, M.A. (Wales), 1934, B.Litt. (Oxon.), 1935. Appts. incl: Prof. of Philos., Bangor, 1947-55; Prof. of the Hist. & Philos. of Religion, King's Coll., Univ. of London; Leverhulme Fellow, 1954-55; Vis. Prof., Bryn mawr Coll., Pa., U.S.A., 1958-59, Yale, 1964-65, Univ. of Miami, 1968, Boston Univ., 1969; Robert McCahan Lectr., Presby. Coll., Belfast, 1960; Wilde Lectr. in Nat. & Comparative Relig., Univ. of Oxford, 1960-63; Edward Cadbury Lectr., Univ. of B'ham, 1962-63; Vis. Lectr., Ctr. for the Study of World Religs., Harvard, 1963; Ker Lectr., McMaster Divinity Coll., Ont., 1964; Owen Evans Lectr., Univ. Coll., Aberystwyth, 1964-65; Firth Meml. Lectr., Univ. of Nottingham, 1966; Gifford Lectr., Univ. of Edinburgh, 1966-68; L.T. Hobhouse Meml. Lectr., Univ. of London, 1966-68; Elton Lectr., Geo. Wash. Univ., 1969; Otis Meml. Lectr., Wheaton Coll., 1969; Commem. Preacher, Univ. Southampton, 1958; Commem. Lectr., Cheshunt Coll., Camb., 1960 & Westminster Coll., 1964; Drew Lectr., London, 1973. etc. Pres. var. learned socs. Has written num. publs. on philos. & religion. Recip., Hon. D.D., St. Andrews, 1964. Address: 1 Normandy Pk., Normandy, nr. Guildford, Surrey, U.K. 1, 3, 43, 109, 128.

LEWIS, Jordan D., b. 9 Aug. 1937. Scientist; Researcher Director. Educ: B.S.E. (Engrng. Phys.), 1960, (Engrng. Maths.), 1960; M.S.E. (Nuclear Engrng.), 1963, (Info. & Control Systems Engrng.), 1963; Ph.D., 1966. Appts: Battelle Dev. Corp., 1966-72; Dir. of Applied Technol. Progs., Battelle-Columbus Labs, 1972-73; Dir., Expmtl. Technol. Incentives Prog., Nat. Bur. of Standards, 1973-. Mbrships: Sigma Xi, 1962; Chmn., Task Force on Fed. Civilian Technol. Policy, AAAS; Exec. Off., Ind. Sci. Sect. & Coun. Mbr., ibid; Assoc. Acad. for Contemporary Problems & Inst. of Pub. Admin. Many publs. Recip. Predoct. Fellowship, Atomic Energy Commn., 1964. Address: Director, Expmtl. Technol. Incentives Prog., Nat. Bur. of Standards, Washington, DC 20234, U.S.A. 2, 14, 130, 139.

LEWIS, Lawrence Vernon Harcourt, b. 13 Mar. 1932. Civil Servant, Educ: Univ. of the W. Indies; Int. Inst. for Labour Studies. Appts: Asst. Acct., 1957; Acct., Min. of Communications & Works, 1963; Admin. Asst., Min. of Finance, 1965; Sr. Personnel Off., 1966; Sr. Trng. Off., 1967; Sr. Asst. Sec., Min. of Educ., 1969; Dir., Data Processing, 1970; Acct. Gen., 1971; Permanent Sec., Min. of Finance, 1973-. Mbrships. incl: Nat. Union of Pub. Wkrs. (Past Pres.); Caribbean Pub. Serv. Assn. (Past Pres.); Nat. Ins. Bd., 1968-; Natural Gas Corp., 1973; Chmn., Bd. of Dirs., Barbados Savings Bank, 1973; Dist. Treas., S. Caribbean for Meth. Ch. in the Caribbean & Ams. Hon: King's Scout, 1950. Address: Min. of Finance & Planning, Govt. Headquarters, Bay St., Bridgetown, Barbados, W. Indies. 109.

LEWIS, Leon Ferdinand Earl, b. 24 July 1908. Psychiatrist. Educ: Univ. Coll., London, U.K., 1927-30; Univ. of Manchester, & Royal Infirmary, Manchester, 1930-34. Appts. incl: Med. Off., St. Ann's Hosp., Trinidad, 1943-63; Specialist-Suptng. Med. Off., ibid, 1951-63; Hon. Assoc. Lectr., Univ. of West Indies, St. Augustine, 1969-. Mbrships. incl: 2nd V.P.,

Trinidad & Tobago Assn. Mental Hlth.; Pres., Caribbean Fedn. Mental Hlth.; Past Pres., Trinidad & Tobago Br., British Med. Assn. Contbr. num. articles & papers in field & Ed.-in-Chief, Group Tensions & Mental Health, 1971. Hons. incl: Fndn. Fellowship, Royal Coll. of Psychiatrists, England, 1971; Fellowship, Royal Coll. Physicians, Edinburgh, 1971; Chaconia Gold Medal, Govt. of Trinidad & Tobago, 1971. Address: 40A Ariapita Ave, Woodbrook, Trinidad, West Indies. 109.

LEWIS, Marguerite Garber, b. 23 July 1911. Civic Worker. Educ: B.A., Coll. of Wooster, 1933; M.A., Univ. of Mich., 1936. Appts. incl: Pres., Nat. Fedn. Motion Picture Couns., & Ed. of Newsreel; Coord., Community Serv. Courses, Div. of Special Courses, Tex. Christian Univ.; Bd. of Mgrs., Tex. Congress of Parents & Tchrs. Mbrships. incl: AAUW; Delta Sigma Rho; Pi Kappa Delta. Hon. Life Mbrships: N.Y. State Congress of Parents & Tchrs., 1959; Larchmont-Mamaroneck Motion Picture Coun., 1961; Tex. Congress of Parents & Tchrs., 1973. Hons. incl: Disting. Alumni Award, Coll. of Wooster, 1971; Cert. Outstanding Serv., Ft. Worth City Coun. of PTAs., 1973. Address: 6254 Cabaret St., San Diego, CA 92120, U.S.A. 5, 7, 138.

LEWIS, Mary Genevieve, b. 28 Aug. 1911 Reference Librarian. Educ: B.A., M.A. Northwestern Univ., 1933, '35; B.S., Columbia 1938. Appts: Ref. Asst., Ref. Libn., Oak Park Pub. Lib., Ill., 1935-37, '38-43; Hd., Ref. Dept. 1938-43, '45-50; Instr., Engl., & Hd. of Dept. Warren Wilson Coll., Swannanoa, N.C. 1950-61; Ref. Libn., Stetson Univ., DeLand Fla., 1962-73. Mbrships. incl: Am. Lib. Assn. Fla. Lib. Assn.; Chmn., W. Volusia Chapt., Am Red Cross. Contbr. of article, Library Orientation for Asian College Students, to profl. jrnl., Coll. & Rsch. Libs., 1969. Address 135 W. Minnesota Ave., DeLand, FL 32720 U.S.A. 5, 7, 15, 42.

LEWIS, Mostyn, b. 27 Oct. 1889. Insurance Broker. Educ: McGill Univ., Montreal, Canada Appts. incl: Dir. & Sec.-Treas., British Canadian Canners, Ltd., 1912; V.P., ibid, 1913; Serv. Capt. RAF, WW I; Sec.-Treas., Int. Corp. of Canada, Ltd., 1918; Gen. Broker, ins. bus. 1923-; Dir., Royal Agencies, Ltd.; Dir. Investment Fndn. Ltd.; Dir., Sir Henry N. Bate Realty Corp. Ltd.; Dir., United Bond & Share Ltd.; Gov. & Hon. Treas., Montreal Diocesan Theol. Coll., 1943-73; Dir., Montreal City & Dist. Savings Bank & Montreal City & Dist Trustees Ltd., 1953-1970; Hon. Treas., The Ch Home (Anglican), 1953-72; Pres., Montrea Sailors' Inst.; Councillor & Hon. Asst. Treas. Montreal Mus. of Fine Arts; Gov., Montrea Gen. Hosp. Mbrships. incl: St. David's Soc. Montreal; Past-Pres., ibid; Westmount Br. Canadian Red Cross; Past-Pres., ibid; Canadian Inst. Int. Affairs; Royal Montreal Golf Club Former Capt. & oldest Mbr., ibid; Fndr-Mbr. Indoor Tennis Club, Montreal, Past-Pres., ibid Address: The Linton Apt. 79, 1509 Sherbrook St. W., Montreal H3G 1M1, Canada. 88.

LEWIS, Ota Irene Harris, b. 25 Aug. 1896 Professor of Languages. Educ: A.B., Univ. of Louisville, 1921; M.A., W.Va. Univ., 1941 Grad., Ohio State Univ. & Univ. of Wis. Appts Tchr., Langs., Hunter, N.Y., 1922; Jennings La., 1923; Bogalusa, 1924; Tchr., Pub. Schls. Charleston, W.Va., 1925-39; Prof., Langs., Rio Grande Coll., Ohio, 1946-47; Lang. Tchr. Danville, 1956-59; Lang. Tchr., Castalia 1960-62. Mbrships. incl: Regent, Hetuck Chapt., Neward, Ohio, DAR, 1966-68; AAUW Pres., Coll. Womens Club, Mt. Vernon

1970-71; Geneaol. Rsch. Chmn., Knox Co., DAR; Life, Knox Co. Hist. Soc.; Knox Co. Chmn., Ohioana Lib. Assn.; Hist. Bldgs. Preservation Comm., Knox. Co.; Am. Red Cross; State Officers Club, DAR of Ohio, 1966. Contbr., DAR Mag., 1970. Recip., Latin Schlrship, Univ. of Wis., 1956. Address: 1004 E. Gambier Ave., Mt. Vernon, OH 43050, U.S.A.

LEWIS, Ruth Elizabeth Young, b. 13 Sept. 1918. Teacher. Educ: B.S., Ala. State Coll.; M.S., Am. Univ., Wash. D.C.; Additional studies at Atlanta Univ., Tuskegee Inst. & Colo. State Univ. Appts. as Tchr. at: Henry Co. Trng. Schl., Abbeville, Ala.; Claflin Schl., Columbus, Ga.; Am. Dependent Schl., Sagamahara, Japan; S. Girard H.S., Phoenix City, Ala.; Am. Dependent Schl., Bamberg, German Fed. Repub.; Carver H.S., Columbus, Ga.; Currently, Chmn., Lang. Arts Dept., ibid. Mbrships. incl: Dean of Pledgees, Grad. Advsr., Alpha Kappa Alpha; Recording Sec., Links, Inc.; Prog. Coord., Jack & Jill Mothers Club; Bd. of Dirs., Adult Comm., YMCA. Hons. incl: Finer Womanhood Award, Omega Psi Phi, Columbus, Ga., 1968; Serv. Award, Alpha Phi Alpha, Columbus, 1972. Address: 4608 Dawn Court, Columbus, GA 31907, U.S.A. 125.

LEWIS, Ruth Hollingsworth Edwards (Mrs. Frank Pierson Lewis), b. 25 Dec. 1912. Free-lance Journalist; School Teacher; Secretary. Educ: B.A., Rollins Coll., Winter Pk., Fla.; Univ. of Southwestern La., Lafayette; George Peabody Coll. for Tchrs., Nashville, Tenn.; Univ. of Grenoble, France. Appts: Sec. to Pres., 1st Nat. Bank, Abbeville, La., 5 yrs.; Asst. to Mgr. of Div. of Employment Interviewing, U.S. Employment Serv., New Orleans, La., 1 yr.; Tchr., Pub. Schls. of La., 8 yrs.; Libn., Pub. Schls. of La., 1 yr. Mbrships. incl: Nat. Promoter, Patroness, Nat. Conven., Wash. D.C. & 9th Annual Conf., Southeastern Region, Birmingham, Ala., 1959; Sr. Pres., Marquis de Lafayette Soc., La.; Nat. Soc., Children of the Revolution; Galvez Chapt., Lafayette, La.; Chmn., Nat. Defense Comm., DAR; Sist. Parlementarian, La. Fedn. of Women's Clubs; Pi Beta Phi; La. Tchrs. Assn. Co-author: Woman in the Life of the World, 1933. Contbr. articles to reviews, etc. Address: 107 W. Oak St., Abbeville, LA 70510, U.S.A. 129, 130, 138.

LEWIS, Stanley J., b. 5 July 1927. Record Distributor & Record Company Executive. Appts.: Owner, Stan's Record Serv. Inc., Shreveport, La., 1948-; Pres., Su-Ma Publishing Co. Inc. (BMI), Jewel Record Corp., Stan's Record Shops, Stan's Record Serv. of Fla. Inc., Shreve Advt. Corp., Lenny Publishing Co. Inc. (ASCAP), Pollyday Publishing Co. Inc. (BMI), Paula Record Co., Ronn Record Co., Soul Power Record Co. Mbrships: Nat. Assn. of Record Mfrs.; Nat. Assn. of TV & Radio Announcers; Broadcast Music, Inc.; Am. Fedn. of Musicians; Progressive Men's Club; Kts. of Columbus. Writer of songs, inclng: Susie Q & I'll Be Home. Address: 728 Texas St., P.O. Box 1125, Shreveport, LA 71163, U.S.A. 2.

LEWIS, Thomas A., Sr., b. 12 May 1918. Investment Banker; Stock Broker. Educ: Bus. & Commerce Courses, Coll. of St. Thomas, St. Paul, Minn., 1937-38, De Paul Univ., Chgo., 1938-39, Schl. Of Finance, Northwestern Univ., ibid, 1946-47. Appts. incl: Cpl. to Capt., U.S. Army, 1942-46, w. campaigns in Tunisia, Italy & Southern France; Salesman, Municipal & Corporate Bonds, Stock Broker, White, Weld & Co., Chgo., 1958-67; Investment Banker, Stock Broker, Dir., V.P., F.S. Moseley & Co., ibid, 1967-; V.P., Moseley, Hollgarten & Estabrook;

Dir., E-Systems Inc., Dallas, Tex.; Elimiware; Miamill Corp. Mbrships. incl: Trustee Bd. of Dirs., St. Joseph's Coll., Rensselaer, Ind.; Chmn., Bd. of Trustees, Coll. of St. Catherine, St. Paul, Minn. & St. Xavier Coll., Chgo.; Bd., Cath. Charities, Archdiocese of Chgo.; Citizens Bd., Loyola Univ., Chgo. Hons. incl: Kt. of Justice, MII. & Hospitaller Order of St. Lazarus of Jerusalem; LL.D., St. Joseph's Coll., Rensselaer, Ind., 1963; var. mil. awards, inclng. Infantry Hall of Fame, Ft. Benning, Ga., 1969. Address: Penthouse, 21 Spinning Wheel Rd., Hinsdale, IL 60521, U.S.A. 22, 49, 120, 131.

LEWISOHN, Marjorie G., b. 28 Nov. 1918. Physician. Educ: A.B., Univ. of Mich., Ann Arbor, 1940; M.B., Johns Hopkins Univ., Balt., Md., 1943; M.D., ibid, 1944; Intern, Hosp. for Women of Md., Balt., 1944; Res. Pathol., Presby. Hosp., Pitts., Pa., 1944-45; Asst. Res. Physn., Chest Serv., Bellevue Hosp., N.Y.C., 1945-50; Rsch. Fellow & Asst. Res. in Chest Diseases, N.Y. Hosp., Cornell Med. Schl., 1947; Asst. Res. Physn., 1st Med. Div., Columbia Univ. Serv., Bellevue Hosp., 1950-51. Appts. incl: Asst. Clin. Vis. Physn., Chest Serv., Bellevue Hosp. & 1st Med. Div., columbia Univ. Div., 1951-55; Pvte. Prac., Internal Med. & Chest Diseases, N.Y.C., 1952-; Clin. Instr. in Med., Cornell Med. Schl., 1955-66; Clin. Asst. Prof. of Med., ibid, 1966-; Asst. Attng. Physn. to Out-Patients, N.Y. Hosp., 1966-. Mbrships. incl: N.Y. Co. Med. Soc.; N.Y. State Med. Soc.; Am. Med. Assn. Publs: Co-author, 6 articles in med. jrnls. Hons. incl: Mbr., Royal Soc. of Hlth., London, U.K., 1969; Harvey Soc., 1952; N.Y. Acad. of Med., 1954. Address: 45 East End Avenue, N.Y., NY 10028, U.S.A.

LEWIS-SMITH, Anne Elizabeth (Mrs.), b. 14 Apr. 1925. Poet; Journalist. Appts. incl: womans page, Stamford Mercury, 1962-69; Chmn., Poetry Day, London, 1967, 70; Engl. Dir., World Poetry Day; Steering Comm., E. of Engl. Arts Comm., 1969-70; Dir., World Poetry Day; Ed., Aerostat; Asst. Ed., Envoi. Mbrships: Comm., Brit. Balloon & Airship Club, 1972-; V.P., Studi e Scambi Int.; London Press Club; PEN; Poetry Soc.; Dublin Balloon Club. Publs: Seventh Bridge, 1963; The Beginning, 1964; Flesh & Flowers, 1967; Dandelion Flavour, 1970; contbr. to num. poetry mags. & anthols. Recip., Medal of Hon., Studi e Scambi Int., 1970. Address: Primrose Cottage, Peppard Common, Henley on Thames, Oxon., U.K. 3, 11, 138.

LEY, Alice Chetwynd (Mrs. Kenneth J. Ley). Novelist. Educ: Dip. in Sociol., London Univ. Appts: Lectr., Creative Writing, Harrow Coll. of F.E., 1961-; Lectr., Sociol. & Soc. Hist., ibid, 1968-71. Mbrships: Past Chmn., Romantic Novelists' Assn.; Soc. of Women Writers & Jrnlsts.; Jane Austen Soc. Publs. incl: The Jewelled Snuff Box, 1959; The Guinea Stamp, 1961; Master of Liversedge, 1966; Toast of the Town, 1968; A Season at Brighton, 1971; Tenant of Chesdene Manor, 1974. Hons: Gilchrist Medal, London Univ., 1962. Address: 42 Cannonbury Ave., Pinner, Middlesex HA5 ITS, U.K. 30, 138.

LIAGRE BÖHL, Franz Marius Theodor de, b. 16 Aug. 1882. Professor Emeritus. Educ: Litt. D., Dr.phil., Leipzig, Germany, 1908; Lic. Theol., Bonn Univ., 1911; Dr. Theol., ibid, 1915; Postgrad. study at Leyden Univ., Holland. Appts: Prof. Hebrew Lang. & Antiquities, Groningen Univ., Holland, 1913-27; Prof. Assyriol., Leyden Univ., ibid, 1927-53; Prof. Emeritus, 1953. Mbrships: Royal Netherlands Acad. Scis., Amsterdam; Royal Acad. Scis. Belgium; German Archaeol. Inst., Berlin; Hon. mbr. Univs. of Rostock,

Germany & Debrecen, Hungary. Publs. incl: Engl. translations of King Hammurabi of Babylon in the setting of his time, 1946; Accadian Chrestomathy, 1947; Dutch translations & commentaries on books of Genesis, 2 vols.; Exodus and the Psalms, 2 vols., 2nd ed., '69; The Babylonian Epic of Gilganosh, 3rd ed., '58. Hons: Degrees from Bonn & Louvain Univs., 1915 & 1947; Kt., Order, Netherlands Lion, 1951. Address: 125 Langstr. Milsbeek/Gennep, L.., Netherlands.

LICHTENWALTER, Myrl Carl, b. 11 Oct. 1900. Educator; Biologist; Archivist. Educ: A.B., Univ. of Mich., 1923; M.A., Univ. of Southern Calif., 1929. Appts. incl: Tchr., Carlsbad H.S., N.M., 1923-24; Gallup H.S., 1924-27; Prin., Fulton Elem. & H.S., Ind., 1927-29; Prin., Elem. Schl., Kokomo, Ind., 1929-31; Tchr., ibid, 1967-68; Archiv., Archives Repository of Nat. Assn. Biol. Tchrs., 1966-. Mbrships. incl: Pres., Chgo. Biol. Round Table, 1937-38; 1st Pres., Nat. Assn. Biol. Tchrs., 1938; Bd. of Dirs., ibid; Hon., Edit. Advsry. Bd., Am. Biographical Inst. Contbr. & Guest Ed., num. publs., & papers presented to profl. socs. Recip. many hons. Address: 5061 N. St. Louis Ave., Chicago, IL 60625, U.S.A. 8, 15, 22, 28, 57, 120.

LIDDY, Martin Aloysius, b. 14 June 1905. Dental Surgeon. Educ: A.B., Seton Hall Univ.; D.D.S., Univ. of Maryland. Appts: Pvte. Prac., Elizabeth, N.J., 1933-; Staff, Alexian Brothers Hosp., ibid; Major, U.S. Army, WW II. Mbrships: Am. Dental Assn.; N.J. Dental Assn.; Union Co. Dental Soc.; Psi Omega; Suburban Golf Club, Union, N.J. Address: 250 Monmouth Rd., Elizabeth, NJ 07208, U.S.A.

LIDMAN, Hans Gustav Otto, b. 22 Aug. 1910. Author. Published over 40 books, inclng. The Crane's Cry, 1959; Adventures in the North, 1963; My Happy Years, 1964; The Sun & the Frost, 1965; Comrade in the North, 1966; Scraps of Grace, 1968; A Thousand Wings, 1970; Bites in the North, 1971; Wandering in Tiveden, 1972; Travel in the Sun, 1973. Mbrships: Pres., Ovanaker Folk Assn.; Bd. Mbr., Art Assn. of the Province of Gavleborg, & Folk Assn. of Gavleborg; Assn. Swedish Authors; Assn. Authors of Norrland; Hon. Mbr., Nation Gastrike-Halsinge, Uppsala. Hons. incl: Medal, Gustaf Adolf Acad., Uppsala, 1952; Plaqutte, Nat. Assn. Educative Art, 1955; Silver Cup for Cultural Achievement, Savings Bank of Gävleborg Province, 1961. Address: Box 28, 828 00 Edsbyn, Sweden.

LIDMAN, J. Kirby, b. 12 July 1930. Aeronautical Engineer; Highway Engineer; Applied Mathematician. Educ: Grad., Iowa State Univ., 1961. Appts: Aerodynamicist, B & C Specialty, Inc., Ames, Iowa; Proj. Engr., Iowa State Hwy. Commn., ibid; Pvte. Cons.; Profl. Registration in Aeronautical Enrng., State of Iowa. Mbrships: AIAA; Assoc. Fellow, British Interplanetry Soc.; Soc. for Indl. & Applied Maths.; Air Force Assn.; Nat. Aeronautics Assn.; Soaring Soc. of Am.; Expmtl. Aircraft Assn. Address: 607 Carroll Ave., Ames, IA 50010, U.S.A. 8, 28.

LIEBERMAN, Elizabeth Koller, b. 10 Oct. 1914. Editor; Private Press Specialist. Educ: B.S., Univ. of Ill., 1935. Appts: Assoc. Ed., Advt. Age, Chgo., 1936-40; Co-Proprietor, Herity Press, San Francisco, now at New Rochelle, N.Y., 1952-; Libn., Orinda Pub. Lib., Calif., 1953-55; Proofreader, Stanford Univ. Press, 1955-57; Registrar, Int. Register of Pvte. Press Names, White Plains, N.Y., now at New Rochelle, 1959-; Copy Ed., Cowles Book Co.,

N.Y.C., 1966-71; William Morrow & Co., N.Y.C., 1971-. Mbr., Moxon, Goudy & Westchester Chappels of private press proprietors. Ed., The Check-Log of Private Press Names, annual publ., 1959-. Address: 7 Stony Run, New Rochelle, NY 10804, U.S.A.

LIEBERMAN, J. Ben (Jay Benjamin), b. 17 Nov. 1914. Business Executive. Educ: B.A. (Hons.), Univ. of Ill., 1935; Ph.D., Stanford Univ., 1952; grad. work, Columbia Univ. Appts. incl: Sunday Ed., Evansville (Ind.) Courier, 1936-38; Dir. Info. Servs., Cmdr. USN, Wash., 1942-46; Copy Ed. & Asst. to Gen. Mgr., San Francisco Chronicle, 1948-52; Economist, Stanford Rsch. Inst., 1955-57; Co-Proprietor, Herity Press, 1952-; Assoc. Prof. Mgt., Columbia Grad. Schl. of Bus., 1960-61; Pvte. Prac., Int. Communication Cons., 1964-67; V.P., Hill & Knowlton, Inc., 1967-. Pres., Popular Printing, Inc., 1960-; Mbrships. incl: Fndr. & 1st Chmn., Goudy Soc. Inc., & Am. Printing Histl. Soc.; Bd. Mbr., Am. Inst. Graphic Arts, & The Typophiles; AAAS; Phi Beta Kappa; Sigma Delta Chi. Publs. incl: Printing as a Hobby; Types of Typefaces; Simple Printing. Holder 3 patents. Recip., USN Commendation Medal. Address: 7 Stony Run, New Rochelle, NY 10804, U.S.A. 14, 24.

LIEBMAN, Emmanuel, b. 26 Mar. 1925. Lawyer. Educ: B.S. in Econs., Univ. of Pa., 1950; J.D., Rutgers Univ., 1954. Appts: Admitted to N.J. Bar, 1954; U.S. Tax Ct., 1955; U.S. Supreme Ct., 1960; D.C., 1972; Prac. of law, specializing in fed. taxation; Ptnr., Liebman & Flaster, profl. corp. Mbrships: Exec. Comm., Taxation Sect., N.J. State Bar Assn. 1967-70; Chmn., Comm. on Bus. Taxes, ibid, 1967-69, 71-73; Chmn., Comm. on Fed. Taxation, Camden Co. Bar Assn., 1964, '68-70; Nat. Panel of Arbitrators; Am. Arbitration Assn.; S. Jersey Chmbr. of Comm.; Kiwanis; Camden City Club. Address: 409 East Marlton Pike, Cherry Hill, NJ 08034, U.S.A. 6, 16, 128.

LIEBSCHER, Victor, b. 28 Oct. 1909. Attorney General. Educ: Dr. juris, Univ. of Vienna, Austria, 1932. Appts: Law Prac., Vienna area, 1932; Judge, Burgenland, 1936; Pub. Prosecutor, Vienna, 1938; Served WWII; Atty. Gen., Supreme Ct., 1954; Procurator Gen., ibid, 1971. Mbrships: Int. Juristen Kommission; Gesellschaft für Strafrecht & Kriminologie; Akademie für Rechtsvergleichung. Co-author, 100 Jahre österreichischen Strafprozessordnung 1873-1973 (w. Müller), 1973. Recip., Grand Silver Medal of Hon. for servs. to the Repub., 1970. Address: Liechtensteinstrasse 23, 1090 Vienna, Austria.

LIEBSCHNER, Gary Keith, b. 5 Feb. 1940. Industrial Engineer. Educ: B.S., Geneva Coll., Beaver Falls, Pa., 1962; M.S., Ohio Univ., Athens, 1974. Appts: Engrng. Assoc., Indl. Engrng., Western Elec. Co., Columbus, Ohio, 1962-65; Engrng. Assoc., Indl. Engrng., for same, res. at Hawthorne, Chgo., 1965-70; Engrng. Assoc., 1970-71, Indl. Engr., Columbus, Ohio, 1971-. Mbrships. incl: Directory Ed., Columbus Chapt., Am. Inst. of Indl. Engrs., 1971-72, Hons. & Awards Comm., 1970-71, Annual Conf. Comm. Sec., 1970-72; Math. Soc. of Am.; Ohio Acad. of Sci.; Chapt. Alumni Sec., Tau Kappa Epsilon, 1964-68; Chmn., Bd. of Deacons, Community Presby. Ch., Broadview, Ill., 1970. Ordained Deacon, 1969. Author of engrng. tech. reports. Address: 3326 Columbus Ct., Apt. 11, Columbus, Ohio 43209, U.S.A. 8, 9, 131, 139.

LIED, Finn, b. 12 Apr. 1916. Manager of Research. Educ: Oslo Univ., Norway; M.S. Elec.

Engrng., Trondheim Univ.; Post-grad. Studies, Cambridge Univ., U.K. Appts: Capt., Norwegian Army, 1943; Scientist-Chief Sci. Off., Norwegian Defence Rsch. Establishment, 1947-57; Dir., ibid, 1957-; Chmn., Bd. of Dirs., Inst. for Atomic Energy, 1963-; Pres., Advsry. Grp. for Aerospace Rsch. & Dev., 1967-; Min. of Ind., 1971-72; Chmn., Exec. Comm., Royal Norwegian Coun. for Sci. & Indl. Rsch., 1973-. Mbrships: Norwegian Acad. of Sci. & Letters, Oslo; Norwegian Acad. Tech. Scis., Trondheim. Num. Publs. in fields of Ionospheric phys., Radio wave propagation, Electronics, Rsch. policy. Address: Norwegian Defence Research Establishment, P.O. Box 25, N-2007 Kjeller, Norway. 43.

LIFSHEY, Earl, b. 6 Oct. 1901. Newspaper Columnist; Author. Educ: B.C.S., Schl. of Commerce, N.Y. Univ. Appts: Var. exec. positions, retail merchandising field; Mng. Ed. & Columnist, Home Furnishings Daily, Fairchild Publs. Inc., N.Y.C., 1934; V.P., Advt. & P.R., Comprehensive Fabrics Inc., N.Y.C., 1952-59; Dir. P.R., Electrolux Corp., N.Y.C., 1954; Columnist, Home Furnishings Daily, 1959-. Publs: More & More It's Door to Door, 1948; The Houseware Story, 1973. Num. columns & articles, Home Furnishings Daily & other publs. Hons. incl: Plaque Award, Direct Selling Assn., 1965; Inst. of Appliance Mfrs. Assn. Citation, 1965; Man of Yr. Citation, Time Mag., & Nat. Assn. Radio-TV Dealers, 1966. Address: 3333 Northeast 36th St., Ft. Lauderdale, FL 33308, U.S.A.

LIGGERO, John G., b. 15 June 1921. High School Counselor. Educ: B.S. in Econ., Siena Coll., Flushing, N.Y., 1955-57. Schl. Admin., State Coll. of N.Y. at Albany, 1949-51; Permanent Cert. in Guidance, Queens Coll., Flushing, N.Y., 1955-57. Currently Guid. Dir., Glen Cove H.S., Glen Cove, ibid, since 1951. Mbrships: NEA; N.Y. State United Tchrs.; N.Y. State & L.I. Personnel & Guidance Assns.; Glen Cove Tchrs'. Assn. Publs: A Successful Approach to High School Counseling, 1968; regular contbr. to profl. jrnls. & local newspapers. Recip., Bronze Star Medal, 1945; European-Africa-Middle Eastern Serv. Medal w. Bronze Arrowhead 1945. Address: 67 Highwood Rd., Oyster Bay, NY 11771, U.S.A. 6, 30.

LIGHTFOOT, Neil R., b. 22 Sept. 1929. Professor; Author; Lecturer. Educ: B.A., 1952, M.A., 1955, Baylor Univ.; Ph.D., Duke Univ., 1958. Appts: Abilene Christian Coll., Tex., 1958- Asst., Assoc. Prof.; Prof., Bible & Biblical Langs: Grad. Advsr. in New Testament. Mbrship: Soc. of Biblical Lit. Publs: How We Got the Bible; Lessons from the Parables: Filmstrips—How We Got the Bible, & Now That I Am A Christian. Address: Box 7778, Stn. ACC, Abilene, TX 79601, U.S.A. 13, 30, 125.

LIKERT, Rensis, b. 5 Aug. 1903. Social Scientist. Educ: A.B., Univ. of Mich., 1926; Ph.D., Columbia Univ., 1932. Appts. incl: Instr., Asst. Prof., N.Y. Univ.; Dir., Morale Div., U.S. Strategic Bombing Survey; Dir., Survey Rsch. Ctr., Univ. of Mich., 1946-49, Dir., Inst. for Social Rsch., 1949-70, Dir. Emeritus, 1971-, Prof. of Psychol. & Sociol.; Chmn. of Bd., Rensis Likert Assn. Inc., 1971-. Mbrships. incl: Fellow, Am. Psychol. Assn.; Dir., ibid, 1950-53; AAAS; Sigma Xi; Phi Kappa Phi; Tau Beta Pi. Publs. incl: Morale & Agency Management, 1940; Some Applications of Behaviorial Research (Co-ed.), 1957; The Human Organization: Its Management & Value, 1967. Contbr., articles, jrnls. Hons. incl: Outstanding Achievement Award, Am. Soc. Trng. & Dev.,

1969; Exceptionally Disting. Achievement Award, Am. Assn. Pub. Opinion Rsch., 1973. Address: 860 Mokolua Dr., Kailua, HI 96734, U.S.A.

LILIUS, Patrik Johan Arvid, b. 1 Mar. 1920. Chief of Department, Finnish Employers' Confederation. Educ: Licentiate in Soc. Scis. Appts: Sec., Swedish People's Party, 1957-71; Hd., Dept., Finnish Employers' Confedn., 1971-; Bd. Mbr., sev. Finnish cos. Mbrships. incl: Bd., Helsinki City Orch., 1953-72; Chmn., Finland Chamber Music Soc., 1950-53. Contbr., Hist. of Finnish Parliament in the 19th Century. Hons: Kt., 1st class, Order of the White Rose of Finland; Cross of Liberty, 4th class, w. swords. Address: Finnish Employers' Confederation, Eteläranta 10, 00130 Helsinki 13, Finland. 43.

LILJENQUIST, L. Blaine, b. 5 Apr. 1912. Association Executive. Educ: B.S., Univ. of Idaho, 1938; J.D., Geo. Wash. Univ., 1959. Appts: Agric. Ext. Agt., 1939-40, Economist, 1941; Personnel Off., U.S. Dept. of Agric., 1942-44; w. Western States Meat Packers Assn. Inc., 1946-70, Pres. & Gen. Mgr., 1961-70. Mbrships: Ordained High Priest & Bishop, Ch. of Jesus Christ of Latter Day Sts, 1951; Chmn., Bd. of Dirs., Youth Dev. Fndn., Inc.; Former Pres., Wash. Soc. of Assn. Execs., Nat. Assn. Execs. Club. Former Ed. & contbr., meat industry publs. Recip. of award. Address: 1234 Meyer Ct., McLean, VA 22101, U.S.A. 7, 16, 128.

LILLEY, Tom, b. 13 Aug. 1912. Banker. Educ: B.A., Harvard Coll., 1931-34; M.B.A., Harvard Bus. Schl., 1935-36. Appts: Mbr., Indl. Dept., Lehman Bros., N.Y.C., 1936-40; Burlington Mills, Greensboro, N.C. & N.Y.C., 1941-42; Assoc. Prof. & Asst. Dir. of Rsch., Harvard Bus. Schl., Boston, Mass., 1943-48; Finance Staff, Ford Motor Co., Dearborn, Mich., 1948-49; Ford Div., ibid, 1949-54; Asst. Controller & Mgr., Prod. Planning Int. Group, 1954-65; Asst. Gen. Mgr., & V.P., until 1965; Dir., Export-Import Bank of the U.S., Wash. D.C., 1965-72; Dir., Continental Ill. Ltd., London, U.K., 1973-. Mbrships: Phi Beta Kappa, 1934; Dir., Nat. For. Trade Coun., 1957-65; Dir., Int. Road Fedn., 1960-65; Dir., Nat. Export Expansion Coun., 1961-65; Trustee, U.S. Coun. of Int. Chmbr. of Comm., 1961-65; Trustee, Pan Am. Dev. Fndn., 1971-; Trustee, Inter-Univ. Rsch. Ctr., Inc., 1973-. Author of rsch. publ., Problems of Accelerating Aircraft Production during World War II, Harvard Bus. Schl. Address: 1522 34th St. N.W., Wash. DC 20007, U.S.A.

LILLFORD, Ralph, b. 6 Nov. 1932. Painter. Educ: Doncaster Coll. of Art, 1948-52; Royal Coll. of Art, 1954-57. Appts: Lectr., Slough Coll. of Technol., Isleworth Polytechnic, Borough Rd. Coll. of Educ., City Literary Inst., Doncaster Coll. of Educ., Ealing & Wimbledon Schls. of Art, Maidstone, Cardiff & Cheltenham Colls. of Art; Vis. Lectr., Vic. & Albert Mus. Mbr., Royal Soc. of British Artists, 1962-67, Councillor, 1965-67. Exhibs. incl: Royal Acad.; Royal Coll. of Art; Royal Soc. of British Artists; Univ. of Durham. Work in Pub. Collects: British Mus.; Imperial War Mus.; Royal Acad. Fine Arts; Leicester, Coventry & W. Bromwich Co. Couns. Works in pvte. collects., U.K., U.S.A., Holland. Address: 221 Jersey Rd., Osterley, Middlesex, U.K. 19, 133.

LILLY, Eli, b. 1 Apr. 1885. Company Executive. Educ: Degree in Pharm., Phila. Coll. of Pharm. & Sci., 1907. Appts: Efficiency Commnr., Eli Lilly & Co., 1907-09, Supt., Mfg. Div., 1909-15, Gen. Supt., 1915-20, V.P.,

1920-32, Pres., 1932-48, Chmn. Bd. Dirs., 1948-61, 1966-69, Hon. Chmn., 1961-66, 1969-; Chmn. of Bd., Lilly Endowment Inc. Mbr., Hon. Mbr., Past Off., var. profl. & acad. orgs. Publs: Prehistoric Antiquities of Indiana, 1937; The Little Church on the Circle, 1957; Early Wawasee Days, 1960, 2nd edit., 1965; Schliemann in Indianapolis (ed.), 1961. Hons. incl: Remington Medal, 1958; Bishop Philander Chase Award, 1965; Alexander Graham Bell Award, 1966; Proclamation by Gov. of Ind. of 1 Apr. 1969 as Eli Lilly Day, his 84th birthday; 13 acad. degrees. Address: 5807 Sunset Ln., Indpls., IN 46208, U.S.A.

LILLYWHITE, John Wilson, b. 12 July 1914. Meteorologist. Educ: B.Sc., Adelaide Univ., Australia, 1936; Australian Bur. of Meteorol. Trng. Schl., 1937; Australian Administrative Staff Coll., 1963. Appts: Area Meteorological Off., RAAF, Meteorological Servs., Darwin, 1943-44, Townsville, 1945 & New Guinea, 1946; Supervising Meteorologist, Australian Bur. of Meteorol., Analysis 1949-51, & Trng. 1952-53; Regional Dir. for Victoria, 1954-58; Asst. Dir. (Servs.) of Bur., 1958-; Acting Dir. of Meteorol., num. occasions, 1960-. Mbrships: Australian Administrative Staff Coll. Assn.; Returned Servs. League; Assn. of Profl. Scis., Australia. Contbr. to meteorological tech. jrnls. Address: 19 Millicent St., Rosanna, Victoria, Australia, 3084. 23.

LILOIA, Michael P., b. 26 July 1920. Dentist. Educ: Grad., Univ. of Md. Dental Schl., 1943. Appts: Served to Capt., USAAF, 1943-46; Pvte. prac. dentistry, Belleville, N.J., 1946-; Mbr. of Staff, Essex Co. Hosp., Belleville. Mbrships: Psi Omega; Essex Co., N.J. & Am. Dental Assns.; Fouchard Dental Soc.; Gargas Odontological Soc.; Am. Legion; Nutley Elks Lodge No. 1290; Amvets Nutley Post 30. Address: 35 Essex St., Belleville, NJ 07109, U.S.A. 6.

LIM, Manuel b. 6 Aug. 1899. Lawyer. Educ: A.B., Ateneo de Manila, 1917; LL.B., Coll. of Law, Univ. of Philippines, 1921; LL.M., Coll. of Law, Univ. of Santo Tomas. 1936; D.C.L., ibid, 1937. Appts. incl: Mbr. (Past V.P. & Dir), Philippine Bar Assn., 1921-; (Past Pres. & Dir.) Lawyers League of Philippines, 1932-; & Am. Bar Assn., 1935-; Dean (Fndr.) & Law Prof., Coll of Law, Ateneo de Manila Univ. 1936-41; Mbr. Philippine Commn. of Jurists, Int. Commn. of Jurists, The Hague, Netherlands, 1957- & many other int. law orgs.; Mbr. (Past Gov.), Philippine Constitution Assn., 1963-; Dir., Area IV Manila, Integrated Bar of the Philippines, 1973-; w. 11 law firms, successively, latest being Ferry & Assocs.; Has held num. govt. posts, 1934- inclng. Vice-Chmn. (1968-) & on Bd. of Vis., 8 Forces colls., acad., etc. in Philippines; currently holding posts w. 7 fndns.; has held exec. posts in num. bus. firms. 13 bus. posts held currently. Mbr. of num. assns., societies, clubs. etc. Inclng: Bd. of Consultation, Philippine Int. Rels., 1947-; Gov., Philippines-China Friendship Assn., 1966-; Pres., Phil. Motor Assn. Recip. 9 mil. decorations, over 13 .hons. inclng. Grand Off. Order St. Gregory the Gt., Pope Pius XII, 1950 & many testimonials. Address: 103 Magallanes Ave., Magallanes Village, Makati Rizal, D-708, Philippines. 34, 101.

LIM, Wasim, b. 9 May 1929. Artist. Educ: Grad., Ctrl. Acad. of Arts, Peking, 1951-56. Appts: Instr., Shensi Provincial Coll. of Fine Arts, Sian, China, 1956-59; Ct.-painter, Pres. Palaces, Repub. of Indonesia, Jakarta & Bogor, 1961-67. Represented in permanent collects: Indonesia State & Pres. Palaces, Jakarta & Bogor. Exhibs. incl: Exhib. of Creative Artistic Work, Bandung, 1960; Charity Exhib. for the Calamity of Waterfloods, Bandung, 1960; Yin Hua Art Exhibs., Jakarta, 1960, 61 & 62; Devi Sartika Mem. Exhib., Jakarta, 1968; Indonesian Artists Exhib., Jakarta, 1969; 12 Painters Exhib., Jakarta, 1974. Mbrships: Bd., Soc. of Chinese Artists in Indonesia, 1960-68. Publs: Paintings & Statues from the Collection of President Sukarno of Indonesia (asst. ed.), 1964. Address: Jalan Tavip V/69, Jakarta, Indonesia.

LIMBACHER, James L., b. 30 Nov. 1926. Librarian. Educ: B.A. & M.A., Bowling Green State Univ.; M.S. in Ed., Ind. Univ.; M.S. in Lib. Sci., Wayne State Univ. Appts: Asst. Dir., News Bur., Bowling Green State Univ.; Film Evaluation Staff, Ind. Univ.; AV Libn., Henry Ford Centennial Lib., 1955-. Mbrships: Pres., Educ. Film Lib. Assn., 1966-70, & Am. Fedn., of Film Socs.; Alpha Tau Omega; Omicron Delta Kappa; Theta Alpha Phi. Publs: Using Films, 1967; Four Aspects of the Film, 1968; Shadows on the Wall, 1968; Feature Films on 8 & 16, 1971; Film Review Annual; The Song List, 1972; Film Music: From Violins to Video, 1973; Over 200 radio, TV, theatrical & film scripts. Contbr. articles to film publs. Hons: Gold Medal, Atlanta Film Festival, 1972. Address: Morley Manor, Dearborn, MI 48124, U.S.A. 8, 13, 14, 30.

LINAM, Ronald Hampton, b. 17 Nov. 1935. Professional Investor. Educ: B.B.A., Baylor Univ., 1958; B.S.I.E., Southern Meth. Univ., 1961. Appts: Indl. Engrng. Cons., 1959-61; Dir. of Investments, Transport Ins. Co., Transport Life Ins. Co., Transport Mgmt. Co., 1961-70; Registered Profl. Investor & Investment Advsr., 1970-. Mbrships: Bd. of Trustees, Dallas Bapt. Coll., & Chmn., Dev. Comm.; Financial Analysts Fedn.; Dallas Assn. Investment Analysts; Am. Inst. Indl. Engrs. Address: 2003 Adolphus Tower, Dallas, TX 75202, U.S.A. 2, 7.

LINARAS, Loucas, b. 11 Dec. 1918. Greek State Administrator; Author. Educ: Law Schl., Athens Univ. Appts. incl: Cmdr., Nat. Resistance Org., V-V 707 Byron, 1941-45; Dir., Pol. Bur., Min. Nat. Educ. & Relig., 1949-50; Cons. of Min. to Prime Min.'s Off., 1956-59; Asst. Supvsr. & Press Dir., Central Serv. Citizens' Problems, 1960-64; Chief, Directorate of Assistance & Examination Citizens' Problems, 1965-69; Dir. Admin. & Staff, Min. Culture & Scis., 1972-, Dir. Fine Arts, Congresses, Exhibs. & Publs., 1973-. Mbr., var. learned socs. Publs. incl: Greek Blood; Poetic Voice; Artistic Creation, 1946; Critic & Poetry, 1948; Requiem, 1951; Pantanassa, 1952. Literary criticisms, studies, monographs, poems. Hons. incl: Grand Cross, Order of Phoenix, 1966; Golden Cross, Warriors of Europe, 1973; Grand Cross, Guard of Holy Sepulchre, 1973. Address: 11 Pl. Carytsi, Athens, Greece. 43.

LINARES, Julio Ernesto, b. 7 Aug. 1930. Lawyer. Educ: Studied Law & Pol. Scis., Univ. of Panama; Dr. in Law, Univ. of Madrid, Spain; Studied Int. Law & Politics, Int. Univ. of Soc. Studies, Rome, Italy. Appts. incl: Prof., Int. Pub. Law, Univ. of Panama, 1958-; Vic. Dean, Law Fac., ibid, 1969-72; Dean i/c, ibid, 1971; Sr. mbr., Nat. Coun. for For. Rels., 1963-64; Treasury & Finance Min., 1963-64; Bd. of Govs., Interamerican Dev. Bank, 1963-64; Pres., 5th Govs. Assembly, ibid, 1964; Mbr., Bd. of Govs., Int. Bank for Reconstruction & Dev., 1963-64; For. Affairs Min. i/c, 1964. Mbrships. incl: Int. Law Assn.; Instituto Hispano-Luso-Americano de Derecho Int.; Am. Soc. of Int. Law; Soc. for Int. Dev.; Nat. Bar

Assn. Author of publs. in field. Recip. of hons. Address: Apartado 8517, Panama 6, Republica de Panama. 136.

LINATI BOSCH, Jose Antonio, b. 18 Jan. 1926. Lawyer. Educ: Univ. of Barcelona, Spain. Appts: Gen. Mgr., Soc. Gen. de Aguas de Barcelona; Bd., Centro de Estudios Investigacion y Aplicaciones del Agua; V.P., Standing Comm. on Pollution of Surface Water, Int. Water Supply Assn.; Exec. Bd., Int. Water Supply Assn. Mbrships: Hon., British Waterworks Assn.; Int. Assn. for Water Law; Int. Law Inst., The Hague. Address: Soc. Gen. de Aguas de Barcelona, P° San Juan, 39, Barcelona 9, Spain.

LINCK, Michael Andrew George, b. 21 Sept. 1926. Insurance Executive. Appts: Mgr., N. British & Mercantile Ins. Co., N. Rhodesia, 1958-60, Fedn. of Rhodesias & Nyasaland, 1960-62; Mgr., Commercial Union Assurance Grp. of Cos., Ctrl. Africa, 1962-70; Dpty. Gen. Mgr. for Canada, Commercial Union Assurance Grp., 1971-72; Gen. Mgr. for Canada, ibid, 1972-; Pres. & Dir., Canada Accident & Fire Assurance Co.; Chmn., Planned Investments Corp., Planned Investment Mgmt. Ltd.; Trustee, BM-RT Realty Investments. Mbrships: incl: Fellow, Chartered Ins. Inst., 1961-; Dir., Ins. Bur. of Canada; Canadian Underwriters' Assn.; V.P., ibid; Past-Pres., Ins. Assn. of Ctrl. Africa, Ins. Inst, Salisbury, Rhodesia, Motor Insurers Bur. of Ctrl. Africa; Past-Chmn., Ctrl. African Insurers Comte; Royal O'seas League, London, U.K. Address: 1212 Pine Ave. W., Apt. 1602, Montreal, Quebec, Canada. 88.

LINDÄLV, Blof, b., 3 Sept. 1887. Educator. Educ: Cert., Tchrs. Training Schl., 1915; Appts: Tchr., Elementary Schl., Gothenburg, Sweden, 1915; Lectr., Tchr. Training Schl., 1920-32; Prin., ibid, 1932-53. Mbrships: Bd., Nordic Folk H.S., Kungälv; Pres., Working Comm., ibid, 1958-68; Majornas Rotary Club; Pres., ibid, 1957; Samfundet för hembygdsvard & Kulturminnesföreningen Gathenhielm. Publs. incl: Skolornas uppslagsbok, 21st edit., 1972; Fornfynd & fornminnen i norra Halland, 2nd. edit., 1968; Kulturminnen i Majorna, 1972; Om fynden på vinden i Majornas växelundervisningskola, 1972; Ed., Skola & Samhälle, 1953-64. Hons: Kt., Order of St. Olof, Norway, 1947; Kt., Order of Vasa, 1949; Ph.D., Univ. of Gothenburg, 1964; Prize for Eminent Rsch., Royal Acad. of Gustaf Adolf, Uppsala, 1967; Honourable Prize, City of Gothenburg, 1973. Address: Fyradalersgatan 38, S 413 19 Göteborg, Sweden.

LINDEMAN, Jack, b. 31 Dec. 1924. Writer; Educator. Educ: B.S., W. Chester State Coll., U.S.A., 1949; Miss. Univ. Appts: Publr. & Ed., mag., Whetstone, 1955-61; Instr., African Studies Ctr. Lincoln Univ., Pa., 1963-64; Mod. Engl. Fac., Temple Univ., 1964-65; Engl. Fac., Kutztown State Coll., 1969-. Mbr. Am. Acad. Poets. Publs: Twenty-One Poems, 1963; Conflict of Convictions, 1968; Contbr. poetry, essays to var. publs. Address: R.D.1 Christiana, PA 17509, U.S.A. 6, 30.

LINDEMANN, Helmut, b. 10 Dec. 1912. Publicist. Educ: Kiel, Hamburg, Exeter (UK) & Berlin, 1931-35; Dr.iur., Berlin, 1936. Appts: For. Corres., London, Amsterdam, Athens, Stockholm, 1938-45; Co-fndr., Christophors-Stift (Port. Rsch. Acad., now at Heidelberg), 1945; Free-lance Publicist, 1948-; Ed., Neues Hochland, 1972. Publs: Generäle machen Politik, 1952; Konrad Adenauer, 1965; Das antiquierte Grundgesetz, 1966; Die Sache mit der Nation, 1970; num. transls. from Engl.

& French (James Burnham, Madariaga, Harold Nicolson, Maurice Paleologue, Lewis Mumford, etc.). Hons: Joseph Drexel Prize, 1957; German Jrnlsts. Prize, 1964. Address: 8993 Nonnenhorn, Postfach 22, German Fed. Repub. 92.

LINDEN, Kathryn Bertha, b. 24 Jan. 1905. Specialist in Audiovisual Education. Educ: B.S., Schl. of Gen. Studies, Columbia Univ., 1953; M.A., Tchrs. Coll., ibid, 1956; Ph.D., N.Y. Univ. Schl. of Educ., 1972. Appts. incl: Dir., Audio-Visual Educ., E. & W. Assn., 1944-46; Chmn., E. & W. Film Comm. & Co-prod. of filmstrip series written & narrated by Pearl Buck, 1945-48; Cons., Audio-Visual Prog., Am. Nurses' Assn., 1948-53; Dir., Am. Nurses' Assn. & Nat. League for Nursing Film Serv., N.Y., 1953-70, Exec. Prod., 20 films, 8 filmstrips; Exec. Sec., Taraknath Das Fndn., N.Y., 1959-71, Dir., 1972-; Exec., Nursing Educ. Alumni Assn., Tchrs. Coll., Columbia Univ., 1974-; Mbrships: incl: Chmn., Audiovisual Conf. of Med. & Allied Scis., Chgo., 1960-62, Prog. Chmn.,1963-66; Chmn., film forum sessions, Am. Film Assemblies, N.Y., 1960-67. Articles, var. jrnls. Recip., Plaque for Outstanding & Dedicated Serv., Audiovisual Conf. of Med. & Allied Scis., 1974. Address: 504 W. 110th St., N.Y., NY 10025, U.S.A. 5, 6, 22, 130, 132.

LINDENBERG (TCHELISTCHEFF), Wladimir, b. 16 May 1902. Neurologist; Psychiatrist. Univ. of Bonn, German Fed. Repub.; Univs. of Heidelberg & Vienna, Austria. Appts: Ship's Dr., African, Asian, S. Am. voyages, 1929-30; Asst., Hosp. for Brain Injuries, Bonn, 1930-35; Detention, Nazi prisons & concentration camps, 1936-41; Hd. Dr., Brain Injuries Hosp., Berlin, 1946-59; currently, Pvte. Prac., Neurol. & Psych., Berlin. Mbrships: Freier deutscher Autoreuverband; Fürst Donnersmarck Stiftung. Publs. incl: Die Menschheit betet, 1956; Mysterium der Begegnung, 1959; Gespräche am Krankenbett, 1959; Briefe an Eine Krankenschwester, 1962; Jenseits der fünfzig, 1970; Uber die Schwelle, 1972; sev. autobiographical novels. Hons: Walter Poppelveuter Medaille; Literatur preis der VDK. Address: Beyschlagstr 13a, 1 Berlin 27, German Fed. Repub.

LINDER, Robert J., b. 29 Oct. 1937. Orchestral Conductor; Music Professor. Educ: Mus.B.Educ., Univ. of Houston, 1959; Mus.M., ibid, 1962; student w. Pierre Monteux, 1963; Tanglewood Conducting student, 1964. Appts: Tchr. & Band Dir., Cypress Fairbanks Ind. Schls., 1960-68; Conductor, Houston Youth Symph., 1960-67, Palmer Hughes Accordion Symph., 1962-64, Houston Civic Symph., 1970-, TV Specials for NBC & CBS, 1972-73; film soundtrack, So Sad About Gloria, 1973; Conductor or Asst. Conductor, Houston Gilbert & Sullivan Opera Soc., 1961-; Asst. Conductor of Opryland, U.S.A., 1974. Mbr., profl. orgs. & fraternities. Contbr., Music Educators Jrnl., 1974. Lectures, Int. Exchange Schls., Austria, France, Yugoslavia. Hons. incl: Tchr. of Yr., Cypress-Fairbanks ISD, 1967. Address: 8602 Birdwood, Houston, TX 77036, U.S.A. 125.

LINDGREN, (Claes) Lennart, b. 4 Nov. 1915. General Maternity Hospital Chairman & Director; Associate Professor of Obstetrics & Gynaecology. Educ: M.D., Caroline Inst., Stockholm, Sweden, 1944; D.Sc., ibid, 1956. Appts: Assoc., Prof., Caroline Inst., Stockholm, 1956-61; Assoc. Prof., Univ. of Umeå, 1961-67; Dir. & Chmn., Gen. Maternity Hosp., Stockholm, 1967-. Mbrships: Swedish Soc. of Med.; Swedish Soc. of Ob. & Gyn. Publs: The lower parts of the uterus during labour, 1955;

Physiology of the cervix during labour, 1968; Der Biomekanismus der cervixdilatation während der Geburt, 1971; Biodynamics of the cervix during pregnancy & labour, 1973. Address: Allmänna B.B., Fiskartorpsvägen 15, 114 86 Stockholm, Sweden. 43.

LINDGREN, Ethel J., b. 1 Jan. 1905. Scientific Editor; Research Worker. Educ: Smith Coll., U.S.A., 1923-24; Newnham Coll., Cambridge, U.K., 1924-27; M.A., Ph.D. (Cantab). Appts. incl: Rsch. Fellowship, Newnham Coll., Cambridge, 1936-39; Hon. Ed., Jrnl. of the Royal Anthropological Inst., 1938-47; Ed.-in-Chief, Wartime Soc. Survey, 1940-41; Liaison Off. w. Allied Govt. Rsch. Orgs., Royal Inst. of Int. Affairs, 1941-45; Univ. Lectr. in Soc. Anthropol., Cambridge, 1950-52. Mbrships: Fndng. Fellow, Lucy Cavendish Coll., Cambridge; Vice-Chmn., Anglo-Swedish Soc. & China Soc., London; Former V.P., Royal Anthropological Inst. Author of publs. in geographical & anthropological fields, inclng. The Herd of Reindeer in Glenmore, 1960, '66. Address: Sunbourn, Harston, Cambridge CB2 5NZ, U.K. 3, 47.

LINDHOLM, Einar, b. 20 July 1913. Physicist. Educ: B.S., Lund Univ., 1935; Ph.D., Stockholm Univ., 1942. Appts: Assoc. Prof. of Phys., Univ. of Stockholm, 1942-47; Tchr., High Schl., 1949-50; Assoc. Prof. of Phys., Chalmers Inst. of Technol., 1950-56; Prof. of Phys., Royal Inst. of Technol., 1956-; Chmn., Phys. Dept., ibid, 1963-. Contbr. num. articles to sci. jrnls. Has developed new theories in field. Address: Physics Dept., Royal Inst. of Technol., S-100 Stockholm, Sweden.

LINDINGER, Asger Juul Linding, b. 13 Oct. 1916. Shipowner & Consul General. Educ: M.Sc., For. Trade; Cand. art, Archaeology; Master, 2nd Class, Navigation. Appts: Pres., Lindinger Holding Co. Ltd., Lindinger Agro Co. Ltd., Lindinger Trading Co. Ltd., Lindinger Int. Ltd., Lindinger Machine Works Ltd., Lindinger Contracting Co. Ltd., Lindinger Shipping Co. Ltd., Lindinger Ferry Co. Ltd., Kolding Korn Ltd., Havneby Shipping Agency Ltd.; Lindinger Shipyard Ltd., Lindinger Hotel Establishment, Lindinger Linien GmbH, Hamburg, Germany, Navis GmbH, Westerland; Hon. Consul General, Guatemala. Mbrships: Br. & Export Orgs.; Coun., Corps Consulaire; Adventurer's Club, Denmark. Hons: Off., Order of the Quetzal, Guatemala, 1964; Crowned Cross, Phys. Culture, Netherlands, 1969; Hon. Citizenship, Phila., U.S.A., 1961; Hon. Chief of Police, Pa., 1961. Address: Rødovrevej 239, DK-2610 Rødovre, Denmark. 43, 134.

LINDLEY, Walter Cary, b. 17 May 1922. Advertising & Importing Executive. Educ: B.A., DePaun Univ., Greencastle, Ind. Appts: w. Chgo. Tribune, 1946-52, WGN Radio, 1952-54, Honolulu Star Bulletin, 1954-57, Fawcett McDermott 1957-61; Dir. of Advt., Bank of Hawaii, 1961-66; Sr. Acct. Exec., Fawcett McDermott, 1968-; Owner, Clark de Castro S.A.R.L., Import Firm, Paris, France; Author; Land developer. Mbrships: Advt. Agcy. Assn. of Hawaii (Pres., 1971); Oahu Country Club; Sales & Marketing Execs. of Hawaii; Honolulu Advt. Club; Honolulu Wine & Food Soc.; Les Amis des Vins; Retd. Lt. Cmdr., USNR. Contbr. of articles on wine & food to var. mags. Address: 21 Craigside Pl., Apt. 4E, Honolulu, HI 96817, U.S.A. 78.

LINDER, Maximilian Paul. Teacher; Lecturer; Art & Technical Consultant; Company Director. Educ: Univ. of Technol., Sydney, Australia; Marconi Schl. Electronics,

Sydney; Metropol. Bus. Coll.; S.C.C., Tech. Coll. in Electricity. Appts: Asst. to Sec., Local Govt. & Shires Assn., N.S.W.; Tchr., St. Charles' Schl., Waverley; Lectr., Dept. of Educ., Adult Classes, Waverley; Mng. Dir., Grant & Lindner Pty. Ltd. & Percentage Pools Pty. Ltd.; Tech. Cons., ibid. Address: P.O. Box 69, Woollahra, N.S.W., Australia 2025. 133.

LINDO, Victor Edward Rudolphus Alexander, b. 12 Aug. 1931. Medical Practitioner. Educ: M.B.B.S., Univ. Coll. of W. Indies, London Univ., 1959. Appts: Intern, Univ. Coll. Hosp. of the W. Indies, 1960; Res. Pathologist, ibid, 1961, Rsch. Asst., Pathol. Dept., 1962-63, Registrar, Chem. Pathol., 1964-69; Hon. Pt.-Time Clin. Asst., Pathol. Dept., Royal Free Hosp., London, U.K., 1963-64; Asst. Med. Off., Chapelton Hosp., Jamaica, W. Indies, 1969-. Mbr., British Med. Assn. & Med. Assn. of Jamaica. Publs. incl: Serum & Urine Proteins in Proteinuria of Pregnancy, 1968. Recip., var. med. awards & schlrships. Address: Chapelton, Jamaica, W. Indies.

LINDOP, Patricia Joyce (Esdale), b. 21 June 1930. Professor of Radiation Biology. Educ: B.Sc. (Hons.), Med. Coll., St. Bartholomew's Hosp., London, 1951; M.B., B.S., 1954; Ph.D., 1960; D.Sc., 1974. Appts: House Physn., St. Bartholomew's Hosp., Children's Dept., House Surg., St. Mary Abbots Hosp.; Rsch. Asst., Dept. of Physiol., Med. Coll., St. Bartholomew's Hosp.; Sr. Lectr., then Rdr. in Radiobiol., Med. Coll., ibid; Prof. & Hd., Dept. of Radiobiol., 1970-; Coun. Mbr., British Inst. of Radiol., & Westfield Coll. Mbr., Fellow & Off., profl. orgs. Publs. incl: Radiation & Ageing (co-ed.), 1966; Progress & its Risks, History of the 20th Century, 1972; var. sci. papers & articles; book chapt. contbns. Hons. incl: Ciba Fndn. Award, 1957; William Gibson Rsch. Schlrship., Royal Soc. of Med., 1957-59. Address: Dept. of Radiobiol., Medical College of St. Bartholomew's Hosp., Charterhouse Sq., London EC1M 6BQ, U.K. 1, 47, 56.

LINDQVIST, Ake E., b. 14 Feb. 1914. Architect. Educ: Grad., Dept. of Arch., Stockholm Univ., 1939; Grad., Dept. of Arch., Royal Swedish Acad. of Arts, 1942. Appts: Own firm, 1944-; Guest Lectr. in Arch. at: Ill. & Syracuse Univs., 1959; Turlane Univ., New Orleans, 1963; Ill. & Circle Campus Univ., Chgo., 1965. Commnd. by UNESCO for work on new Damascus Univ., Syria, 1958; Commnd. by Coun. of Europe for basic planning of swimming pools throughout Europe, 1967-68. Mbrships: Nat. Soc. of Swedish Archts.; Bldg. Assn.; Swedish Technol. Assn.; Int. Working Grp. for Sports Bldg., Cologne, 1969-. Author num. archtl. articles. Hons: 1st Prize in·4 archtl. competitions & 3rd Prize in int. archtl. competition for Stockholm Univ., 1961. Address: Adolf Fredriks Kyrkogata 12, 111 37 Stockholm, Sweden. 43.

LINDSAY, Edward Russell. Administrator; Teacher. Educ: B.S.E.D., Univ. of Tex., Austin; M.A., La Sierra Coll. (now, La Sierra Campus of Loma Linda Univ.); Advanced study, Baylor Univ. Appts. incl: Counselor, McLennan Community Coll., Waco, Tex., Assoc. Prof. of Tech. Maths., Tex. State Tech. Inst., Waco, Tex.; Mgr. of Student Affairs, James Connally Tech. Inst., Waco, Tex.; Tchr. of Maths. & Baseball & Football Coach, Eisenhower H.S., Rialto, Calif.; Tchr. of Maths. & Football & Tennis Coach, Bloomington H.S., Bloomington, Calif.; Tchr. of Maths. & Reading, Calallen Jr. H.S., Corpus Christi, Tex. Mbrships. incl: Chmn., Legislative Comm., Rialto Educ. Assn., 1966; Legislative Contact for Calif. Tchr.'s

Assn., 1966; Pres.-Elect, Rialto Educ. Assn., 1967; Phi Delta Kappa, 1970; V.Chmn., Heart of Tex. Chapt., Tex. Personnel & Guidance Assn., 1971; Ballot Security Chmn. for Falls, Hill, Limestone & McLennan Co.'s in 1972 Gen. Election; Treas., Tex. Jr. Coll. Tchr.'s Assn., 1973; active mbr., Jaycees, Ch., jr. baseball & charitable orgs. Hons. incl: Commissioned, Tex. Col., 1969. Address: 1001 N. 63rd St., Waco, TX 76710, U.S.A. 125.

LINDSAY, Maurice, b. 21 July 1918. Journalist; Broadcaster; Author; Poet. Educ: Scottish Nat. Acad. of Music, U.K., 1936-39. Appts. incl: Drama Ctitic, Scottish Daily Mail, Edinburgh, U.K., 1946-47; Music Critic, Bulletin, Glasgow, U.K., 1946-60; BBC, Glasgow; Free-lance Broadcaster, 1946-61; Ed., Scots Review, 1949-50; Prog. Controller, Border TV, Carlisle, 1961-62; Prod. Controller, 1962-64; Features Exec. & Sr. Interviewer, 1964-67; Dir., The Scottish Civic Trust, 1967. Mbrships: Saltire Soc., Hon. Publs. Sec., 1948-52, Hon. Life Mbr., 1972-; Glasgow Western Club. Author of prose & poetry & edited many books. Written librettos for 2 operas & commentaries for 2 films. Contbr. to Grove's Dictionary of Music & Musicians. Recent Poetry Publs. incl: Snow Warning, 1962; One Later Day, 1964; This Business Of Living, 1968; Comings & Goings, 1971; Selected Poems 1942-1972, 1973. Prose Publs. incl: The Burns Encyclopedia, 1959, revised & enlarged edit., 1970; The Discovery Of Scotland, 1964; Portrait Of Glasgow, 1972; A General History Of Scottish Literature & Lowland Scotland Villages in prep. Hons: Rockefeller Atlantic Award for The Enemies Of Love, 1946; Holder of Territorial Decoration. Address: 11 Gt. Western Ter., Glasgow G12 OUP, U.K.

LINDSAY, Robert William Ludovic, b. 18 Aug. 1905. Commissioned Officer (Retired). Educ: Royal Mil. Coll., Sandhurst, 1923-24. Appts: 2nd Lt., Grenadier Guards, 1925-30; Capt., seconded to Trans Jordan Frontier Force, 1930-34; retd. to Reserve, 1937; recalled from Reserve, 1939; Capt.-Brevet Major, Grenadier Guards, U.K. & Middle E., 1940-43; seconded Trans Jordan Frontier Force, 1943-45; Retd., 1945; Mbr., Australian House of Reps., seat of Flinders, Vic., 1954-66. Mbrships. incl: Guards Club, London; Melbourne Club, Vic.; Rotary Int. Recip. of O.B.E., 1971. Address: Netherplace, Frankston, Vic., Australia 3199. 23.

LINDSKOG, (Gustav Uno) Birger, b. 23 Sept. 1914. Associate Professor. Educ: B.A., Stockholm, Sweden, 1942; B.D., 1945; M.A., 1946; Ph.D., Uppsala, 1954. Appts: Asst., Bd. of Educ., 1944; Asst. Prof. of Social Anthropol., Uppsala, 1954; Sr. Lectr. in Sociol., Uppsala, 1966; Assoc. Prof. of Sociol. & Social Anthropol., ibid, 1969. Mbrships: Assn. Current Anthropol., Chgo.; Hon. Mbr., Varmlands nation, Uppsala; Assoc., Letterstedtska foreningen, Stockholm. Author of profl. books & articles. Address: Dept. of Sociol., Drottninggat. 1 A, 752 20 Uppsala, Sweden.

LIN-FU, Jane S., b. 21 Nov. 1928. Physician; Pediatrician. Educ: M.D., Univ. of Santo Tomas, Manila, Philippines, 1955; Rotating Internship, Jewish Hosp. & Med. Ctr., Brooklyn, N.Y., U.S.A., 1955-56; Pediatric Res., ibid, 1956-58; Fellowship in Pediatric Neurol., 1958-60; Rotating Res., Pediatric Hematol., Cardiol. & Chest Diseases, Kings Co. Hosp., N.Y., 1961. Appts: Pediatric Cons. to Children's Bur., U.S. Dept. of Hlth., Educ. & Welfare, 1963-69; Pediatric Cons. to Maternal &

Child Hlth. Servs., USPHS, ibid, 1969-73; Pediatric Cons. to Offs. of Clin. Servs., ibid, 1973-; Fed. Cons. to White House Conf. on Children, 1970. Mbrships: Dipl., Am. Bd. of Pediatrics; Fellow, Am. Acad. of Pediatrics; Med. Soc. of Dist. of Columbia. Author of num. publs. on childhood lead poisoning, & other pediatric pub. hlth. problems. Recip. of hons. Address: 6420 Hollins Dr., Bethesda, MD 20034, U.S.A. 5, 6, 138.

LING, James Thomas, b. 21 May 1944. Assistant to Chairman & President, Omega-Alpha, Inc. Educ: Southern Meth. Univ.; N. Tex. State Univ.; N.Y. Inst. of Finance. Appts; V.P. & Dir., Ling & Co., Inc., 1964-70; V.P., Sec. & Dir., ibid, 1971-; Asst. to V.P. & Sec., Omega-Alpha, Inc., Dallas, Tex., 1971-73; Asst. to Chmn. & Pres., ibid, 1973-. Mbrships: Dallas Assn. of Securities Dealers, 1965-71; Army Nat. Guard Assn. of Tex., 1965-71; Brook Hollow Golf Club, 1964-. Address: Omega-Alpha, Inc., P.O. Box 50046, Dallas, TX 75250, U.S.A. 7.

LINGLE, James Boal, b. June 27 1896. Rancher. Educ: Grad. Susquehanna Univ., Pa., 1917; Pa. State Coll., 1918-19. Appts. incl: Mgr., Sunny Ridge Farms, A.P. Irwin, Chadd's Ford Junction, Pa., 1926-27; Mgr., Breidablik Dairy Farm, Wilmington, Del., 1928-31; Mgr., Guernsey Cattle Sales, Chester Co. Guernsey Breeders' Assn., 1935-37; Mgr., Homestead Guernsey Cattle & Dairy, Salisbury, Md., 1936-37; Mgr., Wye Plantation, Queenstown, Md., 1937-71; Cons., Int. Exec. Serv. Corps, 1971-. Mbrships: Am. Angus Assn.; Eastern Shore Md. Angus Assn.; Eastern Guernsey Breeders' Assn.; Md. Angus Assn.; Past-Dir., ibid; Nat. Assn. animal Breeders; Ad Hoc Comm., ibid, 1960-; Meth. Ch. Publs: Num. publs. in cattle breeding, production & testing. Hons: Cert. of Merit in Agric., Univ. of Md., Coll. Pk., 1958. Address: c/o International Executive Service Corps, 545 Madison Ave., N.Y., NY 10022, U.S.A. 6.

LINN, Ruby Wilnslow (Mrs. LaVon P. Linn), b. 6 Nov. 1910. Dietitian. Educ: B.S., Dimmons Coll., Mass., 1932; M.A., Instn. Mgmt., Columbia Univ., N.Y., 1951; Postgrad. at other univs. w. U.S. Army, 1936-. Appts. as Chief, Food Serv. Div. incl: Tripler Gen. Hosp., Honolulu, 1951-54; Murphy Gen. Hosp., Waltham Gen. Hosp., Mass., 1954-56; U.S. Army Hosp., Ft. Benning, Ga., 1956-58 & Walter Reed Gen. Hosp., Wash. D.C., 1958-63; Retd. as Lt. Col., A.M.S.C., 1963. Mbrships: Sec., D.C. Dietetic Assn., 1961-63; Chmn., Civil Defence Comm., 1963-64, etc.; Treas., D.C. Home Econs. Assn., 1965-69; Chmn., Finance Comm., 1969-70, Comm. on Aging, 1971-72; Am. dietetic Assn.; Am. Home Econs. Assn.; Chmn., Crafts Advsry. Comm., Food Servs. Supvsns. Prog., Pub. Schls., D.C.; Bd. of Trustees, Plimoth Plantation, Mass., 1971-, & Utd. Meth. Retirement Ctr., E. Providence, R.I., 1972-; Mil. Surgs. Assn. Past Ed., D.C. Dietetic Assn. Bulletin & Contbr. to profl. publs. Decorated Legion of Merit, 1963. Address: 2647 S. Kent St., Arlington, VA 22202, U.S.A. 5, 22.

LINNANE, Anthony William, b. 17 July, 1930. Professor. Educ: B.Sc., Univ. of Sydney, Australia, 1951; M.Sc., ibid, 1953; Ph.D., 1956; D.Sc., 1972. Appts: Demonstrator, Sydney Univ., 1952-53; U.S.P.H.S. Post-doct. Fellow, Univ. of Wis., U.S.A., 1956-58; Lectr., Sr. Lectr., Biochem., Univ. of Sydney, 1958-62; Reader in Biochem., Monash Univ., 1962; Prof. of Biochem., ibid, 1965; Assoc. Dean, Fac. of Med., 1974. Mbrships: Pres.-Elect, Australian Biochem. Soc., 1973; Sec., Australian Biochem.

Soc., 1962-66; Australian Soc. Microbio.; Cell Bio. Soc.; Australian Soc. for Med. Rsch.; Nat. Comm. for Biochem., 1970; Fellow, Australian Acad. Scis.; Rep., Int. Union Biochem., 1973. Contbr. to profl. publs. Address: Biochem. Dept., Monash Univ., Clayton, Vic., Australia 3168. 23.

LINNELL-FFRENCH, Phyllis Marjorie, b. 16 June 1921. Artist. Educ: Studied w. Caroline Weir, Melbourne, Australia, Melbourne Nat. Gall., Sir John Longstaff, Melbourne, Dr. George Wang Wu, Shanghai, China, Max Meldrum, Melbourne, & Corcoran Gall., Wash. D.C., U.S.A. Own pvte. classes, 1943-53. Mbr., Burr Artists. Solo exhibitions incl: Proud's, Sydney, Australia, 1944; Wellon's Gall., N.Y. U.S.A., 1953; Galerie de Bonnecaze, Algiers & Paris, 1953; Grifé Escoda, Barcelona, Spain, 1954; Charles Barzansky Galls., N.Y., 1959; Exhibition of 69 works for the benefit of The Ch. of St. Vincent Ferrer 1929-69; Waldorf Astoria, 1969. Num. portrait & other commns.; Many other exhibitions. Hons: 1st Prize for Pastel Study, "Fuschia", Canterbury Horticulture Soc., Melbourne, Australia, 1929; 1st Prize for Watercolor Study, "Gladioli", Caroline Weir, 1932; Woman of the Week Award, Balt., Md., 1946. Address: 118 W. 57th St., N.Y., NY 10019, U.S.A. 37.

LINNENBERG, Clem Charles, Jr., b. 20 May 1912. Economist. Educ: B.A. (Hons.), M.A., Univ. of Tex., 1933; Ph.D., Yale Univ., 1941. Appts. incl: Chief of Div. Stats. & Studies, Off. Voc. Rehab., U.S. Dept. Hlth., Educ., & Welfare, 1959-62; Economist, U.S. Pub. Hlth. Serv., 1962-69; Independent Cons. Economics & Stats., 1969-. Mbrships: Am. Pub. Hlth. Assn.; Phi Beta Kappa; Pi Sigma Alpha; Sigma Delta Pi. Publs. incl: How Shall We Measure Economic Benefits from Public Health Services?, 1964; Economics in Program Planning for Health, 1966; Organizing & Staffing for the Program Planning Function, 1967. Address: 3812 Benton St., N.W., Wash. DC 20007, U.S.A. 7, 14.

LINNETT, John Wilfrid, b. 3 Aug. 1913. University Vice-Chancellor. Educ: M.A., St. John's Coll., Oxford, U.K.; D.Phil., ibid; Henry Fellow, Harvard Univ., U.S.A., 1937-38. Appts: Jr. Rsch. Fellow, Balliol Coll., Oxford, 1939-45; Fellow, Queen's Coll., ibid, 1945-65; Demonstrator, Chem., ibid, 1945-62; Rdr., Inorganic Chem., ibid, 1962-65; Prof., Phys. Chem., Cambridge, 1965-; Master, Sidney Sussex Coll., ibid, 1971-; Vice-Chancellor, Cambridge Univ., 1973-75. Mbrships: Fellow, Royal Soc., 1955-; Pres., Faraday Div., Chem. Soc., 1971-73; V.P., ibid, 1971-; Gen. Mbr., Coun., Royal Inst. of Chem., 1970-. Publs: Wave Mechanics & Valency, 1960; Electronic Structure of Molecules: a new approach, 1964. Recip., Award of Merit, City of Coventry, 1966. Address: The Master's Lodge, Sidney Sussex Coll., Cambridge, U.K.

LINNIG, Frederic J., b. 30 Mar. 1913. Scientist (Chemist). Educ: A.B., Bucknell Univ., Pa., 1939; M.S., Univ. of Md., 1944. Appts: Chem., Nat. Bur. of Standards, U.S. Govt., Wash. D.C., 1943-68; Chem., Maritime Admin., ibid, 1968-70; Rsch. Sci., Kappe Assoc., Rockville, Md., 1970-. Mbrships: Am. Chem. Soc.; Dir., Div. of Rubber Chem. of ACS, 1963-66; Divs. of Polymer Chem., Analytical Chem. & Plastics & Organic Coatings; Charter Mbr., Wash. Rubber Grp. (Nominating Comm. & Finance Comm.) Contbr. to var. sci. jrnls. Address: 731 Wilson Ave., Rockville, MD 20850, U.S.A.

LINOWITZ, Sol M., b. 7 Dec. 1913. Lawyer; Diplomat. Educ: A.B., Hamilton Coll., 1935; LL.B., Cornell Law Schl., 1938; J.D., ibid. Appts. incl: Ptnr., Law Firm, Rochester, N.Y., 1958-66; U.S. Ambassador, Org. of Am. States, 1966-69; U.S. Rep., Inter-Am. Comm. Alliance for Progress, 1966-69; Sr. Ptnr., Coudert Bros., Law Firm, 1969-. Fellow, Am. Acad. Arts & Scis. Mbrships. incl: Chmn., Nat. Coun., For. Policy Assn.; Chmn., Nat. Urban Coalition; Coun. For. Rels.; Bd. of Dirs., Time, Inc. & Marine Midland Banks, Inc.; Bd. of Govs., Am. Jewish Comm.; Exec. Comm., U.S. Coun. Int. Chmbr. of Comm.; Chmn., Bd. & Exec. Comm., Gen. Counsel, Xerox Corp., until 1966; Bd. of Trustees, Mutual Life Ins. Co. of N.Y.; Active mbr., many other civic & profl. orgs. Author of articles in profl. jrnls. Recip. of 23 hon. doct. degrees, var. Am. colls. & univs., 1963-73. Address: 1 Farragut Square S., Wash. DC 20006, U.S.A. 2, 16, 34, 128.

LINSEY, Mae Cannon Mills, b. 30 Apr. 1930. Educational Consultant. Educ: B.A., Knoxville Coll., Tenn.; M.A., Univ. of Ga., 1969; further study, ibid, 1970-71, 1972, '73, '74. Appts: Hist. & Civic Tchr., jr. high schls.; Intern, Tchr. Corps., Atlanta Pub. Schls., Ga.; Early Childhood Instructional Generalist, Early Childhood Educ. Lead Tchr., Staff & Prog. Dev., ibid; Early Childhood Educ. Prog. Cons., Ga. State Dept. of Educ., Atlanta; Mbr. & Chmn., var. educl. comms. & subcomms. Mbrships. incl: Knoxville Coll. & Univ. of Ga. Alumni Assns.; Delta Sigma Theta; Nat. & Ga. Assns. of Interdenominational Ministers' Wives; Mbrship. Chmn., World Fellowship Comm., YWCA, Knoxville, Tenn. Recip., var. profl. & community serv. awards. Address: 2059 W. Cedar Ln. S.W., Atlanta, GA 30311, U.S.A. 125.

LINTON, Calvin Darlington, b. 11 June 1914. University Professor & Dean. Educ: B.A., Geo. Wash. Univ., 1935; M.A., Johns Hopkins Univ., 1939; Ph.D., ibid, 1940. Appts: Assoc. Prof., Engl., & Chmn. Dept., Queens Coll., N.C., 1940-41; Asst. Prof., Geo. Wash. Univ., 1945-46; Assoc. Prof., ibid, 1946-48; Prof., 1948-; Dean, Coll. Arts & Scis., Geo. Wash. Univ., 1956-; Lectr., Inst. Renaissance Studies, Folger Shakespeare Lib., 1971. Mbrships: Am. Sec., Modern Humanities Rsch. Assn., 1963-; Vice Chmn., Comm. on Higher Educ., Middle States Assn., 1962-70; Prog. Comm., MLA, 1968-71; Pres., Eastern Assoc. of Deans, 1967; Int. Assn. Univ. Profs. Engl., 1965-; Pres., Cosmos Club, 1973. Publs: 4 books on writing; 50 articles on lit., critical, relig. & educ. topics. Address: 5216 Farrington Rd., Wash. DC 20016, U.S.A. 2, 7, 13, 15, 30, 131.

LINTON, Ronald Melvin, b. 7 May 1929. Political Scientist; Journalist; Planning Executive. Educ: B.A., Mich. State Univ., 1951. Appts. incl: Sec., Dept. Workmen's Compensation, Mich., 1955-56; Labour Ed., Courier Jrnl., Louisville, Ky., 1956-60; Asst. to Sen. John. F. Kennedy, 1960; Profl. Staff Mbr., U.S. Senate Comm. of Aging, 1960-61; Dir., Econ. Utilization Policy, Dept. of Defense, 1961-63; Staff Dir., U.S. Senate Comm. of Pub. Works, 1963-66; Dir., Spec. Projs., Urban Am. Coord., Nat. Urban Coalition, 1966-68; Pres., Linton Mields & Coston Inc., 1969-; Vis. Prof., Urban Environmental Studies, Rensselaer Polytech. Inst., 1970-71. Fellow, Am. Pol. Sci. Assn. Mbrships. incl: Chmn., Dept. of Hlth. Educ. & Welfare Task Force on Environmental Hlth.; Chmn., Govng. Bd., D.C. Gen. Hosp.; Exec. Bd., Wash. Ctr. of Metropolitan Studies. Publs: Terracide: America's Destruction of Her Living Environment, 1970; num. articles in profl. jrnls. Address: Linton, Mields & Coston

Inc., 1015 18th St., N.W., Suite 200, Wash. DC 20036, U.S.A. 30.

LIPMAN, Ira Ackerman, b. 15 Nov. 1940. President of Guardsmark, Inc. Educ: Ohio Wesleyan Univ. Mbrships: Former Chmn., Nat. Alliance Businessmen; Memphis Int. Assn. of Chiefs of Police; Am. Soc. of Indl. Security; Economic Club; Ridgeway Country Club. Recip., Hon. LL.D., John Marshall Univ. Address: 4490 Park Ave., Memphis, TN 38117, U.S.A. 6, 7, 16.

LIPOVETSKY, Leonidas E.B., b. 2 May 1937. Concert Pianist. Educ: Piano studies w. Wilhelm Kolischer, Montevideo, Uruguay, & Rosina Lhevinne & Martin Canin, N.Y.; Artist's Dip., Kolischer Conservatory, Montevideo; Mus. B., M.S., Juilliard Schl. of Music, N.Y.; B.Arch. & additional studies, Schl. of Arch., State Univ. of Montevideo; Cert. d'Etudes & Dip., Alliance Française, Montevideo. Appts. incl: Piano Fac., Fla. State Univ., Tallahasse, U.S.A., 1969-; Profl. orchl. debut, Montevideo, 1959; U.S.A. formal debut, Pan Am. Union, Wash. D.C., 1965; Recitals in all S. Am. capitals, 1966; N.Y. orchl. debut, Nat. Orchl. Assn., 1967; Guest artist, UN Staff Day Festival, UN Gen. Assembly Hall, 1969; European debut, var. European capitals, 1969; 2nd European tour, 1970; N.Am. tour, 1971; Spanish tour w. Czech Philharmonic Orch., 1972; Recitals & orchl. appearances, U.S.A. & Spain, 1973; Soloist on tour w. Czech Philharmonic Orch., Czechoslovakia, & Southeastern tour, U.S.A., 1974. Mbrships. incl: Am. Fedn. of Musicians; Capital City Kiwanis Int. Num. radio & TV recordings. Recip. of many hons. Address: 826 E. Park Ave., Tallahassee, FL 32301, U.S.A. 52, 125.

LIPPERT, Albert, b. 23 Apr. 1925. Executive. Educ: B.B.A., City Coll., 1949. Appts: Asst. Buyer, Goldrings, 1949-51; Buyer & Merchandise, Mangel Stores Corp., 1951-67; V.P., Weight Watchers Int. Inc., 1967-68; Chief Exec. Officer, ibid, 1968-. Mbrships. incl: Dir., Weight Watchers Fndn. Inc., 1968-; Dir. & Treas., W.W. Twentyfirst Corp., 1968-; Dir., Gt. Eastern Ins. Co., 1969-71; Advsr., Ranking Minority Mbr., N.Y.S. Comm. of Banks.; Chmn., Congressional Action Comm., Gt. Nech Chmbr. of Comm., 1970-. Fndr., Past Grand Master, Kts. of Pythias, Belmont. Hons: Mil. award, WWII; Man of Yr. Award, N.Y. Coun. for Civic Affairs, 1968. Address: Sousa Drive, Sands Point, NY 11050, U.S.A. 2, 6, 16.

LIPPITT, Elizabeth, b. 13 Jan. 1912. Free-lance Writer, Singer & Monologuist. Educ: Mills Coll.; Univ. of Calif. Mbrships. incl: Metropolitan Club; Olympic Club; Nat. Advsry. Bd.; Am. Security Coun.; Commonwealth Club; League of Men Voters; Nat. Assn. of Railroad Passengers; Defenders of Wildlife; 52 Veterans Assn.; Am. Conservative Union; Guide Dogs for Blind; Royal Humane Soc., London, U.K.; Comm. for Humane Legislation; Korean Fndn. Publs: Contbr. since 1953 of articles on nat. affairs to 100 papers inclng: Chicago American; Miami Herald; St. Louis Globe-Democrat; Jackson News; Montgomery Advertiser; Houston Chronicle. Writer & Performer of Satirical Monologues. Hons: 5 times Winner, Congress of Freedom Award for articles on nat. affairs. Address: 2414 Pacific Ave., San Francisco, CA 94115, U.S.A. 5, 22, 57, 120, 128, 132.

LIPPITT, Ronald O., b. 21 Mar. 1914. Professor of Psychology & Sociology. Educ: B.S., Springfield Coll., 1936; M.A., 1938; Ph.D., 1940, State Univ. of Iowa. Appts. incl: Boy Scouts of Am., 1941-44; USPHS, 1944-45;

Chief of Trng., Fed. Security Agcy., 1945-46; Rsch. Ctr. for Grp. Dynamics, MIT, 1946-48; Rsch. Ctr. for Grp. Dynamics, Inst. for Soc. Rsch., 1948-64; Ctr. Prog. Dir., for Rsch. on Utilization of Sci. Knowledge, Univ. of Mich., 1964-. Mbrships: Pres., Learning Resources Corp.; Pres., Soc. Sci. Educ. Consortium; Fellow, Nat. Inst. for Applied Behavioral Sci.; Am. Educl. Rsch. Assn.; Soc. for Rsch. in Child Dev.; Soc. for Applied Anthropol.; Fellow, Am. Sociol. Assn. Publs: Autocracy & Democracy (c-author), 1972; Images of Potentiality (co-author), 1973. Address: Inst. for Soc. Rsch., CRUSK, Univ. of Mich., P.O. Box 1248, Ann Arbor, MI 48106, U.S.A. 1.

LIPPMAN, Monroe, b. 10 Dec. 1905. University Professor; Theatre Director. Educ: A.B., Univ. of Mich., 1926; M.A., ibid, 1929; Ph.D., 1937; post grad. study, Harvard Univ. & Univ. of Iowa. Appts: Instr.-Assoc. Prof., Hd. of Dept. of Speech & Drama, Southwest Tex. State Univ., 1929-35; Instr.-Prof., Chmn. Dept. of Theatre, Tulane Univ., 1937-67; Prof., Chmn., Dept. of Drama, N.Y. Univ. (Schl. of the Arts), 1967-70; Prof. of Theatre, Chmn., Dept. of Theatre, Univ. of Calif., 1970-73; Prof. Emeritus, ibid, 1973-; Exec. Dir., Le Pitit Theatre du Vieux Carre, New Orleans, 1946-53; Vis. Prof. &/or Guest Dir., Univ. of Tex., Mt. Holyoke Coll., Univs. of Mich., Minn., Denver. Mbrships. incl: Pres., Am. Theatre Assn., 1950; Pres., Southwest Theatre Conf., 1954; Bd. Dirs. sev. times, ANTA; Bd. Trustees sev. times, Nat. Theatre Conf.; Pres., Nat. Collegiate Players, 1946-47; Bd., Theatre Lib, Assn., 1967-70. Dir. of approx. 125 theatrical prods. in univ. & community theatres. Author of some 25 articles & essays. Recip. var. grants & fellowships. Address: 1631 Ransom Rd., Riverside, CA 92506, U.S.A. 2, 13, 128.

LIPSCHUTZ, Alexander, b. 28 Aug. 1883. University Professor. Educ: Univ. Berlin, Zurich, Göttingen; M.D., Univ. of Göttingen, 1907; Expmntl. Rsch. w. Prof. Max Verworn. Appts. incl: Lectr., Fac. of Med., Univ. of Bern, Switzerland, 1915-19; Prof.-Dir., Physiol. Inst., Univ. Dorpat, Tartu, Estonia, 1919-26; Univ. of Concepcion, Chile, 1926-36; Dir., Inst. Exp. Med. Nat. Hlth. Serv., Santiago, Chile, 1937-60; Expt. Rsch., until 1972; Chief of Mission, Sociol. Rsch., Fuegian Indians, S. Chile & Argentina, 1946-. Mbrships. incl: Acad. mbr., Fac. Med., Univ. of Chile, 1952; Hon., Acad. of Scis., Chile; Hon., Royal Soc. Med., London, U.K. Publs. incl: Internal Secretion of Sex Glands, Bern, 1919, Engl., 1924, Spanish, 1928; Steroid Hormones & Tumors, U.S., 1950, Japanese, 1953; Steroid Homeostasis & Turmorigenesis, Engl., 1957, Japanese, 1959; Czech, 1956; Problema Racial en la Conquista de America, 2nd edit. 1967; Perfil de Indoamerica de Nuestro Tiempo (Antologia 1937-62), 1968; Seis Ensayos. Filosoficos Marxistas (1959-68), 1970; Los Muros Pintados de Bonampak-Ensenanzas Sociologicas, 1971. Contbr. to profl. publs. Recip. num. awards & hons. for physiol. & sociol. rsch. Address: Av. Hamburgo 366, Santiago, Chile. 2, 14, 50, 55.

LIPSON, Goldie (Goldman) S., b. 18 Nov. 1905. Artist; Writer; Lecturer; Teacher. Appts. incl: Textile & Wallpaper Designer, 1938-40; Art Tchr., YWCA, Bronx, N.Y., 1940-41, Mt. Vernon Schl. of Fine Arts, 1945-57, Studio Work Shop, New Rochelle, 1957-60; Dir. & Art Tchr., YMYWHA, 1946-53. Mbrships. incl: Bd. Dirs., Artist Equity, N.Y., 1951-69; Nat. Assn. Women Artists (prog. & mbrship. comm., on juries of exhibs., 1944-69); Comm. on Art Educ., Mus. of Modern Art, 1948-49; Bd. Dirs., Y Camps, Lake Tiorati, Bear Mt., N.Y.; Fla. Fed. of Art (Bd. Mbr.; publicity chmn.,

1970-72); Publs. incl: Moods & Nudes, 1960; Rejuvenation Through Hatha & Water Hatha Yoga, 1963; Rejuvenation Through Yoga, 1965; Beyond Yoga, 1965. One Man Exhibs. incl: Up-Town Gall., 1942; Barzansky Galls., 1945-67. Hons. incl: Top Prize, Westchester Co. Ctr. for oil; Justice Louis D. Brandeis Medal for art work contbn., 1955. Address: Lake of the Hills, Lake Wales, FL 33853, U.S.A. 5, 6, 55, 125, 138.

LIPSON, Menzie, b. 15 Feb. 1915. Scientific Research Worker, Educ: B.Sc., Sydney Univ., Australia, 1935; Ph.D., Leeds Univ., U.K., 1948. Appts: F.W. Hughes Pty. Ltd., Sydney, 1935-37; Div. of Animal Hlth., Commonwealth Scientific & Indl. Rsch. Org., Sydney, 1937-39; Div. of Indl. Chem., ibid, 1939-41; Ctrl. Wool Comm., Sydney, 1941-45; Int. Wool Secretariat Rsch. Fellow, Univ. of Leeds, U.K., 1945-48; Off.-i/c., Wool Rsch. Lab., Commonwealth Scientific & Indl. Rsch. Org., Geelong, Australia, 1948-58; Chief, Div. of Textile Ind., ibid, 1958-. Mbrships: F.T.I., Manchester, U.K.; Soc. of Dyers & Colourists; Fellow, Royal Australian Chem. Inst.; Past Pres., Rotary Club of Geelong. Publs: Approx. 90 scientific papers in textile rsch. & wool prod. Recip., Rsch. Fellowship, Int. Wool Secretariat, 1946. Address: CSIRO Division of Textile Industry, P.O. Box 21, Belmont, Vic., Australia 3216. 23, 128.

LIPTON, Stephen, b. 7 Dec. 1928. Professor. Educ: Univ. of Liverpool, U.K. Appts: Lectr., Univ. of Liverpool, 1953-54; Sr. Sci. Off., Rothansted experimental Stn., Harpenden, 1954-59; Reader, Univ. of N.S.W., Sydney, Australia, 1959-67; Prof. of Stats., Univ. of Qld., Brisbane, ibid, 1969-; Fndn. Coun. Mbr., Griffith Univ., Qld., 1970-. Mbrships: Fellow, Brit. Computer Soc.; Royal Statl. Soc.; Pres., A/Asian Region, Biometrics Soc., 1970-73; Australian Statl. Soc.; Australian Math. Soc.; Qld. Univ. Club. Contbr. to profl. jrnls. Address: Univ. of Qld., St. Lucia, Qld. Australia 4067. 23, 128.

LIST, deGraffenried Woolley, (Mrs. D. Clarence List), b. 12 Dec. 1902. Artist. Educ: Geo. Wash. Univ., Wash. D.C., 1921-22; Arch., Nat. Acad. of Design, 1924-27; Pa. Acad. of Fine Arts, 1927-30. Appts: Designer, Walking & Dancing Marionettes, 1932-39; Archtl. Drawings & Illustration, TWA, Wash. D.C., 1943-45; Illustrator, Nat. Educ. Assn., ibid, 1945-56; Free-lance Portrait Painter, Mural Painter, Restorer of Paintings & Photographs, Photographer, Illustrator, Designer of Brochures & Profl. Puppeteer, 1956-. Mbrships: Colonial Dames of Am.; Pilgrims of St. Mary's; Nat. Soc. of Arts & Letters; Chmn., Art. Schlrship Contest, ibid, 1973; Chmn., Arch. Schlrship Contest, ibid, 1974. Paintings incl: Mural painting, First Mass Held on St. Clement's Island, 1634; Similar painting hanging in Chapel, St. Mary's Island, Cornwall, U.K., exhibited London, 1973; over 200 Portraits in Oil & Pastel. Hons: Cresson Traveling European Art Schlrship, Pa. Acad. Fine Arts, 1929; Nat. Recognition for Walking Marionettes, 1938, Dancing Marionettes, 1946. Address: 3613 Chevy Chase Lake Drive, Chevy Chase, MD 20015, U.S.A. 5, 6.

LITKENHOUS, E.E., b. 19 May 1907. Company President; University Professor of Chemical Engineering. Educ: B.S., Univ. of Louisville, 1930; M.S., ibid, 1931; Ph.D., Univ. of Minn., 1934; sev. additional Univ. courses. Appts. incl: Grad. Asst., Univ of Louisville, 1930-31; Grad. Asst., Univ. of Minn., 1931-34; Rsch. Dept., Goodyear Tire & Rubber Co., Akron, Ohio, 1934-36; Asst. Prof. of Chem.

Engrng., Univ. of Louisville, 1936-38; Assoc. Prof. of Chem. Engrng., ibid, 1938-41; Assoc. Prof. & Hd., Dept. of Chem. Engrng., Vanderbilt Univ., 1941-44; Prof. & Hd., ibid, 1944-60; Exec. Dir., Div. of Indl. Rsch., ibid, 1953-56; Rsch., Oak Ridge Nat. Labs., (Summer), 1955; Prog. Dir., Engrng. Scis., Nat. Sci. Fndn., 1956-57; Rsch., Boeing Airplane Co., Seattle, Wash., (Summer), 1959; Exec. Dir., Univ. of Ky., Div. of Rsch. & Dev., 1960-62; Ky. Contract Team, USAID to Indonesia, Cons. Rsch. Tchng., Bandung Inst. Technol., Indonesia, 1962-63; Dir., Palm Beach Grad. Engrng. Ctr., Univ. of Fla., W. Palm Beach, Fla., 1963-68; Specialist, Univ. Ext. Continuing Educ., Univ. of Wis., Madison, Wis., 1968-70; Pres., Litkenhous Enterprises, Nashville, Tenn., 1970-. Address: 4411 Harding Place, Nashville, TN 37205, U.S.A.

LITTELL, Bertha Felder (Mrs. Leland E. Littell), b. 28 Mar. 1910. Retired Legal Executive. Educ: Draughon's Bus.Coll., Jackson, Miss.; Hinds Jr. Coll., Raymond, Miss., 1969-70. Appts: Legal Secy. for 14½ yrs.; Clerk for US Govt. Lending Agcy.; Signatory, Kan. City Title Ins. Co.; Sec.-Treas., Lawyers Corp. & 1st United Meth. Ch. Mbrships: 1st V.P., Pass Christian Gdn. Club; Pub. Chmn., Miss. Gulf Coast Coun. of Gdn. Clubs; Bus. & Profl. Women's Club; Treas., Gulfport Womans Club; Young Adult Sunday Schl. Tchr.; Former Lay Mbr. to Annual Conf., Seashore Dist.; Former Den Mother; Asst. Treas, United Meth. Women; Seashore Dist. Supts. Cabinet; Coun. on Mins. & United Meth. Women; Former Millsaps Coll. Coord., Jackson, Miss. Publs: Prayers in Tarpon-Beacon Newspaper; book in progress. Sketches & makes oil paintings. Address: 435 McClung St., P.O. Drawer J, Pass Christian, MS 39571, U.S.A. 125.

LITTELL, Katherine M. (Mrs. Norman M. Littell). Lawyer. Educ: B.A., Tulane Univ., 1921, M.A., 1922, LL.B.; Univ. of Oxford, U.K. Appts: Admitted to La. Bar; Bar of Supreme Ct., 1933 (w. N. Littell); co-Fndr., Am. Youth Hostels; Asst. to N. Littell (Asst. Atty. Gen.), Dept. of Justice, Lands Div., World War II; co-fndr., Nat. Comm. against Nazi Persecution of Minorities; Bd. of Dirs., One World (later U.N.); Bd., & V.P., Children's Hosp., Wash. D.C., during 20 years. Mbrships: V.P., Women's Nat. Democratic Club (past Chmn., Speaker's Comm.); Sulgrave & 1925 F St. Clubs. Collaborator in publ. of Axis Rule Over Occupied Europe, by R. Lemkin, inclng. first use of "genocide" Recip. of Award of Honor, Wisdom Soc. Address: 1824-1826 Jefferson Pl., N.W., Wash. DC 20036, U.S.A.

LITTELL, Norman M., b. 8 Sept. 1899. Attorney-at-law. Educ: B.A., Wabash Coll., Crawfordsville, Ind.; Christ Church Coll., Oxford, 1921-23; Harvard Law Schl.; LL.B., Wash. Univ. Law Schl., 1929. Appts: Asst. Solicitor, Dept. of Interior, & Special Asst. to U.S. Att. Gen., as Rep. of Nat. Petroleum Administrative Bd. for 6 NW States, 1934-35; Partner, Evans, McClarron & Littell, Seattle, Wash., to 1939; Special Asst. to U.S. Att. Gen. to litigate U.S. vs. N. Pacific Railway Co.; Asst. Atty. Gen. of U.S., Hd. of Lands Div.,939-44; Chmn., comms. on For. Investment Laws, Int. Bar Assn., Inter-Am. Bar Assn., Am. Bar Assn., 1948-61. Mbrships: 1925 F Street Club; Sec., Oxford Soc., Wash., D.C.; Int. Bar Assn.; Am. Bar Assn.; Anne Arundel Co., Maryland, Bar Assn.; D.C., Fed., & Va. State Bar Assns. Contbr. to var. profl. jrnls.; author of num. papers presented to Bar Assns. & reports to comms. of Congress. Hons. incl: Rhodes Schlrship. to Oxford, U.K.; Wisdom Award of Hon., The Wisdom Soc.; Beverley Hills, Calif.

Address: 1824-26 Jefferson Place, N.W., Wash. D.C. 20036, U.S.A. 2.

LITTLE, Edward Grant, b. 13 Dec. 1921. College Professor. Educ: A.B., Hiram Coll., Ohio, 1949; M.A., Univ. of Mich., Ann Arbor, 1950; Ph.D., Mich. State Univ., E. Lansing, 1969. Appts: Instr., French, Hiram Coll., Ohio, 1950-51; Transl.-Interpreter-Instr., Lowry AFB, Denver, Colo., 1952-53; Lang. Supvsr., AF Intelligence, Nuremburg, Germany, 1954-57; Asst. Prof., French & Tech. Writing, Gen. Motors Inst., Flint, Mich., U.S.A., 1957-58; Asst. Prof., Engl., Supvsr., Tech. Writing, Tri-State Coll., 958-60; Asst. Prof., Engl. & For. Langs., Lansing Community Coll., Mich., 1960-64; Asst.-Assoc. Prof., Engl., French, Comp. Lit., Ga. Southern Coll., Statesboro, 1964-74. Mbrships. incl: Pres. Elect & Pres., Phi Kappa Phi, 1972-74; Pi Delta Phi, Ga. Southern Coll.; MLA; S. Atlantic MLA; AAUP; Fac. Senate, Ga. Southern Coll., 1971-73; Fac. Club, Ga. Southern Coll., 1973-74. Recip., scholastic hons. Address: 107 Terrell Dr., Statesboro, GA 30458, U.S.A. 13, 125.

LITTLE, Ervin D., Jr., b. 16 Jan. 1925. Public Relations Consultant. Educ: B.A., Univ. of Mich., 1949; M.A., Univ. of Mo., 1951. Appts: Assoc. Ed., Elec. Dealer, Chgo., Ill. 1951-56; Asst. Ed., World Books Ency., Chgo., 1956-57; Supvsr., P.R., Spector Freight System, Inc., 1957-60; Writer, Jam Handy Org., Detroit, Mich., 1960-64; Asst.Dir., P.R., Mich. Blue Shield, 1964-67; Dir., Community Rels., Wyandotte Gen. Hosp., 1967-74; P.R. Cons., Dewey Little & Assocs., 1974-. Mbrships: Pres., Mich. Hosp. P.R. Assn., 1971, Mich. Hosp. Audio Visual Coop., 1972; P.R. Soc. of Am.; Pres. Elect, Southeastern Mich. Hosp. P.R. Assn., 1974; Treas., Sigma Delta Chi, 1948; Acad. of Hosp. P.R.; Detroit Press Club; Am. Soc. of Hosp. Dirs. Hons. incl: 3 awards, MacEachern P.R. Contest, 1970, '71; 3 awards, Pulse Patient Rels. Contest, 1969. Address: 2902 Glenview, Royal Oak, MI 48073, U.S.A. 8, 24.

LITTLEJOHN, James DeWitt, b. 21 June 1931. Editor; Association Executive. Educ: B.A., Tex. Christian Univ., Ft. Worth, 1954; grad. study, Univ. of the S., Sewanee, Tenn., 1955-56. Appts. incl: Asst. Mgr., Gtr. Florence (S.C.) Chmbr. of Comm., 1961-63; Executive Dir., Hilton Head Island Chmbr. of Comm., Ed. of Islander Mag., & Pres. Chmn., Sunlit Enterprises. Ltd., 1969-. Mbrships. incl: Am. Chmbr. of Comm. Executives; Southern Assn. Chmbr. of Comm. Executives; U.S. Chmbr. of Comm.; Hilton Head Island Rotary Club. Poems under name of Jaime Juanito in var. publs. Contbr. of num. columns, features & news stories to var. newspapers & jrnls. Address: P.O. Box 5647, Hilton Head Island, SC 29928, U.S.A. 7, 125.

LITTLEJOHN, Naomi Smith (Mrs. H.T. Littlejohn), b. 15 Dec. 1893. Home-Maker. Educ: Var. Workshops, Home & Child Care; num. courses relig. study. Mbrships: Past-Pres., Iris Garden Club, Rose Garden Club, United Daughters of Confederacy, Home Demonstration Club, Alathean Sunday Schl. Class; Sr. Counselor, United Commercial Travelers Aux.; Horticulture Chmn., Spartanburg Garden Coun.; Am. Legion Aux. (Past-Sec.); DAR; First Bapt. Ch. (Chmn. Womans Missionary Union Circle); Gold Star Mothers; num. other civic orgs. Publs: Num. Poems in local newspapers & Garden Club Yrbooks. Active Participant in num. city beautification projs. Hons: Four Star Pin (4 sons in WWII), Gov., S.C.; Runner-Up, Spartanburg Mother of Yr., 1946; Cert. of Appreciation for Patriotic Participation as Voluntary Registrar, 1948; num. Horticultural Awards. Address: P.O. Box 2723, Spartanburg, SC 29302, U.S.A. 125.

LITZENBERG, Dorothy P., b. 18 Dec. 1938. Realtor; Insurance Agent. Educ: Misericordia Coll., Dallas, Pa., U.S.A. Appts: Sec., Realtor & Gen. Agent, A.C. Litzenberg & Son, Realtors & Insurers; Owner & Prin. Realtor, Sunnycroft Realty; Sec., Cecil County Land Corp.; Sec., Cecil Enterprises, Inc. Mbrships: Sec., Harford Cecil Ins. Agents Assn., 1972-74; Past V.P. & Sec., Cecil Co. Bd. of Realtors; Chmn., Mbrship. Comm., & Deleg., Cecil Co. Bd. of Educ.; Cecil Co. Histl. Soc. Address: Sunnycroft, 407 Delaware Ave., Elkton, MD 21921, U.S.A. 2.

LIU, James Jo-Yü, b. 14 Apr. 1926. University Professor. Educ: B.A., Fu Jen Univ., Peking, 1948; Nat. Tsing Hua Univ., Peking, 1948; M.A., Univ. of Bristol, 1952; Wadham Coll., Oxford Univ., 1950-51. Appts: Lectr. in Chinese, London Univ. Schl. of Oriental & African Studies, 1951-56; Hong Kong Univ., 1956-59; Assoc. Prof., Engl., New Asia Coll., Hong Kong, 1959-61; Asst. Prof., Chinese, Univ. of Hawaii, 1961-64; Vis. Assoc. Prof., Chinese, Univ. of Pitts., Pa., 1964-65; Assoc. Prof., Chinese Lit., Univ. of Chgo., 1965-67; Prof. of Chinese, Stanford Univ., 1967-; Chmn., Dept. of Asian Langs., 1969-. Mbrships: Assn. for Asian Studies; Am. Oriental Soc. Publs. incl: The Art of Chinese Poetry, 1962, 3rd ed., 1970, Japanese transl., 1972; The Chinese Knight-errant, 1967; The Poetry of Li Shang-yin, 1969; Major Lyricists of the Northern Sung, 1974; Chinese Theories of Literature, in press; contbr. chapt. on Chinese lit. to Half the World, the History & Culture of China & Japan (Arnold Toynbee, ed.), 1973. Hons: Brit. Coun. Schlr., 1951; Guggenheim Fellow, 1971; Am. Coun. of Learned Socs. Grant, 1971-72. Address: c/o Dept. of Asian Langs., Stanford Univ., Stanford, CA 94305, U.S.A. 1, 13, 30.

LIU, Ts'un-yan, b. 11 Aug. 1917. Professor of Chinese. Educ: B.A., Peking, Repub. of China, 1938; B.A. (Hons.), Ph.D., D.Litt., London, U.K., 1954, '57, '69. Appts. incl: Lectr., Govt. Evening Schl. of Higher Chinese Studies, Hong Kong, 1950-62; Sr. Lectr.-Dean of Fac. of Asian Studies, Australian Nat. Univ., 1962-. Fellowships: Royal Asiatic Soc., 1957; Royal Econ. Soc., 1959; Fndn. Fellow, Australian Acad. of Humanities; Oriental Soc. of Australia Sydney, 1970; Coun. Mbr., ibid, 1970. Mbrships. incl: Hong Kong Br., Royal Asiatic Soc., 1960; Coun. Mbr., Assn. Taostic Rsch., Tokyo, 1968. Publs: Four Historical Plays, 1959; Ch'ing-ch'un (tril.), 1968; I Love Long Summer Days (play), 1973; Contbr. var. publs. & jrnls. Recip. of Hon. Litt. degree, Yeungnam Univ., 1972. Address: Australian Nat. Univ., Canberra, A.C.T., Australia, 2600.

LIU, Wu-Chi, b. 27 July, 1907. University Professor; Author. Educ: B.A., Lawrence Coll., Wis., 1928; Ph.D., Yale Univ., Conn., 1931; London Univ., U.K., 1931-32. Appts. Prof., Engl. & Chmn., Dept. Nankai Univ., Tientsin, China, 1932-41; Vis. Prof., Yale Univ., U.S.A., 1951-53; Prof., Chinese & Dir., Chinese Lang. & Area Ctr., Univ. of Pitts., 1960-61; Prof., Chinese, Ind. Univ., 1961-; Chmn., Dept. ibid, 1962-67. Mbrships: Am. Oriental Soc.; Assn. Asian Studies; Edit. Comm., Tsing Hua Jrnl. of Chinese Studies. Publs: More than 10 books in Chinese; in English; Confucius, His Life & Time, 1955; A short History of Confucian Philosophy, 1955; An Introduction to Chinese Literature, 1965; Su Man-Shu 1972. Recip. of

Acad. hons. Address: Dept. East Asian Lang. & Lit., Indiana Univ., Bloomington, IN 47401, U.S.A. 2, 13, 15, 30, 128, 131.

LIVADAS, Gregory, b. 8 Jan. 1894. Professor of Tropical Medicine; Public Health Officer. Educ: M.D. (cum laude), Univ. of Naples, 1915; Dip., Superior Schl. Malariol., Rome, 1928; Master Pub. Hlth., Johns Hopkins Univ., Balt., U.S.A., 1934. Appts. incl: Mil. Serv., to Capt., 1916-23; Dir., malaria field stn., 1928-30; Malaria Cons., Schl. of Hygiene, Athens, 1931-36; Prof. Tropical Med. & Malaria, ibid, 1936-59, Dir., 1938-49; Tech. Advsr., Min. of Hlth., 1951-56; Expert of Malaria, WHO for Afghanistan, Liban, Syria, Jordan, Cameroons, Madagascar, 1955-61. Mbr., var. med. socs. Publs. incl: Elements of Malariology, 1936; Malaria in Greece, Research Control, 1941; Malaria, 1955. Over 100 med. papers & articles. Hons. incl: Cmdr. of Phoenix Royal Order of Greece, 1953; Merite Camerounais Medaille de Premiere Classe, 1959; new insèct species designation, Elianella Livadasi, 1959. Address: Patission Ave. 183, Athens, Greece. 43.

LIVERANI, Giuseppe, b. 17 Sept. 1903. Museum Curator. Educ: Dipl., Faenza Ceramics Schl., 1922; Tchng. Qualification in Hist. of Italian Ceramics, 1967. Appts. incl: Dir., Int. Ceramic Mus. Collect., 1953; Lectr., Hist. & Technique of Ceramics, Italian Inter-Univ. Inst., 1928-42; Ed., Faenza review; Dir., ibid, 1953; Prof., & Dir. Lab. of Restoration, Inst. of Art, Faenza, 1934; Lectr., Univ. of Florence, 1967, & Univ. of Pisa, 1969. Mbrships. incl: Nat. Hist. Comm. of Emilia Romagna; Clementina Acad., Bologna; Torricelliana Acad., Faenza; Incamminati di Modigliana Acad., Moustiers, France; English Ceramic Circle, London. Publs. incl: Ll Reale Istituto d'arte per la ceramica in Faenza, 1941; La maiolica italiana dalle origini sino alla comparsa della porcellana europae, 1957; Selezione di opere del Museo Internazionale delle ceramiche di Faenza, 1964. Hons. incl: Kt. of Italian Repub., 1947; sev. profl. awards. Address: Via Martiri Ungheresi 4, Faenza, Italy. 43, 133.

LIVERSIDGE, Henry Douglas, b. 12 Mar. 1913. Journalist; Author. Appts: London Corres., Yorks. Post, U.K.; News Ed., Sunday Chronicle; Asst. Ldr. Writer, Daily Mail, London; London Corres., Continental Daily Mail, Paris; Staff Writer & For. Corres., Reuters (accompanied Arctic & Antarctic expeditions); Sr. Ed., Ctrl. Off. of Info. Publs: White Horizon; The Last Continent; The While Killers; The Third Forst; St. Francis of Assisi; Lenin; Joseph Stalin; Peter the Great; St. Ignatius of Loyola; The White World; (forthcoming) Queen Elizabeth II. Address: 56 Love Lane, Pinner, Middx., HA5 3EX, U.K.

LIVESCU, Jean, b. 3 June 1906. Professor. Educ: Licenciate Iasi, 1937; Postgrad. studies, Univs. of Marburg/Lahn, 1938 & Berlin, 1940-42; Dr.phil., Strasbourg Univ., 1942. Appts: Asst. Iasi-Prof. Iasi, 1938-55; Prof., Bucharest Univ., Rumania, 1955-; Dean, Fac. Letters-Rector, Univ. of Iasi, 1947-55; Vice-Rector-Rector, Bucharest Univ., 1956-63; '68-72; V. Min. Educ., 1963-68; V.P.-Pres., Rumanian Nat. Commn. for UNESCO, 1965-; Mbrships: V.P., Rumanian Soc. Philol. Scis.; Corres. Mbr., Rumanian Acad. Scis.; Leading Comm., Int. Lenau-Gesellschaft. Publs. incl: Studies & essays on German & Austrian Lit. (the German Petrarchism, Grimmelshausen, Herder, Goethe, Schiller, Romanticism, Lenau, A. Zweig, L. Renn); anthols.; Studies on hist. of lit. criticism (Gervinus) & on educl. & univ.

problems. Address: Dionisie Lupu 65, Bucharest, Rumania.

LIVINGSTON, Virginia Wuerthele-Caspe (Mrs. Afton M. Livingston), b. 28 Dec. 1906. Physician; Educator; Writer. Educ: B.A., Vassar Coll., Poughkeepsie, N.Y., 1930; M.D., N.Y. Med. Schl., Bellvue, 1936. Appts: Indl. Physn., WWII; Schl. Physn., Newark State Tchrs. Coll.; Assoc. Prof., Biol., Rutgers Univ., 1948-53; Currently Assoc. Prof., Microbiol., Univ. San Diego, Calif. Mbrships: Pres., U.S.D. Aux.; Pres., Children's Adoption Soc., 1968; V.P., La Jolla Br., Nat. Assn. Am. Pen Women; Vassar Alumnae; Opera Guild; Soc. Servs. League; AMA; Calif. & S.D. Med. Assn.; Med. Women's Assn.; Am. Soc. Microbiols.; S.D. Symph. Assn. Publs: Cancer, A New Breakthrough; Demonstration of Progenitor Cryptocides in the Blood of Patients with Collagen & Neoplastic Diseases (article) Co-author), etc. Address: 8492 Prestwick Dr., La Jolla, CA 92037, U.S.A. 5, 9, 14.

LIZER, Harlan DeLos, b. 1 Dec. 1910. Cartographic Draftsman; Artist. Appts. incl: Draftsman, Hwy. Dept., N.M., 1937-38; Draftsman, State Engr. Off. of N.M., 1938-42; Chief Draftsman, ibid, 1942-67, at retirement. Mbrships: Pres., Santa Fe Chapt., Artists Equity; Santa Fe Art Assn.; Santa Fe Chapt., Designer-Craftsmen, & Santa Fe Symph., Orchestra Sect.; V.P., Santa Fe Arts & Crafts Guild; Chmn., Santa Fe Ctr., Arts & Crafts Assn. Paintings in var. pvte. collects. Hons: Var. awards N.M., State Fair; Eastern N.M. Fair; Mus. of N.M. Address: 976 Acequia Madre, Sante Fe, NM 87501, U.S.A.

LJUNG, (Per) Ove (Poul), b. 18 May 1918. Lieutenant General. Educ: Royal Mil. Acad., Sweden, 1938-39; Royal Staff Coll. of the Armed Forces, 1946-48; Gen. Course, Royal Nat. Defence Coll., 1959; Chief Course, ibid, 1967. Appts. incl: Capt.-Col., Gen. Staff Corps, 1950-66; Major-Gen., 1966; Lt.-Gen., 1969; C.O., Grenadiers of Royal Life Regiment, 1964-66; Chief, Army Staff & Gen. Staff Corps, 1966(-68); Master Gen. of Ordnance, Acting Chief, Royal Army Material Admin. & Chief, Army Ordnance Corps, 1966-68; Chief, Army Material Dept., Material Admin. of Armed Forces, 1968-69; Commanding Gen., Mil. Command East & Commandant Gen., Stockholm, 1969-74; Dir. Gen., Material Admin., Armed Forces, 1974-. Mbrships: Chmn., Ctrl. Jt. Consultation Bd., Armed Forces; Royal Acad. of Mil. Scis.; Nat. Personnel Coun. Contbr. to daily press & profl. jrnls. Hons: Cmdr. Grand Cross, Royal Swedish Order of the Sword; Cmdr. Grand Cross, 2nd Class, Meritorial Order, W. German Fed. Repub.; Cmdr. Grand Cross, Royal Danish Order of Dannebrogen. Address: Försvarets materielverk, S-104 50 Stockholm 80, Sweden. 134.

LJUNG, Ragnar, b. 12 Dec. 1906. County Librarian. Educ: M.A., Lib. Schl., 1930. Co. Libn., Karlstad, Sweden, 1946-74. Mbrships: Pres., audio-visual team of S.A.B. (Lib. Assn. of Sweden); Pres., co. theatre assn. of Wärmland; Pres., theatre assn. of Karlstad; Central bd., föreningen Norden; Rotary, Karlstad. Publs: Ed., I Värmland, 2nd edit. 1958; Ed., Svenska stadsmonografier: Värmlandsstäderna, 1952; Articles in newspapers & periodicals; Progs. in Swedish broadcasting co. Hons: Plaquette, adult educ. org., 1970; Riddare av Nordstjärneorden, 1973. Address: Märbackagatan 21, 654 61 Karlstad, Sweden.

LJUNGBERG, Sven, b. 15 Dec. 1913. Artist. Educ: Acad. of Art, Stockholm,

Sweden, 1934-43; Study Travels, France, Italy, Netherlands, & USSR. Collective Swedish exhibs., U.S.A. & Europe. Separate Exhibs: Moscow; Leningrad; Kiev. Monumental works in fresco & mosaic incl: Kapellkrematoriet Värnamo, 1957-58; Församlingshemmet, ibid, 1956; Ljungby Kyrka, 1965; Arbetarrörelsens historia i Sverige, Stockholm, Folkets Hus, 1966-69; Skogägarnas Hus, Växjö, 1968; Stadsbiblioteket, Gothenburg, 1967. Theatre Decorations, Dramatiska Teatern, Stockholm, 1951, 1967. Mbrships. incl: Akademien för de Fria Konsterna, 1968; Konstnärernas Riksorg.; Grafiska Sällskapet; Dir., Kungliga Konsthögskolan, Stockholm, 1972. Represented in num. museums. Hons. incl: Jenny Lind Travel Schlrship., 1939-40; Bonnier's Schlrship., 1951-57; Big State Schlrship., 1962-63; State Art Salary, 1968-. Address: Cosmorama, Strandgatan 7, 34100 Ljungby, Sweden. 134.

LJUNGQVIST, Arne Gunnar, b. 23 Apr. 1931. Professor. Educ: M.D., Karolinska Inst., Stockholm, Sweden, 1959. Appts: Asst. Physn., Clinical Pathol., 1959-61; Asst. Physn., Pediatrics, Gynaecol., Surg. & Anaesthesiol., 1961-64; Asst. Prof., Pathol., 1964-67; Prof. of Pathol., 1967-; Vice Dean, Med. Fac., Karolinska Inst., Stockholm, 1972-. Mbrships: Swedish Amateur Athletic Assn.; Pres., ibid, 1973-; Int. Soc. of Nephrol.; Swedish Div., Int. Acad. of Pathol.; Sec., ibid, 1968-70; Affiliate, Royal Soc. of Med.; Pathol., Cardiol. & Nephrol. Divs., Swedish Med. Soc. Publs: Num. papers & reports in field of pathol., particularly renal & cardi-vascular pathol. Address: Dept. of Pathology, Karolinska Hospital, S-10401 Stockholm 60, Sweden.

LLERA SANTOS, Félix José, b. 23 July 1939. Anatomist. Educ: B.S. cum laude, Univ. of Puerto Rico, 1960; D.M.D., Schl. of Dentistry, ibid, 1964; Postdoctoral Fellowship for Human Gross Anatomy, Neuroanatomy & Adv. Neuroanatomy, 1964-65. Appts: Tchr., Med. Gross Anatomy, Univ. of Puerto Rico, 1965-66; I/c.Phys. Therapy Students, ibid, 1966-67; I/c. Gross Anatomy Course for Dental Students, 1968-70; Asst., Postgrad Course in Anatomy, Richmond, Va., 1970; Asst. Prof. of Anatomy, Schl. of Med., Univ. of Puerto Rico, 1970-. Mbrships: Dental Grads. Sco. of the Puerto Rico Schl. of Dentistry; Coll. of Dental Surgs.; Alpha Beta Chi. Elected Grand Master, Puerto Rico Chapt., Delta Sigma Delta, 1964. Address: Munoz Barrios 7, Ciora, PR 00639, Puerto Rico. 7.

LLEWELLYN, Anne Birdsong, b. 1st Sept. 1920. Instructor of Homebound & Hospitalized Children. Educ: B.A.E., Univ. of Fla., Gainesville, 1956; M.A., Stetson Univ., DeLand, Fla., 1972. Appts: Elem. & kindergarten tchr.; Gen. Sci. Tchr., jr. high schls.; Grad. Asst., Stetson Univ. Mbrships: Phi Kappa Phi; Delta Kappa Gamma; Pilot Club, Int.; Assn. for Childhood Educ., Int.; NEA; Fla. Educators Assn.; Volusia Educ. Assn.; Textbook & Curriculum Chmn., Classroom Tchrs. Div. Speaker on Russian, E. German & Comp. Educ. & related subjects, tchrs. grps., students, workshops & clubs. Hon. Dir. for Fla. Educ. Assn. Austrian Tchr. Exchange Prog., 1973. Address: 1511 N. Atlantic Ave., Daytona Beach, FL 32018, U.S.A. 125.

LLEWELLYN-JONES, Frank, b. 30 Sept. 1907. University Administrator; Professor of Physics. Educ: B.A., Merton Coll., Oxford, 1929; M.A., D.Phil., ibid, 1931; D.Sc., 1955. Appts. incl: Demonstrator, Wykeham Dept. Phys., Univ. of Oxford, 1929-32; Sr. Scientific Off., Royal Aircraft Establishment, 1940-45;

Lectr., Dept. of Phys., Univ. of Wales, 1932-40, Prof., 1945-, Hd. Dept. of Phys., 1945-65; Scientific Advsr., Civil Defence, (Wales) 1952-59, Sr. Advsr., 1959-; Vice Prin., Univ. Coll. of Swansea, 1954-56, 1960-62, Acting Prin., 1959-60, Prin., 1965-. Mbr. & Off., acad. orgs. Publs. incl: The Physics of Electrical Contacts, 1957; The Glow Discharge, 1966. Papers, scientific jrnls. Hons. incl: C.B.E., 1965; 1st Ragnar Holm Scientific Achievement Award, Chgo., 1971. Address: University College of Swansea, Singleton Pk., Swansea, SA2 8PP, U.K. 1, 32, 128.

LLEWELYN OWENS, Joan Margaret, (Mrs. D. Anthony Venner), Author; Journalist; Career Consultant. Educ: Cheltenham Ladies' Coll. Appts: Educ. Off., WRNS, 1946-49; Careers Cons., Daily Telegraph, 1970-. Mbrships: Inst. of Jrnlsts.; Soc. of Authors; Nat. Book League. Publs. incl: The Graduate's Guide to the Business World; Travel While You Work; Working in the Theatre; Margaret Becomes a Doctor; A Library Life for Deborah; Contbr. to periodicals in U.K., U.S.A., Scandinavia, Belgium, N.Z. & Australia. Address: Ashley Cottage, Linden Grave, Walton-on-Thames KT12 1EY, Surrey, U.K. 3.

LLORCA VIVES, (Fr.) Bernardin, S.J., b. 3 Feb. 1898. Catholic Priest. Educ: Ph.D., Colegio S. Ignacio, Sarriá-Barcelona, Spain, 1923; Th.D., Ignatiuskolleg, Valkenburg, Holland, 1927; Dr. Hist., Munich Univ., W. Germany, 1932. Prof. Humanities, Monasterio Veruela, Zaragoza, Spain, 1920-23; Prof. Ecclesiastical Hist., Christian Archaeol. & Patrol., Fac. Theol., Colegio S. Ignacio, Sarriá-Barcelona, Spain, 1932-48; Pontifical Univ. of Salamanca, 1948-68. Mbr. Assn. P. Francisco Suárez, Coimbra-Madrid, Spain. Publs: Historia de la Iglesia Catolica, 1967; Manual de Historia Eclesiástica, 1966; Nueva Visión de la Historia del Cristianismo, 1956; Compendio de Historia de la Iglesia Católica, 1862; La Inquisición en España, 1956; Bulario Pontificio de la Inquisición espanola, 1949 & others, incldg. many articles & studies in field. Prof. Emeritus, Fac. Theol., Soc. of Jesus, San Cugat del Vallés, Barcelona, Spain & of Pontifical Univ. of Salamanca. Address: Fac. de Teologia, Colegio S. Francisco de Borja, San Cugat, Barcelona, Spain, 43, 102.

LLOYD, Alan Grahame, b. 26 Sept. 1926. Professor of Economics. Educ: B.Ec., Univ. of Sydney, N.S.W., Australia; M.Sc.Agr., Univ. of Melbourne, Vic. Appts: Econs. Rsch. Off., N.S.W. Dept. of Agric., 1949-59; Sr. Lectr., Agricl. Econs., Univ. of Melbourne, 1959-67; Prof., Agricl. Econs., ibid, 1969-; Warden, Derrimut Agricl. Rsch. Station & Coll., 1970-. Mbrships: Comm., Vic. Br., Econs. Soc. of Australia, 1962-64; Exec. Comm., & Publs. Comm. of Jrnl., Australian Inst. of Agricl. Sci., 1963-66; Publs. Comm., Australian Jrnl. of Agricl. Econs., 1963-64 & 1968; Councillor, Australian Agricl. Econs. Soc., 1963-65, 1967-70, & 1972, V.P., 1967-68. Pres., 1969; Edit. Comm., Australian Econ. Review, 1969-73, Edit. Cons., 1973-; Trustee, Comm. for Econ. Dev. of Australia. Publs: 44 papers & contbns. to books. Address: School of Agriculture & Forestry, University of Melbourne, Parkville, Melbourne, Vic., Australia 3052.

LLOYD, Geoffrey Ernest Richard, b. 25 Jan. 1933. University Lecturer. Educ: B.A., King's Coll., Cambridge, U.K., 1954; M.A., 1958; Ph.D., 1958. Appts: Fellow, King's Coll., Cambridge, 1957-; Sr. Tutor, ibid, 1969-73; Asst. Lectr., Classics, Cambridge Univ., 1965-67; Lectr., ibid, 1967-. Mbrships: Hellenic

Soc.; Royal Anthropol. Inst. Publs: Polarity & Analogy: Two Types of Argumentation in Early Greek Thought, 1966, 71; Aristotle: The Growth & Structure of His Thought, 1968; Early Greek Science: Thales to Aristotle, 1970; Greek Science After Aristotle, 1973; Ed., Hippocratic Writings; num. articles in learned jrnls. Address: King's Coll., Cambridge, CB2 1ST, U.K.

LLOYD, Herbert Mervyn, b. 29 Nov. 1912. Solicitor; Public Relations Officer. Educ: Univ. Coll. of S. Wales & Monmouthshire. Appts: Admitted a Solicitor of Supreme Ct., 1937; Spickett & Sons, 1937-39; Capt. Royal Artillery, 1939-45; Gen. prac., Ptnr., C. James Harwicke & Co., Cardiff, 1945-50; Area Sec. for S. Wales, Law Soc.'s Legal Aid & Advice Scheme, 1950; Under-Sec., Sec., Law Soc. P.R., 1957-64; P.R. Off., Port of London Authority, 1964-; Dir., Port Publng. Co. & Mernian Ltd., 1967-. Num. mbrships. incl: Exec. Coun. Mbr., Chmn., Brit. Grp., Int. P.R. Assn.; Fellow, Past Treas., Inst. of P.R.; European Ctr. for P.R.; Freeman of City of London; Fellow, Chartered Inst. of Transport; Fellow, Royal Soc. of Arts; Fndr. Exec. Coun. Mbr., Brit. Acad. of Forensic Scis.; Nat. Union of Jrnlsts.; Int. Bar Assn.; Exec. Comm., World Wildlife Fund. Publs: Legal Limits of Journalism, 1968; Public Relations, 1971. Address: Port of London Authority, World Trade Centre, London E.1, U.K. 24.

LLOYD, William Nelson, b. 24 July 1920. Attorney. Educ: Cumberland Univ.; Univ. of the South, Sewanee; Law, Univ. of Tenn; J.D., Van Der Bilt Univ. Appts: Judge, Court of General Sessions, Marshall Co., Tenn., 1950-58; Delegate, Dem. Nat. Conven., 1964; Mbr., Constitutional Conven. of Tenn., 1965-70. Mbrships: Bd. Govs., Tenn. Trial Lawyers, 1965-; Comm., Nat. Awards, Am. Trial Lawyers Assn.; Fellow, ibid; Comm. Mbr., Am. Bar Assn.: Am. Judicature Soc.; Am. Soc. of Law & Sci.; Ex Ruler, BPOE; SAE Fraternity; Tenn. Histl. Soc., etc. Hons. incl: (Military) Silver Star; three DFC's; Personal Cit.; Presidential Unit Cit.; Navy Unit Cit.; Battle stars, etc. Address: 220 West Church St., Lewisburg, TN 37091, U.S.A. 2, 7.

LLOYD-JONES, Peter Hugh Jefferd, b. 21 Sept. 1922. Classical Scholar. Educ: Christ Ch., Oxford, U.K. Appts: Fellow, Jesus Coll., Cambridge, 1948-54; Asst. Lectr., Univ. of Cambridge, 1950-52; Lectr., ibid., 1952-54; Fellow & E.P. Warren Praelector in Classics, Corpus Christi Coll., Oxford, 1954-60; Student of Christ Church, Oxford, 1960-; Regius Prof. of Greek, Univ. of Oxford, 1960-. Mbrships: Fellow of the British Acad.; Pres., Int. Comm., Homeric Soc., Greece; Hon. Greek Humanistic Soc. Publs: Appendix to Aeschylus, Loeb Classical Library, 1957; Menandri Dyscolus, Oxford Classical Text, 1960; Translation of P. Maas: Greek Metre, 1962; Translations of: Aeschylus: Agamemnon, Libation-Bearers & Eumenides, 1970; The Justice of Zeus, (Sather Classical Lectures, 41), 1971. Hon. Doct. of Humane Letters, Univ. of Chgo., 1970. Address: Christ Church, Oxford, U.K. 1, 34, 128.

LOBB, John Cunningham, b. 31 May 1913. Company Director. Educ: B.A., Univ. of Minn., 1934; LL.B., Univ. of Wis., 1937. Appts: Pres., H.M. Byllesby & Co., Chgo., Ill., 1962-63; Exec. V.P., Int. Telephone & Telegraph, N.Y.C., 1963-67; Ptbr., Donaldson, Lufkin & Jenrette, Inc., N.Y.C., 1969-70; Pres., Northern Elec. Co. Ltd., 1971-73; Pres. & Chief Exec. Off., ibid, 1973-; Bd. Chmn., Microsystems Int. Ltd., Northern Telecom, Inc., Boston, Mass.,

Bell-Northern Rsch., Ottawa, Canada, Nedco Ltd., Montreal, & Nevron Inds. Co. Ltd., Montreal; Dir., Bell Canda, Montreal, Continental III. Ltd., London, U.K., Northern Elec. Co. (Ireland), Ltd., Galway, Northeast Electronics Corp., Concord, N.H., U.S.A., & LTM, Inc., Boston, Mass. Mbrships. incl: St. James's Club of Montreal; Forest & Stream Club, Dorval. P.Q.; Mt. Royal Club, Montreal; Country Club of Fla.; Duquesne Club, Pitts., Pa.; Cornell Club of N.Y. Address: Northern Electric Co. Ltd., 1600 Dorchester Blvd. W., Montreal, P.Q., H3H 1R1, Canada. 2, 88.

LOBKOWICZ, Nicholas, b. 9 July 1931. University Professor & Rector. Educ: B.A., Collegium Maria Hilf, Schwyz, Switz., 1950; Univ. of Erlangen, German Fed. Repub. Ph.D., Univ. of Fribourg, Switz., 1958. Appts: Chief Asst., Inst. of E. European Studies, Fribourg, 1958-60; Assoc. Prof., Philos., Univ. of Notre Dame, Ind., 1960-67; Prof., Pol. Theory & Philos., Univ. of Munich, 1967-; Dir., Inst. for Pol. Sci., ibid, 1968-70; Dean of Philosophical Fac. I & Rector of Schl. of Pols., 1970-71; Rector Magnificus, 1971-(re-elected, 1973). Mbrships: Bd. of Dirs., Bundesinstitut für Int. und Osteuropäische Studien, Cologne, 1972-; Am. Metaphys. Assn.; Deutsche Gesellschaft für Osteuropakunde; Assn. for Symbolic Logic. Publs. incl: Marxismus-Leninismus in der CSR, 1961; Das Widerspruchsprinzip in der zeitgenössicschen Sowjetphilosophie, 1961; Theory & Practice, From Aristotle to Marx, 1967; Ed. & Contbr., Marx & the Western World, 1967; Co-Ed., Studies in Soviet Thought, Zeitschrift für Politik & Münchenner Studien zur Politik; articles in profl. publs. Hons: Sr. Fellowship, Nat. Endowment for the Humanities, USA, 1967; offered (not accepted) Cardinal O'Hara Chair for Philos., Univ. of Notre Dame, Ind., USA. Address: 8 München 81, Westpreussenstr. 7, Munich, German Fed. Repub. 13, 92.

LOBUE, Ange Joseph, b. 12 Aug. 1937. Physician. Educ: B.S. (Pharm.), Univ. of Miss., 1960; M.D., Schl. of Med., La. State Univ., 1964; Master of Pub. Hlth., Schl. of Pub. Hlth., UCLA, 1969; Res., Depts. of Psych. & Preventative & Soc. Med., Schl. of Med., UCLA, 1969-72. Appts. incl: Registered Pharm., Briargrove Pharmacy, Houston, Tex., 1960; Gen. Med. Prac., Permanente Med. Grp., San Fran., Calif., 1965; Med. Off., 6th Convalescent Med. Ctr., Civic Action Coord. & Grp. Surg., 35th Engr. Grp., Port Surg., Cam Ranh Bay, & Cmdng. Off., 161st Med. Detachment, (all US Army, Vietnam), 1965-66; Med. Off., Oakland Army Terminal, Calif., 1966-67; Planning Coord., Calif. Comm. on Regional Med. Progs., San Fran., 1967-68; Sr. Pub. Hlth. Physn., Venice Youth Clin., Dept. of Hlth., Co. of L.A., 1969-71; Pvte. Prac., Asst. Clin. Prof., Dept. of Psych., Schl. of Med., UCLA & num. cons., attng. & exec. positions, 1972-; Staff Psych., Cedu Fndn., Running Springs, Calif., 1974-. Mbrships. incl: Acad. of Psychosomatic Med.; AAAS; AMA; Fndng. Fellow, Am. Geriatrics Soc.; Delta Omega; Kappa Psi; Phi Chi; Fellow, Royal Soc. of Hlth.; World Med. Assn.; Am. Psych. Assn. Publs: The Electric Couch (in preparation); contbr. to profl. jrnls. Address: 2080 Century Park E., Suite 1107, Los Angeles, CA 90067, USA. 9.

LOCHAK, Paul J., b. 8 Sept. 1929. Managing Nuclear Engineer. Educ: B.A., M.A., Cornell Univ., U.S.A., 1948-50; Rsch. Fellow, Harvard Univ., U.S.A., 1950-53. Appts: Mgr., Nuclear Projs., France, Belgium, Italy, for Gibbs & Hill, Inc., N.Y.C., U.S.A., 1955-60; Mgr., Power Projs., India, Pakistan, 1960-63; Dir., Gibbs & Hill (France), Paris, 1965-72;

Pres., Société Internationale de Technologie (formerly Gibbs & Hill), Paris, 1972-. Mbrships. incl: Assn. des Ingenieurs Civils de France; Soc. Harvard Engrs. & Scis.; Cercle Interallie, Paris; Harvard Clubs of N.Y. & Paris; Am. Club of Paris. Recip., Nat. Defense Serv. Medal, U.S.A. Address: 61 Rue des Belles Feuilles, Paris 16°, France. 43, 91.

LOCHNER, H. Allen, b. 14 Aug. 1912. Lawyer. Educ: A.B., Temple Univ., Phila., Pa., 1936; LL.B., Univ. of Pa. Law Schl., 1939. Appts: Assoc. Atty., Arthur T. Vanderbilt, Newark, N.J., 1939-42; Assoc. Atty., predecessor of Rogers & Wells, N.Y.C., 1942-53; Ptnr., Rogers & Wells & predecessors, 1953-. Mbrships: Pres., Univ. of Pa. Law Schl. N.Y. Alumni Soc., 1967-68; Am. Bar Assn.; N.Y. State Bar Assn.; Trustee, Marble Mens League Fndn.; Order of Coif; Ed. Bd., Univ. of Pa. Law Review, 1938-39. Address: c/o Rogers & Wells, 200 Park Ave., N.Y., NY 10017, U.S.A. 6.

LOCKE, Irene Vivian Fisher (Mrs. John Loor Locke), Civic & National Worker. Educ: Pvte. Schls. Activities: Arranged sponsor for 1st Fellowship in Cardiovascular Rsch., Univ. of Wash. Schl of Med.; Full-time volunteer (King Co. Chmn., Women's Div., then Wash. State, Women's Div.), War Bonds Div., U.S. Treas. Dept., 1941-51; Mbr., Wash. State Heart Assn.; Bd. & Fndng. Comm., Nat. Citizen's Comm. for Mental Hlth., 1963-; Assoc. Dir., Wash. Coun., Nat. Emergency Comm., Nat. Coun. on Crime & Delinquency; Bd. Trustees, Intercollegiate Studies Inst., 1968-; Nat. Advsry. Bd., Am. Security Coun., 1970-; Nat. Assn. for Female Execs., 1972-; Treas.-Asst. Sec., Bd. Trustees, O.D. Fisher Investment Co.; Co-Chmn., Asst. Sec., Asst. Treas., Trustee, O.D. Fisher Charitable Fndn.; Charter Donor, Help Hospitalized Veterans, 1973. Mbrships. incl: Jr. League of Seattle (num. offs.); The Early Am. Glass Club; Life, Past Bd. Mbr., Seattle Children's Home; Past V.P. & Bd. Mbr., Sunset Clyb; Past Bd. Mbr., Seattle Girl Scout Coun.; Children's Orthopedic Hosp. (sev. past offs.); Pres. Lib. Comm., Am. Christian Coll.; Past Bd. Mbr. & V.P., Seattle Vis. Nurse Serv. Hons. incl: Ph.D., Hamilton State Univ., 1973; 2 Citations, Sec., U.S. Treas. Dept.; Sev. Wash. State Treas. Citations. Address: 2148 Broadmoor Dive E., Seattle, WA 98112, U.S.A. 5, 9, 57, 128, 138.

LOCKE, Richard van de Sande, II, b. 17 Apr. 1937. Investment Banker. Educ: B.S., Bucknell Univ., 1958. Appts: Staff Mbr., Kidder, Peabody & Co., 1959-64; Gen. Ptnr., Eastman Dillon Union Securities & Co. 1964-72; Snr. V.P., Blyth Eastman Dillon & Co. Inc., 1973-. Mbrships. incl: N.Y. Stock Exchange; Am. Stock Exchange; N.Y. Assn. Commerce & Industry; Municipal Forum of N.Y.; Municipal Finance Offts. Assn. on U.S. & Canada; Lambda Chi Alpha; Theta Alpha Phi. Address: 14 Wall St., N.Y., NY 10005, U.S.A. 5, 117.

LOCKE, (Mrs.) Ruby Alley, b. 5 Oct. 1900. Licensed Practical Nurse; Poet. Educ: Mt. Sinai Hosp. L.P.N. Schl., 1958. Appts: Aide, Lakeland Hosp.; Pvte. nursing; Owner & Supvsr., Locke's House of Rest, 1940-64; Supvsr., Rest Homes, 1964-70; Night Supvsr., var. rest homes, 1965-. Mbrships: Fla. State Poetry Soc., Miami; Cath. Women's Club. Books of Poetry pubd. every yr. 1967-73, incl. poems in Int. Hall of Fame Poets—5 books; 9 Muses—2 books; Selected Poems—6 books; Murfey Award Books—6 books; Glen Coffield Creative Poetry Review—all poems awarded prizes or honourable mentions. Address: 321 So. Mo. Ave., Lakeland, FL 33801, U.S.A. 11, 128.

LOCKHART, Patt (Patricia Ann) (Mrs. John T. Lockhart Sr.), b. 28 Apr. 1937. Phot-journalist; Public Relations; Broadcaster. Educ: Univ. of Tenn., Chattanooga, 1961-63; Nashville State Inst., 1971. Appts. incl: Photo-jrnlist, 1971-; P.R. for books & civic clubs, 1972-; Asst. to Donia Craig Dickerson, Art Broker, 1972-73; Owner, Pal Features, 1973; Radio Prog. Hostess, Country Express, U.S.A., WGSY-FM, Peru, Ill., 1973-74. Mbrships. incl: V.P., Nat. League Am. Pen Women, 1972-74; Pres., Sigma Chapt, Beta Sigma Phi, 1972-73; DAR; Tenn. Womens Press & Authors; Tenn. Outdoor Writers Assn.; Assn. of Great Lakes Outdoor Writers; Nat. Writers Club; Country Jusic Assn. Inc. Publs: (columns) In and Around Capital Hill; Scouting News; Let's Go Outdoors; Antiques; contbr. to many newspapers. Hons. incl: Nat. Police Officers Assn. Am., 1973; Girl of the Yr. Award, Sigman Chapt., Beta Sigma Phi, 1973. Address: 40 8th St., LaSalle, IL 61301, U.S.A. 76, 125, 138.

LOCKLEY, Ronald Mathias, b. 8 Nov. 1903. Naturalist; Author. Appts: w. Naval Intelligence & Min. of Supply, 1939-45; Field Rchr. for Nature Conservancy, 1955-60; Self-employed. Mbrships: Fndr., W. Wales Naturalist's Trust, Chmn., now V.P.; Fndr. & Chief Ed., Nature in Wales (jrnl.); served on num. Nature & Conservational couns. for Engl. & Wales Publs: sole author, about 36 books & monographs, inclng: Animal Navigation, 1967; Traveller's Guide to the Channel Islands, 1968; The Book of Bird-Watching, 1968; The Island, 1969; Man Against Nature, 1970; The Naturalist in Wales, 1970; Ocean Wanderers, 1974; collaborated on 4 books inclng: Bird-Ringing (w. Rosemary Russell), 1953; Sea-Birds (of the North Atlantic) (w. James Fisher), 1954; contbr. & ed. of anthols.; contbr. num. sci. articles on sea-birds, seals & rabbits to jrnls. Has made nature films for cinema & TV inclng: Private Life of the Gannet (w. Julian Huxley), one of 1st nature films to win Oscar; Shearwaters for Yorkshire TV, 1974. Address: Cole Park, Malmesbury, Wiltshire, U.K. 1, 3.

LOCKSHIN, Samuel D., b. 10 Mar. 1908. Registered Professional Industrial Engineer. Educ: B.I.E., Ohio State Univ., 1930; Profl. Engr., 1935. Appts: Profl. Mgmt. Cons., M.P. Pfeil Co., Dayton, Ohio, 1933-38; V.P., Dominion Elec. Corp., Mansfield, Ohio, 1938-52; Pres., Plymouth Metal Prods. Co., Galion, Ohio, 1942-46; Pres., Royal Master Prods. Co., Marion, Ohio, 1946-48; V.P., Hampden Specialty Prod. Co., E. Hampton, Mass., 1952-67; Pres., Prest-Wheel of Ariz., Parker, Ariz., & Pres., Prest-Wheel Inc., S. Grafton, Mass., 1967-71; Int. Execs. Serv. Corp., N.Y.C., 1971-. Mbrships: Nat. Soc. of Profl. Engrs.; Mass. Soc. of Profl. Engrs.; Ohio Soc. of Profl. Engrs.; Nat. Soc. of Indl. Engrs.; Masonic Order; Melha Shrine. Author of articles in field. Hons: Outstanding Sr., "Younger Award", Ohio State Univ., 1930; 2nd Prize, Apollo Award Metal Furniture Design, 1965. Address: Baker Hill, Northampton, MA 01060, U.S.A. 6, 9.

LOCKWOOD, Earl Forrest, b. 5 July 1930. Engineering Executive. Educ: B.S., Univ. of Kentucky, 1956; Schl. Nuclear Sci. & Engrng., Argunne Nat. Lab., 1958. Appts. incl: Mitre Corp., 1959-68, Assoc. Dept. Hd., 1962-65, Dept. Hd., 1965-68; Prog. Mgr., R.C.A. Corp., 1968-. Mbrships: Am. Soc; M.E.; Am. Nuclear Soc.; A.M.A. Author, num. sci. publs.

(classified). Address: 244 Concord Rd., Wayland, MA 01778, U.S.A.

LODOLINI, Elio, b. 24 Jan. 1922. Archivist & University Professor. Educ: Grad., Pol. Sci; Grad., Law; Dipl. Paleography & Archivism. Appts. incl: Jrnlst., 1940-50; Publr., 1957-; State Archivist, Lazio, Umbria & Le Marche, 1950-61; State Archivist, Rome, 1961-70; Dir., State Archives, Ascoli Piceno, 1954-62; Dir., State Archives, Ancona, 1962-64; Dir., Archives & Cultural Affairs Dept., Min. of Interior, 1970-72. Mbrships: Nat. Hist. Deleg. of Le Marche, Ancona; Assn. Brazilian Archivists, Rio de Janeiro; Nat. Hist. Deleg. of Umbria, Perugia; Nat. Hist. Deleg. of Abruzzi, l'Aquila; Inst. Int. & Comp. Agrarian Law, Florence; Argentinan Archivist Assn. Publs. incl: La illegittimatà del governo Badoglio, Storia costituzionale del'quinquennio rivoluzionario' 25 luglio 1943 - 1° gennaio 1948, 1953; Testi e documenti per la storia del diritto agraria in italia, secoli VIII-XVIII, 1954; Guida delle fonti per la storia dell' Africa a sud del Sahara esistenti in italia, Vol. 1, 1973. Address: Via di Novella 8, 00199 Rome, Italy. 43.

LOENING, Sarah Larkin (Mrs. Albert P. Loening), b. 9 Dec. 1896. Author. Mbrships. incl: Past. Pres., Southampton Garden Club; Past Chmn., Gardeners of St. John; Past Pres., Cathedral Guild of St. John the Divine, N.Y.C.; Past Chmn., Hampton Chapt., Am. Red Cross; Nat. Soc. of Colonial Dames; Nat. Colonial Dames of N.Y.; Pen & Brush; Colony Club; Cosmopolitan Club; Huguenot Soc. Publs: Three Rivers, 1934; The Trevals, a Tale of Quebec, 1936; Radisson, 1938; Dimo, 1940; Joan of Arc, 1951; The Old Master, 1958; Zulli, 1960; The Old Master & Other Tails, 1967; Mountain in the Field, 1972. Assoc. Off., Am. Order of St. John of Jerusalem, 1971. Address: 1 E. 66th St., N.Y., NY 10021, U.S.A. 5, 6.

LOERKE, William Carl, b. 13 Aug. 1920. College Professor & Administrator. Educ: A.B. (magna cum laude), Oberlin Coll., 1942; M.F.A., Princeton Univ., 1948; Ph.D., ibid, 1957. Appts: Instr. & Asst. Prof., Brown Univ., 1949-59; Asst. Prof., Bryn Mawr Coll., 1959-64; Prof., Univ. of Pitts., Pa., 1964-71, Chmn., Fine Arts Dept., 1964-68; Dir. of Studies & Prof. of Byzantine Art, Harvard Univ., Dumbarton Oaks, 1971-. Mbrships: Medieval Acad. of Am.; Coll. Art Assn.; Mng. Comm., Am. Schl. Classical Studies, Athens; Bd. Dirs., Int. Ctr. of Medieval Art. Contbr., Art Bulletin, 1961, New Cath. Ency., 1967. Hons. incl: Fulbright Rsch. Fellowship, Am. Acad., Rome, Italy, 1952-53; Danforth Tchr. Fellowship, 1956-67; Baldwin Seminar Lectr., Oberlin Coll., 1967. Address: Center for Byzantine Studies, Dumbarton Oaks, 1703 32nd St. N.W., Washington, DC 20007, U.S.A. 2, 13.

LOEWENSTEIN, George W., b. 18 Apr. 1890. Medical Director. Appts. incl: Prof., Berlin Acad. for Prevention of Mortality of Newborns & Infants; Lectr., Acad. for Postgrad. Trng. Fed. Employees, Germany; Prof., Peoples Univ., Berlin; Med. Cons., N & Ctrl. Fla., U.S.A.; Re. & Permanent Cons., Int. Abolitionists Fed., ECOSOC, UN; Hlth. Off., Pinellas Co. Pub. Hlth. Dept. Mbrships. incl: Charter Fellow, Am. Acad. Family Physns.; Life mbr., Am. Acad. of Sports Med.; Am. Pub. Hlth. Assn.; Am. Acad. on Mental Retardation. Author of num. papers on preventive med., stats., econs., pub. hlth. & law. Hons. incl: Cert. of Commendation from Pres. Nixon, 1970; 50 yrs. Goldpin, AMA, 1970; 50 yrs. Goldpin Am. Red Cross, 1970; Serv. to Mankind Award, Sertoma Club; Americanism Medal DAR; Jr.

Womens Award for Contbns. to For. Affairs; Community Serv. Award, Am. Acad of Family Physns. Address: 1007 Woodside Dr., Clearwater, FL 33516, U.S.A. 6, 54.

LOEWENSTEIN, Jordan M., b. 24 Oct. 1929. Advertising Executive. Educ: B.S., L.I. Univ., 1971. Appt: Pres., Accredited Mailing Lists, Inc., N.Y.C. & Wash. D.C. Mbrships: Bd. of Dirs., Mail Advt. Club, Wash. D.C., 1965-73, Pres., 1972; Bd. Mbr., Offs. Serv. Club, Wash. D.C., 1970-74, V.P., 1974; Fndng. Mbr., Mailing List Brokers Profl. Assn. Address: 5272 River Rd., Suite 780, Washington, DC 20016, U.S.A. 40.

LOEWY, Raymond, b. 5 Nov. 1893. Industrial & Commercial Designer. Educ: D.F.A., Univ. of Cinn., & Art Ctr. Coll., L.A. Appts: Art Dir., Westinghouse Elec. Co.; started pvte. firm industrial design, 1929; Chmn., Raymond Loewy/William Snaith, Inc. Cons. in var. fields of commercial design, & to NASA on Space Stn. Habitability; Fellow, Industrial Designers Soc. of Am. Mbrships. incl: Soc. Mech. Engrng.; Soc. Automotive Engrs.; Am. Soc. Space Medicine. Publs: The Locomotive—its Aesthetics; Never Leave Well Enough Alone. Hons: Cmdr., French Legion of Honor; Croix de Guerre (4 citations); Interallied Medal; Fellow, British Royal Soc. of Arts, London, 1937; 1000 Makers of the 20th Century, London, 1969. Address: 110 E. 59th St., N.Y., NY 10022, U.S.A. 2.

LÖFGREN, Oscar Anders Valfrid, b. 13 May 1898. Professor Emeritus. Educ: Studentexamen, 1916; Fil.kand., 1920; Fil.mag., 1924; Fil.lic., 1927; Fil.dr., 1927. Appts: Docent, Semitic Langs., Univ. of Uppsala, Sweden, 1927; Lector, Latin & Greek, Gymnasium of Kristinehamn, 1941; Prof., Semitic Langs., Univ. of Göteborg, 1951, Univ. of Uppsala, 1956; Emeritus Prof., 1964-. Mbrships: Kungl. Vetenskaps-och Vitterhets-Samhället i Göteborg, 1951; Kungl. Humanistiska Vetenskaps-Samfundet i Uppsala, 1957; Nathan Söderblom-Sällskapet, 1958. Publs. incl: Die äthiopische Ubersetzung des Propheten Daniel, 1927; Jona, Nahum, Habakuk, Zephanja, Haggai, Sacharja u.Maleachi äthiopisch, 1930; Ein Hamdain-Fund, 1935; Arabische Texte zur Kenntnis der Stadt Aden im Mittelalter, Abu Mahrama's Adengeschichte, I-II, 1936-50; Ibn al-Muğâwir, Descriptio Arabiae meridionalis, 1-2, 1951-54; al-Hamdäni, al-Iklîl. I, 1-2, 1954-65; Translator, Det apokryfiska Johannesevangeliet, 1967. Recip., Th.D., 1971. Address: Övre Slottsgatan 14 C, 752 35 Uppsala, Sweden. 43, 134.

LOFTUS, (Colonel) Ernest Achey, b. 1 Jan. 1884. Schoolmaster. Educ: B.A., M.A., Trinity Coll., Dublin, Repub. of Ireland; B.Sc., London Univ., U.K.; Licentiate Coll. Preceptors (Tchrs. Dip.). Appts: Asst. Master, Palmer's Schl., Gray's, Essex, U.K., 1906-19; Dpty. Hd., Boys' H.S., Southend-on-Sea, 1919-20; Dpty. Dir. Educ., Co. Borough of Southend-on-Sea, 1920-22; Headmaster, Barking Abbey Schl., Essex, 1922-49; Educ. Off., Kenya, Malawi & Zambia. Currently tchng. at Munali Schl., Zambia; Active serv. in WW I & II. Mbrships: F.R.G.S.; F.R.S.A.; M.R.S.T.; Royal Soc. Lit.; Fndr., Essex Playing Fields Assn.; served as local Councillor & on mil. & univ. bodies; Past Pres., V.P., many Essex socs. Publs. incl: A History of Barking Abbey (w. H.F. Chettle); Education and the Citizen; History of a Branch of the Cole Family; A Visual History of Africa; A Visual History of East Africa. Hons: O.B.E., 1929; T.D.; 1930; D.L. (Co. of Essex), 1929.

Address: Polwicks, W. Tilbury, Essex, U.K. 1, 3.

LOFTUS, Martin L., b. 9 June 1911. Librarian. Educ: B.S., Univ. of Wash., 1932; A.B., ibid, 1933. Appts: Jr. Libn., Univ. of Wash., 1933-37; Ref. Asst., N.Y. Pub. Lib., 1937-46; Tech. Libn., VA, N.Y., 1946; Libn., Int. Monetary Fund & Int. Bank for Reconstruction & Dev., Jt. Bank Fund Lib., Wash. D.C., 1946-. Mbrships: Trustee, Pub. Affairs Info. Serv., 1964-; Treas., U.S. Book Exchange, 1964-65; Treas., Special Lib. Assn., 1951-52; ALA; Am. Soc. Info. Sci.; Int. Dev. Assn.; Cosmos Club; Phi Beta Kappa. Publs: International Monetary Fund: Select bibliographies, 1946-73. Address: Jt. Bank Fund Lib., 19th H Sts., N.W. Wash. DC 20431, U.S.A.

LOGAN, (Sir) Douglas William, b. 27 Mar. 1910. Barrister-at-Law; University Principal. Educ: B.A., Univ. Coll., Oxford, U.K., 1932; M.A., B.C.L., ibid, 1935; D.Phil., 1939; Harvard Law Schl., U.S.A. 1935-36. Appts: Asst. Lectr., London Schl. of Econs., 1936-37; Fellow, Trinity Coll., Cambridge, 1937-43; Prin., Min. of Supply, 1940-44; Clerk of the Ctr., Univ. of London, 1944-47; Prin., ibid, 1948-. Mbrships: Called to the Bar, Middle Temple, 1937; Dpty. Chmn., Assn. of Commonwealth Univs., 1961-62 & 1963-67; Chmn., ibid, 1962-63; Hon. Treas., 1967-; Athenaeum Club, 1952-; Hon. mbr., Pharmaceutical Soc. Hons. incl: Chevalier de la Legion d'Honneur, 1957; Knighted, 1959; LL.D., 6 univs.; F.D.S.R.C.S., 1958; F.R.I.B.A., 1971; Coun. for Nat. Acad. Award, 1972. Address: Univ. of London, London WC1 E7HU, U.K.

LOGAN, Henry Leon, b. 15 Mar. 1896. Consulting Electrical Engineer. Educ: Inst. of Polytech., Birmingham, U.K.; P.E., Columbia Univ., N.Y.C., U.S.A.; SUNY. Appts: Asst. to Chief Engr., 1919; Engrng. Cons., 1927; Dir., 1946-71; V.P., Rsch., 1949; Chmn., Bd., Holophane Co. Inc., N.Y.C., 1969-71; Currently in pvte. prac. Fellowships: Nat. Bd. Examiners in 20 yrs. & Chmn., Illumination Grp., 4 yrs., IEEE; Illuminating Engrng. Soc.; Illuminating Engrng. Soc., U.K. Mbrships. incl: Hon. Life, Mexican Inst. of Illumination; Life, U.S. Comm., Congress Int. d'Eclairage; Past, Inter-Soc. Colour Coun.; Soc. for Photobiol. Author of 227 tech. papers in engrng. & sci. jrnls. Hons. incl: Gold Seal Award, Bldg. Rsch. Inst., 1965; Gold Medal Award, Illuminating Engrng. Soc., 1965; Master Kt., Sovereign Mil. Order of Malta, 1965; Kt., Order of the Holy Sepulchre, 1967. Address: 5 Hewitt Ave., Bronxville, NY 10708, U.S.A. 2, 6, 14, 16, 49, 51, 64, 128, 131.

LOGAN, Lee Robert, b. 24 June 1932. Orthodontist. Educ: D.D.S., Northwestern Univ., 1956; M.S., ibid, 1961. Appts: Served to Lt., USNR, 1956-58; Pres., Lee R. Logan, D.D.S. Prof. Corp. Mbrships: var. offs. inclng. Chmn., Pub. Rels., Pacific Coast Soc. of Orthodonts., 1970; Am. Assn. Orthodonts.; Angle Soc. Orthodonts.; San Fernando Dental Soc: Hlth. Week Chmn., 1962; Chmn. of Coun. on Profl. Servs., 1972; Pres., Pacific Coast Soc. Orthodontists, Southern Sect., 1974-75; Am. Dental Assn.; G.V. Black Soc.; Chtr., Fndn. on Orthodontic Rsch.; Fellow, Int. Coll. of Applied Nutrition; S. Calif. Acad. of Nutritional Rsch.; L.A. Speakers Club; Int. Platform Speakers; L.A. Tennis Club; Braemar Country Club. Contbr. to sev. articles to profl. jrnls. Recip. of Dipl., Am. Bd. of Orthodonts, 1967. Address: 18250 Roscoe Blvd., Northridge, CA 91324, U.S.A. 9.

LOGAN, William Philip Dowie, b. 2 Nov. 1914. Physician. Educ: M.D., DPH, Univ. of Glasgow, Scotland, U.K.; Ph.D., Univ. of London. Appts. incl: Chief Med. Statn., Gen. Register Office of England & Wales, 1951-60; Dir., Div. of Hlth. Stats., WHO, Geneva, Switzerland, 1961-. Fellowships: Royal Coll. of Physns., London; Royal Stat. Soc.; Royal Soc. Med. Mbr., Int. State. Inst. Contbr. of articles, reports & chapts. to med. jrnls. & textbooks in field of epidemiol. & hlth. stats. Address: WHO, 1211 Geneva 27, Switzerland. 1, 43, 103, 128.

LOGARAS, George, b. 26 Sept. 1912. Physician; Professor of Experimental Pharmacology. Educ: Univ. studies in Athens, Greece; Leipzig, Germany; Univ. Coll., London, U.K.; Karolinska Inst., Stockholm, Sweden; Grad. in med., Athens Univ. Appts: Asst., Lab. of Experimental Pharmacol., Athens Univ., 1933; Cons., ibid, 1934-46; Assoc. Prof., ibid, 1947; Prof., Dept. of Experimental Pharmacol., Aristotelian Univ. of Thessaloniki, 1960; Dean, Aristotelian Univ. of Thessaloniki Med. Schl., 1968-69, '73-76. Mbrships: Royal Soc. of Med.; Sec. Gen., Hellenic Biochem. Soc.; Soc. Française de therapeutique de Pharmacodynamie; KolloidGesellschaft, Germany; Interdepartmental Comm. on Nutrition of Nat. Defence, Wash.; European Grp. of Nutritionists; Hellenic Narcotics Commn.; Fndr. Mbr., Hellenic Soc. for Environment & Hlth. Author & co-author of num. profl. reports & papers, inclng. Observations on 246 cases of acute poisoning by parathion in Greece, 1971; Potentiation of drug-induced neuromuscular blockade by certain antibiotics, 1973; Absorption & excretion studies of the antibiotic cephradine on human subjects, 1973; D.D.T. & the Pollution of Man. Ed., Annual Scientific Review of the Medical Faculty; Co-Ed., Folia Biochemica Greca & other med. jrnls. Translator of sev. books from French & English on Biological and Med. Problems. Hons: Laureate, Athens Acad. Address: L. Kaftanzoglou 8, Salonica 363, Greece.

LOHNE-KNUDSEN, Christofer, b. 4 Sept. 1908. Psychiatrist. Educ: Med. degree exam., Univ. of Oslo, 1935; Masters degree in Public Health, Oslo, 1936; Approved specialist in Psychiatry, 1946; U.N. Fellowship for studying psychiatric admin., laws & instns. in U.K., Holland, Belgium & Switz., 1951-52. Appts: Local Med. Off. in rural dists., 1935-37; Asst. Physn. at Gen. Hosps., 1938-40 & at Lier Mental Hosp., 1940-42, & at Oslo Univ. Psychiatric Clin., 1942-45; Dpty. Supt., Oslo Univ. Mental Hosp., Gaustad, 1945-48; Asst. Prof. Psych., 1946-48; Psych. Cons. at General Hosps. in Oslo, 1942-62; Psych. Cons. for the Royal Min. of Justice, 1947-57; Dir. of the Psych. Div., The Hlth. Servs. of Norway, Royal Min. of Soc. Affairs, 1948-. Mbrships: Norwegian Med. Assn.; Norwegian, Scand. & World Psych. Assns.; Norw. & Int. Assns. for Mental Hlth.; Cons., Norw. Soc. for Mental Retarded; Scand. League for Mental Retarded. Contbr. to profl. books, jrnls., Periodicals & newspapers. Mbr., Editl. Bd., Int. Jrnl. of Mental Hlth. Hons: Norw. Red Cross Badge of Hon., 1958; Norw. Womens Hlth. Assn. Badge of Hon., 1971. Address: Helsedirektoratet, Akersgaten 42, Oslo-Dep, Oslo 1, Norway. 43.

LOIMARANTA, Aarre Kalervo, b. 7 June 1913. Educationalist; Deputy Mayor of Helsinki. Educ: M.A., Univ. of Helsinki, Finland, 1936. Appts: Sr. Tchr. of Maths. & Phys., Suomalainen Secondary Schl., Helsinki, 1952-61; Dpty. Mayor (Educ. & Cultural Affairs), City of Helsinki, 1961-; Officiating Hd. of Div., Bd. of Educ., 1952, 1954 & 1955.

Num. mbrships. incl: Commn. of Finnish People's Party, 1951-62, Chmn., Helsinki Municipal Org., 1952-62; Chmn., Finnish Municipal Assn., 1960-62; City Coun. of Helsinki, 1954-61; Exec. Bd., Union of Finnish Towns, 1958-61; Comm. of Fedn. of Civil Servants of Finland, 1954-61, Chmn. of Study Ctr., 1956-62; Sec., Assn. of Pvte. Schl. Tchrs. of Finland, 1952-61; Comm. of Ctrl. Fedn. of Finnish Secondary Schl. Tchrs., 1951-61. Publs: Articles in sev. jrnls.; Histl. accounts of pub. educ. org. Hons. incl: Cmdr. of Order of Lion of Finland; Order of Cross of Liberty, Class 3 & 4; Order of White Rose of Finland; Kt. of 1st Class, Icelandic Order of Falcon; Grand Kt. w. Star, Cmdr. of Order of the Lion & Sun of Iran. Address: Risto Rytin tie 28 C 30, 00570 Helsinki 57, Finland. 43, 90, 134.

LOÏZOS, Antonios A., b. 11 July 1916. Civil Engineer; University Rector & Professor; Professor Honoris Causa Universidade Federal do Rio de Janeiro. Educ: Dip. Civil Engrng., Tech. Nat. Univ., Athens, Greece, 1937; Dr. Engrng., 1948; Postgrad. Studies, Ecole des Ponts et Chausées, Paris, London, Germany, Italy, 1950-54. Appts: Engr., Min. of Transport, 1942-50; Lectr., Nat. Tech. Univ. of Athens, 1941-51; Asst. Prof., 1952; Assoc. Prof., Dept. of Fndns. Engrng. & Bridges Design & Dir., Fndns. Engrng. & Soil Mechs. Inst., Nat. Tech. Univ. of Athens, 1955-64; Full Prof. (Ord.), ibid, 1964-; Dean, Civil Engrng. Fac., Nat. Tech. Univ. of Athens, 1968-70 & 1973; Rector, ibid, 1970-73; Prof., Applied Mechs., 1951-62, Prof., Pub. Works, Air Force Schl. of Engrng., 1951-67; Spec. Educ. Advsr., Merchant Marine Schls., 1957-69; Prof., Soil Mechs. & Fndn. Engrng., H.S. of Engrng. of Greek Army, 1967-; Counselor, Greek Nat. Railways, 1967-70, Min. of Pub. Works, 1970-72, Corinth Canal Soc., 1970-74, Nat. Mortgage Bank of Greece, 1974-; Greek rep. at var. int. confs. in field. Mbrships. incl: Int. Soc. Soil Mechs. & Fndn. Engrng.; Pres., Hellenic Soc.; Int. Soc. Rock Mechs.; Int. Soc. of Large Dams; Assn. Int. des Ponts et Charpentes; RILEM; Greek Humanitarian Soc.; CRE; V.P., Greek Sect., Int. Assn. for Fed. Union. Contbr. to tech. jrnls. Hons. incl: Argent Cross w. Swords, Order of Phenix, 1947; Golden Cross, Order of Geo. I, 1959; Cmdr., Order of Phenix, 1966; Kt. Comdr. (Grand Off.), Order of Phenix, 1973; Golden Medal of Athens, 1971; Argent Medal of 150 anniv. of Independence, 1972; Medal of Except Actes, 1946. Address: 51 Posseidonos Ave., Pal. Phaliron, Athens, Greece. 43, 50.

LØKSE, Olav, b. 9 Oct. 1910. Educator. Educ: M.A., Univ. of Oslo, Norway, 1938; Univ. Coll., Southampton, U.K., 1937; Oriel Coll., Oxford, 1946; Univ. of Chgo., U.S.A., 1952-53. Appts: Tchr., Kongsberg Gymnas, Norway, 1939; Tchr., Ullern Gymnas, Oslo; Prin., Finnsnes Gymnas, 1946. Mbrships: Chmn., Dist. 12, Norsk Lektorlag, 2 yrs.; Rotary Int.; Borough Coun.; Chmn., local schl. bd. Publs: Outrageous Fortune, 1960; book reviews; articles, etc, on lit., cultural hist., folklore & educ. Hons: British Coun. Bursary, 1937; Storms stipendfond, Oslo Univ., 1946; Smidth-Mundt-Fulbright, 1952; Norges Allmenvitenskapelige forskningsråd, 1956. Address: Finnsnes Gymnas, 9323 Finnfjordbotn, Troms, Norway. 134.

LOLIS, Sophocles D., b. 9 June 1908. Professor. Educ: M.A.; Dip. of Theol., Schl. of Theol., Univ. of Athens, Greece; Ph.D., ibid, 1945. Appts: Prof., Athens Coll., 1935-48, Higher Clerical Coll., Rizareios Schl., 1950; Dir., Holy Synod's Press Bur., Greek Orthodox Ch. & Ed., Ch. mags., Church & Theol.,

1949-56; Prof. & Sub-Dean, Marasleios Pedagogic Acad., Athens, 1950-59; Prof. of Psych., Higher Clerical Coll., Penteli, ibid, 1953-56; Dean, Pedagogic Acad., Ioannina, 1959-; Asst. Prof., Univ. of Thessaloniki, 1954-57; Assoc. Prof., ibid, 1957-. Mbrships: Christian Archaeol. Soc., Athens; Soc. of Byzantine Studies, ibid; Assn. Medieval Culture; Epirotic Soc. of Athens; Soc. of Epirotic Studies, Ioannina; Rizareios Schl. Alumni Assn.; Deleg. of Greek Govt., 1st Panhellenic Conven. of Greek Pedagogic Acads., Nicosia, Cyprus, 1961. Publs. incl: Psychology, 1956, '67; Dogmatic Essays A, 1976. Recip., hons. Address: Angelos Sikelianos St. 6, P.O. Box 7, Ioannina, Greece.

LOMBARDINI, Siro, b. 3 July 1924. Professor. Educ: Econ. Degree, Cath. Univ., Milan, Italy; Post-grad., Schl. Econ., London Univ., U.K., 1949; Chgo. Univ., U.S.A., 1950-51; Libera docenza in Econ., 1954. Appts: Lectr., Cath. Univ., 1951-56; Modena Univ., 1954-58; Prof., Cath. Univ., 1957-63; Turin Univ., 1963-; Vis. Prof., Cambridge Univ., U.K., 1964; Condr. seminars, Paris, France; Harvard, U.S.A.; Leningrad, U.S.S.R.; Dir., Rsch., regional plans for Umbria & Turin; Mbr. Tech. & Sci. Comm. for Nat. Planning, 1963-; Min. for State Enterprises, 1973-; Pres., Cons. Commn. for price policy. Mbrships: Econometric Soc.; Assn. Italiana degli Econ. Accad. delle Sci. di Torino. Publs. incl: Concorrenza, monopolio e sviluppo, 1971; Corso di Economia Politica, vol. I, 1971; Modern Monopolies in economic development in the corporate economy, 1971; Monopolio e concorrenza nella politica economica, 1973; Economia e societa (in press); Contbr. to Giorno. Recip. Marzotto Prize for book La programmazione economica. Address: Via Roaschia 137, Chieri, Torino, Italy. 50.

LONDON, Hoyt Hobson, b. 12 Oct. 1900. University Professor. Educ: B.S., N. Tex. State Univ., 1924; M.A., Univ. of Mo., 1929; Ph.D., Ohio State Univ., 1934. Appts. incl: Prof., Ind. Educ., Ga. Southern Coll., 1935-37; Prof., Miss. State Univ., 1937-38; Prof., Univ. of Mo., Columbia, 1938-71; Prof. Emeritus, ibid, 1971-. Mbrships. incl: Past Pres., Life, Am. Voc. Assn.; Gen. Chmn., Miss. Valley Ind. Arts Conf., 1961-71; Past Pres., Life, Nat. Assn. Ind. & Tech. Educs.; Life, NEA; Sec.-Treas., Chmn., Legislative Comm., Mo. Voc. Assn., 10 yrs. Publs: Principles & Techniques of Vocational Guidance, 1973; num. articles in profl. publs. Hons. incl: Disting. Serv. Award, Coll. of Educ., Univ. of Mo., 1971; Fac.-Alumni Award, ibid, 1971; Citation of Merit, Coll. of Educ. Alumni Assn., 1974. Address: 2106 Valley View Dr., Columbia, MO 65201, U.S.A. 2.

LONG, Alfred B., 4 Aug. 1909. Retired, Part-Time Consultant. Educ: S. Pk. Jr. Coll., 1928-29; Univ. of Tex., 1941-43, '56-57; Lamar State Coll. Tech., 1947-56. Appts: w. Sun Oil Co., Beaumont, Tex., 1931-68; from Driller, Civ. Engrng. Surveyor & Draftsman to Engr., Prod. Lab., 1931-59; Regional Supvsr., 1960-68, Ret; Currently, Cons. Mbrships. incl: A.P.I.; U.S. Power Squadron; Soc. Wireless Pioneers; Soc. of Petroleum Engrs. of AIMME; Am. Assn. of Geols.; IEEE; Assn. for Computing Machinery; Houston Geol. Soc.; Gulf Coast Engrng. & Sci. Soc. Inventor, various oil well devices. Hons. incl: Spec. Citation for Outstanding Serv. on Behalf of Engrng. Profession, Gulf Coast Engrng. & Sci. Soc. Address: P.O. Box 7266, Beaumont, TX 77706, U.S.A. 7, 14.

LONG, Anton V., b. 11 June 1914. Educator. Educ: B.A., M.A., Univ. of N.M.;

B. Litt., Oxford Univ. Appts: Instr., N.M. Inst. of Mining & Technol., 1947-49; Tchr., Bursar, The Priory Schl., Half-Way Tree, Jamaica, 1952-59. Mbrships. incl: Chmn., Bd. of Trustees, Naples (N.Y.) Pub. Lib., 1962-74; Past Chmn., Ont. Coop. Lib. System Bd. of Trustees; Phi Kappa Phi. Publs: Jamaica & the New Order, 1827-1847, 1956; The Poems of Alice Lavinia Long (Ed.), 1967. Address: R.D.1, Box 203, Naples, NY 14512, U.S.A. 6.

LONG, Gerald, b. 22 Aug. 1923. Managing Director, Reuters. Educ: Emmanuel Coll., Cambridge Univ. Appts: joined Reuters, 1948; Corres. in Turkey, 1953-54; News Ed., Paris, 1955-56; Chief Rep. in Germany, 1956-60; Asst. Gen. Mgr. (w. special responsibility for Europe), 1960-63; Gen. Mgr., ibid, 1963; Chmn., Visnews, 1968; Mng. Dir., 1973. Directorships: Reuters Pension Fund Ltd.; Visnews Ltd.; Reuters Centenary Fund Ltd.; Reuters S.A., Zurich; Vereinigte Wirtschaftsdienste GmbH, Frankfurt; Comercial Telegrafica SA, Madrid. Hons: Cross of Cmdr. of Royal Order of Phoenix, Greece, 1964; Cmdr. of the Star of Hon. of Ethiopia, 1972; Order of the Grand Office of the Rep. of Italy, 1973. Address: Reuters Ltd., 85 Fleet St., London EC4P 4AJ, U.K. 1, 2, 12, 43.

LONG, James Alexander, b. 26 Dec. 1926. Broadcast Executive. Educ: B.Sc., N.C. Agric. & Tech. State Univ., Greensboro; M.A., Univ. of Mich.; Wayne State Univ., Detroit. Appts. incl: Hd., Engl. Dept., Foch Jt. H.S. Detroit, 1963-65; Counselor, Cooley H.S. Detroit, 1966-68; Asst. Prin., ibid, 1968-70; Prin., Northwestern H.S., Detroit, 1970-72; Gen. Exec. & Coord. of Trng., Storer Broadcasting Co., Miami Beach, Fla., currently. Mbrships: V.P., Nat. Alumni Assn., N.C. A&T State Univ.; Phi Delta Kappa; Alpha Phi Alpha; Comm. Co-chmn., Broadcasters Educ. Assn.; Detroit Chmbr. of Comm.; Booker T. Wash. Bus. Assn. Hons. incl: Community Serv. Award Northwestern H.S. PTA, 1972; Resolution for Disting. Serv., Common Coun., City of Detroit. Address: 17359 Prairie St., Detroit, MI 48221, U.S.A. 130.

LONG, James Franklin, b. 23 Sept. 1937. Heating & Air Conditioning Contractor. Educ: USAF H.S.; Heating & Air Conditioning Schls. of Lennox Inds. Inc. Appts: Sales & Serv., Western Auto Assn. Store, 1953-55; USAF, 1955-59; Ptnr., Long Construction Co., 1960-; Ptnr., Custom Comfort Heating & Air Conditioning, 1971-. Mbrships: Batesburg-Leesville Jaycees, 1959-; Pres., ibid, 1965-66, 1973-74, & past holder all other offs.; Pony League Baseball; Local Commnr., ibid, 1966, '67; Asst. Engr., Leesville Volunteer Fire Dept., 1970-; Am. Red Cross Bloodmobile Wkr., 1973-; 1st Bapt. Ch. of Leesville. Hons: Var. Awards, Batesburg-Leesville Jaycees; Am. Red Cross Bloodmobile Award, 1974. Address: P.O. Box 94, Leesville, SC 29070, U.S.A. 117, 125.

LONG, Katherine Scott Hamilton, b. 12 July 1908. Teacher. Educ: B.A., Univ. of Wash., 1929; M.A. (Hons.), Univ. of Chgo., 1950. Appts: Tchr., Renton, Wash., 1930-31, Juneau H.S., Alaska, 1933-39, Winslow H.S., Wash., 1939-40, Kennewick H.S., Wash., 1940-43; Tchr., & Chmn., Soc. Studies Dept., Kelso H.S., Wash., 1943-73; Coord., Soc. Studies Curriculum, 1963-73. Mbrships. incl: Kelso Educ. Assn.; Pres., ibid, 1954-55; Dist. Dir., Wash. Coun. Soc. Studies, 1960-73; Am. Field Serv.; Southwest Wash. Coord., 1960-; AAUW; Pres., Cowlitz Co. Br., ibid, 1946-48; Life Mbr., NEA; Pi Sigma Alpha; Pi Lambda Theta; Delta Kappa Gamma; V.P., ibid,

1972-74, Pres., 1974-. Contbr., Wash. State Educ. Jrnl. Hons. incl: Learned Soc. of Educ. Grant, Univ. of Wash., 1968; AAUW Name Grant, 1973. Address: 1006 Cowlitz Way, Kelso, WA 98626, U.S.A.

LONG, Newell H., b. 12 Feb. 1905. Professor of Music. Educ: A.B., Ind. Univ., 1928; M.S., N. Western Univ., 1934; M.A., 1939, Ed.D., 1965, Ind. Univ. Appts. incl: Maths. Tchr., laGrange H.S., Ind., 1925-26; Trombonist, Dance Orch., France, 1928-29; Music Dir., Thornton Fractional Twp. H.S. Calumet City, Ill., 1932-35; Dir. of Instrumental Music, Pub. Schls., Bloomington, Ind., 1935-39; Prof., Brasses & Music Educ., Schl. of Music, Ind. Univ., 1935-; Vis. Prof., Univ. of Western Australia, 1972. Mbrships. incl: Pres., N. Ctrl. Div., music Educators Nat. Conf., 1949-51; Pres., Nat. Assn. of Coll. Wind & Percussion Instrs., 1955-57; AAUP; Phi Beta Mu; Kappa Kappa Psi; Phi Mu Alpha (Province Gov., 1964-66). Author of instrn. books. Compositions for band incl: American Rhapsody; Salute to Corelli; Stephen Foster Rhapsody. Winner of music awards. Address: 1304 East Univ., Bloomington, IN 47401, U.S.A. 8.

LONG, Paul, b. 28 Jan. 1916. News Commentator. Educ: N. Tex. Univ., 1932-34; Dallas Little Theatre Drama Schl., 1936. Appts: Free Lance Radio, N.Y., 1937-39; Staff radio in Tex., La. & Ark. (KFRO, KELD, KTBS, KWKH) News, Sports & Prod., 1940-42; Pilot, USAAF, 1942-46; Newscaster, KDKA & KDKA-TV, Pitts., 22 yrs.; News Anchorman, Commentator, WTAE, 1968-. Mbrships: Press Club; Aero Club; Fellows Club; Am. Fed. Radio & TV Artists; Aviation Writers Assn.; Gen. Fund Raising Chmn., ibid, 1972-73; W. Pa. Heart Assn.; Big Brothers, Allegheny Co. Hons. incl: AFTRA Award as Pitts. Outstanding TV Newsman, 1967, '70, '71; Man of the yr. in communications, Pitts. Jaycees, 1970; Theta Sigma Pi Award as Printer's Devil in Jrnlsm., 1971. Address: WTAE-TV, 400 Ardmore Blvd., Pittsburgh, PA 15230, U.S.A. 6.

LONG, Paul J., b. 27 May 1927. Physicist; Administrator; Artist; Writer; Genealogical Researcher. Educ: B.S., Tenn. Tech. Univ., 1950; M.S., Univ. of Tenn., 1970; Dip., Famous Artists Schls. & Art Instrn., Inc. Appts: Off. Wkr., Steam Plant Constrn., Combustion Engr. Inc., 1950; Supvsr., NDT Radiography Lab.-Supvsr., Pilot Plant Op.-Rsch., Mats. Characterization-Lab. Supvsr., NDT & Metallurgical Labs., Union Carbide Nuclear Div. Y-12 Plant, Oak Ridge, Tenn., 1951-; Currently Dept. Hd. i/c Staff Grp. Engrs. & Scis., ibid. Mbrships. incl: Past Chmn., Oak Ridge Chapt., Am. Soc. Nondestructive Testing; Am. Phys. Soc.; Deacon, Glenwood Bapt. Ch., Oak Ridge, 1973-; Registered Profl. Engr., Tenn., 1972-. Publs. incl: Our Hill Country Heritage, Vol. I, 1970, Vol. II, 1972; var. articles & reports. Art exhibs. in num. local shows. Address: Hines Valley Rd., Rte. 2, Box 159-A, Lenoir City, TN 37771, U.S.A.

LONG, William Henry, b. 15 Jan. 1914. Marketing Research. Public Opinion Research & Advertising. Educ: A.B., Duke Univ., 1935; Grad. Schl. of Arts & Scis., ibid, 1936-37. Appts: Pres., W.H. Long Marketing, Inc., Greensboro, N.C., 1945-; Publr., Long Advertising & Marketing Publs., ibid, 1958-; Managing Dir., World Marketers Network, ibid, 1962-. Mbrships. incl: Cmdr., Mil. & Hospitaller Order of St. Lazarus of Jerusalem; Sons of the Am. Revolution; Am. Industrial Dev. Coun.; Southern Industrial Dev. Coun.; Am. Marketing

Assn.; Navy League of U.S.; U.S. Chmbr. of Comm.; U.S. Naval Inst. Publs: The Long System of Advertising Service Fees, 1959, 4th edit. 1971; State Development Advertising Reports, 1958; City, Area & Foreign Advertising Reports, 1965; The Renaissance of Freedom, 1974; The Disciplined Society (forthcoming 1975); articles in gen. & profl. mags. Address: 122 Keeling Rd. E., Greensboro, NC 27410, U.S.A. 7, 16.

LONGBOTHAM, Charles Norman, b. 6 July 1917. Artist. Educ: H.M.S. Conway, Birkenhead. Appts: Off., Merchant Navy, 1934-39; RNR, 1940-45; Model-maker, Coun. of Indl. Design, 1946; Free-lance Model-maker, Landscape Artist, 1946-. Mbrships: Art Workers Guild; Pres., Art Club, Royal Water-Colour Soc.; Assoc., Royal-Water Colour Soc. One-man exhibs., London, 1965, '68, '70, '72; Permanent collects., Commonwealth Inst., London; Shell Mus., London; Pilkington Glass Mus., Lancs.; Philips Evoluon, Holland; Churchill Mus., Brunei, Borneo; Imperial War Mus. Exhibs: Royal Water-Colour Soc. Gall., London; Var. galls., London, provinces. Address: Tunbeck Cottage, Alburgh, Harleston, Norfolk IP20 0BS, U.K.

LONGFORD, (Countess) Elizabeth, b. 30 Aug. 1906. Writer. Educ: Lady Margaret Hall, Oxford Univ. Appts: Trustee, Nat. Portrait Gall., London; Advsry. Bd., Victoria & Albert Mus., London; Trustee, Schlrs. & Writers Int. Mbrships. incl; Chmn., Judges Panel, Catherine Pakenham Mem. Award; Labour Party; Nat. Book League; Byron Soc.; Catholic Housing Assn.; Family Welfare Assn.; Fellow, Royal Soc. Lit. Publs: Jameson's Raid; Points for Parents; Victoria R.I.; Wellington—The Years of the Sword; Wellington—Pillar of State. Hons: James Tait Black Mem. Prize, 1964; Yorkshire Post Book of the Yr., 1969. Address: 18 Chesil Ct., Chelsea Manor St., London SW3 5QP, U.K. 1, 5.

LONGSTRETH, William Walter. College Professor; Writer. Educ: B.A., Rollins Coll., 1956; M.S., Univ. of Calif., L.A., 1965. Appts: Tchng. Asst., UCLA, 1965; Asst. Prof., Harbor Coll., 1966-; var. course, UCLA Ext. & L.A. City Coll. Mbrships: The Founders; Coral Casino Beach Club; SAR; Sigma Nu; Engl. Speaking Union; Manuscript Soc.; Fndr., Viva, a patriotic org. Address: 430 Hot Springs Rd., Santa Barbara, CA 93108, U.S.A. 59.

LONGTON, Peter A., b. 6 Dec. 1923. University Professor. Educ: M.A., Merton Coll., Oxford, U.K.; Postgrad. Dip., Anthropol. Appts: Served in WWII, 1943-47; Univ. Demonstrator, Phys. Anthropol., Cambridge, 1954-57; Operational Rsch. Off. in Ind., British European Airways & Shell-Mex & B.P., 1957-62; Proj. Mgr. in U.K. firms for indl. consultancy, 1962-66; Prof., Marketing, Univ. of W.A., Australia, 1966-; Dean, Fac. of Econs. & Commerce, ibid, 1970-72; Vis. Prof., Stanford Univ., U.S.A., 1969; OECD Cons. in Mgmt. Sci. to Turkey, 1973. Mbrships: Fellow, Royal Anthropological Inst.; Operational Rsch. Soc., U.K.; Past State Pres., Operational Rsch. Soc. of Australia; Past State Pres., Australian Market Rsch. Soc. Author, var. papers in profl. field. Address: 64 Beatrice Rd., Dalkeith, W.A., Australia 6009. 23.

LØNNING, Per, b. 24 Feb. 1928. Bishop, Church of Norway. Educ: Cand. theol., 1949, Dr. theol., 1955, Dr. philos., 1959, Univ. of Oslo. Appts: Asst. Pastor Lilleborg Ch., Oslo, 1951-53; Lectr., Oslo Tchrs. Trng. Coll., 1954-64; Dean, Bergen Cathedral, 1964-69; Bishop, Borg Diocese, 1969-; Mbr. of

Parliament for Oslo, 1957-65. Mbrships: Past Chmn., Ch. of Norway Assn. of Pastors; Past Mbr., City of Oslo Schl. Bd.; World Coun. of Chs.—Youth Cons., Assembly, Evanston, Ill., U.S.A., 1954, Deleg., Assembly, Uppsala, 1968, Mbr., Structure Comm., 1968-71; Assoc. Ed., Lutheran World, 1966-71; Chmn., Nordic Ecumenical Inst.; Mbr., Norwegian Broadcasting Coun.; Liturgical Commn. of Ch. of Norway; Guest Lectr., var. univs., sems., U.S.A., 1960, '65, '73. Publs: (In Engl.): The Dilemma of Contemporary Theology, 1962; Pathways of the Passion, 1965; Off the Beaten Path, 1966; The Fourth Candle, 1972; In Swedish, var. books, 2 vols. of radio speeches, collects. of sermons, essays. Address: Bjarne Aas gate 7, Box 265, 1601 Fredrikstad, Norway. 43.

LOOK, Kenneth W., b. 17 Apr. 1939. Corporate Executive; Pharmacist. Educ: B.S., Pharm., 1961, M.S., 1968, Ph.D., 1974, Pharm. Admin., Univ. of Wis.; Postgrad. study, Univ. of Nottingham, U.K. Appts: Retail & Hosp. Pharmacist, Wis. & Tex., 1963-69; Capt., U.S. Army, 1963-65; Tchng. Asst., Univ. of Wis., 1968-69; Marketing Rsch. Mgr., Searle Labs., G.D. Searle & Co., 1969-70; Corp. Marketing Rsch. Mgr., G.D. Searle & Co., Skokie, Ill., 1970-. Mbrships: Am. Pharmaceutical Assn.; Am. Marketing Assn.; Past V.P., Rho Chi, Univ. of Wis.; Kappa Psi; Past Pres., Sigma Phi Epsilon, Univ. of Wis. Contbr. to Am. Jrnl. Pharmaceutical Educ. Hons: Rotary Fndn. Fellowship, Univ. of Nottingham, U.K., 1962-63; Am. Fndn. for Pharmaceutical Educ. Fellow, 1967-68; Charles R. Walgreen Fellow, 1968-69. Address: 1848 N. Hudson Ave., Chicago, IL 60614, U.S.A. 8.

LOOMBA, Rajinder, b. 14 Dec. 1936. Professor of Electrical Engineering. Appts. incl: Assoc. Prof., Elec. Engrng., San Jose State Coll., Calif., 1962-66; Prof., ibid, 1966-; Dir., Ctr. for Interdisciplinary Studies, 1966-67; Dir. for Manpower Rsch. Grp., 1967-. Mbrships. incl: C'wealth. Club of Calif.; V. Chmn., Profl. Grp. on Educ., San Fran. Sect., IEEE. Publs. incl: An Examination of the Engineering Profession, 1967; 20 articles, surveys & reports. Recip., Fed. Grant to study engrng. manpower problems, by U.S. Govt. Address: 1774 Potrero Dr., San Jose, CA 95124, U.S.A. 9, 14, 16, 22, 74.

LOOMIS, Linn Wilbur, b. 19 Dec. 1939. Social Studies Teacher. Educ: B.A., Hiram Coll., Ohio, 1962; Ed.M., Hendend Kent State Univ., Ohio, 1969. Appt: Tchr., Secondary Level, Newcomerstown Bd. of Educ., Ohio, 1962-. Mbrships: Nat. Honor Soc., 1958-; Alpha Phi Omega, 1958-60; Pres., Newcomerstown Lions Club, 1969-71; Pres., Newcomerstown Tchrs. Assn., 1972-73; Treas., Isleta United Meth. Ch. Young Adult Class, 1973-74; Soc. for Preservation & Encouragement of Barber Shop Quartet Singing in Am., 1974-. Hons. incl: Tchrs. Continuing Contract in Soc. Studies, Newcomerstown, 1968; Permanent Cert. for tchng. Soc. Studies on Secondary Level in Pub. Schls., 1973. Address: Route 3, Shady Bend Division, Newcomerstown, OH 43822, U.S.A. 130.

LOOZ-CORSWAREM, (Comte) Arnold Gabriel Henri de, b. 4 Sept. 1895. Cavalry Officer. Educ: Ypres Cavalry Schl. Appts: Lt. Col., Cavalry; Reporter, var. int. congs., Int. Aeronautical Fedn. & Int. Tourism Alliance. Mbrships: V.P., Aero Club; Pres., Belgian Fedn. of Aviation Clubs; V.P., 1st Lancers Fraternity 1st Regiment, Guides; Belgian Aero Club; var. archaeological & heraldic socs. Publs: Ce que j'ai vu de la guerre 14-18; La première liaison aerienne Belgique Congo par la Lybie; Les Grand Axes Nord-Sud à travers le Continent Africain; 1940 Journal d'un Commandant d'Escadron; Livre de famille; Livre d'Or des Soldats Chevaliers de l'Ordre de Leopold; Buvrines, Passé et Present. Hons. incl: Grand Off. of Phoenix, Greece; Cmdr., Order of Leopold I; Off., ibid & Order of the Crown. Address: Château, 7133 Buvrinnes, Belgium. 43.

LOPEZ, Vernon Lister, b. 1 Jan. 1911. Barrister-at-Law. Educ: Dip. in Pub. Admin., London, U.K.; Called to Bar, Middle Temple, U.K., 1948; Admitted to Bar in Jamaica, 1948. Appts: Acting Clerk of Cts., St. James, 1949; Seconded as Magistrate & Acting Judge, Supreme Ct., Turks & Caicos Islands, 1950-52; Clerk of the Cts., Jamaica, 1952-56; Resident Magistrate, Jamaica, 1956-66; Acting Puisne Judge, Supreme Ct., ibid, 1966-69; Puisne Judge, ibid, 1969-. Mbrships: Jamaica Rifle Assn.; Fndr.-Mbr., Jamaica Coll. Lodge 7254 (E.C.); Past Master, ibid; Past Dist. Grand Sr. Warden (E.C.). Address: 32 Manor Park Drive, Kingston 8, Jamaica, West Indies. 96, 110.

LÓPEZ-CALO, José, b. 4 Feb. 1922. Musicologist. Educ: License in Philos., Univ. of Comillas, 1949; License in Theol., Fac. of Granada, 1956; Master in Gregorian Chant, Pontifical Inst. Sacred Music, Rome, Italy, 1959; Dr. in Musicol., ibid, 1962. Appts: Musical Councellor Vatican Radio, 1962-70; Gen. Sec., Int. Sacred Music Soc., 1963-68; Asst., Chair of Musicol., Pontifical Inst. Sacred Music, Rome, 1964-65, Prof. of Musicol., 1965-70, Vice-Rector, 1967-70; Prof. of Hist. of Music, Univ. of Santiago de Compostela, Spain, 1973-. Mbr., nat., for., int. orgs., music & fine arts. Publs. incl: Catalogo Musical del Archivo de la Santa Iglesia Catedral de Santiago, 1972; Presente y Futuro de la Música Sagrada, 1967; Scripta Musicologica of Msgr. Anglés (3 vols.), 1974. Co-contbr., Grove's Dictionary of Music & Musicians. Address: Primo de Rivera 31, Santiago de Compostela, Spain. 21, 43.

LØPPENTHIN, Bernt Hartvig Ove Fabricius, b. 13 May 1904. Chief Librarian. Educ: Gen. Cert., 1929; M.D., 1929; Mag. Scient., 1934. Appts. incl: Physn./Zoologist, 1933-36; Winter Expedition to Iranian Gulf, 1937-38; Libn., Univ. Lib., Copenhagen, 1938; Hd., Loan Dept., ibid, 1950; Ed., bibliography Index Medicus Danicus, 1957-66; Chief Libn., 1966-. Mbrships: Comm., Dansk Ornithologisk Forening, 1930-61; Ed., periodical of Danish Ornithological Soc.; Hon. Sec., ibid; Int. Ornithological Comm., 1938; Corres. Fellow, Am. Ornithological Union, 1959. Publs. incl: List of Danish Vertebrates, Birds, 1950; Danish breeding Birds: Past & Present (Danish w. Engl. summary), 1967. Recip., Knight of Dannebrog, 1969. Address: 14 Torvevej, DK-2740 Skovlunde, Denmark.

LORCH-FALCH, Ewen, b. 19 June, 1934. Lecturer. Educ: Cand. philol., Univ. of Oslo, Norway; Minn. Univ., U.S.A. Appts: Journalist, Nå, illustrated mag., Oslo, 1954-55; Publr. & Ed., Bygdenes By, weekly newspaper, Steinkjer, 1955-59; Tchr., var. Schls., Norway, 1959-; Lectr., Elverum Gymnas, Elverum; Fndr. & Ldr., Det Frie Samfunns Brevskole Correspondence Schl., ibid; Publr., Det Frie Samfunns Forlag, ibid. Mbrships: Chmn., Sociological Study Circle, Elverum; Norwegian Soc. of Authors, Oslo; Norwegian Authors' Ctr., ibid; Norwegian Br., PEN. Publs: Poems: Før Midnatt, 1964; Vår Tanke - Vår Skjebne, 1966; Under ein ny himmel, 1968; Anthols:

Gruppe 66, 1966; Trondsk Lyrikk 1966; Gruppe 67, 1967; Trondske Lyrikk, 1967; Biography: Bertram Dybwad Brochmann & Samtiden, 1971. Contbr. to press & mags., 1954-. Hons: Prof. J.S. Welhaven's Award, 1971. Address: Elverum Gymnas, 2400 Elverum, Norway. 134.

LORD, Columbus Ellis, b. 30 Apr. 1897. Architect. Educ: B.S., Mass. Inst. Technol., 1923; Registered Archt., Va. Registered Profl. Engr: Va., D.C., Mass., Vt. Appts. incl: Engr. w, Office, Chief of Engrs., U.S. Army, Wash. D.C., 1941-47; Prin. Engr. for Air Facilities, Defense Dept., Wash. D.C., 1947-67; Cons. Archt. & Engr., Arlington, Va., 1967-. Mbrships. incl: Am. Inst. Archts.; Am. Soc. Civil Engrs.; Nat. Soc. Profl. Engrs.; Hwy. Rsch. Bd. of Nat. Acad. Scis.: Va. Acad. Sci.; AAAS; Nat. Aeronautic Assn.; Soc. Am. Mil. Engrs. Address: 2000 N. Adams St., Apt. 329, Arlington, VA 22201, U.S.A. 7.

LORD, Doreen Mildred Douglas, b. 25 Sept. 1904. Writer; Journalist. Publs. incl: The Yellow Flower; Kiwi Jane; To Win Their Crown; The Cypress Box; Children at Count of St. Peter; (under pen name Doreen Ireland) Joan at Seascale; Margery the Mystery; Lynette at Carisgate; Spirit of Wearde Hall; (Poetry) Verse of Vectis; Sequence; Solent Shore Songs; Pilgrim Scrip; Heading South; Gleanings; Along the Trail; var. translations from French; contbr. to mags. & hymnals. Mbrships: Romantic Novelists Assn.; London Womens Press Club; Soc. of Women Writers & Jrnlsts. Hons: 2nd Prize, Simon Dare Award, Romantic Novelists Assn., 1960; Cath. Women of Yr., 1970; Douglas Lord Fndn., Univ. of Southern Miss. Address: Flat 2, 11 Campbell Rd., Southsea, PO5 1RH, Hants., U.K. 137.

LORD, Jack, b. 30 Dec. 1930. Actor; Artist; Writer. Educ: B.S., N.Y.U. Exhibs. incl: Corcoran Gall., Nat. Acad. Design; Brooklyn Mus. Repr. in collections incl: Met. Mus. Art; Cinn. Art Mus.; Mus. of Mod Art., N.Y.C. Broadway appearances: Traveling Lady; Cat on a Hot Tin Roof. Films incl: Tip on a Dead Jockey; God's Little Acre; Doctor No. TV appearances incl: Gunsmoke; Dr. Kildare; Invaders; Fugitive; Man from UNCLE; Virginian; Ironside; Hawaii Five-O. Creator of TV. Shows; Pres. Lord & Lady Enterprises, Inc., 1968-. Hons. incl: St. Gaudens Plaque, 1948; Fame Award, 1963; Cowboy Hall of Fame, 1963. Address: c/o Hawaii Five-O, Diamond Hd. Rd, Honolulu, HI 96816, U.S.A. 2, 78.

LORD, Joseph Henry, b. 22 Apr. 1919. Geologist. Educ: Univ. of Western Australia; B.Sc.; M.Aus. Appts: Geologist, Geological Survey of Western Australia, 1946-53; Sr. Geologist, Commonwealth Bur. of Mineral Resources, Darwin, Northern Territory, 1953-56; Chief Geologist, New Consolidated Gold Fields (Asia) Pty. Ltd., Sydney, N.S.W., 1957-61; Dir., Geological Survey of Western Australia. Mbrships. incl: Fellow, Geological Soc. of London; Former Chmn., Perth Br., Australasian Inst. of Mining & Metallurgy; Former Chmn., W.A., Div., Geological Soc. of Australia; Former Pres., Royal Soc. of Western Australia; Hon. Assoc., Western Australia Mus. Author of geological articles. Address: Geological Survey of Western Australia, Mineral House, 66 Adelaide Terr., Perth, W.A., Australia 6000. 23.

LORD, Marion Manns (Mrs.) b. 17 Dec. 1914. Educ: B.S., Northwestern Univ., 1936; M.Ed., Harvard Univ., 1962; M.A., Ph.D., Univ. of Wis., 1968. E.B. Fred Fellow. Appts:

Legislator, N.H. Gen. Ct., 1957-62; Dean of Women, Dir. of Counseling, New England Coll., 1962-64; Educ. Prog. Specialist, Bur. of Higher Educ., U.S. Off. of Educ., 1968-71; Rsch. Analyst, Prof., Barriers to Women's Continuing Educ.. 1971-. Mbrships: Am. Sociol Assn.; Treas., DCSS (Comm. on Status of Women in the Profession); Am. Psychol. Assn.; D.C.P.A.; Federally Employed Women; Am. Pol. Sci. Assn.; Nat. Coun. of AdministrativyWomen in Educ.; Nat. Assn. of Women Deans & Counselors; Order of Women Legislators; Am. Assn. for Higher Educ.; League of Women Voters (held most offs. in N.H.); R & D Comm., Fedn. Orgs. Profl. Women; AAUW; Pi Lambda Theta. Recip. var. acad. hons., fellowships & scholarships, also community awards. Address: 800 4th St. S.W., S-718, Wash. DC 20024, U.S.A. 5, 7, 131.

LORENZO, (Noble Don) Achille di, b. 13 May 1909. Patrician of Sessa, Italy; Majordomo to Mgr. the Duke of Castro, Head of the Royal House of Bourbon—the Two Sicilies; Landowner. Descended from Giovanni Angelo de Laurentio, Ch. of St. John of Jerusalem, & from Count Girardo de Laurentio, Baron of Lauri, Palme & Staviano, Viceroy in Germany of Emperor Henry VI (12th century). Publs. incl: Ed., Bollettino Ufficiale del Corpo della Nobiltà Italiano; Num. articles on hist. & geneal. of noble families. Mbrships: Circolo Nazionale dell'Unione Naples; Assn. of Italian Nobility; Int. Com. for Orders of Chivalry, Edinburgh, U.K. Hons: Chevalier & Sec., Supreme Order of St. Janvier, House of Bourbon—the Two Sicilies; Bailli (Magistrate) & Grand Chancellor, Order of H.M. Constantinien de St.-Georges; Chevalier of Hon. & Piety, Order S. & M. of Malta; Off., Order of St. Maurice & St. Lazarus; Legion of Merit; 2 Bronze Stars & Medal of Merit, U.S.A.; Croix de Guerre for Mil. Valour; 2 Croix de Guerre for Merit. Address: 113 Parco Margheritor, Villa di Lorenzo, 80121 Naples, Italy.

LORIMER, Eleanor Kathleen, b. 5 June 1897. Art Gallery Director, retired. Educ: Guildhall Schl. of Music, London, U.K., pt.-time for 5 yrs.; Johannesburg Tech. Coll. Dept. of Art, S. Africa. Appts: Supvsr., Sheltered Workshop schemes & exhibitions, Soc. Welfare Dept., Johannesburg, Transvaal, 1942-49; Asst. to Dir., Johannesburg Art Gall., 1949-56; Dir., King George VI Art Gall., Port Elizabeth, 1956-72. Mbrships. incl: Former Organising Sec., Comm. mbr. & exhibitor, S. African Acad.; Chmn., Port Elizabeth Soc. & Ed. of its mag., Looking Back, 1960-72; Comm. mbr., Outeniqua Naturalists & Histl. Soc., Knysna, Cape, 1972-; Former Coun. mbr., S. African Museums Assn. Publs: Grandmother Goes Greyhound, 1966; Panorama of Port Elizabeth, 1971. Contbr. to jrnls. Paintings in Africana Mus., Johannesburg & in pvte. collects. New large hall built on to King George VI Art Gall., Port Elizabeth, named Eleanor Lorimer Hall, 1972. Address: P.O. Box 421, Knysna 6570, Cape, S. Africa. 39, 133, 138.

LORING, Kathryn Douglass (Mrs.). Journalist. Educ: Southern Meth. Univ., Dallas, Tex., 1924-25; Univ. of Okla., Norman, 1925-26. Appts: Soc. Reporter, Okla. City Times, 1926-27; Soc. Reporter & Feature Writer, Chgo. Tribune, 1942-56; Soc. Reporter & Columnist, ibid, 1956-60; Front Views & Profiles Columnist, Restaurant Columnist & Critic, 1960--71; Restaurant Columnist & Critic, 1971-. Mbrships: Chgo. Press Club; Arts Club Chgo.; Confrerie de la Chaîne des Rôtsseurs; Connoisseurs Int.; Chgo. Coun. on For. Rels. Address: 905 Austin, Evanston, IL 60202, U.S.A. 5, 8, 138.

LORING, Nancy, b. 13 May 1906. Musician; Writer. Educ: A.B., Radcliffe Coll., 1929; Harvard Grad. Schl. of Educ. (conducting), w. Archibald T. Davison; Pvte. study, voice & singing, Percy Rector Stevens, N.Y.C., Laura Littlefield, Boston, Gertrude Tingley, ibid, repertory & singing, Gerald Moore, London, U.K., Coenraad V. Bos, N.Y.C. Appts: Dir., Music, Sunset Hill Schl., Kan. City, Mo., 1932-39; Dir., Bach & Handel Chorus, Kan. City, Mo., 1934-38; Asst. in Nursery Schl, Dept. of Educ., Mt. Holyoke Coll., 1940-41; Dir., Choral Music, Concord Acad., 1942-60; Dir., Concord Chorus, Mass., 1945-58. Mbrships: V.P., Radcliffe Choral Soc., 1928-29; Soloist, Choral Soc, Harvard Glee Club, 1928-32, Columbia Univ., 1931, Wellesley Coll. Choir, 1948. Solo Recitals: N.Y.C., 1941; Boston, 3; Kan. City, Mo., 1. Author of sev. original compositions & arrangements inclng. 1 vols. of music for ch. solos. Contbr. of poems to jrnls. Address: Box 1157 Duxbury, MA 02332, U.S.A. 5, 6, 7, 130.

LORRANCE, Arleen, b. 26 Feb. 1939. Author; Group Facilitator. Educ: B.A., Brooklyn Coll., N.Y. Univ., 1963; M.F.A., ibid, 1971; Doctoral work in process, U.S. Int. Univ., San Diego, Calif. Appts: Profl. Actress, 1957-63; Prog. Dir., Camp H.E.S., N.Y., 1961-63; Human Rels. Dir., Jefferson H.S., Brooklyn, N.Y., 1970-71; Acting Chairwoman, Speech-Theatre Dept., ibid, 1970-71; Coord., Cultural Activities, San Diego Community Coll., 1971; Exec. Dir., Bishop Pike Fndn., Santa Barbara, Calif., 1972; Currently, Exec. Dir., The Love Proj., San Diego, Calif., & Co-Ed.,The Seeker Newsletter, San Diego. Mbrships: Actors Equity Assn.; Screen Actors Guild; Am. Fedn. of TV & Radio Artists. Publs: The Love Project, 1972; Buddha from Brooklyn, forthcoming; Channeling Love Energy (w. Diane K. Pike), forthcoming. Address: The Love Proj., 4470 Orchard Ave., San Diego, CA 92107, U.S.A. 5.

LOSHBAUGH, Billie Scarborough (Mrs. Dean Loshbaugh), b. 24 Apr. 1927. Clinical Laboratory Technologist; Director of Clinical Laboratory. Educ: B.S., Okla State Univ.; Med. Technol. Dip., Geo. Wash. Univ. Schl. of Med., 1950; Univ. of Hawaii, 1973. Appts: I/c sev. depts., Tchr., Univ. of Okla. Med. Schl.,Clin. Lab., 1950-51; set up 2 labs. in small towns, 1952-55; Dir., Clin. Lab. & EEG, Childrens Med. Ctr., Tulsa, 1956-72; currently, lab. mgmt. & genetics work. Fellow, Royal Soc. Hlth., London. Mbrships. incl: Am. Soc. Clin. Pathols.; Region 7 Prog. Ch., Am. Soc. Med. Technols., 1972; Past Bd., Pres. & current Schlrship Chmn., Okla. Soc. Med. Technols.; Pres., Southern EEG Soc.; Alph Mu Tau; Chmn., Fellowships Comm., Tulsa Br:, AAUW, 1973-74; Knife & Fork Club. Contbr. to profl. jrnls. Address: 1915 E. 52nd St., Tulsa, OK 74105, U.S.A. 125, 138.

LOSS, David Edward, b. 13 Mar. 1938. College Administrator. Educ: B.S., M.B.A., Northeastern Univ., 1961-63; Certified Pub. Acct. Appts: Instr. of Acctng., Northeastern Univ., 1961-63; Asst. Prof. Acctng., Univ. of Bridgeport, 1963-70; Assoc. Prof., Acctng.-Acting Dean, Schl. of Bus., Central Conn. State Coll., 1970-. Mbrships. incl: Publs. Comm., Edit. Bd., Conn. Soc. Certified Pub. Accts., 1970-; Bd. Dirs., Edit. Comm., Nat. Assn. Accts., 1967-; Comm. Chmn., Assoc. Dir., ibid, 1966-67; Am. Inst. Certified Pub. Accts.; Am. Acctng. Assn. Contbns. newspapers & profl. publs. on taxation & var. aspects bus. admin. Recip., Univ. Fellowship, Northeastern Univ., 1961-63. Address: Central Conn. State Coll., New Britain, CT 06053, U.S.A. 6.

LOTT, George M., b. 1 Sept. 1897. Physician-Psychiatrist. Educ: A.B., Univ. of Mich., 1922; M.D., Univ. of Colo., 1925; Cert. in Psych., Am. Bd. of Psych. & Neurol., 1936. Appts. incl: Intern, Colo. Psych. Hosp., 1927 & Henry Ford Hosp., Detroit, 1928-29; Asst. Res. Physn., ibid, 1929-30; Rschr., Spinal Fluid & Encephalagrams, Colo. Psychopathic Hosp., 1930; Asst. Med. Off., & sometime Chief, Med. Serv., Boston Psychopathic Hosp., 1930-31; Dir., Bur. of Child Guidance & R.I. State Psych., 1932-36; Psyc., Bd. of Educ., Bur. of Child Guidance, N.Y.C., 1036-39; in Pvte. Prac., Jamaica, N.Y.C. & Psych., L.I. Home, Amityville, L.I., N.Y., 1939-41; Tchr., Mental Hygiene & Child Guidance, Pub. Hlth. Nurses & Child Welfare Workers; Ed., Newsletter Bulletin, Suffolk Co. Med. Soc., N.Y., 1943-46; Univ. Psych., Pa. State Univ., Univ. Park., 1947-62; ret to Pvte. Cons.; Psych., Vineland Tr. Schl., N.J., 1963-65; Psych. Cons., Clearfield Hosp., Pa., 1965-67 & York Mental Hlth. Clin., Pa., 1967-69. Publs: Story of Human Emotions, 1958; num. articles in sci. publs. Address: 617 E. Foster Ave., State College, PA 16801, U.S.A. 54. 112.

LOUGHRAN, William Cyril, b. 14 Mar. 1929. Manufacturing Company Executive & Public Relations Consultant. Educ: A.B., Nichols Coll., Dudly, Mass., 1950. Appts: Serv. w. U.S. Navy & U.S. Army; Owner & Pres., Shore Mfg. Co., Spring Lake, N.J., 1951-; Pres., Loughran Gardens Inc., real estate holding, ibid, 1960-; Ptnr., Loughran & Loughran, Pub. Rels. Counsel, ibid, 1970-. Patent: Christening Bottle. Mbrships. incl: Cub Scout Exec. Comm., Monmouth Coun., Boy Scouts of Am.; Treas., ibid, 1969-72; Chmn., Seagirt, N.J. Scoutfund Drive, 1970-72; Chmn., Carnation Ball, Seagirt, N.J., 1965-74; Repub. Finance Comm. for Gov., 1969; Exec. Dir., Gov.'s Inaugural Ball, 1970; Trustee, Roman Cath. Ch. Hons: Judge (N.J.), Fifty State Bicentennial Medal Collection, 1972. Address: 637 Oceanfront, Sea Girt, NJ 08750, U.S.A. 6.

LOUKES, Harold, b. 1 Mar. 1912. Teacher. Educ: M.A., Dip. Ed., Jesus Coll., Oxford Univ. Appts. incl: Reader in Engl., Univ. of Delhi, India; Headmaster New Schl., Darjeeling; Reader in Educ., Univ. of Oxford; Fellow, Jesus Coll., Oxford. Publ: Friends Face Reality, 1954; Secondary Modern, 1956; Friends and Their Children, 1958; The Discovery of Quakerism, 1960; Teenage Religion, 1961; New Ground In Christian Education, 1965; The Quaker Contribution, 1965. Hons: Justice of the Peace. Address: Oxford Univ. Dept. of Educ. Studies, 15 Norham Gdns., Oxford, U.K. 30.

LOUROS, Nicholas, b. 6 Mar. 1898. Emiritus Professor, Obstetrics & Gynaecology. Educ: M.D., Bern Univ., Switzerland, 1919; Asst., Dept. of Pathol., Vienna Univ., Austria, 1919-21; Asst., Dept., of Surg., ibid, 1921-22; Asst., Depts. of Ob. & Gyn., Munich & Berlin Univs., Germany, 1922-25; Appts. incl: Prof. & Dir., Dept. of Ob. & Gyn., Athens Univ., 1935-68; Med. Dir., State & Univ. Maternity Hosp., 1954-68; Counsellor on Maternal & Child Hlth. at W.H.O., Geneva, 1963. Mbrships: Acad. of Athens; Pres., Obstetrical & Gynaecol. Soc. of Athens, 1938-47; Fndr. & Pres., Hellenic Eugenics Soc., 1955; Fndr. & Greek rep. of Int. Fertility Assn.; Royal Soc. of Med. (London); & num. for profl. assns. Author, num. publs. in field. Hons: Physn. to late King Paul; Cons. Gynaecologist during reign of King Constantine II; World Pres.-Elect of Int. Coll of Surgs.; Hon. LL.D., Birmingham Univ.; Medal of German Soc. of Emperor Wilhelm, 1937; Order of Disting. Servs., 1946; Highest Order of

Greek Red Cross, 1946; Off. of Legion d'Honneur, 1948; Award of Inst. de France for scientific works, 1950; Grand Cmdr., Order of the Phoenix, 1965; Grand Commander of King George I, 1967. Address: 5 Semitelou Street, Athens (611), Greece.

LOUSSE, Emile (Odon Jean Joseph Ghislain), b. 10 Oct. 1905. Professor Emeritus. Educ: Dr. in Philos. & Letters, 1926; LL.D., 1929; Archivist-Palaeograph, 1929. Appts: Prof. Louvain Univ., Belgium 1929-71; Civilian Prof. War Coll., Brussels, 1950-; Lectr., Inst. Cath. des Hautes Etudes Commerciales, Brussels, 1955-; Prof. emeritus, Louvain Univ., 1971-. Mbrships: Fndr., Past Sec., V.P. & Pres., now Hon. Pres., Int. Commn. for Hist. Rep. & Parliamentary Instns.; Fndr. & Pres., Belgian Sub-Commn. for Hist. of Rep. & Parliamentary Instns., 1950-; Corres. Fellow, Am. Soc. Legal Hist. Author num. histl. publs. Hons: Prix Gobert, Acad. des Inscriptions et Belles-Lettres, Paris, France, 1944; Médaille d'argent du Secrétaire du Conseil de l'Europe, 1958; Cmndr. de l'Ordre de Léopold avec ruban à rayure d'or, 1961; Croix civique de Première Classe 1940-45, 1961; Grand-Off. de l'Ordre de la Couronne de Belgique, 1968; Plaque d'argent de Grand-Off. de l'Ordre du Mérite brabançon, 1973. Address: Av. de Cortenberg, 115, B-1040 Brussels, Belgium. 87.

LOUTZENHISER, James Kenneth, b. 15 Jan. 1931. Physician; Psychiatrist. Educ: B.S., Univ. of Pitts., 1952; M.D., ibid, 1956. Appts. incl: Instr., Film Course, Univ. of Mo., Kan. City, 1968-73; Lectr., Nat. Meetings in US, inclng. Nat. Coun. of Family Rels., 1970, & Showarama, 1969, '70, '71. Mbrships: AMA; Am. Psych. Assn.; 1st Film Chmn., Mo. State Coun. on Arts; Pres., Kan City Film Critics Circle, 1966-74; Chmn., Mo. State Coun. Arts Film Comm., 1965-70; Am. & Brit. Film Insts.; Nat. Cinephile Soc.; Am. Fed. Film Socs.; Pres., Kan. City Film Critic's Circle; Film Chmn., Nelson-Atkins Art Gall., ibid. Contbr. of film reviews to jrnls. & mags. in field. Address: 6400 Prospect, Room 108, Kan. City, MO 64132, U.S.A. 125, 130.

LOVATT, Arthur Kingsbury, Jr. Manufacturing Company Executive. Educ: B.S., Univ. of Southern Calif., 1941; M.B.A., Queens Univ., 1943. Appts: Leaseman, Shell Oil Co., L.A. Calif., 1946-51; Dir. Indl. Rels., Willys-Overland Motors Inc., ibid, 1952-55; Asst. to Pres. & Gen. Mgr., Pastushin Aviation Corp., ibid, 1955-57; Pres., Lovatt Assocs., ibid, 1957-66; Pres. & Gen. Mgr., Lovatt Technol. Corp., Santa Fe Springs, Calif., 1966-; Dir., Lovatt Technol. Corp., Lovatt Inds. Inc. & other Cos. Mbrships: Mason (Past Master); Shriner, Al Malaikah Temple, L.A.; Scottish Rite Mason, Pasadena Lodge, Calif.; Past Cmdr., Am. Legion, 1946; Republican State Ctrl Comm., 1964-; Univ. of Calif. Alumni Assn.; Am. Soc. of Metals; Nat. Histl. Soc.; Fndng. Assoc., Int. Oceanographic Fndn.; Smithsonian Assocs.; Am. Ordnance Assn.; L.A. Chmbr. of Comm. Inventor & Developer, Banadizing, Timadizing & Sheradizing Processes. Address: 13649 E. Valna Drive, Whittier, CA 90602, U.S.A.

LOVE, Eric Russell, b. 31 Mar. 1912. Mathematician. Educ: B.A., Univ. of Melbourne, Australia, 1933; B.A., Cambridge Univ., U.K., 1935; Ph.D., ibid, 1938. Appts. incl: Sr. Lectr., Univ. of Melbourne, 1940-41 & 1945-49; Assoc. Prof., ibid, 1950-52; Prof., Pure Maths., 1952-; Dean, Fac. of Arts, 1960-62; Hd., Dept. of Maths., 1963-71. Mbrships: Fellow, Trinity Coll., Cambrdige, 1948-49; London Math. Soc., 1938-; Cambridge

Philosophical Soc., 1949; Australian Math. Soc., 1956-; Math. Assn. of Victoria, 1950-. Contbr. to num. profl. jrnls. inclng: Proceedings of London Math. Soc.; Jrnl. of London Math. Soc.; Proceedings of Am. Math. Soc.; Jrnl. of Australian Math. Soc.; Proceedings of Am. Math. Soc.; Jrnl. of Australian Math. Soc. Hons. incl: Schlrship., Trinity Coll., Cambridge, 1936-38; Smith's Prize, Cambridge Univ., 1938. Address: Dept. of Maths., Univ. of Melbourne, Parkville, Vic., Australia 3052. 23.

LOVELACE, James Cameron, b. 29 Apr. 1920. Hotel Management; Real Estate Board; Public Relations. Educ: Dalhousie Law Schl. Alumnus Class, 1948; Ryerson Polytech. Inst. (CAB), 1961 (cum laude). Appts: Active serv., RCAF, WWII; Aide-de-Camp, Lt.-Gov., N.S., 1945-48; Retd. Squadron Ldr., 1961; Exec., New Bus. Dev., All Canada Radio & TV Ltd., Toronto, Canada, 1961-62; Var. advt. mgmt. posts, Ont. & N.S., 1962-70; Pres., Time-Space Ltd. (advt. & mgmt. advsry. co.), 1970-72; Hotel Mgmt., 1972-; Pub. Rels. Off., Canadian Red Cross, 1969; Mbr., Real Estate Bd., Cape Breton, N.S., 1972-; Protocol Off., Sydney, N.S., 1972-; Dir., Sydney Housing Authority, 1973-; Chmn., Constituency Advsry. Grp., Fed. Labor Intensive Prog., 1974; Govt. of Canada Rep., Ct. of Citizenship, 1974-. Mbrships. incl: Phi Kappa Pi; Alumnus Dalhousie Univ.; Former Alderman, Sydney, N.S. & num. civic comms., soc. & histl. orgs. Designer Chains of Office & sev. other civic commns. Hons. incl: D.F.C., 1972; Canadian Forces Medal, 1957. Address: 804 Cabot Road, 500 King's Rd., Sydney, N.S., Canada, B1S 1B2.

LOVELL, (Sir) (Alfred Charles) Bernard, b. 31 Aug. 1913. Astronomer. Educ: B.Sc., Univ. of Bristol, U.K., 1934; Ph.D., ibid, 1936. Appts. incl: Lectr., Phys. Labs., Univ. of Manchester & Jodrell Bank Experimental Stn., Cheshire, 1945; Sr. Lectr., ibid, 1947; Rdr., Physics, 1949; Prof., Radio Astronomy & Dir., Nuffield Radio Astronomy Labs., Jodrell Bank, 1951-. Mbrships. incl: V.P., Int. Astronomical Union, 1970-; Pres., Royal Astronomical Soc., 1969-71; Fellow, Royal Soc., 1955; Hon. For. Mbr., Am. Acad. of Arts & Scis.; Hon. Life Mbr., N.Y. Acad. of Scis.; Hon. Mbr., Royal Swedish Acad.; Hon. Fellow, Soc. of Engrs.; Hon. Fellow, F.I.E.E. Author of num. books inclng. The Story of Jodrell Bank, 1968; Out of the Zenith, 1973; The Origins & International Economics of Space Exploration. Hons. incl: O.B.E., 1946; Knighted, 1961; LL.D., 2 univs.; D.Sc., 5 univs. Address: Nuffield Radio Astronomy Labs., Jodrell Bank, Macclesfield, Cheshire, SK11 9DN, U.K.

LOVELL, (Capt.) William John, b. 14 Nov. 1921. Mechanical & Aeronautical Engineer; Retired Captain, R.A.N. Educ: Royal Naval Coll., Dartmouth, U.K.; Royal Naval Engrng. Coll., Keyham. Appts: Marine & Aircraft Engr., & Maintenance Test Pilot, Royal Australian Navy; Dir. of Aircraft Maintenance & Repair, ibid; Australian Naval Attaché, Djakarta; Chief Staff Off. (Tech.), Flag Off. Comm., E. Australia Supt. Tech. Planning & Servs., Garden Island dockground. Mbrships: Inst. of Mech. Engrs., U.K.; Coun. Mbr., United Servs. Instn. of N.S.W.; Imperial Servs. Club, Sydney; Royal Australian Navy Sailing Assn. Kingsford Smith Mem. lect. to Royal Aeronautical Soc., Sydney, Australia, 1967. Recip., Indonesian Naval Star, class 3. Address: 278A Edinburgh Rd., Castleway, N.S.W., Australia, 2068. 23.

LOVELY, Thomas Dixon, b. 2 Apr. 1931. Educational Management Administrator. Educ: B.A., Adelphi Univ., Garden City, N.Y., 1955; M.A., ibid, 1957; Profl. Admnstr. Cert., CUNY.

Appts: Treas., Pepsi-Cola Dist. Corp., 1955-58; Adj. Prof., Speech Communication, Brooklyn Coll., CUNY, 1958-; V.P., Star Management Corp., 1967-; Prin., City Schl. Dist., Long Beach, N.Y., 1970-; V.P., L.I. Enterprise Corp., 1973-. Mbrships: Bd. of Trustees, Adelphi Univ., Garden City, N.Y.; Exec. Comm. of Univ. Trustees; N.Y. State Regents Conf.; AAUP; Empire State Chap., Sons of Am. Revolution; Am. Speech & Hearing Assn. Address: 52 Locust St., Garden City, NY 11530, U.S.A.

LOVERIDGE, (Hon.) Della Lisonbee (Mrs. Elmo S. Loveridge), b. 9 Aug. 1904. Teacher; Retired State Legislator. Educ: Brigham Young Univ., U.S.A.; Boston Tech. Inst., Mass. Appts: Elected to Utah State Legislature, 1941-45; Owner & Instr., Adv. Hair Design, Superior Beauty Coll., 1947-50; Mgr., Darrell's Adv. Hair Design Coll., 1950-56; Elected to Utah State Legislature, 1959-71; Minority Whip & Floor Ldr., 1969-71; Utah State Advsry. Coun., Welfare Commn., 1945-48, 1960-63, 1967-71; Gov.'s Coun. on Aging, 1959-63; Deleg. Nat. White House Conf. on Aging, Wash. D.C., 1961; Nat. Conf. on Rehab., ibid, 1971; Mbr. & Deleg., Democratic State Ctrl. Comm. for 15 yrs.; Utah State Legislative Coun., 1960-63; Deleg., Pres. Kennedy's Comm. on Retardation, Denver, Colo. & num. others. Mbrships. incl: Ward Pres. & State & Regional Dir. of Gleaners in Mutual Improvement Assn., Latter Day Saints Ch.; Charter Pres. & org., State Democratic Women's Clubs, 1958-60. Names Outstanding Bus. Woman, Bus. & Profl. Women's Clubs, 1957. Address: 2336 S. 3rd East, Salt Lake City, UT 84115, U.S.A. 2, 9.

LOVERIN, Charles Robert, b. 28 June 1933. Educator. Educ: B.S., Bridgewater State Coll., 1960; M.Ed., ibid, 1963; Univ. of Mass., 1966. Appts: Hist. Tchr., Asst.-Hd. Football Coach, Freshman Basketball Coach, W. Bridgewater Jr.-Sr. H.S., Mass., 1960-61, Asst. Prin., 1967-68; Asst. Prin., Rockland H.S., Mass., 1968-72; Staff Mbr., Hanson Schl. Comm., Mass., 1969-72; Prin., Joseph Case H.S., Swansea, 1972-. Mbrships: NEA; Nat. & Mass. Assns. Secondary Schl. Prins.; MASSP Athletic Commn.; Mass., Swansea & Bristol Co. Tchrs. Assns.; Past Pres., S. Shore Asst. Prins. & League Football Coaches Assns.; Swansea Lions Club; Past Mbr., Rockland Rotary Club. Hons. incl: Mbr. of Guard for Pres. Kennedy, Summer White House, Hyannisport, Mass., 1959-65; Yearbook Dedicatee, W. Bridgewater H.S., 1966, Rockland H.S., 1972. Address: 457 Dillon Ln., Swansea, MA 02777, U.S.A.

LOW, Jean Barclay (Mrs), b. 8 Dec. 1903. Lecturer; Writer Educ: M.A., Univ. of Glasgow. Appts: Univ. tutor, Engl. Lang.; Univ. Lectr., Econ., to H.M. Forces, WWII; Pub. Lectr., Home & Colonies Race Rels.; Chmn., Nat. Advsry. Comm. (Scotland) Educ. for Vocational Homecraft Trng. & Employment. Mbrships: Fed. Univ. Women; Fellow, Royal Econ. Soc.; Soc. of Authors (Scottish Comm.); Glasgow Univ. Grads. Publs: No Green Pastures; articles in newspapers & educl & lit. jrnls. Address: 35 The Paddocks, Oatlands Chase, Weybridge, Surrey KT13 9RL, U.K. 3.

LOW, William Charles, b. 23 Aug. 1909. Retired Colonial Civil Servant. Educ: Schol., Ormond Coll., Univ. of Melbourne, Australia; M.A., ibid; Clare Coll., Cambridge, U.K. Appts: w. British Colonial Civil Serv., Nigeria, Cameroons, Sierra Leone, 1938-58; Prin., Govt. Secondary Schl., Afikpo, Nigeria, 1952-58; Lay Rdr., Diocese of the Niger. Mbrships: Hon. Fellow, The Heraldry Soc., U.K.; Fellow, Heraldry Soc. of Australia; Melbourne Cricket

Club, 1925-. Publs: White Flows the Latex, Ho!, musical comedy accompanying Indl. Exhib. in Kumba in 1942 & designed to stimulate local prod.; A Roll of Australian Arms, 1971. Address: Afikpo Hill, Melbourne Rd., Ballarat, Vic., Australia 3350. 23.

LÖWBEER, Hans, b. 26 Mar. 1923. University Chancellor. Educ: LL.B., Univ. of Stockholm, Sweden, 1947. Appts: Civil Servant, Min. of Educ., 1950-56; Under Sec. of State, ibid, 1957-64; Dir. Gen. & Chmn., Swedish Nat. Bd. of Educ., 1964-69; Chancellor, Swedish Univs., 1969-. Mbrships: Swedish Deleg., Educl. Comms., OECD & Coun. of Europe, 1958-64; Educl. Planning Coun., 1964-; Bd., Swedish Collective Bargaining Off., 1965-; Govt. Educl. Comm., 1968; Swedish Govt. Rsch. Advsry. Bd., 1969-; Chmn., Bd., Royal Dramatic Theatre, 1964-; Swedish Bd., Nordic Soc., 1964-; Chmn., Cultural Fndn., Sweden-Finland, 1965-; Gov. Bd., Ctr. for Educl. Rsch. & Innovation, OECD, 1971-; Chmn., Coord. Comm., Bds., Premises & Equipment Planning, 1972-. Address: Off. of Chancellor of the Swedish Univs., Box 16334, 103 26 Stockholm, 16, Sweden. 2,*43.

LOWE, Velma Wooldridge, b. 14 Feb. 1910. Teacher. Educ: A.B., Univ. of Tenn., 1932; M.S., ibid, 1934; postgrad. work, Univ. of N.C. Appt: Asst. Prof., Schl. of Technol., Dept. of Bus. Educ. & Off. Admin., E. Carolina Univ., Greenville, N.C., 1937-. Mbrships: Sec., E. Carolina Chapt., AAUW; Pi Omega Pi; NEA; N.C. Educ. Assn.; Nat. Bus. Educ. Assn.; N.C. Bus. Educ. Assn.; Treas., Rho Zeta Bldg. Assn. of Chi Omega Fraternity. Recip., E. Carolina Yr. Book Citation. Address: P.O. Box 2805, Greenville, NC 27834, U.S.A. 125.

LOWI, Theodore J., b. 9 July 1931. University Teacher & Author. Educ: B.A., Mich. State Univ., 1954; M.A., Yale Univ., 1955; Ph.D., ibid, 1961. Appts: Instr.-Asst. Prof., Cornell Univ., 1959-65; Assoc. Prof.-Prof., Pol. Sci., Univ. of Chgo., 1965-72; John L. Senior Prof. of Am. Instns., Cornell Univ., 1973-. Mbrships. incl: Am. Pol. Sci. Assn.; Exec. Coun., ibid, 1974-; Yale Grad. Alumni Assn.; Exec. Comm., ibid, 1973-; Midwest Pol. Sci. Assn.; Exec. Coun., ibid, 1969-72. Publs. incl: At the Pleasure of the Mayor, 1964; Ed., Legislative Politics, U.S.A., 1962, 3rd edit. 1973; Private Life & Public Order, 1968; The End of Liberalism, 1969, 2nd edit. 1974; The Politics of Disorder, 1971; Poliscide, 1974; Incomplete Conquest, 1974; Ed., The Pursuit of Justice (w. Robert Kennedy). Hons: J. Kimbrough Owen Award, Am. Pol. Sci. Assn., 1962; Fellowship, Soc. Sci. Rsch. Coun., 1963; Guggenheim Fellowship, 1967; Doct. Humanities, Oakland Univ., Mich., 1972. Address: Dept. of Government, Cornell Univ., Ithaca, NY 14850, U.S.A. 2, 14, 30.

LÖWING, Folke, b. 13 Mar. 1899. Water Rights Court Judge (Retired). Educ: LL.B., Univ. of Stockholm, 1923. Appts: Ct. Prac., Northern Swedish Judicial Dist., 1923-25; Pub. Prosecutor, 1927; Dpty. Judge, 1932; Judge Referee (Rdr. to Supreme Ct.), 1936-41; Justice of Svea Ct. of Appeal, 1938; Judge, Northern Region Water Rights Ct., Umeå, 1941-58, Lower Northern Region Water Rights Ct., 1959-67. Mbr. & Chmn., Umeå Musical Soc., 1961-70. Publs: The Large Hydro-Electric Schemes, 1948, 7th edit., 1964; Infringement of Qualified Public Rights to Enter Private Land, 1949; Power Plants: Features of the Hydro-Electric Schemes, 1955. Hons: Cmdr., Royal Order of Northern Star, 1956; Norrland Soc.'s Award of Hon. (Norrland Bear), 1966.

Address: Norrlandsgatan 29, 902 48 Umeå, Sweden; 43.

LOWNDES, George Alfred Norman, b. 5 Apr. 1897. Civil Servant; Education Service Administrator. Educ: Litt. B., St. Johns Coll. Oxford. Appts: Asst. Prin., Bd. of Educ., 1919-27; Asst. Pvte. Sec. to Pres., Bd. of Educ., 1927-33; Staff Prin., Technol. Dept., Bd. of Educ., 1933-34; Asst. Educ. Off., Finance & Gen. Purposes, London Co. Coun., 1934-38; Asst. Sec., Min. of Hlth., 1938-45; Dir., British Families Educ. Serv. in Germany, 1949-52; Subsequent return to serv. w. London Co. Coun.; retirement, 1962. Mbrships: Standing Conf. on Studies in Educ., 1961-; Hist. of Educ. Soc. Publs. incl: The Silent Social Revolution, 1937; The English Educational System, 1955; The Silent Social Revolution 1895-1965, 1969. Active as lectr., univs. & colls. of educ. Hons. incl: M.C., 1918; Leverhulme Rsch. Award, 1965. Address: 29 The Green, Marlborough, Wiltshire, U.K.

LOWRANCE, Edward Walton, b. 17 June 1908. Professor. Educ: B.A., Univ. of Utah, Salt Lake City, 1930; M.A., ibid, 1932; Ph.D., Stanford Univ., Palo Alto, Calif., 1937; Univ. of Kan. Schl. of Med., Lawrence, 1944-46. Appts. incl: Rockefeller Rsch. Asst. Exptl. Embryol. Schl. of Biol. Scis., Stanford Univ., 1934-36, '37-38; Instr.-Assoc. Prof. Zool., Univ. of Nev., Reno, 1938-49; Acting Assoc. Prof., Anat., Univ. of Kan. Schl. of Med., Lawrence, 1944-46; Asst. Prof. Anat., Univ. of S.D. Schl. of Med., Vermillion, 1949-50; Assoc. Prof.-Prof. Anat., Univ. of Mo. Schl. of Med., Columbia, 1950-; State Sec., Mo. State Anat. Bd., 1969-; Mbrships: Am. Assn. Anats.; AAAS; Sigma Xi; Phi Kappa Phi; Western Soc. of Naturalists; AAUP. Author num. sci. articles for var. profl. publs. Hons. incl: Rosenberg Rsch. Fellowship, Stanford, 1936. Address: Dept. of Anat., M-306, Univ. of Mo. Med. Ctr., Columbia, MO 65201, U.S.A. 8, 14, 15, 50, 120.

LOWRANCE, Janet Elizabeth, b. 14 Feb. 1941. Librarian; Musician. Educ: A.A., Stephens Coll., Columbia, Mo., 1b61; B.F.A., ibid, 1963; Mus.M., Eastman Schl. of Music, Univ. of Rochester, N.Y., 1965; Doctoral Work in Music, Ind. Univ.; M.A., Univ. of Miss., Columbia, 1970. Appts. incl: Ref. Libn., Stephens Coll., 1968-70; Asst. Humanities Libn., Southern Ill. Univ., 1970-72; Ref. Sect., Carbondale Pub. Lib., Ill., 1972-. Hons. incl: Honors Award for Outstanding Musician, Stephens Coll., 196?. Address: P.O. Box 102, Carbondale, IL 62901, U.S.A. 57, 138.

LOWREY, Russell H., b. 21 Mar. 1942. Orthodontist. Educ: B.S., Univ. of Ala., 1963; D.M.D., Schl. of Dentistry, ibid, 1967; Cert. of Orthodontics, 1971. Appts: Capt., USAF Dental Corps, 1967-69; Pvte. Prac. of Orthodontics, Huntsville, Ala., 1971-. Mbrships: Am. Assn. of Orthodontists; Southern Soc. of Orthodontists; Ala. Soc. of Orthodontists; Am. Dental Assn.; Ala. Dental Assn.; Eighth Dist. Dental Soc.; Royal Soc. of Hlth.; Lambda Chi Alpha; Psi Omega. Address: 2319 Whitesbury Dr., Huntsville, AL 35801, U.S.A. 7, 125.

LOWREY, Thomas Jefferson, b. 4 July 1927. Physician. Educ: B.S., Southern Meth. Univ., Dallas, Tex., 1950; M.D., Univ. of Tex., Galveston, 1954. Appts. incl: Gen. pvte. prac., Yukon, Okla., 1957-; Staff Mbr., Parkview Hosp., El Reno, Okla., Deaconess Hosp., & Bapt. Hosp., Okla. City; Chief of Staff, Parkview Hosp., El Reno, 1966-68; Pres., Okla. City Dist., Am. Acad. Family Prac., 1971.

Mbrships: Fellow, Am. Acad. Family Prac.; Pres., ibid, 1971; Dipl., Am. Bd. Family Prac.; AMA; Okla. State Med. Assn.; Pres., Canadian Co. Med. Assn.; Theta Kappa Psi; Alpha Omega Alpha; Lions Club. Elder, Yukon 1st Christian Ch. Address: 716 Kingston Dr., Yukon, OK 73099, U.S.A. 7.

LOWTHER, Frank E., b. 3 Feb. 1929. Research & Development Engineer & Physicist. Educ: Graduated, Ohio State Univ., 1952. Appts: Employed in Missile & Radar Rsch. & Dev., Raytheon Mfg. Co., rising to Chief Analytical Engr., White Sands Proving Grounds, 1952-57; Inter-Continental Ballistic Missile Rsch. & Dev., w. direct responsibility to USAF & NASA, Gen. Electric Co., 1957-65; Fndr. & Dir., Purification Scis. Inc., 1965-71. Holder of Patents in Ozone Technol. in 20 Countries. Mbrships: Assoc. Fellow, Am. Inst. Aeronautics & Astronautics; Sr. Mbr., Inst. Electrical & Electronics Engrs.; Pi Mu Epsilon. Publs: Num. Papers & Reports. Hons: Feature Article on work in Celestial Mechanics; Time Mag., 1962; Gen. Mgrs. Award, Gen. Electric Co., 1964; New Ozone Generator named the Lowther Cell by W.R. Grace & Co. Address: 64 Boone Trl., Severna Park, MD 21146, U.S.A. 6.

LOY, (Rev.) Carl, b. 19 Apr. 1908. Minister. Educ: A.A., Campbellsville Coll., Ky., 1948; Southern Bapt. Theol. Sem., Louisville, 1950; Corres. courses, Southwestern Bapt. Sem., New Orleans Theol. Bapt. Sem., Moody Bible Inst., Am. Schl. & Gospel Music Inst., Dallas, Tex., 1951-71. Appts: Pastor, rural chs., Adair, Russell Cos., 1931-40; Jamestown Bapt. Ch., Ky., 1940-47; Good Hope Bapt. Ch., Campbellsville, 1947-55; Main St. Bapt. Ch., Williamsburg, 1955-72; Mt. Vernon Bapt. Ch., Jamestown & Pierces Chapel Bapt. Ch., Fairplay, 1972-74. Mbrships. incl: Moderator, Russell Co., E. Lynn, Mt. Zion Bapt. Assns.; Ky. Bapt. State Mission Bd., 1954-55, 60-63, 67-70; Bd. Dirs., Southeastern Ky. Bapt. Hosp., Corbin, Ky., 1959-72. Author of sermons, articles & poems. Composer of over 200 hymns & gospel songs. Hons. incl: Cup., PBWC, Williamsburg, Ky. for outstanding serv. to ch. & community, 1962; Ky. Col., 1971. Address: 502 Jamestown St., Columbia, KY 42728, U.S.A. 125.

LU, Milton Ming-deh, b. 12 Nov. 1919. Plastic Surgeon. Educ: Coll. of Med. & Dentistry, W. China Union Univ., 1936-46; Strong Mem. Hosp., Univ. of Rochester, U.S.A., 1946-51; Barnes Hosp., Wash. Univ., St. Louis, Mo., 1951-54. Appts: Ward Surg., VA Hosp., Lebanon, Pa., 1955; Plastic Surg., Lancaster Gen. Hosp., St. Joseph's Hosp., Crippled Children Hosp., Elizabethtown & Coatsville Hosp., Hershey Hosp., Jennersville Hosp., Good Samaritan Hosp., Lebanon Valley Gen. Hosp. Mbrships: Lancaster Co. & City Med. Soc.; Pa. Med. Soc.; AMA; Robert Ivy Soc. Plastic Surgs. Contbr. to med. profl. jrnls. Address: 628 N. Duke St., Lancaster, PA 17602, U.S.A. 6.

LUBEGA, Matiya, b. 26 Dec. 1933. Diplomat. Educ: Makerere Univ., Uganda; B.A., London, U.K.; M.A., Mich. State Univ., U.S.A.; Carnegie Fellowship in Diplomacy, Columbia Univ. Appts: Income Tax Off., 1959; Asst. Sec., Min. of For. Affairs, 1962; 1st Sec. & Acting High Commnr. of Uganda to Ghana, 1963-65; Alternative Rep. to UN Security Coun., 1966-67; Under Sec., Min. of For. Affairs, 1967-69; Ambassador of Uganda to U.S.S.R., 1969-71; currently Ambassador to Ethiopia. Mbrships: Friendship & Exchange (Whitby, U.K.); Int. Tennis Club, Addis Ababa. Recip., Repub. Medal, Uganda, 1972. Address:

Uganda Embassy, P.O. Box 5644, Addis Ababa, Ethiopia.

LUBIN, Georges, b. 24 Jan. 1904. Man of Letters. Appts: Asst. Prof., var. colls. & lycées; Hon. Asst. Dir., Société Générale (bank). Mbrships: Pres., Soc. of Friends of Maurice Rollinat; Bur., Literary Hist. Soc. of France; Bur., Int. Assn. of French Studies; Soc. of Men of Letters; Ctr. Acad. Publs: A la gloire du Berry, 1926; Le Vert Paradis, 1926; La Terre a soif, 1934; Changer de peau, 1936; Maxime Rasquin, 1951; Michou, 1951; Correspondance de George Sand, 10 vols., 1964-73; George Sand en Berry, 1967; George Sand en Brenne, 1967; Oeuvres autobiographiques de George Sand, 2 vols., 1970-71; Album Sand, 1973; num. contbns. to jrnls. Hons: Chevalier, Legion of Hon., 1970; Award, Acad. Française, 1965, '70; Prix de l'édition critique, 1967. Address: 50 Quai Alphonse Le Gallo, 92100 Boulogne-sur-Seine, France. 91.

LUBNICKI, Narcyz, b. 19 Feb. 1904. Philosopher. Educ: Ph.D., Sorbonne, Paris, 1929; Ph.D., Univ. of Warsaw, 1932. Appts: Counsellor, Min. of Educ., Polish Nat. Liberation Comm., 1944-45; Assoc. Prof. thru' Prof., Maria Curie-Sklodowska Univ., Lublin, Poland, 1944-; Hd. of Chair of Philos., ibid, 1944-; Pro-Rector, ibid, 1962-65; Mbr., Philos. Scis. Comm., Polish Acad. of Scis., 1960-. Mbrships. incl: Pres., Soc. Spinozana Polonica, Lodz, 1930-39; Pres., Philos. Soc., Lublin, 1945-. Publs. incl: Descartes and Modern Materialism, 1957; The Art of Correct Thinking, 1963; Science and Mysticism, 1969; An Outline of Roman Ingarden's Philosophy, 1972. Hons. incl: Golden Cross of Merit, 1946; Off.'s Cross, Order of Polonia Restituta, 1964; Ensign of the Millenium of the Polish State, 1965. Address: ul. Sowińskiego 8/4, 20-040 Lublin, Poland.

LUCAS, Carol. Gerontologist. Educ: B.S., Wm. & Mary Coll., 1949; M.A., Tchrs. Coll., Columbia Univ., 1951; Ed.D., ibid, 1953. Appts: Instr., Tchrs. Coll., Columbia Univ., 1960-64; Dir., Special Pilot Study in Gerontol., 1960-64; Exec. Dir., Five Towns Golden Age Club, 1964-66; Dir., Servs. for the Aging, Hempstead, N.Y., 1967-; Pres., N.Y. State Coun. of Regional Assns. Clubs & Ctrs. for Older Persons; Co.-Chmn., Region II (Nassau-Suffolk Cos.) White House Conf. on Aging. Fellowships: Royal Soc. Hlth. U.K.; Nat. Recreation & Pks. Assn. Publs. incl: Recreation & Total Rehabilitation, 2nd edit., 1971; Recreation in Gerontology. Articles, var. jrnls. Recip., Cert. of Merit for Disting. Serv. in Int. Geriatrics. Address: Services for the Aging, Town of Hempstead, Town Hall, Hempstead, NY 11550, U.S.A. 5, 6, 22, 132.

LUCAS, Colin Cameron, b. 15 Dec. 1903. Biochemist. Educ: B.A.Sc., Univ. of B.C., Canada, 1925; M.A.Sc., ibid, 1926; Ph.D., Univ. of Toronto, 1936. Appts: Prof. of Chem., Brandon Coll., 1926-27, 1929-34; Rsch. Fellow, Univ. of Toronto, 1927-29, 1934-35, Asst.-Prof.-Assoc. Prof., Banting & Best Dept. Med. Rsch., ibid, 1934-46; Prof., ibid, 1946-69; Prof. Emeritus, 1969-. Mbrships. incl: Royal Soc. of Canada; Fellow, ibid, 1959; Rapporteur, Sect. IIIC3 ibid, 1965-69; Am. Chem. Soc.; Am. Soc. of Biol. Chemists; Chem. Inst. of Canada; Fellow, ibid, 1947; Treas. Toronto Sect., ibid, 1950; Edit. Bd., ibid, 1958-63; Councillor, ibid, 1961-63; Canadian Biochem. Soc. Publs: Over 90 Papers on medico-chem. topics. Final phases of work summarized in Fatty Livers & Lipotropic Phenomena, in Progress in the Chem. of Fats & other Lipids, Volume 10 Part 1, 1967. Hons:

D.Sc., Acadia Univ., 1964. Address: P.O. Box 951, Wolfville, Nova Scotia, Canada. 6, 14, 50, 88.

LUCAS, Georgia B. Investment Manager; Poet. Educ: Univ. of Tex. Mbrships. incl: Nat. League Am. Pen Women; Acad. Am. Poets; Poetry Soc. of Tex.; Kwill Klub; Past Pres., ibid; Magna Charta Dames; State Chap., Daughters of Am. Colonists; Local Chap., DAR; Austin Arts Coun.; Advsry. Bd., Austin Salvation Army; Bd. Mbr., Austin Community Nursery; St. David's Women's Grp.; Past Pres., ibid. Author of Prelude (Poems). Contbr. newspapers, jrnls. & publs. inclng: Tex. Literary Quarterly; College Book of Verse; Poetry Digest; Poets of the Lone Star State; Go; Drug Topics; The Bright Scrawl; Visions in Verse. Num. progs. poetry NBC TV & Radio. Recip., sev. State awards. Address: 1801 Lavaca, Apt. 7c, Austin, TX 78701, U.S.A. 5, 11, 113, 132.

LUCAS, Laurent, b. 15 Apr. 1920. Councillor; Consultant. Appts: Municipal Councilor, Le Croisic, France, 1949; Sec., Mgmt. Comm., Penhoet Workshops, 1949; Asst. to Mayor, Le Croisic, 1953; Permanent Sec., CFTC Metallurgical Fedn., 1954; Mbr., Confed. Bur., ibid, 1966; Mbr., Econ. & Soc. Coun. Sect., 1963-64; Pres., Nat. Union of Pension Instns. for Salaried Wkrs., 1964-; Pres., Assn. or Supplementary Pensions, 1967-68; Econ. & Soc. Cons., French Confedn. of Labour, 1969-; Pres., ibid, 1971-. Mbrship: Friends of Wilton Pk. Recip., Chevalier, Legion of Hon. Address: 31 Rue des Maronites, 75020 Paris, France. 91.

LUCAS, Suzanne (Mrs. L. Lucas), b. 10 Sept. 1915. Artist. Educ: Edinburgh Univ., U.K.; Univ. of Grenoble, France; Univ. of Munich, Germany; Berlin Schl. of Art, ibid, Mbrships: Royal Soc. Miniature Painters, Sculptors & Gravers (coun.); Fellow, Royal Horticultural Soc.; Soc. of Miniaturists (coun.); V.P., Dorset Co. Arts & Crafts Assn.; Soc. of Women Artists; Sherborne Art Club; R.S.P.B.; C.P.R.E.; Nat. Trust; World Wildlife Fund. One Man Exhibs: The Cooling Galls., London, 1954; Evening News Show, Olympia, ibid, 1954; Sladmore Gall., 1973. Exhibited regularly at Royal Acad., Paris Salon, Royal Inst. of Painters in Watercolour. Hons: Medaille de la Resistance, Grenfell Medal, 1955; Silver Grenfell Medals, 1971, '73. Address: Ladyfield, Bourton, Dorset SP8 5AT, U.K. 19, 133.

LUCCHESI, Jane Chisholm, b. 27 Sept. 1912. Library Supervisor. Educ: B.S., Coll. St. Scholastica, Duluth, Minn., 1954; M.A.L.S., Univ. of Mich., Ann Arbor, 1965; Attended 1st paperback conf. in U.S.A., Columbia Univ., N.Y., 1965; Workshops. Communications & Lib. Supvsn., Univ. of Mich, 1966 & 1968. Appts: Elem. Tchr., 1948-59; Tchr.-Libn., Jeffers H.S., 1959-68; Lib. Supvsr., Adams Twp. Schls., 1968-74. Mbrships. incl: ALA; Mich. Lib. Assn.; Mich. Assn. for Educ. Media; Houghton-Hancock Bus. & Profl. Women's Club; Life mbr., Univ. of Mich. Alumni Assn.; Delta Kappa Gamma. Contbr. of articles in field. Recip., dedication of Sr. Class Yrbook., Jeffers H.S., 1964. Address: Jeffers H.S. Lib., Painesdale, MI 49955, U.S.A. 5, 138.

LUCE, Henry, III, b. 28 Apr. 1925. Publisher. Educ: B.A., Yale Univ., 1945. Appts. incl: Hd., Time Inc. New Bldg. Dept., 1956-60; Asst. to Publr., Time, 1960-61; Asst. to Publr., Fortune, 1961; Circulation Dir., Fortune Archtl. Forum, House & Home, 1961-64; Assoc. Dir., Rsch. & Dev., Time Inc., 1964-65; Dir., ibid, 1965-66; London Bur. Chief, 1966-68; Publr., Fortune, 1968-69; Publr., Time, 1969-; V.P., Time Inc., 1964-; Dir., ibid, 1967-. Mbrships. incl: Trustee, Princeton Theol.

Sem. & Coll. of Wooster; Pres., Henry Luce Fndn., Inc.; various soc. clubs. Author of various articles. Address: Time Inc., Time & Life Bldg., N.Y., N.Y. 10020, U.S.A. 2, 6, 16.

LUCK, Anthony. Journalist; Educator. Educ: B.A., Pedagogical Technicum, Kremenchuk, Ukraine, 1930; M.A., Pedagogical Inst., Voroshilovgrad, ibid, 1938; Ph.D., Innsbruck Univ., Austria, & Ukrainian Free Univ., Munich, Germany, 1955. Appts.: Pedagogue & Jrnlst., Russia & Ukraine, 1938-41; Jrnlst. & Student, Innsbruck & Munich, 1945-49; Free Lance Jrnlst., N.Y., U.S.A., 1949-52; Instr., Syracuse Univ., N.Y., 1953-57; Ed., U.S. Info. Agcy., Wash., D.C., 1957-. Mbr., Shenandoah Assn. Publs: Portrait of Stalin, 1952; Contbr. to num. Am. & for. mags. & newspapers. Recip. of many prizes & awards for tchng. & jrnlsm. Address: 1202 Holton Ln., Takoma Pk., Wash., DC 20012, U.S.A. 3, 6, 7, 57, 131.

LUCKENBACH, Edgar Frederick, Jr., b. 17 May 1925. President & Chairman of the Board, Luckenbach Steamship Co. Inc. Educ: Grad., Adv. Mgmt. Prog., Harvard Univ., Cambridge, Mass., 1962. Appts: Marine Underwriter, Marine Off. of Am.; Asst. Marine Supt., States Marine Lines; Pres. & Chmn. of Bd., Luckenbach Steamship Co. Mbrships. incl: Am. Bur. of Shipping; Chmn., Marine Transportation Rsch. Bd., Nat. Acad. of Scis.; Int. Oceanographic Fndn.; Chmn., Ctr. for Maritime Studies; Advsry. Bd. of Grad. Schl. of Bus. Admin., L.I. Univ.; Dir., Navy League of the U.S.; Gov., India House; Advsry. Comm., N.Y.-N.J. Port Preparedness Planning, Port of N.Y. Authority; U.S. Chmbr. of Comm.; U.S. Naval Inst.; Trustee & Mbr., Exec. Comm., Webb Inst. of Naval Arch.; Nat. Cargo Bur.; Advsry. Bd., Columbia River Maritime Mus. Publs. incl: articles on The Perpetual Crisis of Soviet Communism, in U.S. Naval Inst. Proceedings; & on Logistics, in Ency. Americana. Hons. incl: Third Annual U.S. Naval Intelligence Award; Naval Intelligence Reserve Disting. Serv. Medal; Kt. of Order of St. John of Jerusalem; Maltese Cross. Address: Luckenbach Steamship Co. Inc., 120 Wall St., N.Y., NY 10005, U.S.A.

LUCKEY, Carl Freeman, Jr., b. 4 Mar. 1941. Art Dealer; Art Investments Consultant. Educ: Ga. Tech. Schl. of Arch., 1959-61; B.S., 1964.; Sewannee Mil. Acad., 1958-59; B.S. in Chem. & Biol., 1964, Serv. as Capt., USAF. 1964-70. Mbrships: Tenn. Valley Art Assn., 1970-; Bd. Mbr., ibid; Chmn., Bd., 1972-; Chmn., Bd., Tenn. Valley Mus. of Art; Int. Profl. Picture Framers Assn.; Pres., S.E. regional, Beta Beta Beta. Hons. incl: Disting. Flying Cross, 1967, 68; 12 Air Medals, 1967-68; Decorated as mbr. of Outstanding Unit, USAF, 1967; num. art awards. Address: The Sunluck Gall., Grant Plaza, Florence, AL 35630, U.S.A.

LUDBROOK, John. b. 30 Aug. 1929. University Surgeon. Educ: B.Med. Sc., Univ. of Otago, N.Z., 1950; M.B., B.S., ibid, 1953; Ch.M., ibid, 1961. Appts. incl: Sr. Lectr.-Prof., Surg., Univ. of N.S.W., Australia, 1964-68; Prof. of Surg., Univ. of Adelaide, 1969-; Vis. Surg., Royal Adelaide Hosp., 1969-; Cons. in Surg., Queen Elizabeth, Queen Victoria & Adelaide Children's Hosp., 1969-; Vis. Prof., Harvard Med. Schl. & Duke Univ. Med. Ctr., U.S.A., 1972. Mbrships. incl: Fellow, Royal Australasian Coll. of Surgs.; Coun., Bd. of Examiners, of Edit. Comm., ibid; Fellow, Royal Coll. of Surgs., U.K. Publs. incl: Aspects of Venous Function in the Lower Limbs, 1966; Guide to House Surgeons in the Surgical Unit, 1964, 5th edit. 1973; An Introduction to

Surgery; 100 Topics, 1971, Italian edit. 1973. Hons. incl: Scott Mem. Gold Medal for Anatomy, 1949; Colquhoun Medal for Systematic Med., 1953; Leverhulme Rsch. Fellowship, St. Mary's Hosp. Med. Schl., London, 1957; Travelling Fellowship, Carnegie Corp. of N.Y., 1967. Address: Univ. of Adelaide Dept. of Surgery, c/o Royal Adelaide Hospital, Adelaide, S.A., Australia 5000. 23, 128.

LUDLUM, Robert, b. 25 May 1927. Novelist. Educ: B.A. (Hons.), Wesleyan Univ., Middletown, Conn.,˜1951. Appts: War Serv., U.S. Marines, S. Pacific, 1944-45; Actor, Broadway & TV, 1952-58; Theatrical Prod., Broadway & Playhouse in the Mall, Paramus, N.J., 1958-69. Mbrships: The Players, Gramercy Pk., N.Y.; Authors League; Am. Nat. Theatre & Acad.; Actors Equity Assn.; Novels: The Scarlatti Inheritance, 1971; The Osterman Weekend, 1972; The Matlock Paper, 1973; Under pseudonum Jonathan Ryder, novel, Trevayne, 1973. Hons: Artistic Citation, Actors Equity Assn., 1962; Scroll of Achievement, Am. Nat. Theatre & Acad., 1965; Book of Month Club Selections, 1971-1973. Address: c/o Henry Morrison, Inc., 311½ W. 20th St., N.Y., NY 10011, U.S.A. 30, 44.

LUDWIG, Reiter (Berthold Dietrich), b. 7 Jan. 1895. Professor of History. Appts: Served WWI; Prof., State Acad. for Technol., Vienna, Austria, & Technologisches Gerwerbe-Mus., Vienna. Mbrships: Hon. mbr., Grillparzer soc.; Raimund soc.; Richard Kralik soc.; Study group for archaeol., Vienna; "Una Voce", Vienna; Fndr. mbr., & mbr., sci. study group for archaeological rsch. in Austria, Vienna. Publs. under name Reiter Ludwig incl; Handbuch der Geschichte Osterreichs, 1955; Das Geheimnis des Silbergitters, 1965. Publs. under pseudonym Berthold Dietrich incl: Der Kampf um den Frieden, histl. drama, 1932; Der Feuerreiter. Recip. of hons. Address: Schreibersweg 86, Vienna 1190, Austria.

LUEBBERT, Karen Merritt (Mrs. Jack R. Luebbert), b. 3 Oct. 1942. Librarian. Educ: B.A., Webster Coll., 1964; M.S.L.S., Case Western Reserve Univ., 1967. Appts: Acting Libn., Webster Coll., 1965-68; Dir. of Libs., ibid, 1968-, Affirmative Action Off., 1974-; Chmn., Learning Resources Coun. of Higher Educ. Co-ordinating Coun. of Metropol. St. Louis, 1973. Mbrships: Edit. Bd., EDUCOM, 1967-68; ALA; Mo. Lib. Assn.; Freedom to Read Fndn.; Mo. Assn. for Affirmative Action in Higher Educ.; Beta Phi Mu; Pi Delta Phi. Address: Webster Coll. Lib., 470 E. Lockwood, St. Louis, MO 63119, U.S.A.

LUEBKE, Mary Ellen Carr Handwork, b. 6 May 1928. Media Specialist. Educ: B.S., Bethel Coll., Mishawaka, Ind., 1961; M.L.S., Ball State Univ., Muncie, Ind., 1971; Additional studies, Valparaiso Univ., 1953 & Ind. Univ., 1962. Appts: WSBT-TV, 1954-55; Tchr., S. Bend Community Schls., 1961-65; Media Specialist, ibid, 1965-. Mbrships: Local Pres., NEA; Local Pres., Assn. for Childhood Educ.; Ind. State Tchrs. Assn. Comms.; ALA; Ed., Periodical, Ind. Schl. Lib. Assn.; Delta Kappa Gamma; Ind. Advsry. Coun., Title III E.S.E.A., 1968-70. Ed. of article on Lib. Educ. in Ind. Hoosier Schl. libs. Address: 2701 Arrowhead Dr., S. Bend, IN 46628, U.S.A. 5, 138.

LUEDECKE, William Henry, b. 5 Apr. 1918. Mechanical Engineer. Educ: B.S. Mech. Engrng., Univ. of Tex., 1940; Exec. Trng. Prog., Westinghouse Elec. Corp., 1944; Nat. Resources Conf., Indl. Coll. of the Armed Forces, 1955. Appts. incl: M.E., Columbian Gasoline Corp.; M.E., Off. of Supvsr. of shipbuilding, USN

Dept.; Gen. Supvsr., Factory Mgrs. Staff, N. Am. Aviation Co.; M.E., Airtemp Div., Chrysler Corp., L.A.; V.P.-Gen. Mgr., Electro-Mechanics Co., Austin, Tex.; Owner, Luedecke Engrng. Co., & Luedecke Investment. Num. mbrships. incl: Nat. Soc. of Profl. Engrs.; Tex. Soc. of Profl. Engrs.; Past Pres., Local Chapt., Am. Soc. of Heating, Refrigerating & Air Conditioning Engrs.; Econ. Dev. Coun., Austin, Tex., Chmbr. of Comm. Chmn., Advsry. Coun., Nat. Fedn. of Independent Bus.; State Dir., Tex. Barbed Wire Collectors Assn., 1969-71, & Fndr., Austin Post, 1970; Masonic Lodge; Rotary Int.; Rotary Club of W. Austin. Recip., Man of the Yr. Award, Tex. Barbed Wire Collectors Assn., 1971. Address: 3403 Foothill Parkway, Austin, TX 78731, U.S.A. 7, 16, 26.

LUFT, Rolf, b. 29 June 1914. Professor of Endocrinology & Medicine. Educ: M.D., 1940; Ph.D., 1944; Prof. of Endocrinol., 1961; Prof. of Endocrinol. & Medicine, 1968. Appts. incl: Dir., Dept. of Endocrinol., Karolinska Hosp., Stockholm, Sweden. Mbrships: Pres., Swedish Soc. for Med. Scis., 1971; Fellow, Royal Acad. of Scis., 1973-; Mbr. Nobel Comm. for Physiol. & Med., (1961) 1973-; Pres., Int. Diabetes Fedn., 1974-. Publs. incl: over 400 sci. papers in fields of endocrinol., internal med., physiol., biochem., molecular med. & neurosurgery. Hons: Elliott Proctor Joslim Medal, New England Diabetes Assn., 1968; Paul Langerhaus Medal, Deutsche Diabetesgesellschaft, 1972; Anders Jahre Med. Prize & Gold Medal, Univ. of Oslo, Norway, 1973. Address: Dept. of Endocrinol., Karolinska Hosp., S-10401 Stockholm, Sweden. 50.

LUING, Gary A., b. 24 Apr. 1937. Professor of Accounting. Educ: B.S., Stetson Univ., Deland, Fla., U.S.A.; M.A.S., Univ. of Ill.; C.P.A., State of Fla. Appts: Chief, Statistical Review Sect., XVIII Airborne Corps; Auditor, Arthur Andersen & Co.; Prof., Acctng., Fla. Atlantic Univ., Boca Raton; Asst. Dean-Dean, Coll. of Bus. & Pub. Admin., ibid. Mbrships: Am. Inst. of Cert. Pub. Accts.; Chmn., Jrnl. Comm., Fla. Inst. of Cert. Pub. Accts.; Am. Acctng. Assn.; State Income & Bus. Taxation, Nat. Tax Assn.; Acctng. Rsch. Assn.; AAUP; Certification Comm., Am. Soc. of Assn. Execs. Publs: Readings in Taxation; Ed., The Florida Certified Public Accountant; Contbns. to profl. jrnls. Address: College of Business & Public Administration, Florida Atlantic University, Boca Raton, FL 33432, U.S.A.

LUISI, Hector, b. 19 Sept. 1919. Lawyer; Diplomat. Educ: Uruguayan Naval Acad.; Inst. Alfredo Vazquez Acevedo, Montevideo; LL.B., Schl. of Law & Soc. Scis., Univ. of Repub.; Dip. in Comparative Legal Studies, St. John's Coll., Cambridge. Appts: Pvte. Atty., 1944-; For. Affairs Advsr. to Pres. Oscar Gestido, 1964-66; elected Senator of the Repub., & appointed Min. of For. Affairs, 1967; Amb. to U.S.A., 1969-. Mbrships: Bd. of Interm. Bar Assn.; Metrop. Club, N.Y. & Wash. D.C. Author of sev. articles. Prin. in drafting of revised Constitution . of Uruguay approved & promulgated by plebiscite, 1967. Hons: OBE, 1966; Grand Cross Order of Isabel la Católica, Spain, 1967; Grand Cross Order of Merit, Chile, 1968; Grand Cross Order El Sol, Peru, 1968; Grand Cross Order of Bright Star, Repub. of China-Taiwan, 1968. Address: 7419 Beverly Rd., Bethesda, MD 20014, U.S.A. 2.

LUKE, Peter (Ambrose Cyprian), b. 12 Aug. 1919. Playwright; Author; Producer; Director. Educ: Eton; Byam Shaw Schl. of Art, London U.K.; Atelier Andre Lhote, Paris, France. Appts: Rifle Brigade, 1940-46; Sub.-ed. Reuters, 1947; Wine Trader, 1947-57; Story

Ed., ABC-TV, 1958-63; Drama Prod., BBC-TV, 1963-67; Free-lance Writer, 1967-. Mbr. of Writers Guild of Gt. Brit. Publs. Hadrian VII (play), 1968, 2nd ed., '69; Sisyphus & Reilly, 1972. Prods. incl; Plays: Small Fish Are Sweet (ABC-TV, 1958); Roll on Bloomin' Death (ABC-TV, 1961); Devil a Monk W'd Be (BBC-TV, 1966); Films: A Portrait of Sean o Riada, Irish Composer (BBC-TV, 1967); Black Sound-Deep Song (BBC-TV, 1968); Recip. of Prix Italia for prod. of Silent Song, A dramatization of the Andalusian poetry of Federico Garcia Lorca, BBC-TV, 1967. Address: La Almona, El Chorro, Malaga, Spain, 2, 3.

LUKE, William Edgell, b. 9 June 1909. Industrialist. Appts: Dir., Mng. Dir., Chmn., Lindustries Ltd., 1938-; Army Serv. to Major, Intelligence Corps, 1940-46; Dir., John Veckie Ltd., Canada, 1950-; Chmn., Linen Thread Co. Inc., U.S.A., 1952-58; Chmn., Indl. Advsrs. to the Blind, 1962-67; Dir., Powell Duffryn Ltd., 1965-; Banicers Trust Int. Ltd., 1973-. Mbrships: Fellow, British Inst. Mgmt.; Coun. Mbr., Aims of Industry; Chmn., U.K. S. Africa Assn.; Trustee, S. Africa Fndn.; Travellers Club; Royal Thames Yacht Club; Cavalier Soc. Author articles indl. mgt., & S. African trade & investment. Recip., Order of Crown of Yugoslavia, 1945. Address: Trevor House, 100 Brompton Rd., London, S.W. 3., U.K.

LUKESCH, (Monsignor) Anton, b. 29 Dec. 1912. Professor of Ethnology; Roman Catholic Priest. Educ: Dr. of Law, Univ. of Graz, Austria, 1936; Ordained 1948; Dr. Theol., Univ. of Graz, 1950. Appts: Missionary, Superior of Missions & Ethnolog. (Anthropol.) Rschr., Indian tribes, Ctrl. Brazil, 1952-59, 1967-71; Dir., Caritas, Soc. work, Graz, 1959-67; Prof., Missol., Univ. of Graz, 1965; Expedition, River Xingu, Brazil, & discovery of Asurini tribe 1971; Prof., Ethnol. & Missol., Univs. of Graz & Vienna, 1972-. Mbrships: Austrian Ethnol. Soc.; Soc. for Sci. of Relig. Contbr. to num. profl. jrnls. Hons: Monsignor, Rome 1965; Official da Ordem Nacional do Cruzeiro do Sul, Brazil, 1971. Address: Mannagettaweg 19, 8010, Graz, Austria.

LUM, Wanza Sueas (Mrs. Eddie G. Lum Jr.), b. 1 Feb. 1922. Librarian. Educ: B.S., E. Tex. State Coll.; M.S.L.S., E. Tex. State Univ. Appts: Grad. Asst., Lib. ETSU, summer, 1963; Co. Schl. Tchr., Red River Co., Tex., 12 yrs.; City Libn (Pub. Libn.), Mt. Pleasant, Titus Co., Tex., 4 yrs. Mbrships: TSTA; Treas., PTA, Avery ISD, Tex., Detroit ISD, ibid; Tex. Lib. Assn.; Red River Co. 4-H Club Leader, 4 yrs.; Bapt. Ch.; Chmbr. of Comm., Titus Co.; Bus. & Profl. Womens Org. (sec.), ibid; Altrusia Int., Mt. Pleasant (treas.); Bd. Dirs., Charter Mbr.; Well Baby Clin., Titus Co.; Friends of Lib.; Titus Co. Sr. Citizens Comm., ibid. Address: 905 E. 1st, Mt. Pleasant, TX 75455, U.S.A. 125.

LUMPKIN, Donavon Dale, b. 5 Apr. 1922. Educator. Educ: B.S., N. Tex. State Univ., Denton, 1942; M.Ed., ibid, 1951; Ed.D., Univ. of Southern Calif., L.A., 1959; Postdoctoral work in Reading, Syracuse Univ., N.Y., 1961. Appts. incl: Tchr. & Instr., Tex. Pub. Schls. & N. Tex. State Univ., 1942-50; Tchr., Calif. Pub. Schls., 1951-54; Cons. in Reading & Developmental Lang. Arts, Monterey Co. Off. of Educ., Salinas, Calif., 1954-63; Dir., Reading Ctr., & Prof. of Educ., Ball State Univ., Muncie, Ind., 1963-74. Mbrships: Treas., Ind. State Coun. & Muncie Area Coun., Int. Reading Assn., 1970-73; Coll. Reading Assn.; Nat. Reading Conf.; NEA; Ind. State Tchrs. Assn.; Int. Coun. on Educ. Tchrs.; Nat. Coun. of

Tchrs. of Engl.; Ind. Right-to-Read Task Group, 1970-73; Ind. State Comm. on Reading, 1964-66. Author of articles & papers presented at Int. Reading Assn. Nat. Convens. Recip. of hons. Address: The Reading Ctr., Ball State Univ., Muncie, IN 47306, U.S.A. 131, 141.

LUMSDEN, Ian Gordon, b. 8 June 1945. Museologist & Curator. Educ: Grad., McGill Univ., Montreal, Canada. Appts: Curator, Art Dept., N.B. Mus., St. John, Canada, 1969; Curator, Beaverbrook Art Gall., Fredericton, N.B., 1969-. Mbrships: Sec.-Treas., Canadian Mus. Assn., 1973-; Treas., Canadian Art Mus. Dirs. Org., 1973-; Sec., Advsry. Comm. to Atlantic Provinces Regional Conservation Lab., Canadian Conservation Inst., 1972-; Chmn., Atlantic Provinces Art Circuit, 1970-72; Canadian Conf. of the Arts; Am. Assn. of Mus.; Coll. Art Assn. of Am. Publs: Nineteenth Century New Brunswick Landscape Painting, 1969; Esther Warkov, 1970; The Figure in Canadian Painting, 1972; Contbns. to art jrnls. Address: Beaverbrook Art Gallery, P.O. Box 605, Fredericton E3B 5A6, N.B., Canada. 133.

LUNDBERG, Bo Klas Oskar, b. 1 Dec. 1907. Aeronautical Administrator & Designer. Educ: Hudiksvalls Läroverk & Royal Inst. of Technol., Stockholm. Appts. incl: Designer, Test Pilot, AB Svenska Järnvagsverkstäderna, Aeroplanavdelningen, Linköping, 1931-35; Asst. Inspector, Bd. of Civil Aviation, Stockholm, 1937-38; Chief Designer J-22 Fighter, Royal Air Bd., 1940-44; Chief, Structures Dept., Aeronautical Rsch. Inst. of Sweden, 1944-47, Dir. Gen., 1947-67, Aviation Cons., 1967-. Mbrships. incl: Fellow, Royal Aeronautical Soc.; Fellow, Royal Swedish Acad. Engrng. Scis.; AAAS. Num. profl. papers, reports & articles. Hons. incl: Thulin Silver Medal, 1948, Gold Medal, 1955; Monsanto Aviation Safety Award, 1963; Carl August Wicander Gold Medal, 1966. Address: Gubbkärrsvägen 29/9, S-16151 Bromma, Sweden. 34, 43.

LUNDBLADE, Hobert Philip, b. 12 Oct. 1929. Dentist; Endodontist. Educ: B.S., Univ. of Minn., 1952; D.D.S., ibid., 1954; M.S.D., 1955. Appts: Capt., U.S. Army Dental Corps, 1955-58; Practice of Endodontics, San Antonio, Tex., 1958-; Instr. Dental Assts., San Antonio Coll., 1961-68; Alderman & Mayor, City of Castle Hills, Tex., 1968-. Formed first Dept. of Endodontics in Armed Forces, 1955. Mbrships. incl: Fndr. & 1st Pres., San Antonio/Austin Dental Study Grp., 1960; Var. Offs. & Pres., San Antonio Dist. Dental Soc., 1962-74; Tex. Dental Assn.; Am. Assn. Endodontics; Alamo Area Coun. of Govts.; Bexar Co. Coun. of Mayors. Contbr. to profl. jrnls. Lectr. at num. Tex. dental socs. Hons. incl: Fellow, Am. Coll. Dentists, Int. Coll. Dentists. Address: 1019 Shook Ave., San Antonio, TX 78212, U.S.A. 7.

LUNDBOHM-REUTERSVÄRD, Britt I.M., b. 16 Apr. 1917. Artist (Painter). Educ: Studied Art, Grande Chaumière, Paris, France, 1939; B.A., Univ. of Stockholm, Sweden, 1954. Mbrships: Women's Assn. of Swedish Artists; Assn. Swedish Artists; Club Int. Féminin, Paris, France; Int. Artists Grp. Roter Reiter, Munich, Germany. Pioneer of Action Painting in Scandinavia (1950s) & introduced tachism into Swedish Informal Art. Major Works: La Méduse de la Lune; The Whirl of Terror (Mus. of Modern Art, Stockholm); The Soot-Cyclone (Norrkoeping Mus.). Permanent Collects: Mus. of Modern Art, Tokyo; Nat. Gall., Oslo; Statens Mus. for Kunst, Copenhagen; Nat. Mus. Fine Arts, Stockholm. Exhibs: Munich, 1957; Hamburg, 1959; Stockholm, 1959, 1967, 1970,

1973; Paris, 1961; Tokyo, 1962; Osaka, Japan, 1962-63; Swedish Art Exhib. Touring Europe, 1964; London, 1964; Paris, 1964. Address: Clemenstorget 10, S-222 21 Lund, Sweden. 133.

LUNDE, Asbjorn Rudolph, b. 17 July 1927. Lawyer. Educ: A.B., Columbia Coll., Columbia Univ., N.Y.C., 1947; LL.B., J.D., Columbia Univ. Law Schl., 1949. Appts: admitted to N.Y. Bar, 1949. admitted to U.S. Fed. Bar; Assoc., Kramer, Marx, Greenlee & Backus, 1950-58; Ptnr., ibid, 1958-68; Pvte. Prac. of law, N.Y., 1968-; num. dirships. of educl. & charitable fndns. Mbrships: Am., N.Y. State Bar Assns.; Assn. of the Bar of City of N.Y.; Metropol. Opera Club, N.Y. Address: 230 Park Avenue, N.Y., NY 10017, U.S.A. 6.

LUNDERVOLD, Arne Johannes Steinvard, b. 21 Feb. 1915. Professor of Medicine. Educ: Grad., Oslo Univ., 1943; Inst. of Physiol. & Pharmacy, ibid, 1945-50; Rsch. Fellow, Neurophysiol., U.K., 1948-49, Univ. Mus., Oxford, & Nat. Hosp., London; Montreal Neurol. Inst., McGill Univ., Canada, 1951; Columbia Univ., Mass. Gen. Hosp., Yale Univ. & Univ. of Calif., U.S.A., 1951; Dr.Med., 1951; Specialist in Clin. Neurophysiol., 1957. Appts: Gen. Prac., 1943-45; Hd., Dept. of Clin. Neurophysiol., Oslo Univ., 1954-; Vis. Prof., Ind. Univ., 1954, Minn. Univ., 1960, Cairo Univ., 1961-62, Univ. of Wis., 1963, Univ. of Okla., 1963, Ain Shams Univ., 1964; Hd., Int. Course, Oslo Univ. & NORAD; Hd., Int. Course in Clin. Neurophysiol., Vis. Prof. & Tech. Advsr., Israel, Egypt, Turkey, Korea, Thailand, Iran & India, 1967-73. Mbrships: Fndr., Norwegian Soc. of Phys. Med.; Fndr., Pres., Norwegian Soc. of Clin. Neurophysiol.; Soc. of Neurological Scis. in Norway; Pres., ibid, 1967-73; Corres. Mbr., Am. Cong. of Rehab. Med.; Norwegian Neurological Soc.; Deleg., Int. Fedn. of Socs. for Electroencephalography & Clin. Neurophysiol.; Int. Sr. Amateur Golf Soc.; Fulbright Alumni Assn. Publs: Electromyographic Investigations of Position & Manner of Working in Typewriting, 1951; num. articles in field of clin. neurophysiol. Invited by Acad. of Scis., USSR, to lecture in Moscow & Leningrad. Hons: incl: Fellow, Royal Soc., London, 1972. Address: EEG-laboratoriet, Rikshospitalet, Pilestredet 32, Oslo 1, Norway. 134.

LUNDSTRÖM, Rolf, b. 25 July 1913. Physician. Educ: Med. studies, Uppsala & Lund Univs., Sweden. Appts: Physn.-Asst. Prof. Clin. Epidemiol., Karolinska Inst., 1941-; Int. Campaign Against TB, Chief of Mission to Austria, 1948-50; Cons., Paediatrics, Royal Med. Bd., 1951-58; Temporary Advsr., European Office of WHO on Rubella prevention, 1972. Mbrships: Chmn., Med. Assn., Comm. of Sodermanland, 1968-; Royal Soc. of London; N.Y. Acad. Scis.; Swedish Soc. Med.; Past Pres., Rotary Club of Eskilstuna-Kloster. Author over 100 articles in paediatrics, bacteriol. & infectious diseases, incl. a Monograph: Rubella in Pregnancy, 1962. Hons: Silver Medal of Swedish Red Cross, 1950; Kt. of Order of Northern Star, 1969. Address: Djurgårdsvägen 26, 633 50 Eskilstuna, Sweden. 43.

LUNSFORD, Angeline Eloise (Brooks), b. 7 June 1913. Teacher. Educ: B.S., Univ. of Montevallo, Ala., 1933. Appts: Tchr., var. schl. systems, Ala., 1933-37; Supvsr., Soc. & Home Mgmt., U.S. Dept. of Agric., 1940-42; Casewkr., Dept. of Welfare, State of Ala., 1948-54; Off. Mgr., Life Ins. Co. of Ala., 1965-69. Mbrships: AAUW; Prog. Chmn., Sec., V.P., Pres., Chautauqua Club, Montgomery,

Ala., var. occasions; Prog. Chmn., V.P., Pres., Better Homes Club, Montgomery, var. occasions; Pres., V.P., Camelia Garden Club, Montgomery, var. occasions; Univ. of Montevallo Alumni Assn. Address: 2775 Pelzer Ave., Montgomery, AL 36109, U.S.A. 125.

LUNSFORD, James Taylor, b. 14 Nov. 1911. United States Marshal. Educ: Auburn Univ., Ala. 1931-32; Univ. of Ala. 1934-35; Univ. of Ala. Law Schl., 1935-36. Appts: Mgr., Lunsford Mercantile Co., Hackleburg, 1937-41; Pub. Safety Off., U.S. Tenn. Valley Authority, 1941-44; Spec. Agt., U.S. Dept. Labor, Birmingham, 1944-45, U.S. Dept. Agric., Montgomery, 1945-46; Mayor, City of Hamilton, Ala., Owner, Ins. & Real Estate bus., 1946-54; State Dir., U.S. Dept. Agric. Farmers Home Admin. Ala., 1954-61; Asst. Dir. P.R., Life Ins. Co. of Ala., 1961-69; U.S. Marshal, Montgomery, Ala., 1969-. Mbrships: Pres., Civitan Club; Chmn., Profl. Fed. Admnstrs. Club; Sec., Life Underwriters Assn.; Co. Chmn., State Exec. Comm. & Co. Comm. Mbr., Repub. Party of Ala.; Bd., Alabama R.R. Corp., Rural Fire Ins. Co. of Ala. (& V.P.). Author of articles on local govt., publ. 1950. Recip. of profl. awards. Address: 2775 Pelzer Ave., Montgomery, AL 36109, U.S.A. 57, 125.

LUPINE, Elmer Alan Roy, b. 19 Nov. 1908. Civil Engineer. Educ: B.S., Ala. Univ., U.S.A., 1931; C.E., Roosevelt Grad. Coll., Chgo., Ill. 1944; Postgrad. work, Columbia Univ., 1936-38. Appts: Civil Engr., Ala. State Highway Dept., Tuscaloosa, 1931-32; w. Carl B. Call, Archt., N.Y.C., 1933-34; Off. Borough Engr., ibid, 1934-39; Mbr. staff, Dept. Engrng., San Juan, Puerto Rico, 1939-40; Civil Engr., Design Div., Dept. Navy, Atlantic Div. Naval Facilities Engrng. Cmnd., 1940-60; Facilities Mgmt., 1961-69; Facilities Planning 1969-. Mbrships: Fellow, Am. Soc. C.E.; var. comms.; Norfolk Boat Club. Address: 212 86th St. Virginia, Beach, VA 23451, U.S.A.

LÜPKE, Gerd, b. 19 May 1920. Writer. Educ: Oberrealschule. Appts: Jrnlst; Ed.; Free-lance Writer. Mbrships: Union of German Writers; Int. Acad., N.Y. Publs. incl: Mecklenburg-Vorpommern; Dome, Kircker und Klöster in Mecklenburg; Tag und Traum; Der Witz der Mecklenburger; approx. 60 radio plays, 1600 radio progs. & 40 TV films. Hons: 6 Literary Awards, 1957-73; Prof. h.c., Repub. of San Marino, 1955; Bundesverdienstkreuz, German Fed. Repub., 1972. Address: 293 Varel 1. 0, Lange Strasse 4, German Fed. Repub. 43, 92.

LUPPER, Edward, b. 4 Jan. 1936. Painter. Educ: Parsons Schl. of Design, N.Y.C.,; Calif. Coll. Arts & Crafts; San. Fran. Art Inst. & State Coll. Mbrships: Sierra Club, San. Fran.; Am. Mus. Natural Hist.; Nat. Audubon Soc.; Nat. Wildlife Fedn.; Marines Mem. Club. Exhibs. incl: Balt. Mus. of Art; Tucson Art Ctr.; Ft. Worth Art Ctr.; San Fran. Mus. of Art. Work in pub. & pvte. collects. Publs: Calendar, 1973, reprods., 1974; contbr. to var. mags., 1967-74. Recip. of Huntington Hargford Fellowship, 1964. Address: 1255 Pacific Ave., San Fran., CA 94109, U.S.A. 37.

LUPTON, David Walker, b. 12 Oct. 1934. Librarian. Educ: B.S., 1956, M.S., 1960, M.S.L.S., 1963, Univ. of Wis. Appts: Tchng. & Rsch. Asst., Ethnol. Dept., Univ. of Wis., 1959-60; Asst., Entolmol. Dept., B.P. Mus., Honolulu, Hawaii, 1960-61; Asst. Life Sci. Libn. & Asst. Serials Libn., Purdue Univ., 1963-68; Hd., Asst. Prof., Serials Dept., Colo. State Univ. Lib., 1968-. Mbrships: Colo. Lib. Assn.; Colo. Field Ornithologists; Colo. Geneal.

Soc.; Entomol. Soc. of Am.; Am. Birding Assn.; Beta Phi Mu. Publs: Articles on libs., ornithol., geneal. & entomol.; Ed., Colo. Field Ornithologist, 1969-, Ptarmigan, 1970-, Luptonian, 1974-. Address: 2808 W. Horsetooth Rd., Ft. Collins, CO 80521, U.S.A.

LUPTON, Mary Hosmer, b. 2 Jan. 1914. Rare book search service owner & operator. Educ: B.S., Univ. of Va., 1940. Appts: Ptnr., Wakefield Press, Earlysville, Va., 1940-55; Owner, operator, Wakefield Forest Bookshop, Earlysville, 1955-65, Forest Bookshop, Charlottesville, Va., 1965- & Wakefield Forest Tree Farm, 1955-. Mbrships. incl: Writers Advsry. Panel, Va. Ctr. for the Creative Arts, 1973-; Corres. Sec., Charlottesville-Albemarle Civic League, 1963-64; Sec., Instructive Vis. Nurses Assn., 1961-62; Chmn., Pub. Info., Charlottesville Chapt., Va. Mus. of Fine Arts, 1970-74; AAUW; DAR; New England Hist. Geneal. Soc.; Am. Forestry Assn. Author of article on Va. mockingbird in Va. Wildlife, 1973. Address; La Casita Blanca, Route 1, Box 50-B, Charlottesville, VA 22901, U.S.A. 5, 138.

LUSKY, Lois Freese, b. 28 Sept. 1931. Public Relations & Advertising Executive. Educ: N.D. State Schl. of Sci., 1952; Univ. of Denver, Colo., 1953-55. Appts: Staff Asst., U.S. Nat. Bank, 1953-58; Asst. P.R. Dir., ibid, 1958-60; P.R. Dir., ibid, 1960-63; Account Exec., Sam Lusky Assocs. Inc., 1963-65; Exec. V.P., ibid, 1965-. Mbrships: P.R. Soc. of Am.; V.P., Colo. Chapt., ibid, 1966; Past-Dir., Colo. Indl. Press Assn.; P.R. Counsel, Boys' Clubs of Denver; Publicity Chmn., Status of Women, Gov.'s Commn., 1969-71; Bd. of Dirs., Auraria Community Ctr.; P.R. Commn., United Fund Agcy. Contbr. to var. trade & profl. publs. Hons: Lulu (L.A. Women's Advertising Club) Citation, 1971. Address: Sam Lusky Associates, Inc., 811 First National Bank Building, Denver, CO 80202, U.S.A. 5, 132, 138.

LUTAYA, (Bishop) Fesito, b. 26 Jan. 1899. Bishop. Educ: King's Coll., Budo, 1918-21; Mukono Coll. for Ordination, 1929-30; Ridley Hall, Cambridge Univ., U.K., 1947-48. Appts: Asst. Schl. Tchr., Masindi Sec. Schl., Bunyoro, Uganda; Headmaster, ibid, 1922-28; Deacon, Mukono Parish, 1930-31; Kabwobe Parish, Ankole, Uganda, 1931-32; Ibande, ibid, 1932-38; Vicar, Namirembe Cathedral, Kampala, 1938-41; Chap., Mukono Theol. Coll., 1942-45; Rural Dean, Mubenda Dist., 1946-47; Cambridge, Ely Diocese, U.K., 1947-48; Canon & Sub-Dean, Namirembe Cathedral, Kampala, Uganda, 1948-51; Asst. Bishop, Uganda, 1952-60; Bishop, W. Buganda, 1960-. Mbr. Bible Soc. Hons. incl: 2 Brit. silver medals & 1 Brit. gold medal, 1954-55. Address: Mityana Singo, P.O. Box 1, Mityana, Uganda, E. Africa.

LUTER, Yvonne Marie-Louise, b. 26 Feb. 1928. Journalist. Educ: B.A., Bryn Mawr Coll., 1949; M.A., Columbia Univ., 1958. Appts: Am. Ed., Stern Mag., 1951-; Am. Ed., Mortensens Forlag, 1960-; Am. Ed., Sondags-B.T., 1965-; Edit. Dir., Bertelsmann Publng. Grp., 1969-. Mbrships: For. Press Assn.; York Club. Address: 60 E. 56th St., N.Y., NY 10022, U.S.A. 132.

LUTOMSKI, Halina Josefa, b. 4 Feb. 1929. Dance Educator; Choreographer. Appts. incl: Prod., Dancecapades, 1948-; Fndr., Artistic Dir. & Choreographer, Elmira-Corning (N.Y.) Ballet Co., 1955-; Dir.-Fndr., Schl. of Dance Arts, Elmira & Corning; Choreographer, Dance Records Co. N.Y. Ballet Rep. to Nat. Coun. of Dance Tchrs. Orgs.; Supvsr., arranger, 15 long-playing records for Roper Dance Records

Inc. to date. Recip., Stevben Cristal & Gold Award, City of Elmira, 1969. Address: 933 Fassett Rd., Elmira, NY 14905, U.S.A. 5, 6.

LUTOUR, Lou, b. in St. Louis, Missouri, U.S.A. Poet-Monologuist, Educator, Broadcaster, Journalist, Lecturer & Columnist. Appts. incl: Community Rels. Coordinator, P.S. 83, Manhattan-a More Effective Schl., Tchr. of Mentally Retarded, N.Y.C. Schl. System; Fndr., Global News Syndicate, N.Y.C., 1945-; Own Radio Show, 1953-; Pub. Rels. Cons. & Practitioner; Famed Writer of Global Portraits Column, etc. Previous appts: Fndr., La Cheerios Inc., 1948; Fndr. & Org., Teen-Town, 1951; Radio Commentator, WHOM, N.Y.C., 1951-55; Pub. Rels. Cons., Nat. Beauty Culturists League, Inc., 1958. Life Mbr., Int. Platform Assoc.; Nat. Guild of Career Women, Nat. Coun. of Negro Women; Am. Poets Fellowship Soc.; Am. Assoc. of Univ. Women; Poetry Soc. of London, U.K. (Chmn., Eastern Ctr., 1967-); Fndr. World Poet Resource Ctr. Hons. incl: U.S. Army 7th Service Comman Citation, 1942; Women of the Year, Zeta Phi Beta Sorority, 1959-60; Int. Goodwill Ambassador, Bermuda 1963; N.Y. Worlds Fair Citation, 1965; Career Woman of the Year 1967; Unsung Heroine (named by Amsterdam News, N.Y.) 1967; Poet in Residence of the Monologue Stage, 1967; Laurel Wreath, United Poets Int., 1967; APFS Gold Cup, 1968; Publs. incl: Int. Hon. Poet Laureate, World Congress of Poets, Manila, 1969 etc. The Power and the Glory (poems); many booklets, poems, newspaper articles, and the special column, Global Portraits, Silhouettes of Rhythm & Portraits of Rhythm. Address: 1270 Fifth Ave., Apt. 2F, New York, NY 10019, U.S.A. 5, 6, 11, 57.

LUTZ, George W., b. 17 Dec. 1916. Realtor; Appraiser; Builder. Appts. incl: Asst. Bus. Mgr., Boys Schl., Port Deposit, Md., 1941; Serv. U.S. Army, to Major, 1946; Corporate Mbr., Susquehanna Trading Co. Inc., Havre de Grace, Md., 1947; Fndr. & Ptnr., Construction Co., N.E., Md., 1950; Pres., Cecil Co. Chmbr. of Comm., 1961-62; Commnr., Town of N.E., Md., 1964; Pres., Cecil Traders, Inc., 1966; Bd. Dirs., Harford Mem. Hosp., Havre de Grace, 1966-; Chmn. Advsry. Bd., Havre de Grace Br., Augusta Bldg. & Loan, 1967-73; Sec., Cecil Co. Bd. Realtors, 1970-71; V.P., Cecil Co. Chapt., Md. Home Bldrs. Assn., 1970-73. Mbrships. incl: Nat. Assoc. Real Estate Appraisers; Nat. Inst. Real Estate Brokers. Recip. sev. mil. awards. Address: 710 S. Main St., N.E., MD 21901, U.S.A.

LUTZ, Kenneth William, b. 8 Jan. 1934. Financial Publisher; Company Executive. Educ: B.S., N.Y. Univ., 1955; M.B.A., Grad. Schl. of Bus., ibid, 1962. Appts: Rsch. Mgr., RHM Assocs., 1959-62; Assoc. Ed., Financial World Mag., 1962-63; Pres., Trendline Div., Standard & Poor's Corp., 1963-. Mbrships: N.Y. Soc. Security Analysts; Boy Scouts of Am.; Delta Sigma Pi; Alpha Beta Gamma. Contbr. of articles to financial publs. Address: 5 Morningside Rd., Ardsley, NY 10502, U.S.A. 6.

LUTZ, Willard Kauffman, b. 10 Aug. 1936. Dentist. Educ: A.B., Bridgewater Coll., 1958; D.D.S., Med. Coll. of Va., 1965. Appts. incl: Pub. Hlth. Dentist, 1965-66; Staff, Page Mem. Hosp., 1969-; Cons. Dentist, Rappa Hannock Co., Va., 1966-. Mbrships: Am. Dental Assn., 1961-; Va. Dental Assn., 1961-; Valley Dental Soc.; Am. Endodontics Soc.; Soc. for Preventive Dentistry; Am. Profl. Prac. Assn.; Life, Delta Sigma Delta; Luray Chmbr. of Comm., 1971-; Sec., Jaycees; Pres., V.P., Luray Jaycees; Pres., Warren Co. Heart Assn.; Bd. Dirs., Warren Co. Recreation Assn.; Bd. Dirs.,

Cancer Soc.; Charter Pres., Page Valley Kiwanis Club, 1972; V.P., St. Mark's Ch. Coun., 1970-73; Supt., St. Mark's Sunday Schl., 1973-74; Charter Pres., Boys Club of Luray; Local PTA Pres., 1973-74. Hons: Merit Award, Va. Heart Assn., 1967; Outstanding Jaycee of Yr., 1972; Outstanding Young Man, Luray Jaycees, 1972; Past Pres.'s Award, Jaycees, 1972. Address: P.O. Box 306, Luray, VA 22835, U.S.A. 7, 57.

LUUKKANEN, Vilho Olavi, b. 16 July 1912. Finnish Army Officer (Lt. Colonel). Educ: Finnish Mil. Acad.; Commercial Coll. of Helsinki, Finland. Appts. incl: Staff Off., Div. 23, 1939-40; Infantry Co. Cmdr. & Chief of Staff, Infantry Regiment 35, 1941-45; Chief of Operative Staff, Infantry Div. 6, 1944; var. Staff appts. in mil. dists. of Finland, 1945-67; retired, 1967; Financial Mgr., Karjalan Liitto r.y., Helsinki, 1968-71. Mbrships: Lions Club, Helsinki. Hons: Finnish Cross of Freedom 3rd (2) & 4th Class; Kt., Order of Finnish Lion 1st Class; Mem. Medal, 1939-40, 1941-45. Address: Vuorenpeikontie 5 A 109, 00820 Helsinki 82, Finland.

LUXARDO de FRANCHI, Nicolò, b. 23 Oct. 1927. Distiller. Educ: Univ. of Padova, Italy. Appts: w. Girolamo Luxardo s.p.a., distillers, Torreglia-Padova, 1947-, Gen. Mgr., 1951, Pres. & Chmn. of Bd., 1963; Pres., Econ. Comm. for Small Inds., Gen. Confedn. of Italian Inds., Rome. Mbrships. incl: Societa Ligure di Storia Patria, Genoa; Deputazione di Storia Patria Provincie Permensi, Parma; Councillor, Societa Dalmata di Storia Patria, Rome; V.P., Istituto Italiano dei Castelli, Veneto, Rome. Publs: Storia del Maraschino, 1952; Considerazioni sulle Marasche, 1961; sev. histl. contbns., var. publs. Hons. incl: Mbr., Order of Merit, Italian Repub., 1962, Off., 1965, Cmndr., 1967, Kt. Cmndr., 1973; Gold Medal, Chmbr. of Comm., Padova; Gold Medal, Associazione degli Industriali, Padova; Kt. of Mil. & Souvrain Order of Malta. Address: Via Luca Belludi 19, 35100 Padova, Italy. 43, 95.

LUXENBERG, Benjamin, b. 24 Sept. 1897. Barrister. Educ: Read law, 1913-18; Called to Bar of Ont., Canada. Appts: Vice Chmn., Bankruptcy Comm., Metropolitan Toronto Bd. of Trade, 1952-70; Dir., Boosey & Hawkes (Can.) Ltd., A & A Selmer Ltd., Beare & Son Ltd.; Counsel, Gardiner Roberts, Toronto. Mbrships: Mexican Acad. Int. Law; Bd. of Coun., Ont. Sect., Canadian Bar Assn., 1955, 61, 65; Int. Law Assn.; Life, Mt. Sinai Masonic Lodge, 1968; Life, Law Soc. Upper Canada, 1970; Life, York Co. Law Assn. Publs: Special Lectures on Bankruptcy, 1956; var. articles. Hons: Silver Medal & Christopher Mem. Schlrship., 1918; Created K.C., 1935. Address: 1 Highland Ave., Toronto, Canada.

LYBECK, (Carl Mikael) Sebastian, b. 3 Aug. 1929. Poet. Educ: Åbo Acad., Finland, 1947-49; Finnish Cadet Schl., Helsinki, 1949-51; Jrnlst. trng., ibid., 1951-52; Helsinki Univ. (lit., philos.), 1953-54. Appts. incl: Poet since 1945; sev. profl. tours in W. Germany & Scandinavia, 1960-; active in Writers' Ctr., Sweden, inclng. num. lecture tours, 1967-; an initiator of Coop. Writers' Publ., Sweden, 1970-. Mbrships: Writers' Socs. of Sweden, Norway, Finland. Publs. incl: Poems: Jorden har alltid sitt ljus, 1958, Dikter fran Lofoten, 1961, Liten stad vid havet, 1963, Mitt i den nordiska idyllen, 1973; children's books: Latte Igelkott reser till Lofoten, 1957, Als der Fuchs seine Ohren verlor, 1966, När Elefanten tog Tanten, 1967; num. translations in sev. langs.; reviews, poems, etc. publd. in many countries. Recip., sev. schlrships. from Finland & Sweden & Writers' Orgs. Address: Morgonbrisvägen 2 C, S-451 00 Uddevalla, Sweden. 134.

LYCHE, Johan Magnar, b. 16 Apr. 1911. Agricultural Society Director. Educ: Cand. agric., Agricl. Univ. of Norway; practical & theoretical agricl. studies, U.S.A. & European Univs. Appts. incl: Gen. Sec., Norwegian 4H Clubs, 1936-39; Dir., Tomb Coll. of Agric., 1939-52; Dir., Ostfold Agricl. Soc., 1952-; Lectr. & Censor, Ext. Serv. Mbrships: Scandinavian Assn. of Agricl. Scis.; Hon. Mbr., Norwegian 4H Clubs, Pres., 1956-70; Norwegian Price Coun. (Norwegian Antitrust Law), 1954-69; Dpty. Mbr., Norwegian Plmnt., 1945-52; Pres., Norwegian Assn. Civil Agronomes, 1954-59; Bd. Mbr., Norwegian Coll. Grads, 1956-60 & Norwegian Civil Servants, 1956-60. Publs: Pedagogy of Extension Service I & II; Sarpsborg, 1965 & 1966. Hons: Royal Award, Norwegian Underground Mil. Serv., 1940-45. Address: Snorresgt 10, 1700 Sarpsborg, Norway.

LYELLS, Ruby Elizabeth Cowan Stutts (Mrs. M.J. Lyells). Librarian; Group Worker; Retailer. Educ: B.S., Alcorn A & M Coll., Lorman, Miss., 1929; B.S. (Lib. Sci.), Hampton Inst., Va., 1930; M.A., Grad. Lib. Schl., Univ. of Chgo., Ill., 1942. Appts. incl: Hd. Libn., Alcorn A & M Coll., 1930-45; Hd. Libn. Jackson State Coll., Miss., 1945-47; Dir., Student YM-YWCAs, Negro Colls. in Miss., 1947-50; Libn., Carver & Coll. Park Brs. Jackson Municipal Libs., 1951-54; Exec. Dir., Miss. State Coun. on Human Rels., 1955-59; Co-owner-Mgr., MLS Serv. Co., Jackson, Miss., 1959-69. Mbrships. incl: Pres., Jackson Area Coun. on Human Rels.; League of Women Voters (var. posts, inclng. State Coord. for wkly. TV series Learn with the League); Life, NAACP; Nat. Assn. Colored Women's Clubs; Past Pres., Miss. State Fedn. of Colored Women's Clubs; Life, Nat. Coun. of Negro Women; AAUW (Area Rep. for Int. Rels.); Nat. Planning Bd. White House Conf. on Aging, 1972; Jackson Chmbr. of Comm. & Civic Art Ctr.-Planetarium; Miss. & Southeastern Region Lib. Assns. Author, num. articles, papers & speeches concerning libs., educ., emancipation of women & negros. Hons. incl: Regional Outstanding Citizen Award, Alpha Kappa Alpha Sorority, 1959, & Southeastern Fedn., 1967, '69; Club Woman of the Yr., Miss. State Fedn., 1965; Outstanding Achievement Award, Nat. Assn. of Colored Women's Clubs, 1970; H.H.D., Prentiss Inst., 1968. Address: 1116 Montgomery St., Jackson, MS 39203, U.S.A. 15, 42, 57, 125, 130.

LYNCH, Etta Lee, b. 19 Sept. 1924. Writer. Educ: Famous Writers Schl., Westport, Conn.; Okla. Univ. Schl. of Profl. Writing. Mbrships: Author's Guild; Nat. League of Am. Pen Women; South Plains Writers' Assn. (Pres., V.P.). Publs: The Power Behind the Comb; Help is Only a Prayer Away; Over 100 articles & short stories. Author of Screenplay for Educl. TV, 1964. Hons: Shamrock Fiction Award, 1966. Address: 5101 41st St., Lubbock, TX 79414, U.S.A. 132, 138.

LYON, Elinor Bruce (Mrs. Peter Wright), b. 17 Aug. 1921. Writer. Educ: Lady Margaret Hall, Oxford Univ., Publs: 18 books for children, published in U.K., U.S.A., Germany, Sweden, Spain, Denmark. Latest works: Strangers at the Door; The Wishing Pool. Address: 2 Horton Crescent, Rugby, Warwicks, U.K. 3.

LYON, George Cook, b. 5 Oct. 1904. Priest; Physician; Educator. Educ: B.S., Midwestern Univ., 1930; M.D., ibid, 1959; Ph.D., 1964;

M.S., Boston Univ., 1937; Ph.D., T.A.E.C., 1970; D.D., ibid, 1970; LL.D., 1971. Appts: Psychotherapist, 1964-72; Ordained Priest, 1970; Fndr., N.Y.'s Gracie Inst.; Fndr. & Pres., Palm Beach, Fla., Psychotherapy Ctr.; Prior, Order of St. John of Jerusalem, P.B.; Pres., Thomas A. Edison Coll. Mbrships: Fellow, ACCH, MAMC, ACCA, AIGP, ASP, AABS; NPA; NISS, FPI; AIH; DEO; APS; Dipl., Am. Bd. Examiners in Psychotherapy. Author, Comprehensive Clinical Psychotherapy, 1971. Hons: Gold Medal, Nat. Inst. Soc. Sci., 1968; Profl. Cross, Order of St. John of Jerusalem, 1970; Award, Am. Coll. Med. Hypnosis, 1972, Nat. Inst. Sexual Educ., 1972, Am. Inst. Hypnosis, 1972. Address: 3475 S. Ocean Blvd., Palm Beach, FL 33480, U.S.A.

LYONS, Beulah Mae (Mrs.), b. 27 Jan. 1912. Christian Science Practitioner. Educ: Newspaper Inst. of Am., 1970. Appts: Christian Sci. Practitioner, 1950-; Mbr., Bd. Dirs., 4 chs.; Charter Mbr., Christian Sci. Soc., Elba, Ala.; Charter Mbr., Advsr., Coe Coll. Christian Sci. Org., Cedar Rapids, Iowa; Mbr., 1st Ch. of Christ Sci., Boston; Mbr., 1st Ch. of Christ Sci., Cedar Rapids, Iowa; Mbr., Christian Sci. Assn., Leslie Leland; C.S.B., Toledo, Ohio, 1944. Mbrships: Nat. Wildlife Assn.; Charter, Marine Corps League Aux Toledo, Ohio, 1942; Life Pres.; V.P. & Charter, Rockford Ill.; Hon. Life, Daughters of Am., 1942. Address: 2875 Mt. Vernon Rd. S.E. Cedar Rapids, IA 52403, U.S.A. 5, 8, 22, 57, 120, 128, 132, 138.

LYONS, Dennis John, b. 26 Aug. 1916. Government Scientist. Educ: Queen Mary Coll., London Univ. Appts: Aerodynamics Dept., Royal Aircraft Establishment, 1937; Hd., Experimental Projs. Div., Guided Missiles Dept., RAE, 1941; Hd., Ballistic Missile Grp., GW Dept., 1951; Hd., Weapons Dept., RAE, 1956; Dir., Road Rsch. Lab., Min. of Transport, 1962; Dir. Gen., Rsch., Dept. of Environment, 1971. Mbrships: Hon. Mbr., Instn. of Highway Engrs. Hons: C.B., 1972. Address: Dept. of Environment, 2 Marsham St., London SW1P 3EB, U.K. 1.

LYONS, Gordon Jarvis, b. 13 Sept. 1922. Industrial Realtor; Consultant. Educ: Grad., Univ. of Toronto Schls., 1941; Univ. of Toronto (Arts), 1941-42. Appts. incl; Royal Canadian Naval Volunteer Reserve, 1943-46; Pres., S.E. Lyons & Son Ltd., Toronto, Ont., Canada; former Dir., Toronto Real Estate Bd. Mbrships: former Dist. V.P., U.S.A. & Canada Soc. of Industrial Realtors; former Pres., Ctrl. Canadian Chapt., Soc. of Industrial Realtors. Mbrships: former Dir., Naval Offs. Assn. of Canada & Toronto Jr. Bd. of Trade; Kiwanis Club of Toronto Inc.; Royal Canadian Mil. Inst. Address: 1514 Kenneth Drive, Mississauga, Ontario, L5E 2Y5, Canada. 88.

LYONS, Harold A., b. 14 Sept. 1913. Professor of Medicine. Educ: B.S., St. John's Univ., 1935; M.D., L.I. Coll. of Med., 1940. Appts. incl: Dir., Pulmonary Disease Serv., Kings Co. Hosp. Ctr., Brooklyn, 1953-; Dir., Cardiopulmonary Lab., SUNY, Downstate Med. Ctr., 1953-; Cons. in Internal Med., VA Hosp., Brooklyn, 1955-; Cons.-Lectr., US Naval Hosp., 1958-; Cons., Mercy Hosp., L.I., 1957-; Cons., Community Hosp. at Geln Cove, 1968-; Cons., Brookdale Med. Ctr., 1959-; Prof., Med., SUNY, 1959-; Int. Advsry. Comm., Aspen Emphysema Conf., 1973-; Cons., USPHS Hosp., Staten Island. Fellowships incl: Am. Coll. Chest Physns.; N.Y. Acad. of Med.; AMA. Mbrships. incl: V.P., Brooklyn T.B. Hlth. Assn.; Dipl., Examiner, Am. Bd. Internal Med.; AAAS; AAUP; Past Pres., Brooklyn Soc. Internal Med.;

N.Y. Acad. Scis.; Comm., N.Y. Heart Assn.; Adirondack Mt. Club; Adirondack 46'ers; Meetings Comm., Biomed. Engrng. Soc., 1973-. Author of approx. 130 publs. in field. Recip. of hons. Address: Downstate Med. Ctr., SUNY, 450 Clarkson Ave., Brooklyn, NY 11203, U.S.A. 6, 14, 17, 28, 128, 130.

LYONS, Phillip M., b. 22 Nov. 1941. Insurance Executive; Real Estate Broker. Educ: McNeese State Univ., Lake Charles, La., U.S.A. Appts: Admin. Trainee, Am. Nat. Ins. Co., 1965; Asst. Mgr., Policy Issue Dept., ibid, 1966-67; Mgr., 1967-69; Methods Analyst, 1969-72; Mgr., Policyholders Serv. Div., 1972-; Real Estate Broker, 1966-. Mbrships. incl: Thespian Club; Dir., Galveston Jaycees, 1971-72 & 1973-74, State Dir., 1972-73; Co. Chmn., Special Events, Am. Cancer Soc., 1973; Elks; Solicitor, United Fund, 1965-69, Loaned Exec., 1970-72. Hons. incl: Outstanding Mbr., Thespians, 1958; Best Male Actor, Thespians, 1959; Sparkplug of the Yr., Jaycees, 1972-73; Roadrunner of the Yr., Jaycees, 1972-73. Address: 1602 Bayou Shore Dr., Galveston, TX 77550, U.S.A. 7.

LYONS, (Sir) William, b. 4 Sept. 1901. Business Executive. Appts: Fndr. in ptnrship., Swallow Sidecar Co., (now Jaguar Cars Ltd.), 1922; Chmn. & Chief Exec., Jaguar Cars Ltd., Daimler Co. Ltd.; Chmn., Coventry Climax Engines Ltd.; Guy Motors (Europe) Ltd.; Henry Meadows Ltd.; Dpty. Chmn., British Leyland Motor Corp. Ltd. Fellow, Royal Soc. Arts. Mbrships. incl: Pres., Fellowship of the Motor Ind., 1957-59; Pres., S.M.M.T., 1950-51; Pres., M.I.R.A., 1954; Pres. Motor Trades Benevolent Fund, 1954; Apptd. Royal Designer for Ind., Royal Soc. Arts. Kt. Bach., 1956. Address: Jaguar Cars Ltd., Coventry, Warwicks, U.K.

LYSEK, Pawel, b. 27 Aug. 1914. Librarian; University Professor. Educ: B.A., Univ. of Cracow, Poland; Birmingham Univ., U.K.; M.A. & M.A.L.S., Kent State Univ., Kent, Ohio, U.S.A. Appts: Educl. Organizer, Polish Min. of Educ., U.K.; Cleveland Pub. Lib., U.S.A.; Assoc. Prof. & Ref. Libn., Queens Coll. Lib., N.Y. Mbrships: Phi Beta Kappa; Polish Inst. of Arts & Scis., N.Y. & London; Polish Writers' Assn. in Exile, London. Publs: Polish Libraries before, during & after World War II (on micro-cards); Poland's Northern & Western Territories, 1973; Novels: Z Istabnej w swiat, 1960; Poszlo na marne, 1965; Przy granicy, 1966; Twarde zywobycie Jury Odcesty, 1970; Marynka cera gajdosza, 1973. Recip., Wiadomosci Award, Polish Acad. in Exile, 1970. Address: 16 Valley View Ct., Huntington, NY 11743, U.S.A.

LYSUN, Gregory, b. 24 Oct. 1924. Artist; Teacher; Picture Restorer. Educ: Art Students League of N.Y.C. Appts: Art Dir., Darthmuthe, Mass., 1951-52; Instr., Painting & Drawing, Westchester Art Workshop, N.Y., 1969-; Y.M./Y.W.H.A., Scarsdale, 1972, New Britain Art League, Conn., 1969-73, Singers Resort Hotel, Spring Valley, N.Y., 1972-. Y.W.C.A., White Plains, 1973-; Chmn., Arts Dept., Fairview-Greenburgh Community Ctr., 1972-. Mbrships: Am. Artists Profl. League; Allied Artists of Am.; Life, Art Students League N.Y.C.; Conn. Acad. of Fine Arts; Guild Hall Artists. Solo exhib., Berkshire Mus., Pittsfield, Mass., 1971; num. grp. exhibs. in U.S.A. Works in collects. of Butler Inst. Am. Art, Ohio, Art Students League, Berkshire Mus., Mass. Portraits commnd. of Murray D. Safanie, Wilmer Wright. Restorer of noted paintings. Recip. of num. art awards. Address: 481 Winding Rd. N., Ardsley, NY 10502, U.S.A. 37.

M

MAAS, Anne G. Physician. Educ: Med. Schl., Leiden, Netherlands; Wilhelmina Gasthuis Univ. Hosp., Amsterdam; Internship, Fla., U.S.A.; Residency in rehabilitation med., Columbia Presby. Hosp., N.Y., ibid. Appts: med. work in phys. rehabilitation & drug addiction, Amsterdam & N.Y. Address: E. Middle Patent Rd., Box 202, Bedford, NY 10506, U.S.A.

MABEY, Richard Thomas, b. 20 Feb. 1941. Writer; Broadcaster. Educ: B.A., St. Catherine's Coll., Oxford, 1960-63; M.A., Oxon., 1971. Appts: Lectr., Soc. Studies, Dacorum Coll. of Further Exuc., 1963-65; Sr. Ed., Penguin Books (Educl. Div.), 1966-73. Mbrships: Coun., Herts. & Middlesex Trust for Nature Conservation; Suffolk Naturalist's Soc.; Norfolk Naturalist's Trust; Royal Soc. for Protection of Birds; Bot. Soc. of Brit. Isles. Publs: The Pop Process, 1970; Children in Primary School, 1972; Food for Free, 1972; The Unofficial Countryside, 1973; The Pollution Handbook, 1974; contbr. articles to var. jrnls. Broadcasts regularly. Address: c/o Richard Scott Simon, Lit. Agts., 36 Wellington St., London WC2E 7BD, U.K.

MABROUK, Ahmed Fahmy, b. 30 Sept. 1923. Research Chemist. Educ: B.Sc., 1945, M.Sc., 1950, Cairo Univ., Egypt; Ph.D., Ohio State Univ., Columbus, U.S.A., 1954; Courses, Mgmt. & Bus. Admin. Appts. incl: Chem., Min. of Agric., Egypt, 1945-46; Instr., Dept. of Gen. & Organic Chem., 1946-48, Agricl. Inds. Dept., 1948-51; Fac. of Agric., Cairo Univ.; Lectr., Assoc. Prof., Agricl. Inds. Dept., ibid, 1955-58; Postdoct. Fellow, 1958-60, Assoc. Rsch. Chem., 1960-61, Am. Meat Inst. Fndn., Univ. of Chgo., Ill., U.S.A.; Proj. Ldr., Rsch. & Prin. Organic Chem., Northern Utilization Rsch. & Dev. Div., Agricl. Rsch. Serv., U.S.D.A., Peoria, Ill., 1961-65; Grp. Ldr., Flavor Chem. Grp., Food Lab., U.S. Army Natick Labs., Mass., 1964-; Abstractor, Chem. Abstracts, 1954-65. Mbrships. incl: Egyptian, Am. & Brit. Chem. Socs.; Sigma Xi; Egyptian Oil & Soap Technols. Assn. (Bd. of Dirs., 1956-60); Ed. Bd., Jrnl., ibid, 1956-60. Contbr., articles in profl. jrnls. Hons: Schol. awards; Scientific Dir.'s Silver Key Award for Rsch., Natick Labs., 1968. Address: Flavor Chemistry Grp., Food Lab., U.S. Army Natick Labs., Natick, MA 01760, U.S.A. 6, 14, 22, 28, 131.

MABROUK, Barbara Elaine, b. 2 Dec. 1927. Physical Therapist. Educ: A.A., Ventura Jr. Coll., Calif., 1948; B.S., Ohio Univ., Athens, 1949; Phys. Therapy course, U.S. Army, Women's Med. Specialist Corp, San Antonio, Tex., 1950-53; M.A., Ohio State Univ., Columbus, 1955. Appts: 1st Lieut., Women's Med. Specialist Corp (P.T.), U.S. Army, 1950-53; Ohio State Univ. Hosp., Columbus, 1953; Ill. Central Hosp., Chgo., 1958; V.A. Hosp., Chgo., Ill., 1959. Recip., B.A., Ohio Univ., Athens, 1950. Address: 9 Wildewood Terr., Framingham, MA 01701, U.S.A. 132, 138.

MCAFEE, Horace J., b. 17 July 1905. Lawyer. Educ: A.B., Southern Meth. Univ., Dallas, Tex., 1926; J.D., Columbia Univ. Law Schl., N.Y.C., 1931. Appts: admitted to N.Y. Bar, 1932; w. Simpson Thacher & Bartlett, attys., N.Y.C., 1931-; Ptnr., ibid, 1944-54; Sr. Ptnr., 1954-; Dir., Sybron Corp., Rochester, N.Y. Mbrships: Assn. of Bar of City of N.Y.; N.Y. State Bar Assn.; N.Y. Co. Lawyers Soc.; Am. Judicature Soc.; Irvington-on-Hudson, N.Y., Zoning Bd. of Appeals, 1951- (Chmn.,

1955-); Pres., Irvington Pub. Lib., 1961-62 (Sec., 1948-61); Ardsley Country Club; Ardsley Curling Club; Marco Polo Club; Downtown Assn.; Tex. Club; Ch. Club of N.Y.C.; Camp Fire Club of Am., N.Y.C. Republican; Episcopalian. Address: Stoneleigh, Mattheissen Park, Irvington-on-Hudson, NY 10533, U.S.A.

McALEECE, Donald John, b. 26 May 1918. University Professor. Educ: Gen. Elec. Co. Machinist-Toolmaker Apprentice Course, 1936-40; Undergrad., Ind. Univ.; B.S.M.E., Purdue Univ., 1952; M.A., Ball State Univ., 1968; Ph.D. candidate, Walden Univ., 1974. Appts: Tool & Die-Maker Journeyman, 1940-42; Tool & Die Designer, 1942-46; Test Engr., U.S. Army, 1946-47; Tool & Methods Planner, 1947-49; Mfg. & Prod. Engr. & Cons., 1952-66; Lectr., Purdue Univ., 1963-66; Asst. Prof., ibid, 1966-70; Assoc. Prof., 1970-74; Engrng. Cons., Franklin Elec. Co., 1970; Adv. Safety Rsch. Cons., Ford Motor Co., 1972. Mbrships. incl: Region VI Off., Am. Soc. Mech. Engrs., 1969-74; Co-Chmn., Campus Film Series Bd., 1969-74; Fac. Advsr., Soc. of Automotive Engr.'s Student Br., 1970-74; Fac. Senate, 1971-74; Fac. Rep., Black Students Affairs Comm., 1969-72; AAUP; Soc. Am. Mill. Engrs.; Pi Tau Sigma. Contbr. to Univ. publs. Hons. incl: R.R. Teetor Award, Soc. of Automotive Engrs., 1972; Outstanding Fac. Advsr. Citation, ibid, 1973. Address: 4426 Dicke Rd., Ft. Wayne, IN 46804, U.S.A. 14, 120.

McALISTER, Michael Ian, b. 23 Aug. 1930. Investment Banker. Educ: Collegio Aldridge, Rio de Janeiro, Brazil; M.A., St. John's Coll., Oxford, U.K., 1954. Appts. incl: Pvte. Sec., H.R.H. The Duke of Windsor, 1959-61; Investment Dir., Ionian Bank, London, U.K., 1961-68; Dpty. Chmn. & Chmn., Slater Walker, Australia, 1969-71; Pres., Australian Stock Exchanges, 1972-. Mbrships. incl: Fellow, Inst. of Mgmt.; Assoc., Securities Inst. of Australia; Inst. of Chartered Accts., England & Wales; Inst. of Chartered Accts., Australia. Publs. incl: Regular contbr. to Financial Press on capital markets, stock exchanges; Contbr. to Australian Stock Exchanges Jrnl. Hons. incl: F.C.A., 1969; F.A.I.M., 1972; A.S.I.A., 1972. Address: 631 Old Northern Rd., Dural, N.S.W., Australia, 2158. 1, 23, 32.

McALISTER, Joseph Charles, b. 25 Aug. 1928. Civil Engineer. Educ: B.C.E., CCNY, 1953; Postgrad., Columbia Univ., 1956-57; Reg. P.E. Va. Appts: Supt., Raymond Concrete Pile Co., 1953-55; Soils & Fndn. Design Engr., U.S. Army Corps Engrs., N.Y. Dist., 1955-57; Chief, Paving Sect., 1957-62; Chief, Fallout Shelter Updating Sect., 1962-63; Constr. Engr., 1963-68; Asst. Area Engr. S. N.J. Area, Wrightstown, N.J., 1968-71; Chief Off. Engr., Sect. Secaucus Area, 1971-73; Civil Engr., Construction-Mgmt. Br., N. Atlantic Div., U.S. Army Corps of Engrs., 1973-; w. AUS, 1946-49. Mbrships. incl: N. Shore Civic Assn.; Civil Congress of S.I.; Rosicrucian Order AMORC; Am. Soc. Civil Engrs.; Pres., Solution to all UN & World Problems Fndn., Inc.; S. Shore Democratic Club; Banner Club. Co-Author, Solutions to all United States & World Problems, 1970. Hons: Sustained Superior Performance Award, C.E., 1963; Suggestion Awards, 1969; Civic Congress of S.I. Achievement Award, 1973. Address: 125 Shirley Ave., Staten Island, NY 10312, U.S.A. 6, 22, 57.

McARTHUR, Estelle Irene (Mrs. Malcolm A. McArthur), b. 1 Apr. 1918. Librarian. Educ: Univ. of Calgary, Canada, 1960-61, 65-66; B.Educ., ibid, 1973; Univ. of Lethbridge, 1969,

71. 73; Medicine Hat Coll., 1969-72. Appts: Dental Asst., Dental Clin., Medicine Hat, 1938-39; Sec., Canadian Pacific Railway, 1940-46; Merrill, Lynch, Pierce, Fenner, Beane, N.Y., 1946-47; Pvte. Sec., J. Demster, Medicine Hat, 1948-56; Pvte. Sec., J.H. Yuill, 1956-58; Co-Owner, New Medalta Caramics, 1958-59; Sec., N.Y. Nitro Chems., 1959-60; Tchr., Medicine Hat Schl. Div. 4, 1961-65; Libn., 1966-; V.P., Malcolm Investments Ltd., Blairmore, 1962-. Mbrships: Sec., Canadian Cancer Soc., 1948-58; Ladies Aux., Medicine Hat Shrine Club; Order of the Eastern Star. Address: 138 First St., S.W., Medicine Hat, Alta., Canada.

MACAULAY, Alice Ittner (Mrs.). Physican. Educ: B.A., Barnard Coll.; M.D., N.Y. Med. Coll., Flower & 5th Ave. Hosps., 1950; Postgrad. studies in Internal Med., N.Y. Univ., 1950; Intern & Res., Grasslands Hosp., 1950-56. Appts: Tchr., Engl. & Speech, N.Y.C. Second. Schls.; Actress, summer stock, Columbia Lab. Players, Old Vic Theatre; Dir., Ambulatory Servs., Grasslands Hosp., 1956-; Physn. i/c. Hypertension Clins., ibid, 1957-; Dpty. Hosp. Adminstr.; Chmn., Pharm. & Therapeutics Comm., Grasslands, 1958-; Hosp. Rep., Comm. on Dev. of Regional Hlth. Ctrs.; Qualified Cons., Internal Med., 1956-; Coord., Home Care Servs., 1957-; Cons. Physn., i/c of Med. Affairs, Westchester Community Coll., 1969-; Chmn., Westchester Heart Assn. Comm. on Hypertension, 1973-. Mbrships: Former Pres., Med. Hon. Soc. & Alpha Sigma Iota; Westchester Acad. of Med.; N.Y. State Med. Soc.; Am. & Westchester Heart Assn.; N.Y. State Lung Soc. Publs: Author or Co-Author of num. articles & tchng. exhibs. on Hypertension, Diabetes Therapy, Pre-menstrual Syndrome & Peripheral Vascular Disease. Address: Hudson House, Ardsley-on-Hudson, NY 10503, U.S.A. 5.

MACAULAY, John Alexander, Q.C. Barrister. Educ: Univ. of Man. & Man. Law Schl., Canada; Called to Bar of Man., 1919. Appts. incl: Mbr., Aikins MacAuley & Thorvaldson, Winnipeg; Pres., Gen. Assets Ltd.; V.P., Canada Safeway Ltd.; Pres., MacDonalds Consolidated Ltd.; Dir., Gtr. Winnipeg Gas Co. Mbrships. incl: Pres., Canadian Bar Assn., 1953-54; Pres., Canadian Red Cross Soc., 1950-51; Chmn., Bd. of Govs., League of Red Cross Socs., Geneva, Switzerland, 1953-65. Hons. incl: K.C., 1931; LL.D., Univ. of Man., 1954; LL.D., Univ. of Winnipeg, 1970; Red Cross received Nobel Peace Prize which he was Pres., 1962; Polonia Restituta; C.C., 1967. Address: 1125 Wellington Cres., Winnipeg, Man., Canada.

MACAULAY, Marion Evelyn, b. 16 Mar. 905. Educator. Educ: B.A., Sydney Univ., Australia; M.Ed., ibid; MACE. Appts: Hd. Mistress & Prin., N. Newtown Infants Demonstration Schl.; seconded Lectr. in Educ. in Tchrs. Colls.; p/t Staff, Univ. of N.S.W. & Lit. Sect. in Adult Educ., Sydney Univ.; Australian Deleg., Int. Confs. of Univ. Women, London, 1953, Karlsruhe, '68; Nat. Coun. Women, Bangkok, 1970, Vienna '73; State Deleg., Australian Confs., ibid. Mbrships: State Sr. V.P., 1964-65, Life Mbr., N.S.W. Univ. Women's Grad. Assn.; Life Mbr., Int. Coun. of Women; Asst. Sec., Nat. Coun. of Women; Life Mbr., State Sr. V.P., 1961-65, NSW NCH; Royal Hist. Soc. of N.S.W.; Life Mbr. & Pres., 973; Past Pres., Hurstville Hist. Soc.; Addtl. Comm., Dunmore Lang. Coll., Macquarie Univ.; Comm. of Convocation, Sydney Univ., 1954- & ndn. Mbr., ibid, Macquarie Univ.; Fndn. Mbr., NSW Chapt., Aust. Coll. of Educ.; Fndn. mbr., Coun. for Educl. Admin.; Convener of Educ.,

Capt. Cook bi-Centenary Pageant of Endeavour. Publs: The Teaching of literature to Young Children (Fisher Lib.); Research on Children's TV (Mitchell Lib.). Recip., Coronation Medal for Educ., 1953. Address: 17 McLeod St., Hurstville, N.S.W., Australia 2220. 23, 138.

MCAULIFFE, Ronald Edward, b. 25 July 1918. Senator, Australian Parliament. Appts: Serv., Australian Army, Middle East & New Guinea, WWII; Senator, Australian Parliament; Mbr., Senate Standing Comms. on Ind. & Trade, For. Ownership & Control, Finance & Govt. Ops.; Chmn., Comm. of Pub. Accounts, Australian Parliament, 1973. Mbrships: Queensland Rugby League; Pres., ibid; Australian Rugby League; Dpty. Chmn., ibid; Australian Labor Party; Convention Deleg., Qld. Br., ibid. Address: Commonwealth Parliament Office, Commonwealth Bank Bldg., 5 Nerang St., Southport, Qld., Australia 4215. 23.

MCAVOY, George Edward, b. 19 July 1920. Hotel Executive; Government Official. Educ: Grad., Geo. Wash. H.S., N.Y.C. Appts: Bell Boy-Mgr., Acheson Hotels, DeWitt & Littleton Hotels, Lewiston, Me., 1940-49; U.S. Army, 1942-46; Pres., Treas., Gen. Mgr., Littleton Hotel Co., N.H., 1949-69; Pres., Littleton Indl. Dev. Corp., 1960-; Agt., Dir., V.P., Peoples Nat. Bank, Littleton, 1965-; Co-ptnr., 1967, Exec. Dir. i/c ops., Crawford House, Crawford Notch, N.H., 1969-72; Pres., Organizer, Crawford Notch Steam Railroad, Inc., 1971-; Mbr.; Gov.'s Staff; Coord. of Fed. Funds, 1973; State Coord. Off. for Disaster, 1972, '73; Commnr., Off. of Manpower Affairs; Chmn., State Histl. Preservation Bd. Num. mbrships. incl: Past Pres., Littleton Chmbr. of Comm.; Past Pres., N.H. Hotel-Motel Assn.; Chmn. of Bd., New England Innkeepers Assn.; Past., Littleton Rotary Club; V.P., White Mtn. Region Assn.; Newcomen Soc.; 32nd deg. Mason; BPOE; Shrine; Hons: Fellow, Pres.' Coun., Am. Inst. of Mgmt., 1970. Address: Bethlehem Rd., Littleton, NH 03561, U.S.A. 6.

McBAIN, Ed. Crime Novelist, See Evan Hunter.

McBAIN, Hugh, b. 7 Dec. 1920. Lecturer; Educator; Writer. Educ: Univ. of St. Andrews. Appts: Locomotive Engr., 1936-41; SET-Instr., R.E. & R.A.E.C., 1941-45; Tchr. & Lectr. in Engl.; Ed., Gleam (mag.) for Glasgow Educ. Auth. Mbrships: Writers Guild of Gt. Britain; Int. PEN; Educ. Inst. of Scotland; Glasgow Soc. of Musicians. Publs: The Undiscovered Country (novel); short stories for mags.; stories, features, talk shows & plays, B.B.C. radio, Glasgow; articles in The Scotsman. Has composed symphonic works, Protergon & Deutergon & piano work, Trigon. Address: 72 Novar Drive, Glasgow, G12 9TZ, U.K. 3.

MACBETH, Norman Lindsay, b. 30 June 1924. Journalist. Educ: M.A., Christ's Coll., Univ. Coll., N.Z. Appts. incl: Messenger boy, The Press, Christchurch, 1941; Subsequently Reporter, Timaru Corres., Commercial Ed., ibid, 1955-64; Asst. Ed., 1965-73; Ed., 1973-; Pt.-time Lectr. in Econs., Lincoln Agricl. Coll., 1964-67; Former Dir., Wood Bros., Ltd., Christchurch (flourmillers) & subsidiary co., Prairie Gold Prods. Ltd. (chicken Processors); Dir. (former Chmn.), Bus. & Econ. Rsch. Ltd., Wellington, & assocd. & subsidiary cos. Mbrships: N.Z. Assn. of Economists; Former Chmn., Christchurch Br., Econ. Soc. of Australia & N.Z.; Former Pres., Old Collegians Cricket Club. Hons: Imperial Rels. Trust Bursary to U.K., 1958; Prize for Econ. Jrnlsm., Commercial Bank of Australia, 1965; U.S. State

Dept. grant, 1966. Address: The Press, P.O. Box 1005, Christchurch, New Zealand.

McBRIDE, Lucia, b. 20 Oct. 1907. Radiographer; Retired Educator. Educ: Mills Coll., Calif., 1927-29; Geneva, Switzerland, 1929-30; Cleveland Coll., 1931-32; B.S., Western Reserve Univ., 1936; Grad. Studies, Iowa State Univ., 1939-40. Appts: Past Tchr., Pub. & Pvte. Schls., Cleveland; Hd., Pre-Schl. Dept., Laurel Schl., ibid, 1936-38; Hd., Brotenahl Nursery Schl., 1941-42; Bd. Mbr., Tchr., Advsr., N.Y.C. Pre-Schl., 1944-50; Radiol. Dept., Roosevelt Hosp., 1948-72; Hd., Beisler Suite X-Ray Dept., 1967-72; Lectr. at Ed. Conventions, W. Reserve Univ. Mbrships. incl: Am. Soc. Radiol. Technols.; Former Mbr., Exec. Bd., N.Y. State Coun. of Roent Ray Technol.; Past Bd. Govs., N.Y. State Soc. Radiol. Technols.; Engl. Speaking Union; AAUW; Am. Assn. Med. Assts.; Pres., & Bd. Mbr., Plato-Pythagorean Coun., Inc.; Fellow, Am. Geog. Soc.; N.Y. Zool. Soc; N.Y.C. Colony Nat. Soc. of New England Women; New Netherland Chapt., DAR; N.Y. Geneal. & Biographical Soc.; Women's Nat. Repub. Club & many others. Contbr. to educl. & sci. jrnls. Address: 264 West 73rd St., New York, NY 10023, U.S.A. 5, 6, 22, 128, 129, 132, 138.

MACCABE, Gladys. Artist; Art Critic; Lecturer; Journalist. Educ: Brookvale Collegiate Schl., Belfast; Ulster Coll. of Art & Design; Var. continental galls. Appts: Lectr., Carnegie U.K. Trust. & Irish Schl. of Landscape Painting; Set Designer, Lyric Theatre, Belfast; Artist, Sunday News, & Belfast News-Letter; Art Critic, Christian Sci. Monitor; Soc. Ed., Ulster Tatler. Mbrships: Royal Inst. of Oil Painters; Fellow, Royal Soc. of Art; Watercolour Soc. of Ireland; Fndr., Past Pres., Ulster Soc. of Women Artists; Past V.P., Royal Ulster Acad.; Writers & Press Club, London; Nat. Union of Jrnlsts. Two-man exhibs, w. husband: London, Dublin, Edinburgh, Belfast; One man exhib: Belfast. Grp. exhibs: Paris Salon; Royal Scottish Acad.; Arts Coun. of N. Ireland; Soc. of Women Artists, London. Num. radio, TV progs. Permanent collects: Imperial War Mus., London; Irish Arts Coun.; Queen's Univ., Belfast; Ulster Mus.; Ulster Folk Mus. Hons: Cert. of Merit for Disting. Work, Bd. of Eds., I.W.W.A.A. Address: 19 Mountcharles, University Rd., Belfast 7, Northern Ireland. 19, 133.

McCABE, Joseph E., b. 23 Apr. 1912. Educator; Clergyman. Educ: A.B., Muskingum Coll., 1937; M.A., Ohio State Univ., 1940; B.Th., Princeton Theol. Sem., 1943; M.Th., 1947; Ph.D., Univ. of Edinburgh, U.K., 1951. Appts. incl: Min., Presby. Ch., Lambertville, N.J., U.S.A. 1946-53; Crict of Student Homiletics, Princeton Theol. Sem., 1951-56; Sr. Min., Presby. Ch., Chestnut Hill, Phila., 1953-58; Pres., Coe Coll., Cedar Rapids, Iowa, 1958-70; Chancellor, ibid, 1970-. Mbrships. incl: Past Pres., Presby. Coll. Union; Past Chmn., Bd., Assoc. Colls. of Midwest; Bd. Trustees, Princeton Theol. Sem. Publs. incl: Challenging Careers in the Church, 1966; Your First Year at College, 1967; Reason Faith & Love, 1972; Better Preaching, Better Pastoring, 1973. Recip., 4 hon. degrees. Address: Coe Coll., Cedar Rapids, IA 52402, U.S.A. 2, 8.

MACCABE, (Robert) Max(well), b. 16 Aug. 1917. Artist; Art Critic; Lecturer. Appts: Art Critic, Are News & Review; Lectr., Carnegie U.K. Trust. & Irish Schl. of Landscape Painting; Set Designer, Lyric Theatre, Belfast, Northern Ireland; Valuer, Wks. of Art. Mbrships: Watercolour Soc. of Ireland. Two-man exhibs. (jointly w.

wife), London, Dublin, Edinburgh, Belfast. Wks. also shown in grp. exhibs., U.K., Repub. of Ireland, Northern Ireland, U.S.A. & Canada, & reproduced in sev. jrnls. Wks. purchased by Ulster Mus. & by num. pvte. persons & firms. Appeared on radio & TV art progs., London, Dublin, & Belfast. Address: 19 Mountcharles, Belfast BT7 1NY, Northern Ireland. 19, 133.

McCABE, Thomas J., b. 28 Nov. 1941. Mathematician. Educ: A.B., Providence Coll. 1964; M.S., Univ. of Conn., 1966; grad. work in computer sci., Univ. of Md. Appts: Capt., U.S. Army Intelligence, 1967-69; Systems Analyst Mathn., Nat. Security Agcy., Ft. Meade, Md., 1969; Adjunct Fac., Howard Community Coll., Columbia, Md., 1970; Cons., Computer Systems & Math. Technol., 1970; Lectr., Inst. for Advanced Technol., Wash. D.C., 1973. Mbrships: Assn. for Computing Machinery; Math. Assn. of Am. Wildlake Tennis Club, Columbia, Md. Contbr. to: NSA Tech. Jrnl. Hons: Burke Mem. Schlrship, R.I., 1960; 1st Place in Computer Info. & Sci. Inst. Essay Contest, 1971; Nat. Crytologic Fellow, 1973. Address: 5380 Mad River Lane, Columbia, MD 21044, U.S.A. 6.

McCAFFREE, Mary Katherine, b. 24 Feb 1933. Physician. Educ: Cottey Coll., Nevada Mo., 1951-52; A.B., Univ. of Mo., Columbia 1956; M.D., Univ. of Mo. Med. Schl., 1963 Intern, St. Luke's Hosp., St. Louis, Mo. 1963-64; Resident Intern Med., Univ. of Mo Med. Schl., 1964-67. Appts: Pract. of Med. specializing in internal med., St. Joseph, Mo. 1967-70, Jefferson City, Mo. 1971-; Mbr. o Staff, Mem. Hosp. Jefferson City, 1971-; Mbr of Staff, St. Mary's Hosp., ibid, 1971-, Staf Sec. 1973-. Mbrships: Am. Coll. Physns.; Am Med. Assn.; Mo. Med. Assn.; Cole Co. Med Assn.; Am. Soc. Internal Med.; Mo. Soc Internal Med.; Southern Med. Assn.; Am. Hear Assn.; Am. Philatelic Soc.; Cole Co. Histl. Soc. Univ. Mo. Alumni Assn.; Delta Delta Delta Publ; Co-Author, Pseudo DNA Autosensitivit in Jrnl. of Am. Med. Assn. Apr. 1966. Address 903A SW Blvd., Jefferson City, MO 65101 U.S.A. 5.

McCAIN, William David, b. 29 Mar. 1907 Archivist; Educator. Educ: B.S., Delta State Coll., 1930; M.A., Univ. of Miss., 1931; Ph.D. Duke Univ., 1935. Appts. incl: Dir., Dept. o Archives & Hist., State of Miss., 1938-55; Pres. Univ. of Southern Miss., 1955-. Mbrships. incl Fndng. Mbr. & Past Pres., Soc. of Am. Archivs (& Fellow); Sec., Bd. of Trustees, Miss. State Dept. of Archives & Hist., 1938-55; Pres., Miss Lib. Assn.; Royal Soc. of Arts; Chmn., Miss Commn., Am. Revolution Bicentennia Commn., 1970. Publs: The US & the Republi of Panama, 1937; The Story of Jackson: A History of the Capital of Miss., 1821-1951 1953; Ed., Jrnl. of Miss. Hist., 1939-56 Co-author, An Outline of Four Generations o the Family of Henry Fox (1768-1852) & Hi Wife, Sarah Harrell Fox (1772-1848) of Sout Carolina & Mississippi, 1971. Recip. of hon. D Litt., Miss. Coll., 1967. Address: Southern Stn. Box 1, Hattiesburg, MS. 39401, U.S.A. 2, 7, 13 15, 121.

McCALL, Charlie Campbell, b. 23 Mar 1895. Lawyer. Educ: Grad., Ga. Mil. Acad 1914; studied Law, Univ. Ala. & privately 1915-17; LL.B., Georgetown Univ., Wash. D.C 1921; LL.M. & M.P.L., ibid, 1922; LL.M. & M.P.L., 1922 & S.J.D., 1936, Nat. Univ., Wash D.C.; LL.M., Am. Univ., 1923; Grad., U.S. Schl Mil. Govt., Univ. Va., 1944; Grad., Personne Mgmt., USAF Schl. Applied Tactics, 1945 Appts: Lt. & Capt., Cavalry, Regular U.S Army, 1917-23; Private Sec. to Congressman

1919-20; Capt. & Maj. Cavalry Reserve, 1920-33; Capt., Judge Advocate, U.S. Regular Army, 1921-24; State Examiner, Pub. Accs., Ala., 1924-26; Maj., Cavalry, Ala. Nat. Guard, 1925-33; State Atty. Gen., 1927-31, & Asst. Atty. Gen., 1931-32, Ala.; Counsellor, Reconstruction Finance Corp., Wash. D.C., 1932-33; Counsel Asst. & Gen. Counsel, U.S. Pub. Works Admin., 1933-48; Acting Gen. Counsel, Puerto Rico Reconstruction Admin., 1937; Maj. & Lt. Col., U.S. Army Reserve & Air Force Reserves, 1942-55; Asst. & Assoc. Gen. Counsel, Fed. Works Agcy., Wash. D.C., 1945-48; Private Law Pract., Ala., 1948-49; Chief Financing Atty., Slum Clearance, Div. Law, Housing & Home Finance Agcy., 1949-58; Special Counsel & Asst., Gen. Counsel, ibid, 1954-58; Private Law Pract., Va., 1959-. Mbrships. incl: Bars of U.S. Supreme Ct., 1926, Ala., 1920, D.C., 1920, Va., 1957; U.S. Ct. of Claims, 1926; U.S. Tax Ct., 1948; Bar Assns. Am., Va., D.C., Birmingham Ala.; Scottish Rite (32) & Shrine; Sigma Nu Phi; Chi Psi Omega; Sec., 1928, Pres., 1929, U.S. Nat. Assn. Attys. Gen. Publs. incl: num. State Statutes, 1932-54; currently working on Scottish Family Hists. Hons. incl: Fac. Prize, Georgetown Univ. Law Schl., 1922; Intercollegiate Debating Prize, Nat. Univ., 1922. Address: 8525 Crestview Drive, Fairfax, VA 22030, U.S.A. 2, 6, 7, 16, 51, 85, 131.

MacCALLUM, Elizabeth Pauline, b. 20 June 1895. Foreign Service Officer. Educ: 1st class Tchng. Cert., Calgary Normal Schl., Alta., Canada, 1916; M.A., Queen's Univ., Kingston, Ont., 1919; grad. study, Columbia Univ., N.Y.C., 1921-22 & 24-25. Appts. incl: Asst. Sec., Soc. Serv. Coun. of Canada & Asst. Ed. 'Social Welfare', 1922-24; Mbr., Rsch. Dept., For. Policy Assn., N.Y., 1925-31; Writing & lecturing for World Peace Fndn. & the League of Nations Assn. in U.S. & League of Nations Soc. in Canada & Canadian Inst. of Int. Affairs, 1935-36; Hd. of Int. Affairs Lit. Serv., League of Nations Soc. in Canada, 1936-40; Helped estab. educl. libs. for Canadian servicemen under auspices of Canadian Legion Educl. Servs., 1940-42; at Dept. of External Affairs, 1942-60 as Specialist in Middle Eastern Affairs; Advsr. to Canadian Delegs. to San Fran. Conf., 1945, the U.N. Gen. Assemblies, 1947, '51, '52, '57; also the 4th World Hlth. Assembly in 1951; temp. duty in Canadian Embassy, Athens, 1951; Charge d'Affaires in Beirut, Lebanon, 1954-56; Histl. Div., 1957-60, 65-67, 71-. Publs: The Nationalist Crusade in Syria, 1929; Rivalries in Ethiopia, 1935; articles in leading newspapers. Recip. var. hons. inclng. LL.D., Queen's Univ., 1952, Officer, Order of Canada, 1972. Address: 145 Clarendon Ave., Ottawa, Ont. K1Y 0R4, Canada. 88.

McCAMPBELL, Virginia Ruth (Mrs. Joe Tilford), b. 29 Mar. 1924. American. Educational Specialist. Commun. Serv.: (past) Neighborhood Chmn., Am. Cancer Soc.; Mbr., Water Safety Comm., Am. Red Cross; Ldr., Girl Scout Trp.; Mbr., Reg. Bd., Lifetime Sports Proj.; Mbr., Defense Advsry. Comm., Women in the Servs., 1967-70; Treas., Pensacola Ladies Golf Conf., 1971-72; (present) Gtr. Pensacola Area Tennis Assn.; Mbr., Naval Reserve, U.S.N.R. Address: (bus) 4321 Skyline Dr., Knoxville, TN 37914, tel. 477-1124; (pvte.) Apt. P-102, 5655 N. 9th, Pensacola, FL 32504, U.S.A.

McCANN, M. Colleen, b. 8 Oct. 1934. Dietitian; Assistant Professor. Educ: B.S., Seton Hall Coll.; Dietetic Intern. Shadyside Hosp., Pitts., Pa.; M.P.H. in Nutrition, Univ. of Pitts. Appts: Student Dietitian, hosps. in Pa.; Chief Dietitian, Lawrence A. Flick State Hosp., Pa.; Dir., Dietetic Intern. Prog., Pa. State Univ.; Dir., Instn. Food Rsch. & Servs. Prog., & Asst. Prof., ibid; Cons., var. instns. & orgs. Mbrships. incl: Var. offs., inclng. Mbr., Nat. Comm. for State Assns., Am. Dietetic Assn.; Am. Pub. Hlth. Assn.; Past Pres., other offs., Pa. Dietetic Assn.; Pres., Ctrl. Pa. Dietetic Assn.; Chmn., Voc. Servs., Altrusa Int.; Mbr., Gov.'s Citizen's Coun. on Status of Women in Pa. Contbr. to profl. jrnls. Hons: Kappa Omicron Phi Award, 1956. Address: Apt. 4, 164 E. McCormick Ave., State Coll., PA 16801, U.S.A.

McCANTS, Jesse Lee, Sr., b. 13 Feb. 1936. Banker; Educator; Urban Planner. Educ: B.S., Ala. State Univ., Montgomery, U.S.A.; M.S., Tenn. State Univ., Nashville. Appts. incl: Tchr., Engl., Hist., & Econs., Pub. Schl. System, Chattanooga, Tenn.; Exec. Dir., Chattanooga Model Cities Prog.; Fndr., Chmn., Bd. of Dirs. & Pres., Security Savings & Loan Assn. of Chattanooga; Asst. Dir., Minority Bus. Dev. Prog., Chattanooga Chapt., Nat. Bus. League; Fndr., Chmn., Bd. of Dirs., & Chief Exec. Off., Peoples Bank of Chattanooga. Mbrships. incl: Gtr. Chattanooga Area Chmbr. of Comm.; Nat. Bankers Assn., Inc.; Tenn. Bankers Assn.; Am. Savings & Loan League; Chmn., Fed. Policy Comm., Chattanooga Chapt., Nat. Bus. League; First Bapt. Ch. of Chattanooga; Big Brothers Assn.; Advsry. Bd., Chattanooga State Area Voc. Tech. Schl.; Kappa Alpha Psi. Hons. incl: Young Man of the Yr. Award, Harrison, Tenn., Jaycees, 1971. Colonelcy, Gov. of Tenn., 1972. Address: 4710 Cordelia Lane, Chattanooga, TN 37416, U.S.A. 125.

McCARLEY, Mack Burl, b. 6 Nov. 1939. Civil Engineer. Educ: B.S.C.E., Univ. of Ala.; further studies, Univs. of Tenn. & Wis. & U.S. Merchant Acad. Appts: Engrng. Staff, Ala. Hwy. Dept., 1960-62; Civil Engr., Div. of Water Control Planning, Tenn. Valley Auth., 1962; Staff Engr., Utility Relocations Staff, ibid, 1965; Asst. Supvsr., Utility Relocation & Records Sect., Maps & Surveys Br., 1966; Supvsr., ibid, 1970; Asst. to Chief, Maps & Surveys Br., 1971. Mbrships. incl: Am. Soc. Civil Engrs.; Tenn. Soc. Profl. Engrs.; Chattanooga Engrs. Club; Tenn. Order of Engr.; Bd. of Dirs., Chattanooga Jaycees, 1969-70; Instr., Am. Red Cross, 1964-; Chi Epsilon. Publs: Staff, Tenn. Valley Engrs., 1963-67. Hons: Presidential Award of Honor, Chattanooga Jaycees; Outstanding Young Mbr., Am. Soc. Civil Engrs., 1970. Address: 207 Haney Bldg., 311 Broad St., Chattanooga, TN 37401, U.S.A. 125.

McCARRAN, (Sister) Mary Margaret Patricia, b. 22 July 1904. Research Historian; College Teacher. Educ: Mus.B., Mount St. Mary's Coll.; B.A., Coll. of Holy Names; M.A., Cath. Univ. of Am.; Ph.D., ibid. Appts: Instr. of Music in Southern & Northern Calif., 1924-46; Assoc. Prof., Hist. & Pol. Sci., Coll. of Holy Names, 1952-63; Lectr., Northern & Southern Calif., 1953-69; Dir. Off. Rsch., Coll. of Holy Names, 1954-; Collector & Ed., Senator Pat McCarran's papers, 1965-; Chmn. of Bd., Washoe State Rehab., 1973-. Mbrships: Nev. Alcoholism Assn. (Fndng. Pres. 1971-73); Ctr. for Study of Presidency; Hispanic Am. Soc.; British Hist. Soc.; Pi Beta Phi; Pi Gamma Mu. Publs. incl: Idea of Progress in Gospel of Wealth, 1945; Fabianism in the Political Life of Britain, 1952; The Fabian Transmission, in Hoover Inst., Stanford, Calif., 1958. Hons: Award of Merit, DAR, 1957; Award for God & Country, Wanderer Forum. Address: McCarran Ranch, Hwy. 80, Via Sparks, NV 89431, U.S.A. 5, 132.

McCART, Warren A., b. 17 Aug. 1926. District Manager, Field Engineering NCR. Educ: Benson Polytech. H.S.; NCR Tech. Serv. Schls.; NCR Mgmt. Courses. Currently Dist. Mgr., Field Engrng. NCR. Mbrships: Chapt. Chmn., Crusade Chmn., Vice Chmn., Am. Cancer Soc.; Past Deacon, Past Elder, W. Park Presby. Ch.; Chief Ranger, Independent Order of Foresters; Rotary Club. Recip. of Award for 25 yrs. w. NCR, 1971 & of Outstanding Achievement Award, Am. Cancer Soc., 1971. Address: 4125 75th St., Urbandale, IA 50322, U.S.A. 130.

McCARTER, Thomas N., III, b. 16 Dec. 1929. Investment Counselor. Educ: Princeton Univ., N.J., 1952. Appts: Sales Exec., Mack Trucks Inc., N.Y.C., 1952-59; Ptnr., Kelly, McCarter, D'Arcy Investment Counselors, ibid, 1959-62; V.P.-Sec.-Dir., D'Arcy, McCarter, Chew, 1962-66; V.P. & Dir., Trainer Wortham Co., Inc., 1967-71; Exec., V.P., 1972-; Pres., 700 Park Ave. Corp., 1965-74; N.Y.C. Chmn., Bd. Trustees, Christodona Fndn., N.Y.C.; V.P. & Charter Trustee, Dalton Schl., N.Y.C.; Trustee, Children's Aid Soc., ibid; Mbr., Pres's. Coun. Mus. of N.Y.C. Mbrships. incl: Cmdr., N.Y. State, Mil. Order Loyal Legion of U.S., 1964-66; Pres. & Trustee, Loyal Legion Fndn., N.Y.C.; Sr. Vice Cmdr., Nat. Cmdng. in Chief, 1972-; various clubs & orgs. Address: 169 E. 78th St., N.Y., NY 10021, U.S.A. 6, 16, 128.

McCARTHY, Edward William, b. 7 June 1920. Chemical Engineer. Educ: B.Chem.E., Polytechnic Inst. of Brooklyn. Appts: Chief Chem., Vulcan Rubber Products, 1938-52; Tech. Dir., Chemprene Inc., 1952-. Mbrships: Nat. Aeronautic Assn.; Tau Beta Pi; Phi Lambda Upsilon; Pres., Dutchess Co. Pilots Assn. Holder 2 U.S. Patents, 1 British Patent. Hons: Purple Heart, 1944; Bronze Star w. Oak Leaf, 1945; N.Y. State Conspicuous Serv. Medal, 1946; Am. Inst. Chemists Medal, 1952. Address: 21 Wasson Dr., Poughkeepsie, NY 12603, U.S.A. 6.

McCARTHY, Mary, b. 21 June 1912. Writer. Educ: B.A., Vassar Coll., 1933. Appts: Ed., Partisan Review, 1937-38, Theatre Critic, 1937-48; Instr. in Lit., Bard Coll., 1945-46; Instr. in Engl., Sarah Lawrence Coll., 1948. Mbrships: Nat. Inst. Arts & Letters (U.S.); Am. Acad. Arts & Scis.; Phi Beta Kappa. Publs: The Company She Keeps, 1942; The Oasis, 1949; Cast a Cold Eye, 1950; The Groves of Academe, 1952; A Charmed Life, 1956; Memories of a Catholic Girlhood, 1957; The Stones of Florence, 1959; On the Contrary, 1961; The Group, 1963; Mary McCarthy's Theatre Chronicles, 1963; The Writing on the Wall, 1970; Birds of America, 1971; The 17th Degree, 1974; The Mask of State: Watergate Portraits, 1974. Hons: Horizon Award, 1949; Guggenheim Fellowship, 1949-50, 1959-60; Nat. Inst. of Letters Grant, 1957. Address: Main St., Castine, MA, U.S.A. 2, 30, 34, 128.

McCARTY, Lois Reeves (Mrs. Fred C. McCarty), b. 3 Nov. 1907. Owner & Operator of women's ready-to-wear business. Appts: Mgr., Millinery Dept., Orange Belt Emporium, Pomona, Calif., 1929-36; Opened own bus., (millinery & lingerie), ibid, 1936; added ladies: ready-to-wear, ibid, 1937; Owner & Operator until 1948; Opened store, Escondido, Calif., 1948. Mbrships: Eastern Star; White Shrine; Pres., Palomar Dist. Womens Club, Calif. Fedn., 1972-74; State Bd., Calif. Fedn. Womens Club, 1972-74; Chmbr. of Comm., 1948-74; Soroptimist Club (org., 3 soroptimist clubs, Riverside, 1948, Escondido, 1949, Vista, 1951; charter Pres., Escondido Soroptimist); Bus. & Profl. Womens Club (Pres., 1935-36); Woman's Club of Escondido (Pres., 1962-63). Address: El Norte Parkway, Escondido, CA 92025, U.S.A. 5, 138.

McCAULEY, William Alexander, b. 14 Feb. 1917. Composer; Conductor. Educ: Mus.B., Univ. of Toronto; Mus.M., Mus.D., Eastman Schl. of Music, Rochester, N.Y., 1960. Appts. incl: Dir. of Music, Crawley Films, Ottawa, 1949-60, O'Keefe Ctr., Toronto, 1960-, N.Y. Univ., 1961-69, Seneca Coll., Toronto, 1970-; Conductor of N.Y. Symph. Orch. 1972-. Compositions incl: Five Miniatures for Flute & Strings; Concerto Grosso for Brass Quintet & Symph. Orch.; Metropolis; Fantasy on Canadian Folk Songs; many choral compositions & arrangements of folk songs; composition of over 160 film scores. Hons. incl: Sr. Fellowship, Canada Coun., 1957; 1st Award, Alba. Centennial Competition for Composition, 1967. Address: 16 Overbank Cres., Don Mills, Ont., Canada.

Mc CAUSLAND, Robert Linsley, b. 27 June 1929. Recreation Director. Educ: B.Sc., W. Va. Univ., 1958; working on deg., Mich. State Univ.; Cert. Camp Dir., Am. Camping Assn. Appts: Dir., Profl. Entertainment Div. (mil.), HQ USAF, Europe, 1951-54; 1st Youth Activities Dir. (civilian), ibid, 1955-60; Exec. Comm., Bd. of Trustees, Leysin Am. Schls., SA., 1960-70; Assoc. Dir., Int. Ranger Camps, 1960-70; Owner, Dir., Village Camps, SA., 1970-. Mbrships: former Pres., European Rec. Soc.; Nat. Rec. & Parks Assn.; Am. Camping Assn.; Int. Rec. Assn.; W. Va. Univ. Recs. Assn. Also semi-profl. wildlife photog., giving lectrs. & displays at mus. in Germany, Switzerland & U.S.A. Hons: Special Citation Award, 1963 & Presidential Citation Award, 1972, both European Rec. Soc. Address: Chalet Seneca, CH-1854 Leysin, Switzerland.

McCAWLEY, Austin, b. 17 Jan. 1925. Psychiatrist. Educ: Grad., Univ. of Glasgow, 1948. Appts: Sr. Clin. Dir., Inst. of Living, Hartford, Conn., 1963-66; Med. Dir., St. Vincent's Hosp., Harrison, N.Y., 1966-72; Dir. of Psych., St. Francis Hosp., Hartford, Conn., 1972-. Mbrships: Fellow, Am. Psych. Assn.; Charter Fellow, Am. Coll. of Psychs. Contbr. to profl. jrnls. Address: 87 Pilgrim Rd., West Hartford, CT 06117, U.S.A. 6.

McCLAIN, Harriett Anderson (Mrs. Jacob J. McClain), b. 17 Mar. 1907. Teacher; High School Counselor. Educ: B.S., Rust Coll.; M.S., Miss. State Univ.; Postgrad. study, Univ. of Ill., Tchrs. Coll., Columbia Univ. Appts. (all in Miss.): Prin., W. Shady Grove, Shiloh, Oak Grove & Pine Grove Elem. Schls.; Asst. Supt. of Women, Rust Coll.; H.S. Counselor, Lexington Attendance Ctr., Lexington. Mbrships: Rust Coll. Alumni Assn.; Life Mbr., Miss. State Univ. Alumni Club; Am., Miss., 3rd Dist., Holmes Co. Tchrs. Assns.; Am., Miss., Personnel & Guidance Assns.; Nat. Retd. Tchrs. Assn.; Sunday Schl. Tchr., Sr. Choir Pres., Asia Bapt. Ch.; Co-chmn., March of Dimes. Author of Rust Coll. band prod., Rusty Toe Joe, Miss. State 1st prize winner; A Field Project, proposed guidance prog. for Lexington Attendance Ctr. Hons: Cert., Initial Schl. Lunch Inst., State of Miss.; Citations, 3rd Dist. Tchrs. Assn., Miss. Tchrs. Assn.-NEA; Plaque, Miss State Alumni Assn. Address: 129 Cemetery St., Lexington, MS 39095, U.S.A.

McCLAIN, Jacob Joshua, b. 14 Jan. 1908. High School Principal. Educ: A.B., Jackson Coll.; B.S., Alcorn Coll.; M.Ed., Univ. of Ill. Appts: Prin., Holy City Elem. Schl., Mt. Zion Elem. Schl.; Veterinarian Instr., Milestone Voc. Schl.; Prin. & Agric. Tchr., Richland Voc. Schl.;

Prin., Lexington (Miss.) Attendance Ctr., 14 yrs., retd. 1973. Mbrships: Nat., Miss. Tchrs. Assns.; Nat., Miss. Assns. of Secondary Prins.; Life, Nat. Retd. Tchrs. Assn.; Am. Assn. of Retd. People; Phi Beta Sigma; Life, Jackson Coll., Alcorn Coll., Univ. of Ill. Alumni Assns. Hons. incl: Miss. & NEA Meritorious Serv. Award, 1972; White House invitation, Pres. Johnson, Congressional Medal of Honor Ceremony; Appreciation for Servs. rendered Holmes Co. Pub. Schls., Lexington Attendance Fac., 1973; Cert. of Appreciation, U.S. Army Recruiting Stn., 1973. Address: 129 Cemetery St., Lexington, MS 39095, U.S.A. 130.

McCLAREN, Adrian Wallace, b. 30 Dec. 1923. English Consultant. Educ: B.A., Lambuth Coll., 1951; M.A., Memphis State Coll., 1956; Postgrad. study, Peabody Coll. for Tchrs., Scarritt Coll., Engl. Inst., Memphis State Univ. Appts: Tchr., Engl., Memphis Schls., 15 yrs.; Tchr., Advanced Placement Engl.; Cons., Engl., Memphis Bd. of Educ. Mbrships: Pres., Tenn. Coun., Tchrs. of Engl.; Past Pres., Tenn., W. Tenn., Memphis Educ. Assns.; NEA; Deleg., Nat. Coun., Tchrs. of Engl.; Sec., V.P., Lions Club Int. Memphis Little Theatre. Contbr. to profl. jrnls. Hons: Winning essays, local papers, 1972; Mbr., Quill & Scroll. Address: 1467 Wilbec St., Memphis, TN 38117, U.S.A. 46, 125.

McCLEAN, Bates DeLos, b. 10 Oct. 1919. Public Relations Officer. Educ: B.S., Temple Univ., 1949. Appts: Corres., United Press Int., 1949-53; Oil Industry Info. Comm., 1953-55; Atlas Powder Co., ICI, 1955-62; E. I. DuPont de Nemours Co., 1962-. Mbr., P.R. Soc. of Am. Address: Parnassus, R.D.1, W. Chester, PA 19380, U.S.A.

McCLEAVE, Mansel Philip, b. 7 Aug. 1926. Baptist Minister; Educator; Author; Poet. Educ: Hampton Inst., Va.; Dip., N.Y. Schl. of Floral Designing; B.S., M.S., Agric. & Tech. Coll. of N.C.; D.D., Friendship Coll., Rock Hill, S.C.; further study, Univ. of N.C., Chapel Hill, & N.C. State Univ., Raleigh. Appts: Instr. of Horticulture & Plant Sci., N.C. Agric. & Tech. State Univ., 1953-; Dir. of Plant Sci. Greenhouses, ibid; Pastor, 1st Bapt. Ch., Silver City, N.C., 1957-70 & Edwards Grove Bapt. Ch., Libert, N.C., 1958-. Mbrships. incl: Vice Moderator, Deep River Missionary Bapt. Assn. of N.C.; Gen. Bd., Gen. Bapt. State Convention of N.C.; AAUP; Comm., Inst. Rep. Boy Scouts of Am.; Advsry. Bd., Home Hlth. Servs., Randolph Co. Hlth. Dept.; Greensboro N.C. Mins. Fellowship; Int. Black Writers Conf.; Fndr./Org., W. Liberty Improvement Assn.; Phi Beta Sigma; Am. Horticultural Soc. Publs: A Scrapbook for Baptist Church Leaders, 1957; The Story of the Deep River Missionary Baptist Association of North Carolina from 1916-61; num. poems & articles. Hons. incl: Plaque, Outstanding Mbr., W. Liberty Improvement Assn., 1973; cited by Town Bd. of Liberty for Outstanding Serv. to Town & Community, 1972. Address: 913 Borders Terr., Greensboro, NC 27401, U.S.A. 125.

McCLELLAND, David Frantz, b. 19 Apr. 1925. Educator. Educ: A.B., Grove City Coll.; M.A., Westminster Coll.; Pa. State Univ.; Univs. of Vt. & Pitts. Appts: Chmn., Dept. of Soc. Sci., Grove City Pub. Schls., 1946-62; Assoc. Prof., Pol. Sci., Grove City Coll., 1962-; Chmn., Dept. of Pol. Sci.; Supvsr., Soc. Sci. Student Tchrs. Mbrships: Am. Pol. Sci. Assn.; N.Y. Acad. of Soc. Scis.; N.Y. Acad. Scis.; Nat. Coun. for Soc. Scis.; Nat. Assn. for Higher Educ.; Pa. Coun. for Soc. Scis.; Omicron Delta Kappa. Hons: John Hay Whitney Fellow, Williams Coll., 1955; Fulbright Tchr., India,

1957; Geo. Wash. Medal, Freedoms Fndn., Valley Forge, Pa., 1959. Address: Crawford Hill, Grove City Coll., Grove City, PA 16127, U.S.A. 6, 14, 22, 57.

McCLELLAND, William Grigor, b. 2 Jan. 1922. Business School Director. Educ: Balliol Coll., Oxford Univ. (lst cl. PPE, 1948); Administrative Staff Coll., Henley. Appts: Dir., Laws Stores Ltd., 1948-; Mng. Dir., ibid, 1950-65; Chmn., 1966-. Sr. Rsch. Fellow in Mgmt. Studies, Balliol Coll., Oxford Univ., 1962-65; Dir., Manchester Bus. Schl., 1965-; Prof. of Bus. Admin., ibid, 1967-. Publs: Studies in Retailing, 1963; Costs & Competition in Retailing, 1966. Address: Manchester Business Schl., Booth St. W., Manchester M15 6PB, U.K. 1.

McCLINTOCK, Bettie Lou Brown (Mrs. Hoyt Mingus McClintock), b. 21 Apr. 1930. Pediatrician. Educ: B.S., Baylor Univ., Waco, Tex., 1952; M.D., Schl. of Med., ibid, Houston, Tex., 1955; Intern., Bethany Hosp., Kan. City, Kan., 1955-56; Pediatric Res., Children's Mercy Hosp., Kan. City, Mo., 1958-60; Dipl., Am. Bd. Pediatrics, 1963. Appts: Pediatrician, McClintock Pediatric Clin., 1960-; Dist. Hlth. Dir., N.M. Hlth. & Soc. Serv. Dept., 1968-. Mbrships: Clovis Mem. Hosp. Med. Staff, 1961-; Sec., N.M. Pediatric Soc., 1970-73; Fellow, Am. Acad. of Pediatrics; AMA; N.M. Med. Soc.; Past Sec., Curry-Roosevelt Co. Med. Soc.; Ctrl. Bapt. Ch. Nursery Comm.; Soroptimist Int. Bus. Womens Club; AAUW. Hons: Outstanding Student Award, HS Graduation, 1948. Address: 1633 Prince St., Clovis, NM 88101, U.S.A. 5, 17, 57, 120, 130, 138.

McCLOSTER, Delena B.T. (Mrs. C. McCloster), b. 31 Aug. 1900. Civic Worker; Protestant Minister. Educ: Ctrl. Tex. Coll., Waco, 1917-19. Appts. incl: Pres., Watts-Willowbrook Coord. Coun., Rays of Sunshine Assn., Watts Chmbr. of Comm., Watts Dist. Co. Hlth. Coun.; Bd. of Dirs., Greater Watts Econ. Dev. Corp., & Community Christian Ch. Urban Dev.; Chmn. of Housing, Citizens Planning Coun.; Instr., Adult Class, Compensatory Educ. Dept., Drew Jr. High Schl. Mbr. of Num. Civic Orgs. inclng: Community Christian Ch. Disciple of Christ, Social Assurance Dev. Ctr. (Pres.); S. Ctrl. Multipurpose Hlth. Servs. Corp. (Chmn., Standing Rules Comm., Past Sec., Past Parliamentarian, & Past Chmn. of Screening Comm. of Bd. of Dirs.); S. Dist. Hlth. Ctr. (Pres.). Contbr. of Articles to var. Newspapers inclng: Star Review News; Pulse. Hons. incl: Outstanding Mother of the Yr., 1968; A.R.C., 1951; Award of Nat. Coun. of Negro Women, 1971; Community Beautiful Award. Address: 9209 Belhaven St., L.A., CA 90002, U.S.A. 5, 138.

McCLOUD, Billy G., b. 25 Jan. 1933. Associate Professor of Music. Educ: A.B., Western Ky. Univ., 1954; M.A., Univ. of Ky., 1961; Additional study at num. Univs. Appts. incl: Supvsr. of Music, Tarrant Schl. System, Birmingham, Ala., 1954; Dir. of Instrumental Music, Jenkins Indp. Schls., Jenkins, Ky., 1956; Dir. of Music, Virgie Schls., Virgie, Ky., 1958; Asst. Prof. of Music, Pikeville Coll., Pikeville, Ky., 1966; Assoc. Prof. of Music, ibid, 1968; Chmn., Music Dept., ibid, 1969; Dir., U.S. Fed. Summer Progs. for Children Aged 12-19, "Cultural Enrichment & Dev.", 1967 & 1968; Guest Instr., App. State Univ., Summers, 1973, 1974. Mbrships. incl: Music Educators Nat. Conf., State Chmn.; Ky. Music Educators Assn., State Bd. of Dirs.; Pike Co. Music Educators Assn., Pres., 1958-65; S.E. Music Educators

Assn., Pres., 1958-60; Eastern Ky. Music Educators Assn., Pres., 1964-68, 1972-75; Pikeville Concert Assn., V.P.; Jenny Wiley Drama Assn., Bd. Dirs.; Pikeville Lions Club, Bd. Dirs.; Phi Delta Kappa, 1964-; NEA; AAUP; Ky. Educ. Assn.; Christian Ch., Mbr., Deacon, Bd. Mbr. & Pianist. Hons. incl: Ky. Col. Appts., 1963; Pikeville Coll. Disting. Fac. Award, 1972. Address: 150 Park St., Pikeville, KY 41501, U.S.A. 125.

McCLURE, Denis, b. 23 Apr. 1914. Management Consultant. Educ: New Zealand Coll. of Pharm.; Auckland Univ. Appts: Var. offs., Pharm. Mgmt., 1936-39; Indl. Chem., McSkimming Inds., Ltd., 1939-42; Sgt., Med. Corp., N.Z. Army, 1942-43; Chief Chem., Consolidated Brick & Pipe Investments, Ltd., 1943-45; Tech. Mgr., ibid, 1945-50; Prin., D. McClure & Assocs., Mgmt. Consultants, Auckland, 1950-; Governing Dir., McClure Rsch. Servs., Ltd., ibid, 1955-. Mbrships: Hon. Fellow, N.Z. Inst. of Mgmt.; Past Auckland Pres., Past Nat. Pres., Educ. Liaison Off., Nat. Grading Comm., Nat. Educ. Comm., Exec. Comm., Auckland, & other offs., ibid; Hon., Assoc., N.Z. Inst. of Chem.; Councillor, Inst. of Mgmt. Consultants, N.Z.; Past V.P., ibid; Corporate, Am. Mgmt. Assn.; Exec. Mgmt. Club, N.Z.; Assoc., Brit. Inst. Mgmt.; Pharmaceutical Soc., N.Z.; Former, Univ. Appts. Bd., Auckland; Mbr. & Former Elder, Mt. Albert Bapt. Ch., ibid; Former, Creative Educ. Fndn., U.S.A.; YMCA, Auckland, N.Z. Publs: Edits. for Modern Manufacturing; Former ed., Contbr. of papers & edits., Management Mag.; Special Corres., var. jrnls. Address: P.O. Box 15-036, Auckland 7, New Zealand. 38.

McCONAGHY, Joseph William, b. 11 Aug. 1932. Health Administrator; Certified Public Accountant. Educ: B.S., Fordham Univ., 1960; M.P.H., Univ. of Mich., 1974; U.S. For. Serv. Inst. 1964-65. Appts: Corporate Officer, sev. small businesses, 1956-64; Supvsr., Chase Manhattan Bank, 1957-60; Sr. Staff Mbr., Price Waterhouse & Co., 1960-64; U.S. For. Serv. Officer, 1964-70; Sr. Corp. Auditor, United Fruit Co., 1970-72; Dir., Fiscal Affairs, RCCHC (BU Med. Ctr.), 1972-73; Admnstr., ibid, 1973-. Mbrships: Am. Inst. CPAs; N.Y. State Soc. CPAs; Nat. Assn. Accts.; Nat. Assn. Neighborhood Hlth. Ctrs. Hons: Vietnam Civilian Serv. Award, 1969; Schlrship, Univ. of Mich. Schl. of Pub. Hlth., 1972, 73, 74. Address: P.O. Box 56, Scituate, MA 02066, U.S.A. 6, 22, 128, 130.

MacCONNAILL, Michael Aloysius, b. 27 July 1902. Professor of Anatomy. Educ: M.B., B.Ch.; B.Sc., M.Sc., D.Sc., Queen's Univ. of Belfast; M.A., Nat. Univ. of Ireland. Appts: Demonstrator in Anatomy, Queen's Univ., Belfast, 1927-29; Lectr., Univ. of Sheffield, 1930-42; Prof., Univ. Coll., Cork, 1942-73, Prof. Emeritus, 1973-; Vis. Lectr., Eastern Canadian Med. Schls., 1966; Vis. Prof., Ghana Med. Schl., 1968. Mbrships: incl: Sr. Fellow, British Orthopaedic Assn.; Fellow, Royal Anthropological Inst.; Royal Irish Acad. Publs. incl: An Cholann Bhes., 1949; Synovial Joints, 1961; Muscles & Movements, 1969. Var. publs., anatomy, anthropol., biomechanics, anthropaedic surg., Irish, Engl., French, Spanish, Italian. Hons. incl: Med. Travelling Studentship, Queen's Univ., Belfast, 1929. Address: 19 Bishopscourt Dr., Bishopstown, Cork, Repub. of Ireland.

McCONCHIE, Edwin Max, b. 24 June 1918. Civil Servatn. Educ: B.A. (Hons)., Trinity Coll., Univ. of Melbourne, 1949; postgrad. studies, London Univ. of Melbourne, 1949; postgrad.

studies, London Univ., 1950-51. Appts: Asst. Dist. Off., H.M. Colonial Serv., Nigeria; Asst. Sec., Fed. Pub. Serv. Commn., Nigeria; Asst. Sec., Min. of Natural Resources, Nigeria; subsequent posts at Nigerian Min. of Labor & Welfare, & Min. Transport; Nigerian Exchange Control Off., Min. of Finance; British Vice-Consul to Spanish Guinea at Fernando Pó; Asst. Sec., Australian Dept. of Educ. & Sci.; ex-officio member of sev. Commonwealth Advsry. Comms. Mbrships: Australian Coll. of Educ; Southern Cross Club, Canberra. Address: Dept. of Education, Phillip Offices, Canberra A.C.T., Australia. 23.

McCONICA, James Kelsey, b. 24 Apr. 1930. Historian Educ: B.A., Univ. of Sask., Canada, 1951; B.A., Oxford Univ., U.K., 1954; M.A., ibid, 1957; D.Phil., 1953; M.A., Univ. of Toronto, Canada, 1964. Appts. incl: Entered Congregation of St. Basil, Ont., 1964; ordained to priesthood, 1968; Assoc. Prof., Pontifical Inst. of Medieval Studies, Toronto, 1967; Prof., ibid, 1971-; Prof. of Hist. of Ideas, Ctr. for Medieval Studies, Univ. of Toronto, 1971-; Assoc. Dir., ibid, 1973-. Mbrships. incl: Fellow, Royal Histl. Soc.; Am. Histl. Assn.; Renaissance Soc. of Am.; Mbr. of Coun., Am. Soc. for Reformation Rsch., 1973-; Canadian Assn. of Rhodes Schols.; Coun. mbr., Oxford Histl. Soc., 1970-. Author of books & articles in field. Recip. of hons. Address: Pontifical Inst. of Mediaeval Studies, 59 Queen's Park Crescent, Toronto, Canada, M5S 2C4. 6, 13, 30.

McCONNELL, Glenn B., b. 10 Mar. 1901. Retired Colonel, College Professor. Educ: B.S., U.S. Mil. Acad., 1924. Appts: 2nd Lt., U.S. Army, 1924; advanced to Col., ibid, 1942; Retd., 1954; Coll. Prof., 1956-; Asst. Prof., Dept. of Engr. Graphics, Coll. of Engrg., Iowa State Univ.; retd., 1971. Mbrships. incl: Assn. of Grads., U.S. Military Acad. Address: 1425 Harding Ave., Ames, IA 50010, U.S.A. 8.

McCONNELL, James Robert, b. 25 Feb. 1915. Senior Professor. Educ: M.A., Univ. Coll., Dublin, 1936; B.C.L. (Canon Law), S.T.L. (Theol.), Lateran Univ., Rome, Italy, 1936-40; D.Sc. Mat., Royal Univ. of Rome, 1941; D.Sc. (on publd. work), Nat. Univ. of Ireland, 1949; Ordained, Priest Roman Cath. Ch., 1939. Appts: Prof., Mathl. Phys., Maynooth, 1945-68; Vis. Prof., Fordham.Univ., N.Y., U.S.A., 1959-60, Laval Univ., Quebec, Canada, 1964, SUNY, Stony Brook, U.S.A., 1973; Sr. Prof., Theoretical Phys., Dublin Inst. Adv. Studies, 1968-. Mbrships: Royal Irish Acad., 1949-, (Sec., 1967-72, V.P., 1972-73); Corresponding, Inst. de Estudios Avanzados, Cordoba, Argentina, 1968-; Rep. of Ireland, Int. Math. Union, 1962, Int. Union of Pure & Applied Phys., 1966; Fellow, Brit. Inst. of Phys., 1968-; Fndr. Mbr., 1st Coun., European Phys. Soc., 1968-70. Author, Quantum Particle Dynamics, (2 edits. & Russian translation), 1958; 40 rsch. papers, theoretical phys. & maths. Address: Dublin Inst. for Adv. Studies, 10 Burlington Rd., Dublin, 4, Ireland. 50.

McCORISON, Marcus Allen, b. 17 July 1926. Librarian. Educ: A.B., Ripon Coll, Wis., 1950; M.A., Univ. of Vt., Burlington, 1951; M.S., Schl. of Lib. Serv., Columbia Univ., 1954. Appts: Chief of Rare Books, Dartmouth Coll. Lib., 1955-59; Hd. of Special Collections, Univ. of Iowa, 1959-60; Libn.-Dir., Am. Antiquarian Soc., Worcester, Mass., 1960-. Mbrships. incl: Chmn., Independent Rsch. Libs. Assn.; Treas., Bibliographical Soc. of Am.; Am. Antiquarian Soc.; Mass. Historical Soc.; Org. of Am. Histns.; Beta Phi Mu. Publs: Vermont Imprints, 1778-1820, & supplements, 1968-73; The 1764 Catalogue of the Redwood Library Company of

Newport, Rhode Island; Ed., The History of Printing in America, by Isaiah Thomas. Num. contbns. in learned jrnls. Address: Am. Antiquarian Soc., 185 Salisbury St., Worcester, MA 01609, U.S.A. 2, 6, 13.

McCORMICK, William Edward, b. 9 Feb. 1912. Industrial Hygienist. Educ: B.S., Pa. State Univ., 1933; M.S., ibid, 1934. Appts: H.S. Tchr., Centre Hall, Pa., 1935-37; Rsch. Chemist, Willson Products Inc., Reading, Pa., 1937-43; Army Capt., Commissioned Corps, U.S. Pub. Hlth. Serv., 1943-46; Ga. Dept. of Pub. Hlth., Atlanta, 1946; Mgr., Environmental Control, B.F. Goodrich Co., Akron, Ohio, 1946-73; Mng. Dir., Am. Indl. Hygiene Assn., ibid, 1973-. Mbrships: Am. Indl. Hygiene Assn.; Pres., ibid, 1964; Am. Chem. Soc.; AAAS; Ruber & Plastics Sect., Nat. Safety Coun.; Past Gen. Chmn., ibid; F. & A.M., Scottish Rite, Shrine. Publs: Num. articles in Indl. Hygiene in profl. jrnls. Address: American Industrial Hygiene Association, 66 S. Miller Rd., Akron, OH 44313, U.S.A. 8, 128.

McCOWN, Hilda Rainey (Mrs. John Robert McCown), b. 11 May 1914. Homemaker. Educ: Grad., Anderson Coll., S.C. Active in Farm Bur. for nearly 30 yrs. Mbrships. incl: Pres., Lake Co. W.M.U., 5 yrs.; Pres., Clermont (Fla.) Woman's Club, 3 yrs.; Pres., Bapt. Women, 1st Bapt. Ch., 5 yrs.; Chmn., Fla. Farm Bur. Fedn. Women; Sec., Daughters of Confederacy; Charter Mbr., Wives' Club, Retd. Offs.' Assn.; Charter Mbr., V.P., Clermont Garden Club; Continues to participate in num. other soc., relig., educl. & hlth. orgs. Hons: United Appeal Award; Disting. Serv. Award, Kiwanis Int.; Nat. Policy Bd., Leadership Fndn., Wash., D.C. Address: 475 Minnehaha Ave., Clermont, FL 32711, U.S.A. 125.

McCOY, John Roger, b. 11 June 1916. Veterinarian. Educ: Undergrad. Coll., Rutgers Univ., 1934-35; V.M.D., Profl. Schl., Univ. of Pa., 1940. Appts. incl: Sr. Veterinary Insp., N.J. Bur. of Animal Ind., Trenton, N.J., 1947-48; Rsch. Prof., Bur. of Biological Rsch., Rutgers Univ., N.B., N.J., 1950-70; Adjunct Rsch. Prof., ibid, 1970-; Prof., Comparative Pathol., & Dir. of the Vivarium, Coll. of Med. & Dentistry of N.J., Rutgers Med. Schl., Piscataway, N.J., 1970-; Cons. to var. pharmaceutical, food & cosmetics mfrs. Mbrships. incl: House of Delegs., Am. Veterinary Med. Assn., 1959-63; Exec. Bd., ibid, 1963-69; Chmn., of Bd., 1966-69; Pres.-elect, 1970-71; Pres., 1971-72; Select Comm. on GRAS Substances, Fedn. of Am. Socs. for Experimental Biol.; AAAS; Am. Animal Hosp. Assn.; Am. Assn. of Lab. Animal Sci.; Am. Veterinary Radiol. Soc.; Am. Pub. Hlth. Assn.; AAUP; Int. Soc. for Comparative Leukemia Rsch. Author of articles in field. Recip. of hons. Address: 1007 River Rd., Piscataway, NJ 08854, U.S.A. 6, 14, 28.

McCOY, Ralph E., b. 1 Oct. 1915. Librarian. Educ: A.B., Ill. Wesleyan Univ., 1937; B.S.L.S., Univ. of Ill., 1939, M.S., 1950, Ph.D., 1956. Appts. incl: Asst. Libn., Coll. of Agric., Univ. of Ill., 1938-39; Ed. of Publs. and Admin. Asst., Ill. State Lib., Springfield, 1939-43; Libn., Q.M. Tech. Lib., Ft. Lee, Va., 1946-48; Libn. (Asst. Prof.), Inst. of Labor & Indl. Rels., Univ. of Ill., 1948-55; Dir. of Libs., Southern Ill. Univ., Carbondale, 1955-70; Dean of Lib. Affairs, ibid, 1970-. Mbrships. incl: ALA; Assn. of Coll. & Rsch. Libs., Pres., 1966; Ill. Lib. Assn., Pres., 1960; Ill. State Histl. Soc., Bibliographical Soc. of Am., Beta Phi Mu; Phi Kappa Phi; AAUP: UN Assn. Publs. incl: Freedom of the Press; An Annotated Bibliography, 1968; Theodore Schroeder, A

Cold Enthusiast, 1973; Personnel Administration for Libraries, 1953. Hons. incl: First annual award, Ill. Lib. Assn., 1961; Intellectual Freedom Award, ibid, 1969; Scarecrow Press Award, ALA, 1969; Joseph L. Andrews Bibliographic Award, Am. Assn. of Law Libs., 1969. Address: 1902 Chautauqua St., Carbondale, IL, U.S.A. 2, 13.

McCOY, Robert Baker, b. 26 Mar. 1916. Book Publisher. Educ: B.S. & M.S., Northwestern Univ., Chgo., 1945-52. Appts. incl: Employee, U.S. Govt. Civil Serv., 1940-53; Exec. Ed., Book Dept., Popular Mechanics Magazine Co., 1953-59; Mng. Ed., H.S. Text Books, J.B. Lippincott Co., Chgo., 1959-60; Publng. Cons., Loyola Univ. Press, ibid, 1959-60; Exec. Dir., H.S. Text Books, Lyons & Carnahan, 1960-62; Pres. & Chmn. of the Bd., Rio Grande Press, Inc., H.Q., N.M., 1962-. Mbrships: Hist. Socs. of Tex., Ariz., N.M., Calif. & Colo.; Nat. Honor Soc., 1935; Westerners Int. Publs. incl: many men's mags., e.g. Argosy & Esquire & scholastic jrnls.; also contbr. of non-fiction articles. Address: The Rio Grande Press, Inc., La Casa Escuela, NM 87535, U.S.A.

McCOY, Wilda Anderson (Mrs. Kenneth E. McCoy), b. 9 Dec. 1916. Educator. Educ: B.A., La. State Univ., Baton Rouge, 1937; M.Ed., Nicholls State Univ., Thibodaux, 1970; Tulane Univ., New Orleans, 1971. Appts: Tchr., Jefferson Davis Parish, Fenton & Elton, La., 1937-41; Tchr., Indian Serv., U.S. Govt., 1942-46; Elem. Tchr., Starkville & McComb, Miss., 1947-55; Elem. Tchr., E. Baton Rouge & Jefferson Parishes, La., 1955-69; Asst. Prin., Elem. schl., Jefferson Parish, 1969-71; Prin., Norbert Rillieux Elem. Schl., 1971-. Mbrships. incl: NEA; Miss. Educ. Assn.; La. Tchrs. Assn.; La. Educ. Assn.; Int. Reading Assn.; Prins. Assn.; AAUW; Bus. & Profl. Womens Club; Am. Red. Cross; 4-H Club Ldr.; La. Coop. Ext. Home Econ. Advsry. Comm.; La. Coop. Ext. Advsry. Bd. for Nutrition Prog. Address: 141 Oak Ave., Westwego, LA 70094, U.S.A. 130.

McCOY, William Reuben, b. 2 July 1940. Civil Engineer. Educ: B.S.C.E., Clemson Univ., S.C., U.S.A., 1962; M.S., ibid, 1963. Appts: Capt., U.S. Pub. Hlth. Serv. Commn. Corps, 1963-65; Proj. Engr., Lyon Assocs., & AAEOI, S.-E. Asia, 1966-67; Pres. & Treas., Enwright Assocs., Inc., Greenville, S.C., 1974; Vice Chmn., S.C. Sect., Profl. Engrs. in Pvte. Prac.; Nat. Soc. of Profl. Engrs.; Master Mason. Address: Enwright Associates, Inc., P.O. Box 5287, Station B, Greenville, SC 29607, U.S.A. 7.

McCRACKEN, Jarrell F., b. 18 Nov. 1927. President of Word, Inc. Educ: B.A., Baylor Univ., 1950; M.A., ibid, 1953. Appts: worked way thru' schl. by working at local radio stan.; began co., then called World Records, in 1951, to meet requests for recordings of a talk, The Game of Life, in which he combined his ministerial interests w. his interest in sportscasting by backing a talk on the battle between good & evil w. sound effects; Co. incorporated, & div., Word Books, added, 1961; Other divs. Sacred Songs & Word Tours. Mbrships: Bd. of Dirs., Waco Chmbr. of Comm., San Marcos Acad., & Baylor Univ. Ex-Students Assn.; Chmn., Civic Affairs, Waco Advancement Comm.; V.P., Youth for Christ Int.; Pres., Record Ind. Assn. of Am.; Former Pres., Waco Symph. Assn.; Dir., Waco YMCA & Nat. City Bank. Hons: LL.D., John Brown Univ., 1969; Outstanding Young Man in Waco, 1961; one of Five Outstanding Young Men in Tex., 1961. Address: c/o Word, Inc., P.O. Box 1790, Waco, TX 76703, U.S.A.

MacCRACKEN, Nell Elizabeth, b. 7 Jan 1934. Travel Industry Executive. Educ: Univ. of Tex., 1951-52; Am. Univ., 1952-53; Cours de Civilisation Française, Sorbonne, Paris France, 1953-54; Univ. of Mexico, summer, 1954. Appts: Special Travel Cons., Van Slycke & Reeside Travel, 1960; Asst. to Pres.,Ober Travel, 1960-62; V.P., Dupont Travel Serv., 1962-64; Travel Cons., Georgetown Travel Serv., 1964-66; Coord. for Special Tours, Ambassador Travel, 1967-69; V.P., now Pres., & Owner, Crystal World Travel, 1969-. Mbrships: Sec., Regional coll. Serv. Comm., Young Repub. Nat. Fedn., States of Tex., Ark., La., Miss. & Panama Canal Zone, 1951; Bd. of Dirs., Wash. Ballet Guild, 1957-60; Archaeol. Inst. of Am., 1971-; Am. Soc. of Travel Agents, 1971; Arlington Chmbr. of Comm.; African Safari Club; Bd. of Dirs. Travel Agents United, 1973-; Soroptimist Int.; Oriental Inst., Univ. of Chgo., 1974-. Hons: Cert., D.C. Fedn. Women's Clubs, 1958; Cert. of Award for outstanding Serv., Int. Eye Fndn., 1969. Address: The Wyoming, 2022 Colombia Road, N.W., Washington DC 20009, U.S.A.

McCRANEY, Willard Kary, b. 4 Aug. 1904. Public Accountant. Educ: B.A., La. Coll., Pineville, 1927; Special Courses, Higher Acctcy. Mbrships: Nat. Soc. Pub. Accts. (Asst. State Dir., Mbr. By-Laws Comm.); Tex. Assn. Pub. Accts. (Past-Pres. & Past-Pres. E. Tex. Area); Assn. of Schl. Bus. Officials of U.S.A. & Canada; Tex. Assn. Schl. Bus. Officials; Exchange Club, Tyler, Tex. (Past-Pres.); Kts. of Phthias (Past Chancellor Cmdr., Tyler Chapt.); Bapt. Ch. (Past Pres. N.-E. La. Trng. Union Convention). Publs: Contbng. Author, Portfolio of Accounting Systems for Small & Medium Sized Businesses. Address: P.O. Box 896, Tyler, TX 75701, U.S.A. 7, 125.

McCRARY, Mary Jane King (Mrs. Carl McCrary), Realtor; Historian. Educ: Furman Univ. (formerly Greenville Women's Coll.); Grad., Tift Coll., 1918. Appts: Tchr. of Pub. Schl. Music, Brevard Schls., 1923-25; Owner & Mgr., Walker Ins. Agcy., 1928-52; Realtor. Mbrships: Nat. Real Estate Bd.; Brevard Realtors; Blood Chmn., Transylvania Red Cross; N.C. Am. Revolution Bicentennial Comm.; Chmn., Transylvania Co. Hist. Commn., 1960-73; Brevard Music Lovers Club; League of Am. Pen Women; Western N.C. Hist. Assn. Publs: History of St. Philip's Episcopal Church, 1959; History of Transylvania County, 1973. Recip. Blue & Purple Ribbons for paintings & ceramics. Address: 228 Maple St., Brevard, NC 28712, U.S.A. 7.

McCREA, William Hunter, b. 13 Dec. 1904. Emeritus Professor of Astronomy. Educ: Trinity Coll., Cambridge, 1923-28; M.A., Ph.D., Sc.D., Cambridge; Univ. of Göttingen, 1928-29. Appts. incl: Prof. of Maths., Queen's Univ., Belfast, 1936-44; Prof. of Maths., Royal Holloway Coll., Univ. of London, 9144-66; Rsch. Prof., Theoretical Astronomy, Univ. of Sussex, 1966-72; Emeritus Prof., ibid, 1972-. Mbrships: Fellow, Royal Soc., 1952-; Royal Irish Acad., 1939-; Fellow, Royal Soc. of Edinburgh, 1931-; Fellow, Royal Astronomical Soc., 1929-; Sec., ibid, 1946-49; Pres., 1961-63; For. Sec., 1968-71; Pres., Math. Assn., 1973-74; Pres., Sect. A., British Assn., 1966; Fellow, Imperial Coll. of Sci. * Technol., 1967-; Deutsche Akademie der Naturforscher Leopoldina, 1972-. Publs: Relativity Physics, 1935; Analytical Geometry of Three Dimensions, 1942; Physics of the Sun & Stars, 1950; The New Cosmos, by A Unsöld, translation 1969. Contbr. to num. sci. jrnls. Recip. of hons. Address: 87 Houndean Rise, Lewes, Sussex BN7 1EJ, U.K. 1.

McCREADY, Warren Thomas, b. 8 Feb. 1915. Professor. Educ: M.A., Univ. of Chgo., 1949; Ph.D., ibid, 1961. Appts: Lectr., Ind. Univ. (Gary Ctr.), 1950-53; Queen's Univ., Kingston, Ont., Canada, 1954-56, Univ. of Toronto, 1956-60; Asst. Prof., ibid, 1960-64; Assoc. Prof., 1964-69; Prof. of Spanish, 1969-. Mbrships: Canadian Assn. Hispanists; Assn. Int. de Hispanistas; Am. Assn. Tchrs. of Spanish & Portuguese; Am. Cryptogram Assn. (V.P., 1961-62; Pres., 1962-63). Publs. incl: La heraldica en las obras de Lope de Vega y sus contemporaneos, 1962; Bibliografia tematica de estudios sobre el teatro antiquo espanol, 1966; Lope de Vega: El mejor mozo de Espana, 1967. Address: Dept. oj Hispanic Studies, Univ. of Toronto, Toronto, Ont., M5S 1AI, Canada. 6, 13.

McCREDIE, Hugh George, b. 30 June 1921. Accountant; Secretary. Educ: LL.B., Univ. of Sydney, Australia, 1948. Appts: Asst. Registrar, Univ. of Sydney, 1950-59; Pt.-time Lectr., ibid, 1954-60; Dpty. Registrar, 1960-67; Registrar, 1967-72; Sec., 1972. Mbrships: Fellow, Australian Soc. Accts., Chartered Inst. Secs. & Admnstrs.; Assoc. Australasian Inst. Cost Accts.; Hon. Sec., N.S.W. Rhodes Schlrship. Selection Comm.; Sec., Rothmans Univ. Endowment Fund; Hon. Treas., Dunmore Lang Coll., Macquarie Univ., Wesley Coll., Sydney Univ.; Australian Comm. on Profl. Qualifications, Generalist Sect.; Pres., Australian Univs. Sports Assn., Univ. of Sydney Sports Union, 1961, '62. Contbr. of articles to profl. jrnls. Recip., Carnegie Travelling Schlrship., Brit. Coun. Schlrship., 1963. Address: Univ. of Sydney, N.S.W., Australia 2006.

McCULLOCH, Etta S. Smith, b. 23 Nov. 1912. Nurse; Educator. Educ: State Tchrs. Coll., Bloomsbury, Pa.; Mt. Sinai Hosp. Schl. of Nursing, N.Y.C.; B.S., Fla. State Univ., Tallahassee; M.S., ibid; Doctoral candidate, to be completed 1974. Appts: Gen. Duty, Hd. Nurse, Asst. Night Supvsr., O.B. Supvsr., Dir. of Nursing, Parkchester Gen. Hosp., N.Y.C., 7 yrs.; Dir. of Nursing, Westchester Square Hosp., Bronx, N.Y., 8 yrs.; Instr., Orange Co. Voc. Schl. of Practical Nursing & Hd., Dept. of Hlth. Occupation, 12 yrs. Mbrships: Past Pres., Orlando Chapt., Altrusa Int.; Past Pres., Dist. 14 7NA. Am. Nursing Assn.; N.L.N.; A.V.A.; NEA (now UTP); Iota Lambda Sigma. Author of Accountabiﬁty in Practical Nursing Education, a 10 yr. follow up study of 496 grads. of 1 schl.; Inventor of process of Terminal Sterilization of Infant Formula. Recip., Nat. Salute for Pioneering Within Nursing, O.R. Reporter, 1970. Address: 717 Lake Shore Dr., Eustis, FL 32726, U.S.A. 5, 125, 138.

McCULLOUGH, John Phillip, b. 2 Feb. 1945. Educator. Educ: B.S., Ill. State Univ., 1967; M.S., 1968; Ph.D., Univ. of N.D., 1971; Cert. Data Educr., 1972; Cert. Bus. Educr., 1973. Appts. incl: Grad. Rsch. Asst., Univ. of N.D., 1969-71; Asst. Prof., Bus., W. Liberty State Coll., 1971-72; Assoc. Prof., Mgmt., ibid, 1972-; Chmn., Dept. of Mgmt. & Admin. Systems, 1974-; Ajd. Assoc. Prof., Bus., Wheeling Coll., 1972; Lectr., Bus., W. Va. Univ., 1972; Lectr., Bus., W. Va. Northern Community Coll., 1972-; Instr., Am. Inst. of Banking, 1971-. Mbrships. incl: Past Pres., Delta Pi Epsilon; Chapt. Advsr., Alpha Kappa Psi; Delta Mu Delta; Exec. Comm., Soc. for Humanistic Mgmt.; Ctrl. Unit Exec., Cath. Bus. Educ. Assn.; Dir., Special Insters Grp. for Cert. Bus. Educrs. Publs: American Business Law Concepts in the Code of Canon Law, 1972; Primer in Supervisory Management, 1973. Hons. incl: Alpha Kappa Psi Disting. Serv.

Award, 1973; Alpha Kappa Psi Civic Award, 1974. Address: Dept. of Management of Admin. Systems, W. Liberty State Coll., W. Liberty, WV 26074, U.S.A.

McCULLOUGH, Roland Alexander, b. 29 Nov. 1917. Banker. Educ: A.B., Wofford Coll., Spartanburg, S.C., 1939; A.M., 1942. Appts. incl: Mng. Ed., Spartanburg Herald-Jrnl., 1944-50; Asst. to Gov. James F. Byrnes of S.C., 1950-54; Admin. Asst. to U.S. Senator Strom Thurmond, Wash. D.C., 1955-57; V.P.-Sr. V.P., S.C. Nat. Bank, 1957-69; Mbr., Bd. Dirs., Export-Import Bank of the U.S., 1969-. Mbrships. incl: Am. Soc. Newspaper Eds.; Pres., S.C. Assoc. Press Mng. Eds. Assn., 1958; S.C. Press Assn.; Assoc., S.C. Broadcasters Assn., 1957-69; Assoc. Press Mng. Eds. Assn.; Past, Bank Mktng. & P.R. Assn.; Past, P.R. Soc. Am.; State Chmn., Fndn. for Commercial Banks, 1960; Past V.P. & Dir., James F.Byrnes Fndn.; U.S. Chmbr. of Comm. Address: 7711 Bridle Path Lane, McLean, VA 22101, U.S.A. 2, 7, 16, 24, 114, 125.

McCUSKER, (Sister) Mary Laurette, b. 18 Jan. 1919. College Administrator. Educ: B.A., Western Md. Coll., 1942; M.S.L.S., Columbia Univ., 1952; D.L.S., ibid, 1963. Appts: Libn., Annapolis H.S., Md., & McDonogh Mil. Schl., Md., 1942-46; Asst. Prof., Iowa State Tchrs. Coll., 1948-59; Vis. Prof., Lib. Sci., Univ. of Minn., 1958-59; Assoc. Prof., Grad. Schl. of Lib. Sci., Rosary Coll., 1963-67, Dir., 1967-69, Dean, 1970-. Mbrships. incl: ALA, 1942-; Cath. Lib. Assn., 1942-; Iowa Lib. Assn., 1947-59; AAUP, 1949-59; Ill. Lib. Assn., 1963-; Chgo. Lib. Assn., 1968-; Ill. State Lib. Advsry. Comm., 1968-. Articles & book reviews, var. jrnls. & publs. Ed. & contbr., books, lib. sci. Advsr., Nat. Central Lib, Taiwan, 1969. Address: Graduate School of Library Science, Rosary College, 7900 W. Division St., River Forest, IL 60305, U.S.A. 2, 5, 138.

McCUTCHAN, Philip Donald, b. 13 Oct. 1920. Author. Educ: Royal Mil. Coll., Sandhurst, U.K. Appts: Lt., RNVR, 1940-46; Asst. Purser, Orient Steam Navigation Co., 1946-49; In London Off., Anglo-Iranian Oil Co., 1949-52; Asst. Master, Preparatory Schls., 1952-54; Fulltime Author, 1954-. Mbr., Crime Writers Assn. (Comm. 1963-67, chmn. 1965-66). Publs. incl: Whistle & I'll Come; The Kid; Storm South; Gibraltar Road; Redcap; The Man from Moscow; Warmaster; Moscow Coach; The Dead Line; Skyprobe; The Screaming Dead Ballons; The All-Purpose Bodies; This Drakotny; The Oil Bastards; Pull My String; Call for Simon Shard; Coach North; Iron Shard. Creator of characters Commander Shaw & Simon Shard. Under Pseudonym Duncan MacNeil: Drums Along the Khyber; Lieutenant of the Line; Sadhu on the Mountain Peak; The Gates of Kunarja; The Red Daniel; Subaltern's Choice. Address: c/o Barclays Bank Ltd., 90 Osborne Rd., Southsea, Hants, PO5 3LW, U.K. 3, 30.

McCUTCHEON, Otty Earle, b. 24 Mar. 1911. Physician. Educ: Grad., Tchrs. Coll., Fredericton, N.B., 1930; Univ. of N.B.; D.D.S., McGill Univ., Montreal, 1949; L.R.C.S.& P., Royal Coll. of Surgs., Dublin, 1956; M.D., Univ. of Western Ont., London, Ont., 1959. Appts: Tchr., N.B. Schls., 1930-38; Dentist, Sask., 1950-52; Staff Psych. & Dir. of Unit, Mendocino State Hosp., 1969-71; Chief Psych. Res., Univ. of Sask. Hosp., 1971-72; Staff Psych., Dammasch State Hosp., Wilsonville, Ore., 1972-. Mbrships: Am. Psych. Assn.; Can. Psych. Assn.; Am. Acad. of Psychosomatic Med.; Calif. Med. Assn.; AMA; Royal Soc. of Hlth., London; For. Grads. Assn.; N.W. Pacific

Neuropsych. Assn.; Med. Coun. of Gt. Brit. & Ireland. Address: P.O. Box 38, Wilsonville, OR 97070, U.S.A.

McDANIEL, Claudette Black (Mrs. Sylvester W. McDaniel) b. 12 Dec. 1939. Occupational Therapist; Public Relations Director. Educ: B.A., Va. Union Univ., 1964; Richmond Profl. Inst. Appts: Dir., P.R., Radio Stn. W.A.N.T., Richmond, Radio Stn. W.E.N.Z., 1966-; Instr.-Supvsr., Dept. of Occupational Therapy, Med. Coll. of Va., 1960-. Conductor, creative workshop, Va. State Penitentiary. Mbrships: Nat. & Va. (Chmn., Scholarship Comm.) Therapeutic Recreation Socs; Nat. Recreation & Pk. Assn.; Va. Recreation & Pk. Soc. (Chmn., recruiting, Ctrl. Dist.); Nat. Coun. Coll. Women; Bd. of Dirs., Med. Coll. Va., Drug Treatment Prog.; Richmond Chapt., Am. Red Cross & N.A.A.C.P.; Richmond Area Assn. Retarded Children; People's Pol. & Civic League; Alpha Phi Zeta. Soloist & singer w. Va. Choirs. Address: 105 E. 15th St., Richmond, VA 23224, U.S.A. 5, 138.

McDANIEL, Madge Beatrice, b. 2 June 1904. Teacher. Educ: A.B., W. Va. Univ.; Fairmont State Coll.; Grad. work, W. Va. Univ.; George Coll. for Tchrs. Appts: Tchr., Ziesing Schl., Harrison Co., W. Va., 2 yrs.; Galloway Schl., Barbour Co., 1 yr.; Elem. Supvsr., Webster Springs Schls., 2 yrs.; 1st Grade Tchr., Ziesing Elem. Schl., 43 yrs.; w. Headstart & Early Child Dev. Prog., Harrison Co. Schls., 5 summers. Mbrships: Life Mbr., W. Va. Congress of Parents & Tchrs., W. Va. Assn. of Classroom Tchrs.; State Pres., Alpha Delta Kappa & W. Va. Reading Coun.; Bd. Mbr. & Sec., State Assn. of Classroom Tchrs.; Sec., W. Va. Assn. of Retired Schl. Employees & State Div., AAUW; V.P., local YWCA, W. Va. Histl. Soc., Woman's Club of Bridgeport & Family Serv. of Harrison & Marion Cos.; Treas., Co. Histl. Soc. & W. Va. Commn. on Children & Youth; Pres., W. Va. Sr. Citizen's Coun.; Bd. of Mgrs., W. Va. Congress of Parents & Tchrs. Hons: Harrison Co. Tchr. of the Yr., 1964; Mary Titus Award ofr Profl. Courage, W. Va. ACT; name given to Community Playfield, Spelter, W. Va. Address: 511 Stout St., Bridgeport, WV 26330, U.S.A. 5, 125.

McDANIEL, Willie Leonard, b. 21 June 1936. Minister. Educ: A.B., Livingstone Coll., Salisbury, N.C., U.S.A., 1960; Master of Divinity, Hood Theol. Sem., 1963. Appts: Min., Soldiers Mem. A.M.E. Zion Ch., Salisbury, N.C.; Pt.-time Chap., VA Hosp., Salisbury. Mbrships: Past Pres., Essex Co. Educ. Assn.; Past Pres., Essex Co. Tchrs. Assn.of VEA, & past mbr., Bd. of Dirs., Dist. A. Bd. of Dirs., Essex Co. Civic League; Bd. of Dirs., Salisbury Rowan Civic League; NAACP; Camp Dorothy Walls; Rowan Cooperate Christian Min.; Essex Recreational Assn.; V.P., Salisbury-Rowan Democrat Party; Pres., Friends of the Lib., Livingstone Coll.; Bd. of Dirs., Mental Hlth. Advsry. Bd.; Family Life Coun.; Omega Psi Phi; Prince Hall Masons. Recip., Citizenship Award, Concord, N.C., 1955. Address: 212 W. Liberty St., Salisbury, NC 28144, U.S.A. 125.

McDARRAH, Fred William, b. 5 Nov. 1926. Photographer; Writer. Educ: B.S., N.Y. Univ., U.S.A., 1954. Appts: Staff Sgt., U.S. Army, 1944-47; Contbr., Village Voice newspaper, N.Y.C., 1959-; Picture Ed., ibid, 1971-; Ed., Exec. Desk Diary, 1962-64; Guest Lectr., sev. Camera Clubs & Schls. of Photography. Mbrship: Am. Soc. of Mag. Photographers. Publs: The Beat Scene, 1960; The Artist's World in Pictures, 1961; Greenwich Village, 1963; New York, New York, 1964; The New

Bohemia (w. J. Gruen), 1966; Sculpture in Environment, 1967; Guide for Ecumenical Discussion (w. J.J. Young), 1970; Museums in New York, 1973; 23 articles in jrnls. Photos shown, Soho Photo Gall. Exhib., 1973. Recip., num. awards for news & feature photos. Address: 505 W. Broadway, N.Y., NY 10012, U.S.A. 6, 30, 130, 131.

McDOLE, Robert David, b. 30 Dec. 1925. Educator. Educ: B.Ed., San Diego State Coll., 1961; M.A., ibid, 1967; Postgrad. work at Univ. of Southern Calif. Appts: Tchr., 5th Grade, Brawley Schl. Dist., Calif., 1959-65; Tchr., 7th & 8th Grade, boys' P.E., ibid, 1965-66; Tchr., 6th grade, Palm Springs Unified Schl. Dist., Calif., 1966-67; Hd. Tchr., ibid, 1967-68; Tchng. V.P., San Jacinto Unified Schl. Dist., Calif., 1968-69; Elem. Schl. Prin., ibid, 1969. Mbrships. Charter, Assn. of Calif. Schl. Admin.; Pres., V.P., Bldg. Rep., Brawley Elem Thrs. Assn.; Bldg. Rep., Palm Springs Tchrs. Assn.; Hd. Coach, Masonic Lodge, Brawley. Contbr. to Calif Schl. Bds. Jrnls.; Educator. Recip. of Doctor of Dedication to Children, San Jacinto Elem. Schl., Calif, 1973. Address: 37-O11 Ferber Driv., Cathedral City, CA 92234, U.S.A. 116, 131.

MACDONALD, A. Angus, b. 22 July 1909. Artist. Educ: Trinity Coll., Univ. of Toronto, Canada; National & Tate Galls., London, U.K.; Louvre & other Galls., Paris, France. Appts: Interior Designer, Robert Simpson Co., Toronto; Hd. of Design & V.P., Indl. Advertising Agency, Ltd., ibid; Designer of Books & Jackets, Longmans Green, Canada, Ltd.; Fabric Designer, Sheraton Hotels; Employed on Pvte. Commns., 1953-. Past-Mbr: Royal Canadian Acad.; Ont. Soc. of Artists. Works in Glass incl: Mural in Glass Layers, Canada House, N.Y.C., 1958 (initiated technique of using glass pieces without lead or concrete); Windows, St. James' Cathedral, Toronto & St. Luke's Cathedral, Sault Ste. Marie, Ont. Painted Murals incl: Guaranty Trust Co., Windsor., Ont.; King Edward Hotel, Toronto. Num. works in Pvte. Collects. Hons: Commissioned to do over 100 paintings, Credit Valley Schl. of Nursing, Missisauga, Ont., 1968. Address: 131 Northwood Drive, Willowdale, Ontario, Canada. 88.

McDONALD, Eva Rose, b. 30 Mar. 1909. Author. Educ: S. London Commercial Coll., Anerley. Mbrships: Soc. of Authors; Life Mbr., Nat. Book League; Cats Protection League. 25 Historical Novels: Lazare the Leopard; Dark Enchantment; The Rebel Bride; The Prettiest Jacobite; The Captive Lady; The Maids of Taunton; The Black Glove; The Reluctant Bridegroom; The Runaway Countess; The Gretna Wedding; The Austrian Bride; The Lost Lady; The Wicked Squire; The French Mademoiselle; Lord Byron's First Love; Shelley's Springtime Bride; The White Petticoat; The Spanish Wedding; The Lady from Yorktown; Regency Rake; The Revengeful Husband; Lament for Lady Flora; Lord Rochester's Daughters; November Nocturne, Roman Conqueror (both in preparation). Address: Wyldwynds, 105 Bathurst Walk, Iver SL0 9EF, Buckinghamshire, U.K. 3, 138.

McDONALD, Hugh Joseph, b. 27 July 1913. Biochemist; Educator. Educ: B.Sc., McGill Univ., 1935; M.S., Carnegie-Mellon Univ., 1936; D.Sc., 1939. Appts: Instr., Chem., Ill. Inst. of Technol., 1939-41; Asst. Prof., ibid, 1941-43; Assoc. Prof., 1943-46; Prof., 1946-48; Prof. & Chmn., Dept. of Biochem. & Biophys., Loyola Univ., Stritch Schl. of Med., 1948-;

Cons., Argonne Nat. Lab., 1946-; Manhattan Proj., Columbia Univ., 1943; Cons., Dept. of Pub. Hlth., State of Ill., 1968-. Fellow, AAAS. Mbrships. incl: Am. Chem. Soc.; Am. Soc. Biol. Chems.; Am. Assn. Clin. Chems.; Charter, Soc. Exptl. Biol. & Med.; Sigma Xi. Author of 170 publs. in field. Address: Dept. of Biochem. & Biophys., Loyola Univ. Stritch Schl. of Med., Maywood, IL 60153, U.S.A. 2, 14, 15, 25, 28, 50, 88.

MacDONALD, Ian Charles, b. 17 Sept. 1915. Journalist. Educ: B.Ed., Univ. of Alta., Edmonton, 1949; M.Ed., ibid, 1956; Banff (Alta.) Schl. of Advcd. Mgmt. Appts. incl: Reporter, Edmonton Jrnl., 1935-40, 1945-46, 1948; Edit. Writer & Sr. Edit. Writer, ibid, 1949-65; Publr. & Edi., Med. Hat News, 1966-; Off., Southam Press Ltd., 1966-. Mbrships. incl: Dir., Med. Hat Exhib. & Stampede Co.; Corres. Sec., Dir., Med. Hat Musical Theatre, Past Pres., 1968-70; Dir. & Sec., Cypress Skiers Assn.; Hon. Life Mbr., Exec. Mbr., Alta. Div., Canadian Authors Assn.; Commonwealth Press Union; Int. Press Inst.; Am. Newspapers Publrs. Assn.; Canadian Daily Newspapers Publrs. Assn.; Canadian Press. Publs: Alberta-A Natural History, 1967; contbns. to educl. jrnls. & others. Address: Medicine Hat News, 4 Sixth Ave., S.E., Medicine Hat, Alta., T1A 7E6, Canada. 9.

McDONALD, Minnie Otilla Oates, b. 17 July 1924. Secretary-Bookkeeper. Educ: Partial course in acctng., Int. Assn. of Accts.; Currently taking course in tax educ., Federated Tax Serv. Appts: Served w. USMC, 1945-46; Clerk Typist, Casualty Div., WWII; Assembly & repair work, Quantico Marine Base, 1944; Assembly & repair work, Bowen & Co.; Bookkeeper machine operator, Suburban Trust Co., 1½ yrs.; Supvsr., ibid, 1951-55; Hd. Bookkeeper, Bank of Bethesda, 1955-58; Bookkeeper-Sec., Devlin Lumber & Supply Corp., 1955-. Mbrships. incl: Color bearer, Veterans of For. Ladies Aux. Post 350, 1969; Sr. V.P., ibid, 1970; Pres., 1971; Conductress, Hosp. Chmn., Bethesda Naval Hosp., 1972; Pres., Drug Abuse & Cancer, 1973-. Hons. incl: Buddy Poppy Award for outstanding work, 1972; Cert. of merit for ldrship., State of Md. V.F.W., 1972. Address: 2511 Randolph Rd., Silver Spring, MD 20902, U.S.A.

MACDONALD, Neil Murray, b. 27 Nov. 1921. Telecommunications Engineer. Educ: Engrng. Cadetship, Dept. of Postmaster-Gen., Australia, 1938-41; B.S., Melbourne Univ. 1940. Appts: Telecommunications Engr., Dept. of Postmaster-Gen., Australia, 1942-60; Ed. & Ed.-in-Chief, Telecommunication Jrnl. of Australia, 1949-63; Asst. Dir.-Gen., Long Line Equipment, ibid, 1960-63; Asst. Dir., Services, 1963-65; Sr. Asst. Dir.-Gen., Transmission & Servs., 1965-69; 1st Asst. Dir.-Gen., Industrial Rels., 1969-71; 1st Asst. Dir.-Gen., Engrng. Works, 1971-. Mbrships: Fellow, Inst. of Engrs., Australia; Indl. Rels. Soc. Australia; Royal Automobile Club of Vic. Contbr., Journal, Institution of Engineers, Australia; The Telecommunication Journal of Australia. Address: Postmaster-Gen.'s Dept., 199 William St., Melbourne, Vic., Australia 3000. 23.

MACDONALD, Nestor J., b. 15 Dec. 1895. Professional Manager. Educ: Columbia Univ., 1918. Appts: w. Thomas & Betts Co., Elizabeth, N.J. for entire career, 1920-, as Salesman, 1920-27, Sales Mgr. 1927-31, V.P. Sales 1931-41, Dir. 1941-74, Exec. V.P. 1942-60, Pres. 1955-65, Chmn. of Bd. & Chief Exec. Off., 1965-74. Mbrships: Nat. Elec. Mfg Assn. (Pres. 1961-62); St. Andrews Soc., N.Y State (Pres. 1969-70); Kessler Inst., Orange

N.J. (V.P. 1960-74); Pres., Grand Father Mountain Highland Games, Linville, N.C., 1960-74; Union League Club, N.Y.C.; Canadian Club, N.Y.C.; Baltusrol Golf Club, N.J.; St. Andrews Golf Club, U.K. Widely quoted in indl. mags. Hons: McGraw Award, 1958; Man of Yr. Award, 1960. Address: 36 Butler St., Elizabeth, NJ 07207, U.S.A. 2.

McDONALD, Pauline Williams. Educator, Author & Lecturer. Educ: Grad., State Univ. Coll. of Educ., Oneonta, N.Y.; State Kindergarten-Elementary Teaching Credential, 1928. Appts. incl: Tchr., Kindergarten, Huntington, L.I., N.Y., 1928-36; Organizer & Dir., Nursery Schl., ibid, 1936-39; Dir., Nursery Schl., Herkimer, N.Y., 1941-45; Tchr., Child Care Ctr., Westchester, Calif., 1946; Kindergarten Tchr., Culver City Schl. System, Calif., 1947-49; Owner & Dir., Palms Tiny Tot Nursery Schl., L.A., 1949-. Mbrships. incl: Pre-Schl. Assn. of Southern Calif.; V.P., ibid; Pres., Los Angeles Chapt., ibid; Mayor's Comm. for Hlth. & Welfare, Culver City; Culver City Child Guidance Clin.; Treas. & 1st V.P., ibid.; Bd., W. Area Planning Coun., L.A. Publs: Co-author, Creative Art for Home & School, 1961, revised edit. 1974; Co-author, Learning Begins At Home, 1969. Hons: Plaque, Pres. Pre-Schl. Org., 1959-61. Address: 5243 Shenandoah Ave., Los Angeles, CA 90056, U.S.A.

MCDONALD, (Tallulah) Dale, b. 26 Dec. 1944. Private Secretary. Educ: High Pt. Coll., N.C.; King's Bus. Coll., Charlotte, N.C. Appts: Sec.-Bookkeeper, Aiken Black Tire Serv., Hickory, N.C., 1965-66; Sec.-Bookkeeper, Brushy Mtn. Motor Co., 1966-68; Sec. to Owner-Mgr., MSA Personnel, 1968-72; Sec. to Dist. Forester, Catawba Timber Co., Div. of Bowaters Co. (N. Am. Div.), 1972-. Mbrships: Hickory Chapt., Nat. Secs. Assn. (Int.); Recording Sec., ibid, 1970-71, Pres., 1971-73, Corres. Sec., 1973-74. Nomination, Sec. of the Yr., Hickory Chapt., Nat. Secs. Assn. (Int.), 1974. Address: 352 9th St., N. W. Hickory, NC 28601, U.S.A. 76, 125.

MACDONALD, William C., b. 19 May 1927. Educationalist & School Administrator. Educ: A.B. Boston Univ., Mass., 1948; M.Ed., Bridgewater State Coll., Mass., 1953; Dr.Ed., Fla. Univ. Appts: Tchr., Lawrence Acad., Groton, Mass., 1948-51; Asst. Prin., Bicknell Jr. H.S., Weymouth, Mass., 1951-63; Assoc. Prof., Bridgewater State Coll., 1963-68; Asst. Supt., Marshfield Pub. Schls., Mass., 1967-68; Supt., Bethel Pub. Schls., Conn., 1968-; Assoc. Prof., Fairfield Univ., Conn., 1968-. Mbrships. incl: Am. Assn. of Schl. Admnstrs.; Secondary Schl. Prins.' Assn.; NEA; Mass. Tchrs. Assn.; Conn. Tchrs. Assn.; Past Pres., Bd. of Dirs., Weymouth Tchrs. Assn.; Pres., Danbury Area Supts. Group; Exec. Bd., Conn. Assn. of Pub. Schl. Supts.; Supts.' Advsry. Comm., Fairfield Univ.; Chmn., Bd. of Dirs., Marshfield Town Lib.; Bd. f Dirs., Bethel Chmbr. of Comm. Hons. incl: Nat. Sci. Fndn. Awards, Boston Coll., 1958 & 1959; Weymouth Kiwanis Award for Disting. Serv. in Educ., 1965. Address: 15 High St., Winchester, MA 01890, U.S.A.

MacDONALD-DOUGLAS, Ronald Angus, Author; Journalist; Actor-Manager. Appts: Mbr., Sir Nigel Playfair's Cos., London, U.K. & Sir Philip Ben Greet's Shakespearean Cos.; Toured w. own cos. & Dir., many repertory Seasons; Fndr., Inverness Little Theatre; Dir., Prods., Olympia Theatre, Dublin; Appeared at Abbey Theatre; Mng. Ed., Catalyst Mag. Mbrships: Life, PEN; Life, Soc. of Authors; Radiowriters Assn.; League of Dramatists; Hon. Pres. & Dir., For. Affairs Bus., Scottish

Nationalist 1320 Club. Publs: Strangers Come Home; The Sword of Freedom; The Scots Book; The Irish Book; The Closed Door; The Red Laugh; The Woman Beyond; contbr. to many publs. Address; Tigh an Uillt, Wilton Dean, by Hawick, Co. Roxburgh, U.K. 3, 137.

McDONELL, John Alexander, b. 25 Feb. 1926. Educator. Educ: B.A., M.Sc., Ph.D., Univ. of Melbourne, Australia. Appts: Demonstrator, Lectr., Sr. Lectr., Phys. Dept., Univ. of Melbourne, 1949-61; Warden, Deakin Hall & Exec. Warden, North-East Halls, Sr. Lectr. in Phys., Monash Univ., 1962-72; Dir., Ctr. for Continuing Educ., ibid, 1973-. Mbrships: F.Inst.P.; F.A.I.P.; M.A.C.E. Co-author, Modern Physics, 2nd. edit., 1971. Address: Ctr. for Continuing Educ., Monash Univ., Clayton, Vic., Australia, 3168.

McDONNELL, Virginia B. (Mrs. John H. McDonnell), b. 24 Nov. 1917. Author; Registered Nurse. Educ: Samaritan Hosp. Schl. of Nursing; Russell Sage Coll., N.Y. Appts: Night Supvsr., Male Surg. Ward. N.Y. Postgrad. Med. Schl. & Hosp.; Co-dir., Gore Mt. Ski Schl., N. Creek, N.Y.; Columnist The Knickerbocker News, Albany; Reporter, Feature Writer, Columnist & Women's News Ed., Macy-Westchester Rockland Chain of newspapers; Mbr., N.Y. State Wintersports Coun., 1950-56; Free-lance Writer, 1962-. Mbrships: Mystery Writers of Am.; Authors' Guild & League; Huguenot-Thomas Paine Histl. Assn. of New Rochelle; IBS. Publs. incl: West Point Nurse; Nurse with the Silver Skates; Olympic Duty; County Agent; The Irish Helped Build America; Ski Trail Mystery; Trouble at Mercy Hospital; Storm over Garnet; Annapolis Nurse; Foster Pups; Miscalculated Risk; Silent Partner; Long Shot; Deep Six; etc. Honoured by Leukemia Soc. for help in fight to conquer leukemia. Address: 79 Hudson Park Road, New Rochelle, NY 10805, U.S.A. 5, 6, 30, 57, 132, 138, 140.

McDONOUGH, Roger Henry, b. 24 Feb. 1909. Librarian. Educ: A.B., Rutgers Univ., 1934; B.S., Columbia Univ. Schl. of Lib. Serv., 1936. Appts: Ref. Libn., Rutgers Univ., 1934-37; Libn., Free Pub. Lib., New Brunswick, N.J., 1937-47; State Libn., N.J., 1947-. Mbrships: Pres., ALA, 1968-69; Rutgers Univ. Press Coun., 1958-; Trustee, N.J. Histl. Soc., 1958-; Trustee, Westminster Choir Coll., Princeton, N.J., 1966-; Princeton Univ. Lib. Advisory Coun., 1970-. Hons: Litt.D., Rutgers Univ., 1956. Address: N.J. State Lib., 185 West State St., Trenton, NJ 08625, U.S.A. 2, 6.

McDORMAND, Thomas Bruce, b. 15 Mar. 1904. Clergyman; Educator. Educ: B.A., Acadia Univ., Wolfville, N.S., Canada, 1929; B.D., Univ. of Alta., Edmonton, 1935; Th.D., Victoria Univ., Toronto, Ont., 1951. Appts. incl: Sev. Pastorates, N.S. & Alta., 1929-38; Dir., Christian Educ., Bapt. Union of Western Canada, 1938-42; Ed., Canadian Bapt. Publs., 1942-48; Gen. Sec., Bapt. Conven. of Ont. & Quebec, 1948-55; Gen. Sec., Bapt. Fedn. of Canada, 1955-59; Exec. V.P., Acadia Univ., 1959-61; Pres., Eastern Bapt. Sem. & Coll., Phila., Pa., U.S.A., 1961-67; Gen. Sec., Atlantic United Bapt. Conven., 1967-70. Mbrships. incl: Pres., Bapt. Fedn. of Canada, 1970-73; V.P., Bapt. World Alliance, 1970-75; Campaign Chmn., YMCA, 1974. Publs: The Art of Building Worship Services, 2 Vols., 1942-48; The Christian Must Have an Answer, 1959; Judson Concordance to Hymn, 1965; Num. articles in religious jrnls.; Hymns. Hons: D.D., McMaster Univ., Hamilton, Ont., 1951; LL.D., Judson Coll., 1965; L.H.D., Sioux Empire Coll., 1966; D.D., Eastern Bapt. Theological Sem.,

Phila., 1971. Address: 50 Elmwood Drive, Amherst, N.S., Canada. 2.

McDOUGALL, Cyril John, b. 10 Oct. 1907. Master Builder; Business Executive. Appts: Chmn., McDougall-Ireland Pty.Ltd; Dir., Morton Investments Pty. Ltd; Mulgrave Industries Pty. Ltd; New Oakleigh Motors Pty. Ltd; Past Pres., Victorian Employers Fedn.; Australian Coun. of Employers' Fedns; Master Builders' Assn. of Victoria; Master Builders' Fedn. of Australia. Mbrships: Melbourne Cricket Club; Royal Automobile Club (Victoria); Huntingdale Golf Club. Fellow, Australian Inst. of Builders & Inst. of Builders, London. Address: 17/1 Park Tower, 201 Spring St., Melbourne, Vic., Australia, 3000. 23, 34, 128.

MacDOUGALL, Ellis C., b. 23 Feb. 1927. Criminal Justice Consultant. Educ: B.A., Davis & Elkins Coll., W. Va., 1950; M.A., N.Y. Univ., 1952. Appts: Probation Off., Soc. Wkr., Supt., S.C., 1951-58; Dpty. Warden, S.C. Penitentiary, 1958-61; Dir. of Correctional Inds., S.C. Dept. of Correction, 1961-62; Dir. of Corrections, State of S.C., 1962-68; Commnr. of Corrections, State of Conn., 1968-71; Dir. of Corrections, 1971; Commnr., Ga. Dept. of Offender Rehab. & Corrections, 1972-73. Mbrships. incl: Am. Correctional & Southern States Prison Assns.; Past Pres., ibid; Nat. Advsry. Commn. Criminal Justice Standards & Goals; Adjunct Assoc. Prof., Univ. of Ga. Contbng. Ed., Manual of Correctional Standards. Hons. incl: Liberty Bell Award, Conn. Bar Assn., 1970; LL.D., Davis & Elkins Coll., 1972. Address: 1258 Ragley Hall Rd. N.E., Atlanta, GA 30319, U.S.A.

MacDOUGALL, Hartland Molson, b. 28 Jan. 1931. Banker. Educ: Lower Canada Coll.; Bishop's Coll. Schl.; LeRosey & McGill Univs. Appts: Joined Bank of Montreal, served in sev. Montreal brs., 1953-57; Acct. & Asst. Mgr., London, Ont., 1958-60; Asst. Mgr., Vancouver, B.C., 1960-64; Mgr., 10th Ave. & Granville St., Vancouver, 1965-66; Apptd. Mgr., Calgary Br., 1966 & Sr. V.P., Alta. Div., 1968; Sr. V.P., Ont. Div., 1969; Exec. V.P., Res. in Toronto, 1970 & Exec. V.P., Hd. Off., 1973. Mbrships. incl: Royal Trust Co. Advsry Bd.; Toronto Redev. Advsry. Coun.; V.P. & Dir., Comite Canada Comm.; V.P. & Dir., Canadian Arthritis & Rheumatism Soc.; Dir. & Treas., Canadian Horse Coun.; Dir., Canadian Equestrian Team; V.P., Empire Club; Dir. & Mbr. Exec. Comm., Jr. Achievement of Canada; Dir., St. Michael's Hosp.; Gov., Stratford Shakespearean Festival Fndn. of Canada; Gov. Upper Canada Coll.; Vancouver Club. Address: Bank of Montreal, 3rd Floor, Hd. Off., 129 St. James St. West, Montreal, P.Q., H2Y 1L6, Canada. 2, 16, 32, 88.

MCDOUGALL, John Frederick, b. 16 Nov. 1907. Company President. Educ: B.Sc. Civil Engrng., Univ. of Alta., Canada; M.Sc. Civil Engrng., McGill Univ., Montreal. Appts: Asst. Mgr., McDougall & Secord, Ltd., 1937-51; Sec.-Trea., ibid, 1942-47; V.P., ibid, 1948-52; Pres. & Gen. Mgr., ibid, 1952-; Edmonton Advsry. Bd., Royal Trust Co., 1962-; Dir., Royal Trust Co., 1971-. Mbrships. incl: Canadian Coun. of Profl. Engrs.; Pres., ibid, 1964-65; Assoc. of Profl. Engrs. of Alta.; Registrar, ibid, 12 yrs.; Councillor, ibid, 3 yrs.; Edmonton Town Planning Appeal Bd. 11 yrs.; Chmn., ibid, 1 yr.; Engrng. Inst. of Canada; Fellow, Royal Commonwealth Soc.; Edmonton Chamb. of Comm.; Alta. & N. West Chamb. of Mines & Resources; Edmonton Symph. Soc.; Edmonton Chamber Music Soc.; Edmonton Opera Soc.; Historical Soc. of Alta.; Friends of

Univ. of Alta; Edmonton Club. Address: 1101 Empire Building, 10080 Jasper Ave., Edmonton, Alberta, T5J 1V9. Canada. 88.

McDOWELL, Frank, b. 30 Jan. 1911. Professor of Surgery; Editor & Author of Surgical Publications. Educ: A.B. (cum laude), Drury Coll., 1932; M.D. (cum laude), Wash. Univ., 1936; Sc.D., Drury Coll., 1973. Appts. incl: Gen. Surg. Res., Barnes Hosp. & Wash. Univ., St. Louis, 1936-39; Fellow in Plastic Surg., Wash. Univ., 1939-41; Instr.-Prof. of Clin. Surg., Wash. Univ. Schl. of Med., 1939-69, Instr.-Prof. of Maxillofacial Surg., Schl. of Dentistry, 1940-69; Prof. of Surg., Univ. of Hawaii Schl. of Med., 1967-; Ed.-in-Chief, Plastic & Reconstructive Surg. Jrnl., 1967-; Prof. of Clin. Surg., Stanford Univ. Schl. of Med., 1974-. Mbr. & past off., var. med. orgs. Co-author, books on surg. Contbr., num. articles, surg. jrnls., & chapts., var. textbooks on surg. Hons. incl: 1st Dow Corning Int. Award for Excellence in Plastic Surg., 1971. Address: Alexander Young Building, Honolulu, HI, U.S.A. 2, 8, 9, 14, 17, 50.

McDOWELL, May Ross (Mrs.), b. 11 May 1898. Manufacturing Executive. Educ: E. Tenn. State Univ.; LL.B., E. Tenn. Law Schl. Appts. incl: Sec., Johnson City Foundry & Machine Co., Tenn., 1932-46; V.P., ibid, 1946-68, Pres.-Treas., 1968-; Prac., law, 1935-43; Bd. of Mayor & Commnrs., Johnson City, 1957-65 Vice Mayor, Johnson City, 2 yrs.; Mayor, ibid 2 yrs. Mbrships. incl: Wash. Co., Tenn. & Am. Bar Assns.; Nat. Assn. Women Lawyers; Nat Lawyers Club, Wash. D.C.; Sarah Hawkins Chapt., DAR; Colonial Dames of the XVII Century; Bus. & Profl. Womens Club. Contbr to newspapers & mags. Hons. incl: Ky. Col. LL.D., Steed Coll. of Technol.; Cert Meritorious Serv., U.S. Labor Dept., 1963 Outstanding Citizen, Civitan Int., Appalachian Dist., 1970. Address: 426 Highland Ave., P.O Box 1038, Johnson City, TN 37601, U.S.A. 5 7, 16, 22, 114, 128.

McDOWELL, Robert J., b. 25 Feb. 1920 Music Store Executive. Educ: B.S.B.A., Wash Univ., 1941. Appts: Lt. s.g. & PT Boat Cmdr. USNR, 1942-46; Expeditor, Front Rank Furnace Co., 1946-47; Special Promotion Mgr., Witte Hardware Co., 1948-49; Ptnr. Western Sales Co., 1950-51; Br. Store Mgr. Ludwig Music House Inc., 1952-55; Pres. Ludwig Music House Inc., 1955-; Pres., St Louis Band Instrument Co., 1963-70; Pres. Aeolian Co. of Mo., 1970-. Mbrships: Past Pres. Nat. Assn. of Music Merchants; Past Chmn. of Bd., Better Bus. Bur. of Gtr. St. Louis; Pas Chmn., Music Ind. Nat. Promotion Comm. Pres., Rotary Club of St. Louis; Past Chmn. Associated Retailers of Music; Past Pres., loca chapt., Sigma Nu; V.P. & Dir., Sunset Country Club. Hons: 1st Hon. Mbr., Nat. Assn. o Young Music Merchants, 1973. Address: 1516 Minmar Dr., Warson Woods, MO 63122, U.S.A 8.

McELROY, George A., b. 25 May 1922 Educator; Journalist. Educ: B.A., Tex Southern Univ., Houston; M.A., Univ. of Mo. Columbia; Adv. Study, State Univ. of Iowa Appts: Special Corres., Houston Post, 1952-69 Columnist, 1971-; Reporter, City, Sports & Mng. Ed., Houston Informer, 1954-57, Mng Ed., 1973; Tchr., jrnlsm., Houston pub. schls. 1957-69; Special Corres., KPRC TV, Houston 1968; Grad. Tchng. Asst., Univ. of Mo. 1969-70; Instr. in Communications, Univ. o Houston, 1970, Asst. Prof., 1973. Mbrships incl: Sigma Delta Chi; Omega Psi Phi; Nat Newspaper Publrs. Assn.; Am. Assn. Coll Profs.; Am. Legion; Press Club of Houston

Publs: Roy Wilkins As A Journalist, 1970; The Beat of the Tom-Toms, 1973. Hons: Disting. Serv. Awards, Newspaper Fund Inc., 1964, '68; Tex. Jrnlsm. Tchr. of Yr. Award, 1968. Address: 3307 Wentworth St., Houston, TX 77004, U.S.A. 125.

McELVEEN, Thomas Melvin, b. 6 July 1902. International Insurance Adjuster; Marine Surveyor & Appraisor. Educ: B.S., Furman Univ., 1925. Appts: Adjuster, Glen Falls Ins. Grp., 3½ yrs.; Adjuster, Travelers Ins. Co., 10 yrs.; Pres., Thomas M. McElveen Int. Corp., Miami, Fla., La Paz, Bolivia & San Jose, Costa Rica. Mbrships. incl: S.C. Assn. Ins. Adjusters (Pres.); Fla Assn. Ind. Ins. Adjusters (Pres.); Int. Inst. of Loss Adjusters (Fndr. & Pres.); Mason; Am. Orchid Soc.; Univ. Bapt. Ch.; S. Fla. Clams. Contbr. to Trade jrnls. Hons: Col. of Order of Ky., 1969-; Awards from Fla Assn. Ind. Ins. Adjusters, Int. Inst. Loss Adjusters & others. Address: P.O. Box 557605, Ludlum Branch, Miami, FL 33155, U.S.A. 7, 16.

McENTYRE, Peter M., b. 15 Aug. 1917. Chartered Accountant. Educ: B.Com., McGill Univ., Canada, 1939; Chartered Acct., 1941; Chartered Financial Analyst, 1963. Appts: Student, Creak, Cushing & Hodgson, 1939-41; Ptnr., ibid, 1946-48; Royal Canadian Navy Serv., 1941-46; Sec. Treas., St. Lawrence Sugar Refineries Ltd., 1949-63; Pres., Commercial Trust Co. Ltd., 1964-; Bd. Chmn., Canada Cement Lafarge Ltd.; Dir., Ciments Lafarge, Crush Int. Ltd., Markborough Properties Ltd., Sucronel Ltd., Starlaw Investments Ltd., Nelcon Trust Co. Ltd. Mbrships: Alderman, City of Westmount, 1962-68, Mayor, 1969-71; Gov., Concordia Univ.; Chmn., Boys' Clubs of anada Endowment Fund; Univ., St. Jame's, Montreal Badminton & Squash, & Royal Montreal Golf Clubs. Address: 444 Clarke Ave., Westmount, P.Q., H3Y 3C6, Canada. 2, 32, 88.

McEWEN, Colin Ellis, b. 10 Aug. 1904. Educator. Educ: Phoenix Coll., 1923-25; Univ. of Calif., Berkeley, 1927; A.B., Univ. of Ariz., 1930; Ariz. State Univ., 1934. Appts. incl: Tchr., Mt. Trumbull Pub. Schls., Ariz., 1926-27, Gila Bend H.S., 1928-30, Tempe H.S., 1930-32, Phoenix H.S., 1934-37, Long Profl. Schl., Hollywood, Calif., 1946-47, Brawley Pub. Schls., Calif., 1947-49, H.S', Hollywood, Santa Monica, Inglewood, Calif., 1949-; Prin., Nehalem Valley H.S., Ore., 1944-46; Pres. & Chmn., Bd. Educ. Dir., Colin McEwen Schls. Inc., L.A.; Pres., Colin McEwen Schl. of Bus., L.A.; Dir., McEwen Labs., 1964-; Pres. & Chmn., Bd. of Dirs., Colin McEwen H.S., Hollywood, Inc. Mbrships. incl: NEA; Am. Acad. Pol. & Soc. Sci.; Nat. & Calif. Couns. Tchrs. of Engl.; AAAS; Hollywood, Santa Monica, Beverly Hills & Inglewood Chmbrs. of Comm.; Better Bus. Bur., L.A.; Ctr. for Study of Democratic Instns. Address: 1798 N. Highland Ave., Hollywood, CA 90028, U.S.A. 9, 15, 59, 120, 131.

McFADYEN, Neil Mathieson, b. 7 June 1923. Physician. Educ: M.B. & Ch.B., Univ. of Glasgow, 1951. Licensed to practice med., State of Va., 1956. Appts. incl: Jr. Staff Physn., Ctrl. State Hosp., Petersburg. Va., 1955-56, Sr. Staff Physn., 1956; Chief of Serv., Gen. & Forensic Psych., Southwestern State Hosp., Marion, Va., 1956-60; Clin. Dir., Administrative, Forensic & Gen. Psych., Weston State Hosp., W.Va., 1960-61, Supt., 1961-63; Chief, Psych, Serv., V.A. Hosp., Clarksburg, W.Va., 1963-70; Clin. Asst. Prof., Dept. of Psych., W.Va. Univ. Med. Ctr., Morgantown, 1965-69; Chief of Staff, V.A. Hosp., Augusta, Ga., 70-73; Clin. Prof., Dept. of Psych., Med. Coll. of Ga., ibid, 1970-; Dir., V.A. Hosp.,

Battle Creek, Mich., 1973-; Clin. Prof., Dept. Psych., Med. Coll., Ga., 1971-73. Fellowships: Int. Assn. of Soc. Psych.; Am. Geriatric Soc.; Royal Soc. of Hlth. Pres., Aususta-Richmond Co. Coun. on Alcohol & Drug Abuse, 1970-73; Mbrships. incl: World Psych. Assn.; British Med. Soc.; Am. Psych. Assn.; Rotary Club of W. Agusta, Ga., 1970-73. Address: V.A. Hosp., Battle Creek, MI 49016, U.S.A. 6, 125, 128, 131.

McFARLAND, Dalton Edward, b. 23 Sept. 1919. Educator; Writer; Consultant. Educ: B.S., Western Mich. Univ., 1943; M.B.A., Univ. of Chgo., 1947; Ph.D., Cornell Univ., 1952. Appts. incl: Asst. Prof., Mgt., Mich. State Univ., 1952-56; Assoc. Dir., Labor & Ind. Rels. Ctr., ibid, 1956-58; Prof. Mgt., 1959; Chmn., Dept. of Mgt., 1961-71; Currently, Prof., Univ. of Ala. Schl. of Bus., Birmingham. Fellowships: Int. Acad. of Mgt.; US Acad. of Mgt.; Am. Soc. for Applied Anthropol. Mbr., sev. profl. & hon. socs. Publs. incl: Measuring Executive Effectiveness (co-ed.), 1967; Personnel Management: Theory & Practice, 1968; Management; Principles & Practices, 3rd edit., 1970; Readings in Personnel Management, 1971. Address: Univ. of Alabama in Birmingham, Schl. of Business, Univ. Stn., Birmingham, AL 35294, U.S.A. 3, 8, 14, 128, 129.

MACFARLANE, Robert Gwyn, b. 26 June 1907. Pathologist. Educ: M.B. B.S., St. Bartholomews Hosp. Med. Schl., Univ. of London, U.K., 1933; M.D., 1938; M.R.C.S.; L.R.C.P. Appts. incl: Clin. Patnol., Radcliffe Infirmary, Oxford, 1941-67; Rdr., Haematol., Oxford Univ., 1957; Dir., Med. Rsch. Coun., Blood Coagulation Rsch. Univ, 1959-67; Prof. Clin. Pathol., 1965; Emeritus, 1967. Fellowships: Coun., Royal Soc., 1960-61; Royal Soc. Med.; Royal Coll. Physns.; All Souls Coll., Oxford. Mbrships. incl: Haemophilia Soc.; Pathol. Soc. Co-Author, Human Blood Coagulation & its Disorders, 1953, 3rd ed., 1962. Co-Ed: The Functions of the Blood, 1961; The Treatment of Haemophilia & other Coagulation Disorders, 1966. Contbr. to sci. publs. Hons. incl: M.A., Oxford, 1947; C.B.E., 1964; Cameron Prize, Edinburgh Univ., 1968. Address: Park Cottage, Ramsden, Oxford. 1, 50, 128.

McFERRIN, Janie Marie, b. 27 Sept. 1946. Guidance Counselor. Educ: A.B., Erskine Coll., 1968; M.Ed., Univ. of Ga., 1969; Adult Educl. Courses, S.C. State Univ., 1971. Appts: Counselor, Adult Educ., Greenville Tech. Educ. Ctr., 1969; Counselor, Evening Ext. Div., Greenville Tech. Coll., 1973. Mbrships: Hon. Mbr., AAUW, 1965; Alpha Psi Omega, 1965; Phi Kappa Phi, 1969; NEA; S.C. Personnel & Guidance Assn.; Sec., Upper S.C. Chapt., Am. Personnel & Guidance Assn.; S.C. Assn. Pub. Continuing Educ: Assoc. Reformed Presby. Ch. Recip., coll. awards. Address: Lane Apt. 7, Greenville, SC 29607, U.S.A. 125.

McGARRITY, Kelvin A., b 25 Aug. 1907. Gynaecologist. Educ: M.B., B.S., Sydney Univ., N.S.W., Australia, 1931; M.R.C.O.G., London, 1937; F.R.C.O.G., ibid, 1956; F.A.C.S., F.I.C.S., in U.S.A., 1962. Appts. incl: Cons. Gynaecologist at The Women's Hosp., Crown St., St. Vincents Hosp., Nepean Hosp., Windsor Hosp., Katoomba Hosp., & Liverpool Hosp. Mbrships: Australian Coun. of RCOG; Hon. Dir., Cancer Registry of RCOG; Chmn.-Treas., N.S.W. Comm. of RCOG; Vice-Chmn., Cancer Comm. Int. Fed. of G. & O; V.P., 5th World Congress of FIGO, Sydney; Mbr. of Expert Comm. of WHO on Cancer Control; Mbr. of Ovarian Cancer Comm. of WHO. Author,

Synopsis of Gynaecology, 1969. Hons: Efficiency Decoration; Mention in Despatches, WW II. Address: 231 Macquarrie St., Sydney, N.S.W., Australia 2000.

McGARVEY, William George, b. 20 Oct. 1904. Professor of Psychology. Educ: B.S., Ursinus Coll., 1930; Cert in Psychol. & Educ., 1940; M.S., Temple Univ., 1948; Ed.D., ibid., 1953. Appts: Instr. in Transportation-Assoc. Prof. Psychol., SUNY, 1941-56; Prof. of Psychol., ibid., 1956. Mbrships. incl: AAAS; Fedn. of Am. Scientists; N.Y. Acad. of Sci; N.Y. State Psychological Assn; Am. Soc. of Clinical Hypnosis; Hon., Phi Delta Kappa (Temple Univ.), 1952 & Sigma Zeta, 1964. Publs. incl: The First Course in Psychology, 1967; Further Thoughts on The First Course in Psychology, 1968. Hons. incl: Citation, Epsilon Pi Tau, 1969; Citation, Sigma Xi, 1971. Address: State Univ. of New York, Coll. at Oswego, NY 13126, U.S.A. 6, 14, 15, 130.

McGARVEY, William J., Jr., b.5 Nov. 1921. Real Estate Broker. Appts. incl: Staff Mbr., Lockheed Aircraft, 1941-44; Petty Off., USN, 1944-46; self-employed paint distributor, L.A., Calif., 1946-51; Licensed Real Estate Salesman & Broker, 1951-; Chmn., Bd. Dirs., McGarvey-Clark Realty, Fullerton, Calif.; Past Pres. & Dir., Fullerton Bd. Realtors; Mbrships. incl: Past V.P. & Dir., Calif. Real Estate Assn.; Exec. Comm. Mbr., ibid, 1973; Area Mbrship. Chmn., Nat. Inst. Real Estate Brokers; Trustee, Calif. Reas Estate Pol. Action Comm.; Chmn. Chancellor, Dumke Advsry. Coun., Calif. State Univ. & Colls.; Vice Chmn., Pres., Shield Advsry Bd., Calif. State Univ., Fullerton. Recip. num. awards. Address: 1431 N. Harbor Blvd., Fullerton, CA 92635, U.S.A.

McGAUGH, James Lafayette, b. 17 Dec. 1931. Professor. Educ: B.A., San Jose State Univ., 1953; Ph.D., Univ. of Calif., Berkeley, 1959; Postdoct. study, Istituto Superiore di Sanita, Rome, 1961-62. Appts: Asst. Prof. - Assoc. Prof. of Psychol., San Jose State Univ., 1957-61; Assoc. Prof. of Psychol., Univof Ore., 1961-64; Chmn., Dept. of Psychobiol., 1964-67 & 71-, Dean, Schl. of Biol. Scis., 1967-70, Assoc. Prof. of Psychobiol.; 1964-66, Prof., ibid, 1966-, Univ. of Calif., Irvine. Mbrships: Chmn., Comm. on Educ., Soc. for Neurosci., 1972-75; Pres., Univ. of Calif. Irvine Club, Sigma Xi, 1973; Fellow, AAAS & Am. Psychol. Assn.; Int. Brain Rsch. Org.; Ed., Behavioral Biol.; Co-Ed., Advances in Behavioral Biol. Publs: Integrating Principles of Social Psychology (w. J.B. Cooper), 1963; Psychology (w. H.F. Harlow & R.F. Thompson), 1971; Memory Consolidation (w. M.J. Herz), 1972; Ed. Psychobiology, 1971; Ed., The Chemistry of Mood, Motivation & Memory, 1972; The Psychobiology of Convulsive Therapy (ed. w. others); contbr. 125 sci. papers to sci. jrnls. Hons: Abraham Rosenberg Rsch. Fellow,1955; Sr. Postdoct. Fellowship, Nat. Acad. of Sci. & Nat. Rsch. Coun., 1961. Address: Dept. of Psychobiol., Schl. of Biol. Scis., Univ. of Calif., Irvine, CA 92664, U.S.A. 2, 14.

McGEE, Robert C. Jr., b. 24 May 1936. Holding Company Executive. Educ: B.A.E., Univ. of Va., 1960. Appts. incl: Dir., Spectrographic Analysis Lab., U.S. Army, 1961-62; Sales Engr., Sikorsky Div., United Aircraft, 1962-63; Wash. Rep., Hiller Aircraft Co., 1963-65; Dir., Mil. Marketing, Fairchild Hiller Co., 1965-67; Pres., Forge Aerospace Inc., 1967-73; Pres., TLC Millburn Corp., 1973-. Mbrships. incl: Inst. Aeronautics & Astronautics; Am. Helicopter Soc.; Am. Mgmt. Assn.; Assn. of U.S. Army; Nat. Security Indl. Assn.; Pres., Sigma Alpha Epsilon; Theta Tau.

Author, var. tech. papers & newspaper articles. Hons. incl: Army Commendation Award; Aviation Club Meritorious Achievement Award. Address: 1705 DeSales St. N.W., Washington, DC 20036, U.S.A. 6.

McGEE, Ronald Alexander, b. 30 Nov. 1910. College Professor of Physics. Educ: B.A., Miss. Coll., 1937; M.A., Univ. of Miss., 1948; postgrad., Univs. of Tex., Okla., Kan., & Kan. State Coll. Appts: Prin., Tchr. Co. Line Schl. Union, Miss., 1937-39; Mbr., Miss. House of Reps., 1940-44; Tchr., Miss. H.S., Houston, 1940-41; Instr., Electronics, Air Force Tech., Schl., Scott Field, Ill., 1942-47; Tchr., Miss. H.S., Kosciuske, 1947-48; Asst. Prof., Univ. of Miss., 1948-53; Asst. Prof., Southern State Coll., 1953-, Hd., Dept. of Phys., 1953-70; Fndr. & Dir., Southwest Ark. Regional Sci. Fair, 1955. Mbrships. incl: Alpha Epsilon Delta; Sigma Pi Sigma; Am. Phys. Soc.; Am. Inst. Phys.; Dist. Comm. Mbr., Boy Scouts of Am. Author, Exhibitors Handbook (Sci. Fair handbook for schls. of Southwest Ark.). Address: Box 1236, Southern State Coll., Magnolia, AR 71753, U.S.A. 7, 125.

McGEE, William, b. 11 May 1925. Painter; Teacher. Educ: B.F.A., Univ. of N.M., Albuquerque, 1951; M.F.A. Ind. Univ., Bloomington, 1953. Appts. incl: Instr., Painting & Design, Univ. of Cinn., Ohio, 1953-56; Asst. Prof., Brown Univ., Providence, R.I., 1956-60; Asst. Prof. Painting, Hunter Coll., N.Y.C., 1962-68; Asst. Prof., Lehman Coll., CUNY, 1968-. Solo Exhibs. incl: Grace Borgenicht Gall., N.Y.C., 1959; Am. Gall., N.Y.C., 1962; Katonah Gall., N.Y., 1973; Max Hutchinson Gall., N.Y.C., 1973. Mus. Collects. incl: Dallas Mus. of Fine Arts, Tex.; Chgo. Art Inst.; Balt. Mus. of Fine Art, Md.; Tate Gall., London, U.K.; Chrysler Mus. of Art, Richmond, Va.; Albright-Knox Mus., Buffalo, N.Y. Var. pvte. collects., N.Y.C. & Buffalo. Address: Route 116, Purdy Station, NY 10578, U.S.A.

McGEHEE, Doris Boyd, b. 16 Nov. 1925. Cotton Classer. Educ: Miss. Delta Jr. Coll., Moorhead; Cotton Classing Schl., Memphis, Tenn. Appts: Receptionist; Bookkeeper; Cotton Classer, U.S. Dept. of Agric. one of first two women to hold this appt. Mbrships: Pres., Beta Zeta Chapt., Beta Sigma Phi.; V.P., Federated Woman's Club; 4-H Club Ldr., Home Demonstration Ldr.; Girl & Scout Ldr. Active civic wkr., & wkr in 1st Bapt. Ch. Hons: Outstanding Home Demonstration Ldr., 1962; Girl of Yr. Award, Beta Zeta Chapt., Beta Sigma Phi, 1971. Address: 707 River Rd., Greenwood, MS 38930, U.S.A. 125.

McGEORGE, John Alexander, b. 12 Oct. 1898. Medical Practitioner; Barrister. Educ: Sydney Univ.; Sydney Univ. Law Schl.; M.B., Ch.M., 1927; D.P.M., 1932; admitted as barrister, 1952. Appts. incl: Cons. Psych., Dept. of the Atty. Gen. & of Justics; Mbr., Prisons Parole Bd.; Post-grad. Lectr. in Forensic Psych., Univ. of Sydney; Mbr., Brit. Acad. of Forensic Scis. & convenor for Australia for the 3rd. Int. Conf. in these scis.; Lectr., Univ. of N.S.W. & Sydney Law Schl.; currently Sr. Cons. Psych., Royal Australian Navy & Cons. Psych., Royal Prince Alfred Hosp. Mbrships: Air Force Assn.; Australian & N.Z. Coll. Psychs. (resigned); Fellow, Royal Soc. Med. (resigned); past Pres., Australian Physiotherapy Assn. Publs. incl: Reflections of a Psychiatrist; My 500 Murderers; The Psychologist's Views of the News; These Strange People. Hons: J.P., 1955; O.B.E., 1962. Address: 1/151 Kurraba Rd., Neutral Bay, N.S.W., Australia 2089. 3, 23.

McGHEE, Elmer Earl, b. 19 Oct. 1936. Teacher. Educ: B.S., Western Ky. Univ., 1961; M.A., ibid, 1964. Appts: Sci. Tchr. & Asst. Coach, Caneyville H.S., Ky., 1961, Hd. Sci. Tchr., 1964; currently, Tchr., Biol. & Psycbol., ibid, & Athletic Dir. Mbrships: NEA; Ky. Educ. Assn.; Ky. H.S. Athletic Assn.; Grayson Co. Tchrs. Assn.; PTA; Band Boostel; Sponsor, Caneyville Pep Club. Hons. incl: Hon. Man, USN, Caneyville Yearbook Dedication, 1966; Coaches Sportsmanship Award, 1970-71; Ky. Col. Award, 1972; Hon. Band Mbr. Award, 1972-73. Address: P.O. Box 162, Caneyville, KY 42721, U.S.A. 125.

McGHEE, Flora Devaughan (Mrs. Herschel McGhee), b. 10 Aug. 1924. Professional Model; Charm School Instructor. Educ: Univ. of Ala.; Grace Downs Schl. for Models, NYC; John Robert Powers Schl. of Charm, NYC. Appts: Beauty Shop Operator; Owner-Operator, Beauty Shops in Mobile & Birmingham, Ala.; Fndr., 1st charm & modelling schl. for Blacks in Ala.; Distributor, Flo McGhee Charm Schl.-Model Cosmetics. Mbrships: Organizer & 1st Pres., Modern Beauticians Club; Dir., Mobile Co. Southern Beauty Congress; Histn., Modeling Assn. of Am.; Sunday Schl. Tchr., Sr. Girls; Treas., Progressive Ladies Club; Advsr., Mothers Charm Club; Past Recording Sec., Dem. Club. of Jefferson Co.; Charm Dir., Birmingham Urban League; Abigail Chapt., Order of the Eastern Star; Bd. of Dirs., 4th Ave. Br., YMCA; Zeta Phi Lambda, 1967; Beta Psi, Booker T. Wash. Bus. Coll., 1970; Negro Bus. & Profl. Women, 1971; Birmingham Beautification Bd., 1970-71. Contbr. newspaper column. A Model You. Hons: Foxes & Hares Award, 1962; Award of Merit, Pi Lambda Sigma, 1962; Maceo Jennings Award, 1968; Keys to the City of Mobile, Ala.; Mayor Joe Bradley, 1973. Address: Flora McGhee Charm & Modeling Schl., 1614 11th Ave. N., Birmingham, Al 35204, U.S.A. 57, 114, 125.

McGHIE, Gwendolyn M., b. 25 Aug. 1930. Teacher. Appts: Var. tchng. posts, 1952-, inclng. Hope Bay, 1959-60; Preston, St. Mary, 1961-62; Rural Hill, Portland, 1965-66; Bethesda, St. Thomas, 1966-68; Somerset, St. Andrew, 1968-72; Job's Hill, St. Mary, 1972-. Mbrships: Supt., Sabbath Schl.; Sec., Christian Endeavour; Local Ldr., 4H Club; Pres., Sec., P.T.A.; Auditor, Agricl. Soc.; Tchrs. Reading Assn. Address: Job's Hill School, Leinster P.A., St. Mary, Jamaica, W. Indies.

McGILL, Edwin M., b. 17 May 1922. Physician. Educ: B.S., Northwestern Univ., 1944; B.M., ibid, 1946, M.D., 1947. Appts: Pres., Med. Staff, Northwest Community Hosp., 1958, 1960; Chief Ob. & Gyn., ibid, 1962-63, Holy Family Hosp., 1964-65; Active Cons., Med. Staff, Northwest Community Hosp., Arlington Heights, Ill.; Assoc. Cons., Holy Family Hosp., DesPlaines, Ill. Mbrships: AMA; Chgo. Med. Soc.; Ill. Med. Soc.; Am. Bd. of Ob. & Gyn.; Am. Coll. of Ob. & Gyn.; Am. Coll. of Surgs.; Int. Coll. of Surgs.; Royal Soc. of Hlth. Address: 1430 N. Arlington Heights Rd., Arlington Heights, IL 60004, U.S.A.

McGILL, Marthalene Filley, b. 16 Fb. 1902. Civic Worker. Educ: Univ. of Calif., Berkeley; Baker Univ.; Univ. of Kan. Mbrships. incl: Kan. Pres Club; Ed., Kan. Clubwoman; Chmn., Press & Publicity, Kan. Fedn. of Women's Clubs, 1937-39; Nat. Commn. on Christian Higher Educ., 1956-60; Trustee, Kan. Wesleyan Univ., 1950-65; Trustee, Meth. Youthville & Meth. Ch. Boy's Ranch, 1953-64; num. offs., New England Histl. & Genealogical Soc.; num. offs., Conn. Soc. of Geneals.; num. offs., Order of Eastern Star; num. offs., AAUW & DAR;

Daughters of Am. Colonists; Daughters of Fndrs. & Patriots of Am.; PEO; Deleg., Official Rep., World Confs. of Meth. Ch., Oslo, Norway; Life Patron, Woman's Soc. of Christian Serv., Meth. Ch., 1953; U.S. Daughters of 1812; Descendants of Colonial Clergy. Hons: Citation of Appreciation for volunteer serv. in Meth. Ch., 1965. Address: 10741 Venturi Dr., Sun City, AZ 85351, U.S.A.

McGILL, Withell H. (Mrs. Timothy L. McGill), b. 26 Sept. 1929. Teacher. Educ: B.S., Huston-Tillotson Coll., Austin, Tex., 1950; M.Ed., Tex. Southern Univ., Houston, 1959; UCLA, 1952 & 53; Univ. of Wyo., 1962 & 65. Appts: Tchr., Pub. Schls., Hawkins, Tex., 1950-69; Asst. Prof. of Educ. & Reading, 1969-; Sabbatical study leave, E. Tex. State Univ., 1973-74. Mbrships: NEA; Tex. State Tchrs. Assn.; AAUP; Pres., E. Tex. Reading Coun.; IRA; Sustaining Mbr., E. Tex. Area Coun., Boy Scouts of Am.; Friend of Youth; Top Teen Club; Pres., Hawkins Alumnae Chapt., Delta Sigma Theta Inc. Hons: Cert. of Hon., PTA Off., 1971; Parliamentarian, ibid, 1972; PTA Attendance Award, 1965, 66 & 67. Address: P.O. Box 371, Hawkins, TX 75765, U.S.A. 125.

McGINN, Donald, J., b. 1 Apr. 1905. Professor. Educ: A.B., Cornell Univ., 1926; M.A., ibid, 1929; Ph.D., 1930. Appts: w. commercial dept., N.Y. Telephone Co., N.Y.C., 1926-28; Hd., Engl. Dept., Rutgers Prep. Schl., 1930-36; Instr., Rutgers Univ., New Brunswick, N.J., 1936-40; Asst. Prof., ibid, 1940-46; Assoc. Prof., 1946-51; Prof., 1951-73; Prof. Emeritus, 1973-; Prof., Georgian Court Coll., Lakewood, N.J., 1953-. Mbrships: Coll. Coun. on Engl. in Ctrl. Atlantic States (sec.-treas., chmn.); MLA; Phi Beta Kappa; Am. Shakespeare Assn.; Renaissance Soc. Am.; Cath. Commn. on Intellectual & Cultural Affairs (sec., 1960-61; chmn., 1970-71). Publs: Shakespeare's Influence on the Drama of his Age, 1938; The Admonition Controversy, 1949; Literature as a Fine Art, 1959; John Penry & the Marprelate Controversy, 1966. Address: 2 President Ave., Lavallette, NJ 08735, U.S.A. 6, 13.

McGIVERN, James Sabine, b. 27 July 1908. Priest of the Society of Jesus. Educ: Jesuit Sems. in Guelph, Ont., Canada, Montreal, P.Q., Toronto, Ont. & Valkenburg, Holland; B.A., Univ. of Montreal; M.A., Univ. of Toronto; Ph.D., Gregorian Univ. Appts. incl: Chap. to Canadian Armed Forces, 1940-64, retiring w. rank of Major; Asst. & Histn., Martyrs' Shrine, Midland, Ont., 1964-; Ed., Martyrs' Shrine Message, 1965-; Jesuit Archivist, 1964-; Archivist, R.C. Archdiocese of Toronto, 1972-; Prof., Ch. hist., Toronto Schl. of Theol., 1972-. Mbrships. incl: Fellow, Royal Geographical Soc., Fellow, Soc. of Antiquaries (Scot.); Kt. Cmdr., Order of St. Lazarus; Kt. Hospitaller, Order of St. John of Jerusalem; Life mbr., New England Genealogical & Histl. Soc.; Life mbr., Clan Donald Soc. of Canada. Publs. incl: The Jesuit Relation of 1635 (co-author); The Martyrs of New France (co-author); The Story of Royal Engineers in British Columbia. Recip. of hons. Address: Regis Coll., 3425 Bayview Ave., Willowdale, Ont., M2M 3S5, Canada.

McGLAUN, Rithia Anna, b. 24 Dec. 1940. Educator. Educ: B.A., Mercer Univ., 1962; Univ. of Leeds; M.A., Univ. of N.C., Greensboro, 1965; Emory Univ. Appts: Tchr. of Engl., Andrew Coll., 1964; Ga. Southern Coll., 1965-66; Columbus Coll., 1966-. Mbrships: Ga. Coun. of Tchrs. of Engl.; Sigma Mu; Tau Kappa Alpha; Cardinal Key Hon. Soc.; Assn. of Marshall Schlrs. & Alumni; AAUW; S. Atlantic MLA. Publs: A Bright Compulsion (poems), 1972; articles in jrnls. inclng: Safe in Byzantium, Contempera, 1970 & "Aeropigitica" The Breaking Forth of Light, Forum, 1974. Co-Writer (w. Lew Tobin, Boston) of song, Toy Bus to the Kindergarten, 1972. Recip. Marshall Schlrship., 1962. Address: c/o Dept. of Lang. & Humanities, Columbus Coll., Columbus, GA 31907, U.S.A. 125.

McGLYNN, Edna Mary, b. 3 Jan. 1908. College Professor. Educ: A.B., Boston Univ., Mass., 1927; A.M., 1928; Ph.D., Boston Coll., 1934; Ph.D., Georgetown Univ., 1959. Appts: Tchr., Keene Normal Schl., N.H., 1928-36; Prof., Salem State Coll., 1936-; Hd., Hist. & Soc. Sci. Dept., ibid, 1953-72; Prof., Mass. State Coll., Fitchburg, summer, 1937; Prof., Mt. St. Mary Coll., N.H., summers, 1939-41. Mbrships. incl: Phi Beta Kappa; N.E. Hist. Assn.; Delta Tau Kappa. Contbr. to schol. publs. Address: Salem State Coll., Salem, MA 01970, U.S.A.

McGOEY, Noelle Theresa, b. 25 Dec. 1927. Librarian. Educ: B.A., Newcomb Coll., 1947; M.A., Tulane Univ., 1950. Appts: Tchr., Orleans Parish Schl. Bd., 1947-54; Libn., New Orleans Pub. Lib., La., 1954-. Mbrships: La Lib. Assn.; New Orleans Lib. Club. Publs: The Teaching of English in New Orleans. Hons: Nat. Honor Soc., 1943; Oreades, 1945. Address: 317 Seattle St., New Orleans, LA 70124, U.S.A. 5, 138.

McGOUGH, Roger, b. 9 Nov. 1937. Poet. Educ: Hull Univ., U.K. Elected Fellow of Poetry, Univ. of Loughborough, 1973-75. Mbrships: Poetry Soc.; Equity; Songwriters Guild; Performing Rights Soc.; Hon. Pres., Merseyside Poetry Soc. Publs: Frinck, & Summer with Monika; Watchwords; After the Merrymaking; Out of Sequence; Gig; Sporting Relations, forthcoming 1974; Contbr. to Penguin Modern Poets No. 10 & Oxford Book of Twentieth Century English Verse. Address: Windermere House, Windermere Terr., Liverpool 8, U.K.

McGOWAN, Daniel A., b. 4 May 1945. Economist. Educ: B.A., Cornell Univ., Ithaca, N.Y., U.S.A., 1966; M.A., Stanford Univ., Calif., 1968; M.B.A., Bucknell Univ., Lewisburg, Pa., 1969; Ph.D., Pa. State Univ., Univ. Pk., 1973. Appts. incl: Instr. & Asst. Prof., Susquehanna Univ., Selinsgrove, Pa., 1967-71; Instr., Pa. State Univ., 1971-73; Sr. Economist, Michael Baker Jr., Inc., 1973; Asst. Prof., Hobart & William Smith Colls., Geneva, N.Y., 1973-. Mbrships: Phi Beta Kappa; Phi Kappa Phi; Omicron Delta Epsilon; Pi Gamma Mu. Publs: The Use of Theoretical Economics in the Choice of Welfare Projects, 1970; Contbns. to profl. jrnls.; 2 papers (one w. J.D. Smith) read at confs. Address: 98 Hillcrest Ave., Geneva, NY 14456, U.S.A.

McGOWAN, Harold, b. 23 June 1909. Master Builder & Developer; Scientist; Financier; Author; Sculptor; Philanthropist; Patentee. Educ: B'lynn Polytech. & Pratt Insts.; N.Y. Univ.; Hubbard Coll., U.K.; Rose Croix Univ., Calif.; D.Sc., Coll. of Fla. Appts: Pres. & Chmn. of Bd., Atomic Rsch. Inc.; Pres., Harold McGowan Bldrs.; Owner & Developer, Ctrl. Islip Shopping Ctr. & Ctrl. Islip Indl. Park.; developer & Builder of Res. Communities: Brinsley Gdns., Rolling Green, Slater Pk., Clover Green, Maple Acres & Wheeler Acres; Suffolk Co'. Hwy. Commnr. Mbrships: Mensa Int.; AAAS; IEEE; Scientologist OT VII; Explorers Club. Sculptures: Peace; Victory; Eternity; Love & Hate; Appreciation; The Creator. Publs: Green Flight: The Making of a Universalist; The Thoughtron Theory of Life & Matter; The Spirit of Christmas in Words & Sculpture. Cited as Owner of Little League Ball Pks., 25 yrs. Recip., Wisdom Award of Hon., 1970. Address: 28 Second Ave., Ctrl. Islip, NY 11722, U.S.A. 6.

McGOWAN, Lionel James, b. 26 Feb. 1900. Consultant; Corporation Director. Educ: Fac. of Mgmt. Scis., Univ. of Ottawa, Canada, 1918; Schl. of Econs., Univ. of Chgo., U.S.A., 1923. Appts: Dir., The Fndn. Co. of Canada Ltd., 1950-62; Gen. Mgr., ibid, 1955; Pres., 1958; Cons., 1962; Cons. & Chmn., Taylor Woodrow of Canada Ltd., 1963-67; Cons., ibid, 1967-; Chmn., Bd. of Regents Univ., Ottawa, 1958-64; Dir., Allied Chem. Canada Ltd., Montreal, 1958-, Texaco Canada Ltd., Toronto, 1958-, Babcock & Wilcox Canada Ltd., Cambridge, Ont., 1964-, & St. John's Convalescent Hosp., 1948-; Dir. & Vice Chmn., N. York Gen. Hosp., 1964-. Mbrships. incl: Fellow, Inst. of Arbitrators, London; Am. Arbitration Assn., N.Y.C.; Canadian Inst. of Mining & Metallurgy, Toronto; Toronto Br., Royal Commonwealth Soc. Address: 5 York Ridge Rd., Willowdale, Ont., M2P 1R8, Canada. 2, 12, 16, 88.

McGOWEN, Faison Wells, b. 20 July 1903. Retired Accountant. Educ: Kings Bus. Coll.; Inst. of Govt., Univ. of N.C.; Commercial Dip; Certs., Co. Admin. & Property Tax Listing & Assessing. Appts: Dpty. Sheriff-Treas., 1924-28; Co. Acct. & Tax Supvsr., 1929-68. Mbrships. incl: Past Pres., N.C. Assn. of Co. Accts.; Past Pres., N.C. Assn. of Assessing Offs.; Past State Chmn., Int. Assn. of Assessing Offs.; Nat. Assn. Co. Treasurers & Fin. Offs.; Sec., N.C. Comm. for Study of Pub. Schl. Fin., 1957-58; Chmn., Duplin Co. Democratic Exec. Comm., 29 yrs.; Duplin Co. Ind. & Agric. Coun.; Sec., Duplin Gen. Hosp. Bd. of Trustees; Official Spokesman, Co. Hosp. Bldg. Prog., 1968-70; Mason; Charter, Order of the Eastern Star, Co-Ed., Flashes of Duplin's History & Government, 1971. Hons. incl: Merit Award, N.C. Soc. Co. & Local Histns.; Graphic Arts Award, Printers of N.C. & S.C. Address: P.O. Box 446 A, Kenansville, NC 28349, U.S.A. 114, 125, 130, 131.

McGRATH, Harold M(orris), b. 1 June 1916. Educator. Educ: B.A., 1956, M.A., 1957, Ed.D., 1964, Univ. of Northern Colo., Greeley (formerly Colo. State Coll.); Additional studies, Pitt. Tech. Inst., 1970. Appts: Prin., Kuner Schl. Dist., Kersey, Colo., 1951-52; Fellow, 1953-54, Vis. Prof., 1968, Univ. of Northern Colo.; Prof., E. Carolina Univ., Greenville, N.C., 1957-; Dir. of Student. Tchng., Schl. of Technol., Dept. of Off. Admin. & Bus. Educ., ibid, 1964-; Symposium Cons. for Preparation of Mgmt. Personnel, 1968; Instr., Cons., Preparing Handicapped for World of Work. Mbrships: Phi Delta Kappa; Delta Pi Epsilon; Pi Omega Pi; Beta Gamma Sigma; Nat. & Southern Bus. Educ. Assn.; NEA; N.C. Educ. Assn.; Gov., Moose; Civitan; Greeley (Pres.) & Colo.-Wyo. Numismatic Assns. Contbr., article on Teaching Introduction to Business by Closed-Circuit Television, Am. Business Education, 1962. Address: 103 Deerwood Dr., Greenville, NC 27834, U.S.A. 7, 141.

McGREAL, Dorothy Winifred (Mrs. James D. McGreal). Editor; Publisher; Writer. Educ: N.Y. Schl. of Interior Decoration. Appts: Commercial Artist, N.Y.C.; 1st Woman Mgr. in profl. baseball, Stamford (Conn.) Pioneers Baseball Club, 1948; Ed.-Publr., World of Comic Art Publns., Hawthorne, Calif., 1966-; Tchr.-Lectr., Communiversity W., Experimental Coll., Calif. State Univ., Long Beach, 1974.

Mbrships: Past Pres. Fin Arts Assn. of Centinela Valley; Fndr., 1967, Comic Art Histl. Soc.; Friends of Huntington Lib.; Soc. of Mayflower Descendants. Publs: Remembered Dust, 1974. Hons: Pub. serv. awards—Community Chest, 1958; Boy Scouts of Am., 1959; Fine Arts Assn. of Centinela Valley, 1971. Address: 3839 W. 139th St., Hawthorne, CA 90250, U.S.A. 5.

MacGREGOR, (John) Geddes, b. 13 Nov. 1909. University Professor. Educ: D. ès L., Sorbonne, Paris, France, 1951; D.Phil., D.D., Oxford Univ., U.K.; LL.B., Edinburgh. Appts. incl: Rufus Jones Chair of Phils of Relig., Bryn Mawr Coll., Pa., U.S.A., 1949-60; Dean, Grad. Schl. of Relig., Univ. of Southern Calif., 1960-66; Disting. Prof., Philos., ibid, 1966-; Canon Theologian, St. Paul's Cathedral, L.A., 1968-. Fellow, Royal Soc. Lit. Mbrships. incl: Am. Philos. Assn.; Royal Commonwealth Soc.; Royal Zool. Soc. Publs. incl: Introduction to Religious Philosophy, 1959; The Coming Reformation, 1960; The Hemlock & the Cross, 1963; God Beyond Doubt, 1966; A Literary History of the Bible, 1968; The Sense of Absence, 1968; So Help Me God: A Calendar of Quick Prayers for Half Skeptics, 1970; Philosophical Issues in Religious Thought, 1973. Recip., Gold Medal, Commonwealth Club, San Fran., 1963. Address: 876 Victoria Ave., Los Angeles, CA 90005, U.S.A. 1, 2, 3, 9, 13, 15, 30, 43, 59, 72, 108, 118, 128, 130, 140.

McGUINNESS, John Seward, b. 12 Mar. 1922. Managerial Consultant & Actuary. Educ: B.S., Univ. of Calif., Berkeley, 1948; M.B.A., ibid, 1949; Ph.D., Stanford Univ., 1955; Grad., U.S. Army War Coll., 1971; various other courses. Appts: Ins. Clerk, Underwriter, 1939-43; Chief, Automotive Serv. Br., EUCOM Exchange System, 1946-47; Dir., Ins. Top-Mgmt. Rsch. Proj., Stanford Univ., 1951-54; Assoc. Actuary, Allstate Ins. Co., 1955-58; Casualty Actuary, MacArthur Ins. Grp., 1958-61; Budget Dir. & Actuary, Glens Falls Ins. Grp., 1961-64; Pres., John S. McGuinness Assocs., Scotch Plaines, N.J., 1964-. Fellowships: Canad. Inst. Actuaries; Casualty Actuarial Soc.; V.P., Int. Advsry. Coun., Soc. for Advancement of Mgmt. Mbrships: Am. Stat. Assn.; Soc. of Chartered Pro.-Casualty Undrs.; Int. Pres., Soc. of Ins. Rsch., 1972; Am. Acad. Actuaries; Int. Actuarial Assn.; ASTIN; Ops. Rsch. Soc. Am.; Alpha Kappa Psi; Beta Gamma Sigma; Delta Tau Delta. Contbr. to publs. in field. Recip. of Hons. & Ruling Elder, United Presby. Ch. in U.S.A. Address: 15 Kevin Rd., Scotch Plains, NJ 07076, U.S.A. 6, 27.

McGURN, Barrett, b. 6 Aug. 1914. Public Information Director. Educ: A.B., Fordham Univ., N.Y.C., 1935. Appts. incl: Reporter, N.Y. Herald Tribune, 1935-42, 1962-66; Bur. chief, ibid, Rome, Italy, 1946-52, 1955-62; Paris, France, 1952-55; Acting bur. chief, Moscow, U.S.S.R., 1958; War Corres., Pacific, & Wash. bur. chief, YANK Mag., 1942-45; U.S. Embassy press attaché, Rome, 1966-68; U.S. Embassy counselor for press affairs, Saigon, 1968-69; Dpty. spokesman, State Dept., 1969-72; World affairs commentator, U.S. Info Agcy., 1972-73; Dir., pub. info, U.S. Supreme Ct., 1973-. Mbrships. incl: Pres., O'seas Press Club of Am., 1963-65; Pres., Stampa Estera, Italy, 1961 & 1962; Bd. of Govs., Anglo-Am. Press Club, Paris, 1954-55. Author of books & mag. articles. Recip. of hons. Address: 5229 Duvall Dr., Westmoreland Hills, MD 20016, U.S.A. 2, 6, 7, 16, 22, 30, 49, 125, 128, 130.

MACHADO, Fernando Manoel Alves, b. 5 June 1906. Lawyer; Government Economic Adviser. Educ: Doctor in Law & Econ. Scis., Univ. of Coimbra. Appts. incl: Legal Advsr., Mining Bd., Portuguese Min. of Econs.; Pres., Regulating Comm. of Metal Trade, Nat. Comm. of Rosins, Supply Fund, Promotion Export Bd.; Chmn., Portuguese Delegation, GATT Meetings, Geneva; Mbr., Portuguese Delegation, Ministerial EFTA Meetings; Sec. of State for Trade; Portuguese Govt. Rep., Bank of Angola. Author, Letters from Abroad, 1935. Contbr., The Economist, Financial Times, La Revue Française, sev. jrnls. & newspapers. Hons. incl: Kt. Equestrian Order of Holy Sepulchre of Jerusalem; Grand Cross Mil. Order of Christ of Portugal; Grand Cross Order of Merit of Italy; Cmdr., Legion of Honour, France. Address: Travessa do Pinheiro 25-4, Lisbon 2, Portugal. 43.

McHENRY, (Mrs.) Charlotte Swales, b. 14 July 1946. Assistant Professor. Educ: BSN, Miss. Univ. Schl. Nursing, Jackson, U.S.A., 1964-68; Md. Univ. Grad. Schl. Nursing, Balt., 1968-70. Appts: Asst. Prof. Nursing, Univ. S. Miss., Hattiesburg, 1970-71; 1st Lt.-Capt., USAF, Psych./Mental Hlth. Nurse, Therapeutic Community, Eglin, Fla., 1971-73; Asst. Prof. Nursing, Univ. S. Miss., Hattiesburg, 1973-74; Proj. Dir. Nat. Inst. Mental Hlth.-Integration Mental Hlth. Concepts in Nursing Curriculum; Chmn. Cons. & Fac. Enrichment Comm. & Mental Hlth. Nursing; Coord. NSG 120 Series. Mbrships: Am. Nurse Assn.; AAUW; AAUP; Forrest Co. Mental Hlth. Assn.; Miss. Univ. Alumni Assn.; Md. Univ., ibid; Nat. League for Nursing; Pres., Beta Club; Phi Delta Gamma. Author Papers, Mental Health in Occupational Nursing, 1970; Family Development, 1974; Motivating Geriatrics (in progress). Hons. incl: Valedictorian Scholship., 1964; Nat. Inst. Hlth. Traineeship, Sr. Yr., 1967-68; Grad. Prog., 1968-70; Award, DAR, 1964; VA Citizenship Award, 1964. Address: 2902 Hillside Dr., Hattiesburg, MS 39401, U.S.A. 125.

McHUGH, Arona (Mrs. Warren McHugh), b. 8 Aug. 1924. Writer. B.A., Iowa Univ., U.S.A., 1950; M.A., Columbia Univ., N.Y., 1951; M.A., Grad. Fac. Philos., ibid, 1953. Appts: w. Women's Army Corps, U.S. Army, 1944-48; Libn., New Schl. Soc. Rsch., N.Y., 1951-53; Children's Libn., N.Y. Pub. Lib., 1954-56. Mbrships: PEN; Authors Guild. Publs: A Banner With A Strange Device, 1964; 2nd ed., '65, paperback ed., '66; The Sea-Coast Of Bohemia, 1965; 2nd ed., '66, paperback ed., '67; The Luck Of The Van Meers: A Tradition, 1969; The Calling Of The Sea, 1973; paperback ed., '74. Hons; Bernard De Voto Fellowship, Fiction Writing, Breadloaf Writer's Conf., Vt., 1967; MacDowell Colony Fellowship, 1969; Edward Albee Fndn. Fellowship, 1972. Address: c/o Paul Reynolds Lit. Agcy., 599 5th Ave., N.Y.C., NY 10017, U.S.A. 30.

McILHANY, Sterling Fisher, b. 12 Apr. 1930. Editor; Writer. Educ: B.F.A., Univ. of Tex., Austin, U.S.A.; Postgrad., Univ. of Calif., L.A., Calif., & Accademia Belle Arti, Rome, Italy. Appts: Tchng. Asst., Univ. of Calif., L.A.; Sr. Ed., Van Nostrand Reinhold, N.Y.C.; Pres., Art Horizons, N.Y.C.; Ed., Am. Artist, N.Y.C. Publs: Banners & Hangings; Art as Design: Design as Art; Wood Inlay; Num. articles in Am. & European mags. Num. pvte. paintings, some reproduced. Recip., Fellowship for yr.'s study at Accademia Belle Arti, Rome, Rotary Int., 1957-58. Address: 52 Morton St., N.Y., NY 10014, U.S.A. 2, 57.

McILVEEN, Walter, b. 12 Aug. 1927. Heating, Ventilating, Air-Conditioning Engineer. Educ: M.E., Coll. of Technol., Queens Univ., Belfast, U.K., 1948; Heating,

Ventilating & Air-Conditioning Engr., Borough Polytechnic, London, 1951. Appts: Mech. Engr. Apprentice, Davidson & Co., Belfast, 1943-48; Sr. Contract Engr., Keith Blackman Ltd., London, 1948-58; Mech. Engr., Fred S. Dubin Assocs., Hartford, Conn., U.S.A., 1959-64; Chief Mech. Engr., Koton & Donovan, W. Hartford, Conn., 1964-66; Prin., Walter McIlveen Assocs., Avon, Conn., 1966-. Mbrships: Registered Profl. Engr., Conn., Mass., N.J., R.I., Fla., N.Y. Address: 3 Valley View Rd., Weatogue, CT 06089, U.S.A. 6.

MACINNIS, Douglas Evan, b. 28 June 1903. Retired Civil Servant; Pastoralist. Educ: LL.B., Sydney Univ., Australia; Qld. Univ. Appts: Pastoral Exec., N.W. Qld. & N.T.; Pastoralist on own account; Govt. Pastoral Insp., N.Y.; Sr. Legal Officer, Crown Law Office; Dir., Dept. of Lands & Surveys; Dir., Dept. of Lands Surveys & Mines, T.P.N.G.; Sr. Legal Officer, Dept. of Mines, N.S.W. Mbrships. incl: Royal Commonwealth Soc.; Aust. Heritage; N.S.W. & T.P.N.G. Bars; N.T. Legislative Coun., 1950; Legislative Coun. & Exec. Coun., T.P.N.G., 1953-64; Chmn., Papua New Guinea Land Bd., 1952-64; Chmn., Petroleum Advsry. Bd., 1953-64; Chmn., Mining Advsry. Bd., 1953-64. Recip., O.B.E., 1960. Address: 19 Morialta St., Mansfield, Qld., Australia 4122. 23.

McINNIS, Ira Mauria, b. 10 Apr. 1903. Librarian. Educ: B.A., Belhaven Coll., 1924; M.A. in L.S., George Peabody Coll., 1955; Postgrad study, Tulane Univ., Belhaven Coll., Univ. of Miss. Appts: Tchr., Maths., Latin, Engl., Libn., var. elem., H.S., Miss. & Ga., 1924-52; Libn., LaFayette H.S., Ga., 1952-53; Libn., Corinth H.S., Miss., 1953-56; Libn., Miss. Delta Jr. Coll., Moorhead, 1956-71; Libn., French Camp Acad., Miss., 1971-. Mbrships: Histl. Comm., Miss. Lib. Assn.; Southeastern Lib. Assn.; Miss. Educ. Assn.; Past Chapt. Pres., Delta Kappa Gamma; Beta Phi Mu; Order of Eastern Star; Sec.-Treas., French Camp Community Club; Clan McInnis Soc. Hons: Maurine McInnis Room named in new Stanny Sanders Lib., Miss. Delta Jr. Coll., 1973. Address: Box 100, Pickens, MS 39146, U.S.A. 5, 7, 15, 125, 138.

MACINNIS, Marcus Lindsay, b. 9 Aug. 1914. Officer, Royal Australian Air Force, Air Commodore, retired 1973. Educ: B.Econ., Sudney Univ.; R.A.A.F. Staff Coll.; Inst.of Indl. Mgmt. Appts. incl: Joined R.A.A.F., 1939; Dir., Supply & Transport, 1950-52; Cmdng. Off., No. 7 Stores Depot, Toowoomba, Qld., 1954-56; Hon. A.D.C. to H.E. the Gov. Gen. of Australia, Field Marshal Sir William Slim, 1954-56; Staff Off., Equipment HQ, Home Command, 1956-58; Dir., Equipment Policy & Admin. Dept. of Air, 1958-60; Promoted Group Capt., 1960; On exchange w. RAF Cmdng. Off., RAF Hartlebury, Worcs., U.K., 1960-63; Staff Off., Supply HQ, Support Command R.A.A.F., 1963-68; Controller of Equipment Dept., Air Canberra, 1968-73; retd. 1973. Mbrships: Naval & Mil. Club, Melbourne, Vic.; Commonwealth Club, Canberra, A.C.T. Hons: Mention in Despatches, Middle East; C.B.E., 1969. Address: 8 Sheehan St., Pearce, A.C.T., Australia 2607. 23.

MacINTOSH, A.J., b. 10 July 1921. Barrister; Solicitor; Queen's Counsel. Educ: B.A., LL.B., Dalhousie Univ., 1942, '48. Read law w. T.D. MacDonald, Q.C., Dpty. Atty.-Gen. of N.S., 1947-48. Called to Bar of N.S., & Ont., 1948. Appts: Serv. WWII w. R.C.N.V.R.; Joined Blake, Anglin, Osler & Cassels, Toronto, 1948; Ptnr., Blake, Cassels & Graydon, 1955; Dpty. Gov., Hudson's Bay Co.; Dir., Canadian Imperial Bank of Commerce, Brascan Ltd.,

Pilkington Brothers Canada Ltd., John Labatt Ltd., DeHavilland Aircraft of Canada Ltd., Steel Co. of Canada, Ltd., Toronto Star Ltd., George Wimpey Canada Ltd., Canadian Corporate Mgmt., Globelite Batteries Ltd. Mbr. of Toronto Club. Address: Box 25, Commerce Ct. Postal Stn., Toronto, Ont., M5L 1A9, Canada. 2, 88.

McINTOSH, Clement Olando, b. 9 June 1905. Teacher; Notary Public; Farmer. Educ: B.Sc. (Educ.), S.C. State Coll., Orangeburg; Hampton Inst., Hampton, Va.; Benedict Coll., Columbia, S.C.; Claflin Coll., Orangeburg, S.C.; Ga. State Coll., Savannah. Appts: Prin., Edgefield Co. Trng. Schl., Johnston, S.C., Centenary Jr. HS, Marion, S.C., St. Mark Jr. HS, Allendale, S.C., 1939-56, C.V. Bing Elem., Allendale, S.C., 1956-61, Fairfax Trng. HS, Fairfax, S.C., 1961-69, Allendale Middle (C.V. Bing), Allendale, S.C., 1969-72. Mbrships: Pres., Edgefield Tchr. Assn.; Exec. Sec., Agric. Tchrs. Assn.; Secondary Schl. Prins. Assn.; Elem. Schl. Prins. Assn.; S.C. Educ. Assn.; Palmetto Tchrs. Assn.; NEA; Allendale Veterans Advsry. Bd.; Allendale Educ. Assn. Hons. incl: 20 Yrs. Serv. Award, S.C. State Dept. of Agric. Educ., 1954; Walterboro Agric. Dist. Award, 1950; Sr. Class Appreciation Awards, Fairfax HS, 1965; Dedication of Fairfax HS Yrbook., 1964; Disting. Tchrs. Award, Allendale Middle Schl., 1972; Outstanding Serv. Award, Allendale Co. Schl. Bd. of Educ., 1972. Address: P.O. Box 172, Allendale, SC 29810, U.S.A. 125.

McINTOSH, James Colin, b. 18 Aug. 1923. Diplomat. Educ: B.S., Georgetown Univ., Schl of For. Serv., 1948; M.S., Columbia Univ. 1950. Appts: Ref. Libn., Enoch Pratt Free Lib. Balt., Md., 1950-52 & 1954-55; For. Serv. Info Off., US Info. Agcy., 1952-53 & 55-; Lille France, 1952-53; Bonn, Freiburg & Frankfurt German Fed. Repub., 1955-61; Cultural Attaché, Am. Embassy, Ottawa, Can., 1961-62 Dir., Book Tranl. Prog., Am. Embassy, Paris, 1963-65; at HQ, US Info. Agcy., Wash. D.C. 1965-67; Pub. Affairs Off., USIS, Am Embassy, Tunis, Tunisia, 1967-70; Pub. Affairs Off. & Cnslr. of Embassy, Kinshasa, Zaire 1970-72; Dpty. Asst. Dir., W. European Area US Info. Agcy., Wash. D.C., 1972-. Mbrships Am. For. Serv. Assn. Publs. incl: transls. from French to Engl.; contbr. articles to newspapers & profl. jrnls. Recip. Superior Hon. Award, US Info. Agcy., 1965. Address: 7608 New Market Dr., Bethesda, MD 20034, U.S.A. 2.

MacINTOSH, Jay W. (Mrs. William Wood Bell), b. 30 Mar. 1937. Actress; Teacher. Educ: B.F.A., Univ. of Ga., 1961; M.A., ibid, 1962 Appts: Hd., Dept. of Speech & Drama, Brenal Coll., 1962-65; Chmn., Div. of Humanities Gainesville Jr. Coll., 1966-68; Film & TV Actress, 1969-. Films incl: Like It Is; Wild Rovers; J.W. Coop; The Blue Knight; Senior Year; The Healers; Pssst, Hammerman's After You. Mbrships: Phi Beta Kappa; Phi Kappa Phi Zeta Phi Eta; Zodiac Scholastic Soc.; Kappa Alpha Theta; Thalian-Blackfriars Hon. Soc.; Lee Strasberg's Actors Studio; Screen Actors Guild Actors Equity; Am. Fedn. of TV & Radio Artists. Address: 2399 Mandeville Canyon Rd. Los Angeles, CA 90049, U.S.A. 5, 9, 22, 74 75, 76, 132, 138.

McINTOSH, Kenneth Bennett, b. 17 Nov 1927. Methodist Minister; Missionary. Educ B.A., Southern Meth. Univ., Dallas, Tex., 1950 M.Th., Perkins Schl. Theol., ibid, 1952. Appts incl: Meth. Min., N. Tex. Annual Conf., 1951-6 Chicota Circuit, 1951-53, Caddo Mills, Tex. 1953-55, Lake Highlands Meth. Ch., Dallas Tex., 1955-61; United Meth. Missionary

1961-71. Mbrships: Southwest Conf. on Asian Studies; Chinese Lang. Tchrs. Assn., U.S.A.; Tex. Chinese Assn.; Co-Chmn., Chinese-Am. Cultural Assn. of Dallas, Tex.; Southern Meth. Univ. Alumni Assn.; Yale Univ. Alumni Assn. of Hong Kong; Y.M.C.A., Hong Kong; Past Sec., V.P., Young Mens Club of Kowloon, Hong Kong. Contbr. to theol. jrnls. Hons: Disting. Serv. Award, N. Tex. Conf. Town & Country Comm., 1953; U.S. army awards & medals. Address: 3028 Fondren Dr., Dallas, TX 75205, U.S.A. 7, 116.

McINTYRE, James Millar, b. 21 Nov. 1935. Educator; Consultant. Educ: B.S., Fla. State Univ., Tallahassee, U.S.A., 1958. Appts: Rsch. Assoc., Grad. Schl. of Educ., Harvard Univ., Cambridge, Mass., 1967-69; Lectr., Sloan Schl. of Mgmt., MIT, Cambridge, 1968-71; Cons., Human Goals Prog., USN, 1972-; Vis. Prof., Behavioral Sci., Schl. of Law, Univ. of Hawaii, Honolulu, 1973-. Mbrship: Dir., Dev. Rsch. Assocs., Newton Ctr., Mass. Publs. incl: Teaching Achievement Motivation (w. A.Alschuler & D. Tabor), 1970; Organizational Psychology: An Experiential Approach (w. D.Kolb & I.Rubin), 1971, 2nd edit. 1974; Ed., Organizational Psychology: A Book of Readings (w. D.Kolb & I.Rubin), 1971, 2nd edit. 1974; 2 pamphlets. Address: 83 Concord Rd., Sudbury, MA 01776, U.S.A.

MACINTYRE, John Reid, b. 30 May 1916. Medical Practitioner. Educ: M.B.Ch.B., Univ. of Glasgow, U.K., 1938; F.R.F.P.S., (R.F.P.S. Glasgow), 1949; F.R.C.S. (R.C.P.S. Glasgow), 1963; Fellow, Australian Coll. Med. Admnstrs. Appts. incl: Sr. Med. Off., Colony of Island of St. Helena, S. Atlantic, 1952-55; Dist. Med. Off., State Dept. of Hlth. Servs., Tasmania, Australia, 1955-56; Sr. Med. Off., ibid, 1956-66; Chief Med. Off., 1966-67; Dpty. Dir. Gen. of Hlth. Servs., 1967-68; Dir. Gen. of Hlth. Servs. & Permanent Hd., Dept. of Hlth. Servs. 1968-. Mbrships. incl: Fellow, Australian Inst. of Hosp. Admnstrs.; Fellow, Australian Inst. of Mgmt.; Fellow, Royal Soc. of Med.; Nat. Hlth. & Med. Rsch. Coun., 1968-; Hosp. & Allied Servs. Advsry. Coun.; Australian Dental Hlth. Servs. Advsry. Comm.; Royal Soc. of Pub. Admin. Contbr. to British Jrnl. of Plastic Surg. Recip., S.B. St. John, 1970. Address: 9 Grange Ave., Taroona, Tasmania, Australia 7006. 23.

MACKAY, Alastair, b. 27 Sept. 1911. Civil Servant. Educ: M.A. (Hons.), Edinburgh Univ. Appts. incl: Staff Mbr., H.M. Treasury, 1940; Mbr., U.K. Treasury & Supply Delegation, Wash. D.C., 1951-54; Seconded to For. Off. Inspectorate, 1957-59; Financial Advsr., British High Commnr. in India, 1963-67; Under-Sec., H.M. Treasury, 1968-71; Financial & Dev. Sec., Govt. of Gibraltar, 1971-. Hons: Companion of Order of St. Michael & St. George, 1966. Address: Govt. Secretariat, Gibraltar. 1, 41.

McKAY, Arthur Ferguson, b. 1 Dec. 1916. Executive. Educ: B.Sc., McGill Univ., Quebec, 1937; M.Sc., Dalhousie Univ., N.S., 1941; Ph.D., Univ. of Toronto, 1944. Appts. incl: Dir., Rsch. & Dev., Monsanto Canada Ltd., 1954-56; V.P., ibid, 1958; Dir., 1964; Res. Dir., Rsch., Norton Co., Chippewa Ont., 1966-67; V.P., & Mgng. Dir., Norton Rsch. Corp. (Canada) Ltd., 1967-70; Pres., Masury-Columbia Co., Ill., 1970-71; Lectr. & Cons. in Bus. Admin., 1972-; at Grad. Schl. of Bus., Univ. of N.S.W., Australia, 1973. Mbrships. incl: Fellow, AAAS, Chem. Inst of Canada & Royal Soc. of Canada; Plastics Inst. of Engrs. Holds 65 patents. Contbr. about 115 sci. papers to field & publs. on mkt. rsch. Address: c/o Grad School of Business, University of New South Wales, P.O. Box 1, Kensington, N.S.W., Australia, 2033. 8, 14, 16, 88, 128, 139.

McKAY, Ian Lloyd, b. 7 Mar. 1929. Barrister; Solicitor. Educ: B.A., LL.B., Vic. Coll., Univ. of N.Z., 1952. Appts: Ptnr., Swan Davies McKay & Co., Wellington, 1953-67, Sr. Ptnr., 1967-; Dir., Independent Newspapers Ltd., 1970-, Waipipi Ironsands Ltd., 1970-, Ados Chem. Co. Ltd., 1971-, Wellington Publishing Co. Ltd., 1972-; Mbr., Law Revision Commn., 1971-, Wellington Dist. Law Soc. Coun., 1971, N.Z. Coun. of Law Reporting, 1973-; Chmn., Torts & Gen. Law Reform Comm., 1971-. Mbrships: Dominion Councillor, Piping & Dancing Assn. of N.Z. Inc., 195/-73, Life Mbr., 1974-; Chmn., Music Comm., Comunn NA Piobaireachd (N.Z.) Inc., 1958-70, Pres., 1970-; Wellington Pipers Club Inc.; Pres., ibid, 1959-61; Pres., Wellington 22 Club, 1962, Life Mbr., 1972-; Wellington Club; Central Club. Address: P.O. Box 236, Wellington, New Zealand.

MACKAY, James Alexander, b. 21 Nov. 1936. Author. Educ: M.A., Glasgow Univ., U.K., 1958. Appts: Keeper, Philatelic Collections, Brit. Mus., 1961-71; Columnist for The New Daily, 1962-66 & Financial Times, 1967-; Ed.-in-Chief, Int. Ency. of Stamps, 1968-72; Antiques Advsry. Ed., Ward Lock Ltd., 1971-. Mbr., Advsry. Bd., The Investing Professional, N.Y., 1972-; Engl. Lang. Ed., Ward Lock New World Ency., 1973-. Publs. incl: Antiques of the Future, 1970; Small Antiques, 1971; Commemorative Medals, 1970; Airmails, 1870-1970, 1971; Commemorative Pottery & Porcelain, 1971; Coin-collecting for Grown-up Beginners, 1971; Greek & Roman Coins, 1971, 1971; Undiscovered Antiques, 1972; Stamps, Posts & Postmarks, 1973; Coins & Money Tokens, 1973; Medals & Decorations, 1973; Glass Paperweights, 1973. Animalier Bronzes, 1973; Dictionary of Stamps, 1973; Kitchen Antiques, 1973; Source Book of Stamps, 1974; Paper Money, 1974; Collecting Famous Faces, 1974; Stamp Design, 1974; Dictionary of Turn of the Century Antiques, 1974; Robert Bruce, King of Scots, 1974. Address: 2 Mill Loch, Lochmaben, Lockerbie, Dumfriesshire, DG 11 1, U.K.

McKAY, (Mrs.) Kate Curtis, b. 14 May 1905. Teacher; Educator. Educ: B.S., Northeastern State Coll., Tahiequah, Okla. 1935; M.A., George Peabody Coll. for Tchrs. Nashville, Tenn., 1960. Appts: Over 40 yrs. Tchr. at Speake H.S., Hatton H.S., Lawrence Co. H.S.; Prin., Iron Bridge Schl., Ala.; Retired 1970. Mbr. of Order of Eastern Star, Moulton Chapt. 412, Ala. Address: 102 Edna St., Moulton, AL 35650, U.S.A. 57.

MACKAY, Kathleen I. (Mrs. Eric Mackay), b. 17 Nov. 1926. Educator. Educ: B.A., Grove City Coll., Pa., U.S.A.; M.Ed., Univ. of Okla., Norman. Appts: Tchr., Otto Township Schls., Pa.; Tchr., Okla. City Schls.; Ed.-P.R. Dir., Okla. Educ. Assn.; Prof., Miami-Dade Jr. Coll.; Dir., For. Student Prog., Miami-Dade Community Coll.; For. Student Advsr., ibid; Supvsr., Writing Lab. Mbrships: Local Pres., Pilot Club Int., Okla. City; Pres., For. Lang. Assn., Okla.; Cons., NEA. Contbr., Column. N. Bay Village News. Address: 7525 W. Treasure Drive, Miami Beach, FL 33141, U.S.A. 2, 125.

MACKAY, (The Hon.) Kenneth Charles, b. 29 Oct. 1920. Judge. Educ: B.C.L., McGill Univ., Canada, 1950; M.C.L., 1951. Appts. incl: Dir., Legal Aid Bur., 1956-61; Crown Atty., 1960-65; Lectr., Fac. of Law, McGill Univ., 1961-69; Councillor, Canadian Bar Assn., 1963-65; Chmn., Maritime Law Sect., 1963-65;

Municipal Judge & Recorder, Hampstead, 1965-69; Judge of Superior Ct., P.Q., 1969-. Mbrships. incl: Hon., Canadian Maritime Law Assn., 1969-; Treas., Montreal Advocates Benevolent Assn., 1972-; Pres., St. Andrews Soc., Montreal; Gov., MacKay Ctr. for Deaf & Crippled Children; Dir. & Hon. Sec., Queen Elizabeth Hosp. Montreal; Jacques Viger Commn. for 'Vieux Montreal'. Author, The St. Andrew's Society: A Brief History, 1973. Hons: Col., 78th (Old) Fraser Highlanders, 1970; Kt. Cmdr., St. John of Jerusalem, 1971. Address: Court House, Rm. 15.23, 1 Notre Dame St. East, Montreal, P.Q., K2Y 1B6, Canada.

McKELLAR, Kenneth, b. 23 June 1927. Singer. Educ: B.Sc., Univ. of Aberdeen, U.K.; Royal Coll. of Music, London. Appts: Prin. Tenor, Carl Rosa Opera Co., 1953-54; Freelance Artist, TV, Radio, Recording, Concert Platform thru' the World; Dir., Radio Clyde Ltd. Mbrships: Fellow, Royal Soc. of Arts; Hon. Pres., Tenovus, Scotland; Saints & Sinners, Scotland. Publs: Romantic Scotland of Kenneth McKellar; Var. songs & setting. Recip. of Henry Leslie Prize for singing, 1952. Address: Marchrie Mhor, 39, Victoria Rd., Lenzie, Glasgow, G66 5AR, U.K. 4.

MACKELLAR, Michael John Randal b. 27 Oct. 1938. Parliamentarian. Educ. incls: B.Sc. Agr., Sydney Univ., 1960; M.A., Balliol Coll., Oxford Univ., U.K., 1964. Appts: Asst. Organiser, Agricl. Bur. of N.S.W., Australia. 1961-67; Asst. Prin. Ext. Off. (Grp. Ext.), N.S.W. Dept. of Agric., 1967-69; Lectr. in Agricl. Ext. Methodol. (p/t), Univ. of N.S.W., 1968, Univ. of Sydney, 1967-68; Mbr., Coun. of Australian Nat. Univ., 1970-; Mbr., Select Comm., on Wildlife Conservation, 1970-72; Mbr., Jt. Standing Comm. For. Affairs & Defence, 1970-; Mbr., Jt. Comm. Pub. Accts., 1973-; Dpty. Chmn. of Comms., House of Reps., 1973-; Parliamentary Sec., Ldr. of the Opposition, 1973-; Mbr., 1st Australian Parliamentary Delegation to China, 1973. Mbrships: Australian Inst. of Agricl. Sci. (Treas., N.S.W. Br., 1962); Royal Soc. of N.S.W.; Commonwealth Parliamentary Assn.; Australian Club. Recip. of Leader Grant, U.S. State Dept., 1972. Address: Parliament House, Canberra, A.C.T., Australia. 23.

McKELVEY, Robert Kenneth, b. 3 Feb. 1922. Research Psychologist. Educ: B.A., Univ. of Mo., U.S.A. 1947; M.A., ibid, 1948; Ph.D., Univ. of Wash., 1951. Appts: Tchng. Assoc., Univ. of Wash., 1948-51; Rsch. Psychologist, USAF, 1951-58; Rsch. Psychologist Chief, Human Factors Br., Fed. Aviation Agcy. Systems Res. & Dev. Serv., 1958-66; Dir., Injury Control Rsch. Lab. USPHS, DHEW, 1966-73; Instr., Ext. Div., 1970-; Adjunct Prof. of Industl. Engrng., Univ. of R.I., 1973-. Mbrships. incl: Am., & E. Psychol. Assns.; Human Factors Soc.; Soc. of Engrng. Psychols.; Bristol Histl. Soc. Author & Co-author of num. profl. contbns. Hons: Psi Chi (Psychol.), Phi Beta Kappa, 1947; Alpha Pi Zeta (Social Sci.), Sigma Xi, 1948. Address: 9 Sandra Drive, Bristol, RI 02809, U.S.A. 6, 54, 130.

McKELVY, Gertrude, b. 18 June 1903. Accountant. Educ: B.S., Kan. State Tchrs. Coll., Emporia, Kan., 1927. Appts: Tchr., var. pub. schls., Anthony, Kan., 1921-24; Bookkeeper, Dighton Auto Co. (Ford Garage), Kan., 1931-47; Sec. to Harry S. Conner, Kan. State Rep., 1936-41; Pvte. Prac. as Acct., 1948-; Sec. Mgr., Dighton Chmbr. of Comm., 1952-. Mbrships: Lane Co. 4-H Ldr., 1931-41; Chmn., Lane Co. Chapt., Crippled Children Soc., 1947-;

Chmn., Lane Co. Chapt., Am. Red Cross, 1952-. Address: Dighton, KS 67839, U.S.A. 5.

MACKEN, Mark, b. 19 Sept. 1913. Sculptor; Director of Academy of Fine Arts. Educ: Royal Acad. of Fine arts, Antwerp, Belgium; Nat. Higher Inst. of Fine Arts, Antwerp. Appts: Tchr., Drawing Prof., Sculpture, Royal Acad. of Fine Arts, Antwerp; Dir., ibid, & Dir., Nat. Higher Inst. of Fine Arts. Mbrships. incl: Royal Acad. of Scis., Letters & Fine Arts of Belgium; Advsry. Bd., Mus. of Sculpture, Antwerp; Pres., Supervisory Bd. for Fine Arts; Royal Comm. for Monuments & Landscape; Nat. Comm. on Plastic Arts, UNESCO; Nat. Advsry. Comm. on Fine Arts. Sculptures incl: Num. war mem.; Belgian Govt. bldgs.; Ch., Minn., U.S.A.; Portrait & free sculptures. Num. hons. incl: Van Ierius & De Keyser Prizes, Nat. Higher Inst. of Fine Arts, Antwerp; Cmdr., Order of the Crown; Kt., Order of the Crown; Off., Order of Leopold II; Grand Prize of Rome, 1938; Egide Rombaut Prize, 1955. Address: Mutsaertstraat 29, B-2000 Antwerp, Belgium.

McKENDRICK, Frances Pleasant (Mrs. John D. McKendrick), Nursing Education. Educ: Dip., St. Elizabeth's Hosp., Schl. of Nursing, 1931; Obl. & Pediatric Nursing, Johns Hopkins Hosp., Schl. of Nursing; 1931; Postgrad. Cert. in Pediatric Nursing, Bellevue Hosp. Schl. of Nursing, 1933; Summer Course in Nursery Schl. Mgmt., Nat. Child Rsch. Ctr., Wash. DC, 1935; Summer Course in Staff Nursing, Crippled Children's Hosp., Richmond, Va., 1937; Cert. Pub. Hlth. Nursing, Wm. & Mary Coll., Schl. of Pub. Hlth. Nursing, Richmond Ext., 1938; 6 credits, Oncological Nursing, N.Y. Univ, 1955; B.S., M.S. Rehabilitation Counseling, Va. Commonwealth Univ., 1957-60. Appts. incl: Coordinator of Nursing of Children, Admissions Counselor, Schl. of Nursing, Johnston-Willis Hosp., 1960-. Mbrships. incl: Bd. Mbr., Am. Red Cross Nursing Serv.; Am. Nurses Assn.; Bd. Mbr., Va. Nurses Assn.; Nat. League for Nursing; Va. League for Nursing, Pres., 1971-73, 1973-75, Ed., Newsletter; DAR. Contbr. to profl. jrnls. Hons: Award, 35 yrs. as Red Cross Volunteer, Tchng. & Disaster serv. Address: 103 Dundee Ave., Richmond, VA 23225, U.S.A. 125.

McKENZIE, Frances Leonie Pettersen, b. 27 Apr. 1911. Educator. Educ: B.A., Fla. State Univ., Tallahassee, 1948; M.S., ibid, 1951; One further yr. of coll. Appts: Classroom Tchr., Ensley Schl., Pensacola, Fla., 1929-34, Brentwood Schl., Pensacola, 1934-35, Hallmark Schl., Pensacola, 1935-44, 1945-54; Elem. Prin., Turner-Lee-Day Schl., 1954-61, Montclair Elem. Schl., 1961-74. Mbrships. incl: Corres. Sec., Delta Kappa Gamma, Int. Soc. for Women Ldrs. in Educ.; 1st Pres., Pensacola Alumni Chapt., Kappa Delta Pi, 1954-56; Pres., Escambia Co. Elem. Prins.' Assn., 1962-63; NEA; Fla. Elem. Prins. Assn.; Escambia Co. Educ. Assn.; Montclair PTA; Hon. Life mbr., Fla. Congress of Parents & Tchrs.; Var. offs., Immanuel Luth. Ch., Pensacola. Paintings. incl: Autumn Trees; Mountain Lake Lamp Light; Yellor Roses. Recip., Cert. of Appreciation, Perdido Bay Dist. of Scouts. Address: 3719 N. Palafox St., Pensacola, FL 32505, U.S.A. 5, 125.

MCKENZIE, Gordon Graham Calder, b. 17 July 1916. Surgeon. Educ: M.B.B.S., Univ. of Melbourne, Australia, 1940; M.S., ibid, 1947; Appts: Res. Med. Off., Royal Melbourne Hosp., 1941; Surg. to Outpatients, Prince Henry's Hosp., Melbourne, 1948-54; Asst. Surg., Royal Melbourne Hosp., 1949-54; Surg. to Outpatients, ibid, 1954-67; Surg. to Inpatients,

1967-. Mbrships: Fellow, Royal Australian Coll. Surgs., Royal Coll. Surgs. (Eng.); Australian Med. Assn.; Melbourne Club; Melbourne Cricket Club. Contbr. of articles to profl. jrnls. Address: 4 Ruhbank Ave., Balwyn, Vic., Australia 3103, 23.

MACKENZIE, Peter Boyd, b. 31 July 1930. Australian Government Trade Commissioner. Educ: Waverley Coll., Sydney; Royal Mil. Coll., Duntroon; B.Econ., Univ. of Queensland, Brisbane; P.S.C., Australian Staff Coll., Fort Queenscliff. Appts. incl: Lt., Capt., Major, Australian Staff Corps., Royal Australian Regiment, 1951-65; Asst. Australian Govt. Trade Commnr., Cairo, 1966; Acting Australian Govt. Trade Commnr., Beirut, Bahrain, 1967; Australian Govt. Trade Commnr., Kuala Lumpur, 1968-70, Malta, 1971-72, Rome, 1973-. Mbrships. incl: Imperial Serv. Club, Sydney. Address: Australian Embassy, Via Alessandria 215, 00198 Rome, Italy. 23.

MACKENZIE, William Richard, III, b. 1 Mar. 1924. Architect; Builder; Land Developer. Educ: B.A., Bus. Admin., N.Western Univ., Evanston, Ill.; M.A., Fine Arts, Paris, France; Ph.D., Sorbonne Univ., Paris; Special Additional Work, Design & Real Estate Land Planning, Univ. of Southern Calif., W. L.A., U.S.A. Appts: Pres., Chmn. of Bd., RAHMAC Corp., Ore.; Pres., Rivervale Antiques, Inc., Importers, ibid; Past Mbr., Bd. of Dirs., Nat. Soc. of Interior Designers, Deer Isle Granite Corp., Me. Mbrships: Univ. Clubs, Chgo., Ill. & L.A., Calif.; Christian Scientist; Petroleum Club of Tulsa, Okla.; Rogue Valley Country Club; Conf. Dir., Bd. of Dirs., Am. Inst. Archts.; Bd. of Dirs., Nat. Ski Assn. of World; Million Miler w. United Air Lines & w. Pan Am. World Air Lines, Clipper Club. Address: 5000 Rogue River Hwy., Gold Hill., OR 97525, U.S.A. 2.

McKEOWN, James Edward, b. 3 Sept. 1919. Educator; Sociologist. Educ: B.A., M.A., Wayne State Univ., 1941, '45; Ph.D., Univ. of Chgo, 1949. Appts. incl: Instr., Soc. Sci., St. Xavier Coll., 1945-48; Asst. Prof., Sociol., N.M. Highlands Univ., 1948-52; Asst Prof., DePaul Univ., Chgo., 1952-55; Assoc. Prof., ibid, 1955-57; Prof., 1957-70; Coord. in Insts. in Youth Welfare, Delinquency Control, & Alcoholism Control, 1961-70; Chmn., Dept. of Sociol., 1962-70; Chmn., Inter-Dept. Progs., Soc. Scis., 1963-70; Cons. Sociol., Pt.-time Pvte. Prac., 1959-70; Prof. of Sociol., Univ. of Wis.-Parkside, 1970-; Exec. Comm., Soc. Sci Div., 1970-. Mbrships incl: Pres.-Elect & Prog. Chmn. Ill. Sociol. Assn., 1969-; Pres., ibid, 1970; various positions, AAUP; Wis. Social. Soc. Publs: Study Guide for Economics, 1957, '60, '64, '70; The Changing Metropolis (w. Tietze), 1964-71; College Study Guide for Sociology, 1968. Contbr. to jrnls. & to Britannica Book of Year, 1968, '69, '70, '71, '72. Address: 1469 N. Sheridan Rd., Kenosha, WI 53140, U.S.A. 2, 8, 14, 15, 22, 28, 30, 50.

MACKERRAS, Alan Charles, b. 17 Nov. 1925. Orchestral Conductor. Educ: N.S.W. Conservatorium of Music, Australia; Acad. of Music, Prague, Czechoslovakia. Appts: Prin. Oboist, Sydney Symph. Orch., Australia, 1943-46; Conductor, Sadler's Wells Opera, London, U.K., 1949-53; Prin. Conductor, BBC Concert Orch., 1954-56; Guest Conductor w. most British & European orchs., 1957-66; First Conductor, Hamburg State Opera, Germany, 1966-70; Musical Dir., Sadler's Wells Opera, 1970-; Conducted num. Am. orchs; Metropol. Opera debut, 1972. Publs: Ballet arrangements: Pineapple Poll; The Lady & the Fool. Address: 10 Hamilton Terrace, London NW8 9UG, U.K.

McKESSON, John Alexander, b. 29 Mar. 1922. Diplomat. Educ: B. ès L., Univ. of Paris, France, 1939; A.B., 1941, M.A., 1942, Columbia Univ., N.Y.C.; Appts: Counselor & Dpty. Chief of Mission, Am. Embassy, Dakar, Senegal, 1964-67; Dir., Off. of Ctrl. African Affairs, Dept. of State, 1968-70; Am. Ambassador, Libreville, Gabon, 1970-. Mbrships: Phi Beta Kappa; Metropolitan Club, Wash. D.C. Hons: Cmdr., Nat. Order of Senegal, 1967; LL.D., Eastern Mich. Univ., 1972. Address: Dept. of State, Wash. D.C., U.S.A.

McKESSON, Malcolm Forbes, b. 24 July 1909. Painter; Scenic Designer; Sculptor. Educ: B.A., Harvard Univ., 1933; M.A., N.Y. Univ., 1953. Appts. incl: Lt. & Capt., U.S. Army, 1943-45; Substitute Art Tchr., N.Y. Bd. of Educ., 1955-60. Pres., Composers, Authors & Artists of Am., 1967-69; Bd. of Dirs., Scottish-Am. Fndn. Many one-man shows & grp. exhibs. in U.S.A. & abroad, inclng. Gall. Internationale, N.Y.C., Lynchburg Art Ctr., Va. Mbrships. incl: Life, 7th Regiment, N.Y. Nat. Guard; Green Room Circle of Onteora Theatre; N.Y.C. Harvard Club; Art Chmn., Barnard Club; Anthropol. Soc. of N.Y. Hons. incl: Twilight Pk. Art Assn. annual exhibit awards, 1955-58; Nat. & Int. Awards, U.S., France, Monaco etc. Address: 22 E. 29th St., New York, NY 10016, U.S.A.

MACKEY, Benjamin Franklin, b. 1 Dec. 1904. Politician; County Judge. Appts: Police serv., Little Rock, Ark., 1937-58; Sheriff of Pulaski Co., Ark., 1963-68; Co. Judge, ibid, 1969-. Mbrships. incl: Bd. of Dirs., Nat. Sheriffs' Assn., 1967-68; V.P., Ark. Law Enforcement Assn., 1968; Pres., Ark. Sheriffs' Assn., 1968; Chmn., Am. Cancer Soc. Crusade Fund Dr. for Pulaski Co., 1974; Mbr. of var. Masonic Lodges. Hons. incl: Hon. Degree of Kt. Cmdr., Ct. of Hon., Ark. Consistory 1, Scottish Rite Masons, 1959; Hon. Degree of Red Cross of Constantine. Address: 819 McAdoo, Little Rock, AR 72205, U.S.A. 125.

McKIBBIN, JoeAnn Lucille Kowalczk (Mrs.), b. 16 Oct. 1929. Civic Worker. Mbrships: San Antonio Chapt., Women of the Moose No. 1075; former Sr. Regent, Jr. Regent & Collegiant, Eagles Lodge; worked w. Girl Scouts for 8 yrs. & Boy Scouts for 6 yrs.; Pres. of LaSalle P.T.C. (Cath. H.S.); Vet. Christmas Pty. for 3 yrs.; U.S.O. Volunteer for 4 yrs. Address: 7224, Westbriar Dr., San Antonio, TX 78227, U.S.A. 125.

MACKIE, Shirley Marie, b. 25 Oct. 1929. Musician; Educator. Educ: B.Mus., La. State Univ., 1949; M.Mus., 1950; Studied w. Darius Milhaud & Nadia Boulanger. Appts: Profl. Clarinetist & Composer, 1950-; Band Dir., Forney H.S., Tex., 1954; Asst. Prof., Music, Mary Hardin-Baylor Coll., Belton, 1954-57; Lectr., Clinician, 1954-; Music Coord., McLennan Co. Dept. of Educ., 1959-70; Fndr. & Conductor, Chmbr. Orch. of Waco, 1966-69; Band Dir., McLennan Co. Schls., 1970-; Publr. of Music, 1968-; Pvte. Tchr., Music, 1950-. Fellow, Intercontinental Biog. Assn. Mbrships. incl: Music Tchrs. Nat. Assn.; Music Educrs. Nat. Conf.; Tex. Music Tchrs. Assn.; Tex. Music Educrs. Assn.; Tex. Composers Guild; Sigma Alpha Iota; Phi Kappa Phi. Compositions incl: Dance in the Brazos Brakes; Concatenation; Gemini's Journey (ballets); Mister Man (opera); Sinfonietta; Passacaglia (orch.); Requiem (chorus & orch); Aria; Latin Duo (piano). Contbr. to music publs. Address: 1815 Colonial Ave., Waco, TX 76707, U.S.A. 125, 132, 138.

McKINLAY, Janet Zimmerman, b. 30 July 1906. Library Administrator. Educ: B.S.,

Syracuse Univ., 1930; M.L.S., Grad. Schl. of Lib. Serv., Columbia Univ., 1932. Appts: Asst. Libn., Glen Rock Pub. Lib., N.J., 1932, Libn., 1932-41; Post Libn., Ft. Monmouth, N.J., 1941-46; Command. Libn., Gov.'s Island, N.Y., 1946, 1st Army Libn., 1946-47; Chief Army Lib. & Serv. Club, 1947-48; Acting Hd., Pub. & Schl. Lib. Servs. Bur., N.J. State Lib., 1949-52, Hd., 1952. Mbrships. incl: Pres., Chapt. of Gtr. Trenton, People-to-People Inc.; Bd. of Mgrs., Exec. Comm. Mbr., Mercer Co. Unit, Am. Cancer Soc.; Burlington Co. Cultural Heritage Commn.; Mbrship. Comm. Mbr., YWCA. Hons. incl: Decoration for Exceptional Serv. to Armed Forces, 1949; Commn., Ky. Col., 1965. Address: 10 Woodland Rd., Sylvan Glen, Bordentown, NJ 08505, U.S.A. 5, 6, 42.

McKINLEY, Jimmie Joe, b. 23 July 1934. Librarian. Educ: Bachelor Jrnlsm. (cum laude), Univ. of Tex., 1955; M.S., Univ. of Ky., 1964. Appts: Asst. Libn., Bethel Coll., McKenzie, Tenn., 1961-63, Ref. Libn., 1963-70, Acting Hd. Libn., 1970-71. Mbrships: ALA; Assn. Coll. & Rsch. Libs.; Carroll Co. (Tenn.) Histl. Soc.; Sigma Delta Chi. Address: P.O. Box 2106, Longview, TX 75601, U.S.A. 7.

McKINNEY, George, b. 1 July 1925. Community Development Consultant. Educ: B.S., Sam Houston State Univ., Huntsville, Tex.; Studies in Educ., Grad. Schl., E. Tex. State Univ., Commerce; Grad., Am. Mgmt. Assn. of N.Y. Appts: Flying Off., USAAF, WWII; Flying Off., USAF, Korean War; H.S. Tchr. of Chem. & Bio.; Mgr., Electric Utility Co.; Community Dev. Cons. Mbrships: Pres., Rotary Club, Crockett, Tex.; Pres., Southeastern Community Dev. Assn.; Tex. Industrial Dev. Coun.; Tex. State Rural Dev. Comm. Address: P.O. Box 1707, Dallas, TX 75221, U.S.A.

McKINNEY, Harold Wellington. b. 12 Mar. 1913. Banker; Writer; Consulting Editor. Educ: B.S.L., J.D., Univ. of Minn., Mnpls., 1941. Appts: Served to Cmdr., USN, 1942-53; Naval Atty. Gen. of Guam, 1948-50; Admitted to Calif. Bar, 1946; U.S. Supreme Ct., 1951; U.S. Ct. of Mil. Appeals, 1951; Pvte. Prac. of Law, San Fran., Calif., 1953-59; Asst. Ed., Commerce Clearing House, Inc., 1960-61; Sr. Mng. Ed., Matthew Bender & Co., Inc., 1962-71; Trust Communications Off. (Statewide), Bank of Am., 1971-; Free-lance Writer, Cons. Ed., 1971-. Mbrships: Sigma Alpha Epsilon; Commonwealth Club of Calif.; Marines Mem. Club (San Fran.); Am. Conservative Union; Am. Security Coun.; Inst. for Am. Strategy. Publs: Probate of Wills & Administration of Descendants' Estates; California Forms of Pleading & Practice (Contbng. author of num. articles); Commercial Transactions (Mng. Ed. & contbng. author of 2 vol. set); California Points & Authorities (Contbng. author). Address: Bank of Am. Ctr., P.O. Box 37000, San Fran., CA 94137, U.S.A. 9.

McKINNEY, Linda Lea Bess (Mrs. Philip A. McKinney Jr.), b. 9 Apr. 1944. Owner, bridal shop, Educ: Ind. Univ., Bloomington, 1962-67. Appts; Sec., Standard Life Ins. Co., 1962-67; Publicity Mgr., Ind. Univ. Press, Bloornington, 1967-72; Owner, Baskin-Robbins 31 Ice Cream, Nashville, Ind., 1971-; Owner & Cons., Bridal Elegance, ibid, 1973-. Mbrships: Ind. Fedn. Bus. & Profl. Women's Clubs (1st V.P., Brown Co. Chapt.); Bd. Dirs., Brown Co. Chmbr. of Comm. Recip., Young Careerist Award, Brown Co. BPW, Nashville, Ind., 1973. Address: P.O. Box 173, Nashville, IN 47448, U.S.A. 5.

MACKINNON, Ewen Daniel, b. 11 Feb. 1903. Grazier. Educ: B.A., New Coll., Oxford Univ., 1924. Appts: Mbr., Australian Parliament, 1949-66; Chmn., Jt. Parliamentary Comm. on For. Affairs, 1962-65; Temporary Chmn. of Comms., 1962-66; Australian Ambassador to Argentina, 1967-70, to Peru & Uruguay, 1968-70. Mbrships. incl: Melbourne Club (Pres., 1972-73); Royal Melbourne Golf Club; Royal Melbourne Tennis Club; Vic. Racing Club. Recip., C.B.E., 1966. Address: Langi Willi, Linton, Vic., Australia 3360. 23.

McKUEN, Rod, b. 29 Apr. 1938. Author; Singer; Composer. Appts. incl: Pres., Stanyan Records; Discus Records; New Gramophone Soc.; Mr. Kelly Prods.; Montcalm Prods.; Stanyan Books; Cheval Books; Friendship Books; Rod McKuen Enterprises. Songs incl: Jean; If You Go Away; Seasons in the Sun; Doesn't Anybody Know My Name; Natalie; Champion Charlie Brown; A Boy Named Charlie Brown; The Beautiful Strangers; Bend Down & Touch Me; The Ever Constant Sea. Classical compositions incl: Symph. No. 1; Concerto for Guitar & Orch.; Concerto for Four Harpsichords; Ballad of Distances, Suite for Orch. Film Scores incl: Joanna, 1968; The Prime of Miss Jean Brodie, 1969; Me, Natalie, 1969. Publs: And to Each Season, 1972; Beyond the Boardwalk, 1973; Come to Me in Silence, 1973. Mbr., var. orgs. Recip., Grand Prix du Disc, 1966. Address: P.O. Box G, Beverly Hills, CA 90213, U.S.A.

McLACHLAN, Ian Douglas, b. 23 July 1911. Company Chairman. Educ: Royal Mil. Coll., Duntroon, Australia. Appts: Imperial Defence Coll., 1954; Dir., Flying Trng., RAF, 1955-56; AOC Trng. Cmd., RAAF, 1957-59; Dpty. Chief of Air Staff, 1959-61; Australian Defence Advsr., Wash. D.C., U.S.A., 1962-63; Air Mbr., Supply & Equipment, Australian Air Bd., 1964-68; Chmn., Mainline Corp. & Chmn., Ponolbin Winemakers; Dir., Capitol Motors & Reef Oil NL; Cons., Northrop Corp., U.S.A. Mbrships: Royal Sydney Golf Club; Elanora Country Club; Melbourne Cricket Club; Royal Canberra Golf Club; Naval & Mil. Club, Melbourne. Hons. incl: Disting. Flying Cross, 1941; CBE, 1954; Companion of the Bath, 1966. Address: 2 Eastbourne Rd., Darling Pt., Australia 2027. 23.

MacLAMROC, James Gwaltney Westwarren. Lawyer, Financier, Philanthropist. Educ: B.A., Univ. of N.C.; J.D., Yale Univ. Bus. interests incl: Owner & Developer, Lamrocton (suburban residential area); Pres., The Lamrocton Co.; WKIX Broadcasting Co., Tri Cities Broadcasting Co., Golden Strand Broadcasting Co. Mbrships: Former Chmn., Comm. on Magistrates & Traffic Cts., State Advsr. for N.C. to Comm. on Improvement of Justice of Peace Cts., Am.Bar Assn.; Am. Judicature Soc.; N.C. State Bar; Former Exec. Comm., 1st V.P., Chmn., comms., N.C. Bar Assn.; Greensboro Bar Assn.; Bar of Supreme Ct. of US; N.C. State Highway Commn., Author, MacLamroc Plan for major N.C. east-west highways and of Guilford County Thorofare Plan; Co. Histn. of Guilford Co.; Carolina Charter Tercentenary Commn.; Exec. Comm. & Chmn. of Fin. Comm.; Guilford Co. Comm., N.C. Confed. Centennial Commn. & N.C. Am. Revolution Bicentennial Commn.; Guilford Co. Bicentennial Commn., Exec. Comm.; N.C. Civil War Roundtable; Sigma Chi; Phi Delta Phi; Admiral, N.C. Navy; Ky. Col.; Sons of Confed. Veterans, Commdr., N.C. Div.; Soc. of War of 1812; Pres., N.C. Soc., Sons of Am. Revolution; Soc. of Colonial Wars in State of Va.; 1st Gov., Soc. of Colonial Wars in State of N.C.; Jamestowne Soc.; Soc. of Descendants of Colonial Clergy; Order of Ams.

of Armorial Ancestry; Nat. Soc. of Ams. of Royal Descent; Order of Crown in Am.; Baronial Order of Magna Charta; Order of Three Crusades; Mil. Order of Crusades; Order of Crown of Charlemagne; Pilgrims of US; Engl. Speaking Union; 1st V.P. & Exec. Comm., State Lit. & Hist. Assn. of N.C.; Va. Hist. Soc.; Va. Geneal. Soc.; New England Hist. Geneal Soc.; Soc. of Geneals., U.K.; Harleian Soc., U.K.; Ulster-Scot Hist. Soc.; Scottish Geneal. Soc.; Scottish Record Soc.; V.P., N.C. Soc. for Preservation of Antiquities; Assn. for Preservation of Va. Antiquities; Exec. Comm., Archaeol. Soc. of N.C.; Pres., Bd. of Trustees, Greensboro Hist. Mus.; Standing Comm. on Hist., Scenario & Title, Greensboro Sesquicentennial Celebration Pageant; Bd. of Dirs., Dolley Madison Mem. Assn.; Hist. Hillsborough Commn., Chmn., Fin. Comm.; Advsry. Comm., N.C. Soc. of Local & Co. Histnrs; Nat. Trust for Hist. Preservation; Newcomen Soc. in N.C.; Nat. Comm. & Chmn., N.C. Comm., Yale Law Lib. Fund; Legis. Comm., N.C. Lib. Assn.; Greensboro Community Coun.; Former Bd. of Dirs. & Exec. Comm., Greensboro Chmbr. of Comm.; Chmn., Gtr. Greensboro Planning Bd.; Gtr. Greensboro Arterial Rds. Commn.; Panel, Am. Abritration Assn.; Originator of the movement to remove the remains of Gov. William R. Davie, "Father" of the Univ. of N.C., to the campus at Chapel Hill; Donor, MacLamroc Collection of Ancestral Family Portraits (Elizabethan) to N.C. Museum of Art; Inventor, MacLamroc Alphabet; Greensboro Country Club; Sedgefield Country Club; Yale Club of N.Y.; Episcopalian; Mason; Shriner.Author of newspaper, TV & radio articles on many subjects. Married Maxine Pugh, Palm Beach, Fla.; Sons: Alan G. W. MacLamroc & Brian G.W. MacLamroc. Address: Box 1588, Greensboro, NC 27402, U.S.A. 7, 16.

McLARTY, Cleylon L., b. 10 Apr. 1923. Educator. Educ: Mus.B., Univ. H.S., Oxford, Miss., 1951; M.Ed., ibid, 1958; Ed.D., Univ. of Miss., Oxford, 1963. Appts. incl: Asst. Dean of Students, Dir. of Dev., Univ. of Ga., Athens, 961-62; Assoc. Prof. & Dir., Proj. to Strengthen Developing Insts., Delta State Coll., Cleveland, Miss., 1962-66; Prof. Educ. & Coord., Rehab. Counseling Prog., Ark. State Univ., 1966-. Mbrships. incl: Bd. Mbr., Mid.-S. Educational Rsch. Assn., & Abilities Unlimited; Am. Educational Rsch. Assn. & Special Grp. on Systems Analysis; Ark. Educational Rsch. & Dev. Coun; Nat. Rehab. Assn.; Phi Delta Kappa; Kappa Delta Pi. Contbr. to sev. books on educational techniques. Address: Box 898, Ark. State Univ., State Univ., AR 72467, U.S.A. 7.

MCLAUGHLIN, Alexander C.J., b. 3 June 925. Engineer. Educ: B.S.C.E., Va. Polytech. Inst.; Grad. Studies, Columbia Univ. Appts: Asst. Struct. Engr., Struct. Engr., Opr. Engr. Area Engr., Standard Vacuum Oil Co.; Pipeline Engr., Trans Arabian Pipeline Co.; Chief Pipeline Engr., Andian Nat. Corp.; Sr. Engr., Chief Proj. Engr., Chief Engr. (South), Sr. Hd. Engr., Sr. Process. Engr., Am. Oil Co.; Operations Mgr., Distrib. Mgr., Singapore Petroleum Co.; Constructn. Supvsr., Iran Pan-Am. Oil Co. Mbrships: Fellow, Am. Soc. Civil Engrs. (Pipeline Comm.); Nat. Assn. Corrosion Engrs.; U.S. Coast Guard Aux. (Trng. Off.); Pathfinder Club, London; Moose Singapore Swim Club; Singapore Am. Club; Singapore Petroleum Club; Pan-Am. Club, Tehran; Tehran Shi Club. Address: c/o Iran Pan-Am. Oil Co., P.O. Box 2213, Tehran, Iran.

McLAUGHLIN, Donald Hamilton, b. 15 Dec. 1891. Mining Geologist & Engineer. Educ:

B.S., Univ. of Calif., Berkeley, U.S.A., 1914; A.M., Harvard Univ., 1915; Ph.D., ibid, 1917. Appts. incl: Chief Geologist, Cerro de Pasco Copper Corp., Peru, 1919-25; Prof., Mining Engrng. & Mining Geol., Harvard Univ., 1925-41; Cons. Geologist, Homestake Mining Co., 1926-45; Prof., Mining Engrng., Univ. of Calif., Berkeley, 1941-43; V.P., & Gen. Mgr., Cerro de Pasco Copper Corp., 1943-45; Pres. & Chief Exec. Off., Homestake Mining Co., 1944-61; Bd. Chmn., ibid, 1961-70; Hon. Chmn. & Chmn., Exec. Comm., 1970-; Num. other directorships incl: Int. Nickel Co. of Canada Ltd., 1948-73, & Advsry., Wells Fargo Bank, 1960-68. Num. mbrships. incl: Am. Acad. of Arts & Scis.; Pres., Soc. of Econ. Geologists; Pres., Mining & Metallurgical Soc. of Am.; Coun., Geological Soc. of Am.; Am. Geophys. Union; Dir., Coun. for Econ. Dev. Hons. incl: Rand Medal, Am. Inst. of Mining, Metallurgical & Petroleum Engrs., 1961; LL.D., Univ. of Calif., Berkeley, 1966. Address: Homestake Mining Co., 650 California St., 9th Floor, San Francisco, CA 94108, U.S.A. 2, 14, 34, 50.

McLAUGHLIN, Edward Thomas, b. 9 Apr. 1916. Agrologist. Educ: B.Sc.A., Ont. Agricl. Coll., 1937. Appts. incl: Mgr., A.E. McKenzie Co. Ltd., Toronto, Ont., 1950-62; V.P., Rudy Patrick Seed Co., Kan. City, Mo., 1962-64; Sec. & Gen. Mgr., Canadian Seed Growers' Assn., Ottawa, Ont., 1964-. Mbrships. incl: Agricl. Inst. of Canada; Ont. Inst. of Profl. Agrologists; Canadian Soc. of Agronomy; Dir., Royal Agricl. Winter Fair, Toronto; Executive Comm., Assn. Official Seed Certifying Agcys.; Dir., Rapeseed Assn. of Canada. Hons. incl: Appointed Pres., Canadian Seed Trade Assn., 1958-59; Hon. Appts., Agricultural Rsch. Inst. of Ont., 1962; Hon. Mbrship., Soc. Commercial Analysts Assn. of Canada. Address: Canadian Seed Growers Assn., Box 8455, Ottawa, Ont. K1G 3T1, Canada.

McLAUGHLIN, Sybil Ione, b. 24 Aug. 1928. Clerk of Parliament. Educ. incl: La Salle Univ., Chgo.; 3 months attachment, House of Commons, London & Stormont, N. Ireland, 1966; Grenada & Trinidad & Tobago Parliaments, W. Indies, 1971. Appts. incl: Sec. to Commnr., Cayman Islands, 1958-59; Clerk of Executive Coun., Cayman Islands, 1959-67; Clerk of Legislative Assembly, 1959-. Mbrships: Sec., Cayman Islands Br. Commonwealth Parliamentary Assn.; Cayman Islands Christian Endeavour Union; George Town Pub. Lib. Comm. Author of Brief Constitutional History on the Cayman Islands, 1971. Recip. of M.B.E., 1967. Address: P.O. Box 890, Legislative Dept., Legislative Assembly Bldg., Grand Cayman, Cayman Islands, Br. W. Indies. 109.

McLAURIN, Henry J., b. 22 Feb. 1904. Insurance Agency Executive. Educ: A.B., Presby. Coll. of S.C., 1925. Appts: w. Equitable Life Ins. Co., Cinn., Ohio, 1925-27; Asst. Mgr., Detroit, 1927-39; Gen. Agent, Detroit Aetna Life Ins. Co., 1943-58; Dir., Pres., G-M Underwriters, Inc., 1948-, McLaurin & Co., actuarial cons., Detroit & Jacksonville, Fla., 1943-. Mbrships. incl: Pres.' Comm. for employment of handicapped, 1964; Gov.'s Comprehensive State Hlth. Planning Advsry. Coun., 1968; State Advsry. Bd., Phase 11, Econ. Stabilization Prog., 1972; Dir., Garden City Hosp., 1968; Bd., Cheboygan Hosp., 1973; Pres., Mich. Chapt., Arthritis Fndn., 1948-63 (Bd. Chmn., Dir., 1963). Hons. incl: Mich. Chapt. Arthritis Fndn. Fndrs. Award, 1971; Gov.'s Disting. Citizen of Mich., 1971. Address: 924 Mason St., Dearborn, MI 48124, U.S.A. 16.

MacLEAN, Donald Angus, b. 15 Mar. 1927. Professor of Oceanography & Ecology; Educational Administrator. Educ: 5 univ. degrees, inclng. Ph.D. Appts: Classroom Tchr., Calif., 1956-59, Curriculum Dir., 1959-60. Adminstr., Univ. Demonstration Schl., 1960-62, Coord. Schl. Curriculum, 1962-70; Univ. Prof., Calif., 1962-, Dir., Floating Marine Lab. Progs., 1970-, Asst. Co. Supt. of Schls., Orange Co., 1972-. Author, The Sea: A New Frontier. Over 150 profl. publs. Writer & prod., 58 nat. TV progs., oceanography & nuclear energy. Former co-ed. & cons., Jacques-Yves Cousteau Films for Educ. Hons. incl: L.A. Educator of Yr. Award, 1960; San Diego Ind. Educ. Coun. Award, Outstanding Contbn. Sci. & Engrng., 1965. Address: Office of the Orange County Superintendent of Schools, 1250 S. Grand Ave., Room 211, Santa Ana, CA 92705, U.S.A.

McLEAN, James Hannis, b. 25 Mar. 1920. University Professor. Educ: B.S., Livingstone Univ., 1941; M.B.A., Univ. of Ala., 1948; J.D., Emory Univ., 1958; Ph.D., Ohio State Univ., 1967. Appts. incl: Asst. Prof., Ga. State Univ., 1956-57; Assoc. Prof., Univ. of Tenn., 1957-67; Asst. Dir., Educ., AICPA, 1961-62; Asst. Instr., Ohio State Univ., 1964-65; Prof., Va. Polytech. Inst. & State Univ., 1967-. Mbrships. incl: Am. Inst. CPA's; Va. Soc. CPA's; Chmn., Profl. Dev. Comm., Tenn. Soc. CPA's, 1961; Roanoke Estate Planning Coun.; Beta Gamma Sigma; Beta Alpha Psi; Delta Sigma Pi; Pres., Belmont II Ruritan Club, 1970. Contbr. to profl. jrnls. Address: Rt. 4, Box 836, Christiansburg, VA 24073, U.S.A. 125.

McLEAN, John Ross, b. 19 July 1905. Communications Adviser. Educ: B.A., Univ. of Man., Canada, 1926; M.A., ibid, 1927; B.A., Balliol Coll., Oxford, U.K., 1929; B.Litt., ibid, 1931. Appts. incl: Asst., Dpty. then Govt. Film Commnr., Nat. Film Bd. of Canada, 1939-50; Mbr., Secretariat, UN Preparatory Conf., 1945; Hd., Films & Visual Info. Div., UN Educl., Sci. & Cultural Org., 1950-56; Writer & Broadcaster, Ottawa, 1957-60; Rsch. Dir., Programmes, Bd. of Broadcast Govs., 1960-68; Special Advsr., Policy, Canadian Radio TV Commn., 1969-73 & Nat. Commn. for UNESCO, 1973. Mbrships.: Canadian Pol. Sci. Assn.; Canadian Insts. of Int. Affairs; Canadian Assn. of Rhodes Schlrs. Address: 33 First Avenue, Ottawa, Ont. K1S 2G1, Canada 88, 128.

McLEAN, Naomi Catherine. Certified Registered Public Stenographer; Business Teacher. Educ: Grad., Phyllis Wheatley Bus. Inst., 1935; Instrs. Cert. Machine Shorthand, Schl. Div., Skokie Ill., 1961; B.S., Ctrl. Christian Coll. Appts. incl: Owner, Operator, McLean's Stenographic & Tutoring Serv., Winston-Salem, N.C., 1939; Newspaper Columnist, Afro-Am. Newspapers, Balt., 1945-; Substitute Commercial Instr., N.C. Coll., Durham, 1945, 71-72; Instr., Ch. Conf. Inst. Mbrships. incl: Sec., Livingstone Coll. Alumni Assn.; Sec., NAACP, State Assn.; Sec., local Assn.; Bus. & Profl. Womens Club; Livingstone Coll. Alumni Assn.; Southeastern Bus. Coll. Assn. Publs: My Experience Serving the Public in General; contbr., The Carolina, newspaper; var. poems. Hons. incl: Named Woman of the Yr., Iota Phi Lambda, 1958; Cert. for Outstanding Accomplishments, 1972. Address: 3731 Spaulding Dr., Winston-Salem, NC 27105, U.S.A. 5.

McLEAN, Richard Thorpe, b. 12 Apr. 1934. Artist. Educ: B.F.A., Calif. Coll. of Arts & Crafts, Oakland, U.S.A., 1958; M.F.A., Mills Coll., Oakland, 1962. Appts: Tchr., Painting & Drawing, Calif. Coll. of Arts & Crafts, 1963-65;

Tchr., Fac., San Fran. State Univ., 1965-. One-man shows; Lucien Labaudt Gall., San Fran., 1957; Art Ctr., Richmond, Calif., 1963; Berkeley Gall., Berkeley, Calif., 1964; Valparaiso Univ., Ind., 1965; Berkeley Gall., San Fran., 1966 & 1968; Univ. of Omaha, Neb., 1967; O.K. Harris, N.Y.C., 1971 & 1973. Num. grp. shows, many cities in U.S.A., Japan, Australia, N.Z., Gt. Britain, Germany & Italy, 1969-73. Address: 6471 Oakwood Drive, Oakland, CA 94611, U.S.A.

McLEMORE, Ethel Ward, b. 22 Jan. 1908. Geophysicist; Teacher of Chemistry & Mathematics. Educ: B.A., Miss. Woman's Coll., 1928; M.A., Univ. N.C., 1929; Grad. work, Univ. Chgo., 1932; Colo. Schl. of Mines, 1941-42; Southern Meth. Univ., 1962-63. Appts. incl: Cons. Geophysicist, 1948-; Rsch. Geophysicist, United Geophysical Co., 1942-46; Hd. Sci. Dept., Hockaday Schl., 1957-58, & Tchr. Chem., 1969-70; Hd. Sci. Dept., Ursuline Acad., 1963-67. Mbrships. incl: Am. Math. Soc.; Math. Assn. Am.; Soc. Industrial & Applied Maths.; Am. Geophysical Union; AAAS; Soc. of Sigma Xi. Contbr. to var. scientific publs. Address: 11625 Wander Ln., Dallas, TX 75230, U.S.A. 5, 7, 28, 132.

McLEOD, J.K.A., b. 19 Dec. 1930. Mining Engineer. Educ: B.Engrng., St. Mark's Coll., Univ. of Adelaide, S. Australia. Appts: Mt. Lyell Mining & Railway Co., 1959-67; Asst. Mgr., Mineral Dev., Utah Dev. Co., Melbourne, 1967-68; Mgr., Min. Dev., ibid, 1968-70; Mgr., Blackwater Mine, 1970-72; Dev. Mgr., Brisbane, 1972-73; Mgr., Queensland Coal Ops., Brisbane, 1974. Mbrships: Mbr. of Coun., Australasian Inst. of Mining & Metallurgy; Mbr. of Coun., Capricornia Inst. of Advanced Educ., Rockhampton; Blackwater Country Club; Brisbane Cricketers' Club. Address: c/o Utah Dev. Co., Box 1389, G.P.O., Brisbane, Qld., Australia 4001, 23.

MACLEOD, Joseph Todd Gordon, b. 24 Apr. 1903. Author; Ret'd Broadcaster & Play Producer. Educ: M.A., Balliol, Oxford, 1945; Called to the Bar, Inner Temple, 1928. Appts: Dir., Cambridge Fest. Theatre. 1933-36; Announcer, BBC, 1938-45; Mng. Dir., Scottish Nat. Film Studios, 1946-47; Convener of Drama, Goethe Fest. Soc., 1948-49. Mbrships: Coun. Mbr. for sev. yrs., Soc. for Theatre Research; Exec. Comm. sev. yrs., Soc. for Cultural Relations, etc. Publs. incl: Beauty & the Beast, 1927; The Ecliptic (poem), 1930; Foray of Centaurs (poem), 1931; Overture to Cambridge (novel), 1936; The New Soviet Theatre, 1943; A Job at the BBC, 1947; A Soviet Theatre Sketchbook, 1951; The Passage of the Torch (poem), 1951; A Short History of the British Theatre (Italian ed.), 1958; People of Florence, 1968; The Sisters d'Aranyi (biog.), 1969; An Old Olive Tree (poems), 1971; also poetry under pseudonym Adam Drian. Hons. incl: Silver Medal, Royal Soc. of Arts, 1944; Scottish Arts Coun. Award, 1952 & 72; Mbr., British Actors Equity. Address: Via delle Ballodole 9/7, Trespiano, Florence, Italy. 1, 128.

McLEOD, Peter, b. 6 Dec. 1936. Baptist Minister. Educ: B.A., Grand Canyon Coll., Phoenix, Ariz.; B.Divinity, New Orleans Bapt. Theological Sem., La. Appts: Min., 1st Bapt. Ch., Ft. Oglethorpe, Ga., 1964-66; Assoc. Min., 2nd Ponce de Leon Bapt. Ch., Atlanta, Ga., 1966-68; Min., Ctrl. Bapt. Ch., Lexington, Ky., 1968-69, 1st Bapt. Ch., Waco, Tex., 1969-. Mbrships. incl: Rotary Int.; Baylor Univ. Bds. of Trustees & Dev.; Human Welfare Commn., Waco; Providence Hosp. Serv. Bd.; Red Cross Int. Bd.; Educl. Studies Commn., Tex. Bapt.

DICTIONARY OF INTERNATIONAL BIOGRAPHY

Convention; New Orleans Alumni; Pres., ibid, 1970-71. Articles & sermons, var. Bapt. publs. Sermons recorded for nat. distribution. Creator & prod., radio talks prog. for young people. Recip., Alumnus of Yr. Award, Grand Canyon Coll., 1969-70. Address: 5101 Meadow Wood, Waco, TX 76710, U.S.A. 46, 117, 125.

McLERRAN, Stanford J., b. 8 Dec. 1925. Accountant. Educ: Bus. Admin., Yakima Bus. Coll. 1950. Appts; Cost Acct., Ross Packing Co., Selah, Wash., 1946-55; Self-employed, ibid, 1955-65; Internal Auditor, Douglas Nuclear Inc., Richland, Wash., 1966-73; Tax & Ins. Specialist, ibid, 1968-; Sec.-Treas. & Dir. of Fin., Meads Foods Inc., Selah, Benton City, Yakima, Wash., Umatilla & Hermiston, Ore., L & R Food Markets, Grandview, Wash., Meads Mgmt. Servs. Inc., Selah, Wash.; Treas. & Dir. of Fin., Dietzen's Inc., Moses Lake, Yakima, Wapato·& Sunnyside, Wash., 1969-; Cert. Pub. Acct., 1965. Mbrships. incl: Fin. Mgmt. Assn.; Am. Inst. of Cert. Pub. Accts., 1965-; Wash. State Soc. of Cert. Pub. Accts., 1965-; Mbrship. Dir., 1971, Awards Chmn., 1972, Assoc. Prog. Dir., 1970, Tri-Cities Chapt., Nat. Accts. Assn.; Pres., Selah PTA, 1951-53; Treas., Selah Jr. Chmbr. of Comm., 1952-53. Address: 525 Holly, Richland, WA 99352, U.S.A. 9, 57, 139.

McLOUGHLIN, Donald, b. 13 Mar. 1926. Legal Consultant. Educ: B.A., LL.B., Univ. of Western Australia. Appts: Barrister & Solicitor in pvte. prac., Perth, W.A., 1951-56; Magistrate, Fiji, 1956-63; Judicial Commnr., W.P.H.C., Pitcairn, 1957-59; Commnr. of Customs & Chmn., Income Tax Ct. of Review, Fiji, 1961-63; Legal Advsr. to Gov. of Pitcairn, Henderson, Ducie & Oeno Islands, 1964-; Solicitor-Gen., Fiji, 1963-71; Commnr. for Law Revision, ibid, 1965-68; Legal Cons. to Govt. of Fiji, 1971-, to Govt. of Papua, New Guinea, 1972-. Publs. incl: Co-Ed., Laws of Fiji, revised edit., 1967; Ed., Law of Pitcairn, Henderson, Ducie & Oeno Islands, revised edit., 1971; accounts of the dev. of the system of govt. & laws on Pitcairn Island in 19th. & 20th. Centuries, Jrnl. of Fiji Soc. Address: 3 James Rd., Swanbourne, W.A., Australia 6010. 23.

MACMAHON, Arthur Whittner, b. 29 May 1890. Professor. Educ: B.A., Columbia Coll., 1912; M.A., ibid, 1913; Ph.D. Columbia Univ., 1923. Appts: Instr., Columbia Coll., 1913-23; Asst. & Assoc. Prof., ibid, 1923-29; Prof., ibid, 1930-1958; tchr., Turkey, India, S. Am., E. Africa. Mbrships: Phi Beta Kappa; Pres., Am. Pol. Sci. Assn., 1947. Publs: Statutory Sources of New York City Government, 1923; Departmental Management, 1927; Federal Administrators, 1939; Administration of Federal Work Relief, 1941; Administration in Foreign Affairs, 1953; Federalism Mature & Emergent, 1955; Delegation & Autonomy, 1961; Administering Federalism in a Democracy, 1972; Liberating Controls, 1973. Recip. LL.D. 1959. Address: 21 Glengary Rd., Poughkeepsie, NY, U.S.A. 1.

McMICHAEL, Sylvia (Betty) Hearn, b. 16 Aug. 1933. Property Investor; Company Director; Operatic Soprano; Author. Educ: Univ. of Hawaii. Appts. incl: Soprano, Madame Butterfly, Palacio de la Bellas Artes, 1950, & The Red Mill, Operetta, 1951-52; Concert & TV appearances, 1953-63; Real Estate Broker, Calif. & Hawaii, 1955-; Investment properties & syndications, 1963-; Post, Advt. Dept., Hawaii Tribune Herald, 1966-68;. Builder-Owner, Condominiums & Resorts, S. Pacific, 1968-; Pres., 4 U.S. Corps., Dir., 3 British Cos. & 2 French Cos., 1972-; Modernizer, European Castles into Residences, 1972-; Soprano, Hawaii Opera Theatre, 1973-; Breeder, horses &

hunting dogs, France, 1973-; V.P., Cinematics Ltd., 1973-. Mbrships. incl: Am. Chapt., Int. Finance Comm.; Int. Fedn. of Realtors; Chmn., Lurcy-Levis Winter Music Festival, 1974; Opera Players of Hawaii. Publs: Poor Howard, 1955; Death of a Playboy, 1965; Touring in Hawaii, 1966; 7 other books. Address: 1166 Waiholo Place, Honolulu, HI 96821, U.S.A. 5.

McMILLAN, Ann Endicott. Musician. Educ: B.A., Bennington Coll., Appts. incl: Music Ed., RCA Victor Recording Co., 1949-55; Prog. Dir., French Broadcasting System, N.Y.C., 1958-64; Dir. of Orch. Lib., Carl Fischer Music Publrs., 1964; Mgr., Green Mountain Gall., & Music Cons., Mus. of Contemporary Crafts, 1968-69. Mbrships: Am. Music Ctr.; Audio Engrng. Soc. Compositions incl. film scores, Black & White, 1972, Turn of the Year, 1973, music for play Choose a Spot on the Floor, 1972, Glass Reflections, for chamber orch., 1973. Concerts incl. Nashville, Tenn., N.M., & Munich, Germany, 1972, N.Y.C., 1973 & '74, Radio Nacional de Venezuela, 1973. Author of broadcast radio-essays & articles in profl. jrnls. Recip. of grants & awards, incl. Guggenheim Fellowship, 1972, '73. Address: 273 W. 10th St., N.Y., NY 10014, U.S.A.

McMILLAN, James, b. 30 Oct. 1925. Journalist; Author. Educ: M.A. (Hons.), Glasgow Univ. Appts: Reporter, Scottish Daily Express; Asst. Ed., Evening Citizen, Glasgow; Chief Ldr. Writer, Daily Express, London; TV & Radio Broadcaster to Canada, on Canadian Broadcasting Corp. network. Mbrships: Trustee, Cobham & Oxshott Med. Aid Fund, Famington Educl. Trust; Tyrrells Wood Golf Club; London Press Club. Publs: The Glass Lie, 1965; The American Take-Over (co-author), 1968; The Honours Game, 1969; Anatomy of Scotland, 1970; Root of Corruption, 1972; The British Genius (co-author), 1973. Address: Thurlestone, Fairmile Pk. Rd., Cobham, Surrey, U.K. 3, 139.

McMILLAN, Kenneth George, b. 28 Mar. 1916. Presbyterian Minister of Religion. Educ: B.A., Univ. of Toronto, 1939; B.D., D.D., Knox Coll., ibid, 1946-61. Appts: Min., Drummond Hill Presby. Ch., Niagara Falls, Ont., Canada, 1944-50; Min., St. Andrew's Presby. Ch., Guelph, Ont., 1950-57; Gen. Sec., Canadian Bible Soc., 1957-; Bible Soc. work in over 100 countries; Lectr. at Canadian & Int. Confs. Mbrships: Gen. Comm. United Bible Socs.; Canadian Coun. Chs.; Empire Club of Toronto. Author of What but They Grace, 1960. Address: 69 St. Leonards Ave., Toronto, Ont., Canada, M4N 1K4.

MACMILLAN, Malcolm Kenneth, b. 21 Aug. 1913. Journalist; Former Member of Parliament. Educ: Univ. of Edinburgh, U.K. Appts: M.P. for Western Isles, 1935-70; Chmn., Scottish Parliamentary Labour Party, 1945-51; Chmn., Govt. Advsry. Panel on Highlands & Islands, 1947-55; Chmn., All Party Parliamentary East West Trade Comm. of both Houses, 1966-70; Mbr., Scottish Advsry. Comm. on Civil Aviation, 1948-55; Mbr., P.O. Advsry. Coun., 1945-48; Mbr., Scottish Econ. Conf. Author, The Heart is Highland (verse). Address: 11 Cross St., Coulregrein, Stornoway, Isle of Lewis, U.K. 1, 34, 41, 128.

McMILLEN, Barclay Doster, b. 7 Mar. 1931. Professor; Lawyer. Educ: A.B., Kent State Univ., Ohio, 1953; J.D., Harvard Law Schl., 1957. Admitted to practice, Mass., Ky., D.C., U.S. Dist. Ct. of Mass., U.S. Dist. Ct. of Appeals for D.C. & U.S. Supreme Ct. Appts: Assoc., Ogden, Galphin & Abell, Louisville, Ky., 1957-58; Law Clerk, Ct. of Appeals of

Ky., Frankfort, 1958-59; Trial & Appellate Atty., Fed. Power Commn., Wash. D.C., 1959-61; Pvte. Prac. of Law, Wash. D.C., Wash. Counsel for sev. cos., on Bd. of Dirs., Olney Theatre Corp., on Bd. of Dirs., V.P. & Gen Counsel, U.S. Petroleum, Inc., 1961-67; appointed to Small Bus. Admin. Advsry. Coun., 1965; in Pvte. Prac. of Law, Hyannis, Mass., 1967-; Prof. of Pol. Sci., Kent State Univ., 1967-71, & Cape Cod Community Coll., 1971-; has made extensive radio, TV & guest speaker appearances. Mbrships: Am., Fed. & Fed. Power Bar Assns.; AAUP; Harvard Club of Boston; Congressional Country Club, Wash. D.C. Hons: Outstanding Educator Award, 1971. Address: 290 W. Main St., Hyannis, MA 02601, U.S.A.

McMULLAN, W.P., Jr., b. 20 Nov. 1925. Banker. Educ: B.S., Univ. of Miss., 1948; M.B.A., Wharton Schl. of Finance, Univ. of Pa., 1949. Appts. incl: V.P. -Pres., Newton County Bank, Miss., 1950-57; State Comptroller, Dept. of Bank Supervision (Miss.), 1957-60; V.P. -Vice Chmn., Deposit Guaranty Nat. Bank, Jackson, Miss., 1960-; Pres. & Chief Operating Off., Deposit Guaranty Corp., ibid, 1973-; Directorships in Miss. incl. Deposit Guaranty Nat. Bank, Newton Co. Bank, Bay Springs Bank, Merchants & Planters Bank, Standard Life Ins. Co., Magna Corp. Mbrships. incl: Am. & Miss. Bankers Assn. Address: P.O. Box 1200, Jackson, MS 39205, U.S.A. 2, 125, 128.

McMULLEN, John Joseph, b. 10 May 1918. Naval Architect; Transportation Consultant; Shipping Executive. Educ: B.S., U.S. Naval Acad., 1940; M.S., MIT, 1945; Doct. Tech. Sci., Swiss Fed. Inst. Technol., Zurich, Switzerland, 1950. Appts: Chief, Off. Ship Construction & Repair, Maritime Admin., U.S. Dept. of Commerce, Wash., D.C., 1954-57; Pres., John J. McMullen Assocs., Inc., N.Y., 1957-68; Bd. Chmn., ibid, 1971; Bd. Chmn., Pres., Chief Exec. Off., U.S. Lines, N.Y., 1968-70; Dir., Richton Int. Corp., Norton Lilly & Co. Inc., Hudson Engrng. Co. Perth Amboy Dry Dock Co., MPR Assocs. Inc., Pacific Marine Corp., Santa Ana Shipyards Corp., N.V., Cornell & Underhill, Inc., Dubai Dry Dock Co. Mbrships. incl: Am. Soc. Naval Engrs.; Bd. Mgrs.. Am. Bur. Shipping. Author of tech. papers. Recip., hons. Address: John J. McMullen Assocs. Inc., One World Trade Ctr., Suite 3047, N.Y., NY 10048, U.S.A. 2, 6.

MacNAB, Bruce E., b. 12 Feb. 1930. Heavy Industry Corporate Executive. Educ: B.D., Denison Univ., 1952; M.B.A., Ohio State Univ., 1959; Ph.D., ibid, 1965. Appts: U.S. Navy Off., 1953-57; Mgr., N. Am. Rsch. & Engrng., 1960-65; Cons., U.S. Dept. of Defense, Weapon Systems Mgmt. Ctr., Wright-Patterson Air Force Base, Dayton, Ohio, 1965-66; Dir. of Marketing. Buckeye Int., 1966-70; Corporate Dir. of Marketing, Jeffrey Galion Inc., 1970-74; Mgr. Marketing, Engrng. Works Div., Dravo Corp., Pitts., Pa., 1974-. Mbrships: Am. Marketing & Mgmt. Assns.; Newcomen Soc.; Masonic Order; Beta Theta Pi. Contbng. author, bus. publs., inclng. Marketing Managers Handbook, 1974. Address: Dravo Corp., 4800 Grand Ave., Neville Island, Pittsburgh, PA 15225, U.S.A. 8.

McNEESE, Betty Allison (Mrs. Robert L. McNeese). Educator. Educ: B.A., Northwestern State Univ., Natchitoches, La.; M.Ed., Univ. of Miss., Oxford; Ed.D., ibid. Appts: Instr.; Counsellor; Supvsr. of Instrn.; Dir. of Secondary Educ. Mbrships: Past Pres., La. Coun. for Soc. Studies; Bd. of Trustees, La. Coun. for Econ. Educ.; Affiliate Ldr., Nat. Coun. of Tchrs. of Engl. Publs: The Creative

Individual; The Story of American Education; Elementary Story Starters; Advanced Story Starters; Stories of States-Each State's History. Recip. Phi Alpha Theta Award, 1944. Address: Caddo Parish Schl. Bd., Box 37000, Shreveport, LA 71130, U.S.A. 46, 125.

McNUTT, Effie Curtis, b. 15 Dec. 1906. Poet; Teacher. Educ: B.A., Northeastern State Coll., Tahlequah, Okla., 1934; M.A., ibid., 1956. Retired as tchr. after over 40 yrs. Published 2 books of poetry: A S Spark of Diety, 1957; Ambrosial Wines, 1960. Mbrships: Reading & Evaluation Comm. Mbr., Ala. State Poetry Soc.; World Poetry Soc. Intercontinental; Int. Poetry Soc.; Am. Poetry League; Nat. Writers Club; Poetry Soc. Tex.; Order of Eastern Star, Tahlequah, Okla.; Order of White Shrine of Jerusalem, Muskogee, Okla. Hons: Nat. Fedn. State Poetry Socs, Inc., Certs. of Merit; W. Va. Poetry Soc. Award (Third), 1972; Beaudoun Gemstone Award - Mystic 1972 (eth Hon. Mention). Address: Route 3, Box 184, Danville, AL 35619, U.S.A. 11, 57.

MCNUTT, Sara Jean, b. 24 Nov. 1932. Educator. Educ: B.S., Ctrl. Mich. Univ., 1954; M.A., Mich. State Univ., 1961. Appts. incl: Tchr., bus. subjects, Oak Pk. Sr. H.S., Mich., 1959-62; Grad. Asst., Univ. of Wyo., Laramie, 1963; Instr., ibid, 1963-65; Pt.-time Instr., acctng., Mid-Mich. Community Coll., Harrison, 1969-70; Asst. Prof., acctng., data processing, Ctrl. Mich. Univ., Mt. Pleasant, 1965-. Mbrships: Nat. & Mich. Bus. Educ. Assns.; Int. Soc. Bus. Educ.; Soc. Data Educators; former mbr., Am. Acctng. Assn.; Smithsonian Instn.; AAUW; Chmn., Mich. Bus. Educ. Roundtable, Higgins Lake Conf., 1967. Contbr. of articles to profl. jrnls. Recip., Ph.D., Colo. State Christian Coll., 1973. Address: 1211 Glen Ave., Mt. Pleasant, MI 48858, U.S.A. 5, 34.

MACOMBER, Allison R., b. 5 July 1916. Sculptor-teacher. Educ: Mass. Coll. of Art, w. Cyrus Dallin & Raymond Porter; work for Sir Henry Kitson. Appts: Assoc., Gorham Corp. Foundry, many yrs.; Artist-in-Residence, Boston Coll., 1963-. Mbrships: Hon. Mbr., Fall River Art Assn., Mass.; Mass. State Senate Art Commnr.; Past Pres., Utopian Club, Providence, R.I. Sculptor, portraits, medals, mems. & archtl. works in bronze & stone, U.S.A. & abroad. Exhbs. incl: Pa. Acad.; Nat. Sculpture Soc. Major works incl: 6 bronze doorways, Trenton Cathedral, N.J.; 12' figure of Christ in limestone, Ch. of the Holy Name, Taftsville, Conn.; Cardinal Cushing Mem., Boston, Mass.; Babe Ruth bronze portrait plaque. Address: Mulberry Cottage, Segregansett, MA 02773, U.S.A. 6, 37, 133.

McPECK, Dorothy Ellis Mooney (Mrs. E.K. McPeck), b. 23 Mar. 1909. Antiques Dealer; Appraiser; Restorer of Early American Houses. Educ: Antioch Coll., Yellow Springs, Ohio; Student Dietitian, Miami Valley Hosp., Dayton, Ohio, 1926-28; Wilfred Beauty Acad., 1930; U.S. Ordnance Ammunition Inst. Schl., 1943; Bryant Stratton Bus. Coll., 1945. Appts. incl: U.S. Govt. Explosive Chemist & Instr. in Ammunition Handling, 1940-42; U.S. Ordnance Surveillance Insp., 1942-45; Early Am. Antiques Dealer, Restorer & Appraiser, New Cumberland, Pa., 1947-48, Chester Depot, Vt., 1948-65, Windsor, Vt., 1965-71; Restorer of Early Am. Houses, Old Stone Village, Chester Depot, Vt. & "Birch Hill", Windsor, Vt.; Early Am. Antiques Appraiser, Winter Pk., Fla., 1971-. Mbrships. incl: Appraiser Assn. of Am.; DAR; Sr. Treas., Battle Thomas Creek, Children of the Am. Revolution; Antique Assns. of Vt. & N.H.; Early Am. Glass Club. Publs. incl: History of The Old Stone Village, Chester Depot,

Vermont, 1951; Early American Silver Spoons and Their Makers, 1960. Recip. of hons. Address: 1259 Lakeview Dr., Winter Park, FL 32789, U.S.A. 5, 130, 132, 133.

MacPHERSON, Janet Taylor Wolfenden. Homemaker; Civic worker. Educ: B.S., Univ. of Pa.; M.A., ibid, Additional grad. work, Columbia Univ. Mbrships. incl: Bd. Dir., Oak Ridge, Tenn. Chapt., AAUW; 1957-59; Pres., League of Women Voters of Oak Ridge, 1961-63 & of Tenn., 1967-69; Bd. Dir., Oak Ridge Civic Music Assn., 1963-66; Nat. Comm. for Better Schools, 1967-70; Tenn. Comm., 1970 White House Conf. on children & Youth, 1969-70; Chmn., Youth Comm. of Oak Ridge, 1969-70; Bd. Dir., Awareness House of Oak Ridge Inc., 1970-73; State Planning Comm., Air Quality Project for Tenn., 1970-71; Oak Ridge City Charter Commn., 1972-74. Ed., This Is Oak Ridge, Tennessee, 1961. Address: 102 Orchard Circle, Oak Ridge, TN 37830, U.S.A. 5, 7, 125, 132.

MACQUARRIE, Heath Nelson, b. 18 Sept. 1919. Member of Canadian Parliament; Educator. Educ: B.A., Univ. of Man., 1947; M.A., Univ. of N.B., 1949; McGill Univ., 1949-51. Appts. incl: Lectr., Pol. Sci., McGill Univ., 1949-51; Prof., Pol. Sci. & Int. Rels., ibid, 1952; Rockefeller Rsch. Assoc., Univ. of Toronto, 1955-56; Instr., Int. Rels., Carleton Univ., 1963-64; M.P. for Hillsborough, P.E.I., 1957-. Mbrships. incl: Canadian Pol. Sci. Assn.; Am. Pol. Sci. Assn.; Int. Pol. Sci. Assn.; Canadian Hist. Assn.; Nat. V.P., Progressive Conservative Party of Canada, 1953-55; Chmn., Canadian Br., Commonwealth Parliamentary Assn., 1960-61; Chmn., Privileges & Elections Comm., House of Commons, 1958-61. Author of num. articles. Ed., Robert Laird Borden: His Memoirs, 1969. Recip., var. rsch. awards. Address: House of Commons, Ottawa, Ont., Canada.

MCQUOWN, Margueritte Robinson (Mrs. J. B. McQuown), b. 28 Sept., 1905. Businesswoman; Administrator. Appts: Prod. Chmn., Am. Red Cross (World War II), Allegany Co.; Standing Mgr., Campaign Pol. H.Q. for Democratic Party, State of Md.; Sec., Nat. Conf. of Christians & Jews, Allegany Co., 1959-; Owner/Operator, News & Book Concession, Ft. Cumberland Hotel, Md. Mbrships: State Off., Democratic Women's Clubs of Md., Chmn., Allegany Co., Md.; Nat. Democratic Women's Club, Wash. D.C.; State Chmn., Citizenship Prog., (State of Md.); Anti-Vivesect. Club, Chgo. Recip. of Am. Red Cross citation, outstanding serv., 1960-66. Address: P.O. Box 1285, Cumberland, MD 21502, U.S.A. 5, 125.

McREE, Johnson, Jr., b. 11 June 1923. Certified Public Accountant. Educ: Hampden-Sydney Coll.; B.S., Wash. & Lee Univ.; C.P.A, Va., 1950. Appts: Staff Acct., T. Coleman Andrews & Co., 1948-51; Sr. Staff Acct., Auditor, City of Richmond, Va., 1951-52; Sr. Staff Acct., Baker, Brydon, Rennolds & Whitt, 1952-54; Off. Mngr., Manassas, Va., 1954-58; Res. Ptnr., Off. Mgr., 1958-61; Comptroller, Treas., Dir., Georator Corp., 1961-63; Sr. Ptnr., Brydon, McRee & Smith, 1963-72; Sole Practitioner, Johnson McRee Jr. T/A Brydon, McRee & Smith, Manassas, 1972-. Mbrships. incl: Treas., Dir., Tax Coun., Wash. D.C.; Va. Mbr., Nat. Assn. of Mfrs.; Am. Inst. of CPAs; Va. Soc. of CPAs; Treas., N.C. Soc. of the Cinn.; Iota, Pi Chapts., Kappa Alpha; Fndr., Dir., Potomac River Jazz Club; New Orleans Jazz Club; Dir., Past Pres. Gtr. Manassas Chmbr. of Comm.; Prod., Pres. & Treas., Manassas Jazz Festival, 1966-; Pres., Fat Cat's Jazz Records. Vocalist, kazoo, on num. jazz records. Address: P.O. Box 458, Manassas, VA 22110, U.S.A. 7.

MC RITCHIE, Alexander Ian, b. 16 June 1915. Engineer; Heat Treatment Specialist & Consultant. Educ: St. Kilda Coll., Melbourne; S. Melbourne Tech. Schl. Appts. incl: Chief Instr., Spencer Gulf Aero Club, Whyalla & Port Pirie, 1939-40; Squadron Ldr., RAF, U.K., 1940-46; Co-Fndr. & Mng. Dir., Watts McRitchie Engrng. Co. Pty. Ltd., 1946-64; Mng. Dir., Melbourne Heat Treatment & Metallurgical Servs. Pty., Ltd.; Chmn. of Dirs., Bradley Engrng. Co.; Dir., Grant McRitchie Motor Cycles. Mbrships. incl: Hon. Fed. Sec., Australian Inst. Metals; Pres., Australian Inst. Metals, Vic., 1962, 1970; Am. Soc. Metals; Royal Aeronautical Soc. Num. papers, tech. publs. Hons. incl: D.F.C., 1942; Locality of McRitchie, Whyalla, S.A. named in his hon.; Gun sight design adopted by RAF; Portrait hung in Royal Acad., 1945. Address: 9 St. Helen's Rd., Hawthorne E., Melbourne, Vic., Australia 3123. 23.

MACRYMICHALOS, Stephen John, b. 20 Jan. 1902. Underwriter; Manager of Insurance Company. Educ: LL.D., Athens Univ., Greece. Appts: Pres., Assn. of Marine Ins. Cos. Operating in Greece, 1940-44; Pres., Bd. Dirs., PROODOS Hellenic Ins. & Reinsurance Co., S.A., 1941-; Pres., Bd. Dirs., Macrymichalos Bros. S.A., 1941-; Pres., Assn. Ins. Cos. Operating in Greece, 1964-68; V.P., Insurers' Union of Greece, 1969-72. Mbrships: Rotary Int. (Gov., Dist. 197, Greece, 1960-62; Pres., Rotary Club of Athens, 1954-55, '55-56); Royal Philatelic Soc. of London (Fellow & Rep. in Greece); Hellenic Philatelic Fed. (Pres.); Hellenic Philatelic Soc. (Fndr. & Pres., 1924-); Athens Club (Sr. Mbr.). Publs. incl: Greece—Economic & Insurance Conditions, 1972, 1973; Bottomry Loan, 1971; Tsakonian Marriage Contracts in the 18th & 19th Centuries, 1967; A Forgotten British Philhellene, Sir Edward Fitzgerlad Law, 1974. Recip., hons. Address: 61 Diamantidou St., Psychiko, Athens, Greece. 43.

McTAGGART, Douglas G., b. 30 Sept. 1931. Insurance Executive. Educ: B.A., Vic. Coll., Univ. of Toronto, 1954. Appts: Life Underwriter—Agcy. Mgr., Canada Life Assurance Co., 1956-63; Prin. own Agcy., Crown Life Ins. Co., Toronto, 1963-69; Pres. & Dir., Planned Ins. Portfolios Co. Ltd., 1969-. Mbrships. incl: Life Ins. Mgmt. Assn.; Past Dir. & Off., Life Underwriters Assn.; Past Chmn., Ins. Sect., United Appeal; Canadian Tax Fndn; Royal Canadian Inst.; Royal Ont. Mus.; Art Gall. of Ont. Winner sev. profl. cups; C.L.U. designation, 1963. Address: Planned Ins. Portfolios Co. Ltd., 797 Don Mills Rd., Don Mills, Ont., Canada. 88.

MACUCH, Rudolf, b. 16 Oct. 1919. Professor of Semitic Languages. Educ: Fac. of Evangelical Theol., Bratislava, Czechoslovakia, 1939-43; study of Semitic Philol., Fac. des Lettres, Ecole Pratique des Hautes Etudes & Ecole Nat. des Langs. Orientales Vivantes, Paris, France, 1945-47; Ph.D., Fac. of Philos., Comenius Univ., Bratislava, 1948. Appts. incl: Assoc. Pastor, Slovak Evangelical Luth. Ch., Trencín & Krajné, 1943-45; Rsch. Fellow, Inst. of Semitics, Comenius Univ., Bratislava, 1948-50; Assoc. Prof., Fac. of Letters, Univ. of Teheran, Iran, 1954-63; Prof. of Semitics, Freie Univ., Berlin, Germany, 1963-. Mbrships: Am. Oriental Soc.; Deutscher Palastina-Verein; Deutsche Morgenländische Gesellschaft. Publs. incl: Islam & Christianity, 1950; A Mandaic Dictionary (w. Lady E.S. Drower), 1963;

Handbook of Classical & Modern Mandaic, 1965; Grammatik Des Samaritanischen Hebräisch, 1969; num. papers & book reviews in profl. jrnls.; book in press & one in prep. Address: Reichensteiner Weg 8-10, 1000 Berlin 33, Germany. 43, 92.

McVEIGH, Miriam Temperance. Fine Artist; Painter. Educ: Grade Schl. Schlrship., John Herron Art Inst., Indpls., Ind.; Elmer Tafflinger Studio, ibid; Studied w. Clifton Wheeler & Eugen Neuhaus, Calif. Coll. Arts & Crafts; B.F.A., Oakland, Calif.; Acad. Goetz, Paris, France. Appts: Studio Galls., Oakland, Calif. & Indpls., Ind.; Currently, St. Petersburg, Fla. Mbrships: Eastern Star; Free Painters & Sculptors, London, U.K. Works represented in: Mus. Monbart, Dijon, France, & in collects. of Mr. R. Janseck, Orlando, Fla.; Mr. Garfield & Mr. John T. Webb, Ont., Canada; Mr. Marshall Field, Sarasota, Fla. & Chgo., Ill. Hons: Hoosier Salon, Indpls., Ind., 1954; num. others inclng. Festival of States, Ligoa Duncan Gall., N.Y., 1972; Galéries Raymond Duncan, Paris, France, 1972; Palmes d'Or du Mérite Belgo-Hispanique, Brussels, Belgium, 1973; One-Woman Show, Galérie Int., N.Y., 1974. Address: 8200 14th St. N., St. Petersburg, FL 33702, U.S.A. 37.

MACVEY, J.W.. b. 19 Jan. 1923. Industrial Chemist; Author. Educ: Dip., Applied Chem., Univ. of Strathclyde, Glasgow, U.K., 1950. Appts: Rsch. Chemist, I.C.I. Ltd., Nobel Div., Stevenston, Ayrshire, 1956-61, 1962-66; Plant Supt., ibid, 1961-62; Tech. Abstractor, 1966-70; Tech. Info. Off., Nobels Explosives Ltd., Ardeer, Ayrshire, 1970-. Mbrships: Fellow, Royal Astronomical Soc., 1958-; Fellow, British Interplanetary Soc., 1956-; British Astronomical Assn.; Astronomical Soc. of the Pacific, San Fran., Calif., U.S.A.; Radio Soc. of Gt. Britain. Publs. incl: How We Will Reach the Stars, 1969; Whispers from Space, 1973; Earth Visited? , forthcoming. Address: Mellendean, 15 Adair Ave., Saltcoats, Ayrshire, KA21 5QS, U.K. 30, 131, 137.

McWHERTER, Iris Guenell, b. 29 June 1946. Social Worker; Educator. Educ: B.A., Ctrl. State Univ., Wilberforce, Ohio, 1967; Masters in Soc. Work, St. Louis Univ., 1969; currently Ph.D. Cand., ibid. Mbrships: Coun. of Soc. Work Educ.; Nat. Assn. of Soc. Workers; Childcare Assn.; Urban League Guild. Address: 2900 Market St., E. St. Louis, IL 62207, U.S.A. 125.

MADDEN, Robert E., b. 16 Sept. 1925. Surgeon. Educ: DePaul Univ., Chgo., Ill., U.S.A., 1946-48; B.S., Med. Schl., Univ. of Ill., 1950; M.D., ibid, 1952; M.S., Grad. Schl., Univ. of Ill., 1952; Intern-Asst. Res.-Res., Rsch. & Educl. Hosps., Univ. of Ill., 1952-58. Appts: Asst. in Surg., Univ. of Ill., 1954-57; Assoc. in Surg., ibid, 1957-58; Sr. Surg., Nat. Cancer Inst., Bethesda, D.C., 1959-60; Asst. Prof., Surg., N.Y. Med. Coll., 1961-66; Assoc. Prof., ibid, 1966-71; Prof., 1971-. Mbrships: Fellow, Am. Coll. of Surgs.; N.Y. Surg. Soc.; Fellow, Royal Soc. of Med., London, U.K.; Fellow, Am. Coll. of Chest Physns.; Am. Soc. of Clin. Oncol.; Am. Assn. for Cancer Rsch.; V.P., N.Y. Cancer Soc., 1973-74; Am. Fed. for Clin. Rsch.; Pi Gamma Mu. Publs: Approx. 50 rsch. papers (some co-author) in profl. jrnls., books, & presented at confs. Address: 1249 Fifth Ave., N.Y., NY 10029, U.S.A.

MADDISON, Angus, b. 6 Dec. 1926. Economist. Educ: B.A., M.A., Selwyn Coll., Cambridge Univ., U.K.; McGill Univ., Montreal, Canada & Johns Hopkins Univ., Balt., U.S.A. Appts. incl: Prin. Administrator, Org. for European Econ. Co-operation, Paris, 1953-57; Hd., Econs. Div., ibid, 1958-62; Dir., Dev. Dept., OECD, Paris, 1963; Fellow, OECD Dev. Ctr., Paris, 1964-67; Dir., 20th Century Fund Study on Econ. Dev., 1967-69; Vis.-Prof., Univ. of Calif., Berkeley, 1968 & Sir George Williams Univ., Montreal, 1969; Fellow, Harvard Univ. Ctr. for Int. Affairs, 1969-71 & Advsr. to Govt.'s of Pakistan, Ghana & Brazil; Cons., Directorate for Scientific Affairs, OECD, Paris, 1971-72; Hd., Staff Grp. on Econ. Analysis & Resource Allocation, ibid, 1972-. Publs. incl: Economic Growth In The West, 1964, (sev. langs.); Economic Growth In Japan & The U.S.S.R., 1969, (sev. langs.); Economic Progress & Policy In Developing Countries, 1970. also Spanish edit.; Class Structure & Economic Growth: India & Pakistan Since The Moghuls, 1972; Economic Performance & Policy In Europe 1913-70, 1974; author, co-author & ed. num. reports & contbns. in books & jrnls. in profl. field. Address: OECD, 2 Rue André Pascal, Paris 16, France. 2, 12.

MADDOX, Cecil Jr., b. 6 Mar. 1931. Minister; Educator. Educ: B.S., Tenn. A & I State Univ., Nashville, 1959; M.A., Murray State Univ., 1968. Appts: Min., African Meth. Episcopal Ch.; Asst. Schl. Prin.; Tchr. Mbrships; Pres., Co. Tchrs. Assn.; V.P., local Tchrs. Assn.; NEA; Ky. Educ. Assn.; Better Rels. Grp.; PTA; Citizen Advsry. Comm.; Boy Scouts; Ky. H.S. Athletic Assn.; local & state Democratic Campaign Worker; local recreation bd.; NAACP. Hons: China Serv. Ribbon, 1952; Korean Serv. Medal, 5 stars, 1955; Nat. Defense Serv. Medal, 1955; U.N. Serv. Medal, 1955. Address: 414 Taylor St., S. Fulton, TN 42041, U.S.A. 125.

MADDOX, George L., b. 2 July 1925. Professor of Sociology. Educ: B.A., Millsaps Coll., 1949; M.A., Boston Univ., 1952; Ph.D., Mich. State Univ., 1956. Appts: Prof., Millsaps Coll., 1956-60; Assoc. Prof., Sociol., Duke Univ., 1960-66; Prof., ibid, 1966-; Hd., Div., Med. Sociol., Med. Schl., 1966-; Dir., Duke Ctr., Study of Aging & Human Dev., 1972-. Mbrships: Fellow, Am. Sociol. Assn.; Comm. Chmn., Gerontol. Soc.; Div. Chmn., Soc. for Study of Soc. Problems; AAAS; Sec., Am. Sect., Int. Assn. Gerontol. Author, book chapts. & Articles, profl. publs. Address: P.O. Box 3003, Duke Univ. Med. Ctr., Durham, NC 27710, U.S.A.

MADDOX, Lucy Jane, b. 6 Apr. 1922. Library Director; Professor of English. Educ: A.B., Seattle Pacific Coll., Wash., U.S.A., 1944; M.A., Colo. State Coll., 1948; M.A.L.S., Univ. of Mich., Ann Arbor, 1956; Ph.D., ibid, 1958. Appts. incl: Dean of Women & Asst. Prof., Speech & Engl., Spring Arbor Coll., Mich., 1948-51 & 1952-53; Assoc. Prof., Speech & Engl., Seattle Pacific Coll., Wash., 1951-52; Libn., & Assoc. Prof., Engl., Owosso Coll., Mich., 1958-59; Prof., Engl. & Speech, & Chmn., Div. of Lit., Langs., & Fine Arts, ibid, 1958-59; Dir.-Instr., Lib. Techns. Prog., Ferris State Coll., Big Rapids, Mich., 1959-62; Lib. Curric. Coord., Spring Arbor Coll., Mich., 1962-63; Dir. of Lib., & Prof., Engl., ibid, 1963-; Pt.-time Lectr., Lib. Sci., Univ. of Mich., Ann Arbor, 1958-65. Mbrships: Chmn., Dist. II, Mich. Lib. Assn., 1967-68; Conf. of Christianity & Lit.; Mich. Acad.; Assn. for Gen. & Liberal Studies; Beta Phi Mu; Alpha Kappa Sigma. Address: 174 E. Harmony Rd., Spring Arbor, MI 49283, U.S.A. 2, 8, 15, 138.

MADEIRA, Sheldon Spencer Rothermel. Educator, Retired. Educ: A.B., Elizabethtown Coll.; M.S., Pa. State Univ.; Ph.D., Univ. of Pa. Appts. incl: Expert on all levels of pub. & pvte.

educ.; Pioneer, remedial reading progs. in Am.; Dir., Developmental Reading Prog., State Reading Prog., Pa.; Pub. Instrn. Off., w. positions as Curriculum Planning Specialist Dir. of Grad. & Profl. Educ.; Cons., European Coll.; Advsr. to State bodies, inclng. Curr. Cmmn., Med. Bd., Pharmacy Bd., Dental Bd., Engrg. Bd. Mbrships. incl: Salvation Army; Overseas Blind; Care; Proj. Hope; Phi Delta Kappa; NEA. Author of num. profl. manuals. Hons: Citation, C'wealth Supt.; Citation C'wealth Coun. of Engl. Address: 417 Arlington Rd., Camp Hill, PA 17011, U.S.A. 2, 6, 15.

MADEY, Richard, b. 23 Feb. 1922. University Professor. Educ: B.E.E., Rensselaer Polytech. Inst., Troy, N.Y., 1942; Ph.D., Univ. of Calif., Berkeley, 1952. Appts. incl: Chief, Applied Phys. Subdiv., Rsch. Div., Chief Staff Scientist, Mod. Phys. & Sr. Scientist, Sci. Rsch. Staff, Repub. Aviation Corp., Farmingdale, N.Y., 1956-64; Prof., Phys., Clarkson Coll. of Tech., 1965-71; Chmn., Dept. of Phys., ibid, 1965; Prof. & Chmn., Dept. of Phys., Kent State Univ., Ohio, 1971-; Cons., U.S. Atomic Energy Commn., 1965-. Mbrships. incl: Fellow, AAAS, N.Y. Acad. of Scis.; Ohio Acad. of Scis.; Am. Phys. Soc.; Am. Nuclear Soc. (var. Comms.); Am. Geophys. Union; Sr. Mbr., IEE; AAUP; Sigma Xi. Author & Co-author num. sci. publs. Holder, 6 U.S. patents. Prin. Investigator, var. Govt. Grants & Contracts. Recip. sev. Hons. Address: Dept. of Physics, Kent State Univ., Kent, OH 44242, U.S.A. 14, 16, 50.

MADGETT, Naomi Long (Mrs.), b. 5 July 1923. Poet; University Professor. Educ: B.A., Wa. State Coll., 1945; M.A., Wayne State Univ., 1956. Appts: Reporter, Mich. Chronicle, 1945-46; Serv. Rep., Mich. Bell Telephone Co., 1948-54; Engl. Tchr. Detroit Pub. Schls., 1955-65, 66-68; Rsch. Assoc., Oakland Univ., Rochester, 1965-66; Lectr., Univ. of Mich., 1970-71; Assoc. Prof., Eastern Mich. Univ., Ypsilanti, 1968-73; Prof., ibid, 1973-. Mbrships. incl: MLA; Coll. Lang. Assn.; Nat. Cohn. Tchrs. of Engl.; Alpha Kappa Alpha; NAACP; AAUP; Poetry Soc. Mich; Delta Kappa Gamma. Publs: (poetry) Songs to a Phantom Nightingale, 1970; One & the Many, 1970; Star by Star, 1970; Pink Ladies in the Afternoon, 1972; (textbook) Success in Language & Literature, 1967; contbr. to num. anthols. Hons. incl: Disting. Engl. Tchr. of the Yr., Metropolitan Detroit Engl. Club, 1967; Soror of the Yr. Award, Alpha Rho Omega Chapt., Alpha Kappa Alpha, 1968. Address: 16886 Inverness Ave., Detroit, MI 48221, U.S.A. 5, 11, 30.

MADRAZO GARAMENDI, Manuel, b. 16 Mar. 1922. Chemist; Educator. Educ: Nat. Schl. of Chem. Scis., Nat. Univ. of Mexico; Trinity Coll., Univ. of Toronto, Canada. Appts: Dir. & Cons., Control Quimico, 1939-; Adv. Min. of Pub. Works, 1954-64; Sec., Nat. Schl. of Chem. Scis., Nat. Univ. of Mexico, 1954; Dir., ibid, 1947-54, Dir., Fac. of Chem., 1965-70; Gen. Sec., Nat. Univ. of Mexico, 1970-73; Pres., Quimica Interamericana S.A., 1961-. Mbrships: Fndr., Pres. Chem. Soc. of Mexico & Consejo Nat. de Educ. Quim.; Hon. Mbr., Assoc. Farm. Mex. & As. Quim. de Guayas; Mex. Inst. of Chem. Engrng.; Mex. Hist. Soc.; Am. Chem. Soc.; AAAS; Corres., As. Venezolana de Quim.; Corres., Sociedad Quimica de Perú. Publs: Tratado de Química Inorgánica de Bargalo (co-author); articles in sci. jrnls. Hons. incl: Order of Palmes Acad., France, 1957; Nat. Order of Merit, ibid, 1967; Permio Nacional de Quimica Manuel Andres Del Rio, 1964; Award Inst. Mex. de Ing. Quim., 1969; Das Grosse Verdienstkreuz, German Fed. Repub., 1973. Address: Durango 283, Mexico 7 D.F., Mexico.

MADRIGAL, José Antonio, b. 18 July 1945. Professor. Educ: B.A., Mich. State Univ., U.S.A.; M.A., ibid; Ph.D., Univ. of Ky. Appts: Mich. State Univ., 1967-68; Univ. of Ky., 1968-70; Auburn Univ., Ala.; 1970-. Mbrships: AATSP; Comediantes; SMLA; Alahispania; Nat. Geographic Soc.; Mich. State Univ. Romance Lang. Club; Sigma Delta Pi. Publs: El Salvaje y La Mitologia, El Arte y La Religion, 1974; El Concepto Filosofico del Hombre Primitivo desde La Antigüedad hasta El Renacimento (in progress); Ed., Alahispania; num. articles, book reviews & papers to confs. on Spanish & Spanish Am. Lit., Hist. & Cuban culture & pol. affairs. Hons: Highest evaluated Prof. at Ky. & Auburn Univs.; Chosen by Lang. Dept. as nominee for Prof. of yr. for Univ. Address: 950 Rustic Ridge Rd., Auburn, AL 36830, U.S.A. 125.

MADSEN, Stephan Tschudi, b. 25 Aug. 1923. Antiquarian. Educ: La Sorbonne, 1946-47; M.A., Univ. of Oslo, 1950; Ph.D., ibid, 1957. Appts: Keeper, Nat. Gall., Oslo, 1950-51, Vigeland Mus., 1951-52; Asst. Prof., Univ. of Oslo, 1953-58; Chief Antiquarian, Ctrl. Off. of Hist. Monuments, Norway, 1959-; Keeper, Akershus Castle, 1961-; Vis. Prof., Univ. of Calif., 1966-67; Regents Prof., ibid, 1973. Mbrships: Sec.-Gen., Archtl. Heritage Yr., Norway, 1965; Norwegian Acad. of Sci. & Letters, 1965-; Coun., Victorian Soc., London, 1966-; Sec., Soc. for Protection of Norwegian Monuments, 1959-69. Publs: To Kongeslott, 1952; Vigelands Fontenerelieffer, 1953; Stoler og Stiler, 1955; Sources of Art Nouveau, 1956; Akershus Slott, Restaurering, 1964; Rosendal, 1965; Chateauneuf's Works in London & Oslo, 1966; Art Nouveau, 1967; Verneideer krysser Atlanteren, 1969; Karl Johansgate, 1970; Akershus Castle, 1973; Art Nouveau, Cuader nos summa-nueva vision 30, 1969; contbr. to jrnls. in field. Hons: Brit. Coun. Schlrship., 1952-53; Spanish State Schlrship., 1957-58; Oslo Municipality Prize, 1972; The Nansen Fund, 1972. Address: Riksantikvaren, Akershus Festning, Oslo 1, Norway. 43.

MAEDA, Yoshinori, b. 31 Jan. 1906. Journalist. Educ: Grad., Tokyo Imperial Coll. of For. Langs. Study (Tokyo Univ. of For. Langs. Study); Rome Univ., Italy. Appts: Advsr., Sci. & Technol. Agcy., 1973, Min. of For. Affairs, 1974, Min. of Int. Trade & Ind., 1974. Mbrships: Hon. Advsr., Nippon Hoso Kyokai, 1973, NHK Symph. Orch.; Hon. Pres., Asian Broadcasting Union, 1973; Hon. Chmn., Int. Broadcast Inst., 1972; Panel, Satellite Use for TV, UNESCO HQ; Co-Chmn., Jt. Comm., US-Japan Cultural Exchange; Pres., Nat. Assn. of Gymnastic Games, Japan; Tokyo Club; Tokyo Ctrl. Rotary Club. Publs: Memory of Defeated War; Turkey; contbr. for Balkan area, Japan Ency. Hons: Grand Off., Italian Govt., 1960; Grand Decoration in Gold for Servs. to the Repub. of Austria, 1960; Golden Medal of Cultural Merit, Italian Govt., 1964; a pair of Silver Cups, Japanese Govt., 1965; Off., Order of the Legion of Honor, French Govt., 1967; Order of the Yugoslav Star w. Golden Wreath, 1968; Cyril and Methodii 1st Class, Bulgarian Govt., 1968; Cmdr.'s Cross, Order of Merit, German Fed. Repub., 1969; Star Grand Cordon, Afghanistan, 1969; Grand Off., Hon. Acad. Order of St. Francis, Fac. of Law, Univ. of Saò Paulo, Brazil, 1969; K.B.E., 1970; Grand Off., Royal Order of the Pole Star, Sweden, 1972; Gwangwha Medal, Order of Diplomatic Serv. Merit, Repub. of Korea, 1973. Address: Gaien Suzuki Bldg. 3F, No. 22, 2-7 Kitaaoyama Minato-ku, Tokyo 107, Japan.

MAEMORI, Shoichi, b. 7 Jan. 1916. Shipping Company Executive. Educ: Grad.,

Fukushima Commercial Coll. of Japan, 1937. Appts: Chief of Archives & Documents Sect., Okinawa Civil Admin., 1947-50; Mng. Dir., Ryukyu Kaiun Kaisha (RKK) Steamship Line, 1950-64; V.P., Okinawa Stevedoring & Forwarding Co., 1964-72, Pres., 1972-. Mbr., Naha W. Rotarians. Address: 230 Matsugawa, Naha, Okinawa, Japan.

MAESTRE MORATO, Joaquin, b. 12 Feb. 1927. Public Relations Consultant. Educ: P.R. & Human Relations courses at Insts. in Spain. Appts. incl: Proprietor, Advt. Co., Alicante, Spain, 1952-56; Dir., Danis, S.A., Barcelona, Spain, 1956-60; Fndr. & Pres., S.A.E. de Relaciones Públicas, Barcelona, 1960-; gives lectures & speeches. Mbrships. incl: V.P., Comm. of Hogarotel & mbr. since fndn., 1962-; Overseas Assoc., Inst. of P.R., 1961-; Accredited Mbr., P.R. Soc. of Am., 1962-; Spanish Deleg., Int. P.R. Assn., 1963-; Fndr. & former Pres., Exec. Comm., Agrupación Española de Relaciones Públicas; Spanish Deleg., mags., Int. P.R. Review & Int. P.R.; V. Chancellor, Chaîne des Rôtisseurs, 1971-; Prof., Escuela de Altos Estudios Empresariales, Barcelona Univ. Publs. incl: chapt. on Spanish P.R., Hand Book on International Public Relations; articles in P.R. Advt. & marketing mags. Hons: Silver Medal, French Assn. P.R., 1960; Silver Medal, Hogarotel, 1960. Address: Balmes, 184, Barcelona-6, Spain. 24.

MAGARIÑOS, Victor, b. 1 Sept. 1924. Painter. Educ: Nat. Schl. Fine Arts, Buenos Aires, Argentina. Appts. incl: Instr., Nat. Schl. Fine Arts. Mbrships. incl: Fndr., Young Grp. of Painters, 1946; Pres., Argentinian Comm., Int. Assn. Fine Arts, Paris (UNESCO), 1958. Works in museums incl: Nat. Mus. Fine Arts, Buenos Aires; Mus. Mod. Art, ibid; Mod. Art Mus., N.Y., U.S.A.; Albright-Knox Art Gall., Buffalo, N.Y.; also exhibd. in Argentinian & int. pvte. collects. Hons: Grants from French Govt., 1951, U.S. State Dept., 1964; Enrique Prins Prize, Nat. Acad. Fine Arts of Argentina, 1947. Address: Los Talleres, Pinamar, Pcia. Buenos Aires, Argentina. 34.

MAGARIÑOS de MELLO, Mateo Jorge, b. 14 Mar. 1914. Lawyer; Diplomat. Educ: Dr., Law & Soc. Scis., Univ. of the Repub., Montevideo, Uruguay. Num. appts. incl: Lawyer, 1945; Under Sec., For. Affairs, 1959-61; Pres., Confs. creating LAFTA, 1959; Ambassador, Geneva, Switzerland, 1964-67; Ambassador, Bern, 1968-69; Ambassador, Sweden, 1969-72; Hd., Dept. of Environment, Min. of For. Affairs, Montevideo, 1973; Vice Chmn., Uruguayan Delegation, UN Conf. on Environment; Prof., Latin Am. Econ. Integration, Int. Fac. of Comparative Law, Strasbourg, France, & Latin Am. Inst., Fac. of Econ. Scis., St. Gallen, Switzerland. Mbrships. incl: Exec. Sec., Nat. Inst. for Preservation of Environment; Fndr. & Pres., Judo Fedn. of Uruguay; Sanmartiniano Inst. Publs: El Gobierno del Cerrito, 1843-1851, 3 vols., 1949-59; Les Organisations Régionales Latinaméricaines d'Intégration, 1971; Apuntes para una Teoria General del Derecho Ambiental, 1973-74; 3 other books. Recip., sev. for. orders & medals. Address: Echevarriarza 3396, Montevideo, Uruguay.

MAGAZZINI, Gene (Gino), b. 5 Nov. 1914. Artist. Educ: Leonardo da Vinci Art Schl., N.Y.C.; Brooklyn Coll., ibid; Art Students League of N.Y. Appts: Free-lance Painter specialising in Oils & Murals, Brooklyn, N.Y. Mbrships: Salmagundi Club (jury of awards, 1972-74; admissions comm., 1972-74; curator's comm., 1969, '70, '72, '73); life mbr., Art Students League of N.Y. Inc.; Allied Artists of

Am. Inc.; Nat. Art League (jury of awards, 1969); Knickerbocker Artists (jury of awards, 1974); Artists Fellowship Inc.; Am. Artists Profl. League (jury of awards, 1966); Burr Artists, Inc. (P.R. chmn., 1969-74). Rep. in Collects: Dr. T. Edward Hanley Collect., Bradford, Pa.; Norton Walbridge Collect., La Jolla, Calif.; Ambassador James S. Kemper Collect., Chgo., Ill.; Dpty. Mayor Spangenberg of Berlin Collect. Hons. incl: 1st Prize, Nat. Art League, 1972; Gold Medal, ibid, 1971. Address: 249 Euclid Ave., Brooklyn, NY 11208, U.S.A. 37.

MAGEE, Bryan, b. 12 Apr. 1930. Writer; Broadcaster. Educ: M.A., Oxford Univ.; Fellowship in Philos., Yale Univ. Appts: Lectr. in Philos., Balliol Coll., Oxford, 1970-71. Mbrships: Aristotelian Soc.; British Soc. for Philos of Sci.; Royal Inst. of Philos.; British Soc. of Aesthetics; Wagner Soc. of Authors; Equity; Critics' Circle. Publs: Crucifixion & Other Poems; Go West Young Man; To Live in Danger; The New Radicalism; The Democratic Revolution; Towards 2000; One in Twenty; The Television Interviewer; Aspects of Wagner; Modern British Philosophy; Popper. Address: 12 Falkland House, Marloes Road, London W8 5LF, U.K. 3, 4, 58.

MAGENHEIMER, Cathryn Cecile (pen name Kay Magenheimer) b. 5 Mar. 1908. Accountant; Real Estate Broker; Poet. Educ: N.Y. State Coll. for Tchrs. (now SUNY), Albany, N.Y., 1925-26, 1940-31; Hunter Coll., N.Y.C., 1938. Appts. incl: Personal Sec., & exec offs., subsidiary cos., Consolidated Film Inds. Inc., N.Y.C., 1932-36; Off. Mgr., Charles H. Kenney Studios, Inc., 1937-42, H.A. Florsheim Co., 1942-49; Clerk, Dept. Pub. Works, N.Y. State Govt., Babylon, N.Y., 1949-54, var. clerical posts, L.I. State Pk. & Recreation Commn., 1954-68, H. Account Clerk, 1968-; Broker-Owner, Bond Realty, Hauppauge, N.Y., 1968. Mbr., profl. & literary orgs. Poetry Publs. incl: Love's Stigmata, 1963; Ah, Camelot (in preparation). Hons. incl: Publr's. Best Book of Poetry Award, 1963; Nat. Poetry Contest Award, 1974; Engrossment of poem, Ask Not..., accepted for John F. Kennedy Mem. Lib. Address: 228 Atlantic Pl., Hauppauge, NY 11787, U.S.A. 5, 11, 57.

MAGER, Artur, b. 21 Sept. 1919. Aerospace Company Executive. Educ: B.S., Univ. of Mich., 1943; M.S., Case Inst. of Technol., 1951; Ph.D., ibid 1953. Appts: Aero Rsch. Sci., NACA Lewis Labs., 1946-51; Rsch. Sci., Marawardt Corp. 1954-60; Dir., Nat. Engrng. Sci. Co., 1960-61; Dir., Spacecraft Scis., Aerospace Corp., 1961-64; Gen. Mgr., Applied Mech. Div., 1964-68; V.P., Gen. Mgr., Engrng. Sci. Ops., 1968-. Mbrships. incl: Fellow, Am. Inst. Aerons. & Astrons.; AAAS; Gesellschaft Angewandte Mechanik; Technion Soc.; Am. Phys. Soc.; Am. Soc. M.R.; L.A. Chmbr. of Comm. Aerospace Comm., 1972; Bd. of Trustees, Exceptional Children's Fndn., 1968-; Sigma Xi. Contbr. to jrnls. Hons: Univ. of Mich. Disting. Alumni Award, 1969. Address: c/o Engrng. Sci. Ops., Aerospace Corp., P.O. Box 92957, Los Angeles, CA 90009, U.S.A. 9, 14, 16, 120, 131.

MAGER, Gerald, Court of Appeal Judge. Educ: B.A., Univ. of Miami, Fla.; LL.B., J.R.D., Law Schl., ibid; further studies Law Schl., Geo. Wash. Univ. Appts: Asst. Atty. Gen. of Fla., 1959-67; Gen. Counsel to Gov. of Fla., 1967-70; Judge, 4th Dist. Ct. of Appeal, Fla., 1970-. Mbrships: Chmn., Fla. Advsry. Coun. on Mental Retardation, 1965-67; Interstate Oil Compact Commn., 1967-69; Interagency Law Enforcement Planning Coun., 1968-69; Fla.

Judicial Coun., 1970-; Am. Bar Assn.; Am. Judicature Soc.; Fla. Bar Hons. incl: Cert. of Appreciation, Radio Free Europe, 1963-66; Fla. Jaycees Governmental Affairs Award, 1965; Fla. Jaycees State Good Govt. Award, 1968. Address: 4th Dist. Ct. of Appeal, 1525 Palm Beach Lakes Blvd., P.O. Box A, W. Palm Beach, FL 33402, U.S.A. 2, 7, 117.

MAGGAL, (Rabbi) Moshe M., b. 16 Mar. 1908. Rabbi; Author; Lecturer; Journalist. Educ: Nat. Rabbinical Sem., Budapest, Hungary, 1933; Rabbinical Ordination, 1934; Univ. of Zurich, Switzerland, 1935; Hebrew Univ., Jerusalem, Israel, 1936. Appts. incl: Rabbi, Temple Beth Kodesh, Canoga Park, Calif., 1959-61, Congregation Ahavath Israel, Hollywood Calif., 1966-; Assoc. Ed., Heritage Newspaper, L.A., Calif., 1958-60; Lectr., Free Enterprise Spkrs. Bir., Coast Fed. Savings & Loan, L.A., Calif., 1971-. Mbrships. incl: Fndr. & Pres., Nat. Jewish Info. Serv., 1960-; Pres., Beverly Hills Zionist Org., 1973-; Exec. Bd. Mbr., Southern Pacific Region, Zionist Org. of Am., 1973-; U.S. Assn. of UN. Publs: Acres of Happiness, 1967; Voice of Judaism newspaper, 1960-. Recip. of hons. Address: 5174 W. 8th St., L.A., CA 90036, U.S.A. 9, 30, 55, 69, 94, 128, 131.

MAGIN, Wolf, b. 21 Sept. 1927. Graphic Designer. Appts. incl: Specialist in Graphic Design, WKS Mannheim; Dir., ibid, 1967-68; Hdmaster, ibid, 1968-69; Rep. Dir., ibid, 1969-71. Mbrships: Berufsverband Bildeuder Kunstler e.v., Baden, Wurttemberg. Exhibs. incl: Posters Exhib., Mannehim, 1959; Rep. Exhib., German Commercial Art After 1945, Berlin, 1962; Posters Exhib., Toulon, France, 1965; Staatliche Museen Preu B. Kulturbesitz der Kunstbibliothek Berlin, 1969; Lib. of Congress, Wash., U.S.A., 1969; Muzeum Narodowe, Warsaw, Poland, 1970; Mahrische Gall., Brno, Czechoslovakia, 1970. Publs: Gebraudisgraphik, 1958, 1966; International Poster Annual, 1957-58, 1958-59, 1960-61, 1961-62, 1963-64, 1966-67, 1969-70; Graphis Annual, 1968, Graphis, 1968; Catalogue 4 Internationale Biennale For Graphik Design, Brno. 1970; Modern Publicity, 1973. Address: Ifflandstrasse 8, 6800 Mannheim 1, German Fed. Repub.

MAGINNIS, Iva Anna Appleyard (Mrs. John J. Maginnis), b. 13 Mar. 1893. Tax Consultant. Educ: A.B., Vassar Coll., Poughskeepsie, N.Y., 1914; Boston Univ., 1918; Pace & Pace Berlitz Schl. of Langs. Appts: Acct., Chief Clerk., Off. Mgr., Mgr. of Tax Dept., Charles H. Tenney & Co., Boston, Mass., 1917-36; Owner, I.A. Appleyard, Tax Cons., ibid, 1936-. Mbrships. incl: New England State Tax Officials Assn.; Assoc. Mbr., Assn. of Mass. Assessors; Mass. Soc. of Mayflower Descendants; Col. Timothy Biglow Chapt., DAR; Gov. William Bradford Compact; Vassar Club of Boston; Coll. Club of Boston; Pres., Worcester Co. Vassar Club, 1943-45; Worcester Art Mus.; Worcester Sci. Mus.; Worcester Fndn. for Experimental Bio.; Int. Wine & Food Soc.; Les Dames d'Escoffier; Chevalier of the Confrerie du Taste-Vin, France; Bald Peak Colony Club (N.H.); Seigniory Club (Canada). 1st Woman Holder of Card for Prac. before Internal Revenue Serv. of U.S. Treasury Dept. Address: 53 Elm St., Worcester, MA 01609, U.S.A. 5, 132, 138.

MAGNER, (Rev. Monsignor) James Aloysius, b. 23 Oct. 1901. Catholic Priest, Educator & Author. Educ: B.A., St. Mary of the Lake Sem., Mundelein, Ill., 1923; M.A. ibid, 1924; S.T.D., Urban Univ., Rome Italy, 1928; Ph.D., Academia S. Thomas Aquinas, ibid, 1929. Appts: Ordained Priest, 1926; Prof., Engl. & Italian, Quigley Prep. Sem., Chgo.,

1929-40; Curate, S. Dominic, S. Gertrude & S. Laurence Chs., ibid, 1929-40; Vice Rector, Bus. & Finance (Procurator), Cath. Univ. of Am., Wash. D.C., 1940-68; Dir., CUA Press, ibid, 1940-68; Assoc. Ed.-in-Chief, The New Cath. Ency., 1962-68. Mbrships. incl: Fndr., Charles Carroll Forum; Exec. Sec., ibid, Chgo., 1939-64, Wash., 1941-66; Cath. Anthropoligical Conf.; Treas., ibid, 1962-68; Cath. Commn. for Intellectual & Cultural Affairs; Exec. Comm., ibid, 1951-54. Publs. incl: This Catholic Religion, 1930; The Latin American Pattern, 1943; The Art of Happy Marriage, 1947; Mental Health in a Mad World, 1953; The Catholic Priest in the Modern World, 1957. Ed., Cath. Univ. of Am Bulletin, 1940-56. Hons: Cmdr., Order of Isabel la Catolica, Spain, 1952; Domestic Prelate, Pope Pius XII, 1957. Address: P.O. Box 2853, Palm Beach, FL 33480, U.S.A. 2, 7, 15, 49.

MAGNO, Pompeo, b. 30 Nov. 1908. Jurist; Barrister; Professor of Law. Educ: Univ. of Rome, Italy. Appts: Prin., law prac., Rome; Italian Rep., space problems, UNO; Prof., of Aeronautical & Space Law; Pres., Istituto Italiano Diritto Spaziale, Section Italienne du Conseil International Droit Spathial; Pres., Associazione Romana Proprietà Edilizia, V.P., Confedilizia; Dir., Int. Inst. of Space Law. Mbrships: Istituto Internazionale Studi Giuridici; Int. Commn. of Jurists; Società Italiana Organizzazioni Internazionali. Author, var publs., legal aspects, aeronautical & space problems. Address: 251 Via Giulia, Rome, Italy.

MAGNUS, Francis Michael, b. 19 Aug 1943. Life Assurance Underwriter. Educ: Grad., St. George's Coll., 1961. Appts: Med. Sales Rep., 1961-64; Med. Sales Supvsr., 1964-67; Underwriter, Dominion Life Assurance Co., 1967. Mbrships: Dir., Jamaica Family Planning Assn; Coun. Mbr., Western Hemisphere of Int. Planned Parenthood Fedn; Vice-Chmn., Jamaica Motoring Club; Life Underwriter Assn. of Jamaica; Past Dir., Kingston Jaycees. Address: P.O. Box 223, Kingston, Jamaica, W. Indies.

MAGNUSSON, David N., b. 5 Sept. 1925. Professor of Psychology. Educ: B.A., Univ. of Stockholm, 1955; Ph.D., ibid, 1957. Appts: Elementary Schl. Tchr., 1946-52, 1953-54; Schl. Psychologist, 1954-55; Rsch. Asst., Psychol. Labs., Univ. of Stockholm, 1955-58, Univ. Lectr., 1959-65, Assoc. Prof. & Hd. of Unit of Applied Psychol., 1964-69, Prof. & Hd. of Psychological Labs., 1969-. Mbrships. incl: Swedish Psychological Assn.; Sec., ibid, 1957-58, V.P., 1959-60, Pres., 1961-62; Bd. Mbr., Swedish Assn. Univ. Profs., 1969-, Pres., 1970-; AAAS. Publs: A Study of Ratings Based on TAT, 1959; Maladjustment & Structure of Intelligence, 1963; Test Theory, 3rd edit., 1969; Psychology, 5th edit. Kt., Order of N. Star. Address: Psychological Laboratories, University of Stockholm, Box 6706, S-113 85 Stockholm, Sweden. 43, 134.

MAGREZ, Michel A.G., b. 4 June 1925. Professor of Law; Social Security Administrator. Educ: Dr. of Laws, Licenciate of Notarial Sci., Grad. of Soc. Law, Univ. of Liege, 1948-49. Appts: Legal Advsr., Federation generale du travail, Belgium, 1949-54; Dir., Caisse nationale de compensation pour allocations familiales, 1954-60; Dpty. Gen. Adminstr., Nat. Off. Family Allowances of Wage Earners, 1960-; Lectr., Fac. of Law, Free Univ. of Brussels, 1960-65, Prof., 1965-; Dir., Labour Inst., Free Univ. of Brussels, 1960-; Gen. Reporter., Permanent Comm. Legal Aspects of Soc.

Security, Int. Soc. Security Assn., Geneva, Switzerland. Mbr., var. profl. orgs. Author, books & articles, legal aspects soc. security. Hon. Off. of Order of Leopold II. Address: Clos des Essarts, 2 - 1150 - Brussels, Belgium, 43, 87.

MAHABIR, Bisram Sooknanan, b. 21 Jan. 1937. Medical Practitioner; Venereologist. Educ: M.B., B.S., Grant Med. Coll., Bombay, India, 1963; D.V.D., Bombay Univ., 1965; D.D.V. (C.P.S.), Appts: Med. Off., J.J. Grp. Hosps., & G.T. Hosp., Bombay; Med. Off., Sangre Dist. Hosp., Trinidad, W.I.; Pt.-time Med. off., Dermatol. Clin., Gen. Hosps., Port of Spain & San Fernando, 1967-; Specialist Med. Off., Venereol., V.D. Div., Minn. of Hlth., Trinidad & Tobago, 1968-. Mbrships: Trinidad & Tobago Med. Assn., Bd., & Coun.; Fellow, Dermatological Soc. of London; Life Mbr., Am. Med. Soc. of Vienna. Author, booklet, V.D. educ. Contbr., med. jrnls. & newspapers. TV & radio progs. on V.D. Recip., Fellowships for study of V.D., U.S.A., 1970, 1974. Address: V.D. Division, Caribbean Medical Centre, Wrightson Rd., Port of Spain, Trinidad, W. Indies.

MAHABIR, Dennis Jules, b. 14 Apr. 1920. Journalist; Author. Appts: Ed. & Publr., Observer, Trinidad, 1941-46; Ed. & Publr., Spectator, Trinidad, 1947-65; Ed. & Publr., Enterprise, Trinidad, 1965-; Pol. Analyst, Radio Trinidad, 1948-73; Chmn., Panel Discussions, Trinidad TV 1962-66; Cons., Ind. Dev. Corp., 1965-66; Lectr., Ctr. for Multiracial Studies, Barbados; Org., Trinidad participation in Canadian Exposition, 1967. Mbrships. Councillor, Port of Spain, Trinidad, 1956-68; Mayor, 1957-60; Pres., Port of Spain Rotary Club, 1963; Pres., Trinidad YMCA, 1958-68; Pres., Trinidad Press Club, 1964-69; Pres., Trinidad Art Soc., 1958-61. Publs: Selected Essays, 1958; The Cutlass is Not for Killing, 1970. Address: Dhein's Bay House, Carenage, Trinidad, W. Indies.

MAHABIR, Diana Mary, b. 14 Feb. 1941. Company Executive. Appts: Pt.-time Lectr., Univ. of the W.I., St. Augustine Campus, Trinidad, 1964-69; Trng. & Admnstrve. Off., Employers' Consultative Assn. of Trinidad & Tobago, 1966-69; Dir., ibid, 1969-; Chief Exec. Off., Caribbean Employers' Confed., 1969-; Bd. Dirs., Nat. ins. Scheme, Mbr., Registration, Recognition & Certification Bd., Sec., Nat. Steering Comm. for Mgmt. Dev., Mbr., Bus. Advsry. Comm. to Mgmt. Studies Prog., Univ. of the W.I., St. Augustine, Mbr., Trinidad & Tobago Tripartite Comm. on Population & Family Planning & Mbr., Int. Labour Org. Panel of Cons. on the Problems of Women Workers, 1969-. Mbrships. incl: V.P., Dev. Fndn. of Trinidad & Tobago; Asst. Dir., SERVOL (pvte. community dev. prog.); Pres., U.N. Assn. of Trinidad & Tobago, Port of Spain chapt. Address: The Employers' Consultative Assn., Old Fort Bldg., S. Quay, Port of Spain, Trinidad, W. Indies.

MAHABIR, Winston Jules, b. 17 Sept. 1921. Psychiatrist. Educ: McGill Univ., Montreal, Canada, 1941-44; Med., ibid, 1944-48; Psych., Edinburgh, U.K. & Vancouver, Canada. Appts: Lectr., Sociol., McGill Univ., 1943-44; Min. of Hlth., Govt. of Trinidad & Tobago, 1956-61; Asst. Prof., Psych., Univ. of B.C., Canada, 1967-; Dir., Crease Clin. of Psychol. Med., 1970-. Mbrships: V.P., Trinidad & Tobago Med. Assn., 1955-56; Alpha Omega Alpha Hon. Med. Soc.; Pres., Riverview Hosp. Med. Staff Org., 1971-73; Queen's Pk. Cricket Club, Trinidad; Vancouver Lawn Tennis Club, B.C., Canada. Publs: History of the Psychedelic Drug Experience, 1966;

Politics in a Multi-Racial Society, 1965; Speech to Commonwealth Parliamentary Association, New Delhi, India, 1957. Hons: Trinidad Govt. Open Schlrship., Univ. Study Abroad, 1940; num. schlrships., McGill Univ., Canada, 1941-48; Won all debating awards, McGill Univ., 1941-48; Music Festival Winner, Tenor Class, Trinidad, 1952. Address: 5950 N.W. Marine Dr., Vancouver 8, B.C., Canada. 136.

MAHAFFIE, Isabel Cooper (Mrs. Charles Delahunt Mahaffie), b. 22 Aug. 1892 . Artist. Educ: Bryn Mawr Coll., 1909-10 Tchrs. Coll. & Barnard Coll., Columbia Univ., 1910-12; Art Students' League, 1912-15; pvte. studies & summer sketch classes w. Alon Bement, 1913-17. Appts: Staff Artist, Dept. Tropical Rsch., N.Y. Zool. Soc., 1917-25, making 5 expeditions to Rsch. Stn., British Guiana, 2 to Galapagos Islands & 1 to Asphalt Lake, Venezuala; Intermittantly working at Am. Mus. of Nat. Hist., 1923-27; executed 15 color plates (sci. subjects) for Encyclopaedia Britannica, 1927-31. Mbrships: Hon. Life, N.Y. Zool. Soc., 1922-; Comopolitan Club, N.Y.C.; Sec., Wash. Watercolor Soc.; Miniature Painters, Sculptors & Gravers Soc. of Wash., 1969-70; Arts Club of Wash.; Friday Morning Music Club. Contbr. articles to Atlantic Monthly. Exhibs. of Animal Paintings of British Guiana, Wembley Empire Exposition, U.K., 1924, & Corcoran Gall. of Art, Wash., 1927. Hons. incl: Muir S. Jamison Award for Best Landscape, Min. Soc. of Wash., 1961; num. other prizes & hon. mentions. Address: 6104 Highboro Drive, Bethesda, MD 20034, U.S.A.

MAHALINGAM, Vaithilingam, b. 8 July 1931. Librarian. Educ: B.A., Calcutta, India, 1956; B.L.S., McGill Univ., Montreal, Canada, 1958; Doctoral Candidate, Schl. of Lib. Serv., Columbia Univ., N.Y. Appts: Libn., Ceylon Inst. of Sci. & Indl. Rsch., 1958-65; Fulbright Schlr., Schl. of Lib. Serv., Columbia Univ., 1965-68; Asst. Hd., Cataloguing Div., Queen's Univ., Kingston, Ont., Canada, 1968-. Mbrships Sec., Ceylon Lib. Assn., 1960-61; Educ. Off., ibid, 1961-62 & 1963-64; Exec. Comm., 1960-64; Pres., Profl. Libns. Assn. of Queens, Queens Univ., Kingston, Ont., 1973-74; L.A.R.C. Author of articles in jrnls. Hons: Canadian Colombo Plan Schlrship., McGill Univ., Montreal, 1957-58; Fulbright Schlrship., Columbia Univ., 1965-68. Address: Cataloguing Div., Douglas Lib., Queen's Univ., Kingston, Ont., Canada.

MAHAN, Gertrude E., b. 5 Aug. 1888. Teacher; Librarian; Journalist. Educ: Damrosch Music Art Schl., N.Y.C., 1906-07; B.A., Kan. State Tchrs. Coll., Emporia, 1948; M.S., Lib. Sci., ibid, 1950. Appts: Pvte. Tutor, Port Lavaca, Tex.; Tchr., Rural Schls., Seward Co.; Libn., Liberal H.S.,- Kan., 1943-54; Admin. Libn., Mem. Lib., Liberal, 1955-72; Book Ed., S.S. Daily Times, Liberal, 1973-. Mbrships. incl: State Pres., Schl. Libns.; Pres., Pub. Lib. Sect., Kan. Lib. Assn.; ALA; Pres., Liberal Educ. Assn.; Pres., Bus. & Profl. Women; Liberal Women's Club; Delta Kappa Gamma; Bd., Am. Red Cross; AAUW. Contbr. to: Nat. Lib. Bulletin; Kan. State Reading Cir.; High Book Lists. Hons: Woman of the Yr., Soroptimists; Meritorious Serv. Award, Chmbr. of Comm., 1968; Plaque of Appreciation, Liberal Mem. Lib., 1973. Address: 613 S. Lincoln, Liberal, KS 67901, U.S.A.

MAHESH, Virendra B., b. 25 Apr. 1932. Research Scientist; Educator. Educ: B.Sc., Patna Univ., India, 1951; M.Sc., Delhi Univ., 1953; Ph.D., ibid, 1955; D.Phil., Oxford Univ., 1958. Appts: James Hudson Brown Mem. Fellow, Yale Univ., 1958-59; Asst. Rsch. Prof.

of Endocrinol., Med. Coll. of Ga., 1959-63; Prof. of Endocrinol., 1966-70; Regents Prof., 1970-; Dir., Ctr. for Population Studies, Med. Coll. of Ga., 1971-; Chmn., Dept. of Endocrinol., 1972-. Mbrships: Ed. Bd., Steroids, 1963-; Chem. & Biochem. Socs., UK; Soc. for Expmtl. Biol. & Med.; Endocrine Soc.; Soc. of Biol. Chems.; Soc. of Gynecol. Investigation; N.Y. Acad. of Scis.; Int. Soc. for the Study of Reproductive Physiol.; Sigma Xi; AAUP; Soc. for the Study of Reproduction; Int. Soc. for Neuro-endocrinol.; Int. Assn. for Clin. Rsch. in Human Reproduction; Int. Assn. for Lab. Animal Sci. Contbr. chapts. to sev. books & over 250 papers & articles to sci. jrnls. Hons. incl: Rubin Award, Am. Soc. for the Study of Sterility, 1963; Billings Silver Medal for work on Gonadal Dysgenesis, 1965. Address: Med. Coll. of Ga., Dept. of Endocrinol., Augusta, GA 30902, U.S.A. 14, 28, 50, 125.

MAHFOOD, Richard Albert, b. 28 June 1931. Barrister-at-Law, Queen's Counsel. Educ: LL.B. Univ. Coll. of London, 1954; Middle Temple, 1951-54. Appts: Called to Bar, 1954; Called to Inner Bar, 1965. Chmn., Jamaica Law Jrnl. & Jamaica Unit Trust; Dpty. Chmn., Jamaica Telephone Co. & W.Indies Sugar Co; Dir., Pan Jamaica Investment Trust Ltd. Mbrships; Fndr. Mbr. & Past Pres., Jamaica Jr. Chamber, 1960-61; Jamaica Independence Celebrations Comm., 1962. Hons: 1st in Bar Final Examinations, Trinity Term, 1954; Independence Celebrations Comm. Medal. Address: 32½ Duke St., Kingston, Jamaica. 96, 109.

MAHLANGU, Alex, b. 16 June 1929. Journalist. Educ: A level pvtly. w. London Univ.; U.K. Dip. in Jrnlsm. Appts: Asst. Ed., Bantu Mirror, 1951-53; Ed., ibid, 1953-60; Special Corres., African Parade Mag. & Daily News (publd. in Salisbury, Rhodesia); Ed., Mufulira Mirror, Zambia, 1961-73; Dist. Ed., Mining Mirror, Zambia, 1973-. Mbrships: Comm., Gamma Sigma Club; Guild of Rhodesian Jrnlsts.; Brit. Assn. of Ind. Eds.; Sec., Matebeleland & Bulawayo African Football Assn.; Comm., Mufulira Adult Educl. & Cultural Club; Comm., Mufulira Dist. Publicity Assn. Recip. Award for contribution to advancement of jrnlsm., 1971-72. Address: KMEC, P.O. Box 308, Kafue, Zambia. 34, 135.

MAHMOUD, Shah, b. 23 Dec. 1939. Professor of Business Administration. Degrees: B.B.A.; M.B.A.; Ph.D. Appts: Grad. Asst., Columbia Univ., N.Y.C., U.S.A., 1964-66; Rutgers, The State Univ. New Br., N.J., 1966-68; N.M. State Univ., Las Cruces, 1966-71; Prof., Bus. Admin., Appalachian State Univ., Boone, N.C., 1971-. Mbrships: Am. Mgmt. Assn.; Financial Mgmt. Assn.; Am. Marketing Assn. Publs: Articles in profl. jrnls. Hons: Award, Bur. of Econ. Rsch.; Schlrship. Toledo Univ., Ohio; Schlrship., Afghanistan Govt. Address: Appalachian State University, Boone, NC 28607, U.S.A. 2.

MAHOLICK, Leonard T., b. 18 Apr. 1921. Psychotherapist; Physician. Educ: Franklin & Marshall Coll., Lancaster, Pa., 1934-41; B.S., Univ. of M.D., College Park, 1944; M.D., Schl. of Med., ibid, Baltimore, 1946; Univ. of Vienna Austria, 1960; Jung Inst., Zurich, Switzerland, 1965; workshops & seminars. Appts: incl: Intern, Emory Univ. Fellow, Psych., Austen Riggs Ctr., Stockbridge Mass., 1950; Dir., Mental Hlth. Clin., Savannah, Ga., 1950-52; Pvte. Prac., Psychotherapy, Columbus, 1952-73 & Atlanta, Ga., 1973-; Dir., Bradley Ctr. Inc., ibid, 1952-73; Cons. Dir., Wiregrass M.H. Clit., Dothan, Ala., 1964-73; Cons., M.H. Clin.

La Grange, Ga., 1966-70, Columbus Pub. Mntal Hlth., 1970-73, Nat. Inst. Mental Hlth., Wash. D.C., & Atlanta, Ga., 1964-68, Voc., Rehab. & Soc. Security Admin., 1963- & num. other bds. & Agcies. Mbrships. incl: AMA; Fellow Am. Psyc. Assn. & Am. Assn. for Grp. Psychotherapy; Am. Pub. Hlth. Assn. & Royal Soc. of Hlth. Publs: Opening Doors for Troubled People (co-author), 1963; The Mental Health Counselor in the Community (jt. author), 1968; The Purpose in Life Test (co-author); The Conflicted Man, 1974; num. articles in profl. jrnls. Address: 2905 Peachtree Rd. N.E., Atlanta, GA 30305, U.S.A.

MAIER, Norman R.F., b. 27 Nov. 1900. Professor of Psychology; Industrial Consultant. Educ: A.B., M.A., Univ. of Mich.; grad. work, Univ. of Berlin, 1926-27; Ph.D., Univ. of Mich., 1928. Appts. incl: Nat. Rsch. Coun. Fellow, Univ. of Chgo., 1929-31; Instr.-Prof., Univ. of Mich., 1931-71; Cons., European Productivity Agcy., Europe, 1959-60; Retired, 1971. Mbrships. incl: Am. Psychol. Assn.; AAAS; Psychonomic Soc.; Sigma Xi. Publs. incl: Principles of Human Relations, 1952; The Appraisal Interview, 1958; Creative Management (w. J.J. Hayes), 1962; Psychology in Industrial Organizations, 1973. Active contbr. to scientific jrnls. Hons: Newcomb-Cleveland Prize, AAAS, 1938; Henry Russel Award, Univ. of Mich., 1939. Address: 1111 Fair Oaks, Ann Arbor, MI 48104, U.S.A. 2, 8, 10, 50, 51, 128.

MAINGOT, Rodney. Consulting Surgeon; Writer. Educ: St. Bartholomew's Coll. & Hosp., London, U.K. Appts. incl: Capt., Royal Army Med. Corps, WWI; House Surg., St. Bartholomew's Hosp.; Sr. Surg., Royal Waterloo Hosp., London; Sr. Surg., Victoria Hosp., Southend-on-Sea; Sr. Surg., Southend Gen. Hosp.; Cons. Surg., Royal Free Hosp., London; Vis. Cons. Surg. & Guest Prof., 6 countries; Ed. in Chief, British Jrnl. of Clin. Prac., 1958-. Mbrships: Fellow & former Coun. Mbr., Royal Soc. of Med., Past Pres., Sect. of Surg.; Sr. Fellow, Assn. of Surgs. of Gt. Britain & Ireland; Brighton & Hove Medico-Chirugical Soc. Publs. incl: Postgraduate Surgery, 6 vols., 1936-39; The Technique of Gastric Operations, 1940; Abdominal Operations, 1940, 6th ed., 2 vols., 1974; Techniques in British Surgery, 1950; The Relationship of Art & Medicine, 1974; Contbns. to sev. books. Hons. incl: Mentioned in Despatches, 1918; Sydney Body Gold Medalist for Advs. in Surg., 1958. Address: 25 Wimpole St., London W1M 7AD, U.K. 1, 3, 128.

MAIR, George Brown, b. 27 May 1914. Surgeon; Author; Travel Journalist; Lecturer; Explorer. Educ: Glasgow Univ.; Edinburgh Royal Coll. Surgs. Appts. incl: Asst. Prof. Surg., Univ. of Durham, 1945-46; Res. Surg., Law Hosp., Scotland, 1947-53; Dir., Med. Clin., Grangemouth, 1953-68. Mbrships: Guild of Travel Writers; Crime Writers' Assn.; Mystery Writers of Am.; Int. PEN; Fellow, Royal Scottish Geographical Soc.; Soc. of Authors. Publs. incl: The Day Khruschev Panicked; Destination Moscow; Confessions of a Surgeon; Arranging & Enjoying your Package Holiday; David Grant spy series; Surgery of Abdominal Hernia. Address: Kinneil House, Polmont, FK2 0XZ, U.K. 3, 30, 43, 139.

MAIR, William Austyn, b. 24 Feb. 1917. University Professor. Educ: Clare Coll., Cambridge, U.K. Appts: Dir., Fluid Motion Lab., Univ. of Manchester, 1946-52; Prof., Aeronaut. Engrng., Univ. of Cambridge, 1952-; Hd., Engrng. Dept., ibid, 1973; Fellow, Downing

Coll., 1953-. Fellow, Royal Aeronaut. Soc. Author of papers on aerodynamics in sci. jrnls. Recip., C.B.E., 1969. Address: 74 Barton Rd., Cambridge, CB3 9LH, U.K. 1.

MAISCH, Erich (Karl Friedrich), b. 14 Dec. 1910. Federal Residing Judge. Educ: Univ. of Berlin; 1st Juridical exam.; 2nd Juridical exam.; J.D. Appts. incl: Asst. Judge, 1942; Judge, Provincial Ct., 1944; Mil. serv. & war captivity, 1942-48; Councillor of Govt., Min. of Econs., Freiburg, Baden, German Fed. Repub., 1 9 5 0 - 5 1 ; Chmn. of Chmbr., Oberversicherungsamt & Ct. for War victims, Freiburg, 1951-53; Prin., Oberversicherungsamt & Ct.-Soc., Konstanz, 1953-54; Chmn. of Senate, Ct. of Appeal for Soc. Affairs, Stuttgart, 1954-56; Dir., Ct. for Soc. Affairs, Karlsruhe, 1956-57; Pres. of Senate, Ct. of Appeal for Soc. Affairs, Stuttgart, 1957-61; Fed. Judge, Supreme Ct. of Judicature for Soc. Affairs, Kassel, 1961-71; Pres. of Senate, ibid, 1971-; Chmn., Coun. of the Justices, ibid. Publs. incl: Inaugural Dissertation & sev. publs. on legal accident insurance. Address: Oberbinge 13, D-35 Kassel-Kirchditmold, German Fed. Repub. 43, 92.

MAITLAND, Barbara Anne, b. 19 Oct. 1940. Educator. Educ: A.B., B.S. in Educ., Mo. Valley Coll., 1962; NDEA Inst., Loyola Univ., 1963; M.A., Univ. of Mo., 1966; NDEA Inst., Rennes, France, 1968. Appts: Tchr., Ctrl. Community H.S., De Witt, Iowa, 1962-64; Asst. Instr., Univ. of Mo., 1965-66; Instr., Wartburg Coll., 1966-67; Chmn., Dept. Foreign Langs., Thomas Jefferson H.S., Iowa, 1967-. Mbrships: Delta Zeta; Alpha Psi Omega, 1960; Kappa Delta Pi, 1961; Pi Lambda Theta, 1966; Sigma Tau Delta, 1961; Am. Coun. on Tchg. of Foreign Langs. (charter); Am. Assn. Tchrs. of French (Exec. Coun., Iowa Chapt.); NEA, Nat. Deleg., 1972; Iowa State Foreign Lang. Articulation Comm.; Cedar Rapids Foreign Lang. Tchrs. (Pres. 1972). Address: 1631 Park Towne Ct., N.E., Cedar Rapids, IA 52402, U.S.A. 46, 57, 120, 138.

MAJEKODUNMI, Moses Adekoyejo, b. 17 Aug. 1916. Medical Practitioner. Educ: Trinity Coll., Dublin; M.A., M.D., 1941; M.A.O., 1949; F.R.C.P.I., 1955. Appts: House Physn., Nat. Children's Hosp., Dublin, 1941-43; Sr. Specialist i/c Govt. Maternity Hosp., Lagos, Nigeria, 1949-50; Sr. Specialist Obstrn., Nigerian Fed. Govt. Med. Servs., 1949-60; Senator, & Ldr. of Senate, Nigeria, 1960-66; Fed. Min. of Hlth., 1961-66; Admnstr. for Western Nigeria, 1962; Med. Dir. & Chmn., Bd. of Govs., St. Nicholas Hosp., Lagos, 1967-. Mbrships: Pres., Soc. of Obs. & Gyn. of Nigeria; Fellow, Royal Soc. of Med., London; Fellow, Royal Soc. of Tropical Med. & Hygiene; Pres., Trinity Coll. Dublin Assn. of Nigeria; Nigeria Med. Assn. Num. publs. incl: Premature Infants: Management & Prognosis, 1943; Effects of Malnutrition in Pregnancy & Lactation, 1957; Behold the Key (play), 1944. Hons: C.M.G., 1963; LL.D., Trinity Coll. Dublin, 1964; D.Sc., Lagos, 1974; F.M.C.O.G.; D.C.H.; L.M. (Rotunda). Address: St. Nicholas Hosp., 57 Campbell St., P.O. Box 3015, Lagos, Nigeria. 34.

MAJEWSKI, Andrzej, b. 15 June 1936. Painter; Stage Designer. Educ: Acad. of Fine Arts, Krakow, Poland, 1953-59; Schlrship. for study Italy & France, 1961-62. Appts: Ldng. Stage Designer, Slowacki Theatre, Krakow, 1960-62, Great Theatre, Warsaw, & Warsaw Opera, 1965-. Mbrships: Polish Union of Plastic Artists. Paintings: Allegorical landscapes, portraits; Stage design for num. operas, ballets, plays, inclng: L'Enfant Prodigue, Le Sacre du Printemps, 1962; Stravinsky's Orphée, 1963, Verdi's Otello, 1969, Strauss' Electra, 1971, Gt. Theatre of Warsaw. Samson & Delilah, Cologne Opera, 1968; Salome, Covent Garden, London, 1970; Jeu de Massacre, Burg Theatre, Vienna, 1971; La Passione, Teatro Piccolo, Milan, 1972; Strauss' Electra, Hamburg, 1973; One man exhibs: Wright-Hepburn-Webster Gall., London, 1969, '70. Hons: Polish Min. of Culture & Art Prize 3rd Class, 1962; Gold Medal for Orphée, Stravinsky Biennial, Novy Sad, 1966; Gold Medal, ibid, Stravinsky Quadrennial, Prague, 1967; State Prize 1st Class, 1967. Address: ul Potacka 60 m 5, Warsaw, Poland.

MAJOR, Jane Rebecca Hatcher (Mrs. William L. Major), b. 19 Sept. 1919. Private Piano Teacher. Educ: Organ Dip., Averett Jr. Coll., 1938; B.S., Mary Wash. Coll., 1940; grad. work., Univs. of Richmond & Va., Richmond Profl. Inst., Va. Commonwealth Univ., Madison Coll., Cath. Univ. of Am. Appts: Tchr., Caroline H.S., 1940-41, 1944-45, Henrico Co. Pub. Schls., 1949-50; Music Dir., Westover Hills Meth. Ch., 1950-53, Fairmount Meth. Ch., 1953-56; Asst. Organist, Grace & Holy Trinity Episcopal Ch., 1956-67; Piano Tchr., Collegiate Schl., 1968-. Mbrships: incl: Bd. Dirs., Mary Wash. Coll. Alumni Assn.; Pres., Richmond Chapt. ibid, 1957-59, Nat. V.P., 1957-59; Bd. Mbr., Richmond Musicians' Club, 1973-; 1st Pres., Richmond Music Tchrs. Assn., 1973-; Nat. Music Tchrs. Assn. Recip., Davenport Key Award, Averett Coll. Address: 9000 River Rd., Richmond, VA 23229, U.S.A. 138.

MAKAR, Boshra Halim, b. 23 Sept. 1928. Professor of Mathematics. Educ: B.Sc., Cairo Univ., 1947; M.Sc., 1952; Ph.D., 1955. Appts: On Fac., Cairo Univ., U.A.R., 1947-60; Assoc. Prof., 1960-65; Vis. Assoc. Prof., Am. Univ. of Beirut, Lebanon, 1966; Assoc. Prof., Mich. Technol. Univ., U.S.A., 1966-67; Prof., St. Peter's Coll., 1967-. Mbrships: Am. Math. Soc.; N.Y. Acad. of Sci.; AAAS; AAUP; N.J. Acad. of Sci.; Life Mbr., Poetry Soc. of London. Author of about 20 publs. on theory of functions of a complex variable, algebra & functional anal. Hons: Sir Myles Lampson's Prize, 1942; Ahmad Maher Pasha's Mem. Prize for best univ. grad., Sohag, 1947. Address: St. Peter's Coll. Math. Dept., Jersey City, NJ 07306, U.S.A. 6, 8, 14, 57, 129, 131.

MAKAR, John, b. 22 Jan. 1912. Attorney; Publisher. Educ: B.S., Northwestern State Univ. of La., 1938; LL.B., J.D., La. State Univ., 1941. Appts: State Supvsr., Mich., FWA, Div. of Rsch. & Stats., 1941-42; Dir. of For. Claims Serv., Germany & Denmark, 1944-46; Gen. Counsel, Comptroller, State of La., 1952-58; Atty. at Law, 1941-; Publr., newspapers in New Orleans, La., area; Bd. Mbr. & Off., Jefferson Democrat, Inc. (Pres.), Guide Newspaper Corp. (Sec.), Sr. Citizen Ctr., Soushatta, La. (Sec.), Makar Publs. (Owner), & Courtland Communications, Cleveland, Ohio. Mbrships: Am., La. & Dist. Bar Assns.; Nat. Pres., Assoc. Ct. & Commercial Newspapers, 1966-67; La. Press Assn., 1962-; Lt. Gov. of Dist., Pres. Natchitoches Club, Kiwanis Int.; Soc. of Am. Magicians; Int. Brotherhood of Magicians; Shrine; Am. Legion; Veterans of For. Wars; Disabled Am. Veterans. Compiler of La. Law on Off. of State Comptroller. Hons: over 27 awards for public speaking; Nathan Burkan Mem. Award in Copyright Law. Address: P.O. Box 775, Natchitoches, LA 71457, U.S.A. 46, 125.

MÄKINEN, Viljo Salmari, b. 9 July 1920. Sculptor. Educ: Turku Soc. of Art Drawing Schl.; studies, Italy & France, 1960, '64 & '68,

Greece, 1973. Appt. as ceramic artist & sculptor, 1939-64; Free-lance, 1964-. Mbrships: Turku Soc. of Artists, 1945-59; Finnish Union of Sculptors; Acad. Int. de la Ceramique, Geneva, Switzerland. Works in following Museum collects.: Ariana, Geneva; Ateneum, Helsinki; Taide museo, Turku; Hämeenlinna; Gualdo Tadino, Umbria, Italy; Pittsburgh, U.S.A. Recip., Finnish & foreign prizes. Address: Parrantie 16 E., 20300 Turku 30, Finland.

MAKOTOKO, Seth Peete, b. 6 Aug. 1925. Medical Practitioner; Politician. Educ: M.B., Ch.B., Witwatersrand Univ., 1948-53. Appts: Med. Supt., var. hosps., Lesotho, 1955-63; Prison Med. Off., Med. Supt., Nat. Leper Hosp., 1956; Sec. Gen., Marematlou Freedom Party, 1963, Pres., 1964; Unofficial Lesotho Rep. at inaugural OAU Conf., 1963; 1st Pres., Senate House of Parliament, 1965; Lesotho Opposition Defeg., UN Decolonisation Comm. Session, 1966; currently, Pvte. Med. Prac., Leribe, Lesotho. Address: P.O. Box 73, Leribe, Lesotho, Republic of S. Africa.

MALAGODI, Giovanni, b. 12 Oct. 1904. Former Bank Official; Politician; Farmer. Educ: Dr. juris, Univ. of Rome. Appts: Staff Off., Banca Commerciale Italiana, 1928-33, Jt. Central Mgr., 1933-37, Central Mgr., 1947-62; Gen. Mgr., Banque Francaise et Italienne pour l'Amerique du Sud, 1937-47; Min. Plenipotentiary, Econ. & Financial Cons., Min. of For. Affairs, Rome & Italian deleg. to OEEC, NATO, ILO, 1944-53; Liberal Party Dpty. for Milan, Italian Parliament, 1953-; Gen. Sec., Italian Liberal Party, 1954-72, Pres., 1972-; V.P., Liberal Int., London, 1954-58, 1966-; Pres., 1958-66; Cabinet Min. of Treasury, Italian Govt., 1972-73. Mbrships: Società del Giardino, Milan; Nuovo Circolo degli Scacchi, Rome. Publs: Le ideologie politiche, 1928; Rapporto sull'emigrazione, 1953; Massa non Massa, 1962; Liberalismo in cammino, 1965. Address: Via Frattina 89, Rome, Italy.

MALECH, Robert G., b. 17 July 1932. Engineer. Educ: B.E.E., CCNY, 1954; M.E.E., Polytechnic Inst. of Brooklyn, 1958. Appts: Airborne Instruments Lab., Melville, N.Y., 1954-59; Sr. Proj. mbr., Missile Electronics Div., Radio Corp. of Am., Burlington, Mass., 1959-61; Chief Engr., Dorne & Margolin, Inc., Bohemia, N.Y., 1961-65; Pres., Malech Electronics, Inc., N.Y.C., 1965-70; Pres., Dorne & Margolin, Inc., 1971-; Pres., Dynaport Electronics, Inc., 1970-. Mbrships. incl: Chmn., L.I. Chapt., G-AP, 1964-65; Sec., Nat. G-AP Symposium, 1964; Sr. mbr., IEE; Profl. Engrs., Mass.; Charter mbr. & Past Bd. mbr., Assn. of Old Crows. Holder of U.S. Patents. Author of papers in field. Address: Dorne & Margolin, Inc., 2950 Veterans Mem. Hwy., Bohemia, NY 11716, U.S.A. 6, 16.

MALIK, Charles Habib, b. 11 Feb. 1906. Professor. Educ: B.A., Am. Univ. of Beirut, 1927; M.A., Harvard Univ., U.S.A., 1934; Ph.D., ibid, 1937. Appts: incl: Tchr., Prof., Admnstr., Am. Univ. of Beirut, 1927-; Vis. Prof., Dartmouth Coll., N.H., U.S.A., 1960, Harvard Univ. Summer Schl., 1960; Prof., Am. Univ., Wash. D.C., 1961-62; Min., Ambassador of Lebanon, Wash. D.C., 1945-55; Min. of For. Affairs, Lebanon, 1956-58; Min. of Educ. & Fine Arts, 1956-57; M.P., 1957-60; Signatory for Lebanon, Charter of UN, 1945; Mbr., Chmn., var. Lebanese delegns., UN; Pres., UN Gen. Assembly, 1958-59; Pres., UN Econ. & Soc. Coun., 1948; Pres., UN Security Coun., 3 mos., 1953, 1954; Chmn., UN Commn. on Human Rights, 1951, 1952. Mbrships. incl: Bd. of Dirs., Woodrow Wilson Fndn., 1961-63;

Advsry. Comm., Int. League for the Rights of Man; Int. Comm., Inst. of Man & Sci.; Grand 1st Magistrate, Holy Orthodox Ch.; Fndg. Mbr., Lebanese Acad.; Pres., Bd. of Trustees, Orthodox Schl. of the Annunciation of Beirut; V.P., United Bible Socs., 1967-72; Commnr., Commn. of Chs. on Int. Affairs, World Coun of Ch.; Pres., World Coun. of Christian Educ., 1967-71. Publs: Problem of Coexistence, 1955; Christ & Crisis, 1962; Man in the Struggle for Peace, 1963; Ed. w. intro., God & Man in Contemporary Christian Thought, 1970; Ed. w. intro., God & Man in Contemporary Islamic Thought, 1972; sev. books & pamphlets in Arabic; Contbr. of num. articles on Philosophical, theol., religious, pol., UN, & int. matters, Am., European & Near Eastern jrnls. & mags. Hons. incl: Decorated by 12 govts.; Recip., num. hon, degrees & num. Fellowships; Gold Medal, Nat. Inst. of Soc. Scis., N.Y. Address: Am. Univ. of Beirut, Beirut, Lebanon. 57, 139.

MALIK, Gunwantsingh Jaswantsingh, b. 29 May 1921. Diplomat. Educ: B.Sc., Gujarat Coll., Ahmedabad, India; M.A., Univ. of Cambridge, U.K. Appts: Second Sec., Indian For. Serv., Brussels, Belgium, 1948-50, & Addis Ababa, Ethiopia, 1950; Under-Sec., Min. of External Affairs, 1950-52; First Sec. & Charge d'Affaires, Buenos Aires, Argentina, 1952-56; First Sec., Tokyo, Japan, 1956-59; Asst. Commnr. & Counsellor, Singapore, 1959-63; Dir., Min. of For. Trade, 1963-64; Jt. Sec., Min. of External Affairs, 1964-65; Ambassador, Manila, Philippines, 1965-68; Ambassador, Dakar, Senegal, 1968-70; Ambassador, Santiago, Chile, 1970-; Accredited in Ecuador & Colombia, 1970-72, & Peru, 1970-73. Mbrships: Nat. Liberal Club, London, U.K.; Delhi Gymkhana Club; Club de Golf Los Leones, Santiago. Address: Embassy of India, 871 Triana, Santiago, Chile. 34.

MALIN, Irving, b. 18 Mar. 1934. Professor. Educ: B.A., Queens Coll., 1955; Ph.D., Stanford Univ., 1958. Appts. incl: Acting Instr., Engl., Stanford Univ., 1955-56, '57-58; Instr., Engl., Ind. Univ., 1958-60; Instr., Engl., CCNY, 1960-63; Asst. Prof., Engl., 1964-72; Prof., 1972-. Mbrships. incl: MLA; Am. Studies Assn.; Authors Guild; PEN; Phi Beta Kappa. Publs. incl: William Faulkner: An Interpretation, 1957; New American Gothic, 1962; Jews & Americans, 1965; Saul Bellow's Fiction, 1969; Nathanael West's Novels, 1972; Isaac Bashevis Singer, 1972; Ed., Psychoanalysis & American Fiction, 1965, Saul Bellow & the Critics, 1967, Truman Capote's, In Cold Blood: A Critical Handbook, 1968; Co-Ed., Breakthrough: A Treasury of Contemporary Jewish Literature, 1964; Co-Ed., The Achievement of William Styron, 1974; Ed., The Achievement of Carson McCullers. 1974. Address: 96-13 68th Ave., Forest Hills, NY 11375, U.S.A. 2, 6, 15, 30, 129.

MALIN, Morton Victor, b. 21 Jan. 1922. Information Scientist. Educ: A.B., Univ. of Chattanooga; M.A., Vanderbilt Univ.; Ph.D., Univ. of Md. Appts. incl: Histn., Nat. Pk. Serv., 1947-49; Sr. Rsch. Analyst, Univ. of Pitts., 1954-56; Rsch. Assoc., ibid, 1959-61; Staff Assoc. & Dpty. Hd., Nat. Sci. Fndn., Govt.-Univ. Staff, Off. of Econ. & Manpower Studies, Nat. Sci. Fndn., 1961-66; V.P., Corporate Dev., Inst. Scientific Info., 1966-. Mbrships. incl: AAAS; Am. Soc. for Info. Sci.; N.Y. Acad. Sci.; Soc. for Hist. of Technol.; Phi Alpha Theta; Phi Kappa Phi. Recip. fellowships, Univ. of Md. Publs: Var. scientific papers & reports. Address: 648 Vassar Rd., Strafford, PA 19087, U.S.A. 6.

MALINOWSKY, Harold Robert, b. 7 Dec. 1933. Assistant Director of Libraries. Educ: Midland Coll., Fremont, Neb., 1951-52; B.S., Univ. of Man., 1955; Post-grad. study, ibid, 1960-61; M.A., Univ. of Denver, 1963. Appts: Gulf Oil Corp., Monahans, Tex., 1955-57; Prod. Engnr., ibid, 1959-60; Lib. Asst., Univ. of Kan. Libs., 1961-62; Student Asst., Univ. of Denver Lib., 1962-63; Asst. Sci. & Engrng. Libn., Univ. of Kan. Libs., 1963-64; Sci. Libn., Univ. of Denver Lib., 1964-67, & Univ. of Kan. Libs., 1967-69; Asst. Dir. of Libs. for Pub. Servs., ibid, 1969-; Former Instr. of Lib. Sci., Univ. of Denver; Former Instr. of Sci. Bibliography, Univ. of Kan.; Instr. in Lib. Sci., Kan. State Tchrs.' Coll., Emporia. Mbrships: Former Pres. of Local Chapt., Special Libs. Assn.; Chmn., Nat. Educ. Comm.; Former Pres., Geosci. Info. Soc.; Mt. Plains Lib. Assn.; Former Pres. of Local Chapt., Am. Soc. for Info. Sci.; Tau Beta Pi. Author, Science & Engineering Reference Sources, 1967. Ed., Sci.-Technol. Sect., Am. Reference Books Annual, 1969-; Ed. Bd., Geosci. Documentation. Address: 2214 Hillcourt, Lawrence, KS 66044, U.S.A.

MALITZA, Mircea, b. 20 Feb. 1927. Professor of Mathematics. Educ: M.S., Ph.D., Fac. of Scis., Univ. of Bucharest. Appts: Dir. of Lib., Romanian Acad., 1950-55; Counsellor, Romanian Mission to UN, 1956-60; Dir., Min. for For. Affairs, 1961-62; Vice Min. for For. Affairs, 1962-70; Min. of Educ., 1970-72; Counsellor of Pres. of Romania, 1972-; Prof., Fac. of Maths., Univ. of Bucharest. Deleg., UN Gen. Assembly, 1956-69, & int. confs. of UNESCO, UNCTAD & disarmament. Mbrships: Romanian Acad. for Soc. & Pol. Scis.; Corres. Mbr., Romanian Acad.; Romanian Union of Writers; Past Sec.-Gen., Romanian Assn. for Int. Law & Int. Rels. Num. publs. incl: Diplomacy, Schools & Institutions, 1970; The Theory & Practice of Negotiations, 1972; The Theory of Graphs, 1972; Non-linear Programming (co-author), 1973; Landmarks, 1967, The Phinx, 1969, Living Stones, 1973 (essays). Hons: Romanian Acad. Award 'Gh. Tzitzeica' for Maths., 1973. Address: Str. Mihàil Moxa 3-5 Bucharest, Romania.

MALLEA, Eduardo, b. 14 Aug. 1903. Writer. Appts: Staff Mbr., La Nación; Ed., Lit. Mag., ibid, 1930-55; Amb. to UNESCO, Paris, 1956-58. Mbrships: Club Náutico Olivos; Círculo de Armas, Buenos Aires; Corres. Mbr., Acad. Goetheana de San Pablo, Brazil, 1949, Hispanic Soc. of Am., 1964; Argentina Acad. of Letters, 1960. Publs. incl: Cuentos para una Inglesa Desesperada, 1926; Fiesta en Noviembre, 1938; La bahia de silencio, 1940; El sayal y la púrpura, 1941; El retorno, 1946; La torre, 1951; Chaves, 1953; Simbad, 1957; Posesion, 1958; La razón humana, 1959; La guerra interior, 1963; Poderío de la novela, 1965; El resentimiento, 1966; La barca de hielo, 1967; La red, 1968; La penúltima puerta, 1969; Gabriel Andaral, 1971; Trista piel del universo, 1971; En la crecienta oscuridad, 1973. Hons: 1st Nat. Prize of Letters, 1945; Gt. Prize of Hon., Argentine Soc. of Writers, 1948; Fundación Vaccarós Prize, 1960; Cmdr., Order of Arts & Letters, Govt. of France, 1964; Dr.h.c. in Humane Letters, Univ. of Mich., Ann Arbor, 1968. Address: Posadas 1120, Buenos Aires, Argentina.

MALLEN, Saul T., b. 18 Dec. 1914. Industrialist. Educ: J.D., Northeastern Univ., Boston, Mass., 1937. Appts: Exec. Mgr., Exec. V.P., Sec. & Treas., Dir., 1938-; Chmn., 1942-; Sport-Wear Mills, Inc.; Off., Dir., Chmn., Windsor Hosiery Mills, Inc., 1956-; Off., Dir., Chmn. (Co-fndr.), Int. Yarn Corp., 1963-; Knitco, Inc., 1968-70; Co-Fndr., Cons., Amtex,

Inc., 1970-; Cons., Roston Mills, Inc., 1972-. Mbrships: Mass. Bar Assn., 1938-; Patron, Bright Schl., Chattanooga, Tenn.; Patron (Dir., 1953-61), McCallie Schl.; Charter, Dir., Cleveland Regional Speech & Hearing Ctr.; Ochs Mem. Temple, Chattanooga (Dir., 1965-67); Pioneered dr. establishing 1st blood bank, McMinn Co., Tenn.; Jewish Community Ctr.; Nat. Assn. Am. Hosiery Mfrs.; Am. Soc. Yarn Mfrs.; Mason, 32 degree Shriner; Elk; B'nai B'rith; Valleybrook Golf & Country Club. Recip., num. tournament trophies, bowling & golf, 1940-. Address: 3408 Harcourt Dr., Chattanooga, TN 37411, U.S.A. 7, 16, 22.

MALLERY, Sylvia E., b. 10 Mar. 1934. Professor of Social Science. Educ: B.A., Syracuse Univ., 1955; Ed.M., Harvard Univ., 1957; Profl. Dip., Tchrs. Coll., Columbia Univ., 1970. Appts: Instr., SUNY, Cobleskill, 1958; Asst. Prof.-Prof., ibid; Instr., Summer Schl., Tchrs. Coll., Columbia Univ., 1966. Mbrships: U.S. Nat. Comm. for Early Childhood Educ., 1969-; Life Mbr., Nat. Assn. for the Educ. of Young Children; Kappa Delta Pi; Pi Lambda Theta. Hon: Advsry. Mbr., Marquis Biog. Lib. Soc., 1973. Address: 12 Washington Ave., Cobleskill, NY 12043, U.S.A. 5, 6, 138.

MALLESON, (The Lady) Constance (Colette O'Neil), b. 1895. Actress; Writer. Educ: Dresden; Paris; RADA, London. Leading roles in: Le monde où l'on s'ennuie, Queen's, London; l'Enfant Prodigue, Kingsway; Orphans of the Storm, Lyceum; Helen, in Euripedes' The Trojan Women; Masefield's The Faithful, Stage Soc.; var. repertory productions; Miles Malleson's Young Heaven, Hull & London, 1925; leading lady on Sir Frank Benson's Farewell Tour. Toured w. Dame Sybil Thorndike & Sir Lewis Casson. Mbrships: Howard League for Penal Reform; Summerhill Soc; Pvte. Libs. Assn; Anti-Slavery Soc.; Soc. for the Preservation of Ancient Bldgs.; Nat. Trust; Conservation Soc. Publs: After Ten Years, 1931; Fear in the Heart, 1936; In the North (Autobiographical Fragments), 1936-46, 1947; Queen Margaret of Norway (translation), 1954; Ed., As the Sight is Bent, 1964; Contrb. to: Bertrand Russell: Philosopher of the Century, 1967; Contbr. to The Guardian, The Countryman, Helsingin Sanomat. Address: c/o Williams & Glyn's Bank, Kirkland House, Whitehall, London S.W. 1, U.K. 1.

MALLIEN, Emil, b. 1 July 1911. Company Director. Educ: Dr. of Law; Dr. of Econs; Harvard Bus. Schl. Alumnus. Appts. incl: Lawyer, Antwerp, Belgium; Mgr., Kredietbank, Brussels, Belgium; Pres., Financia S.A. (Antwerp), Europa Fund Ltd., (Montreal, Canada) & Inmorcy S.A., (Vera, Spain). Publs. incl: 3 books in Flemish Lang. Address: 9 Dennenlaan, 2020 Antwerp, Belgium.

MALLING OLSEN, Erik, b. 20 May 1923. Educator; Senior Veterinary Officer. Educ: Vet. examen., Royal Vet. & Agric. Univ., 1947; Dr.med.vet., 1942. Appts: Asst., Vet. Prac., 1947; Scientific Asst., Vet. & Agric. Univ., 1947-52; Lab. Chief, 1952-56; Sr. Vet. Off., Danish Vet. Serv., 1956; Hd., Dept. for Milk Control & Anti-Mastitis Campaign, ibid; External Examiner, Physiol. & Biochem., Vet. examen, 1965. Mbrships: Danish Vet. Assn.; Sec., Hygienic Comm. & mbr. & chmn., var. comms., ibid. Publs. incl: On Coliform Bacteria in Milk, with Special Reference to the Detection, 1952; Vejledning for veterinaerstuderende ved kursus i bakteriologi, 1952; The effects of radioactive fallout on food & agric., 1963; Folgerne for landbruget af radioaktivt nedfald, 1965; Contbr. to var. profl. publs. Recip., Prof. C.O. Jensen Prize for scientific work in milk bacteriol. Address: Lyngbývej 387 C, 2820 Gentofte, Denmark. 134.

MALMQUIST, Eve Jarl Theodor, b. 15 Nov. 1915. Professor of Educational Research. Educ: Ph.D., Stockholm Univ., 1958. Appts. incl: Dir., Nat. Schl. for Educl. Rsch., Linköping, 1958-68; Prof. of Educ., Tchrs. Coll., Linköping Univ., 1968-. Mbr. edit. advsry. bds. inclng. Reading Rsch. Quarterly; The Slow Learning Child; The Irish Jrnl. of Educ. Mbrships. incl: Pres. of Swedish Coun., & Dir., Int. Reading Assn.; Pres., Int. Acad. Music. Publs. incl: Reading & Writing Disabilities, Analysis & Methodology, 1971; The Teaching of Reading in the Elementary Schools, 1973. Hons. incl: Int. Award for Oútstanding Contbn. to Reading Rsch., World Congress, Sidney, Australia, 1970; Hon. Life Mbrship., Int. Reading Assn., Newark, N.J., U.S.A., 1970. Address: Drottninggatan 35, 582 27 Linköping, Sweden. 43, 134.

MALMROS, Frans Jacob, b. 4 Nov. 1925. Shipowner; Consul. Educ: Higher Commercial School of Malmö, Sweden, 1947; The Stockholm School of Economics, 1948-50. Married w. two children. Appts. incl: Managing Director, Malmros Rederi AB; Consul of Denmark; Board Member, Malmros Rederi AB, AB Olson & Wright, The Frigoscandia Group, AB Atlanttrafik, Munksjö AB, Invevestment AB Öresund, Skanska Banken, Försäkrings AB Skandia, (Southern Zone) Swedish Shipowners' Association, Northern Shipowners' Defence Club, The Swedish Steamship Assurance Club, Lloyd's Register of Shipping (Swedish Committee), The Swedish Ships' Mortgage Bank. Mbrships. incl: The 1001 Club; Travellers' Club. Hons. incl: Knight of the Order of the Dannebrog, 1966; Knight of the Order of Vasa, 1971. Address: Västra Vallgatan 22, S-231 00 Trelleborg, Sweden.

MALO, (Very Rev.) Albert-Adrien, O.F.M., b. 12 Apr. 1894. Biblical Sciences Specialist. Educ: Univ. Laval, P.Q., Canada, 1914-21; Postgrad. Studies, Rome, Italy, 1921-24; Lector generalis, Biblical scis., 1924. Appts: Tchr., Jerusalem, 1924-25; Tchr., Studium Franciscain, Montreal, Canada, 1925-40, Montreal Univ., 1939-53; Ldr., Cath. Hour, CBC, 1939-52; Prof., Diocesan Grand Sem., Sask., 1932-35; Radio Lectr., Biblical Archaeol.; Lectr., Rome, Italy, Lourdes, France, Fatima, Portugal & Zagreb, Yugoslavia. Mbrships. incl: Fndr., Widows Assn. of Montreal, Inc., 1959; Fndr., Pres., Cath. Assn. of Biblical Studies of Canada, 1942; Emeritus Mbr., ibid, 1947; Co-Fndr., Soc. for Mariological Studies; Int. Mariological Acad., Rome; Chap., Scouts, P.Q. Publs. incl: Autobiographie en images; num. books on theol. subjs. Hons. incl: Silver Medal, Pope Pius XII, 1964; Medal of State of Israel, 1966; Hon. Guest, Israel, 1965; Kt., Holy Sepulchre, Jerusalem, 1973. Address: 2010 W. Dorchester, Montreal H3H 1R6, P.Q., Canada.

MALONE, Edwin Scott, III, b. 25 Mar. 1938. Radio, Television & Public Relations Consultant. Educ: B.A., Southern Meth. Univ., Dallas, Tex., 1960. Appts: V.P., Radio Servs., Southern Bapt. Radio & TV Commn., Ft. Worth, Tex.; Ptnr., COMAL PR Cons., Arlington, Tex.; Pres., Ed Malone Enterprises, Arlington. Mbrships. incl: Past Pres., Relig. PR Coun. & Vernon Sertoma Club; Gov.'s Deleg. from Tex., White House Conf. on Children & Youth; Am. Coll. of Radio Arts & Scis.; Am. Acad. of Arts & Scis. of TV; Soc. of Am. Travel Writers; Relig. Heritage of Am.; SAR; Sons of War of 1812. Publs: The Douglas Geneaology;

The Malone Genealogy; The Mystery of the Temple; Religious Landmarks of America; scripts for radio & TV; contbr. rsch. & writing to relig & Masonic publs. Hons: Ph.D., Burton Sem., 1967; Geo. Wash. Medal, Freedoms Fndn., 1966 & 74; Citation, N.J. Conf. of Mayors, 1965; Commodore, Okla. Navy; Admiral, Neb. Navy; Ky. Col.; Lt.-Col., Gov.'s Staff, Ga.; Hon. Cowboy, Wyo.; Hon. Sec. of State, Mont.; Ark. Traveler; Order of White Buffalo, S.D.; Lt.-Col., N.M.; Commandeur, Sovereign Greek Order of St. Dennis of Zante; Chevalier, Sovereign Order of Crown of Thorns. Address: 1902 Mossy Oak, Arlington, TX 76012, U.S.A. 2, 125.

MALONE, Marvin Herbert, b. 2 Apr. 1930. Pharmacologist; Educator; Editor; Author. Educ: B.S., Univ. of Neb., Lincoln, 1951; M.S., ibid, 1953; Grad. study, Rutgers Univ., N.B., N.J., 1954-55; Ph.D., Univ. of Neb., Lincoln, 1958. Appts. incl: Rsch. Asst., Pharmacodynamics, E.R. Squibb Inst. Med. Rsch., N.B., N.J., 1953-56; Asst. Prof., Univ. of N.M., Albuquerque, 1958-60; Assoc. Prof., Univ. of Conn., Storrs, 1960-69; Cons., Drug Plant Labs., Univ. of Wash., Seattle, 1960-64, Natural Prods. Rsch. Labs., Rockville, Md., 1967-70, Atlas Chem. Ind., Wilmington, Del., 1968-72; Prof., Univ. of the Pacific Stockton, Calif., 1969-. Mbrships. incl: Fellow, Am. Fndn. for Pharmaceutical Educ., 1956-58; Fellow, Am. Inst. of Chemists, 1969-; Am. Soc. Pharmacol. Exptl. Therap.; Am. Soc. Pharmacognosy; Sr. mbr., Acad. Pharmaceutical Scis.; Int. Soc. Biochem. Pharmacol.; AAUP. Publs. incl: Bucolics & Cheromanics (book), 1963; Conversation Piece (pamphlet), 1959; Ed., The Wormwood Review, 1961-. Recip. of Hons. Address: 722 Bedford Rd., Stockton, CA 95204, U.S.A. 9, 11, 14, 15, 28, 131.

MALOO, Man Chand, b. 3 May 1939. University Professor. Educ: Bachelor of Commerce, 1960; Master of Commerce, 1962; M.B.A., 1966; DBA Student, Fla. State Univ., Tallahassee. Instr., S.C. State Coll., Orangeburg, 1966-68; Asst. Prof., Fla. A & M Univ., Tallahassee; currently, Asst. Prof., Tuskagee Inst., Ala. Mbrships: Am. Acctng., Finance & Econ. Assns. Contbr., articles, econs., var. jrnls. Donor, Anop Kumar Mem. Gold Medal to Jodhpur Univ., India, for annual award to topmost student in MBA prog. Hons: Meritorious Award, Indian Govt., 1956; Merit Schlrship., Govt. of Rajasthan, India, 1956-62; Centennial Award, Atlanta Univ. Address: School of Applied Sciences, Tuskegee Institute, Tuskegee, AL 36088, U.S.A.

MALTZ, Albert, b. 28 Oct. 1908. Writer. Educ: A.B., Columbia Univ., 1930; Yale Schl. of Drama, 1930-32. Appt: Exec. Bd. Mbr., Theatre Union, 1933-37. Mbrships: Authors' League of Am.; Writers Guild of Am., W.; American PEN; Hollywood Ten, 1947. Novels: The Underground Stream; The Cross and the Arrow; The Journey of Simon McKeever; A Long Day in a Short Life; A Tale of One January. Short Story Collects: The Way Things Are; Afternoon in the Jungle. Film Scripts: This Gun for Hire; Destination Tokyo; Pride of the Marines; Cloak & Dagger; Naked City; Two Mules for Sister Sara. Plays: Merry Go Round (co-author); Peace on Earth (co-author); Black Pit. Hons. incl: O. Henry Mem. Award for Best Short Story, 1938; Special Award, Acad. Motion Picture Arts & Scis., 1945. Address: c/o Author's League of America, 234 W. 44th St., N.Y., NY 10036, U.S.A. 1, 3.

MALUGANI, Anita C., b. 14 Oct. 1917. Foreign Language Instructor. Educ: A.B., Mary Baldwin Coll., 1939; M.A. Equiv. Appts:

Spanish Instr., Chmn., Dept. of For. Langs., Fair Lawn H.S., N.J.; Instr., Spanish & French, Chmn., Dept. of For. Langs., Bogota H.S., N.J. Contbr. to N.Y. Times Mag. Sect. Hon: Fulbright Grant, Coll. Classique de Jeunes Filles, Ajaccio, Corsica. Address: 777 Midland Rd., Oradell, NJ 07649, U.S.A. 5, 6, 22, 130.

MALURA, Oswald, b. 9 Oct. 1906. Artist. Educ: Art schl., Munich, Germany, 1925; Studied at Akademie der Bildenden Künste, Munich, 1925-30; Travel, study, India, 1930-33. Appts: Free-lance painter, Munich, & active in own art schl., 1933-40; Served WWII; Reopened art schl., constructed modern gall., 1946-50; Travel study, S. America, 1951-55; Lectr., & active in gall., 1955-65. Mbrships: Verband Bildender Künstler, Munich; Munich Künstlergenossenschaft. Paintings in town gall. & state collect., Munich. Publs: Als Maler durch Indien, 1949; Indische Plastik im Völker Museum in München, in Die Weltkunst. Hons: Mondsch travel grant, Akademie der bildenden Künste, Munich; Swabian art prize for painting, Munich, 1964. Address: Hohenzollernstr. 16, 8000 Munich 40, German Fed. Repub. 43.

MANACORDA, Mario Alighiero, b. 9 Dec. 1914. University Professor. Educ: Scuola Normale Superiore, Pisa; Dr.'s Degree, Univ. of Pisa. Appts: Prof. of Italian & Latin in the Dicei, 1939-66; Ed., Riforma della Scuola, review, 1965-; Prof. of Educ., Siena, 1966-71, Univ. of Cagliari, Sardinia, 1967-69, Univ. of Florence, Italy, 1972. Mbr. & Sec., Assn. for Defense & Promotion of the Nat. Schl., 1950-60. Publs: Marxism & Education, Vols. I-III, 1964-66; Marx & Education Today; The Educational Idea by Gramsci; The "Paideia" of Achilles. Address: Via Giuseppe Ferrari 12, Rome, Italy. 95.

MANALAYSAY, Reuben Gonzaga, b. 6 Oct. 1915. University Professor. Educ: B.S.Ed., Philippine Union Coll., 1938; B.A., ibid, 1939; M.A., Far Eastern Univ., 1946; M.Ed., Univ. of the Philippines, 1950; Ed.D., Ind. Univ., U.S.A., 1951. Appts. incl: Hd., Dept. of Educ., Philippine Union Coll., 1945-51; Dean, ibid, 1951-52; Pres., 1952-64; Prof. of Educ., Walla Walla Coll., U.S.A., 1964-66; Prof. of Educ. & Psychol., Acadia Univ., Canada, 1966-; Professorial Lectr., Far Eastern Univ., 1957-64; Arrelano Univ., 1960-64. Mbrships. incl: V.P., Philippine Assn. of Grad. Assn.; Phi Delta Kappa; Canadian Psychological Assn.; Am. Educl. Rsch. Assn.; Canadian Educl. Rsch. Assn. Author of publs. in field. Recip. of hons. Address: Acadia Univ., Wolfville, N.S., Canada. 6, 14, 141.

MANCE, Julian Clifford, Jr., b. 10 Oct. 1928. Musician; Composer. Educ: Roosevelt Univ., 1947. Appts: Accompanist, late Dinah Washington, 1954-55; w. Dizzy Gillespie Band, 1958-61; Formed own grp., 1961; own music publng. co. Mbrships: Broadcast Music Inc.; Nat. Acad. Recording Arts & Scis. Recorded 17 record albums. Compositions: Jubilation; The Uptown; Happytime; That Mellow Feeling; Harlem Lullaby; var. blues tunes. Author, How to Play Blues Piano, 1967. Hons: New Star, Melody Maker Jazz Poll, 1960; Int. Jazz Critics Poll, 1961. Address: P.O. Box 5029, F.D.R. Stn., N.Y., NY 10022, U.S.A.

MANDELBAUM, Bernard, b. 12 Jan. 1922. Rabbi. Educ: B.A., Columbia Coll., 1942; M.Hebrew Lit., 1946; Ph.D., 1953. Ordained Rabbi, 1946; Rabbinical Schl. Registrar, 1946-53; Dean of Students, Rabbinical Schl., 1951-61; Provost, Jewish Theol. Sem. of Am., 1961-66; Pres., ibid, 1966-. Publs: Pesikta de Rab Kahana; Assignment in Israel; Choose Life.

Hons: D.D.; Israel Davidson Award, Medieval Hebrew Lit.; Lamport Award for Outstanding Work in Homiletics. Address: The Jewish Theological Seminary of America, 3080 Broadway, N.Y., NY 10027, U.S.A. 6.

MANDELLI, Carlo, b. 16 Aug. 1912. Free-lance Sculptor; Art Master. Educ: Accademia di Belle Arti, Venice. Appts: Art Master, liceo Artistico, Venice, 1957-60; Prof. of Ornamental Sculpture, Accademia di Belle Arti, Venice, 1960-. Mbrships: Chmn., Org. & Selection Comms., Int. Biennale of Small Bronzes, Padua, 1955-74, Biennale Triveneta d'Arte, Padua, 1955-74; Org. Comm., Artisti Italiani, 1964-74; Chmn., Selection Comm., Nat. Exhib., 1974; Chmn., Exhib. Urbani Nat. Prize, 1974; Lyons Club. Sculptures in galls., museums & pub. bldgs. inclng. Galleria d'Arte Moderna, Venice; Museo Civico, Padua; Min. of Treasury of Min. of Educ., Rome. Also pvte. collects., Padua, Rome, Venice. Hons. incl: Gold Medal, Sacred Art, Padua, 1958; 3 Gold Medals, 1965; 2 Gold Medals, 1967; 1st Prize, Nat. Exhib. of Art (Sport), Florence, 1970. Address: Via S. Caterina 2, 35100 Padua, Italy.

MANDZIUK, Michael Dennis, b. 14 Jan. 1942. Artist. Educ: Cass Tech. H.S.; self-taught in fine art. Principal media, acrylic painting & serigraphy. Solo Exhib. J. Walter Thompson Co., Detroit, 1971; Joseph Welna Gall. Chgo., 1974. Exhibs: Tex. Fine Art Assn. Nat. Art Show, 1971, '72; Boston Printmakers Nat. Show, 1972, '74; Butler Inst. of Am. Art, 1973; Drawings U.S.A., Minn. Mus. of Art, 1973. Collects: Minn. Mus. of Art, St. Paul; Pk. Forest, Ill. Art Ctr.; City of Springfield, Ill.; Mfrs. Nat. Bank of Detroit; Boston 1st Nat. Bank; Mich. Bell Telephone Co.; Saginaw Valley Coll., Mich. Address: 17994 Ruth St., Melvindale, MI 48122, U.S.A.

MANGEL, Margaret Wilson, b. 13 May 1912. Professor; Dietitian. Educ: B.A., Home Econs., Ind. Univ.; M.S., Nutrition, Univ. of Chgo.; Ph.D., Food Chem., ibid. Appts: Instr., Univ. of Mo., 1940-43; Asst. & Assoc. Prof., ibid, 1943-50, Prof., 1950, Chmn., 1955, Dir., Schl. of Home Economics, 1960-. Mbrships. incl: Am. Home Econs. Assn.; Am. Dietetics Assn., Past Chmn. Home Econs. Div., Am. Assn. State Univs. & Land Grant Colls.; AAAS; N.Y. Acad. of Sci.; AAUP; NEA; Phi Upsilon Omicron; Phi Beta Kappa; Sigma Xi. Contbr. to num. profl. publs. Address: Schl. of Home Econs., Univ. of Mo.-Columbia, Columbia, MO 65201, U.S.A. 8, 120.

MANGRIOTIS, Dimitrios I., b. 26 Oct. 1897. Honorary Member of Financial Supreme Court of Greece. Educ: Ph.D., Univ. of Athens Schl. of Law, Greece. Appts. incl: Sect. Mgr., Min. of Finance, 1932-41; Dir., Min. of Finance, 1942-51; Mbr., Financial Supreme Ct., 1952-67. Mbrships. incl: Pres., Soc. for Thracian Studies; Pres., Gideous in Greece; Pres., Org. for Amelioration of the Red Cross Nurses; Assoc. Mbr., Bd. of the Red Cross Hosp.; Former V.P., Cert. Pub. Accts. Publs. incl: Books Treatise of Stamp Tax, 1928, '32, '51; Faith & Science, 1940; Christ and Modern Thought, 1949, '65; Bible and Science, 1970; Relations of Two Sexes, 1971. The Art of Administration, 1972. Hons. incl: Medal of Acad. of Athens, 1951; Silver Cross of Phoenix; Golden Cross of King George; Superior Order of Phoenix. Address: Homer St. No. 10, Nea Smirni, Athens, Greece.

MANHATTAN, Avro, b. 5 Apr. 1914. Author. Educ: Sorbonne, Paris, France; London Schl. of Econs., U.K.; Acad. of painting, Venice & Paris; etc. Appts. incl:

one-time Dir., Radio Freedom; Writer on Pol. Warfare, 1940-43; Commentator for special broadcasts to Europe, BBC, 1940-46; Exec. Comm., Dr. Stopes Birth Control Clin., 1953-59; Free-Lance Writer. Mbrships: Royal Soc. of Lit.; Soc. of Authors; PEN Club; Ethical Union; Life, British Interplanetary Soc., & Leicester Secular Soc.; Mark Twain Soc. of Am.; Nat. Secular Soc.; etc. Publd. about 23 books inclng: Of Ants & Men, 1951; Speculations on Time, 1952; The Bewildering Mystery of Mars, 1953 (3 essays); Religious Terror in Ireland, 1971; The Vatican Billions—2000 Years of Wealth Accumulation, 1972; Imperialism & World Freedom, 1972. Hons. incl: Ph.D., Minn. Inst. Philos., 1972; Kt. Templar, Grand Priory of England, 1974. Address: Ansdell Terrace, Kensington, London W8, U.K. 3, 30, 43.

MANKOWITZ, Wolf, b. 7 Nov. 1924. Novelist; Playwright; Film & Television Scriptwriter. Educ: M.A., Cambridge Univ., U.K., 1946. Books incl: A Kid for Two Farthings (also film), 1953; My Old Man's a Dustman, 1956; Expresso Bongo (also play & film), 1960; Cockatrice, 1963; The Penquin Wolf Mankowitz. Films incl: The Bespoke Overcoat (also play), 1955; The Long and the Short and the Tall, 1961; The Millionairess, 1960; The Day the Earth Caught Fire, 1961; The Waltz of the Toreadors, 1962; Casino Royale, 1966; The Twenty-Fifth Hour, 1967; The Assassination Bureau, 1968; The Hebrew Lesson, 1972; The Hireling, 1973. Plays incl: Make Me an Offer, (also film & book), 1952; Pickwick, 1963; Passion Flower Hotel, 1965; The Notorious Cockney Highwayman, 1972. sev. TV scripts. Author of books on art. Producer: The Lion in Love, 1960; This Year, Next Year, 1960; Belle or the Ballad of Doctor Crippen, 1971; Here are Ladies, 1970. Recip., sev. awards for films & plays. Address: Simmonscourt Castle, Ballsbridge, Dublin 4, Repub. of Ireland.

MANLEY, Edna. Sculptor. Appts: Co-fndr. & Tchr., Schl. of Art, Jamaica, W. Indies; Mbr., Edit. Bd., Public Opinion Weekly; Ed., Focus. Mbrships: Bd. of Mgmt., Inst. of Jamaica; London Grp., U.K.; Soc. of Women Artists, London; Contemporary Artists Soc., Jamaica. Statues incl: Lifesize crucifix, All Saints Ch.; The Angel, Kingston Parish Ch.; Over-lifesize Holy Cross; Over-lifesize Paul Bogle. One-man shows: Atlanta, Ga., U.S.A.; U.K.; France; Guyana; Trinidad. Other exhibs.: Germany; Puerto Rico; Canada; U.S.A.; Ireland. Hons: Silver & Gold Medals, Inst. of Jamaica; Key to City of Kingston. Address: Regardless, Washington Dr., Kingston 10, Jamaica, W. Indies. 19, 96.

MANN, Arthur, b. 3 Jan. 1922. Historian, Educator & Author. Educ: B.A., Brooklyn Coll., N.Y.C., 1944; M.A., Harvard Univ., 1947; Ph.D., ibid, 1952. Appts. incl: Instr.-Asst. Prof., MIT, 1948-55; Asst. Prof.-Prof., Smith Coll., 1955-66; Prof. of Am. Hist., Univ. of Chgo., 1966-; Preston & Sterling Morton Prof. of Am. Hist., ibid, 1971-; Vis. Prof., Columbia Univ., Harvard Univ., Salzburg Univ., Austria. Mbrships: Am. Historical Assn.; Org. of Am. Histns.; Exec. Bd., Am. Studies Assn.; Quadrangle Club. Publs. incl: Growth & Achievement: Temple Israel, 1854-1954, 1954; La Guardia, a Fighter Against His Times, 1882-1933, 1959; The Progressive Era 1963; La Guardia Comes to Power: 1933, 1965; Immigrants in American Life, 1968, revised edit. 1974. Contbr. to Dictionary of Am. Biography, var. books & profl. jrnls. Hons; Fellow, Am. Coun. of Learned Socs., 1962-63; Alumni Award of Merit, Brooklyn Coll., 1968.

Address: Dept. of History, University of Chicago, IL 60637, U.S.A. 2, 13, 128.

MANN, Charles S., Sr., b. 17 Apr. 1926. Dentist. Educ: Grad., Stephen F. Austin Univ., Nacogdoches, Tex., 1944; D.D.S., Schl. of Dentistry, Univ. of Tex., Houston, 1947; Postgrad. studies, Univ. of Tenn., 1958, Univ. of Ala., 1959, Walter Reed Hosp., Wash. D.C., 1964, & Letterman Gen. Hosp., San Francisco, Calif., 1968. Appts: Pvte. Prac., Lufkin, Tex., 1947-61; Pvte. Prac., Amarillo, Tex., 1961-66; Dentist, Gary Job Corps, San Marcos, Tex., 1966-70; Pvte. Prac. as Prosthetic Dentist, Austin, Tex., 1971-; Lt. Col. Cmdr., Ctrl. Dental Lab., 425th Med. Detachment, U.S. Army Reserve, Ft. Sam Houston, Tex., 1973-. Mbrships: Am. Dental Assn.; Tex. Dental Assn.; Austin Dental Soc.; Assn. of Mil. Surgs.; Royal Soc. of Hlth.; Reserve Offs. Assn.; Xi Phi Psi. Address: 103 W. Fifth, Austin, TX 78701, U.S.A. 7.

MANN, Clarence Churchill, b. 6 Sept. 1904. Army Officer. Educ: Upper Canada Coll.; Royal Mil. Coll.; Univ. of Toronto, Appts: Lt., Gov. Gen's. Body Guard, Militia, 1923-27; Lt., Royal Canadian Dragoons, Permanent Force, 1927-; Capt., ibid, 1932; Staff Coll., Camberley, 1939; G.S.O.3, HQ 1st Canadian Div., 1939; GSO2, Int. HQ 7 Corps, U.K., 1940; Instr., Canadian Staff Course, E. Grinstead, Sussex; Lt. Col., Cmdng. 8 Canadian Reconnaisance Regiment, 1941; GSO 1, HQ 2 Canadian Infantry Div., 1941; Brigadier, 1942; Dpty. Mil. Force Cmdr. & Sr. Gen. Staff Off., Dieppe Raid, 1942; BGS 1, Canadian Corps HQ, 1942-43; Cmdr., 7 Canadian Infantry Brigade, June-Dec. 1943; Chief of Staff, HQ 1st Canadian Army, 1944-end of WWII; Vice Chief Gen. Staff, Nat. Defence HQ, 1946-49; Retd., 1949. Mbrships: York Club, Toronto, Ont.; Seigniory Club, Montebello, P.Q.; Royal Mil. Coll. Club, Kingston, Ont.; Prominent mbr., Int. Horse Shows & Canadian Army Horse Show Team, 1929-35. Hons: CBE, 1945; DSO, 1942; Cmdr., Netherlands Order of Orange Nassau, w. swords, 1946; Off., Legion of Merit, U.S.A., 1944; CB, 1945. Address: Deers Bush, RR 2, Newmarket, Ont., Canada.

MANN, (Francis) Anthony, b. 10 June 1914. Journalist; Writer. Educ: B.A., Balliol Coll., Oxford. Appts: w. Daily Telegraph, London, 1936-; London Staff, 1936; Vienna & Berlin, 1938; Berlin Corres., 1939; Copenhagen interned, 1940-45; Belsen Trial, Nuremburg Tribunal, Germany, 1945-; Chief Corres., Germany, 1946; Chief Corres., Southern Europe, 1952 & Special Corres. (based in Rome) for num. countries of Africa, Asia & Europe; Chief Paris Corres., 1965; Special Corres., Mediterranean Zone, 1972. Mbrships: Past Pres., Anglo-Am. Press Assn. of Paris; Inst. of Jrnlsts.; For. Press Assn., Rome; Oxford Soc. Publs: Where God Laughed, the Sudan Today, 1954; Well Informed Circles, 1961; Zelezny, Portrait Sculpture 1917-1970, 1970; Tiara (novel), 1973. Recip. Humboldt Medal, German Acad., Munich, 1935. Address: c/o The For. Ed., The Daily Telegraph, 135 Fleet St., London EC4P 4BL, U.K.

MANN, Henry Albert, b. 12 Nov. 1941. Sanitary Engineer. Educ: B.S., Iowa State Univ., 1963. Appts: Inspection Engr., Mt. Coffee Hydroelectric Proj., Liberia, 1965-67; Underwater Inspection Engr., Deep Water Harbour, Nassau, Bahamas, 1965-69; Res. Engr. Construction, Ohio, Ill., & Iowa, 1968-72; Underwater Soil Sampling Inspection, Lake Erie, Ohio, 1972; Proj. Engr., Environmental Pollution Control Design Projs., 1972. Mbrships. incl: Fellow, Am. Congress on

Surveying & Mapping; Nat. Soc. of Profl. Engrs; Muscatine Chapt., Iowa Engrng. Soc.; Chi Epsilon Civil Engrng. Hon. Schol. Soc., 1963. Address: c/o Stanley Consultants, Stanley Bldg., Muscatine, Iowa 52761, U.S.A.

MANN, Kalman Jacob, b. 5 July 1912. Physician. Specialist in Internal Medicine. Educ: Univ. Coll Hosp. Med. Schl., Univ. of London, 1931-37; London Schl. of Postgrad. Studies, 1938; London Schl. of Trop. Med. & Hygiene, 1939; M.D. (Lond.); F.R.C.P. (Lond.); D.T.M. & H., 1939. Appts. incl: Cons. Physn., Min. of Hlth., London, Sect.4, 1943-46; Rsch. Physn. to Med. Rsch. Coun., Pneumoconiosis Rsch. Univ., Penarth, 1946-49; Dpty. Dir., Hadassah Med. Org., Jerusalem, 1949-51; Dir. Gen., ibid, 1951-; Assoc. Prof. in Org. & Admin. of Med. Care, Hebrew Univ - Hadassah Med. Schl., 1966-. Mbrships. incl: Past V.P., Int. Hosp. Fed.; WHO Advsry. Panel of Org. of Med. Care; Chmn., Disability Hlth. Ins. Nat. Planning Comm., Israel Med. Assn Comm. on Reorg. of Hlth. Servs. in Israel, Israel Assn. of Hosp. Dirs.; Bd. Mgmt., Hebrew Univ.- Hadassah Med. Schl. Author w. others, Visits to Doctors, 1970; contbr. to med. jrnls; papers in field publd. in sci. periodicals. Recip., Henrietta Szold Award for achievement in Pub. Hlth., 1973. Address: Hadassah Med. Org., P.O.B. 499, Jerusalem, Israel.

MANN, Maurice, b. 22 Feb. 1929. Economist. Educ: B.A., Northeastern Univ., Boston, 1951; M.A., Boston Univ., 1952; Ph.D., Syracuse Univ., 1955. Appts: Asst. Prof. of Econs., Ohio Wesleyan Univ., 1955-58; Financial Economist, Bur. of Old Age & Survivors Ins., Balt., Md., 1958-60; V.P. & Gen. Economist, Fed. Reserve Bank of Cleveland, 1960-69, Asst. Dir. of Off. of Mgmt. & Budget, Exec. Off. of the Pres., 1969-70; Exec. V.P., Western Pa. Nat. Bank (now Equibank), Pitts., 1970-73; Pres. & Chief Exec. Off., Fed. Home Loan Bank of San Francisco, 1973-. Mbrships. incl: Nat. Coun. Northeastern Univ.; Am. Econ. & Finance Assns.; Am. Mgmt. Assn. Hons: Ford Fndn. Fellowship, 1956; Alumni Citation for Disting. Attainment, Northeastern Univ., 1973. Address: Fed. Home Loan Bank of San Francisco, P.O. Box 7948, San Francisco, CA 94120, U.S.A. 2, 6, 8, 16.

MANN, Peter Henry, b. 5 Sept. 1926. University Lecturer; Researcher. Educ: B.A., Leeds Univ., 1950; M.A., Liverpool Univ., 1952; Ph.D., Nottingham Univ., 1955. Appts: Radio Off., Merchant Navy, 1943-46; Jr. Rsch. Worker, Liverpool Univ., 1950-52; Univ. Rsch. Fellow, Nottingham Univ., 1952-54; Lectr., Sr. Lectr. & Rdr., Sheffield Univ., 1954-. Publs: An Approach to Urban Sociology, 1965; Methods of Sociological Enquiry, 1968; Books & Reading (w. J.L. Burgoyne), 1969; Books, Buyers & Borrowers, 1971; Students & Books, 1974. Address: 10 Whiteley Wood Rd., Sheffield S11 7FE, U.K. 3.

MANN, William Marion, Jr., b. 7 Jan. 1931. Psychiatrist, Educ: B.S., Wake Forest Univ., 1953; M.D., Bowman Gray Schl. of Med., ibid, 1957; Res., NC Bapt. Hosp., Winston Salem, Warren State Hosp., Pa. Appts: Staff Psych., Warren State Hosp., 1966-71; Unit Dir., ibid, 1971-; Clin. Dir., Crawford Co. Mental Hlth. Ctr., Meadville, 1966-70; Med. Dir., Cameron, Elk, McKean, Potter Cos. Mental Hlth.-Mental Retardation Clin. & Psych. Cons., Bradford Hosp., 1970-73; Psych. Cons., Children's Home, Bradford, 1971-72; Cons., Mental Retardation grp. Homes for Adults, Partial Hospitalization Prog. for Mentally Ill, Futures Sheltered Workshop, Field Soc. Servs. for Mentally Ill, Crisis Counseling Telephone Serv., Emergency Servs. for Mental Hlth. Prog., Bradford, 1972-73; Psych. Cons., Alcoholism & Drug Abuse Prog., Port Allegany, Pa., 1972-73; Clin. Dir., CEMP Counseling Ctr. for Problems of Living, Bradford, Pa., 1973-. Mbrships. incl: Mbr., Bd. of Dirs., Pa. Mental Hlth., Inc., 1970-; Warren Co. Mental Hlth. Assn., 1970-, V.P., 1974-; AMA; Am. Psych. Assn.; Pa. Med. & Psych. Socs.; Order of 1st Families of Va.; N.C. Soc. of the Cinn. Plantagenet Soc.; Herald for Soc. of Dscendants of Kts. of Most Noble Order of the Garter. Address: Warren State Hospital, Warren, PA 16365, U.S.A. 138.

MANNEN, Paul Thomas, b. 15 Oct. 1909. Business Executive; Management Consultant. Educ: Mont. State Coll.; Univ. of Wash. Seattle. Appts. incl: Mng. Off: Hilo-Kona Savings & Loan Assn., Hawaii, 1963-70; Hawaii Mem. Gardens Inc., Hilo, 1963-65; Mauna Kea Mem. Pk., 1965-; Hawaii-Hilo Corp., 1964-72; Mauna Kea Corp., Hilo, 1963-; Dir., Ruddle Sales & Serv., ibid, 1965-68 & Ruddle Equipment Co., 1965-68. Mbrships incl: Pres., Calif. State Jr. Chmbr. of Comm., 1944 & Kilauea Coun., Boy Scouts of Am., Hilo, Hawaii, 1972; Pres., Easter Seal Soc. for Crippled Children & Adults, ibid, 1972-73; Master, La Mesa Lodge No. 407 Free & Accepted Masons of Calif., 1933; V.P., San Kiego Conven. & Tourist Bur., Calif., 1959-61; Pres., San Diego & Imperial Cos. Football Offs. Assn., 1950. Address: P.O. Box 576, Hilo, HI 96720, U.S.A. 78.

MANNERS, Norman Donald, b. 10 Dec. 1927. Company Director. Appts: Var. appts. as reporter, feature writer & ed. of newspapers, trade & tech. jrnls., U.K., 1944-54; Serv. in Cameron (Queen's Own), & Argyll & Sutherland Highlanders, 1945-48; Ctrl. Off. of Info., 1954-57; Chief Press Off., Dept. of Scientific & Industl. Rsch., London, 1957-63; Dir. i/c, Parker PR Assocs. Ltd., Dir. Roles & Parker Ltd., 1963-. Mbrships. incl: Assoc., Assn. of British Sci. Writers, 1959-; Inst. of PR, 1965-; Fellow, Inst. of Dirs., 1965-; Bd. of Mgmt., PR Cons. Assn., 1970-73. Author of sev. papers on Public Relations & Information Techniques; Major contbr. to The Science Directory in Basic English, 1965. Address: Parker PR Assocs. Ltd., 22 Red Lion St., London, WC1R 4PX, U.K.

MANNING, Olivia. Novelist & Critic. Publs: The Wind Changes, 1938; The Remarkable Expedition, 1947; Growing Up (short stories), 1948; Artist Among the Missing, 1949; School for Love, 1951; A Different Face, 1953; The Doves of Venus, 1955; My Husband Cartwright (short stories from 'Punch'), 1956; The Great Fortune, 1960; The Spoilt City, 1962; Friends & Heroes, 1965; A Romantic Hero (short stories), 1967; Extraordinary Cats, 1967; The Play Room, 1969; The Rain Forest, 1973. Address: c/o Messrs. William Heinemann, 16 Queen St., London W.1., U.K. 1.

MANNING, Patricia Cripe (Mrs. John T. Manning), b. 27 Aug. 1928. Educator. Educ: B.Sc., Univ. of Tampa, Fla., 1960; M.Ed., Univ. of Fla., Gainesville, 1964; Geo. Peabody Coll., Nashville, Tenn.; Univ. of Southern Fla., Tampa; Doct. Cand., Nova Univ., Ft. Lauderdale, Fla. Appts: Classroom Tchr., Elem., Jr. & Sr. High Schls.; Guidance Cnslr.; Asst. Prof. & Coll. Coord. of Student Tchrs., Fla. Technol. Univ., Orlando, Fla. Mbrships: Past Pres., Gamma Kappa Chapt., State Altruistic Chmn., & Vice-Chmn., Dist. III, Alpha Delta Kappa; Past Pres., ACEI; Fndr. & sev. offs., Brandon Jr. Woman's Club, Brandon, Fla.; Brevard, Fla. & Southern Assns. Children Under Six; Am. Childhood Educ. Int.; Am. Educ. Rsch. Assn.; Mid-S. Educ. Rsch. Assn.;

Nat. Sci. Tchrs. Assn.; AAUP. Publs: An Assessment of the Effects of a Stimulation Game on Individual's Attitudes Toward Inner-City Low Socio-Economic Life Styles. Hons: Outstanding Tchr. Award, 1963, 67; Meritorious Tchr. Award, 1963, 64. Address: P.O. Box 1472, Titusville, FL 32780, U.S.A. 125.

MANNING, Phyllis A. (Mrs. F.J. Manning), b. 2 June 1903. Author-Journalist; Retired Administrative Secretary. Educ: Lasalle Bus. Coll., Pa., U.S.A.; Northern Ariz. Univ., Flagstaff. Appts: Admin. Asst. to Dir. of Finance, City of Miami, Fla., 1933-43; Admin. Asst. to Dir. of Finance, City of Miami, Fla., 1933-43; Admin. Asst. to Hds. of Depts., Yale Univ., New Haven, Conn., Univ. of Miami, Fla., & Northern Ariz. Univ., 1945-62; Writer, Pam's Pantry news column on high altitude cookery, Ariz. Daily Sun, 1958-63. Mbrships. incl: Pres., Pilot Int., 1974-75, Lt. Gov. & Gov., Dist. 14; Pres., Pilot Club, Flagstaff; Pres., Flagstaff Writer's Club; Pres., Ariz. Press Women, 1965-66; Chmn., Coconino Co. Democratic Ctrl. Comm., 18 yrs. Publs: From Sun-Up to Star-Twinkle, 1961; Spirit Rocks & Silver Magic, 1962. Hons. incl: Sr. Citizens Creative Achievement Award, for Spirit Rocks & Silver Magic, Ariz. State Fair Assn., 1964; Citizen of the Yr., & elected to Flagstaff Hall of Fame, 1969. Address: Route 1, Box 876, Flagstaff, AZ 86001, U.S.A. 30.

MANNO, Francis Joseph. University Professor. Educ: Ph.D., Georgetown Univ., Wash. DC, U.S.A. Appts: Analyst, U.S. Govt.; Asst. Prof., Villanova Univ.; Prof., SUNY, Brockport; Gen. Sec., World Org. of Int. Law. Mbrships: Mexican Acad. of Int. Law; Trustee, SW Kan. Hist. Soc.; AAUP; Am. Hist. Assn.; Latin Am. Conf. on Hist.; Am. Acad. of Pol. & Soc. Sci.; Phi Alpha Theta; Univ. Club of Mexico; World Org. Int. Law; UN Comm. Contbr. of num. articles to various publs. Address: State Univ. of New York, Brockport, NY 14420, U.S.A. 6, 13, 14.

MANNUCCI, Edgardo, b. 10 June 1904. Sculptor. Educ: Acad. Delle Belle Arti, Rome, Italy; Individual tuition by Master Sculptors. Appts. incl: Tchr., Rome Acad. of Fine Arts, Italy; Dir., Art Insts. of Cagli, Fano & Ancona. Sculptures incl. Monument to Int. Red Cross, Solferino, Italy. Examples of work in int. Mus.' inclng. Rijksmuseum Kröller-Müller, Otterlo, Netherlands; Nat. Mod. Art Gall., Rome, Italy; Mus.' of Mod. Art, Dallas, Buffalo & N.Y., & Carnegie Inst., Pitts., U.S.A. Address: 91 Via Degli Olimpionici, 00196 Rome, Italy. 43.

MANOFF, Richard Kalman, b. 24 June 1916. Chairman, Advertising Agency. Educ: B.S., CCNY, 1937; M.S., ibid, 1940. Appts. incl: Asst. Dir., War Manpower Commn. for N.Y., 1942; Dir. of Marketing, Welch Grape Juice Co.; V.P. & Chmn., Marketing Plans Bd., Kenyon & Eckhardt, 1952-56; Chmn. & Chief Exec. Off., Richard K. Manoff Inc. Advt. Agcy., specialising in advt. & marketing of packaged goods, 1956-; U.S. Deleg., FAO Conf., Rome, 1966; Special Missions, Agcy. for Int. Dev., U.S. State Dept., to India, 1969, Ecuador & Brazil, 1972; Bd. of Trustees, World Educ. Inc., 1972-; Participant & Lectr., num. Confs. on Advt., Nutrition & Family Planning. Mbrships. incl: Am. Assn. Advt. Agcys.; Past-Gov., ibid; Bd. of Dirs., Nat. Outdoor Advt. Bur., 1970-; Bd. of Govs., Nat. Acad. TV Arts & Scis.; Nat. Planning Coun.; Bd. of Dirs., Planned Parenthood-World Population, 1971-; Mystery Writers of Am. Publs: Papers on Nutrition. Author, over 100 radio plays for var

mystery series. Address: 845 Third Ave., N.Y., NY 10022, U.S.A.

MANOS, George, b. 10 Mar. 1929. Conductor; Pianist; Administrator. Educ: Julliard Schl. of Music. Appts: Pianist, White House, Wash. D.C., 1948-52; Nat. Oratorio Soc., 1957-67; Wash. Bach Festival, 1957-67; Conductor, Nat. Ballet, Arena Stage Prods., 1964-69; Exec. Dir., Wilmington Schl. of Music, Del., 1971-; Fndr., Conductor, & Music Dir., Killarney Bach Festival, Ireland. Fac. Mbr., Am. Univ.; Fac. Mbr., Cath. Univ. of Am., Wash. D.C. Publs: Compositions for voice, chorus, chamber orch. Hons. incl: Commendation, Royal House of Greece, 1955; Ecclesiastic Order for cultural contrbn., Archbishop of Australia, 1957. Address: 6905 Millwood Rd., Kenwood Pk., Bethesda, MD 20034, U.S.A. 7, 117.

MANRAJ, Abdool Shakoor, b. 25 July 1925. Barrister-at-Law; Queen's Counsel. Educ: B.A. Lincoln Univ., Chester Co., Pa., U.S.A., 1948; Dip. in Int. Jurisprudence, Columbia Univ., N.Y., Middle Temple, London, U.K. Law Prac. at Bar, Guyana; Chief Legal Advsr., Guyana United Muslim Party, Int. Commn. of Jurists, 1965; Q.C. (Sr. Counsel), 1969. Mbrships: Guyana Bar Assn., formerly on Exec.; Georgetown Cricket Club; Guyana Motor Racing Club. Address: Temple Chambers, 185 Charlotte & King Sts., Lacytown, Georgetown, Guyana, S. America. 109, 136.

MANSAGER, Felix N., b. 30 Jan. 1911. Business Executive. Appts: Serv. Salesman, Hoover Ltd., 1929; V.P., Sales, ibid, 1959; Exec. V.P. & Dir., 1961; Pres. & Chmn., 1966. Mbrships. incl: Nat. For. Trade Coun., Inc.; Coun. on For. Rels.; Nat. Bus. Coun. Consumer Affairs; Pilgrims U.S.A.; Bd. of Trustees, Ohio Fndn. Independent Colls.; Steering Comm., Strathclyde Univ.; Newcomen Soc. in N.Am.; Hon. mbr., World League of Norsmen; Trustee at Large, Independent Coll. Funds of Am.; Chmn., ibid, 1974; Mbr. & Gov., Ditchley Fndn.; Assoc. Chmn., Nat. Bible Week, 1972; Bd. of Regents, Exec. Comm., Capital Univ., Columbus, Ohio; Rotary Int.; 32nd Degree Mason, Masonic Shrine. Hons: LL.D., Capital Univ., 1967, Strathclyde Univ., Scotland, U.K., 1970; Kt., 1st Class, Order of St. Olav, Norway, 1971; D.H.L., Malone Coll., Canton, Ohio, 1972; Medal of Hon., Vaasa Univ., Finland, 1972; Grand Off., Dukes of Burgundy, 1968; Chevalier, Order of Leopold, Belgium, 1969; Marketing Award, British Inst. Marketing, 1971; Award, Canton Chmbr. of Comm., 1971; C.B.E., 1973; Chevalier, Legion of Hon., France, 1973; Fellow, Univ. Coll., Cardiff, Wales, U.K., 1973. Address: The Hoover Co., N. Canton, OH 44720, U.S.A. 1, 2, 8, 12, 16, 34, 69, 123.

MANTERE, Sampsa Pellervo, b. 11 June 1913. Bank Managing Director. Educ: B.Sc., Univ. of Helsinki, Finland; M.Sc., ibid, 1938. Appts. incl: Asst. to Mng. Ed., Maaseudun Tulevaisuus, 1938-45; Chief, Advsry. Dept., Maataloustuottajain Keskusliitto Pellervo Soc., 1949-50; Mng. Dir., ibid, 1950-56; Vice Chmn., Bd. of Dirs., Pellervo Soc. Market Rsch. Inst., 1950-56; Mng. Dir., Ctrl. Union of Finnish Coop. Banks, 1956-; Vice Chmn., Bd. of Dirs., Ctrl. Bank of Coop. Banks of Finland Ltd., 1967-72; Vice Chmn., Bd. of Dirs. Land & Indl. Mortgage Bank Ltd., 1968-72; Vice Chmn., Bd. of Dirs., Security Fund of the Coop. Banks, 1970-. Num. mbrships. incl: Vice Chmn., Advsry. Comm. of Finnish Financial Instns., 1958-; Vice Chmn., Export Assn. Delegation, 1974-; Bd. of Admin., Kirjayhtymä, 1965-;

Chmn., Bd. of Dirs., Mainosyhtymä Oy, 1950-55; Org. Comm., Finnish Red Cross, 1963-; Ctrl. Admin., Save the Children Assn., 1963-72. Publs: Num. articles in jrnls. Hons: 4 awards, Order of Cross of Liberty; Order of White Rose of Finland. Address: Osuuspankkien Keskusliitto r.y., 23 Arkadiankatu, SF-00100 Helsinki 10, Finland.

MANUWA, (Sir) Samuel Layinka Ayodeji, b. 4 Mar. 1903. Surgeon; Medical Administrator. Educ: King's Coll., Lagos; Univ. of Edinburgh, U.K.; Schl. of Tropical Med., Univ. of Liverpool. Appts: Med. Off., Surg. Specialist, Sr. Surg. Specialist, Dpty Dir., Dir. & Insp. Gen. of Med. Servs., Chief Med. Advsr. to Fed. Govt. of Nigeria, Colonial Med. Serv. in Nigeria, 1927-59; Mbr., Fed. Pub. Serv. Commn. of Nigeria, 1952-; Pro-Chancellor & Chmn., Coun. of Univ. of Ibadan, 1967-. Fellow & Past Pres., var. profl. orgs. Articles, sci. jrnls., tropical med. & surg., pub. hlth. admin., mental hlth. Hons. incl: O.B.E., 1948; C.M.G., 1953; Kt. Bachelor, 1956; C.S.J., 1959; var. acad. degrees & awards, & Nigerian traditional chieftaincies. Address: Fed. Public Service Commission, Independence Bldg., Tafawa Balewa Sq., Private Mail Bag 12586, Lagos, Nigeria. 1, 20, 34, 35, 43, 135.

MANWELL, Reginald Dickinson, b. 24 Dec. 1897. Protozoologist. Educ: M.A., Amherst Coll., 1926; Sc.D., Johns Hopkins Univ., 1928. Appts. incl: Instr., Johns Hopkins Univ., 1929-30; Prof. Zool., Syracuse Univ., 1930-63; Prof. Emeritus & Rsch. Assoc., ibid, 1963-. Past Treas., V.P., & Pres., Soc. of Protozoologists, 1951-63. Past V.P., & Pres., Rocky Mt. Biological Laboratory, Crested Butte, Colo., 1958-68. Trustee, ibid, 1950-. Mbr. many scientific socs. Publs: Author or co-author Practical Malariology; The Church Across the Street; Introduction to Protozoology; Contbr. of num. articles to scientific jrnls. Hons. incl: Annual Rsch. Award, Syracuse Chapt. Sigma Xi, 1959; Sc.D., Syracuse Univ., 1963. Address: Hoag Ln., Fayetteville, NY 13066, U.S.A.

MAO, Yi-Sheng (T.E.Mao), b. 9 Jan. 1896. Engineer; Educator. Educ: B.C.E., Tangshan Engrng. Coll., China, 1916; M.C.E., Cornell Univ., Ithaca, N.Y., U.S.A., 1917; Dr.Eng., Carnegie Inst. of Technol., Pitts., Pa., 1920. Appts. incl: Pres., Hohai Engrng. Coll., Nanking, China, 1924; Prof. & Pres., Nat. Peiyang Univ., Tientsin, 1927; Engrng. Dir., Chien Tang River Bridge, Hangchow, 1933; Pres., Tangshan Engrng. Coll., 1938; Dir., Off. & Bridge Engrs., Kweiyang, 1942; Gen. Mgr., China Bridge Co., Chunking, 1943; Pres., Chiao Tung Univ., Peking, 1949; Dir., Railways Rsch. Inst., Peking, 1951; Chmn., Bd. of Cons. Engrs., Yang-tze River Bridge at Hankow, 1954. Mbrships. incl: Deleg., Nat. Peoples Congress, 1954, 1959, 1964, Standing Comm., 1956, 1959, 1964; Pres., Civil Engrng. Soc. of China, 1953-; Pres., Sci. & Technol. Assn. of Peking, 1960. Publs: Chien Tang River Bridge, Hangchow, 1950; Yang-tze River Bridge at Hankow, 1958; Articles in profl. jrnls. Recip., Achievement Medal, Chinese Soc. of Engrs., 1941. Address: Railways Research Institute, Peking, China.

MAPLES, Evelyn Lucille (Palmer), (Mrs. William E. Maples), b. 7 Feb. 1919. Editor; Writer. Educ: Southwest Mo. State Coll. Appts: Tchr., 1937-38; Proofreader, Herald Publng. House, Independence, Mo., 1953-63; Proofroom Supvsr., Copy Ed. & Asst. Ed., ibid, 1963-. Mbrships: Community Assn. for Arts; Mo. Writers Guild; Good Govt. League. Publs: (Poetry) That Ye Love, 1971; What Saith the Scriptures; (Relig. Juvenile Fiction) Norman Learns about the Sacraments; Jomo the Missionary Monkey; Norman Learns about the Scriptures; Lehi, Man of God; The Brass Plates Adventure; The Many Selves of Ann-Elizabeth, 1973. Author of poems in anthol., Poetic Voices of the Restoration. Writer of 2 plays & contbr. of num. articles, poems & short stories to various relig. periodicals. Recip. Award, Midwestern Books Competition, 1973. Address: c/o Herald Publng. House, Drawer HH, Independence, MO 64055, U.S.A. 5, 30, 130, 132, 138.

MAPLESDEN, Douglas Cecil. b. 30 Oct. 1919. Director of Research. Educ: D.V.M., Ont. Veterinary Coll., 1950; M.S.A. (Nutrition), Univ., of Toronto, 1951; Ph.D., Cornell., 1959. Appts: Assoc. Prof.-Prof., Ont. Veterinary Coll., Guelph, Canada, 1953-60; V.P., Tech. Servs., Stevenson, Turner & Boyce, London, Ont., 1960-63; Dir., Animal Hlth. Rsch. & Dev.-Gen. Mgr., Animal Hlth. Div., CIBA Pharmaceutical Co., Three Bridges, N.J., 1963-69; Dir., Animal Hlth. Rsch. & Dev., E.R. Squibb & Sons Inc., ibid, 1969. Mbrships. incl: N.Y. Acad. Sci; Am. Mgmt. Assn; Am. Veterinary Med. Assn; Am. Soc. of Animal Prod. Author, Handbook of Nutrition, 1962. Address: Three Bridges Road, Three Bridges, NJ 08887, U.S.A. 6, 14.

MAPP, Alf Johnson, Jr., b. 17 Feb. 1925. Author; Historian; University Professor. Educ; Coll. of Wm. & Mary, Williamsburg, Va.; A.B., Coll. of Wm. & Mary, Norfolk, 1961. Appts: Edit. Writer, Assoc. Ed. & Edit. Chief, Portsmouth (Va.) Star., 1933-53; News Ed., Columnist & Edit. Writer; Norfolk Virginian-Pilot, 1953-58; Freelance Writer, 1958-; Lectr.-Instr.-Asst. Prof. Assoc. Prof., Engl. & Am Lit., Creative Writing, Jrnlsm. & Hist., Old Dominion Univ., Norfolk, 1961-. Mbrships. incl: Edit. Bd. Va. Independence Bicentennial Commn., 1968-; Publs. Comm., 350th Anniversary of Rep. Govt. in Western World, 1967-69; Edit. Bd. Jamestown Fndn., 1967-; Va. Writers Club; V.P., Poetry Soc. Va., 1971; Nat Edit. Conf ; Va. Comm. for Lib. Dev.; Dir. YMCA Youth & Govt. Fndn. Publs: The Virginia Experiment; The Old Dominion's Role in the Making of America, 1957; Frock Coats & Epaulets, 1963, '70; America Creates Its Own Literature, 1965; Just One Man; The Widening World of Judson Punaway, 1968. Contbr. to New York Times, learned jrnls. & mags.; film & T.V. scripts. Nominee Pulitzer Prize for Edits., 1953; Recip. Troubadour Gt. Tchr Award, 1969. Address: 225 Grayson St., Portsmouth, VA 23707, U.S.A. 1, 3, 7, 13, 30, 57, 85, 129, 131.

MARAIS, Johannes (Jan) Stephanus, b. 23 Apr. 1919. Banker. Educ: B.Comm.; D.Comm.; F.I.A.C.; F.C.W.A.; Doct. in Econ. Sci., Univ. of Potchefstroom, 1969. Appts. incl: Sec., Mgr ; Dir., major cos. in Fed. Grp.; Fndr., Mng. Dir., Chmn. & Chief Exec. Off., Trust Bank of Africa Ltd.; former Pres. & Chmn., Handelsinstituut; Chmn., Trust Accepting Bank, Trust Growth Fund Admnstrs. Ltd., Trust Finance Corp. Ltd., Trust Property Corp. Grp., Trust Express Grp., Trust Bldg. Soc., S. African Metropolitan Life Assurance Co. Ltd. & Trust Hotels; Dir., Indl. Dev. Corp. of S.A. Ltd., Indl. Selections Ltd., Goodyear Tyre & Rubber Co. & Leyland Motor Corp.; Pres., Univ. of S. Africa Fndn. Mbrships. incl: Bd. Mbr., sev. acad., cultural & profl. bodies. Publs: num. articles & addresses in fields of Econs., Finance & Banking. Hons. incl: Hon. Life Fellowship, Inst. of Admin. & Commerce, S. Africa, 1969; Marketing Man of the Yr., Inst. of Marketing Mgmt., 1969. Address: P.O. Box 2116, Cape Town, S. Africa. 38.

MARANS, Moissaye, b. 11 Oct. 1902. Sculptor; Educator. Educ. incls: Technological Inst. of Bucharest, Roumania, 1923; Univ. of Jassy, 1924; Cooper Union Inst., U.S.A., 1925-27; Nat. Acad. of Design, N.Y., 1927; Pa. Acad. of Fine Arts, Phila., 1928; Cinn. Acad. of Fine Arts, Ohio, 1929-31; Beaux Arts Inst. of Design, N.Y., 1932-33; N.Y. Univ. Appts: Mbr., Edit. Bd., Nat. Sculpture Review, 1952-; Mbr., Panel of Artists-Advisers, U.A.H.C., 1954-; Lectr., Brooklyn Coll., 1955-. Mbrships: Nat. Acad. of Design N.Y.; Allied Artists of Am. Inc.; Fellow, Nat. Sculpture Soc.; Archtl. League of N.Y.; Audubon Artists, Inc. Pub. Commns. & Collects. incl: Carl Linnaeus, Brooklyn Botanical Gdns., N.Y.; Eloquence & Friendship, N.Y. World's Fair, 1939-40; Immaculate Heart of Mary, W. Baden Coll., Ind.; Family at Prayer, Temple Emanu El., Houston, Tex.; The Ten Commandments, First Presby. Ch., Beloit, Wis.; Swords into Ploughshares & Book Against the Sword, Har Zion Temple, Phila., Pa.; Prince of Peace, Ch. Ctr., UN Plaza, N.Y.; Swords into Ploughshares, U.S. Atomic Energy Commn., Wash., D.C.; Four Figures, Smithsonian Instn., Mus. of Natural Hist., Wash., D.C. Recip., num. awards for sculpture inclng: Daniel Chester French Medal, Nat. Acad. of Design, 1967; 2 from the Allied Artists of Am. Inc., 1967, '68; 3 from Nat. Sculpture Soc., 1963, '65, '72; Exhibd. extensively in U.S. & abroad. Address: 200 Clinton St., Brooklyn, NY 11201, U.S.A. 2, 37, 55.

MARAR, Tawfic Salim, b. 14 Nov. 1913. Engineer; Contractor. Educ: grad. as Civil Engr., Univ. St. Joseph/Ecole Superieure d'Ingenieurs, Beirut, Lebanon, 1939. Appts: Civil Engr., Pub. Works, Jordan, 1939, promoted thru' Dist. Engr. & Chief of Tech. Dept. to become Undersec. of State, 1948; civil engrng. contracting firm "Gen. Equipment Co.", estab. "ETS T. MARAR", for contracting & trading in hardware, tools, surveying equipment, sanitary ward, fittings, etc., 1958; Pres., "Middle E. Bldg. Materials Co."; V.P. Amstel Brewery, Jordan. Mbrships: Fndr. & Pres., Engrs. & Archts. Soc. of Jordan, 1948-62; Pres., (Amman), Zone Chmn., Dep. Dist. Gov., Dist. Gov. for Lebanon & Jordan, Lions Club, 1967-68; Sec., Jordan Humanitarian Soc. Has designed & executed schls., hosps., chs., pvte. apts., houses & bldgs. Company has built roads, bridges, phosphate mines, dams in Jordan Valley (jt. venture), water distribution project for Zerka & housing project in Aquaba. Hons: Kt., Order St. Sylvester Pope, 1952; Official, Order of Merit of Italian Repub., 1967; Silver Medal, Kts. of Order of Holy Sepulchre, 1954. Address: P.O. Box 1569, Amman, Jordan.

MARCATANTE, John Joseph, b. 3 Mar. 1930. Educator; Author. Educ: A.B., Brooklyn Coll., N.Y.C., 1955; M.S., Hunter Coll., ibid, 1957. Appts. incl: Instr., Hunter Coll., 1963; Instr., Grad. Schl., Queens Coll., N.Y.C., 1965-67; Asst. Prin., Astoria Intermediate Schl., N.Y.C., 1967-. Mbrships. incl: Executive Bd. Mbr. at Large, N.Y. Soc. Experimental Study of Educ.; Nat. Coun. Tchrs. of English; Coun. Suprvsry. Assns.; N.Y.C. Tchrs. English Assn. Publs: Identification and Image Stories, 1963; American Folklore and Legends, 1967; MacMillan Gateway English Series, 1967; Ed., 14th Yearbook, N.Y. Soc. for Experimental Study of Educ.; Contbr. to var. profl. jrnls.; Poetry in var. publs. Address: 34-51 9th St., Long Island City, NY 11106, U.S.A. 6.

MARCELLETTI, Mario, b. 3 Sept. 1909. Economist. Educ: B.Econs., Bocconi Univ., Milan, Italy, 1932. Appts: Labour Insp.-Chief, Int. Affairs Dept., Min. of Labour, Rome, 1934-48; Div. Mbr., Int. Labour Off., Geneva, Switzerland, 1948-55, Dpty. Dir., Field Off. Latin Am., Lima, Peru, 1955-57; Dir., E.N.I., Rome, 1957-60; Dir., Rels. w. Int. Dev. Progs., Italconsult, 1961-64; Dir., Dev. Assistance Progs., Int. Labour Off., Geneva, 1964-69. Mbrships: Soc. italiana per l'org. int.; Assn. Dév. & Progrés, Paris; Assn. degli italiana dipendenti da organizzazioni int. Publs: Economics of Land Reclamation & Settlement in Sardinia (prizewinner); contbr. to books & profl. publs. Hons: Kt. of the Kingdom, 1937; Cmdr., Order of Merit of Repub., 1971. Address: Riserva S. Antonio, Via Clarice Tartufari 161, 00128 Rome, Italy. 43.

MARC'HADOUR, Germain P., b. 16 Apr. 1921. Roman Catholic Priest. Educ: Ordained Priest, Diocese of Vannes, France, 1944; M.A., Cath. Univ. of the W., Angers, 1945; Docteur ès Lettres, Sorbonne, Paris, 1969. Appts: Tchr., Diocesan H.S., Pontivy, 1945-52; Prof., Medieval Engl., Cath. Univ. of the W., Angers, 1953-; Received into 3rd Order of St. Francis of Assisi, 1954; Fulbright Rsch. Fellow, Yale Univ., U.S.A., 1960-61; Dir., Moreana Quarterly, 1963-; Vis. Lctr., sev. univs., Europe & Am. Mbrships: Fndr. & Int. Sec., Amici Thomae Mori, 1962-; Guillaume Budé Assn., Paris; Renaissance Soc. of Am., N.Y.C.; Cath. Record Soc., London, U.K. Publs. incl: L'Univers de Thomas More (1477-1536), 1963; Thomas More et la Bible, 1969; The Bible in the Works of St. Thomas More, 5 vols., 1969-72; Thomas More, ou la Sage Folie, 1971; Contbns. to books, ency., & jrnls. Hons; Sev. fellowships & dips. Address: B.P. 858, 49005 Angers Cedex, France. 43.

MARCHAL, Maurice Pierre Marie, b. 28 Dec. 1913. Engineer; Port Director. Educ: Polytech. Schl.; Nat. Schl. of Bridges & Rds.; Licence ès scis. Appts: Engr., Bridges & Rds., Montbélird, 1938, Besançon, 1939, Lyon, 1942, Marseille, 1947; Exploitation Chief, Port of Marseille, 1948; Chief Engr., Bridges & Rds., Chief, Commercial Exploitation of Strasbourg Port, & Dpty. to Regional Dir. of Navigation, 1953; Dir. Gen., Strasbourg Port, Chief Engr., Navigation Serv., & Regional Dir. of Navigation, 1961-. Mbrships: Pres. Dir. Gen., SILOSTRA Soc. & La Traction de l'Est; Admin. Couns., num. ports. Author, var. articles on maritime transportation. Hon: Off., Legion of Hon., 1967. Address: 3 Allée Spach, 67000 Strasbourg, France.

MARCHAL, Raymond, b. 11 Mar. 1910. Engineer. Educ: Polytech. Schl.; Nat. Aeronautical Schl.; Nat. Inst. of Nuclear Scis. & Techniques. Appts. incl: Tech. Dir., Nat. Soc. of Study of Construction of Aviation Motors, 1945-54; Dir., Atomic Div., ibid, 1956-64; Scientific Dir., 1964-; Prof., Nat. Aeronautical Schl., 1941-57; Hon. Prof., ibid, 1957-; Prof., Nat. Schl. of Rural Engrng., 1954-66; Hon. Prof., ibid, 1966-; Prof., Nat. Inst. of Nuclear Scis. & Techniques, Saclay, 1963-71. Mbrships. incl: V.P., French Soc. of Encouragement of Nat. Ind.; Improvement Comm., Cath. Inst. of Arts & Trades, Lille, 1963-. Publs. incl: Moteurs d'Avions, 1945; La Thermodynamique. Hons: Cmdr., Legion of Hon., 1969; Aeronautic Medal, 1948; Cmdr., Acad. Palms, 1972; Chevalier, Agricl. Merit, 1964; Inst. Laureate. Address: SNECMA, 22 Quai Galliéni, 92150 Suresnes, France. 43, 50, 91.

MARCIAL, Victor A., b. 23 Feb. 1924. Physician; Radiation Oncologist. Educ: B.S., Univ. of Puerto Rico, 1944; Harvard Med. Schl., U.S.A., 1949; Trng. in Therapeutic Radiol., U.S.A., France, U.K., & Sweden, 1951-55. Appts: Gen. Practitioner, Trujillo

Alto Hlth. Ctr., Puerto Rico, 1950-51; Dir., Cancer Control for Puerto Rico, 1955-65; Prof., Dir., Radiation Therapy Univ. of Puerto Rico Schl. of Med., 1958-; Dir., Radiotherapy & Cancer Div., Puerto Rico Nuclear Ctr., 1958-; Assoc. Dir., Med. Progs., ibid, 1967-. Mbrships. incl: Pres.-Elect, Am. Radium Soc.; Pres., Puerto Rico Radiol. Soc.; Councellor, Radiol. Soc. of N. Am. & Interam. Coll. Radiol.; Pres., X Interam. Cong. of Radiol., etc. Author, over 40 publs. on cancer & radiation therapy. Recip., num. profl. hons. Address: P.O. Box 20581, Rio Piedras, Puerto Rico 00928. 17.

MARCILESE, Mario, b. 27 May 1925. Lawyer; Poet; Writer; Novelist; Literary Critic; Journalist. Educ: Fac. of Law, Nat. Univ. of La Plata, Argentina. Appts: Fndr. & Dir. of review FARO, 1952; Sec., Supreme Ct. of Justice, Province of Buenos Aires, 1962-. Mbrships: Sec., La Plata Br., Writer's Soc. of Argentina, 1956; Jockey Club, Province of Buenos Aires; Students Club of La Plata; num. cultural assns. of Argentina & Spanish-Am. Publs. incl: (Novels) El Fronterizo; El Coyote; Los Ilusos; (Plays) Los pseudos; La máscara viva; La senda. (Poetry) Horas tristes; Cuadro vivo. Articles in newspapers & reviews in Spanish-America, U.S.A. & Europe. Hons: Bicolour Order of Guatemalan Culture; Dip. of Hon., 1966, Cross of Merit, 1967, Panamerican Assn. for Cultural Interchange. Address: Casilla de Correo 217, La Plata, Province of Buenos Aires, Argentina. 136.

MARCILLE, Yves Emile, b. 26 Mar. 1915. Inspector General of Finances. Educ: Fac. of Law, Rennes, France; Licencié en Droit. Appts: Asst., Gen. Insp. of Finances, 1946, Insp., 1948; Under-Dir., State Sec. of Econ. Affairs, 1951; Asst. Dir., ibid, 1953; Tech. Advsr., Cabinets of Edgar Faure, 1952-55; Hd., Price Serv., Min. of Finances & Econ. Affairs, 1955-62; Asst. Deleg. Gen., Profl. Assn. of Banks, 1963, Deleg. Gen., 1965-; Insp. Gen. of Finances, 1969-; V.P., Sicovam, 1972-; Dir., Revue Banque, 1967-. Mbr., Racing-Club of France. Hons: Off., Legion of Hon.; Off., Nat. Order of Merit; Cross, War of 1939-45; Cmdr., Nat. Econ.; Chevalier, Agricl. Merit. Address: 18 Rue La Fayette, 75009 Paris, France. 43, 91.

MARCUS, Jacob Rader, b. 5 Mar. 1896. Educator. Educ: A.B., Cinn. Univ., 1917; Rabbi, Hebrew Union Coll., 1920; Ph.D., Berlin Univ., Germany, 1925; Special study, Paris, France & Jerusalem, 1925-26; Ph.D., Cinn. Univ., U.S.A., 1950; LL.D., Dropsie Coll., 1955. Appts: 2nd Lt., 145th Inf., U.S. Army, 1917-19; Instr. Bible, Rabbinics Hebrew Union Coll., 1920; Asst. Prof.-Prof., Jewish Hist., 1926-59; Adolph S. Ochs Prof. Am. Hist., 1959-65; Milton & Hattie Kutz Disting. Serv. Prof. Am. Jewish Hist., 1965-. Mbrships: Dir. Am. Jewish Archives, 1947-; Am. Jewish Periodical Ctr., 1956-; V.P., Ctrl. Conf. Am. Rabbis, 1947; Pres., 1949; Trustee, Jewish Publ. Soc., Am.; Hon. Pres., Am. Jewish Hist. Soc.; Jewish Acad. Arts & Scis.; Am. Acad. Jewish Rsch.; B'nai B'rith. Publs. incl: The Rise and Destiny of the German Jew, 1934; An Index to Jewish Festschriften, 1937; Studies in American Jewish History, 1969. Hons: Frank L. Weil Award, Nat. Jewish Welfare Bd., 1955; Lee M. Friedman medal for disting. serv. to hist., 1961. Address: 401 McAlpin Ave., Cinn., OH 45220, U.S.A.

MARDELLIS, Anthony, b. 17 July 1920. Professor of Mathematics. Educ: A.B., Univ. of Calif., Berkeley, 1950; M.A., ibid, 1952; grad. work, 1950-55. Appts: Asst. in Math., Univ. of Calif., Berkeley, 1951-55; Instr., Loyola Univ.,

L.A., 1955-56; Asst. Prof., Calif. State Univ., Long Beach, 1956-62; Asso. Prof., ibid, 1962-70; Prof., 1970-. Mbrships: French Math. Soc.; Am. Math. Soc.; Math. Assn. of Am.; Sigma Xi. Publs: The monodromic group & the Picard-Vessiot theory (Bulletin of Am. Math. Soc.), 1957; The monodromic group & the Picard-Vessiot theory 11 (Notices of Am. Math. Soc.), 1959. Address: Dept. of Math., Calif. State Univ., Long Beach, CA 90840, U.S.A 14.

MARDER, Dorie. Artist. Educ: Sorbonne, Paris, France; Art Students League, N.Y., U.S.A. Exhibs. incl: San Fran. Mus.; Nat. Acad. of Design; Brooklyn Mus.; Audubon Artists; N.Y. Univ.; Riverside Mus.; Art U.S.A.; Seattle Art Mus.; Long Is. Univ.; Lehigh Univ.; Mich. State Univ.; Polizzo Vechio, Florence, Italy; Pompeian Pavillion, Naples; Arts Gall., Manila Philippines; Artists Equity Gall., N.Y., U.S.A. Mbrships. incl: Nat. Assn. Women Artists; League of Present Day Artists; Artists Equity Assn. Perm. Collects. incl: Safed Mus., Israel; Norfolk Mus.; Idaho Mus.; U.S. State Dept. Hons: 1st Prize, Graphics, Nat. Assn. Women Artists, 1961; Montag Award, oil painting, Nat. Assn. Women Artists, 1965; 1st Prize, Village Art Ctr., 1955, '58. Address: 223 W. 21st St., N.Y., NY 10011, U.S.A. 5, 6, 37.

MARGETTS, Edward Lambert, b. 8 Mar. 1920. Physician; Educator. Educ: B.A., Univ. of B.C., Canada, 1941; M.D., C.M., McGill Univ., 1944; Dip. Psych., ibid, 1944; F.R.C.P., Canada. Appts: Asst. to Dir., Allan Mem. Inst. of Psych., Montreal, 1949-51; Med. Sup., Mathari Mental Hosp., Nairobi, Kenya, 1955-59; Chief of Serv., Shaughnessy Hosp., Vancouver, Canada, 1964-70; WHO Expert Advsry. Panel & Cons., 1967-; Med. Off. i/c., Mental Hlth. Servs., WHO, Geneva, Switzerland, 1970-72; Prof., Psych., Lectr., Hist. of Med., Univ. of B.C., Canada, 1959-; Hd., Dept. Psych., Vancouver Gen. Hosp., B.C., 1972-. Mbrships. incl: Canadian & Am. Psych. Assns.; Royal Coll. Psych.; Royal Microscopic Soc. Publs: var. tech. papers & book chapts. on psych. int. hlth., hist. of med., & anthropol. Address: Dept. of Psych., Vancouver Gen. Hosp., 700 W. 10th St., Vancouver 9, B.C., Canada. 9, 14, 54.

MARGINSON, Raymond David, b. 13 Dec. 1923. Civil Servant; University Administrator. Educ: B.Com., Dipl. Pub. Admin., Melbourne Univ., Australia; Australian Admnstrve. staff Coll., 1957. Appts: Australian Commonwealth Pub. Serv., 1945-65; Exec. Off., Australian Transport Advsry. Comm., 1945-50; Sr. Finance Off. & Sec., Nat. Security Resources Bd. Comm. on Transport, Postmaster Gen.'s Dept., 1950-61; Exec. Off. to Dir. Gen., ibid, 1961-63; Controller (Finance) & Finance Mbr., H.Q. Tender Bd. & Dpty. Asst. Dir. Gen., 1963-65; V.P., Univ. of Melbourne, 1966; Mbr., Univ. Gov. Coun., 1967. Mbrships. incl: Athenaeum Club; Rotary Club of Melbourne; Univ. House; Chmn., Works of Art Comm., Melbourne Univ. Author of profl. papers. Australian Eisenhower Fellow, 1968. Address: Univ. of Melbourne, Parkville, Vic., Australia 3052. 23.

MARGOLIN, Edythe (Mrs. Gerald J. Margolin). Educator. Educ: B.A., UCLA, 1955; M.A., ibid, 1959; Ed.D., 1963. Appts: incl: Lectr., State Univ., San Fernando, Calif., 1970-71; Vis. Assoc. Prof., Univ. of Miami, Coral Gables, Fla., 1969-70 & 1971-72; Assoc. Prof., Schl. of Educ., Fla. Int. Univ., 1972-. Mbrships: World Org. for Educ. of Young Children; Assn. for Educ. of Young Children; Am. Acad. of Pol & Soc. Sci.; Nat. Assn. for Educ. of Young Children. author of articles in profl. jrnls. inclng. 'Conservation of

Self-Expression in Young Children, Young Children, 1968; 'Young Children's Impressions of the Pupil-Role', Sociocultural Elements in Early Childhood Education, 1974; Selected Articles for Elem. Schl. Prins., 1968. Address: Fla. Int. Univ., Schl. of Educ., Tamiami Trail, Miami, FL 33144, U.S.A. 5, 9, 14, 120.

MARGOLIN, Solomon, b. 16 May 1920. Company President. Educ: B.S., Rutgers State Univ., New Brunswick, N.J., U.S.A., 1941; M.S., ibid, 1943; Ph.D., ibid, 1945. Appts: Rsch. Biologist, Silmo Chem. Co., 1947-48; Sr. Pharmacologist, Asst. Dir.-Dir., Biol. Rsch., Schering Corp., 1948-54; i/c Pharmacol. rsch. & initial clin. pharmacol. in man, Maltbie Labs., Div. Wallace & Tiernan, Inc., 1954-56; V.P., Biol. Rsch., Wallace Labs., Div. Carter-Wallace, Inc., 1956-68; Pres., Affiliated Med. Rsch. Inc. (Biol. Rsch.), Princeton, N.J., 1968-. Mbrships: Am. Soc. Pharmacol. & Expl. Therapeutics; Am. Chem. Soc.; Soc. Expl. Biol. & Med.; N.Y. Acad. Scis.; Soc. Animal Prod.; Endocrin Soc.; Am. Pharmacol. Assn.; Am. Assn. Advmt. Sci. Publs. incl: Profl. jrnl. articles, Effects upon Physiological Systems, (b) Nonbarbiturates, 1963; Selective Inhibition of Dog Spinal Vasoconstrictor Tracts by Mebutamate (w. O.J. Plekss & E.J. Fedor), 1963; Effect of Benzyl N-Benzyl Carbethoxyhydroxamate (W-398) on Experimental Atherosclerosis and Hypercholesteremia (w. F.M. Berger, J.F. Douglas & B.J. Ludwig), 1963. Address: P.O. Box 5700, Princeton, NJ 08540, U.S.A. 6, 14.

MARINO, Domenico, b. 5 Nov. 1910. Lawyer. Educ: Classical studies; Grad. Law, 1933; Grad. Philos., 1942. Appts: Lectr., Hist. & Philos.; Mbr., Fiscal Magistrature, Caltagirone Tribunal; Mbr., Coun. of Order of Lawyers, Caltagirone. Mbrships: Legion d'Oro; Tiberina Acad., Rome; Teatina Acad., Pescara; Ctr. of Logic & Comp. Sci., Bologna; Sicilian Soc. of Nat. Hist., Palermo; Soc. of Nat. Hist. of Eastern Sicily, Univ. of Catania. Publs. incl: Intorno alla natura giuridica del matrimonio dopo il Concordato, 1936; Appunti di filosofia seculativa e pratica, 1946; Kant, tratteggi e rilievi, 1947; Acqueforti, 1949; Le tregue, 1951; Pane Azzimo, 1953; Vetri al sole, 1956; Rosa Rossa, 1974. Recip., Off. of Repub., 1957. Address: Via Giovanni Verga 10, Caltagirone (CT), Italy.

MARINO, Vittore, b. 30 June 1914. Mathematician; Artist. Educ: Grad. Maths., Acad. of Naples, 1945. Appts: Lectr., Maths., Phys., & Art, 1946-; Lectr., Armellini Ind. Tech. Inst., Rome. Mbrships: Tiberina Acad.; Acad. of Sci. & Art, Abruzzo; Mod. Art. Gall., Rome; Archives of Living Art Dict., Rome. Works incl: Portraits of Mio Nonno; M. Picone; Dwight Eisenhower; G. Cannizzaro; Il bacio dell'Aurora; Leda ed il cigno; Le esperidi; A. Vampanignia; Incendio di Castel San Angelo. Recip., Marzotto Prize. Address: Via Mario Musco 73, 00147, Rome, Italy.

MARIUS-MARIN, Popescu, b. 17 Oct. 1927. University Professor of Agronomy; Horticultural Engineer. Educ: Inst. of Agronomy, 1947-51; Dr. in Agronomy, 1965. Appts: Asst. Lectr., & Hd. of practical work, Inst. of Agronomy, Craiova, 1951-65; Prof., Univ. of Craiova, 1966-, Dean, Fac. of Horticulture, 1968-. Co-opted Mbr., Acad. of Agricultural Scis. of Romania, 1970-. Author, 65 scientific publs., inclng. printed courses in fruit-growing & specialized fruit-growing. Recip., Scientific Merit Medal, 1966. Address: Severinului St., Block 11, Apt. 8, Craiova, Rumania.

MARK, D. Arthur, b. 26 Nov. 1905. Appraiser of Antiques & Works of Art; Antiquarian. Appts. & activities: During yrs. after 1926, Mgr., Br. Antiquary, 696 Fulton St. & 115 S. Portland Ave., Brooklyn, N.Y.; Later, Mgr., Harry Mark Antiquary & Art Gall. of Brooklyn, & of its Restoration & Interior Designing Depts.; has carried out restoration & appraisal work for pvte. clients. Address: The Harry Mark Antiquary & Art Gall. of Brooklyn, 753 Fulton St., Brooklyn, NY 11217, U.S.A. 105.

MARK, Phyllis (Mrs. Alan Mark). Artist. Educ: Ohio State Univ. Kinetic Sculptor working in metal. Mbrships: Sculptors League; Archl. League of N.Y. One man Exhibs: Ruth White Gall., N.Y., 1966, '68; Gimpel & Weitzenhoffer Gall., ibid, 1973; Drew Univ., Madison, N.J., 1968; Fontana Gall., Pa., 1972. Collects. incl: Dickerson-White Mus., Cornell Univ.; Syracuse Univ. Perm. Collect.; Lowe Mus., Fla.; RCA Corp. Collect.; Blair Collect.; Am. Nat. Collect., Galveston, Tex. Exhibs. incl: Columbia Univ., 1968; Drew Univ., 1969; N.Y. Archl. League, 1969; Lowe Mus., Fla., 1970; Baruch Coll., N.Y.C., 1970; Morris Mus., N.J., 1970; Hudson River Mus., 1971, '72; Inst. Contemporary Art, Boston, Mass., 1973; N.Y.C. Dept. Cultural Affairs Exhib., World Trade Ctr., 1974; Benson Gall., Bridgehampton, N.Y., 1974. Address: 803 Greenwich St., N.Y., NY 10014, U.S.A. 37.

MARK, Robert (Sir), b. 13 Mar. 1917. Commissioner of Police. Appts: Constable to Chief Supt., Manchester City Police, U.K., 1937-57; Chief Constable of Leicester, 1957-67; Asst. Commnr., Metropolitan Police, 1967-68; Dpty. Commnr., ibid, 1968-72; Commnr. of Police of the Metropolis, 1972-. Mbrships: Standing Advsry. Coun. on the Penal System, 1966; Assessor to Lord Mountbatten's Inquiry into Prison Security, 1966; Advsry. Comm. on Police in Northern Ireland, (the Hunt Comm.), 1969. Hons: Queen's Police Medal for Disting. Serv., 1965; LL.M., Leicester Univ., 1966; Vis. Fellow, Nuffield Coll., Oxford, 1970. Address: New Scotland Yard, Broadway, London SW1H OBG, U.K. 128.

MARK, Shelley Muin, b. 9 Sept. 1922. Economist; Journalist. Educ: B.A., Univ. of Wash., 1943; M.S., Columbia Univ., 1944; Ph.D., Econs., Univ. of Wash., 1956. Appts. incl: Instr., Univ. of Wash., 1946-48; Asst. Prof., Ariz. State Coll., 1948-51; Territorial Economist DPS, Hawaii, 1951-53; Prof., Econs., Univ. of Hawaii, 1953-62; Dir., Econ. Rsch. Ctr., ibid, 1959-62; Dir., Dept. of Planning & Economic Dev., State of Hawaii, 1962-. Num. mbrships. incl: Pres., Coun. of State Planning Agencies; Pres., Western Regional Sci. Assn.; State Sci. Advsr.; Commnr., State Land Use Commn.; State Energy Coord.; Dir., Univ. of Hawaii Rsch. Corp.; Gov.'s Advsry. Comm. on Sci. & Technol.; Bd. Mbr., Coun. of State Govts.; Phi Beta Kappa; Am. Econ. Assn.; Royal Econ. Soc. (England). Publs: The Economy of Hawaii in a Period of National Defense Mobilization; Contbr. to U.S., for. jrnls. Recip., 2 Ford Fndn. Fellowships. Address: Dept. of Planning & Economic Dev., State of Hawaii, P.O. Box 2359, Honolulu, HI 96804, U.S.A. 2, 9, 13, 14, 139.

MARKE, David Taylor. Author; Public Relations Executive. Educ: B.A., M.A., LL.B. Colo. Univ. Appts: Feature & Educ. Ed., Assocd. Press, 10 yrs.; Dir., P.R., Toy Guidance Coun., 4 yrs.; Dir., P.R., Transogram Corp., 3 yrs.; Owner P.R. firm, 7 yrs.; V.P.-Pres., Barber & Baar Assocs. Inc., 1967-73; V.P., P.R. Div.,

George J. Abrams & Assocs., N.Y., 1973-. Mbrships: P.R. Soc. of Am. Author of var. books. Recip. sev. awards, Educ. Writers Assn. Address: George J. Abrams & Assocs., 655 Madison Ave., N.Y., NY 10021, U.S.A. 6, 24.

MARKER, Leonard K., Composer. Educ: Studied composition w. Alban Berg; Acad. of Mus, Vienna, Austria. Appts: Fac., Hunter Coll., NYC., U.S.A.; Staff Composer at Erwin Piscators Dramatic Workshop, etc. Hon. Mbr. of Alban Berg Soc. Publs. incl: Composer of symphony music, motion picture scores; Musicals for Stage, Tilted Hat, Ministry is Insulted, Why do You Lie, Cherie; Co-author w. Olin Downes, Ten Operatic Masterpieces; Contrib., articles N.Y. Times, Opera News, Musical America, etc. Address: 150, Claremont Ave., N.Y., NY 10027, U.S.A. 6, 86.

MARKEY, Gene, b. 11 Dec. 1895. Writer; Retired Naval Officer. Educ: B.S., Dartmouth Coll. Appts. incl: Active Duty, 1st Lt., U.S. Army, 1917-19; Lt.Cmdr.-Rear Admiral, U.S.N., 1941 until retirement, 1955. Mbrships. incl: White's, London; Knickerbocker, N.Y.; The Brook, N.Y. Novels incl: His Majesty's Pyjamas; Amabel; Kentucky Pride; That Far Paraidse; Women, Women, Everywhere. 2 books of caricatures, Literary Lights, & Men About Town, & a profile, Mountbatten. Hons. incl: Legion of Merit; Bronze Star; Legion of Honor (France); Hon. Citizen of Ky., 1957; L.H.D., Rollins Coll. Address: Calumet Farm, P.O. Box 1810, Lexington, KY 40501, U.S.A. 2.

MARKEZINIS, Spyros, b. 9 Apr. 1909. Lawyer. Educ: Grad., Fac. of Law, Univ. of Athens, Greece; Fac. of Pol. & Econ. Sci., ibid. Appts. incl: Legal Advsr. to late King George II, Greece, 1936-46; Legal Advsr. to num. Maritime Cos., Import Cos. & Welfare Inst.; During enemy occupation of Greece, mbr. Supreme Co-ordinating Comm. of Resistance w. Archbishop Chrysnathos & Col.-in-Charge of Army, A. Papagos, 1941-44; elected M.P., Greece, 1946, 1951, 1952, 1958, 1961, 1964; Min. without Portfolio, Mbr. Inner Cabinet, 1949; Min. of Econ. Co-ordination, 1952-54; Ldr. of Opposition, 1954-56; Prime Min., 1973. Legal Publs. incl: The Divorce, 1930; The Head Of State In Modern Democracies, 1935; The Position Of The King In Private Law, 1936; The King As Representing The State From The Point Of View Of International Law, 1938. Pol. & Hist. Publs. inlc: The Road To The People, 1956; Machiavelli & Our Time, 1961; The Political History Of Modern Greece (1928-1964), 8 vols., 5 publd. 1966-73; num. articles & essays in jrnls., encys. & int. newspapers. Hons. incl: num. medals & awards. Address: 5 Lycabettus St., Athens, Greece. 34.

MARKLE, (William) Fletcher, b. 27 Mar. 1921. Film & Television Writer-Director-Producer. Appts. incl: Serv., RCAF, WW II; Contract Scenarist, Orson Welles & Sir A. Korda, London, U.K., 1946; Free-lance Film, Radio & TV Prod. & Dir., 1946-; Dir., Performing Arts, Canadian Pavilion, Expo 67, Montreal, PQ, 1967; Hd., TV Drama, CBC, 1970-. Mbrships. incl: Dirs. Guild of Am.; Dirs. Guild of Canada; Writers Guild of Am.; Prods. Guild of Am.; Acad. of Motion Pictures Arts & Scis.; Acad. of TV Arts & Scis. Radio Series incl: Writer & Actor, Baker's Dozen, CBC, Vancouver, B.C., 1942; Originator, Prod. & Dir., Studio One, CBS, 1947-48. Films incl: Dir., Night into Morning, 1951 & The Incredible Journey, 1963. TV Series incl: Prod. &/or Dir., Studio One, CBS, 1952-53. Father of the Bride, 1956-62; Writer, Host. Prod., Telescope, CBC, 1963-69. Hons: (Studio One) Peabody Award for Radio Drama, 1948;

(Studio One) Christopher Award for TV drama, 1953; (Incredible Journey) Blue Ribbon Award, Box Off. Mag., 1963. Address: 6 Monteith St., Toronto, Canada, M4Y 1K7. 6, 88.

MARKMAN, Sidney David, b. 10 Oct. 1911. University Professor: Art Historian; Archaeologist. Educ: A.B., Union Coll., Schenectady, N.Y., 1934; M.A., Columbia Univ., N.Y., 1936, Ph.D., 1943. Appts. incl: Prof., Art Hist. & Archaeol., Univ. Nacional de Panamá, 1941-45, Duke Univ., N.C. 1947-. Mbrships. incl: Archaeol. Inst. of Am., (V.P., N.C. Chapt., 1947-69); Soc. Archtl. Histns.; Int. Congress of Americanists; Real Acad. de Bellas Artes, Sevilla. Publs: The Horse in Greek Art, 2nd. edit., 1969; San Cristóbal de las Casas y sus monumentos arquitectónicos, 1963; The Colonial Architecture of Antigua Guatemala, 1966; contbr., profl. jrnls. Recip., rsch. grants, Am. Philos. Soc. & Duke Univ. Rsch. Coun. Address: 919 Urban Avenue, Durham, NC 27701, U.S.A. 13, 131.

MARKOVA (Dame) Alicia, b. 1 Dec 1910. Prima Ballerina Assoluta. Appts. incl: Dir., Metropolitan Opera Ballet, N.Y., U.S.A., 1963-; Lectr., Am. univs. & colls., 1963-; Prof., Ballet & Performing Arts, Cinn. Univ., 1971-. Pub. appearances incl: w. Diaghiler Ballet, 1925-29; w. Vic Wells Ballet, London, U.K., 1932-35; w. Markova-Dolin Ballet, 1937-37; w. Monte Carlow Ballet Russe, 1938-41; Prima Ballerina Assoluta, Ballet Theatre, 1941-45; w. Original Ballet Russe, 1946; On Tour w. Dolin, Far E., 1948 & S. Africa, 1949; Co-Fndr. & Prima Ballerina Assoluta, London's Festical Ballet, 1950-52. Guest Prima Ballerina Assoluta w. many famous European ballet cos. & opera houses. V.P., Royal Acad. of Dancing, UK., 1958-. Author of Giselle & I, 1960. Hons incl: C.B.E., 1958; D.B.E., 1963; Hon. Mus.D., Leicester Univ., U.K., 1966. Address: c/o Barclays Bank, 451 Oxford St., London W.1, U.K. 34, 131.

MARKOWSKI, Andrzej, b. 22 Aug. 1924. Conductor & Composer. Educ: Trinity Coll. of Music, London, U.K., 1946-47; Dipl., Conducting, High Music Schl., Warsaw, Poland, 1954; Dipl., Composition, ibid, 1955. Profl. Experience: Asst. Conductor, Poznan Philharmonic, 1955-56; 2nd Conductor, Silesian Philharmonic, Katowice, 1956-58; Chief Conductor, Cracow Philharmonic, 1959-64; Dir., Artistic Leader, Wroclaw Philharmonic, 1965-68; Permanent Conductor, Warsaw Nat. Philharmonic, 1971-; Fndr. & Artistic Leader, Wroclaw Festival Oratorio & Cantata; Conductor in European & Am. tours; Rschr. in Poland on concrete & electronic music for experimental films. Creative Works incl: Music for Ballet, Fantasmoscope; Music for long & short films; Conceived idea & composed music for film, Promenade through Old Town, receiving many int. awards. Hons. incl: Brit. Medal of War, Italy, 1946; Polonia Restituta Order, 1965; Warsaw Min. of Culture Prize, 1969, '71; Polish Composers Union Prize, 1969; City of Wroclaw Serv. Prize, 1968. Address: Aleja Stanów Zjedn. 18/76, Warsaw 03-964, Poland.

MARKS, Charles, b. 28 Jan. 1922. University Professor; Surgeon. Educ: M.B.Ch.B., Univ. of Cape Town Med. Schl., S. Africa, 1945; M.S., Marquette Univ., Wis., U.S.A., 1966; Ph.D., Tulane Univ., New Orleans, 1973. Appts: Cons. Surg., Salisbury Rhodesia, 1953-63; Assoc. Prof., Surg., Marquette Univ. Schl. of Med., U.S.A., 1963-67; Dir., Surg., Mt. Sinai Hosp., 1967-71; Assoc. Clin. Prof., Surg., Case Western Reserve

Med. Schl., 1967-71; Prof., Surg., La. State Univ. Schl. of Med., 1971-. Fellowships: Royal Coll. Surgs., La. State Univ. Schl. of Med., 1971-. Fellowships: Royal Coll. Surgs., U.K.; Am. Coll. Sugrs.; Am. Coll. Cardiol.; Am. Coll. Chest Physns; Royal Coll. Physns., Edinburgh. Mbrships: Am. Thoracic Soc.; SE. Surg. Congress; Pan Pacific Surg. Assn.; Royal Soc. Med. Publs: Applied Surgical Anatomy; The Portal Venous System; A Surgeons World. Named, Clin. Tchr. of the Yr., Aesculapian Soc., 1972. Address: Dept. of Surg., La. State Univ. Schl. of Med., 1542 Tulane Ave., New Orleans, LA 70112, U.S.A. 8, 14, 22.

MARKS, Henry S., b. 26 May 1933. Educational Consultant & Professor Educ: B.B.A., Univ. of Miami, 1955; M.A., ibid, 1956; Univ. of Ala., 1960-64. Appts: Tchr., Jacksonville State Univ., Florence State Univ., Univ. of Ala. in Huntsville; Educ. Cons. & pt.-time Tchr., N.E. Ala. State Jr. Coll. Mbrships. incl: Pres., Southern Region, Regl. Coord. & Popular Culture Assn.; Huntsville Hist. Soc.; Org. of Am. Histns.; Am. Hist. Assn.; Southern, Fla. & Ala. Hist. Assns.; Hakluyt Soc.; Hist. Assn. of S. Fla.; Phi Delta Kappa; Am. Soc. for Pub. Admin: Rotary Club of Huntsville, Ala. Author, The Failure of the United States to Maintain the Independence of Korea and the Effect of the Failure Upon Americans in Korea, 1962, 2nd edit. 1970. Contbr. of articles to publs. in field. Hons. incl: Gov.'s Staff, State of Ala., 1974. Address: 301 Terry-Hutchens Bldg., 102 Clinton Ave. W., Huntsville, AL 35801, U.S.A.

MARKS, Nova Bryant Dickson, b. 28 Aug. 1917. Bilingual Psychological & Educational Counselor. Educ: B.S., Tex. State Coll. for Women, 1939; Hartford Theol. Sem.; Univ. of Tex.; M.A., Tex. Woman's Univ., 1961. Appts: Personnel & Tchng., Am. Inst., United Meth. Ch. Missions, Cochabamba, Bolivia; Instnl. Counselor, Colegio Metodista, Missions S. Am., La Paz, Bolivia; United Meth. Ch., Experimental Educ., Flour Bluff, Tex.; Bilingual Counselor of Elementary Schls. in underdeveloped areas, Austin Pub. Schls., Tex.; Psychological Educl. Counselor. Mbrships: United Meth. Women; Pan. Am. Round Table, Delta Kappa Alpha; DAR; A.P.G.A. Address: 300 E. Berger, Santa Fe, NM 87501, U.S.A. 2, 7, 138.

MARKS, Robert Charles, b. 23 Feb. 1932. Interior Design Educator. Educ: B.S., Roosevelt Univ., Chgo.; Ill., 1953; Dip., Harrington Inst. of Interior Design, ibid, 1956. Appts: Free-lance Interior Designer & Cons Chgo., Ill., 1956-59; Instr. in Interior Design, Harrington Inst. of Interior Design, 1959; Assoc. Dir., ibid, 1960-64; Dir., 1964-68; Dean, 1968- Mbrships. incl: Past Bd., Midwest Chapt., Nat. Soc. of Interior Designers; Am. Inst. of Interior Designer; Inst. of Profl. Designers, London; Am. Inst. of Archts. (Profl. Affiliate); Midwest Regional Chmn. & Bd., Interior Design Educators Coun., 1969-71; Nat. Home Fashions League; Soc. of Archtl. Histns.; Nat. Trust for Historic Preservation; Chgo. Heritage Comm.; Cliff Dwellers Club, Chgo. Address: Harrington Inst. of Interior Design, 410 S. Michigan Ave Ste. 500, Chgo., IL 60605, U.S.A. 8, 120, 133.

MARNITI, Biagia, b. 15 Mar. 1921. Writer; Poet. Educ: Grad. Lit., Univ. of Rome. Appt: Dir., Exec. Off., Nat. Ctr. for Catalogue of Italian Libs. & Bibliographic Info. Mbr., Arcadia Acad., Rome. Publs: Nero amore, rosso amore, 1951; Città, creatura via, 1956; Più forte è la vita, 1957; Giorni del mondo, 1967.

Contbr., var. jrnls. Recip., Lerici Prize, 1956. Address: Via Cola di Rienze 163, 00192 Rome, Italy.

MAROCK; Louise, b. 23 Oct. 1900. Investment Securities Executive. Educ: N.Y.U. Appts: Sec.; Ptnr., W.C. Langley & Co., 1920-35; Executor-Trustee, Chester Dale Estate & other trusts, 1935-. Mbrships: Pres., Silver Cross Philanthropic Soc.; Everglades Club; Beach Club, Palm Beach; Westchester Country Club, Rye, N.Y.; Lake Placid Club. N.Y.; Regency Club, N.Y.C.; Met., N.Y.C. Address: 400 S. Ocean Blvd., Palm Beach, FL 33480, U.S.A. 5, 22, 132.

MAROY, Marcel, b. 29 Apr. 1911. Trade Union Director. Educ: Law Degree, Univ. of Paris, France; Postgrad. Dips., Econs. & Pub. Law. Appts: Nord Steelworks; Min. of For. Affairs; Dir., Fine Steel Prods. Union. Mbrships: Fndg. Pres., Cercle de la Voile de Tromentine; V.P., Nat. Union of Press Attachés; Am. Soc. of Metals; Iron & Steel Inst. Publs: Tech. manuals on rustless & special steels. Hons: Kt., Legion of Honour; Croix de Guerre; Resistance Medal; Volunteer Fighters Medal; Metz Cross; Bronze Star Medal. Address: 5 Villa Chanez, Paris 16, France. 43. 91.

MARPLES, (Lord) Alfred Ernest, (Rt. Hon. the Lord Marples of Wallasey), b. 9 Dec. 1907. Politician; Business Executive. Educ: Stretford Grammar Schl.; Inc. Acct., 1928. Appts: British Army, 1939, Commn., 1941, invalided out Capt., 1944; Fndr., Marples Ridgway & Ptnrs. Ltd., civil engrs., 1945; Conservative M.P. for Wallasey, 1945; Parliamentary Sec., Min. of Housing, 1951-54, Min. of Pensions & Nat. Ins., 1954-55, Postmaster Gen., 1957-59, Min. of Transport 1959-64, Shadow Min. of Technol., 1964-66, Sponsor, Conservative Party Pub. Sector Rsch. Unit, 1967-70; Int. Dir., Purolator Servs. Inc. (U.S.A.), Dir., Purolator Servs. Ltd. (U.K.), 1970-. Mbrships: F.R.S.A., 1969; Pres., Elec. Vehicle Assn. of Gt. Britain, 1973; Pres., Mobile Radio Users Assn., 1974. Author, The Road to Prosperity. Hons: Privy Councillor, 1959; Freeman of Borough of Wallasey, 1970; Life Peer, 1974. Address: 33 Eccleston St., London, SW1W 9NS, U.K. 1, 34.

MARQUEZ, Anibal Roberto, b. 19 May 1914. Doctor in Chemistry. Educ: Pharmaceutical, Dr. in Chem., Univ. of La Plata, Argentina; Sci. Investigator & titular Prof., tchng. profession. Appts: Asst., Adjunct & titular Prof., organic chem., Univ. of La Plata, 1947-73; Hon. Prof., ibid, 1973; Titular Prof., Mil. Schl., 1943-66; Titular Prof., Univ. of Technol.; Sci. Investigator, C.I.T.E.F.A., 1957-58; Assessor Sci., CONICET, 1973-74; Pres., Marquez & Co. (Chem. Prods.), 1958-74; Pres., C.I.N.D.E.F.I. (Nat. Ctr. Investigations & Dev. Indl. Fermentations). Mbrships. incl: Argentine Chem. Assn.; Assn. Fabricantes de Papel; Assn. Argentina para el Progreso de las Ciancias. Author of publs. in field. Address: Entre Rios 1347, Olivos, Pcia. de Buenos Aires, Argentina. 136.

MARRA, Carolyn Christine, b. 10 Oct. 1913. Statistician. Educ: Youngstown Coll. Bus. Schl. Appts: Receptionist, Wean Engrng. Co. Inc., Warren, Ohio, 1935-36; Sec. to Chief Draftsman & Asst. Chief Engr., ibid, 1936-39; Supvsr., Controlled Materials Plan, 1941-45; Supvsr., Accts. Payable Audit, 1945 (co. named changed to Wean Inds. Inc.); currently Statn. for V.P., Sales (co. name changed to Wean-United Inc.). Mbrships. incl: Am. Soc. Women Accts. (charter pres., Youngstown chapt. 72); Past Pres., Warren-Niles Zonta Club,

Zonta Int., Chi Epsilon; Past Sec.-Treas., Friends of the McKinley Mem. Lib. & Mus.; Trustee, Multiple Sclerosis Soc., Tru-Mah-Col chapt., Youngstown, Ohio; Sponsor Xi Eta Chi, Beta Sigma, Niles, Ohio; Nat. Assn. Females Execs. Inc.; Trumbull New Theatre; Int. Hon. Mbr., Beta Sigma Phi. Address: 132 Fulton Ave., Niles, OH 44446, U.S.A. 5, 22, 130, 132, 138.

MARRAS, Efisio Luigi, b. 2 Aug. 1888. Army Corps General. Educ: Royal Artillery Acad; Application Artillery Schl.; War Schl.; Navy War Inst. Appts: Chief of Staff, 5 Army; Mil. Attaché, Italian Embassy, Berlin; Chief of Mil. Mission by German H.Q.; Army Chief of Staff, 1947-50; Defence Chief of Staff, 1950-54; Cahcellor of Order Almerito della Repubblica Italiana, 1954-74. Publs: Artillery During the War 1914-18; Tactical Panorama 1930. Articles in mil. reviews. Hons. incl: Grand Officer. Finnish Order of White Rose, 1930; Cmdr., Order of Sts. Mauritius & Lazar, 1946; Grand Cross, Order of Almerito della Repubblica Italiana, 1952; Grand Cross, Greek Order of Phoenix, 1953; Grand Officer; La Legion d'Honneur, 1954. Address: Via Francesco Siacci 12, 00197 Rome, Italy. 43, 95.

MARREY, Lucien M., b. 7 June 1901. Retired Bank Manager. Educ: Bach. Science & Letters. Appts: Dir., Banque Jordaan, 1934-61; Adminstr., SRPI, 1945-; Adminstr., Vaucluse Automobiles, 1945-; Pres., Societe d'Etudes Petrolieres, 1948-72; Pres., Baker Int. S.A., 1955-72. Mbr., Automobile Club de France. Address: 62 Ave. de New York, Paris 75016, France.

MARROZZINI, Luigi, b. 30 July 1933. Art Dealer; Lecturer. Educ: Grad., Univ. Leonardo da Vinci, Rome, Italy. Appts: Owner & Dir., Galería Colibrí, San Juan, Puerto Rico, 1963-; Jury Mbr., 3rd Int. Miniature Print Show, Pratt Graphics Ctr., 1968; Organizing Comm. Mbr., Sec. Tech. Advsr., San Juan Bienal of Latin Am. Graphic Art, 1970, 1972; Lectr., Technique & Hist. of graphic art. Mbr., Am. Fedn. of Arts. Author, Catalog Raisoneé for the complete Orozco Graphics, 1969. Introductions, var. catalogues of exhibs. at Colibrí Gall. Portfolios, graphic works of Latin Am. & Puerto Rican artists. Address: Box 1734, San Juan, PR 00903, U.S.A.

MARSDEN, Brian Geoffrey, b. 5 Aug. 1937. Astronomer. Educ: B.A., Oxford Univ., U.K., 1959; M.A., ibid, 1963; Ph.D., Yale Univ., U.S.A., 1966. Appts: Asst. in Rsch., Yale Univ. Observ., 1959-65; Astronomer, Smithsonian Astrophysical Observ., Cambridge, Mass., 1965-; Lectr., Astron., Harvard Univ., 1966-; Dir., Ctrl. Bur. for Astronomical Telegrams, Int. Astronomical Union, 1968-. Mbrships: Int. Astronomical Union;V.P., Comm. 20, ibid, 1973-; Am. Astronomical Soc.; Treas., Div. on Dynamical Astron., ibid, 1970-72; Royal Astronomical Soc.; Astronomical Soc. of Pacific; Sigma Xi; British Astronomical Assn. Publs: Ed., The Earth-Moon System (w. A.G.W. Cameron) 1966; Ed., The Motion, Evolution of Orbits & Origin of Comets (w. others), 1972; Catalogue of Cometary Orbits, 1972; Ed., Int. Astronomical Union Circulars, 1968-. Contbr. to astronomical jrnls. Hons: Merlin Medal, British Astronomical Assn., 1965. Address: Smithsonian Astrophysical Observatory, 60 Garden St., Cambridge, MA 02138, U.S.A. 6, 14.

MARSH, John, b. 5 Nov. 1904. Theologian; College Principal. Educ: Yorks. United Theol. Coll. Bradford; M.A., Edinburgh Univ., 1928; Mansfield & St. Catherine's Colls., Oxford Univ.; M.A., D.Phil., Oxford, 1943. Appts. incl: Min., Congreg. Ch., Otley, Yorks., 1934-38; Tutor & Chaplain, Mansfield Coll., Oxford, 1938-49; Prin., ibid, 1953-70; Prof. of Christian Theol., Nottingham Univ., 1949-53. Mbrships. incl: Moderator, Free Ch. Fed. Coun. of Engl. & Wales, 1970-71; Chmn., Jt. Comm. for Union of Congregs. & Presbys., 1965-70; Chmn., Buttermere Parish Coun., 1973-. Publs: The Living God, 1942; Congregationalism Today, 1943; The Fulness of Time, 1952; The Significance of Evanston, 1954; A Year With the Bible, 1957; Contbr. to Essays for Karl Barth, 1957 & Pelican Commentary on St. John, 1967. Hons. incl: D.D., Edinburgh Univ., 1955; CBE, 1964. Address: Rannerdale Close, Buttermere, Cockermouth, Cumberland CA 13 9UY, U.K. 1, 2, 9, 43.

MARSH, John (Henry), b. 17 Aug. 1913. Company Director; Management Consultant; Author; Lecturer. Appts: Dir., Inst. of Personnel Mgmt., London, U.K., 1947-49; Dir., Indl. (Welfare) Soc., 1950-61; Dir.-Gen., British Inst. of Mgmt., 1961-73; Asst. Chmn., ibid, 1973-. Mbrships: Coun., Northern European Mgmt. Inst., Oslo, Norway, 1971-; Exec. Comm., European Coun. of Mgmt.; Coun. for Tech. Educ. & Trng. for Overseas Countries, 1962-; Advsry. Coun., Civil Serv. Coll., 1969-. Publs: People at Work, 1957; Partners in Work Relations, 1959; Work & Leisure Digest, 1960; Ethics in Business, 1970. Named lectures incl: Clarke Hall Lecture, 1957; McLaren Mem. Lecture, 1962; Tullis Russell Lecture, 1967; Frank Geden Foster Lecture, 1973. Hons: D.Sc., Bradford Univ., 1967; C.B.E., 1967. Address: Management House, 43 Parker St., London WC2 5PT, U.K.

MARSHALL, Bryan Edward, b. 24 Oct. 1935. Physician; Researcher; Teacher. Educ: Leeds Univ. Med. Schl., U.K., 1953-59; M.B., Ch.B., 1959; F.F.A.R.C.S., 1962; M.R.C.S., 1963; E.C.F.M.G., 1963; M.D., 1967; M.A., Univ. of Pa., U.S.A., 1971; Dipl., Am. Bd. Anesthesiologists, 1973; Fellow, Am. Coll. Anesthesiologists, 1974. Appts. incl: Registrar, United Cambridge Hosps., U.K., 1961; Elmore Rsch. Schlr., Cambridge Univ., 1963; Rsch. Fellow, Univ. of Pa., U.S.A., 1965; Asst. Prof., ibid, 1968; Assoc. Prof., 1970; Prof. of Anesthesia, 1972-; Prof. of Comparative Anesthesia, 1973-. Mbrships. incl: Assn. of Univ., Anesthetists; Am. Physiological Soc.; Respiration Comm. Mbr.; Am. Soc. of Anesthesiologists; Am. Trauma Soc.; Assn. of Anesthetists, U.K.; Am. Thoracic Soc.; AAAS; AAUP. Author of 60 sci. papers. Hons: Rsch. Prize, Assn. of Aneasthetists, Gt. Britain, 1965; Rsch. Career Dev. Award, N.I.H., Heart & Lung, 1970. Address: Dept. of Anesthesiol., Hosp. Univ. of Pa., 3400 Spruce St., Phila., PA 19104, U.S.A. 6.

MARSHALL, Dara Nusserwanji, b. 25 April, 1906. Professor of Library Science Educ: B.A., Univ. of Bombay, India, 1927, M.A., 1930, Dip. Lib., 1944. Appts: Univ. Libn., Univ. of Bombay; Prof. & Hd., Dept. of Lib. Sci., ibid now Prof. Emeritus. Mbr. of var. profl. socs. Publs: Mughals in India-a Bibliographical Survey, Vol. I., 1967; contbr. to profl. jrnls. Pres., Lib. Confs., India, 1964 & 1969. Recip. of Viceroy's Gold Medal, 1927. Address: 18 Military Sq., Bombay 1, India. 93.

MARSHALL, Eleanor Catherine (Mrs. Paul L. Marshall). Health Therapy Administrator. Educ: Grad., Boston Continuation Schl.; Continuing Educ., Therapeutic Recreation. Appts: Dir., Therapeutic Recreation Prog.,

Elmachri Convalescent Home, Norwich, Conn.; Training Site Dir., ibid; Chmn., Plenary Coun., State Dept. of Hlth; Mbr. & Past Chmn., Regional Prog. Dirs. Mbrships. incl: Pres., Woman's City Club of Norwich; Exec. Bd. Mbr., Conn. State Fedn. of Womans Clubs; Dir., Voluntary Action Ctr., Coun. Ch. Women, Norwich Symph. Assn., United Wkrs. (Pvte. Non-Profit Corp.) Pub. Hlth.; Chmn., Pub. Hlth. Nursing Serv. Comm.; Vice Chmn., Rook Nook Home for Children; Pres., W. Side PTA; Mbr., Citizens' Task Force, Radio Stn. WICH, Norwich, Conn. Nomination, Hon. Mbr., Norwich Jaycee Wives, 1969. Address: 46 Surrey Ln., Norwich, CT 06360, U.S.A. 130.

MARSHALL, John. Carl, b. 25 Feb. 1936. Silversmith-Goldsmith; Teacher. Educ: B.F.A., Cleveland Inst. of Art, Ohio, 1965; M.F.A., Syracuse Univ., N.Y., 1967. Appts: Asst. Prof., Schl. of Art, & Chmn., Metalworking Area, Syracuse Univ., N.Y., 1965-70; Assoc. Prof., Art Dept., Chmn., Metalworking Area, Univ. of Wash., Seattle, 1970-. Mbrships: Educ. Comm., Soc. of N. Am. Goldsmiths; Am. Crafts Coun.; Northwest Designer Craftsmen; Friends of the Crafts; Pacific Northwest Art Ctr. One-man shows: Lowe Art Ctr., Syracuse Univ., 1967; Joseph I. Lubin House, ibid, 1967; Lowe Art Ctr., 1970; Henry Art Gall., Univ. of Wash., Seattle, 1973. Num. other exhibitions. Works incl: Lavabo Bowl & cruets for Altar, Cathedral of Immaculate Conception, Syracuse, N.Y.; Chancellor's Bowl, commnd. by Syracuse Univ. for its Centennial Yr. Hons. incl: Am. Metalcraft Award, Nat. Enamels Exhibition, Craft Alliance Gall., St. Louis, Mo., 1970; Decorative Arts Award, Rochester Finger Lakes Exhibition, Mem. Art Gall., Rochester, N.Y., 1970; 2nd Prize in metalry, 22nd Nat. Decorative Arts & Ceramics Exhibition, Wichita, Kan., 1972. Address: Art Dept., Univ. of Wash., Seattle, WA 98105, U.S.A. 37, 117.

MARSHALL, Margaret Fisher (Mrs. Charles D. Marshall), b. 15 Mar. 1914. Educator. A.B. cum laude, Calif. Univ., U.S.A.; Postgrad. work, ibid & Univ. de Chile. Appts: Hd., Drama Dept. & Instr., Engl., Centerville Union H.S., Calif., U.S.A.; Tchng. Fellow, Am. Lit., Univ. de Chile, Santiago; For. Serv. Clerk, U.S. Embassy, ibid; Asst., Cultural Attaché, ibid; Asst. Headmistress, Rosemary Hall, Greenwich, Conn., U.S.A.; Special Asst., Chmn., Bd. Trustees, ibid; Special Asst., Pres., The Choate Schl. & Rosemary Hall, ibid. Mbrships: Phi Beta Kappa; Sigma Delta Pi; Pi Lambda Theta; Pi Delta Phi; Pres., Greenwich, Conn., Coun. Girl Scouts, Am.; Pres., Greenwich Br., AAUW; Chmn., Cancer Comm., Greenwich Hlth. Assn. Publs: Sor Juana Inés de la Cruz; Eugene O'Neill, El Mercurio; Carl Sandburg, El Mercurio; Autores Contemporáneos Norteamericanos, El Mercurio. Hons: Kraft Prize, 1930; Homenaje del Inst. Chileno Norteam., 1944; Rosemary Medal, 1971. Address: 115 Old Ch. Rd., Greenwich, CT 06830, U.S.A. 5.

MARSHALL, Mary Eleanor, b. 13 May 1939. Physical Education Professor. Educ: B.S., W. Va. Univ., U.S.A., 1961; M.S., Tenn. Univ., Knoxville, 1964; Study for Ed.D. degree, N.C. Univ., Greensboro, 1969-. Appts: Num. short or pt.-time positions w. var. soc. orgs., 1957-65; Phys. Educ. Tchr., Frederick H.S., Md., 1961-63; Phys. Educ. Instr., Towson State Coll., Balt., ibid, 1964-66; Asst. Prof. Phys. Educ., Marshall Univ., Huntington, W. Va., 1966-. Mbr. & holder of positions in num. univ. & extra-mural soc. orgs. in field; Marlin Club Delta. Creative works incl: Dir: Marlin Club Aquatic Art Show, 1962, Dolphin Club Water Carnival, 1961, '62 & Modern Dance Spring

Concert, Marshall Univ., 1972; Performed in Synchronized Swim Show, Tenn. Univ., 1964; Balt. Field Hockey & Lacrosse Assn. Team, 1964-66; U.S. Field Hockey Assn. Regional Championships, Balt., 1965; Presented Lect.-Demonstration on Methods of Teaching Beginning Tennis, 1962; Teaching Modern Dance on the Secondary School Level, 1966. Selected mbrship. Alpha Delta Kappa. Address: 1671 6th Ave., Apt. 5, Huntington, WV 25703, U.S.A. 125.

MARSHALL, William Bly, b. 22 Nov. 1915. Lawyer. Educ: A.B., Yale Univ., 1937; LL.B., Univ. of Pa. Law Schl., 1940. Appts. incl: Lawyer, Cravath, Swaine & Moore, N.Y.; Dir., Tri-Continental Corp., N.Y.C.; Dir., Phelps Mem. Hosp., Tarrytown, N.Y. Mbrships: Am. & N.Y. State Bar Assns.; Bar Assn., City of N.Y.; Ardsley Country Club, Ardsley-on-Hudson, N.Y.; Wall St. Club, N.Y. Hons: Letter of Commendation, U.S. Navy, 1946. Address: 28 Washington Ave., Irvington, NY 10533, U.S.A. 16.

MARSIGLI, Maria Luisa (Marchesa Marsigli Rossi Lombardi), b. 4 May 1922. Writer. Educ: Dr., Classical Lit., Bologna Univ., Italy; Dr., Jurisprudence, Modena Univ., ibid. Lectr. on Italian Hist. & culture; Recent Work: Poems, 1969; La Marchesa e i demoni, 1973. Mbrships: Authors Guild Inc.; Frederick Lewis Allen room in N.Y. Lib., U.S.A.; Nat. Org. for Women; N.Y. Civil Liberties Union; Schaben Int. Address: 225E 72nd St., N.Y., NY 10021, U.S.A.

MARSTON, Doreen. Publishers' Editor; Journalist. Educ: Pvte. Appts: former Engl. Rep., Little, Brown, firm in Boston, Mass., U.S.A., & Alfred Knopf Inc., N.Y.C.; formerly Publrs.'s Ed. w. Hutchinsons of London, & Michael Joseph; currently Publr.'s Ed., Macmillan Ltd., London, & William Collins Ltd., Mbr., PEN Club, London. Former contbr., literary column, Providence Jrnl., R.I., U.S.A. Address: 4 Roberts Mews, Lowndes Pl., London, SW1X 8DA, U.K.

MARTAL, Pierre, b. 21 Dec. 1919. Appraiser of Old Pictures; Picture Restorer. Educ: Menton Secondary Schl. Appts: Picture Restorer for Nat. Museums, 1948; Appraiser, Cts. of Justice, 1958, Sr. Tariff Comm. of Customs, Paris, 1965, Auction-rooms, 1965, French & for. assurance cos. (lloydm etc.). Mbrships: Menton Lawn Tennis Club, 1934-; Pres., ibid, 1962-. Recip., Departmental Drawing Prize, 1935. Address: 1 Sq. Victoria, 06500 Menton, France, 105.

MARTELL, Terrence Foster, b. 29 Jan. 1946. University Professor. Educ: B.A., Iona Coll., 1967; Ph.D., Bus. Admin., Pa. State Univ., 1973. Appts: Asst. Prof., Finance, Univ. of Ala., 1972; Mbr., Grad. Fac., ibid, 1973. Mbrships: Omicron Delta Epsilon; Phi Kappa Phi; Am. Finance Assn.; Financial Mgmt. Assn.; State Sec., Southern Finance Assn. Contbr. to profl. jrnls. Address: Dept. of Finance, Economics & Business Law, Box J, University, AL 35486, U.S.A.

MARTIN, A., b. 8 Sept. 1937. Publishing Executive. Educ: B.A. Stanford Univ., 1959; Grad. Study, ibid, 1959-61. Appts: Ops. Mgr. Emporium, Capwell Corp., 1961-64; Ed., Bus./Economics/Maths., Prentice-Hall, Inc., 1964-70; Gen. Mgr., Educ. Products Div., Milprint Inc. (Philip Morris), 1970-71; V.P., N.Y. Inst. of Finance, 1972-73; Pres., ibid, 1973-. Mbrships: Bay Area Shippers Assn.; Sec.-Treas., ibid; Am. Maths. Assn.; Wall St.

Trng. Dirs. Assn. Address: 2 New York Plz., N.Y., NY 10004, U.S.A. 6.

MARTIN, Anita L., b. 18 Nov. 1905. Professor. Educ: A.B., Univ. of Kan., 1927; M.A., 1937, Ph.D., 1951, Univ. of Wis. Appts: Assoc. Prof., Spanish, Western Coll., Oxford, Ohio, 1954-55; Prof., Spanish, Chmn., Mod. Langs., ibid, 1955-58; Prof., Spanish, Chmn. of Dept., Wilson Coll., Chambersburg, Pa., 1958-61; Residence Dir., Cook Co. Schl. of Nursing, 1961-62; Assoc. Prof.-Prof., Art Hist. & Spanish, Grove City Coll., Pa., 1962-67; Assoc. Prof.-Prof., Fine Arts, Univ. of Pitts. at Johnstown, ibid, 1967-. Mbrships Coll. Art Assn. of Am.; MLA; Delta Kappa Gamma. Contbr. to Cath. Ency. of Am., 1964. Holder of travel-study grants from Univ. of Pitts., summers 1969-73, to visit museums & study works of art in Italy, Netherlands, U.K., France, Greece, Austria, Germany, Switzerland & Belgium. Address: Univ. of Pitts. at Johnstown, Johnstown, PA 15904, U.S.A. 5, 6, 13.

MARTIN, Anthony Vines, b. 27 July 1941. Artist. Educ: H.S.; Self Taught in Art. Married Beverly Ann Martin; 2 sons. Appts: incl: Profl. Artist for 13 yrs. Paintings incl: Texas Home, Jack Brooks, U.S. Congressman; West Texas, Ben Banns; Gate to Nowhere, Mr. Kenneth Franzheim; Kite Flyer, Ann Blyth. Works noted in Houston Post, Houston Chronicle, N.Y. Times, Dallas Times Herald, Dallas Morning News, Wall St. Jrnl., S.W. Art Gall. Mag. Hons. incl: Accepted in Houston Mus. of Fine Arts, 1966-67 & '68-'69, Dallas Mus. of Fine Arts, 1970-71, Jewish Community Ctr. Annual 1968-69, Laguna Gloria Mus., 1968, Rice Univ., Houston, 1969, E. Tex. State Univ., 1970-71; One man shows in DuBose Gall., Houston, Long View Civic Ctr., 1971, San Antonio Jr. League, 1967, Hinkey Gall, N.Y., 1967. Address: Rte. 1, Box 120, Annona, TX 75550, U.S.A. 19, 133.

MARTIN, Bill R., b. 30 May 1941. Lawyer. Educ: Union Univ., Jackson, Tenn., 1959-61; B.S., Memphis State Univ., 1961-63; J.D., Memphis State Univ. Schl. of Law. Appts: Chmn., Henderson Ct. Revenue Comm., 1968, '70, '72, '73; Elected, Henderson Co. Quarterly Ct., 1970-72. Mbrships: Tenn. Bar Assn.; Jackson-Madison Co. Bar Assn.; Commercial Law League Am.; Pres., Lexington Jaycees, 1970; Legal Counsel, Region 14, State of Tenn. Jaycees, 1971-72. Hons: Outstanding Jaycee, Lexington Jaycees, 1970; Over the Top Awards, W. Tenn. Heart Assn., 1970-71, '71-72, '72-73; Cancer Crusade Award, 1969; Cert. of Appeciation, Am. Nat. Red Cross, 1972. Address: 43 North Broad, Lexington, TN 38351, U.S.A. 125.

MARTIN, Cimbro. Musician. Educ: Royal Acad. of Music. Appts: Performer, 1939-; Prof. & Examiner, Hd. of Jr. Dept., Festival Adjudicator, Guildhall Schl. of Music & Drama, 1945-; Fellow, ibid, 1962-. Mbrships: Assoc., Royal Acad. of Music; Inc. Soc. of Musicians; Royal Acad. of Music Club; Brit. Fedn. of Music Festivals. Contbr. articles on technique & interpretation to Music Teacher. Inaugurated a composers' publng. co., direct to the pub. Hons: Thalberg & Elizabeth Stokes Schlr. Address: c/o Guildhall Schl. of Music & Drama, John Carpenter St., London EC4 TCM, U.K. 4.

MARTIN, Cora Arleta, b. 30 Sept. 1923. Equal Employment Opportunity Specialist & Federal Women's Program Coordinator. Educ: Grad., Commercial Dept., Bowling Green Bus. Univ., Ky. Appts: Clerk & Payroll Clerk, War Dept., Tullahoma, Tenn., 1943-46; Payroll

Clerk, VA & Dept. of Agric., Atlanta, Ga., 1946-51; Personnel Rep., U.S. Army Corps. of Engrs., Tullahoma, Tenn., 1951-60; Personnel Specialist & Fed. Women's Prog. Coord., U.S. Army Rocket & Guided Missile Agcy. & U.S. Army Missile Cmd., Redstone Arsenal, Ala., 1960-73; Equal Employment Opportunity Specialist & Fed. Women's Prog. Coord., U.S. Army Missile Cmd., ibid, 1973-. Mbrships. incl: Pres., Tenn. Fed. Bus. & Profl. Women's Clubs, Inc., 1961-63; Parliamentarian, ibid, 1971-72; Pres., N. Ala. Chap., Federally Employed Women, 1971-72; corresp. sec., ibid, 1970-71; Chmn., Bedford Co. Heart Unit. Address: 502 Riverview Dr., Shelbyville, TN 37160, U.S.A. 5, 7.

MARTIN, E.W., b. 31 Apr. 1914. Historian; Critic; Editor. Appts: broadcasts for W. Region of BBC; recently on Radio 3; presented 2 progs. on BBC Further Educ. TV; working on oral hist. survey for Beaford Ctr., Devon. Mbrships: Soc. Welfare Hist. Grp., U.S.A.; Writers' Action Grp., U.K. Publs: The Secret People, 1954; Where London Ends, 1958; Dartmoor, 1958; The Case Against Hunting, 1959; The Tyranny of the Majority, 1961; Country Life in England, 1965; The Shearers & the Shorn, 1966; Comparative Development in Social Welfare, 1972. Hons: Leverhulme Rsch. Fellowship, Univ. of Sussex, 1965-67; Civil List Pension for servs. to lit. & soc. hist., the Queen, 1972. Address: Editha Cottage, Black Torrington, Beaworthy, Devon EX21 5QF, U.K. 3, 30, 139.

MARTIN, Foster Stanley, b. 18 Jan. 1900. Company Director. Appts: Dpty. Chmn., Gilbert Lodge Holdings Ltd.; Governing Dir., Orana Property Ltd. Mbrships: Royal Motor Yacht Club of N.S.W.; Tattersalls Club, Sydney; Rose Bay Bowling Club. Address: 3/3 Longworth Ave., Point Piper, N.S.W., Australia, 2027.

MARTIN, Francis Xavier, b. 2 Oct. 1922. Professor; Priest; Augustinian Friar. Educ: Augustinian Dublin House of Philos., 1942-44 & House of Theol., 1944-46; Univ. Coll. Dublin, 1946-50; L.Ph., Augustinian Coll., Rome, 1947; B.D., Pontifical Gregiorian Univ., Rome, 1952; M.A., Nat. Univ. of Ireland, 1952; Ph.D., Univ. of Cambridge, 1959. Appts. incl: Tutor-Prof. of Medieval Hist., Univ. Coll., Dublin, 1949-; Chmn., Bd. of Hist., ibid, 1968-70; Jt. Ed. of 9 vol. New History of Ireland forthcoming 1976-. Mbrships. incl: Irish Manuscripts Commn., 1963-; Vice-Chmn., Coun., Trustees of Nat. Lib. of Ireland, 1973-. Publs: Giles of Viterbo 1469-1532, 1960; Medieval Studies presented to Aubrey Gwynn (co-ed.), 1961; Friar Nugent, Agent of the Counter-reformation 1569-1635, 1962; The Irish Volunteers 1913-15, 1963; The Howth Gun-running 1914, 1964; 1916 & University College, Dublin (ed.), 1967; The Course of Irish History (co-ed.), 1967; Leaders & Men of the Easter Rising, Dublin 1916 (ed.), 1967; 1916-Myth, Fact & Fiction, Studia Hibernica, 1968; The Scholar Revolutionary, Eoin MacNeill 1867-1945, & The Making of the New Ireland (co-ed.), 1973. Address: c/o Dept. of Medieval Hist., Univ. Coll., Dublin 4, Ireland. 1, 30, 43, 139.

MARTIN, Hugh A., b. 3 Feb. 1914. Company Executive. Appts: Co-Fndr., Marwell Construction Co. Ltd., 1937; Co-Fndr. & Pres., Western Construction & Engrng. Rsch. Ltd. (present); Chmn. of Bd., Canadian Dredge & Dock Co. Ltd., Marwell Dredging Ltd., PeBen Oilfield Servs. Ltd.; Pres., Western Int. Hotel Co. Ltd., Hampshire House Holdings Ltd., Shaughnessy Place Ltd.; Dir., Bethlehem Copper Corp. Ltd., Calgary Inn Ltd., Canada

Dev. Corp., CP Air, Frio Oil Ltd., Interprovincial Steel & Pipe Corp. Ltd., PanCanadian Petroleum Ltd., Western Int. Hotels, Westlea Properties Ltd., W.I.H. Holdings Ltd. Mbrships: Econ. Coun. of Canada; Heavy Construction Assn. of B.C. (Past Pres.); Canadian Assn. for Retarded Children (Hon. Gov., B.C. Sect.); Canadian Coun. of Christians & Jews (Dir.); Western Inst. for the Deaf; Bd. of Trade; Lester B. Pearson Coll. Fund (Reg. Chmn.). Address: 8th Floor 1455 W. Georgia St., Vancouver, B.C., V6G 2T3, Canada.

MARTIN, Ian Holland, b. 1 June 1919. Physician; Psychiatrist; Psychoanalyst. Educ: M.B., B.S., Adelaide Univ., 1942; M.D., ibid, 1952. Appts: Res. Med. Off., Royal Adelaide Hosp., 1942; Surg. Lt., Royal Australian Naval Reserve, 1942-44; Jr. Med. Off., Parkside Mental Hosp., Adelaide, 1945-46, Sr. Med. Off., 1946-48; Dept. Supt., Enfield Receiving House, S.A., 1948-51; Jr. Registrar, Bethlem Royal & Maudsley Hosps., London, U.K., 1949-50; Vis. Psych., Repatriation Dept., Rockingham Home, Kew, U.K., & Repatriation Gen. Hosp., Heidleberg, Germany, 1951-69; Hon. Clin. Asst. Psych., Royal Melbourne Hosp., 1951-58, Hon. Asst. Psych., 1958-67, Hon. Psych., 1967-72; Sr. Vis. Psych., St. Vincent's Hosp., 1973-; currently w. Epworth Hosp., Richmond, Vic. Mbr., profl. orgs. Articles & papers, profl. jrnls. & symposia. Address: Cato Wing, Epworth Hospital, 34 Erin St., Richmond, Vic., Australia 3121. 23.

MARTIN, Jane Elizabeth, b. 1 May 1925. Life Insurance Counselor. Appts: Asst. Off. Mgr., F.W. Woolworth Co., 1941-55; Comptometer Operator, Colonial Oil Co., 1955-57; Asst. Station Mgr., WLOW Radio, 1957-63; Hd., Collect. Dept., Tidewater Assn. of Credit Mgmt., 1963-65; Ins. Counselor, Northwestern Nat. Life Ins. Co., 1965-. Mbrships: Chapt. Dir., Sec., V.P. & (first woman) Pres., Admin. Mgmt. Soc.; Chmn., var. comms., Am. Bus. Women's Assn.; Norfolk Life Underwriters Assn.; Pres., Lydia Bible Class, Ctrl. Bapt. Ch., 1973-74. First woman ins. counselor in Northwestern Nat. Life Ins. Co. to sell over $1 million ins. in one month, Apr. 1973. Hons. incl: Disting. Salesman Award, Sales & Marketing Exec. Club, 1968; Nat. Merit Award, Admin. Mgmt. Soc. Int., 1971; Woman of the Yr., Am. Bus. Women's Assn., 1973. Address: P.O. Box 3013, Norfolk, VA 23514, U.S.A. 125.

MARTIN, John Bartlow, b. 4 Aug. 1915. Author; Professor; Former Diplomat. Educ: A.B., DePauw Univ., 1937. Appts. incl: Free-lance writer, 1938-62; U.S. Ambassador, Dominican Repub., 1962-64; Visiting Fellow in Pub. Affairs, Princeton Univ., N.J., 1966-67; Visiting Prof., Grad. Ctr., CUNY, 1967-68; Prof., Medill Schl. of Journalism, Northwestern Univ., Evanston, Ill., 1968-. Author of 12 books inclng. Why Did They Kill, 1953; The Deep South Says Never, 1957; Overtaken By Events, 1966; The Life of Adlai E. Stevenson (in preparation). Contbr. to many mags. inclng. Harper's Saturday Evening Post, Life, Look. Mbrships. incl: Authors' Guild; Soc. of Mag. Writers; Sigma Delta Chi. Hons. incl: num. mag. awards; Soc. of Midland Authors award, 1967; LL.D. (Hon.), Univ. of Ind., 1971. Address: 185 Maple Ave., Highland Park, IL 60035, U.S.A. 2, 128.

MARTIN, Joseph, Jr., b. 21 May 1915. Attorney. Educ: B.A., Yale Univ., 1936; LL.B., Yale Law Schl., 1939. Appts: Assoc. Caldwalader, Wickersham & Taft, N.Y., 1939-41; U.S. Navy (to Lt. Cmndr.), 1941-46; Ptnr., Wallace, Garrison, Norton & Ray, San Fran., 1946-55; Ptnr., Pettit, Evers & Martin, ibid, 1955-70; 1973-; Gen. Counsel, Fed. Trade Commn., Wash. D.C., 1970-71; U.S. Rep., Geneva Disarmament Conf. (rank, Ambassador), 1971-. Mbrships: Pres., San Fran. Pub. Utilities Commn., 1956-60; Repub. Nat. Comm. Man. for Calif., 1960-64; Dir., Nat. Fair Campaign Pracs. Comm., 1965-; Treas., Repub. Party of Calif., 1956-58; Dir., Patrons of Art & Music, Calif.; Palace of Legion of Hon., 1958-70, Pres., 1963-68; Pacific Union Club, San Fran.; Burlington Country Club; Yale Club, N.Y.; Marco Polo Club, N.Y. Hons: Official Commendation, Outstanding Serv. as Gen. Counsel, Fed. Trade Commn., 1973; Disting. Hon. Award, U.S. Arms Control Disarmament Agcy., 1973. Address: c/o Pettit, Evers & Martin, 600 Montgomery St., San Fran., CA 94111, U.S.A. 2, 9, 16, 32, 59, 128.

MARTIN, Kurt, b. 31 Jan. 1899. Professor; Retired Art Collection General Director. Educ: Dr.phil. Appts. incl: Dir., Staatliche Kunsthalle, Karlsruhe, German Fed. Repub., 1934-56; Gen. Dir., Upper Rhine Mus., Strasburg, 1940-45; Prof. & Dir., Akad. Bild. Künste, Karlsruhe, 1956-57; Gen. Dir., Bayerische Staatsgemäldesammlung, Munich, 1957-64; Hon. Dr., Karlsruhe, 1964. Mbrships: incl: Pres., deutsches Nationalkomm., Int. Coun. of Mus., 1948-64, Emeritus, 1964; German UNESCO Commn. Publs. incl: Verlorene Werke der Malerei in Deutschland in der Zeit von 1939-45, zerstörte & verschollene Gemälde aus Museen & Galerien (w. Marianne Bernhard & Klaus Rogner), 1965; Albrecht Altdorfer: Die Alexanderschlacht, 1965; Schicksale der Isenheimer Altars, 1939-45, in Cahiers d'Alsace, 1967. Organiser & Collaborator, many nat. & int. exhibitions. Recip. of hons. Address: Hermine-Bland-Strasse 3, 8 Munich 90, German Fed. Repub. 92.

MARTIN, LeRoy Jr., b. 4 Jan. 1943. College Professor. Educ: B.A. (hons.) Clark Coll., Atlanta, Ga.; M.A., Ph.D., Univ. of N.C., Chapel Hill. Appts: Instr. of Engl., Tex. Southern Univ., 1968, S.C. State Coll., 1969, 1970; Asst. Prof. Engl., Ga. State Univ., 1970-73, Clark Coll., Atlanta, 1973-; Cons. for Communication Skills, Civil Serv. Commn., 1972-. Mbrships: S. Atlantic Mod. Lang. Assn.; Linguistic Soc. of Atlantic; Southeastern Conf. on Linguistics; Linguistic Circle of Atlanta. Author, paper, Toward a Theory of Perfect Aspects. TV prog., Black Gospel Music, Atlanta, 1971. Hons. incl: Woodrow Wilson Fellowship, 1966-67; Career Tchng. Fellow (UNC), 1967-68; Southern Fellowships Fund Awards, 1968-69, 1969-70. Address: 1715 DeLowe Dr., S.W., Atlanta, GA 30311, U.S.A. 125.

MARTIN, Mabel Irene Lilian, b. 25 Dec. 1886. Painter. Educ: Schl. of Lithog., London. Appts: Art Specialist; Tchr. in Arts & Crafts. Exhibited at: Royal Acad., London; Paris Salon (2 miniatures, 1 oil). Major works: Dover Harbour; miniatures & oil paintings. Featured in art periodicals. Mbrships: formerly Sec., Art Dept., The Three Arts Club; E. Kent Art Soc. (25 yrs.). Address: Cottage 2, Castlemount Rd., Dover, Kent, U.K. 133.

MARTIN, Netta Ferguson (Mrs. J.R.F. Martin). Journalist. Educ: M.A., Glasgow Univ. Appts: Tchr., Jordanhill Schl., Glasgow; Writer, Lucy Ashton Column, Sunday Express; Book Review Columnist. Annabel Mag; Woman's Page Writer, Engl. Sunday Express. Mbrships: Inst. of Jrnlists; Soc. of Authors; PEN; Soc. of British Women Writers & Jrnlsts. Author of Secret of Cavaliers Cave (pending publ.) Recip. of Jubilee Prize Schlrship. in Moral Philos.,

Glasgow Univ., 1952. Address: Rockcliffe, Baldernock Rd., Milngavie, Glasgow; U.K. 3, 131.

MARTIN, R. Keith, b. 5 Sept. 1933. Educator; Registered Professional Engineer. Educ: A.B., Whitman Coll., 1955; M.B.A. (Hons.), CCNY, 1965; Ph.D., Univ. of Wash., 1973. Appts. incl: Div. Mgr., Campus Merchandising Bur. Inc., 1955-56; Sales Rep., IBM Corp., 1956-58; Mgr., Mgmt. Advsry. Servs., Price Waterhouse & Co., 1959-67; Dir., Mgmt. Systems Dept., Univ. of Wash., 1967-71; Pt.-time Lectr., Bellevue Community Coll., 1967-69, Indl. Engrng. Technol., Shoreline Community Coll., 1968-72, Schl. of Bus., Seattle Univ., 1971-72; Lectr., Dept. of Acctng., Univ. of Wash., 1971-73; Asst. Prof., Dept. of Acctcy., Baruch Coll., CUNY, 1973-; Mbr. & Off., var. profl. & advsry. comms. & orgs. Mbrships. incl: Assn. Systems Mgmt.; Pres., ibid, 1970-, var. past offs.; Am. Inst. Indl. Engrs.; var other profl. orgs. Recip., awards. Address: 18 McKinley St., Bronxville, NY 10708, U.S.A. 6, 9, 130, 131.

MARTIN, Riago Joseph, b. 1 Jan. 1905. Educationist. Educ: A.B., Talladega Coll., Ala., U.S.A. M.A., Fisk Univ., Nashville, Tenn.; Dr., Humane Letters, Morris Brown College, Atlanta, Ga.; Allen Univ., Columbia, S.C. Appts: Asst. Prin., Avery Inst., Charleston, S.C.; Sci. Tchr. & Coach, Lincoln Acad., Kings Mountain, N.C.; Prin., Henry Co. Trng. Schl., McDonough, Ga.; Prin., Ctr. H.S., Waycross, Ga.; Prin., Ballard High & Ballard Hudson Sr. High, Macon, Ga.; Dir., Rsch., Ga. Assn. Eductrs., At., Ga. Mbrships: Past Pres., Am. Tchrs. Assn.; Past Pres. Ga. Tchrs. & Educ. Assn.; Past Pres., Bibb Co. Tchrs. & Educ. Assn.; Past Pres., Ga. Coun. of Prins.; Bd. Educ., Bibb Co., Ga.; Past Dir., Nat. Educ. Assn.; Ga. Contbr. to Gorgia Educator. Hons: Outstanding Citizen & Eductr. Award, Bibb Co. Citizens, 1953; Outstanding Ldrship. Award, Am. Tchrs. Assn., 1965; Significan Contbns. to Educ., Ga. Tchrs. & Educ. Assn. Address: 107 Madison St., Macon, GA 31201, U.S.A. 15, 141.

MARTIN, Vernon A., b. 12 June 1928. Realtor; Lecturer. Educ: B.A., Boston Univ., Mass. Appts: U.S. Army, 1946-48; Pres., Vernon A. Martin, Inc., Lynn, Mass., 1952-; Tchr., Lectr.; Cons., real estate; Bd. Dirs., Jr. Achievement Eastern Mass., 1966-70; Chmn., Gtr. Lynn, 1966; State Dir., Am. Cancer Soc., 1966-68. Mbrships: Bd. Dirs., Gtr. Lynn Chapt., A.R.C. Union Hosp.; Gtr. Lynn Chmbr. of Comm.; Pres., ibid, 1969; Gtr. Lynn Bd. Realtors; Pres., Dir., ibid, 1970; Dir., Mass. Assn. Real Estate Bds.; Gtr. Boston, Gtr. Salem Bds. Realtors. Recip., nomination as Realtor of Yr., Mass. Bd. of Realtors, 1969. Address: 555 Boston St., Lynn, MA 01905, U.S.A. 6.

MARTINDALE, Andrew Henry Robert, b. 19 Dec. 1932. University Lecturer. Educ: New Coll., Oxford Univ.; Courtauld Inst. of Art, London Univ. Appts: Lectr., Courtauld Inst. of Art, 1959; Sr. Lectr., Schl. of Fine Arts & Music, Univ. of E. Anglia, 1965; Dean, Schl. of Fine Arts & Music, ibid, 1971-. Mbrships: Fellow, Soc. of Antiquaries. Publs: Man & the Renaissance, 1966; Gothic Art, 1967; The Rise of the Artist, 1972. Address: Schl. of Fine Arts & Music, Univ. of E. Anglia, Norwich NOR 88C, U.K.

MARTINET, André, b. 12 Apr. 1908. Professor. Educ: Licence ès lettres, Sorbonne, Paris, France, 1927; Agrégé, ibid, 1930; Univ. of Berlin, Germany, 1931-32; Docteur ès lettres, Sorbonne, 1937. Appts: Dir., Phonol.

Studies, Ecole des Hautes Etudes, Paris, 1938-47; Dir. of Rsch., Int. Aux. Lang. Assn., N.Y., 1946-49; Prof., Gen. & Comp. Linguistics, Columbia Univ., N.Y., 1947-55; Prof., Gen. Linguistics, Sorbonne, 1955; Dir., Structural Linguistic Studies, Ecole des Hautes Etudes, Paris, 1957. Mbrships. incl: Royal Acad. of Denmark, 1954; Coun., Int. Phonetic Assn., 1946. Publs. incl: La prononciation du fracçais contemporain, 1945; Phonology as Functional Phonetics, 1949; Eléments de linguistique générale, 1960; A Functional View of Language, 1962; Dictionnaire de la prononciation française dans son usage réel, 1973; Studies in Functional Syntax, 1974. Hons. incl: Pres., Int. Linguistic Assn., N.Y., 1972; Mbr., Linguistic Soc. of Am., 1973. Address: 10 Ave. de la Gare, 92330 Sceaux, France.

MARTINEZ, Bernard, b. 25 Jan. 1926. Solicitor of the Supreme Court of Trinidad & Tobago. Educ: St. Mary's Coll., Trinidad. Appts: Legal Dept., Govt. of Trinidad & Tobago; Industrial Rels. Dept., Creole Petroleum Corp., Venezuela. Address: 8 First Ave., Cascade, Trinidad, West Indies.

MARTINEZ, (Maria) Gloria, b. 15 Feb. 1948. Teacher. Educ: B.A., Univ. of Albuquerque, 1970; M.Ed., Univ. of Tex., El Paso, 1972. Appts: Grad. Asst., Univ. of Tex., El Paso, 1970-71; German Tchr., Mayfield H.S., Las Cruces, N.M., 1972; Reading Tchr., 1st Grade Tchr., bilingual prog., Canutillo Elem. Schl., Tex., 1972-. Mbrshps: NEA; Tex. State Tchrs. Assn.; Canutillo Classroom Tchrs. Assn.; Alliance Francaise, 1971-72; Int. Club, Univ. of Albuquerque; Sec., ibid, 1969-70. Address: 9321 Ramirez Ct., El Paso, TX 79907, U.S.A. 120, 130.

MARTINEZ, Julio A. University Lecturer; Librarian. Educ: B.A., Southern III Univ., 1953; M.A.L.S., Univ. of Mich., 1966; M.A., Univ. of Minn., 1971; Ph.D. Cand., Univ. of Calif., 1972-. Appts: Ref. Libn., Genessee Co. Lib., Flint, Mich., 1966; Ref. Libn., St. Clair Shores Pub. Lib., 1967-69; Rsch. Asst., Philos. Dept., Univ. of Calif., San Diego, 1971-. Mbrships: Mich. Lib. Assn.; Pub. Citizen Inc.; United Profs. of Calif. Contbr. to profl. jrnls. Recip., Southern III. Tuition & Activity Award, 1958-61. Address: Dept. of Philos., Univ. of Calif., La Jolla, CA, U.S.A. 139.

MARTINEZ, Luis O., b. 27 Nov. 1927. Radiologist. Educ: B.S., Schl. of Med., Univ. of Havana, Cuba, 1947; M.D., 1954; Am. Bd. of Radiol., 1968. Appts. incl: Intern, Res., Instr., Calixto Garcia Hosp., Havana, 1955-62; Asst.-Chief Radiol,, Curie Hosp., Havana, 1954-62; Res., Jackson Mem. Hosp., Miami, Fla., U.S.A. 1963-65; Fellow, Cardiovascular Radiol., ibid, 1965-66; Sr. Fellow, 1966-67; Asst. Attending Radiol., Mt. Sinai Hosp., Miami Beach, 1968; Assoc. Dir., Dept. of Radiol., ibid, 1969; Instr.-Assoc. Prof., Univ. of Miami Schl. of Med., Jackson Mem. Hosp., 1965-69. Fellow, Am. Coll. of Angiol. & Am. Coll. of Chest Physns. Mbrships. incl: AAUP; AMA; Pan Am. Med. Assn.; N.Y. Acad. of Scis.; Int. Coll. of Surgs; British Inst. of Radiol.; Am. Heart Assn.; Am. Coll. of Radiol.; Chmn., scientific display comms. & soc. progs., Univ. of Miami Schl. of Med., Mt. Sinai Hosp. & Jackson Mem. Hosp. Num. papers publd. in Cuba & USA & presented at confs. Hons: The Angiology Rsch. Fndn.; The Prudue Frederick Co.; The Honors Achievement Award; AMA Physns. Recognition Award for 1971. Address: Mt. Sinai Med. Ctr., Dept. of Radiol., 4300 Alton Rd., Miami Beach, FL 33140, U.S.A.

MARTINEZ-CONESA, Antonio, b. 22 Nov. 1926. Minister; Journalist. Educ: Latin Sem. & Bible Ctr. of Studies, Barcelona, 1949-52; Polytech. Univ., Madrid; Mbr., Fedn. Politécnica Española de Diplomados. Appts. incl: Pastor, 1952-; Fndr., Evangelical Chs., Argentona, 1951, Murcia, 1952, & Barcelona, 1969; Pastor, Villaneuva y Geltrú Ch., 1953-69; Dir., Portavoz mag., 1964-; Pres., Commn. for Evangelical Defense, 1972-; Prof. of Ethics, Ctr. for Evangelical Studies (C.E.E.B.), Barcelona. Mbrships. incl: Pres., Fedn. of Evangelical Free Chs. in Spain, 1971-; Pres., Assn. of Protestant Mins. of Cataluña & Baleares, 1968-; Mbr., Exec. Comm., Spanish Evangelical Coun., 968-; Nat. Comm. for Radio; Fellow, Royal Geog. Soc. Lectr., Contbr. to var. jrnls. Hons: Hon. Litt.D., Defenders Theol. Sem.; Award of the Denomination, Defenders of the Faith of Puerto Rico; elected to Acads. of Human Scis., Dominican Repub. & U.S. of Mexico. Address: Calle Lepanto 256, Entresuelo 4a, Barcelona 13, Spain.

MARTINEZ-DELGADO, Luis, b. 12 Mar. 1896. Lawyer; Historian. Educ: Dr. of law & pol. sci., Nat. Univ. of Colombia, Bogata; study of Int. Law, Paris. Appts: Lawyer; Judge; Ed. & annotator of the Tratado de Pruebas Judiciales, Carlos Martinez Silva. Mbrships: Past Pres., Acad. of Hist., Colombia; Acad. of Lang.; corresp. mbr., Acads. oı Hist., Panama, Venezuela, Ecuador, Dominican Repub., Uruguay, Paraguay, Bolivia; La Renaissance Française; Royal Acad. of Hist., Madrid, Spain. Publs. incl: 10 vols. of the writings of Dr. Carlos Martinez Silva, w. notes & commentaries; Dir. & Mgr., Historia Extensa de Colombia. Hons. incl: Cross of Boyaca; Great Cross of St. Bridget. Address: Carrera 16 A.No.46-21-Bogota, Repub. of Colombia.

MARTÍNEZ-MANAUTOU, Jorge, b. 4 Jan. 1930. Physician. Educ: Univ. of Mex., 1948-53. Appts. incl: Dir., Sci. Rsch., Hosp. de la Mujer, 1966, Syntex Labs., Mex. City, 1959-66; Fndr. & Dir. of Sci. Rsch. Dept., Inst. Mex. del Seguro Soc., 1966-70; Cons., Biol. of Reproduction, Syntex Labs., 1967-71; Rsch. Dir., Ctr. de Investigación sobre Fertilidad & Esterilidad, Mex. City, 1971-; Cons. in Biol. of Reproduction, Alza Rsch., Palo Alto, Calif., U.S.A., 1971-. Mbrships. incl: Fellow, Am. Coll. Physns., U.S.A., Am. Coll. Clin. Pharmacol., ibid. Contbr. to num. profl. books & jrnls. Recip., Carnot Prize, Nat. Acad. Med., 1969. Address: Centro de Investigación sobre Fertilidad & Esterilidad, Bajío No. 203-1, Mexico 7, D.F. Mex.

MARTINEZ MARESMA, Sara (Sara Sofia Martinez). Painter; Educator. Educ: Acad. de San Alejandro, Havana, Cuba, 1929. Prof., drawing & Painting, var. schls., Cuba, 1929-59. One man Exhibs: Dade Fed. Saving, Miami, Fla., U.S.A., 1966; Gables Art Gall., ibid, 1968; Bacardi Gall., 1970. Grp. exhibs. incl: Cuban Mus., Daytona Beach, 1963; Dade Jr. Coll., Miami, 1964; Prog. Cultura Cubana, Miami Univ., 1967; Am. Artists Profl. League, N.Y.C., 1971-72. Mbrships: Am. Artists Profl. League; Miami Palette Club; Fla. Fed. Art. Works incl: Portrait, John F. Kennedy, White House; St. Jose Pignatelli, Ch. Sagrado Corazon, Havana; Cardinal Manuel Arteaga, portrait, Cardinal's Palace, Havana. Hons. incl: Prestige Award, Am. Artists Profl. League, 1969; Dip. of Hon.: Juan J. Remos, Miami, 1973; Gran Order Martiana de Merito Ciudadano, Miami, 1973. Address: 2632 S.W. 30 Court, Miami, FL 33133, U.S.A. 37.

MARTINO, Rocco Leonardo, b. 25 June 1929. Computer & Management Consultant. Educ: B.Sc., Univ. Coll., Univ. of Toronto, 1951; M.A., Dept. of Applied Maths., ibid, 1952; Ph.D., Inst. of Aerospace Studies, ibid, 1956. Appts: Rsch. Assoc., Univ. of Toronto, 1951-56; Dir., UNIVAC Computer Ctrs., Toronto, 1956-59; Prof., Maths., Univ. of Waterloo, 1959-62; Pres., Mauchly Assocs. (Canada) Ltd., 1959-62; Dir., Advanced Systems, Olin Corp., N.Y., 1962-64; Prof. Maths., N.Y. Univ., 1962-65; Dir., Computer Systems, Booz Allen & Hamilton, N.Y. & Chgo., 1964-65; Pres., Info. Inds., Wayne, Pa., 1965-70; Chmn. of Bd., ISI (Canada) Ltd., 1968-70; Pres., XRT, Inc., Villanova, Pa., 1970-; Mbrships: Fndng. Dir., Computer Soc. of Canada, 1959-61; Commodore, Yacht Club of Sea Isle City, N.J.; Var. profl. socs. Num. publs. incl: Heat Transfer in Slip Flows, 1955; Information Management, 1968; Postal Computer Systems, 1974; Num. articles. Hons: 7 undergrad. awards, Univ. of Toronto; Prov. of Ont. Fellowship, 1952; MIT Fellowship, 1952; Univ. of Toronto Fellowships, 1952-55. Address: 512 Watch Hill Rd., Villanova, PA 19085, U.S.A. 6, 14, 88.

MARTINO SAVINO, Francisco, b. 27 Feb. 1916. Urologist. Educ: Licenciate, 1939; Doct. 1941. Appts: Prof. of Urol., Madrid Univ., 1940; Urologist, Red Cross Hosp., Madrid, 1950; Hd. of Urol., Soc. Security of Madrid, 1962-. Mbrships: Royal Acad. of Med. of Zaragoza; Int. Coll. of Surgs. Acad. Médico-Quirúrgica; Soc. de Cirugía. Author of Cancer: Genesis, Pathogenesis & Treatment. Contbr. to num. profl. jrnls. Hons: Prizes awarded by the Ministerio de Educación Nacional, 1953; teh Royal Acad. of Med. of Zaragoza, 1956; the Royal Acad. of Med., Barcelona, 1957; the Exposition of Inventors at Brussels, 1958; the March's Fndn., 1959. Address: Caballero de Gracia, 8, Madrid, 14, Spain. 43.

MARTMER, Edgar Everitt, b. 1 May 1901. Pediatrician. Educ: Liberal Arts, Wayne State Univ., U.S.A.; Coll. Med., ibid. Appts: Assoc. Prof., Pediatrics, Wayne State Univ., 1931-71; Chief, Dept. of Pediatrics, Harper Hosp., Detroit, Mich., 1950-64; Chief of Staff, ibid, 1964-65. Mbrships: Past Pres., Detroit Pediatric Soc.; Past Chmn., Pediatric Sect., Mich. State Med. Soc.; Past Pres. & Treas., Am. Acad. Pediatrics; Asst. Sec., ibid; Past Counsellor, Mich. State Med. Soc. Author, The Handicapped Child. Recip. Clifford Grulee Award, Am. Acad. Pediatrics, 1951. Address: 6935 Curtis Dr., Coloma, MI 49038, U.S.A. 2.

MARTNER, John Garcia, b. 20 June 1920. Physicist. Educ: B.S., Columbia Univ., 1950. Appts. incl: Jr. Engr., Lynch Carriers, Inc., 1952-55; Physicist, Phys. Div., Stanford Rsch. Inst., 1955-66; Physicist, Electromagnetic Techniques Lab., ibid, 1967-70; Pres., Martner Co., Menlo Park, Calif., 1970-. Mbrships: Sr. Mbr., Instrument Soc. of Am., Treas., 1966-67; Sr. Mbr., Commonwealth Club of Calif.; Sci. Rsch. Soc. of Am., 1959-. Contbr. of num. articles to profl. jrnls. Holder of 13 U.S. Patents (9 Pending). Address: 49 James Ave., Atherton, CA 94025, U.S.A. 9, 10, 57, 120, 139.

MARTORANA, Sebastian V., b. 7 Jan. 1919. Professor. Educ: B.S., N.Y. State Tchrs. Coll., Buffalo, 1935; M.A., Univ. of Chgo., 1946; Ph.D., ibid, 1948. Appts: Prof.,Educ., & Cons., Jr. Colls., Wash. State Coll., Pullman, 1948-53; Dean, Gen. Coll., Ferris State Inst., Big Rapids, Mich., 1953-55; Specialist for Community & Jr. Colls., U.S. Off. of Educ., 1955-57; Chief, State & Regional Org., ibid, 1957-63; Asst. Commnr. for Higher Educ. Planning, N.Y. State Bd. of Regents, 1963-65;

Vice Chancellor for Community Colls. & Provost, Vocational & Tech. Educ., SUNY, 1965-72; Rsch. Assoc., Ctr. for Study of Higher Educ. & Prof., Higher Educl, Coll. of Educ., Pa. State Univ., 1972-. Mbrships: Exec. Comm., Bd. of Trustees, Coll. Entrance Exam., 1966-70; Chmn., Nat. Coun. State Dirs. of Community-Jr. Colls., 1967-68 & 70-71; Bd. of Human Resources, Nat. Acad. of Sci., Wash. D.C., 1973; Pres.' Nat. Panel, Priorities in Higher Educ., 1969; NEA; etc. Publs: College Boards of Trustees, 1963; State Boards Responsible for Higher Education (co-author), 1960; Articles in profl. jrnls. Hons. incl: Disting Serv. Awards, U.S. Dept. of Hlth., Educ. & Welfare, 1960. Address: c/o Ctr. for the Study of Higher Education, Pennsylvania State Univ., 119 Rackley Building, University Park, PA 16802, U.S.A. 6, 8, 15, 46.

MARTY, Martin E., b. 5 Feb. 1928. Historian; Editor. Educ: B.D., Concordia Sem., St. Louis, Mo., 1952; S.T.M., Chgo. Luth. Theol. Sem., 1954; Ph.D., Univ. of Chgo., 1956. Appts: Luth. Pastoral Min., 1950-63; Prof., Mod. Ch. Hist., Univ. of Chgo., 1956-; Assoc. Ed., The Christian Centry, 1956-; Assoc. Dean, ibid. Fellow, Am. Acad. Arts & Scis. Mbrships. incl: Pres.; Am. Soc. Ch. Hist., 1971; Hon., Guild for Relig. Arch. & Am. Soc. Ch. Arch. Publs. incl: The Infidel, 1961; The Hidden Discipline, 1963; Varieties of Unbelief, 1964; The Search for a Usable Future, 1969; (w. Dean Peerman) The Modern Schism, 1969; Righteous Empire, 1970; (ed.) The Place of Bonhoeffer, 1962; co-ed. w. Dean Peerman, Annual New Theology, 1964-. Contbr. to num. relig. publs. Recip. of 7 hon. doct. degrees. Address: Swift Hall, Univ. of Chicago, Chgo., IL. 60637, USA. 2, 30, 131.

MARTYN, Laurel (Mrs. Lloyd D. Lawton), b. 23 July 1916. Ballet Director; Choreographer; Teacher. Appts: Soloist, Sadlers Wells Ballet Co., 1935-38; Tchr. for Jennie Brennan, 1938-39; Ballerina & Choreographer, Borovansky Ballet Co., 1940-46; Choreographer, Ballet Victoria, 1946-; Fndr., Victorian Ballet Guild & Artistic Dir., Ballet Victoria, 1946-; Prin. & Tchr., Ballet Victoria Schls., 1946-. Mbrships: Lyceum Club, Melbourne; Prods. & Dirs. Guild of Aust.; Royal Acad. of Dancing Soc.; Imperial Soc. of Tchrs. of Dancing; Aust. Ballet Soc.; Aust. Elizabethan Theatre Trust. Has done about 40 choreographies inclng: Sigrid, 1935; Contes Heraldiques, 1946; En Saga, 1936; The Sentimental Bloke, 1952; Mathinna, 1954; Voyageur, 1956; Sylvia, 1962/63; Once Upon a Whim, 1966. Choreographed 25 Episodes of Dance for TV. Hons: Adeline Genee Gold Medal, Royal Acad. of Dancing, 1935; Royal Acad. of Dancing Choreographic Schlrship., 1935. Address: 49 Bouverie St., Carlton, Victoria, Australia 3053.

MARUYAMA, Masao, b. 22 Mar. 1914. Author. Educ: Imperial Univ. of Tokyo, 1937. Appts: Asst., Fac. of Law, Imperial Univ. of Tokyo, 1937; Prof. of E. Asian Political Theory, ibid, 1950-57. For. Honorary Mbr. of Am. Acad. of Arts & Scis. Author of Thought & Behaviour in Modern Japanese Politics, 1963, (expanded paperback ed., 1969). Hons: Degree of Law, Harvard Univ. & Degree of Letters, Princeton Univ., 1973. Address: 2-44-5, Higashicho, Kichijoji, Musashino, Tokyo, Japan. 2.

MARX, Anne (Mrs. Frederick E. Marx). Poet; Author; Lecturer. Educ: Med. Schls., Heidelberg & Berlin, Germany; Grad. Studies, U.S.A. Publs: Eine Buechlein; Into the Wind of Waking; By Grace of Pain; The Second Voice;

By Way of People; over 800 poems in major mags., newspapers, lit. jrnls., poetry quarterlies & anthols. in U.S. & Europe. Mbrships: Pres., Nat. Assn. of Am. Pen Women, Westchester Co. Br., 1962-64; N. Atlantic Regional Chmn., 1964-66; Officer, Exec. Bd., Poetry Soc. Am., 1965-70; V.P., 1971-72; Poetry Workshop Ldr., Writers Confs., Fairleigh Dickinson Univ., 1964, Wagner Coll., 1965, Iona Coll., 1964, '65, '70; Poetry Soc. G.B.; Acad. Am. Poets.; Nat. Fed. of State Poetry Socs.; Chmn., Poetry Div., Coun. for the Arts in Westchester, 1970. Recip. sev. poetry awards. Address: 315 The Colony, Hartsdale, NY 10530, U.S.A. 2, 5, 6, 11, 30.

MARX, Herbert, b. 8 May 1913. Company Director. Appts: Successively trainee, apprentice, dept. hd., dpty., dir., mng. dir. & chmn., BUHLER-MIAG GmbH, Braunschweig (formerly MIAG Mühlenbau & Industrie GmbH); Dir., J.H. Lerch & Co., GmbH, Hanover; Dir., Lauterberger Blechwarenfabrik GmbH, Bad Lauterberg. Mbrships: V.P., Chmbr. of ind. & trade, Braunschweig; Chmn., export comm., ibid; Export trade comm., German assn. of mech. engrng. insts., Frankfurt/Main; Advsry. mbr., German Bank AG, Braunschweig/Frankfurt. Address: BÜHLER-MIAG GmbH, Ernst-Amme-Strasse 19, 33 Braunschweig, German Fed. Repub. 43.

MARX, Rudolf, b. 22 May 1912. University Professor. Educ: Univs. of Munich, Freiburg im Breisgau & Berlin; State Med. Exam., Univ. of Munich, 1937; Doct., ibid, 1939; Clin. prac., Munich; Inaugurated, Munich, 1954. Prof., Hd., Dept. of internal med., particularly haematol., Munich Univ. Mbrships: Deutsche Arbeitsgemeinschaft für Blutgerinnungs-forschung; Deutsche Hämophiliegesellschaft; German Soc. for Internal Med.; Anglo-German Med. Soc.; Hon. mbr., Soc. Mexicana de Hematologia; Int. Soc. of Blood Transfusion; Advsr., World Fedn. of Hemophilia, Montreal, Canada; Deutsche Gesellschaft für Hämatologie; Soc. Européene d'Hématologie. Author of about 180 articles in med. & haematol. books; Ed. & Co-Ed. of monographs. Recip., E.K. Frey Prize, 1969. Address: 16 Osterwaldstr., Munich 23, German Fed. Repub.

MARYLSKA-LUSZCZEWSKA, Cecylia (Artistic names: Cécile Chem & C.Ch.M.), b. 25 Sept. 1897. Artist; Painter. Educ: Studied in Warsaw, Poland, 1919-22, & in Paris, France, 1922-26. Mbrships: Hon., Acad. T. Campanella, Rome, 1970, Acad. de la Haute-Lutèce, Paris; Cmdr., I.A.G., Monte-Carlo, A.I.A.P., Paris, Z.P.A.P., Warsaw; Deleg. for Northern Europe of "Temple of Arts", N.Y., U.S.A. Religious art & compositions exhibited in Padua, 1963, Monte-Carlo, 1964, Charleroi, 1969, San Remo, 1970, Holstebro, 1970-72, Bologna, 1971, Deauville, 1971, Poitier, 1971, Berlin, 1972. Hons: Grand Prize, for drawing, Warsaw, 1921, 1947; 2 1st prizes, San Remo, 1970; Dip., Monte-Carlo & Deauville, 1971; Silver Medal, Rome, 1970; Gold Medal, Rome, 1972. Address: ul. Piskna 31/37 m 31, 00677 Warsaw, Poland. 133.

MARZIANTONIO, Roberto, b. 24 Mar. 1941. Public Relations Consultant. Educ: Course in Jurisprudence; Dip., Sociology, Public Relations. Appts: Pres., G. & M. Ruder & Finn; P.R. Cons., Milan Stock Exchange, Philips, Wilkinson & Ledsco. Mbrships: Int. P.R. Assn.; Italian Fedn. of P.R. Publs: P.R. manuals. Hons: Best Financial P.R. Consultant, 1973. Address: Via G. Dezza 24, Milan 20144, Italy. 24.

MARZOTTO, Vittorio Emanuele, b. 13 June 1922. Industrialist. Educ: Dr. in Law.

Appts. incl: V.P., Manif. Lane G. Marzotto & F., 1948-52; Pres., Soc. Fondiaria Agric. Ind.-Portugruaro, 1952-55; M.P., 1953-72; Chmn., Bd., Ind. dei Marmi Vicentini S.p.A., 1965-69; V. Chmn., Bd. & Pres., ibid, 1969-; Chmn. Bd., Manif. Lane G. Marzotto & F.S.p.A., 1972-; Chmn. Bd., Aulan S.p.A., 1972-. Mbrships: Bd. Mbr., Compagnia Italjolly S.p.A., Ind. Zignago S. Margherita S.p.A., Marzotto Sud S.p.A., Montedison Fibre S.p.A., Soc. Assicuratrice Ind., Gresicotto S.p.A. & AUS S.p.A. Publs: sev. works in field of Ind., Econs. & Agric. Hons: Cav. Mag. del S.M.O. di Malta; Cav. Ord. del S. Sepolcro. Address: Viale R. Margherita n. 7, 36078 Valdagno (VI), Italy.

MASAKAZU, Tada, b. 25 Jan. 1911. Foundation Director. Educ: B.Sc., Dept. of Biol. Sci., Tokyo Imperial Univ. Appts: Fndr., SOTO Inst., Tokyo, 1934; Dir., SOTO Rsch. of Human Sci.; V.P., Int. Vegetarian Union, 1960; Dir., Micro-biotic Preparation of Foods Corp.; Top Cnslr., YOU-I Club, Japan, 1963; Dir., Yeast Food Co. Ltd., Japan, 1965. Mbrships: Int. Vegetarian Union, London; Int. Acad. of U.S.A., Can. & German Fed. Repub.; Pres., 3rd Democratic Union, Japan. Publs: Introduction of Medicine as a Whole, 1935; Creatism as Human Philosophy, 1945; Remaking of Man through Food & Sex Relations, 1948; Heterogenic Unification of Medicine in East & West, 1950; Character & Human Relations, 1953; Human Health & Dietary Microbes, 1960. Hons: Dr.Sc. & Ph.D., Int. Acad. of U.S.A., Can. & German Fed. Repub. Address: c/o SOTO Inst., 718 Daisen, P.O. Nirayama, SHIZUOKA-Pref., Japan.

MASAVEU y MASAVEU, Jaime. Lawyer; University Professor; Lecturer. Educ: Licence, Law, Univ. of Valladolid, Spain; Doct., Law, Univ. of Madrid; Grad., Italian Lit. & Lang., Italian Inst. of Culture, Madrid; Dip., Univ. of Toma; Adv. Studies, Italy, Germany, Austria. Appts. incl: Prof., Univs. of Oviedo, Madrid, Santiago de Compostela; Prof., Schl. of Criminol., Univ. of Madrid; Dir., Criminol. Lab., ibid; Lawyer, Coll. of Madrid; Mbr., Penitentiary Tech. Coun.; Prof., var. univs. & cultural ctrs. Mbrships. incl: Fndg. Mbr., Int. Assn. of Penal Law; Advsr., Past Treas., Spanish-Am.-Philippine Penal & Penitentiary Inst.; Sec. Gen., Spanish Acad. of Penal Scis. Publs. incl: La Escuela Penal Española; Estudios sobre el Pragmatismo; Derecho Penal; Estudio sobre la personalidad de Enrico Ferri. Recip., num. hons. Address: Velazquez 35, Madrid, Spain. 43, 102.

MASCHHAUPT, Jan Hendrik, b. 26 May 1914. Banker. Educ: Law Degree, Univ. of Amsterdam. Appts: Lawyer, Amersfoort, 1939-41; w. Govt. Offs., The Hague, 1941-47; banking employment w. Nederlandsche Handel-Maatschappij N.V. (now Algemene Bank Nederland N.V.), Amsterdam, 1947-; currently, Dpty. Mbr., Mng. Bd., ibid, & Mbr., Bd. Dirs., sev. subsidiary cos.; Bd. of Dirs., Hobart Brothers A.G. Zug (Switzerland); Mbr., Comité Juridique, Fédération Bancaire de la Cummunauté Economique Européenne; Mbr., Groupe de Travail "Droit des Sociétés", Union des Industries de la Communauté Européenne; Mbr., Comms. of Corporate Law & Econ. Integration, Amsterdam Chmbr. of Comm.; Treas., Vereeniging Handelsrecht. Address: Cannenburg 46, Amsterdam, Netherlands. 1.

MASEFIELD, (Sir) Peter Gordon, b. 19 Mar. 1914. Engineer; Administrator; Writer. Educ: Jesus Coll., Cambridge Univ., U.K. Appts. incl: 1st British Civil Air Attaché, Wash. D.C., 1945-46; Dir. Gen., Long term Planning, British Min. of Civil Aviation; Chief Exec.,

British European Airways, 1949-55; Mng. Dir., Bristol Aircraft Ltd., 1955-60; Chmn., Beagle Aircraft Ltd., 1960-69, British Airports Authority, 1965-71, Project Mgmt. Ltd., 1971-. Mbrships: Royal Aeronautical. Soc. (Pres. 1958-59); British Inst. of Transport (Pres. 1955-56); A.I.A.A. (Hon. Fellow, 1957); Royal Aero Club of U.K. (Chmn., 1968-71). Special lectures incl. Littlewood Mem. Lecture, (S.A.E. & A.I.A.A.), 1971 & "Sight" Lecture, N.Y., 1972. Knighted, 1971. Address: Rosehill, Doods Way, Reigate, Surrey RH2 0JT, U.K. 1, 12.

MASINI, Danilo, b. 7 Dec. 1905. Writer; Publicist; Poet. Educ: Inst. Technico Superiore, Florence & Arezzo, Italy. Appts: on import & export staff of local hat factory. Mbrships: Ordine Nazionale dei Giornalisti (publicist), Rome; Federazione della Stampa, Florence; Sindacato Libero degli Scrittori italiani. Publs: Tu non ignota mai (poems), 1947; Gli Uomini di Dio (poems), 1962; E' un'altra età (poems), 1969; Canti delle Cinque Terre (poems), 1973. Hons: Nat. Prize "Ausonia", Siena, 1947; Nat. Prize "Lucania", Salerno, 1956; Nat. Prize "Città di Enna", Enna, 1973; Lauro d'argento, S. Pellegrino, 1948. Address: Via Piave, 213, 52025 Montevarchi, Arezzo, Italy.

MASINI, Gerardo, b. 8 Aug. 1920. Painter; Art Sociologist. Educ: Econs. Grad., Univ. of Bologna; postgrad. courses, Univ. of Venice. Appts: Dir., Ctr. of Study on Mod. Civility; Promoter, Inst. of Art Sociol.; Dir., Masini Ctrs. of Study (Eurostudy); Dir., Union of Artistic & Cultural Quarter of World; Jt. Promoter, Essentialisme (Universal Artistic Cultural Movement); Rschr., Pub Instruction Min., Repub. of S. Marino; Bd. Mbr., Ctr. of Study & Int. Exchange. Mbr., var. int. & cultural orgs. Publs: The Essentialism of the Modern Art Museum of Paris, 1970; The Essentialism of the Mont-Martre Museum of Paris, 1971. Participant, var. int. exhibs. Work in museums, art galls., pub. & pvte. collects. Recip., num. profl. prizes, medals, dips., & hon. citizenship, Dozza-Bologna, Italy, 1971. Address: 39 Via de Pisis, 44100 Ferrara, Italy. 43.

MASIULIS, Erdivilas, b. 2 Feb. 1922. Architect. Educ: Vytautas the Great Univ., Kaunas, Lithuania, 1944; Stuttgart Tech. Univ., Germany, 1948. Appts: Archtl. Prac., working for Snowy Mtns. Hydro Elec. Authority Archtl. Dept., Sydney, Australia, 1949-54; Archt., schls., chs., municipal bldgs., offs., apts., pks., residences, etc., Chgo., Ill. & Mich. City, Ind., U.S.A., 1955-; Prin., Masiulis & Assocs., archt. & engrs., Mich. City, Ind., 1972-. Mbrships: Towns Planning Commn., Beverly Shores; Bldg. Commn., ibid; Zoning Bd. of Appeals; Former Pres., Lituanica Park Fndn. & designer, Lituanica Park; Am. Inst. of Archts. Designer of Ch. Mural, The Tree of Life, St. Ann of the Dunes Ch., Beverly Shores, Ind.; Contbr. to newspapers & profl. jrnls. Address: P.O. Box 333, Beverly Shores, IN 46301, U.S.A. 57, 120.

MASLINSKI, Antoni, b. 13 July 1917. University Professor. Educ: Univ. of Wilno, Poland; Philos. Magister, Cath. Univ. of Lublin, 1945; Philos. Dr., ibid, 1949; Dr. Habilitatus, Univ. of Warsaw, 1965. Appts: Asst., Cath. Univ. of Lublin, 1946; Adjunct,-ibid, 1949; Asst. Prof., 1958; Chmn., hist. of medieval & modern art, 1966; Chmn., modern art, 1970; Pro-dean, Humanistic Fac., 1967-68 & 1968-69; Assoc. Prof., currently. Mbrships: Sci. Soc., Cath. Univ. of Lublin; Sci. Soc. of Lublin; Winckelmann-Gesellschaft, Stendal, German Democratic Repub.; Comm., art rschs., Polish Acad. of Sci., 1972-74. Author of books & studies in field. Hons: Badge of Millennium,

Millennium Poloniae, 1966; Golden Cross of Merit for pedagogic work, 1973. Address: Balladyny 4 m. 38, skrytka poczt. 10, Lublin 17, Poland. 133.

MASODKAR, Bhaskar Annaji, b. 15 Aug. 1927. Judge. Educ: B.A., M.A., LL.B., Nagpur Univ. Appts: entered Bar as Pleader, 1953; admitted as Advocate, High Ct., Nagpur, 1956; admitted & enrolled as Advocate, Supreme Ct. of India, 1959; Judge, High Ct. of Bombay (State of Maharashtra), India, 1972; Exec. Mbr., High Ct. Bar Assn., 1971-72; Mbr., Bar Coun. of Maharashtra, 1969-72; Exec. Mbr., Univ. of Nagpur, 1969-74; Dean, Fac. of Law, ibid, 1972-74; Chmn., ibid, 1972-74. Mbrships: Govng. Body & Advsr.'s Comm., Laxminarayan Inst. (Technol.), Nagpur; Life Mbr., Exec. Mbr., Mbr. Govng. Body, Women's Educ. Soc., Nagpur; Am. Book Club; Life Mbr., Vidarbha Sahitya Sangh. Publs: Supreme Court on Election Law, Part I; Law of Meetings in India; Supreme Court on Election Law, 1967-1972. Address: 215, Tikekar Rd., Dhantoli, Nagpur, (Maharashtra), India.

MASON, Bruce Edward George, b. 28 Sept. 1921. Writer; Actor. Educ: B.A., Victoria Univ. Coll., Wellington, New Zealand, 1945. Appts. incl: P.R. Officer, N.Z. Forest Serv., 1951-57; Sr. Jrnlist, Dept. of Tourist & Publicity, 1957-59; Ed., Te Ao Hou, Dept. of Maori Affairs, 1960-61; Reviewer & Critic, sev. publs. Mbrships. incl: V.P., Downstage Inc., Wellington, 1964-; Exec., N.Z. Israel Assn., 1972-73. Publs: (plays) The Pohutukawa Tree, 1960, 5th edit., 73; Awatea, 1970; Zero Inn, 1970; (books) Co-auth., Theatre in Danger, 1957; We Don't Want Your Sort Here, 1963; New Zealand Drama, 1973; The End of the Golden Weather, 1962, 3rd edit., 74; (short story) The Glass Wig, 1953. Hons. incl: Winner, competition for new Play, Birds in the Wilderness, Auckland Fest. Soc., 1958; State Schlrship. in Letters, State Lit. Fund, 1973. Address: 14 Henry St., Wellington 3, New Zealand.

MASON, (Sir) Frederick, b. 15 May 1913. Retired Diplomat. Educ: B.A., St. Catharine's Coll., Univ. of Cambridge, U.K., 1935. Appts. incl: 1st Sec., British Embassy, Santiago, Chile, 1946-48 & Oslo, Norway, 1948-50; Asst. Labour Advsr., For. Off., London, U.K., 1950-53; 1st Sec., British Embassy, Bonn, W. Germany, 1953-55; Counsellor, British Embassy, Athens, Greece, 1955-57; & Tehran, Iran, 1957-60; Hd., Economic Rels. Dept., For. Off., London, U.K., 1960-64; Under Sec., Min. of O'seas Dev. & Commonwealth Rels. Off., ibid, 1964-66; British Ambassador to Chile, 1966-70; British Ambassador in Geneva, Switzerland, 1971-73; Dir., New Ct. Natural Resources Ltd., 1973-. Mbrships: U.K. mbr., Int. Narcotics Control Bd., Geneva, 1974-; Travellers' Club; Canning Club; Royal Automobile Club. Hons: Companion, Order of St. Michael & St. George, 1960; Kt. Cmdr., Royal Victorian Order, 1968; Order of Merit Bernardo O'Higgins 1st Class, Chile, 1968. Address: 36a, Cleveland Sq., London W2, U.K. 1, 34.

MASON, Lela Scoville, b. 15 Jan. 1898. Educator. Educ: Dip. in Piano, 1917; Sue Bennett Coll., London, Ky., 1925-26, summer 1929; Cinn. Conservatory of Music & Univ. of Cinn., summers 1920, '28, '37, winter, 1926-27; studied piano w. F.S. Evans, 1926-27 & Corinne B. Harmon, Boston, summer, 1917, '18, '19, '21, '26, '27, '33; B.S., Music, & M.A., Music Educ., Univ. of Ky., Lexington; further studies, ibid. Appts: Supvsr., Pub. Schl. Music, London, Ky., 1919-21, & Kingsport, Tenn.,

1931-32; Dir. of Music, Rule Jr. H.S., Pub. Schls., Knoxville, Tenn., 1927-30, & Picadome High Schls., Fayette Co., Ky., 1934-37; Instr., Music Educ., Ext. Div., Univ. of Ky., 1931, & Summer Schl., ibid, 1935; Instr. Music Educ., Dir. of Vocal Music in Univ. Schls., Supvsr. of Student Tchrs. majoring in Music Educ., Univ. of Ky., 1937-45; Gen. Supvsr., Elem. Schls., Cons. High Schls., Laurel Co. Pub. Schls., Ky., 1945-61; Instr., Engl., Sue Bennett Coll., London, Ky., 1961-63; Instr., Child Growth & Dev., ibid, 1966. Mbrships. incl: Delta Kappa Gamma; Phi Beta; Kappa Delta Pi; Nat. & Ky. Ret. Tchrs. Assns.; DAR; Bd. of Trustees, 1st United Meth. Ch., 1952-; Pres., Laurel Co. Bus. & Profl. Women's Club, 1973-74; Nat. Wildlife Fedn. Contbr. articles to profl. jrnls. Author & Dir. of histl. pageant "The McNitt Defeat in Ky. on Boone's Trace", Aug. 1950, '51 & '57. Hons: Disting. Achievement in Arts Award, Laurel Co. Homecoming Comm., Ky., 1937; Alumni Awards for serv. & achievement, Alumni Assn., Sue Bennett Coll., 1961 & '70. Address: 304 W. 7th St., London, KY 40741, U.S.A.

MASON, Madeline (Mrs. Malcolm Forbes McKesson), b. 24 Jan. 1913. Author; Poet; Critic; Lecturer; Translator. Educ: pvte. schls. & instrs. incl. Arthur Symons, lit.; Ganz & Siloti, music & piano; Ernest Bloch, composition. Appts. incl: Poetry Workshops, Rudolf Steiner Seminars in the Arts; Poetry Soc. of Am.; Anthroposophic Soc. of NY; Schl. of Eurhythmics; Geo. Wash. HS, Alexandra, Va.; curriculum work, readings, lectures, Audio-Visual Dept., Bd. of Educ., NYC; Lectr. throughout US & UK; Co-fndr. w. Geo. Abbe, New England Writers & Readers Conf.; readings at Edinburgh Festival, Scotland, 1953 & Lib. of Congress, Wash. DC, 1956; Advsry. Coun., Int. Who's Who in Poetry & Who's Who of Am. Women; Advsry. Coun. Exec., Nat. Register Prominent Ams.; Poet in Res., Shenandoah Coll., Va., 1971; Edit. Cons., Marquis Who's Who. Mbrships. incl: PEN, London & N.Y.; V.P., Poetry Soc. of Am.; Authors League; Nat. League Am. Pen Woemn; Nat. Poetry Chmn. & 1st V.P., Composers, Authors & Artists of Am.; 1st V.P., Jr. League Art Chmn.; N.Y. Philharmonic Symph. Publs incl: (poetry) Hill Fragments; The Cage of Years; At the Ninth Hour: a Sonnet Sequence in New Form; (fiction) Riding for Texas (under pseudonym Tyler Mason); La Prophete-tr. of Gibran's Prophet. Contbr. of stories, essays & critiques to nat. newspapers & mags. Hons: Diamond Jubilee Award for Poetry, Nat. League Am. Pen Women, 1958; Edna St. Vincent Millay Award for invention of Mason Sonnet, 1968; First Prize Winner, Int. Who's Who in Poetry $3,000 Awards, 1974. Address: Hotel Seville, 22 E. 29th St., New York, NY 10016, U.S.A. 2, 3, 5, 6, 11, 22, 30, 34, 48, 57, 68.

MASON, Philip, b. 19 Mar. 1906. Writer. Appts. incl: Indian Civil Serv., 1928-47; Dir. of Studies in Race Rels., 1952-58; Dir., Inst. of Race Rels., 1958-69; Exec. Chmn., U.K. Coun. for Overseas Student Affairs, 1969-. Publs. incl: (as Philip Woodruff) Call the Next Witness, 1945; Whatever Dies, 1948; Hernshaw Castle, 1950; The Guardians, 1954; (as Philip Mason), Racial Tension, 1954; The Birth of a Dilemma, 1958; Year of Decision, 1960; Common Sense about Race, 1961; Patterns of Dominance & Race Relations, 1970; Race Relations, 1970. Ed., Man, Race & Darwin, 1960; Ed., India & Ceylon: Unity & Diversity, 1967. Hons. incl: O.B.E. Address: The Lyon House, Sherfield English, Nr. Romsey, Hants, U.K. 128.

MASON, (Air Commodore) William Darcy, b. 24 Oct. 1911. Secretary; Administrator.

Educ: Dip. Com., Univ. of Sydney, Australia; B.Com., Univ. of Melbourne; Dip. Ed., Univ. of New Engl., N.S.W.; Imperial Defence Coll., U.K.; Jt. Servs. Staff Coll. Appts. incl: Sr. Equipment Staff Off., 1st Tactical Air Force, Noemfoor, Morotai & Borneo, 1945-46; Staff, Dept. Air, Melbourne, 1946-48, '52-53, '57; Cmdng. Off., No. 1 Stores Depot, ibid, 1950; Cmdng. Off., No. 3 Maintenance Unit, RAF, U.K., 1954-56; Aust. Embassy, Wash., U.S.A., 1958; Sr. Equipment Staff Off., HQ Support Cmd., Melbourne, 1960-69; Sec., Mitchell Coll. Advanced Educ., 1969. Fellow, Aust. Soc. Accts., 1966; Mbr., Aust. Coll. Educ., 1969; Chmn., Western Region, N.S.W., Duke of Edinburgh's Award. Hons: O.B.E., 1954; C.B.E., 1967. Address: Secretary's Residence, Mitchell Coll. of Advanced Educ., Bathurst, N.S.W., Australia 2795. 14, 23, 128.

MASSAQUOI, A. Momolu, b. 16 May 1921. Mining & Metallurgical Engineer. Educ: B.A., Eastern Wash. Coll., U.S.A.; B.Sc., Ore. State Univ. Appts: Asst. Dir., Bur. of Mines & Geol., Monrovia, Liberia, 1951-58; Asst. Dir., Natural Resources & Surveys, 1958-61, Dir., 1961-72; V.P., African Geological Surveys Assn., 1960; Hon. Austrian Consul Gen. to Liberia, 1960-; Pres., UN Econ. Commn. for Africa, 1964-65; Bd. of Dirs., Pub. Utilities Authority, R.L., Chmn., Ad Hoc Meeting, Iron Ore Producers & Consumers, UNCTAD, Geneva, Switzerland, 1970; currently, V.P., Mine Mgmt. Assocs. Ltd. (Mining Concession), Monrovia, Liberia. Mbr., profl. & fraternal orgs. Author, var. articles & pamphlets. Hons. incl: Cmdr., Order of N. Star, Sweden, 1964; Order of Civil Merit, Italy, 1968; Grand Cmdr., Star of Africa, Liberia. Address: Mine Management Associates Ltd., P.O. Box 548, Monrovia, Liberia-WCA.

MASSEY, Donald Wayne, b. 7 Mar. 1938. Micrographer; Thoroughbred Horse Breeder. Educ: Univs. of Hawaii, Honolulu, & Ky., Lexington, U.S.A. Appts: Dir., Microfilm Ctr., Univ. of Ky., 1962-67; . Dir., Photographic Servs., Univ. of Va., Charlottesville, 1967-73; Chmn., Bd. of Workshop V (Handicapped), 1972-73; Pres., Micrographics II, Charlottesville, 1973-. Mbrships: Nat. Microfilm Assn.; Pres., Ky. Microfilm Assn., 1963-67; Pres., Va. Microfilm Assn., 1970-72; Soc. of Reproduction Engrs.; Ky. Histl. Soc. Publs: Contbns. to profl. jrnls. Hons: Outstanding Mbr. Awards, Ky. Microfilm Assn., 1967, & Va. Microfilm Assn., 1972; First Pioneer Award, Va. Microfilm Assn., 1973; Key Award, Workshop V (Handicapped), 1974. Address: Micrographics II, Milton, Route 7, Box 258G, Charlottesville, VA 22901, U.S.A.

MASSEY, Hal, b. 10 Apr. 1921. Administrator. Educ: B.S., Univ. of Fla., 1953; M.Ed., ibid, 1955; Ed.D., Univ. of Md., 1965. Appts: Instr., Educ., Univ. of Fla., 1955-57; Asst. Prof., Educ., N.C. State Coll., 1957-58; Asst. Prof., Educ., Univ. of Fla., 1958-62; V.P. for Acad. Affairs, Daytona Beach Community Coll., 1962-73; V.P. for Admin., ibid, 1973-. Mbrships. incl: Phi Kappa Phi; Phi Delta Kappa; Fla. Assn. of Community Colls.; Am. Assn. of Pub. Jr. Colls.; Am. Vocational Assn.; Fla. Vocational Assn.; NEA; Fla. Educ. Assn.; Am. Indl. Arts Assn.; Fla. Indl. Arts Assn. Hons: Most Outstanding Theta Chi Pledge, 1952; Indl. Arts Soc., Univ. of Fla., 1957. Address: 3064 Liberty St., Daytona Beach, FL 32018, U.S.A. 15, 129, 131, 139.

MASSEY, Joseph Earl, b. 22 Oct. 1897. Writer; Public Relations Director. Educ: A.B. Elon Coll., N.C., 1918; B.Lit., Columbia Univ., N.Y., 1922. Appts: Newsman, New Haven, Conn., Utica, N.Y. & N.Y.C., 1922-29;

Copywriter & Ed. w. N.Y. Telephone Co., 1929-62; Pub. Rels. Dir., East Hudson Parkway Authority, Pleasantville, N.Y., 1963-69. Mbrships: Sigma Delta Chi; Am. Numismatic Soc.; Am. Numismatic Assn:; Past Pres., Kiwanis Club & Westchester Co. Coin Club (N.Y.). Publs: America's Money, 1968; Historic Landmark Journeys in N.Y. State, 1952. Recip. of Award of Merit, Nat. Assn. of State & Local Histns., 1952. Address: 165 Keating Dr. S.W., Largo, FL 33540, U.S.A. 30.

MASSEY, (Mrs.) Mildred Elizabeth Robinson, b. 30 Jan. 1917. Registered Nurse. Educ: Baroness Erlanger Schl. of Nursing, Chattanooga, Tenn., U.S.A., 1936. Appts: Supvsr., Baroness Erlanger Hosp., Chattanooga, 1937-38; Pvte. Duty Nursing, Chattanooga, 1939-40; Hd. Nurse, Crane Co., Chattanooga Div., 1946-51; Supt. of Nurses, Atlas Chem. Inds., Inc., 1953-62; Dir. of Nursing, ICI Am., Inc., 1965-. Num. mbrships. incl: Dir., Am. Bd. of Occupational Hlth. Nurses; Sec., Bd. of Dirs., Tenn. Nurses Assn., Pres., Dist. 4, Sec., Occupational Hlth. Sect.; Am. Assn. of Indl. Nurses; Nat. League for Nursing; Pres. & Sec., Baroness Erlanger Alumni Assn.; Bd. of Dirs., Tenn. Div., Profl. Educ. for Nurses in Tenn. Chapt., Am. Cancer Soc., Fndr., Annual Cancer Conf. for Nurses; Past Matron, Order of Eastern Star; Past High Priestess, Ladies Oriental Shrine of Am. Publs: Papers, tributes, & poems in profl. jrnls. Talks for profl. progs. & workshops. Hons. incl: Baroness Erlanger Alumni Award, 1936; Cert. in Occupational Hlth. Nursing, 1973. Address: 4812 Viola Drive, Chattanooga, TN 37415, U.S.A. 125.

MASSIAH, Valence Irwin, b. 28 Aug. 1918. Pathologist. Educ: B.A., London, U.K., 1944; M.B.B.Ch., Nat. Univ. of Ireland, 1951; Dip. Child Hlth., 1955; D.C.P., London, 1961. Appts. incl: Med. Officer, Min. of Hlth., Trinidad, 1956-57; Grade B Pathol., 1958-59; Registrar, Dept. of Pathol., Hammersmith Hosp.; Grade A, Med. Officer, Min. of Hlth., 1964; Prin. Pathol., ibid, 1969-. Mbrships. incl: Area Surg., St. John Ambulance Brigade, 1962-71; Hon. Sec., Trinidad & Tobago Med. Assn., 1966-72; Pres. Elect, 1973; Chmn., St. John Coun., 1972, '73. Exec. Edit. Bd., Caribbean Med. Jrnl., 1973-. Hons: Serving Brother of St. John, 1971; Officer of St. John, 1972. Address: 14 Braemar Rd., Cascade, Port of Spain, Trinidad, W.I.

MASSIAS, Aubrey Errington, b. 2 Feb. 1935. Company Director. Appts: Clerk—Chief Clerk, Bank of Nova Scotia, 1954-58; Mgr., Bank of Nova Scotia, in Jamaica, 1961-69; Mgr., Bank of Nova Scotia (Jamaica) Ltd., London, England, & Montego Bay, Jamaica, 1969-72; Chmn., Ser-U-Pharmacy & Cafeteria Ltd., Premier Pharmacy Ltd., Liverpool Investments Ltd. & Berkely Investments Ltd; Mng. Dir., Ridgemoor Devs. Ltd., & Aubrey Massias Realty Co. Ltd. Mbrships. incl: Dir., St. Catherine Chmbr. of Comm; Dir., Realtors Assn. of Jamaica; Chmn., St. Catherine Chapt., Georgian Soc. of Jamaica; Jamaica Developers Assn. Ltd. Address: 19 Wellington St., Spanish Town, Jamaica. 109.

MASTROPAOLO, Marie P., b. 25 Apr. 1933. Educator; Editor; Literary Gonsultant. Educ: B.S., W. Chester State Coll., Pa., 1954; M.A., Duke Univ., N.C., 1964. Appts: Engl. Tchr., Shaw Jr. H.S., 1954-56, N. Miami Sr. H.S., 1956-71; Hd. of Engl. Dept., Miami Northwestern Sr. H.S., 1971-. Mbrships. incl: NEA; Nat. Deleg., ibid, 1969; Alpha Delta Kappa; Local Chapt. Pres., ibid, 1959; Dade Co. Classroom Tchrs. Assn.; Assembly of Reps., ibid, 1966-71. Chmn., P.R. Comm., 1970;

AAUW; Fla. Educ. Assn.; Nat., Fla., & Dade Co. Couns. of Tchrs. of Engl. Co-author, publs: The Craft of Poetry; Introduction to Poetry; The Novel. Hons. incl: Educ. Crisis Hon. Roll, 1968; Litt.D., 1974. Address: 367 N.W. 153rd St., Miami, FL 33169, U.S.A.

MATANE, Paulias Nguna (Mace), b. 1932. Educator; Government Official. Educ: Tchr. Trng., 1956; Secondary Educ., 1962. Appts: Asst. Tchr., 1957; Hdmaster., 1958-61; Supvsry. Tchr., 1963-66; Dist. Schl. Insp., 1967-68; Acting Supt., Tchr. Educ., 1969; Mbr., Pub. Serv. Bd., 1969; Acting Dir., Min. of Lands, Surveys & Mines, 1970; Permanent Sec., Min. of Bus. Dev., 1971-. Mbrships. incl: Passenger Transport Control Bd.; Dir., Papua New Guinea Dev. Bank; Dir., Dpty. Chmn., PNG Investment Corp.; Chmn., Duke of Edinburgh Award Scheme; Chmn., PNG Regional Churchill Mem. Trust Selection Comm. Publs. incl: Kum Tumun of Minj, 1966; A New Guinean Travels Through Africa, 1971; Bai Bisnis I Helpim Yum, 1973. Hons. incl: Forsyth Prize, 1954; S. Pacific Commn. Fellowship, 1963; Winston Churchill Fellowship, 1967; UN Dev. Prog. Fellowship, 1973. Address: Box 3383, Port Moresby, T.P.N.G., Australia. 23.

MATELL, Hans, b. 21 Oct. 1925. Architect; Town-planner. Educ: Graduated as archt., Royal Inst. of Technol., Stockholm, Sweden, 1951; French Govt. schlrship, Sorbonne & Atelier d'Art Abstrait, Paris, France, 1952-53; advanced studies, Univ. of Uppsala, Sweden, 1954-57. Appts: Asst*Chief Archt., Province of Uppland, Sweden, 1956-59; Town Archt., Uppland-Bro & Oland, 1960-69; private practice partnership, Anders Nordström arkitektkontor ab., 1970. Supervised housing & town planning on regional & local level. Sev. solo exhibs. of own painting & architecture in Sweden & France. Mbrships. incl: Fndr. Mbr. Swedish Mus. of Architecture, 1962; Fndr. Mbr., 1964, Pres., 1969-70, Swedish Mus. of Architecture; Swedish Nat. Archts. Assn. Publs: Housing at Hydroelectric Powerplants, 1952; The Home—Its New Concept, 1956. Recip., Sev. 1st & 2nd prizes & honours in archtl. competitions, 1962-72. Address: Matell & Nordström arkitektkontor ab, P.O. Box 237, 751 05 Uppsala 1, Sweden.

MATHERNE, Beverly Mary, b. 15 Mar. 1946. Assistant Professor. Educ: B.A., Univ. of Southwestern La., 1969; M.A., ibid, 1971; Ph.D., St. Louis Univ., 1974. Appts: Grad. Tchng. Asst., Engl., Univ. of Southwestern La., 1969-71; Asst. Prof., Engl., ibid, 1974-; Grad Tchng. Asst., Engl., St. Louis Univ., 1971-74. Mbrships: Pres., Gamma Beta Phi, 1968; Sigma Tau Delta; Kappa Delta Phi. Contbr. to learned jrnls. Hons: Inst. of Int. Educ. Schlrship. to Univ. of London, 1973; T.H. Harris Schlrship., 1964. Address: Rt. 1 Box 607, Paulina, LA 70763, USA. 125.

MATHES, David Wayne, b. 23 Apr. 1933. Recording Engineer; Record Producer. Educ: Tenn. State Univ., Nashville; Rutgers Univ., N.J. Appts. incl: Staff-Chief Engr., sev. studios, Nashville, Tenn; currently Pres., Songs of David, Inc., ibid; Owner, Col. Dave Mathes Productions, ibid. Recording artist, NRS Records. Fndr., Nashville Sound Laboratories. Composer, Broadcast Music Inc. Mbrships. incl: Gospel Music Assn.; Country Music Assn.; Am. Soc. of Authors, Compsers & Publrs.; Songwriters Hall of Fame. Compositions incl: Sleepyhead; I'll Be Going Home Tomorrow; Who Can Mend a Broken Heart. Hons: Hon. Order Ky. Cols., 1967; B.A., Sussex Coll. of

Technol., 1973. Address: P.O. Box 653, Nashville, TN 37202, U.S.A.

MATHESEN, John Alfred, b. 10 July 1932. Teacher; Musician. Educ: B.S., Lamar Univ., Beaumont, Tex., U.S.A., 1961; M.M., N. Tex. State Univ., Denton, 1966. Appts: Choral Dir. Tex. Pub. Schls., 1961-66; Choral Dir., Univ. of Tenn. at Martin, 1966-; Choral Clinician & Guest Conductor, S. & S.-E. States. Mbrships: Am. Choral Dirs. Assn.; Am. Choral Fndn.; Past Pres., W. Tenn. Vocal Music Educators Assn.; Phi Mu Alpha; Pi Kappa Lambda; Phi Kappa Phi. Author, The Six Authentic Motets of J.S. Bach: An Analysis in Relation to Performance. Address: Dept. of Music, University of Tennessee at Martin, Martin, TN 38238, U.S.A. 125.

MATHESON, James Adam Louis, b. 11 Feb. 1912. Vice-Chancellor. Educ: M.Sc., Manchester Univ., U.K.; Ph.D., Birmingham Univ. Appts: Lectr., Birmingham Univ., 1938-46; Prof., Civil Engrng., Univ. of Melbourne, 1946-50; Beyer Prof. of Engrng., Manchester Univ., 1950-59; Vice-Chancellor, Monash Univ., 1959-; Chmn., Papua New Guinea Inst. of Technol., 1966-73; Chancellor, ibid, 1973-. Mbrships. incl: Melbourne Club; Fellow, Instn. of Civil Engrs.; Fellow, Instn. of Structural Engrs.; V.P., ibid, 1967-68; Fellow, Instn. of Engrs., Australia; Sr. V.P., ibid, 1974; Chmn., Sci. Mus. of Victoria, 1969-73. Author, Hyperstatic Structures. Hons. incl: Kernot Mem. Medal, 1970; C.M.G., 1972; LL.D., Univ. of Manchester, 1973. Address: Monash Univ., Wellington Rd., Clayton, Victoria, Australia, 3168. 1, 23, 34, 128.

MATHESON, John Ross, b. 14 Nov. 1917. Judge. Educ: B.A., Queen's Univ.; Barrister-at-law, Osgoode Hall; LL.M., Univ. of Western Ont. Appts. incl: Hon. Lt. Col., 30th Field REgiment, Royal Canadian Artillery; Mbr., 24th-27th Parliaments of Canada; Chmn., Standing Comm. on External Affairs, 1963-65; Parliamentary Sec., Prime Min., 1966-68; Created Q.C., 1967; Apptd. Judge, 1968. Mbrships. incl: Life mbr., Nat. Trust for Scotland; Heraldry Soc. of Canada; Royal Econ. Soc.; Canadian Econs. Assn.; Royal Canadian Legion; United Empire Loyalist Assn. of Canada; Fellow, Soc. of Antiquaries of Scotland; Sec., Canadian Amateur Boxing Assn.; Genealogist, Priory of Canada Order os st. John; Trustee, Queen's Univ. Author of The Canadian Flag, Ency. Canadiana. Hons. incl: Named Brockville Citizen of Yr., 1969; Kt. of Justice, Venerable Order of St. John of Jerusalem. Address: 2030 Thistle Cres., Ottawa, K1H 5P5, Canada. 6, 20, 88, 128.

MATHEWS, Anthony Stuart, b. 22 Aug. 1930. Professor of Law. Educ: B.A., LL.B. (cum laude), Ph.D. Appts: Admission as Atty. & Notary Pub., Supreme Ct. of S. Africa, 1953; Prof. of Law, Univ. of Natal, Durban, 1964-; Dean, Fac. of Law, 1966-67, 1971-74; Vis. Schlr., Harvard Univ., U.S.A., 1968-69. Mbrships: Chmn., Pol. Sommn., Study Proj. for Christianity in Apartheid Sco., 1970-73; Nat. Exec. of S. African Inst. of Race Rels., 1973-74; former Mbr., Nat. Exec., Liberal Party of S. Africa. Publs: Law, Order & Liberty in South Africa, 1971; Security Laws & Social Change in South Africa: A Chapter in South Afirca; Sociological Persepctive, 1971. Hons. incl: Carnegie Schlrship., 1968; Butterworths Overseas Legal Fellowship, 1971; Hoernlé Mem. Lectr., 1971. Address: 2 Ferndale Ave., Westville, Natal, S. Africa.

MATHEWS, H. Hume, b. 30 Nov. 1911. Attorney; Engineer. Educ: B.S., Univ.of Md.,

1933; LL.B., Schl. of Law, Georgetown Univ., 1944; J.D., Univ. of Conn., 1944; postgrad. work, Geo. Wash. Univ., & Seton Hall Univ., N.J Appts. incl: Chief Engr., S. Pitts. Coal Co., Morgantown, Va., 1933-35; Patent Examiner, U.S. Patent Off., Wash. D.C., 1936-42; Patent Atty., United Aircraft Corp., E. Harford, Conn., 1942-47; Mgr., Patent Dept., Dir. of Patent, Trademark & Licensing Activities, Food & Drug Counsel, Air Reduction Co. Inc., (Airco Inc), Murray Hill, N.J., 1040. Holder, 4 U.S. Patents. Mbrships. incl: Past Chmn., Nat. Coun. of Patent Law Assns; Past Pres., N.J. Patent Law Assn; Lambda Chi Alpha; Tau Beta Pi; Pi Delta Epsilon; Alpha Psi Omega; Tau Beta Pi Hon. Schol. Engrng. Fraternity, 1932. Address: Scott Rd., R.D.1 Box 70-C, Boonton Township, NJ 07005, U.S.A. 6.

MATHEWS, Piravonu Mathews, b. 12 May 1932. Physicist. Educ: B.Sc., Madras Christian Coll., Univ. of Madras, India, 1952; M.Sc., Univ. of Madras, 1953; Ph.D., ibid, 1956. Appts. incl: Rdr. in Phys., Univ.of Madras, 1956-64; NRC Of Canada Postdoctoral Rsch. Fellow, Ottawa, Ont., 1956-58; Rsch. Fellow, Brandeis Univ., Waltham, Mass., U.S.A., 1958-59; Vis. Sr. Rsch. Assoc., ibod, 1964-65; Prof. of Theoretical Phys., Univ. of Madras, 1964-; Vis. Prof., Univ. of Tex., Austin, U.S.A. 1973. Mbrships: Bd. Govs., Inst.of Math. Scis., Madras, 1966-72. Publs. incl: textbook, Quantum Mechanics (w. K. Venkatesan), in press; num. rsch. publs. Address: Dept. of Theoretical Phys., Univ. of Madras (Guindy Campus), Madras 25, India. 50.

MATHIAS, Peter, b. 10 Jan. 1928. University Teacher; Author. Educ: Jesus Coll., Cambrdige, U.K., 1948-51; B.A., Cambridge, 1951; Harvard Univ., 1952-53. Appts. incl: Fellow, Tutor & Dir. of Studies in Hist., Queens' Coll., Cambridge, 1955-68; Lectr., Hist. Fac., Cambridge, 1955-68; Sr. Proctor, Cambridge Univ., 1965-66; Chichele Prof., Econ. Hist., & Fellow, All Souls Coll., Oxford, 1969-; Vis. Prof., var. univs. inclng. Univ. of Pa., U.S.A., 1972, & Va. Gildersleeve Prof., Barnard Coll., Columbia Univ., 1972. Mbrships: Hon. Treas., Econ. Hist. Soc., 1968-; Chmn., Bus. Archives Coun., 1967-72; U.K. Rep., Coun. of Int. Econ.Hist. Assn.; Vice Chmn., Econ. & Soc. Hist. Comm., S.S.R.C., 1972-; Johnson Club, 1973-; Fellow, Royal Histl. Soc., 1972-. Author of books in field. Address: All Souls Coll., Oxford, U.K. 1.

MATHIAS, Roland Glyn, b. 4 Sept. 1915. Poet; Editor; Literary Critic. Educ: B.A., Jesus Coll., Oxford, U.K., 1936; B.Litt., 1939; M.A., 1944. Appts. incl: Sr. Hist. Master, St. Clement Danes Grammar Schl., London, 1946-48; Hdmaster, Pembroke Dock Grammar Schl., Pembrokeshire, 1948-58; Hdmaster., Herbert Stoutt Schl., Belper, 1958-64; Hdmaster, King Edward's 5 Ways Schl., Birmingham, 1964-69; Pt.-Time Lectr., Univ. Coll., Cardiff, 1970-. Mbrships: Welsh Arts Coun., 1974-; Combined Arts Panel, S.E. Wales Arts Assn., 1973-. Publs. incl: The Flooded Valley, 1960; Whitsun Riot, 1963; Absalom in the Tree, 1971; Vernon Watkins, 1974. Hons: Welsh ARts Coun. Award., 1965; Welsh Arts Coun. Bursary, 1969; Welsh ARts Coun. Prize for Poetry, 1972. Address: Deffrobani, Maescelyn, Brecon, LD3 7NL, U.K.

MATHIS, Eugene Laybronze, b. 23 Jan. 1948. Professor. Educ: B.A., Tuskegee Inst., Ala., USA; M.A., Ata. Univ., Ga., 1971, '74. Appts: Instr., Engl., Voorhees Coll., Denmark, SC, 1968-70; Asst. Prof., Engl., Coord., Freshman Engl., Fac., Asst., Engl., Metro-Ata. Trio Prog., Clark Coll., Ata., Ga., 1970-74.

Mbrships. incl: NCTE; GAE; Ga.-SC Coun. Engl. Tchrs. Assn.; AAUP ℅YMCA; SCLC; Alpha Phi Alpha. Author 2 papers, Teaching the Creative Student, 1974; Black Literature; An Academic Necessity. Hons: Tchr. of Yr. Award, 1972; E.C. Walker Lit. Award, 1967; Missie Jackson Smith Award, 1968. Address: 1631 Stanton Rd., S.W., Apt. F-1, Ata., GA 30311, USA. 125.

MATHIS, James Forrest, b. 28 Sept. 1925. Chemical Engineer; Industrial Executive. Educ: B.S., Tex. A&M Univ., Coll. Station, Tex., 1946; M.S., Ph.D., Univ. of Wis., Madison, Wis., 1950-53. Appts: Asst. Rsch. Chemist, Exxon Corp., affiliated Exxon Co., U.S.A., Baytown, Tex. refinery, 1946; Mgr., Baytown Rsch. & Dev. Labs., 1961; Mgr., Specialty Products, Houston, 1963; V.P., Petroleum Rsch., Esso Rsch. & Engrng. Co., Linden, N.J., 1966; Sr. V.P., Petrochem. Ops., Imperial Oil Ltd., Toronto, Ont. 1968; V.P., Chems. Rsch., Esso Rsch. & Engrng. Co., Linden, N.J., 1971; V.P., Technol. Exxon Chem. Co., Florham Park, N.J., 1973. Mbrships: Profl. Guidance & Awards Comms., Am. Inst. of Chem. Engrs.; Chmn., Awards Comm., ibid, 1963; Am. Chem. Soc.; Pres., Canadian Sect., Soc. of Chem. Ind., 1970; AAAS; Sigma Xi; Tau Beta Pi. Address: Exxon Chem. Co., P.O. Box 271, Florham Park, NJ 07932, U.S.A.

MATHIS, Roy N., b. 3 Jan. 1936. Chaplain. Educ: B.S., Clemson Univ., S.C. 1957; B.A., Tex. Christian Univ., Ft. Worth., 1964; B.D., Southwestern Bapt. Theol. Sem., Ft. Worth, 1966; Dip., US Army Chap. Schl., Ft. Hamilton, N.Y., 1965. Appts: Livestock Specialist, Greenwood Packing Plant, S.C., 1957-63; Cnslr., Southern Tech. Univ., Ft. Worth, Tex., 1963-64; Alumni Records Asst., Southwestern Bapt. Theol. Sem., Ft. Worth, 1964-66; Pastor, Indian Hills Bapt. Ch., N. Little Rock. Ark., 1966-68; Chap., VA Hosp., ibid, 1966-67 & Ark. Nat. Guards, Camp Robinson, 1967-68; Chap. (CPT), US Army, 1968-. Mbrships. incl: N. Pulaski Bapt. Pastors Conf., 1966-68; Kiwanis Int.; Nat. Guard Off.'s Assn. of USA. N. Little Rock Ministerial Alliance, 1967-68; YMCA Bd. of Dirs., 1967068; Assn. of US Army; Mil. Chaps. Assn. Hons: sev. mil. awards inclng. Bronze Star w. OLC, Air Medal w. OLC, Army Commendation Medal; Vietnamese Serv. & Campaign Medals. Address: Rte. Four, Box 351, Gaffney, SC 29340, USA. 117. 125.

MATHON, Reinier Edmond, b. 1 Sept. 1930. Public Relations Manager. Educ: The Netherland Lyceum, The Hague, 1950; Reserve Off. Trng. Schl., Netherlands Army, 1951; Royal Mil. Acad., 1953. Appts. incl: Marketing Off., KLM Royal Dutch Airlines, 1953-63; Market Rsch. Mgr., Dutch Tourist Bd., 1963-65; Co-Dir., Fndn. for P.R., Dutch Agirc. & Horticulture, 1965-70; P.R. & Publicity Mgr., ICI Holland, 1970-. Mbrships. incl: Former Mbr., Nat. Bd. Jr. Chmbr., Netherlands; Bd. Mbr., Dutch Assn. for P.R.; Educ. & Trng. Comm., P.r.; Ctr. Européen des Rels. Pubs.; Chmn., Working Grp. P.R. Crop Protection; Netherlands Rep. on P.R. to Groupement des Fabricatems Phytosanitaires. Publs. incl: Co-author of two books on P.R.; Ed. in Chief of a series of informative leaflets on Dutch horticulture and agric. for educl. use. Co-recip. of Statue of Athens, 1965. Address: ICI Holland BV, P.O. Box NR 1020, 10 Mersey Weg, Rotterdam-Rozenburg, The Netherlands.

MATHOV, Enrique, b. 29 June 1914. Doctor of Medicine. Educ: Grad., Coll. of Med., Buenos Aires Univ., 1939. Appts: Clin. Physn., Rawson Hosp., Buenos Aires, 1940-48; Dir.

Pvte. Clin. of Allergic Diseases, 1950-; Dir., Revista Argentina Alergia, 1954-65; Hd., Allergy Dept., Polyclinic Lanus, 1956-60; Hd., Allergy & Immunopathol. Dept., Polyclinic Finochietto (Avellaneda), 1961-; Free Docent, Med. Dept., Buenos Aires Univ., 1963-64; Dir., Allergia et Immunopathologia, 1972-. Mbr., Fellow 7 Off., var. nat. & for. med. orgs. Publs. incl: Allergy & Immunology (co-author), 1968; Drug Allergy, 1971; Complete Course in Allergy & Immunology, 2 vols., 1973. Num. contbns., clin., allergy & immunol. subjects, med. publs., Argentine, Mexico, U.S.A. & Europe. Address: Cordoba 3431, Buenos Aires, Argentina.

MATIROSSIAN, Aramis, b. May 1920. Specialist in Skin Surgery. Educ: M.D. in Dermatol. Sec. Gen., Iranian Geriatrics Soc. Fellow, Royal Soc. of Med. Mbr., Tehran Lions Club. Author, book on Skin Surgery. Articles in Journal of Tehran Medical School. Address: 70 Ramssar St., Tehran, Iran.

MATLOCK, Damon. b. 7 Aug. 1917. Minister. Educ: B.A., Eastern N.M. Univ., 1949; B.D., Golden Gate Bapt. Theol. Sem. 1951; Grad. Schl., ibid, 1952. Appts: Student Pastor, 1st Bapt. Ch., Arch., N.M. 1945-47, 1st Bapt. Ch. Elida, N.M., 1947-48, Calvary Bapt. Ch., Los Banos, Calif., 1948-50; Pastor, Silverado Bapt. Ch., Napa, 1950-55, El Camino Bapt. Ch., Sacramento, 1955-64, Arden Bapt. Ch., ibid, 1964-71. Mbrships: incl; Exec. Bd., Southern Bapt. Gen. Conven. of Calif., 1951-54, '64-68; Trustee, Golden Gate Bapt. Theol. Sem., Mill Valley, 1964-; Southern Bapt. Fndn. Bd., Nashville, Tenn, 1969-72; served Trans Pacific Crusade, N.Z. 1965, Panama Crusade, 1966, S. Africa Crusade, 1967. Address: 3620 Fair Oaks Blvd., Sacramento CA 95825, U.S.A. 120.

MATOUSEK, Otto Ralph. b. 29 May 1923. Attorney. Appts. incl; Special Asst. Attny. Gen., Homestead, Fla., 1952-64; City Atty., ibid, 1953-61; Dir., Gen. Counsel, 1st Nat. Bank, Fla., & 1st Nat. Bank of Princeton-Naranja; Pres. Chmn., Radio Stn. WIII. Mbrships. incl; Ill., Fla. & Homestead Bar Assns.; Gov. Homstead Moose Lodge, 1971; Dist. Pres. ibid, 1972; Exalted Ruler, Homestead Elks, 1953; State V.P. ibid, 1958; Dist. Dpty. 1959. Address: 234 N. Krome Ave., Homstead, FL 33030, U.S.A. 7.

MATRIGE, Conrad J., b. 12 Oct. 1924. Newspaper General Mkanager & Chief Editor. Educ: Liège Univ. Appts. icnl: Gen. Mgr. & Chief Ed., La Nouvelle Gazette, La Province, & Le Progrès newspapers. Mbrships: Mensa; Lions. Address: La Nouvelle Gazette, 1 Quai de Flandre, 6000 Charleroi, Belgium.

MATSON, Jessie B., b. 18 July 1904. Government Official; Educator; Writer. Educ: A.B., Neb. Univ., 1924; Postgrad. study, Utah Univ., 1945-47. Appts: Writer, Omaha Daily Jrnl., Stockman, 1926-30; Syndicate Writer, Corn Belt Farm Dailies, 1930-34; State Dir., Women's Div. IA Emergency Relief Admin., 1934-35; Dir., Women's Profl. Projs. WPA, 1935-40; Archives Security, Air Force, 942; Fac., Utah Univ., 1945-46; Tchr., Mariannas Islands, 1946-47; Coord., Women's Activities, St. Paul Civil Defense, 1950-70; Tchr., Southern Cross Christian Schl., Miami, 1971-72; Substitute Tchr., var. Co. schls., 1973. Mbrships: Fndr. mbr., St. Paul Coun. Human Rels.; Past Pres., Inter-Club Coun.; 1st St. Paul & Peace River Toastmistress Club; Past Chmn., Ramsey Co. Cancer Assn., Nat. Thanksgiving Day Assn.; Past Nat. V.P., Pub. Affairs, Soroptimist Fedn.; Life mbr. & Past Pres., St.

Paul Club; Theta Sigma Phi; Gamma Alpha Chi; Peo Alpha Phi. Recip. num. awards. Address: 234 SE Beeney Rd., Port Charlotte, FL 33950, U.S.A. 2, 7, 132.

MATSUMAE, Akihiro, b. 16 Apr. 1930. Microbiologist. Educ: Veterinary Dr., Nippon Veterinary & Zootech. Coll., 1952; D.M.S., ibid, 1960. Appts: Asst. Rschr., Antibiotics Lab., Kitasato Inst., 952-60, Assoc. Rschr., Div. Antibiotics & Cancer, 1960-66, Asst. Chief, Dept. of Antibiotics & Cancer, 1966-73, Chief of Mycological Lab., 1973-; Instr., Kitasato Hygiene Tech. Schl., 1961-68, Guest Instr. 1970-; Asst. Prof., Kitasato Univ., 1968-72; Vis. Prof., Mich. State Univ., U.S.A., 1968-70, Coll. of Hygienic Scis., Kitasato Univ., Japan, 1972-. Mbrships: Soc. for Actinomycetes, Japan; Japanese Socs. Bacteriol., Med. Mycol.; Mycological Soc. of Japan; Am. Soc. Microbiol.; Japan Soc. Chemotherapy. Contbr., Japanese Jrnl. Antibiotics, & other profl. publs. Address: Mycological Laboratory, Kitasato Institute, 5-9-1 Shirokane, Minato-ku, Tokyo 108, Japan.

MATSUMOTO, Seiichi, b. 8 Nov. 1916. Physician. Educ: Grad., Fac. Sci., Urawa Nat. Coll., Japan, 1937; Grad., Schl. Med., Tokyo Univ., 1941; Dr. Med. Sci., ibid, 1947. Appts: Asst. Prof., Showa Med. Coll., Japan, 1954-50; Chief, Dept. Maternal Hlth, Aiiku Inst., 1950-54; Chief, Dept. Ob. & Gyn., Kanto Teishin Hosp., 1954-58; P.T. Lect., Ob. & Gyn., Showa Med. Coll., 1950-57; Tokyo Univ., Schl. Med., 1957-58; Prof., Chmn., Ob. & Gyn., Gunma Univ. Schl. Med. Maebashi, 1958-72; Dir., Schl. Midwives, Gunma Univ., 1965-72; Prof., Ob. & Gyn. Jichi Med. Coll., 1972-; Dir., Jichi Med. Coll. Hosp., 1972-. Mbrships: Dir., Japan Ob. & Gyn. Soc.; Dir., Japan Soc. Fertility & Sterility; Dir., Japanese Soc. Maternal Hlth.; Int. Fedn. Gyn. & Ob.; Int. Fedn. Infantile & Juvenile Gyn. (Chmn., Japanese Br.); Int. Planned Parenthood Fedn. Publs. incl: Menstrual Disorders, 1956; Menstruation and Its Disorders, 1962; Physiology of Menstruation, 1964; Maternal Care, 1966; Recent Contraceptive Methods, 1968. Recip. award for paper, Japanese Soc. Ob. & Gyn., 1964. Address: Jichi Med. Schl. Hosp. Minamikawachi-machi, Kawachi-gun, Tochigi-ken, 329-04, Japan.

MATTERSDORF, Leo, b. 12 Sept. 1903. Certified Public Accountant. Appts. incl: Snr. Ptnr., Mattersdorf & Kraemer, 1943-; Advsry. Comm., State Tax Commnr., State of N.Y., 1943-44, 1963-; Advsry. Coun., Tax Inst., 1945-47; Advsry. Comm., Tax Admin., City of N.Y., 1966-69. Mbrships: Past Sec. & Dir., Nat. Tax Assn.; Past Dir., N.Y. State Soc. Certified Pub. Accts.; Am. Inst. Certified Pub. Accts.; Past Pres. & Dir., Amateur Astronomers Assn., Inc., N.Y. Author of Insight into Astronomy (A Key to the Heavens). Recip. of awards & Hon. Life Mbrship., Nat. Tax Assn.-Tax Inst. Am. 1973. Address: 30 Vesey St., N.Y., NY 10007, U.S.A. 6, 16, 51, 128.

MATTHAI, Diego, b. 19 Mar. 1942. Architect; Designer; Sculptor, Painter. Educ: Iberoamerican Univ., Mexico City, 1961-65. Appts. incl: Draftsman, Designer & Planner, sev. archtl. offs., Mexico City, 1962-67; Pvte. Prac., Environmental, Archtl., Theatre, TV, Graphic, & Indl. Designer, Mexico City, 1968-; Prof., Design, Nat. Univ. of Mexico, 1973-. Mbrships: Soc. of Mexican Archts.; Co-fndr., Soc. of Archts. of the Iberoamerican Univ.; Co-fndr., Diseñadores de Mexico. One-man exhibs: Mexico City, 1969, 1971, 1973 & 1974, Guadalajara, 1974, L.A., Calif., U.S.A.,

1973. Other exhibs: Mexico City & Acapulco, Mexico, San Fran., Calif., & Phoenix, Ariz., U.S.A., Nottingham, U.K., 1971-74. Recip., Prize for Monumental Sculpture, Gobierno del Estado de Baja California, 1972. Address: Avenida Mexico 167, Apt. 1, Mexico 11, D.F., Mexico.

MATTHEOU, Chris, b. 10 Apr. 1928. Orthopaedic Surgeon. Educ: Grad., Aristotle Univ. Med. Schl. of Salonica, Greece, 1957. Appts. incl: Orthopaedic Res., Albert Einstein Med. Ctr., Phila., Pa., 1960-62; Children's Orthopaedic Res., Hosp. for Crippled Children, Newark, N.J., 1962-63; Orthopaedic Fellow & Clinical Instr., N.J. Coll. Med., Jersey City Med. Ctr., 1963-65. Pvte. Prac. 1966-. Cons., Passaic Gen. Hosp., St. Mary's Hosp., Beth Israel Hosp., in Passaic, N.J. Certified by Am. Bd. Orthopaedic Surg. Inc., 1969. Mbrships: Fellow, Int. Coll. Surgs., 1969, Am. Coll. Surgs., 1970, Am. Acad. Orthopaedic Surgs., 1971; Mbr., Eastern Orthopaedic Assn., 1971; N.J. Orthopaedic Soc., 1972. Address: 208 Passaic Ave., Passaic, NJ 07055, U.S.A.

MATTHEW, John Britton, b. 16 Sept. 1896. Artist; Educator; Restorer. Educ: A.B., Univ. of Calif., 1921; Hons. Grad., Art Inst., Chgo., 1924; Student of Hans Hofmann, 1930, Leon Kroll, & Millard Sheets. Appts: Art Instr., City Coll., Sacramento, Calif., 1926-60; Art Chmn., ibid, 1935-55; Dir., E.B. Crocker Art Gall., Sacramento, 1950; Exec. Sec., Sacramento Art Ctr., Fed. Art Proj., 1938-41; Lectr., Educl. TV Art Course, 1957; Restorer-Conservator, Sacramento, 1958-73. Mbrships: Art Students League; Art Inst. of Chgo.; Trustee, E.B. Crocker Art Gall., 1950-71, Pres., 1957-60; Pres., Calif. Mus. Assn., 1924; Int. Acad. of Arts, Rome, Italy. Murals: St. Ann's Ch., Columbia, Calif., 1957; Ft. Ord, Calif., for Am. Red Cross, 1946-47. Recip., sev. hons. Address: 1550 12th Ave., Sacramento, CA 95818, U.S.A. 9, 37, 133.

MATTHEWS, John, b. 20 Mar. 1924. Insurance Salesman; Educator; Minister; Principal. Educ: Tougaloo Coll., 1950; Grad. w. Distinctions, Miss. Vocational Coll., Itta Bena, 1961; Courses, Miss. Bapt. Theol. Sem., Univ. of Ala., & Northwestern Univ., Chgo., Ill.; M.Ed., Delta State Coll., 1970. Appts: Ins. Salesman, 1940-; Tchr., all elem. grades & subjects, 1st-8th grades, Hd. Start & Pre-Schl. Classes, Adult Educ. Classes & Classes in Relig.; Prin., E. Sunflower Schl.; Pastor, St. Paul & Chapel Hill Bapt. Chs. Mbrships: NEA; Miss. Tchrs. Assn.; Bell Grove Bapt. Ch.; Trustee, Sunflower Co. Bapt. Assn.; on Bds., Bolivar Co. Bapt. Assn. & Coahoma Co. Brotherhood Assn.; Indianola Biracial Community Rels. Comm.; Nat. Bapt. Convention U.S.A. Inc. Address: P.O. Box 323, Indianola, MS 38751, U.S.A. 125, 130.

MATTHEWS, Philip Albert, b. 2 Mar. 1921. Public Relations & Advertising Officer. Educ: Auckland Univ. Coll., N. Zealand. Appts. incl: various Edit. positions, N. Zealand newspapers & mags., 1938-50; Rep. N. Zealand Inst. of Int. Affairs at Inst. of Pacific Relations Conf., Lucknow, India, 1950; rsch. on relief needs in India, Pakistan & Ceylon, for N. Zealand Coun. of Org. for Relief Servs. Overseas, 1950; Lecture Tour throughout N. Zealand on results of Rsch., 1952-54; Advt. Off., Air N. Zealand, 1955-57; Asst. P.R. Off., Govt. of Fiji, Mbr. Fiji Broadcasting Commn., Bd. Mbr., Fiji Visitors Bur. & establd. 1st P.R. & Advt. Consy., Fiji, 1958-60; P.R. & Advt. Mgr., Fletcher Holdings Ltd., Auckland, N. Zealand, 1961-. Mbrships: Fellow & former Pres., P.R. Inst. of N.Z.; Nat. Coun. Mbr. & former Pres., Assn. of N.Z.

Advertisers; British Assn. Indus. Eds. Publs: num. articles & broadcasts on p.r., advt., Pacific affairs, Race Relations & subsistence gardening. Address: 66 La Trobe St., Pakuranga, Auckland, N. Zealand. 24.

MATTHEWS, Thomas Alexander, b. 3 Aug. 1901. Attorney & Editor. Educ: B.A., Northwestern Univ., 1922; J.D., ibid, 1925. Appts. incl: Asst. city Atty., Chgo., Ill., 1926-27; Counsel, Ill. Municipal League, 1927-65; Pub. Works Commnr., Ill. Div., 1934-37; Counsel, Kreger & Karton, 1969-72; Counsel for following cities, villages & bds. in Ill: Villa Pk., 1934-64; River Forest, 1936-42; Palatine, 1936-61; Hillside, 1938-46; Bellwood, 1938-49; Veterans' Pk. Dist., 1938-49; Berkeley Water Bd., 1938-72; Broadview, 1938-46; Deerfield, 1950-65; Barrington, 1951-67; Stickney, 1957-70; Bridgeview, 1961-63. Mbrships: Annual Fellow, Int. Biographical Soc., 1972-; Ill. Bar; Am. Bar Assn.; Audubon Soc.; Geographic (Nat.) Oceangraphic; Oil Conservation; Am. Forests; Nat. Pks.; Smithsonian Assn.; Osage Hills Gem & Mineral Soc. Inc.; V.P., Inter-galactic Petrol. Soc. Publs. incl: Municipal Ordinances, I vol, 1959, 2 vols, '63, 4 vols, '73; Ed., Current Municipal Problems (qtly.), 1959-; Selected for inclusion in Lib. of Human Resources, Am. Bicentennial Rsch. Inst., 1973. Address: 926 Sandstone Dr., Bartlesville, OK 74003, U.S.A. 7, 8, 16, 22, 57, 125, 128.

MATTIELLO, Roberto, b. 13 Feb. 1934. Painter; Sculptor; Muralist. Educ: Inst. de Educ. por El Arte, Buenos Aires, 1956-59; Pratt Inst., N.Y.C., 1964. Appts: Art Designer, Harrods Ltd., Buenos Aires, 1952-56; Proprietor, Galerie H, Buenos Aires, 1959-63. Works incl: Mural & Interior Design, Olivetti, Buenos Aires, 1958; Ballad (mural on fibreglass), Jack Parker Co., N.Y.C., 1964; Cosmic Voyage (mural, light, sounds), Varig Airlines, Buenos Aires, 1971. Mbrships: Int. Soc. for Non-Verbal Psychotherapy; Int. Soc. for Psychosynteresis, l'Orient, Switzerland, 1973. Recip. Hon. Mention, Segunda Bienal Argentina Arte Sagrado, 1956. Address: 243 E. 31 St., N.Y., NY 10016, U.S.A. 37.

MATTINGLY, James William, Jr., b. 9 Nov. 1920. Executive. Educ: A.B., Univ. of Ky., 1949; Grad. Schl., ibid. Appts: joined Cowden Mfg. Co., Lexington, Ky., 1951; Salesman, 1954-61; Acct. Exec., 1961-67; V.P., Merchandizing, 1968-. Mbrships: Lexington Country Club; Lafayette Club; Lansdowne Club. Recip. Presidential Unit Citation, WWII. Address: 3415 Brookhaven Drive, Lexington, KY 40502, U.S.A. 7.

MATTOO, Brijnath, b. 18 May 1933. Scientist; Forensic Science Administrator. Educ: B.Sc., Jammu & Kashmir Univ., 1950; M.Sc., Poona Univ., 1953; Ph.D., ibid, 1955; D.Sc., 1959. Appts: Post-doctoral Nat. Rsch. Fellow, Poona Univ., 1956-69; CSIR Scientists' Pool Off., 1959; Asst. Dir., Hd. of Phys. Div., Forensic Sci. Lab., Bombay, 1959- 71; Dir., Forensic Sci. Lab., Maharashtra State, Bombay, 1971-. Mbrships: Fellow, Nat. Acad. Scis., India, & Indian Chem. Soc.; Exec. Coun., Indian Acad. Forensic Scis.; Life Mbr., Indian Sci. Congress Assn. Var. publs., sci. jrnls., India, U.K., W. Germany, U.S.A., U.S.S.R. Recip., Study Tour Award, Colombo Plan, 1968-69. Address: Forensic Science Laboratories, State of Maharashtra, Bombay 8, India.

MATTURI, Sahr Thomas, b. 22 Oct. 1925. Educator. Educ: Univ. Coll., Ibadan, 1951-54; Univ. of Hull, U.K., 1956-59. Appts. incl: Univ. Lectr., 1959-63; Prin., Njala Univ. Coll., Sierra

Leone, 1963-; V. Chancellor, Univ. of Sierra Leone, 1968-70; Chmn., W. African Examinations Coun., 1972-. Mbrships: British Mycological Soc.; elected Fellow, Royal Soc. of Arts, London, U.K., 1971-. Hons: C.M.G. for Pub. Servs. to Educ., 1967. Address: Njala Univ. Coll., Pvte. Mail Bag, Freetown, Sierra Leone. 34.

MATUTE, Ana Maria, (Mrs.), b. 26 July 1925. Writer. Appts: Lectr., Ind. Univ., 1965-66; Lectr., Univ. of Okla., 1969. Hon. Fellow, Am. Assn. Tchrs. of Spanish. Corres. Mbr., Hispanic Soc, Am. Publs. incl: Primera Memoria, 1960; El Arrepentido, 1961; Tres y un Sueno, 1961; Historias de la Attamil, 1961; Libro de juegos para los ninos de los otros, 1961; El rio, 1963; Los Soldadoslloran de noche, 1864; Algunos muchachos, 1958; La Trampa, 1969; La torre Vigia, 1971; Olvidado Rey Gudu, 1973; (juvenile) El pais de la pizarra, 1956; Paulina, 1960; El saltamontes verde, 1960; Caballito loco, 1960; El polizon del ulises, 1965. Hons. incl: Prize Lazarillo, 1965; Prize Fastenrath, Royal Spanish Acad., 1969; Runner up, 1970 & Author Highly Commended, 1972, Hans Christian Andersen Award, 1972. Address: Santiago Rusinol 15, Sitges, Barcelona, Spain. 34.

MAUBEUGE, Pierre Louis, b. 8 Feb. 1923. Geologist. Educ: Doct. ès Sci., Univ. of Strasbourg, France; Doct. d'Etat (Geol.) Univ. of Nancy. Appts: Geol. Advsr., la Régie Autonome des Pétroles & Soc. Nat. des Pétroles d'Aquitaine (past); Geol. Advsr., la Chambre Syndicale des Mines de fer de France & l'Inst. de Recherches de la Sidérurgie; Staff, la Carte Geol. de la France. Mbrships: Sec. Gen., Acad. et Soc. Lorraines des Scis.; Inst. Grand Ducal (Luxembourg), Sect. des Scis.; Commn. Int. de Stratigraphie, Pres., Sous Commn. de Jurassique. Publs: num. articles & maps on regional geols.; 23 geol. maps. Hons. incl: Chevalier, Ordre Nat. de Merité, Palmes Acad.; Off. de Merité (Grand Duché). Address: 8 Rue des Magnolias (Parc Jolimont-Trinité), 54220 Malzeville, France.

MAUR, Karin von, b. 8 Nov. 1938. Curator; Art Critic. Educ: Ph.D., Univs. of Tübingen, Paris & Heidelberg. Appts: Asst., Nat. Gall., Stuttgart, 1966-68; Asst., Kunsthalle, Nuremberg, 1968-69; Curator, Oskar Schlemmer Archives, & speciality, French art of 19th & 20th centuries, Nat. Gall., Stuttgart. Mbrships: Verband Deutscher Kunsthistoriker; Deutsches Verein für Kunstwissenschaft; Schweizerisches Kunstinstitut, Zurich. Publc: Oskar Schlemmer—Das plastische Werk (O.S. Sculpture), 1972; Articles in Gazette des Beaux Arts & Beiträge zur Theorie der Künste im 19. Jahrhundert, Band I; Var. catalogues. Address: Oskar Schlemmer Archiv, Staatsgalerie Stuttgart, Konrad-Adenauer-Str. 32, 7000 Stuttgart 1, German Fed. Repub. 133.

MAURER, David W., b. 12 Apr. 1906. Professor of Language & Literature. Educ: B.A., 1928, Ph.D., 1935, Ohio State Univ.; Postgrad. study, Univs. of Mich., Mexico. Appts: Instr., Engl., Ohio State Univ., 1930-36; Prof., Linguistics, Univ. of Louisville, 1936-74; Fulbright Prof., Wilhelmstaat Univ., Münster, German Fed. Repub., 1954-55; Prof., Am. Linguistic Inst., Univ. of Rome, 1955; Staff Lectr., Southern Police Inst., Louisville, 1946-54; Staff Cons. to V.P.,. Joseph P. Seagrams & Son, 1942-50. Mbrships: MLA; Past Pres., Am. Dialect Soc.; Linguistic Soc. of Am.; Acad. of Soc. & Pol. Scis.; Phi Beta Kappa; AAUP. Num. publs. incl: The Big Con, 1963; The American Confidence Man, revised edit of

The Big Con, 1974; Narcotics & Narcotics Addiction, 4th edit., revised w. V.H. Vogel, 1974; The Kentucky Moonshiner, 1974; Fugue in High Octane, 1959, & Soup Up, 1959, TV documentaries; Num. articles in profl. jrnls. Hons: Ky. Prof. of Year, 1948; 2 Fulbright appts.; Rsch. Grant, Instnl. Dev. & Econ. Affairs Serv., Inc., 1972-74. Address: 4124 Nachand Lane, Louisville, KY 40218, U.S.A. 7, 13, 30.

MAURER, Stephen Anthony, b. 8 Mar. 1919. College Administrator. Educ: B.S., Rider Coll., 1949; Temple Univ. Appts. incl: Instr., Rider Coll., 1948-53; Bus. Mgr., ibid, 1953-62, Controller, 1962-66, V.P. for Bus. & Finance, Treas., & Asst. Prof. of Econs., 1966-. Mbrships. incl: Chmn., Assn. of Independent Colls. & Univs. in N.J.; Dir. & Past Pres., Trenton-Mercer Co. Chmbr. of Comm.; Dir., Trenton Area Chapt., Am. Red Cross; Chmn., Licensure & Approval Advsry. Bd., N.J. State Dept. of Higher Educ. Contbr. to profl. jrnls. Hons: Disting. Serv. Award, Kiwanis Club of Trenton, 1971; Brotherhood Award, Nat. Conf. of Christians & Jews, Mercer Co. Chapt., 1973. Address: 533 McClellan Ave., Trenton, NJ 08610, U.S.A. 6, 130.

MAURICE, Julius Hamilton, b. 14 Aug. 1897. Educator. Educ: Gen. Hons. Degree, Univ. of London, U.K.; Post Grad., Inst. of Educ., London; Parliamentary Course, U.K., 1963. Appts. incl: Asst. Master, Nafariwa Coll., 1920-32; Lectr., Tchrs. Coll., 1932-38; Insp. of Schls., 1938-47; Dir. of Educ., Dominica, W. Indies, 1947-55; Lectr., Nafariwa Tchrs. Coll., 1957-59; Emergency Tchrs. Coll., 1959-61; Pres., Senate, Trinidad & Tobago, W. Indies, 1961-71; Mbr., Constitution Commn., 1971-73. Mbrships. incl: Commonwealth Parliamentary Assn., 1961-71; Life Mbr., Hansard Soc. & Blind Welfare Assn.; Sri Aurobindo Soc. Sev. articles and addresses on the hist. & philos. of educ.; publd. locally & abroad. Hons. incl: Trinity Cross; Nat. Golden Award, Tchrs. Union. Address: 4 Prada Street, St. Clair, Port of Spain, Trinidad, West Indies. 1, 2.

MAURIN NAVARRO, Emilio, b. 15 Aug. 1911. Historian; Educator. Educ: Grad. in Law, Univ. Nacional de Buenos Aires. Appts. incl: Tchr.; Schl. of Comm., Univ. Nacional de Cuyo, Argentina, Escuela Normal Sarmiento, San Juan & Nat. Second. Schl. Paula A. Sarmiento, San Juan. Mbrships. incl: Argentinian Assn. of Writers; Provincial Acad. of Hist., San Juan; Cuyo Inst. of Am. Culture; Sarmiento Inst. of Sociol. & Hist., Buenos Aires. Publs: Los Hermanos Arturo y Pablo Berutti, 1964; Contribución a la Historia de la Vitivinicultura Argentina, 1967; El Liderazgo de Cuyo en la Emancipación Continental, 1970; Tres Maestros de la Medicina Argentina, Rawson, Quiroga y Narvarro, 1972; contbr. to reviews, profl. jrnls. & confs. Hons: recip. num. distinctions for hist. works inclng: ''Benefactor de la Cultura Sanjuanian'', Dip. of Hon., 1967. Address: Avda. Rioja 488, Sur, San Juan, Repub. of Argentina. 136.

MAUVE, Thijs, b. 26 Nov. 1915. Painter; Wood-Engraver; Teacher. Educ: Cert., H.B.S. (B), Scheveningen, Netherlands; Cert., Acad. of Art, The Hague. Appts: Free-lance painter & wood-engraver; Tchr.,. Esthetics & Drawing; Lectr., Cultural Soc. Mbrships: Dutch Graphical Soc.; ARTI Art Soc., Amsterdam; Pulchri Studio Art Soc., The Hague; Dutch Bookplate Soc.; Ede Art Soc. Wks. incl: Bookplates; Illustrations for books by Hans Andersen & Turgenev; Watercolors for topographical maps; Oil paintings in bank & pub. bldgs. One-man show: Philip Bell Studios, Georgetown, Va.,

U.S.A., 1955. Num. int., nat., & local exhibs. Permanent exhibs., mus.'s, The Hague, Rotterdam, Amsterdam, & Arnhem. Hons. incl: Bronze Medal & Cert., for "Art at Freedom", Amsterdam, 1945; Dip., int. exhib., Nancy, France, 1946. Address: 2 Hillegondalaan, Lunteren, Netherlands. 43.

MAVROS, Dimitri G., b. 8 Nov. 1943. Economist; Management Consultant. Educ: B.A., Bradies Univ., 1965; M.B.A., CCNY, 1967. Appts: Dir., Stat. Publs., Am. Paper Inst., N.Y.C., 1967; Rschr., Nat. Bur. Econ. Rsch., 1968-69; Dir., Rsch., Spot & Assocs., Athens, Greece, 1969-70; Lectr., Econs., Baruch Coll., CUNY, U.S.A., 1970-71; Exec. Dir., Planning & Rsch. Cons., Athens, Greece, 1971-; Sr. V.P., Dir., Rsch., Spot Advtng. Ltd.; Mng. Dir., Technol. Systems Co.; Dir., Applied Biochem. Scis. Co.; Dir., Publifinter Ltd.; Dir., Intergrp. Ltd. Mbrships: Am. Econ. Assn.; Int. Soc. for Econ. Dev.; Greek Mgmt. Assn.; Am. Acad. Pol. & Soc. Scis.; Int. Advtng. Assn. Author of publs. in field. Hons: Wein Int. Scholar, 1962-65; Fulbright Scholar, 1962-65; Grad. Award, Econ. Theory, CCNY, 1967. Address: 52 Theologou St., Athens 624, Greece. 16.

MaWHINNEY, William T., b. 24 Aug. 1886. Retired Educator; Researcher in Genaelogy. Educ: B.A., Beloit Coll., 1910; M.A., 1926; Dip., Dir. Voc. Ed. by Columbia Univ., N.Y.C., 1927. Appts: Pub. Schl. Tchr. & Prin., 1911-14; Prin. H.S. & Coach, Redfield, S.D., 1914-18; Tchr.-Coach, Milwaukee, Wis., 1919-25; Columbia Univ., 'til 1927; Registrar & Off. Mgr., Gen. Motors Inst., Flint, Mich., 1927-33; Dean, Billings Polytech. Inst., 1933-34; Registrar & Off. Mgr., Gen. Motors Inst., 1934-51. Address: 1518 W. Dayton St., Flint, MI 48504, U.S.A. 15, 16, 130.

MAXIA, Carol Luigi Giuseppe, b. 18 Feb. 1907. Physician; Anthropologist. Educ: M.D., Univ. of Cagliari, Sardinia, Italy, 1933. Appts: Asst., Human Anatomy, Fac. Phys. & Surg., Cagliari, 1934-45; Lectr., Histol. & Embryol., 1935, Human Anatomy, 1942, Anthropol., 1951, Prof., Maths., Phys. & Natural Scis. Fac., 1953; Univ. of Cagliari; Dir., Inst. of Normal Human Anatomy & Expmntl. Morphol., Dir., Anthropol. Scis. Inst., Univ. of Cagliari, 1953-; Dir., Mus. Anthropol., Dir., Anthropol. Scis. Univ. of Cagliari, 1953-; Dir., Mus. Anthropol., Dir., Anthropol. Scis. Univ. of Cagliari, 1953-; Dir., Mus. Anthropol. & Ethnography of Sardinia, Cagliari, 1953; Dean of Scis. Fac., Univ. of Cagliari, 1968-. Mbrships: Pres., Int. Ctr. for Sardinian Studies, Italian Inst. Etnoiatria, Ctr. for Sardinian Speleol.; Academic Acad. Lancisiana, Rome; Academic Acads. Teatina, Abruzzi, Tiberina; French Prehist. Soc.; French Soc. Anthropol.; French Soc. Ethnography; Italian Soc. Anthropol. & Ethnol.; Royal Anthropol. Inst., G.B. & Ireland; Colégio Anatomico Brasilero; Int. Soc. Anthropol.; AAAS, U.S.A. Publs. incl: Gallura, 1962; Grotte della Sardegna, 1964; Breve Stria della Sardegna, 1965; Author & co-author, num. articles in field in profl. jrnls. inclng. Frontiera, Rassegna Medica Sarda, Archivio per l'Antropologia e la Etnologia, Rendiconti del Seminario della Facoltà di Scienze Università di Cagliari, etc. Hons: Order Italian Repub., 1959; Order of Merit, French Repub., 1970; Order of Alphonse X the Wise, 1957; Gold Medal, Acad. Abruzzi, 1970; Gold Medal, Acad. Teatina, 1971; Gold Medal, Ministero Pubblica Istruzione, 1972; Silver Medal, Italian Soc. Dante Alighieri, 1959. Address: Inst. Scienze Antropologiche, via Porcell, 2 Cagliari, Sardinia, Italy. 10, 43, 50, 95.

MAXON, Yale Candee, b. 5 Oct. 1906. Political Scientist. Educ: B.A., Stanford Univ., 1928; M.A., Univ. of Hawaii, 1933; Ph.D., Univ. of Calif., Berkeley, 1952. Appts:'Waimea Jr. H.S., Waimea, Kauai; Puñahou Schl., Honolulu, Hawaii; Dai Shi Koto Gakko, Kanazawa, Japan; Japanese lang. off., USN, w. Int. Prosecution Sect., G.H.Q., S.C.A.P., Tokyo; San Fran. State Coll., U.S.A.; Santa Rosa Jr. Coll.; Oakland City Coll.; Bundesrealschule, Graz, Austria; Merritt Coll. Mbrships. incl: Sec., V.P., Pres., Calif. Roadside Coun.; Northern Calif. Coun.; Pres., UN Assn.; Commonwealth Club; Am. Soc. of Int. Law; World Peace Through Law Ctr.; World Federalists, U.S.A. Publs: Control of Japanese Foreign Policy—A Study of Civil-Military Rivalry—1930-45, 1957. Review of Joseph Yamagiwa's Readings in Japanese Political Science, in Jrnl. of Asian Studies, 1965. Hons: Hopkins Schlrship., 1924; Fulbright Award to Austria, 1961. Address: 820 Euclid Ave., Berkeley, CA 94708, U.S.A.

MAXWELL, Fowden Gene, b. 29 Sept. 1931. University Professor; Head of Department. Educ: Instr. Entomology, Kan. State Univ., 1960-61; Entomologist GS-14 (3), USDA Boll Weevil Lab., Miss. State Univ., 1961-68; Prof. & Hd. Dept. Entomol., ibid, 1968-. Mbrships: Entomological Soc. of Am. (Sec.-Chmn., Section C, 1967-70; Prog. Chmn., Southeastern Br., 1970-71; Mus. Ad Hoc Comm., Awards Comm. SEB, & V.P., Miss. Entomological Soc., 1971-72; Pres. Elect, 1972-73); Mbr. Sec., Agric.'s Comm. on Mechanism of Plant Resistance to Insects & Diseases, 1971-72; Am. Inst. Biological Scis.; Miss. Entomological Soc. & Acad. of Scis.; Agronomy Soc. of Am. Contbr. to num. publs. & papers in field, notably specializing in Host Plant Resistance to Insects & Insect Plant Interactions. Hons: Bussard Award, Entomological Soc. of Am., 1972; Outstanding Educator of Am., 1973; Phi Kappa Phi, 1957; Alpha Zeta, 1957; Gamma Sigma Delta, 1958; Sigma Xi, 1958. Address: Entomology Dept., Drawer Em, Miss. State Univ., Mississippi, MS 39762, U.S.A. 2, 7, 14.

MAXWELL, (Ian) Robert, b. 10 June 1923. Publisher. Appts: Fndr., Publr. & Chmn. of Bd., Pergamon Press, Oxford & London, 1949-69, & Pergamon Press Inc., N.Y., 1949-; M.P. (Labour) for Buckingham, 1964-70; Mbr. Vice-Chmn., Comm. of Sci. & Technol., Coun. of Europe, 1968. Publs: Public Sector Purchasing, 1968; Man Alive (jt. author), 1968. Ed: Information U.S.S.R., 1963; Information Hungary, 1969; The Economics of Nuclear power, 1965. Recip. Mil. Cross, 1945. Address: Headington Hill Hall, Oxford OX3 0BB, U.K.

MAXWELL, K. N. b. 7 Sept. 1924. Broadcaster; Writer; Farmer. Appts: Announcer, Radio Jamaica, 1950-52; Asst., then Govt. Broadcasting Off., 1952-53 & 1953-59; Dir., Rural Progs., Jamaica Broadcasting Assn., 1959-61; Ken Maxwell Assocs. Ltd., Fndr., 1970. Mbrships: Jamaica Press Assn.; Royal Overseas League, U.K. Writer, feature progs. (& producer), poems & short stories for BBC & Canadian Broadcasting Corp., newspaper feature articles, etc. Introduced schls. broadcasts in Jamaica. Address: Dalkeith, Knockpatrick, Manchester, Jamaica, W. Indies.

MAY, (Mrs.) Billie Wilson, b. 11 Oct. 1931. College Instructor; Businesswoman. Educ: B.S., Livingston Univ., Ala., 1955; M.A., George Peabody Coll. for Tchrs., Nashville, Tenn., 1966; postgrad work, Univ. of Ala., Tuscaloosa & Huntsville. Appts: Instr., Bus. Admin.,

Athens Coll., Ala.; Instr. Coord., Manpower Trng. & Dev. Prog.; Instr., Acctng., Calhoun Jr. Coll., Decatur, Ala.; Co-owner, May's Shoes, Huntsville, Ala., May's Nursery & Greenhouses. Mbrships: Omega Chapt., Delta Pi Epsilon; Am. Acctng. Assn.; AAUP. Address: 6112 University Dr., Huntsville, AL 35806, U.S.A. 46, 125.

MAY, Lini, b. 20 Jan. 1930. Educator. Educ: B.A., Columbia Univ., 1951; M.A., 1954; Ph.D., 1963; Cert., Schl. of Int. Affairs Coll., 1959. Appts: Mbr., U.N. Tech. Assistance Admin., 1951-53; Pakistan Mission to the U.N., 1954; Lectr., Hist. of Islam & Judaism, Rutgers Univ., 1962-63; Lectr., N.Y. Theol. Sem., spring, 1972; Fac. Mbr., New Schl., N.Y., 1960-; Adj. Assoc. Prof., Queens Coll., CUNY. Mbrships: Am. Oriental Soc.; Am. Acad. Relig.; Asia Soc.; Pakistan Coun.; Assn. for Asian Studies. Publs: The Evolution of Indo-Muslim Thought after 1857, 70; Mah Iqbal (Iqbal), 1958; My Interview with Maulana Abdul—A La Maududi at Lahore; Maimonides, His Life & Works; The Life & Times of Sir (Dr.) Muhammad Iqbal, 1974; 7 articles on Pakistan & Bangla Desh; contbr. to Islamic Lit. Address: 300 E. 71 St., N.Y., NY 10021, U.S.A. 13.

MAY, Robin (Robert Stephen), b. 26 Dec. 1929. Author; Journalist. Appts: Actor, 1953-63; Artist Agt., 1963-66; Full Time Writer, 1966-; Staff, Look & Learn, 1970-. Mbrships: Soc. of Authors; Nat. Union of Jrnlists; Kan. State Hist. Soc.; Ont. Hist. Soc.; Wyo. State Hist. Soc.; Mont. Hist. Soc.; Neb. State Hist. Soc.; Engl. Westerners Soc. Publs: Opera Mania, 1966; Theatre Mania, 1967; The Wit of the Theatre, 1969; Who's Who in Shakespeare, 1972; Companion to the Theatre, 1973; The American West, 1973; Wolfe's Army, 1974. Address: 23 Malcolm Rd., London, SW19 4AS, U.K. 3, 30.

MAYALL, Michael Marvin, b. 12 Apr. 1939. College Educator-Administrator. Educ: B.A., Ctrl. Wash. State Coll.; M.A., Eastern Wash. State Coll.; Ed.D. Candidate, N. Tex. State Univ.; further studies, Univs. of Ore. & Tex., Tex A & M Univ. Appts: Tchr., Liberty Schl. Dist., 1960-63; Spokane Schl. Dist., 1963-65; Instr., Univ. of Ore., 1965-66; Instr. & Dir., Elcentro Coll., 1966-68; Educl. Cons., 1966-; Assoc. Prof. of Behavioral Scis., Div. Chmn. of Gen. Studies, Tarrant Co. Jr. Coll., Ft. Worth, Tex., 1968-. Mbrships. incl: V.P., Liberty Educ. Assn.; Chmn., Dushane Defense Nat. Educ. Assn.; Life Mbr., NEA; Int. Reading Assn.; AAUP. Publs: Heresy: A Means to an End (co-author), 1969; Administration As a Subversive Activity, 1973. Recip., NDEA Schlrship. for Grad. Study, 1963. Address: 7329 Vanessa Dr., Ft. Worth, TX 76112, U.S.A. 125.

MAYBRAY-KING, (Rt. .Hon. Lord), b. .25 May 1901. Member of House of Lords, London, U.K. B.A., King's Coll., Univ. of London, U.K., 1920; Ph.D., ibid, 1940. Appts: Hd., Engl. Dept., Taunton's Schl., Southampton, U.K., 1921-47; Headmaster, Regent Pk. Schl., 1947-50; M.P., 1950-71; Speaker, House of Commons, 1955-71. F.R.C.P. Publs: (Ed.) Selections from Macaulay, Homer, Sherlock Holmes; Parliament & Freedom; State Crimes; Before Hansard; Songs in the Night. Hons. incl: 6 hon. degrees; F.K.C., 1969; Freeman, Stockton & Southampton. Address: House of Lords, London, S.W.1, U.K. 1, 128.

MAYER, Franz, b. 29 May 1920. Professor in Ordinary at Public Law; Member of Bavarian Administrative Court of Justice. Educ: Univs.

of Bonn & Munich, German Fed. Repub.; J.D., Univ. of Munich, 1951. Appts: Councillor & Sr. Councillor, Govts. of Lower Bavaria & Upper Palatinate, Upper Bavaria & Bavarian State Min. of Interior; Habilitation, Univ. of Wuerzburg, 1958; Lectr., ibid; Prof., Univ. of Regensburg, & Acad. of Administrative Scis.; Speyer; Judge, Bavarian Administrative Ct. of Justice, 1963-; Rector & Prorector, Univ. of Regensburg, 1965-69. Mbr., legal, scientific & rsch. orgs. Publs. incl: Constitutional & Public Law in Bavaria (co-ed.), 3rd edit., 1968; General Administrative Law, an Introduction, 3rd edit., 1972; Law & System of the Public Service (co-author), 4 vols., 1973. Hons. incl: Bavarian Disting. Serv. Order, 1970. Address: Universitätsstr. 31, 84 Regensburg, Bavaria, German Fed. Repub.

MAYER, Hans H., b. 19 Mar. 1907. University Professor; Writer. Educ: Univs. of Cologne, Bonn, Berlin; Grad. in Law, 1929; Ph.D., 1930; State Jury Exam, 1933; Fellow, Postgrad. Inst. of Int. Studies, Geneva, 1935-38. Appts: Pol. exile, 1933-45; Returned to Germany 1945 at invitation of Am. Mil. Govt.; Ed. in Chief, Radio Frankfurt, 1946-47; Docent, Univ. of Frankfurt, 1947-48; Prof., German & Comp. Lit., Univ. of Leipzig, 1948-63; Prof., Univ. of Hannover, 1965-73; Retd., 1973. Vis. Prof., Univs. of Moscow, Stockholm, Berlin (West) Sorbonne, Wis., & Columbia, U.S.A., Coll. de France, Paris. Mbrships: PEN Club; Int. Union of Germanists, 1955-; Dir., Dept. of Lit., Acad. of Fine Arts, Berlin (West); Pres., Int. Brecht Soc. Publs: Books in German, Engl., inclng: Steppenwolf & Everyman, 1971•; Portrait of Richard Wager, 1972. Hons: Nat. Prize, German Democratic Repub., 1955; Lit. Award, W. German Critics, 1966; D.h.c., Univ. of Brussels, 1969; L.H.D. h.c., Univ. of Wis., 1972; Medal of Hon., Coll. de France, 1974. Address: Neckerhalde 41, Tübingen 74, German Fed. Repub. 34, 43, 55.

MAYER, Philippe, b. 15 June 1923. Company Director. Educ: Law degree. Appts: Asst. to European Mgr., TWA, 1946-47; Sales Mgr., Cie. Francaise des Plastiques, 1947-50; Gen. Mgr., Kiddicraft (France), 1950-; Chmn. Mng. Dir., Feralco-Dexion, 1954-; Chmn., Jouet Rationnels, 1953-; Dir., Cie. Generale du Jouet & subsidiaries, 1969-; Dir., Sommer-Alibert. Mbrships: Racing Club of France; Biarritz Golf Club. Hons: Croix de Guerre; U.S. Bronze Star; Chevalier, Legion of Hon. Address: 32 rue Charles Laffitte, 92200 Neuilly sur Seine, France. 43, 91.

MAYER, (Sir) Robert, b. 5 June 1879. Philanthropist; Patron of Music. Appts: was in bus. of Metal-Mining & Commerce, 1879-1929; gave this up to dir. musical movements; Fndr., Robert Mayer Concerts & Youth & Music; on Bds., var. musical & humanitarian orgs. Mbrships: Fellow, Royal Coll. of Music; F.T.C.L.; Athenaeum Club; Royal Automobile Club. Publs: Young People in Trouble, 1945; many articles on music. Hons: Mus.D., Cleveland Inst; LL.F., Leeds; Dr. Sc., City Univ. O.M. German; Order of Crown, Belgium; G.S.M. Address: 2, Mansfield Street, London W1, U.K. 3.

MAYER-LIST, Walter R., b. 3 Mar. 1902. Company Director. Educ: Dip. Ing., Dr. Ing., Univ. of Stuttgart, Germany; Banking & commercial trng., Hamburg & N.Y., U.S.A. Appts: Exec., Bankhaus M.M. Warburg & Co., Hamburg; Gen. Mgr., Bankhaus Merck, Finck & Co., Munich & Berlin; Mng. Ptnr., C.H. Boehringer Sohn, Ingelheim; Mbr., Advsry. Bd., ibid, 1971-; Chmn., Bd. of Dirs., Dr. Karl Thomae GmbH, Biberach; Mbr., Bd. of Dirs.,

Pharma-Investment Ltd., Montreal, P.Q., Canada, Pharma Rsch. Canada Ltd., Pointe Claire, P.Q., Boehringer Ingelheim s.p.a., Florence, Italy, Interam. Bank Corp. S.A., Panama/Nassau, Bankaus Conrad Hinrich Donner, Hamburg. Mbr., List-Gesellschaft, Düsseldorf. Address: An der Saalmühle, D-6507 Ingelheim/Rhein, German Fed. Repub. 43, 92.

MAYLIE, (Mrs.) Anna May Deano, b. 9 Mar. 1920. Restaurateur. Mbrships: Pres., Le Petit Theatre du Vieux Carre (The oldest Little Theatre in US); Treas., Women's Guild, New Orleans Opera House Assn. & Ctrl. Bus. Dist. Assn.; Histn., Overture to Cultural Season; Pubcty. Chmn., Land Marks Soc.; Bd. Mbr., La. Travel Promotion Assn. Address: 1009 Poydras St., New Orleans, LA 70112, USA. 125.

MAYNARD, Henri, b. 20 May 1908. Writer. Appts: Chief, Hon. Prin. Hd. Bur., RATP, Parisian Regional Transport; Former Sec. Gen., French Fedn. of Devotion. Mbrships: Pres., Gaillacois Painters; Int. Comm., Centro Studi e Scambi Int., Rome, Italy; Soc. of Men of Letters of France; Comm., Fedn. of Intellectual Socs., Tarn. Publs: Quelques grains de fantaisie, (poetry); Isidore Gardet, (local hist. study); Jean-Jacques Rigal, (local hist. study). Hons: Silvergilt Medal, City of Paris & Dept. of the Seine; Chevalier, Order of Acad. Palms. Address: 4 Pl. du Barry, 81310 Lisle-sur-Tarn, France. 43.

MAYNARD, Valerie, b. 22 Aug. 1937. Artist; Sculptor; Printmaker. Educ: Seward Park H.S., 1955; Modern Mus.; Elaine Journet Art Schl. Appts: Counselor, Instr., Lectr., Dir., 'Arts for Survival', in community ctrs., parks, schls., colls., jails, in N.Y.C.; Printmaker in Res., Studio Mus., Harlem, N.Y.C. Mbrships: Nat. Conf. of Artists; Studio Mus.; Minisink. One woman exhibs: Am. Int. Coll., Mass., 1971; 350 Broadway, N.Y.C., 1971; Gallery 1199, 1973; Howard Univ., 1973. Pub. collects. incl: Nat. Lawyers Guild; N.Y.C. Hlth. & Hosp. Corp.; IBM, White Plains, N.Y.; Malcolm X Coll., Chgo.; Arnot Mus.; Studio Mus. Work in num. pvte. collects., & in schls. & instns. in Nigeria, Senegal, Tanzania, Trinidad, Jamaica, P.R., Cuba & Canada. In univ. slide & film collects. & videotape. Hons: St. Gaudens Medal for Fine Draftsmanship, 1952; Class Artist Award, 1955; Creative Artists Pub. Serv. Prog. Grants in graphics, 1972, '74. Address: 417 W. 126th St., N.Y., NY, U.S.A.

MAYNE, Richard John, b. 2 Apr. 1926. Writer; International civil servant; broadcaster. Educ: M.A., Ph.D., Trinity Coll., Univ. of Cambridge, U.K. Appts: incl: Offl. of the High Authority, European Coal & Steel Community, Luxembourg, 1956-58, Commn. of European Econ. Community, Brussels, Belgium, 1958-63; Dir., Documentation Ctr., Action Comm. for United States of Europe, Paris, France, 1963-66; Vis. Prof., Univ. of Chgo., U.S.A. 1971-73; Hd., London Off., Commn. of European Communities, 1973-. Mbrships: Trustee, Fed. Trust for Educ. & Rsch., London; Les Misérables, Paris. Publs: The Community of Europe, 1963; The Institutions of the European Community, 1968; The Europeans, 1972; The Recovery of Europe, new edit. 1973; Ed., Europe Tomorrow, 1972; Ed., The New Atlantic Challenge (in preparation). Address: c/o Commn. of European Communities, 20 Kensington Palace Gdns., London W8 4QQ, U.K. 3, 12, 43.

MAYORGA, Gabriel Humberto, b. 24 Mar. 1911. Painter; Sculptor; Printmaker. Educ: Nat. Acad. of Design, N.Y.C.; Art Students League, ibid; Grand Ctrl. Art Schl. Appts: Art Dir.,

Cinerie Mag., 1935-36, Revista Estrellas, 1937-38, Mannequins by Mayorga Inc., 1940-65, & Revista Temas, N.Y.C., 1953-54; Art Instr., Pan-Am. Art Schl., ibid, 1960-73. Mbrships: Aviation Writers & Space Assn., 1958-61; Nat. Assn. of Flight Instrs., 1972-74. Author of Paste Up & Mechanicals Manual, 1973; Illustrator of Revista Estrellas, 1937-38, Theory & Practice of Fencing, 1937, Popular Publs., 1938, Revista Temas, 1953-54, Don Mag., 1960. Works held in Inst. de Ingenieros, Bogota, Colombia; West Point Mus., N.Y.C., & in over 100 pvte. collections; exhibs. at Inst. de Ingenieros, Bogota, 1937; Art Gall. of Barbizon Plaza, N.Y.C., 1955; Mayorga Art Gall., 1960; Int. Exposition, Paris, France, 1962; Int. Art Show, N.Y.C., 1970. etc. Address: Mayorga Art Gall., 331 West 11 St., N.Y., NY 10014, U.S.A. 37, 105.

MAYOUX, Jacques, b. 18 July 1924. Banker. Educ: Ecole Libre des Scis. Politiques; Facs. of Law & Letters, Paris, France; Dip., Ecole des Hautes Etudes Commerciales; Licencié, Law; Licencié ès Lettres. Appts. incl: Tech. Advsr., Min. of Finance, 1958; Dpty. Sec. Gen., Interminl. Comm. on Questions of European Econ. Coop.; Dir. Gen., Caisse Nat. de Crédit Agricole, 1963-, SEGESPAR, 1969-, & SOGEQUIP; V.P., UNIMAT Socs., 1969-, & UNICOMI (Sicomi); Admnstr., French Bank for For. Trade, 1963-; Pres., Union of Studies & Investments, 1967-; Pres., Dir. Gen., EPARGNE UNIE, 1970-; Pres., UNICREDIT, 1971-; Pres., Ctrl. Comm. for Rural Renovation, 1971-; Admnstr., Inst. for Indl. Dev., 1973-, & London & Continental Bankers Ltd., 1974-. Hons: Chevalier, Legion of Hon.; Cmdr., Royal Order of the Phoenix. Address: Caisse Nat. de Crédit Agricole, 91-93 Blvd. Pasteur, CEDEX no. 26, 75300 Paris Brune, France.

MAYRHOFER, Otto K., b. 2 Nov. 1920. University Professor. Educ: M.D., Med. Schl., Univ. of Vienna, Austria, 1944. Appts. incl: Anaesthetist, Columbia Presby. Med. Ctr., N.Y.C., U.S.A., 1949-50; Cert. Specialist, Anaesthesiol., Vienna, 1952; Assoc. Prof., & Hd., Div. of Anaesthesiol., Dept. of Surg. II, Univ. of Vienna, 1955; Prof., & Chmn., Dept. of Anaesthesiol., ibid, 1961- Dir., Dept. of Anaesthesia, Univ. Hosp., Vienna. Mbrships. incl: Pres., World Fedn. of Socs. of Anaesthesiologists, 1973-, Sec., 1964-72; Fellow, Am. Coll. of Anaesthesiologists, 1958; Fellow, Fac. of Anaesthetists, Royal Coll. of Surgs., 1968; Anaesthesia Socs. of Australia, Bulgaria, Gt. Britain & Ireland, German Fed. Repub., Hungary, India, Italy, Peru, Poland, Scandinavia, Spain, W. Africa, & Yugoslavia. Publs: 170 articles in scientific jrnls. Recip., M.D., Med. Univ. of Szeded, Hungary, 1971. Address: Dept. of Anaesthesiology, Spitalgasse 23, A 1090 Vienna, Austria.

MAZIDI, Feisal, b. 2 May 1933. Company President. Educ: B.A., Keele Univ., UK, 1959. Appts: w. Dept. Finance & Econ., 1959; Dir., State Chlorine & Salt Bd.; Dir., Kuwait Oil Co. Ltd., 1960-73; Econ. Asst., Min. Finance & Econ., 1960; Chmn., Econ. & Indl. Comm., 1961; Dir., Kuwait Fund Econ. Dev., Arab Countries, 1962; Mbr., Kuwait Univ. Higher Coun., 1962-64; Chmn. & Mng. Dir., Kuwait Chem. Fertilizer Co., 1964-71; Chmn., Govt. Oil Concession Comm., 1963-65; Govt. Refinery Comm., 1964-66; Kuwait Maritime Mercantile Co., 1965-70; Dir., Petrochem. Inds. Co., 1963-71; Dir., Kuwait United Fisheries Co., 1971-; Pres., Kuwait Assocd. Cons., 1971-. Mbr. Kuwait Econs. Soc. Publs: Natural Gas in Kuwait and its Utilization, 1963; Kuwait As A Base for Petrochemicals, 1965. Recip. Arab League Prize for Paper, Natural Gas in Kuwait and its Utilization, 4th Arab Petroleum Congress, 1963. Address: Kuwait Assocd. Cons., P.O. Box 5443, Kuwait.

MAZIS, Alkinoos, b. 10 July 1904. Educator; General Inspector of Secondary Education. Educ: Grad., Athens Univ., Greece; Dip., Secondary Educ. Coll. Appts: Schoolmaster (Phys.), Aliversion H.S., Euboea, 1927; Schoolmaster, Salonika, 1930-40; Schoolmaster, Varvakion Schl., Athens, 1940-58; Dir., ibid, 1958-64; Hd., Lyceum Athinau Schl., Athens, 1964-74. Mbrships: Past Gen. Sec. & past V.P., Soc. of Greek Physicists; Comms., Soc. of Schl. Book Authors, & sev. other socs. Publs: Atom Fission, How We have come to the Atomic Bomb, 1945; 28 schl. textbooks on phys.; 5 books on phys. & human geog.; Articles in newspapers & scientific jrnls. Hons: Commendation, for study, The Tide of Euripus, Hydrographic Dept., Min. of Naval Affairs; Commendation, for servs. to secondary educ., Min. of Educ.; 6 First Prizes in secondary educ. book competitions. Address: Phylis 165, Athens 821, Greece.

MAZRUI, Ali Al'Amin, b. 24 Feb. 1933. University Professor. Educ: B.A., Univ. of Manchester, U.K., 1960; M.A., Columbia Univ., U.S.A., 1961; Ph.D., Oxford Univ., U.K., 1966. Appts: Prof., Pol. Sci., Makerere Univ., Uganda, 1963-73; Dean, Soc. Scis., ibid, 1967-69; Fellow, Ctr. for Advanced Study in Behavioral Scis., Stanford, U.S.A., 1972-73; Prof., Univ. of Mich., 1973-. Mbrships. incl: Past V.P., Int. Pol. Sci. Assn.; Past V.P., Int. Cong. of Africanists; Dir., African Sect., World Order Models Proj.; Am. Pol. Sci. Assn.; African Studies Assn. of U.S.; African Assn. of Pol. Sci.; Mbr. of Exec., Int. African Inst. Publs. incl: Towards a Pax Africana, 1967; Violence & Thought, 1969; World Culture & the Black Experience, 1974; The Trial of Christopher Okigbo (novel), 1972. Hons: Rockefeller Fndn. Fellowships & Rsch. Grants, 1960-61, 1965-66; Int. Org. Prize, U.S.A., 1964; Northwestern Univ. Book-Author Prize, 1969. Address: Dept. of Pol. Sci., Univ. of Mich., Ann Arbor, MI 48104, U.S.A. 89.

MAZZACCARA di CELENZA, (Marquis) Riccardo, b. 20 Sept. 1908. Sociologist. Educ: studies in jurisprudence, pure philos., sociol., art & the history of Art. Appts. incl: Pres., Italian Inst. of Geneal. & heraldry; Pres., Int. Welfare Commn. for Italians & Veterans; Pres., Nat. Soc. for War Orphans, Milan; Lombard Pres., Nat. Italian Union for transport of the diseased to Lourdes & Italian shrines; Pres., Permanent Int. Commn. for the study of Sociol. Mbrships. incl: capitulary of the Sovereign Mil. Order of Malta; Vice Grand Counllr. of the Sovereign Mil. Order of St. Geo; Noble Guard of His Holiness, the Sovereign Pontiff; Nat. Union of Retired Offs.; Nat. Assn. of Ex-servicemen & veterans. Hons. incl: gold medal of merit of the Italian Inst. of Geneal. and Heraldry; silver medal of the Presidency of the Coun. of Mins. for War Orphans; Bailiff of Justice & Kt. of the Grand Cross of the Sovereign Mil. Order of Constantine; Grand Off. of merit of the Italian Repub.; Grand Off. of merit of the Equestrian order of the Holy Sepulchre of Jerusalem. Address: Piazza del Duomo 20, 20121, Milan, Italy.

MAZZANTINI, Carlo, b. 25 Nov. 1895. University Professor. Educ: Grad. jurisprudence, lit. & philos. Appts: Lectr., Univ. of Turin; Prof., Hist. of philos., Univ. of Genoa, 1929; Lectr., Univ. of Turin, 1959; Prof., Hist. of Philos., ibid, -1971. Mbrships. incl: Soc. for philosophical & religious studies; European Inst. of Human Scis., Urbino; Nat. Union of Retired Italian Offs. Publs. incl: La speranza

nell'immortalita, 1923; Realta e intelligenza, 1929; Spinoza e l'idealismo contemporaneo, 1933; Linee di metafisica spirituale, 1942; Marco Aurelis, 1948; Storia del pensiero antico, 1940 & 1965; Le poesie di un filosofo, 1973. Hons: Gold medal of merit of the Schl. of Culture & Art, 1968; bronze war medal. Address: Corso Palestro 7, 10122 Turin, Italy. 43.

MAZZONE, Domenico, b. 16 May 1927. Sculptor. Works at UN, N.Y., currently; Pvte. studio, Jersey City, N.J. Mbrships. incl: Int. Acad. of Sci., Letters, Art Leonardo da Vinci, Rome, Italy; Ctr. Studies & Int. Exchanges, Rome; Italian Club of UN, N.Y.; Academia Tiberina, Rome; Ethiopia Comply Soc., Boston, U.S.A. Works found in Italian & Am. Museums; Pvte. collects. in U.S.S.R., Switzeralnd, Poland, Italy, France, Egypt, Greece, Canada, U.S.A.; Collectors incl. U Thant, Kurt Waldheim, Richard Nixon, Frank Sinatra, Bob Hope, John Volpe, Sophia Loren, S. Trepczynsky, Victor Lessiowsky. Hons. incl: Silver Medal, Carrara, Italy, 1962; Gold Medal, Int. Grand Prix, Viareggio, Italy, 1972; Bronze Medal of Copernicus, Poland, UN, N.Y., 1973; Acad. of Merit Award, G. Marconi Univ. of Asmara, Ethiopia. Subject of 2 books, Mazzone (ed. M. Pescara), 1969, & The Art of Mazzone (ed. Passantino), 1971. Address: 44 Lembeck Ave., Jersey City, NJ 07305, U.S.A. 2, 37.

MEAD, (Rev.) Jude, C.P., b. 26 May 1919. Catholic Priest of the Passionist Congregation. Educ: B.A., St. Michael Monastery, Sem. Dept., Union City, N.J', 1942; M.A., ibid, 1962. Appts: Spiritual Dir., Passionist Seminarians, Brighton, Jamaica, W. Springfield, Union City, N.J., 1947-52; Assoc. Ed., Sign Mag., 1952-54; Dir., Retreats, St. Gabriel Ret. House, Brighton, Mass., 1958-62; Int. Preacher to clergy, Religious Laity, 1963-; Bd. of Trustees, Mt. St. Joseph Coll., R.I., 1958-58; Instr., Scriptural Theol., ibid, 1958-, Boston Coll. Ext. Dept., 1967-70. Mbrships: Cath. Theol. Soc. of Am.; Cath. Biblical Assn. of G.B.; Cath. Homiletic Soc.; Gen. Chmn., 1971-73, Inter-Community Assn. of Missioners. Publs. incl: Shepherd of the Second Spring 1968; Dove in the Cleft, 1971; Contbr. to the Inner Crusade, 1964 & to The New Cath. Ency., 1967. Prod. & Dir. of film, Modern Crusaders, 1958. Hons: LL.D., Mt. St. Joseph Coll., 1965; Pontifical Cross of Jerusalem (Argent), 1971. Address: St. Joseph Passionist Monastery, 3800 Frederick Ave., Balt., MD 21229, U.S.A. 6.

MEAD, Margaret, b. 16 Dec. 1901. Museum Curator, Educator, Anthropologist. Appts. incl: Adjunct Prof. of Anthrop., Columbia Univ., 1954-; Vis. Prof. Anthrop., Dept. of Psychiatry, Univ. of Cincinnati, 1957; Curator of Ethnology, Am. Mus. of Natural Hist., 1964-; Vis. Prof. of Anthrop., N.Y. Univ., 1965-67, & Yale Univ., 1966-67; Cons. to Div. of Soc. Scis., Fordham Univ. Liberal Arts Coll., Lincoln Ctr., N.Y., 1968; Chmn., Soc. Scis. Div., Prof. of Anthrop., ibid, 1969-70. Has led many expeditions & made many lecture tours since 1925. Author of grt. no. of publs. & films of interest in her field incl: New Lives for Old; Cultural Transforamation-Manus, 1928-53. Recip. numerous awards. Address: Columbia Univ., New York, N.Y., U.S.A.

MEAD, Russell M., Jr., b. 1 Jan. 1935. Educational Administrator. Educ: A.B., Dartmouth Coll., 1956. Appts: Tchr., Woodstock Country Schl., Vt., 1959-62; Tchr., Concord Acad., Mass., 1962-65, Chmn., Engl. & Media, 1965-71, Hd. of Acad., 1971- Mbrships: Fndng. Pres., New England Screen Educ. Assn.; Assn. Am. Rhodes Schlrs. Publs: If a Heart

Rings, 1965; Tell Me Again About Snow White, 1966. Var. articles & poetry, 1958-. Hons: Elinor Frost Playwright, 1955; Rhodes Schlr., 1956. Address: Concord Academy, 194 Main St., Concord, MS 01742, U.S.A. 6.

MEADOR, Lenora McKamie. Elementary Teaching Principal. Educ: B.A., Mary 'Hardin Baylor Coll., Belton, Tex.; M.E., Univ. of Tex., Austin; Assn. Childhood Educ. Workshops, Univ. of Tex.; Reading Workshops, Baylor Univ., Waco. Appts: Elem. Tchr., Grades 4, 5, 6, 10th Grade Spanish; One Tchr. Schl., Grades 1-8, Primary Grade 1; Deleg. to Int. Study Confs. for Assn. Childhood Educ., Kan. City Mo., 1956, Wash. D.C., 1957, L.A., Calif., 1958, Atlantic City, N.J., 1959; Tchng. Prin., 1960-; Headstart Tchr., Summer Progs., 1965-72. Mbrships. incl: Pres., Assn. Childhood Educ. Int., Temple Classroom Tchrs. Assn., Bell Co. Coun. Int. Reading Assn., & Lambda Chapt., Delta Kappa Gamma; Dir., Temple Tchrs. Credit Union. Recip., Boss of Yr. Award, Bell Co. Am. Bus. Women's Assn., 1971. Address: Route 2, P.O. Box 141, Belton, TX 76513, U.S.A. 125.

MEALING, Esther M. (Mollier, Mrs. John P. Mealing), b. 8 Aug. 1916. Artist. Educ: Grad., Dr. Aughon's Bus. Coll.; Art Classes w. Russell Keaton, Jim Miner, Wyndel Taylor & Selma Pov; Columbus Coll. Appts: Sec., T.V.A., Ace Power Co., Corinth for 5 yrs.; Tchr. Art, Wynnton Meth. Ch.; Organist., Christian Ch. of Columbus; Sunday Schl. Tchr. for over 20 yrs.; Dir., Art Display, Chattahooche Valley Fairs, 1972, '73; Artist Publr. of own book, Sketch Book of Century Old Houses of Columbus, Ga., & Vicinity, Vol. I. Mbrships: Pres., Nat. League of Am. Pen. Women; Tres., Muscogee Co. Citizens' Assn. for 6 yrs., Women's Christian Temperance Union for 15 yrs. & Ch., for 7 yrs.; Active in Girl Scouts, leader or co-leader for almost 10 yrs.; Bd., Welfare Dept., later Called Family & Children's Servs., Chmn. Advsry. Bd., ibid. Past Pres., Columbus Artist's Guild; Art Assn., Huntsville, Ala.; Jt. Orgr. & 2nd. Pres., Benning Hills Women's Club. Has won prizes for oil & water colour paintings. Address: 809 Cooper Ave., Columbus, GA 31906, U.S.A. 125.

MEANEY, George b. 16 Aug. 1894. President American Federation of Labor & Congress of Industrial Organizations. Educ: N.Y. Elem. & H.S. Appts. incl: Journeyman Plumber's Certificate, 1915; Elected Bus. Agt., 1922-34; Elected Pres., N.Y. State Fed. of Lab., 1934-39; Sec.-Treas., Am. Fed. of Labor, 1939; Pres., ibid, 1952-55; Pres., AFL-CIO, 1955-. Mbrships. incl: Fed. Prison Inds. Bd; Nat. Merit Schlrship. Corp. Bd. of Govs., Nat. Am. Red Cross; Chmn., Lab. Advsry Comm., Alliance for Prog., AID. Publs: Contbr. to profl. jrnls. Numerous hons. incl: LL.D., Seton Hall, S. Orange, N.J., 1956; Univ. of Pa., 1957; DePaul Univ., 1957; St. John's Univ., 1957; Boston Coll., Mass., 1959; Fordham Univ., 1964; Georgetown Univ., 1965. Address: 815 16th St., N.W., WA D.C. 20006, U.S.A. 7.

MECKLEY, Raymond Henry, b. 13 Oct. 1915. Certified Manufacturing Engineer. Educ: Night Student, Pa. State Coll., 1937-54. m. Ethel R. Wildasin, 1939, 1 s., 2 d. Appts: Chief Engr., Davey Products Inc., Red Lion, Pa., 1951-59; V.P., Flinchbaugh Products Inc., ibid 1959-62; Grp. Ldr., Prod. Engrng., Honeywell Inc., Mpls., Minn., 1962-68; Mgr., Mfg. Engrng., York Div., Am. Machine & Foundry Co., York, Pa., 1968-71; Sr. Mfg. Engr., York Div., Borg-Warner Corp. 1971-. Mbrships: Soc. Mfg. Engrs.; Bd. of Dirs., ibid, 1964-68; Am. Soc. of

Metals. Publs: Contbr. to num. handbooks inclng. Tool Engineer's Handbook; Die Design Handbook; Fixture Design Handbook; Manufacturing, Planning & Estimating Handbook; Numerical Control in Manufacture Handbook; Machining with Carbides & Oxides Handbook; Tooling for Aircraft & Missile Manufacture Handbook; Fundamentals of Tool Design Textbook; Pneumatic Controls for Industrial Application Handbook; Gun Drilling & Trepanning Handbook; High Velocity Forming of Metals Handbook. Holds var. patents, copyrights, & a patent in field, 1953-71. Address: 4233 Webster Dr., York, PA 17402, U.S.A. 6.

MEDCALF, Ian George, b. 12 July 1918. Barrister; Solicitor. Educ: Univ. of W.A., Australia; LL.B., St. George's Coll., ibid. Appts: Sec., Law Soc. of W.A.; V.P., ibid; Lectr., Real Property & Conveyancing, Univ. of W.A.; Sr. Ptnr., Robinson Cox & Co. law firm, Perth; Mbr., Legislative Coun. for Metropol. Province of W.A. Mbrships: Chmn., later V.P., Nat. Trust of Australia, W.A.; Chmn., W.A. Bd., Colonial Mutual Life Assurance Soc. Ltd.; Bds., Elder Smith Goldsbrough Mortgate Ltd. & Perpetual Executors Trustees & Agcy. Co. (W.A.) Ltd.; Past Cmdg. Off., W.A. Univ. Regiment. Past Ed., num. profl. & semi-profl. jrnls. & publs. Hons. incl: Engl. Medal, Univ. of W.A., 1935; Efficiency Decoration, 1962. Address: Parliament House, Perth, W.A., Australia. 23.

MEDLEY, Paul, Jr., b. 9 Mar. 1936. Librarian. Educ: B.A., Southern Meth. Univ., 1958; M.L.S., Grad. Schl. of Lib. Sci., Univ. of Tex., 1969. Appts: Profl. Asst., Pub. Lib., Dallas, Tex., 1959-60; Catalog Asst., Humanities Rsch. Ctr., Univ. of Tex., 1960-61; Vari-Typer Corp., San Antonio, Tex., 1962-64; Lib. Asst., Undergrad. Lib., Univ. of Tex., 1964-66; Pub. Servs. Dir., Pub. Lib., Abilene, Tex., 1966-67; Dir. of Libs., Waco-McLennan Co. Lib., Tex., 1967-; Instr., Dept. of Lib. Sci., Baylor Univ., 1973-. Mbrships: ALA; Chmn., Acquisitions Round Table, & sev. comms., Tex. Lib. Assn.; Chmn., Nominating Comm., Tex. Munical Libns. Assn.; Bd. of Dirs. & Past Pres., W. Tex. Lib. Film Circuit, Inc.; Rotary Club. Address: 1717 Mountainview Dr., Waco, TX 76710, U.S.A. 7.

MEDLIN, Charles Reitzel, b. 9 May 1924. Violoncellist; Music Teacher. Educ: Univ. of N.C., Chapel Hill, U.S.A.; Juilliard Schl. of Music, N.Y.C. Appts: Prin. Cellist, N.C. Symph. Orch.; Indpls. Symph. Orch.; Prin. Cellist, Winston-Salem Symph.; Tchr., Cello & Piano, Schl. of Music, Salem Coll., Winston-Salem, N.C. Mbrship: Am. Fedn. of Musicians. Chosen to play in First World Symph. Orch., under Arthur Fiedler, 1971. Address: 1001 Chestnut Dr., High Point, NC 27260, U.S.A. 125.

MEDVEI, Victor Cornelius, M.D., F.R.C.P., (Lond.) b. 6 June 1905. Physician. Educ: Univ. of Vienna, Austria, 1930; Med. Coll., St. Bartholomew's Hosp., London, U.K., 1938-41; Appts: Lectr. & Chief Asst. on Med. (Profl.) Units, Tchng. Hosps., 1955-56; Sr. Med. Off., 1966-70; Prin. Med. Officer, C.S.D., in charge of British Diplomatic Serv. Med. Servs.; Examining Physn., UN. Mbrships: Pres., V.P. & Treas., Harveian Soc. of London; London Thyroid Club; European Thyroid Assn.; European Assn. Internists; Jt. Sec. Gen., Int. Assn. Physns. Overseas Servs.; PEN; Chmn. & Sec., Soc. of Silver Collectors; Garrick Club. Contbr. of approx. 60 papers to num. med. jrnls. Hons: Buxton Browne Prize & Medal, Harveian Soc. of London, 1948; C.B.E., 1965; Wellcome Trust Grant, 1971. Address: 38

Westmorland Terr., London, S.W. 1, U.K. 3, 131.

MEE, Arlene Driscoll (Mrs. William G. Mee), b. 17 Oct. 1918. Librarian. Educ: Greens Beauty Coll. Appts. incl: Licenced Beautician, Lead, S.D., 1938-41; Licenced Beautician, Belle Fourche, S.D., 1941-44; Bookkeeper, Blue Drug & Jewelry, Spearfish, S.D., 1946-56; Libn., San Manuel Pub. Lib., Ariz., 1959-. Mbrships: Den Mother, Black Hills & Catalina Couns. Cub Scouts of Am., 1952-56, 1958-62; Advsry Bd., Pinal Co., Ariz., Chmn., 1965-72; Am. & Ariz. Lib. Assns.; Pinal Co. Lib. Federation., V. Chmn., 1968-72; Emblem Club, Treas., 1964-69. Address: 1015 1st Ave., San Manuel, AZ, U.S.A. 5.

MEE, John Franklin, b. 10 July 1908. Educator & Editor. Educ: A.B., Miami Univ., 1930; A.M., Univ. of Me., 1933; Ph.D., Ohio State Univ., 1959; LL.D., Miami Univ. 1964. Appts: Assoc. w. Ind. Univ., 1939-; Mead Johnson Prof. ofMgmt.; Dean of Div. of Gen. & Tech. Studies; Chmn., Dept. of Mgmt; other appts. incl. Exec. Office of Pres. of USA; Cmmnr. of Revenue, State of Ind. Mbrships. incl: Phi Beta Kappa; Nat. Pres., Beta Gamma Sigma; Past Pres., Am. Acad. of Mgmt.; Pres., Coun. of Profl. Educ. for Bus.; Chmn., Edit. Bd., Bus. Horizon Jrnl.; Pres., Mee Farms, Inc.; Fellow, Int. Acad. of Mgmt; Sec., Navy Advsry. Bd. for Educ. & Trng., 1973; Indl. Coll. of Armed Forces Advsry. Bd., 1966-68. Publs: Personnel Handbook, 1951; Management Thought in a Dynamic Economy, 1963; Ed., Irwin Series in Management & Behavioral Science Series. Hons: Acad. of Mgmt. Award, 1963; Ky. Col., 1966; Coun. of Sagamores of Wabash, 1964; Taylor Key Award, Soc. for Adv. of Mgmt., 1972; Beta Gamma Sigma Disting. Scholar, 1973. Address: 507 S. Jordan Ave., Bloomington, IN 47401, U.S.A. 2, 8, 13, 14, 15, 16, 30, 128.

MEEHAN, Kathleen Mary, b. 28 Nov. 1904. Teacher. Educ: A.B., Ball State Univ., 1925; M.A., ibid, 1949. Appts: (all in Muncie, Ind.) Soc. Ed., Muncie Star, 1924-25; Tchr., Blaine Elem. Schl., 1925-30; Wilson Jr. H.S., 1930-31; Muncie Ctrl. H.S., 1931-71; Adult Educ. Ctr. of Muncie schls., 1971-73. Mbrships: Past Pres., Administrative Women of Muncie Schls.; Past Ind. Pres., Past Muncie Br. Pres., Nat. League of Am. Pen Women, now Sec., Muncie Br.; Delta Kappa Gamma Soc.; Past Muncie Pres., now Histn., Women in Communications; Women's Press Club of Ind. Publs: Contbr. to periodicals; Feature Writer, Ed. of column, Our Sunday Visitor; Past Ed., Our Muncie Schools. Hons: Woman of Year, Muncie Beta Sigma Phi, 1956; Outstanding Alumni Award, Ball State Univ., 1963; Bus. & Profl. Women's Club Award, 1964; Jrnlsm. Alumni Award, Ball State Univ., 1973. Address: 2125 W. Main St., Muncie, IN 47303, U.S.A. 5, 8, 130.

MEEK, John Millar, b. 21 Dec. 1912. Electrical Engineer. Educ: Liverpool Univ., U.K., 1931-34; Univ. of Calif., U.S.A., 1938-40. Appts: Rsch. Engr., High Voltage Lab., Metropolitan-Vickers, Ltd., 1934-46; Prof., Dept. of Elec. Engrng. & Electronics, Liverpool Univ., 1946-. Fellowships: Instn. of Elec. Engrs. (Pres. 1968-69); Inst. of Physics. Publs: (books) Mechanism of the Electric Spark (w. L.B. Loeb), 1941; Electical Breakdown of Gases (w. J.D. Craggs), 1953; High Voltage Lab. Technique (w. J.D. Craggs), 1953; var. papers in Proceedings of IEE, Inst. of Physics & other learned socs. Hons: Institution Premium, Inst. Elec. Engrs., 1942; Hon. D.Sc., Univ. of Salford, 1971; Hon. Fellow, Japanese Inst. of Elec. Engrs., 1970. Address: Dept. of Elec.

Engrng. & Electronics, Univ. of Liverpool, P.O. Box 147, Liverpool L69 3BX, U.K. 1.

MEEK, Ronald Lindley, b. 27 July 1917. Professor of Economics. Educ: LL.M., Vic. Univ. of Wellington, New Zealand, 1939; M.A., ibid, 1946; PH.D., Univ. of Cambridge, UK, 1949. Appts: Lectr., Econs., Glasgow Univ., Scotland, U.K., 1948-59; Sr. Lectr., ibid, 1960-63; Prof. & Hd., Dept. of Econs., Univ. of Leicester, 1963-. Publs: Studies in the Labour Theory of Value, 1958; The Economics of Physiocracy, 1962. Economics & Ideology, 1967; Figuring Out Society, 1971; (Ed.) Marx & Engels on Malthus, 1953; Quesnay's Tableau Economique, 1971. Address: 27, The Fairway, Oadby, Leicestershire, U.K. 131.

MEEKER, Charles R. Jr., b. 30 Apr. 1913. Management Consultant. Educ: Southern Meth. Univ., 1932-36. Appts: Var. managerial assignments, Interstate Theaters, Dallas, Tex., 1936-44; Mng. Dir., State Fair Musicals, State Fair of Tex., 1944-60, V.P., 1950-60; Mgmt. Cons., 1960-; Pres. & Exec. Prod., Miss Teenage Am. Inc., 1969-. Mbrships. incl: Life Mbr., Press Club of Dallas; Dallas Country Club. Author, var. newspaper & mag. articles, marketing progs. Hons. incl: Exceptional Merit Award, Dallas-Ft. Worth Art Dir.; R.J.O'Donnell Mem. Award for Best Showman. Address: 1145 Empire Central Pl., Suite 134, Dallas TX 75247, U.S.A. 7.

MEEKER, Estella West, b. 13 June 1904. Educator; Lecturer. Educ: A.B., Ky. Wesleyan Coll., Winchester; A.M., George Peabody Coll. for Tchrs., Nashville; Grad. Study, Univ. of Chgo., Univ. of Denver, Univ. of W. Va., Marshall Univ. Appts. incl: Tchr., Kanawha Co. Schls., 1925-41, Charleston W. Va., 1942-44; Instr., Morris Harvey Coll., ibid, 1946-57; Asst. Prof., Engl., W. Va. State Coll., 1949-50, 1955-56; Asst. Prof., Engl. & Dramatics, Montgomery, W. Va., 1958-60; Prof., Engl., Dir., Drama, Southwood Coll., Salembury, N.C., 1965-; Reading Cons., Lectr. Mbrships: AAUP; V.P., AAUW; Worthy High Priestess, White Shrine of Jerusalem; Pres., Wesleyan Serv. Guild; State V.P., Ch. Women United; Local Omicron Pres., Alpha Delta Kappa; Dir., Delta Kappa Gamma, Southwood Coll.; Dir., Alpha Delta Kappa, W. Va. Inst. of Technol.; Lay Speaker, W. Va. Meth. Ch.; Nat. Cons., Nat. Coun. of Chs., 1960. Author, Kentucky in the Writings of Elizabeth Madox Roberts. Address: 129 Maplewood Estates, Scott Depot, WV 25560, U.S.A. 5, 6, 125, 132.

MEEKS, Charles William, b. 4 Apr. 1930. Dental Surgeon. Educ: B.Sc., 1953. D.D.S., 1956, McGill Univ., Canada. Appts: in pvte. Prac.; also pt.-time schl. dentist with St. Mary Parish Coun. Mbrships: Jamaica Dental Assn. (1st V.P., 1965, 1970, Pres., 1972). Address: 55 Hope Boulevard, Kingston 6, Jamaica, West Indies. 109.

MEESCHAERT, Emile, b. 10 Aug. 1910. Stockbroker. Appts. incl: Created Finance Co., 1935 & Soc. d'Etudes Meeschaert, 1948; Tchr., Lille Bus. Schl.; Nominated as Stockbroker to Paris & Marseille Stock Exchanges. Mbrships: Am. Chmbr. of Comm.; Hon. Pres., Ctr. d'Accueil Roubaisien Harmonie des Anciens; Choral Nadaud; Swimming Club of Roubaix. Publs: Financial newsletter, Savoir Acheter. Hons: Off. de la Soc. Nat. d'Encouragement au Bien. Address: 198 Ave. Victor Hugo, Paris 16, France. 43, 91.

MEETZE, Linda Daniel, b. 11 Oct. 1941. Piano & Voice Teacher. Educ: B.S., Winthrop Coll., S.C. Appts: Music Tchr. & Choral Dir.,

Clover Schls., S.C.; Choir Dir., Bethel Presby. & Sherer Presby. Chs.; Interim Dir., Southside Bapt. Ch. Choir. Mbrships: Nat., S.C., & York Co. Educators' Assns.; Cherokee Ave. Bapt. Ch., Sunday Schl. & Ch. Choir; Gaffney Jr. Woman's Club; Ways & Means Chmn., V.P., Pres., Sec., V.P., Cherokee Gladiolus Soc.; Cherokee Singers: Cherokee Hlth. Fndn.; Charter Mbr., Family YMCA; Pres., Past Mbr., Jr. Homer Garden Club. Address: 201 Crestview Dr., Gaffney, SC 29370, U.S.A. 125.

MEGGED, Aharon, b. 10 Aug. 1920. Writer. Educ: Hebrew Gymnasium Hertzlia, Tel-Aviv. Appts: Ed., Massa, literary weekly, 1955-68; Cultural Attaché, Israel Embassy, London, U.K., 1968-71; Columnist, Davar, daily newspaper, 1971-74. Mbrships: Hebrew Writers Assn.; Israel Journalists Assn.; P.E.N. Club. Publs: Spirit of the Seas; Hedva & I; Folks; Fortunes of a Fool; The Escape; Living on the Dead; The Short Life; Evyatar Notes; Midday; Of Stones & Trees; The Second Day. Plays: Far in the Wasteland; Hannah Senesh; Genesis; The Burning Season. Hons: Ussishkin Literary Prize, 1955; Brener Literary Prize, 1957; Shlonsky Literary Prize, 1963; Ussiskin Literary Prize, 1965; Prime Minister's Literary Award, 1973; Bialik Literary Prize, 1974. Address: 26 Rupin St., Tel-Aviv, Israel. 55, 94.

MEGNIN, Donald F., b. 10 Dec. 1928. Professor; Clergyman. Educ: A.B., Syracuse Univ., N.Y., U.S.A.; S.T.B., Boston Univ., Mass.; M.A., Syracuse Univ., Ph.D., ibid. Appts. incl: Lectr., Chulalongkorn Univ., Bangkok, Thailand, 1954-56; Asst. to Dean, Boston Univ. Chapel, 1958-60; Min. i/c, First Ward Meth. Ch., Syracuse, N.Y., 1960-63; Prog. Assoc., S.Asian Studies, Syracuse Univ., 1966-67; Asst. Prof., Slippery Rock State Coll., Pa., 1967-68; Assoc. Prof. & Asst. V.P., Acad. Affairs, ibid, 1968-72; Dir., Int. Educ., 1972; Acting Dean, Schl. of Soc. & Behavioral Scis., 1973-. Mbrships: incl: Chmn., Pa. Consortium for Int. Educ.; Grand Marshall, Fac. & Admin., Slippery Rock State Coll.; Sec., Bd. of Dirs., Regional Coun. for Int. Educ.; Am. Pol. Sci. Assn.; Dir., Franklin Area Schl. Bd. Publs: The Soviet's Challenge to the United States; How Russia Challenges; German Economic Assistance to India; Why Aid? The Case of West Germany & India. Recip., sev. acad. awards. Address: School of Social & Behavioral Sciences, Slippery Rock State College, Slippery Rock, PA 16057, U.S.A.

MEGSON, Barbara Elsie. H.M. Inspector of Schools. Educ: Girton Coll., Cambridge, U.K., 1948-51; B.A., 1951, M.A., 1956, Univ. of Cambridge, Appts: Rsch. Asst. to Prof. W.K. Jordan of Harvard, 1951; Classifier, Hulton Press Illustrations Lib., 1952-53; Asst. Tchr., Cheltenham Ladies' Coll., 1953-62; Hd. of Hist. Dept., Totnes H.S., Devon, 1963-64; Asst. Warden, Devon Ctr. for Further Educ., Dartington, 1965; Admin. Asst., W. Riding, Yorkshire, 1966-67; H.M. Inspector, Dept. of Educ. & Sci., 1968-. Occasional work; Compiled Index. to M.G. Jones' "Hannah More", 1952; in vacs., working on Calendar of Archives & Hist. of Uppark, Hastings, W. Sussex, 1950-62. Mbrships: Histl. Assn; Commonwealth Soc.; Brit. Fedn. Univ. Women. Publs: A Short History of the Lady Eleanor Holles School, 1947; An Informal History of Girton College (w. J.O. Lindsay) 1959; English Homes & Housekeeping 1700-1960, 1968; Children in Distress (w. Alec Clegg) 1968. Address: Dept. of Educ. & Sci., Elizabeth House, York Rd., London, S.E. 1, U.K. 5, 30.

MEHALLIS, George, b. 14 Feb. 1923. Education Administrator. Educ: B.S., M.S.,

Ph.D., Ohio State Univ., 1945, '48, '63. Appts. incl: Ashtabula Harbor H.S., 1945-48; Asst. Prof., assoc. Prof., Chmn., Dept. of Indl. Educ., Univ. of Miami, 1950-64; Instr., Ohio State Univ., 1960-61; Dir., Div. Tech./Voc. Studies, Miami-Dade Community Coll., 1964-; Ed.D Cluster Coord., Nova Univ., Ft. Lauderdale, Fla., 1972-. Mbrships. incl: Fla. Tech. Educ. Assn.; Dir., ibid, 1969-70; Cons. Occupational Progs. Am. Assoc. Jr. Colls., 1966-; Am. Tech. Educ. Assn.; Pres., ibid, 1972; Epsilon Pi Tau; Phi Delta Kappa; Kappa Delta Pi. Hons: Laureate Citation, Hon. Citation, Epsilon Pi Tau, 1956-64. Address: 614 Aledo, Coral Gables, FL 33134, U.S.A. 130.

MEHNERT, Klaus, b. 10 Oct. 1906. Educator; Author. Educ: Univs. of Tubingen & Munich, Germany; Ph.D., Berlin, 1930; Univ. of Calif., Berkeley, U.S.A., 1925-29. Appts: i/c Russian Sect., German Off. for Peace Questions, Stuttgart, W. Germany, 1947-48; Ed. in Chief, Christ und Welt, 1949-54; Ed. in Chief, Osteuropa, 1951-; Radio & TV Commentator, 1950-; Prof., Pol. Sci., Aachen Inst. of Technol., 1961-. Publs. incl: Stalin versus Marx, 1951; Asien Moskau & Wir, 1956; Soviet Man & His World, 1960; Peking & Moscow, 1963; Mao's Zweite Revolution, 1966; Der deutsche Standort, 1967; Peking & the New Left, 1969; China Returns, 1972; Moscow & the New Left, 1974. Recip., Grand Cross of Merit, Germany, 1967. Address: 7291 Schoemberg bei Freudenstadt, German Fed. Repub. 34, 43.

MEHREN, George L., b. 6 July 1913. Business Executive; University Professor; Government Official. Educ: B.Sc. (Econ.)' Calif. Univ., U.S.A.; Ph.D., ibid. Appts: (Univ.) Tchng. Asst.-Instr., Agric. Econ., 1938-42; U.S.N., 1942-45; Asst. Prof-Prof., Agric. Econs., Giannini Fndn. Agric. Econs., 1947-71; Dir., ibid; Chmn., Dept. Agric. Econs., Statewide, Calif. Univ.; Chmn., Statewide Curriculum in Agric. Bus. Mgmt., 1957-62; Prof. Emeritus, Agric. Econs., Calif. Univ., 1971; Govt. appts. incl: U.S. Ambassador, Panama, 1968; Asst. Sec., Agric., 1963-68; Dir., Sci. & Educ., U.S. Dept. Agric., 1965-68; Cons. & Collaborator, var. times between 1949-63; Cons., Agcy. Int. Dev., 1969-70; Cons./Collaborator, Korea, Pakistan, Iran, Mexico, Venezuela, Morocco, Indonesia, 1968-71. Mbr. Alpha Zeta; num. gov. comms. & couns., profl. orgs. & holder var. edit. posts. Author over 500 jrnl. articles, bulletins, rsch. reports & other publs. in field of econ & marketing theory, price analysis & gen. policy. address: 406 Country Lane, San Antonio, TX 78209, U.S.A.

MEHROTRA, Ram Charan, b. 16 Feb. 1922. University Professor & Administrator. Educ: B.Sc., M.Sc., 1st Div., Pub. Examinations; D.Phil., Allahabad Univ., 1948; Ph.D., London Univ., U.K., 1952; D.Sc., ibid, 1964. Appts: Lectr., Allahabad Univ., 1944-54; British Coun. Schlr., London Univ., U.K., 1950-52; Rdr., Lucknow Univ., India, 1954-58; Prof., Gorakhpur Univ., 1958-62, Dean, 1959-62; Prof., Rajasthan Univ., 1962-, Dean, Fac. of Sci., 1962-65, 1972-, Vice-Chancellor, 1968-69. Fellowships: Royal Inst. Chem., 1952-64; Indian Nat. Sci. Acad.; Nat. Acad. of Scis., Allahabad; Indian Chem. Soc., & currently V.P.; Indian Acad. of Scis., Bangalore. Author, some 400 rsch. papers, chem., int. jrnls. Hons. incl: E.G. Hill Mem. Prize, Allahabad Univ., 1949; Sir S.S. Shatnagar Award, chem. rsch., 1965. Address: P4 Univ., Campus, University of Rajasthan, Jaipur-302004, India.

MEIDEN, Walter, b. 12 July 1907. Professor. Educ: A.B., Univ. of Mich., 1931; M.A., Ohio State Univ., 1933; Ph.D., 1945. Appts: Prof. of Romance Langs., Ohio State Univ., 1931-43, 46-; U.S.N.R. Off., Tchr., French, Spanish & German, U.S.N. Acad., 1943-46. Mbrships: MLA. Publs: Beginning French (w. W.S. Hendrix), 1940, 4th edit., 1970; Beginning Spanish (w. Richard Armitage), 1953, 3rd edit., 1972; Onze contes (w. Olin Moore), 1957; Chess Master vs. Chess Amateur (W. Max Euwe), 1963, 2nd edit., 1971; Contes de Michelle Maurois, 1966; The Road to Chess Mastery, 1966; French for Oral & Written Review (w. Charles Carlut), 1968; Jt. Ed., Anouilh's Le voyageur sans Bagage, 1973; Spanish for Oral & Written Review (w. Mario Iglesias), scheduled for 1975; Contbr. w. Norman Cotter, monthly column called Back to Basics to Chess Life & Review. Recip. French Govt. Schlrship., 1946. Address: c/o Dept. of Romance Langs., Cunz Hall, Ohio State Univ., Columbus, OH 43210, U.S.A.

MEIMARIDIS, George Tassos, b. 1 May 1933. Importer; Retail Trader. Educ: Am. Athens Coll., Greece, 1952; Bowdoin Coll., Brunswick, Me., U.S.A., 1953; Schl. of Gen. Studies, Columbia Univ., N.Y., U.S.A., 1955. Appts: Jt. Owner & Gen. Mgr., family bus., import & retail, glassware, chinaware, household fixtures & fittings, retail stores, Athens & Thessaloniki, 1960-. Mbrships: Ligue Franco-Hellenique; Athens Coll. Alumni Assn.; Admin. Mbr., & Ed.-in-Chief, monthly jrnl. ibid, 1970-72. Publs: Was it August?, 1966; Lykabitos, 1972; Lytrotiko, 1973; The Banoons, 1973. Address: c/o Meimaridis & Pirpiroglou, 24 Stadiou St., Athens (132), Greece. 43.

MEIMAROGLOU, Mario, b. 16 May 1916. Educator. Educ: Baccalaureat, France, 1932; Degree, Athens Schl. of Econs. & Bus., 1936; Doct., ibid, 1954. Appts. incl: Assoc. Prof., Athens Schl. of Econs. & Bus., 1959-65; Prof., ibid, 1965-, Rector, 1973-; Advsr. to the Gov., Nat. Bank of Greece, 1968-71. Mbrships: Chmn., Inst. of Cert. Pub. Accts. of Greece, 1967-71; Yachting Club of Greece. Publs: Agricultural Costs, 1954; Budgeting & Budgetary Control, 1957; Cost Behavior and the Break-Even Chart, 1957; Financial Management, 1962. Address: 55 Spefsippou St., Athens, Greece.

MEINHOLD, Peter, b. 20 Sept. 1907. University Professor. Educ: Lic.theol., Berlin, Germany, 1934; inaugurated, Theol. Fac., Univ. of Berlin, 1934. Appts: Asst., Theol. Fac., Berlin, 1934; Curate, ibid; Univ. Lectr., Heidelberg, 1935; Univ. Lectr., Kiel, 1936; Prof., ibid, 1936; Full Prof., 1947; Dir. Kirchlich-Archäologisches Institut, 1947-. Mbr. Pontificia Academia Mariana Internationalis, 1971-. Publs. incl: Konzile der Kirche in evangelischer Sicht, 1962; Okumenische Kirchenkunde. Lebensformen der Christenheit heute, 1962; Caesar's or God's. Conflict of Church & State in modern Society, 1962; Geschichte der kirchlichen Historiographie, 2 vols., 1967; Das Dreieck der Christenheit, 1974. Address: Dorfstede 15, Postfach 3245, D 2300 Kiel-Schulensee, German Fed. Repub.

MEININGER, Herbert, b. 20 Feb. 1907. Publisher; Chief Editor. Educ: Tradesman's Dip. Publisher & Chief Ed., Verlag D. Meininger, Neustadt/Weinstrasse, German Fed. Repub., 1952-. Address: Verlag & Druckerei D. Meininger, Postfach 312, Maximilianstrasse 11-17, 673 Neustadt/Weinstrasse, German Fed. Repub. 1.

MEINKE, Peter, b. 29 Dec. 1932. Writer; Professor. Educ: A.B., Hamilton Coll., N.Y., 1955; M.A., Univ. of Mich., 1961; Ph.D., Univ. of Minn., 1966. Appts: Engl. Tchr., Mtn. Lakes HS, N.J., 1958-60; Instr. in Engl.-Asst. Prof., Hamline Univ. St. Paul, Minn., 1961-66; Assoc. Prof.-Prof., Lit., Fla. Presby. Coll., now called Eckerd Coll., St. Petersburg, Fla., 1966-; Chmn., Lit. Dept., ibid; Dir. of Writing Workshop, 1973-; Dir. of Overseas Prog. for Mid-Fla. Colls., Neuchatal, Switz., 1971-72 (on leave from Eckerd). Mbrships: Delta Kappa Epsilon. Publs: Howard Nemerov (criticism), 1968; The Legend of Larry the Lizard (children's book), 1968; Very Seldom Animals (children's book), 1970; Lines from Neuchatel (poetry), 1974; contbr. over 200 poems, reviews or articles to mags. Hons. incl: 8 awards for poetry; chosen for Poets-in-the-Schls. prog., S.C., 1973-74. Address: Dir., Writing Workshop, Eckerd Coll., St. Petersburg, FL 33733, U.S.A. 7.

MEISELS, Gerhard George, b. 11 May 1931. Professor; Department Chairman. Educ: Univ. of Vienna, 1949-51 & 52-53; M.Sc., Univ. of Notre Dame, Ind., U.S.A., 1952; Ph.D., ibid, 1956. Appts: Postdoct. Rsch. Assoc., USAEC, Univ. of Notre Dame, 1955-56; Chem., Gulf Rsch. & Dev. Co., Pitts., Pa., 1956-59; Instr., Carnegie Tech. Univ., Pitts., 1957-58; Chem., Union Carbide Corp., 1959-62; Asst. Grp. Leader, ibid, 1962-65; Assoc. Prof.-Prof., Univ. of Houston, 1965-; Dept. Chmn., ibid, 1972-. Mbrships: Sec. & Pres., Ramsey, N.J., Jr. Chmbr. of Comm.; Dir., Houston Kennel Club, 1967-; Fndr. & Pres., W. Highland White Terrier Club of S.E. Tex., 1968-; Am. Phys. Soc.; AAAS; Sigma Xi; Am. Soc. for Mass Spectrometry; Fellow, Tex. Acad. of Scis. & Am. Inst. of Chems.; Pres., S.W. Mass Spectrometry Assn.; Dir., Prog. Chmn., Chmn.-elect & Chmn. S.E. Tex. Sect., Am. Chem. Soc. Contbr. about 70 publs to nat. & int. sci. jrnls. & chapts. to books inclng. Chemistry of the Functional Groups, & Fundamental Processes in Radiation Chemistry. Recip. Fulbright Fellowship, 1951. Address: 707 Cowarts Creek Dr., Friendswood, TX 77546, U.S.A. 7, 14, 16, 28, 56, 125.

MEISSINGER, Ruth Annemarie, b. 23 July 1924. Physician; Obstetric & Gynecological Surgeon. Educ: Dr.Med., J.W. Goethe Univ., Frankfurt, Germany, 1949; M.D., 1954. Appts: Med. Off., Int. Refugee Org., Frankfurt, German, 1950-51; Intern, Calif. Luth. Hosp., L.A., U.S.A., 1953-54, Res. in Ob. & Gyn., 1954-57; Ob. & Gyn. Prac., Permanent Med. Grp., Fontana (Calif.) Med. Ctr., 1957-; Staff Mbr., Tchr. of Res. Physns., Kaiser Fndn. Hosp., Fontana. Mbrships: Riverside-San Bernardino Ob. & Gyn. Soc.; Animal Protection Inst. of Am. Inc.; Patron, Humane Soc. of Chaffey Community Inc.; Mus. Chaffey Communities Cultural Ctr., Upland, Calif., 1971-72; Sponsor, W. Edn. Opera Assn., Ontario, Calif., 1971-72. Address: 1790 N. Euclid Ave., Upland, CA 91786, U.S.A.

MEISTER, Emma Agnes, b. 24 Sept. 1915. Educator; Administrator. Educ: B.S., N.Y. Univ., 1950; M.A., ibid, 1954; Postgrad. at var. univs. & colls. Appts: Sec., Prin., Elem. Schl. Pub. Schls., Union City, N.J., 1938-47; Schl. Soc. Wkr., Pub. Schls., ibid, 1948-61; Dir., Special Servs. Dept., 1961-; Instr., Rutgers Univ., 1961-; Dir., Hudson Co. Coun. Soc. Agcys., 1955-60. Mbrships. incl: Union City Juvenile Conf. Comm.; Advsr. to Pres. Kennedy's Comm. on Juvenile Delinquency, Youth & Crime, 1962; Past Pres., Hudson Co. Soc. Wkrs. Org.; N.J. Assn. of Soc. Wkrs.; Nat. Assn. Soc. Wkrs.; Int. & Nat. Confs. on Soc.

Welfare; Union City Educ. Assn.; AAUW; Int. Coun. Exceptional Children; Am. Personnel & Guidance Assn.; Assn. Counselor Educ. & Supvsn. Named Woman of Achievement, Hudson Co., 1965. Address: Bd. of Educ., Dept. of Special Servs., 3912 Bergen Turnpike (32nd St.), Union City NJ 07087, U.S.A. 2, 5, 6, 130, 132, 138.

MEITES, Louis, b. 6 Dec. 1926. Professor of Chemistry. Educ: B.A., Middlebury Coll., 1945; M.A., Harvard Univ., 1946, Ph.D., 1947. Appts: Instr. of Chem., Princeton Univ., 1947-48, Yale Univ., 1948-52, Asst. Prof., 1952-55; Assoc. Prof.-Prof., Polytechnic Inst. of Brooklyn, 1955-68, Chief, Div. of Analytic Chem., 1967-68; Prof. & Chmn. of Dept. of Chem., Clarkson Coll. of Technol., 1968-. Mbrships: Am. Chem. Soc.; A.A.U.P.; Soc. of Sigma Xi; Phi Beta Kappa. Publs: Advanced Analytical Chemistry; Handbook of Analytical Chemistry; Polarographic Techniques; Progress in Polarography; contbr. to num. profl. publs.; Ed., Critical Reviews in Analytical Chemistry & mbr. of edit. advsry. bds. Recip. of Louis Gordon Mem. Award (w. Thelma Meites), 1970. Address: Dept. of Chem., Clarkson Coll. of Technol., Potsdam, NY 13676, U.S.A. 2, 6, 50.

MEIXNER, Mary Louise, b. 7 Dec. 1916. Art Educator & Professor. Educ: B.A. (cum Laude), Milwaukee-Donner Coll., Iowa; M.A., State Univ. of Iowa, Iowa City. Appts: Art Supvsr., pub. schls., Wis., 1938-44; Soc. Dir., State Univ. of Iowa, 1945-46; Tchr., Art Hist., Design, Milwaukee-Donner Coll., 1946-52, Prof., 1950-52; at Eastern Ky. Univ., Richmond, 1952-53; at Iowa State Univ., Ames, 1953-, Prof., Grad. Fac., drawing, painting, color, environmental arts, 1959-. Mbrships. incl: Coll. Art Assn. of Am., 1945-; Midam. Art Assn., 1945-; Intersoc. Color Coun. Solo Exhibs: Iowa, 1957; N.Y.C., 1969; Wis., 1969. Juried shows in var. states, inclng. Iowa, Dak., Ill., Wis. Hons. incl: 1st Award, Wis. State Fair, 1946; Best in Show Award, Denison Art Assn., 1970; Fac., Citation, 1971. Address: 1007 Lincoln Way, Apt. 4, Ames, IA 50010, U.S.A. 37.

MELCHIOR, Mogens Gustav Ivar, b. 14 July 1904. Diplomat; Ambassador. Educ: Univ. of Copenhagen, Denmark. Appts: Danish Diplomatic Serv., 1930-; Mbr., Danish Coun., in Hague Ct. Cas re. Sovereignty over E. Greenland, 1932-33; serv. in many countries; Dpty. Under Sec. of State (Dir. Gen. of Policy), For. Off., Copenhagen, 1957; Amb. to Turkey; Amb. to Yugoslavia; Danish Amb. to Switzerland, 1968-. Hons: Crd. w. Cross of Honour Order of the Dannebrog; Med. for Merit & for. decorations. Address: Danish Embassy, 95 Thunstrasse, Berne, Switzerland. 12, 34, 103.

MELENDEZ, Bermudo, b. 21 Jan. 1912. Professor of Paleontology. Educ: Grad., Natural Scis., 1936; Doctorate, Geol., 1942. Appts: Prof., Geol., Univ. of Granada, Spain, 1945-49; Prof., Paleontol., Univ. of Madrid, 1949-; Vice-Dir., Lucas Mallada Inst., Coun. for Scientific Rsch., Madrid, 1965-; Dir., Dept. of Paleontol., Univ. of Madrid, 1966-; Counsellor, Coun. for Scientific Rsch., 1972-. Mbrships. incl: Pres., Spanish Natural Hist. Soc., 1967; Nat. Comm. of Geol., 1958-; Spanish Assn. for the Progress of Scis.; Geological Soc. of France; AAAS; Soc. of Econ. Paleontologists & Mineralogists. Publs: Tratado de Paleontología (Invertebrados), 2 vols., 1947-50; Paleontología, vol. I, 1970; Geología (co-author), 3rd edit., 1973; La Evolución (co-author), 2nd edit., 1974; Approx. 100 monographs on paleontol. & geol.

Hons: Academician, Academia de Doctores de Madrid; For. Corresponding Assoc., Inst. of Sci., Letters & Arts, Venice, Italy. Address: Departamento de Paleontologia, Facultad de Ciencias, Universidad Complutense, Madrid 3, Spain. 43.

MELI, Salvatore, b. 1 June 1929. Sculptor; Ceramist. Educ: State Inst..of Art, & Fine Arts Acad., Florence, Italy. Appts: Asst. to Prof., Figure & Modelled Decoration, Lyceum of Art, Rome, 1951-54; Tchr., Ceramics, State Inst., Città Castellana, 1954-59; Tchr., Ceramics, State Insts., Rome & Marino, 1959-; Prof., Figure & Medelled Decoration, Second Lyceum of Art, & Tchr., Techniques & New Mats. for Sculpture, Acad. of Fine Art, Rome, 1970-. One-man shows incl: Rome, 1951-65; Palermo, 1954; Rio de Janeiro, Brazil, 1953; L.A. & San Fran. Calif., U.S.A., 1954; N.Y.C., 1955; London, U.K., 1957. Sculptures & Ceramics in permanent collects: Int. Mus., Faenza; Nat. Mus.'s of Ceramics, Messina & Vincenza, Italy; Mus. of Mod. Art, St. Louis, Mo., U.S.A.; Munich Mus., Germany. Num. other exhibs., Europe & Am. Hons. incl: Over 20 Dips. & other awards, 1949-70; 2 Silver Medals, 1952; 8 Gold Medals, 1961-71. Address: Via Appia Antica 65, 00179, Rome, Italy.

MELIN, Karl-Axel, b. 19 Dec. 1915. Head Physician; Medical Director. Educ: Grad., Karolinska Inst., Stockholm, Sweden; Licensed Physn., 1942. Appts. incl: Sev. posts, Clin. for Convulsive Disorders, Stora Sköndal, Stockholm Farsta, 1953-66; Hd. Physn. & Med. Dir., ibid, 1966-; Edit. Bd., int. Jrnl. of Clin. Neurophysiol., 1949-57; Edit. Bd., Social-Medicinsk Tidskrift, 1952-61; Edit. Bd., Int. Jrnl. of Clin. Neurophysiol., 1949-57; Edit. Bd., Social-Medicinsk Tidskrift, 1952-61; Edit. Bd., Int. Jrnl. of Early Childhood, 1972-. Num. mbrships. incl: V.P., Int. League against Epilepsy, 1969-73, Treas., 1973-; V.P., Int. Bur. for Epilepsy, 1966; Assn. de l'Aide A l'Epileptique; Bd., Org. Mondiale pour l'Educ. Préscolaire, 1962, Exec. Comm., 1966-; Bd., Swedish Epilepsy Assn., 1954, Pres., 1970-. Publs: Approx. 200 rsch. papers, reviews & articles on med. educ. & popular med.; 10 papers on artists & graphic art; Ed., Svenska Epilepsia, 1971-. Hons. incl: Int. Bur. for Epilepsy Award, 1967; Bronze Medal, Swedish Red Cross, 1967; Bronze Medal, British Med. Assn., 1969; Gold Medal, Swedish Patriotic Soc., 1973. Address: Stora Sköndals Sjukhus, S-123 85 Farsta, Stockholm, Sweden. 134.

MELLOR, David P., b. 19 Mar. 1903. Professor Emeritus. Educ: .B.Sc., Univ. of Tasmania, 1926; M.Sc., ibid, 1928; D.Sc., 1945; Electrolytic Zinc Co. Rsch. Schlr., 1927; Rsch. Fellow, C'wlth. Solar Observ., Canberra ACT, 1928; Hon. Rsch. Fellow, Calif. Inst. of Technol., Pasadena Calif., 1938. Appts: Lectr., Sr. Lectr., Reader in Chem., Univ. of Sydney, 1929-50; Prof. Chem., Univ. of N.S.W., 1955; Hd., Schl. of Chem., ibid, 1956-68; Dean, Fac. of Sci., 1968-70. Mbrships: Fellow, Royal Aust. Chem. Inst.; Pres., 1941, Hon. Educ. Sec., 1942-48; Bd. of Trustees, Aust. Mus.; Patron, Gemmol. Assn. of Aust. Publs: The Role of Science & Industry (vol. V. C'wlth. Official War Hist.), 1957; Chelating Agents & Metal Chelates (w. F.P. Dwyer), 1964; Evolution of the Atomic Theory, 1971. Hons: H.G. Smith Mem. Medal, Royal Aust. Chem. Inst., 1949; Medal of Royal Soc. of N.S.W., 1954; Dwyer Mem. Medal, Univ. of N.S.W. Chem. Soc., 1969. Address: 20 Pindari Ave., St. Ives, N.S.W., Australia 2075. 23.

MELLOR, John William, b. 28 Dec. 1928. Professor of Agricultural Economics. Educ:

B.Sc., Cornell Univ., Ithaca, N.Y., U.S.A., 1950; M.Sc., ibid, 1951; Dip., Agricl. Econs., Univ. of Oxford, U.K., 1952; Ph.D., Cornell Univ., 1954. Appts. incl: Asst. Prof., Agricl. Econs., Cornell Univ., 1954-58; Assoc. Prof., Agricl. Econs. & Asian Studies, ibid, 1958-65; Assoc. Dir., Ctr. for Int. Studies, Cornell Univ., 1961-66; Acting Dir., ibid, 1964-65; Prof., Agricl. Econs., Asian Studies, Int. Agricl. Dev., Pub. Policy & Int. Dev., 1965-. Mbrships: Am. Econ. Assn.; Am. Agricl. Econs. Assn. Publs: The Economics of Agricultural Development, 1966; Developing Rural India: Plan & Practice (w. T.F' ,Weaver, U.J. Lele, & S.R. Simon), 1968; Article in profl. jrnl. Recip., Award for best published rsch., Am. Agricl. Econs. Assn., 1968. Address: Dept. of Agricultural Economics, Cornell University, Ithaca, NY 14950, U.S.A. 6, 14, 30, 139.

MELO LANCHEROS, Livia Stella. Educator; Writer; Journalist. Educ: Grad. in Jrnlsm., Mass Communications & Educ., Javeriana Univ., Bogota, Colombia. Appts. incl: Fndr. & Hdmistress., Sacred Heart Schl., La Florida, Columbia, 1953; Co-fndr. & Hdmistress., Engl. Gymnasium, Bogota, 1955; Tchr., Police Schl., 1955-61; Full Prof., Technol. Univ. of Cundinamarca; Co-fndr., Gabriela Mistral House of Culture, 1958; Ed., Mundo Femenino, 1954-61; Fndr., sev. charitable assns. & cultural ctrs. Mbrships. incl: Corres. mbr., Antiochian Acad. Hist., Medellin, Colombia, 1970; Int. Schl. Women Jrnlsts. & Writers; Nat. Women's Coun. of Colombia; The Little Parnassus of Bogota. Publs. incl: Valores Femeninos de Colombia, 1966, 2nd. edit., 1967; Contbr. of articles to var. jrnls. & radio progs. & papers on var. aspects of women & history to confs. Hons. incl: Laureat, Dip. & Medal Francisco de Paula Santander, Nat. Govt. of Colombia, 1966; Award, Govt. of Costa Rica, 1967; Dip., V Nat. Congress of Hist., 1969; Dip., 1st Bolivarian week, 1969. Address: Apartado Aereo 8817, Bogota, Colombia.

MELTZER, Bernard David, b. 21 Nov. 1914. Professor of Law. Educ: A.B., Univ. of Chgo., 1935; J.D., 1937; LL.M., Harvard Law Schl., 1938. Appts. incl: Legal Cons., Nat. Defense Commn., 1940-41; Spec. Asst. to Asst. Sec. of State & Acting Chief of For. Funds Control Div., 1941-43; Trial Counsel, Nuremberg War Trials, 1945-56; Counsel, Vedder, Price, Kaufman & Kammholz, Chgo., 1954-55; Professorial Lectr., Univ. of Chgo., 1946-74; Prof., Law, ibid, 1948-72; James Parker Hall Prof. of Law, 1972-. Mbrships: Am. Soc. Arts & Scis.; Am. Law Inst.; Nat. Acad. Arbitrators; Phi Beta Kappa; Order of Coif; Am., Ill. & Chgo. Bar Assn.; Bd. Mgrs., 1972-74. Author of legal publs. Address: Law Schl., Univ. of Chgo., 1111 E. 60th St., Chgo. IL 60637, U.S.A. 2.

MELTZER, Julian Louis, b. 11 Mar. 1904. Writer & Translator; Institution Executive. Educ: Var. schls., U.K. Appts: Staff Asst., Palestine Weekly, Jerusalem, 1921; clerk w. Palestine Police, bank clerk, P.R. Off. & Personal Asst. to Chancellor, Hebrew Univ., Jerusalem, var. periods, 1922-31; Freelance Jrnlst., News Ed., Palestine Post, & For. Corres., N.Y. Times, London Daily Express, Jewish Chronicle, Reuters & Palcor newsagcys., var. periods, 1931-49; Staff Mbr., Weizmann Inst. of Sci., 1949; currently Vice Chmn., Weizmann Nat. Mem. Fndn., Dir., Weizmann Archives, Mng. Ed., Weizmann Letters & Papers of 1st Pres. of Israel, Rehovot. Mbr. & Chmn. of Coun., Friends, of Assaf Harofeh Hosp in Israel. Translator from Hebrew, var. books. Contbr., num. articles, newspapers & mags.

Address: 7 Rehov Leib Jaffe, Talpiot, Jerusalem 93390, Israel. 94.

MENCZEL, Jacob, b. 23 Apr. 1923. Professor of Medicine. Educ: Med. studies, Univ. of Yassi, Rumania, 1945-49; M.D., Hebrew Univ. Hadassah Med. Schl., Jerusalem, 1951; Intern & Res., Hadassah Univ. Hosp., Jerusalem; postgrad. trng., Metabolic Unit, Montefiore Hosp., N.Y., & Hines VA Hosp., Ill., U.S.A., 1961-63. Appts. incl: House Physn.-Chief Physn., Dept. of Med. A., Hadassah Univ., Hosp., Jerusalem, 1953-; Chief, Metabolic Unit for Bone Diseases, Cons. in Internal Diseases, Dept. of Orthopaedic Surg. & Dept. of Oncol., ibid, also Cons., Schl. of Dentistry, 1963-; Hd., Dept. of Med.-Hd., Dept. of Med. & Geriatrics, Rsch. Lab., Shaare Zedek Hosp., Jerusalem; Lectr. in Med.-Full Prof. of Med., Hebrew Univ. Hadassah Med. Schl., 1958-; Vis. Sci., NIH, Bethesda, Md., U.S.A., 1961-63. Mbrships. incl: Israeli Soc. fo; Calcified Tissues; Israeli Assn. for Internal Med.; Soc. of Exptl. Biol. & Med.; IADR; Israeli Soc. for Gerontol. & Geriatrics; Chmn., Prog. Comm., Xth Int. Congress of Gerontol. Contbr. num. pobls. to field. Address: c/o Shaare Zedek Hosp., Jerusalem, Israel 91-000.

MENDE, Herbert G., b. 3 Jan. 1915. Consultant Engineer; Technical Author. Educ: Tech. Acad. & Coll., Berlin; Heinrich-Hertz-Inst. Appts. incl: Probationer, Siemens & Halske, Berlin; Mil. Serv., Air Force, 1937-39; Electronic Engr., Telefunken, Berlin, WWII; Cons. Engr., 1945-; Official Expert in Electronics, Telecommunications & Precision Mech., 1951-. Publs. incl: 22 books & booklets in field of Engrng.; over 1200 articles in tech. jrnls., 1931-. Address: Postf. 1426, D-4812 Bielefeld-Brackwede 1, German Fed. Repub. 43, 92.

MENDELL, David, b. 10 May 1909. Professor; Psychiatrist. Educ: B.S., CCNY, 1929; M.D., Univ. of Vienna, Austria, 1934. Appts. incl: Pvte. Prac., Houston, Tex., 1936-42, 1950-; Clin. Assoc., San Fran. Inst. Psychoanalysis, 1946-50; Assoc. Prof., Baylor Coll., 1951-, & Dir., Postgrad. Grp. Psychotherapy Prog., 1966-70; Assoc. Prof. & Prof., Univ. of Tex., 1959-; Dir., Trng. & Fac. Evaluation, Psychotherapy Assn., 1960-66. Mbrships. Incl: Past Pres., Am. Acad. Psychotherapists; Int. Coun. on Grp. Psychotherapy; Fellow & Past Dir., Am. Grp. Psychotherapy Assoc; Fellow, Am. Psych. Assoc. Contbr. to profl. publs. Lectr., Panel & Workshop mbr. nat. & int., in Psych. & Psychotherapy. Address: 1706 Medical Towers, Houston, TX 77025, U.S.A.

MENDELSON, Marcel L., b. 9 June 1928. University Lecturer. Educ: B.A., Queens Coll., N.Y., 1948; M.A., Yale Univ., 1950; Ph.D., 1955. Appts: Asst. Instr., Yale Univ., 1951-53; Lectr., Queens Coll., N.Y., 1955-56; Lectr., Bar Ilan Univ., Ramat Gan, Israel, 1961-62; Sr. Lectr., ibid, 1962-. Mbrships: Art Advsr., Tel Aviv Mus., 1959-61; Art Advsr., Z.O.A. House, Tel-Aviv, 1966-. Publs: Marcel Janco, 1962; Guillaume Apollinaire, 1968. Address: 27 Reading St., Ramat Aviv, Tel-Aviv, Israel. 94.

MENDES, Paul, b. 19 Oct. 1927. Consultant. Educ: Gen. Acctng., Int. Acctng., Chgo., Ill.; Butler's Bus. Schl., Bridgeport, Conn.; Bus. Admin., Univ. of Bridgeport, Conn.; Warren Inst., Bridgeport. Appts. incl: Ralph Smith Agcy., Stratford, Conn., 1963-65; Educl. Programer Aide, Greater Bridgeport YMCA, Conn., pt.-time 1965-68; Exec. Sec., Chessman Fndn., Bridgeport, 1965-72; CYO-Soc. Action Dept., Min. of Soc. Concerns,

Diocese of Bridgeport, 1972-. Mbrships. incl: Bd. mbr., Greater Bridgeport Red Cross; Past Bd. mbr., Am. Red Cross, Southeastern Coun.; Adult-Prog. Dept. Comm., Bridgeport YMCA; V.P., McKinley Schl. PTA; Chmn., E. End Community Schl., Bridgeport; Pres., Bridgeport Coun., PTA; Chmn., Ctr. for Interim Educ., Bridgeport; Fndr., Chessmen Fndn. Inc., Bridgeport. Housing Cons., num. orgs. Hons. incl: Man of the Yr. Award, Am. Legion, 1963; Community Serv. Award, 1970. Address: 41 Blackman Pl., Bridgeport, CT 06604, U.S.A. 130.

MENDEZ-SANTOS, Carlos, b. 13 Dec. 1936. Assistant Professor of Social Sciences. Educ: B.A., Cath. Univ. of Puerto Rico, 1962; M.S.W., Univ. of Puerto Rico, 1964. Appts. incl: Asst. Prof. of Soc. Scis.; Jrnlst. for sev. Puerto Rican newspapers & writer for Radio progs. Mbrships. incl: Nat. Assn. Soc. Workers; AAUW; Cooperative de Crédito, Cath. Univ. of Puerto Rico, V.P., 1972-73; Pi Gamma Mu, 1964. Publs. incl: Los Immigrantes Puertorriquenos En Los Estados Unidos, 1968, 2nd edit. 1971; Tradiciones Poncenas, 1968, 2nd edit. 1973; Eugenio Maria De Hostos, Sociologo, 1969; Neustra Familia, 1970; Entrada Al Arrabal, 1971; La Gente, 1972; Por Tierras De Loiza Aldea, 1973; Leyendas De Ponce, 1973. Hons. incl: Serrallés Wirshing Co. Lit. Award, 1968; Iberoamerican Poets & Writers Guild Award, 1969; Kts. of Henry Dunant, Puerto Rico Chapt., Am. Red Cross, 1970; Writer of the Decade, Ponce Lions Club, 1971. Address: Box 521 Stn. 6, Cath. Univ. of Puerto Rico, Ponce PR 00731, U.S.A. 117, 125, 136.

MENDOZZA LEONELLI, Cesar, b. 27 July 1913. Lawyer. Educ: LL.D., Univ. of Genoa, Italy, & Ctrl. Univ. of Venezuela; Dr. in Pol. Scis., Univ. of Genoa. Appts. incl: currently Pres., Adriatica Venezolana de Seguros. Address: Gradillas a San Jacinto, Edificio Victor Mendozza, Caracas 101, Venezuela.

MENESES, Obed Jose Guallar, b. 19 Feb. 1924. Lawyer. Educ: Univ. Philippines, Manila, 2 yrs.; LL.B., Far Eastern Univ., ibid; Postgrad. work, Univ. Philippines, ibid. Appts: Prof., Ctrl. Luzon Educl. Ctr., Araneta Univ. Fndn. & Harvard Colls.; Legal Off.-Exec. V.P., Araneta Univ. Fndn., 1950-72; Exec. V.P., Ctrl. Luzon Educl. Ctr., 1972-; Trustee, Manuel V. Gallego Educl., Sci. & Cultural Fndn., 1974-. Mbrships: (Past) V.P., Assn. Colls. Agric., Philippines; Pres. & Gen. Mgr., Meneses Real Estate & Land Dev. Co.; Dir. & Treas., San Beda Alumni Assn. Inc.; Bd. Chmn. & Pres., United Circulation, Inc.; Gov., Philippines Athletic Fedn.; Rizal Coun., Boy Scouts of Philippines; Past Asst. Sec., Rotary Club, Caloocan; Past Chancellor, Kts. Columbus, Malabon Coun.; Trustee & Treas., Our Lady of Victory Charities, Inc. Publs: Business Law, 1957; Farm Laws, 1963; Public Land Law. Hons. incl: Law Valedictorian, Far Eastern Univ., Manila, 1949; Recip. NEC-ICA Grant, Univ. Philippines, 1955-57 & Award, San Beda Coll., 1961 & Araneta Univ. Fndn., 1972. Address: Ctrl. Luzon Educl. Ctr., Cabanatuan City, Philippines A-603.

MÉNETRÉZ, Jean Hugues, b. 18 Feb. 1924. Psychoanalyst; Psychiatrist. Educ: B.A., Univ. de Besancon, Doubs, France, 1942; M.D., C.M., McGill Univ. Med. Schl., Montreal, Quebec, Canada, 1950; 1st yr. of Dip. Course, Psych., ibid, at St. Anne's Hosp., St. Anne de Bellevue, 1954-55; 2nd & 3rd yr. Res. in Psych., N.C. Mem. Hosp., Chapel Hill, U.S.A., 1955-57; Dipl., Psych., Am. Bd. Psych. & Neurol., 1962; Grad., Wash. Psychoanalytic Inst., 1966. Appts.

incl: Mil. serv. as single engine fighter pilot w. Free French Air Force, WWII; Chief, Alcoholic Rehab. Div., D.C. Dept. of Pub. Hlth., 1958-61; Lectr., Psych., Georgetown Univ. Res. in Psych., 1960-62 & Geo. Wash. Univ. Med. Schl., 1960-64; Clin. Asst. Prof., Psych., ibid, 1964-; Mbr., Commn. of Mental Hlth., U.S. Dist. Ct. for D.C.; Instr., Fac. of Wash. Psychoanalytic Inst., 1966-; Short-term Tchr., elective seminar on suitability for psychoanalysis, ibid, 1970- & sev. other short-term seminars, etc.; Past Cons. & Lectr., var. times. Wash. Pastoral Inst., D.C., Inst. Mental Hygiene & Jewish Soc. Serv. Ctr.; Full-time Psychoanalytic & Gen. Adult Psych., Geo. Wash. Univ. Hosp., 1970-. Mbrships. incl: Var. profl. comms.; Fellow, Acad. of Psychoanalysis, 1967-; Wash. Psychoanalytic Soc., 1966-; Fellow, Am. Psych. Assn., 1973-. Address: 7440 Arrowwood Road, Bethesda, MD 20034, U.S.A. 2, 112.

MENEZES, (Sister) Mary Noel, b. 14 July 1930. Religious Sister; University Lecturer in History. Educ: B.A., Coll. Misericordia, Dallas, Pa., U.S.A., 1964; M.A., Georgetown Univ., Wash. D.C., 1966; Ph.D., Univ. of London, U.K., 1973. Appts: Entered Order of Sisters of Mercy, 1947, I/c., Sacred Heart Roman Cath. Girls' Schl., Georgetown, Guyana, 1955-63; Lectr., Coll. Misericordia, 1966; Lectr., Univ. of Guyana, Georgetown, 1967-70; Lectr. & Dir. of M.A. Prog. in Guyanese Hist., ibid, 1973-. Mbrships: Convocation, Univ. of London; Latin Am. Studies Assn.; Am. Histl. Assn.; Phi Alpha Theta; Gamma Pi Epsilon. Lectr. & Broadcaster on the Venezuela-Guyana Boundary Dispute. Recip., Ford Fndn. Fellowship Award, 1970. Address: University of Guyana, Box 841, Georgetown, Guyana. 109.

MENGAL, Paul Charles Justin, b. 29 Mar. 1938. Company Administrator. Appts: Mgr., Trailer Sal. Co.; Admnstr., Mecanic. Co. Mbrships: Conservatoire Africain; C.I.H.O.T.O.M.; S.H.R.R.; Soc. Roy. Arche. Charleroi; S.C.G.D.; Ommegang. Publs. incl: Mémoire sur les tribus Mengal du Baloutchistan, Vol. 1, 1969, Vol. 2, 1973; Rue Mengal; Les origines du Nom Mengal. Address: Bd. Lambermont 350, 1030 Brussels, Belgium.

MENGLIDES, Pandelis Sotirios, b. 20 Sept. 1929. Diplomat. Educ: Law & Econs., Degree, Thessaloniki Univ., Greece, 1958. Appts: Attaché, Royal Greek For. Min., 1958-60; Sec., Greek Embassy, Bucharest, Bulgaria, 1960-62, Sofia, ibid, 1962-63; 3rd Pol. Dept., Royal Greek For. Min., 1963-64; Greek Consul, Liège, Belgium, 1964-66; Rotterdam, Holland, 1966-67; Chargé d'Affaires ad interim, Holland; 1968, Denmark & Norway, 1969-74; Consul-General, Düsseldorf, W. Germany, 1974-; Mbr. Greek Delegns. to Jt. Greek-Rumanian Comm., 1960-62, Nuclear Planning Comm., The Hague, Holland, 1968, 25th Annual Meeting, Bds. Govs., IMF & World Bank Grp., Copenhagen, Denmark, 1970; Rep. Greece, Regional Comm. WHO, ibid, 1972. Hons: Gold Cross, Royal Order of Phoenix, 1970; Gold Cross of Ecumenical Patriarch, 1963; 150th Anniversary, Greek Independence Medal, 1971; Cross, Cmndr., Order of Dannebrog, 1974. Address: Consulate-General of Greece, Kaiserstrasse 30A, 4, Düsseldorf, German Fed. Repub. 2.

MENNINGER, Jeanette Lyle. Editor. Appts. incl: Prin., Prep. Schl., Central Coll., Lexington, Mo.; Reporter, Feature Writer, Book Page, Utica Daily Press, Utica, N.Y.; P.R. Staff, Columbia Univ., N.Y.; Rsch. Proj., Carnegie Fndn. currently, Ed., Bulletin of Menninger Clinic, Topeka, Kans., 1936-; MS & Book Ed., Stone Brandel Ctr., Chicago, Ill.

Fellow, Med. Writers Assoc.; Mbr., Nat. Fed. of Press Women; Kans. Press Women's Assoc.; Trustee, Family Serv. & Guidance Ctr.; Mulvane Art Ctr.; Mbr., Women's Advisory Comm., Int. Christian Univ. of Japan. Author of Love Against Hate (with Dr. K. Menninger); contbr. of articles to newspapers, jrnls., mags. Address: Box 829, The Menninger Foundation, Topeka, KS 66601, U.S.A. 5.

MENNINGER, Karl Augustus, b. 22 July 1893. Psychiatrist. Educ: A.B., Univ. of Wis., 1914; M.S., ibid, 1915; M.D., Harvard Univ., 1917. Appts. incl: Univ. Prof.-at-Large, Univ. of Kan., Lawrence; Disting. Prof., Psych., Univ. of Hlth. Scis., Chgo. Med. Schl., Ill.; Disting. Lectr., Psych., Dept. Psych. & Neurol., Loyola Univ., Chgo.;Mbr. Psychoanalytic Fac., Chgo. Inst. for Psychoanalysis. Fellowships: AMA; Am. Psych. Assn. Mbrships. incl: AAAS; Am. Assn. Child Psychoanalysis, Inc.; Assn. Clin. Pastoral Educ., Inc.; Med. Advsry. Coun., Am. Assn. Rehab. Therapists; Special Cons., Ill. Dept. Mental Hlth.; Cons., Stormont-Vail Hosp., Topeka, Can.;·Chmn., Menninger Fndn.; & num. others. Publs. incl: Man Against Himself, 1938; Manual For Psychiatric Case Study, 1952; Theory of Psychoanalytic Technique, 1958; The Crime of Punishment, 1968. Recip. of many hons., inclng. Edgar B. Allen Gold Medal, Am. Geriatrics Soc., 1971; & 9 hon. degrees. Address: The Menninger Fndn., Box 829, Topeka, KS 66601, U.S.A.

MENON, Mambillikalathil Govind Kumar, b. 28 Aug. 1928. Physicist. Educ: B.Sc., Agra Univ., 1946; M.Sc., Univ. of Bombay, 1949; Ph.D., Univ. of Bristol, U.K., 1952. Appts. incl: Rsch. Assoc., Univ. of Bristol, 1952-53, Sr. Award, Royal Commn. for Exhib. of 1851, 1953-55; Rdr., Tata Inst. of Fundamental Rsch., Bombay, India, 1955-58, Assoc. Prof., 1958-60, Prof. & Dean, Phys. Fac., 1960-64, Sr. Prof. & Dpty. Dir. (Phys.), 1964-66; Dir., 1966-; Chmn., Electronics Commn., Sec., Dept. of Electronics, Govt. of India, 1971-; Pres., Asia Electronics Union, & Indian Acad. Scis., Bangalore; Mbr., Bd. Trustees, Int. Fedn. Insts. for Adv. Study, Stockholm Sweden. Mbr., Fellow & Off., var. sci. orgs. Author, num. sci. publs. Hons. incl: Padma Shri, 1961; Padma Bhushan, 1968. Address: Tata Institute of Fundamental Research, Homi Bhabha Rd., Bombay 400 005, India. 34.

MENSCHER, Barnet Gary, b. 5 Sept. 1940. Steel Company Executive. Educ: B.B.A., Univ. of Tex., Austin, 1963. Appts: V.P., Mktng., Ella Gant Mfg., Shreveport, La., 1964-66; Warehouse Mgr., Dir., Material Control, Gachman Steel Co., Ft. Worth, Tex., 1966-68; Gen. Mgr., Gachman Steel, Houston, 1968-70; Sales Mgr., Gulf Coast Gachman Steel Co., 1971-; Investment Cons., D & L Enterprises, 1966-. Mbrships: Solicitation Comm., United Fund, 1969-; Nat. Alliance of Businessmen Jobs Prog., 1969-; Assn. of ·Steel Distributors; Purchasing Agts. Assn., Houston; Credit Assn., Houston; Tex. Assn. Steel Importers; Phi Sigma Delta; Alpha Phi Omega. Address: 314 Tealwood Dr., Houston, TX 77024, U.S.A. 7.

MENSES, Jan, b. 28 Apr. 1933. Artist; Painting, self-taught, w. study trips France Etching, Acad. of Fine Arts, Rotterdam; Painting, self-taught, w. study trips FRance Italy, Spain, Morocco, 5 yrs.; later rsch., Europe, N. Africa, Israel. Mbrships: Royal Canadian Acad.; Société des Artistes Professionels du Québec. Solo Exhibs. incl: Penthouse Gall., Montreal, 1962; Delta Gall., Rotterdam, Netherlands, 1965; Gall. Moos, Toronto, 1967; Rotterdam Art Fndn., Netherlands, 1974. Num. grp. exhibs., Canada

& abroad. Permanent Collects. incl: Mus. of Mod. Art, N.Y.C., U.S.A.; Nat. Gall. of Canada, Ottawa; Montreal Mus. Fine Arts; Quebec Provincial Mus.; Univ. of Montreal. Works in var. pvte. collects. Recip., many prizes, awards & grants. Address: 5571 Woodbury Ave., Montreal H3T 1S6, P.Q., Canada. 37.

MENZEL, H.H. Werner, b. 8 Oct. 1908. Physician. Educ: Studied med., Cologne & Düsseldorf, Germany; Cert., 1933; Grad., Düsseldorf, 1937; Dr.med., 1941. Appts: Asst., Med. Univ. Clin., Frankfurt/Main, 1933-34; Asst. Dr., Gen. Hosp., Hamburg-Altona, 1934-39, & Med. Univ. Clin., Tübingen, 1939-41; Asst. & Hd. Physn., Med. Univ. Clin. Charité, Berlin, 1941-45; Hd. Physn., Univ. Clin. & outpatients' dept., Hamburg, 1946-53; Chief Physn., Amalie Sieveking Hosp., Hamburg, 1954-; Lectr., Tübingen, 1941; Lectr., Berlin, 1942; Prof., Hamburg, 1948. Mbrships: Deutsche Gesellschaft Innere Med.; Deutsche Gesellschaft für Kreislaufforschung.; Deutsche Gesellschaft für Endocrinol.; Gesellschaft Deutscher Naturforscher & Arzte; N.Y. Acad. of Scis.; V.P., Int. Soc. for Chronobiol., until 1971; Hon. mbr., ibid, 1971. Author of publs. in med. field. Hons. incl: Vesalius Medal, 1964; Ludolph Brauer Medal, 1973. Address: Wiesenkamp 24, Hamburg 67, German Fed. Repub. 92.

MENZEL, Roderich, b. 13 Apr. 1907. Author. Educ: Reichenburg Acad. of Commerce, Reichenberg, Olmütz & Prague. Appts. incl: Contbr., Prager Tagblatt, 1927-38, & Ullstein grp. papers, Berlin, 1931; Mng. Ed., lit. & art, Echo der Woche, Munich, 1948-51; Chief Ed., Das Schönste, Munich, 1955-56; Dpty. Chmn., Knut Hamsun Soc., Mölln, & free-lance writer, 1956-. Mbrships. incl: Int. Club of Germany; Red-White Tennis Club, Berlin. Publs: 3 vols. poems, 1937, 1947, 1957; Als Böhmen noch bei Osterreich war (novel); num. other works inclng. novels for children, memoirs, fairy tale collects., plays & non-fiction works. Recip., var. prizes & medals. Address: D-8132 Deixlfurt/Tutzing, Bavaria. 43, 92.

MENZENSKA, (Sister) M. Jane, CSFN, b. 20 Feb. 1914. Archivist. Educ: A.B., Marywood Coll., Scranton, Pa., 1938; B.S. in L.S., St. John's Univ., Bklyn., N.Y., 1944-46; M.S. in L.S., Drexel Inst. of Technol., Phila. Pa., 1955-58. Appts: Tchr., Nazareth Acad., Torresdale, Phila., Pa., 1938-39, Little Flower Cath. H.S. for Girls, Phila., Pa., 1939-43 & St. Stanislaus Kosta Schl., Bklyn., N.Y., 1943-46; Libn., Nazareth Acad. & pt.-time at Holy Family Tchr. Trng. Schl., Torresdale, Phila. 1946-54 & Holy Family Coll., Phila., 1954-73; Coll. Archivist, ibid, 1974-; Mbrships: Pres. Tri-State Coll. Lib. Coop., 1970-72; Dela. Valley Chapt. of Assn. of Coll. & Rsch. Libs., ALA; Cath. Lib. Assn.; Am. Archives Assn. Publs: Archives & Other Special Collections, A Library Staff Handbook, 1973; Guide to Nazareth Literature, 1873-73, Works Written by & about the Sisters of the Holy Family of Nazareth, in preparation. Address: c/o Holy Family Coll., Grant & Frankford Aves., Philadelphia, PA 19114, U.S.A. 6, 13, 42, 46.

MENZIES, Archibald Norman, b. 10 Sept. 1904. Playwright. Educ: C.E.M.G.S. Melbourne, Aust.; C.E.S.G.S., Sydney. Mbrships: Green Room Club, Savage Club Lords Taveners, London; Société des Auteurs de France. Publs: Between Friends (farce) 1933; A Knight in Vienna (comedy), 1935; A Royal Exchange (musical), 1935; The Astonished Ostrich (comedy), 1936; No Sky So Blue, (musical), 1938; Under Your Hat (musical), 1938; Full Swing (Musical), 1942; Something in the Air, 1943; Gipsy Princess (new book & lyrics, musical), 1944; Under the Gooseberry Bush (comedy), 1945; Quartette in Discord (comedy), 1946; Return Journey (play), 1947; Her Excellency (comedy), 1949; That Woman, (comedy), 1952; Hell's Lagoon (drama), 1953; Take Your Partners (farce), 1954; Universal Uncles (farce), 1956; Tax Free Farce, 1958. Address: The Savage Club, 86 St. James's St., London SW1, U.K. 18, 43, 128.

MENZIES, Arthur Redpath, b. 29 Nov. 1916. Diplomat. Educ: B.A., Univ. of Toronto, Canada, 1939; M.A., Harvard Univ., U.S.A., 1941. Appts: Joined Dept. of External Affairs, 1940; Hd., Canadian Liaison Mission, Tokyo, Japan, 1950-53; High Commnr. to Malaya & Ambassador to Burma, 1958-61; High Commnr. to Australia, 1965-72 & to Fiji, 1970-72; Permanent Rep. & Ambassador to NATO, Brussels, Belgium, 1972-. Address: Canadian Delegation to NATO, Brussels 1110, Belgium.

MENZIES, (The Rt. Hon. Sir) Douglas Ian, b. 7 Sept. 1907. Justice, High Court, Australia. Educ: LL.M., Univ. of Melbourne, 1930. Appts: called to Bar, 1930; appointed King's Counsel, 1948; Privy Councillor, 1963; Law Prac., 1930-58; Sec., Defence Comm. & Chiefs of Staff, 1941-45; Dir., T. & G. Mutual Life Assurance Co., 1948-58; Justice, High Ct. of Australia, 1958-; Lectr., Melbourne Univ. Law Schl., 1939-49; Chancellor, Monash Univ., 1969. Mbrships: Pres., Victoria Div., Heart Fndn. Australia, 1961-62; Nat. Pres., ibid, 1964; Victorian Bar Assn., (Pres., 1958); Hon. Bencher, Inner Temple; Medico-Legal Soc., 1957-58. Author, Victorian Company Law & Practice, 1940. Hons: Jessie Leggatt Schol., J.B. Nunn Prize, Supreme Ct. Prize, Melbourne Univ.; K.B.E., 1958; Fellow, Queen's Coll., Melbourne Univ., 1958-. Address: High Ct. Australia, 450, Little Bourke St., Melbourne, 3000 Victoria, Australia.

MENZIES, Elizabeth Grant Cranbrook, b. 24 June 1915. Author-Photographer. Held One-Man show of photogs., Balt. Mus. of Art, Md. & 3 exhibs., Princeton Univ., 1956. Photogs. have appeared in nat. mags. & educ. books. Woodcuts & photogs. in pvte. collects. & collect. of Graphic Arts, Firestone Lib., Princeton Univ. Mbrships: Stony Brook-Millstone Watersheds Assn.; Nat. Audubon Soc.; N.J. & Princeton Hist. Socs. Publs: Before the Waters—The Upper Delaware Valley, 1966; Millstone Valley, 1969; Princeton Architecture—A Pictorial History of Town & Campus (jt. author), 1967; New Jersey's Early Scottish Ties, in progress; contbr. articles to Encyclopedia Americana & Princeton History, 1974. Hons: N.J. Tercentenary Medal for Photog. of Albert Einstein, 1964; Cit. of Merit, Am. Assn. for State & Local Hist. & Author Award, N.J. Assn. of Tchrs. of Engl., both for Millstone Valley, 1970; Jt. Recip. Award of Merit, Am. Assn. for State & Local Hist. for Princeton Architecture. Address: 926 Kingston Rd., Princeton, NJ 08540, U.S.A. 5, 30, 130, 138.

MENZIES, James Gordon, b. 7 Dec. 1909. Company Director; Retired Banker. Educ: B.Ec., Univ. of Sydney, Australia; F.A.S.A.; F.C.I.S.; A.B.I.A. Appts: Asst. Chief Supt., Commonwealth Savings Bank of Australia, 1952-59; Chief Acct., Reserve Bank of Australia, 1960-62; Dpty. Gov., Ctrl. Bank of Malaysia, 1962-66; Chief Mgr. for Vic., Reserve Bank of Australia, 1966-70; Dir., Thos. Cook & Son (Australasia) Pty. Ltd., 1971-. Mbrships: Treas., Councillor, Indl. Design Coun., Australia, 1970-; Hon. Trustee, Comm. of

Econ. Dev., 1970-; Trustee, Presby. Ch. in N.S.W., 1971-; Chmn., Scottish Hosp. Bd. Author, Postal Savings in South East Asia, 1953. Recip., Johan Mangku Negata, Malaysian Govt. Address: 40 Stafford Rd., Artarmon, N.S.W., Australia 2064. 12, 23, 98, 128, 131.

MENZIN, Margeret Schoenberg (Mrs. Marvin Menzin), b. 17 Nov. 1942. Mathematician; Educator. Educ: B.A., Swarthmore Coll., Pa., 1963; M.A., Brandeis Univ., Waltham, Mass., 1967; Ph.D., 1970. Appts: Programmer, Serv. Bur. Corp., 1963-64; Instr., Maths., Simmons Coll., Boston, 1969-70; Asst. Prof., ibid; Chmn., Maths. Dept., 1971-; Assoc. Prof., 1973-; Dir., Design Technol. Corp., Burlington, 1969-. Mbrships: Am. Math. Soc.; Maths. Assn. Am.; Phi Beta Kappa; Sigma Xi; AAUP; Assn. for Women Mathns. Contbr. to math. jrnls. Address: 26 Mason St., Lexington, MA 02173, U.S.A. 5.

MERCADO, Manuel Odon. b. 7 July 1926. Civil Engineer. Educ: BSCE, Univ. of Ky., 1952; LL.B., Blackstone Schl. of Law, Chgo. & Univ. of Louisville Law Schl., 1964; J.D., Blackstone Schl. of Law, 1970; Dip. Nat. Security Mgmt., Industrial Coll. of the Armed Forces, Wash. D.C., 1972. Appts. incl: Civil Engr., Tippetts, Abbett MacCarthy, Stratton, Engrs., N.Y.C., 1952-59; Civil-Structural Engr., U.S. Army Corps. of Engrs., Alaska Dist., 1959-62, Louisville District, Ky., 1962-65; Gen. Engr. & Admnstr. for Off., i/c Construction, Thailand, A.P.O. San Fran., 1965-69; Gen. Engr., Chesapeake Div., Naval Facilities Engrng. Command, Wash. Navy Yard, Wash. D.C., 1969-. Mbrships: Am. Arbitration Assn.; Am. Socs. Civil & Mil. Engrs; Ky. Soc. of Profl. Engrs; Master Mason. Address: Chesapeake Div., Naval Facilities Engineering Command, Washington Navy Yard, Bldg. 57, Washington D.C. 20374, U.S.A. 6.

MERCER, Ronald E., b. 17 June 1938. Voluntary Organization Manager. Educ: Attended Humboldt Inst., Mpls., Univs. of Colo., Okla., & Notre Dame, & Tex. Christian Univ. Appts: Asst. Traffic Mgr., Marketing, Burlington Truck Lines, Inc., Galesburg, Ill.; Mgr., Chmbr. of Comm., Sidney, Neb., & Scottsbluff, Neb.; Dir., Econ. Dev., Chmbr. of Comm., Salina, Kan.; Mgr., Chmbr. of Comm., Helena, Ark.; Currently, Mgr., Chmbr. of Comm., Big Spring, Tex. Mbrships. incl: Big Spring Rotary Club; Bd. of Dirs., Big Spring United Way; Scoutmaster, Boy Scouts of Am., Buffalo Trail Coun.; Pres., Moss PTA; Bd. of Dirs., W. Tex. Chmbr. of Comm. Mgrs. Assn.; Southern Ind. Dev. Coun. Author, Motor Carrier Transportation & The Industrial Developer, 1969. Named Cert. Indl. Developer, 1973. Address: 1718 Yale, Big Spring, TX 79720, U.S.A. 7.

MERCIECA, Charles, b. 3 Feb. 1933. Professor of Education. Educ: B.A., Loyola Coll., Malta, 1955; B.A., Istituo Filosofico, Milan, 1958; M.S., Kan. State Univ., U.S.A., 1964; B.S., St. Louis Univ., 1965; Ph.D., Univ. of Kan., 1966; D.D., Univ. of Remo, Nigeria, 1973. Appts: Instr., Govt. Elem. Schls., Malta, 1951-55; Supvsr., St. Aloysius Coll., Malta, 1958-61; Instr., St. Marys Pub. H.S., Kan., U.S.A., 1962-64; Assoc. Prof., Calif. State Univ., Fresno, 1966-67; Dir. & Prof., Ctr. for Intercultural Studies, Ala. A&M Univ., 1967-. Mbrships. incl: Fndr., Pres., 1967-70, Sec.-Gen., 1970-, Int. Assn. of Educators for World Peace; AAUP; Philos. of Educ. Soc.; U.S. Chancellor, Delta Tau Kappa; Exec. Coun. Mbr., Emergency Comm. for World Govt. Publs. incl: New Zealand in a Changing World, 1968; Critique of a University, 1973; What

Constitutes Proper Education, 1974. Contbr. to U.S., for jrnls. Hons: Schlrships. to Loyola Univ., 3 yrs.; Philos. Inst. of Gallarate, Italy, 3 yrs.; St. Louis Univ., 4 yrs.; Univ. of Kan., 1 yr. Address: Alabama A&M Univ., Huntsville, AL 35762, U.S.A.

MERCIER, Yannic P., b. 17 July 1933. Investment Banker. Educ: B.A., Hobart Coll., 1956; N.Y. Univ. Schl. of Bus. Admin., 1957. Appts: 2nd V.P., Smith Barney, 1957-66; Blyth Eastman Dillon & Co. Inc., 1966-; Gen. Ptnr., ibid, 1967, Pres., Int. Div., 1968, Sr. V.P. & Dir., 1972. Mbrships. incl: Paris American Club, N.Y.; City Midday Club, N.Y.; Downtown Athletic Club, N.Y.; Westhampton Country Club, N.Y.; Cercle du Bois de Boulogne, Paris; Cercle Interallié, Paris; Sigma Phi Soc., Geneva & N.Y.; Traveler's Club, Paris. Address: 3 Chemin Desvallières, 92410 Ville D'Avray, France. 43.

MERDINGER, Charles John, 20 Apr. 1918. Civil Engineer. Educ: B.S., U.S.N. Acad., 1941; B.C.E., M.C.E., Rensselaer Polytechnic Inst., Troy, N.Y., 1945-46; Ph.D., Brasenose Coll., Oxford Univ., 1949. Appts. incl: Midshipman-Capt., Civil Engr. Corps, U.S.N., 1937-70; Pres., Wash. Coll., Chesterton, Md., 1970-73; V.P., Aspen Inst. Humanistic Studies, Aspen, Colo., & N.Y.C., 1973-1974. Mbrships. incl: Fellow, Am. Soc. Civil Engrs.; Soc. Am. Civil Engrs.; Soc. Am. Mil. Engrs.; Sigma Xi. Author of Civil Engineering Through the Ages. Contbr. Encyclopaedia Britannica, & profl. publs. Hons. incl: Legion of Merit w. Combat V, Combat Action Ribbon, Navy Unit Commedation, 1968; Navy Meritorious Serv. Medal, 1970; Hist. & Heritage Award, Am. Soc. Civil Engrs., 1972. Address: c/o A.M. Kern, 12 Cooke Rd., Lexington, MA U.S.A. 2, 26, 128, 141.

MEREDITH, G. Patrick, b. 10 May 1904. Professor Emeritus. Educ: Univ. of Leeds, 1921-26; Univ. of London, 1929-31. Appts: Schl. Tchr., Switzerland & U.K., 1926-38; Lectr. in Educl. Psychol., Dir., Visual Educ. Ctr., Univ. Coll. of Exeter, 1938-47; Lectr., Prof. Psychol., Univ. of Leeds, 1947-67; Prof. Psychophys., ibid, 1967-69. Retd., 1969. Fellowships: British Psychological Soc.; Royal Astronomical Soc.; Roy Statistical Soc.; Royal Soc. Arts. Mbrships: N.Y. Acad. Sci.; AAAS; Athenaeum Club. Publs. incl: Learning, Remembering & Knowing, 1959; Instruments of Communication, 1966; Dyslexia & The Individual, 1972. Hons. incl: Leon Fellowship Award, 1946; 3 Rsch. Grants, 1954, '65, '70. Address: c/o Dept. of Phys., Univ. of Leeds, Leeds 2, U.K. 1, 128.

MEREDITH, Vana Hutto (Mrs. William David Meredith), b. 5 Nov. 1945. Doctoral Student. Educ: B.S., Univ. of S.C., 1968; M.A.T., The Citadel, 1971; 30 hours doctoral work, Educl. Rsch., Univ. of S.C.; 11 wks., Special Trng. Schls., IBM, 1968-69. Appts: Educl. Servs. Rep., IBM Corp., Columbia & Charleston, S.C., 1968-69; Instr. of Related Subjects, Berkeley-Charleston-Dorchester Tech. Educ. Ctr., N. Charleston, S.C., 1969-72; Admnstv. Asst. to Dir. i/c PR, ibid, 1972-73; full-time doctoral student, 1973- Mbrships: formerly, Am. Vocational Assn., NEA, fac. orgs., Berkeley-Charleston-Dorchester Tech.; Richland Co. Med. Wives Aux., Columbia; Quail Hollow Women's Club, W. Columbia. Publs: Creator & Ed., Poor Richard's Almanac, newsletter; articles in profl. publs. Address: 1709 Ephrata Dr., W. Columbia, SC 29169, U.S.A. 125.

MEREGALLI, Franco, b. 25 Mar. 1913. University Professor. Educ: D.Litt. Appts: Prof. Italian, Univ. of Oviedo, Spain, 1941-43; Prof. Spanish, Univ. of Milan, Italy, 1946-50; Prof. Italian, Univ. of Madrid, 1950-53; Lectr., Italian, Univ. of Göttingen, 1953-56; Dir., Italian Inst., Cologne, 1955-56; Prof. Spanish, Univ. of Venice, 1956-, Protector, ibid, 1967-71, Dean, 1971-73; Vis. Prof., Univ. of Calif., L.A., U.S.A., 1964-65; Vis. Prof., Harvard Univ., 1973. Mbrship: Correspondiente extranjero de la R. Academia Española. 84 publs., Spanish lit. & lit. & pol. rels. between Italy & Spain. Recip., Gold Medal, Pres. of Italian Repub., 1969. Address: Santa Croce 1337, Venice, Italy.

MERHAV, Shmuel Jacob, b. 26 Feb. 1924. Professor of Engineering. Educ: Dipl. Ingenieur, Technion, 1949; Ph.D., Cambridge Univ., 1964. Appts: Sect. Hd., Miniature Electronics & Analog Computers Rsch. & Dev., Sci. Dept., Israeli Min. of Defense, 1950-58; Grp. Ldr., System Analysis & Planning, ibid, 1958-62; Dir. of Rsch. & Dev., ibid, 1964-68, Hd., Control Systems Div., 1969-71; Prof. in Control Systems Engrng., Dept. of Aeronautical Engrng., Technion, 1971-. Mbrships: IEEE; Aeronautical Soc. of Israel; Chmn., Israel Sect., Int. Fedn. of Automatic Control. Contbr. to profl. jrnls. Address: Dept. of Aeronautical Engineering, Technion City, Haifa, Israel.

MERIDA, (Rev.) William D., b. 19 May 1925. Carpentry & Masonry Contractor. Educ: 12th Grade H.S.; courses in art, auto mechanics & masonry. Appts: Pvte., 1st Class, U.S. Army, WWII; Contractor in Carpentry & Masonry; Mbr., Bd. of Dirs., Wash. Co. Hosp., Wash. Exceptional Children's org.; Minister of The Gospel. Mbrships: Master Masons; Pres., Young Men's Progressive Club, Youth Coun., N. Wash., Co. NAACP; Asst. Patron, Order of Eastern Star. Recip., Good Conduct Medal w. 2 Battle Stars, WWII. Address: P.O. Box 2217, Frankville, AL 36538, U.S.A. 130.

MERIKOSKI, Veli Kaarlo, b. 2 Jan. 1905. Professor. Educ: LL.D., Univ. of Helsinki, Finland, 1935. Appts: Asst. Tchr. of pub. law, Helsinki Univ., 1936; Prof. of Admnstrve. Law, ibid, 1941-69; Dean, Fac. of Law, 1947-51; Mbr., High Ct. of Impeachment, 1950-71, Int. Ct. of Arbitration, Hague, 1966-. Mbrships: Pres., Int. Assn. Univs., 1970-75; Min. of For. Affairs, 1962-63; Chmn., Finnish People's Party, 1958-61; Chmn., Union of Finnish Lawyers, 1946-51, '56-58; Finnish Acad. Sci. & Letters. Publs. incl: The Citizen's ABC Book, 1955; Finnish Public Law, vol. 1, 1952, vol. II, 1962; Le Pouvoir discretionnaire de l'Administration, 1958; The System of Legal Protection in Administration, 1969; University-cracy—University Governance, Is It Democracy, 1970; Voice for the Vote, 1972; Necessity for a Constitutional Court, 1973. Address: Urheilutie 15 A 2, 02700 Kauniainen, Finland. 34.

MERINO MORALES, Arturo, b. 25 Feb. 1941. Actor; Radio and Television Director; Professor. Educ: Fac. of Law & Soc. Scis., Univ. of Sonora; Theatre Studies, ibid; Grad., Cinematographic, Theatrical, Radio & TV Inst., Mexico; Seminars on Mass Media. Appts: Sub-Dir., Acad. of Dramatic Arts, Univ. of Sonora; Theatre Dir., Pres., Acad. of Artistic Activities, Ctr. of Scientific & Technological Studies No. 26; Dir., Gen., Radio, TV, & Audiovisual Prod., Univ. of Sonora. Mbrships. incl: Fndg. Mbr., Latin Am. Assn. of TV Educ.; Pres., Los Comancheros, Mexican intellectual grp. Var. theatrical works incl: Cándida, Bernard Shaw; La Vida es Sueño, Calderon de la Barca; The Caretaker, Harold Pinter, etc. Hons. incl: Hon. Mention as major actor, Festival de Otoño, Nat. Inst. of Beaux-Arts, 1968. Address: Justo Sierra 120 final Ote., Colonia Pitic, Hermosillo, Sonora, Mexico. 136.

MERITT, Lucy Taxis Shoe (Mrs. Benjamin Dean Meritt), b. 7 Aug. 1906. Archaeologist. Educ: A.B., Bryn Mawr Coll., 1927; M.A., ibid, 1928; Ph.D., 1935; Fellow, Am. Schl. Classical Studies, Athens, 1929-34; Fellow, Am. Acad., Rome, 1936-37; Rsch. Fellow, ibid, 1949-50. Appts: Asst. Prof.-Assoc. Prof., Art, Archeol. & Greek, Mt. Holyoke Coll., 1937-50; Chief Cnslr. of Students, ibid, 1943-47; Mbr., Inst. for Advanced Study, Princeton, 1948-49, 50-73; Ed., Publs. of Am. Schl. of Classical Studies, Athens, 1950-72; Vis. Prof., Classical Archaeol., Wash. Univ., St. Louis, 1958, 60; Vis. Lectr., Classical Archaeol., Princeton Univ., 1959; Prof., Classical Archaeol., Univ. of Tex., Austin, 1973-74; Vis. Schlr. ibid, 1973-. Mbrships: Mng. Comm., 1937-, Exec. Comm., 1948-52, Chmn., Publs. Comm., 1950-72, Am. Schl. of Classical Studies, Athens; Recorder, 1960-68, 71, Acting Gen. Sec., 1962, Princeton Soc. Sec., 1953-56, Pres., 1963-67, Archaeol. Inst. of Am.; Sec.-Treas., 1940-, Alumni Assn. Am. Schl. of Classical Studies, Athens; Treas., 1942-46, V.P., 1961, Pres., 1962, Classical Soc. Am. Acad. in Rome; German Archaeol. Inst.; U.S.A. Corres., Int. Assn. Classical Archaeol.; Soc. of Archtl. Histns. Publs: Profiles of Greek Mouldings, 1936; Profiles of Western Greek Mouldings, 1952; Etruscan & Republican Roman Mouldings, 1965; num. articles in profl. jrnls. & encyclopaediae. Address: 712 W. 16th St., Austin, TX 78701, U.S.A. 2, 5, 13, 125, 138.

MERIVALE-AUSTIN, (Maj.) Bruce Gardiner, b. 26 Oct. 1920. Industrialist. Educ: Cambridge & London Univs. Appts: 2nd Lt., Black Watch., 1940, served 1940-45 (N. Africa, India & Burma); on staff, Highland District & War Off., 1946-47; Maj., 1948; Asst. Military Attache, Sofia, Bulgaria, 1948-49; on staff, War Office, 1951-52; ret'd 1952. Mbrships: Carlton Club; Pilgrim 1900 Club. Address: 11 Cheyne Row, Chelsea, London S.W. 3, U.K. 41.

MERKADO, Nissim, b. 9 Sept. 1935. Sculptor. Educ: Schl. of Fine Arts, Tel-Aviv, Israel; Nat. H.S. of Fine Arts, Paris, France. Appts: Factory Mgr., Israel; Tchr., Plastic Arts, France. Mbrships: Plastic Arts Fedn. of France; Young Sculptors Comm. One-man shows: Katz Gall., Tel-Aviv, 1960; Zunini Gall., Paris, 1967; Arcanes Gall., Brussels, Belgium, 1973. Other exhibs. incl: Grosvenor Gall., London, U.K., & gals. in France, Belgium, U.S.A., Mexico, Australia. Sculptures acquired by towns: Rouen, France, 1972; Bobigny, France, 1973; Villetaneuse, France, 1974. Hons: First Prize, Young Sculptors, 1969; Rodin Gold Medal, 1970; Bourdelle Prize, 1973. Address: 112 Rue de Turenne, 75003 Paris, France. 105, 133.

MERLAN, Franciszka, b. 4 May 1907. Educator. Educ: Ph.D., Univ. of Vienna, Austria. Appts: Lectr., Pomona Coll., U.S.A., 1946-47; Lectr.-Sr. Lectr., Scripps Coll., 1946-. Mbr. of educl. assns. Publs: Das Problem Des Schöpferischen; contbr. to Music of the Renaissance by Reese, 1954; volume of philos. essays & poetry (in preparation); articles in Int. Congresses of Philos. & Am. Hist. Review 1958-62). Prepared for publ. 2 books & num. articles of Philip Merlan (d.), 1969-73. Address: Scripps Coll., Claremont, CA 91711, U.S.A.

MERRICK, Hugh (Harold A. Meyer), b. 23 June 1898. Author. Educ: B.A., Oxford Univ., J.K., 1922. Appts: Mbr., London Stock Exchange, 1926-39; Asst. Censor, Postal & Telegraph Censorship, 1939-45; Prin., Admiralty, 1945-46, Min. of Civil Aviation, 1946-52; Info. Off., Overseas Rediffusion, 1952-63; Novelist, author & translator, 1942-. Mbrships: Achilles Club; Alpine Club; Nat. Liberal Club; Fellow, Royal Philharmonic Soc. Publs. incl: Pillar of the Sky, 1942; Andreas at Sundown, 1944; Savoy Episode, 1946; The Breaking Strain, 1950; Out of the Night, 1958; The Great Motor Highways of the Alps, 1958; The Perpetual Hills, 1964; Companion to the Alps, 1974. Address: 22 Empire House, London, SW7 2RU, U.K. 3.

MERRILL, David K., b. 18 Oct. 1935. Fine Artist. Educ: Famous Artists Schl., Westport, Conn.; Western Conn. State Coll. Full time free-lance artist. Specialization, Old New England landscapes & studies. Mbrships: Washington & Kent Art Assns., Conn.; Northern Vt. Art Assn., Burlington. Solo exhibs. incl: YWCA, Bridgeport, Conn., 1958; Hoffman Gall., Danbury, Conn., 1968; Wash. Art Assn., Conn., 1971; Stowe Gall., Vt., 1973; Douglas Gall., Stamford, Conn., 1974. Other exhibs. incl: Bridgeport Art League, Conn., 1957; Kent Art Assn., Conn., 1969; Northern Vt. Artists Assn., 1971, 1972; Vt. '73 Exhib., Burlington, 1973. Cornmissions incl: Univ. of Me., Portland, 1971; Monroe Twp., Conn., 1972. Paintings, pvte. & pub. permanent collects. Recip., var. exhib. prizes & awards. Address: P. O. Box 305, Kettletown Rd., Southbury, CT 06488, U.S.A. 37.

MERRILL, Maurice H., b. 3 Oct. 1897. Lawyer; Educator. Educ: B.A., Univ. of Okla., 1919; LL.B., ibid, 1922; S.J.D., Harvard Univ. 1925. Appts: incl: Assoc. Prof. of Law, Univ. of Idaho, 1925-26; Asst. Prof. of Law, Univ. of Neb., 1926-28; Prof. of Law, Univ. of Neb., 1928-36; Prof., Univ. of Okla., 1936-50; Res. Prof., ibid, 1950-68; Emeritus Prof., 1968-; Law Prac., 1922-26; Gen. Counsel, Okla. Assn. of Man. ATTYS, 1971-; Special Justice, Supreme Ct. of Okla., 1965-68; Commnr., Okla. Nat. Conf. of Commnrs. on Uniform State Laws, 1944-. Publs. incl: Law of Notice, 1952; American Casebook Series on Administrative Law, 1954; Public Concern with the Fuel Minerals, 1960. Address: 630 Parrington Oval, Norman, OK 73069, U.S.A. 2, 7, 13, 34, 51.

MERRILL, Merlin Walter, b. 22 June 1914. Methodist Clergyman. Educ: A.B., Neb. Wesleyan Univ., Lincoln, 1940; B.D., Perkins Schl. of Theol. of Southern Meth. Univ., Dallas, Tex., 1944. Appts: Ordination as Deacon, N. Tex. Conf., 1943, Elder, 1945; Assoc. Pastor, 1st Meth. Ch., Wichita Falls, Tex., 1944-47; Pastor, meth. chs., Cotton Valley, La., 1947-50, New Orleans, 1950-53, Mansfield, 1953-58, Minden, 1958-65, Univ. Meth., Lake Charles, 1965-68; Dist. Supt., Lafayette Dist., 1968-71; Pastor, United Meth. Ch., Ruston, La., 1971-. Mbrships. incl: Conf. Bd. of Min., 1971-; Vice Chmn., Conf. Bd. of Educ., 1972-; Chmn., Ruston Ministerial Alliance, 1973-; Bd. of Trustees, La. Moral & Civic Fndn. Hons. incl: Noah Turner Bible & Semetic Lang. Awards, Southern Meth. Univ., 1944; D.D., Centenary Coll., 1974. Address: P.O. Box 1383, Ruston, LA 72170, U.S.A. 116, 125.

MERRILL, Robert Cotton, Jr., b. 13 Oct. 1930. Educator. Educ: Tufts Univ.; New England Conservatory of Music; U.S.N. Schl. of Music; B.B.A., Western New England Coll., 1962; M.Ed., Univ. of Hartford, Conn., 1966. Appts: Served w. U.S.N., 1951-55; Mbr., Admiral's Band, Aircraft Carrier USS Midway, 1952-55; Special Educ. Tchr., Plainville, Conn.,

Pub. Schls., 1965-73; Tchr., Hartford, Conn., Pub. Schls., 1973-. Mbrships: Pres., Plainville Assn. for Retarded Children, 1969-70; Treas., ibid,1970-; Educ. Chmn., Conn. Chapt., Am. Assn. on Mental Deficiency, 1973-; Publicity Chmn., Coun. for Exceptional Children, 1971-73; Hartford Fend. of Tchrs.; New Haven Railroad Tech. Info. Assn.; Gen. Histn. Plainville Histl. Soc. Pi Tau Kappa; Springfield Lodge of Masons. Address: 167 Red Stone Hill, Plainville, CT 06062, U.S.A.

MERRISON, Alexander Walter, b. 20 Mar. 1924. Physicist; University Vice-Chancellor. Educ: B.Sc., Univ. of London, 1944; Ph.D., Univ. of Liverpool, 1957. Appts. incl: Sr. Scientific Off., Atomic Energy Rsch. Establishment, Harwell, U.K., 1946-51; Leverhulme Fellow & Lectr., Univ. of Liverpool, 1951-57; Physicist, European Org. for Nuclear Rsch., Geneva, Switzerland, 1957-60; Prof. of Experimental Phys., Univ. of Liverpool, 1960-69; Dir., Daresbury Nuclear Phys. Lab., Sci. Rsch. Coun., 1962-69; Vice-Chancellor, Univ. of Bristol, 1969-. Mbrships: Fellow, Royal Soc., 1969; Coun., Inst. of Phys. & the Phys. Soc., 1964-66; Fellow, Royal Soc. of Arts, 1970; Gov., Bristol Old Vic Trust, 1969-, Chmn., 1971-; Athenauem Club. Publs: Contbns. to sci. jrnls: on nuclear & elem. particle phys. Hons: Charles Vernon Boys Prize, Inst. of Phys. & the Phys. Soc., 1961; LL.D., Univ. of Bristol, 1971. Address: The University, Senate House, Bristol BS8 1TH, U.K.

MERRITT, Myrtle Agnes, b. 23 Sept. 1925. Professor of Health & Physical Education. Educ: B.A., Northern Iowa Univ., 1946; M.A., Univ. of Iowa, 1951; Ph.D., ibid, 1961. Appts: Phys. Educ. Tchr., Iowa Pub. Schls., Maquoketa, 1946-48; Phys. Educ. Instr., Northern Iowa Univ., 1948-50, 1951-52; Asst. Prof.-Prof., State Univ. Coll. of Arts & Sci., Geneseo, N.Y., 1952-. Mbrships. incl: Var. offs. up to Pres. elect, Pres., Past Pres., C.W. Zone Exec. Bd., N.Y. State Assn. for Hlth., Phys. Educ. & Recreation, 1971-74; Var. offs. up to State Pres. elect, Pres., Past Pres., Assn. of Women in Phys. Educ. of N.Y. State, 1969-72; Sec.-Treas., Eastern Dist. Assn., Am. Assn. for Hlth., Phys. Educ. & Recration, 1971-74; Charter mbr., Nat. Fndn. for Hlth., Phys. Educ. & Recreation; Exec. Bd., Nat. Assn. for Phys. Educ. of Coll. Women, 1973; Charter mbr., Geneseo Chapt., AAUW; Charter mbr., Geneseo Chapt., AAUP; Nat. Jogging Assn. Author of monthly column in The Instructor mag., 3 yrs. Recip. of hons. Address: 12 W. View Crescent, Geneseo, NY 14454, U.S.A. 5, 6, 138, 141.

MERSKEY, (Mrs) Marie Gertrude, b. 10 Oct. 1914. Library Director. Educ: B.A., Univ. of Cape Town, S. Africa, 1959; Dip. of Libnship., Schl. of Libnship., ibid, 1960. Appts: Ref. Libn., Pub. Lib., New Rochelle, N.Y., U.S.A., 1960-63; Rsch. Libn., Consumers Union, Mt. Vernon, N.Y., 1963-66; Asst. to Adult Servs. Cons., Lib. System, Westchester, N.Y., 1966-67; Hd., Union Catalog, ibid, 1968-69; Dir., Pub. Lib., Harrison, N.Y., 1969-. Mbrships. incl: ALA; N.Y. Lib. Assn.; Comm. for Continuing Educ.; Westchester Lib. Assn.; Adult Servs. Advsry. Comm., Westchester Lib. System; V.P., Pub. Lib. Dir's. Assn. of Westchester; Van Riebeeck Soc., Cape Town; Pelham Jewish Ctr., N.Y.; Fndr., Harrison Histl. Soc.; Harrison Hadassah; Harrison Woman's Club. Publs: Num. articles & book reviews. Hons: Red Cross 50 mile swim pins, 1972 & 1973; B'nai B'rith Brotherhood Award, Harrison Lodge 1873, for Harrison Pub. Lib.,

1974. Address: 647 James St., Pelham Manor, NY 10803, U.S.A. 5, 6, 138.

MERSKY, Roy Martin, b. 1 Sept. 1925. Lawyer; Educator. Educ: B.S., Univ. of Wis., 1958; J.D., 1952, M.A.L.S., 1952. Appts. incl: Asst. Libn. Yale Univ., 1954-59; Dir., Wash. State Law Lib., & Exec. Sec., Wash. Judicial Coun., 1959-63; Prof., Law Libn., Univ. of Colo., 1953-65, Univ. of Texas, 1965-; Acting Dir., Jewish Nat. & Univ. Lib., Hebrew Univ. Jerusalem, Israel, 1972-73. Mbrships. incl: Tex. Bd. of Am. Civil Liberties Union; Am. & Wis. Bar Assns.; Tex. Lib. Assn.; A.L.A.; A.A.U.P.; Am. Assn. Law Schls.; Am. Judicature Soc.; Am. Soc. of Legal Hist. Publs. incl: Louis Dembitz Brandeis, 1856-1941; Water Law Bibliography 1947-65; Law Books for Non-Law Libraries & Laymen, 1966; Fundamentals of Legal Research (co-author); assoc. ed. of law jrnls. Address: Univ. of Tex. at Austin, Law Lib., 2500 Red River, Austin, TX 78705, U.S.A. 13, 14, 15, 130.

MERTENS, Jozef Remi, b. 17 Jan. 1921. Archaeologist. Educ: Doct., Univ. of Louvain, Belgium, 1946. Appts: Attaché, Serv. Nat. des Fouilles, Ministère Educ. Nat. et Culture, 1952-57; Conservateur, ibid, 1958-; Hd. of Dept., Univ. of Louvain, 1955; Prof., ibid., 1961-. Mbrships: Koninklijke Vlaamse Akad., Brussels, Belgium, Deutsches archäologisches Inst., Berlin, Germany, 1968; Acad. Pontificia di Archeologia, Rome, Italy, 1970; Club de la Fondation Universitaire, Brussels. Author of reports of excavations in Belgium (Roman Roads, Nivelles, Buzenol, Oudenburg) & Italy (Alba Fucens, Ordona). Hons: Becucci prize, 1964; Officier Ordre de Leopold, 1968. Address: 32 avenue des Genêts, B.1970. Wezembeek-Oppem, Belgium. 87.

MERWIN, John David, b. 26 Sept. 1921. Attorney At Law. Educ: Univ. of Lausanne, Switzerland, 1938-39; Univ. of Puerto Rico, 1939-40; B.Sc., Yale Univ., U.S.A., 1942; J.D., Geo. Wash. Univ. Schl. of Law, 1948. Appts: Served in U.S. Army, 1943-46, 1950-53; Prac. of Law, St. Croix, U.S. Virgin Islands, 1953-57; Govt. Sec., ibid, 1957-58; Gov., ibid, 1958-61; Mgr., Chase Manhattan Bank, Nassau, Bahamas, 1961-65; Exec. V.P., Equity Publng. Co., Orford, N.H., U.S.A., 1965-67; Pvte. Prac., Law, St. Croix, 1967-. Mbrships: Patron, Int. Bar Assn.; Am. Bar Assn.; Virgin Islands Bar; N.H. Bar Assn.; Yale Club of N.Y.C. Author, var. articles in Am. Bar Jrnl. & Virgin Islands Bar Assn. Hons: French Croix de Guerre w. silver star, 1945; U.S. Bronze Star Medal, U.S. Army, 1945. Address: P.O. Box 216, Frederiksted, St. Croix, U.S. Virgin Islands 00840. 2, 128.

MERZBACHER, Claude Fell, b. 29 Oct. 1917. Psychologist; Educator; Consulting Chemical Engineer. Educ: B.S., Univ. of Pa., 1939; M.A., Claremont Grad. Schl., Calif. 1950; Cert. d'Etudes Francaises, Univ. of Poitiers, France, 1951; Ed.D., UCLA, 1962. Appts. incl: Chem. Engr. w. var. Cos.; Instr. Chem., San Diego State Univ.; Chmn., Dept. of Astron., Geol. & Phys. Sci., ibid; Asst. Prof. Phys. Sci.; Lectr., Planetarium & Observatory currently; Prof., Phys. Sci., SDSU; Dir. Psychol. Servs. Ctr., Inc.; Cons., Mgmt. & Ldrship. Creativity; Psychol., Pvte. Prac. Mbrships. incl: Former V.P., local chapt. AAUP; U.S. Candidate for Sci. Prog. Spec. UNESCO; Assoc. Fndr., Calif. Assn. of Chem Tchrs.; San Diego Soc. for Clin. Hypnosis; Bd. of Dirs., Aztec Shops Ltd.; Trustee, Calif. State Colls. Disting. Tchng. Award; AAAS; Am. Chem. Soc.; NEA. Author of Beekeeper's Notebook, 1945. Contbr. of articles & book reviews to profl. jrnls. Address: San Diego State Univ., Dept. of Phys. Sci., San Diego, CA 92115, U.S.A. 9, 28, 141.

MESIBOV, Hugh, b. 29 Dec. 1916. Artist; Professor of Art; Painter; Muralist. Educ: Pa. Acad. of Fine Arts, Phila., U.S.A., 1935-37; Barnes Fndn., Merion, Pa., 1936-40. Appts: Experimental Wkr., Pa. Art Proj., 1937-41; Instr., Art & Ceramics, Lenox Hill Neighbourhood Assn., N.Y.C., 1949-57; Art Therapist, Wiltwyck Schl. for Boys, Esodus, N.Y., 1957-66; Art Instr., Rockland Community Coll., Albany, N.Y., 1963; Asst. Prof., ibid, 1966-71; Assoc. Prof., 1971-. Mbrships: Fellow, Pa. Acad. of Fine Arts; Phila. Watercolor Club. Murals incl: Benjamin Franklin H.S., Phila.;. Univ. of Pa., Phila.; Post Off., Hubbard, Ohio; Temple Beth El, Spring Valley, N.Y. Paintings in num. collects. inclng: Phila. Mus. of Art; Carnegie Lib., Pitts., Pa.; Pa. Acad. of Fine Arts; N.Y. Univ. Collect. of Contemporary Am. Art; Univ. of Ore. Art Mus. Co-inventor, Carborundum Print. Recip., Sev. awards & prizes. Address: 377 Saddle River Rd., Monsey, NY 10952, U.S.A. 6, 37, 105.

MESSEL, Harry, b. 3 Mar. 1922. Professor of Physics. Educ: B.A., Queen's Univ., Ont., Canada, 1948; B.Sc. Ibid, 1948; Ph.D., Nat. Univ. of Ireland, Repub. of Ireland, 1951. Appts. incl: Sr. Lectr., Theoretical Phys., Univ. of Adelaide, Australia, 1951-52; Chair Phys. & Hd., Schl. of Phys., Univ. of Sydney, 1952-; Fndr. & Dir., Sci. Fndn. Phys. ibid, 1954-; Jt. Dir., Cornell-Sydney Univ. Astron. Ctr., 1964-; Sci. Advsr. to Federal Atty.-Gen. & Min. for Customs & Excise, 1973-. Mbrships. incl: AAAS; Elizabethan Trust, Australia; Math. Soc. ibid; Phys. Soc.; Royal Instn. Publs. incl: Num. sci. articles, rsch. papers & books inclng. Abridged Science for High School Students, 2 vols. & Senior Science for High School Students, 3 parts, both 1965. Recip. of num. acad. hons. Address: School of Physics, Univ. of Sydney, N.S.W., Australia 2006. 131.

MESSERLE, Hugo Karl, b. 25 Oct. 1925. Electrical Engineer; Physicist. Educ: B.E.E., Univ. of Melbourne, Australia, 1951; M.Eng.Sc., ibid, 1952; Ph.D., Univ. of Sydney, 1957; D.Sc., Univ. of Melbourne, 1968. Appts: Sr. Demonstrator, Tutor, Univ. of Melbourne, 1951-52; Lectr., Sr. Lectr., Univ. of Sydney, 1952-60; Fulbright Schol., Cornell Univ., N.Y., U.S.A., 1968; Vis. Prof., ibid, 1964; Rdr., Elec. Engrng., Univ. of Sydney, 1960-66; Prof., Elec. Engrng., ibid, 1966-; Hd., Schl., & Prof., ibid, 1970-; Vis. Prof., Inst. für Plasmaforschung, Univ. of Stuttgart, Germany, 1973. Mbrships. incl: Fellow, Inst. Engrs. Australia; Elec. & Electronics Bd., ibid, 1972-, & Bd. of Examiners, 1968-71; Fellow, IREE & IEE. Publs: Dynamic Circuit Theory, 1965; Energy Converstion Statics, 1969; num. scientific papers. Recip., var. profl. hons. Address: Schl. of Elec. Engrng., Univ. of Sydney, N.S.W., Australia 2006. 23.

MESSIA de PRADO, Alberto (Vittorio), b. 10 Oct. 1899. Staff Officer & Major of Cavalry (Retired); Commercial Executive. Educ: Cadet Schl., 1919. Appts: Off., Dragoon Regiment of Nyland (Nylands Dragonregemte), 1920-26; Mng. Dir., AB Nova Oy, Mng. Dir. & Controller, Bank of Oy Henry Auto AB, Chief Salesman, Oy Suomen Autoteollisuus, 1926-39; Gov. of City of Helsinki, 1939-40; Staff Off. to Staff Gen., Mil. Attaché Bur., 1941-44; Atty. Mbrships. incl: Bourse Club of Helsinki, 1927-; Yacht Club of Nyland. Hons: Cross of Freedom, III & IV Class, Finland; Medals, Order of Tammerfors, Order of Filppula, Finland; Order of the Sword, Sweden; Order of

Virtute Militaire, Romania; Bronze Medal, Finnish Team Mbr., Claypidgeon Shooting World Championship, Sweden, 1947. Address: 3 Rödjekärrsbacken, 01620 Martensdal, Finland.

MESSINI, Mariano, b. 12 Sept. 1901. Professor of Therapeutics; Hepatologist. Educ: B.Med. & Surg., Univ. of Padua, Italy, 1924; Qualified in Pharmacol., Therapeut., Med. Hydrol. & Med. Pathol. Appts. incl: Asst., Clin. Med., Univs. of Padua & Rome, 1928-39; Lectr., Pharmacol., 1938; Chair, Med. Fac., Rome Univ., 1939-; Lectr., Occupational Diseases, ibid, 1947; currently, Prof. Therapeut., & Dir., Post-Grad. Schl. of Hepatol. Mbrships. incl: Pres., Comm. of Consultants. Montecatini; Rsch. Comm., Constit. Assembly, 1946; Pres., Italian Med. Soc. for Hydroclimatol.; Italian Soc. of Internal Med.; Chmn., Nat. Inst. of Diabetes & Metabolic Diseases; Rome Med. Acad.; Fndr. Mbr., Union Therapeutique; Sci. Comm., FITCE; Pres., Perm. Comm., Int. Soc. of Med. Hydrol. & Climatol. Publs. incl: Trattato di Terapia Clinica con note di diagnostica, 1940, '42, '44, '56-60; Chemioterapia e Terapia Antibiotica, 1964; Dietetica, 1966. Other books & over 300 med. publs. Fndr., Ed., La Clinica Terapeutica, Epatologia, & La Clinica Termale. Hons. incl: Bronze Medal, Carnegie Fndn., 1925; Guido Bacelli Gold Medal, 1942; Gold Medal, Pub. Hlth., 1963; Gold Medal, Min. of Educ., 1963; Economio Solenne for Treatise on Therapy. Address: Via Rovereto 11, 00198 Rome, Italy. 50.

MESTER, Endre Andrews, b. 20 Nov. 1903. Professor, Surgery. Educ: M.D., 1927; Candidat Med. Sci., 1961; Dr. Med. Sci., 1972. Appts: Asst., III Surg. Clinic, Budapest, 1927; Chief, Dept. Pediatric Surg., St. St. Hosp., Budapest, 1945; Chief of Surg. Dept. & Med. Dir., Bajesy Zsilinszky Hosp., 1947; Prof. of Surg., II Surg. Clin., Semmelweiss Univ., Budapest, 1963-. Mbrships: Bd. of Hungarian Surg. Soc.; Pres., ibid, 1958-66; Corres. Mbr., Surg. Soc. of Lyon; Surg. Soc. of France; Membre titulaire de la Société International de Chirurgie; Hon. Mbr., Int. Soc. of Prostol. 140 publs., gen. surg., in Hungarian, German, Engl. & French. Recip., var. Hungarian scientific decorations. Address: Budapest, 1056, V., Váci-u. 46, Hungary.

MESTER, László, b. 26 May 1918. Research Director; Educator. Educ: Fac. of Chem. Engrng., Tech. Univ., Budapest, Hungary; D. Eng., 1943; D.Chem.Sci., 1956. Appts: w. Tech. Univ., Budapest, 1940-56, Prof., Chem., Natural Products, 1951; Tech. Univ., Berlin-Charlottenburg, 1957-58; Fac. de Pharmacie, Univ. of Paris, 1958-60; Inst. Chimie des Subst. Naturelles, Ctr. Nat. de la Recherce Sci., Paris, 1961-; Tech. Univ. Vienna, Austria, 1962-, Prof., Biochem., 1973; Vis. Sci. NIH, Bethesda, Md., U.S.A., 1961, Inst. Oswaldo Cruz, Rio de Janeiro, Brazil, 1963. Mbrships. incl: Chem. Soc., London; Am. Chem. Soc.; Austrian Chem. Soc.; Chem. Soc. France; Chmn., French Carbohydrate Discussion Grp. Publs: Dérivé Hydraziniques des Glucides, 1967; approx. 120 articles. Decorated Kt., St. John's Order, 1970. Address: Inst. de Chimie des Substances Naturelles, Gif-sur-Yvette-91, France. 15, 122.

MESTER, Ludwig, b. 17 Oct. 1902. University Professor. Educ: Tchrs. Coll., Lübeck, 1923; Coll. for gymnastics, Berlin, 1924; Studied in Berlin, 1928; Dr.phil., Göttingen, 1930. Appts: Asst., Univ. of Berlin, 1924-28; Lectr., gymnastics, Pädagog. Akademien Altona & Frankfurt/Main, 1930-34; Lectr. & Prof., Tchr. Trng. Coll., Weilburg,

1934-39; Prof., gymnastics & young people's welfare, Pädagog. Inst., Weilburg, 1948-63; Prof., Justus-Liebig-Univ., Giessen, & Dir., inst. for tchng. gymnastics, 1964-69; Prof., Univ. of Giessen, & Dir., tchng. dept., sport inst., 1970-71; Emeritus Prof. & mbr., examining bd., 1971- Mbrships. incl: Dir., Arbeitskries für Erziehungsfragen, Beirat des Deutschen Sportbundes, 1955-70; Assoc., Deutsche Lebensrettungsgesellschaft, 1950-67. Author of publs. in field. Recip. of hons. Address: Hainallee 2, 6290 Weilburg, German Fed. Repub. 43, 92.

MESTMAN, Carl, b. 2 Sept. 1930. Dental Surgeon. Educ: B.A., Univ. of Buffalo, 1952; D.D.S., Buffalo Dental Schl., 1958. Appts: Gen. Prac. Dentistry; Lectr. on Occlusion, Manhattan Dental Study Club. Mbrships. incl: Hudson Valley (Treas.) & Orange-Sullivan Dental Study Clubs; Fellow, Soc. of Oral Physiol. & Occlusion, Royal Soc. of Hlth.; Westchester Acad. Restorative Dentistry; N.E. Acad. of Clin. Nutrition; Am. Socs. of Preventive Dentistry & of Children's Dentistry; Am. Assn. for the Study of Headache; Am. Acad. of Implant Dentistry; Gtr. Newburgh Action Comm. (Bd. of Dirs.); Newburgh Jr. Chmbr. of Comm.; Temple Beth Jacob Brotherhood (Pres., 1966-67); Alpha Omega; Masonic·Lodge; Am. Schl. Hlth. Assn. Address: 10 Hideaway Lane, Newburgh, NY 12550, U.S.A. 6.

MESZAROS, Michael Victor, b. 11 Apr. 1945. Sculptor; Architect. Educ: Arch. Degree, Melbourne Univ., Australia, 1967; Churchill Fellowship, Medallion Work & Sculpture in Rome & European Ctrs., 1969; Sculpture w. father, Andor Meszaros. Appts: Arch., R. Inglis & Ptnrs., 1968; Prac. as Sculptor, independent, 1970-. Mbrships: Sec., 1971-73, Sculptors Assn. of Vic.; Australian Deleg., Fed. Int. de la Médaille; Churchill Fellows Assn. of Vic.; Royal S. Yarra Lawn Tennis Club; Assn. Amici della Medaglia. Creative works incl: Num. works w. father, inclng. Mural, Mercy Hosp., Melbourne, ULM Mem., Sydney Int. Air Terminal; num. commissioned portrait, pictorial (1st solo exhib. in Austr., 1970), & prize medallions; Bronze Seahorse fountain, Merimbula, N.S.W.; Wooden Crucifix, New. Offs., St. Patrick's Cathedral, Melbourne; Small Sculpture Biennial, Budapest, Hungary, 1973. Hons: Purchase Prize, Medallion Competition, Gori & Zucchi, Arezzo, Italy, 1968, '70; Dante Medallion Competition, Ravenna, Italy, 1973; 2 Medallions purchased, Royal Dutch Coin Cabinet. The Hague, Netherlands, 1962 & '73. Address: 15 Laver St., Kew, Vic., Australia 3101.

METREY, George David, b. 23 July 1939. Social Worker. Educ: A.B., Marquette Univ., 1961; M.S.W., Fordham Univ. Schl. of Soc. Serv., 1963; Ph.D., N.Y. Univ., 1970. Appts: Soc. Wkr., N.J. Diagnostic Ctr., 1963-64; Asst. Soc. Work Supvsr., ibid,· 1966-70; Dir., Psych. Soc. Work Dept., ibid, 1966-70; Assoc. Prof., Dir., Soc. Work Prog., Kean Coll., N.J., 1970-73; Chmn., Dept. of Sociol. & Soc. Work, ibid, 1973-; Prof., Chmn., Dept. of Sociol. & Soc. Work, 1974; Adj. Assoc. Prof., Fordham Univ. Schl. of Soc. Serv., 1966-; Adj. Assoc. Prof., Rutgers Univ., 1972-. Mbrships: Nat. Assn. of Soc. Wkrs.; Unit Chmn. & Bd. Dirs., Coun. of Soc. Work Educ.; Phi Gamma Mu; Alpha Phi Omega. Address: 42 Devon Dr. East, Piscataway, NJ 08854, U.S.A. 6, 139.

METRO, Patrick Stephen, b. .17 Mar. 1936. Oral Surgeon. Educ: John Carroll Univ., Ohio, 1954-57; D.D.S., Western Reserve Univ. Schl. of Dentistry 1961. Res. Oral Surg., Univ. of Cinn. Gen. Hosp., 1961-64. Mbrships; Dipl., Am. Bd. of

Oral Surg.; Fellow, Am. Dental Soc. of Anesthesiol.; Am. Soc. Oral Surg.; Pres., Delta Sigma Delta, 1960; Ohio Dental Assn.; Am. Dental Assn.; Cleveland Dental Soc.; Westwood Country Club. Contbr. of num sci. articles in dental & oral surg. jrnls. Hons: J.D. Jungman Award, Delta Sigma Delta, 1961; Callahan Mem. Award, Western Reserve Univ. Schl. of Dentistry, 1961. Address: 3730 Rocky River Dr., Cleveland, OH 44111, U.S.A. 8.

METSÄLÄ, Juha Einari, b. 23 May 1925. Conductor; Educator. Educ: B.Pedagogy, Helsinki Univ., Finland, 1953; B.A., 1967; Sibelius Acad. Appts: Conductor, Orch. & Music Ldr., Kemi & Veitsiluoto, 1951-52; Jvyäskylä, 1955-56; Kerava, 1959-; Järvenpää, 1965-; Vis. Conductor, Tampere, Lahti, Turku, etc.; Prin., Adult Evening Schl., Kerava, 1959-. Mbrships: Cultural Comm., Kerava; Kerava Club; Exec. Comm., Lions Club; Exec. Comm., Pohjola-Norden. Composer of pieces for voice, piano, choir, chmbr. music, etc. Author of articles on music & adult education. Ed. Staff, folk music collection, Pelimannisäveliä III, 1973. Hons: 3 prizes in competition compositions, 1951-52; Golden Merit, Soc. of Adult Insts. Address: Sepontie 13, 04200 Kerava, Finland. 134.

METTE, H. Harvey, Jr., b. 19 Mar. 1923. Educator; Musician; Social Scientist. Educ: B.A., Brigham Young Univ., 1946-50; M.M., Butler Univ., 1951-53; Ph.D., N.Y. Univ., 1962-71; Hons. Schol., ibïd, 1972. Appts: Newspaper Mgmt., Brigham Young Univ., U.S.A., 1948-50; Music Tchr., San Juan Co., Utah, 1950-51; Indl. Supvsr., Efficiency Analysis, Kingan & Co., Indpls., Ind., 1951-52; Newspaper Advt., Daily Herald, Provo, Utah, 1952-53; Music Tchr., Duval Co. Schls., Fla., 1953-54; Prof., Jacksoneville Coll. Music, Dir., Div. Music Educ., ibid, 1954-63; Prof., Dir., Instrumental Music, Jacksonville Univ., 1956-63; Band Dir., Bolles Schl., 1954-63; Prof.-Dir., Div. Soc. Scis., 1963-65; Prof., Long Is. Univ., 1965; Brooklyn Ctr., 1966-69; C.W. Post 1969-; Admnstr., Methods, Pracs. & Field Servs., 1965-70; Dir., Tchr. Intern Prog., 1969-72; Schl. Univ. Coord., 1971-73; Prof., Behavioral Analysis, Cultural Diversity, Urban Tchng. & Multi-Lings. & field supvsr., 1973-. Mbr. num. profl. orgs. Author num. works in field. Recip. Post-Doctoral Fellowships, Inst. Ct. Mgmt., 1973, 2 Residential Fellowships, Aspen, Colo., 1973 & Rsch. Fellowship, 1973-. Address: 247 N. 200 East, Provo, UT 84601, U.S.A. 6, 15.

METZGER, Evelyn Borchard (Mrs. H.A. Metzger), b. 8 June 1911. Artist. Educ: A.B., Vassar Coll., 1932; drawing, painting, sculpture studies, U.S.A. & S. Am. Mbrships: Metropol. Mod. Mus.; Archives of Am. Art; Am. Fedn. Art. Solo Exhibs. incl: Gall. Muller, Buenos Aires, 1950; Selected Artists Galls., N.Y.C., 1962; Vassar Coll. Art Gall., 1963; Gall. Belle Chasse, Paris, France, 1963; Norfolk Mus. of Art, Va., U.S.A., 1965; Ga. Mus. Fine Arts, Athens, Greece, 1966; Slater Mem. Mus., Norwich, Conn., U.S.A., 1967; Mexican-Am. Cultural Inst., Mexico City, 1967; Albion Coll., Mich., 1969; Bartholet Gall., N.Y.C., 1973. Permanent Collects. incl: Ariz. State Mus., Tucson; Art Ctr., La Jolla, Calif.; Ga. Mus. Fine Arts; Butler Inst. Am. Art, Columbia Univ., N.Y.C.; Univ. of Me. Recip., Vassar Art Prize, 1932. Address: 815 Park Ave., N.Y., NY 10021, U.S.A. 5, 6, 132, 133.

METZNER, Helmut, b. 15 Sept. 1925. University Professor. Educ: Dr. rer. nat., Univ. of Münster & Göttingen, 1950. Appts: Asst., Univ. of Münster & Göttingen, 1950-55;

Rockefeller Fellow, Univ. of Calif. at Berkeley, U.S.A., 1956-57; Docent, Univ. Göttingen, 1958-60; Prof., Univ. of Tübingen, 1961; Dir., Inst. of Chemical Plant Physiol., ibid, 1964. Mbrships. incl: Gesellschaft Deutscher Chemiker; Gesellschaft Deutscher Naturforscher und Arzte, Phytochem. Soc.; N.Y. Acad. of Scis.; Japanese Plant Physiol. Soc. Publs: Die Zelle: Struktur und Funktion, 1966, 2nd edit., 1971; Progress in Photosynthesis Research, Vol. I-III, 1969; Biochemie der Planze, 1973; Contbr. to num. profl. jrnls. Address: Achalmstr. 11, 74 Tübingen-Pfrondorf, German Fed. Repub.

MEYER, Andreas J., b. 18 Dec. 1927. Publisher. Educ: Apprentice, Heidelberg, Germany, 1948-49; Pol. Econs. & Sociol., Univ. of Hamburg, 1953-56. Fndr., Proprietor & Mgr., Merlin Verlag, (Publrs.), Hamburg, 1957-. Mbrships: Börsenverein Deutscher Verleger & Buch Händlerverbände; Hamburger Künstlerclub Die Insel E.V.; Dramaturgische Gesellschaft Berlin; Norddeutscher Regatta Verein. Publs. incl: num. articles in German newspapers. Address: D3119 Gifkendorf, NR. 3, German Fed. Repub. 45.

MEYER, August R., b. 20 Nov. 1924. Dean. Educ: B.S.E., State Coll. Ark., U.S.A., 1949; M.A., George Peabody Coll. Tchrs.; Ed.D., ibid. Appts: Elem. Tchg. Prin., Camden, Ark., 1949-52; Tchr., Prin. & Dir., Elem. Educ. & Curriculum, Independence, Mo. Pub. Schls., 1952-59; Ext. Instr., Ctrl. Mo. State Coll., Warrensburg, Mo. (summer & evening classes), 1953-55; Lectr. Educ., Univ. Kan. City, Mo. (summers), 1956-57; W. Wash. Coll. Educ., Bellingham (summer)' 1958; Dean. Instrn., Southeast Mo. State Univ., Cape Girardeau, Mo., 1960-. Mbrships. incl: Chmn., Nat. Coun. Accreditation Tchr. Educ. Accrediting Teams at colls. in Mo., Ark., La., Okla., Ala. & Ill.; Pres., Mo. Assn. Supvsn. & Curriculum Dev., 1961; Past Pres., Mo. Reading Circle Comm., Mo. State Tchrs. Assn.; Mo. Gov.'s Conf. on Educ.; Southeast Dist. Tchr. Educ. & Profl. Standards Comm.; Cons., George Peabody Coll. Tchrs., Nashville, Tenn.; Delta State Coll., Cleveland, Miss.; State Coll. Ark.; Nat. Sci. Tchrs. Assn. Address: Southeast Mo. State Univ., Cape Girardeau, MO 63701, U.S.A. 8, 46, 141.

MEYER, Frank H., b. 11 July 1915. Research Physicist. Educ: B.S., City Coll., UCNY, 1936; M.S., Polytech. Inst., Brooklyn, 1951; Okla. State Univ., 1955-60; Wash. State Univ., 1961-62; M.A., Univ. of Minn., 1968. Appts. incl: X-Ray Crystallographer, Textile Rsch. Inst., Princeton, N.J., 1951-53; Rsch. Physicist, Control Rsch., Continental Oil Co., Ponca City, Okla., 1954-60; Sr. Dev. Engr., UNIVAC, Sperry Rand Corp., St. Paul, Minn., 1962-65; Asst. Prof.-Prof., Phys. & Philos., Univ. of Wis.-Superior, 1966-. Mbrships. incl: Am. Phys. Soc.; Am. Crystallographic Assn.; V.P., Superior Chapt., AAUP. Contbr. of articles to profl. jrnls. Ed., Reciprocity. Recip. of various fellowships & awards. Address: Univ. of Wisconsin-Superior, Superior, WI 54880, U.S.A. 14.

MEYER, Harvey, b. 6 Apr. 1929. Architect. Educ: Dip. Structural Technol., SUNY, 1950; B.Arch., Pratt Inst., N.Y.C., 1957. Appts: V. Gruen Assocs., N.Y.C., 1958-60; Skidmore, Owings & Merril, ibid, 1960-62; I.M. Pei & Ptnrs., 1962-66; J.F.N. Assocs., Interior Arch., 1966-70; Staff Archt., E.R. Squibb & Co., Princeton, N.J., 1970-72; Charles Luckman Assocs., N.Y.C., 1972-. Mbrships: Am. Inst. Archts.; Soc. Am. Registered Archts.; Nat. Coun. Archtl. Registration Bds.; Archtl. Assn. London); Am. Arbitration Assn.; Pratt Archtl.

Club; Appalachian Mountain Club. Address: Troy Towers, Apt. 210, 380 Mountain Rd., Union City, NJ 07087, U.S.A. 6.

MEYER, Henry Edwin, b. 23 July 1890. Music Teacher; Choral Director; Fine Arts Administrator. Educ: Tchr. & Artists Dip., B.M., B.S., Ithaca Conservatory of Music; B.A., Southwestern Univ.; M.A., S.W. Tex. Tchrs. Coll.; Studies in Cinn. & N.Y. Appts: Instr., Piano & Theory, Ithaca Conservatory, 1910-11; Instr., Music, Univ. of Minn., 1914; Dir. of Music, Howard Payne Coll., 1918; Dean of Music, Daniel Baker Coll., 1920; Hd., Music Dept. & Dean, Schl. of Fine Arts, Southwestern Univ., 1926-61. Mbrships: Hon. Mbr., Past Pres., Tex. Music Tchrs. Assn.; Hon. Mbr., Past Pres., Tex. Assn. of Music Schls.; Scholia Club, Univ. of Tex.; Rotary; Meth. Ch. Publs: Writer, music review column, The Musicale & The Southwestern Musician, 20 yrs.; Co-Author, Tone the Bell Easy; Author, serial, Beethoven & His Times, & num. articles in music mags. Hons. incl: Mus.D., Southern Schl. of Fine Arts, Houston. Address: 810 E. University Ave., Georgetown, TX 78626, U.S.A.

MEYER, Leopold L., b. 21 June 1892. Company Chairman. Educ: B.A., Tulane Univ., 1912. Appts: V.P., Foley Bros. Dry Goods Co., 1925-45; Chmn. of Bd., Meyer Bros., Inc., Houston, Tex., 1945-. Mbrships. incl: Pres. Emeritus, Tex. Children's Hosp.; Chmn. of Bd. Emeritus, Harris Co. Ctr. for the Retarded; Past Pres., Nat. Retail Credit Assn.; Chmn. of Bd. Emeritus, Houston Civic Music Assn.; Past Pres., Congregation Beth Israel; Past Pres., Houston Crime Commn.; Bd. mbr., Houston Speech & Hearing Ctr., Baylor Coll. of Med., Houston Schl. for Deaf Children, March of Dimes, Tex. Heart Inst., St. Luke's Episcopal Hosp., Houston Arthritis Fndn., Tex. Soc. for Prevention of Blindness. Citations from var. assns. inclng. Nat. Jewish Hosp., 1969, Houston Peace Off. Assn., 1970. Address: c/o Meyer Bros., Inc., 1035 Meyerland Plaza, Houston, TX 77035, U.S.A. 55.

MEYER, Lothar, b. 6 July 1921. Businessman; Author. Educ: Econs. & Pol. Sci., Tech. Univ., Berlin, Germany. Appts. incl: Free-lance Author, 1945-57; Dir., Inst. for Problems of Indl. Rationalization, German Trade Union League (EPA), Municipal Counsellor for Econs; Youth & Sports problems, West-Berlin Burrough Wedding, Cons. & Vis. Lectr., Geotechnol., Inst. of Technol., Atlanta, Ga., U.S.A. & Lectr., Berlin H.S. of Econs., Berlin (latter appts. between 1957-64); Mgr., Atlantik, Ltd. for Admin., Economic Counselling & Info. Mbrships: Mbr. Presidium, Int. Technogeographical Soc.; Mbr. Presidium, Gesellschaft für Weltkunde; Soc. for Scientific Labour Rsch. Comm. for Rationalization of German Economy; Mbr. Presidium, Wappenherold, Genealogical Club; Mbr. Coun. for Prices at Senator for Econs., Berlin; Chmn., Coun. for Environment Problems, Berlin. Publs: Man & Organization, 2nd Vol., 1964; The Economy Of The U.S.A., 1966; Politics, Education & Public Science, 1969. Address: Atlantik GmbH, 1 Berlin 30, Bayreuther Str. 3-4, German Fed. Repub. 42, 92.

MEYER, Marshall T., b. 25 Mar. 1930. Rabbi; Professor; Editor. Educ: A.B., Dartmouth Coll.; M.H.L., Jewish Theological Sem. of Am.; Doctoral studies, Hebrew Univ., Jerusalem, Columbia Univ., N.Y., Union Theological Sem., N.Y. Appts: Sec., Commn. on Jewish Law & Standards, Rabbinical Assembly, N.Y.; Rabbi, Congregacion Israelita de la Republica Argentina; Rabbi & Fndr., Comunidad Bet El, Buenos Aires, Argentina;

Rector & Fndr., Seminario Rabinico Latinomericano, Buenos Aires; Dir. & Fndr., Camp Ramatt, Argentina; Dir., Latin Am. Off., World Coun. of Synagogues, Buenos Aires. Mbrships. incl: Clerical Exec. Comm., Inst. of Mental Hlth.; Argentine Assn. of Family Protection. Ed.-in-Chief, Library of Science & History of Religions; Ed., complete bi-lingual edits., 3 Prayer Books, & Majshavol (Thought), quarterly jrnl. in Spanish. Address: 11 de Setiembre 1669, Buenos Aires, Argentina. 55.

MEYERS, Nechemia, b. 8 June 1930. Journalist; Director. Educ: UCLA, 1948-50; B.A., Hebrew Univ., Israel, 1959. Appts: Sec., World Habonim, 1953; Dpty. Dir., Publs. Sec., Israel Govt. Press Off., 1959-63; w. Weizmann Inst., 1964-; Dir., P.R. ibid, 1968-. Mbrships: Nat. Assn. Sci. Writer, U.S.; AAAS; Israel P.R. Assn.; Past Bd., Assn. of Ams. & Canadians in Israel. Translator, David Ben Gurion's Israel: A Personal History. Regular contbr. to newspapers. Address: P.R. Office, Weizmann Inst. of Sci., Rehovot, Israel. 55, 94.

MEYSHAN (MESTSHANSKI), Josef, b. 26 Dec. 1899. Heart Specialist; Medical Administrator. Educ: Med. Schl., Odessa Univ., U.S.S.R., 1918-22; Dr.'s Degree, Albertus Univ., Koenigsberg, Prussia, 1930. Appts: Asst., Municipal Hosp., Danzig, Germany, 1923-30; Chief Physn., OSE Policlin., 1923-37; Chmn., Tel-Aviv Br., Israel Med. Assn., 1951-54, Hd. of Comm. for Postgrad. Studies, 1951-60, Ctrl. Comm. Mbr., 1952-72; Mbr., Israel Scientific Coun., Hd. of Med. Lib., 1951-68; Expert for Govt. Med. Bd. for German Indemnification Claims, Nat. Inst. Inst., & Min. of Defence, 1960-. Mbr., Fellow & Off., med. & numismatic orgs. Publs. incl: The Disease of Herod the Great, King Of Judaea, 1957; The Death of Agrippa I, 1959; Essays in Jewish Numismatics, 1968. Fndr., Chair of Hist. of Med., Med. Schl., Tel-Aviv Univ., 1973. Recip. of hons. Address: 39 Balfour St., Tel-Aviv, Israel. 55, 94.

MEZZASALMA, Giuseppe, b. 11 June 1913. Medical Doctor. Educ: Messina Univ. Med. Schl., Italy; Cert., Italian Bd. of Cardiol. Appts. incl: Assoc. Prof., Physiol., Milan Univ. Med. Schl., Italy, 1959; Assoc. of Med., ibid, 1962; Chief, Dept. of Cardiopulmonary Physiol., Ospedale Magglore, Milan. Mbrships. incl: Fellow, Deutschen Gesellschaft für Kreislaufforschung, Germany; Fellow, Società Italiana di Cardiologia, Italy; Affiliate Fellow, Royal Soc. of Med., U.K. Contbr. to med. press and profl. jrnls. Address: Via Soperga 10, 20127 Milan, Italy.

MICHAEL, Cyril, b. 22 Jan. 1898. Lawyer; Musician. Educ: Dip., Music, Univ. Ext. Conservatory of Chgo., 1932; LL.B., La Salle Ext. Univ. of Chgo., 1947. Appts. incl: Clerk, U.S. Dist. Ct., Dist. Ct. Commnr., Ct. Interpreter, Spanish, Law Clerk & U.S. Dist. Ct. Judge, 1937-51; U.S. Atty., Dist. of V.I. & Atty. Gen. of V.I., 1951-54; Judge, Police Ct., 1954-57 & Municipal Ct. of St. Thomas & St. John, 1957-65; Presiding Judge, Municipal Ct. of V.I., 1965-; U.S. Commnr., 1955-; Special Assignment by Chief Judge of U.S. Ct. of Appeals for 3rd Circuit to serve as Judge of U.S. Dist. Ct. of V.I., 1970, '71; Hon. Asst. Atty. Gen. of Ga., 1954. Mbrships. incl: Fellow, Int. Biographical Assn.; Col.; Hon. Order of Ky. Cols., 1971; Am. & Nat. Bar Assn.; Puerto Rico Coun.; Examining Comm., 1947-56, Pres., V.I. Bar Assn., 1948-50. Contbr. of articles to newspapers. Recip. of Silver Beaver, Boy Scouts of Am. Address: P.O.Box 297, St. Thomas, VI 00801, U.S.A.

MICHAEL, Kaiser, Jr., b. 28 Sept. 1932. Attorney. Educ: B.B.A., Univ. of N.M., 1955; LL.B., Univ. of Denver, 1957; J.D., ibid, 1970; Grad. work, Northwestern Univ., Schl. of Law, 1961. Appts. incl: Asst. Dist. Atty., Criminal Div., 2nd Judicial Dist. of N.M., Albuquerque, N.M., 1961-62; Ptnr. in law firm of McAtee, Marchiondo & Michael, ibid, 1962-71; Ptnr. in law firm of Mateucci, Franchini, Calkins & Michael, ibid, 1971-; Legal counsel for N.M. Osteopathic Med. Assn.; Legal counsel for Martineztown Citizens Info. Comm., Albuquerque. Mbrships. incl: Pres., Albuquerque Bar Assn., 1972-; Chmn., Albuquerque Chmbr. of Comm. Criminal Justice System Comm.; Bd. of Dirs., Albuquerque Urban Coalition; Am. Bar Assn.; Am. Judicature Soc.; Am. Trial Lawyers Assn. Address: 4317 Royene N.E., Albuquerque, NM 87110, U.S.A. 7, 57.

MICHAEL, Simon George, b. 3 May 1905. Artist; Sculptor; Teacher; Writer; Lecturer. Educ: Wash. Univ., 1923; Detroit Inst. Art, Mich.; Acad. de la Grande Chamière, Paris, France. Appts: Art. Ed., Phoenician Mag., Detroit, Mich., U.S.A.; Instr., Gordon Galls., ibid, & num. Art Guilds & Assns.; Dir. & Instr. Art. Tours, Mexico, Europe & Ctrl. Am.; Lectr., Miami Univ., Oxford, Ohio; Art Demonstrations, Cashocton Mus. Art, Ohio; Simon Michael Schl. Fine Arts, Rockport, Tex.; Fndr., Dir. & Instr., ibid. Mbr. sev. profl. orgs. Creative Works: Var. collects. U.S. & Europe; Exhibs. & Representations incl: Dayton Mus., Ohio; Mus. & Fair Bldg., Shreveport, La.; W. Coll., Oxford, Ohio; Cashocton Mus., ibid; Mt. Vernon Mus., ibid; Miami Univ., Oxford, ibid, San Antonio Woman's Club, Tex.; Corpus Christi Woman's Club, ibid; Wayne Univ., Detroit, Mich.; Chalet Sun Valley, Idaho Scarab Club. Detroit Mich.; Gordon Beer Gall., ibid; Thompson Gall., ibid; Baker Hotel, Dallas, Tex. Recip. many awards. Address: Simon Michael Schl. & Gall. Fine Arts, P.O. Box 1283, Rockport, TX 78382. U.S.A. 125.

MICHAELIDES, Solon, b. 12 Nov. 1905. Composer; Conductor; Musicologist. Educ: Trinity Coll. of Music, London, 1927-30; L'Ecole Normale de Musique, Paris, 1930-34. Appts: Dir., Limassol Conservatoire of Music, Cyprus, 1934-56; Dir., Salonica State Conservatoire, Greece, 1957-70; Dir. Gen., & Prin. Conductor, Salonica State Orch., 1959-70, retirement, Salonica appts., 1970. Past exec. off., musical orgs., adjudicator var. int. musical competitions. Publs. incl: Modern Harmony, 2 vols., 1946; The Neo-Hellenic Folk Music, 1948. Contbr., var. mags. Compositions incl. opera, choral & orchestral works, chamber music, songs, piano pieces. Lects., Greek music, BBC, U.K., 1946-48, Yale & Marshall Univs. U.S.A., 1973. Hons. incl: Cmdr. of Phoenix Royal Order of Greece, 1965. Address: 14-16 Neofytou Metaxa St., Athens 109, Greece. 21.

MICHALOWSKI, Roman Edmund Hugo, b 31 Oct. 1912. Dermatologist; Psychologist Educator. Educ: Phys. Dip., Univ. of Warsaw 1939; Dr. Histol., Univ. of Stefan Batory Wilno 1939; M.A., Univ. of Warsaw, 1952. Appts: Staff, Inst. of Histol., Univ. of Warsaw 1934-38; Asst., Dept. Dermatol., ibid, 1941-49 Asst. Prof., Dermatol. & Venereol., 1949; Cons Dermatologist, 2nd Municipal Hosp., Warsaw 1958-61; Prof. & Dir., Dermatol. Dept., Med Schl., Lublin, 1962-. Mbrships. incl: Bd. Dirs. Polish Dermatol. Soc., 1965-; Polish Psychol Assn.; Corres. Mbr., Int. Soc. Tropica Dermatol., Int. Soc. Cybernetic Med. Publs: Diseases of Buccal Mucosa, 1956, 2nd edit. 1960; Diseases of Hair & Hairy Skin, 1971; var. articles. Recip., Med. Schl. Lublin Awards

1964, '65, '66, '72, '73. Address: Podkowa Lesna, Wrobla 20, Warsaw, Poland. 50.

MICHANOWSKY (Cmdr.) George, b. 9 Mar. 1920. Explorer; Director of Scientific Research. Appts. incl: Fndr. & Pres., Amazonia Fndn., N Y , 1 9 5 2 . Originator, ultraviolet reconnaissance technique for clear ·air turbulence detection, approved for investigation by U.S. Navy Dept. & Air Transport Assn.; Organizer & Dir., 1st aero-photographic survey of prehistoric Tihuanacu ruins; Initiator, infrared & ultraviolet airborne rsch. for archaeol. purposes & gen. Andean studies. Ldr. of num. air & land expeditions to unexplored Upper Amazon & Andes regions, resulting in mapping of legendary River of Writing &· ancient roads. Developer of airborne avalanche warning techniques; Dir. of astrophys. aeronautical & environmental rsch.; Author of concept connecting S. Am. petroglyph w. ancient Vela X supernova explosion, Mbrships: Army-Navy Club (Wash.). Address: Box 651, N.Y., NY 10023, U.S.A.

MICHEEL, Fritz, b. 3 July 1900. University Professor of Chemistry. Educ: Studies chem., Univ. of Berlin, Germany. Appts. incl: Univ. Lectr., Univ. of Göttingen, 1931; Extra Prof., Univ. of Münster, 1936; Lectr., ibid, 1937; Prof., & Dir., Chem. Inst., 1946; Dir., Organic Chem. Inst., 1950. Mbrships: Fellow, AAAS; R h e i n i s c h - W e s t f ä l i s c h e Akad. der Wissenschaften; Gesellschaft Deutscher Chemiker; Gesellschaft Deutscher Naturforschenden & Arzte; Swiss Chem. Soc.; Am. Chem. Soc.; Gesellschaft für biolog. Chemie; N.Y. Acad. of Sci. Publs: Chemie d. Zucker und Polysaccharide, 2nd edit. 1959; Articles in sci. jrnls. in Germany & abroad. Recip., Medal, Soc. de Chimie Bioligique, France, 1970. Address: Auf dem Draun 17, D 44 Münster, German Fed. Repub.

MICHEL, Andreé, b. 22 Sept. 1920. Sociologist; Research Administrator. Educ: Grad. in Law, Univ. of Aix-Marseille; Grad. in Sociol., Univ. of Grenoble, Switzerland; Doctorat d'Etat, Fac. of Letters & Human Scis., Univ. of Paris, France. Appts: Rsch. Assoc., Nat. Ctr. of Scientific Rsch., Paris, 1951-62, 1965-66, Rsch. Dir., Rsch. Grp. on Sex Roles, Family & Human Dev., 1970-; Vis. Prof., Univ. of Algiers, Algeria, 1963-64, Case Western Reserve Univ., U.S.A., 1966-67, Univ. of Ottawa, Canada, 1968-70; Sr. Rsch. Fellow, Family Study Ctr., Univ. of Minn., Mnpls., U.S.A., 1967-68. Mbr., var. profl. orgs. Publs. incl: La sociologie de la famille, 1970; Activite professionnelle de la femme et vie conjugale, 1974. Address: Centre d'Etudes Sociologiques, Centre National de la Recherche Scientifique, 82 rue Cardinet, Paris 75017, France. 50.

MICHELET, Faye Fullerton (Mrs. Charles Jules Michelet, Jr.), b. 13 Oct. 1902. Retired Teacher. Educ: A.B., Univ. of Ill., Urbana, 1926; Audited courses, Univ. of Pitts., 1933; Univ. of Chgo., 1936; Grad. course, Child Psychol., Northwestern Univ., 1938-39. Appts. as Tchr. in pvte. & pub. schls., 1922-37. Mbrships. incl: Nat. Pres., Daughters of the Am. Colonists, 1970-73; Hon. Nat. Pres., ibid, 1973; Nat. Organizing Sec., ibid, 1967-70; Nat. Chmn., Resolutions, 1967; State Chmn., DAR, 1962-64; Pres., Chgo. Chapt., Colonial Dames, XVII Century, 1968-70; Nat. Soc. Sons & Daughters of the Pilgrims; N. Shore Chapt., AAUW; Ill. Histl. Soc.; Ill. Audubon Soc.; Am. Legion Aux; Centurion Club, Iowa Wesleyan Coll., 1974. Author of articles in jrnls. Recip., James A. Harlan Award, presented by Pres., Iowa Wesleyan Coll., Mt. Pleasant, at

Daughters of Am. Colonists Banquet, Wash. D.C., 1972. Address: 1028 Sheridan Rd., Wilmette, IL 60091, U.S.A. 5, 8, 130, 132.

MICHENER, (The Right Hon.) Roland, b. 19 Apr. 1900. Governor General & Commander-in-Chief of Canada. Educ: B.A., Univ. of Alta., Canada, 1920; B.A., Oxford Univ., U.K., 1922; B.C.L, ibid, 1923; M.A., ibid, 1929; Called to Bar, Middle Temple, U.K., 1923; called to Ont. Bar, Canada, 1924. Appts. incl: Lawyer with firm Lang, Michener & others, Toronto, 1924-57; King's Counsel, 1943; Mbr. for St. David, Toronto, Ont. Legislature, 1945-48; Provincial Sec. & Registrar for Ont., 1946-48; Mbr., House of Commons, 1953; re-elected 1957, 1958; Speaker, 1957, 1958; High Commnr. to India, 1964-67; Gov. Gen. & Cmdr-in-Chief, 1967-74. Mbrships. incl: Privy Coun., 1962; Coun., Commonwealth Parliamentary Assn., 1959-61; Gen. Sec., Rhodes Schlrships., Canada, 1936-64; num. civic & bus. orgs. Hons. incl: Chancellor & Prin. Companion, Order of Canada, 1967; Chancellor & Cmdr., Order of Mil. Merit, 1972; Prior for Canada, Order of St. John of Jerusalem, 1967; Kt. of Justice, ibid, 1967; Rhodes Schol., 1919; num. hon. degrees & fellowships. Address: Government House, Ottawa, Canada K1A 0A1.

MICHMAN, Julius, b. 5 Feb. 1909. Dentist. Educ: Dr.med. dent. Dip., Munich, Germany; postgrad. studies in Orthodontics, Periodontics, Prosthodontics & Occlusion, Europe & U.S.A. Appts: Pvte. prac., gen. dentistry, Jerusalem, 1935; Cons., Dental Clin., Hadassah Med. Org., Jerusalem, 1942; Lectr., course on Dental Materials for dental techns., Ort Schl., Jerusalem, 1949-51; Guest Lectr., Prof. Gottlieb's Postgrad. Inst., Tel-Aviv, 1950-52; Chmn., Dept. of Oral Rehab., Hebrew Univ.-Hadassah Schl. of Dental Med., 1955-; Lectr. of Prosthetics & Restorative Dentistry-Full Prof., Oral Rehab., Hebrew Univ., Jerusalem, 1957-. Mbrships. incl: Fellow, Int. Assn. Dental Rsch., Int. Coll. Dentists, Am. Coll. of Dentists, AAAS; Israel Dental Assn.; Int. Dental Fedn.; sev. ed. bds. of profl. jrnls. Contbr. to profl. publs. Hon.: Prize Grabow (W. Langer & Seifert), Israel Dental Assn., 1960; Citation in Special Recognition, Alpha Omega, 1964; Prize of Oral Rehab. in name of late Dr. Zvi L. Abromowski, Israel Soc. of Oral Rehab., 1974. Address: c/o Dept. of Oral Rehab., Hebrew Univ.-Hadassah Schl. for Dental Med. founded by the Alpha Omega Fraternity, Jerusalem, Israel.

MICK, Robert J.H., b. 10 Aug. 1912. Dentist. Educ: D.D.S., Temple Dental Coll., Phila, Pa., U.S.A. Appts: Pvte. Prac., Dentist, Treasure Island, Fla., & Laurel Springs, N.J.; Rsch. Wkr., Foods, Water, & Fluoridation, Africa & U.S.A. Mbrship: Int. Rep., Am. Acad. of Nutrition, 1949. Publs: Articles & papers, mostly on fluoridation, in profl. jrnls. Address: 915 Stone Rd., Laurel Springs, NJ 08021; U.S.A.

MICKELSEN, Olaf, b. 29 July 1912. Educator. Educ: B.S., Rutgers Univ., 1935; M.S., Univ. of Wis., 1937; Ph.D., ibid, 1939. Appts: Chem., Univ. Hosps., Mpls., Minn., 1939-41; Assoc. Prof., Lab. Physiol. Hygiene, Univ. of Minn., 1942-48; w. Nutrition Br., USPHS, 1948-51; w. Nat. Insts. of Hlth., Bethesda, Md., 1951-62; Prof. of Nutrition, Mich. State Univ., 1962-. Mbrships incl: Pres., Am. Inst. of Nutrition; Am. Bd. of Nutrition; British Nutrition Soc.; Sigma Xi. Publs. incl: Nutrition Science and You, 1964; The Biology of Human Starvation (co-author), 1951; More than 170 sci. articles in profl. publs.; Assoc.

Ed., Nutrition Reviews, 1954-. Address: Mich. State Univ., East Lansing, MI 48823, U.S.A. 2, 14.

MICKENS, Edward Frederick, b. 11 Sept. 1924. Traffic Executive. Educ: Grad., Acad. Advance Traffic, 1948; B.S., Rutgers Univ., 1955. Appts. incl: served, U.S.N.R., 1943-46; Rate Specialist, Chevrolet-Bloomfield Div., Gen. Motors Corp., Bloomfield, N.J., 1945-51; Night Supvsr., L.I. Transportation Co., Carlton Hill., N.J', 1946; Traffic Cons., 1949-; Traffic Mgr., Coates Bd. & Carton Co., Inc., Garfield, N.J. & Stroudsburg, Pas., 1951-64; Substitute Tchr., Traffic Mgmt., Fairleigh Dickinson Univ., Teaneck, N.J., 1959-; Sales Serv. Mgr., Coates Bd. & Carton Co., Inc., 1960-64; Gen. Traffic Mgr., ibid, 1964; Gen. Traffic Mgr., Becton, Dickinson & Co., Rutherford, N.J., 1965-. Rsch. work on ICC, p.r. in trucking ind. Mbrships: Nat. Indl. Traffic League; ICC Practitioners Assn. Delta Nu Alpha; Traffic Club of N. Jersey (Pres. Paterson 1962). Address: 90 E. 9th St., Clifton, N.J., U.S.A. 6.

MIDDLEMANN, Werner Gustav, b. 10 Oct. 1909. International Civil Servant. Appts. incl: Exec. Dir., Elec. Appliances & Chem. Inds., 1935-45; i/c Refugees & Expellees, Baden Wurttbg., Germany, 1945-46; U.S. Zone of Occupation, 1947; U.S. & British Zones of Occupation, 1947-49; Permanent Sec., Fed. Min. for Refugees, Expellees & War Victims, 1949-61; Dir., E. Mediterranean Reg., UNICEF, 1961-65; Comptroller, UNICEF, N.Y., U.S.A., 1965-. Mbr., German For. Policy Assn., Bonn, Germany. Address: c/o UNICEF, 866 United Nations Plaza, Room A-6168, N.Y., NY 10017, U.S.A. 34.

MIEGE, Jean-Louis, b. 20 Aug. 1923. University Professor. Educ: Docteur es-Lettres, Sorbonne, Paris, France. Appts: Dir. of Studies, Inst. of Pol. Studies, 1962-; Dir., Ctr. of Rsch. on Mediterranean Africa, 1962-65; Dir., I.H.P.O.M., 1965-; Dir., U.E.R. Mediterranean, 1971-. Mbrships: Overseas Acad. of Scis.; Admin. Coun., Soc. of Econ. & Statl. Studies. Publs. incl: Le Maroc, 5th ed., 1969; Les Européens à Casablanca au XIXè siècle, 1954; Dans la lumière des cités africaines: Casablanca, Mazagan, Mogador, 1956; Le Maroc et l'Europe, 4 vols., 1961-63; L'imperialisme colonial italien, 1968; Une mission française à Marakech, 1969; Documents d'histoire économique et sociale marocaine, 1970; Expansion européene et décolonisation, 1870 à nos jours. Hons: Laureate, Inst. of France; Chevalier, Acad. Palms. Address: I.H.P.O.M., Univ. de Provence, 29 Ave. R. Schuman, 13621 Aix en Provence, France.

MIELKE, Margaret G., b. 17 July 1912. Teacher; Writer; Poet. Educ: Psychol. Testing Grad. Work; Summer Credits, Art, Speech, Drama, Writing, Mont. State Univ., Univ. of Alaska. Appts. incl: Tchr., '1933-37; Indian Schl., 1937-40; Sub. Tchr., 1940-; Poetry Ed., Anchorage Times, 1954-56; Rsch. for Revenue Dept., Motor Vehicles, State of Alaska, 1964-69; Poetry therapy for boys' reform schl., poetry workshops for state schls., 1968-74. Mbrships: 1st Poet Laureate, State Poetry Laureate, 1963-65; State Poetry Councilor; Hon. Life mbr., E.S.A.; Woman's Club of Am.; Kappa Delta; Pan Hellenic. Publs. incl: 1st, 2nd & 3rd anthologies of Alaska Poetry; 100 yrs. of Alaskan Poetry; Haiku Writers of Am.; Gruening's Alaska Reader. Recip. of hons. Address: Box No. 74, Chugiak, AK 99567, U.S.A. 2, 5.

MIELKE, Thelma Jane, b. 14 Dec. 1916. Librarian. Educ: A.B., Elmhurst Coll., 1937;

M.A., Univ. of Rochester, 1939; M.S. Columbia, 1961. Appts. incl: Grp. Wkr., Baden St. Settlement House, 1939-41; Res., Ch. of All Nations, N.Y.C., 1942-43; Libn., Harlem Boys Club, 1943-45; U.N. Corres., Revista, Puerto Rico, 1945-50; P.R., Hill Knowlton, N.Y.C., 1952-54; Ref. Asst. to Sr. Ref. Libn., N.Y. Univ., 1954-63; Ref. Libn., L.I. Univ., Brooklyn, 1963-; Asst. Prof., 1963-65; Assoc. Prof., 1965-. Mbrships: AAUP; ALA; Sec., Exec. Bd., United Fedn. Coll. Tchrs.; Nat. Org. for Women. Ed., Library Leaves, 1964-. Address: 175 W. 12th St., N.Y., NY 10011, U.S.A. 5, 42.

MIESMAA, Tauno Olavi, b. 11 Mar. 1891. Portrait Painter; Professor. Educ: Techl. Inst. of Helsinki; Art study, Univ. of Helsinki under Prof. Eero Jarnefelt, 1912-18, pvte. pupil, 1918-23. Mbrships: Artists Assn. of Finland; Assn. of Finnish Draftsmen; Rotary Club, Helsinki. First exhib., paintings, 1923; Caricatures in daily newspapers, 1920-30; Over 500 portraits. Hons: Pro Finlandia Order, 1964; Professor, 1970. Address: Pohjolankatu 56, 00600 Helsinki 60, Finland. 43, 90.

MIETTUNEN, Helge Leonard, b. 9 Sept. 1916. Broadcasting Programme Planner. Educ: B.A., M.A., Ph.D., Univ. of Helsinki, 1939-49. Appts. incl: Hd. of Programmes (Radio)-Hd. of Programme Planning, Finnish Broadcasting Co. Ltd., 1957-; Docent of Mass Communication-Acting Prof.; Univ. of Tampere, 1964-71; M.P., 1951-58; Finnish UNESCO Comm. Mbr., 1957-65. Mbrships: Union of Reserve Offs., 1936-; Finnish Grp., Interparliamentary Union, 1951-58. Publs. incl: Radio & TV, 1966; Theory of Film, 1969. Contbr. sev. publs. on aspects of film prod. Hons. incl: Liberty Cross IV w. swords, 1940 & 1943, w. oak leaf, 1944; Captain, 1966; Gold Medal (Hon. Mbr.), Finnish Film Assn., 1967. Address: Sateenkaari 1 C 13, 02100 Tapiola, Finland. 43, 90.

MIGAUX, Leon, b. 15 Oct. 1897. Mining Engineer. Appts. incl: Interallied Control Mission, Factories & Mines, Ruhr, 1923-24; Mining Serv., Montpellier, France, 1925-29; Dir., Mining Rsch. & Dev. Bur., & Sherifian Petroleum Co., Morocco, 1929-37; Dir., Schlumberger Elec. Prospecting Co., 1937-42; Dir. Gen.-Presiding Dir., Gen., Gen. Geophysical Co., 1943-67. Mbrships: Pres., French Assn. of Petroleum Techns., 1949-50; Geological Soc. of France; Astronomical Soc. of France; Soc. of Exploration Physicists; European Assn. of Exploration Geophysicists. Publs: Num. articles in profl. jrnls. & contbns. to books. Hons. incl: Croix de Guerre 1914-1918; Kt., Legion of Honour, 1933, Off., 1960; Grand Off., Ouissam Alaouite, Morocco, 1937; Cmdr., Nat. Order of Merit, 1971. Address: 1 Place du Panthéon, 75005 Paris, France.

MIGICOVSKY, Bert B., b. 15 Mar. 1915. Agricultural Scientist. Educ: B.S. Agric., Univ. of Man., 1935; M.S., Univ. of Minn., 1937; Ph.D., ibid, 1939. Appts. incl: Chem. Div., Sci. Serv., Canada Dept. Agric., Ottawa, 1945-55, Hd., Animal Chem. Unit, 1955-59, Chief, Biochem. Sect., Animal Rsch. Inst., 1959-64, Asst. Dir. Gen. & Dir. Gen., Rsch. Br., 1964-68 & 1968-; Special Lectr., Dept. Histol. & Embryol., Univ. of Ottawa, 1961-. Mbrships. incl: Fellow, Chem. Inst. & Agric. Inst. of Canada; Am. Assn. Biol. Chem.; Canadian Biochem. Soc. & Physiol. Soc.; Agric. Inst. Canada; Sigma XI. Contbr., num. sci. jrnls. Int. recognised for new methods in biol. rsch. Recip., hon. degrees. Address: Rsch. Br.,

Canada Dept. of Agric., Ottawa K1A OC6, Canada.

MIGNOTT, T.G., b. 20 May 1922. Farmer. Educ: Durham Coll. Commerce, 1940-41. Appts: Farmer/Mng. Dir., T.G. Mignott & Son Ltd.; Dir., Whitehall Farms, Ltd.; Dir., Four Paths Housing Dev. Ltd. Mbrships: All Island Jamaica Cane Farmers Assn. Ltd., (Chmn.); Mid-Clarendon Dev. Co-op. Soc. Ltd. (Chmn.); May Pen Area Land Authority (Chmn.); Caribbean Cane Farmers' Assn. (1st. Vice-Chmn.); Farmers Federation (Vice-Chmn.); Sugar Authority & Sugar Rsch. Inst. (Ja); Mid-Clarendon Irrigation Authority. Address: 4 North Ave., KGN 4, Jamaica, W. Indies.

MIHANOVICH, Clement Simon, b. 3 Apr. 1913. Professor of Sociology. Educ: B.S., St. Louis Univ., Mo., 1935; A.M., ibid, 1936, Ph.D., 1939. Appts: Grad. Fellow, St. Louis Univ., 1936-38, Instr., Asst. Prof.-Assoc. Prof., 1938-47, Dir., Dept. of Sociol., 1940-64, Prof., 1947-. Mbrships. incl: Am. Sociol. Assn.; Population Assn. of Am.; AAUP. Publs: Principles of Juvenile Delinquency; Current Social Problems; Marriage & the Family; Social Theorists; Papal Pronoucements on Marriage & Family; European Ec. Community (Co-ed.); Glossary of Sociological Terms. Address: St. Louis University, Dept. of Sociology, 221 N. Grand Blvd., St. Louis, MO 63103, U.S.A. 2, 8, 15.

MIKALOW, Alfred Alexander II, b. 19 Jan. 1921. Professional Commercial Deep Sea Diver & Treasure Hunter; Designer of new Marine Diving Equipment. Educ: Columbia Univ., N.Y., 1 yr.; Univ. of Calif. at Berkeley, 2 yrs.; Masters, Rochdale Univ., Toronto, Canada, 2 yrs.; Rutgers Univ., N.J., 1 yr. Is Pres., Dir., Coastal Schl. of Deep Sea Diving, Inc., Oakland, Calif., 1951-. Mbrships: Pres., Divers Assn. of Am.; V.P., Treasure Recovery Inc.; V.P., Calif. Assn. of Pvte. Educ.; Dir., Medic Alert Fndn.; Authors Guild; Explorers Club of San Fran.; Lions Club; Master Mason, Masonic Order, St. Elmo Lodge 697. Publs: Fells Guide to Sunken Treasure Ships of the World (w. H. Reiseberg); Knight from Maine. Winner, Southern Calif. Spear Fishing Contest, 1952. Address: 320-29th Ave., Oakland, CA 94601, U.S.A. 20, 126.

MIKES, George, b. 15 Feb. 1912. Writer. Educ: Budapest Univ., Hungary. Mbrships: Garrick; Hurlingham; Exec., PEN, 1964-67. Publs. incl: How to Be an Alien; How to Scrape Skies; Down with Everybody; Milk and Honey; Eight Humorists; Uber Alles; Italy for Beginners; Switzerland for Beginners; Not By Sun Alone; The Prophet Motive; Boomerang; The Land of the Rising Yen; Any Souvenirs? The Hungarian Revolution; Humour in Memorium; Mortal Passion; With the Duke of Bedford: Book of Snobs and How to Run a Stately Home. Address: 1 b, Dorncliffe Rd., London SW6, U.K. 1, 3, 128, 131.

MIKHAIL, E.H., b. 29 June 1928. Professor of English. Educ: B.A. (Hons.), Cairo, Egypt; Ph.D., Univ. of Sheffield, U.K. Appts: Lectr. & Asst. Prof. Engl., Cairo, Egypt, 1949-66; Prof. Engl., Univ. of Lethbridge, Alta., 1966-. Mbrships: Int. Assn. for Study of Anglo-Irish Lit.; Canadian Assn. for Irish Studies; Mod. Lang. Assn.; Canadian Assn. Univ. Tchrs.; James Joyce Fndn. Publs. incl: The Social & Cultural Settings of the 1890's, 1969; Sean O'Casey; A Bibliography of Criticism, 1972; A Bibliography of Modern Irish Drama 1899-1970, 1972; Dissertations on Anglo-Irish Drama: A Bibliography of Studies 1870-1970,

1973; The Sting and the Twinkle: Conversations with Sean O'Casey, 1974. Recip. 5 Canada Coun. Rsch. Grants, 1967-71. Address: Dept. of Engl., Univ. of Lethbridge, Lethbridge, Alta., Canada. 30.

MIKULEC, Stjepan, b. 11 Nov. 1916. Civil Engineer; University Professor & Administrator. Educ: Fac. of Technol., Univ. of Zagreb. Appts: Dir., Hydro & Civil Engrng. Dept. of Engergoinvest, Sarajevo, 1955-73; Asst. Prof., Civil Engrng. Fac., Univ. of Sarajevo, 1957, Prof., 1961, Dean, 1967-72; Vice Dir., Inst. of Water Resources Engrng., ibid, 1962-67, 1974-; V.P., Univ. Coun., 1969-. Mbrships. incl: Soc. of Engrs. & Techns, 1948-; Yugoslav Comm. on Large Dams; V.P., ibid. 1960-66, 1970-73, Pres., 1966-70; Speleological Fedn. of Yugoslavia; Pres., ibid, 1962-65; Int. Soc. for Rock Mechs., 1969-. Author & co-author, 3 books, water power dev. & its problems. Var. profl. reports & articles, tech. mags. Recip., hons. inclng. 3 medals, Pres. of Repub. of Yugoslavia, 1949, '54, '58. Address: Obala 12, 71000 Yugoslavia.

MILCU, Stefan-Marius, b. 15 Aug. 1903. Professor. Educ: M.D., Bucharest Univ., Rumania, 1928; D.Med. Sci.; Endocrinologist. Appts: Asst., Inst. Anatomy, Fac. Med., Bucharest, 1927-35; Asst., Clin. Endocrinol., 1935; Lectr.-Prof., Endocrinol., 1943-48; Rector, Med. Inst., Bucharest, 1953-55; Dpty. Dir.-Dir., Inst. Endocrinol., 1946-. Mbrships: Gen. Sec.-V.P., Rumanian Acad. of Sci., 1955-74; Deutsch Akad. Naturforscher Halle; Acad. Tiberina Roma; Polska Acad. Nauk; Bulgarian Akad. Sci.; Hungarian Acad. Sci.; Soc. de Biol. de Paris, France; Royal Soc. Med., London, U.K.; Purkynie Soc. Prague, Czechoslovakia; Int. Soc. Endocrinol. Montreal, Canada. Publs. incl: Endocrine Therapeutics, 1964; Clinical Endocrinology (w. others), 1966; Endemic goiter, 2 vols., 1955, '58; Liver & Hormones, 1967; Genetical Endocrinopathies, 1968; Clinical Andrology, 1970 & num. articles in field. Hons. incl: D.H. Causa, Rennes Univ., France, 1968 & Hungarian Med. Univ., 1969; State Sci. Prize, 1964; Rumanian Repub. Star I Class, 1963. Address: Bd. Aviatori 34, Bucharest, Rumania. 1.

MILER, Joseph S., b. 2 Mar. 1911. Telephone Engineer. Educ. in trng. schls. Mbrships: Past Moderator, Abingdon Presbyter; Past Chmn., Wash. Co. Democratic Comm.; Past Pres., Bristol Scottish-Rite Club; Shriner, Kerabela Temple, Knoxville, Tenn.; 32 deg. Mason, Knoxville Scottish-Rite Bodies. Address: 139 Terrace Dr., Bristol, VA 24201, U.S.A. 22, 114, 125.

MILES, Ferdinand Washington, b. 3 Feb. 1921. Educ: B.S., Univ. of Tenn., Knoxville, 1943; M.S., ibid, 1956; postgrad., Ohio State Univ., Columbus, 1949, Univ. of Tenn., 1957-58, Oak Ridge Schl. of Reactor Technol., Tenn., 1958-60. Appts: Chem. Engr., Tenn. Copper Co., Copperhill, 1943-47; W. Va. Pulp & Paper Co., Covington, 1947; Battelle Mem. Inst., Columbus, Ohio, 1948-52; Chem. (Nuclear) Engr., Oak Ridge Nat. Lab., Tenn., 1952-70; Process Engr., Gen. Elec. Co., Morris, Ill., 1970-71; Nuclear Engr., TVA, Knoxville, 1971-. Mbrships. incl: Am. Chem. Soc., 1943-52; Am. Inst. Chem. Engrs., 1952-; Kappa Alpha Pi; Tau Beta Pi; Phi Kappa Phi. Profl. papers & reporters. Ed., Bldg. 3019 Emergency Manual, for Oak Ridge Nat. Lab. Address: 8212 Corteland Dr., Knoxville, TN 37919, U.S.A. 7, 125.

MILES, John Clayton, b. 5 Mar. 1935. Business Executive. Educ: Assoc. Bus. Deg.,

Kan. City Jr. Coll.; Rockhurst Coll.; Qualified, Securities & Exchange Commn. exam, Mo. & Kan. Securities law exams. Appts: Acctng. Mgr., Hesse Corp., 1965; Controller, Econo-Pak Bus., Forms Inc., 1966; V.P., ibid, 1969; Subsidiary Grp. Controller, Angelica Co., 1971; V.P., Gen. Mgr., Saml. Dodsworth Co., 1972; Pres., ibid, 1973; Mgmt. Staff, Avon Prods., Kan. City, Mo., 1973. Mbrships: Chmn. of Bd., Southeastern Jackson Co. Community Mental Hlth. Ctr.; Advsry. Comm., Exec. Comm., Rsch. Hosp. & Med. Ctr.; Nat. Pres., U.S. JCI Senate; Past Pres., Jaycees, Raytown, Mo.; Past Pres., Kan. City Chapt., Project Concern, Inc.; Boy Scouts of Am. Hons: Disting. Serv. Award, 1967; Citation U.N. Assn. of U.S., 1967; Hon Brother of Koho Tribe, S. Viet Nam, Proj. Concern Recognition, 1967; Mental Hlth. Bell Award, 1971. Address: 9401 Ralston, Kansas City, MO, U.S.A. 117, 130.

MILES, Leland, b. 18 Jan. 1924. University Administrator; Professor of English. Educ: A.B. (cum laude), Juniata Coll., 1946; M.A., ibid, 1947; Ph.D., Univ. of N.C., 1949; Post-doctoral study, Duke Univ., 1949. Appts: Chmn., Engl. Dept., Hanover Coll., Ind., 1949-60; Dir., Engl. Prof., Univ. of Cinn., 1960-63, Prof., 1963-64; Dean, Coll. of Arts & Scis., Univ. of Bridgeport, 1964-67; Pres., Alfred Univ., 1967-74, Univ. of Bridgeport, 1974. Mbrships. incl: MLA; Renaissance Soc. of Am.; Am. Assn. Higher Educ. Publs. incl: John Colet & the Platonic Traditions, 1961; Where Do You Stand on Linguistics?, 1964, 2nd edit., 1968. Articles, essays, reviews, & papers. Contbr., book chapts. Fndr., jrnl., Studies in Burke & His Times, 1967. Recip., acad. hons. Address: Alfred University, Alfred, NY 14802, U.S.A. 2, 13, 30, 57.

MILES, Norman Thomas Graeme, b. 16 June 1932. Local Government Official. Educ: B.Ec., Univ. of Sydney, Australia, 1956; Town Clerk's Cert., 1960. Appts: Economist, Staff of Sir Bertram Stevens, 1956; Rsch. Off., Local Govt. & Shires Assns., N.S.W., 1957; Sec., Local Govt. Assn. of N.S.W. & Shires Assn. of N.S.W., 1966; Sec., Australian Coun. of Local Govt. Assns., 1970. Mbrships: Lib. Bd., N.S.W.; Bush Fire Coun., N.S.W.; Hon. Life Mbr., Past Pres., Warringah Lib.; Royal Inst. of Pub. Admin.; Rotary Club, Sydney; Nat. Fitness Coun., N.S.W.; N.S.W. Film Coun. Author, var. articles & address on local govt. problems. Recip., Town Clerks' Soc. Award, 1959. Address: P.O. Box 1557, Sydney, N.S.W., Australia 2001. 23.

MILES, Richard Donald, b. 4 Dec. 1942. Merchant Banker. Educ: B.A., Univ. of Notre Dame, U.S.A., 1964; M.B.A., Wharton Schl., Univ. of Pa., 1968. Appts: Asst. Sec., Int. Banking Chem. Bank, 1968-71; Assoc., Corporate Finance, Kuhn, Loeb & Co., investment bankers, 1971-72; Gen. Mbr., Merill Lynch-Brown Shipley Bank Ltd., London, U.K., 1972-. Mbrships: Overseas Bankers Club: Roehampton Club. Recip., Joseph Wharton Schlrship, 1967-68. Address: 24 Pembroke Sq., London W. 8, U.K.

MILLAR, Robert Neil, b. 11 Jan. 1921. Chartered Engineer; Company Director. Educ: M.A., Emmanuel Coll., Cambridge Univ., U.K.; B. Com., Univ. of S. Africa. Appts: Engr. Off., Royal Navy, 1941-46; Mech. Engr., British Gen. Elec. Co., S. Africa, 1947-51; Chief Mech. Engr., ibid, Australia, 1952-54; Mgr., Atomic Energy Div., Gen. Elec. Co., U.K., 1955-58; Dir., ibid, 1959-68; Mng. Dir., F & T Inds., Ltd., Melbourne, Australia, 1969-. Mbrships: Melbourne Club; Australian Club; Imperial Serv. Club; Naval & Mil. Club; Royal Sydney Yacht Squadron; Fellow, Inst. of Mech. Engrs. & IEE; C.Eng. Address: 16 Kenley Ct., Toorak, Vic., Australia 3142. 23.

MILLER, Arjay, b. 4 Mar. 1916. Industrial Executive; University Administrator. Educ: B.S., Univ. of Calif. at L.A., 1937. Appts: Tchng. Asst., Univ. of Calif. at Berkeley, 1938-41; Economist, Fed. Reserve Bank, San Francisco, 1941-43; Pvte.-Capt., USAF, 1943-46; Asst. Treas., Ford Motor Co., 1947-53, Controller, 1953-57, V.P., Controller, 1957-61, V.P. Finance, 1961-62, V.P. of Staff Grp., 1962-63, Pres., 1963-68; Dean, Grad. Schl. of Bus., Stanford Univ., Calif., 1969-; Mbr., Bd. of Dirs., Ford Motor Co., Levi Strauss & Co., Utah Int. Inc., Wash. Post Co., Wells Fargo Bank. Mbrships: Am. Econ. Assn.; var. soc. clubs. Hons. incl: LL.D., Univ. of Calif., L.A., 1964, Univ. of Neb., 1965, Whitman Coll., 965; B'nai B'rith Nat. Ind. Ldr. Award, 1968. Address: Stanford University, Graduate School of Business, Stanford, CA 94305, U.S.A. 2, 9.

MILLER, Daniel C., b. 8 July 1915. Lawyer. Educ: LL.B., San Fran. Law Schl. Calif., 1946; J.D., ibid, 1968; Trial Atty. Gen Am. Ins. Cos., Assn. of Defense Counsel 1946-52. Appts: Chief, Legal Dept., Gen. Am. Safeco Ins. Cos., San Fran., Calif., 1946-53; Sr Ptnr., Miller, VanDorn & Bowen, 1953-65 currently and incorporated entity in pvte. prac Mbrships: Am. Bar Assn.; Northern Calif. Assn Defense Counsel; Golden Gate Yacht Club Calif, State & San Fran. Bar Assns.; Surety Claims Assn.; Democrat; Opera Guild; Gtr. San Fran. Chmbr. of Comm. Publs: An Introduction to Contract Bond Claims (Pamphlet) 1961 Preservation of Evidence, 1970; (Pamphlet. Mechanical & Engineering Reconstruction of Evidence in Products & Casualty Cases, 1970 Everyman's Guide to Insurance (in preparation). Patentee, jack for raising motor vehicle. Address: Ste. 518, 465 California St. San Francisco, CA 94104, U.S.A. 9.

MILLER, Donald George, b. 30 Oct. 1909 Clergyman; Educator. Educ: A.B., Greenville Coll., 1930; S.T.B., 1933, S.T.M., 1934, N.Y Theol. Sem.; M.A., 1934, Ph.D., 1935, N.Y Univ.; Postdoctoral study, Montpellier, France & Basle, Switzerland. Appts: Tchr., Bible Engl. Pyongyang For. Schl., Korea, 1935-37 Instr., N.Y. Theol. Sem., 1937-38; Pastor Highland Presby. Ch., Street, Md., 1939-41 Asst. Pastor, Highland Park Presby. Ch., Dallas Tex., 1941-43; Walter H. Robertson Prof. of New Testament, Union Theol. Sem. Richmond, Va., 1943-62; Pres., Pitts. Theol Sem., Pa., 1962-70; Pastor, Presby. Ch. Laurinburg, N.C., 1970-. Mbrships: Soc. of Biblical Lit. & Exegesis; Rotary Club. Publs incl: Conqueror in Chains: A Story of the Apostle Paul; The Way to Biblical Preaching The Authority of the Bible. Contbr. to num. periodicals, encys. Hons: Disting. Alumnus Award, Greenville Coll., 1970. Address: Box 862, Laurinburg, NC, U.S.A. 3, 30, 126, 130 139.

MILLER, Donald Richard, b. 30 June 1925 Animal Sculptor. Educ: Grad., Dayton Ar Inst., Ohio, 1951; Atelier Schlrship., ibid 1951-52; Pratt Inst., Bklyn., N.Y., night schl 1955-57; Art Student's League of N.Y., nigh schl., 1957-61; apprenticeship under Ulysses A Ricci, 1956-60. Appts: Studio Asst. to Wm Zorach (Sculptural Relief, Mayo Clin. Rochester, Minn., 1952), Joseph Kiselewski (Relief, Fed. Ct. House, Bklyn., 1961), Wheeler Williams (Mem. Fountain, Kan. City, Mo. 1961), Marshall Fredericks (War Mem. Cleveland, Ohio, 1963), & Julian Harris (Relief.

for Reptile House, Grant Pk. Zoo, Atlanta, Ga., 1964); Instr. in Sculpture, Fashion Inst. of Technol., N.Y.C., 1972-. Works incl: Abstract Torso (Permanent Collect., Dayton art Inst., Ohio), 1954; Pumpkinseed (collect., Wm. A. Farnsworth Art Mus., Rockland, Me.), 1972; 2 Gargoyles for Wash. Cathedral, D.C., 1960; Relief of nocturnal animals for Small Mammals House, Phila. Zool. Gdns., Pa., 1973; 2 Reliefs for aquarium, Cinn. Zool. Soc., in progress; series of 20 medallions for Ducks Unlimited, in progress. Mbrships. incl: Fellow, Nat. Sculpture Soc. & Am. Artists Profl. League; Soc. of Animal Artists. Recip. num. awards for work inclng: Mrs. J. Newington Award, Hudson Valley Art Assn., 1970; Award for Sculpture, Acad. Artists of Springfield, Mass., 1971. Address: 900 Riverside Dr., N.Y., NY 10032, U.S.A. 37.

MILLER, (Mrs.) Elizabeth Jane Barker, b. 24 Aug. 1936. B.S. (magna cum laude) Newberry Coll., S.C., 1959; grad. study, Rollins Coll., Winter Park, Fla., Fla. Inst. Continuing Studies, Tallahassee, Univ. of S.C., Columbia, S.C. State Coll., Orangeburg. Appts: Tchr., Lexington Elem. Schl., S.C., 1959, Springfield Elem. Schl.. Ga.. Park Ave. Elem. Schl., Winter Park, Fla., Allendale-Fairfax H.S., Fairfax, S.C. Bamberg-Ehrhardt H.S., Bamberg, S.C.; Chmn., Dept. of Soc. Studies, Andrew Jackson Acad., Ehrhardt, S.C. Mbrships. incl: U.S. Daughters of 1812; Nat. Histn., ibid, 1973-76; DAR; Delta Kappa Gamma; S.C. Histl. Soc.; Dixie Gdn. Club; Bamberg Am. Legion Auxiliary. Contbr., Sandlapper Mag. Hons. incl: Merit Tchr. Award, Fla., 1963; Star Tchr. Award, S.C., 1971. Address: P.O. Box 37, Ehrhardt, SC 29081, U.S.A. 5, 125.

MILLER, Elva Ruby, (Mrs.). b. 5 Oct. 1907. Educ: College, for 2 yrs.; Pvte. Mus. Study. Cinema Circulus, Univ. of S. Calif.; L.A. Philharmonic Symph. Assn.; Town Hall, 523 W. 6th, L.A.; Calif. Republican Assembly, Griffith Park Hills Univ. Hons. incl: Nomination Award, Nat. Assn. of Recording Arts & Scis. for Hit Album: Mrs. Millers Greatest Hits, 1966; House of Sight & Sound L.A., Calif. for contbr. to Am. Mus. on recordings & radio. Address: 4411 Los Feliz, Los Angeles, CA 90027, U.S.A.

MILLER, Eugene, b. 6 Oct. 1925. Financial Executive. Educ: B.S., Ga. Inst. of Technol., 1945; A.B., Bethany Coll., 1947; M.S., Columbia Univ., 1948; Dip., Oxford Univ., U.K', M.B.A., N.Y. Univ., U.S.A., 1959; LL.D., Bethany Coll., 1969. Appts. incl: Reporter, Greensboro Daily News, N.C., 1948-52; Regional Ed., Bus. Week, Houston, Tex., 1952-54; Asst. Mng. Ed., ibid, 1954-60; V.P., McGraw-Hill, Inc., 1960-68; Sr. V.P., N.Y. Stock Exchange, 1968-73; Sr. V.P., CNA Financial Corp., 1973-. Mbrships. incl: Am. Econs. Assn.; Fndr., Soc. of Am. Bus. Writers; Newcomen Soc.; Alpha Sigma Phi. Publs. incl: Your Career In Securities; many mag. articles. Hons. incl: Adjunct Prof., N.Y. Univ. & Fordham Univ.; Jrnlsm. Award, Columbia Univ., 1962. Address: 310 S. Michigan Ave., Chicago, IL 60010, U.S.A. 2, 16.

MILLER, George William, b. 10 May 1926. Baptist Minister. Educ: B.A., Samford Univ., Birmingham, Ala., 1951; B.D., Southern Bapt. Theol. Sem., 1955; M.Theol., 1956; Cert., Clin. Pastoral Trng., Ga. Bapt. Hosp., Atlanta, 1958; D.Theol., Luther Rice Sem., Jacksonville, Fla., 1970. Appts: Pastor, Cave Springs Bapt. Ch., Attalla, Ala., 1949-51; Mill Creek Bapt. Ch., Bardstown, Ky., 1952-56; West End Bapt. Ch., Gadsden, Ala., 1956-58; Chap., Western Bapt. Hosp., Pudacah, Ky., 1958-62; Sr. Chap. & Dir., Pastoral Care, Bapt. Hosp., Miami, Fla., 1962-;

Adj. Prof., Theol. & Pastoral Care, Luther Rice Sem., Jacksonville, 1970-. Fellow, Am. Coll. Chaps. Mbrships. incl: Fndng. Mbr., Assn. of Clin. Pastoral Educ.; Past Pres., Southern Bapt. Assn. of Hosp. Chaps. Author, Moral & Ethical Implications of Human Organ Transplants, 1971. Contbr. to mags. & newspapers. Address: Bapt. Hosp. of Miami Inc., 8900 S.W. 88th St., Miami, FL 33156, U.S.A.

MILLER, Grace Eleanor Bruno, b. 5 Oct. 1910. Social Worker. Educ: Grad., Dental Assts. Trng. Inst. Appts: Dental Asst., N.J. & Tex., 1936-45; Tchr., Clubwork Course, Evening Div., Polk Community Coll., Winter Haven, Fla., 1972. Mbrships: Fndr. & 1st Pres., Histl. Soc. of Winter Haven; Youth & Educ. Chmn., Advt. Fedn. of St. Petersburg, Fla.; Publicity Chmn., Suncoast Parliamentary Serv. Unit, St. Petersburg; Chmn. Reading Grp., St. Petersburg Woman's Club; Epsilon Sigma Omicron. active soc. wkr., Den Mother, Cub Scouts, St. Petersburg; currently w. Winter Haven Woman's Club, & Histl. Soc. of Winter Haven. Address: 2170-25th Ave. N., St. Petersburg, FL 33713, U.S.A. 57.

MILLER, Harry George. Educationalist. Educ: Univ. of Stockholm, 1961-62; B.A., Carroll Coll., Waukesha, Wisconsin, 1963; M.E., Univ. of Nebraska, 1967; Ed.D., ibid, 1970. Appts. incl: Asst. Prof., Dept. of Secondary Educ., S.Ill. Univ., Carbondale, 1971; Dir., Studies in Adult Educ., Coll. of Educ., ibid, 1972; Acting Chairperson & Assoc. Prof. Dept. of Secondary Educ., 1973; Dir. of num. Workshops; Cons. to var. educational establishments. Mbrships: Ill. Prins. Assn.; Phi Delta Kappa; Pub. Servs. Comm., Mid-Am. Community Educ. Assn.; Pub. Adult & Continuing Educators Assn.; Kappa Delta Pi; S.Ill. Roundtable of Adult Educ.; num. comms. of S.Ill. Univ. of Publs: A Course in American Government, 1969; (w. S.M. Vinocur) A Method for Clarifying Value Statements in the Soc. Studies Classroom; (W. N.Wika) Opinions of High School Students on Factors in Home & School Environment Related to Personal Development, 1969; (w. L.J. Dennis) Strong Confrontation as an Educational Technique, 1971. Contbr. to num. profl. jrnls. Address: 2020 Norwood Drive, Carbondale, IL 62901, U.S.A.

MILLER, Harvey S., b. 13 Nov. 1917. Company President & Welding Engineer. Appts. incl: Time Study Engr. on Welding, Bethlehem Steel Co., 1941-42; Lt. (Sr.), USNR, 1942-45; Foreman & Welding Engr., Back Bay Welding Co., 1945-50; Pres. & Welding Engr., New England Hard Facing Co., Inc., 1950; Pres. & Sales Engr., Nenfco Alloys & Equipment, Inc., 1960-. Mbrships: Rear Commodore, Charlesgate Yacht Club; Past Pres., Archts. & Engrs. Lodge; Rotary Club, Brookline. Author of var. articles in Am. Welding Soc. Handbook, & other tech. papers. Address: 63 Maplewood Ave., Newton Ctr., MA 02159, U.S.A. 6.

MILLER, Helena A., b. 25 Apr. 1913. Professor. Educ: B.A., Ohio State Univ., 1935; B.Sc., ibid, 1935; M.S., 1938; Ph.D., Harvard Univ. & Radcliffe Coll., 1945. Appts. incl: Instr., Botany, Conn. Coll. for Women, New London, 1944-45 & Wellesley Coll., 1945-48; Assoc. Prof.-Prof., Bio., Duquesne Univ., Pitts., Pa., 1948-; Asst. to Dean, title now Asst. Dean Acad. Advisement, Coll. Arts & Scis., ibid, 1966-. Mbrships. incl: Int. Assn. for Plant Taxonomy; Int. Assn. Plant Morphols.; Am. Assn. Univ. Adminstrs.; AAAS; Assn. of Am. Med. Colls.; Am. Inst. of Biol. Scis.; Bot. Soc. of Am.; Soc. for Dev. Bio. Contbr. to profl. publs. hons. incl: Woman of Yr. for Pitts. Area.,

Sigma Lambda Phi, 1959; 1st Lady of Day, radio WRYT, Pitts., 1962. Address: c/o Duquesne Univ., Pittsburgh, PA 15219, U.S.A. 5, 6, 14, 15, 50, 57, 128, 130, 132.

MILLER, Henry (George), b. 13 Dec. 1913. University Vice-Chancellor; Neurological Physician. Educ: M.B., B.S., Univ. of Durham, U.K., 1937; M.D., 1940. Appts. incl: Neuropsych. Specialist, RAF Med. Serv., 1942-46; Hammersmith Hosp. & Nat. Hosp., Queen Square, 1946-47; Asst. Physn., Royal Victoria Infirmary, Newcastle upon Tyne, 1947-64; Hon. Cons. Neurol., ibid, 1968-; Prof. of Neurol., 1964-68; Dean of Med., 1966-68; V. Chancellor, Univ. of Newcastle upon Tyne, 1968-. Fellow, Royal Coll. Physns. Mbrships: Assn. of Physns. of Gt. Britain & Ireland; Hon. For. Mbr., French Soc. of Neurol. Publs: Early Diagnosis, 1961; Modern Medical Treatment, 1963; Medicine & Society, 1973; Jt. Ed., Progress in Clinical Medicine, 1971 & Diseases of the Nervous System, 1972. Address: Vice-Chancellor's Lodge, Adderstone Cres., Newcastle upon Tyne NE2 2HH, U.K. 1, 128.

MILLER, Jack Elius, b. 7 Mar. 1918. Physician. Educ: Glasgow Univ., U.K.; M.R.C.G.P. Appts: House Surg., Kilmarnock Infirmary, Ayrshire, U.K., 1943; Capt., Royal Army Med. Corps., 1943-46; Chmn., Bd. Mgmt., Scottish Physiotherapy Hosp., 1958-71. Mbrships: Chmn., Glasgow Marriage Guidance Coun., 1956-61; Hon. V.P., ibid, 1966-; Hon. V.P., Scottish Marriage Guidance Coun., 1967-; Chmn., Glasgow local med. comm., 1964-66; Scottish Race Rels. Bd., 1967-72; Chmn., Scottish Gen. Med. Servs. Comm., 1969-72; Coun., Brit. Med. Assn., 1964-; Fellow, Royal Soc. Med., Brit. Med. Assn.; J.P., City of Glasgow; Chmn., Assn. Jewish Ex-Servicemen & Women of Scotland, 1952-61, '64-68; Hon. Pres., ibid, 1968-; Pres., Glasgow Jewish Representative Coun., 1971-; Treas., Brit. Med. Assn., 1972-. Ed., Doctors' Handbook, 1963, '72. Address: 158 Hyndland Rd., Glasgow G12 9HY, U.K.

MILLER, Jeanne-Marie Anderson (Mrs. Nathan J. Miller), b. 18 Feb. 1937. Educator. Educ: B.A., Howard Univ., 1959; M.A., 1963. Appts: Instr., Engl., Howard Univ., 1963-; Asst. Dir., Inst. for Arts & the Humanities, ibid, 1973-. Mbrships. incl: Am. Theatre Assn.; MLA; Coll. Lang. Assn.; Am. Studies Assn.; Coll. Engl. Assn.; Nat. Coun. of Tchrs. of Engl.; S. Atlantic MLA; Am. Acad. of Pol. & Soc. Sci.; AAUP; AAUW; Am. Civil Liberties Union; Assoc., Nat. Archives. contbr. to publs. in field. Hons: Adv. Study Fellowship, Ford Fndn., 1970-71, 71-72, 72-73; Fellow, Southern Fellowships Fund, 1972-73, 73-74; Amiri Baraka Award for Theatre Critism, 1972. Address: 1101 3rd St., S.W., Apt. 701, Washington, DC 20024, U.S.A. 5, 13, 57, 129, 130, 138.

MILLER, Joan Ann Glenck (Mrs. William R. Miller), b. 9 Mar. 1941. Information Specialist; Library Administrator. Educ: B.A., SUNY, Albany, N.Y., 1963; M.L.S., ibid, 1964; Post-Mstr.'s work at SUNY, Albany & Rensselaer Polytech. Inst., Troy, NY (RPI) in Lib. Admin., Med. Libnship. & Computer Applications in Lib. Sci. Appts. incl: Rsch. Libn., Character Rsch. Proj., Union Coll., Schenectady, N.Y., 1963-64; Ref. & Circulation Libn., Albany Med. Ctr., Albany, N.Y., 1964; Ref. Libn., SUNY, Albany, Hawley Lib., 1964; Sr. Med. Libn., N.Y. State Med. Lib., N.Y. State Educ. Dept., Albany, N.Y., 1964-68; Assoc. in Instructional Materials in Handicapped Children, N.Y. Special Educ. Instructional Materials Ctr., N.Y. State Educ.

Dept., Albany, N.Y., 1968-72; Assoc. In. Info. Retrieval & Dissemination, NYSEIMC, NYSED, Albany & Admin. Asst., 1972-; Cons. to var. state & local agcys. in area of info. servs., rsch., collection mgmt. for special educ. Mbrships: Coun. for Exceptional Children; N.Y. Lib. Assn.; Assn. for Educl. Communication & Technol.; Med. Lib. Assn.; Upstate N.Y. Chapt., ibid. Publs. incl: profl. reports, articles & num. contbns. in profl. jrnls. Address: 6 Woodridge Ct., Ballston Lake, NY 12019, U.S.A. 5, 6, 42.

MILLER, Joel Robert, b. 22 May 1944. Psychologist. Educ: B.A., Nathaniel Hawthorne Coll., Antrim, N.H., 1967; M.S., Kan. State Coll., 1969; advanced grad. study, Glassboro State Coll., 1970-71. Appts. incl: Psychol. Cons., Cumberland Co. Drug Abuse Clinic, N.J', 1970-72; Staff Clinical Psychologist, Vineland Guidance Ctr., N.J., 1970-72; Chief Psychol. Cons., Rehab. Ctr. Org., Atlantic City, N.J., 1971-73; Assoc. Dir., New Schl. of Psychotherapy, Wash. D.C., 1972-73; Chief Clinical Psychologist, White House Special Action Off. for Drug Abuse Prevention, Div. of the Exec. Off. of the Pres., Wash. D.C., 1972-73. Mbrships: Am. Assn. of Mental Deficiency; Nat. Assn. Schl. Psychologists. Publs: Reduction of Maladaptive Behaviour in a Mentally Retarded Girl; Abnormal Psychology & Modern Life, 4th edit., 1972. Recip., Legion of Honour, Chapel of Four Chaps., Phila., Pa., 1973. Address: 992 E. End, Woodmere, NY 11598, U.S.A. 6.

MILLER, John Peter (Jack), b. 3 Aug. 1928. Journalist. Educ: Welland & Toronto, Ont., Canada. Appts: Sports Ed.-Front Page Ed., Evening Tribune, Welland, Ont., 1948-53; City Hall Reporter—Columnist & Radio TV Ed., on Spectator, Hamilton, Ont., 1953-71; Radio-TV Critic, on Toronto Star, 1971; sr. broadcast critic, Canadian nat. daily newspapers. Mbr., Sigma Delta Chi. Hons: Named leading daily columnist (all categories) in Western Ontario Newspaper Awards, 1968. Address: 44 Charles St.W., Apt. 4703, Toronto, Ont., Canada. 6.

MILLER, Joseph Irwin, b. 26 May 1909. Manufacturer. Educ: B.A., Yale Univ., 1931; M.A., Balliol Coll., Oxford Univ., 1933. Appts: Chmn. of Bd., Cummins Engine Co., Inc., Columbus, Ind.; Chmn. of Bd., Irwin Union Bank & Trust Co., Columbus; Dir., Am. Telephone & Telegraph. Mbrships: Royal Soc. of Arts, London; Exec. Comm., Commn. of Chs. on Int. Affairs, World Coun. of Chs.; Pres., Nat. Coun. of Chs., 1960-63; Exec. Comm. of Ctrl. Comm., World Coun. of Chs.; 1961-68; Fellow, Yale Corp.; Trustee, Ford Fndn., Mus. of Mod. Art, Urban Inst.; Chmn., Special Comm., U.S. Trade w. E. European Countries & Soviet Union, 1965; Chmn., Nat. Advsry. Commn. on Hlth. Manpower, 1966-67; Pres.'s Comm. on Urban Housing, 1967-68; UN Comm. on Multinat. Corps., 1973-74. Address: 301 Washington St., Columbus, IN 47201, U.S.A. 2, 11, 128.

MILLER, Kenneth M., b. 20 Nov. 1921. Electronics Industry Executive. Educ: Ill. Inst., Technol., 1940-41; UCLA, 1961; IBM Exec. Computer Course. Appts. incl: Gen. Mgr., Metrics Div., Singer Co., Bridgeport, Conn. & L.A., Calif., 1962-65; V.P. & Gen. Mgr., Lear Jet Inds. Inc., Detroit, Mich. & Wichita, Kan., 1965-66; Pres. & Dir., Infonics Inc., L.A. 1967-68; V.P. & Gen. Mgr., Computer Inds. Inc., Van Buys, 1968-69; Pres. & Gen. Mgr., Wilcox Elec. Inc., Kan. City, Mo.; V.P. & Dir., World Wide Wilcox Inc., McLean, Va., 1969-72; Pres., Chief Exec., Officer & Dir., Penril Data Communications Inc., Rockville, Md., 1973-.

Mbrships: incl: Sr., IEEE; Sr., Instrument Soc. Am.; AOPA; AMA; AFCEA; ARRL; NAA; SNDT; SEA; AIAA; AFA. Address: 16904 George Washington Dr., Rockville, MD 20853, U.S.A. 6, 8, 9, 14, 16, 128.

MILLER, Lee, b. 14 Oct. 1940. Syndicated broadcaster, Columnist, Author & Platform personality. Educ: B.S., Berry Coll., Mt. Berry, Ga., Univ. of Ga. & Florence Univ., Ala.; Dale Carnegie Ldrship. Prog.; Dale Carnegie Sales Progs.; Sci. of Personal Achievement, Napoleon Hill Acad. Appts: News Dir., WOWL TV, Florence Ala., WMSL TV, Huntsville, Ala. & KFWT TV, Dallas-Ft. Worth, Tex.; Prog. Dir., KWXI Radio; Pres., ITH Prods., Inc.; Anchorman & Prod., KMID, Midland, Tex.; Gen. Mgr., WTHO, Thomson, Ga. Mbrships: Rotary; Sec., Kiwanis; Lions. Publs: Inside the Husk; Be Gentle with Yourself. Radio show, Inside the Husk, syndicated on 127 radio stns. in U.S.A. Contbr. to var. progs. & Mags. Recip., Kiwanis Int. Disting. Serv. Award. Address: 1701 Johnston Ct., Anniston, AL 36201, U.S.A. 57.

MILLER, Louis, b. 9 Apr. 1917. Psychiatrist; Public Health Administrator. Educ: Specialist in Psych. & Pub. Hlth., Univ. of Cape Town, S. Africa, 1934-39. Appts: Army Psych., 6th S. African Div., Egypt, 1943, 7th Base Psych. Ctr., Italy, 1944-45; Chief Psych., Israel Defence Army & Air Force, 1948-49; Dir., Mental Hlth., Israel Min. of Hlth., 1949-54, 1959-69, Chief Nat. Psych., 1969-; Dir., Pub. Hlth. Servs., Hadassah Jerusalem Region, 1954-59. Exec. Mbr., int. med. orgs. Publs: Mental Health in Rapid Social Change (Ed.), 1972; 3 books in press, (Ed. or Jt. Ed.); var. short publs. Ed. Bd. Mbr., Israel Annals of Psychiatry (jrnl.); Ed.-in-Chief, jrnl., Mental Health & Society. Address: Rav Berlin 47, Jerusalem, Israel. 94.

MILLER, Mary Frances, b. 11 June 1919. Automobile Accountant. Educ: Victoris Jr. Coll. Appts: Off. Mgr., Navarra Motors, Key West, Fla., Peebles Motor Co., S. Norfolk, Va., Canada Dry Bottling Co., New London, Conn., Grippo Motor Co., ibid, Snelling Motor Co., Houston, Tex.; Bus. Mgr., Pores', Inc., Ft. Pierce, Fla., Taylor Buick Co., ibid, Dave Snelling Lincoln Mercury, Inc., Houston; Sec.-Treas., Leo Jarnagin Pontiac Co., ibid. Hons. incl: 1st Prize, Automobile Acctng., Ford Motor Co., Gen. Motors Corp., Chrysler Corp., & Am. Motors; Hon. Degree, Colo. Christian Coll. Address: 8354 Ruthby, Houston, TX 7701, U.S.A. 5, 7, 130, 132.

MILLER, Max. b. 28 Jan. 1911. Physician. Engaged in pvte. prac. med. (cardiol.)' N.Y.C., 1940-; Asscod. w. Beth David Hosp., N.Y., 1937-; Dir., Cardiol., 1958-; Pres., Med. Bd., Traf. Hosp., 1964-66; Assoc. Attng. Physn., Lincoln Hosp., N.Y.C.; Instr., 1946-58, Asst. Clin. Prof., 1958-65, N.Y. UNiv. çCons., Mary Manning Walsh Home, N.Y.C., 1955-, etc. Author of num. publs. in var. med. jrnls. Address: 829 Park Ave., N.Y', ,NY 10021, U.S.A. 6.

MILLER, (Max) Cameron, b. 1 Oct. 1908. Author; Actor. Appts. incl: Actor, tours in U.K., 1928-33 & Oxford Repertory, Croydon Repertory & Community Theatres, U.K., 1934-41; Staff Off., U.K', N. Africa & Entertainment Off., Orion, en route to Africa, Army, 1941-45; Dir., Repertory theatre, Leicester, U.K.; BBC Schls. Dept., 1950-63; Actor in Spring 1600 for Emlyn Williams, Exercise Bowler, (Arts & Scala) & in many TV, Stage & Radio prods. Author of Lights That Go Out, 3 act play which toured in 1932, sev. 1 act

plays, radio scripts & a book of reminiscences of touring days in the 30's. Mbrships: BBC Club; Westcliff Cine Club. Address: Graystone, 162 Thundersley Park Rd., Benfleet, Essex SS7 1EN, U.K. 3.

MILLER, Meta Helena, b. 29 Jan. 1897. Professor of Romance Languages (retired)' Educ: A.B., Goucher Coll., 1917; A.M., Ph.D., Johns Hopkins Univ., 1918-22. Appts. incl: Asst. Prof.-Prof. of Romance Languages, Univ. of N.C., Greensboro, 1922-66; Acting Hd.-Hd., Dept. of Romance Languages, ibid, 1953-62; Prof. Emeritus, 1966-. Mbrships. incl: Mod. Lang. Assn.; Am. Archaeological Soc.; World Federalists; Alliance Française; Luth. Acad. of Schlrship.; Kappa Kappa Gamma; Alpha Delta Pi; Tau Psi Omega. Publs: Chateaubriand and English Literature, 1925; Les Natchez (co-author), 1932; French Review Grammar (co-author), 1945. Address: 1908 Walker Ave., Greensboro, NC 27403, U.S.A. 13.

MILLER, Minos D., Jr., b. 9 Sept. 1920. Judge. Educ: B.S., J.D., La. State Univ., 1947; Admitted to La. Bar, 1947. Appts: Atty.-at-Law, Adams & Miller, 1947-53; Judge, 31st Judicial DIst. Ct. of La., 1953-69; Judge, Ct. of Appeal, 3rd Circuit, State of La., 1969-; Served to Lt., USNR., 1941-46. Mbrships. incl: Am., La., S.W.La., Jefferson Davis Parish Bar Assns.; La. Dist. Judges Assn. (past pres.); Am. Judicature Soc.; Am. Legion; Judicial Coun. of La.; Phi Delta Phi; Omicron Delta Kappa; Phi Eta Sigma; Lambda Chi Alpha. Decorated Purple Heart. Address: P.O. Drawer 1309, Jennings, LA 70546, U.S.A. 7.

MILLER, Nels A., b. 26 May 1910. Industrial Designer. Educ: Art Students League, N.Y.C., 1924-26; Cornell Univ., Ithaca, N.Y., 1926-27; Am. Acad. of Art, Chgo., Ill., 1927-29; B.A., Schl. of Design, Chgo., 1943-44; M.A., Univ. of Chgo., 1966. Appts: Furniture Designer, Johnson Chair Co., Chgo., 1929-36; Cons. Designer, Remington Rand, Lib. Bur. Div., 1931-36 & Marshall Field & Co., 1932-36; Ind. Designer, H.T. Roberts Co., 1936-37, & J.P. Seeburg Corp., 1937-56; Cons. Designer, 1956-59; Cabinet Design Supvsr., Hammond Organ Co., 1959-72; Design Cons., ibid, 1972-. Mbrships: Am. Inst. of Mgmt.; Am. Mgmt. Assn.; AAAS; Soc. of Plastics Engrs.; Am. Ordnance Assn.; Am. Craftsmen's Coun. Contbr. articles to mags. Hons: Obelisk, Organ Class, Mahogany Award Competition, 1961, 62, & 63. Address: 262 S. Marion St., Oak Park, IL 60302, U.S.A. 8, 16, 22, 57, 120, 128, 131.

MILLER, O. Neal, b. 5 Feb. 1919. Biochemist; Nutritionist. Educ: B.S., Univ. of Mo., U.S.A., 1941; Ph.D., Harvard Univ., 1950; M.A., Univ. of Mo., 1972. Appts. incl: Asst. Prof.—Assoc. Prof. of Biochem. & Med., Schl. of Med., Tulane Univ., New Orleans, La., 1953-60; Prof. of Biochem., ibid, 1960-68; Cons., Rsch. & Med. Admin., WHO for Med. Educ., India, 1967; Dir., Dept. of Biochem. Nutrition, Hoffmann-La Roche Inc., Nutley, N.J., 1968-; Assoc. Dir. of Biological Rsch., ibid, 1970-. Mbrships. incl: Treas., Am. Soc. for Clin. Nutrition; Fellow, AAAS; Am. Soc. of Biological Chems.; Am. Inst. of Nutrition; Fellow, Southern Soc. for Clin. Rsch.; Soc. of Experimental Biol. & Med.; Food Ind. Liaison Comm., Am. Med. Assn.; Pres., Sigma Xi, 1962. Publs: Author or co-author, 100 contbns. to profl. jrnls., books, & conf. proceedings; Over 100 abstracts. Address: Hoffmann-La Roche Inc., 340 Kingsland St., Nutley, NJ 07110, U.S.A.

MILLER, Orville Crowder, b. 16 August 1897. Educator, Clergyman, Poet, Editor,

Executive. Educ: B.A., Indiana Univ.; M.A., Univ. of Mich.; Litt.D., Free Univ. of Asia; Post-grad., Univ. of Wis., Columbia Univ., Northwestern Univ. Positions held: Educator, Univ. of Pacific, Univ. of Mich., Vanderbilt Univ. Purdue Univ., 1917-45; local Clergyman or State Stewardship Evangelist, Tenn., Ind., Ill., 1942-63; Ed. & Exec. of following since 1963: World Poetry Soc. Intercontinental (Pan-continental Exec. Chancellor & Am. Hemisphere Ed. of its monthly jrnl., Poet); Chancellor for the Americas, Cosmosynthesis League; Hon. Poet Laureate, Ed., United Poets Laureate Int.; Int. Exec. Comm., Centro Studi e Scambi Int.; Corresp., Accad. Leonardo da Vinci & Poesie Vivante; Cornucopia Columnist, Poets Corner; Int. Poets Shrine, etc. Most recent publications incl: Ed., Abraham Lincoln, A Biographic Trilogy in Sonnet Sequences, 3 vols. containing 688 pp., 473 continuity Petrarchan sonnets, w. extensive illustration, annotations & indices, which work has received awards from four continents, 1965; author of Treasured Legacy, 1966; Light Uplift Loaves, 1969. Collections of his poems pub. in five continents and in numerous jrnls. Hons. incl: Int.Gold Medallion & Laurel Wreath, Philippine Pres. Marcos; Karta of Award as Hon. Poet Laureate-Ed. and Distinguished Lyric Poet, United Poets Laureate Int.; Disting. Ed. Service Citation, World Poetry Soc. Intercontinental; Leonardo da Vinci Award for his sonnet, Tree of Paradise. Address: 7 Montclair Rd., Urbana, IL 61801, U.S.A.

MILLER, Pamela Joyce Larayne, b. 11 Nov. 1948. Optometrist. Educ: B.S., Univ. of Redlands, Calif., U.S.A. 1969; B.S., Southern Calif. Coll. of Optometry, 1972; Doctorate of Optometry, ibid, 1973. Pvte. Prac., Optometrist, San Bernardino, Calif., 1973-. Num. mbrships. incl: Calif. Optometric Assn.; Am. Optometric Assn.; L.A. Co. Optometric Soc.; Mensa; Coll. of Optometrists in Vision Dev.; Am. Pub. Hlth. Assn.; DAR; Nat. Histl. Soc.; Nat. Forensic League; Omega Epsilon Phi; Alpha Sigma Pi; Theta Alpha Phi. Publs: Articles in profl. jrnls. Appearances: TV, 1963; 52 radio shows, KCVR Radio, 1964-66. Hons. incl: 5 awards for merit, Nat. Forensic League, 1963-66; 100 Hour Serv. Award, Candystriper, 1966; Outstanding Actress in Radio, 1966; 1st place, Citrus Belt Speech Region Forum in Debate, 1966. Address: 3621 Valencia Ave., San Bernardino, CA 92404, U.S.A.

MILLER, Paul Ingersoll, b. 7 Nov. 1902. Professor. Educ: B.A., Huntington Coll., Ind., U.S.A., 1926; M.A., Univ. of Mich., 1929; Ph.D., Ohio State Univ., Columbus, 1933. Appts: Tchr. in high schls., 1926-30 & 34-35; Asst., Hist. Dept., Ohio State Univ., 1930-33; Tchr., Miami Univ., summer 1934; Asst. Prof., Hist., Battle Creek Coll., 1935-38, Pa. State, 1938-40 & Dickinson Coll., 1940-42; Prof., Wm. Penn Coll., 1942-47; Prof. & Chmn., Hiram Coll., 1947-71; Emeritus Prof., ibid, 1971-; Legislative Sec., Friends Comm. on Nat. Legislation, 1954; Fulbright Lectr., Univ. of Ceylon, Peradeniya, 1957-58 & 61-62; Co-Dir., Friends Ctr., New Delhi, India, 1964-66. Mbrships: Am. Hist. Assn.; Org. of Am. Hist.; Ohio Acad. of Hist. AAUP. Hons: Hiram Coll. Alumni Award for Disting. Serv., 1971; Disting. Serv. Award, Ohio Acad. of Hist., 1972. Address: 17320 Quaker Lane, B 13, Sandy Spring, MD 20860, U.S.A. 13.

MILLER, Philip Francis, b. 27 Apr. 1921. Mechanical Engineer. Educ: Columbia Univ., N.Y., U.S.A., 1941-46; CCNY, 1946-48. Appts: Sec. & Treas., Henry Miller Inds., Inc., 1944-; Pres., Kraftware Corp., 1947-; Pres., N. Am. Plastics Corp., 1952-60; Exec. Dir., Iroquois

Brewing Co., 1965-70; Exec. Dir., Angastura Wuppermann Corp., 1969-; Exec. Dir., Schiff Vitamin & Hlth. Foods, 1969-; Exec. Dir., Leeds Dixon Corp., 1969-; Exec. Dir., Compretec Corp., 1967-72; Exec. Dir., Eagle Lock Corp., 1970-71; Exec. Dir., Champale Corp., 1973-. Mbrships. incl: Premium Club of Am.; Furniture Club of Am.; Housewares Club; Northwood Investment Club; N.Y. Beef Cattlesmen Assn.; 225 Fifth Ave. Club; Pres., Northwood Civic Assn. Holder, Patent for Heat Dissipating Tube Shield. Helped develop first Bazooka gun; Developed Jell Gas Fuse during WWII. Address: 20 Beechwood Rd., Roslyn, NY 11576, U.S.A.

MILLER, (Rev.) Randolph Crump, b. 1 Oct. 1910. Episcopal Clergyman; Seminary Professor. Educ: B.A., Pomona Coll., 1931; Ph.D., Yale, 1936. Appts. incl: Tchr., philos. of relig. & Christian educ., Ch. Divinity Schl. of the Pacific, 1936-52; Prof., Christian Educ., Yale, 1952-64; Horace Bushnell Prof., Christian Nurture, ibid, 1964-; Dir., Christian Educ., St. Paul's, New Haven, Conn., 1956-58, Trinity, New Haven, 1961-71; Ed., Religious Educ., 1958-; Vis. Prof., var. colls. & Univs., 1954-72. Mbr., Religious Educ. Assn. Publs. incl: The Language Gap & God, 1970; Living with Anxiety, 1971; Live Until You Die, 1973; The American Spirit in Theology, 1974. Hons: S.T.D., Ch. Divinity Schl. of the Pacific, 1952; D.D., Pacific Schl. of Relig., 1952; D.D., Episcopal Theological Schl., 1961. Address: 15 Edgehill Rd., New Haven, CT 06511, U.S.A. 2.

MILLER, Robert Cunningham, b. 3 July 1899. Biologist; Oceanographer; Association Executive. Educ: A.B., Greenville Coll., 1920; A.M., Univ. of Calif., 1921; Ph.D., ibid, 1923. Appts: Asst. Prof., Assoc. Prof., Prof., Zool. & Oceanog., Univ. of Wash., Seattle, 1924-38; Vis. Prof., Lingnan Univ., China, 1929-31; Dir., Calif. Acad. of Scis., 1938-63; Sr. Sci., ibid, 1963-. Mbrships: V.P., Sect. Chmn., AAAS; Sec., Pacific Div., ibid, 1944-72; Pres., 1973-74; Past Pres., Oceanog. Soc. Pacific; Nat. Rsch. Coun., U.S. Comm. on Oceanog. of Pacific; Calif. State Marine Comm., 1948-56; Am. Meteorol. Soc. Publs: The Sea, 1966; num. articles in jrnls. & mags. Recip. Fellow's Medal, Calif. Acad. of Scis., 1969. Address: c/o Calif. Acad. of Scis., San Francisco, CA 94118, U.S.A. 2, 3, 14, 50.

MILLER, Robert Earl, b. 23 May 1920. Electronic Engineering Executive. Educ: Pa. State Coll., 1937-39; Geo. Wash. Univ., 1945-55; Univ. of Mich., summer 1953; USNR Midshipmen's Schl., Northwestern Univ., 1943. Appts. incl: V.P., Engrng., Melpar, Inc., Falls Ch., Va., 1960-66; V.P., Melpar Div., Am. Standard, Inc., 1966-68; Sr. V.P., ibid, 1968-70; V.P. & Gen. Mgr., Wash. Systems Div., Control Data Corp., St. Paul, Minn., 1970-71; V.P. & Gen. Mgr., Computer Engrng. Div., ibid, 1971-72; V.P., Small Computer & Communications Dev., 1972-74; Cons., Dept. of Defence, Wash. D.C., on electronics, 1954-71. Mbrships: Sr. mbr., IEEE; Vice Chmn., Wash. Sect., ibid; Sec-Treas., ibid; Exec. Comm.; Sigma Tau. Holder of 2 U.S. Patents. Author of papers in field. Address: Apt. 340, 2800 N. Hamline Ave., St. Paul, MN 55113, U.S.A. 14.

MILLER, Rose Mary, b. 23 Nov. 1911. Educator. Educ: B.S., Middleburg Coll., 1933; Ed.M., Univ. of Vt., 1949; Univ. of Me., 1957. Appts: Tchr., Peacham Acad., V t., 1937-41; Tchr., Exeter H.S., Me., 1941-42; Prin., Peacham Acad., 1942-44; Instr., Vt. Coll., Montpelier, 1944-56; Dean of Women, ibid, 1953-56; Assoc. Prof., Maths., Monmouth Coll.,

N.J., 1957-. Mbrships: Am. & Edinburgh Math. Socs.; AAAS; Math. Assn. Am.; Nat. Coun. Tchrs. of Maths.; N.Y. Acad. Scis.; AAUW; Am. Tchrs. of Maths.; N.Y. Acad. Scis.; N.J. Div. Corp. Rep., AAUW. Address: 220 Ocean Ave., Apt. 12, Long Branch, NJ 07704, U.S.A. 5, 28.

MILLER, Ruth Mary Helen. (Mrs. Ferguson) Physician; Surgeon; Educator. Educ: Rosary Coll., River Forest, Ill.; B.A., 1941, M.D., 1945, Univ. of Wis.; Ph.D., Psychol., Belin Univ., 1959; Grad. Schl., L.A. State Coll., 1956; Cert., N.Y. Polyclin. Med. Schl. & Hosp., 1958; AUS Cmd. & Gen. Staff Coll., 1970. Appts: Concert Pianist thru' Middle W., 1939-41; Intern, 1944-45, Asst. Res. & Res., 1945-47, Chief Res., Neurol., 1947, Goldwater Mem. Hosp., Welfare I., N.Y.C.; Pvte. Med. Prac., Avon Pk., Fla., 1949-51; Capt., M.C., Korean War, 1951-55; Pvte. Prac., Fall River, Mass., 1959-66, Somerset, ibid, 1966-, specializing Family Prac. & Neurol.; Cmdng. Off., 399th Evacuation Hosp., Taunton, Mass., 1970-71; Lt.-Col., M.C., AUS Reserve, 1955-. Mbrships: Fellow, Am. & Int. Colls. Angiol., Am. Geriatrics Soc., Am. Coll. Emergency Physns., Royal Soc. Hlth., U.K.; AMA; Fall River Med. Soc.; Life, Assn. Mil. Surgs.; AUS Reserve; Am. Med. Women's Assn.; Reserve Off. S. Assn.; Order of Eastern Star; Alpha Epsilon Iota; Phi Sigma; Psi Chi; AAUW; Univ. of Wis. & Rosary Coll. Alumnae Assns.; Mass. Citizen's Rights Comm. Address: 161 Johnson St., Somerset, MA 02726, U.S.A. 5, 6, 22, 57, 130, 132, 138.

MILLER, (Mr Justice) Solomon, b. 6 May 1916. Judge of Supreme Court of South Africa. Educ: B.A., Rhodes Univ., Grahamstown, S. Africa, 1935; LL.B., Univ. of Orange Free State, Bloemfontein, 1937. Appts: Prac. at Bar, Bloemfontein, 1938-62; K.C., 1950 (Q.C., 1953); Judge, Supreme Ct., Natal, 1962-; Temporary Judge of Appeal, 1970-71. Mbrships. incl: Past Chmn., Bar Coun. of Orange Free State; Rotary Club, Bloemfontein; Comm., Shakespeare Soc., Bloemfontein; Past Vice Chmn., Ramblers Club, Bloemfontein; Durban Co. Club; Durban Jewish Club; Durban Club; Victoria Club, Pietermaritzburg. Address: Judge's Chambers, Supreme Court, Durban, South Africa. 39.

MILLER, Thelma Delmoor, b. 22 Oct. 1921. Education Coordinator. Educ: N.Y. Univ.; Julliard Schl. of Music; Am. Negro Theatre Schl. of Drama; Hunter Coll; Queens Coll; Univ. of N.C.; Syracuse Univ.; New Schl. for Soc. Rsch. Appts. incl: Queens Soc. for the Prevention of Cruelty to Children, Jamaica, N.Y., 1956-60; Harlem Br., YMCA, 1957-60; Soc. Investigator, Dept. of Soc. Servs., 1949; Supvsr. of Recreation, Callagy Hall Annex, Arvern, 1960-67; Educ. Coord., Jamaica Anti-Poverty Corp., 1967-69; Asst. Dir., York Coll., CUNY Urban Ctr., 1969-71; Asst. to Dean of Continuing Educ. & Urban Affairs, ibid, 1971; Educ. Coord., Ctrl. Brooklyn Model Cities, 1972. Mbrships: Num. bds. & couns. related to soc. work & child guidance, e.g. Chmn., Queens Hosp. Ctr. Community Bd.; Mbr., N.Y. Metropolitan Regional Med. Prog. Advsry Grp.; 1st Vice Chmn., S. Jamaica Steering Comm.; 1st Black Dist. Dir., N.Y. Congress PTA. Address: 120-48 167 St., Jamaica, NY 11434, U.S.A. 138.

MILLER, Virginia Frances Stewart, b. 2 Sept. 1913. Writer. Educ: H.S. & 2 yrs. at coll. Appts: Late Night Mgr., Western Union, Albuquerque, N.M., 2 yrs.; after phys. handicap (polio victim), wkr. w. YMCA, Chgo., Ill. Mbrships: Ch. Women United, Naples, Fla.; Pres., ibid, 4 yrs.; Gadabout Club of YMCA,

Chgo., Ill.; Pres., ibid, 1 yr.; Pres., Collier Co. Republican Club of Naples, Fla.; Sec., ibid, 2 yrs., Mbrship. Sec., 3 yrs. Author, The Goatherder's Wife, 1969. Hons: Most Courageous Woman of Yr. Award, 1970; Ky. Col., 1972. Address: 1236 Michigan, Naples, FL 33940, U.S.A. 125.

MILLER, Walter Richard, Jr., b. 20 Nov. 1934. Banker. Educ: A.B., Dartmouth Coll., 1955; M.B.A., Columbia Univ., 1957; Ph.D., N.Y. Univ., 1965. Appts: Asst. Acct. Exec., McCann-Erickson Inc.; Asst. to Dean, Grad. Schl. of Bus.; Mktng. Instr., Master's Degree Prog. Admnstr., N.Y. Univ.; Dir. Mktng., Mgr., Mktng. Rsch., Mellon Bank N.A. & Mellon Nat. Corp. Mbrships. incl: Mktng & Educ. Comm., Pa. Bankers Assn.; Chmn., Marketing Comm., Interbank Card Assn.; Savings Comm., Am. Bankers Assn.; Am. Mktng. Assn. Publs. incl: Future of Savings Banks in N.Y. State; Marketing for Commercial Banks.; Branch Location Analysis; Planning The Marketing Function; A New Breed of Banker; Planning & Marketing: A Winning Combination; Banking Future -Seen Through the Eyes of a Marketing Man. Recip., Wall St. Jrnl. Award, 1962. Address: Mellon Bank N.A., Mellon Sq., Pittsburgh, PA 15230, U.S.A. 6, 14, 16.

MILLER zu AICHHOLZ, Romedio Gaston von, b. 14 Apr. 1896. Retired Art Dealer. Appts: Served Dragoon Regiment No. 15, Austrian Cavalry, WWI; w. family Bank, liquidated, 1928; Art Dealer in paintings of old masters, 20 yrs. Mbrships. incl: Int. Pan europe Union; Aktion Oesterreich Europa; Volksbewegung für Südtirol/Osterreich E.V'; Former V.P., now hon. mbr., Verband der Osterreicher zur Wahrung der Geschichte Oesterreichs; Oesterreichisher Burgenverein; Bund für Südtirol, Vienna. Author of A Study of the dramatic Life of Archbishop 'Wolf Dietrich'' of Salzburg, in accordance w. the discovery by the author of an important painting portraying the bishop, life size, dated 1604, the only rep. portrait in existence of the famous archbishop, creator & fndr. of the Beauty of Salzburg. Recip., hon. medal, mng. bd., Directory of ''Volksbewegung für Südtirol'', 1970. Address: Am Henmarkt 11, A 1030 Vienna, Austria.

MILLICAN, Edmond Duncan, b. 6 Dec. 1911. Corporation and Association Executive. Educ: grad., Daniel McIntyre Coll. Inst. Appts. incl: Canadian Consolidated Grain Co., Winnipeg, 1929; James Richardson & Son, ibid, 1930; Federal Grain Co. Ltd., 1933; Dir., Manitoba Hosp. Servs. Assn., 1938-42; Chmn. Bd. Dirs., Chmn. Exec. Comm., Pres., Quebec Hosp. Serv. Assn., 1942-; Pres. & Mgng. Dir., Quebec Mutual Life Assurance Co., 1959-; Pres., Canadian Coun. Blue Cross Plans; Pres., Canadian Fedn. Voluntary Hlth. Funds; Dpty. Pres., Int. Fedn. Voluntary Hlth. Serv. Funds; Mbr., Am. Hosp. Assn.; Mbr., Blue Cross Commn. Mbrships. incl: P.Q. Golf Assn.; Pres., ibid, 1956; Gov., Royal Canadian Golf Assn.; Pres., ibid, 1966. Address: 250 Clarke Ave., Apt. 1010, Westmount H3Z 2E5, P.Q., Canada.

MILLINGTON, Terence Alaric, b. 2 Aug. 1922. University Lecturer; UNESCO Consultant; Author. Educ: B.Sc., London Univ., 1948. Appts: RAF, 1942-46, Flt. Lt., Staff Qff., Tech. Signals Br., HQ Transport Cmd., 1943-46; Tchr., Maths., Finchley Co. Grammar Schl., 1949-53; Hd., Maths. Dept., Haverstock Comprehensive Schl., 1953-57, Furzedown Coll., Inst. of Educ., London Univ., 1957-59; Lectr., Maths. Educ., Ctr. Sci. Educ., Chelsea Coll., 1969-74; Cons., UNESCO, Thailand, 1971, '72, Expert in Maths. Educ.,

1973-74; Pt.-time Lectr., Cons., Hendon Tech. Coll., Westminster Coll. of Commerce, & var. profl. orgs. Mbr., Fellow, & Off., profl. orgs. Publs. incl: Dictionary of Mathematics (co-author), 2 edits.; Living Mathematics, Pts. 1—6, 3 edits.; Mathematics Through School (co-author). Profl. papers, educl. TV. Address: 10 Creswick Walk, Hampstead Gdn. Suburb, London NW11 8AN, U.K. 3, 47.

MILLMAN, Herbert, b. 25 Dec. 1909. Social Worker & Administrator. Educ: B.S., Springfield Coll., Mass., 1937; Ed.M., Harvard Univ., 1940. Appts: Club Ldr., Prog. Dir., Day Camp Dir., YM-YWHA, Springfield, 1934-38; Sr. Div. Hd., Camp Wel-Met, N'Y., 1938-; Exec. Dir., YM-YWHA, Brockton, Mass., 1938-43; Field Sec., Nat. Jewish Welfare Bd. in New England, 1943-49, Nat. Dir. Field Serv., 1949-60, Assoc. Exec., 1960-70, Exec. V.P., 1970-; Exec. Dir., Gtr. Boston Coun. of Jewish Community Ctr., 1946-49. Mbr. & Off., var. Jewish & nat. orgs., community & welfare servs. Contbr., chapts. in Goals of Social Welfare, & American Jewish Year Book. Articles, sev. jrnls., soc. work. & Jewish communal serv. Recip., var. citations for work in soc. servs. Address: 15 E. 26th St., N.Y., NY 10010, U.S.A. 2, 6, 55.

MILLS, Ivor Henry, b. 13 June 1921. Professor of Medicine. Educ: Queen Mary Coll., London, U.K., 1940-42; Trinity Coll., Cambridge, 1946-48; St. Thomas's Hosp., London, 1948-51. Appts: Vis. Scientist, NIH, Bethesda, Md., U.S.A., 1956-68; Rdr. in Med., St. Thomas's Hosp., & Hon. Cons Physn., Addenbrooke's Hosp., Cambridge, 1963-. Mbrships: Fellow, Royal Coll. of Physns. & Royal Soc. of Med.; Coun., Royal Coll. of Physns., 1971-; Sec., Soc. for Endocrinol., 1963-70; Exec. Comm., Renal Assn., 1964-67; Med. Rsch. Soc.; Physiol. Soc. Publs: Clinical Aspects of Adrenal Function, 1964; Contbr. of sect., Steroids in Modern Medicine, Part 2, 1972. Recip., MRC (Eli Lilly) Travelling Fellowship, 1956. Address: Dept. of Investigative Med., Addenbrooke's Hosp., Trumpington St., Cambridge CB2 1QE, U.K.

MILLS, John Brent, b. 29 Aug. 1921. Foreign Service Officer. Educ: M.A., Univ. of Cape Town, S. Africa. Appts: Joined S. African For. Serv., 1946; Postings incl: London, 1946-51, Madrid, 1951-53, Rome, 1960-62; Consul; Gen., San Fran., Calif., U.S.A. 1962-68; Under Sec., Dept. of For. Affairs, 1968-71; Ambassador, Canberra, Australia, 1971-. Mbr., Bohemian Club, San Fran. Publs: Waiting For The Sunrise (novel), 1946; Will (play), 1967; Armada (play), 1974. Address: c/o Dept. of For. Affairs, Union Bldgs., Pretoria, S. Africa.

MILLS, Mary, L., b. 23 Aug. 1912. Nurse. Educ: Dip., Lincoln Schl. of Nursing, 1934; Cert. of Pub. Hlth. Nursing, Med. Coll., Va., 1937; M.C.A., Lobenstine Schl. of Midwifery, 1940-41; Beirut Coll. for Women, Lebanon, 1953-56;: Courses at Ind. Univ., Wayne State Univ., N.Y' Univ., Univ. of Colo., etc. Appts. incl: Nat. Communicable Disease Ctr., 1968; Hlth. Care Delivery System, Urban & Rural, in Denmark & Finland, 1970; Hlth. Dev. Prog., U.S. Agcy. Int. Dev., 1946-66. Mbrships. incl: Am. Nurses Assn.; Life, Nat. League of Nursing; Am. Coll. Nurses & Midwives. Hons. incl: D.S., Tuskegee Inst.; Cert of Commendation, Repub. of S. Vietnam, 1964; USPHS Disting. Serv. Award, 1971; Decoration of Cedars, Lebanon; Kt. Official, Liberian Humane Order of Africa, by Pres. Address: 7107 9th St., N.W., Wash. DC 20012, U.S.A. 130.

MILLS, Stella Agnes Alexandra, b. 1 Dec. 1910. Educator. Appts: Jr. Tchr., Trinidad, W.I., 1923; Qualified Tchr., 1930; Sr. Tchr., 1931; Jr. Hd. Tchr., 1957; Prin. I, 1962; Retd., 1970; Vice Prin., La Petite Instn. Pvte. Sec. Schl., St. Joseph. Mbrships: Trinidad & Tobago Red Cross, 1945-; Capt., 3rd Tunapuna Guide Co., 1949-56; Alpha Club; Orpheus Club. Address: 14 Queen St., St. Joseph, Trinidad, W. Indies. 136.

MILLS, William Andrews, 7 Apr. 1910. Certified Public Accountant. Educ: B.S., Univ. of Ga., Athens. Appts: Staff, M. H. Barnes & Co., CPAs, Savannah, Ga., 1934-43; Capt., AUS, 1943-46; Ptnr., Barnes, Askew, Mills & Co., CPAs, Savannah, 1949-61; Ptnr., Haskins & Sells, Int. Acctng. Firm, Savannah, 1961-. Mbrships: Ga. Soc. of CPAs Inc.; La. Soc. of CPAs Inc.; Am. Inst. of CPAs Inc.; N.C. Soc of CPAs; Beta Gamma Sigma; Phi Kappa Phi; Beta Alpha Psi. Address: 802 E. 41st St., Savannah, GA 31401, U.S.A. 2, 7, 16, 125, 128.

MILLS, William Mervyn, b. 23 Feb. 1906. Official Historian (Retired). Educ: King's Coll., London; Sorbonne, Paris. Appts: Script-writer, radio & TV players, BBC; Camp Commandant, HQ Mediterranean Allied Tactical Air Force (Squadron Ldr.), served Tunisia, Sicily, Italy, Corsica & Greece; Squadron Ldr., Admin. HQ 232 Wing; Sr. Histn., RAF, Min. of Defence, Whitehall, London, now ret. Mbrships: Int. PEN Club; Soc. of Authors. Publs: The Long Haul (novel, has been filmed for cinema & TV); Tempt Not the Stars (novel); The Winter Wind (novel); Nelson of the Nile (play); The Tree of Heaven (play); Dance Without Music (TV play); The Queen of Spades (adapted for TV); The Skull (Radio play); The Peter Simple Series (6 plays for radio); The Lost World Series (6 plays for radio); Paul Jones (Radio play); Mexican Gold (radio play); RAF Operations in Libya, the Western Desert & Tunisia July 1942 to May 1943; RAF Operations from Malta June 1940 to May 1943; var. Operational studies & papers. Address: 95 Priory Rd., London N8 8LY, UK. 3.

MILLSAPS, Daniel, b. 30 June, 1919. Artist; Writer; Publisher. Educ: A.B., Univ. of S.C., 1940; Art Students League, 1940-42 & 1946-48. Appts: Practising artist -1965; Book Designer, Harper & Bros., N.Y.C., 1946-48; Art Dir., U.S.A.F., 1951-53; Publr., Wash. Int. Arts Letter, 1962-. Mbr. of Nat. Press Club. Publs: Wounds Pretty, 1949; Community Art Show Guide; Private Foundations Active in the Arts, Vol. 1, 1970; Millions for the Arts: Federal & State Cultural Programs, 1972; Grants & Aid to Individuals in the Arts, 2nd. edit. Hons: Anthony Hampton Award, 1940; 1st Prizewinner, Nat. Print Competition, Va. Mus. of Fine Arts, 1948. Address: Townhouse Four, Harbour Sq., 1321 4th St., S.W., Wash. DC 20024, U.S.A' 7, 7.

MILLSAPS, G. Thelma, b. 28 Mar. 1904. Bookkeeper. Educ: B.A., Maryville Coll., Tenn., U.S.A. Appts: Tchr., Home Econs., Burrville H.S., Tenn.; Tchr., Home Econs., Powell Valley H.S., Tenn.; Tchr., Home Econs. & Spanish, Cedar Creek Acad., Tenn.; Bookkeeper-Treas., & former Dir., Maryville Grocery Co. Mbrships: Charter Mbr. & past Sec., Treas., Histn., & Bulletin Ed., AAUW; Treas. & past Yearbook Ed., Bus. & Profl. Women. Address: 519 Mountain View Ave., Maryvile, TN 37801, U.S.A. 125.

MILLS-ROBERTS, Derek. Commissioned Officer, Irish Guards. Educ: Liverpool Coll.; Oxford Univ. Appts: 1st Battalion, Irish Guards, 1939-42; Cmdr., Lt.Col., 6 Commando

Unit, 1943-44; Cmdr., Brigadier, 1st Commando Brigade, 1944-45; Cmdr., Brigadier, 125th Infantry Brigade, 1946-50. Mbrships: Chmn., N. of England Br., Irish Guards Assn., 1946-74; Guards Club. Author, Clash by Night, 1956. Hons: M.C., 1942; D.S.O., 1943; Bar to D.S.O., 1945; Officier, Legion of Honour, & Croix de Guerre w. palm, France, 1945; C.B.E., 1951. Address: Bryn-Y-Ffynnon, Nr. Bwlchgwyn, Wrexham, N. Wales, U.K. 41.

MILNE, (Charles) Ewart, b. 25 May 1903. Poet; Author. Appts: Student Tchr. & Seaman, 1920-30; Pol. Student, Irish Pol. Movement & Spanish Civil War, 1930-40; Land worker, estate mgr. & smallholder, Ireland, 1941-61; Book Reviewer, Irish Times, Dublin; Staff Mbr., mag., Ireland Today, 1937-40; Book Reviewer, Irish Times Dublin, Staff Mbr., mag., Ireland Today, 1937-40; Book Reviewer, Irish Press, Dublin, 1968-70. Mbrships: Soc. of Authors; Brit. Interplanetary Soc. Publd. Poetry: Forty North Fifty West, 1938; Letter from Ireland, 1940; Jubilo, 1945; Boding Day, 1947; Diamond Cut Diamond, 1950; Elegy for a lost Submarine, 1951; Galion, 1953; Life Arboreal, 1953; Once More To Tourney, 1958; A Garland for the Green, 1962; Time Stopped, 1967; rep. in num. anthols. Author of jrnl. articles. Address: 46 De Parys Ave., Bedford, Beds., U.K. 3, 11.

MILNE, Frank Emmett, b. 31 Mar. 1935. Educator. Educ: B.Sc., Dalhousie Univ., N.S., Canada, 1956; B.Ed., ibid, 1957; M.A., St. Mary's Univ., Halifax, N.S., 1962; Post-grad. Shell Merit Fellow, Cornell Univ., U.S.A. 1965. Appts: Tchr., Maths., Queen Elizabeth H.S., Halifax, N.S., 1957-62; TV Tchr. of Maths., N.S. Dept. of Educ., Halifax, 1962-; Lectr., Maths., Dept. of Educ., St. Mary's Univ., ibid, 1968-; Trustee, Dr. R.E. Marshal Schlrship Fund, 1970-; Judge, TV Educl. Quiz Reach for the Top, Canadian Broadcasting Corp., 1972-. Mbrships: Waegwoltic Club; Pres., ibid, 1967-69; Mason 32°; Master, ibid, 1962-63; Most Wise Sovereign, ibid, 1968-70; Dist. Dpty. Grand Master, ibid, 1970-72; Dalhousie Univ. Alumni Assn.; Pres., ibid, 1969-70; Rotarian; Dir., ibid, 1969-70; N.S. Math. Tchrs. Assn.; Pres., ibid, 1962-63. Hons: Birk's Medal for Ldrship in Student Affairs, 1953. Address: P.O. Box 483, Halifax, Nova Scotia, Canada. 6.

MILNE, R. Eleanor, b. 14 May 1925. Sculptor; Painter. Educ. incl: Sculpture w. Ivan Mestrovićć, Univ. of Syracuse, N.Y., U.S.A. Appts: Tchr., Billings-Bridge Schl. of Art, 1961-62; Sculptor to Canadian Fed. Govt., 1962-; Mbr., Bd. Judges for Art, Canadian Fed. Govt. Mbrships: Assn. Quebec Artists; Am. Craftsmens Coun. Major sculptures in Parliament Bldgs., & Gen. Purpose Off. Bldg. Pub. Wks., Ottawa; Portrait busts in pvte. collects., U.K. & Canada; 12 stained glass windows, Parliament Bldgs., Ottawa; Paintings, sculptures, brush drawings & engravings, pvte. collects. in Canada, U.K', U.S.A. & China. Recip. of Sev. awards. Recip., Centennial Medal for Servs. to Canadian Fed. Govt., 1967. Address: P.O. Box 162, House of Commons, Ottawa, Ont. Canada. 57.

MILNER, Thomas Howard, b. 19 Mar. 1938. Television & Motion Picture Producer; Educator; Writer. Educ: B.A., Univ. of Louisville, Ky., 1960; M.A., Univ. of Fla., 1962; Postgrad. work, Univ. of Louisville, 1968-69. Appts: Drama Critic, Gainesville Daily Sun, Fla., 1960-61; Prof., Dept. of Engl., St. Petersburg Jr. Coll., 1963-; Pres., Piscean Prods., PR & Lit. Agency, 1972-; Pres. & Exec. Prod., Milner Prods. Inc., 1974-. Writer of var. original TV series; co-author, Intentional Walk.

Hons: Woodrow Wilson Fellow, 1960; Hon. Order of Kentucky Colonels, 1959. Address: St. Petersburg Jr. Coll., St. Petersburg Campus, P.O. Box 13489, St. Petersburg, FL 33713, U.S.A.

MILNES, John Herbert, b. 9 Aug. 1913. Fuel Distributing Executive. Educ: Univ. of Toronto (Trinity) Canada. Appts. incl: Pres., Milnes Fuel Oil Ltd., Milnes Holding Co. & Laoc Holding Co. Mbrships: Granite Club; Bd. of Trade; former Pres., Speakers Club of Toronto. Address: 22 Deer Park Cres., Toronto M4V 2C2, Ont., Canada. 6.

MILTON, John R, b. 24 May 1924. University Professor, Editor & Writer. Educ: B.A., Univ. of Minn., 1948; M.A., ibid, 1951; Ph.D., Univ. of Denver, Colo., 1961. Appts. incl: Assoc. Prof. Engl., Jamestown Coll., N.D., 1957-61; Prof. & Chmn., Engl. Dept., ibid, 1961-63; Prof. of Engl., Univ. of S.D., 1963-; Chmn., Engl. Dept., ibid, 1963-65; Fndr.-Ed., S.D. Review, 1963-; Dir. of Creative Writing, Univ. of S.D., 1965-; Vis. Lectr., Univ. of Denver, Colo., N.D. State Univ., Ind. State Univ., Bemidji State Coll., Minn. Mbrships. incl: Western Am. Lit. Assn.; Pres., Governing Bd. & Edit. Bd., ibid; Am. Studies Assn.; Regional Bd., ibid; Rocky Mountain MLA; Sect. Chmn., ibid; Delta Phi Lambda. Publs. incl: The Loving Hawk, 1962; Western Plains, 1964; This Lonely House, 1968; Conversations with Frank Waters, 1971; Oscar How, 1972; The Tree of Bones & other Poems, 1973; Conversations with Frederick Manfred, 1974. Hons: Wurlitzer Fndn. Fellowship, 1965; Story in Best Am. Short Stories, 1969. Address: 630 Thomas St., Vermillion, SD 57069, U.S.A. 30.

MIMS, Lambert C., b. 20 Apr. 1930. Commissioner of Public Works. Appts: in retail & wholesale bus., 1948-65; elected Pub. Works Commn., City of Mobile, 1965, reelected, 1969 & 73; served as Mayor of Mobile, 1968-69, 72-73, will serve again, 1976. Mbrships. incl: Human Resources Comm., Nat. League of Cities; Comm. of Community Dev., Ala. League of Municipalities; 2 terms as Pres., Ala. Pub. Works Assn.; Past Pres., Mobile Co. Municipal Assn.; Kiwanis Club of W. Mobile; Mobile Chmbr. of Comm.; Past Pres., Mobile Camp of Gideons; Bd. of Dirs., Mobile Rescue Mission. Publs: For Christ & Country, 1969. Hons. incl: Mobile's Most Outstanding Young Man, 1965; appointed prin. speaker at sev. Prayer Breakfasts. Address: P.O. Box 1827, Mobile, AL 36601, U.S.A.

MIN, Tony Charles, b. 5 Jan. 1923. Professor of Engineering Mechanics. Educ: B.S. Aero Engrng., Chiao Tung Univ., 1947; M.S., Mech. Engrng., Univ. of Tenn., 1953; Phi. D., Engrng. Sci., ibid, 1969. Appts. incl: Assoc. Prof., Mech. Engrng., Auburn Univ., 1957-64; Rsch. Engr., Oak Ridge Nat. Lab., Ten., summers, 1963, 1964; Cons., ibid, 1963-68; Instr., Engrng. Mech., Univ. of Tenn., 1964-68; Prof., Engrng. Mech., Mich. Technological Univ., Houghton, 1968-; Rsch. Engr., Babcock & Wilcox Rsch. Ctr., summer 1969. Mbrships: Am. Soc. Mech. Engrs.; Am. Acad. of Mech.; Soc. of Engrng. Sci.; N.Y' Acad. of Sci.; Am. Soc. for Engrng. Educ; Am. Phys. Soc.; Sigma Xi; Phi Tau Phi; Tau Beta Pi; Pi Tau Sigma. Contbr. num. papers & reviews to engrng. jrnls. Hons: Sci. Fac. Fellowship at Univ. of Minn., Nat. Sci. Fndn., 1961-63; Int. Travel Grant, ibid, 1961. Address: Department of ME—EM, Michigan Technological University, Houghton, MI 49931, U.S.A. 57.

MINCHEW, Nancy Ruth Anderson, b. 23 Nov. 1939. Kindergarten Teacher. Educ: 12th

Grade H.S.; var. kindergarten tchr. courses & Girl Scout ldrship. classes. Appts: formerly Sunday Schl. & Bible Schl. Tchr.; currently Kindergarten Tchr., 1st United Mech. Ch.'s Schl. of Discovery. Mbrships: Wayne Co. H.S. & Jr. H.S. Band Boosters Clubs; Fellowship, Bapt. Ch.; former mbr., Girl Scouts of Am., & Jaycettes. Formerly active w. Girl Scouts of Am., Troop Ldr., 5 yrs., Neighborhood Chmn., 2 yrs. Address: P.O. Box 164, Jesup, GA 31545, U.S.A. 125.

MINDELL, Bianka G. (Mrs. Max Mindell). Organization Executive. Educ: More Coll.; N.Y. Univ.; Columbia; Hunter Coll. Mbrships: Chmn., Serv. of For. Born, resettlement of war refugees and aid in finding relatives, 1945-47; Chmn., Reception to War Brides, 1945; Chmn., I Am An American Day, Union Coll., 1945, 46; 1st Chmn., Reception for New Ams., 1945-; Lectr., Comparative Religs., 1954-; Chmn., Monthly Birthday Parties w. Prog., Daughters of Sarah Nursing Home, Troy, 7 yrs.; Pink Lady, Ellis Hosp., 3½ yrs.; Pres., Nat. Coun. Jewish Women, 1956-58; Nat. Comm. Community Servs., NCJW, 1965-67; Nat. Comm., Voluntary Trng., NCJW, 1967-68; Sec., World Federalists & Capitol Dist. Chmn.; WF-USA; Hadassah; Planned Parenthood. Address: 1810 Randolph Rd., Schenectady, NY 12308, U.S.A. 5, 55.

MING, Reginald Ewing. Government Youth Adviser. Educ: Bermuda & Swansea Univ. Coll., U.K. Bermuda Govt. Youth Advsr., since leaving Coll. Mbrships. incl: Exec. Coun. Mbr., Bermuda Br., Royal Commonwealth Soc.; Exec. Mbr., Bermuda Coun. of Soc. Scis.; Exec. Mbr., Devonshire Br., Bermuda Welfare Soc.; Exec. Mbr., Bermuda Histl. Soc.; Exec. Mbr., Comm. of 25 for Handicapped Children; Coun. Mbr., Ch. Soc.; Fndr. Mbr., Kiwanis Club; Trustee, St. Matthias Guild Hall; Bermuda Nat. Trust; Bermuda Red Cross Soc.; Bermuda Youth Coun.; Bermuda Assn. of Soc. Wkrs. Author of articles to local newspapers. Hons: Queen's Cert. & Badge of Honour, 1969; Kiwanis Award for outstanding Programming, 1973. Address: P.O. Box 157, Devonshire 4, Bermuda.

MINIFIE, James M., b. 8 June 1900. Writer. Educ: B.A., Univ. of Sask., 1924; M.A., Oriel Coll., Oxford, 1944; LL.D., Univ. of Sask., 1949. Appts: Reporter, N.Y. Herald Tribune, N.Y.C., & Burs. in Paris, Madrid, Rome, London & Wash. D.C., 1929-41; Serv. w. Off. Strategic Servs., U.S.A., N. Africa, & Europe, 1943-45; Free-lance Contbr., C.B.C., from London, Wash. D.C., Toronto, Victoria B.C., 1953-73. Mbrships: Nat. Press Club, Wash. D.C.; Overseas Writers, N.Y.C. Publs: Peace-Maker or Powder-Monkey; Open at the Top; Who's Your Fat Friend? ; Homesteader; Expatriate. Hons: LL.D., 1949; Canada Coun., Grant-in-Aid. Address: 300 Beaumont Ave., Vic., B.C., Canada, V9B 1R1.

MINKOFSKI-GARRIGUES, Horst, b. 23 July 1925. Concert Pianist; Composer. Educ: Music Acad. & Conservatory of Dresden, German Democratic Repub; piano w. Prof. Herbert Wüsthoff, Hermann Werner Finke, Schneider-Marfels, Romana Löwenstein, comp. Karl Knochenhauer. Appts: Formerly Prof., State Music Seminar, Wiesbaden, German Fed. Republic; Num. tours throughout world; Num. recordings. Compositions incl: Variations over a theme by Tchaikovsky, Op.3; Tagebuch Op. 5; Five sketches Op. 6; variations over a Lullaby Op. 9; Two impromptus Op. 11; Two Preludes Op. 12; Sonatina Op. 13; Bilder eines Kindes Op. 16; Après la pluie vient le beau temps Op. 18; Tel qui rit vendredi, pleurera dimanche Op.

19; Canadian landscapes Op. 21; Sonata No. 1 Op. 23; Neuf Ministures Op. 26; Klaviermusik Op. 15; Piano Concerto No. 1 (For two pianos): Eight Miniatures—Expo 67. Address: 205 Edison Ave., St. Lambert-Montreal, P.Q', Canada. 57.

MINNE, Ronn Nels, b. 3 Oct. 1924. Educator; Chemist. Educ: B.S., Northwestern Univ., 1950, A.M., 1951; Ph.D., Harvard Univ., 1960. Appts: Tchr., Chem., Dundee H.S., Ill., 1951-53, Los Alamos H.S., N.M., 1953-54, Culver Mil. Acad., 1954-56 & 1960-65, Phillips Acad., Andover, Mass., 1965-; Vis. Schol., Cambridge Univ., U.K., 1971-72; Served w. U.S. Army, 1942-45. Mbrships: Am. Chem. Soc.; Am. Inst. of Chemists; AAAS; N.Y. Acad. of Sci.; Sigma Xi. Author, Coordination Polymers, 1960. Recip., Prize for Excellence in Teaching, Harvard Univ., 1958-60. Address: Phillips Acad., Andover, MA 01810, U.S.A. 6.

MINSHALL, William Harold, b. 6 Dec. 1911. Research Scientist in Plant Physiology. Educ: B.S.A., Univ. of Toronto, Canada, 1933; M.Sc., 1938, Ph.D., 1941, McGill Univ., ibid, Appts: Grad. Asst., 1933-41, Jr. Botanist, 1941-45, Assoc. Botanist, 1945-48, Botanist, 1948-51, Div. of Bot., Canada Dept. Agric., Ottawa, Ont.; Sr. Plant Physiologist, Rsch. Inst., Canada Dept. Agric., London, Ont., 1951-; Hon. Lectr., Dept. of Plant Sci., Univ. of Western Ont., 1952. Mbrships: Fellow, Weed Sci. Soc. of Am., (Exec. Comm., 1959-66) AAAS; Ont. Inst. Profl. Agrologists (Pres., 1963-64); Agricl. Inst. of Canada (Exec. Coun., 1950-51); Agricl. Pesticide Soc. (Sec.-Treas., 1955-72); Senate, Univ. of Guelph, 1969-73; Pres., Alumni Assn., Ont. Agricl. Coll., 1969-70, Ont. Geneal. Soc., 1971-73, McIlwraith Field Naturalists, 1968-69. Contbr. to scientific jrnls. Address: Rsch. Inst., Canada Agric., Univ. Sub Post Off., London, Ont., N6A 3K0, Canada. 14, 15, 88, 128, 139.

MINTAREDJA, (SH.), Hadja M.S., b. 17 Feb. 1921. Lawyer. Educ: Gadjah Mada Univ., Indonesia; Leiden Univ., Holland; Univ. Indonesia, Jakarta. Appts: Judge, Bandung Ct., Indonesia, 1944-46; Chief, Legal Dept., For. Exchange Control, 1950-55; Pvte. Bus., export, import, banking & ind., 1957-65; Pres., Dir., 2 State Constr. Cos., 1966-68; Min. of State, 1968-71; Min. Soc. Affairs, 1971-. Mbrships: Past Chmn., Partai Muslimin, Indonesia; Fndr., Himpunan Mahasiswa Islam Students Org.; Past Bd. mbr., Muhammadiyah; Past Gen. Exec. Chmn., Partai Persatuan Pembangunan. Publs: Moslem Society and Politics in Indonesia, 1971; Islam and Politics, Islam and State in Indonesia, 1974 & author of many articles in Indonesian mags. & jrnls. Recip. Medal, Bintang Maha Putera II. Address: Jalan Kha. Dachlan No. 21 Kebayoran Baru, Jakarta, Selatan, Indonesia.

MINTER, Merton Melrose, b. 3 Jan. 1903. Specialist in Internal Medicine; Owner of Minter Clinic. Educ: B.A., Univ. of Tex., 1925; M.D., Med. Branch, ibid, 1928; Intern, Rsch. Hosp., Kan. City, Mo., 1928-29. Appts: Bd. of Trustees, S.W. Fndn. for Rsch. & Educ.; Pres., Bexar Co. Med. Soc., 1954, Int. Med. Assembly, 1953, Tex. Diabetes Assn., 1958, & Tex. Acad. of Internal Med., 1959; Chmn., Bd. of Regents, Univ. of Tex, 1959-61; Currently Chmn., San Antonio Med. Fndn. Mbrships. incl: AMA; Tex. Med. Assn.; Am. & Tex. Heart Assns.; Am. Med. Soc. of Vienna; Fiesta San Antonio Commn., Inc.; Order of the Sons of Herman; Order of the Alamo; San Antonio German Club; Rotary Club. Hons: Disting. Alumnus Award, Univ. of Tex., 1970. Address: 1702 Nix Profl. Bldg., San Antonio, TX 78205, U.S.A. 2, 7, 10, 16, 50, 54.

MINTERS, Arthur Herman, b. 22 July 1932. Rare Book & Periodical Dealer. Educ: B.A., Wash. Sq. Coll., N.Y' Univ., 1960; Inst. of Fine Arts, N.Y. Univ., 1960-61. Appts: Asst. to Pres., Paul Gottschalk Inc., booksellers, 1953-56; Founded Arthur H. Minters Inc., N.Y'C., 1957; Pres., ibid, 1969-. Mbrships: Vice Chmn., Middle Atlantic Chapt., Antiquarian Booksellers Assn. of Am., 1965-66, PRes., 1966-67; Int. League of Antiquarian Booksellers Assn. of Am., 1965-66, Pres., Lectured to Art Subsect., Confs. of ALA, 1962 & 1964, at Univ. of Ind., Bloomington, 1967, & to Columbia Univ. Lib. Schl., 1970. Publs: Over 40 catalogs & lists of rare books & periodicals, 1957-73. Recip., Medal for Americanism, For. Legion Navy Post, 1950. Address: 84 University Place, N.Y., NY 10003, U.S.A. 6.

MINTZ, Gilbert Jack, b. 16 July 1925. Retail Trade Executive. Educ: B.S., N.Y. Univ., 1946; Postgrad., Columbia Univ. Schl. of Arch., 1946-48. Appts: Dir., Charm Stores, N.Y.C., 1947-48; Gen. Mgr., New Engl. Trading Corp., 1949-55 & Goldblatts Dept. Store, 1963-65; Sales Prod. Mgr., Goldblatts, 1966-67; V.P., Dir. Sales, Goldblatt Bros. Inc., 1968-; V.P., Dir. Sales & P.R., ibid, 1969-. Mbrships: V.P., Lincoln Belmont Assn., 1959-62; Back of Yards Assn., 1962-63; State St. Coun., 1967-; Fndn. Assn. Univ. of Chgo., Cancer Rsch. Fndn., 1971-. Author of 2 feature articles. Recip., Retail Star Award, 1960. Address: 1707 Clavey Rd., Highland.Park, IL 60035, U.S.A. 34.

MINTZ, Harry. Artist; Educator. Educ: M.F.A., Warsaw Acad. Fine Arts, Poland. Appts. incl: Vis. Prof., Painting, Wash. Univ., St. Louis, Mo., 1954-55; Assoc. Prof., Adv. Painting, Art Inst. Chgo., 1955-70. One man shows incl: Art. Inst. Chgo., 1945; Cowrie Gall., L.A., 1948; Palmer House Gals., Chgo., 1952, 53; John Heller Gall., N.Y., 1952; Gal. Escondida, Taos, N.M., 1953; Cliff Dwellers, Chgo., 1954; Feingarten Galls., Chgo. & L.A., 1961; Adelle Bednarz Galls., L.A., 1970. Grp. exhibs. incl: Art Inst. Chgo., 1934-63; Carnegie Int., Pitts.; Whitney Mus. Am. Art; Venice Biennial; Corcoran Gall. of Art, Wash. D.C.; Palace of Legion of Hon., San Fran.; L.A. Co. Mus. Collects. incl: Art Inst. Chgo.; Whitney Mus., N.Y.; Tel Aviv Mus. of Art, Israel; Rio de Janeiro Mus. of Art. Hons. incl: Num. prizes, Art Inst. Chgo., 1937-62; 1st Prize, Old Orchard Art Exhib. of Chgo. Artist, 1959, '62, '63; 2nd Prize, Sun-Times Exhib. of Chgo. & Vicinity Artist, 1963. Address: 429 Briar Place, Chgo., IL 60657, U.S.A. 2, 37, 55.

MINTZER, Olin Wesley, b. 6 June 1916. Teacher; Research Engineer; Educ: B.S.C.E., Univ. of Tenn., 1942; M.S.C.E., Purdue Univ., 1949; Profl. Engr., Ind. & Ohio; Surveyor, Ohio. Appts. incl: Instr.-Asst. Prof., Purdue Univ., 1947-52; Asst. Prof., Rsch. Assoc., Dir., Camp Case, Case Inst. Technol., 1952-56; Prof., Punjab Engrng. Coll., Chandigarh, India, 1956-58; Assoc. Prof., Civil Engrng., Ohio State Univ., 1958-; Cons., num. govt. & mil. projs. Mbrships. incl: Chi Epsilon; Sigma Xi; var. comms., Hwy. Rsch. Bd.; num. offs. inclng. AIL Comm. Chmn., Am. Soc. Photogrammetry. Publs. incl: Airphoto Interpretation of Soils & Rocks for Engineering Purposes, (co-author), 1953; Manual of Highway Engineering Applications of Photogrammetry, 1959; contbr. to var. manuals; num. profl. articles. Recip., sev. hons. Address: Civil Engrng. Dept., Ohio State Univ., 2070 Neil Ave., Columbus, OH 43210, U.S.A. 8, 26.

MIRABITO, Paul S., b. 7 June 1915. Company President. Educ: Bachelor's Degree, Columbia Univ., U.S.A.; M.B.A., N.Y. Univ.

Appts: Acct., Controller's Div., N.Y.C., 1936-39; w. Haskins & Sells, Cert. Pub. Accts., 1939-42; Dir., Budgets-Controller & Dir., Contracts, Control Instrument Company,Inc., 1942-51; Firm became subsidiary of Burroughs Corp., 1951; Transferred to parent co. as Asst. Controller for Corp., 1951-55; Gen. Mgr., Defense Contracts Org., 1955-60; V.P.-V.P., Admin., 1960-65; V.P. & Grp. Exec., Fed. &. Special Systems Grp., 1965-68; Bd. Dirs., 1968-; Exec. V.P.-Pres., 1968-. Mbrships: Bd. Dirs., Detroitbank Corp. & Detroit Bank & Trust Co.; Bd. Computer & Bus. Equipment Manufacturers Assn.; Nat. Security Indl. Assn.; Econ. Club, Detroit; Past Dir., Greater Phila. Chmbr. of Comm.; Past mbr., Bd. Dirs., Suburban W. Region, 1st PA. Banking & Trust Co. Address: Burroughs Corp., Burroughs Pl., Detroit, MI 48232, U.S.A.

MIRALLES LLADO, Juan, b. 27 June 1912. Painter. Educ: Qualification, Primary Schl. Tchr.; studies, Escuela de Artes y Oficios Artisticos, Majorca. Mbrships: Royal Acad. of Fine Arts, San Sebastian, Spain; Circulo de Bellas Artes de Palma, Majorca. Painter of portraits, landscapes & murals. Solo Exhibs: Barcelona, Spain; Palma, Majorca. Murals, chs., Majorca. Other paintings, pvte. collects., overseas. Address: Lorenzo Vicens, 13-2°, Palma, Majorca, Spain. 43, 102.

MIRAMBEAU, (Gen.) Henri, b. 29 July 1909. Retired Military Officer; Business Executive. Educ: Artillery Schl.; Dip., Gen. Staff Schl.; Breveté, Ctr. des Hautes Etudes Administratives; Auditor, Nat. Defense Inst.; Ctr. of Adv. Mil. Studies. Appts. incl: Entered Mil. Serv., 1933; Cmdr., 40th Artillery Regiment, 1943-45; Pvte. Sec. to Gen. Leclerc, Indochina, & N. Africa, 1945-47; Hd., Army's Scientific Bur., 1948-49; Pvte. Sec. to Gen. Blanc, 1949-54; Pres., Rsch. & Dev. Comm., Mil. Bur. of Standardization, NATO, London, U.K., 1949-55; Chief of Staff, Combined Forces, Algeria, 1955-56; Chief of Staff of the Army, 1956-58; Dpty. Gen., Combined Forces, Sahara, 1958-59; Cmdg. Gen., 13th Infantry Div., Sud-Oranais Zone, 1959-60; Pres., Dir.-Gen., SEPRES, 1968-. Mbr., num. profl. orgs. Recip., var. hons. Address: 191 Bis, Blvd. de la Vanne, 94230 Cachan, France. 43, 91.

MIRASGEZIS, Demosthenes, b. 5 Aug. 1913. Lawyer; Criminologist; Author. Educ: M.D. of Law, Degree in Pol. Sci., Univ. of Athens, Greece. Appts. incl: Lawyer, specializing in cases of Extradition & Int. Penal Law, before all Greek Cts. since 1934 & Supreme Ct. of Greece since 1945. Mbrships: Lawyers Club of Athens; Archaeol. Soc. of Greece; Int. Assn. de Droit Penal; Nat. Coun. on Crime & Deliquency, U.S.A.; Greek Soc. Penal Law. Publs. incl: The Penalty Of Death; The History Of Penal Legislation Of Greece; The Penal Jurisdiction Of The Supreme Court; The Foreign Penal Judgement According To The Greek Legislation; The Legal Remedy Of Reopening A Case in The Penal Procedure; The Stay Of Execution In The Administrative Law; The Control Of Acts Of Administration By The Regular Courts; The Violation Of The Provisions Of The Constitutions; Studies On The Law Of Municipal Employees. Address: Polytechniou St. No. 10, Athens, Greece.

MIRON, Eliahu, b. 18 Sept. 1921. Advocate. Educ: Jerusalem Law Schl. & Tel-Aviv Schl. of Econs; Admitted to Israel Bar, 1946. Appts: Miron, Bension & Prywes, Advocates, Tel-Aviv. Mbrships: Bd. of Dirs., Israel Electric Corp., & Mizrachi United Bank; Bd. of Trustees, Bar-Ilan Univ.; Hon. Counsel, Ort Israel, & Magen David Adom; Trustee,

Morice Polack Fndn.; Exec. Comm., Coun. for Eretz Israel Hayafa; Past Mbr., High Ct. of Zionist Org.; Past Mbr., Ctrl. Comm., Israel Bar Assn.; World Peace through Law Ctr.; Past Dir. Gen., Min. of Interior. Address: 3 Shilo St., Tel-Aviv, Israel. 55, 94.

MIR RAGUE, Raúl Maria, b. 21 Jan. 1939. Agricultural Journalist; Publicity Technician. Educ: Bachelor's, Official Schl. of Jrnlsm., Gen. Press Directorate, Min. of Agric., Spain. Appts: Dir., Jrnl., El Cultivador Moderno (Modern Cultivator): Pres., Grp. of Agric. Publs. in Spain; V.P., Spanish Assn. of Tech. Pres; V.P., Assn. of Spanish Agricl. Publrs. Mbrships: World Assn. of Aviculture Sci.; European Community of Jrnlsts.; Int. Union of Sci. Press, France; Spanish Pres., Commission on Broadcasting & Technique, Int. Fedn. of the Periodical Press; Nautical Club, Comarruga-Vendrell, Tarragona. Contbr. to profl. publs., some in collab. Hons. incl: Chevalier de l'Ordre du Mérite, France; Kt. of Justice, Order of St. John of Jerusalem; Silver Medal of Arts-Scis.-Letters. Address: Amigó, 79, Barcelona 6, Spain. 43.

MISIR, Frank Ramnarine, b. 1 Dec. 1923. Barrister-at-Law. Educ: Naparima Coll., San Fernando, Trinidad; Gray's Inn, London, U.K. Appts: Bar. Coun., 1958-; Queen's Counsel, 1970; Chmn., San Fernando Rent Assessment Bd. Mbrships: Bar Assn.; V.P., ibid, 1964-68; Org. of Commonwealth Caribbean Bar Assn.; V.P., ibid, 1967-68; Justice (Int. Comn. of Jurists), Trinidad; V.P., ibid; San Fernando Rotary Club; Pres., ibid, 1965-66; Administrative Advsr., Rotary Int., 1968-70; Fndr., UN Assn. of Trinidad & Tobago; Pres., ibid, 1966-69; Chmn., Law Assn. of Trinidad & Tobago. Address: 9B Harris Promenade, 4 Archbald St., San Fernando, Trinidad & Tobago, W. Indies.

MISSORI, Alfovino, b. 30 Mar. 1901. Artist. Educ: Schlr., "Reffo" C. Artigianelli, Torino, Italy. Mbrships: Accademia Tibernia, Rome, 1966; Accademia de "i 500" per le Arti, Let ere e Scienze, 1967; Accademia Int. Bur ikhardt di Basilea, 1968; Inst. Int. des Arts et Lettres. Works incl: Cristo e l'Adultera, Discorso della Montagna, 1941; La Voce Che Grida nel Deserto, Santa Fe, Argentina, 1941; Abside di S. Giov. Batt. de Rossi, Rome, 1945; Ritratto di S.F.S. Cabrini, 1947; Gloria Beatificazione di Pio X, Basilica di S. Pietro, Vatican, 1950; Monumento al Filosofo Marco Mastrofini, Montecampatri, 1953; Decorazione: Nuova Farmacia della Scala, Rome, 1956; Ritratto di Giovanni XXIII, 1959; Abside Chiesa di S. Alfonso, Rome, 1964; Santo Volto, 1973. Recip. of hons. Address: Piazza Dante 2, 00185 Rome, Italy. 43.

MISTARDIS, Gasparis, b. 1899. Author; Professor; former Banking Officer. Educ: Grad., Pol. Scis., Univ. of Athens; Dr. of Econ. & Commercial Scis., School of Econs., Athens; Studies in Hist., Geog., Geol., Univ. of Paris, France; Histl. Geog., La Sorbonne; Geol., Coll. de France; Banking, Ecole Scis. Financières; Soc. Scis., Univ. of Lausanne, Switzerland. Appts: Nat. Bank of Greece, 1915-46; Prof., Agrarian Geo., Schl. of Agroecon. Studies, Min. of Agric., 1941-46; Prof., Geoecons. & Geopols., Schl. of Econ. & Commercial Scis., Athens, 1955-63; Prof., Human Geog., Schl. of Telecommunications, 1960-69; Prof., Econ. Geo., Schl. of Jrnlsm. & P.R., 1960-71; Prof., Applied Geog., Ctr. of Demosiology, 1967-. Mbrships. incl: 3rd V.P., Hellenic Geographical Soc., 1968-; Geological Soc. of Greece (Councillor, 1958-63); Hellenic Soc. for Nature Protection (Gen. Sec., 1959-64); Speleological

Soc. of Greece; Hellenic Soc. of Econ. Scis.; Hon., Soc. of Greek Demosiologists (Publicists); Corresng. Mbr., sev. int. commns., working grps., of Int. Geographical Union for Univs. in Colo. (U.S.A.), London (U.K.), Rennes (France), Melbourne (Australia). Contbr. to num. acad. publs. & confs. Recip., 2 prizes, Acad. of Athens, 1928. Address: Sapfo 147 & Tinion, Kallithea (of Athens), Greece.

MITCHELHILL, James Moffat, b. 11 Aug. 1912. Civil Engineer; Industrial Manager. Appts. incl: V.P. & Gen. Mgr., Ponce & Guayama RR, Aguirre, Puerto Rico, 1969-70; Asst. to Gen. Mgr., Land Admin. of Puerto Rico, for Centrals Aguirre, Cortada, Mercedita & Lafayette, 1970-72; Asst. to Gen. Mgr., Corporacion Azucarera de Puerto Rico, Aguirre, 1973-. Registered Profl. Engr., Mont., U.S.A. Licensed Civil Engr., Puerto Rico. Fellowships: Am. Soc. Civil Engrs.; Am. Geographical Soc. of N.Y. Mbrships. incl: Am. Railway Engrng. Assn.; Colegio de Ingenieros, Arquitectos, y Agrimensores de Puerto Rico; Tau Beta Pi. Address: P.O. Box 137, Aguirre, Puerto Rico, 00608. 7, 26.

MITCHELL, Betty Jo, b. 2 May 1931. Librarian. Educ: A.B., Southwest Mo. State Univ., 1952; M.S.L.S., Univ. of Southern Calif., 1967. Appts: Asst. Acquisitions Libn., San Fernando Valley State Coll., 1967-69, Asst. Coll. Libn. for Personnel & Finance, 969-71; Assoc. Dir. Univ. Libs., Calif. State Univ., Northridge, 1971-. Mbrships: Am. & Calif. Lib. Assns.; Assn. Calif. State Univ. Profs; Northridge Exec. Comm., ibid, 1971-72; San Fernando Valley Girl Scout Coun.; Bd. of Dirs., ibid, 1974-77; Pi Beta Chi; Alpha Mu Gamma. Publs. incl: A Systematic Approach to Performance Evaluation of Out-of-Print Book Dealers: The San Fernando State College Experience, 1971; In-House Training of Supervisory Library Assistants in a Large Academic Library, 1973. Address: California State University, 18111 Nordhoff St., Northridge, CA, U.S.A.

MITCHELL, David Ian, b. 31 July 1921. Minister of Religion, Methodist Church. Educ: Caenwood Meth. Theol. Coll., Jamaica, 1943-46; Richmond Meth. Theol. Coll., Surrey, U.K., 1946-47; Union Theol. Sem., N.Y., U.S.A., 1955-56; Tchrs. Coll., Columbia Univ., 1956-58. Appts. incl: Dir., Christian Educ., 1st Meth. Ch., Red Bank, N.J., U.S.A., 1956-58; Circuit Min., Math. Ch., Mackenzie, Mahaica, & Susamacher, Georgetown, Guyana, 1958-60; Gen. Ed. & Dir., Ldrship. Trng., Caribbean Comm. on Joint, Christian Action, 1960-69; Chmn., S. Caribbean Dist. Synod, Meth Ch. in Caribbean & Americas, 1964-69; Lectr., Sociol., Educ. & Relig., Naporima Tchrs. Coll., San Fernando, Trinidad, 1969-72; Assoc. Dir. (Educ.), Christian Action for Dev. in Caribbean, Barbados, W. Indies. Contbr. of Articles to World Christian Education. Hons: Fellow in prog. of Advanced Religious Studies, Union Theol. Sem., N.Y., U.S.A., 1955. Address: CADEC, P.O. Box 616, Bridgetown, Barbados, West Indies. 109.

MITCHELL, Fay J., b. 21 Nov. 1921. Librarian. Educ: B.A., Winthrop Coll., Rock Hill, S.C., U.S.A., 1942; M.L.S., George Peabody Coll., Nashville, Tenn., 1960. Appts: Libn., H.S., Reidsville, N.C., 1943-46; Asst. Circulation Libn., Clemson Coll., S.C., 1946-51; Br. Libn., U.S. Army, Ft. Campbell, Ky., 1951-54; Special Forces Libn., Ft. Bragg, N.C., 1954-56; Acquisitions Libn., Clemson Coll., 1956-61; Hd. Libn., Gardner Webb Coll., Boiling Springs, N.C., 1961-63; Circulation Libn., Appalachian State Univ., Boone, N.C.,

1963-71; Periodicals Libn., ibid, 1971-. Mbrships: ALA; Southeastern Lib. Assn.; Coll. & Rsch. Libs.; AAUP; Mbrship. Chmn., Bus. & Profl. Women's Club; Beta Phi Mu; Sec., Beta Sigma Phi. Address: 114 College St., Apt. 6, Boone, NC 28607, U.S.A. 5.

MITCHELL, George Archibald Grant, b. 11 Nov. 1906. Medical Practitioner. Educ: M.B., Ch.B. and Ch.M., Aberdeen Univ., U.K.; M.Sc., Manchester; D.Sc.; F.R.C.S., England. Appts. incl: Lectr., Anatomy and Surg., Aberdeen Univ., 1930-34; Sr. Lectr., Anatomy, ibid, 1937-39; Served in WWII, 1939-45; Prof., Anatomy, Manchester Univ., 1946-; Dean, Manchester Univ. Med. Schl., 1955-60; Pro-Vice Chancellor, Manchester Univ., 1959-63. Mbrships. incl: Pres., Third European Anatomical Congress, 1973; Chmn., Int. Anatomical Nomenclature Comm., 1970-; Pres., Anatomical Soc. of Gt. Britain and Ireland, 1961-63; Pres., Manchester Med. Soc., 1964-65; Mbr., Ct. of Examiners, Royal Coll. of Surgs., England, 1951-68; Mbr., Bd. of Govs., United Manchester Hosps., 1955-74. Publs. incl: Anatomy of Autonomic Nervous System; Cardiovascular Innervation; Basic Anatomy (w. E.L. Patterson); Contbr. of sects. and chapts. to var. encys; many articles in profl. jrnls. Hons. incl: O.B.E., 1945; Chevalier Order of the Dannebrog, 1966; T.D., 1949. Address: 596 Wilmslow Rd., Manchester, M20 9DE, U.K. 1, 43, 47, 109, 128.

MITCHELL, George Francis, b. 15 Oct. 1912. University Professor. Educ: Trinity Coll., Dublin, Repub. of Ireland. Appts. incl: Prof. of Quaternary Studies, Trinity Coll., Dublin. Mbrships: Royal Irish Acad.; Fellow, Royal Soc.; Pres., Int. Union for Quaternary Rsch., 1969-73. Address: Trinity College, Dublin 2, Repub. of Ireland. 1, 128.

MITCHELL, (Col. Sir) Harold (Paton), b. 21 May 1900. Director of Companies. Educ: Royal Mil. Coll., Sandhurst, U.K.; M.A., Univ. Coll., Oxford; Dr. ès Sciences, Univ. of Geneva, Switzerland. Appts. incl: M.P., Brentford & Chiswick Div. of Middlesex, 1931-45; Dir., London & N. Eastern Railway Co., 1939-47; Hon. Col., 31 A.A. Regiment, City of London Rifles, 1939-48; Command Welfare Off., A.A. Command, 1940-48; Liaison Off. to Polish Forces, France, Belgium & Netherlands, 1944; Hon. Col., 61st (City of Edinburgh) Signal Regiment, T.A., 1947-65; Liaison Off., Order of St. John for Caribbean, 1950-66; Lectr., Hispanic Am. Studies, Stanford Univ., 1959-65; Rsch. Prof., Latin Am. Studies, Rollins Coll., 1965-; Chmn. & Chief Exec., Luscar Ltd. Group, Edmonton, Alta., Canada. Mbrships. incl: Carlton Club; Queen's Body Guard for Scotland. Publs. incl: Europe in the Caribbean, 1963; Caribbean Patterns, 1967. Hons. incl: LL.D., 3 univs.; Fellow, Univ. Coll., Oxford, 1972; Kt. Order of St. John of Jerusalem. Address: Marshall's Island P.O. Box 262, Hamilton 5, Bermuda. 1, 2, 3, 41, 96, 125, 137.

MITCHELL, Hester L., b. 8 Dec. 1915. Librarian. Educ: Univ. of Va., 1937; Regent Inst., London, U.K., 1937; Univ. of N.H., U.S.A., 1939-40, '48, '51; Boston Univ.; Mass. Dept. of Educ., 1946; Univ. of Okla., 1961-64. Appts. incl: Adult Asst., Pub. Lib., Beverly, Mass., 1940-48; Hd., Children's Dept., Pub. Lib., Everett, Mass., 1948-51; Libn., Pub. Lib., Ipswich, Mass., 1951-67; Libn., Addison-Wesley Publ. Co., Inc., 1967-; Book Reviewer, Ref. Servs. Div., ALA, 1969-. Active mbr. many lib. assns. & Am. Security Coun., Wash. D.C.; Common Cause, Wash. D.C. Contbr. to newspapers & periodicals. Address: 88 Stetson Ave., Swampscott, MA 01907, & 7503 N.W. 70th Terr., Ft. Lauderdale FL 33313, U.S.A. 5, 6, 42.

MITCHELL, (Mrs.) Hilliard Jackson, b. 28 Apr. 1916. College Instructor. Educ: B.R.E., Southwestern Bapt. Sem., Ft. Worth, Tex., U.S.A.; M.Ed., Univ. of S.C., Columbia. Appts. incl: Dir. & Org., Weekday Kindergarten, First Bapt. Ch., Joanna, S.C., 14 yrs.; Dir., Weekday Nursery Schl., Larned Lane, Orchard Pk., N.Y.; Cons., Early Childhood Educ., Williamsburg. S.C.; Preschl. Wkr., S.C. Bapt. Conven.; Columbia; Instr., Early Childhood Educ., Univ. of S.C. Mbrships. incl: Pres., Dist. 7, S.C. Assn. on Children Under Six; Assn. for Curriculum Dev.; Nursery-Kindergarten Early Childhood Educ.; S.C. Educ. Assn.; NEA; Southern Bapt. Religious Educ. Assn. Publs: Curriculum mats. for preschl. tchrs., & other articles, in sev. Southern Bapt. Conven. jrnls. Recip., Christian Serv. Award, Woman's Missionary Union, First Bapt. Ch., Joanna, S.C., 1961. Address: University of South Carolina, Education Annex, 916 Main St., Columbia, SC 29208, U.S.A. 125.

MITCHELL, Joseph Stanley, b. 22 July 1909. Physician; Radiotherapist; Professor. Educ: Univ. of Birmingham Med. Schl.; St. John's Coll., Univ. of Cambridge; M.B., B.Chir., Cambridge, 1934; Ph.D., ibid, 1937; M.D., 1957. Appts. incl: Res. Radiol. Off., Christie Hosp., Manchester, 1937; Asst. in Rsch. in Radiotherapy, Dept. of Med., Cambridge Univ., 1938; Radiotherapist, Emerg. Med. Serv., 1939; Med. Off. i/c, Radiotherapeutic Ctr., Addenbrooke's Hosp., Cambridge, 1943; i/c of Med. Investigations, Montreal Lab., Nat. Rsch. Coun., Canada, 1944; Prof. of Radiotherapeutics, Cambridge Univ., 1946; Regius Prof. of Physic, ibid, 1957. Mbrships: FRS; FFR; FRCP; Hon., Deutsche Röntgen-Gesellschaft. Publs: Studies in Radiotherapeutics, 1960; Cancer—if curable, why not cured?, 1971; Ed. of 3 books; Contbr. articles to profl. publs. Hons: CBE, 1951; D.Sc., Univ. of Birmingham, 1958; Durham Lectr., Harvard Univ., 1958; Pirogoff Medal, 1967. Address: Thorndyke, Huntingdon Rd., Cambridge CB3 0LG, U.K. 1, 34.

MITCHELL, Josephine Gray (Mrs. T.A. Mitchell). Musician. Educ: B.S., Tex. Woman's Univ., Denton, U.S.A., 1927; Master's Degree, ibid, 1971. Profl. Experience: Pianist; Accompanist; Tchr.; Lectr.; Adjudicator; Nat. Chmn. & Archivist, Folk Music, Nat. Fedn. Music Clubs; State Chmn., Tex. Composers Guild, conducting annual contests & presenting Tex. Composers Progs., 1950-74; Estab. SW Ctrl. Regional Archive, Folk Music, Ft. Worth Pub. Lib. & Collect. Tex. Music & Manuscripts; As State Music Chmn., Tex. Fedn. Women's Clubs, initiated & placed Ballet in Fine Arts Dept. Mbrships: Past Pres., Preschl. PTA; Ft. Worth Chapt., TWU Alumni; Cecilian, Euterpean & E. Clyde Whitlock Music Clubs; E. Ft. Worth Lady Lions; Polaris Club; Opera Guild; Symphony League; Ft. Worth Women's Club; Fndr., Chmn., Ft. Worth League Composers; Bd. Mbr., Tex. Girls Choir, Youth Orch., Gtr. Ft. Worth. Author 4 books in field & Compiler & Ed., Tex. Composers Guild Handbook, 1966. Recip. num. hons., inclng: Citation, Promotion Tex. Composers, 1966; Merit Award, SAI Music Frat., 1963. Address: 5120 Malinda Ln., Ft. Worth, TX 76112, U.S.A. 4, 5, 7, 79.

MITCHELL, Marion Faulkner, b. 1 Jan. 1914. Librarian. Educ: Meriden Schl. of Nursing, Conn.; Perry Bus. Coll.; Lib. Sci.,

Albany Jr. Coll. Appts: Inspr./Clerk, Army Serv. Forces, 1944-45; Owner & Operator, Local Finance Co., Cordele, Ga., 1948-56; Enumerator, U.S. Dept. of Agric., 1968-71; Libn., Cordele Carnegie Lib., & Lake Blackshear Regional Lib., 1968-; Pres., Wesleyan Serv. Guild. Mbrships. incl: Ga. & Southeastern Lib. Assns.; Vice-Dir., S.W. Dist., Bus. & Profl. Women's Clubs, 1973-74; Mbrship. Comm., Ga. Fedn. of Bus. & Profl. Women's Clubs, 1973-74; Charter Mbr., V.P., Sec., Treas., Cordele Bus. & Profl. Women's Club; Pres., ibid, 1971-73. Hons. incl: Woman of Yr., Crisp Co., 1963; Woman of Yr. in Bus. & Professions, 1972. Address: 705 16th Ave. E., Cordele, GA 31015, U.S.A. 125.

MITCHELL, Martha Joy, b. 29 Mar. 1925. Librarian. Educ: B.A., Tenn. Temple Coll., 1954; B.A., Geo. Peabody Coll. for Tchrs., 1958; M.A. in Lib. Sci., ibid, 1960. Appts: Hd. Libn., Tenn. Temple Coll., Chattanooga, 1954-57, 60-64; Libn., Dalewood Jr. HS, ibid, 1964-66; Hd. Libn., Franklin HS, Nashville, 1966-. Mbrships: NEA; Tenn. Educ. Assn.; Tenn. & Am. Lib. Assn.; Pres., Women's Nat. Book Assn., 1971-73. Hons: Ky. Col. Address: 2406 Blair Blvd., Nashville, TN 37212, U.S.A. 2, 5, 7.

MITCHELL, (Rev.) Robert Sydney, Sr., b. 29 Mar. 1933. Minister of Religion; Educator; Farmer. Educ: A.B., Trevecca Nazarene Coll., 1961; M.A., Austin Peay State Univ., 1964. Appts. incl: Minister, Ch. of the Nazarene, Erin & Griffins Chapel, Tenn., 1961-73; Min., Erin, 1973-; Tchr., Houston Co. Schls., 1961-; Supt., ibid, 1967-71; Dir., Nashville Christian Servs., 1973-. Mbrships. incl: NEA; Erin Civiton Club; Erin Rotary Club. Address: Rte. 3, Box 128A, Erin, TN 37061, U.S.A. 117.

MITCHELL, W(illiam) Morris, b. 13 Apr. 1917. Executive; Explorer; Writer. Educ: B.A., Yale 1939; Ecole Libre des Scis. Politiques, Paris, France, 1939; M.A., Harvard, U.S.A., 1940; Fellow, Magdalen Coll., Oxford, U.K. Appts. incl: Diplomatic Serv., 1941; w. Coord., Inter-Am. Affairs, Wash. & N.Y.; Naval Air Trans. Serv.; various positions w. air firms in Europe & Africa; Stockbroker, 1946-47; Sec., The Mitchell Steel Co., Cinn., 1948; V.P., ibid, 1950; Pres. & Treas., Chmn. of Bd., 1958-65; w. Ridgewood Ordance, Inc.: Sec.-Treas., 1950-55; V.P., Treas., 1955-58; Pres., 1958-63; Chmn. of Bd., 1963-68; Past Chmn. of Bd. & Dir., Lift Trucks, Inc., 1958-72; Past Dir., Cinn. Elect. Equipment Co., 1958-63; Currently: Chmn., Indies Plantations, Ltd.; Dir., James T. White & Co. & Nat. Ency. Am. Biog., N.Y., 1960-; Chmn. & Dir., Sumit, Inc., 1973-; Mbr. of many expeditions to Asia, Africa, Arctic, Antarctic, Ctrl. & S. Am., etc. Publs: Shanghai, A City Divided by War, 1938; A History of the Sino-Japanese Conflict, 1937-39, 1939; A Journey into Sikkim & Bhutan, 1945; Cape to Cairo by Convoy, 1955; A Short History of British North Borneo, 1958; The Lost World of Venezuela, 1959; Tierra del Fuego, 1960; & others; num. articles on exploration, hist., world affairs, etc. Address: "River Hill", Cleves, Hamilton Co., OH 45002, U.S.A. 3, 36, 68, 70, 128, 131, 140.

MITCHELL-GIFT, Caroline Anne Louisa, b. 12 Oct. 1941. Librarian. Eastern Caribbean Regional Lib. Schl., P.O.S.; North Western Polytechnic, London, U.K. Appts: Lib. Asst. I, 1959; Lib. Asst. II, 1963; Libn. I, 1966; Libn. III, 1971. Mbrships: Girl Guides Assn.; Assoc., Lib. Assn., U.K.; Lib. Assn. of Trinidad & Tobago. Address: Central Lib., Scarborough, Tobago, W. Indies. 109, 136.

MITICH, Janice Elizabeth, b. 27 Jan. 1945. Elementary Teacher. Educ: A.A., Eastern Ariz. Coll., 1965; B.S., Northern Ariz. Univ., 1967; Grad. work towards M.S., Univ. of Ariz., 1969-. Tchr., 5th grade, Tucson Pub. Schls., Dist. 1, 1967-. Mbrships. incl: NEA; Ariz. Educ. Assn.; Var. offs., Tucson Educ. Assn.; Phi Kappa Phi; Kappa Delta Pi, 1966-67; Sigma Epsilon Sigma, 1965-66; Pres., Phi Theta Kappa, 1964-65; Riflemen's Assn. Firearm Safety Instr., 1973-; Ariz. Varmit Callers, 1972-. Minor works in water color shown & sold locally. Hons. incl: Fac. Women's Award, Eastern Ariz. Coll., 1965; Outstanding Sr. Woman Award, Northern Ariz. Univ., 1967. Address: 915 E. Halcyon Road, Tucson, AZ 85719, U.S.A. 76, 120, 132.

MITKO, Francis C., b. 16 Mar. 1940. Economist. Educ: B.A., Univ. of Utah, 1964; M.A., San Fran. State Coll., 1970. Appts: Instr., Econs., Golden Gate Coll., evenings, 1969-70; Tax Specialist, Internal Revenue Serv., Alcohol & Tobacco, 1965-67; Economist, U.S. Bur. of Mines, San Fran., 1967-70; Economist, ibid, Arlington, Va., 1970-73; Tariff Commn. Analyst-Economist, U.S. Tariff Commn., Wash. D.C., 1973-. Mbrships: Am. Acad. of Pol. & Soc. Scientists; Am. Econ. Assn.; World Future Soc.; Fndr., Int. Music & Discussion Prog. Publs. incl: Mineral Industry of California, 1970; Mineral Industry of Cuba, 1971; Platinum-Group Metals, 1971. Designed var. forecast methodols. Recip., var. hons. Address: 1416 21st St. N.W., Wash. DC 20036, U.S.A. 7, 130.

MITRA, Sudhansu Bhushan. College Professor. Educ: B.Sc., Calcutta Univ., India, 1933; B.T., ibid, 1940; B.Sc., ibid, 1941; M.A., Cath. Univ. of Am., Wash. D.C., 1967; Ph.D., ibid, 1969; post-doctoral studies, 1969-71. Appts: Rehab. Counselor, Adult Educ. Prog., Dept. Vocatnl. Rehab., Govt. of Dist. of Columbia, Wash. D.C., 1969-70; Lectr., Special Educ., U.S. Dept. of Agric., Grad. Schl., Wash. D.C., 1970-; Lectr., Urban Studies Inst., Morgan State Coll., Balt., Md., 1972-; Asst. Prof., Special Educ.-Assoc. Prof. & Chmn., Dept. of Rehab. Counseling, Coppin State Coll., Balt., Md., 1970-. Mbrships: Am. Assn. on Mental Deficiency; Am. Educnl. Rsch. Assn.; Am. Personnel & Guid. Assn.; Am. Psychol. Assn.; Am. Rehab. Counselling Assn.; Md. Psychol. Assn.; Md. Assn. of Tchr. Eductrs.; Nat. Coun. Univ. Rsch. Admins. Contbr. articles to profl. jrnls. Cons. for Choice, publd. by ALA. Abstractor for Psychol. Abstracts, publd. by Am. Psychol. Assn. Reviewer for Journal of Rehab., publd. by Nat. Rehab. Assn. Address: Coppin State Coll., 2500 W. North Ave., Balt., MD 21216, U.S.A.

MITROVICH, Carol Lee Corbett (Mrs. M.L. Mitrovich), b. 10 Dec. 1938. Housewife; Civic Worker; Volunteer. Educ: Mainland Jr. Coll. Appt: Clerk Typist, Am. Nat. Insurance Co.; Hosp. Volunteer, 1973-74. Mbrships: Beta Sigma Phi (Holde of all offices, 1965-71); Tex. VFW, 1960-74 (Pres., Trustee, Sr. Vice-Chmn.); PTA (Prog. Chmn., 1971-72, Hospitality-Sec. for PTA Coun.); Jr. Girl Scout Ldr., 1972-74; Area Chmn., March of Dimes. Collector of recipes published in var. books; sings at var. occasions. Hons: Cert. of Merit, Voice of Democracy Prog., VFW, & for work done with Youth & Americanism; Sorority Valentine Sweetheart, 1969; Girl of the Year, 1971-72; Mother of the Year, 1972. Address: 1103 Spruce, La Marque, TX 77568, U.S.A. 76, 125.

MITSEM, Sverre, b. 25 Nov. 1907. Chief Editor. Appts: Jrnlist, Nórges Fremtid, Norway, 1930-33; Jrnlist, ABC, 1933-37; Ed., 1937-39; City Ed., Tidens Tegn, 1939-41; Jrnlist, Press

Telegraph, 1941-45; Jrnlist, Tonsbergs Blad, 1945-54; Chief Ed., 1954-. Mbrships: Int. Press Inst.; Assn. of Norwegian Eds.; Bd., Conservative Press Assn. Author, 10 vols. of newspaper articles. Recip., Narvesen Prize for Outstanding Jrnlistic Achievements, 1970. Address: Tonsbergs Blad, 3100 Tønsberg, Norway. 43.

MITSOTAKIS, Constantin K., b. 18 Oct. 1918. Lawyer. Educ: Grad., Law & Pol. Scis., Athens Univ., Greece. Appts: Lawyer, Athens, 1940-; Reserve Off., Greek Army, WWII; Ldr., Nat. Resistance, Crete, twice condemned to death, but exchanged for German prisoners; Dpty., Greek Parliament, 1946-67; Financial Undersec., Min. of Communications & Pub. Wks., 1951; Mln. of Finance, 1963-65; Min. for Econ. Cooperation, 1965-66; Imprisoned, 1967-68; Escaped to W. Europe, 1968; Returned to Greece, 1973. Mbr., Athens Club. Recip., Greek & British Order of Resistance, 1947. Address: Panou Aravandinou St., No. 1, Athens 138, Greece.

MITTEL, John J., Economist; Business Executive. Educ: B.B.A., Univ. City of N.Y. Appts: Rschr., Econs. Dept., McGraw Hill & Co., N.Y.C., 1956; Mgr., Asst. to Pres., Ind. Commodity Corp., J. Carvel Lange Inc. & J. Carvel Lange Int. Inc., 1956-; Corp. Sec., 1958-; V.P., 1964-; Pres., I.C. Investors Corp., 1972-. Mbrships: Trustee, Combined Ind. Commodity Corp. & J. Carvel Lange Inc. Pension Plan, 1962-; J. Carvel Lange Int. Inc. Profit Sharing Trust, 1969-; Grad. Advsry. Bd., Barnard M. Maruch Coll., Univ. City of N.Y., 1971-; Conf. Bd., Am. Stat. Assn.; Newcomen Soc. N.Am.; Union League Club. Publs: How Good a Sales Profit Are You, 1961; The Role of the Economic Consulting Firm; num. mkt. surveys. Address: Rm. 1206, 122 E. 42nd St., N.Y., NY 10017, U.S.A. 6.

MIXON, George Edward, b. 29 Jan. 1919. Family Physician & Surgeon. Educ: A.B. in Sci., Ga. Tech., Atlanta, 1937-41 & Emory Univ., Ga., 1946-47; M.D., Med. Coll. of Ga., Augusta, 1951; Dipl., Am. Bd. Family Prac., 1972; Fellow, Am. Acad. of Family Physns., N.Y.C., 1972. Appts: incl: Serv., Pvte.-1st Lt., WWII, 1941-46; Var. Pub. Hlth. Posts, Irwin Co., Ga., 1962-73; Pvte. Prac., Family Med., Ocilla, Ga. Mbrships: incl: Am. Acad. Family Physns.; Past-Pres., State Chapt., ibid; Ga. Acad. of Gen. (later Family) Prac.; Mbrship. Chmn., ibid, 1967-69; V.P., ibid, 1970; Pres., ibid, 1972; Chmn., Bd. of Dirs., ibid, 1973; Ben Hill-Irwin Co., Ga., Med. Soc.; Pres., ibid, 1963; Ocilla United Meth. Ch.; Mason; British Inter-Planetary Soc.; Phi Rho Sigma. Compiler, 60 Scrapbooks on Space Endeavours, 1957-73. Contbr., The Mixson-Mixon Family, J.L. Mixson, 1972. Hons. incl: 4 Medals, U.S. Army, WWII; Dipl. Cert., Family Prac. Sect., Pan Am. Med. Assn., 1972. Address: 301, S. Cherry St., Ocilla, GA 31774, U.S.A. 7, 17, 22, 125, 126, 129, 131.

MIZRAHI, Abraham, b. 16 Apr. 1929. Physician. Educ: B.S., Manchester Coll., 1955; M.D., Albert Einstein Coll.; Intern, Univ. of N.C., 1960-61; Res., Pediatrics, Columbia Univ., 1961-63; NIH Fellow, Neonatol., ibid, 1963-64. Appts: Dir., Newborn Nurseries, Elmhurst Med. Ctr., & Assoc. Dir., Newborn Nurseries, Mt. Sinai Hosp., N.Y., 1964-66; Staff Physn., Geigy Pharmaceuticals, 1966-68; Assoc. Attng., Fordham Hosp., 1966-; Cons., Misericordia Med. Ctr., N.Y., 1966-; Hd., Cardiovascular, Pulmonary, Renal Sect., Geigy Pharmaceuticals, 1968-71; Sr. V.P., USV Pharmaceuticals, N.Y., 1971-. Mbrships: Dipl., Nat. Bd. of Med. Examiners, & Nat. Bd. of Pediatrics; Fellow, N.Y. Acad. of Med., Am. Soc. for Clin. Pharmacol. & Therapeutics, & Weitzman Inst. of Sci.; AMA; N.Y. Pediatric Soc. Part-author, num. articles in profl. publs. Address: 7 Jason Lane, Mamaroneck, NY 10543, U.S.A. 6, 17.

MJÖSUND, Johan Margido, b. 14 July 1908. Supreme Court Barrister. Educ: Exam. Artium, 1927; Degree Exam. in Jurisprudence, Oslo Univ., 1932. Appts: Barrister, 1933; Mbr., Municipal Coun., Trondheim, 1935-71; Substitute M.P., 1945-49; Barrister, Supreme Ct., 1955-; Chmn., E.C. Dahl Fndn., 1953-; Counsel for Municipality of Trondheim, 1959-; Mbr., num. municipal & state comms. Mbrships. incl: Sec., Norwegian Good Templar Youth Assn., 1931, Chmn., 1932-35; Int. Order of Good Templars; Mbr., Nat. Bd., Norwegian Br., ibid, 1934-, Pres., 1953-73, Mbr., Int. Bd., 1953-, 1st V.P., 1970-; Norwegian Advocate Assn.; Teetotallers Motor-Car Assn.; Norwegian Labour Party. Articles, newspapers, jrnls. Recip., Veteran Medal, Int. Order Good Templars, 1957. Address: P.O. Box 904, 7001 Trondheim, Norway.

MLODOZENIEC, Jan, b. 8 Nov. 1929. Graphic Artist & Designer. Educ: Studies in Applied Graphic Art, Warsaw Acad. of Fine Arts; Dip., Poster Design, 1955. Appts: Free-lance Illustrator, books & mags., Designer, theatre, film & exhib. posters, 1953-; Creator, designs w. own poetic texts, Miesiecznik Literacki, literary monthly, 1966-. Mbr., Polish Union of Plastic Artists, 1956-. Solo Exhibs: Warsaw, 1962, 1969; Vienna, 1963; Prague, 1966; Poitiers, 1968; Lublin, 1969. Hons. incl: Silver Medal, Leipzig, 1965, 1971; Poster & Applied Art Award, Min. of Culture & Art, 1967; Silver Medal, Katowice, 1971; var. competition prizes, awards & dips. Address: Naruszewicza 3 m.7, 02627 Warsaw, Poland.

MNOLIU, Lia, b. 25 Apr. 1932. Engineer. Educ: Grad., Bucharest Inst. of Polytechs., Romania. Appts: Designing Engr., 1956-67; Rsch. Engr., 1967-. Mbrships: V.P., Nat. Coun. Phys. Educ. & Sports, Bucharest; V.P., Romanian Olympic Comm.; V.P., Romanian Olympic Comm.; V.P., Romanian Athletic Fedn.; METALUL Athletic Club, Bucharest. Contbr. Dissertation at 23rd Session Int. Olympic Acad., Greece: 6 Times at the Olympic Games. Hons: Bronze Medal, discus throwing, Olympic Games, Rome, 1960 & Tokyo, 1964; Gold Medal, Mexico City, 1968; Merited Master of Sports Award of Romania, 1964-; Order of Sports Merit, 1st Class, Romania, 1968; Work Order, 3rd Class, Romania, 1952, '60; Star of Socialist Repub. of Romania, 3rd Class, 1973. Address: Romanian Olympic Comm., str. Vasile Conta 16, Bucharest, Romania.

MOAK, Donald Lewis, b. 7 Oct. 1939. Banker. Educ: B.S., Miss Coll., Univ. of Miss., 1961; M.S., ibid, 1963; LL.B., Jackson Schl. of Law, Univ. of Miss., 1965; Ph.D., ibid, 1974. Appts: Asst. Trust Off., Deposit Guaranty Nat. Bank, Jackson, Miss., 1965; Asst. Prof. of Bus., Delta State Coll., Cleveland, Miss., 1969-74; Sr. V.P., Bank of Clarksdale, Miss., 1974-. Mbrships: Miss. State Bar Assn.; Am. Judicature Soc.; Mbrships. Comm., Am. Finance Assn.; Miss. Acad. Economists; Rotary Club; Sigma Delta Kappa; Pi Kappa Alpha, Sec.-Treas., Pi Kappa Alpha Central Delta Alumni Assn. Nomination, Outstanding Alumnus, Zeta Beta Chapt., Pi Kappa Alpha, 1973. Address: Bank of Clarksdale, P.O. Box 1059, Clarksdale, MS 38614, U.S.A. 125.

MOBERG, Carl Gustaf (Gösta), b. 28 Apr. 1894. Explorer; Author. Appts. incl: Expeditions for Swedish & for. museums, inclng. N. Africa, Sahara, Nigeria, Guyana, Alaska, Central Africa, Rio de Oro, 1924-69; Lectr., touring Germany, Denmark, Finland & U.S.A. Mbrships. incl: Geographical Soc. Sweden; Am. Polar Soc., N.Y. Publ. incl: Rädslans Land, 1927; Avensyrens Land, 1929; Farligt Land, 1947; Jagad av indianer, 1957; Bragdernas män, 1959; Num. articles, Swedish & for. newspapers & mags; Mus. collects. incl., Stockholm, Oslo, Finnish, Danish & U.S. nat. museums. Hons. incl: Swedish Linnémedal of Acad. Sci.; Kt. 1st Class, Finnish Lion Order, & Norwegian Order St. Olaf; Cmdr., French Order of Black Star. Address: Narvavägen 7 1, 114 60 Stockholm, Sweden. 134.

MOBLEY, Ora W. (Mrs. Earl R. S. Mobley), b. 16 Mar. 1927. Community Worker. Educ: Barber-Scotia Coll., Concord, N.C.; B.A., Johnson C. Smith Univ., Charlotte, ibid; grad. work, Tchrs. Coll., Columbia Univ., N.Y. Appts. incl: Educ. Coord., Neighborhood Bd. 3, Inc., N.Y., 1965-71; Tchr., Whiteville Elem. Schl., N.C.; Tchr., Div. of Day Care, Soc. Investigator, Dept. of Welfare, N.Y.; 20 yrs. volunteer serv., N.Y.; Fndr., Dir., Ctrl. Harlem Mothers' Assn., Inc.; Currently, Dir., Melrose Community Ctr.; Organizer, many grps. & activities inclng. Mary McLeod Bethune Mem. Servs., St. Nicholas Tenents Org. Mbrships. incl: Chmn., Elem. Poetry Div., World Poets Resource Ctr.; NAACP; Former Sec., Community Schl. Bd. Dist. 5, N.Y.C.; Eastern Ctr., Poetry Soc. of London, U.K.; Bd. of Dirs., Gtr. Harlem Dev. Fndn., N.Y. Hons. incl: Cert of Election, Bd. of Educ., N.Y., 1970; 1st Outstanding Tenant of Yr. Award, N.Y.C. Housing Authority, presented by Hon. Mayor John V. Lindsay, 1966; Community Wkr. & Community Ldr. of Yr. Special Award, Eastern Ctr., Poetry Soc. of London, 1971: Mother of Yr. Award, N.Y.C., 1972. Address: 237 W. 127th St., Apt. 2C, New York, NY 10027, U.S.A. 130.

MOCH, Ronald Wilbur, b. 23 Dec. 1942. Army Officer & Veterinary Pathologist. Educ: B.S., Univ. of Mo., 1964; D.V.M., ibid, 1966; Career Offs. Course, Ft. Sam Houston, Tex., 1970; Master of Liberal Arts, Johns Hopkins Univ., Balt., Md., 1972. Appts. incl: Asst. Chief-Acting Chief, Special Projs. & Food Technol., U.S. Army Med. Serv. Veterinary Schl., Chgo., Ill., 1967-68; Asst. Chief-Acting Chief, Dept. of Combat Serv. Support, ibid, 1968; Precepte, Veterinary Pathol., Med. Resch. Lab., Edgewood Arsenal, Md., 1968-72; Hd., Veterinary Med. Dept., Naval Med. Rsch. Unit No. 3, Cairo, Egypt 1972-. Mbrships. incl: Am. Veterinary Med. Assn.; Am. Assn. of Mil. Surgeons; Unicorn Fraternity. Publs: Guide to Garrison Veterinary Officers, 1967; Co-author, Large Babesia: Infection in a dog in Egypt, (In press); cntbns. to med. jrnls. Hons. incl: Danforth Schlrship, Am. Youth Fndn., 1964; Army Commendation Medal, 1968. Address: Veterinary Medicine Dept., Naval Medical Research Unit No. 3, F.P.O. NY 09527, U.S.A. 7, 117.

MOCHLY, Josef, b. 18 Apr. 1920. Architect. Educ: Arch., Univ. of Rome, 1946; B.Sc., Technion, Israel Inst. Technol., 1952. Appts: Pvte. Prac. as Archt., 1954-; Assoc. Prof., Fac. of Arch., Israel Inst. Technol., 1960-; Mbr., Coun. Indl. Design, 1966; Cons., Lab. Design, for FAO of UN, 1967-; Ptnr., J. Mochly Archts. Ltd., 1968-; Ptnr., J. Mochly, Y. Eldar Archts. Ltd., 1970-. Mbrships: Israel Inst. Archts.; Int. Illuminating Soc. Publs: Lighting Calculation Tables, 1958; Laboratory Design in Secondary Schools. Contbr., Educl. Ency. Jerusalem. Articles & reports, bldgs. & designs, profl. publs. Address: Josef Mochly Architects Ltd., 15 Smolensky St., Haifa, ISrael.

MOCKRIDGE, David George Christopher, b. 21 Sept. 1923. Publisher. Educ: M.A. (Hons.), Literae Humaniores, Brasenose Coll., Oxford Univ., U.K. Appts. incl: Mng. Dir., Iliffe Books Ltd., 1960-65; Mng. Dir., Melrose Press Ltd., London 1969-. Mbrships: All England Lawn Tennis Club, Wimbledon; Int. Lawn Tennis Club of G.B. Address: Newnham's Rough, Horsted Keynes, Sussex, U.K.

MODEEN, Viking Henrik Albert, b. 5 Jan. 1908. Lord Justice of the Supreme Court. Educ: M.A., Fac. of Arts; LL.B. Appts: Extraordinary Clerk, Supreme Ct. of Finland, 1938, Extraordinary Referant, 1946, Notary, 1946, 2nd Sec., 1948, 1st Sec., 1955, Extraordinary Justice, 1961; Justice of the Supreme Court, 1961-. Mbrships: Legal Assn. of Finland; Finnish Jurists' Assn. Hons: Finnish Medal, 1941-44; Cross of Liberty, 4th Class w. swords, 1942; Cmdr., Order of the Lions, 1957; Cmdr., 1st Class, Order of the White Rose, 1966. Address: Fredriksgatan 75, Helsinki, Finland.

MODICA, Alfred J(oseph), b. 22 Jan. 1925. Marketing Communications Management Executive. Educ: LL.B., Blackstone Schl. of Law, Chgo., Ill., U.S.A., 1965; J.D., ibid, 1968. Appts: USMC, 1943-46; Sales Mgr., Electrolux Corp., N.Y.C., 1946-49; Free-lance Marketing Dir., 1949-54; Pres. & Dir., Meadowstone, Inc., N.Y.C., 1954-62; Marketing Communications Cons., 1962-66; Exec. V.P., Seltz Franchising Dev., Inc., N.Y.C., 1967-69; Pres. & Dir., O.F.I. Corp., Maspeth, N.Y., 1969-; Pres. & Dir., Lee Myles Assocs. Corp., Maspeth, 1969-; Exec. V.P. & Dir., Lee Myles Corp., Maspeth, 1969-; Lectr., Workshop seminars, for bus., fed. & state govts., 1970-; Assoc. Ed., Franchising Around the World, 1970-. Mbrships: Int. Franchising Assn.; Am. Acad. of Cons.; Alpha Psi Omega. Publs: Take the Con out of the Franchising Contract; The Funny Side of Owning your own Business; Frustration of Purpose in Franchising. Recip., Ph.D., Ohio Christian Coll., 1970. Address: 700 Scarsdale Ave., Scarsdale, NY 10583, U.S.A.

MOE, Johannes, b. 24 Apr. 1926. Professor of Ship Structures. Educ: B.Sc., Tech. Univ. of Norway, Trondheim, 1952; Lic. Techn., ibid, 1957; Dr. Techn., 1961. Appts. incl: Cons. Engr., Kristiansund, 1953-57; Nat. Sci. Fndn. Fellow, Portland Cement Assn., Chgo., Ill., U.S.A., 1957-59; Mgr., Structural Sect., Norwegian Inst. of Wood Working & Wood Technol., Oslo, 1959-62; Prof., Ship Structures, Tech. Univ. of Norway, 1962-; Rector, ibid, 1972-. Mbrships. incl: Royal Norwegian Acad. of Scis. & Letters; Norwegian Acad. of Tech. Scis.; Int. Ship Structures Congress; Royal Instn. of Naval Archts.; Am. Soc. of Naval Archts. & Marine Engrs; Int. Assn. of Bridge & Structural Engrng.; Int. Assn. of Shell Structures. Author, about 80 publs. on shell theory, theoretical & experimental studies of reinforced concrete & timber structures, & design of ship structures. Address: Technical University of Norway, 7034 Trondheim, Norway.

MOE, Rolf, b. 24 Sept 1917. Managing Director; Electrical Engineer. Educ: M.S., Norwegian Tech. Univ., 1943. Appts. incl: Mgr., Narvik Municipal Electricity Works, 1947-52; Mgr., Midt-Helgeland Power Co., 1952-54; Chief Engr., Skiensfjordens Municipal Power Co., Porsgrunn, 1954-64; Chief Engr.,

Norwegian Assn. of Power Supply Undertakings, 1964-65; Dir. of Electricity, Norwegian Water Resources & Electricity Bd., 1965-71; Mng. Dir., Norwegian Bd. for Testing & Approval of Elec. Equipment, 1971. Mbrships. incl: Norwegian Engrs. Assn; Norwegian Electrotechnical Assn; Pres., Norwegian Electrotechnical Comm. (Nat. IEC Comm). Contbr. to tech. jrnls. & publs. Recip., Participation Medal. Address: NEMKO, Gaustadalleen 30, Blindern, Oslo 3, Norway.

MOFFAT, John Lawrence, b. 4 Dec. 1916. Writer; Lecturer. Educ: Canterbury Univ. Coll., 1935-39; Bristol Univ., U.K., 1946-48; Ph.D., ibid; M.A., N.Z. Appts: Lang. Master, Christchurch Boys' H.S. 1939-53; Prin. Lectr., Post-Primary Lang. Sect., Christchurch Tchrs. Coll., 1954-. Mbrships: Past Pres., Christchurch Classical Assn.; Canterbury Inst. Educ. Rsch.; Orch. Pianist, Christchurch Savage Club; Int. Yoga Tchrs. Assn.; N.Z. Homosexual Law Reform Soc.; Philos. of Educ. Soc. of Australasia; Canterbury Repertory Theatre Soc.; Soc. for Rsch. on Women in N.Z.; N.Z. Assn. Classical Tchrs. Publs: The Structure of English, 1968; A Guide to Study, 1971. Educ. Columnist, var. N.Z. newspapers. Recip., sev. acad. hons. Address: Soul's Repose, 51 London St., Christchurch 1, New Zealand. 131.

MOFFATT, David John, b. 23 July 1939. University Professor. Educ: B.Sc., Univ. of Bristol, U.K., 1961; M.B.Ch.B., 1964. Appts: Lectr., Anat., Univ. of Bristol, 1968; Asst. Prof., Univ. of Iowa Coll. of Med., U.S.A., 1968-71; Assoc. Prof., ibid, 1971-; Dir., Gross Human Anat. for Med. Students, 1973-. Mbrships. incl: Anat. Soc. of G.B. & Ireland; Am. Assn. Anats.; Soc. for Exptl. Biol. & Med.; Nat. Soc. for Performance & Instrn.; Assn. for Study of Med. Educ. Publs: Human Anatomical Terminology; The Peripheral Nervous System; The Cardiovascular System; num. articles in profl. jrnls. Recip., Physns Recognition Award, AMA, 1971. Address: Dept. of Anat., Univ. of Iowa Coll. of Med., Iowa City, IA 52242, U.S.A. 139.

MOFFETT, (Henry Clay) Nick, b. 30 Nov. 1908. Floraculturist & Public Relations Executive, Educ: Fordham Univ., N.Y.C., 1946; Rutgers Univ., N.J., 1947-48. Appts. incl: Sales Mgr., Metropolitan Life, 1939-63; Lectr., Radio & TV Commentator, Gladiolus Culture, 1960-69; Dir. & Judge, All Am. Gladiolus Selections, 1962-72; Chief Finance Off., Woodbury, N.J., 1963-72; Admnstr. & Treas., Pub. Lib., ibid, 1963-72; Chmn., Stabilization Bd., Gloucester Co., N.J., 1968-; Tax Commnr., ibid, 1972-; V.P., Most Co. Inc., Woodbury, N.J. Mbrships. incl: N. Am. Gladiolus Coun.; Accredited Judge, ibid, 1960-; Pres., ibid, 1962-64; Woodbury Rotary Club; Pres., ibid, 1968-69; Gloucester Co. Holy Name Soc.; Pres., ibid, 1948-64; Republican Campaign Mgr., Gloucester Co., 1958-71. Contbr. to Newspapers. Originator of Top Ten Symposium of Outstanding Gladiolus Varieties. Hons. incl: Tiki Award, N.Z. Gladiolus Soc., 1963; Gold Medal Award, N. Am. Gladiolus Coun., 1964; Citizen, Lubbock, Tex., 1963; Outstanding Community Serv. Award, Woodbury, N.J., 1972. Address: 428 Hemlock Ter., Woodbury, NJ 08096, U.S.A. 6.

MOFFETT, Samuel Hugh, b. 7 Apr. 1916. Missionary Educator. Educ: A.B., Wheaton Coll., 1938; Th.B., Princeton Theol. Sem., 1942; Ph.D., Yale Univ., 1945. Ordained, Presby. Ch., U.S.A., 1943. Appts: Asst. Pastor, Conn. chs., 1943-45; Dir., Youth Work, Presby. Bd. of For. Missions, 1945-47; Missionary to China, 1947-51; Fac., Yenching Univ. Peking, &

Nanking Theol. Sem., 1948-50; Vis. Lectr., Princeton Theol. Sem., N.J., 1953-55; Missionary to Korea, 1955-; Prof., Ch. Hist., Presby. Theol. Sem., Seoul, 1960-; Dean of Grad. Schl., 1966-70; Assoc. Pres., 1971-; Dir., Asian Ctr. for Theol. Studies & Mission, 1974-. Mbrships: Councilor, Past Pres., Korea Br., Royal Asiatic Soc.; U.S. Educl. Commn. (Fulbright), Korea, 1966-67; Presby. Histl. Soc.; Bd. of Dirs., Yonsei Univ., Soongjun Univ., Korea, Whitworth Coll., Wash.; Contbng. Ed., Christianity Today. Publs: Where'er the Sun, 1953; The Christians in Korea, 1962; Joy for an Anxious Age, 1966; The Biblical Background of Evangelism, 1968; Contbr. to U.S., Korean mags. Address: G.P.O. Box 1125, Seoul, Korea.

MOFFITT, Donald Anthony, b. 15 May 1936. Journalist. Educ: B.A., Yale Univ., 1958. Appts: Reporter, Houston Post, Tex., 1958-60; Reporter, Wall Street Journal, Dallas, Tex., San Francisco, Calif. & N.Y.C., 1960-68; V.P. & Edit. Dir., Caldwell Communications Inc., N.Y.C., 1968-71; Page-One Copy Ed., Wall Street Journal, N.Y.C., 1971-. Publs: Articles in American Way, Coronet, Investment Sales Monthly, Motorboat, Physicians World, True. Hons: Meyer Berger Award, Columbia Univ. 1970. Address: 39 Jane St., Apt. 5-A, N.Y., NY 10014, U.S.A.

MOFFITT, John, b. 27 June 1908. Editor; Writer; Poet. Educ: A.B., Princeton Univ., N.J., U.S.A., 1928; Grad., Curtis Inst. of Music, 1932. Appts. incl: Monastic Probationer, N.Y. Ctr., Ramakrishna Order of India, 1933-35 & 1939-49; Pvte. Tutor, 1936-39; Monastic Novice, N.Y. Ctr., Ramakrishna Order of India, 1949-59; Monk, ibid, 1959-63; Copy Ed., Am. mag., N.Y.C., 1963-70; Poetry Ed., ibid, 1963-. Mbrship: Authors Guild. Publs: Poetical versions of songs & hymns in The Gospel of Sri Ramakrishna, 1942; This Narrow World, 1958; The Living Seed, 1962; Adam's Choice, 1967; Journey to Gorakhpur, 1972; Escape of the Leopard, 1974; Ed. & Contbr., A New Charter for Monasticism, 1968; Poems & articles on relig. & philos. in sev. mags. & jrnls.; Poems in anthols. Recip., Award for poem, O Men of Might, contest for a new Nat. Anthem for U.S.A., 1929. Address: Rocklands, Gordonsville, VA 22942, U.S.A. 6, 11, 139.

MOGAVERO, I. Frank, b. 12 July 1913. Professor of History. Educ: B.S., Canisius Coll., Buffalo, 1944; M.A., ibid, 1946; Ph.D., Ottawa Univ., Canada, 1950. Appts: Prof. of Hist., Niagara Univ., 1946-; Medaille Coll., 1947-70; D'Youville Coll., 1964-67. Mbrships. incl: Bd. of Mgrs., Buffalo & Erie Co. Hist. Soc., 1963-; Sec., ibid, 1967-; Chmn., Comm. on Markers, 1956; Soc. of Am. Archivists; N.Y. State Hist. Assn. N.Y. State Am. Revolution Bicentennial Commn. Publs: Brief History of the Diocese of Buffalo; Centennial History of Niagara University; Historical Guide to the City of Buffalo. Hons: Dr. of Pedag., Medaille Coll., 1973. Address: 3091 Second Ave., Grand Island, NY 14072, U.S.A. 6, 13.

MOGUL, Ebrahim, b. 1 Mar. 1918. Artist; Painter; Sculptor. Educ: Nat. Dip. in Design, Camberwell Schl. of Art, U.K.; Ecole Nat. Supérieure des Beaux-Arts, Paris, France. Works incl: One Man Exhibs. in St. Imier, 1961, Zurich, 1961, '63, '65, '67, '70, Lausanne, 1963, Geneva, 1972, '73; Grp. exhibs. in Bombay, 1944, London, 1951, Zurich, 1961, '64, '68, '70, Paris, 1950, Geneva, 1962, '70; Publs. incl: Development of Indian Painting, (W. G.A. Molvi), 1941; Contbr. to periodicals. Address: 32 rue des Noirettes, CH-1227 Carouge, Geneva, Switzerland. 133.

MOHAMED SAID BIN MOHAMED, Tan Sri Datuk, b. 31 Oct. 1907. Physician; Politician (ret.'d). Educ: King Edward VII Coll. of Med., Singapore; Postgrad., London Univ. & Rotunda Hosp., Dublin, Repub. of Ireland. Appts: Gogt. Med. Serv., 23 yrs.; Clin. Specialist in Obstetrics, Gen. Hosp., Seremban, Negri Sembilan, 1949-55; Mbr., State Legislative Assembly, Negri Sembilan, 1955-58; Chief Min., Negri Sembilan, 1959-69. Mbrships: Life mbr., Malaysian br., Royal Asiatic Soc.; Brit. Med. Assn.; Royal Commonwealth Soc.; V.P., Malaysian Govt. Pensioners Assn.; UMNO. Contbr. of articles to med. jrnls. Hons: P.M.N., 1966; P.P.T., 1967. Address: 101 Gedong Lalang, Ampangan, Seremban, Negri Sembilan, Malaysia. 98.

MOHAMED SUFFIAN bin HASHIM, b. 12 Nov. 1917. Lawyer. Educ: M.A., Gonville & Caius Coll., Cambridge Univ., U.K. 1939; LL.B., ibid, 1940; Called to Bar, Middle Temple; Cambridge Univ., 1946-47; London Schl. of Oriental & African Studies & London Schl. of Econs., 1947-48; Hon. LL.D., Singapore & Hon. D.Litt, Malaya. Appts. incl: Solicitor Gen., Malaya, 1959; High Ct. Judge, Malaya, 1961; Apptd. Pro-Chancellor, Univ. of Malaya, Kuala Lumpur, 1964-; Chmn., Royal Commn. on Salaries of Pub. Servs., 1965; Judge, Fed. Ct., Malaysia, 1968; Chmn., Comm. to enquire into resignations of acad. staff, Univ. of Malaya, 1968; Chmn., Comm. to draft constitution of Univ. of Sci., Panang & Comm. to draft constitution of Nat. Univ., Kuala Lumpur, 1968; Chmn., Higher Educ. Advsry. Coun., 1972; Chief Justice, Malaya, 1973. Publs: A Malay translation of Malayan Constitution, 1963; An Introduction To The Constitution Of Malaysia, 1972. Hons. incl: S.M.B., by H.R.H., Sultan of Brunei, 1959; J.M.N., 1961 & P.S.M., 1967, by H.R.H., Yang Dipertuan Agung; P.J.K., 1963 & D.I.M.P., 1969, by H.R.H., Sultan of Pahang. Address: Federal Ct., Kuala Lumpur, Malaysia. 34, 98.

MOHAMMED, Isahak, b. 6 June 1926. Medical Practitioner. Educ: M.B., B.S., St. Thomas's Hosp. Med. Schl., Univ. of London, U.K., 1952; Dip. Child Hlth., Royal Coll. Physns., London, & Royal Coll. Surgs., U.K., 1959; Mbr., Royal Coll. Physns., Edinburgh, U.K., 1960. Appts: Registrar, Dept. of Med., Univ. Hosp. of the West Indies, Mona, Jamaica; Specialist Paediatrician, Gen. Hosp., San Fernando, Trinidad. Mbrships: Exec., Trinidad & Tobago Med. Assn. Contbr. to profl. jrnls. Hons: Island Schlrship in Maths., Queen's Royal Coll., Trinidad, 1944. Address: General Hospital, San Fernando, Trinidad, West Indies.

MOHAMMED, Shamshuddin, b. 8 May 1936. Barrister-at-Law; Politician. Educ: London Schl. Econs. & Pol. Sci., U.K.; Admission to Bar, Gray's Inn, London, & Trinidad, W.I., 1964; Appts: Schl. Tchr., Trinidad, 1956-60; Corres., Focus Mag., London, U.K., 1962-64; Jr. Counsel in Chambers, w. Edgar Gaston Johnston, Q.C., Trinidad, 1965-71; Mbr., House of Reps., 1966-, Dpty. Speaker., 1970; Min. of State, Local Govt., 1971; Min. for Community Dev., Youth Affairs, P.R., & Min. of Pub. Utilities, 1973. Mbrships. incl: Pres., Trinidad & Tobago Volley Ball Assn. (N. Zone); Fndr. & 1st V.P., Dreadnought Youth Sports Club & Middlesex Sports Club of San Juan; Gray's Inn & Commonwealth Inst. Debating Socs., London. Ed., var. sports, cultural & religious mags. & publs. Address: Whitehall, Maraval Rd., Port of Spain, Trinidad, W. Indies. 109, 136.

MOHLER, Stanley Ross, b. 30 May 1927. Medical Doctor. Educ: B.A., Univ. of Tex.,

1953; M.A., ibid, 1953; M.D., Med. Br., Univ. of Tex., Galveston, 1956. Appts: Med. Off., Ctr. for Aging Rsch., Nat. Insts. Hlth., U.S. Pub. Hlth. Serv., Bethesda, Md., 1957-61; Assoc. Prof. of Rsch., Preventive Med. & Pub. Hlth., Univ. of Okla. Schl. of Med., 1961-68; Dir., Civil Aeromed. Rsch. Inst., Okla. City, 1961-65; Chief, Aeromed. Applications Div., Off. of Aviation Med., Fed. Aviation Admin, 1965-. Mbrships. incl: Fellow, Aerospace Med. Assn.; V.P., ibid, 1962; Flying Physns. Assn.; Dir., ibid, 1964-67; Fellow, Gerontological Soc., 1958-. Author, Wiley Post, His Winnie Mae & the World's First Pressure Suit, 1971. Num. sci. publs., Aeromed. & allied rsch. Recip., profl. awards. Address: Office of Aviation Medicine, 800 Independence Ave. S.W., Washington, DC 20591, U.S.A.

MOHNS, Edward A., b. 8 July 1903. Presbyterian Minister. Educ: B.A., Southwestern Presby. Univ., Clarksville, Tenn.; B.D., Louisville Presby. Theol. Sem., Ky.; postgrad. work, Univ. of Edinburgh, Scotland & Mansfield Coll., Engl. Ordained Presby. Min., 1927. Appts: Pastor, Greenville, Ala. (along w. Hayneville, Lowndesboro & Good Hope Ch., Benton), Montevallo Presby. Ch., Ala., 2nd Presby. Ch., Newark, N.J., Westminster Presby. Ch., Grand Rapids, Mich., & Westminster Presby. Ch., Seattle, Wash.; Asst. Pastor, 1st Presby. Ch., Pitts., Pa.; Assoc. Pastor, Highland Pk. Presby. Ch., Dallas, Tex.; Ret., 1970. Mbrships: during active ministry, Chmn., num. comms. of Presbyteries & Synods: Moderator, 4 Presbyteries; Trustee, Alma Coll. for sev. yrs.; Sigma Alpha Epsilon; V.P., Alpha Phi Epsilon; Pres., Alpha Theta Phi; Kiwanis Club; formerly, Rotary, Lions & Exchange Clubs. Publs: sermons & articles in Ch. periodicals. Hons: Walter Kennedy Patterson Fellowship in New Testament Greek, for study abroad, Louisville Sem., 1927; D.D., Alma Coll., Mich., 1948. Address: Highover, 2889-2 Ptarmigan Dr., Walnut Creek, CA 94595, U.S.A.

MOHNS, Grace Updegraff Bergen (Mrs. Edward A. Mohns), b. 20 Nov. 1907. Musician. Educ: B.A., Univ. of Minn.; MacPhial Schl. of Music, Mpls.; Southern Meth. Univ., Dallas, Tex., 1968-69. Appts: Recitalist, Pianist, 1923-; Tchr., Piano & Theory, Pub. & Pvte. Schls., Mpls. & St. Paul, Minn., 1930-32; Piano Tchr., 1930-; Organist, Choir Dir., Neward N.J., 1937, Grand Rapids, Mich.; 1947 & Seattle, Wash., 1953; Presby. Bible Class Tchr., 1949-. Mbrships. incl: Jr. League Am.; DAR; Nat. Music Tchrs. Assn.; Delta Gamma; Sigma Alpha Iota. Compositions incl: Thine is the Power; Nocturne; This is God's Gift; Sea Suite; L'Armistice; Anchored Hearts. Thine is the Power chosen as Nat. Theme Hymn, U.S. Presby. Women, 1950-54. Address: Highover, 2889-2 Ptarmigan Drive, Walnut Creek, CA 94595, U.S.A. 5, 7, 79.

MOHR, Walter, b. 21 Oct. 1910. Professor of Medieval History. Educ: Bonn Univ., Germany, & Innsbruck Univ., Austria; Ph.D., 1933. Appts: Lectr., Univ. of Saarbrucken, Germany, 1948-50; Prof., Medieval Hist., ibid, 1950-. Mbr., Int. Commn. for the Hist. of Rep. & Parliamentary Insts. Publs: König Heinrich I, 1950; Studien zur Charakteristik des Carolingischen Königtums im 8. Jahrhundert, 1955; Die Karolingische Reichsidee, 1962; Fränkische Kirche & Papsttum zwischen Karlmann & Pippin, 1966; Waldes von seiner Berufung bis zu seinem Tode, 1971; Over 30 articles in schol. jrnls. Address: Saarbrucken, Blieskastelerstr. 1, German Federal Repub. 43, 92.

MOHRHARDT, Foster Edward, b. 7 Mar. 1907. Librarian. Educ. incl: A.B., Mich. State Coll., U.S.A., 1929; B.S., Columbia Univ., 1930; Dip., Univ. of Munich, Germany, 1932; M.A., Univ. of Mich., 1933; LL.D., Kalamazoo Coll., 1967; D.Litt., Mich. State Coll., 1970; Student at N.Y., Purdue & Indiana Univs. Appts. incl: Asst. Libn., Var. Univ., Coll. & Pub. Libs., 1926-35; Asst. to Chmn., Carnegie Corp. advsry. grps. on coll. libs., 1935-38; Libn., Wash. & Lee Univ., 1938-42; '45-46; Dir., Lib. Serv. VA, 1948-54; Dir., U.S. Dept. Agric. Lib., 1954-68; Prog. Off., Coun. on Lib. Resources, 1968-; Vis. Prof., Univ. of Hawaii, 1972. Mbrships. incl: AAAS, co-Fndr. & Chmn., Sect. T; V.P., 1963; Bd. Dirs., U.S. Book Exchange, Pres. 1958-60; Assn. of Rsch. Libs., Pres., 1966; ALA, Pres., 1967-68; Int. Fedn. of Lib. Assns., V.P., 1965-71. Author, books on lib. & info. sci.; Articles in lib. & educl. jrnls. Hons. incl: Disting. Serv. Award, Dept. of Agric., 1963; Special Medal, Int. Fed. of Lib. Assns., 1972. Address: Coun. on Lib. Resources, Inc., Suite 620, 1 Dupont Cir., Washington, DC 20036, U.S.A. 2.

MOIR, George Guthrie, b. 30 Oct. 1917. Educational & Religious TV Programmes Administrator. Educ: Peterhouse, Cambridge. Appts: Chief Off., St. John Ambulance Brigade Cadets, 1947-50; Co. Councillor, Buckinghamshire, 1949-; Dir., European Youth Campaign, 1950-52; Chmn., then Pres., World Assembly of Youth, 1952-56; Mbr., Gen. synod, Ch. Assembly, 1956-; Educ. Advsr., Hollerith Tab. Machine Co., 1957; Asst. Controller & Exec. Prod., Rediffusion TV, 1958-68; currently Controller of Educ. & Religious Progs., Thames TV. Mbrships: Athenaeum, Nat. Liberal & Nikaean Clubs. Ed. of Publs: Why I Believe, 1964; Life's Work, 1965; Teaching & Television: ETV Explained, 1967; Beyond Hatred, 1969. Author, 2 books, The Suffolk Regiment, Into Television, 1969. Contbr., The Times, Church Times, var. reviews & publs. Recip. of hons. Address: The Old Rectory, Aston Clinton, Aylesbury, Buckinghamshire, U.K. 1.

MOL, Johannis J., b. 14 Feb. 1922. University Professor. Educ: Cert., United Theol. Fac., Sydney, Australia, 1951; B.D., Union Theol. Sem., N.Y.C., U.S.A., 1955; M.A., 1956, Ph.D., Sociol., 1960, Columbia Univ. Appts. incl: Prisoner, German concentration camps, 1943-45; Dpty. Admnstr., Dutch sugar beet ind., 1946-48; Chap. to immigrants, Boneguilla, Australia, 1952-54; Pastor, Bethel Presby. Ch., White Hall, Md., U.S.A., 1956-60; Lectr., Sociol., Univ. of Canterbury, N.Z., 1961-63; Fellow, Sociol., Inst. of Advanced Studies, Australian Nat. Mus., Canberra, 1963-70; Prof., Dept. of Relig., McMaster Univ., Hamilton, Ont., Canada. Mbrships. incl: Past Pres., Canberra Sociol. Soc.; Sec., Comm. on Sociol. of Relig., Int. Sociol. Assn.; Dir., Bd. of Dirs., Relig. Rsch. Assn. Publs. incl: Race & Religion in New Zealand, 1966; Christianity in Chains, 1969; Religion in Australia, 1971; Contbr. to jrnls., books. Hons: Kenneth Edwards Prize, 1951; McFadden Fellowship, Union Sem., 1955-56. Address: McMaster Univ., Arts Div., Hamilton, Ont., Canada L8S 4K1.

MOL, Leo, b. 1915. Sculptor. Educ: Kunst Acad., Berlin, Germany; Acad. of Art, The Hague, Netherlands. Exhibs: Winnipeg Art Gall., 1950-71, '74; Royal Canadian Acad. of Arts, Montreal, Ottawa, Toronto & Winnipeg, 1956-70; Hamilton Art Gall., Ont., 1956-71; Mus. Fine Arts, Montreal, 1959; Allied Artists of Am., Nat. Acad. Galls., N.Y', 1963-64; McMichael Canadian Collect., Kleinberg, Ont.,

1974. Work in Pub. Collects: Hamilton Art Gall., Ont.; McMichael Canadian Collect., Kleinberg, Ont.; Toronto Art Gall.; Winnipeg Art Gall.; Vatican, Rome, Italy. Commns: Monument to a poet, T. Shevchenk, Citizen's Comm., Wash., D.C., 1964; Bust of Rt. Hon. J'G. Diefenbaker, Senate, Ottawa, 1964; Bust of Gen. Dwight D. Eisenhower, Gettysburg, Pa., 1965; Bust of Pope Paul VL, St. Clements Univ., Rome, Italy, 1967; Monument to T. Shevchenko, Citizen's Comm., Buenos Aires, Argentina, 1971. Hons: LL.D., Univ. of Winnipeg, 1974; Allied Artists Medal, Royal Canadian Inst. of Arch., 1960; 1st prize in competition for monument in Wash., D.C., 1962; Jacob C. Stone Prize, Allied Artists of Am., 1963; Canadian Centennial Medal, Candian Fedl. Govt., 1967; 1st prize in competition for monument in Buenos Aires, 1969. Address: 104 Claremont Ave., Winnipeg, Man. R2H 1V9, Canada. 37.

MOLDAVE, Gertrude Eloise. Business Executive. Educ: Secretarial degree, Dominion Bus. Coll., Winnipeg; Canada; Grad., St. Johns Tech., Winnipeg. Appts: Sec., Royal Garment, Winnipeg, 1938-41; Warrant Off., Canadian Women's Army Corps, 1941-45; Employment Off., Unemployment Ins. Commn., Winnipeg, 1945-48; Sec., Bookkeeper, Am. Shippers, L.A., U.S.A., 1948-51; Sec.-Treas. & Dir., ibid, 1951-59; Co-Fndr., Jet Air Freight, Inglewood, Calif., 1960; Sec.-Treas. & Dir., ibid, 1960-73; Dir., currently. Mbrships: Commnr., Bd. of Municipal Arts, City of L.A.; Sec.-Treas., Valley Beth Shalom, Encino, Calif.; Bd. of Govs., ISrael Bond Org.; Bd. of Govs., B'nai B'rith; Nat. Assn. for FEmale Execs. Address: 5325 C White Oak Ave., Encino, CA 91316, U.S.A. 5, 9, 57, 138.

MOLINA, Rafael Rodriguez de la Seda y, b. 23 Sept. 1901. Physician; Internist; Clinical Investigator. Educ: B.S., Univ. of Puerto Rico, 1922; M.D., Med. Coll. of Va., U.S.A., 1926; D.Sc. (Med.), Columbia Univ., N.Y., 1935; postgrad. work, Johns Hopkins Clin., 1931-32 & Columbia Univ., 1934-35; Cert., Am. Bd. Internal Med., 1937. Appts: Instr.-Assoc. Prof., Med. Zool., Schl. of Tropical Med., Univ. of Puerto Rico, San Juan, 1931-41; Chief, Med. Serv., U.S.A. Army Hosp., San Juan, 1942-47 & U.S.A. Veterans Hosp., ibid, 1947-55; Assoc. Chief of Staff for Rsch., ibid, 1955-65; Clin. Prof., Med., Med. Schl., Univ. of Puerto Rico, 1954-; Cons. to Rsch. Prog., VA Hosp., San Juan, 1965-. Mbrships: Chmn., Sci. Comm., Puerto Rico Med. Assn., 1938-41; Fellow, Past Gov. for Puerto Rico, 1948-57, Am. Coll. Physns.; Am. Soc. Tropical Med. & Hygiene; Affiliate, Royal Soc. of Med.; A.F.D.A. Frat., San Juan; Mil. Order of World Wars; Order of San Juan Bautista. Contbr. num. articles & chapts. to publs. in field of Tropical Diseases & Internal Med. Hons: Recip. of hons. Address: No. 12 M. Rodriquez-Serra St., Santurac, PR 00907.

MOLINA-ORANTES, Adolfo. Lawyer. Educ: Grad., Schl. of Law, Univ. of San Carlos de Guatemala, 1943; postgrad. studies, Columbia Univ., N.Y., U.S.A., 1943-44. Appts: Prof., Int. Law, Univ. of San Carlos, 1945; Dir., Dept. of Publs., ibid, 1951-54; Dean, Law Schl., 1954-58; Pres., Guatemalan Bar Assn., 1952-53; Min. of For. Affairs, 1957-58; Counsellor of State, 1964-67, 70-74; Chmn., INter-Am. Juridical Comm. of O.A.S., 1972-74, & Guatemalan Inst. of Hispanic Culture, 1972. Mbrships. incl: Colegio de Abogados de Guatemala; Soc. de Geografía e Historia de Guatemala; Assn. Guatemalteca de Derecho Int.; Rotary Club; Am. Soc. Int. Law Publs: Juridical Considerations on Pacifism, 1943; The

Repression of International Crimes, 1951; Regionalism in International Relations, 1953; The Sedimentation of Public International Law Norms & the Work of United Nations, 1958; Historical Aspects of the Law of Asylum in Guatemala; The Panamerican Operation, 1959; The American Principle of "uti possidetis"; Economic Development of the Counties of the Spanish-Luso-American-Filipino Community in the Frame of International Law; Central American Policies Regarding the Proposed Latin American Common Market; Constitutuional & Conventional Roots of Central American Economic Integration; Jus Cogens in Codified International Law. Recip. num. hons. inclng: LL.D., Univ. of Pa., 1962; Medal Alexandre Gusmão, Hist. & Geog. Inst. of São Paulo, Brazil, 1971; Order of Dom Pedro I, ibid, 1972. Address: 13 calle 6-47, zona 1, Guatemala City, Guatemala.

MOLINA-VALLEJO, Fernando, b. 7 July 1936. Professor. Educ: Lic. Law & Soc. Scis., Cath. Univ. Valparaíso, Chile; M.A., Wis. Univ., U.S.A. Appts: Prof., Constitutional Law, Dir. & Fndr., Inst. de Ciencias Soc. y Desarrollo & V.-Rector, Acad. Affairs, Cath. Univ. Valparaiso, Chile, 1961-67; Vis. Prof., Notre Dame Univ., Ind., U.S.A.; Dir. & Fndr., Pol. Sci. Inst., Cath. Univ., Chile; V.-Rector, Acad. Affairs, Cath. Univ., Chile, 1968-71; Chmn., Soc. Dev. Studies Grp., Inter-Am. Dev. Bank (on leave from Cath. Univ., Chile), 1971-. Mbrships: Past Bd. mbr: Ctr. Interuniv. de Desarrollo Andino & Latin Am. Schlrship. Prog. Am. Univs.; Fndng. mbr: Comisión Nacional de Investigación Científica y Tecnol. & Chilean Assn. Pol. Sci. Publs. incl: Elementos para el estudio de la dimensión communitaria del hombre, 1962; Socialización, 1966; Analytical Theory for the Study of Political Thought, 1967; Bases para la reforma académica de la Universidad Catolica de Chile, 1970; Paradigma para el Análisis de los Gobiernos Universitarios, 1973. Address: Camino de Asis 515, Las Condes, Santiago, Chile.

MOLL, Francesc de Borja, b. 10 Oct. 1903. Professor of Linguistics; Editor. Educ: Humanistic studies, Ecclesiastical Sem. of Minorca; studies of Romance Philol., Majorca & Madrid. Appts: Edit. Staff, Diccionari Català-Valencià-Balear; Fndr., Edit. Moll, 1933; Tchr. of German, Instituto Nacional de Enseñanza Media Ramon Llull, Palma, Majorca, 1938, Tchr. of French, 1957; Prof. of Spanish, Estudio General Luliano, Palma, 1951-; Prof. of Catalan, Barcelona Univ. at Palma, 1968-73. Mbr., var. acad. orgs. Publs. incl: Gramática Italiana, 2 vols., 12 edits., 1937-; Gramática 2 vols., 7 edits., 1938-; Gramática Histórica Catalana, 1952; El Liber Elegantiarum, 1960; Els meus primers trenta anys, 1970. Hons. incl: Prix de M. le President de la Republique Francaise, Perpignan, 1963; Premi d'Honor de les Lletres Catalanes, Barcelona, 1971. Address: Plaza de Espana 86, 3°, Palma, Majorca, Spain. 43.

MOLL, Jan Witold, b. 24 Oct. 1912. Physician; Surgeon. Educ: M.D., Univ. of Warsaw, 1945; Assoc. Prof., 1955; Prof. of Surg., 1961; Full Prof., 1972. Appts: Res. Surg., Municipal Hosp., Radom, 1939-45; w. Surg. Clin., Poznań, 1945-49, Thoracic Surg. Dept., 1959-65; Dir. & Chief Surg., 2nd Surg. Clin., Lódz, 1958-. Mbrships. incl: Pres., Polish Assn. Thoracic Surg., 1965-; Int. Coll. of Surgs.; Am. Coll. of Cardiol.; Presiding Off., Polish Surgs. Assn.; Soc. Int. de Chirurgie; Soc. Européenne de la Chirurgie Cardio-vasculaire. Over 120 scientific publs., Poland, Germany, U.K., France, U.S.S.R. Holder, 5 med. patents. Hons. incl: Scientific Awards of Lódz City,

1962, City of Poznań, 1963; Off.'s Cross, Poland's Resurrection Order, 1965, Cmdr.'s Cross, 1973. Address: Swierczewski 24a 5, Lódz, Poland.

MOLLAND, Jacob, b. 17 May 1909. Professor of Medicine. Educ: Cand. real. (Chem., Maths., Phys., Astron.), Univ. of Oslo., & Cand. med.; advanced studies, Univ. of Uppsala, Sweden, & Yale Univ., U.S.A. Appts: Libn., Univ. of Oslo; Lectr., Clin. Chem., Univ. of Oslo; Rockefeller Rsch. Fellow, Pharmacol.; Prof. of Med. (Pharmacol. & Toxicol.), & Dir., Pharmacological Inst. of Univ. of Oslo; Edit. Staff, Acta Pharmacologica et Toxicologica; Authorized Medico-legal adviser. Mbrships: Am. Soc. Pharmacol. & Experimental Therapeutics; Societas Pharmacologica Scandinavica; Norwegian Pharmacological Soc.; Nordic & Norwegian Pharmacopoeia Commns. Num. publs., chem., bacteriol., pharmacol. Hons: Dr. philosophiae, Univ. of Oslo, 1940, Dr. medicinae, 1948. Address: Pharmacological Institute, University of Oslo, Blindern Oslo 3, Norway.

MOLLER, Hans, b. 20 Mar. 1905. Artist. Educ: local art schl., 1919-27; Berlin Acad. of Fine Arts, 1927-28. Appts: Tchr., Cooper Union Schl. of Art, N.Y., U.S.A., 1944-56. Num. one-man exhibs. inclng: Otto Gerson Gall., N.Y., 1957, 60; Albert Landry Gall., N.Y., 1962; Midtown Galls., N.Y., 1964, 67, 70, 73; Allentown Art Mus., 1969; Norfolk Mus., 1970; Art Alliance, Phila., 1968; Retrospective, "1926-56 thirty yrs. of my paintings", arranged by Olsen Fndn., Guilford, Conn. & exhib. for 7 yrs. at univs., mus. & colls. thru'out U.S.A. In num. grp. exhibs. inclng. U.S. State Dept. "Art in the Embassies" shows in France, Italy, Germany, Sweden & Japan. Paintings in num. perm. collects. inclng: Mus. of Mod. Art, N.Y.C.; Whitney Mus., N.Y.; BKlyn. Mus., N.Y.; Detroit Inst. of Art; Walker Art Ctr., Mpls.; Melbourne Mus., Australia; Von der Heydt Mus. of Wuppertal; U.S. Info. Agcy.; James A. Michner Fndn. IBM Collect. Mbrships: Nat. Acad. of Design, N.Y. Recip. num. awards inclng: Palmer Mem. Prize, Nat. Acad., for a marine painting, 1968; Samuel F.B. Morse Medal, 144th Annual Exhib., Nat. Acad., 1969; Murray Kupferman Prize, Audubon Artists, 1973; Andrew Carnegie Prize, Nat. Acad., for oil painting, 1974. Address: 2207 Allen St., Allentown, PA 18104, U.S.A. 2, 37.

MØLLER, Orla Reinhardt, b. 7 May 1916. Minister of Religion. Educ: Aarhus Univ., Denmark; M.A., Copenhagen Univ., 1940. Appts: Schltchr., 1940-42; Vicar, Danish Ch., 1942-51 & 1956-64; Nat. Gen. Sec., YMCA & YWCA, Denmark, 1951-56; Mbr., Danish Parliament, Copenhagen, 1964-; Min. of Ch. Affairs, 1966-68; Min. of Defence, 1973-. Mbrship: Soc. Democratic Party. Publs: 12 books on relig.; 14 schl. textbooks on relig.; 4 books on youth problems; 1 book on pol. Address: Oldfuxvej 17, 9000 Aalborg, Denmark. 43.

MOLLET, Guy, b. 31 Dec. 1905. Politician; Teacher. Educ: Bach., Maths. & Philos.; Licencié ès-Lettres, Engl. Appts. incl: Tchr., var. lycées-France; Serv. in French Army, 1939-40; POW, 1940-42; Joined Resistance; Sec., Comité de Libération, 1944; Mbr., both Constituent Assemblies, 1945 & '46; V. Premier, 1951, '58; Prime Min., 1956-57; Min. of State (de Gaulle Cabinet), 1958-59; Mayor of Arras; Dpty., Pas-de-Calais; Pres., Univ. Bur. of Socialist Rsch.; Former V.P., Socialist Int.; Former Sec. Gen., Socialist Party S.F.I.O. Publs: Du Français à l'Anglais (Engl. grammar); Bilan et Perspectives Socialistes; 13 mai

1958-13 mai 1962; Les Chances du Socialisme; Le Socialisme selon Tito. Hons: Off., Legion of Hon.; Croix de Guerre; Resistance Medal; Grand Off. & Grand Cross, num. for. orders. Address: 86 rue de Lille, 75007 Paris, France. 34.

MOLLOY, Emmett Edward, b. 6 Aug. 1940. Rehabilitation Counselor. Educ: B.A., Wash. Coll., Chestertown, Md., 1964; M.S., Va. Commonwealth Univ., Richmond, 1969; Postgrad. Rehab. Counseling, Univ. of Va., Charlottesville, 1966-67. Appts. incl: Asst. Prof., Va. Commonwealth Univ., 1968-69; Dir., Info. & Referral, Lancaster Co. Mental Hlth./Mental Retardation, Pa., 1969-70; Voc. Rehab. Specialist, VA Hosp., Perry Pt., Md., 1969-73; Counseling Psychologist, Bur. of Rehab., Nat. Capital Area, Wash. D.C., 1973-; PVte. Prac., Drug Abuse Counseling, 1967-; Pres., Ascension, Inc. Music, Molloy Ltd., etc. Mbrships. incl: Nat. Rehab. Assn.; Nat. Rehab. Counseling Assn.; Theta Chi. Publs. incl: au tres temps, 1973; Contbr. to var. books in field; author of song lyrics. Address: 7308 Forest Rd., Apt. 303, Hyattsville, MD 20785, U.S.A. 6.

MOLOMBY, Thomas, b. 17 June 1918. Solicitor; Notary Public. Educ: Xavier Coll., Kew; Melbourne Univ. Appts: Ptnr., Molomby & Molomby, solicitors, Melbourne, 1946-; Pres., Law Inst. of Vic., 1953-54, 1968-69; Pres., Law Coun. of Australia, 1970-72, Chmn., Comm. on Fair Consumer Credit Laws; Coun. Mbr., Int. Bar Assn., 1970-72, Sect. on Bus. Law, 1973-; Dir., var. pvte. cos. Author, Molomby Report to Govt. of Vic., 1973. Hons: Mention in Despatches, 1943; M.B.E., 1944. Address: 411 Collins St., Melbourne, Australia 3000. 23.

MOLOMUT, Norman, b. 21 Jan. 1913. Oncologist; Immunologist. Educ: B.A., Brooklyn Coll., 1934; M.A., Univ. of Mich., 1935; Ph.D., Coll. of Physns. & Surgs., Fac. of Pure Sci., Columbia Univ., 1938. Appts. incl: Asst.-Assoc. Bacteriologist, Dept. Med., Coll. Physns. & Surgs., Columbia Univ., 1939-46; Chief, Biophys. Br., Aero. Med. Lab., Wright Field, 1942-43; Chief, laboratory Div., Fairmount AAB Hosp., 1943; Air Force Major, Chief, Trng. & Air Sea Rescue Servs., Far E. Air Forces, 1943-45; Dir., Biol. Labs. Inc., Brooklyn, N.Y., 1946-53; Dir., Waldemar Med. Rsch. Fndn., 1946-. Mbrships. incl: Am. Assoc. Immunologists; AAAS; Am. Soc. Cell Biol.; N.Y. Acad. Scis.; Am. Assn. Cancer Rsch. Contbr. var. med. jrnls. & publs. Address: Scientific Dir., Waldemar Med. Rsch. Fndn., Inc., Woodbury, NY 11797, U.S.A. 14, 15, 28.

MONCREIFFE OF THAT ILK (Sir) Iain, b. 9 Apr. 1919. Author; Herald; Historian; Advocate. Educ: Heidelberg Univ.; Germany; M.A., Christ Church, Oxford Univ., U.K.; LL.B., Ph.D., Edinburgh Univ. Presently, Albany Herald. Mbrships incl: Fndr., Puffin's, Edinburgh; Coun., Harleian Soc.; V.P., Heraldry Soc.; V.P., '45 Assn.; Chmn., Scottish Geneal. Soc.; Preas., Duodecimal Soc. of Gt. Britain. Publs. incl: Simple Heraldry; Simple Custom; Blood Royal; The Robertsons; Map of Scotland of Old; The Highland Clans. Hons: Dpty. Lt. for Perthshire; Hon. Sheriff of Perth & Angus. Address: Easter Moncreiffe, Perthshire, Scotland, U.K. 1, 35, 41, 128.

MONCURE, James A., b. 4 June 1926. Educator. Educ: B.A., Univ. of Richmond, Va., 1949; M.A., ibid, 1953; Ph.D., Columbia Univ., 1960. Appts. incl: Instr. in Hist., Univ. of Richmond, 1954-60, Asst. Prof.-Prof. Hist. 1960-74; Assoc.Dean, Univ. Coll., ibid, 1963-68, Fndr. & Dir., Summer Schl. Study

Abroad Prog., 1963-70, Dean, Univ. Coll., 1968-74; V.P., Acad. & Student Affairs, Elon Coll., N.C., 1974-. Mbrships. incl: Am. Hist. Assn.; Va. Soc. Sci. Assn.; Pres., Duntreath Community Assn., 1959-61; Pres. & Fndr. Mbr., Richmond Int. Coun., 1967-69; Omicron Delta Kappa; Phi Alpha Theta; Pi Sigma Alpha. Author, acad. papers & articles. Hons. incl: Bronze Star; Selection as Richmond's Community Ambassador to England, 1954. Address: Elon College, Elon, NC 27244, U.S.A. 2.

MONDESIR, Jones Euphraim Hyacinth, b. 11 Sept. 1915. Educator. Educ: Govt. Trng. Coll., Trinidad, 1949; Moray House Coll. of Educ., Edinburgh, U.K., 1959-60; Reading Univ., ibid, 1966-67. Appts: Asst. Qualified Tchr., Somfriere Boys' Primary Schl., St. Lucia W.I. 1942-55; Acting Insp. of Schls., Min. of Educ., St. Lucia, 1955-58; Tutor, Min. of Educ. Tchng. Serv., ibid, 1958-61; Educ. Off., Min. of Educ., 1962-70; Acting Chief Educ. Off., ibid, 1970-71; Prin., Corinth Jr. Secondary Schl., 1972-. Mbrships: Assn. Coll. Preceptors; Boy Scouts Assn.; Castries Club, St. Lucia; Hd. Tchrs. Assn., ibid. Address: Corinth Jr. Secondary Schl., Castries, St. Lucia, W. Indies 136.

MONE, Louis C., b. 10 July 1936. Clinical Social Worker. Educ: B.A., Univ. of Ariz., 1962; M.S.W., Rutgers Univ., 1965; Cert., Psychoanalytic Psychotherapy, Wash. Square Inst. for Psychotherapy & Mental Hlth., 1970. Appts. incl: Pvte. Prac., Adolescent & Adult Psychotherapy, Marriage & Family Counseling, 1965-71; Soc. Work Cons., Pub. Schls., Borough of Spotswood, N.J., 1967-69; Proj. Dor. & Grp. Therapist, Heart Assn., Middlesen Co.; Edison, N.J., 1968-69; Chief Psychiat. Soc. Wkr., Am. Fndn. Relig. & Psych., N.Y.C., 1969-71; Dir., Profl. Servs., Family Serv. Assn., San Diego Co., Calif., 1971-. Mbrships. incl: Soc. Clin. Soc. Work; Am. Grp. Psychotherapy Assn.; Nat. Assn. Soc. Wkrs.; Delta Chi. Contbr. to publs. in field. Recip. of N.J. Police Trng. Commn. Award. Address: 14102 Recuerdo Dr., Del Mar, CA 92014, U.S.A. 6, 57.

MONET, Jacques, b. 26 Jan. 1930. Historian. Educ: Ph.L., Coll. de l'Immaculee-Conception, Montreal, Canada, 1956; Th.L., ibid, 1967; M.A., Univ. of Toronto, 1961; Ph.D., ibid, 1964; Also studied at Laval Univ., Quebec, & St. Beuno's Coll., N. Wales. Appts: Ordained to priesthood, 1966; Sessional Lectr., Loyola Coll., Montreal, 1965-67; Asst. Prof., Univ. of Toronto & Univ. de Sherbrooke, 1968-69; Assoc. Prof., Univ. of Ottawa, 1969-; Chmn., Hist. Dept., ibid, 1972-. Mbrships: French Lang. Sec., Canadian Histl. Assn., 1969-; Int. Comm., French Lang. Histns. & Geographers, 1970; Huronia Histl. Dev. Coun., 1972-; Inst. d'Histoire de l'Amérique française. Author of articles in books & jrnls. inclng. Colonists & Canadians, Culture, The Month, Canadian Histl. Assn. Annual Report. Address: Dept. of Hist., Univ. of Ottawa, Ottawa, Ont., K1N 6N5, Canada.

MONGUNO, (Shettima) Ali, b. 1926. Government Minister. Educ: Cert., Soc. Anthropol., Edinburgh Univ., U.K. Appts: Educ. Sec., N. Nigeria, 1959; Elected M.P., ibid; Created Shettima & appointed Councillor for Educ., Bornu Native Authority, 1961; Held portfolios for Works & Rural Water Supplies, Social Welfare, etc., between 1961-65; Min. of State (Air Force), 1965; Min. i/c Int. Affairs, 1965-66; Commnr. Trade & Inds., Fed. Mil. Govt., 1967; Currently Fed. Commnr. Mines & Power; Mbr. num. Delegns. to all Continents; Attended annually Gen. Assembly of U.N. &

led Nigerian delegn. to num. int. confs.; Elected Pres., OPEC, 1972, '73; V.P., UNCTAD II, New Delhi, India, 1968; Served on U.N. Comm. on Oman, 1964. Mbrships: Appeals Off., Red Cross, Bornu Br.; Org. Sec., Bornu Local Scout Org.; Chmn., Maiduguri Amateur Football Assn.; Bornu Native Authority Lib. Bd.; Nat. Coun. & Fed. Exec. Comm.; Nigerian Red Cross. Hons: 1st Class Medals from Ethiopia, Sudan, Egypt & Camerouns. Address: Fed. Min. Mines & Power, Commnrs. Off., Lagos, Nigeria, W. Africa.

MONK, Clive Harlie, b. 12 Oct. 1915. Civil Engineer. Educ: Sydney Tech. Coll., Australia. Appts: Civil Engr., Dept. of Main Rds., 1937-46; Shire Engr., Wakool, N.S.W., 1946-52; Gen. Mgr. & Mng. Dir., McDonald Inds., 1953-62; Exec. V.P., Utah Constructions, 1963-64; Mng. Dir., Blue Metal Inds., 1965-; Dir., Ready Mixed Concrete Ltd. Grp.; Chmn., Computer Engrng. Applications Pty. Ltd.; Flight Lt., Royal Australian Air Force. Mbrships. incl: Fellow, Instn. of Engrs., Australia; Past Pres., Employers Fedn. of N.S.W., 1968-70; Past Pres., Australian Fedn. of Civil Engrng. Contractors; Sci. & Ind. Forum, Australian Acad. of Sci.; Fellow, Inst. of Dirs.; Australasian Inst. of Mining & Metallurgy; Fellow, Australian Inst. of Bldg.; Fellow, Australian Inst. of Mgmt. Author, papers to Inst. of Engrs., Royal Inst. of Pub. Admin., & to sev. univs. Hons: Gold Medal, Water Supply Engrng.; George A. Taylor Medal, Local Govt. Engrs. Assn. Address: 104 Stuart St., Blakehurst, N.S.W., Australia 2221. 23.

MONK, Mildred Haltom, b. 7 Feb. 1905. Editor. Educ: B.S., Sam Houston State Tchrs. Coll., Huntsville, Tex., 1933; M.A., Tchrs. Coll., Columbia Univ., 1945; grad. work Chgo. Univ., Tex. Univ. Appts. incl: Publrs. Educl. Cons., The Stock Co., Austin, Tex., 1936-62; Ed., ibid, 1962-65; V.P. & Executive Ed., 1965-70, at retirement. Mbrships: Sec., Tex. Bookmen's Assn., 1946-71; Pi Lamba Theta; Theta Sigma Phi; Kappa Delta Pi. Address: 1104 W. 29th St., Austin, TX 78703, U.S.A. 5, 132.

MONNIER, Alexandre Marcel, b. 25 Aug. 1904. Professor; Laboratory Director. Educ: Fellow, Rockefeller Fndn., Univs. of St. Louis & N.Y., U.S.A., 1929; Dr. ès-Scis. Naturelles, Paris, 1933; Dr. ès-Scis. Phys., ibid, 1934. Appts: w. French Nat. Ctr. of Rsch., 1931-36; appointed Asst. Prof., Sorbonne, 1937; Vis. Prof., Brazil, 1948, 49, 56, 71, 72; appointed Full Prof., Physiol., Paris, 1953; Vis. Prof., Liege, Louvain & Ghent, Belgium, 1951; Halliburton Lectr., King's Coll., London, 1955; Vis. Prof., Rockefeller Inst., N.Y., 1956-62; Dir., Lab. Gen. Physiol., Sorbonne, 1958-. Mbrships. incl: Coun. for Org. of Pure & Applied Biophys., 1961; Pres., Physiol. Soc., 1963; Med. Acad. of Paris; French Physiol. Soc.; Physico-Chem. Soc.; French Electn. Soc. Publs: L'excitation électrique des tissus. Essai d'interprétation Physique, 1934; La Machine Humanine, 1961; Les modèles de la membrane cellulaire, 1972; num. articles in profl. jrnls. Hons: Off., l'Ordre Nat. des Palmes Acad., 1952; Chevalier, Legion d'Honneur, 1957; off., ibid, 1970; Off., l'ordre Nat. Bresilien de la Croix du Sud, 1958; Dr. h.c., Univ. de Pécs, Hungary, 1972. Address: 4, Square Montsouris, 75014, Paris, France.

MONROY MARTINEZ, Juan Antonio, b. 13 June 1929. Journalist; Writer; Preacher. Appts: Preacher, sev. chs., Canary Islands, Tangier, Morocco, & Madrid, Spain, 1953-; Ed., Luz y Verdad mag., Tangier, 1956; Ed., Restauracion, Primera Luz, & Heraldo de la Verdad, monthlies, Madrid, 1966-; Gen. Mgr.,

Irmayol Publishing House, & Christian Bookstore, Madrid, 1967-; Broadcaster, daily 15-minute radio prog., Madrid. Mbrships: gen. Authors Soc. in Spain; Int. Cervantin Soc.; Order of Sancho; Evangelical Press Assn. of Spain; Evangelical Lit. Assn.; Humanistic Sci. Acad. of Mexico & Dominican Repub. Publs: 15 books in Spanish; 10 books translated from Engl. & French. Recip., D.D., Theological Defenders Sem., Puerto Rico. Address: Apartado 2029, Madrid-2, Spain.

MONSEN, Courtenay, b. 24 May 1893. Public Relations. Appts. incl: Sec.-Inst., Kelvin; Reporter, var. papers, N.Y. & Calif.; Sec. Dir., P.R., Pasadena Bd. of Educ., 1928-53; Dean of Admissions, Montecite Schl. for Girls, 1953-56; Dir. P.R. & Publicity, Santa Barbara Chmbr. of Comm., Calif., 1956-67; Dir. P.R., Old Spanish Days in Santa Barbara, 1968-; Dir., Civil Defence, Pasadena Schl. Review, 25 yrs., News & Views, Santa Barbara, 11 yrs. Contbr. educ. jrnls.; Ed., Noticias, Hist. Soc. Quarterly Jrnl. Address: 21 E. Pueblo St., Santa Barbara, CA 93105, U.S.A. 9, 15, 74, 75.

MONTAGU of BEAULIEU (Lord), Edward John Barrington Douglas-Scott, b. 20 Oct. 1926. Peer of Realm; Company Director; Publisher. Educ: New College, Oxford, U.K. Appts: Fndr., Montagu Motor Mus., 1952 which became The Motor Mus. at Beaulieu in June, 1972; Fndr., Motorcycle Mus., 1956; Fndr./Ed., Veteran & Vintage Mag. Mbrships: Pres., Citroen Car Club; Pres., Hist. Commercial Vehicle Club; Pres., Disabled Drivers Club; Chmn., Showbiz Car Club; Fellow, Inst. of Motor Ind. Publs: Motoring Montagus; Lost Causes of Motoring (3 vols.); Jaguar, A Biography; The Gordon Bennett Races; Rolls of Rolls Royce; The Gilt & The Gingerbread; More Equal Than Others. Address: Palace House, Beaulieu, Hampshire, U.K. 131.

MONTANARI, Giuseppe, b. 30 Oct. 1889. Painter. Educ: Brera Acad. of Fine Arts, Milan. Hon. Mbr. of Brera Acad. of Fine Arts. Works exhibited in many Int. collects. Hons: Gold Medal, Min. of Educ., 1925; Carnegie Inst. Prize, 1930; Price Humbert Prize, 1932; City of Milan Prize, 1932; Marini-Missana Prize, 1932; Hon. Dipl., Budapest, 1936; Gold Medal, Paris, 1937; Feltrinelli Prize, Milan, 1957; Gold Medal of Pres. of Repub., 1968. Address: via Conventino 33, 1° Cappella, 21100 Varese, Italy. 43.

MONTCHALIN, Yvonne Cornell, b. 9 Dec. 1909. Lawyer. Educ: J.D., Willamette Univ., Salem, Ore., 1930. Appts: Title Examiner, Home Owner's Loan Corp., 1932-35; City Atty., Camas, Wash., 1945-50; City Atty., Ridgefield, Wash., 1945-50. Mbrships: Am. Bar Assn.; Wash. State Bar Assn.; Am. Judicature Soc.; Bus. & Profl. Women's Club; Touring Club of France; Chichester (England) Yacht Club. Contbr. of articles to var. mags. Address: Route 2, Box 378A, Washougal, WA 98671, U.S.A. 5, 57, 114, 138.

MONTEIRO, Domingos, b. 6 Nov. 1903. Writer; Editor; Publisher. Educ: Grad., Fac. of Law, Lisbon. Appts: Lawyer, specializing in Pol. Law; Ed. & Publr.; Dir., Dept. of Itinerant Libs. of Calouste Gulbenkian Fndn., 1958-. Mbrships: Acad. of Sci. & Arts., Lisbon; Soc. of Geog., Lisbon; Lit. Guild, Lisbon. Publs. incl: Evasão (Evasion, poetry), 1953; Paisagem Social Portuguesa (Outlook of Portuguese Society), 1944; O Livro de Todos os Tempos-História da Civilização (The Book of all Times-History of Civilization, 3 vols.), 1951; Enfermaria, Prisão e Casa Mortuária (Infirmary, Prison & Mortuary), 1943; O Mal e o Bem (Evil

& Good), 1945; Contos do Dia e da Noite (Stories of Day & Night), 1952; Histórias Castelhanas (Castilian Stories), 1955; O Primeiro Crime de Simão Bolandas (The First Crime of Simao Bolandas), 1965; Letícia e o Lobo Júpiter (Laetitia & Jupiter the Wolf), 1972; many works have been trans. into other langs. Hons: Nat. Prize of Novelistics, 1965 & 72; Prize "Diário de Notícias", Lisbon, 1966; Cmdr., Mil. Order of Sant'lago da Espada, Portugal, 1973. Address: Rua D. João V, 16-2° Dto., Lisbon 2, Portugal.

MONTEIRO, José de Gouveia, b. 7 June 1922. Professor of Medicine. Educ: M.D., Coimbra, 1952; postgrad studies, London, U.K., 1952-53, Phila., Pa., U.S.A., 1957-58. Appts: 1st Asst. Prof., Univ. of Coimbra, 1947-52, 1st Asst. Prof., 1952-57, Assoc. Prof., 1957-63, Dir., Ctr. of Gastroenterol., 1960-, Catedratic Prof., 1963-, Univ. Rector, 1970-71. Mbrships: Pres., Portuguese Exec. Comm.; Cumunidade Lusiada de Gastrenterologia, 1968-; Pres., Portuguese Soc. of Gastroenterol.; V.P., ibid, 1968-70; Bockus Int. Soc. Gastroenterol.; Sociedade das Ciências Médicas de Lisboa; Sociedade Portuguesa de Educação Médica. Author, books & num. papers, nat. & for. mags., mainly gastroenterol. & med. educ. Recip., many hons. Address: Centro de Gastrenterologia, Faculdade de Medicina, Universidade de Coimbra, Coimbra, Portugal. 43.

MONTEITH, (Rev.) Lionel, b. 6 Aug. 1921. Psychotherapist; Clinic Director; Ordained Minister of Religion. Educ: New Coll., London, U.K., 1954-57; Dip.Th., Univ. of London; Personal Analysis & Supvsn. w. Dr. P.L. Backus & Psychoanalysis w. Dr. L. Haas. Appts: Chartered Surveyor's pupil, 1939; Ed., Poetry Commonwealth, 1948-53; Min., W. Kensington Cong. Ch., 1957-64; Min. Christ Ch. & Upton Chapel, 1954-68; Chap., St. Mary Abbots Hosp., 1959-64; Prof., Psychoth. Prac., 1959-; Dir., Lincoln Mem. Clin., 1966-; Fndr., Christian Psychotherapy Fndn., 1967-; Min., Cong. Ch., 1957, United Reformed Ch., 1972; Extra Mur. Lectr., Richmond Fell. Coll., 1966-, New Coll., 1966-. Mbrships: Fellow, Int. PEN (Mbr., 1951); Inst. of Relig. & Med.; British Assn. of Soc. Psych. Author of poems, lit. criticism & articles in var. publs. in U.K., U.S.A., Australia, N.Z., S. Africa, India, Argentine. Address: The Lincoln Tower, 77 Westminster Bridge Rd., London SE1 7HS, U.K. 3, 11, 131.

MONTELIBANO, Alfredo, b. 20 Dec. 1905. Businessman. Educ: Univ. of Philippines, Los Baños, Laguna. Appts. incl: Mayor, Bacolod City, 1938; Mil. Gov., Free Govt. of Negros & Siquijor Island, 1942-45; Sec., Dept's. of Nat. Defense & of Interior, 1945-46; Chmn., Import Control Commn., 1951, Nat. Econ. Coun., 1955-56; Adminstr., Off. of Econ. Coordination, 1954-55; Chmn.-Gen. Mgr., Rice & Corn Admin. (Nat. Grains Authority), 1968-71; Chmn. of Bd., Country Bankers' Ins. & Surety Co. Inc., Philippine Pres. Lines, Repub. Real Estate Corp.; Pres., Pacific Wood Preserving Co. ·Inc.; Dir., Rural Bank of Bacolod. Mbr., profl. orgs. & var. clubs. Articles, Econs. & Finance, var. mags. Hons. incl: Cmdr., Legion of Honor, Philippine Govt., 1952; Ph.D., De La Salle Coll., Bacolod City, 1962; many profl. awards. Address: 794 Harvard, Wack Wack Subdivision, Mandaluyong, Rizal, Philippines. 16.

MONTGOMERY, Elizabeth Flanagan (Mrs. Stewart Magruder Montgomery). Housewife; School Teacher. Educ: A.B., Miss. State Coll. for Women, Columbus; N. Western Univ. Schl. of Speech, Evanston, Ill.; Grad. work, Peabody Coll., Nashville, Tenn., Columbia Univ., N.Y.C., Columbia Schl. of Drama, ibid, Univ. of Calif., Berkeley. Appts: Tchr., Dramatics, Elem. grades, H.S. Engl., Cary Schl.; H.S. Engl., Rolling Fork Schl. Mbrships: Life, State Histn., King's Daughters & Sons; Past Pres., Miss. King's Daughters & Sons; Miss. Women's Cabinet Pub. Affairs; Episc. Ch. women, Miss. & Province of Sewanee; Highland Club Aux.; Patron, Delta Debutante Club; Dir., Sec., Miss. Assn. Mental Hlth.; Sharkey Co. Commnr., 5th Region Mental Hlth.; Vicksburg Club Book Reviewer; Pres., Miss. Colonial Dames XVIIth Century; Pres., Gov.'s Trustees, King's Daughters Home, Natchez; Colonial Dames XVIIth Century; Dames of the Ct. of Hon.; Daughters of the Am. Colonists; Daughters of 1812; Soc. Magna Charta; Ams. Royal Descent; Zeta Phi Eta; Daughters of the Confederacy. Hons: Woman of Achievement, Rolling Fork Bus. & Profl. Women, 1965; Outstanding Civic Ldr. of Am., 1967; Outstanding Community Ldr. of Am., 1968. Address: Rte. 2, Rolling Fork, MS 39159, U.S.A. 5, 7, 22, 57, 70.

MONTGOMERY, George C., b. 17 Sept. 1932. Lawyer. Educ: Loyola Univ., 1951; Univ. of S. Calif., 1955; LL.B. & J.D., Loyola Law Schl., L.A., 1956-59. Appts: Pres. & Chmn. of Bd., Montgomery, Bottum, Regal & McNally, 1959-; V.P. & Bd. Mbr., Norso Distributors, & Samoa Investment Co., 1959-; Pres. & Chmn., of Bd., George C. Montgomery Enterprises, Inc., 1968-; Bd. Mbr., Trans Pacific Drug, Ltd., 1971-; V.P. & Bd. Mbr., Biota Int., 1972-. Mbrships: Am. Bar Assn.; Calif. & L.A. Bar Assns.; Am. Judicature Soc.; Phi-Delta-Phi; U.S. Dist. Ct. & Ct. of Appeal, 9th Circuit; U.S. Tax Court. Author, Current Change in the Law of Surety Bonds, 1960. Recip., Patron of Youth Award, 1972. Address: 1100 Glendon Ave., Suite 1250, Los Angeles, CA 90024, U.S.A.

MONTOYA, Carlos Garcia, b. 13 Dec. 1903. Flamenco Guitarist. Spanish Gypsy descent. 1st played guitar age 8. 1st profl. appearance age 14. Appeared w. La Argentina, Paris, 1927. Int. tours since that date. 1st solo recital, N.Y., 1948. 1st concert performance w. St. Louis Symph. Orch., Mo., 1966. Composer of Suite Flamenca, for Flamenco Guitar & Symph. Orch. Solo compositions for guitar incl. Soleares, Granaina, Malaga, Saeta. Hons. incl: Comendador, Spanish Order of El Merito Civil; Hon. Citizen of State of Tex.; Keys to Cities of N.Y., San. Fran., Miami. Address: 345 W. 58th St., N.Y., NY 10019, U.S.A. 1.

MOODY, Carol Martin (Mrs. Richard A. Moody). Radio Television Producer. Educ: B.S., Univ. of Ill., 1939; Mus.B., Ind. Univ., 1958; Mus.M. (in piano), 1966. Appts: John Robert Powers Model, 1937; Dir., Women's & Children's Progs., WHCU Ithaca, N.Y., 1940-41; Actress, Brattle St. Theatre, 1943; Prod., CBS Chgo., 1944-45; Radio Actress, Chgo., 1945; Originator, Owner, Prod., QUIZDOWN, 1945-67 (Quizdown was 1st synd., locally prod. prog. Performed locally in most large cities in country). Mbrships: Nat. Soc. of Arts & Letters; Mu Phi Epsilon; Indpls. Symph. Soc.; Pres., Bloomington Unit, 1951; Friends of Art & of Music; Woman's Club; Investment Club; Fri. Musicale, Prog. Dir., 1969-71; Presby. Ch. Subject of articles in jrnls. inclng. Printers Ink, Variety, Broadcast Mag., Time, Tide, Newsweek & Ed. & Publisher. Address: Red Ridge, R. Route 1, Bloomington, IN 47401, U.S.A. 5, 8.

MOODY, Herbert Henry Gatenby, b. 12 Mar. 1903. Architect. Educ: B.Arch., Univ. of Manitoba, 1926. Appts. incl: Ptnrship. w. Robert E. Moore, F.R.A.I.C., Winnipeg &

Toronto, 1936-; Sr. Ptnr., Moody & Moore & Ptnrs., Winnipeg, until 1968, & currently Cons. to same firm. Archt. for pub. bldgs. inclng: Winnipeg Gen. Hosp.; Dauphin Gen. Hosp.; Hudson Bay Stores across Canada; St. John's Coll., Univ. Coll., & Fac. of Med. Bldgs., Univ. of Man.; Winnipeg Centennial Concert Hall, Mus., & Planetarium. Mbrships: Man. Assn. Archts.; Ont. Assn. Archts. Recip. of Mention in Despatches, Royal Canadian Engrs., WWII. Address: Moody & Moore & Ptnrs., 295 Broadway, Winnipeg, Canada.

MOODY, Louis Smith (Mrs.), b. 10 Sept. 1904. Home Economist. Educ: Bradley Univ.; B.S., Univ. of Wis., 1926; Postgrad. study, Univ. of Chgo.; & Harvard Univ. Schl. of Pub. Hlth. M.S., Pub. Hlth. Nutrition, Simmons Coll., 1947; Postgrad. study, Iowa State Univ. Appts: Home Econs. Tchr., Ashland, (Wis.), H.S. & Special Lectr., Cafeteria Mgmt., Northland Coll., 1927-28; Cafeteria Dir. & Hom Econs. Tchr., Wauwatose, Wis., 1928-33; Dist. Home Mgmt. Supvsr., Farm Security Admin., U.S. Dept. of Agric., Champaign, Ill., 1936-41; Pub. Hlth. Nutritionist, Ill. Dept. of Pub. Hlth., Springfield, Ill., 1941-56; Ext. Advsr., Home Econs., Univ. of Ill. Coop. Ext. Serv., 1959-73; Retd., 1973. Mbrships: Bd. Mbr., Ill. Home Econs. Assn.; Ill. Pub. Hlth. Assn.; Nat., Ill. State Assns. of Ext. Advsrs.; Int., Am. Ill., Home Econs. Assns.; Am. Pub. Hlth. Assn.; Am., Ill. Dietetics Assns.; V.P., Bus. & Profl. Women's Club; Gamma Sigma Delta; Epsilon Sigma Phi. Publs; Contbr. to Nat. Ext. Review. Hons: Fellow, Am. Pub. Hlth. Assn., 1949; Disting. Serv. Award, Nat. Assn. of Ext. Home Economists, 1971; U.S. AID Cert. of Coop., 1972. Address: 612 S. 5th St., Princeton, IL 61356, U.S.A. 5.

MOOK, Barbara Heer Held, b. 9 June 1919. Civic & Patriotic Worker. Educ: Coll. of Wooster, Ohio; Actual Bus. Coll., Akron, Ohio, 1941. Appts: Mus. Docent, Nat. Soc. DAR, Wash., D.C., 1973-; Sr. Nat. Asst. Organizing Sec., Children of Am. Revolution, ibid, 1974-. Mbrships: DAR, 1959- (var. posts inclng. as Recording Sec., Libn. & Regent, Thomas Nelson Chapt., & Mbr., Chmn., Nominating Comm., Potomac Regents Club); Adult Ldr. Activities, Children of Am. Revolution, 1960-64 (inclng. as Sr. Pres., George Johnston Soc. & Sr. State Chmn., Gadsby's Tavern); Adult Ldr. Activities, Girl Scouts, 1951-56 (inclng. as Troop Ldr., Co-Ldr., Neighborhood Chmn. & Mbr., Arlington Prog. Comm.); Nat. Trust for Historic Preservation; Nat. Audubon Soc.; Smithsonian Res. Assocs.; Am. Mus. of Natural Hist.; Nat. Archives Assocs.; Va. Histl. Soc.; Nat. Histl. Soc.; U.S. Capitol Histl. Soc. Address: 5222 Twenty-sixth Rd. N., Arlington, VA 22207, U.S.A. 22, 125.

MOOK, Conrad Payne, b. 2 May 1914. Meteorologist; Retired Government Official. Educ: A.B., Coll. of Wooster, 1939; M.S., Grad. Schl. of Arts & Scis., N.Y. Univ., 1943. Appts: Tchng. Fellow & Instr., Meterol., N.Y. Univ., 1940-43; Rsch. Meteorologist & Forecaster, Weather Bur., 1943-57; Geophysicist, Diamond Ordnance Fuze Labs., 1957-61; Hurricane Rsch. Meteorologist & Forecaster, Weather Bur., Wash., 1961-62; Rsch. Prog. Mgr., Space Vehicle Thermal Control & Vacuum Technol., HQ, NASA, 1962-70. Mbrships: Am. Meteorological Soc.; Chmn., Wash. Br., ibid, 1952-53; Am. Geophys. Union; AIAA; Thermophys. Comm. Mbr., ibid, 1965-68. Tech. papers, storms rsch., clear air turbulence, meteorological stats. Assoc. Ed., Jrnl. of Geophys. Rsch., Official jrnl. of Am. Geophys. Union, 1959-65. Recip., Apollo Achievement

Award, NASA, 1969. Address: 5222 26th Rd. N., Arlington, VA 22207, U.S.A. 7, 14, 125.

MOOKERJEE, Ajit, b. 29 Dec. 1915. Museum Administrator. Educ: M.A., Univ. of Calcutta, 1939; M.A., London Univ., U.K., 1942. Appts: Dir., Indian Inst. of Art in Ind., Calcutta, 1949-59; Lectr., Dip. Course in Museol., Calcutta Univ., 1958-59; Dir., Crafts Mus., New Delhi, 1959-; Chief Exec. Off. & Dev. Commnr., All India Handicrafts Bd.; Paper Seter & Examiner, Museol., Calcutta Univ., Fine Art & Sculpture, Coll. of Art, New Delhi; Examiner, Museol., Baroda Univ. Mbr., profl. orgs. Publs. incl: Folk Art of Bengal, 1939, 2nd edit., 1945; Museum Studies, 1946; Art of India, 1949; Designs in Indian Textiles (Ed.), 1953; Folk Toys of India, 1956; Modern Art in India, 1956; Indian Primitive Art, 1959; Tantra Art, 1966; Indian Dolls & Toys, 1968; Terracottas of Bengal (Ed.)' 1972. Recip., Watumull Fndn. Award, U.S.A., 1962. Address: C-II/117 Moti Bagh, New Delhi-21, India.

MOON, Delmas LaVerne, b. 28 May 1910. Pharmacist; Educator. Educ: Grad., Butler Univ., Indpls., Ind., U.S.A., 1931; Springfield Schl. of Pharmacy; Postgrad., Schl. of Med., Univ. of Ga., Athens. Appts: Clin. Investigator & Med. Researcher, num. hosps. in U.S.A., for 30 yrs.; Sr. H.S. Supt., for 7 yrs.; Fndr. & Exec. Dir., Moonderosa Tech. Ctr. for voc. trng., Spotsylvania, Va. Mbrships. incl: Elks Community Civic Club; Bd. of Deacons, First Bapt. Ch. Hons: Century Note Award, Lakeside Labs., Inc., 1943; Gold Star Award, Lakeside Labs., Inc., 1945; Achievement Award, Kremers Urban Co., 1954. Address: R.R. # 3, Box 126A, Spotsylvania, VA 22553, U.S.A. 125.

MOON, Tylman Redfield, b. 8 Oct. 1934. Architect. Educ: Vanderbilt Univ., 1952-53; Coll. of Wm. & Mary, Va., 1953-54; B.Arch., Univ. of Va., 1958. Appts: Served w. USN, 1958-61; Designer, Archtl. Off., Ernest T. Brown, Plainfield, N.J., 1961-66; Archt., Archtl. Off., Richard J. Chorlton, Princeton, N.J., 1966-68; Owner, Prin., Tylman R. Moon, A.I.A., Archt., Flemington, N.J., 1968-. Mbrships: Elder, Presby. Ch.; Pres., Design Resource, Inc., 1969-; Am. Inst. of Archts.; Dir., Hunterdon Co. Chmbr. of Comm., N.J.; Pres., Flemington Lions Int.; Incorporator, Hunterdon Low Income Housing Corp.; Raritan Twp. Conservation Commn., 1971-72. Variety of archtl. commns. incl. Master Plan of Hunterdon Co. Hons: Alpha Rho Chi Medal, 1958; Scarab, 1957; Omicron Delta Kappa, 1958; Raven Soc., 1958. Address: 122 Main St., Flemington, NJ 08822, U.S.A. 6.

MOONEY, George Austin, b. 23 Nov. 1911. BAnk Executive. Educ: B.S., Fordham Univ Appts. incl: Financial News Ed., N.Y. Times, 1926-54; Supt. of Banks, State of N.Y., 1955-58; Exec. Dir., Investment Co. Inst., 1959-63; Chmn. & Chief Exec. Off., Wash. Fed. Savings & Loan Assn., 1963-. Mbrships. incl: Dir. & Exec. Comm. Mbr., Savings Assn. League of N.Y. State; Legislative Comm., U.S. Savings & Loan League; former Dir. & V. Chmn., Fed. Home Loan Bank of N.Y.; 1st Pres. & Fndng. Mbr., World Trade Writers Assn.; former Gov., N.Y. Financial Writers' Assn.; former Exec. Comm. Mbr., Nat. Assn. Supvsrs. of State Banks; Trustee, Mt. Olivet Cemetry. Contbr. to financial jrnls. & mags. Hons. incl: Fordham Univ. Alumni Assn.'s Annual Award for Outstanding Pub. Serv., 1958; Cert. of Honor, Fed. of Jewish Philanthropies of N.Y., 1966; Cert. of Honor, Young Men's Christian Assn., 1966; Man of the Yr. Award, Real Estate Bd. of the Bronx, 1970; Cert. of Honor, Salvation

Army, 1973. Address: Wash. Fed. Savings & Loan Assn., 1390 St. Nicholas Ave., N.Y., NY 10033, U.S.A. 2.

MOONEY, John Bradford, Jr., b. 26 Mar. 1931. Naval Officer. Educ: USN Acad., 1953. Appts: Off. i/c, Bathyscaph Trieste II, 1964-67; Cmdng. Off., USS Menhadden (SS-377), 1967-68; Deep Submergence Prog., Off. of Chief of Naval Ops., 1968-71; Chief Staff Off., Submarine Dev. Grp. ONE, 1971-73; Cmdng. Off., Naval Stn., Charleston, S.C., 1973-. Mbrships: Mason; Eagle Scout, Active Adult Scouter; Naval Acad. Alumni Assn.; Naval Inst.; Marine Technol. Soc.; Rotary. Hons: Demolay Legion of Hon., 1964; Navy Commendations, 1964, 66 & 68; Meritorious Serv. Medals, 1971 & 74. Address: Commanding Off., Naval Stn., Charleston, SC 29408, U.S.A. 125.

MOONEY, William Tyrrell Jr., b. 28 Jan. 1927. College Professor; Consultant. Educ: A.B., Phys., Univ. of Calif., Berkeley, 1946; M.A., Educ., Stanford Univ., Calif., 1947; M.S., Chem., ibid, 1950; Grad. Work, Univ. of S. Calif. & Univ. of Calif., L.A., 1956-67. Appts. incl: Tchng. Asst., Chem., Stanford Univ., 1948-50; Chem. Fac., El Camino Coll., Torrance, Calif., 1950-54; Dean, Div. of Phys. Scis., ibid, 1954-66; Prof. of Chem., 1966-. Mbrships. incl: Div. of Chem. Educ., Am. Chem. Soc. (Chmn. or Mbr., var. comms.): Advsry. Coun. on Coll. Chem. (var. offices held); Nat. Sci. Tchrs. Assn.; Bd. of Convocators, Calif. Lutheran Coll., 1970-74; Educl. Dir., Solar Energy Soc. of Am, 1974-; Am. Inst. Biol. Scis.; Phi Delta Kappa; Alpha Chi Sigma. Publs: incl: Author, Beginning Chemistry Learning System (5 vols)' 197-73; Co-author, The Education & Training of Chemistry Teachers for Two-Year Colleges, 1969. Hons: Coll. Chem. Tchng. Award, Mfg. Chems. Assn., 1967; Outstanding Educator of Am. Award, 1971, '74. Address: Dept. of Chem., El Camino Coll., 16007 S. Crenshaw Blvd., Torrance, CA 90506, U.S.A.

MOORE, (Sister) Alice Joseph, b. 19 Mar. 1924. College Professor & Administrator. Educ: Ph.B., Siena Heights Coll., 1946; M.A., Cath. Univ., 1949; Ph.D., ibid, 1957. Appts: Prin., St. Brendan's Jr. H.S., San Francisco, Calif., 1949-53; Schl. Supvsr., Mich., Ohio, N.Y., Prof. & Sec., Grad. Coun., Siena Heights Coll., 1957-64; Prof. of Educ. & Dir. of Placement, Barry Coll., Miami, Fla., 1965-, at Loyola, L.A., 1946, '47, & summer only, Our Lady of Mercy Coll., Charleston, S.C., 1965; study of educl. systems in Europe, 1967-68. Mbrships: NEA; Nat. Cath. Ed. Assn.; Am. Assn. Coll. Tchr. Educ.; Fla. Placement Assn. Recip., Tchr. of Yr. Award, 1972. Address: Barry College, 11300 N.E. 2nd Ave., Miami, FL 33161, U.S.A. 138, 141.

MOORE, Archie Lee, b. 13 Dec. 1916. Former World Light Heavyweight Boxing Champion; Social Worker. Appts: w. Civilian Conservation Corps govt. poverty proj., 1935; Started boxing professionally, 1936; Served in WWII; Profl. Fighter, 1942-62; Fndr., Any Boy Can Clubs, Inc., San Diego, Calif., 1965-; Lectr. thru'out world to var. grps.; CAlif. Youth Cons.; Athletic Dir., Buenaventura, Acad., Ventura, Calif. Mbr., NAACP. Co-AUthor, w. Leonard Pearl, Any Boy Can: The Archie Moore Story, 1971. Hons. incl: Freedom Fndn. Award for Outstanding Youth Work, 1968; Edward J. Niel Award for Boxer of the Yr., 1958; Guardian of Freedom Plaque for visiting armed forces in Berlin, Germany, 1973. Address: 3517 E St., San Diego, CA 92102, U.S.A. 30.

MOORE, Bernice Milburn (Mrs. Harry E. Moore), b. 17 June 1904. Administrator; Consultant; Author. Educ: B. Jrnlsm., Univ. of Tex., 1924; M.A., ibid, 1932; Ph.D., Univ. of N.C., 1937. Appts: Cons., Home & Family Educ., Tex. Educ. Agcy., 1941-64; Cons., Hogg Fndn. for Mental Hlth., 1941-64; Exec. Assoc., ibid, 1964-; Coord., Tex. Coop. Youth Study, 1956-64; Dir., Seminar for Chaps., USAF, 1956-66; Assoc. Dir., Philanthropy in the Southwest, 1964-70. Mbrships: Fellow, Am. Sociol. Assn.; Am. Assn. Marriage Counselors; Nat. Assn. for Mental Hlth.; Southwestern Soc. Sci. Assn.; Alpha Kappa Delta; Women in Communication; Philos. Soc. of Tex. Publs: (co-author) Tomorrow'S Parents, 1965; The Crisis of Separation, 1966; Our Youngest Children, 1971; Individual Freedom and the Requirements of Modern Society, 1972 & others. Hons: Bernice Milburn Moore Scholarship in Continuing Educ. for Women, 1970; Moore Bowman Award of Excellence, 1970; Hon. Fellow, Am. Assn. Marriage & Family Counselors, 1973; Disting. Alumnus Award, Ex-Student Assn. Tex. Univ., 1974; & others. Address: Hogg Fndn. for Mental Hlth., P.O. Box 7998, Univ. of Tex., Austin, TX 78712, U.S.A. 5, 7, 14.

MOORE, Carey Armstrong, b. 5 Mar. 1930. College Professor.Educ: A;B.,Gettysburg Coll., Pa., 1952; B.D., Luth. Theological Sem., Gettysburg, Pa., 1956; Ph.D., John Hopkins Univ., Balt.,Md., 1965; Post-doctoral fellow, Hebrew Union Coll., Jerusalem,Israel, 1967-68. Appts: Instr. - Assoc. Prof., Gettysburg Coll., Pa., 1955-68;Prof. of Relig., ibid, 1969- ; Vis. Prof. of Hebrew, Luth. Theological Sem., Gettysburg, 1965-66; Area Supvsr. at archaeological excavations, Gezer, Israel,sponsored by Hebrew Union Coll. & Harvard Uni., summers 1966-68 & 1973. Mbrships. incl: Soc. of Biblical Lit. & Exegisis; Archaeological Inst. of Am.; Am. Schls. of Oriental Rsch.; AAUP;Phi Beta Kappa; Nat. Assn. of Profs. of Hebrew. Author of books, in field; Contbr. to jrnls. Recip., Martin Luther Fellowship, 1958. Address: Dept. of Relig., Gettysburg Coll., Gettysburg, PA 17325, U.S.A. 13, 30.

MOORE, Dan Tyler, b. 1 Feb. 1908. Writer, Lecturer, Administrator. Educ: B.S., Yale Univ., 1931. Appts: Chief, Ohio Div. of Securities (co-author of Ohio Securities Act); Regional Admin., U.S. Securities & Exchange Commn.; Reg. Dir., Fifth Corps Area, Off. of Civilian Defense; Capt., U.S. Army Off. of Strategic Servs.; Major, Chief of OSS Counter Intelligence in Middle East; Pres., Middle East Co.; Pres., China Co.; Currently Dir., General, International Platform Assn.; Writer & Lectr. Mbrships: Yale Club., N.Y.; Union Club, Tavern Club, Hanger Club, Cleveland; Book & Snake; Rowfant Club, Cleveland; Metropolitan Club of Wash. Publs: The Terrible Game; Cloak & Cipher; Wolves, Widows & Orphans; Lecturing For Profit; The Tricks of the Trade (Newspaper Column); Contbr. of many articles to domestic & for. publs. Recip., Teenage Book Award, 1957 & IPA Award for "Best Adventure Speech Being Given in US Today". Address: 2564 Berkshire Rd., Cleveland Heights, OH 44106, U.S.A. 2, 8, 22, 129, 131, 140.

MOORE, Dorothy Christine Sexton, b. 27 Nov. 1912. Educator. Educ: B.S., E. Carolina Coll., Greenville, N.C., 1953, M.S; 1964. Appts: Primary Tchr., Dawson Schl., Scotland Neck, N.C., 1937-39, New Hope Elem. Schl., Roanoke Rapids, N.C., 1939-40, Wm. R. Davie Schl., ibid, 1940-46, Enfield Graded Schl., N.C., 1947-62; Elem. Supvsr., Halifax Co. Schls., N.C., 1962-. Mbrships: Pres., Halifax Co.

Unit, N.C..Educ. Assn.; NEA. Assn. of Sup N.C. Educ Assn. Div. of Supvsrs.; Chapt. Pres., Mbrship. Chmn., Delta Kappa Gamma; Pres., Sec., Treas., Studby Club; Sunday Schl. Tchr., Bàpt. Ch., 25 yrs.; Woman's Club, Recip., var. hons. Address: Rte. 2, Box 32, Enfield, NC 27823, U.S.A. 5, 7, 15, 132.

MOORE, Eleanor Belle Heberlin (Mrs. Franklin D. Moore), b. 26 Oct. 1921. Musician; Civic Worker; Business Executivr. Educ: Old Dominion Univ., 1956-58 ' 69-70; Geo. Wash. Univ., 1964-65 Appts.Violist, Norfolk Symph. Orch., 1936-, Scherzo String Ensemble, 1969, Scherzo String Quartet, 1970- ; w. Bell Ringers of Scherzo, 1972-; held var. exec. positions, the final one being Dir. Wage Admin. & Position Classification Div., Ind. Rels. Dept., U.S. Navy Pub. Works Ctr., 1941-68. Mbrships. incl: Pres., Altrusa Club of Norfolk, 1970-72 & 73-; Corres. Sec., Norfolk Fedn. of Civic Leagues, 1970-; V.P., Bel-Aire Civic League, 1970-; Recip. Sustained Superior Performance Award, U.S.N. Pub Works Ctr., 1958. Address: 1684 Cougar Ave., Norfolk, VA 23518, U.S.A. 5.

MOORE, (The Worshipful Chancellor the Rev.) Evelyn Garth, b. 6 Feb. 1906. Barrister-at-Law; Clerk in Holy Orders; Chancellor. Educ: M.A., Trinity Coll., Cambridge; Cuddesdon Theol. Coll.; Called to Bar, Gray's Inn, 1928. Ordained Deacon & Priest, 1962. Appts. incl: Fellow, Corpus Christi Coll., Cambridge Univ., 1947-; Lectr. Evidence & Criminal Procedure, Coun. of Legal Educ., 1952-67; Chancellor, Vicar-Gen. & Official Prin., Archdeaconries of Lewisham, Southwark & Kingston-on-Thames & Ely; High Bailiff of Ely Cathedral, 1961-;Guild Vicar, St. Mary Abchurch, 1972-; Legal Assessor, RCVS, 1963-68; Ch. Commnr., 1964-; Mbrships. incl: Gov. Bodies of sev. schls.; Pres., Ch's Fellowship for Psychical & Spiritual Studies, 1963-. An Introduction to English Canon Law, 1966; Co-Author, 8th edit., Kenny's Cases in Criminal Law; Jt. Author, Ecclesiatic Law, 3rd edit., Halsbury 's Laws of England; articles and profl. jrnls. Address: 9 Maitland House, Barton Rd., Cambridge, U.K. 1, 41.

MOORE, Florence Agnes, b. 30 Sept. 1922. Librarian. Educ: B.A., B.L.S., Univ. of Ottawa. Appts: Cataloguer- Dir. of Tech. Servs., Lib. of Parliament, Ottawa. Mbrships: Lib. Assn. of Ottawa; Can. Assn. of Law Libns.; Can. Lib. Asnsn. Address: c/o Lib. of Parliament, Ottawa, Ont. K1A 0A9, Canada. 5.

MOORE, Gloria Carole, b. 3 May 1946. Educator. Educ: B.S., Middle Tenn. State Univ., 1964-67; M.Ed., ibid, 1968. Appts: Tchr., Maury Co., 1968-. Mbrships: NEA; Tenn., Middle Tenn. & Maury Co. Educ. Assns.; Int. Reading Assn.; PTA; Pres., Maury Co. & Mid. Tenn. Brs., State Mbrship. Chmn., Assn. for Childhood Education. Int.; Project Chmn., AAUW; Drama Chmn., Maury Co. Creative Arts Guild; Pres., Beta Alpha Chapt., Alpha Delta Kappa; Sec.-Hist., Chautauqua Chapt., Good Cheer Circle of King's Daughters; Sec., Maury Co. Nutrition Coun.; Maury Co. Assn. for Retarded Children & Adults; Maury Co. Mental Hlth. Assn. Hons. incl: Gen. Excellency Student & Most Likely to Succeed, 1964. Address: Trotwood Apts. No. 20, Columbia, TN 38401, U.S.A. 76, 125.

MOORE, Hugh Purfield, b. 2 Aug. 1912. Manager. Educ: B.A., Univ. of N.D., 1933; Univ. of Mich., 1934. Appts: Pres., Acme Electronics, Inc., L.A., 1955-59; Gen. Mgr., Acme Div., Aerovox, L.A., 1959-62; Pres., Computer Equipment Corp., El Monte, Calif., 1962-. Mbrships: Dir. & Chmn. of Bd., Western

Electronic Show & Convention; V.P., Western Electronic Mfrs. Assn.; S. Hills Country Club, W. Covina, Calif.; Sigma Delta Chi; Phi Beta Kappa. Hons: Wescon Award, 1960 & 66; Sioux Award, Univ. of N.D., 1966. Address: 1906 Montezuma Way, West Covina, CA 91791, U.S.A. 9, 16.

MOORE, James Lewis, b. 16 Feb 1908. Newspaper Publisher. Educ: Univ. of Mo., 1925. Appts: Publr., The Toweler, Kannapolis, N.C., 1927; The China Grove (N.C.) Press, 1930; Pres., Treas., & Chmn. of Bd., Kannapolis Publng. Co; Publr. & Gen. Mgr., The Daily Independent, Kannapolis; Retires, 1973. Mbrships Trustee, Independent Student Aid Assn.; Kannapolis Chmbr. of Comm. Author of Cabarrus Re-Born. Address: 205 East E. St., Kannapolis, NC 28081, U.S.A. 7.

MOORE, (James) Mavor, b. 8 Mar. 1919. Playwright; Actor; Producer; Teacher. Educ: B.A. Univ. of Toronto, Canada, 1941. Appts. incl: Chief Prod., CBC TV Eng. Network, 1950-54; Drama Critic, Toronto Telegram, 1958-60; Artistic Dir., Charlottetown Fest., P.E.I., 1963-68; Gen. Dir., St. Lawrence Ctr. for the Arts, Toronto, 1965-7-; Prod., Dir., Canadian Opera Co., Vancouver Fest., Crest Theatre, Neptune Theatre, CBC-TV, etc. 1946-66; Prof., Theatre, York Univ., 1970-. Mbrships incl: Assn. of Canadian TV & Radio Artists; Actors Equity Canada; Dramatists Guild, U.S.A. Publs. incl: (plays) The Ottawa Man, 1958; Getting In, 1971; The Pile, Inside Out & The Store, 1973; Come Away Come Away, 1973; (musicals) Sunshine Town, 1955; The Best of All Possible Worlds, 1956; Johnny Belinda (1968); (opera) Louis Riel, 1967; (poetry) And What do You do, 1960; contbr. to books. Hons. incl: D. Litt., York Univ., 1969; Order of Canada, 1973; Mbr., Canada Coun., 1974. Address: Fac. of Fine Arts, York Univ., 4700 Keele St., Downsview, Ont., Canada. 88.

MOORE, Jane Elizabeth (Ross). Librarian. Educ: A.B., Smith Coll., 1951; M.S.L.S., Drexel Univ., 1952; M.B.A., N.Y. Univ., 1965; Doct. Candidate, Case Western Reserve Univ., 1970-. Appts. incl: Cataloger, Chief Serials Catalogue Libn., Brooklyn Coll. Lib., 1958-65; Asst. Prof., Chief of Catalogue Div., ibid, 1965-70; Assoc. Prof., Chief of Catalogue Div., ibid, CUNY, 1971-; Lectr., Grad. Dept. of Lib. Serv., Queens Coll., 1967-69. Mbrships. incl. Mbrship. Comm. ALA, 1967-71; Pres., Resources & Tech.. Servs. Libns., 1963-64. Address: Brooklyn Coll. Library, City Univ. of New York, Brooklyn, NY 11210, U.S.A. 5, 6,

MOORE, Marece Elizabeth Gibbs. Librarian. Educ: B.S., N.C. Agricl. & Tech. State Univ., Greensboro, 1940; B.L.S., Univ. of Chgo., 1945., Further study, 1948-49. Appts: Instr., N.C. Agricl. & Tech State Univ., 1940-43; Asst. Libn., ibid, 1943-44; Cataloger, Fisk Univ., Nashville, Tenn., 1945-48; Instr., Lib. Sci., ibid, 1945-46; Cataloger, Detroit Pub. Lib., 1949-53; Ref. Libn., ibid, 1953-54; Supvsr., Ref. Servs. Cataloguing, 1955-67; Detroit Area Libn., Burroughs Corp,., 1967-71; Mgr., Corp. Lib., ibid, 1971- ; Pt. - Time Instr., Wayne State Univ., 1970. Mbrships. incl: Chmn., var. comms., Special Libs. Assn., 1969-73; Mich. Chapt. Pres., ibid, 1973-74; Life Mbr., ALA; Life mbr., Delta Sigma Theta; Life mbr., NAACP; Am. Soc. for Info. Serv.; 2nd V.P., Detroit Chapt. Pres., ibid, 1972-74. Recip. of hons. Address: Corp. Lib., Burroughs Corporation, Burroughs Pl., Detroit, MI 48232, U.S.A. 5.

MOORE, Michael J. b. 11 July 1935. Engineer; Computer Designer; Consultant. Educ: B.S., Univ. of Mich., U.S.A., 1956; M.S., State Univ., N.Y., Buffalo, 1962. Appts: Electronics Engr., Bell Aircraft Corp., Buffalo, N.Y., 1956-57; Communications Off., USAF, 1957-59; Electronics Engr., Satellite Design, Philco Corp., Palo Alto, Calif., 1959-60; Computer Design Hd., System Analysis Sect., Mgr., Calif. Off, Computer Systems Dept., Calspan Corp. (formerly Cornell Aeronautical Lab. Inc.), Buffalo, N.Y., 1960-. Mbrships: Sr. Mbr. & Past Chmn., Buffalo Sect., IEEE: Assn. for Computing Machinery; Sigma Xi; Int. Platform Assn. Publs: num. Engrng. reports. Address: 2274 Monticello Rd., Napa, CA 94558, U.S.A.

MOORE, Patrick, b. 4 Mar. 1923. Author. Appts: Bomber Navigator, RAF, WWII; Dir., Armagh Planetarium, 1965-68. Mbrships: Int. Astronomical Union; Fellow, Royal Astronomical Soc.; Dir., Lunar Sect., Brit. Astronom. Assn.; Hon. Mbr., Astronomical-Geodetic Soc. of U.S.S.R.; Astronom. Soc. of the Pacific, etc. Publs: 60 books, mainly astronomical; one light opera (now in rehearsal). Has presented the BBC TV Astronomical Prog., 'The Sky at Night' every month since April 1957. Hons: O.B.E., 1969; Goodacre Medal, 1968; Lorimer Medal, 1962; Guido Horn d'Arturo Medal (Italian), 1971; Hon. doctorate, Univ. of Lancaster, 1974. Address: Farthings, 39 West St., Selsey, Sussex, U.K. 1.

MOORE, Pollard Japhet, b. 21 May 1923. Port Executive. Educ: Post Grad. Dip., Mgmt. Studies, 1965; Bus. Admin., Univ. of W. Indies, 1965; Port Admin., Port of London Authority, 1958. Appts: Mgr., Port Ops., Port Authority, Trinidad & Tobago, 1964-66; Asst. Gen. Mbr., ibid, 1967-68; Gen. Mgr., ibid, 1969; Gen. Mgr., W. Indies Shipping Corp. (Regional), 1969-71; Mng. Dir., Trinidad & Tobago Port Contractors Ltd., 1971-. Mbrships: Int. Assn. of Ports & Harbours; Int. Cargo Handling Assn., U.K.; Tech. Advsry. Sub-Comm., ibid; Trinidad & Tobago Econl. & Statl. Soc.; V.P., Trinidad & Tobago Port Servs. Club. Author, var. short papers on shipping & dock ind. Address: 27A Benjamin St., Diego Martin, Trinidad, W. Indies. 109.

MOORE, R. Albert Jr., b. 10 Feb. 1937. Roman Catholic Priest; Art Instructor & Chairman Art Department; Painter in Polyester Resin. Educ: B.A., St. Mary's Coll., Ky., 1959; S.T.B., St. Mary's Pontifical Univ., Balt., Md., 1961; M.A., Notre Dame du Lac, Ind., 1972; M.F.A., ibid, 1974. Appts: Instr. British Lit., Trinity H.S., 1963-65; Instr. Theol., ibid, 1964-65; Fndr. & Chmn. Dept. Fine Arts, ibid, 1965-; Instr. Art, ibid, 1967-73; Reconstruction Artist, Am. Schl. Oriental Rsch., Jerusalem, sponsored by Furman Univ., 1966 (5000 drawings of ancient city of Ai, c. 1150 B.C.); Rsch. in Polyester Resin as painting medium, Univ. Notre Dame du Lac, 1973-75. Mbrships: Nat. Art Educl. Assn.; NEA; Ky. Art Educl. Assn.; Nat. liturgical Conference. All nat. & int. exhibs., lectrs. & commnd. works handled by Thor Gall., Louisville, Ky. 5000 drawings publd. in attempt to date Biblical Book of Josue. Recip. of grants from Frank J. Lewis Fndn., Chgo. & Riviera Beach, Fla., 1973; Courier Jrnl. & Louisville Times Fndn., 1972; Klein Fndn., Louisville, Ky., 1973. Address: 4011 Shelbyville Rd., Louisville, KY 40207, U.S.A. 37, 105, 125.

MOORE, Sonia, b. 4 Dec. 1902. Theatre Director; Eudcator; Lecturer; Author. Educ: Univs. of Kiev & Moscow, Russia, 1918-20; Drama Studio, Solovzov THeatr, Kiev, 1919-20; STudio, Moscow Art Theatre, 1920-23; Dip., Alliance Française, Paris, 1927; Degrees, Reale Conservatorie de Musica, Santa Cecilia, 1939, & R. Acad. Filarmonica, Rome, 1939. Appts: Dir., Sonia Moore Studio of the Theatre, N.Y.C., 1961-; Fndr., Pres., Artistic Dir., Am. Ctr. for Stanislavski Theatre Art, Inc., 1964-; Lectr., var. seminars, convens., univs., & radio progs. Plays Directed incl: The Cherry Orchard; Desire Under the Elms; The Slave; The Stronger; The Man with the Flower in his Mouth; The Boor; The Marriage Proposal; The Anniversary; The Crucible; A Deed from the King of Spain. Mbr., var. profl. orgs. Publs. incl: The Stanislavski Method, 1960; Stanislavski Today, 1973; contbr. to var. profl. jrnls. Address: 485 Park Ave., N.Y., NY 10022, U.S.A. 5, 44, 130, 132, 138.

MOORE, V.C., b. 25 Jan. 1918. Diplomat. Educ: Victoria Coll., B.C., Canada; Univ. of B.C., Vancouver; Georgia Augusta Univ., Goettingen, Germany. Appts. incl: For. Serv. Off., Dept. of External Affairs, Ottawa, 1948-; 2nd, then 3rd Sec., Canadian Embassy, Bonn/Berlin, 1951-52; Chargé d'Affaires, Vienna, 1954; 2nd Sec., Moscow, 1956; 1st Sec., Chargé d'Affaires, ibid, 1958; Acting Hihg Commnr., Karachi, 1960; Counsellor, 1961 & '63; Chargé d'Affaires, The Hague, 1962; Ambassador, Hd. of Canadian Delegation, Int. Commn. Suprvsn. & Control Viet Nam, Saigon/Hanoi, 1965-67; Dpty. Hd., Off., Econ. Affairs, Ottawa, 1967-68; High Commnr., Jamaica & Canadian Commnr. to British Hondura, & to Commonwealth of Bahama Islands, 1968-72; Dir., Commonwealth Instns. Div., Dept. of External Affairs, 1973-. Mbrships. incl: Royal Commonwealth Soc., Ottawa; Nat. Gallery Assn. Mentioned in Despatches, 1943. Address: 294 Manor Ave., Rockcliffe Pk., Ottawa K1M OH4, Ont., Canada. 128.

MOORER, (Admiral) Thomas Hinman, b. 9 Feb. 1912. U.S. Navy Admiral & Chairman, Joint Chiefs of Staff. Educ: Grad., U.S. Naval Acad., 1933; Designated Naval Aviator (HTA), 1936; GRad., Naval War Coll., Newport, R.I., 1953; Hon. LL.D., Auburn Univ., 1968; Hon. H.H.D., Samford Univ., 1970. Appts. incl: Ensign, 1933; Lt.(Jr. Grade), 1936; Lt., 1940; Lt.Cmdr., 1942; Cmdr., 1944; Capt., 1952; Rear Admiral, 1958; V. Admiral, 1962; Cmdr., 7th Fleet, 1962-64; Admiral, 1964; Cmdr.-in-Chief, Pacific Fleet, 1964-65; Cmdr.-in-Chief Atlantic, Cmdr.-in-Chief U.S. Atlantic Fleet, Cmdr.-in-Chief Western Atlantic Area & Supreme Allied Cmdr. Atlantic, 1965-67; apptd. Chief of Naval Ops. by Pres. Johnson, 1967-69; re-apptd. ibid, by Pres. Nixon, 1969; Chmn., Jt. Chief of Staff, 1970-. Recip. many hons. inclng. 42 medals, 9 individual decorations from U.S., 18 from for. nations, Stephen Dacatur Award for Operational Competence, Navy League of U.S., 1964, Gen. William Mitchell Award, Wings Club, N.Y.C., 1968, Ala. Acad. of Honor, 1969, Frank M. Hawks Award for Outstanding Contbns. to Dev. of Aviation, Am. Legion Air Serv. Post 501, N.Y.C., 1971 & Grey Eagle of U.S. Navy Award at Wash. Navy Yard, 1972. Address: Jt. Chiefs of Staff, Wash. DC 20301, U.S.A.

MOORE-RINVOLUCRI, Mina J. University Lecturer; Educational Administrator. Educ: Liverpool Univ.; Univs. of Ferrand & Strasbourg, France. Appts: Lectr., Univ. Coll., Cardiff, 1938-40, Univ. of Liverpool, 1943-46, 1947-69, Newcastle Sect., Univ. of Durham, 1946-47, Univ. Coll., Cork, Oreland, 1969-74; Dir., UCC Educ. Ctr., Limerick, IReland, until

1974. Mbrships: Life Mbr., MLA, Chmn., 1955; Life Mbr., BFUW; Mod. Lang. Comm. Mbr., Schls. Coun., until 1967, Comm. of Nat. Acad. Awards, until 1969; Nat. Coun. of Women, 1974; Comp. Educ. Soc. in Europe; Gt. Britain Br. Mbr., ibid. Publs: Bernard Shaw et la France, 1934; Oral Work in Modern Languages, 1953; Education in E. Germany, 1973. Articles, var. learned jrnls. Hons: Medaille de Vermeil, Académie Française, 1936; Officier d'Académie, 1946. Address: 45 Lôn Tywysog, Nyddleton Park, Denbigh, N.Wales, U.K. 137.

MOORES, (The Hon.) Frank D., b. 18 Feb. 1933. Business Executive; Premier of Newfoundland and Labrador. Educ: St. Andrew's Coll., Aurora, Ont., Canada. Appts: Dir., Avalon Telephone Co. Ltd.; Dir., Fisheries Coun. of Canada; Dir., Atlantic Provinces Econ. Coun.; Dir., Frozen Fish Trades Assn.; Gov., Coll. of Fisheries Navigation Marine Engrng. & Electronics, St. John's; Elected to House of Commons from Bonavista-Trinity-Conception, 1968; Pres., Progressive Conservative Part of Canada, 1969; Ldr., Progressive Conservative Party, Nfld., 1970; Led his party to victory in Provincial Election, 1971; 1st Progressive Conservative Premier of Nfld. & Labrador, Min. of Fisheries, 1972-. Mbrships. incl: Past Pres., Harbour Grace Recreation Ctr.; Past. Pres., Kiwanis Club; Masonic Order of Carbonear. Address: Premier of Nfld., Off. of the Premier, Confederation Bldg., St. John's, Nfld., Canada.

MOORES, Lawrence Wayne, Jr., b. 21 Apr. 1925. Educator. Educ: B.A., Hist., 1949, M.A., Hist., 1950, Univ. of Maine; Ph.D., Univ. of Sarasota, 1971. Appts: Tchr., Hist., 1950-64; H.S. Prin., 1964-68; Sr. Pupil Servs. Counselor, 1968-; Educl. Cons.*Pvte. Contracts for Educl. Rsch.), 1970-. Mbrships: Masonic Lodge, F. & A.M.; Phi Delta Kappa; USAF Reserves (Lt. Col.); Civil Air Patrol (Lt. Col.); Experimental Aviation Assn. Aircraft Owners & Pilots' Assn.; N.E.A. & Am. Vocatl. Assn. (Life mbrships.). Publs: History of the Ku Klux KLan in Maine (Maine Study Series); Directory of Occupational Education Schools; Resonsibilities of the Clerk of the Works, 1973; Guide to Career Education Schools; article, Old Crate to Cream Puff, in Sports Aviation. Address: 65 Floral Ave., Bethpage, NY 11714, U.S.A.

MOOS, Ruth Carolyn Feinthel (Mrs. Gilbert Ellsworth Moos), b. 17 Apr. 1913. Artist; Author; Musician; Civic Worker. Educ: Cinn. Conservatory of Music, Ohio; Univ. of Cinn., Ohio; St. Lawrence Univ., Canton, N.Y. Appts: Tchr., Piano, Cinn., 1928-31; Commercial Artist, G. Lindemann Sons Printing Co., Cinn., 1928-31; Hd., Tonnage Dept., E. Kahn Sons Co., Cinn., 1932-34; N.Y. Off. Mgr., ibid, 1944-46; Co-owner, Laurentian Mart, Fredonia & Canton, N.Y., 1954-; Owner, Designer, Tatted Originals, 1969-. Mbrships. incl: Life Mbr., N.Y. State Congress of Parents & Tchrs., 1969; 1st V.P., Wheelock PTA, Fredonia, N.Y., 1966-67,'Pres., 1967-69; Publicity Chmn., Am. Cancer Crusade, Pomfret, N.Y., 1967; Alpha Omicron Pi. Contbr. of poems to mags. & reviews. Address: 34 Middlesex Rd., Fredonia, NY 14063, U.S.A. 5, 138.

MORAES, Dom, b. 19 July 1938. Writer. Educ: B.A., M.A., Oxford Univ., U.K. Appts: Features Ed., Nova, London, 1966-68; Assoc. Ed., Asia Mag., Hong Kong, 1971-73. Mbrships: Garrick Club, London, U.K.; For. Correspondent's Club, Hong Kong; Cambridge Club, N.Y., U.S.A. Publs: A Beginning; Poems; Gone Away; My Sons's Father; The Brass Serpent; Collected Poems 1955-65; John Nobody. Hons: Hawkerden Prize,. 1958;

Larnark Prize, 1959; Overseas Press Club Award of Excellence, 1971. Address: 'c/o Asia Mag., 31 Queen's Rd. Ctrl., Hong Kong. 1.

MORALES-MALVA, Juan Alberto, b. 26 Nov. 1919. Chemist; Pharmacist; Professor. Educ: Fac. of Chem. Scis., Valencia; Fac. of Chem. Scis., Santiago, Univ. of Chile; Fellowship, Comm. Ctrl. de Becas, Univ. of Chile, 1959-61. Appts: Chief of Biochem., Fac. of Med., Univ. of Chile, 1953; Dir., Escuelas de Temporada, ibid, 1954-55; Prof., Modern Sci., Fac. of Philos., 1955; Prof., Physiol. & Pathol. Chem., Fac. of Chem. Scis., 1958; Mbr., Misiones Culturales Universitarias, 1958; Chmn., Dept. Physiol. & Pathol. Chem., 1964; Off. Rep. of Univ. of Chile, var. Int. Congresses; Academic Rep., Univ. Senate, 1969, High Univ. Bd., 1970; V.P., Nat. Comm. for Sci. Rsch., 1972. Publs. incl: Estudio de las Proteinas del Suero Humano por medio de la Electroforesis en Papel, 1958; A piedra y lodo, 1958. Address: Casilla 233, Univ. of Chile, Santiago, Chile, S. America 136.

MORALES Y FRAILE, Eladio, b. 22 Sept. 1899. Agronomist. Educ: Escuela Superior de Ingenieros Agronomos, Madrid, 1918-1923. Appts. incl: Ed., Tech. Agrarian Dept., Int. Inst. Agric., Rome, Italy, 1924-27; Supvsr., Banco Hipotecario of Spain, 1929-36; Agricl. Attache, Spanish Embassies in Rome, Athens, Berne, Ankara & Cairo, 1948-56; First Spanish Deleg., FAO. Mbrships. incl: Fndr., Ist Pres., Assn. Agrarian Press, Spain, 1933, & of Assn. of Agrarian Writers of Spain, 1972; Fndr., Int. Fedn. Agronomists, 1932; Co-Fndr., Int. Fedn. Agrarian Credit; Int. Ctr. for Coop. in Agrarian Rsch. Contbr. of num. papers to profl. jrnls. & confs. Hons. incl: Gold Medal, 1V Int. Congress of Agricl. Instruction, Rome, 1934; Kt. Cmdr., Mil. Order of Christ, Portugal; Off., Agricl. Merit, France; Mbr., Acad. Agric., Czechoslovakia. Address: José Ortega y Gasset, 88, Madrid 6, Spain.

MORALIS, Yannis, b. 23 Apr. 1916. Painter; Arts School Professor. Educ: Athens Sch. of Fine Arts; Athens Acad. Schlrship. Student, Ecole des Arts et Metiers, & Metiers, & Ecole des Beaux Arts, Paris, FRance, 1937, & in Rome, Italy, 1937. Appts: Prof., Athens Schl. of Fine Arts, Greece, 1947-; Stage & Costume Designer for Greek Nat. Theatre, Charles Koun's Art Theatre, & Greek Chorodrama. Work shown var. exhibs. inclng. Biennale of Venice, 1958. Etchings & illustrations, var. books. Designer of linear composition for N.W. & S.E. facades, Hilton Hotel, Athens. Recip., Painting Prize, Panhellenique Exhib., Athens, 1940. Address: 9 Deinocratous St., Athens 139, Greece.

MORAN, Martin Joseph, b. 3 Nov. 1930. Company President. Educ: Grad., St. John's Univ., N.Y.C., 1952. Appts: Naval Aviator, USN, 1952-56; Fndr., Pres., Martin J. Moran Co., Inc., N.Y.C., int. fund raising & P.R., 1964-. Mbrships: Bd. of Trustees, Notre Dame Coll. & La Salle Acad.; Mbr., Cardinal's Comm. for Educ., N.Y.C.; Mbr., Zoning Bd. of Appeals, Massapequa Park, N.Y.; Dir., Am. Assn. of Fund Raising Counsel; Navy League; Navy Histl. Assn.; Kts. of Columbus. Hons: Decorated Kt. of Holy Sepulchre by Pope Paul VI, 1968; Kt. of Malta, ibid, 1974; Mbr., Am. Revolution Bicentennial Commn. Address: 1300 Lake Shore Dr., Massapequa Park, NY 11762, U.S.A. 2.

MORANDO DI CUSTOZA, Eugenio Giovanni, b. 9 July 1911. Civil Engineer. Educ: Grad., Engrng., Univ. of Padua, 1934. Appts: Lectr. in explosives & mines, Pavia Off. Schl.,

1942-43; Dir., Tre Venezie Ins. Co., 1960-; Dir., La Fenice Theatre, Venice; Dir., Arena Theatre, Verona; Vice-Pres., A.N.E.C., 1969-; Dir., La Minerva Ins. Co.; Pres., A.G.I.S. Inter-regional Sect. Mbrships: Pres., Lions Club, Verona; Int. Counllr., Lions International; Var. Theatrical Commns. Hons: 'Una vita per il Cinema' Gold Medal, 1967; High Off. of Italian Repub., 1973; Kt. of Italian Repub, 1959. Address: Vicolo S. Zeno in Oratorio 9, 37100 Verona, Italy.

MORAWSKI, Stefan Tadeusz, b. 20 Oct. 1921. Scholar; Educator. Educ: M.A., Univ. of Warsaw, 1945; Ph.D., ibid, 1947; B.A., Univ. of Krakow, 1946, Dip. in English Studies for Foreigners, Univ. of Sheffield, U.K. 1947, Appts. incl: Rdr. & Lectr., Jagiellonian Univ., Krakow, 1947-51; Rsch. work, Nat. Inst. of Arts, Warsaw 1952-58; Asst. Prof. (Chair of Philos.) , Univ. of Warsaw, 1955-58; Assoc. Prof. (Chair of Aesthetics), ibid, 1958-64; Prof. (Chair of Aesthetics), ibid, 1964-68; Hd., Chair of Aesthetics, 1960-68; Dean, Philosophical Fac., 1965-67; Rsch. w work, Inst. of Arts, Polish Acad. of Scis., 1970-. Mbrships: Polish Philosophical Soc.; Am. Soc. of Aesthetics; Jrnl. of Aesthetics & Art Criticism (USA); Praxis, Yugoslavia; Int. Union of Film Critics. Recent Publs. incl: Polish Art Theory Of The Romantic Period, 1962; Between Tradition & The Vision Of Tomorrow, 1964; On A. Malraux's Philosophy of Art, 1966; Assoluto E Forma, 1971, French edit., 1972; Il Marxismo E L' Estetica, 1973; On The Subject Matter & Method Of Aesthetics, Polish edit., 1973; Marx & Engels On Literature & Art (co-author), Address: Al. Waszyngtona 20 m. 21, 03910, Warsaw, Poland.

MØRCH, Otto Johannes, b. 16 Mar. 1922. Danish Parliament Member (Police Officer). Educ: Commercial & Police Schls. Appts. incl: Mbr., Parish Coun., Hornslet, 1962-66; Mbr., Danish Parliament (Folketinget) as Labor rep., 1964-; Mbr., State Couns. for Pub. Work, Wages, Road Transports, State Railways & sev. other pub. & pol. trusts. Address: Skelvangsvej 55-8900 Randers, Denmark. 1.

MØRCH, Tormod, b. 14 Apr. 1910. Professor of Odontology. Educ: Grad., State Dental Sch., Univ. of Oslo, Norway, 1937; Intern, Forsyth Dental Infirmary, Boston, Mass., U.S.A., 1945-46; Ph. D., Univ. of Oslo, 1954. Appts: Rsch. Fellow, Norwegian Inst. of Dental Rsch., Oslo, 1952-62; Prof., Odontol., & Hd., Inst. of Pedodontics, Unic. of Bergen, 1962-; Mbr., sev. nat. & int. dental orgs. & Socs. Publs: Approx. 50 scientific papers, mostly on caries rsch. Hons: Benzow's Prize, 1956; 75th Anniversary Prize, Norwegian Dental Assn., 1959. Address: Faculty of Odontology, University of Bergen, Norway.

MORDINI, Antonio, b. 14 Feb. 1904. Archaeologist; Ethnologist; Explorer. Educ: Florence & Berlin Univs.; Pr.Dz., Berlin. Appts: Archaeol. & Ethnographic Rsch., Lower Amazon, Island of Marajo, French Guiana, 1926-28; Explorations, S. Arabia, 1928-35, 38-39; Sahara Desert, 1932; Socotra Island, 1935-39; Ethiopia, 1928-44; Former Chief, Ethnographical & Archaeol. Serv., Italian E. Africa Govt.; Advsr., Int. Bus. Italia Milan, 1973-74. Mbrships. incl: Corres., Nat. Acad. of Sci., Letters & Arts, Lucca; Corres., French Inst. of Andean Studies, Lima Peru; Accad. del Mediterraneo, Rome; Italian Geog. Soc. Publs. incl: Il Convento di Gunde Gundie, 1954; The Monastery of Debra Damo, Ethiopia, 1959; Le Chiesa de Aramo, 1959; Indagini sul Convento di Gunde Gundie e su problemi di Storia Medioevale Etiopica, 1964. Hons: Cav. Ordine Coloniale della Stella d'Italia, 1933; Encomio

Solenne della della Marina Militare Italiana, 1958. Address: 55051 Barga, Lucca, Italy. 95.

MORENO, J(acob) L(evy), b. 20 May 1890. Psychodramatist; Sociometrist; Group Psychotherapist. Educ: M.D., Univ. of Vienna, Austria, 1917. Num. appts. incl: Pvte. Prac., Psych., Vöslau & Vienna, & Pub. Hlth. Off., Vöslau, Austria, 1919-25; Fndr., Spontaneity Theatre, 1921-25; Pvte. Prac., Psych., N.Y.C', U.S.A., 1928-; Fndr., Impromptu Theatre, N.Y.C., 1929-31; Sociometrist, N.Y. State Trng. Schl. for Girls, Hudson, 1932-38; Fndr. & Physn. i/c., Beacon Hill & Moreno Sanitoria, 1936-68; Adjunct Prof., Sociol., Grad. Schl. of Arts & Scis., N.Y. Univ., 1951-66; Pres., Moreno Acad. Mbrships. incl: Fellow, Am. Psych. Assn.; Pres., Am. Sociometric Assn., 1945; Am. Soc. for Grp. Psychotherapy & Psychodrama; Med. Soc. of N.Y.; AMA; AmSociol. Soc. Publs. incl: Sociometry, Experimental Method & the Science of Society, 1951; Psychodrama, 3 vols., 1959-69; Publr., Daimon mag., 1918, & Impromptu mag., 1931; Ed., Int. Handbook of Grp. PSychtherapy, 1966. Patentee, radio film for electromagnetic sound recording, 1924. Hons. incl: Doctorate, Univ. of Barcelona, Spain, 1968; Golden Dr. Dip., Univ. of Vienna, 1969; Plaque on house, Vöslau, 1969 (where sociometry, psychodrama & grp. psychotherapy originated). Address: 259 Wolcott Ave., Beacon, NY 12508, U.S.A. 2, 6, 14.

MORENO-BAEZ, Enrique, b. 29 Sept. 1908. Professor. Educ: Univ. of La Plata, Argentian; Centro de Estudios Históricos, Madrid; M.A., Univ. of Oxford, 1936; Ph.D., Univ. of Cambrdige, 1943; Dr. en Fil. y Let., Univ. of Madrid, 1948. Appts: Special Lectr.-Univ. Lectr., Spanish, Univ. of Oxford, 1933-38; Lector in Spanish, Univ. of Cambridge, 1939-41; Lectr., Spanish, King's Coll., Univ. of London, 1944-50; Prof., Spanish Lit., Univ. of Oviedo, 1950-54 & Univ. of Santiago de Compostela, 1954-. Mbrships: Assn. Int. de Hispanistas; Corresp. Mbr., Royal Lit. Acad. of Seville, Argentine Acad. of Lit., Royal Spanish Acad., Madrid & Royal Acad. of Fine Arts, Madrid. Publs: Lección y sentidodel Guzmán de Alparache, 1948; Nosotros y nuestros clásicos, 1961, 2nd edit., 1968; Reflexiones sobre el Quijote, 1968, 3rd edit, 1974; Los cimientos de Europa, 1971. Hons: Chevalier, Ordre des Palmes Acad., Paris, 1972. Address: c/o Facultad de Filosofia y Letras, Universidad de Santiago de Compostela, Spain. 43, 102.

MORETON, Russell, b. 20 Feb. 1929. Artist. Educ: Chgo. Inst. of Art., 1948. Exhibs: Exec. Offs., Western White House, San Clemente, Calif.; Ebell of L.A.; Showcase 21, L.A.; Nat. Art Round-Up, Las Vegas, Nev.; Marine Art Show, Anaheim Conven. Ctr., Anaheim, Calif.; Showcase Gall., Laguna Beach, Calif.; Showcase Gall., Prescott, Ariz. Publs: 20 paintings (seascapes & landscapes), Bernard Picture Co. Ltd., N.Y.C.; 4 paintings (Seascapes & landscapes)' Donald Art Co., Port Chester, N.Y'; 14 paintings (seascapes and landscapes), Western Tradition, Boulder, Colo.; 1 seascape, Shedd-Brown Inc., Mpls.; seascape for cover, Reader's Digest, N.Y.C. Hons: 2nd Place Oils & Best of Show, Ebell of L.A., 1970; Best of Show, Showcase 21, L.A.; 1970; 1st Place Oils, Lake San Marcos Invitiational, 1968; 2nd Place Oils, ibid, 1970. Address: Camp Wood Route, Prescott, AZ 86301, U.S.A. 37.

MOREWEDGE, Hosseine, b. 14 Mar. 1912. College Professor; Economic Consultant. Educ: B.A., LL.B., Teheran Univ., Iran; M.A., Ph.D., Columbia Univ., U.S.A. Appts: Br. Mgr., Credit

Dept. Dir., Bank Melli Iran, Bank Rahni Iran, Tehran, Iran; Ed.-in-Chief, Khabardar, weekly jrnl., Iran-America, monthly bi-lang. mag., Tehran; Pvte. Prac., Atty.-at-Law & Econ. Cons., Tehran; currently Econ. (labor) Cons., State of N.Y., N.Y.C., U.S.A., & Prof. of Econs., L.I. Univ., N.Y.; Pvte. Prac., Tax & Labor Cons., N.Y.C. Mbrships. incl: Am., Canadian, Western & Int. Econ. Assns.; Indl. Rels. Rsch. Assn.; Int. Indl. Rels. Assn. Author, The Economics of Casual Labor, 1970. Articles, econs., labor, var. publs. Recip., authorship award, Tehran Univ. Address: 454 Riverside Dr., N.Y., NY 10027, U.S.A.

MOREY, Frederick L., b. 16 Apr. 1924. Professor of English. Educ: B.A., Ashland Coll., 1955; M.A., Univ. of Md., 1966; Doct., Howard Univ., Wash. D.C., 1970. Appts: H.S. Engl. Tchr., 1956-68; Assoc. Prof., Dist. of Columbia Tchrs. Coll., Wash., 1969-. Mbrships: V.P., Nat. Fedn. of State Poetry Socs., 1972-; Pres., Md. State Poetry Soc., 1971-72. Publs: Emily Dickinson Bulletin, 1968-. (author of majority of 25 issues to date); Higginson Jrnl. of Poetry (Co-auhor), 1971-; Dickinson & Other Poems, 1972; The Fifty Best Poems of Emily Dickinson, 1974; The Golden Zero, forthcoming 1974. Invited schlr. for 3 days of ceremonies during issuance of Emily Dickinson stamp, 1971. Address: 4508 38th St., Brentwood, MD 20722, U'S.A. 11.

MOREY, John Alan, b. 30 May 1924. Trade Commissioner. Educ: B.A., B.Econs., M.Econs., Univ. of Sydney, Australia. Appts: Flying Off., Bombadier/Navigator, Royal Australian AF; Bomber Cmd. S.W. Pacific Area & S.E. Asia Cmd., 1942-45; Australian Govt. Trade Commissioner & Counsellor (Commercial), to New Zealand, 1960-66, to Chile, 1968-72, to Poland & German Democratic Repub., 1973-. Mbrships. incl: Auckland Club, Middlemore Golf Club, Auckland, New Zealand; Club de Union, Santiago de Chile; Sydney Univ. Club. Author., Role of the Statutory Marketing Boards in the Organised Marketing of Australia's Primary Products, 1960. Contbr. to learned jrnls. inclng. Economic Record & Public Administration. Recip., Royal Inst. of Pub. Admin. Prize, 1960. Address: C/O Australian Trade Commissioner Serv., Dept. of Overseas Trade, Canberra, ACT, Australia.

MORGAN, Arthur C., b. 3 Aug. 1904. Sculptor. Educ: Beaux Arts Inst. of Design, N.Y.C.; Pvte. Pupil, Gutzon Borglum, Mario Korbel, & others. Appts: Dir., Art Dept., Centenary Coll., Shreveport, La., 1928-33; Fndr., S.Western Inst. of Arts, 1934; Dir., ibid, 1934-. Mbr., Nat. Arts Club, N.Y.C. Works incl: Dr. S.D. Morehead Mem., Centenary Coll.; Henry Miller Shreve Monument, River Pkwy.; Shreve Monolith, Civic Theater; Bronze Bust, John D. Ewing, Shreveport Times Bldg.; Bronze Busts, Dr. George S. Sexton, Dr. John B. Entrikin & Mr. Paul M. Brown, Lib., Centenary Coll.; Van Cliburn Medallion, Symph. House; Heroic Bronze Statue, Chief Justice Edward Douglass White, Nat. Capitol, Wash. D.C.; E. K. Long Monument, Winnfield, La. Fellow, Int. Inst. of Arts & Letters. Address: The Art Inst., 657 Jordan St., Shreveport, LA 71101, U.S.A. 7, 37.

MORGAN, Audley Roy, b. 5 Sept. 1919. Educator; Journalist. Educ: Kings & Birkbeck Colls., Univ. of London, U.K.; B.A.; A.C.P. Appts: Sr. Master, Cornwall Coll., Jamaica, 1944-53; Jamaica Coll., 1953-57; Clarendon Coll., 1957-59; 2nd Master, Rusea's H.S., 1959-61; Sr. Spanish Master, Queens Coll., Guyana, 1961-64; Asst. Prof. & Hd., Spanish Dept., Univ. of Guyana, 1965-66; Hdmaster,

Boys Grammar Schl., St. Vincent, 1966-. Mbrships: Past Dir., St. Vincent Lions Club; Hon. Sec., St. Vincent Scout Assn.; Admin. & Fin. Comm., Caribbean Examinations Coun.; Film Censorship Comm.; Past Master, St. GEorge Lodge 2616 E.C. Contbr. to jrnls. & newspapers. Address: St. Vincent Grammar Schl., Kingstown, St. Vincent, W. Indies. 136.

MORGAN, Barbara Brooks, b. 8 July 1900. Photographer; Writer; Painter. Educ: Art Major Grad., Univ. of Calif., L.A., 1923. Appts: Art Fac. Mbr., Univ. of Calif., L.A., 1925-30; free-lance painting, art photography, & lectr., N.Y.C., 1930-. Mbr., profl. orgs. Publs: Martha Graham (art photographs), 1941; Summer's Children, 1951; Monograph, Barbara Morgan, 1972. Photographs in Permanent Collects: Metropol. Mus. of Art, Mus. of Mod. Art, N.Y.C.; Smithsonian Instn., Wash. D.C.; Nat. Portrait Gall., Wash. D.C.; Mass. Inst. Technol., Cambridge; Princeton Univ. Lib., N.J.; Pasadena Mus. of Arts, Calif.; Univ. of Calif. at L.A.; Amon Carter Mus., Ft. Worth, Tex.; Int. Mus. of Photography, Rochester, N.Y.; Nat. Gall., of Canada, Ottawa. Address: High Pt. Rd., Scarsdale, NY 10583, U.S.A. 37, 128.

MORGAN, David Archibald Stevenson, b. 29 Apr. 1920. Medical Officer, Royal Australian Air Force. Educ: M.B., B.S., Univ. of Adelaide, 1943; D.P.H., Univ. of Sydney, 1968. Appts: Dir. Gen. of Med. Servs., Royal Aust. Air Force, 1971. Mbrships: Past Chmn., AViation Med. Soc. of Aust. & N.Z.; Fndn. Fellow, Aust. Coll. of Med. Admnstrs.; Assoc., Aust. Postgrad. Fedn. in Med. Hons: Off., Order of Brit. Empire Mil. for servs. during Korean conflict. Address: Directorate Gen. of Med. Servs., Dept. of Defence (Air Off.), Russell Offs., Canberra, A.C.T., Australia 2600.

MORGAN, Edwin George, b. 27 Apr. 1920. University Teacher; Author. Educ: Glasgow Univ., Scotland, U.K. Appts: Asst. Lectr., Engl., Glasgow Univ., 1947-50; Lectr., ibid, 1950-65; Sr. Lectr., 1965-71; Reader, 1971-. Publs: Beowulf, 1952; The Cape of Good Hope, 1955; Poems From Eugenio Montale, 1959; Sovpoems, 1961; Starryveldt, 1965; Emergent Poems, 1967; The Second Life, 1968; Gnomes, 1968; Proverbfolder, 1969; Penguin Modern Poets 15, 1969; Twelve Songs, 1970; The Horseman's Word, 1970; Wi the Haill Voice, 1972; Glasgow Sonnets, 1972; Instamatic Poems, 1972; From Glasgow to Saturn, 1973. Hons: Scottish Arts Coun. Publs. Award, 1968; Cholmondeley Award For Poets, 1968; Mem. Medal, Magyar P.E.N. Club, 1972. Address: 19 Whittingehame Court, Glasgow G12 OBG, Scotland, U.K. 3, 30, 131.

MORGAN, Helen Bosart, b. 17 Oct. 1902. Sculptor. Educ: Wittenberg Univ.; Dayton Art Inst.; Chgo. Art Inst. Instr., Springfield Art Ctr., 10 yrs. Mbrships: Fndr. & 1st Pres., Springfield Art Assn.; Nat. Assn. of Women Artists; Altrusa Club. Permanent collects: Cinn. Art Mus., Ohio; Butler Inst. of Am. Art, Youngstown, Ohio; Ohio Univ., Athens; Wittenberg Univ., Springfield, Ohio; Snyder Park, Springfield; Warder Lib., Springfield; Cowling Park, London, Ohio. Recip., 20 Prizes in local & state competitions. Address: 845 E. High St., Springfield, OH 45505, U.S.A. 5, 8, 37.

MORGAN, Jeanette Pauline, b. 29 Aug. 1929. Teacher of English. Educ: B.S., Univ. of Houston, Tex., U.S.A., 1960; M.A., ibid, 1963. Appts: Serv., Women's Army Corps, U.S. Army, 1948-57; Dir., Engl. Writing Lab., Univ. of Houston, 1963-65; Curric. Specialist, Gary Job Corps. Trng. Ctr., San Marcos, Tex.,

1965-66; Chmn., Tchr. Educ. Comm., Dept. of Engl., Univ. of Houston, 1970-72; Dir., Freshman Studies, Dept. of Engl., ibid, 1973-. Mbrships: Chairperson, Comm. on State of the Profession, Tex. Coun. of Coll. Tchrs. of Engl.; Chairperson, Tex. Assn. of Dirs., of Freshman Studies; Liaison Off., Tex. Coun. Tchrs. of Engl.; Nat. Coun. Tchrs. of Engl.; Coll. Engl. Assn.; AAUP; MLA; Phi Kappa Phi; Kappa Delta Pi; Mortar Bd. Publs: Contbns. to anthol., Themes & Writers; Reviews in profl. jrnl. Address: English Dept., University of Houston, Houston, TX 77004, U.S.A. 125.

MORGAN, Kenneth Carol, b. 13 Aug. 1918. Realtor; Builder; Apartment Owner. Educ: B.S., Univ. of Ky., Lexington, U.S.A., 1941; Dental Schl., Univ. of Louisville, Ky., 1941-43. Appts: USN, WWII; Realtor, Lexington, 1946-; Builder, ibid, 1947-; Owner, Shopping Ctr. & Apts., 1960-. Mbrships. incl: Lexington Home Bldrs. Assn.; Lexington Real Estate Bd., 32nd degree Mason, 1957, 33rd degree, 1971; Master, Robert M. Sirkle Lodge 954, Lexington Consistory, 1966; High Priest, Webb Chapt. 6, 1970; Preceptor, Lexington Coun. Kts. Kadosh, 1971-74; Past Pres., 1200 Club, Covington; Deacon & Past Chmn., Bd. of Trustees, Chevy Chase Bapt. Ch.; Alpha Sigma Phi. Recip., Sigma Award, Alpha Sigma Phi, 1941. Address: 1602 Jennifer Rd., Lexington, KY 40505, U.S.A. 125.

MORGAN, (Sir) Morien Bedford, b. 20 Dec. 1912. Aeronautical Engineer. Educ: B.A., St. Catharine's Coll., Cambridge Univ., U.K., 1934; M.A., ibid, 1939. Appts. incl: Dpty. Controller, Aircraft (Rsch. & Dev.), Min. of Aviation, 1960-63; Controller of Aircraft, ibid, 1963-66; Controller, Guided Weapons & Electronics, Min. of Technol., 1966-69; Dir., Royal Aircraft Establishment, Farnborough, Hants., 1969-72; Master, Downing Coll., Cambridge, 1972-; Airworthiness Requirements Bd., Civil Aviation Authority, 1972-. Mbrships. incl: Fellow, Royal Soc. & Royal Aeronautical Soc.; Pres., ibid, 1967-68; Athenaeum Club. Publs. incl: Lectures in Royal Aeronautical Soc. Jrnl., inclng: Supersonic Aircraft-Promise & Problems, 1960, Keeping the Pilot Happy, 1971, A New Shape in the Sky, 1972; num. Reports & Memoranda to Aeronautical Rsch. Coun. Hons. incl: C.B., 1958; Kt. Bach., 1969; Go,d Medal, Royal Aeronautical Soc., 1971; Buck Prize, ibid, 1972. Address: The Master's Lodge, Downing College, Cambridge CB2 1DQ, U.K. 1, 34.

MORGAN, Roy L., b. 14 Nov. 1908. Retired Judge; Consultant on International Trade. Educ: B.S., Univ. of Va., 1930; LL.B., ibid, 1933. Appts: Admitted to Va. Bar, 1932, N.C. Bar, 1941, Japan Bar, 1951; Atty., Dept. of Agric., 1933; Special Agt., FBI, 9134-45; Pvte. Prac., Greensboro, N.C., 1945-47, 1950-; Assoc. Prosecutor, War Criminals, Int. Tribunal, Tokyo, Japan, 1946; Legal Advsr., Counsel, Ford Motor Co., Japan, 1950-55; Am. Advsr., Prime Min., Japan, 1955-56; Chief Justice, U.S. Civil Admin., Appellate Ct. for Far E., 1956-60; Special Asst. to Sec., Commerce, 1960-61; Dir., Off. Field Servs., 1961-67; Hd., U.S. Govt. Trade Missions to Japan, 1962, '68. Mbrships. incl: Chmn., Am. Cancer Soc.; Greensboro City Coun., 1948-50; Bd. of Dirs., Gen. Counsel, Elizabeth Saunders Home, Tokyo, 1951-53; Hon. V.P., Am. Chmbr. of Comm., Tokyo, 1953; Sigma Chi; Phi Alpha Delta; Edit. Bd., Va. Law Review, 1931-33. Author of articles in field. Address: 1720 W. 28th St., Sunset Island 1, Miami Beach, FL 33140, U.S.A. 7.

MORGENSTERN, Otto W., b. 6 Aug. 1919. Economist. Educ: B.A., San. Fran. State Coll.,

Calif., 1953; Ph.D., Univ. of Calif., Berkeley, 1958. Appts. incl: Teaching Asst., Rsch. Economist, Univ. of Calif., Berkeley, 1953-56; Instr., Asst. Prof., Univ. of San. Fran., 1954-66; UN Econ. Expert in regions of Africa, 1962-65, 1972-73; Fulbright Prof., Inst. for Economic Dev. Studies (ISVE), Naples, Italy, 1965; Assoc. Prof. Univ. of Bridgeport, Conn., U.S.A., 1966-71; Cons., UN Industrial Dev. Org., Vienna, Austria1967-68. Vis. Prof., Univ. of Québec, Canada, 1971-72; Vis. Prof., Rhodes Univ., S. Africa 1974-. Mbrships. incl: AAUP; Am. Econ. Assn., Western Econ. Assn.; Econ. Hist. Soc. (UK); Royal African Soc.(U.K.). Publs. incl: profl. papers & reports; Contbr. to profl. jrnls. Address: c/o Dept. of Economics, Rhodes University, Grahamstown, S. Africa. 6, 14.

MORGENTHALER, Helen Marie (Mrs.). Importer; Designer; Colorist. Educ: Univ. of Southern Calif. Appts: Pres., Clara Somers Co., mfrs. women & knotted belts (resort wear) for womens' dress mfg. ind.; Pres., The Morgenthaler Co., mfrs., importers, distributors of fade resistant Oriental Wallcovering. Mbrships. incl: Chmn. of Gift Shop Display, Assistance League of Southern Calif.; Fndr. Mbr., Pasadena Guild Children's Hosp.; Comm. Chmn., Doll Fair; Organizer & 1st Mgr., Childrens Hosp. Thrift Shop (staffed by 5 guilds); Fndr. Mbr., LA Orphanage Guild; Town Hall of LA Resources Coun. of Am.; LA World Affairs Coun. Address: 1730 West Dr., San Marino, CA 91108, U.S.A. 22, 59, 74, 75.

MORIGI, Paolo, b. 4 Mar. 1939. Ethnologist. Appts: Specialist in Primitive Art, Ethnol. & Ethnog.; on expedition, W. Africa; LLiberia, Mali, Ivory Coast, Gabon, Cameroon, & the Congo; Proprietor, Casa Serodine, Ascona/Ticino & Casa Calao, Magliaso-Lugano, Switzerland. Exhibs: African Art, Mus. Civico, Lugano, Switzerland, 1965; Pre-Colombian Art, Mus. delle Ceramiche, Faenza, Italy, 1967; Gall. Flaviana, Locarno, 1966; Gall. Levi, Milan, 1969; Franklin Coll., Lugano, Switzerland, 1971; Gall. Beno. Zurich, 1972; Gall. Caldarese, Bologna, 1972. Mbrships: Segreteria Accademica, Rome; Amici delle Belle Arti, Lugano; Amici Mus. della Ceramica, Faenza. Publs: Meisterwerke Alt-Afrikanischer Kunst, 1968. Address: Casa Calao, Vla ,Fiume, CH 6983 Magliaso-Lugano, Switzerland. 133.

MORIYAMA, Hideo, b. 28 June 1902. Biochemist. Educ: Imperial Univ., Tokyo, Japan, 1925-29; M.D., 1944. Appts: Rsch. staff, Inst. Infectious Diseases, Tokyo Univ., 1929-36; Shanghai Sci. Inst., China, 1936-42; Aeronautical Rsch. Inst., Yokosuka, Japan, 1942-45; Fndr., Shonan Hyg. Inst., Kamakura, 1946. Publs: The Nature of Viruses and the Origin of Life, 1955; Immunity, 1955; Life, its Nature and Origin, 1958; Immunity and Immune Reactions, 1958; Studies on X-Agent (Real Cause of Environmental Pollution Including Photo-chemical Oxidants), 1970; Studies on X-Agent, Continued (The True Cause of Environmental Pollution), 1973 & num. articles; rsch. on immunochem.; viruses; aviation med.; origin of life; unknown phys. factor (X-agent) affecting living & non-living objects. Address: 1439 Kokufu-Hongo, Oisomachi, Kanagawa-ken, Japan. 50.

MORLAN, John E., b. 10 Dec. 1930. Professor of Instructional Technology; Musical Composer. Educ: B.S., Abilene Christian Coll., Tex., 1952; M.A., ibid, 1955; Ed.D., Tex. Technological Univ., 1959. Appts. incl: Coach & Music Tchr., Abilene Christian H.S., 1951-52; USAF Instr., 1953-54; Tchr. & Coach, Lubbock Pub. Schls., 1955-58; Prof., Elem. Educ. &

Instructional Technol., San Jose State Univ., 1959-, Dir., Overseas Projs., Orient & Pacific, 1959-. Mbrships. incl: NEA; Nat. Sci. tchrs. Assn.; AAUP; Phi Delta Kappa. Publs. incl: Preparation of Inexpensive Teaching Materials, 1963, 2nd edit., 1973; Classroom Learning Centers, 1974; Electric Boards You Can Make (co-author), 1974. Num. articles., profl. jrnls. Composer, 12 songs, 1974. Recip., Grad. Fellowship, Tex. Technological Univ., 1959-60. Address: Instructional Technol. Dept., San Jose State Univ., San Jose, CA, U.S.A. 8, 141.

MOROI, Saburo, b. 7 Aug. 1903. Composer. Educ: Dr. Arts (Aesthetics), Tokyo Univ., 1928; Grad., Staatlich Hochschule für Musik (Composition), 1934; studied Composition & Musl. Theory under Prof. L. Schratenholz, Orchestration under Prof. W. Gmeindl, Piano under Prof. R. Schmidt. Appts: Tchr. of Musl. Theory, Tokyo Mus. Schl. & Toyo Mus. Schl., 1929-31; Mus. & Adult Educ. Insp., Min. of Educ., 1946-64; Dir., Tokyo Met. Symph. Orch., 1965-66; Dir., Senzokugakuen Mus. Coll., 1967-. Mbrships: Pres., Japanese-German Mus. Soc.; Hon. Mbr., Japan Mod. Mus. Soc.; Perm. Jury, Japan Mus. Comp. Publs: Historical Reseach of Musical Forms, 5 vols; Analysis of Beethoven's String Quartets; Analysis of Beethoven's Piano Sonatas; Current Romantic Music; Music & Thinking, etc. Compositions incl: 5 symphonies, piano concerto, violin concerto, string trio, piano sonatas, viola sonatas; Fantasy-Oratorio 'Visit of the Sun'. Recip., Grand Prize, Nat. Art Fest., Symph. No.4, 1971, Symph. No.2, 1972. Address: Senzokugakuen Daigaku Mus. Coll., No.290 Hisamoto, Takatsu-ku, Kawasaki-shi, Kanagawa-ken, Japan.

MORONE, Remo, b. 26 Sept. 1913. Lawyer. Educ: Law Deg., Univ. of Turin; Deg. in Pol. Sci., Univ. of Florence. Appts: in Pvte. Prac. of Law; Mbr., Superior Coun., Banca d'Italia, Rome; Pres., Bd. of Dirs., Banca d'Italia, Turin; Mbr. Deputation of the Stock Exchange, Turin; Pres., Albertina Acad. of Fine Arts, Turin. Collector of Mod. Art. Mbrships: V.P., Press Circle, Turin; Past Pres., Turin Rotary Club, Subalpino Circle & Massimo D'Azeglio Assn.; UCID, Turin; Italian Pres., Rotary Interclub Comm.; Assn. Friends of Contemp. Art. Publs: The Project of The Reform of the Companies; The Modern Art Collection. Hons: Gold Medal of Merit in Culture & Art; Sovereign Mil. Order of Malta; War Cross for Mil. Valour; War Cross for Merit. Address: 5 via Mercantini, 10121, Turin, Italy.

MORPURGO, Jack Eric, b. 26 Apr. 1918. Author; Professor. Educ: Univ. of N.B., Canada; Coll. of William & Mary, U.S.A.; Durham & London Univs., U.K. Appts: Lt.-Col., Royal Artillery, 1939-45; Editl. Bd., Penguin Books Ltd.; Asst. Dir., Nuffield Fndn.; Dir.-Gen., Nat. Book League; Prof. of Am. Studies, Univ. of Geneva, Switzerland; Presently, Prof. of Am. Lit., Univ. of Leeds, U.K. Mbrships incl: V.P., Nat. Book League; PEN; Soc. of Bookman. Publs. incl: The Spy (Ed.); Pelican History of the United States (co-author); Homage to America; Impact of America upon European Culture (w. Bertrand Russell & John Lehmann), etc. Recip. of various hon. degrees. Address: Schl. of English, Univ. of Leeds, U.K. 1, 3, 34, 43, 131.

MORRELL, Wayne Beam, Jr., b. 24 Dec. 1923. Artist. Educ: Drexel Inst., Phila., Pa.; Phila. Schl. of Ind. Arts. Appts: Art Dir., Designer, John Oldham Studio, Weathersfield, Conn.; Designs in Paris & Brussels World Fairs. One man show, Wash. Co. Mus. of Fine Arts,

Hagerstown, Md., 1973. Mbrships. incl: Allied Artists of Am.; Salmagundi Club, N.Y.; Conn. Acad. Fine Arts; Am. Artists Profl. League; Am. Vets. Soc. Artists; Rockport; Meridian Arts & Crafts. Illustrator, mag. covers. Hons. incl: Allied Artists Am., 1965-71; Salmagundi Club, 1965-73; Gold Medal, Jordan Marsh, Boston, 1965; Gold Medal, Rockport Art Assn. 1971; Springfield Acad. Artists, 1958-72. Address: Wayne Morrell Gall., 153 Main St., Rockport, MA 01966, U.S.A. 6, 37.

MORRELL, William Bowes, b. 18 Feb. 1913. Newspaper Company Executive. Educ: M.A., Univ. of Cambridge, U.K' Appts: Dir. & Gen. Mgr., Birmingham Gazette & Dispatch Ltd., 1945; Dir. & Gen. Mgr.-Mng. Dir., Westminster Press Provincial Newspapers Ltd., 1953-; (now Westminster Press); Dir., Southern Publg. Co. Ltd., Ings. Property Co. Ltd., Pearson Longman Ltd., Evening Mail Ltd., & Chmn., Turret Press (Holdings) Ltd. & Joseph Rowntree Soc. Serv. Trust Ltd. Mbrships: Coun., Newspaper Soc.; Univ. of York Ct.; Liveryman, Co. of Stationers & Newspaper Makers. Address: 99 S. End Rd., London NW3, U.K. 1, 32.

MORRIS, Alice Lee Banning. Writer; Executive Secretary. Educ: Univ. of Ore.; Multnomah Coll.; Ore. State Univ. Appts: Sec. of Adult EDuc., Multnomah Coll., 1945; Sec. to Registrar, ibid, 1946; Sec. to Pres. for 50th Yr. Celebration, 1947; Dir., Pacific Northwest, Nat. Exec. Bd., Hospitalized Veterans Writing Proj., 1959-73. Mbrships. incl: Gov.'s Advsry. Comm. on Art & Humanities, 1966-69; Nat. Rehab. V.A.V.S.; Dir., Campfire Girls of Am.; State Directory, Ore. Fed. Women's Clubs, 1972-73; Pres., Women's Assn. & Treas., Presby. Ch., 1966-69. Author, The Bells of St. Mary's, 1931. Contbr. to: Beverly Hills Citizen; Wash. Post; Hosp. Mgmt. Mag.; Oregonian Sunday Supplement. Hons. incl: Hollywood Citizen of the Week, 1953; Nat. Rehab. Creative Writing Awards, 1959-68. Address: Alsea, OR 97324, U.S.A. 5, 132.

MORRIS, Arthur Newth, b. 30 Mar. 1903. Executive. Educ: Phila. Bible Coll., 1923-26. Appts. incl: Trng. in sales & mgmt. of set-up bus., Edwin J. Schoettle Co., Phila., Pa., 1925-35; Organizer, folding box bus., in complete charge of this op., 1927; Fndr., southern Box Co., Balt., Md., 1936, forerunner of present Rock City Packaging, Inc.; Currently Chmn. of Bd., Rock City Packaging, Inc. Mbrships: Dir., Presby. Mins. Fund; Trustee, Stetson Univ., Overseeers Bd., Law Ctr. Fndn.; Berry Coll., Queens Coll., Randolph-Macon Mil. Schl., Gordon-Cornwell Theological Sem., Luther-Rice Sem., & Bethune-Cookman Coll.; Arlington Presby. Ch.; Nat. Assn. of Mfrs.; Merchants Club; N.Y. Athletic Club; Chartwell Country Club; Anpls. Yacht Club; River Club; San Jose Country Club; Ponte Vedra Club; Oceanside Golf & Country Club. Recip., LL.B., Bloomfield Coll. & Sem., N.J., 1955. Address: Rock City Packaging, Inc., 3701 Bank St., Balt., MD 21224, U.S.A. 16.

MORRIS, Christopher Hugh, b. 28 Mar. 1938. Journalist; Broadcaster; Author. Educ: St. Alban's Schl., 1948-53. Appts: Reporter, Daily Sketch, London, 1958-61; For. Corres., Daily Express, London, 1961-69, Daily Mirror, 1961-72, Independent TV News, 1961-68, BBC TV & Radio, 1968-72, Daily Mail, 1969-72, Westinghouse Broadcasting, 1969-72; Reporter, BBC, London, 1972-. Mbr., Pathfinder Club. Author, The Day They Lost the H-Bomb. Recip., NCTJ Dip., 1958. Address: 31b Beaumont Ave., St. Albans, Hertfordshire AL1 4TL, U.K. 139.

MORRIS, Desmond John, b. 24 Jan. 1928. Zoologist. Educ: B.Sc., Dept. of Zool., Birmingham Univ., U.K., 1951; Ph.D., Dept. of Zool., Oxford Univ., 1954. Appts: Post-Doctoral Rsch., Dept. of Zool., Oxford Univ., 1954-56; Hd., Granada TV & Film Unit at Zoological Soc. of London, 1956-69; Curator of Mammals, Zoological Soc. of London, 1959-67; Dir., Inst. of Contemporary Arts, London, 1967-68. Publs. incl: Biology of Art; The Mammals; Men & Apes (w. Ramona Morris); The Naked Ape; The Human Zoo; Intimate Behaviour; Patterns of Reproductive Behaviour. Ed., International Zoo Year Book, Primate Ethology. Author, sev. scientific papers. Solo Exhibs: London Gall., 1950; Stooshnoff Gall., 1974. Address: Villa Apap Bologna, Attard, Malta. 1.

MORRIS, Jesse Harry, b. 28 June 1892. Dentist. Educ: D.D.S., Balt. Coll. Dental Surg., 1923. Appts: Prac. gen. dentistry, Webster Co., W. Va., 1923-27, Mineral Co., ibid, 1927-32, Jefferson Co., ibid, 1932-42, Alexander, Va., 1942-47, Charlestown, W. Va., 1948-; Hon. mbr., Staff Charlestown Gen. Hosp. Mbrships: Northern Va. Dental Study Club (hon); Alumni Assns., Fairmont State Coll. & Univ. of Md.; Mason; Kiwanis; Moose, etc. Address: Professional Bldg., Charlestown, WV 25414, U.S.A.

MORRIS, Joseph Paul, b. 27 Dec. 1922. Sales Consultant; Manufacturer's Representative. Educ: Liberal Arts Coll. Mbrships: Histl., Welcome & Colonial Socs. of Pa.; Morris Family Publs. Comm.; Pa. Soc. of Sons of the Revolution; Mil. Order of For. Wars of U.S., Pa. Commandery; C.C. Morris Cricket Lib. Assn.; Zool. Soc. of Phila.; Athenaeum, Phila.; Friends of Independence Nat. Histl. Pk.; PA. Soc. of N.Y. Address: P.O. Box 218, Ambler, PA 19002, U.S.A. 6.

MORRIS, Keith Iles, b. 13 May 1931. Architect. Educ: B.Arch., Univ. of Cape Town, S. Africa, 1953. Appts. incl: Archtl. Ptnrship., Hope, Reeler & Morris; elected Councillor, Zambia Inst. of Archts. Coun., 1964; Mbr., Archts. & Quantity Surveyors Registration Bd., Zambia, 1966-; V.P., Zambia Inst. of Archts., 1971-72; Pres., ibid, 1973-74. Mbrships: Dir., Bd., Zambia Trade Fair; Pres., Lusaka Rowing Club; Ndola Club; Ndola Boating & Sailing Club. Publs: poetry in IN Situ (Zambia Inst. of Archts. jrnl.). Hons: Archtl. Ptnrship. received Design Awards for Domestic, Commercial & Indl. projs., 1968, 1971. Address: P.O. Box 1073, Lusaka, Zambia.

MORRIS, Louise Elizabeth Burton (Mrs. Harry Joseph Morris), b. 6 Dec. 1905. Author; Editor; Certified Genealogist; Heraldist; Lecturer; Clubwoman. Educ: Okla. City Univ.; Special courses, var. univs. Active mbr. w. many offs. in more than 60 geneal., histl. & patriotic orgs. & socs., inclng. State Chmn. (apptd. by Gov. John Connally), Tex. State Magna Carta Comm.; Trustee, Ctrl. Tex. Area Mus., Inc., Salado, Bell Co.; Permanent Chmn., Geneal. Lib., ibid; Dallas Co. Histl. Survey Comm.; Rep.-Geneal., State of Tex., for Soc. of Descendants of King William I, The Conqueror & His Companions at Arms, & for Brit. Am. Soc.; V.P., Augustan Soc., Inc., Tex. State Geneal. Soc.; Charter, Nominations Bd., N. Am., of Royal Blue Book, London, U.K.; Advsry., Marquis Biographical Lib. Soc., Chgo., Ill.; Fellow Malta Heraldic Soc.; Heraldry Soc. of Canada; Fndr.-Fellow, Tex. Histl. Rsch. Inst.; Hon. Fellow, Harry S. Truman Lib. Inst.; DAR; CG; FHG; Hon. Life, Ctrl. Tex. Area Geneal. Soc., Inc.; Hon., Harrison Co. Histl. Soc., Marshall, Tex.; 2nd V.P., S.W. Coun. of

Geneal. & Histl. Socs.; Fellow, Soc. Scottish Antiquities; Life, Royal Soc. of St. George; Nat. Charter Mbr., Smithsonian Assocs.; Nat. Trust for Historic Preservation; Nat. Fedn. Press Women; Tex. Press Women Inc.; many others, past & present. Publs. incl: Instant Historical Programs, 1968; A Compilation of The Registers of The Army, Navy, & Marine Corps of The United States, 1816, 1970; num. papers & articles. Hons. incl: Ph.D., Colo. Christian Coll., 1973; Cert. of Merit, Augustan Soc., Inc., 1968; Mbr. w. rank of Off., Mil. & Hospitaller Order of St. Lazarus of Jerusalem, 1970. Has attended & presented papers at sev. int. congresses, & has conducted num. Geneal. wkshops. Address: Hacienda Tejas, 2515 Sweetbrier Dr., Dallas, TX 75228, U.S.A. 5, 7, 22, 57, 69, 70, 79, 125, 128, 129, 130, 132.

MORRIS, Mary Smith, b. 21 June 1940. Assistant Professor of Music. Educ: B.Mus., Lee Coll., Cleveland, Tenn., 1962; M.A., Univ. of Tenn., Knoxville, 1971. Appts: Instr., Lee Coll., Cleveland, Tenn., 1962-68; Instr., Univ. of Md., Eastern Shore, princess Anne, 1970-72, Asst. Prof., 1973-. Mbrships: Am. Musicological Assn.; Coll. Music Soc.; Sec.-Treas., Nat. Assn. Ch. Musicians of Ch. of God; AAUW; AAUP; Am. Piano Tchrs. Assn.; Wicomico Coun. on Arts; Dir. of Civic Chorus; Organist-Choir Dir., Walker Mem. Ch. of God. Publ., Four Chorale Cantatas of Johann Schelle: A Modern Edition. Hons: Coll. Music Award, 1960; Valedictorian of Coll. Class, 1962. Address: 129 Prince William St., Princess Anne, MD 21853, U.S.A. 76, 125.

MORRIS, Michael Frank, b. 29 Sept. 1936. Sociologist. Educ: B.S., Ariz. State Univ; M.A., Univ. of Tenn. Appt: Asst. Prof., Pensacola JR. Coll., Univ. of W. Fla. Mbrships: Am. Sociological Assn.; Southern Sociological Soc. Contbr., Am. Jrnl. of Sociol. Address: 5655 N. 9th Ave. (N-107), Pensacola, FL 32504, U.S.A. 125.

MORRIS, Raymond E., b. 21 June 1925. Electrical Contractor; Electronic Technical Consultant. Educ: Brooklyn Coll. Appts: Sales Mgr., Harrison Radio, N.Y., 1950-61; Pres., Amatronics Inc., N.Y., 1961-63; Asst. to Pres., Nat. Sales Mgr., Round Hill Assocs., N.Y., 1963-68; V.P., ibid, 1968-71; Pres., Ray Morris Elec. Co., 1971-; Adult Educ. Instr., Radio Theory, Delehanty Inst., N.Y.; Cons., Tech. Inds., N.J. Mbrships: Assoc., Int. Assn. Elec. Insps.; Nat. Fire Protection Assn.; Am. Radio Relay League. Address: Box 94, Park Rd., Yulan, NY 12792, U.S.A. 6, 57.

MORRIS, Robert, b. 21 Nov. 1910. Social Planner. Educ: A.B., Univ. of Akron, Ohio, 1931; M.Sc., Schl. of Applied Soc. Scis., Western Reserve Univ., 1935; D.S.W., N.Y. Schl. of Soc. Work, Columbia Univ., 1959. Appts: Kirstein Prof., Soc. Planning, Brandeis Univ., Mass.; Dir., Levinson Gerontological Policy Inst., ibid; Planning Cons., Nat. Coun. of Jewish Fedns. & Welfare Funds; Dir., Soc. Work Servs., Mid-W. Regional Off., VA; Prin. Welfare Off., UNRRA. Mbrships. incl: Pres., Fellow, Gerontological Soc. of Am.; Fellow, Am. Pub. Welfare Assn. Publs. incl: Centrally Planned Change: Prospects & Concepts, 1964; Urban Planning & Social Policy (w. B. Frieden), 1968; Ed., Encyclopedia of Social Work, 16th ed., 1971; contbr. to var. profl. jrnls. Address: 18 Battlegreen Rd., Lexington, MA 02173, U.S.A. 2.

MORRIS, Robert John, b. 30 Sept. 1914. Lawyer; Editor. educ: A.B., St. Peter's Coll., 1936; J.D., Fordham Law Schl., N.Y., 1939; Admitted, N.Y. State Bar, 1939, U.S. Supreme

Ct., 1952, & Tex. State Bar, 1962. Num. appts. incl: Civil Liberties Lawyer, 1939-71; Off. i/c., Communist Counter-Intelligence, 3rd Naval Dist., 1941-43; Off. i/c., Adv. Sect., Psychol. Warfare Sect., Admiral Nimitz HQ., Guam, 1944-45; Ptnr., Hochwald, Morris & Richmond, 1946-52; Sec.-Treas., Monrovia Port Mgmt. Co., 1946-50; Special Counsel, U.S. Senate Internal Security Subcomm., 1951-53; Chief Counsel, ibid, 1953-54 & 1956-58; Justice, Municipal Ct., 9th Dist., N.Y.C., 1954-55; Pres., Univ. of Dallas, Tex., 1960-62; Pres., Univ. of Plano, Tex., 1964-71 & 1973-; Chancellor, ibid, 1971-; Ed. & Publr., Twin Circle, 1970-72. Mbrships. incl: Pres., Defenders of Am. Liberties, 1962; Chief Justice, World Org. of Human Potential, 1969-; Phi Delta Phi. Publs: No Wonder We Are Losing; Disarmament: Weapon of Conquest; What is Developmental Education? ; Weekly column in 50 nat. newspapers; Contbns. to sev. mags. Hons: LL.D., St. Francis Coll., 1957; Doctor of Humane Letters, Fu Jen Univ., Taipei, Taiwan, 1971. Address: 1237 Ocean Ave., Mantoloking, NJ 08738, U.S.A. 2, 49.

MORRIS, (The Hon. Senator) Shadrach A., J.P. b. 17 Apr. 1931. Banker. Educ: Bahamas & U.S.A. Appt: Pres. & Gen. Mgr., The People's Penny Savings Bank, Ltd. Mbrships: Senator, Jr. Chamber Int; Masonic Order; Rotary Club. Hons: J.C.I. Plaque, for services rendered to the community, 1971. Address: P.O. Box 4421, Nassau, Bahamas.

MORRIS, W.R., b. 8 July 1936. Writer. Educ: Southern Ill. Univ., Carbondale, U.S.A. Appts: Pres., Three Star Records, Lexington, Ala.; Insp. with the Finger, Tenn. Police Dept. Mbrships: Veterans of For. Wars; Country Music Assn., Nashville, Tenn.; Am. Soc. of Authors & Writers. Author, The Twelfth of August. Recip., Outstanding Citizen's Award, Jaycees, 1974. Address: P.O. Box 81, Loretto, TN 38469, U.S.A. 125.

MORRIS, William Coke, b. 21 Feb. 1922. Journalist. Educ: B.A., Emory Univ. Appts: Serv. in U.S. Army, Field Artillery, Europe, WWII; Publicity Dir., Wofford Coll.; Reporter, Atlanta Constitution; Staff Writer, City Ed., 1961-65); Mng. Ed., (1965-73), Greenville (S.C.) Piedmont. Mbrships. incl: S.C. Press Assn.; Treas., Greenville Co. Mental Hlth. Assn.; V'P., Greenville Co. Alston Wilkes Soc.; Bd. Mbr., Greenville Rescue Mission; Greenville Jr. Chmbr. of Comm.; Bd. Mbr., St. Matthew United Meth. Ch.; Sigma Delta Chi. Author, Series of articles on S.C. prison conditions resulting in State Law requiring inspection all prisons, 1967. Hons: S.C. Associated Press Awards, 1955-57, 1969, 1967; William F. Gaines Mem. Award, 1972. Address: 132 Fernwood Ln., Greenville, SC 29607, U.S.A. 7.

MORRISH, Ernest Ivor James, b. 8 Feb. 1914. Lecturer in Education; Author. Educ: B.A., Univ. of Bristol, U.K., 1938; B.A., B.D., Univ. of London, 1946-49; postgrad. studies, St. Catherine's Coll., Oxford, 1938-39. Appts. incl: Hd., Divinity & Soc. Sci. Dept., Purley Grammar Schl., 1949-61; Sr. Lectr. & Tutor Libn., Bognor Regis Coll. of Educ., 1961-67; Prin. Lectr., La Sainte Union Coll. of Educ., Southampton, 1967-. Mbrshipa: Oxford Soc.; British Sociological Assn.; Assn. Tchrs. in Colls. & Depts. of Educ. Publs: Disciplines of Education, 1967; Education Since 1800, 1970; The Background of Immigrant Children, 1971; The Sociology of Education; An Introduction, 1972. Address: 44 Midanbury Ln., Southampton, Hampshire SO2 4HF, U.K. 30.

MORRISON, Harold Abraham, b. 9 Oct. 1919. Journalist; Editor. Educ: B.J., Carleston Univ., Ottawa, Canada, 1947. Appts. incl: Reporter, Ottawa Citizen, 1946-48; Parliamentary Reporter, The Canadian Press, 1948-59; Wash. Corres., ibid, 1959-64; Bur. Chief, London, U.K., 1964-72; For. Ed., 1973-. Mbrships: The London Press Club, U.K.; Nat. Press Club, Wash.; Commonwealth Corres.' Assn., London, U.K.; Carleton Univ. Alumni Assn.; Kt. of Mark Twain Soc.; Commonwealth Press Union, London; Deleg., Int. Press Telecommunications Coun., London. Author of mag. articles, short stories & pol. criticism in var. publs. inclng. Esquire, Weekend Mag. & Canadian Bus. Hons: Award, Govl. Affairs Inst., Wash., 1963; Kt. of Mark Twain Soc. for contbn. to mod. jrnlsm., 1970. Address: 30 Kingfisher Drive, Ham, Richmond, Surrey, U.K. 2.

MORRISON, Kristin Diane, b. 22 Apr. 1934. Teacher; Scholar; Author; Academic Administrator. Educ: B.A., Immaculate Heart Coll., 1957; M.A., St. Louis Univ., 1960; Ph.D., Harvard Univ., 1966. Appts: Instr. in Engl., Immaculate Heart Coll., 1960-61; Prof., S.C. State Coll., 1966-67; Asst. Prof., N.Y. Univ., 1967-69; Asst. Prof., Boston Coll., 1969-71; Assoc. Prof., ibid, 1971-; Acad. Dean & prof. of Engl., Newton Coll. (on leave from Boston Coll.), 1972-74. Mbrships: Danforth Assn.; Soc. for Relig. in Higher Educ.; Am. Assn. for Higher Educ.; Am. Conf. of Acad. Deans; Am. Coun. on Educ. Inst. for Acad. Deans, 1972. Publs. incl: Handbook of Contemporary Drama (w. Michael Anderson, Jacque Guicharnaud & Jack D. Zipes), 1971; In Black & White, 1972; Articles in jrnls. Hons: Woodrow Wilson Nat. Fellowship, 1958; Kent Fellowship, 1964. Address: Engl. Dept., Boston Coll., Chestnut Hill, MA 02167, U.S.A. 30, 138.

MORRISON, Lucille Maud, b. 21 June 1913. Teacher. Educ: St. Joseph's Tchrs. Coll.; Kingston Tech. Home Econs. Trng. Ctr., Jamaica, W. Indies. Appts. incl: Sec.-Treas., Kingston Tchrs. Assn.; Pres., Ctrl. St. Andrew Dist. Tchrs. Assn.; Exec. Comm. Mbr., Kingston Moravian Ch. of the Redeemer; Pres., Jamaica Women Tchrs., 1963-64; Organizing Sec. & Tour Mgr., Ing. Goodwill Assn.; Asst. Dist. Commnr. & Exec. Mbr., Girls' Brigade; Since 1964 has organized and led many tours for tchrs., students & assocs. to all parts of the world. Mbrships. incl: Exec. Mbr., Ancient Order of Foresters, Ct. Surrey. Publr. of mags. for Jamaica Women Tchrs. Assn. & for Int. Goodwill Assn. Hons. incl: Scrolls of Friendship, permanent keys & lifetime mbrships. to some cities; many certs. of merit for disting. serv. Address: 18 Ashbury Ave., Kingston 3, Jamaica, W. Indies. 96, 109, 132.

MORRISON, Robert Jay, b. 1 Dec. 1924. Optometrist. Educ: Pa. State Univ.; O.D., Pa. State Coll. of Optometry, 1948. Appts. incl: Pvte. Prac., Optometry, Harrisburg, Pa., 1949-; Vis. Instr., Contact Lens Dept., Pa. State Coll. of Optometry, 1957-58; Pres., Chief of Consultation & Rsch., Morrison Labs., Inc., Harrisburg, 1957-; Pres., Morrison Rsch., Inc., 1959-; Chmn. of Bd., Union Optics; Assoc. Prof.,Optometry, Pa. State Coll. of Optometry; Asst. Prof. Ophthalmol., N.Y. Med. Coll. Mbrships. incl: Fellow, Am. Acad. Optometry; Dipl., Contact Lens Sect., ibid; Int. Coll. of Ocular Sci.; Central Pa. Optometric Assn.; Chmn., Contact Lenses, ibid; V.P., Eastern Beta Sigma Kappa; Gamma Omega Phi; Zeta Beta Tau; Pi Tau Pi. Publs: Contact Lens Manual, 1959, 1960; Your Contact Lenses, 1960. Contbr. to profl. jrnls. Originator, theory of Myopia Control thru' Contact Lenses. Hons: Man of Yr., Harrisburg Chamb. of Comm., 1966; Kt., Prince Bernhard of Netherlands,

1969; Ph.D. Address: Green & Division Sts., Harrisburg, PA 17110, U.S.A. 28.

MORROW, Glenn D., b. 4 Mar. 1911. Economist. Educ: A.B., Murray State Coll., 1933; M.A., George Peabody Coll., 1940; postgrad., Univ. of Ky., 1941-44, & Univ. of Chgo., 1966-67. Appts. incl: Soc. Sci. Analyst, Finance Studies, Soc. Security Admin., Wash. D.C., 1958-63; Financial Economist, Off. of Economic Advsr., Small Bus. Admin., Wash. D.C., 1963-67; Supervising Economist, Off. Planning, Rsch. & Analysis, ibid, 1967-. Mbrships: Am. Econ. Assn.; Nat. Tax Assn.; Univ. of Ky. Rsch. Club; Beta Gamma Sigma. Address: 4848 Chevy Chase Dr., Chevy Chase, MD 20015, U.S.A. 7, 14, 15, 51.

MORSCHEL, John Robert Gordon, b. 7 Aug. 1920. Plant Pathologist. Educ: H.D.A., Hawkesbury Agricl. Coll., 1940; B.Sc. Agric., Univ. of Sydney, N.S.W., Australia, 1948. Appts: Serv., RAAF, WWII; Dist. Pathologist, Dept. of Agric., Leeton, N.S.W., 1949-55; Plant Quarantine Off., Dept. of Hlth., Canberra, A.C.T., 1955-65; Dir. Plant Quarantine, ibid, 1966-; Chmn., FAO Consultation on Plant Protection Conven., 1973. Mbrships: Australian Inst. of Agric. Sci.; A.C.T. Freedom from Hunger Comm. (Vice Chmn., 1972-73); Past Mbr., Caterpillar Club, U.K. Publs. incl: For N.S.W. Dept. of Agric., 1953-55; Introduction to Plant Quarantine, 1971. Hons: State Jr. Farmer Champion, N.S.W., 1936-37; R.A.S. Schlrship., Hawkesbury Agric. Coll., 1937; Dux, ibid, 1940. Address: Dept. of Health, P.O. Box 100, Woden, A.C.T., Australia, 2606.

MORSE, David A., b. 31 May 1907. Attorney. Educ: Grad., Rutgers Univ., N.J., 1929; Grad., Harvard Law Schl., 1932. Appts. incl: Major, U.S. Army, WWII; Gen. Counsel, Nat. Labor Rels. Bd., 1945; Acting Sec. of Labor under Pres. Truman, 1948; Dir.-Gen., Int. labor Organ, 1948-70; Ptnr., Law Firm Surrey, Karasik & Morse, 1970-; Special Asst. to U.S. Attorney Gen.; Chief Counsel, Petroleum Labor Policy Bd., U.S. Dept. of Interior; Regional Attorney, Nat. Labor Rels. Bd., N.Y.C. Mbrships. incl: Century Assn., N.Y.C.; Union Interalliée, Paris, France; Metropolitan Club, Wash. D.C.; Coun. on For. Rels.; Am. Bar Assn. (Pres., Int. Labor Law Comm.). Contbr. to profl. jrnls. Pierce Lectr., Cornell Univ. Hons. incl: Meritorious Pub. Serv. Award, Sidney Hillman Fndn., 1969; Nobel Peace Prize on behalf of I.L.O., 1969; Gold Medal, UNESCO, 1971; Recip. decorations, Brazil, Gabon, Cameroon, Colombia, France, Italy, Peru; num. hon. degrees. Address: Surrey, Karasik, Morse & Seham, 500 Fifth Ave., 27th Floor, N.Y., NY 10036, U.S.A.

MORSE, Herbert Carpenter, b. 30 Jan. 1911. Economist. Educ: B.A. Oberlin Coll., 1932; Duke Univ.; M.A., M.Phil., Columbia Univ. Appts: Econs. Instr. CCNY, 1937; Econs. Cons., Bowen Engrng., N.J., 1936-38; Rsch. Assoc., Alfred P. Slona Fndn., 1937-38; Asst. Prof., Antioch Coll., 1941-42; Economist, Off. of Price admin., Wash., D.C., 1942-45; Econ. Analyst, Bur. of Internal Revenue, 1945-47; Economist, Swift & Co., Chgo., 1947-66; Economist, Fed. Reserve Bank, Chgo., 1966-; Economist, Bank Holding Co. Task Force, Bd. of Govs., Fed. Reserve System, 1967-68. Mbrships: Fellow, Royal Econs. Soc. (England); Am. Econs. Assn.; Am. Acad. of Pol. & Soc. Sci.; Phi Beta Kappa & Exec. Comm., Chgo. Area Assn.; Past Trustee, Ill. Coun. on Consumer Educ. Hons: Mercer Prize, Oberlin Coll., 1932; Grad. Asstship., Duke Univ., 1932; Univ. Fellow in ECons., Columbia Univ.,

1935-36. Address: 333 S. Kensington Ave., La Grange, IL 60525, U.S.A. 14.

MORSE, Leon William, b. 13 Nov. 1912. Physical Distribution Management Executive. Educ: B.S., N.Y. Univ., 1935; Acad. Advanced Traffic, 1937. Appts: Individual Bus. Traffic Mgmt. Cons., Phila., 1950-58; Gen. Traffic Mgr., W.H. Rorer, Inc., Ft. Wash., Pa., 1958-; Instr., Econs. of Transp., Pa. State Univ., 1963-; Advsry. Coun., Pa. Small Bus. Admin. Mbrships: Fellow, Int. Soc. of Law & Sci.; Traffic & Transp. Club, Phila.; Traffic Clubs, Phila. & Norristown; Am. Soc. Int. Execs.; Canad. Assn. Phys. Distbn. Mgmt.; Assn. ICC Practitioners; Fndr. Mbr., Am. Soc. Traffic & Transp.; Pres., Drug & Toilet Preparation Conf.; Chmn., Del Valley Drug Traffic Assn.; & others. Recip., Del Valley Traffic Mgr. of the Yr. Award, 1963. Address: 500 Virginia Dr., Ft. Washington, PA 19034, U.S.A. 6, 16.

MORSE, Mary Genevieve Forbes (Mrs. Frederick Tracy), b. 8 June 1905. Community Worker; Homemaker. Educ: B.A., La. Polytech. Inst., Ruston, La. Mbrships. incl: Nat. Trust for Hist. Preservation; Pres., Univ. of Va. Hosp. Circle, 1947-49; Bd. of Dirs., 1947-65; Bd. of Dirs., Community Chest, for 2 yrs.; Corres. Sec., Va. DAR, 1953-56; State Chmn., Resolutions, ibid, 1971-74; Va. State Room Comm.; Ed., Va. DAR News Bulletin, 1953-59; V. Regent, 1956-59; State Regent, 1959-62; Nat. Soc. DAR; Nat. Chmn., Nat. Resolutions Comm., 1971-74; V.P. Gen. from Va., 1962-64; Curator Gen. Nat. Chmn. DAR Mus. Comm., 1965-68; Currently DAR Mus. Advsr.; Chap. Gen., 3 yr. term, 1974-; Past Chmn., Bylaws Comm., Daughters of the Colonial Wars State Recording Sec., ibid, in the commonwealth of Va., 1953-56; Pres., 1956-59; Nat. Pres., 1962-65; Nat. Pres., Kappa Delta, 1959, for 4 yrs, Re-elect., 1963; Nat. Ed. 'The Angelos'. 1953-59; Corres. Sec. Gen., Nat. Soc. of Ams. of Royal Descent, 1974; Order of Wash.; Nat. Histl. Soc.; Colonial Dames of Am., Chapt IX-Ky. Publs: Through the Years & Other Poems, 1945; Poems in sev. anthols.; Ed., Monticello Cook Book, 3rd ed., 1950; A History of Kappa Delta Sorority (1897-1972), 1973. Address: Box 6127, Charlottesville, VA 22906, U.S.A.

MORSE, William Eugene, b. 1 Dec. 1893. Attorney-at-Law. Educ: B.S., Univ. of Miss.; LL.B., Columbia Univ., N.Y. Appts: City Prosecuting Atty., Jackson, Miss., 1924; Special Judge, City, Circuit & Chancery Cts.; Gen. Counsel & Atty., Jackson, 1928-45; Mbr., Bar Examining Bd.; Mbr., State Oil & Gas Bd., 1 term; Trustee, Dept. of Archives & Hist., State of Miss., 1964-. Mbrships: Episcopalian; YMCA; Past Pres., ibid; KE Sigma Epsilon; Scribes; Mason; Shriner; V.P., Miss. State Bar, 1939-40 & Pres., 1940-41; Deleg. from Miss. Bar to House of Delegs. of Am. Bar & on Jurisprudence & Law Reform. Publs: Treatise on Edward Mayes, 1941; "Brierfield, The Home of Jefferson Davis", 1969; Compiled & publd. Ordinances of City of Jackson, 1929, revised, 1938; Miss. Annotated Form Book, 1940; Morse Miss. Form Book, annotated, 2 vol. set, 1950, supplemented 1965; Morse Legal Forms Annotated Pocket Supplements, vol. 1 & 2, 1974; Bunkley & Morse on Divorce & Separation, 1957; Wills & Administration in Mississippi, 1968. Address: 782 Belhaven St., Jackson, MS 39202, U.S.A. 7.

MORSE-BOYCOTT, (Rev.) Desmond Lionel, b. 10 Dec. 1892. Clerk in Holy Orders. Appts. incl: Curate, Mayfield, Sussex, Bognor Regis U.K., 1917-18; St. Mary's Somers Town, London, 1919-34; Fndr. & Hon. Prin., St.

Mary-of-the-Angels Song Schl., 1932. Publs: Fields of Yesterday (autobiog.); A Golden Legend of the Slums; They Shine Like Stars, etc. (monograph); The Boy Bishop Book (illus.): A Tapestry of Toil (illus. autobiog.), 1970; A Pilgrimage of Song, 1972. Mbrships: Fellow, Royal Soc. of Arts, & Tonic Solfa Coll. of Music. Address: Walnut Tree Cottage, 79 Ashacre Ln., Offington, Worthing, Sussex BN 13 2DE, U.K. 1, 3, 4.

MORTENSEN, Ralph, b. 29 Jan. 1894. Publisher. Educ: B.A., Augsburg Coll., Mpls., Minn., U.S.A., 1913; Cand. Theol., Augsburg Sem., 1916; S.T.M., Hartford Sem. Fndn., 1918. Ph.D., ibid, 1927. Appts. incl: Gen. Sec., Luth. Bd. of Publ., & Mgr., Luth. Book Concern, Hankow, China, 1930-42; China Rep., Am. Bible Soc., Shanghai, China, 1945-53; Rep. & Travelling Sec., Am. Bible Soc., British & For. Bible Soc., & Nat. Bible Soc. of Scotland, E. Asia, 1954-58; Field Sec., Am. Bible Soc., N.Y.C., 1958-65; Special Sec., ibid, 1966-67; Special Rep., 1968-. Mbrships. incl: Fellow, Royal Asiatic Soc.; Am. Oriental Soc.; Asia Soc.; Tibet Soc.; Past Pres., Shanghai Tiffin Club; Treas., Hymn Soc. of Am.; Chmn., Coordinating Comm. for For. Refugees, Shanghai, 1948-52; Chap. & Asst. Dist. Commnr., S.-E. Dist., Long River Coun., Boy Scouts of Am., 1967-. Hons. incl: Bronze Medal, Centennial Celebration, Augsburg Coll., 1964; Meritorious Serv. Award, Inst. of Chinese Culture, 1972. Address: Riverbound Farm on the Quinnipiac, 1881 Cheshire St., Route 1, Southington, CT 06489, U.S.A. 6, 22, 128, 130, 131.

MORTIMER, John Clifford, b. 21 Apr. 1923. Playwright & Q.C. Educ: Brasenose Coll., Oxford Univ. Called to Bar, 1947. Appts: Queen's Counsel; Mbr., Bd. of Govs., Royal Shakespeare Co.; Bd. Mbr., Nat. Theatre. Mbrships: Garrick Club; Fellow, Royal Soc. of Lit. Publs: (novels) Charade, 1947; Rumming Park, 1948; Answer Yes or No, 1950; Like Men Betrayed, 1953; Three Winters, 1956; (travel, in collab. w. 1st wife) With (Love & Lizards), 1957; (plays) The Dock Brief & Other Plays, 1959; The Wrong Side of the Park, 1960; Lunch Hour & Other Plays, 1960; Two Stars for Comfort, 1962; What Shall We Tell Caroline, 1958; The Judge, 1967; Come As You Are, 1970; A Voyage Round My Father, 1970; I Claudius, 1972; Collaborators, 1973; var. play translations & many film scripts, radio & TV plays, articles for newspapers, mags. & periodicals. Hons: Italia Prize for 'The Dock Brief', 1957; Writers' Guild of G.B. Award for best Brit. original teleplay 'A Voyage Round My Father', 1969. Address: Turville Heath Cottage, Henley-on-Thames, Oxon., U.K. 1, 18.

MORTON, C.P., b. 8 June 1920. Air Conditioning Engineer. Educ: Auburn Univ. Appts: V.P., Construction Servs., Hardy Corp., Birmingham, Ala. Mbrships: Past Pres., Nominating Chmn., Ala. State Poetry Soc.; Ala. Writers Conclave; Vice Chancellor, Nat. Fedn. of State Poetry Socs.; Ariz. State Poetry Soc. Publs: Desiring Stone (poems), 1973. Hons: Num. contest prizes; 1st Prize, title poem, Desiring Stone, Nat. Fedn. of State Poetry Socs. Address: 1732 Shades View Lane, Birmingham, AL 35216, U.S.A. 7, 125.

MORTON, Dixie Evelyn McKamie (Mrs. Harry H. Morton, Jr.), b. 15 Oct. 1921. Registered Dietitian. Educ: Midwestern Univ., Tex., 1940-41; B.S., Tex. Woman's Univ., Tex., 1944; Troy State Univ. courses in educ.; Mstrs. Degree in Home Econs., Foods & Nutrition, Univ. of Ala., 1969. Appts. incl: Dietitian, Lawrence Gen. Hosp., Lawrence, Mass.;

Jackson Hosp., Miami, Fla.; Sec., Lockheed Aircraft Corp., Gifu, Japan; St. Mary's Hosp., Reno, Nev.; U.S.A.F., Istanbul, Turkey; currently, Dietitian, VA Hosp., Montgomery, Ala. Mbrships: Chmn., Coun. on Mins., Trinity United Meth. Ch.; Pres., Montgomery Dist. Dietetic Assn.; Chmn. Elect, Montgomery Co. Nutrition Coun.; Co-Chmn., Legislative Comm., Ala. Dietetic Assn.; Registered, Am. Dietetic Assn.; Phi Epsilon Omicron; Phi Theta Kappa. Hons: Special Award for Communications w. pub., 1967; Dir.'s Commendation, 1970. Address: 111 Camellia Drive, Prattville, AL 36067, U.S.A. 125.

MORTON, Murray Douglas, b. 28 Apr. 1916. Lawyer. Educ: Univ. of N.B., Canada; B.A. & LL.B., Univ. of Toronto; Barrister-at-Law, Osgoode Hall Law Schl., Law Soc. of Upper Canada. Appts: Capt., Canadian Army, WWII.; Sr. Ptnr., Law Firm, Morton & Malo, Toronto, Ont., 1947-70; Elected Mbr., Canadian House of Commons, 1957-62; Q.C., 1959; Judge, Family Div., Provincial Ct., Co. of Simcoe, Barrie, Ont., 1970-. Mbrships: Law Soc. of Upper Canada; Trustee, Toronto Bd. of Educ., 1952-57, Chmn., 1956; Past Pres., Kiwanis Club of W. Toronto; Dir., Kiwanis Club, Kempefeldt Bay; Soc. Planning Bd., Toronto; AF-AM Ionic Lodge No. 21, Toronto; Empire Club, Toronto. Address: Provincial Court, Family Div., County of Simcoe, Box 184, Barrie, Ont., Canada.

MORTON, Wilbur Young, b. 22 May 1915. Assistant Professor; US Navy Commander Educ: B.S., Coll. of Wm. & Mary, 1938; Grad., US Navy Flight Schl., 1939; M.A., E. Tenn. State Univ., 1966. Appts. incl: Air Officer, U.S.S. Siboney, 1949-51; Asst. Plans Off., Supreme Allied Cmdr., Atlantic, 1954-56; Asst. Dir., Air Weapons Rsch. & Dev., Bur. of Ordnance, Wash. D.C., 1956-59; Hd., Ind. Equipment Br., US Naval Weapons & Naval Air Systems Cmd., 1965-66; Asst. Prof., E. Tenn. State Univ., 1971-. Mbrships. incl: Past Pres., PTA, Bristol, Tenn.; Phi Sigma; Delta Sigma Pi; Tenn. Educ. Assn.; AAUP. Hons. incl: Kiwanis Disting. Serv. Award, Bristol, 1964. Address: East Tenn. State Univ., Box 2854, Johnson City, TN 37601, U.S.A.

MORY, Warren H., Jr., b. 3 June 1925. Professor. Educ: Univ. of Scranton; B.S., 1956; M.A., 1961, Ph.D., 1968, Univ. of Ala. Appts: U.S. Army, 1943-45; Supvsr., Costa Rican Br., Int. Correspondence Schls., 1956-57; Chief Admnstr., Costa Rican Chmbr. of Comm., 1957; Dept. Supvsr., Calif. Bank, L.A., 1958-59; Mgr., Colonial Schl. of Dancing, Tuscaloosa, Ala., 1959-61; Prof., Langs., Birmingham-Southern Coll., Birmingham, Ala., 1962-. Mbrships: Nat. Hispanic Soc.; Lions Club Int.; Pres., Birmingham Spanish Club; S.E. Conf. on Latin Am. Studies; Am. Assn. of Tchrs. of Spanish & Portuguese; S. Atlantic Mod. Lang. Assn.; AAUP. Publs: Instrinsic Spanish, 1961. Address: P.O. Box 797, Birmingham-Southern Coll., Birmingham, AL 35204, U.S.A. 125.

MOSAK, Jacob Louis. Economist; UN Administrator. Educ: A.B., Univ. of Chgo., 1935; Ph.D., ibid, 1941. Appts. incl: Sr. Economist, Price Dept., Off. of Price Admin., U.S. Govt., 1941-42, Hd., Fiscal & Monetary Sect., Rsch. Div., 1942-43, Chief, Econ. Analysis & Forecasting Br., 1943-46, Chief, Stabilization Div., Off. of War Mobilization & Reconversion, 1946-47; Sr. Economist & Dpty. Chief, Econ. Stability Sect., UN, 1947-52, Chief, Int. Trade Sect., 1953-55, Asst. Dir., Bur. Econ. Affairs, 1955-59, Sir., Bur. Gen. Econ. Rsch. & Policies, 1959-65, Dir., Ctr. for

Dev. Planning, Projs. & Policies, 1965-, Dpty. to Under-Sec.-Gen. for Econ. & Soc. Affairs, 1967-; Vis. Lectr., Prof. Econs., Columbia Univ., Grad. Facs. of Pol. Scis., 1948-58. Author, General-Equilibrium Theory in International Trade, 1941. Articles, var. econ. & statistical jrnls. Recip., acad. fellowships. Address: 66-18 110th St., Forest Hills, NY 11375, U.S.A. 6, 13.

MOSBY, Håkon, b. 10 July, 1903. University Professor. Educ: Cand. real., Univ. of Oslo, Norway, 1930; Ph.D., ibid., 1934. Appts: Asst. to F. Nansen, 1923-27; Asst. Prof., Geophysical Inst., Bergen, Norway, 1927-47; Prof., ibid., 1947-73; Dean, Fac. of Sci., Univ. of Bergen, 1954-59; Rector, Univ. of Bergen, 1955-71. Mbrships: Pres., Subcomm. on Oceanographic Rsch., NATO, 1960-65; Sci. Comm., NATO, 1965-69; Sec., 1948-54, Pres., 1954-60, Int. Assn. of Phys. Oceanography; Acad. of Sciences, Oslo; Acads. of Sciences, Bergen, Gothenburg, (Sweden), Helsinki (Finland). Num. publs. on atmospheric radiation, evaporation from oceans, heat & salt balance in sea, Mixing of water masses in sea, phys. processes in sea, formation of bottom water, ocean· currents & their determination, oceanographic instrumentation. D.Sc., Univ. of Newcastle upon Tyne, U.K., 1971; Cmdr., Royal Order of St. Olav, 1971. Address: Geophysical Institute, Univ. of Bergen, Allégatan 70, N-5014 Bergen-Universitet, Norway. 34, 43.

MOSCONAS, Theodore, b. 11 Dec. 1892. Librarian. Educ: Univ. of Manchester, Coll. of Technol., U.K. Appts: Mbr., Ed.'s Staff, Greek newspaper Alexandria Tachydromos, 1937-42; Proto Bibliothecarius, Greek Orthodox Patriarchate of Alexandria & all Africa, U.A.R., 1942-68; Libn. Emeritus, ibid, & i/c of Press Off., currently. Mbrships: YMCA, Manchester, U.K., 1918-22; YMCA, Alexandria, 1934-. Publs: Contbr. to British papers inclng. Manchester Guardian, The Near East, during stay in U.K., 1918-22; 40 var. publs. in Greek & Engl. on W. Africa (Sierra Leone, Dahomey & Gold Coast, now Ghana). Hons. incl: Class II, Order St. Mark, Patriarchate Alexandria, 1959; St. Augustine's Cross, Archbishop of Canterbury, 1966; Vatican Benemerenti, 1966; Grand Off. of Merit, Spain, 1973. Address: 45 Rue Canope Camp Caesar, Alexandria, United Arab Repub.

MOSCOVICH, Ivan, b. 14 June 1926. Museum Director. Educ: M.Sc. Mech. Engrng.; B.Sc. Indus. Design. Appts. incl: Hd., Engrng. Dept., Min. of Transport, Yugoslavia, 1949; Rsch. Off., Min. Defence, Israel, 1951; proposed establmt. of 1st Sci. Mus. in Israel & responsible for design & dev. of project, 1959-64; Dir., Mus. in original temp. premises, 1964 & of Lasky Planetarium, 1968 & Main Bldng. of Mus. of Sci. & Technol., opened, 1974. Inventor of tchng. aids & methods, sci. toys & games & kinetic art sculptures inclng: Brain Drain, adult puzzles series; Bits, computer game. One-man, didactic & art exhibs. incl: Cybernetic Serendipity, London U.K.; Indus. Design Centrum Berlin, German Democratic Repub. Mbrships: Int. Comm. of Mus'.; Int. Comm. Transport & Communication Mus'.; Soc. of Tech. Writers & Publrs. Hons. incl: sev. prizes for inventions at didatic & art exhibs. & toy fairs. Address: Mus. of Sci. & Technol., 79 Univ. St., Ramat Aviv, Israel.

MOSCOVIS, Vassilios E., b. 6 Dec. 1913. Professor of Ancient & Modern Greek.' Educ: Degree in Philos. & Philol., Univ. of Athens. Appts: Dir., 3 Hierarchs Lyceum, Piraeus, 1936-39; Prof., IVth Gymnasium, Piraeus,

1939-40; Dpty.-Dir., Municipal Lib. of Athens, 1941-45; Prof., Athens Coll., 1946-71. Mbrships: Soc. of Greek Authors; Art Dir., Popular Ballads, City of Rhodes, 1962-65. Publs. incl: The Salt of the Earth; On the Top of Monte Smith; The Generation Comes; The Unreconcilables; The Last Visitor; Portraits of My House; Denudation; Compositions; Message; Synopsis; Megalinaria; Dodecanesian Ballads. Hons: Prize, City of Piraeus, 1929; Gold Medal, City of Rhodes, 1963; 1st Nat. State Prize for a Novel, 1971. Address: 119 Dodonis, Athens 202, Greece.

MOSELEY, Thomas E., b. 26 Mar. 1933. Administrator; Educator. Educ: B.S., N. Tex. State Univ., 1955; Masters Ed. Admin., Our Lady of Lake, 1967. Appts. incl: Coach/Sci. Tchr., Hondo H.S., Tex., 1963-66; Student Govt. Advsr./Tchr., Robert E. Lee H.S., San Antonio, Tex., 1963-66; Asst. Prin. ibid, 1967-71; Prin., Nimitz Middle Schl., San Antonio, Tex., 1972-74. Mbrships. incl: Tex. State & N. East Tchrs. Assns.; Nat. Educators Assn.; Tex. & Nat. Assns. Secondary Prins.; Optimist Int.; former Pres., N. East Optimist Club & former Mbr. Executive Bd., Optimist Club; Bd. Dirs., San Antonio Boys Club; former State Chmn., PGA & Organizer Jr. Prog.; served on Comms. & Chmn. at Convens. num. educ. & related socs. Contbr. to mags. & jrnls. Hons: Recip. of Sev. Fellowships in Biol./Sci; All Am. Golf Comm., Univ. of Houston, 1968. Address: Nimitz Middle Schl., 5426 Blanco Rd., San Antonio, TX 78216, U.S.A. 57, 125.

MOSELEY, Vince, b. 29 Oct 1912. Physician. Educ: A.B., Duke Univ., 1933; M.D., ibid, 1936. Appts: Intern, Duke Hosp., N.C., 1937-38; Res., ibid, 1938-39; Asst., Duke Schl. Med., 1939-40; Assoc., Univ. of Pa. Schl. Med., 1940-41; Assoc., Univ. of S.C. Med. Coll., 1947; Asst. Prof., ibid, 1947; Assoc. Prof., 1948; Prof., 1949-; Chmn. of Dept. & Physn. in Chief, 1949-61; Dean, Clin. Med., 1961-69; Dir., Div. of Postgrad. continuing educ., 1969-. FACP; FRSH. Mbrships: Pres., Charleston Co. Med. Soc., 1952; Chmn., Med. Sect., Southern Med. Assn., 1951; Gov., S.C. Am. Coll. of Physns., 1968; Chmn., Bd. of Trustees, S.C. Retarded Children's Habilitation Ctr., 1963-68; Retarded Children's Commn., 1969-; Hosp. Advsry. Coun., State Bd. of Hlth., 1963-. Chmn., 1970-73; Bd. Trustees, Palmer Jr. Coll., 1972-. Author of approx 50 articles in field in profl. jrnls. Address: Medical Univ. of South Carolina, 80 Barre St., Charleston, SC 29401, U.S.A. 7.

MOSER, Fritz, b. 18 Jan. 1908. Librarian. Educ: Berlin & Munich Univs., Germany; Phil. D., Univ. of Berlin. Appts. incl: Supvsr., municipal Libs., authors, publrs. & booksellers' affairs, Magistrate, later Senate, Berlin, German Fed. Repub., 1946-52; Dir., Am. Mem. Lib., Berlin, 1952-73, Emeritus, 1973-; Pres., Coun. for Lib. Affairs, Senate of Berlin, 1966-74; Chmn., Coun. for Pub. Libs., 1966-74; Chmn., Lib. Commn. for Regional Planning, 1972-74. Mbrships: Heinrich-Von-Kleist-Gesellschaft (Bd.); Historische Kommision Zu Berlin; Gesellschaft fur Theatergeschichte; Verein Deutscher Bibliothekare; Verein der Bibliothekare an Offentlichen Bibliotheken. Publs. incl: Die Anfänge des Hof Und Gesellschaftstheaters in Deutschland Berlin 1940; Luftbrucke Berlin, 1949; Goethe in Berlin, 1949. Address: Paulsbornerstr. 65, 1 Berlin 33 Grunewald, German Fed. Repub. 2, 43, 92.

MOSER, Isabel Fairclough (Mrs.). Artist; Publicity Writer Educ: N.Y. Univ.; Nat. Acad. Schl. of Design; pvte. tchrs. Appts: Asst. to

Frank Moser (former husband); Free Lance; Publicity Writer; Histn. Mbrships: Pres , 2 yrs., V.P., 2 yrs., Hastings Morning Choral; Bd. of Dirs., Hudson Valley Art Assn., Publicity Chmn., Music Chmn.; Poetry Soc. of London; Southern Vt. Artists; Arts & Culture Coun., Town of Greenburgh, W. Country. Recip. of Awards for water colors, 1943, '45, '48, H.V.A.A. & 1970, Int. Platform Assn., Wash., D.C. Address: 37 Hollywood Dr., Hastings-on-Hudson, NY 10706, U.S.A. 5, 6, 37, 129.

MOSER, Robert McNeil, b. 25 July 1922. Sales Manager. Educ: B.S. Educ., Cumberland Coll., Williamsburg, Ky., 1966; M.A. Educ. & Principalship, Eastern Ky. Univ., Richmond, 1967; Postgrad. studies, Educl. Admin. Appts: Serv., USN, Recruit to Chief Warrant Off., in Atlantic, Pacific, Mediterranean & Asiatic areas, 1940-61; Currently N. Fla. Gen. Sales Mgr., H.T. Moser Co. Inc., Hialeah; Licensed & Ordained Min., Bapt. Pastored Ch. Mbrships. incl: NEA; Ky. Educ. Assn.; Phi Delta Kappa; Retired Off. Assn.; USN Inst; A.A.S.A.; K.A.S.A.; P.D.K. Hons: Phi Delta Kappa Schlrship, Eastern Ky. Univ.; Rep., Eastern Ky. Univ. at Ky.-Tenn. Ldrship Conf. (3 yrs.) & Nat. Biennial Conf. Address: 1451 Cattlemen Rd., Sarasota, FL 33580, U.S.A. 125.

MOSES, Elbert Raymond, Jr., b. 31 Mar. 1908. College Professor(Retired). Educ: A.B., Univ. of Pitts., 1932; M.S., Univ. of Mich., 1934; Ph.D., ibid, 1936. Appts: Instr., Speech, Women's Coll., Univ. of N.C., Greensboro, 1936-38; Asst. Prof., Ohio State Univ., Columbus, 1938-46; Assoc. Prof., Eastern Ill. State Univ., 1946-56; Asst. Prof., Communication Skills, Mich. State Univ., 1956-59; Prof., Speech & Chmn., Dept. Speech & Dramatic Arts, Clarion State Coll., Pa., 1959-71; Retd., 1971; w. U.S. Army in various capacities inclng. Intelligence Corps., 1942-46; Chief Instr., Trng. Br., Signal Schl., Exec. 5th Army HQ, Ft. Monmouth, N.J., 1952-53; Retd., Lt.-Col. in Reserves. Mbrships incl: Am. Speech & Hearing Assn.; AAAS; Assn. Phonetique Int.; Int. Soc. Phonetic Scis.; Speech Assn. Am.; Tau Kappa Epsilon; Phi Alpha Theta; Theta Alpha Phi; Life, Phi Delta Kappa.; Dist. Gov., Rotary Int., Dist. 728, 1973-74. Publs: A History of Palatography Techniques, 1940; Interpretations of a New Method in Palatography, 1940; A Guide to Effective Speaking, 1957; Phonetics: History & Interpretation, 1964. Author of num. articles & monographs. Fulbright Lectr., Cebu Normal Schl., Philippines, 1955-56. Address: 18 Fairview Ave., Clarion, PA 16214, U.S.A. 6, 13, 15, 22, 30, 116, 126, 128.

MOSIER, Rosalind Asch (Mrs. Richard D. Mosier), b. 14 May 1923. Librarian; Artist. Educ: Schl. of Fine Arts, Temple Univ., 1940-43; Barnes Fndn., 1942-43; B.A., Columbia Univ., 1944; M.A., Univ. of Calif., Berkeley, 1950; B.L.S., 1954. Appts: Sr. Children's Libn., Richmond Pub. Lib., Calif., 1954-59; Libn. on special assignment, Oakland Pub. Schls., Calif., 1959-72; Media Specialist, Franklin Schl., ibid, 1972-. Mbrships: Calif. Assn. Schl. Libns.; Assn. Children's Libns., Northern Calif. (Inst. Chmn.); ALA; San Fran. Women Artists; Oakland Art Assn.; Delta Kappa Gamma. Exhibs. incl: San Fran. Mus. Art; Oakland Art Mus.; Richmond Art Ctr.; St. Mary's Coll. Art Gall. Rep. in pvte. collects. Contbr. of articles to profl. jrnls. Recip., Award in painting, Oakland Art Assn., 1971. Address: Franklin Schl., 915 Foothill Blvd., Oakland, CA 94606, U.S.A. 5, 138.

MOSLEY, Mary McKinley Howell, b. 11 Nov. 1926. Librarian. Educ: B.S., Auburn Univ., Ala., U.S.A., 1947; MLn., Emory Univ., Atlanta, Ga., 1968. Appts: Sci. Tchr., Rome City Schls., Ga., 1964-66; Ext. Libn., Tri-Co. Regional Lib., 1966-67; Asst. Libn.-Hd. Libn., Shorter Coll., Rome, Ga., 1968-; Assoc. Prof., Lib. Sci., ibid, 1968-. Mbrships: Pres., Rome Br., AAUW, 1973-75; ALA; S.-Eastern Lib. Assn.; Ga. Lib. Assn.; NEA; Ga. Educ. Assn.; Coosa Valley Lib. Assn.; Chmn., Women's March of Dimes, Floyd Co., 1966; Swimming Instr., Am. Red Cross; Alpha Epsilon Delta; Delta Kappa Gamma. Address: Mildred Arnall Peniston Library, Rome, GA 30161, U.S.A. 5, 7, 138.

MOSS, Charles Basil, b. 13 Sept. 1925. Physician. Educ: B.S., Southwestern La. Univ., Lafayette, 1947; M.D., Univ. of Okla., 1949; Postgrad. study, Am. Acad. of Family Prac. Appts. incl: Staff Physn., W. Tex. Hosp. & Meth. Hosp., Lubbock, Tex., 1952-; Family Prac., Med. Arts Clinic, ibid, 1952-; City-Co. Child Welfare Bd., 1953-56; Staff Physn., Parkdale Sick Children's Clinic, 1960-71; Staff Physn. & Bd. of Dirs., Drug Crisis Ctr., 1970-73; Med. Dir., Am. Red Cross Disaster Prog., 1970. Mbrships. incl: Admin. Bd., St. John's United Meth. Ch., 1952-; Chmn., ibid, 1954; Am. Acad. of Family Prac., 1952-; Local Pres., ibid, 1956; Am. Med. Assn., 1952-. Med. Dir. & Panellist, TV Progs., 1968. Hons: 1st Place, Puissance, Am. Bus. Club Horse Show, 1969; num. awards for horsemanship, 1967-72; Commendation, Am. Red Cross, Lubbock, Tex., 1970; Commendation for Pub. Serv., 2nd Bapt. Ch. ibid, 1972; Awards for Wood Sculpture, S. Plains Fair Assn., 1971-72. Address: 5508 Ave. T, Lubbock, TX 79412, U.S.A. 7.

MOSS, Elikam George, b. 11 June 1940. Engineer. Educ: M.Sc., Southampton Univ., U.K., 1968. Appts: Asst. Engr.-Exec. Engr., Bahamas Telecommunications Corp., 1966-72; Asst. Gen. Mgr., ibid., 1973. Mbrships: Corporate Mbr., Inst. of Electronic & Radio Engrs; Chartered Engr., Coun. of Engrng. Instns., U.K; First V.P., Bahamas Instn. of Profl. Engrs., & Chmn., Joint Grp. of Engrs. Address: Bahamas Telecommunications Corp., P.O. Box N3048, Nassau, Bahamas.

MOSS, Irene Langlands, b. 3 Dec. 1915. School Teacher & Counsellor. Educ: Tchr. Trng. Schl., Vic., Vancouver Island; Univ. of Vic., 3 yrs. Appts: Tchr., rural schl., Sahtlan, Vancouver, 4 yrs.; primary schl., S. Ft. George, B.C.; Schl. Prin., Prince George, B.C., & Tchr., Sr. H.S., 20 yrs.; Tchr., Mission City, B.C., 2 yrs.; Art Tchr. & Girls' Counsellor, Penticton, B.C., 1962-; var. exec. offs., Tchrs. Fedn., over 20 yrs. Mbrships. incl: Capt., 3rd Penticton Co., Girl Guides; Dir., Okanagan Histl. Soc.; Royal Canadian Legion Aux., Prince George, Mission & Penticton; Pks. Bd., Prince George; Fair Dir., Penticton Peach Festival, & currently Treas., Harvest & Grape Fiesta; Commandant, Red Cross Corps, WWII. Hons. incl: Medal of Merit in Guiding, 1949; Long Serv. Cert. in Guiding, 1973. Address: 269 Scott Ave., Penticton, B.C., Canada.

MOSS, James A., b. 27 Mar. 1920. University Professor. Educ: B.A., Fordham Univ. & New Schl. for Soc. Rsch., N.Y.C., 1948; M.A., Columbia Univ., 1949; Ph.D., ibid, 1957. Appts. incl: Asst. Prof. Sociol., Union Coll., Schenectady, N.Y., 1958-63; Specialist on Minorities, U.S. Dept. of State, lecturing abroad, 1962; Pt.-time Lectr., African Studies Prog., Howard Univ., Wash. D.C., 1965-68; Cons., UN Inst. for Trng. & Rsch. & United

Planning Org., Wash. D.C., 1967-68; Sociol. Prof., SUNY at Buffalo, 1967, 1971-73; Vis. Prof. Sociol. & Cons. New Progs., Vassar Coll., N.Y., 1969-70; Prof. Soc. Sci., Medgar Evers Coll., CUNY, 1971-72; Ford Fndn. Cons., African Prog., 1971-72. Mbrships. incl: Rsch. Comm., Coll. Entrance Examination Bd., 1968. Publs: Ed., The Black Man in America: Integration & Separation, 1971; num. articles in profl. jrnls. Hons: Fellow, Woodrow Wilson Int. Ctr. for Schols., 1972-73; Ford Fndn. Travel & Study Award, 1973. Address: 10 Waterside Plz., N.Y., NY 10010, U.S.A. 7, 14, 15, 28, 30.

MOSS, James Earl, b. 2 Feb. 1931. Museum Director. Educ: B.S., Univ. of Mo., Columbia, U.S.A., 1956; M.A., ibid, 1958. Appts. incl: Instr., Am. Hist. & Econs., Columbia Coll., Mo., 1958-61; Asst. to Dir., State Histl. Soc. of Mo. & Assoc. Ed., Mo. Histl. Review, 1961-66; Exec. Dir., Harris Co. Heritage & Conservation Soc., Houston, Tex., 1966-69; Exec. Dir., San Diego Histl. Soc., & Ed., Jrnl. of San Diego Hist., San Diego, Calif., 1969-70 & 1971-; Exec. Dir., Hawaiian Mission Children's Soc., Honolulu, 1970; Dir., Villa Montexuma Hist. & Educ. Ctr., San Diego, 1971-. Publs: Duelling in Missouri History, The Age of Dirk Drawing & Pistol Snapping, 1966; Articles in newspapers & profl. jrnls. Hons: Fidelity Educl. Fndn. Fellowship, 1955; Harry S. Truman Lib. Inst. Fellowship, 1963. Address: San Diego Historical Society, Serra Museum, Library & Tower Gallery, Presidio Pk., P.O. Box 81825, San Diego, CA 92138, U.S.A. 133.

MOSS, Joe, b. 26 Jan. 1933. Sculptor; Professor of Art. Educ: B.A., W. Va. Univ., Morgantown, W. Va., 1955; B.S. requirements for Secondary Tchng., ibid, 1956; M.A., ibid, 1960. Appts. incl: Chmn., Art Dept., Morgantown H.S., W. Va., 1956-60; Instr.-Assoc. Prof. of Art, W. Va. Univ., 1960-70; Vis. Prof. of Art, Univ. of Md., Coll. Park, Md., 1967; Benedum Artist in Residence, Bethany Coll., W. Va., 1967; Assoc. Prof.-Prof. of Art, Univ. of Del., Newark, Del., 1970-; Vis. Rsch. Fellow, Ctr. for Advanced Visual Studies, MIT, Cambridge, Mass., 1973. Work included in num. pub. & pvte. colls. in U.S.A. & recent commns. incl. auditory environment work for Bloomsburg State Coll., Pa., 1973. Recent Exhibs. incl: Sci. Mus. of Franklin Inst., Phila., Pa., 1973; Hall of Sci., N.Y.C., 1974; Calif. Mus. of Sci. & Ind., L.A., 1974. One-Man Shows incl: W. Va. Univ., 1955, 1963; Pa. State Univ., State Coll., Pa., 1965; Univ. of Md., Coll. Park, Md., 1967; Towson State, Balt., Md., 1972; Russell Mus., Gt. Falls, Mont., 1973. Recip. num. awards for painting & sculpture inclng. Arts & Humanities Coun. Purchase Awards for Sculpture, 1967 & 1970 (2 awards). Address: Coll. of Arts & Scis., Dept. of Art, Univ. of Del., Newark, DE, U.S.A. 6, 37, 125, 133.

MOSS, Stephen J., b. 1 Apr. 1935. Dentist; Educator; Lecturer. Educ: B.S., Queens Coll., 1955; D.D.S., Coll. of Dentistry, N.Y. Univ., 1959; M.S., N.Y. Univ., 1963; Postgrad Orthodontic Prog., ibid, 1963-67. Appts: Pvte. Prac., Pediatric Dentistry, 1960-; Instr.-Assoc. Prof. & Chmn., Dept. Pedodontics, N.Y. Univ., 1964-; Adjunct i/c Periodontics, Brookdale Hosp. Ctr., N.Y.C., 1966-; Dir. Dental Affairs, Medcom Inc., N.Y.C., 1969-. Fellowships: Am. Acad. Pedodontics; Am. Coll. Dentists; Royal Soc. Hlth. Mbrships. incl: Dipl., Am. Bd. Pedodontics; Bd. Dirs., Am. Acad. Pedodontics, Assn. Pedodontic Dipls. Prod. 3. films incnlg., Development of the Human Tooth. 1969 & Preventive Dentistry, 1972. Recip., Meritorious Award, Am. Dental Assn. Preventive Dentistry,

1972. Address: 1 Wash. Sq. Village, N.Y. NY 10012, U.S.A. 6.

MOSTOFI, Fathollah Keshvar, b. 10 Aug. 1911. Physician. Educ: A.B. & B.Sc., Univ. of Neb., 1935; Harvard Med. Schl., 1939. Appts. incl: Chief of Laboratory ZI, U.S. Army, 1945-47; Chief, Genitourinary Pathol., VA Special Lab., Armed Forces Inst. of Pathol, 1948-61; Sci. Dir., Am. Registry of Pathol., ibid., 1957-59; Chief of Special & Gen. Pathol. & Chief, Genitourinary Pathol., ibid., 1961-; Hd., WHO Int. Ref. Centre on Tumors of Urogenital Organs, 1965-; Clin. Prof., Pathol., Georgetown Univ. Hosp., Wash., D.C., 1961-; Asst. Prof. of Pathol., Johns Hopkins Hosp., Balt., Md., 1960-. Mbrships. incl: Sec.-Treas., 1952-70, & Pres., 1972, Int. Acad. of Pathol.; Sec., Int. Coun. of Socs. of Pathol.; Am. Assn. of Pathologists & Bacteriologists. Over 100 publs. dealing w. pathol., cancer, tropical diseases, inclng: The Kidney, 1966; Bilharziasis, 1967; The Liver (co-ed.), 1972; Striated Muscle (Co-ed.), 1973. Hons: Special Gold Med. Award, Int. Acad. of Pathol., Dept. of the Army. Address: Armed Forces Inst. of Pathol., Washington, DC 20306, U.S.A. 2.

MOTE, Winnifred K., b. 13 Oct. 1918. Pharmacist. Educ: Drake Univ. Coll. of Pharmacy. Appts: Instr. of Student Nurses, 1946-58; Instr., Drake Univ., Pharmacy Students, Hosp. Pharmacy, 1947-73; Broadlawns Polk Co. Hosp., 1942-73; Dir. of Pharmacy, ibid, 1973. Mbrships: Am. Soc. of Hosp. Pharmacists; Bd. of Dirs., Iowa Soc. of Hosp. Pharmacists, 1969-74; Sec., Pharmacy & Therapeutic Comm., 1967-73; Inst. Prac. Comm., 1969-72; Hosp. Liaison Comm., 1969. Am. Pharmaceutical Assn.; AAUW; Bus. & Profl. Women's Club; Y.W.C.A.; White Shrine Ambassador Club; etc. Hons. incl: Good Citizenship Award, 1959; 15, 20, 25, & 30 Yr. Awards of Serv., Broadlawns Polk Co. Hosp. Address: 3512 S. Union, Des Moines, LA 50315, U.S.A.

MOTT, (Sir) Nevill Francis, b. 30 Sept. 1905. University Professor (Retired). Educ: B.A., St. John's Coll., Cambridge, 1927; M.A., ibid, 1930; studied Theoretical Phys. under R.H. Fowler, Cambridge, & Niels Bohr, Copenhagen. Appts: Lectr., Theoretical Phys., Manchester Univ., 1929; Fellow & Lectr. in Maths., Gonville & Caius Coll., Cambridge, 1930-33; Prof. of Theoretical Phys., Bristol Univ., 1933-53; Cavendish Prof. of Phys., Cambridge Univ., 1953-71; Master of Caius Coll.; Chmn., Nuffield Advsry. Comm. on Phys. Sci. Educ.; Chmn., Bd. of Dirs., Taylor & Francis, Sci. Publrs. Mbrships: F.R.S., London; Fellow, Inst. of Phys.; Pres., Int. Union of Phys., 1947-53; Athenaeum Club. Publs: Theory of Atomic Collisions (w. H.S.W. Massey), 1933; Theory of the Properties of Metals & Alloys (w. H. Jones), 1936; Theory of the Properties of Metals & Alloys (w. H. Jones), 1936; Electronic Properties of Ionic Crystals (w. R.W. Gurney), 1939; Electronic Properties of Non-Crystalline Materials (w. E.A. Davis), 1971; Metal-Insulator Transitions, 1974. Hons: Kt. Bachelor, 1962; D.Sc., Univs. of Louvain, Grenoble, Poitiers, Ottawa, Paris, London, Bristol, Sheffield, Liverpool, Reading, Warwick, Lancaster, Herriot-Watt; Hughes, Royal & Copley Medals. Address: 31, Sedley Taylor Rd., Cambridge CB2 2PN, U.K. 1.

MOTTHEAU, Jacques, b. 19 May 1899. Interior Decorator; Professor of Applied Arts. Educ: Specialist Schl. of Arch., Paris, France. Appts: Pres., Soc. of Decorative Artists, Paris; Pres. & Fndr., Nat. Union of Archtl. & Interior Decorators; Prof., Applied Arts, Am. Schls. of

Arts, Fontainebleau, & Nat. Higher Schl. of Decorative Arts, Paris. Mbrship: Ctrl. Union of Decorative Arts. Interior decorations: Elysée Palace, Min. of For. Affairs, Min. of Justice, Paris, & num. pvte. houses, France & abroad. Publs: 3 books on furniture; Contbns. to tech. jrnsl. Lctr. on contemporary interior decoration. Hons: Off., French Acad., 1937; Chevalier, Légion d'Honneur, 1953; Num. awards at int. exhibs., inclng. Paris, 1937, Brussels, Montreal. Address: 14 Rue Charles VII, 94130 Nogent sur Marne, France.

MOULE, Charles Francis Digby, b. 3 Dec. 1908. Clergyman & Professor. Educ: M.A., Emmanuel Coll., Cambridge Univ., 1934; Ridley Hall, Cambridge. Ordained Deacon, 1933, Priest, 1934. Appts: Tutor, Ridley Hall, Cambridge, 1933-34; Curate, Rigby Parish Ch., 1934-36; V.Prin., Ridley Hall, Cambridge, 1936-44; Fellow, Clare Coll., Cambridge, 1944-; Dean, ibid, 1944-51; Univ. Lectr., Univ. of Cambridge, 1947-51; Lady Margaret's Prof. of Divinity, Univ. of Cambridge, 1951-. Mbrships: Fellow, Brit. Acad., 1966-; Hon. Fellow, Emmanuel Coll., Cambridge, 1972-; Studiorum Novi Testamenti Societas; Pres., ibid, 1967-68; Hon. Mbr., Soc. of Biblical Lit., U.S.A. Publs: An Idiom Book of New Testament Greek, 1953; The Epistles to the Colossians & to Philemon, 1957; Worship in the New Testament, 1961; The Birth of the New Testament, 1962; The Phenomenon of the New Testament, 1967, etc. Hons: D.D., Univ. of St. Andrews, 1958; The Burkitt Medal of the Brit. Acad., 1970. Address: Clare Coll., Cambridge, U.K.

MOULTHROP, James Irwin, b. 10 Apr. 1936. Veterinary Epidemiologist. Educ: D.V.M., Univ. of Ga., Athens, U.S.A., 1961; M.A., Pub. Hlth., Univ. of Minn., Mpls., 1969. Appts. incl: Pvte. Prac., Cambridge, Md., 1961-63; Field Poultry Epidemiologist, Animal Hlth. Div., Dept. of Agric., St. Paul, Minn., 1964-67; Regional Poultry Epidemiologist, Animal Hlth. Div., Dept. of Agric., S.-. U.S.A., 1968-72; Prin. Staff Off., Field Ops., Emergency Progs., Animal Plant Hlth. Inspection Serv., Dept. of Agric., Hyattsville, Md., 1973-. Mbrships. incl: Am. Veterinary Med. Assn.; Am. Assn. of Avian Pathologists; Nat. Assn. of Fed. Veterinarians; AAAS; World Poultry Veterinary Med. Assn.; U.S. Animal Hlth. Assn.; Southern Conf. on Avian Diseases; Vestryman, Grace Ch., Gainesville, Ga. Co-author, sev. contbns. to profl. jrnls. Recip., 2 Certs. of Appreciation, 1972-73. Address: Room 743, CB 1, Emergency Programs Veterinary Services, APHIS, USDA, Hyattsville, MD 20781, U.S.A. 130.

MOULY, George J., b. 16 Sept. 1915. University Professor. Educ: B.A., Univ. of Sask., Can., 1945; B.Ed., ibid, 1946; M.Ed., 1947; Ph.D., Univ. of Minn., U.S.A., 1949. Appts: Tchr. & Prin., Sask. Pub. Schls., 1934-42; Instr. of Math., Univ. of Sask., 1946-47; Assoc. Prof. & Dir., Testing Bur., Univ. of Miami, Fla., 1949-52; Assoc. Prof., Marquette Univ., 1952-56; Prof. of Educl. Psychol., Univ. of Miami, 1956-; Dir., Rsch. Trng. Prog., ibid, 1966-69; Chmn., Dept. of Educl. Psychol., 1969-71. Mbrships: Am. Psychol. Assn.; Am. Educl. Rsch. Assn.; Phi Delta Kappa. Publs: Psychology for Effective Teaching, 1960, 3rd ed., 1973; Test Items in Education (jt. author), 1962; The Science of Educational Research, 1963, 2nd. ed., 1970; Readings in Educational Psychology, 1971. Hons: Outstanding Tchr., Univ. of Miami, 1966; Man of Yr., Gamma Xi Chapt., Phi Delta Kappa. Address: 8121 Erwin Rd., Coral Gables, FL 33143, U.S.A. 2, 14, 130, 139, 141.

MOUNT, Charles Merrill, b. 19 May 1928. Artist. Educ: Columbia Univ., N.Y.C., U.S.A.; Univ. of Calif., L.A.; Columbia Law Schl.; Grande Chaumière Acad., Paris, France. Appts: Tchr., Art Students' League, N.Y.C.; European Agent, Corcoran Gall. of Art, Wash. D.C.; Free-lance Portrait Painter; Lectr., num. art galls. & mus.'s; Expert Cons. on fakes. Mbrships: Fndr. & First Pres., Irish Portrait Soc., Dublin, Ireland; V.P. & Recording Sec., The Burr Artists, N.Y.C. Painter, num. portraits of eminent people & noble families, Europe & Am. Publs: John Singer Sargent, 1955, 3rd edit. 1969; Gilbert Stuart, 1964; Monet, 1967; Over 100 articles in art & other jrnls. Hons. incl: Best Book of the Yr. Accolade, or John Singer Sargent, N.Y. Times, 1955; Guggenheim Fellowship, 1956. Address: 308 Beach 145 St., Neponsit, NY 11694, U.S.A. 37.

MOUNTCASTLE, Vernon Benjamin, Jr., b. 15 July 1918. Neurophysiologist; Educator. Educ: Roanoke Coll.; Johns Hopkins Univ. Schl. of Med. Appts: House Off., Surg., Johns Hopkins Hosp., 1943; USN, 1943-46; Johns Hopkins Univ. Schl. of Med., 1948-; Prof., Physiol., 1959-; Dir. Dept. of Physiol., 1964-. Mbrships: Nat. Acad. of Scis.; Am. Acad. of Arts & Scis.; 1st Nat Pres., Soc. for Neurosci., 1971-72. Publs: Medical Physiology, (ed., major contbr.), 2 vols., 1958; Over 50 articles in profl. jrnls. Hons: Vis. Lectr., Univ. Coll., London, & Coll. de France, Paris, 1959; Penfield Lectr., Am. Univ., Beirut, 1971; Sherrington Lectr., Univ. of Liverpool, 1974. Address: Dept. of Physiol., Johns Hopkins Univ. Schl. of Med., 725 N. Wolfe St., Baltimore, MD 21205, U.S.A. 14, 34.

MOURA-RELVAS, Joaquim de, b. 1 Aug. 1898. Roentgenologist. Educ: Univ. of Coimbra. Appts: Asst. Prof., Med. Fac., Coimbra Univ., 1928-31; Gov. of Coimbra, 1932-33; Mbr., Nat. Assembly, 1935-57; Pres., Order of Physicians of Coimbra, 1953-58; Mayor of Coimbra, 1957-66; Mbrships: Pres., Portuguese Soc. Radiol., 1941-42; Inst. of Coimbra. Publs. incl: Hystero-Salpingography, 1929; Radiotomia Directa, 1939; Intestinal Invagination, 1946, Cholecystometry, 1958. Hons: Gt. Off., Order of Cruzeiro do sul, Brasil, 1962; Cmdr., Order of Christ, Portugal, 1962; Merit Medal, Portuguese Red Cross, 1965. Address: Penedo da Saudade, 30, Coimbra, Portugal. 10, 43.

MOUREAUX, Georges, b. 11 June 1914. Drawing Master. Educ: Univs. of Besançon, Lyon & Paris, France; Ecole Normale Superieure Technique; Dips. in Art, Tchng. Drawing & Tchng. French in For. Countries. Appts. incl: Sketcher & Drawer, ind. & the press; Illustrator, books, reviews, etc.; Drawing Master, Voiron, St. Etienne, Lyon, Oyonnax, Cluses; Ed., La Langue Internationale. Mbrships. incl: Nat. Comm. Against Tobacco; French League Against Vivisection; Soc. for Protection of Nature; Assn. for Protection Against Ionizing Radiation. Contbr. to var. publs. Hons. incl: Chevalier du Merite culturel et artistique, 1967; Priz Montagne Blanche 1968. Address: 11 rue J. Donier, FO 1100, Oyonnax, France, 43. 91.

MOUSOURAKIS, John N., b. 5 Aug. 1944. Bank Executive. Educ: A.B., W. Liberty State Coll., W. Va., 1968; M.A., Vanderbilt Univ., Nashville, Tenn., 1970; A.I.B. course, Univ. of Tenn., Nashville; Schl. for Int. Banking, Univ. of Colo., 1973. Appts: Assoc. Mgr., Asst. V.P., Int. Banking Dept., Hamilton Nat. Bank, Chattanooga, Tenn. Mbrships: Am. Econ. Assn.; Brazilian-Am. Chmbr. of Comm.; Int. Law Soc.; Middle E. Inst. Address: Landmark

Estates, 171 Cecil Lane, Chattanooga, TN 37412, U.S.A.

MOUSSA, Pierre (Louis), b. 5 Mar. 1922. Banker. Educ: Agrégé des Lettres, 1943; Inspecteur des Finances, 1946. Appts: Insp. Finances, 1946-54; Dir. i/c econ. affairs & planning for French Overseas Territories, 1954-59; Dir., Civil Aviation, 1959-62; Dir. of Africa Dept., World Bank, Wash., U.S.A., 1962-65; Pres., Fedn. Française des Socs. d'Assurances, 1966-69; Sr. Exec. V.P., Banque de Paris & des Pays-Bas, 1969; Pres., ibid, 1969-. Publs: The Economic Chances of French & African Community, 1957; The Underprivileged Nations (translated into 7 langs.), 1958; The Economy of the Franc Area, 1960; The United States & the Underprivileged Nations, 1965. Hons: Chevalier, Légion d'Honneur; Off., Ordre Nat. du Mérite & Ordre de Boyaca (Columbia); Commdr., Ordre Nat. Mauritanien; Médaille aéronautique; Commdr., Ordre Nat. Babonais de l'Etoile Equatoriale. Address: Banque de Paris & des Pays Bas, 3 Rue d'Antin, 75083 Paris Cedex 02, France. 34, 91.

MOVCHAN, Julian G., b. 19 Feb. 1913. Journalist; Physician; Author. Educ: Attended Ukrainian Inst. of Jrnlsm. (Kharkiv), 1932-35; M.D., Kharkiv & Lviv Med. Colls., 1937-43; Passed Ohio State Med. Bd. Exam., U.S.A., 1952. Appts: Corres. Staff Mbr. of sev. Ukrainian newspapers 1932-37; Intern, Alexian Bros. Hosp., St. Elizabeth Hosp., N.J., U.S.A., 1949-53; Pvte. Prac., Med., specializing in internal & gen. med., Oakwood & Macedonia, Ohio, 1953-; V.P., Paulding Co. Bd. Hlth., ibid, 1957-60; Corres., Ukrn. & Am. newspapers & rnls. Mbrships: Ohio State Med. Assn.; Summit Co. Med. Soc ; Med. Staff, Bedford Municipal Hosp., Ohio & Chmn., Record Comm. Publs: How to Cure Oneself & Others in Emergency Cases, 1946; Things Worth Knowing, 1966; Doctor's Notes, 1970. Recip. of award from Summit Co. Med. Soc., Ohio, 1964. Address: P.O. Box 133, Macedonia, OH 44056, U.S.A. 8.

MOVIUS, John Dryden, b. 27 May 1930. Engineer. Educ: M.E., Stevens Inst. of Technol., 1953; Stanford-Sloan Exec. Fellow, Grad. Schl. of Bus., Stanford Univ., 1968-69. Appts: Sr. Projs. Mgr., Mpls.-Honeywell Regulator Co., 1957-59; Regional Dir., Ford Motor Co., Aeronautics Div., 1959-63; Corporate Dir., Diversification Plans & Analysis, Northrop Corp., 1963-. Mbrships: Fellow, Brit. Interplanetary Soc.; Sr., Am. Astronautical Soc.; AAAS; Past Off., Nat. Space Club; Southern Calif. Wine & Food Soc.; Cndr., Dir., Les Amis du Vin; Wine Judge, L.A. Co. Fair, 1971-73; Kts. of the Vine; Confrerie u Chevaliers de St. Etienne. Publr. of The Vine Scene. Regional Dir. of Yr., Les Amis du Vin, 1971. Address: 2457 Pesquera Dr., L.A., CA 90049, U.S.A. 75.

MOY, Henry Kwok Leong, b. 30 June 1916. Economist, Statistician & Government Official. Educ: CCNY, 1934; Lingnan Univ., China, 1934-37; B.S., N.Y. Univ., 1939; M.S., Columbia Univ., 1941; Cert., Indl. Coll. of the Armed Forces, Wash. D.C., 1962. Appts: Economist, Off. of Price Stabilization, 1951-53; Economist, Bur. of Labor Stats., Dept. of Labor, 1955-56; Statn., Manpower & Training, Dept. of the Air Force, 1956-62; Statn., Sampling & Surveys, ibid, 1962-66; Economist, Directorate Personnel Studies & Rsch., Dpty. Chief of Staff for Personnel, Dept. of Army, 1966-70; Statn., Directorate Mgmt. Review & Analysis, Off. of Comptroller of the Army, Dept. of Army, 1970-. Mbrships: . Am. Economic Assn.; Treas., Wheaton Coun., Nat. Capital Area, Boy Scouts of Am., 1961-64.

Hons: Superior Performance Award, Dept. of Air Force, 1962; Appreciation Cert., Dept. of Army, 1970. Address: 13402 Lydia St., Silver Spring, MD 20906, U.S.A. 7.

MOYLAN, Harold Carlton, b. 8 Nov. 1933. Economist. Educ: B.A., Univ. of Toronto, Canada, 1964; Mgmt. Trng. Course, Univ. of the W. Indies, 1966; Postgrad. Course in Indl. Mgmt., Carl-Duisberg Gesellschaft, W. Germany. Appts: Admin. Cadet., Min. of Finance, Trinidad, W. Indies, 1964; Economist, Min. of Pub. Utilities, ibid, 1965; Sr. Economist, Pub. Utilities Commn., 1966; Sr. Economist, Min. of Pub. Utilities, 1967-70; Asst. Gen. Mgr., Port Authority of Trinidad & Tobago, 1970-73; Gen. Mgr., ibid, 1973-. Address: 21, Opal Gdns., Diamond Vale, Diego Martin, Trinidad, W. Indies. 109, 136.

MOYLE, Roland (Dunstan), b. 12 Mar. 1928. Member of Parliament. Educ: LL.B., Univ. Coll. of Wales, Aberystwyth, U.K., 1949; M.A., LL.B., Trinity Hall, Cambridge, 1953. Appts: Mbr., Gray's Inn, 1949-; Served w. Royal Welch Fusiliers, 1951-53; Legal Asst., Wales Gas Bd., 1953-55; Asst. Indl. Rels. Off., ibid, 1956; Asst. Irdl. Rels. Off., Gas Coun., 1956-62; Conciliation Rsch. Off., Elec. Coun., 1962-65; Sec., Nat. Jt. Coun. for Admin. & Clerical Staff in Elec. Supply, 1965-66; M.P., N. Lewisham, 1966-; Parliamentary Pvte. Sec. to Chief Sec. to Treasury, 1966-68; Parliamentary Pvte. Sec. to House Sec., 1968-70; Mbr., Select Comm. on Race Rels. & Immigration, 1968-71; Labour's Spokesman on Higher Educ., 1971-. Mbrships: Nat. Union of Pub. Employees; Chmn., Cambridge Univ. Labour Club, 1953; Hon. Sec., British Am. Parliamentary Grp., 1972-. Address: House of Commons, London S.W. 1, U.K. 1.

MOYSTON, Douglas Errington, b. 15 Nov. 1920. Attorney-at-Law. Educ: Articled to late D.V. Silvera, Solicitor, Morant Bay, 1937-42; Admitted to Solicitors Supreme Ct. of Judicature in Jamaica, 1942. Appts: Ptnr. in firm of Silvera & Moyston, 1943-49; Own Prac., 1950-53; Asst. Crown Solicitor, Jamaica, 1953-55; Assoc. ptnr. late N.N. Nethersole, 1956-57; Ptnr. in firm of Dickenson & Moyston, St. Ann's Bay, 1958-61; Own Prac., St. Ann's Bay, 1962-73. Mbrships: Int. Dir., Rotary Club of Ocho Rios; Former Mbr., Kingston Cricket Club & St. Thomas Country Club; Past Sr. Warden, St. Thomas Masonic Lodge. Address: P.O. Box 9, St. Ann's Bay, Jamaica, W. Indies.

MRAZEK, Thelma Stevens (Mrs. James E. Mrazek), b. 22 Sept. 1930. Editor; Writer. Educ: B.A', Duke Univ., Durham, N.C., 1952; M.A., Univ. of Pa., Phila., 1954. Appts: on staff, Congressman Charles E. Bennett of Fla., U.S. House of Reps., Wash. D.C. & Jacksonville, Fla., 1952-53; Intern, Tech. Assistance Admin., U.N., N.Y.C., 1954; Ed. Asst., For. Policy Assn., N.Y.C., 1955-60; Chief Rschr. of Book Series, Time-Life Books, Time, Inc., N.Y.C., 1960-66; Ed., The Challenge of Crime in a Free Society, Pres.'s Commn. on Admnstrn. of Justice (Nat. Crime Commn.), Wash. D.C., 1966-67; Dir., Tech. Info. Servs., Appalacian Regional Commn., Wash. D.C., 1967-71; Free-lance Writer & Ed., 1971-, recent work incls. Ed., Manual for Equal Employment Opportunity in the Construction Industry. Hons: 1st Prize for best tech. mag. prod. by govt. agcy., Fed. Eds. Assn., 1968, 3rd prize, 1969; Resolution of Commendation, Appalachian Regional Commn., 1970. Address: Apt. No. 708, 8811 Colesville Rd., Silver Spring, MD 20910, U.S.A. 5, 138.

MUCHIN, John Serge, b. 25 Nov. 1920. Librarian. Educ: B.Ed. (equiv.), Pervomaisk Pedagogical Inst., Ukraine, 1939; Lt., Moscow Artillery Coll., 1939-41; B.L.S., Univ. of Ottawa, Canada, 1963; M.A., Univ. of Man., 1972. Appts: Artillery Off., U.S.S.R. Army, Moscow, 1941-43; Lectr., UN R.R.A. Tech. Schl., Landshut, Germany, 1946-47; Libn., J. Richardson & Sons, Financial Lib., Winnipeg, Canada, 1963-64; Cataloguer, Univ. of Man. Lib., 1964-65; Slavic Libn. & Cataloguer, ibid, 1965-67; Hd., Special Collects. Dept., 1968-. Mbrships: Canadian Lib. Assn.; Man. Lib. Assn.; Hd., Lib. Comm., Bd. of Dirs., Ukrainian Cultural & Educl. Ctr., Winnipeg; Canadian Assn. of Slavists; Ukrainian Free Acad. of Scis.; Univ. of Man. Fac. Assn. Publs: Slavic Collection of the Univ. of Manitoba Libraries, 1970. Address: Special Collects. Dept., Elizabeth Dafoe Lib., Univ. of Man., Winnipeg, Man., R3T 2N2, Canada.

MUCZYNSKI, Robert Stanley, b. 19 Mar. 1929. Composer. Educ: B.M., De Paul Univ., Chgo., 1950; M.M., ibid, 1952; Summer session study, Acad. of Music, Nice, France, 1961. Appts: De Paul Univ., Chgo., 1955-56; Asst. Prof., Loras Coll., Dubuque, Iowa, 1956-58; Vis. Lectr., Roosevelt Univ., Chgo., 1964-65; Assoc. Prof., Music, Univ. of Ariz., Tucson, 1965-. Mbrships: Am. Soc. of Composers, Authors, Publishers; Am. Fedn. of Musicians. Compositions incl: Symph. No. 1; 1st Piano Concerto; Dance Movements, for orch.; Fantasy Trio for Clarinet, Cello, Piano; Sonata for Cello & Piano; 6 Preludes for Piano. Commercial discs incl: Sonata for Cello/Piano; Film Scores; Piano/Chamber Music of Muczynski. 8 documentary film scores for Univ. of Ariz. Film Dept. Recip. of hons. Address: Route 8, Box 381-B, Tucson, AZ 85710, U.S.A.

MUELLER, (Sister) Gerardine, O.P., b. 16 Sept. 1921. Artist; Teacher. Educ: B.A., Caldwell Coll., N.J.; M.A., M.F.A., Notre Dame Univ., Ind. Mbr. of Relig. Community of Dominican Sisters, 1940-. Appts: Art Instr. St. Dominic Acad., Jersey City, N.J., 1954-63; Fordham Univ., N.J., 1961; Prof. & Chmn., Dept. of Art, Caldwell Coll., N.J., 1963-. Mbrships. incl: Cath. Fine Arts Soc. (Pres., 1969-71; Chmn. 1968 conven.); Nat. Art Educ. Assn.; Am. Craftsmen's Coun.; Art Eductrs. of N.J.; Trustee, Mt. St. Dominic Acad., Caldwell N.J'; Fine Arts Study Comm., N.J. Dept. Higher Educ., 1973; N.J. State Coun. on Arts: Evaluation for Visual Arts Grants, 1974; 1976 Bicentennial Comm., Caldwell Borough. Art Works incl: Designed Chapel, All Saints Ch., Jersey City; Glass Mosaic Murals, Caldwell Coll.; num. exhibs. of work. 1st Place Nat. Miniature Art Exhib., 1971. Address: Caldwell Coll., Caldwell, NJ 07006, U.S.A. 5, 37.

MUELLER, Virginia S., b. 27 Apr. 1924. Lawyer. Educ: B.A., Stanford Univ., 1944; LL.B., Cornell Univ., 1946; Doctor, Fac. Law., Univ. of Paris, France, 1950. Appts: Rsch. Atty., Calif. Ct. of Appeals, 1946-49; pvte. prac., Seattle, Wash., 1951-53; Dpty. Prosecuting Atty., King Co., 1953-56; Tax Div., Wash. Tax Commn., 1956-58; Asst. Counsel, Calif. State Bd. of Equal., 1959; Dpty. Dist. Atty., Sacramento, Calif., 1959-66; Counsel, Legal Aide Soc., ibid, 1966-71; pvte. prac., ibid, 1971-. Mbrships. incl: State Bar Calif.; Wash. State Bar Assn.; Am. Bar Assn.; Int. Cts. Comm. (Vice-Chmn. 1974-); Sacramento Co. Bar Assn.; Fed. Bar Assn. (V.P. 1971-72, 1973); Calif. Trial Lawyers Assn. Phi Alpha Delta. Contbr. to legal jrnls. & League of Women Voters' Calif. Handbook. Hons. incl: Ray Lymnan Wilbur Award, Stanford Univ., 1944; Deleg., Democratic Nat. Convention, 1972.

Address: 3401 Freeport Bldv., Suite 4, Sacramento, CA 95818, U.S.A. 5, 9.

MUENCHINGER, Herman Gustave, b. 25 Sept. 1913. Mechanical Engineer. Educ: B.S. Univ. of R.I., Kingston, U.S.A., 1938. Appts incl: Mgr., Product Design, Am. Screw Co. Willimantic, Conn., 1944-56; Dir. of Rsch. ibid, 1956-62; Dir. of Rsch., Holokrome Co. Hartford, Conn., 1962-67; Chief Product Engr. Continental Screw Co., New Bedford, Mass. 1967-69; V.P., Engrng., ibid, 1969- Mbrships incl: Vice Chmn., B-18 Comm. on Fasteners, & Chmn., Subcomm. 6, Am. Nat. Standards Inst. Past Chmn. in R.I., Am. Soc. for Metals, 1938- Soc. for Mfg. Engrs., Hartford, Conn., 1962-67 Chmn., Bd. of Educ., Chaplin, Conn. Holder approx. 20 U.S. & other patents in threaded fasteners. Author, article in profl. jrnl., 1971 Recip., Award for dev. of Posidriv recessed head fastener, Screw Prods. Tech. Comm. 1962. Address: 15 River View Ave., S Dartmouth, MA 02748, U.S.A. 6.

MUETZELFELDT, Bruno E., b. 7 Feb 1918. Churchman. Educ: Immanuel Coll. Adelaide, Australia; Lutheran Theol. Sem., ibid Appts: Min., Lutheran Ch., Albury, N.S.W. 1939-46; Exec. Sec., Lutheran Youth Dept. 1946-51; Chap., Commonwealth Immigration Ctr. Australia, 1947-51; Dir., Lutheran World Fed./Dept. of World Serv. in Australia & Exec Sec., Bd. of Immigration, Utd. Evangelica Lutheran Ch. in Australia, 1951-60; N.S.W Pres., Utd. Evangelical Lutheran Ch. ir Australia, 1954-60; Sec. for Resettlement & Relief, Lutheran World Fed./Dept. of World Serv. H.Q., Geneva, Switzerland, 1960-61; Dir. Lutheran World Fed./Dept. of World Serv. 1961-. Mbrships. incl: Int. Word Refugee Year Comm., 1960-61; Chmn., Int. Coun. Voluntary Agcys., 1963-65. Hons: D.D., Capitol Univ. Ohio, U.S.A., 1962; Star of Jordan, 1964 Address: Lutheran World Fed./World Serv., 150 rte. de Ferney, P.O. Box 66, 1211 Geneva 20 Switzerland. 23, 34, 128, 139.

MUHITH, Abulmaal Abdul, b. 25 Jan 1934. Development Administrator; Diplomat Educ: B.A. (Hons.), Dacca Univ., 1954; M.A. ibid, 1955; Balliol Coll., Oxford, U.K. 1957-58; M.P.A., Harvard Univ., U.S.A., 1963 Appts. incl: Subdivl. Off., E. Pakistan, 1959-60 Protocol Off., Govt. of E. Pakistan, 1960-61 Dpty. Sec., Transportation Dept., Govt. E Pakistan, 1961-63; Dpty. Sec. & Chief of Prog Planning Commn. of Pakistan, 1964-66; Dpty Sec. to Cabinet, Pakistan Govt., 1966-69; Econ Counsellor, Pakistan Embassy in U.S.A. 1969-71; Econ. Min., Bangladesh Embassy Wash.D.C., 1971-, Chargé d'Affaires, 1972 Mbr., var. orgs. & clubs. Author, The Deputy Commissioner in East Pakistan, 1968, & articles, Bangladesh newspapers. Recip. Tamgha-e-Pakistan Award, Pakistan Govt. 1967. Address: 5006 Edgemoore Ln., Bethesda MD 20014, U.S.A. 2, 22.

MUIR, Laurence Macdonald, b. 3 Mar 1925. Sharebroker. Educ: Scotch Coll. Melbourne, Australia; LL.B., Univ. o' Melbourne, 1949. Appts: Served R.A.N. 1942-46; Barrister & Solicitor, Supreme Ct. o' Vic., 1950; Sharebroker, 1951-; Mbr., Stock Exchange of Melbourne, 1960-; Ptnr., Ian Potter & Co., 1962-; Dir., Australian United Enterprises Pty. Ltd., Ins. Off. of Australia, & James Miller Holdings Ltd.; Alt. Dir. Commercial Union Assce. Co. Mbrships. incl Chmn., Assn. of Independent Schls., Vic. 1972; Comm., Nat. Coun. of Independent Schls., 1969-73; Scotch Coll. Coun., 1963-73 Dpty. Chmn., ibid, 1971-; Bd. Mbr., Alfred Hosp., 1971-; Bd. Mbr., Vic. Div., Nat. Heart

Fndn., 1968-. Recip., Volunteer Reserve Decoration, 1963. Address: Ian Potter & Co., 325 Collins St., Melbourne, Australia 3000. 23.

MUIRHEAD, (Judge) James Henry, b. 24 Apr. 1925. Judge. Educ: LL.B., Adelaide Univ., Australia. Appts: Admitted, Barrister & Solicitor, Supreme Ct., S.A., 1950; Q.C., 1967; Judge, Local & Dist. Criminal Ct., Adelaide, 1970; Acting Justice, Supreme Ct., Papua New Guinea, 1972; Acting Dir., Australian Inst. of Criminol., Canberra, A.C.T., 1973-. Mbrships: Naval Mil. & Air Force Club, Adelaide; Stock Exchange Club, ibid. Address: c/o Australian Inst. of Criminol., Box 28, Woden, A.C.T., Australia. 23.

MUIRHEAD, John Franklin, b. 21 Feb. 1938. Attorney-at-Law. Educ: Articled Clerk, Judah & Randall. Appts: Assoc. Solicitor w. Judah & Randall, Solicitors, 1963-65; Legal Counsel, Kaiser Bauxite Co., 1965-67; Ptnr., Alberga, Milner & Muirhead, Solicitors, 1967-69; Ptnr., Marley, Milner, Soutar & Co., Attorneys-at-Law, Kingston, Jamaica, 1969-. Mbr., Jamaica Bar Assn. Address: P.O. Box 158, Kingston, Jamaica, W. Indies. 109.

MUJEEB, Muhammad, b. 30 Oct. 1902. University Professor of History & Administrator. Educ: Hons. Grad., Mod. Hist., Oxford, U.K., 1922; further studies, printing & langs., Germany, 4 yrs. Appts: Prof. of Hist. & Pol. Sci., Treas., Mgr. of University Press, Jamia Millia Islamia (Nat. Muslim. Univ.), Delhi, India; Vice-Chancellor, ibid, 1948-74; Mbr. & occasional Chmn., govng. bodies, var colls. & schls., Delhi; Deleg., Liberia, China, U.S.S.R.; Alternate Deleg., UN Gen. Assembly, 1949. UNESCO Session, 1954. Mbrships: var. educl., soc., econ. & cultural orgs. Publs. in Urdu incl: The Story of the World: History of Russian Literature. Publs. in Engl. incl: Glimpses of New China; The Indian Muslims; Ghalib. Also 6 plays in Urdu. Recip., Padma Bhushan Award, Govt. of India, 1964. Address: Naseem Bagh, P.O. Jamia Nagar, New Delhi-110025, India. 34.

MUKERJI, Bishnupada, b. 1 Mar. 1903. Teacher & Researcher in Medicine. Educ: M.B.B.S., Calcutta Univ., India, 1927; D.Sc., Univ. of Mich., U.S.A., 1936. Appts. incl: Pharmacologist–Dir., Biochem. Standardisation Lab., Govt., India, 1937-47; Dir., Ctrl. Drugs Lab., Min. of Hlth., 1947-51; Dir., Ctrl. Drug Rsch. Inst., Coun. Sci. & Indl. Rsch., Govt. of India, 1951-63; Dir., Chittaranjan Nat. Cancer Rsch. Ctr., Calcutta, 1963-69; Hon. Cons., Ford Fndn., Calcutta, 1971-73. Mbr. & advsr., var. comms., WHO, FAO & UNESCO, 1950-70. Mbrships: incl: Pres., Indian Assn. Biol. Sci., 1970-, Inst. of Chemists (India), 1971-73, & Asiatic Soc., Calcutta, 1972-74; Gen. Pres., Sci. Cong. Assn., 1962-63; & Indian Pharmaceutical cong. Assn., 1960-62; Pres., Indian Brain Rsch. Assn., 1970-; V.P., Indian Biophys. Soc., 1968-; Past V.P., Nat. Inst. Sci., India. Publs: Indian Pharmaceutical Codex, 1957; Handbook of Tropical Therapeutics, 1955; Pharmacognosy of Indian Root & Rhizome Drugs; Pharmacognosy of Indian Leaf Drugs; Contbr., num. profl. jnls. Recip., many hon. degrees. Address: 54 Gopimohan Dutt Lane, Calcutta 3, India.

MUKWATO, Lifuwa Edwin, b. 23 Oct. 1932. Librarianship. Educ: Cert. Lib., Dip. Lib. (EA), Makerere Univ. Coll., 1964-68. Appts. incl: Welfare Off., 1958-62; Asst. Lib. Off., 1962-68; Regional Lib. Off., (1 mnth.), 1968; Asst. Libn., (1 mnth.), 1968; Chief Libs. Off., 1968-. Mbrships: Zambia Lib. Assn., 'former Chmn., 2 yrs.; Zambia Police Offs. Mess, Lusaka, Zambia; United Nat. Independence

Pty. Publs: Zangi Muchima, 1956; Kwatoku Na Mutwenu, 1959; Ed., Zambia Lib. Serv. Bulletin, 1968-72. Hons: Cert. of Disting. Serv., New Hall JCR, Makerere Univ. Coll., Uganda. Address: P.O. Box 802, Lusaka, Zambia.

MULCAHY, Risteárd, b. 13 July 1922. Physician. Educ: Univ. Coll., Dublin, Repub. of Ireland; Postgrad. study, Nat. Heart Hosp., London, U.K. Appts: Dir., Cardiac Dept. & Coronary Heart Disease Rsch. Unit, St. Vincent's Hosp., Dublin, Repub. of Ireland; Cardiologist, Coombe Lying-In Hosp., ibid. Mbrships. incl: Irish Cardiac Soc.; Brit. Cardiac Soc.; Am. Heart Assn.; Past Pres., Irish Med. Assn.; Past Pres., Irish Heart Fndn.; Assn. Physns. Gt. Britain & Ireland; Am. Pub. Hlth. Assn.; Int. Soc. Epidemiol.; Coun. Epidemiol. Int. Soc. Cardiol.; Royal Soc. Med.; Royal Acad. Med. Ireland; Corrigan Club; Osler Club. Publs: About 100 sci. publs. on prevention of coronary heart disease; About 20 publs. on hist. med. & vocatl. & educl. aspects of med. profession; 1 textbook, The Prevention of Coronary Heart Disease; 6 short books on var. aspects coronary disease. Address: 3 Clyde Rd., Ballsbridge, Dublin 4, Repub. of Ireland.

MULDER, Frederick Sasser, b. 24 Nov. 1932. Government Official. Educ: B.S., Univ. of Ala., 1955; Cert., Univ. of Paris, France, 1955; M.S., N.Y. Univ., 1965; Postgrad., ibid, & New Schl. for Soc. Rsch., 1972. Appts: 1st Lt., U.S. Army, 1956-58; Asst. Battalion Surg.; Instr., Field Med. & Surg., Brooke Army Med. Schl.; State Govt. Official, N.Y. State Dept., Mental Hygiene, 1958-60, Dept. Soc. Servs., 1960-61, Exec. Dept., 1961-; Area Supvsr., Bur. of Census, Dept. of Commerce, U.S. Govt., 1960; Psych. Admitting Official, N.Y.C. Hosp. Corp., 1968-. Mbrships. incl: Fndr. Mbr., Soc. Descendants, Order Kts. of the Garter; Assn. N.Y.C. Recip. of Hons. Address: 96 Duane St., N.Y., NY 10007, U.S.A. 2.

MULDER, George William, b. 30 Dec. 1922. Musicologist; Musician. Educ: A.B., Coll. of Wooster, Ohio; A.M., Columbia Univ.; Amsterdam Conservatory, Netherlands; also attended other univs. Appts: Musician, U.S. Army, 1942-45; Cryptographer, U.S. Army Signal Corps; Asst. to Music Libn., Columbia Univ., N.Y., 1946-48; Asst. Prof. of Music, Western Ill. Univ., Macomb, 1946-68; Instr. in Music, Northwestern Mich. Coll., Traverse City; Organist & Dir. of Music, Bethlehem Luth. Ch., ibid; Pvte. Instr. of Organ & Piano, Interlochen. Mbrships. incl: Am. Musicol. Soc.; Int. Musicol. Soc.; Chapt. Sec., Cherry Captial Area, Am. Guild of Organists; AAUP. Contbr. of articles & reviews to jrnl. of Am. Musicol. Soc. Hons: Danforth Fndn. Award for Tchng. Excellence, 1955; Humanities Award, Danforth Fndn., 1965. Address: Interlochen, MI 49643, U.S.A.

MÜLDNER-NIECKOWSKI, Wieslaw, b. 20 Aug. 1915. Sculptor; Painter; Interior Decorator. Educ: Acad. of Fine Arts, Paris, France; State Higher Schl. of Fine Arts, Poznan, Poland. Mbrships: Provincial Culture Coun., Poznan, 1948-73; Union of Polish Artists (Warsaw Bd. Sculpture Sect.; Vice Chmn., Ctrl. Bd. of Control; Vice Chmn., Warsaw Bd.); Rep. of F.I.D.E.M. for Poland & Mbr., F.I.D.E.M. Ctrl. Bd.; Chmn., Medal Engraving Commn., Ctrl. Bd., Union of Polish Artists; Int. Assn. Art; UNESCO; Fed. Int. de la Medaille, Paris, France; Soc. des Auteurs "ZAIKS". Sculptures incl: A girl with the book; White bear; num. other works in Warsaw & in pub. & pvte. collects. in Europe, India, Canada, U.S.S.R. Hons. incl: French Govt. prize for contrib. to cultural life of Paris, 1960; Accademia del'Arte, Montecatini, 1968.

Address: Filtrowa 79 m. 53, 02-032, Warsaw, Poland.

MULFINGER, George Leonidas, Jr., b. 21 June 1932. Professor; Author; Musician; Lecturer. Educ: B.A., Syracuse Univ., 1953; M.S., ibid, 1962; grad. studies, Harvard Univ., Univ. of Ga. Appts: Hd., Math. & Sci. Dept., Elbridge Ctrl. Schl., N.Y., 1955-57; Sci. Instr., Syracuse-Ctrl. Tech. HS, N.Y., 1957-65; Chmn., Sci. Dept., ibid, 1962-65; Prof. of Phys. & Phys. Scis., Bob Jones Univ., 1965-. Mbrships: Astron. Soc. of Pacific; Am. Phys. Soc.; S.C. Acad. of Sci.; Creation Rsch. Soc.; Bible-Sci. Assn.; Phi Beta Kappa; Sigma Pi Sigma. Publs: The Flood & the Fossils & How Did the Earth Get Here? (pamphlets); Physical Science (co-author), 1974; contbr. chapts. to Why Not Creation?, 1970, The Creation Alternative, 1970 & A Challenge to Education, 1972; contbr. articles to jrnsl. Hons: Nat. Sci. Fndn. Grant to study desalination of seawater, 1964; Creation Rsch. Soc. Grant to study growth rate of stalactites, 1971-. Address: 25 Springdale Dr., Greenville, SC 29609, U.S.A. 28, 125, 130.

MULHALL, Edgar Machen, b. 26 Sept. 1916. Merchant. Educ: Radley Coll., Berks., U.K. Appts: Served in WWII, 1940-46; Pres., Bethell Robertson & Co. Ltd., Nassau, Bahamas. Mbrships: Royal Nassau Sailing Club; Hurlingham Club, Buenos Aires; St. Andrew's Soc., Bahamas. Address: P.O. Box 6340, Nassau, Bahamas. 109.

MULLALLY, Frederic, b. 25 Feb. 1921. Novelist. Educ: Clapham Coll., U.K. Appts: Asst. Ed., Tribune, 1945-47; Pol. Ed., Sunday Pictorial, 1947-50; Publicity Dir., Hulton Press, 1954-56. Mbr, Writers Guild of G.B. Mbr., Soc. of Authors. Publs: Death Pays a Dividend, 1945; Fascism Inside England, 1946; Danse Macabre, 1959; Man With Tin Trumpet, 1961; Split Scene, 1963; The Assassins, 1964; No Other Hunger, 1966; The Prizewinner, 1967; The Munich Involvement, 1968; Clancy, 1971; The Malta Conspiracy, 1972. Address: 44 St. Marks St., Gudja, Malta. 99.

MÜLLER, Carlos Otto. University Professor; Artist. Educ: Grad. in Philos.; Lawyer & Dr. in Law, Univ. of Buenos Aires, Argentina. Appts: Lectr., Fac. Econs., Univ. of Buenos Aires, 1951-; Hd. Dept. of Humanities, ibid; currently, Prof., Nat. Univ. of Technol.; Prof., Univ. of Mar del Plata; Dir., Legal Affairs, Min. For. Trade, 1952-55; Mbr., Guitar Trio Tarrega. Mbrships: sev. Fine Arts Instns. inclng. Impulso & Asociación Estimulo de Bellas Artes. Publs: Author of var. works in fields of law & philos. Solo Exhibs. & Collective Shows; exhibd. in Museums of Fine art of Boca, Santa Fe, Posadas, Bahía Blanca. Hons: Drawing Prize, Posadas Art Exhib., 1948; Hon. mention, Art Exhib. of Santa Fe, 1950. Address: Juncal 2210, Buenos Aires, Argentina. 136.

MÜLLER, (Caspar) Detlef (Gustav), b. 19 July 1927. University Professor. Educ: Friedrich-Wilhelms Univ., Berlin, Germany, 1945-48; Ruprecht-Carls Univ., Heidelberg, 1949-54; Dr. Sanctissimae Theologiae, Heidelberg, 1953; Inaugurated, ibid, 1966. Appts: Stipendiate, Deutsche Forschungsgemeinschaft, 1954-57; Rschr., Heidelberger Akad. der Wissenschaften, 1959-67; Prof., Univ. of Heidelberg, 1961-66; Lectr., ibid, 1967; Univ. Lectr., 1968; Extraordinary Prof., 1972. Mbrships: Theologisches Prüfungsamt der Evangelischen Landeskirche, Baden, 1971; Soc. for Am. Archaeol.; Deutsche Morgenländische Gesellschaft; Deutscher Hochseesportverband Hansa; Deutscher Marinebund. Publs. incl: Die

Homilie über die Hochzeit zu Kana und weitere Schriften des Patriarchen Benjamin I. von Alexandrien, 1968; Grundzüge des christlich-islamishcen Ägypten von der Ptolemäerzeit bis zur Gegenwart, 1969; Num. articles in jrnls. & dictionaries. Address: Bergheimer Str. 25, D-69 Heidelberg, German Fed. Repub. 43.

MÜLLER, Karl Friedrich Horst, b. 1 Apr. 1907. University Professor. Educ: Studied Physics & Maths.; Grad., Physics, 1933; Dr.phil. habil., 1941. Appts. incl: Sci. Asst., central lab., Siemens & Halske A.G., Berlin-Siemensstadt, 1935-39; Asst., Physics Inst., Leipzig, 1939; Lectr., ibid, 1941; Asst., rsch. inst. Teltow-Seehof, Berlin, 1941; Lectr., Phys. Chem. Inst., Marburg, 1946-; Dir., Inst. for Polymer, Marburg, 1960-. Mbrships: Deutsche Bunsengesellschaft; Chmn., comm. on Physics of Polymer, Deutsche Physikalische Gesellschaft, 1951-63; Gesellschaft Deutscher Chemiker; Kolloid-Gesellschaft; Deutsche Rheologen-Vereinigung; Faraday Soc.; Am. Chem. Soc.; Pres., Int. Comm. for Rheol., 1958-63. Publs. incl: Exec. Ed., Kolloid-Zeitschrift, 1943; About 200 sci. papers & articles. Recip., Wolfgang Ostwald Prize, Kolloid Soc., 1963. Address: Schulstr. 26, 355 Marbach-Marburg/L., German Fed. Repub.

MÜLLER, Rudolf O.B., b. 14 Jan. 1898. State Forest Inspector (Retired). Educ: Study of Forestry, Eberswalde, Germany, 1919-22; Qualified by exam. 1924; Ph.D., Univ. of Giessen, 1930. Appts: Forest Mgr., Pomerania, 1924-26; Chief, Bd. of Woods & Forests, Wetzlar/Lahn, 1926-31; Forest Mgmt. Off., Magdeburg, 1931-32; Forest Div. Govt. Dist. Köslin/Pommern, 1932-33; Forest Min., Berlin, 1934-38; Forest Attaché, German Embassy, Bucharest, Rumania, 1938-44; Chief, Poplar Inst., Brühl, Cologne, Germany, 1947-62. Mbr., Ecol. Soc. of Am. Publs. incl: Altstammsorten der Schwarzappelbastarde (w. E. Sauer), Offprint Holz-Zentralblatt, 1957-61; Contbng. Ed., Grundlagen der Forstwirtschaft, 1959; Urteilsgrundlagen für die trichocarpa-Pappel (w. E. Sauer), Offprint Forstpflanzen-Forstsamen, 1969-72; Contbr. to books & profl. jrnls. Hons: H.C. Burckardt Medal, Fac. of Forestry, Georg-August Univ., Göttingen, 1968. Address: Unterfeldstrasse 10, 8173 Bad Heilbrunn, German Federal Repub.

MÜLLER, Sten Eiden, b. 23 Oct. 1921. Publicist; Journalist; Author. Educ: H.S., Thorshavn, The Faroes, Denmark. Appts: Dimmalaetting newspaper, Thorshavn, 1938-45; Politiken newspaper, Copenhagen, 1946-47; Reporter & Asst. Ed., Dimmalaetting, Thorshavn, 1947-71; Pres., Faroese Press League, 1952-; Bd. Mbr., Pub. Ins. Co. of the Faroes; Bd. Mbr., Tourist Coun. of Denmark; Br. Mbr., Faroese-British Soce.; Free-lance writer & P.R. work 1971-. Mbr., Club of Thorshavn. Author, Fem Aar under Union Jack, 1945. Contbr., other publns., inclng. Danmark under Besaettelsen, 1946; Life in the Faroes, 1950. Address: P.O. Box 131, Thorshavn, the Faroes, Denmark. 43.

MÜLLER, Wolfgang (Karl) (pseudonym, W. Müller-Thalheim), b. 24 Apr. 1928. Neuropsychiatrist. Educ: Univs. Innsbruck & Paris; Med. Dr., 1952; Asst., Inst. of Balneol. Gastein, Austrian Acad. of Scis., 1949-52; studies in Neuropsychiatry, Univ. Clins. Innsbruck, Bern/Waldau, Salpetrière, Paris & Rosenhügel Wien, 1952-59. Appts. incl: Neuropsychiatrist Cons., Wels, Upper-Austria, 1959-; Chief, Neurological Dept., Pensionsversicherungsanstalt der Arbeiter, Linz,

1971-. Mbrships: Soc. Int. de Psychopathologie de l'Expression, Membre de Conseil, 1966-; Round Table Club, Wels, Pres., 1964-65; Rotary Club, Wels; German Soc. of Psychopathol. of Expression, Pres., 1972-. Publs: Die Erkrankung des Vincent Van Gogh, 1959; Alfred Kubin In Psychiatrischer Sicht, 1961; Die Bildende Kunst Und Der Begriff Des Abnormen, 1964; Co-ed., Psychopathologie Und Kunst, 1969; Dämonie Und Erotik, 1970. Hons: H. Prinzhorn Prize, 1972. Address: Gross-Str. 8, A-4600 Wels, Austria. 43.

MÜLLER-GANGLOFF, Erich, b. 12 Feb. 1907. Evangelical Academy Director. Educ: Dr.phil., Univs. of Berlin, Innsbruck, Marburg, 1931. Appts. as Libn., Author, Jrnlst., Publicist. Other positions: Co-fndr., Aktion Sühnezeichen, Aktion Weltfriedensdienst & Für Die Hungernden; Chmn., Verein Versöhnungdienste; Chmn., Comenius Clubs, Berlin; Hon. Chmn., ibid, 1970; Adam von Trotthaus student hostel, Wannsee; Christian Peace Conf., Prague; Dir., Evangelical Acad., Berlin. Publs. incl: Dreifaltigkeit des Bösen, 1953; Horizonte der Nachmoderne, 1962; Mit der Teilung Leben, 1965; Im Spannungsfeld, 1967; Vom gespaltenen zum doppelten Europa, 1970; Theologie für Nichttheologen (co-author), 1964. Address: Residenz Kirfürsteneck, Ansbacher Strasse 8 Berlin-Schöneberg, German Fed. Repub.

MÜLLER-MARKUS, Siegfried, b. 15 Sept. 1916. Scientist. Educ: Studied law, pol. sci. & philos., Univ. of Berlin; Dip., Hochschule für Politik, 1938; Grad., 1942. Appts: Russian Interpreter, German Armed Forces, 1940-45; Russian Prisoner of war, 1945-55; Lectr. in dialectical materialismus, Ostkolleg, Cologne, German Fed. Repub., 1956-64; Rockefeller Fndn. Fellow, 1959-60; German Fed. Repub. Schlr., 1960-64; Prof., E. European Inst., Univ. of Freiburg, Switzerland, & Dir., special phys. studies, ibid, 1962-66. Publs: Einstein & die sowjetphilosophie, Vol. I, 1966; Der Aufstand des Denkens. Sowjetunion zwischen Ideologie & Wirklichkeit, 1967; Protophysik. Entwurf einer Philosophie des Schöpferischen, pt. 1, 1970; Wo die Welt nochmal beginnt, 1969; Gott kehrt wieder, 1972; Wen Sterne rufen, 1960; Physik, Glaube, GOTT, 1970; Num. articles on physics & philos. in int. jrnls. Address: Brüelmattstr. 25, CH 4632 Trimbach-Olten, Switzerland.

MULLIKEN, Robert Sanderson, b. 7 June 1896. Distinguished Service Professor of Physics & Chemistry. Educ: B.S., MIT, 1917; Ph.D., Univ. of Chgo., Ill., 1921. Appts. incl: Prof. of Phys., Univ. of Chgo., 1931-61; Prof. of Chem., ibid, 1961; E. de Witt Burton Disting. Serv. Prof., ibid, 1956-61; Disting. Serv. Prof. of Phys. & Chem., ibid, 1961-; Disting. Rsch. Prof. of Chem. Phys., Fla. State Univ., 1964-. Mbrships. incl: Nat. Acad. of Scis.; Am. Acad. of Arts & Scis; Am. Chem. Soc.; Fellow, Am. Phys. Soc. & AAAS; Am. Philosophical Soc.; Royal Soc. of Gt. Britain. Publs. incl: Molecular Complexes: a Lecture & Reprint Volume (w. W.B. Person); contbr. to scientific jrnls. Hons. incl: T.W. Richards Gold Medal, Northeastern Sect., Am. Chem. Soc., 1960; Gilbert Newton Lewis Gold Medal Award, Cal. Sect., Am. Chem. Soc., 1960; Willard Gibbs Medal Award, Chgo. Sect., ibid, 1965; Nobel Prize in Chem., Stockholm, Sweden, 1966. Address: Dept. of Physics, Univ. of Chicago, 1100 E. 58th St., Chicago, IL 60637, U.S.A. 2, 8, 10, 12, 14, 15, 29, 34, 36, 50, 128.

MULLIKIN, Agnes Snyder, b. 11 Feb. 1906. Accountant. Educ: Var. Courses, Calif.

Ext. Schl.; Salinger's Schl. of Dress Design 1963. Personal Details: m. Alfred Mullikin 1954; 1 s. by previous marriage. Appts: Accountant, U.S. Army, 1941-59; Accountant, Fed. Water Pollution Control Administration, 1964-73. Mbrships: Pacific Musical Soc.; Peninsula Symphony; De Young Museum; Legion of Honor; Leonardo da Vinci Soc. Address: 1328 Skyview Drive, Burlingame, CA 94010, U.S.A. 5, 9, 71, 132.

MULLINS, Lance P., b. 8 Aug. 1921. Salesman; Congressman. Educ: Yale Univ., U.S.A., 1945; Northeastern Univ., 1946; Bridgeport Univ., Conn., 1946-48. Appts: V.P., Conn. State Salesmen & Purchasing Assn.; Pres., Carbio-Engrng. Assn., U.F. Conn. Mbrships: Past Nat. Pres., 36th Div., VA; Disabled Am. Veterans; Life, Kts. Columbus. 4 original Bills passed through Congress for Veterans' Benefits. Hons: Serv. Awards, 1941-45; Good Conduct Medal; Combat I Infantry Badge; Purple Heart w. 3 Clusters; Bronze Star w. 3 Clusters; Silver Star w. 1 Cluster; Bronze Arrow Head-Original Darby Ranger; Am. Defense Medal; E.A.M.E. Campaign Medal w. 5 Battle Stars; Pre-Pearl Harbor Medal; Expert (Sub-Machine Gun & All Hand Weapons); Demolition Expert; Judo Expert, Special Espionage Schl.; Civilian Award: Salesman of Yr., Briggs Weaver Inc., Dallas, Tex., 1967. Address: 2727 San Medina, Dallas, TX 75228, U.S.A. 125.

MULVIHILL, James E., b. 24 Sept. 1940. Doctor of Dental Medicine. Educ: A.B., Coll. of the Holy Cross, Worcester, Mass., 1962; D.M.D., Harvard Schl. of Dental Med., 1966; Rsch. Fellow, Periodontol., ibid, 1966-68; Special Student, Harvard Univ. Grad. Schl. of Educ., 1967-68; Rsch. Fellow, Periodontol. & Oral Med., Harvard Schl. of Dental Med., 1968-70; Cert., Periodontol. & Oral Med., ibid, 1970. Appts. incl: Asst. to Dean, Student Affairs, Harvard Schl. of Dental Med., 1968-70 & Asst. Dean, 1970-71; Instr., Periodontol., ibid, 1970-71 & Lectr., 1971; Coord., Harvard-VA Continuing Educ. Prog. for New England, Harvard School of Dental Med., 1970-71; Dean, L.I. Jewish-Hillside Med. Ctr./Queens Hosp. Ctr., S.U.N.Y., Stony Brook, 1971; Asst. Prof., Periodontol., Schl. of Dental Med., ibid, 1971 & Assoc. Prof., Dental Med., 1972; Staff Periodontist, L.I. Jewish-Hillside Med. Ctr., 1972. Mbr. & V.P., Gen. Alumni Assn., Coll. of the Holy Cross, 1971-73. Publs. incl: Many abstracts and articles in jrnls.; Num. lectures and papers presented to var. profl. grps. Hons. incl: Alpha Sigma Nu, 1961; Harvard Odontological Soc. Rsch. Award, 1966; Omicron Kappa Upsilon, 1966; Fellow, AAAS, 1969. Address: L.I. Jewish-Hillside Med. Ctr., New Hyde Park, NY 11040, U.S.A. 6, 46.

MUMFORD, Lawrence Quincy, b. 11 Dec. 1903. Librarian of Congress. Educ: A.B., 1925, M.A., 1928, Duke Univ.; B.S., Columbia Univ., 1929. Appts: Hd., Circulation Dept., Duke Univ. Lib.; Asst., Clumbia Univ. Lib.; Ref. Asst., N.Y. Pub. Lib., 1929; Gen. Asst. i/c Dirs. Off., ibid, 1932-35; Exec. Asst., Coord., Gen. Servs. Div., ibid, 1943-45; On leave of absence, organizer of Processing Dept., Lib. of Congress & Dir, 1 yr.; Asst. Dir., Cleveland Pub. Lib., 1945, Dir., 1950; Libn. of Cong., 1954-. Num. mbrships. incl: Past Pres., Ohio Lib. Assn.; Past Pres., ALA; Bd. of Dirs., Past Pres. Manuscript Soc.; Chmn., Fed. Lib. Comm.; Bd. of Advsrs. Dumbarton Oaks Rsch. Lib. & Collects.; Sponsors Comm., Papers of Woodrow Wilson; Bd. of Advsrs., U.S. Nat. Book Comm.; Nat. Advsry. Comm., Am. Antiquarian Soc.; Brit. Mus. Soc. Hons: Litt.D.—Bethany Coll., Rutgers Univ., Duke Univ., Belmont Abbey Coll.; LL.D.—Union Coll., Bucknell Univ., Univ.

of Notre Dame, Univ. of Pitts., Univ. of Mich.; H.H.D., King's Coll. Address: 3721 49th St., N.W., Washington, DC 20016, U.S.A.

MUMMA, Albert Girard, Jr., b. 2 July 1928. Architect. Educ: B.S., Arch., Univ. of Va., 1951. Appts: Designer, McLeod & Ferrara, Archts., Wash. D.C., 1951-56; Assoc., Deigert & Yerkes, Archts., Wash. D.C., 1956-62; Prin., Mumma & Assocs., Wash. D.C., 1962-. Mbrships: Am. Inst. of Archts.; Wash. D.C. Sect. ibid. Bldgs. incl: Nat. Arboretum H.Q. Bldg., Wash. Bd. of Trade Design Award, 1967. Proj., Silver Spring, Md.; Inverness, 350 Town Houses & Recreation Area, Potomac, Md.; Housing & Recreation areas in Fairfax, Va.; Houses, Penn State, Pa.; Post Off. & Fed. Bldg., Elkins, W. Va.; Enclosed Pools, Wash. D.C.; Pvte. residences, Wash. D.C., Md., Va.; Dept. of Comm. Trade Fairs, Spain, Finland, Japan & El Salvador. Hons: Medal, Am. Inst. of Archts., 1951; Wash. Bd. of Trade Design Award, 1967. Address: 1071 Wisconsin Ave. N.W., Washington, DC 20007, U.S.A. 7.

MUMMENDEY, Richard, b. 14 July 1900. Librarian. Educ: Univ. of Bonn & Munich; Insts. of Technol., Aachen & Hanover; Dr.-Ingenieur, 1925. Appts: Prussian State Lib., Berlin; Lib. Inst. of Technol., Aachen; Dpty. Dir. (retired), Univ. Lib., Bonn. Publs. incl: Language & Literature of the Anglo-Saxon Nations as Presented in German Doctoral Dissertations 1885-1950, 1954; Belles Lettres of the United States of America in German Translations, 1961. Ed., Bonner Beiträge zur Bibliotheks und Bücherkunde, 1-25, 1954-74. Collaborator & contbr., var. publs. Translations from Engl., var. authors inclng. Defoe, Swift, Poe, John Buchan, Nathaniel Hawthorne, Herman Melville. Address: Poppalsdorfer Alice 44, 53 Bonn 1, German Federal Republic. 43, 92.

MUNA, Solomon Tandeng, b. 1912. Politician. Educ: Tchrs. Higher Elementary Cert., 1942; Tchrs. Sr. Cert., 1946; Profl. Tchrs. Dip., Inst. of Educ., London, 1951. Appts: Mbr., Eastern Nigeria House of Assembly, 1951; Min. of Works, 1951-53; Southern Cameroons Min. of Works, 1954-57; Min. of Commerce & Ind. & Min. of Finance, 1958-61; Min. of Transport, Mines, Posts & Telecommunications, Cameroon Fed. Govt., 1961-67; Prime Min., W. Cameroon, 1968-70; V.P. of Fed. Repub., 1970; Min. of State, 1972; elected Pres., 1st Nat. Assembly, United Repub. of Cameron, 1973. Mbrships: Chief Scout of Cameroon, 1970-; Nat. Pol. Bur., Cameroon Nat. Union Party. Hons. incl: Off., Order of Valour, Cameroon; Cmdr., ibid; Off. & Grand Off., Legion of Honour, France; Coronation Medal, U.K.; Grand Cordon, Order of the Star of Africa, Liberia; num. others. Address: National Assembly, Yaounde, United Repub. of Cameroon.

MUNDAL, Maria (Mrs.), b. 10 Nov. 1893. Tapestry Weaver. Educ: summer colls., Norway; Sunni Mundal's Schl. of Weaving, Oslo, Norway, 1919-1920; Britta Dahle's Schl., Sognefjord; studied w. Kristi Meland, 1925-26 & Bertha Frey; Universal Schl. of Handicraft, N.Y.C. Appts: Has given talks on Norwegian customs, costumes & crafts at Columbia Tchrs. Coll., The Dalton Schl., The Am. Folkart Ctr., etc.; Taught 2 seasons at the Chautauqua Inst., N.Y. & 2 yrs. at Countess Zichy Acad. of Art, N.Y.C.; Has given talks on weaving at Meml. Mus., Rochester, N.Y.; twice at Pittsburgh, Pa. & 3 times at Chatauqua—once at the Hall of Philos. One man shows: Norheim Art Gall., Brooklyn, N.Y.; Contessa Studio, Lebanon, Conn.; Bertha L. Knudtsen's Studio, Parkton,

Md. Group Shows incl: Int. Exhib. of Handwork, N.Y.C., 1927-; Cooper Union Mus., N.Y.C.; Int. Textile Exhib., Greensboro, N.C., 1950-52, & many others. Mbrships: Hon., Am. Assn. Popular Arts; N.Y. Guild of Weavers; Norwegian Art & Craft Club; Potomac Craftsmen; Nat. Pen Women; Northern Va. Art Assn.; Hon., Folkart Ctr. Recip. hons. & awards inclng: Blue Ribbon Award, Int. Exhib. of Handwork, N.Y.C., 1961 for 'Antarctic Delegation'. Address: 1105 S. Washington St., Alexandria, VA 22314, U.S.A.

MUNDEBO, (Kurt Allan) Ingemar, b. 15 Oct. 1930. Educator; Politician. Educ: Socionom, 1957; Fil. Lic. (Pol. Sci.), 1964. Appts: Amanuens, Nat. & Communal Admin., 1950-56; Tchr., Folk H.S., 1956-60; Lector, Schl. of Soc. Studies, Stockholm Sweden, 1960-64; Hd. of Dept., Stockholm Univ., 1964-; Mbr. of Parliament, 1965-; Mbr., Nordic Coun., 1969-. Mbrships: Chmn., Working Comm., Swedish Liberal Party; Vice-Chmn., Study Soc. Vuxembolan. Publs: Ny Kris i Befolkningsfrågan?, 1962; Social Administration, 1963; Socialkunskap, 1968; Forvalkinskunskap, 1970. Recip: Kt. of the Nordstjårneorden. Address: Sveriges Riksdag, 100 12 Stockholm 46, Sweden. 43, 134.

MUNFORD, William Arthur, b. 27 Apr. 1911. Librarian. Educ: B.Sc., 1932, Ph.D., 1963, Univ. of London. Appts: Municipal lib. posts, Gtr. London, 1927-34; Borough Libn., Dover, 1934-45; City Libn., Cambridge, 1945-53; Dir.-Gen., Nat. Lib. for Blind, 1954-. Mbrships: Fellow, Past Sec., Lib. Assn.; Chmn., Lib. Comm., Nat. Liberal Club. Publs: 3000 Books for a Public Library, 1939; Penny Rate: Aspects of British Public Library History, 1951; William Ewart, M.P.: Portrait of a Radical, 1960; Edward Edwards: Portrait of a Librarian, 1963; Louis Stanley Jast: A Biographical Sketch, 1966; James Duff Brown: Portrait of a Library Pioneer, 1968. Hons: M.B.E., 1946. Address: Nat. Lib. for the Blind, 35 Great Smith St., London SW1P 3BU, U.K. 3.

MUNIR, Mehmed Nedjati, b. 7 Dec. 1923. Supreme Court Judge. Educ: B.A. (Hons.), St. John's Coll., Cambirdge Univ., U.K., 1946; M.A., ibid; called to Bar, Hon. Soc. Gray's Inn, 1946. Appts: Cyprus Volunteer Force, WWII; Crown Counsel, Tanganyika, 1948-53; Solicitor-Gen., Cyprus, 1953-60; Acting Atty.-Gen., Cyprus, intermittently 1953-60; Legal Advsr., Turkish Cypriot Delegation to Jt. Constitutional Commn. on Cyprus, 1959-60; Turkish Judge of Supreme Constitutional Ct. of Cyprus, 1960-. Mbrships. incl: UN Assn. of Cyprus; Pres., ibid, 1973; Fellow, Royal Commonwealth Soc., London; World Peace through Rule of Law Ctr., Geneva; World Assn. of Judges, Geneva; League of Friends Soc., Nicosia; Rotary Club of Nicosia; V.P., ibid, 1962-63. Hons: O.B.E., 1957; Q.C. for Cyprus, 1957. Address: The Supreme Court, Nicosia, Cyprus.

MUÑIZ, Carlos Manuel, b. 2 Feb. 1922. Diplomat; Lawyer; Professor. Educ: Dr., Law & Soc. Scis., Univ. Nacional de Buenos Aires, Argentina. Appts: Under Sec., Interior & Justice-Under Sec., Interior, Argentina, 1955-56; Ambassador to Bolivia, 1956-59, to Brazil, 1959-62; Min. For. Affairs & Worship, 1962-63; Cand. for Sec.-Gen. of Org. Am. States, 1967; Ambassador to U.S.A., 1971-73; Prof., Pub. Int. Law, Univ. La Plata; Prof., Constitutional Law, Univ. Buenos Aires. Mbrships: Pres., Peruvian-Argentinian Cultural Inst.; Argentina Assn. Pol. Sci.; Soc. Int. Criminol.; Soc. Legislation Comm.; Inter-Am. Bar Assn.; Soc. de Numismatica y Antiguedades de Buenos Aires, etc.; Metropol. Club, Wash. D.C. Circulo de Armas, Buenos Aires; Jockey Club, ibid; Club Frances, ibid, etc. Publs: Foreign Policy in the Nuclear Age, 1969; National Bases for an international Policy, 1969; International Law and Domestic Law, Theories, 1970; Desde esta Tierra, Poems, 1956; Esa Que Llaman Vida, Poems, 1958, etc. Recip. sev. for. hons. Address: Parera 117, Buenos Aires, Argentina. 1, 131.

MUNK, Elie, b. 15 Sept. 1900. Rabbi. Educ: Hildesheimer Rabbinical Sem., Berlin, Germany; Ph.D., Univ. of Marbourg, 1925; Rabbinical Dip., 1926. Appts: Rabbi, Ansbach, Bavaria, 1926-37; Rabbi, Israeli Community of Strict Observants, Paris, France, 1937-; Pres., Yabné Schl.; Pres., Coun. representing traditional Judaism; Pres., Rabbi Yehiel Grp., Paris; Pres., European Union of Orthodox Israeli Communities, 1945-. Publs: Vers l'Harmonie; Rachel, ou le devoir de la femme juive; Rachi commentaire de la Thora; La Voix de la Thora, La Genèse, l'Exode, Le Lévitque, etc.; Le Monde des Prières; La Justice Sociale en Israël. Address: 18 Rue Notre Dame de Lorette, 75009 Paris, France.

MUÑOZ-DONES, Gerardo, b. 2 Feb. 1920. Attorney & Counsellor at Law; Notary Public. Educ: B.A. Educ., Univ. of Puerto Rico, 1943; B.A. Dramatics, Pasadena Playhouse, Calif., U.S.A., 1949; Grad., Coll. of Law, P.R. Univ., 1955. Appts. incl: Admitted to prac., P.R. Supreme Ct., U.S. Dist. Ct. for P.R., Boston Ct. of Appeals & U.S. Customs Ct., 1955; Trial Lawyer & Sub-Dir., Legal Off., Govt. of Capital of P.R., 1956-63; Pvte. Prac. Law, 1963-73; Mbr., Commn. of Public Acts, P.R. Bar Assn. 1963-71; Licensed Authorised Chemist, Bd. of Chemists, P.R., 1965; Dir., Legal Div., Dept. of Educ., San Juan, 1973-; Licensed Real Estate Broker, 1973. Mbrships. incl: Am. Trial Lawyers Assn.; Sec., P.R. Chapt., ibid, 1972; P.R. Tchrs. Assn.; Coll. of Chemists, P.R.; Coll. of Lawyers, P.R.; Am. Bar Assn. Publs: anthols. of Int. Song; articles on legal & gen. subjects. Composer, Musical arrangement for solo guitar, baritone voice & guitar. Hons. incl: Bronze Plate of Merit, Disting. Citizen of Yr., San Lorenzo, P.R., 1973. Address: 219 Fordham-Oxford, University Gdns., Rio Piedras, PR 00927, 136.

MUÑOZ PÉREZ-VIZCAINO, Jesús, S.J., b. 13 Feb. 1908. Priest; University Professor. Educ: Studied Philos. & Theol. in S.J. Univs.; Educl. pracs. in S.J. High Schls.; Dr. of Philos.; Licentiate in Theol. Appts: Admitted to S.J., 1924; Extraordinary Prof., Gen. & Philosophical Psychol., Pontifical Univ. Comillas, Spain, 1941-49; Prof., ibid, 1949-72; Dean, Fac. of Philos., 1961-64; Dean, Fac. of Philos. & Humanities, Cath. Univ. of Cuyo, Argentina, 1972-; Titular Prof., ibid; Participant in num. nat. & int. assemblies & congresses of studies; Priestly activities, preaching, conscience counseling, 1937-. Mbrships. incl: Bd. of Dirs., Philos. inquiry, Superior Coun. of Sci. Rsch., Madrid, Spain; Bd. of Fndrs., Int. Cath. Assn. for Study of Med. Psychol., Fribourg, Switzerland; Bd. of Dirs., Pensamiento, Madrid, 1958-66; Pres., ibid, 1959-62; Int. Coun. of Psychologists, U.S.A. Author of publs. in field. Address: Universidad Catolica, Av. J.I. de la Roza 1516 Oeste, (Opto. Rivadavia), San Juan, Argentina. 43, 102.

MUNRO, Raymond Alan, b. 14 July 1921. Aviator. Educ: LL.B., Ill. Univ.; M.A., Ph.D., Sussex Coll. Appts: Num. Sr. daily newspaper posts, to Ed.-in-Chief, Chatham Daily News, Canada, 1958; Profl. Pilot, 1937-; Serv. RCAF, European theatre, 1940-42; Pres., Munro Aviation to 1971; Mng. Dir., Canada's Aviation Hall of Fame, Calgary, Alta., 1973-; Col., U.S. Nat. Guard. Mbrships: Assoc. Fellow, Canadian Aeronautics & Space Inst.; Companion, Royal Aeronautical Soc.; Canadian Inst. Mining & Metallurgy; AIAA; Am. Inst. Mining Engrs.; Am. Helicopter Soc. Holder, World Record for most northerly parachute descent (on N. Pole), 33 FAI World Records for aerostation, Successful Balloon voyage across Irish Sea. Recip: num. Nat. Records; 30 Nat. & Int. Awards for Newspaper work; num. Hon. Citizenships, Honours, Awards & Decorations from Govts., Soc. & other Grps. for achievements in aviation. Address: 3424 Lane Cres., S.W., Calgary, Alta., Canada. 88.

MUNTHE, Gerhard, b. 28 Apr. 1919. Library Director. Educ: Cand. philol., Univ. of Oslo, Norway. Appts: Deputy Libn., Univ. Lib., Bergen, Norway, 1948-64; Lib. Dir., The Royal Norwegian Soc. for Sci. & Letters, Trondheim, Norway, 1964-70; Lib. Dir., The Royal Univ. Lib., Oslo, 1970-. Mbr., Norwegian Lib. Assn., Pres., ibid, 1965-69. Publs: Karlstad 1905, 1954; Handbok over norsk bibliografi, 1965. Address: Universitetsbiblioteket, Drammensveien 42, Oslo 2, Norway.

MURAKAMI, Ken, b. 29 Apr. 1934. Researcher in Foreign Language Education. Educ: B.A., Osaka Coll. of Econs., 1958; M.A., UCLA, Schl. of Educ., 1960; Rsch. in TESL at UCLS, 1966-67. Appts: Dir., Osaka YMCA Coll. of Bus. & Langs., 1960-66; Dir., Osaka YMCA Engl. Educ. Rsch. I, 1968-. Mbrships: Phi Delta Kappa; Japanese Assn. Coll. Engl. Tchrs. Publs. incl: Seijin no Tame no Eikaiwa Kunren (Dialogs & Pattern Drills for Engl. Conversation), Vol.1, 1968, Vol.2, 1969, Vol.3, 1970, Vol.4, 1971; Jissen Eigo Kyohon (Engl. Structure Drill for Speakers of Japanese), 1969; Konna Hyogen (Such Expressions), 1971; New Experience in English, 1973; Language Aptitude Test for Speakers or Japanese, 1974; many contbns. to educl. & profl. jrnls. Recip., Serv. Award, Westside YMCA, Los Angeles, 1968. Address: Osaka YMCA Engl. Educ. Rsch. Inst., 12 Tosabori, 2-chome, Nishi-ku, Osaka, Japan.

MURAMATSU, Tsuneo, b. 12 Apr. 1900. Psychiatrist; Lecturer. Educ: M.D., Tokyo Nat. Univ. Schl. of Med., 1925; D.Med. Scis., ibid, 1933; Rockefeller Rsch. Fellowship, Harvard Univ., Boston, U.S.A. & Hirnforschungsinstitut, München, 1933-35. Appts: Prof., Psych., Tokyo (pvte.) Med. Coll., 1936-49; & Nagoya Nat. Univ. Schl. of Med., 1950-64; Dean, ibid, 1960-62; Supt., Konodai Nat. Hosp., Ichikawa, Chiba-ken, 1948-50; Dir., Nat. Inst. of Mental Hlth., ibid, 1964-71; Ret., 1971. Mbrships: WHO Expert Advsry. Panel on Mental Hlth., 1958-70; Corres. Fellow, Am. Psych. Assn., 1951-; Pres., Japan Soc. Psych. & Neurol., 1953-54 & Nat. Liaison Coun. for Mental Hlth., 1964-73; Ctrl. Couns., for Correction, Min. of Justice, 1948-, & for Mental Hlth., Min. of Hlth. & Welfare, 1951-71. Publs: Mental Hygiene, 1930; The Japanese—An. Interdisciplinary Research, 1962; Neurosis - Its Essential Nature & Clinical Research, 1972; chapts. in books. Recip. 2nd Order of Merit w. Rising Sun-Double Light Prize for Prolf. contbns., 1971. Address: 18-18 Mejirodai 1-chome, Bunkyo-ku, Tokyo 112, Japan.

MURARO, Michelangelo, b. 8 Aug. 1913. University Professor. Educ: Grad., Univ. of Padua; Studies in Brussels & Priceton. Appts: Prof. of Hist. of Art, Univs. of Padua & Trieste; Off. of Monument Supervision, Venice & Florence; Dir. of Giogio Franchetti Gall. Mbrships: Inst. of Advanced Studies, Princeton;

Olympic Acad., Vicenza; Acad. of Sci., Lit. & Art, Udine; Venetian Athenaeum, Venice. Works: Tipi e architetture delle ville venete, Treviso, 1952; Treasures of Venice, Geneva, 1963; Carpaccio, Florence, 1966; Paolo di Venezia, Milan, 1969. Contbr. to various jrnls., incl. The Burlington Magazine; The Art Bulletin; Gazette des Beaux-Arts; Bollettino dell'Istituto di Studi Bizanti e Post-Bizantini; Ateneo Veneto. Address: Salute 350, Venice, Italy.

MURAT, Dimitri, b. 5 Dec. 1908. Actor; Theatre Director; Stage Manager. Educ: Reinhardt Schule, Berlin, 1928-30; Dipl. Philos., Univ. of Athens, Greece. Appts. incl: Leading Actor, Nat. Theatre of Greece, 1948-50; Dir. & Stage Mgr., Kotopouli Theatre, Athens, 1950-57; formed pvte. Theatre Co., Co. Dimitri Murat, 1957 (since 1967, Co. Dimitri Murat & Voula Zoumboulaki), which has staged many notable performances in which he has played major roles. Mbrships: former Pres., Int. Theatre Inst., Greece; Panhellenic Union of Theatre Dirs. Publs: Miscellanea, 1964; Turning The Pages Of Ancient Texts, 1970; sev. articles in lit. & sci. mags. Hons: Cmdr., Order of Phoenix, Greece; Commendatore dell'Ordine all Merito della Rep. Italy; Goldren Cross of St. Marc; Chevalier de l'Ordre des Arts & des Lettres; Medaglia Italiana al Merito Culturale; 1st Prize, Int. Festival of Lisbon (for performance of Tonight We Improvise). Address: Dinokratous 28, Athens (139), Greece. 43.

MURDOCK, Eugene Converse, b. 30 Apr. 1921. Professor of History. Educ: B.A., Wooster (Ohio) Coll., 1943; M.A., Columbia Univ., 1948, Ph.D., 1951. Appts: Prof. of Hist., Rio Grande (Ohio) Coll., 1952-56; Asst. Prof.-Prof. & Chmn., Dept. of Hist., Marietta (Ohio) Coll., 1956-. Mbrships: Am. Hist. Assn.; Org. of Am. Histns.; Southern Hist. Assn.; Ohio Acad. of Hist. (Exec. Coun., 1970-73); Soc. for Am. Baseball Rsch.; N. Am. Soc. for Sport Hist. (Ed. Bd., 1973-). Publs: Ohio's Bounty System in the Civil War, 1963; Patriotism Limited, 1862-65, 1967; One Million Men; articles & reviews. Address: Dept. of Hist., Marietta Coll., Marietta, OH 45750, U.S.A. 13, 30.

MURESAN, Mircea, b. 11 Nov. 1930. Film Director. Educ: Grad., I.L. Caragiale Inst. of Dramatic & Cinematographic Art, Bucharest, 1955. Appts: Actor, Sibiu Municipal Theatre, 1948-50; Lectr. in film direction, 1968-; Writer for Cinema, mag.; Screenplay Writer. Mbr. & V.P., Romanian Assn. of Film Makers. Films incl: Autumn; Knock Out; The Siege; The Barrier; You're Guilty Too; The Uprising (Winter in Flame); The Axe (Baltagul); A Six Years Long Night, 1970; Blue Gates of the City, 1973. Hons: Rascoala Prize, Cannes Film Festival, France, 1966; Rascoala Prize, Mamais Film Festival, 1966; Venice Film Festival Award, Italy, 1969. Address: Romanian Association of Film Makers, Bd. Gh. Gheorghiu-Dej 65, Bucharest, Romania.

MURGATROYD, Keith. Graphic Design Consultant. Appts. incl: Gov. of Portsmouth & Bolton Colls. of Art, U.K.; Design Studio Mgr., Bennett Williams Ltd., 1950 & W. Hopwood & Co. Ltd., 1953; Asst. Lectr., Manchester Coll. of Art, 1960, Full Lectr., 1961, Sr. Lectr., 1964; Prin. Lectr., i/c of Post Grad. Graphic Studies, Polytechnic, Manchester, 1970; Vis. Full Prof., San Fernando State College, U.S.A., 1971; Dir., Royle-Murgatroyd Design Assocs. Ltd., U.K., 1971-. Mbrships. incl: Fellow, British Soc. of Typographic Designers & Pres., 1969-73; Fellow, Soc. of Indl. Artists & Designers; Inst. of Packaging; Wynkyn De

Worde Soc.; Bd. Mbr., Mgmt. of the Ikon Art Gall.; Graphic Advsry. Panel to the Nat. Coun. for Dips. in Art & Design. Cons. Publs. incl: Modern Graphics. Typographer to: Westminster Abbey; W.R. Royle & Son Ltd.; The Royal Northern Coll. of Music; Salisbury & Wells Theological Coll. Designer to many natl. & int. cos. Hons. incl: 56 awards for Stationery Design, British Stationery Coun., 1967-71. Address: 48 Ridge Cres., Marple, Cheshire, U.K.

MURIO, Jay, Concert & Opera Singer. Educ: B.A., Ark. Coll.; M.A., Univ. of Chgo.; M.M., Am. Conservatory. Appts: Writer, feature stories & edits., 1933-; Soprano, Merrie England, Century of Progress Exposition, Chgo., 1934; Tex. Centennial, 1936; Concerts, Mexico, 1937-40 & throughout U.S.A., 1937-; w. Nat. Opera of Mexico; w. Chgo. Civic Opera. Mbrships: Bd. Dirs., Ill. Opera Guild; Pres., Chgo. Chapt., Nat. Soc. Arts & Letters; Nat. Bd. of Arts & Letters; Delta Omicron. Contbr. to trade jrnls. Recorded Indian & folk music sung by natives. Owner, recreational park, Wis. Address: P.O. Box 244, Oak Park, IL 60303, U.S.A. 4, 5, 8, 132.

MURNAGHAN, Gerald Francis, b. 20 Sept. 1926. Professor of Surgery. Educ: Ch.M., M.D., F.R.C.S., U.K.; Appts. incl: Scottish Hosps. Endowment Rsch. Trust Fellowship in Urol., Univ. of Edinburgh, U.K., 1958-61; Assoc. Prof.-Prof. Surg., Univ. of N.S.W. Sydney, Australia, 1961-; Staff Urologist-Hd. Univ. Dept. of Surg., Prince Henry & Prince of Wales Hosps., ibid, 1961-; Dir. of Surg. & Hon. Urological Surg., Prince Henry & Prince of Wales & Eastern Suburbs Hosps., 1969-; Hon. Cons. Urologist, Royal Hosp. for Women, Paddington, N.S.W., 1969-. Mbrships. incl: Exec. Comm. & Ed., Urological Soc. of Australasia; British Assn. Urological Surgs.; Int. Soc. of Urol.; Surgical Rsch. Soc. Contbr. to med. jrnls. & books. Hons. incl: Lawson Gifford Prize in Obstetrics & Gyn., 1948; Hunterian Prof., Royal Coll. of Surgs., U.K., 1958. Address: 19 Mosman St., Mosman, N.S.W., Australia 2088. 23.

MURPHEY, Milledge, b. 15 Dec. 1912. Entomologist; Professor of Entomology. Educ: B.S.A., Univ. of Fla., Gainesville, 1935; Ph.D., Okla. State Univ., Stillwater, 1953. Appts: Dist. Supvsr., USDA, Gainesville, Fla., 1935-36, Asst. State Supvsr., 1936-37, State Supvsr., Monticello, Fla., 1946-47; Entomologist & Asst. State Entomologist, Ga. Dept. of Entomol., Atlanta, 1937-42; Off., U.S. Army, European Theater of Ops., 1942-46; Supvsr. of Plantation, Sumner, Miss., 1946-47; Asst. Prof.-Prof. of Entomol., Univ. of Fla., Gainesville, 1947-. Mbrships. incl: Ga. Entomol. Soc.; Past Pres., ibid; Fla. State Beekeepers' Assn.; var. fraternities. Scientific publs. & educl. films, beekeeping, vegetable insects, etc. Recip., Prof. of Yr. Award, 1966. Address: 3093 McCarty Hall, Univ. of Florida, Gainesville, FL 32611, U.S.A.

MURPHREE, Charles Quincy, b. 23 July 1931. High School Principal. Educ: B.A., Univ. of Tex., El Paso, 1959; M.Ed., ibid, 1962. Appts: Tchr.; Asst. Prin., Elem. Schl.; Prin. of Intermediate Schl.; Prin. of H.S. Mbrships: NEA; Treas., El Paso Ed. Assn.; Tex. State Tchrs. Assn.; Legislative & Transportation Chmn., 1st Dist., & Hon. Life Mbr., PTA; Publs. Chmn., El Paso Tchrs. Assn.; Kappa Delta Pi; Phi Delta Kappa. Address: 222 Shadow Mt. Dr. 49, El Paso, TX 79912, U.S.A. 125.

MURPHY, A. Marie. Teacher. Educ: B.S., Buffalo State Univ. Coll., N.Y., U.S.A.; Ed.M., State Univ. at Buffalo; Ed.D., ibid. Appts. incl:

Tchr., Sr. H.S., Lockport, N.Y.; Tchr., N. Pk. Jr. H.S.; John E. Pound Elem. Schl.; Lockport Evening Schl.; Niagara Univ. Mbrships. incl: Deleg., N.Y. State House of Delegs., 1954-63; Pres., Lockport City Tchrs. Assn., 1949-50, past V.P., Sec., & Exec. Comm.; Chmn., Tchr. Educ. & Profl. Standards Comm., Lockport Educ. Assn., 1970-71; Past Pres., Niagara Co. Coun. for Soc. Studies; Chmn., Resolutions Comm., N.Y. State Coun. for Soc. Studies, 1966-70; Nat. Coun. of Soc. Studies; N.Y. State Tchrs. Assn.; NEA; Provisional League of Women Voters; Pres., Lockport Coll. Women's Club; Niagara Co. Histl. Soc.; Buffalo Coun. on World Affairs; Pi-State Pres., & Chmn., sev. comms., Delta Kappa Gamma, Pres., Alpha Theta Chapt.; Pi Lambda Theta. Hons. incl: Pi-State Achievement Award, 1968; N.Y. State Tchr. of the Yr. Merit Award, 1969; Nat. Tchr. of the Yr., 1970; Disting. Alumnus Buffalo State, 1970. Address: 97 Price St., Lockport, NY 14094, U.S.A. 130.

MURPHY, Lionel Keith, b. 1922. Barrister; Lawyer. Educ.: B.Sc., LL.B., Sydney Univ., Australia; admitted N.S.W. Bar, 1947, Vic. Bar, 1958. Appts: Q.C., N.S.W., 1960, Vic., 1961; Labour Senator for N.S.W., 1962-; Opposition Ldr., 1967-; Mbr. Australian Delegation to U.N. Conf. on Human Rights, Teheran, 1968. Mbrships: Exec. Int. Commn. of Jurists Australian Sect., 1963-; Coun., Australian Nat. Univ., Canberra. Address: Parliament House, Canberra, A.C.T., Australia 2600. 23, 128.

MURRAY, Anne, b. 20 June 1945. Singer & Entertainer. Educ: Bachelor of Phys. Educ., Univ. of N.B., Fredericton, Canada, 1966. Appts: Tchr. of Hlth. & Phys. Educ., P.E.I., 1966-67; Free-lance Singer & Entertainer, 1967-. Num. TV appearances incl: Glen Campbell Show, C.B.S., U.S.A.; BBC, U.K.; David Frost Show; Dean Martin Show; Anne Murray Specials, Swedish TV. Concert performances incl: Royal Festival Hall, London, U.K.; Palladium, London; Int. Music Ind. Conven., Cannes, France. Num. recordings incl. 7 albums. Famous songs incl: Snowbird; Danny's Song; I'll Be Your Baby Tonight; I'll Never Fall In Love Again. Num. hons. incl: Juno Award for best female vocalist, RPM Mag., Canada, 1970, 1971 & 1972; U.S. Gold Record, for Snowbird, Record Ind. Assn. of Am., 1970; Moffatt Award, for best produced, female, Canada, 1972; Britain's Best Female Artist, British Country Music Assn., 1972; Actra Award for best TV Variety performer, Assn. of Canadian TV & Radio Artists, 1973. Address: P.O. Box 71, Station L, Toronto M6E 4Y4, Ont., Canada.

MURRAY, (Donald Walter) Gordon, b. 29 May 1894. Surgeon. Educ: M.B., Univ. of Toronto, Canada, 1921; Postgrad. studies, London, U.K., N.Y.C., U.S.A., Toronto, 1922-28; F.R.C.S. U.K., 1926; F.R.C.S. Canada, 1931. Appts. incl: Serv., Canadian Field Artillery, WWI; Hunterian Prof., Royal Coll. Surgs., U.K., 1939; Assoc. Prof. Surg., retired, Univ. of Toronto; Grad. Lectr., ibid; Sr. Surg., retired, Toronto Gen. Hosp.; Cons. Surgs., ibid; Med. Dir., Caven Mem. Inst. (now Gardiner Med. Rsch. Inst.), Toronto; Vis. Lectr., num. Hosps. & Instns., Canada & abroad. Initiator, Heart Surg., Brazil, 1950, Australia & N.Z., 1951. Mbrships. incl: Fellow, Am. Surg. Assn.; Charter Fellow, Int. Soc. Angiol.; Fndg. Fellow, Am. Coll. Angiol.; Fellow, Canadian Heart Assn.; Hon. Fellow, Int. Coll. Surgs. & Coll. of Surg., Brazil; N.Y. Acad. of Scis.; Publs. Medicine in the Making, 1960; Quest in Medicine, 1963; Quest in Surgery, 1965; num. papers on original rsch. Assoc. Ed.; var. surg. jrnls. Hons. incl: Medal,

Md. Med. Soc., 1949; Medal, Int. Coll. Surgs., 1952; Companion, Order of Canada, 1967; Centennial Medal, 1967. Address: 56, Sandringham Drive, Toronto 12, Ontario, Canada.

MURRAY, Eric John, b. 7 Mar. 1920. Minister of Religion; Administrator. Educ: B.A., Andrews Univ., Berrien Springs, Mich., U.S.A., 1951; M.B.A., ibid, 1969. Appts: Sec.-Treas., Bahamas Conf. of Seventh-day Adventists, Nassau, Bahamas; Sec.-Treas., E. Caribbean Conf. of Seventh-day Adventists, Barbados, W. Indies; Vice-Chmn., Caribbean Union Coll. Bd., 1965-; Vice-Chmn., Port-of-Spain Community Hosp. Bd., Trinidad, W. Indies, 1965-. Mbr., former Ed. & Past Pres., Caribbean Union Coll. Alumni Assn. Contbr., Seventh-day Adventist Ency., 1966. Address: Caribbean Union Conference of S.D.A. P.O. Box 221, Port-of-Spain, Trinidad, W. Indies. 109.

MURRAY, Haydn Herbert, b. 31 Aug. 1924. Geologist. Educ: B.S., Univ. of Ill., 1948; M.S., ibid, 1950, Ph.D., 1951. Appts: Asst. Prof., Ind. Univ., 1951-57, Prof. & Chmn. of Geol., 1973-; Dir. of Applied Rsch., Ga. Kaolin Co., 1957-60, Mgr. of Ops., 1960-62, V.P. Ops., 1962-64, Exec. V.P., 1964-73. Fellowships: Geological Soc. of Am.; Am. Minerological Soc.; Am. Ceramic Soc.; Tech. Assn. of Pulp & Paper Ind. Mbrships. incl: Clay Minerals Soc.; Pres., ibid, 1965-66; Am. Chem. Soc.; Am. Inst. Mining Engrs. 40 publs., clay & Clay minerals. Holder, 2 U.S. Patents. Hons: Mbrship., Nat. Rsch. Coun. Comm. on Clay Minerals, 1958-63; Pres., Ceramic Assn. of N.J., 1967, & Man of the Yr. Award, 1971. Address: Dept. of Geol., Ind. Univ., Bloomington, IN 47401, U.S.A. 6.

MURRAY, James E., b. 12 June 1932. Lawyer. Educ: B.A., Notre Dame Univ., 1955; J.D., Law Schl., ibid, 1956. Appts: Law Clerk to Hon. Luther M. Swygert, Chief Judge of U.S. Dist. Ct.; Army Judge Advocate Gen. Corps, 1957-60; Ptnr., Hogan & Hartson law firm, 1967; Sr. V.P., Gen. Counsel, Fed. Nat. Mortgage Assn., 1972-. Mbrships: Am., Fed., & D.C. Bar Assn.s; Iowa Bar; U.S. Supreme Ct.; Rotary Club; Barristers; Metropol. Club; Counsellors; Am. Judicature. Soc. Contbr. to: Real Property Probate & Trust Jrnl.; Real Estate Review; Title News. Address: 1133 15th St. N.W., Legal Dept., Wash. DC 20005, U.S.A.

MURRAY, John, b. 14 Oct. 1898. Professor Emeritus; Minister. Educ: M.A., Univ. of Glasgow, 1923; Th.B., Th.M., Princeton Theol. Sem., 1927; Univ. of Edinburgh, 1928-29. Appts: Instr., Systematic Theol., Princeton Theol. Sem., 1929-30; Instr., ibid, Westminster Theol. Sem., Phila., Pa., 1930-37; Prof., ibid, 1937-67; Prof. Emeritus, 1967-; Min. of Orthodox Presbyterian Ch. Mbrships: Trustee, The Banner of Truth Trust, Edinburgh; V.P., Sovereign Grace Union; Lord's Day Observance Soc.; Evangelical Theol. Soc.; Soc. for Parent-controlled Christian Schls. in Scotland; Nat. Assn. for Christian Political Action. Publs: Christian Baptism, 1952; Divorce, 1953; Redemption Accomplished & Applied, 1955; Principles of Conduct, 1957; The Imputation of Adam's Sin, 1959; The Epistle to the Romans, 1959-65; Calvin on Scripture & Divine Sovereignty, 1960; contbr. to num. other theol. books. Hons: Gelston-Winthrop Fellow in Systematic Theol., Princeton Theol. Sem., 1927; Payton Lectrs., Duller Theol. Sem., Pasadena, 1955. Address: Badbea, Bonar Bridge, Ardgay, Ross-shire, IV24 3AR, U.K.

MURRAY, John Joseph, b. 2 July 1915. Historian; College Professor. Educ: A.B., Univ.

of Me., 1937; M.A., Ind. Univ., 1938; Ph.D., UCLA, 1942. Appts. incl: Ed., Douglas Aircraft Co., 1940-45; Instr., Hist., Northwestern Univ., 1945-46; Asst.-Assoc. Prof., Ind. Univ., 1946-54; Prof. & Chmn., Hist. Dept., Coe Coll., 1954-74; Prof., 1974-. Mbrships. icnl: Am. Hist. Assn.; Karolinska Forbundet, Sweden; Kappa Sigma; Phi Kappa Phi. Publs: Essays in European History, 1952; An Honest Diplomat at the Hague, 1956; Amsterdam in the Age of Rembrandt, 1967; George I in the Baltic& the Whig Split, 1969; Antwerp in the Age of Plantin & Breughel, 1970; The Heritage of the Middle West, 1958; many articles & reviews. Hons. incl: Guggenheim Fellowship, 1968-69; Rsch. Fellow, Bank of Paris & the Low Countries, 1972, 73, 74. Address: Dept. of Hist., Coe Coll., Cedar Rapids, IA 52403, U.S.A. 2, 8, 13, 51.

MURRAY, (John) Ralph, b. 17 Apr., 1916. Educator. Educ: A.B., Northwestern State Coll., Alva, Okla., 1937; A.M., Univ. of Southern Calif., 1939; Ph.D., Univ. of Fla., 1952. Appts. incl: Instr.-Assoc. Prof., Engl., Univ. of Miami, Fla., 1941-42, 1945-52; Ensign, U.S.N.R., 1944-45; Asst. Dean & Registrar, Acting Dean, Dir. S. Campus, Univ. of Miami, 1946-50; Asst. to Pres., ibid, 1948-50, 1952; Pres., Greenbrier Coll., Lewisburg, W. Va., 1952-54; Pres. & Prof., Engl., Elmira Coll., N.Y., 1954-; Edit. Bd., Learning Today, 1971-. Mbrships. incl: Int. Assn. of Univ. Pres.; Trustee, W.J. Phillips Fndn., 1961-; Trustee, Am. Ctr. for Students & Artists, Paris, France, 1965-; Regents Advsry. Coun. on Regionalism, 1972-; Elmira Rotary Club; Pres., ibid, 1966-67; Sigma Phi Epsilon; Phi Sigma Pi; Kappa Delta Pi; Phi Kappa Phi; Epsilon Phi. Publs: Secretary's Handbook, 1941; The College & World Affairs, 1964; Non-Western Studies in the Liberal Arts Colleges, 1964; articles on Educ. Hons: Dedication, J. Ralph Murray Athletic-Educl. Ctr., 1973. Address: Elmira College, Elmira, NY 14901, U.S.A. 2, 7, 108, 141.

MURRAY, Kathleen, b. 10 Nov. 1918. University Professor. Educ: St. Anne's Coll., Univ. of Oxford, U.K.; Pontifical Inst., Rome, Italy; Univ. of Strasbourg, France. Appts: Mbr., Community of Sisters of Notre Dame; Lectr., Mediaeval Hist., Liverpool Coll. of Educ., Mt. Pleasant, U.K.; Chmn., Theol. Dept., Notre Dame Coll. of Educ., Glasgow, Scotland; Tutor, Open Univ; Asst. Prof., Theol., Georgetown Univ., Wash., D.C., U.S.A. Author of Confession-Outmoded Sacrament; 1972. Contbr. of articles to various publs. Address: Louisville, Glen Rd., Belfast 11, Northern Ireland.

MURRAY, Warren J., b. 3 Dec. 1936. Professor of Philosophy. Educ: B.A. in Chem., Wis. State Univ., U.S.A., 1962; B.Ph., Laval Univ., P.Q., Canada, 1964; Ph.L., ibid, 1965; Ph.D., 1966. Appts: Analytical Chem., 3M Co., St. Paul, Minn., 1957-61; Rsch. Chem., 1961-63; Prof. of Philos. of Sci., Laval Univ., 1966-; Invited Prof., Faculté de Philosophie Comparée, Paris, France, 1969, 1972, 1973 & 1974. Mbrships: Pres., Soc. for Aristotelian Studies; Am. Phys. Soc.; Canadian Philosophical Assn. Publs: Scientific & Humanistic Education & the Notion of Paideia, 1969; Les Relations de Raison et la Modalité du Jugement dans la Logique d'Aristote, 1969. Recip., For. Exchange Tchng. Grant, P.Q., 1969. Address: Faculté de Philosophie, Université Laval, Quebec, Canada. 6.

MURRAY, William C., b. 15 Mar. 1899. Museum Executive. Educ: A.B., Cornell Univ., 1921. Appts: Treas. & Gen. Mgr., Lincoln Radiator Corp., 1923-28; V.P. & Gen. Mgr., Utica Radiator Corp., 1928-41; Pres., ibid, 1941-55; Bd. Chmn., 1955-62; Munson Williams Proctor Inst., 1955-. Mbrships: Vice Chmn. & Dir., State Ins. Fund, 1940-48; Pres. & Dir., Hosp. Fund Inc., 1952-58, Hosp. Plan Inc., 1955-60; Trustee, Roat Art Ctr., 1958-; Pres. & Dir., Ctrl. N.Y. Community Arts Coun., 1965-; Dir., Oneida Nat. Bank & Trust Co., 1941-. Hons: L.H.D., Hamilton Coll., Clinton, N.Y., 1963; Civic Award, Colgate Univ. Hamilton, ibid, 1958. Address: 1603 Sherman Dr., Utica, NY 13501, U.S.A. 6, 37, 129.

MURRAY SIMPSON, Joan. Writer & Verse Speaker. Educ: Guildhall Schl. of Music & Drama, London, U.K. Appts: 11 yrs. w. Latin-Am. Serv., BBC; Tchr., Writer's Craft, Richmond Adult Coll., Surrey, U.K. Mbrships: Poetry Soc.; Chmn., Prog. Comm., ibid, for many yrs.; PEN Club; Comm., British Uruguayan Soc. Publs: Novels: A Bracelet of Bright Hair; Picaflor & the Vicerory; Poems: Driving at Night; For Rembrandt & Others; High Places Anthol: Without Adam; LP Recording: Meredith's "Modern Love" (w. J. Westbrook). Address: 60 Highfield Ave., London NW 11 9UD, U.K.

MUSCHAMP, (Right Rev.) Cecil, b. 16 June 1902. Retired Anglican Bishop. Educ: B.A., Univ. of Tasmania, Australia, 1923; Th.L., Australian Coll. of Theol., 1925; B.A., Univ. of Oxford, U.K., 1927; M.A., ibid, 1934. Appts. incl: Deacon, 1927; Priest, 1928; Asst. Curate, St. Luke's Ch. Bournemouth, U.K., 1927-30; Asst. Curate, Ch. of SS. Aidan & Alban, Aldershot, 1930-32; Asst. Curate, Withycombe Raleigh, (All SS. Exmouth), 1932-37; Vicar, St. Michael & All Angels, Christchurch, N.Z., 1937-50; Chap., Royal N.Z. Air Force, 1942-45; Bishop of Kalgoorlie, 1950; Asst. Bishop of Perth, 1950-55; Dean of Brisbane, Qld., 1967-72. Mbrships: The Hannan's Club, Kalgoorlie; The Queensland Club; Rotary. Publs: Table Manners; Sin & its Remedy; The Church of England & Roman Catholicism. Address: 9 Samson St., Mosman Park, Western Australia, Australia, 6012. 1, 41.

MUSHKAT, Mario'n, b. 5 Nov. 1914. Professor of International Law. Educ: Dr. of Law & Pol. Sci., Univs. of Warsaw, Poland, & Nancy, France. Appt: Prof. of Int. Law, Univ. of Tel Aviv. Mbrships: Fellow, World Acad. of Art & Sci; Mbr.-Corres., French Polemological Inst.; Merton Prof., Inst. of Pol. Sci., Univ. of Frankfurt. Publs. incl: Theory & Practice of International Relations, 1957; International Co-operation & International Organizations, 1967. Contbr., articles, legal subjects, var. jrnls. & publs. Hons: Naphtali Prize in Legal Sci., 1967; World Peace Through World Law Award, Abijan Conf., 1973. Address: P.O. Box 17027, Tel Aviv, Israel.

MUSIC, Edward Cecil, b. 12 May 1924. Automobile Dealer. Appts: Operated Gulf Serv. Stn., Prestonsburg, 1946-47; Sales Mgr., Ranier Motor Sales, 1947-48; Sales, Valley Motor Car Co., 1948; Purchased & Operated C.H. Smith Motor Co., 1949-53; Promoted Kroger Bldg. & Ky. Motel, 1955; Orgr., B & D Motor Co., 1956-; Music-Colvin Motor Co., 1956; Edsel Car Dealer, 1957; Chevrolet Car Dealer, 1958; Buick Car Dealer, 1959; Pres., Music-Carter-Hughes, Chevrolet, Buick Inc., Music Motor Co., C & M Leasing Co. Inc. Archer-Music Enterprises Inc., Mountain Parkway Chair Lift Inc., Natural Bridge Sky Lift Inc., Jesse James Sky Lift Inc., Abbott Dev. Co. Inc., Daniel Boone Gorge Ests. Inc., Resort Bldrs. & Developers Inc.; Chmn., Archer Park Corp. Mbrships: Past Dir., Tchrs. Nat. Life

Ins. Co.; Chevrolet Dealers Coun.; CA/Prestonsburg Chmbr. of Comm.; Prestonsburg Kiwanis Club; 100 Club BSA—Shriner, El Hasa Temple, Ashland, Ky.; 32° Mason, Lexington, Ky.; Chmn., Bd. Dirs., P'burg Ind. Coun.; Bd. Dirs., P'burg Chmbr. of Comm.; Chmn., Highland Reg. Med. Ctr.; Dir., P'burg Low Rent Housing Prog.; Contbr., 15 area Ch. denominations; Ky. Chmbr. of Comm.; Past Mbr., Ky. Dev. Coun., Municipal Housing Comm., P'burg; Dir., Jenny Wiley Drama Assn.; PA/Dem. Orgr. Support in area for Bert T. Combs in race for Gov., 1959. Address: 341 S. Lake Drive, Prestonsburg, KY 41653, U.S.A. 125.

MUSSELMANN-HELMERINGEN, Erich, b. 7 June 1911. Farmer. Educ: Univ. of Göttingen, Germany; Tech. Univ., Munich; Dip. Landwirt; Dr.agr. Mbrships: Bd. of Dirs., Deutsche Landwirtschaftsgesellschaft; Pres., Bayerischer Bauernverband, Swabia; Bayerischer Senat; Bayerischer Rundfunkrat; Trustee, Bundesforschungsanstalten für Landwirtschaft; Several other orgs.; Corps "Cisario", Munich; Rotary Club Heidenheim, Aalen. Author of publs. in field. Hons: War medals, WWII; Bavarian cross of merit, 1964; Freeman, Tech. Univ., Munich, 1964. Address: Gut Helmeringen, 8882 Lauingen/Do., German Fed. Repub. 43, 92.

MUSSER, Tharon, b. 8 Jan. 1925. Theatrical Lighting Designer. Educ: B.A., Berea Coll., 1946; M.F.A., Yale Univ., 1950. Appts: Lighting Designer for over 60 Broadway Shows inclng.: Long Day's Journey Into Night; J.B.; Five Finger Exercise: The Entertainer: Any Wednesday; Golden Boy; Mame; Applause; Follies; The Sunshine Boys; A Little Night Music; Candide; The Good Doctor. Assocd. w. Am. Shakespear Festival, Stratford, Conn., Nat. Rep. Co., Mark Taper Forum, L.A., Dallas Civic Opera, Tex., Opera Guild of Gtr. Miami. Hons. incl: L.A. Drama Critics Award for "Dream on Monkey Mountain", 1970, "Follies", 1972; Antoinette Perry ("Tony") Award for "Follies", 1972; Disting. Alumni Award, Berea Coll., 1973. Address: 21 Cornelia St., N.Y., NY 10014, U.S.A. 5, 44, 46.

MUSSIVAND, Tofigh Varcaneh, b. 2 Dec. 1942. Engineer. Educ: B.Sc., Engrng. Univ. of Tehran, Iran; M.Sc., Engrng., Univ. of Alta., Edmonton, Canada; Post-grad. Univ. of Fal. U.S.A. Appts: Design Engr.; Karadge Dam Proj. Instrumentation Engr., Dez Dam Proj.; Planning Engr., Alta. Water Resources; Dir., Planning Div., Alta. Water Resources, Dept. of Environment. Mbrships: Alta; Profl. Assn. Engrs.; Am. Water Resources, Assn.; World Fedn. of world Federalists. Publs: Hydrologic. Jump; Methods of Engineering in Irrigation; Soils & Water Relation, translated into Persian; tech. report writing on supply & demand of metal. Hons: Schol. Awards; Engrng. Gold Medal, Univ. of Tehran, 1972. Address: Planning Div., Dept. of the Environment, 5th Floor, Milner Bldg., 10040—104 St., Edmonton, Alberta, Canada, T5J Oz6. 9, 57.

MUSTAD, Ole Mauritz, b. 14 Sept. 1925. Business Executive. Educ: Law degree, Univ. of Oslo, Norway, 1951; M.B.A., Harvard Univ., 1953. Appts: Fndr., Chmn. & Pres., Selco, Oslo, 1956-70; Chmn., Greaker Cellulosefabrik, 1966-70; Chmn., Vestfos Cellulosefabrik, 1967-71; Fndr., Chmn., & Pres., Selco-Holland, 1969-; Chmn., Telox Investronics, Norway, 1969-71; Chmn., Terma Elektronisk Industri, Denmark, 1969-71; Pres., Washington Refrigeration Ltd., U.K., 1973-; Chmn. & Pres., Washington Freezers, Norway, 1973-; Fndr. & Chmn., Fryser. Mat A/S, Norway, 1974-;

Chmn. & Pres., O.M. Mustad A/S, 1974-. Address: Gregers Grams veg 18, Oslo 3, Norway. 43.

MUSTARD, J. F., b. 16 Oct. 1927. Professor. Educ: M.D., Univ. of Toronto, Canada 1953; Jr. Intern, Toronto Gen. Hosp., 1953-54; Ph.D., Cambridge Univ., 1956. Appts. incl: Asst. Prof., Dept. of Pathol., Univ. of Toronto, 1963-65; Rsch. Assoc., Med. Rsch. Coun., 1963-66; Assoc. Prof., Dept. of Pathol., Univ. of Toronto, 1965-66; Prof. & Chmn., ibid, 1966-72; Dean, Fac. of Med., McMaster Univ., Hamilton, 1972-. Mbrships: incl: Bd. Dirs., Canadian Heart Fndn. (chmn., med. advsry. comm., 1972); Pres., Am. Soc. Haematol., 1969-70; Pres., Canadian Soc. Clin. Investigation, 1965-66; Ont. Coun. Hlth. (chmn., hlth. rsch. comm. & jt. rsch. review comm., 1966-73). Contbr. to profl. publs. Hons. incl: Gairdner Fndn. Int. Award, 1967; James F. Mitchell Award for Heart & Vascular Rsch., 1972. Address: Fac. of Med., McMaster Univ., 1200 Main St. W., Hamilton, Ont., L8S 4J9, Canada.

MUTHARIKA, Arthur Peter, b. 18 July 1940. Law Professor. Educ: LL.B., London; LL.M., Yale, 1966; J.S.D., ibid, 1969. Appts: Lectr. in Law, Univ. of Dar es Salaam, Tanzania, 1968-71; UNITAR Lectr. in Int. Law & Diplomacy for Dipls. from Asia & Africa, Makerere Univ., Uganda, summer 1969; Visiting Lectr., Law, Haile Selassie I Univ., Addis Ababa, Ethiopia, spring 1970 & Rutgers Univ. Schl. of Law, Newark, N.J., 1971; Law Prof., Wash. Univ., St. Louis, Mo., 1972-. Mbrships: Am. Soc. of Int. Law; Int. Law Assn.; World Peace Thru' Law Ctr.; African Law Assn. in U.S.A. Publs: International Regulation of Statelessness, 1974. Address: 6924 Millbrook Blvd., St. Louis, MO 63130, U.S.A. 135.

MUTLUAY, Mehmet, b. 22 July 1917. Chemical Engineer. Educ: Grad., Fac. of Chem., Univ. of Istanbul. Appts: Off., Capsule Fac., Kayas, 1944-46; Chem. Engr., Sugar Ind., Alpullu, Eshisehir, Adapazari, 1946-55; Working Mgr., Kayseri & Usah Sugar Fac., 1955-57; Dir., Sugar Facs., Malatya, Erzincan, Usah, Turhal & Eshisehir, 1957-71; Tech. Insp., Gen. Directory, Turkish Sugar Ind., 1971-73. Mbrships: Turkish Chem. Engrs.; Gen. Assembly, Kayseri Sugar Fac.; "Seker Spor" & "Eskisehir Spor" Football Team Comms. Address: Kadiköy Caddebostan Gelengül sok., Yonca apt No 2/1, Daire: 5, Istanbul, Turkey.

MUZUMDAR, Ammu Menon (m. to Dr. Haridas T. Muzumdar), b. 30 July 1919. Educator; Social Worker. Educ: B.A., Annamalai Univ., India, 1940; B.T., Madras Univ., 1943; M.A., Univ. of Chgo. Schl. of Soc. Serv. Admin., U.S.A., 1950; D.S.W., Columbia Univ. Schl. of Soc. Work, 1960. Appts. incl: Sr. Lectr., Fac. of Soc. Work, M.S., Univ. of Baroda, India, 1951-57; Prof. & Dean, ibid, 1960-63; Hd., Mental Hlth. & Psych. Clin., Shri Sayaji Gen. Hosp., Baroda, 1960-63; Prof., Soc. Sci. & Soc. Work, Ark. Mech., Agric., Mech. & Normal Coll., 1963-72; Prof. Soc. Sci. & Soc. Work, Univ. of Ark. at Pine Bluff, 1972-73; Prof. Soc. Work, Univ. of Ark. Grad. Schl. Soc. Work, Little Rock, Ark., 1973-. Fellow, Am. Sociol. Assn. Mbrships. incl: U.S. Comm., Int. Conf. on Soc. Welfare, 1969-73; Assn. for Asian Studies; other profl. orgs. Author of Social Welfare in India: Mahatma Gandhi's Contributions, 1964. Recip. of acad. hons. Address: Univ. of Arkansas, Grad. School of Social Work, Univ. Ave. & 33rd St., Little Rock, AR 72204, U.S.A. 5, 7, 14.

MUZUMDAR, Haridas T., b. 28 Dec. 1900. University Professor. Educ: B.A., Northwestern Univ., 1925; M.A., ibid, 1926; Ph.D., Univ. of Wis., 1930. Appts. incl: Prof. & Chmn., Dept. Sociol. & Econs., N.M. Highlands Univ., 1946-48; Vis. Prof., Ohio Western Univ., 1948-50; Prof. Sociol. & Soc. Work, Cornell Coll., Iowa, 1951-60; Prof. Sociol., Ark. A.M. & N. Coll., 1960-61; Vis. Prof. Sociol. & Soc. Work, Fac. of Soc. Work, Univ. of Baroda, India, 1961-62; Prof. & Chmn., Dept. of Sociol. & Dean. Div. of Arts & Scis., Ark. A.M. & N. Coll., U.S.A., 1963-72; Prof. & Chmn., Dept. Sociol., & Dean, Div. of Arts & Scis., Univ. of Ark. at Pine Bluff, 1972-73; Dean Emeritus, 1973-. Fellow, Am. Sociol Assn., 1966-; Mbrships. incl: Pres., conf. on Asian Affairs, 1953-54; Assn. for Asian Studies, 1967-; Chmn., Ark. Sociol. Assn., 1970-71, '71-72; Ark. Conf. on 1968-. Publs; incl: Mahatma Gandhi: Peaceful Revolutionary, 1952; America's Contributions to Indias Freedom, 1962; Mahatama Gandhi: A Prophetic Voice, 1963; The Grammar of Sociology: Man in Society, 1966; America's Foreign Policy Towards Asia: A Fiasco, 1971. Recip. of Hons. Address: 58 Maryton Park Cove, Little Rock, AR 72204, U.S.A. 7, 14, 125.

MWEMBA, Joseph Ben, b. 28 July 1917. Teacher; Diplomatist & Politician. Educ: Univ. Coll., Ft. Hare, S. Africa; B.A., U.E.D., 1951; Ed.Dip., Ball State Univ., 1960; Studies in dip. affairs, Am. Univ., Wash. D.C., U.S.A., 1964. Appts: Tchr., 1947; '52-60; Mgr. Schls., 1961-62; Educ. Off., 1962-63; Admin. Off., 1964-65; Permanent Sec., Min. Educ., 1965-66; Ambassador Extraordinary & Plenipotentiary & Permanent Rep. of Rep. of Zambia at U.N., 1968-69; Commnr., Tech. & vocatnl. trng., 1968-69; Dpty. Dir., Zambia Nat. Provident Fund, 1969-. Mbrships: African Nat. Congress, 1950-60; United Nat. Independence Party, 1960-; M.P., Zambia Nat. Assembly, 1973; Past V. Chmn., Lusaka Inter-Racial Club; Past Pres., Tchrs. Assn.; Agricl. Soc., Zambia, 1965-; Commercial Farmers Bur., 1973-. Publs: Mubekwabekwa—a Tonga novel: Mukandeke—a Tonga novel. Address: P.O. Box 2144, Lusaka, Zambia, Ctrl. Africa. 135.

MWENDA, Gaston Mundemba, b. 1919. Bible Society Church Relations Secrétary. Educ: Tchr. Trng. Dip., Mulungwishi, Zambia, 1950. Appts: Tchr: Lumbadashi, 1940-41 & 1951-59; Kipushi, 1941-43; Mulungwishi, 1948-49; Kapanga, 1949-50; Lay Preacher, 1957-59; Rural Schls. Supt., 1959-65; Bible Soc. Ch. Rels. Sec., 1966-; Bible Prof. in State Schl., 1969-. Mbrships. incl: Christian Writers of African Fellowship, 1965; Chmn., Zambian Mutual Assn. in Zalre, 1969. Publs: How We Got The Bible (Trans), 1963; Leadership, 1969; What's The Creation? (French), 1972; Our Stewardship, 1972-73; 30 African stories, 1968. Hons: Long Serv. Brass Medal, 1957; Long Serv. Golden Medal, 1968. Address: Zone Ruashi Qt V No 655, Lubumbashi, Repub. of Zaire, Africa. 116.

MYER, Lester Nolt, b. 7 Oct. 1898. Psychologist. Educ: A.B., Elizabethtown Coll., 1923; M.S., Columbia Univ., 1928; Ed.D., Univ. of Pa., 1946. Appts: Tchr., Secondary Schls., Pa., 1916-41; U.S. Army, 1917-18; Jt. Supvsr., Special Educ., Chester Co., Pa., 1941-47; State Dir., Special Educ., Pa., 1947-57; Schl. Psychologist & Cons., Pa., & Delaware (pt.-time), 1957-72; Psychologist (pt.-time) to non-profit pvte. schls., Chester Co., Pa., 1972-. Mbrships. incl: Am. Psych. Assn.; Am. Assn. on Mental Deficiency; Pa. Psych. Assn.; Delaware Psych. Assn.; Contbr., Handbook of Applied Psychology, 2 vols., 1950. Hons: Awards by Pa. Assn. Retarded Children Inc., 1965, & Pa. Fedn. Coun. for Exceptional Children. Address: 503 Price St., West Chester, PA 19380, U.S.A. 6.

MYERS, Alexander Reginald, b. 3 Nov. 1912. Professor. Educ: B.A., 1933; M.A., Univ. of Manchester, 1934; Ph.D., Univ. of London, 1956. Appts: Lectr. in Medieval Hist., Univ. of Liverpool., 1938-41, 46-56; Sr. Lectr., ibid, 1956-59; Reader, 1959-67; Prof., 1967-; in R.N. reaching rank of Lt.-Cmdr., RNVR, 1941-45. Mbrships: Pres., Histl. Assn. of GB, 1973-76; Fellow, 1939, Coun., 1967-73, Royal Histl. Soc.; on Coun., 1950-, Pres., 1967-, Hist. Soc. of Lancashire & Cheshire, 1967-; Fellow, Soc. of Antiquaries of London, 1949. Publs: England in the Late Middle Ages, 1952, 3rd ed., 1971; The Household of Edward IV, 1959; English Historical Documents 1327-1485, 1969; London in the Age of Chaucer, 1972; Parliaments & Estates in Europe to 1789, in press; num. articles, essays & reviews. Recip. sev. schlrships. & fellowships. Address: The Schl. of Hist., The Univ., P.O. Box 147, Liverpool, L69 9BX, UK. 3.

MYERS, Daniel George, b. 22 June 1947. Elementary School Administrator. Educ: B.S., Miss. State Univ., State Coll., U.S.A.; M.Ed., ibid. Appts: Maths. Tchr., H.S., Eupora, Miss.; Maths. Tchr., Carpenter 1 Schl., Natchez, Miss.; Sci. Tchr., Wash. Elem. Schl., Natchez; Asst. Prin., w. Elem. Schl., Natchez; Prin., Ellis Elem. Schl., Yazoo City, Miss. Mbrships: Smithsonian Assocs.; Am. Mus. of Natural Hist.; State Deleg., Miss. Educ. Assn.; Miss. Assn. of Schl. Admnstrs.; Dept. of Elem. Schl. Admnstrs.; Yazoo Educ. Assn.; Friends of Pub. Schls.; Bluff City Lions Club. Address: 750 Wildwod Cove, Yazoo City, MS 39194, U.S.A. 125.

MYERS, Dorothy R., b. 24 Mar. 1921. Occupational Therapist & Recreationist. Educ: Antioch Coll., Ohio; Corcoran Gall. of Art, D.C. Appts: Lead Demonstrator & Field Instr., Allcraft Distributors; Demonstrator & Instr., Wallmar; Occupational Therapy, S. Oaks Psych. Hosp., N.Y.; Recreational Therapy, Ctrl. Gen. Hosp., N.Y.; Recreational & Occupational Therapy, Middle Earth Drug Rehab.; U.S. Agent & Rep. for int. literary agcy., SPILA. Mbrships: Am. Fed. of Arts; Nat. Writers' Club; Am. Crafts Coun.; Artisans' Guild. Painting exhibited at Galerie Internationale, Lynn Kottler & Ligoua Duncan Galls., N.Y.C.; Contbr. to num. gen. & trade publs. Hons: Poetry Award, Am. Poetry Assn., 1942; First Award for Fine Art, Wayne, Pa., 1954; Dartnell Award for Excellence in Bus. Writing, 1970. Address: Box 61, Garden City, N.Y. 11530, U.S.A. 57.

MYERS, Hortense (Mrs.), b. 15 July 1913. Journalist & Author. Educ: B.S., Butler Univ., U.S.A., 1953. Appts: Reporter, Old Trail News, 1934-42; Asst. Ed. & Ed., United Press Int., 1942-; Pol. & State Govt. Reporter, Ind. Bur. Mbrships: Past Pres.: Nat. Fedn. Press Women, Woman's Press Club of Ind. & Indpls. profl. chapt., Women in Communication; Pres., Ind. Profl. Chapt., Soc. Profl. Jrnlsts., Sigma Delta Chi, 1973-74; Educ. Writers Assn.; Wash. D.C. Press Club; Indpls. Press Club; World Assn. Women Jrnlsts. Publs: Co-author, 5 books in Bobbs-Merrill Childhood of Famous Ams. series; The Brother Within: Robert F. Kennedy. Hons: Nat. Headliner Award, Women in Communication, 1967; Frances Wright Awards, Indpls. Women in Communication, 1960; Kate Milner Rabb Awards, Woman's Press Club of Ind., 1964; Ind. Newsman of Yr., Indpls. Press Club; 2 School Bell Awards, Ind. State Tchrs.

Assn. Address: 7839 W. 56th St., Indpls., IN 46254, U.S.A. 5, 8, 30.

MYERS, Legh, b. 11 Nov. 1916. Sculptor. Educ: Pa. State & Lehigh Univs., 1935-39; studied under J. Wallace Kelly, Phila., Pa., 1952-54. Mbrships: Sculptors Guild, N.Y. (Bd. Dirs., 1972-); Audubon Artists, Nat. Acad., N.Y.; Knickerbocker Artists, Nat. Arts Club, ibid. Nat. Annual Exhibs: Audubon Artists Annuals, Nat. Acad., N.Y., 1960, '62, '63, '64, '70-74; Knickerbocker Artists Annuals, Nat. Arts Club, ibid, 1957, '59-63, '68, '70, '71, '72, '73; Allied Artists Annuals, Nat. Acad., 1961, '62; Sculptors Guild Annual Mbrship. Exhibs., N.Y., 1971-73. Rep. in pvte. collects. Num. grp. & 3 one man exhibs. Hons: Margaret Hirsch Levine Mem. Prize for Sculpture, Audubon Artists, 1972; Audubon Artists Medal for Creative Sculpture, 1970. Address: 9 S. Mansfield Ave., Margate, NJ 08402, U.S.A. 6, 37.

MYERS, Robert Manson, b. 29 May 1921. University Professor. Educ: B.A., Vanderbilt Univ., 1941; M.A., Columbia Univ., 1942; M.A.. Harvard Univ., 1943; Ph.D., Columbia Univ., 1948. Appts: Instr. in Eng., Yale Univ., 1945-47; Asst. Prof of Engl., Coll. of Wm. & Mary, 1947-48, Tulane Univ., 1948-54., Univ of Md., 1959-63; Assoc. Prof., Univ. of Md., 1963-68; Prof., ibid, 1968-. Mbrships: MLA; Am. Soc. for 18th Century Studies. Publs: Handel's Messiah: A Touchstone of Tast, 1948; From Beowulf to Virginia Woolf, 1952; Handel, Dryden, & Milton, 1956; Restoration Comedy, 1961; The Children of Pride, 1972. Hons: Nat. Book Award for The Children of Pride, 1973; Fulbright Postdoctoral Rsch. Fellowship (London), 1953-54 & Lectureship (Rotterdam), 1958-59. Address: 2101 Connecticut Ave. N.W., Wash. D.C. 20008, U.S.A. 2, 13, 30.

MYERS, Ronald E., b. 24 Sept. 1929. Neurologist. Educ: B.A., Univ. of Chgo., 1950; Ph.D., ibid, 1955, M.D., 1956. Appts. incl; Rsch. Off., Walter Reed Army Inst. of Rsch., Wash. D.C., 1957-60; Rsch. Fellow, Johns Hopkins Schl. of Med., 1960-63; Chief, Lab. of Perinatal Physiol, Nat. Insts. of Hlth., San Juan, Puerto Rico, 1964-70 & Bethesda, Md., 1970-. Mbrships. incl: Soc. for Gynecol. Investigation; Am. Physiol. Soc.; Eastern Psychol. Assn.; Am. Assn. of Neuropathols.; Soc. for the Neurosciences. Contbr., sci. jrnls. in field of neurol., neuropathol., perinatal physiol., etc. Address: Lab. of Perinatal Physiol., Nat. Inst. of Neurol. Diseases & Stroke, Nat. Insts. of Hlth., Auburn Bldg., Room 106, Bethesda, MD 20014, U.S.A. 2, 14, 28.

MYERS, Sylvie Wendy, b. 25 May 1941. State Registered Nurse; State Certified Midwife. Appts. incl: former Student Nurse-Staff Nurse, Guy's Hosp., London & Student Midwife, Queen Charlotte's Hosp., London, U.K.; Acting Matron, Nurse Tutor, Pub. Hlth. Sister, British Solomon Islands Protectorate. Author of book, Seven League Boots, 1969, about travels through over 100 countries throughout world over a period of 7 yrs. Mbrships: Royal Coll. of Nursing; Guy's Hosp. Nurses' League. Address: 34 Derwent Ave., Hatch End, Pinner, Middlesex, U.K.

MYHRE, Eivind Kristian, b. 4 Aug. 1920. Professor; Doctor of Medicine. Educ: M.D., Univ. of Oslo, Norway, 1949,. Appts: Gen. practice, 1949-50; Gen. Hosp. Serv., 1950-51; Staff, Dept. Pathol., Det Norske Radiumhospital, 1951-54; Staff, Rikshospitalet & Univ. of Oslo, 1954- (Dept./Inst. of Pathol.); Specialist in Pathol., 1962; Prosector of Pathol., 1956; Docent, 1965; Full Prof., 1969. Mbrships: former Chmn., Pathological Soc. of Norway; Norwegian Med. Assn.; Norwegian Med. Soc.; Pathological Soc. of G.B. & Ireland. Publs: Bjøro & Myhre: The P-Pill (mongraph), 1969; Myhre (in coop. w. Bjoro): Hormones & Cervical Cancer. Effect of sex hormones & antifertility compounds on chemically induced carcinoma of the mouse uterine cervix. Comparative morphological & histochemical studies (monograph), 1971 Functional Endometrial Diagnosis (Monograph), 1973; (in prep.) Human Infertility. Monograph in co-operation with scandinavian authors (Myhre chief ed.) Var. articles on endocrine pathol. (clin. pathological relations). Address: Inst. for Pathol., Rikshospitalet, Univ. of Oslo, Oslo 1, Norway.

MYHRE, William Norwood, b. 21 Jan. 1908. Physician. Educ: Wash. State Coll., 1925-26; Gonzaga Univ., Spokane, 1926-27; B.S., M.D., . St. Louis Univ., 1932; Intern, St. Luke's Hosp., Spokane, 1932-33; House Off., Peter Brent Brigham Hosp., 1933-35; Res., ibid, 1925-37; Appts. incl: Active Staff, St. Luke's Hosp., Spokane, Wash.; Staff, Deaconess Hosp., Sacred Heart Hosp. & Holy Family Hosp., Spokane, Wash.; Cons. in Med., Sgruber's Hosp. for Crippled Children. Spokane, & Royal Soc. of Med., London, U.K. Mbrships: AAAS; Am. Soc. for Clin. Investigation; N.Y. Acad. of Scis.; AMA; Fellow, Am. Coll. of Physns.; Fellow, Am. Coll. of Geriatrics; Am. Soc. of Internal Med.; Int. Soc. of Internal Med.; Am. Heart Assn. Hons: Nat. Wildlife Fedn.; Eastern Wash. State Histl. Soc. Address: S. 906 Cowley, Spokane, WA 99202, U.S.A. 9, 10, 17, 54.

MYRES, John Nowell Linton, b. 27 Dec. 1902. University Librarian; Historian; Archaeologist. Educ: B.A., 1924 & M.A., 1928, New Coll., Oxford Univ. Appts: Student, Tutor, Libn., Christ Ch., Oxford Univ. (Lectr. in Early Engl. Hist.); Libn., Oxford Univ., 1948-65. Mbrships: Pres., Lib. Assn., 1963; Pres., Coun. For Brit. Archaeology, 1959-61; Pres., Standing Conf. of Nat. & Univ. Libns., 1959-61; Pres., Soc. of Antiquaries of London, 1970-. Publs: Oxford History of England, vol. I. (w. R.E. Collingwood), 1936; Anglo-Saxon Pottery & Settlement of England, 1969. Hons: LL.D., Toronto, 1954; D. Lit., Reading, 1963 & Belfast, 1965; Fellow, Brit. Acad., 1967; Hon. Student of Christ Ch., 1971; C.B.E., 1972; Hon. Fellow, New Coll., 1973. Address: Manor House, Kennington, Oxford OX1 5PH, U.K. 1.

N

NAAMAN, Mitri Abdallah, b. 16 oct. 1917. Author; Poet; Printing-works Executive. Educ: Bachelor's degree, St. Anne Sem., Jerusalem, Jordan, 1933. Appts: Freelance Author, Poet, & Translator; Dir., Paulist Fathers Printing-works, Harissa & Jounieh, Lebanon, 1933-65; Rep. of St. Paul Printers, Lebanese Master-Printers Union, Beyrouth, 1944-; Dir., St. Paul Bookshop, Beyrouth, 1955-57; Dir., Paulist Instn., Jounieh, 1957-60; Reviser & Typographic Controller, New Concise Arabic Larousse Dictionary, 1965-71. Mbrship: Lebanese Master-Printers Union. Num. publs. incl: At Talaqi ba'dal Firaq, 1933; Fi Sabil ath Tha'r, 1938; Al Oummane, 1940; Al Khaouf minad Deir, 1944; Al Fatat az Zalim, 1946; Minal Geahim ilan Naim, 1952; Haynamat Zikral Habib, 1952; Sev. translations, French books into Arabic or into Lebanese dialect; Articles & poems in jrnls.; Ed. & Revise, sev. literary & schol. works. Recip., 1st class prize grant, French Cultural Delegation, 1925. Address: Sarba (5013), Jounieh, Lebanon. 97.

NADALINI, Louis E., b. 21 Jan. 1927. Artist; Painter. Educ: City Coll., San. Fran., Calif., U.S.A. Appts: Tchr., Pub. Schols. & Privately. Mbrships: Am. Fedn. of Arts; Artists Equity Assn.; E. Bay Artists Assn. 10 one-man shows incl: Village Art Ctr., N.Y.C., 1953; Am. Students & Artists Ctr., Paris, France, 1954; Univ of Calif., Berkeley, 1967. Num. invitational & Juried exhibs. incl: Pa. Acad. of Fine Arts, Phila., 1966; Oakland Art Mus., Calif., 1966, 67, 68, 69, 70; M.H. De Young Mem. Mus., San Fran. Paintings in num galls. & permanent collects. incl: Oakland Art Mus.; Wells Fargo Bank, San Fran.; James Gall., N.Y.C.; Esther Baer Gall., Santa Barbara, Calif.; Univ. of Calif., Berkeley; San Fran. Pub. Schls. Hons: First Prize, YMCA All-city Art Exhib., San Fran., 1939; James D. Phelan Award in Art, San Fran., 1965; Merit of Awards in Art, London, U.K.,1973. Address: 1230 Grant Ave. No. 295, San Francisco, CA 94133, U.S.A. 37, 120, 133.

NADARAJA, Tambyah, b. 27 Dec. 1917. Lawyer; University Dean. Educ:B.A., Trinity Hall, Cambridge; M.A., ibid; Ph.D.; Lincoln's Inn, London, 1937-41. Appts. incl: Lectr., Ceylon Law Coll., 1943-49; Lectr., 1947-50, Reader, 1950-51, Prof. & Hd., Dept. of Law, 1951-68, Dean, Fac. of Arts, 1957-60, Dean, Fac. of Law, 1968-, Univ. of Ceylon. Mbrships. incl: Coun. of Legal Educ., 1969-; Bd. of Review, Dept. of Inland Revenue, Min. of Fin., 1972-; Hindu Religious Affairs Advsry. Comm., Min. of Cultural Affairs, 1972-; Nat. Archives Advsry. Comm., ibid, 1973-; Comm.,Royal Asiatic Soc., Ceylon, 1973-; Pres., Classical Assn. of Ceylon, 1970-71. Publs: The Roman-Dutch Law of Fideicommissa as Applied in Ceylon & South Africa, 1949; The Legal System of Ceylon in its Historical Setting, 1972; articles in var. jrnls. Address: Fac. of Law, Univ. of Sri Lanka, Colombo 3, Sri Lanka.

NADEL, (Oren) Itzhak, b. 8 May 1918. Writer; Editor. Educ: Hebrew Univ., Jerusalem. Appts: Dpty. Ed., Israel State Controller's Publs.; Ed., Educ. Progs.; Israel Russian Lang. Broadcasts. Mbr., Israel Writer's Assn. Publs. (under name Yizhak Oren) incl: Behind the Lines, 1953; The Ventures of Benjamin the Fifth, 1958; Fathers and Sour Grapes, 1964; The Portrait of a Generation as a Dog, 1968; The Buyers of Heaven and Earth, 1970; Challenges, 1972; The Mountain and the Mouse, 1972. Address: 68A Tchernikhovsky Str., Jerusalem, Israel. 55, 94.

NADLER, Joseph Rexwood, Executive Electrical & Mechanical Engineer. Educ: B.S., Auburn Univ.: M.E., M.E.E., Cornell Univ.; further studies Univ. of Cinn. Am. Univ., Istanbul, Turkey. Appts. incl: V.P., Montauk Construction Co., Richmond, Va.; Pres. & Owner, Investment Rsch., inid; Civilian Engr., Asst. to Chief Engr., U.S. Army Transportation Corps; Registered Profl. Engr., Ohio, 1942. Mbrships. incl: Past Pres., Gtr. Richmond Republican Club; Pres., Cornell Univ. Club, Richmond; 1st Sect., Phi Kappa Phi Hon. Soc. Num. contbns. on var. subjects to mags. Hons. incl: Advsry. Comm. Mbr., 350th Anniversary of Jamestown, Va.; Mbr., Va. Citizen's Comm. on Birth-place Restoration for Woodrow Wilson Centennial, Staunton, Va. Address: 2606 Kensington Ave., Richmond, VA 23220 U.S.A.

NAEVDAL, Per Thee, b. 20 May 1919. Ambassador. Educ: B.A.; Defence Coll., Norway. Appts. incl: Mbr., Norwegian Perm. Mission to Un, N.Y., 1954-59; Counsellor, For. Min., Oslo, 1959; Counsellor, Pol. Dept., Min. For. Affairs, ibid, 1961-61; Acting Chief, Norwegian Mi. Mission, Berlin, 1962; Consul, Norwegian Consulate, N.Y., 1962; Counsellor, Norwegian Embassy, Rome, 1964 & Valletta, 1969; Perm. Rep., Norway, Rome, 1969; Ambassador, Norwegian Embassy, Abidjan, 1969; Conakry, Monrovia, Niamey, 1970; Dakar, 1971; Exec. Dir., African Dev. Fund. Hons. incl: Legion of Merit, U.S.A; Comdr., Order del Merito Civil, Spain; Chevalier 11, Order of Vasa, Sweden; Chevalier 1, Order of St. Olav, Norway. Address: Royal Norwegian Embassy, B.P. 607, Abidjan, Ivory Coast.

NAGAI, Shoshichiro, b. 2 Jan. 1914. Professor of Hydraulic Engineering. Educ: Grad., Civil Engrng. Dept., Fac. of Engrng., Hokkaido Imperial Univ., Japan, 1938. Appts: Asst. Prof., Seoul Imperial Univ., Japan (now Korea), 1942-45; Chief, Planning Sect., 3rd Harbour Constrn. Bur., Min. of Transport, Japanese Govt., 1946-51; Prof., Harbour & River Engrng., Dept. of Civil Engrng., Fac. of Engrng., Osaka Univ., 1951-; Dean,Grad. Schl., ibid, 1958-59, & Fac. of Engrng., 1969-72; Mbr. of Meeting of Bd. of Trustees. Mbrships: Japan Soc. Civil Engrs.; Fellow, Am. Soc. Civil Engrs.; Life Mbr., Permanent Int. Assn. of Navigation Congresses. Publs. (in Japanese): Hydraulics; Harbour Engineering. Hons: 1st Prize, Manchurian Soc. of Civil Engrs. for paper 'Mean Velocity Formulas for the Manchurian Rivers', 1942; D. Eng., Hokkaido Imperial Univ., 1951; Supreme Prize, Japan Soc. of Civil Engrs. for 2 papers on constrn. of sea-walls & breakwaters, 1961. Address: 1-9-2, Nogami-Dori, Takarazuka, Hyogo Pref., Japan.

NAHAL, Chaman, b. 2 Aug. 1927. Creative Writer; University Teacher. Educ: M.A., Engl. Lit., Delhi Univ., India, 1948; Ph. D., Nottingham Univ., U.K., 1961. Appts: Lectr., Engl., var. univs., 1949-62; Rdr. in Engl., 1962-; Currently, Chmn., Dept. of Engl., Postgrad. Evening Classes, Delhi Univ., Delhi, India. Publs: Azadi (novel), 1974; My True Faces (novel), 1973; The Narrative Pattern in Ernes Hemingway's Fiction, 1971; Drugs & the Other Self, 1971; D.H. Lawrence: an Eastern View, 1970; A Conversation with J. Krishnamurti, 1965; The Weird Dance (collect. of short stories), 1965. Hons. incl: British Coun. Schol., Nottingham Univ., 1959-61; Fulbright Fellow, Princeton Univ., U.S.A., 1967-70; Assoc. Prof., Engl., Long Island Univ., 1968-70; Lectr., Vis. Prof., Malaysia, 1971, 1971, Japan, 1972, & U.S.A., 1971-73Num mentions in Am. & Indian literary publs. Address: 2/1 Kalkaji Ext., New Delhi-110019, India. 30.

NAIL, Charles Edwin, Jr., b. 17 Sept. 1931. Insurance Company President. Educ: A.B., Amherst Coll., 1954. Appts: Lumbermens Mutual Life Ins. Co., Mansfield, Ohio, 1954-; Bd. of Dirs., 1963; Exec. V.P., 1968; Exec. V.P., Gen. Mgr. & Mbr., Exec. Comm., 1970; Pres., Chief Exec. Off., 1972. Mbrships: Vice Chmn., Am. Mutual Ins. Alliance; Pres., & Trustee, Griffith Fndn. for Ins. Educ.; Convocation Gen. Chmn., Int. Ins. Hall of Fame. Mbr., Exec. Comm., Improved Risk Mutuals; Bd. of Trustees, Ohio Ins. Inst.; Psi Upsilon; Trustee, Ins. Fedn. of Ohio; Rotary Club of Mansfield; Bd. of Dirs., Mansfield Area Chmbr. of Comm. Address: Lumbermens Mutual Insurance Co., 900 Springmill Rd., POB 969, Mansfield, OH 44901, U.S.A. 27.

NAIRN, Charles Edward, b 26 Aug. 1926. Librarian; Clergyman. Educ: B.A., Kent State Univ., Ohio, U.S.A., 1950; M.A. L.S., ibid, 1951; B.D., Oberlin Grad. Schl. of Theol., Ohio, 1958; M.Div., Vanderbilt Univ., Tenn., 1972. Appts. incl: Br. Libn. & Gen. Asst. Lorain Pub. Lib., Ohio, 1955-60; Asst. Prof., Philos. & Relig., & Hd. Libn., Upper Iowa Coll., Fayette, 1960-64; Assoc. Prof., Relig., & Hd. Libn., Findlay Coll., Ohio, 1964-68; Assoc. Prof., Relig., & Lib. Dir., Lake Superior State Coll., 1968-. Mbrships. incl: Am. Philos. Assn.; Bibliographical Soc. of Am.; Metaphys. Soc. of Am.; Soc. of Biblical Lit.; Am. Oriental Soc.; Fellowship of Religious Humanists; Am. Acad. of Relig.; ALA; Fndr., Northwestern Ohio Acad. Lib. Assn., 1964; Co-Chmn., Sault Area Lib. Assn., 1971-. Publs: Some Contributions of Medieval Monastic Libraries to the Preservation & Dissemination of Knowledge; Contbns. to philos. jrnls. Address: 903 Prospect, Sault Ste Marie, MI 49783, U.S.A. 2, 8, 13.

NAITO, Takeshi, b. 17 May 1929. Company Director. Educ: Schl. of Commerce, Osake Univ., Japan, 1950-53; Univ. of Calif. at L.A., U.S.A., 1957-59. Appts: First V.P. & Dir., Seibu Securities, Inc., L.A., 1962-64; Mgr., For. Dept., Yamaichi Securities Co. Ltd., Tokyo, Japan, 1965-67; Dir. & Mbr. of Finance Comm., Yasuda Fire & Marine Ins. Co. of Am., N.Y.C., 1967-; Pres. & Dir., Yamaichi Int. (Am.), Inc., 1967-; Dir.; Yamaichi Int. (Canada) Ltd., 1972-. Mbrships. incl: Boston Stock Exchange; Midwest Stock Exchange; Dir., Nippon Club, N.Y.C.; Dir., Chmbr. of Comm., N.Y.C.; N.Y. Chmbr. of Comm.; Wall St. Club; Bankers Club of Am., Inc. Recip., Cert. of Honor, Money Mgmt. Inst., L.I. Univ., 1973. Address: Yamaichi International (America) Inc., One World Trade Center, Suite 5361, New York, NY 10048 U.S.A. 6.

NAJENSON, Theodore, b. 11 Nov. 1920. Medical Doctor. Educ: M.D., Fac. of Med., Universidad del Litoral, Rosario, Argentine, 1946; Trng. Course in Electrodiagnostics, London Univ., U.K., 1961-62. Appts. incl: Dist. Physn., Kupat Holim, Western Gallilee, 1951-57; Dept. Dir., Loewenstein Hosp., Raanana, 1959-; Hosp. Dir., 1965-; Lectr. for Postgrad. Studies, Hadassah Hosp., Jerusalem, 1960-; Staff Mbr., Neurosurg. Dept., Beilinson Hosp., Petah Tikva, 1963-; Mbr., Sect. for Rehab., Tel Aviv Univ. Med. Schl., 1965-, Sr. Clin. Lectr. on Rehab., 1970-, Hd., Sect. for Rehab., 1973-. Mbr. & Off., var. med. orgs. Articles, var. med. jrnls., papers & reports. Hons: Fellowships, British Coun. & Kupat Holim, U.K., 1961-62, Voc. Rehab. Admin. in Holland, Denmark & U.S.A., 1964, Immanuel Charitable Fndn., U.K., 1972. Address: Loewenstein Hospital, P.O. Box 3, Raanana, Israel. 94.

NAKAGAKI, Masayuki, b. 19 Apr. 1923. Chemist. Educ: B.Sc., Univ. of Tokyo, Japan, 1945; D.Sc., ibid, 1950. Appts: Lectr., Univ. of Tokyo, 1951-54; Prof., Osaka City Univ., 1954-60; Vis. Prof., Wayne State Univ., Detroit, Mich., U.S.A., 1955-57 & 1968-69; Prof., Kyoto Univ., Japan, 1960-. Mbrships: Councillor, Pharmaceutical Soc. of Japan, 1963-66 & 1968-73, Pres., Kinki Chapt., 1973, Dir., 1974-; Chem. Soc. of Japan; Am. Chem. Soc.; Am. Phys. Soc. Author, 19 books & 158 scientific papers. Recip., Prize for physico-chem. studies on permeability of eye lens capsule, Pharmaceutical Soc. of Japan, 1970. Address: Fac. of Pharmaceutical Sciences, Kyoto University, Sakyo-ku, Kyoto 606, Japan. 50.

NAKAYAMA, Shigeru, b. 22 June 1928. Science Historian. Educ: B.Sc., Astron., Univ. of Tokyo, 1951; Ph.D., Hist. of Sci. & Learning, Harvard Univ., U.S.A., 1959. Appts: Ed., Heibonsham, 1951-55; Lectr., Univ. of Tokyo, 1960-; Rsch. Fellow, Harvard Univ., 1972-73; Vis. Fellow, Hiroshima Univ. Ctr. for Rsch. on Higher Educ. Mbrships: Corres. Mbr., Acad. Int. d'Histoire des Sciences; Int. Astronomical Union; Advsry. Ed., Jrnl. for Hist. of Astron.; Nat. Comm. for Hist. & Philos. of Sci. (Japan); Hist. of Sci. Soc. (U.S.A. & Japan). Publs: A History of Japanese Astronomy: Chinese Background & Western Impact, 1969; Chinese Science: Explorations of an Ancient Tradition (co-ed.), 1973; 3 hists. of astron., astrol. & Japanese sci. in Japanese. Address: Coll. of General Education, Univ. of Tokyo, Komaba, Meguro Tokyo, Japan. 30.

NAKI KISSEIH, Docia Angelina, b. 13 Aug. 1919. Nursing Officer. Educ: Gen. Nursing cum Midwifery, Maternity Hosp., Accra, Ghana, 1940-43; Ctrl. Midwives Bd. Cert., Korle bu Accra; S.C.M., Queen Charlotte's Maternity Hosp., London, 1949-50; S.R.N., Nightingale Trng. Schl., St. Thomas' Hosp., London, 1950-53; N.A.C., Royal Coll. of Nursing, London, 1956-60; M.Sc., Boston Univ., Schl. of Nursing, Mass., U.S.A., 1970-71; observed nursing educ., admin. & serv. in 20 countries. Appts. incl: Nursing Supvsr. (Sr. Sister), sometime Dir. of Nursing Serv., Govt. Serv., 1953-58; Dir. of Nursing Serv. (Hosp. Matron), 1958-59; Sr. Dir. of Nursing Serv. (Sr. Matron), 1959-60; Dpty. Chief Nursing Off., Min. of Hlth., Accra, 1960-61; Chief Nursing Off. (Hd. of Nursing Serv.), Min. of Hlth., Accra, 1961-. Mbrships. incl: Pres., Ghana Registered Nurses Assn., 1960-70, & Ghana Girl Guides Assn., 1965-70; Dir., St. Johns Ambulance Assn., 1961-70; Ctrl. Coun., Red Cross Soc., 1960-70; Dist. Supt. St. Johns Brigade, 1965-; WHO Expert Advsry. Panel on Nursing, 1961-; 1st V.P., Int. Coun. of Nurses, 1973-. Contbr. articles to nursing jrnls. Hons: Manya Krobo Meritorious Award, 1964; Ghana Registered Nurses Meritorious Award, 1966; "Serving Sister of the Order of St. John" Queen Elizabeth, 1969. Address: P.O. Box 2101, Accra, Ghana.

NALDER, (Hon.) C.D., b. 14 Feb. 1910. Farmer; Parliamentary Representative. Appts: Farmer; M.P., 1947-; Dpty. Leader, Co. Party in W.A., 1956; Min. for Agric. & War Serv., 1959; Leader, Co. Party in W.A. & Min. for Electricity, 1962; Acting Premier, 1 yr.; Dpty. Premier, 1962-71. Resigned leadership of Co. Party, 1973. Mbrships. incl: V.P., Primary Prods. Assn.; local agricl. soc.; Parents & Citizens Assn.; V.P. elect, W.A. Conf. of Meth. Ch. & lay preacher; Ldr., sev. youth socs.; Warden of W.A. War Mem., 1973-. Address: Parliament House, Perth 6000, Western Australia, Australia. 23.

NALECZ, Maciej, b. 27 Apr. 1922. Professor. Educ: M.S., E.E. Dept., Warsaw Tech. Univ., 1949; D.Sc., ibid, 1959. Appts. incl: Asst. Prof., Chair, Elec. Measurements, Warsaw Tech. Univ., 1949-63; Dpty. Hd. & Hd., Electrotechnical Lab., Polish Acad. of Scis., 1954-61; Postdoctoral Fellowship, Eng. Design Ctr. Case Inst. of Technol., Cleveland, Ohio, U.S.A., 1961-62; Assoc. Prof., 1962; Dir., Inst. of Automatic Control, Polish Acad. of Scis., 1969-72; Corres. Mbr., Pol. Acad. of Scis., 1967; Vis. Prof., Polytech. Inst. of Brooklyn, N.Y., U.S.A., 1967-68; Sec., Div. IV for Tech. Scis., Pol. Acad. of Scis. & Mbr., Presidium, ibid, 1972; Mbr., Pol. Acad. of Scis., 1974. Mbrships: V.Chmn. & Chmn., Comm. of Components of Int. Fedn. of Automatic Control, IFAC, 1966-72; Chmn., Polish Nat. Pugwash Grp., 1972; Mbr., Exec. Coun., IFAC, 1972; Chmn., Continuing Comm. of Pugwash Confs. Sci. & World Affairs, 1974; Chmn., Comm. on Measurements, 1969-72 & Chmn., Comm. on Biomed. Eng., 1972, Polish Acad. of Scis. Author & Ed. many books, monographs & other contbns. in Polish & for. scientific jrnls. Hons. incl: Krzyz Kawalerski Orderu Odrodzenia Polski, 1959; Krzyz Oficerski Orderu Odrodzenia Polski, 1964; Sztandar Pracy II Klasy, 1972. Address: Pol. Acad. of Scis., Palac Kultury i Nauki, Warsaw, Poland.

NANCE, H. Eugene, b. 16 Sept. 1922. Manager & Chief Corporate Executive Officer. Educ: B.S., Wake Forest Univ., 1951; M.A., E. Carolina Univ., 1959. Appts: Self-employed, Motel-Hotel bus., until 1959; Sales Rep.-Sales Mgr.-V.P., Sales, Universal Bus. Machines, Inc., Columbia, S.C., 1959-63; Product Sales Mgr.-Distributor Sales Mgr., Fairchild Davidson, & Dir., Fairchild Camera & Instrument Corp., Commock, L.I., N.Y., 1963-66; Pres., Gen. Mgr., Treas., & Bd. Chmn., Universal Bus. Machines Inc., Columbia, S.C., 1966-. Mbrships: USNR, 1943-46; Spring Valley Country Club; Sigma Pi; Alpha Kappa Psi. Address: Tanglewood Apt. 1307, 7400 Hunt Club Rd., Columbia, SC 29206, U.S.A.

NANDA, Bal Ram, b. 11 Oct. 1917. Historian; Biographer. Educ: M.A., Univ. of the Punjab, 1930. Appts: Exec. Coun. Mbr., Indian Coun. of World Affairs, 1963-69; Dir., Nehru Mem. Mus. & Lib., New Delhi, 1965-; Mbr., UNESCO Int. Round Table on Jawaharlal Nehru, New Delhi, 1966; Mbr., Schl. of Oriental & African Studies Conf. on Partition of India in 1947, at London, 1967, & Gandhi Symposium of the Assn. for Asian Studies at Honolulu, 1969; Mbr. of Int. Seminar on Gandhi, New Delhi, 1970, & Int. Conf. on Leadership in S. Asia, at London, 1974. Publs: Mahatma Gandhi: A Biography, 1958; The Nehrus, 1962; Nehru & the Modern World (ed.), 1967 Socialism in India (ex.), 1971; Gokhale, Gandhi & the Nehrus, 1974. Contbr., Ency. Britannica. Recip., Rockefeller Fndn. Fellowship, 1964. Address: Nehru Memorial Museum & Library, Teen Murti House, New Delhi 110011, India. 3.

NANDELSTADH, Oscar Wilhelm von, b. 28 May 1916. Psychiatrist; Physician. Educ: Matriculation, Univ. of Helsinki, Finland, 1934; Mic. Med., 1944; Specialist Psych., 1948. Appts. incl: Tchr., Mental Hlth. & Psych., Swedish Schl. for Soc. Work & Community Admin., Helsinki, 1945-50; Physn. Supt., Mental Hlth. Dist., Southern Finland, 1950-; Chief Mental Hlth. Off., ibid, 1955-; Psych., Child Guidance Clin., Ekenas, 1952-60; Mbr., many comms. on psych. out-patient & hosp. care & nursing educ., 1957-; Chmn., Soc. Hosp. Psychs., 1962-; Mbr., Bd., Assn. of Mental Hosps., 1962-; Mbr., Bd., League of Child Guidance Clins. of Finland, 1970-. Mbr., var. profl. socs. Rep., Swedish Peoples Party, Ekenas, 1960-; Mbr., Ctrl. Coun., ibid, 1971-. Author of publs. in field. Hons: Liberty Cross w. Sword, 1940 & oak leaf, 1941; Kt., lst class, Order of the Finnish White Rose, 1972. Address: Jägargränd 3 E, 10600 Ekenäs, Finland. 43, 90.

NANNAN-PANDAY, Radjnarain Mohanpersad, b. 21 Oct. 1928. Economist. Educ: Tchr. Trng. Inst., Paramaribo, Surinam, 1942-46; B.A., Punjab Univ., India, 1955; M.Sc., The Hague, Netherlands, 1957; Int. Law Dip., Peace Palace, Netherlands, 1957; Soc. Welfare Policy Dip., ibid, 1958; Dr. Econ., Univ. of Amsterdam, 1959. Appts: Tchr., Surinam, 1946-52; Assoc. Expert, UN (UNTAO), Bangkok, Thailand, 1959-60; Advsr., Rural Dev., Govt. of Surinam, 1961-62; Advsr., Ctrl. Planning Off., ibid, 1963-69; Dir., Community Dev. Off., 1962-69; Min. of Educ., Culture & Community Dev., 1969-71; Min. of Agric., Animal Husbandry & Fisheries, 1971-73; Mbr. of Parliament, 1963-. Mbrships: V.P., Sanatan Dharma, 1963-68; Pres. Gen., ibid, 1968-; Pres. Gen., Hindu-Muslin Org. of Surinam, 1968-. Ph.D. thesis Agriculture in Surinam publd. in book form. Hons: Order of Andres Bello, Govt. of Venezuela, 1971; Kt., Order of Nederlandse Leeuw, Queen of Netherlands, 1974. Address: 239 Dr. Sophie Redmondstraat, Paramaribo, Surinam. 109.

NAPIER, Linda Smith, b. 23 Nov. 1940. Piano Teacher; English Teacher; Librarian. Educ: B.Ed., Miss. Coll., Clinton, U.S.A.; M.L.S., Univ. of Miss. Appts: Sec.; H.S. Tchr.; Kindergarten Asst.; Piano Tchr.; Soc. Wkr. Mbrships: Mortar Bd.; Fortnightly Musicale; Ladies' Ensemble; Woman's Literary Club; Cub Scouts of Am.; Community Theatre; Community Chorus; Hosp. Aux.; PTA; Alpha Lambda Delta; Alpha Chi; Kappa Delta Pi. Contbr. to Gifted Child Quarterly. Address: 1226 W. Jackson St., Tupelo, MS 38801, U.S.A.

NAPIER, Olive Verna Rogers (Mrs. Walter Simpson Napier), b. 2 Oct. 1902. Artist. Educ: Grad., Pa. Mus. Schl. of Indl. Arts, Phila., U.S.A. 1925; later w. Metropol. Mus. of Art, N.Y., Beaux Arts Inst. of Design, 1925. Solo Exhibs: Int. Bldg. San. Fran., Calif., 1965-66. Grp. shows incl. Oakland Art Mus., Calif., 1950-60 & 1962-68; Cunningham Mem. Galls., Bakersfield, Calif., 1955-62 & 1964-67; M.H. deYoung Mem. Mus., San Fran., 1956-60; Nat. Fine Arts Gall., Smithsonian Inst., Wash. D.C., 1960; Fukuoka, Japan-Oakland, Calif.,1964; Crocker Galls., Sacramento, 1964 & 1967, Mills Coll., Oakland, Assn. Western Mus. Travelling Shows: Haggin Galls., Stockton, Calif. Works in num. pvte. collects., U.S.A., Thailand, etc. Num. murals. Art Critic; Lectr.; Demonstrator, Juror, 1955. Num. mbrships. incl: Nat. Wildlife Fedn.; Chmn. Emeritus, Calif. State Expo. & Fair; Artists Advsry. Bd., No Sect., previously chmn. for 10 yrs. Hons. incl: Paintings in opening & dedication, Palace of Fine Arts, San Fran., 1967; Bronze Plaque, Showcase of the Golden State, Calif., Exhib., 1971. Address: 20 via La Cumbre, Greenbrae, CA 94904, U.S.A. 5, 9.

NARAINE, Shiw Sahai, b. 4 Mar. 1924. Civil Engineer; Member of Parliament, Guyana. Educ: B.Sc., Univ. of London; Pub. & Bus. Admin., Univ. of W. Indies; Dip., Hydraulic Engrng., Delft Technol. Univ.; UN Fellowship, Water Resources. Appts: Engr. & Exec. Engr., Pub. Works Dept., Guyana, 1951-57; Dpty. Dir. of Works, 1957-61; Dir. of Drainage & Irrigation, Govt. of Guyana, 1961-64; Chief

Works & Hydraulic Off., Min. of Works & Hydraulics, 1964-70; Tech. Advsr. to Prime Min., 1971-72. Mbrships: 1st Pres., 1969-70, Fellow, Guyana Assn. of Profl. Engrs.; Fellow, Instn. of Civil Engrs., U.K.; Trustee, Maha Sabha, Guyana. Contbr. to profl. jrnls. Hons: Independence Medal, 1966; Golden Arrow of Achievement, 1970. Address: Ministry of Housing, P.O. Box 482, Georgetown, Guyana.

NARANG, Harbans Lal, b. 5 Apr. 1933. Professor. Educ: B.A., Punjab Univ., India, 1958; M.A., Univ. of Delhi, 1961, B.Ed., 1964; M.A., Univ. of Wis., U.S.A., 1966. Appts: Instr., Univ. of Delhi, India, 1962-63; Instr., Univ. of Wis., U.S.A., 1965-68; Asst. Prof., Educ., Univ. of Sask., Regina, Canada, 1968-; Summer Schl. Instr. Univs. of Chgo., P.A., Mich. State & Brandon. Mbrships: Int. Reading Assn.; Phi Delta Kappa; Canadian Soc. Study of Educ.; Canadian Assn. of Profs. of Educ.; Canadian Educl. Rsch. Assn. Author, num. articles & papers in field. Recip., Imperial Oil Travel Grant, 1970. Address: Fac. of Educ., Univ. of Sask., Regina, Sask., S4S OA2, Canada.

NARAYAN, Jagdish, b. 15 Oct. 1945. Engineering Scientist. Educ: B. Tech., Indian Inst. of Technol., Kanpur, 1969; M.S. Univ. of Calif., Berkeley, U.S.A., 1970; Ph.D., 1971. Appts: Rsch. Metallurgist, Lawrence Berkeley Lab., 1971-72; Prin. Investigator, Oak Ridge Nat. Lab., Tenn., 1972-. Mbrships: Am. Phys. Soc.; Am. Soc. Mining & Metallurgical Engrs. Author of 28 sci. publs. Hons: Best Prize for transmission electron microscopy of non-metals, Am. Soc. Metals, 1970; Best Prize, non-metallic mats. & cermets, ibid, 1971; Pres's. Silver Medal, Indian Inst. Technol., Kanpur, 1969. Outstanding Grad. Student, Univ. of Calif., Berkeley, 1971; Hon. Mention, Int. Metallographic Exhib., 1973. Address: Solid State Div., Oak Ridge Nat. Lab., Oak Ridge, TN 37830, U.S.A. 125.

NARDIN, Mario, b. 17 Mar. 1940. Sculptor. Educ: Acad. Belle Arti, Venice, Italy. Appts: Assts. to Guido Manarin, Venice; Asst. to Fiore de Henriquez, London, U.K., & U.S.A.; Asst. to Jacques Lipchitz, U.S.A.; Asst. Mgr., Avent-Shaw Art Foundry, U.S.A.; Asst. Mgr., Joel Meisner Art Foundry, U.S.A. Mbrships: Am. Soc. of Contemporary Artists; Sculptors League of N.Y.; Y.A.A.; Hudson River Mus. Works in collects. of Fordham Univ., Hudson River Mus. & pvte. collects. in U.S.A. & abroad. Hons: New Rochelle Art Assn. Award, 1967; Greenburgh Arts & Culture Comm. Award, 1971; M.A.G., White Plains, 1973. Address: 184 Warburton Ave., Hastings-on-Hudson, NY 10706, U.S.A. 37.

NARAYANAN, Palayil Pathazapurayil, b. 15 Feb. 1923. Trades Union Official. Appts: Var. Trades Union activities, 1947-73; Advsr., ILO Delegn., New Delhi Finance Review Comm., Malayan Union, 1947; 1st Pres., Malaysian Trades Union Congress, 1950-52; '54-55; Cons., Wkrs.' Rep. Asian Employers' Seminar, Population & Family Planning, New Delhi, India, 1971; Panel Mbr./Speaker, Challenge of Youth, Int. Planned Parenthood Fedn. Meeting, Singapore, 1973; Currently, Gen. Sec., Nat. Union Plantation Wkrs., 1954-; Mbr., Gen. Counc. & Exec. Coun., MTUC, 1949-; Pres., Asian Regional Org. Int. Confedn. Free Trade Unions, New Delhi, 1960-66; '69-75; Chmn., World Econ. Comm., ICFTU, 1968-; VP, ICFTU World Body, Brussels, Belgium, 1972-75; Mbr., Advsry. Comm. Rural Dev., Geneva, Switzerland, 1973-78; Chmn., Int., Bldg. & Educ. Comms., Malaysian Trades Union Congress; VP, Int. Fedn. Plantation

Agric. & Allied Wkrs., Geneva, Switzerland. Mbr. num. pub. bds. & educl. comms. Author short stories, poems & var. Trade Union publs. Recip. sev. hons. Address: Plantation Wkrs. House, P.O. Box 73, Petaling Jaya, Selangor, Malaysia.

NARINS, Charles Seymour, b. 12 Mar. 1909. Lawyer; Instrument Company Executive. Educ., B.S., N.Y. Univ., 1929; LL.B., Yale Univ., 1932. Admitted to N.Y. Bar. 1933, Mass. Bar., 1955. Appts. Atty., Curtin & Glynn, N.Y.C., 1932-34, Glynn, Smith & Narins, 1934-47, Probst & Probst, 1937-47, Pres., Dir., Counsel C.L. Berger & Sons, Inc., Boston, 1947-68; Chmn, Berger Instruments Div. High Voltage Engrng. Corp., 1969-74; Dir. & Chmn., Med. Planning, New England Sinai Hosp. Mbrshops. incl; Corp. Norfolk House Ctr., Boston, 1957; Trustee, Graham Jr. Coll., Boston, BoBoston Opera; Boston Ballet Co.; Mbrship. Comm., Boston Symph. Ball., 1965; Am. N.Y., State Mass Boston Bar. Assns.; Assn. Bar City N;Y.; N.Y. Co. Lawyers Assn.; Am. Judicature Soc.; Law Schl. Rep., Assn. Yale Alumni; Pi Lambda Phi. Yale Club, N.Y., Boston, Mass.; Kernwood Country Club, Salem, Mass., Palm Beach Country Club, Fla. Address 37 Williams St., Boston, MA 02119, U.S.A. 6, 16.

NARTKER, John Richard, b. 12 Nov. 1930. Professor of Art; Painter; Ceramic Artist. Educ: B.F.A., Univ. of Dayton, Ohio, 1959; M.F.A., Cranbrook Acad. of Art, Bloomfield Hills, Mich., 1960; further art studies, Japan. Appt: Prof. of Art, Coll. of Mt. St. Joseph, Cinn,. Ohio. Mbrships: Bijutsubunka Kyokai, Japan; Chu Ta Assn. of Arts, Japan; Bd. Mbr., Ohio Designer-Craftsmen, N. Shore Art League, Chgo. Dayton Soc. Painters & Sculptors, Cinn. Ceraminc Soc., Studio San Guiseppe, Cinn.; Am. Craftsmens Coun.; Paintings, prints & ceramics, pub. collects., inclng: USAF Acas., Dayton, Ohio; Battelle Mem. Inst.; Spingletop Rsch. Ctr.; Ist Nat. Bank of Cinn. Wrok in var. pvte. collects. Hons. incl: Magnovox Award, 1962; Invitational Exhibs., Ohio State Capital, 1972, U.S. Capitol, Wash. D.C., 1972, 1973. Address: 352 Robben Ln., Cincinnati, OH 45238, U.S.A. 57.

NASCA, June, b. 19 June 1920. Secretary-Treasurer of Nasca Compound, Inc. Appts: Asst. to Personnel Dir., H.L. Green Stores; Off Mgr., Western Freight Assn.; Sec.-Treas., Nasca Compound, Inc., mfrs. of chems. for printers & lithographers. Mbrships: Comm., Nassau Chapt. Boys Towns of Italy; Pub. Rels. Chmn., Zonta Club Int.; Committeewoman, 64th Electoral Dist., Nassau Co. Democratic Comm. Address: 2346 Windsor Rd., Baldwin, L.I., NY 11510, U.S.A. 5, 6, 16.

NASH, Evelyn Melvena, b. 27 Feb. 1946. Teacher of English & Mathematics. Educ: B.S., Miss. Valley State Coll., 1967; M.A.T.; Miss. State Univ. 1973; Univ. of Mo., Kan. City. Appts: Engl. Tchr., Harris Jr. Coll., Meridian, Miss., 1967-68; Alexander H. Brookhaven, Miss., 1968-69; Alcom A. & M. Coll., Lorman, Miss., 1970; Jr. H. Math., Manuel H.S., Kan. City, Mo., 1970-71; H.S. Engl., ibid, 1971-73. Mbrships: NEA; Miss. Tchrs. Assn.; NCTE. Recip. medal for outstanding singing performance, 1963. Address: 10509 E. 42nd St., Apt. H., Kan. City, MO 64133, U.S.A.

NASH, E. Marie (Mrs.). Social Worker. Educ: Dramatic Art Schl., Boston, Mass.; Dennison Univ., Granville, Ohio; Nelson Bus. Coll., Cinn., ibid; Course in Soc. Welfare, Univ. of Cinn., Appts. & activities; Conducted pvte. classes in Dramatic Art; later, Exec. Dir., Am.

Red. Cross Chapt., Middletown, Ohio, for 3½ yrs.; 1st woman to be Notary Pub. in Butler Co., ibid; Appted. Exec. Sec., Coun. of Soc. Agcys., 1923. Mbrships: Pres., Children's Trng. Soc., now "The Sycamores", Coun. Soc. Agcys., Women's Circle of Altadena, Woman's Civic League, Pasadena, Opera Guild, ibid; Bd. Womens Comm., Symph. Assn, Pasadena, Arts Coun, ibid; Pasadena Hitl. Soc.; Cultural Heritage Comm., apptd. by Bd. Dirs., of Pasadena, Recip., Recognition Day Citation for Outstanding Community Serv., Woman's Civic League, Pasadena, 1971. Address: Bixby Knolls Towers, 3737 Atlantic Ave. Apt. 1111, Long Beach, CA 90807, U.S.A. 57, 120, 128.

NASH, George W., b. 6 July 1930. Neurological Surgeon. Educ: A.B., Univ. of Kan., 1952, M.D., 1955, Res. in Neuro Surg., 1958-62; U.S.A.F. Schl. Aviation Med., 1956. Appts: Inst., Surg., Univ. of Kan., 1962-63; Rsch. Assoc.-Assoc. in Neurol., Univ. of Ariz., 1963-74.; Pvte. prac., Tucson, Ariz. 1963-74. Mbrships. incl: Dipl., Am. Bd. of Neurosurg.; Am. Assn. Neurol. Surgs. Inc.; Fellow, Am. Coll. of Surgs.; Congress of Neurol. Surgs.; Ariz. (Pres. 1974), Western & Rocky Mtn. Neurosurg. Socs.; Ariz. Med. Assn. Bd. of Dirs.; Am. Civil Liberty Union; Nat. Assn. Adv. of Colored People; Royal Soc. of Hlth., U.K.; Fraternal Order of Police; Christian Med. Soc. Publs: Experimental Acceleration Concussion, an Electron Microscopic Study; How Brief the Glory (autobiog., in preparation); contbr. to med. jrnls. Address: 4800 Winged Foot Drive, Tucson, AZ 85718 , U.S.A. 17, 130.

NASH, Patrick Gerard, b. 10 July 1933. Lawyer; Educator. Educ. LL.B., Univ. of Melbourne; LL.M., Univ. of Tas. Appts: Legal Off., Atty. Gen.'s Dept., Commonwealth of Aust., 1956-57; Lectr., Univ. of Tas., 1957-59; Practitioner, Vic. Bar., 1959-62; Sr. Lectr., Univ. of Melbourne, 1962-64, Monash Univ., 1964-66; Fndn. Prof. & Dean of Law, Univ. of Papua & New Guinea, 1966-70; Vis. Prof., Boston Law Schl., U.S.A., 1969; Henry Bourne Higgins Prof. of Law, Monash Univ., 1971-; Vis. Fellow, Trinity Coll., Oxford Univ., U.K., 1973. Mbrships: Vic. Bar; Int. Commn. of Jurists; & Past Pres., New Guinea Br.; World Peace Through Law Ctr.; Law Assn. of Asia & Western Pacific; Soc. of Pub. Tchrs. of Law; Dir., Leo Cussen Inst. for Continuing Legal Educ.; Dir., Trauma Fndn.; Australian Univ. Law Schls. Assn. Publs: Articles in profl. jrnls., textbooks; Monograph, Some Problems of Administering Law in T.P.N.G., 1967. Address: Fac. of Law, Monash Univ., Clayton, Vic., Australia 3168. 23, 128.

NASR, Raja Tewfik, b. 18 Oct. 1929. Professor of Education & Linguistics. Educ: B.B.A., Am. Univ. of Beirut, 1950; M.A., Ed D., Univ. of Mich., 1954,55. Appts. incl: Tchr., Engl., Int. Coll., Am. Univ., Beirut, 1950-52; Instr., Ling., ibid, 1955-57; Dir. of AID/AUB Reg. Ctr. for Engl. Lang. Rsch. & Tchng., 1964-66; Prof., Educ. & Chmn., Dept. of Educ., Beirut Coll. for Women, 1955-71; Mbr. & Chmn., Curric. Comm., ibid, 1955-69; Dir., Summer Schl., 1961-64; Acting Dean of Fac., 1967-68; V.P. for Acad. Affairs, 1968-69; Dir., Acad. Planning, 1969-70; Cors., Pt. IV Engl. Tchng. Proj., Lebanon, 1955-59; Cons., Engl. Lang., Min. of Educ., Jordan, 1966-67. Mbrships incl: Chmn., Synod Bd. of Educ., 1961-68; V.P., Assn. Univ. Tchrs. of Engl. in Arab World; Life Fellow, RSA; Fellow, IBA. Publs: Applied Engl. Grammar, books 1-4, 1968; The Patterns of Engl. (w. Michael Paine), 1970; Teaching & Learning Engl. as a Foreign Lang., 1971; Teaching & Learning Engl., 1972;

A New Secondary Engl. Course, books 1-4, 1973 (w. A. Gilchrist). Recip., Medal. of Educ. (1st class). Address: P.O. Box 4080, Beirut, Lebanon.

NASRALLA, Ronald Victor St. George, b. 28 Nov. 1930. Advertising Director; Promoter; Manager of Bands & Artistes. Appts: Bakery & Restaurant Bus., Jamaica, W.I., 1951; Schl. Tchr., ibid, 1951-53; Salesman, Dry Good Wholesaler, 1954-55; Salesman, Foodstuffs, Drugs & Haberdashery, Advt. & Promotional Mgr. for Co. & Mgr., Pharmacy Store, Restaurant, 1956-59; Dir. & Ptnr., Advt. Assocs. Ltd., 1960-64; Dir. & Ptnr., MacMillan Advt. Ltd., 1965-. Mbrships: Senator, Kingston Jaycees; hon. mbr., Kiwanis Club, Kingston; Constant Spring Golf Club; St. George's Coll. Old Boys' Assn. Recip., Certs. of Merit, Kingston Jaycees, 1966, '68, '69, '71. Address: 7 Norbrook Mews, Kingston 8, Jamaica, W. Indies. 96, 109.

NASSIKAS, John N., b. 29 Apr. 1917. Chairman, Federal Power Commission. Educ: A.B., Dartmouth Coll., 1938; M.B.A., Harvard Grad. Schl. of Admin., 1940; J.D., Harvard Law Schl., 1948. Appts. incl: Sr. Ptnr., Wiggin, Nourie, Sundeen, Nassikas & Pingree, Manchester, N.H., 1953-59; Special Counsel, electric power rates, State of N.H., 1958-59; Chief Counsel, Republican Minority, U.S. Senate Comm. on Commerce, 1968-69; Chmn., Fed. Power Commn., 1969-. Mbrships. incl: Water Resources Coun.; Vice-chmn., ibid, 1970-71; Bd. of Dirs., U.S. Nat. Comm., World Energy Conf.; U.S. Administrative Conf.; Rulemaking Comm., ibid; Pres.'s Cabinet Task Force on Oil Import Control, 1969-70; Coun., Greek Orthodox Archdiocese, N. & S. Am., 1970-72; Exec. Advsry. Coun. of Jr. Achievement, Metropolitan Wash.; Coun., Nat. Harvard Law Schl. Assn.; Am. Bar Assn. Contbr. to legal & pub. utilities jrnls. Hons.: Doct. of Laws, Notre Dame Coll., Manchester, N.H., 1972. Address: Federal Power Commission, 825 N. Capitol St. N.E., Washington, DC 20426, U.S.A.

NATALIS, Ernest Henri Joseph, b. 15 June 1897. Emeritus Professor of Liege State University. Educ: Secondary schl., Nivelles, 1919-21; self-tuition, Psychol., Pedag., Linguistics, Hist., after 1917; Schl. Tchr.'s Cert., Nivelles, 1925. Appts: Elem. Tchr., Vervier, 1917-18; Coo (Stavelot), 1918, Stoumont, 1918-48; Prof., Inst. Psychol. & Educl. Scis., Liege State Univ., 1947-67. Mbr. & Off., educl. & scientific orgs. Publs. incl: La langue swahilie: Cours methodique; Perspectives et suggestions methologiques; Carrefours psychopedagogiques; 7 books, didactics; 12 schl. books, maths. & geog. Num. articles & pamphlets, educ. Hons. incl: Officier de l'Ordre de Léopold, 1954; Grand Officier de l'Ordre de Leopold II, 1959; Grand Officer de l'Ordre de la Couronne, 1965. Address: 56 Route de l'Amblève, B4984 Stoumont, Belgium. 43, 87.

NATH, Rajendra Lal, b. 1 Jan. 1913. Professor of Biochemistry. Educ: B.Sc., Calcutta Univ., 1935; M.Sc., ibid, 1937; Ph.D., London Univ., U.K., 1951. Appts: Tchr., Chem. & Phys., B.W. Med. Schl., Dibrugarh, 1939-47; Lectr., Assam Med. Coll., ibid, 1947-51, Asst. Prof., Chem. & Biochem., 1951-57; Prof., Calcutta Schl. of Tropical Med., 1957-72; Hon. Prof., R.K. Mission, Residential Coll., Narendrapur, W. Bengal, & Hon. Hd., Biochem. Dept., R.K. Mission, Seva Pratisthan, Calcutta. Mbrships. incl: Indian Sci. Congress Assn.; Indian Chem. Soc.; Soc. of Biological Chemists (India); Instn. of Chemists (India);

Indian Assn. Advancement Med. Educ. Num. papers, biochem. rsch. Collaborator, int. jrnl. Enzymologia. Hons: Gold Medal, Calcutta Univ.; Brahmamohan Mallik Gold Medal. Address: R.K. Mission Seva Pratisthan, 99 Sarat Bose Rd., Calcutta 26, India.

NATHAN, Clemens N., b. 24 Aug. 1933. Chartered Textile Technologist. Educ: Scottish Coll. of Textiles, Galashiels, U.K.; Univ. of Leeds. Appts. incl: Chmn., The Cunart Co. Ltd., London; Advsr., E.E.C. Technol. Devs., Shirley Inst.; Chmn., London Sect., Textile Inst., 1971-73; V.P., ibid, 1974; Rep., Textile Inst., Confedn. of British Ind.; Presenter, Jewish case, Human Rights Conf., 1972; Vis. Lectr., sev. higher educ. insts.; Broadcaster, B.B.C. Mbrships. incl: Treas., Anglo-Jewish Assn., 1965-70, V.P., 1970-; Govng. Bd., Consultative Coun. of Jewish Orgs.; Int. Comm. for Defence of Human Rights in the U.S.S.R.; Inst. of Marketing. Publs. incl: A Background to the Italian Textile Industry; The Role of the Textile Agent; Papers on technol. & int. trade; Contbns. to books & trade jrnls. Hons. incl: Cavaliere al Merito, Pres., Italian Repub., 1967; Cart. of Merit, Italian Trade Assn., 1972. Address: c/o The Cunart Co. Ltd., 231 Oxford St., London W.1., U.K. 55.

NATHAN, David, b. 9 Dec. 1926. Journalist. Appts: Theatre Critic, Daily Herald/Sun, 1960-69; Arts & Entertainment Ed., Jewish Chronicle, 1970-. Publs: co-author, Hancock, a biography, 1969; The Freeloader, 1970; The Laughtermakers, a quest for comedy, 1971. Address: 20 The Mount, Wembley Park, Middx., U.K. 30.

NATHAN (Notkovich), Hilel, b. 5 Feb. 1917. Physician; Professor of Anatomy. Educ: M.D., Med. Schl. of Univ. del Litoral, Rosario (Santa-Fe), Argentina, 1941; Intern., Univ. Hosp. Centenario, 1939-40; post-grad. studies in Anatomy & Phys. Anthropol., U.S.A., 1955-56. Appts. incl: Physn., Med. Off., Baron Hirsch Hosp., Dir., Hlth. Dept. Off. & HS Lectr., Anatomy, Physiol. & Psychol., Moises Ville, Argentina, 1941-51; Gen. Practitioner, Kupat Holim (Labor Sick Fund), var. settlements, Negev, 1951-52; Asst-Assoc. Prof., Anatomy, Hebrew Univ. Hadassah Schl. of Med., Jerusalem, 1951-56; Prof., Hd., Dept. of Anatomy & Anthropol., Tel-Aviv Univ. Med. Schl. & Hd., Sect. of Anatomy, Fac. of Continuing Med. Educ., 1966-; Prof. of Anatomy, Schl. of Communication Disorders, Tel Aviv Univ., 1967-. Mbrships. incl: Am. Assn. Phys. Anthropols.; Mexican Soc. of Anatomy; Am. Assn. Anatomists. Has done rsch. in var. fields of Anatomy & Anthropol inclng. works on ancient Israeli skeletons, problems of erect posture, & use of autograft fibers as suture material. Hons: Magnes Prize for specialized studies in U.S.A., Hebrew Univ., 1955; Dr. Federgreen Prize for heart rsch., Hebrew Univ. Med. Schl., 1964. Address: c/o Dept. of Anatomy & Anthropol., Tel-Aviv Univ. Sackler Schl. of Med., Ramat Aviv, Israel. 94.

NATHAN, Shepherd, b. 27 July 1928. Physician. Educ: B.S., N.Y. Univ., U.S.A., 1950; Rockford Coll., Ill., 1950-51; M.D., Schl. of Med., Basel Univ., Switzerland, 1956; Morrisania City Hosp., Bronx, N.Y., U.S.A., 1957; Intern, N.Y. Schl. of Psych., Ward's Island, 1958-61. Appts: Res.-Supvsng. Psych., Ctrl. Islip State Hosp., 1958-64; Clin. Dir., Suffolk State Schl., 1964-65; Clin. Dir.-Dir., King's Pk. State Hosp., N.Y., 1965-70; Pvte. prac., 1964-. Mbrships: A.M.A., A.P.A. (Nat. & Dist. Br.)-Chmn., Hosp. Comm.; Assn. of N.Y. State Mental Hygiene Physns.; Assn. of Med.

Supts. of Mental Hosps. (Nat. & State Br.). Contbr. to profl. jrnls. Hons: Dipl. in Psych. & Neurol., 1970; Fellow, Am. Psych. Soc., 1974. Address: State Hosp., King's Pk., NY 11754, U.S.A. 17.

NATION, David Stanhope Windsor, b. 23 Nov. 1930. Business Executive. Appts: Asst. Acct., Citrus Growers Assn., Kingston, Jamaica, W. Indies; Asst. to Sugar Acct., United Fruit Co., Kingston, Jamaica; Gen. Mgr., Caribbean Hlth. & Gen. Ins. Co. Ltd., Kingston, Jamaica. Mbrships: Kingston Cricket Club; Constant Spring Golf Club; Jamaica Club. Address: c/o Caribbean Health & General Insurance Co. Ltd., 116 Tower St., Kingston, Jamaica, W. Indies. 109.

NATIV, Nissan (name formerly Nissan Notowitz). Stage Director. Educ: Hebrew Univ., Jerusalem: Acting, Habimah Studio, Tel-Aviv; Schl. of Mime Etienne Decroux, Paris; Prodn., Guildhall Schl. of Music & Drama, London; Direction, V.A.R.A. TV, Hilversum, Netherlands. Appts: Actor w. var. theatre cos. in Tel-Aviv, 1946-; Hd., Habimah Schl. of Drama, 1956-58; Stage Dir., var. cos. in Israel, 1960-; Artistic Advsr. to Tel-Aviv Municipality, 1961-62; Fndr. & Prin., Acting Studio (schl. of drama), Tel-Aviv, 1963, & Studio Theatre, Tel-Aviv, 1966-; has directed many radio plays at Kul-Yisrael. Plays directed incl: The Refusal (Y. Haezrachi); Tamed Birds (Benjamin Tammuz); Tchin-Tchin (Francois Billetdoux); A Midsummer Night's Dream (Shakespeare); Eyes in the Hand (Josef Avissar); The Maids (Jean Genet); Drawings for a Theatre (Nathan Zach); The Builders of the Empire (Boris Vian). Mbrships: Secretariat, Israeli Union of Actors & Dir. (Stage, TV, Film & Radio), 1971-. Address: 26 Dov Hos St., Tel-Aviv, Israel. 55, 94.

NATRA, Sonia, b. 28 Apr. 1925. Sculptor; Ceramist; Teacher. Educ: Acad. of Fine Arts; Guguiam Acad.; M.A., Bucharest, Rumania, 1953. Appts: Tchr., var. art schls. & Arts Tchrs. Sem., Min. of Culture, Israel. Mbrships: Rumanian Painters & Sculptors Union, 1947-58; Israeli Artists Assn.; Painters & Sculptors Assn., Tel-Aviv; Israeli Ceramic Artists Assn. Exhibs. incl: Prague; Milao; Warsaw; Berlin; U.S.S.R., U.S.A.; Israel. Permanent Collects incl: Nat. Gall., Bucharest; Prague Mod. Art Gall. Work in pvte. collects., world-wide. Bronze & Stone sculptures, & monumental ceramic works, introducing new art tchng. methods. Contbr., art publs. in her var. fields. Prize-winner, Int. Exhib. of Art, Moscow, 1957. Address: 10 Barth St., Tel-Aviv 69104, Israel, 55, 94.

NATTRASS, Roland, b. 19 May 1904. Obstetrician & Gynaecologist. Educ: M.B., B.S., Univ. of Melbourne, Vic., Australia; Royal Adelaide Hosp., S.A., Australia; Perth Childrens Hosp., W.A., Australia; St. Mary's Hosp., Manchester, U.K.; Mile End Hosp., London, U.K., D.G.O.; F.R.C.O.G. (Eng.); F.A.G.O. (Aust.); Appts: Squadron Ldr. & Specialist Gynaecologist, Royal Australian Air Force, 1939-45; Cons. Obstrn. & Gynaecologist, King Edward Mem. Hosp., Perth; Cons. Gynaecologist, Royal Perth Hosp. Mbrships. incl: State Hlth. Coun. of W.A., 1957-72; Nurses Registration Bd. & Examiner of Midwives Bd., 1954-72; Late Examiner in Ob. & Gyn., Univs. of Perth & Adelaide; W.A. Coun. of Royal Coll. of Obstrns. & Gynaecologists; V.P., Obstetrical & Gynaecological Sect., Australian Med. Congress, Melbourne, 1952; W.A. Cancer Coun.; of Asian & Oceanic Med. Assn. Contbr., sev. British &

Australian med. jrnls. Address: Martalup, 254 St. George's Terr., Perth, W.A., Australia 6000.

NATVIG, Jacob Birger, b. 6 Dec. 1934. Medical Doctor. Educ: M.S., Oslo Univ., Norway 1959; M.D. thesis, Bergen Univ., 1966. Appts; Instern, Orkdal Sanitetsforenings Hosp. & Kvaernes Dist., 1959-60; Mil. Serv., Norwegian Navy, 1961; Res. Physn., Dept. of Pathol. & Dept. of Microbio., Gade Inst., Univ. of Bergen, 1961-64; Asst. Prof., Boegelman Rsch. Inst. for Microbio., ibid, 1964-66; U.S. Pub. Hlth. Int. Postdoct. Rsch. Fellow, Rockefeller Univ., Dept. of Immunol., N.Y.C., U.S.A., 1966-67; Physn. in Chief, Inst. Hd., Inst. of Immunol. & Rheumatol., Rikshospitalet Univ. Hosp., Oslo, Norway, 1967-. Mbrships: Int. Union of Immunological Socs.; Coun. Mbr., Nomenclature & Symposium Comms., Chmn., Clin. Immumol. Comm., ibid; Scandinavian Soc. for Immunol.; Dpty. Coun. Mbr., Chmn., Comm. on Clin. Immunol., ibid; Bd. Mbr., Rikshospitalet Univ. Hosp.; Ctrl. Comm. for Norwegian Rsch. Dept. Coun. Mbr., Norwegian Rsch. Coun. for Sci. Humanities; European Soc. for Clin. Investigation; British Soc. for Immunol.; N.Y. Acad. of Scis.; Chmn., Norwegian Soc. for Immunol. Publs: Studies on the specificities of gammaglobin & antigammaglobulin factors (thesis), 1966; num. articles & papers on basic immunol & immunopathol.; Ed., Scandinavian Jrnl. of Immunol.; Mbr., Edit. Bd., Immunochem., European Jrnl. of Immunol., & Annals of Clin. Rsch. Hons: Norwegian Women's Hlth. Org. Prize for Rsch. in Rheumatol., Univ. of Oslo, 1968; Anders Jahre's Prize for Med. Rsch., 1972; Int. Geigy Rheumatism Prize, 1st Prize, 1973. Address: Inst. of Immunol. & Rheumatol., Rikshospitalet Univ. Hosp., Oslo 1, Norway. 134.

NAUTA, Doede, b. 11 Apr. 1898. Professor Emeritus of Theology. Educ: Grad., Free Univ. of Amsterdam, Netherlands, 1922; Th.D., ibid, 1935. Appts: Asst. Min., Reformed Ch., Alphen aan de Rijn, 1922-27; Min., Reformed Ch., Wernbrugge, 1927-36; Prof., Theol., Free Univ. of Amsterdam, 1936-68; Prof. Emeritus, 1968-. Mbrships. incl: Rijkscommissie voor Vaderlandse Geschiededis; Kerkhistorisch Gezelschap van Christelijke Historiei; Advsr., Synod of Reformed Ch. Publs: Samuel Maresius, 1935; De Nederlandsch Gereformeerden en het Independentisme in de zeventiende Eeuw, 1936; Opera Minora, 1961; Verklaring van de Kerhorde van de Gereformeerde Kerken in Nederland, 1971. Recip., Knighthood, Order of the Lion of the Netherlands, 1955. Address: Vondelstraat 182, Amsterdam 1013, Netherlands.

NAVEH, Z., b. 2 Dec. 1919. Ecologist; University Teacher & Researcher. Educ: MSc.Agr., Hebrew Univ., Jerusalem 1950; Ph.D., ibid, 1960. Appts: Rsch. Scientist, Vulcani Agricl. Rsch. Inst., Israel, 1950-62; Rsch. Fellow, Univ. of Calif., Berkeley, U.S.A., 1958-69; Rsch. Off., Northern Rsch. Ctr. Tengeru, Tanzania, 1963-65; Sr. Lectr. in Agronomy & Ecol., Technion, Haifa, 1965-70; Assoc. Prof., Ecol., ibid, 1970-. Mbrships: Israel Soc. of Ecol.; Israel Soc. of Botany; Nature Protection Soc. of Israel; Int. Soc. of Ecol.; Am. Soc. of Ecol.; Soc. of Israel; Int. Soc. of Sigma Xi; Bnei Brith, Arazim Lodge, Haifa. Author of 72 sci. publs. in profl. jrnls. in Engl., Hebrew & German; Co-author of sev. books in field of Range & Pasture Ecol. & Landscape Ecol. Hons: Henrietta Sxold Award, Hebrew Univ., Jerusalem, 1946; Vis. Scientist Award, Nat. Acad. of Scis., Nat. Rsch. Coun., U.S.A., 1958-60. Address: Fac. of Agricl. Engrng.,

Technion, Israel Inst. of Technol., Haifa 32000, Israel. 94.

NAVIA, Luis Eduardo, b. 28 Jan. 1940. University Professor. Educ: B.A., Queens Coll., N.Y.C.; M.A., Ph.D., N.Y. Univ. Appts: Instr., Mod. Langs., Hofstra Univ., N.Y.; Lectr., Philos., N.Y. Univ.; Instr., Philos., & Hist., Queens Coll., N.U.C.; Asst. Prof. Philos., N.Y. Inst. Technol., 1968-; Ed. Assoc., Jrnl. of Critical Analysis, 1973-. Mbrships: Exec. Comm., L.I. Philosophical Soc.; Am. Philosophical Assn.; AAUP; Schopenhauer-Gesellschaft; Phi Beta Kappa; Sigma Delta Pi. Author, A Guide to Philosophy: A Study Guide, 1973. Contbr., articles, var. jrnls. Hons. incl: Fndrs. Day Award, N.Y.U., 1972; Man of Yr. Award, N.Y. Inst. Technol., 1973; Outstanding Educators of Am. Award, 1974. Address: 17 Gaynor Ave, Manhasset, NY 11030, U.S.A. 13.

NAYIR, Yaşar Nabi, b. 24 Dec. 1908. Journalist; Author; Editor. Educ: Galatasaray Coll., Istanbul. Appts: Controller, Agric. Bank, Istanbul, 1929-31; Writer, var. newspapers, inclng. Hakimiyeti Milli, 1933-36, Ulus, 1936-39; Fndr., Varlik, publishing house, 1946, & Varlik Review. Mbrships: Turkish Union of Writers; Past Sec. Gen., ibid; Pres., Turkish Ctr., Int. P.E.N. Club; Int. Assn. Literary Critics. Publs: Heroes (poetry), 1929; Adam & Eva (novel), 1932; Mete (play), 1932; Turks & Balkans, 1937; Attaturk's Way, 1966; Out Literary Way, 1971; Our World in Change, 1973. Address: Varlik, Ankara Caddesi, Istanbul, Turkey.

NAZARETH, John Maximian, b. 21 Feb. 1908. Advocate. Educ: B.A., Bombay Univ., India, 1929; Called to Bar, Inner Temple, London, U.K., 1933. Appts: Advocate, Supreme Ct. of Kenya, 1935; Temporary Puisne Judge, ibid, 1953; Pres., Law Soc. of Kenya, 1954; Q.C., 1955; Elected Mbr., Kenya Legislative Coun., 1956-60. Mbrships: Pres., E. African Indian Nat. Congress, 1950-52; Pres., Gandhi Mem. Acad. Soc., 1956-59 & 1973-; Govng. Coun., Royal Tech. Coll. of E. Africa (now Univ. of Nairobi), & Chmn., Gandhi Smarak Nidhi Trustees, 1957-; Goan Gymkhana, Nairobi, 1937-; S.V. Indian Gymkhana (now Nairobi Gymkhana), 1951-; Nairobi Scientific & Philosophical Soc., 1972-; Histl. Assn. of Kenya, 1973-. Hons. incl: Special Prize in Criminal Law, Coun. of Legal Educ., London, 1931; Poland Prize, Inner Temple, 1931; Profumo Prize, Inner Temple, 1932. Address: P.O. Box 40532, Nairobi, Kenya.

NAZARIO, Luis Adam, b. 25 Sept. 1909. Dental Surgeon. Educ: B.A., Inter-Am. Univ., San German, Puerto Rico; M. in Th., Evangelical Sem., Rio Piedras, Puerto Rico; M.S., Tulane Univ., New Orleans, La., U.S.A.; D.D.S., Loyola Univ., New Orleans. Mbrships. incl: Am. Dental Assn.; Puerto Rico Coll. of Dentists; Puerto Rico Dental Assn.; Ohio Dental Assn.; Pres. & Fndr., Evangelical Hosp. Assn. of Puerto Rico; Pres. & Fndr., Hlth. Coop. of Puerto Rico; Gerontological Assn. of Puerto Rico; Masonic Lodge Estrella de Luquillo no. 5, San Juan, Puerto Rico. Publs: Principles of Dental Health, 1960; My Student Life in New Orleans, 1969; What is Masonry, 1974; Dir., Soc. Work Mag., 1940-42; Dir. & Ed., Heraldo Sabaneño, 1955-63; Dir., Revista de la Ciudad del Retiro, 1969-73; Contbns. to mags. & newspapers. Hons. incl: Fellow, Acad. of Law & Sci., N.Y., 1963; Worthy Master, Masonic Lodge Estrella de Luquillo no. 5; Grand Lectr., Grand Lodge of Puerto Rico, 1969-73. Address: P.O. Box 6244 Loiza

Station, Santurce, PR 00914, Puerto Rico. 7, 109.

NDEGWA, John, b. 13 July 1928. Librarian. Educ: Loughborough Coll., U.K.; North-Western Polytechnic Schl. of Libnship., London; Univ. Coll., London; M.A.; F.L.A. Appts: Libn., E.A. Lit. Bur., 1956-63; Asst. Libn., Univ. of Nairobi, 1963-64; Dpty. Libn., ibid, 1964-66; Univ. Libn., 1966-. Mbrships: Fellow, Lib. Assn., U.K.; Chmn., E.A. Lib. Assn., 1965-66; Kenya Lib. Assn. Author of Printing & publishing in Kenya; an outline of development, 1973. Address: Univ. of Nairobi, P.O. Box 30197, Nairobi, Kenya. 135.

NEAL, Laurie Frederick, b. 7 May 1913. Professor. Educ: Univ. Coll., Leicester; Univ. of Paris. Appts: Tchr., var. schls., 1937-47; Hdmaster., 1947-49; Sr. Lectr. & Dept. Hd., Dept. of Educ., Univ. of Leeds, 1949-59; Fndn. Prof. of Educ., Univ. of Adelaide, 1959-. Mbrships: Patron, Humanist Soc. of S.A.; Past Pres., Alliance Française of S.A. Publs. incl: Higher Education in Australia, 1965; The preparation of teachers in Australia, 1967; It's People that matter, 1969; Catholic Education: Where is it going? , 1972. Address: Dept. of Educ., Univ. of Adelaide, Adelaide, S.A. Australia 5001, 23.

NEAL, Louise Adelaide, b. 5 Nov. 1906. Professor of Science & Childhood Education. Educ: A.B., Friends Univ., Wichita, Kan.; M.A., Univ. of Colo., Boulder; Ed.D., Univ. of Northern Colo. Appts: Tchr., Elem. Schl; Prin. Tchr. & Sci. Specialist in Elem. Schls., Kan., 1925-46; Sci. Educ. Specialist, Dir. of Rsch. in Sci. for Educ. of Children, Univ. of Northern Colo., 1946-. Fellow, AAAS. Mbrships. incl: Sigma Xi; N.Y. Acad. Sci.; Delta Kappa Gamma; Lambda Sigma Tau; NEA; Colo.-Wyo. Acad. of Sci.; Nat. Coun. for Elem. Sci. Int. Publs: (co-author), Discovering Science in the Elementary School, 1970; articles in educ. jrnls. Recip. of var. hons. Address: Dept. Elementary Education & Reading, Univ. of Northern Colorado, Greeley, CO 80631, U.S.A. 5, 14.

NEAL, Paul Gordon, b. 5 Nov. 1933. Psychiatric Social Worker Educ: B.A., Southern Ill Univ., 1960; M.S.S.W., Schl. of Soc. Work, Univ. of Mo., 1963. Appts. incl: Marriage Counselor & Admnstr., Marital Clin., Forest Hosp., Ill., 1965-67; Pt.-time Pvte. Prac., Psych. & Child Guidance Clin., Palatine, 1963-69; Chief Psych. Soc. Wkr., Mental Hlth. Ctr., McHenry, Ill., 1965-68; Grp. Treatment Cons., Diagnostic Learning Ctr., Arlinton Heights, 1968-69; Soc. Work Supvsr., Schaumburg Schl. Dist. 54, Hoffman Estates, 1968-69; Psych. Soc. Wkr., Springfield Mental Hlth. Cr., Ill., 1969-. & Menard Co. Mental Hlth., Petersburg, ibid, 1972-; Psych. Soc. Wkr., Me. H.S. East, Park Ridge, Ill., 1974-. Mbrships: Nat. Assn. for Soc. Wkrs.; Acad. of Cert. Soc. Wkrs.; Am. Assn. of Marriage Counselors. Address: 49 North Shore Dr., Petersburg, IL 62675, U.S.A. 8, 22, 131.

NEAS, Margaret F. (Mrs. George M. Neas). Pianist & Composer. Educ: Concert Dip., Va. Int. Coll.; Tchrs Cert., Peabody Inst. Conservatory of Music. Appts: Guest Artist on many Radio & TV presentations in N.Y., Tenn., Va., N.C., Fla., Ala., Pa. & Cuba; Piano Soloist at var functions in B'ham. Mbrships: Past Pres., Roanoke Music Tchrs. Assn.; Past Mbr., Nat. Guild of Piano Tchrs.; Gray Lady Hosp. Music Prog., Phila., Pa., 1955-61; Broadcast Music Corp.; Composer Mbr., Am. Music Ctr., N.Y.; Am. Fedn. of Musicians; Nat. Fedn. of Music Clubs; Melodia Music Club; Past Sec., Mu Phi Epsilon. Compositions: Teatime on Fifth

Avenue; Portrait In Satin; Cathy; Tremendous; Harmony In Emerald; Enchantment; Farewell Concerto; In A Rut; Lazy Holiday (all are piano solos incld. on record album "Margaret. Margaret".) Address: 1908-C Vestavia Ct., Birmingham, AL 35216, U.S.A. 5, 7.

NEAT, (Sister) Charles Marie. Professor. Educ: B.A., Coll. of St. Rose, 1935; M.A., Cath. Univ. of Am., Wash. D.C., 1946; Ph.D., ibid, 1954. Appts: Secondary Schl. Tchr., St. Ann's Acad., Albany, 1935-36, St. Peter's Acad., Saratoga, 1939; Coll. Tchr., Coll. of St. Rose, 1939-; Chmn., Dept. of For. Langs., ibid, 1969-74. Mbrships. incl: V.P., Hudson Valley Chapt., Am. Assn. of Tchrs. of German, 1966-69; Sec., ibid, 1957-60; Sec.-Treas., 1971-74; Regional Dir., Nat. German Contest, 1969-71; Sec.-Treas., ibid, 1972-74; Sec., Coll. of St. Rose Chapt., AAUP, 1966-68, 1972-74; Standing Comm. for For. Lang. Requirements & Curric., N.Y. Assn. of For. Lang. Tchrs.; Am. Coun. of Tchng. of For. Langs.; MLA; Assn. of Depts. of For. Langs.; Panelist, Kiamesha Lake Conf., 1969, & Jt. Meeting of N.Y. Assn. of For. Lang. Tchrs. & Ont. Lang. Tchrs. Conf., Toronto, Canada, 1971; Delta Epsilon Sigma; Alpha Chi Chapt., Delta Epsilon Sigma. Contbr. of articles to profl. publs. Address: Coll. of St. Rose, 432 Western Ave., Albany, NY 12203, U.S.A, 5, 6, 13, 15, 28, 129, 132, 138.

NEATBY, Leslie Hamilton, b. 16 May 1902. Professor of Classics. Educ: B.A., 1925, M.A., 1939, Univ. of Sask., Canada; Ph.D., Toronto Univ., 1950. Appts: Prin., Continuation Schl., Shelbrook, Sask., 1930-40; Instr., Classics, Mt. Royal Coll., Calgary, Alta., 1945-47; Hd., Dept. of Classics, Acadia Univ., N.S., 1951-67; Prof., Classics, Univ. of Sask., Saskatoon, 1960-70; Retd. 1970; Histl. Assoc., Inst. of Northern Studies, Univ. of Sask. Mbrships: Past Mbr. of Exec. (2 terms), Classical Assn. of Canada; Past Mbr., Arctic Circle, Ottawa. Publs: In Quest of the North-West Passage, 1958; Link Between the Oceans, 1960; Conquest of the Last Frontier, 1966; Search for Franklin, 1970; Discovery in Russian & Siberian Waters, 1973; Num. articles & reviews. Address: 5 D, 1800 Main St., Saskatoon, Sask. S7H 4B3, Canada. 3.

NEBEL, William Arthur, b. 23 Dec. 1936. Physician; Obstetrician; Gynecologist. Educ: A.B., Univ. of N.C., U.S.A., 1958; M.D., Schl. of Med., ibid, 1962; Intern, Med. Ctr., Duke Univ., Durham, N.C., 1962-63; Res. Physn., Ob. & Gyn., N.C. Mem. Hosp., 1963-67. Appts: Lt.Cmdr., U.S.N.R., & Chief, Gyn. & Oncol., Naval Hosp., San Diego, Calif., 1967-69; Instr., Ob. & Gyn., Schl. of Med., Univ. of N.C., 1969-70; Clin. Instr., ibid, 1970-; Pvte. Prac., Ob. & Gyn., Chapel Hill, N.C., 1970-; Clin. Asst. Prof., Ob. & Gyn., Med. Ctr., Duke Univ., 1973-. Mbrships. incl: Am. Med. Assn.; V.P., Orange Co. Unit, Am. Cancer Soc.; N.C. Med. Soc.; Orange Co. Med. Soc.; Fellow, Am. Coll. of Ob. & Gyn.; N.C. Ob. & Gyn. Soc.; Dipl., Am. Bd. of Ob. & Gyn.; Robert A. Ross Ob. & Gyn. Soc.; Am. Fertility Soc.; Phi Alpha Theta; Alpha Omega Alpha. Publs: Contbns. to profl. jrnls. Address: 1030 Torrey Pines Place, Chapel Hill, NC 27514, U.S.A. 17, 57, 125.

NEBELONG, Bent, b. 19 Oct. 1917. Barrister of the Supreme Court. Educ: Grad. in Law, Univ. of Copenhagen, Denmark, 1943; London Schl. of Economics, U.K., 1947-48. Appts: Mbr., City Coun. of Copenhagen, 1969-; Bd. Mbr., sev. cos. Publs: On Guarantee, 1948; On Sale of Goods Act, II, 1949; contbns. to legal jrnls. Hons: Gold Medal, Copenhagen Univ., for monograph On Guarantee, 1948. Address: 1 A Frederiksberggade, 1459 Copenhagen K, Denmark. 43.

NECUS-AGBA, Benedict Ikwebe, b. 19 Dec. 1938. Educator; Artist. Educ: Ahmadu Bello Univ., Zaria, 1963-64, 1965-66, 1967-68; Univ. of Nigeria, Nsukka, 1966-67. Appts: Headmaster, var. primary schls., Wanokom Touring Area, 1957-59; Headmaster, Ctrl. Schl., Obanliku, 1962; Tutor, Co. Coun. Trng. Coll., Obudu, 1962; Prin., Govt. Secondary Schl., Obudu, 1968-70; Master, St. Thomas' Coll., Ogoja, 1971, Mary Knoll Secondary Schl., Okuku, Ogoja, 1972; Prin., St. Thomas' Higher Elem. Coll., Ogoja, 1973; Pt.-time Lectr. in Engl. Lang., Dept. of Extra Mural Studies, Univ. of Nigeria, Nsukka, 1971-72. Mbrships. incl: Obudu & Ogoja Divs., S.E. State Schlrship. & Loans Bd., 1969-72; Obudu W. Dev. Coun., 1973-74; S.E. State Exec. Coun. & Hon. Commnr. for Natural Resources, 1974-. Author of Pottery in Obudus, 1968. Address: Commissioner for Natural Resources, S.E. State, Nigeria. 135.

NEEDHAM, Lucien, b. 5 Apr. 1929. Musician; Educator. Educ: G.G.S.M. (Lodnon), A.G.S.M., A.R.C.M., Guildhall Schl. of Music, London, U.K. Appts: Conductor, Winnipeg Philharmonic Choir, Canada, 1956-60; Prin. Prog., Voice & Theoretical Subjects, Brandon Univ., Man., 1960-67; Conductor, Western Man. Philharmonic Choir, 1965-67; Sr. Prof., Music, Univ. of Lethbridge, Alta., 1967-; Conductor, Lethbridge Symph. Orch., 1970-. Mbrships. incl: Past Pres., Man. Registered Music Tchrs. Assn.; Inc. Soc. Musicians, U.K.; Canadian Assn. of Univ. Schls. of Music; Canadian Assn. of Univ. Tchrs. Compositions: Christmas Gradual; The Fields Abroad. Author of monographs & articles in profl. publs. Hons. incl: British Coun. Visitors Awards, 1964, 71; Nuffield Fndn. Fellowship, 1965; Canada Coun. Awards, 1966, 71. Address: c/o Univ. of Lethbridge, 805-21 St. S., Lethbridge, Alta., Canada. 4.

NEEMAN, Yuval, b. 14 May 1925. Physicist. Educ: B.Sc., Israel Inst. Technol., Haifa, 1945; Dip. Engrng., ibid, 1946; D.I.C., Imperial Coll., Sci. & Technol., London, U.K., 1962; Ph.D., London Univ., ibid, 1962. Appts: Var. mil., 1946-57; Mil. Air & Naval Attaché, Israel Embassies, U.K. & Scandinavian countries, 1958-60; Sci. Dir., Israel Atomic Energy Commn., 1961-63; Rsch. Fellow & Vis. Prof., Theoretical Phys., Calif. Inst. Technol., Pasadena, U.S.A., 1963-65; Prof., Phys.-Pres., Tel-Aviv Univ., Israel, 1965-; Non-res. Dir. & Prof., Phys., Ctr. Particle Theory, Tex. Univ., Austin, U.S.A., 1968; Num. short-terms appts., Am., Finland & France, 1961-74; Participated 6-Day & Yom Kippur Wars, 1967. Mbr. num. sci. orgs. Creative Works: Discovered Unitary Symmetry Theory of Elementary Particles & 1st Suggestion of Fundamental Triplet Field (leading to quarks); Author 3 sci. books & about 150 sci. jrnl. articles. Hons. incl: Albert Einstein Medal & Award, Phys. Scis., Washington, 1970; D.Sc. hon cause, Yeshiva Univ., NY, 1972. Address: Tel-Aviv Univ., Israel, 5.

NEERGAARD, Else Beate de. Artist. Educ: Acad. Rancon, Paris, France; Acad. Collarossi, Paris; Acad. de la Grande Chaumiere, Paris. Appts: Tchr., Picture Weaving, Art H.S., Holbaek, Denmark, & Sem. for Design Craftsmanship & Arch., Danish Inst. Mbr., Fine Art Painters Assn. Num. exhibs. of tapestries, watercolour paintings, collages & book illustrations, inclng: Copenhagen Mus. of Decorative Arts, Denmark; Danish Soc. of Arts & Crafts; Mus. of Indl. Arts, Copenhagen; Aarhus Town Hall, Denmark; Åbo Art Mus., Finland; Charlottenborg & Artists' Autumn Exhib., Stockholm, Sweden; Gobelin Exhib.,

Saarbrucken, Germany, 1969; Deutsche Kulturamt, Berlin, Germany, 1970; Galerie Internationale, N.Y.C., U.S.A., 1973. Author, Digte og Billedtaepper, 1969. Address: Atelier, Hortensiavej 16st., 1857 Copenhagen V, Denmark. 134.

NEFF, Hans Josef, b. 11 June 1920. Physicist. Educ: Univ. of Karlsruhe, 1939-40, 1946-51; Dipl., 1948; Dr. rer. nat., 1951. Appts: Rsch. Worker, Siemens Co., 1951-55; Lrd., var. laboratories for X-ray rsch., electromicroscopy & Microanalysis, 1955-; Prof., Univ. of Karlsruhe. Mbrships: Deutsche Phys. Gesellschaft; Verein Deutscher Eisenhüttenleute; Deutsche Gesellschaft für Electronenmikroskopie. Contbr. to sci. jrnls. Address: Gruenberger Str. 17A, (7500) Karlsruhe 1, German Fed. Repub.

NEFF, W. Perry, b. 4 Feb. 1927. Banker. Educ: B.A., Williams Coll., 1950; LL.B., Univ. of Wis., 1954; A.M.P. Cert., Harvard Univ., 1969. Appts: V.P., Trust Admin., Chem. Bank, N.Y.C., 1964-67; Sr. V.P., ibid, 1968-71; Exec. V.P., Hd. of Ops., ibid, 1971-; Sr. Admin. Off., Trust & Investment Bank, 1971-; Dir., Petroleum Corp. of Am., 1972-. Mbrships: Bd. of Trustees, Seawanhaka Corinthian Yacht Club, 1963-; Treas., ibid, 1973-. Address: Chemical Bank, 20 Pine St., N.Y., NY 10015, U.S.A.

NEHER, Leon Crist, b. 21 Nov. 1933. Educator; Clergyman; Farmer. Educ: B.A., Inst. of Agric., Anand, India, 1955; B.S., McPherson Coll., Kan., U.S.A., 1957; M.Div., Bethany Theol. Sem., Ill., 1961; M.S., Ohio State Univ., 1962. Appts. incl: Pastor, Ch. of the Brethren, Kan., Mont., Ohio & Ind., 1953-68; Instr. & Asst. Prof., Sociol., Manchester Coll., Ind., 1963-69; Prof., Sociol., Colby Community Jr. Coll., Kan., 1969-72. Mbrships. incl: Pres., Quality Pork Prods. Assn., 1971-; Gen. Bd., Ch. of the Brethren, 1970-; Bd. Dirs., Am. Country Life Assn., 1969-; Rural Sociol. Assn.; Pi Kappa Delta; Phi Alpha Theta; Gamma Sigma Delta. Contbr. to mags. Address: P.O. Box 433, Quinter, KS 67752, U.S.A. 8.

NEHLIL, Jacques, b. 7 May 1917. Physician. Educ: Fac. of Med., Paris. Appts: Intern, Paris Hosps.; Chief., Clin., Paris Fac. of Med.; Hd., Dept. of Neurol., Centre hospitalier 95100 Argenteuil; Dir., Clin. Tchng., Paris Univ. Mbrships: Sr. Mbr., French Lang. Soc. of Neurol. & Soc. of Clin. Neurophysiol. & EEG; Assoc., French Lang. Soc. of Neurosurg. & Am. Acad. of Neurol.; Treas., Soc. of Med. Psychol.; Hon., Argentine Assn. of Biol. Psych.; Assn. of Former Resistance Fighters; Comm., Fencing Sect., Racing Club of France. Publs: La Streptomycine, 1947; L'encephalopathie-porto care, 1967; sev. papers on Neurol. & Psych. Hons: Croix de guerre, 1939-45 war. Address: 8 Square Alboni, F 75016, Paris, France.

NEIDIGH, Pansy M. (Mrs.), b. 1 April 1901. Teacher; Art Supervisor. Educ: A.B., Ctrl. Normal Coll.; Art Trng., summers, 1930-34; M.A., Columbia Univ., 1942; Postgrad. study, Columbia & Univ. of Fla. Appts: Tchr., all grades, schls. in Ind. & Fla., 45 yrs., inclng. Art Supvsr., Richmond, Ind., 19 yrs.; Tchr., Danville Normal, 3 yrs., Ind. Univ., evenings, 10 yrs., summers, Iowa State Tchrs. Coll., & adult evenings classes. Mbrships. incl: Fndr., Art Assn., Leesburg, Fla.; Western Arts Assn.; Nat. Arts Educ. Assn.; Ind. State Tchrs. Assn.; Nat. Tchrs. Assn.; Comm. on Art Educ., Mus. of Mod. Art, N.Y.C.; Delta Kappa Gamma; Sigma Delta Pi; Fla. Fedn. of Art; Nat. Arts Club, N.Y.C. Altrusa Int. Exhibs: Richmond, Ind., galls.; Hoosier Salon, Indpls.; Nat. Arts Club;

Butler Art Inst.; Iowa State Tchrs. Coll.; Columbia Univ. Tchrs. Coll.; Leesburg Arts Fedn. Hons: 2nd Award, Richmond, Ind.; Ribbons, Butler Art Inst., 1941; Sweepstake Tri Color Award, Fla. State Arts Fedn., 1961. Address: 260 Elnor St., Morgantown, IN 46160, U.S.A. 5, 37

NEIHARDT, John Gneisenau, b. 8 Jan. 1881, dec. 3 Nov. 1973. Poet; Author. Educ: Dip. for sci. course, Neb. Normal Coll. (now Neb. State Tchrs. Coll.), Wayne, 1897. Appts: Prof. of Poetry, Univ. of Neb., Lincoln, 1923; Lit. Ed., St. Louis Post-Dispatch, Mos., 1926-38; Honnold Lectr., Knox Coll., 1939; Dir. of Info. Off., Chgo., Ill., U.S. Dept. of Interior, Bur. of Indian Affairs, 1946-48; Lectr., Engl. & Poet in Res., Univ. of Mo., Columbia, 1949-65. Mbrships: Fellow, Int. Inst. Arts & Letters; Nat. Inst. Arts & Letters; Fndng. & Life Mbr., Westerners; Chancellor, Acad. of Am. Poets; V.P., Middle W. Br., Poetry Soc. of Am.; Hon. Companion of Order of Indian Wars of U.S.; Sigma Tau Delta; Phi Beta Kappa. Publs: 26 books inclng: Black Elk Speaks, 1932, transl. into German, Flemish, Dutch, Italian, Danish, Serbo-Croatian, Swedish & Spanish; The Song of the Messaiah, 1935; The Song of Jed Smith, 1941; A Cycle of the West, 1951; When the Tree Flowered, 1951, in U.K., Eagle Voice, 1953; All is But a Beginning (autobiog.), Vol. I, 1972, Vol. II, in progress. Recip. num. hons. & prizes inclng: Gov.'s Award, Neb.'s Poet of Century, 1967; Mari Sandoz Award, Neb. State Lib. Assn., 1971; Poet Laureate of Neb. by designation by act of State Legis., 1921; 1st Sunday in Agu. Annual Statewide Neihardt Day, by proclamation, Gov. of Neb., 1968. 2.

NEIL, Josephine, b. 9 Nov. 1917. Librarian. Educ: B.S., Geo. Peabody Coll., 1939; B.S. in L.S., ibid, 1940: Grad. study, Med. Lib. Admin., Univ. of Chgo. Appts. incl: Intern, Med. Libnship., Tulane Univ. Schl. of Med. Lib., 1940-41; Ref. Asst., Vanderbilt Univ. Schl. of Med. Lib., 1941-43; Chief Libn., Thayer Army. Hosp., 1943-51; Staff Libn., U.S. Army Forces Antilles, San Juan, P.R., 1951-54; Staff Libn., var. U.S. Army commands, Europe, 1954-61; Post Lib. Dir., Ft. Knox, Ky., 1961; Naval Regional Libn., Charleston, S.C., 1961-. Num. mbrships. incl: Var. comms., ALA; Past Pres., Past Dir., Armed Forces Libns. Sect., ALA; Pres.-Elect, S.C. Lib. Assn.; Southeastern Lib. Assn.; English Speaking Union; S.C. Histl. Soc.; Carolina Art Assn.; Navy League; Nat. Trust for Historic Preservation; Hon. mbr., Pi Gamma Mu, Kappa Delta Phi, Sigma Delta Pi. Hons. incl: Hon. Chmn., Medal of Hon. Archives Advsry. Comm., Freedoms Fndn., Valley Forge, 1966-; Num. letters of Commendation, Army & Navy. Address: Ashley Hall Gardens, B-9, 2040 Ashley River Rd., Charleston, SC 29407, U.S.A. 5, 7, 42, 138.

NEILD, Robert Ralph, b. 10 Sept. 1924. Professor of Economics. Educ: Trinity Coll., Cambridge, U.K. Appts: Served RAF, 1943-44; Operational Rsch., 1944-45; Secretariat, UN Econ. Commn. for Europe, Geneva, 1947-51; Econ. Sect., Cabinet Off. & Treasury, 1951-56; Lectr. in Econs., Fellow, Trinity Coll., Cambridge, 1956-58; Ed., Quarterly Econ. Review, then Dpty. Dir., Nat. Inst. of Econ. & Soc. Rsch., 1958-64; MIT Ctr. for Int. Studies, India Proj., New Delhi, India, 1962-63; Econ. Advsr., HM Treasury, 1964-67; Dir., Stockholm Int. Peace Rsch. Inst., Sweden, 1967-71; Prof., Econs., Fellow, Trinity Coll., Univ. of Cambridge, U.K., 1971-. Author, Pricing & Employment in the Trade Cycle, 1964. Address: 5 Cranmer Rd., Cambridge, U.K. 1.

NEILSON, Winthrop C., III, b. 7 Jan 1934. Management Consultant, Investor Relations. Educ: B.A., Harvard Univ., 1956; Security Analysis, New Inst. of Finance, 1962-63. Appts: Asst. Prodr., Rangley Lakes Summer Theatre, 1955; U.S. Army, 1956-59; Reporter, Hearst's Albany Times-Union, N.Y., 1959-60; Pub. Info. Staff Mbr., Consolidation Edison, NYC, 1960-61; Asst. Dir. of PR, Union Serv. Corp., NYC, 1961; Cons., Georgeson & Co., 1961-67; Prin., ibid, 1968; Dir., Guardsman Chem., Am. Stock Exchange, 1968-, & Stockholders of Am., 1972-. Mbrships: Pres.- Chmn., Robert A. Taft, Repub. Club, Queens, 1964-68; Treas., 24 Assembly Dist., Repub. Pty., 1966-68; Charter, Nat. Investor Rels. Inst.; PR Soc.; Bankers, Mtn. Lakes Country, Hasty Pudding, & DU Clubs; formerly w. Am. Newspaper Guild. Publs: "Aunt Jane" series on annual reports; frequent author of TRENDS; contbr. articles to jrnls. Hons: Levertt House Award for outstanding sr., Harvard, 1956; U.S. Army Cert. of Achievement for outstanding activities in German/Am. rels., Stuttgart, German. Fed. Repub., 1959; Writing Award for Humor, Hearst Publs., 1960. Address: 18 Bellville Rd., Mountain Lakes, NJ 07046, U.S.A. 6, 24.

NEL, Barend Frederik, b. 16 Dec. 1905. Professor Emeritus. Educ: B.A., Univ. of Pretoria; M.Educ., ibid; Doct., Univ. of Amsterdam; Dr. Litt. & Phil., ibid, 1935; Dr.Phil., Univ. of S. Africa, 1945. Appts. incl: Sr. Lectr. & Hd. of Dept. of Educ. Psych. & Educ. Sociol., Univ. of Pretoria, 6 yrs.; Prof. of Educ. Psych. & Educ. Sociol., ibid, 1945-70. Mbrships. incl: S. African Acad. Sci. & Art; Fndr. & 1st Chmn. & Hon., S. African Assn. for Advancement of Educ.; Mgmt. Comm., Int. Assn. for Adv. of Educl. Rsch., Gent, 1953-; Assn. for Humanistic Psuchol., San Fran. Author of num. books & articles. Address: 410 Nicolson St., Brooklyn, Pretoria, Repub. of S. Africa.

NELIMARKKA, Eero Alexander, b. 10 Oct. 1891. Artist. Educ: Art Schl., Univ. of Helsinki, Finland, & in Europe & U.S.A. Mbr., socs. of art. One-Man Exhibitions in Finland & Sweden; Num. grp. shows in Europe & China; Major works in Finland, Leningrad Hermitage, U.S.S.R., Sweden, Norway. Hons: Cross of Liberty Class 4, War of Independence, 1918; State 1st Prize for art, 1927; Pro Finlandia & Mannerheim Medal. Address: Töölönkatu 12 A 11, Helsinki 10, Finland.

NELLI, Andrew Edward, b. 19 Dec. 1916. Executive Vice President. Educ: B.S., Fordham Univ., N.Y.C.; M.A., Columbia Univ.; A.M.P., Harvard Univ.; Certified Pub. Acct. Appts: Executive V.P., Carnation Int.; Chmn., Far East Broadcasting Co.; Dir., Caribbean Mfg. Co., Carnation S. Am., Carnation Co. (Malaysia) Sdn. Bhd., Carnation Co. (Singapore) Pte. Ltd., Cia. Pamamena de Alimentos, S. Am., Carnation Philippines Inc., Hanseatische Lebensmittel G.m.b.H., Int. Food Mfg. Co., Premier Milk (Singapore) Pte. Ltd., Solis Industrias de Alimentacion, S. Am. Mbr: Am. Inst. Certified Pub. Accts., States of Calif. & N.Y. Address: 5045 Wilshire Blvd., Los Angeles, CA 90036, U.S.A. 123.

NELLIST, Arthur Ivan, b. 4 Oct. 1926. Architect. Educ: Dept. of Arch., Regional Coll. of Art; Dip. Arch., A.R.I.B.A., F.I.Arb. Appts: Sr. Ptnr., own archtl. firm; Dir., Rsch., Fac. of Arch., Thames Polytechnic, & Sr. Tutor in Profl. Studies. Mbrships: Liveryman, Worshipful Co. of Paviors, London; Life Mbr., City Livery Club, London; Past Pres., Ealing Chmbr. of Comm. Archt. of new hotels, U.K. &

Europe; Churches, sports bldgs., Indl. bldgs., Prototype residential & day care ctrs. for mentally handicapped. Publs: Planning Buildings for Handicapped Children; Contbr. to profl. jrnls. Address: 32 The Mall, Ealing, London W.5, U.K.

NELMES, Archibald Wallace, b. 9 Mar. 1915. Federal Public Servant. Appts: var. appts., P.M.G.'s & Supply Depts., 1930-52; Registrar, Tech. Assistance Admin., U.N., N.Y., U.S.A., 1950-52; Prin. Contracts Off., Aust. Dept. of Supply, 1952-62; Sec. & Exec. Mbr., N.S.W. Contracts Bd., 1962-65; Regional Dir., S. Aust., Aust. Dept. of Supply, 1965-67; Regional Dir. (N.S.W.), Chmn., Dist. Contracts Bd. (N.S.W.) & Mbr., Bd. of Mgmt. (Stores & Transport), ibid, 1967-. Mbrships: Fellow, Royal Inst. Pub. Admin.; Bd. Dir., Rotary Club of Sydney, 1973-74; N.S.W. Leagues Club, Sydney. Address: 1157 Pacific Hwy., Pymble, N.S.W., Australia 2073. 23.

NELSON, Archibald John Alexander, b. 12 Aug. 1911. University Teacher. Educ: Adelaide Tchrs. Coll., Australia; B.A., Adelaide Univ. Appts. incl: London Rep. of Commonwealth Off. of Educ. & Min. of Post War Reconstruction, 1947-48; Off. i/c, Int. Rels., Commonwealth Off. of Educ., & Sec., Australian Nat. Advsry. Comm. for UNESCO, 1949-54; Dir., Univ. Extension, Univ. of New England, Armidale, N.S.W., 1954-71; Professorial Fellow, Adult Educ., ibid, 1971-; Lect.-Conf. tour, Indian Univs., 1971; Mbr., UNESCO Mission to Ethiopia, 1962. Mbrships. incl: Fellow, Australian Coll. of Educ.; Chmn., Australian Assn. of Adult Educ., 1968-69; Int. Congress of Univ. Adult Educ.; Int. Coun. of Adult Educ.; African Adult Educ. Assn. Author of articles on adult educ. & community. Recip. of hons. Address: Univ. of New England, Armidale, N.S.W., Australia 2351. 23.

NELSON, Barbara Lorraine (Czurles) (Mrs. Donald J. Nelson), b. 26 June 1936. School Administrator. Educ: Northwestern Univ., Medill Schl. of Jrnlsm., Evanston, Ill., 1954-56; B.S., Syracuse Univ., N.Y., 1958; Grad. Schl., Jrnlsm., ibid, 1958-59; M.Ed., Educl. Admin., Univ. of Hawaii, 1973. Appts: Grad. Inst. of Photography, Syracuse Univ. Schl. of Jrnlsm., 1958-59; Feature Writer, Photographer, Honolulu Advertiser, 1959; Asst. to Ed., Sunday mag. sect., Honolulu Star-Bulletin, 1959-61; Dir. of mission careers prog., Evangelical Lit. Overseas, 1961-62; Tchr., Engl. & Home Econs., Hawaii Bapt. Acad., Honolulu, 1963-64; Engl. Dept. Chmn., ibid, 1963-67; Secondary Schl. Prin., 1968-73; Elem. Schl. Prin., ibid, 1970-71; Writing Assignment for Southern Bapt. Sunday Schl. Bd., Nashville, Tenn., 1972-73; Music Dir., Pali View Bapt. Ch., Kaneohe, Hawaii, 1971-; Tchr., Engl., Punahou Acad. Honolulu, 1973-. Mbrships. incl: Nat. Assn. Secondary Schl. Prins.; Nat. & Hawaii Educ. Assns.; Coun. Prog. Servs. Comm., Girl Scout Coun. of Pacific; 1st V.P., 1973-74; Exec. Bd., 1974-76; Exec. Bd., Hawaii Bapt. Convention, 1972-75; V.P., Chi Omega, 1968-70; Nat. Assn. for Supvsn. & Curric. Dev.; Theta Sigma Phi; Omicron Nu; Honolulu Chorale; Hawaii Rock & Mineral Soc.; Choir Dir., Chmn., music comm., Pali View Bapt. Ch., Kaneohe, Hawaii; Hawaii Rep. to Nat. Girl Scout Coun., Dallas, Tex., 1972; U.S. Rep., Int. Girl Scout & Girl Guide event, Trondheim, Norway, 1953. Contbr. of Vacation Bible School materials to Bapt. Sunday Schl. Bd., Nashville, Tenn., 1974. Hons. incl: DAR Citizenship Award, 1954; Citizen of Week of Kenmore, N.Y., 1953; Hawaii's Outstanding Young Woman, 1970; Honolulu KGU Citizen of the Day Citations, 1971, 73. Address:

45-233 Koa Kahiko St., Kaneohe, HI 96744, U.S.A. 57, 76, 78.

NELSON, Betty Jean, b. 2 Oct. 1923. Medical Writer/Editor. Educ: B.A., N.Y. Univ., 1944. Appts: Med. Reporter, Med. News, N.Y.C., 1957-61; Pharmacy Ed., Drug News Weekly, 1961-63; Med. Reporter, Antibiotic News, 1963-67; Med. Ed., Urologic Soundings, 1962-72, Geriatric Times, 1967-70; Exec. Ed., Chronic Disease Mgmt., 1971-72; Ed., Urologic Procedures, 1972-; Ed., Surgery in the 70s, 1974-; Sci. Ed., Nat. Multiple Sclerosis Soc., 1972-. Mbrships: Nat. Assn. of Sci. Writers; Am. Med. Writers Assn.; Jrnlsts. Div., AAAS. Publs: Articles in var. med. jrnls.; Contbng. Ed., Hosp. Prac., 1966-72; Contbr., The Expectant Mother. Address: 372 Pacific St., Brooklyn, NY 11217, U.S.A. 5, 6, 132.

NELSON, Charles Lamar, b. 9 June 1917. High School Guidance Counselor; Free-lance Writer; Poet. Educ: B.A.E., Univ. of Miss., 1946; M.A., ibid, 1947. Appts: Classroom Tchr., Prin., & Guidance Counselor, sev. schls. in Miss., Ark., Tenn., Ga., Mo., & Fla.; At present, Guidance Counselor, H.S., Caledonia, Miss. Mbrships: Co-fndr., Natchez Poetry Soc.; Miss. Hist. Soc., Jackson; Past Treas., Miss. Poetry Soc., Jackson; Past Prog. Chmn., Natchez Exchange Club. Publs: The Marble Urn, 1941; William Faulkner: The Anchorite of Rowan Oak, 1973; Poems in Nat. Anthol. of Poetry & in sev. poetry jrnls.; Features & articles in num. mags. & newspapers. Recip., Top Area Mgr. (sales) Award, World Book Ency. & Childcraft, Field Enterprises, Chgo., Ill., 1959. Address: P.O. Box 57, Caledonia, MS 39740, U.S.A. 57.

NELSON, Elizabeth. Educator. Educ: B.S., Ala. State Tchrs. Coll., 1939; M.S., Wayne State Univ., Detroit, Mich., 1948; N.Y. Univ., 1950; Univ. of Heidelberg, German Fed. Repub., 1950; Mich. State Univ., U.S.A., 1961 & 73; Univ. of Md., 1964, 69; Univ. of Paris, France, 1965, 67; Univ. of Neuchatel, Switz., 1969-71; Appts: Tchr., Jefferson Co. Schls., Ala., U.S.A., 1939-45, & Geo. Wash. Carver Schl., Ferndale, Mich., 1945-55; Prin., ibid, 1955-58; Curric. Coord., 1959; Tchr., Bad Kreznach Elem. Schl. (for U.S. Army), Germany, 1962, Vassincourt Am. Elem. Schl., Overseas Dependents Schls., Dept. of Defense, Army, France, 1963-65; Verdun Am. Elem. Schl., ibid, 1966; Shape Int. Elem. Schl., NATO Shape, 1967-74. Mbrships. incl: FIBA; Organizer Pres., Carver Fed. of Tchrs., Ferndale, 1947-54; V.P., Mich. Fed. of Tchrs., 1951-52; Dist. Chmn., ACEI, 1961-62; Sec., Oakland Co. Br., Assn. for Childhood Educ., 1962; Zeta Phi Beta; League of Women Voters; NAACP; YWCA; OEA; NEA; Int. Comm., Shape Int. Elem. Schl., Belgium, 1970-73. Hons. incl: Gov.'s Award for notable contbrns. to educ. & people of Mich., 1955; Zeta of Yr., Zeta Phi Beta, 1960; Subj. of This Is Your Life prog., Carver Tchrs., 1960. Address: Shape Am. Elem. Schl., A.P.O. 09088, Shape, Belgium. 5, 15, 132, 138.

NELSON, Elizabeth Mara Barron, b. 2 Mar. 1920. Librarian. Educ: A.A., Stockton Jr. Coll., 1939; A.B., Our Lady of the Lake Coll., 1963; M.S. Lib. Sci., ibid, 1968; Postgrad. Work, Univ. of Calif. at Davis & Berkeley, Univ. of San Francisco. Appts: Libn., Our Lady of the Lake H.S., San Antonio, Tex., 1963-65; Libn., Madrid Dependent H.S., Rorrejon, Spain, 1965-66; Libn., Royal Oak Dependent Elementary Schl., Madrid, ibid, 1966-67; Libn., Lincoln H.S., Stockton, Calif., 1968-69; Dir. Media Ctr., ibid, 1970-. Mbrships: ALA; Am. Assn. Schl. Libns.; NEA; AAUW; Calif. Assn. Schl. Libns.; Calif. Tchrs. Assn.; Calif. Assn. for

Educl. Media & Technol.; United Fedn. of Doll Clubs; Lincoln Unified Tchrs. Assn.; Stockton Doll Club. Contbr. to profl. jrnls. Hons: Nat. Award, Alpha Beta Alpha Fraternity (Pi Chapt.); Grad. Fellowship Lib. Sci., Dept. of Hlth., Educ., Welfare. Address: 521 Lincoln Rd., Stockton, CA 95207, U.S.A. 5, 138.

NELSON, Esther Marion. Educator; Professor of Education. Educ: B.S., Univ. of Ore., Eugene, U.S.A., 1926; M.A., Columbia Univ., N.Y.C., 1929; Ph.D., ibid, 1939; Postdoctoral Rsch., 1946-48. Appts: Tchr., Educ. & Engl., Dir. of Publicity, & Supvsr., Student Tchng., State Univ. of N.Y., Coll. of Educ., Oneonta, 1931-43; P.R. & Intelligence, Women's Army Corps, U.S.A. & Asiatic-Pacific Theatre of Ops., 1943-46; Gen. Educ. & Rsch., U.S. Naval Operating Base, Guantanamo Bay, Cuba, 1948-50; Assoc. Prof.-Prof., Educ., Univ. of Houston, Tex., 1950-. Num. mbrships. incl: NEA; AAUP; Am. Assn. of Higher Educ.; Histn., Am. Legion, Houston Post 52, 1972-74; AAUW; Kappa Delta Pi; Pi Lambda Theta; Alpha Sigma Omicron. Publs: Analysis of the Content of Student Teaching Courses in State Teachers Colleges, 1939; Assoc., National Survey of the Education of Teachers in the U.S.A., 6 vols., 1931-35; Ed., FEASC Intelligence Bulletin, 1945; Num. contbns. to educl. jrnls. & newspapers. Recip., Num. hons., citations, special awards, plaques, dips., & certs. Address: 4432 Wheeler St., Houston, TX 77004, U.S.A. 5, 7, 15, 22, 57, 125, 128, 129, 130, 132, 138.

NELSON, George J., b. 12 Nov. 1905. Investment Banker Educ: M.A.; London Schl. of Econs., U.K.; Univ. of Cambridge, ibid. Appts. incl: Economist; Pres., Belson Fund, Inc., U.S.A., 1955-; Pres., Tokyo Fund, Inc. Mbrships. incl: Chmbr. of Comm., State of N.Y.; Chmbr. of Comm., Comm. on Finance & Currency; N.Y. Socs. of Security Analysts & For. Analysts; Am. & Metropol. Econ. Assns.; Money Marketeers; N.Y. Assn. of Bus. Economists; The Pilgrims; Ch. Club of N.Y.; Nat. Guild of Chmen; Am. Ch. Union; Episc. Actors Guild of Am.; Nat. Coun. of Metropol. Opera; Am. Friends of Covent Gdn.; Bd. of Dirs., Wine & Food Soc.; Chmn., Mbrship. Comm. ibid; Catarina de Medici Soc.; Japan Soc., Inc.; Engl. Speaking Union; Am. Scandinavian Soc.; Order of Lafayette; Mid-Ocean Club, Bermuda; Annabel's London; Rotarians; St. George's Soc.; France-Am. Soc.; Lucullus Cir.; Accademia Italiana della Cuccina; Commandeur, Confrerie des Chevaliers du Tastevin. Author, Anatomy of Wall Street, 1968. Address: 12 E. 93rd, N.Y., NY 10028. U.S.A. 6, 12, 16, 22, 64, 123, 128, 131.

NELSON, H. Tracy, b. 30 May 1895. Attorney. Educ: Permanent Tchrs. Cert., 1st Grade, State Tchrs. Coll., San Marcos, Tex.; Cert. Pub. Acct., Buford Coll.; LL.B., Jefferson Schl. of Law. Appts: Tchr., Tex. Pub. Schls., 2 yrs.; Ptnr., Nelson & Nelson, Cert. Pub. Accts., 40 yrs.; Tchr., Cert. Pub. Acct. Coaching & Income Tax, YMCA Evening Classes, 2 yrs.; Pvte. Prac., Tax Atty., 6 yrs. Mbrships: Am. Assn. of Atty.-Cert. Pub. Accts.; Am. Bar Assn.; Am. Inst. of Cert. Pub. Accts.; Dallas Petroleum Club; Tex. Astronomical Soc.; Chautauqua Literary Soc.; Pres., Tex. Soc. of Cert. Pub. Accts., 1936-37. Publs: (book) The Heavens & Earth Declare; (songs) Queen of my Heart; Rainbow of Happiness; Nestled among the Roses; My Fondest Dreams; My Mother's Voice; Newspaper Columnist, Today's Tax Talk. Hold sev. patents for airplane inventions. Address: 3161 1st Nat. Bank Bldg., Dallas, TX 75202, U.S.A. 7, 22, 125.

NELSON, Howard C., b. 4 June 1914. Civil Engineer. Educ: B.C.E., Univ. of Fla., 1946. Appts: Res. Hydrographer, Int. Boundary Commn., U.S. Dept. Agric., 1937-40; 2nd Lt.-Major, U.S. Armed Forces, 1941-45, 1950-52; Civil Engr., Pvte. Prac., 1946-48; Design Engr., U.S. Soil Conservation Serv., Dept. Agric., 1949-; Mbr., Martin Co. Planning Bd., 1957-58. Mbrships: Am. Soc. Civil Engrs.; Chapt. Pres., Am. Soc. Agric. Engrs.; Sec. Pres., ibid, 1963-64. Veterans for For. Wars; Chapt. Advsr., Square Dance Clubs, & Bd. Mbr., Pres., ibid, 1964-65, 1968-69. Address: 4118 N.W. 36th St., Gainesville, FL 32605, U.S.A.

NELSON, Howard Duane, b. 31 Mar. 1930. Opera & Concert Baritone Soloist; Singing Teacher; Music Educator. Educ: B.A., Fresno State Coll., Calif., 1956; M.A., Univ. of Wash., Seattle, 1960; D.Mus. Arts, ibid, 1967; vocal trng. w. Vern Delaney, August Werner, Wm. Miller. Appts: Instr., Voice, Univ. of Wash., Seattle, 1959-60; Asst. Prof. Mus., Trinity Coll., Chgo., Ill., 1960-66; Solo Artist, Chgo. Lyric Opera, 1963-66; Ldng. Lyric Baritone, Zurich Opera, Switzerland, 1967-; guest appearances Basle, Cologne & Hamburg, Germany. Hons: 1st Place Award, San Francisco Opera Auditions, 1960; Am. Opera Auditions, Chgo. Area, 1962. Address: Opernhaus Zurich, 8001 Zurich, Switzerland. 4.

NELSON, James Woodrow, b. 29 Mar. 1914. Lawyer. Educ: A.B., Dickinson Coll., 1935; LL.B., Univ. of Pa., 1938. Appts. incl: Admitted to Pa. Bar, 1938; Law Clerk, Supreme Ct. of Pa., Phila., 1939-41; Assoc., McCoy, Brittain, Evans & Lewis, ibid, 1941-46; Serv., U.S. Navy, 1943-45; Sr. Ptnr., Nelson, Campbell & Levine, Altoona, Pa., 1946-; Asst. Sec. & Dir., Boyer Bros., Inc.; V.P. & Dir., Condrin Oldsmobile-Cadillac, Inc. Mbrships. incl: Pa. Bar Assn.; Phila. Bar. Assn., Blair Co. Bar Assn.; Am. Arbitration Assn.; Nat. Panel, ibid, 1963-; U.N. Assn. of U.S.A.; Nat. Legacies Comm., ibid, 1957-67; Altoona City Water & Sewer Authority, 1962-73; Pa. Republican State Comm., 1964-72; Pa. Republican Platform Comm., 1966; Blair Co. Hist. Soc.; Phi Beta Kappa; Order of the Coif. Hons: Bronze Star with Combat V, 5 Battle Stars, U.S. Navy. Address: 1118 26th Ave., Altoona, PA 16601, U.S.A. 6.

NELSON, Robert Eddinger, b. 2 Mar. 1928. Consultant to Not-for-Profit Organizations. Educ: B.A., Northwestern Univ, 1949. Appts. incl: Pub. Info. & Personnel Work, U.S. Army, SHAPE, France, 1951-53; Asst. Dir., Alumni Rels., Northwestern Univ., 1954-55; V.P. & Dir. of P.R., Iowa Wesleyan Coll., 1955-58; Vice Chancellor for Dev., Univ. of Kan. City, 1958-61; V.P., Instnl. Dev., Ill. Inst. Technol., 1961-68; Pres., Robert Johnston Corp., 1968-69; Pres. & Treas., Robert E. Nelson Assocs., Inc., 1969-. Mbr. & Off., num. profl. civic & fraternal orgs. Contbr., Handbook of College & University Administration, 1970. Num. articles, higher educ. & dev. Recip., L.H.D. (Hon.), Iowa Wesleyan Coll., 1969. Address: Robert E. Nelson Assocs. Inc., 100 S. York Rd., Elmhurst, IL 60126, U.S.A. 8, 15, 16.

NELSON, Ruth McLendon (Mrs.), b. 20 Oct. 1910. Prayer Leader; Prayer Counselor. Educ: Salem Coll., Winston-Salem, NC; Duke Univ.; Grad., Bus. Coll. Appts: Ldr., Prayer Seminars, Chs., Retreats & Confs.; Exec. Sec., Dept. of Prayer & Spiritual Life, Asbury Theol. Sem., Ky.; Counselor, Friend & Prayer Ptnr. to many students; Planner & Projector, World Prayer Ctr., Asbury Theol. Sem.; Ldr., Communion Prayer Fellowship; Prayer Grp.

Ldr., Coun. Ring, Tenn. CFO; Coord., Prayer Grps., E. Area Tex., Alive, Inc. Pavilion, Hemisfair, San Antonio; Counselor; Sermons from Sci. Pavilion, Expo '67, Montreal, Canada. Address: Dept. of Prayer & Spiritual Life, Asbury Theological Seminary, Wilmore, KY 40390, U.S.A. 125, 138.

NELSON, Stanley, b. 9 June 1933. Writer; Editor. Educ: B.A., Univ. of Vt., 1957. Appts: Reporter, Burlington (Vt.) Daily News, 1957-58; Tchr., retarded children, Hackensack, N.J., 1958-59; Mutual Funds Rep., Investors Planning Corp., N.Y.C., 1958-62; Sr. Writer, Medica Materia, N.Y.C., 1962-63; Asst. News Ed., Medical World News, 1963-65; Sr. Writer, IMAGE, 1965-66; Sr. Ed., Hospital Practices, 1966-69; Freelance med. writer, var. mags., 1969-. Mbrships: Am. Med. Writers Assn.; Nat. Assn. of Sci. Writers, Jrnlsts. Div.; AAAS; Dramatists Guild; Co-chmn., N.Y. Drama Concept. Publs. incl: The Passion of Tammuz, 1959; Idlewild (poetry), 1970, 2nd edit., 1971; The Brooklyn Book of the Dead (poetry), 1972; Plays-24 prods., N.Y. & London, other U.S. cities; Contbr. to poetry jrnls. Hons: Thomas Wolfe Poetry Award, 1961. Address: 372 Pacific St., Brooklyn, NY 11217, U.S.A. 6, 11, 30.

NELSON, Victor Edwin, b. 1 Mar. 1904. General Surgeon. Educ: A.B., Univ. of Mich., Ann Arbor, U.S.A., 1930; M.D., Med. Schl., ibid, 1932; Dipl., Nat. Bd., 1933; Fellow, Am. Coll. of Surgs., 1947. Appts: Intern & Res. in Surg., Highland Pk. Gen. Hosp.; Jr., Surg. Staff, ibid; Asst.; Assoc.; Attng.; Sr.; Pres., associated med. & surg. orgs.; Mbr., sev. comms.; Staff Phys., Emergency Treatment of Trauma. Num. mbrships. incl: Wayne Co. Med. Soc.; Mich. State Med. Soc.; AMA; Acad. of Surg. at Detroit; Detroit Surg. Soc.; Highland Pk. Physns. Club; Pres., Highland Pk. Gen. Hosp. Staff, 1947; Pres., Acanthus Club, 1957; Fndr., Am. Bd. Abdominal Surgs.; Am. Mus. of Natural Hist.; Am. Assn. of Retired Persons; Engl. Speaking Union; Royal Oak Histl. Soc.; Mich. Assn. of the Professions; Past Cmdr., Circumnavigators Club; Detroit Pres., Alpha Omega Alpha, 1970-74; Phi Kappa Phi. Address: 3025 Crooks Rd., Royal Oak, MI 48073, U.S.A.

NELSON, (Rev.) Wilford Alexander, b. 5 Dec. 1930. Baptist Minister of Religion. Educ: Dip. in Theol., Toronto Baptist Sem., Canada, 1962. Appts: Organizer, Jamaica Clubs, 1966-70; Pastor, Antioch Circuit of Baptist Chs., 1966; Organizer, Nat. Volunteers Org., 1970. Mbrships: Mile Gully Area Citizens Assn; Gen. Sec., Jamaica Baptist Conven: Corres. Sponsor, Antioch & Norway Basic Schls. Ed., The Baptist Witness. Address: Antioch Baptist Church, Troy P.O., Trelawny, Jamaica, W. Indies 136.

NELSON, William Linton, b. 20 Jan. 1900. Retired Rear-Admiral; Mutual Fund Executive. Educ: Wharton Schl., Univ. of Pa. Appts. incl: Employee, Fidelity Phila. (Pa.) Trust Co., 1922-29; w. Investment Corp. of Phila., 1929-41; Organizer, Del Fund Inc., 1938; Dir., ibid, 1938-; Bd. Chmn., 1963-; Pres., 1942, 1946-71; Mng. Ptnr., Del Co. Investment Firm, Phila.; Pres., Decatur Income Fund, 1956-71; Dir., ibid, 1956-; Bd. Chmn., 1963-; Pres., Delta Trend Fund, 1967-71; Dir., Chmn. Bd., ibid, 1967-; Pres., Delchester Bond Fund, 1970-71; Dir., Chmn. Bd., ibid, 1970-; Dir., Del Mgmt. Co., 1952-; Bd. Chmn., ibid, 1952-57, 1963-; Pres., 1957-71; Chmn. Bd., Dir., Delcap Energy Fund, 1972-; Rear-Admiral, USNR, Retd. Mbrships. incl: Securities Ind. Assn.; Investment Co. Inst.; Naval Reserve Assn.; Navy League, U.S.A.; Nat. Assn. Security Dealers Racquet; Phila. Country Club. Hons: Legion o' Merit, Bronze Star; Commend. Ribbon. Address: 7 Penn Ctr. Plaza, Phila., PA 19103, U.S.A. 2, 6, 12, 16, 128.

NELSON-COLE, Olakunle John Theodore, b. 30 Nov. 1913. Physician; Surgeon. Educ: Univ. of Bristol; St. Mungo's Coll. of Royal Infirmary, Glasgow; L.R.C.P. & L.R.C.S. Edinburgh; L.R.F.P. & S., Glasgow; F.M.C.G.P. Nigeria. Appts: House Surg., Gen. Hosp., Lagos, 1947; Med. Off. i/c hosps. in var. parts o' Nigeria, equipped & opened govt. hosp. in Keffi, 1958. Mbrships: Fellow, Med. Coun. o' Nigeria in Gen. Prac., 1971; BMA; Nigeria Med. Assn.; St. Paul's Ch., Breadfruit, Lagos. Address: P.O. Box 57-Iketa, Lagos State, Nigeria. 135.

NEMIRO, Beverly Anderson (Mrs. Jerome Nemiro), b. 29 May 1925. Educator. Educ: B.A., Reed Coll. & Univ. of Colo. Appts. incl: Summer Session Tchr., Seattle Pub. Schls. 1945 & 1946; Fashion Dir., Denver Dry Goods Co., 1948-51; Fashion Model, 1951-58; Fashion Dir., Denver Market Week Assn., 1952-53. Moderator, Your Preschool Child (TV prog.) 1955-56; Tchr., Realities of Writing, Univ. o' Colo., 1970-. Publs. incl: The Complete Book Of High Altitude Baking (w. D. Hamilton) 1961; Colorado A La Carte (w. D. Hamilton) 1963; The Lunch Box Cookbook (w. M. Von Allman), 1965; Colorado A La Carte Series I (w. D. Hamilton), 1966; Where To Eat In Colorado (w. D. Hamilton), 1967; The Busy People's Cookbook, 1971; num. articles on cooking, grooming, fashion, entertaining & mod. living for nat. mags. Mbrships: Bd. Dirs. Colo. Authors' League; Denver Women's Pres Club; Nat. Woman Writers; Authors League & Authors Guild of Am.; Soc. of Mag. Writers Hons. incl: sev. Lit. awards. Address: 470 Westwood Drive, Denver, CO 80206, U.S.A. 5 132, 138.

NEMSCHAK, Franz, b. 27 July 1907. Economist. Educ: Dr.jur., 1931; Postgrad. econ. & sociol. studies. Appts: Econ. lawyer Free-lance Author; Dir., Osterreichisches Inst für Wirtschaftsforschung, 1945-72; Staff Dir. econ. dept., ERP-Büro, Fed. Chancellor's Off. & Mng. Dir., Osterreichische Produktivitätszentrum, 1949-53; Pres. Wirtschaftsund Sozialwissenschaftliche Rechenzentrum, Vienna, 1971-72; Dir., Vienn Inst. for Int. Comparative Econs., 1973-; Bd. o' Dirs., Osterreichisches Inst. fü Wirtschaftsforschung. Publs. incl: Di europäische Integration aus der Perspektiv Osterreichs & der Schweiz, 1964; Osterreich Wirtschaft in den 60er & 70er Jahren, 1970 Recip., Grand Medal of Hon. for servs. t Repub. of Austria. Address: Arsenal Objek 3/II/28, 1030 Vienna, Austria.

NERGER, (Rev.) Edwin Albert, b. 12 Jan. 1916. Lutheran Minister. Educ: Luth' Concordia Coll., Austin, Tex., 1933; St. John' Coll., Winfield, Kan., 1935; Concordia Sem., S' Louis, Mo., 1939. Appts: Asst. Pastor, Trinit Luth. Ch., 1939; Pastor, St. John's Luth. Ch Galveston, Tex., 1940-46; Asst. Pastor, S' Paul's Luth. Ch., Ft. Wayne, Ind., 1946-50 Pastor, ibid, 1950-. Mbrships: Chmn., Bd. o World Relief, Luth. Ch., Mo. Synod, 1953-68 Sec., Bd. of Luth. World Relief, N.Y., 1956 Chmn., Mayor's Commn. on Human Rels. o the City of Ft. Wayne, Ind., 1963-70; Truste The Luth. Fndn., 1967-70; Mbr., Commn. o World Hunger, St. Louis, Mo., 1970-. Publ co-ed., Crossing the Kidron, 1954, Pastor a Work, 1959; contbr. to Portals of Prayer, 1955

'56; Concordia Pulpit, 1951-. Address: 1126 Barr St., Ft. Wayne, IN 46802, U.S.A. 8.

NERY, Eduardo, b. 2 Sept. 1938. Painter; Graphic Artist. Educ: Grad., Fine Arts Acad. of Lisbon; pvte. studies w. Jean Lurçat, Saint-Céré, France. Appts: Tchr., Instituto de Arte e Decoraçao, Lisbon, 1969-72; Jt. Sub-Dir., Tchr., AR.CO-Centro de Arte e Comunicacao Visual, Lisbon, 1973-. Mbrships. incl: World Crafts Coun.; Hon. Mbr., Tommaso Campanella Acad. of Rome, 1970-. Bd. of Dirs., Sociedade Nacionale de Belas Artes 1963-67, 1971-73; Solo Exhibs. incl: Sociedade Nacionale de Belas Artes, 1964, '67, '68; Galeria III, Lisbon, 1970, '72; Centre Cultural Portugais, Paris, 1973. Over 60 grp. exhibs., Portugal, 1959-, & many for. exhibs. Mural & pavement decorations, commercial & pub. bldgs. Works of art in 6 museums, many pvte. collects. Recip., var. painting awards. Address: Ave. Columbano Bordalo Pinheiro, 95-7°, Dto., Lisbon-1, Portugal. 133.

NESBIN, Esther Caroline Winter, b. 5. Aug. 1910. Librarian; Teacher; Administrator. Educ: B.A., Univ. of Buffalo, N.Y., 1931; Cert. Lib. Sci., ibid, 1932. Appts: Lib. Asst., Grosvenor Lib., Buffalo, 1931-42; Instr. Lib. Sci., Univ. of Buffalo, 1939-42; Libn., Temple of the Jewelled Cross, L.A., Calif., 1942-46; Libn. & Instr. in Lib. Sci., Palomar Coll., 1947-; Dir. of Lib. Servs., ibid, 1965-68; Asst. Dean of Instruction for Lib. Servs., ibid, 1969-. Mbrships: Calif. Lib. Assn.; Jr. Coll. Libns. Round Table (Pres. 1966); Calif. State Advsry. Comm. Lib. Techn. Prog., 1967-; Palomar Cactus & Succulent Soc. (Pres. 1958-60); Delta Kappa Gamma (V.P. Zeta Pi Chapt.). Publs: Shaker Literature in the Grosvenor Library, 1940; Library Technology Study Manuals, 4 vols. 1973. Hons: Award for Outstanding Serv. to Educ., Consuelo Lodge, Free & Accepted Masons, 1965, 1972. Address: P.O. Box 102, San Marcos, CA 92069, U.S.A.

NESBITT, (Mrs.) Olive Kathryn, b. 28 Jan. 1907. Librarian. Educ: Erie Br., Univ. of Pitts., 1930-31; Univ. of Buffalo, 1934; Libn.'s Cert., 1941. Appts. incl: Asst., Erie Pub. Lib., 1929-46, 1st Asst., Tech. Div., 1942-46; Sec., Off. Mgr., Libn., Family & Child Serv., Erie, 1947-49; Hd. Libn., Engrng. & Sci. Lib., Lord Mfg. Co., Erie, 1949-61; Libn., Hamot Med. Ctr., Erie, 1963-73; Tchr., Cons., student grps. & new libns. Mbrships. incl: Erie Mental Hlth. Assn.; YMCA; YWCA; Democratic Women's Coun., 1961-, Sec., 1965-67; Am., N.W. Pa., Pa. Lib. Assns.; Erie Special Libns. Assn., Chmn., 1967-69; Am. Soc. for Info. Sci., N.Y.; Sec., League Women Voters. Recip., Cert. of Merit for voluntary work, WWII, Pres. Truman, 1946, '47. Address: 1262 W. 10th St., Apt. 1, Erie, PA 16502, U.S.A. 5, 42.

NESBITT, Renee Jean, b. 10 Mar. 1937. Assistant Dean of Women. Educ: B.A., S.-Eastern La. Coll., Hammond, U.S.A., 1958; M.A., Colo. State Univ., Ft. Collins, 1961. Appts: Pub. Schl. Tchr., 1958-61; Hd. Res., Res. Hall. La. State Univ., Baton Rouge, 1961-62; Coord., Residence Hall Activities, ibid, 1962-65; Asst. Dean of Women, 1965-74; Mbr., Staff Personnel Policy Comm., 1969-74. Mbrships. incl: Pres., La. Assn. of Deans of Women; V.P., Women's Fac. Club; Nat. Assn. of Deans of Women; Past Coed V.P., Student Govt. Assn.; Past Pres., Kappa Rho; Past Pres., Kappa Delta Pi; Alpha Lambda Delta. Address: Drawer BR, Louisiana State Univ., Baton Rouge, LA 70803, U.S.A. 125.

NETHERCUT, William Robert, b. 11 Jan. 1936. Educator. Educ: A.B., Harvard Coll.,

1958; New England Conservatory of Music, Boston, 1959; A.M., Columbia Univ., 1960; Ph.D., ibid, 1963. Appts: Instr., Greek & Latin, Columbia Univ., 1961-66; Asst. Prof., ibid, 1966-67; Assoc. Prof., Classics, Univ. of Ga., 1967-72; Prof., Classics, ibid, 1972-. Mbrships. incl: Archaeological Inst. of Am.; Pres., Athens, Ga. Soc., 1972-73; Chmn., Lecture Comm., Explorers' Club, 1967; Am. Philol. Assn.; Classical Assn. of Mid W. & S. Publs: Invasion in the Aeneid, 1968; The Ironic Priest, 1970; The Imagery of the Aeneid, 1972; & other articles. Hons: var. acad. hons.; Vical Recital, Carnegie Hall, 1966; TV Prog., Ga. Educ. TV. 1970-71. Lectr., Int. Soc. for Homeric Studies, Athens, Greece, 1973 & 1st Int. Conf. on Ovid, Constanta, Romania, 1972. Address: 101 Moss Side, Athens, GA 30601, U.S.A. 6, 15, 22, 125, 126, 128, 130, 131, 139.

NETTLETON, Herbert, b. 6 Jan. 1913. Sales & Communication Consultant. Educ: Special Courses at Harvard Univ; Northeastern Univ.; New England Conservatory of Music; N.Y. Univ. Appts: Supvsr., Jet Engine Div., Gen. Electric Co; Nat. Sales Cons., ibid; Gen. Mgr., Communication Div., Teleprompter Corp., N.Y.C.; Pres., Herbert Nettleton Assocs., Clifton, N.J.; Nat. Sales Mgr., Kalart Victor Corp., Plainville, Conn, Advsr. to Pres. Eisenhower for Farewell TV Speech to the Nation, 1960; Pioneer of multi-media techniques for presentation of info.; Responsible for over 200 Communication & Visual Display Systems thru'out U.S. & O'seas. Mbrships: Dist. Gov., Toastmasters Int.; Fndr., 7 Toastmaster Clubs; Sales Exec. Assn., N.Y.C.; Am. Ordnance Soc. Address: 18 Arcadia Lane, Clifton, NJ 07013, U.S.A. 57.

NEUMANN, Bernhard Hermann, b. 15 Oct. 1909. Professor of Mathematics. Educ: Univ. of Freiburg, Germany; Dr. Phil., Univ. of Berlin, 1932; Ph.D., Univ. of Cambridge, U.K., 1935; D.Sc., Univ. of Manchester, U.K., 1954. Appts: Temp. Asst. Lectr., Univ. Coll., Cardiff, U.K., 1937-40; Pioneer Corps, RA, Intelligence Corps, Army, 1940-45; Lectr., Univ. Coll., Hull, (now univ.), 1946-48; Lectr.-Sr. Lectr.-Rdr., Univ. of Manchester, 1948-61; Prof., Hd., Maths. Dept., Inst. of Adv. Studies, Australian Nat. Univ., 1962-74; Sev. vis. appts., inclng. Vis. Prof., Vanderbilt Univ., U.S.A., 1969-70; Univ. of Cambridge, U.K., 1970. Mbrships: Fellow, Royal Soc., 1959; Australian Acad. of Sci., 1964; Councilor, 1968-71, V.P., 1969-71; Australian Coll. Educ., 1970; Councilor, London Math. Soc., 1954-61, V.P., 1957-59; Councilor, Australian Math. Soc., 1963-, Pres. 1964-66, V.P., 1963-64, 1966-68, 1971-73; Australian Assn. Maths. Tchrs.; Glasgow & Canberra Maths. Assns.; ANZAAS; Am. Math. Soc.; Canadian Math. Congress; Math. Assn. Am.; Wiskundig Genootschap Amsterdam. Author, works on maths., over 90 papers in var. math. jrnls. Hons: Adams Prize, 1952-53; Wiskundig Genootschap te Amsterdam Prize, 1949. Address: Dept. of Maths., Inst. of Adv. Studies, Australian Nat. Univ., P.O. Box 4, Canberra, ACT, Australia 2600. 1, 15, 23, 34, 43, 47, 50, 128, 129, 131, 139.

NEUMANN, Harry George Charles, b. 15 June 1914. Research Microbiologist. Educ: B.A., UCLA, 1938; Postgrad., ibid, 1959; Univ. of Southern Calif., 1940. Appts: w. Dept. of Water & Power, City of L.A., 1940-; Med. Dept., U.S. Army & Med. Admin. Corps (AUS), 1941-45; Rsch. Microbiol., Dept. of Water & Power. Mbrships. incl: Registered Microbiol., Am. Acad. of Microbiol.; Am. Soc. for Microbiol.; S. Calif. Br., ibid; Am. Waterworks Assn.; Engrs. & Archts. Assn. of S. Calif.; Water & Power Assocs., Inc.; Alumni Assn.; UCLA;

Alpha Zeta Chapt. Theta Xi; Past Sec.-Treas., 20-30 Club, Glendale, Calif. Contbr. to profl. jrnls. Hons: EAME; Am. Theatre & Am. Defense Ribbon; 4 Bronze Stars; medals of Rome-Arno, Rhineland, Southern France & Northern Appenines battles & campaigns. Address: Dept. of Water & Power, P.O. Box 111, Los Angeles, CA 90051, U.S.A. 9.

NEUMANN, Hava (Eva), b. 15 Jan. 1920. Scientist. Educ: Univ. of Budapest, Hungary; Hebrew Univ., Jerusalem, Israel; B.Sc., 1947; M.Sc. summa cum laude, 1948; Ph.D., 1964. Appts: Rsch. Wkr., Electron Miscroscopy, Weizmann Inst. of Sci., Rehovot 1949-50; Analytical Chem., Chem. Lab., Min. of Agric. ibid, 1951-52; Weizmann Inst. of Sci., Dept. of Biophys., 1953-; Sr. Sci., 1969-;· Vis. Sci., Chem. Dept., UCLA, 1961-62; Vis. Rsch. Assoc. Prof., Depts. Biochem. & Biophys., Tex A&M Univ., 1967-68; Rsch. Assoc. Prof., Dept. of Med., Univ. of Chgo., 1972-74; Vis. Prof., ibid, 1974-76. Mbrships: European Biochem. Soc.; Israel Biochem. & Chem. Socs.; Am. Chem. Soc. Author of 55 scientific publs. in fields of protein chem., enzymol., leukaemia, mainly in U.S.A. & Europe. Address: Dept. of Biophysics, The Weizmann Inst. of Science, Rehovot, Israel.

NEUMANN, Robert Gerhard, b. 2 Jan. 1915. Diplomat; Educator. Appts. incl: Asst. Prof., Univ. of Calif., L.A., 1947-52; Assoc. Prof., ibid, 1952-58; Prof., 1958-66; Dir., Inst. of Int. & For. Studies, 1959-66; Am. Ambassador, Afghanistan, 1966-73; Am. Ambassador, Morocco, 1973-. Publs. incl: The Government of the German Federal Republic; European Comparative Government; Germany After Adenauer. Hons: Order of the Star, 1st class, Afghanistan, 1973; num. fellowships & awards. Address: American Embassy, Rabat, Morocco. 2, 9, 12, 14, 15, 30, 59, 86, 114, 128.

NEUSTEIN, Abraham. Clergyman; Attorney. Educ: LL.B., St. Lawrence Univ., 1936; Rabbi, Yeshiva Univ., 1940; M.H.L., ibid, 1948; D.H.L., 1953. Appts: Rabbi, Jewish Ctr., Brighton Beach, 1940-; Prin., Yeshiva of Flatbush H.S., 1950-53; Counsel, Hebrew Prins. Assn., 1962-66; Arbitrator, Small Claims Ct., N.Y.C., 1972-; Instr. of Law, CUNY, 1973-. Mbrships: Praesidium, Mizrachi Org. of Brighton Beach; Assn. of Arbitrators of Civil Ct. of N.Y., Small Claims Div.; former V.P., Rabbinic Alumni Assn., Yeshiva Univ.; Speakers Bur. & Family Law Comm., Bklyn. Bar Assn.; Chmn., Seashore Dist. USO; Nat. Assn. of Secondary Schl. Prin. Publs: Life & Works of Bezalel Ashkenazi; Life and Works of Judah Ben Benjamin Anav. Hons. incl: Award, Yeshiva Univ., 1963; Plaque, Bonds for Israel, 1968; Cit., Jewish Nat. Fund, 1969. Address: 235 Dover St., Brooklyn, NY 11235, U.S.A. 6, 55.

NEVIN, (His Hon. Judge) Thomas Richard, b. 9 Dec. 1916. Judge of Crown & County Courts. Educ: LL.B., Leeds Univ., U.K., 1939. Appts: Solicitor's Articled Clerk, 1935-39; Special Constable, 1938-66; Territorial Army, WWII; Lt.-Col., ibid, 1944; Barrister, Inner Temple & N.E. Circuit; Asst. Recorder, Leeds, 1961-64; Chmn., Northern Agricl. Land Tribunal, 1963-67; Recorder, Doncaster, 1964-67; Dpty. Chmn., Quarter Sessions, W. Riding, Yorkshire, 1965-71, E. Riding Yorkshire, 1968-71; Humberside Crown Ct. Liaison Judge; Chmn., Lord Chancellor's Advsry. Comm. Humberside Area; Dir., Bowishott Estates Ltd. Mbrships. incl: Freeman, City of London; Leeds Hosp. Mgmt. Comm., 1965-67; Yorkshire Numismatic Soc.; Pres., ibid, 1968-69; Thoresby Soc. Publs: The

Past Passed On, & other poems, 1939; Hon. Ed., Transactions, Yorkshire Numismatic Soc. 1965-71; articles in legal & numismatic jrnls. Hons: T.D. & bar, 1949; Justice of the Peace, 1965. Address: 11 Kings Bench Walk, Temple, London E.C.4, U.K. 1, 41, 128.

NEVINS, (Rev.) Albert J., b. 11 Sept. 1915. Author; Editor; Publisher. Educ: Venard Coll. Clarks Summit, Pa., 1936; Maryknoll Sem. N.Y., 1942; L.H.D., St. Benedict Coll. Atchinson, Kan., 1963; Ordained Priest, Roman Cath. Ch., 1942. Appts. incl: Dir., World Horizon Films, 1945-68; Ed., Maryknoll Mag. 1955-69; World Campus Mag., 1958-67; Dir. Soc. Communications, Cath. For. Mission Soc. Am., 1960-70; Ed.-in-Chief, Our Sunday Visitor, 1969-; Publr. & V.P., OSV Inc., 1974-. Mbrships. incl: Treas., Tech. Ctr., 1972- & Bd Dirs., Inter-Am. Press Assn., Cath. Press & Latin Am. Studies Assns.; Cath. Assn. Int. Peace Prod., Author, Photographer, num. films. Publs incl: The Catholic Year, 1949; St. Francis of the 7 Seas, 1955; Church in the Modern World 1964; Away to Mexico, 1966; Our American Catholic Heritage, 1972; The World Book of Peoples, 1973. Hons. incl: Nat. Brotherhood Award, 1958; St. Augustine Award, Villanova Univ., 1962. Address: Our Sunday Visitor, Nol Plz., Huntington, IN 46750, U.S.A. 8.

NEVITT, Joyce, b. 18 Nov. 1916. Nurse Educator. Educ: Nursing Educ., Fulham Hosp. London, U.K., 1946-49; B.S. Nursing McMaster Univ., Hamilton, Ont., Canada, 1958 Grad. Study, Harvard Univ., U.S.A., summer 1961; M.A., Columbia Univ., 1963; currently Ed.D. Cand. Appts. incl: Lectr., Pub. Hlth Nursing, Univ. of Western Ont., London Canada, 1958-62; Asst. Prof. & Asst. Hd., Pub Hlth. Dept., Wayne State Univ., Detroit U.S.A., 1963-65; Dir., Schl. of Nursing, Mem Univ. of Nflnd., Canada, 1965-73. Mbrships incl: 1st V.P. & Chmn., Assn. Registered Nurses of Nflnd., 1969-72; var. comms., ibid; Pres. Provincial Br., Nflnd. & Labrador, Canadian Pub. Hlth. Assn., 1970-71; Charter Pres., Bus. & Profl. Women's Club; Nominated Chmn., Can Nurses Assn. Comm. on N. Educ.; Bd. Dirs. Victorian Order of Nurses, St. John's Br. 1973-74; Nflnd.-Labrador Assn. for Aged; Bd Dirs., Canadian Nurses Fndn. Contbr., profl jrnls. & book review, The Canadian Nurse 1969. Recip., acad. hons. Address: 7 Sycamore Pl., St. John's, Newfoundland, Canada.

NEWALL, Venetia June, b. 29 June 1935 Author; Scholar; Folklorist. Educ: Sorbonne Paris, France; St. Andrews Univ., Scotland U.K. Appts: Univ. Extension Lectr. in Folklore London Univ; Hon. Rsch. Fellow in Folklore Univ. Coll., London; Mbr., Int. Edit. Advsry Bd., Studies in Folklore, publd. by Folklore Inst., Ind. Univ., U.S.A.; Gen. Ed. of series County & Regional Folklore of the British Isles Mbrships. incl: Hon. Sec., Folklore Soc; Comm Mbr., Soc. for Folk Life Studies; Am. Folklore Soc; Int. Soc. for Folk Narrative Rsch. Publs An Egg at Easter—A Folklore Study, 1971; The Folklore of Birds & Bees, 1971; The Witch Figure (Ed.), 1973; Folklore, Myths & Legend of Britain (co-author), 1973. Hons: Fellow Royal Soc. of Arts, 1960 & Royal Geographica Soc., 1961; Int. Folklore Prize, Univ. of Chgo. 1971. Address: Dept. of English, Univ. Coll London, Gower St., London, WC1E 6BT, U.K.

NEWBOLD, Jerry McMullan, Jr., b. 25 Sept 1922. Presbyterian Minister. Educ: B.S. Davidson Coll., N.C.; M. Divinity, Union Theol Sem., Richmond, Va. Appts. incl: Presby Paster, Warsaw Presby. Ch., N.C., 1949-52 Supt., Vera Lloyd Presby. Home for Children Monticello, Ark., 1952-56; Exec. Dir., Presby

Children's Home & Serv. Agcy., Dallas, Tex., 1956-73; Exec. Dir., Presby. Home, Lynchburg, Zuni Presby. Trng. Ctr. & New River Valley Children's Home, Radford, all Va., 1973-; Former Chap. (Capt.) N.C. Nat. Guard. Mbrships: Chmn., Bd. of Advsrs., Grp. Child Care Cons. Servs., Schl. of Soc. Work, Univ. of N.C.; Pres., Presby. Child Care Assn.; Pres., Southwestern & Tex. Assns. Execs. of Homes for Children; Tex. Govs. Deleg. to 1970 White House Conf. on Children; Chmn., Planning Comm., Workshop for Personnel of Homes for Children, Univ. of Tex.; Rotary Int. Hons: L.H.D., Austin Coll., Sherman. Tex. Address: 2621 Linkhorne Drive, Lynchburg, VA 24503, U.S.A. 125.

NEWBY, John S., b. 12 July 1915. Structural Engineer. Educ: B.A., Berea Coll., 1939; B.S., Univ. of Ky., 1947. Appts: Bridge Design Engr., Calif., 1947-52; Bldg. Design Engr., U.S. Army, Ga., 1952-58; Gen. Engr., U.S. Army Ordnance, 1958-61; Structural Engr., U.S. Info. Agcy., 1961-. Mbrships: Am. Soc. of Civil Engrs.; Am. Meteorological Soc.; Sigma Pi Sigma; Pi Alpha. Address: 4133 Teton Pl., Alexandria, VA 22312, U.S.A. 7.

NEWELL, Strohm, b. 21 Sept. 1916. Inventor. Educ: H.S.; Self educated. Appts: Former owner, Newfield Machined Parts Co., Hollywood, Calif. & LaMatic Co., N. Hollywood, ibid; Owner, Vanair Co., San Diego. Mbrships: Nat. Trust of Histl. Preservation; 2nd World conf. on Nat. Pks.; Exec. Bd., Friends of Pala Mission Indian Schl.; Smithsonian Instn., Wash. D.C. Patents owned: Elec. Gauge (U.S.A.); Rope Pulling Device (U.S.A., U.K., Canada, France & Mexico); Bolt or Nut Hd. (U.S.A. & Canada); Card Case (U.S.A.) Door Securer (U.S.A.); Device for Securing a Line (U.S.A.); Assembly for Pulling A Line (U.S.A.) Patents pending; 3 in U.S.A., 2 in Japan & 1 in Australia. Address: 2350 Sixth Ave., San Deigo, CA 92101, U.S.A. 9, 74, 120, 130.

NEWGARDEN, Albert, b. 9 May 1930. Editor; Writer. Educ: B.A., Columbia Coll., 1952. Appts: P.R. Assoc., The Diebolo Grp., N.Y.C., 1954; Ed., Am. Mgmt. Assn., ibid, 1955-61; Ed. & Writer, Arthur Young & Co. (CPA's), 1961-; Ed., The Arthur Young Jrnl., 1965-; Dir. of Communications, 1969-; Dir., 1970-. Mbrships: Int. Assn. Bus. Communicators; N.Y. Assn. Indl. Communicators, 1969-72 (bd. govs., 1970-72; exec. V.P., 1971-72); Corporate Communicators Canada. Publs: Accounting & Accountants: A Little Anthology of Words & Pictures, 1969; articles in profl. jrnls.; Ed., The Field Sales Manager, 1960; co-ed., Management Guides to Mergers & Acquisitions, 1969. Recip., Award of Excellence, Int. Assn. Bus. Communicators, 1965, '70. Address: 277 Park Ave., N.Y., NY 10301, U.S.A. 6.

NEWMAN, Harry R., b. 10 Sept. 1909. Surgeon; Urologist. Educ: M.D., Univ. of Toronto, Canada, 1935; M.S., Univ. of Pa., U.S.A., 1940; Cert., Am. Bd. of Urol., 1947; Fellow, Am. Coll. of Surgs., 1946; Fellow, Int. Coll. of Surgs., 1961; Fellow, Am. Urological Assn., 1946. Appts: Asst. Prof., Yale Univ., 1946-; Assoc. Prof., Chief of Urol., Albert Einstein Coll. of Med., N.Y.C., 1955-58; Prof. & Chief of Urol., ibid, 1958-; Chmn. & Prof., 1968-; Major, USAF, 1943-46. Mbrships. incl: Canadian Med. Assn., 1946-; AMA, 1946-; Am. Urological Assn., 1950-; U.S. Mil. Surgs., 1942-46; Univ. Urologists, 1970-. Author of publs. in field. Hons: Disting. schlr. in Urol., Ben Morden Award, Albert Einstein Coll. of Med., N.Y.C., 1972; Honored for initiating &

developing Dept. of 'Urol., ibid, 1955-73. Address: 95 Broadfield Rd., Hamden, CT, U.S.A.

NEWMAN, Mildred Evelyn Hill (Mrs. Russel B. Newman), b. 5 Sept. 1917. Educator; Civic Worker. Educ: Ark. State Tchrs. Coll., 1935-36; Draughons Schl. of Bus., 1942-43. Appts: Tchr., McClelland Elem. Schl., Ark. 1936-38; Prin., Griffithville Elem. Schl., Ark, 1948-39; Tchr. Heber Springs Jr. H.S., Ark, 1941-42; Mgr., Shipping Dept., Ark. Ordinance Plant, Jacksonville, Ark., 1943-44; Sec. to Mgr., Nat. Life & Accident Inst. Co. Little Rock, Ark., 1944-45; Sec. to Transportation Agt., Miss. Pacific Railroad, Hot Springs, Ark., 1945-48. Mbrships incl; Pres., Jr. Forum Club, 1952-54; Charter Mbr., Woman's Soc. of Christian Serv., Meth. Ch., 1941, & United Meth. Ch., 1968; Sigma Chapt. Sponsor & Organizer, Alpha Kappa Chapt., Beta Sigma Phi; Bd. of Dirs., & Transportation Chmn., Henrico Chapt. Am. Red Cross, 1971-; Pres., Aux. Bd., Richmond Cerebral Palsy Ctr., 1974-75. Active in num. other civic orgs. Address: 8913 Norwick Rd., Richmond, VA 23229, U.S.A. 5, 22, 132.

NEWMAN, Paul Anthony, Sr., b. 12 June 1920. Submarine Nuclear Marine Electrician. Educ: Div. of V.P.I., Wm. & Mary Coll., Norfolk, Va., 1950. Appts: Aircraft Gunner, 1943; Mech., 1944, Pilot, 1946; Instr., Search, Survival & Rescue, WWII; Mbr., Sheriff's Posse, Santa Fe, N.M., 1946-50; Dr. of Divinity, Ch. of rsch., 1970; Min. of Bible Hist., 1970; Instr. of 1st Aid, Am. Red Cross, 1971; Dpty. Sheriff, Pearl River, La., 1973. Mbrships. incl: Past Dir., Tidewater Rescue & Survival Serv., Inc., Portsmouth, Va.; Fndr. & Past Dir., Southern Dixie Rescue Rangers Inc., Picayune, Miss.; Past Pilot Mbr., Civil Air Patrol. Hons. incl: Good Conduct Medal; Purple Heart; Air Medal w. 3 Oak Leaf Clusters; Soldiers Medal, 1944. Address: Route 3, Box 296, Picayune, MS 39466, U.S.A. 125.

NEWMARK, Marilyn. Sculptor. Educ: Art & Drawing, Adelphi Coll., 1945-46; Ceramics, Alfred Univ., 1949; Protege of Paul Brown, 1946-58. Mbrships. incl: Fellow, Nat. Sculpture Soc.; Coun. mbr., 1973-75; Mbrship. jury, Soc. of Animal Artists, 1972-74; Fellow, Am. Artists Profl. League; Allied Artists of Am.; Mbrship. jury, Catherine Lorillard Wolf Art Club, 1972-74. Works incl: Cormac, portrait, 1954; Elkridge, portrait, 1955; Peggy Augustus on Waiting Home, portrait, 1960; Am. Gold Cup Medal, 1970; Hacking Home Trophy for P.H.A., 1971; Hobson Perpetual Trophy for Liberty Bell Race Track, 1972; Appaloosa Horse Club Medal, 1973. Hons. incl: Coun. of Am. Artists Socs. Award, Am. Artists Profl. League, 1973; Gold Medal Award, ibid, 1974; Ellin P. Speyer Award, Nat. Acad. of Design, 1974; Mrs. John Newington Cash Award, Hudson Valley Art, 1974. Address: Woodhollow Rd., East Hills, L.I., NY 11577, U.S.A. 37.

NGAI LUEN YOU, (Rev.) Ming Yan or Lun Yau, b. 22 Feb. 1919. Minister of Religion. Educ: B.Sc., 1941, M.Sc., 1958, D.Sc., 1959, Wah Kiu Coll. of Engrng. & Comm., Hong Kong; Ph.D., Int. Free Prot. Episc. Univ., 1963; sev. other docts. & certs. Appts: incl; Comptroller, 1961, Dean of Students, 1962, Kingsway Coll., Hong Kong; Chmn., 1961 & 1962, Dean of Studies, 1963, Dept. of Civil Engrng., Chinese Inst., Kingsway Coll., Pres., James Martin Theol. Sem. & Coll., 1962-; For. Chancellor, Trinity Hall Coll. & Sem., Ill., U.S.A., 1966; Supvsr., Minn., Free Port Episc. Ch. of Hong Kong, 1967; Chancellor, Sussex Coll. of Technol., U.K., 1969; Hon. Fellow,

Curwen Coll., 1973. Mbrships; incl; Fellow, Am. Int. Acad. AAAS; Am. Ministerial Assn. Inc.; Fellow, Ecclesiol. Soc., U.K. has written on child educ. & welfare. Hons. incl: Silver Medal, 1964, Gold Medal, 1965, St. Andrews. Address: 61 Bute St., 2nd Floor, Mong Kok, Kowloon, Hong Kong, China, 131.

NGALANDE, Matiya, b. 2 June 1932. Government Servant. Educ: High Polytech. Inst., Shoubra Cairo, ARE. Appts: Tchr., Mission Schl.; Clerk, N. Rhodesia Govt. (Zambia); Mbr., African Nat. Congress, 1957; Org. Sec., ibid; M.P., Kasemba Constituency, Zambia, 1964; Parliamentary Sec., Min. Housing & Soc. Servs.; Zambia High Commnr., Ghana; Nigeria, 1966-68; M.P. & Min. State i/c Province, 1968-69; Min. State in Min. Trade & Ind.; Off., Pres., i/c State functions & Protocol; Zambia Ambassador, ARE, 1970-74; Kenya, 1974-. Address: Zambian High Commn., P.O. Box 8741, Nairobi, Repub. Kenya, E. Africa.

NGIAM, Tong-fatt, b. 11 Jan. 1917. Educator; Author; Civil Servant. Educ: Univ. of Qld., Australia. Appts: Tchr., Singapore, 1937-39; Staff Mbr., Overseas Chinese Banking Corp., 1939-42; Clerk, Interpreter, Nippon Kazima-Gumi, Ltd. 1942-45; Exec. Officer, Brit. Min. of Defence, Army Dept., 1945-63; w. Brit. Min. of Pub. Bldngs. & Works, Far East, 1964-70 w. HBM Dept of the Environment, ibid, 1970-. Mbrships. Advsr., Singapore Chuang & Ngiam Clansmen's Assn.; Life., Singapore Chinese Chmbr of Comm.; Citizens Consultative Sub-Comm., Joo Chiat Constituency, 1969-70; Chmn., Ngiam Clan Scholarship Fund. Publs: Inspirational Essays with Chinese Translations, 1934-46; Collection of Poems, 1935-37; various articles; Singapore Special Corres., China Weekly Review, 1946-49. Recieved special mention as a regular writer on education (33 yrs). for the Straits Times in Singapore in feature articles "Dialogue between you & the Govt." 1973. Address: 36 Ean Kiam Place, Singapore, 15, 11, 98.

NG'OMA, Philemon, b. 5 Aug. 1927. Postmaster General. Educ: Roma Univ. Coll., Lesotho, Southern Africa, 1963; B.A., Carnegie Coll. Phys. Educ. Appts: Tchr., 1953-62; Dist. Off., 1962-65; Sec., Zambia Pub. Serv. Commn., 1965; Under-Sec., Min. For. Affairs, 1965-66; Under-Sec., Off. of Pres., 1966; Permanent Sec., Prin. Pvte. Sec., Pres. of Zambia, 1966-69; Zambian Ambassador, People's Repub. China, Peking, N. Korea, 1969-; Chmn., Bd. Dirs., Zambia Mail; Ambassador to Italy, 1970-71; Postmaster-Gen., 1971-. Mbrships: Nat. Coun. United Nat. Independence Party; Copperbelt Provincial Sec., Tchrs. Assn., 1953-55; '56-58; Past Gen. Sec., Tchrs. Union; Chmn., Dominican Convent Schl. PTA; Chmn., Zambia Amateur Athletics Assn.; Councillor, Ndola City Coun.; Bd. Dirs., Zambia Trade Fair. Address: GPO, HQ, P.O. Box 1630, Ndola, Zambia, Ctrl. Africa.

NGWENYA, Malangatana Valente, (Artistic name, Malanga), b. 6 Jan. 1936. Painter. Educ: Indl. Schl. Appts: var., inclng. domestic servant, waiter, schl. tchr. Solo Exhibs: Lourenço Marques, Mozambique, 1961, 1970, 1972. Grp. Exhibs. incl: London, U.K., 1963, 1969; Paris, France, 1970; Lisbon, Portugal, 1972; Prague, Czechoslovakia, 1972, 1973. Work includes murals for Portuguese Bank, in Mozambique, Lourenço Marques; Auditorium, Beira; Factories Manufatos & Fabrica Princesa, Lourenço Marques; Hosp. of Univ. of Lourenço Marques. Contbr., poems, Penguin Book of Contemporary Art in Africa. Other contbs., var.

jrnls. Hons: 1st Prize in Mozambique, 1962; Mbr. Hons. Causa, Academia Internazionale Tommaso Campanella, Rome, 1970; Gulbenkian Fndn. Schlrship, 1971. Address: Bairro do Aeroporto, Rua de Camões 359, Lourenço Marques, Mozambique.

NIANIAS, Demetrius George, b. 8 Feb. 1921. Professor. Educ: B.A., Athens Univ., Greece; B.Litt., Oxford Univ., U.K., 1956; D.Phil., Athens, 1965. Appts: Advsr. & Ed., Eugenides Fndn. for Tech. Adv., 1957-66; Sec.-Gen., Min. of Educ.,Mr. Pipinellis' & Mr. Mavromichaelis' Govts., 1963; Min. of Press & Info., 1964; Chmn., State Bd. of Schl. Bldg., 1965-66; Prof. of Philosophy, Athens Nat. Univ. of Sci. & Technol., 1966; Min. of Press & Info., 1966-67. Mbrships: Vice Chmn., Greek Philos. Assn., 1973; Sec.-Gen., Greek Assn. for Aesthetics, 1960-62, '65-69; Advsr., Royal Fndns, 1965-67. Publs. incl: Plato's Theory of Language, 1965; Knowledge & Logos, 1965; Philosophical Studies 1960-64, 1965; The Dimensions of Crisis, Science & Society 20th. century, 1974. Hons: 2 Medals of Disting. Actions in Greek Resistance; Golden Cross, Order of St. George. Address: 39 Cleomenous St., Athens 140, Greece. 43.

NICHOLL, George William Robert, b. 23 Nov. 1907, d. 20 Apr. 1973. Naval Officer & Pilot in Fleet Air Arm; Author. Educ: Pvte. & secondary schls. Appts: Hd., Naval Accident Prevention, Off. i/c Safety & Survival Schl., Lee-on-Solent; retirement from Navy as Lt. Cmdr., 1952; Designer, inflatable rafts, boats, lifesaving equipment, P.B. Cow Ltd., Dunlop Ltd., Avon Rubber Co.; Pvte. Cons., inflatable products. Mbrships: Fellow, Royal Soc. Arts; Assoc., Royal Inst. Naval Archts.; Assn. Royal Navy Offs.; Tech. Advsr., Naval Lifesaving Comm. Publs: Survival at Sea, 1960; The Supermarine Walrus; Inflatable Boats; History of the Aircraft Carrier (for posthumous publ.). Hons: O.B.E., 1952; Samuel Baxter Prize for 1st Book, 1961. Address: Mrs. H.M. Nicholl, Saxons, Turleigh, Bradford-on-Avon. Wiltshire, BA15 2LR, U.K.

NICHOLS, Alonzo Lee, b. 14 May 1908. Minister; Attendance Supervisor. Educ: A.B. & B.D., Allen Univ., Columbia, S.C.; further studies, Tuskegee Inst., Ala. & S.C. State Coll., Orangeburg. Appts: Schl. Prin., 1930-33; Attendance Supvsr., Marion Co. Schls., 1955-74. Mbrships: Treas. for 6 yrs., Chap. for 3 yrs., Beta Alpha Sigma Br., Phi Beta Sigma; Int. Assn. Pupil Personnel Workers; var. positions inclng. Bd. of Dirs., S.C. Assn. of Attendance Supvsrs.; Marion Co. Alcohol & Drug Commn.; Bd. of Dirs., Prog. for Sr. Citizens of Marion Co. Recip. D.D. for outstanding work in African Meth. Episcopal Ch. as repairer & builder of chs., Allen Univ., Columbia, S.C., 1959. Address: P.O. Box 5, Marion, SC 29571, U.S.A.

NICHOLS, Annie Lee Holloway, b. 14 Sept. 1901. Teacher. Educ: A.B., Judson Coll., Marion, Ala., U.S.A., 1923; M.A., Univ. of Ala., 1950. Appts: Tchr., Soc. Studies, Capitol Heights Jr. H.S., Montgomery, Ala., 1923-26; Tchr., Soc. Studies, Jr. H.S., Marion, 1928-31; Tchr., Soc. Studies, Sr. H.S., Marion, 1945-53; Asst. Prof., Hist. & Educ., Judson Coll., 1953-60; Assoc. Prof., ibid, 1960-69. Mbrships: Pres., Perry Co. Tchrs. Assn.; Pres., Marion PTA; State Pres., Judson Coll. Alumnae Assn.; Marion Chapt., AAUW; Ala. Histl. Soc.; Charters Pres., Perry & Hale Co. Chapt., Delta Kappa Gamma; Phi Alpha Theta; Kappa Delta; First woman mbr., Marion City Bd. of Educ., 1966. Publs: Ed., History of Siloam Baptist Church, 1972; Paper given at meeting; Article in jrnl. Hons. incl: Outstanding Achievement Alumnae Award, Judson Coll. Alumnae, 1963; Citizen of the Yr. Award, Civitan Club of Marion, 1973. Address: P.O. Box 234, 1112 S. Washington St., Marion, AL 36756, U.S.A. 80, 125.

NICHOLS, Charles Harold, b. 6 July 1919. Professor of English & American Literature. Educ: B.A., Brooklyn Coll., N.Y., U.S.A., 1942; Ph.D., Brown Univ., Providence, R.I., 1948. Appts: Assoc. Prof., Engl., Morgan State Coll., Balt., Md., 1948-49; Prof., Engl., Hampton Inst., Va., 1949-59; Prof., N. Am. Lit., Free Univ., Berlin, Germany, 1959-69; Prof., Engl., Brown Univ., Providence, R.I., 1969-. Mbrships. incl: MLA; Am. Studies Assn.; AAUP; Edit. Bd., Novel: A Forum of Fiction; Univ. Club, Providence. Publs: Many Thousand Gone: The Ex-Slaves' Account of their Bondage & Freedom, 1963, 2nd ed. 1969; Black Ex-Patriates, 1966; Ed., African Nights: Black Erotic Folk Tales, 1971; Instructor's Manual to Accompany Cavalcade, 1971; Ed., Black Men in Chains: Narratives by Escaped Slaves, 1972; Articles in profl. jrnls. Recip., sev. schlrships., grants, & awards. Address: Box 1852, Dept. of English, Brown University, Providence, R.I., U.S.A. 43.

NICHOLS, Dale, b. 13 July 1904. Artist; Designer; Writer; Lecturer. Educ: Art Inst. of Chgo.; Chgo. Acad. Fine Arts. Appts: Art Dept., John Baumgarth Co., Chgo., 1924; Art Dept., Chgo. Tribune, 1927; Crafton Studios, 1928; Stevens, Sundblom & Stultz Studio, 1932; Pres., Soc. of Typographic Arts, Chgo., 1938; Carnegie Vis. Prof. in Art, Univ. of Ill., 1939-40; Art Ed., Ency. Britannica, 1942-48. Mbrships: Life Fellow, Soc. of Typographic Arts, Chgo. (Dir.; Pres.); Am. Artist League; Pres., Gulf Coast Art Assn., Miss.; life mbr., Brownsville Art League, Tex.; Am. Artist Grp., N.Y.; Assocd. Am. Artists, N.Y.; Tucson Watercolour Club. Publs: A Philosophy of Esthetics, 1938; jrnl. articles. Paintings incl: The End of the Hunt; The Cold Wave. Recip., 137 awards for fine design in printing and 18 for fine art. Address: El Rosario, Antigua G, Guatemala, C.A. 2, 7, 13, 57.

NICHOLS, Jeannette D., b. 27 July 1906. Artist; Art Educator, retired. Educ: I.I.T., U.C.; Schl. of the Art Inst., Chgo.; Individual tuition in Lithography & Mural painting. Appts. incl: Chmn. Art Dept. in sev. Chgo. Pub. H.S.', 1945-71. Exhibd. & won awards in num. Art Shows & Fairs. One Man Shows incl: Crespi Gall., N.Y.C.; Krieg Gall., Ill.; Kottler Galls., N.Y., 1973; sev. in Mich., Ill. & Ind. Work included in num. pvte. & pub. collections inclng. Wash. H.S., Chgo., Ill., Portage Pub. Schls., Ind. & 6 slides of work in Am. Lib. Color Slide Index, N.Y. Mbrships. incl: Life Fellow, Int. Inst. of Arts & Letters; former Pres. & Bd. Mbr., Chgo. Art Educators; Assn. of Artists & Craftsmen of Porter Co.; Gary Artists League; Artist Equity, U.S.A.; served on sev. Juries for Art Exhibs. Publs. incl: mag. articles. Hons. incl: 1st, 2nd, 3rd Purchase Awards, Annual Ceramic Show, S. Bend, 1956; Tri-Kappa Award (Southern Shores), 1967; Print Show (Juried), 1969. Address: 2 Frederick Drive, Gower, MO 64454, U.S.A. 5, 8, 15, 37, 105, 126, 132.

NICHOLS, John Peter, b. 10 Mar. 1906. Public Relations/Publishing Executive; Author. Educ: A.B., Columbia Univ.; Grad. Studies, Northwestern Univ., Evanston, Ill. Appts. incl: Off. USAF, 1943-45; Special PR Counsel, F.W. Woolworth Co., N.Y.C., 1946-50; Mgmt. Cons. (PR/Publishing), N.Y.C., 1951-55; Chief Exec. Off., Am. Electroplaters. Soc. Inc. & Publr.,

Plating Mag., 1956-63; Mgmt. Cons., N.Y.C., 1963-68, 1970-71; Chief Exec. Off., British-Am. Chmbr. of Comm., 1969. Mbrships. incl: Columbia Univ. Club, N.Y.C. (past Gov.); Army-Navy Club, N.Y.C.; The Down Town Club, Newark, N.J.; Sigma Alpha Epsilon. Publs. incl: Retailers Manual of Taxes & Regulations, annually for 33 yrs., created 1936; The Chain Store Tells Its Story, 1940 2nd edit. 1942; History of Woolworth (4 vols.) & Milestones of Woolworth, 1950; Skyline Queen & the Merchant Prince, 1973 paperback 1974. Hons. incl: Citations, U.S. Treasury & U.S. Dept. of Agric., 1942; J.H. VanderVries Pub. Affairs Award, 1942; Certified Assn. Exec., Am. Soc. Assn. Execs., 1973. Address: Spring Valley Rd., Morristown, NJ 07960, U.S.A. 24.

NICHOLS, Paul Lewis, b. 26 Nov. 1911. Civil Engineer. Educ: B.A., Univ. of Nev., 1934; C.E., ibid, 1956. Appts. incl: Proj. Mgr., Terminal Steel Co. Ltd., Honolulu, 1961-62; Civil Engr., Kaiser Engrs. Int., London, U.K., 1963-66; Proj. Engl., ibid, Oakland, Calif., 1966-72; Chief Engr., Vinifera Dev. Corp. subsidiary of Heublein, Inc., Rutherford, Calif., 1972-. Mbrships: Fellow, Am. Soc. Civil Engrs. Publs. incl: Construction of Second Mokelumne Aqueduct, 1947; The Russian River Project & Water Supply for Sonoma County, California, 1956; The Midway Island Project, 1958; Accra Plains Irrigation Feasibility Study, Ghana, Africa (jt. author), 1964; Feasibility Report & Master Plan for Water Supply System for Frost Protection & Irrigation of Vineyards, 1972. Hons. incl: Am. Theatre Serv. Bronze Medal, & Bronze Victory Medal, US Army, 1946. Address: 1475 Yountville Crs. Rd., Napa, CA 94558, U.S.A. 9.

NICHOLS, Paul Raymond, b. 13 May 1918. College Professor. Educ: B.S., Univ. of N.H., 1940; M.A., Univ. of Conn., 1942; A.M., 1949; Ph.D., 1952. Appts. incl: Asst. Prof., Econs., Simmons Coll., 1948-53; Assoc. Prof., ibid, 1953-63; Prof., 1963-72; Chmn., Dept. of Econs., 1965-70; Emeritus, 1972-. Mbrships. incl: Treas., local chapt., AAUP; Am. Econ. Assn.; Am. Stat. Assn.; Phi Kappa Phi; Kappa Delta Pi. Contbr. to profl. publs. Address: 153 Grant St., Needham, MA 02192, U.S.A.

NICHOLS, William Ichabod, b. 27 June 1906. Editor; Publisher; Library Executive. Educ: A.B., Harvard Coll., 1926; Rhodes Schlr., Balliol Coll., Univ. of Oxford, U.K., 1926-27. Appts. incl: Dir., Harvard Univ. News Off., Cambridge, Mass., 1932-34; Sec. & Campaign Mgr., Mayor Richard M. Russell, Cambridge, Mass., 1934; Advt. & Publicity Mgr., Nat. Elec. Power Co., N.Y., 1929-32; Dir., Elec. Dev., TVA, Chattanooga, 1934-37; Ed., Sunset mag., San Fran., Calif., 1937-39; Govt. Cons., 1939-45; Mng. Ed., This Week mag., N.Y.C., 1939-43; Ed., ibid, 1943-55; Ed.-in-Chief & Publr., 1955-65; Publr. & Edit. Dir., 1965-70; Pres., Am. Lib., Paris, France, 1970-72; Cons., Jrnlsm. & Communications, Lib. of Congress, 1970-73; Free-lance Ed., Author, & Lit. Cons., Paris, 1972-. Mbrships. incl: Coun. on For. Rels.; Pilgrims of the U.S.; PEN; Am. Soc. of Rhodes Schlrs.; Chmn., Nat. Book Comm., 1966-68; Sigma Delta Chi. Ed: Words to Live By, 1948; A New Treasury of Words to Live By, 1962; On Growing Up (H. Hoover), 1962; Fishing for Fun (H. Hoover), 1963. Recip., Irita Van Doren Book Award, 1967. Address: 21 Rue de Verneuil, Paris 7e, France. 2, 6, 12.

NICHOLSON, Gerald William Lingen, b. 6 Jan. 1902. Soldier; Military Historian. Educ: B.A., Queen's Univ., Kingston, Ont., Canada, 1931; B. Paed., Univ. of Toronto, Ont., 1935. Appts: Tchr., Elem. & Secondary Schls., Sask.,

1922-42; Prin., Battleford Collegiate, Sask., 1935-40; Serv., Prince Albert Volunteers, 1940-43; Histl. Sect., Gen. Staff, Canadian Army, 1943-61; Dpty. Dir., ibid, 1946-49; Dir., 1959-61. Mbrships: Sec., Canadian Histl. Assn., 1957-61; Canadian Comm., Comité Internationale d'Histoire de la 2eme Guerre Mondiale; Royal United Servs. Inst.; Royal Commonwealth Soc. Publs. incl: Marlborough & the War of the Spanish Succession, 1955; The Canadians in Italy 1943-45, 1956; Canadian Expeditionary Force 1914-1919, 1962; The Fighting Newfoundlander, 1963; The Gunners of Canada, 2 vols., 1967 & 1972; More Fighting Newfoundlanders, 1969; Num. articles on mil. hist. Hons: J.B. Tyrrell Gold Medal, Royal Soc. of Canada, 1968; Canadian Efficiency Decoration. Address: 1101 Bronson Pl., Ottawa, Ont., K1S 4H2. Canada 88.

NICHOLSON, Gunnar Walfrid Enander, b. 11 July 1893. Business Executive. Educ: M. Sc. Chem. Engrng., Chalmers Tech. Univ., Gothenburg, Sweden, 1916. Appts. incl: Mgr. Mills, Southern Kraft Corp., U.S.A., 1931-41; Res. Mgr., Union Bag & Paper Corp., 1941-45; V.P., ibid, 1945-52; Exec. V.P. & Dir., ibid, 1952-56; Pres. & Dir., Tenn. River Pulp & Paper Co., 1956-67; Dir., Rising Paper Co., 1967-; Dir., Olinkraft Corp., 1971-. Mbrships: Tech. Assn. Am. Pulp & Paper Ind.; V.P., ibid, 1944-45; Pres., ibid, 1946; Engrng. Inst. of Canada; Swedish Pulp & Paper Assn.; Swedish Acad. of Engrng. Scis.; Newcomen Soc.; Acad. of Pol. Sci.; Dir. at Large, Nat. Coun. Boy Scouts of Am.; Trustee, Norwich Univ., 1964-; Trustee, Am.-Scandinavian Fndn., 1965-; Church Club; Univ. Club; Union League, N.Y.C. Hons: Gold Medal Award, Am. Pulp & Paper Engrs. Assn., 1954; Comdr. of Vasa, Sweden, 1966; Doct. Engrng., 1968. Address: 200 E. 66th St., N.Y. NY 10021, U.S.A. 2.

NICHOLSON, Hubert, b. 23 Jan. 1908. Writer. Appts: var. in jrnlsm., inclng. Reuters Agcy., 1945-68. Mbrships: Fellow, P.E.N. & I.I.A.L.; Life Mbr., Nat. Union of Journalists. Novels: Face Your Lover; Here Where the World is Quiet; No Cloud of Glory; The Sacred Afternoon; Little Heyday; Sunk Island; Mr. Hill & Friends; Patterns of Three Four: Duckling in Capri; The Lemon Tree; Dead Man's Life; Ella. Memoirs, Half My Days & Nights. Essays, A Voyage to Wonderland. Poems: Date; New Spring Song; The Mirage in the South. Address: Kertch Cottage, 3 Albert Rd., Epsom, Surrey, U.K. 3, 137.

NICHOLSON, Malverse A., b. 28 Feb. 1938. Public Relations & Development Officer. Educ: Norfolk Div., Va. State Coll., 1955-57; grad., Morgan State Coll., 1960; Jrnlsm. Fellowship to Rutgers Univ., summer 1963. Appts: V.P. & former Bd. Mbr., Coll. News Assn. of Carolinas; Bd. Mbr., Mason-Dixon Am. Coll. PR Assn. Mbrships: PR Soc. of Am.; S.C. Div., ibid; S.C. Press Assn.; S.C. Broadcasters Assn.; Gtr. Orangeburg Chmbr. of Comm.; NAACP; Alpha Phi Omega; Alpha Phi Gamma. Hons: Nat. Newspaper Publrs. Assn. Award for News Writing, 1964; Nat. Assn. of Intercollegiate Athletes Souvenir Prog. Award, 1969. Address: P.O. Box 1774, S.C. State Coll., Orangeburg, SC 29117, U.S.A. 125.

NICKERSON, Herman, Jr., b. 30 July 1913. Governmental Administrator. Educ: B.B.A., Coll. of Bus. Admin., Boston Univ., Mass., 1935. Appts: w. US Marine Corps., 1935-70, ret. w. rank of Lt. Gen., served in China, Ctrl. & S. Pacific, Korea, Middle E. & Vietnam, as well as holding peace-time posts in U.S.A., inclng. Fiscal Dir., Marine Corps., 1958-62 & 2 terms, Pres., Am. Soc. of Mil. Comptrollers; Admnstr.,

Nat. Credit Union Admin., 1970-(presidential appointee); Mbr., Comm. on Interest & Dividends, 1972-. Mbrships. incl: Masons; Boy Scouts of Am.; SAR; Am. Legion; Ret. Offs. Assn. Hons; num. mil. decorations inclng. D.S.C. 2 D.S.M. (Navy), Bronze Star Medal & Air Medal; Ky. Col., 1969; Tenn. Squire No. 9396; Boston Univ. Alumni Assn. Outstanding Pub. Serv. Award, 1969; Disting. Achievement Award, Grand Lodge of N.Y. AF&AM, N.Y., 1970. Address: Administrator, Nat. Credit Union Admin., 2925 M St., N.W., Washington, DC 20456, U.S.A. 2, 114, 130.

NICKERSON, Sheila Bunker (Mrs. Martinus H. Nickerson), b. 14 Apr. 1942. Writer. Educ: B.A., Bryn Mawr Coll., Pa., 1964. Tchr., Poetry in Schl. Prog., Juneau, Alaska, 1974. Mbrships: Nat. League Am. Pen Women; Colo. Authors League; Denver Womens Press Club; Past Ed., Poetry Soc. Alaska. Author, Letter from Alaska & other Poems, 1972. Other works in progress. Recip., Colo. Authors League Award for best book of poetry by a mbr., 1972-73. Address: 540 E. 10th St., Juneau, AK 99801, U.S.A.

NICOL, Davidson Sylvester Hector Willoughby. UN Under Secretary General; UN Institute for Training & Research Executive Director; Hon. Consultant Pathologist. Educ: B.A., Christ's Coll., Cambridge Univ., U.K., 1946; Beit Mem. Fellow for Med. Rsch., 1954; Benn Levy Univ. Studentship, Cambridge, 1956; M.A.; M.D.; Ph.D. (Cantab); Fellow, Royal Coll. Path. Appts. incl: Sr. Pathologist, Sierra Leone, 1958-60; Prin., Fourah Bay Coll., Sierra Leone, 1960-68; 1st Vice Chancellor, Univ. of Sierra Leone, 1966-68; Permanent Rep. & Ambassador for Sierra Leone to UN, 1969-71; High Commnr. of Repub. of Sierra Leone, London, Ambassador of Sierra Leone, Norway, Sweden & Denmark, 1971-72; Under Sec.-Gen., UN; Exec. Dir., UN Inst. for Trng. & Rsch.; Hon. Cons. Pathologist, Sierra Leone Govt. Mbrships. incl: Governing Body, Kumasi Univ., Ghana; Pub. Serv. Comm., Sierra Leone, 1960-68; Pres., W. African Sci. Assn., 1964-66; Chmn., W. African Exams. Coun., 1964-69; Conf. Deleg. to UNESCO Higher Educ. Conf., Tananarive, 1963, Commonwealth Prime Mins. Conf., London, 1965 & '69, Singapore, 1971; Hon. Fellow, Christ's Coll., Cambridge, Ghana Acad. of Scis. Contbr. to books & jrnls. in field. Recip. of hons. Address: UNITAR, 801 UN Plaza, N.Y., NY 10017, U.S.A.

NICOLAI, August William, Jr., b. 29 May 1940. Writer. Educ: B.A., Wm. & Mary Coll., Williamsburg, Va., 1961; M.B.A., Pace Univ., N.Y.C., 1969. Appts: Advt. Account Exec., Young & Rubicam Inc., N.Y.C.; Asst. Dir., Sales Promotion, McCall's Magazine, ibid; Copy Dir., Metromedia; Asst. Dir., Communications, Young Presidents' Org.; Mgr., Employer Communications, Am. Standard Inc. Mbrships: Copy Dir., Jr. Div., Advt. Club of N.Y.C.; N.Y. Assn. of Indl. Communicators; Int. Assn. of Bus. Communicators; N.Y. Athletic Club. Publs: Ed., House organ, Young Presidents' Assn.; Ed. mag. YPO Enterprise; Ed., Standard Bearer, House organ, Am. Standard Inc. Contbr. to: Travel & Leisure; The Winged Foot. Recip., Cert. of Special Merit as Ed. of YPO Enterprise, Printing Inds. of Metropolitan N.Y., 1972. Address: 20 E. 35th St., N.Y., NY 10016, U.S.A. 6.

NICOLOV, Dimitar Ivanov, b. 12 Apr. 1924. Archaeologist. Educ: Sofia State Univ., 1950. Appts: Staff Mbr., Stara Zagora Mus., Bulgaria, 1951-63; Sci. Wkr. in Archaol. & Numismatics, 1963-74; Sr. Sci. Wkr., 1974-. Mbrships: State Mus. Coun., Comm. of Culture

& Arts, 1969-; Museums Int. Coun., UNESCO 1970-. Publs. incl: Augusta Traiana-Beroe; The Thracian Villa Rustica at Chatalka-Stara Zagbra District; The Large Landed Possessions in Roman Thracia; The Republican Roman Coins of Stara Zagora District. Hons: Kiril & Metodii Medal, Class II, 1961; Honoured Wkr. of Culture, 1972. Address: Musée Historique Régional, Stara Zagora, Bulgaria.

NIEBELSCHÜTZ, (Baron) Götz von, b. 10 Jan. 1909. Journalist; Diplomatist. Educ: Knights Acad., Liegnitz, Germany. Appts: For. Press Correspondent, Greece, 1933; Attaché, German Legation, Athens, Greece, 1941; Dir., Greek Radio, 1942; Sect. Hd., German Legation, Budapest, Hungary, 1943; Dir., Hungarian Radio, 1944; Cons., Cultural Affairs. Mbrships: Presidential Bd., Writers Assn. of S.W. Germany, 1947. Publs. incl: Greek Mirrors, Tales of New Hellas, 3rd edit.; The Dormouse, the Life of a Sluggard. Hons. incl: Mil. Cross of Merit. Address: Castellano, 02020 Posticciola, Rieti, Italy. 43.

NIELSEN, Erik Lykkegaard, b. 27 Jan. 1917. Surgeon. Educ: Grad., Univ. of Copenhagen, Denmark, 1943; M.D., ibid, 1954. Appts: Intern, 1943-51; Res. Surg., Sundby Hosp., Copenhagen, 1951-54; Sr. Res. Surg., Bispeberg Hosp., Copenhagen, 1955-58; Chief Surg., Ctrl. Hosp., Esbjerg, 1959-; Specialist, Gastro-enterological Surg., 1973-. Publs: Articles on surg. in profl. jrnls. Address: Torvegade 90, 6700 Esbjerg, Denmark.

NIELSEN, Frederik, b. 1 Jan. 1915. Professor of Danish Literature. Educ: M.A., Univ. of Copenhagen, Denmark, 1941; Ph.D., ibid, 1953. Appts: Tchr., Secondary Schls.; Lectr., Univ. of Copenhagen; Critic & Ed. in Chief, Soc. Democratic newspaper, Copenhagen, until 1966; Prof. of Danish Lit., Royal Danish Schl. of Educ. Studies, Copenhagen, 1958-. Publs: Faraos Fede Aar, 1945; Dansk Teater-og Litteraturkritik (Anthol.), 1948; J.P. Jacobsen (Ph.D. dissertation), 1953; Dansk Digtning i Dag, 1957; Hvorfor Leeser Vi?, 1961; Digter og Leeser, 1961; Martin A. Hansen, 1961; Nis Petersen, 1971; Ed., sev. Danish classics; Articles on lit. for Danish For. Min. Address: Hjortholmsvej 26, DK-2830 Virum, Denmark. 43.

NIELSEN, Henning Maegaard, b. 16 Aug. 1917. Government Official for Foreign Affairs; Business Executive. Educ: Bachelor of Econs., Copenhagen Schl. of Econs. & Bus. Admin.; Master of Econs., Univ. of Copenhagen. Appts: Sec., Min. of For. Affairs, 1946, Hd. of Sect., 1954, Min., Trade Dept., 1960, Asst. Under-Sec. of State, 1966; Attache, Danish Embassy, Oslo, Norway, 1949; Vice-Consul & Sec., Danish Embassy, London, U.K., 1950; Counsellor, Danish Embassy, Bonn, German Fed. Repub., 1958; Mng. Dir., Den Danske Landmandsbank A/S., Copenhagen, Denmark. Hons. incl: Kt. 1st Class, Order of Dannebrog; Officier de la Legion d'Honneur, France; Officer of Siamese Crown Order, Thailand; Cmdr., Order of Tunisian Repub. Address: Den Danske Landmandsbank, 12 Holmens Kanal, 1092 Copenhagen K, Denmark.

NIELSEN, Richard Elmer, b. 2 July 1919. Clergyman. Educ: B.A., Samford Univ., Birmingham. Ala., 1950; M.Div., Th.D., New Orleans Bapt. Theol. Sem., La. Appts. incl: Pastor Oakdale Bapt. Ch., Ramer, Ala., 1948-50, Ferris Hill Bapt. Ch., Milton, Fla., 1950-52, Immanuel Bapt. Ch., Hattiesburg, Miss., 1952-58, 1st Bapt. Ch., Cullman Ala.,

1958-67, Capitol Heights Bapt. Ch., Montgomery, ibid, 1970-; Exec. Dir., Ala. Coun. on Alcohol Problems, 1967-70. Mbrships. incl: Southern Bapt. Conven.; Exec. Bd., Ala. Bapt. Conven., 1958-61, '64-67; Admin. Comm., ibid, 1966-67; Bd. Trustees, New Orleans Bapt. Theol. Sem., 1963-72; Bd. Dirs., Ala. Temperance Alliance, 1962-67; Bd. Trustees, Judson Coll., 1961-64. Contbr. to Ency. of Southern Bapts. Recip., Award, Freedom Fndn., .Valley Forge, Pa., 1973. Address: 825 Federal Dr., Montgomery, AL 36107, U.S.A. 125.

NIELSEN, Sivert Andreas, b. 24 Nov. 1916. Diplomat; Banker. Educ: Grad. in Law, Oslo Univ., 1940. Appts: Employee, Bank of Norway, 1940-41; Pol. Prisoner, 1941-45; Dpty. Atty., Oslo Police, 1945-46; UN Sec., 1946-48; Sec., Norwegian Embassy, Wash. D.C., U.S.A., 1948-50; Sect. Chief, Min. Defence, 1950-51, Div. Chief, 1952-55, Under-Sec. Defence, 1955-58, Permanent Rep. & Ambassador to UN, 1958-66; Rep., Advsry. Comm. to Sec.-Gen. UNEF, 1958-66; Norwegian Rep., UN Security Coun., 1963-64; Chmn. & Vice Chmn., Norwegian Delegn., 13th-21st Sessions Gen. Assembly of UN; Gen. Mbr., Bergens Privatbank, 1966-. Recip., R.1 St. O.O., 1964. Address: Bergens Privatbank, P.O. Box 404-sentrum, N-Oslo 1, Norway. 34, 43.

NIEMISTÖ, (Väinö Veli) Pertti, b. 8 Apr. 1931. Barrister; Company Executive. Educ: LL.B., Univ. of Helsinki, Finland, 1957; Barrister at law, 1960. Appts: Lawyer, Union of Finnish Ins. Cos., 1959-61; Mng. Dir. & Chmn., Ed. Dirs., Starch Co., Hameen Peruna Oy, 1961-. Mbrships: exec. comm., Union of Food Ind., 1963-; local exec. comm., Chmbr. of Comm. in Finland, 1962-; exec. comm., Assn. Finnish Starch Ind., 1962-; Bd. Dirs., Ins. Co. Sampo-Tarmo, 1966-; exec. comm., Support of Finnish Defence, 1972-; Chmn., Bd. Dirs., Potatostarch Market centre, Perunajauhokeskus Oy, 1966-; Rotary Club of Hameenlinna. Address: Tammitie 6, Helsinki 33, 00330, Finland.

NIERMAN, Leonardo, b. 1 Nov. 1932. Artist; Sculptor. Educ: Degrees, Nat. Univ. of Mexico. Major Works incl: Mural, Crystal Enigma, Schl. of Commerce, Univ. City, Mexico D.F.; Mural, Golden West Savings, San Fran., Calif.; Mural, Cosmic Meditation, Phus. Bldg., Princeton Univ., N.J. Aurora Borealis, Santa Barbara Mus., Calif.; Volcanic Rock, Mus. of Fine Arts, Boston, Mass. One-Man Shows incl: I.F.A. Galls., Wash. D.C., 1959, '65, '68; Little Gall., Phila., Pa., 1964, '70; Alwin Gall., London, U.K., 1970; El Paso Mus. of Art, Tex., 1971. Grp. Shows incl: Mus. of Mod. Art, Mexico City, 1958, '65, '66, '67, '68; Biennale de Paris, France, 1959, '61, Waddington Galls., Montreal, Canada, 1958, '59, '68; Mus. of Fine Arts, Brussels, Belgium, 1966; Barberini Palace, Rome, 1966; Pitts. Int., Carnegie Inst., Pa., 1964, '67. Work rep'd. in sev. permanent collections inclng: Mus. of Mod. Art, Haifa, Israel; Mus. of Mod. Art, Mexico City; Gall. of Mod. Art, N.Y. Hons. incl: Degree, Univ. of Mexico, 1960; Prize in Contest of Mexican Contemporary Art, Art Inst. of Mexico, 1964; Palme d'Or des Beaux Arts, Monaco, 1969; Silver Medal, Tommaso Campanella Fndn., Italy, 1970; Royce Medal, N.Y., 1970. Mbrships: Int. Biographical Assn., U.K.; Int. Arts Guild, Monte Carlo; Salon de la Plastica Mexicana. Life Fellow, Royal Soc. of Arts, London, U.K. Subject of sev. books. Address: Nuevo Leon 160-701, Mexico 11, D.F. 105.

NIEVES-FALCON, Luis, b. 29 Dec. 1929. Sociologist. Educ: B.A., Univ. of Puerto Rico, W. Indies, 1950; M.A., N.Y. Univ., U.S.A., 1956; Ph.D., London Univ., U.K., 1963. Appts. incl: Secondary Schl. Tchr., 1950-55; Inst., Sociol., Univ. of Puerto Rico, W. Indies, 1959-62; Dir., Educl. Rsch. Ctr., ibid, 1963-67; Dir., Soc. Sci. Rsch. Ctr., ibid, 1971-73; Vis. Disting. Prof., CUNY, U.S.A., 1971-73; Prof., Sociol., Univ. of Puerto Rico, W. Indies, 1973. Mbrships. incl: Alpha Kappa Delta; AAAS; AAUP; Am. Sociological Soc.; N.Y. Acad. of Scis. Publs. incl: Recruitment to Higher Education in Puerto Rico, 1965; Diagnostico de Puerto Rico, 1970; Community Action and Pre-school Education, 1970; Public Opinion in Puerto Rico, 1972; Puerto Rico: Grito y Mordaza, 1972, Clima ideologivo de grupo de jurados, 1972. Hons: Disting. Citizen, 1965 & 1972. Address: 1503 Ashford Ave., Apt. 12-C, San Juan, Puerto Rico. 7, 14, 136, 141.

NIGAM, Raghubar Saran, b. 7 July 1935. University Teacher. Educ: M. Com.; Ph.D.; Dip., Co. Law; Int. Dip., European Integration. Appts: Lectr., Commerce, P.G.D.A.V. Coll., New Delhi, 1958-66; Rdr., Commerce, Univ. of Delhi, 1966-; Hd., Dept. of Commerce, Delhi Schl. of Econs., ibid, 1973-. Mbrships: Delhi Bd. of Tech. Educ.; Ctrl. Coun., Inst. of Chartered Accts. of India; Exec., Northern India Shareholders Assn. Publs. incl: Commonwealth Problems in Britain's Entry into the E.E.C.; Monetary Unification in Europe - genesis of the European Monetary Union; Non-Tariff Barriers to Trade; Enlargement of the E.E.C. Challenges & Opportunities for India. Hons. incl: F.E.E. Fellowship for participation in Seminar for Econ. Educ., 1968; Netherlands Govt. Fellowship, 1970. Address: Hd., Dept. of Commerce, Delhi Schl. of Econs., Univ. of Delhi, Delhi-7, India.

NIGGEMANN, Clara L. (Mrs. Pablo L. Leyva), b. 10 Oct. 1910. Poet; Writer. Appts: Dir., Poetry Sect., El Camagueyano newspaper, Canaguey, Cuba; Dir., poetry prog., radio stn. La Voz del Camagueyano, ibid; Dir., poetry page, Realidades mag., L.A., Calif., U.S.A. Mbrships: Centro Episcopal Latino, L.A.; Past, Ateneo Martiano de Cuba & Rosacruz Order of San Jose. Publs: Canto al Apostol, 1953; contbr., Collection de poetas de la Cuidad de Camaguey, 1958; En La Puerta Dorada, 1973; collab., Mural Poem, 1973. Participant, 7 Poets & 7 Painters Exhib., Western Md. Coll., Westminster, 1973. Hons. incl: Ateneo Martiano de Cuba, 1953; Coll. of Letters & Philos. of Camaguey, 1955; Rosacruz Chapt., Camaguey, 1955. Address: 3434 Angelus Ave., Glendale, CA 91208, U.S.A. 125.

NIGHTINGALE, Mae Wheeler, b. 30 Dec. 1898. Music Educator; Composer- Arranger of Choral Music. Educ: Grad., UCLA, 1919 Postgrad., ibid, 1923, 1926, 1927-28, 1933-34; Postgrad., var. other colls.: Studied piano w. Abby de Averitt, voice w. Bertha Vaughn, violin w. Ludvig Kading. Appts. incl: Dir., L.A. City Schls., 1926-59; Fndr.-Dir., Le Conte Troubadours, 1926-59, Mixed Glee, 1940-59, Alumni, 1934-74; Trng. Tchr., UCLA, Univ. of S.C., Calif. Coll., L.A., 1926-59; Tchr., courses Dev. Adolescent Voice, Coll. Pacific, Stockton, Calif., 1952-, Adams State Coll., Alamosa, Colo., 1955-, & Univ. of Ariz., Tucson, 1961-; Workshops, Decatur, Ga., 1954-, Pueblo, Colo., 1956-, Denver, Colo., 1956-, Galveston, Tex., 1959-, & Kan. City, Mo., 1961-. Mbrships. incl: A.S.C.A.P.; M.E.N.C.; Hon. Life mbr., S. Calif. Vocal Assn.; Hon. Life mbr., Calif. PTA; L.A. Secondary Music Tchrs. Assn.

Composer-Arranger of more than 200 publd. compositions. Recip., Mancini Award, Calif. Music Educators, 1964. Address: Sugar Loaf Box 300, Mtn. Ctr., CA 92361, U.S.A. 4, 5, 59, 132.

NIGRO, Felix Anthony, b. 8 Aug. 1914. Teacher; Author; Consultant. Educ: B.A., Univ. of Wis., U.S.A., 1935; M.A., ibid, 1936; Ph.D., 1948. Appts. incl: Prof., Dept. Pol. Sci., San Diego State Coll., Calif., 1961-65; Prof., Pub. Admin., Univ. of Del., Newark, 1965-69; Currently Prof., Pol. Sci., Univ. of Ga., Athens. Mbrships. incl: Am. Soc. Pub. Admin.; Am. Pol. Sci. Assn.; Int. Personnel Mgmt. Assn.; AAUP. Publs. incl: Public Personnel Administration, 1959; Management-Employee Relations in the Public Service, 1969; Modern Public Administration (w. L.G. Nigro), 1965, 3rd edit. 1973; Ed., Public Administration, Readings & Documents, 1951. Recip., Simon Fellowship, Univ. of Manchester, U.K., 1972. Address: 199 W. View Dr., Athens, GA 30601, U.S.A. 2, 7, 14, 15.

NIIMI, Masami 'Sparky', b. 5 Mar. 1916. President, Hawaiian Flower Exports, Inc Appts: Greenkeeper, Golf Club Mgr., 1931-41; Retail Liquor Store & Bar Mgr., 1941-43; Sgt., U.S. Army, 1943-46; Construction Machinery Operator, 1946-64. Hawaiian Flower Grower & Export, 1964; Advsry. Commn., Flowers & foliages, Hawaii State; Advsry. Counc., Farming, Hawaii Co.; Past Chmn., Parks & Recreation, ibid. Mbrships incl: Pres., Hawaiian Anthurium Marketing Assn., Mtn. View Veterans Club; Hawaii Co. Democrat Party (Past Chmn.); Bd. of Dirs. & Chmn., Community Betterment Volcano Lions Club; Agric. Comm., Hawaii I. Chmbr.; Hilo Shippers' Assn. (Past V.P.); Hawaii Nurseryman Assn.; Comm., Chmn., Boy Scouts; Dir., Puan Hongwanji Mission; Hawaii Farm Bur. Hons. incl: Good Conduct Medla & Pacific Theater Victory Ribbon, U.S. Army, 1945; Disting Serv. Awards, Democrat Party, 1969. Hawaii Co. Ext. Serv., 1972, Boy Scouts Am., 25 yrs., 1972. Address: P.O. Box 249, Mountain View, HI 96771, U.S.A. 78.

NIINI, Heikki Ilmari, b. 4 Feb. 1937. Geologist: Associate Professor. Educ: Cand. Nat. Sci., Helsinki Univ., 1958; Lic. Phil., ibid 1964; D.Sc., 1968. Appts: Studies Asst. in Econ. & Engrng. Geol., Helsinki Univ. of Technol., 1961-65; Engrng. Geologist, Nat. Bd. of Public Rds. & Waterworks, 1965-69; Asst. Prof. of Econ. Geol., Helsinki Univ. of Technol. & Sr. Fellow of the Rsch. Coun. for Tech. Scis., Acad. of Finland, 1969-. Mbrships: Exec. Comm., Int. Assn. of Engrng. Geol., 1972-76, Pres., Engrng.-Geol. Soc. of Finland, 1972, Sec.-Gen., Geol. Soc. of Finland, 1966-67. Contbr. of studies concerning the properties of rocks & their use in Finland to profl. Jrnls. Address: Koukkusaarrentie 7 C 329, SF 00980 Helsinki 98, Finland.

NIJHAWAN, Inder Pal, b. 26 Feb. 1940. Associate Professor of Economics. Educ: B.A., Delhi Univ., 1959; M.A., Delhi Schl. of Econs., ibid, 1961; Ph.D., Univ. of N.C., 1971. Appts. incl: Lectr. & Hd. of Dept. of Econs., Sri Venkateswara Coll., Delhi Univ., 1961-67; Pt.-time Instr. in Econs., Univ. of N.C., 1967-70; Assoc. Mbr. of Grad. Fac. & Asst. Prof.-Hon. Asst. Prof. of Econs., N.C. State Univ., 1970-72; Assoc. Prof. of Econs. & Coord., Fayetteville State Univ., N.C., 1972-. Mbrships: Omicron Delta Epsilon; Am. Econ. Assn. Contbr. articles & reviews to profl. jrnls. Address: Fayetteville State Univ., P.O. Box 156, Fort Bragg, NC 28307, U.S.A.

NIJINSKY-MARKEVITCH, Kyra, b. 19 June 1914. Ballet Teacher; Painter; Choreographer; Dancer. Educ: Grad., Acad. Nationale de la Musique et la Dance, Paris, & Legat Schl. of Imperial Acad. of Dance of St. Petersburg, in London, U.K.; studies w. Max Reinhardt, Berlin. Appts. incl: Former Ballet Mistress & Choreographer, State Opera, Budapest, Hungary, & Verdi Opera House, Florence, Italy; Mbr., Russian Ballet of Monte Carlo, w. Massine, & Max Reinhardt Co., Berlin; Ballet Tchr., own Choreodrama style, Nat. Am. Dancers Affiliation; currently pvte tchr., ballet, Kyra Nijinsky Schl. of the Dance, U.S.A. Mbr., religious orders & orgs. Publs. incl: The Dream of Varlann, 1954; also, a biography. Paintings in galls. & museums, U.S.A., & pvte. collects., U.S.A. & abroad. Address: 2326 Ulloa St., San Francisco, CA 94116, U.S.A.

NIKIFORUK, Gordon, b. 2 Nov. 1922. Dental Educator. Educ: D.D.S., Univ. of Ill. Schl. of Med., 1950; Dept. of Paedodontics, Schl. of Dentistry, ibid, 1948-50; Cert. Paedodontics, Royal Coll. of Dental Surgs., Ont., 1955; Fellow, Royal Coll. of Dentists, Canada, 1966. Appts. incl: Chmn., Div. of Dental Rsch., Univ. of Toronto, 1954-64; Prof., Paediatric Dentristry, Univ. of Calif., L.A. 1964-69; ibid, Chmn., Div. of Paediatric Dentistry, Schl. of Dentistry. 1964-66; Acting Dean, 1968-69; Chmn., Div. of Oral Bio.; Dir., Div. of Biol. Scis., Univ. of Toronto, 1970-; Dean, Fac. of Dentistry, ibid, 1970-. Mbrships. incl: Review Comm. & Coord. Comm., Govt. of Ont.; Int. Assn. Dental Rsch.; Cons., Coun. on Dental Therapeutics, etc. Author, num. publs. in field. Recip., num. hons. Address: Fac. of Dentistry, 124 Edward St., Toronto, Ont., M5G 1G6, Canada.

NIKITIADES, Constantine, b. 4 Feb. 1906. Vice Admiral, Hellenic Navy. Educ: Grad., Royal Naval Coll., 1925. Appts. incl: Lt. Cmdr., Torpedo Dept. Hellenic Navy, 1939; Exec. Off., Destroyer Panther, 1940-41; C.O. ibid, 1940-43; C.O. Destroyer Miaovlis, 1943-44; C.O., Coastal Defence Staff, 1945; Promoted to Cmdr., 1945; Dpty. C.O. Naval Coll., 1946; Naval Off. i/c., Dodecanese Islands, 1947; C.O., Destroyer Dundos, 1948; Capt., Cruiser Elli, 1950-52; C.O., Naval Coll., 1954; Nat. Defence Staff, 1955; N.M.R. of Greece, SHAPE, Paris, France, 1956-59; Promoted to Rear Admiral, 1959; Retired with rank Vice Admiral, 1963. Publs: Underwater Weapons; Articles in mags. Hons: Ordre Militaire (twice); Croix de Guerre (twice); Cross of the Order of George I; Cross of the Order of the Phoenix; O.B.E.; Medals for Bravery. Address: 22 Drosopoulos Square, Filothey, Athens, Greece. 43.

NILES, Doris Kell Kildale (Mrs. Arthur D. Niles), b. 26 July 1903. Educator. Educ: A.B., M.A., Stanford Univ.; Ph.D., 1931; Rsch. Fellow, Harvard Univ., 1930. Appts: Ariz. State Univ., 1931; Humboldt State Univ., 1926-45, 55-58; Univ. Ext., Univ. of Calif., Davis, 1958-. Mbrships: Nat. Audubon Soc.; Nat. Wildlife; Int. Oceanographic Fndn.; Ocianic Soc.; Calif. Native Plant Soc.; Calif. Malacol. Soc.; N.Y. Acad. Scis.; Calif. Acad. Scis.; Phi Beta Kappa; Sigma Xi; Pi Lambda Theta; Sigma Delta Pi. Publs. incl: New Taxonomy for Teachers: Botanical Entomological Zoological; Nature Studies of the Hawaiian Islands; Botanical Survey of the Siskiyou Mts. Royall Victor Fellow, 1928. Address: P.O. Box 307 Loleta, CA 95551, U.S.A. 5, 9, 14, 132.

NILES, John Jacob, b. 28 Apr. 1892. Folk Singer & Composer; Collector & Arranger of Folk Music. Educ: Univ. de Lyon, France;

Cinn. Conservatory of Music, U.S.A. Lectrd. at Curtis Inst. Music, Juilliard, Eastman, Univ. Kan. City, Baker Univ. etc. Mbrships. incl: Am. Soc. Composers, Authors & Publrs.; Am. Folklore Soc.; Am. Dialect Soc. Creative Works: Many songs inclng. The Devil's Questions; The Dreary Dream; King William's Son; The Little Family; Moses and Pharaoh's Daughter; Oh, Judy, My Judy; The Old Lord By the Northern Sea; What Songs Were Sung; Tiranti, My Love; The Lass From The Low Countree; The Water-Cresses; The Rambling Boy; Reward; Let All Mortal Flesh Keep Silence & Venezuela (Choral Works); Black Oak Tree; Fee Simple; He's Goin' Away; I Never Had But One Love; Oh Waly, Waly; Author, sev. books. Recip. hon. docts., Transylvania Univ., Univs. of Louisville & Ky.; Cinn. Conservatory of Music; Theol. Sem. Address: Boot Hill Farm, RFD#7, Lexington, KY 40502, U.S.A. 2,4.

NILSSON, Jan S., b. 23 Jan. 1932. Professor. Educ: Dr. of Technol., Chalmers Univ. of Technol., Göteborg, Sweden, 1962; Ph.D., Univ. of Rochester, N.Y., U.S.A., 1962. Appts: Rsch. Assoc., CERN, Geneva, Switzerland, 1960-62; Asst. Prof., Inst. of Theoretical Phys., Göteborg, Sweden, 1962-65; Prof., ibid, 1965-; Vis. Assoc. Prof., Phys., Univ. of Va., Charlottesville, U.S.A., 1964-65; Vis. Prof., Ctr., of Particle Phys., Univ. of Tex., Austin, 1968-69. Mbrships: Assoc. Sec. Gen., Int. Union of Pure & Applied Phys.; Am. Phys. Soc.; European Phys. Soc.; Swedish Phys. Soc.; Bd. Mbr., ibid, Author, 50 scientific papers in theoretical phys. Hons. incl: Bd. Mbr., Nordic Inst. of Theoretical Phys.; Mbr., Swedish Atomic Rsch. Coun. Address: Inst. of Theoretical Phys., FACK, S-402 20 Göteborg 5, Sweden.

NILSSON, (Lars) Torsten, b. 3 July 1918. Company Executive. Educ: M.B.A. 1945; Ekon. lic., 1964; studies in U.S.A. & Cuba, 1955. Appts: Asst. to Prof. Ulf af Trolle for Swedish Sugar Corp. & Govt., 1946-54; Asst. Dir., Swedish Sugar Corp., 1956-57; Mng. Dir., Sveriges Allmänna Kolonialgrossister SAKO, 1958-73; Advsr., Bd. of Dirs., ASK-Bolagen, 1974-. Mbrships: Bd. of Dirs., Swedish Wholesalers Assn., KIAB-Grossisterna AB, Sveriges Allmänna Kolonialgrossister SAKO. Publs: Food Marketing in the U.S.A.; Choice of Distribution Methods for Sugar (co-author); Sale & Distribution of Sugar in the U.S.A.; contbr. to profl. publs. Address: Kristinebergs gård (Box 45), S-230 30 Oxie, Sweden. 43.

NILSSON, Nils Johan, b. 8 Mar. 1915. University Professor. Educ: Qualified Physn., 1946; Med. Dr., Univ. of Lund, Sweden, 1957; Specialist, Internal Med., 1952; Clin. Physiol., 1966. Appts: Asst., Physiol., Lund, Heidelberg & Berlin, 1937-45; Asst. Physn., Dept. of Röntgen Diagnostics, Lund, 1946-47; Dept. Internal Med., ibid, 1948-52; Asst. Physiol., Marburg & Göttingen, Germany, 1952-56; Asst. Physn., Dept. of Clin. Physiol., Stockholm & Gothenburg, Sweden, 1957-58; Est. Investigator, Swedish Med. Rsch. Coun., 1958-63; Asst. Prof., Physiol., Univ. of Lund, 1957-61; Clin. Physiol., Univ. of Gothenburg, 1961-68; Prof., Clin. Physiol., ibid, 1968-; Hd., Dept. Clin. Physiol., E. Hosp., 1968-. Mbrships: Scandinavian Soc. for Clin. Chem. & Clin. Physiol.; Swedish Soc. for Clin. Physiol. Author of num. publs. in field. Address: Dept. of Clin. Physiol., Vasa Hosp., 411 33 Gothenburg, Sweden. 134.

NIMMO, Derek Robert, b. 19 Sept. 1933. Actor. Educ: Quarry Bank Schl., Liverpool, U.K. Appts: 1st profl. engagement, Hippodrome Theatre, Bolton, 1952; Gaston in

'Waltz of the Toreadors', Criterion Theatre, 1957; Joseph in 'Duel of Angels', Apollo Theatre, 1960; Hubert in 'How Say You', Aldwych Theatre, 1961; Willie Maltravers in 'The Amorous Prawn', Saville Theatre, 1962-63; 'The Irregular Verb to Love', Criterion Theatre; Nicholas Wainwright in 'Charlie Girl', Adelphi Theatre, and in Australia and New Zealand, 1965-72; Good Robber in 'Babes in the Wood', London Palladium, 1972-73. Own TV Series incl: 'Oh Brother'; 'All Gas & Gaiters'; 'If It's Saturday, It Must Be Nimmo'. Mbr., Green Room Club, London, and Garrick Club, London. Hons: Show Bus. Personality of The Year, Variety Club of G.B., 1971; Silver Medal, Royal TV Soc. 1970. Address: c/o The Garrick Club, Garrick Street, London, W.C.2. U.K.

NININGER, Ruth McAninch. Musician; Writer; Educator. Educ: Little Rock Univ., Ark.; Belgian Schl. of Violin, N.Y.C., 1919; Westminster Choir Coll., Princeton, N.J., 1942. Appts. incl: Debut as Concert Violinist, 1918; Organist, First Bapt. Ch., Little Rock, 1919-22; Min. of Music, First, Immanuel, Pulaski Hts. & Pk. Hill Bapt. Chs., ibid, 1919-41; Dir., Ruth Nininger Schl. of Music, 1920-40; 1st Violinist, Ark. State Symph., 1930-38; Singer, 6 Performances w. Westminster Choir, Carnegie Hall, N.Y.C., 1942; State Dir. of Ch. Music, 1941-54; Fac. Mbr., Ridgecrest Music Conf., N.C. & Glorieta Music Conf., N.M., 1945-54; Mbr. Commn. compiling Bapt. Hymnal, 1952; Ch. Music Cons., 1954-72. Mbr. num. musical & civic orgs. Publs. incl: Growing a Musical Church, 1947; Church Music Comes of Age. 1957. Writer & Dir., Film, A Day at Music Camp, 1950. Honoured by Southern Bapt. Ch. Music Dept, Nashville Tenn., 1971. Address: 2643 State St., Apt. 1, Santa Barbara, CA 93105, U.S.A. 5, 138.

NIPITELLA, Alfio, b. 22 June 1913. Painter; Professor of Painting. Educ: Liceo Artistico; Acad. of Fine Arts. Paintings in int. pvte. & pub. Collections. Paintings incl. Martyrdom Of Saint Lucy of Syracuse; The Deposition Of The Cross; Juliette & Romeo; The Dancer; portrait of Giovanni XXIII (in Vatican); portrait, Queen Fabiola of Belgium; portrait of Prince Andrew of Great Britain. Mbr. num. Art Acads. inclng. Tiberina & Legion d'oro, Rome, Italy; Pontzen, Naples, Italy; Free World Int. Acad., Deerbourn, Mich., U.S.A. Mbrships. incl: Unione Cavalleria Cristiana Int. Hons. incl: num. nat. & int. Art Awards. Address: 55/5 Via Regina Elena, Pescara-65100, Italy. 43.

NIR, Isaac, b. 16 June 1916. Pharmacologist. Educ: M.Sc., Ph.D., Hebrew Univ. of Jerusalem, Israel. Appts: Chief, Govt. Lab. for Control. of Pharmaceuticals, Jerusalem, 1949-53; Dir., Inst. for Standardization & Control of Pharmaceuticals, ibid, 1953-65; Hd., Toxicol. Unit, WHO, Geneva, Switzerland, 1957-60; Vis. Rsch. Assoc. Prof., Dept. of Pharmacol. & Therapeutics, Chgo. Med. Schl., Ill., U.S.A., 1963-64; Hd., Clin. Pharmacol. & Drug Monitoring Ctr., Min. of Hlth., Jerusalem, 1965-; Vis. Prof., Dept. of Applied Pharmacol., Hebrew Univ., 1965-70; Assoc. Prof., ibid, 1970-. Mbrships: WHO Expert Advsry. Panels & var. Israeli Comms.; AAAS; Am. Chem. Soc.; Israel Med. Assn.; Israel Chem. Soc. Author of num. publs, in field. Recip., Annual Award, Israeli Chem. Soc. for Basic Rsch. in Chem., 1944. Address: Dept. of Applied Pharmacol., Fac. of Med., Hebrew Univ. Schl. of Pharm., Jerusalem, Israel. 94.

NISCO, John F.A., b. 11 Dec. 1929. Economic Geologist Educ: B.A. Sc., Trinity Coll., Dublin Univ., Ireland. Appts: Subsurface Geologist, Texaco Exploration Co., Calgary, Alta., 1952; Cons. Geologist, Assoc., A.W. McCoy & Assocs., 1955; The Beneventum Syndicate & Beneventum Mining Co., Ltd., 1956; Independent Cons., Canada & S.Am., 1960; Asst. V.P. & Asst. Sec., Empire Trust Co., N.Y. & Empire Int. Corp., N.Y., 1962; V.P., Stockholder & Assoc. Mbr., William D. Witter, Inc., N.Y.; Pres, World Resources Corp., Cupertino, Calif., 1970; Pres., Globex Minerals, Inc. & Gen. Mgr., Globex Minerals, Ltd., 1972; Dir. & Pres., Globex Minerals (Liberia) Inc. & Globex Enterprises Minerals Ltd. Mbrships. incl: Life Mbr., Royal Dublin Soc., Registered Profl. Geologist, Assn. of Profl. Engrs. of Alta.; Soc. of Mining Engrs.; Am. Inst of Mining Engrs. Address: 2627 Hale Dr., Burlingame, CA 94010, U.S.A. 6, 9, 16.

NISKANEN, Erkki Vilho, b. 6 Oct. 1911. Professor. Educ: M.Sc., 1937; D.Sc., 1958. Appts: Asst., Helsinki Univ. of Technol., Finland, 1938-50; Rsch. Engr., State Inst. for Tech. Rsch. in Finland, 1951-60; Dir., Lab. of Statics & Bridge Bldg., Ibid, 1960-63; Prof., Structural Mechanics, Helsinki Univ. of Technol. Mbrships: Finnish Acad. of Tech. Scis.; U.S. Geophys. Union; Chmn. of Bd., Soc. for Steel Constructions in Finland; Code Drafting Comms. of Finnish Standards. Author of num. pbls. in field. Hons: Cross of Liberty III, 1942, & IV, 1940; S.L.K. Cross, 1972. Address: Mäntyviita 3 D 29, 02100 Tapiola, Finland.

NISSAN, Alfred Heskel, b. 14 Feb. 1914. Chemical Engineer. Educ: B.Sc., Univ. of Birmingham, U.K., 1937; Ph.D., 1940; D.Sc., 1943. Appts: Lectr., Dept. of Chem. Engrng., Univ. of Birmingham, 1940-47; Hd., Ctrl. Rsch. & Mbr., Bd. of Dirs., Bowaters Rsch. & Dev. Ltd., 1947-53; Rsch. Prof., Textile Engrng., Univ. of Leeds, 1953-57; Rsch. Prof., Chem. Engrng., Rensselaer Polytech. Inst., Troy, N.Y., U.S.A., 1957-62; V.P. & Corp. Rsch. Dir., Westvaco, 1962-; Hon. Vis. Prof.; Univ. of Uppsala, Sweden 1974. Fellowships; Int. Acad. of Wood Sci. Bd. Dirs., Tech. Assn. of Pulp & Paper Ind., 1968-70. Mbrships: incl: Am. Inst. of Chem. Engrs.; Am. Soc. Mech. Engrs.; Am. Chem. Soc.; Am. Inst. of Chems.; Inst. of Engrng. Educ., State of N.Y., 1970-; Commnr., Engrng., Manpower Commn., Jt. Engrng. Coun., N.Y., 1971-; Bd. Dirs., Ind. Rsch. Inst., 1972-. Ed: Textile Engrng. Processes, 1959; Future Technical Needs & Trends in the Paper Industry, 1973. Address: Westavaco, 299 Park Ave., N.Y., N.Y., NY 10017, U.S.A. 1.

NISSEN, Gerhardt, b. 21 Sept. 1923. Professor of Medicine; Clinic Director. Appts: Dir. & Chief Dr., Städtosche Klink für Kinder- & Jugendpsychiatrie Wiesengrund, Berlin; Prof., Child & Youth Psych., Free Univ., Berlin; Lectr., Psych., Pädagogische Hochschule, Berlin. Mbrships: Deutsche Vereinigung für Kinder- & Jugendpsychiatrie; Deutsche Gesellschaft für Kinderheilkunde; Deutsche E.E.G. Gesellschaft; Deutsche Gesellschaft für perinatale Medizin; Inst. für Psychotherapie Berlin e.V.; Bd. of Dirs., Gesamtverband Deutscher Nervenärzte; Advsry. Bd., Deutsche Gesellschaft für Kinderheilkunde. Author of publs. in field; Co-ed., Zeitschrift für Kinder- & Jugendpsychiatrie, & Musiktherapie, Berlin. Address: Städt. Klínik für Kinder- & Jugendpsychiatrie Wiesengrund, Frohnauer Str. 74-80, 1 Berlin 28, German Fed. Repub. 1.

NISSEN, Rudolf, b. 9 Sept. 1896. Surgeon. Educ: Study of Med., Breslau, Munich, Marburg

Univs., Germany. Appts: Battalion Surg., German Army, 1914-18; Asst., Dept. of Pathol., Univ. of Freiburg, 1920-21; Asst., Surg. Dept., & Instr., Univ. of Munich, 1921-27; Assoc. Surg., Univ. of Berlin Charité Hosp., & Assoc. Prof., 1927-33; Prof., Surg., & Hd. of Dept., Univ. of Istanbul, Turkey, & Chief Surg., 1st Surg. Clin., 1933-39; Rsch. Fellow, Mass. Gen. Hosp., U.S.A., 1939-40; Attng. Surg. & Chief of Div., Jewish Hosp., Brooklyn, N.Y., 1941-52; Chief Surg., Maimonides Hosp., 1944-50; Prof., Surg. & Dept. Hd., Univ. of Basel, Switzerland, & Chief Surg., Bürgerspital, 1952-67; Prof. Emeritus, 1967-. Mbr. num. socs., Europe & U.S., Past Pres. - Int. Coll. of Surgs.; Rudolf Virchow Med. Soc., N.Y.; German Surg. Assn.; Swiss Surg. Assn.; Swiss Soc. of Angiol.; Bavarian, Middle-Rhine Surg. Assns. Publs: 52 books & book chapts; 580 articles; performed 1st total pneumonectomy, 1931. Num. hons. incl: Crown of Acad. Hon., Acad. Coun., Am. Int. Acad., 1952 Master Surg., Int. Coll. of Surgs., 1956; Dr. med. h.c., Berlin Univ., Univ. of Technol., Munich, Univ. of Ankara. Address: Höhenstr. 45, CH-4125 Riehen, Switzerland.

NISSILÄ, Viljo Johannes, b. 21 Aug. 1903. University Professor. Educ: M.A., Univ. of Helsinki, 1927; Ph.D., ibid., 1941. Appts. incl: Sr. Tchr., Helsinki Secondary Lyceum, 1945-61; Lectr. of Onomastics, Univ. of Helsinki, 1948-66; Dir., The Finnish Name Archives, 1958; Asst. Prof., Jyvaskylä Coll. of Educ., 1962-66; Prof., Univ. of Helsinki, 1969-71. Mbrships. incl: Finnish Acad. of Art; Kalevala Soc; Soc. of Finnish Literature; Finno-Ugric Soc; Fndn. for Advancement of Karelian Culture. Publs. incl: Suomalaista nimistöntutkimusta, 1962; Paikannimistömme huolto ja suojelu, 1965; Die Dorfnamen des alten lüdischen Gebietes, 1967; Iin Kansakouluhistoria, 1968; approx. 200 smaller linguistic publs. Recip., Recognition Medal of Kalevala Soc. Address: Pihlajatie 11 A 12, 00270 Helsinki 27, Finland.

NISSIOTIS, Nicolaos, b. 21 May 1925. Professor of Philosophy of Religion. Educ: Univ. of Athens, Greece, 1942-47; Univ. of Zurich, Switzerland, 1948-49; Univ. of Basle, 1951-52; B.A., Univ. of Louvain, Belgium, 1953; D.D., Univ. of Athens, 1956. Appts: Assoc. Dir., Ecumenical Inst., Geneva, Switzerland. 1958-66; Prof., Univ. Ctr. on Ecumenical Studies, 1962-74; Prof., Philos. of Relig., Univ. of Athens, 1965-; Dir., Ecumenical Inst., Geneva, 1966-74; Assoc. Gen. Sec., World Coun. of Chs., Geneva, 1967-71. Mbrships: Gen. Sec., Student Christian Assn., 1969-71; Panhellinios Athletic Club. Publs: Existentialism & Christian Faith (in Greek), 1958; Prolegomena to a Theological Theory of Knowledge (in Greek), 1965; Philosophy of Religion & Philosophical Theology (in Greek), 1965; Orthodoxy in Ecumenical Dialogue (in German), 1968. Hons: Royal Cross of the Greek State, 1966; D.D., Univ. of Aberdeen, U.K., 1967; D.D., Theological Inst. of St. Serge, Paris, France, 1968. Address: Theological Faculty, University of Athens, Athens, Greece. 43.

NISSMAN, Albert, b. 23 Feb. 1930. College Professor. Educ: B.S., M.Ed., Temple Univ., 1952, '56; Ed.D., Pa. State Univ., 1965. Appts. incl: Tchr. - Chmn., Engl. & Soc. Studies Depts., Bristol Township Schl. Dist., Pa., 1953-63; Dir. Profl. Laboratory Experiences, Rider Coll., Trenton, N.J., 1966-70; Asst. Prof., Engl. & Educ. - Assoc. Prof. Educ., Div. of Grad. Studies, ibid, 1970-. Mbrships. incl: Nat. Educ., Assn.; Advsr., Am. Poetry League; Phi Delta Kappa; Phi Kappa Phi. Publs. incl:

Fragments/Figments (Poetry), 1967; Organizing & Developing a Summer Professional Workshop (w. Dr. J. Lutz), 1971; Contbr. poems to var. collects & articles var. jrnls. & publs. Recip., Author Award, N.J. Assn. Tchrs. of Engl., 1968. Address: Schl. of Educ., Rider Coll., Trenton. NJ 08602, U.S.A. 11, 15, 30, 141.

NISTAL, Gerard E., b. 6 July 1920. Marketing Executive. Educ: B.S., La. State Univ.; M.B.A., NY Univ. Appts. incl: Asst. Gen. Mgr., Watchmaster Div. & Dir. of Marketing, Am. Time Div., Mgr., Admin. Bulova Watch Co., Inc., 1960-66; V.P. Robertson & Associates, Inc., NJ, 1966-68; V.P. & Gen. Mgr.-Exec. V.P., Mowbot Inc., Tonawanda, NY, 1968-70; Asst. V.P. & Dir., Marketing, Buffalo Savings Bank, NY, 1971-. Mbrships. incl: Am. Marketing Assn.; Am. Mgmt. Assn.; Am. Acad. of Pol. & Soc. Sci.; Am. Acad. of Advt.; Past State V.P., US Jr. Chmbr. of Comm. & Air Force Assn.; Univ. Clubs, Buffalo, NY & NYC; AIAA; IEEE. Publs: Contbr. to profl., bus., tech., & trade jrnls. Recip. of hons. Address: 63 Center St., E. Aurora, NY 14052, U.S.A. 6.

NITYANANDAN, Perumpilavil Madhavamenon, b. 4 Nov. 1926. Engineer. Educ: B.E. Mech., Coll. of Engrng., Guindy, Madras, 1947; trng. in Prodn. Mgmt., France, 1961. Appts: Apprentice Trng., Hindustan Aircraft Ltd., Bangalore, 1947-48; Lectr. & Workshop Instr., Madras State Engrng. Colls., 1948-54; Asst. Works Mgr. & Plant Engr., Mahindra & Mahindra, Ltd., Bombay (Jeeps & Trailers), 1954-58; Tech. Dir., Gears India (Madras) Pvte. Ltd., 1958-. Mbrships: Comm. for Gearing, Indian Standards Inst.; Zonal Coun., Indian Soc. for Ind. Tribol.; Nat. Productivity Coun., India; Fellow, Indian Inst. of Valuers; former Pres., Alliance Française of Madras & Ind. Manager. Estate Mfr.'s Assn., Guindy, Madras. Publs: The Long Long Days (novel); short stories & humorous articles in Indian & for. mags. Address: "The Wabe", 15, Arundalenagar, Madras-600041, India.

NIVISON, David Shepherd, b. 17 Jan. 1923. Educator. Educ: A.B., Harvard, 1946; M.A., 1948; Ph.D., 1953. Appts: Instr., Chinese, Stanford, 1948-52; Ford Fndn. Fac. Fellow, 1952-53; Instr., Chinese & Philos., 1953-54; Fulbright Rsch. Schlr., Kyoto, Japan, 1954-55; Lectr., Philos., Stanford, 1955-58; Asst. Prof., Chinese & Philos., 1958-59; Assoc. Prof., 1959-66; Prof., 1966-; Chmn., Dept. Philos., 1969-. Mbrships: Assn. for Asian studies; Am. Philos. Assn.; Am. Oriental Soc. (Western Br. V.P., 1964-65, Sec., 1965-70); AAUP (Pres., N. Calif. Conf., 1964-66); Phi Beta Kappa. Publs: The Life & Thought of Chang Hseuh-ch'eng, 1738-1801, 1966. Co-editor, Confucianism in Action, 1959; Contbr. articles to profl. jrnls. Recip., Prix Stanislas-Julien, Inst. de France, 1967. Address: 1169 Russell Ave., Los Altos, CA 94022, U.S.A. 2.

NIXON, Amsay Laurie, b. 1 Apr. 1922. Nurse Anesthetist; Educator. Educ: Registered Nurse, Miss. Bapt. Hosp., Jackson; Cert. Nurse Anesthetist, Univ. of Ala.; B.S., Elem. Educ., Univ. of Southern Miss.; grad. work, Miss. State Univ. Appts: Maternity Supvsr. for 1 yrs.; Orthopedic Surg. Asst. for 8 yrs.; Nurse Anesthetist, Hd. of Dept. for 6 yrs.; Elem. Tchr. for 15 yrs. Mbrships: State Accreditation Commn. for 5 yrs., Miss. Educ. Assn.; Treas. for 3 yrs., PTA; Sec., Dept. of Classroom. Tchrs;. Sec., V.P., Biloxi Educ. Assn.; Chmn., Supvsry. Comm. for 3 yrs., Biloxi Fed. Tchr.'s Credit Union; Miss. State Treas. for 2 yrs., Pres., Zeta Chapt., Alpha Delta Kappa; Kappa Delta Pi; Xi Chapt., Beta Sigma Phi; Master Tchr. in Elem.

Educ.; Dir., Sec., V.P., Miss. Nurse Anesthetist Assn.; Pres., Pilot Club of Biloxi & Gulf Coast Women's Bowling Assn. Designed & wrote a blazon of coats of arms for Miss. Women's Bowling Assn., publd. in Rebel Pin. Hons. incl. 3 times Girl of Yr., Beta Sigma Phi. Address: 319 Washington Ave., Ocean Springs, MS 39564,U.S.A. 125.

NIXON, Colin Harry, b. 9 Mar. 1939. Civil Servant. Educ: Dip. in Sociol., London Univ., U.K. Appts. incl: Dept. of Employment, London, U.K., 1962-. Mbrships: Fellow, Int. Poetry Soc., 1971-; Edit. Bd., ORBIS mag. Author of num. poems publd. throughout world. Address: 72 Barmouth Road, Wandsworth, SW18 2DS, U.K. 11.

NIXON, John William, b. 2 Mar. 1922. Dentist. Educ: Fisk Univ., Nashville, Tenn., 1947; D.D.S., Meharry Med. Coll., ibid, 1951. Appts: Instr., Dept. of Dentistry, Univ. of Ala., Birmingham, 1971-74; John Andrew Dental Clin. Mbrships. incl: Pres., Jefferson Co. Dental Study Club, 1958-61; Pres., Ala. Dental Assn., 1963-64; Am. Dental Assn.; Nat. Dental Assn.; Kappa Alpha Psi; Birmingham Chmbr. of Comm.; Downtown Action Comm., ibid; Operation New Birmingham; Birmingham Concentrated Employment Prog. Publs: Co-auth., Stepping Stone, 1961; God Smiles on a Troubled City, 1963. Hons. incl: Outstanding Community Serv. Award, Birmingham Housing Authority, 1971; NAACP Pres.'s. Award, Ensley NAACP, 1971; Outstanding Community Serv. Award, Birmingham Chapt., Am. Red Cross, 1971. Address: 1728 W. 20th St., Birmingham, AL 35218, U.S.A. 2, 7, 125.

NIZER, Louis, b. 6 Feb. 1902. Attorney. Educ: B.A., Columbia Coll., 1922; LL.B., Columbia Law Schl., 1924. Appts: Sr. Ptnr., law firm of Phillips, Nizer, Benjamin, Krim & Ballon, N.Y.C.; Gen. Counsel to Motion Picture Assn. of Am. Mbrships: N.Y.C. Bar Assn.; Am. Bar Assn.; Am. Soc. Composers, Authors & Publrs.; Lotos Club. Publs: The Implosion Conspiracy; The Jury Returns; My Life in Court (chapt. made into play, A Case of Libel, by Henry Denker); Thinking on Your Feet; "Commentary & Analysis of Official Warren Commission Report"; What To Do With Germany; New Courts of Industry; Between You & Me; articles in var. mags. & law reviews. Paintings exhib. at Permanent Art Gall., Am. Bank & Trust Co. & Hammer Gall., N.Y. Hons: Gold Plate Award, Acad. of Achievement, 1962; Lit. Father of Yr., 1962 & 74; awards at N.Y.C. Bar Assn. Art Exhibs.; sev. hon. degs. Address: c/o Phillips, Nizer, Benjamin, Krim & Ballon, 40 W. 57th St., N.Y., NY 10019, U.S.A. 1, 30, 44, 131.

NNAGGENDA, Francis Xavier, b. 21 May 1936. Bukuumi Sculptor & Painter; Lecturer. Educ: Ecole de Dessin de Paris, France; State Acad. Fine Art, Munich, Germany. Fellow, Inst. African Studies, Nairobi Univ., Kenya, E. Africa. Mbr., Stiring Comm., All-Black Art Festival. Recip Belobigung (Termer Wand), Munich, Germany, 1966. Address: Nairobi Univ., P.O. Box 30197, Nairobi, Kenya, E. Africa.

NOAILLES, Alicia de. Artist; Writer. Educ: N.Y. Schl. of Fine & Applied Arts. Mbrships: Pres., Assn. Mediator Dei, 1952-; Mbr. of Jury, Art Competitions; Assn. Argentina de Cultura Inglesa; A.M.A.C., Socorro; Lectr. on Art. One man exhibs. incl: Galatea, Buenos Aires, 1956, '58; Alcora, ibid, 1960; Wildenstein's Gall., 1961; El Sotano, 1964; Banco Supervielle, 1971; OEA Salon, 1972. Rep. in pvte. collects.

& pub. bldgs. Publs: Book illustrations; Author of Edward T. Mulhall, a XIX century link with Argentina, 1970; El Viaje Detenido, 1973 Address: Juncal 841, Buenos Aires, Argentina.

NOAKES, Michael, b. 28 Oct. 1933. Portrait Painter. Educ: Nat. Dip. in Design, 1954; Cert., Royal Acad. Schls., 1960. Appts: Broadcaster, radio & TV, U.K., U.S.A.; Art Corres., BBC TV prog. Town & Around, 1964-68. Mbrships: Pres., Royal Inst. of Oil Painters; Coun. Mbr., Royal Soc. of Portrait Painters; Gov., Fedn. of Brit. Artists; Past Chmn., Contemporary Portrait Soc.; Nat. Soc. of Painters, Sculptors & Printmakers. Portraits incl: The Queen, Duke of Edinburgh, Queen Elizabeth the Queen Mother, Prince of Wales, Princess Anne, Princess Margaret & Lord Snowdon, Lord Mayor of London, in grp. portrait; Lord Boothby; Alec Guiness; Archbishop Lord Fisher; Robert Morley; Dennis Wheatley. Publs: A Professional Approach to Oil Painting, 1968; Num. articles in art jrnls. Address: The Studio, Doods Park Rd., Reigate, Surrey, U.K. 1, 19, 128, 133.

NOBLE, Alma Nease, b. 16 June 1901. Teacher; Professor Emerita. Educ: A.B., Wittenberg Coll., 1924; A.M., Columbia Univ. 1930; Ph.D., Ohio State Univ., 1938; A.M., Western Reserve Univ., 1942; Postgrad. Work, Univ. of Wis., 1959. Appts. incl: Hd., Lang Dept, Ashand Jr. Coll., Ky., 1938-41; at Marshall Univ., Huntington, W.Va., 1941-69 as Asst. Prof. 1941-45, Hd. Dept. of French, 1945-64; Assoc. Prof. French, 1945-69; Assoc. Prof. French, Morris Harvey Coll., Charleston W.Va., 1969-72; Acting Hd., Mod. Lang. Dept. ibid, 1970-72. Mbrships incl: Am. Assn. Tchrs. of French (Pres. W.Va. Chapt. 1947-48); Mod. Lang. Tchrs. Assn. (Pres. W. Va. Chapt. 1955-56); MLA; Am. Guild of Organists; Eta Stigma Phi; Pi Delta Phi; Delta Kappa Gamma. Publs: A few Poems. Hons. incl: Plaque, 15 yrs. Disting. Serv., Marshall Univ., 1966; Wittenberg Alumni Citation, 1971; Professor Emerita, Marshall Univ., 1973. Address: 301 W. Tenth Ave., Huntington, WV 25701, U.S.A. 5, 6, 13, 15.

NOBLE, Charles MacIntosh, b. 10 June 1896. Civil Engineer. Appts. incl: Cons. Engr., U.S. Engrs., Ala. Highway Dept., 1914-21; Res. Engr., ibid, 1921-23; Res. Highway Engr., N.J. Highway Dept., 1923-25; Engr., Pt. of N.Y. Authority, 1925-38; Special Highway Engr., Pa. Turnpike Commn., 1938-41; Lectr., Yale Univ., 1939-41 & 1947-50; Lt. Cmdr. - Cmdr., Seabees USNR Adv. Base Construction, Alaska & Aleutians, 1942-46; N.J. State Highway Engr., 1946-49; Chief Engr., N.J. Turnpike Authority, 1949-57; Dir. of Highwats, State of Ohio, 1957-59; Cons. Engr., 1959-. Mbrships. incl: Fellow, Am. Soc. Civil Engrs.; Nat. Soc. Profl. Engrs.; Past V.P., Am. Assn. State Highway Officials; Past V.P., Am. Rd. Builders Assn.; Advsry. Coun., Civil Engrng. Dept., Princeton Univ.; Chi Epsilon. Publs: Over 80 contbns. to profl. jrnls. Hons. incl: Legion of Merit Medal, 1944; Bronze Star Medal, 1945. Address: P.O. Box 386, Ponte Vedra Beach, FL 32082, U.S.A. 6, 7, 8, 26, 64.

NOBLE, James Kendrick, Jr., b. 6 Oct. 1928. Security (Investment) Analyst; Naval Reserve Officer. Educ: Princeton Univ., 1945-46; B.S., U.S. Naval Acad., Annapolis, Md., 1950. M.B.A., N.Y. Univ. Grad. Schl. of Bus. Admin., 1961; N.Y. Univ. Schl of Educ., 1962-69. Appts: to Lt., USN, 1950-57, while attached to USS Thomas E. Fraser (DM-24), 1950-51; Student Naval Aviator, 1951-52; Patrol Squad.21, 1952-55; Student, U.S. Naval

Gen. Line Schl., Monterey, 1955-56; Instr., U.S. Naval Acad., 1956-57; trans. to U.S. Naval Rsve, 1957; to Capt., USNR-R, 1973-; Dir., Curric. Info. Ctr., 1972-; to Exec. V.P., Dir., Noble & Noble, Inc., 1957-66; Sr. Publng. Analyst, F. Eberstadt & Co., 1966-69; V.P. & Sr. Analyst, Auerbach, Pollak & Richardson, Inc., 1969-. Mbrships incl: Bd. Educ., Bronxville, 1968-74 & Pres., 1970-72; Bd. Trustees, St. John's Hosp., Yonkers, 1972-; Printing & Publng. Ind. Analysts Assn. & Pres., 1969-71; V.P., N.Y. Chapt., Naval Rsve. Assn., 1968-; Fellow, AAAS; Inst. Chartered Financial Analysts, 1972-; Nat. Inst. Soc. Scis., etc. Publs: Ploob, 1949, 55; The Years Between, 1966; contbr. ot profl. jrnls. Hons: Van Dyke Essay Prize, 1950; Chartered Fin. Analyst, 1972; All Am. Rsch. Team of Instnl. Investor Mag., 1972 '73. Address: 45 Edgewood Ln., Bronxville, NY 10708, U.S.A. 6, 15, 16, 18, 30.

NOBLE, John Appelbe, b. 27 Jan. 1914. Port Phillip Sea Pilot. Educ: Apprentice in Bank Line's M.V. 'Comliebank', 1929-33; 2nd Mate's Cert., Sir John Cass Nautical Schl., London, U.K. 1933; 1st Mate's Cert., London, 1936; Master's (For.-Going Steamship Cert., Wellington, N.Z., 1940. Appts: 3rd Off., Bank Line, 1933-35; 3rd, 2nd & 1st Off., Union Steamship of N.Z. vessels, 1936-51; Master, Union Steamship Co's vessels, 1951-58; Port Phillip Sea Pilot, 1959-. Mbrships. incl: Jrnl. Ed., Co. of Master Mariners of Australia, 1965-71; Australian Soc. of Authors; Royal Histl. Soc. of Vic.; Returned Servs. League of Australia. Publs: Free lance articles for Sydney Bulletin, Auckland Weekly News & other publs., 1957-66; Australian Lighthouse, 1967; Hazards of the Sea, 1970; Port Phillip: Pilots & Defences, 1973; Port Phillip: Melbourne & Geelong Harbours, forthcoming. Address: 8 Agnes Ave., N. Balwyn, Vic., Australia, 3104. 30, 131.

NOBLITT, Katheryn (Marie) McCall (Mrs. A. Spencer Noblitt), b. 10 Feb. 1909. Composer; Piano Teacher; Secretary. Educ: B.M., Greensboro Coll., N.C., 1930. Appts: Tchr., Piano, N.C., 1930-48; Tchr., Piano, Roanoke, Va., 1948-; Pvte. Sec. & Med. Sec., ibid, 1948-59; Co-Pastor w. husband, 2 yrs. & indep. Christian wkr., 1934-. Mbrships: Am. Soc. Composers Authors & Publrs.; Am. Guild Authors & Composers; Va. Music Tchrs. Assn.; Roanoke Valley Music Tchrs. Assn.; Histn., Roanoke Music Tchrs. Assn., 1973-75. Music Tchrs. Nat. Assn.; Am. Piano Tchrs. Assn. Compositions: Waltz Mood, 1957; Jack Frost Surprised Me., 1958; Marh of the Americans, 1961; Twinklin Kays, 1961; The Wind-Up Donkey, 1974. Approx. 125 unpubld. compositions. Address: 4848 Cove Rd., N.W., Lot 1, Roanoke, VA 24017, U.S.A. 5, 57, 138.

NOCHIMOW, Eli, b. 23 July 1908. Physician. Educ: Ph.Ch., Columbia Univ., N.Y., 1930; B.S., 1931; M.D., Midwest Med. Coll., Kan. City, Mo., 1937. Appts: Censor; Bristol Co. Med. Soc., 1962; Chief, Med., Union Hosp., New Bedford, Mass., 1965-73; Hon. Staff, Sr. Lukes Hosp., ibid, 1968-; Med. Dir., Frances P. Mem. Hosp., 1968-73. Fellowships: Am. Acad. Family Prac.; Royal Soc. Hlth. Mbrships. incl: Post Surg., Mass. State Reserve Offs. Assn.; Pres.; Ahavath Achim Congregation; Pres.; Hebrew Free Loan Soc.; V.P., New Bedford Jewish Convalescent Home; Am. Geriatric Soc.; AMA; Jr. Vice Cmdr., Jewish War Vets. Post 154. Hons: Man of the Yr., New Bedford Lions Club, 1970; Gates of Jerusalem Award, 1972. Address: 43 Orchard Terrace, New Bedford, MA 02740, U.S.A. 6.

NOEL, Chris, b. 2 July 1941. Actress. Appts: Schl. of Charm & Modelling, Lake Pk., Fla.; Model, Palm Beach Model Agcy.; Own radio show, A Date w. Chris, Armed Forces Radio Serv., 1966-71. Films incl: Joy in the Morning; Girl Happy; Wild Wild Winter; Beach Ball. TV appearances incl: Tonight (Johnny Carson); Bob Hope Presents; Joe Franklin; Joey Bishop; My Three Sons; What's My Line; Bewitched; Password; Eleventh Hour; Smothers Brothers; Hollywood Palace; Dr. Kildare; Perry Mason; Burke's Law; Art Linkletter. Recordings: Doll House; Mr & Mrs Smith, Monument label. Num. visits, etertaining U.S. Servmen. in S. Vietnam & in U.S. Hosps. Star of 3 films of Vietnam tours. Hons: Miss Nat. Radio, Nat. Assn. of Broadcasters; num. mil. awards. Address: 2030 Delphia St., West Palm Beach, FL 33401, U.S.A. 132.

NÖEL-PATON, Margaret Hamilton, b. 21 Jan. 1896. Writer. Educ: Carey Hall Missionary Trng. Coll., Selly Oak. Appts: Girls' Work Sec., YMCA, India. Mbrships: Nat. YWCA; Soc. of Authors; Edinburgh Film Guild. Publs: (plays) The Hidden People; Fear No More; Choose Ye; More Than Conquerors; Knight of the White Cross; (poems? A Wanderer's Lute; Hevridian Medley; "Choose Something Like a Star"; (biog.) Tales of a Grand-daughter (memoir of the artist Sir Noël Paton.) Plays broadcast only: Pandita Ramabhai; Pernnell of the Afghan Frontier; A Song for Serbia. Address: Braecot, Hopeman, Elgin, Moray IV30 2SL, U.K. 3, 137

NOGUERAS RIVERA, Nicolás, b. 10 Sept. 1902. Educator. President Puerto Rico Free Federation of Labor. Educ: Elem. Tchrs. Cert., Univ. of P.R., 1920; Elam. Engl. Tchr. Cert., 1926; Labor Educ. Inst., 1935. Appts: Tchr., Pub. Schls. of P.R., 1920-35; Pres., Protective Labor Union, Cayey, 1931; Lectr., Dept. of Labor, 1935; Sec.-Treas., Fed. Labor Union, San Juan, 1936; Sec.-Treas., P.R. Free Fedn. of Labor, 1936-52; Pres., ibid, 1951-; Mbr., House of Reps. of P.R., 1932-36; Pres., Factory & Agric. Labor Coun. of P.R., 1938-41; Org. & Pres., Round Table Conf. on Sugar Ind. Problems, 1943-44; Pioneer & Exec. Sec., 1st Statehood Congress of P.R., 1943; Drafter, Labor Unity Charter, 1945; Pres., Prog. & Constitution Commn., 1st Interam. Labor Conf., Lima, Peru, 1948; Org. & Pres., Congress for Plesbicitary Action, 1959-60. Mbrships. incl: Bd. of Appeals, Selective Serv. System, 1942-70; Apprenticeship Coun. of P.R.; Bd. of Dirs., P.R. Tchrs. Assn.; Nat. Security Coun. Publs. Incl: Prospects of the University Reorganization, 1942; Collective Bargaining in the Sugar Industry of Puerto Rico, 1956; Ed. Forty Years of Labor Activities; Fndr. & Dir., Salario (monthly), 1966. Composer of 2 waltzes. Recip. var. hons. inclng: Special Cert. of Appreciation on 5th Anniversary of Signing of Selective Serv. Act., 1967; Certs. of Appreciation, Presidents Roosevelt, Truman, Eisenhower, Kennedy, Johnson & Nixon, from Gen. Hershey, from ex-Gov. Luis A. Ferré & Co. Manuel F. Silverio, State Dir. for P.R. of Selective System; Cert. of 'Meritorious Serv. Award' medal & insignia of Selective Serv. System of US. Address: 173 Taft St., Santurce, PR 00911. 2.

NOJORKAM, Norbert, b. 12 Mar. 1911. Artist; Archaeologist. Educ: Acad. of Fine Arts & Polyglot Inst., Ghent, & Univ. of Ghent, Belgium;The Sorbonne, Paris; Inst. Berenson, Settignano, & Schl. of Fresco, Perugia, Italy. Dir., Sch. of Landscape, Latern St. Martin, 1941-51; Fndr. & Dir., Inst. for Relief of Complete Arts, 1952; Dir., Les Cahiers de l'Irac; Fndr., Fondation Charles Quintet.

Mbrships: Rotary Club, Ghent; Soc. européenne de Culture Venezia. Author, novels, essays, poetry, art criticism, papers in archaeol. Paintings, over 1500 canvasses since 1930, 64 exhibs. Engravings & sculptural work in bronze. Hons: Chevalier de l'Ordre de la Couronne, Belgium; Chevalier All'Me rito della Republica Italiana; Cammandeur Mérite artisanal, France. Address: Zandpoort St. 35B, 9000 Ghent, Belgium.

NOLAND, Kenneth Clifton, b. 10 Apr. 1924. Artist. Educ: Black Mountain Coll., 1946-48 (summers 1950, 51); student, Ozzip Zadkine, Paris, 1948-49. Appts: Tchr., Inst. Contemporary Arts, Cath. Univ. of Wash. D.C., 1950-52. Hons: Recip., 1st Prize, Premio National, International Intituto Torcuato de Tella, Buenos Aires, 1964; Creative Arts Award, Brandeis Univ., 1965; 4th Prize, Corcoran Biennale, 1967. Address: South Shraftbury, VT, U.S.A.

NOLTE, Hendrik Johan, b. 11 Aug. 1915. Architect. Educ: Acad. for Arch., Amsterdam, Netherlands. Mbrships: Bond van Nederlandse Architecten B.N.A.; Pan Am. Fedn. of Archts. Assn.; Inst. of Netherlands Profl. Engrs.; Bd. mbr., Stichting Monumentenzorg, Curacao; Bd. mbr., Federatie Jeugdzorg, Curacao; Bd. Mbr., tech. educ. sect., R.M. Centraal Schoolbestuur; Bond Heemschut; Genootschap Amstelodamum; Kring Het Rembrandthuis; Nat. Geographic Soc.; Stichting De Hollandse Molen; K.N.Z.H.R.M. Archtl. work incls: Schoolbldgs., off. bldgs., interior decoration, residences, hosps., banks, hotels, stores. Address: Lelieweg 9 Mahaai, Curacao, Netherlands Antilles.

NOONAN, Robert Harry, b. 18 Sept. 1924. Musician; Chemist; Educator. Educ: B.S., Northwestern State Coll. of La., 1948; Mus.B. in Music Educ., Centenary Coll. of La., 1963; grad. studies in organic chem. & music. Appts: Horn Player, inclng. 16 yrs. prin., Shreveport Symph. Orch., 25 yrs.; Sr. Chem., Ark. Fuel Oil Co., Shreveport, La., 5 yrs.; Asst. Chief Chemist, Atlas Refinery, Shreveport, 3 yrs.; Dir., Jesuit H.S. Band, Shreveport, 4 yrs.; Instr. in Horn, Centenary Coll., 5 yrs.; currently w. E. Baton Rouge Parish Schl. Bd. Mbrships: Am. Chem. Soc.;Am. Fedn. Musicians; ASTM; Phi Mu Alpha; Gamma Sigma Epsilon. Compositions incl. investiture music, Fanfare & Processional, an Alma Mater, & sev. items chamber music. Recip., music schlrships., 1958, 1959, 1960. Address: 5745 Linden St., Baton Rouge, LA 70805, U.S.A. 139.

NORBECK, (Rev.) Mildred Evelyn, b. 18 Feb. 1904. Missionary; Educator. Educ: A.B., Greenville Co., 1925; Th.B., God's Bible Schl. & Coll., 1943. Ordained Min., Gospel, 1945. Appts. incl: Evangelist & tchr., Free Meth. Ch., Breathitt Co., Ky., 1923-38; Pastor, Fla., 1941-45; Missionary, W. Indies Bible Mission, Haiti, 1945-48; Fndr/Supt. Haiti Inland Mission IcInc., 1949-64; Fndr/Dir., Gt. Commn. Crusades Inc., 1960-. Mbrships: Nat. Assn. Evangelicals; World Evangelical Fellowship; Women's Christian Temperance Union. Publs: The Lure of the Hills, 1931; The Challenge of the Hills, 1947; The Haitian Challenge & Your, 1965; Ed., publr., & contbr., var. publs. in field. Address: Box 55, Intercession City, FL 33848, U.S.A.

NORDAHL, June Olga. Singer & Acress; Songwriter; Journalist. Educ: A.A., B.A., Geo. Wash. Univ., 1959; Georgetown Law Ctr., Wash. D.C., 1959-64; grad. work, Seton Hall Univ., S. Orange, N.J., 1966. Appts. incl: Reporter, Wash. Law Reporter, D.C., 1960-61;

Edit. Staff, Wash. Daily News, 1961-62; Feature Writer, Newspaper Enterprise Assn., Wash. D.C., 1962-63; Supper Club Singer, N.Y. C., Wash. D.C., & S. Am., 1964-; Actress, Sr. Dramatic Workshop Rep. Co., Off-Broadway prods., 1965-67; currently, Contbng. Ed. Am. Bicentennial, monthly mag., Wash. D.C. Author, sev. vols. poetry, & a play, The Black Widow. Composer, songs, inclng. You Are a Miracle, Merci Beaucoup, Summer Rain, Once Upon a Willow. Recip., Mil. & profl. awards. Address: 2060 Mountain Ave., Scotch Plains, NJ 07076, U.S.A. 138.

NORDBERG, Olle, b. 9 June 1905. Painter; Sculpotor. Educ: Swedish Acad. of Art, 1921-26. Works represented in: Swedish Nat. Gall. & Mus.; Mod. Mus. of Art; Prince Eugen's Gall.; Gothenburg Mus.; Ateneum Museum of Art, Helsinki, Finland. Mbrships: Swedish Club for Painters; Nat. Org. of Painters K.R.O. Recip. of Gold Medal, Swedish Art Acad. Address: Furlid, 17010 Ekerö, Sweden.

NORDBERG, Tord, b. 18 Jan. 1898. Archaeologist. Educ: Ph.D., Univ. of Stockholm, Sweden, 1963. Appts. incl: Sec., Royal Acad. of Antiquities, 1925-31; Archaeol., Stockholm City Mus., 1921-37; 1st Archaeol. & Hd., Dept. for Histl. Bldgs., ibid, 1937-60; Archaeol. & Hd., Stockholm City Mus., 1960-64; Ldr. & Sci. Controller sev. archaeol. excavations & Histl. bldg. restorations in Sweden. Publs. incl: Katarina Kyrka, 1944; Karlbergs Slott, 1945; Stockholm I 12 Vandringar, 1946.; Södra Stadshuset i Stockholm, 1964; Västerås slott, 1974. Address: Södermalmstorg 6, 116 45 Stockholm, Sweden. 43.

NORDELL, Bengt T., Jr., b. 16 Jan. 1924. Managing Director. Educ: LL.B., Univ. of Stockholm, Sweden, 1948. Appts: Asst. Sec., Min. of Trade, Stockholm, 1948; Permanent Sec., Swedish Delegation, UN Econ. Commn. of Europe, Geneva, Switzerland, 1950; Asst. Dir., Swedish Textile Fedn., 1951; Dir., Swedish Pig Iron Assn., 1960; Mng. Dir., Grp. Assn. of Swedish Steel Wks., 1971. Mbrships: Sec., Friends of Mining & Steelmaking, 196l; Sällskapet Club, Stockholm; E. Asian Soc., Stockholm; Swedish Horse Breeding Assn. Publs: Num. articles on steel industry & steel market. Address: Tunsäter, 15014 Vagnhärad, Sweden. 43.

NORDEN, Hugo, b. 31 Dec. 1909. Violinist; Composer. Educ: B.Mus., Univ. of Toronto, Can., 1942; D.Mus., ibid, 1948; pvte study. Appts: Lectr., Boston Conservatory of Music, 1943-45; Mus. Ed., Arthur P. Schmidt Co., Boston, 1943-58; Prof., Music Theory, Boston Univ., 1945-. Mbrships: Finonacci Assn.; Am-Scandinavian Fndn.; AAUP; Phi Beta Kappa. Publs Incl: The Technique of Canon; Fundamental Harmony; Fundamental Counterpoint; Form- The Silent Language; Harmony & its Application to Violin Playing. Modulation Re-Defined; num. musical compositions inclng. Fantasia liturgica for clarinet & String quartet, Sonata in A minor for contrabass & piano & 3 Bagatelles for flute & harp; contbr. to mags. Address: 11 Mendelssohn St., Roslindale, MA 02131, U.S.A.

NORDEUS, Rolf, b. 17 May 1915. Managing Director. Educ: Univ. of Econs., Stockholm, 1938; Schlrship., Studies in German Ind., 1952. Appts. incl: Controller, Svenska Diamantbergborra AB, Stockholm, 1938-46; Controller & Financial Mgr., Cloetta, Ljungsbro, 1946-47, Sveriges Slaktosiförbund, 1958-62; V.P. Cloetta, Ljungsbro, 1962-65; Pres. & Mng. Dir., ibid, 1965-73; Dir

Företagskonsultationer, Linköping,1974; Chmn. of the Bd., Riksglass, Straugnas, 1974-, Pamir Skifferbetong AB, 1974-, Brokinds Snicken AB, 1973-, Mbrships. incl: Pres., Rotary Club, Linköping-Malmen, 1971-72, Univ. Educ. Bd., Linköping, 1972-,SNS Soc. of Linköping, 1963-66; Bd., Off. Int. du Cacao et du Chocolat, 1966-73, Swedish Assn. of Advts., 1966-74, Swedish Assn. of Chocolate & Confectionary, 1966-74. Hons: Kt., Royal Swedish Vasaorden, 1971. Address: Guslaf Adolfsgatan 171, 58220 Linköping, Sweden.

NORDLAND, Eva, b. 3 Jan. 1921. Professor. Educ: magistergrad & doct., Univ. of Oslo, Norway, 1955. Appts: Tchr., H.S., Bergen, 1944-55; Lectr., Univ. of Oslo, 1957-; Pres. State Coun. of Tchr. Trng., 1960-69; Mr. & Pres., Bd. of nat. broadcasting, 1955-60; Mbr. & Pres., Nat. coun. of conflict & peace rsch., 1964-68; Mbr., Scandivavian comm. for int. pol., 1966-68; Pres. Nat. coun. of youth problems, 1972-; Asst. Prof. of Educ. Univ. of Oslo, 1963-; Prof. of psychol., Arhus Univ., 1971-72. Mbrships: Int. coun. psychols.; Norwegian Assn. Univ. Women; Int. coun. soc. democratic women. Publs. incl: Values in the Traditional & New School, 1958; Psychology & Mental Hygiene, 1968,'71; Education & the Creative Mind, 1966; Children Outside the Welfare State, 1971. Address: Pedagogisk Forskningsnstitutt, Univ. of Oslo, Oslo, Norway. 134.

NORDLIE, Jens Henrik Throne, b. 18 Jan. 1910. Managing Director. Educ: Mil. Coll., 1932, War Acad., 1938; Sr. Offs. Schl., 1946. Appts: Lt., Norwegian Army 1932; Capt., ibid, 1940; Major, 1944; Gen. Staff, 1938-40; Clandestine Army, 1941-43; High Cmd., Norwegian Forces, London, 1943-45; Tchr., Mil. Coll., 1946-47; Gen Mgr. Narvesen's Kioskkompani, Oslo, 1947-56; Mng. Dir., ibid, 1957-; Author of publs. in field of mil. hist. Hons: U.S. Medal of Freedom, 1946; The Kin's Commendation for brave conduct, London, 1950. Address: Professor Dahls gate 25 D, Oslo 3, Norway. 43.

NORDSTRAND, Nathalie Elizabeth Johnson (Mrs. Robert I. Nordstrand), b. 6 Nov. 1932. Artist. Educ: Barnard Coll., Columbia Univ., 1954; Pvte. Art studies. Appts. incl: Rsch. Assoc., Age Ctr. of New England, Inc., 1955-64; Free lance oil & watercolor Artist, 1964-; Ptnr., Sullivan Nordstrand Gail. Rockport, Mass., 1969-73; Dir. & Clerk,Johnson Green-Houses Inc. Exhibd in num. profl. soc. Art shows & paintings in num.Int. pvte & Pub. collections. Exhibs. incl: Contemporary Am. Painters, Bhu Labai Mem. Inst., Bombay, India; Am. Fortnight, Am. Chmbr. of Comm., Hong Kong, China, 1973; Traveling Exhib., Am. Watercolor Soc., 1969, 1970, 1971, 1972, 1973. Mbrships. incl: Am. Watercolor Soc.; Allied Artists of Am.; Acad. Artists Assn.; Am. Artists Profl. League; Advsry. Mbr., Marquis Biographical Lib. Soc. Contbr. to profl. jrnls. Recent Art Awards incl: Strathmore Paper Co. Best Painting Award, Acad. Artists Nat. Exhib., 1973; Assoc. Mbrs. Award, Watercolor, Allied Artists of Am. Nat. Exhib., 1973. Address: 384 Franklin St., Reading, MA 01867, U.S.A. 2, 5, 6, 37, 57, 129, 132, 138.

NORDSTRÖM, (Judge) Hans Ehrenskjöld, b. 17 Dec. 1914. High Court Judge. Educ: Royal Cadet Schl. for Army Offs. (Reserve), 1936; LL.B., Univ. of Stockholm, Sweden, 1939. Appts. incl': various·appts., Svea·Ct. of Appeal & its Dist. Cts., 1939-58; Acting Advocate Gen., Ethiopia; 1950-5 1; Pres. of Div., Ethiopian High Ct., 1951-52; Pres., Fed.

High Ct. Eritrea, 1953-55; Chief of Personnel, Swedish UN contingent to Palestine, 1957; Pres., District Ct. 1959-60; Counsellor, High Ct., 1961-68; Judge Advocate, Swedish UN contingent to Cyprus, 1964; V.P., Div., Svea Ct. of Appeal, Sweden, 1969-. Mbrships incl: permanent mbr. Swedish UN Assn., Stockholm; Swedish sect., Int. Commn. of Jurists & Swedish Inst. for the Int. Comp. Law. Publs: Mil. Legislation Chapt., You & The Law, 1970; articles on Un Emergency Force, 1957-64; draft, Maritime Ct. Procedure Rules, 1955. Hons: Kt., Royal Order, Northern Star, 1962. Address: Frimärksvägen 35, S-122 47, Enskede, Sweden. 43.

NØRGAARD, Johannes, b. 2 Feb. 1893. Pastor Emeritus; Author; Publisher. Educ: Mission Schl., Denmark, 1911-14; Lang. & Hjorth Coll.; Cand. phil., Copenhagen Univ., 1922; B.D., Colgate-Rochester Divinity Schl., U.S.A., 1927; Postgrad. study, Harvard Grad. Schl. of Arts & Sci., Chgo. Univ. Divinity Schl. Appts: Asst. Min., Oure, Sevndborg, Langeland, Denmark, 1915-19; Pastor, 1st Bapt. Ch., Copenhagen, 1921-43; Pres., Bapt. Theol. Sem., Tølløse, 1943-66; Ed., Bapt. weekly, Baptisernes Ugeblad, 1953-67. Mbrships: Pres., Bapt. Union of Denmark, 1934-39, 1944-49; V.P., Bapt. World Alliance, 1947-50, Mbr., Exec. Comm., 1961; Rep., Baptist Union of Denmark, World Coun. of Churches, & Trustee, Bapt. Theol. Sem., Rüschlikon, Switzerland, 1948-66; Co-fndr., Free Ch. Coun. of Denmark, & of European Bapt. Fedn.; Evangelical Alliance Comm., Denmark, 1930-43. Publs: Num. books, papers, translations, inclng. autobiog., På vej til en livsopgave, 1954; Publr., Forlaget Fraternitas, 1971. Hons: D.D., William Jewell Coll., Liberty, Mo., U.S.A. 1954; Scroll of Hon., Bapt. Theol. Sem., Rüschlikon, Zurich, 1966. Address: Nansensgade 39, 3 Copenhagen K 1366, Denmark. 43.

NORMA, Rafael, b. 14 June 1914. Architect. Educ: Grad., Fac. Arquitectura, Univ. Nal. Aut.Mexico, 1940. Appts: Draftsman, Pub. Hlth. Dept., 1932-36; Archt., S.C.O.P., 1936-39; Justice Dept., 1939-43; Pres., Norma Arqs., 1946-; Arquitectos, S.A. 1959-; Lucentum, S.A., 1964-; Mbr., Bd. Dirs. & Treas., Cred. Ind. Constr., 1964-. Mbr. num. profl. & soc. orgs. Creative Works: Sev. constrs. in Mexican Repub., inclng. Master Plans Agua Prieta, Son., 1950; Tapachula, Chis., 1950; Apt. Bldgs., Mexico City, 1955-64; Lagunilla & Coyoacan Markets, 1955-58; Unidades Seguro Soc. Cosamaloapan, Ver. & Toluca, Mexico, 1963-65; San Luís Potosí Hosp., 1966-69; Ctr. Pop. José Ma. Morelos, Mexico City, 1968-70; Delegación Gustavo A. Madero, ibid, 1971-73. Hons. incl: Special Citation, Am. Inst. Arch., 1971; Fellow, A.I.A., 1966; Fellow, Royal Arch. Inst., Canada, 1972; Dip. Gold Medal, Soc. Arqs., Uruguay, 1969; Hon. mbr., 12 for. archtl. socs. Address: Agustín Ahumada 310, Mexico 10, D.F. Mexico. 2.

NORMAN, John L., b. 20 May 1928. College Professor of Music. Educ: A.B., Northeastern State Coll., Tahlequah, Okla. 1950; M.Mus., Univ. of Okla., Norman, 1957; PhD., Mich. State Univ., 1968. Appts: Inst., Music, Billings Pub. Schls, Okla., 1950; Inst., Piano, Conservatory of Music, Albany, Ga., 1954; Inst., Music, Ft. Hays State Coll., Kan., 1957; Inst., Music, Mich. State Univ., 1960; Instr., Music, Coll. of the Desert, 1962; Chmn., Dept. of Music, ibid, 1967. Mbrships. incl: Life Mbr., Phi Mu Alpha; Charter, Calif. Assn. Profl. Music Tchrs.; Pres., ibid, 1970-73; Pres., Music Tchrs. Nat. Assn. Contbr. to profl. jrnls. Address: Dept. of Music, Coll. of the Desert, Palm Desert, CA 92260, U.S.A.

NORMAN, Michael John Thornley, b. 2 Oct. 1923. Professor. Educ: B.Sc., Ph.D., Univ. of Reading, U.K. Appts: Grassland Rsch. Inst., Hurley, U.K. 1951-56; Div. of Land Rsch., Commonwealth Sci. & Indl. Rsch. Org., Australia, 1956-70; Dept. of Agronomy & Horticultural Sci., Univ. of Sydney, ibid, 1970-. Mbrships: Fellow Australian Inst. Agricl. Sci.; Tropical Grassland Soc.; Sydney Assn. Univ. Tchrs. Contbr. of articles to profl. jrnls. Recip., F.A. Brodie Mem. Prize, 1967. Address: Dept. of Agronomy & Horticultural Sci., Univ. of Sydney, Sydney, N.S.W., Australia 2006. 23.

NORMAN, Theodore, b. 14 Mar. 1912. Composer; Guitarist; Violinist. Educ: Studied music in Germany, Italy & Spain; Studied w. Adolph Weiss, Willy Hess, Aurio Herrero. Appts: 1st Violinist, L.A. Philharmonic, 1935-42; Lectr. & Tchr. of classical guitar, UCLA, 1968-; Recordings of Schoenberg Serenade (Guitar) & Bonley "Le Marteau Sans Maitre" (Guitar). Mbr., Am. Soc. of Composers, Authors & Publishers. Inventor of over 200 devices for helping the handicapped, double arm harness for hemiplegias etc., used in hosps. in U.S.A. & Europe. Publs. incl: Music for the Young Guitarist; Music for the Guitar Soloist; Music for the classical guitar, Book I for Beginners, Book II for Intermediate Players. Compositions incl: 24 Caprices of Paginini transcribed for guitar; 8 pieces of Igor Stravinsky transcribed from piano for 2 guitars. Address: 451 Westmount Dr., L.A., CA 90048, U.S.A.

NORMANN, Carl-Edvard, b. 26 Jan. 1912. Professor of Church History. Educ: Cand. Theol., 1936; Cand. Phil., 1939; Lic. Theol., 1944; Dr. Theol., 1948. Appts: Lectr. of Ch. Hist., Lund, Sweden, 1948; Rsch. Lectr., ibid, 1955; Prof. Ch. Hist., Univ. of Lund, 1960-; Mbr., Ch. Synod of Sweden, 1968. Mbrships: Royal Soc. for Publn. of Documents on Scandinavian Hist.; Royal Acad. Sci. & Humanities, Lund. Publs. incl: Cleri comitialis cirkulär 1723-1772, 1952; Lundastiftets prästerskap & 1731 års kyrkoordningsförslag, 1954; Enhetskyrka & upplysningsideer, 1963. Hons: Westrup Prize, Royal Acad. of Sci. & Humanities, Lund, 1948; Oscar II Schlrship, 1957. Address: Institutionen för kyrkohistoria, Finngatan 10, 223 62 Lund, Sweden. 134.

NORMAN-WILLIAMS, Charles Modupe, b. 4 June 1911. Medical Practitioner; Company Director. Educ: Edinburgh Univ., U.K.; M.B.; Ch.B. (Edin.); L.R.C.P.; L.R.C.S. (Edin.); L.R.F.P.S. (Glasgow); D.P.H. (Engl.), 1952. Appts: Chief Med. Advsr., Fedl. Govt. Nigeria, 1958-61; Dir. Hlth. Servs., WHO for Region of Africa S. of Sahara, 1961-66; Chmn., Lagos State Pub. Serve. Commn., 1968-. Mbrships: Chmn., St. John's Ambulance, Lagos State Coun.; Chmn., 400 Club Nigeria; Chmn., Lagos Race Club; Trustee & Chmn., Metropolitan Club, House Comm.; Trustee & Past Chmn., Yoruba Tennis Club; Trustee, Lagos Lawn Tennis Club. Address: Motunde House, 6 Hagley St., Yaba, P.O. Box 34, Lagos, Nigeria.

NØRREGAARD, Georg Pedersen, b. 24 Aug. 1904. University Professor; Historian. Educ: Cand. Mag., Univ. of Copenhagen, 1928; King's Coll., London, U.K., 1930-31; Ph.D. Univ. of Aarhus, 1948. Appts. incl: Asst. & collaborator, Inst. Hist. & Econ., Copenhagen, 1928-38; Prof., Univ. of Aarhus, 1963-. Mbrships. incl: World Federation Sci. Wkrs. (Exec. Coun., 1954-65, V.P. 1957-65); Danish Assn. for Protection of Sci. Work, (Bd., 1950-64, Chmn., 1962-64); Royal Danish Soc. for Nat. Hist., 1967. Publs. incl: Entreprenørforeningen 1892, 1942; Danske

Ingeniører fra Teknika, 1945; Freden i Kiel 1814, 1964; Danmark mellem Øst og Vest 1824-39, 1969; & others. Hon: Ridder af Dannebrog, 1972. Address: Dag Hammarskjölds Alle 1, 2100 Copenhagen Ø, Denmark. 43, 134.

NORRIS, Dorothy E. Koch (Mrs.) b. 12 Jan. 1907. Professor of Health, Physical Education & Recreation. Educ: A.B., Oberlin Coll., 1930; M.A., Tchrs. Coll., Columbia Univ., 1936. Profl. Dip. Tchrs. Coll., ibid, 1961. Appts. incl: Instr. & Asst. Prof., Hlth. & Phys. Educ., Tchr. of Dance, Univ. of Tenn., Knoxville, 1936-41; Asst. Prof., Assoc. Prof., Prof., Phys. Educ., Sargent Coll., Boston Univ., Cambridge, Mass., 1941-57; Dir., Hlth., Physl. Educ. & Recreation Admin., YWCA, Wilmington, Del., 1958-59; Assoc. Prof., Hlth. Phys. Educ. & Rec., State Univ. Coll. at Buffalo; 1959-68; Prof. ibid, 1968-. Mbrships. incl: Pi Lambda Theta; Kappa Delta Pi; Am. Assn. Hlth. Phys. Educ. & Rec. Am. Assn. for Phys. Educ. of Coll. Women; N.Y. State Tchrs. Assn.; N.Y. State Assn. for Hlth. Phys. Educ. & Rec.; Ballet Guild of Buffalo, Pi Lambda Theta; Kappa Delta Pi; NEA; Publs. incl: Keynotes to Modern Dance (w. Reva P. Shiner), revised 3rd edit., 1969; Three LP records to accompany above book, 1966; Co-Author, educ. manuals; contbr. of articles to profl. jrnls. Address: 2691 Elmwood Ave., Apt. 3. Kenmore, NY 14217, U.S.A. 2, 5, 6, 22, 30, 138, 141.

NORRIS, Paul Edmund, b. 9 Nov. 1918. Pharmacist; Toxicologist. Educ: B.S., 1941, M.S., 1942, Ph.D., 1951. Univ. of Mich.; Upjohn Fellow in Pharm. Chem., ibid, 1941-44. Appts: Off. (Lt., Jr. Grade), USN Bomb Disposal, Pacific Fleet, 1944-46; Rsch. Asst. to Dr. F. F. Blicke, Ergot Substitute Proj., Univ. of Mich., 1946-48; Instr. in Pharm., ibid, 1948-51; Asst. Prof. Pharm., ibid, 1951-54; Prod. Dev. Chem., Proctor & Gamble Co., 1954-64; Toxicol., ibid, 1964-. Mbrships: Dir. Fulton Cryogenics, Inc., Cinn., Ohio, 1964-; Bd. of Educ., Finneytown Schl. Dist., ibid, 1957-61; Soc. of Toxicol.; Am. Pharm. Assn. (Pres., Cinn. Br., 1958-59); Am. Chem. Soc.; Fellow, AAAS; Sigma Xi; Rho Chi; Phi Lambda Upsilon; Acad. Pharm. Scis.; Ohio State Pharm. Assn. Author & co-author, sci papers, area of synthetic drugs, dental caries rsch., clin. test methods. Holder of Dental Patents, U.S. & abroad. Address: 476 Beech Tree Dr., Cincinnati, OH 45224, U.S.A. 8.

NORRMAN, Märta Axelsdotter, b. 18 Oct. 1916. Lecturer in Physical Education. Educ: Physical Master Degree, Stockholm, Sweden, 1937; B.A., Lund, 1946. Appts: Tchr., var. schls., 1938-47; Trainer, Girl Guide Movement, 1947-49; Tchr., Jönköping Tchr. Trng. Coll., 1949-51; Tchr., Kalmar Tchr. Trng. Coll., 1951-62; Lectr., Malmö Tchr. Trng. Coll., 1962-. Mbrships. incl: Chief Commnr., Swedish Scout & Guide Assn., 1957-64; Pres., Swedish Girl Guide Coun., 1964-72; World Comm. Mbr., World Assn. of Girl Guides & Girl Scouts, 1966-; Guildmaster of Sweden, 1970-; Communal Coun. Mbr., Bara, Sweden. Address: Fasangatan 2, 23040 Bara, Sweden. 134.

NORTH, Eleanor B., b. 6 July 1898. Educator; Poet; Lecturer. Educ: B.A., M.A., Pa. State Univ.; Oxford, Cambridge, London Univs., U.K.; Harvard Univ. & Breadloaf Schl. of Engl., U.S.A.; Sorbonne, Paris, France. Appts. incl: Prof., Lit., Juniata Coll.; Prof., Youngstown Univ. & Berry Coll.; Vis. Prof. of Shakespeare; Sponsor, Summer Lit. Pilgrimages for coll. & univs. students, Europe, many yrs.; Lectr., lit., educ. & relig. orgs. Mbrships. incl:

Int. Poets' Shrine; Shakespeare Fndn.; Am.
Poetry League; Int. Poets; World Poetry Assn.;
Poetry Soc. of Australia; United Poets; MLA;
AAUP; Am. Philos. Soc.; AAUW; Delta Kappa
Gamma; Soc. for Women Educators; Sigma Tau
Delta. Publs. incl: (poetry) Star Dust, 1930;
Fall of Dew, 1936; Grace Notes, 1952; My
Heart Sings, 1969; High Tide, 1973; (other)
Reading & Personal Guidance, 1942; contbr. of
poems to num. anthols. & mags. Hons. incl:
Philos. Schol., Harvard, 1942; Schol.,
Cambridge Univ., 1930; Lit. Medal, Int. Acad.,
Rome, Italy, 1968; Recip., literary rsch. grants;
Cons., Int. Poetry Soc., U.K.; Poem placed on
plaque, Berry Coll., Ga. Address: 204 E.
Hamilton Ave., State College, PA 16801,
U.S.A. 5, 6, 11, 15, 57, 68, 138.

NORTHACKER, Alfred Austin, b. 2 May
1915. Business Executive. Educ: N.Y. Univ.,
Pratt Inst. of Technol., CCNY, & Univ. of
Houston, Tex.; B.B.A., M.B.A., Ph.D. Appts:
Purchasing Agt., M.W. Kellogg Co., N.Y.C.,
1936-51, 1954-57; European Procurement
Coord., Kellogg Int. Corp., Dortmund, German
Fed. Repub., 1951-54; Mng. Dir., Kellogg
Refinery Consultants Ltd., & Deutsche Kellogg
Industriebau GmbH, Dusseldorf, 1957-73; Dir.
of Procurement, M.W. Kellogg Co., Hackensack,
N.J., U.S.A., 1973-. Mbrships: Pres., Metropol.
Purchasers Assn., N.Y.C.; V.P., Am. Chmbr. of
Comm. in Germany, Dusseldorf.; num. other
profl. orgs., U.S.A. & Europe. Articles,
comments & book reviews, int. purchasing &
bus. ops. Hons. incl: Ambassador & Hon.
Citizen, City of New Orleans, La., 1972; Cert.
of Merit, Am. Chmbr. of Comm. in Germany,
1973. Address: M.W. Kellogg Co., 411
Hackensack Ave., Hackensack, NJ 07601,
U.S.A. 92.

NORTHEY, John Frederick, b. 3 May 1920.
Professor of Public Law; University
Administrator. Educ: B.A., LL.B. (N.Z.), Vic.
Univ. of Wellington; LL.D., Univ. of Auckland;
D.Jur., Univ. of Toronto, Canada. Appts: Sr.
Lectr. in Law, Univ. of Auckland, 1951-54,
Prof. of Pub. Law, 1954, Dean, Fac. of Law,
1965-. Mbrships: N.Z. Law Revision Commn. &
Pub. & Admin. Law Reform Comm.; N.Z.
Coun. of Legal Educ.; N.Z. Inst. of Int. Affairs.
Publs. incl: Introduction to Company Law, 7th
edit., 1971; Commercial Law in New Zealand,
(co-author), 5th edit., 1974; Law of Contract,
1974. Edit. Bd. Mbr., Univ. of Toronto Law
Jrnl., N.Z. Univ.'s Law Review, Recent Law.
Hons. incl: Canada Coun. Fellowship, 1962;
Carnegie Travel Grant, 1962. Address: Faculty
of Law, University of Auckland, Private Bag,
Auckland, New Zealand.

NORTHUP, William O'Dell, b. 4 Dec. 1930.
Educator. Educ: B.Sc., Rio Grande Coll., 1960;
M.A., Marshall Univ., 1962; Postgrad., Ohio
Univ. Appts: Maths. Instr., N. Gallia H.S.,
1960-62; Guidance Coun., Jackson H.S.
1962-63; Dir. of Guidance, Gallipolis City
Schls., 1964-66; Local Supt., N. Gallia H.S.,
1966-70; Supvsr. of Guidance, Gallia Co. Schls.,
1972-73, Gallia-Jackson-Vinton JVSD, 1973-.
Mbrships. incl: Pres., Bd. of Dirs., Gallia-Meigs
Action Agency; Lt.-Gov., Div. 9, Kiwanis; Sec.,
Bd. of Dirs., Gallipolis Kiwanis Club;
Sec.-Treas., Kiwanis Youth Fndn.; Master,
Masonic Lodge; Class Orator, Ancient Accepted
Scottish Rite; Educ. Chmn., Gallia Co. Am.
Cancer Soc.; Bd., Gallia Co. Safety Comm.
Recip. State Farmer Award, 1948. Address:
Route 3, Box 121, Gallipolis, OH 45631,
U.S.A. 130.

NORTON, Aloysius A., b. 31 July 1920.
Professor. Educ: B.S., U.S. Mil. Acad., W.
Point, N.Y., U.S.A., 1944; B.A. Columbia

Univ., 1950; Ph.D., Univ. of Madrid, Spain,
1954. Appts: USAF, 1944-52; Prof., Seton Hall
Univ., S. Orange, N.J.; Chmn., Humanities,
Dickinson State Coll., N.D.; Prof., Incarnate
Word Coll., San Antonio, Tex.; Cdr., U.S.
Merchant Serv. & Prof., U.S. Merchant Marine
Acad., Kings Pt., N.Y. Mbrships: Int. Inst. for
Strategic Studies; W. Pt. Soc. of N.Y.; Nat.
Coun. of Tchrs. of Engl. Publs: Christian
Approach to Western Literature; A Study of
Mark Twain's Huckleberry Finn; Literary
Craftsmanship. Recip., Rsch. Fellowship,
Harvard Univ., 1973-74. Address: U.S.
Merchant Marine Academy, Kings Point, NY
11024, U.S.A. 6.

NORTON, Ernest, b. 3 Feb. 1910.
Company Director. Educ: Portsmouth Tech.
Coll.; Royal Dockyard Coll. Appts: Mng. Dir.,
Yarrow & Co. Ltd.; Dpty. Chmn. & Mng. Dir.,
Yarrow (Shipbuilders) Ltd.; Dpty. Chmn.,
Yarrow Engrng. (Glasgow) Ltd.; Dpty. Chmn.,
Y—ARD Ltd.; Dir:, yarrow (Africa) Ltd.; Dir.
Y—ARD (Australia) Pty. Ltd.; Dir., Yarrow
Africa Maritime Consultancy Ltd., Yarrow
(Trng.) Ltd. & Scottish Computer Servs. Ltd.
Mbrships: Fellow, Inst. Mech. Engrs., Inst.
Marine Engrs. & Royal Inst. Naval Arch.; Inst.
Engrs. & Shipbuilders in Scotland; Am. Soc.
Mech. Engrs; Am. Soc. Naval Engrs.; Soc. Naval
Archts. & Marine Engrs.; Hon. Membr., City &
Guilds of London Inst.; Inst. of Dirs. Publs:
Leonardo da Vinci Lecture, 1959; Thomas
Lowe Gray Lecture, Inst. of Mech. Engrs.,
1972; articles in trade jrnls. Hons: B.E.M., 1946
& C.B.E., 1961 for servs. to R.N. in field of
Warship Design. Address: c/o Yarrow & Co.
Ltd., Scotstoun, Glasgow, G14 OXN, UK. 12,
32, 41, 43, 128, 139.

NORTON, Paul F., b. 23 Jan. 1917.
Teacher. Educ: B.A., Oberlin Coll., Ohio,
U.S.A., 1938; M.F.A., Princeton Univ., N.J.,
1947; Ph.D., ibid, 1952. Appts: Asst. Prof., Pa.
State Univ., 1947-53; Assoc. Prof., ibid,
1953-58; Assoc. Prof. & Chmn., Dept. of Art,
Univ. of Mass., Amherst, 1958-64; Prof., Univ.
of Mass., 1971-. Mbrships. incl: Coll. Art Assn.;
Archaeological Inst. of Am.; Nat. Trust, U.K.;
Nat. Trust, U.S.A.; Fellow, Royal Soc. of Arts;
Soc. of Archtl. Histns.; Pioneer Am. Soc.;
Societe Francaise d'Archeologie. Publs:
Contbns. to books & ency.; Articles & reviews
in profl. jrnls. Recip., sev. fellowships & grants.
Address: 57 Woodside Ave., Amherst, MA
01002, U.S.A. 2, 13, 30, 37, 133.

NORVILLE, D.O., b. 26 Dec. 1944.
Business Executive. Appts: Civil Servant, St.
Lucia, W. Indies, 1963; Travelling Salesman in
Caribbean, Bergasse & Co., 1965; Salesman,
Singer Sewing Machines, 1967; Ins. Agt.,
Guyana & Trinidad Mutual Ins. Co., 1968; Mng.
Dir., D.O. Norville & Co. Ltd., 1972-. Mbrships:
Sec., Shamrock Sports Club, 1963; Asst. Sec.,
St. Lucia Jaycees, 1968; 1st V.P., Mental Hlth.
Assn., 1972; Gen. Sec., United Wkrs. Party
(Govt. Party), 1972-. Address: P.O. Box 177,
Castries, St. Lucia, W. Indies.

NOSS, John B., b. 5 Oct. 1896. College &
Seminary Professor. Educ: A.B., Franklin &
Marshall Coll., Lancaster, Pa., 1916; B.D.,
Lancaster Theol. Sem., 1922; Ph.D., Univ. of
Edinburgh, U.K., 1928. Appts: Pastor, Bethany
Reformed Ch., 1922-26; Asst. Prof., Relig.,
Franklin Marshall Coll., 1928-31; Prof., ibid,
1931-45; Prof., Philos., 1945-62; Adj. Prof.,
World Religs. & the Christian Faith, Lancaster
Theol. Sem., 1958-; Lectr., Hist. of Relig.,
Union Theol. Sem., N.Y., 1951-64. Mbrships:
Am. Philos. Assn.; Am. Acad. Relig.; Phi Beta
Kappa; AAUP. Publs. incl: Living Religions,
1967; Man's Religions, 4th edit., 1968. Recip.,

D.D., Franklin & Marshall Coll., 1964. Address: 509 N President Ave., Lancaster, PA 17603, U.S.A. 13.

NOSSEK, Arnold Pavel, b. 6 Feb. 1899. Company Director. Educ: Acad. of Int. Commerce, Vienna, Austria. Appts. incl: Retail Dept., Bata Shoe Co., 1922; Dpty. Mgr., ibid, 1939-1944; Gen. Mgr., Nederlandse Schoen en Lederfabricken Bata, Best, Holland, 1944-62; Dir. sev. Cos., 1962-. Mbrships: Rotary Int. Hons: Freeman (Citizen), Municipality of Best, Holland, 1952; Off., Order Oranje Nassau, 1960. Address: Arnold P. Nos Seklaan 14, Best, Netherlands. 43.

NOTARBARTOLO, Albert. Painter; Writer; Editor. Educ: Nat. Acad. Fine Arts, N.Y.C., 1950; apprenticeship w. Ignacio La Russa, 1951-53; N.Y. Univ. & New Schl. for Soc. Rsch., 1953-57. Appts: Pvte. Instr., Painting & Composition, 1967; Art Instr., YMHA, N.Y.C. & Riverdale, N.Y., 1972; Currently Mng. Ed., Art Workers News. Mbrships: Am. Chem. Soc.; Overseas Press Club. Solo Exhibs: Univ. of Puerto Rico, 1965; 1966; Hemisphere Gall., N.Y.C., 1973. Gen. Exhibs. incl: Mus. of Mod. Art, N.Y.C.; Nat. Gall. of Art, Wash. D.C.; Del. Art Mus.; Nat. Gall. of Canada, Ottawa; Nat. Acad. Fine Arts, N.Y.C.; N.Y. Histl. Soc., N.Y.C.; Univ. of Ohio; Mus. of Fine Arts, Houston, Tex. Hons. incl: 1st Prize, N.Y. Intercultural Soc., 1951; HUD Nat. Community Art Competition, Wash. D.C., 1973. Tapestry Commn., Aubusson, France, 1973. Address: 215 W. 98th St., N.Y., NY 10025, U.S.A. 37.

NOTARO, Anthony, b. 10 Jan. 1915. Sculptor. Educ: Rinehart Schl. of Sculpture, Md. Inst., Balt., 1939. Tchr., Edgewood Schl., Greenwich, Conn., 1943-48. Exhibs. incl: NAD, N.Y.C.; Nat. Sculpture Soc.; Audubon Artists, Allied Artists Am.; Nat. Arts Club. Works incl: Vietnam Mem., Seton Hall Univ.; Henry Wadsworth Longfellow Medal, Hall of Fame for Gt. Ams., N.Y. Univ.; 1st Transcontinental Railroad Medal, Nat. Commemorative Soc. Mbrships: Nat. Sculpture Soc.; Allied Artists Am.; Am. Artists Profl. League. Hons. incl: Mrs. Louis Bennett Prize, Nat. Sculpture Soc., 1961; Nat. Competition to design N.J. Tercentenary Medal, 1962; Coun. of Am. Artists Award, 1967. Address: 14 Brookfield Way, Mendhom, NJ 07945, U.S.A.

NOTERMANS, Jef, b. 30 Apr. 1898. Retired Lecturer in Dutch Language & Literature. Educ: Headmaster's Cert., 1921; private tutorials; Fac. of Law, Univ. of Batavia, Java, 1932-37; Doct., Univ. of Leuven, Belgium, 1938; Univ. of Leiden, Netherlands, 1965-69. Appts. incl: Lectr., Hollands-Chinees Inst., Batavia, 1931-34; & Canisius Coll. & Pedagogische Akad. van de Ursulinen, ibid, 1934-37; King William III Lectr., 1939-41; Infantry Reserve Off.; Lectr., Univ. of Indonesia, 1945-47; Dir.-Gov. Hogere Burger School, Batavia, 1947-49; Tchr., 1949-69. Mbrships. incl: Maatschappij der Nederlandse Letterkunde, 1957-; Koninklijke Zuidnederlandse Maatschappij vcr Taai-en Letterkunde en Geschiedenis, 1938-; Nederlandse Genootschap voor Leraren, 1931-; Pres., Stichting Mathias-Kemp-Prijs. Author of num. publs. on Dutch lang. & lit. inclng. Vijf Charters van vóór 1300 in zogenaamd Maaslandse taal, 1970; Rondom de Maaslandse Dichter en Minnezanger Heinric van Veldeke. Contbr. to num. schol. jrnls. inclng. De Nieuwe Taalgids; Levende Talen; Tijdschrift voor Taal en Letteren. Hons. incl: Ridder, Crde van Oranje-Nassau, 1946; Juliana-Boudewijn-Prijs, 1969; Ridder, Kroonorde van België. Address:

Athoslaan 1 D-Biesland, Maastricht, Netherlands.

NOTHMAN, Martin M., b. 14 May 1894. Physician. Educ: Philos., Univ. of Breslau, Germany, 1912-14; M.D., ibid, 1919. Appts: Asst. Med., Medical Clin., Breslau Univ., 1920-26; Privatdocent, Internal Med., Breslau, 1925; Rsch. Fellow, Pharmacol. Inst., Graz Univ., Austria, 1926; Assoc. Prof., Internal Med., Univ. of Breslau, 1930; Phys.-in-Chief., Med. Dept., Jewish Hosp., Leipzig, 1932-38; Instr., Tufts Univ. Med. Schl., Boston, U.S.A., 1939; Asst. Clin. Prof., ibid & at Postgrad. Div., 1951; Prof., Internal Med., Germany, 1954; Staff Mbr., New England Med. Ctr. Hosp., Boston; Beth Israel Hosp. & Boston Dispensary. Mbrships. incl: Fellow, Royal Soc. of Hlth; Med. Assn. of Israel; Am. Soc. for Biol.; Am. Soc. for Advancement of Sci. Author, 2 monographs, 1937, 1947; Contbr. num. articles to med. jrnls. Num. discourses at meetings. Address: 94 Williston Rd., Brookline, MA 02146, U.S.A.

NOTMAN, Aubrey Reid, (Mrs. John D. Notman), b. 21 Apr. 1915. Home Economist. Educ: B.S., N.M. Coll. of Agric. & Mech. Arts, 1938; M.Ed., Colo. State Univ., 1962. Appts: Co. Home Agt., Coop. Ext. Serv., N.M. State Univ., 1938-73; w. WAC, 1943-45. Mbrships: Am. Econ. Assn.; Pres., N.M. Econs. Assn., 1959; Pres., N.M. Assn. Ext. Home Econs., 1947-48; Councilor, Western Region, Nat. Assn. Ext. Home Econs., 1949-50; Life, Epsilon Chapt., Epsilon Sigma Phi; Adult Educ. Assn.; Albuquerque Home Econs.; Pres., Belen Club, Pilot Int., 1965-66. Hons. incl: Disting. Ext. Award, N.M. Coll. Agric. & Home Econs., 1972; U.S. Dept. of Agric. 35 yr. Serv. Award, 1973; N.M. State Univ. Meritorious Serv. Award, 1973. Address: P.O. Box 207, Los Lunas, NM 87031, U.S.A. 5.

NOTOWIDIGDO, Musinggih Hartoko, b. 9 Dec. 1938. Operations Research Executive. Educ: B.M.E., Geo. Wash. Univ., 1961; M.Sc., N.Y. Univ., 1966. Appts: Engrng. Cons., Dollar-Blitz's Assn., 1962-64; Sr. Ops. Analyst, Am. Can Co., 1966-69; Prin. Analyst-Mgr., Ops. Rsch. & Analysis Dept., Borden Inc., N.Y.C., 1969-. Mbrships: Inst. of Mgmt. Sciences; Am. Statistical Assn; Ops. Rsch. Soc. of Am; Am. Mgmt. Assn. Recip., Int. Student Soc. Prize, 1961. Address: c/o Borden Inc., 277 Park Ave., 40th Floor, N.Y., NY 10017, U.S.A. 6.

NOTT, Kathleen Cecilia (Mrs.). Author. Educ: King's Coll., London; Somerville Coll., Oxford; B.A. Appts: V.P., Engl. Ctr., Int. PEN; Ed., Int. PEN Bulletin of Selected Books. Mbrships: PEN; Univ. Women's Club. Publs: (poetry) Landscapes & Departures; Poems from the North; Creatures & Emblems; (novels) Mile End; The Dry Deluge; Private Fires; An Elderly Retired Man; (criticism) The Emperor's Clothes; A Soul in the Quad; Philosophy & Human Nature; The Possibilities of Liberalism (forthcoming); (gen.) A Clean Well-Lighted Place; (jt. author) Objections to Humanism; What I Believe. Recip. Arts Coun. of Gt. Britain Awards, 1968 & 73. Address: 5 Limpsfield Ave., Thornton Heath, CR4 6BG, Surrey, U.K. 3, 30.

NOUSE, Charles Dale, b. 12 Jan. 1921. Advertising & Public Relations Director. Educ: Univ. of Mich., 1939-41; Columbia Univ., 1957. Appts: Advt. Salesman, Ann Arbor, (Mich.) News, 1945-46; Washten aw Co. Postr-Tribune, 1947-48; Reporter, Columnist, Mich. City (Ind.) News-Dispatch, 1948-50; Ed., The Beacon, Mich. City, 1949-50; Ed., Newsletter, Detroit Round Table Christians & Jews,

1952-53; w. Detroit Free Press, 1950-63; Edn. Ed., 1954-56; Asst. City Ed., 1956-58; Edit. Writer, 1958-63; Asst. Dir., P.R. & Advtng., Mich. Blue Cross, 1963-. Mbrships: Commodre Grosse Pointe Sail Club, 1973; R.R. Dir., Detroit River Yachting Assn., 1974. Author, History of Grosse Pointe Sail Club, 1974. Contbr. to mags. & jrnls. Hons: Serv. Award, Detroit Coun., P.T.A., 1957; Detroit Page One Award, Detroit Newspaper Guild, 1958; num. yacht racing trophies. Address: 324 Belanger Ave., Grosse Pointe Farms, MI, U.S.A. 8.

NOVAK, Cornelius Dan Zacharia (pseudonym Dan Zacharia), b. 24 Feb. 1928. Journalist; Writer. Educ: Econ. Higher Acad. & Law Fac., Bucharest Univ., Romania, 1945, '49-50; Fac. of Jrnlsm., Romanian Mil. Acad., 1950-51. Appts. incl: Mng. Dir., Documentary Ctr. Ltd., Tel Aviv, Israel, 1963-64; Ed., Hebrew review "Lemaaneich Gvirti", ibid, 1967-68; Ed., Freemasonic review "Aurora", 1969-73; Ed., "Detailed Bibliography of Environmental Dept., Israel Inst. Petroleum, 1970-74. Mbrships. incl: Pro-Venerable, Masonic Lodge "Hashachar", Tel Aviv, 1973; Int. Fedn. Free Jrnlsts. Publs. incl: Mocanii (The Transylvanian Peasants), 1955; Two Misogynic Plays, 1967. Recip., masonic hons. Address: 53 Ashkenasi St., Shikun Dan, Tel Aviv, Israel. 55.

NOVAK, Eva (Chava). Journalist; Theatre & Cinema Critic. Educ: Higher Schl. of Drama, Brasov, Rumania, 1945-48. Appts: Jrnlst., review "The Woman", Bucharest, Rumania, 1948-49; Gen. Sec., off. of review "The Peasant Woman", Bucharest, 1949-51; Writer, Rumanian Broadcasting Corp., Bucharest, 1951-52; Jrnlst., 2nd Ed., Red Cross Reviews, Bucharest, 1953-57; Critic, theatre & cinema Ed., newspapers "Davar" & "Omer", Tel-Aviv, Israel, 1960-74. Mbrships: Profl. Union of Artists, Jrnlsts. & Writers, Rumania, 1945-48; Jrnlsts. Union of Rumania, 1948-59; Istael Fedn. of Jrnlsts., 1963-74; Literary Fund, Writers Union of Rumania, 1953-59; Literary cenacles "Eliezer Steinbarg" & "Menora", Israel, 1960-61 & 1963-69. Publs: Stories & features; Co-author, short plays; Several hundred newspaper articles. Hons: Dishon Prize for Jrnlsm., Israel Nat. Fedn. of Jrnlsts., 1961; Schlrship., Pub. Coun. for Culture & Arts, Israel, 1963. Address: 53 Ashkenasi St., Shikun Dan, Tel-Aviv, Israel. 55.

NOVELL, Earl Kenyon, b. 13 Sept. 1925. Risk Management Executive. Educ: Univ. of Conn.; Admiral Billard Acad., New London, Conn.; Air Force Finance Schl., Maxwell Field, Ala.; Retail Credit Mgmt. Schl., Atlanta, Ga. Appts: Mgng. Dir., Marta Ins. Mgrs., 1972; Dir., Ins. & Safety, Perini Corp., Framingham Mass.; Rep., Employers Ins. of Wausau; Mgr., Retail Credit Co., Boston; Rsch. Photographer, USN Underwater Sound Lab., New London; Aerial Photographer, Photo Lab. Chief, U.S.; Lectr., Constrn. Ins. & Safety; Safety Advsry. Bd., Rapid Transit Dev. Corp.; Exec.Comm.-Heavy Constrn., Nat. Safety Coun. Mbrships: Am. Soc. Ins. Mgmt.; Am. Soc. Safety Engrs.; Flotilla Off., U.S. Coast Guard Aux.; Kts. of Columbus Coun. 3716; Am. Legion; VFW. Address: 3755 Dunwoody Club Dr., Dunwoody, GA 30338, U.S.A.

NOVIDOR, Benjamin, b. 17 Aug. 1917. Motel Executive. Educ: Rochester Bus. Inst., Rochester, N.Y. Appts: Owner-Mgr., New Central Meat Markets, Elmira, Elmira Hts., Corning & Ithaca, N.Y., 1940-60, Queen City Wholesale Provision Co., 1960-65, Charlesmont Construction Co., Elmira, 1944-, Red Jacket

Motel, 1956-, Red Jacket Restaurant, 1965-; Builder, Developer & Sec.-Treas., Nate's Floral Estates Inc. Mobile Home Park, Ithaca, N.Y. Mbrships: Active United Jewish Appeal Drive, 1944-50; N.Y. State Hotel & Motel Assn.; Dir , N.Y. State Motel Assn., 1960-64; Ch. Co. Chmbr. of Comm. Address: P.O. Box 489, Elmira, NY 14902, U.S.A. 6.

NOVOTNY, Ann Margaret, b. 3 Oct. 1936. Editorial Research Consultant; Writer. Educ: B.A., McGill Univ., Montreal, Canada, 1957; M.A., ibid, 1960. Appts: Edit. rschr. for Collier's Ency., Cntrl. Feature News, Grolier's Ency. Int., The N.Y. 1964-65 World's Fair Corp., Time Inc. Books Div., 1961-65; Dir. & Fndr. of Rsch. Reports, an edit. rsch. cons. serv., N.Y.C., 1965-. Mbrships: Sec., Am. Soc. of Picture Profls. Inc., 1969; Pres., ibid, 1970; N.Y. Histl. Soc. Publs. incl: White House Weddings (w. Wilbur Cross), 1967; Why Do They Act That Way? (simplified edit. of Black Race), 1970; Strangers at The Door: Ellis Island, Castle Garden, & The Great Migration to America, 1972, 1974; Articles in Publishers Weekly & Special L braries. Address: P.O. Box 80, New Lebanon Ctr., NY 12126, U.S.A. 5, 6, 138.

NOVOTNY, Elmer Ladislaw, 27 July 1909. Artist; Professor & Director, School of Art. Educ: Dip., Cleveland Inst. of Art, Ohio, U.S.A.; B.A., Western Reserve Univ., Cleveland; M.A., Kent State Univ., Ohio; Special studies at Slade Schl., Univ. of London, U.K. Acad. of Zagreb, Yugoslavia, Yale Univ., U.S.A. Appts: Instr. in portraiture, Cleveland Inst. of Art, 1934; Instr. in Art, Kent State Univ., 1936; Asst. Prof.-Prof. of Art, ibid, 1938-45; Chmn., Dept. of Art, 1946; Dir., Schl. of Art, 1948-74. Mbrships: Life Fellow, Int. Inst. of Arts & Letters; Alpha Beta Delta, Art Frat.; Kappa Delta Pi, Educ. Hon.; Omicron Delta Kappa, Ldrship. Hon. Author, Byways in Southern Europe-A Portfolio of Drawings with Comments, 1968. Paintings in Mus. Collects. incl: Wingaersheek Beach, Butler Inst. of Am. Art; Brown & Blue, Cleveland Mus. of Art; 2 Weeks with Pay, Akron Art Inst. Hons. incl: Prizes Cleveland Mus. of Art, 1930-38; Jurors Award, Akron Art Inst., 1952; Disting. Prof. Awars, Kent State Univ., 1964. Address: 7317 Westview Rd., Kent, OH 44240, U.S.A. 2, 8, 37.

NOVOTNY, Jiří, b. 29 Apr. 1911. Architect. Educ: Czech Tech. Univ. Fac. Arch. & Bldg., Prague, 1930-35; Appts: Stage Designer, 1933-35; Archt., 1935-49; Chief Archt., Ctr. of Town Planning, Stavoprojekl, 1949-51; Chief Town Planner of Master Plan, Capital City Prague, 1951-. Mbrships: Rep. Union Czech. Archts. in Int. Union Archts.; Exec. Comm., Union Czech. Archts., -1971; jury of int. comps., Vienna, 1968, '70, Brussels, 1969. Author, New Housing in Prague, 1965. Hons. incl: Prize of Prague, 1958; Award for Merits in Construction, 1965. Address: Náměstě Svobody 1, 16000 Prague 6, Czechoslovakia.

NOYAN, Mehmet Ismet Turgut, b. 14 Apr. 1916. Professor of Chemical Engineering. Educ: Am. Coll.-Haydarpasa Lisesi, Istanbul, Turkey, 1930-35; Fac. of Sci., Univ. of Istanbul, 1935-39; D.Sc., 1949-52. Appts. incl: Works Engr., Pasabahce Glassworks, Istanbul, 1941-43; Tech. Mgr., Imperial Chem. Inds. Ltd., ibid, 1943-58; Prof. & Chmn., Dept. of Chem. Engrng., Boğaziçi Univ., 1958-; Sr. V.P., Robert Coll., 1965-69; Cons., Indl. Dev. Bank of Turkey, Istanbul, 1958-71; Cons., State Planning Dept., Ankara, 1962-65; Lectr., Fac.

of Chem., Univ. of Istanbul, 1967-; Cons., Soda Fabrikasi T.A.S., Mersin, 1971-72; Cons., Turkish Glass Factories, 1971-72. Mbrships. incl: Chem. Soc. of Turkey, Istanbul, 1941-; Turkish Phys. Soc., 1951-; Chmbr. of Chem. Engrs., Ankara, 1955- & Pres., 1955; Soc. of Chem. Ind., London, U.K., 1951-; Turkish Cancer Soc., Istanbul, 1963-; Société de Chemie Ind., Paris, France, 1965-. Contbr. to mags., symposiums, and profl. jrnls. Hons. incl: 25 yrs. Serv. Award, Turkish Chmbr. of Chem. Engrs., Ankara, 1964. Address: Dept. of Chem. Engrng., Boğaziçi Univ., Bebek/Istanbul, Turkey.

NOZOE, Tetsuo, b. 16 May 1902. Professor Emeritus. Educ: Grad., Tohoku Imperial Univ., Sendai, Japan, 1926; D.Sc., Osaka Imperial Univ., 1936. Appts: Rsch. Off., Formosan Govt., Taihoku, 1926; Asst. Prof., Taihoku Imperial Univ., 1929; Prof., Nat. Taiwan Univ., Taipei, Repub. of China, 1945, Tohoku Univ., Sendai, Japan, 1948; Emeritus Prof., Tohoku Univ., 1966. Mbrships. incl: Pres. elect, Chem. Soc. of Japan; Chem. Soc., London, U.K.; Swiss Chem. Soc.; For. Mbr., Royal Acad. Scis., Sweden; Hon. mbr., Chinese Chem. Soc., Repub. of China; Hon. mbr., Pharmaceutical Soc. of Japan. Author of many papers & sev. monographs in special field of organic chem. Hons: Chem. Soc. Award, 1944; Asahi Newspaper Cultural Award, 1952; Japan Acad. Award, 1953; Order of Cultural Merits, Japanese Govt.; 1958; Hon. Citizenship of Sendai City, 1958. Address: No. 811, 2-5-1, Kamiyoga, Setagaya-ku, Tokyo 158, Japan.

NULMAN, Seymour Shlomo, b. 6 Sept. 1921. Rabbi; Dean; Community Leader. Educ: Yeshiva Univ.; Ordained Rabbi, 1942; Rabbinical Sem. of Am., 1943; M.A., Columbia Univ., 1944. Appts: Rabbi, E. Side Torah Ctr., 1943-, Slutzker Synagogue, 1944-; Dean, Yeshivah Konvitz, 1945-, Talmud Torah Jacob David, 1941-; Chap., Jewish Teamsters Assn., 1941-, Nat. Slutzker Landsmanshaft Orgs., 1945-, Beekman-Downtown Hosp., 1973-. Mbrships. incl: Chmn., Nat. Conf. Hebrew Day Schl. Prins., Jacob David Assn., Jewish Community Coun., E. Side, N.Y., Multi-Serv. Ctrs., Community Dev. Bd., N.Y.C.; Pres., Yehudah Wolf Inst., 1939-45. Publs. incl: Torah Presentation Program, 1973; Tree of Life Program, 1973. Hons. incl: Hon. dedication of Torah Scroll, E. Side Torah Ctr., 1973; Talmud Soc. Award, Torah Umesorah, 1973. Address: 268 E. Broadway, N.Y., NY 10002, U.S.A. 55.

NUMATA, Makoto, b. 27 Nov. 1917. University Professor. Educ: Grad., Botany, Tokyo Univ. of Lit. & Sci., 1942; D.Sc., Kyoto Univ., 1953. Appts: Asst. Prof., Chiba Normal Schl., 1945; Lectr., Tokyo Univ., of Lit. & Sci., 1948; Asst. Prof., Chiba Univ., 1950; Prof. of Ecol., ibid, & Prof., Agric. Rsch. Inst. Tohoku Univ., 1964; Dean, Fac. of Sci., Chiba Univ., 1968-74. Mbrships. incl: Pres., Weed Soc. of Japan; Chmn., Grassland Proj. & Conservation Sect., Japanese IBP Comm.; Commn. on Ecol., I.U.C.N.; Coun., Ecol. & Botan. Socs. of Japan. Publs. incl: Standpoint of Ecology, 1958; Weed Flora of Japan, 1968; Biological Flora of Japan, 2 vols., 1969; Life of Plants, 1972; Nature Conservation & Ecology, 1973; Ed., New History of Biology, 1973; Ed., Flora & Vegetation of Japan, 1974. Hons: Award for Educl. Servs., Gov. of Chiba Prefecture; Award for Servs. in Natural Conservation, Min. of Educ. Address: Lab. of Ecol., Fac. of Sci., Chiba Univ., Yayoicho, Chiba 280, Japan.

NUNES, Louis Emmanuel, b. 1 June 1924. Businessman. Educ: Study of Law, Netherlands, 1 yr. Appts: British Army, WWII;

Freight Mgr., KLM Royal Airlines, Neth. Antillies; w. Curacao Trading Co.; Dir., Ceteco Antillian Corp.; Est., own bus.; Currently, proprietor, 3 boutiques. Mbrships: Cariari Int. Country Club, San Jose, Costa Rica; Past Pres., Soc. di Comerciantenan. Address: P.O. Box 768, Willemstad, Curacao, Netherlands Antillies. 109, 136.

NUNEZ, Frank. Librarian. Educ: B.A., Eastern Ky. Univ.; M.S.L.S., Univ. of Ky. Appts: Admin. Asst. to Libn., Dir. of Circulation, of Acquisitions & of Summer Sessions, Eastern Ky. Univ., 1963-68; Coord. of Lib. Servs., ibid, 1968-. Mbrships: ALA; Southeastern & Va. Lib. Assns.; Vis. Comm., Southern Assn. of Schls. & Colls. Address: Route 2, Box 242B, Cedar Bluff, VA, U.S.A.

NUNZIATO, Ralph Joseph, b. 19 Sept. 1920. Business Executive. Educ: Bachelor of Aeronautical Engrng., Coll. of Engrng., N.Y. Univ., U.S.A., 1942. Appts: Col., U.S.A.F., 1942-60; Assoc., Laurance S. & David Rockefeller, N.Y.C., 1960-65; Asst. Mgr., New Investment Dept., Standard Oil Co., N.J., & V.P., Jersey Enterprises, Inc., 1965-67; V.P., Emerson Elec. Co., St. Louis, Mo., 1967-70; V.P., Amcord, Newport Beach., Calif., 1970-72; Pres. & Chief Exec. Off., Optics Technol., Inc., Redwood City, Calif., 1972-. Mbrships: Assoc. Fellow, Am. Inst. of Aeronautics & Astronautics; Univ. Club, N.Y.C.; Kenwood Golf & Country Club, Wash. D.C. Recip., Legion of Merit U.S.A., 1955. Address: 181 Forest Lane, Menlo Park, CA 94025, U.S.A. 9.

NUORTEVA, Pekka Olavi, b. 24 Nov. 1926. Educator; Museum Curator. Educ: M.Sc., Helsinki Univ., 1951, D.Sc., 1955. Appts. incl: Docent. Zool., Helsinki Univ., 1955-; Curator, Zool. Mus., ibid, 1958-; Lectr., Vet. H.S., Helsinki, 1967-; Mbr., Finnish Coun. for Protection of Water, 1969-71, Environmental Coun. 1970-, Commn. for Protection of Baltic, 1973. Mbrships. incl: Finnish League for Protection of Nature (Pres. 1967-70); Societas Biol. Fennica Vanamo (Ed.), 1953-61; Nordic Agric. Assn. Publs: Atlas of Finnish Animals, 1-2, 1955-57; Animals in Colour, 1956; Popularized Insect Physiology, (ed.), 1963; Principles of Zoology (w. S-L Nuorteva), 1966; Eläinoppi, 1-2 (co-author), 1968-69; contbr., num. sci. publs. & writer, articles on environmental problems. Recip. of var. awards. Address: Ida Ekmanintie 5 Y 199, SF-00400 Helsinki 40, Finland. 90, 134.

NURMESNIEMI, Antti Aarre, b. 30 Aug. 1927. Interior & Product Designer. Educ: Inst. of Indl. Design, Helsinki, Finland, 1950. Appts. incl: Design Off., Oy Stockmann Ab, Helsinki, 1949-50; Archt. Off., Viljo Rewell, ibid, 1951-55; Archt. Off., Giovanni Romano, Milan, Italy, 1954; Owner, Interior & Product Design Off., Helsinki, Finland, 1956-; Tchr., Inst. of Indl. Design, 1964-69; Lectr., Indl. Art Inst., Tokyo, Japan, 1965; Chmn., Bd. of Dirs., Inst. of Indl. Design, Helsinki, Finland, 1969-. Mbrships. incl: Finnish Assn. of Designers ORNAMO, Pres., 1967-; Finnish Soc. of Crafts & Design; Assn. of Finnish Interior Designers SIO; Am. Inst. of Interior Designers. Works incl: Ch. at Herttoniemi & Hyvinkaa, 1959-60; Hallapyora, Vanhan Kellari, Kaivopiha, Holvari restaurants, theatre restaurant at Joensuu City Hall, Rauta Grilli, 1958-71; PSP, Rovaniemi & Vaasa Banks; Off. of Gen. Mgr. of WHO, Geneve, Switzerland; Off. of the Trade Commnr. for Finland, Hamburgh, 1964-71; Participated in num. exhibs. Hons. incl: Silver Medal, Triennale of Milan, Italy, 1957; Grand Prix, 1960 & '64; Lunning Price, 1959, Order of the Lion. Address: Studio Nurmesniemi, Kalliolinnantie 12, E., Helsinki 14, Finland.

NURNEY, (Mrs.) Geraldine (Prentiss) Latham, b. 28 Dec. 1907. City Librarian Emeritus. Educ: Sacramento Jr. Coll., Calif., 1927; A.B., Univ. of Calif., Berkeley, 1930; J.H./Elem. Tchng. Credential, Cert. in Libnship., San Jose State Coll., Calif., 1931; var. courses & certs. Appts: Libn., Dir. of Reading, Lit. & Visual Educ., Elem. Schls., Coronado, Calif., 1931-32; Children's Libn., San Jose Pub. Lib., Calif., 1932-43; City Libn., Dir. of Libs., ibid, 1943-70; Retd., 1970. Mbrships: Life Mbr., Soroptimist Club; Sec.-Treas., ibid, 1947-48, 2nd V.P., Prog. Chmn.; Pres., San Jose Bus. & Profl. Women's Club, 1946-47; AAUW; Life Mbr., Univ. of Calif. Alumni Assn.; Adult Educ. Senate, San Jose Unified Schl. Dist., 1950-59. Contbr. to Ency. Americana & El Padre. Presented weekly lib. prog. of book reviews & interviews, Radio KEEN, San Jose, 1947-50. Recip., var. hons. Address: 3584 Irlanda Way, San Jose, CA 95124, U.S.A. 5, 9, 57, 59, 132.

NUTTER, Daniel Gerald, b. 7 June 1928. Australian Public Servant (Foreign Affairs). Educ: B.A., Univ. of Sydney, N.S.W., Australia; Dip. Diplomatic Studies, Canberra Univ. Coll. Appts: Diplomat, Bonn & Berlin, Germany, 1952-56; Diplomat, Saigon, Vietnam, & Vietiane, Laos, 1958-59; Chargé d'Affaires, Vientiane, 1961; Diplomat, Tokyo, Japan, 1961-63; Dpty. High Commnr., Delhi, India, 1965-68; Australian Govt. Observer, Vietnam Elections, 1967; Asst. Dir., Commonwealth Secretariat, London, U.K., 1968-70; Min., Saigon, 1970-71; Asst. Sec., S. East Asia Br., Canberra, 1971-73; Hd., Nat. Assessments Staff, Canberra, 1973-. Mbr: Classical Soc., Canberra. Address: Dept. of Defence, Building 10, Canberra, A.C.T., Australia 2600. 23.

NUZUM, Katherine B., b. 29 Dec. 1907. Teacher; Author; Free-lance Writer. Educ: B.S., Pa. State Univ., U.S.A. Appts: Tchr., Soc. Studies, Art, & Engl., Pub. Schls., Pa., Calif., & Ala.; Supervising Prin., Schl., Pa., 1941-43; Off., WAVE, U.S. Navy, Wash. D.C., WWII & Korean War; Feature writer & Photographer, The Baldwin Times, Fairhope Courier, & Foley Onlooker, Ala., 1971-. Mbrships. incl: Pres., Pensters, 1970-72; NEA; AAUW; Int. Club; Ala. Histl. Soc.; Baldwin Co. Histl. Soc.; Eastern Shore Art Assn.; Sev. State & local tchrs. orgs. Publs: A History of Baldwin County; Contbns. to sev. jrnls.; Photos in mags. TV appearance, WKRG, Mobile, Ala. Recip., Awards for feature articles, Ala. Press Assn., 1968, 1969, & 1970. Address: 41 Winter Haven, Fairhope, AL 36532, U.S.A. 125.

NWANSI, (Chief) John Obiukwu Njoku (H.H. Ike III of Ikeduru), b. 20 Sept. 1933. Traditional Ruler. Appts: U.A.C. Sales Asst. (Managerial), 1955-60; Judicial Off., 1960-74; Traditional Ruler (Ike III of Ikeduru), 1970-.

Mbrships: Owerri Diocesan Synod Deleg., Mbr. Archeaconry Bd. & Diocesan Finance Comm., & C.M.S. Parish Treas.; H.M. Prisons Visitor; Fed. Nigerian Pub. Serv. Bd.; Chmn. & Organiser, Mbaitoli/Ikeduru Divisional Festival of Arts Comm.; Divisional Sports Comm.; Sec., Owerri Govt. Second. Schl. Old Boys Assn.; Life Chorister; Anglican Youth Fellowship; 1st Aider & Blood Donor, Brit. Red Cross Soc.; formerly in schl. Boxing & Lawn Tennis Clubs, Sr. Lit., Art, Sci. & Music Socs. Address: Umuiyi-Akabo Postal Agcy., Owerri, Nigeria.

NYE, Robert, b. 15 Mar. 1939. Poet; Critic. Appts: Poetry Ed., The Scotsman, 1967-; Poetry Critic, The Times, 1971-. Publs: Juvenilia 1, 1961; Juvenilia 2, 1963; Doubtfire (novel), 1967, N.Y. ed., 1968; Tales I Told My Mother (short stories), 1969; Darker Ends, 1969; Agnus Dei, 1973; Two Prayers, 1974; Five Dreams, 1974; The Seven Deadly Sins, 1974; rep. in num. anthols.; contbr. critical articles, reviews, etc. to num. periodicals; prepared eds. of Sir Walter Raleigh, Swinburne, & William Barnes. Hons: Gregory Award for Poetry, 1963; Scottish Arts Coun. Bursary & Publication Award, 1970; James Kennaway Mem. Award, 1970; Scottish Arts Coun. Bursary, 1973. Address: c/o Calder & Boyars Ltd., 18 Brewer St., London W1, U.K. 3, 11.

NYLES, Robert David, b. Tientsin, China, 21 Mar. 1926. Psychologist. Educ: St. John's Univ., Shanghai, 1946; B.A., Univ. of Calif., Berkeley, 1949; M.A., Univ. of London, U.K., 1955; Ph.D., ibid, 1956; postgrad., Inst. of Psych., Maudsley Hosp., Univ. of London; Clinique Psych. Ste.-Anne, Univ. of Paris; Nat. Inst. Mental Hlth.; Trng. in Analytic Psychol. w. Prof. C.A. Meier, Clin. & Rsch. Ctr. for Jungian Psychol., Zurich, Switzerland; pvte. prac. as Analyst-. Appts: Chief Clin. Psychol., & Dir., Psychol. Dept., N.J. State Hosp., Trenton, U.S.A., 1962-63; Dist. Psychol., Maui Co., Wailuku, Hawaii, 1965-66; Pvte. prac., analytic psychotherapy, Princeton, N.J., 1962-63, Wailuku, Hawaii, 1965-66, Zurich, Switzerland, 1966-68, & Berkeley, Calif., 1964-65; & 1968-. Address: 1735 Highland Pl., Berkeley, CA 94709, U.S.A. 9.

NYREN, Dorothy., b. 29 Sept. 1927. Librarian. Educ: B.A., Boston Univ., 1952; M.A., 1954; M.S., Simmons Coll., 1960. Appts: Dir., Young Lib., Daytona Beach, Fla., 1955-57; Town Lib., Concord Mass., 1959-64; Chief Libn., Northbrook Pub. Lib., Ill., 1965-69; Coord., Adult Servs., Brooklyn Pub. Lib., N.Y., 1970; Chief, Central Lib., 1971-. Mbrships: Councillor, ALA; Exec. Bd., PLA; N.Y. Lib. Assn.; Phi Beta Kappa. Publs: Modern American Literature, 1960, 61, 63, 69; Modern Romance Literature, 1968; Community Service, 1970; Voices of Brooklyn, 1973. Address: Ctrl. Lib., Ingersoll Bldg., Grand Army Plaza, Brooklyn, NY 11238, U.S.A. 5, 30, 138.

O

OAKLEY, Stewart Philip, b. 21 Apr. 1931. University Lecturer. Educ: B.A., Oxford Univ., U.K., 1952; Dip.Ed., 1953; M.A., 1956; Ph.D., London, 1061. Appts: Tutor, Hist., Univ. of Exeter, 1959-60; Asst., Hist., Univ. of Edinburgh, 1960-62; Lectr., Mod. Hist., ibid, 1962-69; Vis. Prof., Scandinavian Hist., Univ. of Minn., U.S.A., 1966-67; Lectr., Schl. of European Studies, Univ. of E. Anglia, 1969-73; Sr. Lectr., ibid, 1973-. Mbr., Hist. Soc. Publs: The Story of Sweden, 1966, 69; The Story of Denmark, 1972; articles in field. Address: Schl. of European Studies, Univ. of E. Anglia, Univ. Plain, Norwich NOR 88C, U.K. 3, 30.

OANCIA, David, b. 6 Dec. 1929. Journalist. Educ: Sir George Williams Univ., Montreal, Canada. Appts: Began writing for publ., 1952; Based in London, travelled through Europe, N. Africa & Middle E., 1959-62; Only N. Am. Corres. based in Peking, China, during cultural revolution, 1965-68. Publd. articles on dev. of European Econ. Community, Algerian war & Arab-Israeli Conflict. Reports on Chinese Cultural Revolution publd. widely in N. Am., Europe, Asia, & Australia. Recip., Nat. Newspaper Award, 1967. Address: Apt. 36, 4326 Sherbrooke St. W., Westmount, P.Q., Canada.

OBAID, R.M.S., b. 12 Oct. 1936. Professor. Educ: B.Sc., Cairo Univ., Egypt, 1958; Ph.D., Birmingham Univ., U.K., 1962. Appts: Lectr., Fac. of Sci., Riyadh Univ., 1963; Dean, ibid, 1963-72; Hon. Rsch. Fellow, Birmingham Univ., 1972-73; Prof. of Phys. Chem., Riyadh Univ., Saudi Arabia, 1973-. Mbrships: Chem. Soc.; Faraday Soc.; Royal Inst. Chem. Address: Chem. Dept., Fac. of Sci., Riyadh Univ., Riyadh, Sauid Arabia.

O'BEIRNE-RANELAGH, Elaine Lewis. Educator; Librarian. Educ: Vassar Coll., M.S., Columbia Univ., 1937; M.A., Indiana Univ., 1943; Postgrad. study, Univ. of Rome, Trinity Coll., Dublin. Appts: Libn., Brooklyn Pub. Lib., N.Y., 1938-45; Writer, ASCAP, 1945-46; Adjudicator, Cork Film Festival, 1956; Mbr., Schlrship. Exchange Bd., Dublin, 1957-59; Libn., USAF, & Lectr., European Div., Univ. of Md. Engl. Dept., 1959-; Co-dir., Cambridge (U.K.) Conf. of Am. Women Grads., 1966-68. Mbrships: N.Y. Lib. Club; V.P., Contbng. Ed., N.Y. Folklore Soc.; Ind. Folklore Soc.; ALA; Special Lib. Assn.; Armed Forces Libns. Assn.; Phi Beta Kappa. Publs: Himself & I, 1958; Wentworth Hall, 1975; Contbr., N.Y. Times Mag. & Book Review, 1958-. Hons: Inst. Int. Fndn. Fellowship, 1935-36; Citation, Inst. of Educ. by Radio, 1944; Guggenheim Fellow, 1947-48; Trustee, Schlrship. Exchange Bd., 1957-59. Address: Huccaby, Long Rd., Cambridge, U.K. 5.

OBENG, Letitia Eva Takyibea (Mrs.), b. 10 Jan. 1925. Research Scientist; Research Institute Director. Educ: B.Sc., Univ. of Birmingham, U.K., 1952; M.Sc., ibid, 1962; Ph.D., Univ. of Liverpool, U.K., 1964. Appts. incl: Lectr., Coll. of Technol., Kumasi, 1952-57; Rsch. Staff, Nat. Rsch. Coun. & Ghana Acad. of Scis., Ghana, 1960-65; Dir., Rsch. Inst. of Aquatic Biol., Coun. for Scientific & Indl. Rsch., Ghana, 1965-. Mbrships: Fellow, Ghana Acad. of Arts & Scis. & Royal Soc. of Arts, U.K.; Affiliate, Royal Soc. Tropical Med. & Hygiene; Chmn., Bd. Dirs., Electricity Corp. of Ghana. Publs. incl: num. scientific papers. Hons: Silver Medal, after delivering Caroline Haslett Mem. Lecture,

Royal Soc. of Arts, 1972. Address: P.O. Box 49, Achimota, Ghana. 135, 138.

OBENSHAIN, James Warner, b. 19 July 1916. Division Superintendent of Schools. Educ: Grad., Va. Polytechnic Inst., 1939; M.Ed., Univ. of Va., 1960. Appts: Tchr., Vocational Agric., Fincastle H.S., 1941-54; Prin., ibid, & H.S. Supvsr., 1954-59; Supt., Botetourt Co. Schls., 1959-. Mbrships: Deacon & Trustee, Fincastle Bapt. Ch.; Past Pres., Fincastle Rotary Club; Charter Pres., Fincastle Ruritan Club; Dist. Gov., Ruritan Nat.; Phi Delta Kappa. Recip., Honorary State Farmer Degree. Address: P.O. Box 101, Fincastle, VA 24090, U.S.A. 7, 85.

OBERLANDER, Marek, b. 14 Sept. 1922. Artist. Educ: Acad. of Fine Arts, Warsaw, Poland. Appts: Cultural Ed., Po Prostu, Nowa Kultura, & Wspokczesnosc, literary & artistic publs., Warsaw, 1955-63. 1 Man Exhibs: Warsaw, 1959; Wroclaw & Zakopane, 1961; Stockholm, Sweden, 1963. Grp. Expositions: Poland; U.S.S.R.; Czechoslovakia; China; India; Canada; U.S.A.; Denmark; Sweden; Germany. Represented in num. permanent collects. inclng: Nat. Mus. of Warsaw; Jewish Mus. of Warsaw; Revolutionary Mus. of Warsaw; Nat. Mus. of Stockholm; Mod. Art Mus. of Stockholm; Lublin Mus.; ABF Collect., Stockholm; Swenska Hnadelsbauken Collect., Stockholm. Pvte. Collects. incl: France; Poland; U.S.A.; Germany; Sweden; Holland; Israel; Finland; Czechoslovakia; U.S.S.R.; Brazil; Switzerland. Recip., Pro Prostu Prize, 1955. Address: Le Provence II, 140 Ave. Cyrille Besset, 06100 Nice, France.

OBERMAN, Moishe David, b. 3 Mar. 1914. Publisher. Educ: St. Louis Coll. of Pharmacy, 1931-33. Appts. incl: Publr., Scrap Age (int. ind. publn.), 1942-; Publr., Waste Age (mag. serving solid waste ind. internationally), 1969-; Publr., Mill Trade Jrnl. (weekly newspaper devoted to recycling & paper stock ind.), 1963-. Mbrships: Exec. Dir., City of Springfield Area Dev. & Tourism Commn., 1963-68; Pres., Emde Realty Corp., 1957-63; Pres., Execs. Inc., 1963-67; Exec. Sec., Midwest Scrap Dealers Assn., 1941; Am. Soc. of Assn. Execs.; Nat. Press Club, Wash. DC, Pres., 1946-47; Pres., Jr. Chmbr. of Comm., 1946-47; Springfield Assn. of Comm. & Ind.; Treas., N. Shore Investment Club, 1968 & N. Suburban Synagogue Beth El, 1970-71. Hons: Meritorious Award for outstanding contbns. to Iron & Steel Ind., St. Louis Steel Assn., 1961. Address: 3 Sons Publng. Co., 6311 Gross Pt. Rd., Niles, IL 60648, U.S.A. 40, 55.

OBERMAYER, Herman J., b. 19 Sept. 1924. Newspaper Publisher. Educ: A.B., Dartmouth Coll., 1948; Univ. of Geneva, Switzerland. Appts: Reporter, L.I. Daily Press, Jamaica, N.Y., 1950-53; Classified Advt. Mgr., New Orleans Item, 1953-55; Promotion Mgr. & Asst. to Publr., New Bedford Standard-Times, 1955-57; Ed. & Publr., Long Br. Daily Record, N.J., 1957-71; Ed. & Publr., Northern Va. Sun, 1963-. Mbrships. incl: Exec. Comm., Nat. Capital Coun., Boy Scouts of Am.; Nat. Press Club, Wash. D.C.; Advt. Club of Wash.; Am. Newspapers Publrs. Assn.; Labor Rels. Comm. & Edit. Comm., Southern Newspapers Publrs. Assn.; Am. Soc. Newspaper Eds.; Arlington Co. U.S. Bicentennial Commn.; Sigma Chi; Rotarian; Ocean Beach Club, Elberon, N.J.; Trustee, Arlington Chapt., Am. Red Cross. Contbr. of articles to var. newspapers & jrnls. Address: 1227 N. Ivy St., Arlington, VA 22210, U.S.A. 6, 16, 128, 131.

OBERMAYER, Klaus, b. 5 May 1916. Professor of Constitutional, Administrative & Ecclesiastical Law. Educ: Univ. of Munich, 1946-48; Clerk at Ct. & Admin. Agcys., 1948-50; Grad. Dr. of Law, 1956; Habilitation, 1958. Appts: Serv. w. Coun. Luth. Regional Ch. of Bavaria, 1951; Civil Serv., Bavarian Min. of Interior, 1952; Chief Councillor to Govt. or Upper-Bavaria, 1952-60; Prof., Law Schl., Univ. of Erlangen-Nürnberg, 1960-, Dir., Inst. Ch. & Pub. Law of Univ., 1961-, Prochancellor of Univ., 1961-63, Dean of Law Schl., 1964-66, 1971-72, Mbr., Acad. For. Off. of Univ., 1965-, Chief of Off., 1968-70, 1972-. Contbr., legal publs. & profl. jrnls. Address: Institut für Kirchenrecht und Öffentliches Recht, D-8520 Erlangen, Hindenburgstr. 34, German Fed. Repub.

O'BRIEN, Cyril Cornelius, b. 22 Mar. 1906. Research Scientist; Psychologist; Educator; Musicologist. Educ: B.A., St. Mary's Univ., N.S., Canada, 1926; L.Mus., McGill Univ., Montreal, 1931; M.A., Mt. Allison Univ., N.B., 1932; B.Paëd., Univ. of Toronto, Ont., 1934; B.Mus., Laval Univ., Quebec City, 1937; D.Paed., 1937, D.Mus., 1950, Univ. of Montreal, P.Q.; Ph.D., Univ of Ottawa. Appts. incl: Tchr. & Prin., schls. in N.S., 1927-47; Asst., Assoc. & Prof., Educ., Marquette Univ., Milwaukee, U.S.A., 1947-63; Lectr., Univ. of Alta., Edmonton, Canada, 1968-; Pres., Adan Rsch. Co. Ltd., ibid, 1969-; Organist & Choremaster, chs. in N.S. & Toronto, 1929-47, 1933-34; Var. cons. positions, educ. & psychol. Fellowships: Am. Psychol. Soc.; Royal Statl. Soc., London, U.K.; AAAS; Life, Int. Inst. of Arts & Letters. Corres. Accademician, Accademia Tiberina, Rome, Italy, 1973. Publs. incl: 130 articles in sci. & profl. jrnls.; Contemporary Studies in Industrial Psychology, 1969. Hons. incl: Kt. Cmdr. of Magistral Grace of St. Bridget of Sweden, 1968. Address: P.O. Box 666, Edmonton, Alta., T5J 2K8, Canada. 2, 8, 9, 14, 15, 22, 49, 51, 112, 129, 130, 139.

O'BRIEN, Katharine Elizabeth. Educator. Educ: A.B., Bates Coll.; A.M., Cornell Univ.; Ph.D. Brown Univ. Appts: Chmn., Maths. Dept., Coll. of New Rochelle, N.Y., 11 yrs.; Hd. of Maths. Dept., Deering H.S., 31 yrs.; Lectr. in Maths., Brown Univ., 5 summer sessions; Lectr. in Maths., Portland Campus, Univ. of Me., for 12 yrs. Mbrships: Phi Beta Kappa; Sigma Xi; N.Y. Acad. of Scis; Math. Assn. of Am.; Poetry Soc. of Am.; Bates Key; Soc. of Bowdoin Women; Portland Coll. Club. Publs: Sequences, 1966; Excavation & other verse, 1967. Contbr. to var. profl. jnls. inclng: Bulletin of Am. Math. Soc.; Am. Math. Monthly; Maths. Mag.; Maths. Tchr. Verse contbns. to jrnls. inclng: Saturday Review; Christian Sci. Monitor; N.Y. Herald Tribune; Ladies Home Jrnl. Hons: Sc.D.Ed., Univ. of Maine, 1960; L.H.D., Bowdoin Coll., 1965. Address: 130, Hartley St., Portland, ME 04103, U.S.A. 5, 11, 14, 57.

O'BRIEN, Michael Joseph. Advertising Executive. Appts: Radio Actor, Writer, Dir. & Prod., Ireland; Post in Price Gourlay, Vancouver, B.C., Canada, 1938; V.P., Gourlay Advertising, ibid, 1940; Pres., O'Brien Gourlay (later O'Brien Advertising Ltd.), 1942-; O'Brien Consultants Ltd. & other Co's; Pub. Rels. Cons. & Advsr. to num. large corps. & orgs. Mbrships: Bd. of Govs., Vancouver Gen. Hosp.; Past Chmn., Special Names Div., Community Chest; Past Dir., Children's Hosp., Vancouver; Past Dir., Borstal Inst., Past V.P., Vancouver Better Bus. Bur.; Dir., Vancouver Opera Assn.; Exec., Pacific Region, Canadian Coun. of Christians & Jews; Canadian Bd. of Trade Club; Vancouver Club. Address: 825-1445 Marpole Ave., Vancouver 9, B.C., Canada.

O'BRIEN, Richard Desmond, b. 29 May 1929. Professor. Educ: B.Sc., Univ. of Reading, U.K., 1950; Ph.D., 1954, B.A., 1956, Univ. of W. Ont., Canada. Appts: Soil Specialist, Ont. Agric. Coll., Guelph, 1950-51; Chem., Pesticide Rsch. Inst., London, Canada, 1954-60; Postdoct. Fellow, Nat. Rsch. Coun. (Canada), Inst. of Animal Physiol., Babraham, Cambridge, U.K., 1956-57; Vis. Assoc. Prof., Entomol., Univ. of Wis., U.S.A., 1958-59; Assoc. Prof., 1960-64, Prof., 1964-65, Insecticide Chem., Cornell Univ.; Chmn., Deot. of Biochem., 1964-65, Sect. of Neurobio. & Behavior, 1965-70, Dir., Div. of Biol. Scis., 1970-, ibid; Guggenheim Fellow, Naples, Italy, 1967-68. Mbrships. incl: Am. Chem. Soc.; Biochem. Soc., U.K.; Entomol. Soc. of Am.; Fellow, AAAS; Sigma Xi; Am. Soc. Neurochem.; Soc. for Neuroscis.; Fndr. & Ed., Jrnl. of Pesticide Biochemistry & Physiology. Publs: Toxic Phosphorus Esters, 1960; Radiation, Radioactivity & Insects, 1964; Insecticides—Action & Metabolism, 1967; Co-ed., Biochemical Toxicology of Insecticides, 1970; Co-author, life on Earth, 1973; author or co-author of num. articles in profl. jrnls. Recip., Int. Award for Rsch. in Pesticide Chem., Am. Chem. Soc., 1970. Address: Stimson Hall, Cornell Univ., Ithaca, NY 14850, U.S.A. 128.

O'BRIEN, Warren Sylvester, b. 24 Mar. 1898. Photographer. Educ: Univ. of Wis., Milwaukee; pvte. instruction in Latin, Art, Aviation, Astronomy. Appts: Sole owner & Mgr., photographic studios, 62 yrs. Mbrships. incl: Profl. Photographers of Am.; Soc. of Motion Picture Engrs.; Wis. Histl. Soc.; Milwaukee Astronomical Soc.; Bd. Mbr., ibid, 1953-59; Milwaukee Advt. Club; Am. Legion. Publs. incl: Photography, 1961; Adventures Along the Cumberland, 1964; Aviation in Waukesha County, 1969. Contbr., Landmark, quarterly mag. Recip., var. profl., aviation, soc. servs. awards. Address: 315 Oakland Ave., Waukesha, WI 53186, U.S.A.

O'CAIN, James Howard, b. 10 Aug. 1921. Educator; Employee Relations Negotiator. Educ: B.A., Univ. of Ark., Little Rock; M.S.E., Ouachita Bapt. Univ., Arkadelphia, Ark. Appts: Tchr., Am. Hist., Ctrl. H.S., Little Rock, Ark., 1962-71; Exec. Dir., Prince William Educ. Assn., Manassas, Va. Mbrships: Advsry. Coun., Dept. Classroom Tchrs., NEA; Assn. Classroom Tchrs., Ark. Educ. Assn. (bd. dirs.; pres.); Va. Educ. Assn.; Nat. Coun. Soc. Studies; Am. Histl. Soc.; Mason; life mbr., Ark. Congress of Parents & Tchrs. Author, "College Opportunities for Students", in The Golden Key, jrnl. of Phi Theta Kappa, 1962. Address: 10131 Brandon Way, Manassas, VA 22110, U.S.A. 125, 130.

OCEPEK, Drago, b. 1 Jan. 1927. University Professor; Mining Engineer. Educ: Mining Engr. Degree, Fac. of Mining & Metallurgy, 1953; Dr. of Tech. Sci., 1960. Appts. incl: Asst., Fac. of Mining & Metallurgy, 1954; Dozent, Fac. of Natural Sci. & Technol., 1960; Prof., ibid, 1970; Dean, ibid, 1969-72; Pres., Fed. Comm. for For. Cultural Activities, 1973; currently Mbr., ibid. Mbrships: Engrng. Assn. of Yugoslavia; AAAS. Author of num. publs. in profl. field. Hons: Prize, Sklad Borisa Kidriča for tech. & sci. publs. in mech. processes, 1973. Address: 61000 Ljubljana, Prijateljeva 11/a, Yugoslavia.

OCHS, Verna Love (Mrs. Alfred Louis Ochs), b. 25 June 1910. Business Executive. Educ: Univ. of Minn., 1933; Mpls. Bus. Schl., 1936; Patricia Stevens Schl. of Fashion Merchandising, 1969-70. Appts: V.P., Ochs Dept. Store, Faribault, 1944-; V.P., Sec., Ochs

Bldg. Corp., 1944-; Pres., ibid, 1969-72. Mbrships. incl: Exec. Sec., Minn. Coun. Cath. Women, 1933-45; Archdiocesan Coun. Cath. Women, 1933-50; V.P., Faribault Community Concerts, 1952-72; Pres., Minn. Hosp. Aux., 1970-72; Vol. Blood Bank A.R.C., 1944-70; Mpls. Chapt. House, 1940-44; Mpls. League Cath. Women; Daughters of Isabella; Dir., United Fund, Faribault, 1964; Univ. of Minn. Alumni Club. Recip., Scroll award, Faribault Chmbr. of Comm., 1972. Address: 406 7th St., N.W., Faribault, MN 55021, U.S.A. 5.

OCHSENSCHLAGER, Edward L., b. 5 Apr. 1932. Educator; Archaeologist. Educ: B.S., Columbia Univ., 1954; M.A., N.Y. Univ., 1961. Appts: Dir., Classical Excavations, Thmuis, Egypt, 1965-; Am. Field Dir., Jt. Yugoslav-Am. Excavations, Roman Sirmium, Yugoslavia, 1969-; Asst. Field Dir., al-Hiba Excavations, Iraq, 1968-; Asst. Prof., Classics, Brooklyn Coll., CUNY, 1968-70, Assoc. Prof., 1971-, Chmn., Dept. of Classics, 1973-; Dir., Archaeol. Rsch. Inst., ibid, 1973-; Mbr., Columbia Univ. Seminar on Archaeol. of Eastern Mediterranean, 1973-. Mbrships: Exec. Comm., N.Y. Soc., Archaeol. Inst. of Am.; Am. Rsch. Ctr. in Egypt; Am. Schls. of Oriental Studies; Am. Soc. of Orientalists; Societas Archaelogica Yugoslaviae; Explorers Club. Publs: Co-Ed., Sirmium, Archaeological Investigations in Syrmian Pannonia; Contbr. to var. profl. jrnls. Recip., var. rsch. grants. Address: Dept. of Classics, Brooklyn Coll., Brooklyn, NY 11210, U.S.A. 6.

OCHSNER, Bjørn, b. 4 Apr. 1910. Librarian. Educ: Studied philos., Berlin, 1931-33; M.A., Copenhagen Univ., Denmark, 1939. Appts: State Mus. of Art, 1941-44; Hd. of Dept. of Maps, Prints & Photographs, Royal Lib., Copenhagen, 1944-; Co-examiner, Danish Schl. of Libnship.; Co-examiner in Philos., Univs. of Copenhagen, Arhus & Odense, Denmark; Sec. at Univ. Ext., Copenhagen, 1944-46. Mbrships: Comm., Soc. of Danish Cultural Hist., 1957-73; Co-fdr., 1950, & Exec. Mbr., Nat. Comm. for Collection of Old Photographs; Assn. of Libns. at Schol. & Scientific Libs., 1954-60, (Chmn. 1955-60); Chmn., Booktrade Soc.'s. Comm. to select Books of Yr., 1954-73; Chmn., ibid, 1969-73. Publs: Photographers in & from Denmark until the year 1900, 1956, 2nd. ed., 1969; Photographs of Hans Andersen, 1957; Early Photographs of Architecture & Views in two Copenhagen Libraries, (co-author), 1957 (in English); Photography in 100 Years from a Danish point of View, 1962; Contbr. to num. encys., manuals & jrnls. Address: The Royal Lib., Christians Brygge 8, DK-1219 Copenhagen K., Denmark. 43.

O'CONNELL, Daniel Patrick, b. 7 July 1924. Barrister-at-Law. Educ: Sacred Heart Coll., Auckland, N.Z.; Univ. of Auckland; B.A., Trinity Coll., Cambridge, U.K.; LL.M., N.Z.; Ph.D., LL.D., Cantab. Appts: Rdr. in Law, Univ. of Adelaide, 1953-62; Prof., Int. Law, ibid, 1962-72; Chilele Prof. of Int. Law, Oxford Univ., U.K., 1972-. Mbrships. incl: Assoc. de l'Inst. de Droit Int.; Rapporteur, State Succession Comm., Int. Law Assn., 1961-; Chmn., Australian Deep Sea Mining Comm., etc. Publs: The Law of State Succession, 1956; International Law, 1965, '71; State Succession in Municipal Law and International Law, 1967; Richelieu, 1968. Kt. of Grace & Devotion, Order of Malta, 1957. Address: All Souls Coll., Oxford, U.K.

O'CONNELL, James J., b. 7 Feb. 1933. Realtor. Educ: B.S., Bus. Admin. & Economics, Lewis Coll., Lockport, Ill., 1958; advanced

studies, Purdue & DePaul Univs.; Licensed Real Estate & Ins. Broker. Appts: Ptnr., Strand Realty Co., Joliet, Ill., 1958-59; Owner & Pres., ibid, 1959-; Dir. 1964, V.P. 1966, Southwest Suburban Bd. of Realtors; Chmn. Transportation, Des Plaines Valley Improvement Assn., 1965-; On Joliet Will Co. Bd. of Realtors as 2nd V.P. 1970, Sec.-Treas, 1971, Pres. 1972; Commnr., Joliet Land Clearance Commn.; Commnr. to Joliet Port Authority, Will Co. Bd., 1973-79. Mbrships: Jr. Chmbr. of Comm. (Holder num. Offs. inclng. Nat. Pres., Jr. Chmbr. Int. Senate); Joliet Flying Club (past-Sec.); Keep Joliet Beautiful; Joliet Exchange Club; active wkr., good causes. Carried out comprehensive indl. survey of Lemont, Ill., 1963. Hons: Disting. Serv. Award, Jr. Chmbr. Int. Senate, State of Ill., 1974. Address: 69 W. Jefferson St., Joliet, IL, U.S.A.

O'CONNELL, Philip R., b. 2 June 1928. Lawyer; Corporate Executive. Educ: B.A., Manhattan Coll., 1949; Ll.B., Columbia Law Schl., 1956; Adv. Mgmt. Prog., Harvard Bus. Schl., 1967. Appts: w. Dewey, Ballantine, Bushby, Palmer & Wood, law firm, N.Y., 1956-64; Gen. Counsel & Div. Mgmt., Wallace-Murray Corp., 1964-70; Pres., Universal Papertech Corp., 1970-71; Sec., Champion Int. Corp., 1972-. Mbrships: U.S. Supreme Court Bar; N.Y. Bar; Am. Bar Assn.; Assn. of Bar of City of N.Y. Address: 777 3rd. Ave., N.Y., NY 10017, U.S.A. 2, 6, 16.

O'CONNOR, Frank Roderic Gerald Vincent, b. 18 Jan. 1925. Assistant Director, Irish Government Information Services. Educ: Irish Mil. Coll., Curragh, Kildare, Ireland; Post Grad. Studies, Trinity Coll., Dublin Univ. Appts. incl: Joined Army, 1943; Commnd. Infantry Corps, 1944; A.D.C. to G.O.C., Eastern Cmd.; 1949-52; Cmd. Libn., ibid, 1948-52; Capt., 1954; Chief of Staffs, Br. Army HQ, 1957; Resigned Regular Commn., 1960; Marketing Advsr., Coras Tractala/Irish Export Bd.; Info. Off., Irish Export Bd., London, 1961-64 & N.Y., U.S.A., 1964-68; Asst. Dir., Govt. Info. Servs., Dublin, Ireland, 1969-; Gov., Sutton Pk. Schl., Co. Dublin, 1969-71. Mbrships. incl: Pres., Irish-Iranian Soc., 1969-; Trinity Coll., Dublin Assn.; Life Mbr., The Irish Assn.; Inst. of Pub. Admin.; Inst. of Profl. Civil Servants & Chmn., Info. Offs. Br.; Life Mbr., Mil. Hist. Soc., Ireland. Publs. incl: A Survey of The Middle East, 1968; Press Relations in the Public Service, 1973. Hons. incl: Emergency Serv. Medal with Bar, 1945; Order of Cyrus the Gt. Address: Govt. Inf. Servs., Govt. Bldgs., Dublin 2, Repub. of Ireland.

O'CONNOR, James Ignatius, (S.J.), b. 30 July 1910. Clergyman; Educator. Educ: Xavier Univ., 1930-35; W. Baden Coll., 1935-38, '40-'44; Cath. Univ. of Am., 1945-46; Gregorian Univ., Rome, Italy, 1946-48; Litt.B., 1934; M.A., 1935; Ph.L., 1938; S.T.L., 1944, J.C.B., 1946; J.C.L., 1948; J.C.D., 1950. Appts: Entered Soc. of Jesus, 1930; Ordained, 1943; Prof., Canon Law, W. Baden Coll., Ind., U.S.A., 1948-64; Prof., Canon Law, Bellarmine Schl. of Theol., Chgo., Ill., 1964-; Canonical Cons., Cath. Hosp. Assn. of U.S.A., 1953 Mbrships: Canon Law Soc. of Am.; Canadian Canon Law Soc. Publs. incl: Introduction to the Divine Office; Dispensation From Irregularities to Holy Orders; Canon Law Digest, Vols., 4, 5, 6, (co-author); Canon Law Digest for Religious, Vol. 1 & annual suppls. (co-author). Contbr. to ency. & jrnls. Address: 2345 W. 56th St., Chicago, IL 60636, U.S.A. 8, 13, 15, 30, 49, 120, 128, 131.

O'CONNOR, Louise Leslie (Worley), Librarian. Educ: B.A., Coe Coll., Cedar Rapids,

Iowa; M.A., State Univ. of Iowa, Iowa City, 1937; M.A., Univ. of Denver, Colo., 1962. Appts: Tchr., H.S., E. Peoria, Ill., 1938-39; Tchr., Latin & Engl., York H.S., Elmhurst, Ill., 1939-43; Field Cons., Iowa State Lib., Des Moines, 1962-64; Dist. Libn., Rim-of-the-World Schl. Dist., Lake Arrowhead, Calif., 1964-67; Lib. Chmn., Naperville Central H.S., Ill., 1967-72. Mbrships: NEA; AAUW; Eta Sigma Phi. Author of hymn, A Missionary Prayer (music adapted from Brahms, arrangement by Leslie Oren Worley). Recip., 2000 Schlrship., Iowa State Lib., to Univ. of Denver, Colo., 1961-62. Address: Cedar Circle 2806, 3000-J St. S.W., Cedar Rapids, IA 52404, U.S.A. 5, 138.

O'CONNOR, Mary Catherine, Librarian. Educ: B.A., Queen's Univ., Kingston, Ont., Canada; B.L.S., Univ. of Toronto Lib. Schl. Appts: Ref. Libn., Douglas Lib., Queen's Univ., Kingston, 1940-43; Rsch. Libn., Nylon Div., Canadian Inds. Ltd., 1943-47; Cataloguer, Univ. of Sask. Lib., 1948; currently, Chief Libn., Ft. Frontenac Lib., Nat. Defence Coll. & Canadian Land Forces Cmd. & Staff Coll. Mbrships: Mil. Lib. Div., Special Libs. Assn.; Canadian Lib. Assn.; Trustee Div., Ont. Lib. Assn.; Info. Scis. Assn. of Canada. Author, article on Nat. Defence Coll., Canadian Defence Quarterly, 1971. Address: Ft. Frontenac Lib., Kingston, Ont., K7K 1X8 Canada.

O'CONNOR, (Robert) Patrick, b. 26 Aug. 1925. Editor-in-Chief. Educ: Univ. of Pitts. 1943; Cath Univ. of Am., 1946-50. Appts: Dir., Co-fndr., Rochester Arena Theater, N.Y., 1950-52; Sec., M.C.A. Talent Agcy., N.Y.C., 1953-54; Salesman, Official Films, 1954; Pres., O'Connor Prods., TV Films, N.Y.C., 1954-55; Sec., Ivan Oblensky, book publr., 1960; Sr. Ed., Popular Lib. Publrs., 1963-66; Ed.-in-Chief, Silver Screen Mag., 1965-67; Sr. Ed., New Am. Lib., 1967-71; Ed.-in-Chief, Curtis Books, 1971-73; Ed.-in-Chief, Popular Lib. Publrs., 1973-. Mbrships: Treas., Nat. Tap Dance Fndn. Publs: The Prayers of Man (Ed.), 1962. Address: 74 W. 38th St., N.Y., NY 10018, U.S.A.

O'CONNOR, Tommie Louise (Mrs. Robert R. O'Connor), b. 23 Aug. 1930. Speech Pathologist; Special Education Supervisor. Educ: B.S., Univ. of Southern Miss., Hattiesburg, U.S.A., 1951; M.S., ibid, 1958. Appts. incl: Tchr., Pre-schl. Handicapped Speech Class, Meridian, Miss., 1953-67; Special Educ. Supvsr., Meridian Pub. Schls., 1967-70; Speech Pathologist, Separate Schls., W. Pt., Miss., 1970-72; Pres., & Prog. Dir., Clay Co. Assn. for Retarded Children, Inc., W. Pt., 1972-. Mbrships. incl: Chmn., Special Educ. Div., Miss. Educ. Assn.; Exec. Comm., Miss. Title III State Advsry. Coun.; State Conven. Chmn., Miss. Assn. for Retarded Children; State Legislative Comm., Am. Speech & Hearing Assn.; Pres., Miss. Speech & Hearing Assn.; Past State Sec./Treas., Coun. for Exceptional Children; Chapt. Pres., Pilot Club Int.; Sec./Treas., Delta Kappa Gamma. Publs: Contbns. to jrnls. Recip., sev. awards & certs. of appreciation. Address: 909 E. Main, West Point, MS 39773, U.S.A. 76, 125.

OCVIRK, Otto G., b. 13 Nov. 1922. Professor of Art; Artist; Author. Educ: Dipl., Cass Tech. H.S., Detroit, Mich.; B.F.A., State Univ. of Iowa; M.F.A., ibid. Appts: Instr. of Art, Bowling Green State Univ., 1950; Asst. Prof. of Art, ibid, 1955; Assoc. Prof. of Art, 1960; Prof. of Art, 1965. Mbrships: Coll. Art Assn. of Am.; Mid-Am. Art Assn.; Dir. of the 1971 Annual Conf., ibid; Delta Phi Delta. Publs: Art Fundamentals, Theory & Practice,

co-author, 1st ed., 1960, 2nd ed., 1968. Hons: over 24 awards for prints, paintings & sculpture included in Art Exhibs. & Museums throughout the U.S.A., 1948-58; Broadcast Media Award, WBGU-TV, Color II - Course Dir., 19th Annual Broadcast Ind. Conf., 1969, San Francisco, Calif; Included in 1970 Ed. of Outstanding Educators of Am., 1970. Address: 231 Haskins St., Bowling Green, OH 43402, U.S.A.

ODAKA, Kunio, b. 17 Oct. 1908. Professor of Economics. Educ: B.A., Univ. of Tokyo, 1932; D.Litt., ibid, 1947. Appts: Assoc. Prof.-Prof. of Sociol., Univ. of Tokyo, 1945-69, Chmn., Dept. of Sociol., 1956-69, Chmn., Grad. Schl. of Sociol., 1963-65, 1967-68, Prof. Emeritus, 1969-; Rsch. Fellow in Soc. Rels., Harvard Univ., U.S.A., 1953-54, Rsch. Fellow in E. Asian Studies, 1970-72; Vis. Schlr. & Rsch. Assoc. in Indl. Rels., Univ. of Calif. at Berkeley, 1958-59. Mbr. & Off., profl. orgs. Publs. incl: Occupational Sociology, 1941; Sociology: Its Nature & Themes, 1949; Sociology Today, 1958; Industrial Sociology, 1963; Work Ethics, 1970; Toward Industrial Democracy: Management & the Workers in Modern Japan, 1974. Hons. incl: Nikkei Keizai Tosho Bunka Literary Prizes, 1959, '66. Address: 2-2-5 Honkomagome, Bunkyo-ku, Tokyo 113, Japan.

ODDO, Paul Charles, b. 9 Feb. 1915. Book Publisher. Educ: B.B.A., St. John's Univ., 1936; M.A., Bus. Mgmt., Columbia Univ., 1937; Hamilton Inst. of Advanced Bus. Mgmt. Appts: H.S. Tchr., Accting. & Bus. Mgmt.; Pvte. Acct.; V.P., Educl. Cons., Grolier Soc.; Free-lance publrs.' cons.; Pres., Oddo Publshng, Inc., Fayetteville, Ga. Mbrships: Rotary Int.; ALA; Am. Booksellers Assn.; Int. Reading Assn.; Iota Alpha Sigma. Hons: Hidalgo de Calificado Nobleza al Servicio del Estado de Nuevo Mexico, 1968. Address: Storybook Acres, P.O. Box 68, Fayetteville, GA 30214, U.S.A. 125.

ODEKU, E(manuel) Latunde, b. 29 June 1927. Neurological Surgeon. Educ: B.S., Coll. of Liberal Arts, Howard Univ., Wash. D.C., U.S.A., 1950; M.D., Coll. of Med., ibid, 1954; Postgrad., Univ. of Mich., Ann Arbor, 1954-60. Appts. incl: Instr., Neuroanatomy & Neurosurg., Coll. of Med., Howard Univ., 1961-62; Prof., Surg. (Neurosurg.), Fac. of Med., Univ. of Ibadan, Nigeria, 1965-; Dean, ibid, 1968-70; Cons. Neurosurg., Univ. Coll. Hosp., Ibadan, 1962-. Mbrships. incl: Fellow, Am. Coll. of Surgs.; Sec., Surg. Bd., & Fellow, Med. Coll. in Surg., Nigeria; Treas., Nigerian Chapt., & Fellow, Int. Coll. of Surgs.; Fellow, W. African Coll. of Surgs.; Am. Assn. of Neurological Surgs. (Harvey Cushing Soc.); Past Pres., Nigerian Soc. of Neurological Surgs.; Pan-African Assn. of Neurological Scis.; N.Y. Acad. of Scis.; Kappa Pi. Publs: Twilight—Out of the Night (poems), 1964; Whispers from the Night (poems), 1969; Over 90 articles in profl. jrnls. & contbns. to books. Hons. incl: Disting. Alumni Award, Howard Univ., 1973. Address: Neurosurgery Unit, Surgery Dept., Faculty of Medicine, University of Ibadan, Ibadan, Nigeria. 17, 46.

ODELBERG, C.V. Wilhelm, b. 1 July 1918. Chief Librarian. Educ: Grad., Uppsala Univ., Sweden, 1944; Ph.D., Stockholm Univ., 1954. Appts: Royal Lib., Stockholm, 1947-56; Ctrl. Office, Nat. Antiquities, 1957-59; Keeper, Libs., Archives & Mus. Collections, Royal Swedish Acad. of Scis., 1959-. Mbrships: Chmn., Swedish Assn. of Special Libs., 1961-; Royal Manuscripts Soc., 1960; Royal Navy Soc., 1963; Bd., Royal Patriotic Soc., 1963; Soc. for Naval Rsch., 1959; Assn. for Biographical Studies, 1962; Linnaean Soc. of

Sweden, 1969; Assn. for Humanist Studies, 1970; Genealogical Soc., 1971. Publs. (in Swedish) incl: Life & Times of Vice-Admiral Carl Olof Cronstedt, 1954; The History of Sicily, 1957; The Surrender of Sveaborg, 1958; Sev. papers on hist., hist of scis., & bibliography; Ed., Les Prix Nobel, 1968. Hons: Order of Dannebrog, Denmark, 1952; Kt., Order of the N. Star, 1963; Cmdr., Order of the Lion of Finland, 1969. Address: Royal Swedish Academy of Sciences, 104 05 Stockholm 50, Sweden.

ODER, Charles Rollin Lorain, b. 1 May 1897; d. 18 Feb. 1972. Geologist. Educ: A.B., Univ. of Va., 1928; M.A., ibid, 1929; Ph.D., Univ. of Ill., 1933. Appts. incl: Field Geologist, Va. Geological Survey, 1927-28 & Tenn. Survey, 1929-34; H.Q. Mascot & Tenn. Geologist, Lead & Smelting Co., St. Louis, Mo., 1934-39, Chief Geologist, 1939-63, Cons., 1963-70. Discovered & identified fossils some of which are on display in Smithsonian Inst., Wash., D.C. Mbrships. incl: U.S.N., 1917-1919; Mbr. & Past Pres., Jefferson City Civitans; Past Pres., Community-Coll. Coun. Carson-Newman Coll.; Philatelic Soc. of Am.; Geological Soc. of Am.; Soc. Econ. Geologist; Am. Inst. of Mining Engrs. & Petroleum Geologists; Tenn. Acad. of Sci. Author of many publs. in mags., bulletins & newspapers. Hons. incl: Thomas Jefferson Literary Soc., Univ. of Va., 1927-29; Sigma Xi, 1929; Phi Beta Kappa, 1928. Address of widow: Dandridge Hwy., Jefferson City, TN 37760, U.S.A. 14, 125.

ODERMATT, Oscar, b. 16 Apr. 1914. Lawyer; Notary. Educ: Law Fac., Univ. of Berne, Switzerland; Dip., lawyer, clerk, notary, 1938. Appts: Former Sec., Justice Dept., Canton Soleure; Vicarious judge of Youngsters; Chief, Serv. of Right Depts. justice, police & mil., Canton Soleure; Legal Counsel, Swiss Soc. rule of law. Mbrships: Automobil-Club; Swiss Juridical Soc.; Swiss Soc. of Criminol.; Chaine des Rotisseurs. Publs: Jugendstrafrecht in der Schweiz; Zerfall unseres Rechts; Rechtsliches Gehör im Verwaltungsverfahren; Ständerat; Neues Adoptionsrecht. Recip., hon. as excellent quartermaster-sergeant in mil. serv. Address: Ambassadorenhof, CH-4500 Soleure, Switzerland. 43, 103.

ODNOPOSOFF, Adolfo, b. 22 Feb. 1917. Educator; Concert Artist. Educ: Licence E'Enseignement & Licence de Concert, Ecole Normale de Musique, Paris, France. Appts: Fndr. Mbr., Israel Philharmonic Orch., 1936-38 & Nat. Conservatory of Music, Lima, Peru, 1938-40; Prof., Nat. Conservatory of Music, Lima, 1938-40; Fndr., "CuartetoChile" of Univ. of Chile, 1941-44; 1st Cellist, Havana Philharmonic Orch., 1944-58; 1st Cellist Nat. Symph. Orch., Mexico City, 1958-61; Prof., Nat. Conservatory of Music, ibid, 1958-63- Judge for Pablo Casals Int. Competitions, 1964-; Prof. of Cello & Chamber Music, Conservatory of Music, Puerto Rico. Mbr. of Violoncello Soc., N.Y. Named "Best Performer", Music Critics Assn. in Mexico City, 1959. Address: Conservatory of Music of Puerto Rico, Hato Rey, PR 00918, U.S.A. 4.

ODNOPOSOFF, Ricardo, b. 24 Feb. 1914. Concert Violinist. Educ: Studied w. Aaron Klasse, Argentina; Hochschule für Music, under Carl Flesch, Berlin, Germany, 1928-32. m. Irmtraut Baum, 1965; 1 d. Appts. incl: Num. concerts all over the world; University Professor, Masterclass, Hochschule fur Musik, Vienna, Austria, 1956-; Professor, Masterclass, Hochschüle für Musik, Stuttgart, Germany, 1964. Mbrships. incl: Wiener Phulharmoniker; Conservatoire de Bruxelles. Hons. incl: Pour le Merite, Argentina; Medaille Mon Hwa Po Chang (Arts et Lettres), S. Korea; Chevalier de l'Ordre des Arts et Lettres, France; Officier de l'Ordre des Arts et Lettres, Austria; Grosses Verdienstkreuz des Verdienstordens der Duetschen Bundesrepublik; Several prizes. Address: Singerstr. 27, A 1010 Vienna, Austria. 1, 21.

O'DOHERTY, Eamonn Feichin, b. 10 Feb. 1918. Catholic Priest; Professor. Educ: M.A., Nat. Univ. of Ireland, 1939; B.D., Lateran Univ., Rome, 1941; Ph.D., Cambridge Univ., 1945, Appts: Lectr. in Logic & Psychol., Univ. Coll., Dublin, 1945; Prof., ibid, 1949; Vis. Prof., The Seton Psych. Inst., Balt., Md., U.S.A., 1962-68; Vis. Prof., Cath. Univ. of Am., 1962; Forwood Lectr., Univ. of Liverpool, 1965-66; Acting Registrar, Univ. Coll., Dublin, 1972-74. Mbrships. incl: Fellow, Brit. Psychol. Soc., Psychol. Soc. of Ireland; former V.P., Royal Irish Acad.; Ergonomics Rsch. Soc. Publs. incl: Consecration & Vows, 1971; Vocation, Formation Consecration & Vows, 1972; The Religious Formation of the Elementary School Child, 1973; The Religious Formation of the Adolescent, 1973. Address: Dept. of Psychol., Univ. Coll., Dublin 4, Repub. of Ireland. 1, 30.

ÖDÖN, Szakács, b. 20 Sept. 1912. Judge. Educ: Doct., Law & Pol. Sci., 1942. Appts: Judge, Dist. Ct., Mako, 1942, & Co. Ct., Szeged; Pres., Co. Ct., Debrecen, 1951-53 & Szeged, 1953-55; Ldr., Criminal Dept., Min. of Justice, 1955-56; Pres., Budapest Metrop. Ct., 1957-62; V.P., Supreme Ct. of Hungarian Peoples Repub., 1962-68; currently Pres., ibid. Address: c/o Supreme Ct. of the Hungarian Peoples Repub., Budapest, I. Fö-u 1, Hungary.

O'DONNELL, James Francis, b. 17 Nov. 1927. Public Relations/Public Affairs Executive. Educ: B.A., Fordham Univ., 1949; M.A., ibid, 1952. Appts. incl: Special Agt., U.S. Army Counter Intelligence Corps, 1953-55; Instr., Engl. & Speech, Univ. of Md. accredited U.S. Army Course. USAFI, Kobe, Japan, 1954-55; Confidential Asst., Dist. Atty of Queens Co., 1956-65; Special Asst., Pres. of the City Coun., N.Y.C., U.S.A., 1966-69; Special Asst., Comptroller Beame (now Mayor-elect), ibid, 1970; Dir., Corporate Communications & Mgr., Proj. Servs., L.I. Lighting Co., 1970-. Mbrships. incl: Bd. of Dirs., Queens Chmbr. of Comm.; Chmn., City Charter Comm. to report 1975 on revision of N.Y.C. Charter; Vice Chmn., Legislative Comm. of Chmbr.; Advsry. Comm. on Communications Arts, St. John's Univ.; Exec. Dir., United Democrats for Humphrey in N.Y. State 1968 campaign for Pres. of the U.S. Publs. incl: Catholic Mind, 1959; Reviewer of books for Sign Mag., Union City, N.J. Hons. incl: Schlrship., All Hallows Inst., 1941. Address: 147-23 Jasmine Ave., Flushing, NY 11355, U.S.A. 24.

O'DONNELL, Stanley Denis, b. 10 Nov. 1911. Secretary for Foreign Affairs, Rhodesia. Educ: Univ. of Sydney, Australia. Appts: Pub. Prosecutor, Juvenile Ct., Sydney, 1939; Dir. of Soc. Welfare, Rhodesia, 1961; Dpty. Sec., Min. of Labour & Soc. Welfare, ibid, 1964; Sec. for For. Affairs, 1967. Mbrships: Chief Commnr., Boy Scouts Assn. of Rhodesia, 1964; Dpty. Commnr. Gen., Rhodesian War Fund, 1962; Pres., Bulawayo Rotary Club, 1956-57, Salisbury Rotary Club, 1966-67; Salisbury Club; Salisbury Country Club. Hons: Independence Commemorative Decoration, 1970; Silver Wolf, Boy Scouts Assn., 1970. Address: Private Bag 185H, Salisbury, Rhodesia. 23.

ODOR, Dorothy Louise, b. 25 May 1922. Anatomist. Educ: B.A., Am. Univ., Wash. D.C. 1945; M.S., Univ. of Rochester, N.Y., 1948; Ph.D., ibid, 1950. Appts: Instr., Dept. of Anatomy, Univ. of Wash., 1950-56; Asst. Prof., Dept. of Anatomy, Univ. of Fla., 1956-60; Assoc. Prof., 1960-61; Asst. Prof., Bowman Gray Schl. of Med., 1961-65; Assoc. Prof., 1965-69; Assoc. Prof., Med. Coll. of Va., 1969-73; Prof., 1973-. Mbrships: Sigma Xi; Am. Assn. of Anatomists; Am. Soc. for Cell Bio.; Southern Soc. of Anatomists; AAAS; Soc. for Study of Reprod.; Reticuloendothelial Soc.; Am. Inst. of Biol. Scis.; N.Y. Acad. of Scis.; Va. Acad. of Scis. Pilot Int. Contbr. of 24 papers to profl. jrnls. Address: Dept. of Anatomy, Med. Coll. of Va., Va. Commonwealth Univ., 1200 E. Broad St., Richmond, VA 23219, U.S.A. 5, 14, 132.

O'DOWD, Michael Conway, b. 27 Feb. 1930. Manager. Educ: St. John's Coll., Johannesburg; B.A., Witwatersrand Univ., 1950; LL.B., ibid, 1953. Appts: Mgr. & Alternate Dir. of Anglo Am. Corp. of S.A. Ltd.; Dir. of num. other cos. inclng. Botswana RST Ltd., Bamangwato Concessions Ltds., Highveld Steel Co., Vanadium Corp. Ltd. & Pres., Brand Gold Mining Co. Ltd. Mbrships: Standing Comm. of Associated Ch. Schls. & of Bd. Govs. of St. John's Coll., St. Mary's Waverley, St. Martin's, Rosenttenville; Coun. of Educ., Witwatersrand & The 1820 Settlers Nat. Monument Fndn. Publs: The Achievements of Japan, 1970; Sir John Adamson-Better than they Knew, 1972; Through the Eye of a Needle, 1971; Second Henry Hare Dugmore Lecture, 1971. Address: Anglo-Am. Corp. of S.A. Ltd., P.O. Box 61587, Marshalltown, Transvaal, S. Africa.

O'DWYER, (Rev.) James F., b. 3 Dec. 1939. Catholic Priest; Marriage Counselor. Educ: Ordained, St. Patrick's Sem., Thurles Co., Tipperary, Ireland, 1965; M.A., M.Div., St. Patrick's Sem., Menlo Pk., Calif., U.S.A. Naturalized U.S. Citizen, 1970. Appts: Assoc. Pastor of Parishes, Stockton, Calif.; Diocesan Dir., Stockton Curia Legio Mariae, H.S. Vocations, Ecumenism, Religious of the Virgin Mary; Diocesan Chap., Handicapables. Mbrships: Life Mbr., Calif. State Marriage Counseling Assn.; Bd. of Dirs., Casa Mana Inn; Chap., Ct. Francesca Cabrini Cath. Daughters of Am.; Chap., Coun. Juan Crespi Kts. of Columbus; Chap., Young Men's Inst. Publs: St. Vincent Pallotti, 1963; Dreams of Destiny, 1970; To Live for Others, 1971; The Face of Love, 1971; Apollo, 1973. 1st Recip., Kiwanis Ministerial Award for outstanding servs. to Ch., faith, community & mankind, 1969. Address: 2445 Country Club Blvd., Stockton, CA 95204, U.S.A. 30, 57.

OEI TAT HWAY, b. 12 Apr. 1923. Patents & Trademarks Lawyer. Educ: Univ. of Leiden for 3 yrs.; Law Fac., Netherlands. Appts: w. Oei Tat Hway e.s., Patent & Trade Mark Attys., Jakarta, since graduation. Mbrships: Bd., All Indonesian Swimming Assn.; A.I.P. P.I. Address: 5, Kali Besar Barat, Jakarta-Kota. P.O. Box 2102 DKT, Jakarta, Indonesia.

OESCH, Wilhelm Martin Johann, b. 9 Nov. 1896. Pastor & Professor of Systematic Theology. Educ: Grad., Concordia Sem., St. Louis, Mo., 1922; Divinity Schl., Univ. of Chgo.; Heard lects. of Adolf Schlatter at Univ. of Tübingen, Germany, intermittently for sev. yrs. Appts. incl: Luth. Pastor, · Stuttgart, Germany, 1922-34, then London Pastor, U.K.; Lehrbeauftragter, Ev.-Luth. Freikirche, called to unite all Luth. Free Chs. of Germany, 1945; Tchr., systematic theol., Luth. Theol. Univ.,

Oberursel, 1947-68; Prof. Emeritus, ibid, 1968-; Ed.-in-Chief, "Lutherischer Rundblick", global theological quarterly, 1953-72; Assoc., ibid, 1972-; O'seas negotiator, U.S.A., 1959-62. Mbrships. incl: Advsry. mbr., synodical meetings, Selbständinge Evangelisch-Lutherische Kirche, German Fed. Repub.; Acting Pres., Humanistische Gesellschaft im Oberen Taunuskreis. Author of num. publs. in field. Hons: D.D., Concordia (now Luther) Sem., Adelaide, S. Australia; Solus Christus, Festschrift, 1971. Address: Dornbachstr. 13, 637 Oberursel, German Fed. Repub. 43, 92.

OFFENHARTZ, Edward, b. 1 Mar. 1928. Aerospace Executive. Educ: B.S.M.E., Polytech. Inst., Brooklyn, 1948; Postgrad., Univ. of Va., 1949-50; P.M.D., Harvard Univ., 1970. Appts: Aero Rsch. Scientist, NACA, Langley, Va., 1948-56; Rsch. Engr., Grp. Ldr., Proj. Engr., Sr. Proj. Engr., Proj. Mgr., Proj. Dir., Avco Corp., Wilmington, Lowell, Mass., 1956-67; Proj. Dir., Asst. Gen. Mgr. Ops., Perkin-Elmer Corp., 1967-70; Prog. Dir., Special Proj., ELMS Prog. Mgr., Grumman Aerospace Corp., 1970-. Author, num. papers presented at var. aerospace symposia & articles publd. in profl. jrnls. Address: 4 Glen Lane, Weston, CT 06880, U.S.A.

OFFERLE, Mildred, (Mrs. Martin A. Offerle), b. 3 Jan. 1912. Teacher. Educ: Duluth Tchrs. Coll., 1932; B.S., Mankato State Coll., 1966. Appts: Tchr., Rural Mapleton, 1932-33; Elem. Tchr., Barnum, Minn., 1933-38; Tchr., Madelia Elem. Schl., 1964-. Mbrships: League of Minn. Poets; Nat. Poetry League; Hon. Rep., Centro Studi E Scambi Internazionali; Minn. Rep., World Poetry Soc., Intercontinental. Publs: Crystal Wells, 1950; The Long Cry, 1960; Moods & Thoughts, 1970 (in poetry display of XXI Rassegna Internazionale D'arte Contemporanea, La Scala Gall. of art, Florence). Address: 105 3rd St. S.W., Madelia, MN 56062, U.S.A. 131.

OFIESH, Gabriel Darrow, b. 3 May 1919. University Professor. Educ: B.S., Univ. of Pitts., 1941; M.S., Columbia Univ., 1946; Ed.D., Denver Univ., 1959. Appts. incl: Assoc. Prof. of Psychol., Dir. of Cadet Counseling, USAF Acad., 1959-61; Prof. & Hd., Dept. of Psychol., ibid, 1961-62; Chief, Trng. Methods Div., Asst. Chief of Staff for Trng. Dev., HQ Air Trng. Command, Randolph AFB, Tex., 1962-64; Dir., Trng. Methods Directorate, ibid, 1964; Student, Ind. Coll. of Armed Forces, 1964-65; Chief, Evaluation Div., Air War Coll., Air Univ., 1965; Chief Cons., Educ. Technol., Office of Econ. Opportunity, 1965; Dir., Trng. Methods Study, Comprehensive Trng. Educ. Prog., Office of Asst. Sec. of Defense, 1965-66; Prof. of Educ., Dir. of Ctr. for Educ. Technol., Cath. Univ. of Am., 1966-71; Prof. of Continuing Educ., Adjunct Prof. of Educ., ibid, 1971-. Mbrships. incl: AAUP; Am. Psychol. Assn.; NEA; Am. Educ. Rsch. Assn.; Assn. for Supvsn. & Curric. Dev.; Edit. Bd., educ. Screen & Audiovisual Guide; Int. Soc. for Programmed Instruction. Contbng. Ed., Educational Technology mag.; Sr. Ed., series of audio cassette tapes for Educational Technology. Author of num. papers, books, articles, in field. Hons: Legion of Merit, USAF; DFC; Air Force Assn. Citation of Hon.; Jt. Servs. Commendation Medal. Address: 4031 27th Rd. N., Arlington VA 22207, U.S.A. 6, 7, 14.

OFOSU-APPIAH, L.H., b. 18 Mar. 1920. Director. Educ: B.A., Hertford Coll., Oxford, U.K., 1948; M.A., 1951; Dip., Anthropol., Jesus Coll., Cambridge, 1949; British Schl. Archaeol., Rome, 1951 & Athens, 1963. Appts. incl: Lectr., Classics, Univ. Coll., Gold Coast,

1949; Sr. Lectr., 1959; Assoc. Prof., 1962-64; Fulbright Schlr., 1964-66; Edgar B. Stearn Univ. Prof., Humanities, Dillard Univ., 1965-66; Dir., Ency. Africana Secretariat, Accra, Ghana, 1966-; Chmn., Ghana Lib. Bd., 1967-72. Fellow, Ghana Acad. Arts & Scis.; Hon. Sec., 1969-70. Mbrships incl: Chmn., Ghana Housing Corp., 1969-72; Classical Assn. G.B.; Classical Assn. Ghana. Publs. incl: Slavery: A Survey, 1969; People in Bondage, 1971; The Life of Lt. General E.K. Kotoka, 1972; Ed. & Author, Introduction to Journey to Independence & After, 3 vols., 1970, 71, 72; The Life & Times of Dr. J.B. Danquah, 1973. Address: Ency. Africana Secretariat, P.O. Box 2797, Accra, Ghana. 30, 135.

OGATA, Robert, b. 16 Feb. 1934. Art Teacher. Educ: B.A., Fresno State Univ.; Grad. studies, ibid, Appts: Art Tchr., Dept. of Defense Dependent Schls., Munich; Art Tchr., Fresno H.S.; Lectr., East Asian Studies Dept., Dominguez Hills State Coll., L.A.; Instr., Ceramics, Potters Studio, Fresno; Art Tchr., Sierra H.S. One man exhibs: Plum Tree Gall., Fig Tree Gall., Tulare Co. Art Mus., Dominguez Hills State Coll. (all in Calif.). Grp. exhibs: num. Calif. art shows; German-Am. Inst., Regensberg, Germany; Ward-Nasse Gall., N.Y.C.; Leiland Art House, Taipei, Taiwan. Address: 6590 N. Sherman, Fresno, CA 19710, U.S.A.

OGDEN, Ernestine Sally, (Stanbery) (Callahan) (Mrs. Wm. Carl Ogden), b. 3 May 1922. College Professor; Accountant; Researcher. Educ: B.A., Stanford Univ., Calif., 1952; M.A., Adams State Coll., Colo., 1962. Appts. incl: w. U.S. Govt., Wash., DC & Rheims, France; Acct., Daniel, Daniel, Ennis & Co., Tulsa, Okla.; Acctng. Off., Alamosa Abstract Co., Ala.; Prof. of Engl., Adams State Coll. & Southern Colo. State Coll.; Hd., Tchr. Trng., Colo.; U.S. Postal Serv., Grove, Okla. 1973, '74. Mbrships. incl: AAUP; Stanford Alumni; Pres., Am. Legion Auxiliary; Nat. Coun. Tchrs. of Eng.; Driver, Am. Red Cross; Colo. Educ. Assn.; AAUW' Author, An Effective Method of Instruction and Selected Content for Instruction in a Composition Course for College Freshmen, 1962. Ed. of: Freshman English, TV SCSC, 1966; A Look at Colorado Cultures, 1968; Countdown, 1969, etc. Contbr. of poems & articles to various jrnls. Recip. of many hons. Address: P.O. Box 652, Grove, OK 74344, U.S.A.

OGDON, Thomas Hammer, b. 16 Apr. 1935. Advertising Executive; Management Supervisor. Educ. B.A., Amherst Coll., 1957. Appts: Copy Trainee, Ted Bates Advt., 1957-58; Copywriter, Grey Advt., 1958-61; Copywriter, Benton & Bowles Advt., Inc., 1961-62; Creative Grp. Hd., ibid, 1962-63; Account Exec., 1963-66; V.P. & Account Supvsr., 1966-71; Sr. V.P., Mgmt. Supvsr., 1971-. Mbrships: Psi Upsilon; Univ. Club of N.Y.; Round Hill Club, Greenwich, Conn.; Bd. Dirs., Gtr. N.Y. YMCA (counseling & testing); Fndr., Stanwich Club, Greenwich, Conn.; Trustee, Northwich Dev. Corp., 1967. Address: Benton & Bowles, Inc., 909 3rd Ave., N.Y., NY 10022, U.S.A. 2, 6, 57, 130.

OGER, Ghislain, V., b. 23 Oct. 1935. Cultural Centre Director, Educ: B.A. degree, philos. & sociol. of developing countries. Appts: Tchr., maladjusted children: Provincial Commnr., Social & Youth Action, Belgian Congo; Dir., African Cultural Ctr, Brussels, Belgium; Dir., Belgian Cultural Ctr., Kinshasa, Zaire; Attache, Belgian Embassy, Kinshasa. Mbrships: Scouts; Lions Club. Publs: Jeunesse Organisée & Non-organisée dans un Pays d'Afrique; Les Centres Culturels, Voies de Coopération au Developpement. Address: Chaussée de la Hulpe, 22, 1180 Brussels, Belgium. 43.

OGG, Wilson Reid, b. 26 Feb. 1928. Lawyer; Civic & Cultural Leader. Educ: A.B., Univ. of Calif., Berkeley, 1949; J.D., Boalt Hall Schl. of Law, ibid, 1952. Appts. incl: Pvte. Law Prac. & Cons., 1955-; Trustee & Sec., 1st Unitarian Ch, Berkeley, 1957-58; Rsch. Atty., Legal Ed., Dept. of Continuing Educ. of the Bar, Univ. of Calif. Ext., 1958-63; Arbitrator, Am. Arbitration Assn., 1963-; Pres. & Bd. Chmn., Calif. Soc. Psychical Study Inc., 1963-65; Edit. Cons., Bancroft-Whitney Co., 1965-66; Contbng. Author, Matthew Bender & Co., Inc., 1968-; Ordained Min., Universal Life Ch., 1969-. Fellow, Int. Acad. Law & Sci. Mbrships. incl: Soc. for Psychical Rsch., U.S.; Pacific Film Archive; Univ. Art Mus. Coun.; Town Hall of Commonwealth Clubs of Calif.; San Fran. Press Club; Fac. Club, Calif., Berkeley; San Fran. Symph. Assn.; San Fran. Mus. Art; Mechs. Lib. Publs. incl: Legal Aspects of Doing Business; Under Government Contracts & Subcontracts, 1958; California Practice Handbook, 1959. Hons: Commendation Ribbon w. Medal Pendant, 1954; D.D, Universal Life Ch.; 1969; D. Relig. Humanities, ibid, 1970. Address: 8 Bret Harte Way, Berkeley, CA 94708, U.S.A. 9, 16, 22, 57, 59, 74, 120, 128, 130, 131, 133.

OGLIASTRO, Jacques Marie Jean, b. 21 May 1910. Journalist. Educ: Lic. in law; Dip., Ecole Libre des Scis. Pols. Appts: Preparation of Concours des Affaires Etrangéres (pre-WWII): Jrnlst., Radiodiffusion Française, 1944-47; Diplomatic Corresp., Le Figaro, 1945-; Chief of Diplomatic Serv. & Dpty. For. Ed., ibid, 1965-. Mbrships: Exec. Comm., Assn. de la Presse Diplomatique Française, 1958- (Pres., 1970-71); Bugatti Owners' Club; Etrier Perigordin. Hons: Off. de la Legion d'Hon.; Croix de Guerre; Ufficiale dell'Ordine Al Merito della Repubblica Italiana; Cmdr. du Nichan Iftikhar. Address: 8 Rue de Varize, Paris I6, France. 43, 91.

OGUZMAN, Kemal, b. 15 Dec. 1927. Professor of Law. Educ: Grad., Law Fac., Univ. of Istanbul, 1950; S.J.D., ibid, 1955. Appts: Rsch. Asst., Univ. of Istanbul, 1950-51; Rsch., Law Facs., Lausanne & Paris, 1955-56; Assoc. Prof., 1957, Prof., 1965-. Fac. of Bus. Admin., Univ. of Istanbul; Mbr., Fac. Exec. Bd., Fac. Rep., Senate of Istanbul Univ., 1969-73; Vice Rector, 1973-. Mbrships: Int. Soc. for Labour & Soc. Legislation; Assn. Henri Capitan. Publs: Num. books, articles, inclng: Strike & Lockout from Juristic Viewpoint, 1964, 2nd edit., 1967; Text Book on Civil Law, 1971; Relations between Employer & Employee through Case Method, 1973. Address: Istanbul Üniversitesi, Hukuk Fakültesi Istanbul, Turkey.

OHANYAN, Agop, b. 31 July 1932. Dentist. Educ: Physn. in Stomatol., Inst. of Med. & Pharm., Bucharest, Rumania, 1961; D.D.S., Loma Linda Univ. Schl. of Dentistry, Calif., U.S.A. 1968. Appts: Chief Physn., Div. of Stomatol., Corabia State Polyclin. & Hosp., 1961-63; Pvte. Prac., Dentistry, Sunnyside, N.Y., 1968-; Mbr., Med. Staff, Cath. Med. Ctr., Brooklyn & Queens; Attng. Dentist, Dept. of Dentistry, St. John's Hosp., Queens, N.Y. Mbrships: N.Y. State of Am. Dental Assns.; Armenian Rumanian Assn.; Loma Linda Alumni Assn.; N.Y. Bell Raquet Club. Publs. incl: Maxillary Cyst Complications, 1961; Nutrition of Denture Wearers, 1968. Hons. incl: Highest Grad. Award, Part I, Nat. Bd. for

Dentistry, Loma Linda, 1966, & Part II, 1968. Address: 65-75 Fitchett St., Rego Park, NY 11374, U.S.A. 6.

O'HEARN, William J., b. 8 Sept. 1890. Dentist. Educ: grad., Univ. of Md. Dental Schl., 1916; Northwestern Univ. Appts: pvte. prac., 1933, '16-57; Mbr., Dental Staff, Hillcrest Hosp., Pittsfield, Mass., 1945-, St. Lukes Hosp., ibid, 1945-; Mbrships: State Histl. Comm., Dental Soc., 1969; Pittsfield Campaign Chmn., Nat. Fndn. March of Dimes, 1952, '53, '70; Pres., Goodwill Inds., Pittsfield, 1955-65; Trustee, Opportunities Craftshop for the Handicapped, Unitarian Ch., 1957-; Cmdr., Am. Legion, Pittsfield, 1943-; Hon. Soc. of Am. Legion, 40-8 Grand Chef de Gare of Mass., 1959. Named Dentist of the Yr. by Dist. Dental Soc., 1958. Address: 10 Silver St., Pittsfield, MA 01201, U.S.A. 6.

OHIRA, Masahiko, b. 11 July 1914. University Professor. Educ: M.D., Univ. of Kyushu Schl. of Med., Japan, 1939; Postgrad. course of med. sci., ibid, 1946-48; Dr. Med. Sci., 1952; M.P.H., Univ. of Pitts. Grad. Schl. of Pub. Hlth., 1955. Appts: Rsch. Fellow, Dept. of Hygiene, Univ. of Kyushu, Schl. of Med., 1939; Naval serv. as physn., 1939-45; Rsch., Dept. of Hygiene, Univ. of Kyushu, Schl. of Med., 1945-50; Asst. Prof. of Hygiene, ibid, 1950-57; Prof. & Chief, Dept. of Hygiene, Okayama Univ., Med. Schl., 1957-. Mbrships: Trustee, Japanese Soc. for Hygiene; Bd. of Dirs., Japan Assn. of Indl. Hlth.; Trustee, Japanese Soc. of Pub. Hlth.; Permanent Commn., Int. Assn. of Occupational Hlth.; Permanent Comm., YMCA, Japan. Author of 8 articles & 3 monographs in field. Recip., Min. of Labor Prize in appreciation of co-operative works in field of occupational hlth., 1973. Address: c/o Dept. of Hygiene Okayama Univ. Med. Schl., 2-5-1, Shikata-cho, Okayama City 700, Japan.

OHLMAN, Maxwell, b. 9 June 1918. Investment Counselor & Financial Publisher. Educ: B.A., Columbia Coll. N.Y.C., 1939. Appts: Rsch. Analyst, Acct. Exec., Standard & Poor's Corp., Franklin Cole & Co., Inc., W.E. Burnet & Co., Thomson & McKinnon, Walston & Co., Arthur Wiesenberger & Co., Edwards & Hanly, Laird, Bissell & Meeds, 1943-63; Advsry. Dir., All Funds Inc., N.Y.C., 1961-67; Sr. Ptnr., Maxwell Ohiman & Co. N.Y.C., 1963-68; Pres. 1968-72; Pres., Info. & Rsch. Servs., Inc., N.Y.C. & Roslyn, N.Y., 1964-; Pres., Columbia Mgmt. Cons. Corp., Wilmington, Del., 1967-69; Chmn., Kennedy, Ohlman & Co., Inc., 1966-67; Prin., Ohlman Schl. of Finance, 1968-70. Mbrships. incl: Advsry. Bd. Provident Mgmt. Corp., Wilmington, Del., 1961-68; Cmdr., Nassau Co. Civil Defense; Phila-Balt-Wash. Stock Exch.; Assoc. Mbr., Boston Cinn. & Montreal Stock Exchs.; N.Y. Soc. Security Analysts, Inc. Publs. incl: Washington Ahead of the News, 1968-70; Trends in Natural Resources Shares, 1971-72; Inflation Shelters, 1970-71; Financial Prospective, 1968-69; Ohlman's Report on Financial Planning Companies, 1969-70; Originated "Industry Lineup" series for Forbes Mag., 1952. Address: 7 Dick's Lane, Roslyn, NY 11576, U.S.A. 16.

ÖHMANN, Emil, b. 25 Jan. 1894. University Professor of German Philology. Educ: M.A., 1915, Dr.phil. (Helsinki), 1918. Appts: Univ. Rdr., German Philol., Helsinki, Finland, 1921-25; Prof., Turku, 1925-44; Prof., Helsinki, 1944-63. Mbrships: Academia Scientiarum Fennica, 1932-; Sec. Gen., ibid, 1948-65; Pres., 1965-66; Hon. mbr., 1972; Societas Scientiarum, 1952-; Pres., Soc. Neo-philologique de Helsinki, 1960-72; Hon.

mbr., ibid, 1972; Hon. mbr., Koninklўke Vlaamse Acad. voor Taal en Letterkunde; Corres. mbr., Akad. der Wissenschaften, Göttingen, German Fed. Repub., Kongelige Danske Widenskabernes Selskab, Copenhagen, Denmark, Kungliga Vitterhets Historie & Antikvitets Akad., Stockholm, Osterreichische Akad. der Wissenschaften, Vienna, Deutsche Akad. der Wissenschaften, Berlin. Hons. incl: Dr.phil., Univ. of Freiburg im Breisgau, 1961, Univ of Berlin, 1963, Univ. of Turku, Finland, 1970; Brothers Grimm Prize, Univ of Marburg, 1961. Address: Pihlagatie 50, 27 Helsinki, Finland.

OHRENSTEIN, Roman Abraham, b. 12 June 1920. Educator; Economist. Educ: M.A., Univ. of Munich, Germany, 1948; Ph.D., 1949; M.A., Jewish Theol. Sem., Am., 1955; Ordained, Rabbi, 1955. Appts. incl: Rabbi, Auburn, N.Y., 1955-57; Pittsfield, Mass., 1957-60; Atlanta, Ga., 1960-62; N.Y.C., 1962-66; Prof., Econs., SUNY, Nassau Community Coll., Garden City, N.Y., 1964-; Campus Chap., ibid, 1970-; Prof., Econs., Soc. Sci. Dept., Am. Coll., Jerusalem, Israel, 1968-. Mbrships incl: Am. Econ. Assn.; AAUP; Coll. Coun., Am. Coll., Jerusalem, 1967-72; Nat. Exec. Comm., Am. Profs. For Peace in the Middle E., 1971-72; Nat. Bd. Dirs., Jewish Rights Coun., 1972-; Publs: Inventories During Business Fluctuations, 1973; articles in profl. mags. Recip., State Univ. Fellowship Award, 1968, 70. Address: 28-74 208th St., Bayside, NY 11360, U.S.A. 6.

OINAS, Felix J., b. 6 Mar. 1911. University Professor. Educ: M.A., Tartu Univ., Estonia, 1930-35, '36-37; Budapest Univ., Hungary, 1935-36; Heidelberg Univ., W. Germany, 1946-48; Ph.D., Ind. Univ., 1950-51, '52. Appts: Lectr. of Finno-Ugric, Budapest Univ., Hungary, 1938-40; Vis. Lectr. in Estonian, Baltic Univ., Hamburg, W. Germany, 1946-49; Lectr. in Slavic, Ind. Univ., U.S.A., 1952-53; Instr., ibid, 1953-55; Asst. Prof., 1955-61. Assoc. Prof., 1961-65; Prof., 1965-; Publs: The Language Teaching Today (Ed), 1960; The Development of Some Propositional Cases, 1961; Basic Course in Estonian, 1966, '67, '68; Estonian General Reader, 1964; Studies in Finnic-Slavic Folklore Relations, 1969; The Study of Russian Folklore (w. S. Soudakoff), 1974. Recip., Rsch. Grant, Nat. Endowment for the Humanities, 1974. Address: Dept. of Slavic Langs. & Lit., Ballantine Hall 502, Ind. Univ., Bloomington, UN 47401, U.S.A. 8, 13, 15.

OISO, Toshio, b. 2 Apr. 1908. Institute Director. Educ: Ph.D., Med. Fac., Kyoto Imperial Univ., 1935; M.D., ibid, 1942. Appts: Rsch. Mbr., Nat. Inst. of Nutrition, 1935-38; Admnstv. Official, Min. of Hlth. & Welfare, 1938-50; Chief of Hlth. Sect. Govt. Personnel Auth., 1950-53; Chief of Nutrition Sect., Bur. of Pub. Hlth., 1953-63; Cnslr. of Sci. & Tech., Min.'s Secretariat, 1963-65; Dir., Nat. Inst. of Nutrition, Tokyo, 1965-. Mbrships: V.P., Xth Int. Congress of Nutrition, 1975; Dir., Kanto Regional Off., Japanese Soc. of Food & Nutritions Coun., Educ. Min., Min. of Justice & Min of Hlth. & Welfare; Panel, WHO Advsry. Panel on Nutrition, Malnutrition Panel, USA-Japan Coop. Med. Sci. Prog.; Hon. Mbr., Am. Inst. of Nutrition. Has carried out nation-wide nutrition survey & publd. data anually, 1946-. Contbr. publs. to field of nutrition. Hons: Min.'s Awards, Min. of Hlth. & Welfare, 1948, 63 & 69; Hon. Citizen of New Orleans, U.S.A. Address: c/o Nat. Inst. of Nutrition, Toyamacho-1, Shinjuku-ku, Tokyo, Japan.

OJALA, (Kauko) Aatos, b. 6 Jan. 1919. University Professor. Educ: Cand.phil., 1944, Dr.phil. (Helsinki), 1954; Greifswald Univ., 1944; Stockholms Högskila, 1945; Bedford Coll., Univ. of London, U.K., 1950-52; Yale Univ., U.S.A., 1955-56. Appts: Lectr. in Aesthetics & Modern Lit., Helsinki Univ., 1956-; Acting Asst. Prof., ibid, 1960; Prof. of Lit., Jyväskylä Univ., 1960-; Dean, Sect. of Hist. & Philol., ibid, 1966-68; Guest Lectr., Leningrad & Moscow Univs., U.S.S.R., 1959. Mbrships: Ed.-in-Chief, Parnasso, 1959; Ed., Jyväskylä Studies in Arts, 1970-; Vice Chmn. of Bd. of Communal Theatre of Jyväskylä, 1961-71; Bd. mbr., Finland Dept., Scandinavian Summer Univ., 1963-72; Bd. mbr., Literary Schlrs.' Assn., 1963-; Chmn. of Bd., Finnish-British Soc. of Jyväskylä, 1969-70. Author of publs. in field. Hons: Cmdr., Order of Finnish Lion, 1969; CE IV w. swords, 1942. Address: Tiedepolku 4 C 12, 40720 Jyväskylä 72, Finland. 90, 134.

OJTOZY, Ernest, b. 18 Oct. 1897. Engineer. Educ: B.S., M.E., 1944. Appts. incl: Exec. Engr. - Dir., Chem. Factory, Villa Mella, Dominican Repub., 1951-67; Tech. Advsr., Sect. of Armed Forces, & Prof., Mil. Acad., & Naval Acad., Dominican Repub., 1968-. Mbrships. incl: Charter Coll. of Engrs., Dominican Repub.; Dominican-Am. Cultural Inst.; Alliance Française en Republique Dominicaine; Assn. of Am. Engrs. (ASHRAE), N.Y., U.S.A. Publs: Instrnl. manuals & textbooks, Hungary & Dominican Repub. Hons. Incl: Cmdrs., Cross of Italy, 1940; Kt., Order of Merit (Hungary), 1942. Address: c/o. Intendencia General M.B.F.A., P.O. Box 1216 - Pellerano Alfau 2, Santo Domingo, Z.P.I., Dominican Repub. 136.

OKA, Hiko-Ichi, b. 22 Dec. 1916. Research Official. Educ. B.Agr., Fac. of Agric., Hokkaido Univ., Sapporo, Japan, 1940; D. Agr., ibid, 1954. Appts. incl: Asst. Rschr., Ohara Inst. for Agricl. Rsch., Kurshiki, Japan, 1940-42; Rsch. Asst. under Prof. E. Iso, Taiwan Univ., 1942-43; Prof., Taichung Agricl. Coll. (under Japanese Govt.-Gen. for Taiwan), 1943-45; Prof., Taiwan Provincial Coll. of Agric. (under Chinese Govt.), 1945-54; Rschr., Nat. Inst. of Genetics, Japan, 1954-; Hd., Applied Genetics Dept., ibid. Mbrships: Bd. Mbr. & Ed., Soc. for Advancement of Breeding Researches in Asia & Oceania; Japanese Genetics Soc.; Japanese Breeding Soc. Publs. incl: over 100 articles in scientific jrnls. Hons: Japan Agricl. Sci. Prize, 1963; Indian Jrnl. of Genetics Prize, 1964. Address: Nat. Inst. of Genetics, Misima City, 411 Japan. 50.

OKA, Masao, b. 5 June 1898. Professor of Ethnology. Educ: Grad., Fac. of Humanities, Tokyo Imperial Univ., 1924; Ph.D., Vienna Univ., 1932. Appts. incl: Prof., Showa Med. Coll., Tokyo, 1928-35; Mbr., Comm. of Anthropol. & Ethnol., Japan Sci. Coun., 1946-;Guest Prof., Vienna Univ., 1938-40; Chief, Inst. of Japanol., ibid, 1938-40; Guest Lectr., Budapest Univ., 1939-40; Gen. Mgr., Nat. Inst. of Ethnol., Tokyo, 1943-45; Prof. of Ethnol., Tokyo Metropolitan Univ., 1951-60; Dir., Nat. Inst. for Study of Langs. & Cultures of Asia & Africa, Tokyo, 1964-72; Chief, Dept. of Folklore & Ethnol., Cultural Properties Protection Commn., Min. of Educ., 1965-. Mbrships. incl: Japanese Soc. of Ethnol., 1934-; Chief Dir., 1950-58; Japanese Soc. of Anthropol.; Hon Fellow, Royal Anthropological Inst. of Great Britain & Ireland, 1966-; Int. Union of Anthropological & Ethnological Scis., Pres., 1964-68, Pres., 8th Int. Congress, 1968, Hon. Pres., 1968-73, Hon.

Mbr., 1973-. Author of may publs. in profl. field. Hons: Ehrenkreuz für Wissenschaft Und Kunst. 1 Klasse, Austria, 1966. Address: 4 - 10 - 15, Narita Higashi, Suginami-ku, Tokyo, Japan. 1.

O'KELLEY, Harold Ernest, b. 20 Mar. 1925. Corporate Executive. Educ. B.E.E., Auburn Univ., Ala., 1947; M.S., Univ. of Fla. 1952. Appts: Assoc. Prof. & Rsch. Assoc., Elec. Engrng., Auburn Univ., 1948-57; V.P., Gen. Mgr., Radiation Inc., 1957-68; V.P., Progs., Harris-Intertype Corp., 1968-72; Group V.P., ibid, 1972-73; Pres., Chief Exec. Off., Dir., Datapoint Corp., 1973-. Mbrships: Bd. of Dirs., Computer Inds. Assn.; Sr. Mbr., IEEE; Am. Mgmt. Assn.; Am. Ordinance Assn.; AIAA; Bd. of Govs., Brevard Hosp.; Pres., Civitan Club; Kiwanis Club. Contbns: Pulse Cross Monitor, Electronics; 21 inch Oscilloscope, Electronics; Ground Stn. for Tiros Weather Satellite, Electronics. Address: 300 Geneseo Rd., San Antonio, TX 79209, U.S.A. 7.

OKER-BLOM, Nils Christian Edgar, b. 5 Aug 1919. Professor; Physician. Educ; M.D., Univ. of Helsinki, 1948; post-doctoral studies, Copenhagen, 1947, Stockholm, 1948; Schl. of Med., Yale Univ., 1949-50, Rockefeller Fndn. Fellow, 1960. Appts: Prof. of Virol., Univ. of Helsinki, 1957; Med. Advsr., Sigrid Jusëlius Fndn., 1957-; Dean, Fac. of Med., Univ. of Helsinki, 1968-69; Vice-Dean, ibid, 1969-70. Mbrships. incl: Sec. - Pres., Finnish Med. Assn., 1953-70; V.P. Pub. Hlth. Assn., Folkhälsan, 1962-; V.P., European Assn. Against Poliomyelitis & Other Virus Diseases, 1969-; Sec., Virol. Sect., Int. Microbiological Soc., 1970-; V.P., Int. Union Biological Scis., 1970-. Author or Co-author, over 100 official med. reports & papers. Hons: Hugo Standertskjöld Award for Cancer Rsch., 1960; Honoris Causa, Univ. of Uppsala, 1967. Address: Dept. of Virol., Univ. of Helsinki 9, Haartmaninkatu 3, 00290 Helsinki 29, Finland. 134.

OKEZIE, Josiah Onyebuchi Johnson, b. 26 Nov. 1924. Medical Administrator; Nigerian Government Minister. Educ: Yaba Coll. of Med., 1944-47; Univ. Coll., Ibadan, 1948-49; Royal Coll. Surgs. of England & Ireland, 1955-57. Appts. incl: Asst. Med. Off., Civil Serv. of Nigeria, 1950-54; Fndr.,Ibeku Ctrl. Hosp.,Umuahia-Ibeku; Med. Supt., ibid, 1958-69; Independent Mbr., Eastern Nigeria House of Assembly, 1961-66; Ldr., Republican Party, 1964-66; Sr. Med. Off. i/c. of Queen Elizabeth Hosp., Umuahia-Ibeku, 1970; Fed. Commnr. for Hlth., 1970-71; Mbr., Fed. Exec. Coun. of Nigeria, 1970-; Fed. Commr., Agric. & Natural Resources, 1971-. Mbr. & past off., med. orgs. Publs: The Evolution of Science, 1959; Atomic Radiation, 1961. Address: Federal Ministry of Agriculture & Natural Resources, 34-36 Ikoyi Rd., Lagos, Nigeria.

OKORIE, Kalu Chima, b. 25 Feb. 1923. Librarian. Educ: Higher Coll., Yaba (w. Achimota Coll., Accra), 1942-43; Schl. of Libnship., Coll. of Further Educ., Loughborough, U.K. 1949-50; Schl. of Libnship., North-Western Polytech., London, 1950-51; Inst. of Educ., London Univ., winter term, 1951-52. Appts. Lib. Asst., Brit. Coun., Lagos, 1944-46; Sr. Lib. Asst., Lagos Pub. Lib., 1946-47; Asst. Libn., ibid, 1947-49; Libn., Lagos Municipal Lib., 1952-55; Libn., Eastern Nigeria Govt., Enugu, 1955-56; Regional Libn., Dir. of Lib. Servs., Eastern Nigeria Lib. Servs., Eastern Nigeria Lib. Bd., 1957-70; Dir. of Lib. Servs., E. Ctrl. State Lib. Bd., 1970-. Mbrships. incl: W. African Lib. Assn.; Councillor, Nigerian Lib. Assn.; Hon. Treas., Eastern Nigeria Festival of the Arts, 1959-62, currently on Exec.

All Sts. Schl. Provisional Comm., 1970-71; Enugu Sports Club, 1959-; E. Ctrl. State Automobile Assn. Contbr. num. articles to publs. & jrnls. in field. Hons: M.B.E., 1961 & O.O.N., 1964, for outstanding pub. serv. in field of pub. libnship. Address: 9A Abakaliki Rd., Enugu, Nigeria.

OKOSHI, Eugenia Sumihe Ushiyama. Artist. Educ: Seattle Univ., 1954-56; Schlrship. Henry Frye Mod. Art Mus., Seattle, 1957-59; New Schl. of N.Y., 1968. One man exhibs: Miami Mus. of Mod. Art, Miami, Fla., 1970; Gall. Int., N.Y.C., 1970; Wesbeth Gall., N.Y., 1972. Grp. exhibs. incl: Japanese Contemp. Artists Show, Pitts., Pa.; Raymond Duncan Gal., Paris, France; Bohman Art Gall., Stockholm, Sweden; Woolman Hall Gall., New Schl., N.Y.C., U.S.A.; Painters & Sculptors Soc., N.J.; Union Carbide Gall., N.Y.C. Mbrships: Burr Artists Corp., N.Y.; Japanese Artists Assn.; Westbeth Graphics Assn. Works incl. painting, graphics & flower arrangement. Collects. incl: Miami Mus. of Mod. Art; Lowe Gall., Univ. of Miami. Hons: 2nd Prize, Ikenobo Flower Arrangement Competition, Ueno Mus. of Fine Art, Tokyo, Japan, 1950; Hon. Mention, Art Exhib., Puyallup Fair, Wash., 1959; 2nd Prize, Beauty Ind. Art Exhib., Hotel Statler Hilton, N.Y., 1964. Address: Westbeth Studio G226, 643 W. St., N.Y., NY 10014, U.S.A. 37.

OKSALA, Arvo Alfred, b. 2 July 1920. Professor & Ophthalmologist. Educ: Cand. med., Helsinki Univ., Finland, 1943; Lic. med., ibid, 1947; Specialist in Ophthalmol., 1950; M.Sc.D., 1951. Appts. incl: Lectr., 1955-61; Prof., Clin. Ophthalmol., 1961; Chief Physn., Dept. of Ophthalmol., Middle Finland Ctrl. Hosp., Jyväskylä; Prof. & Chief Physn., Dept. of Ophthalmol., Turku Univ. Hosp.; Dean Med. Fac., Turku Univ., 1971-. Mbrships. incl: Societas Internationalis pro Diagnostica Ultrasonica in Ophthalmologia; V.P., 1967-69, Pres., 1969-71, Hon. Mbr., 1971, ibid; Finnish Acad. of Scis.; Hon., Am. Inst. of Ultrasound in Med. Publs. incl: Studies on Interstitial Keratitis Associated with Congenital Syphilis Occurring in Finland, 1951; Co-ed., Ultrasonics in Ophthalmology, 1967. Contbr. to med. & Ophthalmol. books & jrnls. Hons. incl: K.K.K. Lundsgaard Prize & Gold Medal, 1969; Anders Jahre's Prize & Gold Medal, 1970. Address: Dept. of Ophthalmology, Turku Univ. Hosp., 20520 Turku 52, Finland. 43, 90.

OLDIN, Gunnar Emil Olof, b. 4 Feb. 1932. Journalist; Author. Educ: Drama Schl., Stockholm, Sweden. Appts. incl: Jrnlst., 1952-57; TV Prod., 1957-62; Film Prod., 1963; free-lance Jrnlst. & Author, 1963-; Mbr. Cultural Comm., Co. of Stockholm, 1974-. Mbrships: former Sec., Swedish Film Acad.; former Sec. Swedish Film Jrnlsts. Assn.; former Pres., Swedish Boxing Assn.; former bd. Mbr., Swedish Actors' Soc.; Lion's Club. Publs. incl: Fakta Om Film, 1957; Har Kulturen Rad Med Oss, 1970; Gambling, 1973; Tusen Och Ett Skratt, 1974; Charlie I Vart Hjärta, 1974. Hons: Prize for Outstanding Achievement in Swedish Films, 1962. Address: Ringvägen 10, S - 117 26 StockholmSweden. 43.

OLDING, Raymond Knox, b. 7 Mar. 1929. Librarian. Educ: B. Econs., Univ. of Adelaide, S. Australia, 1964. State Libn. of S. Australia, 1970-. Mbr. Lib. Assn. of Australia (Pres., S. Australian Br., 1963, Fellow, 1967, Bd. of Examiners, 1970-). Publs: Readings in Library Cataloguing (Ed.), 1965; Wyndham Hulme's Literary Warrant & Information Indexing, 1968. Address: State Lib. of S. Australia, Box 419 G.P.O., Adelaide, S.A., Australia, 5001. 23.

OLDINGER, Bengt (Anders Valter), b. 3 Nov. 1911. Artist (Signature Bengtolle to 1966, then Oldinger). Educ: Acad. André l'Hote, Paris, France, 1947 & 1951. Num. study & profl. tours throughout Europe, N. Africa, U.S.A., Soviet Union, Far East, 1936-. Exhibs. incl. Acad. Royale, Stockholm, Sweden, 1958. Galerie Paul-Ambroise, Paris, France, 1959, '67, Gall. des Beaux Arts, Gothenburg & Amals Konsthall Sweden, 1968. Works represented in Royal Collect. of Sweden & Musée de Tessin, Paris, France. Recip. of Dip. of Hon., Monte Carlo, 1966. Address: Backebogatan 30, 12657 Hägersten, Sweden.

OLDS, Elizabeth, b. 10 Dec. 1896. Artist; Author. Educ: Univ. of Minn.; Minn. Schl. of Art. Author & Artist, children's books: Feather Mountain; Deep Treasure; Riding The Rails; The Big Fire; Plop Plop Ploppie; Little Una. Hons: Recip. num. awards, graphic & watercolor works; John Simon Guggenheim Fnd. Fellowship, 1926-27. Address: Brown Hill Road, Tamworth, NH 03886, U.S.A.

O'LEARY, (Sister) Mary Margaret. Teacher. Educ: B.A., Notre Dame Univ., Md.; Cert. of Theol., ibid, M.Ed., Boston Coll.; Grad. work, Tufts Univ. Tchr., Latin & Maths., Mission H.S., Boston, Holy Angels Acad., Ft. Lee, N.J.; Tchr., Latin, Girsl Cath. H.S., Malden, Mass.; Tchr., Engl. & Latin, St. Thomas Aquinas H.S., Dover, N.H.; Tchr., Engl., Girls Cath. H.S., Dover. Mbrships: Chmn., Boston Archdiocesan Latin Contests; Mbr. of Comm. for Curric. Planning: Mbr. of Exec. Bd., New England Classics; N.H. Coun. of Tchrs. of Engl. Address: 2 Fellsway East, Malden, MA 02148, U.S.A. 5, 132.

O'LEARY, Wilfred L., b. 3 July 1906. Educator. Educ: A.B., Boston Coll., Mass., 1929; A.M., ibid, 1930; Ed.M., State Coll., Boston, 1938; Ed.D., Calvin Coolidge Coll., 1954. Appts: Master, Boston Latin Schl., 1934-42, 1946-48; Hd., Hist. Dept., Jeremiah E. Burke H.S., Dorchester, Mass., 1948-57; Asst. Prof. Educ., Calvin Coolidge Coll., 1952-57; Headmaster, Roslindale H.S., Mass., 1957-64; Headmaster, Boston Latin Schl., 1964-. Mbrships. incl: Headmasters' Assn.; V.P., ibid, 1972-73; Advsry. Bd., Scholastic Mag., 1960-64; Mass. Advsry. Coun. on Educ.; Past-Mbr., New England Hist. Tchrs. Assn.; Sec.-Treas., ibid, 1952-64; V.P., ibid, 1965; Pres., ibid, 1966-67; Boston Headmasters' Assn.; Pres., ibid, 1964-65; Libn., Boston Latin Schl. Assn., 1964-; Am. Hist. Assn.; Nat. Coun. Soc. Studies Tchrs. Hons: Commendation Medal, USAF. Address: 4 Calvin Road, Jamaica Plain, MA 02130, U.S.A. 2, 6, 13, 128, 139.

OLESA MUÑIDO, Francisco-Felipe, b. 24 Apr. 1925. Professor of Law. Educ: Bachelor of Law, Univ. of Barcelona, 1944; Dr. of Law, Central Univ. of Madrid, 1949. Appts: Prof., Law Fac., Univ. of Barcelona; Prof., Spanish Naval War Coll.; Prof., Inst. Criminol., Univ. of Barcelona; Lawyer at Bars of Madrid & Barcelona; Advsr., ins., reins., maritime, aviation corps. & firms. Mbr. of Sociedad de Estudios Internacionales y Coloniales. Publs. incl: Induccion y auxilio al suicidio, 1958; Principios de Organización Aerea, 1967; Estructura de la infracción penal en el Código Español vigente, 1971. Hons. incl: Comendador de la Orden de Africa; Medalla Commemorativa de Lepanto; Medaille de l'Academie de Marine, France; Hai-Feng Medal, China. Address: Via Layetana 159, 3 A, Barcelona (9), Spain. 43.

OLHEISER, (Sister) Mary David, b. 13 Jan. 1918. Educational Administrator. Educ: B.A.,

Holy Names Coll., Spitane, Wash., 1942; M.A., St. Louis Univ., 1952; Ph.D., Boston Coll. Grad. Schl., Mass., 1962. Appts: Elementary Tchr., Tacoma, Wash., 1942-50; Instr. in Educ., Coll. of St. Benedict., St. Joseph, Minn., 1952-59, Prof. & Chmn. of Coll., 1962-72, V.P. for Acad. Affairs & Dean of Fac., 1972-. Mbrships: Order of St. Benedict; Chmn. & Sec., Educ. & Psychol. Sect., Am. Benedictine Acad.; NEA; Am. Assn. Colls. for Tchr. Educ.; Vis. Team mbr., Nat. Accreditation of Colls. for Tchr. Educ.; Nat. Assn. Women Deans. Hons. incl: Educators' European Discovery Tour, 1970; A.C.E. Grant for Inst. of Deans, 1972. Address: College of St. Benedict, St. Joseph, MN 56374, U.S.A. 5, 138.

OLIPHANT, Keith Morris, b. 13 Jan. 1909. Retired Commercial Company Manager. Appts: Sev. posts, Elder Smith Goldsbrough Mort Ltd., London, U.K., 1926-46; Mgr., ibid, 1947-73; Lt.-Col., Royal Australian Artillery, 1939-45; Dir., London Woolbrokers (Holding) Ltd., 1958-63. Mbrships: R.S.L. of Australia, 1967-; Rep. of R.S.L., British Commonwealth Ex-Servs. League Coun., 1952-64; Exec. Comm., British Commonwealth Ex-Servs. League, 1955-73, Treas., 1964-73; Naval, Mil. & Air Force Club, Adelaide, S.A., Australia; E. India, Sports & Pub. Schl. Club, London, U.K. Recip., Efficiency Decoration. Address: 175 Greenhill Rd., Parkside, Adelaide, S.A. Australia 5063. 23.

OLIVER, Eli Leslie, b. 4 May 1899. Economist. Educ: Hamline Univ., St. Paul, Minn., 1914-17; B.A., Univ. of Minn., 1918; Grad. Fellowship, Philos., ibid, 1919. Appts. incl: on staff, Fed. Trade Commn., 1918, 20, 22; on Fac., Univ. of Pa., 1920-21 & Brookwood Coll., N.Y., 1921-22; w. Jt. Bur. of Studies, Ladies' Garment Ind., 1923; Hd., Offs. of Labor Bur., Inc., Chgo., Cleveland, San. Fran., Wash.; Rsch. Dir., Brotherhood Railway Clerks, 1928-37; Hd., Labor Rels. Br., Off. Prod. Mgmt. & War Prod. Bd., 1941-42; mbr., Textile Workers Assignment Bd., 1951; Cons., M.S.A., 1951-53; Fac., Salzburg Seminar, 1961, & Seminar, Puerto Rico Univ., 1963; US Deleg., I.L.O., Geneva, 1966, O.E.C.D., Rome, 1963; Deleg., I.T.F. World Congresses, Brussels, Vienna, Berne, Helsinki, Copenhagen, Mexico City, Stockholm; made studies of transportation in Latin Am. (Argentina, Peru, Guatemala, Costa Rica) for O.A.S., & India for US AID, 1968. Mbrships: Royal Econ. Soc.; Am. Econ. Assn.; Am. Stat. Assn.; Acad. Pol. & Soc. Sci.; Ind. Rels. Rsch. Assn.; Am. Arbitration Assn. Specialist in Labor Rels. Publs: Report of President's Committee on National Recovery Administration (co-author); num. studies on transportation problems; articles in profl. jrnls. address: c/o Labor Bur. of Middle W., 1200 15th St. N.W., Washington, DC 20005, U.S.A. 2, 7.

OLIVERA, D. Miguel Alfredo, Writer; Professor. Educ; Lang. Study, Oxford Univ., U.K., 1938; Prof. of Philos. & Letters; Law Studies. Appts. incl: Prof., Humanities Fac., Univ. of La Plata, Argentina & Ingl. Inst. of Santo Tomas Moro, Buenos Aires; Fndr., Dir., Lib. of Argentinian Soc. of Writers; 3 times Pres., Argentinian PEN Club; Fndr., Dir., Agonia Polyglot review, 1939-46. Mbrships: Fellow, PEN Engl. Ctr.; Fellow, Dickens Fellowship of London. Publs. incl: Hojas Secas (poetry), 1937; La Ifigenia de Goethe, 1939; Teatro Inglés del siglo XX (w. P.O. Dudgeon), 1958; Camila O'Gorman (Argentinian tragedy), 1959; Sapphó, o de la Educación, 2nd ed., 1973; Oda a Leandro, 1970; El Collar de la Paloma (poetry), 1974; var. translations.

Address: Calle Basarilbaso 1396, Buenos Aires, Argentina.

OLIVERO, Humberto, b. 23 Aug. 1918. Civil Engineer; Sanitary Engineer. Educ: Civil Engineer, Univ. of Guatemala, 1943; M.S., Harvard Univ., 1945. Appts: Chief Design Engr., Servicio Cooperativo Interamericano de Salud Publica, Guatemala; Cons Engr., var. authorities, Guatemala; Cons., Panamerican Hlth. Org. & WHO, var. occasions; Dir. & Prof., Dept. Sanitary Engrng., Schl. of Engrng., Univ. of San Carlos, Guatemala & Dean, Schl. of Engrng.; currently, Chief, Sanitary Engrng. Sect., Inter-Am. Dev. Bank, Wash. D.C., U.S.A. Mbr., var. profl. orgs. Profl. articles, papers & reports, var. publs. Hons. incl: Presidente Consejo Directivo Organización Panamericana de la Salud; Int. Pres., Inter-Am. Assn. Sanitary Engrng.; V.P., Am. Assn. Pub. Hlth. Address: Inter-American Development Bank, 808 17th St., Washington, D.C. 20577, U.S.A.

OLIVETTI, Alfred C., b. 13 Sept. 1942. Executive; Broker. Educ: B.A., Colby Coll., 1964. Appts. incl: Sole Admnstr., ECO Elettro-Controlli Sp.A., 1971-; Pres., RSM Sp.A., 1972-; Broker, dealing specifically in Co. Sales, Oil & Commodities. Address: Via Asclepiade 82, 00124 Casal Palocco, Rome Italy.

OLLEY, Robert Edward, b. 16 Apr. 1933. Professor of Economics. Educ: B.A., Carleton Univ., Ottawa, Ont., 1960; M.A., Queen's Univ., Kingston, Ont., 1961; Ph.D., ibid, 1969. Appts. incl: Dept. Mgr., Retail Lumber Outlets, 1952-60; Hd. Tutor, Introductory Econ. Hist., Queen's Univ., Kingston, 1961-63. Asst. Prof., Univ. Of Sask., Saskatoon, 1963-67, 1968-69, Assoc. Prof., 1968-71, 1973-. Dir., Royal Commn. Consumer Problems & Inflation, Saskatoon, Winnipeg & Edmonton, 1967-68; Econ. Advsr., Bell Telephone Co. of Canada, Montreal, 1969-71, 1971-73, 1973-. Mbr. & Off. var. profl. orgs. Publs. incl: Consumer Credit in Canada (co-author), 1965; An Oil Railway to the Arctic (co-author), 1972. Contbr., profl. articles, jrnls. & other publs. Recip., var. academic Fellowships & grants. Address: Dept. of Econs. & Pol. Sci., Univ. of Sask., Saskatoon, Canada.

OLMSTED, George Bice, b. 28 Apr. 1918. Retired Physicist. Educ: A.B., Depauw Univ., Greencastle, Ind., 1939; Postgrad., Univ. of Wis., Madison, 1939-41; Pt.-time, Univ. of Md., College Pk., 1946-48. Appts: Physicist, USN Ordnance Lab., White Oak, Md., 1941-48; Physicist, Off. for Atomic Energy, Air Force Dept., Wash. D.C., 1948-58; Asst. Tech. Dir., USAF Tech. Applications Ctr., Alexandria, Va., 1958-72; Scientific Advsr., Western Delegation, Conf. of Experts on Nuclear Test Cessation. Geneva. Switzerland, 1958. Mbrships: Am. Phys. Soc.; Am. Geophysical Union; Phi Beta Kappa, Sigma Xi. Hons: Exceptional Civilian Service Awards, USAF, 1955, 1958. Address: 1117 Westmoreland Rd., Alexandria, VA 22308, U.S.A. 7.

OLSEN, Jørgen Lykke, b. 10 May 1923. Professor of Physics. Educ: Trinity Coll., Dublin, Irish Repub.; Corpus Christi Coll., Oxford, U.K. Appts: Assoc. Prof., Low Temperature Physics, Swiss Fed. Inst. of Technol., Zurich, 1961; Prof., Experimental Physics, especially Low Temperature Physics, ibid, 1972; Chmn., Dept. of Physics, 1972-74. Mbrships: Pres., Swiss Phys. Soc., 1973-75; Var. other sci. socs.; United Oxford & Cambridge Univs. Club. Publs: Electrons in Metals; Num. publs. in sci. jrnls. Address: Laboratorium für

Festkörperphysik, Eidg. Technische Hochschule Zurich, CH-8049 Zurich, Switzerland.

OLSEN, Kaare Ritter, b. 16 June 1922. Engineer. Educ: B.Eng., McGill Univ., Montreal, 1948. Appts: V.P., Chief Engr. & Dir., Atlas Construction Co. Ltd., 1948; Pres. & Dir., G.M. Gest Ltd., & Subsidiaries, 1969-; Pres. & Dir., Fathom Oceanol. Ltd., 1970. Mbrships: Corp. Engrs. of Quebec; Corp. Engrs. of Ont; Corp. Engrs. of Nflnd; Engrng. Inst. Canada; Associated Am. Soc. of Civil Engrs; Marine Technol. Soc; Naval Offs. Assn; Hudson Yacht Club; Viking Ski Club; Royal Oak Tennis Club; Montreal Amateur Athletic Assn. Address: 4781 Ste-Catherine St. W., Montreal, P.Q. H3Z 1S7, Canada. 32, 88.

OLSON, Bonnie Waggoner Breternitz, b. 30 May 1916. Civic Worker. Educ: A.B., Univ. of Chgo. Appts. incl: Soc. Wkr., Am. Red Cross, Chgo., 1942-44, Sacramento, Calif., 1944. Amarilla, Tex., 1945; Exec. Sec., Econometrica, Cowles Commn. Rsch. in Econs., 1945-47; Mbr., Colo. Springs Community Coun., 1956-58, Chmn., Children's Div., 1956-58; Chmn. ad hoc comm., El Paso Citizens' Comm. for Nat. Probation & Parole Survey, Juvenile Procedures & Detention, 1957-61; Mbr., Children's Advsry. Comm., Colo. Child Welfare Dept., 1959-63, Chmn., 1961; Deleg., White House Conf. on Children & Youth, 1960, '70; Mbr., Colo. Springs Human Rels. Commn., 1968. Mbrships. incl: Am. Acad. Pol. & Soc. Scis.; Coun. on Relig. & Int. Affairs. Recip., Lane Bryant Annual Nat. Awards Citation for Pub. Serv., 1952. Address: 31 Broadmoor Ave., Colorado Springs, CO, U.S.A. 5.

OLSON, Dean A., b. 10 Nov. 1918. Engineer; Company Executive. Educ: B.S.M.E., Univ. of Ill., 1941. Appts. incl: Co. Cmndr., 4th Ordnance Corps, U.S. Army, 1942-45; Pres. & Bd. Chmn., Rockford Acromatic Products Co., Ill., 1949-, & Die Max Products Co., ibid, 1952-; Chmn. of Bd., Aircraft Gear Corp., Chgo., Ill., 1966-; Dir., Barrett Cravesn Co., Northrbook, ibid, 1968-, & Ill. Nat. Bank & Trust Co., 1972-; Dir., Howard H. Monk & Assocs., Inc., Rockford, Ill., 1974-. Mbr. of many Bds. & Comms. inclng: Ill., Gov's. Advsry. Coun., 1970-; Advsry. Bd. of Ctr. for Strategic & Int. Studies, 1970-; Chgo. Coun. on For. Rels., 1971-; Fndng. Past Pres., Jr. Achievements in Rockford; Sec. of Navy's Advsry. Bd. on Educ. & Trng., 1972-; Navy League of U.S., Dist. Columbia Coun., 1973-. Other mbrships. incl: Brit. Inst. of Dirs., London, England, 1966-; Beta Gamma Sigma, 1967. Chgo. Pres. Org., 1968-. Hons: U.S. Victory Medal, WWII; U.S. Asiatic Pacific Campaign Ribbon w. Bronze Star, ibid. Asiatic Army of Occupation Medal (Korea). Address: 611 Beacon St., Rockford, IL 61111, U.S.A. 8, 16, 120, 128, 131.

OLSON, Gerald Walter, b. 22 Mar. 1932. Associate Professor. Educ: B.S., 1954, M.S., 1959, Univ. of Neb.; Ph.D., Univ. of Wis., 1962. Appts. incl: Party Chief, Wis. Geological & Natural Hist. Survey & Rsch. Asst., Univ. of Wis., 1959-62; Soil Technologist, Asst. Prof.-Assoc. Prof. Soil Sci. in Resource Dev., Cornell Univ., 1962-; Advsry. Bd., Environmental Geol. Digest, Univ. of Kan., 1968-71; Sec.-Treas., Empire State Chapt., Soil Conservation Soc. of Am., 1969-71; Cons. on num. soil surveys & progs. for planning & engrng. firms, archaeol. expeditions, univs., nat. & int. comms., inclng. FAO, Rome, Italy, & FAO/Soil Inst. of Iran, 1972; Vis. Soil Sci., Kan. Geolog. Survey, 1973. Mbrships. incl: Am. Soc. of Agronomy; Sci. Soc. of Am.; Int. &

British Socs. of Soil Sci.; Fellow, AAAS; Gamma Sigma Delta; Sigma Xi; Phi Sigma Kappa. Author of about 70 surveys & reports dealing w. soil sci., resource dev. & environment. Address: 701 Bradfield Hall, Cornell Univ., Ithaca, NY 14850, U.S.A. 14, 50, 57, 129, 130.

OLSON, James C., b. 23 Jan. 1917. University Professor. Educ: A.B., Morningside Coll., Sioux City, Iowa, 1938; M.A., Univ. of Neb., 1939; Ph.D., ibid, 1942; LL.D., Morningside Coll., 1968. Appts. incl: Instr., Northwest Miss. State Tchrs. Coll., Maryville, 1940-42; Dir., Neb. State Histl. Soc., Lincoln, 1946-56; Lectr.-Prof., Univ. of Neb., 1947-68, Chmn., Dept. of Hist., 1956-65, Assoc. Dean, Grad. Coll., & Dir., Grad. Prog. Dev., 1965-66, Dean, Grad. Coll., & Univ. Rsch. Adminstr., 1966-68, Vice Chancellor for Grad. Studies, 1968; Chancellor, Univ. of Mo., Kan. City, 1968-. Mbr. & Off., var. profl. orgs. Publs. incl: History of Nebraska, 1955, 2nd edit., 1966; Red Cloud & the Sioux Problem, 1965. Contbr., encys., histl. publs. & jrnls. TV educl. progs. Hon. Fellow, Univ. of Neb., 1959-60. Address: University of Missouri-Kansas City, Kansas City, MO, U.S.A.

OLSON, Jane Virginia, b. 14 Dec. 1916. Science Editor. Educ: B.A., Univ. of N.M., 1939. Appts: Edit. Asst., Atlantic Monthly, 1942-46; Copy Ed., Vogue, 1946-49; Tech. Ed., Ill. State Geol. Survey, 1949-55; Sci. Ed., Yale Univ. Press, 1958-69; Ed., American Scientist, 1969-. Mbr., League of Women Voters. Address: American Scientist, 345 Whitney Ave., New Haven, CT 06511, U.S.A. 5, 138.

OLSON, Rolf Yngve Hallin, b. 4 Nov. 1934. Educator. Educ: B.A., Univ. of Mont., 1961; M.A., ibid, 1964. Appts: Reporter, Anchorage Daily Times, Alaska, 1961-62; Copy Ed., Idaho Falls Post Register, 1964-65; News Ed., Wallingford Post, Conn., 1965-66; Ed., Assoc. Press, Helena Mont., 1966-67; Mng. Ed., Bozeman Daily Chronicle, ibid, 1967-68; Asst. Prof., Engl. & Communications, Mont. State Univ., 1968-; Dir. & Hd. Instr., Mont. Outdoor Ldrship. Exped. (MOLE), 1970-. Mbrships: Gallatin Sportsmen's Assn.; Am. Qtr. Horse Assn.; Nat. Rifle Assn. Publs: Mont. Outdoors Column, Bozeman Chronicle, Gt. Falls Tribune, etc., 1966-69; Contbr. of articles to other sports jrnls. Recip. of medals & awards. Address: Windy Ridge, W. Yellowstone, MT 59758, U.S.A. 9.

OLUWASANMI, Hezekiah Adedunmola, b. 12 Nov. 1919. University Administrator. Educ: B.A., Morehouse Coll., Ata., Ga., U.S.A., 1951; M.A., Ph.D., Harvard Univ., Cambridge, Mass., 1951-55. Appts: Lectr.-Sr. Lectr., Dept. Agric. Econs., Ibadan Univ., Nigeria, 1955-62; Warden, Mellanby Hall, ibid, 1955-57; Dpty. Master-Master, Sultan Bello, 1958-66; Prof.-Dean, Fac. Agric., Ibadan Univ., 1962-66; V.-Chancellor, Univ. Ife, 1966-; Nat. & int. econ. advsr. & cons. Mbrships: W. Nigeria Econ. Planning Comm., 1961-62; W. Nigeria Econ. Advsry. Coun., 1966-71; Coun., Univ. Ghana; Bd. Govs., Int. Dev. Rsch. Ctr., Ottawa, Canada; Zambia Univ. Grants Comm.; Bd. Trustees, Int. Inst. Tropical Agric., 1971-72; Nigerian Econ. Soc.; Agric. Soc., Nigeria; Int. Assn. Agric. Econs.; Chmn., Comm. V-Chancellors Nigerian Univs.; Assn. C'wealth. Univs. Publs. incl: The Role of Agriculture in Nigerian Economic Development, 1963; Agricultural Education at the University of Ibadan, 1963 (conf. papers); Peasant Farming and Technical Change, 1966 (jrnl. article). Recip. Hon. D.Sc., Univ. of Nigeria, Nsukka,

1971. Address: Univ. Ife Campus, Ile-Ife, Nigeria, W. Africa.

O'MALLEY, Raymond Morgan, b. 15 Aug. 1909. University Lecturer. Educ: Trinity Coll., Cambridge, U.K., 1928-31; London Day Trng. Coll., 1931-32. Appts: Asst. Master, Dartington Hall Schl., 1932-59; Dpty. Headmaster, ibid, 1948-59; Univ. Lectr. in Educ., Cambridge; Fellow, Selwyn Coll., ibid. Mbrships: Inc. Soc. of Authors, Playwrights & Composers; Assn. of Univ. Tchrs. Publs: One-Horse Farm, 1949; Rhyme & Reason, w. Denys Thompson, 1957; English One-English Give, w. Denys Thompson, 1955; The Key of the Kingdom, I-IV, w. Denys Thompson, 1961; Tell, I & II, w. Denys Thompson, 1972; Introducing Chaucer, 1967. Address: 8 Hills Ave., Cambridge CB1 4XA, U.K.

O'MEARA, Sara Elizabeth Buckner (Mrs. Robert E. O'Meara), b. 9 Sept. 1934. Actress (as Sara Buckner). Educ: B.A., Drama, Sorbonne, Paris, France. Mbrships: Fndr. & Chmn. of Bd., Int. Orphans, Inc.; Past Pres., Spastics Children's League, LA., Calif.; Off., Nat. Assistance League; L.A. World Affairs Coun.; Advsry., Mayor of L.A. Coun.; Advsry. Bd., Educl. Films, Inc., Relig. Film Enterprises. Hons. incl: III Amphibians Force, USMC; Award for outstanding assistance rendered to serv. action fund & CARE, USMC Reserve; Award for P.R. between Japan & U.S.A. Japanese Govt.; Cross of Merit, Knightly Order of St. Brigitte; Commendation for work on behalf of children, L.A. City Bd. of Supvsrs.; Postulant, Mil. & Hospitaller Order of St. Lazarus of Jerusalem, 1974. Address: 5425 Shirley Ave., Tarzana, CA 91356, U.S.A. 54, 74, 75.

OMORI, Takeo Kensei, b. 15 Apr. 1910. Business Executive; President of Institute of Hypnotism & Psychology. Educ: B.Engrng., Aeronautical Dept., Fac. Engrng., Tokyo Univ., 1933; Postgrad. studies, Stanford Univ., U.S.A., 1940. Appts: Lt.Col., Japanese Army, 1944; w. Tokyo Kikaika Kogyo Co. Ltd., 1950-; Chmn. of Bd., ibid, 1974-; Pres., Omori Co., Ltd.; Pres., Inst. of Hypnotism & Psychol. Mbrships: Kojunsha; Standing Comm., Japan Rocket Soc.; Pres., Tokyo Tama Rotary Club. Publs: The "Yutto" ism, induction technique, healing, getting well & the "Satori." Recip., Testimonial, All Japan Ski Fedn., 1972. Address: 1-30-34 Chitosedai, Setagaya, Tokyo 157, Japan.

O'NEAL, Jewell, b. 25 Jan. 1928. Bank Executive. Educ: B.A., Jackson State Univ., 1973. Appts. incl: Teller & Bookkeeper, 1st Nat. Bank Ctrl. Br., Helenwood, Tenn., 1953; Asst. Cashier, ibid, 1961-65; Cashier, ibid, 1965; Currently Asst. V.P. & Br. Mgr., ibid. Mbrships: Nat. Assn. Bank Women, Chmn., 1972; Oneida Bus. & Profl. Women's Club, Sec., 1969; Oneida Bank Assn., Pres., 1965; Cancer Fund Drive, Oneida, Chmn., 1965. Hons: Ky. Col., 1970. Address: Route 3, Box 172, Oneida, TN 37841, U.S.A. 125.

O'NEAL, Maston Emmett, Jr., b. 19 July 1907. Attorney at Law. Educ: Marion Mil. Inst., Ala.; Davidson Coll., N.C.; Lamar Schl. of Law, Emory Univ., Ga. Appts: Notary Public & ex officio Justice of the Peace, Decatur Co., Ga., 1934-40; Solicitor Gen., Albany Judicial Circuit of Ga. (Prosecuting Attorney for six Cos.), 1941-65; Rep., Second Congressional Dist. of Ga., U.S. House of Representatives, 1965-70. Mbrships: First Pres., Solicitors General Assn. of Ga.; Former Dir., Nat. Assn. of Co. & Prosecuting Attorney. Address: P.O.

Box 127, Bainbridge, GA 31717, U.S.A. 2, 7, 125.

O'NEAL, Lt. Col. Robert Palmer, b. 20 Sept. 1912. Aeronautical Engineer; Aircraft Maintenance Officer. Educ: A.B., M.A., Occidental Coll., L.A., Calif., 1935, '36; Grad., var. trade & profl. shcls., incl. U.S. Air Force Schl.; Westinghouse Turbo-Jet Schls.; McDonnell Aircraft Corp.; Class A Tchrs. Cert., N.C., 1947. Appts. incl: Rep., Bur. of Aeronautics, Pratt & Whitney Aircraft Corp., 1941-43; w. U.S. Marine Corps, 1944-; Instr., Prin. of Engine Testing, & Asst. to Power Plant Div. Off., 1944-46; Off. i/c, & Instr., Trade Maths., Naval Apprentices Schl., MCAS, Cherry Point, N.C., 1946; Proj. Admnstr. & Plant Engr., 1950-52; Prod. Control Off., 1952; Asst. Prod. Off., 1952-53; K-3 Korea 1st Marine Aircraft Wing (MAW) Projs. & Planning Off., Air Installations Off., Liason Off., K-3 5th Air Force & 8th Army Prod. Engrng. & Aeronaut. Engrng., 1953-54; Staff Duties to Overhaul and Repair, & Overhaul Repair Off., ibid, 1955-56; Instr.,Supvsr., Trng. Prog., 1957; Asst. A/C Maint. Off., Quality Control Off., Dir., Interim Rework, Dir., JATO Installation Prog., 1st MAW, 1958-59; Material & Aircraft Maint. Off., SOES, 1959-62; Aircraft Maint. Off., Mag. 24, 2ns MAW F4B (Phantom II, Mach II), Cherry Point, 1962-67; Flew N. America Defense Missions, Cuba, 1963; Mbr., Atlantic Task Team, F4B, 1962-64; 1st Marine Fighter, A/C Squad., S. Vietnam, 1965; Prod. Off., Japan Aircraft Corp., Atsugi, Japan, Marine Liason Off., CFUP Staff, COMFAIR WEST PAC., 1967-69; Aircraft Maint, Marine Liason Off., CFUP Staff, COMFIR WEST PAC., 1967-69, Aircraft Maintenance Officer, S. Vietnam, MAG-13 121 MAW, 1969-70; currently FM/FLANT, Staff, AWSS, Norfolk, Va. Mbrships. incl: Am. Inst. Aeronaut. & Astronaut.; AAAS; Am. Ordnance Soc.; Am. Chem. Soc.; Soc. of Am. Mil. Engrs. Recip. hons. for aircraft maint. Address: FM FLANT, Staff AWSS, Norfolk, VA 23511, U.S.A. 7, 14, 28, 57.

O'NEIL, Lloyd, b. 17 July 1928. Publisher. Appts: Angus & Robertson Ltd., 1945-51; Cassell & Co. Ltd., 1951-55; Mgr., Jacaranda Pres Pty. Ltd., 1955-60; Fndr. & Mng. Dir., Lansdowne Press Pty. Ltd., 1960-69; Gen. Mgr., F.W. Cheshire Pty. Ltd., 1968-69; Fndr. & Mng. Dir., Lloyd O'Neil Pty. Ltd., 1969-; Assocd. Cos., George Philip & O'Neil Pty. Ltd., John Currey, O'Neil Pty. Ltd., G.C.O. Pty. Ltd., Colorcraft Ltd., Hong Kong. Mbrships: Dpty. Chmn., Nat. Lit. Bd. of Review, 1967-; Past Pres., Australian Book Publishers Assn.; The Savage Club, Melbourne; The Jrnlst.'s Club, Sydney; The Royal S. Yarra Lawn Tennis Club, Melbourne. Address: 337 Auburn Rd., Hawthorn, Vic., Australia 3122. 23.

O'NEIL, Mary Ann, b. 11 May 1906. Teacher & Principal. Educ: B.S., Western III. State Coll., Macomb, III., 1945; M.A., ibid 1954. Appts: Tchr., Liverpool Township Five-Five Rural Schl., 1925-26; Monterey Rura Schl., Banner Township, 1926-36, Univ. of III Ext. Ctr., 1946-47; Bradley Univ. summer & evening Sessions, 1961-72, Spoon River Coll. Canton, III.; Tchr., Evening Div., 1961-67 Canton Union Schl. Dist. 66, 1961-70, Prin. 1936-72. Mbrships: Kappa Delta Pi; Fulton Co Pres. & V.P., Alpha Delta Kappa; Pi Lambda Theta; AAUW; Int. Reading Assn.; Nat. Coun of Engl. Tchrs.; Sec., Western III. Div., 'Prins Assn.; III. Prins. Assn.; Western III. Alumn Assn.; Life Mbr., NEA; Canton Educ. Assn. PTA; III. Educ. Assn. Hons. incl: Fulton Co Tchr. of the Year, 1965; Outstanding Tchng Performance in Maths. & Sci., Grad Tchr. Mag.

1967. Address: 50 West Ash St., Canton, IL 61520, U.S.A. 130.

O'NEILL, Hugh Breffni, b. 5 July 1922. Physician & Osteopath. Educ: St. Thomas' Hosp., London, U.K., 1939-41, '46-51. Appts: House Physn., Casualty Off. & House Surg., Margate Gen. Hosp., Kent, 1951-52; Jr. Registrar, Radiotherapy Det., St. Thomas' Hosp., 1952; Staff Physn., King Edward VII Mem. Hosp., Bermuda, 1953-; Med. Referee, St. Brendan's Hosp., ibid, 1954-61; Locum Res., Univ. of Md. Hosp., Balt., U.S.A., 1955; Locum, Paediatric House Physn., Radcliffe Hosp., Oxford, U.K., 1958; London Coll. Osteopathy, U.K., 1971-72. Mbrships: Bermuda Med. Soc.; Bermuda Br., R.A.F.A. Club; Bermuda War Vets. Assn.; M.R.C.S.; L.R.C.P. Address: Russell Eve Bldg., Church St., Hamilton, Bermuda.

O'NEILL, Luis, b. 12 Oct. 1888. Librarian; Author. Appts. incl: Under Libn., Insular Lib., Puerto Rico, 1912-16; Lib., 1916-19, Dir., 1919-55, Carnegie Lib, ibid; Retired, 1955. Publs: La Biblioteca Publica Moderna; Arca de Recuerdos (Poems); Eugenio Maria de Hostos (Biog.); Ed., "Patria", "Los Catorce", etc. Mbrships: Pres., Puerto Rico Inter Am. Assn.; Puerto Rico Lib. Assn. Address: 123 O'Neill St., Hato Rey, Puerto Rico 00918 7, 10.

ONG, (Rev.) Walter Jackson, S.J., b. 30 Nov. 1912. Clergyman; Professor of English; Professor of Humanities in Psychiatry. Educ: B.A., Rockhurst Coll., 1933; M.A., St. Louis Univ., 1941; S.T.L., ibid, 1948; Ph.D., Harvard Univ., 1955. Appts: Entered S.J., 1935, Ordained Priest, 1946; Instr., Engl., Regis Coll., 1941-43; Instr., Engl.-Assoc. Prof., St. Louis Univ., 1953-59; Prof., Engl., 1960-; Prof., Humanities in Psych., ibid, 1970-. Mbrships: Nat. Coun. on Humanities; White House Task Force on Educ., 1971-73; Advsry. Bd., Guggenheim Mem. Fndn.; Bd. Mbr., Nat. Humanities Fac.; Seminar Ldr., Ctr. for Study of Democratic Instns., Aspen Inst. for Humanistic Studies, & others; Fellow, Am. Acad. of Arts & Scis. Am. Renaissance Soc.; MLA; Cambridge Bibliog. Soc., U.K. Publs. incl: Frontiers in American Catholicism, 1957; Ramus, Method & the Decay of Dialogue, 1958; American Catholic Crossroads, 1959; The Barbarian Within, 1962; In the Human Grain, 967; Rhetoric, Romance & Technology, 1971. Ed., var. works, & contbr. to jrnls. Hons. incl: Chevalier, Ordre des Palmes Académiques, France; Chmn., Nat. Selection Comm., Fulbright Prog., Study in France. Address: St. Louis Univ.,St. Louis, MO 63103, U.S.A. 2, 3, 8, 13, 15, 49, 128.

O'NIANS, Henry Melmoth, b. 8 May 1923. Art Gallery Proprietor. Educ: Royal Mil. Coll., Sandhurst; B.A., Trinity Coll., Oxford. Proprietor, Hal O'Nians Gall. Exhibs: Old Master Drawings, 1963, '64, '65 (2 exhibs.), '66, '67; Dutch, Flemish & Italian Old Master Paintings, 1963; 17th Century Dutch Marine Paintings, 1964, '65; Old Master Paintings, 1967, 1967-68, 1968, '69, '72, '73. Mbrships: Army & Navy Club; Trinity Coll. Soc. Address: 6 Ryder St., St. James's, London SW1Y 6QB, U.K. 133.

ONIANS, Richard Broxton, b. 11 Jan. 1899. Scholar; Researcher; Writer. Educ: B.A., M.A., Liverpool Univ., U.K.; Ph.D., Trinity Coll., Cambridge. Appts: Lectr., Latin, Liverpool Univ., 1925-33; Prof. of Classics, Univ. of Wales, Swansea, 1933-35; Hildred Carlile Prof. of Latin, Univ. of London, 1936-66; Emeritus Prof., ibid, 1966-. Mbrships: Coun., Assn. of Univ. Tchrs., 1945-53; Exec.

Comm., ibid, 1946-51; Chmn., London Consultative Comm., ibid, 1946-48; Chmn., Nat. Campaign Comm. for Expansion of Higher Educ., 1948-53; Chmn., Jt. Standing Comm. & Conf. on Library Coop., 1948-60; Exec. Comm. & Finance Comm., Nat. Ctrl. Lib., 1947-53. Publs. incl: The Origins of European Thought about the Body, the Mind, the Soul, the World, Time, & Fate: New Interpretations of Greek, Roman & kindred evidence, also of some basic Jewish & Christian Beliefs, 1951, enlarged edit., 1954; Contbr. to classical jrnls. Hons: Oration Prize, Trinity Coll., Cambridge, 1924; Hare Prize, Univ. of Cambridge, 1926. Address: Stokesay, 21 Luard Rd., Cambridge CB2 2PJ, U.K. 1.

ONICESCU, Doina, b. 31 Mar. 1926. Medical Doctor. Educ: Fac. of Med., Bucharest, Romania. Appts: Assoc. Prof., Docent, Dept. of Histol., Fac. of Med., Bucharest. Mbrships: Gen. Sec., Romanian Soc. of Histochem. & Cytochem.; Gen. Sec., 5th Int. Cong. of Histochem. & Cytochem., Bucharest, 1976; Assn. of Anatomists, France; Soc. of Psychoneuroendocrinol ; Int. Grp., Scientific Rsch. on Stomatology. Contbr. to profl. jrnls. Address: Fac. of Med., Dept. of Histol., Bul. Dr. Petru Groza 8, Bucharest, Romania.

ONICESCU, Octav, b. 20 Aug. 1892. Professor. Educ: Univ. of Bucharest, 1914; Doct., Rome, Italy, 1920. Appts: Prof., Coll. Manastirea Dealu, 1914-22; Prof., Univ. of Bucharest, 1922-62; Dir., Inst. of Stats., Actuariat & Calculus, ibid, 1932-42; Rector, Int. Ctr. of Mech. Scis., Udine, Italy, 1968-. Mbrships. incl: Acad. R.S. Romaine; Pres., Soc. Romana de Stüute, 1938-42. Publs. incl: Principes de Logique & de Philosophie Mathématique, 1971; Mécanique Statistique, 1971. Recip., Prize of the State for gen. activity, 1969. Address: Strada Soimarestilor 9, Bucharest V1, Romania.

ONOKPASA, Benedict Etedjere, b. 21 June 1928. Teacher. Educ: St. Thomas Coll., Ibusa, 1947-49; Forest Schl., Ibadan, 1951-52; Fourah Bay Coll. (Univ. of Durham), Freetown, 1954-57; B.A., Univ. of Durham, 1957. Appts. incl: Forest Asst., 1952-54; Administrative Off. (Asst. Sec.), Min. of Finance, 1958; Geog. Tchr., Loyola Coll. & Ibadan City Acad., 1959-61; Econs. Tchr., Urhobo Coll., Effurun, 1962-63; Fndr., Trinity Coll., Okwidieuw, 1964; Prin., ibid, 1964-72; currently working on an Agricl. proj. to be registered as a co. Mbrships: Fndr./Pres., African Dramatic Soc., 1962; Sec., Urhobo Orthography Comm., 1963; Fndr., Onokpasa-Akemu Schlrship. Scheme, 1966-72; NCNC Pty., 1962-66. Publs: Modern Urhobo Readers, Books I-IV; Urhobo Poems, 1962; The Hero Of Sharpville, 1962. Hons: Botany Prize, Forest Schl., Ibadan, 1952. Address: Trinity Cottage, P.O. Box 27, Adeje, via Warri, Nigeria. 135.

ONWUMECHILI, Cyril Agodi, b. 20 Jan. 1932. University Professor. Educ: B.Sc., 1953, B.Sc. (Special in Phys.), 1954, Univ. Coll., Ibadan, Nigeria; Ph.D. (London), 1958; Dipl., Univ. of Chgo., 1960; F. Inst. P. (Britain), 1969. Appts: Lectr Grades, Univ. Coll., Ibadan, 1958-62; Prof., Phys.-Dean, Fac. of Sci., Univ. of Ibadan, 1962-66; Director of Observs. at: Ibadan, 1960-66, Zaria, 1960-63, Kontagora, 1962-66, Sokoto, 1966; Prof., Hd. Dept., Univ. of Nigeria, Nsukka, 1966-; Dean, Fac. of Scis., ibid, 1970-71; Dean, Fac. of Phys. Scis., 1973-; Vis. Prof., Geophys., Univ. of Alaska, U.S.A. 1971-72; Cons., Inst. Space Rsch., Sao Jose dos Campos, Nat. Rsch. Coun. of Brazil. Mbrships. incl: Rep. of Africa, Int. Comm. for Int. Yrs. of Quiet Sun, 1963-67 (ICSU); Comm. Co-Chmn.,

Int. Assn. Geomagnetism & Aeronomy, 1973-;
C'wealth Consultative Comm. on Space Rsch.,
1963-66; Am. Geophysical Union, Treas., W.
African Sci. Assn., 1961-65; Chmn., Nigerian
Nat. Comm., Int. Union of Geodesy &
Geophys., 1963-70. 1st Ed.-in-Chief, Nigerian
Jrnl. Sci., 1965-67; Contbr. to num. sci. publs.
Fndn. Fellow, Sci. Assn. of Nigeria, 1974.
Address: Dept. of Physics., Univ. of Nigeria,
Nsukka, Nigeria. 55, 135.

OOI ENG HONG, b. 10 Sept. 1918.
Executive Secretary. Educ: Sultan Abdul
Hamid Coll.; Assoc., Chartered Inst. of Secs.,
U.K.; Fellow, British Assn. of Accts. &
Auditors; Fellow, Soc. of Commercial Accts.;
Fellow, British Soc. of Commerce; Mbr., Inc.
Assn. of Cost & Indl. Acct.; Assoc., Inst. of
Commercial & Indl. Mgrs.; Fellow, Malaysian
Soc. of Inc. Accts. Appts. incl: Acct., United
Transport Co., Sdn. Berhad, 1947-65; Exec.
Sec., ibid, 1965-; J.P., Kedah, 1967; Pres.,
Malaysian Chinese Assn., Alor Setar Div. &
Kampong Ward Br., Alor Setar; Chmn., Bd. of
Dirs., Kuala Kedah Transport Co., Sdn. Berhad;
Chmn., Bd. of Govs., St. Michael Secondary
Schl. & St. Nicholas Convent Schl., Alor Setar;
Chmn., Bd. of, Mgrs., St. Michael Primary Schl.,
ibid; Dir., Oriental Marines Inds., Sdn. Berhad,
Trio Paper Mill, Alor Setar Transport & Trading
Co., Perlis Transport Co. & Bas Bandaran Alor
Setar. Mbrships. incl: Univ. of Malaya Ct.,
Penang Port Commn. Consultative Comm., Bd.
of Govs., Sultan Abdul Hamid Coll. & Keat
Hwa Middle Schl., Alor Setar; Bd. of Mgrs.,
Sekolah Menengah Telok Chengai, Iskandar
Schl. & Long Chuan Chinese Schl., Alor Setar.
Hons. incl: Kedah Installation Medal, 1960;
Kedah Meritorious Serv. Decoration Medal,
1965; Malaysian Commemorative Medal, 1965;
Pingat Pangkuan Negara, 1968; Setia Mahkota
Kedah, 1971. Address: 6-A Lorong Patani, Alor
Setar, Kedah, Malaysia.

OOLIE, Samuel Alan, b. 11 Aug. 1936.
Food Service Company Executive. Educ: B.S.
Metallurgy, MIT, 1958; M.B.A., Harvard Bus.
Schl., 1961. Appts: V.P., Drinx Plus Co. Inc.,
Rutherford, N.J., 1962-68; Pres., ibid, 1968-;
Pres., Food Concepts Inc., Rutherford, 1972-;
Exec. V.P., fnt pies inc., ibid, 1972-. Mbrships:
Harvard Bus. Club of N.J. (Past Pres. & Dir.);
Young President's Org.; Automatic Merchandise
Coun. of N.J. Address: 50 Green Pl., North
Caldwell, NJ 07006, U.S.A. 6.

OOSTBURG, Baltus Franklin Julius, b. 20
Aug. 1928. Medical Doctor. Educ: Dip. as Asst.
Tchr., Paramaribo, Surinam, 1944; M;D., M.Sc.,
Med. Schl., ibid, 1945-53; Schl. of Pub. Hlth. &
Administrative Med., Columbia Univ., U.S.A.,
1962-63. Appts. incl: Chief, Div. of
Helminthol. & Med. Serv. of Interior, Bur. of
Pub. Hlth., Surinam, 1960-62, 1963-64; Med.
Advsr., Brokopondo Bur., ibid, 1964-67; Min.
of Hlth., 1967-69; Lectr. in Parasitol., Fac. of
Med., Univ. of Surinam, 1969-; Dpty. Dir., Bur.
of Pub. Hlth., 1969-73; Dir., ibid, 1973-.
Mbrships. incl: Treas., Surinam Med. Assn.;
Sec., Fac. of Med.; Am. Soc. of Tropical Med.
& Hygiene; Netherlands Assn. for Tropical
Med.; Nat. Commnr. for Trng., Boy Scouts of
Surinam; Pres., Surinam Olympic Comm.
Contbr. to med. jrnls. Hons: Silver Jacob's Rod,
Boy Scouts Assn. of Netherlands, 1966.
Address: Bureau of Public Hlth, P.O. Box 487,
Paramaribo, Surinam. 109, 136.

OPARIN, Alexander, b. 2 Mar. 1894.
Biochemist. Educ: Grad., Moscow Univ., 1917;
grad. prog. course, ibid, 1917-21. Appts. incl:
Tchr., Dept. Plant Pathol., Moscow Univ.,
1921-25, Asst. Prof., 1925-27; Prof., Dept.
Indl. Biochem., Mendeleew Inst. Chem.

Technol., Moscow, 1929-31; Dpty. Dir., Inst. of
Biochem., Acad. Sci. U.S.S.R., 1935-46, Hd.
Dept. Plant Biochem., 1942-60, Dir., A.N. Bach
Inst. of Biochem., 1946-; Prof., Moscow Inst.
for Food Technol., 1937-49. Mbr. & Off., var.
profl. orgs. Publs. incl: The Origin of life on he
Earth, 1938. 3rd edit., 1957; Life, its Nature,
Origin & Development, 1961; The Chemical
Origin of Life, 1964, Genesis & Evolutionary
Development of Life, 1968. Hons. incl: Order
of Cyril & Methodius, Bulgaria, 1972; Medal,
Supreme Coun. Sci. Rsch., Spain, 1973; Lenin
Prize, 1974; 5 Orders of Linin. Address:
Leninsky pr. 33, Moscow, U.S.S.R. 1.

OPPENHEIMER, John F., b. 13 Nov. 1903.
Editor. Educ: Hochschule fuer Politik, Berlin.
Appts: Mbr., Exec. Br., Centralverein deutscher
Staatsbuerger juedischen Glaubens, Darmstadt,
Frankfurt, Stettin & Berlin, 1924-29 & 35-38;
Hd., Lit. Promotion, Ullstein & Propyläen
Publng. House, Berlin, 1930-33; Hd., Book
Distribution Dept., ibid, 1934-35; Ptnr.-Pres.,
Wallenberg & Wallenberg, Inc., N.Y., 1940.
Publs: Contbr. articles on theatre & Jewish
affairs to newspapers & mags., 1921-38; Lit.
Ed., C.-V.-Zeitung, Berlin; Originator & Co-Ed.,
Philo-Lexikon, Handbuch des juedischen
Wissens, 1934, 37; Ed., Philos-Atlas, Handbuch
fuer die juedische Auswanderung, 1938; Ed. for
Mod. Biog., Universal Jewish Encyclopedia, 10
vols., 1938-42; Ed.-in-Chief, Lexikon des
Judentums, 1967, 70. Address: 36-35 193rd
St., Flushing, NY 11358, U.S.A. 55.

OPPENHEIMER, Max, Jr., b. 27 July 1917.
University Professor. Appts. incl: Lt. Col.,
GS12, U.S. Army; Intelligence & Ctrl.
Intelligence Agcy., 1951-56, 1956-58; Assoc.
Prof., Fla. State Univ., 1958-61; Prof., Chmn.,
Univ. of Iowa, 1961-67; Prof., Chmn., SUNY
Coll. at Fredonia, 1967-73; Prof., ibid, 1973-.
Publs. incl: Outline of Russian Grammar, 1962;
Theory of Molecular Excitons (trans. from
Russian), 1962; Theory of Ship Waves & Wave
Resistance (trans. from Russian), 1968.
Authors of num. articles & review on Russian &
Mod. Langs. Recip., SUNY Rsch. Award, 1973.
Address: 10 Lowell Pl., Fredonia, NY 14063,
U.S.A. 2, 13, 15.

OPSTAD, Steinar, b. 20 May 1941.
Information Executive. Educ: Grad. in
Pedagogics, Sociol., & P.R. Appts: Journalist;
Editor; Chief Editor; Tchr., Jrnlsm. & Sociol.;
Mng. Chief, Info. Dept.; Pvte. Pedagogical
Advsr. Mbrships: Norwegian P.R. Assn.; Bd.
Mbr., Periodical Press Eds. Assn.; Norwegian
Polytech. Assn. Publs: Pleie Vårt Rykte, 1967;
Informasion i Praksis, 1971. Contbr., profl. &
trade jrnls. Address: Selvbyggerveien 163,
N-Oslo 5, Norway.

ORATA, Pedro T., b. 27 Feb. 1899. Retired
Educator. Educ: B.S. (Educ.), Univ. of Ill.,
1924; M.S. (Educ.), ibid, 1925; Grad. work,
educl. psychol., Univ. of Chgo., 1925, Tchrs.
Coll., N.Y., 1926; Ph.D., Ohio State Univ.,
1927. Appts. incl: Div. Supt. Schls., Isabela &
Sorsogon, 1930-33; Instr., Coll. of Educ., Ohio
State Univ., 1934-36; Curr. Cons. for Sioux
Indians, Kyle, S.D. for U.S. Off. of Indian
Affairs, Dept. of Interior, 1936-37; Tech. Asst.,
U.S. Off. Educ., Wash., D.C., 1938-39; Special
Cons., ibid, 1939-41; Tech. Asst., Nat. Coun.
Educ., Philippines, 1941-43, '46-47; Tech.
Asst.-Acting Exec. Off., Nat. Commn. of Educl.
Sci. & Cultural Matters, 1947-48; Sec. &
Chmn., Bd. Cons., Jt. Congressional Comm. on
Educ., 1948, Prog. Specialist, Tchr. Trng. &
Curr. Dev., UNESCO, 1948-60; Dean, Grad.
Schl. & Dir. Curr. Dev., Philippine Normal
Coll., 1960-65, Dean Emeritus, ibid, 1965;
Lectr., Univs. throughout Australia, 1969.

Mbrships: Am. Educ. Rsch. Assn.; Soc. for Advancement of Educ.; Nat. Soc. for Study of Educ.; John Dewey Soc.; Southeast Asia Inst.; Philippine Soc. for Curr. Dev.; Philippine Assn. of Grad. Educ.; Kappa Delta Pi; Pi Mu Epsilon; Sigma Delta Sigma; Phi Kappa Phi; Kappa Phi Kappa; Phi Delta Kappa. Has been responsible for num. educ. innovations, inclng. dev. of community schl. concept on Indian Reservation in U.S.A., as well as in the Philippines. Recip. of hons. for servs. to educ. Address: Barrio High School, Preschool & Community Coll. Office, Urdaneta, Pangasinan, Philippines. 15, 101, 129, 131, 139, 141.

ORCHARD, Dennis Frank, b. 21 May 1912. Chartered Civil Engineer. Educ: B.Sc., Ph.D., D.I.C., Imperial Coll., London, U.K., 1933-37. Appts: Min. of Works, U.K., 1939-46; Rd. Rsch. Lab., 1946-50; Harlow (New Town) Dev. Corp., 1950-54; Acting Engr. in Chief, firm of cons. engrs. to Ghana Govt., 1954-57; Fndn. Prof., Hwy. Engrng., Univ. of N.S.W., Australia, 1957-; Cons., U.N., 1966-67. Mbrships: Instn. of Civil Engrs.; Instn. of Structural Engrs.; Instn. of Municipal Engrs.; Fellow, Instn. of Engrs., Australia; Fellow, Inst. of Transport; Chmn., 2 comms., Standards Inst. of Australia; Rd. Pavements Comm., Australian Rd. Rsch. Bd. Publs: Concrete Technology, Vol. I, Properties of Materials, Vol. II, Practice; num. papers publd. by profl. bodies. Hons: Telford Prize, Miller Prize, James Forest Medal, Instn. of Civil Engrs.; Richard Pickering Prize & Gold Medal, Rees Jeffreys Prize, Inst. of Municipal Engrs.; Sanford E. Thompson Award, Am. Soc. for Testing & Mats. Address: Univ. of N.S.W., P.O. Box 1, Kensington, N.S.W., Australia. 3, 23, 128.

ORDJANIAN, Nikit, b. 22 Feb. 1918. Engineering Executive. Educ: B.E., Pribram Schl. of Mines, Czechoslavakia, 1938; M.M.E., Freiberg Bergakademie, Germany, 1941; Dr.Sc., ibid, 1944. Appts: Asst. to Pres., Mining & Ind. Dev. Co., N.Y.C., 1947-50; Pres., Columbia Tech. Corp., N.Y.C., 1950-. Mbrships: Am. Inst. Mining Engrs.; Y.Y. Athletic Club. Tech. papers, German & U.S. profl. mags. Address: 71-49 170 St., Fresh Meadows, NY 11365, U.S.A. 6, 14.

ORDOÑEZ, Georges, b. 20 Mar. 1907. Mining Engineer; Geologist. Educ: Engr. of Mines degree, Colo. Schl. of Mines, Golden, Colo., 1929. Appts. incl: Pvte. prac. as Cons. Geologist, Mexico, D.F., 1941-44; Field Engr., Kennecott Copper Corp., Silver City, N.M., 1944-50; Asst. Chief Geologist, Kennecott Copper Corp., N.Y.C., 1951-52; Chief Geologist, ibid, 1952-54; Mgr., Cia. Minera Kenmex, S.A. Mexico, D.F., 1954-61; Cons. Geologist, Mexico, D.F., 1961-; Prof., Econ. Geol., Univ. of Mexico, D.F., 1960-62; Dir., Minas de San Luis, S.A., Minera Frisco, S.A. Mbrships. incl: Pres., Mexico Sect., Am. Inst. of Mining, Metallurgical & Petroleum Engrs., 1956-57; Geological Soc. of Am.; V.P., Soc. of Econ. Geologists, 1967; Coun. mbr., ibid, 1967-68; Soc. Geologica Mexicana. Author of publs. in field. Recip., Disting. Achievement Medal, Colo. Schl. of Mines, 1964. Address: Sierra Gorda 54, Mexico 10, D.F. Mexico.

ORFORD, Herman Eglon, b. 20 July 1890. Stock Clerk; Department Storekeeper. Appts: Postal Dept., Diamond & Gold; Prospector, Sea Defence, Casting Concrete Pilings; w. Demerara Bauxite Co. Ltd., 28 yrs.; Ret'd., 1950. Mbrships: Churhmen's Union Cricket; Asst. Sec., MacKenzie Sports; Cath. Guild Club; YMCA; Red Triangle. Address: 11-11 Durban st., Workmanville, Georgetown, Guyana, S. America.

ORGLAND, Ivar, b. 13 Oct. 1921. University Lecturer; Author. Educ: Grad., Educ., Dept. of Educ., 1947; Master, Univ. of Oslo, 1949; Doct., Univ. of Iceland, 1969. Appts. incl: Lectr., Univ. of Iceland, 1952-60; Univ. of Lund, Sweden, 1962-69, Oslo Coll. of Educ., 1969-73, Univ. of Oslo, 1973-. Mbrships. incl: P.E.N. Club; Norwegian Assn. of Authors & Assn. of Translators; Norwegian, Icelandic & Swedish Tourist Assns. Publs: many boks of poetry, 1950-73; Stefán frá Hvítadal (biography), 1962; Nyare nynorsk lyrikk (ed. anthol.), 1969; anthols. w. translations, 20 c. Icelandic poets, Davío Stefánsson, Stefán frá Hvítada, Tómas Guomundsson, Steinn Steinarr, Hannes Pétursson, Jóhannes úr Kötlum, Snorri Hjartarson, Jón úr Vör. Recip., Order of Falcon, Iceland, 1955 & other awards. Address: Lerkevegen 27, 1370 Asker, Norway.

ORIO, Francisco Frederico, Jr., b. 8 Apr. 1921. Agriculturist. Educ: Imperial Coll., Tropical Agric., Trinidad, W. Indies; Ohio State Univ., U.S.A. Appts: Farm Demonstrator & Agricl. Off., Civil Serv.; Cultivation Mgr., Belize Sugar Inds. Ltd.; Agricl. Supt., ibid. Mbrships: Past Pres., Belize Cattle Raisers' Assn. & Orange Walk Rotary Club. Hons: St. John Medal, Serving Brother, 1971; MBE, 1973. Address: Belize Sugar Inds. Ltd., P.O. Box 52, Belize City, Belize, Ctrl. Am.

ORLICH, Margaret Roberta Carlson, (Mrs. Eli Orlich), b. 27 Feb. 1917. Educator & Speaker. Educ: B.S., M.A., Univ. of Minn. Appts: H.S. Prin., 1941-5; Supervising Tchr., Univ. of Minn., Duluth; Tchr., Govt. & Economics, 1955-73; Professional Speaker, 1960-73. Mbrships. incl: Nat. Coun. of Women; Coun., Nat. Pres. of Women's Clubs; Am. Acad. of Pol. & Soc. Sci.; Alpha Delta Kappa; Exec. Bd., ibid, 1967-75; Int. Grand Pres., ibid, 1971-73; Int. Fedn., Bus. & Profl. Women's Clubs, Inc.; var. offs., ibid; Int. Assn. Univ. Women; Bd. Dirs., ibid; U.N. Assn; Fndr., Head of Lakes Chapt., ibid, 1962. Publs. incl: Ed., Glimpses of the Orient, 1970; Ed., Stop Drinking & Driving; UNESCO Around the World; Newsletters, U.N. Assn., Alpha Delta Kappa, Bus. & Profl. Women's Clubs; num. articles & TV appearances. Hons. incl: Nat. Award, U.N. Assn., 1965; Disting Serv. Awards, Mayor of Duluth, Minn., Civic Serv., 1967, 1969; Nat. U.N. Fellowship Award, Nat. Fedn. Bus. & Profl. Women's Clubs, 1970. Address: 421 Anderson Rd., Duluth, MN 55811, U.S.A. 57.

ORME, William John, b. 26 Jan. 1935. Solicitor. Educ: St. Paul's Coll., Sydney Univ., Australia. Appts: Ptnr., Smithers, Warren & Tobias, Solicitors; Chmn., Dirs., Dier Computer Corp. Ltd.; Chmn., Dirs., Nixdorf Computer Pty. Ltd. Mbrships: Solicitors Admission Bd.; Australian Soc. Accts.; Pres., Australia Jr. Chmbr. of Comm., 1967; Exec. V.P., Jr. Chmbr. Int., 1969; Dir., Young Mens Christian Assn., Sydney; Tattersalls, Sydney. Address: Smithers, Warren & Tobias, 175 Castlereagh St., Sydney, Australia. 23, 128.

ORMEROD, (Major Sir) (Cyril) Berkeley, b. 3 Oct. 1897. Public Relations Director (Retired). Educ: Royal Mil. Acad., Woolwich, 1915-16. Appts. incl: Active army serv., 1917-18; promoted Major, 1918; invalided, 1926; Foster & Braithwaite, London Stock Exchange, 1928-39; Dir. P.R., British Press Serv., British Info. Servs., Wash. D.C. & N.Y., U.S.A., 1940-62; U.K. Deleg., U.N. Conf., San Francisco, 1945; Press Advsr. to Royal Party, U.S. visit of H.M. The Queen & H.R.H. Prince Philip, 1957; Retired 1962. Mbrships. incl: Royal Inst. of Internal Affairs; Cavalry Club;

Travellers Club, Paris; Knickerbocker Club, N.Y. Author of Dow Theory Applied to the London Stock Exchange, 1938. Hons: K.B.E.; Fellow, British Inst. P.R.; Life Mbr., Assn. of Radio & TV News Analysts (U.S.A.). Address: Sigrist House, P.O. Box N. 969, Nassau, Bahamas. 1.

ORMS, Betty Jane, b. 9 July 1921. Librarian. Educ: B.S. Art Educ., Ind. Univ., 1944; M.Ed. Art Educ., Pa. State Univ., 1952; M. Lib. Sci. & Info. Sci., Univ. of Pitts., Pa., 1965; Adv. Cert. Lib. Sci., ibid, 1970. Appts: Art Supvsr., Ferndale Schl. Dist., 1944-52. Employed Greater Johnstown Schl. Dist., Pa. as Art Instr., 1952-66, Libn. 1966-68, Ctrlized, Processor of Libs. 1968-73, Elementary Lib. Coord. 1973-. Mbrships. incl: Community Concerts; United Fund Campaigns; YWCA (Bd. of Dirs. 1949-53); NEA; Pa. State Educ. Assn.; Nat. Art Educ. Assn.; Pa. Art Educ. Assn. (Sec. 1949-59); Allied Artists of Johnstown; Beta Sigma Phi; Beta Phi Mu; Delta Kappa Gamma. Works incl: Unity of Churches (Oil Painting); Sunlit Alley (Water Colour). Hons. incl: Awards from Allied Artists of Johnstown: First Oil 1947, First Black & White 1948, Best of Show 1949, First Watercolor 1952. Address: 1096 Edson Ave., Johnstown, PA 15905, U.S.A. 5, 6, 138.

ORR, David Alexander, b. 10 May 1922. Corporation Executive. Educ: Arts, Law degs., Trinity Coll., Dublin. Appts: Unilever Ltd., 1948-; Mgmt. Trainee, 1948; Prod. Mgr., Gen. Advt. Mgr., Lever Brothers Ltd., London, 1950-55; Marketing Dir., Vice Chmn., Hindustan Lever Ltd., Bombay, 1955-60; Overseas Comm., Unilever Ltd., London, 1960-63; V.P., Pres., Lever Brothers Co., N.Y., 1963-67; Bd. of Dirs., Unilever Ltd. & Unilever NV.; Detergents Coord., 1967-70; Vice Chmn., Unilever Ltd., 1970-. Mbrships: V.P., Liverpool Schl. of Tropical Med.; Jt. Co-chmn., Netherlands Brit. Chmbr. of Comm.; Trustee, Leverhulme Trust; Fellow, Brit. Inst. of Mgmt.; Trustee, Ctr. for Southern African Studies, York Univ.; Lansdowne Club, London. Hons: M.C. & Bar., WWII. Address: Unilever House, Blackfriars, London, EC4P 4BQ, U.K.

ORR, Joella Allen. Public Library Director. Educ: B.S., Tex. Womans Univ., Denton, 1960; M.L.S., ibid, 1964. Appts: Libn., Lewisville Independent Schl. Dist., 1960-67; Cataloguer, Main Lib., Tex. Womans Univ., 1967-69; Dir., Denton Pub. Lib., Tex., 1969-. Mbrships: Tex. Lib. Assn. (Chmn. Dist. 7, 1972-74); Pub. Lib. Assn. N. Tex. (Pres. 1970-72); N. Ctrl. Tex. Film Coop. (Bd. of Dirs. 1970-72); DAR (Libn. Benjamin Lyon Chapt.); ALA; Pub. Lib. Admnstrs. N. Tex.; Tex. Municipal League; Southwestern Lib. Assn.; Bd. of Dirs., Denton Co. Hlth. Planning Coun. Address: 1509 Kendolph Drive, Denton, TX 76201, U.S.A. 5.

ORR, Robin (Robert Kemsley), b. 2 June 1909. Musician. Educ: Royal Coll. of Music, U.K.; M.A., Mus.D., Cambridge Univ. Appts. incl: Asst. Lectr., Leeds Univ., 1936-38; Organist, St. John's Coll., Cambridge, 1938-51, Fellow, 1948-56; Univ. Lectr., Cambridge, 1947-56; Prof., Royal Coll. of Music, 1950-56; Prof., Music, Glasgow Univ., 1956-65; Prof., Music, Cambridge, & Fellow, St. John's Coll., 1965-; Chmn., Scottish Opera, 1962-; Dir., Arts Theatre, Cambridge. Mbrships. incl: Composers' Guild of Gt. Britain; Inc. Soc. of Musicians; Chmn., Cambridge Univ. Opera Soc., 1967-74. Compsoitions incl: Festival Te Deum, 1950; Oedipus at Colonus, 1950; Spring Cantata, 1955; Symphony in One Movement, 1963; Full Circle (Opera), 1967; Journeys & Places, 1971; chamber music, songs, ch. music, etc. Hons:

CBE, 1972; D.Mus., Glasgow, 1972; FRCM, 1965; Hon. R.A.M., 1966; Organ Schol., Pembroke Coll., Cambridge, 1929-32. Address: c/o Univ. Music Schl., Cambridge, U.K. 1, 4, 21, 35, 43, 128, 139.

ORR, Wendell Eugene, b. 23 July 1930. Bass Singer; Opera & Choral Conductor; Educator. Educ: B.S., Lawrence Coll., 1952; B.Mus., Lawrence Coll., Conservatory, 1955; M.Mus., Univ. of Mich., 1957; Pvte. study, Rome, Italy, 1961-62, Edinburgh Int. Festival, U.K., 1961, London, 1967, Blossom Festival Schl., 1970, Studies w. Chase Baromeo, Giovanni Manurita, Josef Blatt, Pierre Bernac, Hilde Beal, Eugene Bossart, Burton Garlinghouse. Appts: Instr., Music, Wis. State Coll., 1958-63; Instr., Music, & Dir., Opera Theatre, Kan. State Tchrs. Coll., 1963-64; Asst. Prof., Music, Dir., Opera Workshop, & Dir., Newhampshiremen male chorus, Univ. of N.H., 1964-69; Asst. Prof., Music, Dir., Youngstown State Univ. Men's Chorus, Dana Schl. of Music, Youngstown State Univ., 1969-; Dir. of Music, 1st Christian Ch., Youngstown, Ohio, 1969-. Mbrships: Nat. Assn. of Tchrs. of Singing; Ctrl. Opera Serv.; Am. Choral Dirs. Assn.; Ohio Educ. Assn.; Nat. Trust for Historic Preservation; Pi Kappa Lambda. Appearances as soloist & conductor in opera, oratorio, recital, & on radio & TV on E. Coast & in Midwest areas of U.S.A. Address: 109 Elmland Dr., Poland, OH 44514, U.S.A. 15, 57, 126, 131.

ORR, William Newton, b. 18 Dec. 1908. Dentist. Educ: D.D.S., Tex. Dental Coll., 1930. Appts: Pvte. Prac., Littlefield, Tex., 1930-67; Houston Dental Pub. Hlth., Tex., 1968-; Dir., Model C Cities Dept., 1971-. Mbrships. incl: Charter Mbr., S. Plains Dental Soc., 1932; Pres. ibid, 1945; Tex. Dental Assn.; Alternate, ibid, 1940; Deleg., ibid, 1941; V.P., ibid, 1960-61; Fellow, Am. Coll. of Dentists, 1961; Tex. Coll. of Dentistry Alumni Assn.; Pres., ibid, 1967-68; Meth Ch.; Bd. of Trustees, ibid, 30 yrs.; Sunday Schl. Supt., ibid, 5 yrs.; Chmn., Finance Comm., ibid, Mason. Served on var. Comms., Boy Scouts of Am., 19 yrs.; Rotary Club; Chmn., Youth Comm., ibid, 16 yrs.; V.P. & Program Chmn., ibid, 1965; Pres., ibid, 1966. Hons: Citizen of the Year, Littlefield, Tex., 1965. Address: 10118 Holly Springs, Houston, TX 77042, U.S.A. 7.

ORT, Paul Lanning, b. 31 May 1917. Real Estate Counselor & Appraiser. Educ: grad., Jordan Engrng. Schl., 1938. Appts: w. Thomas Motors, Hackettstown, N.J., 1938-40; William G. Vey & Sons, 1940-42; Proprietor, Paul L. Ort, Hackettstown, 1945. Mbrships. incl: Chmn., Hackettstown Parking Authority, 1956-; Past Chmn., Juvenile Conf. Commn., Hackettstown; Past Pres., 1st. Aid & Rescue Squad; Past Chmn., Hackettstown Zoning Bd. of Adjustment, Hackettstown Planning Bd.; Bd. Dirs., Retarded Children Assn., Warren Co. Unit.; Nat. Inst. Real Estate Brokers (dist. rep.); Nat. Assn. Real Estate Appraisers; Past Pres., Warren Co. Bd. Realtors; Past V.P., N.J. Assn. Real Estate Bds.; Past Cmdr., Vets. For Wars; Chmn., Advsry. Bd., Nat. Community Bank of N.J., Hackettstown Off.; Past Dir., N.J. Presby. Homes. Hons: Ph.D., Hamilton State Univ.; Community Serv. Award, Warren Co. Realtors, 1970. Address: 410 Moore St., Hackettstown, NJ 07840, U.S.A. 6, 16, 22, 128, 130, 131.

ORTEGA ALVAREZ, Elpidio Jose Francisco, b. 28 Apr. 1930. Civil Engineer; Archaeologist. Educ: Qualification as Civil Engr., Universidad Autonoma of Santo Domingo, 1957; Techniques of Archaeol., I.V.I.C., Caracas, Venezuela, 1963. Appts. incl: Construction Engr., Min. of Works, Dominican

Repub., 1957-60, Road Engr., 1960-65, Engr. i/c. Stats. Sect., 1966-67; Supvsr., Tavera Dam construction, 1968-71; Supvsr., construction of Museo del Hombre Dominicano, 1971-73. Mbrships. incl: Dominican Assn. of Anthropol.; Caribbean Assn. of Anthropol.; Dominican Assn. of Geog.; Colegio Dominicano de Ingenieria y Arquitectura y Agrimensuras. Contbr. articles, profl. jrnls., civil engrng. & archaeol. Address: Calle N. N° 4, Augustina, Santo Domingo, Dominican Republic.

ORTIZ, Silvia. Advertising Executive. Educ: M.Philos. & Arts, Univ. of Havana, Cuba, 1954; M.Advt., ibid, 1956; Mus.M., Iranzo Conservatory, Havana, 1950. Appts: Copywriter, Godoy & Cross, Cuba, 1954-59 & Publicidad Alvarez Perez, ibid, 1959-60; Creative Hd., Int. Mktg., Puerto Rico, U.S.A., 1961-67; Creative Dir., Spanish Advt. & Mktng. Servs. Inc., N.Y.C., 1967-. Mbr. of Spanish Inst., N.Y. Contbr. of articles to var. Latin Am. mags. Hons: El mundo Newspaper Advt. Award, 1965 & '66; Int. Film & TV Fest. of N.Y., 1973. Address: 40-05 Hampton St. Apt. 503, Elmhurst, NY 11373, U.S.A.

ORTLIP, Paul Daniel, b. 21 May. 1926. Artist. Educ: Art Students League, N.Y.C.; La Grande Chaumiere, Paris. Appts: Official Artist, U.S.N.; Instr., Montclair Acad., N.J., 1957-58; Instr., Montclair Mus., 1958-59; Artist-in-Res., 1956-57, Art Curator, 1967-72, Fairleigh Dickinson Univ. Mbrships: Portraits Inc., N.Y.C.; Life Mbr., Art Students League; Allied Artists of Am.; Salmagundi Club; N.J. Water Color Soc. Pub. collects: U.S.N. Art Collect; Pentagon, Wash., D.C.; Bergen Community Mus., N.J.; Fairleigh Dickinson Univ.; Bergen Co. Court House; N.J. Coll. of Med.; As U.S.N. Official Artist, portraits of Gemini 5 Astronauts; Appollo 12, 17, Astronauts; Mem. portrait, John F. Kennedy, Fairleigh Dickinson Univ. Lib.; Exhibs. incl: Salon l'Art Libre, Paris, 1950; Nat. Acad. of Design, 1952; Allied Artists of Am., 1960-71; Smithsonian Instn. Hons. incl: 1st Prize, Oils, N.J. State Exhib., Am. Artists Profl. League, 1960; Franklyn Williams Award, Salmagundi Club, 1967; Artist of Year. Hudson Artists, Jersey City Mus., 1970. Address: 95 Main St., Fort Lee, NJ 07024, U.S.A.

ORY, Robert Louis, b. 26 Nov. 1925. Biochemist. Educ: B.S., Loyola Univ., New Orleans, La.; 1948; M.S., Univ. of Detroit, Mich., 1950; Ph.D., Tex. A. & M. Univ., Coll. Stn., 1954; Appts. incl: Sr. Biochemist, Seed Protein Pioneering Rsch. Lab., 1958-67; Acting Hd., ibid, 1967-68; Fulbright-Hayes Rsch. Schol., Dept. Biochem., Polytechnic. Inst. of Denmark,Lyngby, 1968-69; Hd., Protein Properties Investigations, Oilseed Crops Lab., Southern Regional Rsch. Lab., 1969-72; Rsch. Ldr., Protein Properties Rsch., Oilseed & Food Lab., S. Regional Rsch. Ctr., New Orleans, 1972-. Mbrships. incl: Am. Chem. Soc.; Pres., La. Sect., ibid, 1968; Div. of Biological Chem., ibid; Div. of Agric. Food Chem., ibid; Sigma Chi. Contbr. to books & profl. jrnls. Hons. incl: Student Coun. Gold Medal Award, Loyola Univ., New Orleans, 1948; Nutrition Fndn. Rsch. Asstship. Award, Tex. A. & M. Univ., 1950-54. Address: Oilseed & Food Lab., Southern Regional Research Center, P.O. Box 19687, New Orleans, LA 70179, U.S.A. 7, 14, 15, 28, 125.

OSARA, Nils Arthur, b. 29 Nov. 1903. Forestry Educator & Administrator. Educ: Bachelor, 1924, Master, 1926, Dr. of Forestry, 1936, Helsinki Univ., Finland. Appts: Asst. Prof., 1924-26, Assoc. Prof., 1937-70, Helsinki Univ.; Rsch. Off., 1928-36, Prof. Forest Econs.,

1938-47, Forest Rsch. Inst., Helsinki; Off., 1936-37, Mng. Dir., 1947-52, Ctrl. Forestry Org. "Tapio"; Min. of Agric. & Supply, Finnish Govt., 1943-44; Dir. Gen., State Bd. Forestry, 1952-60; Dir., Forestry & Forest Products Div., FAO, 1962-68; Retired 1968; Sr. Advsr., Jaakko Pöyry & Co., 1973-; Bd. Officers or Mbr., sev. indls. cos., banks, ins. cos., civic orgs. Mbr. or hon. mbr. sev. acads., socs., etc. U.S.A., U.K., Scandanivia & Finland. About 120 profl. & rsch. publs. on forestry admin. & econs. Recip of hons. from Finland, Sweden, Norway, Denmark, German Federal Repub. Address: Lauttasaarentie 29, 00200 Helsinki 20, Finland. 12, 90.

OSBORN, Arthur Walter. Author; Retired Executive. Appts: Rep. for British firm in Dutch E. Indies, 1913-14; Exec., British firm in Australia, 1920-54; Commnd. Off., British Royal Field Artillery WWI; Wounded in France. Publs. incl: The Superphysical, 1937, reprint in preparation, The Expansion of Awareness, 1955, paperback, 1967; The Future is Now, 1961, 2nd. edit., 1964, paperback, 1967; The Axis & the Rim, 1963; The Meaning of Personal Existence, 1966, paperback, 1967 The Cosmic Womb, 1969; What are We Living For? in preparation; 4 titles translated into Italian & Spanish. Hons.: M.C.; Twice Mentioned in Despatches. Address: 1 Marne St., S. Yarra, Vic., Australia 3141. 23.

OSBORN, Elodie Courter, b. 11 Dec. 1911. Museum Curator. Educ: B.A., Wellesley Coll., 1933; Sorbonne Univ., Paris, France. Appts: Fndr. & later Dir., Dept. of Circulating Exhibits, Mus. of Modern Art, N.Y.C., 1933-47; Bd. of Dirs., Flaherty Fndn.; Bd. of Dirs., MacDowell Fndn.; Mbr., N.Y. Film Coun. Mbrships: Fndr., Salisbury Film Soc., Conn. (Pres. 1948-74); Former Mbr., Shakespeare Soc., Wellesley Coll.; Cosmopolitan Club, N.Y.C. Films: Fall, 1970; Calder's Plane, 1974. Address: RFD 1, Box 140, Salisbury, CT 06068, U.S.A. 2, 6.

OSBORN, (Sir) Frederic J., b. 26 May 1885. Town Developer; Writer on Planning. Appts: Clerk in London Offs., 1901-12; Mgr., Housing Soc., Letchworth Gdn. City, 1912-17; Estate Mgr., Welwyn Gdn. City, 1919-36; Fin. Dir., Radio Mfg. Co., 1936-60. Mbrships. incl: Hon. Sec., Town & Country Planning Assn., 1936-61, curently Pres.; Hon. Treas., Int. Fedn. or Housing & Planning, 1944-62, now V.P.; Fabian Soc.; V.P., Royal Inst. of Town Planners; Hon. Mbr., Am. inst. of Planners. Publs: New Towns After the War, 1918, 2nd ed., 1942; Green-Belt Cities, 1946, 2nd. ed., 1969; Can Man Plan? & Other Verses, 1959; The New Towns, Answer to Megalopolis (w. A. Whittick), 1963, 3rd ed., 1974; Letters of Lewis Mumford & Frederic Osborn (ed. M.R. Hughes), 1973. Hons: Kthood., 1956; Silver Medal, Am. Assn. of Planning Officials, 1960; Gold Medal, Royal Town Planning Inst., 1963; Howard Mem. Medal, 1968. Address: 16 Guessens Rd., Welwyn Gdn. City, Herts., AL8 6QR, U.K. 1, 3, 12, 41.

OSBORN, Malcolm E., b. 29 Apr. 1928. Tax Attorney, Insurance Company Executive & Professor. Educ: B.A., Univ. of Me., Orono, 1952; J.D., Schl. of Law, Boston Univ., Mass., 1956; LL.M., Taxation, ibid, 1961. Appts. incl: Asst. V.P. & Tax Counsel, Security Life & Trust Co. & affiliated Cos., Winston-Salem, N.C., 1964-72; V.P. & Tax Counsel, Integon Life Ins. Co. & other Integon Grp. Cos., Winston-Salem, 1972-; Adjunct Prof., Guilford Coll., Greensboro, N.C., 1965-68, Am. Inst. for Property & Liability Underwriters Inc., 1969-70; Adj. Prof., Fed. Taxation, Ins. & Bus.

Law, Univ. of N.C., Greensboro, 1969-; Adj. Prof., Income Tax, Am. Coll. Life Underwriters, 1973-. Mbrships. incl: Am. Bus. Law Assn.; Chmn. Comm. on Fed. Taxation, ibid, 1972-; Am. Bar Assn.; Chmn., Subcomm. Ins. Co. Tax Deductions, ibid, 1967-; Fed. Bar. Assn.; Phi Eta Kappa. Contbr. to profl. jrnls. Hons. incl: 2nd Place, State of Me. Bar Examination, 1956; Guest Lectr., num. Colls. & Instns. Address: 3639 Kirklees Rd., Winston-Salem, NC 27104, U.S.A. 7.

OSBORN, Robert Chesley, b. 26 Oct. 1904. Artist. Educ: Univ. of Wis., 1922; Ph.B., Yale Univ., 1928; British Acad., Rome, Italy, 1929; Acad. Scandinav, Paris, France, 1930. Appts: Tchr., Hotchkiss Schl., Lakeville, Conn., 1930-35; Free-lance Artist, 1935-. Cartoonist 1939-; Lt.-Cmdr., U.S.N., producing cartoons for instrn. of naval aviators, 1941-46. Mbrships: Elizabethan Club, Yale Univ.; Scroll & Key, ibid; Fellow, Berkely Coll., ibid, 1958, Century Club, N.Y.C. Publs. incl: War Is No Damn Good, 1946; Osborn on Leisure, 1955; The Vulgarians, 1962; Mankind May Never Make It, 1970; A Festival of Phobias, 1972; Illustrator, 45 books; Contbr. cartoons to num. mags. inclng. New Republic. Hons: Legion of Merit, U.S.N., 1946; Disting. Pub. Serv. Award, ibid, 1958; Gold Medal, Soc. of Illustrators, 1959; Yale Art Assn. Medal. Address: RFD 1, Box 140, Sslisbury, CT 06068, U.S.A. 2, 6, 29.

OSBORNE, Clive Debenham, b. 18 Apr. 1909. Architect. Educ: Schl. of Arch., Sydney Tech. Coll., Australia, 1928-33; Dip., Arch., A.S.T.C., 1933. Appts: w. archtl. firms, A.W. Anderson & Messrs. Budden of Mackay, 1933-36; w. Messrs. Howard Lester & Ptnrs., Archts., & Archtl. Div., RAF, London, 1937-38; w. Messrs. L.M. Perrott & Ptnrs., Archts., Melbourne, 1939; Archt., i/c. Sect. Designing Australian Munition Factories, Allied Works Coun., Pacific Region, 1940-48; Designing Archt., Australian Govt. Dept. of Works, Melbourne, 1949; Asst. Dir., Arch., ibid, 1953, Dir. on Arch., 1958, 1st Asst. Dir.-Gen., Arch., 1964; Australian Govt. Rep., Adelaide's Lord Mayor's Vic. Sq. Redev. Comm., 1968; var. overseas archtl. missions, 1952-73. Mbrships. incl: Life Fellow, Royal Australian Inst. of Archts., 1970. Responsible for designs inclng. Royal Australian Mint & Sydney Int. Passenger Terminal. Hons. incl: MBE, 1963. Address: Dept. of Works, 17 Yarra St., Hawthorn, Vic., Australia 3122. 23.

OSBORNE, Colin Porter, Jr., b. 15 Jan. 1921. Dentist. Educ: Emory Univ., Atlanta, Ga.; Southern Dental Coll., ibid; Schl. of Dentistry, Chapel Hill, N.C. Mbrships. incl: N.C. Dental Soc. (comm. chmn., prosthetic dental serv., 1956-67; Pres., 1968-69; exec. comm., 1966-71); Pres., Dist. Offs. Coun., 1969-70; 4th Dist. Dental Soc. (chmn., clin. comm., 1954-56; exec. comm., 1960-65; Pres., 1964-65); Dental Fndn., Schl. of Dentistry, Chapel Hill, N.C., 1960-; Fed. Dentaire Int.; Assn. Dentists for children; Acad. Gen. Dentistry; Flying Dentist Assn.; Royal Soc. for promotion of hlth.; Lumberton Kiwanis Club (Dir., 1952-53; Pres., 1954); 1st Bapt. Ch. (Sunday Schl. Tchr.; Choir Mbr.; Deacon); N.C. Symph, Soc. & Contbr. of articles to profl. jrnls. Recip. sev. commendations for profl. servs. Address: 2405 Rowland Ave., Lumberton NC 28358, U.S.A. 7.

OSBORNE, John, b. 12 Dec. 1929. Playwright & Actor. Actor in many roles & writer for the theatre since 1957. Mbrships: Coun., English Stage Co.; Garrick Club; Savile Club; Royal Soc. of Arts. Plays Published: Look back in anger, 1957; The Entertainer,

1957; Epitaph for George Dillon (w. A. Creighton), 1958; The World of Paul Slickey, 1959; Luther, 1961; Plays for England, 1963; Inadmissible Evidence, 1965; A Bond Honoured, 1966; A Patriot for Me, 1966; Time Present: The Hotel in Amsterdam, 1968; West of Suez, 1971; Hedda Gabler, 1972; A Sense of Detachment, 1973; A Place Calling Itself Rome, 1973; TV Plays: A Subject of Scandal & Concern, 1961; The Right Prospectus, 1970; Very Like a Whale, 1971; The Gift of Friendship, 1972; Film Script: Tom Jones, 1964. Hons: Doct., Royal Coll. of Art, 1970. Address: 25 Gilbert St., London, W.1., U.K. 1, 18.

OSBORNE, Leon H., b. 14 Aug. 1925. Artist; Instructor. Educ: A.A., San Diego City Coll.; B.A., San Diego State Univ., Calif.; M.A. ibid. Appts: Art Instr., San Diego State Univ., 1968-69; Currently, Art Instr., Fresno City Coll.; One-man shows incl. Fresno Art Ctr., 1970; grp. shows incl. Nat. Print Show, 1969. Mbrships: Pres., Fig Tree Gall., Fresno; Phi Kappa Phi. Recip., Schlrship for Outstanding Art Student, 1968. Address: 3044 W. California Ave., Fresno, CA 93706, U.S.A. 9.

OSEN, Kirsten Kjelsberg, b. 20 July 1928. Professor of Morphology. Educ: Cand. med., Oslo, 1954; Dr. med., ibid, 1970; Specialist Pathol., 1963. Appts: Res. Physn., Dept. of Pathol., Tromso Univ.; Prorector, Dept. of Anatomy, ibid,; Prof. of Morphol., 1971-. Mbr., Norwegian Coun. for Sci. & the Humanities, Oslo, Norway. Author, The cochlear nuclei in the cat, Felis domestica, & the common propoise, Phocaena phocaena (thesis), 1970 & var. publs. in the field. Address: Univ. of Tromsø, Inst. of Med. Biol., P.O. Box 977, 9001 Tromsø, Norway. 134.

O'SHEA, Phillippe Patrick, b. 23 Mar. 1947. Librarian; Numismatist. Educ: St. Patrick's Coll., Wellington; Vic. Univ. of Wellington. Appts: Libn., N.Z. Treasury, 1967-; Numismatic Advsr., ibid, 1967-; Archivist, Order of St. Lazarus of Jerusalem, Bailiwick of N.Z., 1969-; Acting Sec., Monetary & Econ. Coun., 1970. Mbrships. incl: Royal Numismatic Soc. N.Z.; Nat. Sec., ibid, 1965-71, Ed., 1966-72, V.P., 1972-, Fndr., Otago Br., 1968; Coun. Mbr., Friends of Nat. Mus.; N.Z. Acad. Fine Arts. Publs. incl: A Short Biography of Professor Sir John Rankine Brown, KBE, MA, LLD, FNZIA, 1965; The Royal Humane Society of New Zealand, 1971. Contbr., N.Z. overseas jrnls. & newspapers. Hons. incl: Mbr. Companionate of Merit, Order of St. Lazarus, 1972; Fellow, Royal Numismatic Soc. of N.Z., 1972. Address: P.O. Box 2021, Wellington, New Zealand. 133.

OSHIMA, Shotaro, b. 28 Sept. 1899. Emeritus Professor of English Literature. Educ: Waseda Univ., Tokyo, 1918-23; Merton Coll., Oxford, U.K., 1937-39. Appts: Prof. Engl. Lit. Waseda Univ., Tokyo, 1935-70, Prof. Emeritus 1971-; Advsry. Bd. Mbr., Study of Anglo-Irish Literature, 1969-, & Yeats Studies: An International Journal, 1970-. Mbrships: Pres. Yeats Soc. of Japan, 1965-; Pres., Japan-Ireland Friendship Soc., Tokyo, 1967-69; Dir., Japan Poets Club, 1970. Publs. incl: W.B. Yeats: A Study, 1927; Studies in English Prose & Verse, 1935; Poetic Imagination in English Literature, 1953; W.B. Yeats, the Man & Poet, 1961 Poems: Journeys & Scenes, 1968; Poems, 1973. Occasional articles, Irish writers Yeats & Synge. Address: Dept. of Literature, Waseda University, Toyamacho, Shinjuku, Tokyo, Japan.

OSMANSKI, Frank Alexander, b. 22 Oct. 1913. Retired Government Official. Educ: U.S. Mil. Acad., W. Pt., N.Y., 1931-35; Univ. of Heidelberg, Germany, 1935; Harvard Univ., U.S.A., 1953-55, 1958-59; Ph.D. Candidate, Univ. of S.C. Appts. incl: Artillery Cmdr., 2nd Inf. Div., 1961-62; J-4 MACV, Vietnam, 1962-65; Comm. Gen., U.S. Army Supply & Maintenance Cmd., Wash. D.C., 1965-66; U.S. State Dept. Agcy. for Int. Dev., 1966-70; Vietnam Bur., 1966-68; USAID & MACV, Vietnam, 1968-72; Retd. U.S. State Dept., 1972. Mbrships. incl: Delta Sigma Rho; Soc. for Adv. of Mgmt.; Assn. of U.S. Army. Author, articles in mil. publs. Hons: Cum Laude Soc., 1931; Daughters of 17th Century Award, 1935. Address: P.O. Box 656, Beaufort, SC 29902, U.S.A. 2, 128.

OSOGO, (Hon.) J.C.N., b. 10 Oct. 1932. Teacher. Educ: Railway Trng. Schl.; Kagumo Tchrs.' Trng. Coll. Appts: Tchr., Sigalame Schl., 1955, Withur Schl., 1958, Boarding Schl., 1957, Ndenga Schl., 1958, Port Victoria Schl., 1959; Headmaster, Kibasanga Schl., 1960, Nangina Schl., 1961-62; Elected Mbr., Kenya House of Reps., 1963; Asst. Min. for Agric., 1963-66; Min. for Info. & Broadcasting, 1966-69; Min. for Commerce & Ind., 1969-73; Min. for Local Govt., 1973-. Mbrships: Chmn., Kenya Union of Tchrs., Ctrl. Nyanza, 1958-62; Chmn., Kenya Soc. Guild, Nangina Schl., 1961-62; Patron, Kenya YHA, 1970-. Hons: Elder, Order of the Golden Heart, Kenya; Order of Star of Africa, Liberia; Grand Cordon of Star of Ethiopia; Grand Cross of the Yugoslav Flag (1st class). Address: P.O. Box 30004, Nairobi, Kenya.

OSORIO LUQUE, Antonio, b. 13 Oct. 1913. Painter. Educ: Lessons w. Benito Quinquela Martin, Cleto Giochini, Gaston Jarry & Juan Carlos Yramain. Creative works incl: Participated in Tucuman State Exhib. of Art, Argentina, 1932; Works sent to competitive salons at La Plata, Rosario, Mar del Plata, Buenos Aires, Santiago del Estero, Santa Fe, Catamarca & Salta; Works displayed in the Amigos del Arte, Van Riel & Galeria Arentina Galls.; Collection of his best work was sent to the Art Acad. of Berna, Switzerland. Mbrships. incl: Pres., Amigos del Arte Soc.; Sociedad Argentina de Artistas Plasticos; Sociedad Estimulo de Bellas Artes, Sociedad Circulo de Bellas Artes. Hons. incl: First Prize, Chmbr. of Dptys., Tucuman, 1938 Special Prize, Salon Independiente, ibid, 1939; 3rd Prize, Santiago del Estero, 1942; First Prize, Salta, 1953; Prize Ezequiel Leguina, Nat. Exhib., Buenos Aires, 1962; Prize Martin Malharro, Salon Municipal, ibid, 1963. Address: Díaz Vélez 4567, Buenos Aires, Capital Federal, Argentina.

OSTASHINSKY, Eliakum, b. 16 Feb. 1909. Agronomist. Educ: Univ. of Toulouse, France; Portici Univ., Naples, Italy; (Dr.'s degree). Appts: Mgr., Hanotaiah Co., Tel-Aviv, Israel, 1931-40; Mgr., Agricl. Dept., Farmers' Fedn. of Israel, 1940-46; Mayor, Rishon-Le-Zion, 1946-50; Mgr., Agricl. Dept., Israel Citrus Marketing Bd., 1950-53; Mng. Dir., Carmel Wine Co. & Wine Cellars, Rishton-Le-Zion & Zicron-Jacob, 1953-. Mbrships: Advsry. Comm., Bank of Israel; Directorate, Bank Leumi Le-Israel Ltd.; Presidium, Israel Farmers'- Fedn. Contbr., num. articles on agricl. problems & politics in Israel Press. Address: Societe Cooperative Vigneronne des Grandes Caves Ltd., P.O. Box 2, Richon-Le-Zion, Israel. 94.

ØSTERGAARD, Torsten Emil, b. 16 Apr. 1911. Chief Physician. Educ: Med. Examination, Univ. of Copenhagen, Denmark, 1938; Specialist in Psych., 1946, Neurol.,

1948; M.D., Univ. of Copenhagen, 1948. Appts: Asst. Physn., Med., Neurol. & Psych. Depts., var. Hosps., 1938-51; Chief Physn., Montebello Hosp. for Nervous Disorders, Elsinore, 1951-73; Chief Physn., Montebello daughter Hosp., Benalmádena, Malaga, Spain, 1974-; Cons., num. Hosps. & Cts. Mbrships: Danish Med. Soc.; Danish Neurological Soc.; Danish Psychiatric Soc.; Rotary Club, Elsinore; Pres., ibid, 1960-61; Elsinore Golf Club; Hon. Mbr., Orphei Dränger men's choir, Uppsala, Sweden, 1964-. Publs: Respirationscentrets folsomhed ved melankoli, 1948. Contbr. of num. articles on neurosis to med. jrnls. Broadcaster & Lectr. to popular audiences on med. subjs. Address: Montebello Benalmádena, Benalmádena Pueblo, Malaga, Spain. 43.

OSTERWEIS, Rollin Gustav, b. 15 Aug. 1907. Historian; Educator. Educ: B.A., Yale, 1930; M.A., ibid, 1943; Ph.D., 1946. Appts: Instr. in Hist., Yale, 1943-46; Asst. Prof., ibid, 1948-54; Assoc. Prof., 1954-68; Prof. of Hist. & Oratory, 1968-; Lectr. of Debating, Pub. Speaking, Pol. Union, Yale, 1948-. Mbrships: Am. Histl. Assn.; Org. Am. Histns.; Conn. Acad. Arts & Scis.; Elizabethan Club, Yale; Authors' Club, London, U.K.; New Haven Colony Histl. Soc. (pres., 1962-67); New Haven Preservation Trust (pres., 1971-); Pres., Yale Fac. Club, 1970-72. Publs. incl: Romanticism & Materialism in the Old South, 1949; Three Centuries of New Haven, 1638-1938, 1953; The Myth of the Lost Cause, 1865-1900, 1973. Address: 396 St. Ronan St., New Haven, CT 06511, U.S.A. 6, 13.

OSTFELD, Alexander M., b. 13 Feb. 1930. Advertising Executive. Educ: B.S./B.A., Washington Univ., 1951; M.S.C. cand., St. Louis Univ. Grad. Schl., Mo., 1953-56. Appts: Dir. of Marketing, Emerson Elec. (Lighting Subsidiary), 1955-60; V.P., Compton Advt. Inc., 1960-65; Assoc. Dir., Leo Burnett Co. Inc., 1965-68; V.P. & Dir., McCann-Erickson Inc., 1968-72; V.P. & Dir., Kenyon & Eckhardt Inc., 1972-73; V.P. & Dir., Draper Daniels Inc., 1973-. Mbrships. incl: Comm. Co-Chmn., Exec. Club of Chgo.; Int. Visitors' Ctr., Chgo. Coun. on For. Rels.; Lectr., Am. Mgmt. Assn.; Sec., Am. Marketing Assn. Publs. incl: Effect of Government Action on Food Product Advertising; The Decline in Interviewing Response to Interviews & Questionnaires; Employing the Computer to Develop Usable Psychographic Data; The Effect of Advertising on Sales. Hons: Prize, Readers. Digest, 1967; Chicago Radio Award, 1971. Address: 391 Poplar Ave., Elmhurst, IL 60126, U.S.A. 8, 40, 57.

OSTIGUY, Jean P.W., b. 4 Mar. 1922. Business Executive. Educ: Coll. Jean de Brébeuf; Fac. of Comm., Univ. of Montreal; Grad., Royal Mil. Coll. of Canada, Kingston, 1942. Appts. incl: Casgrain & Co., 1948-56; Crang & Ostiguy Inc., formerly known as Morgan, Ostiguy & Hudon, 1956-; Dir., CP Air, Canadian Pioneer Ins. Co., Civitas Corp. Ltd., Dominion Life Assurance Co. of Canada, Ford Motor Co. of Canada, Laura Secord Candy Shops Ltd., Scottish Canadian Assurance Corp., Sintra Ltd., Gen. Accident Assurance Co. of Canada; Exec. Dir., Canadian Imperial Bank of Comm. & Kerr Addison Mines Ltd. Mbrships. incl: Pres., La Maison des Etudiants Canadiens a Paris, 1964-; Dir., Canadian Coun. of Christians & Jews, 1967; Jt. Chmn., Centennial Comm., Montreal Stock Exchange, 1972-74; Advsry. Comm. of the Min. of Ind., Trade & Comm., 1971-74; Dir., Régie de la Place des Arts, Montreal, 1969-73; Bd. of Govs., Royal Victoria Hosp., 1972-; Gov., Hockey Canada, 1973-. Hons. incl: Star of Italy; Ordre de Malte; Canadian Overseas Serv. & Clasp; 39-45 Star;

War Medal. Address: Crang & Ostiguy Inc., 500 west, St.-James St., Montreal, H2Y 1S3, P.Q., Canada. 32, 88.

OSTRANDER, Linda Woodaman (Mrs. Edmund Ostrander), b. 17 Feb. 1937. Composer; Teacher. Educ: B.Mus., Oberlin Conservatory, 1958; M.A., Smith Coll., 1960; Doct. of Musical Arts, Boston Univ., 1972. Appts: Lectr., Adelphi Suffolk Coll., 1961-63; Adjunct Asst. Prof., Southampton Coll., L.I. Univ., 1963-64; Tchng. Fellow, Univ. of Ill., Urbana, 1964-65, Boston Univ., 1969-72; Chmn., Dept. Fine, Creative, Performing Arts, Bunker Hill Community Coll., Charlestown, Mass., 1973-74. Mbrships: Am. Music Ctr.; Am. Soc. Univ. Composers; MENC. Compositions & Performances incl: Duet (piano), Boston Univ., 1970, '72; Three for Eight (2 pianos, 8 hands), Portland, Me., 1969; Concerto Grosso No. 2 (Portland Symph.), 1969; Suite for Chamber Orchestra No. 2. Address: 48 Atwood Rd., Southboro, MA 01772, U.S.A. 5, 7, 138.

OSTREM, Carl T., b. 27 Feb. 1899. Dentist. Educ: grad., Coll. of Dentistry, Univ. of Ia., 1923. Appts: Tchr., pub. schl., Williams, Ia., 1917-18; Pvte. prac., Ankeny, ibid, 1923-36, Des Moines, 1936; Pvte. 1st Class, M.C., U.S. Army, 1918-19; Cmdr., Dental Corps., U.S. Navy, 1943-46. Mbrships: Ia. State Bd. Dentistry, 1962-72 (chmn., 1 yr.; sec., 8 yrs.); Fellow, Am. Coll. Dentists; Charter Mbr. & Past Pres., Am. Prosthodontia Soc.; Am. Dental Assn.; Ia. State Dental Assn.; Past Pres., Des Moines Dist. Dental Soc.; Reserve. Offs. Assn., Navy League; Charter Mbr., Equilibration Soc.; Fed. Dentaire Int.; Pierre Fauchard Acad.; Delta Sigma Delta; Delta Upsilon; Elder, St. John's Lutheran Ch. (past Coun. Mbr.); Mason; Shrine; Bohemian Club; Des Moines Club. Contbr. of articles to profl. jrnls. Address: 704 Equitable Bldg., Des Moines, IA 50309, U.S.A. 8.

OSTROWSKY, Abbo, b. 23 Oct. 1885. Painter; Etcher; Art Instructor. Educ: Schl. of Fine Arts, Odessa, Russia; Nat. Acad. of Design, N.Y.C., U.S.A. Appts: Fndr. & Dir., Educl. Alliance Art Schl., N.Y.C., 1914-55, Dir. Emeritus, 1955. Mbrships. incl: Allied Artists of Am., N.Y.C.; Socs. of Am. Etchers & Am. Graphic Artists; Am. Fedn. of Art. Solo Exhibs. incl: Anderson Galls., N.Y.; U.S. Nat. Mus., Wash. D.C.; Balt. Art Mus. Grp. Exhibs. incl: Art Inst. of Chgo.; L.A. Art Assn.; Metropol. Mus. of Art, N.Y.; Nat. Bezalel Mus., Jerusalem; Mus. of Western Art, Moscow, U.S.S.R.; Vic. & Albert Mus., London, U.K.; Tokyo Mus., Japan. Works in permanent collects., U.S.A., France, U.S.S.R., Israel. Hons: Kate Arms Award, 1937; Henry Wineman Landscape Prize, 1961. Address: 95-28, 67th Ave., Rego Pk., NY 11374, U.S.A. 37.

OSTROWSKI, Avi, b. 19 Aug. 1939. Conductor. Educ: grad. from following acads: Musical Tchrs. Inst., Tel-Aviv, 1956-58; Rubin Acad. of Mus., Tel Aviv, 1958-61; Staats Akademie fur Musik und Dartstellende Kunst, Vienna, 1966-68; Academia Chigiana, Siena, 1968. Appts: Began Conducting in Israel 1968; Appointed Permanent Conductor, Israel Broadcasting Service Choir, 1965; Musical Dir. & Permanent Conductor, Haifa Symph. Orch., 1969; Founded the Kibbutz Chamber Orchestra & is its permanent Conductor & Musical Dir.; has conducted in France, Denmark, Holland, Austria, Italy, Rumania, U.S.A. & at annual Israel Festival. Recip., 1st Prize, Int. Comp. for Young Conductors "Nicolai Malko Competition", 1968. Address: 12 Shalem St., Ramat Chen, Ramat Gan, Israel.

OSTROY, Joseph, b. 4 Jul. 1917. Educator. Educ: B.A., Wash. Sq. Coll., U.S.A., 1952; M.A., N.Y. Univ., 1953; Prof. Dip., Columbia Univ. Tchrs. Coll., 1966. Appts: Newspaper work on various dailies, 1943-45; City Ed., Homestead Daily Messenger, Pittsburgh, Claremont Daily Eagle, N.M., 1945-49; Production, Promotion & Publicity, L. Kruger & Co., 1954-62; Instr. of Engl. Jrnlsm., Dramatics, Pub. & Pvte. Schls., 1962-65; Dir. of Guidance, Dannemara H.S., 1966-67; Asst. Prin., Dir. of Vocational Educ. Counseling, Brewster C.S. Dist., 1969-; H.S. Guid. Couns. & Dir., Coll. Counseling, Roosevelt Pub. Schls., N.Y., 1969-; Nat. Coord., P.R., Am. Schl. Counselor Assn., Div. APGA; Mbr., Educ. Resources Info. Ctr. Mbrships. incl: Deleg. of N.Y.S. Schl. Counselors Assn. to A.S.C.A. Assembly & to APGA Assembly, 1967-71; Advsry. Comm., N.Y. State Senate, Comm. on Hlth. & many profl. orgs. Publs: Columnist & Ed., for profl. publs. Commentator on Guidance, Radio Station, WPUT, N.Y. Recip., Writer of the Yr. Award, Am. Schl. Couns. Assn., 1971. Address: 453 W. Walnut St., Long Beach, NY 11561, U.S.A. 6, 22, 57, 128, 131.

OSTRY, Sylvia (Mrs. Bernard Ostry), b. 3 June 1927. Economist. Educ: B.A., McGill Univ., Canada, 1948 M.A., 1950; Ph.D., Cambridge Univ. & McGill, 1954. Appts. incl: Assoc. Prof., Univ. of Montreal, 1962-64; Cons., Manpower Studies, Econ. Coun. of Canada, 1964-65; Dir., ibid, 1969-72; Dir., Special Manpower Studies, Dominion Bur. of Stats., 1965-69; Chief Statn. of Canada, Stats. Canada, 1972. Fellow, Am. Stat. Assn. Mbrships. incl: Am. Econ. Assn.; Soc. Sci. Rsch. Coun. of Canada; Econs. Vis. Comm., Bd. of Overseers, Harvard Coll., 1973-. Publs: (co-auth.) Labour Policy & Labour Economics in Canada, 1962; An Analysis of Post-War Unemployment, 1964;; (Co-Ed.), Regional Statistical Studies, 1966; (Ed.), Canadian Perspective in Economics, 1972; num. articles & papers. Hons. incl: Women of Distinction Award, Soroptomist Fed. of the Ams., 1970; num. hon. degrees. Address: Stats. Canada, Tunney's Pasture, Ottawa, Ont., K1A OT6, Canada. 5, 6.

OSTWALD, Michael, b. 10 Aug. 1926. Artist & Graphic Artist. Educ: Hochschule für Bildende Künste, Berlin-West, Germany, 1945-51. Works: Dichter besuche, 1964; Ick bin jejen allet; Der Kudamm is keen Muhdamm; 22 drawings in Robert Gilbert, Dürch Berlin fliesst immer noch die Spree; 36 portraits in Wilhelm Duwe, Deutsche Dichtung des 20. Jahrhunderts. Address: Postfach, 1 Berlin 33, German Fed. Repub.

OSZE, Andrew Eösze, b. 14 Jan. 1909. Sculptor. Educ: Acads. of Art, Budapest, Hungary & Rome, Italy. Appts: Prof., Cath. Univ. of Lima, Peru & Escuela de Bellas Artes, Cuzco, ibid, 1962-64. Mbr., Coll. Art Assn. Works appear in num. collects. throughout the world. Has held exhibs. in U.S.A., Italy, Brazil, Hungary, Rumania & Peru. Works incl: St. Francis Chap., N.Y.C. Book Illustrations incl: Gilgamesh (a graphic interpretation, 90 drawings); Ziusuora's Baro (20 illustrations); Uesurü Gyökeren (10 drawings). Recip., grants to travel to Italy, Peru, France, Spain & Germany. Address: 652 W. 163rd St., Apt. 37, N.Y., NY 10032, U.S.A.

OTHMER, Donald Frederick, b. 11 May 1904. Educator; Chemical Engineering Consultant. Educ: B.S., Univ. of Neb., 1924; M.S., Univ. of Mich., 1925; Ph.D., ibid, 1927. Appts. incl: Instr., Polytech. Inst., Bklyn., 1932-33; Prof., ibid, 1933-; Hd., Dept. Chem.

Engrng., 1937-61; Disting. Prof., 1961-; Cons. & Licensor of process patents for desalinating sea water, sewage treatment, petrochemicals pigments, extractive metallurgy, plastics pipeline heating etc., to num. cos. & govt. depts., U.S., Belgium, Burma, Canada, S. Am., Denmark, U.K., Germany, France, India, Israel, Japan, etc., 1931-; Cons. to: UN; WHO; U.S. Dept. of Interior; U.S. Dept. HE & W; Off. of Saline Water; U.S. Army Chem. Corps, Ordnance Corps & Sci. Advsry. Bd.; USN; U.S. State Dept., & many cos. Fellowships: AAAS; N.Y. Acad. Scis.; Am. Inst. Chems.; Am. Soc. Mech. Engrs.; Am. Inst. Chem. Engrs.; Am. Inst. Cons. Engrs.; Sigma Xi. Mbrships: Am. Chem. Soc.; Soc. de Chimie Ind. (Pres. 1973); Chemurgic Coun.; Panel Arbitrators, Am. Arbitration, Assoc. Publs: Kirk-Othmer Ency. of Chemical Technology (Co-ed.), 56 vols. 1st, 2nd, Spanish Edits.; Fluidization (Ed.), 1956; Fluidization & Fluid Particie Systems (Co-author), 1960; Advsry. Bd., Chem. Eng. Handbook; Over 300 sci. publs. in jrnls. 100 patents. Lect. Tours, many countries. Hons: Tyler, AIChE,, 1958; Barber-Coleman, Am. Soc. Engrng. Educ., 1958; Scroll of Merit, Am. Inst. Chems., 1970. Hon. Degrees: Univ. of Neb.; Univ. of Concepcion, Chile. Address: 333 Jay St., Brooklyn, NY 11201, U.S.A. 2, 6, 10, 12, 14, 15, 16, 26, 28, 30, 34, 50, 51, 64, 128, 131

OTTENBERG, Perry, b. 14 Nov. 1924. Physician; Psychiatrist. Educ: A.B., Harvard Coll., 1948; M.D., Harvard Med. Schl., 1952. Appts: Sr. Attng. Psych., Inst. of Pa. Hosp., 1965; Assoc. Clin. Prof., Dept. of Psych., Univ. of Pa., 1970. Mbrships: Phila. Assn. for Psychoanal.; Phila. Psych. Soc.; Pa. Psych. Soc. Am. Psych. Soc.; Coun. Soc. Issues; Grp. for Adv. of Psych.; Soc. Issues Comm.; Phi Beta Kappa. Author of sev. papers. in field. Address: 111 N. 49th St., Philadelphia, PA 19139, U.S.A.

OTTERSEN, Ottar, b. 13 Aug. 1918. Headmaster. Educ: Cand. theol., Univ. of Oslo, Norway, 1947; Practicum theol., 1948; Theol.kand., Univ. of Uppsala, Sweden, 1947. Appts: Ordained, 1948; Clergyman, Swedish Nat. Ch. & Norwegian Sunday Schl. Sec., Oslo, Norway, 1948-50; Diocesan Curate, Straengnaes, 1950-55; Curate, Diocesan Cons., Nat. Ch.; Stockholm, 1955-58; Hdmaster., Pedagogical Inst., Stockholm, Christian Educ. Assn., Swedish Ch., 1958-67; Mbr., Nat. Investigation Comm. on Sexual Behavior, 1964-; Hdmaster., Adult Educ., Educl. Assn. of Swedish Ch., 1967-; Bd. Mbr., Sweden's Radio & TV Co's. Comm. for Adult Educ.; Chmn., Bd., Inst. for Sci. of Educ., Lulea, Karlstad, Kalmar, Gothenburgh, Jönköping & Lund. Mbrships: Freemason; St. Erik, degree IIX. Publs. incl: De Viktigaste aaren, 1958; Att vara foersamlingsfadder, 1970; De lyckliga aaren, 1974. Address: Sveriges Kyrkliga Studieförbund (SKS), Box 1125, 111 81 Stockholm, Sweden.

OTTLEY, Robert Carlton, b. 14 Oct. 1914. Community Development Administrator. Educ: Grad. in Soc. Sci., Liverpool Univ., U.K., 1947. Appts: Dir., Community Dev., Govt. of Trinidad & Tobago; Seconded to UN as Community Dev. Advsr., 1965-66; retirement from Govt. off., 1968; Mbr., Penal Commn. on Reform of Prison Serv. in Trinidad & Tobago, 1972-. Mbrships: Exec. Mbr., Trinidad & Tobago Histl. Soc.; Pres., Trinidad & Tobago Handicraft Cooperative Soc. Publs. incl: Story of Port of Spain; Spanish Trinidad; Story of Tobago; Slavery Days in Trinidad; Story of San Fernando; Police Force; Sayings of Trinidad & Tobago; Jokey Stories of Trinidad & Tobago.

Hons: Queen Elizabeth Medal; Gold Medal of Merit, 1st Class, Govt. of Trinidad & Tobago, 1968. Address: 18 Claude Ave., Fairview, Diego Martin, Trinidad, W. Indies.

OTTO, John Neal, b. 17 Oct. 1941. Farmer; Stockman. Educ: B.S., Okla. State Univ., 1964; Pub. speaking course, Dale Carnegie; Currently involved in co. short course. Owner & operator of own bus. Mbrships: V.P., Agronomy Club; Soils Club; Future Farmers of Am.; 4-H Club; Guard, Warden Dpty Grand Kt., & Grand Kt., $3°$ Knights of Columbis; $4°$ Knights of Columbus; Farmers Union. Hons: Am. Legion Schl. Award, 1958; Hon. Citizen of Boystown, 1968-71. Address: Rt. 1, Kildare, OK 74642, U.S.A. 125.

OTTOSON, Lars-Henrik, b. 13 Dec. 1922. Company Director; Writer; TV Producer. Educ: Norra Latin H.S., Stockholm. Appts: Jrnlst., 1941-45; For. Corres., London, 1946-49; BBC European Serv. Commentator, 1946-49; Advt. & P.R. Mgr., Ford, Sweden, 1950-52; Film Dir. & Ldr., Sci. Exped. to Ctrl. Africa, 1953-57; own Advt. Agency, Sweden, 1958-; Political Commentator & News Rdr., Swedish TV (free-lance), 1959-66, etc.; Pres., U.S. Affiliated Corps., 1973-. Mbrships: Chmn., Swedish Advt. Agencies Assn., 1959-66; Chmn., Swedish Safari Club; Bd. Mbr., Int. Club, 1960-64; Chmn., Bahamas-Scandinavian Club, 1965-71; Explorers Club, N.Y.; Travelers Club & of Publicists' Club. Publs: Mara Moja; Kabissa; The Trip to Lambarene; a series of Guide Books to U.K. & the Continent; Dir. & Author of the Film 'Gorilla'; regular contbr. to Swedish newspapers & mags. & travel talks on Swedish Radio. Address: 1111 Crandon Blvd. A107, Key Biscayne, FL 33149, U.S.A.

OUIMET, J. Robert, b. 9 Apr. 1934. Industrialist. Educ: M.Comm. (Econs.), Schl. of Commerce, Univ. of Montreal, Canada; Master of Pol. & Soc. Sci., Int. Univ. of Fribourg, Switzerland; M.B.A., Columbia Univ., N.Y.C., U.S.A. Appts: Dir. of Marketing, J. René Ouimet Ltd., Montreal, 1960-64; V.P. of Marketing, ibid, & Cordon Bleu Ltd., 1964-66; V.P. & Chief Exec. Off., J. René Ouimet Enterprises Ltd., Cordon Bleu Ltd., J. René Ouimet Ltd., Cordon Bleu Int. Ltd., & J.R. Ouimet Canada Ltd., 1966-; Pres., Buffet Foods Corp. Ltd., 1972-. Mbrships: St. Denis Club, Montreal; Coral Beach & Tennis Club, Bermuda. Address: J. René Ouimet Ltd., 8585 Jeanne-Mance St., Montreal, P.Q., H2P 2S8, Canada. 2, 6, 32.

OULD, William James Lee, b. 10 Apr. 1912. Business Executive. Fellowships: Australian Soc. of Accts; Chartered Inst. of Secs; Australian Inst. of Mgmt; Inst. of Dirs; Inst. of Dirs. in Australia. Appts: Cost Acct., Wiluna Gold Mines, 1936-41; Acct., Allied Bruce Small, 1942-43; Sec., John McIlwraith Inds., Ltd., & all subsidiaries, 1943; Mng. Dir., ibid, 1953; Chmn., 1969-; Chmn., Gen. Inds. Ltd., & all subsidiaries; Chmn., Walloo Pty. Ltd. Mbrships: Athenaeum Club; Pres., W. Brighton Club; Kelvin Club; Healesville Country Club; R.A.C.V., (all Melbourne, Vic.); R.A.C.A., Sydney, N.S.W. Address: John McIlwraith Industries Ltd., 34 York St., Richmond, Vic., Australia 3121. 23.

OURIVIO, José Carlos Mello, b. 23 Feb. 1933. Civil Engineer. Educ: Colégio Santo Inácio; Civil Engrng., Escola Nacional de Engenharia; Mgmt. Studies, Pontifícia Universidade Católica. Appts: Trainee-Pres., H.C. Cordeiro Guerra S.A.; Pres., Veplan-Residência, Empreendimentos e Construçoes S.A.; Pres., RESIDENCIA,

Companhia de Crédiot Imobiliário. Mbrships: Exec. Comm., Int. Union of Bldg. Socs. & Saving Assns.; V.P., Sindicato da Construçao Civil do Estado da Guanabara; Gen. Sec., XIII Int. Meeting of IUBSSA, Associaçao Brasileira das Entidades de Crédito Imobiliário e Poupança (ABECIP); Rio de Janeiro Country Club; Jockey Club of Brazil; late Clube do Rio de Janeiro. Address: Rua Buenos Aires, 68–21°–Rio de Janeiro-G.B.–Brazil. 136.

OUTHWAITE, Leonard, b. 12 July 1892. Anthropologist; Explorer. Educ: Yale Coll., 1915; Univ. of Calif., Berkeley, 1916; Pre-med., Columbia Univ., Coll. Physns. & Surg. Appts: Exec. of U.S. Govt., WWs I & II, 10 yrs., inclng. Sec. & Tech. Dir., Pres. Roosevelt's Commn. on Demobilization resulting in "G. I. Bill of Rights", 1943-44; Sec. & Tech. Dir., Pres. Comm. on Hosps., 1944-45; Author of Cons.; Bus. Exec.; Exec., L.S. Rockefeller Mem., Rockefeller Fndn., etc. Mbrships. incl: Life Fellow, Int. Inst. of Arts & Letters; Life Fellow, Explorers Club, N.Y. (Former Ed. & V.P.); Union Club, N.Y., 1923-; Ends of the Earth, N.Y.; Newport Reading Room. Publs. incl: Many mag. articles & tech. reports; Fndr. & Ed., Jrnl. of Personnel Rsch.; Atlantic Circle: Around the Ocean with the Winds & Tides, 1931; Unrolling the Map (Hist. of Exploration), 1935, revised 1938, '72. Address: Beachmound, Bellevue Ave., Newport, RI 02840, U.S.A. 2, 6, 22, 128.

OVERBECK, Alfred E. von, b. 8 Mar. 1925. University Rector. Educ: Licence en Droit, 1948; Bar. Cert., 1952; LL.D., Univ. of Fribourg, Switzerland, 1961. Appts: Practised at Bar, 1953-56; Sec., then 1st Sec., Permanent Off. of La Hague Conf. on Int. Pvte. Law, 1956-65; Swiss Deleg., 12th Session, ibid, & special Comm. on Maintenance Obligations, 1972 & '73; i/c. Tchng. Int. Law, Univ. of Zurich, 1962-68; Prof., Int. Pvte. Law, Civil Procedure & Commercial Law, Univ. of Fribourg, 1965-; Vis. Prof., Univs. of Glasgow, U.K. & Switz., 1967-68; Pres., Reform Commn. for Legal Studies, 1969-; Rector, Univ. of Fribourg, 1971-. Mbrships. incl: Gvng. Coun., Int. Instn. for Unification of Pvte. Law, Rome; Pres., Comm. for Founding a Swiss Inst. of Comp. Law; Fed. Commn. of Experts for the Revision of Family Law; Pres., Swiss Br., Int. Law Assn. Contbr. of num. articles to legal jrnls. Address: Route Fort-St-Jacques 14, 1700 Fribourg, Switzerland.

OVERBY, George Robert, b. 21 July 1923. Educator. Educ: B.A., Fla. State Univ., 1951; M.Ed., Univ. of Fla., 1959; Sp.Ed., ibid, 1963; Ph.D., Fla. State Univ., 1966. Appts: Tchr. & Prin., elementary & secondary schls., 1956-63; Assoc. Prof., instns. of higher educ., 1966-71; Prof. & Chmn., Dept. of Educ., Shelton Coll., 1971-74; Pres., Freedom Univ., 1974-. Mbrships. incl: Christian Warriors for Christian Educ. Inc.; Univ. Profs. for Academic Order Inc.; Am. Assn. of Christian Schls.; Christian Educators Assn. of Southeast; William Holmes McGuffey Histl. Soc.; Kappa Delta Pi; Phi Delta Kappa. Publs. incl: A Critical Review of Selected Issues Involved in the Establishment & Functioning of the National Council for Accreditation of Teacher Education from its Origin through 1965; Gen. Ed., Christian Educator. Num. hons. incl: Presidential Unit Citation, USN, WWII; Precision Flying Award, USN; Life Ins. Underwriter's Award; Address: Post Drawer C, Cape Canaveral, FL 32920, U.S.A. 6, 7, 129, 130, 139, 141.

OVERHOLSER, Ronald, b. 25 June 1942. Actor; Scriptural Character Impressionist. Educ: Johnson Bible Coll., Knoxville, Tenn.,

1964; Cinn. Bible Sem., 1968-70. 1st appearance, child actor, Ch. pageant, Wash., Ind., 1955; serv. USN, Naval Air Stn., Brunswick, Me., 1960-63; var. employment, clerical & manual, 1963-66; 1st profl. appearance, as Judas Iscariot, Englewood Christian Ch., Indpls., 1964; Narrator, The Good Life, N. Am. Christian Conf., Cinn. Riverfront Stadium, 1972; solo performances as The Messiah, Paul of Tarsus, & the 12 Disciples, Ga., Ill., Ky., Mich., Mo., N.C., Pa., Tenn., Va., var. chs., schls, colls. Address: 425 Grand Ave., Cinn., OH 45205, U.S.A. 57.

OVERMAN, Frances Elizabeth Henson. Free-lance Writer; Educator. Educ: B.A., Murray State Univ., Ky.; Grad. studies, Northwestern Univ., Univ. of Wis. Appts: Tchr., Ky. Elementary & Secondary Schls.; Tchr., Oak Ridge Schls., Tenn., 1944-45, 1957-59; Tchr. Deleg. to Ky. & Tenn. Educl. Assns. Mbrships. incl: Fellow, Intercontinental Biographical Assn.; Advsry. Mbr., Marquis Biographical Lib. Soc.; Int. Comm., Fine Arts Sect., Centro Studi E Scambi Internazionali; Academia Leonardo da Vinci, Rome; past mbr., var. community orgs. Contbr., articles, profl. jrnls. Recip., Community Serv. Award, 1972. Address: 109 Pelham Rd., Oak Ridge, TN 37830, U.S.A. 5, 7, 32, 57, 125, 129, 138, 140.

OVERSTREET, Bonaro W., b. 30 Oct. 1902. Educator & Author. Educ: Univ. of Calif., Berkeley, 1925; Tchrs. Cert., 1926; Grad. work, Columbia Univ., 1929-30. Appts: incl: Tchr., Creative Writing, Arts Guild, N.Y.C., 1933-36; Rsch. Assoc., Am. Assn. of Adult Educ., 1939-40; Instr. in Adult Educ., Univ. Ext. Divs., Univs. of Mich. Ala., Tex., Calif., Hawaii, Free-lance author & Lectr. Mbrships. incl: Am. Adult Educ. Assn.; Va. Adult Educ. Assn.; Mental Hlth. Assn. of Va.; Nat. Press Club; Theta Sigma Phi; Phi Beta Kappa; Sigma Delta Pi, Num. publs. incl: Poetic Way of Release, 1931; Brave Enough for Life, 1941; Courage for Crisis, 1943; Freedom's People; 1945; Understanding Fear, 1951; w. H.A. Overstreet: The Mind Alive, 1954; The War Called Peace, 1961; The F.B.I. in Our Open Society, 1969. Hons. incl: Special Citations, Merrill Palmer Inst., Nat. Conf. of Christians & Jews; P.L. Schneider Award for serv. to adult educ. Address: 3409 Fiddler's Green, Falls Church, VA 22044, U.S.A. 2, 3, 5, 7, 138.

OVIDIU, Papadima, b. 23 June 1909. Professor. Educ: Philos. & Letters Dept., Bucharest Univ., Romania, 1928-31; Postgrad. schlrship., Alexander von Humboldt Fndn., 1937-39; Dr., Philos. & Letters, Bucharest Univ., 1945. Appts: Asst. Lectr., Folklore & Mod. Hist., Romanian Lit. Dept.; HS Tchr., Romanian, 1931-33; Asst. Lectr., Romanian Lit. Depts., Bucharest Philos. & Letters Dept. & Bucharest Schl. Econs., 1933-35; Tchr., Romanian, var. HSs, 1935-40; Edit. Sec., Royal Fndns. Mag., 1940-46; Asst. Lectr.-Hd., Rsch., Philol. Dept. Bucharest, 1941-49; Rsch. Wkr.-Hd., Folklore & Romanian Lit. Dept., G. Calinescu Lit. Hist. & Theory Inst.; Supvsr., doct. papers; Rector, M. Eminescu People's Univ. Lit., Bucharest, 1971-73. Mbrships: Writers' Soc., SRR; Scis. Soc., SRR; Int. Soc. Folk-Narrative Rsch., Göttingen, W. Germany. Author num. publs. on Romanian Lit. & Folklore. Hons. incl: Prize, A Romanian View of the World, Romanian Acad., 1942; Prize, Cezar Bolliac (monograph), SRR Acad., 1968. Address: Strada Aviator Stephan Sanatescu No. 38, Bucharest I, Romania.

OWEN, Eunice Pauline Stewart (Mrs. Mauldin J. Owen), b. 3 Aug. 1929. School Teacher. Educ: A.B., N. Greenville Jr. Coll.,

Tigerville, S.C.; B.A., Furman Univ., Greenville, S.C.; M.A., Fla. State Christian Coll., Ft. Lauderdale, Fla.; Grad. work, Clemson Univ., S.C. Univ. of S.C. Appts. incl: former 5th Grade Schl. Tchr., Phoebus, Va.; former 2nd Grade Schl. Tchr., Lebanon Schl., Pendleton, S.C.; 11th & 12th Grade Sponsor & Counselor, Pendleton, S.C.; 1st Grade North Fant, Anderson, S.C. Mbrships: EQV Lit. Soc.; Swartz Rose Club; Alpha Psi Omega; NEA; SCEA; ACEA; SS Tchr., Calvary Bapt. Ch.; BSU Exec. Coun.; YWA Coun.; Kappa Delta Epsilon; Theatre Guild. Publs: poems in mag., The Hornet & book in press. Address: Rt. 2, Liberty, SC 29657, U.S.A. 125.

OWEN, George Earle, b. 26 Mar. 1908. Clergyman; Educator; Church Executive. Educ: B.A., D.D., Bethany Coll., W. Va.; M.A., Univ. of Chgo.; B.D., Union Theol. Sem., N.Y.C.; Ed.D., ibid & Columbia Univ. Appts. incl: Min., Pa., Va. & N.Y.C., 1925-40; Vice Dir., Hd., Ch. Hist. Dept., Fac. Evangelica de Teologia, Buenos Aires, Argentina, 1943-48; Hd., Philos. Dept., Union Theol. Sem., Manila, Philippines, 1951-55; Dean, Coll. of Missions & Exec. Sec., Missionary Selection & Trng., 1955-57; Exec. Chmn., Div. of Gen. Depts., 1957-68; United Christian Missionary Soc., Indpls., U.S.A.; Asst. to Gen. Min. & Pres., Christian Ch., 1968-; Bd. Trustees, Tougaloo Coll., 1962-; Exec. Comm., ibid; Advsry. Coun., Am. Bible Soc., 1969-73. Mbrships. incl: Alpha Kappa Pi; Alpha Delta Pi; Phi Delta Kappa; Tau Kappa Alpha; Pres., Irvington Hist. Soc., 1970-72 Nat. & Ind. Couns. of Family Rels.; Bd. Relig. in Am. Life, 1967-; Futurist Soc.; Indpls. Coun. on World Affairs. Publs. incl: Alpha Kappa Pi Pledge Manual (w. others); Education for Mission & Change, 1969; Ed., Yrbook & Directory of the Christian Church, 1970-; Faith & Freedom, 1953; num. articles & poems. Hons: Disting. Serv. Award, Disciples of Christ Chs., Tagalog Area, Philippines, 1954; Disting. Mins. Pin, 1974. Address: 5354 Julian Ave., Indpls., IN 46219, U.S.A. 2, 22, 57, 82, 128.

OWENS, Byrns Lezelle, b. 27 Apr. 1933. Educator; Minister. Educ: B.A., Stetson Univ., 1954; B.D., 1959, Th.D., 1965, New Orleans Bapt. Theol. Sem.; Grad. study, Memphis State Univ. Appts: Tchr., Ext. Div., Stetson Univ.; Pastor, Bapt. churches in La., Tenn., Fla., 20 yrs.; Acad. V.P., Luther Rice Sem., Jacksonville, Fla. Mbrships: Pi Alpha Theta; Civitan Int. Publs: Frederic George Kenyon as Papyrologist; Conservative Theology & Academic Excellence. Hons: Grad. Fellowship, New Orleans Bapt. Theol. Sem., 1959. Address: Box 997, Keystone Heights, FL 32656, U.S.A. 125.

OWENS, Chester Daniel, b. 27 Dec. 1907. Educator. Educ: A.B., Bucknell Univ.; M.A., N.Y. Univ. Appts: Tchr., Supvsr. of Educ., Woodbourne Corr. Inst., 1937-45; Dir. of Educ., Elmira Reformatory, 1943-53; Asst. Supt., Reception Ctr., Elmira, 1953-63; Supt., ibid, 1963-; Instr., var. courses, Elmira Coll., St. Lawrence Univ. Mbrships. incl: Hon. Mason; Rotarian; Past Pres. & hon. life mbr., Corr. Educ. Assn. of Am. Corr. Assn. Contbr. of articles to profl. jrnls. Past Ed., Jrnl. of Corr. Educ. Mbr., editl. bd., Jrnl. Criminal Psychopathol., Jrnl. of Clin. Psychopathol. & Psychotherapy. Recip., Meritorious Serv. Award, N.Y. Coun. of Deliberation, 1960. Address: 109 Orchard Knoll Dr., Horseheads, NY 14845, U.S.A. 6.

OWENS, Martha Armistead (Mrs. Joseph James Owens, Jr.), b. 12 Jan. 1930. Librarian. Educ: B.Mus. Ed., Madison Coll., Harrisonburg, Ba., 1951; Lib. Cert., Wm. & Mary Coll.,

Williamsburg, Va., 1967; post-grad. work, Univ. of Va., 1970-71; M.Sc., Second. Schl. Admin., Old Dominion Univ., Norfolk, Va., 1973. Appts: Tchr. & Libn., Music & Chorus, Broad Creek Jr. HS, Norfolk Co., 1951-53; Tchr., Grade 4, Ingleside Elem., ibid, 1954-55; Tchr., var. grades, Oceana, John B. Dey & Linkhorn Elem. Schls., Va. Beach, Va., 1956-61; Tchr., Engl., Frank Cox HS, ibid, 1961; Libn., 1st Colonial HS, 1966-69 & Floyd E. Kellam HS, 1969-. Mbrships. incl: Am., Va. & Va. Beach Lib. Assns.; Nat., Va. & Va. Beach Educ. Assns.; AAUW. Publs: Pilot Study-The Effectiveness of a Wireless Audio Library Learning System Utilizing Cassette Tapes & Sound-Slide Programs; Handbook—Using Libraries & Library Resources, Guide to Research. Hons: State Rsch. Grant for Pilot Study expmtl. prog., 1970-72; James Bland Music Schlrship. for piano performance, Lions Club, 1948. Address: 1712 S. Woodhouse Rd., Va. Beach, VA 23454, U.S.A. 5, 7, 138.

OWREN, Paul A., b. 27 Aug. 1905. Physician. Educ: Grad., Med. Schl., Univ. of Oslo, Norway, 1931; Res., Oslo City Hosp., Aker Hosp., & Univ. Hosp., 1939-45 & 1948-49; Rsch. Fellow, Lister Inst. of Preventive Med., London, U.K., 1946-47. Appts: Asst. Prof., Med., Univ. of Oslo, 1947-48; Prof., ibid, & Hd., Med. Dept., Rikshosp., Oslo, 1949-69; Dir., Inst. for Thrombosis Rsch., Univ. of Oslo, 1956-65. Num. mbrships. incl: Chmn., Norwegian Soc. for Internal Med., 1953-56; Chmn., Malthe Fndn. for Clin. Rsch., 1954-60; Chmn., Med. Sect., Norwegian Rsch. Coun. for Sci. & Humanities, 1958-61; WHO Expert Advsry. Panel in cardiovascular diseases; Royal Norwegian Soc. of Scis.; Norwegian Acad. of Sci. & Letters; Fellow, Am. Coll. of Physns.; Gov., Am. Coll. of Chest Physns., 1966-74; V.P., Int. Soc. of Haematol., 1950-54; V.P., Int. Coll. of Angiol., 1965-. Publs: The Coagulation of Blood: Investigations on a New Clotting Factor, 1947; About 200 articles in profl. jrnls. Hons. incl: Cmdr., Royal Order of St. Olav, 1953; Cmdr. w. Star, Royal Order of St. Olav, 1970. Address: Bjerkaasen 44, 1310 Blommenholm, Norway.

OXLEY, P.L.B., b. 8 Jan. 1930. Professor. Educ: Leeds Coll. Technol., U.K. (Pt.-time),1950; Leeds Univ., 1951-57. Appts: Lectr., Mech. Engrng., Manchester Coll. Sci. & Technol., U.K., 1958-61; Sr. Lectr., Prod. Engrng. Dept., Coll. Aeronautics, Cranfield Inst. Technol., 1961-65; Prof., Indl. Engrng.-Sir James Kirby Prof., Prod. Engrng., Univ. N.S.W., 1965-; E.A. Taylor Vis. Prof., Mech. Engrng., Birmingham Univ., U.K., 1969 (6 mths.). Mbrships: Fellow, Instn. Engrs., Australia; Fellow, Instn. Prod. Engrs.; Instn. Mech. Engrs.; College Int. Pour l'Etude Sci. des Techniques De Prod. Mecanique. Author rsch. papers in profl. jrnls. & articles in The Guardian, Engrng., Engrs. Digest, etc. Hons: F.W. Taylor Medal, CIRP, 1964; Water Arbitration Prize, Instn. Mech. Engrs., 1969; Paul Henderson Mem. Prize, ibid, 1970. Address: Univ. N.S.W., Schl. Mech. & Indl. Engrng., P.O. Box 1, Kensington, N.S.W., Australia 2033. 23.

OYAGI, Charles Kazuo, b. 28 Jan. 1903. Educator; Librarian. Educ: Ed.B., Univ. of Hawaii, 1939. Appts: Instr., Voc. Educ., 1926; Tchr., Elem. Schl., State of Hawaii, 1926-65; Libn. & Art Instr., 1937-41; Libn. & Audio Visual Coord., Elem. Schl., 1941-65; Retd. 1965. Mbrships. incl: Charter mbr., Kauai Tchrs. Fed. Credit Union; Committeeman, Pres., Treas., & Mgr., ibid, 1998-; 1st Pres. of Chapt., Nat. Dir., Pres., State Credit Union League; Lihue Christian Ch., Moderator of Ch.,

Trustee, Finance Chmn.; Past Worshipful Master, Treas. & Sec., Kauai Lodge, Masonic Lodge; Grand Standard Bearer, Grand Lodge of Calif., 1969. Hons. incl: 1st place among 7000 chapts. of credit union movement in Int. Credit Union Day Publicity Contest, 1957; Sr. Citizen of the Yr., 1974. Address: P.O. Box 1306, Lihue, HI 96766, U.S.A. 9, 130.

ÖZBUDUN, Ahmet Halûk H., b. 9 Sept. 1924. United Nations Senior Political Affairs Officer. Educ: B.A., Robert Coll., Am. Coll., Istanbul, Turkey, 1944; B.A., Yale Coll.; M.A., Yale Univ.; Postgrad. work, ibid. Appts. 1949-74; UN Asst. Pol. Affairs Off.; Lt., Turkish Army; UN Pol. Affaris Off.; Pol. Affaris Off., UN Commn. for Korea; UN Assoc. Pol. Affairs Off.; Pol. Affairs Off., UN Commn. for Korea; UN 1st Pol. Affairs Off.; Prin. Sec., Rep. of UN Sec.-Gen. & Custodian of UN Mem. Cemetery in Korea, UN Commn. for Korea; UN Sr. Pol. Affairs Off., Dept. of Pol. & Security Coun. Affairs, Pol. Affairs Div., Pol. Studies & Advsry. Servs. Mbrships: Columbia Univ. Seminar on Peace, 1950-; Prog. Comm., ibid, 1970-71; Fac. Assoc.; seminar on UN, CUNY, 1967-73; Pres., Yale Univ. Int. Club, 1947-49. Stained glass work exhibited at UNICEF Art Exhibition, UN, 1974. Address: P.S.C.A., UN, N.Y., NY 10017, U.S.A.

P

PAAVONSALO, Matti Aimo, b. 29 Nov. 1934. Director; Columnist. Educ: M.Pol. Sci., Helsinki Univ., Finland, 1957; Lic. Pol. Sci., ibid, 1969. Appts: Ed., Assoc. Press, 1957; Uutiskeskus (press agcy.), 1957-58; Pol. Ed., Uusi Suomi, 1958-61; Columnist, ibid, 1961-; Information Chief, Osuuspankkien Keskuspankki Oy (Ctrl. Bank, Coop. Banks, Finland, Ltd.), 1961-67; Dir., Osuuspankkien Keskusliitto r.y. (Ctrl. Union, Finnish Coop. Banks), 1967-. Mbrships: Planning Comm., Intellectual Nat. Defence; Finnish UNICEF Comm.; Marketing Excs. Grp.; Information Comm., Finnish Financial Instns.; Finnish Pol. Sci. Assn.; Helsinki Finnish Club. TV & Radio Broadcaster. Address: Mellstenintie 17 B 15, 02170 Haukilahti, Finland. 43.

PABLO, Narcisa C. (Mrs. R.L. Alcala), b. 7 July 1938. Physician. Educ: A.A., Letran Coll., Manila, Philippines; M.D., Univ. of Santo Tomas, Manila. Appts: Rotating Intern, St. Barnabas Med. Ctr., N.J.; Med. Res., Brooklyn-Cumberland Med. Ctr., Brooklyn, N.Y., & Misericordia Hosp., Bronx, N.Y.; Fellow, Renal & Electrolyte Sect., Dept. of Med., Brookdale Hosp. Medical Ctr., Brooklyn, N.Y.; Fellow, Nat. Kidney Fndn.; Physn., Kings Co. Hosp. Ctr., Brooklyn, N.Y.; Asst. in Med. & Renal on Assoc. Staff, Dept. of Med., & Asst. Attending, Dept. of Community Hlth. Servs., Brookdale Hosp. Med. Ctr., Brooklyn, N.Y. Mbrships: Int. Soc. of Nephrol.; Am. Fedn. for Clin. Rsch.; Am. Soc. of Nephrol.; N.Y. Soc. of Nephrol.; Nat. Kidney Fndn.; Med. Soc. of Co. of Kings & Acad. of Med. of Brooklyn; Philippine Med. Assn. in Am. Co-author of 5 articles in med. jrnls. Address: 130 Clarkson Ave., Brooklyn, NY 11226, U.S.A.

PACE, Antonio, b. 7 July 1914. University Professor. Educ: A.B., Syracuse Univ., N.Y., 1935, Ph.D., Princeton Univ., 1943. Appts: Instr., Romance Langs., Syracuse Univ., 1939-42; Instr., Phys., ibid, 1943-44; Asst. Prof.-Prof., Romance Langs., ibid, 1945-67; Prof. of Italian, Univ. of Wash., 1967-. Mbrships: Am. Assn. Tchrs. of Italian (Pres., 1959-60); MLA (Modern Italian Sect.: Sec., 1951, Chmn., 1952; Sci. & Lit. Sect: Sec. 1952, Chmn., 1953); Phi Beta Kappa. Publs: Antonio Pucci, Il Contrasto delle Donne: A Critical Edition, 1944; Co-Author, The Leopold von Ranke Manuscripts of Syracuse University, 1952; Benjamin Franklin & Italy, 1958. Contbr. to profl. jrnls. Hons: Grants, Am. Philosophical Soc., 1944-48, 1951, 1958, 1960; Guggenheim Fellow, 1948-49, 1959-60; Nat. Sci. Fndn., 1959; Kt. Order of Merit, Italy, 1963. Address: Dept. of Romance Langs. & Lit., Univ. of Washington, Seattle, WA 98195, U.S.A.

PACE, Eulala Watson, b. 16 Oct. 1928. Credit Union Executive-Manager & Treasurer. Educ: Grad., Southeastern Credit Union Schl.; Oglethrope Univ., Atlanta, Ga., 1 yr.; Univ. of Ga., Athens, 2 yrs. Appts: Supvsr. of Acctng., Lyman Printing & Finishing Co.; Asst. Off. Mgr., Wamsutta Mills, Lyman S.C.; Asst. Mgr., Lyman Fed. Credit Union; Mgr., ibid. Mbrships. incl: Nat. Credit Union Exec. Soc.; Past Sec., S.C. Coun., Credit Union Exec. Soc.; V.P., ibid; Sec. (2nd term), S.C. League Bd. of Dirs.; Bd. of Dirs., Credit Union Acctng. Ctr., & Lyman Fed. Credit Union; Pres., Young Womans Club; PTA Pres., Dist. 5 Schl. Coun.; Sec., Treas., Advsr., Lymann's Club. Hons: Lyman Fed. Credit Union Woman of the Yr., 1971-72, 1972-73; Piedmont Area Chapt. of Credit Unions Woman of the Yr., 1971-72, 1972-73;

S.C. Credit Union Ldr. of the Yr., 1972-73; Nat. Credit Union Admin. Merit Award, 1974. Address: 104 Briarwood Dr., Lyman, SC 29365, U.S.A. 125.

PACE, Eunice, b. 8 June 1906. Nursing Educator. Educ: B.S., George Peabody Coll., Nashville, Tenn., U.S.A., 1948; M.P.H., Univ. of N.C., 1955. Appts. incl: Mbr., State Bd. of Hlth. Staff, Lincoln & Madison Cos., Miss., 1935-49; Nurse, Outpatient Dept., VA Hosp., Jackson, Miss., 1949-54; Asst. Prof., Nursing, Med. Ctr., Univ. of Miss., 1955-62; Assoc. Prof., Schl. of Nursing, Univ. Med. Ctr., 1962-64; Dir., Dept. of Nursing, Miss. Delta Jr. Coll., 1964-65; Dir., Dept. of Nursing, Hinds Jr. Coll., Raymond, Miss., 1965-73. Mbrships. incl: Fellow, Am. Pub. Hlth. Assn.; First V.P., Pub. Hlth. Nursing Sect., Am. Nurses Assn., 1964-66; First V.P., Clinton-Raymond Br., AAUW, 1971-73; First V.P., Miss. Nurses Assn., 1950-52; Nat. League for Nursing; WHO; Pres., Alpha Chapt., Beta Sigma Phi; Kappa Delta Pi. Author, article in Southern Regional Educ. Bd.'s Nursing Coun. Report, 1972. Address: 4436, Forest Pk. Drive, Jackson, MS 39211, U.S.A. 5, 7, 125.

PACE, George Gaze, b. 31 Dec. 1915. Architect. Appts: Cons. Archt. to Dioceses of Llandaff, Sheffield, Wakefield, Bradford, York, & Monmouth, U.K.; Cons. Archt. to Cathedrals of Lichfield, Llandaff, Sheffield, Durham, Chester, Liverpool, Newcastle, & Southwark; Surveyor, St. George's Chapel, Windsor Castle; Cons. Archt., Historic Ch. Preservation Trust, & York Civic Trust. Mbrships. incl: Fellow, Royal Inst. of British Archts.; Fellow, Soc. of Antiquaries of London; V.P., New Chs. Rsch. Grp.; Athenaeum. Publs: The Church & the Arts, 1960; Making the Building Fit the Liturgy, 1962; The York Aesthetic, 1968; Bishophill: York, 1974; 2 other books; Articles in encys. & ecclesiological jrnls. Hons. incl: Robert Mitchel Gold Medal, Royal Inst. of British Archts., 1936; Asphitel Prize, Royal Inst. of British Archts., 1938; M.A., conferred by Archbishop of Canterbury, 1961; Cmdr., Royal Victorian Order. Address: 18 Clifton Green, York YO3 6LW, U.K. 1, 41, 43, 128, 131.

PACEVICUITE, Irene, b. 26 Oct. 1918. Artist. Educ: Dip., Acad. of Fine Arts, Kaunas, Lithuania; Dip., Acad. of Fine Arts, Vienna, Austria. Mbrships: Acad. of Fine Arts, Vienna, 1945; Int. Burckhardt Acad., San Gallo, 1969; Teatina Acad., Pescara, 1971; William Marconi Acad., Rome, 1971; Tiberina Acad., Rome; Gentium Pro Pace Acad., Rome, 1973; Tommaso Campenella Acad., Rome. Works to be found in var. museums & pvte. exhibs. in Italy, U.S.A. & Lithuania. Hons. incl: Kaunas Acad. of Fine Arts Prize, 1938; Min. of Educ. Prize for Best Artist, Kaunas, 1938; Arte Sacra Silver Medal, Lucca, 1955; Hon. Dip., Viareggio, 1955; Special Prize, Int. Grand Prix of Painting & Sculpture, Monte Carlo, 1962; Silver Medal, Italian Art Exhib., Zurich, Switzerland, 1965; Silver Medal, Rome, 1966; New Kaleidoscope Trophy, Rome, 1969; Gold Medal, Teatina Acad., Rome, 1971; Silver Medal & Dip., Eva Arte Exhib., Rome, 1973. Address: Via dei Torriani 23, 00164 Rome, Italy. 43, 105, 133.

PACHAI, Bridglal, b. 30 Nov. 1927. Professor of History. Educ: B.A. & M.A., Univ. of S. Africa, Pretoria; Ph.D., Univ. of Natal, Durban. Appts: Tchr., Natal Educ. Dept., 1947-61; Lectr., Hist., Univ. of Cape Coast, Ghana, 1962-65; Sr. Lectr. & Hd., Hist. Dept., Univ. of Malawi, Zomba, 1965-68; Prof., Hist., & Hd., Hist. Dept., ibid, 1968-; Dean, Schl. of

Soc. Sci., Univ. of Malawi, 1973-. Mbrships. incl: Chmn., Ladysmith Indian Child Welfare Soc.; Chmn., Ladysmith Br., Natal Indian Tchrs. Soc.; Trustee, Malawi Mus. Bd.; Chmn., Edit. Bd., Jrnl. of Soc. Sci.; Edit. Bd., Transafrican Jrnl. of Hist.; Comm. for African Studies in Southern Africa. Publs: The History of Indian Opinion, 1961; The International Aspects of the South African Indian Question, 1860-1961, 1971; Malawi, the History of the Nation, 1973; Livingstone, Man of Africa, 1873-1973, 1973; Ed., 3 other books. Address: Univ. of Malawi, Chancellor College, P.O. Box 280, Zomba, Malawi. 135.

PACHECO de AMORIM, Diogo, b. 7 Nov. 1888. University Professor. Educ: Mil. Schl., Lisbon; M.Sc., Univ. of Coimbra, Portugal, 1913; Ph.D., ibid, 1914. Appts: Asst. Prof., 1912; Auxiliary Prof., 1918; Full Prof., 1919; Dpty., Nat. Assembly (Parliament), sev. legislatures. Mbrships. incl: Academia das Ciências de Lisboa; Pres., Instituto de Coimbra; Pres., Centro Académico de Democracia Cristã; Fndr., Mbr., Centro Catolico Portugues, 1915. Publs. incl: Cálculo das Probabilidades, 1914; A Nova Geraçao, 1918; Sobre o determinante de Wronsky, 1923; Aritmetica Racional, 1931; Finanças e Economia, 1936; A Chefia da Europa, 1945; Da Cultura geral do universitário, 1951; Medida das Matrizes, 1972. Hons. incl: King's Medal for Serv. in Cause of Freedom, 1947; Com. S. Gregorio Magno, Vatican, 1959. Address: Cruz de Celas, Coimbra, Portugal. 43.

PACHTMAN, Elliott A., 8 Aug. 1919. Pathologist; Biochemist. Educ: A.B., Univ. of Colo., 1947; M.S., Univ. of Ill., 1953; Ph.D. Georgetown Univ., 1958. Appts. incl: Var. rsch. posts, 1938-58; Chmn. & Rsch. Prog. Dir., Nat. Drug Co., Phila., 1958-61; Assoc. Lab. Dir., Beth-EL Hosp., Brooklyn, 1961-62; Dir., Clin. Lab. Sect., Veterans Hosp., Phil., 1962-65; Assoc. Dir. of Labs., Long Island, 1965-66; Dir. of Biochem., Albert Einstein Med. Ctr., Phil., 1966-. Mbrships: Am. Chem. Soc.; A.A.A.S.; Clin. Chemists; Chromatography & Am. Microbiol. Socs.; Nat. Registry in Clin Chem.; Lab. Dirs., N.Y.C. Contbr. to sci. jrnls. Recip. of rsch. awards. Address: 1603 Longshore Ave., Phila., PA 19149, U.S.A. 6, 14, 28.

PACIFICO, Larry, b. 26 Oct. 1923. Dentist. Educ: Grad., Lafayette Coll., 1952; Grad., Univ. of Pa., Schl. of Dental Med., 1958. Appts: Served w. U.S.A.A.F., WWII; Currently Dr. of Dental Surg. Mbrships: Am. Dental Assn.; F. & A. Masons. Recip., Bronze Star, 1944. Address: 48 N. Third St., Bangor, PA 18013, U.S.A. 6.

PACIORKIEWICZ, Tadeusz, b. 17 Oct. 1916. Composer; Organist; Teacher. Educ: Warsaw Conservatoire, Poland, 1936-43. Appts: Fndr. & Headmaster, Musical Schl., Plock, 1945-49; Tchr., High & Higher Musical Schls., Lodz, 1949-59; Prof. Harmony, Counterpoint instrumentation & Composition, State Musical Acad., Warsaw, 1954-59; Dean, Fac. Composition, Theory & Conducting, 1962-69; Schl. Rector, 1969-71. Mbrships: Polish Composers Assn.; ZAIKS Assn. Composers & Publrs.; Frederick Chopin Assn.; Warsaw Musical Assn. Creative Works incl: 1st Symphony, 1953; 2nd Symphony, 1957; 1st Piano Concerto, 1952; 2nd Piano Concerto, 1954; A Concerto for Violin & Orch., 1955; A Concerto for Organs & Orch., 1967; A Concerto for Trombone & Orch., 1971; A String Quartet, 1960; A Quintet for Flute, Oboe, Clarinet, Horn & Bassoon, 1963; Music for Harp & Wind Quintet, 1963; A Trio for the Oboe, Clarinet & Bassoon, 1963; A Trio for the

Flute, Alt Horn & Harp, 1965; A Short Suite for 4 French Horns, 1971. Recip. Hons. Address: ul. Jasnorzewskiej Marii 9 m.25, 01-863 Warsaw, Poland.

PACKARD, Henriette Lehman (Mrs. William Albert Packard) Artist. Educ: N.Y. Univ. Art Schl.; Brooklyn Mus. Art Schl., N.Y.; New Schl. of Soc. Rsch., N.Y.C. Mbr: Artists' Equity, N.Y.C. Has exhibited Paintings & Sculpture at: N.Y. Univ.; Brooklyn Mus.; Bass Mus.; New Schl. of Soc. Rsch.; var. N.Y. Galls. Lecturer on Art. Contbr. to: The Villager, N.Y.C.; The Daily Pennsylvanian, Phila; The Cherry Lawn Chronicle. Recip. 2nd Prize, Brooklyn Mus. Address: The Seasons South, 5001 Collins Ave. Apt. 15 H, Miami Beach, FL 33140, U.S.A. 105, 133.

PADGETT, George Arthur, b. 17 Feb. 1932. Lawyer; Company Executive. Educ: A.B., Hamilton Coll., N.Y., 1954; LL.B., Georgetown Univ. Law Ctr., Wash. D.C., 1960. Appts; Admitted to Bar, Wash. D.C., 1960, N.J., 1961; Assoc. Atty., Covington & Burling, Wash. D.C., 1959-60, Pitney, Hardin & Kipp, Newark, N.J., 1961-65; Asst. Sec.-Sec. & Corp. Counsel, Lionel Corp., N.Y.C., 1965-; Dir., Lionel Morsan, Inc., N.J., Sterling Power Systems Inc. & Western Hydraulics, Inc., Calif. Mbrships: Am., N.J. & Essex Co. Bar Assns.; Am. Soc. of Corp. Secs. Address: 21 Woodland Rd., Short Hills, NJ 07078, U.S.A. 6.

PADLEY, Walter Ernest, b. 14 July, 1916. Politician. Educ: Ruskin Coll., Oxford. Appts: Pres., Union of Shop, Distributive & Allied Workers, U.K. 1948-64; Min. of State for For Affairs, 1964-67; M.P. for Ogmore, Glamorgan. Mbrships: Nat. Exec., Labour Part, 1956-; Chmn., ibid, 1965-66; Chmn., Int. Comm., 1963-71; Rep., Socialist Int., 1960-72. Publs: The Economic Problems of the Peace, 1954; Am I My Brother's Keeper, 1945; Britain—Pawn or Power, 1946; U.S.S.R.—Empire or Free Union, 1947. Address: 73 Priory Gdns., Highgate, London N6, U.K. 1, 34.

PADOVANO, Anthony Thomas, b. 18 Sept. 1934. Professor. Educ: A.B., Seton Hall Univ., S. Orange, N.J., 1956; S.T.B., Gregorian Univ., Rome, Italy, 1958; S.T.L., ibid, 1960; S.T.D., 1962; Ph.L., Int. Univ. of St. Thomas, Rome, 1962; M.A., Univ., 1971. Ordained Cath. Priest, 1959. Appts. incl: Prof. of Systematic Tehol., Darlington Sem., Mahwah, N.J., 1962-; Prof. of Am. Lit., Ramapo Coll. of N.J., ibid, 1971-; Vis. Prof., var. univs.; Parish Asst., St. Catharine's, Glen Rock, N.J., 1963-. Mbrships. incl: Cath. Theol. Soc. of Am.; Mariological Soc. of Am.; Cons., Nat. Cath. Off. for Radio & TV; Nat. Fedn. of Priests Couns. Publs. incl: American Culture and the Quest for Christ, 1970; Dawn Without Darkness, 1971; Free to be Faithful, 1972; Eden and Easter, 1973. Address: Ramapo Coll. of N.J., Mahwah, NJ 07430, U.S.A. 2, 6, 13. 131.

PAGE, Charles Hunt, b. 12 Apr. 1909. Sociologist. Educ: A.B., Univ. of Ill., 1931; Ph.D., Columbia Univ., 1940. Appts. incl: Instr., Sociol., CCNY, 1933-41; Asst. Prof.-Prof., Smith Coll., Mass., 1946-52; Prof., Dept. Chmn., ibid, 1953-60; Prof., Dept. Chmn., Princeton Univ., 1960-65; Prof., Provost, Adlai E. Stevenson Coll., Univ. of Calif., Santa Cruz, 1965-68; Prof., Univ. of Mass., Amherst, 1968-. Mbrships. incl: Am. Sociological Assn.; Coun., ibid, 1955-61, Exec. Comm., 1958-60; Eastern Sociological Soc.; V.P., ibid, 1956-57, Pres., 1965-66. Publs: Class & American Sociology, 3rd ed., 1969; Society: An Introduction Analysis (w. R.M. MacIver),

1949; Freedom & Control in Modern Society (w. M. Berger & T. Abel), 2nd ed., 1964; Sociology & Contemporary Education, 1964; Sport & Society (w. J. Talamini), 1973. Recip., var. hons. Address: 7 Hampton Terr., Northampton, MA 01060, U.S.A. 2, 14, 15, 50, 128.

PAGE, James Hutcheson, b. 16 Aug. 1916. Advertising & Marketing Executive. Educ: B.A., Univ. of Va., 1940. Appts: Employee, J. Walter Thompson Co., N.Y., 1946, Dir. of Int. Media, 1948; Far E. Publr., Army Times Publishing Co., Tokyo, Japan, 1952, Newsweek, Tokyo, 1954; Japanese Rep. for J. Walter Thompson Co., 1952-56; Fndr., Tokyo Br., J. Walter Thompson Co., 1956., V.P. & Gen. Mgr. until resignation 1964; Pres., Int. Market Cons. Inc., 1965-; Dir., Interprogres Ltd., & Hancock Inds. Inc., 1970; Exec. Dir., Falcon P.R. & Adv. Inc., 1974-. Mbrships: For. Corress. Club, Tokyo; Am. Club, Tokyo; Mayflower Soc.; Pres., Univ. of Va. Alumni Assn. of Japan; Kappa Alpha Fraternity. Columnist, Japan Bus. News, 1966-67. Hons: Am. Legion Award, 1936; Am. Red Cross Cert. of Hon., 1960. Address: Int. Market Consultants Inc., Central P.O. Box 1967, Tokyo 100-91, Japan.

PAGE, Marilyn Jane Brooks (Mrs. Dean Edwin Page), b. 25 Mar. 1945. Registered Nurse & Homemaker. Educ: Dip., Gordon Keller Schl. Nursing, Tampa, Fla., U.S.A.; Fla. Univ., Gainesville; Tampa Univ., Fla. Appts: Staff Nurse, Tampa Gen. Hosp., 1967-70; Off. Nurse w. pvte. pracs., 1970-71; Surg. Nurse, St. Joseph's Hos., 1971-. Mbrships: Past Pres., V.P., Treas. & Soc. Chmn., Tampa City Coun., Beta Sigma Phi; Lambda Zeta Chapt., ibid; Past V.P. & Pres., Student Nurse Assn., Fla. Dist. 4; Faith Assembly Order, Rainbow for Girls No. 85; Astron Chapt. No. 254, Eastern Star. Hons: Order of Rainbow for Girls: Grand Page, 1963, Grand Rep., Ky., 1963-64 & Hon. mbr., Grand Assembly, Ky., 1964; Most Outstanding Mbr., Faith Assembly, No. 85 ORG, Grand Lodge, F & A Masons, Fla., 1964; Majority Degree, Supreme Assembly, Int. Order; Miss Student Nurse of Yr., 1966; Girl of Yr., Lambda Zeta Chapt., Beta Sigma Phi, 1972; Attendant & Master of Ceremonies, Grand Cross of Color, 1974. Address: 7001 Applewood Ct., Tampa, FL 33615, U.S.A. 76, 125.

PAGE, Patti (Mrs., nee Clara Ann Fowler), b. 8 Nov. 1927. Entertainer. Appts. incl: Ptnr., Page-Rael Assocs., Pattack Inc. & Page-Rael Realty Co.; Pres., Egap Music Co.; V.P., Lear Music Co. Publd. Once Upon a Dream, 1960. Hons. incl: Cash Box Best Record Award, 1951; Cash Box Female Vocalist Award, 1951, 1952, 1954, 1957; ASCAP Achievement Award, 1971, 1972; Billboard Achievement Award, 1973. Address: Page-Rael Associates, 8899 Beverly Blvd. 407, Los Angeles, CA 90048, U.S.A. 2, 22, 132.

PAGE, Robert Griffith, b. 25 Mar. 1921. Professor of Medicine & Pharmacology. Educ: A.B., Princeton Univ., 1943; M.D., Univ. of Pa. Med. Schl., 1945; Intern, Res. in Med., Univ. of Pa. Hosp., 1945-49. Appts: Asst. Instr.-Assoc. in Pharmacol., Univ. of Pa., 1949-53; Vis. Prof., Pharmacol., Med. Coll., Univ. of Rangoon, Burma, 1951-53; Asst. Prof., Assoc. Prof., Med., Univ. of Chgo., 1953-68; Dean, Fac. of Med., Med. Coll. of Ohio, 1967-74; Prof., Med. & Pharmacol., ibid, 1968-; Provost, ibid, 1972-74. Num. mbrships. incl: Fellow, Coun. Mbr., AAAS; Acad. of Med., Toledo, Ohio; Fellow, Am. Coll. of Physns.; Fellow, Am. Coll. of Cardiol.; Past Mbr., Bd. of Dirs. & Exec. Comm., Am. Heart Assn.; AMA; N.Y. Acad. of Scis.; Soc. of Sigma Xi; Past V.P., Chgo. Heart

Assn. Publs: Preparation for the Study of Medicine (co-author), 1961; Psychological Aspects of Medical Training (co-author), 1971; Num. sci. papers, articles in encys.; Lectr. Address: Dept. of Med., Med. Coll. of Ohio, P.O. Box 6190, Toledo, OH 43614, U.S.A.

PAGET, Edward Robert Hugh, b. 5 June 1910. Representative of the British Council. Educ: B.A., Keble Coll., Oxford Univ., U.K., 1933; M.A., ibid, 1945. Appts. incl: Rep., British Coun. in Northern Caribbean, 1942-48; Chmn., Brit. Coun. Student Policy Comm., 1949; Brit. Coun. Area Off., Oxford, U.K., 1948-50; Lecture Tour for Brit. Coun., W. Africa, 1949-50; Dir., Brit. Coun., Hans Cres. House, London, U.K., 1950-54; Rep., Brit. Coun., in Netherlands, 1954-63, in Poland, 1966-69 & in Australia, 1969-74. Mbrships: Co-Fndr. & Hon. Sec., Jamaica Histl. Soc., 1943-48; Ed., Jamaican Histl. Review; Chmn., Community Educ. Comm., Jamaica, 1945; Coun. of Royal African Soc., 1954; Fndr. & Pres., Needham Market Soc., U.K.; Publs: To The South There Is A Great Land, 1970; Ed., All The World's A Stage, 1973; articles in sev. mags. Hons: O.B.E., 1960. C.B.E., 1972. Address: Tudor House, Needham Market, Suffolk, U.K. 23, 128.

PAGET, John Arthur, b. 15 Sept. 1922. Mechanical Engineer. Appts. incl: Chief Draughtsman, Gutta-Percha Rubber, Ltd., Toronto, Canada, 1946-49, Viceroy Mfg. Co., Toronto, 1949-52; Supvsg. Design Engr., C.D. Howe, Co. Ltd., Montreal, 1952-58; Sr. Design Engr., Combustion Engrng., Montreal, 1958-59; Sr. Staff Eng. Gen. Atomic Co., La Jolla, Calif., U.S.A., 1959-; currently working on the HTGR Gas Turbine Power Plant Proj., G.A. Fellow, Inst. Nuclear Engrs. Mbrships. incl: Am. Soc. Mech. Engrs.; Canadian Soc. for Mech. Engrng.; I. Mech. E.; SAME; Inst. Nuclear Engrng. Soc. for Hist. of Technol.; Newcomen Soc. Publs: Contbr. to profl. jrnls. in field. Address: c/o Gen. Atomic Co., P.O. Box 81608, San Diego, CA 92138, U.S.A. 2, 9, 15, 28, 56.

PAGNIN, Beniamo, b. 27 Aug. 1904. University Professor. Educ: Grad., Lit. & Philos. Appts: Lectr., Latin Palaeog. & Medieval Hist., Univ. of Pavia; Dir., Inst. of Palaeog. & Diplomatics, ibid; Dir., Richerche Medievali. Mbrships. incl: Patavina Acad. of sci., Lit. & Art; Nat. Hist. Comm. of Venice & Lombardy. Works. incl: Richerche sulla scrittura gotica, 1932; Littera Bononiensis; La cronica padue e lombardie di Guglielmo Cortusio (sec. XIII). Hons: Lincei Prize; Hon. Citizen of Pontida; Dipl. & Gold Medal for culture & art. Address: Viale Liberta' 61, 27100 Pavia, Italy.

PAI, Ei Whan (Edward W.), b. 30 June 1904. Diplomat; Economist. Educ: B.S., Coll. of Bus. Admin., Northeastern Univ., Boston, Mass., U.S.A., 1935; M.B.A., Grad. Schl. of Bus. Admin., N.Y. Univ., 1937. Appts. incl: Staff, For. Econ. Admin., Wash. D.C., 1944; Asst. Dir., Dept. of Finance, Mil. Govt., Seoul, Korea, 1946; Financial Advsr., Nat. Econ. Bd., ibid, 1947; Gov., Bank of Korea, Seoul, 1960; Korean Ambassador to Japan, 1961; Korean Ambassador to Argentina, Chile, Paraguay, Uruguay, & Bolivia, 1965; Korean Ambassador to U.K., Malta, & Gambia, 1967; Ambassador-at-Large & Special Envoy of the Pres. of Repub. of Korea, 1971; Pres., Overseas Econ. Rsch. Inst., Seoul, 1973-; Mbr., Pres.'s Coun. of Econ. & Scientific Advsrs., 1974-. Mbrships. incl: Pres., Korean Chmbr. of Comm., Honolulu, Hawaii, & Pres., Far Eastern Trading Co., 1950-60; Patron, UN Assn., U.K., 1968-71. Publs. incl: Conversational Korean, 1944; Japanese Public & War Finance, 1945;

Korea Today, 1969; A Coming of Age, 1970; 3 other books. Recip., LL.D., Northeastern Univ., Boston, 1972. Address: Overseas Economic Research Institute, C.P.O. Box 5864, 10th Floor, KTA Bldg., 10-1, 2-ka, Hoehyun-dong, Chung-Ku, Seoul, Korea. 12.

PAIGE, Richard E., b. 30 Dec. 1904. Inventor; Engineer. Educ: Voltaire Schl. of Music; Grand Ctrl. Schl. of Art. Appts: 1st Profl. Idea Man, Advtng., 1929; Fndr., 1st sci. rsch. into folding of paper; Est. 1st trng. prog. for Cardboard Engrs., 1932; Guest Lectr., Pratt Inst. & Am. Mgmt. Assn.; Cons., Bethlehem Steel Co., Proctor & Gamble Co., Hallmark Cards Inc., Container Corp. Am., Gift Box Corp. Am., Gen. Elec. Co. Author, Complete Guide to Making Money with Your Ideas & Inventions. Contbr. to mags. Wrote 1st singing commercial for radio, 1923. Holder of 150 U.S. patents. Hons. incl: Silver Plaque, Folding Paper Box Assn.; Top Packaging Design Award, Packaging Design Mag. Address: 215 E. 68th St., N.Y., NY 10021, U.S.A. 6, 128.

PAINTER, Floyd Eugene, b. 17 May 1920. Archaeologist; Editor. Appts: Laborer, Archtl. proj., Chichen Itza, Yucatan, Mexico, 1938; Contract Archt., Norfolk Mus. Arts & Sci., Va., 1955; Archt., ibid, 1956-59; Lectr., Arch. & Hist., Civic orgs., clubs, etc., 1955-; Lectr., TV Educ. Prog. (TV Schl.) Arch. & Hist., 1957-58; Lectr., Arch. & Hist., Norfolk Schl. System, 1964; Contract Archt., Norfolk Histl. Fndn., 1966; Contract Archt., Isle of Wight Histl. Soc., 1972; Instr., Arch., Adult Educ. Prog., Old Dominion Univ., 1972-73; Contract Archt., Assn. Preservation Va. Antiquities, 1974; Asst. Ed., Popular Archaeology, 1973-. Mbr. sev. soc., assns. & confs. in field. Publs. incl: Major archaeol. papers: The Helmet Site; The Chesopean Site; The Last of the Nottoway; The Mussel Eaters of Waratan; Paleo Man's Tool Kit; The Meherrin River Cache; The Cattail Creek Fluting Tradition; Excavation at the Thoroughgood House; The Long Creek Midden; Excavations at the Willoughby-Baylor House; Concentric Rectangles. Address: 7507 Pennington Rd., Norfolk, VA, U.S.A. 2, 7, 130.

PAINTON, Ivan Emory, b. 7 Aug. 1909. Painter; Poet; Art Instructor. Educ: Northwestern State Coll., Alva, Okla.; Okla. Bapt. Univ., Shawnee; pvte. art studies w. Albert E. von Strode. Appts: Art studio, 1930; employment in theatre, stock & vaudeville, 1932-35; decoration & design, 1936-39; turkey breeding, 1939-34; shop owner, 1945-; ranch owner; 1947-68; Owner, New Studio, 1955-; Art Tchr., 1964-; Fndr., Orion Cemetary Fndn. Mbr. & Fellow, var. art, poetry & mineral. socs. Publs. incl: Basic Art, 1967; Whispers in the Night (Love Poems), 1971. Paintings incl: Little Face; The Protector; Revenge; Nocturnal Fantasy; Autumn Call. Originator of Rock Art Portraits. Solo exhibs. incl: Wash. D.C.; Okla. City; Phoenix, Ariz.; Lincoln, Neb. Hons. incl: Ph.D., Colo, Christian Coll., 1973; var. hons. & awards. Address: Orion, Fairview, OK 73737, U.S.A. 7, 11, 22, 57, 125, 128, 130, 131, 133.

PAIR, Henry Tazwell, Jr., b. 30 Mar. 1928. Banker. Educ: B.B.A., Ga. State Coll. of Bus. Admin., Atlanta. Appts: w. Citizens & Southern Nat. Bank, Atlanta, 1946-68; Adj. Gen. Corp., U.S. Army, 1953-55; w. Bank of Cumming, 1968-. Mbrships: Past Local Pres., Kiwanis Club; Shriner; Vets. of For. Wars; Royal Order of Moose; Deacon, Bapt. Ch.; Forsyth Co. Chmbr. of Comm. Address: P.O. Box 35, Cumming, GA 30130, U.S.A.

PÄIVÄNSALO, Paavo Rafael, b. 3 July 1918. Educator. Educ: Ph.Mag., 1941; Ph.D.,

1949. Appts: Sr. Tchr., Relig., Psychol. & Philos., Helsinki 2nd Lyceum, Finland, 1950-; Lectr., Educ. & Didactics, Helsinki Univ., 1953-; Prof., 1972-. Chmn., Finnish Assn. for Educ. Sociol., 1947-. Publs. incl: Punishment in Secondary Schools, 1953; About the Laplanders Methods of Nursing & Educating Children, 1953; Social Life Among Secondary School Pupils, 1965; Experimental Research of Discipline in Secondary Schools, 1966; Measurement of Scientific Competence, 1968; The History of Educational Research in Finland before 1970; School System in Finland & in the Neighbouring Countries, 1971; Some Characteristics of Educational Research, 1973. Address: Kuusisaarentie 13, Helsinki 34, Finland. 134.

PAJIC, Svetomir, b. 24 Nov. 1932. Veterinarian. Educ: D.V.M., Vet. Med. Schl., Belgrade, Yugoslavia, 1957; D.V.M., Hannover, W.Germany, 1964; Ph.D., Univ. Hannover, ibid, 1964; Specialisation in Food Bacteriol., ibid, 1964; Food Hygiene Schl., Univ. Chgo., Ill., U.S.A., 1965. Appts: Vet. Praxis, Obrenovac, Yugoslavia., 1958-59. Vet. Insp. in Charge, Osijak, ibid, 1960-62; Cons. in Meat Ind., Luebek, W. Germany, 1959-60; Vet. Praxis, Lensahn, ibid, 1962-63; Vet. Meat Insp., USDA, 1964-68; Supvsng. Vet. Med. Off., ibid, 1968-. Mbrships: Am. Vet. Med. Assn.; Nat. Assn. of Fed. Vets.; Am. Pub. Hlth. Assn.; Lions Club & Chess Club, Ill. Author of The Contents of Calcium & Protein in the Blood of Dogs with Fractures, 1964, Address: 1702 Jay Ln., St. Charles, IL 60174, U.S.A. 8.

PAJULA, Jaakko Ilmari, b. 9 Aug. 1928. Lawyer. Educ: LL.B., 1953; LL.M., 1962; Attorney-at-Law, 1957. Appts: Hd., Legal Div., Secretariat-Chmn., Bd., & Pres., Finnish Soc. Ins. Instn., 1962-; Mbr., Sickness Ins. Comm. 1961-64; Sec. to Soc. Commn., Diet, 1962-63; Mbr. Delegn. Sickness Ins. Matters, 1964-67, Chmn., 1967-; Mbr., Comm. Pharmaceutical Ind. & Servs., 1967-68, Chmn., 1969-70; V-Chmn., Young People's Assn. For. Policy, 1962-65, Chmn., 1966-68; Chmn., Enlarged Bd. Kiipula Rehab. Fndn., 1971-; Chmn., Enlarged Bd. Kiipula Rehab. Fndn., 1971-; Chmn., Enlarged Bd. Finnish Rheumatic Fndn., 1972-; Bd. Mbr., Finnish Invalid Fndn., 1969-73; Bd. Mbr., Occupational Hlth. Fndn., 1967-; V.-Chmn., Socio-Pol. Prog. Comm., Min. Soc. Affairs, 1966-68; Mbr., Students' Hlth. Care Fndn.'s Delegn. & Admin. Bd., 1969-, etc. Publs: Code of Statutes: Sickness insurance and national pensions legislation, 1968; Articles in var. periodicals dealing w. soc. ins. legislation; Ed.-in-Chief, Sosiaalivakuutus (Soc. Ins.), 1968-. Recip. Cmndr., Order of Lion Award, 1971. Address: Alkutie 36 F, 00660, Helsinki 66, Finland. 43, 90.

PALADIN, David Chethlahe, b. 4 Nov. 1926. Artist; Educator. Educ: Chgo. Art Inst.; Univ. of N.M. Appts: Chmn., Am. Indian Designer Craftsmen, 1965-68 (Pres., ibid, 1968-69); Dir. of Fine Arts, Prescott Coll., Ariz., 1971-74; Dir., Renaissance Arts Workshop, ibid, 1974. Mbrships: Am. Crafts Coun.; Artists Equity; Nat. Art Educ. Assn.; Acad. Parapsychol. & Med.; Coun. of Am. Indian Artists. Paintings in Pub. Collects: Wm. Penn Men. Mus., Harrisburg, Pa.; U.S. Dept. of the Interior, Wash. D.C.; UNICEF, U.N., N.Y.; Bowers Mem. Mus., Santa Ana, Calif.; City of Phoenix, Ariz.; City of Scottsdale, ibid; City of Harrisburg, Pa. Tapestries, City of Phoenix Civic Ctr., 1972. Hons: Special Purchase, 1st. & Grand Awards, Scottsdale Nat., 1968, '69, '70; Carnegie Medal, 1969. Address: 2206 Sandia Ln., Prescott, AZ 86301, U.S.A. 37.

PALANDER, Viljo Viktor, b. 13 Feb. 1907. Managing Director. Educ: Dip. in econs., Commercial H.S., Helsinki. Appts: Clerk in bank, & textile factory; Export Sales Mgr., granite works; Commercial Mgr., bldg. assn. & bldg. contractor co.; Ptnr., Mng. Dir., Pirkan Rakennustoimisto Oy, bldg. contractors, Tampere, Finland. Mbrships: Fndn. Mbr., Chmn., local econ. assn., Tampere; Commercial Club, Tampere; Philately Soc., Tampere; Sec., Kulju Hunting Club, Chaine des Rotisseurs sect., Tampere. Hons: Hon. Medal of Econs., 1958. Address: Näsilinnankatu 21 A 20, 33210 Tampere 21, Finland. 43.

PALANISWAMI, Appiche Gounder, b. 15 Apr. 1925. Teacher; Director, Legal Studies. Educ: B.A., St. Joseph's Coll., Madras Univ., India; B.L., Law Coll., ibid; M.L., P.PA. (Dip.), ibid. Appts: Advocate, High Ct., Madras, India, 1952-; Pt.-time Lectr., Madras Law Coll., 1955-56; Prof.-Prin., ibid, 1956-58; Dir., Legal Studies, Tamilnadu State, 1958-. Mbrships: Pres. Madras Univ. Fac. Law; V.P., All-India Law Tchrs. Assn.; Exec. Comm., Indian Law Inst. (TV) & Indian Commn. Jurists; Syndicate, Madras Univ. Publs: Int. Law (Tamil); Ed., Yr. Book Legal Studies, 1957-62; Contbr. articles to The Indian Yr. Book Int. Affairs; Jrnl. Trad. Culture, Madras Univ.; The Yr. Book Legal Studies; Ceylon Univ. Law Coll. Jrnl. Recip. Prize Rs. 1000, for book International Law, as best of yr., Tamil Vazharchi Kazhganu, Tamilnadu Govt. Address: Dir. Legal Studies, Law Coll., Chepauk Triplicane P.O., Madras, India.

PALESTRANT, Simon S., b. 8 July 1907. Writer; Educator; Lecturer; Photographer. Educ: Cooper Union Art Schl., 1926; Pratt Inst., 1929; Yale Univ. Drama Schl., 1930; B.S., N.Y. Univ., 1935; M.S., CCNY, 1937; Inst. of Fine Arts, N.Y., 1938; China Inst., 1961, '68. Appts. incl: Artist, Illustrator & Cartoonist, 1926-60; Tchr. & Supvsr., Secondary Schls. & Colls., 1929-69; Lectr., Art, Tech. Subjects & Travel, 1936-67; TV & Radio Guest, 1940-66; Author, Writer, Columnist & Ed., 1942-69. Mbrships. incl: Mystery Writers of Am.; Int. Mark Twain Soc.; Nat. Acad. TV Arts & Scis.; Crime Writers Assn. of Gt. Britain; Hypo Camera Club, 1972-; Metrop. Camera Club Coun., 1973-; AAUP. Publs. incl: Toymaking, 1951; Lamp & Lampshade Making, 1952; Car-Owner's Fix-It Guide, 1952; Mechanisms & Machines, 1956; Papercraft, 1957; Games on the Go. 1960 & 1974. Permanent Palestrant Collect., Univ. of Southern Miss., Hattiesburg, 1967-. Address: 185 W. End Ave., N.Y., NY 10023, U.S.A. 3, 15, 30, 35, 131.

PALÉUS, Sven Paul, b. 25 Jan. 1917. Professor. Educ: M.D., Karolinska Inst., Stockholm, Sweden, 1955. Appts: Asst. Physn., Karolinska Sjukhuset & Serafimerlasarettet, Stockholm, 1945-46; Mbr., Sci. Staff, Biochem. Dept., Nobel Med. Inst. (head, Prof. H. Theorell), 1947-70; Asst. Prof.-Assoc. Prof., Biochem., Karolinska Inst., 1955-70; Prof., ibid, 1971-; Active employment, Södersjukhuset, Stockholm. Mbrships: Swedish Assn. of Chemists; Swedish Assn. of Physns.; N.Y. Acad. of Scis. Author of about 50 sci. publs., mainly concerning different hemo-proteins. Recip., Medal, Soc. of Biological Chem., France, 1964. Address: Blodverksamheten, Södersjukhuset, S-100 64 Stockholm 38, Sweden.

PALMER, Agnes Mae High (Mrs. D.D. Palmer). Chiropractor; Portrait Sculptress. Educ: Dr. of Chiroprac., Palmer Coll. of Chiroprac., 1938, Pvte. tutoring in voice, 1938-. Appts: Pvte. prac. as Chiroprac. Dr., W. Chester, Pa., 1938-43; Portrait Sculptress, 1967-; Pt.-time Soloist, W. Chester Presby. Ch., 1939-42. Mbrships: Past Pres., Davenport Etude Club, St. Katharine's Mothers Club, Davenport; supreme Kiatrus, Sigma Phi Chi; Life mbr., Nat. Assn. of Music Clubs, St. Luk's Hosp. Aux., Davenport, Mercy Hosp. Aux., Davenport; Assoc., Naples Community Hosp. Aux., Naples, Fla.; Daughters of Nile; Eastern Star; Eldorado Country Club; Union League Club, Chgo., Ill.; Lake Shore Club, Chgo.; Hole-in-Wall Colf Club, Naples, Fla. Publs: Aim (poem), 1927; An Ideal Man—Lincoln, 1928. Sculptured Portraits incl: Robert Kennedy; D.D. Palmer II (candidate for 1st Prize, Nat. Acad. of Sculpturing, 1967); Philip D. Adler. Address: 5 Forest Road, Davenport, IA 52803, U.S.A. 5, 8, 132.

PALMER, Edward Henry, b. 12 Feb. 1932. Housing Developer & Consultant. Educ: A.B., Hanover Coll., Ind.; S.T.B., Yale Univ.; Grad. work, Northwestern Univ. Appts: Off., Community & Tenant Rels., Chgo. Housing Authority, 1960-62; Exec. Dir., Trumbull Pk. Community Ctr., 1962-64, & Hyde Pk./Kenwood Community Conf., 1964-66; Pres., Soc. Planning Assocs. & Real Estate Data Co., 1966-70; Pres., SPA/REDCO, Inc., 1970-; Chmn. & Pres., Mark VII Corp., 1971-; V.P. & Bd. Mbr., Perkins & Will, Inc., Archts. & Engrs., 1972-. Mbrships. incl: Nat. Assn. Housing & Redev. Offls.; Am. Inst. of Housing Cons.; Urban & Regional Info. Systems; Univ. Club; Cliff Dwellers Club; Quadrangle Club. Publs: Urban Renewal—The New on community org. to var. jrnls. Address: SPA/REDCO, Inc., One E. Wacker Dr., Chgo., IL 60601, U.S.A. 8.

PALMER, Ernest William, b. 28 July 1916. Solicitor; Company Director. Educ: LL.B., Adelaide Univ., Australia; Appts: Cons., Wallman & Ptnrs., Barristers & Solicitors; Chmn., Beneficial Finance Corp. Ltd.; Dpty. Chmn., Ralph McKay Ltd.; Dir., Beach Petroleum, Argo Investments Ltd., Yellow Cab Fleet Ltd. Mbrships: Fellow, Australian Soc. Accts., Australian Inst. Mgmt.; Rep. for Australia, Int. Game Fish Assn.; life mbr., Game Fishing Assn. of Australia; Law of Sea Comm., Int. Law Assn. Royal Geog. Soc., S.A.; Royal Adelaide Golf Club; Naval, Mil. & Air Force Club, Adelaide; Stock Exchange Club, ibid. Author of articles on game fishing in var. books & mags. Hons: A.W. Bennett Prize, Adelaide Univ., 1939; Stow Prize Winner, ibid, 1937-39. Address: 29 Tarlton St., Somerton Park, S.A., Australia, 5044. 23.

PALMER, James Edward, b. 15 Sept. 1936. Dentist; Dental Educator. Educ: Grinnell Coll., Iowa; B.S., Maths., Howard Univ., 1961; D.D.S., Coll. of Dentistry, ibid, 1969. Appts: Served to Capt., U.S. Army, 1961-65; Instr., Dept. of Pedodontics, Coll. of Dentistry, Howard Univ., 1965-. Mbrships: Nat. Dental Assn.; Robert T. Freeman Dental Soc. Address: 5001 5th St., N.W., Wash. DC 20011, U.S.A. 7.

PALMER, Jerry L., b. 16 Sept. 1934. Recreational Therapist. Educ: B.S., Okla. State Univ.; Johnson Coun. Community Coll.; Kan. Univ. Med. Ctr. Appts. incl: former Dir., Commercial Sales, WBBZ Radio; Former Dir. P.R., Int. Supreme Coun., Order of DeMolay; Recreational Therapist for emotionally disturbed youth; Feature Writer & Photographer Int. DeMolay Cordon (mag.). Mbrships. incl: Fndr. & Directing Chief, Warbonnet Indian Dancers; Hon. Warrior, Tribe of Mic-O-Say; Hon. Mbr., Koshare Indian Dancers, Colo.; Kasiki, Tribe of Tacala Sunka; P.R. Soc. of Am.; Phi Delta Theta Fraternity; Fndr. & 1st Pres., Sigma Epsilon Sigma. Hons.

incl: DeMolay Legion of Honor, 1969; Silver Bow, Boy Scouts of Am., 1972. Address: 2616 W. 79th St., Prairie Village, KS 66208, U.S.A. 24.

PALMER, John Alfred, b. 22 May 1926. Professor; Administrator. Educ: B.A., Univ. of Wash., 1950; M.A., Cornell Univ., 1952; Ph.D., ibid, 1962. Appts: Instr., Engl., Cornell Univ., 1957-62; Asst.—Full Prof., Engl., Calif. State Univ., LA, 1962-; Chmn., Dept. of Engl., ibid, 1967-69; Dean., Schl. of Letters & Sci., 1969-70; V.P. for Acad. Affairs, 1970-. Mbrships: Off., local chapts., AAUP & A.C.S.C.P.; Phi Beta Kappa; Phi Kappa Phi; MLA. Publs: Joseph Conrad's Fiction, 1968; Twentieth-Century Interpretations of "The Nigger of the 'Narcissus'," 1969. Address: V.P. for Acad. Affairs, Calif. State Univ., Los Angeles, CA 90032, U.S.A. 30, 130, 140.

PALMER, Per Albert Johannes, b. 20 July 1914. Managing Director. Educ: M.B.A., Norwegian Univ. of Econs. & Bus. Admin., Bergen, 1941. Appts. incl: V.P., Economies, Norwegian Airlines, 1946-47; w. Orkla Grube A.B. Mining Co., 1947-; Pres., Orkla Industrier A.S., 1959-; Chmn. of the Bd., Orkla Exolon; Bd. Mbr., Orkla Grube A.B. & Fosdalens Bergverk; Mbr., Bd. of Reps., Elkem-Spigerverket, Idun, Kosmos, Norcem, Norgas, Norsk Hydro & Storebrand. Mbrships. incl: Ctrl. Bd., Norwegian Employers Assn.; Ctrl. Bd., Norwegian Fedn. of Inds.; Chmn., Norwegian Fedn. of Mining Cos.; Bd. Mbr., Sulphur Inst., Wash. D.C.; Bd. Mbr., Norwegian-Am. Chmbr. of Comm.; Norske Selskab, Oslo; Den Norske Klub, London. Address: 7340, Lokken Verk, Norway.

PALMER, Robert Leland, b. 29 Jan. 1916. Gospel Ministry. Educ: B.A., La. Coll., Pineville, U.S.A., 1937; Th.M., Southern Bapt. Theol. Sem., Louisville, Ky., 1941; Th.D., ibid 1944; Postgrad. study, Union Coll., Barbourville, ibid; Tenn. Univ., Knoxville. Appts: Fellow, Southern Bapt. Theol. Sem.; Pastors: Longview Hts. Bapt. Ch., Memphis, Tenn.; Napoleon Ave. Bapt. Ch. New Orleans, La.; Baldwyn Bapt. Ch., Miss. 1st Bapt. Ch., Murfreesboro, Tenn; 1st Bapt. Ch., Williamsburg, Ky.; Assoc. Prof. Engl. & Relig., Cumberland Coll., ibid. Mbrships. incl: Denominational Bds: Exec. Bds., La., Miss. Tenn. & Ky. Bapt. Convens.; Trustee, Belmont Coll., Nashville, Tenn. & Cumberland Coll., Ky. Southern Bapt. Hosp. Annuity Bd.; S.B.C.; Southern Bapt. Fndn.; Southeastern Ky. Bapt. Hosp. Corbin, Ky. Publs: Author articles Ency. of Southern Bapts., 1958; num. book reviews & articles, Quarterly Review & other Southern Bapt. publs. Ldr., workgrp., Exceptional Children, Family Life Conf., 1963. Address: 818 Walnut St., Williamsburg, KY 40769, U.S.A. 46.

PALMER, Sidney J(ewell), b. 18 Nov. 1928. Television Producer-Director; Composer; Conductor; Opera Director. Educ: B.Mus., Univ. of Tex., U.S.A., 1947; Fellowship, Juilliard Schl. of Music, N.Y.C., 1947-48; M.Mus., Univ. of Tex., 1949. Appts: Concert Pianist; Conductor, New Braunfels Symph., Houston Symphonette, Ark. State Symph., & Little Rock Philharmonic; Guest Conductor & Opera Dir., num. cos.; Artistic Dir., Hot Springs Lyric Theatre & Columbia Lyric Theatre; Radio Prod., KHOU, KLAR, & KARK; TV Prod. Dir., KARK-TV; Exec. Prod. & Prod. Mbr., WIS-TV; Exec. Prod., Pub. TV & Educl. Servs., S.C. Educl. TV Network; Artist-in-Residence, Columbia Coll., S.C.; Arts Critic; TV Cons. to the Arts. Mbrship: Sec., TV Programmer's Conf. TVPC NAEB. Compositions: Symph. for

Strings; Concerto for Orch.; Harp Concerto; Cantata, Seven Last Words of Christ; Royal Wedding Overture; Choral, instrumental, & Vocal works. Recip., sev. awards & prizes for compositions & TV prods. Address: 3101 Barnes Spring Rd., Columbia, SC 29204, U.S.A. 7, 125.

PALMER, William Marvin, b. 13 July 1918. Magazine Executive. Educ: L.L.B., Atlanta Law Schl., Univ. of Ga., 1950; Grad., Signal Corps., U.S.A., 1941; U.S.A.F. Flying Trng., 1943 & in Turkish, U.S.A. Lang. Schl., 1951. Appts: Admitted, Ga. Bar, 1951 & Fed. Dist. Ct., Northern Dist. of Ga.; in Advtng. & Promotion, Huntsville Daily Times, Ala., 1957-60; P.R./Advtng. Dir., Ga. Press Assn., Atlanta, 1960-62; Advtng./Promotion, Kan. City Star, Mo., 1963-67; Ed., Chief Exec., Electronics Digest Mag. (int.), Tandy Corp., Ft. Worth, Tex., 1967-72 & Ed., Radio Shack Intercom Mag. (int.), 1967-; Nat. Mag. Coord., Radio Shack Div. Mbrships: Am. Bar Assn.; V.P., Ft. Worth Chapt., Int. Assn. Bus. Communicators; Antique Wireless Assn., U.S.A.; Canadian Vintage Wireless Assn., Toronto. Author, Great Men in Electronics, 1970. Recip. Air Medal w. silver cluster, 1944. Address: 7325 Bursey Rd., Smithfield, TX 76080, U.S.A. 16.

PALOHEIMO, Erkki Ensio, b. 18 May 1911. Civil Engineer. Educ: Helsinki Tech. Univ., final examination 1932. Appts: Constructor, Oy Palmberg Ab., Helsinki, 1934-41, Construction Chief, 1941-50; Vice Mng. Dir., 1950-53; Major, Finnish Army, 1941; Pvte. Cons. Engr., 1953-56; Mng. Dir., Oy KreuTo Ab., Helsinki, 1956-71, Pres., Bd. of Dirs., 1971-. Mbrships. incl: Finnish Tech. Soc.; Finnish Concrete Soc.; Finnish Genealogical Soc.; Bourse Club in Helsinki. Hons: Finnish Cross of Liberty III & IV; Cross of White Rose I. Address: Vähäniityntie 14, 00570 Helsinki 57, Finland.

PALSSON, Halldòr, b. 26 Apr. 1911. Agricultural Director. Educ: B.Sc., Agric., Edinburgh Univ., U.K., 1936; Postgrad. work, Schl. of Agric., Cambridge & Inst. of Animal Breeding & Genetics, Edinburgh; Ph.D., Edinburgh Univ., 1938. Appts. incl: Chief Advsr. on Sheep Prod., Agricl. Soc. of Iceland, 1937-62; Scientific Off., Dir., Physiol. of Reproduction, Growth & Meat Prod., Dept. of Agric., Univ. Rsch. Inst., Reykjavik, Iceland, 1942-61; Sr. Scientific Off., Physiol. of Growth & Meat Prod., Ruakura Animal Rsch. Stn., Hamilton, New Zealand, 1961-62; Dir., Agric., Agricl. Soc. of Iceland, 1962-. Mbrships: Soc. Scientiarum Islandica; Royal Agricl. Soc. of England; Natural Hist. Soc. of Iceland; Nat. Rsch. Coun., Iceland; Bd. of Dirs., Sec., Icelandic Sci. Fndn. Author or co-Author of num. sci. & tech. papers in jrnls. Hons: Kt., Order of the Falcon, 1965; Kommandör af Dannebrogordenen, 1973. Address: The Agricultural Soc. of Iceland, Box 7080, Reykjavik, Iceland. 134.

PALSSON, Hermann, b. 26 May 1921. University Reader. Educ: Univ. of Iceland; Univ. Coll., Dublin, Ireland. Appts: Lektor, Icelandic, Univ. of Edinburgh, U.K., 1950, Lectr., 1954-62, Rdr., 1967-; Vis. Prof., Old Icelandic & Old Irish, Toronto Univ., Canada, 1967-68. Publs: Njal's Saga, 1960; Sagnaskemmtun Islendinga, 1962; Hrafnkels Saga of Freysgydlinger, 1962; Eftir Thjodveldid, 1965; The Vinland Sagas, 1965; King Harald's Saga, 1966; Hrafnkels sögu, 1966; Gautrek's Saga & Other Medieval Tales, 1968; Halgafell, 1968; Laxdaela Saga, 1969; Art & Ethics in Hrafnkel's Saga, 1970; Legendary Fiction in Medieval Iceland (co-author), 1970; Hrafnkel's Saga & Other Icelandic Stories, 1971; Hrolf Gautreksson, 1972; Addor-Odd, 1973; Eyrbyggja Saga, 1973; Grettir's Saga, 1974. Address: 14 Royal Terrace Mews, Edinburgh 7, U.K. 3.

PALUMBO, Pier Fausto, b. 3 Nov. 1916. University Professor. Educ: Grad., Litt. & Philos., Univ. of Rome; post-grad, studies, Univ. of Berlin. Appts: Lectr., Mediaeval Hist., Univ. of Rome, 1941-; Prof., Univ. of Bari, 1945-56; Prof., Univ. of Lecce, 1956-60; Prof., Univ. of Salerno, 1958-; Ed. of various jrnls. Mbrships: Pres. of Hist. Soc. of Terra d'Otranto & of Ctr. of Salentine studies; Pres. of soc. of Puglian Nat. Hist., 1947-63; Roman Soc. of Nat. Hist., 1942-; Fndr. & Gen. Sec., Labour Studies Inst., 1944-53, Fndr. of Italian Sect. of European League of econ. co-operation & of "European Movement" for Italy; Gen. Sec. of Nat. Union of Musicians. Publs. incl: Lo scisma del MCXXX, 1942; La cancelleria di Anacletoll, 1945; Vomini, tempi, paesi dall' antico al nuovo, 1947 & 1961; Studi medievali, 1949 & 1965; L'organizzazione del lavoro nel mondo artico ed altri saggi, 1942 & 1967; Per la storia delle relazioni tra le due sponde adriatiche, 1962; Patrioti, storici e erudite salentini e pugliesi, 1974. Address: Via G. B. Martini 6, 000198, Rome, Italy.

PAMILLA, Jeanne R., Orthopedic Surgeon. Educ: B.S., St. John's Univ., 1964; M.D., Woman's Med. Coll. of Pa., 1968. Appts. incl: Intern, Lenox Hill Hosp., N.Y.C., 1968-69; Gen. Surg. Res., ibid, 1969-70; Orthopedic Surg. Res., ibid, 1970-73; Cerebral Palsy Fellowship, Hosp. for Special Surg., Cornell Med. Ctr., 1973-74; Instr. in Surg., Cornell Med. Schl., 1973-75; Sr. Fellow in Children's Orthopedics, Hosp. for Special Surg., 1974-75; Orthopedic Cons., Dept. of Hlth., N.Y.C. Mbrships: Candidate in Am. Coll. of Surgs.; Am. Acad. of Cerebral Palsy; Am. Med. Women's Assn.; Alumnae Assn., Woman's Med. Coll. of Pa. & Ed., Iatrian, assn.'s yrbook., 1968. Hons: Physns. Recognition Award, 1970, 1973. Address: 77-17 62 St., Glendale, N.Y., NY 11227, U.S.A. 5, 6, 138.

PANA, Sasa, b. 8 Aug. 1902. Physician; Writer. Educ: Fac. Med. & Surg., Bucharest, Romania. Appts: Mil. Dr.; Chief Physn., Clin. Med., Bucharest Garrison; Adjunct, Chief Physn., Mil. Hosp., ibid; Chief Physn., Bucharest Garrison; Ret'd. as Col., 1960. Mbrships: Writers' Union, Romania; Writers' Assn., Bucharest; Dada Movement & Surrealism, Paris, France; Int. Acad. Poetical Interchanges, Geneva, Switzerland; Acad. des Marches, St. Pee-sur-Nivelle, France. Author 10 vols. poems, 3 prose poems, 5 vols. novels, sketches & essays, inclng. The Talisman Word, 1933; For Liberty, 1945; That was formerly . . . and will no more be, 1949; Sadism of the Truth, 1970; Chief Ed., var. periodicals & reviews, 1928-47. Hons. incl: Ordinul Meritul Cultural Class I-a. 1972; Medalia Eliberarea de sub jugul fascist, 1949; Ordinul Steaua R.P.R.cl.V-a, 1954 Medalia Meritul Militar Clasa I-a 1956; Medalia Muncii, 1959. Address: Str. Dogarilor, 36 (of. postal 9), Bucharest, Romania.

PANAYOTOPOULOS, John M., b. 23 Oct. 1901. Professor. Educ: Athens Univ., Greece. Appts: Prof. Philol., 1923-38; Prof., Dir., Hellenikon Ekpedeftirion, 1938-; Prof. Ecole Normale, 1947-63. Mbrships: Pres., Bd. mbr., Comm. on Arts, Nat. Theatre; Bd. Dirs., Nat. Gall.; Bd. Dirs., Gen. Sec., Comm. Expansion Cultural Books; V.P., Gen. Book Stores of Greece; Community European Writers; Int. Union Art Criticism; Int. Confedn. Jrnlsts. & Writers of Tourism. Publs. incl: The Seven Sleepers, 1956; Africa Awakes, (a travel book) 1963; The Contemporary Man, 1966; The Hard Times, 1972; Humble Life; 11 other novels; 5 books on poetry; 9 other travel books & 1 on hist. neohellenic lit. Hons: Palamas Prize, Book on Palamas & studies on the poet, 1947; Nat. Award Prizes, novel, 1956; travel book, 1963; essays, 1966, '72. Address: 14 Nikiforou Lytra St., Palaion Psychikon, Athens, Greece.

PANG, Herbert George, b. 23 Dec. 1922. Ophthalmologist. Educ: B.S., Northwestern Univ., Ill., 1944; M.D., ibid, 1947; Internship, Queen's Hosp., Honolulu, 1947-48; N.Y. Univ. Post Grad. Med. Schl. (Ophthalmol.), 1948-49; Res. at. other hosps. Appts. incl: Pvte. Prac., Honolulu, Hawaii, 1956-; Cons., Bur. of Crippled Children, ibid, Kapiolani Maternity Hosp. & Leahi Tuberculosis Hosp.; Courtesy Staff, Kuakini Hosp., Children's Hosp., Castle Mem. Hosp. & Queen's Hosp., Honolulu; Active Staff, St. Francis Hosp., ibid; Tchr., Fac., Am. Acad. of Ophthalmol. & Otolaryngol.; Asst. Clin. Prof. of Ophthalmol., Univ. of Hawaii Schl. of Med. Mbrships. incl: Chmn., var. comms., Honolulu Med. Soc., Pres., Hawaiii Eye, Ear, Nose & Throat Soc., 1960; AMA; Am. Coll. of Surgs.; Pres., Eye Study Club, N.Y. Contbr. of sev. articles to profl. jrnls. Address: 1374 Nuuanu Ave., Honolulu, HI 96817, U.S.A. 9, 78.

PANOFF, Robert, b. 16 Aug. 1921. Electrical Engineer. Educ: B.S.E.E., Union Coll., 1942; Registered Profl. Engr., D.C. Appts. incl: assoc. w. dev. of mod. submarine for 25 yrs. & w. atomic power dev., 1949-; Civilian Engr., Elec. Sect., Bur. of Ships., 1947-49; Assoc., Naval Nuclear Propulsion Hdqtrs., posts inclng. Hd., Ship Application Sect. & Sr. Submarine Project Off., Nuclear Propulsion Divs. & Asst. Mgr., Naval Reactors, U.S. Atomic Energy Commn., 1950-64; Prin. Off. & Dir., MPR Assoc., 1964-. Mbrships. incl: N.Y. Acad. of Scis.; Naval Rsch. Advsry. Comm. Lab. Advsry. Bd. for Naval Ships; Tau Beta Pi. Publs: Professional Development in a Small Engineering Firm, 1967; classified reports & articles in profl. jrnls. Hons: D.Sc., for work in dev. of naval nuclear propulsion, Allegheny Coll., 1959; Navy Dept. Civilian Serv. Awards. Address: c/o MPR Associates Inc., 1140 Connecticut Ave., N.W., Washington DC 20036, U.S.A. 2, 14, 50, 131.

PANTELIDIS, (Gen.) Menelas of George, b. 2 Dec. 1895. Retired Lieutenant General. Educ: Mil. schl., 1916-18; Superior Acad. of War, 1930; Ecole des Commandants, Ecole d'Application, France, 1926-27; Sr. Offs.' Schl., U.K., 1946. Appts. incl: Nat. Resistance during occupation of Greece, 1942-44; Cmdr., regiment of Valtos, 1943; Gen. staff, 1945; Chief of staff, II Div., 1946-47; Brigadier against the communists, 1947-49; Cmdr., II Div., 1950-51; Cmdr., Greek expeditionary forces, Korea, 1951-52; Chief of staff, 1st Army, 1952-53; Cmdr., Cyprus Army, 1960-68. Mbrships: Union Int. Resistance Deportes; Union Resistance pour une Europe Unie; Pres., Greek Resistance Assn., 1957-58. Author of many articles about the mil. value of Cyprus & the Cyprus problem. Hons. incl: Golden Medal of Bravery, War Cross, 4 times; War Cross of France, Medal of Korea, 1952; British D.S.O., Legion of Merit, U.S.A., 1952. Address: Efroniou 25, Athens 516, Greece.

PANUSH, Louis, b. 16 Feb. 1910. Educational Administrator. Educ: B.S., Wayne Univ., 1934; M.A., ibid, 1935. Appts. Incl: Hd. of Sci. & Math. Depts., Northeastern H.S., 1952-57, Henry Ford H.S., 1957-58; Instr. in Hebrew Lang. & Lit., Wayne State Univ.,

1945-58; Asst. Prin., Mackenzie H.S., 1958-63; Prin., Western H.S., 1963-. Mbrships. incl: Fellow, AAAS; Bd. Dirs., Zionist Org. of Detroit, 1947-; V.P., ibid, 1965-68; Pres. 1968-70; Phi Delta Kappa; Pres., Zionist Fed. of Detroit, 1971-72; Fndng. V.P., ibid, 1970-71. Contbr. of articles to profl. jrnls.

PANYARACHUN, Sern, (Phya Prichanusat) b. 27 June 1890. Educator. Educ: Manchester Univ., U.K., 1908-10. Appts: Sci. Tchr., later Hd.-Master, Royal Pages Coll., Bangkok, 1910-15; Hd.-Master, Royal Pages Coll., Chiengmai, 1916; Dir. of Schls. under H.M. the King's patronage, 1919; Dir.-Gen. Post & Telegraph Dept., 1920; Prof., Chulalongkorn Univ., Bangkok, 1920-26; Hd.-Master, Vajiravudh Coll., Bangkok, 1926-33; Under-Sec. of State, Min. of Educ., 1933; Civil Serv. Commnr., 1948; Cultural Cnslr., Royal Thai Embassy, London, 1949; Chmn., Coun. of World Affairs & Int. Law, Thailand, 1968, 69, 70; Fndr. & Ed., The Saim Chronicle (in Engl.); Fndr., Phim Thai & Siam Nikorn (in Thai), The Morning Express (in Engl), Suparb Satri (in Thai) & The Bangkok Post (in Engl.); Chmn., Laem Thong Bank, & World Travel Serv., Ltd., Bangkok; Dir., S.E. Ins. Co., Ltd., Bangkok. Mbrships: Fndr. & 1st Pres., Press Assn. of Thailand, 1941-43; Life, Old Salopian Club & Old Engl. Students Assn.; Skal Club of Bangkok. Publs: Tale of Two Princes. Hons: Order Chula Chom Klao; Order White Elephant; Order Crown of Thailand; Ky. Coll., 1970. Address: 28 Soi 18 Sukhumwit, Bangkok, Thailand.

PAOLETTI, Pietro, b. 31 Jan. 1934. Physician; Neuro-Surgeon. Educ: M.D., Univ. of Milan, 1957. Appts. incl: Asst. Prof., Univ. of Milan, 1959-62; Rsch. Fellow, Harvard Univ., U.S.A., 1962-63; Prof. of Neurosurg., Univ. of Cagliari, 1970-; Dir., Neurosurg. Clin., Univ. of Pavia, Italy, 1971-. Mbrships: Congress of Neurol. Surgs. Inc., U.S.A.; N.Y. Acad. of Scis.; Soc. for Study of Hydrocephalus & Spina Bifida, Cambridge; Italian Soc. for Neurosurg. Publs. incl: Progress In Neurological Surgery, Vol. 1, 1966, Vol. 2, 1968, Vol. 3, 1969, Vol. 4, 1971, Vol. 5, 1973; Experimental Biology Of Brain Tumors, 1972. Hons: Victor Emanuel II Award, 1960; Bertarelli Prize, 1962. Address: Univ. of Pavia, Piazza 60661, 27100 Pavia, Italy.

PAOLETTI, Rodolfo, b. 23 Aug. 1931. University Professor. Educ: M.D., Schl. of Med., Univ. of Milan, 1955. Appts: Asst. Prof., Pharmacol., Univ. of Milan, 1955; Hd. of Lab., ibid, 1960; Assoc. Prof., Pharmacol., 1962; Dir., Dept. of Pharmacol., Univ. of Cagliari, 1967-70; Dir., Dept. of Pharmacol. & Pharmacognosy, Fac. of Pharm., Univ. of Milan, 1970-. Mbrships: Sci. Sec., Exec. Ed., "Pharmacol. Rsch. Communications", Italian Pharmacol. Soc.; V.P., Italian Heart Fndn.; Biochem. Soc., London; Royal Soc. of Med., London; N.Y. Acad. of Scis.; Italian Soc. for Atherosclerosis, Milan; Fndng. Mbr., European Grp. of Atherosclerosis, Cambridge; Int. Cardiol. Fedn., Geneva; Publs: num. monographs & articles to field of biochem. pharmacol.; Ed. of series, Lipid Pharmacology, Advances in Lipid Research, Advances in Experimental Medicine & Biology & Progress in Biochemical Pharmacology; Ed. or on Ed. Bd. var. jrnls. Sci. Sec. for sev. int. congresses. Recip. num. prizes. Address: c/o Inst. of Pharmacol. & Pharmacognosy, Univ. of Milan, Via A. Del Sarto 21, 20129 Milan, Italy. 50.

PAPACHATZIS, Georgios, b. 21 Mar. 1909. University Professor: Counsellor of State. Educ: Dr. of Law & Pol Sci., Fac. of Law,

Athens Univ. Appts: Barrister-at-Law, 1927-29; Auditor, Council of State, 1929, Mâitre des Requêtes, 1937, Counsellor of State, 1949, V.P., Supreme Admin. Ct., 1963; Asst. Prof., Fac. of Law, Athens Univ., 1936-39; Full Prof., Pantios Grad. Schl. Pol. Scis., 1939, Vice Rector, 1963, Rector, 1964-65; Mbr., Tribunal of Conflicts, Athens, 1950-61. Mbrships. incl: Pres., Soc. Pub. Admin. Studies, Athens, 1951-64; Int. Inst. Admin. Scis., 1951-. Publs. incl: Christianity & Culture, 1953; Studies Upon Administrative Contentions & Disputes, 4th edit., 1961; Administrative law & Public Administration in Greece, 4th edit., 1965. Recip., sev. hons., Greece & Italy. Address: Iofontos St. 7, Athens 516, Greece. 43.

PAPACONSTANTINOU, Theophylactos, b. 10 July 1905. Author & Journalist. B.A., Univ. of Athens, Greece, 1927; M.A., ibid, 1930. Appts. incl: Ed. & Contbr., Great Hellenic Ency., Athens, 1928-34; Sub-ed., Proix, Athens, 1936-43; Press Dir., Hellenic Info. Serv., Cairo, Egypt, 1943-44; Ldr. Writer, Eleftheria, Athens, 1945-63; Radio Commentator, Nat. Broadcasting Inst., Athens, 1950-53 & 1959-64; Ldr. Writer, Meddimvrini, Athens, 1963-67; Min. of Educ., Greek Govt., 1967-69; Contbr., Acropolis, Athens, 1972-; Coun. Mbr., Nat. Bank of Greece, 1972-. Mbrships. incl: Int. Fedn. of Jrnlsts.; Union of Athens Daily Newspaper Jrnlsts.; Hellenic Soc. for Humanistic Studies. Num. publs. incl: Falsifications of Marxism in Greece, 1931; Introduction to Dialectics, 1933; Against the Current, 1949; Ion Dragoumis & Political Prose, 1957; Problems of Our Era, 1960; 6th edit., 1972; The Battle of Greece, 1966, 2nd edit., 1971; Political Education, 1969, 2nd edit., 1970. Hons. incl: Cmdr., Royal Order of Phoenix, 1965; Gold Medal of City of Athens, 1971; Kt. Cmdr., Royal Order of George I, 1972. Address: 23 Agias Philotheis, Philothei, Athens, Greece. 34, 43.

PAPACOSTAS, George A., b. 4 Aug 1932. Professor of Philosophy. Educ: B.A., Hunter Coll., CUNY, 1959; M.A., N.Y. Univ., Ph.D. ibid., 1968. Appts: Asst. Prof.-Prof. of Pol. Sci., Calif. State Coll., Pa., 1964-69; Chmn., Dept of Humanities, York Coll. of Pa., 1969-72; Prof. of Philos., York Coll. of Pa., 1969-. Mbrships. incl: Am. Philosophical Assn; Am. Pol. Sci. Assn; Am. Soc. Int. Law; NEA; AAUP; Phi Delta Kappa; Delta Tau Kappa. Publs: The Development of International Arbitral Tribunals, 1961; George Gemistos-Plethon: A Study of His Philosophical Ideas & His Role as a Philosopher-Teacher, 1968. Contbr. to var. academic publs. Hons: Selected as Univ. Honours Schol., & awarded N.Y. Univ. Fndrs. Day Cert., 1968. Address: 3205 E. Market St., York, PA 17402, U.S.A. 6, 111.

PAPADOPOULOS, George S., b. 17 Jan. 1926. Economist. Educ: Athens Univ. & Schl. of Econs. Appts. incl: Chief, Admin. Dept. of Prime Min., 1952-54; Prof., Nat. Defence Schl. Naval Coll., etc. & Radio & TV Commentator on Internal Econs., 1954-74; Dir. in Min. 1958-60; Special Advsr., Min. of Press, 1960-61, Min. of Finance, 1961-63, & Prime Min., 1965-67. Mbrships. incl: Press. & Fndr., Studies Soc. of Hellenic Econ. Dev., 1961-74; Counsellor, Hellenic Dept. of European Ctr. of Documentation & Information. Publs: Economics of U.S.S.R., Eastern Europe & China, 1957; International Economic Struggle, 1958; Atlantic Economy, EEC & Greece, 1962; A New Theory of Economic Strategy, 1963; Programs, Plans & Free Economy, 1964; Strategy & Economy in the Balkans, 1965; New Tendencies of World Economic Strategy, 1969; The Role of Science in Industrialization, 1972; Introduction to the Basic Statutory

Deficiencies of the Athens Agreement, 1973; articles in newspapers, jrnls. etc.; TV lectr. series, EEC West & East, 1970. Address: 44, Panepistimiou St., Athens, Greece.

PAPADOPOULLOS, Theodore H., b. 6 Mar. 1921. Historical Research Administrator. Educ: Acctng. Bus. Mgmt.; Classical studies; Medieval & Mod. Greek Hist. & Lit.; Ethnol. Appts: Mng. Acct. & Auditor; Hon. Consul Gen. of Greece, Zaire; Fellow, Cyprus Rsch. Ctr., 1963, Dir., 1967. Mbrships: FRAI, London; Hon. Fellow, Soc. of Histl. Studies, Athens; var. learned socs. Publs. incl: Studies & Documents Relating to the History of the Greek Church & People under Turkish Domination, 1952; Social & Historical Data on Population (1570-1881), 1965; Texts & Studies of the History of Cyprus (Ed.). Ed., Epeteris, annual of Cyprus Rsch. Ctr. Hons: Order of St. Mark, Patriarchate of Alexandria; Order of Phoenix, Greece; Chevalier de la Légion d'Honneur, France. Address: Cyprus Research Centre, P.O. Box 1436, Nicosia, Cyprus.

PAPAGEORGIOU, Apostolos, b. 17 Dec. 1906. Supreme Court Advocate Greece. Educ: Univs. of Munich & Athens. Appts: Advocate, Cts. of 1st Deg., 1936, Ct. of Appeal, 1940 & Supreme Ct., 1945; Acting Gov. Gen., Ionian Islands, 194? ; Sec. Gen., Min. of Justice, 1952-54; Legal Cons., Econ. Dev. Financing Org., 1955-64; Vice-Gov., Hellenic Ind. Dev. Bank, 1967; Dir., Nat. Mortgage Bank of Greece, 1969-72; Chmn., Econ. & Soc. Coun., 1970-72; Min. for Energy, 1973. Mbrships: Athens Club; Royal Yacht Club. Publs: num. articles & commentaries in var. legal jrnls. Co-Responsible for ed. conduct of Archives of Penal Sciences, 1937-40. Address: 5, Xanthippos St., Athens 139, Greece. 43.

PAPAIOANNOU, Yannis A., b. 7 Jan. 1910. Composer. Educ: Dip., Piano, Hellenic Conservatory, Athens, 1934; Dip., Harmony, Counterpoint, Fugue & Composition, ibid, 1934; UNESCO Schlrship. to study at sev. music ctrs. in Europe, worked w. A. Honegger for 1 yr. in Paris. Appts: Prof., Hist. of Music. Nat. Coll. of Anavryta, Athens, 1951-61; Prof., Musical Composition, Hellenic Conservatory, Athens, 1954-. Mbrships: Pres., Hellenic Assn. for Contemp. Music & Greek Sect., Int. Soc. for Contemp. Music (I.S.C.M.), 1965-; Bd. of Dirs., Union of Greek Composers, Athens; Soc. Hellenique d'Esthetique. Has composed num. works inclng. 5 symphs.; Pygmalion, symph. poem for orch; Vassilis Arvanitis, symph. legend for orch.; works for solo instruments & small ensembles; Four Orpheus Hymns, for narrator & instrumental ensemble; works for solo voice w. instrumental ensemble; choral works; theatre & ballet music. Hons: Prize for 3rd symph., Concours Musical Int. Reine Elisabeth de Belgique, Brussels, 1953; Gottfried von Herder Prize, Germany, 1970. Address: Eptanissou Str. 5, Athens 801, Greece. 43.

PAPALAMBROU, Apostolos, b. 22 May 1916. Jurist. Educ: Dip., Econs. & Pol. Sci., Univ. of Athens, 1935; Dip. of Law, ibid, 1936. Appts: Lawyer, 1937; Rapporteur, coun. of State, Athens, 1946; Jr. Mbr., Coun. of State, 1951, Councillor of State, 1959, V.P., Coun. of State, 1969-73. Mbrships: Soc. of Admin. Studies; League of Greek Jurists for Study of Procedural Law. Publs. incl: Some Aspects of the Jurisdiction of the Council of State, 1958; Interpretative Laws & Authentic Interpretation, 1959; Administrative Agencies & Administrative Tribunals, 1962; Jurisdiction of the Council of State in Precuniary Disputes, 1963; Vague Concepts & Control of Legality, 1966. Recip., Cross of the Order of Phoenix,

1961. Address: Iphigeneia St., Kallithea, Athens, Greece. 43.

PAPANEK, Jan, b. 24 Oct. 1896. Diplomat; Government Minister. Educ: LL.D., Univ. of Paris, France, 1923; LL.D., Charles Univ., Prague, Czechoslovakia, 1928. Appts. incl: Organizer, Br. Off., Czechoslovak Legions of Min. Nat. Defense, 1919; Mbr., Min. of For. Affairs, Prague, 1922; Commercial Attache, Czech. Legation, Budapest, Hungary, 1925; Sec. of Czech Legation, Wash. D.C., U.S.A., 1926-31; Parliamentary Sec., Min. For. Affairs, Prague, 1933; Czech Consul, Pitts., Pa., U.S.A., 1935; Czech. Min. Plenipotentiary, N.Y.C., 1942; Deleg., UN Conf., San Francisco, 1945, & Comm. Mbr., drafting UN Charter; Permanent Rep. for Czechoslovakia, & Ambassador at UN; Acting Pres., Econ. & Soc. Coun. of UN, 1947. Mbr. & Off., var. relief & humanitarian orgs. Author, sev. books. Articles, newspapers & mags. Broadcasts. Recip., LL.D.(Hon.), Hobart Univ. Address: 77 Sprain Valley Rd., Scarsdale, NY 10583, U.S.A.

PAPATSONIS, T.C., b. 30 Jan. 1895. Financier; Civil Servant; Author. Educ: Grad., Law & Pol. Sci., Univ. of Athens, Greece; B.A., France. Appts. incl: Sev. posts, inclng. Sec.-Gen. & Gen. Dir., Min. of Econs., Athens; Greek Rep., 30 int. convens.; Negotiator, trade agreements with Germany, Roumania, & U.K.; Dpty. Chmn., Commercial Bank of Greece. Mbrships. incl: Acad. of Athens (Letters & Fine Arts), 1968-; Pres., Greek Soc. of Esthetics; V.P., Bd., Royal Theatre, 1954-65; Chmn., Bd., Nat. Gall., 1955-65. Num. publs. incl: Selection A (poems), 1934; Selection B (poems), 1936; Ursa Minor (poems), 1944; Pilgrimage of an Ascent to Mount Athos, 1950; Moldovalachia Legendary, 1955; The Four Dimensions of the World (essays); Translations into Greek of works by Edgar Allan Poe, Chaucer, Aragon, Paul Claudel, Anouilh, & others; Contbns. to sev. reviews. Hons. incl: French Legion of Honour, 1929; Cmdr., Order of Crown of Italy, 1935; Cmdr., Order of Phoenix, 1952; Cmdr., Order of George I, 1955; Nat. Poetry Prize, Greek State, 1963. Address: Anagnostopoulo Str. 9, Athens 136, Greece. 12, 35.

PAPAVLACHOPOULOS, John, b. 23 Dec. 1914. Civil Servant. Educ: Grad., Univ. of Thessaloniki, 1937; studied admin. subjects in U.K. Appts. incl: Pres., Supreme Coun. for Civil Servs., 1967, now Hon. Pres. ibid; Gov. of Agric. Bank, 1967; Min. of Agric., 1969-71; Mbr., Constitutional Comm., 1967. Mbrships Admin. Coun. Nat. Bank of Greece; Vice Chmn., "The King Paul" Nat. Inst. Publs: Public & Local Administration in England & in Greece; Aspects of Administrative & Professional Organization. Hons: Commendation Medal; Gold Cross & Cross of the Supreme Taxiarchon, both Order of King Geo. I; Cross of the Taxiarchon, Order of the Phoenix; Gold Cross of the Holy Patriarch for the Millennium of the "Aghion Oros." Address: 48 Fok. Negri St., (803) Athens, Greece. 43.

PAPE, Donna Lugg, b. 21 June 1930. Juvenile Book Author & Free-lance Writer. Educ: Grad. courses in creative writing & art. Photo-jrnlst., 1959-65. Mbrships: Nat. Writers Club; Wis. Regional Writers Assn.; Past Pres. & Sec., Sheboygan Co. Writers Club. Publs. incl: Gerbil for a Friend; The Pape Series of Speech Development; The Best Surprise of All; Splish, Splash & Splush; Toby Zebra & the Lost Zoo; I Play in the Snow; Bumper Bear's Bus; Whoever Heard of a Lost Policeman; The Seal Who Wanted to Ski; Mary Lou, The Kangaroo; My Fish Got Away; Leo Lion Looks at Books; Mrs. Twitter, The Sitter; Mr. Mogg in the Log; Count on Leo Lion; Greeting cards written for major & minor greeting card cos; Contbr. to jrnls. Recip., 1st prize, Wis. Regional Writers' Assn. Juvenile writing contest, 1964. Address: 1734 S. 15th St., Sheboygan, WI 53081, U.S.A. 30, 76.

PAPE, Rainer Emil Eduard Wilhelm, b. 5 Mar. 1926. Museum Director. Educ: Univ. of Wurzburg, German Fed. Repub., 1949-50; Ph.D., Univ. of Kiel, 1955. Appts: Ex-serviceman, 1944-45; Prisoner of war, U.S.S.R., 1945-46; Asst., Städtische Mus., Herford, 1955; Commissary Dir., ibid, 1956; Dir., 1957; Additional Dir., Stadtarchiv, Herford, 1964; Mus. Advsr., 1965; Hd. Mus. Advsr., 1970. Mbrships. incl: Historischer Verein für die Grafschaft Ravensberg, 1951; Hansischer Geschichtsverein, 1953; Bd. of Dirs., Herforder Verein für Heimatkunde, 1955-; Verein für Westfälische Kirchengeschichte, 1957. Publs. incl: Das alte Herford, Bilder aus vier Jahrhunderten, 1971; Anton Fürstenau, ein Kaufmann & Diplomat der Reichsstadt Herford im 17. Jahrhundert, 1973; Herforder Geschichtsquellen, 1968. Address: Weddigenufer 76, 49 Herford, German Fed. Repub. 133.

PAPENHEIM, (Paul) Felix (Theodor), b. 19 Dec. 1916. Company Executive. Educ: Humanistisches Gymnasium; Dipl. Ing., Tech. H.S., Danzig, 1940; Dr. Rer. Pol., Univ. of Munich, 1948. Appts: Reserve Off., 1941-45; Govt. Bd. of Works, 1943; Deutsche Diat Aktiengesellschaft, 1948-; Dir., Spare Parts Div., ibid, 1948-; Bd. Mbr., ibid, 1966-. Recip., Cavaliere Ufficiale des Italienischen Verdienstordens. Address: 7107 Neckarsulm (Württ.), Marktstr. 17, German Fed. Repub.

PAPIN, Joseph, b. 2 Oct. 1914. University Professor. Educ: Ph.L., Berchmanianum Philos. Fac., Nijmegen, Netherlands, 1937; Ph.D., ibid, 1939; ordained, 1942; S.T.D., Univ. of Nijmegen, 1946; Postgrad. studies, Univ. of Louvain, Belgium, 1946. Appts. incl: Docent Univ. of Nijmegen, 1946; Prof., St. Procopius Coll., Lisle, Ill., U.S.A., 1948-50; Prof. & Dept. Chmn., De Paul Univ., Chgo., 1950-53; Prof., Univ. of Notre Dame, Ind., 1953-63; Prof. & Dir., Chmn., Grad. Studies, Villanova Univ., Pa., 1963-; Vis. Prof., Loyola Univ., Chgo., 1954; Vis. Prof., Valparaiso Univ., 1962. Mbrships. incl: Int. Mariological Pontif. Acad., Rome, Italy; Am. Philos. Assn.; Theological Soc. of Am.; Acad. Pol. Scis.; AAUP; Pres., Middle European Club, 1950. Publs. incl: The Dynamics in Christian Thought, Vol. 1, 1968; The Dynamics in Christian Action, Vo.. II, 1969; Openness to the World, Vol. III, 1970; The Pilgrim People's Vision, Vol. IV, 1971; The Eschaton: A Community of Love, Vol. V., 1972; The Church & Human Society at the Threshold of the Third Millenium, Vol. VI, 1972; Man's Religious Quest, Vol. VII, 1973; Theological Folia, Biblical Studies, Vol. 1, 1973; Speculative Studies, Vol. II, 1973, Moral & Liturgical Studies, Vol. IV, 1973; Eschatological Studies, Vol. IV, 1973; Ecclesiological Studies, Vol. V, 1973; Historico–Patriological Studies, Vol. VII, 1974; Interdisciplinary Studies, Vol. VIII, 1974; Index of Names & Concepts, Vol. IX, 1974; Transcendence & Immanence, 1972; Wisdom & Knowledge, 1973; Festschrift in Honour of Joseph Papin, 1973; Christian Encounter, 1974. Hons: Gold Medal, Imperial Byzantine Univ., Madrid, 1951; Bene Merenti, Pius XII, 1954; Vatican Deleg., 1945; Fellow, Intercontinental Biographical Assn., 1974. Address: Villanova Univ., Vallanova, PA 19085, U.S.A. 3, 8, 13, 15.

PAPINEAU-COUTURE, Jean, b. 12 Nov. 1916. Composer. Educ: B.A., Coll. of Jean de Brébeuf, Montreal, P.Q., Canada, 1937; Mus.B., New England Conservatory of Music, Boston, Mass., U.S.A., 1941. Appts. incl: Sec., Acad. of Music, Quebec, 1947-54; Asst. Prof., Fac. of Music, Univ. of Montreal, 1963; Vice-Dean., ibid, 1967; Dean, 1968-73. Mbrships. incl: Past Pres., Canadian Coun. of Music; Pres., Canadian League of Composers, 1957-59 & 1963-66; Sec., Canadian Music Soc., 1959-66; Pres., Quebec Soc. of Contemporary Music, 1966-72; Pi Kappa Lambda. Compositions incl: Symph., 1948; Violin Concerto, 1952; Piano Concerto, 1965; Num. other orchestral, chamber, solo instrumental, & choral works, songs, & ballet music. Publs: Contbns. to music jrnls.; Papers read at meetings. Num. hons. incl: Mus.D., Univ. of Chgo., Ill., 1960; Calixa-Lavallée Prize, St. Jean-Baptiste Soc., Montreal, 1962; Mus.D., Univ. of Sask., 1967; Canadian Medal of Serv., 1968. Address: 657 Avenue Rockland, Montreal 154, P.Q., Canada. 2, 88.

PAPPAS, Charles Nicholas, b. 14 Jan. 1936. Dentist. Educ: Univ. of Colo., Boulder, 1953-55; D.D.S., Dental Schl., Northwestern Univ., Chgo., Ill., 1959. Appts. Capt., U.S. Army Dental Corps, 1960-62; Assoc. in Prac. of Dentistry, S. Weymouth, Mass., 1962; Pvte prac., Weymouth Heights, ibid, 1962-65; Pub. Hlth. Dentist, Dept. of Hlth. & Hosps., Boston, 1965-70; Clin. Instr., Tufts Univ. Dental Schl., ibid, 1965; Assoc. Prac., Weymouth, 1965-68 & Brookline, Mass., 1969; Clin. Instr., Operative Dentistry, Harvard Schl. of Dental Med., 1967-71; Practising Clin. Dentist, ibid, 1970-71; Clin Rsch. Asst., Forsyth Dental Ctr., 1972; Assoc. in Restorative Dentistry, Univ. of Pa., 1972-. Mbrships. incl: Lambda Chi Alpha; Xi Psi Phi; Am. Dental Assn.; Mass. Dental Soc.; Phillips Brooks Soc. Publ: Self-Control of Tooth Decay (pamphlet), 1967. Address: 4001 Spruce St., Philadelphia, PA 19104, U.S.A. 6.

PAPPAS, Tassos, b. 21 Mar. 1921. Writer. Appts: Ed., var. newspapers & mags.; Collaborator, Theatrical Div., EIR (Nat. radio org.), adapting many plays for radio from Greek & int. repertoire; 1 of 1st collaborators w. cultural mag. Theatro, K. Nitsos; w. newspaper, Ta Nea, 1961-73. Mbr., Bd. & Trustee, Ligue des Hommes de Lettres Helleñes, 1943-. Publs: Poetry: Fota Messa sti Thiella (Lights in the Storm), 1946; Ta Tragondia Tow Pathanares (The Songs of Pathanares), 1948; Messinveinos (Meridian), 1960; Dir., Techni kai Zoi (Culture & Life), 1943 (ceased publ. during Nazi occupation). Recip. Greek Poetry Prize Veairon ton Dodeka (The Prize of 12), 1961. Address: Konstantinoupoleos 13, Ymittos, Athens TT457, Greece.

PAPPENHEIM, (Count zu) Rudolf, b. 25 Dec. 1910. Airline Executive. Appts. incl: Dir., Accident Claims Tribunal, Am. Arbitration Assn., N.Y.C.; Exec. Sec., Interamerican Arbitration Assn. & pro tem Int. Arbitration Tribunal; Regional Mgr., Lufthansa German Airlines, Wash. D.C., 1955; Dir., Govt. Affairs, ibid, 1968-. Mbrships: Order of St. John; Metropolitan Golf Club, Wash. D.C.; Kenwood Golf & Country Club, Bethesda, Md. Address: 5011 Sedgwick St. N.W., Washington, DC 20016, U.S.A.

PAQUIN, Nancy Ann, b. 3 Nov. 1939. Digital Computer Systems Analyst. Educ: B.A. Univ. of Vt., Burlington, 1961; M.A., Am. Univ., Wash., D.C, 1965; Ph.D. Canad., ibid. Appts: Computer Programmer Data Processing & Maths. Section, Bur., Radiological Hlth., U.S. Pub. Hlth. Serv., 1961; Systems Analyst, 1962; Sr. Systems Analyst, 1963; Chief, Systems

Design & Programming Unit, 1964; Asst. Dir., 1966; Special Projs. Systems Analyst, Off. of the Dir., Div. of Dental Hlth, 1967-. Fellow, Int. Biog. Assn., 1972, 73, 74. Mbrships. incl: Am. Soc. Info. Sci.; Assn. Computing Machinery; Pi Sigma Alpha, 1964. Contbr. of articles to specialized jrnls. Recip. Staff and Sandal, Jr. Women's Hon., Univ. of Vt., 1960. Address: 16513 Walnut Hill Rd., Gaithersburg, MD 20760, U.S.A. 57, 76, 132, 138.

PARANTELA, Aldo, b. 2 Jan. 1929. Surgeon. Educ: M.D., Univ. of Rome, 1951; Bds.-Gen.-Surg., 1957, Cardiovascular Surg., 1959, Thoracic Surg., 1960; Tchng. qualifications—Surg. Semeiol., 1958, Thoracic Surg., 1959, Surg. Pathol., 1962, Surg. Clins., 1964. Appts: Asst., Surg. Clin., Univ. of Rome, 1952-58; Asst. Prof., Surg. Clin., Univ. of Perugia, 1958-68; Assoc. Prof., ibid, 1968-74. Mbrships: Int. Soc. of Surg.; Int. Soc. of Cardiovascular Surg.; Past Sec. Gen., Int. Coll. of Surgs.; Italian Soc. of Surgs.; Italian Soc. of Thoracic Surg.; Rotary Club. 120 publs. Hons: Academician, Acad. Tibernia, Rome, 1972; Unione della Legion d'Oro, Rome, 1973; Min. of For. Affairs Schlrship., 1954; NATO Schlrship., 1962. Address: 4705 Troy Rd., Springfield, OH 45502, U.S.A. 2, 43.

PARASCOS, Edward Themistocles, b. 20 Oct. 1931. Consultant; Business Executive; Engineer. Educ: B.M.E., CCNY, 1956; M.M.E., ibid, 1958; Completed studies towards Ph.D., N.Y. Univ., 1967. Appts: Design Engr., Curtiss Wright Aero Div., 1956-57; Sr. Design Engr., Ford Instrument Co., 1957-61; Supvsr., Reliability Engrng., Kearfott Div., Singer, 1961-63; Cons. Engr., Am. Power Jet Co., 1963-64; Mgr., Reliability Engrng., Perkin Elmer Corp., 1964-66; Dir., System Effectiveness, CBS Labs., 1966-72; Cons., QA&R, Con Edison Co. Inc., 1972-; Pres., Dir. Engrng., Dipar Cons. Servs. Ltd., 1971-; Pres. Bd. Chmn., LAPA Trading Corp., 1973-. Mbrships. incl: Sr. Mbr., Chapt. Chmn., Regional Dir., Am. Soc. for Quality Control; Sr. Mbr., Inst. of Environmental Scis. Author, num. papers & articles in field. Address: 30-02 83rd St., Jackson Hts., NY 11370, U.S.A. 6, 22.

PARASKEVOPOULOS, Stephen-Constantine A., b. 21 May 1926. Architect; Professor. Educ: Dipl. Arch. Eng., Nat. Tech. Univ. of Athens, Greece, 1951; M.Arch., Univ. of Mich., Ann Arbor, U.S.A., 1954. Appts: Pvte. Prac., Archt. & Cons., 1951-; Assoc. & Dir., various rsch. projs., Archtl. Rsch. Lab., Univ. of Mich., 1954-; Sev. tchng. posts, ibid, 1955-64; Prof., Arch., 1964-; Chmn., Doctoral Prog. in Arch., 1971-; Guest Lectr., sev. univs., 1963-. Mbrships: Am. Inst. of Archts.; U.S. Bldg. Rsch. Inst.; Tech. Chmbr. of Greece; Archtl. Soc. of Greece. Publs: Rsch. papers & synopses in profl. jrnls., books, & newspapers; Papers presented at nat. & int. confss. & meetings of profl. orgs. Address: Architectural Research Laboratory, University of Michigan, Ann Arbor, MI 48104, U.S.A. 2.

PARDO, Luis Pérez, b. 26 Aug. 1915. Professor. Educ: Dr.Econ.; Fellow, Del Amo Fndn., LA, Calif., U.S.A. Appts: Official Transl., Engl., French & Italian; Prof., Econ. Geog. & Structure, Schl. of Commerce, Univ. of Barcelona, 1943-; Sec., ibid, 1947-53; Dir., 1962-73; Mbr., Nat. Coun. of Educ.; City Councillor, Barcelona, until 1976. Mbrships: Real Soc. Geográfica Madrid; Am. Geog. Soc., N.Y.; Int. Soc. for Bus. Educ. Hons: Economienda con Placa, Orden Civil Alfonso X el Sabio. Address: c/o Escuela Estudios

Empresariales, Universidad de Barcelona (14), Spain.

PARELIUS, Nils Monrad, b. 24 May 1912. Public Prosecutor. Educ: Grad., Law, Oslo Univ., Norway, 1937. Appts: Asst. Dist. Judge, 1939-41; Sec. to Prof. Dr. Jon Skeie, 1942; Judge, 1945; Depty. to Dir. of Pub. Prosecutions, 1946; Pub. Prosecutor, Dir. of Pub. Prosecutions Off., 1946-50; Pub. Prosecutor, Möre & Romsdal, Sogn & Fjordane cos., 1950-. Mbrships. incl: Chmn., Romsdal Hist. Soc., 1958-; Hon., 1971; Chmn., Romsdal Dist. Grp., Municipal Cultural Defence, 1958-; Chmn., Molde & Romsdal Defence Union, 1972-. Publs. incl: Pre-Historic Relics in Midsund, 1967; Pre-Historic Relics in Sandöy, 1969; Molde & Romsdal During the War, 1940-45, 1970; Rambles in the Pre-History of Romsdal, 1971; Co-author, From the Campaign in Norway, 1940; Contbr. to var. jrnls. Hons. incl: Norwegian War Participant Medal, 1945; H.M. the King's Gold Medal of Merit, 1969; Order of the Yugoslav Flag w. Silver Wreath, 1973. Address: 6400 Molde, Norway. 134.

PARIS, Dorothy. Artist; Painter. Mbrships. incl: Exec. Bd., Nat Assn. of Women Artists, V.P., 1972-74; Exec. Bd., Am. Soc. of Contemporary Artists, Treas., 1965-66, First V.P., 1965-67, Pres., 1967-69; Sec., U.S. Comm., Int. Assn. of Art, 1969-73; Treas., Conf. of Am. Artists, 1971. One-man shows: Zak Gall., Paris, France, 1950; Van Dieman-Lilienfeld Galls., N.Y.C., U.S.A., 1951; Barzansky Galls., N.Y.C., 1954; Bodley Galls., N.Y.C., 1959. Paintings in num. permanent collections inclng: Dallas Mus., Tex.; Evansville Mus., Ind.; Brandeis Univ., Mass.; Mus. of Art, Birmingham, Ala.; N.Y. Univ. Art Collection; Art Mus., Phoenix, Ariz.; Mus. of Mod. Art, Miami, Fla.; Mus. of Art, Oakland, Calif.; Musée de Cannes, France. Other exhibs. incl: Mus. of Mod. Art, Tokyo, Japan; Mus. of Fine Arts, Mexico; Ga. Mus. of Art; World's Fair, 1965; Villa Communale, Naples, Italy, 1972. Address: 88 7th Av. S., New York, NY 10014, U.S.A. 2, 5, 6, 37, 132, 138.

PARISH, H(ayward) Carroll, (jr.), b. 13 Feb. 1920. Educator. Educ: A.B., Univ. of Calif., L.A., 1949; M.A., 1950; Ph.D., 1958; Fulbright Rsch. Fellow, Waseda Univ., Japan, 1958-59. Appts: L.A. Co. Youth Commnr., 1938-42 (pres., 1938); Asst. Prof., Univ. of Calif., Berkeley, 1946-47; Attaché, Calif. State Legislature, 1947; Assoc. Prof., Naval Sci., UCLA, 1952-54; Assoc. Dean, ibid, 1962-66; Dean, 1966-71; Provost & Trustee, Miller Community Coll., L.A., 1971-. Collab., Inst. Int. Rels., Aoyama Gakuin Univ., Tokyo, 1960-; Lectr., Asian Studies, Univ. of Southern Calif., U.S.A., 1961. Fellowships: Int. Inst. Arts & Letters, 1961; AAAS, 1963; Augustan Soc., 1967-. Mbrships. incl: Chmn., Perm. Secretariat, ASPAC, 1970-; Pres., Am. Siam Soc., 1954-; Pres., Nat. Assn. Student Financial Aid Admin., 1970-71; Chmn., Coun., Japan Am. Soc. of Southern Calif; Lif, Siam Soc. Soc. of Southern Calif; Life, Siam Soc. (Bangkok); Chancellor, Western Region, Pi Gamma Mu; Life Mbr., Naval Order of the U.S.A., Life Mbr., Navy League; Jonathan Club; Capt., U.S. Naval Reserve. Publs: Canada & The United Nations, 1950; Co-auth., Thailand Bibliography, 1958; num. articles. Hons: Disting. Serv. Award, Nat. Assn. Student Financial Aid Admins., 1971; Diamond Award, Japan Am. Soc., 1962; Order of Golden Merit, Japanese Red Cross Soc., 1970; Nat. Hon. Key, Pi Gamma Mu, 1973; Kt. Grand Officer, Order of St. John Baptist of Am., 1970; Kt., Cmndr. Order of Kts. Hospitaller of St. John of Jerusalem, 1972; Kt. Military & Hospitaller Order of St. Lazarus of

Jerusalem. Address: 633 24th St., Santa Monica, CA 90402, U.S.A. 9, 14, 15, 22, 59, 70, 74, 75.

PARKER, Edgar Turner, b. 29 Dec. 1938. Engineer. Educ: B.S.E.E., Univ. of Tenn., Knoxville, 1962; M.S.E.E., Fla. State Christian Coll., Ft. Lauderdale, 1972; Ps.D., Coll. of Divine Metaphys., Indpls., Ind., 1971. Appts: Profl. Engr.; Cert. Fallout Shelter Analyst. Engrng. Trainee, U.S. Army Ballistic Missile Agcy., Redstone Arsenal, Ala., 1958-60; NASA, Geo. Catlett Marshall Space Flight Ctr., Huntsville, ibid, 1960-62; Aerospace Technol., ibid, 1962-67; Electronic Engr., U.S. Army Missile Cmd., Redstone Arsenal, Ala., 1967-68, U.S. Army Materiel Cmd. HQ, Wash. D.C., 1968-70; U.S. Army Computer Systems Cmd., Ft. Belvoir, Va., 1970-73, Naval Coastal Systems Lab., Panama City, Fla., 1973-. Mbrships: Nat. Hon. Soc., 1957; Eta Kappa Nu, 1961; Tau Beta Pi, 1962, Qualified & selected for participation in Univ. of Tenn. Coop. Schlrship. Prog., 1958-62. Address: 6104 Boat Race Rd., Panama City, FL 32401, U.S.A. 7.

PARKER, Edith Lee Boone Hartley, b. 20 Feb. 1928. Business Executive. Educ: Eastern N.M. Univ., 1945-46; Grad., St. Mary's Schl. Radiologic Technol., 1962. Appts: X-Ray Technologist, St. Mary's Hosp., 1962-64; Owner, Lee Anne Dress Shoppe, 1964-66; V.P.-Sec., Swan Drug Store, Inc., 1967-. Mbrships: Am. Registry Radiologic Technologists; Am. Soc. Radiologic Technologists; Ocotillo Club (Past Treas.); Am. Assn. of Retail Druggists. Address: 6939 E. Crestline Dr., Tucson, AZ 85715, U.S.A. 5, 9, 16.

PARKER, Ernest William, Jr., b. 23 Mar. 1930. Certified Public Accountant. Educ: B.A. in Bus. Admin., Univ. of Mont., 1951. Appts. incl: Ptnr., Randall, Emery, Campbell & Parker, Spokane, Wash., 1954-; Trustee & Exec. Comm., Deaconess Hosp., 1968-; Chmn., Spokane Transit Commn. Authority, 1968-; Ptnr., Coopers & Lybrand, 1973-. Mbrships. incl: Pres., Spokane Chapt., Wash. Soc. Cert. Pub. Accts., 1962; Pres., Wash. Soc. of Cert. Pub. Accts., 1970; Coun. Mbr., Am. Inst. of Cert. Pub. Accts., 1972-; Kiwanis; Alpha Kappa Psi; Phi Delta Theta. Hons: Ten Outstanding Young Men of Wash., 1963; Disting. Community Serv. Award, Spokane Jr. Chmbr. of Comm., 1963; Youth Silver Serv. Award, YMCA of Inland Empire, 1969; Disting. Serv. Award, Kiwanis Club of Spokane, 1960, 62, 66, 68, & 72. Address: 3515 S. Lee St., Spokane, WA 99203, U.S.A. 9, 117.

PARKER, Gilbert Norman, b. 19 Oct. 1902. Banker. Educ: Columbia Univ., NY, U.S.A., 1925-27; Columbia Grad. Schl. Bus., 1952-53. Appts: Acct., 1927-43; Sec.-Treas., Alaska Airlines, 1943-46; Chmn., Pres.-Sr. Chmn., Nat. Bank Gulf Gate, Sarasota, Fla., 1963-; Dir. & 1st Regional V.P., Southwest Fla. Banks, Inc., 1973-; Pres., 301 Realty Corp., 1967-. Mbrships: Past Chmn., Sarasota Co. Pub. Hosp. Bd.; Past V.-Chmn., Sarasota Co. Pub. Housing Authority; Sarasota Chmbr. of Comm., U.S. Coast Guard Aux.; U.S. Power Squadron; Sarasota Yacht Club; Field Club; Elks Club; Bay Is. Siesta Assn.; Save Our Bays Assn., Inc.; Am. Contract Bridge Club; Audubon Soc.; Humane Soc., Sarasota Co.; Am. Forestry Assn.; Century Club, Sarasota Mem. Hosp.; Ringling Mus. of Art; Repub. Nat. Finance Comm.; G.S. Alumni Assn., Columbia Univ.; Sarasota Co. Civic League; Planned Parenthood Assn., Southwest Fla.; Oceanographic Soc.; Boys Club; Fla. Sheriffs Boys Ranch & Girls

Villa. Address: P.O. Box 5117, Sarasota, FL 33579, U.S.A.

PARKER, Jack Royal, b. 25 Apr. 1919. Chemical Engineer; Engineering Executive; Industrailist. Educ: CH.E., Polytech. Inst. of Brooklyn, 1943; D.Sc.(Hon.) Pacific Int. Univ., 1956. Appts. incl: Ptnr., Dir. & Chief Proj. Mgr., The Parco Co., N.Y.C., 1947-; Fndr., Past Dir. & Pres., Vernitron Corp.; Dir., V.P. & Fndr., Refinadora Costarricense de Petroleo, SA, San José, Costa Rica, 1963-; Pres., Par-Con Inc.; V.P., Parkise Realty Inc.; Parco Chem. Servs. Inc., 1965-; Peruviana Del Sur, SA, (Peru), 1965-; Guyano Oil Refining Co. (British Guiana), 1966-; Pres., Royalpar Inds., Inc.; Cons., Stone & Webster Engrng. Corp.; Todd Shipyards Corp.; Lever Brothers Co., etc. Reckp. of many patents in U.S. & abroad w. respect to chem. engrng. & design, Inventor of Lazy Golfer; Lectr., One World Club, Cornell Univ. Mbrships. incl: Am. Inst. Chem. Engrs.; Am. Soc. Mil. Engrs.; Am. Petroleum Inst.; U.S. Naval Inst.; Inst. of Engrng. Designers; Fellow, AAAS. Author of Aircraft Carrier Gasoline Systems, 1945; Contbr. of articles to tech. jrnls. Recip of Hon. Ph.D., Pacific Int. Univ., 1965. Address: 106 The Mews, Haddonfield, NJ 08033, U.S.A. 2, 6, 16, 25, 26, 64, 69.

PARKER, James Varner, b. 27 June 1925. Curator; Administrator. Educ: Assoc. Art; B.F.A.; M.A. Appts: Curator of Educ., Dir. of Arts/Crafts, currently Curator of Art & Asst. Dir., Heard Mus. of Anthropol./Primitive Art; Instr., Phoenix Community Coll., Glendale Community Coll., Phoenix, Ariz. Mbrships: Ariz. & Nat. Art Educ. Assns.; Past Pres., Ariz. Artists Guild; Fndng. Pres., Ariz. Watercolor Assn. Works in Collect.: Carl Hayden H.S., Dr. & Mrs. Dean Nichols, Sen. Barry Goldwater, Mr. & Mrs. Eugene C. Pullian, Gtr. Ariz. Savings/Loan Co., Heard Mus., & Alhambra H.S., all in Phoenix; City of Phoenix Fine Arts Collect.; S.E. Mo. Univ.; Ctrl. H.S., Mo. Hons: Nat. Vets. Art Award, Calif., 1953; Ariz. State Fair, 1958, 60 & 61; Tucson Arts/Crafts Ctr. Award, 1960; Phoenix Art Jus., 1960. Address: 2433 West Sweetwater Ave., Phoenix, AZ 85029, U.S.A. 37.

PARKER, Josephus Derward, b. 16 Nov. 1906. Farmer & Corporation Executive. Educ: N.C. Univ., 1924-25; Univ. of the South, 1925-28; Tulane Univ., 1928-29. Appts: Chmn., Bd., J.D. Parker & Sons, Inc., 1955-; Parkers Tree Farms, Inc., 1956-; Pres., Brady Lumber Co. Inc., 1957-62; V.P. & Dir., Atlantic Limestone, Inc., 1970-; Owner, Op., Parker's Airport, Eagle Springs, N.C., 1940-62; Capt., Civil Air Patrol, 1944-47. Mbrships: Past mbr: Lions, Moose & Plymouth Country Clubs; Wilson Country Club. Address: P.O. Box 405, Elm City, NC 27822, U.S.A. 2, 7.

PARKER, Levan Grady, b. 21 Dec. 1940. Headmaster. Educ: B.S., Samford Univ., 1965; M.S., ibid, 1970; additional study, Univs. of Miami & Ala., Southwestern Bapt. Theol. Sem. Appts: Tchr., Am. Hist., & Basketball & Baseball Coach, Ragland HS; Asst. Prin., Talledaga Co. Trng. Schl.; currently Hdmaster., Westminster Christian Schls.; Interim Pastor, 1st Bapt. Chs., Glencoe, Ragland & Gallent, Bellevue Bapt.; Goodyear Hts. Bapt. & White Springs Bapt. Chs. Mbrships: NEA; Ala. Educ. Assn.; Nat. Assn. Second. Schl. Prins.; Phi Kappa Phi; NASSA; AHSCA; Rotary; Bd., Southern Assn. of Christian Schls.; Pi Gamma Mu; Alpha Kappa Psi; E. Gadsden Bapt. Ch. Hons: Alpha Kappa Psi Schlrship., 1964; Cert. Pub. Accts. Award, 1965; Fellowship in Multi-Cultural Admin., Univ. of Miami, 1969.

Address: P.O. Box 544, Gadsden, AL 35901, U.S.A. 117, 125.

PARKER, Oscar Cecil, b. 24 Oct. 1924. Social Worker. Educ: Dip., Univ. of Paris, France, 1947; B.A., L.I. Univ., N.Y., U.S.A., 1949; M.S.W., Mich. State Univ., 1959. Appts: Psych. Soc. Wkr., Childville, Inc.; Supvsng. Soc. Wkr., Spofforol Juvenile Ctr.; Dir., Soc. Serv., Mamida Juvenile Ctr.; N.Y.C. Human Resources Admin., Off. of Staff Dev. & Trng., Spec. Servs. for Children; Trng. Specialist, Spec. Servs. for Children. Mbrships: Nat. Assn. Soc. Wkrs.; Acad. Cert. Soc. Wkrs.; N.Y. State Welfare Conf. Recip. of profl. h ons. Address: Morrisinia Stn., P.O. Box 43, Bronx, NY 10456, U.S.A. 6, 57.

PARKER, Stirling George James, b. 11 May 1912. Architect. Educ: Melbourne Univ., Australia. Archt., Commonwealth of Defence, 1939, Commonwealth of Works, 1940-45; Suptng. Archt., Commonwealth of Works, 1956; Asst. Dir. Gen. (M & S), ibid, 1964. Mbrships: Fellow, Royal Australia Inst. Archts.; Ergonomics Soc. of Australia & N.Z.; Int. Hosp. Fed.; Royal Automobile Club of Vic.; Healesville Country Club. Recip., Schlrships; M.B.E., 1970. Address: Commonwealth Dept. of Works, 17 Yarra St. Hawthorn, Vic., Australia. 23.

PARKER, Sydney Richard, b. 18 Apr. 1923. Professor of Electrical Engineering. Educ: B.E.E., CCNY; M.S., Stevens Inst. of Technol., Hoboken, N.J.; Sc.D., ibid. Appts. incl: w. Adv. Dev. Grp., Radio Corp. Am., 1952; Dept. of Elec. Engrng., CCNY, 1956-65; Prof., Univ. of Houston, Tex.; Prof. & Chmn., Dept. of Elec. Engrng., Naval Postgrad. Schl., Monterey, Calif., 1966-. Mbrships. incl: IEEE; N.Y. Acad. Scis.; AAAS; Sigma Xi; Tau Beta Pi; Eta Kappa Pi. Publs: Principles of Control Systems Engineering, 1960; over 50 tech. papers. Address: Dept. of Elec. Engrng., Monterey, CA 93940, U.S.A.

PARKINSON, Ariel, b. 12 July 1926. Painter; Designer. Educ: B.A., Scripps Coll., 1942; M.A. Univ. of Calif., 1943; art studies, San Francisco Art Inst., & Academie Montmartre; also w. sculptors Morescalchi & Lisk. Appts: Tchng. Asst., Univ. of Calif., 1946-47; Instr., Mills Coll., 1947-48, Calif. Coll. of Arts & Crafts, 1949-50; Commns. from Drama & Music Depts., Univ. of Calif., 1961-71. Mbr. & past Off., var. waste recovery orgs. Solo Exhibs. incl: Oakland Art Gall., 1951; Gumps Gall., San Francisco, 1953, '59, '61, '64, '67, Mus. of Art, 1962, '64. Permanent Collects. incl: Davison Art Ctr.; Univ. of Calif. at L.A.; Smithsonian Instn.; Lincoln Ctr. Lib. & Mus., N.Y. Work in pvte. collects. Settings & costumes, var. theatrical prods., Univ. of Calif. & San Francisco Opera. Address: 1001 Cragmont, Berkeley, CA, U.S.A.

PARKINSON, Thomas I. Jr., b. 27 Jan. 1914. Lawyer. Educ: B.A., Harvard Coll., 1934; LL.B., Univ. of Pa. Law Schl., 1937. Appts: Assoc. (then Ptnr.), Milbank, Tweed, Hadley & McCloy (law firm), 1946-56; Ptnr. in investment Firm of Penington, Colket & Co., 1956-58; Ltd. Ptnr., ibid, 1958-69; Pres. Inch. Corp. & assoc. cos., 1951-. Mbrships: Dir., Pine St. Fund, N.Y.C., 1963-; Trustee, Exec. & Finance Comms., Milbank Mem. Fund, ibid; Mgr., Exec. & other Comms., State Communities Aid Assn.; Pilgrims, U.S.A.; Am. Bar Assn.; Dir., 1949-53, For. Policy Assn.; Assn. of the Bar of City of N.Y.; Knickerbocker Club, Union Club & Down Town Assn., all of N.Y.C.; Piping Rock Club (Locust Valley, N.Y.) off., Metropol. Unit Fndn.; Off., British

War Relief Soc. (inactive); Phi Beta Kappa. Recip. of King's Medal, 1947. Address: 25 Broadway- Rm. 659, N.Y., NY 10004, U.S.A. 6, 12, 16, 123.

PARKS, Albert F., b. 27 June 1909. U.S. Government Executive. Educ: A.B., Ark. Coll., Batesville, U.S.A., 1929; Tenn. Univ. Grad. Schl., Knoxville, 1929-30; M.S., N.Y. Univ. Grad. Schl., 1931; Tenn. Univ. Med. Col., Memphis, summer, 1935. Appts: Tchng. Fellow, Tenn. Univ., 1929-30; N.Y. Univ., 1930-31; Hd., Chem. Dept., Ark. Coll., 1931-36; Jr. Seafood Insp., U.S. Food & Drug Admin., 1936-37; Jr. Chem., U.S. Customs Lab., 1937-43; Mil. serv., Lt. (jg), USNR, 1943-46; Asst. Chief Chem., U.S. Customs Lab., 1946-49; Asst. Chief, Tech. Servs., Bur. of Customs, 1949-59; Asst. Chief, Tech. Serv.-Dir., Off. Trade & Ind., U.S. Tariff Commn., 1959-. Mbrships: Past Pres., D.C. Chapt., Am. Inst. Chems.; Am. Chem. Soc.; Reserve Offs. Assn. (USNR, Lt. Cmmndr.); Am. Soc. Quality Control; Alpha Chi Sigma; Alpha Lambda Tau. Author num. papers in field, inclng: Cinnabar—It's Occurence & Distribution in Arkansas, 1933; What the Freshman in College Chemistry Needs to Know, 1934; Technical Information of the U.S. Customs Service, 1955; 53 vols., Summaries of Trade & Tariff Information series. Recip. hons. Address: U.S. Tariff Commn., Wash. D.C., 20436, U.S.A. 2, 14, 57.

PARKS, D.C., b. 17 Oct. 1913. Author; Lecturer; Executive; Foundation President; Retired Farmer, Rancher & Hereford Breeder. Appts. incl: Ptnr., Land Developer, Parks Brothers, 1934-59; Owner, Parks Hereford Ranch, 1954-. Breeder of num. Hereford Cattle Champions. Participant to many cattle shows. Pol. activities incl: Campaign Mgr., Robert G. Charlton for Assembly, 1962; Alternate Mbr., Repub. Ctrl. Comm., Kern Co.; Calif. Repub. Assembly; Repub. State Ctrl. Comm. of Calif. Mbrships. incl: Charter, Bakersfield Chapt. FFA, 1928; Charter, 1st Pres., Old River Harvest Club, 1940; Am. & Calif. Hereford Assns.; Kern Co., Calif. & Nat. Cattleman's Assns.; Fndr., Bd. of Dirs., Jr. Hereford Breeder of Kern Co., 1958; Calapproved Seed Assn.; Kern Co. Farm Bur.; Chmn., Narcotics Comm., S. Bakersfield Lions Club, 1962-63; num. other community activities. Author, Narcotics and Narcotics Addition, 1969. Recip. of many hons. & awards. Address: 2639 Belle Terrace, Bakersfield, Calif. 93304, U.S.A. 59, 125.

PARKS, James Dallas, b. 25 Aug. 1906. Artist; Art Teacher. Educ: B.S., Bradley Univ., Peoria, Ill., U.S.A.; M.A., State Univ. of Iowa, Ames; Chgo. Art Inst., Ill. Appt: Hd., Art Dept., Lincoln Univ., Jefferson City, Mo. Mbrships: Coll. Art Assn. of Am.; Nat. Art Educ. Assn.; Pres., Mo. Coll. Art Conf., 1955-56; Pres., Nat. Conf. of Artists, 1955-56; Alpha Phi Alpha. Co-author, comprehensive exam, art hist. majors for educl. testing serv.; Princeton Univ., N.J., 1969. Painter, mural, Early Presidents of Lincoln University. Exhibs. incl: City Art Mus., St. Louis, Mo.; Rockhill Nelson Mus., Kansas City, Mo.; Joslyn Mus., Omaha, Neb.; Univ. of Iowa, Ames; Bradley Univ., Peoria, Ill.; Howard Univ., Wash. D.C.; Fisk Univ., Nashville, Tenn. Recip., First Prize in Sculpture, Mo. State Fair, 1945. Address: 923 E. Dunklin St., Jefferson City, MO 65101, U.S.A.

PARKS, Rena Ferguson, b. 17 Jan. 1888. Adult Educator; Poet. Educ: Univ. of Ore.; Ore. State Univ.; Univ. of Pa. Appts: Tchr., Creative Writing, 7 yrs.; Educ. Cons., City Bur. of Hlth., 11 yrs.; Workshop serv. for Portland

Verseweavers Soc., 8 yrs.; Assoc. Ed., The Country Bard, N.J., 4 yrs., Currently Assoc. Ed., Driftwood Mag., Ore., 11 yrs. Mbrships: Ore. State Poetry Assn. Publs: The Changing Land (37 poems), 1966; Furrows in the Sun (51 poems), 1972; Miniature Profiles (31 poems), 1972; Contbr. to num. mags. inclng. Driftwood Mag., Portland Oregonian Verse, Univ. of Portland Review, Review Moderne, Paris, Oregon Jrnl., The Country Bard. Recip. of var. awards. Address: 709 S.W. Clay, Apt. 15, Portland, OR 97201, U.S.A. 11.

PARMER, Dan Gerald, b. 3 July 1926. Veterinarian. Educ: L.A. City Coll.; Dr. of Vet. Med., Auburn Univ., Ala. Appts: Serv. WWII w. USN; 5th USAF Vet. Chief of Servs., Morocco, 1955; Prof., Highlands Univ., 1959; Pvte. Prac., 1960-. Mbrships: Chmn., ISVMA Civil Defense, 1968-70; Pres., SCVMA, 1968, Bd. of Govs., CVMA, 1968-71; Ill. Acad. of Vet. Prac.; Mason, 32 Degree; Shriner; V.P., Kiwanis Int., 1972-73; V. Cmdr., Veterans For Wars. Contbr. of articles to profl. jrnls. Recip., Vet. Appreciation Award, State VMA & Univ. of Ill. Schl. of Vet. Med., 1971. Address: c/o Scottsdale Animal Clin., 7953 S. Cicero Ave., Chicago, IL 60652, U.S.A. 8, 139.

PARNAS, Joseph, b. 14 June 1909. University Professor; Microbiologist. Educ: Acad. of Veterinary Med., Lvov, Poland, 1933; V.M.D., ibid, 1939. Prof., State Veterinary Inst., Pulawy, until 1939; Prof., Acad. of Veterinary Med., Lvov, 1939-41; Off., Polish underground, WWII; Prof. & Vice Chancellor, Marie Curie Univ., Lublin, 1945-52; Prof., Acad. of Med., Lublin, 1952-68; Prof., State Veterinary Serum Inst., Copenhagen, Denmark, 1969-74. Mbrships: Fellow, Royal Soc. of Med., London, U.K.; Fellow, Royal Soc. of Tropical Med. & Hygiene, London; Expert, WHO, Geneva, Switzerland; Am. Soc. of Microbiol.; Belgian Soc. of Tropical Med., Antwerp; Hon. Pres., Int. Assn. of Rural Med., Paris, France; Sec., Vet. Med. Comm., Polish Acad. of Scis., Cracow, 1949. Author of 4 books & 345 papers publd. in U.S.A., U.K., france, Germany & Poland. Hons. incl:: Charles Darwin Medal, Acad. of Scis., Moscow, 1964; Dr. of med., Brno, U.S.S.R., 1968. Address: 27 Bülowsvej, DK-1870 Copenhagen, Denmark.

PARNIGOTTO, Enrico, b. 6 July 1908. Sculptor; Art Master. Educ: Liceo Artistico, Venice, Italy, 1932, Dip., Accademia di Belle Arti, Venice, 1936. Hd., Art Depts., different state schls., 1937-73. Mbrships: Associazione Pittori e Scultori, Padua; Assn. A.N. Des Anisethiers. Sculpture: Museo Civico, Padua; Museo Civico, Faenza; Statue of A. Mantegna, Prefettura, Padua, 1956; Portrait of A. Boito, Pub. Gardens, Padua, 1958; Figure, Astronomical Observ., Asiago, 1954; 3 portraits, Univ. of Padua, 1956-64; Altarpiece, Altichiero Ch-ch-Padua, 1970; Altar Silverwork, Abano Duomo, 1969; About 40 portraits for pvte. collects.; One-man shows in Milan, Rome, Padua, Venice, Trieste, Monaco, Vienna; Group Exhibs. in Paris, Moscow, Warsaw, Lima, Nancy & Italy; Exhibs. at XX, XXI, XXII, XXVII Biennale, Venice, Int. Exhibs. of small bronzes, Padua, var. yrs., 1956-73; Pottery Exhib., Faenza, 1958. Hons: Int. Prize for Portrait, XXVIII Venice Biennale; Prize, Terra cotta, Faenza, 1958; Gold Medal, Int. Exhib., Paris, 1937. Address: Via Damiano Chiesa 4, 35100 Padua, Italy.

PARR, Charles Henry III, b. 3 Oct., 1921. Company Executive. Educ: B.A., Univ. of Ill., 1942; N.Y. Trade Schl., 1945; Cooper Union, 1946. Appts. incl: Bd. of Dirs., Crippled Childrens Hosp., 1951-66; Marketing Dir.,

Eldon Mfg. Col., L.A., 1952-55; Chmn., Bd., Chief Exec. Off., coleman-Parr Inc., Calif., 1956-66; Chmn., Bd., Assoc. Marketing Cons. Inc., 1963-66; Guest Lectr., Univ. Calif. L.A., 1963-64, San Fernando State Coll., 1964, New. Coll., Sarasota, 1968; Pres., U.S. Dev. Land Co., Beverly Hills, 1963-64, Eichler Corp., San. Fran., 1966-67, U.S. Home Townelife, Sarasota, Century II Corp., 1972-; Sr. V.P., Dir., 1st Dev. Corp. Am., 1967-72. Mbrships. incl: Nat. Home Builders Assn.; Am. Mgmt. Assn.; Int. Advt. Assn.; Mason. Publs: Physical Properties of Phenalic Resins, 1953; Marketing & Merchandising Your Homes, 1961; contbr., ed., mag. features. Address: 3215 Pine Valley Drive, Sarasota, FL 33580, U.S.A. 7.

PARRY, Hugh Jones (pen-name, James Cross), b. 10 Mar. 1916. Research Sociologist; Writer. Educ: A.B., Yale Univ., 1937; M.A., Columbia Univ., 1939; Ph.D., Southern Calif. Univ., 1949. Appts. incl: Assoc. Dir.-Dir., Opinion Rsch. Ctr., Univ. of Denver, 1947-49; Assoc. Dir.-Dir., Troop Attitude Rsch., U.S. Armed Forces, Europe, 1950-52; Proj. Dir., Reactions Analysis Br., U.S. High Commn. for Germany, 1952-55; Rsch. Off. in France-Dir. Rsch., Western Europe, Off. of Intelligence & Analysis, U.S. Info. Agcy., 1955-65; Assoc. Dir. & Rsch. Prof. of Sociol., Soc. Rsch. Grp., Geo. Wash. Univ., 1966-. Fiction publs. incl: Root Of Evil, 1957; The Dark Road, 1959; The Grave Of Heroes, 1961; To Hell For Half A Crown, 1967; num. short stories in int. mags. & newspapers & anthologies. Non-Fiction publs. incl: Public Opinion In Western Europe (w. L.P. Crespi), 1953; contbns. in Public Opinion & Propoganda, 1954 & American Sexual Behaviour, 1955; num. articles in profl. jrnls. Mbrships. incl: Phi Beta Kappa, 1949; num. profl. assns. Hons. incl: num. lit. awards. Address: c/o Soc. Rsch. Grp., Geo. Wash. Univ., 2401 Virginia Avenue, NW, Wash. D.C. 20037, U.S.A. 2, 14.

PARRY, Shedden Chalmers Cole (See CHALMERS PARRY, Shedden)

PARSLEY, Andrew Mentlow, b. 7 Mar. 1908. Southern Baptist Minister; Teacher. Educ: Bapt. Bible Inst.; B.S., Sul Ross Univ., Alpine, Tex.; Post-Grad. work, ibid, Univ. of Tex., El Paso & Tex. Tech. Univ., Lubbock. Appts: Missionary, remote mountain areas of Tenn., Mixico & Tex.; Pastor, Tenn., N.M. Ariz. & Tex. chs.; Tchr., Comstock, Tex. (Math. & Sci.), Presidio, Tex. (5th Grade), Odessa, Tex. (Math.) & remote villages on Mexican border; worked w. Flying Ambasadores; Currently a Resource Tchr. Mbrships: Tex. State Tchrs. Assn.; Tex. Class Room Tchrs. Assn.; Elem. Prin. & Supvsrs. Assn.; former mbr., Rotary Club; Ldr., Boy Scouts of Am. & Royal Ambasadores; Young People's Dir., Bapt. Trng. Union. Paints in oils. Contbr. poems & essays to var. publs. Address: Box 161, Tornillo, TX 79853, U.S.A. 125, 129, 130, 131.

PARSLEY, John C., b. 20 June 1939. Chief of Police. Educ: S.W. Tex. State Coll.; Victoria Police Acad. Basic Law Enforcement Course; Tex. Dept. of Pub. Safety Trng. Schls.; FBI Trng. Schls. Appts: Patrolman, Gonzales Police Dept., 1962-64; Asst. Chief of Police, ibid, 1964-71; Chief of Police, 1971-. Mbrships: Tex. Police Chiefs Assn.; Optimist Club of Gonzales, Zone 10, S. Ctrl. Tex. Dist., Optimist Int. (Pres., V.P., Sec. & Treas. of local club). Hons: Honor Grad., Victoria Police Acad. 14th Session, 1973; Outstanding Leadership as Club Pres. Award, Optimist Club of Gonzales, 1971. Address: 110 St. Joseph, Gonzales, TX 78629, U.S.A. 125.

PARSLOW, Thomas, b. 12 Mar. 1920. Solicitor General for Queensland. Educ: LL.B., Univ. of Qld., 1950; Appts. incl: Petty Sessions Offs., Qld., Australia, 1935-39; Crown Law Off., ibid, 1946-; Barrister-at-Law, 1950; Crown Prosecutor, 1952-60; Asst. Crown Solicitor, 1960; Asst. Parliamentary Draftsman, 1960-63; Sr. Asst. Crown Solicitor, 1963-68; Crown Solicitor, 1968-71; Q.C., 1971; Solicitor General, 1971-; Dpty. Cmdr., Royal Qld. Regiment; Brigadier, 1973-. Mbrships: Utd. Serv. Club; State Serv. Club; Patron, Sandgate Returned Soldiers Club, Sandgate Returned Soldiers Bowling Club. Hons. incl: Australian War Medal; Efficiency Decoration & 2 bars. Address: Treasury Bldg., Queen St., Brisbane, Qld., Australia 4000. 23.

PARSONS, Eileen Elizabeth, b. 16 Oct. 1942. Editor & Project Manager, Management Consulting Field. Educ: A.B., Barnard Coll., Columbia Univ., 1965; Freshman, Miami Univ., Oxford, Ohio, 1960-61; Postgrad., writing sem., N.Y. Univ.; Music course, Harvard Univ. Ext.; Studied voice w. Orva Hoskinson, San Fran. Appts: Ed., Coemar Mgmt. Info. Ctr.; Ed., Asst. United Presby. Ch. (COEMAR) Off. for Communications, N.Y., 1965-66; Free-lance Writer, N.Y., 1966; Ed., Sterling Inst., Boston & Wash. D.C., 1966-69, Behavioral Sci. Ctr., ibid, 1969; Cons. Ed., Boston, 1969-70; Prog. Dev. Specialist, Louis A. Allen Assocs., Inc., Palo Alto, Calif., 1971-73; Ed., Real Estate Rsch. Corp., 1973-. Mbrships. incl: Lamplighters, San Fran. Gilbert & Sullivan Theatre; 1st Congl. Ch., United Ch. of Christ, San Fran.; Contbr., Peninsula Conservatory of Music; Alpha Lambda Delta. Contralto Soloist & TV debut w. San Mateo Co. Choral Soc., 1974. Recip., DuBois Bookstore Award for freshman writing, 1960. Address: 1113 Chula Vista Ave., 6, Burlingame, CA 94010, U.S.A. 132, 138.

PARSONS, Margaret A., b. 21 July 1933. Medical Entomologist. Educ: B.S., Univ. of Mass., Amherst, 1956; M.S., ibid, 1963. Appts. incl: Profl. Asst., Dept. of Entomol. & Plant Path., Univ. of Mass., 1960; Tech. Asst., Dept. of Zool., ibid, 1959-61; Civilian Entomologist, 3rd U.S. Army Med. Lab., Ft. McPherson, Ga., 1962-63; Med. Entomologist, NCDC, Atlanta, Trng. Br., 1963-65; Med. Entomologist, Ohio Dept. of Hlth., 1965-. Mbrships. incl: Sigma Xi; Entomol. Soc. of Am.; Am. Mosquito Control Assn.; Pres., Ohio Mosquito Control Assn., 1970-72, V.P., 1969; Ohio Pub. Hlth. Assn.; Am. Inst. of Biol. Scis.; Am. Soc. of Parasitologists; Acarol. Soc.; Nat. Wildlife Fed. Contbr. of articles to profl. jrnls. Address: Ohio Dept. of Hlth., 1571 Perry St., P.O. Box 2568, Columbus, OH 43216, U.S.A. 5, 8.

PARTIN, Robert E., b. 22 June 1927. Artist; University Professor. Educ: B.A., UCLA, 1950; Fellowship, Yale-Norfolk Art Schl., Norfolk, Conn., 1955; M.F.A., Columbia Univ., 1956; Fellowship, Tamarind Lithog. Workshop, Indpls., 1963. Appts. incl: Instr. in Art, Univ. of Ky., Lexington, 1957; Asst. Prof.-Assoc. Prof. of Art, Univ. of N.C., Greensboro, 1957-66; Prof. of Art, Calif. State Univ., Fullerton, 1966-. Exhibs. incl: All-City LA Art Festival, 1967; 10-Yr. 1-man Retrospective, Calif. State Coll., Dominguez Hills, 1968; Centennial Exhib., San Fran. Art Inst., 1971; Viewpoints 5, Dana Arts Ctr., Colgate Univ., Hamilton, N.Y., 1971. One-man Shows: Orlando Gall., Encino, Calif., 1971; 58-F Plaza Sq. Gall., Orange, Calif., 1973. Mbrships: Coll. Art Assn. of Am.; Southeastern Coll. Art Conf.; Phi Delta Kappa; Ephebian Soc., LA. Contbr. to The Choral Jrnl. Hons. incl: Ford Fndn. Purchase Prize, Whitney Annual, Whitney Mus.

of Am. Art, N.Y.C., 1963; Purchase Prize, S. Coast Art Show, Ringling Mus. of Art, Sarasota, Fla., 1961; Painters of the Southeastern U.S., Univ. of S. Fla., Tampa, 1962, N.C. Annual, N.C. Mus. of Art, Raleigh, 1958, 64 & 65; Prize, Calif. S. 7, Fine Arts Gall. of San Diego, 1969. Address: Dept. of Art, Calif. State Univ., Fullerton, 800 N. State Coll. Blvd., Fullerton, CA 92634, U.S.A. 9, 15, 37, 105, 133.

PASCAL, David, b. 16 Aug. 1918. Artist. Educ: Artists Schl., N.Y. Appts: Instr., Graphic Jrnlsm., Schl. of Visual Arts of N.Y., 1955-58; Free-lance Illustrator, N.Y. Times, New Yorker, Esquire, Playboy, Evergreen Review, Punch, Paris-Match, Stern, etc. Mbrships: For. Affairs Sec., Nat. Cartoonists Soc., 1963-; former Am. Rep. of Icon; Cartoonists Guild. Publs: Ed., Comics, The Art of the Comic Strip; The Silly Knight (author-illustrator). One-man shows of Comics Paintings, Graham Gall., N.Y., 1973, Mus. of São Paulo, Brazil, 1973 Pavillon de l'Humour, Terre des Hommes, Montreal, Can. Hons. incl: Best Illustrator's Award, Nat. Cartoonists Soc., 1969; Silver T-Square Award, ibid, 1972. Address: 133 Wooster St., N.Y., NY 10012, U.S.A. 2, 30, 37.

PASKINS, Cloyd Woodrow, b. 30 Sept. 1914. Educator. Educ: B. Ed., Eastern III. Univ.; M.A., Duke Univ., N.C.; Doctoral Fellow, Walden Univ., Fla.; Grad. Studies, Univ. of Calif., Berkeley; La. State Univ.; Univ. of Pitts.; Interam. Univ. Saltillo, Mexico; Syracuse Univ., N.Y. Appts: Tchrs., Fla. Secondary Schls., 12 yrs.; Ala. State Tchrs. Coll., Troy, 1943-44; E. Ctrl. Jr. Coll., Miss., 1944-46; Elon Coll., N.C., 1946-48; Ala. State Tchrs. Coll., Jacksonville, 1949-50; Troy State Univ., Ala., 1958-. Fellow, Am. Sociol. Assn. Mbrships: Am. Hist. Assn.; Nat. Coun. Soc. Studies; Pres., S.W. Fla. & Palm Beach Co. Coun. for the Soc. Studies; Southern Sociol. Assn.; Pi Gamma Mu; Phi Alpha Theta; Hons: Tchng. Fellowship, La. State Univ., 1944; Asian Fellowship, Syracuse Univ., 1956. other profl. orgs.; Address: 419 Collegedale Ave., Troy, AL. 36081, U.S.A. 7, 13.

PASNICK, Raymond Wallace, b. 29 Apr. 1916. Public Relations Director; Editor. Appts: Ed., Aluminum Wkrs. Jrnl., New Kensington, Pa., 1936-37; Publicity Dur., Aluminum Wkrs. of Am., Pitts., 1937-44; Asst. Ed., Steel Labor, 1944-46; Midwest Ed., Midwest Dir. of Educ., United Steelwkrs. of Am., Chgo., 1946-62; Nat. Ed., Dir. Communications, ibid, 1962-65; Dir., P.R., Ed., Steel Labor, Pitts., 1965-. Mbrships: Pub. Mbr., Chgo. Bd. of Educ., 1955-66; Pres., Int. Labor Press Assn., 1972-73; Treas., Chgo. Newspaper Guild, 1948-56, V.P., 1957; Am. Fedn. of Tchrs. Hons. incl: Civil Rights Award, Jewish Labor Comm., Chgo., 1962; Tchrs. Hons. incl: Civil Rights Award, Jewish Labor Comm., Chgo., 1962; Man of Yr., Nat. Frontiersman, Chgo., 1963. Address: 5 Gateway Ctr., Pitts., PA 15222, U.S.A. 2, 6.

PASQUAY, Wolfgang, b. 10 Feb. 1931. Pianist. Educ: Studied piano w. Prof. Leopolder; Studied theory w. Prof. Kurt Thomas. Career: Debut in Stuttgart, 1945; Founded own piano trio, 1950, & performs much chmbr. music in concerts; Num. solo performances; Work w. radio stns. such as Munich, Frankfurt, Cologne, R.S.I., Radio Paris; Debut in Paris w. 3 piano concerts, 1961; Concerts in U.K., Ireland, Austria, France & Switzerland; Performances w. Berlin Symph. Orch., L'Orch. Sinfonico della Radio Svizzera Italiana, L'Orch. de la Radiodiffusion TV Francaise. Compositions: Variationen über ein Thema von Distler für Klavier; Variationen und Finale über ein Thema von Lortzing für Oktett.

Recip., Hallischer Jugendpreis for composition, 1943. Address: Schrodtberg 39, D 5650 Solingen 1, German Fed. Repub. 43.

PASSANI, Emile, b. 7 Feb. 1905. Composer; Conductor; Pianist. Educ: Conservatoire Nat. Supérieur de Paris. Composer of num. works for orchestra, theatre, ballet, chamber music, piano, voice, choir. Hons: Chevalier, Légion d'Honneur; Chevalier du Mérite Nat.; Off., Ordre des Palmes Académiques. Address: Les Gravettes, 83220 Le Pradet, France.

PASSOW, A(aron) Harry, b. 9 Dec. 1920. University Professor. Educ: B.A., S.U.N.Y., Albany, 1942; M.A., ibid, 1947; Ed.D., Columbia Univ., 1951. Appts. incl: Instr., Maths., N.Y.S. Coll. for Tchrs., Albany, 1948-50; Prof. Educ. & Rsch. Assoc., Tchrs. Coll., Columbia Univ., 1950-72; Prof. Educ., ibid, 1972-, Chmn., Dept. of Curriculum & Tchng., 1968-. Mbrships. incl: Assn. for Supervision & Curriculum Dev.; Nat. Soc. for the Study of Educ.; Comparative Educ. Soc.; Am. Educl. Rsch. Assn. Publs: Author, co-author or Ed. of: Reacing the Disadvantaged Learner; Opening Opportunities for Disadvantaged Learners; Developing Programs for Disadvantaged Learners; Education in Depressed Areas; about 100 articles or chapts. in books. Address: Tchrs. Coll., Columbia Univ., N.Y., NY 10027, U.S.A. 6, 30.

PASTORE, Pasquale, b. 19 July 1908. Magistrate. Educ: Grad. in law, pol. & social sci. Appts: Dir. Gen. of Min., of Defence; Counllr. of the Audit Off., 1969-. Mbrships: Lions Club; Serra Club; Kivanis Club; Int. Assn. of Sci. Experiments in Tourism, Berne. Publs: Il regime amministrato dei beni di interesse militare; Il problema dell'accasermamento con particolare riferimento all'odiema legislazione; Beni destinati alla difesa nazionale; L'arbitrato negli appalti di opere pubbliche; considerazioni sulle pubbliche relazioni nell'Amministrazione dello stato; Gli interessi pubblici nella disciplina giuristica italiana dei rifugi alpini. Hons: High Off. of the Order of the Italian Repub.; Kt. of the Order of St. Sepulchre of Jerusalem. Address: Via dei Prati Fiscati 221, 00141, Rome, Italy. 43.

PATERNOSTO, Pedro Guillermo, b. 29 June 1899. Professor of Chemistry. Educ: Dr. in Chem. & Pharmacol., Univ. of La Plata, Buenos Aires, Argentina. Appts: Lectr., Fac. of Chem. & Pharmacol., Univ. of La Plata, 1921-55; Prof. of Chem., ibid; Prof., Indl. Schl. of La Plata; Dpty. Dean, Fac. of Chem. & Pharmacy, Univ. of La Plata; 1950; Dean, ibid, 1952; Pro Vice Chancellor, 1952; Emeritus Prof., Fac. of Exact Scis. Mbrships. incl: Argentinian Sci. Soc.; V.P., Argentinian Acad. of Pharmacol. & Biochem.; Hon. Life mbr., Argentinian Assn. of Chem.; Argentinian Assn. for Sci. Progress. Publs. incl: La influencia del Zircomio sobre algunos caracteres biologicos de los microbios, 1924; El Yoduro de Potasio obtenido por doble descomposicion, 1938; Carburo de Aluminio, su obstencion a partir del Negro de Humo y Polvo de Aluminio; Sev. Chem. textbooks; Articles in profl. jrnls. Address: Calle 2, no. 786, La Plata, Argentina. 136.

PATERSON, Arthur Spencer. Consultant Psychiatrist. Educ: Hons., Classics & Philosophy, Oriel Coll., Oxford; M.D. (Hons), Edinburgh; postgrad., Johns Hopkins Univ., Md., U.S.A.; Rsch. Inst. for Psych., Munich, Germany. Appts. incl: House Physn. to Prof. of Clin. Med., Edinburgh Univ., 1928; Asst. Physn., Glasgow Royal Hosp., 1929-30; Psych.,

Cassel Hosp., Penshurst, 1933-36, Asst. Psych., Middlesex Hosp., London, 1936-46; Chief., Dept. of Psych. & Psychiatric Lab., Lectr., Med. Schl., W. London Hosp., 1946-66; Pvte. Prac., London, 1966-. Mbrships. incl: Fellow, Royal Soc. Med; Corres. Fellow, Am. Psychiatric Assn. & Pavlovian Soc.; Sec., Int. Soc. Clin. & Experimental Hypnosis, 1967-73. Author, Electrical & Drug Treatments in Psychiatry, 1963. Contbr., over 100 articles, sci. jrnls.. Hons. incl: Honeyman-Gillespie Lectr., Edinburgh Univ., 1948; Goldman Lectr., N.Y. Med. Coll., 1964. Address: 2 Devonshire Pl., London W.1, U.K. 1, 43, 128, 131.

PATERSON, Michael Hugh Orr, b. 7 Dec. 1927. Curator of Museums & Art Galleries; Further Education Lecturer; Art Restorer. Educ: Manchester & Edinburgh Univs., U.K.; B.A. (Manc), 1951; Dip. of Mus.' Assn., specializing in Fine Art, 1955. Appts. incl: Trainee/Asst., City Art Gall., Birmingham, 1953-54; Asst. in charge of Mus.' & City Art Gall., Hereford, 1954-56; Asst.-in-charge, Municipal Art Gall. & Mus.', Oldham, 1956-57; Asst. Keeper of Art, City Mus.', Leicester, 1957-58; Curator, Russell Cotes Mus. & Art Gall. & Rothesay Mus., Bournemouth, 1958-66; Curator of Mus.' & Art Galls. in London Borough of Enfield, 1966-. Mbrships. incl: Fellow, Royal Soc. of Arts; Fellow, Mus.' Assn.; Mbr. & Voluntary Lectr., Nat. Trust, Nat. Art-Collections Fund. Publs. incl: Art & The Bible; The Theatre In Art; Painters Of Wessex; 19th Century French Paintings; Guidebook To Forty Hall, 1971; 18th Century Cordials & Their Contents, in press; Mus. & Art Gall. catalogues. Address: Forty Hall, Forty Hill, Enfield, Middlesex, EN2 9HA, U.K. 19.

PATERSON, Thomas Ferguson, b. 31 Jan. 1923. Public Servant. Educ: B.A., Univ. of Melbourne, Australia; B.Comm., ibid. Appts: Trng. Off., Commonwealth Off. of Educ., 1947-55; Investigator, Dept. of Works, 1955-57; Insp., Sr. Insp. & Asst. Commnr., Commonwealth Pub. Serv. Bd., 1955-69; Pub. Serv. Bd. Rep., Org. & O'seas conditions, Australian High Commn., London, U.K., 1969-72, Asst. Commnr., Mgmt. Systems, Pub. Serv. Bd., 1973. Mbrships: Royal Inst. of Pub. Admin.; Royal Canberra Golf Club; Canberra Southern Cross Club. Address: Off. of the Pub. Serv. Bd., Canberra, A.C.Y., Australia. 2600. 23.

PATKIN, Benzion, Educ: Univ. of Moscow, U.S.S.R., 1920-22. Appts. & Mbrships. incl: Zionist Youth Org., Akhdut Utkhiya & student's org., Gekhaver, U.S.S.R.; Exec. Mbr., Moscow Maccabi sports org. & later Fed. Russian Comm., Maccabi sports org. until 1924; re-organized & deleg. sev. nat. confs., Maccabi org., Ness-Ziona, Eretz Israel; Havurat Hadarom, Ness-Ziona; Co-Fndr., Ivriah, Australia, 1929; Co-Fndr., State Zionist Coun., Vic. & Vic. Zionist Org., 1936, V.P. latter, 1936-37, Hon. Sec. of both, 1938-42; Exec. Mbr., State Zionist Coun., Vic., sev. occasions; Co-Fndr., Friends of Hebrew Univ., 1936; Initiated trade w. Eretz Israel & assoc. sev. Israeli cos., 1937-; Exec. Mbr., Victorian Jewish Advsry. Bd., later Bd. of Deputies, 1938-51 & Fndn. Chmn., Educ. Comm. ibid, 1943-50; Fndr., Pro-Magen David Adom org., Australia, 1940, Mt. Scopus Coll., 1947 & Pres., ibid, 1948-52; Exec. Mbr., Zionist Fedn. of Australia & New Zealand, Hon. Sec., 1940-45; Exec. Mbr., Exec. Coun. of Aust. Jewry, 1945-49 & Fndn. Chmn., Educ. Comm., 1947-49; Australian Corres., Tel-Aviv daily newspaper, Haboker, 1946-49; Organizer & Mgr., Knitting Factories in Galilee, Israel, for immigrants, on behalf of Israel Min. of Trade & Ind., 1961;

Co-Fndr., Australian Friends of Israeli Philharmonic Orch., 1938, Sr. Exec. V.P., 1963-; Pres., Briti Ivrit Olamit (World Hebrew Union), Vic., var. periods 1958-74 & Pres., Brit Ivrit Olamit, Australia, 1965-; Exec. Mbr., UN Assn. of Australia, Vic. Div., 1966-69; Hon. Life Mbr., var. orgs. Contbr. to var. publs. in Australia & abroad. Publs: Heritage & Tradition, 1972. Address: 2/313A Dandenong Rd., Windsor, Melbourne, Vic., Australia 3181. 55.

PATRAM, Sarah Lee, b. 22 Jan. 1922. Nursing Education. Educ: Dip., Petersburg Hosp. Schl. of Nursing, 1943; B.A., Bridgewater Coll., 1947; B.S.N.Ed., Univ. of Va., 1952; M.S.N., Cath. Univ. of Am., 1959. Appts. incl: Hosp. & Pvte. Duty Nursing, Va., 1945-51; Dir. Nursing Serv., Randolph Hosp., Inc., Asheburo, N.C., 1952-53; Dir., Burlington City Schl. Practical Nursing, 1953-55; Sr. Instr.-Coordinator, Schls. of Practical Nursing, Miners Mem. Hosp. Assn., Harlan, KY., 1955-57; Dir., Schl. Practical Nursing, Miners Mem. Hosp. Assn., Williamson, W. Va., 1958-62; Asst. Dir. of Nursing, Mem. Med. Ctr., Williamson, 1962-64; Assoc. Prof. & Chmn., Dept. Nursing Educ., Marshall Univ., Huntington, W. Va., 1964-. Mbrships. incl: Am. Nurses Assn.; W. Va. Nurses Assn., Chmn., Happy Mem. Schlrship. Fund, former Dist. Pres. & Parliamentarian & Chmn. num. Comms.; AAUW; AAUP; Alumni Assns., Univ. of Va., Cath. Univ. of Am. & Petersburg Gen. Hosp., former Treas. Publs: book reviews in Jrnl. of Practical Nursing; papers presented to Nursing orgs. Recip. of awards. Address: Prichard Bldg., Huntington, WV 25701, U.S.A. 5, 6.

PATRASSI, Gino, b. 30 Aug. 1904. University Professor; Director of Medical Clinic. Educ: Master's Degree, Univ. of Florence, Italy, 1927. Appts: Assoc. Prof.-Prof., Univ. of Florence; Prof., Univ. Padova of Cagliari, Padua; Dir., Med. Pathol. Inst., Padua, 1949-63; Ed., Acta Medica Patavina, 1951-; Dir., Splenopathol. Ctr., Padua, 1954-; Dir., Med. Clin., Padua, 1963-. Mbrships: Italian, German, & Int., Socs. of Internal Med.; Swiss Gastroenterological Assn.; Int. Assn. for Study of the Liver; Venetian Inst. of Scis., Letters & Arts. Publs: La Questione del Morbo di Banti; La Pletora Portale; L'Ipertensione Renovascolare; Le Iperlipoproteinemie. Hons: War Cross ofr Mil. Valour; Gold Medal for Achievement, 1971. Address: Via Vescovado 23 a, Padua, Italy.

PATRICK, Douglas Arthur, b. 17 Mar. 1905. Philatelic Writer; Curator of Philately. Educ: Pvte. French Schl.; Engl. & Jrnlsm. w. Profl. McKeon, 6 yrs.; Fine Art, Hamilton Art Schl.; Sealy Art Schl.; Leonard Hutchinson Art Schl.; Mattice Art Schl., Hamilton, Ont., Canada. m. Mary Powell 1929, 1 s. Robert. Appts- Free-lance work, merchandise display, newspaper advt. prod. & mfg. of point-of-sale mats., 1929-52; Introduced Stamp Collectors' Radio Prog., CBC Stamp Club, Trans-Canada Network, 1950-71; Advt. Rep., Globe & Mail, 1952-70; Writes weekly stamp column, ibid, 1952-. Mbrships. incl: Fellow, Royal Philatelic Soc., London, Royal Philatelic Soc., Canada; Coun., Am. Philatelic Cong., 1965-74; Collectors Club of N.Y. Publs. incl: (all in coop. w. wife) Stamp Collecting—The Greatest Hobby in the World, 1952; Postage Stamps & Postal History of the United Nations, 1956; Canada Stamp Album, 1959; International Guide to Stamps & Stamp Collecting, 1962; Fascination of Stamps, 1970; Musson Stamp Dictionary; over 3200 newspaper columns. Hons. incl: Bronze Award, Int. Philatelic Show, Poznan,

Poland, 1973; var. Fellowships. Address: 1616 Applewood Rd., Mississauga, Ont., Canada. 6, 30.

PATRICK, (Mrs.) Nesta, b. 29 Aug. 1923. Educational Administrator for the Mentally Handicapped. Educ: Sr. Cert. in Res. Work w. Children, Bristol Univ., U.K., 1962; Dipl. in Soc. Policy & Admin., Univ. of Wales, 1968; Bachelor of Profl. Studies, Pace Univ., N.Y., U.S.A., 1973; M.B.A., ibid, 1974. Appts. incl: Soc. Welfare Off., Govt. of Trinidad & Tobago, 1950; Supvsr. of Servs. for Mentally Handicapped, St. Ann's Hosp., 1958; Fndr., Schl. for Retarded Children, Lady Hochoy Home, Trinidad, 1961; Prin., Schl. for Mentally Handicapped, St. Ann's Hosp., 1967; Cons., Govt. of Trinidad & Tobago, & Caribbean Mental Retardation Assn. for Southern Caribbean & S. Am. Mbr. & Off., var. profl. & community orgs. Author, var. profl. publs. Active participant, profl. seminars & confs. Hon. Mbrship., U.S. Pres.'s Comm. on Mental Retardation in U.S.A. Address: 7, 4th St., Mt. Lambert, Trinidad, W. Indies. 136.

PATRINACOS, Nicon Demetrius, b. 19 Mar. 1911. Clergyman; Educator. Educ: B.A., Univ. of Qld., Australia, 1945; M.A., 1947; D.Phil., Oxford Univ., 1950. Ordained Priest, Greek Orthodox Ch., 1936; Archimandrite, 1937. Appts: Hd., Greek Orthodox Communities, Qld., Australia, 1937-48; Hd., community of St. Louis, Mo., U.S.A., 1950-53; Tchr., psychol. of relig., Univ. of Wash., ibid, 1950-53; Dean, Greek Orthodox Schl. of Theol., Boston, Mass., 1953-55; Tchr., philos., St. Basil's Inst., Garrison, N.Y., 1961-63; Chmn., Archdiocesan Greek Orthodox System of Educ., U.S.A., 1968-. Publs: The Orthodox Sacraments, 1963; The Individual & His Orthodox Church, 1970; The Orthodox Liturgy, 1973; Ed., The Orthodox Observer, 1967-72. Address: 20 Salem Rd., White Plains, NY 10603, U.S.A. 6.

PATTERMANN, William, b. 1 Oct. 1903. Industrial Company Executive. Educ: Commerical Acad., Vienna. Appts: Dir., Pilot Stainless Steel Co., Birmingham, U.K., 1934-38; Mng. Dir., Anglo-Styrian Steel Co. Ltd., 1938-39; Dir., Schoeller Bieckmann Steel Works, Vienna, Austria, 1939-45; Prin. & Owner, firm of W. Pattermann, Vienna, 1945-. Publs: Pattermann's Practical English, 1945; Pattermann's English Phrase Book & Dictionary, 1950. Address: Rudolfinergasse 18, 1190 Vienna, Austria.

PATTERSON, Harry Thomas, b. 11 June 1920. Theatre & Festival Administrator. Educ: B.A., Trinity Coll., Univ. of Toronto. Appts. incl: Fndr. & Gen. Mgr., Stratford Shakespearean Festival, Canada; Cons., W. Indian Festival of Arts; Fndr. & Gen. Mgr., Dawson City Gold Rush Festival, Yukon Territory, Canada; Co-fndr (w. Douglas Campbell), Canadian Players Ltd; Exec. Prof., Irish Arts Theatre; Fndg. Pres., Nat. Theatre Schl. of Canada, Montreal; Dir., Special Projects, Mediavision Inc., Toronto. Hons: Canadian Arts Coun. Annual Award, 1954; N.Y. Shakespearean Soc. Annual Award, 1955; Am. Shakespearean Festival Award, 1955; President's Award, Canadian Cou. of Authors & Artists; Off. of the Order of Canada, 1967. Address: Mediavision Inc., 17 Hazelton Ave., Toronto, Ont., Canada, M5R 2E1. 18.

PATTERSON, Josie Mildred (Lee), b. 18 Aug. 1927. Associate Professor of English. Educ: B.A., Southwest Tex. State Coll., 1949; M.A., Baylor Univ., 1954, 1967. Appts: Tchr., Pub. Schls., Tex., 1946-57; Assoc. Prof. Engl.,

Howard Payne Coll., Brownwood, Tex., 1962-. Mbrships: Coll. Conf., Tchrs. of Engl. of Tex.; AAUW; Sigma Tau Delta; Dist. XI Engl. Assn.; Fac. Women's Club (Pres. 1973-74); Coggin Ave Bapt. Ch., Brownwood, Tex. Hons: Outstanding Fac. Woman of Yr. Award, Assn. of Women Students, Howard Payne Coll., 1966, 1969. Address: 2201 Eleventh, Brownwood, TX 76801, U.S.A. 2, 5, 119, 132.

PATTERSON, Keith Evan, b. 3 June 1925. Artist-Painter; Art Educator; Musician. Educ: Auckland Tchrs. Trng. Coll., N.Z.; Auckland Univ. Appts. incl: Art Tchr., Mount Roskill Intermediate Schl., Auckland, 1957-61; Dir., Art & Music Dept., Am. Schl. of Barcelona, Spain, 1964-72; Tchr., i/c of Art, Music & Biol. Progs., Am. H.S., Barcelona, 1973. Mbrships: Auckland Soc. of Arts, N.Z.; Pena Flamenca de Antonio Mairena Hospitalet, Spain. One-man shows incl: Galeria Fort, Tarragona, Spain, 1969; La Galerie, Paris, France, 1971; Barroc Design Studio, Sitges, Spain, 1971; Galeria Nova, Barcelona, 1972; Premio Miro, Barcelona, 1973; Tom Maddock Fine Art Gall., Barcelona, 1973. Works in pub. & pvte. collects. Flamenco Guitar Recitals incl: Mainz, German Fed. Repub., 1966; Peniscola, Spain, 1967; Barcelona, 1970. Hons. incl: Textile Prize, Bienal de Terrasa, 1973; 2nd Prize, Ciudad de Hospitalet, 1973. Address: Calle Capitan Arenas 70, Barcelona 17, Spain.

PATTERSON, Lucy Phelps, b. 21 June 1931. Social Worker; Educator. Educ: B.A., Howard Univ., Wash. D.C.; Master's Degree, Grad. Schl. of Soc. Work, Denver; further study, Univ. of Tex., Austin. Appts: w. U.S. Depts. of Navy & Commerce, 1950-54; Casewkr., Dept. of Pub. Welfare, Dallas Co., Tex., 1954-61, Casework Supvsr., 1963-68, Dir., Inter-Agcy. Proj., 1968-71; Dir., Dallas Co. Child Care Coun., 1971-73; Planning Dir., Community Coun. of Gtr. Dallas, 1973-; Mbr., City Coun. of Dallas, 1973-; Asst. Prof., N. Tex. State Univ., 1974-. Mbrships. incl: Charter & Bd. Mbr., Nat. Assn. Soc. Wkrs.; N.Tex. Assn. Black Soc. Wkrs.; Acad. Certified Soc. Wkrs.; Pres., Top Ladies of Distinction; Sec. & Exec. Comm. Mbr., Am. Lang. Assn. Profl. reports & articles, var. jrnls. Recip., var. soc. serv. awards. Address: 2779 Almeda Dr., Dallas, TX 75216, U.S.A. 125.

PATTERSON, Margaret Cleveland (Mrs.), b. 13 Apr. 1923. Assistant Professor of English. Educ: A.A., Sullins Coll., Va.; B.A., Wellesley Coll., 1944; M.Ed. (w. cert. in Lib. Sci.), Univ. of Fla., 1965; Ph.D., ibid, 1970. Appts: Legal Sec., Nuremburg War Trials, 1945-46; Grad. Asst., Engl. Dept., Lib., Univ. of Fla., 1965-70; Asst. Prof., Engl. Dept. & Div. of Continuing Educ., ibid, 1970-; Dir., Writing Prog., Freshman Minority Students, & Assoc., Carnegie Prog., Exchange Minority Students, 1972-. Mbrships: Assoc. Bibliog., Bibliog. Comm., MLA, 1972-; ALA; Life Mbr., Hopkins Soc.; AAUP; AAUW; Phi Kappa Phi; Pi Lambda Theta. Publs: 3 cores. courses, 2 surveys of Engl. Lit. & 1 on children's lit., 1970-73; num. articles in jrnls. Hons: NDEA Grant, 1969; Carnegie Grants, 1971, 74; Outstanding Tchr. Award, Univ. of Fla., 1972. Address: c/o Engl. Dept., Anderson Hall, Univ. of Fla., Gainesville, FL 32601, U.S.A. 13, 125.

PATTERSON, (The Hon.) Percival James, b. 10 Apr. 1935. Attorney-at-Law. Educ: B.A., Univ. of W. Indies, London, 1958; LL.B., London Schl. of Econs., 1963; Called to Bar, Middle Temple, 1963; Admitted to Jamaican Bar, 1963. Appts: Exec. Comm., Peoples Nat. Pty., 1964; V.P., ibid, 1969; Senate, 1968-70; Leader of Opposition in Senate, 1968-70; Mbr.,

House of Reps. for S.E. Westmorland, 1970; Min. of Ind. & Tourism, 1972; Min. of Ind., Commerce & Tourism, 1973; Jamaica's Rep., Coun. of Mins., Caribbean Common Mkt. Recip. Hugh Parry Prize for Excellence in Law or Contract & Leverhulme Schlrship. to read for Law Deg., London Schl. of Econs. Address: c/o Ministry of Industry, Commerce & Tourism, 2 National Heroes Circle, Kingston, Jamaica.

PATTERSON, Robert Otis, Jr., b. 13 Sept. 1924. Business Executive. Educ: A.B., Engl. Lit.; studied var. Univs. inclng. Columbia Univ.; Candidate, M.B.A., Adelphi Univ., N.Y., 1973-. Appts. incl: USAF Serv., 1943-45, 1947-54; Dir., Armed Forces Radio & TV Serv. Network, USAF Northeast Air Command; Continuity Writer, Columbia Broadcasting System, 1947-; Contbng. Ed., New York Times, 1954-57; Assoc. Ed., Volume Feeding Mgmt. Mag., N.Y., 1955-57; Prin., Knox Manning-Patterson-Gebers-Kadin, L.A., 1961-64; Fndng. Ed., Institutional Distribution Mag., N.Y.C., 1964-68; Account Supvsr., Bronhill Assocs. Inc., N.Y.C., 1968-70; Managing Dir., Int. Foodservice Distributors Assn., N.Y.C., 1971-. Mbrships. incl: Writers Guild of Am.; Int. Food Edit. Coun.; Civil Air Patrol; Air Force Assn.; The Masquers (Hollywood). Contbr. to num. mags. Radio Prog: Broad Horizons (CBS), 1946-48. Hons. incl: J.H. Neal Award for Bus. Journalism, Am. Bus. Press, 1967. Address: Int. Foodservice Distributors Assn., 51 Madison Ave., N.Y., NY 10010, U.S.A.

PATTERSON, (Mrs.) Zella Justina Black, b. 20 May 1909. Home Economist; Family Living Specialist. Educ: B.S., Langston Univ., Okla.; M.S., Colo. State Univ., Ft. Collins; Further study, Calif. Univ., Berkeley; Okla. State Univ., Stillwater. Appts. incl: Vocatl. Home Econs. Instr., Suprvsng. Tchr., Home Econs. student tchrs., Langston Univ. H.S., 1937-46; Home Econs. & Soc. Sci., Langston City H.S., Okla., 1946-47; Vocatl. Homemaking Tchr., ibid, 1947-60; Foods & Clothing Instr. & Dormitory Dir., Freshmen Women, Langston Univ., Okla., 1960-63; Clothing Instr., Home Econs. Tchr., Educ. & State Advsr., New Homemakers of Am., ibid, 1963-65; Asst. Prof.-Assoc. Prof., Home Econs., 1966-; Chmn., Dept. Home Econs., 1966-; Mbr., Langston Univ. Rsch. Team, USDA Proj. Study for Rural Youth in Logan Co., 1967-71; Family Living Specialist in coop. w. Okla. State Univ. & U.S. Dept. Agric., 1971-72. Contbr. to: Jrnl. Home Econs.; Southwestern Jrnl. Mbrships: Am. Home Econs. Assn.; Okla. Home Econs. Assn.; Am. Vocatl. Assn.; Okla. Vocatl. Assn.; V.P., Home Missionary Soc., Chmn., Pub. Rels. Comm. & Sec., Building Fund, New Hope Bapt. Ch.; Int. Biographical Assn.; Okla. Educ. Assn.; Am. Educ. Rsch. Assn.; Home Econs. Educ. Assn.; Higher Educ. Alumni Coun.; Nat. Coun. Negro Women; Langston Univ. Alumni Assn.; Colo. State Univ. Alumni Assn.; Alpha Upsilon Omega Chapt.; Alpha Kappa Alpha; Smithsonian Assn.; Order, Eastern Star; Past Treas., Chmn., Art Comm. & Bicentennial Commn. Proj. Langston Beautiful Club. Hons: Woman of Yr., Langston Beautiful Club, 1959; Award, Outstanding achievements, Higher Educ., Langston Univ., 1972. Address: P.O. Box 96, Langston, OK 73050, U.S.A. 125, 139.

PATTESON, Joseph Drury, Jr., b. 14 Dec. 1933. Professor. Educ: B.A., Wheaton Coll., 1955; B.D., Southwestern Bapt. Theol. Sem., 1960; Th.D., ibid, 1965; M.A., Univ. of Chgo., 1969. Appts: Ptnr., Patteson & patteson Stately Homes, 1957-70; Instr. in Philos. & Relig., Judson Coll., 1966-67; Assoc. Prof. of Philos. & Relig., Carson-Newman Coll., 1969-. Mbr. Am.

Acad. of Relig. Address: Box 65, New Market, TN 37820, U.S.A. 2, 7.

PATTISON, Rose Mary (Smith), b. 5 Mar. 1919. Educator. Educ: B.S., Home Econs. & Biol. Scis., W. Va. Univ., Morgantown; M.A., Higher Educ., Ohio State Univ., Columbus, 1965; Grad. courses in Adult Educ., Northern Ill. Univ., DeKalb, 1972-73. Appts. incl: Tchr., Ohio, 1951-59; Tech. Asst., Instr. & Guidance Counselor, Schl. of Home Econs., Ohio State Univ., 1959-65; Dir., , Adult Basic Educ., State Dept. of Pub. Instrn., Ind., 1966-69; Dir., Div. of Adult Educ., Black Hawk Coll., Moline, Ill., 1969-; Cons.-Examiner, Commn. on Instns. of Higher Educ., N. Ctrl. Assn. of Colls. & Secondary Schls., 1971-; Mbr. of Cons. Network, Nat. Assn. for Pub. Continuing & Adult Educ., 1970-. Mbrships. incl: Var. offs., Nat. Assn. for Pub. Continuing & Adult Educ., 1965-, Adult Educ. Assn., U.S.A., 1965-; NEA; Am. Assn. Jr. Colls.; Author of publs. in field. Hons. incl: Recip., Alfred J. Wright Award, Ohio State Univ., 1964. Address: 5533-34 Ave., Moline, IL 61265, U.S.A. 5, 120.

PATTON, Robert Lawrence, b. 20 Dec. 1921. Operations Analyst. Educ: B.A., Univ. of Tulsa, 1942; B.D., Garrett Bible Inst., Northwestern Univ., 1944; M.Sc., Okla. State Univ., 1956; Grad. study, Univ. of Chgo., Univ. of Calif. at L.A., Boston Univ., Appts: Chap., USNR, 1945-46, 1950-52; Instr., Univ. of Tulsa, 1946-48; Staff, MIT, 1955-57; Computer Systems Specialist, Systems Dev. Div., Rand Corp. & Systems Dev. Corp., 1957-59; Grp. Engr., Douglas Aircraft Co., 1959-63; Dir., Alva Lee Mgmt. Servs., 1959-; Engrng. Specialist, I.Y. & T., 1963-65. Mbrships: MENSA; Masons. Address: P.O. Box 772, Pacific Grove, CA 93950, U.S.A. 9, 14, 116.

PAUCKER, George, b. 25 Sept. 1910. Manager; Author. Educ: Univ. of Munich, Germany. Appts: Parliamentary & Press shorthand writer, 1932-39; Capt., WWII; Free-lance author, 1945-54; Dir., Berufsfortbildungswerk, German Trade Union, Düsseldorf, 1954-67; Dir., Europasprachklub, Düsseldorf-Munich, 1967-74; Co-Fndr., Kings Schl. of Engl. (United Lang. Schls.), London, 1966; Fndr. & Proprietor, Notizschriftverlag Georg Paucker, Düsseldorf. Mbrships: Co-Fndr., Deutscher Stenografenbund, 1947; Co-Fndr., Gesellschaft für praktisches Auslandswissen, Düsseldorf-Cologne; Europäische Sprach- & Bildungszentren, Zurich. Initiator of reform of German stenogrpahy; Inventor of Deutsche Notizschrift, abbreviation system of longhand; Publisher of num. articles & books on shorthand. Recip. of hons. Address: Lindacher Str. 1, 8 Munich 60, German Fed. Repub.

PAUL, Elizabeth V., b. 17 Jan. 1909. Writer. Mbrships. incl: Bd. of Dirs., UAPA; Rosicrucian Order, Ancient Mystical Order Rosae Crucis; AAPA. UAPPA. Contbr. to var. newspapers incing. Worcester Gazette, Worcester, Mass., & Cape Girardeau Evening Newspaper, Cape Girardeau, Mo. Hons. incl: Cert. of Merit, Laura Publrs.; Cert. of Merit from ref. book publrs. Address: 300 High St., Winchendon, MA 01475, U.S.A.

PAUL, Herbert Morton, b. 17 July 1931. Business Executive. Educ: B.B.A., Bernard Baruch Coll.; J.D., Harvard Law Sch.; M.B.A., Grad. Schl. of Bus., N.Y. Univ.; LL.M., Grad. Schl. of Law, ibid. Appts: Ptnr.-Dir., Tax Servs., N.Y. Off. of Touche Ross & Co.; Adjunct Prof., N.Y. Univ. Mbrships: Chmn., ed. Taxation Comm., N.Y. State Soc. of Certified Pub. Accts.; Taxation Div., Am. Inst. of Certified Pub. Accts.; Nat. Assn. of

Accounts; V.P. & Chmn., Comm. for Tax Shelters, N.Y. Univ. Tax Study Group; Empire State Chmbr. of Comm.; Comm. on Trusts & Bequests, Rockefeller Univ.; Advsry. Bd., Bur. of Nat. Affairs, Tax Mgmt.; Advsry. Bd., Int. Inst. on Tax & Bus. Planning; Bd. of Trustees, Assocd. Y's of N.Y. Publs: Ordinary & Necessary Expenses; Advsry. Tax Ed., The Practical Acct.; Contbng. Ed., Fed. Income Taxation of Banks;. 10 articles. Address: 775 Oakleigh Rd., N. Woodmere, NY 11581, U.S.A. 6, 32, 46, 131.

PAUL, Ouida Fay, b. 18 Jan. 1911. Music Educator; Conductor. Educ: A.B., Huntingdon Coll., Ala., 1930; B.S. in Pub. Schl. Music, 1933; Grad. work, Duke Univ., 1931; M.A., Tchrs. Coll., Columbia Univ., 1943; Ed. Din. Mus. & Mus. Ed., 1957; Class & pvte. voice lessons from Harry R. Wilson, 1942-64; Postdoctl. studies, Univ. of Ill., 1968; Additional studies at other univs. Appts. incl: Asst. Prof. of Music Educ., Univ. of Fla., 1949-61 & Univ. of Hawaii, 1961-68; Choir Dir., 1st Presby. Ch., Gainesville, ibid, 1950-61 & Community Ch. of Honolulu, 1969; Music Instr., Leeward Community Coll., 1968-; Occasional pvte. voice students, choral adjudications, guest conductor, soloist etc. in Ala., N.C., Fla. & Hawaii. mbrships. incl: var. offs., Hawaii Music Educators Assn.; Chi Delta Phi; Pi Lambda Theta; Delta Kappa Gamma; Beta Sigma Phi; United Meth. Ch.; AAUW; NEA; Deleg. to Int. Conven. of Altrusa Int., 1963, 73; Tri Sigma, 1930. Contbr. of poetry & articles to mags & profl. jrnls. Address: 5740 Haleola St., Honolulu, HI 96821, U.S.A. 78.

PAUL, Per-Edvard Axel, b. 9 May 1919. Financial Manager; Company Executive. Educ: Dr. Econs., Swedish Schl. of Econs., Helsinki. Appts. incl: Hd. Acct., Ins. Co. Fennia-Patria, 1946-51; Hd. Clerk, Finland's Paint & Varnish Factory, 1951-66. Financial Mgr., 1966-68, Vice Mng. Dir., 1968-70; Expert, Econ. Coun. of Finnish Govt., 1958-59, Goods Ins. Bd., 1961-62; Auditor, Nat. Pension Inst., 1964-; Pres. of Bd., Finnish Astra Org., 1968-; Hd., Financial Dept., Oy Scan-Auto Ab., 1970-73, Financial Mgr., 1973-; Bd. Mbr., Oy Kontram Ab., 1972-; Supvsr., Nordiska Föreningsbanken, 1973-. Mbr., var. bus. & religious orgs. & comms. Publs. incl: The Trade on the East (co-author), 1971; Business & Community (co-author), 1972; The Foreign Trade of Finland, 1972. Econs. Commentator, Finnish TV 1964-. Radio 1968-. Address: Oy Scan-Auto Ab., Sturegatan 27, 00550 Helsinki 55, Finland. 43, 90.

PAUL, Robert, b. 22 Nov. 1931. Lawyer. Educ: B.A., N.Y. Univ., 1953; LL.B., Columbia Univ., 1958. Appts: Ptr., Paul Landy & Beiley, Miami, Fla., 1964-; Ptr., Morrison Paul Stillman & Beiley, N.Y.C., 1970-; Chmn., Bd. Dirs. & Gen. Counsel, Republic Nat. Bank, Miami, 1968-; Dir., Amcourt Systems Coral Gables; Ptnr., Landy, Paul, Morrison & White, London, U.K., 1973-. Mbrships: Am. Bar Assn.; Inter Am. Bar Assn.; N.Y. Bar Assn.; Fla. Bar Assn.; Dade Co. Bar Assn. Address: 700 Alhambra Circle, Coral Gables, FL 33134, U.S.A. 7.

PAULO, Zeferino Ferreira, b. 24 Apr. 1909. Physician; Scientific Information Researcher; Institute Director. Educ: M.A., 1933; Schlr., Inst. for Higher Culture & Inst. Français ou Portugal, France, 1941-42. Appts: Free Prof., Fac. of Med., Oporto, 1934-38; For. Asst., Fac. of Med., Lyon, France, 1941; created & directed Portuguese Med. Bibliog. Off., Inst. for Higher Culture, Min. of Nat. Educ. Off., 1944; created & directed Med. Bibliog. Off., Civil Hosps. of Lisbon, Min. of Interior, & Sci.

Documentation Ctr. of IAC (1st in Portugal, nat. mbr. of FID) 1945; created & directed (currently Dir.), Sci. Info. & Documentation Ctr. (CDCU), Overseas Min., coordinating Documentation Off. of Overseas Min. & those of Overseas Provinces (Angola, Mozambique), 1957-; Sci. Councillor, Coun. Presidency, J.N.I.C.T., for Nat. Serv. of I.C.T., 1969. Mbrships: Pres., Sci. Info. Sect., S.G.L.; Int. Commns., FID/E T & FID/DC; former V.P., FID. Publs. incl: Bibliografia Médica Portuguesa (10 vols.), 1940-56; Publicações Periódicas Estrageiras inventariadas nas Bibliotecas Portuguesas (7 vols.); Classificaçao Decimal Universal (5 vols.); Bibliografia Científica da Junta de Investigações do Ultramar (13 vols.), 1938-70. Hons: Hon. Citizen of Brazil, 1968; Ordre de la Sante Publique, France, 1945. Address: CDI, Ministério do Ultramar-2. Piso -Av. Ilha da Madeira-Restelo-Lisbon-3, Portugal.

PAULSEN, Frederik, b. 31 July 1909. Research Director. Educ: Univs. in Graz, Frankfurt, Kiel & Basel; Dr. Med. Basel. Appts. incl: Endocrinologist, Organon, Oss, Netherlands, 1935; Endocrinologist, A.B. Pharmacia, Stockholm, Sweden, 1936; Dir., Nordiska Organon, Stockholm, 1945; Asst. Prof. in Pharmacol., Univ. of Lund, Sweden, 1950; Fndr., Owner & Rsch. Dir., Ferring A.B., Malmo, Sweden, 1953-. Mbrships: Fndr. & 1st Sec., Swedish Soc. Endocrinol.; N.Y. Acad. of Scis.; Fndr. & Chmn., N.-Frisian Inst.; Frisian Coun. Publs: num. works on Frisian Hist. & Lang., Endocrinol. & related fields. Address: 2271 Alkersum/Föhr, Nordfriesland, German Fed. Repub. 43.

PAULSON, Arvid, b. 14 Feb. 1888. Actor; Author; Translator. Appts: Asst. Ed., SVEA, Worcester Mass., 1906-07; Actor, Swedish Cos., N.Y. & Eastern States, 1908-10; Actor, Stage, Radio, TV, NYC, 1910-50. Mbrships. incl: Vets. For. Wars; Actors Equity Assn.; PEN; N.Y. Univ. Fac. Club; 1st Eds. Club; Am. Transls. Assn.; Norwegian Am. Mus. Author of The Story of Don Quixote (w. C. Edwards), 1922. Transl. of: Eyes That Cannot See (Albert Gnudtzman); In Confidence (Alvilde Prydz), 1923; Poverty (Hans Alin), 1925; Letters by Strindberg to Harriet Bosse, 1959; A Dream Play, 1960; To Damascus, 1960; Hedda Gabler; The Master Builder; John Gabriel Borkman; When the Dead Awaken, 1962; Lucky Per's Journey; The Keys of Heaven; To Damascus I-III; The Ghost Sonata, 1965; The Outlaw; Creditor; Pariah; Simoon; Debit & Credit; The First Warnings in the Face of Death; Mother-love; Playing with Fire; The Pelican; The Bond; Miss Julie; The Stronger, 1969; The Father; Comrades; Crimes & Crimes; Easter, 1960; The Strindberg Reader (stories, essays, poems, excerpts from plays & novels, letters, etc.), 1969; The Natives of Hemso, 1966; The Scapegoat, 1967; The Dance of Death, 1971; Days of Loneliness, 1971; Strindberg's World-Historical Plays, The Nightingale of Wittenbeg (Luther), Through Deserts to Ancestral Lands (Moses), Hellas (Socrates), The Lamb & the Beast (Christ), 1970; Late Plays of Henrik Isben, 1973. Contbr. of poetry & articles to Swedish & Am. publs. Hons. incl: 1st Recip. of Gold Medal of Swedish Acad. for transl. of Swedish Lit., 1964; D.Litt., Upsala Coll., 1973. Address: 5606 Ninth Ave., Bklyn., NY 11220, U.S.A. 2, 6, 128, 130, 131.

PĂUNEŞCU, Eugeniu, b. 24 Dec. 1925. Physician. Educ: Fac. Physics & Chem., Univ. of Bucharest, Rumania, 1944-48; M.D., Fac. of Med., ibid, 1952; Prin. in microbiol., 1959; D.Sc., 1969; Fellow, WHO advanced course of clin. chem., 1971. Appts: Asst. Rschr., "Dr. I.

Cantacuzino" Inst. of Microbiol. & Epidemiol., Bucharest, 1948-52; Chief of Lab., San. & Anti-epidemic Ctr., Bucharest, 1952-53; Gen. San. Insp., Min. Food Ind., 1953-56; Chief of Lab., Fac. of Med., Dept. TB., 1954-57; Sr. Rsch. Wkr., TB Rsch. Inst., Bucharest, 1956-63; Hd., Dept. Immunochem. & Radioisotopes, ibid, 1963-. Mbrships: Sec., Union of Med. Socs., Rumania, 1959-64; Int. Union against Tuberculosis; Exec. Comm., Commn. of Biochem., Acad. of Rumanian Socialist Repub., 1968-; Exec. Comm., Commn. of Immunol., Acad. of Med. Sci., Bucharest, 1971-. Author of sci. monographs & 150 short publs., results of rsch. Hons: Medal for distinction in sanitary work, 1956; Dr. V. Babes Prize, Rumanian Acad., 1960. Address: Tuberculosis Rsch. Inst., Sos. Viilor 90, Bucharest 28, Rumania.

PĂUŞESCU, Exacustodian, b. 20 Nov. 1928. Physician; Pathophysiologist. Educ: Physn. w. Exceptional Dip., Inst. of Med. & Pharm., Bucharest, 1954; Dr. in Med. Scis., 1966. Appts: Asst. Fellow, Asst. at Chair of Physiopathol., Inst. of Med. & Pharm., Bucharest, 1955-60; Hd. of Dept. Experimental Pathol., Orvan Transplantation & Special Clin. Investigations, Fundeni Clin. Hosp., Bucharest, 1960-. Mbrships: Int. Union of Immunological Socs.; European Soc. for Experimental Surg., European Dialysis & Transplant Assn.; Balkan Med. Union; Union of Socs. of Med. Scis. of Romania; German Assn. of Clin. Med. Author, 5 med. monographs & over 120 papers. Address: Department of Experimental Pathology, Fundeni Clinical Hospital, Soseaua Fundeni 37, Bucharest, Romania. 50.

PAVASARS, Raimunds, b. 10 May 1902. Physician. Educ: M.D., Latvian Univ. Med. Schl., 1927; Dr. Med. Habil., 1938; Post-grad courses, Germany & Vienna, Austria, 1929 & 1930's. Appts. incl: Asst., Univ. Clins.; Asst. Prof., Fac. of Med. Schl.; i/c. Orthopedic Serv. Latvian Red Cross Hosp., Riga; Cons., Mil. Hosp., ibis; i/c. Ctrl. Sick Bay Meesen, Lubeck & Rehab. Ctr., Eversburg/Osnabruck, Germany Res. Physn., Southside Hosp., Bay Shore, N.Y. U.S.A., Pownal State Schl, Me., & State VA Hosp., ibid; I/c. Ctrl. Sick Bay Meesen, Lubeck Rehab., VA Hosps., Bath, N.Y., 1959-62; Hosp in Tomah, Wisc., 1962-74. Mbrships. incl: Am Cong. of Rehab. Med.; Int. Assn. of Phys. Med. Assn. of Mil. Surgs., U.S.A.; Am. Soc. of Med Hydrol.; V.P. & Ed., Latvian Med. & Denta Assn.; Latvian Assn. of Univ. Profs.; Am Latvian Assn. Publs. incl: The Amputation Stump & Prostheses, 1937. Address: VA Hosp. Tomah, WI 54660, U.S.A. 8, 28.

PAWAR, Sheelwant Bapurao, b. 19 Oct 1932. University Professor. Educ: B.Com. B.A., LL.B., Univ. of Bombay, India; M.B.A. Ph.D., Univ. of Utah, U.S.A. Appts: Rsch Asst., Bur. of Econ. & Bus. Rsch., Univ. o Utah, Salt Lake City, 1963-66; Assoc. Prof. Bus. Admin., Coll. of Bus., Idaho State Univ. Pocatello, 1967-. Mbrships: Am. Bus. Law Assn.; Alpha Kappa Psi; Nat. Geog. Soc Co-Author, Population Characteristics of Sal Lake Metropolitan Area, 1964. Author of var papers. Recip., sev. fellowships. Address Campus Box 8359, Idaho State Univ. Pocatello, ID 83209, U.S.A.

PAWLEY, Thomas Désiré, III, b. 5 Aug 1917. University Professor. Educ: A.B., Va State Coll.; A.M., Univ. of Iowa, 1939, Ph.D 1949; post-doct. study, Univ. of Mo. Appts Instr., Prairie State Coll., 1939-40; Instr.-Assoc Prof., Lincoln Univ., 1940-52, Prof., 1952 Chmn. Div. of Humanities & Fine Arts, 1966 Hd., Dept. of Speech & Theatre, 1969-; Vis Prof., Univ. of Calif., Santa Barbara, 1968

Northern III. Univ., 1971. Mbrships: Nat. Assn. of Dramatic & Speech Arts (Pres. 1953-55); Am. Theatre Assn. (Advsry. Comm. 1953-55); Am. Coll. Theatre Festival Ctrl. Comm., 1971-; Speech & Theatre Assn. of Mo.; Comm. on Int. Exchange of Persons (Advsry. Comm. in Theatre Arts). Publs. incl: The Black Teacher & the Dramatic Arts (w. W. Reardon) 1970; a play & articles in theatre publs. Recip. of awards. Address: 1014 Lafayette St., Jefferson City, MO 65101, U.S.A. 2, 8, 13, 125.

PAWLOWSKI, Gareth Lee, b. 1,1 Sept. 1939. Aircraft Blueprint Control. Appts: USN, 1959-63; w. Lockheed Calif. Co., Burbank, Blueprint Control Room, 1963-. Mbr. USN Inst., Annapolis, Md. Author Flat-Tops and Fledglings, A History of the American Aircraft Carriers, 1971. Address: 145 "A" N. Lamer, Burbank, CA 91506, U.S.A. 30.

PAXTON, Alice Adams (Mrs. James L. Paxton Jr.), b. 19 May 1914. Artist; Interior Architect; Designer. Educ: Peabody Inst. of Music, Balt., Md.; Parson's Schl. of Design, N.Y.; Studied portrait painting w. J. Laurie Wallace, Augustus Dunbler, Sylvia Curtis, Milton Wolsky, Frank Sapousek. Appts. incl: Designer, interior Dowd Mem. Chapel, Boys' Town, Neb., 1942; Tchr., art classes, Alice Paxton Studio, Omaha, Neb., 1957-64; Dir., Paxton-Mitchell Co., Omaha, Neb. Mbrships: Charter mbr., Assocd. Artists of Omaha; Bd. mbr., Jr. League of Omaha, 1946-54; Joslyn Art Mus.; Omaha Club; Omaha Country Club. Exhibitions: Wash. Co. Mus. of Fine Arts, Hegerstown, Md. (Arch.); Joslyn Art Mus., Omaha, Neb.; Annual Exhibition, Cumberland Valley Artists, Hagerstown; Permanent collects. in Omaha. Contbr. of room portraits, var. profl. publs., & of articles & photographs, Popular Home Mag., 1958. Recip. of hons. Address: 3623 Jackson St., Omaha, NB 68105, U.S.A. 5.

PAYNE, Arnold Pershing. Educational Administrator. Educ: B.S., Univ. of Tex, U.S.A., 1948; M.Ed., ibid, 1950; Postgrad., Univ. of Houston, Tex., 1962-66; Ph.D., Tex. A & M Univ., 1973. Appts: Off., USAF, 1943-45; Coach & Prin., H.S., Eagle Lake, Tex., 1948-55; Prin., Aldine Jr. H.S., Houston, 1955-65; Curriculum Dir., Fed. Prog., Aldine, Houston, 1965-66; Prin., H.S., Tivoli, Tex., 1967-68; Grad. Asst., Tex. A & M Univ., 1968-69; Curriculum Coord., Windham Schl., Tex. Dept. of Correction, 1969-70; Prin., H.S., Calvert, Tex., 1970-71; Asst. Schl. Supt., Calvert, 1971-73; Admin. Asst. to Schl. Supt., Gonzales, Tex., 1973-74. Mbrships: Tex. Assn. of Schl. Prins.; Tex. PTA; Tex. State Tchrs. Assn.; Tex. Assn. of Schl. Admnstrs.; Phi Delta Kappa. Initiated first special educ. (retarded) prog, & first bilingual educ. prog., 1969-70. Hons. incl: Admiral, Tex. Navy, Gov. of Tex.; Recognition for outstanding community serv., Houston, Tex.; Honorable discharge, Capt., USAF, 1966. Address: P.O. Drawer H, Gonzales, TX 78629, U.S.A.

PAYNE, Charles W., b. 31 Jan. 1911. Public Relations Counsellor. Educ: Univ. of Evansville; B.A., Wittenberg Univ., 1932; Grad. studies, Northwestern Univ., 1951-53. Appts. incl: Mgr., Acme Newspictures, Newspaper Enterprise Assn., United Press Newspictures, 1946-53; V.P., Selvage & Lee Inc., 1953-67; Mgr., Wash. Rels., Ins. Info. Inst., 1967-. Mbrships: Pres. & Fndr., Mt. Prospect (III.) Park Dist.; Sigma Delta Chi.; Nat. Press Club; Chgo. Press Club; 32 Degree Mason; Shriner; Chgo. Press Photogs. Assn.; Luth. Ch.; Co-Treas., Comm. to Help Others. Recip. Geo. Wash. Medal, Freedoms Fndn. Address: 536 Marshall Rd. S.W., Vienna, VA 22180, U.S.A. 8.

PAYNE, James Edward, b. 23 Dec. 1944. Industrial Engineer. Educ: B.S., Okla. State Univ., 1968; further studies, Okla. City Univ. Appts: Indl. Engr., Tinker Air Force Base, Okla., 1968-; Dir. & V.P., J.B. Payne & Assoc. Inc., Enid, Okla., 1969-; Registered Profl. Engr., Okla., 1972-. Mbrships: Okla. & Nat. Socs. of Profl. Engrs.: Am. Inst. Indl. Engrs.; Am. Soc. Mech. Engrs.; AIAA; Treas., Okla. State Univ. Chapt., ibid, 1967; Tinker Soc. Profl. Engrs. & Scis.; Tinker Mgmt. Club; Okla. Co. Foster Parent Assn.; Highland Pk. Elem. PTA; Tinker Men's Golf Club; Desert Oaks Country Club; Order of the Engr. Hons: Outstanding Job Performance Recommendations, 1971, 1973; Nomination, Air Force Logistics Command Incentive Orientation Prog., 1973. Address: 4201 Corbett Dr., Del City, OK 73115, U.S.A. 125.

PAYZIN, Hüseyin Sabahattin, b. 13 Sept. 1916. Medical Doctor. Educ: M.D., Fac. of Med., Univ. of Istanbul, 1940; Alumnus, Harvard Univ. Schl. of Pub. Hlth., U.S.A., 1956. Appts: Specialist, Bacteriol. & Infectious Diseases, Ctrl. Inst. Hygiene, Ankara; Chief, Dept. of Biol. Control, R.S. Ctrl. Inst. of Hlth., until 1950; Lectr., Ankara Med. Fac., 1949; Asst. Prof., Microbiol. until 1957, Prof., 1957-, Univ. of Ankara; Guest Rsch. Worker, Rocky Mtn. Lab., U.S.A., & Salk Vaccine Evaluation Prog.; Dir. Gen., Profl. Educ., Min. of Hlth. (pt.-time), 1960-63; Dean, Fndr., Diyarbakir Med. Schl., 1969-72. Mbrships: Fndr. & 1st Pres., Turkish Family Planning Assn., 1960-64; Fndr., Microbiol. Assn., Ankara; Int. Comm., Int. Med. Assn. for Study of Living Conditions & Hlth.; WHO Virus Diseases Panel; Int. Comm. Nomenclature, Int. Microscopy Assn.; Kocatepe Mosque Constrn. & Maintenance Assn.; Assn. for Responsibility of Sci. Publs: 7 books in Turkish inclng. Türkiye'nin Sağlik Insangücü ve Ortak Pazar ile mukayeseli olarak III. (w. T. Büyüksarac) (proposed plan for new med. schls. in Turkey, 1973-95), 1972; num. articles in profl. jrnls. on viruses, med. educ., etc. Hons. incl: Medal, Med. Assn. for Study of Living Conditions & Hlth., Portugal. Address: c/o Ankara Universitesi Tip Fakültesi, Sihhiye, Ankara, Turkey.

PEAD, James Harold, b. 3 Apr. 1924. Real Estate Agent; Company Director. Appts: A.C.T. Advsry. Coun., 1955- (chmn., 1964-; dpty. chmn., 1961-64); Canberra Hosp. Mgmt. Bd., 1955-59, '61- (dpty. chmn., 1967-); A.C.T. Nat. Fitness Advsry. Coun., 1956-67; Dir. Travelana Holdings Ltd., 1960-62; A.C.T. 3rd. Party Premiums Advsry. Comm., 1969- (chmn., 1971-); A.C.T. Electricity Authority 1963-67, '70-; A.C.T. Totalisator Agcy. Bd., 1973; Chmn., Interim Bd., Belconnen Trust, 1973; Dir., Canberra Lakes Carotel Pty. Ltd., Canberra Press Pty. Ltd.; Chmn., Dirs., Community Broadcasters Pty. Ltd.; Dir., Tysulin Pty. Ltd.; P.M.'s Dept., 1941-42; R.A.A.F., 1942-46; Dept. External Affairs, 1946-54. Mbrships: Yowani Country Club; A.C.T. Jockey Club; Manuka Football Club. Recip., M.B.E., 1972. Address: A.C.T. Advsry. Coun. Chmbrs., S. Bldg., Civic Offs., London Circuit, Canberra City, A.C.T., Australia 2601, 23.

PEAKS, Mary Jane, b. 19 Aug. 1916. Dentist; Orthodontic Specialist. Educ: D.D.S., Univ. of Pa., 1939; Cert. in Orthodontics, Columbia Univ., N.Y.C., 1974. Appts: Jr. Asst. Surg., N.Y. Postgrad. Med. Schl. & Hosp., N.Y.C., 1942-46; Pvte. Prac., Dentistry, N.Y.C., 1939-52; Pvte. Prac., Orthodontics, Garden City, N.Y., 1952-. Mbrships: Am. Assn. Orthodontists; Am. Soc. Composers, Authors & Publrs.; Fellow, Royal Soc. Hlth.; Charter Mbr.,

N.Y. Assn. of Professions; Songwriters Hall of Fame; Am. Guild Authors & Composers; N.Y. Soc. Orthodontists: Am. Dental Assn.; Soroptimists Int. Composer, words & music, I Told a Lie, 1954. Address: 152 W. 11th St., N.Y., NY 10011, U.S.A. 5, 6, 138.

PEARCE, Brian Louis, b. 4 June 1933. Librarian; Editor; Poet. Educ: Acton Co. Schl., 1944-49. Appts. incl: Ref. Libn., Twickenham Pub. Libs., 1958-61; Libn., Acton Tech. Coll., 1962-66; Ed., Expression One, jrnl. of Richmond Poetry Grp., 1965-67; Tutor-Libn., Twickenham Coll. of Technol., 1966-; Ed., Quarto Poets Series, 1973-. Mbrships. incl: PEN; Poetry Soc.; Fndr. Mbr., Richmond Poetry Grp., 1961; Chmn., Hounslow Chess Club, 1973-. Publs: The Eagle & the Swan, 1966; The Argonauts & other poems, 1970; The Art of Eric Ratcliffe, an appreciation, 1970; Requiem for the Sixties, 1971; Twickenham Eyot (Ed., anthol.), 1973. Contbr. var. jrnls. inclng. Enigma, Envoi, The Guardian, Tribune. Award, 5th-6th places, Poetry Soc.'s one-act verse play contest, 1964. Address: 72 Yeathfield S., Twickenham, Middlesex, TW2 7SS, U.K. 11.

PEARCE, Dorothy DeL. (Mrs. Charles Wellington Pearce), b. 22 Mar. 1927. Civic Worker. Educ: B.A., Barnard Coll., Columbia Univ., NY, U.S.A., 1947. Appts: Rsch. Asst., Cardiac Catheterization Lab., Bellevue Hosp., NY, 1948-50; Rsch. Asst., Cornell Medical Coll., NY, 1950-55; Exec. Rsch. Libn., Shell Chem. Co., Houston, Tex. & NY, 1955-57. Mbrships. incl: Bd. Govs., New Orleans Opera House Assn. Women's Guild, 1965-; Soc. Hostess, 1966-; Histn., 1969-; Chmn., Uptown Subscription Comm., 1967-69; Children's Concerts Comm., 1964-66; Tour Comm., New Orleans Spring Fiesta Assn., 1966-67; Opera Orientation Comm., New Orleans Opera House Assn., 1964-; Registrar, Hostess, 1965; Thrift Shop Rep. Soc. NY Hosp. Women's Aux., 1959-60; Fund Raising Comm., DePaul Hosp. Women's Aux., 1968, Vol. Crippled Children's Hosp. Guild, 1965-66; La. Coun. Performing Arts, 1967-; Gallier Hall Women's Comm., 1967; Bd., Community Concerts Assn., New Orleans; Fund Raising Comm., Hotel Dieu Women's Aux., 1968. Address: 6145 St. Charles Ave., New Orleans, LA 70118, U.S.A. 5, 7, 125, 130, 132, 138.

PEARSE, Ronald William, b. 23 Nov. 1931. Business Executive. Educ: Univ. of Toronto Schl. of Bus., Canada; Univ. of Waterloo. Appts: Sales Mgr., Quaker Oats Co. of Canada Ltd., 1958-65; Product Mgr., ibid, 1965-66; Marketing & Sales Mgr., Kitchens of Sara Lee, 1966-67; V.P., Sales & Marketing, ibid, 1967-69; Exec. V.P., Gen. Mgr., ibid, 1969-70; Dir., Brampton Chmbr. of Comm., Frozen Food Assn., & Grocery Products Mfrs. of Canada; Pres., Chief Exec. Off., Mng. Dir., Kitchens of Sara Lee (Canada) Ltd., 1970-. Mbrships: Bd. of Trade, Metropol. Toronto; Canadian Chmbr. of Comm.; Am. Inst. of Mgmt.; Canadian Club; Am. Marketing Assn.; Toronto Sales & Marketing Execs.; Dir., Chmn., Finance Comm., YM-YWCA; Tent 28 Canada, Variety Clubs Int.; Progressive Conservative Assn. of Canada; Lodge 192, AF & AM, GRC; Brampton Golf & Country Club; Brampton Curling Club; Assn. of Canadian TV & Radio Artists. Address: 38 Richmond Dr., Brampton, Ont., Canada.

PEARSON, Betsy Decelle (Mrs.). Educator. Appts. incl: Assoc. Prof. to Dr. Lucien Dehoux, Ecole des Scis. Sociales, Liège; Belgium; Collaborator to Mr. Rene Ledent, Lab. de Biometrie Experimentale, Liège; Vol. Tchr.,

Talented Youth Prog. & Fyre Inst.; Hd., For Lang. Dept., Chattanooga H.S., Tenn., U.S.A. Pres., Am. Assn. Tchrs. of French, Tenn., 1968 Advsry., Marquis Lib. Soc. Address: 938 McCallie Ave., Chattanooga, TN 37403, U.S.A. 5, 7, 22, 57, 68, 130.

PEARSON, Donald Stuart, b. 19 Feb. 1905. University Professor; Engineer; Mathematician Author. Educ: B.S., Case Western Reserve Univ., 1929; M.S., 1933; Ph.D., St. Andrews Univ., 1958. Appts. incl: Prof. & Chmn., Elec. Engrng. Dept., Ohio Northern Univ., 1938-43 Grad. Fac., Mich. State Univ., 1945-49; Pa. State Univ., 1949-65; Emeritus Prof., ibid, 1965; Design Engr., Special Prods. Div., Westinghouse Elec. Corp., 1943-45; Prof. Maths. Prof., Lorain Community Coll., 1965-; Acting Hd., 1970-71. Mbrships incl: IEEE, Counselor, Life, ASEE; AAUP; Emeritus Mbr. Eta Kappa Nu; Life, Phi Delta Kappa; Theta Chi; Sigma Tau Delta. Publs: Creativeness for Engineers, 4th edit., 1961; Creative Image, 1959; Basic Energy Converters, 1962; contbr. to sci. jrnls. Hons. incl: Fellow, St. Andrew's, Ohio Northern Univ.; Lee Gold Medal Rsch. Award, 1958. Address: 8886 Westlawn Blvd., Olmsted Falls, OH 44138, U.S.A. 2, 6, 14, 15, 22, 26, 28, 69, 127, 129, 130.

PEARSON, Helen R. (Mrs. Russell S. Parks). Author; Educator. Educ: A.B., Indiana Univ. 1926; M.A., 1931; Postgrad., Univ. of Chgo., 1938-42. Appts: Tchr., Maths., Arsenal Tech. H.S., Indpls., 1942-61; Hd., Math. Dept., Arlington H.S., ibid, 1961-65; Lectr., Purdue Univ., Indpls. campus, 1966-68. Mbrships: Nat. Coun. Tchrs. Math.; AAAS; Ctrl. Assn. Sci. & Math. Tchrs.; NEA; Phi Beta Kappa; Phi Lambda Theta; Delta Kappa Gamma. Co-author, math. text books. Named Outstanding Woman Educator, Pi Lambda Theta, 1956. Address: 6246 N. Olney St., Indianapolis, IN 46220, U.S.A. 5.

PEARSON, Herbert Daniel, b. 3 July 1911. School Administrator. Educ: B.S., E. Tex. State Univ., 1934; M.S., ibid, 1949; advanced study, Univ. of Tex., & Southern Meth. Univ. Appts: Tchr./Coach, Honey Grove, Tex., 1934-36, Garland, Tex., 1936-37; Prin., Elem. Schl., Garland, 1937-45; Supt., Garland Schl. Dist., 1945-53; P.R. Dir., Star Engraving Co., Northeast Tex., 1953-56; Prin., Maple Lawn Elem. Schl., Dallas, Tex., 1956-59, Thomas C. Marsh Jr. H.S., Dallas, 1962-64, W.T. White H.S., 1964-66; Asst. Supt. Bus. Servs. & Sec., Bd. of Educ., Dallas, 1966-. Mbrships. incl: Assn. Schl. Bus. Officials of U.S. & Canada; Dir., Tex. Assn. Schl. Bus. Officials; Am., Tex., & Dallas Assns. Schl. Admnstrs. Hons. incl: Naming of H.D. Pearson Chapt., Garland H.S. Future Tchrs. of Am., in his hon. Address: 10620 Creekmere Dr., Dallas, TX 75218, U.S.A. 130.

PEARSON, Manuel Malcolm, b. 5 Feb. 1911. Physician. Educ: A.B., Brown Univ., 1932; M.D., Jefferson Med. Coll., 1936; Intern., 1936-38, Res., 1938-49, Phila. Gen. Hosp.; Rockefeller Fellow in Psych., Inst. of Pa. Hosp., 1940-41. Appts: Staff Psych., Inst. of Pa. Hosp., 1946-; Vis. Chief, Psych., Phila. Gen. Hosp., 1947-; Assoc. Prof., Psych., Grad. Schl. of Med., Univ. of Pa., 1951; Psych. Cons., Valley Forge Army Hosp., 1956; Prof., Clin. Psych., Schl. of Med., Univ. of Pa., 1966. Mbrships: Past Pres., Phila. Psych. Soc.; Examiner, Am. Bd. of Neurol. & Psych.; Past Pres., Delaware Valley Grp. Therapy Assn.; Life Fellow, Am. Psych. Assn., & Task Force Comm. on Suicide & Jt. Congress, Australia, 1975; AMA; Am. Assn. for Rsch. in Nervous & Mental Diseases. Publs: Streker's Fundamentals of Psychiatry, 6th edit., 1963; Contbr. of chapts. to encys.; 40 sci. papers. Address: 111 N. 49th St., Philadelphia, PA 19139, U.S.A.

PEARSON, Nels Kenneth, b. 2 May 1918. Manufacturing Executive. Appts: Assembly Line Supt.-Toolmaker-Co. Fndr. & Pres., Wauconda Tool & Engrng. Co. Inc.; Co. Fndr., Kenmode Tool & Engrng. Co. Inc.; Allied Tool & Die & Mfg. Co. Inc.; Mbrships. incl: Bd. Dirs., III. Region & Chief Judge, Mbr. of Comm. for Nat. Awards, Antique Automobile Club Am.; Treas., McHenry Co. Educ. & Trng. Comm.; Veteran Motor Car Club; Classic Car Club; Independent Order of Vikings; Am. Soc. Tool & Mfg. Engrs.; Horseless Carriage Club. Author of articles in antique automobile publs. Recip. numerous awards for perfection of restoration of antique automobiles, 1962-. Address: 125 Dole Ave., Crystal Lake, IL 60014, U.S.A. 8.

PEARSON, Norman, b. 24 Oct. 1928. Chartered Town Planner; Planning Consultant; Land Economist; Geographer; Political Scientist. Educ: B.A., Univ. of Durham, U.K., 1951. Appts. incl: Navigator, G.D. RAF, Flying Officer, U.K., Canada, NATO, 1952-53; Planning Asst., London Co. Coun., Archt.'s Dept., 1953-54; Dir. of Planning & Sec.-Treas., Hamilton-Wentworth Planning Area Bd., Ont., 1956-59; Dir. of Planning, Town of Burlington Planning Dept., 1960-62; Planning Cons., pvte. prac., 1962-; Special Lectr. in Planning, Geog. Dept., McMaster Univ., Hamilton, 1957-62; Special Lectr. Planning, Geog. Dept., Waterloo Luth. Univ., 1960-63; Special Lectr., Planning, Ont. Agric. Coll. & Univ. of Guelph, 1963-67; Asst. Prof., Geography & Planning, Univ. of Waterloo, 1963-67; Assoc. Prof., Geog., Univ. of Guelph, 1967-72; Chmn., Ctr. for Resources Dev., ibid, 1967-71; Dir., ibid, 1971-72; Prof., Pol. Sci., Univ. of Western Ont., 1972-. Mbrships. incl: Fellow Royal Econ. Soc.; Life, ibid, 1966; Fndr. Mbr., Brit. Sociol. Assn.; Fellow, Royal Town Planning Inst. U.K., 1972; Town Planning Inst. of Canada; Chartered Town Planner, U.K.; Canadian Assn. Geogrs.; Am. Geog. Soc.; Life, Royal Ont. Mus.; Lambda Alpha; (Sec.-Histn., Simcoe Chapt., 1973-); Soc. for Int. Dev.; 1st Pres., Bruce Trail Assn., 1963; Hon. Pres., ibid, 1966-; Int. Inst. for Municipal Scis.; Canad. Pol. Sci. Assn.; Trustee, Nat. & Provincial Pks. Assn. of Canada, 1970-; Humanities Assn. of Canada, 1970; Canadian Assn. for Latin Am. Studies, 1967; Ont. Coop. Prog. in Latin Am. & Caribbean Studies, 1967; Comm. (A1004) on Soc., Econ. & Environmental Factors of Transportation, Hwy. Rsch. Bd., U.S.A., 1969-; Edit. Bd., Int. Assn. for Grt. Lakes Rsch., 1972-; Canadian Univ. Rep., Soc. Scis. Econs. & Legal Aspects Comm. of Rsch. Advsry. Bd., Int. Jt. Commn., 1973-; Coun., Town Planning Inst. of Canada, 1957-62. Publs: Co-Ed., Regional & Resource Planning in Canada, 1963; Co-Author, An Inventory of Joint Programmes & Agreements Affecting Canada's Renewable Resources, 1964; Co-Ed., The Pollution Reader, 1968-; Co-Ed., revised & enlarged edit. of Regional & Resource Planning in Canada, 1970; Contbr. to num. other periodicals & books. Wrote script for CBC-TV film, The Great Lakes, in series, The Nature of Things, 1971. Recip. President's Prize, Royal Town Planning Inst. U.K., 1957. Address: Dept. Pol. Sci., Coll. of Soc. Scis., Univ. of Western Ontario, London 72, Ont., Canada.

PEARSON, Welton Dennis. Prosthodontist. Educ: Union Univ., Albany, N.Y., U.S.A.; Grad., Coll. of Dentistry, Univ. of Tenn., 1936; Cert. in Prosthodontics, Tenn. State Bd. of Dental Examiners; Dipl., Am. Bd. of Prosthodontics. Appts. incl: Pvte. Prac., Jackson, Tenn., 1937-42; 1st Lt.-Lt.Col., U.S. Army Dental Corps, U.S.A., U.K., Belgium, France, & Germany, 1942-47; Pvte. Prac., Prosthodontics, Chattanooga, Tenn., 1947-. Num. mbrships. incl: Fellow, Am. Coll. of Prosthodontics; Am. Denture Soc.; S.-Eastern Acad. of Prosthodontics; Crippled Children's Serv., Tenn. State Dept. of Pub. Hlth.; Bd., Chattanooga-Hamilton Co. Speech & Hearing Ctr.; Nat. Rehabilitation Assn.; Assn. of Mil. Surgs. of U.S.; Am. Soc. of Dentistry for Children; Delta Sigma Delta. Hons. incl: Purple Heart ETO Medal with 3 Bronze Stars; Am. Campaign Medal; Wisdom Award of Honor, 1972. Address: 938 McCallie Ave., Chattanooga, TN 37403, U.S.A. 22, 57, 125, 131.

PEASE, Oliver James, b. 23 Nov. 1896. Horticulturist; Connoisseur. Originator, Iris Versicolor Settosa in Blue, Purple, Red, Magenta, Mauve, Pink, etc.; Raised thousands of Hemerocallis; Mailman; Over 400 different kinds of flowers. Mbrships: Chap., Men's Garden Club, Mohawk Valley, N.Y.; Am. & Engl. Iris Socs.; Mbr., many other hort. orgs.; Republican; Meth. Ch. Recip. of Awards for Best French Iris & Best Collection Hemerocallis World's Fair, 1940. Address: Rte. 1, N. Rd., Iris Rd., Dolgeville, NY 13329, U.S.A.

PEAT, Grace Sims (Mrs.), b. 19 July 1913. Realtor. Educ: J.D., Univ. of Ala. Appts. incl: Legal Sec., 1932-35; Admin. Sec., Univ. of Ala., 1935-41; Admitted to Ala. Bar, 1941; Gen. Asst., Harold R. Peat Inc., Lectr. Bur., N.Y.C., 1941-47; Mng. Dir., 1947-55; Owner, Mgr., Grace Sims Peat, Personal Rep. Lectrs., personal appearance attractions, N.Y.C., 1955-; Pres., Skyward Realty Co., N.Y.C., 1967-. Mbrships: The Real Estate Bd. N.Y. Inc.; Nat. Assn. Real Estate Bds. Address: 410 E. 57th St., N.Y., NY 10022, U.S.A. 2, 5, 6, 16.

PECCORINI, Francisco L., b. 27 Nov. 1915. Professor of Philosophy. Educ: Humanities, Collegio de San Ignacio de Loyola, Spain; M.A., Colegio de San Francisco Javier, Burgos, ibid; Ph.D., Philos., Univ. of Comillas, ibid. Appts. incl: Prof., Philos., Nat. Univ., San Salvador, C. Am., 1959-62; Asst. Prof., Philos., Univ. of San Diego, Calif., U.S.A., 1963-66; Asst. Prof., Philos., Calif. State Univ., Long Beach, 1966-67; Assoc. Prof., Philos., ibid, 1967-72; Prof., 1972-. Mbrships: Acad. de Hist., El Salvador; Medieval Acad. of Am., Cambridge, Mass.; Medieval Assn. of the Pacific; Pacific Sect., Am. Philos. Assn. Publs. incl: El Ser y los seres según Santo Tomás de Aquino, 1962; El hombre en perspectiva ontológica, 1963; Los Fundamentos Ultimos de los Derochos del Hombre, 1964; A Method of Self-Orientation to Thinking (An Essay on Kant), 1970; La Voluntad del Pueblo en la Emancipación de El Salvador, 1972; articles in philos. jrnls. inclng: Transcendental Apperception & Genesis of Kant's Theological Convition & The Ontological Route in the Light of Marcel & Sciacca, both in Giornale di Metafisica. Address: 10059 Los Caballos Ct., Fountain Valley, CA 92708, U.S.A. 9, 13.

PECHÉ, Dale Clifford, b. 28 Nov. 1928. Artist. Educ: Long Beach City Coll., Long Beach, Calif; B.P.A., Art Ctr. Coll. of Design, L.A., Calif., 1951; special studies w. sev. Profs. Work included in many pub. & pvte. collections, 2 paintings purchased by Lezius-Hiles Co. for their 1973 & 1974 Fine Arts Calendar, Duncan McIntosh Greeting Cards purchased reproduction rights to ''Joyous Mother'' for 1974 Christmas Card, & McCleary-Cummings, Co., Inc., purchased 2 paintings for their Artists of Am. Calendars. Painting, "Sorrowful Mother" accepted for Vatican. Exhibs. incl: Challis Galls., Laguna Beach, Calif. inclng. 2 One-Man shows; 52nd Annual Exhib., Calif. Nat. Water Color Soc., 1972; W. Coast Americana Realists, Muckenthaler Cultural Ctr., 1972; Inland Exhib., San Bernardino Art Assn., 1972; Galleries Choice Exhib., Chaffey Coll. Mus., Alta Loma, Calif., 1973. Mbrships: Calif. Nat. Watercolor Soc., 1972-. Hons. incl: Indl. Graphics Inst., L.A., 25 awards, 1956-71; N.Y. Art Dir.'s Show, N.Y., 12 awards, 1958-71; L.A. Art Dir.'s Show, L.A., 2 awards, 1962-72; Orange Co. Advt. Club, Orange Co., 20 awards, 1962-72. Address: Challis Galls., Laguna Beach, CA 92652, U.S.A. 37.

PECK, Anne Elliott Roberts, b. 17 Dec. 1935. Journalist; Teacher. Educ: B.A., Wellesley Coll., 1957; M.A., Columbia Univ. Appts: P.R. Asst. to ed., Mademoiselle Mag., 1954; Contbng. & Features Ed., Newsfront Mag., 1959-63; Engl. Tchr., Masters Schl., Dobbs Ferry, N.Y., 1963-65; Sports Feature Writer, Reporter Dispatch newspaper, White Plains, N.Y., 1969; Local Reporter, Times Union newspaper, Albany, N.Y., 1972-73. Mbrships: DAR; Bd. of Dirs., Schenectady, N.Y. Chapt., AAUW; Bd. of Dirs., Jr. League of Scarsdale, N.Y., Inc.; Art Comm., Schenectady Mus. Art & Sci.; Bd. Dirs., & Sec., N.Y. State Legislative Forum; Bd. Dirs., Schenectady Br., Planned Parenthood. Hons: Feature Writing Contest Winner Mademoiselle Mag., 1954, Vogue Mag., 1957. Address: 100 Steeplechase Rd., Devon, PA 19333, U.S.A. 5, 6, 132, 138.

PECK, Jean Marie, b. 15 Nov. 1925. Librarian; Nurse. Educ: Dip., Millard Fillmore Hosp. Schl. of Nursing, Buffalo, N.Y., 1946; B.S. (Nursing Admin.), Univ. of Buffalo, 1956; M.S. (Lib. Sci.), Syracuse Univ., 1961. Appts: Staff Nurse, N.Y. Hosp., 1946-47, Millard Fillmore Hosp., Buffalo, 1948, 1949, Cedars of Lebanon Hosp., L.A., Calif., 1948-49, Dartmouth Coll. Infirmary, Hanover, N.H., 1949-50, Veterans' Admin. Hosp., Buffalo, 1951-54; Nursing Serv. Suprvsr., Buffalo Gen. Hosp., 1956-60; Libn., Mich. State Univ., E. Lansing, 1961-66; Libn./Suprvsr., Univ. of Calif., Berkeley, 1966-. Mbrships: Am. & Calif. Lib. Assns.; Golden Gate & Nat. Audubon Socs.; Pt. Reyes Bird Observatory; Beta Phi Mu; Sierra Club. Address: The Library, Univ. of California, Berkeley, CA 94720, U.S.A. 5, 138.

PECK, (Mrs.) Marion Skeen Coleman, b. 14 Oct. 1913. Staff Aide to U.S. State Governor. Educ: Bus. Schl., Tarpon Springs, Fla. Appts. incl: Wire Ed., Pol. Reporter, Assocd. Press, Nashville, Tenn., 1942-44; Acting Chief, Photo Div., Off. of War Info. (U.S.A.), London, U.K., 1944-45; Wire Ed., Asscd. Press of Am., London, U.K., 1945-46; Dpty. Dir., P.R. Off., Off. of Mil. Govt. for Germany (U.S.A.) & Press & Publs. Off., U.S. State Dept., Berlin Sect., Germany, 1946-53; Pres., Hixson Pike Fire Dept., Inc., Hixson, Tenn., 1955-73; Dir., Pub. Info., Tenn. Dept. of Mental Hlth., 1965-71; Speechwriter & Rschr. for Gov., Tenn., 1971-. Mbrships: Accredited Mbr., P.R. Soc. of Am. & Middle Tenn. Chapt.; Smithsonian Assocs.; Republican Pty.; Protestant Ch. Hons. incl: Citation for Serv. in Blockaded Berlin, Pres. Truman, U.S.A., 1948; sev. Citations, work for handicapped children & adults. Address: 6712 Currywood Drive, Nashville, TN 37205, U.S.A.

PECKHAM, John Munroe III, b. 25 July 1933. Real Estate Investment Broker; Author; Lecturer. Educ: A.B., Tufts Univ.; Columbia Schl. of Law. Appts: Pres., Data Realty Corp; Pres., Data Real Estate Investment Corp.; Pres.,

Data Real Estate Mgmt. Corp. Mbrships: V.P., Gov., Nat. Inst. of Real Estate Brokers; Dir., Mass. Assn. of Real Estate Fedn.; Gtr. Boston Real Estate Bd.; Dir., Int. Real Estate Fedn.; Nat. Assn. of Real Estate Bds.; Urban Land Inst.; Nat. Inst. of Real Estate Mgmt.; Dir., Gtr. Boston Rental Housing Assn.; Nat. Assn. of Home Bldrs.; Nat. Apt. Owners Assn.; Gtr. Boston Chmbr. of Comm.; Omega Tau Rho. Publs: Master Guide to Income Property Brokerage, 1969; 101 Questions & Answers on Investing in Real Estate, 1971; var. articles in "Real Estate Today", Nat. Inst. of Real Estate Brokers. columnist, Boston Herald Traveler, "Investing in Real Estate", Real Estate Investment Newsletter, Data Realty Corp., monthly 1968-. Address: 358 Chestnut Hill Ave., Boston, MA 02146, U.S.A. 130.

PECORARO, Peter Blaise, b. 3 Feb. 1931. Dentist. Educ: B.S., Providence Coll., 1953; D.D.S., Univ. of Md. Dental Schl., 1957. Appts: Staff Mbr., Joseph Samuels Dental Clin., R.I. Hosp., 1957-60; Staff, Kent Co. Mem. Hosp., 1957-; Sec., Dental Staff, ibid, 1970-73; Prac., Dentistry, W. Warwick, 1957-60; Coventry, 1960-. Mbrships: Quidnessett Country Club, N. Kingston, R.I.; Am. Dental Assn.; Am. Acad. Oral Med.; R.I. State Dental Soc.; Kent. Co. Dental Soc.; R.I. Soc. Dentistry for Children; Kts. of Columbus; XI Psi Phi. Recip., Schlrship, R.I. Conservatory of Music, 1944-46. Address: 433 Country View Dr., Warwick, RI 02886, U.S.A.

PEDICORD, Harry William, b. 23 Mar. 1912. College Professor; Clergyman. Educ: A.B., Wash. & Jefferson Coll., 1933; M.A., 1934; Th.B., Princeton Theol. Sem., 1937; Ph.D., Univ. of Pa., 1949. Appts: Asst. Pastor, 1st Presby. Ch., Bridgeport, Conn., 1937-38; Exec. Min., Ch. of the Covenant, Erie, Pa., 1938-42; Pastor, 1st Presby. Ch., Bridgeport, Pa., 1942-47; Pastor, Hiland Presby. Ch., Pitts., 1947-63; Chmn., Dept. of Engl. & Speech, Thiel Coll., Greenville, 1963-. Fellow, Consular Law Soc. Mbrships: Fndr., Am. Soc. Theatre Rsch., 1956; Chmn., 1962-70; Plenary Comm., Int. Fed. of Socs. for Theatre Rsch., 1970-; MLA; Soc. for Theatre Rsch., G.B. Publs. incl: The Theatrical Public in the Time of Garrick, 1954; Course of Plays, 1740-2: An Early Diary of Richard Cross, Prompter to the Theatres, 1958. Hons: D.D., Waynesburg Coll., 1949; D.Litt., Wash. & Jefferson Coll., 1961; Citation, Consular Law Soc., 1970. Address: Dept. of Engl. & Speech, Thiel Coll., Greenville, PA 16125, U.S.A.

PEDIO, Tommaso, b. 17 Nov. 1917. University Professor; Lawyer. Educ: Dr.jur. Appts: Keeper, Potenza State Archive; Judiciari Auditor; Currently lawyer (barrister) & Prof., modern hist., Bari Univ., Italy. Mbrships: Sec., Deputazione Storia Patria della Lucania; Bd. of Dirs., Societa di Storia Patria per la Puglia; Nat. Coun., Ist. It. di Storia del Risorgimento. Publs. incl: Per la Storia del Mezzogiorno d'Italia nel l'eta medievale—Note ed appunti, 1968; Avviamento allo studio della storiografia medievale—I: Dalla caduta dell'Impero Romano d'Occidente alla deposizione di Carlo il Grosso, 1969; Il 1799 in Terra di Bari, 1970; Gli Spagnoli alla conquista dell'Italia, 1970; Napoli e Spagna nella prima meta del Cinquecento, 1971; Storia della Storiografia del Regno di Napoli nei sec. XVI e XVII, 1973; L'eta di Pietro il Grande, 1973; Contbr. to several daily papers & jrnls. Hons: Prize, Lions Centenario Unita d'Italia, 1961; Prize, Basilicata, 1972. Address: via Pretoria 210, 85100 Potenza, Italy.

PEDROSO, Antonio Alvarez, b. 15 June 1910. Professor. Educ: D.C.L., Havana Univ., Cuba, W. Indies, 1934; Ph.D. & Litt.D., ibid, 1938. Appts. incl: Prof., Havana Inst., 1938; Prof., Latin Am. Hist., Univ. of Havana, 1942-60; Prof., Latin Am. Hist. & Lit., Univ. of Villaneuva, Havana, 1946-59; Cuban Vis. Schol., St. Louis Univ., U.S.A., 1961-62; Prof., Latin Am. Lit., Marshall Univ., Huntington, W. Va., 1962-63; Prof., Spanish, Kutztown State Coll., Pa., 1963-. Mbrships. incl: Cuban Acad. of Hist.; Ateneo de la Habana, Lit. Soc.; Am. Assn. of Tchrs. Spanish & Portuguese. Publs. incl: Estudios Americanistas, 1944; La Civilización Maya, 1946; La Civilización Incaica, 1947; La Doctrina de Monroe y su evolucion Historica, 1948; La Politica Francesa en Alemania, 1940; Caracter de los Viajes de Descubrimiento en el Sigle XVI, 1943. Address: 1939 Woodlawn St., Apt. 7, Allentown, PA 18104, U.S.A. 6, 13.

PEDUSSIA, Aldo, b. 21 Dec. 1922. Municipal Administrator. Educ: Grad. in Acctcy.; Dr. Econs. Appt: Jt. Gen. Mgr., & Admin. Mgr., Turin Municipal Aqueduct. Mbrships: Accademia Tiberina, Rome; Giant's Club, Turin. Author, Municipal Organizations: Reality & Problems, 1974. Contbr., econs., tech. publs. Hons: Kt. of Merit, Italian Repub., 1962; Chevalier au Merite Interallie, French Repub., 1965. Address: Corso Brescia 29, 10152 Turin, Italy.

PEEK, Heather Elinor, b. 27 Feb. 1916. Archivist. Educ: B.A., St. Hilda's Coll., Oxford; M.A., ibid & Cantab. Appts. incl: Rsch. Asst., Nat. Register of Archives, Histl. Manuscripts Comm., 1947-48, Ctrl. Coun. Care of Chs., 1949-50; Record Searcher, Leicestershire & Oxfordshire Vic. Co. Hists., & Engl. Place-Name Soc., 1951-55; Dpty. Keeper, Archives, Univ. of Cambridge, 1955-58, Keeper, 1958-. Mbrships. incl: Royal Archaeological Inst; British Records Assn.; Oxford Soc.; Comm. Mbr., Devon Cambridge Soc. Co-author, The Archives of the University of Cambridge: An Historical Introduction, 1962. Contbr., var. acad. jrnls. Hons: F.S.A., Scotland, 1951; A.R. Hist. S., 1953; F.S.A., London, 1960; F.R. Hist. S., 1962. Freedom of City of London, by Redemption, 1974. Address: Taintona, Moretonhampstead, Newton Abbot, Devon. TQ13 8LG, U.K. 132, 133.

PEEL, Bruce Braden, b. 11 Nov. 1916. Librarian. Educ: B.A., Univ. of Sask., Canada, 1944; M.A., ibid, 1946; B.L.S., Univ. of Toronto, 1946. Appts: Tchr., Pub. Schl., Sask.; Libn. i/c of Adam Shortt Collect., Univ. of Sask., 1946-51; Chief Cataloguer, Univ. of Alta. Lib., 1951-54; Asst. Chief Libn., ibid, 1954-55; Acting Chief Libn., 1955-56; Libn. to the Univ., 1969-. Mbrships: Pres., Canadian Lib. Assn., 1969-70; Histl. Soc. of Alta.; Pres., Bibliographical Soc. of Canada, 1970-72; Heraldry Soc. of Canada. Publs: The Saskatoon Story, 1882-1952 (w. Erick Knowles), 1952; A Bibliography of the Prairie Provinces to 1953, 1956 Supplement, 1963; A Bibliography of the Prairie Provinces to 1953: with a Biographical Index, 2nd edit. 1973; Steamboats on the Saskatchewan, 1972; Ed., Librarianship in Canada, 1946-67, 1967. Address: 11047 83rd Ave., Edmonton, Alta., Canada. 2, 12, 42, 88.

PEEL, P.D., b. 16 July 1907. Stipendiary Magistrate. Educ: Sr. Univ. Exam., Qld., Australia; Solicitors Bd. Exam. Appts: Clerk of Ct., var. places, Qld.; Stipendiary Magistrate, Mining Warden & Coroner, ibid; Solicitor, Supreme Ct. of Qld. Mbrships: Dir., Mbr., Bd. Mgmt., Qld.; Rugby Football League, Inc.; Qld. Irish Assn.; Qld. Rugby League Club; Past

Brothers Leagues Club; Life Mbr., N. Qld. Rugby League; Past Pres., Stipendiary Magistrates & Wardens Assn. of Qld., Survey Corps. Ex-servicemen's Assn., Qld. Br. Address: 205 Raymont Rd., Alderley, Qld., Australia 4051.

PEELER, Herman Ray, b. 13 Dec. 1926. Textile Company Executive. Educ: Catawba Coll., 1943-44. Appts: Credit Mgr., Norman's Furniture, Salisbury, N.C., 1952-56; Mgr., 1957-63; Gen. Mgr., furniture div., Salisbury & Lumberton, N.C., 1959-63; Sec., 1964-; Asst. Treas., Credit Mgr., Norman's Custom Draperies, 1956-61; Sec.-Treas., R.W. Norman Co., Inc., drapery & bed spread mfg., Salisbury, 1968-; Dir., 1955-. Mbrships: bus. Div., United Fund, 1962; Pres., Salisbury Spencer Furniture Dealers Assn., 1959; Ch. coun. (Lutheran), 1957-60. Address: 225-227 N. Main St., Salisbury, NC 28144, U.S.A. 7

PEEPLES, Dolly June, b. 20 June 1931. Social Worker. Educ: B.S., Northwestern Univ., 1952. Mbrships: AAUW; Bus. & Profl. Women's Club; Lion's Aux.; Legion Aux.; Outagamie Co. Histl. Soc.; Fox Valley Symph. League; Outagamie Drug Coun.; Jr. Drug Coun.; FISH; Pres., Appleton Women's Club, 1971-72; Pres., 8th Dist., Fedn. of Women's Clubs, 1972-74; Fndr., State of Wis. Chapt., Dialogue; Chmn., ibid; Mbr., Nat. & Int. Bds.; Pres., City PTA; YMCA Indian Scout Prog. Work involves helping blind, aged, young, handicapped & needy. Author of articles in jrnsl. Hons: Woman of the Yr., N. Central Wis., 1971-73; Christian Mother of the Yr., 1971, 1972 & 1973; Clubwoman of Yr., Women's Dept., Post-Crescent. Address: 1705 S. Outagamie St., Appleton, WI 54911, U.S.A.

PEEPLES, Maija Woof (Maija Gegeris Zack Peeples) Mrs. Earl Peeples), b. 21 Nov. 1942. Artist. Educ: B.A., Univ. of Calif., Davis, 1964; M.A., 1965. Appts: Instr., Art, Laney Coll., Oakland, Calif., 1968-69; Instr., Univ. of Calif., Davis, 1971-72; Sierra Coll., Rocklin, 1971-73. One man exhibs: Candy Store Gall., Folsom, Calif., 1965-73; Nelson Gall., Univ. of Calif., Davis, 1972; Solano Community Coll., 1972; Matthews Art Ctr., Tempe, Ariz, 1971; Ariz. Arts Commn. toured The World of Wool, 1971; Sigi Kraus Gall., London, U.K., 1970; Hansen-Fuller Gall., San Fran., 1969; La Jolla Art Mus., 1967. Grp. exhibs. incl: Crocker Art Mus., Oakland Mus. & Sao Paulo, Brazil, 1972; San Fran. Mus. Collectables, 1973; Sea of Japan Expositions, 1973-74. Collects. incl: Crocker Art Gall.; LaJolla Mus. of Art; San Fran. Mus. of Art. Address: 2586 Richard Drive, El Dorado Hill, CA 95630, U.S.A. 37.

PEER, Shlomo, b. 27 June 1923. Civil Engineer; Professor; Researcher. Educ: B.Sc., Fac. Civil Engrng., Technion, I.I.T., Israel, 1954; C.E., ibid, 1955; Dr. Ing., Technische Hochschule, Stuttgart, W. Germany, 1963. Appts: Hd., Dept. Constr. Mgmt. & Econs., Bldg. Rsch. Stn., Technion, I.I.T., 1963-; Cons., Bldg. Ops. & Econs. Sect. Div., Bldg. Rsch., CSIRO, Australia, 1970-; Hd., Constr. Mgmt. Studies, Fac. Civil Engrng., Technion, I.I.T.; Cons., govtl. & pvte. orgs., 1973-. Mbrships: CIB Working Grps.; Information Processing Assn., Israel; Ops. Rsch. Soc., Israel; Int. Union, Testing & Rsch. Labs. for Materials & Structures; Int. Assn. Housing Sci. Publs: Vorfertigung auf der Baustelle, 1964 & author & co-author 8 sci. papers, inclng. Unproductive Time in Building Operations (w. T.R. North), 1971; Mobile VTR Laboratory (w. A. Warszawski), 1971. Recip. Goldstein Prize, for rsch. Factors Affecting Construction Time,

1971. Address: Technion, Israel Inst. Technol., Bldg. Rsch. Stn., Haifa, Israel.

PEERY, Paul Denver, b. 9 Aug. 1906. Retired Army Officer; Author; Musician; Teacher of Creative Writing. Educ: B.S., U.S. Mil. Acad., West Point, 1928. Appts: Cmdnt., West Point Prep. Schl., Ft. Scott, Calif., 1932-34; Battery Cmdr., HQ, & Adjutant, 41st Coast Artillery Corps, Ft. Kamehameha, 1934-35; Retired from U.S. Army due to phys. disability, 1935; Hd., own Creative Writing Schl., 1935-; Tchr. of Organ & Recitalist, 1935-; Cons. Carillonneur, Maas-Rowe Carillons, L.A., Calif., 1946-; sev. times Vis. Lectr. & Recitalist, Claremont Coll.; has made about 50 records of chimes & played at most dedicatory carillon recitals in Southern Calif., 1946-. Mbrships: Lib. Bd., Coronado, Calif. (& twice Pres. of Bd.), 1942-56; Am. Guild of Organists. Publs: Chimes & Electronic Carillons, 1948; Billy Casper: Winner, 1969; over 200 columns, articles & short stories publd. in U.S.A. & abroad. Address: 1413 Tenth St., Coronado, CA 92118, U.S.A. 9, 30, 51.

PEGGE, Cecil Denis, b. 7 Dec. 1902. Author. Educ: Eastbourne Coll.; Magdalene Coll., Cambridge Univ., U.K. Appts. incl: Tchr., Engrng. Dept., Cambridge Univ., 1940-51; Gen. Sec., Cambridge Univ. Educl. Film Coun., 1946-55; Rsch. on Film & Simulactics, Inst. of Experimental Psychol., Oxford, 1960-61; Juror of poetry, made Univ. Rsch. film & essay films now w. British Film Inst. & written & lectured on Walter de la Mare. Publs. incl: Construction (Prose), 1930; Bombay Riots (prose), 1932; Obsidian (poetry), 1934; The Fire (poetry), 1943; The Flying Bird (poetry), 1955; Tribute (poetry), 1966; Contbns. in Fear No More (Anthol.), 1941 & many literary jrnls. inclng. Poetry Review, Poetry Australia, New Headland, Blackwoods Mag., Contemporary Review, the New Humanist, Sight & Sound, Univ. Film Jrnl. & Nature; Broadcast in 'Midland Poets'; num. film articles in film & other media jrnls. Mbrships: Soc. of Authors; Poetry Soc.; Cambridge Union Soc. Address: c/o Barclays Bank Ltd., Benet St., Cambridge, U.K. 3, 11, 30, 139.

PEILE, Misomé, b. 22 Mar. 1907. Painter. Educ: Pvte. study; Art Student, Rome, & St. Ives Schl. of Painting with Leonard J. Fuller, Enragh Mooney. Appts: Lectr., Hist. of Art, Adult Educ. Classes, Cornwall, & P.N.E.U. Schl., Cornwall. Mbrships: Fndr. Mbr., & Chmn., Penwith Soc. of Artists in Cornwall, 1947; Fndr. Mbr., Taurus Artists, London, 1960; Newlyn Soc. Publs: Broadsheets, Penwith Soc.; Art Critic, Cornish Press. One man exhibs: Drian Gall., London; R.W.S. Gall., London; Newlyn Gall., Penzance; S.S. Paraguay Star at sea. Grp. exhibs: Empire Art Loan; Coll. of Higher Educ., London; Chelsea Town Hall; Scottish Nat. Gall. Retrospective, w. Sculptor D. Mitchell, Nat. Mus., Valetta, Malta, 1973. Purchases: The Ascension of Christ, Carbis Bay Meth. Ch.; P. & O. Steamship Co.; Cornwall Co. Coun. Address: Stanmar, Ursuline Sisters St., G'Mangia, Malta, G.C. 19, 43.

PEJOVIC, Ilija, b. 25 May 1919. Physician. Educ: M.D., Fac. of Med., Univ. of Belgrade, Yugoslavia, 1944; Internship, Main Mil. Hosp., Belgrade, 1944-48; Fla. License, 1962; Am. Bd. in Internal Med. (written part), 1963. Appts. incl: Schlrship. in Cardiol., Paris, France, 1952-53; Residencies in Internal Med., Atlanta, Ga. & Houston, Tex., 1953-56; Asst. Med. Dir., Tuberculosis Hosp., Decatur, Ala., 1957-58; Staff Physn., W.T. Edwards Tuberculosis Hosp., Tampa, Fla., 1958-63; Chief of Clin. Servs., ibid, 1963-66; Med. Supt., ibid, 1966-.

Mbrships: AMA; Fla. Med. Assn.; Am. Thoracic Soc.; Fla. Thoracic Soc.; Hillsborough Co. Med. Assn.; Gulf Coast TB-RD Assn., Bd. Mbr., RD (Respiratory Diseases); Fla. Lung Assn. (Deleg.); Family Servs. Assn. Advsry. Comm., Bd. Mbr.; Foster Grandparents Prof., Bd. Mbr. Co-author of num. scientific papers. Hons. incl: Award (Recognition), Lib. of Human Resources of Am. Bicentennial Rsch. Inst., 1973. Address: 2715 W. Virginia Ave., Tampa, FL 33607, U.S.A. 2, 7, 125.

PEJSAK, Jan, b. 24 Nov. 1913. Painter. Educ: London, 1953-58; Univ. of Stefan Batory, Poland. Exhibs: London, 1955; Munich, 1960; Salon Basio, Monte Carlo, 1962-63; London, 1969; Palme d'Or des Beaux Arts, 1969 & 70; Int. Festival of Paintings & Graphic Art, 1970; Int. Noel Galerie 1971 Vallombreuse, Biarritz, France, 1971-72; Exhib. Nat. Galerie Mouffe, Paris, 1972; Assn. of Polish Artists in Gt. Britain, London, 1972; Palme d'Or des Beaux Arts, Monte Carlo, 1973. Mbrships: Int. Assn. of Plastic Arts; Int. Assn. of Art; Int. Arts Guild. Hons: Silver Medal, Acad. Int. Tomasso Campanella, 1971; Gold Medal, ibid, 1972. Address: 4 Lilac Grove, Westbury, Wilts. BA13 3NL, U.K. 105, 133.

PEKARSKY, Robert L., b. 8 Feb. 1922. Oral & Maxillofacial Surgeon. Educ: A.B., Univ. of Rochester; D.D.S., Western Reserve Dental Schl., 1945; Dipl., Bd. of Oral Surg., State of N.Y.; Trng. prog. in Forensic Dent., N.Y.C., 1971. Appts. incl: Pvte. Prac. Rochester, N.Y., 1947-; Asst. Oral Surg., The Genesee Hosp., affil. w. the Univ. of Rochester Schl. of Med. & Dentistry, 1948-; Sr. Attng. Oral Surg., Rochester Gen. Hosp., 1948; Attng. Oral Surg., The Highland Hosp., 1952- & The Park Ave. Hosp., 1949-; Cons. Oral & Maxillofacial Surg., State of N.Y. & Rochester State Hosp., 1953- & Baden St. Hlth. Ctr., 1949-60; Chief of Oral Surg. & Dept. of Dentistry, Lakeside Meml. Hosp., Brockport, N.Y., 1960-; Cons., Rochester Hemophilia Soc., 1954-71; Cons. in Oral Surg., The Eastman Dental Ctr., 1967-; Chief of the Dental Serv. & Oral Surg., The Eastman Dental Ctr., 1967-; Chief of the Dental Serv. & Oral Surg., Park Ave. Hosp., 1969-; Attndg. Oral Surg., Myers Community Hosp., N.Y., 1966- & Newark-Wayne Community Hosp., N.Y., 1966-; Cons. in Oral Surg., Queens Med. Ctr., Honolulu, 1973. Mbr. of sev. profl. assns. & on var. comms. Currently conducting rsch. in Acupuncture. Address: 63 Niuhi St., Honolulu, HI 96821, U.S.A.

PELL, Claiborne de Borda, b. 22 Nov. 1918. Politician. Educ: Princeton Univ.; M.A., Columbia Univ. Appts: U.S. Coast Guard Reserve, 1941- (currently Capt.); Off., U.S. State Dept. & For. Serv., 1945-52; Investments, Pol., & refugee work (V.P., Int. Rescue Comm.), 1952-60; U.S. Senator, 1960-. Mbrships: Hope Club of Providence; Knickerbocker, Brook & Racquet & Tennis Clubs, N.Y.; Metropolitan Club, Wash.; Travellers of Paris. Publs: Megalopolis Unbound; Challenge of Seven Seas (co-author); Power and Policy. Recip. of 12 hon. docts.; Legion of Honour, France, 1960; Grand Cross of Kts. of Malta, 1965; awards of merit in Italy, Portugal & Liechtenstein. Address: U.S. Senate, Wash. DC, U.S.A. 2, 12.

PELLEGRINI, Alessandro, b. 8 Oct. 1897. University Professor. Educ: Grad. in Letters, Scientific & Literary Acad., Milan, 1920. Appts: Pvte. Schlr. until 1950; Prof. German Lang. & Lit. & French Lang. & Lit., Univ. of Catania, 1950-58, Univ. of Pavia, 1958-72; retirement as Prof. Emeritus, 1973. Mbrships: Rotary Club, Milan, 1958-; Instituto Lombardo di Scienze e Lettere, Milan, 1960-; Officier d'Académie de France. Publs. incl: André Gide, 1937; Baudelaire, 1938, 2nd edit., 1944; Novecento Tedesco, 1942; Strindberg, 1944; Incontri in Europa, 1947; F. Hölderlin, sein Bild in der Forschung, 1965; Wieland e la classicità tedesca, 1968; Memorie per un nuovo giorno, 1972; Tre Cattolici liberali, 1972. Contbr. essays, criticism, reports, Italian & for. newspapers & jrnls. Address: Via Francesco Sforza 15, Milan, Italy. 43, 95.

PELS, Albert, b. 7 May 1910. Artist; Art Instructor; Commercial Art School Director. Educ: Cinn. Art Acad., U.S.A.; Cinn Univ. Appts: Instr., Fine Arts, Commercial Art; 26 yrs., Owner & Dir., State-licensed commercial art schl.; Book Illustrator. Audubon mbr., Salmagundi. Creative Works: Fine Art pntngs. exhib. nat. mus., inclng. Carnegie Inst., Corcoran, Nat. Acad., Boston, etc., Pa., etc.; World tour sponsored by Butler Mus., Ohio (28 pntngs., Collect., ibid, Pa.; Murals: Ct. House, Wilmington, Delaware; Post Office, Normal, Ill.; Anniston Marine Base; Italian steamship lines. Recip. 1st Prize, W. Va. Mus., etc. Address: Albert Pels Schl. Art, Inc., 2109 Broadway, N.Y., NY 10023, U.S.A. 19.

PEMBERTON, John Edward, b. 27 May 1930. Chartered Librarian. Educ: B.A., Mod. Langs., Manchester Univ., U.K., 1951; Fellow, Lib. Assn., 1956. Appts: Libn., UN Info. Servs., Manchester, 1955-57; Info. Off., Normalair Ltd., 1957-58; Libn., Tech. Lib., Liverpool City Libs., 1958-59; Sr. Documentation Off., Technical Info. Co., 1959-61; Libn., Int. Lib., Liverpool, 1961-66; Sub-Libn., Univ. of Warwick, 1966-73; Libn., Univ. Coll. at Buckingham, 1973-. Mbrships: Chmn., ASLIB Soc. Scis. Grp. & Mbr., ASLIB Meetings Comm.; Cons., The Open Univ. & Soc. Sci. Rsch. Coun. Publs: How to Find Out in Mathematics, 2nd edit., 1969; How to Find Out About France, 1966; British Official Publications, 2nd edit., 1973; The National Provision of Printed Ephemera in the Social Studies, 1971; European Materials in British University Libraries, 1973. Also Ed., Harvester/Primary Social Sources, & Routledge Student Literature Guides; Contbr. to num. profl. jrnls. Address: Univ. College at Buckingham, Bank House, 2 Bridge St., Buckingham, Bucks., U.K.

PEÑALOZA, Walter, b. 7 Dec. 1920. Philosopher; Educator. Educ: San Marcos Univ., Lima, Peru, 1938-40; Ph.B., Ph.D., ibid, 1943, '46. Appts: Tchr.-Sub-Dir., Anglo-Peruvian Schl., 1940-45; Prof. Greek, San Marcos Univ., 1944-47; Vis. Prof. Theory of Knowledge, Univ. Rio Piedras, Puerto Rico, 1948-51; Peruvian Ambassador, W. Germany, 1963-69; i/c. seminars, San Marcos Univ., 1946-73; Dir., Evaluation of Univs., Nat. Coun. Univs., 1969-74; Mbr., Nat. Commn. Educl. Reform, 1969-71; Dir., 1st Course for Teacher-Trainers in the Educl. Reform, 1970-71; Mbr., Nat. Commn. Study of Teacher Status, 1971-72; Cons., Educ., Inter-Am. Dev. Bank, 1972-73; Mbr., Superior Bd. Educ., Min. Educ., 1973-. Mbrships: Peruvian Soc. Philosophy; Tchrs. Assn. Puerto Rico. Publs. The Evolution of Greek Knowledge, 1946; A Study on Knowledge, 1955; Inferential Knowledge and Transcendental Deduction, 1962; The Discourse of Parmenides, 1973; articles on educ. & tchrs.' educ. Recip. sev. hons. Address: 330 Calle Ciro Alegria, Urb. El Rosal, Miraflores, Lima, Peru.

PENDELL, Thomas Roy, b. 28 May 1912. Methodist Clergyman. Appts. incl: Exec. Sec., Nat. Coun. of Meth. Youth, 1938-40; Pastor,

Holbrook (Ariz.), Newport Beach, San Diego, San Gabriel, Anaheim, Sherman Oaks & Riverside, (Calif.). Deleg., World Conf. of Christian Youth, Amsterdam, 1939; Ldr., Meth. Youth Reconstruction Proj., Nurnburg, 1950; Ldr., Overseas Seminars to Europe, Soviet Union & Middle East, 1958, '62, '65; Dean, annual Meth. Pastors' Schl., 1958, '59. Mbrships. incl: Nat. Coun., Am. Fellowship of Reconciliation, 1967-69; Chmn., Div. of World Peace, S. Calif., Ariz. Conf. Bd. of Christian Soc. Concerns, 1964-71; Deleg., World Congress of Peace Forces, Moscow, Soviet Union, 1973; Var. local & co. ch. couns. & min. assns. Contbr. of articles to var. publs. Address: 6951 Malibu Dr., Riverside, CA 92504, U.S.A. 9, 59, 74, 116.

PENDERGRASS, Margaret E., b. 9 Aug. 1912. Librarian. Educ: B.S., Hampton Inst., Va., 1934; External classes, Univ. of Ill., Champaign, 1967 & 1968; Cert., La Salle Extension Univ., Chgo., Ill., 1972. Appts. incl: Cataloger, Juvenile Books, Ill. State Lib., Springfield, Ill., 1950-57; Hd., Juvenile Dept., ibid, 1957-70; Ref. Libn. & Hd., Children's Book Reviewing Ctr., 1970-73; Juvenile Cataloger & Order Person, Juvenile Dept., 1973-. Mbrships. incl: ALA; Vice Chmn., Children's Sect., Ill. Lib. Assn., 1956-57; Chmn., ibid, 1957-58, Cath. Lib. Assn., Belleville, Springfield Diocese; Bd. of Dirs., Springfield Chapt., NAACP. Contbr. of articles to Ill. Libs., Lib. Lit. & Lib. Nodes (staff paper). Hons: Urban League pin for 10 yrs. serv., 1972; Community Serv. Award, NAACP, 1974. Address: 2001 S. 11th St., Springfield, IL 62703, U.S.A. 5, 138.

PENDLETON, Don(ald) Eugene (pseudonyms: Dan Britain & Stephen Gregory), b. 12 Dec. 1927. Novelist. Appts: Radioman, USN, 1942-47, 1952-54; Agt.-Telegrapher, Southern Pacific Railroad, 1948-57; Controller, Fed. Aviation Agcy., 1958-61; Engrng. Admnstr., Aerospace, Martin-Marietta Corp., ICBM Dev. & Deployment, 1961-67; Author, self-employed, 1967-. Mbrships: Authors League of Am.; Authors Guild, Inc.; Brown Co., Ind., Metaphysical Soc.; Speaker, ibid, 1970-71. Publs. incl: (under name Don Pendleton) Revolt! , 1968; The Olympians, 1968; Cataclysm: The Day the World Died, 1969; 1989: Population Doomsday, 1970; The Executioner Series, inclng. War Agaisnt the Mafia, 1969, The Death Squad, 1969, Battle Mask, 1970, Miami Massacre, 1970, Continental Contract, 1971, Assault on Saho, 1971, Nightmare in New York, 1971, Chicago Wipe-Out, 1971, Vegas Vendetta, 1971, Caribbean Kill, 1972, California Hit, 1972, Boston Blitz, 1972, Washington IOU, 1972, San Diego Siege, 1972, Panic in Philly, 1973; The Truth About Sex, 1969; Ed., Metaphys. Jrnl., Orion, Lakemont, Ga., 1967-69. Address: Scott Meredith Literary Agcy., Inc., 580 Fifth Ave., N.Y., NY 10036, U.S.A. 8, 30, 57.

PENDON, Ruben Gil, b. 3 Sept. 1929. Journalist; Evangelist. Educ: Psychol., Jrnlsm., Theol., univ. level. Appts: Early career in pol.; Evangelical Minister, 9 yrs.; Newspaper Columnist & Writer, 2 yrs.; Columnist in religious jrnls.; Exec. Sec., Iberian Congress on Evangelism, & Evangelical Press Assn. Mbr., Royal Geographical Soc. Contbr., articles, var. publs. Hons: State Medal for Pol.; Hon. Mbr., Cuban Ministers; Hon. Citizen, State of Tex., U.S.A.; Dr. of Humanities; Man of the Yr. in Relig., City of Alicante, 1972. Address: Apartado 3071, Madrid, Spain.

PENGELLEY, Harold Owen, b. 29 June 1924. Agriculturist. Educ: McGill Univ.,

1942-43, 1946-48. Appts: Ptnr., Pengelley & Robison, 1948-53; Mng. Dir., Clifton Hill Estates Ltd., 1953-; Chmn., Serge Island Cane Farmers Assn., 1959-69, Serge Island Factory Ltd., 1969-, & Sugar Ind. Authority, 1972-73. Mbrships: Past Master, St. Thomas Lodge 4338 (E.C.); V.P., Eastern Jamaica Anglers Assn.; Vice Chmn., Jamaica 4H Clubs; Pres., St. Thomas Gun Club; Jamaica Rifle Assn.; Royal Jamaica Yacht Club; Jamaica Club; St. Andrew Club. Address: Clifton Hill, Port Morant P.O., Jamaica, W. Indies. 109.

PENGLAOU, Michel, b. 31 Mar. 1925. Painter; Art Teacher. Educ: B.A., Univ. of Paris, France; Nat. H.S. of Fine Arts, Paris. Appts: Tchr. & Pres., Bretoncelles Art Ctr., Nogent-le-Rotrou, 1966; Tchr., Acad. of Nat. Bank of Paris, 1967-; Tchr., E.N.T.A., Photo-Cinema-TV. Mbrships: Comm., Soc. of Independents; Nat. Fine Arts Soc. Paintings acquired by Min. of For. Affairs; Towns of Paris & Nevers; & num. pvte. collects. in France, Belgium, Netherlands, U.S.A., & Canada. Participant, restoration of Chateau of Versailles. Hons: Prize, Art Lovers, 1955; Prize, Town of Fontainebleau, 1955; Grand Prize, Gen. Coun. of Seine-et-Marne, 1957. Address: 18 Ave. de Breteuil, 75-Paris 7, France. 43.

PENG-YOKE, Ho, b. 4 Apr. 1926. University Professor. Educ: Raffle's Coll., Singapore; Univ. of Malaya, ibid; B.Sc., 1950; M.Sc., 1951; Ph.D., 1959; D.Sc., 1969. Appts: Asst. Lectr.-Lectr., Phys., Univ. of Malaya, 1951-60; Rdr. in Hist. of Sci., Univ. of Singapore, 1960-64; Prof., Chinese Studies, Univ. of Malaya, Kuala Lumpur, 1964-73; Dean of Arts, ibid, 1967-68; Fndn. Prof. & 1st Chmn., Schl. Mod. Asian Studies, Griffith Univ., Brisbane, Qld., Australia, 1973-. Fellow, Inst. Phys., London, U.K., 1971-. Author of num. articles, papers, reviews & contbr. to books, especially in fields of Chinese sci. & culture. Hons: Malayan Union Schlrship., 1946-49; Fedn. Schlrship., 1949-50; Shell Rsch. Fellowship, 1950-51; Edward Hume Lectrship., Yale Univ., 1969; Carnegie Fndn. of N.Y. Grant, 1965; State Dept. Coun. of Ldrs. & Specialists Travel Grant, 1967; Asian Fellow, Australian Nat. Univ., 1972. Address: Schl. of Modern Asian Studies, Griffith Univ., Nathan, Qld., Australia 4111. 23, 98.

PENISTON, Eugene Gilbert, b. 23 June 1932. Psychologist. Educ: A.B., Ctrl. State Univ., Wilberforce, Ohio, 1953; M.Ed., S. Dakota State Univ., Brookings, 1962; Ed.D., Okla. State Univ., Stillwater, 1972. Appts: Child Clin. Psychol., Lutheran Homes, Muscatine, Ia., 1960-63; Schl. Psychol., Forest Lake Area Schls., Minn., 1963-65; Chief Schl. Psychol., Clarence Ctrl. Pub. Schls., N.Y., 1965-69; Evaluation Coord. & Schl. Psychol., Coop. Educ. Serv. Agcy., Wis., 1971-73; Chief, Psychol. Serv., Petersburg Trng. Schl. & Hosp., 1972-; Assoc. Prof. (part time), Psychol. Dept., Va. State Coll., Petersburg, 1973-. Mbrships: Am. Psychol. Assn.; Am. Schl. Psychol. Assn.; Am. Grp. Psychotherapy Assn.; Am. Psychotherapy Assn.; Am. Educ. Rsch. Assn.; AAAS; Nat. Schl. Psychol. Assn.; Phi Delta Kappa; Am. Educ. Psychol. Assn. Publs: Guidance & Counseling at Lutheran Homes, 1961; Individual Counseling Program, 1962; num. articles, reports etc. in profl. jrnls. Hons: Excellent Grad. Award, 1970; Award of Recog., Nat. Assn. Schl. Psychols. Address: 17 Ivy Lane, Petersburg, VA 23803, U.S.A. 8, 120, 126, 131, 140.

PENN, Erta V. (Mrs.), b. 24 Mar. 1909. Speech Pathologist; Educator. Educ: A.B., Fresno State Univ., 1931; M.A., 1961. Appts:

Music Tchr.; Classroom Tchr.; Speech & Hearing Therapist; Psychmetrist; Tchr., Orthopedically & Phys. Handicapped Children; Glee Club Dir.; Drama Coach. Mbrships: Phi Kappa Phi; Past Pres., Ctrl. Calif. CSHA; Past Pres., Kings Co. CEC; Ctrl. Calif. Nurses Assn.; Past Pres., Kings Co. Easter Seal Assn.; Life, NEA; CTA; AAUW; Pres., St. Thomas Womens Guild; Democratic Womens Club; Rebeccah Lodge. Author, A Handbook for the Remedial Speech Program, 1952. Address: 27 Garden Highway, Yuba City, CA 95991, U.S.A. 120, 130.

PENNINGTON, Albert Joe, b. 29 Oct. 1950. Author; Farmer. Educ: Grad., Van Buren H.S., Mo., 1968. Mbrships: V.P., Carter Co. Ext. Assn.; Am. Angus Assn.; Nat. Rifle Assn. of Am. Publs: Ozark National Scenic Riverways (co-author), 1967; Big Boy, The Story of a Dog, 1970; Num. articles in newspapers, mags. Address: Rte. 1, Fremont, MO 63941, U.S.A.

PENNINGTON, Eunice, b. 16 Feb. 1923. Author; Librarian. Educ: B.S.E., Ark. State Coll., Jonesboro; M.L.S., George Peabody Coll., Nashville, Tenn. Appts: Tchr., Carter & Shannon Cos.; Free-lance Jrnlst.; currently regional libn., Current River Regional Lib. System. Mbrships: Mo. State Histl. Soc.; ALA; Mo. Lib. Assn.; Nat. Ozarks Scenic Riverways Histl. Assn. (Pres.); Friends of the Lib.; Ozark Community Coun.; Past Chmn., Carter Co. Save the Children Fed.; Hon. life Mbr., Nat. Eugene Field Poetry Soc. Publs: History of Carter County, 1959; History of the Ozarks, 1971; Perry, the Pet Pig, 1966; Ozark National Scenic Riverways, 1967; Master of the Mountains, 1971; num. jrnl. articles. Recip., Dipl. of Educ., Colo. Christian Coll. Address: Route 1, Fremont, MO 73941 U.S.A. 130, 128.

PENNINGTON, Lillian Boyer (Mrs.), b. 2 Apr. 1904. Teacher; Artist; Author. Educ: Grad., Shippensburg State Coll., Pa., 1926; Manhattan Schl. of Music, N.Y.C., 1937-39; Studied Art, CCNY, 1 yr., Nat. Acad., 1963-66, var. masters. Appts. incl: Dir., Jr. Prog., Summer Camp, Keeseville, N.Y., 1943-49; Tchr., Barnard Schl.. N.Y.C., 1944-45; Tchr., Riverdale Country Schl., ibid, 1947-58, 1960-64. Mbrships. incl: Pikes Peak Br., Nat. League Am. Pen Women; Pikes Peak Artist Assn.; Colo. Springs Art Guild; Assoc., Am. Watercolor Soc. Publs: The Choo Choo Train, 1958; Reading for Beginners, 1963; Treasure House of Bedtime Stories, 1963; Snafu the Littlest Clown, 1972, Schl. & Lib. Edit., 1973; num. literary & artistic contbns. to educl. jrnls., 1951-. Hons: Maggie Award, 1959; 1st Prize, Primary Activities Contest, Scott Foresman Inc., 1963; num. Awards for Paintings & Photographic Slides. Address: 900 Saturn Drive, Apt. 901, Colorado Springs, CO 80906, U.S.A.

PENNISTEN, John William, b. 25 Jan. 1939. Consulting Actuary. Educ: A.B., Hamilton Coll., Clinton, N.Y., U.S.A., 1960; Nat. Sci. Fndn. Fellow, Harvard Univ., 1960-61. Appts: Actuarial Asst., New England Mutual Life Ins. Co., Boston, Mass., 1965-66; Asst. Actuary, Mass. Gen. Life Ins. Co., Boston, 1966-68; Actuarial Assoc., John Hancock Mutual Life Ins. Co., Boston, 1968-71; Asst. Actuary, George B. Buck Cons. Actuaries, N.Y.C., 1971-. Mbrships: Assoc., Soc. of Actuaries; Am. Math. Soc.; Math. Assn. of Am.; Phi Beta Kappa. Recip., WWII Occupation Medal, Berlin, Germany. Address: 135 Willow St., Brooklyn, NY 11201, U.S.A. 6.

PENSER, (Per) Wilhelm (Julius), b. 29 May 1901. Advocate; Politician. Educ: LL.M., Univ.

of Lund. Appts: Swedish Ct. Prac., 1924-25; then Assoc., Hedener & Penser, lawfirm, Eslöv, & subsequently holder of firm, 1954-; Mbr., Swedish Bar Assn., 1928-, Bd. Mbr., 1951-57, Pres., Södra Avdelningen, 1956-66; Councillor, Eslöv City, 1935-, Vice Chmn., 1959-66, Chmn., 1966-70; Mbr., Co. Coun. of Skåne, 1960, Exec. Comm. Mbr., 1961-, Vice Chmn., 1969-70. Mbrships: Travellers' Club at Malmö; New Soc. of Letters at Lund. Author, var. juridical essays. Hon. Cmdr., Royal Order of VASA. Address: Box 201, Södergatan 2, 241 00 Eslöv, Sweden. 43.

PEPELASIS, Adamantios, b. 6 Sept. 1923. Professor of Economics. Educ: B.A., Athens Schl. of Econs.; L.S.E.; Ph.D., Univ. of Calif, Berkeley, U.S.A. Appts: Asst. Prof., SUNY, Buffalo, 1954-57; Assoc. Prof., Univ. of Calif., 1959-63; Depty. Gov., Agricl. Bank of Greece, 1963-67; Cons., FAO-UN, 1968; Prof., Econs., & Hd., Va. State Univ., 1971-. Mbrships: Am. Econ. Assn.; Royal Econ. Assn.; Pub. Choice Soc.; Pelerin Soc.; Econ. Hist. Soc. Publs. incl: Economic Development: Analysis & Case Studies, 1962, 2nd edit., 1965; Essays in Economic Development, 1965; Old Trends in New Economic Thought, 1974; Num. articles in profl. jrnls. Hons: Cmdr., Order of Phoenix, 1965; Fellow, Soc. Sci. Rsch. Coun. Address: Dept. of Econs., Va. State Univ., Blacksburg, VA 24061, U.S.A. 43.

PEPPARD, Coral Maryette, b. 24 Jan. 1946. Educator. Educ: SUNY, Brockport; A.B., Tompkins-Cortland Community Coll., 1971; B.A., SUNY, Empire, 1973; full-time Masters student, SUNY, Cortland. Appts: Tchr., Adult Educ. Classes, Bd. of Coop. Educl. Servs. Mbrships: Am. Assn. for Higher Educ.; AAUW; Cortland Country Club; State Vice-Chmn. PR, DAR; Order of Eastern Star; Cortland Co. Hist. Assn.; Am. Studies Assn.; Nat. Coun. of Admnstv. Women in Educ. Publs: Illusion of Reality. Address; 33 Pearl St., Cortland, NY 13045, U.S.A. 130, 138.

PEPPARD, Sara Elizabeth (Mrs. Robert E. Peppard). Personnel Administrator. Educ: B.A., Empire State Coll., 1973; Currently working on Master's degree, State Univ. Coll., Cortland. Appts: Coord. Vets. Affairs, State Univ. Coll., Cortland; Registrar for Local Bd. 56, Selective Serv.; Personnel Officer, Guthrie Clin., Robert Packer Hosp., Syare, Pa. Mbrships: Regent, State Vice Chmn., P.R. & State Chmn. Elect of Resolutions, DAR; Am. Assn. Higher Educ.; AAUW; Am. Coll. Personnel Assn.; Am. Studies Assn.; Cortland Co. Hist. Soc.; Grad. Student Club, SUNY, Cortland; Nat. Coun. Admin. Women in Educ.; Huguenot Soc.; Cortland Coll. Alumni Assn. Address: 33 Pearl St., Cortland, NY 13045, U.S.A. 130.

PEPPÉ, Rodney Darrell, b. 24 June 1934. Author; Artist; Graphic Designer. Educ: Eastbourne Schl. of Art, U.K.; Central Schl. of Arts & Crafts, London. Appts: Art Dir., S.H. Benson, London, 1959-64; Art Dir. for TV Accounts, J. Walter Thompson Co. Ltd., 1964-65; Cons., Ross Foods Ltd., London, 1965-72; Free-lance Graphic Designer & Illustrator, 1965-; Cons., Syon Park, 1972-73. Mbr., St. Edward's Schl. Soc. Publs: The Alphabet Book, 1968; Circus Numbers, 1969; The House That Jack Built (Author & Illustrator), 1970; Hey Riddle Diddle! , 1971; Simple Simon, 1972; Cat & Mouse, 1973. Illustrator: The Little Painter, 1971; Odd One Out, (in press). Hons. incl: Nat. Outdoor Advt. Award, 1962; Bronze Star & Silver Star, Inst. of Packaging, 1967-68. Address: 21 Denmark Ave., Wimbledon, London SW19 4HF, U.K. 30

PEPPER, Beverly, b. 20 Dec. 1924. Sculptor. Educ: Grad., Pratt Inst.; B.A., Art Students League, N.Y., 1941; Studied painting w. Fernand Leger & Andre L'Hote, Paris, France, 1949; Student, Cordon Bleu, 1951. One-Man Exhibitions incl: Hayden Ct. & Plaza, MIT, Cambridge, U.S.A., 1969; Albright-Knox Art Gall., Buffalo, 1969; Studio Marconi, Milan, Italy, 1970; Piazza della Rotonda, Milan, 1970; Galerie Hella Nebelung, Düsseldorf, German Fed. Repub., 1971; Piazza Margana, Rome, Italy, 1971; Parker St. Gall., Boston, U.S.A., 1971; Qui Arte Contemporanea, Rome, 1972; Marlborough Galleria d'Art, Rome, 1972; Temple Univ. Abroad, Tyler Schl. of Art in Rome, 1973; Group Exhibitions incl: Am. Artists in Italy, U.S.I.S., Rome, 1969; Basle's Fair, Switzerland, 1970; Mus. of Modern Art, Rome, 1974; Civic Community Ctr., Phila., 1974; 12 major sculpture commns.; Works in permanent collects.; Author of 5 cookery books. Address: Castello di Torreolivola, Torregentile di Todi (PG), 06059, Italy. 5, 37.

PEPPER, Charles Willis, b. 1 Aug. 1932. Publisher. Educ: B.A., Southern Meth. Univ., 1954. Appts: USAF, 1955-57; Exec. Trng. Prog., Wyatt Food Stores, Dallas, 1958; Var. positions, Holt Rinehart & Winston, Inc., 1959-69; Pres., Am. Book Co., 1969-72; Pres., Educ. Div., Litton Educl. Publishing, Inc., 1972-(The Educ. Div. incls. Am. Book Co., D. Van Nostrand Co. & McCormick Mathers Publishing Co.). Mbrships: V.P., Glenridge N.J. Schl. Bd.; N.J. State Advsry. Coun. for Educl. Prog. Dev.; Exec. Comm., Schl. Div., Assocd. Am. Publishers; Lambs Club; Glenridge N.J. Country Club; Newcomen Soc. Address: 176 Ridgewood Ave., Glenridge, NJ 07028, U.S.A. 2, 6.

PEPPER, John J., b. 17 Feb. 1928. Advocate. Educ: B.A. & B.C.L., Loyala Coll., McGill Univ., Montreal, P.Q., Canada. Appts. incl: Read Law w. Hon. F. Philippe Brais, Q.C. & A.J. Campbell, Q.C., 1949-53; Called to Bar of P.Q., 1953; Assoc., Brais & Campbell (now Campbell, Pepper & Laffoley), 1953; Mbr., Bar of P.Q. & Montreal; Coun. Mbr., Canadian Bar Assn.; Special Fed. Crown Prosecutor, 1954-57; Dir., Legl. Aid Bur., Bar of Montreal, 1962-63; Sec., Ins. Sect., P.Q. Br. of the Canadian Bar Assn., 1963 & Pres., 1965; Sec., Montreal Bar Assn., 1963-65; Mbr., Bd. of Discipline, Bar of P.Q., 1968-; Pub. Info. Bur., Bar of P.Q., 1971-; Pres. & Dir., Soges Inc.; Sec. & Dir., Ultramar Canada Ltd., Golden Eagle Canada Ltd., & Marwest Hotel Co.; Sec.-Treas. & Dir., Broadcast Relay Serv. Canada Ltd.; Dir., W.I.H. Holdings Ltd.; Western Int. Hotels Ltd.; The Odeon Cinemas Ltd.; Mercury Press Co.; Bd., Rediffusion Inc.; Dir. & Sec., St. Mary's Hosp. Fndn. Address: Campbell, Pepper & Laffoley, 1 Place Ville Marie, Suite 1414, Montreal, P.Q., H3B 2B3, Canada. 88.

PERAGLIE, Bruno R., b. 4 Oct. 1928. Medical Doctor; Obstetrician; Gynaecologist. Educ: Univ. of Turin, Italy; Med. Schl., Univ. of Ferrara-Bologna. Appts: Internship, Elizabeth Gen. Hosp., N.J., U.S.A.; Res., Anaesthesiol., Hahnemann Med. Coll., Phila, Pa., 1 yr.; Res., Gyn. & Ob., N.J. Coll. of Med., 3 yrs.; Res., Gynaecological Oncol., ibid, 1 yr.; Former chief res. Gyn. & Ob., Mortland Med. Ctr., Univ. of N.J. Mbrships: Jr. mbr., Am. Colls. of Ob. & Gyn. & of Surgs.; Past mbr., N.Y. Acad. of Sci.; Fellow, Am. Socs. of Fertility & Sterility & of Cancer Cytol.; Past Pres., Local Unit, Am. Cancer Soc.; AMA; Italian Med. Assn.; Tex. Med. Assn.; Former Chmn., Ob. & Gyn., Brownsville Med. Ctr.; Past Dir., Fndn. of Love, Cath. Charity, Inc.; Dir.,

Valley Zoological Soc.; Pres. Elect, Cameron-Willacy Co. Med. Soc.; Pres., Merril-Peraglie Profl. Assn. Contbr. sev. articles, papers to profl. publs. Recip. of Price Award, Am. Coll. of Ob. & Gyn. Address: 495 Owens Road, Brownsville, TX 78520, U.S.A. 125.

PERCY, (Commodore) Robert H., b. 27 Nov. 1929. Officer, Royal Australian Navy. Educ: Royal Australian Naval Coll., 1943-47; Australian Army Staff Coll., 1963-64. Appts: Cadet Midshipman, 1943; Midshipman, 1947; Sub-Lt., 1948; Lt., 1951; Lt.-Cmdr., 1959; Cmdr., 1963; Capt., 1968; Commodore, 1973; C.O., HMAS Parramatta, 1964-65; Dir., Australian Jt. Anti-Sub. Schl., 1966-68; Dpty. Dir., Jt. Ops. Staff, Dept. of Defence, 1968-71; C.O., HMAS Perth, 1971-73; Australian Naval Attaché, Wash., D.C., 1973-. Hons: Royal Humane Soc. Bronze Medal for Saving Life at Sea, 1955. Address: Embassy of Australia, 1601 Mass. Ave., NW, Washington, DC 20036, U.S.A. 23.

PERDON, Henri, b. 22 Jan. 1915. Engineer. Educ: Civil Engr., Mines, Ecole Nat. Supérieure des Mines, Paris, France, 1938; Thermic Schl. Appts: Engr., Ctrl. Off. for Rational Heating, 1945-52; Sec. Gen., French Inst. of Combustibles & Energy, 1952; Dir., ibid, 1966-; Sec. Gen., Revue Gen. de Thermique 1962-. Mbrships: Sec. Gen., French Soc. of Thermicists, 1960-; Sec. Gen., Alumni Assn. of Thermic Schl., 1945-; Treas., Interprofl. Ctr. for Tech. Study of Atmospheric Pollution; Fuel Inst., London, U.K.; French Archaeol. Soc. Publs. incl: num. papers in jrnls. & confs; Conférence Internationale sur la Pollution Atmospherique, 1973. Hons. incl: Off., Nat. Order of Merit; Chevalier, Acad. Palms; Combatant Cross, 1939-45. Address: Inst. Français des Combustibles & de L'Energie, 3 Rue Henri-Heine, 75016 Paris, France. 43, 91.

PEREA-ROSELLÓ, Pedro Luis Tomás, b. 18 Sept. 1906, d. 9 Dec. 1971. Lawyer; Professor of Law. Educ: Pre-law studies, Columbia Univ., N.Y., U.S.A., 1924-28; LL.B., Univ. of Puerto Rico, 1933; B.A., ibid, 1938. Appts. incl: Pvte. Law Prac., Mayaguez, P.R., 1933-43, '46-49; Instr., Soc. Scis., & Humanities, Univ. of P.R., 1943-46; Instr., Asst. Prof., Assoc. Prof., Cath. Univ. of P.R., Ponce, 1951-61; Prof., Law, Schl. of Law, ibid, 1961-71. Mbrships. incl: Am. & P.R. Bar Assns.; Am. Soc. of Int. Law; Advsry. Commn. on Hist. of Inst. of P.R. Culture; Epsilon Omicron Chapt., Phi Alpha Theta; P.R. Alpha Chapt., Pi Gamma Mu; AAUP; Columbia Coll. Chapt., Phi Lambda Alpha; Charter, Columbia Univ. Club of P.R.; Am. Soc. for Legal Hist.; Columbia Law Schl. Alumni Assn. Publs. incl: Articles on hist., law & philos.; Los Periódicos y los Periodistas de Mayaguez, 1962; Ensayos de Historia del Derecho 1963; Poems publd. in reviews, etc. Winner of literary awards. Address of Mrs. Perea-Rosello: Avenida Las Américas 33, Condominio Torruella, Apt. 403, Ponce, Puerto Rico 00731. 15, 109, 136.

PEREGRINE, David Seymour, b. 9 June 1921. Astronomer. Educ: A.B., UCLA, 1950; post-grad. study, Univ. of Calif. at Berkeley, 1956-59. Appts: Photogrammetric Cartographer, U.S. Geol. Survey, 1951-56; Sr. Physicist. N.Am. Aviation, Space Div., 1960-66; Exec. & Sci. Specialist, Chrysler Corp., Space Div., 1966-68; Cons., 1968-. Fellow British Interplanetary Soc. Mbrships: Am. Astronom. Soc.; Am. Soc. of Photogrammetry. Contbr. to Astrophys. Jrnl. Co-author of environmental manuals on Moon, Venus, & Mars. Address: 190 S. Marion St. Pkway., Denver, CO 80209, U.S.A. 9, 14, 131, MCL.

PÉRÈS, Gabriel, b. 1920. Professor of Physiology; Laboratory Director. Educ: D.Sc. & D.V.S., Univ. of Lyons, France. Appts: Supvsr., Nat. Veterinary Schl., Lyons, 1947; Supvsr., Fac. of Scis., Univ. of Lyons, 1956; Lectr., ibid, 1959; Prof., Physiol., & Dir., Michel Pacha Inst., 1961-. Mbrships. incl: French Physiological Assn.; Biol. Soc.; N.Y. Acad. of Scis.; AAAS; Gen. Sec., Lyons Comparative Med. Soc., Acad. of Var. Publs: Fndr. & Ed., Annals of Michel Pacha Inst.; Num. articles & rsch. papers in profl. jrnls. Hons. incl: Off., Order of Acad. Palms; Kt., Order of Agricl. Merit; Volunteer Combattants Cross. Address: 3 Rue du Musée Guimet, 69006 Lyons, France. 43.

PEREZ, Rodolfo Paras, b. 7 Apr. 1934. Artist; University Professor; Writer. Educ: B.F.A., Univ. of Philippines, 1957; M.F.A., Univ. of Minn., 1961; M.A., ibid, 1962; Ph.D., Harvard Univ; 1971. Appts. incl: Art Dir., Panorama Mag., Philippines, 1956-59; Tchr., Univ. of Minn; 1959-60 & Boston Univ., 1969; Assoc. Ed., Filipino Heritage, 1972-73; Assoc. Prof., Coll. of Fine Arts, Univ. of Philippines; Art Cons. to Woman's Home Companion (mag.) & Galerie Bleue, Philippines. Work exhibtd. in pvte. & pub. collects., throughout Europe & U.S.A. One-Man Shows incl: Boris Mirski Gall., Bostn, 1969; Luz Gall., Makati, Philippines, 1969, 1971. Publs. incl: sev. monographs on Filipino Artists. Contbr. to profl. mags & jrnls. Mbrships. incl: Life Mbr., Phi Kappa Phi; Assn. Int. des Critiques des Art; Life Mbr., Philippine Fulbright Schlrs. Assn.; Coll. Art Assn., 1965-70; Art Assn. of Philippines, 1962, 1st V.P. Hons. incl: Mbr. Design Team, Philippine Pavilion, N.Y. World's Fair; Gold Medal Award, I Mostra Int. della Grafica, Florence, Italy, 1969. Address: Galerie Bleue, Rustan, Ayala Ave., Makati, Rizal, Philippines. 133.

PEREZ GUTIERREZ, Mariano, b. 11 Sept. 1932. Priest; Professor of Music. Educ: Dip., Composition, Piano, Organ, Conserv. of Music, Madrid, Spain; Univ. Santiago de Compostela; Lic. in Art, Univ. of Seville; Lic. in Law, Univ. Pontificia de Comillas, Madrid. Appts. incl: Monk, Chapel Choir Master, Sem. Prof., Diocesan Dir. of Sacred Music, Santiago de Compostela, 1964; Prof., Harmony, Santiago de Compostela Conserv., 1965; Prof., Esthetics & Hist. of Music, Conserv. of Music, Univ. of Seville, 1969; Dir. of Studies, ibid, 1972; Sub-Dir., ibid, 1974. Mbr., var. profl. orgs. Compositions incl: Elegia cromatica for violin & piano; Canto a Santiago. Publs. incl: Musica Sagrada y Lenguas Modernas, 1967; La Estetica Musical de S. Agustin & la Luz del Libro I de su 'De Musica'. Recip., num. hons. Address: Catedratico del Conservatorio Superior de Musica Jesus del Gran Poder 49, Seville, Spain. 43.

PEREZ-SOTO, Armando, b. 12 Feb. 1936. Physician. Educ: B.S., Univ. of Puerto Rico, 1957; M.D., 1961. Appts: Intern, Univ. of Puerto Rico Hosp., 1961-62; Cmdng. Officer, 19th Med. Detachment, Stuttgart, Germany, 1964; Cmdng. Officer, 732th Med. Detachment, ibid, 1964-66; Asst. Prof., Internal Med., Arecibo Municipal Hosp., Puerto Rico, 1966-67; Pvte. prac., 1967-. Mbrships: AMA; Univ. of Puerto Rico Schl. of Med. Grads. Address: P.O. Box 1813, Arecibo, Puerto Rico 00612. 7, 136.

PERFALL, Arthur G., b. 26 Apr. 1927. Banker; Communicator. Educ: B.A., Hofstra Univ., Hempstead, N.Y., 1951. Appts. incl: Org. & Staff Writer, Seafarers Int. Union, AFL, N.Y.C., 1951-54; Reporter, for. corresp., feature ed., picture ed., mng. ed., assoc. ed.,

Newsday, Inc., Garden City, NY., 1954-72; V.P. & Dir., P.R., Franklin Nat. Bank, N.Y.C., 1972-; Sr. V.P. i/c Corporate Mktng., ibid, 1973-; Adjunct Lectr. in jrnlsm., C.W. Post Coll., L.I. Univ., Brookville, N.Y., 1962-64. Mbrships. incl: Overseas Press Club of N.Y.; Nat. Headliners Club; Sigma Delta Chi; Acad. Pol. Sci.; Am. Acad. Soc. & Pol. Scis.; U.S. Naval Inst. Author of articles in var. mags. Hons. incl: Pulitzer Prize, 1970; Sigma Delta Chi Disting. Serv. to Jrnlsm. Awards, 1968, '71. Address: The Harbour Club, 15 Milligan Rd., W. Babylon, NY, U.S.A. 6, 16.

PERFLER, Olaf K., b. 30 Nov. 1940. University Professor. Educ: Law Schl., Vienna, Austria; Ph.D., Vienna Univ.; Cambridge Univ. Appts: Instr., Am. Int. Schl., Vienna; Asst. Prof., Sacramento State Coll., Calif., U.S.A.; Assoc. Prof., Calif. State Univ., Sacramento. Mbrships. incl: Exec. Coun., FLAGS, 1968-73; Chmn., German Sect., 1968-70; 1st V.P., 1970-71; Pres., 1971-72; Dir., Bd. CFLTA, 1972-73; PAPC; AATG; FLANC; FASSC; FACSUS. Publs: Die Entwicklung der lyrischen Sprachkunst bei Josef Weinberber. 1967; Contbr., Dizionario della Letteratura Tedesca; Contbng. Ed., Ring Rund, Vienna; var. other articles. Address: 5226 Mississippi Bar Drive, Orangevale, CA 95662, U.S.A. 120.

PERIĆ, Berislav, b. 7 Aug. 1921. University Professor (Educator). Educ: Univ. of Zagreb Law Schl., 1945-49; LL.D., ibid, 1954. Appts. incl: Prof., Theory & Philos. of Law; Dir. for Theory of Law, Sociol. & Constitutional Law, Univ. of Zagreb Law Schl.; Ed.-in-Chief, Collected Papers (Zbornik), Univ. of Zagreb Law Schl. Mbrships: Int. Assn. or Philos. of Law & Soc. Philos. Publs. incl: Problem Of Autonomy-Heteronomy Of Law, 1955; Methodology In The Science Of Law, 1958; Science Of Law & Dialectics, 1964; Structure Of Law, 1965. Major rsch. work in fields of Solidarism in Theory of Law, Some Elements of Law's Evolution, Structuralism (from innocent notion to pretentious philos.), Technol., Human Personality & New Social Relationship, Hegel's Heritage & Dialectic Philos. of Man & The Role of Dailectic in Acquisition of Knowledge of Law. Hons: Bozidar Adzija Prize of Sabor (Parliament Croatian) for book, Science of Law & Dialectics, 1964. Address: Ružmarinka 15, 41 000 Zagreb, Croatia, Yugoslavia.

PÉRINET, Jean-Pierre-Gérard, b. 7 Oct. 1945. Company Managing Director; Perfumer. Educ: Bachelor's degree. Appts: Mng. Dir., Codipar; Commercial Dir., Rose-Valois Perfumes; Fndr., Perinay Perfume Co., 1974. Mbrships: Int. Cultural Rels. Ctr.; Rolls-Royce Enthusiasts Club. Address: 6 Rue Alsace Lorraine, Boulogne 92100, France.

PERKINS, Gloria Okes (Mrs. Everett Dan Perkins), b. 5 Jan., 1932. Journalist. Educ: B.J., Univ. of Mo., 1953; postgrad. work in counseling, Univ. of Ill., 1963. Appts: Ed., News-Times, Webster Groves, Mo., 1953-54; P.R. Dir., St. Louis Co. Lib. System, 1955; P.R., YWCA, Rockford, Ill.; 1956; Speaker & Bible Tchr., Rockford, 1958-68; Ed., The Jonquil mag., Epsilon Sigma Alpha Int., 1969-74; Dir. of Publs. ibid, 1971-74; Bd. of Dirs., ESA Serv. Corp. Mbrships: Keeper of Archives, Theta Sigma Phi; Delta Tau Kappa; Pres. of Bd., Child Evangelism Governing Coun., Rockford; V.P., Penpointers; Gov. Bd., Faith Evangelical Free Ch., Ft. Collins, Colo. Contbr. articles & poems to mags. & newspapers. Address: 201 Annabel Lane, Fort Collins, CO 80521, U.S.A. 5, 138.

PERKINS, Richard Burle, b. 1 July 1923. Realtor. Educ: Oberlin Coll.; Univ. of Mich.; DePauw Univ.; B.A. Appts: Territorial Mgr., Hulman & Co., Terre Haute, Ind., Gen. Mills, Springfield, Ill., Proctor & Gamble, Okla. City; Dist. Mgr., DCA Food Inds.; Pres., Gold Seal Donuts Inc., Houston, Tex.; Div. Mgr., Nat. Oats Co., Houston; Gen. Mgr., Seven-Up Bottling Corp., Houston; Mgr., Apt. Systems Off. Servs. Inc., Houston; Owner, Dick Perkins Co., Houston. Mbrships: Pi Sigma Alpha; Boy Scouts of Am.; Pres., Mem. Plaza Civic Club; Houston Home Builders Assn.; Tex. Assn. of Realtors; Houston Chmbr. of Comm. Recip. Unit Citation, U.S.M.C., 1944. Address: 5915 Havenwoods Dr., Houston, TX 77066, U.S.A. 2.

PERKINS, Robert Lee, b. 23 June 1930. Professor of Philosophy. Educ: A.B., Stetson Univ., DeLand, Fla., 1951; B.D., Southern Bapt. Theological Sem., Louisville, Ky., 1954; M.D., Ind. Univ., Bloomington, 1959; Univ. of Copenhagen, Denmark, 1959-60; Ph.D., Ind. Univ., Bloomington, 1965. Appts: Tchng. Asst., Ind. Univ., 1957-59; Asst. Prof., Murray State Coll., 1960-61; Assoc. Prof., ibid, 1961-65; Asst. Prof., Southern Ill. Univ., 1965-66; Assoc. Prof. & Chmn., Dept. of Philos., of S. Ala., 1966-70; Prof. & Chmn., ibid, 1970-. Mbrships. incl: Søren Kierkegarrd Selskabet, Copenhagen, 1959-; Chmn., Local Comm. T, AAUP, 1963-64; Pres., Local Chapt., ibid, 1964-65; Sec., Hegel Soc. of Am., 1968-72; Int. Hegel Gesellschaft; Søren Kierkegaard Soc., Osaka Univ.; Eastern Div., Am. Philosophical Soc., 1968-. Author of book, Søren Kierkegaard, & of reviews. Hons. incl: Travel Grant to Paris, France, 1969, & Study Grant, 1972-73, Am. Coun. of Learned Socs. Address: Dept. of Philos., Univ. of S. Ala., Mobile, AL 36688, U.S.A.

PERLIS, Alan J., b. 1 Apr. 1922. Computer Scientist. Educ: B.S., Carnegie Inst. Technol., 1943; M.S., MIT, 1949; Ph.D., 1950. Appts. incl: Rsch. Mathn., Proj. Whirlwind, MIT, 1952; Asst. Prof., Maths., Purdue Univ., 1952-56; Assoc. Prof.-Prof. & Chmn., Dept, Maths., Dept., Computer Sci., Carnegie Inst. Technol., 1956-71; Eugene Higgins Prof., Computer Sci., Yale Univ., 1971-. Pres., Assn. for Computing Machinery, 1962-64. Author of tech. publs. Hon. incl: Ph.D., Davis & Elkins Coll.,1968; D.Sc., Purdue Univ., 1973. Address: Yale Univ., Dept. of Computer Sci., 10 Hillhouse Ave., Dunham Lab. Room 308, New Haven, CT 06520, U.S.A.

PERNA, George Donald, Sr., b. 24 Aug. 1911. Management Consultant. Educ: Ph.D. & D.B.A., Northeastern Univ., Boston, Mass., U.S.A., Boston Univ., Harvard Univ., Univ. of Mass., Hamilton State Univ., & Colo. Christian Coll. Appts. incl: Publicity & Drama Writer, Ed., Publr., Hyde Pk. Gazette-Times, Milton-Mattapan News, 1945-51; Pres., Norfolk Press, Inc., 1946-51; Prod. Mgr., Nat. Pneumatic Co. & Holtzer-Cabot Div., 1951-56; Mgmt. Engr., Dyer-Lundberg Assocs., Cons. Engrs., 1956-58; Systems Mgr., Systems & Procedures, Raytheon Co., 1958-63; Mgmt. Systems AVCO Corp., DIPG Mgmt. Ctr., Corporate Systems Mgmt., 1963-; Chmn., New Engl. Systems Seminar; Course Inst., Integrated & Adv. Mgmt. Systems, Northeastern Univ. Mbrships. incl: Systems & Procedures Assn.; Coun. Pres., Am. Inst. of Mgmt.; Nat. Contracts Mgmt. Assn.; Nat. Mgmt. Assn.; Mgmt. Dev. Seminars; Gen. Chmn., Norwood Red Cross. Recip., Sev. awards. Address: 8 Kennedy Ln., Walpole, MA 02081, U.S.A.

PERPIÑÁ Y GRAU, Román, b. 10 Sept. 1902. University Professor. Educ: Intendente Mercantil, Schl. of Advanced Bus. Studies, Barcelona & Bilbao, 1920; Dr. Econ., Univ. de Deusto, Bilbao, 1929; studies in Frankfurt-am-Mein & Berlin, 1925-26; study trips., France, Belgium, Germany, Switz., Italy & U.K. Appts: Chief of Studies, Compañia Hispano Am. de Electricidad (CADE), Barcelona, 1927-29; Dir., Ctr. of Econ. Studies, Valencia, Spain, 1929-36 & 39-40; Prof., Int. Bus. Law & Int. Econs., Schl. of Advanced Bus. Studies, Valencia, 1934-36; Mbr., Permanent Commn. of Nat. Econ. Coun. of Spain., 1940-; Pres., Econ. Mission, Spanish Guinea, 1941-; Prof., Econ. Structure & Econ. Theory, Pol. & Econ. Scis. Fac., Madrid, Univ., 1945-55; Prof., Econ. Philos., Philos. Fac., Pontifical Univ. of Salamanca & Dir. of Cursos económico-sociales, 1950-; on UNESCO Mission for Econ. Sci., Schl. of Econs., Managua, Nicaragua, 1955-56; V.P., Mediteranean Coun. of Soc. Studies, Athens & Catania, 1963-65; Prof. Population Studies, Inst. of Pol. Studies, Madrid, 1971-74. Mbrships. incl: Real Acad. de Ciencias Económicas y Financieras; Consejo Superior de Estadística; V.P., Real Congregación de la Virgen de Montserrat; Town Coun. of Valencia. Publs: Política del Carbón, 1935; Crisis económica y dericho internacional, 1935; De colonización y economía en la Guinea española, 1945; De Estructura económica y Economía hispana, 1952; La crisis de la economía liberal; Corología. Teoría estructural y estructurante de la Poblición, 1954; Corología de la población de Nicaragua, 1958, Origen y Ocaso de las Talasocracias, 1965; De Economía hispana. Infraestructura. Historia, 1973; Determinantes económico-políticos de grandes espacios, 1973; De lo liberal y de los pueblos, 1974. Recip. sev. hons. Address: Alcalá, n- 21, Madrid, 14, Spain. 43, 102.

PERRAULT, Guy, b. 25 Sept. 1927. Professor. Educ: B.Sc.A. & Mining Engr., Ecole Polytech., Montreal, Canada, 1949; M.Sc.A., Univ. of Toronto, 1951; Ph.D., 1955. Appts: Field Engr., Iron Ore Co. of Canada, 1949-52; Norancon Exploration Ltd., 1953; Moneta Porcupine Mines Ltd., 1954-56; Asst. Prof., Ecole Polytech., Montreal, 1956-57; Assoc. Prof., ibid, 1958-65; Prof., 1965-; Chmn., Dept., Geol. Engrng., 1966-72. Fellowships: Mineral. Soc. Am.; Royal Soc. Canada. Mbrships. incl: Pres., Mineral. Assn. Canada, 1967-68; Geol. Assn. Canada; Assoc. Tech. Ed., Canadian Spectroscopy, Spectroscopy Soc. Canada, 1966-71; Sci. Counselor, French Soc. Mineral & Crystallog., 1971-. Author of tech. publs. Recip., Prix Sci. du Quebec, Govt., P.Q., 1971. Address: Ecole Polytech., C.P., 501 Montreal, P.Q. H3X 3TB, Canada.

PERRAULT, Paul Eugene, b. 29 Oct. 1930. Company Executive; Design Engineer. Educ: Univ. of Wash., Seattle. Appts: Application Engr., Steber Lighting Corp., L.A., Calif., 1960-63; Mktng. Mbr., Shalda Lighting Prods., Burbank, ibid, 1963-65; Mgr., Lighting Fixture Div., Radiant Lamp Corp., E. Windsor, N.J., 1965-68; Eastern Regional Mgr., Shalda Lighting Prods., Burbank, 1968-70; Corp. V.P., Pemco Corp., Phila., Pa., 1970-73; Pres., Rsch. Assocs., Seattle, 1973-. Mbrships. incl: Past Dir. at Large, Nat. Electrical Mgrs. Assn.; Illuminating Engrng. Soc.; Pres., E. Windsor Republican Club, 1966, '67; Fndng. Mbr. & Past V.P., E. Windsor Concerned Citizens Comm., Inc. Address: 313 W. McGraw, Seattle, WA 98119, U.S.A. 6.

PERREAULT, Germain, b. 23 May 1916. Banker. Educ: Montreal, Canada. Appts: Montreal Stock Exchange, & Garneau Ostiquy & Co., 1937-39; joined Hd. Off., Bank Canadian Nat., Montreal, P.Q., 1939; Asst. Mgr., Investment Dept., ibid, 1947; Asst. Gen. Mgr.—Chief. Gen. Mgr., 1964-71; V.P. & Chief Gen. Mgr., 1972-; Pres., Canagex Ltd; Dir., Bank Canadian Nat; Compagnie Immobilière BCN Limitée; Société de la caisse de retraite de la Banque Canadienne Nationale; Domco Industries Ltd; Laurentian, Mutual Assurance Co; Commerce Gen. Ins. Co; Canadian Mercantile Ins. Co; Corporation d'Expansion Financière. Mbrships. incl: Exec. Coun., Canadian Bankers' Assn; Quebec Hosp. Serv. Assn; Régie de la Place des Arts. Address: Bank Canadian National, 500 Place d'Armes, Montreal, P.Q. H2Y 2W3, Canada. 2, 32, 34, 88.

PERRENOUD, Jean-Frédéiic, b. 18 Apr. 1912. Composer. Educ: Licentiate, Theol., Univs. of Neuchatel, Geneva, & Basle, Switzerland; Musical Studies, Geneva. Mbrship: Assn. of Swiss Musicians. Compositions incl: 4 symphs. & other works for orch.; 2 piano concertos; Ballade for violin & piano; Ballade for cello & piano; 7 albums of lieder for voice & piano; music for solo piano. Address: 11 Clos-Brochet, 2000 Neuchatel, Switzerland. 103.

PERRET, François-Albert, b. 18 May 1904. Keeper of Archives. Educ: Collegium Stans; Univs. of Paris & Geneva; Licence en droit, Univ. of Geneva, 1929. Appts: Sec., Oeuvre Saint-Justin, Fribourg, Switzerland, 1930-35; Compiler & Publisher, Fontes ad Historiam Regionis, Planis, Nieder-Rätien, 1936-39; Municipal employee, Mels & Pfäfers, 1939-42; Compiler of records, 1942-48, Asst., Staats- & Stiftsarchiv, St. Gallen, 1948-58; State Archivist & Canton Libn., St. Gallen, 1958-68; Fndn. Archivist, St. Gallen, 1968-. Mbrships: Alliance Francaise, St. Gallen; Dante Allighieri, St. Gallen; Historischer Verein des Kantons St. Gallen. Publs. incl: Urkundenbuch der südlichen Teile des Kantons St. Gallen, Vols. I & II, 1961-; Liber viventium Fabariensis, Stiftsarchiv St. Gallen, Fonds Pfäfers Codex I (Co-ed. w. Prof. Dr. Albert Bruckner & Prof. Dr. Hans Rudolf Sennhauser), 1973. Hons: 1st Culture Prize, Sarganserland, 1964; Ufficiale dell'Ordine "Al merito della Repubblica italiana", 1968. Address: Stiftsarchiv St. Gallen, Regierungsgebäude, CH-9001 St. Gallen, Switzerland.

PERRET, Gene, b. 3 Apr. 1937. Humorist; Comedy Writer. Appts: Hd. Writer for Phyllis Diller; Monolog Writer for Bob Hope; Hd. Writer, The New Bill Cosby Show; Staff Writer, The Jim Nabors Show, Laugh In, & Carol Burnett Show. Mbr., Writer's Guild of Am., W. Publs: Comedy Writing for Today's Audiences, 1972; Contbn., Getting Started in Comedy Writing, to How to Make Money in your Spare Time by Writing. Nominated for Writer's Guild Award, for the New Bill Cosby Show, 1973. Address: 1485 Westhaven Rd., San Marino, CA 91108, U.S.A.

PERRET, Henri, b. 9 Mar. 1930. Engineer. Appts. incl: with Union des Mines, Sotemi, Pechtney, Alsthom, 1958; Engr., Sté. Le Matériel électrique, S.W., 1960-; Dir., Evening Study Ctr. for North Africans in Paris, 1965-; Municipal Councillor, Chanceaux-près-Loches. Address: 9 rue Jasmin, 75016 Paris, France. 91.

PERRETTA, Charlotte Anne, b. 14 July 1942. Attorney. Educ: B.A., Coll. of St. Elizabeth, Morristown, N.J., 1964; LL.B., Suffolk Univ. Suffolk Univ. Schl. of Law, Boston, Mass., 1967. Appts: Mass. Pub. Defenders Comm., 1967-69; Asst. Dist. Atty.,

Middlesex Co., Mass., 1969; Assoc., Crane, Inker & Oteri, 1970-73, Ptnr., 1973-; Mbr., Mass., Conn., Mass. Fed. Dist. Ct., U.S. Ct. Appeals 1st Circuit, & U.S. Supreme Ct. Bars. Mbrships: Am., Mass., Boston Bar Assns. Contbr., var. legal jrnls. & publs. Recip., var. acad. citations. Address: 20 Ashburton Pl., Boston, MA 02108, U.S.A. 5.

PERRIN, C. Robert, b. 13 July 1915. Artist. Educ: Schl. of Practical Art, Boston, Mass. Appts: Free-lance Artist, Illustrator, 1938-42; 1945-64; U.S. Army, 1942-45; Owner & Watercolorist, C. Robert Perrin Gall., Nantucket, Mass. Mbrships: Am. Watercolor Soc.; Rockport Art Assn.; Guild of Boston Artists; Art Assn. of Nantucket; Boston Watercolor Soc. Publs: Whopper, The Tale of A Nantucket Whele, & Further Adventures of Whopper & Winnie (co-author, illustrator). Hons. incl: Schlrship., Schl. of Practical Art, 3 yrs., Purchase Prize, Boston Soc. of Independent Artists, 1952; William Pulicover Award, N. Shore Arts Assn., 1955; Critics Award, Art Dirs. Club of Boston; Paul H. Allen Mem. Award, Copley Soc.; 2 Firsts, Art Assn. of Nantucket shows, 1973. Address: 500 Washington St., Nantucket Is., MA 02554, U.S.A. 6, 37.

PERRY, Arthur Augustus, b. 9 Mar. 1916. Business Administrator. Educ: N.Y. Univ., 1938-40; Seton Hall Univ., 1947-48; Newark Coll. of Engrng., 1954; Rutgers Univ., 1957-61. Appts: Acct., White, Weld & Co., N.Y.C., 1937-41; Acct., Asst. Treas., Ivers-Lee Co., Newark, N.J., 1941-58; Treas., Asst. Controller, Asst. Sec., ibid, 1958-68 (Mbr. of Mgmt. & Exec. Comms., Bd. Dirs. & The Exec. Comm); Dir. of Indl. Rels., Ivers-Lee Div. of Becton, Dickinson & Co., N.J., 1968-71; Mgmt. Cons., 1971-72; Asst. to the V.P. & Treas., Drew Univ., Madison, N.J., 1972-. Mbrships: Am. Mgmt. Assn.; NJ Purchasing & Personnel Assns.; Assn. of Indl. Mgmt.; Treas., Dir., Lion Tamer, Newark Ctrl. Lions; Dir., West Essex Chmbr. of Comm., etc. Address: 7 Wilmer St., Apt. 1, Madison, NJ 07940, U.S.A. 6, 16, 128.

PERRY, David T., b. 6 Nov 1946. Preacher. Educ: A.B., Asbury Coll., Wilmore, Ky; grad. studies, Asbury Theological Sem., Wilmore, Ky; Southern Baptist Theological Sem., Fort Worth, Tex. Appts. incl: Min. to Young People, United Meth. Ch., Cynthiana, Ky., 1968-70; Min. of Revival, Castle Hills 1st Bapt. Ch., San Antonio, Tex., 1971; Min. of Young Adults, Univ. Bapt. Ch., Fort Worth, Tex., 1972; Dir. of Outreach, Paul Anderson Youth Home Inc., Vidalia, Ga., 1973; Pastor, United Meth. Ch., Wrens, Ga., 1974-. Mbr., Int. Kiwanis Club. Publs: Rolling for Jesus, 1971; Retreat For a Spiritual Advance! , 1972. Address: P.O.Box 503, Wrens, GA 30833, U.S.A. 30, 57.

PERRY, Edmund Franklin, b. 18 May 1923. Professor of Comparative Religions. Educ: A.B., Univ. of Ga., Athens, U.S.A., 1944; B.D., Emory Univ., Atlanta, Ga., 1946. Appts: Dir., Wesley Fndn., Ga. State Coll., Atlanta, 1946-48; Instr. & Asst. Prof., Relig., Duke Univ., Durham, N.C., 1950-54; Assoc. Prof. & Chmn. of Dept., Hist. & Lit. of Religs., Northwestern Univ., Ill., 1954-60; Prof., Comparative Religs., ibid, 1960-; Chmn., Int. Studies Coun., & Dir., Richter Int. Schlrs. Prog., 1973-. Mbrships. incl: V.P. & Pres. Elect., Am. Theol. Soc., 1974-75; Exec. Comm., Am. Soc. for Study of Relig., 1959-60 & 1968-70, Ed., Newsletter, 1968-71; Int. Assn. for Hist. of Religs.; Am. Acad. of Relig., Literary Ed., Jrnl., 1964-68. Publs. incl: Confessing the Gospel Mark Preached, 1957; The Gospel in Dispute, 1958; The Sangha of the Tiratna (w. S. Ratnayka), 1974; Articles in profl. jrnls. & encys. Hons. incl: LL.D., Vidyodaya Univ. of Ceylon, 1968; Hays-Fulbright Prof., Comparative Religs., Sri Lanka, 1968-69. Address: Northwestern University, 619 Clark St., Evanston, IL 60201, U.S.A. 2, 8, 13.

PERRY, Edward J., b. 20 Aug. 1923. Superintendent of Public Schools. Educ: B.A., Syracuse Univ., N.Y., 1948; Schl. Admin., Grad. Schl., ibid; Schl. Admin., Grad. Schl., Colgate Univ., N.Y. Appts: Served w. USAAF, S. Pacific, WW II; Tchr., Phys. Educ., 1948-60; Prin., Elementary Schl., 1960-63; Prin., Secondary Schl., 1963-66; Dpty. Supt. of Schls., Utica, N.Y., 1966-68; Supt., Utica Pub. Schls., 1968-. Mbrships incl: Advsry. Coun., Nat. Alliance of Bus. Men; Exec. Bd., Mohawk Valley Chief Schl. Offs.; Voc. & Occupational Educ: Comm., Region 10; N.Y. State Chief Schl. Admnstrs.; Mayor's Advsry. Coun., Utica, 1969-71; Bd. of Dirs., Blue Cross; Kappa Phi Kappa. Publs: Administrative Training Program in the Utica Public Schools, 1968; School Districts with Notable Reading Programs, 1971; articles in local press. Address: 13 Elizabeth St., Utica, NY, U.S.A.

PERRY, Esther Mary (Izzo). Librarian. Educ: 4 yrs. H.S.; 1 yr. jr. coll.; pvte. studies, lib. sci. & cataloging. Appts: Timekeeper, Teletype Corp.; Asst., Northlake Lib., Ill., Cataloger, 4 yrs., Lib. Dir., 1962-73. Mbrships: Sec., Northlake PTA; Am. & Ill. Lib. Assns.; Lib. Admin. Conf. of N. Ill.; Suburban Lib. System; Northlake Garden Club. Address: Northlake Public Library, 231 N. Wolf Rd., Northlake, IL 60164, U.S.A. 5, 34.

PERRY, G. Neil, b. 22 Nov. 1909. Economist. Educ: B.A., Univ. of B.C., Canada; M.P.A., A.M., Ph.D., Harvard Univ., U.S.A. Appts. incl: Dir., Bur. of Econs. & Stats., B.C. Govt. & Advsr. on Dominion-Provincial Fiscal Rels., 1938-47; Chief, Trade & Payments Div., Exchange Restrictions Dept., Int. Monetary Fund, Wash. D.C., 1950-52; Canadian Alternate Exec. Dir., Bds. of Int. Monetary Fund & Int. Bank for Reconstruction & Dev., 1952-54; Assisted Dir. (Ops.), Int. Bank for Reconstruction & Dev., Wash. D.C., 1956-60; Dean, Fac. Commerce & Bus. Admin., Univ. of B.C., 1960-65; Dpty. Min., Educ., B.C., 1965-70; Asst. Dpty. Min., Manpower & Immigration, Govt. of Canada, 1970-73; Prof., Dir., Schl. of Pub. Admin., Univ. of Vic., 1973-. Mbr., num. profl. orgs. Publs. incl: Bridging the Gap Between Education & the World of Work, 1973; Contbr. to var. publs. in field. Recip., num. hons. Address: Schl. of Pub. Admin., Univ. of Vic., P.O. Box 1700, Vic., B.C., Canada. 50, 88.

PERRY, Glen Crossman Hayes, b. 1 Oct. 1903. Public Relations Consultant. Educ: A.B.; Mod. Langs., Princeton Univ., 1926. Appts: Asst. Space Buyer, H.E. Lesan Advt. Agcy., N.Y.C., 1926-27; Reporter, Corres., N.Y. Sun, inclng. Police H.Q., 1927-37, Wash. D.C. Bur., 1937-44; Asst. Dir., P.R. Dept., E.I. du Pont de Nemours & Co., 1944-65; Dir., ibid, 1965-68; P.R. Cons., ibid, 1968-. Mbrships. incl: Nat. Press Club, Wash. D.C.; N.Y. Chapt., Sons of the Revolution; P.R. Soc. of Am. Publs: Watchmen of the Sea, 1938; Contbr. to periodicals & profl. jrnls. Hons: Navy. Dept. Commendation for Serv. as Corres., WW II, 1946; Inaugural Award, Community Rels. Commendation, Mfg. Chemists Assn., 1966; Hall of Fame, Practical P.R., 1961, '63, '66; Presidential Citation, P.R. Soc. of Am., 1966, '68. Address: 10 Lighthouse Way, Darien, CT 06820, U.S.A. 2, 6, 12, 24.

PERRY, Hart, b. 18 June 1918. Investment Banker. Educ: M.A., Univ. of Chgo., 1940. Appts: Var. exec. posts, Dev. Loan Fund, & w. Bur. of Budget, Wash.; w. Sogen-Swiss Int. Corp. (Investment Banking), N.Y.C., 1961-, Treas., 1962-64, Sr. V.P., 1964-66, Financial Exec. V.P., & Mbr., Bd. of Dirs., 1966-73, Pres., 1973-; Bd. of Trustees, Univ. of Chgo. & Bard Coll.; Bd. of Dirs., Horn & Hardart Co., For. Policy Assn. Mbrships: Treas. & Trustee, Asia Soc.; Coun. on For. Rels., Conf. Bd., Coun. of Financial Execs., Overseas Dev. Coun. Address: Sogen-Swiss International Corporation, 20 Broad St., N.Y., NY 10005, U.S.A. 2.

PERRY, Jerry Wayne, b. 5 Oct. 1940. College Teacher. Educ: B.A., Baylor Univ., Waco, Tex., 1962; M.A., Univ. of Tex., Austin, 1964; Ph.D. cand., Tex. Tech. Univ., Lubbock. Appts: Instr., Engl., St. Patrick's Coll., Asaba, Nigeria, 1964-66; Instr., Govt., Wayland Bapt Coll., Plainview, Tex., 1966-69; Instr., Govt., Angelo State Univ., San Angelo, Tex., 1969-71; p/t Instr., Govt., Tex. Tech Univ., Lubbock, 1972-73. Mbrships: AAUP; Am. Pol. Sci. Assn.; Southwestern Soc. Sci. Assn.; Southern Pol. Sci. Assn.; Law & Soc. Assn. Address: 3410B-49th St., Lubbock, TX 79413, U.S.A.

PERRY, Reginald Carman. Professor of Philosophy. Educ: Dip., Mem. Univ. Coll., St. John's Nfld., Canada; B.A., Mt. Allison Univ., Sackville, N.B.; B.D., Vic. Univ., Toronto, Ont.; M.A., Ph.D., Toronto Univ., ibid; Postdoct. rsch., Harvard Univ., Cambridge, Mass., U.S.A. Appts: Tchr. & Prin., Nfld. schls., Canada; Min., United Ch. of Canada; Instr., Syracuse Univ., N.Y., U.S.A.; Asst. Prof., Okla. A. & M. Coll., Stillwater; Assoc. Prof., Ark. A., M. & N. Coll., Pine Bluff; Prof., Univ. of Ark. at Pine Bluff. Mbrships; Ark. Philosophical Assn.; Former, AAUP; Am. Philosophical Assn.; Publs: Articles in The Philosophical Quarterly, Mind, Ratio, & Australasian Jrnl. of Philosophy, inclng. Assertion & Postulation in the 'Material Logic', in Mind, Oct. 1971. Address: P.O. Box 4064, Univ. of Ark. at Pine Bluff, Pine Bluff, AR 71601, U.S.A. 7.

PERSCH, Ruth Lucille Kelly, b. 3 Nov. 1892. School Teacher; Educational Administrator. Educ: B.S., Univ. of Southern Calif., L.A., 1939; M.S., ibid, 1941; Ed.M., 1946. Appts. incl: Tchr., grades 2-8, rural schls., Chesterfield, Ind., 1911-12, Houston, Tex., 1912-14; Tchr., var. High Schls., Calif. Adult Depts., inclng. L.A., Burbank, Glendale, Pasadena City Coll., 1935-42, & San Simon, Ariz., 1942-43; Tchr., Engl. grades 9-12, Chino H.S., Calif., 1943-58; Counselor, & Hd., Jr. Coll. Div., Calif. Inst. for Women, 1956-58; Tchr., Carrizo Springs H.S., Tex., 1958-60, Lytle H.S., Tex., 1960-70. Mbrships: incl: AAUW, 1939-; Nat. Fedn. Bus. & Profl. Women's Clubs, 1941-71; Nat. Retired Tchrs. Assn., 1958-; Kappa Kappa Iota. Instructional & rsch. papers & reports. Recip., var. awards for schol. & community servs. Address: 6701 Blanco Rd., 726, San Antonio, TX 78216, U.S.A.

PERSHADSINGH, Raam Shankar, b. 27 Dec. 1924. Attorney-at-Law. Educ: B.A., Toronto Univ., Canada, 1946; LL.B., London Univ., 1948; Bar Finals, Middle Temple. Appts: Pvte. Prac. of Law; Queen's Counsel. Mbrships: Chief Justice, Univ. of Toronto Moot Ct.; Chmn., Bd. of Govs., Vere Tech. H.S.; Bd. of Govs., Mona Prep. Schl.; Fndn. Mbr., Little Theatre; Club India; E. Indian Progressive Soc.; Jamaican Bar Assn. Ltd.; Gen. Legal Coun.; Fndn. Mbr., Sanatan Dharma Mandir; Panel to frame Jamaica (Constitution) Order in Coun., 1962. Hons: Schlrships. & Bursaries, 1934-36,

& at Univ. of Toronto, Canada, 1942-46. Address: 63 Duke St., Kingston, Jamaica, W. Indies. 136.

PERSONÈ, Luigi Maria, b. 30 June 1902. Writer. Educ: Grad., Litt., Univ. of Florence, 1923. Appts: Schl. Tchr., Italian Lit., Florence; Lectr., Lit., Cherubini Mus. Conservatoire, ibid. Mbrships: Cherubini Nat. Acad., Florence; Tiberina Acad., Rome; Lions Club. Works: La belle statuine, 1930; Il Primo Passo, 1930; Sisto quinto, 1935; Incontri, 1942; Paesi come uomini, 1942; Stare al mondo, 1942; L'Arte di saperla lunga, 1952; Pittori toscani del Novecento, 1952; Tempo da lupi 1960; Antonio Fogazzaro, 1961; Scrittori Italiani moderni e contemporanei, 1968; Pensatori liberi nell'Italia contemporanea, 1970; Il teatro italiano della Belle Epoque, 1972; Gli angeli giocano a palla, 1972; Lo spirito di Alessandro Manzoni, 1973; I signori del quarto potere, 1973. Contbr. to var. jrnls. Hons: Rustichello Prize; Florence Lit. Prize; Panzini Prize. Address: Via San Gallo 123, Florence 50129, Italy.

PERTICA, Horacio Nicanor, b. 23 Oct 1936. Computer Company Executive. Educ: B.S., Mil. Coll., Buenos Aires, 1955; B.S. in Physics, Univ. of Buenos Aires, 1958; Doct. Maths., 1960; post-grad. studies, Systems Rsch. Inst., 1965; Int. Mgmt. Schl., Netherlands, 1973. Appts: Univ. Buenos Aires, 1958-66; IBM Argentina, Buenos Aires, 1962-67; Cath. Univ. of Buenos Aires, 1964-66; IBM World Trade Co., N.Y.C., 1967-; Univ. Bridgeport, Conn., 1967-69; Mgr., Data Base, 1969-; CCNY, 1970-; Pace Univ., 1974-. Mbrships: AAAS; Am. Math. Soc; London Math. Soc., Hon., Argentinian Chem. Soc., 1960. Contbr., articles & reports to profl. publs. Address: RFD 2, Brundage Ridge Rd., Bedford, NY 10506, U.S.A. 6.

PETER, John Edward, b. 23 Dec. 1934. Architect. Educ: B. Arch., Okla. State Univ., 1958; Licensed Archt., Okla., Kan. & Tex.; Nat. Coun. of Archtl. Registration Bds. Cert. Appts: Pvte. Prac., Okla. City, Okla., 1962-68; Woodward, ibid, 1968-. Mbrships: Woodward Dance Club; Skyhawk Flying Club; Woodward Chmbr. of Comm.; Woodward Indl. Team; Dist. Commnr., Boiling Springs Dist.; V.P., Boiling Springs Dist., Boy Scouts of Am., Mooreland Chmbr. of Comm.; Woodward Coin Club; Pres., N.W. Guidance Ctr.; Deleg., Okla. Episcopal Ch. Gen. Convention, 1973, 74; Pres., Woodward Elks Rodeo, 1971 & '72; Lions Int.; B.P.O.E.; Mayors Comm. for Hire the Handicapped, Okla. City; Past Mbr., Goodwill Inds. Advsry. Bd.; Past Mbr., Lakeside Country Club; Treas., St. John's Episc. Ch.,1969-75; Voom; Past Mbr., Diocese Comm. for Clergy Placement: Corp. Mbr., Am. Inst of Archts. Address: 911 35th St., Woodward, OK 73801, U.S.A. 7, 16, 22, 125, 131.

PETER, Lily. Farmer; Writer. Educ: B.S., Memphis State Univ., 1927; M.A., Vanderbilt Univ., 1938; Chgo. Music Coll.; Juillard Schl. of Music, N.Y. Operator of 2 plantations of approx. 8,000 acres, Eastern Ark. & ½ interest in 8,400 acre ranch, Southern Okla. Publs: The Green Linen of Summer, 1964: The Great Riding, 1966; many poems & feature articles on local hist., music & art in nat. publs. Mbrships: Nat. League Am. Pen Women; DAR; Nat. Fed. of Music Clubs; Little Rock Musical Coterie; Poets' Roundtable of Ark.; Poetry Socs. of Tex., Tenn. & Ga.; Sigma Alpha Iota; Southern Ginners' Assn.; Farm Bur.; Nat. Soybean Assn.; Bd. of Dirs., Ark. Arts Ctr.; Nat. River Acad.; Hon. Trustee, Moravian Music Fndn.; Ark. Authors', Composers' & Artists' Soc.; Delta

Kappa Gamma. Hons. incl: Kenneth Beaudoin Gemstone Award, 1966-67; Poet Laureate, Ark., 1971; Ark. Democrat Woman of the Year Award, 1971. Address: Marvell, AR 72366, U.S.A. 5, 7.

PETERFI, Istvan Stefan, b. 8 Mar. 1906. Professor. Educ: Fac. Sci., Cluj Univ., Romania, 1927-32; Lic., Nat. Scis., 1933; Dr., Nat. Scis., 1937. Appts: Preparatory Asst., Botanics, Univ. Cluj, 1929-35; Asst. Lectr.-Prof., Plant Physiol., ibid, 1936-; Dean, Fac. Scis., ibid, 1945-46; V.-Rector, ibid, 1947-48; 1959; 1974. Mbrships: Corres. mbr., Acad. Romanian People's Repub.; Presidium, ibid, 1963-; V.P., 1974-; Exec. Comm., Int. Union Biol. Scis. Author 180 sci. papers, inclng. The Physiological basis of growth and development of the plants, 1954; Plant nutrition, 1956; Co-author, Handbook of Plant Physiology, 1957; 2nd ed. '64; Agricultural Botany, 1965; Co-author, Plant Physiology, 1972. Hons: Emil Racovita Prize, publ. on Plant Nutrition, Acad. Romanian People's Repub., 1956; Hero, Socialist Labour, 1971; Merited Sci., 1972. Address: Universitatea Babeş-Bolyai, Str. M. Kogălniceanu nr. 1, Cluj, Romania.

PETERMANN, Andreas, b. 27 Sept. 1922. Physicist. Educ: Lic. es Phys. & Maths., 1950; Ph.D., Phys., 1952; Asst. to Prof. Stueckelberg. Appts: Asst., Swiss Atomic Energy Commn., 1952-53; Asst. to Prof. Rosenfeld, Univ. of Manchester, UK, 1953-55; Rsch. Assoc., Niels Bohr Inst., Copenhagen, 1955-57; Fellow, CERN, Geneva, 1957-60; Permanent Staff Mbr., ibid, 1960-. Discoverer of Renormalization Grp. Contbr. rsch. articles to profl. jrnls. Address: c/o CERN, 1211 Geneva 23, Switzerland. 43, 103.

PETERS, (Mrs.) Gloria Cache Poindexter, b. 5 Apr. 1907. Psychologist. Educ: A.B., Miami Univ., Fla., U.S.A; Postgrad. work, ibid. Appointed Employees Rels. Off., Corps Army Engrs., Gt. Lakes Div., 1944-46. Mbrships: Pres., Miami Br., AAUW; 1958-60; Sec.-Treas., ibid. 1960-65; Pres.-elect., Fla. Div., ibid; Ex-Community Rep., Nat. AAUW Assn. Bd.; Legislative & Valutes Comms., ibid, 1965-71; State Sec., Nat. League Am. Penwomen. Author Series of stories & articles in profl. publs. Hon: Named annual endowment for $75,000 for S. Am. women to do post-doct. work in U.S. Address: 3305 Alhambra Cir., Coral Gables, FL 33134, U.S.A.

PETERS, Robert Parkin. College Administrator; Minister of Religion. Educ: Magdalen Coll., Oxford; Univ. of Manchester; Univ. of Lancaster. Appts: Pastoral Work & Schl. Tchr. until 1965; Supvsr., Engl. Studies, Pembroke Coll., Cambridge, 1965-66; Vis. Asst. Prof. Hist., Hope Coll., Mich., U.S.A., 1966-67; pvte. acad. rsch. work, Oxford, 1967-69; Prof. Hist., U.S. Univ. in England, 1969-70; Pt.-time Fac. Mbr., Univ. of Birmingham, 1971-73; curently Prin., St. Aidan's Coll., Willey, Broseley, Salop. Mbrships: Fndn. Mbr., Ecclesiastical Hist. Soc.; Renaissance Soc. of Am.; Soc. Renaissance Studies Gt. Britain; Educ. Comm., Order of Christian Unity. Author, Oculus Episcopi: Administration in the Archdeaconry of St. Albans, 1580-1625, 1973. Ed., contbr., author of introductions, var. publs., ecclesiastical hist. Address: St. Aidan's College, Willey, Broseley, Salop, TF12 5JP, U.K.

PETERS, William Lee, b. 27 June 1939. Associate Professor of Entomology. Educ: B.A., Univ. of Kan., 1960; M.A., Univ. of Utah, 1962; Ph.D., ibid, 1966. Appts: Assoc. Prof., Fla. A & M Univ. & Adjunct Assoc. Prof., Fla.

State Univ., 1967-; Rsch. Assoc., Fla. Dept. of Agric., 1968-; Asst. Entomol., Univ. of Fla., 1968-70; Prof. & Entomol., ibid & Coord., USDA, Fla. A & M Univ., 1970-. Mbrships. incl: Entomol. Soc. of Am.; Soc. of Sytematic Zool.; Am. Entomol. Assn.; Entomol. Soc. of Wash.; Fellow, Royal Entomol. Soc. of London; Sigma Xi; Phi Sigma; Asst. Ed., Eatonia, 1968-. Publs: num. articles & monographs; ed. of 1 book. Hons. incl: Pennock Award in Entomol., 1962; Chmn., 1st Int. Conf. on Ephemeroptera, 1970. Address: Lab. of Aquatic Entomol., Univ. P.O. Box 111, Fla. A & M Univ., Tallahassee, FL 32307, U.S.A.

PETERSEN, Orval Lyman, b. 24 Mar. 1924. Educator. Educ: B.S., Univ. of Wash., U.S.A., 1950; B.A., 1951; M.Ed., 1956; Ed.D., Stanford Univ., 1958; Ph.D., St. Gabriel Univ., 1963. Appts. incl: Aircraft Engine Mechanic, Flight & Engine Control Insp., Boeing Airplane Co., Seattle, Wash., 1942-47; Pt.-time Clerk, Microfilm Records, Univ. of Wash., Registrar's Off., 1947-51; Sci. & Maths. Tchr., Schl. Dist., No. 201, Sunnyside, 1951-59; Sci. Maths. Coord., Montclair H.S., 1959-64; Pt.-time Sci. Instr., Uplant Coll., 1963-64; Dir., Curriculum Servs., Chaffey Union High Dist., Ontario, Calif., 1964-66; Asst. Supt., ibid, 1966-. Mbrships. incl: Calif. Assn. Supvsn. & Curric. Dev.; Calif. Educ. Data Processing Assn.; Nat. Sci. Tchrs. Assn.; NEA; Am. Educ. Rsch. Assn.; Contbr. to num. educ. publs. Address: 903 W. Bonnie Brae Ct., Ontario, CA 91762, U.S.A. 15, 120,

PETERSEN, Roland Conrad, b. 31 Mar. 1926. Painter; Educator. Educ: A.B., Univ. of Calif., Berkeley, 1949; M.A., 1950. Appts. incl: Instr., Fine Arts, Wash. State Univ., Pullman, 1952-56; Fac., Art Dept., Univ. of Calif., Davis, 1956-; Currently, Assoc. Prof. One man exhibs. incl: City Lib., Sacramento, 1961; Calif. Palace of Legion of Hon, San Fran., 1961; Gumps Art Gall., ibid, 1962; Staempfli Gall., N.Y., 1963, 65, 67; Crocker Art Gall., Sacramento, Calif., 1965; De Young Mus., San Fran., 1968; Bednarz Galls., L.A., 1969, 70, 72, 73; Nat. Travelling Exhib., 1968; Artists Contemp. Gall., Sacramento, 1969, 72. Participant in num. grp. exhibs. Mbrships. incl: Delta Phi Delta; San Fran. Art Assn. & Art Inst.; Bay Printmakers Soc.; Juror, num. exhibs. Collects. incl: Smithsonian Instn.; De Young Mus., San Fran.; Mus. of Mod. Art, N.Y.; Phila Mus. of Art; Fine Arts Gall., San Diego; Whitney Mus. of Am. Art, N.Y. Recip., num. art awards. Address: Art Dept., Univ. of Calif., Davis, CA 95616, U.S.A. 2, 9, 37, 131, 133.

PETERSON, John, b. 21 Aug. 1921. Management Consultant. Educ: B.S., MIT, 1943. Appts: w. export div., E.I. duPont de Numours & Co., Wilmington, Del., 1946-48; w. chem. div., FMC, W.R. Grace, Drew Chem Co.; Pres., Drew Foods Co., St. Louis; Exec. V.P., Drew Chem. Co., ibid, 1966-68; Fndr., Pres., John Peterson & Assocs., 1968-71; V.P., ops., Falstaff Brewing Corp., 1971-72; reestab. John Peterson & Assocs., Pres., 1972-. Mbrships. incl: Mayor, City of Frontenac, Mo., 1969, '71, '73; Dir., Fargo Holding Co., Fargo-Wilson-Wells Co.; Bd. Dirs., Frontenac Civic Dev. Assn.; V.P., Knox-Ariz.; Am. Chem. Soc.; Am. Inst. Food Technols.; Soc. Plastics Engrs.; Margarine Mfg. Assn. (bd. chmn, 1968); Int. Oil Mill Supts.; Dir., Bridlespur Hunt. Address: 41 Countryside Lane, St. Louis, MO 63131, U.S.A.

PETERSON, Martha, b. 1916. Educational Administrator. Educ: B.A., M.A., Ph.D., Univ. of Kan. Appts: Instr. in Maths., Univ. of Kan; Asst. Dean of Women, Dean of Women, Univ. of Kan., 1946-56; Dean of Women, &

subsequently Special Asst. to the Pres., Univ. of Wis., Madison, 1956-67, Dean for Student Affairs, 1963-67; Pres., Barnard Coll., Columbia Univ., N.Y.C., 1967-. Mbrships. incl: Bd. of Dirs., Coun. Financial Aid to Educ., & Overseers of Bowdoin Coll.; Chmn., Empire State Fndn. Independent Liberal Arts Colls.; Nat. Bd. on Grad. Educ.; Past Pres., Nat. Assn. Women Deans & Counselors, 1965-67. Hons. incl: L.H.D., Chatham Coll., 1968, Med. Coll. Pa., 1970, Molloy Coll, 1971, Mundelein, Coll., 1972; DD.L., Columbia Univ., 1968, Douglass Coll., 1968, Hofstra Univ., 1969, Austin Coll., 1972. Address: Barnard Coll., Columbia Univ., N.Y., NY 10027, U.S.A.

PETERSON, Oscar Emmanuel, b. 15 Aug. 1925. Concert Jazz Pianist. Educ: Conservatory of Music, Montreal, P.Q., Canada. Mbrships: Masons; Bd. of Trade; Pres., Toronto Jazz Club. Compositions incl: Canadiana Suite; Hymn to Freedom; Jazz Studies; Children's Tune; Interludes for TV, movies, & theatre. Num. hons. incl: Achievement Award, Lakeshore Lions Club of Toronto, 1966; Gold Rose Award, France, 1968; Testimony of Gratitude, Mexico, 1969; Toronto Civic Medal, 1971; LL.D., Carleton Univ., Ottawa, Ont., 1973; Order of Canada, 1973; Golden Disc Award, Japan; 5 nominations for recording best album of the yr., Nat. Acad. of Recording Arts & Scis. Address: 2421 Hammond Rd., Mississauga, Ont. L5K 1T3, Canada. 88.

PETERSON, Russell W., b. 3 Oct. 1916. Government Official. Educ: Grad., Univ. of Wis., 1938; Ph.D., ibid. Appts. incl: w. DuPont Co., 1942-68; Adv. thru' mgmt. assignments to Dir., Dev. Dept., Rsch. & Dev. Div., ibid; Bd. Chmn., Textile Rsch. Inst., Princeton, N.J.; Gov. of Del., 1969-73; Chmn., Nat. Advsry. Commn. on Criminal Justice Standards & Goals, 1971-73; Chmn., Comm. on Crime Reduction & Pub. Safety, Nat. Govs.' Conf., 1971-72; Chmn., Educ. Commn. of the States, 1971-72; Chmn., Exec. Comm., Nat. Commn. on Critical Choices for Am., 1973-; Chmn., Coun. on Environmental Quality, Exec. Off. of the Pres., 1973-. Mbrships. incl: Gtr. Wilmington Dev. Coun.; Correctional Coun.; Citizens Crime Commn., etc. Author, sev. articles. Num. Hons. incl: Conservationist of the Yr., Nat. Wildlife Fedn., 1971; Phi Beta Kappa. Address: Coun. on Environmental Quality, 722 Jackson Pl. N.W., Wash. DC 20006, U.S.A. 2.

PETERSON, Victor Herbert, b. 9 Oct. 1916. Public Relations Executive. Educ: B.A., Beloit Coll., Wis.; M.A., Univ. of Chgo. Appts: Tchr., Kingsport H.S., Tenn., 1939-42; Mng. Ed., Indpls. Times, Ind., 1942-54: Mgr., Info., Mobil Oil Corp., 1954-67; Dir., P.R., Hooker Chem. Corp., N.Y.C., 1967-69; V.P., Mfg. Chem. Assn., Wash. D.C., 1969-. Mbrships. incl: Phi Beta Kappa; Nat. Press Club; Overseas Press Club; Sigma Delta Chi; Sigma Alpha Epsilon. Author, MCA 1872-1972 A Centennial History. Address: 2306 California St., N.W., Washington, DC 20008, U.S.A. 2.

PETERSON, Vivian A., b. 15 Oct. 1919. College Librarian. Educ: B.A., Augsburg Coll., 1941; M.A., Univ. of Denver, 1949; Postgrad. study, Columbia Univ., N.Y.C. Appts: H.S. Tchr. Libn., Minn., 1941-48; Asst. Libn., Univ. of Colo. Med. Schl., 1948; Series Cataloguer, Iowa State Univ. of Sci. & Technol., 1949-52; Catalogue Libn., Asst. Prof., Lib. Sci., Luther Coll., Iowa, 1952-60; Hd. Libn., Assoc. Prof., Lib. Sci., Midland Luth. Coll., Fremont, Neb., 1960-. Mbrships: Past Pres., Neb. Lib. Assn.; Past Sec., Assn. of Luth. Coll. Facs.; Past Pres., Decorah Br., AAUW; Past V.P., Midland Luth.

Coll. Br., AAUP; Past Sec. Coll. Sect., Iowa Lib. Assn.; ALA; Mountain Plains Lib. Assn. Contbr. to profl. jrnls. Hons: Educ. Fund Grant, Luth Ch. in Am., 1968; Mbr., Cardinal Key Nat. Scholastic Hon. Soc., 1968; Field Study Seminar Grant, Comparative & Int. Educ. Assn. & Phi Delta Kappa, 1972. Address: 1434 N. Platte, Fremont, NB 68025, U.S.A. 5, 8, 42, 132.

PETERSON, Vivian Woodward, b. 30 Jan. 1886. Educator. Educ: B.A., B.Ec., Univ. of Sydney, Australia; Sydney Tchrs. Coll.; Sydney Conservatorium of Mus. Appts: Tchr., Primary, 1901-16, Secondary, 1916-32, N.S.W. Dept. of Educ.; Asst. Supvsr. Mus., N.S.W. State Schls., 1932-38; Sr. Lectr., Mus., Sydney Tchrs. Coll., 1938-50; Broadcasted Schl. Mus. lessons; Conductor, Bathurst Choral Soc., 1921-25; Bathurst Mus. Soc., 1923-25; Hurlstone Choral Soc., Sydney, 1925-52; Chorus Master, ibid, concerts w. Sir Malcolm Sargent, Eugene Ormandy; Otto Klemperer, Sir Thomas Beecham, Sir Eugene Goossens & others; Ch. Choir Master, num. Congs., 1911-. Mbrships: Arts Coun. of Australia; Past Pres.-Mus. Dir., Cronulla & Dist.; var. sporting orgs. Recip., M.B.E., 1971. Address: 14 Pozieres St., Cronulla, NSW 2230, Australia. 4.

PETERSON, William Theodis, b. 15 June 1930. Educator; Magistrate. Educ: B.S., M.Ed., Tuskegee Inst.; workshops, Bank St. Coll. of Educ. & Auburn Univ. Appts: Boys' Phys. Educ. Instr., HS, 1957 & Elem. Schl., 1959; Elem. Art Instr., 1967; Elem. Prin., 1969; Councilman, City of Tuskegee, Ala., 1967; Municipal Judge, ibid, 1973. Mbrships: NEA; Ala. Educ. Assn.; Macon Co. Tchrs. Assn.; Ala. League of Municipalities; Pershing Rifle Nat. Mil. Honor Soc. Has done num. paintings in tempera & poster paint, inclng. Golden Gate Bridge. Designed & constructed Historic Tuskegee for Blue & Grey Pageant Parade, Montgomery, Ala., 1972. Dir. & produced Macon Co. Art Show of Elem. Art, 1969 & Schl. of Home Econs., Head Start Trng. Ctr. Art Show, 1968. Recip. sev. awards inclng: Prairie Farms Schl. Appreciation Award, 1973; Macon Co. Blue Ribbon Ed. Study, 1973. Address: P.O. Box 143, Tuskegee, AL 36083, U.S.A.

PETRUSHKA, Shabtai Arieh, b. 15 Mar. 1903. Composer; Conductor. Educ: Tech. Univ., Berlin-Charlottenburg, Germany; Stern's Conservatory, Berlin. Appts. incl: Arranger, Deutsche Grammophon Gesell. & U.F.A. Film Co., 1938-48; Misician, Conductor & Arranger, Palestine Broadcasting Serv., 1948-58; Asst. Dir., Music, Israel Broadcasting Authority, 1958-68; Dir., Music, ibid, 1969-; Lectr., Rubin Acad. of Music, Jerusalem. Mbrships. incl: Israel Composers League; Soc. Authors Composers & Music Publrs., Israel. Compositions incl: 5 Oriental Dances; 3 Movements for Orch.; 4 Movements for Band; Piccolo Divertimento for Symph. Band; Israel Sings: Fantasia for Symph. Band; Trio for Strings; Trio for Flute Clarient & Bassoon. Recip., Am-Israel Soc. Music Awards, N.Y., 1957. Address: 13 Abba Hilkia St., 93183 Jerusalem, Israel. 94.

PETTERSSON, Bengt Karl, b. 30 May 1915. University Professor. educ: Fil.Mag., Uppsala Univ., Sweden, 1938; Fil.Dr., ibid, 1958. Appts: Lectr., Uppsala Univ., 1958-66; Prof., Umeå Univ., 1966-. Mbrships. incl: num. botanical socs.; Bd. Mbr., Svenska Botaniska Föreningen, & Edit. Staff, Jrnl., Svensk Botanisk Tidskrift; Swedish Union of Authors; AAAS. Publs. incl: Photogeographical Excursions in Gotland, 1950; Gotlands orkidéer, 1951; The Vallhagar Country: Some Natural Features Relating to its History, 1955; Gotska Sandön, 1959. Num. newspaper articles. Hons. incl: Linnaeus Prize, Royal Soc. Sci., Uppsala, 1959; var. Medals & Awards for achievements in field of nature conservancy. Address: Sect. of Ecological Botany, Umeå Univ., S-901 87 Umeå, Sweden.

PETTEY, Ruth Briscoe (Mrs. Joe Pettey), b. 1 Sept. 1902. Retired Teacher. Educ: B.S., Florence State Univ., 1946; Grad. study, Univ. of Ala., 1947. Appts: Grade Tchr.,Morgan Co. Schls., 1921-25; Grade Tchr., Decatur, Ala., Pub. Schls., 1925-42; Employment Interviewer, U.S. Employment Serv., 1942-46; H.S. Tchr., Gen. Continuation (Veterans), 1946-62; H.S. Tchr., Priceville H.S., 1962-64. Mbrships: Pres., 4 yrs., also V.P. & Sec., Ctrl. Garden Club; AAUW; Women's Chmbr. of Comm.; ArtsCoun.; Decatur Fedn. of Garden Clubs; Ctrl. United Meth. Ch.; Sunday Schl.; Womens Soc.; Ala. Retd. Tchrs.; Nat. Retd. Tchrs.; Ala. Educ. Assn. Address: 1302 Tower St., Decatur, AL 35601, U.S.A. 125.

PETTY, James Milton, b. 12 July 1941. Painter; Teacher. Educ: B.S., Campbellsville Coll., Ky., 1962; grad. studies, Geo. Wash. Univ., D.C., Va. Commonwealth Univ., Richmond. Appts: Instr., Engl., Charlotte Hall Schl., Md.; Instr., Engl., Art, Speech, & Dir. of Drama, Randolph-Macon Acad., Front Royal, Va.; Prof. of Painting & Speech, Dir. of Drama, Shenandoah Coll. & Conservatory of Music, Winchester, Va.; Instr. of Art, Milton M. Somers Schl., La Plata, Md.; Special Instr., Wayside Theatre, Middletown, Va., 1967. Mbrships. incl: NEA; Delta Psi Omega; V.P., ibid, 1961. Exhibs. by invitation: Gall. Int., N.Y.C.; Gall M., Pitts., Pa., 1972. Works in collects: "Bryant Park", Shenandoah Coll.; "Queen Cnarlotte", Charlotte Hall Schl. Recip., Best Actor Award, Campbellsville Coll., 1962. Address: 5064 Silver Hill Ct., No. 204, Saitland, MD 20028, U.S.A. 125.

PETTY, Keith, b. 13 June 1920. Attorney. Educ: B.A., Univ. of Idaho, Moscow, 1942; J.D., Leland Stanford Jr. Univ., 1948. Appts: Pacific Tel. & Tel., San. Fran., 1948-50; John F. Forbes & Co., CPAs, 1950-54; Petty & Olsen, 1960-63; Petty, Andrews & Olsen, 1963-64; Petty, Andrews, Olsen & Tufts, 1964-68; Petty, Andrews, Olsen, Tufts, Jackson & Sander, 1968-73; Petty, Andrews, Tufts & Jackson, 1973-. Mbrships. incl: CPA; Calif. & Idaho Bar Assn.; Bankers Club; Cwlth. Club; Univ. Club. Participant in minority grp. help progs. Lectr., Practising Law Inst. Seminars, Venture Capital & to var. grps. on taxation. Address: Petty, Andrews, Tufts & Jackson, 650 California St., San Francisco, CA 94108, U.S.A. 9.

PETZOLD, Joachim (Oskar Maz), b. 26 Aug. 1928. University Professor of Theoretical Physics. Educ: Studied biol., Humboldt Univ., Berlin, 1947-49; Studied physics, Free Univ., Berlin, 1949-56; Physics Dip., Berlin, 1953; Dr.rer.nat., ibid, 1956; Inaugurated, Univ. of Heidelberg, 1961. Appts: Asst. Prof., Free Univ., Berlin, 1957-59; Asst. Prof., Univ. of Heidelberg, 1959-62; Assoc. Prof., Univ. of Marburg/Lahn, 1962-63; Full Prof., ibid, 1963-. Mbrships: Lions Int., Club Marburg, German Fed. Repub.; Sect. Marburg, Deutscher Alpenverein. Author or co-author of 23 articles & papers in var. jrnls. Address: Dept. of Physics, Univ. of Marburg, Mainzer Gasse 33, D 355 Marburg/Lahn, German Fed. Repub, 43,92.

PETZOLDT, Adie Sylvester, b. 29 June 1909. Accountant; Business Administrator.

Educ: B.A., Elmhurst Coll.; B.D., Eden Theol. Sem.; M.A., Wash. Univ. Appts: Min., Evangelical Reformed Ch., 1931-40; Fin. Officer, Nat. Youth Admin., 1940-43; Controller Sec., Gates Radio Co., 1943-63; Dir.-Dir. Sec., Gates Acceptance Corp & Hampshire Corp., 1954-64; Owner, Quincy Timberlodge Co., 1963-. Mbrships. incl: Pres.-Dir., Quincy Human Rels. Coun.; Pres., Quincy Chapt.,World Fed., U.S.A.; Chmn., Spiritual Assembly of the Baha'is; Trustee, Fndn. for Freedom & Democracy in Community Life; Dir., United Citizen Comm. for Freedom of Res. in Ill. Publs: Truth or Tradition; Jehovah God's Chronological Scales. Address: 2500 Vermont St., Quincy, IL 62301, U.S.A. 120, 129, 130.

PEUGNIEZ, Jack Hugues Christian, b. 2 Nov. 1910. Shipping Company Director; International Shipping Arbitrator. Appts: Radio Off., French Merchant Marine, 1934-36; w. Soc. Navale Caennaise, Caen, France, 1937; i/c Commercial Dept., Marseille Br., ibid, 1941; Mgr., Paris, 1945-72; Mgr., Somarco Paris, Gennevilliers, Port of Paris, 1948-71; Chmn., Somarfran Rouen, 1963-, Cie Franco Finlandaise de Navigation Paris, 1963-, Somarco London Ltd., London, 1963-, Mng. Dir., Belfranline, Antwerp; Dir., Rotrama, Rotterdam; Pres., Baltic & Int. Maritime Conf., Copenhagen, 1963-67. Mbrships. incl: Pres., Assn. des Consignataires des Ports de Paris; V.P., Chmbr. Syndicale des Courtiers d'Affretements, Paris; Dir., Comm. Ctrl. des Armateurs de France, ibid, Port Autonome de Paris, Chmbr. Arbitrale Maritime de Paris; Nat. Counsellor for French For. Trade; Dpty. Mbr., Conseil Superieur de la Marine Marchande, Paris; Fellow, Inst. Chartered Shipbrokers, London, Inst. Arbitrators, ibid. Hons. incl: Chevalier, Legion d'Hon.; Off. duMerite Maritime. Address: Le Coteau, 37 380 Crotelles, France.

PEVSNER, Isaiah, b. 11 Jan. 1896. Advocate. Educ: Law Fac. of Univ. Appts: Lectr., Int. Law & Stats., 1921-25; Admitted to Palestinian (now Israeli) Bar, 1928. Mbrships: Ctrl. Comm., Int. Fedn. of Human Rights, Paris, France; Pres., Israel Assn. for Human Rights; World Coun., Int. Assn. of Jewish Lawyers & Jurists; Fndr. & former Chmn., Israel Assn. for UN; Fndr., former Chmn., Jewish Demographic S-ty; Pub. Coun. for family problems, Prime Min.'s Off.; Pres., Coun. of Premarriage Advsr.; Active in Zionist Movement & Bnei Brith; Decalogue Soc. of Lawyers, Chgo., Ill. Publs: (Publr.) Our Cooperative Law; Israel Commercial Law; Income Tax Law; Israel & Human Rights; Palestine Directory; Chess Magnum; Triangles—educl. game; Articles in Hebrew, Engl. & Russian. Address: 3 Joseph Eliahu, Tel-Aviv, Israel. 94.

PEVSNER, (Sir) Nikolaus (Bernhard Leon), b. 30 Jan. 1902. Emeritus Professor of History of Art. Educ: Univs. of Leipzig, Munich, Berlin & Frankfort, Germany; Ph.D., 1924. Appts. incl: Asst. Keeper, Dresden Gall., 1924-28; Lectr., Hist. of Art & Arch., Geottingen Univ., 1929-33; Slade Prof. of Fine Art, Univ. of Cambridge, U.K., 1949-55; Fellow, St. John's Coll., Cambridge, 1950-55, Hon. Fellow, 1967-; Emeritus Prof. of Art, Birkbeck Coll., Univ. of London. Mbrships. incl: Chmn., The Victorian Soc.; Historic Bldgs. Coun.; Advsry. Bd. on Redundant Chs.; Royal Fine Art Commn. Publs. incl: Italian Painting from the end of the Renaissance to the end of the Rococo, 1927-30; An Enquiry into Industrial Art in England, 1937; An Outline of European Architecture, 1942; The Buildings of England,

45 vols., 1951-; Studies in Art, Architecture & Design, 1968. Hons. incl: Kt., 1969; CBE, 1953; var. hon. degrees & fellowships. Address: 12 Bloomsbury Sq., London WC1B 3QU, U.K. 1.

PEW, George Thompson, b. 30 Mar. 1917. Retired Aviation & Transportation Executive. Educ: Grad., MIT., U.S.A., 1939. Appts: Sun Oil Co., 1939-50; Chmn., Aero Design & Engrng. Co., 1950-57; Chmn. & Pres., ibid, 1957-58; Pres., 1958-61; Pres., George T. Pew Enterprises, 1961-; Chmn., PaR Truck Leasing, Inc., 1961-; Joe Hodges Transportation, Inc., 1963-71. Mbrships. incl: AIAA; Am. Defense Preparedness Assn.; Sportsman Pilots Assn., Inc.; Quiet Birdmen; Nat. Pilots Assn.; Merion Cricket Club, Haverford, Pa.; Bay Hd. Yacht Club, Bay Hd., N.J.; Phila. Aviation Country Club, Ambler, Pa.; Union League of Phila. Address: 231 Cheswold Hill Rd., Haverford, PA 19041, U.S.A. 2, 128.

PEYER, Jean B, b. 4 Apr. 1946. Historian. Educ: B.A., CUNY, 1967; M.A., ibid, 1969; Ph.D., Grad. Ctr., CUNY, 1974. Appts: Lectr., Queens Coll., CUNY, 1969; Asst. Ed., Hamilton Papers, Columbia Univ. Press, 1972-73; Rschr., Columbia Broadcasting Corp., 1973; Sr. Rsch. Asst., Grad. Ctr., CUNY, 1973-74; Adjunct Prof., Queens Coll., CUNY, 1974-. Mbrships: Am. Histl. Soc.; Inst. Early Am. Hist. & Culture; N.Y. Histl. Soc.; Phi Alpha Theta; Sec., Queens Coll. Chapt., ibid, 1967. Hons. incl: NDEA Fellowship, 1971-72; var. rsch. assistantships. Address: 150-15 Barclay Ave., Flushing, NY 11355, U.S.A.

PEYER, Joan B., b. 4 Apr. 1946. Data Processing Systems Analyst. Educ: B.A., Queens Coll., CCNY, 1967; M.A., ibid, 1969. Appts: Tech. Rep. for Time Sharing Systems, RCA Corp., 1969-71; Data Processing Mgr. & Tech. Time Sharing Cons., Bd. of Higher Educ., CCNY, 1971-72; Mgr. in Data Processing, Bank Off., Chem. Bank, N.Y. Corp., 1972-. Mbrships: N.Y. Histl. Soc.; Nat. Honor Soc. for Second. Schls., 1963; Queens Coll. Chapt., Phi Alpha Theta, 1967. Contbr. to jrnls. Address: 150-15 Barclay Ave., Flushing, NY 11355, U.S.A.

PEYRONNET (Comte de), Gérard, b. 29 Sept. 1922. Government Official. Educ: École Polytech. Appts: Currently, Commissaire Controleur Gen., Min. Finances. Mbrships: Jockey Club; Assn. de la Noblesse Française. Hons: Chevalier, Légion d'Honneur; Chevalier, Ordre du Mérite. Address: 1 Rue Le Notre, Paris XVI, France. 43.

PEYSTER, William François de, b. 13 Aug. 1917. Diplomat. Educ: Licence en Droit; Dip., Ecole des Scis. Politiques, Paris, France. Appts: Pol. Observer, Trieste, 1946-49; Gen. Sec., French Delegation, Interallied Reparation Agcy., Brussels, 1950-51; Sec., then Counsellor, French Embassy, Madrid; Counsellor, Copenhagen & London, 1960-67; Asst. Dir. for Econs. & twice Secretariat Gen. of Nat. Defense, 1968-72. Mbrships: French Numismatic Soc.; Am. Numismatic Soc. Author, article on medieval & Venetian numismatics. Hons: Chevalier, Legion of Hon., 1957; Off., Order of Merit, 1967; Grand Off., Spanish Merit, 1959; Cmdr., Danebrog, Denmark, 1963. Address: 52 Ave. Charles de Gaulle, 92 200 Neuilly sur Seine, France. 43, 91.

PEYTON, Sarah Margaret, b. 29 Dec. 1895. Physician. Educ: A.B., Goucher Coll., Md., 1916; M.D., Johns Hoplins Med. Schl., 1923. Appts. incl: Intern, New England Hosp. for Women & Children, Boston, 1924; Gen. Prac.,

Crisfield, Md., 1925-74; Mbrships: Johns Hopkins Med. & Surg. Soc.; AMA; Md. Med. Fac.; Fellow, Am. Acad. of Family Prac.; Phi Beta Kappa, Goucher Coll., 1916. Hons. incl: Citizen of the Yr., Crisfield Chmbr. of Comm., 1948; Crisfield Sarah Peyton Day, Kiwanis Award, 1970; Sr. Citizen Award, Somerset Co., Md., 1973. Address: 33 W. Main St., Crisfield, MD., U.S.A.

PFAENDER Ann McLelland (Mrs) b. 6 Mar. 1903. Librarian. Educ: Lib. Trng. Schl., Multnomah Co. Pub. Lib,; Night classes & ext. divs., Univ., of Ore., Portland Univ. of Hawaii, Honolulu; New Schl. for Soc. Rsch., N.Y.C. Appts.; Childrens & Br. Libn., Portland Ore., 1920-25; Asst. Childrens Libn.-Hd. Childrens Libn., Lib. of Hawaii, 1925-41; Book Mobile Surveyor, Multnomah Co. Lib. (on loan from Lib. of Hawaii) 1941; worked in hosp. lib.; worked in H.S. libs., Iolani, Punahou Schls. 1945-47; Asst. Dir., Kokokahi Camp, 1950-55; Dir., Relig. Educ., 1956-60; Dean of Women, Mid-Pacific Inst., 1960-66; Hd., Schl. Lib. Hawai Prep. Acad. Kamuela, 1967-; Cataloger, acquisitons, Sem. Lib., Arab-Christian Bapt. Sem., Beirut, Lebanon, 1974. Mbrships: Camp Comm., Girl Scouts, 1956-59; Hawaii Lib. Assn. & ALA, 1929-69 (Pres., Hawaii Lib. Assn., 1937, '50); Am. Camping Assn., 1950-55; Imiola United Ch. of Christ (Congl.) Kamuela; Womans Bd., Missions for Islands of Pacific (1956-67, Tchr., Sunday Schl.; Comm. for republ. of Hymnal in Hawaian; Cum Laude Soc., Hawai Prep. Acad.; Womens Comm., Japan Int. Christian Univ. Fndn., Tokyo, Offs. in N.Y.C.; Deleg., State of Hawai, Singapore Conf., 1974; Int. Assn. Schl. Libns.; Kobe Coll. Corp., Nishinomiya, Japan. (Offs. in Chgo. Ill., U.S.A.). Chosen one of two reps. from Hawaii to go to Europe w. grp. of 24 Am. women visting chs. in Wales, Scotland & England, U.K. & observing refugee work in Austria (for World Coun. of Chs., Geneva, Switzerland). in Near E. (for U.N.) in India & Hong Kong, 1959. Made 2 subsequent world tours, visiting Orient, Israel, Austrailia, N.Z., etc. Pubs. incl: book, Miss Library Lady, to recruit young people for lib. work, 1954; Articles for Childrens Religion, periodical in Boston, Mass.; article on story telling, Library Jrnl. Address: c/o Hawaii Prep. Acad., Kamuela, HI 96743, U.S.A. 78.

PFAFFLIN, James Reid, b. 3 Dec. 1930. Environmental Engineer; University Professor. Educ: B.S., Ind. State Univ.; B.E.S., Johns Hopkins Univ.; M.S., ibid; Ph.D., Univ. of Windsor, Ont., Canada. Appts: Fac. Civil Engr., The Cooper Union; Fac. Civil Engr., Polytech. Inst. of Brooklyn; Fac. Civil Engr., Univ. of Windsor; Fac. of Civil Engrng., Stevens Inst. of Technol. Fellow, Royal Soc. Hlth., U.K. Mbrships: Assoc., Inst. of Fuel, U.K.; Canadian Soc. Civil Engrs.; Engrng. Inst. of Canada; Raritan Yacht Club. Tech. Bd., Am. Boat & Yacht Coun. Co-ed. The Encyclopedia of Environmental Science & Engineery, 2 vols., 1927. Author of some 20 tech. papers. Address: 173 Gates Ave., Gillette, NJ 07933, U.S.A. 22.

PFEFFER, Leo, b. 25 Dec. 1910. Attorney; Educator. Educ: B.S., CCNY, 1930; J.D., Law Schl., N.Y. Univ., 1933. Appts. incl: Legal Prac., N.Y.C., 1933-; Pvte. Tchr. of Law, ibid, 1933-45; Lectr., New Schl. for Soc. Rsch., 1954-58; Lectr., Mt. Holyoke Coll., 1956-60; Gen. Counsel, Am. Jewish Congress, 1958-64, Special Counsel, 1964-; Yeshivah Univ., 1962-63; Prof. Constitutional Law, Prof. Pol. Sci., & Chmn. of Dept., L.I. Univ., 1964-; Vis. Prof. Constitutional Law, Rutgers Univ., 1965. Mbr. & Off., var. legal, educl. & religious orgs. Publs. incl: Church, State & Freedom, 1953;

Creeds in Competition, 1958; This Honorable Court, 1965. Contbr., var. books, encyclopedias, law reviews & jrnls. Recip., var. civic awards. Address: 191 Willoughby St., Brooklyn, NY 11201, U.S.A. 2, 55.

PFEIFER, Melvin George, b. 8 Jan. 1928. Engineer. Educ: B.M.E., Marquette Univ., Milwaukee, Wis., 1951; Registered Profl. Engr. No. 2696, N.H. Mbrships: Am. Soc. of Mech. Engrs.; Am. Ordnance Assn; Am. Soc. of Naval Engrs; Nat. Security Ind. Assn; Delta Tau Delta; Knights of Columbus. Sev. papers presented at profl. conventions. Address: Bloody Brook Rd., Amherst, NH 03031, U.S.A. 6.

PFEIFFER, Mildred Clara Julia, b. 16 Aug. 1910. Physician. Educ: B.S., Univ. of Pa., Phila., 1933; M.D., 1936; M.P.H., 1945. Appts. incl: Chief, Med., Womens Hosp., Phila., 1939-52; Practol. & Charter Mbr., Drs. Hops., 1940-48; Instr., Proctol., Grad. Hosp., Univ. of Pa., 1940-48; Vis. Asst. Chief Med., Phila. Gen. Hosp., 1940-49; w. Pa. Dept. of Hlth., 1952-73; Dir., Div. of Planning, Evaluation, Rsch., ibid, 1963-70; Dir., Chronic Diseases Div., 1970-73. Mbrships. incl: Am. Coll. Physns.; Am. Coll. Chest Physns.; AMA; Alpha Omega Alpha; Delta Phi Alpha; Am. Geriatric Soc.; Phila. Cool. of Physns.; Harrisburg Acad. of Med.; Am. Pub. Hlth. Assn. Contbr. to med. publs. Hons. incl: 1st prize, Alcoholism, APHA, 1956; Disting. Serv. Citation, Heart of the Am. Home Convocation, Drexel Inst. of Technol., 1953. Address: 358 Valley Rd., Merion Stn., PA 19066, U.S.A. 5.

PFEIFFER, Reuben John, b. 7 Aug. 1901. Architect. Educ: B.S., Univ. of Ill., U.S.A., 1924; Postgrad., Columbia Univ., N.Y.C., 1931. Appts: Archt., Henry C. Ulen, Lebanon, Ind., 1928-30; i/c. Houston, Tex., Off., Alde B. Dow, Archt., Midland, Mich. Mbrships: Sec.-Treas., Tex. Soc. of Archts., 2 yrs.; Chmn., Houston Div., Inter-Profl. Commn. on Child Dev., schl. plant study, 1 yr.; Sec.-Treas., Santa Fe Chapt., Am. Inst. of Archts., 1971; Gorgoyle, Univ. of Ill.; Sigma Tau. Address: 114 Placita de Oro, Santa Fe, NM 87501, U.S.A. 9, 63.

PFISTER, Hans Oscar, b. 22 Feb. 1905. Doctor; Psychiatrist. Educ: Study in Zurich, Paris. Appts: Asst. Dr., Psych. Clins., Univs. of Zurich, Berlin; Regimental Med. Off., 1939-45; Med. Dir., Cantonal Psych. Clin. Herisall Appenzell A.RH., 1941-43; Chief Med. Off., City of Zurich, 1945-71. Mbrships: Chmn., League Against Rheumatical Diseases, Canton Zurich; Chmn., Swiss Mental Hlth. Soc.; Chmn., Commn. of Hygiene, Swiss Soc. of Pub. Utility. Contbr. to num. profl. jrnls. Address: Hohensteinweg 28, CH-8055 Zurich, Switzerland.

PFLUG, Günther, b. 20 Apr. 1923. Librarian. Educ: Studies in Philos., Maths. Univs. of Cologne, Bonn & Paris, 1944-51; Trng. in Libnship., Univs. of Münster, Aachen & Cologne, 1953-55. Appts: Subject Libn., Univ. of Cologne, 1955-61; Asst. Libn., ibid, 1961-62; Libn., Univ. of Bochum, 1963-74; Dir., Lib. Ctr., North-Rhine-Westphalia. Publs: Henri Bergson: Quellen und Konsequenzen einer induktiven Metaphysik, 1959; Elektronische Datenverarbeitung in der Universitätsbibliothek Bochum, 1968; Bibliotheksarbeit haute, 1973. Hons: Prof., Philos., Univ. of Bochum, 1966. Address: Hochschulbibliothekszentrum des Landes Nordrhein-Westfalen, Berrenrather Str. 138, 5000 Cologne, German Fed. Repub.

PFRIEMER, Udo, b. 2 Sept. 1909. Publisher. Educ: Univs. of Berlin, Munich &

Riga; Hochschule für Politik, Berlin; Dip., Pol. Econ., Munich, 1932. Appts: Lexicographer; Ed., periodicals "Bad & Küche", "Elektro-Neuheiten", "Heizungsbau" "Abwassertechnik", "Haus—Hof—Strasse"; Ed., catalogues in many branches; Proprietor, publishing house Udo Pfriemer Verlag, Munich, 1948-. Mbrships. incl: Börsenverein des Deutschen Buchhandels; Gesellschaft für Deutsche Sprache; Deutscher Normenausschuss; Rationalisierungskuratorium für Wirtschaftlichkeit; Abwassertechnische Vereinigung; Assn. of Contracting Plumbers, N.Y., U.S.A. Publs: Gemeinschaft, Wesen, Art & Idee, 1950; Sanitäre Einrichtungen, 1953; Essays in own & other jrnls. Address: Landwehrstrasse 68, D-8000 Munich 2, German Fed. Repub. 43.

PHARES, Gail Jay, b. 28 Dec. 1919. College Dean. Educ: B.A., Chico State Coll., Calif, 1951; M.A. ibid, 1952; Ed.D., Univ. of Southern Calif, 1962; Appts.; Tchr., Ind. Arts Automechs., Maryville, H.S., Calif, 1952-54; Woodworking, Drafting, Burbank City Schls., ibid, 1954-56 Supvsr., Ind. Educ., ibid, 1956-65; Grad. Instr., (p/t.) Calif. State Coll., L.A., 1963-64, (summers), Colo. State Univ., Ft. Collins, 1964-65; Dean, Applied Scis., Metropolitan State Coll., Denver, Coll., 1965-72; Dean, Schl. of Prof. Studies, ibid, 1972-. Mbrships. incl; Trustee, Nu Field Chapt. (Colo.) Epsilon Pi Tau; Phi Delta Kappa; NEA; Am. Voc. Soc.; Am. Ind. Arts Assn.; Nat. Geog. Soc.; Bd. of Dirs., EduCon.; Univ. Aviation Assn.; Sr. Mbr., Civil Air Patrol; Alpha Eta Rho. Publs. incl; School Equipment & Tool Guide (co-author) 1967; Industrial Arts in the Elementary Schools (co-author). Recip. Fulbright Lectship., Iran, 1974-75. Address: Schl. of Profl. Studies, Metropolitan State Coll., 250 West 14th Ave., Denver, CO 80204, U.S.A. 15, 46, 60, 120, 126.

PHAUP, Bernard Hugo, b. 17 July 1912. Minister. Educ: Central Wesleyan Coll., Central, S.C. Appts: Ordained to Min., Wesleyan Meth. Ch., 1936; Pastor, churches in Va. & N.C., 1932-46; Gen. Evangelist, 1946-48; Pastor, Charlotte, N.C., 1948-53; Pres., N.C. Conf., Wesleyan Meth. Ch., 1953-59; Elected Gen. Supt., Wesleyan Meth. Ch., 1959-68; Elected Gen. Supt., The Wesleyan Ch., 1968-; Bd. of Admin., ibid, 1955-; Chmn. of Bd., 1959-69; Chmn., Bd. of Trustees, all ch. corps.; Chmn., Bd. of Mgrs., Hephzibah Children's Home, Macon, Ga.; Denominational Rep., Nat. Assn. of Evangelicals & The Lord's Day Alliance Bd. of Dirs. Mbr., Exec. Comm., Christian Holiness Assn. Recip., D.D., Houghton Coll., Houghton, N.Y., 1961. Address: 229 Cannon St., Thomasville, NC 27360, U.S.A. 2, 7, 8, 125, 128, 131.

PHELPS, Flora Lewis. Editor; Anthropologist; Photographer. Educ: A.B., Bryn Mawr Coll., 1938; A.M., Columbia Univ., 1954. Appts: Acting Dean, Cape Cod Inst. of Music, E. Brewster, Mass., 1940; Assoc. Soc. Sci. Analyst, U.S. Govt., Wash. D.C., 1942-44; Adjunct Instr. Anthropol., Rutgers Univ., 1954-55; Mbr. of Staff of Américas Magazine, 1960-, Ed. Engl. Edit., 1970-. Mbrships: Soc. of Woman Geographers; Am. Anthropol. Assn.; Am. Ethnol. Soc.; Anthropol. Soc. of Wash.; AAAS. Publs: Num. articles on Latin Am. Art, Anthropo., Arch., & Educ. Address: Américas Magazine, Organization of American States, Washington, DC 20006, U.S.A. 2, 5.

PHIEBIG, Albert Jakob, b. 2 Jan. 1908. Bookseller. Educ: LL.M., Univ. of Berlin, Germany, 1931; Postgrad., Columbia, U.S.A., 1940, N.Y. Univ., 1941. Appts: German judge in trng., 1930-33; Chief statistician, Reichsvertretung der Juden in Deutschland, 1933-38; Statistician & rsch. analyst, Soc. agencies, N.Y.C., U.S.A., 1939-42; Rsch. analyst, later cons., Off. of Strategic Servs., Wash.-N.Y., 1943-45; Am. rep. of for. publishers & ordering agt. for Am. & for. libs., 1947-. Mbrships: Antiquarian Booksellers Assn. of Am.; Am. Booksellers Assn.; Pewter Collectors Club of Am.; Pewter Soc., U.K.; Chevalier, Chene des Rotisseurs. Author of many articles in pre-WWI German jrnls. Address: P.O. Box 352, White Plains, NY 10602, U.S.A. 6.

PHIFER, James R., b. 10 Nov. 1944. Historian. Educ: B.A., Univ. of Colo., 1966; M.A., 1969; Ph.D., Cand. Appts: Asst. Prof., Wayne State Coll., 1968-; Dir., Neb.-G.B. Summer Inst., 1972. Mbrships: Am. Hist. Assn.; Histns. of Early Mod. Europe; Phi Alpha Theta. Contbr., Mid-West Review, 1974. Hons: Neb. Coun. of the Humanities Rsch. Award, 1970; Neb. Bd. Dirs. Rsch. Grant, 1971-72. Address: Wayne State Coll., Dept. of Hist., Wayne, NB 68787, U.S.A.

PHILBERTH, Bernhard, b. 26 Mar. 1927. Physicist; Philosopher. Educ: Univ. of Munich, Germany. Pvte. prac. as physicist & engr. Mbrships. incl: Chieti, Acad. of Sci., Italy; Acad. of Scis., Belles-Lettres & Arts, Besancon, France; Phys. Soc. of Japan; Int. Glaciological Soc.; German Soc. for Polar Rsch. Publs: Christiliche Prophetie & Nuklearenergie, 1961, 18th ed. 1974; Der Dreiene, 1970, 3rd ed. 1974; Num. contbns. to books & sci. jrnls. Author, project for disposal of atomic waste in polar ice-caps. Discoverer, Zeitgradient relativistic vector. Holder, over 40 patents (some jointly with K. Philberth) in field of electromagnetism, incl. Philberth Transformer. Address: D-8031 Puchheim-München, Peter Roseggerstrasse 6, German Federal Repub. 43.

PHILIP, John Robert, b. 18 Jan. 1927. Physicist & Mathematician. Educ: B.C.E., D.Sc., Melbourne Univ., Australia. Appts: Rsch. Asst., Melbourne Univ., 1947; Engr., Queensland Irrigation Commn., 1948-51; Rsch. Sci.-Sr. Prin. Rsch. Sci., Commonwealth Sci. & Indl. Rsch. Org., 1951-63; Chief Rsch. Sci. & Asst. Chief, CSIRO Div., Plant Ind., 1963-71; Chief, CSIRO Div., Environmental Mechanics, 1971-; Vis. positions: Vis. Sci., Cambridge Univ., U.K., 1954-55; Rsch. Fellow, Calif. Inst. Technol., U.S.A., 1957-58, Vis. Prof., Ill. Univ., 1958, '61; Nuffield Fndn. Fellow, Cambridge Univ., U.K., 1961-62; Rsch. Fellow & Fulbright Schol., Harvard Univ., U.S.A., 1966-67; Vis. Prof., Fla. Univ., 1969; Vinton-Hayes Fellow, Harvard Univ., 1972. Mbr. num. profl. assns. Publs: About 130 sci. papers in field. Hons: Robert E. Horton Award, Am. Geophys. Union, 1957; 1st recip. David Rivett Medal for phys. scis., 1966. Address: CSIRO, P.O. Box 821, Canberra City, A.C.T. 2601, Australia. 1, 23, 50, 128, 139.

PHILIP, Lotte (Brand), (Mrs. Otto H. Förster), b. 27 May 1910. Art Historian. Educ: Univs. of Munich, Heidelberg, Freiburg i Br., Hamburg; Ph.D., Freiburg, 1938. Appts: Artist Designer in N.Y. & Providence, R.I., 1941-60; Instr. of Art Hist., N.Y. Univ., 1960; Lectr., 1961; Asst. Prof., 1962; Assoc. Prof., 1965; Full Prof., City Univ. of N.Y., Queens Coll., 1968. Mbrships: Coll. Art Assn. of Am.; The Renaissance Soc. of Am.; Vereeniging van de Nederlandse Kunsthistroici. Publs: Stephen Lochner's Hochaltartar von St. Katharinen zu Köln, 1938, Hieronymus Bosch, 1955; The Peddler by Hieronymus Bosch, a Study in Detection, Nederlands Kunsthistorisch

Jaarboek, 1958; Raum und Zeit in der Verkündigung des Genter Altares, Wallraf-Richartz Jahrbuch, 1967; The Ghent Altarpiece & the Art of Jan van Eyck, 1971. Hons: Fulbright, 1957-58; Bollingen 1962 & '63. Address: 58 W. 68th St., N.Y., NY 10023, U.S.A. 43.

PHILIPPATOS, George C., b. 2 Nov. 1938. Educator. Educ: B.S., M.B.A., Ph.D., N.Y. Univ; post-doct. studies, Yale Univ. & MIT. Appts. incl: Lectr., Coll. Arts & Sci., N.Y. Univ., 1964-65; Dir., Computer Ctr., Iona Coll., New Rochelle, N.Y., 1965-68; Dean, Schl. Bus. Admin., ibid., 1968-69; Prof. & Hd., Dept. of Finance, Pa. State Univ., 1969-; Assoc. Ed., Decision Sciences, & Jrnl. of Bus. Rsch. Mbrships. incl: Regional Pres. (Midwest), Am. Inst. for Decision Sciences, 1971-72; Nat. Coun. Mbr., ibid, 1972-73; Pres., Alpha Iota Delta, Nat. Hon. Sco. in Decision Sciences, 1972-73; Am. Economic Assn.; Am. Finance Assn; Inst. of Mgmt. Sci; Beta Gamma Sigma; Alpha Iota Delta. Publs: Financial Management, 1973; Essentials of Financial Management, (in preparation). Contbr., articles on bus. & financial subjects to profl. jrnls. Recip., Fndrs. Day Award, N.Y. Univ., 1962 & 1966. Address: 487 Sierra Lane, State College, PA 16801, U.S.A. 2, 14.

PHILLIPS, David Chilton, b. 7 Mar. 1924. University Professor. Educ: Univ. Coll., Cardiff, Univ. of Wales, 1942-44 & 47-51. Appts: Post doctoral Fellow, Nat. Rsch. Labs, Ottawa, Canada, 1951-53; Rsch. Officer, Nat. Rsch. Lab., Ottawa, 1953-55; Rsch. Wkr., Davy-Faraday Lab. of the Royal Instn., London, 1956-66; Prof. of Molecular Biophysics, Oxford Univ., 1966-. Mbrships: Fellow, Royal Soc., 1967; Mbr. of Coun., ibid, 1969-70 & 71-73; V.P., 1972-73; Fellow, Inst. of Physics (Chmn. of the Crystallography Grp.), 1971-; Biochem. Soc. (Comm. Mbr., 1969-71); Brit. Biophys. Soc. Contbr. of sci. papers to jrnls. in field. Hons: Feldberg Prize, 1968; Krebs Medal, Fed. of European Biochem. Soc., 1972; CIBA Medal of the Biochm. Soc., 1972. Address: Lab. of Molecular Biophysics, Dept. of Zoology, South Parks Rd., Oxford OX1 3PS, U.K. 1, 34, 47, 128

PHILLIPS, David Leslie, b. 19 Nov. 1938. Mayor. Educ: Assoc. Sci., Franklin Tech. Inst., 1961; Dip., Boston Archtl. Ctr., 1965; Int. Acad. Fine Arts, Salzburg, Austria, 1965; Urban Affairs, Harvard Univ., 1967-68. Appts: Archtl. Draftsman, var. firms, 1961-65; City Planner, Lynn, Mass., 1967-68; Commnr., Pub. Works, ibid, 1969-72; Mayor, Lynn, 1973-; Designed sev. homes & schls., New England, 1965-70; Lectr., Problems of City Govt; Served w. U.S. Army, 1958. Mbrships: Am. Pub. Works Assn.; Am. Water Works Assn.; Lynn Dept. Hds. Assn.; Essex Co. Hwy Assn.; Lynn Jr. Chmbr. of Comm. Author, It's a Small World, 1967. Hons: Pub. Serv. Awards, Gtr. Lynn Bd. Realtors, 1970, Lynn Merchatsn Assn., 1971; Awards, Lynn Jr. Chmbr. of Comm., 1969-71; Young Man of Yr., ibid, 1973; Recognized as 1 of nation's experts in field of Solid Waste Mgmt., Am. Pub. Works Assn., 1973; Featured in cover story, Am. City Mag., 1971. Address: 23 Greystone Pk., Lynn, MA 01902, U.S.A. 6.

PHILLIPS, Earl, b. 28 May 1933. Psychologist. Educ: B.A., Howard Univ., Wash. D.C., 1961; M.A., Columbia Univ., 1962; post-grad. studies at Georgetown & Columbia Univs. Appts: Exec. Dir., Morris Co. Urban League, Morristown, N.J., 1966; Assoc. Exec. Dir., Urban League, N.Y.C., 1967; Assoc. Dir., Nat. Urban Coalition, Wash.D.C., 1969; Pres.,

Urban League, Essex Co., N.J., 1970; Exec. Dir., Anti-Crime Commn., Newark, N.J., 1972; Dir. of Housing, Newark, 1973-; Lectured at var. univs., inclng. Rutgers's, Cornell, Howard, & Seton Hall. Mbrships. Incl: Bd. of Trustees, N.J. Welfare Coun., Edison Coll., N.J. Educ. Opportunity Fund, & N.J. Eye Inst. Contbr., articles in var. publs. Hons. incl: Citation of Merit, Nat. Multiple Sclerosis Soc., 1961; Pres. of U.S. Cert. of Appreciation for Nat. Selective Service System Mbrship., 1968. Address: 57, Sussex Ave., Newark Housing Authority, Newark, NJ. U.S.A. 2, 6.

PHILLIPS, Gilbert Paul, b. 12 Apr. 1919. Executive Director, Australian Mining Industry Council. Educ: B.Sc.Agr., Univ. of Sydney, N.S.W., Australia, 1941; M.P.A., Harvard Univ., U.S.A., 1950. Appts: Asst. Dir., Bur. of Agricl. Econs.; Special Commercial Advsr., Australia House, London, U.K.; Dpty. Sec., Dept. of Trade & Ind., Australia; Exec. Dir., Australian Mining Ind. Coun. Mbrships: Australasian Inst. of Mining & Metallurgy; Comm., Commonwealth Club, Canberra; Sci. Club, Melbourne; Mining Club of Sydney; Comm., Canbera Polo Club; Pres., A.C.T. Div., Nat. Heart Fndn.; Royal Canberra Golf Club. Recip., O.B.E., 1965. Address: 9 Baudin St., Forrest, A.C.T., Australia 2603. 23.

PHILLIPS, Harper Trenholm, b. 28 Aug. 1928. Professor of Fine Arts. Educ: Hampton Inst., w. Vicktor Lowenfeld, 1945-46; B.S., Ala. State Coll., Montgomery, 1951; M.A., N.Y. Univ., 1957. Appts. incl: Ala. State Coll., Montgomery & Mobile, 1952-56; Hampton Inst., Va., 1957-59; Grambling Coll., La., 1966-67; Manhattan Community Coll., N.Y., 1968-72; Bergen Community Coll., Paramus, Horace Mann-Lincoln Inst. of Experimentation—Ben. Franklin Project, 1966-67; Manhatan Community Coll., N.Y., 1968-72; Bergen Community Coll.,P aramus, N.J., 1968-. Works. incl: Mural, The Inner City, N.Y. State Youth Servs. Res., Bklyn., 1973; Fine Creative Relief Paintings, McDonalds Restaurant, 125th St., NYC; Lullabye (in collect. of artist); Fishermen, Joseph Gilliard, Hampton Inst. Works in collects. of: Atlanta Univ.; Howard Univ.; Jackson State Coll. Mbrships: N.J. Cultural Coun.; Bergen Co. Mus. Comm.; Chmn., Nat. Conf. of Artists, 1962-64; N.J. Educ. Assn.; NEA; AAUP. Recip. many awards inclng: Best in Show, Emancipation Centennial Xavier Univ., 1963; 1st, Southwestern Artists & Writers Conf., Univ. of Southwestern La., 1963; 1sts, Mobile Art Festival, 1953, 54. Address: c/o Bergen Community Coll., Four Hundred Paramus Rd., Paramus, NJ 07652, U.S.A.

PHILLIPS, Helen C. Historian. Educ: B.Lit., Coll. of St. Elizabeth, Convent Stn., N.J., 1923; M.A., Columbia Univ., N.Y., 1944; Cert. grad. study, Oxford Univ., U.K., 1947; Cert. grad. work, Harvard Univ., Cambridge, Mass., 1958. Appts. incl: Tchr., hist. & Supvsr., Soc. studies, Rumson H.S., 1943-46; Hd. Dept. of Soc. studies, Rumson Country Day Schl., 1946-49; Chief, Mus. & Histl. Off., Fort Monmouth, N.J., 1952-67; Officially estab. U.S. Army Signal Corps Mus., 1954. Mbrships. incl: Am. Histl. Assn.; Nat. Trust for Historic Preservation; Nat. Trust for England & Scotland; Soc. Am. Archivists. Publs: History of Rumson, N.J., 1944; Fort Monmouth History & Place Names, 1954, '60; Historical Sketch of the U.S. Army Signal Corps., 1960-1966; 1966; History of the U.S. Army Signal Center & School, 1919-67, 1966; History of Red Bank of the Navesink, 1974. Recip., LL.D., Coll. of St. Elizabeth, Convent Stn., N.J., 1969. Address: 146 Maple Ave., Red Bank, NJ 07701, U.S.A. 5, 6, 13, 22, 128, 130, 132, 138.

PHILLIPS, Kathleen Barbara (Mrs. Hayward Clinton Phillips), b. 27 Aug. 1925. Real Estate Broker. Educ: W. Va. Wesleyan Coll.; B.A., W. Va. Univ. Appts: Child Welfare Wkr.-Juvenile Ct. Wkr., W. Va. Dept. of Welfare, Charleston, 1948-61; Substitute Tchr., Lewis Co. Schl. System, Weston, W. Va.; Realtor. Mbrships: 1st V.P.-Pres., Weston Br., AAUW; Div. Chmn., State Nominating Comm., ibid; Bd. of Dirs., Lewis Co. Chmbr. of Comm., 1973-74; Weston Ctrl. PTA; 1st V.P., Rachel Chapt. 47, Order of the Eastern Star; St. Matthew United Meth. Ch.; United Meth. Women's Assn.; Roster Chmn., Weston Br., AAUW; Status of Women Chmn., ibid. Contbr. to Allied Youth Mag. & The Clarksburg News. Address: 658 Locust Ave., Weston, WV 26452, U.S.A. 125.

PHILLIPS, Margaret Mann (Mrs. Charles William Phillips), b. 23 Jan. 1906. University Lecturer. Educ: Somerville Coll., Oxford, 1924-28; B.A., Oxon., 1927; M.A., 1931; Doctorat d'université, Paris, 1934. Appts: Asst. Lectr. in French, Univ. of Manchester, 1934-36; Dir. of Studies in Mod. Langs. & Lectr. in French, Newnham Coll., Cambridge, 1936-45; Asst. Lectr., King's Coll., London, 1959-60, 63-64; Reader in French, ibid, 1964-68; Hon. Lectr., Univ. Coll., London, 1971-. Mbrships: F.R.S.L., 1951-64; Teilhard de Chardin Soc.; Amici Thomae Mori; Soc. for French Studies; Soc. for Renaissance Studies. Publs: Erasme et les Débuts de la Réforme française, 1934; Outgoing, 1936; Within the City Wall, 1943; Erasmus & the Northern Renaissance, 1949; The Adages of Erasmus, 1964 (Erasmus on his Times, 1968); Chapts. in Courants religieux et humanisme, 1959, Erasmus & the Reformation, 1969 & Erasmaus, 1970; articles in var. reviews, jrnls., quarterlies, etc. Hons: Prix Bordin, Acad. des Belles-Lettres, 1934; Medal of Coll. de France, 1969. Address: 103, Ditton Rd., Surbiton, Surrey, U.K. 3, 137, 138.

PHILLIPS, (Mrs.) Marjorie, b. 25 Oct. 1894. Artist. Educ: Art Students League, N.Y.C., U.S.A. Appts: Assoc. Dir., Phillips Collect., Mus. Modern Art & its sources, 1925-66; Dir.-Dir. Emeritus, ibid, 1966-. Mbrships: Cosmopol. Club, N.Y.C.; Sulgrave Club, Wash. D.C., Creative Works: Exhib. pntngs., Carnegie Insts., Mus. Fine Arts, Carnegie Inst., Pa.; 2 1-man exhibs., Kranshaar Galls., N.Y.C., Durand Ruels, ibid; 4 shows, Durlashee Galls., ibid; 5 shows, Corcoran Gall. & Phillips Collect., Wash. D.C.; exhibs. also at Denver, Colo.; Santa Barbara Mus., Calif.; Marlborough Fine Arts Galls., London, U.K.; Pntngs. owned by Corcoran Gall.; Whitney Mus.; Yale Mus. Fine Arts; Katherine Dreiser Collect., Boston Mus. Fine Arts. Hons: Dr. Fine Arts, Smith Coll., Northampton, Mass.; Govt. Award, Pa. Univ. Schl. Art. Address: 2101 Foxhall Rd. NW, Wash DC 20007, U.S.A. 2, 5, 132.

PHILLIPS, Mary Elizabeth Hargrove (Mrs. Andrew G. Phillips), b. 23 Mar. 1935. Educ: B.S., Clark Coll., Ata., Ga., U.S.A.; M.A., Columbia Univ., N.Y.C.; Postgrad. studies, Pa. State Univ., Univ. Pk.; Ed.S., Ga. State Univ., Ata., Ga. Appts: Tchr., Ata. Pub. Schls., 1957-66; Adult Basic Educ. Proj., Jt. Fed., State, City Proj., 1966-67; Tchr., Ata. Pub. Schls., 1967-72; Family Serv. Wkr., Jt. Fed., City, State Proj., 1972; Tchr., Ata. Pub. Schls., 1973-. Mbrships: Past Chmn: Subcomm. Pub. Affairs & Admin., Phyllis Wheatley Br., Y.W.C.A., Comm. Evaluation Instrl. Prog. in Reading, Miles Elem. Schl., Ata., Ga. & Admin. Comm. Instrl. Dev. Team, ibid; Past Chmn., Soc. Action Comm. & Past Co-Chmn., Am.

Coun. Human Rights, Alpha Kappa Alpha; Past Pres. & Treas., Wataushi Civic & Soc. Club; Girl Scouts Advsr., Ata. Pub. Schls., 1962-63, '70-71; Chmn., Standardized Testing Prog., Ata.'s Bethune Schl., 1964-65; Student Newspaper Advsr., Miles Elem. Schl., Ata., Ga., 1967-72 & Minnie Howell Elem. Schl., ibid, 1973. Address: 3415 Laren Lane, S.W. Atlanta, GA 30311, U.S.A. 76, 125.

PHILLIPS, Orie Leon, b. 20 Nov. 1885. Judge. Educ: Knox Coll., 1 yr.; J.D., Univ. of Mich. Law Schl., 1908. Appts: Asst. Dist. Atty., 8th Dist., N.M., 1912-16; U.S. Dist. Judge, 1923-29; U.S. Circuit Judge, 10th Judicial Circuit, 1929-; Chief Judge, 1940-56. Mbrships: Am. Law Inst.; Am., Colo. & N.M. Bar Assns.; Pres., Rotary Club; Pres., Denver Club; Cherry Hills Country Club. Publs: Kennecote Lectures Series 1955-56. Author, 'Conduct of Lawyers & Judges'. Contbr. to various publs. in field. Hons: Gold Medal & Citation, Am. Bar Assn., 1950; Gold Medal, Freedoms Fndn., 1950, '55. Address: Gulf Shore Colony Club, Apt. 15, Naples, FL 33940, U.S.A. 2, 7.

PHILLIPS, Walter Ray, b. 19 Mar. 1932. Educator; Attorney. Educ: B.A., Univ. of N.C., Chapel Hill., 1954; Vanderbilt Univ., 1954-55; LL.B., Emory Univ., 1957; LL.M., ibid, 1962; LL.D., 1970. Appts. incl: Atty., Jones, Adams, Paine & Foster, W. Palm Beach, Fla., 1957-58 & Powell, Goldstein, Frazer & Murphy, Atlanta, Ga., 1959-61; Bankruptcy Judge, Atlanta, 1961-64; Asst. Prof., Law, Univ. of N. Dakota, 1964-65; Sterling Fellow, Yale Univ., 1965-66; Prof., Law, Fla. State Univ., 1966-68; Prof. & Assoc. Dean., Tex. Tech. Univ. Schl. of Law, 1968-71; Staff Atty., then Dpty. Dir. & Admnstrv. Off., Commn. on Bankruptcy Laws of the U.S., Wash. D.C., 1971-73; Prof., Law, Univ. of Ga., 1973-. Mbrships: Am., Fla., Ga. & Tex. Bar Assns.; Am. Judicature Soc.; Phi Alpha Delta. Publs: Florida Law & Practice, 1960; Encyclopedia of Georgia Law, 1962. Debtors' & Creditors' Rights, 1966; The Law of Debtor Relief, 1969. Recip. sev. acad. awards. Address: c/o School of Law, University of Georgia, Athens, GA 30601, U.S.A. 7, 125, 131.

PHIRI, Bentley Martin Ndonde, b. 5 May 1940. Administrator. Educ: B.Soc.Sci., Univ. of Malawi. Appts: Customs Off., Min. of Finance, 1970-71; Traditional Cts. Commnr. for Ctrl. Region, 1971-72, Traditional Cts. Commnr. for Northern Region, Min. of Justice, 1972-. Mbrships: Students Representative Coun., Univ. of Malawi Students Union, 1965-67; Financial Sec., ibid, 1965-67; Chmn., Pax Romana, Chancellor Coll., 1968-70; Asst. Ed., Economica Africana, 1967-69; Sec.-Treas., Histl. Soc., 1966-69. Author of Independent African Churches in Nkhata Bay District, 4th yr. hist. seminar paper presented in Univ. of Malawi, 1970. Address: Min. of Justice, P.O. Box 66, Mzuzu, Malawi.

PHIRI, John Daniel, b. 2 Feb. 1932. Farm Manager; Flue Cured Tobacco Grower. Educ: Lyacium Corres. Coll. Appts: Gen. Clerk & Motor Car Driver, Rhodesia; Schl. Tchr., Nyasaland, 1954-55; Police Constable, N. Rhodesia (now Zambia), 1955-57; Chief Admnstv. Clerk & Labour Off., Falicon Mines Ltd., Dalney Mine, Chakari Gatooma, Rhodesia, 1957-63; Tobacco Grower, Kansungu Flue Cured Tobacco Auth., 1963-71. Mbrships: Growers Rep., Zomba, Malawi HQ, Min. of Agric., 1968-71; Br. Sec., A.N.C. N. & Southern Rhodesia, 1956-63; Br. Sec., Independence Celebration Sec. for Areas & Malawi Congress Pty. Areas Sec. for Mziza, Miszi & Chigoda

Areas, 1964-68. Address: Sable Creek Farm, P.O. Box 74, Kasungu, Repub. of Malawi.

PHOCAS, George John, b. 1 Dec. 1927. Lawyer; Businessman. Educ: A.B., Univ. Chgo., 1950; J.D., 1953. admitted to N.Y. State Bar, 1955, U.S. Supreme Court Bar, 1962. Appts: Assoc., Sullivan & Cromwell, N.Y.C., 1953-56; Counsel to Creole Petroleum Corp., subsid. Standard Oil Co., N.J., Caracas, Venezuela, 1956-60; Int. Negotiator, Standard Oil Co., N.J., N.Y.C., 1960-63; Sr. Ptnr., Casey, Lane & Mittendorf, London, U.K., 1963-73; OF Counsel, 1973-; Exec. V.P., Occidental Petroleum, 1973-; advsr. to U.S. deleg. UN ECAFE, Teheran, 1963. Mbrships: Law Soc., London; Brit. Inst. Comparative Law; Am. Soc. Int. Law, Assn. of Bar of City N.Y.; Am. Bar Assn.; Nat. Aero Assn.; Psi Upsilon. Address: 56 Grosvenor St., London W1, U.K. 6.

PHOON, Wai-On, Professor; Medical Practitioner. Educ: Univ. of Singapore; Inst. of Child Hlth., London, U.K.; Univ. of Edinburgh, ibid; London Schl. Hygiene & Tropical Med. Appts: Asst. Lectr., bacteriol., Univ. of Malaya; Med. Off., Singapore Govt.; Lectr., paediatrics, Univ. of Singapore; Med. Off., Shell Eastern Petroleum Ltd.; Prof. & Hd., Dept. of Soc. Med. & Pub. Hlth., Univ. of Singapore, 1970-; Vice Dean, Fac. of Med., ibid, 1971-; Mbr.; Family Planning & Population Bd., Singapore; Med. Coun., ibid; Examiner, Royal Soc. of Hlth. Bd. for Singapore; External Examiner in Pub. Hlth., Univ. of Hong Kong. Mbrships. incl: Pres., Singapore Med. Assn.; Fellow, Royal Colls. Physns., Edinburgh & Glasgow, Fac. of Community Med., U.K.; Pres., Soc. of Occupational Med., Singapore. Publs. incl: ed., Health & Safety at Work, 1971; co-author, Comprehensive Human & Social Biology, 1973. Address: Dept. Soc. Med. & Pub. Hlth., Univ. of Singapore, Outram Hill, Singapore 3, Repub. of singapore. 98.

PICKARD, Andrew E. Educator; Citrus Grower & Processor. Educ: Tchrs. Coll., St. Cloud, Minn.; Univ. of Minn., Mpls.; La Salle Univ., Chgo., Ill. Appts: Prin., Pub. Schls., Willow River, Minn.; Supt. of Schls., Cokato, Minn., Hinckley, ibid; Pres., Collegiate Bus. Inst., Mpls.; Conductor, summer schls. for tchrs., Mpls.; Currently, Citrus Grower; Planted over 2000 acres of citrus fruits; Now bldg. subdivs. in 3 cos. in Ctrl. Fla. Mbrships: Pres., orgs. of citrus ind. in Fla.; Odd Fellows Lodge; 320 Mason; Shriner; Pres., Kiwanis Club, Mpls.; Dist. Gov., Kiwanis, Minn., N.D. & S.D. Publs: Rural Education, A Manual for Teachers; Textbooks, Industrial Work for Boys, Industrial Work for Girls, Industrial Booklets. Address: P.O. Box 2667, Orlando, FL, U.S.A. 7.

PICKEL, Carol, b. 9 Mar. 1909. Diamond Importer & Exporter. Educ; 2 yrs. of coll. Mbrships: Finance Chmn., Zionist Org. of Am.; Gen. Coun., World Zionist Org.; Diamond Bourse of Antwerp; on Bd., Diamond Dealers Club of N.Y.; Diamond Trade Assn. of N.Y.; Diamond Bourse of Israel; Edgwood Country Club, River Vale, N.J.; Vanderbilt Tennis Club, N.Y.C.; Manhattan Skating Club. Address: 650 Park Ave., N.Y., NY 10021, U.S.A.

PICKELL, Charles Norman, b. 18 Dec. 1927. Clergyman. Educ: B.A., Juniata Coll., Pa., U.S.A., 1949; B.D., Western Theol. Sem., 1952; Th.M., Pitts.-Xenia Theol. Sem., 1957; M.Div., Pitts. Theol. Sem., 1971; Postgrad. study, Harvard Univ., Andover-Newton Theol. Schl., Princeton Union, & Columbia Theol. Sems. Appts: Pastor, Presby. chs., Atlantic City, N.J., Monongahela, Pa. & Newton, Mass., 1952-63; Guest Lectr., Practical Theol., Gordon Divinity Schl., 1958-63; Pastor, Wallace Mem.

United Presby Ch., Hyattsville, Md., 1963-70; Co-Pastor, Vienna Presby. Ch., Va., 1970-. Min. of Presby. Ch. & United Presby. Ch., U.S.A. Num. mbrships. incl: Trustee, Gordon Coll. & Gordon Divinity Schl.; Am. Soc. of Ch. Hist.; Presby. Histl. Soc.; Commnr. to Gen. Assmbly, United Presby. Ch., U.S.A., 1966. Publs: Preaching to Meet Men's Needs, 1958; A Commentary on Colossians, 1965, 2nd edit., 1973; Works Count Too! 1966; The Presbyterians, 1972; Also ed. & contbr. to Presbyterianism in New England, 1962, & contbr. to God's Minute, 1969. Author of articles & poetry in ch. jrnls. Hons: D.D., Sterling Coll., Kan., 1964. Address: Vienna Presbyterian Church, Box 351, Vienna, VA 22180, U.S.A. 6, 7, 30.

PICKENS, William G., b. 27 Dec. 1927. Professor. Educ: B.A., Morehouse Coll., Atlanta, 1948; M.A., Atlanta Univ.; Ph.D., Univ. of Conn., Storrs, 1969. Appts. incl: Tchr., Engl. & Soc. Studies, Barnard-Brown Schl., Hartford, Conn., 1954-57; Tchr., Engl., Weaver H.S., ibid, 1957-67; Mbr., Engl. Curric. Team to dev. new curric., 1967-68; Chmn., Engl. Dept., Weaver H.S., 1968-70; Chmn., Dept. Engl. & Linguistics, Morehouse Coll., 1970-. Mbrships: MLA; Coll. Lang. Assn.; AAUP; Atlanta Area Engl. Club. Contbr. of articles to profl. jrnls. Ed., A Guide to Personal English, 1968, General English, Grades 9 & 10, 1969, Program of English Studies, Grades 9 through 12, 1970, Trends in Southern Sociolinguistics, 1974. Address: 855 Fair St., S.W., Atlanta, GA 30314, U.S.A. 125.

PICKERING, Edward Davies, b. 4 May 1912. Publisher. Appts: incl; Mgng. Ed., Daily Mail, 1947-49; Daily Express, 1951-57; Ed., Daily Express, 1957-62; Dir., Beaverbrook Newspapers Ltd., 1956-65; Edit. Dir., The Daily Mirror Newspapers Ltd., 1964-68; Chmn., ibid, & Int. Publng. Corp. Newspaper Div., 1968-70; currently Chmn. IPC Mags. Ltd. Mbrships. Press Coun., 1964-69, 1970-; Garrick Club. Address: Chmn., IPC Magazines, Tower House, Southampton St., London WC2E 9QX, U.K. 1.

PICKERING, (Sir) George White, b. 26 June 1904. Physician. Educ: Pembroke Coll., Cambridge, U.K.; St. Thomas Hosp.; M.B., 1930; M.D., 1955. Appts. incl: Prof., Med., Univ. of London & Dir., Med. Clin., St. Marys Hosp., 1939-56; Regius Prof., Med., Oxford Univ., 1956-68; Master, Pembroke Coll., ibid, 1969-. Fellowships: Royal Soc.; Royal Coll. Physns. Mbrships. incl: Pres., Pres., Brit. Med. Assn., 1963-64; For. Assoc., Nat. Acad. Scis., Wash., 1970; AMA; Royal Coll. Physns., Edinburgh & Dublin. Publs: High Blood Pressure, 1955, 68; The Nature of Essential Hypertension, 1961; The Challenge to Education, 1967; Hypertension: Causes Consequences & Management, 1970. Hons. incl: D.Sc., Durham, 1957, Danrmouth, U.S., 1960 & Hull, 1972; Sc.D., Trinity Coll., Dublin, 1962. Address: Master's Lodgings, Pembroke Coll., Oxford, U.K. 1.

PICKETT, Doyle C. b. 15 July, 1930. Business Executive. Educ; B.A., Wabash Coll., Crawfordsville, Ind.; M.B.A., Ind. Univ., Bloomington. Appts: Grad. Asst. Dept. of Mgmt. Schl. of Bus., Ind. Univ.; Exec. Trainee, Employment Interviewer, Staff Asst. to Gen. Merchandise Mgr., Off. & Asst. Store M r. L. S. Ayres & Co., Inc, Indpls, Ind.; Mgmt. Analyst, Cummins Engine Co., Inc. Colombus, ibid; Admin. Asst. to Pres., Mgr. Special Projs. & Approval Prog., The Baker & Taylor Co., Momence, Ill & Somerville, N.J. Mbrships. incl: Kiwanis Club of N. W. Indpls. (Charter Pres.,

1958-59, Dir., 1960-61) Ind. Dist., Kiwanis Int. (Zone Chmn. Mbrship. & Attendance Comm., 1960-61); Masonic Order; Christian Ch.; Delta Tau Delta; Pi Delta Epsilon; Alpha Phi Omega; Blue Key Fraternity. Hons: Soldier of the Month. Nat. Defence Serv. Medal, 1955; Winner of Schlrships. & Boy Scouts Awards. Address: 240 Gt. Hills Rd., Somerville, NJ 08876, U.S.A. 8, 16.

PICKETT, Eunice MacFarlane Cowan (Mrs. John D. Pickett) b. 31 Aug. 1899. Accountant. Educ: B.B.A., Boston Univ., 1920; Northeastern Univ.; Bentley Coll. Appts: Collection Clerk, Nat. Shawmut Bank, 1929-20; Bkkppr., Linn Realty Serv., 1920-24; Bkkppr., Bonelli Adams Co., 1925-33; Acft., W. Robert Cowan & Co., 1928-55; Report Ed., Charles F. Rittenhouse & Co., 1942-45; Acct. Mass. Soc. for the Prevention of Cruelty & Am. Humane Educ. Soc., 1945-47; Asst. & Treas. ibid, 1947-67; Dir., Am. Fondouk Maintenance Comm., 1964-. Mbrships. Pres., Boston Chapt., Am. Soc. Women Accts., 1960-62; Pres., Boston Club, Zonta Int., 1964-66; Order of Eastern Star, 1928-; Hons. Nat. Humane Key, 1955; Exec. Profl. Hall of Fame, 1966. Address: 68 Pine Lane, Westwood, MA 02090, U.S.A. 5, 6.

PICKRELL, Eloise N., b. 21 Oct. 1911. Librarian. Educ: B.A., Occidental Coll., 1935; M.S., Univ. of S. Calif., 1942. Appts. incl: Soc. Wkr., WPA, Pasadena, Calif., 1934-35; Dean of Women, & Tchr., physical educ., Newport H.S., Calif., 1935-37; Long Beach Pub. Lib., 1938-48; Children's Libn., Allentown (Pa.) Free Lib., 1948-50; Lion., St. Mary Co. Lib., Leonardtown, Md., 1950-56; Hd. Libn., Naval Air Stn./Naval Air Test Ctr, Patuzent River, Md., 1956-. Active off. & mbr. of num. civic orgs. & assns., inclng. Exec. Dir., Girl Scouts of Am., Long Beach, 1944-45; Dir., Mentally Retarded Day Care Ctr., 1960-66; Pres., Citizens Schlrship. Fndn., 1967; Chmn., Md. Congress PTA Lib. Servs., 1969-. Address: P.O. Box 168, Leonardtown, MD 20670, U.S.A.

PICON-PARRA, Roberto, b. 18 Jan. 1926. Lawyer; Professor of Philosophy of Law. Educ: Ph.B., Ctrl. Univ. of Venezuela, Caracas, 1941; Dr. of Pol. Scis., ibid 1949. Appts: Mbr., Bar, Fed. Dist., 1949; Atty., Escritorio Pizani, 1950-52; Atty., Escritorio Maury, 1952-; Asst. Prof., Philos. of Law, Ctrl. Univ. of Venezuela, 1950-58; Aggregate Prof., ibid, 1958-63; Assoc. Prof., 1963-69; Titular Prof., 1969-. Mbrships: Dir., Venezuelan Assn. for Philos. of Law; Dir., Libn.-Archivist, & Legal Advsr., Venezuelan Inst. of Geneal.; Asociación de Hidalgos a Fuero de Espana, Madrid. Publs: El Derecho y Los Usos Sociales, 1950, 2nd ed. 1963, Ideas para una Metafisica Futura, 1964; Introduccion a la Ontologia del Derecho, 1969. Recip., Hon. Dip., Ctrl. Univ. of Venezuela, 1950. Address: Escritorio Maury, P.O. Box 573, Caracas, Venezuela.

PIECH, Paul Peter, b. 11 Feb. 1920. Artist. Educ: Brooklyn Coll., N.Y., 1939; Cooper Union Schl. of Art, N.Y., 1939-42, 1945-47; Chelsea Schl. of Art, London, U.K., 1948-51. Appts. incl: Art Dir., Columbia Record Co., U.S.A., 1945-46; Art Dir., Dorland Int. Advt., 1947; Art Dir., W.S. Crawfords, London, U.K., 1951-58; Art Dir., Service Advt., London, 1958-68; Sr. Lectr. Graphics, London Coll. of Printing, 1968-74; Sr. Lectr. Graphics, Leicester Polytechnic, 1969-73. Mbrships: Fellow, Soc. Typographic Designers, London U.K.; Int. Typographl. Ctr., U.S.A.; British Printing Soc.; Soc. of Artists-Craftsmen.; London Chapel of Pvte. Press Printers; Assn. of Small Presses. Works incl: War & Misery, 1959; Poem To

Rene, 1963; Taurus Tribute to Martin Luther King, 1968; London, Oh Captain My Captain!, 1970; Proverbs of Hell, Please Listen, 10 War Poems of Wilfred Owen, America. Hons. incl: Christian Sci. Monitor Poster Award, U.S.A., 1947; Int. Advt. Award, U.S.A., 1961; Blake Grant, Ill. State Coll., 1974. Address: 2 Willow Dene, Bushey Heath, Herts. WD2 1PS, U.K.

PIEPER, (Otto) Hans (Friedrich Henry Ernst), b. 1 Mar. 1913. Scientific Chief. Educ: 'Leopoldimun' Detmold, Univs. of Münster & Tübingen, Germany, 1935-38; Dr. phil., Münster, 1938. Appts: Town archives, Münster, 1939-45; Served WWII; Active at firm, Büssing Automobilwerke AG, Braunschweig, 1953-62; Werner von Siemens Inst., Munich, 1962-. Mbrships: Sci. & Histl. assn. of Lippe: Soc. & econ. hist. assn., Munich; Soc. for Technikgeschichte in V.D.I., Düsseldorf; Soc. of philatelic examiners, Munich; Study group, new handbook for philately. Publs. incl: Aus der Geschichte der Nachrichtentechnik von der Antike bis zur Gegenwart, 1973; Articles in jrnls. inclng. Technikgeschichte, Lippische Blätter für Heimatkunde, Automobiltechnische Zeitschrift. Recip. of hons. Address: Hausnerstrasse 17, D 8011 Kircheim über Munich, German Fed. Repub. 43.

PIERCE, Florence Wayne (Mrs. Richard L.). Clinical Psychologist. Educ: B.A., Seton Hill Coll., Greensburg, Pa., 1939; M.A., Univ. of Pitts., Pa., 1942; Doctoral Prog., ibid; Postgrad. Prog., Univ. of S. Fla., Tampa. Appts: State Psychologist, Mich.; Psychologist for Child Guidance Clin., St. Petersburg, Fla.; Counselor, Cons., Tchr., Cath. Schls.; Pinellas Co.; Schl. Psychologist, Pinellas Co. Schls., St. Petersburg, Fla. Mbrships: Am. Psychological Assn.; Fla. Psychological Assn.; Fla. Assn. of Schl. Psychologists; Charter mbr., Tampa Bay Psychological Assn.; Signa Kappa Phi, 1939. Author of articles Parents Are People, Too, & Preparing Your Child For School. Address: 1205 Royal Palm Dr. South, St. Petersburg, FL 33707, U.S.A. 125.

PIERCE, M. Scheffel, b. 27 Feb 1922. Higher Education & Communications Specialist. Educ: B.S.Ed., Phys. & Chem., Kent State Univ., Ohio, 1943; M.S., Speech, Univ. of Wis., Madison, 1952; Ph.D. Speech, ibid, 1958. Appts. incl: Instr., Speech, Maths., Soc. Studies, Bath. H.S. Ohio, 1946-48, Speech, McKinley H.S., Canton, ibid, 1948-50; Asst. Prof., Speech, 1950-54; Acting Dean of Men, 1952-53; Baldwin-Wallace Coll., Berea, Ohio; Asst. Prof., Speech, Beloit Coll., Wis., 1955-56; Speech Dept. Gen. Motors Inst., Flint, Mich., 1956-58; Asst. Prof., Speech, Ctrl. Mo. State Coll. Warensburgh, 1959-62; Exec. Dir., Neb. Educl. TV Coun. for Higher Educ; 1965-68; Asst. Prof., Speech, 1962-64, Jrnlsm, 1963-64; Fac. Coord. for Closed-Circuit TV, 1964-68; Univ. of Neb.; Dir., Instrnl. Resources, State Univ. Coll., Plattsburgh, N.Y., 1968-73; Exec. Dir., N.E. N.Y. Educl. TV Assn., 1968-74; Mbr., Bd. Trustees, ibid, 1974-; Coord. & Mentor, Empire State Coll., N. Country Unit, Plattsburgh, 1973-. Mbrships. incl; Exec. Comm., Adirondack Coun., Boy Scouts Am.; Bd., Clinton Co. N.Y. Chapt., Am. Red Cross. Publs. incl; co-author, Communication to Industry, 1958; articles in var. jrnls. Recip. Disting. Serv. Alumni Award in Broadcasting, Kent State Univ., 1971. Address: 34 N. Main Street, Peru, NY 12972, U.S.A. 6, 13, 15, 126, 131.

PIERCE, Ralph, b. 14 Apr. 1926. Consulting Engineer. Educ: B.S. in Elec. Engrng., Northwestern Univ., Chgo., Ill., 1946.

Profl. Engr. Registrations in 8 States. Appts: Test Engr. at Am. Elec. Heater Co., 1946-47; Sr. Assoc. Engr., Underground Lines Dept. of Detroit Edison Co., 1947-52; Hd. & Sec., Utility Dept., Geo. Wagschal Assocs., Cons. Engr., 1952-58; Ptnr., Pierce, Yee & Assocs., 1958-72; Mng. Ptnr., Harley Ellington Pierce Yee, Assocs., Archts., Engrs. & Planners, 1972-; V.P., Sec., Treas., Pierce, Yee & Assocs., Ltd., Windsor, Canada, 1968-. Mbrships: Nat. Soc. Profl. Engrs.; Am. Inst. Elec. Engrs.; Am. Inst. Architects; Engrng. Soc. of Detroit; Illuminating Engrng. Soc. Hons: Mbr. of Dept. of Commerce Mission to Yugoslavia; Chmn., Airport Lighting Comm., IES. Address: 26111 Evergreen Rd., Southfield, MI 48076, U.S.A. 16.

PIERCE, Raymond Kenneth, b. 13 July 1924. Principal. Educ: A.B., Franklin & Marshall Coll., 1948; Ed.M., Temple Univ., 1955. Appts. incl: Tchr., Soc. Studies, Solanco H.S., Quarryville, Pa., 1948-51 & at E. Lampeter H.S., Lancaster, Pa., 1951-53; Tchr., Engl. & Soc. Studies, Coun. Rock Jr.-Sr. High, Newtown, Pa., 1953-55; Instr., Secondary Educ., Temple Univ., Phila., Pa., 1955-58; Asst. Prin., Franklin Delano Roosevelt Jr. High, Bristol, Pa., 1958-61 & Prin., 1961-63; Prin., Delhaas High, ibid, 1963-65; Proj. Dir., Bucks Co. Youth Corps., Doylestown, Pa., 1965-67; Dir., Child & Youth Study Servs., ibid, 1967-69; Prin., N. Penn H.S., Lansdale, Pa., 1969-. Mbrships. incl: Montgomery Co. Prins. Assn., Pres., 1973-74; Am. Assn. for Supvsn. & Curric. Dev.; Nat. Soc. for the Study of Educ.; Nat. Assn. of Secondary Schl. Prins.; Pa. Assn. of Secondary Schl. Prins., Life Mbr., NEA. Publs. incl: Observing An Individual Student At A Learning Task; Ed. & Publr., PEP CAPSULES. Hons; incl: Kappa Phi Kappa; Minute of Appreciation, Friends Serv. Assn., 1965; Legion of Honor, Chapel of Four Chaps., 1965. Address: N. Penn H.S., 1340 Valley Forge Rd., Lansdale, PA 19446, U.S.A. 6.

PIERCE, Wallace Lincoln, b. 4 Mar. 1912. Retired Merchant. Educ: B.S., Harvard, 1934. Appts: Serv. WWII; Lt.-Lt. Cmdr. U.S.N.R.; w. S.S. Pierce Co., 1934-, as Clerk of Corp., V.P., 1947-54; Pres., 1954-68; Chmn., Bd., 1967-69; Hon. Chmn., Bd., 1970-72; Cons., 1972-; Pres. S.S. Pierce Realty Co., Pierce Co., Inc., 1967-; Trustee, Franklin Suffolk Savings Bank, Wm. Underwood Co., Watertown, Mass.; Dir., New England Merchants Nat. Bank, Trustee Univ. Hosp., Michael Anagnos Agricl. Coll., Konista, Greece; Mbr., Corp., Boston Children's Aid Soc.; Bd. Dirs., Chmn. Exec. Comm., Robert Breck Brigham Hosp. Mbrships: Nat. Assn. Wholesale Grocers (Past Dir.); Boston Retail Trade Bd. (Past Dir., V.P.); Am. Inst. Food Distribution (Regional Dir.); Am. Soc. for Friendship w. Switzerland (Dir., Fndr., Boston Chapt.) Recip., Ordre Merite, France; Navy Commendation Medal. Address: 60 Fernwood Rd., Chestnut Hill, MA 02167, U.S.A.

PIERHAL, Armand, b. 27 July 1897. Writer. Educ: Engrng. Schl., Univ. of Lausanne, Switzerland, 1910-20; Music Studies, Genéva, 1920-22; Piano Studies w. Blanche Selva & Composition w. Nadia Boulanger, Paris, 1922. Appts. incl: Personal Sec. to Jacques Rivière, dir. of Nouvelle Revue Française, 1924-25; Literary Sec. to Jacques-Emile Blanche, 1925-42; Special Envoy of Figaro, Nazi Cong., Nurenburg, 1935; Literary Critic, Art Critic, Nouvelles Littéraires, Annes, Temps Présent, L'Aube, La Revue de Genève, Radio-Paris, etc. Mbr., var. profl. socs. Publs. incl: (novels) Jeunes Morts chéris des Dieux, 1938; La Chartreuse de Tonar, 1956; (essays) Le Combat de Poitiers, 1949; (poetry) Maximes

Alexandrines, 1969. Hons. incl: 2 awards, Acad. Française; Chevalier, Legion of Hon. Address: 234 Blvd. Pereire, 75017 Pâris, France. 43, 91.

PIERRE-NOEL, Louis Vergniaud, b. 2 Aug. 1910. Graphic Designer. Educ: Ecole Tech. de Damien, Univ. of Haiti; Columbia Univ., N.Y.C., U.S.A.; Casa de Moneda, Buenos Aires, Argentina; Acad. de la Grande Chaumière, Paris, France. Appts: Graphic Designer, Dept. of Educ., Haiti; Stamp Designer for Haiti Postal Admin., Port-au-Prince; Scientific Illustrator, Am. Mus. of Natural Hist., N.Y.C., U.S.A.; Art Cons., Pan Am. Union (UNESCO), Wash. D.C., Haiti Govt. Tourist Bur., N.Y.C.; Art Dir., Pierre-Noel Studio d'Art, Wash. D.C.; Visual Media Techn., Pan Am. Hlth. Org. (WHO), ibid. Mbrships: Nat. Assn. Indl. Artists, Wash. D.C.; Indl. Int. Graphics, Calif.; Wash. Tech. Inst. Advt. Design Advsry. Comm., Wash. D.C.; Int. House Alumni Assn., N.Y.C.; Mus. of Mod. Art, ibid; Masonic Lodge, Mt. Liban No. 22, Haiti. Hosp: Haiti Stamp Design Award for UN Victims of the War, 1944; Haiti Gold Medal Award for stamps commemorating 200th Anniversary of Fndn. of City of Port-au-Prince, 1949; Mead Paper Co. Award for Haiti Govt. Tourist Travel Folder, Wash. D.C., 1958; UN 1st Award for 20th Anniversary Commemoration Stamp Design, 1965; Nat. Assn. Indl. Artists Award for Tribute to John F. Kennedy, allegoric portrait of the Pres., Wash. D.C., 1965; UN Stamp Disign Award for Cessation of Nuclear Testing, N.Y.C., 1966; Nat. Assn. Indl. Artists Award, for World Hlth. Day, Poster, Man & His Cities, 1966, for poster commemorating 20th Anniversary of WHO, Hlth. in the World of Tomorrow, 1968; Haitian Am. Citizens Soc. Award of Merit for disting. Contbn. in field of graphic arts 1970; UN 1st Hon. Mention for stamp design for World Hlth., Your Heart is Your Hlth., 1972; Pan Am. Hlth. Org. commemorative stamp, 70th Anniversary, issued by Haiti Govt., 1973. Address: 4706 17th St., N.W., Washington, DC 20011, U.S.A.

PIERS, (Rear Admiral) Desmond William, b. 12 June 1913. Retired Naval Officer. Educ: Royal Mil. Coll. of Canada, 1930-32; Royal Naval Staff Coll., 1949; Nat. Defence Coll. of Canada, 1951-52. Appts. incl: Cmdng. Officer, destroyers, WWII; Dir., Naval Plans & Ops., Ottawa, 1949-51; Asst. Chief of Staff, SACLANT, 1953; Cmdnt., Royal Mil. Coll. of Canada, 1957-60; Asst. Chief, Naval Staff, Ottawa, 1960-62; Cmdr., Canadian Defence Liaison Staff, Wash., 1962-66; Canadian Mil. Rep., NATO, 1962-66; Retd., 1967. Mbrships. incl: Canadian Corps. of Cmdnrs.; Navy League Canada; Atlantic Coun. Canada; Canadian Civil Liberties Assn.; Canadian Inst. Int. Affairs; Heritage Trust, N.S.; Kt., St. Lazarus of Jerusalem. Hons. incl: Disting. Serv. Cross, 1943; Canadian Forces Decoration; 1939-45 Star; Atlantic Star; Africa Star. Address: The Quarter Deck, Chester, N.S., BOJ 1JO, Canada. 41, 88.

PIERSEL, W. Guthrie, b. 25 Mar. 1899. Educator. Educ: A.B., Ohio Wesleyan Univ.; A.M., Univ. of Chgo.; Ed.D., Ind. Univ. Appts. incl: Instr., Marietta Coll., Ohio, 1929-33; Statn., Ill. Tax Commn., 1938-40; Statn., Dept. of Pub. Safety, State of Ill., 1940-47; Chief Rsch. Analyst, Pub. Safety Div., G-2, Tokyo, Japan, 1949-52; Personnel Dir., Horace Mann Ins. Co., 1952-55; Rsch. Analyst, Dept. of Pub. Safety, Ill., 1955-61; Rsch. Cons., 1962-; Ed., Gifted Tchrs. Books, 1968-. Mbrships. incl: Phi Delta Kappa; AAAS. Publs. incl: Photo-Math I,II, (w. D. Piersel); Photo-Phonics, I,II,III; Photo-Cabulary, I,II. Address: 2 W. 152 St., Harvey, IL, U.S.A. 28.

PIERSON, George Wilson, b. 22 Oct. 1904. Historian; Professor of History. Educ: B.A., Yale Univ., 1926; Ph.D., ibid, 1933. Appts. incl: Instr., Engl., Yale Univ., 1926-27; Instr., Hist., ibid, 1929-30, 1933-36; Asst. Prof., 1936-39; Assoc. Prof., 1939-44; Prof., 1944-46; Learned Prof., 1946-73; Dept. Chmn., 1956-62; Emeritus, 1973-; Dir., Div. of Humanities, 1964-70; Grad. Pres., Phi Beta Kappa, 1965-73; Histn., Univ. of Yale, Mbrships. incl: Phi Beta Kappa; Fellow, Davenport Coll., Yale, 1933-; Fellow, Am. Acad. of Arts & Scis., 1973-; Century Assn., 1939-; Am. Histl. Assn. Publs. incl: Tocqueville and Beaumont in America, 1938; Yale: The University College, 1921-37, 1955; The Education of American Leaders: Comparative Contributions of U.S. Colleges and Universities, 1969; The Moving American, 1973. Hons. incl: The Warren Mem. High Schlrship. Prize, Yale Univ., 1926; Guggenheim Fellowship, 1955-56; Wilbur Lucius Cross Medal, Yale Grad. Schl. Assn., 1973. Address: 1691 Yale Stn., New Haven, CT 06520, U.S.A. 2, 6, 13.

PIETARINEN, Aarne, b. 18 Nov. 1902. General Manager; Retired Major General, Educ: Matriculation, Finland, 1923; Cadet Schl., 1924-26; Schl. of Artillery, 1928; Battle Schl., 1932; Mil. Acad., 1935-37. Appts: Adjutant, Battery Cmdr., & Course Dir., Non-commnd. Offs. Schl., Field Artillery Regiment (KTR 1), 1926-35; Artillery Educ. Off., Reserve Offs. Schl., 1928-30; Chief of Educ. Off., Divisional Staff, 1937-39; Chief, Ops. Off., Winter War, 1939-40; Mil. Dist. Staff Cmdr., 1940-41; Chief of Staff, & Infantry Regiment Cmdr., 8th Div., Continuation War, 1941-44; Bur. Chief. Gen. Staff of the Armed Forces, 1944-48; Chief of Staff, Light Brigade, 1948-52; Hd. of Dept., Gen. Staff, Instr., Mil. Acad., & Chief Topographical Off., 1952-59; Hd. of Ordnance, Gen. Staff, 1959-62; Bd., Lapua Cartridge Factory.; Mbr., N. Karalia Deleg.; Rep., Retail Trade Trng. Fndn.; Security Mgr., Kesko Oy; Gen. Mgr., Osakeyhtiö Pientare. Mbrships: Olympic Comm. (Alternate); Hd., Mil. Div., Survey Bd.; Rationalisation Bd., Min. of Defence; Chmn., Riders of Häme; Hon., Liperi Reserve Offs. Assn., etc. Hons: Cmdr., Order of the Lion, 1956; Cross of Liberty, 2nd Class, 1944, etc.; Kt., Order o the White Rose, 1939; Olympic Medal, 2nd Class, 1952; Iron Cross, 2nd Class, Germany, 1941. Address: Hämeentie 152 C 64, 00560 Helsinki 56, Finland. 43, 134.

PIETZ, Emil Theodore, b. 28 Oct. 1904. Psychologist; Counselor. Educ: Ph.B., Redfield Coll., 1932; B.A., Yankton Coll., 1933; M.A., Univ. of S.D., 1936; Grad. work towards doct., various univs. Appts. incl: Ordained Min., United Ch. of Christ; Pastor, Grandview Congregational Ch., Denver, Colo., 1950-58; Counselor & Chap., State Ind. Schl. for Boys, Golden, Colo., Rehab. Counselor III, Colo. State Reformatory, Buena Vista, 1958-63; Fed. Civil Soc. Worker, USDB Army Dept., Ft. Leavenworth, Kan. 1966; Currently, ret'd. & Pastor, First Cong. Ch., Tonganoxio. Mbrships. incl: Psych. Assn. of Ctrl. States; Lincoln & Denver Ministerial Assns.; Denver Probations Parole Correctional Assn., 1955-63; Alpha Kappa Delta. Author of many articles. Recip. of sev. Hons. Address: 1007 N. 2nd St., Apt. 6, Aberdeen, SD 57401, U.S.A.

PIGADIOTIS, Costas, b. 21 May 1915. Bank Clerk; Poet. Educ: Grad., Pantios Coll. Econ. & Pol. Sci., Greece. Chief, Dept., Agric. Bank, Greece. Mbr. Assoc. Lit. Men. Publs: Author, 4 collects. poems: Unpaved Streets, 1966; Musing, 1968; Residence unknown, 1970; Luggage (2 eds.), 1972. Address: N.

Kazantzaki 74 St., Zografou, Athens (T.T. 625), Greece.

PIGGE, Helmut, b. 28 Sept. 1919. Television Producer; Author. Educ: Univ. of Berlin; Univ. of Munich; Ph.D. Appts. incl: Art-Dir., Regensburg, 1946-49; Actor & Dir., Zimmertheater Aachen, 1953-55; TV Prod. & Writer, S. German Radio Stuttgart, 1955-61; Bavaria Atelier GmbH Munich, 1961-. Author of Geschichte Und Entwicklung Des Regensburger Theaters, 1954 & sev. TV plays inclng: Frieden Unserer Stadt, 1960; Oberst Chabert, 1963; Sieben Wochen Auf Dem Eis, 1967; Schleicher, 1967; Operation Walkure, 1971. Hons: Goldene Kamera; Adolf Grimme Prize, Marl; Silberne Nymphe, Monte Carlo. Address: Waldschulstr. 43, 8 Munich 82, German Fed. Repub. 43, 92.

PIGUET, J. Claude, b. 13 July 1924. Professor of Philosophy. Educ: B.A., Univ. of Lausanne, Switzerland, 1945; Ph.D., ibid, 1948. Appts: Tchr., H.S., Neuchâtel, 1949-59; Lectr., Univ. of Lausanne, 1959-65; Vis. Lectr., Tech. H.S., Darmstadt, Germany, 1962; Ordinarius for Philos., H.S., St. Gallen, 1965-73; Vis. Prof., Univs. of Montreal & Quebec, Canada, 1968-71; Prof. of Philos., Univ. of Lausanne, 1973-. Mbrships: Edit. Comm., Revue de Théologie et Philosophie; Pres., Swiss Philosophical Soc., 1969-71; Swiss Acad. of Humane Scis.; European Cultural Soc. Publs: Découverte de la Musique, 1955; Le Vocabulaire de la Philosophie, 1957; De l'Esthetique à la Métaphysique, 1959; L'Oeuvre de Philosophie, 1960; Entretiens sur la Musique (w. E. Ansermet), 1964; Entretiens sur la Musique (w. F. Martin), 1967. Address: Villa Vogelsberg, CH-9240 Uzwil, Switzerland. 2, 43.

PIJPER, Guillaume Frédéric, b. 6 Apr. 1893. Professor. Educ: Litt.D., Univ. of Leyden, The Netherlands, 1924. Appts: Govt. Advsr. on Islamic Affairs, Dutch Indies, 1925-51; Prof. of Arabic, Univ. of Jakarta, 1940-51; Prof. of Arabic, Univ. of Amsterdam, 1955-63; Dir., Inst. for the Modern Near E., Amsterdam, 1956-65. Mbr., Doctrina & Amicita Club, Amsterdam. Publs: Het Boek der Duizend Vragen (the book of the thousand questions), 1924; Fragmenta Islamica (studies on Islam in Indonesia), 1934; Islam & the Netherlands, 1957; jrnl. articles. Hons: Kt., Order of Netherland Lion, 1950; Off., Order of Orange-Nassau, 1940. Address: Haringvlietstraat 17, II Amsterdam, The Netherlands. 43, 100.

PIKOULIS, Stelios D., b. 3 Mar. 1917. Chemical Engineer. Educ: Grad., Nat. Tech. Univ. of Athens, Greece, 1940; Dr. Chem. Engrng., Nat. Univ. of Athens, 1969. Appts. incl: Posts, Min. of Reconstruction & Min. of Pub. Works, 1947-62; Greek Govt. Deleg., Econ. Commn. Europe, UN, 1947-50; Rep., Min. of Pub. Works & Tech. Chmbr. of Greece, Congresses for Bldg. Rsch., 1951-; Prof. of Bldg. Mats., Tech. Schl. for Army Offs., Instr. Bldg. Mats., Tech. Univ. of Athens, & Cons. Chem. Engr., 1957-; Mbr., Bd. of Dirs., Nitrogenous Fertilizer Ind. S.A., 1967-. Mbrships. incl: Bd. of Dirs., Tech. Chmbr. of Greece; V.P. & Gen. Sec., Hellenic Assn. for Environmental Protection; Past Pres., Greek Assn. of Chem. Engrs.; Union of Greek Chems.; Pres., Air Pollution Control Comm., 1967-70; Long Term Prog. for Dev. of Greek Economy State Comm., 1971-72. Publs: 19 tech. papers. Recip., Decoration, Greek State. Address: 6 Raidestou St., Nea Smyrni, Athens, Greece. 43.

PILET, Paul-Emile, b. 26 July 1927. Professor of Plant & Cell Biology. Educ: D.Sc., Lausanne Univ.; Postdoct. Fellow, Calif. Inst.

of Technol., U.S.A.; The Sorbonne, Paris. Appts: Prof., Univ. of Lausanne; Assoc. Prof., Univ. of Paris; Dir., Inst. of Plant Biol. & Physiol., Univ. of Lausanne. Mbrships. incl: Fndr. & Pres., Swiss Soc. Plant Physiol.; Edit. Comm., Dealectica, Physiologie vegetale, Plant Sci. Letters; Gen. Sec., Int. Assn. Plant Physiologists. Publs: Les phytohormones de croissance, 1961; La cellule, 1968; Les parsis cellulaires, 1971. Dir., 2 monographies, Physiologie végétale; Ultrastructure et fonctions cellulaires. 200 papers on biological & biochem. control of cell growth. Recip., Dr. hon. causa., Univ. of Toulouse, 1967. Address: Inst. Plant Biol. & Physiol., Place de la Riponne, 1005 Lausanne, Switzerland.

PILKINGTON (Lord) William Henry, b. 19 Apr. 1905. Glass Manufacturer. Educ: Magdalene Coll., Cambridge, U.K. Appts: Hon. Life Pres., Pilkington Brothers Ltd., Chancellor, Univ. of Technol., Loughborough, 1966; Dpty. Lt. of Lancashire, 1968; Dir., Bus. Int., 1968; Pres., British Shippers' Coun., 1971, British Plastics Fedn., 1972. Mbrships: Fellow, British Inst. of Mgmt., Royal Soc. of Arts; United Oxford & Cambridge Univs. Club; Hon. Liveryman, Glass Sellers' Co.; Royal Nat. Rose Soc. Publs: Chmn.'s Reports, Royal Commn. on Doctors & Dentists' Remuneration, 1960 & Comm. on Broadcasting, 1962. Hons: Knighted, 1953; Life Peerage, 1968; Docts., Univs. of Manchester, 1959, Liverpool, 1963, Loughborough (Technol.), 1966, Kent, 1968. Address: Windle Hall, St. Helens, Lancashire, U.K. 1, 32, 34.

PILSON, (Mrs.) Isabel Wilkins, b. 1 Dec. 1909. Elementary Teacher & Principal. Educ: B.S., GSCW, Milledgeville, Ga., U.S.A.; M.S., Ga. Univ., Athens, Ga.; 6th Yr. Cert. Admin., ibid. Appts: Elem. Tchr., Cave Springs, Ga., 1928-30; Rome, Ga., 1930-44; Prin., Neely Schl., ibid, 1945-55; Elm St. Schl., ibid, 1955-. Mbrships: Bd. Dirs., Rome Girls Club & Holly House Inc.; All local, Dist., State & nat. profl. orgs., as tchr. & prin.; Iota Chapt., Psi State, Delta Kappa Gamma; Kappa Delta Pi; Life mbr., Nat. Congress Parents & Tchrs. Hons: 5-yr. serv. award, Rome Girls Club, 1972; 40-yr. serv. award, Rome Bd. Educ., 1972. Address: 103 E-5th Ave., Rome, GA 30161, U.S.A. 125.

PIÑAR, Blas, b. 22 Nov. 1918. Notary; Lawyer; Politician. Educ: Grad. Law, Madrid Univ., Spain; Dr., Law, ibid. Appts. incl: Pub. Notary; Mbr., Nat. Coun. Movement; Mbr., Spanish Cortes (Parliament). Mbrships: Fndr. Pres., Fuerza Nueva (mag. & pol. grp.); Pres., Antonio Rivera Fndn., Madrid Univ. Publs: La Legitimacion por Concesion Real; La Prestacion Alimenticia en Nuestro Derecho Civil; La tutela: Principios y Organos; Contbr. pol. jrnls.; Lectr. Hons: Gt. Cross Civil Merit; Gt. Cross O'Higgins; sev. other decorations, Latin Am. countries & Vatican; Hispanic Fraternity Award, Jrnlsm. Address: P^o Gen. Martinez Campos, 41, 2° Madrid 10, Spain.

PINCHER, (Henry) Chapman, b. 29 Mar. 1914. Journalist. Educ: B.Sc., Univ. of London, U.K., 1935; Mil. Coll. of Sci., Inst. of Educ. Appts: Staff, Liverpool Inst., 1936-40; Serv. w. Royal Armoured Corps, & Rocket Div., Min. of Supply, WWII; Defence, Sci. & Med. Ed., Daily Express, 1946-, Asst. Ed. & Bd. Mbr., 1973-. Publs: Breeding of Farm Animals, 1946; A Study of Fishes, 1947; Into the Atomic Age, 1947; Spotlight on Animals, Evolution, It's Fun Finding Out (w. B. Wicksteed), 1950; Sleep, & How to get more of it, 1954; (novels) Not with a Bang, 1965; The Giantkiller, 1967; The Penthouse Conspirators, 1970; Sex in our Time,

1973; author of num. articles in sci. & agric. jrnls. Recip. of Granada Award, Jrnlst. of the Year, 1964. Address: Lowerhouse Farm, Ewhurst, Surrey. 1.

PINCK, Louis Aaron, b. 20 June, 1894. Research Chemist (Retired). Educ: B.S., N.Y. Univ.; M.S., Geo. Wash. Univ., Wash. D.C. Appts: Chemist, U.S. Nitrate Plant, Muscle Shoals, Ala., 1918; Rsch. Chem., U.S. Dept. of Agric. Wash. D.C. & Beltsville, Md., 1921-64; now ret. Holder of patents in field of chem. fertilizers. Mbrships: Fellow, AAAS; Am. Chem. Soc.; N.Y. Acad. of Sci.; Am. Soc. of Agron. Publd. over 50 sci. papers. Address: 5805 Bradley Blvd., Bethesda, MD 20014, U.S.A. 6, 7, 14, 55.

PINCKNEY, Neal T(heodore), b. 26 July 1935. Psychologist; Professor. Educ: A.B., Univ. of Southern Calif., 1958; Univ. of Southern Calif., 1958-61; D.Phil., Oxford Univ., U.K., 1966. Appts. incl: Dir., Guidance Servs., U.S. DESEA, U.S. Defense Dept., Japan, 1966-67; Assoc. Prof., Educ. Psychol., Calif. State Univ., Sacramento, U.S.A., 1967-; Cons. Psychol., Calif. Hwy. Patrol., 1967-. Mbrships. incl: Am. Psychol. Assn.; Brit. & Japanese Psychol. Assns.; Am. Educ. Rsch. Assn. Phi Delta Kappa. Author of 2 books & over 25 papers in field. Address: Dept. of Behavioral Scis. in Educ., Calif. State Univ., 6000 J St., Sacramento, CA 95819, U.S.A.

PINES, Kapai, b. 25 Jan. 1926. Journalist; Author. Educ: Columbia Univ. Schl. of Jrnlsm., 1947-49; Tchrs. Courses, Kibbutz Movement, 1951, 53; Schl. of Econs., Tel-Aviv Univ., 1956-58. Appts: Free-lance writer, contbng. articles to var. newspapers & periodicals, 1945-46; For. Corres., Davar Daily, 1947-48; Sec., Ed. Bd., Contbr., Hebrew Popular Encyclopedia, 1955; Hd., Div. of Publn., Volcani Inst. of Agric., 1956-62; w. Maariv & Omer Dailies & Weekly Dvar Hashavau, 1958-60; Ed., Mada (Sci.), 1962-, & Contbr. of num. articles & columns on pol., econ. & sci. topics. Mbrships: Int. Sci. Writers Assn.; Conf. of Biol. Eds.; Israel Assn. of Amateur Astrons. Publs: What's What in the Histadrut, 1955; Who's Who in the World, 1959; Ptach Dah, 1961; The Enlarged Dictionary of Foreign Words in Hebrew, 1974; Transl., Engl. to Hebrew of var. books; Transl., Rewriter & Ed., The Negev, the Challenge of a Desert (Evenari, Shanan & Tadmor), 1971. Address: Beit Pines, Ramat Motza, Jerusalem, 95744, Israel. 55.

PINHEIRO E ROSA, José António (pseudonyms, Valadares, A'lvaro de or Pais, A'lvaro), b. 5 May 1908. Director of Municipal Library & Museum, Faro; Teacher; Author. Appts: Tchr., Sem., Faro, Portugal; Tchr., Colls., ibid; Tchr., Tech. Schls., Lagos & Faro; Organist, Cathedral, Faro; Dir., Municipal Lib. & Mus., ibid. Mbrships: ICOM: APOM. Publs. incl: Visit to the Collection of Ferreira d'Almeida, 1970; Rembrandt na coleccao Ferreira d'Almeida, 1971; Procissoes de Faro, 1972; Roteiro das Ruinas de Milreu, 2nd edit., 1974. Musical Compositions: Responsoria in Officiis Majoris Hebdomada; Missa in honore visitationis B.M. Virginis; songs. Address: Biblioteca e dos Museus Municipais, Faro, Portugal. 105, 133.

PINNEY, Don Ovid, b. 12 Sept. 1937. Educator. Educ: B.S., Univ. of Ill., Urbana, U.S.A., 1959; M.S., Okla. State Univ., Stillwater, 1961; Ph.D., Ibid, 1963. Appts: Sec., Int. Intercollegiate Livestock Coaches Assn., 1970; V.P., 1971; Pres., 1972; Official Judge for num. beef & swine shows Mbrships: Am. Soc. of Animal Sci.; Sigma Xi; Alpha Gamma Rho. Phi Kappa Phi; Phi Eta Sigma; Gamma Sigma Delta; Alpha Zeta; Nat. Multiple Sclerosis Soc. Publs: Livestock Evaluation, 1971; Contbns. to profl. jrnls.; M.S. & Ph.D. theses. Hons. incl: William Gultas Mem. Award, Coll. of Agric., Univ. of Ill., 1959; Ralston Purina Rsch. Fellowship Awards, 1959, 60 & 61; State Farmer Degree, Okla. Assn. of Future Farmers of Am. 1969. Address: Dept. of Animal Sciences & Industry, Okla. State Univ., Stillwater, OK 74074, U.S.A. 7, 14.

PIÑOL, Joaquín, b. 26 Nov. 1908. Writer. Educ: Ph.D., Univ., Crtl. Española, Madrid, Spain. Appts. incl: Tech. Sec., Min. of Pub. Educ., 1931; Lib. Advsr., New Editorial Lib., Madrid, 1931-36, & '44-50; Prof. of Spanish, Nat. Cervantes Inst., Madrid, 1932-36; Editing Sec., Ilustración Moderna Ibero-Americana, 1928-30; Collaborator, Unión Radio, ibid; Chief Ed., Aquí Está & Editing Sec., Síntesis (mag), 1946-50; Collab, Clarín, Atlántida, La Nación, Buenos Aires, Argentina, 1951-; currently Lit. Critic, La Prensa, Buenos Aires; Dir., Miguel de Unamuno, Lib., 1966-. Mbrships: Treas, PEN Club, 1967, 1972; Pres. Press Commission, ibid., Argentinian Writers' Soc.; Publs. incl: El Libro de mis Horas, 1936; El Libro de mi Noche, 1964. Hons. incl: Cross of Mil. Merit, 1938, SADE, 1964. Address: Boedo 908, Buenos Aires, Argentina.

PIÑON, Manuel Tiana, O.P., b. 2 Feb. 1924. Priest; Educator; Professor of Philosophy. Educ: Ph.D., Pontifical Univ. of St. Thomas Aquinas, Vatican City, 1954. Appts: Sec. Gen., Letran Coll., Manila, Philippines, 1954-57; Asst. Prefect of Libs., Univ. of Santo Tomas, Manila, 1957-59; Prof., Philos., ibid, 1957-; Dir., H.S. Dept., 1959-; Hd., Dept. of Philos., 1965-68; Dean., Fac. of Philos., Ecclesiastical Facs., 1966-; Dir., Univ. of Santo Tomas Coop., 1965-; Supvsr., ibid, 1970-; Chmn., Univ. Coun., 1971. Publs: Judgment on Agrarian Reformatory Expropriations, 1960; Being & Reality, 1972; Fundamental Logic, 1973; 2 pamphlets; Articles in profl. jrnls. Address: University of Santo Tomas, España, Manila, Philippines D-403.

PIPPARD, (Alfred) Brian, b. 7 Sept. 1920. University Professor. Educ: B.A., Clare Coll., Cambridge, U.K. 1941; M.A., ibid, 1945; Ph.D., ibid, 1949; Sc.D., ibid, 1966. Appts: Scientific Off., Radar Rsch. & Dev. Estab., Gt. Malvern, 1941-45; Demonstrator in Phys., Univ. of Cambridge, 1946; Lectr., Phys., ibid, 1950; Rdr., Phys., ibid, 1959-60; John Humphrey Plummer Prof. of Phys., ibid, 1960-71; Cavendish Prof. of Phys., ibid, 1971-; Fellow, Clare Coll., ibid, 1947-66; Pres., Clare Hall, ibid, 1966-73. Fellow, Royal Soc., 1956-. Publs: Elements of Classical Thermodynamics, 1957; Dynamics of Conduction Electrons, 1962; Forces & Particles, 1972; paper in Proceedings of Royal Soc. Hons: Hughes Medal, Royal Soc., 1959; Holweck Medal, 1961; Dannie-Heineman Prize 1969; Guthrie Prize, 1970. Address: Cavendish Lab., Madingley Rd., Cambridge CB3 OHE, U.K. I.

PIRBHAI, (Count Sir) Eboo, b. 15 July 1905. Representative of H.H. The Aga Khan in Africa. Appts: Mbr., Nairobi City Coun., 1938-43; Mbr., Legis. Coun., Kenya, 1952-60; Pres., Muslim Assn.; Chmn., Aga Khan Supreme Coun., Africa; Pres., Aga Khan Supreme Coun. for Europe, Canada & U.S.A.; Mbr. other official bodies. Mbrships: Reform & Landsdown Clubs. Hons: O.B.E., 1946; K.B., 1952; granted title Count by Aga Khan 1954; Brilliant Star of Zanzibar, 1956. Address: P.O. Box 40898, Nairobi, Kenya. I, 34.

PIRKLE, Alica Andrea Head (Mrs. David A. Pirkle), b. 28 June 1941. Teacher. Educ: B.S., Tift Coll., Forsyth, Ga., 1963. Appts: Tchr., La Mesa-Spring Valley Schl. Dist., La Messa, Calif., 1963-65; Tchr., Oglethorpe Co. Schl. System, Lesington, Ga., 1965-66; Tchr., 3rd grade, Oneonta City Sch. System, Ala., 1966-67; Tchr., 1st grade, ibid, 1967-70; Tchr., 2nd grade, 1973-. Mbrships Incl: Chmn., Community Coord. Child Care Comm.; Sec., Citizens Advsry. Comm.; NEA; Sec., V.P., Pres., Amicus Study Grp.; P.T.A.; Am. Cancer Soc. Named one of 4 disting. Young Women, 1972. Address: 41 Pine Circle, Oneonta, AL 35121, U.S.A. 46, 76, 125.

PIRLO-HÖDL, Sieghilde, b. 5 Feb. 1905. Artist. Educ: Acad. der bildenden Künste, Munich, Germany; Acad. Grand Chaumière & Colarossi, Paris, France; Portrait Schule Prof. Eugen Spiro, Berlin. Mbrships: Berufsvereinigung bildender Künstler Osterreichs; Tiroler Künstlerschaft, Innsbruck; Salzburger Kunstverein, Salzburg. Purchases incl: Staatliche Graphische Sammlung "Albertina", Vienna; Kultus-Ministerium, Vienna; Tiroler Landes-Regierung, Innsbruck; Landeshauptstadt Innsbruck; Var. offs., schls. & assns. Var. pvte. purchasers in Austria & abroad. Publs: Osterreichische Kunst, 1937-38; Bergland, 1935-41; Tirol Kunst, Volk & Leben, 1969-70; La Revue Moderne des Arts, Paris 1971. Recip., title of Prof., Pres., Repub. of Austria, 1974. Address: Morsbacherstrasse 15, A 6330 Kufstein (Tirol), Austria. 86, 133.

PIROTTO, Armando Diego, b. 12 Nov. 1907. Lawyer. Educ: Univ. of Montevideo, Uruguay; Fac. of Philos. & Letters. Buenos Aires, Argentina, & Madrid, Spain; Oriental Inst., Univ. of Naples. Appts. Incl: Nat. Dpty., 1934-42; Dir., Soc. Provision Bank, 1943; Catedratico, Fac. of Humanities, Montevideo, 1948-74; Prof., Inst. of Profs., Uruguay, 1952-74; Hon. Dir., Histl. Mus. of City of Montevideo, 1969. Mbrships. incl: Exec. Comm., Int. Comm. on Histl. Scis.; Real Academia de la Historia, Madrid. Publs: Francisco de Vitoria, 1943; Philippe II et la Saint-Barthélemy, 1939; Acuña de Figueroa, 1968; Andrés Bello, 1932. Hons. incl: Grand Off., Order of Infante D. Enrique of Portugal; Grand Off., Crown of Belgium, Condor of Los Andes of Bolivia; Hon. Mbr., num. socs. Address: Paysandú 963, Montevideo, Uruguay.

PISAR, Samuel, b. 18 Mar. 1929. International Lawyer; Author. Educ: Queen's Coll. & Melbourne Univ., Australia, 1953; Harvard Univ., U.S.A., LL.M., 1955; S.J.D., 1959; Univ. Paris, France, LL.D., 1969. Appts: w. Oswald Burt & Co., Solicitors, Melbourne, Australia, 1953-54; Legal Counsel, Off., Dir-Gen., UNESCO, Paris, France, 1956-58; Law Off. Hays, Busby & Rivkin, N.Y., Wash. & Paris, 1959-60; Mbr., Pres. Kennedy's Task Force on For. Econ. Policy, 1960-61; Advsr., Jt. Econ. Comm. of Congress, Wash., 1962; Prof. & Sr. Ptnr., Int. Law Offs., Paris, France, 1962-. Mbrships: Wash. D.C. & Calif. Bars; Barrister-at-Law, Gray's Inn, London, U.K.; Counseil Juridique, Paris, France. Publs: A New Look At Trade Policy Toward The Communist Bloc, 1961; Coexistence And Commerce, 1970; 2nd ed., '71; Les Armes De La Paix, 1971; Transactions Entre l'Est Et L'Ouest, 1972; Num. articles on econ., pol. & legal topics. Hons: Interne, UN, N.Y., 1955; Addison Brown Prize, Harvard Univ., 1956; Chmn., Int. Confs. East-West Trade & Indl. Coopn., N.Y., 1969; Vienna, 1971; Warsa, 1972; Budapest, 1973. Address: 20 Place de la Madeleine, 75008, Paris, France. 43, 91, 92.

PISCHEDDA, Giovanni, b. 11 July 1918. University Professor. Educ: Grad. of Univ. of Rome, 1940; Libero Docente in Italian Lit., 1956; Preside di Liceo, 1956. Appts: Prof. of Italian Lit., Univ. of Aquila; Dir., Inst. Dialectol., Univ. Roseto. Mbrships. incl: Acad. Tiberina; Acad. of Sci., Lettere & Arti, Milan. Publs. incl: Tematica Dantesca, 1955, 1969; Classicita provinciale, 1956; L'orrido e l'ineffabile nella tematica dontesio, 1958; L'elegia nello Tematica dantesca, 1966; about 500 other publs. Hons: Cmdr., Order of Merit of Repub. of Italy; Grand Cross of Cavaliers of Colombo, Brazil. Address: Villa Eclisse, Aquila, Italy. 43.

PITIS, Marcella-Eugenia (Mrs. Ion Pitis) b. 12 June 1914. Medical Endocrinologist. Educ: M.D., Fac. of Med., Bucharest, Rumania, 1939; Docent Dr. Med. Sci., 1962. Appts: Asst., Inst. of Med. & Pharmacol., Bucharest, 1940-47; Lectr., 1947-50; Asst. Prof.-Prof., Inst. of Endocrinol. Contbr. to sci. publs. Recip., var. 1950-; Hd., Clin. Rsch. Dept., 1947-70; Dir. Adjoint, 1970-. Mbrships: Acad. Med. Scis.; V.P., Rumanian Soc. Endocrinol.; Int. Soc. Endocrinol., Gerontol. & Comparative Endocrinol. Contvr. to sci. publs. Recip., var. distinctions & medals. Address: Inst. of Endocrinol. C.I. Parhon, Bd. Aviatorilor, No. 34, Bucharest, Sector, 1, Rumania.

PITMAN, Naomi K., b. 22 June 1908. Pediatrician. Educ: M.D., Loma Linda Univ., Calif., 1931-35; Intern, L.A. Gen. Hosp., Calif., 1935-36; Res., L.A. City Maternity Hosp., 1936, San Luis Obispo Hosp., Calif., 1936-37. Appts. Incl: Schl. Hlth. Serv. & Pvte. Prac., 1937-41; Inst., Loma Linda Univ., 1937-41, Asst. Prof. - Assoc. Prof., 1960-73, Dir., ICU Nursery, Loma Linda Univ. Hosp., 1972-73, Sr. Attng. Pediatrician, Univ. Hosp., 1973; Staff, Chulumani Hosp., Bolivia, 1943-45; Dir., Guyarmarin Hosp., Bolivia, 1946-48; Pediatric Res., White Mem. Hosp., L.A., Calif., U.S.A., 1948-50; Assoc. Prof. Pediatrics, Madison Hosp., Tenn., 1951-60; Dir., L.A. Co. Premature Follow-Up Clin., 1960-66; currently tchng. Newborn Med., Autonomous Univ. of Guadalajara, & Ramon Garabay Hosp., Mexico. Mbr., profl. orgs. Recip., Hon. Plaque, Dept. Pediatrics, Loma Linda Univ. Schl. of Med., 1973. Address: Apartado 5-414, Guadalajara Jalisco, Mexico. 5, 17, 138.

PITTARD, Jean-Jacques Léonard, b. 14 Apr. 1906. Engineer; Scientific Journalist. Educ: Lic., Natural Scis.; Engr.-Prospector Dip.; Docteur és scis. Appts: var. prospecting expeditions, Europe & Morocco; Dir. of Mines, Oubangui; Engr.-Advsr., Gold & Diamond Mines, Ctrl. Africa; Hd., Scientific Rsch. Mission, Africa; Corres., var. newspapers; Explorer, Swiss Speleol. Soc. Mbrships. incl: Swiss Natural Scis. Soc.; Acad. Soc. of Geneva. Publs. incl: Le gisement d'asphalte de Volland-Pyrimont; La recherche de l'or dans la région de Genéve; Une nouvelle station lacustre dans le Leman Thérapeutiques indigénes de la lèpre in Oubangui-Chari; Une grotte m'a dit. . . ; Le rôle des cavernes dans le folklore savoyard. Hons. incl: Fndr., Assn. of Eng.-Prospectors. Address: 36 Ave. Eugene-Pittard, CH 1206 Geneva, Switzerland.

PITTENGER, Norman, b. 23 July 1905. Clergyman; Author; Professor. Educ: Princeton Univ.; Oxford Univ., U.K.; Gen. Theol. Sem., N.Y.; S.T.B.; S.T.M.; S.T.D. Appts: Instr., Gen. Sem., N.Y., 1935-52; Prof., ibid, 1952-65; Mbr., Divinity Fac., Cambridge Univ., U.K. 1966-. Mbr., some-time Pres., Am. Theol. Soc. Publs. incl: Process Thought & Christian Faith; God in Process; Time for Consent: Making

Sexuality Human; Life in Christ; Christology Reconsidered. Hons: Doct., Berkeley Divinity Schl., 1952; Doc., Gen. Sem., N.Y., 1966. Address: King's Coll., Cambridge, U.K.

PITTENGER, Richard Morgan, b. 12 Oct. 1912. Public Relations Practitioner. Educ: Grad., Interview & Classification Prog. U.S. Naval Stn., Bainbridge, Md.; Educ. Prog., Farmers Grp. Inc. Appts. incl: Publicity Dept., RKO Studios, 1930-37; Publicity Dept., 20th Century Fox Studios, 1937-42; Chief Petty Off., U.S. Coast Guard, 1942-44 inclng. Lend-Lease to War Shipping Admin., 1944-46; Ken Murray Prods., 1946-49; V.P. P.R., Farmers Ins. Grp., 1949-; Chmn of Bd., Farmers Ins. Grp. Safety Fndn., 1969-; Instr., P.R., Schl. of Pub,. Admin., Univ. of Southern Calif., 1969-. Mbrships. incl: Cmdr., Am. Legion Post 707; Dir of Special Events, L.A. Co. Coun. of the Am. Legion; Chmn., Ways & Means Commn., Am. Legion, Dept. of Calif.; Coord., Nat. Govs. Conf., Colo. Springs, 1969; Dir.-at-Large, Portland Rose Festival; Exec. Sec., Doolittle Raiders' Reunion; Bd. of Govs., Arthritis Fndn.; Past Mbr., Bd. of Consultors, Wilshire Ct. Chmbr. of Comm. Prod. & Dir., Stage, TV, Film & Outdoor Shows. Recip. of Special Serv. Award, Delinquency Control Inst. of Schl of Pub. Admin., Univ. of Southern Calif., 1973 Address: 4680 Wilshire Blvd., Los Angeles, CA 90010, U.S.A 24, 27.

PITTS, Donald Lee, b. 15 Dec. 1940. Attorney at Law. Educ: Grad., Bluefield State Coll., Bluefield W. Va., 1965, N.C. Ctrl. Univ., Durham, 1970; Duke Univ, Durham, N.C. Appts: Engl. Tchr., Clarkesville H.S., Va., 1967-68; Law Students' Civil Rsch. Counsel Intern, 1968-69; Legal Assistance Fndn. for Community Dev., Durham, N.C., 1969; Staff Asst., Durham Legal Aid Clin., 1969-70; Dir., Legal Servs., Raleigh Co. Community Action Assn., 1970-72; Acting Dir., ibid, 1972. Pvte. Prac., 1972; Gen Counselor, Beckley Urban Renewal Authority, 1972-; Vis. Lectr. on Civil Rights, Univ. of W. Va., 1972 & 72; Pres., Miss Black Teenage W. Va. Pageant Inc., 1972-73, Denise Enterprises Cons. Assn., 1973. Mbrships. incl: NAACP, 1960; CORE, 1961; Appalachian Aide, Southern Christian Ldrship. Conf., 1961-69; Bd. of Dirs., Law Students' Civil Rights Rsch. Coun., 1966-70; Bd. of Dirs., Dirs. Planning League for Action NOW, Durham, N.C., 1968-69; Bd. of Dirs., Raleigh Co. Civic League, 1971-. Publs: Handbook for Welfare Rights Organizers in the State of North Carolina, 1968; contbr. to Profiles in Black, radio stn. WOAY, 1974. Hons. incl: Man of the Yr. Award, We Exist, 1969; W. Publ. Award for Ct. Excellence, 1970; Cert. of Appreciation, Kiwanis Club, Beckley, W. Va., 1972. Address: 415 S. Fayette St., Beckley, WV 25801, U.S.A. 6, 125.

PITZALIS, Giovanni Battista, b. 14 Apr. 1906. Italian Government Official; Master of Public Law. Educ: Grad. in Law. Appts: Nat. Coun. Mbr., Christian Democrat Party, & Dpty., Italian Parliament, 1953-72; Superior Dir. & Inspr., Tech. Inst. Br., Min. of Pub. Educ.; Mbr., Permanent Parliamentary Commns. on Educ & Art. Constitutional & For. Affairs; Mbr. & Sec., Parliamentary Commn. of Investigation of Crime in Sardinia; Mbr., Nat. Commn. on Reform in Pub. Admin.; Sec. Gen., & Nat. Coun. Mbr., Fedn. of State Dirs.; Sec. Gen., MPE Dependent Grads. Hons: Cavalier of Sovereign Mil. Order of Malta; Merit Cmdr. of Repub. of Italy. Address: Viale O. Atlantico N.244, 00144, Rome, Italy.

PIZANI BURNAY, José Eduardo, b. 17 June 1924. Theatre Director; Antique

Collector. Educ: Lyceum Course, Fac. of Law; Theatre Course, Nat. Conservatory of Lisbon, Portugal, 1954. Appts. incl: Assocd. w. many Theatres inclng. Monumental Avenida, Trindade, Nacionald Maria & w. films & TV inclng. prog. for Portuguese TV entitled The Arms & The Man, 1958; Asst. Dir., Portuguese Opera Co., Teatro da Trindade (FNAT), Lisbon, 1967-; Antique Collector, mainly of European Arms & Armour, Toby-Jugs, Walking Sticks, Rings, Masonic Objects & Decorations, Amulets, Talismen & engraved Gems & Seals. Mbrships: V.P., Portuguese Acad. Antique Arms; Arms & Armour Soc., London, U.K.; Acad. di San Marciano, Torino, Italy; Gremio Literario, Lisbon; Soc. Jules Verne Paris, France. Publs. incl: Le Noel Sur La Place, 1960; Catalogue of Fire-Arms, Pizani Burnay Collection, 1963; articles & translations. Hons. incl: Nat. Conservatory Award, Lisbon; Eduardo Brazão Award; Augusto Rosa Award. Address: 3 Rua Direita, Paco Do Lumiar, Lisbon 5, Portugal. 43, 105, 133.

PIZZIRANI, Guglielmo di Zancati, b. 11 Mar. 1903. Diplomat. Educ: Studies in jurisprudence. Appts: Consul, Locarno, Switzerland, 1948; Counsellor, Embassy in Paris, 1951-58; Chef. Adj., Min., NATO, 1958-61; Cons. Gen., Toulouse, France; Cons. Gen., Lugano, Switzerland & Min. Plenipotentiary, Canton of Tessin, ibid 1963-68. Mbrships: Nuovo Circolo degli Seacchi; Golf Club of Rome. Author of sev. articles for specialist Italian publs. Hons: Grand Off. of Italian Repub.; Off., Légion d'Honneur. Address: 142 Via Ripetta, Rome, Italy.

PLACE, Marian Templeton (Mrs. Howard T. Place), b. 1910. Librarian. Educ. B.S.L.S., Univ. of Minn.; B.A., Rollins Coll. Appts: Children's & Schl. Libn., num. locations; currently, Dir., Adult Servs., Jackson Co. Lib. System, Medford, Ore. Mbrships: Ore. & Mont. Lib. Assns.; Ore. & Southern Ore. Histl. Socs.; P.E.O.; Western Writers of Am. Publs: under own name & pen name of Dale White has publd. 40 books, 3 for adults & 37 for teen-aged children. Hons: 2 times winner, Best Western Juvenile Novel, & 2 times winner, Best Western Juvenile Non-fiction, Western Writers of Am.; 4 Lit. Guild Selections. Address: Box 548, Jacksonville, OR 97530, U.S.A. 30.

PLACER, Alejandro Eliso, b. 9 June 1931. Civil Engineer. Educ: Land Surveyor, Fac. of Engrng., Univ. of Buenos Aires, Argentina, 1958; Civil Engineer, ibid, 1963. Appts. incl: various positions-Hd., Opl. Radiological Protection Dept. & Dpty. Hlth. Phys. Mrg., Comisión Nacional de Energia Atómica, 1958-; Lectr., acad. courses, ibid, 1958-; Sec., Advsry. Bd. on Radioisotopes Applications; Advsr. on Radiodosimetry, Clinica Pueyrredón, 1959-. Dept. of High Energy, Univ. Hosp. Jose de San Martin, 1967- & Inst. Acevedo, 1969-; Lectr., acad. courses, Univ. of Montevideo, Uruguay & Cuyo, Buenos Aires, Tucuman, Sur, Litoral ỹ Rosario, Argentina; attended num. confs. on atomic radiations, nuclear med., hlth. phys. etc.; Advsr. to Argentine Delegn., UN Sci. Comm. on Effects of Atomic Radiations, 1961-65, 1967 & 1972. Mbrships. incl: Fndr., Argentine Assn. Biologia y Med. Nuclear, 1963, V.P., 1970, Pres., 1971. Recent Publs. incl: Aspectos Radiosanitarios En La Evaluación De Emplazamientos De Centrales Nucleares 1970; Diagrama Para El Empeleo Práctico Del Concepto De Dosis Standard Nominal, 1973. Address: Ayacucho 1497-6°-A--, Buenos Aires (53), Argentina. 136.

PLAMBECK, Charles Randolph, b. 20 Oct. 1932. Civil Engineer. Educ: Calif. Inst. of

Technol., Pasadena, 1950-52; UCLA, 1953-55; Kokusai Gakkyu Kai, Tokyo, Japan, 1959. Appts: Surveyor, Co. of L.A., 1957-58; Civil Engr., ibid, 1960-64; Construction Supt., Baize Int. Inc., Seoul, Korea, 1959; Sr. Construction Engr., Arabian Am. Oil Co., Saudi Arabia, 1965; Chief Master Planner, Adrian Wilson Assocs., Tokyo, Japan, 1966-67; Sr. Civil Engr., Daniel Mann Johnson & Mendenhall, L.A., 1968; Owner, Charles Plambeck Assocs. & Coastal Dev. Co., Fallbrook, Calif., 1967-. Designer or Constructor of num. bldgs. or facilities inclng: Seoul Int. Airport, 1959; Master Plan of Air Base, Chu Lai, Vietnam, 1966; Calif. Rancho Mobile Village, Warner Springs, 1971. Mbrships: Nat. Soc. Profl. Engrs.; Am. Soc. Civil Engrs.; Calif. Water Quality Control Fedn.; Far. E. Soc. of Archts. & Engrs.; Soc . of Am. Mil. Engrs. Address: 1002 N. Orange Ave., Fallbrook, CA 92028, U.S.A. 9.

PLANCKE, Robert Léone René, b. 28 May 1911. University Professor. Educ: Dr. of Philos. & Letters, Univ. of Ghent, Belgium, 1933; Licentiate in Educ., ibid, 1939. Appts. incl: Prof., Hist. of Educ. & of Comp. Educ., Fac. of Psychological & Pedagogical Scis., Univ. of Ghent, 1946-; Pres.-Dir., Int. Secretariat for the Univ. Study of Educ., Ghent, 1953-; Dean, Fac. of Psychological & Pedagogical Scis., Univ. of Ghent, 1952-54; V.P., Univ. of Ghent, 1961-71; Dir., Ctr. for the Study of the Hist. of Educ., Ghent, 1961-; Vice-Rector, Univ. of Ghent, 1971-73; Pres., Ctr. for the Comp. Study of Higher Educ., Ghent, 1971-; Hon. V.P., Univ. of Ghent, 1971-; Hon. Vice-Rector, ibid, 1973-. Mbrships. incl: Pres. of Coun., Int. Assn. for the Advancement of Educl. Rsch., 1957-73; Hon. Pres. of Coun., ibid, 1973-; Bd. of Admin., Belgian Nat. Fndn. for Sci. Rsch., 1967-; Int. Bur. for the Study of Problems relating to the Tchng. of Greek & Latin. Author of num. publs. in field, of hist. of educ. & classical philol. Recip. of mil., civil & acad. awards. Address: A. Baertsoenkaai 3, 9000 Ghent, Belgium. 87.

PLASIL, Franz, b. 28 Mar. 1912. Retired Civil Servant & Professor. Educ: Comm. Univ., Prague, Czechoslovakia & St. Gallen, Switzerland. Appts. incl: M.P., Bohemia, 1945-51; Econ. Affairs Officer, U.N., 1951-72; Spec. Asst., Exec. Dir., UN Ind. Dev. Org., 1967-72; Vis. Prof., Univ. of Turin, Italy, 1960-65; Prof., Dean, Fac. of Econ. & Soc. Sci., Nat. Univ. of Rwanda, 1966-67; Hon. Advsr., Austrian Inst. of Econ. Rsch., Vienna, Austria, 1968-73; Cons., IBM Austria & Austroplan & Austrian Engrng. Co. Ltd., Vienna. Contbr. to var. jrnls. Hons: Revolutionary Medal, Czech., 1945; St. Sava Order, Yugoslavia Iron Crown Order, Rumania; Grand Medal of Hon., Austria, 1973; Prize, Theodor Körner Fndn., 1959, 65. Address: Haemeaustr. 19/7, A 1190 Vienna, 19, Austria. 86.

PLASS, Herbert Fitz Randolph, b. 17 July 1912. Physician. Educ: S.B., MIT, 1934; S.M., ibid, 1935; M.D., Harvard Univ., Mass., 1939; Intern, Univ. Hosp., Cleveland; Res., New Engl. Med. Ctr. Hosp., Boston & Univ. of Minn. Hosps., Mpls.; Cert., Am. Bd. Internal Med., 1947. Appts: Flight Surg., Capt., USAAF, 1942, '46; Clin. Prof., Internal Med., Univ. of Minn. Mbrships: AMA; FACP; FACCP; Minn. Acad. of Med.; Mpls. Acad. of Med.; Am. Soc. of Internal Med.; AMI; Boylston Soc. Contbr. of 20 articles in sci. jrnls. or Symposia. Address: 1935 Med. Arts Bldg., Mpls., MN 55402, U.S.A. 8, 22.

PLASTOW, David Arnold Stuart, b. 9 May 1932. Company Director. Educ: Culford Schl.,

Bury St. Edmunds, U.K. m. Barbara Ann May, 1954; 1 son, 1 daughter. Appts. incl: Motor Car Div., Rolls-Royce Ltd., Crewe, 1958; Factory Sales Mgr., 1960-63; Marketing & Contracts Mgr., 1963-67; Marketing Dir., 1967; Mng. Dir., Motor Car Div., Rolls-Royce Ltd., 1971; Mng. Dir., Rolls-Royce Motors Ltd., 1972. Mbrships. incl: V.P., Soc. of Motor Mfrs. & Traders; Automobile Golfing Soc. Address: Rolls-Royce Motors Ltd., Pym's Ln., Crewe, Cheshire, CW1 3PL, U.K. 34, 123.

PLATEN. (Baron) Carl Henrik G:son von, b. 14 Dec. 1913. Business Executive & Ambassador. Educ: B.P., M. Pol. Sci.; Lund University, Sweden; London · Schl. of Economics, U.K.; Sorbonne, Paris, France. Appts: Entered For. Serv. 1939; served in Moscow, Rome, Ankara, Washington, D.C., Geneva, Paris: Rep. to U.N. & other int. orgs., Geneva, 1959; Ambassador, ibid, 1960-63; Ambassador at Large & Negotiator, UN Disarmament Conf., 1963; Swedish Rep., OECD, Paris, 1964-72, UNESCO, 1965-72; Chmn., OECD Ind. Comm., 1966-72; Chmn., Nya Asfalt AB, 1967; Chmn., A. Johnson & Cie., Paris, 1973-; Chmn., BINAB AB, Gothenburg, Sweden, 1973-. Publs: Diplomati & Politik, 1966; articles on int. pol. & economic problems. Address: 124 Blvd. Maurice Barrès, 92200 Neuilly-sur-Seine, France. 34, 43.

PLATON, George, b. 1 Apr. 1910. Pianist; Composer; Professor of Piano. Educ: student of Thisseas Pindios, Alecos Condis & Marcios Varvoglis, Greek Conservatory. Educ: Prof., Piano, Greek Conservatory, 1935-; Dir., Greek Conservatory, Sparti, 1932-33 & Heraklion, Crete, 1936-38; Pianist, Orch. of Royal Palace, 1949-64; Pianist (Maestro Sostituto), Nat. Opera of Athens; has given many recitals in Athens & other Greek cities. Mbrships: Union of Greek Composers; Union of Profs. of Conservatory; Panhellenic Union of Musicians; V.P., Union of 'Friends of Music', Greece, 1954-58. Has composed num. works which have been performed by Symph. Orch. of Athens, Orch. of Greek Radio & TV, & in recitals in Greece, Germany, France, U.K, U.S.A. Russia & Spain. Works. incl: 2 Sonatas for Violin & Piano; Sonata for Piano; Minoic Seremony (music for chorodrama officially played in Crete & Salonica by 'Lyceum of Greek Ladies'). Address: Asclipiou 169-171, Athens 705, Greece. 43.

PLATTOR, Emma E. Professor. Educ: B.A., Bklyn. Coll., 1952; M.A., ibid, 1956; Ed. D., Univ. of Rochester, 1966. Appts: Tchr., N.Y.C. Pub. Schls., 1952-56; Dir., Guidance Dept., Secondary Schl., Plainview, N.Y., 1956-59; Test Dev., N.Y. State Educ. Dept., 1959-60; Schl. Admnstr., Plainview N.Y., 1960-63; Lectr., Schl. of Educ., Univ. of Rochester, 1963-64; Asst. Prof., Schl. of Educ., Auburn Univ., Alá., 1964-66 & Ctr. for Tchr. Educ., Tulane Univ., 1966-68; Cons., Ford Fndn. Proj., New Orleans, La., 1966-68; Assoc. Prof., Fac. of Educ., Univ. of Calgary, Canada, 1968-. Mbrships. incl: Pres., Calgary Film Soc.; Sec., Canadian Coun. of Tchrs. of Engl. & Alta. Engl. Coun.; Edit. Bd., Jrnl. of Educ. Thought; Phi Beta Kappa; Kappa Delta Pi. Publs: The Leaf Not the Tree-Teaching Poetry Through Film & Tape (multi-media set), 1971; Action English 1, 1973; Writing, Editing Polishing, scheduled for 1975; articles in profl. jrnls. Has done 2 TV series: Eyes, Ears, Nose Against the World (w. tchrs. guide), 1971 & What If (w. tchrs. guide), 1973. Address: c/o Fac. of Educ., Dept. of Curric. & Instrn., Univ. of Calgary, Calgary, Alberta, Canada T2N 1N4. 138.

PLAUT, Berta Gertrud, b. 20 June 1898. Retired Librarian. Educ: B.L.S., Columbia Univ., 1943. Appts. incl: Cataloger, U.S. Nat. Lib. of Med., 1945-46; Hd. Libn., Temple Emmanuel, N.Y. 1946-49; Cataloger, N.Y. Pub. Libs., 1949-52; Cataloger to Incunabula, Bryn Mawr Coll. Lib., 1952-53; Cataloger, For. Langs. & Rare Books (Fac. Status), W. Va. Univ. Lib., 1953-63. Mbrships. incl: Am., W. Va. & Special Lib. Assns.; Bibliographic Soc. Am.; AAAS; AAUW; Centro Studi e Scambi Int., Rome (Recip., Dip. of Merit; Morgantown Art Assn. (Artists of Month. Dec. 72-Jan. 73); Bibliographical Soc., Univ. of Va.; Smithsonian Assoc., Nat. Hist. Soc., Gettysburg, Pa. Contbr. to W. Va. Libs. Radiations. Participant in art exhibs. inclng: I.P.A., Wash. D.C., 1970, 72, 73; Oil painting in 'Panorama Ind. D'Art Contemporaine' (in series 'Cahiers d'Art de l'Academie Leonardo Da Vinci). Recip. of Award, Personalities of the South. Address: 236 S. High St., Apt. 3, Morgantown, WV 26505, U.S.A. 5, 6, 22, 28, 42, 57, 125.

PLEASANTS, Arthur Ben, b. 4 Aug. 1940. Poet; Teacher. Educ: B.A., Hofstra Univ.; Grad., Univ. of Calif. at L.A. Appts: Tchr., Engl., Brentwood, N.Y., 1962; Theatre Reviewer, L.A. Times, 1968-69; Tchr., L.A. City Schls., 1970-. Mbrships: Phi Sigma Kappa; Conservative Christian Anarchists Soc.; Fndr., Jacobin. Publs: The Gluttons (play), 1968; Tao in the Winter Mountains, 1972; 53 Stations in the Tokaido, 1973; Transcontinental, 1974. Contbr. to num. periodicals. Address: 321 S. Doheny, Beverly Hills, CA 90211, U.S.A.

PLENGE, Erich, b. 15 Sep. 1910. Newspaper Publisher. Educ: Dip., Univs. of Heidelberg & Bonn, 1930-33. Appts: Publr., Diepholzer Kreisblatt, Schröder & Plenge, Diepholz; Publr. & Ed., Alt-Hannoverscher Volkskalendar annual; Assoc., Alfred Wegenr Steel, Emden/Ostfriesland. Mbrships: Verband Nordwestdeutscher Zeitungsverleger im Bundesverband Deutscher Zeitungsverleger; Rotary Club, Diepholz. Contbr. to Diepholzer Kreisblatt & Alt-Hannoverscher Volkskalender. Address: 2828 Sulingen i.Han., Postfach 117 - Lindenstrasse 13, German Fed. Repub. 43, 92.

PLESCH, Arpad, b. 25 Mar. 1889. Royal Consul of Hungary. Educ: Doctor in Law, Universities of Budapest, Hungary, Paris, France, Berlin, Germany, & Oxford, U.K. Married to Countess Maria Wurmbrand-Stuppach. Appts. incl: Royal Consul of Hungary; Board Member, I.G.Farbenindustrie, Frankfort, German Fed. Rep. Mbrships. incl: Yacht Club de France; St.-James's Club, London, U.K. Publs. incl: La Clause Or; The G Clause, Die Oesterrlishische Volkerbundanleihe; Mille et Un Livres Botaniques de la Collection Arpad Plesch. Address: P.O. Box 168, Monte-Carlo, Monaco. 91.

PLESCH, Peter Hariolf, b. 14 Feb. 1918. University Reader in Chemistry. Educ: Trinity Coll., Univ. of Cambridge, U.K.; Sc.D.; ibid, 1970; Ph.D., Univ. of Manchester, 1946. Appts: Rsch. Chem., Brit. Pottery Rsch. Assn., 1940-42, Cefoil, Ltd., 1942-44; Asst. Lectr., Univ. of Manchester, 1946-50; Lectr., Sr. Lectr., Rdr., Univ. of Keele, U.K., 1951-73. Mbrships: Fellow, Royal Inst. of Chem., 1952; Chem. Soc.; Soc. Chem. Ind.; World Acad. Arts & Sci.; Soc. Psychical Rsch.; Oriental Ceramic Soc. (twice on Coun.); Glass Collectors Circle; 4-man Comm., Carl Duisberg Stiftung zur Fortbildung von Deutschen Studierenden der Medizin, 1957. Publs: Ed., 2 Chem. Rsch. Monographs; has written more than 80 papers in learned jrnls. on var. aspects of chem., & 12 on non-chem. subjects, inclng. antique glass & Chinese Ceramics. Recip., Visitor of Yr. Award, Royal Australian Chem. Inst., 1971. Address: Chem. Dept., Univ. of Keele, Newcastle, N. Staffs., ST5 5BG, U.K. 105.

PLETSCHER, Els, b. 23 June 1908. Sculptress. Educ: Studios of Ernst Dallmann & Alfons Magg; Studied in Paris, Florence & Zurich. Mbr., Zontians Club. One-man exhibitions: Mus. Allerheiligen Schaffhausen, Stein/Rhein; Galleria Spinetti & Galery 14, Florence; Feuerthalen Zurigo Forli; Pontassieve Roma; Group exhibitions in Switzerland, U.S.A. & Italy, inclng. Mostra dellow Sport, 20 premio Biennale, Fiorino, Florence. Works incl: Statue in bronze, Hosp., Schaffausen, Zürcher Kantonalbank; Madonna, grande place Vals.; Donna senza maschera, Schaffhausen theatre. Hons. incl: Georg Fischer Prize, 1960; 1st Prize, la donna nell'Arte, Florence, 1971; Int. Prize for 'Crescendo', Massa, 1972, & for 'Bar', Carrara, 1973. Address: Monte Muscoli, 50014 Fiesole, Florence, Italy.

PLITT, Jeanne Given (Mrs F. C. Plitt, Jr.), b. 27 Aug. 1927. Librarian. Educ: A.B., Univ. of Md., 1949; M.S.L.S., Cath. Univ., 1968. Appts: Army Special Servs. Libn., 1949-52; Lib. Asst., Alexandria Lib., Va., 1958-60; Tchr., Fairfax, Va., 1960-62; Ref. Libn., Alexandria Lib., 1962-68; Asst. Dir., ibid, 1968-70; Dir., 1970-. Mbrships: Va. Lib. Assn.; Chmn., Libns. Tech. Comm., Coun. of Govts., 1970-71; Little Theatre Assn., Alexandria Assn.; Zonta Club Int. (sec., Alexandria Chapt., 1972-73; Govng. Bd. Dirs., ibid, 1973-74); PTLA, Civic Assn. Address: Alexandria Lib., 717 Queen St., Alexandria, VA 22314, U.S.A.

PLOMLEY, Roy. Playwright & Broadcaster. Appts: Copy-writer, London Advt. Agcy.; Actor, all forms of entertainment from Grand Opera to Pantomime; Res. Announcer, French radio stns., Radio Normandy, Poste Parisien & Radio Int., 1936-40; Produced progs. for these stns., recording in London & Paris; Produced first film in U.K. made especially for TV. Mbrships incl: Chmn., Exec. Comm., Radio & TV Writers Assn., 1957-59; Chmn., Provisional Comm. of Radiowriters Assn., 1960; Chmn., Exec. Comm., Radiowriters Assn., 1960-62. Author of 15 plays inclng: Home & Dry, 1964; The Lively Oracles (w. John Allegro), 1965; Moonlight Behind You, 1967; You're Welcome to my Wife, adap. from French, 1971; Just Plain Murder, 1972. Has devised many popular radio series inclng. Desert Island Discs. Address: 91 Deodar Rd., London SW15 2NU, U.K.

PLÖNES, Heino (Friedrich), b. 16 June 1924. Industrial Manager. Educ: Cologne Univ., Germany. Appts: Confidential Clerk-Dir., H.G. Essener Steinkohle, Mannesmann AG.; Dir., Mannesmann-Export AG. Mbrships: V.P., Düsseldorfer Aero-Klub e.V.; Steuben-Schurz-Gesellschaft E.V., Düsseldorf. Hons: Hon. Citizen, City of New Orleans, 1973; Kt. of Grace, Sovereign Order, St. John of Jerusalem, Kts. of Malta, 1973; Gold Medal, Arts, Scis., Letters, Paris, France, 1972; Consul, Ville de Cannes, 1972; Chev., Ordre de la Courtoisie Française, 1971. Address: Drakestrasse 3, D-4000 Düsseldorf, 11 German Fed. Repub.

PLOUVIER, Philippe, b. 25 Nov. 1929. Director of Companies. Kenyon Coll., Gambia, Ohio, U.S.A., 1950; Diplomè de L'Institut d'Etudes Politiques de Paris, 1952. Appts: Mng. Dir., Tissages de Conflans Faverney (France), & Ets. J. Haffner S.A., until 1963; Finance Mgr., PAULSTRA S.A. grp. of cos., Dir. of subsidiaries, S. Africa, Belgium, Spain, until

1970; Mng. Dir., Pradoval S.A., Sierra Nevada, Granada, Spain, until 1973; currently, Dir., SICEO, BLAVIER, & Mng. Dir., A.L.F.A., mgt. consultancy co. Address: 3 Rue Antoine Arnauld, 75016 Paris, France. 91.

PLOWDEN, Gene Daley, b. 1 Feb. 1906. Newspaper Reporter; Author. Educ: B.S., Clemson Univ. Appts: Sports Ed., Sarasota Daily Tribune, Fla., 4 yrs.; Reporter, United Press, 1938-43; USN, in communications, then Ed., Navy News, 1943-45; Reporter, Assocd. Press, 1945-69; Ed., Greyhound Racing Record, 1969; currently writer, books & mag. articles. Mbrships. incl: Dir., Circus Histl. Soc.; Circus Fans Assn.; Nat. Turf Writers Assn.; Variety Club; Sigma Delta Chi. Publs. incl: History of Hardee County; Those Amazing Ringlings and Their Circus; This is Horse Racing (co-author); The Jones Boys (co-author); Her Name Was Ulelah. Hons: Special Citation, Fla. Legislature, 1967; Kentucky Colonel, 1968. Address: 720 S.W. 20th Rd., Miami, FL 33129. U.S.A.

PLUM, Dorothy Alice, b. 16 June 1900. Librarian, Educ: A.B., Vassar Coll., 1922; B.L.S., N.Y. State Lib. Schl., 1926. Appts: Asst., N.Y. State Lib., 1923-26; Asst., Columbia Schl. of Lib. Serv., 1926-27; Ref. Libn., Vassar Coll., 1927-45; Bibliographe, Vassar Coll. Lib. 1945-65; Archivist for Centennial, Vassar Coll., 1960-61; Lib. Cons., 1965-. Mbrships: Am. & N.Y. State Lib. Assns.; Essex Co. Histl. Soc. (Trustee. 1970-); Clinton Co. Histl. Assn.; Trustee, Keene, N.Y. Pub. Lib., 1969-; Adirondack Mountain Club (chmn., bibliography comm., 1958-73). Publs. incl: co-author, The Great Experiment, 1961, The Magnificent Enterprise, 1961; Ed., Adirondick Bibliography, 1958, 10-yr. Supplement, 1972. Address: E. Hill, Keene, NY 12942, U.S.A. 5.

PLUMBE, Wilfred John, b. 14 Jan. 1915. Librarian. Appts: Libn., Rsch. Div., Min. of Agric., Sudan Govt., 1949-52; Asst. Libn., Univ. of Malaya, Singapore, 1953-56; Libn., Nigerian Coll. of Arts, Sci. & Technol., Zaria, 1956-59; Univ. Libn., Univ. of Malaya, 1959-62, Ahmadu Bello Univ., Northern Nigeria, 1962-66, Univ. of Malawi, 1966-73, Univ. of Guyana, 1973-. Mbrships: Lib. Assns. of Malaysia (Life Mbr.), Malaya (Past Pres.) & Nigeria (Past Pres.) Publs: Kingdom of earth; poems, 1939; African poems, & others, 1951; Preservation of books in tropical & subtropical countries, 1964; contbr. to num. profl. publs. Address: Univ. of Guyana, Box 841, Georgetown, Guyana, S. America. 135.

PLUMER, Edna Holland, b. 19 Jan. 1911. Artist. Educ: Lebanon Schl. of Nursing, N.Y.C.; Canal Zone Coll., Repub. of Panama; Studied art w. Frances Greening, Elva Fairchild, & Pete Johnson; Creative Writing, Clemson Coll., S.C. Mbrships: Balboa Women's Club; Past Pres., ibid; Sec., Balboa Women's Club; Chmn., Little Gall., Tivoli Hotel, Panama; Nat. League of Am. Pen Women; Intercontinental Biog. Assn.; Inter-Am. Women's Club; Soroptimist Club. Exhibs. of Art: Camden Art Show, 1963, 1964; Nat. League of Am. Penwomen Art Shows; 1-Man Art Show, Little Gall., Tivoli Hotel, Panama & in S.C. Hons. incl: Prize for Still Life, Camden Art Show, 1963; Hon. Mention, ibid, 1964. Address: P.O.Box 727, Camden, SC 29020, U.S.A. 132.

PLUMMER, (Sir) (Arthur) Desmond (Herne), b. 25 May 1914. Chartered Surveyor. Educ: Hurstpierpoint Coll.; Coll. of Estate Mgmt. Appts: Mbr. of St. Marylebone Borough Coun., 1952-65 (Mayor 1958-59); Mbr. of London Co. Coun. for St. Marylebone,

1960-65; Mbr. of Gtr. London Coun. for Cities of London & Westminster, 1964-; Ldr. of Opposition, GLC, 1966-67; Ldr. of GLC, 1967-73; Ldr. of Opposition, 1973-; Mbr. of Inner London Educ. Authority, 1964-; Mbr. South Bank Theatre Bd., 1967-; Mbr. of Standing Conf. on S.E. Planning, 1967-; Mbr. of Transport Co-ordinating Coun. for London, 1967-69; Mbr. of Local Authorities Conditions of Service Advice Bd., 1967-71; Mbr. of Exec. Comm. of Int. Union of Local Authorities, 1967-73; Mbr. of St. John Coun. for London, 1971-; Mbr. of Exec. Comm. of Nat. Union of Conservative & Unionist Assns., 1967-. Fellow, Royal Inst. of Chartered Surveyors; Hon. Fellow, Fac. of Archts. & Surveyors. Publs: Time for Change in Greater London, 1966; Report to London, 1970; Planning & Participation, 1973. Hons: Territorial decoration, 1950; Dpty. Lt. of and for Gtr. London, 1970. Address: 4 The Lane, Marlborough Pl., London NW8 OPN, U.K. 1, 41.

PLUNK, Dolores Maxine (Mrs.), b. 22 Dec. 1926. Educator; Rancher. Educ: B.S., Black Hills State Univ., Spearfish, S.D., 1961; M.A., Tex. Womens Univ., Denton, 1964. Appts. incl: Asst. Prof., Sam Houston State Univ., Huntsville, Tex., 1964-65; Guest Lectr., Tchr. Workshop for Tchrs. of Trainable Retardates, 1972. Asst. Prof., Ctrl. Mo. State Univ., 1965-. Mbrships incl: AAUP; Am. Assn. Univ. Women; Am. Assn. for Hlth. Phys. Educ. & Recreation; Ctrl. Dist. Assn. for Hlth. Phys. Educ. & Recreation; Ctrl. Dist. Assn. for Hlth. Phys. Educ. & Recreation; Mo. Assn. for Hlth. Phys. Educ. & Recreation; Am. Dance Therapy Assn; Kappa Delta Pi; Pi Lambda Theta. Author of 2 papers: Movement & Creativity; A Way to Learn, & Repetition of Temporal Experiences, published 1972. 6 TV tapes produced for Tchr. Educ. Address: Rte. 3, Warrensburg, MO 64093, U.S.A. 5, 8, 22, 132, 138.

POCHOLLE, Georges, b. 26 Mar. 1901. Telecommunication Engineer. Educ: Higher Nat. Schl. of Telecommunications, Paris, France. Appts: Engr.-Chief Regional Engr., Dept. of Telecommunications; Seconded to Secretariat Gen. of Nat. Defence, 1950-56; Chief Telecommunication Engr., 1958; Pres., Civil Telecommunications Comm., 1963; Retired 1966; Pres., La Liaison des Transmissions, 1968-72. Mbrships: French Soc. of Electns., Electronicians & Radioelectns.; French Astronautical Soc.; Radio & Electronic Elders Assn. Publs: Rsch. papers in profl. jrns. Hons. incl: Croix de Guerre, 1939-45; Off., Legion of Honour, 1962; Cmdr., Nat. Order of Merit, 1966. Address: 17 Rue Julien Certain, 78220 Viroflay, France. 43, 91.

PODOSKI, Joseph Junosza, b. 3 Apr. 1900. Electrical Engineer; Economist (ret.'d). Educ: M.S., Warsaw Polytech. Inst., Poland, 1929; M.A., UCLA, U.S.A., 1949. Appts: Sec., Polish Commn., Int. Intellectual Cooperation, 1924-29; Sec. Gen., Polish Nat. Exhib., Poznan, 1929; Sec. Gen., Dir., Assn. Polish Electrical Engrs., 1929-39; Dir., Polish Info. Ctr., Govt. in Exile, U.S.A., 1941-45; Assoc. Prof. of Econ., Immaculate Heart Coll., L.A., Calif., & L.A. State Coll., 1947-53; Sr. Rsch. Specialist, Lib. of Congress, Wash., D.C., 1963-69. Mbrships: Life Mbr., IEEE; Am. Econ. Assn. Publs: Guidance & Control; Power conditioning devices; analytical survey. Hons: Polish Cross of Merit, 1938; French Golden Palmes Academiques, 1929. Address: 3732 Windom Pl., N.W., Wash., DC 20016, U.S.A. 6.

POERTNER, John Paul, b. 28 Aug. 1940. Assistant Professor of Mathematics. Educ:

A.A., Lincoln Coll., 1960; B.S., Northern Ill. Univ., 1962; M.S., Ill. State Univ., 1967; Grad. study, Univ. of Ill., 1972. Appts. incl: Maths. Tchr., San Jose H.S., 1962-67; Maths. Tchr., Lincoln Comm. H.S., 1967-68; Asst. Prof., Lincoln Coll., 1968-; Dir., Ctrl. Ill. Econ. Dev. Corp., 1971. Mbrships: Logan Co. Assn. for Mental Hlth., Pres., 1973, V.P., 1974; Ctrl. Ill. Econ. Dev. Corp., Pres., 1971, Bd. Mbr., 1971-74; Nat. Coun. of Tchrs. of Maths.; AAUP; Math. Assn. of Am.; Am. Statistical Assn.; 1st Presby. Ch., Deacon, 1967-69 Ch. 1969, Trustee, 1971-73 Ch. 1973, Elder, 1974. Hons: Nat. Sci. Fndn. Grants, 1964, 1974. Address: 420 Coll. Ave., Lincoln, IL 62656, U.S.A. 117.

POGGI, Emile, b. 6 July 1912. Ski Instructor; Mountain Guide. Appts: Instr. in skiing, Breuil & Sestrière; Dir., Ski Schl., Clavière; mountain guide, (rescued sev. mountaineers on Mont Blanc, 1933); currently, Tchr. of skiing at Sestrière & Dir./Proprietor, Hotel Edelweiss, Serre-Chevalier. Address: Hotel Edelweiss, Chantemerle/Serre-Chevalier, France.

POGUE, Mary Ellen (Mrs. L. Welch Pogue), b. 27 Oct. 1904. Genealogist; Homemaker. Educ: B.F.A., Univ. of Neb., Lincoln, U.S.A., 1926; Conservatory of Music, Boston, Mass., 1926-29; Kemp Stillings Violin Master Class, N.Y.C., 1939-40. Appts: Mbr., Potomac String Ensemble, 1948-; Histn., Gov. William Bradford Compact, 1966-. Mbrships: Vice Chmn., Montgomery Co., Md., Vicotry Garden Ctr., 1946-47; Pres., Bethesda Community Garden Club, 1946-48; Bd., Montgomery Co. YWCA, 1946-50 & 1952-55; Mayflower Soc.; Nat. Genealogical Soc.; Columbia Histl. Soc.; League of Women Voters; Pres., P.E.O., 1957-59; Pres., Mortar Bd., 1965-67; Delta Omicron; Alpha Rho Tau. Publs: Ed., Favorite Menus & Recipes of Mary C. Edgerton of Aurora, Nebraska, 1963; Ed. & Compiler, Edgerton-Coe History, 1965. Recip., Cert. of Merit, Gov. William Bradford Compact, 1970. Address: 5204 Kenwood Ave., Chevy Chase, MD 20015, U.S.A.

POGUE, Ralph E., b. 1 Dec. 1929. Attorney. Educ: Roosevelt Univ., Chgo., Ill.; LL.B., Cumberland Univ., Lebanon, Tenn.; J.D., Samford Univ., Birmingham, Ala. Appts: Mbr., Bd. of Dirs., Tenn. Tombigbee Water Mgmt., for State of Miss., 1964-72; Co. Campaign Mgr. for Gov. Paul B. Johnson, 1964, for Gov. John Bell Williams, 1968; Mbr. Gov.'s Commn. on Law Enforcement, 1968-72; City Atty., Aberdeen., Miss., 1968-72 Atty., Urban Renewal Agcy., Aberdeen, 1968-72, Aberdeen-Monroe Co. Hosp., 1968-, for Town of Prairie, Miss., 1968-72, Town of Gattmen, Miss. 1969-73; Mbr., Bd. Dirs., Tombigbee Water Valley Authority; Deleg., Democratic Nat. Conven., 1972. Mbr., var. legal orgs. Hon. Mbr. Gov.'s Statt. of Cols., 1964-72. Address: Lakewood Dr., Aberdeen, MS 39730, U.S.A. 125.

POHJANPALO, Jorma. Managing Director. Educ: D.Sc., Helsinki Schl. of Econs., Finland. Appts. incl: var. positions, P.R. & the press, 1931-39; var. ind. & trade assns., 1941-52; Exec. Dir., Finnish Plastics Assn., 1942-67; Mng. Dir., ibid, 1967-73; Mng. Dir., Finnish Maritime League, 1950-54. Mbrships incl: Charter Mbr., Lions Club, Helsinki; Pres., 1963-64; V.P., Suomi-Serra, Assn. for Finns Abroad. Publs. incl: Handbook for Business Life, 1946, 3rd ed., 1953; Commercial Dictionary in Six Languages, 1956; The Sea and Man, 1969; Finnish Shipping & Shipbuilding,

1971. Hons. incl: Kt., 1st Class, Order of the Lion; Cross of Liberty 4th class with swords. Address: Uvilantie 19 g, 00350 Helsinki 35, Finland.

POHL, Jacques P.H., b. 2 Apr. 1909. University Professor. Educ: Royal Mil. Schl., Belgium; Roman Philol., Univ. of Brussels; Licencié en philos. & lettres, 1935; Doct., 1950. Appts. incl: Prof., secondary & tech. levels, 1936-63; Lectr., Univ. of the Congo, Elisabethville, 1960; Lectr.-Prof., Univ. of Brussels, 1960-; Pres., Roman Philol. Sect., ibid & Scientific Coun., Inst. of Phonetics; Vis. Prof., var. univs. Mbrships. incl: Int. Coun. of French Lang.; Roman Linguistic Soc.; Belgian Club of Linguistics. Publs. incl: Temoignages sur la syntaxe du verbe dans quelques parlers français de Belgique, 1962; Symboles et langages, 2 vols., 1968; L'Homme et le signifiant, 1972; Co-Author, Bibliographie de Linguistique romane, 4th ed., 1973. Proposed the term 'demolinguistics' to designate the sci. of facts pertaining to linguistics & demography. Recip., sev. hons. Address: Les Orangers, 16 A Ave. L. Wiener, B-1170 Brussels, Belgium.

POIDEVIN, Leslie Oswyn Sheridan, b. 28 Jan. 1914. Physician & Surgeon. Educ: Fac. of Med., Sydney Univ., Australia, 1932-37; Res. Med. Off., Royal Prince Alfred Hosp., Sydney, 1938-39; M.D., Univ. of Adelaide, 1960; M.S., ibid, 1965. Appts: Capt., Australian Infantry Force, 1940-46; Pvte. Gen. Prac., Scone, N.S.W., 1946-51; Dir. of Obstetrics, Univ. of Adelaide, 1951-57; Rdr., Dept. of Ob. & Gyn., ibid, 1957-69; Pvte. Prac. in Gyn., 1969-. Mbrships: Fellow, Royal Coll of Obstetricians & Gynaecologists; Adelaide Club; Angus Soc. of Australia; Capt., Sydney Univ. Lawn Tennis Club, 1932-37. Publs: Caesarean Section Scars, 1965; Over 30 papers in med. jrnls. Hons: Mention in Despatches, Pacific Zone, 1939-45; Life Gov., Postgrad. Med. Fedn. in Australia, 1973. Address: Wirraninna, Morphett Vale, S.A., Australia, 5162.

POIGNANT, Karl Erik Lennart, b. 22 Mar. 1930. Editor. Educ: Tchr. Examination, Linköping, 1953; Royal Swedish Defence Acad., Stockholm, 1955; studies in Psychol., U.S.A., Mexico, U.K. Appts: Tchr., Norrköping; Radio & TV Prod., Educ. Dept., Swedish Broadcasting; P.R. Off., Swedish Battalion, Congo; News Reporter, Swedish Broadcasting; P.R. Off., UNFICYP, Cyprus; P.R. Mgr. Fecit AB; Freelance Ed., Swedish Broadcasting & different newspapers; P.R. Cons. Mbrships: Publicistklubben; Rotary, Ätvidaberg; Sec., Ätvidaberg Golf & Football Clubs. Contbr., Strategies Psychologiques d'Enterprises, 1970. inc: Films. About Swedish Soccer, 1970; Swedish P.R. Assn. Hons. In the Serv. of Peace Award, UN, 1962, 1964; P.R. Film of the Yr. Award, 1970. Address: Jägarstigen 2, 597 00 Ätvidaberg, Sweden. 24.

POLAN, Nancy Moore (Mrs. Lincoln M. Polan). Artist. Educ: A.B., Marshall Univ., 1936; Huntington Galls. One man exhibs: Charleston Art Gall., 1961, 67, 73; Huntington Galls., 1963, 66, 71; N.Y. World Fair, 1965; W. Va. Univ., 1966; Carroll Reese Mem. Mus., 1967. Grp. Exhibs. incl: Nat. Arts Club, 1962-73; Am. Watercolor Soc. & Annual Framed Travelling Exhib., 1972-73; Allied Artists Am.; Pa. Acad. Fine Arts; Patron at Premi Int. Dibiux Joan Miro; Florence, Italy, 1971; Siena, 1973; Int. Platform Assn. Art Exhib., 1973. Mbrships incl: Nat. Arts Club, N.Y.C.; Leonardo da Vinci Acad.; Centro Studi e Scambi Int; Allied Artists Am. Fed. Arts; Sigma Kappa. Work reproduced, La Revue Moderne, Paris, 1961, 66. Recip., num. awards inclng. Norton Award, Chautauqua Am. Art. Address: 2 Prospect Dr., Huntington, WV 25701, U.S.A.

POLANO, Germano, b. 11 Aug. 1910. Admiral and Nuclear Engineer. Educ: Grad., Naval & Mech. Engrng., Univ. of Genoa, 1936; Grad., Electrotech. Ind. Engrng., Univ. of Pisa, 1951; post-grad. studies in Nuclear Sci,. Appts: Chief Engrng. Instr., Naval Acad., 1945-; Prof. of Thermodynamics, ibid; Asst., Physics, Engrng. Fac., Univ. of Pisa; Hd., Arsenal, Venice; Hd. of Engrng., Mil. Nuclear Ctr., S. Piero a Grado; Gen. Mil. Dir., ibid, 1962-66; Projects Chief, Navy Dept., Rome, 1966-73; Vice-Pres., INSERAN Naval Ctr; Pres., EXCO Nuclear Engrng, Milan, 1973-. Mbr. of Soc. of Italian Archts. & Engrs., 1937-. Works; Course of nuclear terrestrial and naval installations, 1958; Thermodynamics and naval machines, 1965; Nuclear installations for military & naval propulsion; Nuclear Energy and Progress, 1971; Contbr. to Nuclear Engrng. jrnl. Hons. incl: Two bronze war stars & war cross; Order of Italian Kts; Cmdr. of Italian Repub., 1968. Address Via Roma 109/1V°, 57100 Leghorn, Italy.

POLEK, Mittie Plymale Johnson (Mrs. Joseph E. Polek), b. 12 Nov. 1905. Real Estate -Insurance. Educ: Drawns Bus. Coll.; Instrument Flying Schl. for USAF Offs. course; Real Estate Course under H. Bemis Lawerence, Louisville, Ky. Appts. incl: Acctng. Asst. to Admin. Off., Fed. Pub. Housing Authority w. Regional Offs. in Wash. DC & N.Y.; Instrument Flying Schl. for Offs., Scott AFB, Ill.; Fiscal, Cost & Commercial Acctng., ibid; Cost Acctng. for reimbursement of Mil. personnel, Olathe Naval AB, Kan.; Bookkeeper, reorganizing & establishing new system, Off.'s Club, Grandview, AFB, Mo.; Real Estate Salesman, 1956-57; Established own bus. after sucessfully taking Mo. Real Estate Test & currently run co. jointly w. son, Johnson Polek Realtor's, Mo. & Belton, Mo. Mbrships. incl: Am. Bus. Womens Assn.; Better Bus. Bur. of Gtr. Kan. City area; Dir. & former Sec., Treas. & Pres., Midwest Mo. Bd. of Realtors; Pilot Club Int., Ft. Smith, Ark.; Treas., St. Johns Episc. Ch., Ft. Smith, Ark.; Treas., Grandview AFB NCO Wives Club; Trustee, Belvidere Height Lot Owners Assn. Address: 6206 E. 149th St., Grandview, MO 64030, U.S.A.

POLIDORI DI CASTEL PORNELLO, Goffredo, b. 17 Mar. 1916. Journalist; Writer. Educ: tech. studies, Torino & Milan; Cert. Capt. of Ocean-going Vessels, Nautical Inst. G. Caboto, Gaeta. Appts: Capt. of Artillery (Seren), Israel Army, 1st Independence War of Israel, 1948; Jrnlst. (Reporter - Ed.), daily newspaper, 1949-; author of only interview granted by Moshé Pijade, V.P. of Presidium of Repub. of Yugoslavia, which was transmitted by BBC & Radio Am., Oct. 1949. Publs: Jerusalem Without God., 1962; The Seed of Hatred, 1967; num. other lit. works. Hons: Ot Komeniut (mil. decoration of 1st War of Independence), Israel Army. Address: Via del Babuino, 160, Rome, Italy. 43, 95.

POLIN, Claire. Musician. Educ: Mus.B., Mus.M., Mus.D., Phila. Conservatory; further studies, Temple Univ., Juilhard Schl., Tanglewood. Appts: Prof., Composition, Musicol., Flute, Phila. Conservatory, 1949-64; Lectr., Art Hist., Assoc. Prof., Musicol., Theory, Composition, Am. Music, Flute. Mbrships. incl: Bibliotheque Int. de musique Contemporaire; Int. & Am. Musicologic Soc.; Am. Soc. Univ. Composers; AAUP; Am. Music Ctr. Publs: Music of the Ancient Near East,

1954; Flute Method (w. Wm. Kincaid), 5 vols. Articles, int. jrnls., Welsh, Hebrew, Am. music. Compositions incl: String Quartet III; Symphony II (Korean); 1st Flute Sonata; Journey of Owain Madoc, for brass & percussion. Hons. incl: Leverhulme Fellow, Univ. of Wales, 1968-69; Award Commn., Ga. State Univ., 1970; Acad. Study Grant, Rutgers Univ., 1973-74. Address: Music Dept., Rutgers Univ., Camden, NJ 08102, U.S.A. 5, 6, 13, 55, 132.

POLINGER, David H., b. 16 Mar. 1927. Radio & TV Executive. Educ: B.A., Duke Univ., 1949; M.A., N.Y. Univ., 1971. Appts. incl: USN, 1944-46; Dir., Latin Am. Div., Voice of Am., N.Y.C., 1951-52; V.P. & Gen Mgr., var. TV stns., Puerto Rico & N.Y.C., 1953-59; Exec. V.P., Lewis & Polinger Advt. Agcy., Wash. D.C., 1959-60; Nat. Defense Exec. Reserve, Dept. of Defense, 1960-; Civil Air Patrol, 1961-; Communications Cons., CATV Ops., radio & TV, 1961-; Pres., Friendly Frost Broadcast Div., Westbury, N.Y., 1961-70; V.P. Ops., Bell TV Inc. (OTC), N.Y.C., 1970-72; Pres., Suburban Broadcasting Corp (OTC), Central Islip, N.Y., 1973-. Mbr. & Off., var. profl. & community orgs. Holder of Fed. Communications Commn. 3rd Class License, Radio-Telephone License, & Pvte. Pilot License. Recip., Armstrong Mem. Rsch. Fndn. Award, 1968. Address: WSNL-TV, Suburban Broadcasting Corp., Central Islip, NY 11722, U.S.A. 6.

POLITIS, Charles J., b. 23 Jan. 1914. Industrialist. Educ: Schl. of Law, Athens Univ., Greece; B.A., N.Y. Univ., U.S.A.; Grad., Athens Schl. of Music; Grad., N.Y. Schl. of Music. Appts: Concert Pianist; Post w. 20th Century Fox; Major, U.S. Airforce; Mbr., ML Mission to Greece; Post w. UNRAA; Chief Liaison, UNRRA - Greek Govt.; Fndr., APCO Inds. S.A.; Chmn., Bd. of Dirs., & Gen. Mgr., Hellenic Milk Inds. S.A. 'EVGA'. Mbrships: Sec. Gen., Am.-Hellenic Chmbr. of Comm.; Bd. of Govs., Propellor Club, Athens; Yachting Club of Greece; Athens Lawn Tennis Club. Athenian Club. Owner, extensive collect. of ancient Greek art. Recip., sev. mil. awards. Address: 5 Herodou Attikou, Athens, Greece.

POLIVKA, Joan Hickey. International Relations Consultant. Educ: B.S., Univ. of Wis., Lawrence Univ.; Postgrad. work, Oxford Univ., U.K., Univ. Coll., Dublin, Ireland, Univ. of Wis., U.S.A. & Marquette Univ., Milwaukee, Wis. Appts. incl: Former P.R. Asst. to Pres. of large indl. org., Milwaukee, Wis.; Former Community Rels. Coord., Int. Inst. of Milwaukee Co. & Int. Hospitality for city; Organizer & Admnstr. prog. for cultural exhange for Sister Cities int. exhange proj., Mnpls., Minn. Mbrships. incl: U.S. Dept. of State Advsry. Comm. on Int. Orgs.; Status of Women Chmn., Zonta Int.; Co-Fndr. & Bd. Chmn., Peace Corps Serv. Coun. of Minn.; Women's Advsry. Comm., Minn. State Dept. of Human Rights; Co-Fndr. & Chmn., Mnpls. Commn. on Human Rels., Int. Comm.; Nat. P.R. Chmn., Nat. Assn. for For. Student Affairs; Fndg. Comm. mbr.; State-wide Minn. Int. Hospitality Comm.; Charter mbr., Irish Am. Cultural Inst. Publs. incl: Evaluation of Informal Learning Experiences of the International Student in the U.S.; The Child of the Working Mother. Recip. of hons. Address: 405 W. Minnehaha Parkway, Mnpls., MN 55419, U.S.A. 5, 138.

POLK, Lilian Graham, b. 18 June 1901. Teacher, retired. Educ: B.A., H. Sophie Newcomb Coll., Tulane Univ., New Orleans; Doct. level work, Columbia Univ., N.Y.C.; Mstr.'s Degree in Speech, La. State Univ., 1939. Appts. incl: 3rd Grade Tchr. & Sports Coach,

Fairfield Ave. Schl., Shreveport, La., 1925-31; Tchr., Claiborne Ave. Schl., Shreveport, 1931-35; Hist. & Eng. Tchr., Byrd H.S., Shreveport, 1935-50; Tchr., Fair Park H.S., Shreveport, 1950-66; Hd., Speech Depts., Byrd & Fair Park H.S.'; active organizer & participant many extra-curricular schl. activities inclng. Dir., plays, Speech & Debate coaching, Sports coach & work w. handicapped children. Since retirement, artist, exhibiting at sev. One-Man shows, local State & regional shows. Mbrships. incl: Fndr., La. Conclave of Alpha Chapt., Kappa Kappa Iota; Off., NEA; Matthew Agee Chapt., Colonial Dames of the XVII Century; former Pres., Shreveport Chapt., Nat. Daughter's Of Am. Revolution; La. Div., Magna Charta Dames; former Pres., Chapt. 237, United Daughter's of the Confederacy; Off., Nat. Soc. of Arts & Letters. Publs. incl: translation of book, Les Pénsées by Lucienne Holland McKay; num. articles in profl. jrnls.; Ed. & wrote poetry for Newcomb Arcade, Coll. quarterly mag.; Biography, Brigadier Gen. Charles Clark, in prep. Exhibiting Artist, Ark., Tenn., La. & Tex. Address: 4525 Finley Drive, Shreveport, LA 71105, U.S.A.

POLK, Otis C., Jr., b. 15 Mar. 1928. School Administrator. Educ: B.S., Mary Allen Coll., Crockett, Tex., 1950; M.S., Prairie View A & M Coll., 1959; grad. studies, Tex. Christian & Midwestern Univs., & Bishop Coll. Appts: Maths. & Sci. Tchr., Wichita Falls Independent Schls. Dist., Tex., 1959-60; V.P., Wash. H.S., 1960-67; V.P. & Coach, Eastside Jr. H.S., 1967-69; Prin., Hirschi Jr. H.S., 1969-73, New Northwest Jr. H.S., 1973-. Mbrships. incl: Wichita Falls Human Rels. Comm., 1962-; E.Side Community Dev. Assn.; Bd. Dirs., Ctrl. YMCA, 1968-; Kiwanis, 1971-; Bd. Mbr., 1972-74, Past Chmn., Youth Servs. Comm.; TASSP; NASSP. Contbr., poetry, local newspapers. Hons. incl: Serv. to Youth Award, Ctrl. YMCA, 1967-68; Boy Scout Serv. Award, 1968; Nat. Conf. Christian & Jews Annual Brotherhood Award, 1973. Address: 1400 Normandy Dr., Wichita Falls, TX 76303, U.S.A. 125.

POLKINGHORNE, John Charlton, b. 16 Oct. 1930. Professor of Physics. Educ: Trinity Coll., Cambridge, U.K. Appts: Lectr., Math. Phys., Edinburgh Univ., 1956-58; Lectr., Applied Maths., Cambridge Univ., 1958-65; Rdr., Theoretical Phys., ibid, 1965-68; Prof., Math. Phys., ibid, 1968-. Publs: Co-Author, The Analytic S-Matrix, 1966; Contbr. of articles on theoretical elem. particle phys. to various jrnls. Address: DAMTP, Silver St., Cambridge, U.K. 1.

POLLACK, Joan Diehl (Mrs. Eugene L. Pollack), b. 3 Sept. 1931. Psychologist. Educ: A.B., Barnard Coll., 1953; M.A., Columbia Univ., 1959; Ph.D., 1963. Appts: Lab. Asst., Columbia Univ., Electronics Rsch. Lab., 1953-55; Jr. Psychol., ibid, 1955-58; Rsch. Asst., IBM Rsch. Ctr., Yorktown Heights, N.Y., 1959; Staff Psychol., Dunlap & Assocs. Inc., Stanford, Conn., 1960; Asst. Psychol., Columbia Univ., 1959-62; Asst. Rsch. Zool., UCLA, 1963-70. Mbrships: Am. Psychol. Assn.; Western Psychol. Assn.; Human Factors Soc.; Barnard Coll. Club of L.A.; Sigma Xi; Psi Chi. Contbr. to profl. publs. Address: 30214 Cartier Dr., Palos Verdes Peninsula, CA 90274, U.S.A. 5, 9, 59.

POLLARD, Donald Pence, b. 13 Sept. 1924. Glass Designer & Painter. Educ: B.F.A., R.I. Schl. of Design, Providence, 1949; Brown Univ., 1942-43. Appts: Ensign, USNR, Pacific Ops., 1943-46; Trainee, Reed & Barton

Silversmiths, 1949; Sr. Designer, Steuben Glass, 1950-. Mbrships: Alumni Govng. Bd., R.I. Schl. of Design, 1960-70; Alumni Trustee, 1968-70. Works incl: Vase of Three Presidents, Engraved Globe & Eisenhower Stele, collect. Pres. Dwight D. Eisenhower; Voyage, Collect. Pres. Kennedy; Genesis, Collect. Pres. Kubitshek, Brazil; Great Ring of Canada, Collect. Canadian Govt.; Saying of Confucius, Collect. Gen. Chiang Kai-Shek; pvte. & pub. collects., U.S.A., Europe & Asia. Address: 200 E. 66th St., N.Y., NY, U.S.A. 37.

POLLARD, Patience Howell, (Mrs. Clarence O. Pollard), b. 17 Oct. 1898. Poet; Lecturer. Educ. incl: Miss. St. Coll. for Women, 1920; Robertson Schl. of Personality, Wash., D.C.; UCLA Tchr's Cert., Woodrow Schl. of Dramatics, Dallas, Tex.; Univ. of Calif.; Metro-Goldwyn-Mayer Studios, w. Dir., of Tone Prod.; Laguna Schl. of Art & Design, Calif. Appts: Radio performer; Transcript artist; Coach of Dialect; Lectr. on Poetry & Color in fashion, designs etc.; Monologuiste; Writer of stories, articles, monologues. Mbrships: Prog. Chmn., Oak Cliff Fine Arts, Dallas, Tex. & Civic Assn.; Upper Derby, Pa.; V.P., Woman's Club, Santa Monica Bay, Calif.; Poetry Curator, Ebell, L.A.; Regent, DAR, Hemet, Calif.; Pres., Colonial Dames of XVII Century, Hemet Br. League of Am. Pen Women; IPS; Nat. Writer's Club. Publs: (Poetry) Forgetting All Else, Memory is Bold, Armed With Song; 44 Families. Address: 41734 Crest Drive, Hemet, CA 92343, U.S.A. 5, 57, 59, 132.

POLUNIN, Nicholas, b. 26 June 1909. Scientific author & editor; Explorer. Educ: Christ Church Coll., Oxford, U.K., 1928-32; Yale Univ., U.S.A., 1933-34; New Coll., Oxford, 1934-36; Rsch. Assoc., Harvard Univ., U.S.A., 1936-37; M.S. (Yale), M.A., D.Phil., D.Sc. (Oxon). Appts. incl: Fielding Curator & Keeper of Univ. Herbaria, 1938-57; Demonstrator & lectr. in Bot., Oxford 1938-47; Macdonald Prof. of Bot., McGill Univ., Montreal, Canada, 1947-52; Prof., Plant Ecol. & Taxonomy, Hd. Dept. of Bot., Dir. of Univ. Herbarium & Bot. Gdn., Univ. of Baghdad, Iraq, 1956-58; Guest Prof., Univ. of Geneva, Switzerland, 1959-61; Prof. of Bot., Dean & Fndr., Fac. of Sci., Univ. of Ife., Nigeria, 1962-66; Ed., World Crops books., 1954-69; Biol. Conservation, 1967-74, Environmental Conserv., 1973-. Mbrships. incl: Life Fellow, Linnean Soc.; Royal Geog. Soc. & Royal Hortic. Soc.; AAAS. Publs. incl: Russian Waters, 1931; Botany of the Canadian Eastern Arctic, 2 vols., 1947, 48; Circumpolar Arctic Flora, 1959; Ed., The Environmental Future, 1972; 200 rsch. & review papers etc. Recip., Rolleston Mem. Prize, 1938. Address: 15 Chemin F.-Lehmann, 1218 Grand-Saconnex, Geneva, Switzerland. 1, 2, 34, 50, 128.

POMROCK, Zvi Abraham, b. 31 Mar. 1931. Advocate. Educ: Tel Aviv Schl. of Law & Econs., 1952-53; M.Jur.; Hebrew Univ. of Jerusalem, 1957. Appts: Pvte. Prac. as Advocate, 1964-; Mbr., Disciplinary Tribunal, Israel Bar Assn., 1969-. Mbr., Israel Bar, 1960-. Contbr., literary review Keshet, 1970. Address: 56 Achad-Haam St., Tel-Aviv, Israel. 55.

PONDER, Norman Alaric, b. 13 Sept. 1938. Real Estate Executive. Educ: A.S., Arlington State Coll., 1959; B.S., Univ. of Tex., 1962; Masters Prog., Okla. State Univ., 1965-66; Exec. Dev. Prog., Cornell Univ., 1970; Real Estate Inst., N.Y. Univ., 1973. Appts. incl: V.P. & Dir., Ft. Wayne Bank Bldg., Inc., ibid, 1970-73; Dir., Cities Serv. Realty, Inc., 1968-73; V.P., ibid, 1969-73; Dir., Citgo

Atlanta, Inc., 1968-73; V.P., ibid, 1970-73; Dir., Chesebrough Bldg. Co., 1969-73; V.P., ibid, 1969-73; Dir. & V.P., Sixty Wall St., 1969-73; Dir. & V.P., Cities Serv. Tulsa, Inc., 1970-73; Dir. & V.P., Holgate Dev. Corp., 1970-73; Dir., Sixty Wall Tower, Inc., 1969-73; V.P., ibid, 1970-71; Pres., 1971-73; Mgr., Carlton Shopping Ctr. Co., Dallas, Tex., 1973-. Mbrships. incl: Int. Coun. of Shopping Ctrs., Am. Mgmt. Assn.; Real Estate Bd. of N.Y., Inc.; Nat. Assn. of Real Estate Bds. Rycip., Presidential Award of Hon., Jaycees, Bartlesville, Okla., 1964. Address: 9229 Raeford Dr., Dallas, TX 75231, U.S.A. 6.

PONOMAREW, Serge, b. 20 Aug. 1911. Painter; Sculptor. Educ: Fine Arts Schl., Wilno & Paris. Art work incls: (sculpture) L'Age-Atomique; Paradis Perdu—Solitude; Tête de Cheval; St. Paul; Ste. Vierge et l'Enfant Jesus; Crucifix; Méditation; La Joie; (paintings) L'Homme dans Cosmos; Christ; Ste. Vierge; Dante; Self Portrait; Vision; Poésie Lyrique; Génie-Temps-Espace; var. animals, still-lifes, landscapes, religious works & portraits; (medals) W.H. Wollaston; Kepler; Copernicus; Sienkiewicz; Rimsky-Korsakov; St. Paul; Borodine; Montmartre; Apolcalypse; Kosciuszko; Thon. etc. Hons. incl: Silver Medal for Encouragement of Progress; Medal for Arts, Scis. & Letters; Prize for Oil Painting, XXV Grand Prix d'Arts, Lyon, 1973; Dip. of Hon., Int. Aquitaine Salon, 1973. Address: 16 bis Rue Bardinet, 75014 Paris, France.

PONSONBY, Doris Almon (Mrs. John Rybot), b. 23 Mar. 1907. Author. Appts. incl: Sub.-Ed., Oxford Times, Oxford Evening Times, 1928-29; Feature Writer, Hong Kong Sunday Heralds, 1935-36. Mbrships. incl: W. Country Writers Assn.; Life, London Lib.; Nat. Book League. Publs. incl: (biogs.) Call a Dog Hervey; The Lost Duchess; A Prisoner in Regent's Park; (fiction) The Gazebo; Strangers in My House; Family of Jaspard; The Bristol Cousins; Bells Along the Neva; An Unusual Tutor; The Forgotten Heir; The Heart in the Sand; (non-fiction, as Doris Rybot) My Kingdom for a Doneky; A Donkey & a Dandelion; It Began Before Noah. Address: c/o Curtis Brown Ltd., 1 Craven Hill, London W2 3EW, U.K. 3, 131.

POOLE, John Bayard, b. 17 May 1912. Lawyer; Broadcasting Executive. Educ: Univ. of Chgo; LL.B., Detroit Coll. of Law. Appts: Ptnr., Poole, Littell & Sutherland, Detroit, 1936; Sec., V.P., Dir., Gen. Counsel, Storer Broadcasting Co., 1945-55; Chmn., Exec. Comm., Capital Cities Broadcasting Co., 1960-64; Chmn., Poole Broadcasting Co. (WJRT-TV, Flint, Mich., WPRI-TV, Providence, WTEN-TV, Albany), 1964-; Dir., Mich. Bank (N.A.), Detroit, 1964; Mich. Nat. Bank, Lansing, 1967-; Dir., Detroit Educ. TV Fndn., 1968; Dir., Gleaner Life Ins. Soc., 1969-; Dir., White Motor Corp., Cleveland, 1973; Mich. Nat. Corp., Detroit, 1974-. Mbrships. incl: Cat Cay, Bahamas, N. Key Largo, Fla., Indian Creek Country Clubs; Marco Polo Club, N.Y. Address: 1700 N. Woodward, Box K, Bloomfield Hills, MI 48013, U.S.A. 2, 8, 16, 36.

POPE, Andrew Jackson, Jr., (Jack), b. 18 Apr. 1913. Justice, Supreme Court of Texas. Educ: B.A., Abilene Christian Coll., 1934; LL.B., Univ. of Tex., 1937. Appts: Judge, 94th Judicial Dist. Tex., 1946-50; Justice, Ct. of Civil Appeals, 1950-65; Justice, Supreme Ct. of Tex., 1965-; Chmn., Appellate Judges Conf., 1972. Mbrships. incl: State Bar of Tex. (offices held); Am. Bar Assn.; Am. Judicature Soc., Am. Soc. for Legal Hist.; Grand Chancellor, Kts. of

Pythias, 1946. Contbr. to profl. jrnls. Hons: Silver Beaver Award, Boy Scouts of Am., 1961; Rosewood Gavel Award, St. Mary's Schl. of Law, 1962; Alumni of Yr., Abilene Christian Coll., 1965; Annual Law Award, Optimist Club, Corpus Christi, Tex., 1965. Address: Supreme Ct. of Tex., Box 12248, Capitol Stn., Austin, TX 78711, U.S.A. 2, 114.

POPHAM, Robert Earle, b. 10 Feb. 1925. Medical Anthropologist. Educ: B.A., Univ. of Toronto, Ont., Canada, 1947; M.A., ibid, 1949. Appts: Rsch. Assoc., Pharmacol., Univ. of Toronto, 1949-51; Instr., Anthropol., ibid, 1953-54; Rsch. Vis., Finnish Fndn. for Alcohol Studies, Helsinki, Finland, 1958-59; Special Lectr., Med. Anthropol., Univ. of Toronto, 1961-62; Hd., Rsch. Div., Addiction Rsch. Fndn. of Ont., Toronto, 1967-. Mbrships: Soc. for Med. Anthropol.; WHO Expert Advsry. Panel on Drug Dependence. Publs: Statistics of Alcohol Use & Alcoholism in Canada 1871-1956 (w. W. Schmidt), 1958; Liver Cirrhosis Mortality as a Means to Measure the Prevalence of Alcoholism (co-author), 1960; A Decade of Alcoholism Research (w. W. Schmidt), 1962; Alcohol & Alcoholism, 1970; 53 rsch. papers. Recip., Jellinek Mem. Award for Contbns. to the Study of Alcoholism, Amsterdam, 1972. Address: Addiction Research Foundation, 33 Russell St., Toronto, Ont., Canada.

POPJAK, G.J., b. 5 May 1914. Physician; Educator; Professor of Biochemistry. Educ: M.D., Royal Hungarian Francis Joseph Univ. of Szeged, 1938; Postgrad., Med. Schl., Univ. of London, U.K., 1939-41. Appts. incl: Lectr., Dept. of Pathol., St. Thomas's Hosp. Med. Schl., London, 1941-47; Mbr., Sci. Staff, Nat. Inst. Med. Rsch., London, 1947-53; Dir., M.R.C. Exptl. Radiopathol. Rsch. Unit, Hammersmith Hosp., London, 1953-62; Jt. Dir., Chem. Enzymol. Lab., Shell Rsch. Ltd., Sittingbourne, Kent, 1962-68; Prof. of Biochem., UCLA, U.S.A., 1968-. Mbrships: Fellow, Royal Soc., London, 1961-; Biochem. Soc., U.K.; Fellow, Royal Soc. of Med., London; Fellow, Royal Inst. of Chem., London, 1955-; British Med. Assn.; Hon. mbr., Am. Soc. Biol. Chemists; AAAS; For. mbr., Royal Flemish Acad., Belgium, 1955; Am. Acad. of Arts & Sci., 1971; Hon. mbr., Alpha Omega Alpha, 1971. Author of num. articles on biochem. in jrnls.; Ed., 3 books; Monograph, 1955. Hons. incl: Stouffer Prize, U.S.A., 1967; Davy Medal, Royal Soc., London, 1968. Address: 511 Cashmere Terr., L.A., CA, U.S.A. 1, 2, 128.

POPPER, (Sir) Karl Raimund, b. 28 July 1902. Emeritus Professor. Educ: Ph.D. Univ. of Vienna, Austria; M.A., New Zealand; D.Litt., London, U.K. Appts: Sr. Lectr., Philos., Univ. of Canterbury, N.Z., 1937-45; Rdr., Logic & Sci. Method, Univ. of London, U.K., 1946-49; Prof., Logic & Sci. Method, ibid, 1949-69. Fellow, Brit. Acad. Mbrships. incl: For. Hon., Am. Acad. Arts & Scis.; Hon., Phi Beta Kappa; Int. Acad. for Philos. of Sci.; Hon., Royal Soc. New Zealand. Publs. incl: The Poverty of Historicism, 1957; The Logic of Scientific Discovery, 1959; Conjectures & Refutations, 1963; Objective Knowledge, 1972. Hons: Kt., 1965; Prize, City of Vienna, 1965; Sonning Prize, Univ. of Copenhagen, 1973. Address: Fallowfield, Manor Rd., Penn, Bucks., U.K. 1, 3, 30, 34, 139.

POPRICK, Mary Ann, b. 25 June 1939. Psychologist. Educ: B.A., M.A., De Paul Univ., Chgo., 1960, '64; Ph.D., Loyola Univ., Chgo., 1968. Appts. incl: Intern, Elgin State Hosp., Ill., 1961-62; Staff Psychol., ibid, 1962, Ill.

State Trng. Schl. for Girls, Geneva, 1962-63, & (Pt.-time), Mt. Sinai Hosp., Chgo., 1963-64; Lectr., Loyola Univ., 1964-67; Asst. Prof.-Assoc. Prof., Lewis Univ., Lockport, Ill., 1967-; Chmn., Dept. of Psychol., ibid, 1968-72; post-doct. Intern, Ill. State Psych. Inst., Chgo., 1972-73. Mbrships. incl: AAAS; AAUP; Am., Ill. & Midwestern Psychol. Assns.; Delta Epsilon Sigma; Kappa Gamma Pi; Psi Chi. Contbr. to Jrnl. of Personality & Soc. Psychol., 1968. Address: 547 Marquette Ave., Calumet City, IL 60409, U.S.A. 5, 8, 14, 128, 132.

PORRERO DE CHAVARRI, Fernando R., b. 22 Dec. 1917. Diplomat. Educ: Dr. in Law, Prof. Int. Law, Univ. of Madrid. Appts: Entered diplomatic serv., 1942; Served in Embassies of Spain in Brussels (Belgium), Lisbon (Portugal), Athens (Greece), Paris (France), Libya; formerly Dir. European Pol. Affairs & Dir. Gen. Pol. Affairs w. For. Off.; Currently, Ambassador of Spain, Athens. Hons. incl: Grand d Croix du Mérite Civil, Spain; Ordre du Mérite, Germany; Ordre de l'Etoile, Ethiopia; Ordre du Phenix, Greece; Ordre du Christ, Portugal; Ordre de Beinfaisance, Portugal; O'Higgins, Chile; Collier de St. Jacques, Portugal; Cmdr. Charles III, Spain; Cmdr., Legion d'Honneur, France. Address: Embassy of Spain, Vassilissis Sofias 29, Athens, Greece.

PORTELA-LOMBA, Maneul B., b. 7 Mar. 1925. Certified Public Accountant. Educ: B.B.A.; Postgrad. studies, Univ. of Puerto Rico; C.P.A., 1954. Mbrships: Phi Delta Gamma (sec., treas., v.p., Pres.); Mason; Shriner; Puerto Rico Inst. C.P.A.'s (Bd.); Am. Inst. Accts.; Rio Piedras Lions Club (past pres.); Dist. Gov., Lions Int. 1972-73; Pres., P.T.A., Episcopalian Cathedral Schl.; Advsry. Commn. to Hon. Sec. of Instrn., Commonwealth of Puerto Rico on Vocational Guidance. Hons: Hon. Citizen of Indpls., Ind., U.S.A., 1970; Silver Anniversary Dedication of the Conven., Phi Delta Gamma, 1970. Address: P.O. Box G.P.O. 1240, San Juan, Puerto Rico.

PORTER, Agnes Louise, b. 14 Feb. 1932. College Professor. Educ: B.A., Pa. State Univ., 1954; M.A., Univ. of Pitts., 1959; Ph.D., Ohio State Univ., 1964. Appts. incl: Tchng. Asst. in Speech, Univ. of Pitts., 1956-57; Instr. in Speech, Marshall Univ., 1959-61; Asst. in Speech, Ohio State Univ., 1961-64; Asst. Prof. of Speech, Southern Conn. State Coll., 1965-69; Assoc. Prof. of Speech, ibid, 1969-. Mbrships: former Dir. of M.S. in Speech Communication, 1968-73; Speech Assn. of Conn., Sec., 1967-69; V.P., 1969-71; Pres., 1971-73. Publs: Ed., W. Va. State Speech Jrnl., 1960-61; Ed., Southern Conn. State Coll. Speech Jrnl., 1966-. Address: Speech Dept., Davis Hall, Southern Conn. State Coll., 501 Crescent St., New Haven, CT 06515, U.S.A. 5, 13, 129, 130, 138.

PORTER, Arthur Thomas, b. 26 Jan. 1924. Educationalist. Educ: B.A., Fourah Bay Coll., Sierra Leone, W. Africa, 1944; B.A., Cambridge Univ., U.K., 1950; Postgrad. Cert., Educ., London Univ., ibid, 1951; Ph.D., Boston Univ., Mass., U.S.A., 1959. Appts: Asst., Dept. Soc. Anthropol., Edinburgh Univ., U.K., 1951-52; Lectr., Hist.-V.P., Fourah Bay Coll., Univ. Coll., Sierra Leone, 1954-64; Prin., Univ. Coll., Univ. E. Africa, Nairobi, Kenya, 1964-70; UNESCO Field Staff Off., Educl. Planning Advsr., Min. Educ., Kenya, 1970-74; V.-Chancellor, Univ. Sierra Leone, Freetown, W. Africa, 1974-. Consultative Dir., Int. African Inst., London, U.K. & Fellow, Royal Soc. Arts, ibid. Author var. profl. jrnl. & newspaper articles. Hons: Sierra Leone Independence Medal, 1961;

L.H.D., Boston Univ., Mass., U.S.A., 1969; LL.D., Royal Univ., Malta, 1969; Yugoslav Flag w. Golden Star on Necklace, 1970; Silver Medal, Royal Soc. Arts, U.K.; Hon. Mbr., Phi Beta Kappa, Epsilon Chapt., Boston Univ., Mass., U.S.A., 1972. Address: Univ. Sierra Leone, Pvte. Mail Bag, Freetown, Sierra Leone, W. Africa.

PORTER, Bernard Harden, b. 14 Feb. 1911. Author. Educ: B.S., Colby Coll., Waterville, Me., 1932; Sc.M., Brown Univ., Providence, R.I., 1933. Author, over 50 books, inclng: Boys Book of Physics, 1939; Map of Chemistry, 1941; Doldrums, 1941; The Union of Science & Art, 1948; Rocket Data Book, 1956; H.L. Mencken, 1957; Physics for Tomorrow, 1959; F. Scott Fitzgerald, 1960; Scandinavian Summer, 1961; I've Left, 1963; Mathematics for Electronics, 1965; Cut Leaves, 1966; Knox County, 1969; The Box, 1969; Reminiscences, 1970; Hand Coated Chocolates, 1972; Contemporary Italian Painters, 1973; Trattoria Due Formi, 1973; The Books of Dos, 1973; The Very, Very Dead (in preparation); Where (in preparation). Mbrships: Soc. for Programmed Instrn; Soc. of Int. Dev; Int. Poetry Soc. Address: 41 Ocean Drive, Rockland, ME 04814, U.S.A. 6, 9, 30.

PORTER, Elmer Johnson, b. 5 May 1907. Professor of Art. Educ: B.A.E., Chgo. Art Inst., Ill., U.S.A., 1930; M.A., Ohio State Univ., Columbus, 1938. Appts: Art Instr., McKinley H.S., Cedar Rapids, Iowa, 1930-37; Art Instr., Hughes H.S., Cinn., Ohio, 1938-46; Prof. of Art, & Chmn., Art Dept., Ind. State Univ., Terre Haute, 1946-73; For. Student Advsr., ibid, 1967-72. Mbrships. incl: Pres., Art Educ. Assn. of Ind., 1952-63, Sec. Treas., 1954-67; Exec. Coun., Western Arts Assn.; Nat. Art Educ. Assn.; Regional Chmn., Nat. Assn. of For. Student Affairs, 1968-69; Coll. Art Assn.; Pres., Pen & Brush Club, 1947 & 1970, Treas., 1958-; Phi Delta Kappa; Int. Sec., Kappa Pi, 1972-. One-man exhibs: Chgo.; N.Y.C.; Cinn.; Columbus, Ohio; Indpls., Ind.; Richmond, Ind.; Bath, Me. Awards: Indpls. Art Assn.; Columbus Art League; Hoosier Salon of Chgo.; Richmond, Ind., Art Assn. Address: 3115 Margaret Ave. E., Terre Haute, IN 47802, U.S.A. 2, 8, 19.

PORTER, Enid Mary. Museum Curator. Educ: B.A., Univ. Coll., London, U.K.; Dip. Ed., Cath. Trng. Coll., Cavendish Square, London. Appts: Teaching posts in Grammar Schls.; Curator, Cambridge & Co. Folk Mus., 1947-. Mbrships: Former Comm. Mbr., The Folklore Soc., The Soc. for Folk Life Studies, Cambridge Preservation Soc. Publs: Cambridgeshire Customs & Folklore; East Anglian Folklore. Ed., Tales From the Fens & More Tales From the Fens, by W.H. Barrett; Fenland Memories, Sixty Years a Fenman, Fenland Railwayman, Fenland Molecatcher, by A.R. Powell. Contbr. to var. jrnls. inclng: Folklore; Jrnl. of Folk Life Studies. Winner, Coote-Lake Medal for Rsch. in Folklore, 1968. Address: Museum Cottage, Northampton St., Cambridge CB3 0AD, U.K. 1.

PORTER, Eric Richard, b. 8 Apr. 1928. Actor. Educ: Wimbledon Tech. Coll. Appts. incl: 1st profl. appearance, Arts Theatre, Cambridge, 1945; 1st London appearance, Saint Joan, 1946; Bristol Old Vic Co., 1954, 55-56; Old Vic Co., 1954-55; Royal Shakespeare Co., 1960. Roles incl: Barabbas, The Jew of Malta; Shylock, Merchant of Venice; Ossip, The Government Inspector; King Lear; Dr. Fuastus. Films incl: The Pumpkin Eater, 1964; Kaleidoscope, 1966; Nicholas & Alexandrea, 1971; Antony & Cleopatra, 1972; The Day of the Jackal, 1973; The Belstone

Fox, 1973. Many TV appearances. Hons: Best Actor, Evening Standard Drama Award, 1959; TV Actor of the Year, Guild of TV Prods. & Dirs., 1967. Address: c/o Int. Famous Agcy Ltd., 11-12 Hanover St., London, W.1., U.K. 1, 34, 128.

PORTER, Harry Culverwell, b. 9 Nov. 1927. University Lecturer. Educ: B.A., Corpus Christi Coll., Cambridge, 1948; M.A., ibid, 1953; Ph.D., 1956. Appts: Rsch. Fellow, Corpus Christi Coll., Cambridge, 1956; Proctor Fellow, Princeton, 1956-57; Lectr. in History, Univ. of Toronto, 1957-59; Asst. Prof., Univ. of Calif., Berkeley, 1959-60; Fellow. of Selwyn Coll., Cambridge, 1960-72; Asst. Lectr. in Hist., Cambridge, 1961; Lectr. in Hist., Cambridge, 1966. Sr. Treas., Cambridge Univ. Footlights Club, 1961-. Publs: (libretto) Daisy Simpkins, 1953; The Literary Delinquent, 1954; The Dutch Uncle, 1956. Other publs: Reformation & Reaction in Tudor Cambridge, 1958; Erasmus & Cambridge (w. D.F.S. Thompson), 1963; Puritanism in Tudor England, 1970. Recip., Archbishop Cranmer Prize, Cambridge Univ., 1952. Address: Fac. of History, West Road, Cambridge, U.K.

PORTER, William L., b. 23 May 1918. Financial Advisor. Educ: B.S., Am. Univ., 1949; LL.B., Wash. Coll. of Law, ibid, 1954, J.D., 1968. Appts. incl: Agent, Internal Revenue Serv., Treasury Dept., 1948-59; Sr. Acct., M.B. Hariton & Co., Wash. D.C., 1959; Mbr., Pub. Serv. Commn., Dist. of Columbia, 1966-70; Treas., Ctr. for Community Change, 1970; Prof., Wash. Tech. Inst., 1970; Financial Cons., Min. of Pub. Utilities & Housing, Govt. of Jamaica, 1971; Mng. Ptnr., Wash. Off., Lucas, Tucker & Co., 1972; Cons., Potomac Elec. Power Co., Wash. D.C., 1973. Mbrships. incl: Fndg. Mbr., Edit. Staff, Am. Univ. Intra-Mural Law Review; Municipal Finance Comm., Metropolitan Wash. Bd. of Trade; Treas., Bd. of Govs., D.C. Inst. of Cert. Pub. Accts.; Am. Inst. of Cert. Pub. Accts.; Wash. Bar Assn.; NAACP; AAUP; Omega Psi Phi; Bd. of Dirs., Wash. Home Rule Comm.; etc. Address: 907 Sixth St. S.W., Apt. 701 & 703, Washington, DC 20024, U.S.A. 7, 130.

PORTERFIELD, Rosella French, b. 28 Dec. 1918. Librarian. Educ: A.B., Ky. State Univ., Frankfort, U.S.A., 1940; M.A., Univ. of Cinn., Ohio, 1957; Lib. Certification, Univ. of Ky., Lexington, 1965. Appts: Tchr., Elem. Schls., Erlanger, Ky., 1940-54; Prin. & Primary pt.-time Tchr., 1954-59; Libn., 1959-; Tchr., Headstart Prog., Covington, Ky., 1965. Mbrships: Sec.-Treas., N. Ky. Libns. Assn., 1968; Treas., Erlanger-Elsmere Educ. Assn., 1971-72; Ky. Libn. Assn.; Organist, Bapt.-Zion Bapt. Ch., 1956-; Pres., Community Homemakers Club, 958-59; Tau Sigma. Author, History of Zion Baptist Church (1872-1972). Responsible for field project, Adapting the Primary Program to Underprivileged Children in a Small School. Address: Box 37, Chambers Rd., Walton, KY 41094, U.S.A. 5.

PORTMANN, Georges, b. 1 July 1890. Professor of Otolaryngology; Member of Parliament. Educ: Collège de Perpignan; Lycée de Cherbourg; Faculté de Médecine de Bordeaux. Appts: Prof., Clin. of Otorhinolaryngol., Fac. of Med., Bordeaux, 1926-63, Dean of Fac., 1949-55, Hon. Dean., 1955-; Senator of the Gironde, 1932-40, 1955-71, V.P. of Senate, 1959-62. Mbrships. incl: Académie de Médecine, Paris; Pres., l'Association Française pour la Communauté Atlantique; V.P., l'Alliance Française. Publs. incl: L'Allemagne dans les tranchées de la paix, 1935; Le Crépuscule de la paix, 1955;

Réflexions sur un monde dérégle, 1962; Notes de politique socio-économique, 1972; also 18 med. books. Hons. incl: Croix de Guerre, 1914-18; Grand Officier de la Légion d'Honneur, 1933; Commandeur des Palmes académiques; many for. awards & hon. degrees. Address: 226 Blvd. St. Germain, 75007 Paris, France.

PORTOGHESI, Paolo, b. 2 Nov. 1931. Architect & Writer. Educ: Grad., Rome Univ., Italy, 1957. Appts: Prof., Fac. Arch. & H.S. for grads. for Restoration of Monuments, Rome Univ., 1961-66; Prof., Hist. Arch.-Dean, Fac. Arch., Politecnico di Milano, 1967-71. Mbrships: Accad. di San Luca, 1966; High Coun. Pub. Works, Italian Min., 1965-. Creative Works incl: Books: Guarino Guarini, 1955; Michelangelo as an Architect, 1964; Borromini in the European Culture, 1964; The Infancy of Machines, 1965; Bernardo Vittone, 1966; Roma Barocca, 1966; Borromini, Architecture as a Language, 1967; Rome of the Renaissance, 1970; Archtl. Works: E.N.P.A.S. Bldg., Lucca, 1959; Baldi House, Rome, 960; Andreis House, Scandriglia, 1963; Michelangelo Exhib., Rome, Palazzo delle Esposizioni, 1964; Tech. Indl. Inst., L'Aquila, 1968; Sacra Famiglia Ch., Salerno, 1968; Swimming Pool, Marbella, Spain, 1972; Khartoum Int. Airport, Sudan, 1973, et al.; Participator num. archtl. exhibs. Hons: Nat. Award, Italian Inst. Arch., 1963; Gold Medal, Manzu Fndn., Min. Pub. Works. Address: Via Gregoriana, 25, Rome, Italy.

PORTTEUS Elnora M. (Mrs. Paul Portteus). Librarian; Educational Supervisor. Educ: B.S., Univ. of Wis., 1941; M.A., Kent State Univ., 1954. Appts: Asst. Libn., Fed. Reserve Bank of Cleveland, Ohio, 1942-43; Asst., Ind. Rels. Counselors, N.Y., 1947-48; Findlay, Ohio, City Schls., 1949-58; Prof., Schl. of Lib. Sci., Kent State Univ., Ohio, 1958-65; Directing Supvsr., Schl. Libs., Cleveland, Ohio, 1965-. Mbrships: ALA; W.N.B.A.; Pres., Am. Assn. of Schl. Libns., 1972-73, V.P., 1971-72; Chmn., Right to Read Comm., 1971-72; Ohio Lib. Assn., Serv. to Schls. Roundtable Chr., 1958; Pres., Ohio Assn. of Schl. Libns., 1957-58, V.P., 1956-57, Rec. Sec., 1954-55; Bd. Mbr., Soc. Studies Chmn., Ohio Div. of AAUW; Beta Phi Mu; Delta Kappa Gamma. Contbr. of articles to profl. jrnls. Hons. incl: Ohio Lib. Assn. Libn. of the Year, 1972. Hons: Ency. Brit. Schl. Lib. Award, 1st Place, 1967; John Cotton Dana Award, 1967; '69. Address: Woodhill Quincy Ctr., Cleveland Pub. Schls., 10600 Quincy Ave., Cleveland, OH 44106, U.S.A. 5, 8, 130.

PORZIO, Ralph, b. 27 Aug. 1914. Lawyer; Author; Lecturer. Educ: A.B., Drew Univ., Madison, N.J., U.S.A.; J.D., Harvard Univ. Appts: Admitted to Prac., N.J. Fed. Cts. & U.S. Supreme Ct.; Sr. Ptnr., Porzio, Bromberg & Newman, Morristown, N.J.; Counsel, Bd. of Trustees, Int. Coll. of Angiol.; Assoc. Ed., Lex et Scientia—The Int. Jrnl. of Law & Sci. Num. mbrships. incl: Am. Bar Assn.; Bar Assn. of N.J.; Pres., Bar Assn. of Morris Co., 1970-71; Am. Judicature Soc.; Am. Coll. of Legal Med.; V.P. & Fellow, Int. Acad. of Law & Sci.; Assn. of Trial Lawyers of Am.; N.J. Assn. of Schl. Attys.; Trustee, Drew Univ.; Bd. of Educ., Town of Boonton, N.J. Publs: The Transplant Age—Reflections on the Legal & Moral Aspects of Organ Transplants, 1969; Contbns. to profl. jrnls. Lectured at sev. int. meetings of scientists, physicians, & lawyers. Hons: Citation for Writings Advancing the Am. Way of Life, Freedoms Fndn.; Outstanding Achievement Award in the Arts, Drew Univ. Address: 123 Glover St., Boonton, NJ 07005, U.S.A. 6, 16.

POSADA, Rafael, b. 17 Apr. 1927. Professor. of Spanish. Educ: B.S., Pedagogical & Technol. Univ. of Colombia, S. Am., 1945; M.A., 1967, Ph.D., 1969, Ind. Univ., U.S.A. Appts: Instr., For. Langs., Gimnasio Moderno, 1946-57; Asst. Prof., Spanish, Nat. Univ., Bogotá, Colombia, 1958, Univ. of the Andes, ibid; Chmn., Spanish Dept., Univ. of the Andes, 1964; Fellow, Inter-Am. Prog. of FL Tchng. & Linguistics, Summer Linguistics Inst., Ind. Univ., 1964; Asst. Prof., Spanish, Ball State Univ., Muncie, Ind., 1969-. Mbrships: Linguistic Soc. Am.; Am. Assn. Tchrs. Spanish & Portuguese; MLA of Am.; Romance Lang. Assn.; Kiwanis Int. Publs: 2 books in preparation in area of FL tchng. of lit. analysis thru' linguistics; Contbr., learned articles to var. jrnls. Address: P.O. Box 1145, Muncie, IN 47305, U.S.A.

POSELL, Elsa Z. Author; Librarian. Educ: B.S., Temple Univ., U.S.A.; B.L.S., Drexel Univ.; M.L.S., Case Western Reserve Univ. Appts: Tchr. Libn., Aldan Pub. Schls.; Chief, Mus. Dept., D.C.; Pub. Lib. Rdrs. Advsr., Cons. in Adult Educ., Cleveland Pub, Lin., Lib., Canterbury Schl., Cleveland Hts., Ohio, 1953-; Lectr., Schl. of Lib. Sci., Case Western Reserve Univ. Mbrships: ALA; Ohio Assn.; Schl. Libns.; Women's Comm., Cleveland Orch.; Advsry. Bd., Schl. Lib. Sci., Kent State Univ.; Nat. Book Assn. Publs. incl: True Book of Horses, 1961; American Composers, 1963; Beginning Book of Seashells, 1969; Russian Authors, 1970; This is an Orchestra, 1950, complete revision, 1973. Address: 2469 Kingston Rd., Cleveland Hts., OH 44118, U.S.A.

POSNANSKY, Merrick, b. 8 Mar. 1931. Archaeologist. Educ: B.A. & Ph.D., Univ. of Nottingham; Dip. in Prehistoric Archaeol., Peterhouse, Cambridge. Appts: Warden of Prehistoric Sites of Royal Nat. Pks. of Kenya, 1956-58; Curator, Uganda Mus., 1958-62, Asst. Dir., Brit. Inst. of Hist. & Archaeol., E. Africa, 1962-64; Lectr. in Hist.-Dir. of African Studies, Makerere Univ. Coll., Kampala, Uganda, 1964-67; Prof. of Archaeol., Univ. of Ghana, Legon, 1967-; Vis. Fellow, Clare Hall, Cambridge, 1974; Vis. Prof., UCLA, 1966 & Syracuse Univ., 1969. Mbrships. incl: Fndr. Pres., Mus. Assn. of Middle Africa, 1969-71; V.P., Mus. Assn. of Tropical Africa, 1971-74; Pres., 1964, Ed., Uganda Jrnl., 1962-66, Uganda Soc.; Fellow, Brit. Inst. of Hist. & Archaeol. in E. Africa; Hon. Life Mbr., Kenya Hist. Soc. Publs: Prelude to East African History, 1966; Myth & Methodology, the Archaeological Contribution to African History, 1969; The Origins of West African Trade, 1971; articles in num. jrnls. Address: c/o Dept. of Archaeol., Univ. of Ghana, P.O. Box 3, Legon, Ghana. 89.

POSNER, Bernard, b. 26 Aug. 1916. Public Relations Practitioner. Educ: A.B., Univ. of Cinn., Ohio, U.S.A., 1938; M.A., Am. Univ., Wash. D.C., 1957. Appts: Asst. Dir., Pub. Info., VA, 1946-60; Adjunct Prof., Am. Univ., 1958-; Exec. Dir., Pres.'s Comm. on Employment of the Handicapped, Wash., D.C., 1960-. Mbrships. incl: P.R. Soc. of Am.; Nat. Rehabilitation Assn.; Bd. of Dirs., Woodley House, Wash. D.C.; Nat. Multiple Sclerosis Soc. Contbr., Chapts. to 4 books. Hons. incl: Belle Greve Award, Nat. Rehabilitation Assn.; Pres.'s Award, Nat. Assn. for Retarded Citizens; Communications Award, Am. Psychological Assn. Address: President's Committee on Employment of the Handicapped, Washington DC 20210, U.S.A.

POSNER, Michael Vivian. b. 25 Aug. 1931. University Teacher. Educ: Balliol Coll., Oxford Univ. Appts: Rsch. Off., Inst. of Econs., Oxford Univ.; Univ. Lectr. in Econs., Cambridge, 1958-; Fellow & Dir. of Studies in Econs., Pembroke Coll., ibid, 1960-; Dir. of Econs., Min. of Power, 1966-67; Econ. Advsr. to H.M. Treasury, 1967-71; Vis. Prof., Brookings Instn., U.S.A. 1971-72; Cons., World Bank & Int. Monetary Fund, 1971-. Publs: Italian Public Enterprise (co-author), 1966; Fuel Policy, 1973. Address: Pembroke Coll., Cambridge Univ., Cambridge, U.K. 1, 3.

POSNIAK, Abraham Oscar, b. 13 June 1909. Physician; Educator. Educ: B.S., Univ. of Liege, Belgium, 1932; M.D., Univ. of Lausanne, Switzerland, 1938; Intern, Brugmann Hosp., Brussels, Belgium, 1939-40. Num. appts. incl: Pvte. Prac., internal med., 1940-50; Res. Physn., Bellevue Med. Ctr., N.Y. Univ., U.S.A., 1951-53; Chief, Children's Rehab. Div., Bird S. Coler Hosp., N.Y.C., 1955-60; Cons., ibid, 1963-; Asst. Prof., Phys. Med., N.Y. Med. Coll., 1956-63; Assoc. Clin. Prof., ibid, 1964-; Chief, Children's Rehab. Clin., Metropol. Hosp., N.Y.C., 1957-60; Attng. Physn., Med. & Rehab., St. Clare's Hosp., N.Y.C., 1958-. Mbrships. incl: AMA; Fellow, Am. Acad. of Phys. Med. & Rehab.; Dipl., Am. Bd. of Phys. Med. & Rehab.; Am. Acad. of Cerebral Palsy; Profl. Advsry. Bd., United Cerebral Palsy Assns.; Am. Coll. of Physns.; Pres., Med. Alliance in N.Y., 1963-65; Pres., Fedn. of Am.-European Med. Socs., 1966; N.Y. Acad. of Med.; N.Y. State Med. Soc. Address: 150 E. 61st St., N.Y., NY 10021, U.S.A. 6, 17, 54.

POSPISIL, Leopold Jaroslav, b. 26 Apr. 1923. Educ: B.A., Olomouc, Czechoslovakia, 1942; J.U.C., Charles Univ., Prague, Czechoslovak, 1948; B.A., Willamette Univ., Salem, Ore., U.S.A., 1950; M.A., Univ. of Ore., Eugene, 1952; Ph.D., Yale Univ., 1956; Hon. Sc.D., Willamette Univ., Salem, Ore., 1969. Appts. incl: Instr. in Anthropol. & Asst. Curator, Yale Univ., 1956-57; Asst. Prof. & Asst. Curator, ibid, 1957-60; Assoc. Prof. & Assoc. Curator, ibid, 1960-65; Prof. & Curator, ibid, 1965-; Dir., Div. of Anthropol., Peabody Mus., ibid, 1966-. Mbrships: Fellow, Am. Anthropol. Assn.; Fellow, Sigma Xi; Fellow, Czechoslovak Acad. of Arts & Scis., Wash. DC; Fellow, N.Y. Acad. of Scis.; Archaeol. Soc. of Conn. Publs: The Kapauku Papuans Of West New Guinea, 1963; Anthropology Of Law, 1971; The Ethnology Of Law, 1972; num. articles & book reviews in profl. jrnls. Hons. incl: sev. Fellowships & Rsch. Grants. Address: 554 Orange St., New Haven, CT 06511, U.S.A. 2, 29, 139.

POSSATI, Mario, b. 7 Apr. 1922. Company President. Educ: B.S., Mech. Engrng., Univ. of Bologna, 1946. Appts: Tech. Mgr., Officine Macaferri, Bologna, 1946-49; Gen. Mgr., Baschieri & Pellagri, Bologna, 1949-52; Fndr., Pres., Apparecchi Elettronici Marposs, Bologna, 1952-; Pres., Marposs Finike Italiana S.A.S. (electronic gauge co.), 1968-. Mbrships: Bd. of Dirs., Cassa di Risparmio di Bologna; Rotary; Profl. Engrs. Assn. of Italy; Soc. of Mfng. Engrs., U.S.A.; Engrng. Soc. of Detroit, U.S.A. Address: c/o Marposs Finike Italiana s.a.s., Via Saliceto 13, Bentivoglio, Bologna, Italy.

POSTEL, Michel, b. 7 Apr. 1926. Company Executive. Educ: Baccalauréat (Philo.), Lycée de Biarritz; Ecole Supérieure de Commerce de Paris. Appts: Fndr. & Mng. Dir., Franco-Indian Pharmaceuticals Ltd., Bombay, India; Mng. Dir., Griffon Labs. Ltd., Bombay. Fndr. Mbr., Prince of Wales Mus., Bombay. Fndr. & Ed., La Médecine en France, review med. & pharmaceutical news & articles, 1952-. Recip.,

Chevalier de l'Ordre National du Mérite, 1968. Address: 8 Rue Tastova, 64200 Biarritz, France. 34, 43.

POTH, Harry Augustus, Jr., b. 5 Nov. 1911. Lawyer. Educ: B.S., Univ. of Pa., Phila., U.S.A., 1933; LL.B., ibid, 1936. Appts: Assoc., Reid & Priest, N.Y.C., 1937-48, Ptnr., ibid, 1949; Mng. Ptnr., Wash. D.C. Off., 1949-58; Advsr., elec. pub. utility matters, Greek Govt., 1953-54, & Pakistan, 1962-63; Dir., Bayrock Utility Securities, Inc. Mbrships. incl: Nat. Coun., For. Policy Assn.; Coun., Fed. Power, N.Y., Chmn., Comm. on Taxation & Acctng. of Pub. Utility Law; Am. Bar Assn.; Edison Elec. Inst.; Am. Soc. for Int. Law; Zeta Psi. Publs: Contbrns. to Pub. Utilities Fortnightly, & Am. Bar Assn. Annual Report. Hons: Bronze Star Medal, 1945; Cross of Merit, Ordine Militario di Malta, 1964. Address: Reid & Priest, 40 Wall St., N.Y., NY 10005, U.S.A. 6.

POTOTSCHNIG, Heinz (Heinrich) Rudolf Karl, b. 30 June 1923. Physician; Author. Educ: Studied at Univs. of Berlin, Graz & Innsbruck; Dr.med., Innsbruck, 1948. Appts: Med. prac.; Publisher, Der Bogen. Mbr., PEN Club. Publs: Books: Schatten Schrägen ins Licht; Nachtkupfer; Den Rest Teilen die Sterne; Lotungen; Der Himmel war Lila; Die Grünen Schnäbel; In Alten Maszen; Lyrik; Die Grenze; Radio Plays: Ludwig Uhland; Das Ohr des Erhabenen; Wenn es sein muss, meine Dame; Begegnung im Sand. Hons: Peter Rosegger Prize, 1964 & 1969; Theodor Körner Prize for Lit., 1965 & 1971; Ludwig Ficker Prize, 1967; Dramatists' Prize, Baden-Baden Stadttheater, 1968; Frontkämpferkreuz mit Schwertern am Bande Rot-Weiss; Golden Medal for special servs., O.K.B. Address: Ghegastrasse 5, A-9500 Villach, Austria. 43.

POTT, Pieter Hendrik, b. 3 Oct. 1918. Professor of Museology; Museum Administrator. Educ: Indol., Univs. of Utrecht & Leiden; D.Litt., Ph.D., Univ. of Leiden, 1946. Appts: Keeper, Kern Inst. (for Indian Archaeol.), Leiden, 1945-47; Keeper, Indian Dept., Rijksmuseum voor Volkenkunde, Leiden, 1947-54; Dir., Rijksmuseum voor Volkenkunde, Leiden, 1955-; Prof , Univ. of Leiden, 1974-. Mbrships: Societe Asiatique, Paris; Masonic orgs. Publs: Introduction to the Tibetan Collection, National Museum of Ethnology, Leiden, 1951; Naar wijder horizon: kaleidoscoop op one beeld van de buitenwereld, 1962. Contbr., Art of the World Series, 1964. Off. in the Order of Oranje-Nassau, 1965. Address: c/o. Rijksmuseum voor Volkenkunde, P.O. Box 212, Leiden, Netherlands. 43, 100, 133.

POTTER, (Mrs.) Alta McLean Clifford. Former State Official; Account Executive. Educ: Calif. Univ., U.S.A. Appts: Owner/Mgr., Alta Clifford—Beautiful Clothes, Long Beach, Calif.; Legislative Pol. Campaign Mgr., 1942-44; '50-; Bus. Mgmt.-Pub. Rels. Counselor, L.A., 1945-53; Vocatl. Counselor, Woodbury Coll. Bus. Admin., 1953-55; Dpty. Dir.-Chief on Div., Off. Civil Defense, L.A., 1955-58; Rep. L.A. & Calif., Nat. Strategy Conf., Civil Defense, Wash. D.C., 1958; Chief, Div., Indl. Welfare, Dept. Indl. Welfare, Calif., 1959-60; Investment Securities Broker, 1961-. Mbrships: Calif. State Exec. Comm.; Nat. Bus. & Profl. Women's Club; Chmn., L.A. area, Calif. Cancer Rsch. Assn.; Nat. Pub. Rels. Forum; Am. Inst. Mgmt. Assn. Hons: Observer (guest U.S. Chmbr. of Comm.), UN, San Fran.; Mayor's Advsry. Comm.; Gov. Brawus' Advsry. Comm. on Legislation; Elected Repub. Candidate, Calif. Legislature, 1944. Address: 740½ So. Mansfield Ave., L.A., CA 90036, U.S.A.

POTTER, Charles Wilbur. Realtor. Educ: Pratt Inst. of Technol., 2 yrs.; Brooklyn Coll., 1 yr.; Cartoonists & Illustrators Schl., N.Y., 1 yr.; Wash. Schl. of Art, 1 yr. Appts: Machine Tool Design & Maintenance Bus.; N.Y.C. Firefighter; Special Asst. to House Mgr., N.Y. Met. Opera; Mun.Bch. Lifeguard; Real Estate Bus.; Town Mayor, Lantana; Tchr., Adult Educ. Prog. Mbrships: Pres., Lantana Chmbr. of Comm.; Pres., Lantana Republican Club; Pres., Lantana Rotary Club; Pres., Hypoluxo Is. Property Owners Assn.; Fraternal Order of Police Assocs.; Sons of the Am. Revolution; Am. Legion; Coast Guard Aux. Instr.; Bd. of Realtors Assoc., Lantana Art Guild. Publs: cartoons in mags. Hons: Elected to Lantana Town Coun., 1967-70, & Mayor, 1973-76; 1st Rdr., 1st Ch. of Christ Scientist; Cert. to teach Real Estate Law in Palm Beach Co. Adult Educ. System, etc. Address: 805 Pelican Ln., Lantana, FL 33462, U.S.A. 125.

POTTER, Fred Allan, b. 6 Jan. 1916. Free-lance Writer; Poet. Educ: Ext. Dept., Christian Writer's Inst., Wheaton Coll., Ill., U.S.A. Mbrships: Okla. Writer's Fedn.; Poetry Soc. of Okla. Publs: Contbr. to Anthology of American Poetry, 1962, American Poets' Anthology, 1962. Address: 2528 N. Trosper Dr., Oklahoma City, OK 73161, U.S.A. 11.

POTTER, Richard Charles, b. 9 Aug. 1924. Librarian; Library Consultant; Gold Archivist. Educ: B.A., St.Ambrose Coll., 1951; M.A., Fla. State Univ., 1957; Pre-Flight Dip., US Naval Schl., 1949. Appts: w. US Marines, 1943-46; Deck Off., US Navy, 1952-54; HS Tchr., 1951-52, '54-55; Night Schl. Libn., Pensacola Jr. Coll., 1957-58; Consulting Libn., Pensacola News-Journal, 1959-70; Schl. Libn., Escambia Co., Fla., 1957-; Currently, also free-lance Cons., pt.-time. Histn.-Statn., Monsanto-PGA Golf Tournament. Contbr. of articles to local & regional profl. jrnls. & newspapers. Address: 404 Clairmont Dr., Forest Park, Pensacola, FL 32506, U.S.A. 42.

POTTER, Robert Ellis, b. 16 Mar. 1937. Librarian. Educ: B.Sc., Univ. of Tenn., 1961; Basic Army Admin. Schl., 1959; Univ. of Southern Calif. Lib. Schl., 1963-64. Appts: Lib. Asst., Univ. of Tenn., 1959-61; 1962-63; Copyreader, Knoxville News-Sentinel, 1961-62; Lib. Aide, L.A. Co. Lib. System, El Monte, Calif., 1963-65; Ref. Libn., in charge of Bus. Sci. Coll., John F. Kennedy Lib. in Hialeah, Fla, 1966-. Mbrships. incl: Pres., Dade Co. Lib. Assn., Fla., 1970-71; V.P. Prog. Chmn., 1969-70; Sigma Delta Chi; ALA; Fla., Public & Southeastern Lib. Assns.; Univ. of Tenn. Alumni Assn., Gtr. Miami Chapt., Bd. Govs. 1973-75; V.P. 1974-; Hist. Assn. of Southern Fla.; Mus. of Sci. & Planetarium in Dade Co. Fla; Assn. of Coll. & Rsch. Libs.; Co-Chmn., City of Hialeah Lib. Div. Pre-Tem. Staff Comm., 1974-; Archivist, Dade Co. Lib. Assn., 1974. Publs: Sports Ed., Orange & White Student Newspaper, Univ. of Tenn., 1958; Copy Ed., 1960; Ed., SORT Bull., Am. Lib. Assn., 1971-; DCLA Newsletter, 1971-. Title & Key Word Index to Small Business Administration Bibliography Series, 1972. Address: City of Hialeah Lib. Div., 190 West 49th St., Hialeah, FL 33012, U.S.A. 7, 42, 139.

POULAKOS, Kyriakos, b. 14 Oct. 1925. Economist. Educ: Schl. of Econs. & Bus. Admin., Athens Univ., Greece; Postgrad. studies, London Schl. of Econs. & Pol. Sci., U.K. Appts: Nat. Bank of Greece, 1947-50; Financial Mgr., Cambas Co. (Wine & Spirits), 1950-55; Gen. Mgr. (& Finance), Gen. Cement Co., Athens, 1955-64; Econ. Advsr. to Gov., Nat. Bank of Greece, 1965-68; Dpty. Chmn. of

Bd. & Mng. Dir., Cambas Co., Chmn. of Bd. & Mng. Dir., Radio Springs Kamena Vourla Ltd., Bd. mbr., Am. Plaster Corp., Hellenic Dairy Inds. Co. Ltd. (EVGA), Hellenic Cement Ind. (CHALYPS), Oil Refineries of Greece, 1968-. Mbrships: Assn. of Grads. of Athens Schl. of Econs.; Soc. of Studies for Econ. Dev. Author of econ. studies & articles in local publs. Recip., Gold Key to N.Y.C., U.S.A., 1973. Address: 17 Faidrou St., Athens 501, Greece. 43.

POULSEN, Hemming Engelund, b. 26 Aug. 1921. Professor. Educ: M.D., Copenhagen Univ., Denmark, 1947; Clin. trng., Inst. of Pathol. Anatomy. Appts: Pathol. in Chief, Sundby Hosp., Copenhagen, 1957, Kommimehospitaler, ibid, 1965; Docent, Univ. of Copenhagen, 1962; Prof., Royal Dental Schl.; Prof. of Pathol. Anatomy, Univ. of Copenhagen, 1971. Mbrships: Chief, Int. Reference Ctr. for Classification of tumours of the uterus, World Hlth. Org., 1963-; Chief of Collaborating Ctr. for precancerous lesions of the oral cavity, ibid, 1967; European Assn. for study of the liver (int. working grp., 1967); Int. Acad. of Pathol. Author on num. sci. publs. Address: Frederiksberg Alle 54I, 1820 Copenhagen V, Denmark. 134.

POULSEN-HANSEN, Alfred Gerhardt, b. 7 Jan. 1915. Doctor. Educ: M.D., Univ. of Copenhagen, Denmark, 1941; Dip., Tropical Med. & Hygiene, Univ. of Liverpool, U.K., 1948; Dip., Pub. Hlth., London Schl. of Hygiene & Tropical Med., 1952. Appts. incl: Intern & Res., var. hosps. in Denmark, 1941-44; Med. Off., Tanganyika Territory, 1948-51; Med. Off., WHO, Kandahar, Afghanistan, 1955-57, Manila, Philippines, 1958-60; Asst. Med. Off., Middlesex Co. Coun., Hlth. Area 3, U.K., 1962-63; Cons., Inst. of Ophthalmol., Iran, Iraq, Jordan, 1963; Dpty. Med. Off. of Hlth., Asst. Med. Off., Harlow & Epping Urban Dist. Coun. Epping & Ongar Rural Dist. Coun. Essex Co. Coun., U.K., 1963-65; Sr. Med. Off., London Borough of Lewisham Coun., 1965-69; Prin. Med. Off., London Borough of Hackney Coun., 1969-; Specialist, Community Med., Barking & Havering Area Hlth. Authority, 1974-. Mbrships. incl: Hon. Sec. to City Div., BMA; Fndr. Mbr., Fac. of Community Med., Royal Coll. of Physns., 1972; Danish Med. Assn.; Royal Soc. Tropical Med. & Hygiene. Address: 24 Noel Rd., London N1 8HA, U.K. 134.

POUND, Leland Earl, b. 23 July 1945. Newspaper Editor. Educ: B.A., Univ. of Calif., Riverside, 1967; Brigham Young Univ., Provo, Utah. Appts: Profl. Genealogical Rsch., 1968-69; Asst. to Mgr., J.J. Newbury Co., Buena Park, Calif., 1968; Reporter, Fullerton Daily News Tribune, Fullerton, ibid, 1968-70; Ed., News-Times, Placentia, 1970-. Mbrships: V.P., Kiwanis Club, Placentia, 1972 (treas., 1972-); Orange Co. Calif. Genealogical Soc. (Ed., quarterly publ., 1971-); Univ. of Calif. Riverside Alumni Assn. (publs. comm., 1 yr.). Author, History of Glabe Family, 1969. Hons. incl: Placentia Jaycees Award of commendation, 1970; City of Placentia serv. awards, 1972, '73. Address: 110 Orange Grove Ave., Placentia, CA 92670, U.S.A. 16.

POUNDS, Jessie L., b. 7 July 1909. Educator; Coach; Librarian. Educ: B.S. in Phys. Ed., N.W. Tchrs. Coll., Okla., 1937; M.S. in Hlth., Phys. Ed. & Rec., A & M Coll., ibid, 1942; Postgrad. work at other univs. Appts. incl: Tchr. & Coach, Knowles Schl., Beaver Co., Okla., 1937-40 & Laverne Schl., Harper Co., ibid, 1940-42; Phys. Educ. Instr. & Coach, Woodward Jr. H.S., 1942-58; Phys. Educ. Instr., Tchr., Coach & Libn., Quinault H.S.,

Amanda Pk., Wash., 1958-71; Olympic Coach, 1953. Mbrships. incl: Recording Sect., Delta Kappa Gamma; Kappa Kappa Iota; var. offs. & Fellow, Nat. Assn. for Hlth. Phys. Educ. & Recreation; Wash. Educ. Assn.; Nat. U.S. Olypmpic Comm., Trng. & Field for Girls, 1956-60. Publs. incl: Co-author, Oklahoma State Physical Education Syllabus, 1952; articles in profl. jrnls. Address: Box 68, Quinault, WA 98575, U.S.A.

POUPKO, (Rabbi Dr.) Bernard A. Rabbi. Educ: Yeshiva Univ. Coll., CCNY, Columbia Univ.; Ph.D., Univ. of Pitts.; Ordination as Rabbi, Theological Sem. of Yeshiva Univ. Appts. incl: Rabbi w. life tenure, Shaare Torah Congregation, Pitts., 1942-; Volunteer Civilian Chap., U.S.A. Air Corps Cadet Units, Duquesne Univ., Pitts., Pa., WW II; Chmn., Rabbinical Fellowship of Gtr. Pitts., & Rabbinical Bd. Gtr. Pitts.; Co.-Chmn., Int. Comm. of Schlrs.; past Nat. Pres., Religious Zionists of Am.; Co.-Fndr., Chmn. Fac. & Personnel Comm., Hillel Acad., Pitts. Mbr. & Off., var. profl. orgs. Publs. incl: In the Shadow of the Kremlin; Forms of Jewish Adult Religious Education. Author, over 300 articles & 400 sermons in U.S.A. publs. & abroad. Recip., var. awards for religious servs. Address: 2523 Beechwood Blvd., Pittsburgh, PA 15217, U.S.A. 55.

POWELL, Charlene (Mrs.), b. 5 June 1911. Educator. Educ: B.S., Murray State Univ., 1936; M.A., ibid, 1960. Appts: Tchr., Lone Valley & Colvert City, 1929-35; Tchr., TVA Schl., Gilbertsville, 1939-42, '46-47; Chemist & Supvsng. Chemist, Ky. Ordnance Works, 1942-45; Prin., Forley Elem. Schl., Paducah, Ky., 1947-; Admnstr. & Supvsr., Adult Basic Educ., 1967-. Mbrships: Pres., McCracken Co. Educ. Assn., 1960; V.P. ibid, 1959; Sec., McCracken Co. Tchrs. Credit Union, 1960-; Hon. Life Mbr., PTA; Treas., Reidland-Farley Volunteer Fire Assn. Recip. of hons. Address: 3730 Old Benton Rd., Rte. 8, Paducah, KY 42001, U.S.A. 57, 125, 130, 138.

POWELL, Charles Kenneth, b. 11 Aug. 1939. Attorney. Educ: B.S., Clemson Univ., 1961; LL.B., Univ. of S.C., 1964. Appts: Page, S.C. House of Reps., 1961-64; Campaign Adie, Floyd Spence, Republican Candidate, 1962; Candidate, Richland Co. Repubn. Ticket, House of Reps., 1966; Cand., State Senate, ibid, 1968; Chmn., Repubn. Pty., ibid, 1970; Chmn., Credentials Comm., S.C. Repubn. Convention, 1970; Election Law Study Comm., ibid, 1970; Organiser, precincts 2nd Congressional Dist. for S.C. Repubn. Pty., 1968; Sr. Ptnr., Law Firm, Powell & Smith; Chmn., S.C. Repubn. Pty., 1971-72. Mbrships. incl: Bd. Dirs., Am. Cancer Soc., Richland Co.; Organiser & 1st Advsr., S.C. Teenage Repubns.; Legal Counsel, Young Ams. for Freedom; Third Degree Mason; Blue Key Nat. Hon. Soc., Clemson Univ.; Wade Hampton 273, Sons of Confedeate Veterans. Address: P.O. Box 5247, Columbia, SC 29250, U.S.A. 46, 117, 125.

POWELL, John Rolfe, Sr., b. 23 Mar. 1915. Certified Public Accountant. Educ: Grad., LaSalle Ext. Univ.; Bachelor of Accts., Wheelers Bus. Coll., B'ham, Ala.; Univ. of Ala., N.Y. Univ. Tax Inst. & Southern Fed. Tax Inst. Appts: w. Bolling P. Starke, ins. agcy., 1934-40; Prac. Pub. Acct., 1941-; Dir. in var. corps.; one of 4 organizers of Investors Fed. Savings & Loan Assn., Montgomery, Ala. Pres., Montgomery Chapts. of Ala. Soc. of C.P.A.s, 1961-62, Nat. Assn. of Accts., 1967-68 & Ala. Assn. of Pub. Accts., 1953-54; Montgomery Estate Planning Coun.; Rotary Int.; Civitan; Am. Inst. C.P.A.s. Address: 1345 Glen Gratten

Ave., Montgomery AL 36111, U.S.A. 7, 16, 128, 131.

POWELL, Roy James, b. 18 Feb. 1934. Educational Administrator. Educ: B.Ed., Univ. of Miami, 1966; M.Ed., Fla. Atlantic Univ., 1967; Ph.D., Univ. of Miami, 1971. Appts: Sci. Tchr., Youth Manpower Trng. `Prog., Miami, Fla., 1963; Curric. Writer, Dade Co. Pub. Schls., Miami, 1963-64; Tchr., ibid, 1964-65, Rschr., 1965-66; Rsch. Assoc. & Dir. of Bus. Affairs, Fla. Migratory Child Survey Ctr., Univ. of Miami, 1968-69; Chmn., Dept. of Elec. Engrng. Technols., Miami-Dade Community Coll., Miami, 1969-. Mbrships: Am. Soc. for Engrng. Educ.; Am. Tech. Educ. Assn.; Fla. Assn. of Community Colls.; Med. Electronics & Data Soc.; IEEE; Phi Delta Kappa. Publs: Electronics Instructor's Guides, 2 vols., 1965; Radio and Television Instructor's Guide (ed. & contbr.), 1965; Electricity Instructor's Guide (ad. & contbr.), 1965; Migrant Children in Florida (contbr.), 1969. Address: 850 Palm Springs Mile, Apt. 414, Hialeah, FL 33167, U.S.A. 7.

POWELL, William R., b. 20 Nov. 1932. Educator. Educ: B.S., Ind. State Univ., 1954; M.S., ibid, 1957; Ed.D., 1962. Appts: Tchr., Elem. Schl., Speedway, Ind., 1956-60; Instr., Ind. Univ., 1960-62; Asst. Prof. & Dir., Reading Ctr., Ball State Unive., 1962-64; Prof. & Dir., Ctr. for Reading Rsch. & Instrn., Univ. of Ill., Urbana, 1964-72; Dean, Schl. of Educ., Univ. of Evansville, Ind., 1972-. Mbrships: State Chmn., Ind., 1962-64 & Ill., 1964-65, Int. Reading Assn.; Pres., Ill. Coun., Int. Reading Assn., 1968-69; Pres., Ind. Profs. of Reading Educ., 1975-76; Am. Educl. Rsch. Assn.; Nat. Coun. Tchrs. of Engl.; Phi Delta Kappa; Nat. Coun. Measurement in Educ. Publs: Co-Ed., Elementary Reading Instruction-Selected Materials, 1974; contbr. articles to profl. jrnls. Hons: Disting. Tchng. Award, Ind. Univ. Fndn., 1962; Leadership Award, Alpha Chapt., Phi Delta Kappa, 1962. Address: Dean, Schl. of Educ., Univ. of Evansville, P.O. Box 329, Evansville, IN 47702, U.S.A.

POWELL, William Roland, b. 16 Mar. 1923. Administrative Clerk. Educ: CUNY, 1941-43; Wayne State Univ., Detroit, Mich., 1951; Pa. State Univ., 1960-62. Appts: Ldr., Dance Band, N.Y.C., 1937-42; Pub. Acct., Wash. D.C., 1963-66; Admin. Clerk, Defense Gen. Supply Ctr., Richmond, Va., 1966-. Mbrships: Am. Acctng. Assn.; Past, Int. Assn. of Machinists. Compositions: The Man-Made Hell Suite in G minor; The Blood of the Lamb; Undaunted; Martin's Dream. Inventor, Compass Caliper, measuring instrument for machinists. Hons: Cert. as Charter Mbr., U.S. Defense Supply Agcy.; Letter of Appreciation, Defense Supply Agcy. Address: 3324 Parkwood Ave., Richmond, VA 23221, U.S.A. 125, 130.

POWELL-SMITH, Vincent, b. 28 Apr. 1939. Academic Lawyer; Author; Trade Association Executive. Educ: Univ. of Birmingham, U.K.; Inns of Ct. Schl. of Law, London; LL.B., LL.M.; D.Litt. Appts. incl: Legal Advsr., John Hilton Bur., 1964-66; Cons., ibid, 1966-; Jt. Sec., Demolition Ind. Conciliation Bd., 1971-; Mbr., Jt. Advsry. Comm. for Safety in Hlth. in Construction Inds. Mbrships: Vice-Chancellor, Order of Crown of Stuart; Registrar, Mem. of Merit of King Charles the Martyr; Fellow, Royal Soc. of Arts. Publs. incl: Casebook on Contract, 2nd edit. 1972; The Building Regulations Explained & Illustrated, 4th edit. 1973; The Law of Boundaries & Fences, 2nd edit. 1974. Contbr. to Architects' Jrnl., 1972. Hons. incl: Off. de l'Ordre de Mérite Juridique; Grand Cross, Order of St. Sava; Freeman, City

of London. Address: 2 Bankart Ave., Leicester LE2 2DB, U.K. 3, 43, 139.

POWERS, Margaret Pauline Serritelli (Mrs. Raymond Allen Powers), b. 16 May 1947. Woman's Editor. Educ: A.A. Pasadena City Coll., Calif., 1967; B.A., Calif. State Univ., L.A., 1970. Appts: Jrnlist., Edit. Dept., Alhambra Post-Advocate, 1967; Woman's Ed., ibid, 1969. Mbrships: V.P., Corres. Sec., Serv. Comm. Chmn., Alhambra-San Gabriel Soroptimist Club; Bd. of Dirs., P.R. Chmn., San Gabriel Community Boys' Club; Charter Mbr., Southern Calif. Press Club; Alhambra Day Nursery Assn. Hons. incl: Award, La Chime Bus. & Profl. Women's Club, 1970; San Gabriel Valley Pilot Club Award, 1970; San Gabriel Valley Symph. Assn. Women's Comm. Award, 1971; Ring of Truth Award, Copley Newspapers, 1971. Address: 512 Cortez Rd., Arcadia, CA 91006, U.S.A. 5, 117, 138.

POWERS, Marilyn (Mrs. Jason Berger), b. 23 May 1925. Artist. Educ: Mass. Coll. of Art, 1942-45; w. Karl Zerbe, Boston Mus. Schl., 1945-49; travelled & painted in Europe, 1949-52. Appts: Pvte. Tchr. (master-student relationship), Direct Vision Atelier; Pres., Direct Vision Inc., Revolutionary Art Movement against dehumanization & the impersonal in art (inclng. painters, poets, writers & composers). Works incl: portraits commissioned by Baroness Evakelety, Mathilde Goodwin Bird, Warren Bennis (Pres., Univ. of Cinn.), John Warren (Bayard) Deknatel, John Sullivan (Provost, State Univ., Buffalo), & François Truffaut; landscape paintings of Normandy, S. of France, New Engl. & Mexico. Recip. grant from Mass Coun. on Arts & Humanities, Flemming Mus., Vermont. Address: 40 University Rd., Brookline, MA 02146, U.S.A. 5, 37.

PÖYRY, Jaakko (Veikko Emanuel), b. 6 Aug. 1924. Engineer; Company Director. Educ: M.Sc., Tech. Univ. of Helsinki, Finland, 1948. Appts: Design Engr., Paper Machine Dept., Oy Wärtsilä Ab, Helsinki, 1947-49; Dir., Pulp & Paper Machine Dept., ibid, 1949-56; Mng. Dir., Oy Tekno-Invest Ab, Helsinki, 1956-58; Mng. Dir., Murto & Pöyry, cons. engrs., Helsinki, 1958-61; Mng. Dir. & Bd. Chm., Jaakko Pöyry & Co. Oy, cons. engrs., Helsinki, 1961-. Mbrships. incl: Finnish Paper Engrs. Assn.; Engrng. Soc. of Finland; Finnish Assn. of Cons. Engrs.; Finnish Acad. of Tech. Sci.; Royal Swedish Acad. of Engrng. Sci.; Swedish Assn. of Pulp & Paper Engrs; Brazilian Pulp & Paper Tech. Assn. Publs: Articles on forest inds. econs. in profl. jrnls. Hons: Lampén Gold Medal of Merit, Finnish Paper Engrs. Assn., 1971; Jaakko Pöyry & Co. Oy awarded Export Prize, Pres. of Finland, 1967; & Recognition Prize for meritorious work, Engrng. Soc. of Finland, 1971. Address: P.O. Box 30, 00380 Helsinki 38, Finland.

PRADT, Robert W., b. 4 Sept. 1928. Publisher. Educ: B.S., Univ. of Wis., U.S.A.; Grad. study, Art & Psychol., ibid; Art, Schl. of Art Inst. of Chgo.; Restoration, Conservation of Paintings, Art Objects under J.C. Fenner Bridgem. Appts: Pres., Bd. Chmn., A.R. Pragare Co., Inc., Publrs.; Art Dir., Nueller Color Plate Co., Milwaukee, & Country Beautiful Fndn., Waukesha; Fine Arts Appraiser, Conservator, Free-lance & for Bresler Galls., Milwaukee. Mbrships: Art Inst. of Chgo.; Milwaukee Art Ctr. Friends of Art; U.S. Chmbr. of Comm.; Kiwanis Club, Ctrl. Wauwatosa. Publs: Art Dir. & Designer, The Beauty in Great America; Publr., Designer, Artist Source Book Series, & others. Address: 8444 Ravenswood Cir., Wauwatosa, WI 53226, U.S.A. 37.

PRAETORIUS, Cecilia W., b. 22 Sept. 1912. Executive Secretary. Educ: Grad., H.S., U.S.A.; Corres. Courses in Spanish, Jrnlsm. Appts: Sec. to Dist. Mgr., X-Ray Dept., Gen. Electric Co., 18 yrs.; Legal Sec., Western Girl, 3yrs.; Sec. to Dir., Div. of Nursing, Charity Hosp. of La., 3 yrs. Mbrships: Pres., Gentilly Ter. Chapt. 990, Am. Assn. of Retd. Persons; St. Bernard Jubilees; Jefferson Golden Agers; Hazel Pl. Soc. Club. Publs: Fantasy & Emotion (poetry). Also contbr. to periodicals. Hons: Poetry Pageant, 1969. Address: 9029 Camille Dr., New Orleans, LA 70123, U.S.A. 11, 57.

PRAGER, H. Lee, b. 11 July 1935. Executive. Educ: B.S., Engrng., MIT, Cambridge, 1957; M.B.A., Marketing, Xavier Univ., Cinn., Ohio, 1963. Appts: Sales Engr., Goodyear Tire & Rubber Co., Akron, Ohio, 1957-60; Sales Rep., Lightolier Inc., Cinn., Ohio, 1961-63; Market Dev. Specialist, U.S.I. Film Products, Stratford, Conn., 1963-65; Product Mgr., Extrudo Film Corp. (Div. of Std. Oil Co. of N.J.), 1965-68; V.P. & Gen. Mgr., Amerace Corp., Wheel Products Div., Butler, N.J., 1968-; Pres., Prager Land Trust, 1969; Pres., Interdeck Dev. Corp., 1970. Mbrships: Am. Marketing Assn.; Soc. Plastic Engrs.; Chequesset Country Club, Wellfleet, Mass. Contbr. of sev. bus. & tech. articles to trade publs. Address: 2233 Old Farm Rd., Scotch Plains, NJ 07076, U.S.A. 16.

PRAKASH, Om, b. 18 Aug. 1927. University Professor & Dean. Educ: B.Com., Univ. of Allahabad, India; M.Com., ibid; Ph.D.; Litt.D. Appts: Asst. Prof., Univ. of Allahabad, 1947-62; Prof. & Hd., Dept. of Commerce, Panjab Univ., Chandigarh, 1962-63; Prof., Hd. of Dept., & Dir./Dean, Schl. of Commerce, Univ. of Rajasthan, Jaipur, 1963-, now Sr. Prof.; Vis. Prof., attached inter alia to Karl Marx Univ. of Econs. & Ctr. for Afro-Asian Rsch., Hungarian Acad. of Scis., Budapest, Hungary, 1969. Mbrships: Treas., Indian Jrnl. of Econs., 1950-54; Mng. Ed., ibid, 1954-62; Chmn., Commercium (Bi-annual rsch. jrnl.; Schl. of Commerce), since establishment 1965-; Asst. Sec. (1st), Indian Commerce Assn., 1948-51; Edit. Bd., Indian Jrnl. of Commerce, sev. terms; Lions Club, 1967-71. Author of some 12 books & over 70 papers. Recip., Int. Prize of $500, Comm. for Econ. Dev., N.Y., U.S.A., 1958. Address: P-2, Univ. Campus, Jaipur 4, Rajasthan, India.

PRANICH, Chittra (Mrs. Kachorn Pranich), b. 21 Jan. 1933. Government Official; Librarian. Educ: B.A., Fac. of Art, Chulalongkorn Univ., Bangkok, 1956; M.A. in Lib. Sci., Cert. in Pub. Admin., Ind. Univ., U.S.A., 1958. Appts: Lectr., Engl. Lang., Tech. Coll., Bangkok, 1956; Asst. Libn., Fac. of Pub. Admin., Thammasat Univ., Bangkok, 1958-59; Univ. Libn., ibid, 1959-. Mbrships: Thai Lib. Assn.; ALA; Family Planning Assn. of Thailand. Address: Thammasat Univ. Library, Prachand Rd., Bangkok 2, Thailand. 5.

PRASAD, Bhairo, b. 13 July 1927. Barrister-at-Law. Educ: Tchrs. Cert., 1946; Entered Hon. Soc. of Gray's Inn, London, U.K., 1949; Qualified as Barrister-at-Law, 1950; Called to Utter Bar, London, 1951. Appts: Schl. Tchr., 1943-48; Commenced law prac., 1951; Prosecuted for the Crown, 1959-61; Currently in pvte. prac. Mbrships: Pres., Berbice Bar Assn., 1959, '61, '63, 1967-69; Ldr., Berbice Bar, 1970-; Councillor, New Amsterdam Town Coun., 1970-74; Chmn., Parliamentary Comm., New Amsterdam, ibid, 1971-73; Finance Comm., ibid, 1970-72; Chmn., Finance Comm., ibid, 1973; Berbice Reading Soc.; Lions Int.Club. Hons. incl: Schlrship., Govt. Tchrs. Trng.Coll., 1946; Queen's Counsel, Letters Patent, 1969; Mayor, New Amsterdam, 1974. Address: Lot 5, Main & Coburg St., New Amsterdam, Berbice, Guyana. 109.

PRASAD, Braj Nandan, b. 23 Oct. 1923. University Reader. Educ: Grad., Benares Hindu Univ., Varanasi, India, 1945; M.Sc., ibid, 1947; Ph.D., London Univ., U.K., 1959. Appts: Tchr. & Rschr., Algol., Agra & Saugar Univs., India, 1945-51; Lucknow Univ., ibid, 1951-; Off. i/c, Prin. Investigator, var. aspects Phycol., Hydrobiol. & Algal Cytol., w. Coun. Sci. & Indl. Rsch., New Delhi, U.P. State Coun. Sci. & Indl. Rsch. etc. Mbrships: Fellow, Linnean Soc., London, U.K.; Life Fellow, Nat. Acad. Scis., India & Indian Botanical Soc.; Int. Phycol. Soc.; Brit. Phycol. Soc; Current Sci. Assn., India; Edit. Bd., Phycol. Soc., India; Indian Sci. Congress Assn. Author 38 papers & reports, var. aspects Phycol., esp. Algal cytogenetics, taxonomy & Algae of India. Recip. Malaviya Gold Medal, outstanding achievement in studies, Benares Hindu Univ., 1945. Address: Dept. Botany, Lucknow Univ., Lucknow, UP, India.

PRAST, Johannes Werner, b. 26 June 1917. Electronics Engineer. Appts. incl: Sr. Electronics Engr., U.S.A.F. Air Univ., Schl. of Aviation Med., Randolph Field, Tex., 1947-53; Prog. Mgr., Group Supvsn., Secure Cmd. Systems, Bell Aircraft Corp., Buffalo, N.Y., 1953-59; Chief Systems Engr., Mil. & Electronics Div., Wurlitzer Co., 1959-62; Dir. of Adv. Systems, Sierra Rsch. Corp., Buffalo, 1962-; Pres. & Rsch. Dir., Prast Rsch. Assocs., Inc. Mbrships. incl: 1972 Wkshop. Panel on Lower-Limb Orthotics, Nat. Acad. of Scis., Nat. Rsch. Coun.; Chmn., Distributed Air Traffic Control Study Group, Air Traffic Contrl Advsry. Commn., U.S. Dept. of Transportation; Alternate Deleg., Radio Tech. Commn. for Aeronautics; President's Aviation Advsry. Commn. Contbr. to profl. jrnls. Recip., Cert. of Appreciation, U.S. Dept. of Transportation, 1969. Address: 1094 Stony Point Rd., Grand Island, NY 14072, U.S.A. 6.

PRATER, Jesse Wallace, b. 23 Mar. 1932. Dentist. Educ: Univ. of Louisville, Ky.; Grad., Dental Schl., ibid, 1962. Appts: Dental Cons., Bur. of Crippled Children & Div. of Vocational Rehab., State of Fla., 1971-; Cons. Ed., Dental Mgmt. Mag., 1971-; Lectr. on Dental Prac. Mgmt. & Tech. Dentistry. Mbrships. incl: Fellow, Royal Soc. of Hlth., 1973; Alpha Epsilon Delta, 1957; Am. Dental Assn.; Psi Omega; Pres., Fla. Chapt., Am. Soc. of Preventive Dentistry; Am. Acad. of Dental Prac. Admin.; Fla. Dental Assn.; Fla. W. Coast Dental Soc.; Am. Equilibration Soc.; Fed. Dentaire Int.; Pierre Fauchard Acad.; Charter Mbr., Southern Acad. of Clin. Nutrition; Seroma Club; etc. Publd. Ways to Better Days in Your Practice. Address: 2630 W. Waters Ave., Tampa, FL 33614, U.S.A. 7, 57.

PRATT, Ewart Arthur, b. 20 Mar. 1919. Company Director. Educ: B.Sc., Univ. of Pa., 1942 Appts: Chmn., Steers Ltd., St. John's, Newfoundland; Pres., Pratt Reps. (Nfld.) Ltd., Steers Exports Ltd., J.C. Hudson Co. Ltd., Colonial Bus. Properties Ltd.; V.P., Steers Ins. Agcys. Ltd., Standard Mfg. Co. Ltd.; Dir., Canadian Nat. Railways, Pratt Invesment Co. Ltd., Standard Mfg. Co. Ltd., Nfld. Steamships (1965) Ltd., Purity Factories Ltd., Nfld. Light & Power Co. Ltd.; Mbr., St. John's Advsry. Bd., Canada Permanent Trust Co.; Councillor, Nfld. Bd. of Trade, 1950-52, '64-65; V.P., ibid, 1966;

Pres., 1967. Mbrships. incl: Dir., Nat. Coun., Canadian Chmbr. of Comm., Canadian Coun., Int. Chmbr. of Comm.; Bd. Govs., Coll. of Fisheries, St. John's, Nfld.; Advsry. Bd., Inst. Soc. & Econ. Rsch., Mem. Univ. of Nfld.; Pres., Nfld. Br., Canadian Mental Hlth. Assn., 1970. Address: c/o Steers Ltd., Water St., St. John's, Newfoundland, Canada.

PRATT, Louis Hill, b. 11 Aug. 1937. Educator. Educ: B.S., Savannah State Coll., Ga., U.S.A., 1958; M.A., Tchrs. Coll., Columbia Univ., N.Y.C., 1967; Ph.D., Fla. State Univ., Tallahassee, 1974. Appts: Chmn., Dept. of Bus. Educ., Todd-Grant H.S., Darien, Fla., 1958-60; Instr., Dept. of Engl., Sol C. Johnson H.S., Savannah, Ga., 1960-62 & 1964-69; Asst. Prof., Dept. of Engl., & Dir., Freshman Composition, Fla. Agricl. & Mech. Univ., Tallahassee, 1969-. Mbrships: AAUP; Coll. Lang. Assn.; Seven Hills Toastmasters Club, Tallahassee; Phi Delta Kappa; Alpha Phi Alpha. Recip., sev. schlrships. & fellowship. Address: 1415 Charlotte St., Tallahassee, FL 32304, U.S.A. 125.

PRECA, Giorgio, b. 25 June 1909. Professor; Artist; Painter. Educ: Studied at Govt. Schl. of Art, Malta; Accademia di Belli Arte, Rome, Italy. Appts: Prof., British Acad., Rome, 1939; Dir. of Fine Arts, Mus. of Malta. Hon. Pres. of Modern Art, Malta. Personal exhibitions in Malta, in Italy, Biennale of Venice, 1952; Exhibition at Commonwealth Art Gall., London, U.K., 1966; Chronological Art exhibition, Palasso Braschi del Commune, Rome, 1974; Sacred art paintings in Malta & Rome; Life paintings incl. H.H. Pope Pacelli, Grand Master of Order of Malta; Works in U.K. & other countries. Address: 6 Via Giulio Ventianique int. 26, 00136 Rome, Italy. 43.

PREE Bernice Wilson, b. 1 July 1913. Publishing Company Executive. Educ: Fleisher Voc. Schl., Phila., Pa., 1939; Drexel Inst., Phila., 1951-52; Wharton Schl., Univ. of Pa., 1956. Appts: Counselor, Martha Falkner Schl. for Girls, Darling, Pa., 1947; Sales Rep., P. Lorillard Co. Inc., N.Y.C., 1947-50; Lectr. in Salesmanship, William Penn Bus. Inst., Phila., 1949; var. offs. & appts., inclng. Advt. Dir., V.P. i/c Promotions, Bd. of Dirs. of Co., Phila. Tribune Newspaper Co., Pa., 1950-73. Mbrships. incl: P.R. Chmn., Nat. Bus. & Profl. Women's Assn.; Financial Sec. & Statistician, Assn. Bus. & Profl. Women of Phila. & Vicinity; Sales Assn. of Phila. Author of poems. Hons. incl: Disting. Serv. Award, NAACP, 1962; Dedication & Disting. Serv. Award, Phila. Tribune Co., 1969; Outstanding Achievement Award, 1970. Address: 6925 Anderson St., Philadelphia, PA 19119, U.S.A. 5, 57, 138.

PREGEL, Boris, b. 24 Jan. 1893. Executive. Appts. incl: Expert Cons., Office of the Chief of Staff, U.S. Army, 1944; Prof., Dean of Scis., Ecole Libre Des Hautes Etudes, N.Y.C.; For. V. Prof. of Rsch., Manhattan Coll.; Prof. Emeritus, U.T.Ł. Luxembourg, 1973; Gen. Del. for the U.S., Société d'Encouragement au Progrès-Paris, France & Société d'Encouragement pour la Recherche et l'Invention, Paris; Gen. Del. for N. Am., Institut Int. pour les Problèmes Humains du Travail; Chmn. of the Bd., Canrad Precision Industries, Inc, 1969-73; Hon. Chmn. of the Bd., Canrad-Hanovia, Inc., 1973. Trustee, Mbr., Bd. of Govs., Pres. & ordinary Mbr. of many profl. assns. inclng: Life Fellow & V.P. of Bd. of Govs., N.Y. Acad. of Scis., 1970-73; Chmn. of the Hon. Life Govs. of the Bd., ibid, 1974. Inventions & Patents incl: Use of Radioactive Materials in Motors with Internal Combustion, 1929; Aerial Exploring of Radioactive Deposits (in collab.), 1944; Radioactive Relays (in collab.), 1945; Alpha Ray Source & Method of Preparation (in collab.); Industrial Production of Actinium, 1949. Publs. incl: Peacetime Uses of Atomic Energy, 1947; Energy, Economy & Society in Transition, 1959; America Faces the Nuclear Age, 1961. Recip., num. medals, awards, decorations & hons. Address: 50 Rockefeller Plaza, suite 1009, N.Y., NY 10020, U.S.A. 2.

PREGER, Andrea, b. 20 Mar. 1912. Pianist. Educ: studies w. Max Pauer, Leipzig Conservatory; Grad., Acad. of Music, Ljubljana; LL.D., Fac. of Law, Zagreb. Appts: Sec. & Hd., Music Dept., Chief Ed., Music Prof., Radio Belgrade, 1944-51; Prof., Acad. of Music, Belgrade, 1954-. Fnded. Belgrade Trio w. Alexander Pavlović (violin) & Viktor Jakovcić ('cello), 1963; has toured most European countries, U.S.A., Canada & U.S.S.R. w. trio. Has given concert tours in Yugoslavia, Israel, Greece, Austria, Italy, France, Belgium, Norway, Denmark, German Fed. Repub., Hungary, Rumania, Czechoslovakia, Bulgaria, U.S.S.R., U.S.A. & Canada. Has recorded for Club français du disque & RTB Belgrade. Mbrships: 1st Sec. Gen., Assn. of Concert Artists of Yugoslavia; sev. times Mbr. of Coun. & V.P. of Assn. of Concert Artists of Serbia. Hons: October Prize, City of Belgrade, 1964; Order of Repub. w. Silver Wreath, 1972. Address: 22, Svet. Markovića, 11000 Belgrade, Yugoslavia. 55.

PREISER, Gert Richard, b. 18 Feb. 1928. University Professor. Educ: Univs. of Frankfurt (Main) & Heidelberg, German Fed. Repub., 1946-53; Dr. phil., Kiel, 1957. Appts: H.S. Tchr., 1954-56; Ed., Hippocrates Lexicon (Thesaurus Linguae Graecae, Hamburg), 1957-62; Lectr. in Greek & Latin langs., Univ. of Hamburg, 1962-66; Sci. Off., Senckenberg Inst. of Hist. of Med., Frankfurt (Main), 1966-70; Lectr. in Hist. of Med., 1969-70; Prof., Univ. of Frankfurt (Main), 1971-; Vice Chancellor, ibid, 1971-73. Mbrships: Int. Soc. of Hist. of Med.; Soc. for Hist. of Scis.; Mommsen-Gesellschaft; Chmn., Hochschulverband, Hesse, 1973-. Author of articles on med. hist., 1966-71. Recip., Senckenberg Prize, 1969. Address: Rollossweg 36, D-6900 Heidelberg 1, German Fed. Repub.

PREJES, Genevieve Barbara, b. 29 Oct. 1918. Medical Records Administrator; Medical Records Consultant. Educ: Dip., St. Mary's Hosp. Schl. for Med. Record Libns., Brooklyn, NY., 1956; Mbr., Am. Med. Record Assn., registered nationally, RRA, 1956; B.S., Boston Coll., Chestnut Hill, Mass., 1961; Cert., St. Louis Univ. Prog. of Continuing Educ. in Hosp. Exec. Dev., 1970. Appts. incl: Med. Records Libn., New Britain Mem. Hosp; Conn., 1952-54; Asst. Med. Record Libn., Sancta Maria Hosp., Cambridge, Mass., 1957-61; Chief Med. Record Libn., ibid, 1961-66; Hosp. Admnstr., ibid, 1966-72; Med. Records Admnstr., Bon Secours Hosp., Methuenn, Mass., 1972-; Med. Records Cons., Georgetown, Mass., 1973-. Mbrships: Nominee, Am. Coll. of Hosp. Admnstrs.; Mass. Med. Record Assn.; Mass. Hosp. Assn & New England Hosp. Assembly. Hons. incl: Plaqued Commendation Resolution, State Senate of Commonwealth of Mass., 1972; Plaque & Citation, Gov. Francis Sargent, Commonwealth of Mass., 1972. Address: 21 Howe St., Apt. 21, Methuen, MA 01844, U.S.A. 5, 132, 138.

PRENSKY, Sol D., b. 27 Jan. 1903. Educator; Engineer. Appts. incl: Test Engr., Curtiss-Wright Co., Carlstadt, N.J., 1952-54; Electronics Engr., Otis Elevator, Brooklyn, 1954-55; Assoc. Prof., Elec. Engrng. Dept.,

Fairleigh Dickinson Univ., Teaneck, N.J., 1956-70; Now Assoc. Prof., Emeritus, ibid, 1970-. Publs: Electronic Demonstration Manual, 1945; Electronic Voltmeters, 1962; Electronic Instrumentation, 1963, 2nd ed. '71; Advanced Electronic Instruments, 1970; Manual of Linear Integrated Circuits, 1974. Recip., Grant from Nat. Sci. Fndn. for In-Serv. Inst. in Electronics, 1965. Address: Fairleigh Dickinson Univ., Teaneck, NJ 07666, U.S.A. 6, 15.

PREOBRAJENSKA, Vera Nicolaevna, b. 27 Apr. 1926. Pianist; Composer. Educ: B.A., San Fran. State Univ., 1953; M.A., Bernadean Univ., Las Vegas, Nev., 1972; Ph.D., ibid, 1973; studied w. Darius Milhaud, Ernst Bloch, Frederick Jacobi, Roger Sessions, Alexander Tcherephine, Ernst von Dohnanyi & Dmitri Shostakovitch, 1945-61. Appts. incl: Concert Mgr., Musical Artists of Am., 1959-61; Asst. Tchr. & Phys. Educ. Women's Dance Pianist, Univ. of Calif. (& Ext.), Berkeley, 1965-68; Chmn., Dept. of Music, Bernadean Univ., Las Vegas, 1973-; Tchr., Corres. Courses, Ext., ibid, 1974-. Mbrships: Am. Music Ctr., N.Y.C.; Am. Soc. of Univ. Composers, N.Y.C.; Contemporary Californian Composers. Publs. incl: Piano Jazz (Blues) Sonata, Op. 1; Violin & Piano Sonata, Op. 1; Seven Piano Mazurkas; Five Classic Art Songs; Clara Milltch Ballet Score; Rhapsodie for 2 Pianos; String Quintet Suite; The Money Lender; Piano Sonata, Op. 2; Jazz (Blues) Symphony; Suite of Orchestral Pieces; Russian Art Songs. Hons. incl: Russian Texts commnd. for Liturgical Chorales, 1960, 62, 65, 66, 67 & 69; Cantata commnd. by The Orthodox Press, 1972. Address: 5423 Ygnacio Ave., Oakland, CA 94601, U.S.A. 5, 138.

PRESCOTT, David Samuel, b. 18 July 1938. Attorney; Developer Legal Education Programs. Educ: B.A., Calif. State Coll., Long Beach, 1961; J.D., Calif. Coll. of Law, 1969. Appts: Dpty. Pub. Defender of L.A. Co., 1969-70; Dpty. Dist. Atty., Riverside Co., 1970-71; Asst. Dean, Schl. of Law, Univ. of W. L.A., 1971-; Dean, Schl. of Paralegal Studies, ibid, 1971-; Orig.-Fndng. Advsr., Am. Paralegal Assn., 1972. Mbrships: Co-Chmn., Sub-Comm. on Legal Assts. of the Econs. of Law Off. Mgt. Comm., Am. Bar. Assn.; Calif State Bar Assn.; L.A. Co. Trial Lawyers Assn. Contbr. to Lawyers Newsletter & L.A. Co. Bar Bulletin. Recip. of Am. Jurisprudence Award for Excellence in 7 subjects, 1964-68. Address: Univ. of West L.A., 11000 W. Washington Blvd, Culver City, CA 90230, U.S.A.

PRESCOTT-PICKUP, Vernon Edmund, b. 27 Sept. 1923. Art Publisher; Writer; Public Relations Consultant. Educ: Univ. Coll. of Wales, Aberystwyth, 1941-42; RAF, 1941-43; pvte. art studies. Appts. incl: War Serv., Coastal Cmd. & Radar, R.A.F., 1941-47; Ptnr., Scenart Display (Visual Aids for Ind.), 1947-49; P.R. Off., Area Sec., Aims of Ind. Ltd., E. Midlands Area, 1949-57; Publicity & Advt. Mgr., Coseley Grp. of Cos., 1958-67; Dir., Coseley Engrng (Int.) Ltd., 1962-67, Coseley Engrng. Servs. Ltd., 1963-67; Mng. Dir., Ind. Marketing Servs. Ltd., 1965-67; Chmn. & Mng. Dir., Prescott-Pickup & Co. Ltd., 1967-. Mbrships. incl: Fndr. & Pres., Julian Soc.; profl. & lit. orgs. Originator & inventor, lithographic colour reprod. system. Contbr., var. profl. & specialist publs., newspapers. Radio & TV broadcasts. Recip., var. profl. awards. Address: Rodwin, Allscott, Telford, Salop TF6 5EQ, U.K. 24.

PRESS, Harold Alan, b. 5 Aug. 1909. Physician Educ: B.S., Tufts Univ., 1932; M.D., Tufts Univ. Coll. of Med., 1936. Appts: Dir., Prog. Analysis Staff, Dept. of Med. & Surg.,

VA, Wash., D.C., 1945-51; Exec. Dir., Pres.'s Commn. on Hlth. Needs of Nation, 1952; Asst. Dir., Med. Servs., Nat. Fndn. Infantile Paralysis, 1953-55; Exec. Ed., Yorke Med. Publs., N.Y.C., 1962-63; Med. Dir., Breon Labs. Inc., ibid, 1963-66; Dir., Profl. Communications, Merck Sharp & Dohme, W. Pt., Pa., 966-72; Dir., Mgmt. Appraisal Staff, Dept. of Med. & Surg. VA, Wash., D.C., 1972-. Author of var. publs. in the med. field. Address: 3809 Queen Mary Dr., Olney, MD 20832, U.S.A.

PRESTON, Kendall, Jr., b. 22 Oct. 1927. Engineer; Scientist. Educ: B.A., Harvard Coll., 1950; M.S., Grad. Schl. of Arts & Scis., ibid, 1952. Appts: Acting 1st Sgt., U.S. Army, Mediterranean Theatre of Ops., 1946-47; Mbr., Tech. Staff, Special Systems Dept., Bell Telephone Labs., Murray Hill, N.J., 1952-60; Mgr., New Prod. Dev., Rsch. Engrng. Dept., Perkin-Elmer Corp., Norwalk, Conn., 1960-61; Sr. Staff Scientist, Rsch. Div., ibid, 1961-72; Sr. Staff Engr., Optical Technol. Div., ibid, 1972-74; Prof. of Engrng. & Bio-Engrng., Carnegie-Mellor Univ., Pitts., Pa., 1974-. Mbrships: AAAS; Biol. Engrng. Soc., U.K.; Biomed. Engrng. Soc.; Harvard Engrs. & Scientists; Pres., Student Chapt., ibid, 1952; IEEE; Vice Chmn., Conn. Sect., ibid, 1963; Exec. Comm., 1964-66; Chmn., Conn. Chapt., Profl. Tech. Grp. of Electronic Computers, 1966-67; N.Y. Acad. of Sci.; var. pvte. clubs. Publs. incl: Coherent Optical Computers, 1972; Contbng. Author, Computer Technique in Biomedical Engineering, 1973. Advances in Optical & Electron Misroscopy, 1973, Computers & Automata, 1972, Automated Multiphasic Health Testing, Image Processing in Biological Science, 1968, & Optical & Electro-Optical Signal Processing, 1965; Contbr. to num. profl. jrnls. inclng. cover story, Scientific American, 'Automatic Analysis of Blood Cells', Nov. 1970. Holds var. patents in U.S., U.K., W. Germany, Japan, & Canada. Hons: Cum Laude Soc., 1945; Fellow Award, IEEE, 1973. Address: Dept. of Elec. Engrng., Schenley Park, Pittsburgh, PA 15213, U.S.A. 6.

PRESTWOOD, Alvin Tennyson, b. 18 June 1929. Lawyer. Educ: B.S., Ala. Univ., 1951; LL.B., ibid, 1956; J.D., ibid, 1970. Appts: Served to 1st Lt., inf. AUS, 1951-53; Admitted to Bar, 1956; Law Clerk, Supreme Ct., Ala., 1956-57; Asst. Atty-Gen., ibid, 1957-59; Commnr., Ala. Dept. Pensions & Securities, 1959-63; Pvte. prac., Montgomery, Ala., 1963-65; Ptnr., Volz, Capouano, Wampold & Prestwood, 1965-; Chmn., Gov.'s Comm., White House Conf. on Aging, 1961; Mbr., Advsry. Comm., Dept. Hlth., Educ. & Welfare, 1962; Sec., Nat. Coun. State Pub. Welfare Admnstrs., 1962. Mbrships: Pres., Morningview Schl. PTA, 1970; Chmn., Bd. Mgmt., E. Montgomery YMCA; Chmn., Am. Nursing Home Assn. Legal Comm.; Bd. Dirs., Montgomery Bapt. Hosp.; Chmn., Exec. Comm. & Legislative Comm., Montgomery Co. Bar; Am., Ala. & Montgomery Co. Bar Assn.; Farrah Order Jurisprudence; Kappa Sigma; Phi Alpha Delta; Pres., Exchange Club, Greater Montgomery, Ala. Contbr. articles to profl. jrnls. & on Edit. Bd., Ala Law Review, 1955-56. Recip. hons. Address: 350 Adams Ave., P.O. Box 1910, Montgomery, AL 36103, U.S.A. 2.

PREUSS, Roger, b. Waterville, Minn., U.S.A. Painter; Graphic Artist. Paintings owned by mus. & major collects. throughout world. Works represented by Merrills Gall. of Fine Arts, Taos, N.M. & Wildlife of Am. Art Gall., Mpls., Minn. Mbrships: Fellow, Soc. of Animal Artists, Int. Inst. of Arts & Letters & Am. Artists Profl. League. Paintings reprod. in 15 books & 45 major periodicals inclng. Nat.

Wildlife, Look & Today's Art. Hons.: recip. 26 major art awards inclng: 1st Award, Nat. Art Print of Yr., 1971; 1st, Fed. Duck Stamp Design; 1st, Limited Ed. Graphics, 1974. Address: c/o Wildlife of Am. Gall., Box 556-Y, Minneapolis, MN 55440, U.S.A. 8, 10, 19, 22, 29, 37, 57, 68, 105, 120, 130, 133, 139.

PREVIN, Andre George, b. 6 Apr. 1930. Conductor; Composer; Pianist. Educ: Berlin Conservatory, Germany; Paris Conservatory, France; Univ. of Calif., U.S.A. Appts: Composer, Conductor, var. film studios, U.S.A., 1950-62; Music Dir., Houston Symph. Orch., 1957-69; Prin. Conductor, London Symph. Orch., 1968-; Music Dir., London S. Bank Summer Music Fest., 1972-74. Mbrships: Garrick; Savile; British Composers Guild; Dramatists Guild. Compositions: Cello Concerto; Guitar Concerto; Music for Strings; Overture to a Comedy; Piano Preludes; Paraphrase on Theme by Walton; Two Serenades for Violin; Woodwind Quintet. Author, Music Face to Face. Hons: Acad. Awards, 1960, 61, 63, 64; Gramophone Soc. Awards, 1958, 60, 61, 66; Hon. GSM, 1971; Brit. TV Critics Award, 1972. Address: c/o London Symph. Orch., 1 Montague St., London, W.C.1, U.K. 2, 4, 21, 34.

PRICE, Donald C., b. 6 Aug. 1931. Lecturer. Educ: Western Reserve Univ., Cleveland; Schl. of P.R., Cleveland Advt. Club; Dale Carnegie Schl. of Human Rels. Appts: Warranty Admnstr., Spitzer Motors, Cleveland; Serv. Dir., Bill Scher Motors, ibid; Warranty Admnstr., Fleishman Motors, ibid. Mbrships. incl: Bd. of Govs., Chmn., Admissions Control, Int. Platform Assn.; Publicity Dir., Cleveland Br. 17, USN Fleet Reserve Assn.; Americanism Chmn., Brook Pk. Am. Legion Post 610. Lectures: You Auto Know; Ashes to Victory (Out of the Rising Sun, Ordeal at Wake, & Midway to Victory). Hons. incl: Award for 'You Auto Know', Int. Platform Assn., 1973; Num. awards for 'Out of the Rising Sun'. Address: 14096 Kathleen Dr., Brook Park, OH 44142, U.S.A. 57.

PRICE, George Cadle, b. 15 Jan. 1919. Politician. Educ: St. John's Coll.; Univ. of the People. Appts: Belize City Councillor, 1947-62, Mbr., Legislative Coun., 1954-61, Exec. Coun., 1954-57, Assoc. Mbr., Natural Resource Coun., 1954-57, Mayor, Belize City, 1957-62; Pres., Gen. Wrkrs. Union, 1951-54; Fndr., & Gen. Sec., Peoples' United Party, 1950-57, Party Ldr., 1957-; Mbr., House of Reps., 1961-, 1st. Min., 1961-65, Mbr., Security Coun., 1961-, External Affairs Comm., 1961-, Premier, 1965-; Chmn., Dev. Finance Corp., 1962-. Mbr. & Pres., St. John's Coll. Alumni Assn., 1954-58. Recip., Outstanding Citizen Award, St. John's Coll. Address: c/o. Chief Information Officer, Belmopan, Belize, Ctsl. Am.

PRICE, George Raymond, Jr., b. 30 Nov. 1925. Architect. Educ: B.S., Clemson Univ., S.C., U.S.A., 1950. Appts. incl: Lyles, Bissett, Carlisle, & Wolff, Columbia, S.C., 1954-57; George R. Price, Gen. Contractor, Columbia, S.C., 1957-63; Califf, Geiger & Price, Archts., Columbia, S.C., 1963-65; Jones & Fellers, Archts.-Engrs., Augusta, Ga., 1965-68; George R. Price, Archt., Augusta, Ga., & Aiken, S.C., 1968-73. Num. mbrships. incl: Am. Inst. of Archts.; Guild for Religious Arch.; Pres., Construction Specification Inst., 1971; Pres., Carolina Opera Guild, 1970-71; Bd. of Dirs., & Treas., Aiken Civic Ballet, 1971-; Fndr., Aiken Arts Coun., 1972; Augusta Chmbr. of Comm.; Richmond Co. Histl. Soc.; Columbia Mus. of Art; Sertoma Int.; S.C. Republican Party; Scout Master Troop 100; Order of the Arrow; Coun.

on Aging. Co-inventor, Quick-set Story Pole (Bricklaying aide). Hons. incl: Sev. WWII Serv. Medals; Sev. Scouting Awards. Address: 455 Sumter St., Aiken, SC 29801, U.S.A. 7, 57, 125, 129, 130, 131, 139.

PRICE, (Brig. Gen.) John Herbert, b. 5 July 1898. Consultant Industrialist. Bishop's Coll. Schl., Lennoxville, P.Q., Canada; Royal Mil. Coll., Kingston, Ont. Served as Commissioned Off., Canadian Royal Field Artillery, in France & Belgium, in WWI. Returned to Canada & entered firm of Price Brothers & Co., 1919. Served as Lt.-Col. Cmdng. Royal Rifles of Canada in Hong Kong, & taken as prisoner of war, WWII. Returned to Canada 1947. Retired from Price Brothers & Co., as V.P., 1947. Currently Brig. Gen., Hon. COT, Sherbrooke Hussars; Dir., Sev. Companies. Canadian Delegate at UN, 1961-62. Mbrships. incl: Pres., Quebec Garrison Club; Chmn., Mount Royal Club, Montreal; Gov., Montreal Gen. Hosp., Royal Victoria Hosp. & Montreal Rehab. Inst. Hons: Military Cross, 1918; O.B.E. (Mil), 1945; D.C.L.(Hon), Bishops Univ., 1962; Off., Order of Canada, 1968; Outstanding Citizenship Award, Montreal Citizenship Coun., 1968. Address: 1455 Sherbrooke St. W., Montreal, P.Q., Canada, H3G 1L2. 32, 88.

PRICE, Joseph Henry, b. 6 June 1924. University Teacher. Educ: Pembroke Coll., Oxford, U.K., 1941-42, '47-48; B.A., M.A., Univ. of Oxford, 1948. Appts: War serv., Major, 16th Punjab Regiment, 1942-47, Seconded to Indian Civil Serv., 1946; w. Home Civil Serv., War Off., 1949-50; Lectr., Univ. Coll. of the Gold Coast (Ghana); 1950-60; Sr. Lectr. & Sr. Tutor, Univ. Coll. of Ghana, 1960-61; Hd., Dept. of Govt., Dean, Fac. of Econs., & Soc. Studies, Univ. of Ife, Nigeria, 1961-66; Lectr., Pols., Univ. of Bradford, U.K., 1966-70, '73-; Lectr., Overseas Administrative Studies, Univ. of Manchester, 1970-73; Advsr. to Govt. of Bahamas on Recruitment & Trng. of Sr. Civil Servants, 1970-. Mbrships. incl: Co. Councillor, W. Riding Co. Coun., 1970-; Co-opted, Nat. Advsry. Comm. on Educ.; Brit. & Nigerian Insts. of Mgmt.; Fellow, African Studies Assn.; Int. Pol. Sci. Assn. Publs. incl: The Gold Coast General Election of 1951, 1951; Political Instutions of West Africa, 1967; Comparative Government, 1970. Address: The Old Vicarage, Cragg Vale, Hebden Bridge, Yorks. HX7 5TB, U.K. 3, 137.

PRICE, Lee George, b. 1 Sept. 1940. Government Official. Educ: A.A., Geo. Wash. Univ., 1961; A.B., ibid, 1963; Postgrad. studies, Am. Univ., 1963-65. Appts: Sr. Trust Acct., 1st. Nat. Bank of Wash., Wash., D.C., 1964-66; Mgmt. Intern, Internal Revenue Serv., ibid, 1966; Prog. Analyst, Off. of the Comptroller of the Navy, Dept. of the Navy, 1967-. Mbrships: Am. Soc. Mil. Comptrollers; Am. Soc. Pub. Admin.; Fed. Govt. Accts. Assn. Address: 2315 Ashboro Dr., Chevy Chase, MD 20015, U.S.A. 7.

PRICE, Lewis Owen, b. 16 Apr. 1914. Educator. Educ: Elmira Bus. Inst., N.Y., 1936; A.B., Syracuse Univ., N.Y., 1950; Fellowship, Pol. Sci. Dept., Maxwell Grad. Schl., ibid.; Fulbright Schol., Univ. of the Philippines, Quezon City; Grad. work, Syracuse & Buffalo Univs. Appts. incl: Proprietor, educl. film serv., 1936-41; Clerk, N.Y. State Legislature, 1936-41; Intelligence & Med. Brs., U.S. Army, 1942-46; Pastoral duties, Ctrl. N.Y. Conf. of Meth. Ch., 1954-56; Lay missionary, Tchr., Admnstr. & Chmn., Personnel Comm., Philippine Wesleyan Coll., Cabanatuan City, Philippines, 1957-65; V.P., Chmn. Student Activities Comm., & Dir., Relig. Educ., ibid.,

1962-67; Tchr., Alfred Agric. & Tech. Coll., N.Y., 1968-. Mbrships. incl: Vice-Chmn., Alfred Accreditation Comm. Phi Beta Kappa; Alpha Kappa Delta; Pi Gamma Mu; Philippine Geographical Soc. Has prepared & presented slide lectures on Far East inclng: The Rural Philippines; Exciting Bangkok; Hongkong Today. Recip., Philippines YMCA Awards. Address:- P.O. Box 263, Hornell, NY 14843, U.S.A. 57.

PRICE, Wilson Titus, b. 28 Mar. 1931. Educator; Author. Educ: B.Sc., Wash. State Univ., Pullman; M.S., Univ. of Pitts., Pa., 1958; Calif. State Univ., San Jose, 1962. Appts: Engrng. Analyst, Westinghouse Electric Corp., Sunnyvale, Calif., 1958-61; Engrng. Cons., Lockheed Missiles & Space Co., ibid, 1962-64; Dir., Data Processing Dept., Merritt Coll., Oakland, Calif., 1962-; Editl. Cons. for data processing textbooks, Holt, Rinehart & Winston, N.Y., 1965-73. Mbrships: Calif. Tchrs. Assn.; Assn. for educl. data systems. Publs. incl: Elements of IBM 1130 Programming, 1968; Introduction to Data Processing,, 1972; Introduction to Data Processing, Student Guide, 1972. Address: Merritt Coll., 12500 Campus Dr., Oakland, CA 94619, U.S.A.

PRIDDY, Barbara Cecil, b. 2 Oct. 1927. Associate in Prayer Breakfast Movement. Educ: B.A., Wheaton Coll., Ill.; Grad. work, Young Life Inst. Appts: Tchr., Hutchinson' Schl. for Girls, Memphis, Tenn., 1949-52; Staff, Young Life Campaign (Youth Org.), 1952-67; Assoc., Prayer Breakfast Movement, 1967-. Bd. Advsr., Welcome to Wash. Int. Club, 2 yrs. Address: 4750 Chevy Chase Dr., Chevy Chase, MD 20015, U.S.A.

PRIESING, Dorothy M. (Mrs. Edward R. Priesing), b. 31 July 1910. Pianist; Composer; Professor of Music. Educ: Grad. in Piano, Julliard Inst. of Musical Art, 1930; Postgrad. in Piano, ibid, 1932; B.S., Columbia Univ., 1932; M.A., ibid, 1933; Study w. pvte. tutors. Appts. incl: former Asst. in Music for 5 yrs., Tchrs. Coll., Columbia Univ.; former Instr. of Theoretical Subjects & Piano sev. yrs., Julliard Inst. of Musical Art; former Hd., Piano Dept., Frances Shriner Jr. Coll., Ill.; Prof. of Music, Montclair State Coll., N.J. Mbrships: ASCAP; SAI. Publs. & Comps.: Language Of the Piano (w. L. Tecklin); Basic Piano For the College Student (w. R. Hayton & A. Zimmerman); Choral works & an Invocation for Band. Hons: Issac Newton Seligman Prize in Chmbr. Music Comps., 1933. Elizabeth Sprague Coolidge Prize in Chmbr. Music Comps., 1934. Address: 42 Llewellyn Rd., Montclair, NJ 07042, U.S.A. 5.

PRIEST, Melville Stanton, b. 16 Oct. 1912. Hydraulic Engineer. Educ: B.S., Univ. of Mo., 1935; M.S., Univ. of Colo., 1943; Ph.D., Univ. of Mich., 1954. Appts. incl: Instr.-Assoc. Prof., Cornell Univ., 1941-55; Prof., Hydraulics, Ala. Polytech. Inst., 1955-58; Hd., Civil Engrng., Auburn Univ., 1958-65; Dir., Water Resources Rsch. Inst., Miss., 1965-. Mbrships. incl: Exec. Comm., Pipeline Div., Am. Soc. of Civil Engrs., 1972; Am. Water Resources Assn., 1973; Int. Assn. for Hydraulic Rsch.; Permanent Int. Assn. of Navigation Congresses; Sigma Xi. Author of num. tech. papers in profl. publs. Address: P.O. Box 541, Starkville, MS 39759, U.S.A. 2, 14.

PRIESTLEY, Charles Henry Brian, b. 8 July 1915. Meteorologist. Educ: B.A., Cambridge Univ., 1937; M.A., ibid, 1942; Sc.D., 1953. Appts: Tech. Officer & Sr. Meteorologist, U.K. Met. Off., 1939-46; Chief of Div. of Atmospheric Physics, CSIRO, Australia,

1946-72; Chmn. of Environ. Physics. Rsch. Labs., ibid, 1971-. Mbrships: Exec. Comm., 1954-60, V.P., 1967-, Int. Assn. of Meteorol. & Atmospheric Physics; Mbr., Advsry. Comm., 1964-69, Chmn., 1967-68, World Met. Org. Fellowships: Royal Soc. of London; Coun., 1958-60, V.P., 1959-60, Australian Acad. of Sci. ; Inst. of Physics; V.P., Royal Met. Soc., 1957-59. Publs: Turbulent Transfer in the Lower Atmosphere, 1959; approx. 70 papers in Sci.; Inst. of Physics; V.P., Royal Met. Soc., 1967; Int. Met. Org. Prize, 1973. Address: CSIRO Environ. Physics Rsch. Labs., P.O. Box 77, Mordialloc, Vic., Australia, 3195. 23, 128, 129, 139.

PRIESTLEY, John Boynton, b. 13 Sept. 1894. Author. Educ: M.A., Trinity Hall, Cambridge. Appts: Serv. w. Duke of Wellington's & Devon Regiments, 1914-19; Deleg., UNESCO Confs., 1946-47; Chmn., Int. Theatre Conf., Paris, 1947, Prague, 1948; Chmn., British Theatre Conf., 1948; Pres., Int. Theatre Inst., 1949; Mbr., Nat. Theatre Bd. Num. books incl: Figures in Modern Literature, 1924; Adam in Moonshine, 1927; The Good Companions, 1929 (dramatised w. E. Knoblock, 1931); Angel Pavement, 1930; Dangerous Corner (play), 1932; Cornelius (play), 1935; Time & the Conways (play), 1937; I Have Been Here Before (play), 1937; Let the People Sing, 1939; Black-Out in Gretley, 1942; They Came to a City (play), 1943; Daylight on Saturday, 1943; Three Men in New Suits, 1945; An Inspector Calls (play), 1946; The Linden Tree (play), 1947; The Olympians (opera), 1949; (w. Jacquetta Hawkes) Dragon's Mouth (play), 1952; Mr. Kettle & Mrs. Moon (play), 1955; The Glass Cage (play), 1957; Literature & Western Man, 1960; Saturn over the Water, 1961; (w. Iris Murdoch) A Severed Head (play), 1963; Man & Time, 1964; It's an Old Country, 1967; The Prince of Pleasure & His Regency, 1969; The Edwardians, 1970. Subject of num. books & articles. Hons: Litt.D.; LL.D; D.Litt. Address: Kissing Tree House, Alveston, Stratford-on-Avon, U.K. 1, 3, 18, 34.

PRIESTLEY, (Sir) Raymond Edward, b. 20 July 1886. Educator. Educ: Attended Bristol, Sydney & Cambridge Univs. Appts: Geologist, Shackleton Antarctic Expedition, 1907-09, Scientist, Northern Party Scott Antarctic Expedition, 1910-13; Served in WW I; Fellow, Clare Coll., Cambridge, 1923-34; Sec., Bd. of Rsch. Studies, Cambridge Univ., 1923-34, Gen. Bd., 1926-34; Sec.-Gen., Facs., ibid, 1934; Vice-Chancellor, Melbourne Univ., Australia, 1935-38; Vice-Chancellor, Prin., Birmingham Univ., U.K., 1938-52; Chmn., Royal Commn. on Civil Serv., 1953-55; Dir., Falkland Islands Rear Base, 1955-59. Mbrships: Pres., British Assn. for the Adv. of Sci., 1956; Hon. Fellow, Clare Coll., Cambridge; Pres., Royal Geog. Soc., 1961-63. Hons: Fndrs. Medal, Royal Geog. Soc., 1959; Chevalier, Ordre de la Couronne, Belgium. Publs: Antarctic Adventure; Scott's Northern Party; Breaking the Hindenburg Line; History of Signal Service in France, etc. Address: Barn Hill, Bredon's Norton, Tewkesbury, Glos., U.K. 34.

PRIETO LORENZO, Antonio, b. 2 May 1923. Public Health Officer. Educ: Normal Schl., 1941; M.D., Fac. of Med., & Dr. Pharm., Fac. of Pharm., Univ. of Madrid; Med. Corps. of Pub. Hlth., ibid, 1955. Appts: House Surg., Hosp. Clin., Fac. of Med., Univ. of Madrid; Asst. Prof., Trop. Med.; Mbr., Inst. Tropical Med.; Asst. Prof., Microbiol. & Parasitol.; Sub-Chief., Sanatorio Nacional de Trillo; Chief, Servs. of Radiol., Bd. of Pub. Hlth; Sub.-Chief, Epidemiol.; Chief, Tech. & Planning Bur., Nat.

Pub. Hlth., Mbrships. incl: Spanish Soc. of Hygiene & Preventive Med.; Soc. of Specialists in Clin. Analysis; Nat. Assn. of Med. Writers. Publs: Los artrópodos vectores de enfermedades infeciosas y parasitarias en el hombre; La anquilostomiasis en la huerta del Jarama; Parasitologia y clínica de las Helmintiasis humanas, 1952; Estudio biográfico del Dr. Claudio Delago y Amestoy, 1971; Fiebre tifoidea y saneamiento en España (6 vols.), 1973; Civilaciones, ensayos y pensamientos, 1973; over 108 sci. publs. & 125 lit. essays in jrnls. Hons: Rubio Prize, Royal Nat. Acad. of Med.; Prizes, Provincial Assembly of Guipúzcoa & Provincial Comm. of Madrid, 1956, 53 & 55; Kt., Nat. Order of Merit Carlos J. Finlay, 1954; Cmdr., National Order of Health, 1971. Address: Dirección General de Sanidad, Plaza de España, 17, Madrid, Spain.

PRIETO Y FERNANDEZ DE LA LLANA Carlos, b. 19 May 1898. Lawyer; Industrialist. Educ: Grad., Law, Univ. of Oviedo, Spain. Appts: Hd., Legal Dept., Compañía Fundidora de Fierro y Acero de Monterrey, S.A., Latin Am.'s oldest integrated steel co., 1923; Chmn., Fundidora Monterrey, S.A., 1945-73; Chmn., Ctrl. Financiera, S.A., 1941-73; Chmn., Fábrica de Ladrillos Industriales y Refractarios Harbison Walker Flir, S.A. (refractories co.), 1927-73; Chrm., Latin Am. Iron & Steel Inst., 1961-65. Mbrships: Banco de México, S.A.,1939-73; Banco Nacional de México, S.A; Celanese Mexicana, S.A.; Gen. Rubber, Mexico, Asociación Hipotecaria Mexicana, 1934-73; Cementos del Norte, S.A.; other cos.; Sponsor, Instituto Nacional de Cardiología, 1967-73; Instituto Mexicano de Recursos Naturales Renovables, 1960-73, Orquesta-Sinfónica de la Universidad, 1960-73, Centro Mexicano de Excritores, 1954-73; Univ. Club, 1930-73; Club de Banqueros; Club de Industriales; Société Francaise de Métallurgie, 1962-73; Am. Iron & Steel Inst., 1963-73; Iron & Steel Inst., 1964-73; Japanese Iron & Steel Inst., 1965-73; Instituto Latino Americano del Fierro y del Acero, 1966-73; Sociedad Nuevoleones de Historia Natural, 1966-73; Mbr.-at-Large, Int. Iron & Steel Inst.; Int. Advsry. Comm., Chase Manhattan Bank, 1969-72; Sociedad de Ingenioros de México, 1970-73. Has taken part in num. int. congresses on steel matters, expecially in Latin Am. & has played an active role in the dev. of steel incl. in Mex. Has established tropical botanical gdn. & malacol. mus. on coast of Gulf of Mexico (Tecolutla). Publs: La Minería en el Nuevo Mundo, eds. 1967, '68 (Mining in the New World, Engl. ed., 1973); El Oceano Pacifico, Navegantes Españoles del Siglo XVI, 1972. Hons: Kt., Legion of Honor, 1951; Francisco R. Miranda, Venezuelan decoration; LL.D., Law Schl., Oviedo Univ., Spain. Address: Altavista 147, San Angel, México 20, D.F., Méxcio. 105.

PRIMIANO, Bernard, b. 12 Nov. 1940. Educator. Educ: B.A., Jersey City State Coll.; M.A., New Schl. for Soc. Rsch.; Ph.D. Cand., N.Y. Univ. Tchr., Soc. Scis., Union City Bd. of Educ., N.J., 1962-. Mbrships: V.P., Union City Educ. Assn., 1967; Dir., Communications, 1967-71; Pres., 1973-; Int. Phenomenol. Soc.; Am. Acad. Pol. & Soc. Sci. Contbr., NJEA Review, 1967. Dean's List student, last two yrs. as undergrad. Address: 208 Lafayette Ave., Cliffside Park, NJ 07010, U.S.A. 130.

PRINCE, Evelyn Ioma, b. 5 Feb. 1914. Nurse; Physical Therapist. Educ: Basic Nursing, St. Thomas, U.S. Virgin Islands, 1930-33; Orthopedic Nursing, Tchrs. Coll., Columbia Univ., 1947-49; Phys. Therapy, Coll. of Physns. & Surg., ibid, 1949-50; Pediatric Nursing,

Tchrs. Coll., 1955-56. Appts: Student Nurse, 1930-33; Staff Nurse, 1933-37; Hd. Nurse, Maternity Serv., 1942-45; Staff Nurse, Surg. Serv., 1945-48; Orthopedic Nurse, Phys. Therapist; Crippled Children Nurse Cons., 1956-. Mbrships. incl: Am. Nurses Assn.; Past Pres. & Bd. Dirs., Virgin Islands Nurses Assn.; Currently, Treas.; Pres., Virgin Islands Chapt., Am. Phys. Therapy Assn.; Chmn., Bd., Virgin Islands Bd. of Phys. Therapists; Womens League of St. Thomas. Hons: Award, Virgin Islands Nurses Assn.; Past Pres., Award, ibid, 1973. Address: P.O. Box 703, St. Thomas, U.S. Virgin Islands, 00801.

PRINCE, Richard Edward, b. 5 Jan. 1920. Engineer; Historian; Author. Educ: B.S., Ga. Schl. of Technol., Atlanta, U.S.A., 1942. Appts: Marine Engr., U.S. Merchant Marine, WWII; Engr., Turbine Locomotive Design, Union Pacific Railroad; Engr., Locomotive Maintenance & Inspn., ibid. Mbrships: Am. Soc. of M.E.'s; Railway & Locomotive Hist. Soc.; World Ship Soc.; Steamship Hist. Soc. of Am. Publs. incl: Louisvile & Nashville Steam Locomotives; Steam Locomotives & History—Georgia Rail Road & West Point Route; Southern Railway Steam Locomotives & Boats; Atlantic Coast Line Rail Road; Nashville Chattanooga & St. Louis Railway; Seaboard Air Line Railway; Norfolk Southern Rail Road, 1973. Address: 8909 Broadmoor Dr., Omaha, NB 68114, U.S.A.

PRINCE (de Saint-Gilles), Moussa, b. 27 Sept. 1925. Lawyer; Professor. Educ: Degrees & Docts. incl: Licencié en Droit Français; Dr. Civil Law; Dr. Econ. & Soc. Sci.; Ministerial Trng. Coll, Sheffield, U.K.; Criminal Law, Vancouver, Canada; Prof. Agrégé., Inst. Rivadavia, Buenos Aires, Argentina; Ph.D., Am. Int. Acad., N.Y. & Wash., U.S.A.; Dr. Sociol. & Dr. Law, Rome, Italy; D.Hist., Un. Philo-Byzantine Acad., Madrid, Spain. Appts: Fellowship., U.N. Econ. Rels. & Soc. Defense, Benclux, 1949; Chancellor, Lebanese T.U.C.; Hon. Chargé d'Affaires to Lebanon, V.-Prin., Free Fac. de France; Rep. Répub. de St.-Marin; Consul of Paraguay in Beirut; Int. Ctr., Studies on Counterfeit, Madrid. Mbrships. incl: Comm., Int. Synd. of Petrol, 1952; Pres., Young Lawyer's Int. Assn.; Int. Soc. of Criminol.; Lodge Libano-Americaine, Beirut. Publs. incl: Qui Est Responsable? ; Or & Sang, 1949-51; Elixir des Enquêteurs, 1952; Assurance-Crime, 1964; Génocide, (5 vols), 1973-74. Hons. incl: l'Ordre du Mérite de la Répub. Italienne; Chevalier de l'Ordre de St. Marin; Médaille d'Or de l'Ordre du Mérite Libanais. Address: Abdelwahab Inglisi-Ferneyni St., Ferneyni BLDG, Beirut, Lebanon.

PRINGLE, Burt E., b. 11 Feb. 1929. Artist; Designer. Catham Acad., Savannah, Ga., 1943. Appts. incl: Display & Advtng. Dir., Haltiwanger's, Columbia, S.C., 1950-52; Lourie's, ibid, 1950-52; Burke's Nashville, Tenn., 1955-56; Rosenblum's, Jacksonville, Fla., 1956-. One man exhib., Norton Gall. & Schl. of Art, W. Palm Beach, Fla., 1968. Mbrships: Am. Fed. Arts; Fla. Watercolor Soc.; Jacksonville Art Mus.; St. Augustine Art Assn.; Past Pres., Art Dirs. Club of Jacksonville; Past Pres., Jacksonville Chmbr. of Comm. Display & Advtng. Comm. Commnd., U.S. Army Mural, Stuttgart, Germany, 1954. Designer: U.S. Postage Stamps, 1966; Virgin Island Commemorative Post Card, 1967. Recip., 15 Honorariums, UN for Philatelic designs, 1966-. Address: 7028 Altama Rd., Jacksonville, FL 32216, U.S.A. 7, 37.

PRINGLE, Mia Kellmer. Psychologist. Educ: B.A., Birkbeck Coll., Univ. of London, U.K., 1944; Ph.D., ibid, 1950; Postgrad. dip. in educl. psychol. Appts: Tchr., Nursery & Primary Schls., 1940-45; Sr. Educl. & Clin. Psychologist, Hertfordshire, 1945-50; Lectr.-Sr. Lectr., Educl. Psychol., Univ. of Birmingham, 1950-63; Dpty. Hd., Dept. of Child Study, ibid, 1952-63; Dir., Nat. Children's Bur., 1963-. Fellowships: British Psychological Soc.; Royal Soc. of Med.; Royal Soc. of Arts. Mbrships. incl: Chmn., Assn. for Child Psychol. & Psych.; Sec. of State Advsry. Coun. for Handicapped Children. Publs. incl: Able Misfits, 1970; Deprivation & Education, 1971; The Needs of Children, 1974. Hons: Henrietta Szold Award for servs. to children, 1970; D.Sc., Univ. of Bradford, 1972. Address: Nat. Children's Bur., 8 Wakley St., Islington, London EC1V 7QE, U.K. 1, 43, 128, 129, 138.

PRINGLE, Robert William, b. 2 May 1920. Physicist; Managing Director. Educ: B.Sc., Ph.D., Edinburgh Univ., U.K. Appts: Lectr., Natural Philos., Edinburgh, 1945; Asst. Prof. of Physics, Manitoba, 1949; Prof. & Chmn., Physics, ibid, 1953; Chmn. & Mng. Dir., Nuclear Enterprises, Edinburgh, 1956-. Fellowships: Inst. of Physics, 1948; Am. Phys. Soc., 1950; Royal Soc. of Canada, 1955; Royal Soc. of Edinburgh, 1964. Mbrships. incl: Economic Coun. for Scotland, 1971-; Bd. Nuclear Physics (S.R.C.), 1972-; Sci. Rsch. Coun., 1972-. Author of papers on nuclear spectroscopy & nuclear geophysics in U.K. & U.S. sci. jrnls. Recip., O.B.E., 1967. Address: Westridge, 91 Ravelston Dykes, Edinburgh, EH12 6EY, U.K. 1.

PRINI, Pietro, b. 14 May 1915. University Professor. Educ: Grad., Univ. of Pavia, Italy; Fellow, Almo Collegio Borromeo; Fellow, Sorbonne, Paris, France. Appts: Tchr., Greek Philos., Univ. of Genoa, Italy, 1954-59; Prof., Philos., Univ. of Perugia, 1959-64; Prof., Hist. of Philos., Univ. of Rome. Mbrships: Pres., Italian Soc. Philos.; Pres., Soc. Int. Meetings, The World of Tomorrow; Mng. Comm., Italian Radio & TV; Acad. du Monde Latin, Paris. Publs: G. Marcel e la metodologia dell'inverificabile, 1950, 2nd edit., 1972; Esistenzialisions, 1952, 3rd edit., 1972; Verso una nuova ontologia, 1957; Discorse e situazione, 1961; Umanesimo programmatico, 1965; Cristianesimo 3 ideologia, 1974. Address: Piazza Carracci 1, Rome, Italy.

PRIOR, Tula Mims (Mrs. Alfred F. Prior Sr.). Civic Volunteer. Educ: Southern Conservatory of Music; Cert. Dirs. Bridge Course. Appts. incl: Airport Reception Volunteer for Wash. Int. Ctr. working in conjunction w. Dept. of State to help orientate For. Vis.' to U.S.A.; Local & Nat. Charity work inclng. Dir. local Charity Bridge games. Mbrships: former mbr., League of Women Voters; 1st Meth. Ch.; Laurel Bridge Soc.; Democratic Club. Hons: Annual Recognition for support of org. by holding weekly Charity Bridge games, Laurel Volunteer Rescue Squad Inc., 1964-. Address: 128 Lafayette Ave., Laurel, MD 20810, U.S.A. 125.

PRISANT, Giséle, b. 22 May 1939. Painter. Educ: Higher Nat. Schl. of Fine Arts, Paris, France; Grande Chaumière Studios, & Goetz Studio, Paris. Mbrships. incl: Soc. for Arts, Scis., & Letters; Soc. for the Encouragement of Progress; Paternoster Corner Acad.; Violette Legion; Lutetia Acad.; Fedn. of Graphic & Plastic Arts. One-man shows: Duncan Gall., Paris, 1969 & 1973; Reflets Gall., Lyon, 1970; Corner Gall., London, U.K., 1972. Permanent Exhib: European Painters Gall., Cannes, 1972-.

Grp. exhibs. incl: Sev. major exhibs., Paris; Carlton Gall., Cannes, 1963 & 1964; Borel Gall., Deauville, 1968; Taft Hotel, N.Y.C., U.S.A.; Waldorf Astoria, N.Y.C.; Int. Festival, Toulon, France, 1971; Off. Salon, Montélimar, 1972, 73 & 74. Creator, Sillonnism style of painting, 1963. Paintings acquired by Toulon Mus., Ovar Mus., Portugal, & pvte. collects. Num. hons. incl: Silver Medal, Soc. for Arts, Scis., & Letters; Gold medals & trophies, Exhibs. in N.Y.C., U.S.A., Nice, & Cannes, France. Address: 17 Rue Guy de Maupassant, 06400, Cannes, France.

PRITCHARD, Jack Alfred, b. 2 July 1940. Educator. Educ: Rensselaer Poly. Inst., Troy, N.Y., 1958-60; A.B., Wilkes Coll., Pa., 1962; M.S., Univ. of Iowa, 1968; Ph.D. Candidate, Lehigh Univ., Pa., 1974. Appts: Instr., Wyoming Sem., Kingston, Pa., 1962-66; Tutor, Parsons Coll., Iowa, 1966-67; Asst. Prof., Iowa Wesleyan Coll., Mt. Pleasant, 1967-69; Tchng. Asst., Lehigh Univ., Pa., 1969-71; Instr., Wyo. Sem., 1971-. Mbrships. incl: AAUP; Am. Math. Soc.; Assn. of Symbolic Logic; Nat. Coun. Tchrs. of Maths.; Luzerne Co. Tchrs. of Maths.; Alpha Tau Omega; Masons; Cum Laude Soc. Publs: (booklet) Slide Rule Operations; article on new maths. Address: Wyoming Sem., Kingston, PA 18704, U.S.A. 6.

PRITCHETT, Lewis, b. 16 Apr. 1921. Company Director; Public Relations Consultant. Appts: Jrnlst., News Agcy. Press Assn. Midlands; Film Publicist, Associated British Cinemas Ltd.; Acct. Dir., Ripley Preston & Co. Ltd. (Advt. Agency); Holdings Dir., The Toon & Heath Org. (Advt. Agency), 20 yrs.; Mng. Dir., Protah Ltd. (P.R. Consultancy), 20 yrs. Mbrships: Inst. of Practitioners in Advt.; Inst. of P.R., 1955-. Publs: History of the Morgan Motor Car; var. contbns. to newspapers. Address: The Toon & Heath Org., Warwick Rd., Knowle, Solihull, Warwicks., U.K. 34.

PRITTIE, (Hon.) Terence Cornelius Farmer, b. 15 Dec. 1913. Writer; Journalist. Educ: M.A., Univ. of Oxford, U.K., 1936. Appts. incl: Off., Rifle Brigade, WWII; Correspondent, Manchester Guardian, Germany, 1946-63; Diplomatic Correspondent, The Guardian, 1963-70; Dir., Britain & Israel, 1970-. Mbrships. incl: Royal Inst. for Int. Affairs; Travellers Club; Exec., Angle-Israel Assn. Publs. incl: South to Freedom; Mainly Middlesex; Second Innings; Lancashire Hotpot; Germany Divided; Germans against Hitler; Israel, Miracle in the Desert; Konrad Adenauer. A Study in Fortitude; Moselle; Willy Brandt, 1974; 3 other books; Britain & Israel, monthly jrnl. Hons: M.B.E. (Mil.), 1945; Federal German Cross of Merit, 1st class, 1972. Address: 9 Blithfield St., London, W.8., U.K. 2, 35, 41.

PRITZKER, Lee, b. 1 July 1896. Writer; Bibliographer; Art Dealer. Educ: Tech. H.S., Toronto, Canada; London Schl. of Econs., U.K.; Schl. of Jrnlsm., ibid; apprentice in art bus. mainly in Europe. Appts: Serv. WW I w. Canadian Expeditionary Force; Art Dealer for past 35 yrs., bibliographer & cataloguer to firm in Toronto handling rare literary property. Mbrships: Past Pres., Canadian Vegetarian Union; Past V.P., Int. Vegetarian Union; Toronto Vegetarian Assn.; Royal Canadian Legion Br. 256. Author of num. articles, mainly on lit. & the vegetarian credo for publs. inclng. World Forum, London; Vancouver Sun; Dr. Shelton's Hygienic Review; The American Vegetarian; The Auctioneer, Toronto; The Ottawa Citizen. Address: Box 293 Oakville, Ont. L6J 5A2, Canada. 133.

PROBST, David A., b. 8 July 1920. University Administrator. Educ: B.S., Univ. of Pitts., 1943; M.S., ibid, 1945, Univ. of N.C., 1950-52, Mellon Schl. Indl. Mgmt., 1952; Ph.D., Northwestern Univ., 1953. Appts: Petroleum Engrng., Gulf Oil Corp., Venezuela-U.S.A., 1940-50; Petroleum Economist, Shell Oil Co., Venezuela, 1953-58; Investment Advsr., Standard Oil (N.J.), N.Y.C., 1959-63; Dir., Corporate & Govt. Rels., Princeton Univ., 1964-; Exec. V.P. & Dir., Demat Corp., Princeton; Exec. V.P. & Trustee, Univ. Properties Holding Corp., Princeton; V.P. & Dir., Coll. of Petroleum & Minerals Fndn. Mbrships: Cm. Assn. Petroleum Geologists; Am. Statistical Assn.; Geological Soc. of Am.; Elizah Mitchell Hon. Soc.; Sigma Xi; Sigma Tau; Sigma Gamma Epsilon; Phi Beta Kappa; Princeton Club of N.Y. Address: P.O. Box 39, Princeton Univ., Princeton, NJ 08540, U.S.A. 6, 14.

PROCTOR, William Con, Jr., b. 6 Dec. 1925. Industrial Engineering Executive. Educ: B.S.M.E., N.C. State Univ., 1950. Appts: Engine Sales Promotion, N.C. Equipment Co., Raleigh, N.C., 1950-51; Equipment Sales, Fla.-Ga. Tractor Co., Lakeland, Fla., 1952-53; Sales Engr., A.E. Finley & Assoc., Raleigh, N.C., 1954-60; Plant Design Engr., Superior Stone Co., Raleigh, 1961; V.P. & Mgr., Engrng. Resources, Rea Construction Co., Charlotte, N.C., 1961-. Mbrships. incl: Chmn., Environmental Comms., Nat. & Carolina Asphalt Pavement Assns.; Dir., Carolinas Air Pollution Assn. Publs. incl: Good Housekeeping at Hot Mix Plants, 1972; Fabric Filters & the Hot Mix Asphalt Plant, 1973. Designer, rock crushing, ready mix concrete & hot mix asphalt plants. Recip., Bronze Star, U.S. Army, 1945. Address: P.O. Box 27067, 6001 Old Dowd Rd., Charlotte, NC 28208, U.S.A.

PROFANT, Wenzel, b. 21 July 1913. Sculptor. Educ: Reggio instituto d'arte, Florence. Appts: Atelier, Esch/Alzette, 1930-40; Lt.-Paratrooper, Allied Armies, 1941-44; Atelier Schifflange, & Drawing Tchr., 1945-50; at Luxembourg, 1951. Exhib: Biennale Internazionale di Scultura, Carrara; Biennale voor Beldhouwkunst, Stad Antwerpen; Mostra Internazionale di Bianco e Nero, Lugano. Mbrships: Deleg., 3rd Congress, Int. Assn. of Plastic Arts, Vienna, & 4th Congress, Int. Assn. of Plastic Arts, NYC; Fellow, Mbr. of Coun., Int. Inst. of Arts & Letters; Comm., Nat. Comm. of Plastic Arts, Luxembourg. Address: 193 A, rue de Neudorf, Luxembourg, Grand Duchy of Luxembourg. 43, 133.

PROKOSCH, Frederic, b. 17 May 1908. Writer. Educ: Ph.D., Yale Univ., 1933; King's Coll., Cambridge, U.K.; Rsch. work in Chaucerian MSS, 1933-38. Publs. incl: The Asiatics (novel), 1935; The Seven who Fled (novel), 1937; The Carnival (poems), 1938; Night of the Poor (novel), 1939; Death at Sea (poems), 1940; The Skies of Europe (novel), 1942; Chosen Poems, 1944; Age of Thunder (novel), 1943; The Idols of the Cave (novel), 1946; The Medea of Euripides, 1947; The Sonnets of Louise Labe, 1947; Storm & Echo (novel), 1948; Nine Days to Mukalla (novel), 1953; A Tale for Midnight (novel), 1955; A Ballad of Love (novel), 1960; The Seven Sisters (novel), 1962; The Dark Dancer (novel), 1964; The Wreck of the Cassandra (novel), 1966; The Missolonghi Manuscript (novel), 1968. Hons: Harper Prize, 1937; Monroe Prize, 1942; Guggenheim & Fulbright Fellowships, 1936 & 1951. Address: Ma Trouvaille, 06 Plan de Grasse, France. 1.

PROPES, Aron Zvi, b. 25 May 1904. Educator. Educ: Univ. of Prague. Appts: Hd., Zionist Youth Org. Betar-Brith Trumpeldor, Latvia, Poland, Rumania, U.S.A., 1923-49; Mbr., action comms., World Zionist Org. & Deleg. to Zionist World Congresses; Mbr., World Exec. of Betar, 1929-49; Hd., ibid, 1940-49; Hd., Interministerial comm. for pilgrims & i/c Int. Convens. in Israel, Civil Serv., Israel, 1949-; Fndr. & Dir., The Zimriya (int. assembly of choirs), Int. Harp Contest, Israel Int. Music & Drama Festival; Fndr. & Dir., Int. Youth City, Israel. Past Pres., Order Zeev Jabotinsky; Publs: Biography of J. Trumpeldor; handbook on how to organize int. congresses; translations from Russian into German of Z. Jabotinsky's feuilletons. Recip., State of Israel Fighters Award. Address: 4 Shadal St., Tel Aviv, Israel. 55, 94.

PROPES, Moshe, b. 18 Oct. 1922. Painter; Sculpture; Educator. Educ: Avnj & Schwarzman Studios; Grand Shomer Acad. of Arts, Paris. Appts: Painter-Tchr., Art, Avni Inst. for Art & Sculpture. Paintings on show in pvte. mus. & galls. in Israel & abroad. Participated in Bianela san Paulo, 1957. Mbrships: Israel Artists Assn. Hons: Dizengoff Prize; Hahistadrut Prize; Educ. Dept. Prize. Address: 8, Burla St., Tochnit "L", Tel Aviv, Israel.

PROPST, Elmer Allen (A1), b. 11 Jan. 1926. Pilot; Instructor; Crop Duster; Now disabled. Educ: Albany H.S., 1944; Home Studies for Aviation, equivalent to 2 yrs. coll.; Has successfully completed examinations for law schl. admission. Appts: Flight Operator; Airport Owner; Pilot Instructor, trng. in metrology & insecticides; Handling Chem. & Field Advsr. in chems.; Aviation Cadet, WWII, Aerial Combat 15th AAF, Italy; Operator, Propst Air Serv. Mbrships: Past Kiwanian; Elks; Chmbr. Comm.; Past Pres., Linn. Co. Rural Property Owners Protective Assn.; Ore. Aviation Trades Assn.; Am. Legion; Filed Candidature for Gov. Ore.; Fire Control by Air; Air Searches for Lost Children. Hons: 4 Bronze Battle Stars; Presidential Unit Citation; I.B.A. Passport, 1973. Address: 253 S.E. Scravel Hill Rd., Battle Ground Meadows, Albany, OR 97321, U.S.A. 57, 120, 139.

PROPST, Mary Frances (Thomas) (Mrs. Noel L.), b. 29 Oct. 1917. Librarian. Educ: B.Sc., Longwood Coll., Va., 1939; A.B., Lib. Sci., Coll. of Wm. & Mary, 1949. Appts: Tchr., Pub. Schls., Va., 1939-45; Libn., Hist. Rsch. Dept., Colonial Williamsburg, Va., 1946-47; Libn., Southside Regional Lib., Boydton, Va., 1948-. Mbrships: Chmn., Regional Lib. Sect., Va. Lib. Assn., 1951-52; Dist. Rec. Sec., Clarksville Bus. & Profl. Women's Club, 1968-70; Sec., Women's Comm., Va. Farm Bur., 1954-55; Co. Exec. Comm., Assn. for Preservation of Va. Antiquities, 1968-; Boydton Fedn. Women's Clubs; Pres. & num. other offs.; Finchley Home Demonstration Club; Delta Kappa Gamma; Chmn., Mecklenburg Co. Bicentennial Commn. Address: Rte. 1, Box 156, Boydton, VA 23917, U.S.A. 5, 85, 138.

PROSS, Harry, b. 2 Sept. 1923. University Professor; Author; Journalist. Educ: Dr. Phil., Heidelberg, 1949; Hoover Lib., Columbia Univ., New Schl. (Commonwealth Fund Fellow), 1952-53. Appts. incl: Writer & Jrnlst., 1945-; Mng. Ed., Ost-Probleme, 1949-52; Ed., Deutsche Rundschau, 1955-60; Ed.-in-Chief, Radio Bremen, 1963-68; Co.-Ed., Neue Rundschau, 1963-69; Full Prof., Dir., Inst. f. Publizistik, Freie Univ. Berlin, 1968-; Guest Lectr., sev. acad. instns. Mbrships: PEN, 1959; sev. profl. & learned socs. Publs. incl: 17 books in fields of contemporary hist. & pol. communications. Address: Hagenstr. 56, D 1 Berlin 33, German Fed. Repub. 43, 92.

PROUGH, George Harrison, b. 27 Dec. 1911. Educator. Educ: B.S., Ball State Tchrs. Coll., 1933; M.S., Ind. Univ., 1941. Appts: Tchr., Coach, Prin., Lancaster Central Schl., 1935-43; Tchr., Coach, Mishawaka, Ind. Pub. Schls., 1943-. Mbrships. incl: Exec. Sec., St. Joseph Co. 4-H Fair, S. Bend, Ind., 1957-58; Dir., Ind. Assn. of Co. & Dist. Fairs, 1962-66; V.P., ibid, 1967; Pres., 1968; Charter mbr., Am. Federation of Tchrs.; Pres., Mishawaka Educ. Assn., 1964-67; NEA; Pres., Mishawaka Rotary, 1964; Dir., ibid, 1970-72; Ball State Alumni; Phi Sigma Epsilon; Special Dpty. Sheriff, St. Joseph Co. Fraternal Order of Police; Ind. State Lodge. Hons. incl: Award of Distinction, Ind. Assn. of Co. & Dist. Fairs, 1968; Award, Mishawaka Educ. Assn., 1967. Address: 2327 Homewood Ave., Mishawaka, IN 46544, U.S.A.

PRUDEN, Ida Mae, b. 7 Jan. 1922. Medical Technologist. Educ: B.S., Univ. of Ky., Lexington, 1950. Appts: Med. Technol., Owensboro Daviess Co. Hosp.; Med. Technol., Union Hosp., Terre Haute, Ind.; Blood Bank Supvsr., Good Samaritan Hosp., Vincennes; Clin. Instr., Med. Technol. Schl., ibid; Med. Technol., Our Lady of Mercy Hosp., Owensboro, Ky. Mbrships incl: Pres., All-Am. City Charter Chapt., Am. Womens Bus. Assn.; Am. Soc. for Med. Technols.; Ky. Soc. for Med. Technols.; Past Pres., Western Dist. Soc. for Med. Technols.; Bapt. Ch. Dorothy Carnegie Grad., 1966. Address: 102 E. 22nd St., Owensboro, KY 42301, U.S.A. 125.

PRUETT, Robert Thomas, b. 30 Nov. 1933. Consulting Engineer. Educ: B.S., Civil Engrng., Univ. of Ky., Lexington, 1957; M.S., ibid, 1959; Postgrad. Study, Scarritt Coll., Nashville, Tenn., 1959-60. Appts: Design & Field Techn., Howard K. Bell Engrs., Lexington, Ky.; Design & Dev. Engr., Irving Air Chute Co., ibid; Rd. Design Engr., Mich. State Hwy. Dept.; Tech. Missionary, Rhodesia, 1960-62; Bridge Design Engr., Mich. State Hwy. Dept., Lansing; Structural Dev. Engr., I.L.C. Inds., Dover, Del.; Owner, Robert Thomas Pruett Cons. Engrs., ibid. Mbrships. incl: Am. Soc. Engrs.; Dir., Del. Land Surveyors Assn. 1st Del. engr. to design & use sand filters as after treatment following secondary sewage treatment on small treatment plants. Recip., var. awards. Address: 285 Old Mill Rd., Dover, DE 19901, U.S.A. 6.

PRULLETTI, Rita Geada, (pen-name, Rita Geada), b. 7 Sept. 1934. Educator & Writer. Educ: M.A., 1956, Ph.D., 1957, Univ. of Havana, Cuba; Post-doct. rsch., OAS Fellowship, Univ. of Buenos Aires, Argentina, 1961-62. Appts: Instr., Spanish, Jr. H.S., Artemisa, Cuba, 1954-57; Asst. Prof., Lang. & Lit., Pinar del Rło Coll., 1957-60; Instr., Wicomico Sr. H.S., Md., U.S.A., 1966-70; Assoc. Prof., Span. & Span.-Am. Lit., Southern Conn. State COll., New Haven, Conn., 1970-. Mbrships: M.L.A.A.; Am. Assn. Tchrs. of Spanish & Portuguese. Publs. (poetry): Desvelado Silencio, 1959; Cuando Cantan las Pisadas, 1967; Mascarada, 1970; contbr. to: Caracola, Spain; Norte, Amsterdam, Netherlands; Il Giornale dei Poeti, Rome, Italy; Punto Cardinal, Fla., U.S.A.; etc. Recip., 1st Prize, Carabela de Oro, for Mascarada, 1969. Address: 25 Woodcrest Rd., Seymour, CT 06483, U.S.A. 138, 140.

PRUNTY, Paul Edward, b. 9 Oct. 1943. Maintenance Machinist. Educ: Fairmont State Coll., W. Va. Appts: Maintenance Machinist,

Westinghouse Elec. Corp., 1962-74; US Army Reserves for 6 yrs., honorably discharged w. rank of Staff Sgt., 1970; Deleg. from Co. of Marion, W. Va. House of Delegs., 1972-. Mbrships: Int. Union Elec., Radio & Machine Workers, AFL-CIO-CLO; Nat. Rifle Assn.; SAR; US Eastern Ski Assn.; Elks; Moose Lodge No. 9; Sierra Club; Tech. Advsry. Bd., Nature Conservancy; Bd. of Dirs., Citizens United to Restore the Environment & Stream Improvement Assn. of Marion Co.; Young Repubs. of W.Va. & Marion Co.; Admin. Bd., Diamond St. United Meth. Ch. Hons: Disting. Serv. Award, Fairmont Jaycees, 1974. Address: Rt. 6, Box 237, Fairmont, WV 26554, U.S.A. 125.

PRYOR, Keith Cowes, b. 4 Aug. 1913. Business Executive; Livestock Breeder. Educ: St. George's Coll., Quilmes, Argentina; London Polytechnic, U.K. Appts. incl: Livestock Broker, 1932-33; Exec. Swift & Co., Argentina, 1934-40; Rep., British Min. of Food, in Argentina, 1941-45; Exec. Swift & Co., Argentina, 1946-57; Mng. Dir. in Argentina, Int. Packers Ltd., Chicago, Ill., U.S.A., 1958-67; Dir., King Ranch Argentina, La República S.A., Co., Pilagá S.A., Timbó S.A. & Ombu S.A., 1968-74. Mbrships: Chmn., British & Am. Benevolent Soc.; Trustee & mbr. Comm. of Mgmt., Buenos Aires British Hosp.; Trustee, mbr. Bd. of Govs. & former Chmn., St. George's Coll., Quilmes, Argentina; Am. Soc. of River Plate; Sociedad Rural Argentine; Anglo-Argentine Soc.; Buenos Aires Jockey Club; Hurlingham Club, Argentina; Am. Club, English Club & Swedish Club, Argentina. Address: Florida 890–25, Buenos Aires, Argentina.

PRYOR, William Y., b. 24 Oct. 1908. Counsellor at Law retired. Educ: B.A., Columbia Univ., 1931; J.D. N.Y. Univ. Law Schl., 1934; admitted to N.J. Bar, 1936, Bar of Supreme Court, U.S.A., 1946. Appts: Counsellor at Law, N.J., 1935-72 (retired); Offs., Newark, 1935-59, Montclair, 1959-72. Mbrships: V.P., Verona, N.J. Schl. Bd., 1936-40; St. Nicholas Soc., N.Y.C.; Soc. Colonial Wars; Sons of the Revolution; Sons of Am. Revolution Society War of 1812; Order of Crusades; Acorn Soc.; Herieitary Order Descendants Colonial Govs. (past Gov. Gen.); Sovereign Mii. Order Temple of Jerusalem (past Grand Prior); Newcomin Soc. of N. Am.; Huguenot Soc.; Mason; Shriner; Royal Order of Scotland. Hons: Grand Croix, Order of Temple, Portugal, 1965; Minute Man Award, SAR, 1963. Address: 64 Fellswood Dr., Essex Fells, NJ 07021, U.S.A. 6.

PUCCIO, Guido, b. 1 Mar. 1894. Writer; Traveller; Educator; Journalist. Educ: Laurea Degree, Univ. of Venice. Appts: Jrnlst., often travelling as "Special Envoy", posts incl: "Redacteur", La Tribuna, Rome, & other papers; Corres. from Italy to London Daily Express for 10 yrs. & from London to La Tribuna. Mbrships: Assn. di critici letterari italiani; Sindacato Libero Scrittori Italiani. Publs. incl: Al Centro della Macchina Sovietica; Parole sulla Sabbia (poems); Albre Parole sulla Sabbia (poems); Esperienze nord-americane; I Poeti Laureati d'Inghilterra; Customs on the Other Side of the Channel; Calabria Sicilia 1840-; Avventure d'un pittore inglese (A.J. Strutt) nel Mezzogiorno borbonico; Shakespeare negli Archivi di Chancery Lane; Frai Lapponi nomadi; Viaggio nella memoria di un giornalista (Dal boia d'Inghilterra ai misteri di Hong Kong); The Son (play in 3 acts); num. essays & articles. Hons: Gold Medals, Min. of Educ., 1971 & "Assn. Stampa romana";

Commendatore della Corona d'Italia. Address: 28, Via Severano, Rome, Italy. 43.

PUCKETT, Ruby Parker, b. 26 Nov. 1932. Director of Dietetics. Educ: B.S., Auburn Univ., Ala., 1954; 1 yr. dietetic internship, Henry Ford Hosp., Detroit, Mich.; Presently working on master's degree, Univ. of Fla., Gainesville. Appts: Staff Dietitian, Houston, Tex., 1955-56; Only dietitian, Meridian, Miss., 1957-58; Asst. Dir., Jackson, Miss., 1960-61; Dir., Dietetics, Knoxville, Tenn., 1961-63, Eustis, Fla., 1963-68, & Gainesville, Fla., 1968-. Mbrships. incl: Var. offs., inclng. Reviewer for Position Papers, 1973-, & Task Force for Administrative Dietetics, 1974-, Am. Dietetic Assn.; Var. offs. up to Pres., Fla. Dietetic Assn.; Fellow, Royal Soc. of Hlth., U.K., 1971-; Educ. Comm., Am. Soc. of Hosp. Food Serv. Admnstrs., 1968-71; Charter mbr., Nutrition Educ. Soc., 1970. Author of articles & papers in field of dietetics. Recip. of hons. Address: Dept. of Dietetics, Shands Tchng. Hosp. & Clins., Box 770, Univ. of Fla., Gainesville, FL 32610, U.S.A. 5, 138.

PUCKLE, Owen Standidge, b. 2 June 1899. Research Engineer (Electronics); Author; Lecturer. Appts: Standard Telephones & Cables, Transmission Measuring Equipment, Oscillographs, 1923-29; Tests on 1st Transatlantic radio telephone serv., secret telephony w. Berlin, & 19 cm. radio telephony, U.K. & Italy (S.S. Elettra), Marconi's Wireless Telegraphy Co., 1929-31; Dev. of velocity modulation tv system, Puckle time base & radar equipment, A.C. Cossor Ltd., 1931-45; Tech. Dir., Radio & TV, Sobell Ltd., 1945-48; Dev., mobile radio telephones & marine radio, Rep. on British Radio Mfrs. Assn., Rep on Computer Soc. i/c Tech. Writers, Liaison w. Armed Servs., & Chief Lectr., Elec. & Musical Inds. Ltd., 1948-60. Mbrships. incl: FIEE; Fellow, Royal TV Soc.; Hon. Mbr., British Numerical Control Soc.; Fndr., V.P., Beaconsfield & Dist. Histl. Soc.; Past Chmn., Beaconsfield Urban Dist. Coun. Publs. incl: Time Bases, 1943; Numerical Control of Machine Tools (w. J.R. Arrowsmith), 1964. Contbr. to num. jrnls. & newspapers. Hons: M.B.E.; IEE Radio Sect. Premium (w. L.H. Bedford), 1934; IEE Duddell Premium, 1942. Address: Pigeon House Cottage, Grove Rd., Beaconsfield, Bucks. HP9 1UP, U.K. 43.

PUDNEY, John Sleigh, b. 19 Jan. 1909. Writer. Appts. incl: Prod. & Writer on staff of BBC, 1934-37; Corres., News Chronicle, 1937-41; RAF, 1941-45; Dir., Putnams, publrs., 1953-63. Mbr., Savile Club. Publs. incl: (Verse) Ten Summers, 1944; Selected Poems, 1945; Collected Poems, 1957; The Trampoline, 1959; Selected Poems, 1967-1973, 1973; (Novels) Jacobson's Ladder, 1938; Estuary, 1947; The Net, 1952; Thin Air, 1961; The Long Time Growing Up, 1971; (Non-fiction) Who Only England Know, 1943; The Thomas Cook Story, 1953; A Pride of Unicorns, 1960; Bristol Fashion, 1960; The Golden Age of Steam, 1966; Brunel & His World, 1973; (Official) The Air Battle of Malta, 1944; Laboratory of the Air, 1948; also collected stories & books for boys & girls; (Film scripts, etc.) Elizabeth is Queen, 1953; May Wedding, 1960; Mission of Fear, 1966; Ted, TV Play, 1971. Address: 4 Macartney House, Chesterfield Walk, Greenwich Pk., London SE10 8HJ, U.K. 1, 3, 34, 128.

PUGACZ, Yitzhak, b. 13 Sept. 1919. Artist. Educ: Art Course, Gottingen Univ., Germany, 1946; Grad., Bezalel Art Acad., Jerusalem,

Israel, 1950. Appts. incl: Tchr. & Lectr., num. Schls. & Art instns., Jerusalem, 1948-60; Mbr., Planning Bd., Israel's 10th Anniversary, 1957; Lectr., Bezalel Art Acad., Jerusalem, 1960-74. Mbrships: Israeli Comm. Mbr., UNESCO, 1957-60; Gen. Sec., Jerusalem Artist's Comm., 1965-66; Chmn., Israeli Coun. of Painters & Sculptors Assn., 1970-72. From 1950, paintings exhibd. in num. shows in Israel & abroad inclng. One Man Exhib., representing Israel, Tours, France, 1963. From 1957-60, work included dimensional wire sculptures & murals & from 1964-69, designer of goblets & medals. Publs. incl: paintings for Picture & Poem (co-author). Hons. incl: Jerusalem Prize, 1960; Guest of Min. des Affaires Etrange, Paris, Direction Gen. des Affaires Coulturelles, 1964. Address: 5 Pinsker St., Jerusalem, Israel. 55.

PUGH, Clifton Ernest, b. 17 Dec. 1924. Artist. Educ: Nat. Gall., Vic., Schl. of Painting, Australia, 1949-51. Appts: Served in AIF, 1943-47; Chmn., Victorian Alp. Arts & Culture Policy Comm., 1972-73; Mbr., Australian Coun. for the Arts, 1973. Mbr., Victorian Amateur Turf Club. Books in Collaboration: Yellow Jacket Jock, w. Colir Thiele, 1969; Death of a Wombat, w. Ivan Smith, 1972; Wombalong, w. Judith Pugh, 1974. Hons: Represented in all state Nat. Art Galls., Australia; Also represented in London Univ., Malaysian Nat. Gall., Leningrad Ballet Collect., all Australian univs. & collect. of Queen Elizabeth II; Subj. of sev. books inclng. Clifton Pugh, by Noel Macainsh, 1962 & Involvement, by Andrew Grimwade, 1968; Bendigo Art Prize, 1958; Vizard Wholohan Award, 1958; Crouch Prize for Watercolour, 1960; Archibald Prize for Portraiture, 1965, 1972, 1973. Address: Dunmoochin, Cottlesbridge, Vic., Australia. 23.

PUGH, John Charles, b. 9 Jan. 1919. University Professor. Educ: B.A., Cantab., U.K., 1940; M.A., ibid, 1944; Ph.D., London, 1954; A.R.I.C.S., 1950; F.R.I.C.S., 1970. Appts: Royal Engrs., 1941; Surveyor, Colonial Survey Serv., Nigeria, 1942; Lectr. in Geog., Univ. Coll., Ibadan, 1949; Dean, Fac. of Arts, ibid, 1950-52; Sr. Lectr., 1955; Rdr. in Geog., King's Coll., London, 1956; Prof., ibid, 1964; Hd., Dept. of Geog., 1966; Dean, Fac. of Natural Sci., 1970-72. Fellowships: Royal Soc. of Arts; Royal Geographical Soc.; Geological Soc. of London; Royal Commonwealth Soc. Mbrships. incl: Inst. of British Geographers; Geographical Assn. Publs. incl: Short Geography of West Africa (w. A.R. Perry), 1960; West Africa (w. W.B. Morgan), 1969; Surveying for Field Scientists, 1974. Address: Dept. of Geog., Univ. of London King's Coll., Strand, London WC2R 2LS, U.K. 3.

PUGLIESE, Peter Francis, b. 25 July 1914. Attorney & Counselor-at-Law. Educ: A.B., Grove City Coll., U.S.A., 1935; J.D., Univ. of Pa. Law Schl., Phila., 1941; J.S.D., Schl. of Law, N.Y. Univ., 1951; Mbr., Bars of N.Y., Pa., & Fed. Cts. Appts. incl: Law Prac. w. Donovan, Leisure, Newton & Lumbard, N.Y.C., 1941-55; Pvte.-Capt., Off. of Strategic Servs., WWII; Gen. Atty., Bell Telephone Co. of Pa. & Diamond State Telephone Co. of Del., Phila., 1955-. Num. mbrships. incl: Am. Bar Assn. Assn. of Bar of N.Y.C.; Pa. State Bar Assn. Phila. Bar Assn.; Am. Judicature Soc.; Fndr., Pres., & Chmn., Bd. of Trustees, Am. Inst. for Italian Culture; Exec. Bd. & Past Vice Chmn., Comm. of Seventy; Exec. V.P. & Dir., Pa. Grand Opera Co.; Exec. Comm., Cardinal's Comm. of the Laity, Archdiocese of Phila. Exec. Comm., Prisoners' Family Welfare Assn of Phila. Hons. incl: 2 Decorations conferred by Repub. of Italy; Civic Award of Merit

Columbus Sq. Assn., Phila, 1969. Address: One Parkway, Philadelphia, PA 19102, U.S.A. 6, 22, 131.

PUGNALIN, Albino, b. 10 Aug. 1893. Lawyer. Educ: Doct. in Law & Soc. Scis. Appts. incl: Under-Sec., Min. of Pub. Works, 1916; Min. in Japan, 1918; Min. in Ecuador, 1922; Ambassador Extraordinary & Plenipotentiary, ibid, 1946-49; Prof. of Hist. of Argentinian Inst. Mbrships. incl: Pres., Argentine-Colombia Cultural Inst.; V.P., Bolivian Inst., Argentine; Hon. Mbr., Acad. of Hist., Costa Rica; Bolivar Soc., Ecuador. Publs. incl: El Universo, el Planeta y el Hombre; Perfiles Japoneses. Hons: Grand Cross, Order of Merit, Ecuador; Cmdr., Order of S. Sivestre Papa. Address: Esmeralda 1,386, Buenos Aires, Repub. of Argentina.

PUGSLEY, Cynthia Durance (Mrs.), b. 3 Oct. 1940. Librarian. Educ: B.A., Univ. of Toronto, Canada, 1962; M.L.S., McGill Univ., 1967. Appts: Ref. Libn., Sir George Williams Univ., Montreal, 1967-69; Serials Cataloguer, Carleton Univ. Lib., Ottawa, 1969; Hd., Serials Dept., ibid, 1969-72; Hd., Serials Dept., Univ. of Waterloo Lib., 1972-73; Asst. Libn., Planning & Systems, ibid, 1973-. Mbrships: Chmn., Subgrp. on Union List of Serials, Canadian Union Catalogue Task Grp.; Canadian Lib. Assn.; Canadian Assn. of Coll. & Univ. Libs.; ALA; Am. Soc. for Info. Serv. Recip., H.W. Wilson Schlrship, 1967. Address: Univ. of Waterloo Lib., Waterloo, Ont. N2L 3G1, Canada. 5.

PULLAN, Clarence Thomas Norrell, b. 21 Jan. 1914. Company Director. Educ: Univ. of Western Australia; F.A.S.A.; A.C.I.S.; F.A.I.M. Appts: Australian Corps of Signals, 1940 45; Asst. Gen. Mgr., Swan Portland Cement Ltd., 1945-52; Mng. Dir., ibid, 1952-61; Mng. Dir., Plaimar Ltd., 1961-. Mbrships: Export Dev. Coun., 1960-66; V.P., Assocd. Chmbrs. of Mfrs. of Australia, 1970-72; Pres., W. Australian Chmbr. of Mfrs., 1970-72; Mfg. Inds. Advsry. Coun., 1971-; Permanent Mbr., Fuel & Power Advsry. Coun., W. Australia, 1972-; Nat. Steering Comm. on Trng., 1972-73. Hons: Efficiency Medal w. clasp, 1970; O.B.E., 1972. Address: 103 Melvista Ave., Nedlands, W.A., Australia. 23.

PULLEE, Ernest Edward, b. 19 Feb. 1907. Art & Design Education. Educ: Royal Coll. of Art, London, U.K., 1926-30. Appts. incl: Staff Mbr., Cheltenham Coll. of Art, U.K., 1930; Prin., Gloucester Schl. of Art, 1934; Prin., Southern Coll. of Art, 1939; Prin., Leeds Coll. of Art, 1945; Prin., Leicester Coll. of Art, 1956; Chief Off., Nat. Coun. for Dips. in Art & Design, 1967-. Mbrships: Fellow, Royal Soc. of Arts; Pres., Nat. Soc. for Art Educ., 1945, 1959; Chmn., Assn. of Art Instns., 1959; Nat. Advsry. Coun. for Art Educ.; Chelsea Arts Club; Hon. Fellow., Manchester Coll. of Art, 1961. Mbr. of New English Art Club & paintings exhibd. in London & provincial galls. inclng. Royal Acad., London, U.K. Works in many pub. & pvte. collections inclng. City of Leeds Art Gall. & W. Riding of Yorkshire Collection. Contbr. to profl. & acad. jrnls. Hons. incl: C.B.E., 1967. Address: 91 Park Meadow, Hatfield, Herts., U.K. 1.

PULLEIN-THOMPSON, Josephine Mary Wedderburn. Writer. Mbrships. incl: Children's Writers Grp. Comm., Soc. of Authors; Exec. Comm., Int. PEN; Comm., Crime Writers Assn., 1971-72; British Horse Soc.; Vis. Commnr., Pony Club; Dist. Commnr., Woodland Pony Club. Publs. incl: (crime novels) Gin & Murder, 1959; They Died in the Spring, 1960; Murder

Strike Pink, 1963; (hist. anthol.) Horses & Their Owners, 1970; (books for children) Racehorse Holiday, 1971; The Trick-jumpers; Show-jumping Secret; Patrick's Pony; How Horses are Trained; Learn to Ride Well; The Radney Riding Club; Proud Riders, 1973, etc.; (under pseudonym Josephine Mann) A Place with Two Faces. Recip., Ernest Benn Publng. Award, for All Change, 1961. Address: 16 Knivet Rd., London SW6 1JH, U.K. 3, 30, 131.

PUMPHREY, Fred Homer, b. 31 July 1898. Educator. Educ: A.B., 1920, B.E.E., 1921, E.E., 1927. Appts. incl: Tech. Engr., Staten Is. Edison Corp., 1924-27; Instr., State Univ. of Iowa, 1927-28; Prof., Elec. Engrng., Rutgers Univ., 1928-45; Major, Lt. Col., U.S. Army Signal Corps, WWII, & Chief, Sci. Curric. Sect., Army Specialized Trng. Prog., 1943-44; Engr., Educl. Serv. Div., Gen. Elec. Co., 1945-46; Hd. Prof., Elec. Engrng. Dept., Univ. of Fla., 1946-58; Dean of Engrng., Auburn Univ., 1958-69; Dean Emeritus, 1969-. Mbrships: Fellow, IEEE; Chmn., var. comms., Am. Soc. for Engrng. Educ.; Nat. Soc. of Profl. Engrs.; Phi Beta Kappa; Sigma Xi; Tau Beta Pi; Etta Kappa Nu; Omicron Delta Kappa; Phi Eta Sigma; Phi Kappa Phi. Hons: D.Sc., Ohio State Univ., 1962; Outstanding Serv. Award, 1962, Ala. Engr. of Year, 1969, Nat. Soc. of Profl. Engrs. Address: 706 Cary Drive, Auburn, AL 36830, U.S.A. 2, 26.

PUMPIAN, Paul Allen, b. 8 Dec. 1926. Pharmacist; Attorney. Educ: B.S., Univ. of Md. Coll. of Arts & Sci., 1948; B.S., Schl. of Pharm. ibid, 1950; J.D., Schl. of Law, 1953. Appts. incl: Asst. Prof., Univ. of Md. Schl. of Pharm, 1953-56; Sec., Wis. State Bd. of Pharm., 1958-66; N.J. Bd. of Pharm., 1971-; Dir., Off. of Legislative & Govl. Serv., U.S. Food & Drug Admin., 1967-69; Adjunct Prof., St. John's Univ. Schl. Pharm., 1972-; Columbia Univ. Coll. Pharm. Sci, 1973-. Mbrships. incl: Fed. Bar Assn., (Pres., Milwaukee Chapt.); Am. Pharm. Assn. (Chmn., Educ. & Legislation Sect.); Am. Assn. of Colls. Pharm. (Sect. Chmn.). Ed., Laws Governing Pharmacy, Remington's Pharm. Sci. (13th edit.) & Practice of Pharmacy (12th edit.) Contbr., num. profl. publs. Recip. awards for profl. servs. Address: 381 Broad St., Newark, NJ 07104, U.S.A. 6, 7, 8.

PUNCH, Lulworth Darrell, b. 8 Aug. 1898. Civil Servant. Appts. incl: Jr. Clerk, Trinidad Govt. Railways, 1919; 3rd Class Clerk, Warden's Off., Eastern Cos., 1932; 2nd Class Clerk, Lands & Surveys Dept., 1941; Control Bd., ibid, 1945; Asst. Warden, Dist. Admin., Toco, 1947; Warden, Caroni, 1951. Mbrships. incl: Area Commnr., Trinidad & Tobago Boy Scouts Assn.; Pres. & Sec., Lynette Lit. & Soc. Club; Sec., Toco Lit. & Debating Club; Sec., Child Welfare League. Publs. incl: Scouting Memories, 1963; A Journey to Remember, 1968. Hons. incl: Medal of Merit, 1944; Companion, Imperial Serv. Order, 1958; Silver Acorn, 1961; Golden Poui for Scouting, 1970; Gold Medal of Merit, Trinidad Govt., 1972. Address: San Antonio St., San Juan, Trinidad, West Indies.

PUNT, (Rev.) Martin A. Pastor (Retired). Educ: A.B., Ctrl. Coll., Pella, Iowa, 1927; M.Div., Western Theol. Sem., Holland, Mich., 1930. Pastorates: The 2nd Reformed Ch., Rochester, N.Y., 1930-42; The Old Saratoga Reformed Ch., Schuylerville, ibid, 1942-44; The 1st Reformed Ch., Hasbrouck Hts., N.J., 1945-65; The Reformed Ch., Bronxville, N.Y., 1965-73. Appts: Chancellor & Dir., Youth Confs., Reformed Ch. in Am., 1934-49; Missioner, Nat. Preaching-Tchng.-Reading Mission, Dept. of Evangelism, Reformed Ch. in

Am., 1962-65. Mbrships. incl: Bd. of Trustees, Ctrl. Coll., Pella, 1951-56 & Northwestern Coll., Iowa, 1962-64; Bd. of Supts., N.B. Theol. Sem., 1933-38 & 1965-67; Bd. of Theol. Educ., Reformed Ch. Am., 1967-70; Served on var. Comms., Bd. of Educ., Reformed Ch. Am.; Rep., ibid, Comm. on Mat. Resources & Planning of Ch. World Serv., Nat. Coun. of Chs., 1963-. Address: P.O. Box 1645, Poughkeepsie, NY 12601, U.S.A. 6, 130.

PURBECK, Luca Gutmann, b. 13 July 1914. Company Director. Educ: Berlin Univ., Germany; Inst. of Jrnlsm., Berlin, 1932-33. Apprentice, Klasing & Co., Publrs., Berlin, 1933-34; Hambros Bank Ltd., London, U.K., 1936-37; Dir., Brieger & Co. Ltd., ibid, 1938-39; News Ed., Assoc. Press of Am., 1944-46; Fndr. & Mng. Dir., Mayborn Prods. Ind., 1946; Mng. Dir., Dylon Int. Ltd., 1959; Dir., Dylon-France S.A., Paris, 1959; Dylon-Japan K.K., Tokyo, 1971; Dylon-Nederland N.V., Driebergen, 1965; Pres., Dylon-France/SAFCO S.A., Paris, 1974. Mbrships: Wentworth Golf Club, Surrey; Soc. of Dyers & Colourists; Reform Club; Royal Automobile Club. Oil paintings & Sculptures exhibited at Royal Acad., London. Address: Dylon Int. Ltd., Worsley Bridge Rd., Lower Sydenham, London SE26 5HD, U.K. 16, 32.

PURBRICK, Eric Stevens, b. 4 Aug. 1903. Grazier; Vigneron. Educ: B.A., Jesus Coll., Cambridge Univ., U.K., 1925; M.A., ibid, 1929; Called to Bar, Inner Temple, London, 1929. Honorary appts: Dpty. Mbr., Australian Wine Bd., 1950-64; Pres., Viticultural Soc. of Victoria, 1955-58; Fndr. & Coun. Mbr., Wine & Brandy Prods. Assn. of Victoria, 1955-68, & Pres. 1964-67; V.P., Fed. Wine & Brandy Prods. Coun. of Australia, 1964-67. Mbrships. incl: Melbourne Club; Australian Club; Vic. Racing Club; Jr. Carlton Club, London; Cmdr., Confrerie des Chavaliers du Tastevin. Author, The Story of a Vineyard—Chateau Tahbilk, 1960. Recip., Royal Greek Red Cross Medal, 1946. Address: Chateau Tahbilk, Tabilk, Vic., Australia 3607. 23.

PURCELL, Hugh D. b. 26 Apr. 1915. Rancher; Retired Major, USAR. Educ: Univ. of Wash., Seattle; Art Ctr., L.A.; Otis Art Inst., ibid; Command & Gen. Staff Schl., Fort Leavenworth. Mbrships: Valley Hunt Club, Pasadena; Calif. & L.A. Yacht Clubs, L.A. Publs: United States Naval Institute Proceedings; Essex Institute Historical Collections. Address: 3353 Padaro Lane, Carpinteria, CA U.S.A.

PURCELL, John Michael, b. 28 Apr. 1922. Professor of Business Administration. Educ: B.S., Bloomsburg State Coll., Pa., U.S.A., 1949; M.A., N.Y. Univ.; Ed.D., Columbia Univ., N.Y. Appts. incl: Mil. Serv., U.S. Army, 1943-46; Cost Acct., Foster-Wheeler Corp., N.Y.C., 1951-52; Jr. Instr.-Instr.-Asst. Prof.-Assoc. Prof.-Prof. Bus. Admin., SUNY, Farmingdale, 1952-63; Assoc. Dean-Dean of Instr., ibid, 1963-67; V.P., Coll. & Acad. Affairs, 1967-73; Prof. Bus. Admin., 1973-. Mbrships. incl: Nat. Off. Mgmt. Assn.; Treas.; Suffolk Co. Bus. Tchrs.; Rotary; Rsch. Comm., Delta Pi Epsilon; Kappa Delta Pi; Phi Sigma Pi; Phi Delta Kappa. Publs. incl: Co-author, Modern Business Communication, 1963; Ed., Purchasing, 1964; Var. rsch. papers & surveys. Hons. incl: Commendation, Cmdng. Gen., WWII; Nat. Off. Mgmt. Int. Award, 1961; Outstanding Coll. Instr. Award on L.I., Nat. Off. Mgmt. Assn., 1962. Address: 16 Walland Ave., Farmingdale, NY 11735, U.S.A. 22.

PURDY, Cecil John Seddon, b. 27 Mar. 1906. Writer. Educ: B.A., Sydney Univ., Australia. Appts: Ed., Australasian Chess Review, 1929-45; Chess World, 1946-67; Chess Ed., Sunday Telegraph, Sydney, 1961-. Mbr. Sydney Univ. Union. Publs: How Euwe Won, 1935; The Return of Alekhine, 1937; Among These Mates; Guide to Good Chess, 1952; How Fischer Won, 1972; Chess Made Easy (w. G. Koshnitsky), 23 eds., 1942. Hons: Chess Championships: New Zealand, 1925; N.S.W., 1929; 1934-39; 1960; 1962; Australia, 1935-38; 1949-52; E. Asia & Oceania, 1960-63; Corres. Chess Champion, Australia, 1941, '47; 1st World Champion, Corres. Chess, 1953-58; Awarded title, Int. Chess Master, Fide, 1951; Grand Master, Corres. Chess, ibid, 1953; Record holder, 3 Corres. Chess tourneys. Address: 10/205 Greenwich Rd., Greenwich, N.S.W., Australia 2065.

PURDY, Harold John, b. 14 June 1914. Minister of Religion. Educ: A.B., Salem Coll., W. Va., U.S.A., 1936; D.D., ibid, 1948; B.D., Southern Bapt. Sem., Louisville Ky., 1942. Appts: Pastor, Barnes Mem. Bapt. Ch.; Clarksburg, W. Va.; First Bapt. Ch. Madison, W. Va.; Deer Pk. Bapt. Ch., Louisville, Ky.; First Bapt. Ch., Madisonville, Ky.; First Bapt. Ch., Bowling Green, Ky.; Belmont Hts. Bapt. Ch., Nashville, Tenn. Mbrships: Pres., Tenn. Bapt. Conven.; Trustee, Belmont Coll., Nashville; Exec. Comm., Southern Bapt. Conven.; Dir., Western Recorder; Kiwanis Club Int. Publs: The Blessed Man; Times & Seasons; Portraits in the Book of Romans; Contbns. to jrnls. Hons. incl: Disting. Serv. Award, Kiwanis Club Int., 1970; Disting Serv. Citation, Southern Bapt. Conven. 1973. Address: Greenville Pike, Drawer 607, Madisonville, KY 42431, U.S.A. 7.

PURDY, Milton Wessells, b. 14 Aug. 1915. Manufacturing Corporation Executive. Educ: Univ. of Wis., 1944; Alexander Hamilton Inst., 1963; Syracuse Univ., 1967-68; Univ. of Me., 1970-71. Appts: Maintenance Engr., Union Bag & Paper Corp., Hudson Falls, N.Y., 1938-46; var. posts, Sandy Hill Corp., ibid, 1947-50; Prod. Coord.-Asst. V.P., ibid, 1950-68; V.P., 1968-. Mbrships: Nat. & N.Y. State TAPPI; Canadian Pulp & Paper Assn; Paper Ind. Mgmt. Assn; Sales & Marketing Executives Int. Address: Nottingham Dr., R.D.1, Glens Falls, NY 12801, U.S.A. 6.

PURNELL, William Ernest, b. 23 Sept. 1911. Chemical Engineer. Educ: Sydney Tech. Coll., Australia. Appts: Prod. Mgr., Kenworth Rubber Co. Pty. Ltd., 1934-38; Mgr., Chems. Dept., A.S. Harrison & Co. Pty. Ltd., 1938-41; Rubber Tech. Off., Commonwealth of Australia, 1941-45; Mbr., Australian Sci. & Tech. Mission to Germany, 1945-47; Counsellor, UNESCO, Dept. of Natural Scis. Paris, 1947-50; Dir., Middle E. Sci. Coop. Off., Cairo & Istanbul, 1950-55, S.E. Asia Sci. Coop. Off., Jakarta, 1955-57; Dir., Sci. & Technol. Careers Bur., 1957-61; Exec. Sec., Royal Australian Chem. Inst., 1961-. Mbrships. incl: Am. Chem. Soc.; Fellow, Royal Australian Chem. Inst., Royal Soc. Arts; Royal Soc. of Vic.; Instn. Chem. Engrs. Publs. incl: co-author, The Question of International Research Laboratories, 1948, Scientific Liaison, 1949. Address: Royal Australian Chem. Inst., 191 Royal Parade, Parkville, Vic., Australia 3052. 23, 34, 131.

PURVIS, Edna O'Shields (Mrs. John W. Purvis), b. 27 Sept. 1916. Banker. Appts: Bank Off. & Exec. i/c New Accounts & Custodian of official records, 1st. Nat. Bank, Mobile, Ala. Mbrships: Bapt. Clubs; Int. Trade Club;

Bienville Club, Mobile; Nat. Assn. Bank Women. Address: 1 Camilla Ct., Mobile, AL 36606, U.S.A. 5.

PURVIS, Lois Allene (Mrs. James Pittman Purvis), b. 26 Nov. 1929. Newspaper Editor. Educ: Hardin-Simmons Univ., Abilene, Tex., 1948-49; Univ. of N.M., Albuquerque, 1950; Coll. of Artesia, N.M., 1969-70. Appts: on Oil Desk, The Odessa Am. newspaper, Tex., 1955-57; Gen. Reporter, Encinitas Coast Dispatch, Calif., 1961-64; City Ed., Artesia Daily Press, N.M., 1966-69; Ed., ibid, 1970-71; Artesia Corres., El Paso Times, Tex., 1964-68; Regional Ed. & Edit. Writer, Roswell Daily Record, N.M., 1971-. Mbrships: N.M. Press Assn.; N.M. Press Women. Recip. 19 awards for writing & picture layout, 1968-71. Address: c/o Roswell Daily Record, 2301 N. Main St., P.O. Box 1897, Roswell, NM 88201, U.S.A. 5, 138.

PUSTER, Frances Garnett (Mrs. James G. Puster), b. 14 July 1911. Travel Agency Owner; Photographer & Writer. Educ: Advt., Int. Corres. Schls.; N.Y. Inst. of Photography; Cert. in basic banking, Am. Bankers Assn. Appts: Hd. Teller, Nat. City Bank of Rome, Ga.; Dept. Hd., Collection Dept., ibid, 1956-68; Fndr., World Travel Agcy., Rome, Ga., 1951; Currently, Owner & Mgr., Travel Agcy. Mbrships. incl: Nat. Assn. of bank Women; Am. Soc. of Travel Agts.; Photographic Soc. of Am.; Nat. Audobon Soc. Contbr. of articles to profl. jrnls. & newspapers. Hons. incl: Winner in window display, Am. Express, U.S.A. & Canada, 1965; Winner in color photography (print), Ga. State Fair, 1971. Address: P.O. Box 488, Rome, GA 30161, U.S.A 5, 16, 57

PUTNAM, Helen B. (Mrs.), b. 21 Aug. 1914. Editor; International Affairs Specialist. Educ: B.A., Smith Coll., 1936; M.A., N.Y. Univ. Appts: Vice Chmn., Art for Bonds Exhib., 1944-45; Rsch., Ed., Writer, Atomic Energy Commn., 1949-51; For. Affairs Off., Dept. of State, 1951-53; Rancher, Mexico, 1953-57; Sec. to Pres., Am. Overseas Fin. Co., 1959-60; Dir., Org. Rels. U.S. Commn. for Refugees, 1960; U.S. Deleg., Triennial Conf., Pan Pacific & S.E. Asia Women's Assn., Island of Tonga, S. Pacific, 1964; Asst. Dir., Int. Students Ctr., N.Y. Univ., 1962-64; Chmn., The Conservation Ctr., 1965-67; Dir., Corres. Sec. Pan Pacific S.E. Asia Women's Assn., 1967-; Ed., Publr., African Life, 1972; Goord., Citizens Comm., Radiation Control, 1970-71. Mbrships. incl: Dir., Children of India Fund; AAAS; Acad. of Pol. Sci.; Dir. & Assoc. Dir., Ctr. for Energy Info.; Am. Acad. of Pol. & Soc. Sci.; Ctr. for Study of Democratic Instns.; Am. Civil Liberties Union. Ed., Energy in the Future, 1953. Contbr. to art jrnls. Hon. Citizen, Repub. of Korea, 1968. Address: 340 E. 51st St., N.Y., NY 10022, U.S.A. 5, 6, 138.

PUTT, Arlene May, b. 27 Mar. 1926. Professor of Nursing. Educ: Dip., Schl. of Nursing, Temple Univ., 1948; B.S., Temple Univ., Phila., Pa., 1950; Ed.M., ibid, 1953; Ed.D., Univ. of Ariz., Tucson, 1969. Appts. incl: Instr. in Nursing, Univ. of Mich., Ann Arbor, 1954-57; Asst. Prof., ibid, 1957-61; Asst. Prof.-Assoc. Prof., Univ. of Ariz., Tucson, 1962-67, 1969-70; Prof., ibid, 1970-; Prin. investigator, conf. to plan a collaborative study of fatigue, Div. of Nursing, U.S. Pub. Hlth. Serv., 1971-73. Mbrships: Sigma Xi; AAAS; AAUP; Am. Assn. Higher Educ.; Am. Nurses Assn.; Nat. League for Nursing; Phi Lambda Theta; AAUW; Ariz. Diabetes Assn.; Ariz. Heart Assn.; Common Cause. Author of articles in jrnls. inclng. Nursing Research, The Catholic Nurse, Modern Hospital, Nursing Outlook.

Recip., Special Predoctoral Fellowship, U.S. Pub. Hlth. Serv., 1967-69. Address: 7821 E. Elida St., Tucson, AZ 85715, U.S.A. 5, 138.

PYATT, Jeanne Wells (Mrs. Glen Crawley Pyatt), b. 30 Dec. 1927. Customer Representative & Traffic Manager. Educ: Gardner Webb Coll., 1947; Gaston Coll. Appts: Prod. Scheduler, Uniroyal Inc., 1960-68; Customer Rep. & Traffic Mgr., McNeill Inds., High Shoals, N.C., 1968-. Mbrships: Pres., Beta Sigma Phi, 2 yrs.; V.P., Sec., 2 yrs.; Chmn., var. comms.; Organizer & 1st Pres., Beta Sigma Phi City Coun., 1964-65; Pres., Coun., 1973-74; Charter & an Organizer, Faith Missionary Bapt. Ch.; Life, N.C. Assn. for the Blind; Gardner Webb Coll. Alumni Assn.; Gastonia Community Concert Assn. Named Beta Sigma Phi Girl of the Yr., 1964-65, 72-73. Address: Rt. 6, Box 243, Gastonia, NC 28052, U.S.A. 125.

PYBURN, Mary Ethel Abernathy, b. 10 Sept. 1921. Educator; Social Worker. Educ: B.S., Kan. State Coll., Pittsburg, Kan., 1943; M.S.W., Atlanta Univ., Ga., 1949; B.S., Macalaster Coll., St. Paul, Minn., 1957; Grad. work, Univ. of Chgo. & Univ. of Minn. Appts. incl: 2nd Grade Tchr., Douglass Elem. Schl., Kan. City, Kan., 1944-48; Vis. Tchr., Walker St. Schl., Atlanta, Ga., 1948; Family Case Worker, Atlanta Ga. Welfare Dept., 1949; 2nd Grade Tchr., Lincoln Elem. Schl., Kan. City, Kan., 1949-53; Family Case Worker, St. Paul Family Serv., St. Paul, Minn., 1953-54; 2nd Grade Tchr., Madison Elem. Schl., Mpls., Minn., 1955-; Night Classes, Edina Minn. Adult Armchair Educ., 1968-70; Adult Educ., Horace Mann Elem. Schl., Mpls., Minn., 1969. Mbrships. incl: AAUW, 1955; City of Mpls. Educ. Assn., 1955-; Tchr. Rep.; NAACP, 1943-; NEA, 1943-; Alpha Kappa Alpha, 1942-; Sec., 1968, State Pres., 1970-71, Ivy Leaf Reporter, 1972-; Minn. ACE, Pres., 1974; Mpls. ACE, Treas., 1965-68, Pres., 1969-70, Legislative Chmn & Photographer, 1972-74. Hons: Nominee, Hon. Ph.D., Hamilton State Univ. & Tchr. of the Yr., Minn., 1974. Address: 4209 Scott Ter., Edina, MN 55416, U.S.A. 5, 138.

PYM, Christopher, b. 13 Jan. 1929. Administrator. Educ: Trinity Coll., Cambridge, U.K. Works w. Robert Matthew, Johnson-Marshall & Ptnrs., archts. & engrs., London. Councillor, Hansard Soc. for Parliamentary Govt., 1972-. Author of books on Cambodian subjects; Contbr. to Int. Affairs (Chatham House) & others. Address: 132 Bromley Rd., Beckenham, Kent, U.K.

PYROS, John A., b. 29 Feb. 1929. Theatre & Film Curator. Educ: B.A., Brooklyn Coll., 1953; M.A., Geo. Spelvin Coll., 1963; Ph.D., N.Y. Univ., 1973. Appts. incl: Asst. Prof., Southern Univ. & Lincoln Univ.; Assoc. Prof., Cumberland Co. Coll.; Dir. of Theatre, Boys Club of N.Y.; Fndr., Phila. Film Co-operative, 1973. Mbrships: Coun. of Small Mag. Eds. & Publrs.; AAUP; Assn. of N.J. Univ. Profs.; Am. Theatre Assn. Publs: Le Voyage (play), N.Y. Univ. Jrnl. Film Reviews; Take One (essay), Baton Rouge Advocate Book Reviews; Cineste (essay), L'esprit Poetry; Small Press Review (essay), Theatre Jrnl.; Dramatika (Ed./Publr.); Nicket Review (essay); Film articles in Nola Express, 1973, Sneak Preview, 1974, The Drummer, The Smith; Paper given at Temple Univ., 1974; Homage to Nobby Brown (play), produced at Southwork Theater, Phila., 1974. Hons: CCLM Award for edit. excellence, Dramatika; Henry A. Spangler Film Criticism Award, 1974. Address: Dramatika, 390 Riverside Dr., N.Y., NY 10025, U.S.A. 130.

Q

QUANT, Natalie Lois, b. 10 Oct. 1914. Accountant; Tax Collector. Educ: Special acctng. courses, Cornell Univ. & U.S. Army Schl. of Acctng., Indpls. Appts: Schenectady Co. Tax Collector, Duanesburgh, N.Y., 1938-42; Acctng. Techn., Schenectady Army Depot, N.Y., 1943-65; Schoharie Co. Soc. Servs. Offs., N.Y., 1967; Sec., Off. Mgr., Bookkeeper, Jamaica Builders Supply Corp., Esperance, N.Y., 1967-72; Town Clerk-Tax Collector, Registrar of Vital Stats., Esperance, 1971-. Mbr., Esperance Presby. Ch.; Pres., ibid, 1964-73. Recip., Sustained Superior Performance Award, for serv. at Schenectady Army Depot, 1943-65. Address: 30 Main St., Esperance, NY 12066, U.S.A. 5.

QUASTEL, Judah Hirsch, b. 2 Oct. 1899. Professor of Biochemistry. Educ: Imperial Coll. of Sci., London, 1919-21; Ph.D., Trinity Coll., Cambridge, 1924; D.Sc., Univ. of London, 1926; A.R.C.S., 1921. Appts: Fellow, Lectr. & Demonstrator in Biochem., Trinity Coll., Cambridge, 1924-29; Dir. of Rsch., Cardiff City Mental Hosp., Wales, 1930-41; Dir., Unit of Soil Metabolism, Agric. Rsch. Coun., U.K., 1941-47; Prof. of Biochem., McGill Univ., Montreal, 1947-66; Prof. of Neurochem., Univ. of B.C., Vancouver, 1966-. Mbrships. incl: Fellow, Royal Soc., London, Royal Soc. of Canada, Royal Inst. of Che,.; Past Pres., Canadian Biochem. Soc, Montreal Physiol. Soc.; etc. Publs. incl: Methods in Medical Research (ed. & co-author); Neurochemistry (co-ed. & co-author), Hons. incl: 2 Hon. Docts.; Companion, Order of Canada. Address: Div. of Neurological Studies, Univ. of British Columbia, Vancouver 8, B.C., Canada. 1, 14, 34, 50, 68, 88, 131.

QUDSI, F., b. 15 Oct. 1927. University Professor. Educ: D.D.S., Syrian Univ. Coll. of Dentistry, 1949; Dip., Prosthetic Dentistry, N.Y. Univ., U.S.A., 1955; M.Sc., Georgetown Univ., 1957. Appts: Dean, Dental Coll., Baghdad Univ., Iraq, 1963-69; Vis. Prof., Georgetown Univ. U.S.A., 1969; Vis. Prof., Howard Univ., Wash. D.C., 1969-71; Chmn., Prosthetic Dept., Coll. of Dentistry, Baghdad Univ., Iraq, 1971-. Fellow, Int. Coll. of Dentists. Mbrships: Pres., Iraqi Dental Soc., 1965-69, 70-; Pres., 6th Arab Dental Congress, Baghdad, 1968; Med. Assocs. Club; Al-Mansoor Club. Publs: Introduction to the Dental Science, 1952; Facial Prosthesis, 1968; articles in profl. jrnls. Recip., Cert., Outstanding Citn. Tchr., Howard Univ., 1971. Address: 44-6 Med. ect., Al-Yarmock City, Baghdad, Iraq.

QUEIROZ, José Carlos, b. 15 Nov. 1937. Designer of architectonics; Painter. Educ: Vale do Paraiba Schl. of Fine Arts, 1962-67. Appts: Architectonic design, Aerospatial Tech. Ctr., Sao Jose dos Campos, 1963-; Tehr., artistic design, vale do Paraiba's Schl. of Fine Arts, 1968-69. Mbrships: Paulista Assn. of Fine Arts; artistic grp., Free Atelier of Sao Jose dos Campos Municipal Prefecture, 1969. Paintings incl: As Tres Mulatas (the three brunettes); Cangaceiro (Brazilian bandit); Capoeira (a Brazilian dance-and-fight); Naufragos (Shipwreckeds). Hons. incl: 1st. Prize, 1 Salon of Work of São Jose dos Campos, 1967; Bronze Medal, Paulista Salon of Fine Arts, São Paulo, 1971. Address: Rua Humaitá N. 95, São José dos Campos, São Paulo, Brazil. 133.

QUEST, Arthur Eugene, Jr., b. 9 Oct. 1914. Company Executive. Educ: B.S., W. Tex. State Univ., 1939; post-grad., Southern Meth. Univ.,

1944; Hon. Ph.D., Hamilton State Univ., 1973. Appts. incl: Am. Tel. & Tel., 1941-43; Engr., Tex. Hlth. Dept., 1943-45; Ptnr., A.E. Quest & Sons Mfrg. Co., Lubbock, Tex., 1946; Owner, Cotton Farm, Lorenzo, Tex., 1960-; Dir., Trinity Valley Ranch Co., Rosser, Tex., Big D. Dev., Dallas, Tex., Inter-Continental Corp., Dallas, Corps. Great S.W., Dallas & Great S.W. Life Ins. Co., Houston, Tex.; Pres., A.E. Quest & Sons Mfrg. Co. Inc., 1974; Owner Cotton Farm, Ralls, Tex., 1974. Mbrships. incl: Fndr., A.E. Quest Jr. Student Loan Endowment Fund, W. Tex. State Univ., 1952; Pres., S. Plains Shrine Club; W. Tex. State Univ. Ex-Students Assn., 1959-, Pres. Publs: Composer, Religious Hymn. Hons. incl: Bd. of Regents, 1969 & Appreciation Award, 1970, W. Tex. State Univ.; Col., Tex. Army, 1972; Outstanding Citizen's Award, Lubbock, Tex., 1972. Address: 3311 46th St., Lubbock, TX 79413, U.S.A. 7, 16, 57.

QUEST, Charles Francis, b. 6 June 1904. Painter; Printmaker; Educator. Educ: Wash. Univ. Schl. of Fine Arts, St. Louis, Mo., 1924-29; Paris, 1929; Spain, France & England, 1960. Appts: executed murals in pub. bldgs., libs. & sev. large chs., 1930-45; Instr., Wash. Univ. Schl. of Fine Arts, St. Louis, 1945, now Prof. Emeritus. Works purchased by Metropolitan Mus., N.Y.C.; Mus. of Mod. Art, N.Y.C.; Chgo. Art Inst.; Phila. Art Mus.; Lib. of Congress; St. Louis Art Mus.; Bklyn. Mus.; British Mus.; Victoria & Albert Mus., London; Bibliotheque Nat., Paris; Nat. Mus., Stockholm; Nat. Mus., Jerusalem; Nat. Gall. of Australia; etc. Exhib. in 90 mus. & galls. in U.S.A., France, Germany & Italy. Represented in permanent collects. of 40 mus. Mbrships. incl: Soc. of Am. Graphic Artists; Life Mbr., St. Louis Club; The Print Club of Phila.; Phila. Colour Print Soc. Hons: 53 prizes 1923-, inclng. Bklyn. Mus., 1949; Lib. of Congress, 1952; Rensselaer Hist. Mus., Troy, N.Y., 1967; Soc. of Am. Graphic Artists, 1968 & 71. Address: 200 Hillswick Rd., Tryon, NC 28782, U.S.A. 2, 8, 15, 37, 105, 125.

QUIGLEY, Carroll, b. 9 Nov. 1910. Professor of History. Educ: A.B., Harvard, 1933; A.M., 1934; Ph.D., 1938. Appts. incl: Instr. & Tutor, Hist., Harvard, 1938-41; Lectr., Georgetown Univ., Schl. of For. Serv., Wash. D.C., 1941-47; Prof., ibid, 1947-; Cons. & Lectr., govt. agcys. & armed forces, 1951-; For. Serv. Inst., Dept. of State, 1961-; Civil Serv. Commn., 1964-; U.S. Dept. of Agric. Grad. Schl., 1966-. Mbrships. incl: Am. Hist. Assn.; Am. Anthropol. Assn.; AAAS; Am. Econ. Assn.; Soc. for Gen. Systems Rsch.; Coun., Int. Soc. for Comparative Study of Civilizations. Publs: Evolution of Civilizations, 1961; Tragedy & Hope: A History of the World in Our Time 1895-1965, 1965; The World Since 1939: A History, 1968; Weapons Systems & Political Stability: A History; many articles & papers. Hons. incl: Vicennial Medal, Georgetown Univ., 1961; 175th Anniversary Medal of Merit, ibid, 1964. Address: 4448 Greenwich Parkway, N.W., Washington, DC 20007, U.S.A. 2, 13.

QUIHALLALT, Oscar Armando, b. 4 July 1913. Engineer. Educ: Fac. Exact Scis., Buenos Aires Univ., Argentina, 1940-44; Cert. Ext. Ballistics, A.B. Bofors, Sweden, 1945-48. Appts: Prof., Ext. Ballistics, Tech. Inst., Buenos Aires, Argentina, 1948-; Pres., Argentina Atomic Energy Commn.; 1954-73; Pres., Argentina Delegn. Conf. Statute Int. Atomic Energy Agcy., N.Y., U.S.A., 1956; Gov., Argentina Bd. Govs., I.A.E.A., Vienna, Austria, 1957-73; Pres., Tech. & Budgetary Comm.,

Vienna & Tokyo, Japan, 1960, '65; Pres., Gen. Conf., Vienna, Austria, 1961; Pres., Bd. Govs., I.A.E.A., 1967-68; Pres., Inter-Am. Nuclear Energy Commn., Wash., U.S.A., 1962-63; Mbr., Argentina Nat. Advsry. Comm. Sci. & Technol., 1967-73; Sr. Advsr., I.A.E.A. for study of Nuclear Power Stns., Iran, 1974-. Mbr. sev. sci. orgs. Publs. incl: 14 sci. & tech. papers on Exterior Ballistics, 1940; The Nat. AEC Progress in Nuclear Energy, 1959; Feasibility study of a Nuclear Power Station (Co-author), 1966. Recip. sev. hons. inclng. Sarmiento Prize, 1952 & decorations from France, Spain, Germany & Italy. Address: Juez Tedín 2875, Buenos Aires, Argentina.

QUILLEN, James H(enry), b. 11 Jan. 1916. United States Representative. Educ: Navy Indoctrination, Dartmouth Coll., Hanover, N.H., 1942. Appts. incl: Mbr., Tenn. State Legislature, 1955-63; Elected to U.S. House of Reps., 1962; Now serving 6th term, ibid. Mbrships: Am. Legion; Veterans of For. Wars; Sons of the Am. Revolution; Lions Club. Hons. incl: LL.D., Steed Coll., Johnson City, Tenn., 1963. Citations & Awards, all Nat. Veterans' Orgs., Veterans of World War I, Am. Legion, Veterans of For. Wars, AMVETS, & Disabled Am. Veterans, 1963-73; Sons of the Am. Revolution Award, 1972. Address: 102 Cannon House Off. Bldg., Wash. DC 20515, U.S.A. 2, 7, 12, 22, 114.

QUILTY, Francis C., b. 28 Feb. 1904. Lawyer. Educ: B.A., Coll. Univ. of Wis., 1925; J.D., Univ. of Wis. Law Schl., 1928; Judge Advocate Schl., Univ. of Mich., 1943; study of Articles of War, Geneva Conven., Int. Law; sev. Univ. Law courses, towards M.L. degree. Appts. incl: Pvte. Prac., Law, Milwaukee & Madison, Wis., specializing in Trial work in City of Milwaukee; Lobby work before Wis. legislature; 2 yrs., Judge Advocate Gen. Dept. performing legal work w. Air Transport Command; Pvte. Prac., State of Mo., 20 yrs. Mbrships: former Pres., Kan. City Social Hlth. Soc.; Wis. Bar Assn., 1928; Admitted, Mo. Bar, 1950; Kan. City Bar Assn., Mbr., Bus. & Commercial Law Sect.; Corp. Law Comm., Mo. State Bar; Commercial Law League of Am.; Kts. of Columbus, 4th Degree. Contbr. to profl. jrnls. Address: 402 Argyle Bldg., Kansas City, MO 64106, U.S.A.

QUINCY, Guy, b, 5 Sept. 1929. Departmental Director of Archives. Educ: Ecole Nat. des Chartes; Dipl., Archivist-Paleographer. Appts: Custodian, Deptl. Archives, Constantine, 1955; Dir., Archive Servs., La Corrèze, 1963-; Custodian, Antiquities & Objets d'Art, ibid, 1964-73. Mbrships: V.P. (1963-70), Mbr. (1970-), Commn. of Sites of La Corrèze; Soc. des Lettres, Scis. & Arts, ibid; Soc. Hist. & Régionaliste du Bas-Limousin; Soc. Sci. Hist. & Archaeol., La Corrèze; Soc. des Scis. Hist. & Naturelles de l'Yonne. Publs: Les Métiers d'Auxerre du milieu du XVII siécle à la Révolution (thesis); Répertoire de documentation nord-africaine. Suppléments 1, 1956, & 2, 1958; var. hist. articles. Hons: Chevalier des Palmes Académiques; Chevalier des Arts & des Lettres. Address: Archives départementales, rue Souham, 19012 Tulle, France. 43, 91.

QUINTANA, Epaminondas, b. 19 Aug. 1896. Physician. Educ: San Carlos Univ., Guatemala, 1914-23; Post-grad. study, Paris, France, 1928-30; Berlin, Germany, 1930; Calif. Univ., Berkeley, U.S.A., 1944-45. Appts. incl: Mil. surg., Guatemalan Army, 1917-27; Gen. Prac., 1927-37; Hd., Propaganda Sect., Dept. Pub. Hlth., Guatemala, 1938-42; Hd., Div. Hyg. Educ., Inst. Am. Affairs, 1945-50; Chief Off.,

Hyg. Educ. var. ctrs., Guatemala, 1950-65; Dir., Indigenist Inst., Guatemala, 1965-70. Mbrships: Paediatricians Assn., Guatemala; Coun. Welfare, Nicaragua; Fndr. & Sec., League against TB; Fndr., Assn. Prevention Heart Diseases & Assn. Mental Hyg.; Fndr. & Pres., Assn. Med. Writers; Dndr. & Pres., Assn. Weiters & Friends Nat. Book. Publs. incl: Higiene Escolar, 1923, Higiene de la Finca Rural, 1940; Profilaxis y Educación de la Tuberculosis, 1941; Educación Higienica Escolar, 1952; 2nd ed., '54; El Agro Uberrimo (fiction), 1964; 2nd ed., '68; Historia de la Generación de 1920, 1971; Cantos a la Patria (poems), 1972; La Obra Inicial de Miguel Angel Asturias, 1974. Recip. hons. Address: Calzada Raúl Aguilar Bátres, 12-31, zona 12, Guatemala City, Guatemala.

QUINZADA, Antenor, b. 12 Nov. 1896. Attorney & Counsellor at Law. Educ: B.A., Nat. Inst. of Panama, 1918; LL.B., Fordham Univ., N.Y., U.S.A., 1926; J.D., N.Y. Univ., 1928. Appts: Sec., Vice-Consul & Gen. Consul of Panama, N.Y., 1918-29; Prof., Civic, Econ. & Mercantile Laws, Panama Official Colls., 1929-36; Prosecuting & Corp. Counsel, City of Panama, Dpty. to Nat. Assembly of Panama, 1936-40; Prof., Mercantile Law, Panama Univ., 1940-44; Alternate Magistrate, Superior Labor Ct. of Panama, 1960-68; Legal Counsel, Panama Nat., 1960-64; Counsel for Min. of Treasury, Int. Revenue & Financial Affairs Dept., 1964-68; Asst. to legal firms in U.S.A., Canada, U.K., France, Italy, Spain, Greece, Switzerland, & almost all Latin Am. countries. Mbr., Union Club of Panama, until 1968. Publs. incl: The Panama-American Annual Commercial Guide, 1928. Address: Apartado 473, Panama 1, Panama, Repub. of Panama.

QUIRK, (Sister) Mary Richardine, B.V.M., b. 8 June 1908. Educational Administrator. Educ: A.B., Clarke Coll., Dubuque, Iowa, U.S.A., 1945; M.A., Marquette Univ., Milwaukee, Wis., 1953; Ph.D., Cath. Univ. of Am., Wash. D.C., 1965. Appts: Tchr., Parochial schls., Ill., Colo., Iowa., & Neb., 1928-47; Prin., St. Francis Xavier Schl., Kan. City, Mo., 1947-50; Provincial Superior, Sisters of Charity, Blessed Virgin Mary, 1950-56; Educ. Dept., Mundelein Coll., Chgo., Ill., 1956-58; Assoc. Sec., Elem. Schl. Dept., Nat. Cath. Educ. Assn., 1958-64; Dir., Grad. Div., Clarke Coll., 1964-. Mbrships. incl: Nat. Sister Formation Comm., 1954-63; Edit. Advsry. Bd., Cath. Ency. for Schl. & Home, 1958-64; Exec. Comm., Coun. of Nat. Orgs. for Children & Youth, 1964-66; AAUW. Publs: Co-author, Laidlaw History Series for Catholic Schools, 1963-65; Contbns. to book & encys. Received in Pvte. Audience with Pope Paul VI, 1972. Address: Graduate Division, Clarke College, Dubuque, IA 52001, U.S.A. 5, 8, 15, 138, 141.

QURESHI, Anwar Iqbal, b. 10 Apr. 1910. Economist. Educ: B.A., Punjab, India, 1930; M.A., ibid, 1932; M.Sc., London, U.K., 1934; Ph.D., Trinity Coll., Dublin, Irish Repub., 1935; Travelling schlrship. to Australia, N.Z. & S. Africa, 1933; Fellowship, Mussoori Univ., visited Canada & U.S.A., 1934. Appts. incl: Dpty. Econ. Advsr. to Govt. of Pakistan, 1947-51; Advsr., Int. Monetary Fund, Latin Am., Middle & Far Eastern Depts., 1951-55; UN Pub. Finance Expert to Libyan Govt., 1953; Financial & Econ. Advsr., Min. of Finance & Nat. Econ., Jeddah, S. Arabia, 1955-59; Econ. Advsr. & (Ex-Officio) Addl. Sec. to Pakistan Govt., retd. 1971; Chief Economist, Sabasun Tech. Servs., 1974-; Rep., Pakistan, Meeting of Asian Dev. Bank, 1965-66. Mbrships: Pres., Pakistan Econ. Assn., 1965; Sec., Indian Econ. Assn., 1944-47; Edit. Bd., Indian Econ. Jrnl., 1939-46. Author of publs.

in field. Recip., Sitara-i-Quaid-i-Azam, 1965. Address: Sabasun Tech. Servs., 54 Main Gulberg, Lahore, Pakistan. 34.

QURNELL, Kenneth L., b. 28 Nov. 1910. Athletic Director. Educ: B.A., East Carolina Univ., Greenville, N.C.; M.A., George Peabody Coll., Nashville, Tenn., 1939; var. other univs. Appts: Football Coach & Phys. Ed. Tchr., Trinity, Ala., 1939-41; Football Coach & Hist. Tchr., Burlington, 1941-42; USAF, 1942-46; Coach & Tchr., Burlington, 1946-; currently Athletic Dir. & Tchr. of Driver Educ. at Cummings H.S. Mbrships: Elks Lodge; Moose Lodge; Kiwanis. Hons: 8 trophies for undefeated teams in football & basketball; Awards, N.C. Coaches Assn. for 35 yrs. of serv. in Athletics, 1968. Address: 233 Waverly Way, Burlington, NC 27215, U.S.A.

R

RABAU, Erwin M., b. 15 Nov. 1899. Physician. Educ: Grad. in Med., Univs. of Berlin, & Heidelberg, Germany, 1922; Post-grad. work, Robert Koch Inst., Berlin & Patholl. Inst., Municipal Hosp. Berlin-Moabit, 1923. Appts. incl: Asst., Surg. Dept.-Dpty. Chief, Gyn. Dept., Municipal Hosp. Berlin-Mohabit, Germany, 1924-33; Edit. work, 2 German Med. Jrnls., 1928-33; Dir., Municipal Maternity Ctr. for Prenatal Care, Tiergarten Dist., 1930-33; Specialist in Gyn. & Ob., Kupath-Cholim Outpatient Clin., Tel-Aviv, Israel, 1934; Dir., Dept. of Gyn. & Ob., Beilinson Hosp., Petach-Tikva, 1936-47; Hd., 1st Sterility Clin., ibid, 1939; Dir., Gyn. & Ob. Dept., Hayarkon Hosp., 1947-49; Dir., Dept. of Ob. & Gyn., Tel-Hashomer Govt. Hosp., 1950-68; Assoc. Clin. Prof. of Gyn & Ob., Hebrew Univ. Med. Schl., Jerusalem, 1959; Cons. in Gyn., Malben Instns., Israel (Israel Jt. Org.), 1955-65; Assoc. Vis. Prof., Ob. & Gyn., Tel-Aviv Univ. Med. Schl., 1968. Mbrships. incl: Hon. Mbr., Turkish Gyn. Soc., 1956 & Sinai Med. Assn., Teheran, 1964. Publs: num. sci. works in sev. langs. in field of Gyn. & Ob. Address: 21, Levy Itzhak St., Tel-Aviv, Israel.

RABINOWITZ, Kurt, b. 1916, d. 5 Feb. 1974. Physician; Institutional Administrator. Educ: Ph.D., Hadassah-Hebrew Univ. Med. Schl., Jerusalem, 1947, M.D., 1956, M.P.H. 1961. Appts: Dir., Vaccine Prod. Inst., Govt. Central Labs., Min. of Hlth., Jerusalem, 1941-48, Dir., Dist. Hlth. Lab., 1948-55, Dpty. Dir., Regional Hlth. Servs., 1960-74, Fndr. & Hd., Unit for Prevention of Cross-Infections in Hosp., 1966-74. Mbrships: Israel Med. Assn., & Exec. Mbr. of Jerusalem Br.; Israel Microbiological Assn. Num. profl. articles, papers & reports, var. med. & sci. publs. Hons: Maimonides Award, 1955; PLH Grant from CDC, U.S.A., in recognition of Dr. Rabinowitz' disting. pioneer servs. in prevention of cross-infections in hosps., 1971-73. Address: Dr. Sonja Bergner-Rabinowitz, Public Hlth. Lab., Ministry of Health, Jerusalem, Israel.

RABINOWITZ, (Rabbi) L.I., b. 24 May 1906. Rabbi; Editor. Educ: M.A., Ph.D., London Univ., U.K.; Rabbinical educ: Tree of Life, Yeshivah, ibid; Chief Rabbi Hertz, England & Chief Rabbi A.1. Kook, Israel. Appts: Rabbi, Shepherds Bush Synagogue, London, U.K., 1926-28; S. Hackney, ibid, 1928-32; Cricklewood, ibid, 1932-38; Sr. Jewish Chap., Middle East, 1939-44; Brit. Liberation Army, 1944-45; Chief Rabbi, S. Africa, 1945-61; Prof. Hebrew Lit., Univ. Witswatersrand, 1945-61; Dpty. Ed.-in-Chief, Ency. Judaica, 1967-71; Ed., Ency. Yr. Book, 1971-. Publs: The Social Life of the Jews of Northern France in the XII-XIV Centuries, 1938; The Herem Hayyishub, 1945; The Radanites, 1948; Vols. of Sermons: Out of the Depths; Sparks from the Anvil; Sabbath Light; Light and Salvation. Address: 6 Mapu St., Jerusalem 94-189, Israel.

RABKIN, Leo, b. 21 July 1919. Artist. Educ: Univ. of Cinn., Ohio; w. Inglehart, Tony Smith & Baziotes, N.Y. Univ., N.Y.C., 1948-52. Appts: Tchr., var. subjects inclng. remedial reading & typing, often in special schls.; Sculptor, Painter & Printer. Exhibs: Painting & Sculpture Biennials, Whitney Mus., 7 shows; New Talent Show, Mus. of Mod. Art, 1960; Light/Motion/Space, Walker Art Ctr., Mpls., Minn., 1967; A Plastic Presence, San Fran., Milwaukee & N.Y.C., 1970; Retrospective Show, Storm King Art Ctr., Mountainville, N.Y., 1970. Watercolors in many collects.

inclng: Mus. Mod. Art; Guggenheim Mus.; Whitney Mus. of Am. Art, N.Y.C.; U.S. State Dept.; John D. Rockerfeller III; Savings Banks Assn. Prints in Smithsonian, Wash. & Bklyn. Mus. Sculptural Constructions (acrylic): Mus. Mod. Art; Whitney Mus.; N.C. Mus. of Art; Univ. of Calif., Berkeley; var. pvte. collects. Hons: Ford Fndn. Award for watercolor, 1961; 1st prize, Silvermine Guild for Arts, 1961; Popular Award for Sculpture First Ann Westchester, 1967. Address: 218 West 20th St., N.Y., NY 10011, U.S.A. 37.

RABON, Florence Graham (Mrs. Wright Coxwell Rabon, Jr.) b. 22 July 1906. Writer. Educ: B.Sc., Fla. State Coll. for Women. Appts: Mgmt; Analyst, USN Dept., 1941-70; Writer, The Miami Herald, 1958-. Mbrships. incl: Alpha Kappa Delta; Phi Alpha Theta; Publicity Chmn., Key West City Panhellenic; Past Pres., Beta Sigma Phi Int.; Pub. Rels. Chmn;. Order of the Rose; Bd. of Dirs., Key West Community Concerts Assn.; Bd. of Dirs. & Pub. Rels. Chmn., Key West Coun. of Heart Assn.; Charter Sec. Key West Art & Hist. Soc.; Am. Legion Aux.; Alpha Xi Delta; Key West Coun. Navy League; Key West Country & Woman's Clubs. Contbr. to The Miami Herald & Key West Citizen. Recip. of Outstanding Citizen Award, Am. Legion, 1958. Cert. Appreciation Bus. & Profl. Woman's Club & Easter Seal Soc. for Crippled Children & Adults, 1972. Address: 1622 Laird St., Key West, FL 33040, U.S.A. 132.

RACE, George Justice, b. 2 Mar. 1926. Physician; Educator. Educ: M.D., Univ. of Tex., S.W. Med. Schl., 1947; M.Sc., Univ. of N.C, 1953; Ph.D., Baylor Univ., 1969. Appts: incl: Asst. Prof./Prof., Univ. of Tex. S.W. Med. Schl., 1955-; Chief, Pathol., & Dir., Lab., Baylor Univ. Med. Ctr., 1959-; Prof., var. Depts., ibid, 1962-; Dean, A. Webb Roberts Ctr., 1973-. Mbrships. incl: Fellow, Am. Acad. Forensic Sci., Fellow, AAAS; Int. Acad. Pathol.; AAUP; AMA; Archaeol. Inst. Am.; N.Y. Acad. Sci. Author, Laboratory Medicine (4 volumes) 1973. Contbr. num. profl. publs. Hons: Award, Rsch. Contbn. Angiol., N.Y., 1968; Award of Honor, Am. Cancer Soc., N.Y., 1971. Address: Roberts Ctr., Continuing Educ., Baylor Univ. Med. Ctr., 3500 Gaston Ave., Dallas, TX 75246, U.S.A. 2, 50.

RACHWAL, Walter A., b. 8 Oct. 1925. Certified Public Accountant. Educ: Walsh Inst. of Acctcy., 1946-49; B.B.A., Univ. of Detroit, 1956; M.B.A., Univ. of Detroit, 1967. Appts: Dir., Bd; Bradbury-Kenrick Assocs., Inc., 1964: V.P., ibid, 1965; Trustee, ibid, & Employee Deferred Profit Sharing Trust, 1965; Chmn., Prog. Mutual Fund, ptnrship., 1967. Mbrships: Am. Inst. of CPA's; Mich. Assn. of CPA's; Am. Acctng. Assn., Am. Inst. of Mgmt. Hons: D.I.B. Cert. of Merit for dist. serv. to bus. & comm., 1967; Dipl. for Dist. Achievement, Two Thousand Men of Achievement, 1969; Mbr. of Eminent Dist., Nat. Register of Prom. Ams. Address: 6833 Oakman Blvd., Dearborn, MI 48126, U.S.A. 8, 16, 57.

RADCLIFFE, Lynn James, b. 14 Apr. 1896. Methodist Clergyman. Educ: B.A., Wesleyan Univ., 1919; D.D., ibid, 1962; Grad. Schl., Harvard Univ., 1922; M.Div., Boston Univ., 1924; D.D., Syracuse Univ., 1937. Appts: Pastor of Meth. Churches, Coll. Ave. Somerville, Mass., 1921-35, 1st, Syracuse, N.Y., 1935-41, 1st, Oak Park, Ill., 1941-48, Hyde Park Community, Cinn., Ohio, 1948-61; Preacher, 35 U.S.A. states & 12 other countries. Mbrships: Trustee, Ohio Wesleyan Univ., 1950-61; 5 supreme Meth. Gen. Confs., 1940-60; Meth. Coord. Coun., 1960-64;

Organizing Bd., Meth. Theological Schl., Ohio, 1952-56; Pres., Coun. of Churches, Syracuse, 1939-41, Cinn., 1949-50; Morris Country Golf Club; Rotary Club; Scottish Rite Masons. Publs: Making Prayer Real, 1952; With Christ in the Garden, 1959; With Christ in the Upper Room, 1960; Seven Steps of Spiritual Progress, 1959. Recip., Medal of the Yr., Ohio Lib. Assn., 1953. Address: 21 Ferndale Rd., Madison, NJ 07940, U.S.A. 6.

RADHU, Asha Nand, b. 17 Sept. 1916. Cinema Owner. Educ: B.A., Vidya Ratna; Doct., Vaidya Kaviraj. Appts: Owns 2 cinemas; regularly engaged as Hindi writer; active soc. wkr.; Fndr., Shri S.D. Mahabir Dal Radju Lin., Sambhal, Dist. Moradabad, Upper Province, India. Mbrships: Pres., Hindi Sahitya Niketan; Pres., Shri Kalki Vishnu Mandir, Sambhal; Mgr., Azad Pub. Lib; of var. socs. & orgs. in Sambhal. Hons: Ajat Shatroo (an award meaning 'Who has no enemy'); Gold & Silver Medals awarded by Punjabi Sabha for social work. Address: Radhu Road, Sambahl, Dist. Moradabad, U.P., India.

RADOVICH, Donald, b. 3 Jan. 1932. Painter; Naturalist; Professor. Educ: B.F.A., Univ. of N.M., 1956; M.A., ibid, 1960; Postgrad., San Miguel de Allende, Mexico. Appts: Illustrator, Naturalist, N.M. Dept. of Game & Fish, Santa Fe; Illustrator, Sandia Corp. A.E.C. Contract Wkr., Albuquerque, N.M.; Asst. Prof., Painting, Western State Coll., Gunnison, Colo. Mbrships: Pres., Fac. Welfare Comm., Western State Coll.; Interim Pres., Fac. Affairs Coun., ibid; Pres., Gunnison Valley Naturalists, 1965. Illustrator of: New Mexico Birds & Where to Find Them, by S. Ligon; New Mexico Wildlife Mag. (num. covers) Commissions incl: Paintings of N.M. Bird, Mammal, Fish, & Tree for State Capitol Bldgs., Santa Fe; pvte. commns. Num. 1-man exhibs. Invited to participate in 4th Int. Game Conservation Int. Art Exhib., San Antonio, Tex., 1973. Address: 518 N. Main St., Gunnison, CO 81230, U.S.A. 63.

RADZINOWICZ, (Sir) Leon, b. 15 Aug. 1906. Professor. Educ: M.A., Geneva, Switzerland; LL.D., Cracow, Poland; LL.D., Rome, Italy; LL.D., Cambridge, U.K. Appts: Adjunct Prof., Geneva & Warsaw; Dir., Dept. of Criminal Sci., Univ. of Cambridge; Dir., Inst. of Criminol. & Wolfson Prof. of Criminol., ibid; Adjunct Prof., Univs. of Yale, Columbia, Pa., Rutgers, & Va., U.S.A. Mbrships: V.P., Govng. Body, Int. Assn. of Criminal Law, Int. Soc. for Soc. Defence, & British Soc. of Criminol.; Hd., UN Soc. Defence Sect.; Chmn., Criminol. Coun., Coun. of Europe; Pres., British Acad. of Forensic Scis. Publs: History of English Criminal Law, 4 vols., 1948-; In Search of Criminology, 1961; Ideology & Crime, 1966; James Fitzjames Stephen, 1957; Crime & Justice, co-ed., 3 vols., 1971; Ed., Cambridge Studies in Criminology. Hons. incl: Kt. Bach., 1970; Coronation Medal, 1953; Chevalier, Ordre de Leopold, Belgium, 1930; Fellow, Trinity Coll., Cambridge & British Acad.; Hon. Fellow, Silliman Coll., Yale; James Ames Prize, Harvard Law Schl. Address: 21 Cranmer Rd., Cambridge, U.K. 1, 3, 34, 41.

RAE, Matthew Sanderson, Jr., b. 12 Sept. 1922. Attorney. Educ: A.B., Duke Univ., U.S.A., 1946; LL.B., 1947; Stanford Univ. Law Schl. Appts: Asst. to Dean, Duke Law Schl., 1947-48; Assoc. Attny., Off. of Karl F. Steinmann, Balt., Md., 1948-49; Nat. Field Rep., Phi Alpha Delta, 1949-51; Rsch. Atty., Calif. Supreme Ct., 1951-52; Assoc. Atty., 1953-54; Ptnr., Darling Hall Rae & Gute, 1955-. Mbrships. incl: Pres., Calif. Repub. League,

1966-67; Supreme Justice, Phi Alpha Delta, 1972-74; Pres., Legion Lex., 1969-71; Chmn., State Bar of Calif. Jrnl. Comm., 1970-71; V.-Chmn., State Bar of Calif. Probate & Trust Law Comm., 1973-; Repub. State Ctrl. Comm., 1966-; V.-Pres., Calif. Town Hall, 1973-; Fellow, Am. Coll. Probate Counsel, 1963; Phi Beta Kappa, 1943; Omicron Delta Kappa, 1943; Rotary Int.; Commonwealth Club; World Affairs Coun.; Chancery Club. Contrbr. of articles to profl. jrnls. Address: 523 W. 6th St., Ste. 400, L.A., CA 90014, U.S.A. 9, 16, 22, 57, 59, 75, 114, 120, 128, 130, 131.

RAE, Norman Frederick, b. 5 Dec. 1931. Administrator; Radio Producer; Dramatic Critic. Educ: B.A., Univ. of Oxford, U.K., 1954: M.A.; Univ. of London, U.K., 1956. Appts: Asst. Sec., Banana Bd., Kingston, Jamaica, 1956; Sec. & Admin. Mgr., ibid; Special Writer on Fine Arts, Theatre, Cinema & Dance, The Daily Gleaner, Kingston, Jamaica, 1956-70. Theatre Dir. of num. Jamaican & other plays. Prod. of radio progs. incing. serial, A Time to Remember. Recip., Seprod Jrnlsm. Award, for radio prod., The Hertiage Now, 1969. Address: 1A Hillman Rd., Kingston 8, Jamaica, W. Indies. 96.

RAE, Thomas b. 14 Mar. 1928. Master Printer. Mbr., Editorial & Advisory Bd., D.I.B. Dir., Thomas Rae Ltd., 1953 and The Signet Press, 1956-67; owner, Grain-aig Press, 1967. Mbr. of Coun., Glasgow Bioliog. Soc.; Mbr., Edinburgh Bibliog. Soc. & Pvte. Libs. Assoc. Publs. incl: Andrew Myllar, a Short Study of Scotland's First Printer; The Book of the Private Press (compiled w. G. Handley-Taylor); Some Notes on Wood Engraving by Thomas Berwick (ed.). Address: 23 Union St., Greenock, Scotland, U.K. 3, 11, 43.

RAEDER, Arthur O., b. 15 Sept. 1915. Orthodontist. Educ: D.D.S., N.Y. Coll. of Dentistry, 1937; Postgrad. Orthodontic Cert N.Y. Univ., 1941. Appts: Instr., N.Y. Coll. of Dentistry, 1937; Postgrad. Orthodontic Cert Orthodontics, 1950-53; Pres., N.Y. Univ. Orthodontics Soc. 1952-53; Dir., Orthodontic Clin., Univ. Hosp., Bklyn, 1965-69. Presl. Appt., Examining Dentist, 1942. Mbrships. incl; Dipl. Am. Bd. of Orthodontics; Fellow, N.Y. Acad. of Scis.; Has served on var. commns.; Am. Dental Assn.; Am. Assn. of Orthodontists; Pan-Am. Med. Assn.; Dental Sci. Chmn., City Schis & Oral Hlth Comm. of Gtr. N.Y.; Alpha Omega; Mason (Shriner); Past High Priest of Royal Arch Masons 147; Coun. Judges, Annual City-Wide Sci. Fair, N.Y.C.; State Coun. on Dental Trade & Lab. Rels. of Dental Soc. of State of N.Y. Author of papers and articles in profl. jrnls. Recip. of Congressional Medal of Merit, & of Presl. Citation, 1945. Address: 615 Eastern Parkway, Brooklyn, NY 11216, U.S.A, 2, 6, 14, 28.

RAEKALLIO, Jyrki Arno Johannes, b. 27 Mar. 1929. Professor. Educ: M.D., Schl. Med., Helsinki Univ., Finland, 1954; Post-grad. work, Dept. Forensic Med., ibid, 1956-62; Med. Akad., Düsseldorf, German Fed. Repub., 1958-59; John Hopkins Univ., Balt., Md., U.S.A., 1963. Appts: Asst. Physn-Sr. Lectr., Forensic Med., Helsinki Univ., 1956-63; Assoc. Prof.-Prof., Forensic Med. Turku Univ., 1962-. Mbrships: Past Secs., Scandinavian Soc. Forensic Med.; V.P., Int. Acad. Legal Med.; Fellow, Royal Microscopical Soc., Oxford, U.K.; Italian Soc. Legal Med.; Corres., Deutsche Gesellschaft für Rechtsmedizin & Am. Acad. Forensic Scis.; Fellow, Am. Acad. Cellular Biol.; Histochem. Soc., U.S.A. Publs: Histochemical Studies on Vital & Post-Mortem Skin Wounds, 1961; Die Altersbestimmung mechanisch bedingter

Hautwunden mit enzymhistochemischen Methoden, 1965; Enzyme Histochemistry of Wound Healing, 1970; about 150 articles in sci. jrnls. Address: Linnankatu 13 b 13, SF-20100, Turku 10, Finland. 43, 50, 90, 134.

RAFSKY, Jessica C. (Mrs. Murray Rafsky), b. 18 Sept. 1923. Financial Analyst; Art Collector. Educ: Geo. Wash. & N.Y. Univs. Appts: Mbr., N.Y. Univ. Law Review. Mbrships: Friend of Tate Mus.; Brit. Mus.; Contbng. Mbr., Mus. of Primitive Art & Asia Soc., N.Y.; Assoc., Guggenheim Mus.; Sustaining Mbr., Mus. of Mod. Art & N.Y. Pub. Lib.; Assoc., Metrop. Mus. of Art; Friend of Whitney Mus.; Assoc., UN. Address: 200 E. 62 St., N.Y., NY 10021, U.S.A. 37.

RAGGI, Carlos Manuel, b. 10 Oct. 1910. Educator. Educ: B.A., B.S., Havana Inst., Cuba, 1927; Ph.D., Univ. of Havana, 1934. Appts: Esc. Superior Admin. Pub., 1940-48; Dir., Gral. de la Seguridad Soc., 1942-45; Univ. Mac. J. Marti, 1952-58; Assoc. Prof., Lit. & Latin Am. Hist., Russell Sage Coll., U.S.A., 1963-. Mbrships: Diputado, Havana Bar Assn., 1935-44; Exec. Sec., Circulo de Cultura Panamericana, 1963-. Publs. incl: Seguridad Social en Cuba, 1944; Sociedad, Democracia y Trabajo, 1935; Apuntes Lit. Siglo de Oro, 1966. Hons: Nat. Award, Best Jr. Book, Havana, 1938. Address: 16 Clark Ave., Troy, NY 12180, U.S.A. 6, 13.

RAGLAND, Jack Whitney, b. 25 Feb. 1938. Professor; Artist. Educ: B.A., Arizona State Univ., Tempe, 1960; M.A., ibid, 1964; Grad. study, pntng., Drawing, Art Hist., Calif. Univ., L.A., 1961-64; Akad. für Angewandte Kunst-Vienna, Austria & Graphische Bundes-Lehrund Versuchsanstalt, ibid, 1970-71. Mbrships: Coll. Art Assn. of Am.; Mid-Am. Coll. Art Assn. Creative Works: 12 solo exhibits; num. grp. shows; Pntngs. or Prints in permanent Collects. at Albertina Mus., Vienna, Austria; Arizona State Univ., Tempe, U.S.A.; Graphische Bundes Lehr-und Versuchsanstalt, Vienna, Austria; Kunsthaus, Basle, Switzerland; L.A. Co. Mus., Calif.; Phoenix Mus., Arizona; Simpson Coll., Indianola, Iowa; Unity Ctr., Des Moines, ibid; Works of art reprod. in Applause, mag. for the Arts, 1971; Prize Winning Paintings, Book II, 1962. Recip. hons., inclng. Grand Purchase Prize, Arizona Annual Exhib., Phoenix, 1961; Hon. Mentions, 5-state competition, Tucson, Arizona, 1961 & Arizona State Fair, Phoenix, 1962. Address: 1005 Ann Parkway, Indianola, IA 50125, U.S.A. 2, 37.

RAGNARSSON, Jón Edwald, b. 24 Dec. 1936. Advocate. Educ: LL.M., Univ. of Iceland, Reykjavik, 1966; Bar exam, 1966; Admitted to bar, Supreme Ct. of Iceland, 1973. Appts: Jrnlst. & Pol. Ed., Morgunbladid newspaper, Reykjavik, 1960-63; Asst. to Mayor, Reykjavik, 1966-69; Attorney, own law firm, Reykjavik, 1969-; Dir., Gamma s.f.; Attorney, U.S. Govt. & USN in Iceland, 1973-74. Mbrships. incl: Pres., Vardberg Assn. of Atlantic Cooperation, 1971-72; Exec. Comm., Atlantic Assn. of Young Pol. Ldrs., 1972-74; Pres., Nat. Union of Icelandic Students, 1962-63; Bd., Univ. of Iceland, 1963-64; V.P., Nat. Assn. of Young Independence Party Mbrs., 1965-68; Icelandic Bar Assn.; Pres., Jr. Chmbr. of Comm. of Iceland, 1972-73. Publs: Num. articles on law, pol. & int. rels. in mags.; Ed., sev. mags. Address: Reykjavik, P.O. Box 579, Laugavegur 3, Iceland. 43.

RAGSDALE, (Ouida) Zane Oakley, b. 16 Jan. 1921. Director of School Programs for Handicapped. Educ: B.S., Memphis State Univ.,

Tenn., U.S.A.; M.S., Univ. of Tenn. Appts: Pub. Schl. Tchr., Gibson Co., Child Welfare Wkr. Tenn. Dept., of Pub. Welfare; Psychiatric Soc. Wkr, Chattanooga Guidance Clin., Chief Psychiatric Soc. Wkr., Jackson Mental Hlth. Ctr.; Field Soc. Wkr., Western State Psychiatric Hosp.; Schl. Soc. Wkr., Gibson Co. Schls., Tenn. Dept. of Educ.; Dir., Comprehensive Schl. Progs. for Handicapped of Gibson Co. Num. mbrships. incl: Chmn., Mental Hlth. Comm., N.-W. Tenn. Comprehensive Hlth. Planning Coun.; Sec., Econ. Dev. Prog., Gibson Co.; Sec., Bd. of Dirs., Gibson Co. Child Dev.Ctr.; Memphis State Univ. Fndn. Century Club; Nat. Assn. of Soc. Wkrs.; Acad. of Cert. Soc. Wkrs.; NEA; Coun. for Exceptional Children; Pres., Trenton Club; Am. Assn. for Retarded Children & Adults. Author, Care of the Mentally Ill in Tennessee, 1952. Recip., Engraved Award, Gibson Co. Child Dev. Ctr., 1973. Address: Route # 3, Dyersburg Rd., Trenton, TN 38382, U.S.A. 57, 125.

RAHBAR, Muhammad Daud, b. 6 Apr. 1927. University Professor. Educ: B.A. (Hons.), Punjab Univ., 1945; M.A., ibid, 1947; Ph.D., Cambridge Univ., U.K., 1953. Appts: Tchng. Fellow, McGill Univ., Montreal, Canada, 1954-56; Specialist i/c Chair of Urdu & Pakistan Studies, Ankara Univ., Turkey, 1956-59; Vis. Prof., Hartford Sem. Fndn., Conn., U.S.A., 1960-62, Assoc. Prof., 1962-66; Vis. Assoc. Prof., Wis. Univ., 1966-68; Assoc. Prof., World Religs., Boston Univ. Schl. of Theol., 1968-. Mbrships: Am. Oriental Soc.; Am. Soc. Study of Religs. Publs. incl: Nuskhahâ-i-Wafâ, 1960; God of Justice: A Study in the Ethical Doctrine of the Qur'an, 1960; The Cup of Jamshid, 1974. Hons. incl: McLeod Punjab Arabic Schirlship, Punjab Univ., 1947-48. Address: 745 Commonwealth Ave., Boston, MA 02215, U.S.A.

RAHILLY, Maurice F., b. 4 Jan. 1924, Librarian. Educ: B.S., Boston Coll., 1951; M.S., Simmons Coll., 1952; Boston Univ., 1951-52; Univ. of Pitts., 1957-58. Appts. incl: Asst., then Libn., Boston Pub. Lib., 1947-52; Asst. Libn SUNY Maritime Coll., 1953-56; Asst. Libn., Libn. & Documents Custodian, Westinghouse Atomic Power Div., Forest Hills, Pa., 1957-63; Chief Rsch. Libn., AVCO Missile Systems Div., Wilmington, Mass., 1963-67; Proj. Mgr., Info. Dynamics Corp., Reading, Mass., 1967-68; Libn., Div. Libs. & Special Collections, Northeastern Univ., Boston, 1970-. Mbrships. incl: Planning Comm., Mass. Lib. Assn., 1973-74; Edit. Staff, Soc. Tech. Writers & Publrs., 1965-66; Tech. Info. Adv. Comm., Nat. Security Ind. Assn.; num. offs., SLA; Am. Bankers Assn. Ed. & compiler of bibliographies. Address: 360 Huntington Ave., Boston, MA 02174, U.S.A. 42.

RAHME, Habib S., b. 15 Dec. 1924. Engineer; Scientist. Educ: Ecole d'Ingenieurs, Beirut, Lebanon; B.S., M.S., Univ. of Okla., U.S.A.; Ph.D., Univ. of Calif., Berkeley;Cert. in Numerical Analysis, Univ. of Mich.; Cert. in Indl. Pollution, S.U.N.Y. Appts. held as Rsch. & Chief Engr., Sr. Rsch. Sci., Mgmt. Advsr., Corp. Cons., Dir. of Scis. & Sr. Staff Cons. Mbrships: A.I.M.E.; Soc. of Petroleum Engrs.; Columbia Seminar on Water Resources & Pollution; A.A.A.S.; Am. Acad. of Ocean Scis.; Tau Beta Pi; Sigma Tau; Pi Epsilon Tau; Pi Mu Epsilon; Sigma Gamma Epsilon. Writer of num. profl. papers. Address: 40 Meadowbrook Road, Syosset, NY 11791. U.S.A. 6.

RAIKE, Virginia (Mrs. Sydney R. Raike), b. 7 Jan. 1914. Educ: Northwestern Univ., Evanston, Ill., 1931-34. Mbrships: Gov.'s Commn. on Status of Women, 1970-71; Chmn.,

Jt. Comm., PTA, III., 1970-71; Pres., III. PTA, 1970-72; Jt. Comm., Nat. PTA & Nat. Coun. of Juvenile Ct. Judges, 1970-72; III. Comm. on Schl. Governance, 1972; Bd. Dirs., Inst. for Sex Educ., Chgo., 1973-; Regional V.P., Nat. PTA, 1973-75; Cert. Parliamentarian, Am. Inst. of Parliamentarians; Assn. Schl. Admnstrs.; III. Assn. of Schl. Bds.; III. Educ. Assn.; Alpha Epsilon Phi; Chgo. Woman's Aid; Friends of Am. Writers; Nat. Coun. of Jewish Women; Nat. Comm. for Support of Pub. Schls.; Common Cause. Publs: monthly articles, III. PTA Bulletin. Hons: Hon. Life Mbr., III. PTA, 1957 & Nat. PTA, 1963; Book of Recognition, III. PTA, 1962. Address: 580 Hawthorne Pl., Chicago, IL 60657, U.S.A. 5.

RAJALA, Toivo Juhani, b. 11 Sept. 1920. Museum Director. Appt: Dir., Nastolan Kotiseutu Museo (Parish Mus. in Nastola), 1959-. Mbrships: Suomalaisen Kirjallisuuden Seura (Finnish Lit. Soc.); Museo Liitto; Suomen Muinaismuistoyhdistys (Finnish Antiques Soc.). Contbr. to local newspaper, 1968; Kotimaa lehden mielinidepanelin jasenyys, 1969. Hons: Mem. Medal of Winter War & Home Guard Cross; Mem. Medal of Continuation War; Silver Medal of Merit, Seurasaari Fndn.-Nat. Mus., 1963; Award for the Study of Museums, 1964; Cross of Merit, Nat. League of Fire Servs., 1966; 50 Yr. Jubilee Medal, Kansallinen Kokoomus, 1968; Silver Medal of Commendation, Finnish Boy Scout Org., 1968; Blue Cross, 1969, etc. Address: Lustiglullevägen 12a, 591 00 Motala, Sweden. 133.

RAJAN, Mannaraswamighala Sreeranga, b. 4 Aug. 1920. University Professor. Educ: M.A., Univ. of Mysore, India, 1943; M.A., Columbia Univ., N.Y., U.S.A., 1952; D.Litt., Mysore Univ., 1963. Appts. incl: Prof. & Hd., Dept. of Commonwealth Studies, Indian Schl. of Int. Studies, New Delhi, 1962-71; Dir., ibid, 1965-70; Same acad. & administrative positions, Schl. of Int. Studies, Jawaharlal Nehru Univ., New Delhi, 1970-71; Prof., Int. Org., ibid, 1971-; Asian Fellow, Australian Nat. Univ., Canberra, 1971-72; Hd., Ctr. for Int. Studies, Jawaharlal Nehru Univ., currently. Attended var. int. confs. Publs. incl: India in World Affairs 1954-56, 1964; Non-alignment, India & the Future, 1970; Ed., Studies in Politics: National & International, 1970; Ed., India's Foreign Relations during the Nehru Era: Some Studies, forthcoming; Ed., Int. Studies, 1964-74; Articles in learned jrnls. Hons: Chancellor's Gold Medal, Univ. of Mysore, 1943; Fulbright & Smith-Mundt Fellowships, Columbia Univ., U.S.A., 1950-52. Address: Schl. of Int. Studies, Jawaharlal Nehru Univ., Ferozeshah Rd., New Delhi 1, India.

RAKETTE, Egon H(elmut), b. 10 May 1909. Government Adviser; Author. Educ: Int. Hochschule für Gestaltung; Ecole libre des scis. sociales, Paris, France; Verwaltungsakad. Breslau. Appts: Provincial Official, Breslau; Saw-mill employee, Schwäb. Hall; Expert Advsr., Ministerpräsidentenbüro, Wiesbaden; Ctrl. govt. advsr., Bonn. Mbrships: Künstlergilde, Esslingen; Chmn., Wangener Kreis, 1950-69; Hon. Chmn., ibid, 1969-; Bd. of Dirs. (at times), Ost- & Mitteleuropäischer Arbeitskreis; Chmn., West-Ost-Kulturwerk e.V., 1953-60; Chmn. of Coun., ibid, 1960-72; V.P., 1973-. Publs. incl: Novels: Drei Söhne; Planwagen; Anka; Heimkehrer; Mit vierundzwanzig liegt das Leben noch vor uns (short stories); Hier und anderswo (poems); Sev. anthols. Hons. incl: Gold Eichendorff plaque, 1969; 3rd Prize, Erzähler-Wettbewerb, Cologne, 1972; Distinction, Erzähler-Wettbewerb, Düsseldorf, 1973.

Address: Hainbuchenweg 4, D 5486 Remagen-Oberwinter, German Fed. Repub. 43, 92.

RAKNES, Ola, b. 17 Jan. 1887. Psychotherapist. Educ: M.A., Univ. of Oslo, Norway, 1915; Also studied at Sorbonne, Paris, France; Ph.D., Univ. of Oslo, 1928; Appts: H.S. Tchr., 1913-15, 1916-17, 1922-27; Jrnlst., 1915-16; Lectr., Sorbonne, Paris, 1917-21, Univ. Coll., London, U.K., 1921-22; Psychoanalyst, 1929-37; Orgone Therapist, 1937-; Guest Prof., Univ. of Fla., Gainesville, & Univ. of N.M., Albuquerque, 1971. Mbrships: Trustee, Wilhelm Reich Fndn., 1950-56; Am. Assn. for Med. Orgon., 1950-58; Fellow, Am. Coll. of Orgon., 1968-; Hon. mbr., Det Norske Samlaget & Studentmallaget, Oslo. Publs: Fransk-Norsk Ordliste, 1914; Chapters in Norwegian Literature (w. I.C. Grondahl), 1923; Motet med det Heilage (thesis), 1927; Engelsk-Norsk Ordbok, 1927; Fransk-Norsk Ordbok, 1939-42; Fri Vokster, 1949; Wilhelm Reich & Orgonomy (translated into Italian, Danish & German), 1970. Address: Nilserudkleiva 22, Oslo 8, Norway.

RAKOTOBE-ANDRIAMARO, Ny Sampandrofia, b. 12 Nov. 1912. Pastor; Evangelical Mission President. Educ: Fac. of Letters & Fac. of Theol., Univ. of Strasbourg, France; Dip. of Theol., Litt.D., ibid. Appts: Pastor, Ch. Manarintosoa-Finoana, Madagascar, 1946-; Fndr., 1st Protestant Orphanage in Madagascar, 1949; Chmn., Mission Evangélique de Tananarive, 1955-; V.P., E. Africa Christian Alliance, Kenya; V.P., Int. Coun. of Christian Churches, Amsterdam, The Netherlands; Tchr., practical theol., Superior Instn. of Evangelical Theol., Tanarive; Hd., Secondary Schl., Manarintsoa-Finoana. Pres., Acad. Andriananpoinimerina (Acad. of Letters). Author of 26 books (novels, poetry, theol.), & 2 books of religious psalmodies; Chief ed. of 3 reviews. Recip. of hons. Address: Ambohimanoro, Tananarive, Madagascar.

RALEY, Sicily Belle. Telegraph Office Manager; Hostess-Cashier. Educ: Houston Co. Schls.; Southern Coll. of Telegraphy, Newnan, Ga. Appts: Morse Operator & Mgr., var. offs., Western Union Telegraph Co., 1919-24, Off. Mgr., Andalusia, 1924-51; Pvte. Sec., Gen. Adjustment Co. Inc., 1953-61, var. ins. adjusters, inclng. T.B. Graddy, Wayne Trammell, W.M. Ward, 1962-65; Hostess-Cashier, Leon Restaurant, Dothan, Ala., 1965-. Mbrships: Charter Pres., Dir., Pilot Club, Andalusia, 1947-52; Pilot Club, Dothan; Pilot Club Int., 1947-, Gov., Dist. 2, 1950-51, Vice Chmn., P.R. Comm., 1969-71, Chmn., P.R. Comm., 1971-72. Ed., Soundings, jrnl. of Pilot Int. Dist. 2, 1967-72. Hon. Award, Woman of Yr., Phi Sigma Alpha, Iota Chapt., 1972. Address: 1105 Moates St., Dothan, AL 36301, U.S.A. 125.

RALPH, Henry A.J., b. 21 Jan. 1901. Diplomat. Educ: Am. Inst. of Banking. Appts: Ambassador Extraordinary & Plenipotentiary, Order of Malta, 1973; Envoy Extraordinary, Costa Rica; Pres., World Banking Corp.; Exec. Off., Dir., Bank of Am. Mbrships. incl: Pilgrims, U.S.A.; Am. Club, London, U.K. Author, Consultants View on Bank Management, 1971. Hons. incl: Magistral Kt., Sov. Mil. Order of Malta, 1954; Kt. Grand Cross, Equestrian Order of the Holy Sepulchre, Vatican, 1956; Grand Silver Medal of Hon., Austria, 1957; Grand Cross, Order of Reuben Datio, Nicaragua, 1958; Kt. 'Off., Order of Merit, Italy, 1958; Grand Cross of Merit, 1960, Grand Cross Magistral Grace, 1972, Order of Malta; Orden del Centenario, Nicaragua, 1970, etc. Address 5255 Cribari Lane, Sane Jose, CA 95135, U.S.A. 128.

RAMALINGASWAMI, Vulimiri, b. 8 Aug. 1921. Medical Scientist. Educ: M.B., B.S., Andhra Univ., India, 1944; M.D., ibid, 1946; D.Phil., Oxford Univ., U.K, 195l; D.Sc., ibid, 1967. Appts: Pathol., Indian Coun. of Med. Rsch., Nutrition Rsch. Labs., Coonoor, S. India, 1947-54; Asst. Sec., & Dpty. Dir., Indian Coun. of Med. Rsch., 1954-57; Prof., Pathol. & Hd. of Dept., All-India Inst. of Med. Scis., New Delhi, 1957-69; Dir. & Prof. of Pathol., ibid, 1969-; Annual Ciba Fndn. Lectr., London, 1963; Maude Abbott Lectr., Int. Acad. Pathol., 1964; Vis. Prof., Harvard Schl. of Pub. Hlth., 1970; Jacobson Lectr., Univ. of Newcastle-upon-Tyne, 1971. Mbrships: For. Assoc., Nat. Acad. of Scis., U.S.A.; Hon. Fellow, Am. Coll. of Physns.; Fellow, Royal Coll. of Physns., London, Indian Nat. Sci. Acad., & Indian Acad. of Med. Sci.; Prs., Indian Assn. Pathols., 1971-72; V.P., Indian Assn. for Advancement of Med. Educ., 1971-. Contbr. about 130 publs. mostly articles, but also reviews, chpts. in books & monographs, on var. hlth. & nutritional problems in India & other developing countries. Recip. many awards inclng. Med. Coun. of India Silver Jubilee Rsch. Award, 1974. Address: c/o All India Inst. of Med. Scis., Ansari Nagar, New Delhi-110016, India.

RAMATI, Yohanan Joseph, b. 17 Nov. 1911. Economist. Educ: M.A., Lincoln Coll., Oxford Univ., U.K. Appts. incl: Dir., State of Israel Bonds (Israel Off.), Jerusalem, 1952-; Dir.-Gen., Negev Ceramic Materials Ltd., 1953-54, Mng. Ed., The Israel Economist & Jerusalem Contbr. to The Economist, The Banker, The Jewish Observer & Middle E. Review, all London, U.K., 1955-; Councillor, Jerusalem Municipality, 1959-69; Dpty.-Chmn., Town-Planning & Bldg. Permits Comm., 1959-67; Mbr., City Exec., 1959-67; Chmn., Pub. Works & Water Comm., 1960-65; Chmn., Assessments Comm., 1965-67; Dir., Yohanan Ramati, Investment Cons.' & Real Estate, Jerusalem, 1970-. Mbrships: Oxford Soc.; Oxford Union Soc., former Mbr. Standing Comm.; Jerusalem Econ. Club. Publs: Ed.; Economic Growth In Developing Countries - Material & Human Resources, 1974. Musical Comps. incl: Concerto for Clarinet & Chmbr. Orch. op. 4; 2 duos for Violin & Violancello, op. 6; Sonata for Piano, op. 7; Trio for Violin, Viola & Violancello, op.10. Address: Yohanan Ramati, Investment Cons.'& Real Estate, 4 Ein Rogel St., Jerusalem, Israel.

RAMBERT, Gordon Arthur, b. 6 Mar. 1922. Management Consultant. Educ: B.S., Lehigh Univ., Bethlehem, Pa., U.S.A. Appts: Pvte. Prac., Mgmt. Cons., 1951-55; Personnel Mgr., Jamestown Malleable Iron Corp., N.Y., 1955-58; Mgr., Wage & Salary Admin. (Compensation), Burroughs Corp., Todd Div., Rochester, N.Y., 1958-64; Personnel Dir., & Asst. Sec., Consolidated Vacuum Corp., Rochester, 1964-66; V.P. Indl. Rels., Joslyn Mfg. & Supply Co., Chgo., Ill., 1966-70; Pres., People Dynamics, Inc., Lake Bluff, Ill., 1970-; Pres., Rambert, Allen & Barker, Div. People Dynamics, Inc., 1970-; Lectr., var. Univ. & Mgmt. seminars. Mbrships: Bd. of Dirs., Am. Soc. for Personnel Admin., Nat. Treas., 1970-71; Indl. Rels. Comm., Nat. Assn. of Mfrs.; Bd., Indl. Rels. Assn. of Chgo.; Chmn., Nat. Conf., Graphic Arts Indl. Rels. Execs. Address: 415 Park Lane, Lake Bluff, IL 60044, U.S.A. 8.

RAMDAS, Lakshminarayanapuram Annanthakrishna, b. 3 June 1900. Scientific

Researcher. Educ: B.A., Presidency Coll., Madras, India, 1920; M.A., Univ. Coll. of Sci., Calcutta, 1923; Ph.D., Calcutta Univ., 1926. Appts. incl: Dir. of Agricl. Meteorol. Meteorol. Off., 1932-53; Dty. Dir.-Gen. of Observatories, India Meteorol. Dept., Poona, 1953-56; Rsch., Nat. Physical Lab., New Delhi, 1956-65; Hd., Heat & Power Div., ibid, 1956-62; Scientist Emeritus, 1965-. Mbrships: Fellow, Indian Acad. of Scis., 1934; India Nat. Sci. Acad., 1935; Royal Meteorol. Soc.; London, U.K., 1936; Nat. Acad. of Sci., Allahabad, India, 1948; Profl., Am. Meteorol. Soc., 1961; Int. Soc. of Biometeorol; India Geophys. Soc., 1967; World Acad. of Art & Sci. Author, Crops & Weather in India, 1960. Contbr. w. others to over 400 rsch. publs., in Indian & overseas jrnls., Hons: M.B.E., Brit. Govt. of India, 1946; Padma Shri, Pres. of India, 1958. Address: Endeavour, C-14, Inderpuri, New Delhi, 110012, India.

RAMEL, (Baron) Stig U.M., b. 14 Feb. 1927. Diplomat; Institutional Administrator. Educ: LL.B., 1952. Appts: Mbr., Swedish Min. For. Affairs, 1953; Swedish Embassy, Paris, France, 1954-56; Mbr., Permanent Swedish Delegation to OECC, 1956-58; Swedish Embassy, Wash. D.C., U.S.A., 1958-60; Hd., Shipping Sect., Min. of For. Affairs, 1960-64, Dpty. Hd., Coun. for Swedish Info. Abroad, 1964-66; V.P., & Pres., Gen. Swedish Export Assn., 1966-72; Pres., Nobel Fndn., 1972-. Chmn. & Bd. Mbr., sev. indl. cos. & socs. Address: Nobel Foundation, Sturegatan 14, S-114 36 Stockholm, Sweden.

RAMLØV, Preben, b. 11 Aug. 1918. Author; Critic, Educ: Tchrs. Exam., 1940; Scandinavian Philol. & Folklore, Univ. of Copenhagen, until 1946. Appts: Tchr., Educ. Staff., Frederiksberg, Copenhagen, 1941-63, Assoc. Prof., Danish Lit. & Lang., Copenhagen Trng. Coll. for Tchrs., 1967; Literary & Theatre Critic, var. Danish Newspapers & periodicals, 1940-, currently w. Christian Daily News, Copenhagen, 1967-; Reader for var. Danish publrs., currently Gyldendal, 1967;- Prodr., Danish State Broadcasting & TV, 1945-. Mbrships: Bd., Danish Writers' Assn. & Danish Critics' League. Publs: Kaj Munk (biog.), 1947; The Story of Hans (novel), 1959; The Sons of the Lord Chancellor (novel), 1961; Danish Literature I-III (anthol.), 1961-62; Danish Folk Tales, 1964; The Story of Danish Literature, 1965; Massa Peter (novel), 1967; Slaves & Brothers (hist.), 1968; Childrens & Young People's Literature, 1969-71 & accompanying Textbooks, 1970-; On reading Folk Tales, History & Problems, 1974. Hons: Danish State Art Fndn. prizes, 1967, 68, 69 & 72; Danish Acad. Prize of Hon. for Massa Peter, 1967. Address: 11, Dysseager, 2720 Vanløse, Copenhagen, Denmark. 134.

RAMM, Eva, b. 23, Nov. 1925. Author; Editor. Educ: Cand. Psychol., Univ. of Oslo, Norway, 1955. Appts: Schl. Psychologist, Nesodden, Norway, 1956-68; Ed., Sykepleien (Jrnl. of Norwegian Nurses Assn.), 1973-. Mbrships: Norwegian Assn. of Authors; Past Chmn., Norwegian Assn. of Children & Young People's Authors. Publs: Med stov pa hjernen (With Dust on the Brain), 1958, translations in 6 Langs., filmed, 1959; Engel pa vidvanke, 1962; Kvinnekall og Mannefall, 1965; Noe ma gjores, 1968; En gang var himmelan bla, 1970; Mors tre hoder, 1973. Address: Norsk Sykepleierforbund, Box 5136, Sognsveien 72, Oslo 3, Norway. 134.

RAMO, Simon, b. 7 May 1913. Engineering Executive. Educ: B.S., Univ. of Utah, 1933; Ph.D., incl: Calif. Inst. of Technol., 1936.

Appts. Incl: Dir., Phys. Sec., Electronics Rsch. Lab., General Electric Co., 1936-46; V.P. & Dir., Ops., Hughes Aircraft Co., 1946-53; Exec. V.P. & Co-Fndr., The Ramo-Wooldridge Corp., 1953-58; Scientific Dir., U.S. Intercontinental Ballistic Missile Prog., 1954-58; Pres., Bunker-Ramo Corp., 1964-66; Dir., TRW Inc., 1954-; Exec. V.P., ibid, 1958-61; V. Chmn. of Bd., 1961-; Chmn., Exec. Comm., 1969-; var. directorships. Mbrships: Num. advsry. couns. & comms.; Nat. Acad. of Scis.; Am. Philos. Soc.; Int. Acad. of Astronautics; Fndng. Mbr., Nat. Acad. Engrng.; Eta Kappa Nu; Epsilon Eta Sigma; Phi Kappa Phi; Sigma Pi Sigma; Sigma Xi; Tau Beta Pi; Theta Tau; Phi Beta Kappa. Fellowships. incl: Am. Acad. of Arts & Scis.; AAAS; Am. Astronautical Soc.; IEEE; Am. Phys. Soc. Author or co-author, publs. in field. Ed. of & Contbr. to textbooks, tech. publs., num. articles. Holder of 25 patents. Num. hons. inclng. sev. doctorates. Address: I Space Pk., Redondo Beach, CA 90278, U.S.A.

RAMOS, Marcos Antonio, b. 19 Sept. 1944. Baptist Minister & College Teacher. Educ. incl: B. Litt., Matanzas Inst., Cuba; Ph.D., Latin Am. Univ.; D.D., Defenders Theological Sem., Rio Piedras, Puerto Rico; Dip. Hispanic Studies, Inst. of Spanish Philol., Saltillo, Mexico. Appts. incl: Bapt. Min., licensed 1967, ordained 1971; Pastor, Spanish Bapt. Ch., S. Miami Hts., Fla., 1970-; Prin., Calvary Bapt. Ch. Schl., Miami, 1971-; Literary Critic, America Libre Mag., Miami, 1972-; Instr., Ch. Hist., Miami Christian Univ., 1973-. Mbrships. incl: PR Comm., Am. Lung Assn., Dade & Monroe Co., Fla.; Evangelical Theological Soc.; Am. Soc. Ch. Hist.; Am. Medieval Acad. Publs: A History of Protestantism in Cuba; articles in Spanish Lang. newspapers. Hons. incl: Hon. Lt-Col., Nat. Guard, State of Ga., 1971; Commendation, Mayor of Dade Co., Fla., 1972; Dip. of Honor Lincoln Marti, U.S. Dept. of Hlth. Educ. & Welfare, 1973; 7 Hon. Degrees. Address: 2836 SW 23rd St., Miami, FL 33145, U.S.A. 125.

RAMOS GOMEZ, Oscar Gerardo, b. 27 Nov. 1928. University Professor. Educ: Licence, Philos., Javeriana Univ., Bogota, Colombia; Grad. Courses, Fla, Southern Coll., U.S.A., 1954, Ctrl. Univ. of Spain, 1955, Univ. of Chgo., U.S.A., 1959-60, Univ. of Tex. at Austin, 1962, & Stanford Univ., 1963; Ph.D., Javeriana Univ., Colombia, 1955; Magister, Indl. Admin., Valle Univ., Cali, 1970. Appts. incl: Sec. of Educ., Cali, 1957-59; Prof., Philos., Valle Univ., 1957-59; Hd., Humanities Dept., ibid, 1959-60; Sec. Gen., ibid, 1960-66; Dean, Fac. of Philos., Letters & Hist., Div. of Humanities, 1960-71; Prof., Dept. of Letters; Dean of Educ., Univ. of San Buenaventura. Mbr., num. profl. orgs. Publs. incl: Delina, vida amarosa de Jose E. Caro, 1955; Poseia, 1962; num. articles. Recip., num. hons. Address: Universidad del Valle, Cali, Colombia.

RAMRATTAN, Evans, b. 20 Aug. 1940. Civil Engineer. B.Sc., Civil Engrng., Univ. of Wales, Cardiff. Appts: Master, Presentation Coll., Trinidad, 1958; Naparima Coll., Trinidad, 1959-60; Engr., Dept. of Mech. & Bldg. Engrng., John S. Donaldson Tech. Inst., Trinidad, 1964-;. Mbrships: Examiner Nat. Exam. Coun. for Voc. & Tech. Educ.; Trinidad, Tobago; Comm., Techn. Trng., Trinidad, Tobago; Assn. of Profl. Engrs., Trinidad & Tobago; Past Acting Pres., Christian Endeavour Union of Trinidad & Tobago, & Deleg., 6th Area 1 Conf., Am. Samoa, 1972; Ldr., Student Christian Movement. Address: 16 Poona Rd., Williamsville, Trinidad, W. Indies. 136.

RAMSDEN, Samuel Raymond, b. 10 Oct. 1913. Administrator. Educ: Lic. Theol., Coll.

St. John the Evangelist, Morpeth, NSW. Appts: Curate of Parkes, 1937; Rector, Geurie, 1939; Chap., RAAF, 1942-46; Dept. of Civil Admin., Papua, New Guinea, 1946-47; Asst. Sec., Servs. Canteens Trust Fund, 1949-57; Elected Qld. Parliament, 1957 (resigned 1971); Full time Adminstr. & Chief Exec. Off., Multiple Handicapped Assn. of Qld., 1971-. Wide Parliamentary experience as Sec., Parliamentary Liberal Party, Sec. of the Jt. Government Parties, Temporary Chmn. of committees, etc. Mbrships: Fellow, Royal C'wealth Soc.; Qld. Area Pres., Parliamentary Assn. Conf., Uganda, 1967; All Party Parliamentary Mission to S.E. Asia, 1964; Past Chmn., Brisbane Missions to Seamen; Past Chmn., Metropolitan Fire Brigade Bd.; V. Patron, Legion of Ex-Servicemen; Chmn., Qld. Coun. of Soc. Serv. & Chmn., Q.C.S.S. Coordinating Comms.; J.P.; Hon. Life Mbr., Multiple Handicapped Assn. of Qld., 1972; Life Fellow, Intercontinental Biog. Assn., 1974. Has written many artcles, reports & bulletins concerned with the Multiple Handicapped Assn. of Qld; Free-lance writer. Address: 16 Tandara St., Rochedale, Qld. Australia, 4123. 23, 131, 139.

RAMSEY, Gordon Clark, b. 28 May 1941. Alumni Administrator. Educ: B.A., Yale Univ., New Haven, Conn., U.S.A., 1963. Appts: Instr., Engl., Alumni Dir., & Asst. to Headmaster, Worcester Acad., Mass., 1963-69; Record Critic, The Am. Organist, 1966-68; Bd. Sec., Yale Alumni Fund, New Haven, 1969-71; Asst. Exec. Dir., Assn. of Yale Alumni, New Haven, 1972-. Mbrships: Yale Club of N.Y.C.; Am. Guild of Organists. Publs: Agatha Christie, Mistress of Mystery, 1967; Num. articles on boy choir tradition in music jrnls. Address: 901-A Yale Station, New Haven, CT 06520, U.S.A.

RAMSEY, Russell Wilcox, b. 29 May 1935. Army Officer; Director of Special Programs; Author. Educ: B.S., U.S. Mil. Acad. W. Pt., N.Y., U.S.A., 1957; M.A., Univ. of Southern Miss., Hattiesburg, 1963; Ph.D., Univ. of Fla., Gainesville, 1970. Appts. incl: Lt.-Capt., U.S. Army, 1958-66; Major, U.S. Army, Reserve Offs. Trng. Corps Prog., Univ. of Fla., 1967-; Admnstr., Alachua Co. Pub. Schls., 1970-74; Lectr., Armed Forces Staff Coll., Univ. of Fla., 1970-74; Commnr., Gainesville City Commn., 1973-. Mbrships. incl: Am. Histl. Assn.; Conf. on Latin Am. Studies; Am. Legion. Veterans of For. Wars; Phi Alpha Theta; Phi Delta Kappa. Publs. incl: Some Keys to the Vietnam Puzzle, 1968; Peasant Revolution 1950-54, 1969; Insurgency in Latin America: The Colombian Experience, 1946-65, 1971; Community Involvement in the Problems of Neglected & Delinquent Youth, 1971; 3 other books. Hons. incl: Combat Infantry Badge, 1965; Bronze Star Medal, 1966; Meritorious Serv. Medal, 1970. Address: 1930 NW 11th Rd., Gainesville, FL 32605, U.S.A. 125.

RAMSEY, Sally Ann Seitz, b. 15 Feb. 1931. Political Scientist. Educ: B.A., Ohio State Univ., 1952; M.A., ibid, 1955; St. Mary Coll., Kan., 1962; Grad. Study, Ohio State Univ., 1963-66, Fla. State Univ., 1970. Appts: Rsch. Engr., Sr. Rsch. Engr., N. Am. Rockwell Corp., Columbus, Ohio & Downey, Calif., 1962-67; Rsch. & Info. Off., Dept. of Urban Affairs, Admin. Specialist, Dept. of Dev., State of Ohio, 1967-68; Assoc. Planner, Div. of State Planning, Dept. of Admin., State of Fla., 1968-. Mbrships: Am. Soc. for Pub. Admin.; Am. Pol. Sci. Assn.; Kappa Kappa Gamma. Publs: Co-Author, Representation & Reapportionment: The Case of Ohio, 1965; Contbr. to State Government Administration, Vol. III, 1968. Hons: Pi Sigma Alpha, 1953;

Ohio Legislative Internship, 1964-65. Address: P.O. Box 3643, Tallahassee, FL 32303, U.S.A. 5, 7.

RANASINHA, (Sir) Arthur Godwin, b. 24 June 1898. Retired Civil Servant; Banker; Diplomat. Educ: Trinity Hall, Cambridge, 1919-21; Selected Cand. for Indian Civil Serv., Hons. Deg. (B.A.) (Ext.), London Univ., 1920. Appts. incl: Dist. Judge, Avisawella & Badulla, 1928-33; Sec. to Min. of Agric. & Lands, 1933-36; Pub. Trustee, 1936-44; Custodian of Enemy Property, 1939-44; Supt. of Census & Dir. of Stats., 1945-47; Sec. to Leader of State Coun. on Pol. Mission to London, 1945; Land Commnr., 1947; Perm. Sec., Min. of Agric. & Lands, 1948; Sec. to Cabinet & Perm. Sec., Min. of Finance Planning Commn., 1950-54; Gov., Ctrl. Bank of Ceylon, 1954-59; Amb., Italy, Greece & Israel, 1959-61; Chmn., People's Banking Commn., 1965-66; Taxation Commn., 1966-68. Mbrships: Former Pres., Classical Assn. of Ceylon, Pol. Sci. Assn., Ceylon Stats. Soc. & Ceylon Turf Club; Royal Asiatic Soc. Publs: General Report on Census of Ceylon, 1946; Memories & Musings, 1972; articles in jrnls. & newspapers. Hons: C.B.E., 1947; C.M.G., 1948; Kt. Bach., 1954; Kt. Grand Cross, Order of Merit of Italian Repub., 1961; Kt. of Mark Twain, 1971. Address: 99/1, Rosmead Place, Colombo, Sri Lanka. 1, 34.

RANDALL, Dudley (Felker), b. 14 Jan. 1914. Librarian. Educ: B.A., Wayne Univ., U.S.A., 1949; M.A.L.S., Univ. of Mich. Appts: Libn., 1951-54, Instr., Lincoln Univ., 1952; Libn., Morgan State Coll., 1954-56, Wayne Co. Federated Lib. System, 1956-69; Ed./Publr., Broadside Press, 1965-; Libn. & Poet in Res., 1969-, Instr., Univ. of Detroit, 1970-; Instr., Univ. of Mich., 1969-. Mbrships: ALA; Comm. of Small Mag. Eds. & Publrs.; New Detroit, Inc. Comm. on the Arts; Mich. Coun. for the Arts Literary Advsry. Panel. Publs: Poem Counterpoem; For Malcolm; Cities Burning; Black Poetry; Love You; The Black Poets; After the Killing. Hons: Tompkins Award, Poetry & Fiction, 1962, Poetry, 1966, Wayne State Univ.; Metropol. Detroit English Club Citation, 1972; Kuumba Liberation Award, 1973. Address: 12651 Old Mill Pl., Detroit, MI 48238, U.S.A.

RANDALL, (Lillian) Paula, b. 21 Dec. 1895. Sculptor; Contralto Singer; Poet; Lecturer; Retired Biochemist. Educ: Univ. of Southern Calif.; Mnpls. Inst. of Arts; Otis Art Inst.; Pvte. sculpture classes; Iowa State Tchr.'s Coll., Cedar Falls; Minn. State Univ.; Ellsworth Coll., Iowa Falls, Iowa; Detroit Conservatory of Music; McPhail Schl. of Music, Mnpls., Minn.; Univ. of Colo.; B.A.; M.A.; Ph.D. Appts. incl: Asst. Ed., several poetry mags.; Mgr., Hillcrest Hosp., Tex.; Hd., Biochem. Dept., Scripps Clin., LaJolla, Calif., & Huntington Mem. Hosp., Pasadena, Calif.; Hd., Randall Med. Lab., Pasadena, 20 yrs.; Sculptor, studio at home, 1949-; Mbr., fac., Pasadena Schl. of Fine Arts, 1967-68; Lectr., currently. Mbrships. incl: Am. Chem. Soc.; Nat. Soc. of Clin. Photographers; Nat. Assn. of Psychical Rsch.; Past Pres., Pasadena Chapt., Nat. Audubon Soc.; Acad. of Am. Poets. Publs: Poetry in var. anthols. & jrnls.; Co-author, cancer rsch. work publd. in Am. Jrnl. of Clin. Pathol. Recip. of awards for sculpture. Address: 441 Ramona Ave., Sierra Madre, CA 91024, U.S.A. 37, 59, 132.

RANDELL, Gladys Marie Rue, b. 9 June 1907. Teacher; Management Analyst; Social Worker. Educ: State Tchrs Coll., Valley City, N.D.; Standard Curric. Dip.-Life Cert., Public Schls.; B.Sc., Univ. of Minn.; Univ. of So. Calif.; Cert., Supvsry. Mgmt.; Aircraft Inspection

course, Univ. of Mich.; Personnel trng. courses, Air Techl. Cmd., Detroit. Appts: Elem. & H.S. Tchr.; Position Classifier, Fed. Govt. (field & staff levels), U.S. & Japan; Conducted surveys & evaluated positions in the legal, medical, engrng., signal & other command H.Q. servs. requiring top secret security certification; Re-assigned as Asst. to the Chief, Salary & Wage Div., Civilian Personnel Sect., H.Q. Japan Logistical Cmd.; Assigned to Comtroller Section as Mgmt. Analyst; Soc. Wkr., State of Fla. Mbrships. incl: Pres., Tampa Br., AAUW, 1969-71. Hons. incl: Woman of the Yr. Award, President's Round Table Womens Serv. Clubs, AAUW, 1972. Address: 208 South Manhattan Ave., Tampa, FL 33609, U.S.A. 125.

RANIVILLE, Francis Oliver, b. 19 Oct. 1920. Industrialist; Poet. Appt: Asst. Sec., Rainville Co. (Indl. Belting). Mbrships. incl: Past Treas. & Past Chap., Bards of Grand Rapids, Mich.; United Poets Laureate Int.; N.Y. Poetry Forum, Inc.; Eastern Ctr. Br., N.Y.C. London Poetry Soc.; World Poetry Soc. Intercontinental; The Poet's Guild, Idaho Falls; Hymn Soc. of Am. Publs: Poems in num. mags., & anthols. Hons. incl: World Contest Winner, Hymn Soc. of Am., 1966; UN Day Award of Honor, 1969; Magnum Cum Laude World Poet Award, World Poetry Soc. Intercontinental, 1970, Gold Medal, Int. Poet's Shrine, 1971. Address: P.O. Box 1524, Grand Rapids, MI 49501, U.S.A. 11.

RANKIN, Alexander Gormaly, b. 18 Sept. 1916. Chartered Accountant. Educ: B. Comm., Univ. of Toronto, Canada, 1938. Appts. incl: Asst. to Col. W. Eric Phillips, Fin. Analyst, Pres., Grew Boats Ltd., Sec.-Treas., Henry A. Martin, Mgt. Cons., Gen. Mgr., Univ. of Toronto Press., 1947-52; Comptroller, Univ. of Toronto, 1951-55; V.P.-Sec.-V.P., Fin., B.C. Forest Prods. Ltd., 1955-67; V.P., Univ. of Toronto & Dpty. Chmn., United Dominions Corp. (Canada) Ltd. & Dir., Weldwood of Canada Ltd., 1967-. Fellow, Ont. Inst. Chartered Accts. Mbrships incl: Vancouver Club; Bd. of Trade, Metropolitan Toronto; Bd. Trustees, United Community Fund of Gtr. Toronto. Address: Univ. of Toronto, Rm. 232, Simcoe Hall, Toronto, M5S 1A1, Canada.

RANKIN, James Gerald D'Arcy, b. 19 May 1930. Physician. Educ: M.B.Ch.B., Univ. of Sydney, Australia, 1954. Appts. incl: Fellow in Med., Royal Prince Alfred Hosp., 1960-61; Vis. Fellow in Med., Columbia Univ. Coll. of Physns. & Surgs. & Presby. Hosp., N.Y., U.S.A., 1962-63; 2nd Asst., Univ. of Melbourne Dept. of Med., St. Vincent's Hosp., 1964-69; Physn. i/c, Univ. of Melbourne Dept. of Med., Alcoholism Clin., ibid, 1964-68; Dir., Summer Schl. of Alcohol Studies, ibid, 1966-69; Sr. Physn., Alcoholism Clin., St. Vincent' Hosp., 1968-69; Dir. & Hd. of Med., Clin. Inst., Alcoholism & Drug Addiction Rsch. Fndn., Ont., Canada, 1970-; Assoc. Prof. of Med., Univ. of Toronto, ibid, 1970; Cons. Physn., Toronto Western Hosp., 1971-. Mbrships: Fellow, Royal Australasian Coll. Physns. & Surgs.; Certificant, Royal Coll. Physns. & Surgs., Canada. Author, num. profl. papers. Address: Addiction Rsch. Fndn. Clin. Inst., 33 Russell St., Toronto, Ont. M5S 2S1, Canda. 23.

RANNEY, Helen M., b. 12 Apr. 1920. Physician; Professor of Medicine. Educ: A.B., Barnard Coll., 1941; M.D., Coll. of Physns. & Surgs., Columbia Univ., 1947; Med. Intern, Presby. Hosp., N.Y., 1947-48; Med. Res., ibid, 1948-50. Appts. incl: Cons. in Hematol., N.J. VA Hosp., E. Orange, 1958-70; Assoc. Prof., Med., Yeshiva Univ., 1960-65; Assoc. Vis. Physn., Bronx Municipal Hosp., 1960-70; Vis.

Physn., ibid, 1963-70; Prof., Albert Einstein Coll. of Med., 1965-70; Prof., SUNY, Buffalo, 1970-73; Prof. & Chmn., Dept. of Med., Univ. of Calif., San Diego, 1973-. Mbrships. incl: Pres. elect, Am. Soc. of Hematol.; Recorder, Assn. of Am. Physns.; Am. Soc. for Clin. Investigation; Am. Soc. of Biological Chemists; Harvey Soc.; Phi Beta Kappa; Hematol. Study Sect., M.I.A.M.D., Nat. Insts. of Hlth., 1971-; Nat. Acad. of Scis., 1972; Inst. of Med., 1973. Author of num. articles in med. jrnls. Hons: Joseph Mather Smith Prize, Columbia Univ., 1955; Dr. Martin Luther King, Jr. Med. Achievement Award for Outstanding Contbn. in Field of Sickle Cell Anemia, 1972. Address: Dept. of Med. 8110, Univ. Hosp., 225 W. Dickinson St., San Diego, CA 92103, U.S.A. 5.

RANOSCHY, Aleksander, b. 22 June 1918. Educator. Educ: Univ. of Poland; Melbourne Univ., Australia; B.E.; M.A.; A.T.T.I. (Dip.); M.A.C.E. Appts: Mgr., Utd. Polish Oil & Natural Gas Ind., 1944-45; Dir. i/c, Res. Team of 100 Scis. in hydrogenation of coal & synthetics, Schwarzeheide, Germany, 1946; Designer, org., & 1st Dir. & Prin., Int. Refugee Org. Rehab. Ctr. & Voc. Trng., Passau, ibid, 1947-48; Field Insp., I.R.O. assembly ctrs., Area No. 4 H.Q. U.S. Zone; Sci Master, Vic. Educ. Dept.; Lectr., Mercer House Tchrs. Coll., 1960-63; Vice Prin., Mt. Scopus Coll., 1965-71. Mbrships. incl: Hdmasters. Conf., Independent Schls. of Australia; Pres., B'nai B'rith Harmony Lodge, Melbourne, 1965-66; Australian Coll. Educ.; Chmn., Dpty. Hdmasters. Assn., Hdmasters. Conf. Schls., Vic., 1969. Address: Unit 64, 3 Rockley Rd., S. Yarra, Melbourne, Vic., Australia, 3141. 23.

RANSDELL, Lena Gibbs, b. 26 July 1903. Elementary Teacher; School Librarian. Educ: B.S. Educ., Spalding Coll., Louisville, Ky., 1969; M.S. Lib. Sci., ibid. Appts: Elementary Schl. Tchr., V.H. Engelhard Schl., Louisville Independent Schls., 1945-66; Libn., ibid, 1966-72. Mbrships: NEA; Ky. Educl. Assn.; Ky. Assn. Schl. Libns.; Ky. Assn. Audio-Visuals; Assn. Childhood Educ.; Louisville Lib. Club; Ky. Histl. Soc.; Filson Club, Ky.; DAR (Regent, John Marshall Chapt.); Cumberland Trace Chapt., Daughters of Am. Colonists; Tenn. Chapt., Daughters of Fndrs. & Patriots of Am.; Col. Zachary Taylor Chapt., U.S. Daughters of 1812; Crescent Hill Woman's Club, Louisville, Theta Chapt., Delta Gamma Int. Publs: New Directions New Dimensions; Elementary Programs in Ky., Off. of Curriculum Dev., Bur. of Instruction, Ky. Dept. of Educ., 1970. Address: 124 S. Crestmoor Ave., Louisville, KY 40206, U.S.A. 5, 138.

RANSLEY, (Chev.) George John. Appts. incl: Sec., Malta Police, 1919-41; Commnr. of Gozo & Reg. Protection Off., 1942-44; Dir. of Prisons, 1944-60; Govt. Film Censor, 1960-61; Former Pres., Malta Transport Union; Lectr., St. Joseph's Colls. & Lyceum. Mbrships. incl Sec.-Gen., Malta Employers' Assn., 1963-66; Employers' Deleg., Int. Labour Conf. Geneva, Switzerland, 1963-66; Fndr., Nat. Brigade, 1930; Hon.Treas., Save the Children Fund; VP, Malta Soc. of Arts, Mfrs. & Commerce, 1961-65; Pres., Lions Int., 1958-59, 1972; Chmn., Child Arts Exhibn. 1961-65;VP, Malta Soc. for the Blind, 1962-; Chancellor, Coun. Sovereign Mil. Ord. of Malta, 1973-. Publs: Shorthand System in Maltese, 1929; History of Shorthand, 1940; A New System of Shorthand (English & Maltese), 1942; Textbook on Typewriting. Hons. incl: Sev. mil. awards, 1919-45; Kt. of Magistral Grace Sovereign Mil. Ord. of St. John of Jerusalem, 1948; Kt. of Merit, Sovereign Mil. Ord. St. George of Constantine, 1952; Kt. Imperial Sovereign Ord.

of St. Constantine, 1956; Dip. of Hon. for Community Serv., 1973. Address: 51, Windsor Ter., Sliema, Malta. 99,129.

RANSOM, Raymond Lincoln, b. 10 Jan. 1916. Recreation Director. Educ: A.B., Claflin Univ., 1942; M.S., S.C. State Schl. of Grad. Work, 1956. Appts: Asst. Prin., Wayne Co. Trng. Schl., Jesup, Ga., 1949-50; Prin., Geo. Wash. Carver Schl., Ford Fndn., Richmond Hill, ibid, 1950-53, Lee St. H.S., Blackshear, 1953-65; Prin., Geo. Wash. Carver Elem. Schl. & Asst. Prin., Geo. Wash. Carver H.S., Douglas, 1965-68; Assoc. Dir., City Dept. of Recreation, Waycross, 1968-. Mbrships. incl: Chap., Phi Beta Sigma, 1941; Bryan Co. Tchrs. Assn. (Pres., 1951-52); Pierce Co. Tchrs. Assn. (Pres., 1957-58); NEA. Pres., Minority Grp., U.S. Labor Dept.; Chmn., Waycross Centennial Participation Comm., 1974. Address: 1404 Quarterman St., Waycross, GA 31501, U.S.A. 125, 129, 131.

RANTA, Tauno Uolevi, b. 25 Apr. 1920. Confederation Director. Educ: M.Pol.Sci., Helsinki Univ., Finland, 1946. Appts: Statistical Sec., Wage Dept., Soc. Min., 1946-47; Sec.-Chief, Statistical Dept., 1947-63; Dir., Econ. & statistical activities, 1963-; U.N. Expert in Indonesia, 1962-63. Mbrships: Finnish Econ. Assn.; Soc. Policy Assn. (Mbr. Bd., 1966-71); Finnish Statistical Assn.; ADP Assn. (Mbr. Bd., 1958-62. Author articles var. publs. Address: Orisaarentie 4D, 00840 Helsinki 84, Finland. 90.

RAO, Chatrathi Purushottama, b. 23 June 1934. Teacher. Educ: B.Com., Andhra Univ., India, 1954; M.Com., ibid, 1956; I.C.A.M.E. Cert., Stanford Univ., Calif., U.S.A., 1963-64; Ph.D., Univ. of N.C., Chapel Hill, 1968. Appts: Lectr., Andhra Univ., 1958-63; Asst. Prof., Bus. Admin., N.C. Coll., Durham, U.S.A., 1967-68; Asst. Prof., Marketing, Indian Inst. of Mgmt., Ahmedabad, 1968-69; Chmn., Dept. of Marketing, ibid, 1969-70; Coord., Marketing Exec. Dev. Progs., 1969-70; Asst. Prof., Marketing, Univ. of Ark., Fayetteville, U.S.A., 1970-72; Assoc. Prof., ibid, currently. Mbrships: Beta Gamma Sigma; Am. Marketing Assn.; Southern Marketing Assn.; Assn. for Consumer Rsch.; Acad. of Int. Bus.; Southwestern Marketing Assn.; Southern Case Rsch. Assn.; Purchasing Mgmt. Assn. Publs. incl: Export Marketing: Problems, Practices & Impact, 1970; Articles in acad. & profl. jrnl. in U.S.A. U.K. & India. Hons. incl: Marketing Cert. for acad. work on Pinto Proj., Ft. Marketing Corp., 1971; Rsch. grant, Grad. Schl. of Bus., Univ. of Ark., 1973-74. Address: Dept. of Marketing & Transportation, Coll. of Bus. Admin., Univ. of Ark., Fayetteville, AR 72701, U.S.A. 14, 125.

RAO, John O. Hospital Chief of Staff. Educ: B.S., Fordham Univ.; N.Y. Univ. Schl. of Med., 1935. Appts: Res., Pathol. St. Vincent's Hosp., N.Y.C., 1936; Med. & Surg., Bellevue Hosp., N.Y.C., 1937-38; Fellow, Radiol., N.Y. Univ. of Med., 1938; Asst. Res., N.Y. Mem. Hosp. for Cancer, 1938-39; Res., Brooklyn Cancer Inst., Kings Co. Hosp., N.Y., 1939-41; Dir. of Labs. & Blood Bank, Mercy Hosp., Detroit, Mich., 1941-43; Med. Dir., ibid, 1944-46; Med. Dir., Osceola Hosp., 1947-72; Chief of Staff, Community Hosp., Kissimmee, Fla., 1973-. Mbrships: Dipl., Am. Bd. of Radiol., Xray & Radium Therapy; AMA; Deleg., Fla. Med. Assn., 1973; Pres., Osceola Co. Med. Soc., 1972; N.Y. Acad. of Med.; Am. Cancer Soc.; Instr. & Dir., Osceola Co. Comm. for Emergency Med.; Nominee, Am. Coll. of Hosp. Admnstrs. Author of papers in field.

Address: 800 N. Central Ave., Kissimmee, FL 32741, U.S.A.

RAPELI, Toivo, b. 12 July 1903. Dean; Provost. Educ: Degree in Theol., 1927, ordained as min., pedagogics exam., 1st class hons., 1944; became dean, 1947. Appts: Army chap., 1927-32; Sec., Evangelical Students Fedn., 1932-33; Dir., Evang. Hosp. Folk H.S. 1933-38; Rector, Muola Parish, 1938-48; Dir. Finnish Luth. Evang. Assn., 1947-73; Retired 1973. Mbrships. incl: Bd., Evang. Hosp. Folk H.S., 1933-; Mgmt. & Exec. Comms., Karelian League & Karelian Trust, 1944-; Bd., Finnish Luth. Evang. Assn., 1947-; Mgmt. Comm., Evang. Students Fedn., 1947-70; Finnish Comm., Luth. World Fedn., 1948-58; Chmn., Finnish Ch. Publrs., 1949-73; Past Bd. of Comm. mbr., num. other relig. orgs. Author of num. publs. incl. Ensin Jumalan valtakunta, 1962 (transld. into Japanese); Nâin taistelevan Israelin, 1969; Monikasvoinen itä, 1972; Etelâmeren helmi, 1973; A book on S. Am. in preparation; Past Ed. & Contbr. to num mags. Participant in confs. all over world. Address: Dosentintie 7 C 15, Helsinki 33, Finland.

RAPER, William Burkette, b. 10 Sept. 1927. Educational Administrator. Educ: A.B., Duke Univ., Durham, N.C., 1937; B.D., Duke Univ. Schl., 1952; M.S., Fla. State Univ., Tallahassee, 1962. Appts. incl: Pastor, Free Will Bapt. Chs., 1946-54; Pres., Mt. Olive Coll., N.C., 1954; Cons., Am. Assn. Community & Jr. Colls. Progs. w. Developing Instns., 1968-71; Mbr., Commn. Student Personnel of Am. Assn. Community & Jr. Colls., 1968-71, Chmn., 1970-71; Regional Coord., U.S. Off. of Educ., Prog. w. Developing Instns., N. & S.C., 1968-70; Dir., Educ. Profns. Dev. Act Grant for Strengthening Dev. Pvte. 2-Yr. Colls., 1970-72. Mbr., N.C. State Educ. Assistance Authority, 1972-. Mbrships. incl: N.C. Assn. Colls. & Univs.; Pres., ibid, 1969-70. Hons. incl: LL.D., Atlantic Christian Coll., 1960; Kellogg Fellowship, Fla. State Univ., 1962. Address: 619 W. Main St., Mt. Olive, NC 28365, U.S.A. 2, 15, 108.

RAPISARDA, Emanuele, b. 29 June 1900. University Professor. Educ: Dr. ès lettres. Appts: Prof., Fac. of Letters, Catania Univ., Italy; Dir., Univ. Inst. of Catania Educ.; Fndr. & Dir., Orpheus & Nuovo Didaskaleion reviews. Mbrships: Fndr., Dir., Ctr. of Study of Ancient Christianity; Sec. Gen., European Movement for Defense of Latinity. Publs: Arnobio; Prometeo di Eschio; Boezio; Dranconzio; Prudenzio; Gregorio Nazianzeno; Filemone Comico. Hons. incl: Gold Medla, Cultural, Fine Arts, & Tchng. Merit. Address: Via G. Battista Grassi 11, Catania, Italy.

RAPKE, Trevor George, b. 2 Sept. 1909. Judge of the State of Victoria. Educ: B.A., LL.B., Univ. of Melbourne, Vic., Australia. Appts: Judge, Co. Ct., Vic., 1958-; Judge Advocate Gen., Royal Australian Navy, 1964-. Hon. Prof., U.S.N. Justice Schl., 1964-. Mbrships: Victorian Jewish Bd. of Deputies; Pres., ibid, 1955-57; Athenaeum; Pres., ibid, 1956; V.P. Dir. & Fndg. Mbr., Vic. Br., Nat. Heart Fndn.; Fndn. Coun., Churchill Fndn. Contbr. to legal publs. Hons: Queen's Counsel, High Ct. of Australia & Victorian, N.S.W. & Tasmanian Bars. Address: Judges' Chambers, Law Courts, Melbourne, Victoria, Australia 3000. 23, 128.

RAPOPORT, Azariahu, b. 13 May 1924. Journalist. Educ: Hebrew Univ. of Jerusalem; Cinema, Theatre, Film & TV trng., The Habimah Studio, Tel Aviv, N.Y. Univ., U.S.A., C.B.S., N.Y., & WGBH, Boston. Appts: Actor

w. Habimah & in films, 1949-55; Writer, arts column & reviews, Maariv (Tel Aviv Daily), 1955-70; Dir. & Prod., narrated & emceed progs. & special events, Israel Broadcasting Authority's radio & TV, 1955-70; Writer for Variety & Billboard, Special Councillor for profls. who wish to settle in Israel, Hd. Off., Israel Aliyah Ctr., N.Y.C., 1970-73; Consul & Press Off., Israeli Consulate Gen., N.Y.C. Mbrships: Off., Israel Press Assn.; Union of Cinema Critics; Israeli Br., I.T.I.; Off., WWII Israeli Veterans Assn. Translator of Engl. & Am. plays & songs by Aznavour, Cole Porter, & others. Address: Israeli Consulate Gen., 800 2nd Ave., N.Y., NY 10017, U.S.A. 94.

RAPP, Janet L(orraine) C(ooper), b. 3 Nov. 1921. Physiologist. Educ: B.Sc., N.J. Coll. for Women, 1943; Fellow, Nat. Carbon Co., Rutgers, 1943-44; M.S., Univ. of Ill., 1945; Fellow, ibid, 1947-48; Ph.D., 1948. Appts: Asst., Botany Dept., Univ. of Ill., 1944-47; Asst. Prof., Biol. Dept., Doane Coll., Crete, Neb., 1948-49; Dir. of Rsch., Archem Corp., Crete, 1949-51; Asst. Prof., Doane Coll., 1951-52; Dir. of Rsch., Feed Serv. Corp., Crete, 1953-. Mbrships: Am. Chem. Soc.; Am. Soc. for Animal Prod. Author of feed serv. communiques; Holder of patents for feeding ruminants. Recip.; Serv. to Mankind Award, Crete Seratoma Club, 1974. Address: 430 Ivy Ave., Crete, NB 68333, U.S.A. 14.

RAPP, William Frederick, b. 24 Mar. 1918. Entomologist. Educ: B.Sc. Rutgers Univ., N.J., U.S.A.; M.Sc., Univ. of Ill. Appts: Tchng. Asst., Univ. of Ill., 1944-47; Asst. Prof., & Chmn., Biol. Dept., Doane Coll., Crete, Neb., 1947-51; Pres., Archem Corp., 1949-52; Entomologist, State Dept. of Hlth., Neb., 1952-. Mbrships: Entomological Soc. of Am.; Am. Mosquito Control Assn.; Am. Ornithologists' Union; Ed.; Bulletin, Railroad Station Histl. Soc. Publs: Papers & articles on ornithol., entomol., pub. hlth., railroad & postal hist. Recip., Arthur Sidney Bedell award, Fedn. of Sewage & Indl. Waste Assn., 1955. Address: 430 Ivy Ave., Crete, NB 68333, U.S.A. 8, 14.

RAS, Florence A. School Dirctor. Educ: B.A., Barat Coll., Lake Forest, Ill.; M.A., Northwestern Univ., Evanston, Ill.; M.Ed., Fla. Atlantic Univ., Boca Raton. Appts: Tchr. of Deaf, West Palm Beach, Fla., 1960; Tchr., Ft. Lauderdale Oral Schl., 1958-65; Asst. Dir., ibid 1962-64; Dir., 1964-; Confraternity of Christian Doctrine, 1963-64; Chmn., Speechreading Classes, Broward Co., Fla., 1966-68; Mbr., Advisory Comm. for Workshops & Facilities, State Dept. of Educ. Div., Vocational Rehab., 1967-68; Dir., Young Deaf Adult Club, Ft. Lauderdale, 1967-68; Ldr., Girl Scouts; Volunteer Wkr., Am. Red Cross. Mbrships: Bd. Dir., Broward Co. Speech & Hearing Assn., 1965-70; Pres., Bd. Dir., ibid, 1967-68; NEA; Fla. & Am. Speech & Hearing Assns., etc. Address: 3100 S.W. 8th Ave., Ft. Lauderdale, FL 33315, U.S.A. 5, 7, 125, 129, 130, 132, 138.

RASCH, Georg William, b. 21 Sept. 1901. Professor Emeritus. Educ: M.Sc., 1925; Ph.D., 1930; Rockerfeller Fellow, Univ. Coll., London, U.K., 1935-36. Appts. incl: Asst. Prof., Maths., Univ. of Copenhagen, Denmark, 1925-40, Assoc. Prof., Biometrics & Math. Stats., 1938-62. Lectr., Educl. & Psychological Stats., Dept. of Psychol., 1944-59, Full Prof., Fac. of Soc. Scis., 1962-72; Hd., Dept. of Biostats., State Serum Inst., 1940-56 & Inst. of Stats., 1962-72; Rsch. Prof., Danish Coun. for Soc. Rsch., 1972-; Cons., Psychological Serv. of the Defense, 1952-70; Danish Inst. for Educl. Rsch., 1955- & Danish Meteorological Inst.,

1968-. Mbrships. incl: Int. Statistical Inst., 1948; Biometric Soc.; Charter Mbr., Danish Soc. for Theoretical Stats., 1971; Danish Statistical Assn., 1962. Publs. incl: Matrix Algebra and Its Application to Difference and Differential Equations, 1939; Papers in profl. jrnls. Recip., Kt. of the Dannebrog, 1969. Address: Bredebovej 33, 3, DK 2800 Lyngby, Denmark.

RASKIN, Marcus Goodman, b. 30 Apr. 1934. Political Philosopher. Educ: A.B., Univ. of Chgo., 1954; J.D., ibid, 1957. Appts: Legislative Advsr., House of Reps., 1958-61; Special Staff, Nat. Security Coun., White House, 1961-63; Cons. to Exec. Off. of Pres., 1963-65; currently Co-Dir., Inst. for Policy Studies & Gen. Ed., Encyclopedia of Soc. Reconstruction. Publs: Limits of Defense, 1962; Vietnam Reader, 1965, 1967; After Twenty Years, 1965; An American Manifesto, 1971; Washington Plans and Aggressive War, 1971; Being and Doing, 1971, 1973. Recip. Univ. of Chgo. Alumni Award, 1971. Address: Co-Director, Inst. for Policy Studies, 1520 New Hampshire Ave., N.W. Washington, DC 20036, U.S.A.

RASMUSSEN, Mogens Viktor, b. 17 June 1923. Economics & Public Relations Consultant. Educ: M.A., Univ. of Aarhus, Denmark, Appts. incl: Econ. Corres. in London, U.K. for grp. Danish Newspapers, 1948-51; former Ed. & Hd., Information, Danish Employers' Confederation; Prod., films about Labour & Community Relations for Ind. & Vocational Trng. bodies, 1951-60; Hd., A.P. Moller (Int. P.R. Co.), 1961-62; Cons., 1962 . Mbrships: Danish Lawyer & Economists Assn.; Danish Writer's Assn.; sev. Danish & Int. P.R. Assns. Publs. incl: Co-Ed., publs. for Danish Productivity Coun.; articles in Scandinavian & Am. newspapers & mags.; books in Danish Lang. on Labour & P.R.; Publr. & Ed. sev. books on Econs., Educ. & Pol. Address: Rungstedvej 113, 2960 Rungsted Kyst, DK Denmark. 16.

RASMUSSEN, Phyllis Joanne, b. 20 June 1942. Librarian. Educ: B.A., Dana Coll., 1964; M.A. in Lib. Sci., Univ. of Minn., 1966. Appts Libn. Co. Lib. Servs. & Pub. Servs., Elsinore & Copenhagen, Denmark, 1967-68; Asst. Libn., C.A. Dana-LIFE Lib., Dana Coll., 1969-72; Libn., Cataloguer, Dutch-Scandinavian Sect., Shared Cataloguing Div., Lib. of Cong., Wash., D.C., 1972-. Mbrships: ALA; D.C. Lib. Assn.; Sec., Lib. of Cong. Profl. Assn.; Mbrship. Chmn., Am. Scandinavian Fndn.; Soc. for Advancement of Scandinavian Studies; AAUW; Alpha Chi. Hons: Am. Luth. Ch. Future Fac. Fellowship, 1964. Address: 3200 Curtis Dr., Marlow Hts., MD 20031, U.S.A. 5.

RASPÉ, Gerhard J.O., b. 20 Jan. 1928. Biochemist. Educ: Dip. in Chem., Tech. Univ., Braunschweig, German Fed. Repub., 1951; Fellowhip, Consejo Superior de Investigaciones Cientificos, Madrid, 1952; Dr. rar. nat./Ph.D., 1953. Appts: Asst. Prof., Organic Chem., Tech. Univ., Braunschweig, 1954-55; Vis. Sci., Squibb Inst. of Med. Rsch., N.J., U.S.A., 1956; Rsch. Asst., Main Rsch. Lab., Schering AG, Berlin; Hd., Div. of Biochem. Microbiol., ibid; Hd., Main Rsch. Labs, ibid; Mbr., Bd. of Mgmt. i/c Rsch., ibid. Mbrships: Advsry. Comm., Educ. & Sci., Min. of Educ. & Sci., Bonn.; Bd. Mbr., Coun. for Sci. & Educ.; Mbr. of Senate, Max Planck Soc.; Bd. Chmn., Max Planck Inst. for Molecular Genetics; Bd. Mbr., Max Planck Inst. for Cell Biol., Wilhelmshaven; Bd. Mbr., Inst. for Molecular Biol. rsch., Stöckheim; N.Y. Acad. of Sci. Publs: Num. articles in profl. jrnls: Holder, U.S. & German patents; Ed.,

chapts in advances in the Biosciences, vols. I-XII. Address: Müllerstr. 170-72, 1 Berlin 65, German Fed. Repub. 43, 92.

RASPELLI, Giuseppe, b. 26 Mar. 1907. Journalist. Educ: Dipl. Acctcy., Tech. Inst., Piacenza; Studies at Cath. Univ. of Milan; Dipl., Syndical Schl., Milan. Appts: Acct., Nat. Credit Bank, 1924-30; Acct., Hospitallers Inst., Milan, 1931-65; Nat. Sec., Hospitallers Trade Union. Mbrships: Lo Scoltenna Soc. of Sci., Lit., & Art, Frignano; Order of Jrnlists., Milan; Lomard Assn. Jrnlists., 1929-; Coll. of Accts., Milan. Publs: Dizionario dei Chitarristi e liutai italiani. Contbr., var. jrnls. inclng: Svegliarino; Quaderni di poesia; Stirpe Italica; La Signorina; Academia; Libertà; Gazzetta di Modena; La Stampa; l'Ambrosiano; Buonsenso. Hons: Kt. Off., Equestrian Order of St. Maria the Glorious, 1948; Silver Medal, Tripoli Festival, 1930; Gold Medal, Lombard Assn. Jrnlsts., 1970. Address: Via G.A. Amadeo 3, 20133 Milan, Italy. 43.

RASPONI DALLE TESTE, Lanfranco, b. 11 Dec. 1914. Writer. Educ: Law studies, Univ. of Florence, Italy; B.A., Univ. of Calif. at Berkeley; M.S., Univ. of Columbia. Appts. incl: Reporter & Feature Writer, N.Y. Times; Travel Writer, Am. Vogue, Am. Harpers Bazaar, Town & Country & House & Garden; former Pres., Rasponi Assoc. (P.R. Co.), N.Y.C.; former Pres., Sagittarius Gall. (contemporary Art), N.Y.C. Publs. incl: The International Nomads, 1966; The Golden Oases, 1968. Address: Palazzo Rasponi dalle Teste, Piazza Kennedy, Ravenna, Italy.

RATCLIFF, John, b. 22 Jan. 1914. Architect; Town Planner; Painter. Educ: Dijon & Gottingen Univs.; Gen. hons. dipl., Archl. Assn. Schl. of Arch. Appts: Min. of Twon & Country Planning, U.K.; Dpty. Dir., Arch. Festival of Britain, 1951; Dpty. Controller, Construction, ibid; Ptnr., Howard V. Lobb & Ptnrs. Mbrships: Fellow, R.I.B.A., R.T.P.I.; Fellow & Past Chmn., Free Painters & Sculptors; Past Pres., Franco-British Union Archts.; Reform Club. Archl. Works incl: British Govt. Pavilion, Burssels Int. Exhib., 1958; City & Guilds of London H.Q.; Dungeness B Nuclear Generating Stn.; Town Plan for Ankara (Int. Competition); Paintings: Passepied series; Indica series; Rigaudon series; Micro series; Microman series; Portraits of James Huskisson Esq., Dr. Jean Riach, Dr. Charles Bryson. Contbr. to profl. jrnls. Hons: O.B.E., 1952; 3rd. Prize, Brussels Int. Exhib., 1958. Address: Terrace Cottage, 132 Richmond Hill, Richmond, Surrey TW10 6RN, U.K. 19, 133.

RATCLIFFE, John Spurgeon, b. 30 Mar. 1918. University Professor. Educ: M.Sc.; Ph.D. Appts: Lectr., Sydney Tech. Coll., Australia 1946-51; Sr. Lectr., Univ. of N.S.W., 1952-60; Assoc. Prof., ibid, 1961-64; Prof., ibid, 1965-; Assoc. Prof., Univ. of Newcastle, 1965; Chem. Engr., Broken Hill Propane Co. Ltd., 1935-45; Warden, Int. House, Univ. of N.S.W.; J.P., N.S.W.; Cmdr., Royal Australian Naval Reserve. Mbrships. incl: Tech. Advsry. Comm., State Pollution Control Commn., N.S.W.; Instn. Chem. Engrs.; Instn. Engrs., Australia; Fellow, Instn. Radio & Electronic Engrs. Author, papers publd. in tech. jrnls. in fields of chem. reaction engrng., low temp. carbonisation, wheat drying, spouted bed technol., chlorination, nuclear technol. Recip., Chem. Engrng. Award, Instn. of Engrs., Australia, 1970 & 1975. Address: Univ. of N.S.W., Kensington, N.S.W., Australia 2033. 23, 128.

RATCLIFFE, Myron Fenwick, b. 5 June 1902. Investment Management Executive; Banker. Educ: B.Sc., III. Univ., U.S.A., 1925. Appts: w. Goldman, Sachs & Co., N.Y.C., 1925-33; Admin., Financial Codes NRA, 1934-35; Syndicate Mgr., Lehman Bros., N.Y., 1936-49; Ptnr., Bache & Co., Chgo., III., 1949-56; Bd. Govs., Midwest Stock Exchange, 1949-56; Pres. & Dir., Miami Corp., Chgo., III., 1956-; Pres. & Dir., Cutler Oil & Gas Corp., ibid, 1956-; Chmn., Bd. & Dir., Nat. Blvd. Bank of Chgo., ibid, 1956-; Dir. Nat.-Standard Co., Niles, Mich. Mbrships: Trustee, III. Children's Home & Aid Soc.; Mason; Bond Club, Chgo.; Chgo. Club; Casino Club, Chgo.; Mid-Am. Club, ibid; Eldorado Country Club, Palm Desert, Calif.; Indian Hill Country Club, Winnetka, III.; Exmoor Country Club, Highland Pk., ibid; Old Elm Club, Ft. Sheridan, ibid. Recip. Legion of Merit. Address: 410 N. Mich. Ave. (Rm. 590), Chgo., IL 60611, U.S.A. 2, 8.

RATH, Hildegard Julie (Mrs. Herman Gross), b. 22 Mar. 1909. Artist; Painter; Writer; Lecturer. Appts: Fndr. & Dir., European Schl. of Fine Arts, N.Y.C., until 1954; Lectr. in Art, all N.Y. Muss., 1960-62; Great Neck Pub. Schl. Adult Educ., North Shore Art Assn. Roslyn, N.Y., 1960-62; North Merrick H.S., N.Y. etc. Mbrships: Assn., Pub. Schl. Adult Eductrs.; Artists Equity, N.Y.; Knickerbocker Artists, N.Y., North Shore Art Assn.; Southern Vt. Art Assn., Landesverband Württ. Künstler, Stuttgart, Germany; Württembergischer Kunstverein, Stuttgart; Landesverband Württembergischer Künstler, Tübingen. Creative Works: Over 800 Pntngs. & Graphics in Metropolitan Mus., N.Y., etc.; N.Y. Pub. Lib.; Lib. of Congress, Wash. D.C.; Kultministerium Stuttgart, Germany & Pvte. Collects. in Am. & elsewhere. Hons. incl: Dr. Blaicher Award, Stuttgart, 1938; Grumbacher Award of Merit, Fla., U.S.A., Int., 1952; Salon of 50 States, N.Y., 1962; Prix de Paris, 1963. Address: 3 Cypress Ave., Kings Point, Gt. Neck, NY 11024, U.S.A. 2, 5, 37.

RATHMAN, Richard Fielding, b. 24 Sept. 1912. Educator. Educ: A.B., Leland Stanford Jr. Univ., Palo Alto, Calif., 1935; A.M., ibid, 1938; Dip. in French Civilization, Sorbonne, Univ. of Paris; Doct. of Univ., Univ. of Paris, 1951; var. post-grad. studies, Mills Coll., Oakland, Calif., Laval Univ., P.Q., Can., San Jose (Calif.) State Coll, Deutsche Sommerschule am Pazifick, Portland, Ore., & others. Appts: Tchr., var. subjects, Jr. HS-Jr. Coll. levels, Ore. & Calif., 1941-48, Engl. & Dramatics, Gardnerville, Nev., 1951-52, Engl., French & Audio-Visual Prog., Minot, N.D., 1954-55, Music, Livingston, Calif., 1952-53; Substitute Tchr., var. subjects, Second. Schls., Calif., 1957-59; Assoc. Prof., Music, French, German & Spanish, Bethel Coll., McKenzie, Tenn., 1959-64; Asst. Prof., French, Moorehad State Coll. Ky., (now a univ.), 1964-66, & MacMurray Coll., Jacksonville, III., 1966-68; Asst. Prof.-Assoc. Prof., French, Morris Brown Coll. (Atlanta Univ. Ctr.), Ga., 1968-. Mbrships. incl: NEA; MLA; Nat. Assn. Tchrs. of French; Coll. Lang. Assn.; AAUP; Tenn. Philol. Assn.; var. ch. choirs, amateur symph. orchs. & bands, 1929-. Composer of sev. musical works inclng: Let There Be Light (oratorio), 1949; Proavda Vitezi—Truth Triumphs, a tribute to Czech. people & their leaders. Address: 4054 Pepperdine Dr., Decatur, GA 30034, U.S.A. 7, 13.

RATZ, Georg Otto, b. 22 Mar. 1917. International Sports Consultant; Former Barrister. Educ: Dr.jur., Pazmany Peter Univ., Budapest, Hungary, 1939. Appts incl: Barrister, Budapest; Hon. Judical Counsellor, Govt. Pest;

Legal Advsr., Munich, Germany; Star Mgr., Int. Football. Mbrships incl: Hon., sev. European football clubs. Publs. incl: The influence of the Magna Charta on the Hungarian Tripartitum of Verboczy, 1939. Address: CH-4125 Riehen, Aussere Baselstr. 204, Switzerland. 92, 103.

RAUCHE, Gerhard (Albin), b. 2 Nov. 1920. Professor of Philosophy. Educ: Philological State Exam, Univ. of Leipzig, Germany, 1948; Ph.D., Univ. of S. Africa, 1956; D.Litt., Univ. of Cape Town, 1966. Appts: H.S. Tchr., Germany & S. Africa, 1948-53; Lectr., Tchr. Trng. Colls. for Africans, 1953-56; Prin., German H.S., Johannesburg, 1957-59; Sr. Lectr. & Hd., Dept. of Philos., Univ. of Ft. Hare, 1960-61; Prof., ibid, 1962-69; Dean, Fac. of Arts, 1966-67; Prof., Univ. of Durban-Westville, 1969-; Dean, Fac. of Arts, ibid, 1970-71, 1974. Mbrships: Royal Soc. of S. Africa; Engl. Acad. of Southern Africa; Philosophical Soc. of Southern Africa; Medieval Soc. of Southern Africa; Pres., Soc. for the Advancement of Philos. in Southern Africa, 1961-63. Publs. incl: Truth & Reality in Actuality, 1971; The Choice (Quo vadis, homo?), 1973; Abdication of Philosophy—Abdication of Man, forthcoming; Num. articles in var. sci. jrnls. Recip. of hons. Address: Dept. of Philos., Univ. of Durban-Westville, Private Bag 4001, Durban, Natal 4000, Repub. of S. Africa.

RAUHAMAA, (Armas) Ylermi, b. 24 May 1923. Dentist. Educ: Licentiate of Dental Surgery. Appts: Inst., Dental Schl., Univ. of Helsinki, Finland, 1952-61; Mbr., Bd. of Govs., Schl. of Dental Techns., 1959-. Chmn., 1968-71; Chmn., Postgrad. Studies, Finnish Dental Soc., 1960-67; Chmn., Bd. of Dirs., Hammasvaline Oy., 1962-; Bd. of Dirs., Regulus Oy., & Orion-Yhtymä. Mbrships: Int. Coll. Dentists; Finnish Dental Assn.; V.P., ibid, 1956-59; Corres. Mbr., Gothenburg Dental Soc., Odontological Soc. of Finland; Delta Sigma Delta. Author, sev. publs., dental prosthetics. Hons: Cross of Liberty, 4th Class w. Sword; Bronze Badge, Finnish Dental Soc.; Silver Badge, Finnish Dental Assn. Address: Mariankatu 12, 00170 Helsinki 17, Finland 43, 90, 134.

RAULT, Joseph Matthew, Jr., b. 24 Feb. 1926. Company President. Educ: S.B., MIT, 1948; Georgetown Univ. Law Schl., 1948; LL.B. (now D.S.), Tulane Univ., 1950. Appts: Mbr. of Law Firm, Terriberry, Rault, Carroll, Martinez & Yancey, 1951-59; Pres. & Owner, Independent Oil Prod. & Real Estate Developer, Joseph M. Rault, Jr., Inc., 1959-; & Rault Petroleum Corp., 1962-; Pres. & Owner, The Lamplighter Club, Inc., 1967-; Owner, The Rault Ctr., 17-storey off./apt./Club bldg., 1967-72, Hotel, 1972-; Pres. & Owner, Real Estate Dev., Lake Hillsdale Estates, Inc., 1970-; Pres. & Owner, Hotel & related enterprises, The Domed Stadium Hotel, Inc., 1972-; Co-owner, Oakbrook Village, 1972-; Pres. & Owner, Lake Hillsdale Inn, Inc., 1973-; Pres., Rault Petroleum Corp. of Venezuela, Constructora-Otila, S.A., Mexico (For. Oil Prod.). Mbrships. incl: Bd. of Dirs., Chmbr. of Comm., New Orleans Area; Gen. Chmn., U.S. Savings Bond 25th Anniversary Campaign, Greater New Orleans Area; Chmn., New Orleans Railroad Terminal Bd.; Am. Petroleum Inst.; Am. Bar Assn. Address: The Rault Ctr., 1111 Gravier St., New Orleans, LA 70112, U.S.A. 7, 22.

RAUM, Otto Friedrich, b. 29 Apr. 1903. University Teacher. Educ: Tchrs. Coll., Germany; B.A., 1934; Dip. in Anthropol., 1935, Dip. in Educ., 1936, Ph.D., Educ., 1938,

London Univ. Appts: Lectr., Tchrs. Trng. Coll., Marangu, Tanzania, 1928-34, Umpumulo, Natal, 1938-40; Prin., Hermannsburg H.S., Natal, 1943-48; Prof., Educ., Univ. Coll. Fort Hare, Cape Province, 1949-59; Prof., Anthropol., ibid, 1960-68; Prof. Emeritus, 1969-. Contbr. to num. profl. jrnls. Hons: Carnegie Corp. Travel Grant to U.S.A., 1955; Ranke Gesell. Prize, Hamburg, German Fed. Repub., 1965. Address: Bahnhofstr. 2, D-8051 Langenbach, German Fed. Repub.

RAURAMO, (Mauno) Heikki, b. 26 Apr. 1914. University Administrator. Educ: LL.B., Univ. of Helsinki, 1939; Pol.D.h.c., ibid, 1971. Appts: Notary of Consistory, Univ. of Helsinki, 1945, Amanuensis of Consistory, 1946, Bursar, 1947-48, Sec. Gen. & Hd. of Rector's Off., 1949-70, Dir. of Admin., 1970-. Mbrships: Sec., Fac. of Soc. Scis., Univ. of Helsinki, Sec., Univ. Salary Comm., 1947-48, Comm. Mbr., 1949; Univ. Admin. Reform Comm., 1950-54, 1965; Bd. Mbr., Fed. Admin. of Disabled War Veterans' Fndn., 1958-67, 1st Vice Chmn., 1962-67. Author, Högre utbildning och forskning i Finland, 1961. Contbr. higher educ., var. publs. & newspapers. Hons. incl: Order, 1st Class, White Rose of Finland, 1953; Disabled War Veterans' Fedn. Silver Badge, 1954, Gold Badge, 1960, Cross of Merit, 1965; Kt. Cmdr., Order of Lion of Finland, 1961. Address: Ritokalliontie 11, 003300 Helsinki 33, Finland. 43.

RAUSCHART, Edward A. b. 17 Oct. 1924. Psychologist. Educ: B.S., N.Y. Univ., 1949; M.A., ibid, 1950; Profl. Dip. in Special Educ., Columbia Univ., 1959; Ed.D., E. Coast Univ., Fla. Appts: Schl. Psychol., N.Y. & N.J., 1950-61; Coord., State Rsch. Project Able, Suffern, N.Y., 1961-64; Dir., Pupil Personnel Servs., Portchester, N.Y., 1964-67 & Psychol. Servs., Glen Ridge, N.J., 1967-71; Psychol. Cons., title I Proj., Measuement of Tchr. Attitudes,1961; Evaluator, Metropol. Schl. Study Coun. Quality Measurment Proj., 1966-67; Chmn., Psychol. Servs., Clarkstown Schls., 1971-. Mbrships: Past V.P., Featherstone Chapt., Coun. for Exceptional Chldrn., Columbia Univ.; Past Pres., Nassau Co. Assn. of Schl. Psychols.; Am., N.Y. State & Essex Co. Psychol. Assns.; Nat. Assn. of Tests & Measurements; Nat. Assn. of Schl. Psychols. Contbr. articles & monographs to profl. publs. Recip. Community Serv. Awards. Address: 41 Glenbrook Road, Monsey, NY 10952, U.S.A.

RAUTALA, Pekka, b. 16 Apr. 1918. Physicist. Educ: Dip. Engr., Helsinki Tech. Univ., Finland, 1946; D.Sc., MIT, U.S.A., 1951. Appts. incl: Engr., Oy Vuoksenniska Ab, 1947-48; Instr., MIT, 1949-50; Asst. Prof., ibid, 1951-53; Lectr., Helsinki Tech. Univ., 1953-55; Prof., Purdue Univ., Lafayette, Ind., 1955-60; Dir. of Rsch., Vuorikemia Oy, 1960-61; Chief Physicist, Outokumpu Oy, 1962-. Mbrships: V.P., Finnish Acad. of Tech. Sci., 1967-69, Pres., 1969-71; Assn. Franco-Finlandaise pour la Recherche Scientifique et Technique. Publs: Sev. sci. & tech. papers. Hons: Freedom Cross 4, 1944; Badge of Merit, Assn. of Finnish Engrs., 1970; Cmdr., Sun & Lion Order, 1970; Gold Medal, Finnish Acad. of Tech. Scis., 1972. Address: Outokumpu Oy, Inst. of Physics, 02100 Tapiola, Finland. 43, 90.

RAUTAVAARA, (Kaj) Tapio, b. 8 Mar. 1915. Singer. Educ: Violin Study, Finnish Folk Conservatory; Film & Theatre Schls.; Study of Singing. Appts. incl: Warehouse & Off. Employee, Coop. Wholesale (OTK), 1935-49; Free-lance Singer, 1949-. Mbrships: Finnish Wkrs. Sports Org. (Hon. 1962-); Finnish Archery Assn. (Hon. 1971-); Lions Club.

Singing Tours, U.S.A. & Canada, 1959-60, 1972; Num. Records inclng. 6 Golden Discs. Composer & Lyricist, num. songs. inclng. 2 song Albums. Actor, 25 Films. Num. appearances at European Sports Meetings (Javelin & Archery). Hons: Gold Medal, Javelin, Olympic Games, London, U.K., 1948; Finnish Javelin Champion, 1944, 1945, 1947, 1948, 1949; Champion, Finnish Wkrs. Sports Org., 7 times; Finnish Archery Champion, 1955; World Archery Champion, Finnish Team, Brussels, Belgium, 1958; Medal of Freedom, 1 & 2; Silver Cross Finnish Sports, 1965; 1st Class Cross w. Buckle, Order of Finnish Lion. Address: Teinintie 4, 00640 Helsinki 64, Finland. 43.

RAUTAVAARA, Toivo Fredrik, b. 27 Feb. 1905. Professor of Agriculture. Educ: Dr.Sc.(Agr. & Forest.), Helsinki Univ., Finland. Appts: R & D Dir., Huhtamaki Corp. (food industry); Hd. Rsch. Bur. of Horticulturists' Assn.; Hd., Bur. for Horticulture, Admin. of Agric; retired, 1972. Mbrships. incl: Pres., Finnish Mycological Soc., Soc. for Combating Obesity, & Union of Civic Orgs. against Alcoholismus; V.P., Int. Assn. for Rsch. on Civilization Diseases, & World Union for Protection of Life. Author, scientific textbooks & articles. Hons. incl: Kt., 1st Class, Order of the White Rose; Cmdr., Lion Order; Golden Emblems, Horticulturists' Assn. & Nature Conservation Assn. Address: Mannerheimintie 56 B 15, SF 00260 Helsinki 26, Finland. 43.

RAUTKARI, Mauri Tapio, b. 17 Jan. 1932. Forest Engineer. Educ: M.A., forestry, Helsinki Univ., Finland, 1956; Int. Mktng. Inst., Harvard Bus. Schl., Boston, U.S.A., 1961. Appts: For. Trade Dept., Rauma-Repola Oy, hd. off., Helsinki, 1953-58; Sales Mgr., Woodworking Dept., ibid, Rauma, 1959-60; Mng. Dir., Oy Penola Ab (subsid. of Chr. Olsen AS, Copenhagen), Helsinki, 1962-67; Mng. Dir. & Chmn. of wholesale house, Lahjatukku Oy, 1967-. Mbrships: P.R. Soc., Finland; Finnish For. Trade Assn.; Sales & Advt. Assn.; Jr. Chmbr. of Comm. Address: Ilkantie 1, 00320 Helsinki 32, Finland. 43.

RAUX, Henri Frédéric, b. 29 June 1913. Chief Curator of Libraries. Educ: Licence ès lettres; Dip., Superior Studies. Appts: Curator, Nat. Lib. of Paris, 1945-52, 1955-62; Fndr. & Dir., Turkish Nat. Inst. of Bibliography, 1952-54; Dir., Lib. of Int. Contemporary Documentation & Mus. of the 2 World Wars, 1963-69; Dir., Interuniv. Lib., Paris A, 1970-. Publs. incl: Répertoire de la Presse et des publications périodiques françaises Parait depuis 1958; num. articles in profl. reviews. Hons: Chevalier, Legion of Hon.; Off., Nat. Order of Merit; Off., Acad. Palms; Cross of War of 1939-45. Address: 2 Rue Cujas, 75005 Paris, France. 43, 91.

RAVEN, Peter Hamilton, b. 13 June 1936. Botanical Garden Director; University Professor. Educ: A.B., Univ. of Calif., Berkeley, 1957; Ph.D., UCLA, 1960. Appts: Nat. Sci. Fndn. Postdoctoral, British Mus. (Natural Hist.), 1960-61; Botanist & Curator, Rancho Santa Ana Botanical Garden, Claremont, Calif., 1961-62; Asst. Prof.-Assoc. Prof., Dept. Biological Scis., Stanford Univ., 1962-71; Dir., Mo. Botanical Garden & Prof., Biol., Wash. Univ., St. Louis, Mo., 1971- Mbrships. incl: Ed.-in-Chief, Brittonia (jrnl. of Am. Soc. of Plant Taxonomists), 1963-66; Interim V.P., Assn. of Systematic Collects., 1972-; Edit. Bd., Memoirs of N.Y. Botanical Garden, 1966-; Edit. Comm., Am. Inst. of Biological Scis., 1966-; Systematics & Biogeog. Subcomm., U.S. Int. Biological Prog., 1967-; Edit. Comm., Flora Neotropica, 1965-; 1st V.P., Soc. for the Study of Evolution, 1969, 1972; Am. Soc. of Naturalists; Int. Assn. of Plant Taxonomists. Author of 3 books inclng. The Biology of Plants (w. Helena Curtis) & over 100 publs. in tech. jrnls. Recip., A.P. DeCandolle Award for best taxonomic paper of the period, for monograph of Camissonia, Geneva, 1970. Address: 2315 Tower Grove Ave., St. Louis, MO 63110, U.S.A. 14.

RAVENSCROFT, Leonard Ellis, b. 28 May 1913. General Manager. Educ: Footscray Tech. Coll., Australia. Appts: Adjutant, Supply & Transport Serv., 7th Australian Div. M.E., 3rd Australian Corps, 1940-44; Asst. Western Australian Mgr., British Phosphate Commnrs., 1945-53; Western Australian Mgr., ibid, 1953-59; Asst. Gen. Mgr., 1959-64; Dpty. Gen. Mgr., 1964-66; Gen. Mgr., 1966-; Gen. Mgr., Christmas Island Phosphate Commn. Mbrships: Past Pres., Fremantle, Legacy; Australian Club, Melbourne; Australian Inst. of Mgmt.; Australian Soc. of Sr. Edecs.; Naval & Mil. Club, Melbourne. Address: 20 Barina Cres., Croydon, Vic., Australia. 23.

RAVERA ONETO, Cecilia. Painter. Educ: Fac. of Arch., Turin Univ., Italy. Mbrships: Accademia Tiberina, Rome; Accademia Teatina per la Scienze, Pescara; Accademia dei Cinquecento, Rome; Accademis di Paestum, Salerno. One-man shows incl: Galleria Rotta, Genoa, 1954; Galleria S. Babila, Milan, 1959; Galleria Bolzani, Milan, 1960; Centro Artistico Gioventu Italiana, Genoa, 1963; Galleria Vinciana, Milan, 1964; Galleria Rotta, Genoa, 1965; Galleria Ca'Vegia, Lecco, 1967; Galleria Martano, Torino, 1967; Galleria Abba, Brescia, 1967; Galleria Carlevaro, Genoa, 1970; Galleria Agrati, Monza, 1971; Galleria Flacovio, Palermo, 1971. Num. group collects. Paintings in pub. & pvte. collects. Co-illustrator, Trenta favole, 1971. Recip. of 44 prizes. Address: Via Puggia 55, 16131 Genoa, Italy.

RAVESON, Betty Rich (Mrs. Sherman H. Raveson), b. 16 June 1913. Editor; Writer. Educ: A.B., Columbian Univ., N.Y., 1934. Appts: East Chester Ed., Yonkers Herald-Statesman, N.Y., 1940-42; Night Bur. Mgr., United Press., Albany, N.Y, 1942-43; Ed. Columnist, Delray Beach, Fla., 1942-43; Palm Beach Illustrated, 1959-62; Columnist, Palm Beach Daily News, 1963-69; Monthly Contbr., Palm Beach Life, 1963-74; Ed., Palm Beach Voice, 1969-70; Ed. & V.P., Mtn. Living Mag., Franklin, N.C., 1970-. Mbrships: N.C. Press. Assn.; Atlanta Press Club; Gold Coast Press Club. Author article in Palm Beach Life Mag., June, 1974. Recip., Outstanding Achievement Award, Fla. Gold Coast Press Club, 1962. Address: P.O. Box 290, Franklin, NC 28734, U.S.A. 5, 125, 132.

RAWLS, Walter Cecil, Jr., b. 13 Sept. 1928. Lawyer & Company Executive. Educ: A.B. Univ. of Mo., 1951; J.D., Wash. Univ., St. Louis, Mo. 1958. Appts: Gen. Agt, France, A. Trust Life Ins. Co. 1953-54; Trial & Co. Law Prac., 1958-; Dir., GA—FLA Oil & Ref. Co. Inc., 1968-; Dir., F.I.D. Int. 1971; Ptr. RAWB & Co., 1967-; Pres., Biomagnetics Int. Inc., 1973-; Dir., Int. Film Corp., 1974-; Dir., Funds Inc., 1974-; Dir., Canvi-Andor, 1973-; Dir., British W.I. Capital Reserves Ltd., 1973-. Mbrships: Jacksonville, Fla. & Am. & Int. Bar. Assns.; Am. Judicature Soc.; Am. Trial Law Assn.; Arbitrator, Am. Arbitration Assn.; Pres., Metropolitan Dinner Club of Jacksonville; Capital Hill Club; Univ. Club; English Speaking Union; Am. Archaeol. Soc.; Advsry. Coun., Wash. Univ. Law Schl. St. Louis, Mo., 1970-. Publs. History of the Bar, 1965; (co-Auth.) Energy Crisis & Solution, 1970. Recip., Hon.

D.Sc., Davis Coll., 1973. Address: 6962 Almours Dr., Jacksonville, FL 32217, U.S.A. 7, 16, 57, 130.

RAWLINS, Joseph Thomas, Jr., b. 7 Nov. 1936. Artist; Voice Teacher. Educ: A.A., Univ. of Fla., Gainesville, 1957; B.Mus., La. State Univ., Baton Rouge, 1959; M.Mus., ibid, 1961; Summer study, Univ. of Fla., 1962; Doctoral study, N. Tex. State Univ., Denton, 1969-70; Mus.D., La. State Univ., Baton Rouge, 1972. Appts. incl: Asst. Prof., Music, Dir., opera workshop, voice, Auburn Univ., Ala., 1965-69; Grad. Fellow in choral-voice, Dir., Campus Chorale & Tchr. of voice, N. Tex. State Univ., Denton, 1969-70; Grad. Asst. in opera, La. State Univ., Baton Rouge, 1970-71; Auburn Univ., 1971-; Assoc. Prof., ibid, 1972-; Recitalist-performer, 11 leading operatic roles; Presenter of concerts, operas, recitals & oratorios for nat. profl. music convens.; Recitals over Ala. Educl. TV Network & 13-state network of radio stns.; Guest appearances w. Memphis Symph., Columbus (Ga.) Symph., State Symph. of Fla. & others. Mbrships: Nat. Voice Comm., Music Tchrs. Nat. Assn.; Nat. Assn. of Tchrs. of Singing; Pi Kappa Lambda; Phi Mu Alpha Sinfonia. Recip. of hons. Address: Music Dept., Auburn Univ., Auburn, AL 36830, U.S.A. 125, 130, 131.

RAWN, Stanley R., Jr., b. 3 Feb. 1928. Executive. Educ: B.S., Calif. Inst. of Technol., 1952; M.S., ibid, 1953. Appts: Rsch. Engr., Chevron Rsch. Corp., Standard Oil Co. of Calif.; V.P., Deerfield Oil Corp. & Pioneer Lands Corp.; Pres., Pentagon Petroleum, Inc.; Vice Chmn. of Bd., KCA Drilling Grp., Ltd.; Chmn. & Pres., Pan Ocean Oil Corp. Mbrships: The River Club, N.Y.; Sigma Xi. Address: Pan Ocean Building, 645 Madison Ave., N.Y., NY 10022, U.S.A. 6, 16.

RAY, Cyril, b. 16 Mar. 1908. Writer; Educ: Jesus Coll., Oxford Univ. Appts: w. Manchester Guardian, 1936-44 (War Corres., mentioned in despatches); BBC, 1944-46; UNESCO Missions, 1945-50; Sunday Times, 1949-56 (Moscow Corres., 1950-52); Asst. Ed., The Spectator, 1958-62; The Observer, 1962-. Pres. The Circle of Wine Writers. Publs: Scenes & Characters from Surtees; From Algiers to Austria; The History of 78 Division; The Pageant of London; Merry England; Regiment of The Line; The Story of the Lancashire Fusiliers; The Gourmet's Companion; Morton Shand's Book of French Wines (rev. & ed.); Best Murder Stories; The Wines of Italy; In A Glass Lightly; Lafite; The Story of Chateau Lafite - Rothschild; Bollinger; The Story of Champagne; Cognac; The Complete Imbiber, Vols. 1-12 (Ed.). Recip. var. hons. Address: Delmonden Manor, Hawkhurst, Kent TN18 4XJ, U.K. 1, 3, 30.

RAY, Dorothea Hammers (Mrs. Walter E. Ray), b. 28 Apr. 1917. Analyst. Educ: Tex. Womens Univ.; Univ. of Houston. Appts. incl: Former Tchr., 2nd Grade, Cove Schl., Orange Co., Tex.; Analyst, E.I. du Pont de Nemours & Co., Inc., Sabine River Works, 1948-. Mbrships. incl: Orange Bus. & Profl. Women's Club, Inc., Pres., 1970-71; Tex. Fed. B.P.W. Clubs Dist. 14, Dist. Dir., 1971-72, 1972-73; Nat. Fed. B.P.W.; Sports Car Club of Am., Locensed Race Control Official; Provisional Mbr., Nat. Parliamentarians Assn.; Tex. Women's Pol. Caucus; Bd. Trustees, Southeast Tex. Chapt., Nat. Multiple Sclerosis Soc., Drive Chmn., Orange, 1972, 1973; 1st Bapt. Ch., Orange. Hons: Best Dist. Dir. Award, 1972 & Cooperating Award for Dist. Dirs., 1973, Tex. Fed. B.P.W. Clubs; B.P.W. Fndn. Ldrship Award, 1973. Address: 1213 W. Wrenway, Orange, TX 77630, U.S.A. 57, 125.

RAY, John Walker, b. 12 Jan. 1936.
Physician specialising in Ear, Nose, Throat &
Facial Plastic Surgery. Educ: A.B. Marietta
Coll., Ohio, 1956; M.D., Ohio State Univ. Coll.
of Med., Columbus, 1960. Appts: Internship,
Dept. of Surg., Ohio State Univ. Hosps.,
1960-61; Capt., USAF, Off. in Charge, EENT
Dept., Lockburne AFB, 1961-63, Active
Reserve, 1963-67; Res., Asst. & Asst. Instr.,
Dept. of Otolaryngol., Ohio State Univ.,
1963-67; Clin. Instr. ibid, 1971-; Pvte. Prac.,
Zanesville, Ohio, 1967-; Mbrships. incl: Phi Beta
Kappa; Alpha Omega Alpha; Dipl., Am. Bd. of
Otolaryngol.; Fellow, Am. Coll. of Surgs.;
Fellow, Am. Acad. of Ophthalmol. &
Otolaryngol. Fellow, Am. Soc. of Ophth. &
Otolaryng. Allergy; AMA: Ohio State Med.
Assn.; Muskingum Co. Acad. of Med.; Columbis
Ophth. & Otolar. Soc.; Pres., Muskingum Co.
Unit. of Am. Cancer Soc., 1971-73. Author of
num. articles in med. & surg. lit. Collaborator,
surg. motion picture "Laryngectomy & Neck
Dissection", 1964. Address: 2927 Bell St.,
Zanesville, OH 43701, U.S.A. 8, 17, 117.

RAYBURN, Deannie E., b. 19 Mar. 1939.
Nuclear Medicine Technologist. Educ: Register
Radiological Technol.; Registered Nuclear Med.
Technol., La. State Univ. Med. Schl. in assoc.
w. Schempert Mem. Hosp. Licensed Notary
Public, Caddo Paris, State of La. Address: 134
Ardmore Ave., Shreveport, LA 71105, U.S.A.
125.

RAYBURN, Robert Gibson, b. 14 Jan.
1915. Clergyman & Educator. Educ: A.B.,
Wheaton Coll., Ill.; Th.B., Th.M., Omaha
Presby. Theol. Sem., Neb.; Th.D., Dallas Theol.
Sem., Tex. Appts: Pastor, 1st Presby. Ch.,
Bellevue, Neb. & 1st Presby. Ch., Gainesville,
Tex.; U.S. Army Chap., W.W. II (European
Theatre) & in Korean War; Pastor, Westminister
Presby. Ch., Gainesville, Tex. & Coll. Ch. of
Christ, Wheaton, Ill.; pres., Highland Coll.,
Pasadena, Calif., Covenant coll., Lookout Mt.,
Tenn. & Covenant Theol. Sem., St. Louis, Mo.
Mbrships: Evangelical Theol. Soc.; Mil. Chap's
Assn.; Hymn Soc. Am; Moderator, Reformed
Presby. Ch.'s Gen. Synod 1954. Publs: Fight
the Good Fight; What About Baptism. Hons:
D.D., Geneva Coll., Beaver Falls, Pa., 1974.
Address: 12330 Conway Rd., St. Louis, MO
63141, U.S.A. 8, 30.

RAYBURN, Russell Howard, b. 21 Sept.
1902. Educator; Administrator. Educ: B.S.,
Ind. State Univ., Terre Haute, 1929; M.S., ibid,
1933; postgrad. work at sev. univs. Appts. incl:
Tchr. & Prin., Ind. Public schls., 1921-51; Var.
admin. posts, Ind. State Schls., 1951-56; Supt.
of Schls., Hendiricks Co., Ind., 1956-59;
Planning Cons. & P.R., Lennox, Mathews,
Simmons & Ford, Arct. Engrs., Indpls.,
1959-61; Asst. Prof., Educ. & Supvsr., Student
Tchrs., Ind. Ctrl. Coll., Indpls., 1961-65;
Emeritus, ibid, 1970; Tchr., Wash. H.S., Indpls.,
1969-71, Ret., 1971; Coord. Plainfield
Community Schl., Release Weekday Relig.
Educ. Prof., 1972-. Active Mbr. many educl.
fraternal & community orgs. inclng; Past Pres.,
Ind. Sec. Prins., Assn.; Lay Leader, N.W. Conf.
Medh. Ch., 1956-68; Trustee Ind. Ch. Ctr., Inc.,
1969-; 32 deg. Mason; Ctrl. Ind., Rep., Heritage
of Am. Inc., 1967-; etc. Recip. num. awards.
Address: 215 Hobbs Street, Plainfield, IN
46168, U.S.A. 8, 15, 82, 116, 129, 131.

RAYMOND, Diana Joan (Mrs. Ernest
Raymond), b. 25 Apr. 1916. Novelist. Publs:
Joanna Linden, 1952; The Small Rain, 1954;
Between the Stirrup & the Ground, 1956;
Strangers' Gallery, 1958; The Five Days, 1959;
Guest of Honour, 1960; The Climb, 1962;

People in the House, 1964; The Noonday
Sword, 1965; Front of the House, 1967; Are
You Travelling Alone, 1969; The Best of the
Day, 1972; Incident on a Summer's Day, 1973.
Hons: 2 books (The Small Rain & The Five
Days) were Book Soc. Fiction Choice, 1954 &
59. Address: 22 The Pryors, East Heath Road,
London NW3 1BS, U.K. 3.

RAYMOND, Ernest, b. 31 Dec. 1888
Novelist. Edic: Chichester Theol. Coll. (aff
Durham Univ.). Ordained decon, 1914 & priest,
1915. Appts: Chaplain, Royal Army Chaplains'
Dept., 1915-19; served, Gallipoli, Sinai, France,
Mesopotamia, Persia & Russia. Mbrships:
Councillor, Soc. of Authors; Fellow, Royal Soc.
of Lit.; Pres., Int. Dickens Fellowship, 1971.
Publd. 54 novels, 3 books of "belles lettres", 2
plays & 7 biogs. Hons: Kt. Off., Order of Merit,
Italy, 1964; Off., O.B.E., for servs. to lit., 1972;
Gold Medal of British Book Guild for novel We,
The Accused, 1935; Am. Lit. Guild Alt. Choice
for novel, Gentle Greaves, 1972. Address: 22
The Pryors, East Heath Road, London NW3
1BS, U.K. 1, 3.

RAYNOR, (The Very Rev.) John P., S.J., b.
1 Oct. 1923. University President. Educ: B.A.,
St. Louis Univ., 1947; M.A., ibid, 1948; Ph.L.,
1949; S.T.L., 1956; Ph.D., Univ. of Chgo.,
1959. Appts: Instr., St. Louis Univ. H.S.,
1948-51; Asst. Prin., ibid, 1951; Instr.,
Marquette Univ., 1960; Asst. Dean, Coll. of
Liberal Arts, ibid, 1960; Asst. to V.P., Acad.
Affairs, 1962-65; Pres., 1965-. Mbrships. incl:
Past Pres., Wis. Assn. Fndn. Indep. Colls. & Univs.;
Pres., Wis. Assn. Indep. Colls. & Univs.; Bd. of
Dirs., Assn. Jesuit Colls. & Univs.; Past Pres.,
Nat. Assn. Urban Univs; Phi Beta Kappa; Alpha
Sigma Nu; Phi Delta Kappa. Recip., LL.D.,
Cardinal Stritch Coll., 1973. Address:
Marquette Univ., 615 N. 11th St., Milwaukee,
WI 53233, U.S.A.

RAYNOR, Robert Albert, b. 30 July 1907.
Company Director. Educ: Adelaide Univ.,
Australia, 1926; Melbourne Univ., 1932; Dip.
of Commerce. Appts. incl: Mng. Dir. of sev.
Cos. inclng. President Foods Corp. Pty. Ltd.,
Robert Raynor Pty. Ltd., Safrana Investments
Pty. Ltd., Safrana Nominees Pty. Ltd., Robesta
Corp. Pty. Ltd. Mbrships. incl: Life Mbr., The
Nat. Gall. Soc. of Vic., Melbourne; Life Mbr.,
The Australian Nat. Mem. Theatre, St. Kilda.
Hons. incl: Gall. of Prints & Drawings has been
named the Robert Raynor Gall., Nat. Gall. &
Cultural Ctr., Melbourne. Address: 24 Douglas
St., Toorak, Melbourne, Australia, 3142. 23.

RAZAFIMBAHINY, Jules A., b. 19 Apr.
1922. Ambassador. Educ: Grad., Law & Econ.
Scis. Schl. Paris Univ., France, 1953; Grad.,
Paris Coll. des Scis. Soc. et Econ. Appts. incl:
Attaché, Pres.' Cabinet, French Union
Assembly, Palais de Versailles, France, 1950-52;
Chmn., Comm. of countries assoc. w. EEC, Soc.
& Econ. Coun., Common Market & Euratom,
Brussels, Belgium, 1958-60; Tech. Counsellor,
Min. of State, Madagascar-Tananarive, 1960-61;
Sec.-Gen., Malagasy For. Off., Tananarive,
Madagascar, 1964-65; Ambassador
Extraordinary & Plenipotentiary, Gt. Britiain,
Italy, Greece & Israel, 1965-67; U.S.A.,
1970-73; Belgium, Holland, Luxembourg &
Switzerland, 1973-; Permanent Rep., EEC,
Brussels, Belgium & UN, Geneva, Switzerland,
1973-. Mbr. sev. econ. orgs. Author 2 econ.
publs. Hons. incl: Cmdr: Ordre Nat. Malgache,
1969, Ordre Nat. de la Répub. Islamique de
Mauritanie, 1963, Ordre Nat. de la Répub. de
Tchad, 1964, Ordre du Léopard de la Répub.
du Zaire, 1969 & sev. others. Address: Ave. de
Tervueren, 276, 1150 Brussels, Belgium. 34, 43.

RAZAFINDRALAMBO, Edilbert Pierre, b. 3 Oct. 1921. Chief Justice. Educ: Licencié ès lettres, Sorbonne, Paris, France; Cert. d'aptitude à la profession d'avocat, Paris; Dr. en droit, Paris; Studied at Cambridge Univ., U.K. Appts: Advocate, Ct. of Appeal, Paris, 1948-60; Prin. Sec. of Advocate of Conseil d'Etat & Cour de Cassation, Paris, 1951-60; Dpty. Atty. Gen., Ct. of Appeal, Tananarive, Madagascar, 1961; Advocate Gen., Supreme Ct. of Madagascar, 1961-62; Pres. of Chmbr., ibid, 1962-67; Chief Justice, 1967-. Mbrships. incl: Chief, Malagasy experts on French-Malagasy negotiations for gen. treaty, Paris-Tananarive, 1973; I.L.O. Comm. of Experts on Application of Convens. & Recommendations Gen. Reporter, 1964-; Pres., Malagasy Soc. of Judicial studies; World Assn. of Judges; Am. Soc. of Int. Law. Author of publs. in field. Hons: Off., Ordre Nat. Malagasy; Off., Ordre Nat. du Mérite Francais; Off., Ordre du Croissant Vert des Comores. Address: Supreme Ct., P.O. Box 391, Tananarive, Madagascar. 135.

RAZAFINIPARANY, Andriantefison Honore, b. 19 Feb. 1932. Professor. Educ: Licence es Scis., Univ. Clermont Ferrand, France; Dip. of Geol., ibid; Dr. Nat. Scis., ibid. Appts: Asst. Prof., Geol. Fac. Scis., Tananarive, Madagascar, 1960-63; Geol., Survey, ibid, 1963-64; Dir., Geol. Survey, Madagascar, 1965-74; Prof., Geol. Fac. Scis., Univ. Madagascar, Tananarive, 1971-. Mbrships: Pres., Malagasy Nat. Comm. Geol.; Corres. mbr.; Malagasy Acad. Publs: Etudes des Massifs Granitiques de Meynac et d'Egletons de leurs enclaves, 1960; Constitution et Origine des Principaux types de Charnockites à Madagascar, 1969; Les Charnockites du socle précambrien de Madagascar, 1969 (sci. papers). Address: Fac. des Scis., Univ. de Madagascar, B.P. 906, Tananarive, Madagascar.

RAZIN, Shmuel, b. 1 Feb. 1929. Professor of Microbiology. Educ: M.S., Hebrew Univ., Jerusalem, 1955; Ph.D., ibid, 1958; post-doct. Fellow, Reading Univ., U.K., 1958-59. Appts: Jr. Asst. Prof., Hebrew Univ., 1953-71; Sr. For. Sci. Fellow, Nat. Sci. Fndn., Univ. of Conn., U.S.A., 1964-65; Vis. Sci. Nat. Insts. of Hlth., Bethesda, Md., 1969-70; Chmn., Inst. of Microbio., Hebrew Univ.-Hadassah Med. Schl., Jerusalem, Israel, 1973-. Mbrships: Sec., Israel Microbiol. Soc., 1966-69; Soc. for Gen. Microbio.; Am. Soc. for Microbio.; Israel Biochem. Soc.; Sigma Xi. Contbr. to profl. jrnls. Hons: Abraham Back Award for Disting. Sci. Work, Hebrew Univ.-Hadassah Med. Schl., 1969. Address: c/o Dept. of Clin. Microbiol., The Hebrew Univ.-Hadassah Med. Schl., Jerusalem, Israel.

RAZZAK, Muhammad A., b. 23 Apr. 1928. Physician; Professor. Educ: M.B., B.Ch., Fac. Med., Cairo Univ., U.A.R., 1950; D.M., 1956, ibid; M.D., 1957, ibid; Fellow, Nuclear Med., 1960. Appts: Tutor, Med., Fac. Med., Cairo Univ., U.A.R.; Hd., Unit Med. Rsch., Atomic Energy Estab., ibid; Asst. Prof., Med., Fac. Med., Cairo; Rsch. Assoc., Case W. Reserve Univ. Cleveland, Ohio, U.S.A.; Lectr., Nuclear Med. Inst., Cleveland; Prof., Internal Med., Fac. Med., Cairo Univ.; Expert, Int. Atomic Energy Agcy., Albania. Mbrships: Egyptian Med. Assn.; Soc. Nuclear Med., U.S.A.; Am. Coll. Physns. Author, Textbook of Nuclear Medicine Technology. Recip. Nat. Award Med. Rsch., A.R.E., 1970. Address: 16 El Nil St., Gizah, U.A.R.

READ, Sylvia. Actress; Author; Poet. Educ: Royal Acad. of Dramatic Art, U.K. Appts: Actress, BBC TV & Radio; Actress, playing leading parts for Theatre Roundabout, under auspices of British Coun., The Arts Coun. of Gt. Britain & Scottish Arts Coun., 1964-; Dir. & Script-Writer for Theatre Roundabout. Works: The Poetical Ark (poetry); Travelling Actors (poetry); Burden of Blessing (novel); A Cage of Arms (novel); Harvest (unpubld. play); Ed., Here & Now (4 edits.); Ed., Anthologies. Address: 859 Finchley Rd., London, NW11 8LX, U.K.

READY, William Bernard, b. 16 Sept. 1914. University Librarian & Professor of Bibliography. Educ: B.A., Univ. Wales, U.K., 1937; Dip.Ed., Oxford Univ., ibid, 1946; M.A., Man. Univ., Canada, 1948; M.L.S., Univ. W. Ont., ibid, 1970; Dip. Paleography & Archives. Appts: Lib. Asst., Cardiff Pub. Lib., Wales, U.K., 1933-39; Lectr., Berkeley Univ., Calif., U.S.A., 1950-51; Asst. Dir., Libs. & Lectr., Engl., Sanford Univ., 1951-56; Univ. Libn., Marquette Univ., 1956-66; Univ. Libn. & Prof., Bibliography, McMaster Univ., Hamilton, Ont., Canada, 1966-. Mbrships: Am. Assn. Archivists; Am. Lib. Assn.; Canadian Lib. Assn.; Inst. Profl. Libns. Ont.; Lib. Assn. Gt. Britain; Ont. Coun. Univ. Libns.; Royal Soc. Canada. Publs: The Great Disciple, 1951; The Poor Hater, 1958; The Tolkien Relation, 1965; Necessary Russell, 1969; Notes on The Hobbit and Lord of the Rings, 1971. Hons: $1,000 Short Story Award, Atlantic Monthly, 1948; Hon. Roll of Am. Short Story, 1952; Thomas More Award & Citation, 1960; Clarence Day Award (Libn. of Yr.), Am. Lib. Assn. Address: McMaster Univ. Lib., Hamilton, Ont., Canada.

REAGAN, Marie Adele, b. 26 Apr. 1926. Physician. Educ: B.S., Univ. of Pitts., 1948; M.D., Schl. of Med., ibid, 1953; Harvard Grad. Schl. of Med., 1963. Appts: Sec., Ob.-Gynecol. Dept., St. Francis Gen. Hosp.; Gov.'s Abortion Commn., State of Pa. Mbrships: AMA; Fellow, Am. Coll. of Ob.-Gynecol.; Pa. Med. Soc.; Pitts. Ob.-Gynecol. Soc.; Pitts. Med. Soc.; Cath. Physns. Guild. Address: 220 N. Dithridge St., Pitts., PA 15213, U.S.A. 5, 6.

REAGIN, Ynez Morey (Mrs. Charles E. Reagin), b. 3 Mar. 1913. Graphoanalyst; Educator. Educ: B.S., Colo. State Univ., Ft. Collins, 1934; Grad. courses, var. coils.; Tchng. Cert., Colo. State, 1951; Cert. of Graphoanalyst, Int. Graphoanalyst Soc., 1958; Var. further certs. Appts. incl: Tchr., Engl., Pub. H.S., Canon City, Colo., 1958-59; Instr., Graphoanalysis, pvte. classes, Canon City, 1962-; Guest Instr., var. State Chapts., Int. Graphoanalysis Soc., 1966-72; Instr., psychol., Adult Educ. Prog., Canon City, 1970-; Instr., Graphoanalysis, ibid, 1974-. Mbrships. incl: Int. Graphoanalysis Soc., Inc., 1957-; Charter mbr., Colo. State Chapt., ibid, 1957-; Nat. Fedn., Bus. & Profl. Women's Club; Int. Fedn. Univ. Women, 1957-; AAUW, 1957-; Pres., Canon City Br., ibid, 1968-70. Contbr. to the Jrnl. of Graphoanalysis & The Int. Altrusan. Hons: Pres.'s Merit Award, Int. Graphoanalysis Soc., 1969; 1st place, Altrusa Publicity Award, Dist. 10, 1971-72. Address: 610 Burrage Ave., Canon City, CO 61212, U.S.A. 5, 138.

REBBECK, Denis, b. 22 Jan. 1914. Shipbuilder; Marine Engineer. Educ: B.A., Pembroke Coll., Cambridge, 1932-35; M.A., ibid, 1939; M.A., Dublin, Ireland, 1945; B.Litt., ibid, 1946; M.Sc., Belfast, 1946; Ph.D., ibid, 1950. Appts. incl: Dir., Dpty. Mng. Dir., Mng. Dir., Chmn., Harland & Wolff Ltd., Belfast, 1935-70; Dir., Shipbuilding Corp. Ltd., 1963-73; Colvilles Ltd., 1963-67, Nat. Commercial Bank of Scotland Ltd, 1965-69; Special Cons., Swan Hunter Grp., 1970-; Dir., Royal Bank of Scotland Ltd., 1969-; Chmn., John Kelly Ltd., Belfast, 1969-, Belships Co.

Ltd., London, 1972-, Iron Trades Employers Ins. Assn. Ltd., 1972-. Mbrships. incl: Pres., Shipbldg. Employers Fedn., 1962-63; Gen. Comm., Lloyd's Register of Shipping, 1962-; Belfast Harbour Commnr., 1962-; Coun., Royal Instn. of Naval Archts., 1964-72; Pres., Glencraig Curative Schls. for Mentally Handicapped Children, 1953-70. Contbr. to var. jrnls. Num. hons. incl: CBE, 1952; JP, Belfast, 1949; DL, ibid, 1960; Akroyd Stuart Award, Inst. of Marine Engrs., London, 1943. Address: The White House, Craigavad, Co. Down, N. Ireland.

REBIN, Norman Kenneth, b. 20 Apr. 1938. Orator; Educator; Commentator. Educ: Master. Soc. Sci., Univ. of Stockholm, Sweden; B.A., Univ. of Sask., Canada; Grad., For. Serv. Trng. Prog. & Career Assignment Prog., Govt. of Canada; Grad., Reisch Am. Schl. of Auctioneering. Appts: Sprvsr., Adult Educ., Govt. of Sask.; Off. i/c Immigration, Canadian Diplomatic Serv., New Delhi, India; Aide to Citizenship Min., Govt. of Canada; Vis. Prof., Oral Communication & Grp. Dynamics, Univ. of St. Paul, Ottawa, Canada; Serv. 3 Fed. Task Forces. Mbrships. incl: Canadian Deleg., & Acting Chmn., Exec. Comm., World Fedn. UN Assns., Luxembourg; Co-Chmn., Int. Twinning Prog.; Exec., Sask. Coun. Pub. Affairs & Canadian Inst. Int. Affairs. Publs: Forgotten Christmas, 1971; Kimmy the Dinghy, 1973. Sev. TV & radio prods. Manuals, tapes & films on communicative arts. Recip., JC Citizen Award, 1973. Address: 7 Pilgrim St., Aylmer E., Quebec, J9H 3T1, Canada. 57.

RECHNITZ, (The Rev. Canon) Wilhelm Lawrence, b. 24 Oct. 1899. Priest, Church of England (retd.); Scholar; Poet. Educ: Friedrich-Wilhelms Univ., Berlin, Germany; Dr. phil., Berlin, 1924; State exam., ibid, 1925; Higher Libn.'s Dip., Leipzig, 1930. Appts. incl: Headmaster, St. Paul's Mission Schl., Moa Island, 1948-50; Tutor, St. Francis Coll., Brisbane, 1953, & Ridley Coll., Melbourne, Australia, 1953; Chap., Edward River Mission, 1954-56; Priest, St. Paul's Mission, Moa Island, 1956; Rector, Murray Island, 1956-60, & Yorke Island, 1960-66; Asst. Priest, Badu Island, 1966-71; Rector, Yam Island, 1971-72; Retd., 1972. Mbrships: Fndr. & Literary Sec., later V.P., St. Paul's Coll. Literary Soc. (Pauline Group), 1946-; Int. Schutzverband deutscher Schriftsteller, Zurich, 1955-. Author of books & articles. Hon: Canon of All Souls' & St. Bartholomew's Cathedral, Thursday Island, 1969. Address: St. John's Home, Exmouth St., Toowong, Brisbane, Australia 4066. 43.

REDFORD, Donald Kirkman, b. 18 Feb. 1919. Barrister-at-Law. Educ: L.L.B., King's Coll., Univ. of London. Appts: Practice at bar; Joined, Manchester Ship Canal Co., 1946; Appointed to Bd., ibid, 1966; Mng. Dir., 1970; Chmn. & Mng. Dir., 1972, Chmn., Nat. Assn. of Port Employers, 1972-; Deputy Chmn., British Ports Assn., 1973-. Mbrships: St. James's Club, Manchester; Royal Birkdale Golf Club. Address: The Manchester Ship Canal Co., Ship Canal House, King St., Manchester M2 4WX, U.K. 1.

REDMAN, J(ohn) James, b. 19 May 1919. Auditor; Teacher; Coach. Appts. incl: Tchr. & Prin., High Schls., Ohio, 1943-50; Sec. to Pres., Albert Radmon & Assocs., cons. engrs., 1950-56; Prof., Bliss Coll., 1955-; Hd. Basketball Coach, ibid, 1956-, Athletic Dir., 1961-; Dpty. Auditor, Franklin Co. Auditors Off.; Tabulator, Franklin Co. Bd. of Elections. Mbrships. incl: Hon. Pres., Buckeye Intercoll. Conf.; Pres., Ohio Poetry Day Assn.; AAUP; Ohio Bus. Tchrs. Assn.; Advsr., Phi Kappa

Gamma Frat.; Former Orgr., Gra-Y Clubs, Franklin Co.; Past Pres., Verse Writers Guild of Ohio & Columbus Br., Ohio Poetry Soc.; Former State V.P., Ohio Poetry Soc.; Lukemia Soc. of Am., Franklin Co. Chapt. Ed., Ohio Varsity Sports Mag., Youth & Poetry Columns; Contbr. to lit. publs. Hons. incl: Serv. Award Winner, Columbus Br. of The Ohio Poetry Soc.; Five-time schlrship. winner; Nationally publd. poet with All-Am. rating; Citations from U.S. Pres., Gov. of State, Mayor of Columbus, etc. Address: 1403 W. Third Av., Apt. A, Columbus, OH 43212, U.S.A. 9, 57, 126, 129, 130, 139.

REDMON, Martha A., b. 16 Nov. 1902. Librarian. Educ: B.A., Eastern Ky. Univ.; Univ. ot Ky. Appts: Ky. Pub. Schls., 1928-46; Ctrl. H.S., Lima, Ohio, 1946-51; Ill. Pub. Schls., 1951-69. Mbrships: Delta Kappa Gamma; Ill. Lib. Assn.; Ill. Educ. Assn.; Pres., Northern Ky. Lib. Dept., Ky. Educ. Assn.; Daughters of the Am. Revolution; Colonial Dames of the XVII Century. Contbr. of story & articles to mags. & jrnls. Address: 900 N. Lake Shore Dr., Apt. 1001, Chgo., IL 60611, U.S.A. 42.

REDMONT, Bernard Sidney, b. 8 Nov. 1918. Foreign Correspondent; Broadcaster. Educ: B.A., CCNY, 1938; M.S., Grad. Schl. of Jrnlsm., Columbia Univ., 1939. Appts. incl: Staff Corres., Bur. Chief, U.S. News & World Report, Buenos Aires & Paris, 1946-51; Columnist, Continental Daily Mail, Paris, France, 1951-53; Chief Corres., Engl.-lang. World News Serv., Agence France-Presse, Paris, 1953-65; European Corres., Paris News Bur. Chief, Westinghouse Broadcasting Co. (Grp. W. News), Paris, 1962-; makes frequent guest appearances on BBC TV & radio & var. French radio & TV stns.; Lectr. on For. Affairs, Mbrships: Sec.-Gen., Anglo-Am. Press Assn. of Paris, 1974-; Overseas Press Club of Am., N.Y.; Nat. Press Club, Wash. D.C. Contbr. num. articles to mags. & documentary series to radio on France, Middle E., Africa & Latin Am. Hons. incl: Best Radio Reporting from Abroad, Overseas Press Club, for Vietnam Peace Story, 1968-69, & for Oct. 1973 Middle E. War Coverage, 1973-74; Chevalier, Legion of Hon., France, 1974. Address: 61 Ave. du Gen. Leclerc, 92100 Boulogne-sur-Seine, France. 2.

REDPATH, Norma, b. 20 Nov. 1928. Sculptor. Commissioned works in Baillieu Lib., Univ. of Melbourne; Reserve Bank of Australia, Adelaide & Brisbane; Vic. Coll. Pharmacy, Melbourne; Arts Ctr. of Vic. Exhibs. incl: Grp. of Four, Schl. of Archt., Univ. of Melbourne, 1953-55; Olympic Games Exhib., Melbourne, 1956; Mildura Open Air Sculputre Exhib., 1961, '64; Young Painters & Sculptors, Tokyo, 1965 Australian Pavilion, Montreal, Expo' 67 Solo exhibs: Gallery A, Melbourne, 1963; Rudy Komon Gall., Sydney, 1970. Work in following collects: Nat. Gall. of Vic., Melbourne; Art Gall. of N.S.W.; W.A. Art Gall., Perth; Newcastle City Gall., N.S.W. Featured in num. art publs. Hons. incl: O.B.E., 1970; Meyer Fndn. Grant, 1970; Fellowship, Creative Arts, Australian Nat. Univ., 1972. Address: c/o Abbott, Stillman & Wilson, 406 Lonsdale St., Melbourne, Australia 3000. 23, 128, 133.

REDPATH, (Robert) Theodore (Holmes), b. 17 Aug. 1913. University Teacher; Writer. Educ: B.A., St. Catharine's Coll., Cambridge, U.K., M.A., St. John's Coll., ibid, 1939; Ph.D., ibid, 1940; Called to Bar, Middle-Temple, 1948. Appts: Fellow, Asst. Lectr., Engl., Trinity Coll., Cambridge, 1950; Asst. Lectr., Univ. of Cambridge, 1951; Univ. Lectr., ibid, 1954; Tutor, Trinity Coll., ibid, 1960-70; Sr. Lectr., ibid, 1970-. Mbrships: Cambridge Union Soc.;

Steward, ibid, 1960-70; Univ. Pitt Club; Hon. Treas., ibid, 1963-69; Pres., ibid, 1969-; Travellers' Club (Hon.); Société Européenne de Culture; Aristotelian Soc. Publs: Ed., The Songs & Sonets of John Donne, 1956; Tolstoy, 1960; Co-Ed., Shakespeare's Sonnets, 1964; Romantic Perspectives, 1964; Sixty-five Sonnets of Shakespeare, 1967; The Young Romantics & Critical Opinion, 1807-24, 1973. Recip., Charles Oldham Shakespeare Schlrship., Univ. of Cambridge, 1934. Address: 49 Madingley Rd., Cambridge, U.K. 3.

REED, Clyde T., b. 12 Sept. 1891. Educator. Educ: A.B., Campbell Coll., Holton, Kan., 1914; Grad. work, Chem., Univ. of Chgo., 1916; M.A., Wash. Coll, 1918; Grad. work, Educl. Admin., Univ. of Tex.; M.S., Cornell Univ., 1937. Appts. incl: Prof., Maths. & Sci., Athletics Coach, Graceland Coll., Lamoni, Iowa, 1914; Prof., Chem. & Bio., Parsons Coll. Fairfield, ibid, 1916; Prof., Chem., Wash. Coll., Chestertown, Md., 1918; Robert Coll., Turkey, 1918; Hd. of Sci. Dept., Tex. Woman's Coll., 1923; Hd., Dept. of Bio., Tex. Coll. of Arts & Inds., 1927-38; Prof., Hd., Dept. of Bio., Univ. of Tampa, Fla., 1942-61; Retd., 1962; Dir., Mus. of Sci. & Natural Hist., ibid, 1962-. Mbrships. incl: Life, NEA; Fellow, AAAS (Past Coun. Mbr.); Hon. Life Fellow & twice Pres., Tex. Acad. of Scis.; Hon. Life, Fla. Assn. of Sci. Tchrs. Author of sci. publs. Recip., Gold Medal, Univ. of Tampa, for outstanding contbn. to the Univ. Address: Mus. of Sci. & Natural Hist., 1101 E. River Cove, Tampa, FL 33604, U.S.A. 14, 15, 28.

REED, Dallas John, b. 23 May 1929. Sociologist; University Professor. Educ: B.A., Univ. of Mont., Missoula, 1951; M.A., 1955; Ph.D., Univ. of Minn., Mpls., 1968; Rutgers Univ., N.J., 1973. Mbrships: Instr., Univ. of Mont., 1959-61; Instr.-Assoc. Prof., Ida. State Univ., 1961-70; Chmn., Dept. of Sociol., ibid, 1962-70; Dir., Rsch. & Educ. Computer Ctr., 1965-67; Cons., local, state & fed, activities; Assoc. Prof., Univ. of Nev., Las Vegas, 1970-. Mbrships. incl: Gov's. State Advsry. Bd. of Alcohol & Drug Abuse; Exec. Comm., Southern Nev. Drug. Abuse Coun., 1973-; Profl. Dev. Comm., Western Corrections Assn., 1965-70; Gen. Chmn., WICHE Soc. Serv. Insts., 1965-66; Pi Gamma Mu; Alpha Kappa Delta. Publs. incl: Cons. Reviewer, Choice: Books for College Libraries, 1966-; A Survey of Correctional Manpower in Idaho, 1969. Address: Dept. of Sociol., Univ. of Nev., Las Vegas, NV 89154, U.S.A. 9, 14, 120, 130.

REED, (E.) Hal, b. 22 Feb. 1921. Artist; Sculptor; Writer; Teacher. Educ: Trade Tech. Coll., L.A.; Art Ctr. Schl. Design; Art League, San Fran.; individual tuition. Appts. incl: Fndr., Art League, L.A., 1965 & Instr., color, composition, anatomy, perspective & advanced painting, ibid, 1965-; Juror, Calif. State Fair, Sacramento, 1968 & L A. Annual All City Art Festival, 1970. Work in pub. & pvte. collect. inclng. State of Calif. Gov.'s Off., Sacramento & L.A. City Hall Permenent Collect Sculpture Commns. incl: Robert Fulton Medal for Nat. Commemorative Soc. & Eleanor Roosevelt Medal for Soc. Commemorative de Femmes Celebres. Exhibs. incl: Nat. Open, Miniature Painters, Sculptors & Gravers Soc., Wash. DC, 1972; Nat. Open, Miniature Art Soc., N.J., 1972; Am. Artist's Profl. League, N.Y., 1972. Mbrships. incl: Fellow, Am. Artist's Profl. League & Am. Inst. Fine Arts, 1967. Publs: How To Compose Pictures 7 Achieve Color Harmony, 1969-72. Hons. incl: Best in Sculpture & Col. King Award, Miniature Painters & Sculptors Soc., Wash. DC, 1972; Best in Sculpture & Purchase Award, Nat.

Open, Miniature Art Soc., N.J., 1972; WWII Battle & Bronze Stars for Disting. serv. in Army Engrs. Address: 18237 Jovan St., Reseda, CA 91335, U.S.A. 37.

REED, Frank Fremont, II, b. 15 June 1928. Lawyer. Educ: A.B., Univ. of Mich., Ann Arbor, 1952; J.D., 1957. Appts: Off. of Post Judge Advocate, U.S. Army, Ft. Benjamin Harrison, Indpls., 1952-54; Admitted, Ill. Bar, 1958; U.S. Dist. Ct., 1958; U.S. Patent Off., 1960; Assoc., Byron Hume, Groen & Clement, 1958-61; Marks & Clerk, 1961-63; Own Prac., Chgo., 1963-; Dir., Western Acadia Inc. (Western Felt Works), 1960-; Chmn., Exec. Comm., 1969-71. Mbrships. incl: Dir. & Sec., Chgo. Fndn. for Theater Arts, 1959-64; Am., Ill. Chgo. Bar Assns.; Chgo. & Patent Law Assns.; Chmn., By-Laws Comm., 1962; Am. Judicature Soc.; Phi Alpha Delta; Repub. Precienct Capt., 43rd Ward, Chgo., 1972-; Univ. Club Chgo.; Boy Scouts Am., 1964-70. Ed., Faurot Family Newsletter, 1973-. Contbr., Am. Geneal. Address: 1500 Lake Shore Dr., Chgo., IL 60610, U.S.A. 8.

REED, H. Owen, b. 17 June 1910. Composer; Author; Educator. Educ: Univ. of Mo.; B.M., 1934, M.M., 1936, B.A., 1937, La. State Univ.; Ph.D., Eastman Schl. of Music; Study, var. subjects. w. Howard Hanson, Roy Harris, Aaron Copeland, Leonard Bernstein. Appts: Mich. State Univ., E. Lansing, 1939-; Chmn., Theory & Composition; Acting Hd., Music Dept., 1957-58; Prof., Music, & Chmn., Dept. of Music Composition. Mbrships. incl: Music Tchrs. Nat. Assn.; Past Pres., Mich. Composers Club; ASCAP; Assoc. Mbr., Am. Music Ctr.; Am. Soc. of Univ. Composers; Kappa Sigma; Compositions incl: Choral & orchestral works; Folk operas; Band works; Ballets; Chamber music; Songs. Publs. incl: A Workbook in the Fundementals of Music, 1947; Basic Music Workbook, 1954; Basic Contrapuntal Technique (co-author), 1964; Scoring for Percussion (co-author), 1969. Hons. incl: Guggenheim Fellowship, 1948-49; Res. Fellowship, Huntington Hartford Fndn., Calif., 1960; Res. Fellowship, Helene Wurlitzer Fndn., N.M., 1967; Annual ASCAP Awards. Address: Mich. State Univ., Dept. of Music, E. Lansing, MI 48824, U.S.A. 8, 13, 15, 128, 129, 130, 139.

REED, Kenneth G., b. 17 Dec. 1917. President and Chief Executive Officer of Apexco, Inc. Educ: Grad., Univ. of Tex., 1936; Postgrad., S. Meth. Univ. & Univ. of Alberta, Canada. M. Virginia C. Reed; one daughter, one son. Appts. incl: Dist. Landman & Exec. V.P., Amerada Petroleum Corp., 1948-71; Pres. & Chief Exec. Off., Apexco Inc., Tulsa, Okla., 1971-; Mbr., Bd. of Dirs., Apache Corp., Mpls.; Dir., First Nat. Bank & Trust Co., Tulsa, Okla. Mbr., Southern Hills Country Club & Tulsa Club. Address: Apexco, Inc., P.O. Box 2299, Tulsa, OK 74103, U.S.A.

REED, Philip G., b. 17 Jan. 1908. Illustrator; Wood engraver; Typographer. Educ: Grad., Art Inst. of Chgo., 1930. Appts: Fndr., Dir., Broadside Press, 1930-39; Dir., Monastery Hill Press, 1939-43; Fndr., Printing Off. of Philip Reed, 1946-; Assoc., A. & R. Roe, Printers, St. Joseph, Mich., 1959-73; Art Dir., Cons. Engr. Mag., 1959-73; Fndr., Philip Reed, Printer, 1973-. Mbr., Cliff Dwellers, Chgo., Ill. Book Illustrations incl: Thoreau, The Wild Apple; Dickens, A Christmas Carol; The 7 Voyages of Sinbad the Sailor; Mother Goose & Nursery Rhymes. Hons. incl: 43 awards, printing for commerce (A.I.G.A.), 1939-; 6 awards, Top Honor Books, Chgo. Book Clin. Address: 191 Michigan Ave., Benton Harbor, MI 49022, U.S.A. 8.

REED, Victor, b. 1 Feb. 1926. Teacher. Educ: A.B., Harvard Coll., 1947; A.M., Harvard Univ., 1948; Ph.D., Columbia Univ., 1964. Appts: Lectr. in Engl., CCNY, 1950-55; Lektor, Univ. of Helsinki, 1955-56; Instr. in Engl., Fairleigh Dickinson Univ., 1958-60; Asst. Prof., ibid, 1961-63; Asst. Prof., Lehman Coll., CCNY, 1964-68; Assoc. Prof., ibid, 1969-; Vis. Asst. Prof., Univ. of Mass., 1968. Mbr., MLA. Publs. incl: A Casebook on Shakespeare's Sonnets (co-author), 1964; The Case of Aaron Burr (co-author), 1960. Broadcast, Le roman contemporain aux Etate-Unis, Canadian Broadcasting System. Address: Lehman Coll., Bronx, NY 10468, U.S.A. 13.

REEDIJK, Cornelis, b. 1 Apr. 1921. Librarian. Educ: Grad., State Univ. of Leyden, 1948; Dr.'s degree, 1956. Appts: Staff Mbr., Municipal Lib., Rotterdam, 1945, Keeper, 1953, Chief Libn., 1958; Chief Libn., Royal Lib., The Hague, Netherlands, Dir., State Mus. Meermanno-Westreenianum, The Hague, & Dir., Mus. & Documentation Ctr. for Netherlands Lit., 1962; Chmn., State Advsry. Comm. Lib. Affairs, & Prog. Dev. Grp., Int. Fedn. Lib. Assns. Mbrships: Royal Netherlands Acad. Scis. & Letters; Soc. Netherlands Lit.; Dutch Soc. of Scis. Publs: Poems of Desiderius Erasmus (Ed.), 1956; Das Lebensende des Erasmus, 1958; translation (w. Alfred Kossmann), Alice's Adventures in Wonderland & Through the Looking-Glass. Var. articles, studies & papers. Address: Nieuwe Parklaan 7, The Hague, Netherlands. 43, 100.

REEDY, Ruth (Mrs.), b. 22 July 1915. Librarian. Educ: Northwestern State Univ.; B.A., La. Coll., 1935; B.S.L.S., Univ. of Ill.; Postgrad. study, La. State Univ. Appts: Libn., Rayville H.S., La., 1937-42; Libn., Lake Charles H.S., La., 1942-61; Mats. Ctr. Libn., McNeese State Univ., La., 1961-72; Dir. of Libs., ibid, 1972-. Mbrships: Past Pres., La. Assn. of Schl. Libns.; Past Pres., Lake Charles Tchrs. Assn.; Past Pres., La. Lib. Assn.; Exec. Dir., Nat. Lib. Week, La., 1964; Past Exec. Sec., Lib. Dev. Comm. for La.; ALA; Life, NEA; Southwestern Lib. Assn.; Past Pres., Alpha Phi Chapt., Delta Kappa Gamma. Contbr. to profl. jrnls. Address: 1808 18th St., Lake Charles, LA 70601, U.S.A. 5.

REENPÄÄ, Yrjö, b. 18 July 1894. Professor emeritus. Educ: Dr.med.; Prof., Physiol. Prof., Physiol., Univ. of Helsinki, Finland. Mbrships: Finnish Acad. of Scis.; Heidelberger Akademie der Wissenschaften; Debresen Acad. of Scis.; The Kant-Gesellschaft; Hon. mbr., Physiological Soc. of Germany, 1960, The Scandinavian Physiological Soc., 1965, & Finnish Physiological Soc., 1964; Finnish Physns. Assn. "Duodecim"; Hon. Pres., Finnish Cultural Fndn., 1968. Publs: Allgemeine Sinnesphysiologie; Aufbau der allgemeinen Sinnesphysiologie; Wahrnehmen, Beobachten, Konstituieren; Ueber das Körperseele-Problem, in Neue Anthropologie Bd. V. Hons: Cross of Liberty, 4th Class, 1918, 3rd Class, 1940, 2nd Class, 1944; Cmdr., 1st Class, Order of Finland's White Rose, 1962; Grand Cross, Order of Finland's Lion, 1967; Dr.phil., Univ. of Helsinki. Address: Hietalahdenranta 17 A, 00180 Helsinki 18, Finland.

REES, Albert Lloyd George, b. 15 Jan. 1916. Scientist. Educ: B.Sc., Univ. of Melbourne, 1936; M.Sc., ibid, 1938; D.Sc., 1948; Ph.D., Univ. of London, 1941; Dip., Imperial Coll., 1941. Appts. incl: Rsch. & Dev., Philips Elec. Inds., U.K., 1941-44; Ldr., Chem. Phys. Sect., C'wlth. Sci. & Ind. Rsch. Org., Australia, 1944-58; Asst. Chief, Div. of Ind. Chem., ibid, 1954; Chief, Div. of Chem. Phys.,

1958-; Chmn., Rsch. Labs., 1961-70. Mbrships. incl: Exec. Comm., 1963-73, V.P., 1967-69, Pres., 1969-72, Int. Union of Pure & Applied Chem.; Feloow, 1954, Coun., 1963-68, 68-73, Australian Acad. of Sci.; Fellow, 1948, Coun., 1957-59, Pres., 1967-68, Royal Australian Chem. Inst.; Coun., Inst. of Defence Sci., 1965-71. Publs: Chemistry of the Defect Solid State, 1954, Russian ed., 1956; articles in learned jrnls. Hons. incl: Rennie Medal, 1946; H.G. Smith Medal, 1951; Leighton Mem. Medal, 1970. Address: 9 Ajana St., N. Balwyn, Victoria, Australia 3104. 23, 34, 128.

REES, Mina (Mrs. Leopold Brahdy), b. 2 Aug. 1902. Mathematician; Educational Administrator. Educ: A.B., Hunter Coll., 1923; A.M., Columbia Univ., 1925; Ph.D., Univ. of Chgo., 1931. Appts. incl: Instr.-Prof. & Chairman Fac., Hunter Coll., 1926-43, '53-61; Tech. Aide & Exec. Asst. to Chief, Applied Maths. Panel, OSRD, 1943-46; Hd., Maths. Br.-Dir., Math. Scis. Div., Off. Naval Rsch., 1946-53; Prof. & Dean of Grad. Studies-Provost Grad. Div., CUNY, 1961-69; Pres., Grad. Schl. & Univ. Ctr., ibid, 1969-72; Pres. Emeritus, ibid, 1972-. Mbrships. incl: var. offs., AAAS & Coun. Grad. Schls; Am. Math. Soc.; Math. Assn. of Am.; Comm. on Profl. Scientific & Tech. Manpower, U.S. Dept. of Labor; Bd. Dirs., Assocd. Hosp. Serv. of N.Y.; Senator at Large, Phi Beta Kappa; Hon. Advsr., British Univs. Summer Schls. Contbr. num. articles in field. Recip. of num. awards & hon. degrees. Address: Grad. Schl. & Univ. Ctr., CUNY, 33 W. 42 St., N.Y., NY 10036, U.S.A. 2, 5, 6, 14.

REES, William Linford Llewelyn, b. 24 Oct. 1914. Professor of Psychiatry. Educ: Univ. Coll., Cardiff, U.K.; Welsh Nat. Schl. of Med., ibid; Inst. of Psych., Univ. of London. Appts: Physician-in-Charge, Dept. of Psychol. Med., St. Bartholomew's Hosp., 1959-; Prof. of Psych., St. Bartholomew's Hosp. Med. Coll., Univ. of London, 1966-. Mbrships: Treas., World Psychiatric Assn.; Sr. V.P., Royal Coll. of Psychs; Fndn. Fellow, ibid, 1971; Pres., Soc. of Psychosomatic Rsch.; Pres., Sect. of Psych., Royal Soc. of Med.; Chmn., Mental Hlth. Grp., British Med. Assn; Athenaeum; Disting. Fellow, Am. Psychiatric Assn.; Hon. Mbr., Swedish Psychiatric Assn & Soc. of Biol. Psych.; Hon. Fellow, Eastern Psycho-analytic Assn., 1973 & All Union Soc. for Neurol. & Psych., USSR, 1972. Publs: A Short Textbook of Psychiatry; over 120 contbns. to profl. jrnls. Hons. incl: Freeman, City of London; Alfred Sheen Prize, 1969; David Hepburn Medal in Anatomy; Pirogov Medal, Acad. Med. Sci., Moscow, 1968. Address: Dept. of Psychological Medicine, St. Bartholomew's Hospital, London EC1A 7BE, U.K.

REES-MOGG, William, b. 14 July 1928. Journalist. Educ: Balliol Coll., Oxford, U.K. Appts: Chief Ldr. Writer, Fin. Times, 1955-60; Asst. Ed., 1957-60; City Ed., Sunday Times, 1960-61; Pol. & Econ. Ed., 1961-63; Dpty. Ed., 1964-67; Ed., The Times, 1967-. Mbr., Garrick Club. Address: c/o The Times, Printing House Sq., London, EC4, U.K. 1.

REEVES, Elton Traver, b. 23 Sept. 1912. Professor of Management. Educ: B.S., Univ. of Idaho; M.A., Univ. of Wash.; 2 yrs. Grad. Work, La. State Univ. Appts: Tchr., Pub. Schls., 11 yrs.; 27 yrs. Experience in 5 Cos. in Indl. Rels. Trng. & Mgmt. Dev.; Asst. Prof., Univ. of Wis., Ext., 1969-72; Assoc. Prof., ibid, 1972-. Mbrships: Am. Soc. for Personnel Admin.; Smithsonian Assocs.; Club Int., Chgo. Publs: Management Development for the Line Manager, 1969; The Dynamics of Group

Behavior, 1970; So You Want to be a Supervisor, 1971; So You Want to be a Manager, 1971; So You Want to be an Executive, 1971; How to Get Along with Almost Everybody, 1973. Address: 432 N. Lake St., Room 321, Madison, WI 53706, U.S.A. 8, 30, 57.

REEVES, Emma Barrett (Mrs. Jonathan Floyd), b. 17 Nov. 1901. Educator. Educ: B.A., Hardin Simmons Univ., Abilene, Tex., 1924; M.A., Tex. Technol. Coll., Lubbock, 1949; Leland Stanford Jr. Univ., Palo Alto, Calif., 1927. Appts: H.S. Tchr., 1923-24, 24, 25; Tchr., Engl., Tex. Technol. Coll., 1949-66; Retd. Mbrships. incl: Sigma Tau Delta; Recording Sec., Tech. Chapt., AAUP, 1965; Delta Kappa Gamma; AAUW; State Regent, Am. Soc. Magna Charta Dames, 1974-75; Chap., E. Tex. Colony, ibid, 1970-72; State Chap., Am. Soc. Colonial Dames, 1970-72; Org. Sec., 1972-74; DAR; State Recording Sec., Tex. State Geneal. Soc., 1973-75. Publs. incl: Kehey Clansmen & Their Kin, Slay, Summerall, Smith; A Few Barrett Kin; Smith Studies: Tennessee to Texas. Recip., Award, Tex. State Soc., Colonial Dames, 1970. Address: 1620 Redbud St., Nacogdoches, TX 75961, U.S.A. 125.

REFSUM, Erling, b. 17 June 1902. Chief Public Health Physician. Educ: M.D., Univ. of Oslo, Norway, 1927. Appts: Asst., Norwegian Univ. Clinics & Vardaasen Sanatorium; First Asst., Glittre State Tuberculosis Hosp.; Chief Physn. & Dir., ibid; Sr. Med. Off., Oslo Pub. Hlth. Serv., 1946-72; Chief Med. Off., Scandinavian Med. Ctr., Seoul, Korea, 1962-63; Edit. Bd., Acta Tuberculosis Scandinavica. Pres., Norwegian Scientific Tuberculosis Soc., 1953-55. Publs: Thoracoplasty in the Treatment of Cavernous Tuberculosis of the Lung; Extrapleural Pneumothorax in the Treatment of Cavernous Tuberculosis of the Lung; Various studies of tuberculosis morbidity in Oslo, Norway, and Seoul, Korea. Hons: Dr.Med., Univ. of Oslo, 1951; Kt. First Class, Order of Vasa; Cmdr., Order of Civil Merit (S. Korea). Address: Suhmsgate 20 B, Oslo 3, Norway. 43, 134.

REFSUM, Helge, b. 15 Feb. 1897. High Court Judge. Educ: Cand. jur., Oslo Univ., Norway, 1921. Appts: Barrister, 1921; Sec., Dept. of Soc. Affairs, 1921-25; Dpty. Commnr., Police, 1926-39; State Atty for Nordland, 1939-40; State Atty., Möre & Romsdal & Sogn & Fjordane, 1945-50; Judge, Gulating Ct. of Appeal, Bergen, 1950-67; 1st Dpty. Mbr., Nobel Comm. of the Norwegian Storting, 1953-66; Elected Mbr., ibid, 1966-72; Trustee, Nobel Fndn., 1968-73. Mbrships. incl: Hon., Assn. for Local Hist. for Co. of Romerike; Corres., Royal Gustav Adolfs Acad. Contbr. to var. publs. Hons. incl: Plaque, Norwegian Ski Club, 1967; Cndr., Order of the Falcon, I, 1971; Medal La productividad agricola al servicio de Mexico—Trigos Mexicanos para el mundo. Address: Vilhelm Bjerknesvei 70, 5030 Landås, Bergen, Norway. 134.

REFSUM, Sigvald, b. 8 May 1907. Professor; Physician. Educ: M.D., Univ. of Oslo, 1932; Dr. Med., ibid, 1946. Appts: Prof., Neurol., Univ. of Bergen, 1952-54 & Univ. of Oslo, 1954-; Vis. Prof., Univ. of Ill., Chgo., U.S.A., 1949, Univ. of Minn., Mpls., 1950 & 64; Univ. of Calif., San Fran., 951-52, Univ. Ill.-Presby.-St. Luke's Hosp., Chgo., 1969; Vis. Sci., Nat. Insts. of Hlth. Bethesda, Md., 1960; Vis. Prof. & Tech. Advsr., Norwegian Agcy. Int. Dev., Thailand, 1966-67; currently Physn.-in-Chief, Neurol. Dept., Rikshospitalet, Oslo. Mbrships: Pres., Norwegian Acad. of Sci.

& Letters, 1956; Pres. & V.P., 1970-75; Hon., Am. Acad. of Neurol. Am. Neurol. Assn., Assn. of British Neurols. Deutsche Gesellschaft für Neurol. Norsk Neurologisk Forening, Soc. Ital. di Neuro., Svenska Neurologsällskapet (Sweden), Soc. Peruana Psiquat. Neurol. Neurocir., & Soc. Neurol., Cordoba, Argentina; Steering Comm., World Fedn. of Neurol. Pres., 1973-; Hon., Spanish & French Neurol. Socs. Publs: Heredopathia actactia polyneuritiformis (thesis, describing new disease later called Refsum's disease), 1946; Genetic Aspects of Neurology, 1955, 3rd edn., 1971; Clinical Examination of the Nervous System, in 12th edn. On Edito. Bd., Handbook of Clinical Neurology & sev. neurol. jrnls. Hons: Monrad-Krohn's Prize for Neurol. Rsch., 1948; Kt., 1st Class, Royal Order St. Olav. Address: c/o Rikshospitalet, Oslo 1, Norway. 43, 50, 134.

REGAN, Edward J., b. 14 July 1919. Corporate Director of News Services. Educ: Marquette Univ.; B.S., B.A., Wash. Univ., 1948; Grad. Schl. ibid. Appts: Asst. Paymaster, Fruco Construction Co., St. Louis, Mo., 1940-41; USAF, 1943-45; Chief Copy Ed., St. Louis Globe-Democrat, 1946-56; Supvsr. of Community Rels., McDonnell Aircraft Corp., 1956-67; Mgr., News Servs., McDonnell Douglas Corp., 1967-73; Corporate Dir. of News Servs., ibid, 1973-. Mbrships: Chmn., Dev. & P.R. Coun. & Mbr., Athletic Advsry. Bd., St. Louis Univ.; Past Mbr., P.R. Comm., St. Louis Archdiocean Schls.; P.R. Soc. of Am.; Aviation/Space Writers Assn.; St. Louis, Community Chmbrs. of Comm.; 4th Deg., Kts. of Columbus; Nat. Press Club; Aviation Club. Address: 13224 Heirloom Ct., Creve Coeur, MO 63141, U.S.A. 8, 24.

REGESTER, Robert Thomas, b. 15 June 1903. Hydraulic & Sanitary Consultant. Educ: Grad., Balt. Polytech. Inst., U.S.A., 1921; B.E., Johns Hopkins Univ., 1925. Appts: Design Engr., sewerage & treatment works, serving cities of Balt., Columbus, Ohio & others, inclng. Cleveland rate studies & Wash. Suburban Sanitation Comm.; Advsry. Engr., Balt. Co. & City to study jt. sewerage problems; Planned water supply & other facilities at many mil. posts; Expert Cons., flood pumping problems, U.S. Army Engrs.; Approved drainage structures, N.J. & Ohio turnpikes; Hydraulic & Sanitary Cons., municipal water & sewerage works. Mbrships: Past Pres., Ctrl. Ohio Sect.; ASCE. ACEC; AWWA (life mbr.); APWA; TBP; USNI; Registered profl. engr., 13 states. Recip. Rudolph Hering Medal, ASCE, 1942. Address: Rte. 3, Box 301, Edgewater, MD 21037, U.S.A. 6, 16.

REGGIO, Vito Anthony, b. 17 Dec. 1929. Management Consultant. Educ: Grad. study, Middlebury Coll., 1948; B.S., Purdue Univ., 1952; Exchange Fellowship, Univs. of Ala., Tenn. & Ky., 1952-53. Appts: incl: Jr. Engr., Rochester Gas & Elec. Co., 1950; Designer-Draftsman, Globe Construction Co., 1951; Rsch. Analyst, Dept. of Revenue, Commonwealth of Ky., 1952; Adjutant Gen. Corps., U.S. Army, 1953-55; Wage & Salary Admin. Specialist, Off. Indl. Rels., U.S. Navy, 1955-56; Assoc. Prin., Bus. Rsch. Corp., 1956-60; Dir., Org. & Personnel Mgmt. Cons. Dept., Ebasco Servs. Inc., 1960-; invited Speaker & Lectr., to profl. socs. num. occasions. Mbrships: Western Soc. of Engrs.; Am. Mgmt. Assn.; Am. Compensation Assn.; Indl. Rels. Assn. of Chgo.; Am. Soc. for Personnel Admin.; Nat. Soccer Coaches Assn. cf Am. Co-fndr., Midwestern Collegiate Soccer Conf., 1st Sec.-Treas., Publs: rsch. results & num. contbns. in profl. jrnls. Hons. incl: sev. Schlrships & Fellowships. Address: 441 S. 6th Ave., La Grange, IL 60525, U.S.A. 8, 16.

REGO, Raul, b. 15 Apr. 1913. Teacher; Journalist. Educ: Sem., Viana do Castelo, Portugal; Orly, France. Appts. incl: Liceum Tchr. until 1940; Sub-Ed., Jornal do Comércio, 1940-71; Translator at Reuters until 1961; Sub-Ed., Diário de Lisboa, 1961-71; Dir. pol. evening newspaper, Republica, Lisboa, Portugal, 1972-; Candidate, Democratic Opposition in Deputies elections, Portugal, 1965, 1969 & Poo. prisoner sev. occasions. Publs. incl: Duas Cartes Inédites De Alexandre Herculano, 1953; Christáos Novos E Christáos Velhos Em Portugal, 1956, 2nd edit. 1973; Monografia De S. Jośe De Godim, 1961; Horizontes Fechados, 1969, 2nd edit., 1970; Os Politicos E O Poder Económico, 1969; O Ultimo Regimento Da Inquisicáo De Portugal, 1971; Continuidade, 1973. Mbrships: Sindicato Nat. dos Jrnlst.; Casa da Imprensa, Pres., 1965, 1966. Address: Rua Conde de Ficalho, 24, Lisbon, 5, Portugal.

REGULINSKI, Judy Peyer, b. 4 Apr. 1946. Data Processor. Educ: B.A., Queens Coll., CUNY; M.A., ibid; M.B.A., Baruch Coll., ibid to be completed 1975. Appts: Systems analyst/programmer, RCA Info. Systems, N.Y.C., 1960-70; Sr. systems analyst, Hostos Community Coll., N.Y.C., 1970-72; Data Processing Trng. Mgr., Abraham & Straus, N.Y.C., 1972-. Mbrships: Math. Assn. of Am., 1967-; Ambulance attendant, Flushing Community Volunteer Ambulance Corps, 1968-73. Address: 12 Long Hill Rd., Smithtown, NY 11787, U.S.A. 5.

REHAK, James Richard, b. 2 Jan. 1938. Orthodontist. Educ: B.S., Univ. of Ill., 1966-68; Orthodontic Cons., Dept. of Operative Dentistry. Mbrships: Fellow, Royal Soc. Hlth.; Am. Assn. of Orthodontists; Ill. State Assn. of Orthodontists; Chgo. Ill. & Am. Dental Assns.; Omicron Kappa Upsilon. Publs: Resection of The Inferior Alveolar Nerve in the Albino Rat, Jrnl. Dental Rsch., 1963; Corrective Orthodontics, Dental Clins. of N. Am., 1969. Recip. of Stanley D. Tylman Award for Oral Reconstruction, 1962. Address: 1465 Michele Dr., Palatine, 1L 60067, U.S.A. 8, 57.

ŘEHÁK, Svatopluk, b. 20 Jan. 1926. Professor. Educ: M.D., Charles Univ. Med. Schl., Hradec Králové, Czechoslavakia, 1951; Ph.D., 1958; D.Sc., 1964. Appts: Staff, Charles Univ. Dept. of Ophthalmol., Hradec Králové, 1951-; Sr. Lectr., ibid, 1952, Assoc. Prof., 1960; Prof., Ophthalmol., 1967; Hd., Univ. Eye Dept., 1970; Dean, Med. Fac., 1963-68. Mbrships: Advsry. Bd., Univ. of Edusstion, 1963-67; Regional Expert for Ophthalmol., 1957-58, 1972-; Pres., Comm. for awarding D.Sc. for Ophthalmol., 1972, V.P., Czech Ophthalmol. Soc., 1973-. Author of over 120 sci. papers about exptl. & clin. problems of glousoma. Hons: Deyl's Prize for rsch. in ophthalmol., 1961; Mem. Medal, Charles Univ., Prague, 1965; Hus's Mem. Medal, 1965; State Prize for Excellent Work, 1967; Mem. Medal, Med. Fac., Hradec Králové, 1970. Address: Univ. Eye Dept., 50036 Hradec Králové, Czechoslovakia.

REHKOPF, Charles Frederick, b. 24 Dec. 1908. Clergyman; Church Executive. Educ: B.S., Washburn Coll., Topeka, Kan., 1932; Episc. Theol. Schl., Cambridge, Mass., 1935. Appts: Civil Engr., Kan. Engrng. Co., Topeka, 1927-29; Rector, Trinity Episc. Ch., El Dorado, Kan., 1935-44 & St. John's Episc. Ch., St. Louis, 1944-52; Archdeacon, Exec. Sec., Dir. of Admin., Archivist & Historiographer, Ecumenical Off., Diocese of Mo., 1953-. Mbrships: Ed., Historiog. Newsletter, Ch. Histl. Soc.; Soc. Am. Archivists; Press Club of Gtr. St.

Louis; Fndr., Conf. of Diocesan Execs. Author of Missouri's Episcopal Church (chapts. in Bulletin of Mo. Histl. Soc.). Hons: Exec. of Yr., Conf. of Diocesan Execs., 1971; Ecumenical Citation, Metropolitan Ch. of Fedn., 1966. Address: 1210 Locust St., St. Louis, MO 63103, U.S.A. 8.

REHNBERG, (John) Bertil (Sanne), b. 5 July 1917. University Lecturer. Educ: B.A., Uppsala, Sweden, 1939; D.D., 1966; B.D., Lund , 1944; Lic. Divinity, 1952; Ordained, 1966. Appts: Asst., Ch. Hist. Archives, Lund Univ., 1949; Tchr., Ystad & Malmö, 1955-58; Sr. Master, Sec. Grammar Schl., Umeå, 1958 & Malmö, 1960; Lectr., Ch. Hist., Uppsala Univ., 1966 & Lund Univ., 1967. Publs; The Ecclesiastical Estate & the Religious Debate 1786-1800, 1966; contbr. to profl. publs. Address: Ernst Ahlgrensgatan 3 B, 217 59 Malmö, Sweden. 134.

REIBLICH, G. Kenneth, b. 4 May 1905. Educator. Educ: B.A., Johns Hopkins Univ., 1925; Ph.D. (Pol. Sci.J, 1928; J.D., N.Y. Univ., 1929; LL.M., Columoia Univ., 1937. Appts. incl: Prof. of Law, Univ. of Md., 1930-44; 1949-63; Atty., Consolidated G.E.L. & P. Co., Balt., 1944-49; Cons., ibid 1949-55; Bd. of Dirs., Safe Harbor Water & Power Co., 1949-55; Mbr. of Bd., Patuxent Inst., Md., 1954-63; Prof. of Law, Univ. of Ariz., 1963-; Mbr. of N.Y. Bar, 1930. Md., 1935; Ariz., 1968; Supreme Ct. of U.S., 1952. Mbrships. incl: Am. Bar. Assm.; Am. Law Inst. Publs. incl: A Study of Judicial Administration in Maryland, 1929; Cons. & Advsr. to West's Md. Law Ency. (25 vols., 1960-62); Annual Summary of Terms of U.S. Supreme Ct., 1953-. Recip. of fellowships & awards. Address: 4661 E. Don Jose Dr., Tucson, AZ 85718, U.S.A. 6, 9, 126.

REICH, Barbara Held (Mrs. Robert E. Reich), Real Estate Broker; Building Restorer. Educ: Pvte. study in Voice, Wash. DC & N.Y., 1940-45; Georgetown Univ., 1943-44; Grad., Wash. Coll. of Music, 1944. Appts. incl: Asst. Dir., Luth. Innermission Soc., N.Y. for United Luth. Ch. of Am., 1945-46; Dir., Choir, Georgetown Luth. Ch., 1946-64; Pres., Barbara Held Inc. (restoration & preservation of old bldgs.), 1955-. Mbrships: Wash. Bd. of Realtors; Assoc., Smithsonian Inst.; Capital Hill Restoration Soc.; Victorian Soc.; English Speaking Union; Aux. Bd., Episc. Home for Boys; Nat. Trust for Preservation of Historic Houses. Hons: Award winner w. husband for restoration of residential & commercial bldgs., Capital Hill Restoration Soc. Address: Barbara Held Inc., 222 7th St. S.E., Wash. DC 20003, U.S.A. 5.

REICHAW, Meir, (formerly Marian Reichbach), b. 20 Dec. 1923. Mathematician. Educ: Univ. of Wroclaw, Poland, 1946-50; M.Sc., ibid, 1950; Ph.D., 1956. Appts: Dpty. Asst. & Asst., Dept. of Maths., Polytechnic of Wroclaw, 1948-51; Sr. Asst., ibid , 1951-53; Adjunct, 1953-57; Lectr. & Sr. Lectr., Technion, Israel Inst. of Technol., Haifa, Israel, 1957-63; Assoc. Prof., ibid, 1963-69; Prof., 1969-. Mbrships: Israel Math. Union; Am. Math. Soc. Contbr. of about 30 papers to var. math. jrnls., inclng: Fundamenta Mathematicae; Pacific Jrnl. of Maths.; Studia Mathematica; Israel Jrnl. of Maths. Awarded Sr. For. Sci. Fellowships, Nat. Sci. Fndn. of U.S.A., 1970. Address: Shderot Hazvi 32, Haifa, Israel.

REICHENTAL, Frank, b. 6 May 1895, d. 2 Apr. 1971. Artist. Educ: Art Acad., Leningrad & Budapest. Prof., Schl. of Applied Arts, Bratislava, 1933-39. Mbrships: Melecka Beseda Slovenska; Masaryk Acad., 1934; Slovakischen

Kunstlerverbandes, Bratislava, 1947; Acad. for Arts & Scis., Bratislava, 1947; Designing Artist, World Fedn. of UN, 1968-71. Exhibs. in Leningrad, Vienna, Dresden, Paris, Prague, Bratislava, Budapest, N.Y., Miami, Chgo., Toronto, Israel; Paintings in museums in Austria, U.S.S.R., U.S.A., Israel, Czechoslovakia; Pvte. Collects. in Czechoslovakia, Hungary, Austria, Germany, U.K., Australia, Israel & U.S.A. Recip., Prize for Oil Painting, Hecksher Mus., U.S.A., 1963, Falls River Nat. Exhib., U.S.A., 1964. Address: 197-20 89 Rd., Hollis, NY 11423, U.S.A.

REICHERT, Robert George Chase, b. 25 Mar. 1921. Architect; Organist; Teacher. Educ: Bach. arch., Univ. of Minn., 1948; m.arch., Harvard Univ., 1951; MIT, Boston; Mac Phail Coll. music, Univ. of Minn., Mpls.; Royal Coll. Organists, London, U.K. Appts: Designer, var. archl. firms, Boston, Mpls. & Seattle, 1937-53; Prof. of Arch., Univ. of Wash., Seattle, 1948-64; Pvte. Prac., 1953-; Organist, 4th. Ch. of Christ, Sci., Seattle, 1967-. Mbrships: Colleague, Am. Guild Organists; Mason. Address; 5735-25th N.E., Seattle, WA 98105, U.S.A.

REICHMAN, Fredrick Thomas, b. 28 Jan. 1925. Painter. Educ: B.A., Univ. of Calif., Berkeley; M.A., ibid; San Fran. Art Inst., Calif. Appts. incl: Instr. in Art, San Fran. Art Inst., 1952; Lectr. in Art, Univ. of Calif., Berkeley, 1954; Dir. of Art Classes, Jr. Ctr. of Art, Univ. of Calif. at Davis, 1962-64; Instr. in Art, Univ. of Calif. Ext., San Fran., 1966-. Exhibd. in num. Grp. shows. Paintings in many Pub. Collects. inclng. San Fran. Mus. of Art, Bank of Am. World Headquarters, San Fran. & Continental Telephone Co., Wash. DC. Commns. incl: murals, Stanford Univ. Med. Schl., Palo Alto, Calif., 1961 & San Fran. Art Festival, Civic Ctr., 1968. One Man Shows incl: Gall. 8, Paris, France, 1958; Benson Gall., Bridgehampton, L.I., N.Y., 1966, 1972; Santa Barbara Mus. of Art, Calif., 1974. Hons. inc: Taussig Traveling Fellowship, Univ. of Calif., 1952; Artist's Coun. Prize, San Fran. Art Assn., 1952, 1954; Art Festival, City & Co. of San Fran., 1964, 1968. Address: 1235 Stanyan St., San Fran., CA 94117, U.S.A. 37.

REID, Charles Frederick, b. 25 Apr. 1898. Emeritus Professor. Educ: A.B., Colgate Univ., 1923; A.M., Columbia Univ., 1929; Ph.D., ibid, 1940. Appts: Supervising Prin., Victor H.S., N.Y., 1925-29; Asst. to Pres., Carnegie Fndn., 1929-31; Fac., Schl. of Educ., City College, CUNY, 1931-68; currently, Prof. Emeritus; Vis Prof., Summer Session, Univ. of Puerto Rico, 1941; Worcester State Coll., Mass., 1948; Ore. State Bd. of Higher Educ., 1949; Profl. Lectr., Univ. of the Philippines, 1953-55. Mbrships: Educ. Survey Commn., Holyoke, Mass., 1929; Panama Canal Zone, 1930; Rsch. Asst., Hoover Nat. Advsry. Commn. on Educ., 1930; Sr. Specialist, Roosevelt Advsry. Commn. on Educ., 1937; Trustee, Hastings on Hudson, N.Y., 1948-52; Mayor, 1957-59; served w. U.S. Army, WWI & II & w. USAF, Korean War; Fellow, AAAS; Life Mbr., Am. Assn. of Schl. Admnstrs. Publs: Education in the Territories and Outlying Possessions of the United States, 1941; Overseas America, Headline Book No. 35, 1942. Hons. incl: Recip. of Gold Medal, Univ. of the Philippines, 1955. Address: 176-02 Kildare Rd., Jamaica, NY 11432, U.S.A. 6, 15, 51.

REID, Ethna Robinson, b. 19 Oct. 1927. Educator. Educ: B.A., Univ. of Utah, 1948, M.S., 1959, Ph.D., 1965. Appts. incl: Tchr.-

Prin., Salt Lake City & Granite Schl. Dist. Schls., 1948-63, Supvsr. & Specialist, 1963-66; Fndr. & Dir., Reading Clin., Granite Schl. Dist., 1965-, Exemplary Ctr. for Reading Instrn., 1966-; Lect., Westminster Coll., Salt Lake City, 1966-69; Adjunct Asst. Prof., Univ. of Utah, 1970-. Cons. to num. educ. ctrs. & projects. Mbrships. incl: Granite Admnstrs. & Supervsrs. Assn.; Ogden Utah & Nat. Educ. Assns.; Delta Kappa Gamma; Int. Reading Assn.; Utah Nature Soc.; num. educl. & community serv. comms. Publs: Improving the Elementary School Principalship, 1961; contbr. to num. educl. publs. Speaker at many educ. confs. & workshops. Address: 4225 Helaman Cir., Salt Lake City, UT, U.S.A. 5, 15, 126, 138, 141.

REID, John Kelman Sutherland, b. 31 Mar. 1910. Minister of Religion & Professor of Theology. Eudc: Univs. of Edinburgh, Heidelberg, Marburg, Basle, Strasbourg. Appts: Prof. of Philos., Univ. of Calcutta, 1935-37; Min. of Craigmillar Pk. Parish Ch., Edinburgh, 1939-52; Chaplain to the Forces, 1942-46; Prof. of Theol., Univ. of Leeds, 1952-61; Prof. of Systematic Theol., Univ. of Aberdeen, 1961-; Jt. Ed., Scottish Jrnl. of Theol., 1948-; Hon. Sec., Jt. Comm., New Engl. Bible, 1947-. Mbrships: Soc. for Study of Theol.; Societas Novi Testamenti Studiorum. Publ incl: The Biblical Doctrine of the Ministry, 1955; The Authority of Scripture, 1957, 63; Our Life in Christ, 1963; Presbyterians & Unity, 1966; Christian Apologetics, 1969; var. translations. Recip., C.B.E., 1970. Address: Don House, 46 Don St., Aberdeen AB2 1UU, U.K. 1, 3, 139.

REID, John Madden, b. 10 Feb. 1924. Management consultant. Educ: M.A., Univ. of Aberdeen, U.K., 1951. Appts: Planning asst., Chiswick Prods. Ltd., 1951-52; Rsch. Asst., Marketing Dev. Co. Ltd., 1952-53; Personal Asst. to Mng. Dir., Haworth's Fabrics Ltd., 1953-55; Trade advsr., Irish Export Promotion Bd., 1955-59; Mng. Dir., Merchandise & Marketing Consultants Ltd., 1959-62; Mng. Dir., Kiernan & Co. (U.K.) Inc., 1962-65; Chmn. & Mng. Dir., Exec. Search Ltd., 1965-; Chmn., Exec. Search Int. Ltd., 1972-; Pres. Dir. Gen., Exec. Search Int. S.A., Paris, France, 1973-. Mbrships: Chmn., Fulham Soc., 1972-; Hurlingham Club. Author of articles & lects. on Exec. Recruiting. Address: 7 Bradbourne St., Parson's Green, London, SW6 3TF, U.K. 16.

REID, Kenneth Grahame, b. 7 May 1923. Company Director. Educ: B.A., Lincoln Coll., Oxford, 1946; M.A., ibid, 1948. Appts: Lt., Royal Navy, U.K., 1941-46; MacAndrews & Co. Ltd., Shipowners of London, Spain, 1949; Mgr., ibid, Barcelona, Spain, 1958-60; Asst. Gen. Mgr. for Spain, 1960-62; Gen. Mgr. for Spain, 1962; Chmn., MacAndrews Tours S.A., Madrid & Barcelona, 1964; Chmn., Finanzas y Consignaciones S.C.E., Madrid, 1964; Bd., MacAndrews & Co. Ltd., 1965. Mbrships: Pres. Brit. Chmbr. of Comm., Spain, 1971-73. Chmn., U.K./Spain Freight Assn., 1973-74; Naval Club, London; Real Club, Nautico de Barcelona; Davenant Soc., Oxford (sec., treas., pres.). Contbr. of articles to profl. jrnls. Hons: Cmdr., Order of Cisneros, Spain, 1965; O.B.E., 1973. Address: Calle Musitu, 29-31, Barcelona 6, Spain. 43, 102.

REID, Mildred I. Novelist; Creative Writing Instructor. Educ: Columbia Univ.; Temple Univ. Dir., Mildred I. Reid Writers' Colony, Contoocook, N.H. Mbrships: Nat. League of Am. Pen Women; Press Club. Publs: Writers: Here's How! ; Writers: Help Yourselves! ; Writers: Let's Plot! ; Writers: Make it Sell! ; Writers: Try Short Stories! ; Writers: Learn to Earn! ; Writers: Why Stop Now! ; The Devil's

Handmaidens (novel); Over Fool's (novel). Address: Mildred I. Reid Writers' Colony, Contoocook, NH, U.S.A. 5, 6, 8, 138.

REID, Silburn M., b. 22 Apr. 1927. Minister of Religion. Educ: Grad., Ministerial Course, W. Indies Coll., 1949; B.Th., ibid, 1960; M.A., Systematic Theol., Andrews Univ., Mich., U.S.A., 1961. Appts: Pastoral work, 1950-51; Publng. Sec., W. Jamaica Conf. of Seventh Day Adventists, 1951-53; Pastoral work, 1954-59; Lay Activities Sec., Sabbath Schl. Sec., Exec. Sec., W. Jamaica Conf., Seventh Day Adventists, 1962-66; Pres., ibid, 1966-73. Mbr., Rotary Int., Montego Bay, Jamaica. Address: W. Jamaica Conference of S.D.A., P.O. Box 176, 30 Church St., Montego Bay, St. James, Jamaica, W. Indies. 136.

REID, (Rev.) William Alexander, b. 19 July 1943. Minister, Church of God. Educ: A.A., Lee Coll., Cleveland, Tenn., U.S.A., 1963; B.A., Univ. of Md., Coll. Pk., 1966. Appts. incl: Tchr., Balt. City Pub. Schls., 1966-70; Pastor, Ch. of God, Damascus, Md., 1967-70; Pastor, Ch. of God, Bridgeville, Del., 1970-72; Dir., Youth & Christian Educ., Delmarva, D.C., 1972-; Ordained in Ch. of God, 1974. Mbrships. incl: State Youth & Christian Educ. Bd., 1968-72; Chmn., State Bd. of Educ., 1972-74; Institutional Rep., Boy Scouts, 1967; V.P., Lee Coll. Alumni, 1969-70, Pres., 1971-72. Publs: Articles in Ch. of God Lighted Pathway. Hons. incl: Dist. Youth Dir. of the Yr. Award, 1971; Citation of Achievement, Gen. Youth Dept. Ch. of God, 1973. Address: P.O.Box 98, Simpsonville, MD 21150, U.S.A. 117, 125.

REID, William James, Jr., b. 2 Nov. 1927. Physicist; College Professor. Educ: A.B., Erskine Coll., 1949; M.A., Duke Univ., 1958; Ph.D., Clemson Univ., 1967. Appts: Instr., Chem., 1949-51, Field Rep., 1951-52, Asst. Prof., Phys., 1956-62, Assoc. Prof., Phys., 1966-68, Erskine Coll.; Prof., Phys., Dept. Hd., Jacksonville State Univ., 1968-. Mbrships: Sigma Xi; ODK; Sigma Pi Sigma; Phi Lambda Upsilon; Am. Phys. Soc.; S.Eastern Sect., ibid; Ala. Acad. of Sci.; Pi Kappa Phi; Pres., Fac. Senate, Jacksonville State Univ., 1971-72; Fac. Senator, 1971-73. Publs: The Polarography of Some Azo Compounds; The Effect of Strain Upon the Superconducting Transition Temperature of Vacuum Deposited Indium Films. Recip., Disting. Serv. Award, Young Man of Yr., Abbeville, S.C., 1960. Address: Dept. of Phys. & Engrng., Jacksonville State Univ., Jacksonville, AL 36265, U.S.A.

REIFSCHNEIDER, Mollie, b. 3 Sept. 1907. Executive. Educ: Compton Coll., 1950-51; B.A., Univ. of Calif. at L.A., 1952. Appts: Pres., Manchester Tank & Equipment Co., 1947-71; Chmn. of Bd., ibid, 1971-. Mbrships incl: Southeast Coun. on Alcoholism & Drug Problems, Downey, Calif., (BD. of Dirs. 1973-, Chmn. Bd. of Dirs. 1974); Bd. of Dirs., Lynwood Youth Employment, Calif. S.East-Rio Vista YMCA, Huntington Pk., U.S.O., L.A.; United Way Inc., L.A.; Pres., Edward Reifschneider Fndn., 1968-; Lynwood & U.S. Chmbrs. of Comm.; Soroptimist Club (Pres. Lynwood-South Gate, 1952); Town Hall, L.A.; Southeast Mental Hlth. Serv.; Pub. Affairs Comm.; Nat. LP-Gas Assn.; San Moritz Club, Grestline. Hons: Outstanding Serv. Award, United Way, 1963; Outstanding Citizen Award, Jr. Chambr. of Comm., 1968; Youth Helping Hand Award, Lynwood Unified Schl. Dist., 1971. Address: 7148 Nada St., Downey, CA 90242. 5.

REILLY, James D., b. 30 Sept. 1908. Mining Engineer. Educ: Correspondence courses, Mining Engrng. Appts: Chmn. of Bd., Reilly Chevrolet & Cadillac; Chmn. of Bd., Pike Natural Gas; Chmn. of Bd., St. Clair Oil; Past Pres., Hanna Coal Co.; V.P., Consolidated Coal Co. Mbrships: Past Pres., Ohio Coal Assn.; Past Pres., Soc. of Mining Engrs.; Pres.-Elect, Am. Inst. of Mining; Assn. of Metallurg. & Petroleum Engrs. Publs: 20 Years of Safety in Coal Mining; The Future of Young Mining Engineers. Hons: Chevalier, Legion of Hon., France. Address: 219 E. Main St., St. Clairsville, OH 43950, U.S.A. 2, 12.

REILLY, Robert Neil, b. 6 Sept. 1907. Otolaryngologist. Educ: M.B., B.S., Adelaide Univ., Australia, 1933; Dip., Laryngol., Melbourne, 1947; Fellow, Royal Austral. Coll. Surgs., 1954. Appts. incl: Hon. Clin. Asst., ENT Dept., Royal Adelaide Hosp., 1947-49; Hon. Asst. Surg., ibid, 1949-55; Hon. Surg., 1955-67; Hon. Cons. Surg., 1967-; Lectr., Diseases of ENT, Nurses Bd. of S. Aust., 1952-; Hon. ENT Surg., Townsend House Schls. for. Blind & Deaf, 1952-64; Cons. Otologist & Dir., Deafness Guidance Clin., Dept. Pub. Hlth., 1956-; Lectr., Univ. of Adelaide, 1963-67. Mbrships. incl: Advsry. Panel, Deaf & Hard of Hearing Children to Min. of Educ.; 1955-; Fndn. Mbr., Exec., Asia Oceania Assn. Otolaryngol. Socs., 1967-; Chmn., ibid, 1972; Fndn. Chmn., Comm., Care of Hearing Impaired Children, Int. Fed. Otolaryngol. Socs., 1969-; Aust. Med. Assn.; Asvsry. Comm. on Noise, Dept. of Pub. Hlth., 1964-; Chmn., Hearing Impairment Comm., Standards Assn. of Australia; Acoustics Comm. on Noise, Int. Org. Standardization. Contbr. to profl. jrnls. Address: Elizabeth House, 231 North Terrace, Adelaide, S.A., Australia 5000. 23.

REIMEN, Gustave, b. 26 July 1918. Conservatory Principal. Educ: Conservatory of Music, Esch/Alzette, Grand Duchy of Luxemburg, 1930-37; Royal Conservatory of Music, Brussels, Belgium, 1937-40. Appts: Prof., Conservatory of Music, Esch/Alzette, 1938-65; Music Critic, Tageblatt, Esch, 1950-65; Music Master, Hubert Clement Coll., Esch, 1952-65; Prin., Conservatory of Music, Esch/ALzette, 1965-. Mbrships: Artistic Commn., Union Grand-Duc Adolphe, Luxemburg Music Fedn., 1965-72; Mbr. of Juries, Royal Conservatory of Brussels, Conservatories of Luxemburg City, Metz, etc., & of contests of Luxemburg & Belgium Music Fedns.; Lions Int. Club. Publs: Music criticisms, music essays & articles collected in 12 vols.; Publisher, Annuaire du Conservatoire d'Esch-sur-Alzette. Hons: Silver Medal of Arts, Scis. & Letters, Paris, France, 1960; Chevalier, Ordre du Mérite Luxembourgeois, 1966; Chevalier, Ordre Grand-Ducal de la Couronne de Chêne, 1972; Off., Ordre de la Couronne de Belgique, 1973; Médaille spéciale en vermeil de l'Union Grand-Duc Adolphe, 1974; Off., Ordre d'Orange Nassau, 1974. Address: 20 North St., Esch-sur-Alzette, Grand Duchy of Luxemburg.

REIMENSCHNEIDER, Joseph Donald, b. 11 May 1934. Township Manager. Educ: B.S., Bus. Admin., Drexel Univ., 1957; M.G.A., Univ. of Pa., 1959. Appts: Town Mgr., Northumberland, H.H., 1959-61; Twp. Mgr., Aston Twp., Pa., 1961; Twp. Mgr., E. Whiteland, Pa., 1962-. Mbrships: Assn. of Pa Municipal Mgrs.; Int. City Mgmt. Assn.; Am. Soc. Pub. Admin.; Am. Soc. Planning Officials; Nat. Municipal League; Past Pres., Exton Frazer Rotary Club & K.D. Markley PTA; Past Chmn., Gt. Valley Schl. Dist. PTA; Cubmaster, Frazer Cub Scout Pack 176. Recip., Scouter's Key,

Boy Scouts of Am., 1973. Address: 30 Woodview Rd., Malvern, PA 19355, U.S.A. 6.

REIMER, Donald Ross, b. 12 July 1934. Physician; Anesthesiologist; Psychiatrist. Educ: B.A., 1958, M.D., 1962, Univ. of Colo.; Internship, U.S. Naval Hosp., Boston, Children's Hosp. Med. Ctr., ibid, U.S. Naval Hosp., Boston, 1963-65; Fellow in Psychiatry, Menninger Fndn., Topeka, Kan., 1971-73. Appts: Asst. Chief in Anesthesiol., U.S. Naval Hosp., Boston, 1966-68; Chief Anesthesiol., U.S. Naval Hosp., Key West, Fla., 1968-69; Instr. in Anesthesiol., Schl. of Med., Boston Univ., 1966-68. Mbrships. incl: Int. Anesthesia Rsch. Soc.; Am. Soc. Anesthesiol. (Fellow, 1968); AMA; Am. Psychiatirc Assn. & Kan. Br., ibid; Kan. Soc. Anesthesiol.; Acad. Psychosomatic Med.; Phi Rho Sigma; Dipl., Am. Bd. Anesthesiol., 1969, Pan Am. Med. Assn., 1972. Publs: Malignant Hyperpyrexia; The Methohexital-Methylphenidate Interview Technique; The Use of Operant Conditioning Techniques to Chronic Hospitalized Schizophrenic Patients; Anesthesiologists, Why; papers & articles, var. med. jrnls. Recip., Presidential Unit Citation, 1968. Address: 234 Greenwood Ave., Topeka, KS 66606, U.S.A. 8, 17, 57, 112, 131.

REIMONDO, (Sister) M. Sylvia, S.S.J. Professor of English & American Literature, Educ: B.S., M.A., Canisius Coll. High Schls., 12 yrs.; Hd., Dept. of Engl., Mr. Joseph Tchrs. Coll. (now Medaille Coll.), 25 yrs.; Hd. Dept. of Engl., Vic. Acad., Lackawanna, N.Y., 5 yrs.; Tutor, Schl. of Nursing, O.L.V. Home, Lackawanna, N.Y. Mbrships. incl: Charter Mbr., N.Y. State of Engl. Coun.; State Dir., Promotion, Buffalo Area Tchrs. Assn.; Ed., NYSEC Newsletter, 10 yrs.; 1st Pres., V.P. repng. Colls., Exec. Comm., BAETA; var. offs., sev. other educl. orgs. Co-author, Arts & Skills, in 4 vols. Contbr., schol. mags. & profl. publs. Hons: Fellowship, N.Y. State Engl. Coun., 1962; var. educl. citations. Address: 790 Ridge Rd., Lackawanna, NY 14218, U.S.A. 5, 13, 30, 140.

REINER, Mary Elisabeth Wells (Mrs. John Paul Reiner), b. 19 Apr. 1931. Teacher; Civic Worker. Educ: B.A., Middlebury Coll., 1953; M.A., N.Y. Univ., 1955; Dipl., Russian Inst., Columbia Univ., 1960; M.A., ibid, 1960. Appts: Asst. Dean, N.Y. State Univ., 1957-59; Lectr. in Russian, ibid, 1958-59; Asst. Prof. of Govt., Notre Dame Coll., Staten Island, 1960-62; Non-Govtl. Del. to the U.N. for World Assn. of Girl Guides & Girl Scouts, 1968-; Tchr., Marymount Schl. for Girls, 1973-74; Assoc. Ed., NGO-UNICEF Newsletter. 1973-. Mbrships: Bd. Mbr., N.Y. Jr. League, 1967-69; DAR; City Gardens Club of N.Y.; Comm. on Progs. for the Aging, 1971-73; Lect., Metropolitan Mus. of Art. N.Y.C., 1971-72. Contbr. to profl. jrnls. Address: 151 Avenue B, N.Y., NY 10009, U.S.A. 5.

REINHARDT, Kurt, b. 18 Feb. 1920. Professor of Medicine; Head Physician. Educ: State exams. 1945; Inaugurated, 1958. Appts: Hd. Physn., X-ray & nuclear med. dept., Kreiskrankenhaus, Völklingen-Saar, 1958-; Prof., 1964-. Mbrships: Deutsche Röntgengesellschaft; Int. Commn. on Radiol.; Asst. Ed., Newsletter, I.C.R.E. Author of over 150 publs. in med. jrnls. & of monographs & handbook articles. Address: Am. Kirschenwäldchen 32, 662 Völklingen/Saar, German Fed. Repub. 43, 92.

REINHOLD, (Mrs) Miriam Caroline (Hood), b. 13 Aug. 1925. English & Speech Teacher. Educ: B.S., Phillips Univ., Enid, Okla., U.S.A.,

1956; M.A., ibid, 1958; Postgrad., Baylor Univ., Waco, Tex., 1961-62; Appts: H.S. Tchr., Pub. Schls. of Kan., 1957-60; Instr., Engl. & Speech, Southwestern Coll. of the Assemblies of God, Waxahachie, Tex., 1960-. Mbrships: Roger Williams Family Assn.; SAR; Sec., Ellis Co. Chapt., AAUW, 1971-73; Sec., Tex. Jun. Coll. Speech & Theater Assn., 1961-63; Tex. Jun. Coll. Tchrs. Assn. Contbr., The Hood Familes, chapt. in Prairie Progress in West Central South Dakota, 1968. Address: 108 Villanova Court, Waxahachie, TX 75165, U.S.A. 125.

REININGHAUS, Ruth (Mrs.), b. 4 Oct. 1922. Artist; Art Instructor; Advertising Manager. Educ: Hunter Coll.; Nat. Acad. of Design (Nell Boardman Schlrship. Award), 1962-63; Frank Reilly Schl. of Art. (Robert Lehman Schlrship Award), 1966; N.Y. Univ. (Schlrship. Award), 1967. Appts. incl: Jr. Chemist, Sheffield Labs.; Draftsman, Allied Control Co., Inc.; Engrng. Aide, ibid; Internal Sales Rep., ibid; Advt. Asst., ibid; Advt. Mgr., Elec. Testing Labs., Inc.; Art Instr., Banker's Trust, N.Y. & Kitteredge Club for Women, N.Y. Oil Paintings. Inc.: Le Tableau de Quatre Sens, 1972; Crailsheim, Germany (Street scene), 1973: La Bouilloire A Thé, 1973; Peonies, 1974. Grp. Shows, Far Gall. & Hammer Galls., N.Y., 1974. Mbrships. incl: Salmagundi Club of N.Y. (Art Club), 1973-, Bd. Dirs., 1974 (1st women elected in Club's hist.); Fellow, Am. Artists' Profl. League; Fellow, Hudson Valley Art Assn.; Allied Artists of Am., Assoc.; Advt. Women of N.Y., 1973; Am. Advertising Fedn., 1973; Alpha Delta Pi; Musical Box Soc. Int. Hons. incl: Claude Parson's Mem. Award for a floral painting. 1974. Address: 418 E. 88th St., N.Y., NY 10028, U.S.A. 5, 37.

REINL, Harry Charles, b. 13 Nov. 1932. Commissioned Civil Servant. Educ: Dip., Ordnance Schl., APG, Md., 1953; A.M., Geo. Wash. Univ., 1968; Grad. Schl., U.S. Dept. of Agric., 1966. Appts: U.S. Army, 1st Lt., 1953-55; Reserve Commissioned Off., ORDC, 1955-62; SRC, 1958-62; Labour Economist, Manpower Admin., U.S. Dept. of Labor, 1962-68; CSC (disabled), 1968-. Mbrships: AEA; ASC; Nat. Bd. Sponsors, Inst. Am. Strategy; Taxation with Representation; Nat. Trust for Historic Preservation; Sponsor, Nat. Police Hall of Fame; Assoc., Smithsonian Instn.; Geo. Wash. Gen. Alumni Assn. Recip., Intercontinental Biographical Assn. Award. Address: Apt. 4-F, 3505 Wayne Ave., Bronx, NY 10467, U.S.A. 6, 7, 57, 125, 130, 131.

REINSCH, James Leonard, b. 28 June 1908. Executive. Educ: B.S., Commerce, N.Western Univ., 1934. Appts: Pres., Cox Broadcasting Corp.; Chmn., Cox Cable Communications. Mbrships: Rotary Club, Atlanta; Capital City Club, ibid; Peachtree Gold Club, ibid; Burning Tree Club, Wash. D.C.; Int. Radio & TV Soc., N.Y.; Broadcast Pioneers; Nat. Capital Democratic Club, Wash. D.C.; Sigma Delta Chi. Publs: Radio Station Management, 1948; Co-author of revised ed. 1960. Hons: Disting. Bus. Mgmt. Award, Emory Univ., 1968; Gold Medal Award, Int. Radio & TV Soc., 1973. Address: Cox Broadcasting Corp., 1601 W. Peachtree St., N.E., Atlanta, GA 30309, U.S.A. 7.

REINTON, Lars, b. 29 Mar. 1896. Professor. Educ: Cand. Philos., Univ. of Oslo, Norway 1928; Ph.D., ibid, 1940. Appts: Coll. Prof., 1929-56; Bd. of Dirs., Noregs Boklag, publrs., 1941-63; Rsch. Fellow, Inst. for Comp. Cultural Rsch., 1943-61; Ed., Heimen, 1955-66; Rsch. Fellow, Norwegian Govt., 1956-; Lectr. on Agricl. Hist., Norwegian Univ. of Agric., 1962-69. Mbrships. incl: Norwegian Acad. of Scis.; Pres., Comm. on Planning Norwegian Inst.

of Local Hist., 1950; Pres., Assn. of Township & City Hist., 1945-70; Pres., Friends of the Norwegian Theater, 1946-57. Publs: Sev. books inclng. Den Norroene Litteraturen, 1946. Saterbruket i Noreg, 3 vols., 1955-61, Fridtjof Nansens Kongerike (w. H. Björnsrud), 1961; Articles in profl jrnls. & yearboks Recip., Kt., First Class, Royal Order of St. Olav, 1970. Address: Skjerstadvegen 2C, Oslo 3, Norway. 43, 134.

REIS, Mary Barrett (Mrs. Lincoln Reis). Writer; Editor. Appts: Writer, Columbia Univ. Press, 1939-41; Brit. Publs., 1944-46; Freelance Ed., 1947-. Mbrships: V.P. & Bd. Trustees, Murray Hill Comm.; Exec. Comm., Democratic Party, 1959-61. Contbr., stories & articles to New Yorker, Sat. Review, Discovery, etc. Address: 15 Park Ave., N.Y., NY 10016, U.S.A. 5, 6.

REITMEISTER, Louis Aaron, b. 2 Feb. 1903. Philosopher; Author; Poet. Appts: Assoc. Ed., Lewis Copeland Co., 1928-31; Cons., Indian Nat. Congress, 1928-31; Fndr., Einstein Coll. of Med., N.Y.C., 1959; Freelance. Mbrships. incl: Am. Acad. Pol. & Soc. Schis.; Smithsonian Instn.; Am. Humanist Assn.; Oceanic Soc.; Defenders of Wildlife; Nat. Audubon Soc.; Am. Mus. of Natural Hist. Publs. incl: Paradise Found, 1926, 2nd edit., 1927; Music & Philosophy, 1930; If Tomorrow Comes, 1934; An Appeal to Common Sense, 1938; Nature of Power, 1943; Nature & Philosophy of Friendship, 3 vols., 1948; By the Way, 1953; A Philosophy of Freedom, 1970; My Credo, 1973. Num. publs., poetry. Hons. incl: Fellow, Int. Inst. Arts & Letters; Mbr., Eugene Field Soc. Address: 100 Hicks Ln., Gt. Neck, NY 11024, U.S.A. 2, 30, 55.

REITZEL, Alma Burns (Mrs. Charles Reitzel), b. 23 Mar. 1915. Media Specialist; Educator. Educ: Rutherford Coll., N.C., 1932-33; B.S., Appalachian State Univ., Boone, N.C., 1936; M.S. in L.S., Univ. of N.C. at Chapel Hill, 1964; var. summer courses. Appts: Tchr., French & Engl., Pilot H.S., Thomasville, N.C., 1942-44; Tchr., Engl. & French, Sherrill's Ford, H.S., N.C., 1945-47 & Blackburn H.S., Newton, 1947-53; Tchr., Engl. & Latin, Fred T. Foard H.S., Newton, 1953-62; Libn., Francis Garrou H.S., Valdese, N.C., 1964-74; Chmn., Media Ctr., Eastern Burke Sr. H.S., 1974-. Mbrships: ALA; Am. Assn. Schl. Libns.; N.C. Lib. Assn.; N.C. Assn. of Educators; Nat. Coun. of Tchrs. of Engl.; NEA; Am. Assn. Tchrs. of French. Author, Prison Libraries (in preparation). Address: Rural Route 3, Box 750, Newton, NC 28658, U.S.A. 5, 138.

REKHESS, Jaakov, b. 22 June 1906. Building & Development Executive; Immigration Administrator. Educ: Commercial H.S. Appts: Dir., Jewish Agcy. Offs., Haifa, & Dir., Emigration Depts., France & Italy; Chmn. Bd. of Dirs., Acre Dev. Soc. Ltd.; Mbr., var. dev. & bldg. cos.; Mbr., City Coun. of Haifa. Pres., Independent Liberal Party in Haifa. Articles, Zionist problems & immigration to Israel, var. periodicals & newspapers. Address: Ave. Hanadiv No.2, Haifa, Israel.

RELIS, Rochelle R. (Mrs. Bernard Bardach), b. 21 June 1914. Actress; Singer; Painter; Decorator. Educ: Acad. Fine Arts, Lwow, Poland. Appts: Opera, Musical & Dramatic Theatre, Poland, 1934-; Theatre, Music Halls, Radio, TV, Concert Recitals, Vienna, Berlin, Munich, Hamburg, Paris, Marseilles, Brussels, Antwerp, Zurich, London, 1946-; Radio, TV, Concert Recitals, U.S.A. & Canada, Musical Theatre, Broadway, N.Y., U.S.A., 1953-.

Mbrships: Am. Fedn. TV & Radio Artists; Nat. Acad. TV Arts & Scis.; Am. Guild Variety Artists; Hebrew Actor's Union; Smithsonian Instn.; Berkshire Art Assn., Berkshire Mus., Tx. Fine Arts Assn., Laguna Gloria Art Mus. Paintings in collects. inclng: LBJ Mem. Lib., Austin; Bertrand Russell House, Nottingham, U.K.; Synagogues Mus., Graz, Austria. Sev. one man exhibs., U.S.A. Hons: M.F.A., 1971; sev. art awards, 1967-. Address: 45-35 44th St., L.I. City, NY 11104, U.S.A. 2, 37, 105.

REMICK, Oscar E., b. 24 Aug. 1932. Baptist Minister. Educ: A.B., Eastern Bapt. Theol. Sem., 1957; B.D., ibid, 1957; M.A., Univ. of Pa., 1957; Fulbright Fellowship to study in Heidelberg, Germany, 1958-59; Ph.D., Boston Univ., 1966. Appts. incl: Min., 1st Congregational Ch. (United Ch. of Christ), Paxton, Mass., 1963-66; Asst. Prof., Philos., Assumption Coll., Worcester, Mass., 1966 Co-Dir., Ecumenical Inst. of Relig. Studies, ibid, 1968; V.P., Acad. Dean & Coord of Acad. Affairs; ibid, Prof., 1969; V.P., Worcester Area Coun. of Chs., 1969, Pres., 1971; Pres., Chautauqua Inst., N.Y., 1971-. Mbrships. incl: Dir., First Nat. Bank, Y.M.C.A.; Am. Philosoph. Assn.; Am. Acad. of Pol. & Soc. Sci.; Am. Acad. of Relig.; num. local educ. Christian comms. Author of Responding to God's Call, 1970. Contbr. to religious jrnls. Recip. of hons. Address: Chautauqua Inst., Chautauqua, NY 14722, U.S.A. 2, 6, 117, 130.

REMINGTON, George Clifford Thomas, b. 19 July 1899. Dealer in Music, Pianos, & Organ; Retired Naval Officer. Educ: Yale Coll., New Haven, Conn., U.S.A., 1918-20. Appts: Lt., USNR, 1940; Active duty, Phila. Navy Yard, Pa., 1941-44; Lt.-Cmdr., 1942; Overseas duty, U.S. 7th Fleet, 1944-45; Inactive duty, 1945-50; Retired from USNR, 1950. Mbrships. incl: Past Gov., Soc. of Colonial Wars in the State of Fla.; Pa. Soc.; Past Gov., Fla. Soc. of the Order of Fndrs. & Patriots of Am.; Past Pres., Sons of the Am. Revolution; Mil. Order of For. Wars; Mil. Order of World Wars; Corinthian Yacht Club of Pa.; Beach Club, Palm Beach. Address: 520 Everglades Island, Palm Beach, FL 33480, U.S.A.

REMIREZ, Richard Joseph Fernandez, b. 28 Nov. 1934. Professor of Foreign Languages. Educ: B.A., De La Salle Coll., 1952; M.A., Univ. of Ark., 1970; Ph.D., Univ. of Holguin, 1957. Appts. incl: Prof. of Spanish Lit., De La Salle Coll., 1956-57; Asst. Prof. of For. Langs., Wofford Coll., Spartanburg, S.C., 1964-72; Assoc. Prof., ibid, 1972-. Mbrships: MLA; Am. Assn. Tchrs. of Spanish & Portuguese, S.C. Chapt. Pres., 1967-68, 1968-70; Sigma Delta Pi, Gamma XI Chapt. Sponsor 1966-; St. Paul' Mens Club. Publs: Lang. Communication, rsch. in press. Hons: Sigma Delta Pi Recognition Award, 1968. Address: 368 Fairlane Drive, Spartanburg, SC 29302, U.S.A. 125.

REMPT, Jan Dirk, b. 14 Sept. 1907. Journalist; Writer. Educ: Leyden Univ., Netherlands. Appts: Reporter w. local newspaper, 1927-28; Asst. Pub. Rels. Off., Philips Industries, Eindhoven, 1928-29; Reporter, Sub-Ed., sev. Dutch newspapers, 1929-40; Mbr., Parliamentary Gall., The Hague, 1930-40; Snr. Press Liaison Off., Dept. of Agric., 1940-48; Ed.-in-Chief, Nederlands Studieblad, Dir. & Ed., Int. Econ. Press Agcy., 1948-51; Corres., Australia, for Provincial Daily Newspapers Assn., The Hague; num. appts. in field in Australia; Dir. & Ed., Dutch Int. Press, Sydney, 1951-. Mbrships: Australian Jrnlsts. Assn.; Australian Soc. of Authors; P.E.N. Int. - Sydney Ctr.; World Poultry Sci. Assn.,

Australian Br.; Farm Writer's & Broadcasters' Soc. Publs. incl: Aan de Rand der Wereld: Een Hollandse Emigrant in Australia, 1953; All about Australia (co-author), 1952; Emigratie: Kansen voor jonge Nederlanders in het Buitenland, 1947; Televisie: Verleden, Heden en Toekomst, 1949 & num. articles in field. Address: 55-57 Fowler Rd., Illawong via Menai, Sydney, Australia 2234, 3.

RENAY, Liz, b. 14 Apr. 1926. Actress; Artist; Writer. Appts Model, N.Y.C., 1953-55; Nightclub Entertainer, ibid, 1955-57; Stage & Screen Actress, Hollywood, 1957-73; Nightclub Entertainer, 1970-73; appeared in 18 films; Stage & TV appearances; Columnist, Nat. Insider. Mbrships: Screen Actors Guild; Am. Fed. TV & Radio Actors; Am. Guild Variety Artists. Publs: How to Attract Men; Moods (record album of poetry); My Face for the World to See. Hons. incl: Winner, Most Exciting Face in N.Y. Contest, 1955; 1st Prize, Nat. Arts Fair, Madison Sq. Garden, N.Y. 1967; 1st Prize, Art L.A., 1969. Address: 1645 North Ogden Drive, Hollywood, CA 90046, U.S.A.

RENDA, Francesco, b. 18 Feb. 1922. Lecturer in modern history. Appts. incl: Communist Sect. & Chmbr. of Labour, Cattolica Eraclea, 1944; Provincial Chmbr. of Labour, Agrigento, 1948; Sicilian Regional Agric. Wkrs. Fedn., 1950; Sicilian Regional Assembly, 1951-67; Communist Fedn. of Agrigento, 1952; Regional Comm. of Miners, 1954; Sicilian Regional Sec., C.G.I.L., 1957; Nat. Coun. of Econ. & Labour, 1958; Regional Pres., Nat. League of Coops. & Nat. Ins., 1963; Senator of Repub., 1968; Mbr., Sicilian Soc., of Nat. Hist., Palermo. Publs: Il movimento contadino nella società Siciliana, 1956; l'Emigrazione in Sicilia, 1963; La Sicilia nel 1812, 1963; Risorgimento e classi popolari in Sicilia, 1820-21, 1968; Socialisti e cattolici in Sicilia, 1900-04, 1971; Bernardo Tanucci e i beni dei gesuiti in Sicilia, 1974. Address: Via Onorato 44, 90139 Palermo, Italy.

RENDELL, Kenneth W., b. 12 May 1943. Antiquarian Manuscript Dealer. Appts: Fndr., Pres., Kenneth W. Rendell (Numismatics), Medford, Mass., 1955-61; Pres., Betken Luggage Mfg. Co., Somerville, ibid, 1958-62; Fndr., Pres., Kingston Galls., Inc., Somerville, 1961-67; Pres., Kenneth W. Rendell, Inc., ibid, 1967-; Dir., Kenneth W. Rendell Ltd., (U.K.), 1967-, & Japan, 1967-; Appraisal Cons., Boston Univ., Boston Pub. Lib., Harvard Univ. Lib., Harvard Music Lib., Columbia Univ., Syracuse Univ., Wis. State Histl. Soc. Mbrships: Pres., The Manuscript Soc.; Chmn., New Engl. A.B.A.A.; Grolier Club. Contbr. of many articles to profl. jrnls. Address: 154 Wells Ave., Newton, MA 02159, U.S.A. 6.

RENFREY, (The Rt. Rev.) Lionel Edward William, b. 26 Mar. 1916. Clerk in Holy Orders. Educ: B.A., Univ. of Adelaide, Australia; Th.L., St. Barnabas' Theol. Coll., Australian Coll. of Theol. Appts: Ordained Deacon, 1940, Priest, 1941; Prospect, Ch. St. Cuthbert's, 1940; 43; Mission Chap., Mid-Yorke Peninsula, 1943-44; Warden, Brotherhood of St. John Baptist, 1944-47; Priest i/c. St. Edward's, Kensington Gdns., 1950-56; Rector, St. James', Mile End, 1957-63; Ed., Adelaide Ch. Guardian, 1961-65; Rural Dean, Western Suburbs, 1962-63; Organising Chap., Bishop's Home Mission Soc., 1964-66; Archdeacon, Adelaide, 1965-66; Acting Archdeacon, Eyre Peninsula 1965-67; Examining Chap. to Bishop of Adelaide, 1965-; Bishop's Vicar, Cathedral Ch. of St. Peter, 1966-73; Dean of Adelaide, 1966-; Consecrated Bishop, 1969. Publs: Father Wise, A Memoir, 1950; A Short History of St.

Barnabas' Theological College, 1965. Recip., sev. awards. Address: 18 King William Rd., North Adelaide, S.A., Australia 5006. 23.

RENGOS, Polycleitos, b. 10 Apr. 1903. Artist; Professor of Fine Arts. Educ: Grad., Fine Arts Sch., Athens, Greece; Acad. de la Grande Chaumière, Paris, France; Louvre Mus., Paris, France; Prof. D. Galaris's Studio. Appts. incl: Prof. of Fine Arts, Thessaloniki, Greece; Hd., Dept. of Drawing & Design, Univ. of Thessaloniki, 1950-69; Since 1926 exhibd. in over 60 int. One-Man & Grp. shows. Exhibs. incl: Biennale Alexandria, Egypt; Biennale Ancona, Italy; Biennale Cracovia, Poland; Salon d'Automne, Paris, France; Salon de l'Art Libre, Paris; Salon of Contemporary European Painters, N.Y., U.S.A. Mbrships: Macedonian Soc., Techni; Rotary Club. Thessaloniki. Hons: Off., French Acad., 1952; 1st Prize, Mural Painting, St. Demetrius Cathedral, 1959; Medal Vermeil, Art Sci. Lettres, Paris, 1964; Prize & Medal of Honor, Salon de l'Art Libre, Paris, 1965; Gold Medal for Greece, Annual d'Art Grafica Ancona, Italy, 1966; Dip. w. Golden Medal, 2nd Biennale Ancona, 1968; Silver Cross of Order of Phoenix, Greece, 1971. Address: 6 Acheropeetou St., Thessaloniki, Greece.

RENI-MEL, Léon, b. 10 Apr. 1893. History of Art Professor; Painter. Educ: Pub. & pvte. drawing schls. Appts: Official painter, French War Dept.; Lectr., Am. Colls. & Univs., inclng. Bradford Coll., Mass., Columbia Univ. Metropol. Mus. of Art, N.Y.C.; Fndr. & Pres., Centre d'art Francais, Paris, 1920. Mbrships: Pres., Soc. de l'Ecole Francaise, Paris, 1973-74; Presse artistique francaise; Acad. du Languedoc, France; Jury & Comm., Soc. des artistes Francais; Grand Palais Champs Elysées, Paris. Work incls: Surrender of the German armies to the Field Marshal Montgomery of Alamein, 1945; Author of var. portraits & a valuable collect. of marines, landscapes, mil. & Indian scenes, 1922-73; Author of Vers l'Asie & en Asie, 2 large mural paintings, Chapelle des Missions Etrangeres, Paris, 1960-65. Recip. of hons. Address: 6 Ave. du Gen. Balfourier, Paris 75016, France. 43, 91, 133.

RENOFF, Paul Vernon, b. 17 July 1911. Electrical Manufacturing Company Executive. Educ: B.E., Johns Hopkins Univ., 1932; grad. work, Balt. Polytech. Inst. Appts. incl: Ptnr., Houghton & Renoff, 1935-45; Ptnr., Paul V. Renoff Co., 1945-66; Pres., Renoff Assocs., Inc., 1966-. Mbrships: Engrng. Soc., Balt.; Inst. of Elec. & Electronic Engrs.; Johns Hopkins Club; Md. Acad. of Sci.; Md. Histl. Soc.; Chartwell Country Club; U.S. Power Squadron; various Civic & Community orgs. Address: 4326 Roland Ct., Balt., MD 21210, U.S.A. 6, 16.

RENOUD, Dorothy (Mrs. David Francis Renoud), b. 11 Aug. 1933. Circulation Director. Educ: Var. bus. courses. Appts: File Clerk - Sales Serv. Mgr., Reinhold Publishing Corp., 1951-62; Circulation Dir., United Tech. Publs. Inc., Div. of Box Broadcasting Co., 1962-. Mbrships: V.P., Ladies Aux., Long Beach (N.Y.) Vol. Fire Dept.; Nat. Bus. Circulation Assn.; Fulfilment Mgrs. Assn. Hons: Charles J. Fraundorf Award, 1973. Address: 527 W. Chester St. Long Beach, NY 11561, U.S.A. 5, 138.

RENSE, Paige. Editor. Educ: B.A., Calif. State Univ., LA; Postgrad. work, UCLA, U.S.A. Ed., Archtl. Digest Mag. (53 yrs. old) 4 yrs. Address: 5900 Wilshire Blvd., Suite 820, LA, CA 90036, U.S.A.

RENTON, (Sir) David Lockhart-Mure, b. 12 Aug. 1908. Member of Parliament; Barrister; Queens Counsel. Educ: M.A., B.C.L., Univ. Coll., Oxford, U.K. Appts: Called to the Bar, 1933; Elected to Bar Coun., 1939; M.P., 1945-; Dpty. Chmn., Quarter Sessions, 1954; Queens Counsel, 1954; Min. of State, Home Off., 1961-62; Bencher, 1962; Recorder, 1963-71. Mbrships: Senate, 1966; Coun. for Legal Educ., 1967; Vice-Chmn., ibid, 1969-73; Royal Commn. on the Constitution, report publd. 1973; Privy Coun., 1962; Chmn., Comm. on Preparation of Legislation, 1973; Carlton Club; Past Pres., Conservation Soc. Hons: Territorial Efficiency Decoration, 1946; D.L., 1962; K.B.E., 1965. Address: House of Commons, London S.W.1, U.K. 1, 41.

RENVALL, Eeva Helmi Elina (Mrs. Pentti Renvall), b. 17 June 1917. Textile Artist. Educ: At Univ., 1936-37; Turku Art Schl., 1937; Inst. Indl. Art, 1943; Åbo Akad., 1951-54. Appts: Councillor, Kaunianinen, Finland, 1968-; Mbr., Ch Comm. Art, 1968-; Culture Comm., Kauniainen, 1967. Mbr. Ornamo Texo. Creative Works: Exhibited in sev. Finnish & for. exhibs., inclng. Wall Hangings, Mus. Mod. Art, N.Y., U.S.A., 1968-69; 1-Woman exhibs., Helsinki, Finland, 1965, '71, '74; Turku, 1971, '74; Oslo, Norway, 1967; Stockholm, Sweden, 1970, '74; Warsaw, Poland, 1970; Copenhagen, Denmark, 1973; Works in num. pub. estabs. & in Assn. Indl. Art Mus., Helsinki. Recip. Awards, Swedish- Finnish Fnds. for Culture, 1970 & Fndn. Danish-Finnish Jt. Work, 1973. Address: Bredantie 26, 02700 Kauniainnen, Finland, 138

REST, (Rev.) Friedrich O. (Fred), b. 28 Aug. 1913. Minster of the Gospel. Educ: B.A., Elmhurst Coll., Ill., 1935; B.D., Eden Theological Sem., Webster Groves, Mo., 1937. Appts: Pastor, United Ch. of Christ, Jasper, Ind., 1937-41, Dayton, Ohio, 1941-48, Hermann, Mo., 1948-55, Evansville, Ind., 1955-64, Rochester, N.Y., 1964-70, Houston, Tex., 1970-. Mbr. & Off., var ch. & welfare orgs. Publs: Our Christian Symbols; Worship Services for Church Groups; Worship Aids for 52 Services; The Cross in Hymns; You've Got a Point There. Contbr., mags. Host pastor, TV prog., Pastor's Study, 12 yrs. Recip., Hon. degree, D.D., United Theological Sem. Address: 9022 Long Point Rd., Houston, TX 77055, U.S.A. 125.

RETZEPIS, George, b. 1 May 1913. Professor. Educ: Fac. of Med., Univ. of Athens, Greece; Univ. of Vienna; Univ. of London. Appts: Dir., Diagnostic X-ray Dept., Hosp. Sotizia, Athens, 1947-48; Dir., Dept. of Radiol., 404 Mil. Hosp., 1949; Prof. of Radiol., Univ. of Athens, 1952-. Mbrships: Hellenic-British League; Sci. Comm., Annales de Radiol., Paris, France; Soc. française de la Tuberculose; Austrian Röntgen Ray Soc. Contbr. of articles to profl. jrnls. Hons: Laureate, Acad. of Athens, 1935; Cross of war, 1940; Medallist for excellent actions, 1949; Cross of silver w. sword of King George II, 1950. Address: 5 Neophytou Vamva, Athens 138, Greece. 43.

RETZER, William Raymond, b. 1 Apr. 1913. Industrial Hygiene Engineer. Educ: B.S.C.E., Lehigh Univ., 1934. Appts: w. Du Pont Corp., 1934-36; w. Pulmosan Safety Equipment Corp., 1936-40; w. Ky. Hlth. Dept., 1940-42; Major, USAAF, 1942-46; w. Md. Hlth Dept., 1946-47; Indl. Hygiene Engr., Caterpillar Tractor Co., worldwide 1947-; Cons. in field. Mbrships: Dipl., Am. Bd. Indl. Hygiene; Am. Indl. Hygiene Assn.; Am. Pub. Hlth. Assn.; Advsry. Bd., State of Ill. Dept. of Labour; Comm. of Indl. Hygiene; Mayor's Commn. on Noise; Bd. Dirs., Lake Camelot, 1973-; Willow Knolls C.C.; Blue Lodge, F & AM No. 396; Scottish Rite, Peoria; Mohammed Temple; Shrine; Recip. of hons., prizes & award. Address: 1317 W. Moss Ave., Peoria, IL 61606, U.S.A. 22, 68, 120, 128, 131.

REUSS, Carl (Frederick), b. 7 June 1915. Sociologist; Denominational Executive. Educ: B.S., Univ. of Va., 1934; M.S., ibid, 1935; Ph.D., 1937. Appts. incl: Prof. of Sociol., Capital Univ., 1944-48; Dean of Fac., Wartburg Coll., 1948-51; Exec. Sec., Bd. for Christian Soc. Action, Am. Luth. Ch., 1951-60 Exec. Dir., Commn. on Ch. & Soc. ibid, 1961-; Dir., Rsch. & Anal., Am. Luth. Ch., 1974-. Mbrships: Am. Sociol. Assn.; Nat. Coun. on Family Rels.; Rural Sociol. Soc.; Soc. for Study & Soc. Problems; Deleg., Luth. World Fed. Assemblies; Deleg., World Coun. of Chs. Assembly, Uppsala, 1968; V.P. for Relig. Ldrs., Nat. Safety Coun. 1973-; Exec. Comm. & Bd. Dirs., ibid. Publs: (Ed.) Conscience & Action, 1971; contbr. to Luth. Ency., 1965; articles in relig. & sociol. publs. Address: 422 S. 5th St., Minneapolis, MN 55415, U.S.A. 8, 14, 120, 128.

REUTER, George S., Jr., b. 9 Feb. 1920. Educator. Appts. incl: Prof. of Educ., Dept. Hd. & Dir. of Rsch., Ark. A&M Coll.; Dean of Coll. & Dir. of Summer Session, Minot State Coll., N.Dak.; Rsch. Dir., Am. Fed. of Tchrs.; Prof. of Educ., Grad. Schl. of Educ., Southern Ill. Univ., Edwardsville; Pres., Sioux Empire Coll., Hawarden. Iowa; Supt. of Schls., R-I, Enlarged, New Madrid Co, Mo., 1970-. Author of 13 books inclng.: Democracy and Quality Education (co-author), 1965; For Conscience Sake, 1959; The Philosophy of General Education, 1954; Achieving Quality Education, 1971; Emergency School Assistance Program Seminars, 1972. Mbr., Harvard Club of Chgo. Ordained Baptist Deacon. Address: P.O. Box 376, Portageville, MO 63873, U.S.A. 8, 15, 57, 120.

REUTER, Helen Hyde (Mrs. George S. Reuter, Jr.). Counselor; Psychologist. Educ: B.A.; Westmar Coll.; A.M., Univ. of S.D. Appts: U.S. Postmaster; Elem. Tchr.; Community Coll. Tchr.; H.S. Counselor; Schl. Psychol. Mbrships incl: AAUW; Psi Chi; Alpha Chi; Napus; Bapt. Ldr.; Portageville P.E.O. Publs: One Blood (co-author), 1964; Democracy and Quality Education, 1965; sev. profl. articles, incl. The Learning Improvement Ctr., Guidance Bulletin, State Dept. Mo., Nov. 1972. Hons: Woman of the Yr., Monticello, Ark., 1960; L.H.D., 1966. Address: P.O. Box 376, Portageville, MO 63873, U.S.A. 22, 208

REVELL, John Robert Stephen, b. 15 Apr. 1920. Professor of Economics. Educ: London Schl. of Econs., U.K., 1947-50; B.Sc., London, 1950; M.A., Cantab., 1960. Appts: Rsch. Off., Dept. of Allied Econs., Univ. of Cambridge, 1957-63; Sr. Rsch. Off., ibid, 1963-68; Fellow, Fitzwilliam Coll., Cambridge, 1965-68; Tutor, ibid, 1965-67; Sr. Tutor, 1967-68; Prof. & Hd., Dept. of Econs., Univ. Coll. of N. Wales, Bangor, 1969-. Mbrships: Royal Econ. Soc.; Soc. Universitaire Européenne de Recherches Financiéres; Int. Assn. for Rsch. in Income & Wealth; Royal Commonwealth Soc. Publs: The Owners of Quoted Ordinary Shares; a Survey for 1963 (w. J. Moyle), 1966; The Wealth of the Nation, 1967; Changes in British Banking: the Growth of a Secondary Banking System, 1968; Financial Structure & Government Regulation 1952-1980, 1972; The British Financial System, 1973. Address: Dept. of Econs., Univ. Coll. of N. Wales, Bangor, LL57 2AB, U.K.

REVOL, Guy-Charles, b. 3 Oct. 1912. Sculptor; Medallist. Educ: B. Lettres & Philos., Ecole Nat. Supérieure des Beaux-Arts, Paris, France. Appts: Tchr., l'Ecole Supérieure des Arts Appliqués, Paris, 1963, a l'Ecole Polytech., 1973. Mbrships: Hon. Gen. Sec., Syndicat Nat. des Sculpteurs Statuaires Professionels Créateurs; Racing Club de France. Work represented in collects. in var. countries, inclng: France, U.S.A., Iran; creator of busts & statues of the Shah of Iran, Pres. Bourguiba, Pres. Tsiranna, Pres. Bokassa; designer of num. sculptures for new educl. & community bldgs. & of many comemorative medals. Hons: Off., l'Ordre des Arts et Lettres, 1965; Ordre Seppase de lére classe, Iran; Chevalier de la Légion d'Honneur, 1969. Address: 112 Blvd. Malesherbes, 75017 Paris, France. 43, 91.

REYES-GUERRA, Antonio, Jr., b. 4 Aug. 1919. Dentist. Educ: B.S., St. Josephs Coll., 1938; B.C.C.L.L., Univ. of El Salvador, 1939; D.D., ibid, 1943; Internship & Residency, Oral Surg., Rosales Hosp., San Salvador, 1943-45; D.D.S., Univ. of Pa., 1947; Grad. Schl. of Med., ibid; Dipl., N.Y. Bd. of Oral Surg., 1956. Appts: incl: Dir., Dental Div., Dept. Pub. Hlth., San Salvador, 1944; Clin. Instr., Dept. of Oral Surg., Columbia Univ. Coll. of Physns. & Surgs., 1952-53; Chief Oral Surg., Shaw A.F. Base, Sumter, S.C., 1953-55; Assoc. Attng. Oral Surg., Polyclin. Hosp., 1955-62 & Lincoln Hosp., N.Y.C., 1955-65; Dir., Dept. of Dentistry & Oral Surg., Lawrence Hosp., Bronxville, N.Y., 1970-; presented papers num. profl. confs. & lectured to many profl. grps. Mbrships. incl: Fellow, Royal Soc. of Hlth., Exec. Sec. & former Pres., Am. Soc. for the Advancement of Gen. Anesthesia in Dentistry; former Pres., Bastchester Dental Soc.; 9th Dist. Dental Soc.; Am. Dental Assn.; N.Y. Acad. of Oral Pathol.; Westchester Acad. of Med.; Int. Fedn. of Dentistry. Publs: El Tratamiento De Las Fracturas De Los Maxilares Y La Mandibula Y El Cigoma, 1970. Recip., sev. awards for servs. to Dentistry. Address: 475 White Plains Rd., Eastchester, NY 10707, U.S.A. 130.

REYNOLDS, Carroll Foster, b. 14 Oct. 1910. Librarian. Educ: B.S. in Phys. Educ., W. Va. Univ., 1932; B.L.S., Columbia Univ., 1935; M.A., Univ. of Pittsburgh, 1940; Ph.D., ibid, 1950. Appts. incl: Ref. Libn., Okla. State Univ., 1938-40; Acquisitions Libn.-Asst. Libn., Univ. of Pittsburgh, 1940 44; Dir. of Evening Classes, ibid, 1947-57; Dir., Falk Lib. of Hlth. Profns., 1957-; Rockefeller Fndn. Vis. Libn., Fac. of Sci., Mahidol Univ., Bangkok, Thailand, 1967-68; Asia Fndn. Cons. on Hlth. Scis. Libs. in Bangladesh, 1973-. Mbrships. incl: Treas., & Chmn. of Int. Comm., Med. Lib. Assn.; Chmn., Biological Div., Special Lib. Assn.; ALA; Sigma Delta Pi; Delta Mu Delta; Phi Chi Theta. Publs: Contbns. to profl. jrnls. & to Proceedings, Third Int. Congress of Med. Librarianship, 1970. Address: Falk Library of the Health Professions, Univ. of Pittsburgh, Pittsburgh, PA 15261, U.S.A. 2, 6, 42.

REYNOLDS, (Eva Mary) Barbara, b. 13 June 1914. University Teacher. Educ: Univ. Coll., London Univ., U.K. Appts: Asst. Lectr. in Italian, London Schl. of Economics, London; Lctr. in Italian, Cambridge Univ.; Warden of Willoughby Hall, Rdr. in Italian Studies, Nottingham Univ. Mbr., Univ. Women's Club. Publs. incl: The Linguistic Writings of Alessandro Manzoni, 1950; Cambridge Italian Dictionary, 1962; (w. Dorothy L. Sayers) Dante, Paradise, trans., 1962; Dante, Vita Nuova, trans., 1969. Hons: Edmund Gardner Prize for Servs. to Italian Culture, 1963; Silver Medal, Italian Govt., 1963; Silver Medal, Province of Vicenza, for serv. to Anglo-Italian Cultural Rels. Address: Dept. of Italian Studies, Univ. of Nottingham, Nottingham, U.K. 1, 138.

REYNOLDS, Georgina Ann, b. 12 Nov. 1945. Group Editor, Melrose Press, Chief Editor, Dictionary of International Biography, 1970-. Appts incl: P.A. to Ldn. O'Seas Mgr., Australian Consilidated Ind. Ltd., London, 1963-64; Shrm. Asst. Antiference Ltd., 1964--65; Asst. to Chmn., Exec. Marketing Cons. Ltd., 1965-67; Edit. Asst., D.I.B., 1967; Sec., Alberta & Southern Gas Co. Ltd., Alta., Canada, 1967-68; Exec. Ed., Dictionary of Caribbean Biography, U.K., 1968-70; Registrar, D.I.B., ibid Grp. Ed., Melrose Press, 1970-73; Cons. Ed., ibid. Address: c/o Melrose Press, 3 Market Hill, Cambridge, U.K.

REYNOLDS, James R. (Jim), b. 30 Aug. 1937. Publisher. Educ: Tex. Tech. Univ. Appts: Ed. & Co-owner, The Lockney Beacon, Lockney, Tex.; Sec.-Treas. & Stockholder, Balnco Offset Printing Inc., Floydada, Tex.; Publisher, Ed. & Owner, The Crosbyton Review, Tex. Mbrships. incl: Dist. 2-T2 Gov.'s Cabinet, Lions Int., 7 yrs.; Zone Chmn., ibid, 3 yrs.; Dpty. Dist. Gov., 2 yrs.; Med. Chmn., 2 yrs.; Chmn., Dist. 2-T2 to S. Plains Kidney Fndn. (founded by Lions); Dist. 2-T2 Coaches All-Am. Football Game Comm.; Dir. & Immediate Past Pres., Crosbyton Chbr. of Comm.; Boy Scouts Comm. & Merit Badge Counselor; Tex. Press Assn.; Panhandle Press Assn.; W. Tex. Press Assn. Author of articles publd. in sev. jrnls. Hons. incl: Over 25 Tex. Press Assn., Panhandle Press Assn. & W. Tex. Press Assn. Awards in jrnlsm., advt. & photographic categories in past 6 yrs.; Outstanding Pres.'s Award, Lions Dist. 2-T2, 1965. Address: 113 W. Aspen, Crosbyton, TX 79322, U.S.A. 125.

REYNOLDS, (Rev.) John P., b. 23 Apr. 1925. Ordained Priest. Educ: St. Joseph Sem. Coll., 1938-44; Notre Dame Sem. Univ., 1944-46; M.Ed., Loyola Univ. of the S., 1952; Ordained, 1949. Appts: Assoc. Dir., St. Ann's Nat. Shrine, New Orleans, La., 1949-65, Sodalities Archdiocese of New Orleans, 1950-55; Asst. Ed.-in-Chief, Cath. Action of the South, 1966-62; Dir., St. Patrick's Cemeteries, 1965-68; Administrative Dir., Mbr. of Bd. & Treas., Clarion Herald, 1962-; Pastor, St. Patrick's Ch., New Orleans, 1965-; Bd. of Dirs., Ozanam Inn, 1966-; Supt. Schl. 'Food Servs., Archdiocese of New Orleans, 1967-. Mbrships: Nat. Cath. Press Assn., 1955-; Press Club of New Orleans, 1966-; Kappa Delta Pi, 1952. Address: 724 Camp St., New Orleans, LA 70130, U.S.A. 49, 125.

REYNOLDS, Margaret Norene, b. 15 June 1914. Librarian. Educ: B.A., Dalhousie Univ., Halifax, N.S., Canada 1935; B.L.S., McGill Univ., Montreal, Quebec, 1938. Appts: Asst. Libn., Royal Bank of Canada., Hd. Off., Lib., Montreal, P.Q., 1939-42; Chief Libn., Canadian Legion Educl. Servs., Ottawa, 1942-44; O'seas Libn., ibid, London, U.K., 1944-46; Dir., Canadian Book Ctr., Halifax N.S., 1948-50; Dir. of Libs., Canada Dept. of Agric., Ottawa, 1950-. Mbrships: Special Libs. Assn., N.Y.; Am. Soc. of Info. Sci.; Canadian Assn. of Info. Sci. Hons: Coronation Medal, 1953; Centennial Medal, 1967. Address: c/o Canada Dept. of Agric., Sir John Carling Bldg., Ottawa, K1A OC5, Canada. 88.

REYNOLDS, Philip Alan, b. 15 May 1920. Professor. Educ: The Queens Coll., Oxford, U.K., 1937-40; B.A., (Oxon), 1940; M.A., (Oxon), 1950. Appts. incl: Woodrow Wilson Prof. of Int. Pols., Univ. Coll. of Wales, Aberystwyth, 1950-64; V.P., ibid, 1961-63;

Vis. Prof. in Int. Rels., Univ. of Toronto, 1953; Vis. Prof. in Commonwealth Hist. & Instns., Indian Schl. of Int. Studies, New Delhi, 1958; Prof. of Pols. & Pro Vice Chancellor, Univ. of Lancaster, 1964-; Sr. Pro Vice Chancellor, ibid, 1973-. Mbrships: Chmn., British Co-ordinating Comm. for Int. Studies; Int. Pol. Sci. Assn.; Royal Inst. of Int. Affairs; U.K. Pol. Studies Assn.; Conflict Rsch. Soc.; Univ. Assn. for Contemporary European Studies in Politics, National & International, 1970; Introduction to International Relations, 1971. Address: Dept. of Politics, Univ. of Lancaster, Lancaster LA1 4YT. U.K. 3, 30, 128.

REZNIK, David, b. 5 Aug. 1923. Architect. Educ: Grad., Univ. of Brazil, 1948. Appts: Off. Post, Archt. Zeev Rechter, Tel-Aviv, Israel, 1951-56; Ptnr., Archt. H. Rau, Jerusalem, 1956-58; Pvte. Prac., Jerusalem, 1958-; Lectr., Fac. of Arch., Technion, Haifa, 1962-63; Assoc. Prof., ibid, 1966-69. Chmn., Assn. of Engrs. & Archts. in Israel, Jerusalem Br., 1971-74. Bldgs. incl: Hatzor Mus., Kibbutz Ayelet Hashachar, Israel; Kennedy Mem., Jerusalem; Journalists Assn. Bldg., Jerusalem; Dr. Israel Goldstein Synagogue (w. H. Rau), Jerusalem; Van Leer Fndn. Bldg. (w. S. Powsner), Jerusalem; The Soldier's House (w. A. Spector & M. Amisar), Jerusalem; Israel Pavillion (w. A. & A. Sharon), Montreal World's Fair, Canada, 1967; Israel Pavillion, N.Y. World Fair, U.S.A., 1964. Hons: Progressive Arch. Award, for Israel Pavilion, N.Y., 1964; Zeev Rechter Award, for Israel Goldstein Synagogue, 1965. Address: 4 Narkiss St., P.O. Box 346, Jerusalem, Israel.

RHEA, Claude H., b. 26 Oct. 1927. Dean, School of Music. Educ: B.A., Wm. Jewell Coll., 1950; B.Mu.Ed., 1953, M.Mu. Ed., 1954, Ed.D., 1958, Fla. State Univ. Appts: Dean, Schl. of Ch. Music, New Orleans Bapt. Theol. Sem., 1954-63; V.P. for Admin. Affairs & Chmn., Div. of Fine Arts, Houston Bapt. Coll., 1963-67; Cons., Ch. Music & Mass Communications, For. Mission Bd., Southern Bapt. Conv., 1967-69; Dean, Schl. of Music, Samford Univ., Ala., 1969-. Mbrships incl: Am. Assn. of Univ. Admnstrs.; Nat. Conf. of Arts in Educ., Music Educators Nat. Conf.; Nat. Coun. of Fine Arts Deans; Phi Eta Sigma; Phi Kappa Phi. Publs: Books - A Child's Life in Song, 1964; Claude Rhea's Favorite Gospel Songs, 1966; The Lottie Moon Cookbook, 1969; Num. recordings incl: Claude Rhea Sings, Sacred Masterpieces, Blesses Assurance, Majestic Themes. Hons. Incl: Citation of Achievement, Wm. Jewell Coll. 1961; Citation, City of Houston, 1965; Chmn., Music Comm., Billy Graham Ala. Crusade, 1972; Guest soloist, var. symph. orchs. Address: Schl. of Music, Samford Univ., Birmingham, AL 35209, U.S.A. 15, 46.

RHEA, Emerlee Lena(Craine), (Mrs. Lyle Gordon Rhea), b. 20 Dec. 1936. Educator; Drama Coach. Educ: A.B., Drury Coll., Springfield, Mo., 1959; Grad. work, Dallas Theatre Ctr., Tex., 1961-64. Appts: Tchr., Engl., Speech-Drama, Tucson Pub. Schls., 1959-61; Tchr., Engl., Reading, Speech-Drama, Rolla Jr. H.S., Mo., 1964-71, Drama Coach, 1964-71; Tchr., Engl., Theatre, Freshman H.S. & Sr. H.S., ibid, 1972-, Drama Coach, 1972-; Edit. Staff, Summer Theatre Directory, Am. Theatre Assn., 1969-; Directed sev. plays for Childrens Theatre, Rolla, 1966-72. Mbrships: Childrens Theatre Assn.; U.S. Inst. for Theatre Technol.; Coterie Littie Theatre; Chapt. Pres., Alpha Phi, 1958-59; Mbr., Cultural Comm., AAUW, 1972-73; Am. Nat. Theatre & Acad.; Mo. State Tchrs. Assn.; Chmn., Welfare Comm., Rolla Community Tchrs. Assn., 1970-71, P.R. Comm., 1972; Rolla Theatre Arts Players. Address: Route 1, Box L-189, Rolla, MO 64501, U.S.A. 8, 120.

RHINEBURGER, Kenneth Bruce, b. 10 Apr. 1912. Realtor; Lecturer; Pharmacist; Consultant. Educ: Univ. of Ark.; Memphis State Univ.; B.S., Univ. of Tenn. Appts: Realtor & Lectr., Real Estate & La. Ante Bellum Plantation Mansions, Memphis State Univ. Auth. on Southern Antebellum Classic Mansions. Mbrships: Memphis Bd. of Realtors, 1951-; Chmn., Educ. Comm., Realtors, 1958-59; Bd. of Dirs., Bd. of Realtors, 1959-60; Tenn. & Nat. Assns. of Realtors; Nat. Inst. of Real Estate Brokers; Non-res. Fac., Jt. Univ. Ctr., Memphis State Univ./Univ. of Tenn., 1956; Sigma Nu; Mbr. & Licensee in Ark. to practice Pharm.; Propagation of Faith; St. Jude Soc.; Benedictine Soc. of Perpetual Adoration; Charter, Med. Serv. Soc. of Am.; Delta Sigma; Kappa Iota Delta; Sigma Nu. Hons: Van Vleet Cert. for outstanding scholastic work, Univ. of Tenn., 1935; num. Outstanding Salesman Awards; int. recognition in Real Estate Advt., Howard Parrish Mag. Address: 376 Perkins Extended, Suite 208, Memphis, TN 38117, U.S.A. 125.

RHODE, Gotthold K.S., b. 28 Jan. 1916. University Professor. Educ: Studied Hist., Geog. & Slavic Langs., Univs. of Jena, Munich, Konigsberg, Breslau; Dr. Phil., Breslau, 1939; Habilitation, Hamburg, Germany, 1952. Appts. incl: Mil. Serv. & Scientific Wkr., Inst. of E. European Studies, Breslau, 1939-45; Asst., Hist. Sem., Hamburg, Germany, 1946-52; Rsch. Work, J.G. Herder Inst., Marburg, Germany & Lectr., E. European Hist., Marburg Univ., 1952-57; Assoc. Prof., E. European Hist., Univ. of Mainz, Germany, 1957; Prof., ibid, 1962-; Vis. Prof., Kan. Univ., U.S.A., 1969. Mbrships. incl: Verbd. d.Hist. Deutschlands; Bd. of Dirs., J. G. Herder-Forschungsrat, 1964-; Pres., Studiengesellsch. f. Fragen mittel-und osteurop. Partnerschaft, 1963-; Am. Assn. for the Adv. of Slavic. Publs. incl: Bradenburg-Preussen u.d. Protestanten in Polen, 1941; The Genesis of the Oder-Neisse-Line, Sources & Documents (w. W. Wagner), 1959; Ed., East Europe Monographs (w. J. Hauptmann), 1969, Gesch.d.Stadt Posen, 1953; Num. articles in handbooks, encys. & periodicals. Recip. Georg Dehio Prize for Hist. of Culture and Ideas, 1973. Address: Kapellenstr. 8, Mainz-Gonsenheim, German Fed. Rep. 92.

RHODES, Francis Arlington, b. 23 June 1908. Educator. Educ: B.A., 1930; M.A., 1946, Ed.D., 1948, Univ. of Fla.; Postdoct. work in Schl. Admin., Columbia Univ., 1949. Appts. incl: Supt. of Schls., Tallahassee & Leon Co. (combined systems), 1937-45; Mil. Serv., 1942-45; Lt. Cmdr., USNR, 1942-46., inclng. 20 months' serv. w. Cmdr. of Serv. Squadron, S. Pacific; Assoc. Prof., Educ., Miss. State Univ., 1948-51; Specialist in Surveys, Fla. State Dept. of Educ., 1951-60; Hd. of Survey Sect., 1953-60; Vis. Prof., Educ., Fla. State Univ., summer sessions, 1954-60; Assoc. Prof., Educ., Fla. State Univ., 1960-61; Dean, Coll. of Educ., Miss. State Univ., 1961-70; Admnstr., Tchr. Educ., Fla. Dept. of Educ., 1971-72; Vis. Prof., Rollins Coll., 1972-. Mbrships: incl: Pres., Grad. Coun., Phi Kappa Tau; Bd. of Dirs., Rotary; Kts. of Columbus, 4th Degree; Am. Legion; SAR (Former Pres.); Educ. Comm., Starkville Chmbr. of Comm.; Miss., Fla. & Tallahassee (Pres.) Histl. Socs. Author of publs. on educ. Address: 909 Washington St., Tallahassee, FL 32303, U.S.A. 2, 7, 15, 108, 128, 130, 131, 141.

RHODES, Marion, b. 17 May. 1907. Artist; Retired Lecturer in Art. Educ: Huddersfield Art Schl., U.K.; Leeds Coll. of Art; Ctrl. Schl. Arts & Crafts, London; Cert., Univ. of Oxford, 1930. Appts: Pt.-time, Huddersfield Art Schl.;

Scunthorpe Grammar Schl.; West Ham H.S.; Pt.-time Lectr., Berridge House Trng. Coll.; Enfield Co. Schl. Fellowships: Royal Soc. of Painters, Etchers & Engravers; Royal Soc. of Arts; Soc. of Ancient Monuments. Mbrships: Hon. Life, Soc. of Graphic Artist; Assn. Artistes Francais; Manchester Acad. Exhibs. incl: Royal Acad., London, 1954; Royal Soc. of Artists; Paris Salon, France; Walker Art Gall., Liverpool; S. London, Leeds, Bradford, Huddersfield Galls.; S. Africa; USA. Works in permanent exhib. incl: British Mus. Print Room; Bradford Art Gall., Huddersfield Art Gall., etc. Works reproduced in Teach Yourself Etching; The Sunday Observer; Manchester Guardian, etc. Recip. of many hons. for work. Address: 2 Goodwyn Ave., Mill Hill, London, NW7 3RG. U.K. 1, 43, 128.

RHODES, Patricia Mary. Painter. Educ: Langs., Montreux, Switzerland; Calder Coll. of Domestic Sci.; Art, Univ. of Liverpool, U.K. Serv. WWII. Grp. Exhibs. incl: Liverpool Open Exhib., 1959, '67; Tour of Municipal Galls., England & Wales, 1960; Paris Salon, 1960-71; Bradford Open Exhib., 1961; Salon Bosio, Monte Carlo, 1962; 2nd. Biennial of Int. Art, Les Sardes, 1963; Rassegna Int. of Contemp. Art, 1969; New Engl. Art; Flower Paintings, Royal Inst. of Oil Painters; Nat. Soc.; Soc. of Women Artists; Royal Inst. of Painters of Watercolour. Major works: Rhododendron, watercolour, pvte. collect.; Mixed Spring Flowers, oil, pvte. collect.; Alabaster & Fruit, oil; Farmhouse in Denbighshire, oil. Mbrships. incl: Exec. Comm. & Coun., Sandon Studios Soc., Liverpool, 1959; House Sec., 1961; Centro Studi e Scambi, Rome, Italy, 1970; Hon. Rep., 1971; English Speaking Union; Num. hosp., soc. & animal welfare comms.; Formby Ladies Golf Club Coun., 1949-52, '66-69. Contbr. to art jrnls. Hons: Medal & Dip., Centro Studi e Scambi Int., Rome, 1970; Silver Medal, Accad. Tommaso Campanella, ibid, 1970; Dip. of Hon., Int. Salon, Biarritz, 1970. Address: The Rowans, Blundellsands, Liverpool L23 6UW, U.K. 133.

RHYNE, Charles Sylvanus, b. 29 Mar. 1932. College Professor. Educ: Tyler Schl. of Fine Art, Temple Univ., Phila., Pa., 1950; Wittenberg Coll., Springfield, Ohio, 1950-54; Univ. of Chgo., Chgo., Ill., 1954-60; Courtauld Inst. of Art, London, U.K. Appts: Instr., Art Hist. & Humanities, Reed Coll., Portland, Ore., 1960-62; Asst. Prof., ibid, 1962-66; Assoc. Prof., 1966-73; Chief Rdr., Advanced Placement Prog. in Hist. of Art, 1970-. Mbrships: Nominating Comm. for Bd. of Dirs., Coll. Art Assn. of Am., 1971; Soc. of Archtl. Histns.; Friends of the Courtauld Inst., London; Portland Art Mus.; Ore. Histl. Soc. Hons. incl: Fulbright Fellowship, London, 1962-64; Sr. Fellow, Humanities Rsch. Ctr., Reed Coll., 1967-68; Fellowship, Nat. Endowment for Humanities, 1972-73. Address: Reed Coll., Portland, OR 97202, U.S.A. 13.

RIBA, Paul Francis, b. 25 Jan. 1912. Painter. Educ: Pa. Acad. of Fine Arts, Phila.; Grad., Cleveland Inst. of Art, Ohio, 1936. Appts. incl: Tchr., Cleveland Inst. of Art, 1949-62. Work includes murals, illustrations, paintings, fabric & wallpaper designs, archtl. & interior designs. Commns. incl: Cleveland Airport (mural), 1937; Statler Hotels (series of murals); Ind. Univ. (fabric design). Exhibd. in num. Mus.' & shows inclng. Carnegie Int., Pitts., Pa., 1947, 1948, 1949, 1952, N.Y. World Fair, Art in U.S.A., N.Y. & Seattle World Fair. Represented by Grand Ctrl. Art Galls., N.Y., Palm Beach Galls., The Gall., Ft. Lauderdale, Oehlschlaeger Galls., Chgo. & Sarasota, Foster Harmon Gall., Naples, Italy & Brian Riba Gall.,

Palm Beach. Works in num. pub. & pvte. collects. inclng. White House, Wash. DC, Smithsonian Instn., Wash. DC, Ill. State Mus., Springfield & Art Mus. of the Palm Beaches, Fla. Mbrships: Fellow, Royal Soc. of Arts, London, U.K., 1973; Artist's Guild, Art Mus. of the Palm Beaches, Bd. Mbr., 1972. Hons. incl: num. Art awards & prizes; paintings selected for representation in Fine Am. Art Calendar, 1962-66. Address: 112 Worth Ct. S., W. Palm Beach, FL 33405, U.S.A. 37.

RIBALTA, Martin, b. 17 Feb. 1907. Business & Organizational Administrator. Appts: Pres., Hijo de J. Ribalta S.A., 1947; V.P., Banco Credit Andorrá, 1953; V.P., Banco Popular Español, 1956; Pres., TELERASA ZENITH, 1960; Pres., TEIN, S.A., Real Estate & Bldgs, 1966; Pres., URPISA, S.A., HOLDING, 1968; Pres., TELECRONO, S.A., 1974. Mbrships: Pres., Hosp. de la Santa Cruz y de San Pablo; Am. Chmbr. of Comm. for Spain; Camara Oficial del Comerceio e Industria. Address: Balmes 429, 6°, 1ª, Barcelona 6, Spain.

RIBEIRO, Eurico Branco, b. 29 Mar. 1902. Surgeon. Educ: M.D., Med. Schl., Univ. of São Paulo, Brazil, 1927. Appts: Surg. in chief, Railroad Assns.; Gen. Surg., Caixa da Estrada de Ferro Sorocabana, Caixa of São Paulo Railway, Soc. of Chaufeurs; Dirs., Sanatorio São Lucas; Pres., Fndn. for Progress of Surg. Mbrships. incl: Fellow, Int., Am. & Brazilian Colls. of Surgs., Int. Coll. of Digestive Surg., Acad. of Scis., N.Y.; Past Pres., Rotary Club, & Med. Acad., São Paulo, Fndr., Brazilian Soc. of Writer Doctors; Sec., P.E.N. Club, São Paulo. Publs. incl: Estudos Cirurgicas, 6 vols.; Medico, Pintor e Santo, 4 vols.; Lucas, o medico, escravo; A cascase dos nervos na Lepra; Litiase do apendice; Rotary em evoluçao; Rotary aos 50 anos. Hons. incl: profl. awards; Hon. Citizen, Curitiba City, Brazil; Hon. Mayor, San Antonio Tex., U.S.A. Address: Caixa Postal 1574, 01000 São Paulo, S.P., Brazil.

RIBEIRO, Pedro Freire, b. 1 Sept. 1913. Professor of History. Educ: Bach. Legal & Soc. Scis., Univ. of Rio de Janeiro, Brazil, 1936; Bach. Geog. & Hist., Univ. of Brazil, 1942, Lic., 1943; Doct., Soc. Scis., ibid, 1946; D.Sc., Univ. of Estado da Guanabara, 1955. Appts: Prof., Ancient Hist., Univ. of Estado da Guanabara, 1942, Hist., Mil. Coll., Rio de Janeiro, 1944, Hist. of Civilization, Univ. of Brazil, 1948, Diplomatic Hist. & Contemporary World Pols., Min. of Foreign Affairs, 1947, Brazilian Studies, Univ. of San Marcos, Lima, Peru, & Cultural Attaché, Brazilian Embassy, Lima, 1957; Prof., Am. Hist., Univ. Fed. Fluminense, 1971; Dean, Inst. of Human Scis., Univ. of Guanabara, 1969-. Publs. incl: The Clisthenes Reform & the Athenian Democracy; Basis of the Imperial Politics of the Achaemenians; In Praise of the Learned Scribe. Hons. incl: Cmdr., D.S.O., Peru, 1960. Address: Avenide Maracanã, 1500 apt. 401, Muda. Rio de Janeiro, Estado da Guanabara, Brazil. 136.

RIBERA, François, b. 17 May 1930. Poet; Writer; Lecturer; Dancing Instructor. Educ: Docteur ès lettres, Sorbonne, Paris, France. Pres., Cultural Ensemble Les Damoiseaux; Vice Consul of Mexico, Lyons, France. Mbrships: Inst. Int. de Culture; Assn. Int. des Ecrivains Latins. Publs: Parfums d'Espagne (poems); Preludes pour ma Guitare (poems); Rythmes d'Orient (poems); La Danse Chretienne (essay); Les Ballet de Cour de la Renaissance en Savoie. Hons: Chevalier Commandeur d'Isabelle la Catholique, Spain; Palmes Académiques; Chevalier Commandeur de l'Ordre de la Couronne d'épines; Mérite artistique et culturel;

Gold Medal of Arts, Scis., Letters; Chevalier du Mérite Nat. Français. Address: 22 Rue Crillon, 69006, Lyons, France. 43.

RICCIARDI, Anthony, b. 5 June 1922. Dentist. Educ: B.A., Upsala Coll., E. Orange, N.J., U.S.A., 1951; D.D.S., Temple Univ. Schl. of Dentistry, Phila, Pa., 1958; Intern & Res., Mountainside Hosp., Montclair, N.J., 1958-60. Appts: Lt. Col., USMCR, WWII, 1942-48; Korea, 1952-54; Dental Staff, Mountainside Hosp., 1960; Schl. Dentist, Westfield Schl. System, N.J., 1960-61; Dental Staff, St. Elizabeth's Hosp., Elizabeth, N.J., 1963; Cons., Implants Int., N.Y.C., 1971. Mbrships: incl: Am. Dental Assn.; Am. Acad. of Implant Dentistry; Int. Coll..of Oral Implantol.; Fellow, Acad. of Gen. Dentistry; Fellow, Royal Soc. of Hlth.; Inst. for Adv. Dental Rsch.; Inst. for Endosseous Implants; Plainfield Dental Soc.; Pres., Nat. Gymnastic Clin., 1963; Pres., Nat. Gymnastics Judges Assn., 1963. Publs: Articles in dental jrnls. Address: 200 E. Dudley Ave., Westfield, NJ 07090, U.S.A. 6.

RICE, Arthur Henry, b. 6 Sept. 1900. Editor; Author; Educator; Educ: A.B., Ctrl. Mich. Univ., Mt. Pleasant, 1925; M.A., Univ. of Mich., 1934; Ph.D., 1947. Appts: Reporter & Dept. Ed., Saginaw Daily News, 1919-23; Alumni Sec. & Jrnlsm. Div. Hd., Ctrl. Mich. Univ., 1926-29; Ed., Mich. Educ. Jrnl. & Dir., P.R., Mich. Educ. Assn., 1929-47; Ed., Mich. Educl. Planning Comm., 1935-36., The Nation's Schls., 1947-63; Editl. Cons. & Writer, 1963-; Vis. Prof., Northwestern Univ., Evanston, Ill., 1948-60, summer fac., Univ. of Mich., 1947, '48, Univ. of Dela., 1954, Univ. of Colo., 1952, '56, Houston Univ., 1956; Prof. of Educ. & Coord., Instrnl. Systems in Tchr. Educ., Ind. Univ., 1964-70. Mbrships: Pres., Educl. Press Assn. of Am., 1948 (V.P., exec. comm., 1949-50); Sem. Cons., Nat. Schl. P.R., 1962. Publs. incl: Ninety Guides to Better Public Relations, 1946; co-author, Better Public Relations for Rural & Village Schools, 1946. Recip., LL.D., Ctrl. Mich. Univ., 1950; Address: 3705 Cameron Ave. R. 12, Bloomington, IN 47401, U.S.A.

RICE, Beverly Ann (Mrs. Larry T. Rice), b. 2 Feb. 1934. Company Vice President. Educ: B.S., Textile Merchandising, Schl. of Bus., Ind. Univ., Bloomington, 1956. Appts: Mgr., Coll. Bd.-Asst. to Fashion Dir., L.S. Ayres & Co., 1956; Buyer, Gown Room Dresses, ibid, 1959; Fashion Dir., 1965; Divisional Mdse. Mgr., Better Apparel, 1966; Divisional V.P., 1969. V.P., Merchandising, L.S. Ayres & Co., 1973-. Mbrships: Beta Sigma Pi; Alpha Omicron Pi; I.U. Alumni Assn.; I.U. Womens' Club; N. Grp., Indpls. Symph. Orch.; Sustaining Mbr., Indpls. Mus. of Art; Indpls. Mus. of Art Alliance; Bd. of Fellows, Northwood Inst.; Indpls. Womens' Chmbr. of Comm.; N.Y. Fashion Grp.; Bd. of Dirs., Tanner of N.C., 1974-. Address: 4532 N. Pennsylvania St., Indianapolis, IN 46205, U.S.A. 5.

RICE, (Boone) Douglas, Jr., b. 24 Mar. 1942. Classical Guitarist; Composer; Editor; Educator. Educ: B.Mus., Cornish Schl., 1969; 5 yrs. at Univ. of Wash.; studied guitar w. Chris Jordan, Alice Artzt, Theory w. John Cowell & conducting & composition w. Lockrem Johnson. Appts: Fac., Helen Bush Schl., 1966-69 & Cornish Schl., 1970 & 73; Affiliated Fac., Bellevue Community Coll.; V.P. & Guitar Ed., Puget Music Publs., Inc.; Adjudicator, Wash. State Music Educs. Assn., 1972. Mbrships: on Bd. & Auditions Chmn., Seattle Music Tchrs. Assn.; Guitar Chmn., Wash. State Music Tchrs. Assn.; Seattle Classic Guitar Soc.; Broadcast Music, Inc. Am. Mus. Ctr.; Am.

String Tchrs. Assn. Compositions incl: Divertimento No. 1; Sonata Concertante for Flute & Guitar; In Bethlehem that Night—a Christmas Cantata for narrator, small chorus, guitar, harp & organ; num. other chmbr. works. Address: 410 E. Roy St., Seattle, WA 98102, U.S.A. 130.

RICE, Denis Timlin, b. 11 July 1932. Lawyer. Educ: A.B., Princeton Univ., 1954; J.D., Univ. of Mich. Law Schl., 1959. Appts: Assoc., Pillsbury, Madison & Sutro, San Fran., 1959-61, Howard & Prim, San Fran., 1961-63; Ptnr., Howard, Prim, Rice, Nemerovski, Canady & Pollak, 1964-. Mbrships: Univ. Club., San Fran.; Bankers Club, San. Fran.; Olympic Club, San Fran; Corinthian Yacht Club, Tiburon, Calif.; Tiburon Peninsula Club; Nassau Club, Princeton, N.J.; Am. Bar Assn.; Fed. Bar Assn. Contbr. to profl. jrnls. Recip. Freedom Fndn. Medal, 1956. Address: 117 Hacienda Dr., Tiburon, CA 94920, U.S.A. 9.

RICE, Mabel McCullough, b. 8 Jan. 1904. Motor Company Executive; Land Developer. Educ: B.B.L., Law. Appts: w. McCullough Motor Co., Mt. Ayr, Iowa & Groundbirch, B.C., Canada, Dir. 1936-74, Pres. 1948-; Dir., McCullough Implement Inc., 1962-72; Dir., McCullough Motor Co. Ltd., 1969-73; Dir., Iowa Grain Co., Ringdeck Corp., Mount Ayr Dev. Corp. Mbrships: Dir., Ringgold Co. Hosp.; Bus. & Profl. Women's Club; Democratic Party; Meth. Ch.; Worthy Matron, Order of Eastern Star. Hons. incl: 50 Yr. Mbrship Card, Eastern Star; Life Mbr., Iowa Trapshooting Assn.; Airman Cert., 1945-74. Address: 117 E. Madison, Mount Ayr, IA 50854, U.S.A. 5, 138.

RICE, Maurice B., Jr., b. 24 Feb. 1924. Multi-line Insurance. Appts: Instr., Submarine Schl., USN; Asst. Dist. Mgr.-Dist. Sales Mgr., Life Ins. Co.; Sr. Instr., Life Underwriter Coun. (8 yrs.); Pres.-Educ. Chmn., Odessa Assn., Life Underwriters; Coord.-Hd. Instr., Casualty Ins. Course, Odessa Coll., Tex. Mbrships: Nat. Assn. Life Underwriters; Bd. Dirs. & Educ. & Trng. Chmn., Odessa Assn. Life Underwriters; Deacon & Bible Schl. Tchr., Sherwood Bapt. Ch. Developed Final Exam., Casualty Course, Odessa Coll., Tex., approved by Tex. State Bd. Ins. Address: 1207 E. 10th St., Odessa, TX 79761, U.S.A. 125.

RICE, Michael, b. 21 May 1928. Company Director. Appts: Chmn., Michael Rice & Co. Ltd., London, U.K., 1955-; Chmn., Consultancy Pracs. Comm., & Dir., Pub. Rels. Cons. Assn., 1969-. Mbrships: Int. P.R. Assn.; Coun., London Symph. Orch. Trust; Egypt Exploration Soc.; Treas., Comm. for E. Arabian & Gulf Studies; British Film Inst.; Inst. of P.R.; Inst. of Dirs. Publs: The Arab Case in the Conflict with Israel, 1967; Articles on Archeol., P.R., & Politics. Address: 23, 100 Lancaster Gate, London, W2, U.K.

RICE, Myrtle (Mrs. John Rice), b. 19 Nov. 1897. Teacher (Retired). Educ: B.A., Catawba Coll., 1945; Grad. work, Univ. of Fla., 1950-51. Appts: Tchr., N.C., 16 yrs.; Tchr., Fla., 16 yrs. Mbrships: Flagler Co. Schl. Bd., 1963-; Bd. Chmn., ibid, 1969-; Hon., Delta Kappa Gamma (Rho Chapt.) Flagler Co. Chmbr. of Comm.; Bd. of Dirs., Fla. Schl. Bds. Assn.; Sec., N. Coastal Div., Children's Home Soc. of Fla., 1965; Fla. Educ. Assn.; Nat. Retired Tchrs. Assn. Address: Rte. 1, Box 152, St. Augustine, FL 32084, U.S.A. 5, 57, 130, 132.

RICHARD, Corinne Genevieve (Mrs. Albert A. Richard). Educator. Educ: B.Ed., B.A., Washburn Univ., Topeka, 1953; M.Ed., Univ. of Kan., 1960; Grad. work, ibid & Kan. State

Univ. Appts: Tchr., rural schls., Nemaha & Jackson Cos., Kan., 1930-44; Co. Supt. of Pub. Instrn., Jackson Co., Kan., 1944-49 & 1963-69; Elem. Schl. Prin., Holton & Basehor, Kan., 1949-59; Tchr., Counselor & Supt. of Schls., Netawaka, Kan., 1959-63; Counselor & Elem. Schl. Prin., N. Jackson U.S.D. No. 335, Circleville, Kan., 1969-70; Elem. Schl. Prin., U.S.D. No. 338, Valley Falls, Kan., 1970-71; Secondary Schl. Counselor & Remedial Reading Specialist, ibid, 1971-; Owner, A-C Servs., 1967-. Mbrships. incl: Gov., Dist. 20, Pilot Club Int., 1972-73; Internal Affairs Coord., ibid, 1974-75; Sec., & Bd. of Dirs., Holton Chmbr. of Comm., 1967-; NEA. Author of articles in newspapers. Hon: Charles Kettering Fellows, 1967. Address: Route 3, Box 167, Holton, KS 66436, U.S.A. 5.

RICHARD, St. Clair Smith, b. 16 Nov. 1910. Writer; Editor. Educ: Grad., Pulitzer Schl. of Jrnlsm., Columbia Univ., N.Y.C. Appts. incl: Corres., United Press Int., N.Y., 1960-66; Instr., Jrnlsm., Good Counsel Coll., 1962-64; Ed., Independent Herald, Westchester, 1963-66; P.R. Dir., Westchester Lib. System, 1966-71; P.R. Counsel, Westchester Democratic Comm., & Legislative Asst., Democratic Ldr., Co. Bd. of Legislators, 1972-74. Mbrships: Vice Chmn., Nat. Soc. Bill of Rights; Bd. mbr., Mt. Vernon Chapt., UN Assn.; Bd. mbr., Afro-Am. Cultural Fndn.; Bd. mbr., Westchester Alumnae Chapt., Delta Gamma; Bicentennial Comm., Mt. Vernon, N.Y.; Westchester Co. Assn. Publs. incl: Women in the News; Public Relations—Who Needs it? ; Do It Yourself Publicity; Recip. of hons. Address: Halo House, Box 85, Larchmont, NY 10539, U.S.A. 5, 42, 138.

RICHARDS, Christine-Louise, b. 11 Jan. 1910. Artist; Composer; Musician; Publisher. Educ: Studied piano, U.S.A., 1923-29; Studied piano w. Maria Landes, Munich, Germany, 1929-30. Appts. incl: Fndr., Owner, Pres., Blue Star Music Publishing Co., New Berlin & Morris, N.Y., U.S.A. Mbrships: Phila. Art Alliance; Pa. Acad. Fine Arts; Am. Fed. Musicians; Nat. Assn. for Am. Composers & Conductors; Metropolitan Mus. of Art. Publs: The Blue Star Fairy Book of Stories for Children; The Blue Star Fairy Book of More Stories for Children; many songs; 'Cynthia' (Portrait Painting) shown in Artists U.S.A., 1970-71 (Art Book). Has exhibited, printed & published own original works at Stockbridge, Mass. Art Assn. shows & at 4 one-man exhibs at Stockbridge in 1947-48-53-54 & at Oneonta, N.Y. in 1960-61. Address: Springslea, P.O. Box 185, Morris, NY 13808, U.S.A. 5, 6, 57, 128, 131.

RICHARDS, Eleanor King (Mrs. Charles Donald Richards), b. 22 Sept. 1933. Dietitian. Educ: B.Sc., Auburn Univ., Ala., U.S.A., 1955. Appts: Tchr., Gadsden City Schls., Ala., 1955-56; '58-59; Dietitian, Bapt. Mem. Hosp., Gadsden, 1960-62; Chief Dietitian, W. State Hosp., Bolivar, Tenn., 1962-64; Bapt. Mem. Hosp., Gadsden, 1965-; Instr., Home Econs., Jacksonville State Univ., Ala., 1969; Dir. & Sec.-Treas., Leslie C. King Co. Inc., Real Estate, Gadsden, 1970-. Mbrships: Sect. Chmn., Ala. Dietetic Assn.; Pres., Gadsden Dietetic Assn.; Pres., S.E. Hosp. Conf. Dietitians; Pub. Rels. Chmn., Pilot Int., Dist II; Pres., Pilot Club, Gasden, 1970; Am. Dietetic Assn.; DAR; James Gadsden Sec., Antiquarian Soc. Address: 309 Casey Dr., Gadsden, AL 35903, U.S.A. 125.

RICHARDS, George Armsby, b. 26 Oct. 1903. Barrister-at-Law. Educ: Univ. Tutorial Coll., London, U.K.; Inns of Ct. Law Schl., ibid. Appts: Called to Bar, Middle Temple, 1940; Chmn., Rent Restriction Bd., Trinidad & Tobago, 1946; Stipendiary Magistrate, Trinidad & Tobago, 1947; Sr. Magistrate, ibid, 1956-61; Mbr., Senate, ibid, 1961-69; Atty. Gen. & Min. for Legal Affairs, ibid, 1962-64; Chmn., Peoples Nat. Movement, 1963; Chmn., Law Commn. of Trinidad & Tobago, 1970-71; Chmn., Trinidad & Tobago External Telecommunications Co., 1970; Chmn., Commonwealth Telecommunications Coun., 1970-73. Author, var. parliamentary & official papers. Hons: Q.C., 1963; Trinity Cross, Order of the Trinity. Trinidad & Tobago, 1970. Address: 5 Camaca Rd., Valsayn Pk., Trinidad, W. Indies.

RICHARDS, Horace Gardiner, b. 21 Mar. 1906. Geologist. Educ: A.B., Univ. of Pa., 1927; M.S., ibid, 1929; Ph.D., 1932. Appts. incl: Rsch. Assoc., N.J. State Mus., Trenton, 1934-40; Rsch. Assoc.-Chmn., Dept. of Geol., Acad. of Natural Scis., Phila., 1937-72; Hon. Curator of Quaternary Geol., ibid, 1972-; Lectr., Univ. of Pa., 1949-71; Sr. Rsch. Assoc., Lamont Geol. Observ., 1962-. Mbrships. incl: Fellow, Geol. Soc. of Am.; Paleontol. Soc.; Am. Assn. of Petroleum Geols.; Permanent Sec., Atlantic Coastal Plain Geol. Assn.; Pres., Int. Assn. for Quaternary Rsch., 1969-. Publs. incl: Record of the Rocks, 1953; Geology of the Delaware Valley, 1956; The Story of Earth Science, 1959; Annotated Bibliography of Quaternary Shorelines, 1965, supplement, 1970. Hons: Pres.'s Award, Am. Assn. of Petroleum Geols., 1945; Disting. Alumnus Award, Penn Charter Schl., 1971. Address: c/o Acad. of Natural Scis., 19th & Parkway, Philadephia, PA 19103, U.S.A. 6, 14.

RICHARDS, L.J., b. 12 Sept. 1908. Engineer; Executive. Educ: B.S., Okla. State Univ., 1933; Adv. Mgmt. Prog., Harvard Univ., 1952. Appts: Engr., Okla State Hwy. Dept., 1935-37; Geophys., Continental Oil Co., 1937-48; Chief Geophys., Hudson's Bay Oil & Gas Co. Ltd., 1948-52; Asst. Gen. Mgr., ibid, 1952-54; V.P., 1954-65; Dir., 1957-65; Pres. & Chief Exec. Off., 1965-70; Petroleum Cons., Pres., Quintana Exploration Co. & Quintana Properties Inc., 1970-. Mbrships. incl: Gov., Past Chmn., Canadian Petroleum Assn.; Past, Nat. Advsry. Comm. on Petroleum; Dir., W. Canadian Resources Trust Fund; Past Dir., Peace River Oil Pipe Line Co., Echo Bay Mines, Hudson's Bay Oil & Gas Co. Ltd. Address: Suite 2330, 355 4th Ave., S.W., Calgary, Alta., T2P OJ1, Canada. 2, 88.

RICHARDS, Neil Orrett. Architect & Town Planner. Educ: Grad. Dip. in Arch., & Acad. Cert. in Planning & Urban Design, Archtl. Assn., London, U.K., 1968. Appts: Archt.-Planner, Town Planning Div., Jamaican Govt. Serv., W. Indies, 1969; Asst. Govt. Town Planner, ibid, 1971; Guest Ed., Jamaica Archt. Mag., 1971; Fndr. & Prin., Neil O. Richards & Assocs., Archts. & Planners, Kingston, 1972-. Mbrships: Archtl. Assn., London; Asst. Sec., Jamaican Soc. of Archts., 1970. Publs: Articles in newspapers & profl. jrnls; The Growth & Problems of Metropolitan Kingston, Jamaica, 1967. Hons: Caribbean Cement Co. Award, 1972; Inst. of Jamaica Award, 1973. Address: 10 Oxford Terrace (Suite 2b), Kingston 5, Jamaica, W. Indies.

RICHARDS, Paul Westmacott, b. 19 Dec. 1908. University Professor. Educ: B.A., Trinity Coll., Cambridge, U.K., 1930; M.A., 1934; Ph.D., 1936; Sc.D., 1954. Appts. incl: Univ. Lectr., Cambridge, 1945-49; Prof., Bot., Univ. Coll. of N. Wales, Bangor, 1949-; Vice Prin., ibid, 1965-67; Bullard Fellow, Harvard Univ., U.S.A.; 1964-65. Fellowships: Linnean Soc.; Inst. of Biol. Mbrships. incl: Pres., Brit. Ecol. Soc., 1961-63; Pres., Brit. Bryol. Soc., 1949-51.

Publs: A Book of Mosses, 1950; The Tropical Rain Forest, 1952, 73; The Life of the Jungle, 1970. contbr. to sci. jrnls. & encys. Recip., C.B.E. Address: Schl. of Plant Biol., Univ. Coll. of N. Wales, Bangor, U.K. 50.

RICHARDS, R(ebekah) Ruth, b. 6 Jan. 1907. Educator. Educ: A.B., DePauw Univ., 1927; M.A., Univ. of Mich., 1932; Ph.D., Univ. of Chgo. 1949. Appts. incl: Instr.-Asst. Prof., Ohio Wesleyan Univ., Delaware, 1943-45; Asst. Prof., Wells Coll., Aurora, N.Y., 1947-48; Assoc. Prof. Ill. State Normal Univ., 1948-52; Tchr., Shortridge H.S., Indpls., 1953-72. Mbrships incl: Sigma Xi; Sigma Delta Epsilon; 2nd V.P., Caroline Scott Harrison Chapt., DAR, 1973-75; Soc. of Mayflower Descendents. Author of sic. publs. Address: 4923 A Adams Blvd., N. Dr., Indianapolis, IN 46220, U.S.A. 5, 8, 14, 15.

RICHARDSON, A.W., b. 23 Dec. 1922. Public Servant. Educ: B.A. (Hons), Univ. of Western Australia; Fellow, Commonwealth Inst. of Valuers Inc. Appts. incl: Chief Admin. Off. & Property Off., State Housing Commn. of Western Australia, 1950-60; Dir. of Lands & Surveys, Valuer Gen., Chmn. of var. Bds. & Commns., & Mbr. of Legislative Coun., Northern Ty., 1960-67; Asst. Sec., Dept. of External Territories, 1967-73; Asst. Sec., Commonwealth Dept. of Housing, 1973; Gen. Mgr., Monarto Dev. Commn., S.A., 1973-. Published sev. reports & appraisals on Govt. projs. Mbrships: Economics Soc. of Australia & N.Z; Commonwealth Parliamentary Assn. Address: Monarto Dev. Commn., 129 Green Hill Rd., N. Unley, S.A., Australia 5061. 23, 128.

RICHARDSON, Angus Victor, b. 17 Nov. 1913. Accountant. Appts: Off. Boy, Humes Ltd., Australia, 1929; Off. Mgr., Hume Inds. (Far E.) Ltd., Singapore, 1938; Acct., Humes Ltd., Perth, 1938, Melbourne, 1944; State Mgr., ibid, Sydney, 1954, Chief Sales Mgr., 1957, Asst. Gen. Mgr., 1959, Dpty. Gen. Mgr., 1964, Gen. Mgr., 1971, Mng. Dir., 1972. Mbrships: Fellow, Australian Soc. of Accts.; Assoc., Inst. of Sales & Marketing; Fellow, Australian Inst. of Mgmt.; Pres., Melbourne Rotary Club; Australian Club. Address: Humes Ltd., 185 William St., Melbourne, Vic., Australia 3000. 23.

RICHARDSON, Artemas Partridge, b. 24 May 1918. Landscape Architect. Educ: B.A., Williams Coll., Williamstown, Mass., 1940; B.S., Iowa State Coll., Ames, 1947. Appts. Incl: Ptnr., Olmsted Bros., 1950-61; Ptnr., Olmsted Assocs., 1961-64; Pres. & Treas., ibid, 1964-; Mbr. Planning Bd., Needham, Mass., 1956-62; Chmn., 1958-61; Mbr., Conservation Commn., ibid, 1963-64; Mbr. & Chmn., Mass. Bd. Registration Landscape Archts., 1968-73; Licensed Landscape Archt. in 12 states. Fellowships: Am. Soc. Landscape Archts.; Boston Soc. Landscape Archts. Mbrships. incl: Trustee, Trustees of Reservations, Mass., 1963-; Advsry. Commn., Boy Scouts Am., 1971-; Delta Phi; Tau Sigma Delta; Pi Gamma Alpha. Works incl: Univ. of Miss., Miss. State Univ.; Rock Creek Park, Md.; Armco Assn. Club Recreational Park, Ohio; Wickham Park, Conn; Design for Am. Mil. Cemetery, Cambridge, U.K; Master planning for num. insts. Recip., Silver Beaver Award, Boy Scouts Am., 1967. Address: 99 Warren St., Brookline, MA 02146, U.S.A. 6.

RICHARDSON, (Sir) John (Samuel), b. 16 June 1910. Consultant Physician. Educ: Univ. of Cambridge & St. Thomas's Hosp. Med. Schl., London, U.K.; M.B., B.Ch., Univ. of Cambridge, 1936; M.D., ibid, 1940; M.R.C.P., 1937; F.R.C.P., 1948. Appts: Physn., St.

Thomas's Hosp., London, 1949- & King Edward VII Hosp. for Offs., 1964-; Cons. Physn. to Army, 1964-. Mbrships: Gen. Med. Coun., 1967-; Chmn., Coun. for Postgrad. Med. Educ. for England & Wales, 1972-; Past Chmn., Jt. Cons. Comm., 1967-72; Past Pres., British Med. Assn., 1970-71, Royal Soc. of Med., 1969-71, Int. Soc. Internal Med., 1966-70; Master, Soc. Apothecaries, 1971-72. Publs: The Practice of Medicine, 2nd edit., 1960; Connective Tissue Disorders, 1963; Anticoagulant Prophylaxis & Treatment (co-author), 1965; Articles in med. jrnls. Hons. incl: M.V.O., 1943; Created Kt., 1960; Created Baronet, 1963. Address: Alvechurch, 1 Hillcrest Road., London W5 2JL, U.K. 1, 35, 43, 128.

RICHARDSON, Joseph Thomas, b. 20 Oct. 1926. Dental Educator. Educ: Middle Tenn. State Coll., 1947-48; D.D.S., Coll. of Dentistry, Univ. of Tenn., 1951; M.A., The Citadel, 1972. Appts: Lt., USNR Dental Corps, 1952-54; Pvte. Prac. of Gen. Dentistry, 1954-70; Res. Dentist, Tenn. Orphans Home, 1958-70; Maury Co. Bd. of Hlth., 1967-70; Chmn., ibid, 1968-70; Assoc. thru' Assoc. Prof., Dept. of Crown & Bridge Dentistry, Coll. of Dental Med., Med. Univ. of S.C., 1970-. Mbrships: Pres., 6th Dist. (Tenn.) Dental Soc., 1962-63; V.P., ibid, 1961-62, Alternate Deleg., 1970; Coun. on Mbrship., Tenn. State Dental Assn., 1958-61; V.P., Student Coun., Univ. of Tenn., 1950-51; Grand Master Psi Omega, 1949-50; Student Senate, Middle Tenn. State Coll., 1947-48. Contbr. to profl. jrnls. Recip. Outstanding Clin. Instr. Award, Med. Univ. of S.C., 1972. Address: 444 Wade Hampton Dr., Charleston, SC 29412, U.S.A. 7.

RICHARDSON, Lee, b. 11 Sept. 1926. Actor. Educ: Grad., Goodman Theatre. Appts: Leading Actor, N.Y. Shakespeare Festival 1962, Minn. Theatre Co., Tyrone Guthrie Theatre, Am. Shakespeare Festival, 1970-; Mbr., Nat. Endowment of the Arts, 1963-70; Prof., Yale Univ., 1970-72. Mbrships: Players Club, N.Y.C.; Penthouse Club, Mpls., Minn. Stage Appearances incl: Summer & Smoke; St. Joan; Volpone; Orthello; Vivat, Vivat, Regina; Death of Bessie Smith; Plays for Bleeker St.; King Lear; Merchant of Venice; Jockey Club Stakes; Arturo Ui; House of Atreus; Hamlet; Richard III; Twelfth Night; Uncle Vanya; Cherry Orchard; Skin of our teeth; Homecoming; Glass Menagerie; Doctor's dilemma; The Miser; Caucasian Chalk Circle. Address: R.F.D. 1, Redding Rd., Weston, CT 06880, U.S.A.

RICHARDSON, Luns Columbus, b. 29 Apr. 1928. College Administrator. Educ: B.A., Benedict Coll., Columbia, S.C., 1949; M.A., Tchrs. Coll., Columbia Univ., N.Y.C., 1958; Further studies, var. colls. Appts. incl: Dean of Men & Chap., Denmark Regional Tech. Inst., Denmark, S.C., 1949-64; Dir. of Compensatory Prog. of Educ., Dir. of Basic Studies, Assoc. Dean of Fac., Dir. of Institutional Self-Study, Dean of Admissions & Records, & Acting Pres., successively, Benedict Coll., Columbia, S.C., 1967-73; V.P., Voorhees Coll., Denmark, S.C., 1971-; To take off. as Pres., Morris Coll., Sumter, S.C., 1974. Mbrships: Am. Assn. for Higher Educ.; NEA; S.C. Educ. Assn.; Am. Acad. of Pol. & Soc. Scis.; Nat. Assn. of Secondary Schl. Prins.; Omega Psi Phi; Alpha Kappa Mu. Author of articles in educl. jrnls. Hons: H.H.D., Morris Coll., Sumter, S.C., 1973; Dr. of Pedagogy, Benedict Coll., Columbia, S.C., 1973. Address: Morris Coll., Sumter, SC 29150, U.S.A. 125.

RICHARDSON, M. Dwight, b. 20 Nov. 1949. Educational Administrator. Educ: B.A, Tenn. Technological Univ., Cookeville, U.S.A., 1971; M.A., ibid, 1972; Postgrad., Univ. of

Tenn., Knoxville. Appts: Grad. Asst., Tenn. Technological Univ., 1971-72; Prin., Elem. Schl., 1972-73; Coord., Fed. Progs., Sevier Co., Tenn., 1974-; Post, Field Enterprises, Inc.; Owner, Tanglewood Enterprises, Sevierville, Tenn. Mbrships. incl: Tenn. Educ. Assn.; S.C. Educ. Assn.; E. Tenn. Educ. Assn.; AAUP; E.Tenn. Histl. Soc.; Tenn. Histl. Soc.; Overton Co. Histl. Soc.; Fort Loudoun Assn.; Nat. Schl. Pub. Rels. Assn.; Masonic Lodge # 197; Kappa Delta Pi. Address: P.O. Box 68, Sevierville, TN 37862, U.S.A. 125.

RICHARDSON, Martha, b. 22 Apr. 1917. Nutrition Analyst. Educ: Univ. of Mo. Appts. incl: Instr., Home Econs., Univ. of Mo., Columbia, 1950-53; Hd. of Foods & Nutrition, Asst. Prof. Home Econs., Univ. of Utah, Salt Lake City, 1953-55, Acting Hd. of Dept., 1954-55; Assoc., U.S. Dept. of Agric., 1954-, currently Nutrition Analyst, Consumer & Food Econs. Div., Agric. Rsch. Serv., Hyattsville, Md. Author, num. profl. publs. Hons: Fellowship, Univ. of Mo., 1950; Distng. Alumnae Award, Centennial Celebration of Admission of Women to Univ. of Mo., 1968. Address: Consumer & Food Economics Div., Agricultural Rsch. Serv., 317 Federal Ctr. Bldg., Hyattsville, MD, U.S.A. 5, 7, 14, 15, 28.

RICHARDSON, Sam Scruton, b. 31 Dec. 1919. Principal, Canberra College of Advanced Education. Educ: B.A., Trinity Coll., Oxford Univ., U.K., 1946; M.A., 1947; Barrister-at-Law, Lincoln's Inn, London, 1958; LL.D., Ahmadu Bello Univ., 1967. Appts: Commnd. Off., Royal Marines, 1940-46; Dist. Commnr., Sudan Pol. Serv., 1946-54; Dist. Off., H.M. Overseas Civil Serv., 1954-58; Commnr. for Native Courts, Atty.-Gen.'s Chmbrs., N. Nigeria, 1958-61; Dir., Inst. of Admin., Zaria, ibid, 1961-67; Dpty. Vice-Chancellor & Ag. Vice-Chancellor, Ahmadu Bello Univ., ibid, 1962-67; Prof. of Pub. Admin. & Vice-Chancellor, Univ. of Mauritius, 1967-68; Prin., Canberra Coll. Adv. Educ., Australia, 1968-. Mbrships. incl: Utd. Oxford & Cambridge Univs. Club, London; Soc. of Pub. Tchrs. of Law. Publs. incl: co-author, The Native & Customary Courts of Nigeria, 1966; Notes on the Penal Code, 1960, '67. Hons: O.B.E., 1960; C.B.E., 1965. Address: Canberra Coll. Adv. Educ., P.O. Box 381, Canberra City, A.C.T., Australia, 2601.

RICHARDSSON, Richard Long. Economist. Educ: grad., Icelandic Coll. of Commerce, 1948, Univ. of Iceland, 1953. Appts: Treas., Indl. Bank of Iceland, 1953-55; Exec. Rep. to Norway for Icelandic Airlines, 1956; Hd., Icelandic State Tourist Bur., U.S.A., 1957-59; Treas., Icelandic Airlines, Inc., 1959-69; V.P., Rodin Enterprises, 1969-73; Treas., Douglas Gibbons, Hollyday & Ives, Inc., 1973-; Icelandic News Rep. to U.N., 1956-59; Mbr., Bd. of Zoning Appeals, Tuxedo Park, 1965-; Treas., Bd. of Educ., Tuxedo, 1966-68. Mbrships: Tuxedo Club; St. Anthony Club; U.S. Court Tennis Assn., Inc.; Yacht Club of Reykjavik; Reykjavik Golf Club; Past Pres., Icelandic Soc. Address: Tuxedo Park, NY 10987, U.S.A. 6, 16.

RICHEY, Robert W., b. 14 Aug. 1912. Professor; Author. Educ: B.S., B.S. in Educ., Wilmington Coll., Ohio, 1929-33; M.A., Ohio State Univ., 1937; Ph.D., ibid, 1941. Appts. incl: Asst. Prof., Ind. Univ., Bloomington, 1946-49; Assoc. Prof., ibid, 1949-53; Prof. of Educ., 1953-; Dir. of summer sessions, 1959-; Dean, Continuing Educ., 1970-. Mbrships. incl: V.P., Assn. Univ. Summer Sessions, 1967; Pres., ibid, 1968; Recorder, 1969-; Pres., N. Ctrl. Conf. on Summer Schls., 1968; Nat. Assn. of Univ. Ext.; AAUP; Phi Delta Kappa; Hon. mbr.,

Blu Key. Publs. incl: Planning for Teaching; An Introduction to Education, 1952, '68, '73; Co-author, Year-Around Operation in American Universities, 1963. Address: Office of Summer Sessions, Ind. Univ., Bloomington, IN 47401, U.S.A. 8, 15, 30.

RICHMAN, Mel-Pah Jacqueline. Teacher. Educ: B.A., Life Tchng. Cert., Southeastern State Coll., Durant, Okla.; Grad. study, Okla. Univ., Norman, & Okla. City Univ. Appts. as Piano Coach & Tchr., grades 1-12; Operator w. husband, cattle ranch Seokla, McCurtain Co. Mbrships. incl: Pres., Tom Schl. PTA; Volunteer Ldr., Youth Activities, Conservation & Hlth.; Tchr., Sunday Schl.; Dist. Dir., Okla. Bus. & Profl. Women's Club, 2 terms; Idabel Bus. & Profl. Women's Club Okla.; Fac. mbr., Nat. Piano Tchrs. Guild; Nat. League for Nursing; Instr., Red Cross Home Nursing; Sec., McCurtain Co. Home Demonstration Coun.; Chmn., Farm Bus. Women; Lib. Bd., Foreman, Ark.; McCurtain Co. Cattlemen's Assn.; Dir., McCurtain Co. Histl. Soc.; Okla. Deleg., White House Conf. on Children & Youth, 1960; Okla. Deleg., Nat. Conf. on Rural Children & Youth, 1963. Hons. incl: Farm Woman of the Yr., 1958; Emerald Clover 4-H Award, 25 yr. ldrship., 1972. Address: Rt. 1, Box 49, Foreman, AR 71836, U.S.A. 125.

RICHMOND, John, b. 10 Dec. 1907. Attorney. Educ: B.S., Univ. of Calif., Berkeley, 1928; M.S., 1934; LL.B., Oakland Coll. of Law, 1942. Appts. incl: Pres., Richmond Enterprises, 1928-; Atty., ibid, 1946-; Atty., San Fran. Bay area, 1946-. Mbrships incl: Calif. State Bar; Am., Fed. & Alameda Co. Bar Assns.; Nat. Lawyers Club; Vets for For. Wars; United Vets Coun. of Berkeley; Am. Judicature Soc.; AAAS; Am. Acad. of Pol. & Soc. Sci.; Am. Fisheries Soc.; Int. Oceanographic Fedn.; Nat. Hist. Soc.; Smithsonian Assocs.; Izaak Walton League Am.; Mason. Recip., Hon. Ph.D., Hamilton State Univ., 1973. Address: 1611 Bonita Ave., Suite No. 2, Berkeley, CA 94709, U.S.A. 9, 16, 22, 57, 59, 128, 129, 131.

RICHNER, Thomas Benjamin, b. 5 Nov. 1911. Concert Pianist; Organist; College Professor. Educ: B.M., West Va. Univ., U.S.A.; M.A., Columbia Univ.; Ed.D., ibid; Int. Organ Course, Helmut Walcha. Appts: 13 Piano Recitals (inclng. 6 Mozart Recitals), Town Hall, N.Y., U.S.A.; Fac., Manhattan Schl. of Mus., 1945-46; Fac., Tchrs. Coll., Columbia Univ., 1945-68; Prof. of Mus., Douglas Coll., Rutgers Univ., 1959-; Dir., Colby Coll. Ch. Mus. Inst.; Organist, 1st Ch. of Christ Scientist, Boston, Mass. Mbrships: Nat. Arts Club; Life Mbr., Sinfonia, The Bohemians, Am. Guild of Organists, St. Wilfrid Club; Mus. Tchrs. Nat. Assn. 2nd Concert Tour of Far East, 1973. Publs: Orientation for Interpreting Mozarts Piano Sonatas (book), second printing 1972); Techniques for Piano & Organ—A Comparative Study (Am. Guild of Organists Quarterly & The Piano Teacher); The Pianos of Mozart's Day, Piano Quarterly (article), 1973. Hons. incl: Mus.D., Colby Coll., 1958; H.H.D., Lander Coll., Greenwood, S.C., 1971. Address: 21 Caroline Ave., Setauket, L.I., NY 11733, U.S.A. 4.

RICHTER, Curt Paul, b. 20 Feb. 1894. Psychologist. Educ: B.S., Harvard, 1917; Ph.D., Johns Hopkins, 1921. Appts: Dir. of Psychobiological Lab., Phipps Psych. Clin., Johns Hopkins Hosp., 1922; Prof. Emeritus, Psychobiol., Johns Hopkins Med. Schl., 1960. Mbrships: Nat. Acad. of Scis.; Am. Philosophical Soc.; Am. Acad. of Arts & Scis.; Century Assn., N.Y.C.; Inst. for Advanced Study, 1957-58; Phi Beta Kappa; Hon. mbr.,

Am. Neurological Soc., Harvey Soc. Author of Biological Clocks in Medicine & Psychiatry. Hons: Annual award, Am. Psychological Soc.; Warren Medal, Soc. of Experimental Psychol., 1950; Disting. citizen of Denver, 1958. Address: Phipps Psychiatric Clin. 318, Johns Hopkins Hosp., Balt., MD 21205, U.S.A. 2, 34.

RICHTER, Horst-Eberhard, b. 28 Apr. 1923. Psychoanalyst; Professor of Psychosomatic Medicine. Educ: Med., Psychol. & Philos., Berlin, 1943-49; Trng. in Psychoanalysis, ibid, 1949-54; Trng. in Psych., 1955-58; Dr.med.; Dr.phil. Appts: Dir., Psychoanalytic Inst., Berlin, 1959-62; Dir., Psychosomatic Clin., Univ. of Giessen, 1962-. Mbrships: German Paychoanalytic Assn.; P.E.N. Int. Publs: Eltern, Kind und Neurose, 1963 (transl. into French & Italian); Herzneurose, 1969 (transl. into Italian); Patient Familie, 1970 (transl. into Engl., French, Italian, Danish, Dutch & Swedish); Die Gruppe, 1972 (transl. into Engl. French, Italian, Dutch & Swedish); Giessen-Test, 1972; Lernziel Solidaritoit, 1974. Recip. Rsch. Prize, Swiss Psychosomatic Soc., 1970. Address: Ludwigstrasse 76, 63 Giessen, German Fed. Repub.

RICKERT, Russell Kenneth, b. 6 Feb. 1926. Professor of Education. Educ: B.S., W. Chester State Tchrs. Coll., Pa., 1950; M.S., Univ. of Delaware, 1953; Ed.D., N.Y. Univ. 1961. Appts: Sci. Tchr., Queen Ann's Co., Md., 1950-52; Sci. Tchr., Seaford, Del., 1952-55; Phys. Instr., Salisbury State Tchrs. Coll., Md., 1955-56; Asst. Prof.-Prof., W. Chester State Coll., Pa., 1956-64; Prof. & Chmn., Dept. of Sci., ibid., 1964-68; Prof. & Chmn., Dept. of Phys., 1968-69; Prof. & Dean, Schl. of Sci. & Maths., 1969-. Mbrships: AAAS; Am. Assn. Phys. Tchrs; AAUP; Nat. Sci. Tchrs. Assn. Author, Introduction to Astronomy & Space Exploration, 1974. Address: 921 Baylowell Drive, W. Chester, PA 19380, U.S.A. 14.

RICKLETON, David, b. 8 Nov. 1916. Engineer. Educ: Brooklyn Polytech. Inst.; Pratt Inst. Appts: Draftsmen, Engr., Cons., V.P., Aeronca Inc., Environmental Control Grp. Mbrships: Am. Soc. of Heating, Refrigerating and Air Conditioning Engrs.; Dir., Pres., 1974. Nat. Soc. of Profl. Engr.; Publs: (papers) Psychometrics or Dual Duct Systems, 1963; Analysis of Terminal Unit Systems, 1967; Terminal Equipment for Air Systems, 1969; Variable Volume Stystems Equipment, 1969; (Energy Conservation Aspects of Variable Volume Systems, 1972; Variable Air Volume Systems, 1972.) Address: 3413, Highview Rd., Charlotte, NC 28210, U.S.A. 7.

RICKMAN, Emily Elizabeth Jones. Home Economics Education Assistant State Supervisor. Educ: B.S., Longwood Coll. & Univ. of Va., 1927; M.A., Geo. Peabody Coll., 1947; Further study, Duke Univ. & Va. Polytechnic Inst. Appts: Tchr., home econs., Va. Pub. Schls., 18 yrs.; Asst. to State Supvsr. of home econs. in planning & administering State Prog. working w. 900 tchrs., 1945-73; Mbr. of team to asst. schl. div. to impliment standards of quality & set up Objectives for Schl. Divs.; Asst. in conducting state & local workshops & confs. for tchrs.; Asst. to State Supts. in planning & equipping home econ. depts. Mbrships. incl: Nat. Assn. for Supvsrs.; Am. Home Econs. Assn.; Am. Voc. Assn.; Bus. & Profl. Women's Club; Life mbr., Va. Retd. Tchrs. Assn.; Hon. mbr., Future Homemakers of Am., 1973; Hon. mbr., Piedmont Fedn., ibid, 1973. Address: 128 Forest Lawn Dr., Danville, VA 24541, U.S.A. 125.

RIDDELL, Gordon, b. 4 Aug. 1940. Bank Director. Appts: Trust Off., E.D. Sassoon Banking Co. Ltd., London, U.K. & Nassau, Bahamas; Sec., Royal Bank Trust Co. Ltd.; Sr. V.P. & Dir., Sterling Bank & Trust Co.; Notary Pub., Cayman Islands, W. Indies, 1969. Mbrships. incl: Fellow, Inst. of Bankers; Overseas Bankers Club; British Inst. of Mgmt.; Fellow, Inst. of Admin. Mgmt.; Fellow, Inst. of Dirs.; W. India Comm.; Royal Commonwealth Soc.; British Standards Inst.; Past Sec., Cayman Islands Hotel Assn.; Jamaica Club, Kingston, Jamaica. Contbr. to bus. publs. Paintings in pvte. collections. Address: Westmeston Lodge, Westmeston, Sussex, U.K. 109.

RIDDLE, Lindsey Grant, b. 11 Aug. 1910. Professional Engineer. Profl. Registered Engr. of La. Apts: Studio Supvsr., WHB Broadcastig Co., Kan. City, MO., 1933-46; Chief Engr., Stephens Broadcasting Servs., Inc., New Orleans, La. 1946-48; V.P., - Chief Engr., Royal Street Corp., 1948-73; Cosmos Broadcasting of La., Inc., 1973-. Mbrships: Chmn., Broadcast Servs. Sub-Comm, La., La. Ind. Advsry. Comm., 1967-; Nat. Assn. of Broadcasters Tech. Advsry. Comm., 1969-71; Nat. Assn. of Broadcasters Tech. Comm., 1971-73; Assn. Broadcasting Engrng. Standards; Sr., IEEE Assoc., Fed. Communications Cons. Engrs.; Nat. Soc. Profl. Engrs.; La. Engrng. Soc.; New Orleans Engrng. Club; Radio Pioneers; Amateur Radio Deita DX Club; VHF Club of New Orleans; City of New Orleans Engrng.; Armed Forces Radio Servs., Amateur Radio Extra Class License, W5JG; Pres., Royal Street Radio Club; Amateur Radio Replay League; Tech. Advsry. Delgado Coll. of New Orleans; Young Mens Bus. Club, New Orleans,; Chambr. of Comm., ibid; Lakewood Property Owners Assn.; S. Ctrl. Mod. Lang. Assn.; 1st Class Radiophone FCC Permit. Publs: Articles in Broadcasting Engineering, Mar. 1970, Radio-Electronics, Aug. 1970. Technician Engineer, June, 1971. Address: 5646 Bellaire Dr., New Orleans, LA 70124, U.S.A. 7.

RIEDEL TELGE, Claudio, b. 2 Feb. 1932. Industrialist; Diplomat. Educ: B.A., Univ. of Chile; Univ. San Carlos, Guatemala. Appts: Capt., Chilean Army; Civil Attaché, Chilean Embassy, Guatemala, 1960-71; Chilean Chargé d'Affaires, ibid, 1968-69; Chilean Deleg. (alternate), 24th. Gen. Assembly, U.N., N.Y., U.S.A., 1969; Hon. Consul of Paraguay, Guatemala, 1968-; Pres., Obras & Montajes S.A., Guatemala; Bd., Tecnico Mercantil Temsa, Marpica S.A., I TT, Guatemala, S.A., Flota Mercante Gran Centroam., Flomerca. Mbrships: Soc. for Int. Dev., Wash.; Guatemala Country Club; Camara de la Contruccion, Guatemala. Contbr. of articles to Guatemalan jrnls. Hons: Kt. Cmdr., Quetzal Order, Guatemala, 1964; Nat. Order of Merit, Kt., Ecuador, 1966; 1st. Class Nat. Order of Merit, German Fed. Repub., 1969; Kt. Cmdr. Order of Merit, Ecuador, 1971. Address: P.O. Box 927, Guatemala City, Guatemala, C.A. 136.

RIEDL, John Orth, b. 10 June 1905. College Professor & Dean. Educ: A.B., Marquette Univ. 1927; A.M., 1928; Ph.D., 1930. Appts. incl: Assoc. Prof., Philos., Marquette Univ., 1944-46; Prof. & Dean, Grad. Schl., ibid 1954-60; Prof. Philos., 1960-66; Chief, Cath. Affairs, U.S. Mil. Govt., Germany, 1946-48; Chief, Educ. Br., ibid, 1948-49; Chief, Educ. Br., Off. of US High Cmd. for Germany, 1949-52; Off. & Dir., Pub. Affairs Field Ctr., Freiburg, 1952-53; Rsch. Writer. 1953-54; Dean i/c, Queensborough Community Coll., U.S.A., 1966-67; Dean, Fac., ibid, 1966-. Mbrships. incl: Am. Cath. Philos. Assn.; AAAS; Am. Cath. Educ. Assn.; AAUP. Publs. incl: Exercises in

Logic, 1st Series, 1935; 2nd Series, 1947; A Catalogue of Renaissance Philosophers, 1940; The University in Process, 1965; Chapts. in books, articles, etc. Address: 42-19, 219 St., Bayside, NY 11361, U.S.A. 2, 6, 8, 13, 15, 30, 49.

RIEMSCHNEIDER, Randolph, b. 17 Nov. 1920. University Professor. Educ: Dip. Chem., 1941; Dr.rer.nat., 1943; Inaugurated for Chem., Univ. of Berlin, 1947. Appts. incl: Lectr., organic & physiological chem., Fac. of Natural Sci., Fac. of Med., Free Univ. of Berlin, 1948-54; Assoc. Prof., ibid, 1954-58; Extraordinary Prof., 1958; Dir., Inst., of Biochem., 1962-; Dir.-Coord., Central Inst. of Chem., Universidade Fed. de Santa Maria, Brasil, 1964-. Mbrships: Gesellschaft für Biologische Chemie; Hochschulverband; Lion Club; A.D.U.C. Publs. incl: Biochemisches Grundpraktikum, 1970; Aula pratica de Bioquimica 1, 1970; Organizacao e Estabilecemento do Instituto Central de Quimica, 1970; Articles in sci. jrnls. Hons: Doct., Universidad Fed. de Santa Maria, 1973; Prof., ibid, 1973. Address: Postfach 136, 1 Berlin 19, W. Berlin, German Fed. Repub. 43, 92.

RIES, Edward Richard, b. 18 Sept. 1918. Petroleum Explorationist. Educ: A.B., Univ. of S.D., Vermillion, 1941; M.S., Univ. of Okla, Norman, 1943; Ph.D., ibid, 1951; Geol., Harvard Univ., Cambridge, Mass., 1946-47. Appts. incl: Jr. Geologist, Carter Oil Co., 1943-44, Geologist 1944-49; Sr. Geologist, Standard Vacuum Oil Co., Calcutta, India, 1951-53; Regional Geologist, Standard Vacuum Petroleum Maatschappij, Palembang, Sumatra, Indonesia, 1952-59; Geological Advsr., Far E., Africa & Oceania, Mobil Petroleum Co., N.Y., 1962-65, Europe & Far E., Mobil Oil Corp., ibid, 1965-71; Regional Explorationist, E. & S.E. Asia, Mobil Oil Corp., Dallas, Tex., 1971-73; Sr. Regional Explorationist, Asia-Pacific, ibid, 1973-. Mbrships. incl: Am. Assn. Petroleum Geologists; AAAS; Phi Sigma Xi; Soc. of Exploration Geophysicists. Publs: Articles in scientific jrnls.; Geology of the Princely State of Tripura, India, 1952; Parameters & Methods for Basin Hydrocarbon Evaluation, 1973. Winner of Schol. Awards. Address; 6009 Royal Crest Dr., Dallas, TX 75230, U.S.A. 6, 7, 14.

RIGATTO, Mario, b. 12 Jan. 1930. Physician; Researcher; Professor. Educ: M.D., Univ. Fed. do Rio Grande do Sul, Brazil, 1953; Docente-Livre, ibid, 1961; Post-grad. trng., Cornell Univ., N.Y., U.S.A., 1957, Columbia Univ., ibid, 1958-59; Univ. de São Paulo, Brazil, 1961; Rsch. work, London Univ., U.K., 1966; Karolinska Inst., Stockholm, Sweden, 1967. Appts: Instr.-Assoc. Prof., Prof. & Rschr., Univ. Fed. do Rio Grande do Sul, Brazil, 1954-; Kellogg Fndn. Fellow, Cornell Univ., N.Y., U.S.A., 1957 & Columbia Univ., ibid, 1958-59, Vis. Prof., London Univ., U.K., 1966 & Rsch. Fellow, Karolinska Inst., Stockholm Univ., Sweden, 1967 as Brazilian Min. of Educ. & Wellcome Trust Fellow; V.P., Fundação de Amparo à Pesquisa, State of Rio Grande do Sul; Rschr.-Lectr., Conselho Nacional de Pesquisas. Mbr. sev. profl. assns. Publs: Fisiopatologia da Circulação Pulmonar, 1973; Volume Residual Pulmonar. Contribuição ao Seu Estudo (thesis), 1961; 80 papers in profl. jrnls. Recip. many hons. inclng. Prize Azevedo Sodre, Acad. Nacional de Med., 1971. Address: Ave. Lajeado 879, 90000 Porto Alegre, RS Brazil.

RIGAU-MARQUES, Jose M., b. 15 Oct. 1925. Physician. Educ: B.S., Tulane Univ. of La., U.S.A., 1946; M.D., Univ. of Madrid,

Spain, 1955. Mbrships: Treas., Eastern Med. Soc., Puerto Rico; Treas., Puerto Rico Med. Assn.; Vice Speaker, House of Delegs., ibid; Speaker, ibid; Pres., Puerto Rico Med. Assn., 1972-73; Pres., Assoc. Puertorriquena Graduados Universidades Espanolas, 1971-72; Bd. mbr., ibid, 1972-73; Bd. Mbr., Puertorican Inst. of Spanish Culture, 1971-73. Recip., Kt. of Grace, Sovereign Order of St. John of Jerusalem. Address: Llorens Torres St. 432, Floral Park, Hato Rey, PR 00917.

RIGG, Margaret R. Artist; Calligrapher; Graphic Designer; Educator. Educ: Art courses, Carnegie-Mellon Univ., Pitts., Pa., 1946-50; B.A., Fla. State Univ., Tallahassee, 1951; M.A., Presby., 1955; M.F.A. work, Chgo. Art Inst., 1963. Appts: Staff Artist, Bd. of Publs., Fla. State Univ., Tallahassee, 1950-53; Art Ed., Motive mag., Nashville, Tenn., 1955-65; Artist-in-Res., Fla. Presby. Coll., St. Petersburg, Fla., 1965-66; Assoc. Prof., Art, Eckerd Coll., St. Petersburg, 1966-. Mbrships: Fellow, Soc. for Arts, Relig. & Culture; Fla. Artist Grp.; Resource Comm., Highlander Folk Ctr., Tenn.; Soc. of Women Calligraphers; Artists Concerned (for representation of Black Am. & Indian Am. Artists). 30 one-woman exhibitions in U.S.A., 1950-74; Int. Exhibitions in Seoul, Korea, Osaka & Kyoto, Japan, Turku, Finland, Muskat, Oman; 5 liturgical appts. for var. chs.; Monumental outdoor sculpture design for Contemporary Prayer Garden, Scarritt Coll., Nashville, Tenn.; Num. grp. shows. Hons. incl: Sr. Rsch. Schlr. Grant in Calligraphy, Korea, 1972; Stone Lectureship, Art & Relig., Princeton Theological Sem., N.J., 1973-74. Address: 4260 Narvarez Way S., St. Petersburg, FL 33712, U.S.A. 125, 138.

RIGGAN, James Gordon, b. 1 Jan. 1914. Presbyterian Clergyman. Educ: B.A., Davidson Coll., 1939; B.D., Union Theol. Sem., Va., 1942; D.D., Eastern Neb. Christian Coll., 1972. Appts: Organizer & Pastor E. Ocean View Presby. Ch., Norfolk, Va. 1941-49 & '67-; Supply Pastor, Calvary Presby. Ch., ibid, 1945-49; Fndr. & Pastor, Bayside Presby. Ch., Va. Beach, 1948; Mission Pastor, 1st Presby. Ch., Huntington, W.Va., 1949 50; Organizer & Pastor, Enslow Pk. Presby. Ch., ibid, 1949-54; Pastor, Macon Rd. Presby. Ch., Memphis, Tenn., 1954-67; Moderator of Norfolk Presbytery, 1944; Moderator, Kanawha Presbytery, 1951; Commnr. to Gen. Assembley Presby. Ch., U.S., 1945, '52, '69; Chmn., Exam. Comm., Norfolk Presby., 1969-71. Mbrships: Philanthropic Lit. Soc.; Delta Phi Alpha; Eta Sigma Phi; Minl. Assns.; etc. Contbr. to The Earnest Worker. Hon. D.D., Eastern Neb. Christian Coll., 1972. Address: 9547—9th Bay St., Norfolk, VA 23518, U.S.A.

RIGGS, B. Lawrence, b. 24 Mar. 1931. Physician. Educ: B.S., Univ. of Ark., Little Rock, 1951; M.D., ibid, 1955; M.S., Univ. of Minn., Mpls., 1962. Appts: Res., Fellow, Mayo Grad. Schl., 1958-61; Res. & Asst. to Staff, Mayo Clin., 1961-62; Cons., Internal Med., ibid, 1962-67; Instr., Internal Med., Mayo Grad. Schl., 1962-67; Asst. Prof., ibid, 1967-71, Assoc. Prof., 1971-74; Prof., Med., Mayo Med. Schl., 1974-. Mbrships: Am. Fed. for Clin. Rsch., Midwestern Counsellor, 1968-71; Ctrl. Soc. for Clin. Rsch.; Am. Coll. of Physns.; AMA; Am. Soc. Clin. Investigation; Ctrl. Clin. Rsch. Club; N.Y. Acad. of Scis.; Orthopedic Rsch. Acad. Author of over 67 articles in sci. jrnls. on calcium & bone metabolism. Hons. incl: Kappa Delta award, Am. Acad. of Orthopedic Rsch. for rsch. on musculoskeletal system; Travelling Fellowship, Royal Soc. Med. Fndn., 1973. Address: 1324-8th St., S.W., Rochester, MN 55901, U.S.A.

RIGGS, Karl A., Jr., b. 12 Aug. 1929. Professor & Geologic Consultant. Educ: B.S. (Hons.), Mich. State Univ., 1951; M.S., ibid, 1952; Ph.D., Iowa State Univ., 1956. Appts: Pvte. Prac., Geologic Cons., 1952-; Instr. & Rsch. Assoc., Iowa State Univ., 1952-56; Sr. Rsch. Technologist, Mobil Field Rsch. Lab., Dallas, Tex., 1959; Dir., Nortex Oil & Gas, Dallas, Tex., 1960-64; Asst. Prof. Geol., Western Mich. Univ., Kalamazoo, 1966-68; Cons., Cabot Corp., 1968-; Assoc. Prof. Geol., Miss. State Univ., 1968-. Mbrships. incl: Am. Inst. Chemists; Fellow, Legislation Comm., ibid; Fellow, Geological Soc. of Am.; Clay Minerals Soc.; var. hon. fraternities. Publs: Num. profl. co. reports, papers, & abstracts; Abstractor, Mineralogical Abstracts & Geoscience Abstracts. Address: RFD 5, 140 Grandridge Rd., Starkville, MS 39759, U.S.A. 7, 125.

RIGGS, Myrton Meredith Richmond, b. 8 Jan. 1899. Newspaper Editor & Publisher. Educ: LL.D. & Dr. of Letters, Ctrl. Mich. Univ., Mt. Pleasant. Appts. incl: Bus. Mgr., Northern Auto Co., 1918, J.B. Lund's Sons Machine Co., 1919-25; Bus. Mgr., Advt. Mgr., Ed. & Publsr., Cheboygan Daily Tribune, 1926- & Owner of Cheboygan Daily Tribune, Cheboygan Weekly Observer, The Weekender, Gt. Northern Printing Co.; Mbr., Advt. Coun., Mich. Dept. of Econ. Dev.; Gen. Chmn., Cheboygan Co. Centennial Comm.; Mbr., State Exec. Bd. for Michigan Week; Chmn., Cheboygan Co. Red Cross; Pres., Northern Mich. Dev. Coun.; Trustee, Dir., Community Mem. Hosp. Mbrships. incl: Fndr., Am. Music Camp; Fndr. & Chmn. of Bd., Community Meml. Hosp.; Pres., Cheboygan Indl. Assn., 1956-. Hons. incl: Mich. Econ. Dev. Dept. New Frontiers Award, 1955; Cheboygan H.S. Nat. Boys Club Hon. Soc. Hall of Fame, 1971. Address: 332 Benton St., Cheboygan, MI, U.S.A.

RIGGSBY, Dutchie Sellers (Mrs. Ernest D. Riggsby), b. 26 Oct. 1940. Educator. Educ: B.S., Troy State Coll., Ala., 1962; M.S., ibid, 1965; Geo. Peabody Coll. for Tchrs., Nashville, Tenn., 1963; AA Tchng. Cert., Auburn Univ., Ala., 1968; Ed.D., ibid, 1972; post-grad. course, Univ. of Calif., Berkeley, 1974. Appts: Tchr., 5th Grade, Highland Gdns. Schl., Montgomery, Ala., 1962-63, & 6th Grade, Troy City Schls., Ala., 1963-67; Instr., Educl. Media Ctr., Auburn Univ., Ala., 1968-69; Dir., Aerospace Sci. Workshop, Vis. Prof., Univ. of Puerto Rico, Rio Piedras, summer, 1972 & 73; Dir., Media Servs., Columbus Coll., Ga., 1972-. Mbrships: PR Comm., Ala. Acad. of Sci., 1972-74; Ga. Acad. of Sci.; Assn. for Educl. Communications & Technol.; Kappa Delta Pi; Alpha Delta Kappa; Gov's Comm. on Pub. Safety, 1964-70. Publs: over 32 profl. articles in jrnls.; sev. slide-tape presentations for Dept. of Family & Children Servs., Columbus & Columbus Coll.; 4 Super 8mm films. Hons: STAR Award, Nat. Sci. Tchrs. Assn., 1968. Address: 2214 Coventry Dr., Columbus, GA 31904, U.S.A. 5, 15, 22, 125, 126, 129, 130, 132, 138.

RIGTRUP, Kenneth, b. 13 Mar. 1936. Lawyer. Educ: B.S. in Acctng., Univ. of Utah, Salt Lake City, 1960; J.D., Coll. of Law, ibid, 1962. Appts: Clerk to Hon. Chief Justice, Chief Justice, Utah Supreme Ct., 1962; Admitted Utah State Bar, 1962; Ptnr., Rigtrup & Hadley, Salt Lake City, Utah, 1963-65; Ptnr., Rigtrup Hadley, Livingston & Newman, ibid, 1965-67; Hearing Examiner, Utah State Indl. Commn., 1972-; Ptnr., R & R Enterprises, Investors Associated, Ltd., & Rigtrup Investment Co.; Mbr., Gov.'s Comm. Unemployment Handicapped, Utah, 1974-80. Mbrships: Sect. on Ins., Negligence & Compensation law. Am.

Bar Assn.; Utah State Bar Assns.; Exec. Comm., Salt Lake Co. Bar Assn., 1970-; Am. & Utah Trial Lawyer's Assns.; Bd. of Govs., 1969-, & V.P., 1972, UTLA; Copy & Rsch., Ed., 1961-62, Utah Law Review, 1960-62; Delta Sigma Pi; Treas., Delta Theta Phi.; Life mbr., Disabled Am. Veterans; Past Treas., Evergreen Swimming & Tennis Club. Author of articles in Utah Law Review, Univ. of Utah, Coll. of Law. Address: 466 E. 500 S., Salt Lake City, UT 84111, U.S.A. 9.

RIMPAU Edward L., b. 26 Nov. 1898. Realtor (retired). Educ: A.B., Stanford, 1921. Appts: Realtor, L.A., 1922-70; Mbr., L.A. Realty Bd., 1924-70; Dir., ibid, 1947-51. Mbrships: Co-Incorp., Miracle Mile Assn., 1941; Dir., ibid, 1941-67; Pres., 1947-52; L.A. Co. Courthouse Comm., 1955-59; Reserve & Ret'd Offs. Assns.; Am. Legion; Dir., Property Owners Tax Assn. of Calif., 1956-; Dir., Hosp. Charity Fund, 1960-. Served. w. USNRF, WWI, & w. USNR, WWII, now Lt. Cmdr. Ret. Address: 435 S. Curson Ave., Apt. M-H, Los Angeles, CA 90036, U.S.A. 9, 16, 59.

RINGWALD, Donald Charles, b. 3 Apr. 1917. Financial Manager. Appts: w. Fiscal Serv., U.S. Veterans Admin., 1948-74; Currently, Financial Mgr., ibid. Mbrships: Pres., Steamship Histl. Soc. of Am., Inc., 1973-; Dir., ibid, 1959-65, 1971-; Ed., quarterly jrnl., Steamboat Bill, 1955-60; Ed. in Chief, ibid, 1961-66; Trustee, Hudson River Marine Mus., 1971-; N.Y. Histl. Soc.; Sons & Daughters of Pioneer Rivermen; World Ship Soc.; Great Lakes Histl. Soc.; Great Lakes Maritime Inst.; Marine Histl. Soc. of Detroit; Canal Soc. of N.Y. State; Ulster Co. Histl. Soc.; Albany Co. Histl. Assn. Publs: Hudson River Day Line, 1965; Day Line Memories, 1971; The Mary Powell, 1972; Contbr. to newspapers & periodicals; Lectures on hist. of Hudson River steam navigation. Address: P.O. Box 7015, Albany, NY 12225, U.S.A. 6, 30, 131.

RINTOUL, Walter, b. 29 July 1913. Analytical Chemist. Educ: B.Sc., Ph.D., Edinburgh, U.K. Appts: Chemist, I.C.I., 1937-39: Colonial Serv., Straits Settlements of Malays, 1939-53; Official Analyst, Malayan Racing, 1953-; Lectr., Univ. of Singapore, 1956; Mng. Dir., Singapore Testing Lab., 1960; Chmn. of Bd., Healthy Products Ltd., 1967. Mbrships. incl: Fellow, Royal Inst. of Chem., Royal Soc. for the Promotion of Hlth.; Profl. Mbr., Inst. Food Technologists; V.P., Dist. Gov., Singapore Nat. Heart Assn.; Fndr. Pres., Singapore Nat. Inst. Chem.; Coun. Mbr., Singapore Nat. Kidney Fndn.; Singapore Nat. Acad. Sci.; Past Pres., ibid; Pres., Rotary Club of Singapore, 1965-66. Address: 32 New Race Course, Bukit Timah Rd., Singapore 11.

RIOJA y FERNANDEZ de MESA, Mariano, b. 16 Apr. 1915. Newspaper Publishing Executive. Educ: Degree in Econs., Univ. of Duesto, Bilbao, Spain; Degree in Econs. & Pol. Scis., Univ. of Madrid. Former Appts: Lectr. in Econs., Official Schl. of Jrnlsm., Madrid; Mbr., Bd. of Publrs., Editorial Sevillana S.A.; Mbr. of Spanish Parliament. Present Appts. incl: Mbr., Bd. of Publrs., La Editorial Católica S.A., Madrid; Pres., Nat. Grp. of Spanish Newspapers; V.P., Spanish Audit Bur. of Circulations; Mbr., Bd. of News Agcy. EFE; Lectr. in Econs., Ch.'s Schl. of Jrnlsm., Madrid. Contbns., var. jrnls., econ. & financial subjects. Kt. Cmdr. of Order of Civil Merit. Address: Editorial Católica, Mateo Inurria 15, Madrid, Spain.

RIORDAN, Kim Justine, b. 17 May 1932. Real Estate Manager. Educ: B.S., Mills Coll., Oakland, Calif.; Stanford Univ., Palo Alto,

Calif.; Postgrad. work in Radio & TV, Sacramento State Univ., Calif. Appts: Chmn., Calif. State Kennedy for Pres. Delegation, 1968; Co-chmn., Sacramento Co. Kennedy for Pres., 1968; Mgr., Sacramento Kennedy HQ, 1968; Deleg., Democratic Nat. Conven., Chgo., 1968; Radio Interviewing; Newscasting. Mbrships: Women's Athletic Club, San Francisco; Sierra View Country Club, Roseville, Calif. Address: 589 Woodlake Inn, 500 Leisure Ln., Sacramento, CA 95815, U.S.A. 57, 114, 120.

RIPINSKY, Michael M., b. 23 Mar. 1944. Archaeologist. Educ: A.B., Univ. of Calif, Berkeley, 1966; postgrad. studies, ibid, Berkeley & Los Angeles. Appts: Rsch. Asst., Am. Mus. of Natural Hist., 1964; Fac. Mbr., Dept. of Geog.-Anthropol., Calif. State Coll., Hayward, 1969-70; Sr. Rsch. Anthropologist, Hadassah Med. Schl., Hebrew Univ., Jerusalem, 1971. Mbrships. incl: Soc. Am. Archaeol; Archaeological Inst. of Am; Am. Anthropological Assn; Hist. of Sci. Soc. Contbr. to var. academic publs. Hons: Ruth Benedict Grant for Rsch. Assistantship., Dept. Anthropol., Am. Mus. Natural Hist, 1964; Grant-in-Aid, Univ. of Calif, 1969. Address: Materials Dept., Schl. of Engineering & Applied Science, 6531 Boelter Hall, Univ. of Calif., Los Angeles, CA 90024, U.S.A.

RIPLEY, Herbert Spencer, b. 29 June 1907. Psychiatrist. Educ: A.B., Univ. of Mich., 1929; M.D., Harvard Univ., 1933; N.Y. Hosp., Cornell Univ. Med. Ctr., 1934-38; Cert. in Psychoan., Columbia, 1949. Appts. incl: Asst. Attng. Psych., N.Y. Hosp., 1938-42 & 1946-49; Asst. Prof. of Psych., Cornell Univ. Med. Coll., 1946-49; Prof. & Chmn., Dept. of Psych., Univ. of Wash., 1949-69; Prof. of Psych., ibid, 1969-; Attng. Psych., Univ. Hosp.; Cons., Seattle, VA Hosp. & Children's Orthopaedical Hosp. & Med. Ctr. Mbrships: Fellow, former Coun. mbr., Am. Psych. Assn.; Fndng. Fellow, Bd. of Regents, Am. Colls. of Psychs. & Psychoans.; Am. Psychoan. Assn.; Rainier & Coll. Clubs, Seattle, Wash.; Harvard Club, N.Y.C.; Pi Kappa Alpha; Alpha Omega Alpha, 1950; Sigma Xi, 1951. Author, num. publs. in field. Recip., Bronze Star Medal. Address: Dept. of Psychiatry, School of Medicine, Univ. of Washington, Seattle, WA 98195, U.S.A. 2, 14, 28, 120.

RIPPEL, Florence Lena, b. 13 May 1902. Educator; Musician; Youth Organiser. Educ: B.S., Univ. of Pa., 1927; M.A., ibid, 1930; UCLA, 1940-41; Univ. of S. Calif., 1952-53. Appts. incl: Tchr. of Mus., Stetson Jr. HS, 1938-50; Co-owner Ripple Schl. of Music, 1938-49; Soc. Wkr., St. Agnes Settlement House, Phila., 1949-52; Reading Cons., Stetson Jr. HS, 1950-52; Cons., Lynwood Unified Schl. Dist., 1952-; Oboist, Phila. Women's Symph. Orch., 1950-52; Dir., Choir, Lutheran Ch. of the Master, LA, Calif., 1952-55; Organizer & Dir., Moreno Valley Youth Orch., 1960-; Conductor & Organizer, Moreno Valley Youth Marching Band, 1965-. Mbrships: Life, PTA; Matinee Musical, Phila.; Phila. Music Club. Recip. of various hons. Address: 140 N Sunset Place, Monrovia, CA 91016, U.S.A. 5, 9, 22, 59, 71, 128.

RISCHIN, Moses, b. 16 Oct. 1925. Professor. Educ: A.B., Brooklyn Coll., U.S.A., 1947; A.M., Harvard Univ., 1948; Ph.D., ibid, 1957. Appts: Lectr., Brooklyn Coll., 1949-53; Instr., Am. Civilization, Brandeis Univ., 1953-54; Lectr., New Schl. Soc. Rsch., 1955-58; Asst. Ed., Notable American Women, 1959-60; Asst. Prof., Long Is. Univ., 1958-59; Lectr., UCLA, 1962-64; Assoc. Prof.-Prof., San Fran. State Univ., 1964-. Mbrships: V.P., Immigration Hist. Soc., 1973-; Pelzer Mem.

Award Comm., OAH, 1970-74; Am. Histl. Assn.; Org. Am. Histns.; Am. Jewish Histl. Soc. Publs: An Inventory of American Jewish History, 1954; Our Own Kind, Voting by Race, Creed or National Origin, 1960; The Promised City, 1962; The American Gospel of Success, 1965; 2nd ed., '74; Ed., A Liberal Between Two Worlds, 1969; Immigration and the American Tradition, 1974; Ed., Minority History series. Hons: Fellow, Am. Coun. Learned Socs., 1966-67; Guggenheim Fellow, 1967-68; Fulbright-Hays Fellow, Uppsala Univ., Sweden, 1969. Address: Hist. Dept., San Fran. State Univ., San Fran., CA 94132, U.S.A. 13.

RISOM, Albinus, b. 1 Mar. 1897. Architect; Credit Association Director. Educ: Grad., Royal Danish Acad. of Fine Art. Appts: Pvte. Prac. as Archt., 1930-; Bldg. Expert, Credit Assn. for House Owners in Copenhagen, 1950, Dir., 1954; Cons. Archt., var. indl. orgs. Mbr., Acad. Instn. Arch. Archt., villas, apartment houses & factories, Copenhagen & suburbs. Hon. Kt. of the Dannebrog. Address: Limfjordsvej 21, DK-2720 Copenhagen, Denmark. 43.

RISSANEN, Toivo, b. 31 Dec. 1920. Executive. Educ: M.S., Inst. Technol., Helsinki, Finland. Appts: Rsch. Asst., Finnish Ctrl. Lab., 1948-50; Hd. of Lab., Sanoma Oy, 1950-51; Tech. Mgr., ibid, 1951-56; Mng. Dir., Herttoniemen Syväpaino Oy, 1956-57, Banknote Printing House, Bank of Finland, 1957-; Graphic expert, U.N., Tehran, 1955, Am. Type Fndrs., Arnoldo Mandadori, Italy, 1955; Lectr., Coll. of Technol., Helsinki, 1950-56; Specialist Educator in Helsinki, Bank of Thailand, 1970. Mbrships: Finnish Tech. Soc.; Graphical Club; Finnish Chem. Soc.; Tech. Assn. Graphic Arts, U.S.A.; Inst. of Printing, U.K.; Graphic Arts Tech. Fndn., U.S.A. Contbr. of articles to profl. jrnls. Hons. incl: Kt. 1st. Class, Order of the White Rose; Pro Philatelia, 1972. Address: Rauhankatu 19, 00170, Helsinki 17, Finland. 43, 134.

RISTOW, Walter W., b. 20 Apr. 1908. Geographer; Librarian. Educ: B.A., Univ. of Wis., 1931; M.A., Oberlin Coll., 1933; Ph.D., Clark Univ., 1937. Appts: Instr. in Geog., E. Wash. Coll. of Educ., 1935-37; Hd., Map Room & Chief, Map Div., N.Y. Pub. Lib., 1937-46; Asst. Chief, Assoc. Chief, Chief, Geog. & Map Div., Lib. of Congress, Wash. D.C., 1946-. Mbrships: Sec., Assn. of Am. Geographers, 1949-51; Am. Cong. on Serv. & Mapping; AAAS; Nat. Coun. for Geog. Educ.; ALA; Spec. Lib. Assn.; Soc. for Hist. of Discoveries; Cosmos Club. Author of articles in profl. geog., cartography, hist. & lib. jrnls. Address: Geog. & Map Div., Lib. of Congress, Wash. DC 20540, U.S.A. 2, 7, 14, 42.

RITCHIE, Eris Alton, Jr., b. 18 Apr. 1935. College Administrator; Businessman. Educ: B.S., Abilene Christian Coll., Tex., 1957; M.Ed., ibid, 1961. Appts: Band Dir., Tex. Pub. Schls., Trent, 1957-59 & Cisco, 1959-67; Band Dir. & PR Dir., Cisco Jr. Coll., 1968-73; PR Dir., ibid, 1973-; operates summer camps for baton twirlers, cheerleaders & girls' dance-drill teams, Cisco, Houston, Dallas & San Antonio; Owner, Women's Fashion Store, Cisco. Mbrships: Past Pres., Cisco Chmbr. of Comm. & Cisco Rotary Club; Blue Key Club; Drum Major of Band, Abilene Christian Coll.; Pres., Kappa Delta Pi. Has made num. public & TV appearances w. bands. Hons: Community Serv. Award, Cisco Chmbr. of Comm., 1964; Outstanding Citizen Award, ibid, 1968. Address: 1307 Park Dr., Cisco, TX 76437, U.S.A. 7, 22, 46, 117, 125.

RITCHIE, George Stephen, b. 30 Oct. 1914. Hydrographer. Educ: Royal Naval Coll., Dartmouth, 1928-31. Appts: Cmmd. of H.M. Survey Ships, H.M.S. Challenger, 1949-51, H.M.N.Z.S. Lachlan, 1953-56, H.M.S. Dalrymple, 1958-59 & H.M.S. Vidal, 1964-66; Hydrog. of the Navy, U.K., 1967-72; Pres., Dir. Comm., int. Hydrog. Bur., Monaco, 1972-. Mbrships: Pres., Royal Inst. of Navigation, 1970-72 & Hydrog. Soc., 1972; Hakluyt Soc.; Soc. for Nautical Rsch.; Reform Club, London; Monte Carlo Club; Fellow, Royal Instn. Chartered Surveyors. Publs: Challenger—The Life of a Survey Ship, 1957; The Admiralty Chart-British Naval Hydrography in the Nineteenth Century, 1967; num. papers in sci. jrnls. Hons: D.S.C., 1942, C.B., 1968; Silver Medal, Royal Soc. of Arts, London, 1970; Gold Medal, Royal Geog. Soc., London, 1972. Address: c/o International Hydrographic Bureau, Ave. Pres. J.F. Kennedy, Monte-Carlo, Monaco. 1, 41.

RITCHIE, L. Edwin. Novelist; Columnist; Poet; Painter. Educ: studied Fine Arts, Pratt Inst., N.Y., Am. Schl. of Design, Grand Ctrl. Schl. of Art. Appts: incl: Assoc. w. ad agcy., Madison Ave., N.Y.; sev. Govt. posts; Int. Citizen, Conf. & P.R. Div., UN. Publs: A Rose in December, 1967, reissued as A Light in Eden, 1972; The Spy Syndrome, 1969; Winter, 1972; novel about contemp. adolescent scene in Am. forthcoming; satirical novels, Godiva Marlow, 1967, & Insomniacs' Cabaret, 1970, publd. under name of Voltaire Lewis; poems incl. Elegy for November 22nd, 1963, The Token, 1972; Park Bench, a column in var. L.I. weeklies, 1965-. Paintings incl: Objects from a Nuclear Century Studio (oils). Recip. sev. prizes for paintings. Address: P.O. Box 205, Floral Park, NY 11002, U.S.A. 30.

RITOV, Israel, b. 5 Apr. 1895. Labour Official. Educ: Talmudic Coll. (Yeshiva), Leeda, Lithuania, 1908-1909; Univ. of Yekaterinoslav Law Schl., Ukraine, 1919-20. Appts: Dir., Palestine Immigration Off., Warsaw, 1921-32; Sec., Histadrut (Gen. Labour Fedn.) Ctr. for Ind., Serv. & Transport Coops., Tel Aviv, 1933-69; Mbr. Histadrut Gen. Coun., 1941-63; Mbr., Palestine (later Israel) Govt. Coop. Coun., 1934-; Mbr., Int. Comm. of Workers' Productive Socs., Int. Coop. Alliance, 1957-. Mbrships: formerly active in Zionist-Socialist movements in Poland & Russia; Mapai (now Labour Pty.) Exec. Comm., Israel, 1934-; World Zionist Coun., 1947-; Bd. of Dirs., World Keren Hayesod-United Jewish Appeal, 1949; etc. Publs. incl: (in Hebrew) Cooperation in Eretz Israel, 1947; The Voice of Cooperation, 1949; Chapts., The History of Zeirei Zion-Socialist Zionists, 1964; Brief History of the Warsaw Jewish Community, 1971; Ed. sev. other books & jrnls.; contbr. many articles to newspapers, Israel, Poland, Russia & U.S.A. Recip. sev. awards inclng Dan Bus Coop., 1969. Address: 62 Reines St., Tel-Aviv, Israel. 55, 94.

RITSCHEL, Karl Heinz, b. 20 Jan. 1930. Journalist. Educ: Dr.phil. & cand. jur., Univ. of Vienna, Austria. Appts: Free-lancer, until 1954; Buld-Telegraf, Vienna, 1954-55; Kleine Zeitung, Graz, 1955-56; Bild-Telegraf, Vienna, 1956-58; Osterreichischer Wirtschaftsverlag, 1959; Salzburger Nachrichten, 1959-; Ed. in Chief, ibid, 1964-. Mbrships: PEN Club; V.P., Presseclub Concordia. Publs. incl: Eine Stadt erzählt: Salzburg—Anmut & Macht, 1970; Kreisky: Der Pragmatiker-Sozialdemokrat ohne Dogma, 1972; Standpunkte. Dommentare & Reportagen, 1973; Unbekanntes Italien—Le Marche, die Marken, 1974; China, 1974. Hons. incl: Leopold Kunschak prize for jrnlsm., 1970; Award, Fedn. Int. des Redacteures en Chef,

Paris, 1970. Address: Bergstr. 12, 5020 Salzburg, Austria. 43, 86.

RITTER, Gary, b. 25 Apr. 1938. Company Executive. Educ: B.S., C.U.N.Y., 1960; St. John's Univ. Schl. of Law, 1961-64. Appts: Cert. Pub. Acct., N.Y.; Pres., Digitax, Inc., 1968-71, Digital Analysis, 1971-, Data Systems of Am. Inc., 1973-, Caribe Cons. Corp., 1972-, Trans-Caribbean Hotel & Country Club, Haiti, W. Indies, 1974. Mbrships: Am. Inst. of C.P.As.; N.Y. State Soc. of C.P.As. Address: 267 Fox Hollow Rd., Woodbury, NY 11797, U.S.A.

RITTER, Jesse Paul, Jr., b. 16 Oct. 1930. Professor of English; Writer. Educ: B.A., Kan. State Tchrs. Coll., 1955; M.A., Univ. of Ark., 1956; Ph.D., ibid, 1967. Appts: Assoc. Prof., Eastern Wash. State Coll., 1957-59; Instr., N. Tex. State Coll., 1960-62; Assoc. Prof., Northern Ill. Univ., 1963-68; Dir. of Freshman Engl., San Fran. State Univ., 1968-73; Prof. of Engl., ibid, 1973-; Contbng. Ed. & Columnist, Pacific Sun weekly newspaper. Mbrships. incl: V.P., Am. Fedn. of Tchrs., Local 1352, 1968-69; Sec.-Treas., Engl. Coun. of Calif. State Colls. & Univs., 1971-73. Publs: Santa Rita (screenplay), 1970; Beyond Survival, 1972; Ed., Focus/Media, 1973; A Catch-22 Casebook, 1973. Contbr. to: Life Mag.; Rolling Stone; The Village Voice; The Bay Guardian; The Vonnegut Statement, 1973. Address: 222 Floribel Ave., San Anselmo, CA 94069, U.S.A. 13.

RITTER, Rupert, b. 5 Apr. 1900. Attorney at Law. Educ: Agricl. H.S. in Vienna; Tech. H.S., Munich; Univs. of Vienna & Innsbruck; LL.D., Univ. of Innsbruck, 1937. Appts: commercial activities, 1925-35; Law prac., Liechtenstein, 1937-38; Sec. to His Highness the Reigning Prince of Liechtenstein, 1938-45; Law prac., 1946-; Pres., Administrative Ct. of Liechtenstein, 1949-57; Pres. of the High Constitutional Ct., 1960-. Mbrships: Assn. of World Peace through Law Ctr.; Histl. Soc. of Liechtenstein, 1920-. Publs: var. works on Liechtenstein Law & History. Hons: title 'Fürstlicher Hofrat', 1945; Knight's Cross of Liechtenstein, 1956. Address: Brandiserweg 22, Vaduz, Liechtenstein. 12, 43.

RIVERO CERVERA, Jose Antonio, b. 17 July 1931. Engineer. Educ: B.M.E., Univ. of Miami, 1953; B.E.E., ibid, 1953; B.B.A., 1963. Appts: Fndr. & Pres., Jose Rivero & Assocs., Ltd., Cons., Guatemala City, 1967; Fndr. & Chmn. of Bd. & Pres., Co. de Distribucion Centroam., S.A., ibid, 1969; Fndr. & Dir., Co. Procesadora de Alimentos, S.A. (COPSA), 1971; Pres. & Dir., Aguirre Corp. of Puerto Rico & Exec. V.P. & Trustee, Aguirre Co., 1970-74; Pres., Rodriguez Portela & Cia, 1974. Mbrships: Colonia Espanola de Cienfuegos (Cuba Dir.); Register Profl. Engrs., State of La.; Am. Mgmt. Assn.; Am. Soc. Agricl. Engrs.; Sigma Delta Kappa; Omicron Delta Kappa; Pres., Phi Iota Alpha; Fndng. Mbr., Am. Chmbr. of Comm., Guatemala; Assn. de Gerentes de Guatemala. Address: G.P.O, Box G4825, San Juan, PR 00936, U.S.A.

RIVET, Albert Lionel Frederick, b. 30 Nov. 1915. University Professor . Educ: B.A., Oriel Coll., Oxford, U.K., 1938; M.A., 1947. Appts: Asst. Archaeol. Off., Ordnance Survey, 1951-64; Lectr. in Classics, Univ. of Keele, 1964-67; Rdr. in Ramano-British Studies, ibid, 1967-. Prof. of Roman Provincial Studies, 1974-. Fellowships: Soc. of Antiquaries, 1953; Corres. Fellow, German Archaeological Inst., 1960; Soc. of Antiquaries of Scotland (served on Coun. & edited Proceedings, 1961-64).

Mbrships: Soc. for the Promotion of Roman Studies, 1964 (served on Coun. & Review Ed., Britannia, 1970-); Royal Archaeological Inst. (served on Coun. & Exec. Comm.). Publs: Ordnance Survey Map of Roman Britain (Compiler), 3rd edit. 1956; Town & Country in Roman Britain, 1958, 2nd edit. 1964; Ordnance Survey Map of Southern Britain in the Iron Age (Compiler), 1962; The Roman Villa in Britain (Ed. & Co-author), 1969; The Iron Age in Northern Britain (Ed.), 1966; Contbr. to many books & jrnls. dealing w. the Iron Age & Roman period. Address: Dept. of Classics, The University, Keele, Staffs., ST5 5BG, U.K. 139.

RIVETT, Rohan Deakin, b. 16 Jan. 1917. Journalist; Author; Commentator. Educ: B.A., Queens Coll., Melbourne, Australia, 1937; Postgrad. study, Balliol Coll., Oxford, U.K., 1938-39; Study of UN, Wash. & N.Y., 1955. Appts. incl: Melbourne Herald, 1946-47; Corres. for Australian papers in China, 1947, in London & Europe, 1948-51; Ed. in Chief & Dir., News Ltd., 1951-60; Commentator on Int. Affairs, Australian Broadcasting Commn., 1946-; Columnist, Canberra Times, 1964-; Columnist, Nation Review Weekly, 1970-74. Mbrships. incl: Australian Journalists Assn.; Councillor, Australian Soc. of Authors, 1966-; Fellow, Australian Writers, 1970-; Hon. Life mbr., Int. Press Inst., 1963. Publs. incl: Australian Citizen: Herbert Brookes 1868-1963; Writing about Australia, 1965; Australia This Land These People (co-author), 1973. Recip. of hons. Address: 147 Wattle Valley Rd., Camberwell, Victoria, Australia 3124. 3, 12, 23, 34, 128.

ROANE, Philip R., Jr. Virologist. Educ: B.S., Morgan State Coll.; M.S., Schl. of Hygiene & Pub. Hlth., Johns Hopkins Univ.; Ph.D., Dept. of Microbiol., Univ. of Md. Appts: Fellow, Dept. of Microbiol., Schl. of Med., Johns Hopkins Univ., 1958-60; Asst., ibid, 1960-64; Virologist, Microbiol. Assocs., Inc., Bethesda, Md., 1964-72, Dir., Quality Control. ibid, 1967-72; Asst. Prof., Dept. of Microbiol., Schl. of Med., Howard Univ., 1972-; Vis. Sci., Inst. of Microbiol., Ferrara, Italy. Mbrships: Soc. of Sigma Xi; Am. Soc. for Microbiol.; Am. Assn. of Immunologists. Contbr. to num. profl. jrnls. Hons: Var. rsch. grants, Howard Univ., 1972-74; Nat. Inst. of Hlth. Grant, 1973-74. Address: 3327 Mt. Pleasant St., N.W., Washington, DC 20010, U.S.A. 7, 14, 125.

ROBBINS, June (Pen name Julie of Colo. Springs). Registered Nurse. Educ: B.A., Relig. Educ.; B.A., Arts & Scis. Appts: Psych. Nurse; Regular Staff Duty Nurse, Med., Surg., Pediatrics, etc.; Civil Serv. Nurse; Pvte. Duty. Mbrships: Pikes Peak Poetry Fellowship Soc.; Colo. State Poetry Fellowship Soc.; World Poetry Soc.-Intercontinental; Nat. League Am. Pen Women. Work used on radio stns., Va. & Ark. Publs: Poems publd. in mags., newspapers & anthols., inclng. Major Poets, Moon Age Poets Anthol., Voices Int., Tempo, Canada, Pegasus, N.S.; Poetry & Peanut Butter, 1970. Has travelled in Europe, N. Africa, Mexico, Canada, etc. Hons: Award, Am. Poetry Fellowship Soc., 1970; Sev. hon. mentions, Moon Age Poets Anthol., Skylines, Pikes Peak Poetry Soc. Address: 105 Everett Dr., Colo. Springs, CO 80911, U.S.A. 132.

ROBBINS, Keith, b. 9 Apr. 1940 University Teacher. Educ: Magdalen Coll., Oxford, 1958-61; St. Antony's Coll., ibid, 1961-63. Appts: Lectr. in hist., Univ. of York, U.K., 1963-71; currently Prof. of hist., Univ. Coll. of N. Wales, Bangor, ibid. Fellow, Royal Histl. Soc. Publs: Munich, 1938, 1968; Sir Edward

Grey, 1971. Address: Dept. of Hist., Univ. Coll. of N. Wales, Bangor, Caerns., U.K.

ROBBONE, Joseph, b. 16 June 1916. Director of Music Conservatoire. Educ: Grad., Econ. & Actuarial Maths.; Dipl. Mus. Composition. Appts: Pres., Viotti Int. Mus. Competition; Pres., Viotti Opera Co.; Pres., Deutsch Opernacademie; Dir., Viotti Mus. Conservatoire; Dir., Les Semaines Musicales de St. Vincent. Mbrships: Tiberina Acad., Rome; Rotary Club, Vercelli. Works. incl: Requiem per il Partigiano Ignoto; Impressione Guerresca; Trittico Sacro; Visitatio Sepulcri; I canti della Sermenza; Sinfonia da chiesa; Concerto da Chiesa in La Minore; Don Giovanni; Partita per violino e viola. Recip., Kt. of Italian Repub. Address: Piazza Sant' Eusebio 12, 13100 Vercelli, Italy. 43.

ROBECHEK, Philip John, b. 23 Feb. 1914. Surgeon. Educ: A.B., Adelbert Coll., Case Western Reserve Univ., 1937; M.D., Med. Schl., ibid, 1940; Surg. Trng., St. Lukes Hosp., Cleveland, Ohio. Mbrships: Dipl. Am. Bd. Surg., 1947; Fellow, Am. Coll. Surgs., 1948; Pres.-Elect, Ohio Chapt., ibid; Past Pres., Ohio State Med. Assn.; Ohio Deleg. to AMA; Cleveland Surg. Soc.; Past Pres., Acad. of Med., Cleveland. Publs: num. articles on med. in profl. jrnls. Address: 3461 Warrensville Ctr. Rd., Cleveland, OH 44122, U.S.A. 8, 17.

ROBERT-GORSSE, François, b. 10 June 1923. Bank Director. Educ: Dip., Inst. of Pol. Studies. Appts: Lt., French Naval Reserve; Post, Lazard Frères & Cie., 1948-52; Post, French Nat. Coun. of Mgmt., 1952-55; Admin. Dir. Gen., Banque Monod-La Hénin; Dir., Finance Dept., Banque de Suez; Dir., Finance Dept., Mining Union; Admnstr., Gen. Bills of Exchange Co.; Admnstr., Real Estate Rsch. & Promotion Co.; Admnstr., Investment Management & Counselling Co.; Admnstr., Valois Soc.; Admnstr., Financial Management & Counselling Co.; Admnstr., Permali Co. Mbrships: French Soc. of Financial Analysts; Polo Club of Paris; Automobile Club of France; Racing Club of France. Hon: Chevalier du Mérite Militaire. Address: 11 Avenue de Suffren, 75007 Paris, France.

ROBERTS, B.K., b. 5 Feb. 1907. Justice, Supreme Court of Florida. Educ: J.D., Univ. of Fla., 1928. Appts. incl: Law prac., Tallahassee, 1928-49; 3 yrs. serv., WW II, inclng. U.S. Shipping Commnr., Port of Jacksonville, Lt. Cmdr., USCGR, 1944-45; V.P., Tallahassee Bank & Trust Co., 1948-49; Justice, Fla. Supreme Ct., 1949-; Chief Justice, 3 terms; 1st Dpty. Chmn., Nat. Conf. of Chief Justices, 1972-73. Mbrships. incl: Past Pres., Fla. Heritage Fndn.; Pres., Fla. State Univ. Fndn. Inc.; Bd. of Counselors, Fla. Presby. Ch.; Chmn., Fla. Judicial Coun.; Past Pres., Tallahassee Bar Assn.; Past V.P., Fla. State Bar Assn.; Fellow, Am. Bar Fndn.; Am. Bar Assn., Patron, Int. Bar Assn.; Fla. Constitution Revision Comm., 1966, & Chmn., Subcomm. on Human Rights. Hons: Freedoms Fndn. of Valley Forge Awards Jury, 1962; Disting. Citizens Award, Stetson Law Coll.; Chmn., Judicial Admin. Commn., 1971-72; LL.D., Univ. of Miami, 1954. Address: Supreme Court Bldg., Tallahassee, FL 32304, U.S.A.

ROBERTS, Clara Irene (Broadway) (Mrs Philip Carey Roberts), b. 29 Dec. 1914. Civic Worker. Educ: Licensed Voc. Nurse, Memphis Tech. Schl., Tenn., U.S.A., 1956. Mbrships: Treas., Lenna P. Hart Circle King's Daughters, 1961; Sec., Recreation Servs. for Handicapped, Inc., 1964 & 1966, Exec. Bd., 1964-67. Hons: Certs. of Appreciation, Recreation Servs. for

Handicapped, Inc., 1965, 1966, & 1967; Named Volunteer of the Yr., Recreation Servs. for Handicapped, Inc., 1965 & 1966; Plaques, Memphis Jaycees, 1965 & 1966. Address: 5452 N. Suggs Drive, Memphis, TN 38117, U.S.A. 5, 57, 138.

ROBERTS, Denys Tudor Emil, b. 19 Jan. 1923. Barrister. Educ: Wadham Coll., Oxford, U.K., 1942; M.A., 1948; B.C.L., 1949. Appts: Crown Coun., Nyasaland, 1953; Atty. Gen., Gibralter, 1960; Solicitor Gen., Hong Kong. 1962; Atty. Gen., ibid, 1966; Colonial Sec., 1973. Mbrships: Lincolns Inn., 1950; M.C.C., Hong Kong. Publs: Smugglers Circuit; Beds & Roses; The Elwood Wager; The Boner of the Wayingas; How to Dispense with Hangers. Hons: O.B.E., 1960; C.B.E., 1970; Q.C., Gibraltar, 1960 & Hong Kong, 1964. Address: Victoria House, Barker Rd., Hong Kong. 1, 3.

ROBERTS, Eirlys Rhiwen Cadwaladr, b. 3 Jan. 1911. Journalist. Educ: B.A., Girton Coll., Cambridge, U.K. Appts: Sub-Ed., Amalgamated Press; Mil. then Pol. Intelligence, 1943-45; P.R., UNRRA, Albanian Mission, 1945-47; Info. Div., Treasury, 1947-57; Mbr., Consumers' Comms. for G.B., England & Wales; Dpty. Dir., Consumers' Assn.; Dir. Gen., European Bur. of Consumer Orgs.; Rsch. Dir., Rsch. Inst. for Consumer Affairs. Mbr., Econ. & Soc. Comm., EEC. Author, Consumers, 1966. Recip., OBE, 1971. Address: Consumers' Assn., 14 Buckingham St., London WC2N 6DS, U.K. 1.

ROBERTS, Fay Ingram, b. 18 Jan. 1907. Writer; Civil Servant. Educ: Tex. Tech. Univ., Lubbock, Tex. Appts: incl; Tchr., Rural Schls. of W. Tex., 1925-32; w. U.S. Civil Serv., 1950. Mbr., Poetry Soc. Tex. Publs: incl; In White Starlight (poems), 1962; Chinaberries (song); The Dusty Way; Saga (TV Screen Plays); Appeared in Anthol., Best Am. Poems. 1967; Int. Who's Who in Poetry Anthol., 1972. Address: 2912 Hubby Ave., Waco, TX 76707, U.S.A. 11, 57, 128, 132, 138.

ROBERTS, Frank Lester, b. 8 Sept. 1895. Physician. Educ: B.A., Univ. of Minn., Mpls., U.S.A., 1918; M.A., ibid, 1919; M.B., 1921; M.D., 1922; Ph.D., Johns Hopkins Univ., Balt., Md., 1936. Appts: Co. Hlth. Off., Gibson Co., Tenn., 1924-37; Prof., Preventive Med., Coll. of Med., Univ. of Tenn., 1948-55; Assoc. Dean, ibid, 1955-59 & 1961-66; Med. Educator to Iran, U.S. State Dept., 1959-61; Dir., Venereal Disease Div., Memphis Shelby Co. Hlth. Dept., Tenn., 1966-. Mbrships: Fellow, Am. Coll. of Physns.; Pres., Tenn. State Pub. Hlth. Assn., 1952; Alpha Omega Alpha; Sigma Xi; Delta Omega. Publs. incl: Growth of Children below Average Weight; Vital Capacity of the Negro Child; Vital Capacity of Children Infected with Hookworm; Changes in the Mamary Glands during Latter Half of Pregnancy; The Ecology of the Medical Graduate (w. M.K. Callison); Diagnosis & Treatment of Gonorrhea; Syphilis in Shelby County; What is a Man? Address: 172 Kimbrough Place, Memphis, TN 38104, U.S.A. 2, 14, 128.

ROBERTS, Irene, b. 27 Sept. 1929. Writer. Publs: Over 70 books, some under pseudonyms Iris Rowland, Irene Shaw, Elizabeth Hare, & Roberts Carr, inclng: The Throne of Pharaohs, Surgeon in Tibet, The Lion & The Sun, & The Shrine of Fine. Address: Alpha House, Higher Town, Malborough, Kingsbridge, Devon, TQ7 3RL, U.K. 3, 30.

ROBERTS, Percival Rudolph, III, b. 2 Nov. 1935. Art Educator; Poet. Educ: A.B., 1957, M.A., 1962, Univ. of Del.; Ed.D., Ill. State Univ., 1968; Litt.D., Free Univ. of Asia, 1967.

Appts: incl: U.S. Naval Off., 1958-60; Art Instr., Stanton Schl. Dist. & Dela. Art Ctr., Univ. of Del., 1960-65; Lectr., Art, Ill. State Univ., 1966-68; Chmn., Art Dept., Bloomsburg State Coll.; Cons. to Renaissance Coll., 1967. Mbrships. incl: Eastern Rep., Higher Educ. Sect., NAEA, 1968-72; V.P., Pres., Del. Assn. Art Educ., 1965; Chmn. Art Commn., DSEA, 1963-65; Nat. & Pa. Art Educ. Assns., 1968; Poetry Soc. U.K.; Acad. Am. Poets, 1960-; Am. Poetry League; UPLI, 1965; Am. Poets Fellowship Soc., 1965-70; Omicron Delta Kappa; Kappa Delta Pi. Solo art exhibs. incl: U.S. Fine Arts Registry Concurrent Exhib., 1967; Nat. Design Ctr., N.Y.C., 1968; Haas Gall. of Art, Bloomsburg State Coll., 1969; Mansfield State Coll., Pa., 1970; Susquehanna Univ., 1971. Publs. incl: World Echoes, 1966; Centaurian Flight, 1968; Out, Out Brief Candle, 1969. Rep. at large for Voices Int., etc., plus essays, books. Hons. incl: 9th Poet Laureate of Del., 1965; Am. Poets Gold Cup, Am. Poets Fellowship Soc., 1967; Ship Award, NAEA, 1965; 1st Prof. Educator's Award, DSEA, 1965; Outstanding Young Man of Am. US JC. Address: RD 5, Bloomsburg, PA 17815, U.S.A. 6, 8, 11, 15, 117.

ROBERTS, Roland Douglas, Jr., b. 8 Jan. 1937. Architect. Educ: Bachelor of Sci. of Arch., Rice Univ., Houston, Tex.; Postgrad., Okla. Univ. Appts: Designer, Grayson Gill Inc., Dallas, 1961, Smith & Warder, Grand Prairie, Tex., 1964-65; Tchr., Univ. of Tex., Arlington, 1963-64; Archt., Leman H. Wilson, Tulsa, Okla., 1965-67, Brush, Hutchison & Swinn, Nashville, Tenn., 1968-70; Owner of archtl. firm, Nashville, 1970-; has designed sev. notable chs., off. bldgs. & appt. bldgs. in Nashville, Tenn., Winston-Salem, N.C., Kissimmee, Fla., & Shelbyville, Tenn. Mbrships: Nashville Jr. Chmbr. of Comm.; Nashville Area Chmbr. of Comm.; Am. Concrete Inst.; A.I.A.; Tenn. Soc. of Archts.; Illuminating Engrng. Soc.; Guild for Relig. Archts.; Construction Specifications Inst.; etc. Address: 845 Forest Hills Dr., Nashville, TN 37220, U.S.A.

ROBERTS, Walter Orr, b. 20 Aug. 1915. Solar Astronomer. Educ: A.B., Amherst Coll., 1938; M.A. Harvard Univ., 1940; Ph.D., ibid, 1943. Appts. incl: Established & directed solar coronagraph stn., Harvard Coll. Observ., Climax, Colo., 1940-46; Dir., High Altitude Observ., Boulder, Colo., 1946-60; Prof. of Astro-Geophysics (on indefinite leave), Univ. of Colo., 1957-; Dir., Nat. Ctr. Atmospheric Rsch., Boulder, 1960-68; Pres., Univ. Corp. for Atmospheric Rsch., 1967-. Mbrships. incl: Bd. of Dirs., AAAS, 1963-68; Pres., ibid, 1968; Advsry Comm., World Meteorol. Org.; Trustee, Amherst Coll., Kettering Fndn., Max. C. Fleischmann Fndn. & MITRE Corp. Contbr. of articles to profl. jrnls. Recip. of num. hon degrees. Address: Univ. Corp. for Atmospheric Rsch., P.O. Box 1470, Boulder, CO 80302, U.S.A. 2, 9, 14, 34, 128.

ROBERTS, William Howard, b. 13 Jan. 1922. Manufacturing Executive. Educ: B.S., Northwestern Univ., 1943; M.S., ibid, 1949. Appts: Instr. Mech. Engrng., Northwestern Univ., 1944-49; Asst. Prof., N.Y. Univ., 1949-52; Systems Dev. Mgr., Carrier Corp., 1952-61; York Div., Borg-Warner Corp., 1961-69, Pres., 1965-69; Grp. V.P., Am. Standards Inc., 1969-72; Asst. to Grp. Exec., Singer Co., 1972-73; V.P. & Gen. Mgr., Valves & Fittings Div., Crane Co., N.Y.C., 1973-. Mbrships: Sigma Xi; Pi Tau Sigma; Tau Beta Pi. Co-author, Modern Heating & Air Conditioning, 1959. Recip., Laskowitz Award, N.Y. Acad. of Sci., 1968. Address: 655 Pk. Ave., N.Y., NY 10021, U.S.A.

ROBERTSON, Bruce McNeil, b. 6 Apr. 1922. Real Estate—Investor. Educ: studies in Real Estate. Appts. incl: served in Marine Corp, WWII; Chmn., Planning Commn., Manhattan Beach, 15 yrs.; City Councilman, Manhattan Beach, 1966-67; Acting Mayor, ibid, 1967; Mbr., League of Calif. Cities; Mbr., Coordinating Coun. of L.A., Calif., 1966-67; Cattle Rancher, Idaho, 1971-74; Planning Commn., Gooding, Idaho, 1973-74; Coun. of Govt's Mbr., Wood River Resource Area (4 cos.), Idaho, 1974. Mbrships. incl: Charter Mbr., Rotary Int., Manhattan Beach, Calif.; Chmn., Red Cross, Manhattan Beach; Sepulvada Businessmen's Assn., 1949-67; S. Bay Bd. of Realtors; Lifetime Hon. Mayor, Hon. Police Dept. & Hon. Fire Chief. Hons. incl: Life Lifetime Hon. Mayor Award, 1967; Lifetime Hon. Fire Chief Award, 1967; Lifetime Hon. Police Chief Award, 1967; Outstanding Community Rose & Scroll Award, 1968; Community Ldr. of Am. Award, 1972. Address: Route II, Box 208, Gooding, ID 83330, U.S.A. 130.

ROBERTSON, Constance Pierrepont Noyes (Mrs.), b. 27 Sept. 1897. Author. Educ: Univ. of Wis. Mbrships: N.Y. State Histl. Soc.; Onondaga Histl. Assn.; Madison Co. Histl. Soc.; Engl. Speaking Union; Authors League of Am. Publs: Enchanted Avenue, 1931; Five Fatal Letters (pseud. Dana Scott); Seek-No-Further, 1938; Salute to the Hero, 1943; Fire Bell in the Night, 1944; The Unterrified,1946; The Golden Circle, 1951; Six Weeks in March, 1953; Go & Catch A Falling Star, 1957; Oneida Community, 1851-1876; An Autobiography, 1970; Oneida Community, 1876-1881; The Breakup, 1972; Address: Struan House, Kenwood, Oneida, NY 13421, U.S.A. 30.

ROBERTSON, Edna Gertrude Weatherford, b. 21 July 1920. Master Certified Graphoanalyst; Questioned Document Examiner. Educ: Univs. of Calif., 1955-56, Md., 1956-57, Ala., 1957-58; Fla. State Univ., 1958-59, 1961-62, 1970; Gulf Coast Community Coll., Panama City, var. periods, 1958-70; Univ. of W. Fla., 1972-; Master's Degree in Graphoanalysis, Int. Graphoanalysis Soc. Inc., Chgo., Ill., 1972. Appts. incl: Tchr., pub. schls., Ala. & Fla., 1957-59 (provisional); Lectr., civic, bus. & educl. orgs.; Licensed & Ct. Qualified Questioned Document Examiner; Treas., Fla. Graphoanalysts Inc.; Questioned Document Workshop Instr.; Tchr., Handwriting Analysis, 1971-. Mbr., profl. orgs. Var. profl. publs. Recip., Cert. of Award for Meritorious Servs., Int. Congress & Inst. of Graphoanalysis, 1973. Address: 4111 Mariner Dr., Panama City, FL 32401, U.S.A. 125.

ROBERTSON, Edwin J., b. 28 Sept. 1905. Chemical Engineer. Educ: B.S., Iowa State Univ., Ames, 1934. Appts. incl: Rsch. & Tech. Div. (New Prod. Dev.), Process Dev. & Heat Transfer), Wilson & Co., Inc., 1934-70; Ind. Cons., Frich & Co., Waynselica, 5 months, 1970; Legal Cons., 1970-. Mbrships. incl: Organizer, Chmn., Nat. Meat Products Comm., Ind. Engrs. for participation in int. activities of Am. Soc. Heating, Refrigerating & Air Conditioning Engrs., 1968-; Sect. Hd., 11 Nat. Comms. on Food Sci. & Food Refridg., 1963-66; Club 371, Toastmasters Int., Chgo.; Fellow Am. Inst. Chems.; Am. Chem. Soc.; Inst. of Food Technols.; Intersoc. Rep. on World Engrng. Centennial Planning Coun., 1952. Author of Prepackaged Frozen Meats, ASRE Jrnl., 1950 & of other articles & lectures. Recip. of Disting. Serv. Award, Am. Soc. Heating, Refrig. & Air Cond. Engrs., 1963. Address: 614 Fullerton Parkway, Chgo., IL 60614, U.S.A. 8, 16, 51, 57, 128.

ROBERTSON, Franklin Lee. Civil Engineer. Educ: Freed-Hardeman Coll., Henderson, Tenn.; Univ. of Tenn., Martin; B.S., Civil Engrng., Tenn. Technol. Univ., Cookeville, 1964. Appts: Civil Engr., constrn., Forcum-Lannom Inc., Dyersburg, Tenn., 1964; Asst. Sec. & Dir., ibid, 1970-; Licensed Profl. Engr., State of Tenn., 1969-. Mbrships: Pres., W. Tenn. Chapt., Tenn. Soc. of Profl. Engrs., 1972; Dir., Tenn. Soc. of Profl. Engrs., 1973-; Tau Beta Pi. Address: 2030 Crossgate Rd., Dyersburg, TN 38024, U.S.A. 7, 125.

ROBERTSON, Fred R., b. 24 Nov. 1914. University Professor. Educ: B.S., Univ. of Tenn., Knoxville, Tenn., 1939; M.S., ibid, 1948; Dr. PA, Harvard Univ., Cambridge, Mass., 1956. Appts. incl: former Asst. Co. Agricl. Agent, Univ. of Tenn.; U.S. Navy Off., WWII; former Instr., Coll. of Agric., Univ. of Tenn.; former Economist, Tenn. Valley Authority; former Asst. to Dir., Coop. Ext. Serv., Penn. State Univ.; former Dir., Coop. Ext. Serv., Auburn Univ.; V.P. for Ext., Auburn Univ. Mbrships: Alpha Gamma Rho Fraternity; Epsilon Sigma Phi Frat.; Gamma Sigma Selta Frat.; Omicron Delta Kappa Frat. Publs: num. profl. papers & articles. Hons: Superior Serv. Award, TVA, Test Demonstration Assn., 1969; Progressive Farmer Mag. Man of the Yr., 1970; Ala. Farm Bur. Serv. to Agric. Award, 1970; Outstanding Ldrship Award, Ala. Marketing Assn., 1970; Man of the Yr. Award, Ala. Crop Improvement Assn., 1971. Address: 208 Samford Hall, Auburn Univ., Auburn, AL 36830, U.S.A. 46, 125.

ROBERTSON, James David, b. 13 Oct. 1922. Professor. Educ: B.S., Univ. of Ala., 1942; M.D., Harvard Med. Schl., 1945; Ph.D., MIT, 1952. Appts. incl: Asst. Prof. of Pathol. & Oncol., Dept. of Pathol. & Oncol., Univ. of Kan. Med. Schl., Kan. City, 1952-55; Hon. Rsch. Assoc., Dept. of Anatomy, Univ. Coll., London, U.K., 1955-60; Assoc. Biophys., Rsch. Lab., McLean Hosp., 1960-63; Biophys., ibid, 1964-66; Asst. Prof. of Neuropathol., McLean Hosp., Dept. of Neurol. & Psych., Harvard Med. Schl., 1960-63; Assoc. Prof., ibid, 1964-66; Prof. & Chmn., Dept. of Anatomy, Duke Univ. Schl. of Med., 1966-. Mbrships. incl: Phi Eta Sigma; Phi Beta Kappa; Sigma Xi; Electron Microscopy Soc. of Am.; Am. Assn. Anatomists; Int. Acad. Pathol.; Anatomical Soc. of Gt. Brit. & Ireland; Physiol. Soc.; Rsch. Defense Soc.; Int. Assn. Cell Bio. Publs: The Ultrastructure of Synapses. The Neurosciences, 1971; jrnl. articles. Address: Dept. of Anatomy, Duke Univ. Schl. of Med. Durham, NC 27710, U.S.A. 2, 54.

ROBERTSON, Norman, b. 15 July 1909. Company Director. Educ: Melbourne Univ. Australia. Appts: Gen. Mgr. & Gov. Dir., Colorprint Pty. Ltd.; Mng. Dir. & Chmn. of Dirs., Mac Robertson (Australia) Ltd.; Dir., Mac Robertson Miller Airlines, Ensign Holdings Ltd.; Pres., Vic. Chmbr. of Mgrs., Assocs. Chmbrs. of Mgrs. of Australia; Mbr., Export Dev. Coun., Decimal Currency Bd. Metric Conversion Bd.; currently Dir., Nat. Mutual Life Assn. of Alasia, Mbr. of Coun., Inst. of Pub. Affairs & Bus. Advsr. to Australian Army. Mbrships: Fellow, Australian Inst. Mgmt.; Inst. Adv. Motorists; Athenaeum Club, Melbourne. Hons: C.B.E. Address: Apt. 8, 58 Clarendon St., E. Melbourne, Vic. 3002, Australia. 12, 123.

ROBERTSON, William B., b. 31 Jan. 1933. Special Assistant to Governor of Virginia. Educ: B.S., Elem. Educ., B.S., Secondary Educ., Bluefield State Coll.; Virginia. Educ: B.S., Elem. Educ., B.S., Secondary Educ., Bluefield State Coll.; M.S., Radford Coll., 1965.

Appts: Tchr., Roanoke (Va.) schls., 10 yrs.; Elem. Supvsr., 2 yrs., ibid; Special Asst. to Gov. Linwood Holton, 1970-. Mbrships. incl: Nat. Advsry. Hwy. Safety Comm.; Pres., S.W. Va. Community Dev. Fund; Speaker's Bur., Roanoke Fine Arts Ctr.; Dir., Cath. Family & Children's Serv., Roanoke; NEA; Va., Roanoke Educ. Assns.; Va. State Supvsrs.; Assoc., Roanoke Jaycess & Advsr., U.S. Jaycees; Bd. of Trustees, Roanoke Valley United Fund; Speaker's Bur., U.S. Pres.' Comm. on Mental Retardation. Hons. incl: Outstanding Young Educator in Roanoke, 1965; Num. hons, Roanoke, Va., Pa., Wash., D.C., Jaycess; Life Mbr., Va. Jaycees, 1969; Hon. Citizen of New Orleans, La., 1971; Annual Brotherhood Award, Nat.. Conf. of Christians & Jews, 1972; Gov. Man of Year, Nat. Bus. League, 1973; Citizen of Year, Small Bus. Admin., 1973. Address: 4800K Terrace View Apts., Blacksburg, VA, U.S.A. 7, 57, 117, 125, 130, 131.

ROBERTSON, William Douglas Gordon, b. 18 Feb. 1912. Journalist. Educ: St. Peter's Coll., Adelaide, Australia; Adelaide Univ.; N.Y. Univ., U.S.A. m. Dorothea Margaret Dixon, 1950, 1 d., Deborah, 1958. Appts: Ed., Aircraft Mag. (Herald & Weekly Times), Melbourne. Mbr., Naval & Mil. Club, Melbourne. Recip., OBE, 1963. Address: Herald & Weekly Times Ltd., 61 Flinders Lane, Melbourne, Vic., Australia. 23.

ROBILLARD, Jennifer K. Executive Director; Sociologist. Educ: Univ. of Mass., Amherst, 1959; Muskingum Coll., New Concord, Ohio, 1962; Penn. State Univ., Univ. Pk., 1964; Univ. of Md., Coll. Pk., 1973. Appts: Tech. Acct., U.S. Ordnance, Springfield, Mass., 1951-58; Asst. Comptroller, Continental Air Cmd., L.I., N.Y., 1959-60; Exec. Dir., Marketing Art & Cultural Artifacts, Eastern Shore Arts & Crafts Ctr., Princess Anne, Md., 1971-; V.P., Ex Officio, Federated Garden Clubs of Md., Inc., Balt., 1973-; Dir., Dist. III, ibid, 1973-. Mbr. & Off., soc. & welfare clubs & orgs. Publs. incl: Herb Culture, 1966; Favorite Recipes, 1967; Flowers In the Kitchen, 1972; Around the Kitchen, 1973. Recip., var. awards conservation, flower arrangement & design. Address: Hillcreek, 1305 Milldam Rd., Towson, MD 21204, U.S.A.

ROBILLARD, Raymond Alfred, b. 26 Jan. 1923. University Administrator. Educ: Acctng., Bay Path Inst., Springfield, Mass., 1941; Admin., Sawyer's Schl. of Bus., L.A., Calif., 1942; B.B.A., Northeastern Univ., Boston, 1952; Landscape Arch., Nat. Landscape Ins., L.A., 1954 Comptrollership, Univ. of Toledo, 1955; M.B.A., Univ. of Mass., Amherst, 1959. Appts: U.S. Mil. Intelligence attached to French Army, 1942-46; Costs & Budgets Dir., Holyoke Care & Paper Co., Springfield, Mass., 1946-52; Supvsry. Acct., Springfield Armory, Mass., 1952-59; Mgr., Admin. & Financial Control Surface Communications Div., Radio Corp. of Am., Camden, N.J., 1959-62; Finance Mgr., Martin-Marietta Corp., Balt., Md., 1962-65; Controller & Asst. Treas., AAI Corp., Balt., Md., 1965-67; Lectr., Loyola Coll., Balt., 1963-68; Lectr., Johns Hopkins Univ., 1965-70; Bus. Mgr., Eastern Shore Campus, Univ. of Md., Princess Anne, Md., 1967-. Mbrships. incl: Financial Execs. Inst., N.Y.C.; Pres., Princess Anne Area Chmbr. of Comm.; Rotary Club; Nat. Assn. of Coll. & Univ. Bus. Offs.; Delmarva Indl. Dev. Assn., Easton, Md.; Advsry. Coun., Somerset Co., Md., Bd. of Educ.; Educl. TV Planning Coun., Md.; Fndr., Dir., Pres., Eastern Shore Arts & Crafts Ctr., Princess Anne; Arts & Crafts Comm., Wye Inst., Queenstown, Md.; Dir., Adult Educ., Cambridge, Ohio, YMCA;

Chmn., Cost Grp., Coated & Processed Paper Assn.; Johns Hopkins Club. Publs: Teletype Standard Operating Procedures for Military Government, 1945; The Break-Even Point, 1948; Distribution Cost Accounting, 1950; Survey of Paper Converting Industry Cost Accounting, 1951; Army Industrial Fund Accounting, 1956; Union Financial Accounting & Reporting, 1959; Role of Capitalism in a Democratic Society, 1959; The Soviet Approach to International Relations 1959. Hons. incl: var. mil. hons.; Man of Yr., Marylander & Herald Newspaper, Md. Address: Hillcreek, 1305 Milldam Rd., Towson, MD 21204, U.S.A. 6.

ROBIN, Reginald de Quetteville, b. 17 Jan. 1919. Shipping Executive. Educ: B.Comm., Univ. of Melbourne, Australia. Appts: Investigating Cost Acct., Commonwealth Bank of Australia, 1950-51; Controller, Parts & Accessories Div., Ford-Australia, 1955-56; Exec. Positions, Australian Nat. Line., 1956-66, Gen. Mgr., Chief Exec. Off., 1967-; Dir., Australian Maritime Inds. Ltd., 1966-67, A.C.T.A. Pty. Ltd., Freightbases Pty. Ltd., Terminal Properties of Australia Pty. Ltd., Through Transit Marine & Mutual Assurance Assn.; Chmn., P.A.D. Shipping Australia Pty. Ltd. Mbrships: Australian Club; Naval & Mil. Club; V.R.C.; M.C.C.; R.A.C.V. Address: Australian National Line, Box 2238T, G.P.O., Melbourne, Vic., Australia 3001. 23, 128.

ROBINETT, Leslie White, b. 13 June 1913. Civic Worker. Appts. incl: Chmn., Fine Arts Dept., Woman's Club of Ft. Worth, 1959-61; Sec., 1962, Dir., 1962-, Van Cliburn Int'l. Quadrennial Piano Competition of Ft. Worth. Mbrships: Bd. of Dirs., Ft. Worth Symphony League, 1966-68; Bd. of Dirs., Tex. Christian Univ. Fine Arts Guild. Address: 3704 Country Club Circle, Fort Worth, TX 76109, U.S.A. 5, 7, 22, 57, 128, 129, 132, 133, 138.

ROBINSON, Annie Laurie, Educator. Educ: B.S., Jackson State Univ., Miss.; Boston Univ.; Univ. of Wis. Appts: Tchr., Sci., Engl. & Music, St. John H.S., Wesson, Miss., 1947-48; Tchr., Music, Ctrl. Miss. Coll., Kosciusko, 1948; Tchr., Sci., Jackson Pub. Schls., 1948-73. Mbrships. incl: Jackson Tchrs. Assn.; 8th Educl. Dist. Assn.; Dept. Classroom Tchrs. Assn.; NEA; Nat. Sci. Tchrs. Assn.; Nat. Assn.; Biol. Tchrs.; AAUP; MTA-NEA State Tchrs. Assn. Organiser, Sci. Fairs, City of Jackson. Hons. incl: Personality of the Yr., Jim Hill H.S. Students, 1960, MTA-NEA State Sci. Fair Disting. Serv. Award, 1971; Cert. for Outstanding Serv., Students of Ctrl. H.S., 1972; Nominated NABT Outstanding Biol. Tchr. Award, 1973. Address: 1018 E. View St., Jackson, MS 39203, U.S.A. 125.

ROBINSON, Antony Meredith Lewin, b. 11 Oct. 1916. Librarian. Educ: B.A., Rhodes Univ., Grahamstown, 1937; Dip. in Libnship., Univ. Coll., London, U.K., 1939; Ph.D., Univ. of Cape Town, 1961. Appts: Asst. Libn., Natal Univ. Coll., Durban, 1940-42, Univ. of Cape Town, 1943-45; Dpty. Libn., S. African Lib., Cape Town, 1945-61, Dir., 1961-; Lectr. in Bibliography, Schl. of Libnship, Univ. of Cape Town, 1962-; Mbr., Nat. Lib. Advsry. Coun., 1972-. Mbr., Fellow & Off., profl. & learned orgs. Publs. incl: Thomas Pringle's Narrative of a Residence in South Africa, (1835), (ed.), 1966; The Letters of Lady Anne Barnard to Henry Dundas, from the Cape & elsewhere, 1793-1803 (ed.), 1973. Contbr., Standard Ency. of Southern Africa, Dictionary of S. African Biography, var. jrnls. Hon. Visitor, Carnegie Corp. of N.Y., U.S.A., 1965. Address:

S. African Library, Queen Victoria St., Cape Town 8001, S. Africa. 30, 39, 139.

ROBINSON, Barry, b. 17 June 1938. Journalist; Gerontologist. Educ: Schl. of Pub. Communication, Boston Univ., 1956-60; New Schl. for Soc. Rsch., N.Y.C., 1962-. Appts. incl: Asst. to Ed.-Publr., Cape Shore Publng. Co., Portland, Me., 1959-60; Reporter-Photographer, Franklin News-Record, N.J. 1960-61; News Ed.-Writer-Photog., Citizen of Morris Co., 1961-62; Entertainment & Books Ed., Asbury Park Press., 1962-67; Free-lance Jrnlist. Communication Cons., N.Y.C., 1967-70; Editl. Cons. & Spec. Projs. Writer, Colonial Penn Grp., N.Y.C. & Assn. of Retd. Persons Nat. Retd. Tchrs. Assn., Wash. D.C., 1970-. Mbrships: Gerontol Soc., U.S.A.; World Future Soc.; Nat. Press Photog. Assn. Publs: On the Beat: Policemen at Work, 1968; Collab., Options for Older Americans, 1971. Recip., News & Feature Photo Award, N.J. Publrs. Assn., 1962. Address; 20th Floor, 555 Madison Ave., N.Y., NY 10022, U.S.A. 6.

ROBINSON, Brian John, b. 4 Nov. 1930. Radio Astronomer. Educ: B.Sc., 1952, M.Sc., 1953, Univ. of Sydney, Ph.D., University of Cambridge, U.K. 1958. Appts: Dir. of Rsch., Australian Nat. Radio Astronomy Observatory. Mbrships: Fellow, Aust. Inst. of Physics & Royal Astronomical Soc.; Sr., IEEE; Int. Astronom. Union; Aust. Nat. Comm. for Radio Sci. Author, 70 Scientific papers. Hons: Univ. Medal (Sydney), 1952; Royal Soc. Rutherford Schlrship., 1953; Premium, Inst. of Elec. Engrs. (London), 1963. Address: CSIRO Div. of Radiophysics, Epping, 2121, Australia. 50.

ROBINSON, Dollye Mary Emily, b. 11 Dec. 1929. Music Teacher & Administrator. Educ: B.S., Jackson State Coll., Miss., U.S.A., 1948; B.Mus., N.W. Univ. Schl. Music, Evanston, Ill.; M.Mus., ibid; Post-grad. work, Boston Univ. Coll. Music, Mass.; Ph.D., N.W. Univ. Schl. Music, Evanston, Ill. Appts: Music Counselor & Dir., Music Progs., Cir. Pines Ctr., Cloverdale, Mich., summers, 1948, '49; Music Tchr., Choir Dir. & Co-Dir., Bands, Alexander Schl., Brookhave, Miss., 1948-52; Instr., Music & Asst. Dir., Bands, Jackson State Coll., ibid, 1952-54; Asst. Prof., Music, Asst. Dir., Bands-Assoc. Prof., Music, Hd., Dept. Music, Acting Chmn., Fine Arts Area, ibid, 1955-67; Prof., Music, Hd., Dept. Music, Chmn., Div. Fine Arts, Chmn., Fac. Personnel Comm.-Dir., Instl. Self-Study Prog., Instl. Rep., AACTE, Jackson State Univ., Miss., 1967-74; SACS Vis. Comm. Mbr., S. Assn. Schls. & Colls. Mbrships. incl: Pres., Miss. Intercoll. Opera Guild; Chmn., Bd. Dirs., Opera/South; Chmn., Arts Educ., Miss. Arts Commn.; Pi Kappa Lambda. Author num. reports, Self-Study Prin. Recip. num. hons. Address: 1018 Eastview St., Jackson, MS 39203, U.S.A. 5, 125.

ROBINSON, Enders Anthony, b. 18 Mar. 1930. Geophysicist. Educ: S.B., MIT, 1950; S.M., ibid, 1952; Ph.D., ibid, 1954. Appts. incl: Dir., Geophysical Analysis Grp., MIT, 1952-54; Assoc. Prof., Univ. of Wis., 1958-62; Dpty. Prof., Uppsala Univ., Sweden, 1960-64; V.P., Digicon Inc., Houston, Tex., 1965-70; Geophysical Cons., Houston, Tex., 1970-. Mbrships: Soc. of Exploration Geophysicists; European Assn. of Exploration Geophysicists. Publs: Infinitely Many Variates, 1957; Random Wavelets & Cybernetic Systems, 1962; Statistical Communication & Detection, 1967; Multichannel Time Series Analysis, 1967. Contbr. of num. rsch. papers to sci. jrnls. Hons: Best Paper Award, 1964, Disting. Lectr., 1967 & Medal Award, 1969, all Soc. of Exploration Geophysicists; Schlumberger Award, European

Assn. of Exploration Geophysicists, 1969. Address: 100 Autumn Ln., Lincoln, MA 01773, U.S.A. 7, 14, 125.

ROBINSON, Francis Arthur, b. 28 Apr. 1910. Assistant Manager, Metropolitan Opera. Educ: B.A., Vanderbilt Univ., Nashville, Tenn., 1932; M.A. ibid, 1933. Appts. incl: Reporter-Sunday Ed., Nashville Banner, Tenn., 1933-38; Co. Mgr. & Press Rep., Playwrights' Co., 1938-40, Cornelia O. Skinner, 1938-40; Press Rep., Katharine Cornell, 1940-42; 1945-48; Tour Dir., 1948, Box Office & Subscription, 1950-62, Asst. Mgr., 1952-, Chief, Press Dept., 1954-, Metropolitan Opera, N.Y.C. Mbrships' incl: Assn. of Theatrical Press Agents & Mgrs.; Tenn. Soc. in N.Y.; Past-Pres., Kentuckians; Bd. of Trust. Vanderbilt Univ.; Trustee, Manhattan Schl. of Music; The Players. Publs: Caruso: His Life in Pictures, 1957, reprinting TV scripts, record album notes. Radio Broadcaster. Hons: Cavaliere, Order of Merit, Italy, 1970; Doct. Letters, Westminster Choir Coll., Princeton, 1969; Handel Medallion, 1972; Award of Merit, Lotos Club, 1972. Address: Metropolitan Opera House, Lincoln Center, N.Y., NY 10023, U.S.A.

ROBINSON, Francis Edwin, b. 24 Dec. 1909. Banker. Educ: B.A., Univ. of N.H., 1931; M.A., Engl., ibid, 1933. Appts: Sec. N.H. Farm Bur. Fedn., 1934-40; U.S. Govt. serv., 1940-44; Asst. to Pres. & Dir., Pub. Info., Univ. of N.H., 1944-52; Exec. Staff, New England Coun., 1952-61; Exec. V.P. N.H. Assn. of Savings Banks, 1961-73; Pres., Durham (N.H.) Trust Co., 1973-; Dir., Financial Life Ins. Co. (N.Y.), 1971-. Mbrships: Newcomen Soc. in N. Am. Publs: Isaac Hill (biog.). Hons: Ernest Thompson Fairchild Prize, Univ. of N.H., 1931; Dir., N.H. Assn. of Savings Banks; Trustee, Berwick Acad., 1973. Address: Roundabout House, RFD 2, Durham, NH 03824, U.S.A. 15, 24.

ROBINSON, (Rev.) Frank M., b. 27 Sept. 1944. Minister. Educ: Va. Union Univ., Richmond, U.S.A. Appts: Dir., Afro-Am. Experience, 1965-67; Dir., Nassau Co. Black Hist. Mus., 1967-68; Admin. Asst., M.C.A.P., 1968-70; Dir., Martin Luther King Jr. Community Ctr., Rockville Ctr., N.Y., 1970-. Mbrships: Vice Chmn., E.O.C. Bd., Rockville Ctr.; Vice Chmn., Stable Inn Dev. Corp.; Exec. Bd., T.Y.C. Youth Progs.; Recreation Advsry. Comm., Village of Rockville Ctr. Recorded "A Sense of Touch", 1966. Recip., Martin Luther King Award, for outstanding serv. to Rockville Ctr. E.O.C., 1969. Address: 6-D Meehan Lane, Rockville Centre, Long Island, NY 11570, U.S.A. 130.

ROBINSON, George Reginald Gray, b. 29 Mar. 1909. Banker. Educ: Merton Coll., Oxford, U.K. Appts: Schlmaster, 3 yrs.; Sec., Bank of Bermuda Ltd.; Dir., var. cos.; Servd. sev. Govt. bds. Mbrships: Myrmidon Club, Merton Coll.; Sec-Treas., Bermuda Lawn Tennis Club; Rear-Commodore, Royal Hamilton Amateur Dinghy Club; Chmn., Paget W. Br., United Bermuda Party. Author of articles & verse. Hons: Bermuda Govt. Schlrship, 1927; Rhodes Schlrship, 1928. Address: P.O. Box 127, Paget 6, Bermuda. 109.

ROBINSON, Gilbert Kelly, b. 31 Dec. 1900. Professor of History & Philosophy. Educ: A.B., Univ. of Mo., 1923; B.D., Yale Univ., 1927; Ph.D., Univ. of Chicago, 1934. Appts. incl: Pastor, Fed. Ch., Sturbridge, Mass., 1927-28; Educ. Rsch., Yale, 1929-30; Soc. Trends Study, U.S. Govt., 1930-31; Urban Rsch., Victor Lawson Fund, Chicago Theol. Sem., 1931-37; Tchr. of Sociol., Franklin Coll., Ind., 1937;

Prof., Sociol. & Philos., Ctrl. Coll., Fayette, Mo., 1937-39; Fac., Harris Tchrs. Coll., St. Louis, Mo., 1939-70; Chmn., Dept. Soc. Scis., ibid, 1948-70. Mbr. of profl. socs. Contbr. of articles to profl. jrnls., inclng: Ethics, Cosmology & Religious Faith, Jrnl. of Relig., 1935; The Catholic Birth Rate, Am. Jrnl. of Sociol., 1936; Trends in the Ethnic Composition of the U.S. Population, Jrnl. of Soc. for Soc. Rsch., 1936; Nationality Origin & Relig. Background, Am. Jrnl. of Sociol., 1939. Hons. incl: Downs Prize, Yale, 1926; Selected to give 1st & 2nd series of radio broadcasts for St. Louis Pub. Schls., 1944-46; Cert. of Merit for Dist. Serv. as Tchr., Scholar & Guidance Counselor, 1969. Address: 315 Charlene Dr., St. Louis, MO 63122, U.S.A. 13, 15, 57.

ROBINSON, Helene Margaret. Professor of Music, Piano. Educ: B.A., Univ. of Ore., Eugene; M.Mus., Northwestern Univ., Evanston, Ill.; Postgrad. study, Univ. of Southern Calif., L.A. Appts: Asst. Prof., Music, Piano; Assoc. Prof., Hd. of Piano Dept., Southern Ore. State Coll., Ashland; Asst. Prof., Music, Piano, Calif. State Coll., Fullerton; Assoc. Prof., Univ. of Calif., Santa Barbara; Prof. of Piano, Ariz. StateUniv., Tempe. Mbrships: State Chmn. of Student Mbrship. & of Piano Comm., Mus. Educs. Nat. Conf.; Phi Beta; Mus. Tchrs. Nat. Assn.; OMTA & ASMTA; V.P., Ariz. Music Tchrs. Assn. Publs: Basic Piano for Adults (Coll. Text), 1964, 12 prints.; Intermediate Piano for Adults, Vol. 1, 11, 1970; Teaching Piano in Classroom & Studio, 1967; Articles in many mags. Address: Music Dept., Ariz. State Univ., Tempe, AZ 85281, U.S.A. 2, 52, 130.

ROBINSON, Jack Fay, b. 7 Mar. 1914. Clergyman. Educ: A.M., Univ. of Mont., 1936; B.D., Cozer Theological Sem., 1939; A.M., Univ. of Chgo., 1949. Appts: Pastor, American Falls, Idaho, 1939-41; Hyde Park YMCA, Chgo., 1942-44; Pastor, Council Grove, Kan., 1944-49, Chebanse, Ill., 1948-51; Fellow in Hist., Univ. of Chgo., 1951-52; Educ. Lib., ibid, 1952-54; Pastor, Argo, Ill., 1954-58, St. Charles, Ill., 1958-64, Plymouth Ch., Lansing, Mich., 1964-66; Dir., Darrow Community Ctr., Chgo., 1966; Tchr., Chgo. Bd. of Educ., 1966-68; Pastor, Waveland Ave., Chgo., 1967-; Tchr., Wilmette Pub. Schls., 1968-72. Mbrships: Am. Soc. Ch. Hist.; Ill. Conf., United Ch. of Christ (V.P., 1963-64); Gen. Bd., Ch. Fedn. of Greater Chgo., 1972-. Publ: The Growth of the Bible, 1969. Address: P.O. Box 4578, Chicago. IL 60680, U.S.A. 8, 57, 128.

ROBINSON, James McNulty Ainslie, b. 10 Sept. 1931. Educator; Consultant; Lecturer. Educ: B.Sc., Wash. Univ., St. Louis, 1954; M.B.A., ibid, 1956; Ph.D., Ohio State Univ., 1965. Appts: Dir., McNulty's Ltd., 1952-; Asst. Prof., Marketing, Wash. Univ., 1958-60; Pres., James McNulty Robinson Marketing Mgmt. Servs., Toronto, Canada, 1961-67; Assoc. Prof., Bus., Univ. of Calgary, 1967-68; Prof., ibid, 1968-; Dean, Fac. of Bus., 1967-72; Pub. Lectr., Bus. Orgs., 1972-; Pres., Sentinel Enterprises, 1973. Mbrships. incl: Coun., Banff Ctr., 1970-72; Bd., Banff Schl. of Adv. Mgmt., 1967-73; Ind. Expansion Comm., City of Calgary, 1971 '72 '73; Past Sec.-Treas., Coun. for Profl. Educ. for Bus.; Past Exec. Sec., Am. Assn. Collegiate Schls. of Bus.; Chmn., Sub-comm. on Rsch., Indl. Expan. Comm., Calgary, 1972-73; Chmn., Indl. Expansion Comm., City of Calgary, 1974; Am. Marketing Assn., etc. Contbr. to profl. publs. Two manuscripts in process. Address: 2308 Uxbridge Dr., N.W., Calgary, Alberta, Canada T2N 3Z6, 2, 14, 88, 139.

ROBINSON, John Alexander III, b. 23 Apr. 1942. Company President. Educ: B.S., Ala. Univ., U.S.A., 1967. Appts: Asst. to Pres., Am. Southern Publg. Co., 1966-67; Marketing-Unit Marketing Rep., IBM Corp., 1967-72; State Campaign Mgr., Govship. Ala. (on leave, IBM Corp.), 1973; Pres., RoBen, Inc., 1973-; Fndr., Ptnr., Southern Properties, Ltd., 1974-. Mbrships. incl: S.E. Regional Dir., Young Democrats of Am., 1972; State Pres., Young Democracts of Ala., 1972-; State Off., Ala. Jaycees, 1972, '73, '74; State Dir., L.Q.C. Lamar Soc., 1972-; Pres., Huntsville Chapt., L.Q.C. Lamar Soc., 1972; Past Pres., V.P. & Treas., Family Counseling Assn., Huntsville/Madison Co.; Pres., N. Ala. Multiple Sclerosis Soc., 1972; V.P., N. Ala. T.B. Assn., 1972; State Dir., Ala. Lung Assn., 1973-; Past Pres. & V.P., Civic Club Coun., Huntsville/Madison Co.; Past Treas., Voluntary Action Ctr., Huntsville/Madison Co. Hons: 1 of 5 Outstanding IBM Employees in U.S. for Community Involvement, 1968; Disting. Serv. Award, Huntsville Jaycees, 1972; 1 of 4 Outstanding Young Men of Ala., 1972. Address: 12008 Carnelot Dr., Huntsville, AL 35803, U.S.A. 114, 117, 125.

ROBINSON, John Desmond, b. 20 Jan. 1910. Journalist; Newspaper Director. Appts: Reporter, Natal Mercury, S. Africa, 1929; Reporter, Daily Telegraph, London, U.K., 1930-31; Capt., S.A. Artillery, served N. Africa & Italy, WW II; Sub-Ed., Natal Mercury; Asst. Ed., ibid, 1946; Dir., 1949; Ed., 1959; Chmn., Ed.-in-Chief & Mng. Dir., 1970; Dir., S. African Assocd. Newspapers, 1973. Mbrships: Dir., S.A. Press Assn.; Durban Club; Durban Country Club. Author of sev. pol. pamphlets. Address: P.O. Box 950, Durban, S. Africa.

ROBINSON, John Thomas, b. 6 Dec. 1920. Advertising Executive. Educ: B.S., Northeast Mo. State Tchrs. Coll., U.S.A. Appts: Prod., B. Altman & Co., N.Y.C., 1956-57; Prod., Bonwit Teller, 1957-58; Prod. Mgr., Bergdorf Goodman, N.Y.C., 1958-66; Advt. Mgr., ibid, 1966-69; Advt. Dir., 1969-; Pres., The Ad Galley, Inc., Advt. Agcy. Mbr., Sigma Tau Gamma. Exhib. of paintings, Nena's Choice Gall., Bergdorf Goodman, N.Y.C. Address: 305 E. 72nd St., New York, NY 10021, U.S.A. 6, 34, 40, 46, 130.

ROBINSON, Leacroft Heriot Ulysses, b. 20 July 1916. Barrister-at-Law. Educ: 2nd Class Hons. in Bar Finals, Gray's Inn, London, U.K.; 1948; Appts: Coun. Mbr., W. Indian Bar Assn., 1957-60; Q.C., 1959; Pres., Bar Assn. Jamaica, 1967-73; Mbr., Wooding Comm. on Legal Trng., 1967; Mbr., Advsry. Comm. to Min. of Legal Affairs, on Fusion of Legal Profns., 1969-71; Pres., Org. of Commonwealth Caribbean Bar Assns., 1970-72; Atlantic Region Rep., Commonwealth Legar Bur., 1970-73; Chmn., Gen. Legal Coun., Jamaica, 1971-; Coun. Legal Educ., W. Indies, 1971-; Chmn., Jamaica Law Revision Comm., 1972-; Atty. Gen. of Jamaica, 1972-. Hons: Gold Medal, Jamaica Civil Serv. Assn., 1969; Appt. as Senator, Upper House of Jamaican Parliament, 1972. Address: Attorney General's Chambers, P.O. Box 456, Kingston, Jamaica. 96.

ROBINSON, Marie Josephine, b. 21 Jan. 1915. Professor of Speech. Educ: B.L.I., Emerson Coll., Boston, Mass., 1935; M.A., Mich. State Univ., E. Lansing, 1944; Ph.D., Northwestern Univ., Evanston, Ill., 1960. Appts: Dir., Plays & Contests, Speech, Drama, Lockport Sr. H., N.Y.; Hd., Dept. of Speech & Drama, State Tchrs. Coll., Bemidji, Minn.; Instr., Syracuse Univ., N.Y.; Prof. of Speech, Ill. Wesleyan Univ., Bloomington; Dir. of

Forensics, ibid, 1950-72; Vis. Lectr., var. colls. & univs. Mbrships. incl: Speech Communication Assn.; Pres., Ill. Speech & Theatre Assn., 1962-63; Am. Theatre Assn.; Am. Forensic Assn.; Past Pres. & Sec.-Treas., Ill. Wesleyan Univ. Chapt., AAUP; Charter mbr. & Sec., N.Y. State Speech Assn.; Past Sec. & Pres., Ill. Wesleyan Univ. Chapt., Phi Kappa Phi; Theta Alpha Phi. Author of articles & chapts. in books. Recip., var. educl. awards. Address: Ill. Wesleyan Univ., Bloomington, IL 61701, U.S.A. 5, 8, 13, 14, 15, 120, 126, 138.

ROBINSON, O(liver) Preston, b. 25 June 1903. Professor; Editor & Business Executive. Educ: A.B., Brigham Young Univ., 1928; M.S., D.C.S., N.Y. Univ., 1928-35. Appts. incl: Prof. & Hd., Dept. of Mktng., Univ. of Utah, 1947-50; Ed. & Gen. Mgr., Deseret News Publ. Co., 1950-64; Pres., Brit. Mission, Ch. of Jesus Christ, London, 1964-67; Gen. Mgr., Deseret Press, 1967-. Mbrships. incl: V.P., Rotary Int.; Bd. of Advsrs., Chmbr. of Comm.; Pres., Yough Tobacco Advsry. Coun. for Utah, 1970-; Pres., Timpanogos Club of Utah, 1973-74. Publs. incl: Biblical Sites in the Holy Land, 1963; The Challenge of the Scrolls, 1963; Successful Retail Salesmanship, 1966; Store Salesmanship; Retail Store Operation & Management; Israel's Bible Lands, 1973. Hons. incl: Outstanding Civilian Serv. Award, Dept. of U.S. Army, 1964; Merit Honor Award, Univ. of Utah, 1972. Address: 670 E., Three Fountains Dr., Murray, UT 84107, U.S.A. 2, 9.

ROBINSON, Prezell Russell, b. 25 Aug. 1922. Coll. President. Educ: A.B., St. Augustine's Coll., Raleigh, NC U.S.A., 1946; M.A., Cornell Univ., Ithaca, NY, 1951; Ed.D., ibid, 1956. Appts: Served w. US Army, WW II; Tchr., Bettis Jr. Coll., Trenton, SC, 1946-48; Registrar-Tchr., Acting Prin., HS, Acting Dean, Jr. Coll., Instr., Soc. Sci. & Dir., Adult Educ., Voorhees Jr. Coll., Denmark, SC, 1948-56; Cornell Univ. Fellowship, spring, 1954; Rsch. Fellowship, ibid, summers, 1955, '56; Dean, Prof., Sociol.-Pres., St. Augustine's Coll., Raleigh, NC, 1964-; US Fulbright Lectrng. Fellowship, India, 1965; Dir., var. Insts. sponsored by Nat. Sci. Fndn., 1959-66; Periods further study, Pres. Inst., Pa. State Univ., summer, 1968; Vis. Fellowship, Wm. James Schl., Behavioral Scis., Harvard Univ., summer, 1973. Mbrships: Phi Beta Lambda; Alpha Kappa Mu; Delta Mu Delta; Phi Delta Kappa; Phi Kappa Phi; num. acad. assns. & educl. advsry. comms. Author num. profl. jrnl. articles & papers. Recip. num. hons. Address: St. Augustine's Coll., 1315 Oakwood Ave., Raleigh, NC 27611, U.S.A.

ROBINSON, Ray, b. 8 July 1905. Author & Journalist. Appts: Contbr. to Daily & Sunday Telegraph, London; The Times of India, Bombay; New Australian Ency., Sydney; The Cricketer, England; Australian Cricketer, Melbourne; Sportsweek, Bombay. Mbrships: Australian Jrnlsts.' Assn.; Australian Soc. of Authors; Jrnlsts.' Club, Sydney; Cricketers' Club, Sydney. Publs: Between Wickets, 1946; From the Boundary, 1950; The Glad Season, 1955; The Wit of Sir Robert Menzies, 1966; Cricket's Fun, 1968; The Wildest Tests, 1972. Address: Cricketers' Club, 254 George St., Sydney, Australia. 3, 23.

ROBINSON, (Sir) Robert, b. 13 Sept. 1886. Organic Chemist. Educ: M.A.; Fellow, Royal Inst. of Chem.; D.Sc., Victoria. Appts. incl: Prof. of Organic Chem., Manchester, 1922-28; Prof., Univ. Coll., London, 1928-30; Waynflete Prof. of Chem., Oxford Univ., 1930-35; Dir., Shell Chem. Co. Ltd., 1955- & Shell Rsch. Ltd., 1967-. Mbrships. incl: Hon. Fellow, Magdalen

Coll., Oxford, 1956- & Weizmann Inst. of Sci., Rehovot, Israel; Pres., British Assn. for Advancement of Sci., 1955; Pres., Soc. of Chem. Ind., 1958-59; Fellow, ibid, 1920-; Pres., Royal Soc., 1945-50; Fellow, ibid; Hon. mbr., Inst. of British Engrs. Author of over 600 sci. memoirs, mainly in Jrnl. of Chem. Soc., & of book on Structural Relations of Natural Products, 1955. Hons. incl: Nobel Prize for Chem., 1947; D.Sc., 14 univs.; LL.D., 6 univs. Address: Grimm's Hill Lodge, Grimm's Hill, Bucks., U.K. 1, 2, 34, 50, 131.

ROBISON, James E., b. 22 Nov. 1915. Company Director. Educ: B.B.A., Univ. of Minn., 1938; M.B.A., Harvard Univ. Grad. Schl. of Bus. Admin., 1940. Appts. incl: Served WW II; Exec. V.P., Textron Inc., 1950-53; Pres., Chief Exec. Off. & Dir., Indian Head Inc., N.Y.C., 1950-53; Pres., Chief Exec. Off. & Dir., Indian Head Inc., N.Y.C., 1953-67; Chmn. of Bd. & Chief Exec. Off., ibid, 1967-72; Mbr., Exec. Comm., 1967-; Chmn., Finance Comm., 1971-; Chmn., Bd. of Trustees, Pension & Profit Sharing Trusts. Dir., var. cos. inclng. Am. TV & Communications Corp., 1971-, Continental Oil Co., 1971-, Thyssen-Bornemisza Group NV (Supvsry. Bd.), 1973-. Mbrships. incl: Trustee, Air Force Aid Soc., 1968-; Finance Comm., ibid, 1969-; Dir., Bus. Comm. for the Arts, 1973-; Trustee, Calif. Inst. of Technol., 1970-; Vis. Comm., Harvard Univ. Grad. Schl. of Bus. Admin., 1966-72, 1973-; Dir., Manhattan Eye, Ear & Throat Hosp., 1969-. James E. Robison Professorship, Harvard Univ. Grad. Schl. of Bus. Admin. endowed in his hon., 1973. Address: Indian Head Inc., 1211 Ave. of the Americas, N.Y., NY 10036, U.S.A. 2.

ROBLES, Esther Waggoner (Mrs. Robert Holtz Robles). Educ: Calif. Univ., L.A., U.S.A.; Alliance Francaise; Paris Univ., France. Appts: Owner, Esthers Alley Gall., 1947- (changed to Esther-Robles Gall., 1954); Judge, num. exhibs., inclng. Annual Kern Co. Pks. & Recreation Dept. Art Festivals; Future Masters series (3 events), Music & Fine Arts Commn., L.A. Jr. Chmbr. of Comm., 1968, '69; Org., num. travelling art shows, Western Assn. Art Muss., 1964-; Cons., Calif. Arts Commn. Comm. to Investigate Taxation in the Arts, 1966; Fndr., Org. & Pres., The Art Sponsors, Inc.; Advsr., Fed. Visual Arts Proj. (Title III), 1967; Tour, John Battenberg work to San Bernardino, Ynyo, Mono; Lectr., Cons.; Advsry. Art Panel, Commnr., Internal Revenue Serv., 1970-72. Mbrships: Graphic Arts Coun., L.A. Co. Mus. of Art, 1968-; Fashion Coun., ibid, 1969-; Alumni Assn., Calif. Univ., L.A.; W. Assn. Art Muss.; Publs: Articles on art; Art cores., L.A. newspapers at Venice Biennale, 1960, '68; Tour & Catalogue, Robert Cremean, Calif. Arts Commn. Tour, 1966; Resonne, Claire Falkenstein Catalogue, Mod. & Ill. Univs., 1969; Ed., The Lively Arts. Address: Esther-Robles Gall., L.A., CA, U.S.A. 37.

ROBSON, (Dame) Flora KcKenzie, b. 28 Mar. 1902. Actress. Educ: Royal Acad. of Dramatic Art. First stage appearance, 1921. Num. theatre performances in London incl: Old Vic Season, 1934; Mary Tudor, 1936; Man About the House, Message from Margaret, 1948; The Winter's Tale, 1951; The Return, 1953; No Escape & A Kind of Folly, 1955; The House by the Lake, 1956-58; The Aspern Papers, 1959; Time & Yellow Roses, 1961; The Importance of Being Earnest, 1968; Ring Round the Moon, 1969. Overseas appearances incl: Lady Macbeth, N.Y., U.S.A., 1948; The Aspern Papers, S. Africa, 1960; The Corn is Green, S. Africa, S. Rhodedesia, 1962. Films incl: Fire Over England, Wuthering Heights, Caesar & Cleopatra, Black Narcissus, Saraband for Dead Lovers, Romeo & Juliet, High Tide at Noon, The Gipsy & the Gentleman, 55 Days at Peking, Those Magnificient Men in their Flying Machines, Fragment of Fear, Alice in Wonderland. Former Pres., Royal Acad of Dramatic Art. Hons. incl: D.B.E., 196U; D.Litt., Durham Univ., 1959, Wales, Oxford, 1974; D.Lit., London, 1971; Best Actress, Film Weekly Award, 1937, Evening Standard Award, 1959. Address: 14 Marine Gdns., Brighton BN2 1AH, Sussex, U.K. 1.

ROCA-PUIG, Ramon, b. 23 Mar. 1906. Professor. Educ: Doct., Sacred Theol., Pontifical Univ., Tarragona, Spain, 1928; Doct., Classical Philol., Cath. Univ. of the Sacred Heart, Milan, Italy, 1939; Doct., Philos. & Letters, Univ. of Salamanca, Spain, 1958. Appts: Prof., Greek, Conciliar Sem., Barcelona, 1940; Prof., Greek Philol., Pontifical Univ., Salamanca, 1950; Dir., St. Luke the Evangelist Fndn. & Papyri Barcinonenses Collect., 1954; Prof., Univ. of Barcelona, 1959-63. Mbrships: Int. Assn. of Papyrologists; Egypt Exploration Soc., London. Publs. incl: Un papir grec de l'Evangeli de sant Mateu, 1962; Himne a la Verge Maria, Psalmus responsorius, Papir llat1 del segle IV, 1965; Contbr. to num. profl. jrnls. Address: Consejo de Ciento 381, 1°, 2ª, Barcelona 9, Spain. 43.

ROCCI LUPI, Ottavio Alberto Renato, b. 23 Apr. 1905. Business Executive. Educ: Doct. in Econ. Scis., Univ. of Genoa. Appts: Spanish Rep., Italcable, Rome, 1938-45; Mgng. Dir., Neotecnica S.A.E., Madrid, 1959-; Pres., Eurobags Iberica S.A., Cieza (Murcia) Spain, 1973-. Mbrships: Automobile Club of Spain, Madrid; Royal Country Club, Madrid; Hunting Club, Madrid. Contbr. to tech. jrnls. Hons: Mil. Medal; Medal of the Campaign, Spanish Civil War; Kt. of Hon. of the King of Italy; Kt. of Grace and Devotion, Order of Malta. Address: Paseo Pintor Rosales, 30, Madrid 8, Spain. 1.

ROCKE, Russell Alan, b. 8 Feb. 1945. Advertising Agency President; Writer. Educ: B A., Tulane Univ., New Orleans, La., 1967; J.D., ibid, 1968. Appts: Vista Lawyer, Wash. D.C. & N.Y.C., 1969-70; Pres., Sales Ammunition Inc. (Advt. & Sales Promotion Agcy.), 1970-; Co-Ed. & Publr., The Baritaria Review; Mbr., Bd. of Dirs. & Co-Publr., The New Orleans Review of Books. Publs: The Grandiloquent Dictionary, 1972; Author & Publr., 1968-; of Pamphlets: Negro Historical Calendar, Puerto Rican Historical Calendar, Mexican Histor ical Calendar, Native American Historical Calendar. Hons: Glendy-Burke Oratorical Gold Medal, Tulane Univ., 1965. Address: Cragsmoor, NY 12420, U.S.A. 30.

ROCKLIN, Raymond, b. 18 Aug. 1922. Sculptor. Exuc: Cooper Union Art Schl., N.Y.; Educ: Alliance Art Schl., N.Y. Appts: Vis. Artist, Univ. of Calif., Berkeley, 1959, Am. Univ., Wash. D.C., & Bull State Tchrs. Coll., Muncie, Ind. Prin. works incl: Wall Brass, Whitney Mus. of Am. Art, N.Y.; Bronze, "Revelation", Temple Israel, St. Louis, Mo. Mbrships: Sculptor's Guild; Fedn. of Mod. Painter's Sculptors. Hons: Fulbright Grant to Italy, 1952-53 & Yaddo Grant for Sculpture, 1956. Address: 232B Watch Hull Rd., Peekskill, NY 10566, U.S.A. 37, 105.

ROCKWELL, Theodore III, b. 26 June 1922. Chemical Engineer. Educ: B.S., Princeton Univ., 1943; M.S., ibid, 1944; Grad. courses, Oak Ridge. Appts: Process Improvement Engr., Pilot Plant of Electro-magnetic Separation Plant, Manhattan Proj. for Atomic Bomb, Oak Ridge, Tenn., & later, Hd., Shield Engrng. Group, Oak Ridge Nat. Lab., 1944-49; Admiral

Rickover's Naval Reactors HQ Org., 1949-64; Dir., Nuclear Technol. Div., ibid, 1953-55; Tech. Dir., 1955-64; Prin. Off. & Dir., MPR Assocs., 1964-; Rsch. Assoc., Johns Hopkins Univ. Ctr. of For. Policy Rsch., 1965-68; Cons., Jt. Congressional Comm. on Atomic Energy, 1967. Mbrships: Chmn., Atomic Indl. Forum Reactor Safety Task Force; Advsry. Group on Artificial Heart Prog., Nat. Insts. of Hlth., 1966; Advsry. Coun., Princeton Univ. Dept. of Chem. Engrng., 1966-72; Cosmos Club. Author, co-author & ed. of publs. in field. Recip. of hons. Address: MPR Assocs., Inc., 1140 Connecticut Ave., N.W., Wash. DC 20036, U.S.A. 2, 14, 50, 56.

ROCKWOOD, Vivian V., b. 9 Apr. 1911. Professor of Home Economics. Educ: B.A., State Univ. of Iowa, 1933; M.A., Columbia Univ., 1938; R.D., 1969; P.D. Profl. Dip., Columbia Univ., 1963. Appts. incl: Instr., Home Econs. & Dietitian, Keene State Coll., N H., 1938-42; Dir. Commons & Instr., Home Econs., R.I. State Univ., 1942-43; Assoc. Prof., Hd., Home Econs., Keene State Coll., 1943-53; Prof., Hd., Home Econs., Wichita State Univ., Kan., 1953-58; Prof., Chmn., E. Tenn. State Univ., 1958-. Mbrships. incl: Fac. Rep., E. Tenn. State Univ., NEA, 1970-73; num. offs., Am. Home Econs. Assn.; Charter, Past Pres., Am. Dietetic Assn.; Kappa Omicron Phi, Kappa Rho Chapt.; Delta Kappa Gamma; DAR; AAUW; AAUP; NEA; many others. Address: 1902 Kenwood Dr., Johnson City, TN 37601, U.S.A. 6, 15, 125, 129, 138.

RODBORD, Joseph Harrison, b. 27 Oct. 1913. Counselor. Educ: 3 Masterates; 16 Doctorates; 1 Bishopric; 22 var. dips. Appts. incl: Aux. Police Off., U.S. Civil Defense, Wash. D.C. & other places, 1941-74; Counselor, Mental, Phys., Spiritual, Profl. Servs.-Man7, Perryville, Md., 1964-74; Notary Pub., State of Md., 1969-74; Field Rsch. Corres., World Field Rsch., Mineola, N.Y., 1969-74. Mbrships. incl: Charter Mbr., Nat. Opportunity Rsch. Serv.; Princeton, N.J., 1972-74; Permanent Mbr., British Guild of Drugless Practitioners, London, U.K.; Profl. Mbr., Natural Therapeutics Assn.; Dane Hill, Sussex, U.K.; Life Mbr., Lambda Sigma Delta, Denver, Colo., U.S.A.; Alpha Psi Omega; Am. Counselors Soc.; Life Mbr., Int. Inst. of Criminol.; Life Mbr., Colnel, Highway Radio Patrol Int., St. John, N.B., Canada; Advsry. Mbr., Am. Security Coun., Wash. D.C. & Boston, VA. Recip. of num. hons. Address: Broad St. Aside P.O., Perryville, MD 21903, U.S.A. 130.

RODECK, Heinrich F.J., b. 1 Nov. 1920. Pediatrician. Educ: M.D. Univ. Munich; Univs. Halle (Saale), Münster, Würzburg. Appts: Sci. Asst., Inst. Physiol., Univ. Munster, 1946-48, Inst. Biochem., 1948-50; Sci. Asst., Children's Clin., Univ. Düsseldorf, 1950-60, Asst. Prof., ibid, 1956-; Asst. Prof., Inst. Anatomy, Univ. Kiel, 1955; Vis. Lectr., Inst. de Médecine et de chirurgie experimentales Univ. of Montreal, Canada, & med. instns., U.S.A., 1959; Med. Dir., Children's Hosp., Datteln, Germany, 1960-. Mbr., var. med. socs. Publs. incl: Diabetes insipidus u. primäre Oligurie, 1955; Physiology & Pathology of the Hypothalamo-Neurohypophyseal System, 1967; Epiphysis cerebri, 1971. Recip., MORO Prize, German Soc. Pediatrics, 1959. Address: Vestischen Kinderklinik, D-4354 Datteln/Westf., Lloydstr. 5, German Fed. Repub. 43, 92.

RODELL, Marie, b. 31 Jan. 1912. Literary Agent. Educ: B.A., Vassar Coll., Appts. incl: Asst. to Ed., William Morrow & Co.; Fiction Ed., Modern Age Books; Hd., Mystery Dept.,

Duell, Sloan & Pearce; currently own Literary Agcy. Mbrships: former V.P. & Bd. Mbr., Soc. of Author's Reps.; Author's Guild; Advsry. Bd., Rachel Carson Trust for the Living Environment. Publs: 3 novels under pseudonym; Mystery Fiction: Theory & Technique; articles & short stories. Hons:Edgar (Mystery Writers of Am.), 1948. Address: 141 E. 55 St., N.Y., NY 10022, U.S.A. 5.

RODEMAN, Frederick Ernest, b. 29 Jan. 1938. Banking Executive. Educ: B.S. in Bus., Ind. Univ., Bloomington, 1959; Postgrad., DePaul Univ., Chgo., 1968-71; Am. Inst. of Banking, 1972. Appts¨ Auditor-C.P. A., Andersen & Co., 1959-67; Acctng. Mgr., A. B. Dick Co., 1967-72; Audit Mgr., Beloit State Bank, 1972-. Mbrships: Am. Inst. Cert. Pub. Accts. (Cert. Pub. Acct b State of Ind., 1965); Am. Inst. of Banking; Sigma Delta Chi. Address: 2372 Tara Ct., Beloit, WI 53511, U.S.A. 8.

RODENBERG, Rudolf, b. 20 Oct. 1929. Professor. Educ: Bamberg Univ., Germany, 1949; Master, Theoretical Phys., Göttingen Univ., 1955; Ph.D., Heidelberg Univ., 1956. Appts: Asst., Tübingen Univ., Germany, 1956-62; Frankfürt/Main Univ., 1962-65; Prof. Phys., Okla. State Univ., Stillwater, U.S.A., 1965-66; Technische Hochschule, Aachen, Germany, 1966-74; Vis. Prof. Phys., Ctr. Brasileiro de Pesquisas Fisicas, Rio de Janeiro, Brazil, 1973. Mbr. Am. Phys. Soc. Publs: 144 papers in field, inclng. Radio of the cross sections for the (e,N)—and ge,N)—process, 1960; Spin zero mesons and broken chiral Su(3) x SU(3) (w. P. Zerwas), 1970; Polarization of the recoil protons in the elastic electron-proton scattering process, (w. U. Guenther), 1971; Estimate of the mass of the ninth pseudoscalar meson, w. P. Zerwas, 1970; On the quark-parton fragmentation functions (w. F. Cleymans), 1974. Address: Diepenbenden 28, 51 Aachen, German Fed. Repub.

RODGERS, Ellen Davis (Mrs. Hillman P. Rodgers), b. 13 Nov. 1903. Educator; Club Woman; Planter; Author. Appts. incl: Critic Tchr., Trng. Schl., Memphis State Univ., 1924-26; Prof., Early Childhood Educ., ibid; Prin., Arlington H.S., 1928-29; Lausanne Schl. for Girls; State Elem. Supr., W. Tenn., 1938-40; Mbr., Shelby Co. Bd. of Educ., 1961-65; Dir., Tenn. Schl. Bds. Assn., 1963-65; First Shelby Co. (Tenn.) Histn., 1965-; Organizer, Pleasant Hill Cemetary Assn., 1937; Pres., ibid, 1937-. Mbrships: Int. Hon. Mbr., Beta Sigma Phi; active mbr., num. profl. & civic orgs. Publs. incl: The Romance of the Episcopal Church in West Tenessee, 1964; The Holy Innocents, 1965; Education-Then, Now & Yon, 1971; The Great Book, Calvary Protestant Episcopal Church, Memphis, 1832-1972, 1973. Contbr. of many articles to mags. Address: Davies Plantation, Brunswick, Memphis, TN 38134, U.S.A. 5, 131.

RODNEY, William, b. 5 Jan. 1923. University Professor; Historian. Educ: B.A., Univ. of Alta., Canada; M.A., Univ. of Cambridge, U.K.; Ph.D., Univ. of London. Appts: Rsch. Officer, Govt. of Canada, Ottawa, 1952-62; Prof., Hist., Royal Roads Mil. Coll., Victoria, 1963-. Fellow, Royal Hist. Soc. Mbrships. incl: Am. Assn. for the Adv. of Slavic Studies; Canadian Hist. Assn.; Canadian Assn. of Slavists; Chmn., Victoria Br., Canadian Inst. of Int. Affairs, 1965-68. Publs. incl: Soldiers of the International: A History of the Communist Party of Canada, 1968; Kooterai Brown: His Life & Times, 1969. Recip. D.F.C. & Bar, 1944-45 & Univ. of B.C. Medal for popular

biography. Address: Dept. of Hist., Royal Roads Mil. Coll., Victoria, B.C., Canada. 13, 30.

RODOPOULOS, Panteleimon-Evaggelos, b. 1929. University Professor; Clergyman. Educ: Lisc. Theol., Univ. of Athens; B.Litt., Oxford Univ., U.K.; Dr.Theol., Univ. of Athens. Appts. incl: Chap., Greek Army, 1952-53; Parish Priest, Greece, U.K., German Fed. Repub., 1954-58; Vicar Gen., Archdiocese of Thessaloniki, Greece, 1958-63; Asst. Prof., Univ. of Thessaloniki, 1960-63, Assoc. Prof.-Prof., 1966-; Dean of Holy Cross Greek Orthodox Theological Schl., Brooklyn, U.S.A., 1963-66; Dean of St. John of Damascus Theological Schl., Balamand, Lebanon, 1972-. Mbr., var. religious orgs. Publs. incl: The Sacramentary of Serapion; The Anaphora of the Liturgy of St. Mark; The Consecration of the Eucharistic Gifts; Contemporary Pastoral Principles. Address: University of Thessaloniki, Greece. 43.

RODRIGUES, W. J., 22 Nov. 1921. Chartered Surveyor. Educ: Queen's Coll., Guyana, 1933-38; Qualified Land Surveyor, Guyana Legislation; Coll. of Estate Mgmt., London, U.K., 1954-59; Assoc., Royal Instn. of Chartered Surveyors, 1959. Appts. incl: Govt. Surveyor, Land Survey, Pub. Serv. of Guyana & Served in Pub. Works Dept., Lands & Mines Dept., Hydrographic Survey Sect. Transport & Harbours Dept., 1938-47; Sr Staff Surveyor, Lands & Surveys Dept., St. Lucia, W. Indies, 1947-59; Chief Valuation Off., Govt. of Guyana & Hd., Valuation Off., Min. of Local Govt., 1959-73; Pvte. Prac. as Chartered Surveyor, 1973. Appts. incl: Fellow, Royal Instn. of Chartered Surveyors, England & Assoc., 1959; Corres. Sec., RICS for Chartered Surveyors, Guyana; Exec. Comm., Commonwealth Assn. of Surveying & Land Econ., 1969-73; Fellow, Royal Soc. of Hlth., England & Rating & Valuation Assn., England; Guyana Assn. of Surveyors; Royal Commonwealth Soc., U.K. Presented paper on the surveying profn. in the Commonwealth Caribbean to the 13th Int. Cong. of Surveyors, Wiesbaden, Germany, 1971. Address: 64 Fifth Ave., Subryanville, Georgetown, Guyana, S. America.

RODRIGUEZ, Alirio, b. 4 Apr. 1934. Painter. Educ: Art Courses, Escuela de Artes Plásticas de Caracas, Venezuela & Inst. of Art, Rome, Italy; Study of Mosaics, Rome & Ravenna. Appts: Hd., Fine Art Dept., Escuela de Artes Plásticas Cristóbal Rojas-Caracas, Venezuela; Prof., Design, Painting, etc., ibid; Prof., Painting, Inst. Pedagógico, Caracas; Tchr., Educ., Caracas. Advsr., Directiva, Athenaeum, Caracas. Author of articles & essays on art in var. reviews. Hons. incl: Arturo Michelena Prize, Valencia, 1963; Design Prize, Athenaeum, Caracas, 1963; 1st Prize, Design, Ctrl. Univ. of Venezeula, 1965; Acquavella Prize, Caracas, 1968; Nat. Prize for Painting, Venezuela, 1969; Federico Brandt Prize, Caracas, 1966; Prize, Venezuelan Assn. of Archts., ibid, 1965. Address: Avenida Anauco Edificio Titania Entrada B Apt. B-43; San Bernardino, Caracas 101, Venezuela, S. Am. 136.

RODRIGUEZ, Juan Francisco, b. 3 Jan. 1897. Minister; Seminary President. Educ: Grad., Ciales Bible Coll., P.R. Appts: Pastor of Protestant Chs.; Pub. Schl. Tchr., Dominican Repub.; Ed., Spanish Defender, a religious publ. in Latin Am. based in Rio Piedras, P.R.; Missionary, Dominican Repub.; Fndr., Defenders Theological Sem., Rio Piedras (instn. began as Bible Inst., 1934, full Sem., 1948); Pres., ibid, since fndn.; Gen. Supt., Evangelical

Chs., P.R. Mbrships: P.R. Assn. of Jrnlsts. & Writers, 1950-; Acad. of Humanities, Dominican Repub. & Mexico; Hon. mbr., Bd. of Dirs., Cuban Protestants in Exile Assn. Publs. incl: El Privilegio de Llorar; El Camino de la Felicidad; Above All Nations is Humanity. Hons. incl: D.D., 2 univs.; Hum.D., Kan. Theological Sem., U.S.A.; Dip., United Fund, Miami, Fla. Address: Arizmendi 200, Rio Piedras, PR 00928.

RODRIGUEZ, Ramon J., b. 6 May 1938. Educator; Administrator. Educ: B.S., N.Y. Univ., 1961; M.S., CUNY, 1966. Appts: Asst. Dean of Students for Special Progs.; Acting Dean of Students; Dir., Educl. Opportunity Prog.; Dir., Special Servs., Off. of Educ., Farmingdale Univ., N.Y.; Tchr., Indl. Arts; Prog. Dir., Cath. Charities of Emotionally Disturbed; Dir., Weekend Tutoring Prog. Mbrships. incl: Past Mbr., Fac. Senate Comm. on Expanding Educl. Opportunities; N.Y. State Guidance Counselors Assn.; Past Comm. Mbr., Admission Recruitment Employment Comm., Farmingdale Univ. Hons. incl: Innovative Tchng. & Counseling Award for work on Comm. on Expanding Educl. Opportunities for disadvantaged students, 1972; Middle States Award; Cert. of Hon., Educl. Opportunity Prog. students, SUNY, Farmingdalee, 1972. Address: Off. of Special Progs., State Univ. at Farmingdale, Farmingdale, NY 11735, U.S.A.

RODRIGUEZ MARIN, Ranulfo Aureliano, b. 16 June 1922. Lawyer; University Professor; Politician. Educ: B.A., Univ. of Narino, Colombia, 1948; Licentiate, Econ. & Soc. Scis., ibid, 1950; J.D., 1953; Dr., Int. Scis., Ctrl. Univ., Quito, Ecuador, 1954. Appts. incl: Gen. Sec., Ctrl. Univ., Ecuador, 1948-74; Prof., Constitutional Law, Cath. Univ. of Ecuador, Quito, 1952-70; Presidential Asst., Repub. of Ecuador, 1955-56; Lectr., Law, Police Schl. & Infantry Schl., Ecuador; Prof., Law, Ctrl. Univ., Ecuador, 1960-64; Dpty. Min., Ind. & Commerce, Ecuador, 1961; Mbr., Supreme Ct., Ecuador, 1961. Mbrships. incl: Pres., Assn. of Former Grads. of the Schl. of Int. Scis.; Gen. Sec., Acad. of Lawyers of Ecuador; Bd., Conservative Assn. of Ecuador. Publs: Poems in anthols., jrnls. & reviews. Address: Carrera Ponce de León No. 339, Quito, Ecuador.

RODRUCK, Robert Calvin. b. 2 Sept. 1896. Cattle Breeder; Business Executive. Appts: Breeder of Scottish Highland Cattle; Owner R&F Ranch, Chehalis, Wash.; Bd. Chmn. & Chief Exec. Off., The Pacific Underwriters Corporation, Seattle, Wash. Mbrships: Pres., Wash. State Power Users Assn.; Pres Coun., Am. Inst. Mgmt.; Highland Cattle Soc. of Scotland; Coll. Club, Seattle; Chmbr. of Comm.; Elks Club. Contbr. of articles to trade jrnls. & local newspapers. Recip. Earl Coe Award, 4H Clubs, 1969. Address: 211-6th Ave. N., Seattle, WA 98109, U.S.A. 128.

ROE, Anne (Mrs. George G. Simpson), b. 20 Aug. 1904. Psychologist; Educator. Educ: B.A., Univ. of Denver, 1923; M.A., 1925; Ph.D., Columbia Univ., 1933. Appts. incl: Dir., Study of Scis. Rsch. Grant, USPHS, 1947-51; Adj. Prof., Psychol., N.Y. Univ., 1957-59; Lectr., Educ. & Rsch. Assoc., Harvard Grand. Schl. of Educ., 1959-63; Prof., Educ., ibid, 1963-67; Emerita, 1967-; Dir., Ctr. Rsch. on Careers, 1963-66; Sec.-Treas., Simroe Fndn., 1968-. Fellow, Am. Psychol. Assn. Mbrships. incl: Dipl., Am. bd. Examiners in Profl. Psychol.; Am. Personnel & Guidance Assn. Publs: Quantitative Zoology; The Making of a Scientist; The Psychology of Occupations; Co-Ed., Behavior & Evolution; num. papers. Hons. incl: Univ. of Denver Alumni Assn.

Award for Disting. Profl. Achievement, 1972; Sc.D., Kenyon Coll., 1973. Address: 5151 E. Homes St., Tucson, AZ 85711, U.S.A. 5, 14, 28.

ROE, Claude Leighton, b. 26 Feb. 1916. Clergyman; Executive Director. Educ: B.S. cum laude, Baldwin Wallace Coll., 1939; B.D., Oberlin Grad. Schl. Theol., 1946; S.T.M., ibid, 1949. Appts: Pastor, 2nd Presby. Ch., E. Liverpool, Ohio, 1946-48; Glenville Presby Ch., Cleveland, Ohio, 1948-55; Ctrl. Presby. Ch., Montclair, N.J., 1955-58; 1st Presby. Ch., Whippany, ibid, 1958-62; Asst. Exec. Dir., Presby. Homes, Synod of N.J., 1962-72; Exec. Dir., Copeland Oaks, Sebring, Ohio, 1972-. Mbrships: Fellow, Am. Coll. Nursing Home Admnstrs.; Pres., N.J. Ann. Homes for Aged, 1966-70; Bd. Am. Assn. Homes for Aging, 1968-72; Nat. Coun. of Aging; Acad. Relig. & Mental Hlth.; Soc. Sci. Study Relig.; Nat. Geriatrics Soc.; Menninger Fndn.; Mensa; Mason. Contbr. to profl. jrnls. Address: 800 S. 15th St., Sebring, OH 44672, U.S.A.

ROE, Derek Arthur, b. 31 Aug. 1937. Archaeologist. Educ: B.A., Peterhouse Coll., Cambridge Univ., U.K., 1961; M.A. Cantab., ibid, 1964; M.A. Oxon, 1965; Ph.D. Cantab., 1968. Appts. incl: Lectr. in Prehistoric Archaeol., Univ. of Oxford, U.K., 1965-; Sec., Palaeolithic & Mesolithic Rsch. Comm., Coun. for British Archaeol., 1965-; Mbr. Edit. Bd., World Archaeol., 1967-; Fellow, St. Cross Coll., Oxford Univ., 1970-; Gov., St. Edward's Schl., Oxford, 1970-. Mbrships: Prehistoric Soc., Coun. Mbr. Publs: A Gazetteer Of British Lower & Middle Palaeolithic Sites, 1968; Prehistory: An Introduction, 1970, U.K. paperback edit., 1971, U.S. paperback edit., 1972. Contbr. to profl. jrnls. Hons: Exhibr. Schol., 1958 & Lady Ward Rsch. Studentship, 1961, Peterhouse Coll., Cambridge Univ. Address: Dept. of Ethnol. & Prehistory, Univ. of Oxford, Parks Rd., Oxford OX1 3PP, U.K. 3.

ROEBUCK, John Athey, b. 22 June 1920. Executive, Author, Group Staff Personnel Officer. Appts. incl: U.K. Agent, Corresp. & Int. Comt. Chmn., Pen-Prints Inc., 1952-; Engrng. Admin., Nationalised Ind.; Dir. (U.K.) Curry Electronics (U.S.A.); Mgmnt. Services Exec., int. group of cos., 1965-. G.G.G.G. Grandson of Dr. John Roebuck, fndr. of Carron Co., 1718-1794; G.G. nephew of Rt. Hon. John A. Roebuck, P.C., Q.C., M.P., 1802-1879. G.G. nephew of Miss Florence Nightingale, O.M. Family motto 'Free'. Mbrships. incl: Fellow, Royal Soc. of Arts, London, 1950; Assoc. Mbr., Faculty, Taylor Univ., 1953; Philosophical Soc. of England, 1953; Fndr., Chmn., The Arts Club, S. Elmsall, 1950; Int. Coun. of Leaders & Scholars, 1969; Arts Theatre Club, London, 1965. Publs. incl: The Life Mind Man; E. Tenebris Lux; Philosophy for Everyman; Accepted Principles of Planned Maintenance in Indsutry; The Roebuck Story (in collab. w. cousin, The Hon. A. N. Roebuck, Q.C.). Hons: Ph.D., Taylor Univ., U.S.A., 1951; M.Ph.S. of Eng., 1953; Int. Award of Hon, 1st Int. Congress of Drs., 1969. Address: 'Inglenook', Stockingate, S. Kirkby. Pontefract, Yorks., U.K. 3, 11, 30, 43.

ROED, Ole Torleif, b. 4 Nov. 1911. Judge; Attorney. Educ: Cand. juris, Oslo Univ., Norway, 1935; Fac. of Law & Carnegie Endowment for Int. Peace, Paris, France, 1935-37. Appts: Dpty. Judge, Norway, 1938-39; Asst. to Atty. Gen., 1940-43; w. Min. of For. Affairs for Post War Negotiations, 1945-48; Sec., Norwegian Deleg., Inter-Allied Reparation Conf., Paris, 1945; Counsellor, Norwegian Deleg. to Peace Conf., Paris & other delegs.; Advocate of Supreme Ct. in Pvte. Prac., 1948-; Deleg., European Convention for Protection of Human Rights, 1950; Rdr., Int. Law, Oslo Univ.; Cons., Int. Law, Int. Nobel Peace Prize Comm., 1947-58; Mbr., Norwegian-Swedish Int. Commn., 1952-56. Pres., Norwegian Assn. of Int. Law, 1954-. Author of legal publs. Address: Uraneinborg terrasse 5, Oslo 3, Norway.

ROEDERER, Louis J. M., b. 15 July 1920. Lawyer; Professor; Writer. Educ: Bach., Law & Econs., Univ. of Lyon, France; Licencié, ibid; Ph.D., N.Y. Univ., U.S.A., 1971. Appts. incl: Legal Counsellor, Paris, France, 1946-50; Legal Advsr. & Acting Gen. Counsel, UN Relief & Works Agcy. for Palestine Refugees, Beirut, Lebanon & N.Y., U.S.A., 1950-55; Chmn., For. Langs. Dept., Stony Brook Schl., N.Y., 1955-64, Montclair State Coll., N.J., 1964-66; Grad. Advsr., Dept. of For. Langs., ibid, 1966-68; Chmn., French Dept., ibid, 1969-70; Assoc. Prof., For. Langs, & Lits., Montclair State Coll., 1964-. Mbrships. incl: Union Française; Pres., Int. Christian Assn. Publs. incl: Modern Language & Modern Living (w. Dr. Cordasco), 1968; Microfilm of doct. thesis, Le Divin et le Theatre Contemporain en France, 1971. Address: Box 84, Port Murray, NJ 07865, U.S.A. 6.

ROEMER, Elizabeth, b. 4 Sept. 1929. Astronomer; Professor of Astronomy. Educ: B.A., Univ. of Calif., Berkeley, U.S.A., 1949; Ph.D., ibid, 1955. Appts. incl: Astronomer, USN Observ., Flagstaff, Ariz., 1957-66, Acting Dir., ibid, 1965; Assoc. Prof., Astron., Lunar & Planetary Lab., Univ. of Ariz., Tucson, 1966-69; Prof., Astron, ibid, 1969-. Mbrships. incl: Chmn., Wkng. Grp. on Orbits & Ephemerides of Comets, Comm. 20, Int. Astronomical Union, 1964-, V.P., Commn. 6, 1973-; Coun., Am. Astronomical Soc., 1967-70, Vice Chmn., 1973, Chmn., 1974; Fellow, AAAS, Coun., 1966-69 & 1972-73; Fellow, Royal Astronomical Soc., London, U.K.; Am. Geophys. Union; Phi Beta Kappa; Sigma Xi. Publs: Articles & observation results in profl. jrnls.; Contbns. to symposia & encys.; TV & radio sci. presentations. Hons. incl: Lick Observ. Fellowship, Univ. of Calif., 1952-54; Minor planet no 1657 named Roemera by discoverer, P. Wild, 1965; Benjamin Apthorp Gould Prize, U.S. Nat. Acad. of Scis., 1971. Address: Lunar & Planetary Laboratory, Univ. of Arizona, Tucson, AZ 85721, U.S.A. 2, 5, 9, 14.

ROESSEL, Eugene Jules, b. 16 Feb. 1918. Shoe Company Executive. Educ: B.A., Wash. Univ., St. Louis, Mo., 1939. Appts. incl: V.P., Wohl Shoe Co., St. Louis, Mo., 1939-62; USAAF, 1942-45; V.P., Interco, Inc., St. Louis, 1962-66; V.P. & Dir., Freeman Shoe Co., Beloit, Wis., 1967-69; Exec. V.P. & Dir., ibid, 1969-73; Pres. & Dir., ibid, 1972-. Mbrships: Old Warson Country Club, St. Louis; Univ. Club, St. Louis; Ledges Country Club, Roscoe, Ill.; Ocean Reef Club, Key Largo, Fla. Hons: Purple Heart Air Medal & D.F.C., USAAF. Address: 7335 McCurry Rd., Roscoe, IL 61073, U.S.A. 16.

ROETERS VAN LENNEP, Frederik Theodoor, b. 31 Mar. 1919. Economic Adviser. Educ: Kennemer Lyceum, Overveen; Advanced Textile Schl., Tilburg. Appts: Int. Textile Imports & Exports; Adviser, Textile Industry; Bd. Dirs., Investment Fund; Pres., Netherlands-Japan Inst.; Swiss Corres., Reformatorisch Dagblad, Apeldoorn, & De Wachter Sions, Utrecht. Mbrships. incl: Co-Fndr., Hon. Sec., Netherlands—Ulster & Netherlands—Japan Socs.; Co-Fndr., V.P.,

Netherlands—Thailand Soc.; Execs. Int. Lausanne; Schweizer Heimatschutz, Zurich; ORT-Suisse, Geneva; Assn. Amis du Musée d'horlogerie, Le Locle. Contbr., pol., relig., Dutch, Japanese & Irish newspapers. Candidate, Pol. Reformed Party, for Mbrship., Dutch Lower House, 1967. Address: Petit Bellaria, CH 1814 La Tour-de-Peilz, Switzerland.

ROGERS, Dorothy. Psychologist; Writer. Educ: B.A., Univ. of Ga., 1934; M.A., ibid, 1936; Ph.D., Duke Univ., 1947. Appts: Pub. schls., Birmingham, Ala., 1935-44; Prof., Psychol., State Univ. Coll., Oswego, N.Y., 1946-. Mbrships: Am. Psychological Assn.; Assn. of Child Psychol. & Psych.; Eastern Psychological Assn.; Assn. of Women Psychologists; Phi Beta Kappa; Phi Kappa Phi; Kappa Delta Pi. Publs. incl: Issues in Adolescent Psychology, 2 edits.; Psychology of Adolescence, 2 edits.; Issues in Child Psychology; Readings in Child Psychology; Child Psychology; Adolescence: A Psychological Perspective; Educational Psychology, forthcoming; Issues in Educational Psychology, forthcoming. Recip., Educators Award, Delta Kappa Gamma Int. Soc., 1957. Address: 5143 Franklin Ave., Oswego, NY 13126, U.S.A. 5, 6, 14, 15, 28, 30, 128, 132.

ROGERS, Gladys T. (Mrs. Wilburn Knox Rogers) Educator & Counselor. Educ: B.Sc., Univ. of Southern Miss., 1940; Life Credential Pupil Personnel Servs., San Diego State Coll., 1965. Appts. incl: Organizer & Dir., Lincoln Jr. H.S. Reading Ctr., 2 yrs.; Tchr., Oceanside Schl. Dist., 1953-63; Schl. Coun., Lincoln Jr. H.S., 1963-. Mbrships. incl: Oceanside Elem. Tchrs. Assn. (Pres., 1970-71); Oceanside Tchrs Assn. (1st V.P., 1969-70); Delta Kappa Gamma, (Beta Delta Pres., 1969-71). Author of articles in var. newspapers. Appeared on T.V. Hons. incl: San Diego Co. Tchrs. Assn., Who's Who Award, 1971; Commendation for Meritorious Serv., N. Co. Area Dirs. for San Diego Co. Tchrs. Assn., 1972. Address: 1826 Burroughs St., Oceanside, CA 92054, U.S.A. 5, 9, 132.

ROGERS, Jumelle Haile (Mrs. Francis Drake Rogers), b. 3 Sept. 1908. Secretary. Educ: B.A., Winthrop Coll., Rock Hill, S.C., 1928; Univ. of S.C. Appts: Exec. Sec., Marlboro Co. T.B. Assn.; Off. Mgr., Farm & Seed Loan Off., Marlboro Co.; Sec., Co. Agric. Agcy. of Marlboro Co.; Personal Sec. to pastors of the 1st Presby. Ch., Bennettsville, S.C. Mbrships: Life Mbr., Women of the Ch., Presby. Ch., (Pee Dee Presbytery, 1957-, Synod of S.C., 1973-); Pres., Women of the Ch., Synod of S.C., 1972-74, Jr. Charity League of Bennettsville, Lit. Club & Gdn. Club; Pres., V.P., Treas. & Sec., Women of the Ch., Bennettsville Presby. Ch.; Dean, Synodical Trng. Schl., Clinton S.C. Presby. Coll., 1973; Rep. for S.C. Women of the Ch., Gen. Assembly of the Presby. Ch., Ft. Worth, Tex.; V.P., Columbia Friendship Circle, Columbia Theol. Sem., Decatur, Ga.; Sec., Mission Haven, ibid; Women's Advsry. Coun., Presby. Ch., U.S.; Nomination Comm., Synod of the S.E.; Promotion & Stewardship Comms., Synod of S.C.; Supt., Kindergarten & Primary Depts. & Tchr. in a Presbytery-wide Trng. Schl., Bennettsville Presby. Ch.; Sec. & Treas., Marlboro Co. Cancer Soc.; Marlboro Histl. Soc.; United Daughters of the Confederacy; Mental Hlth. Assn.; Heart Assn. Hons: Silver Gift, 8 Presbyterial Pres., of S.C., 1973; Church Supper & Silver Gift, Bennettsville Presby. Ch., 1973. Address: 711 E. Main St., Bennettsville, SC 29512, U.S.A. 125, 130.

ROGERS, Kathryn T., b. 30 June 1908. Reading Specialist. Educ: B.S., Southeastern State Univ., Durant, Okla.; M.Ed., E. Tex. State

Univ., Commerce, Tex.; Postgrad., Okla. Univ., Okla. State Univ. & Central State Univ. Appts. incl: Reading Tchr., 1st grade; Reading Specialist, Orientation Ctr., Moore, Okla.; Reading Specialist, Proj. STAY (Schl. To Aid Youth). Mbrships. incl: NEA; Reading Steering Comm. on Okla. Curric. Improvement Commn. State Dept. of Educ.; Int. Reading Coun.; Guest Panel mbr., Prog. of State Reading Assn. Conven., 1972; Int. Platform Guests, 1972; Kappa Kappa Iota. Hons: Tchr. of the Yr., Moore, Okla., 1967-68; Guest Spkr., State Audio-Visual Conf., Okla. City, Okla.; 1972. Address: 1005 S. Howard, Moore, OK 73160, U.S.A. 129, 130.

ROGERS, King Walter Jr., b. 19 Aug. 1912. Business Executive. Educ: B.A., Univ. of Tenn., 1934; Harvard Bus. Schl., 1934-36. Appts: U.S. Army, WWII; Pres., K.W. Rogers & Son, Inc., (Grocers), 1943-; Pres. & Dir., Tipton Co. Utilities, Inc., Ardmore Telephone Co., Inc.; Sec. & Dir., Crockett Telephone Co. Inc., United Telephone Co. Inc.; Dir. & Finance Comm. Mbr., 1st Citizens Nat. Bank, Dyersburg, 1st Fed. Saving & Loan Assn.; Dir., Edenton-Lamb Co. (Who. Grocers). Mbrships. incl: Dir. & Exec. Comm. Mbr., Hosp. for Crippled Adults, 1957-69; Mbr. of Dyersburg Elec. Bd., 1958-; Dist. Gov., Rotary Int., 1960-61, Counselor, 1961-62; Bd. Mgrs., Meth. Hosp. in Memphis, 1972-. Hons. incl: Silver Beaver Scouting Award, 1968; Outstanding Bus. Man's Award, Dyersburg Chmbr. of Comm., 1970-71. Address: 408 W. Ct. St., Dyersburg, TN 38024, U.S.A. 7.

ROGERS, Mary Read (Mrs. Glenn K.), b. 9 Apr. 1904. Writer; Librarian (retd.). Educ: A.B., Baker Univ., Baldwin, Kan., 1924; Grad. work & music, Kan. Univ. & Univ. of Wyo. Appts: H.S. Tchr., Kan. & Wyo, Schls.; Dir., teenage prog., Cheyenne YWCA; Dir., P.R., & Ed., all publs., State Lib. Mbrships. incl: Zonta Int.; Former Nat. Chmn., now Div. Chmn. of Continuing Educ., ESO, Lib. Servs. & Literacy, Gen. Fedn. of Women's Clubs; Nat. Bd., Nat. Congress of Parents & Tchrs.; Nat. Bd., Nat. Fedn. of Press Women, 1969-; State Pres., Wyo. Fedn. of Press Women, 1969-71; Nat. Assn. of Parliamentarians; Nat. Assn. of Am. Conductors & Composers; Cultural Arts Chmn., State Bd., AAUW; Var. offs., ALA: Am. Assn. of Schl. Libns. Publs. incl: 4 solos for low voice; Ed., Wyo Lib. Roundup, 1959-72; Ed., The Outrider, 1966-72; Articles in jrnls. & state newspapers. Hons. incl: Award for meritorious serv., Wyo. Presswomen, 1974. Address: 312 E. Pershing Blvd., Cheyenne, WY 82001, U.S.A. 5, 9, 15, 42, 126.

ROGERS, Paul, b. 10 July 1909. University Professor; Consulting Engineer. Educ: Dr. Engrng., Rumania; Dip. Engrng., France. Appts: Designer, Chief Structural Engr., var. firms, Chgo., Ill.; 1940-53; Cons. Engr., Pvte. Prac., L.A., Calif., 1953-; currently Prof. of Civil Engrng., Calif. State Univ., L.A. Mbrships. incl: Fellow, Am. Soc. Civil Engrs., Am. Concrete Inst.; Nat. Soc. Profl. Engrs.; Société des Ingenieurs Civils de France; Int. Assn. Bridge & Structural Engrng; Structural Engrs. Assns. of Calif. & Ill. Publs. incl: Civil Engineering Practice, Vol.III, 1958; Reinforced Concrete Design for Buildings, 1973. Sci. papers & articles. Hons. incl: Gold Medal, ASCE, 1953; Eminent Engr. Award, ISPE, 1963; var. other profl. awards. Address: California State University, 5151 State University Dr., Los Angeles, CA 90032, U.S.A. 2, 26, 122.

ROGERSON, Jean Ethel. Investor; Civic Worker. Educ: Univ. of W.A., Australia. Appts. incl: V.P., Aust. Fed. of Univ. Women, 1951,

'61; Mbr., Senate, Univ. of Western Aust., 1956-; Convocation Warden, ibid, 1961-65, '72-; Mbr., Coun., St. Catherin's Coll., 1954-74; Trustee, Univ. Women's Coll. Fund, 1959-; Mbr., Adult Educ. Bd., 1962-63; Mbr., Aust. Nat. Comm., Vic. League for C'wealth Friendship, 1962-64; Mbr., W.A. State Adv. Comm., Aust. Broadcasting Commn., 1962-65; Mbr., Prog. Planning & Activities Comm., Tech. Trng. Yr., 1966, 1965-66; Patroness, Ctrl. Dists. Police & Citizend Youth Club, 1967-; Educ. OFficer, Aust. Fed. of Univ. Grads., 1968-70; Deleg., Univ. W.A., 10th C'wealth. Univs. Congress, 1968; Deleg., W.A. Br. Australian Inst. Int. Affairs, Nat. Conf., Topic Advance, Australia–Where? ; Pres., Friends Univ. Lib., W.A., 1970-; VP., Aust. Univ. Grads. Conf., 1971-; V.Chmn., St. Catherine's Coll. Coun., Univ. W.A., 1971-74; VP, WA Br., Aust. Inst. Int. Affairs, 1971-. Address: 699 Beaufort St., Mt. Lawley, W.A., Australia 6050. 23, 128.

ROGGE, O. John, b. 12 Oct. 1903. Lawyer. Educ: A.B., Univ. of Ill., 1922; LL.B., 1925, S.J.D., 1931, Harvard Law Schl. Appts: Special Counsel, Securities & Exchange Commn., 1937-38; Asst. Gen. Counsel i/c Litigation, ibid, 1938-39; Asst. U.S. Atty. Gen., i/c Criminal Div. of Dept. of Justice, 1939-41; Special Asst. to U.S. Atty. Gen., 1943-46. Mbrships: Comm. on Int. Criminal Jurisdiction, Am. Bar Assn.; Assn. of Bar. of City of N.Y.; N.Y. Co. Lawyers Assn.; Egypt Exploration Soc., London; Phi Beta Kappa. Publs: Our Vanishing Civil Liberties, 1949; Why Men Confess, 1959; The First & the Fifth, 1960; The Official German Report, 1961; Contbr. to books & profl. jrnls. Hons: Ed., Harvard Law Review, 1924-25. Address: 777 Third Ave., N.Y., NY 10017, U.S.A. 2, 6, 139.

ROHLFS, Ruth Alexandria Swanberg (Mrs. Marcus Rohlfs). Voluntary Church & Welfare Worker. Educ: Univ. of Wash.; Union Theological Sem. Appts. incl: V.P., Nat. Bd. of Am. Bapt. Women, 1958-61; Mbr., Bd. Am. Bapt. Home Mission Socs., 9 yrs., Nat. Pres., 1968-71; Mbr., Am. Bapt. Convention Gen. Coun. & Exec. Comm.; 1968-71; Pres., Am. Bapt. Convention, 1971-72; Admin. Asst., Univ. of Wash. YMCA; Past Pres., Seattle YWCA Bus. & Profl. Club, Nat. YWCA Bus. & Profl. Coun. & Assembly, & Univ. of Wash. YWCA Advsry. Bd.; Mbr., Nat. Bd. YWCA, 12 yrs.; Mbr., Exec. Comm. & Gen. Bd. Am. Bapt. Chs. U.S.A.; Dir., Religious Educ., 1st Bapt. Ch. Author, History Turns a Page. Contbr. to book, Meditations for Women. Num. articles, var. mags. Recip., var. serv. awards. Address: 4303 54th Ave. N.E., Seattle, WA 98105, U.S.A. 5.

ROHR, Martin, b. 24 Jan. 1907. Postal Service Administrator; Jurist. Educ: Law Studies, Univs. of Berlin & Leipzig; Judicial Assessor's Examination, Berlin, 1936. Appts: Post Off. Admnstr., Berlin; Oldenburg, Coblenz, Tübingen; Hd. Divl. Admnstr. (retd.), Tübingen, Hanover. Contbr. of articles, geneological rsch. & chess, var. publs. Hons: Chess Championships, Elbo-Aller Chess Soc., 1949, Tübingen, 1954. Address: Pappelweg 3, 3001 Anderten-Hannover, German Federal Republic. 43, 92.

ROHRBAUGH, Lewis Henry, b. 2 July 1908. Educator; Administrator; Consultant. Educ: Ph.B., Dickinson Coll.; Cornell Univ.; Ph.D., Univ. of Pa.; Wharton Grad. Schl. of Finance & Commerce, ibid; Grad. Schl., U.S. Dept. of Agric. Appts. incl: Dir., Mission to Iraq, U.S. Dept. of State, 1951-54; V.P. & Provost, Univ. of Ark., 1954-59; V.P. for Acad. Affairs, Boston Univ., 1959-62; Acad. V.P., Boston Univ., Dir., Boston Univ. Med. Ctr.,

Exec. V.P., Univ. Hosp., Prof. of Hlth. Mgmt., Coll. of Bus. Admin., Prof. of Hlth. Admin., Schl. of Med., 1962-73 (Emeritus in all since retirement in 1973); Cons. in Org. & Mgmt., Arthur D. Little, Inc., Univ. of Mich., Nat. Sci. Fndn., Assn. of Schls. & Colls. of Optometry, Mass. Coll. of Optometry, etc., 1973-. Mbrships. incl: Incorporator, Univ. Hosp.; Trustee, ibid, 1962-73; Trustee, Maine State Couns. of Hlth. Facilities & Mental Hlth. Facilities, 1968-; Assoc., Acad. Hlth. Ctrs.; Pres., ibid, 1969-70; Bd. of Dirs., 1966-72; Trustee, New Engl. Primate Ctr., 1964-73. Address: No. 2 Sea St., Rockport, ME 04856, U.S.A. 2, 6, 22, 128, 130.

RÖHRER, Heinz, b. 23 Mar. 1905. Emeritus College President; Professor. Educ: Dr.med.vet., Univ. of Leipzig, Germany, 1928; Inaugurated, Univ. of Cologne, 1941. Appts. incl: Dpty. Dir., Staatl. Vet. Unters. Amt., Berlin, 1925-36; Dir., Staatl. Vet Unters. Amt., Cologne, 1936-42; Dir. & Prof., Reichsforschungsanstalt, Insel Riems, 1942-45; Sci. Tech. Dir., Asid Serum Inst., Dessau, 1945-48; Pres., Friedrich Loeffler Inst., Insel Riems, 1948-70; Prof., Univ. of Griefswald, 1950-. Mbrships: Akad. der Wissenschaften, German Democratic Repub.; Sec., Sect. of Vet. Med., Akad. der Landwirtschaftswissenschaften, ibid, 1956-65; Senator, Deutsche Akad. der Naturforscher-Leopoldina; Fellow, Royal Soc. of Med., London, U.K.; Corres. mbr., World Fedn. of Neurol.; Hon. mbr., Wissenschaftliche Gesellschaft für Veterinärmed., German Democratic Repub., Polnische Gesellschaft für Veterinärmed. Author of books & over 100 articles in jrnls. Recip. of hons. Address: Horstenweg 1, 183 Rathenow-West, 183, German Democratic Repub.

ROHRLICH, George F., b. 6 Jan. 1914. Social Economist. Educ: Dr. Jur., Univ. of Vienna, Austria, 1937; Dip., Consular Acad. of Vienna, 1938; Ph.D., Harvard Univ., U.S.A., 1943. Appts. inch: Sr. Staff mbr., Int. Labour Off., Geneva, Switzerland, 1959-64; Prof., Soc. Econs. & Policy, Univ. of Chgo. Schl. of Soc. Serv. Admin., 1964-67; U.S. Govt. Cons. on Income Maintenance, pt.-time 1965; Prof., Pol. Econ. & Soc. Ins., Temple Univ. Schl. of Bus. Admin., 1967-; Fndr. & Dir., Inst. for Soc. Econs. & Policy Rsch., ibid; External Collaborator to Puerto Rico's Commn. on Universal Hlth. Ins., 1973. Mbrships. incl: Int. Soc. for Labor Law & Soc. Legislation; Charter mbr., Indl. Rels. Rsch. Assn.; Assn. for Soc. Econs.; Am. Risk & Ins. Assn.; AAUP. Author of books & articles in field. Recip. of hons. Address: Schl. of Bus. Admin., Temple Univ., Phila., PA 19122, U.S.A. 14, 30.

ROJO, Trinidad A., b. 25 May 1902. Sociologist; Labor Economist; Author; Businessman. Educ: A.B., M.A., Univ. of Wash. Appts. incl: Gen. Mgr., Pan-Am. Co.; Bd. Chmn., Pan-Pacific Fndn.; Lectr., Univ. of Wash.; Rsch. Fellow, Stanford Univ., Calif. Mbrships. incl: S.-E. Asian-Am. Coun.; Am. Nat. Honorary Soc. in Social; Past Pres., Cannery Wkrs. & Farm Laborers Union; V.P., Seattle Congress of Indl. Orgs.; Maritime Fndn. of the Pacific; Panel, 12th Regional Dist., U.S. War Labor Bd.; Alpha Kappa Delta. Publs: Sev. plays, inclng: At Stake; Living Dead Man; Roots of Red Rebellion; Sev. poems. Hons: Sarusal Schlrship, 1935; Decano Schlrship, 1937; Victor Royal Rsch. Fellowship, Stanford Univ., 1945-46. Address: 213-215 Maritime Bldg., 911 Western Ave., Seattle, WA 98104, U.S.A. 57.

ROLFE, Sidney E., b. 20 June 1921. Economist. Educ: B.A., Ph.D., Univ. of Chgo. Appts: Chief Econ., C.I.T. Financial Corp., N.Y.; Fac. of Econ., Princeton & Columbia Univs.; currently Rsch. Assoc., MIT, Cambridge, Prof. of Finance, L.I. Univ., Brookville, N.Y. & Pres., Charles Dev. Corp., N.Y. Mbrships: Fellow, Soc. Sci. Rsch. Coun., 1949-50, Am. Coun. of Learned Socs., 1948. Publs: co-author, The Great Wheel: The World Monetary System, 1973; The International Corporation, 1969; co-author, The Multinational Corporation in the World Economy, 1970; Gold and World Power, 1967; Capital Markets, 1967. Address: 860 United Nations Plaza, N.Y., NY 10017, U.S.A. 6, 14.

ROLFSEN, Wilhelm Münter, b. 11 May 1913. Educ: Norwegian War Schl., 1932; Law Degree, Univ. of Oslo, 1937. Appts: Barrister, 1941; Lt., Norwegian Forces in Sweden, 1944; Capt., ibid, 1945; Barrister, Supreme Ct. of Norway, 1952; Mbr., Bd. of Dirs., several Norwegian oil, bus. & ind. cos. inclng. A.S. Norgear, OY Norfinn A.S., Kristiansund, &c. Mbrships: Norwegian Bar Assn.; Norske Selskab, Oslo; Ctrl. Staff of the Mil. Home Forces, 1943. Publs: From Oscarsborg to Hegra, 1945; Usynlige Veier, 1946. Produced 3 films: The Shetland Bus, 1954; Nine Lives (We Die Alone), 1957: Venner (Friends), 1961. Hons: Norwegian Medal w. star; King Geo. V Commendation for Brave Conduct. Address: Huk aveny 8, Bygdø, Oslo 2 Norway. 43.

ROLLWAGEN, Jack Robert, b. 25 Aug. 1935. Anthropologist. Educ: B.A., Univ. of Wash. 1957; Ph.D., Univ. of Anthropol., Univ. of Ore., Predoct. Fellow, Nat. Defense Educ. Act, 1962-65; Postdoct. Fellow, Nat. Inst. of Mental Hlth., 1968-69. Postdoct. Fellow, Dept. of Anthropol., Univ. of Calif., Berkeley, 1968-69. Appts: Chmn., Dept. of Anthropol., State Univ. Coll., Brockport, N.Y., 1970-; Publr. & Ed., Urban Anthropol. (jrnl.) & Urban Anthropol. Newsletter, 1972-; Pres., Inst. for the Study of Man. Inc., 1973-; Asst. Prof., Dept. of Anthropol., Cath. Univ. of Am., Wash. D.C; Asst. Prof., Dept. of Anthropol., Portland State Univ., Ore. Mbrships. incl: Sec.-Treas., Northeastern Anthropol. Assn, 1972-; Fellow, Am. Anthropol. Assn. Contbr. to var. jrnls. & profl. publs. Address: Dept. of Anthropology., SUNY College at Brockport, NY 14420, U.S.A.

ROLONTZ, Robert, b. 14 Dec. 1920. Publicity & Advertising Executive. Educ: B.S., Schl. of Gen. Studies, Columbia Univ., N.Y., 1952; Grad. Schl., Soc. Scis., ibid, 1952-54. Appts: Served w. USAF, 1942-45; Reporter, Billboard Mag., 1951-55; Record Prod., RCA Victor Records, 1955-58; Music Ed., Billboard Mag., 1962-63 & Music Bus. Mag., 1964-65; Dir., Advt. & Publicity, Atlantic Records, 1965; V.P., ibid, 1969; Dir. of Corp. Info., Warner Communications, Inc., 1974. Mbrships: Fndr. & V.P., Music Reporter's Assn., 1935-55; Record Ind. Assn. Am.; Nat. Assn. Recording Arts & Scis. Contbr. of articles to jazz mags. inclng. 'The Rock & Roll Revival-Evolution', 1970, & The Music Revolution, 1974. both in Record World Mag. Recip. of Air Medal w. clusters for missions over Europe. Address: c/o Warner Communications, 75 Rockefeller Plaza, N.Y., NY 10019, U.S.A. 2, 16.

ROLPH, C.H., b. 23 Aug. 1901. Writer. Appts: Chief Insp., City of London Police, 1921-46; Editl. Staff, New Statesman, 1948-70; Ed., The Author, 1956-60; Dir., Statesman Publng. Co., Ltd., 1965-; Parole Bd. for England & Wales, 1967-69. Mbrships: Soc. of Authors; PEN Club; V.P., Howard League for

Penal Reform; Inst. for Study & Treatment of Delinquency; Trustee, Koestler Award. Publd. 14 books inclg: Law & the Common Man, 1967; Books in the Dock, 1969; Kingsley: The Life Letters & Diaries of Kingsley Martin, 1973. Address: Rushett Edge, Grafham Bramley, Surrey, U.K. 1, 3.

ROLSTON, Margaret Elizabeth, b. 10 Mar. 1910. Realtor & Insurance Agent; Property Manager. Appts. incl: Organizer, Regional Gov. & 1st Pres., Women's Coun., Mo. Real Estate Assn.; Sec., Adair Co. Red Cross, 11 yrs., Organizer of ARC Grey Lady Serv., & Mbr., ARC Blood Unit Lab., 20 yrs.; Mbr., Collegiate Nursing Comm. & P.R. Comm., Kirksville Coll. Osteopathic Med., 1972; Dir., Adair Co. Ctr. for Exceptional Children; currently Co-owner, Rolston & Rolston, realtors, & Owner & Mgr., real estate dev. & multi-family rental units; Dir., Kirksville Chmbr. of Comm., & Chmn., Civic Events. Mbrships. incl: Omega Tau Rho; El Kadir Jewels (Wives of Shriners); Local, State & Nat. Bds. of Realtors. Address: 804 Shannon Ln., Kirksville, MO 63501, U.S.A. 5.

ROLSTON, Rodrick R., b. 7 Aug. 1931. Sociologist. Educ: B.A., Manchester Coll., 1954; M.D., Bethany Sem., 1958; M.A., Northern Ill. Univ., 1960; Ph.D., Iowa State Univ., 1966. Appts. incl: Tchr., Geneva Pub. Schls., Ill., 1958-60; Instr., Manchester Coll., 1961-63; Asst. Dir., Ctr. for Community Rsch., Bradley Univ., 1966-68; Asst. Prof., Univ. of Wis., Platteville, 1968-73; Assoc. Prof., Sociol., Ind. Univ., South Bend. Mbrships incl: Am. Sociol. Assn.; Midwest Sociol. Soc.; Nat. Coun. on Family Rels.; Alpha Kappa Delta; Ind. Coun. on Family; Deleg., Wis. Congress on Aging. 1973. Contbr. to publs. in field. Recip., Nat. Sci. Fndn. Grants, 1961, 72, 73. Address: 52330 Kenilworth Rd., South Bend, IN 46637, U.S.A. 14, 130.

ROMAN, Marian, b. 2 Feb. 1920. Artist; Painter. Educ: Acad. de Beaux Arts, Danzig, 1946-48, Acad. de Beaux Arts, Warsaw, 1949-52; 1st Prize for Painting & Drawing, Acads. of Danzig & Warsaw. One-Man Shows: Paris, 1961, '62, '63, '67, '68; N.Y., U.S.A. 1968. Group Exhibs: Salon d'Automne, 1961-73; Salon Artistes Français, 5 times; Salon des Indépendants, 6 times; Casino d'Aix en Provence, Lyon, Galérie d'Art Reflets, Nice, 1971. '72, '73; Exhib. of French & European Painters in U.S.A, N.Y., 1974; Rio de Janeiro, 1967. Mbrships: Salon Artistes Français; Salon d'Automne. Other works incl: Abstract Painting, Landscapes, Portraits, Views of Paris. Recip. of num. hons., inclng. Silver Medal, Soc. des Artistes Français, 1972. Address: 10 Rue Seveste, Paris 18, France.

ROMANO, Liboria Elizabeth (Mrs. Dominic C. Romano), b. 17 July 1899. Writer; Editor. Educ: A.B., Hunter Coll., N.Y.C., 1955; M.A., ibid, 1958. Appts: Column. Staten Island Transcript, 1949-51; Column, Writers' Voice, 1958-63; Ed., Manhattan Pen Woman, 1942-68. Mbrships. incl: Nat. League Am. Pen Women (past Pres, Mannattan br.); World Poetry Soc.; AAUW (1 term book review chmn., N.Y.C. br.); All Arts Assn. (prog. chmn.); Centro Studie Scambi Int. (Hon. Rep.); Hon. Life Mbr., World Poets Resource Ctr.; Sigma Tau Delta; Iota Tau Alpha. Publs. incl: Coney Island & Other New Poems, 1970; Selected Essays, 1971. Recip. D.Litt. 1959. Address: 1455 81st. St., Brooklyn, NY 11228, U.S.A. 9, 11.

ROMANO Pacheco, Arturo, b. 29 Sept. 1921. Anthropologist. Educ: M.D. cum laude, Nat. Schl. Anthropol. & Hist., Mexico. Appts: Prof., Nat. Schl. Anthropol. & Hist., 1949-;

Asst. Rschr.-Chmn., Dept. Photography, Nat. Mus. Anthropol.; Dir., Dept. Prehist., Inst. Nat. Anthropol. & Hist.; Sec.- Dir., Nat. Mus. Anthropol.; Dir., Dept. Phys. Anthropol.; Dir.-Admin. Dir., Nat. Mus. Anthropol.; Currently Dir., Dept. Phys. Anthropol. Mbrships: Soc. Mexicana de Antropol.; Soc. Mexicana de Hist. y Filos. de la med.; Soc. de Georgrafia e Hist. de Guatemala; Am. Assn. Phys. Anthropols.; Soc. Am. Archaeol. Author num. publs. on Mexican archaeol. (burials); prehispanic human craneol., Mexican palaeoanthropol.; intentional cranial deformation in prehispanic epoch. Address: Dept. de Antropol. fisica, Reforma y Gandih, Mexico 5, D.F. Mexico. 2.

ROMANOS, George, b. 29 Oct. 1908. Barrister & Solicitor. Educ: Dip., Law Schl., Univ. of Athens, Greece. Appts: Pvte. Prac., Barrister & Solicitor, Athens; Mbr., Legislative Comm., Min. of Justice, & Prof., Pantios School for Pol. Sci. & Finances, Athens, 1937-40; M.P., 1952-56; Undersec. of State, Min. of Coordination, 1954; Mbr., Greek Comm., Coun. of Europe, 1954-56; Legal Counsel for City of Athens, 1961-70. Mbrship: Athens Bar. Publs: Report on the Budget 1954, 1954. Sev. reports on bills, Greek Parliament; Papers in Greek law reviews. Recip., Medal of the Greek Resistance, 1947. Address: 5 Alex. Soutsou St., Athens 134, Greece.

ROMAO, Emanuel Alexis, b. 22 July 1921. Barrister-at-Law. Educ: Attended Gray's Inn, London, U.K.; Intermediate Arts, London; LL.B.; Degree of Utter Barrister. Appts: Acting Magistrate, 1956; Acting Crown Counsel, 1957; Crown Counsel, 1958; Sr. Crown Counsel, 1960; Acting Prin. Legal Advsr., 1962-63; Acting Dir., Pub. Prosecutions, 1964; Chief Counsel to Commns., 1965; Dir., Pub. Prosecutions, 1966. Mbrship: V.P., Guyana Chess Assn. Hon: Sr. Counsel, 1968. Address: 1 Sea Wall Flats, Eve Leary, Kingston, Georgetown, Guyana. 109.

ROMAY, (Mrs.) Angela (Quincy) Marchese, b. 14 May 1906. Educator; Singer; Librarian (music). Educ: A.B., Tufts Univ., 1924; A.M., Boston Univ., 1949. Appts. incl: Asst., Music Dept., Tufts Coll., 1930-33; Cataloguer, Record Lib., ibid, 1933-47; Music Libn., 1945-47; Hd., Spanish Dept., Choate Schl., Brookline, Mass., 1947-49; Tchr., French & Latin, Plainville H.S., 1949-50; Tchr., Spanish & Latin, Winthrop (Mass.) Sr. H.S., 1950-60; Tchr., Spanish, French & Latin, Wellesley (Mass.) Sr. H.S., 1960-63. Tchr., Spanish & French, Burlington (Mass.) Sr. H.S., 1963-73. Mbrships. incl: AAUW; NEA; Mass. Tchrs. Assn.; Pan Am. Soc. N.E.; Am. Assn. Tchrs. of French; Classical Assn.; Treas., N.E. Chapt., Am. Assn. Tchrs. Spanish & Portuguese, 1951-52; Chmn., Spanish Conf., N.E. Modern Lang. Assn., 1959. Publs. incl: Horses! Horses! (one-act play); Rodolphus (in Latin); Translator of lyrics of popular music into Latin, Spanish & French. Address: 74 Curve St., Wellesley, MA 02181, U.S.A. 5, 6, 62, 128, 138.

ROMBACH, Otto, b. 22 July 1904. Author. Educ: Tchr. Trng. Coll. Appts. as civil servant, feuilleton ed. & free-lance author. Mbrships: Deutsche Akademie fûr Sprache & Dichtung, Darmstadt. PEN Club, German Fed. Repub.; Hon. mbr., Acad. Berrichonne, Bourges, France; Rotary Club. Publs. incl: Novels: Adrian, der Tulpendieb (translated several times, made into 6 part TV film); Der junge Herr Alexius (translated several times); Vittorino oder Die Schleier der Welt; Anna von Oranien (translated into Dutch); Der gute Kônig René; Travel essays: Agyptische Reise;

Alte Liebe zu Frankreich; Italienische Reisen; Deutsch-französosche Vignetten; Wieder in Frankreich; Autobiography: Vorwärts, rückwärts meine Spur, 1974. Hons: Swabian Poets' Prize; Grand Cross of Merit, German Fed. Repub.; Hon. Citizen (prof.), Bietigheim/Württemburg. Address: Marbacherstrasse 11, 712 Bietigheim Württemburg, German Fed. Repub.

ROMBEY, Nobert August, b. 13 Nov. 1910. Art Antiquarian; Graphic Artist; Painter. Educ: Business Schl.; studied w. W. Renfordt (Painting & Etching), I. Engelhardt (Model Drawing), Th. Hucke (Portrait Drawing), W. Kamprath (Graphics). Appts: Commercial training & advt. work; Art Dealer & Expert; Arranger of Art Exhibs.; Restorer of Graphic works. One-Man exhib: Art House Wunsch, Osnabrück, 1932. Major work: Picture of an Old Man (oil). Address: Jacobstr. 7a, 45 Osnabrück, German Fed. Repub. 105, 133.

ROMERO, Patricia Watkins, b. 28 July 1935. Historian. Educ: B.A., Ctrl. State Univ., Ohio; M.A., Miami Univ., Ohio; Ph.D., Ohio State Univ. Appts. incl: instr., Ctrl. State Univ., 1965-66; Rsch. Asst., Assn. for Study of Afro-Am. Life & Hist., 1965-68; Assoc. Ed., Negro Hist. Bulletin, 1966-68; Vis. Prof., Findlay Coll., Findlay, Ohio, 1969, Ed.-in-Chief, United Publg. Co., Wash. DC, 1968-70; Rsch. Assoc. for African Affairs & Educ., Assn. for Study of Afro-Am. Life & Hist., Inc., 1970-72; Vis. Lectr., Univ. of S. Fla., Tampa, Fla., 1972-74; Cons. to Chgo. Bd. of Educ., Ohio State Bd. of Educ., Publrs. & Encys. Mbrships: African Studies Assn.; Am. Histl. Assn.; Assn. for Study of Afro-Am. Life & Hist., Fellowship, 1968-69. Publs: Negro-Americans In The Civil War (w. Charles H. Wesley); I, Too, Am. America: A Documentary History (Ed.); In Black America: 1968 The Year Of Awakening; In Pursuit Of African Culture (Ed.); num. articles & reviews. Address: Univ. of S. Fla., Dept. of Hist., Tampa, FL 33617, U.S.A. 138.

ROMERO, Redentor, b. 25 Aug. 1929. Symphony Conductor. Educ: Grad., Univ. of the Philippines, 1950; Postgrad. studies at San Fran. State Coll., San Fran. Conservatory of Music, Mills Coll., Music Acad. of the W. & Am. Symph. Orch. League, 1953-57. Appts: Conductor & Music Dir., Nat. Philharmonic Orch., Manila, & Guest Conductor in U.S.S.R., Europe, U.S.A., Far E., Australia & N.Z., 1960-; concert tour as Violinist, Far E., 1958-59; Concertmaster, Berkeley Symph. Orch., Monterey Symph. Orch. & San Fran. Symph. Orch., appearances as solo violinist, 1953-57; Fndr. & Conductor, Guam Symph. Orch., 1950-52. Mbrships: V.P., Philippine Fubright Schlrs. Assn.; Music Chmn., R.P.-U.S.S.R. Friendship Soc.; Assoc. Mbr., Philippines Overseas Press Club; Rotary Club of Pasay; Makati Gdn. Club; Nat. Rifle & Pistol Ass.; Merville Pk. Tennis Club. Contbr. to var. jrnls. Hons: Most Outstanding Alumnus & Most Disting. Jubilarian, Arellano High Schl., 1972; 24 Most Outstanding Young Men of the Philippines, Asia Mag., 1963. Address: Music Director & Conductor, National Philharmonic Soc. of the Philippines, Metropolitan Theatre Bldg., Plaza Lawton, Manila, Philippines.

ROMLEY, Frederick J., Jr. (Profl. name, Derek Romley), b. 6 June 1940. Architect. Educ: B.A., Harvard Univ., 1957; B.Arch., Yale Schl. of Art & Arch., 1964; M.Arch., ibid, 1965. Appts. incl: w. Michael Folliasson, Arch., Paris, France, 1965-66; w. NDP Design Assocs., Lima, Peru, 5 months, 1966; w. Paul Rudolph,

Arch., NYC, 1967-68; Design Instr., Pratt Inst., Bklyn., N.Y., 1969-71; w. Richard Meier, Arch., NYC, 1969-70; w. James Stirling, Arch., London, U.K., summer, 1970; w. Edward Barns, Arch., NYC, 1970-71; w. Carla Venosta, Arch., Milan, Italy, 6 months, 1971; w. Jack Coble, Arch., NYC, 1972-73; Chief Designer, Leach-Kehoe-Ticer, AIA, Oxnard, Calif., 1973-74; currently planning & designing many projects w. Scott Ellinwood, Arch., Rasmussen & Love, AIA, San Buenaventura, Calif. Projects incl: Prefecture of Police, Seine-St.-Denis (w. Michel Folliasson); Nightclub, Beach Club & Shopping Ctr. for Braniff Airlines, Lima, Peru (w. NDP Design Assocs.); Endow Labs., Yale Schl. of Art & Arch. (w. Paul Rudolph); Westbeth Artists' Lofts (w. Richard Meier). Contbr. of weekly column on Arch. to N.Y. Herald; articles in var. profl. & gen. interest mags. Address: 1156 Pittsfield Lane, San Buenaventura, CA 93003, U.S.A.

ROMO—ARREGUI, Josefina, b. 27 May 1913. Professor of Classical Languages & Literature; Writer. Educ: A.M., Ph.D., Univ. of Madrid, Spain; further studies, France, Italy, Portugal. Appts: Owner & Dir., family publishing house, Madrid; Proff. Spanish & Spanish-Am. Lit., Univ. of Madrid, 1947-58; Disting. Schlr., Columbia Univ., N.Y., U.S.A., 1958-60; Vis. Lectr., City Coll., CUNY, 1960-63; Prof. Romance & Classical Langs. & Lit., Univ. of Conn., 1963-. Mbrships: Pres., Academia de la Lengua espanole, N.Y.; V.P., Ateneo Puertorringneño, N.Y.; AATSP; ACTFL; Amigos de la Argueologia, Madrid. Publs. incl: Cantico de Maria Sola, 1950; Isla sin Tierre, 1954; Poemas de America, 1967; Autoantologia, 1968. Hons. incl: Academician, Academia de Doctores, Madrid; Medal of Merit, Repub. of Ecuador. Address: University of Connecticut, Storrs, CT 06268, U.S.A. 13, 15.

ROMOSER, Ruth Amelia (Mrs. Edward L. Romoser), b. 26 Apr. 1916. Painter; Sculptor. Educ: Grad., Balt. Art Inst.; studied w. Stephen Berge (oils), Reuben Kramer (sculpture); sculpting course, Corbera of Spain; workshops w. Robert Motherwell & Joseph Ruffo (graphics). Commns. incl: Portraits; Murals for pvte. homes; paintings for 12 prodns., Actors Studio M., Coral Gables, Fla. Works in pub. collects: Miami Mus. of Mod. Art, Fla; Lowe Mus., Univ. of Miami, Fla.; Miami Herald; Nat. Catdiac Hosp., Miami, Fla.; Int. Gall., Balt. Md. Mbrships: Pres., Blue Dome Art Gellowship, 1972-74; Fla. Artist Grp. Inc.; WAIT; Lowe Mus.; Miami Art Ctr. Hons: 8th Annual Hortt Meml. Award, Ft. Lauderdale Mus. of Art, 1967; Design Derby Award, Designers, Decorators Guild, 1969; ARTSPO, Coral Gables, Fla., 1970; Artists Grp. Inc. Award, Fla. Atlantic Univ., Boca Raton, 1973. Address: 8025 S.W. 64th St., Miami, FL 33143, U.S.A. 5, 37.

RÖMPÖTTI, Kalevi, b. 29 Apr. 1917. Physical Education Instructor. Educ: B.Sc., Helsinki Univ., Finland, 1948; Postgrad., Stanford Univ., Calif., U.S.A., 1955-56. Appts: Coast Artillery Off., Mil. Acad., Helsinki, 1943-45; Nat. Track & Field Coach, 1948-53; Hd. Instr., Phys. Educ. & Sports, Finnish Armed Forces, 1953-63; Chief, Phys. Educ. Off., Gen. HQ., Helsinki, 1963-; Prof., Track & Field, Phys. Educ. Inst., Helsinki Univ., 1953-70. Mbrships. incl: European Track & Field Coaches Assn., 1969-; Chief, Finnish Delegation, Conseil Int. Du Sport Militaire, 1963-; Comm. for Scientific Coaching, Finnish Ctrl. Sports Fedn., 1968-; Bd., Finnish Sport Coll., 1970-; Int. Gemeinschaft der Olympiateilnehmer, 1973-. Publs: How to Run Victories & Break Records, 1973; Contbns. to sev. profl. jrnls. & chapts. in books. Hons. incl: Cross of Liberty, 3rd Class with Swords, 1943; Olympic Medal of Helsinki Olympic Games, 1952; Kt. Cross of Ordo Constanti Magni, 1960; Silver Cross of Finnish Sports, 1963; Golden Cross of Finnish Sports, 1968. Address: Box 25, 00131, Helsinki 13, Finland. 134.

RONAN, Colin Alistair, b. 4 June 1920. Author; Editor; Lecturer. Educ: B.Sc., Astron., Imperial Coll., Univ. of London; M.Sc., Hist. & Philos. of Sci., Univ. Coll., ibid. Appts: Sci. Asst. to Exec. Sec., Royal Soc., 1949-60; Free-lance Author & Ed., 1961-. Mbrships. incl: Fellow, Coun. Mbr., Royal Astronomical Soc.; Past Dir., Histl. Sect., Brit. Astronomical Assn.; Int. Astronomical Union; Brit. Soc. for Hist. of Sci.; Int. Sci. Writers Assn.; Assn. of Brit. Sci. Writers. Publs. incl: Man Probes the Universe, 1964; Their Majesties' Astronomers, 1967; Invisible Astronomy, 1969; Lost Discoveries, 1973; Contbr. to Ency. Britannica & Dictionary of Scientific Biography. Address: 39 New Rd., Barton, Cambridge CB3 7AY, U.K. 3.

RONTY, Bruno George, b. 10 June 1922. Operatic Tenor; Corporate Executive. Educ: B.A., Lyceum of Humanities, U.S.S.R., 1940; M.A., Conservatory of Music, U.S.S.R., 1941. Opera, concerts, radio, U.S.S.R., 1940-42, Europe & U.S.A., 1945-50; concerts, occupied Europe, 1942-45; concerts, U.S.A., 1973-. Appts: Dir., Polish Min. of Culture, & Cultural Off. w. Polish Army for Min. of Defence, 1945; Pres., Colosseum Records, Inc., U.S.A., 1950-; Pres., Musicart Int. Ltd., U.S.A., 1958-; Pres., Musica Nostra et Vostra, Nat. Corp. of Am., 1973-. Mbrships: Nat. Mbr., -Smithsonian Assocs.; YMCA. Musical articles, translations of operatic libretti. Hons. incl: 1st Prize, Int. Artist Contest, U.S.S.R., 1940; Grunwald Corss, Poland; Polonia Restituta, Poland. Address: 49 W. 72 St., N.Y., NY 10023, U.S.A. 2, 6.

ROOD, Larry Eugene, b. 18 Oct. 1936. Teacher. Educ: B.A., Otterbein Coll., Westerville, Ohio, U.S.A., 1958; Ohio State Univ. Appts: State Treas., Ohio Athletic Dirs.; Football Basketball, Baseball Official; Fac. Mgr., Westland H.S. Mbrships: Pres., ABC Bowling, 1972; Regional Pres., Cols. Westgate, 1973; O.E.A.; N.E.A.; Ki of Pi; Past Bd. Mbr., OHSADA; United & Method. Ch. Author, The Generation Gap Can be Bridged. Recip. Driver Educ. Safety & O.I.I. Seminar Awards. Address: 233 Amity Rd., Galloway, OH 43119, U.S.A. 130.

ROOK, Alvin Gordon, b. 15 Feb. 1923. Research Chemist. Educ: B.S., Chem. Engrng., Univ. of Calif. at Berkeley, 1949. Appts: Sr. Rsch. Chem., Fibreboard Corp., Pabco Paint Div., (now Napko Corp.), 1949-71; Mgr., Prod. Dev., Napko Corp. (Calif.), 1971-. Mbrships: Bd. of Dirs., Past Pres., Fedn. of Socs. for Paint Technol. & Chmn., var. comms.: Western Coatings Socs.; Past Pres., Golden Gate Soc. for Coatings Technol.; Am. Chem. Soc.; AAAS; Alpha Chi Sigma; Past Treas., Paint Rsch. Inst.; Past Pres., Golden Gate Cinematographers; Concertmaster, San Fran. Park & Recreation Symph.; Int. Violin, Guitar Makers & Musicians Assn. Contbr. to profl. jrnls. Hons: Outstanding Serv. Awards—Golden Gate Soc. for Coatings, 1970, Fedn. of Socs. for Paint Technol., 1973; Harrison & Crossfield Award, 1970. Address: Napko Corp. (Calif.), P.O. Box 1910, Fremont, CA 94538, U.S.A. 15, 28, 131.

ROOT, Paul Ray, b. 24 Oct. 1932. Educator. Educ: B.S.E., State Coll. of Ark., 1958; M.S.E., ibid, 1959; Ed.D., Univ. of Ark., 1964. Appts: Tchr., Greenbrier H.S., Ark.,

1958-59, Hot Springs H.S., 1959-62; Asst. Prof. Hist., Ouachita Bapt. Univ., Arkadelphia, Ark., 1964-68; Assoc. Prof. & Dept. Chmn., 1966-68, Educ. Cons., Ark. Tech. Assistance & Consultative Ctr., 1972-; Asst. Prof. Hist. & Educ., Ark. State Univ., Jonesboro, 1968-69; Prof. Educ., & Chmn., Div. of Educ. & Psychol., Oakland City Coll., Ind., 1969-72. Mbrships: Ark. Educ. Assn.; NEA; Conf. of Faith & Hist.; Phi Delta Kappa. Author, Leadership, Some Things to Ponder. Recip.,Community Serv. Award, 1972. Address: 1075 Phelps Cir., Arkadelphia, AR 71923, U.S.A.

ROOTHAM, Jasper St. John, b. 21 Nov. 1910. Banker; Author. Educ: St. John's Coll., Cambridge, U.K.; M.A., 1936; Sandhurst, 1941. Appts: Asst. Prin. Min. of Agric., 1933-34; Colonial Off., 1934-36; Treasury, 1936-40; Prin., ibid, 1939; Asst. Pvte. Sec. to Prime Min., 1938-39; War Serv., 1940-46; Successively Acting Asst. Advsr., Asst. Chief Cashier, Asst. Advsr., Advsr. to Gov., Chief of O'seas Dept., Asst. to Gov., Bank of England, 1946-67; A Mng. Dir., Lazard Bros. & Co. Ltd., 1967-; also Dpty. Chmn., Agricultural Mortgage Corp., Dir., British Sugar Corp. & Chmn., D.E.K. Printing Machines Ltd., Weymouth. Mbrships: A t h e n a e u m ;   N o r t h e r n   C o s . (Newcastle-upon-Tyne) O'seas Bankers. Publs: Miss-Fire, 1946; Demi-Paradise, 1960; Verses 1928-72, 1973. Address: Lower Farm, Hadstock, Cambridge, U.K. 1, 3, 43.

ROPER, Edmund George, b. 12 June 1917. Educator; Economist. Educ: B.A., Univ. of London, U.K., 1951; M.S., Cornell Univ., Ithaca, N.Y., U.S.A., 1956. Appts: Headmaster, Primary Schls., 1940-45; Jr. Tutor, Mico Tchrs. Coll., 1945-46; Master, Jamaica Schl. of Agric., 1947-57; Registrar & Sr. Master, ibid, 1958-60; Prin., St. Elizabeth Tech. H.S., 1961-64; Prin., Kingston Tech. H.S., 1965-. Mbrships: Chmn., Nat. Indl. Trng. Bd., 1970-72 & 1972-; Chmn., Apprenticeship Bd., 1966-; Examinations Bd., Min. of Educ., 1973; First V.P., St. Elizabeth Football Assn., & St. Elizabeth Cricket Bd. of Control, 1963 & 1964; Dist. Chief Ranger, Jamaica Dist., Ancient Order of Foresters, 1972-73. Hons: Govt. Exhibitioner, 1936; Justice of the Peace, 1963-73. Address: 32 Vermont Ave., Kingston 8, Jamaica, W. Indies. 96. 109.

ROPER, William Leon, b. 6 May 1897. Writer; retired Journalist. Educ: Drury Coll., Springfield, Mo. Appts: incl: Commercial Artist, St. Louis, Mo., 1918; Jrnlst., L.A. Times, L.A. Examiner & num. other newspapers; S. Calif. Publicity Dir., U.S. Senator William F. Knowland, 1946; Ed., Tex. City Sun, 1949; Publicity Dir., Lt. Gov. Goodwin J. Knight, 1950; free-lance writer, 1953-. Publs. incl: William Spry-Man of Firmness (w. L. Arrington), 1971; Roy Rogers-King of the Cowboys, 1971; Sequoyia & His Miracle, 1973; Consumer Power In Action (w. T. Drury), 1973; A Treasury of Success Unlimited (co-author), 1966; short stories & articles in over 100 U.S. & U.K. mags. Mbrships. incl: Hon. Bd. of Trustees, Gen. John H. Forney Hist. Soc.; Counselor, Pomona Valley Writers' Club (Calif.). Hons: Purple Heart Decoration, 1919; WWI. Mil. medals. Address: 11843 Monte Vista Ave., Chino, CA 91710, U.S.A. 30.

ROQUEMORE, (Mrs.) Lois Evelyn Masterson, b. 14 July 1903.. Teacher; Floral Designer; Writer. Educ: Univ. of N.M., Albuquerque, 3 yrs.; A.B., N.M. Highlands Univ., Las Vegas, 1940; M.A., ibid. Appts: Tchr., San Jon & Logan, N.M. schls., 2 yrs.;

Farmington City Schls., N.M.; Las Vegas City Schls. & N.M. Highlands Univ. Educ. Dept., 20 yrs.; El Paso City Schls., until retirement in 1973; Univ. Tchr. & Florist during the summer. Mbrships. incl: Sigma Sigma Sigma; Organist & Pianist, Bapt. Ch.; Pres., Tex. Press Women, Dist. 1, El Paso; Pres., El Paso Writers' League; AAUW; World Poetry Soc.; Tex. & Nat. Fed. of State Poetry Socs.; Avalon Poets. Contbr. of num. poems, stories, articles to popular, educl., religious jrnls. & in children's mags. Rep. in num. anthols. Contbr. to broadcasts. Hons. incl: Top Hons. in El Paso Writers' League Contest, 1973; Chosen Poet of the Yr., by J. Mark Press, 1973. Address: 1401 Randolph, El Paso, TX 79902, U.S.A. 5, 11, 125.

RØRHOLT, Bjørn Arnold, b. 27 Aug. 1919. Consulting Electronic Engineer. Educ: Mil. Acad., 1940; Tech. Univ., Trondheim, Norway; M.Sc., Harvard Univ., U.S.A., 1948. Appts: Engr., Norwegian Army Signals Trng. Ctr., 1950; Chief, Tech. Br., Norwegian Defense Communications Agcy., 1953; Dir., ibid, 1958; Dir., A/S Telox, 1969; Chief, Electronics Br., Norwegian Army Meterial Command, 1972. Mbrships: Pres., Norwegian Aero Club, 1957-59; Pres., Mental Barnehjdp, 1965-; Inst. of Navigation (Royal Geog. Soc.), London, U.K. Author of var. articles on navigational electronics in several countries; Holder of several U.S., Norwegian & Int. patents in electronics; Designer of mech. analogue model of ionospheric radio wave refraction & of radio sets & communications for the Kon-Tiki Expedition. Hons: D.S.O., 1942; Norwegian War Cross w. sword, 1942. Address: Eiksveien 70, 1345 Østerås, Norway. 43.

ROSA, Guilherme, b. 17 Mar. 1906. Executive; Editor. Appts. incl: Former Dir., Water & Elec. Bd., Viana do Catelo, Portugal; Econ. Cons., Banco Portugues del Atlantico; Currently, Financial Dir., Companhia Vidreira Nacional (COVINA), Dir., mag. "Actividades Economicas", Pres., mag. "Jornal do Technico de Contas e da Empresa". Mbrships: Int. Sci. Assn. of Acctcy. & Econs., Portugal; Fndr. & Dir., Rotary Club, Viana do Castelo; Fndr. & Dir., Circulo de Cultura Musical, Viana do Castelo. Author of about 60 publs. inclng: Sobre o Balanco do Estado Portugues; Sobre Concorrencia em Ambito Internacional; Sobre termos de Viabilidade Economica de Empresas de Producao; Num. articles in jrnls. Address: Rua Rodrigo da Fonseca, 62 4° Esq., Lisbon 1, Portugal. 43.

ROSACK, (Rev.) Edward Victor, b. 23 Dec. 1925. Catholic Priest. Educ: B.A., St. Procopius Coll., Lisle 111, 1950; Sem., St. Procopius 1950-54 & SS. Cyril & Methodius, Pitts, Pa., 1950-54; O.E.S.B., Pontifical Oriental Inst., Rome, Italy, 1955. Ordained, 1954. Appts: Past Apostolic Admnstr., Byzantine Cath. Diocese of Pitts.; Past Mbr., USSCC Advsry. Coun.; Chancellor, Consultor, ex officio mbr. of Priests' Pension Plan Bd., Mbr. of Exec. Comm. for Golden Jubilee Yr. Celebration, Chmn. of Golden Jubilee Yr. Comm. on News Coverage, Archdiocese of Munhall (Byzantine Ruthenian Rite); Past Ed., Byzantine Cath. World; Mbr., Admnstv. Bd., Pa. Cath. Conf.; V.P. & Mbr., Bd. of Delegs., Christian Assocs. of S.W. Pa.; Pastor, St. Mary's Ch., Ambridge, Pa. Mbrships: Hist. Soc. of Western Pa.; Pa. Histl. Assn. Hons: named Papal Chamberlain, 1965; named Papal Prelate, 1970. Address: 624 Park Rd., Ambridge, PA 15003, U.S.A. 49.

ROSCH, Paul J., b. 30 June 1927. Physician. Educ: B.A., Brown Univ., 1948; M.A., N.Y. Univ., 1950; Fellow, Inst. of Experimental Med. & Surg., Univ. of Montreal,

1951; Intern., Res., Internal Med., Johns Hopkins Hosp., 1954-56; Res., Fellowship Internal Med., Walter Reed Army Med. Ctr., 1956-58. Appts: Chief, Endocrine Sect., Dept. of Metabolism, Walter Reed Army Inst. of Rsch.; Asst. in Med., Johns Hopkins Hosp.; Asst. Clin. Prof., Med., N.Y. Med. Coll. & Mt. Sinai Hosp. Schl.. of Med., N.Y.C. Mbrships: Fellow, Life Mbr., Am. Coll. of Physns.; Pres., Westchester Diabetes Assn.; Pres., Yonkers Acad. of Med.; Pres., Westchester Chapt., N.Y. Soc. of Internal Med.; Dipl., Am. Bd. of Internal Med., Endocrine Soc., N.Y. Acad. of Scis., Am. Coll. of Cardiol., Am. Diabetes Assn. Publs: Co-author, 12 med. texts; Contbr. to profl. jrnls. Address: 124 Park Ave., Yonkers, NY 10703, U.S.A. 6, 17.

ROSE, Bea, b. 22 Jan. 1921. Professor of Philosophy. Educ: B.A., Univ. of Calif., San Fran.; M.A., San Fran. Theol. Sem., San Ansilmo; Tchng. Credential, Redlands Univ., 1950. Appts: Innovation of Release Time Relig. Educ., Antelope Valley, 1944; Dir. of Relig. Educ., Calvary Presby. Ch., Riverside, 1945-50; Tchr. of Engl., Chaffet H.S., 1951-54; Prof. of Philos., Chaffey Coll., Alta Loma, 1954-; Chmn., Soc. Sci. Div. of Chaffey, 1966. Author of article on Ldrship. for Presby. Life Mag., 1949 & of Pamphlet, 'Who's Listening' Address: Box 448, Mt. Baldy, CA 91759 U.S.A. 2, 9.

ROSE, Beatrice Schroeder, b. 15 Nov. 1922. Harpist; Educator. Educ: Inst. of Musical Art, N.Y.C., 1940, '41; Mannes Coll. of Music, N.Y.C., 1942-44. Appts. incl: Concert & radio debut, N.Y. World's Fair, 1939; Assoc. Harpist, Radio City Music Hall Orch., N.Y.C., 1944-50; var. radio & solo performances, N.Y. area, 1944-51; Concert Artist,, Italy, U.S.A. & Canada, 1952, '53, Prin. Harpist, Houston Symph. 1953-; Fac. Mbr., Univ. of Houston, 1953-; Soloist under Stokowski, as mbr. Contemporary Music Soc., 1959, '60; Fndr. & Dir., Houston Harp Ensemble. Mbrships. incl: Am. Harp Soc.; Tex. Music Educators Assn. Co-author, Outline of Six-Year Harp Course for Elementary, Jr. & Sr. High School. Book of compositions, Enchanted Harp. Hons: 1st Prize, Fed. Music Clubs Contest, 1936; Winner, N.Y. Hour of Music Award, 1945. Address: 1315 Friarcreek Ln., Houston, TX 77055, U.S.A. 5, 7, 125, 138.

ROSE, Brian Waldron, b. 2 Sept. 1915. Educator. Educ: Trinity Coll., Dublin; Univ. of Witwatersrand, S. Africa; Univ. of S. Africa. Appts: Lectr., Engl., Univ. of S. Africa; Lectr., Communication Studies, Univ. of Witwatersrand; Lectr., Educ., Mt. Holyoke Coll., Mass., U.S.A.; Hd. of Dept., Educl. Studies, Jo-burg. Coll. of Educ., Johannesburg. Lectr., Bus. & Mgmt., Human Rels. Mbrships: Royal Commonwealth Soc., London; Int. & Comparative Educ. Soc., U.S.A.; S. African Inst. of Race Rels.; S. African Inst. of Int. Affairs; Past Chmn., PEN in S. Africa. Publs. incl: No Mean City; Modern Trends in Education; S. African Educational Documents; Education in Southern Africa; Modern Narrative Verse; Radio features & prods. Hons: Oppenheim Bursary, 1962; S. Africa-U.S.A. Ldrship. Award, 1963-64. Address: 81 Greenside Rd., Greenside, Johannesburg, S. Africa.

ROSE, Gerhard (August Heinrich), b. 30 Nov. 1896. Physician; Professor of Hygiene & Tropical Medicine; Factory Owner. Educ: Studied med., Kaiser Wilhelm Acad. & Univs. of Berlin & Breslau, Germany; German med. licence, 1921; M.D., Breslau, 1922; Chinese med. licence, 1932. Appts. incl: Prof., Robert

Koch Inst., Berlin, & Dir., Dept. for Tropical Med., ibid, 1936-45; V.P., Robert Koch Inst., State Inst. for the control of epidemic diseases; Cons. for hygiene & tropical med. to surg. gen., German Air Force, WWII; Prisoner of war, 1945-55; Chief Rep., Hermann Heye, Hamburg, German Fed. Repub., 1956; Chmn., ibid, & Heye Glass Works "Schauenstein", Obernkirchen, 1957-64; Rschr. into solid waste disposal, recycling of glass, environmental problems & donor insemination on humans in childless marriage, 1964-. Mbrships. incl: Deutsche Gesellschaft für Hygiene & Mikrobiologie; Deutsche Glastechnische Gesellschaft; Life mbr., Chinese Med. Assn.; Fellow, Royal Soc. for Tropical Med., 1933-39. Author of books & about 150 papers in field. Recip. of hons. Address: Vor den Büschen 46, 4962 Obernkirchen, German Fed. Repub. 43, 92.

ROSE, Wesley H., b. 11 Feb. 1918. Music Publisher; Gramophone Record Manufacturer. Educ: B.S., Walton Schl. of Comm., Chgo., 1939. Appts: Acct., Standard Oil Co. Ltd., Whiting, Ind., 1939-45; w. Acuff-Rose Publs. Inc., 1945-; Pres., ibid, 1954-; Fndr., Hickory Records & Acuff-Rose Artists Corp.; Prod. of Hand Williams recordings, MGM; Prod., Columbia, Warner Bros., RCA Victor, Epic, Cameo-Parkway & other labels. Mbrships: Bd., Am. Soc. of Composers, Authors & Publrs. (ASCAP); Fndg. Bd. Mbr., Country Music Assn.; Bd., Nat. Music Publrs. Assn.; Bd., Nashville Area Chmbr. of Comm.; Bd., 1st Am. Nat. Bank; Nat. Pres., Nat. Acad. of Recording Arts & Scis. (NARAS), 1971. Address: Acuff-Rose Publications, Inc., 2510 Franklin Rd., Nashville, TN 37204, U.S.A.

ROSE, William Erle, b. 16 Nov. 1902. Teacher; Author. Educ: Vic. Univ. of Wellington, N.Z.; M.A., Hist., Auckland Univ., 1946. Appts: Tchr., State Primary Tchng. Serv.; RNZAF Educl. Servs., WWII; Sr. Secondary Asst., Southbridge Dist. H.S., Canterbury, N.Z., 1946; Hd., Soc. Studies, Hutt Valley Mem. Tech. Coll., 1950; Hd., Engl. & Soc. Studies, Wellington Tech. Coll., 1957; Retd. 1960; J.P., 1967. Mbrships: Sub-comm. on Appreciation of Sci., Royal Soc. of N.Z.; N.Z. Inst. of Int. Affairs; Standing Comm., UN Assn. of N.Z. Publs: It Happened that Day, N.Z. 1900 to 1930; Hortopp, 1970; Num. articles in N.Z. mags.; Bulletins & booklets; Ed., World Affairs, mag. of N.Z. UN Assn., 1964-. Hons: Prince Konoye Silver Medal, Japanese Soc. for Int. Cultural Rels., 1938. Address: 149 The Ridgeway, Mornington, Wellington 2, N.Z. 38.

ROSEBURY, Theodor, b. 10 Aug. 1904. Author. Educ: C.C.N.Y.; N.Y. Univ.; D.D.S., Univ. of Pa., 1928. Appts: Fellow in Biochem., Columbia Univ., N.Y., 1928-30, Instr.—Assoc. Prof., Dept. of Bacteriol., 1930-51; Proj. Dir., Camp Detrick, Md., 1943-45; Prof., Bacteriol., Wash. Univ., St. Louis, 1951-66, Emeritus, 1966-. Mbrships: Am. Soc. Microbiol.; Fellow, A.A.A.S.; Soc. Experimental Biol. & Med.; Amer. Venereal Disease Assn.; Harvey Soc.; Sigma Xi. Publs. incl: Experimental Air-Borne Infection, 1947; Peace or Pestilence, 1949; Microorganisms Indigenous to Man, 1962; Life on Man, 2nd. edit., 1970; Microbes & Morals, revised edit. in preparation; contbr. of about 150 reports to tech. jrnls. & sev. chapts. in books. Address: Conway, MA 01341, U.S.A.

ROSELAND, Paul Luther, b. 11 May 1917. Educator; Artist; Interior Designer. Appts. incl: Assoc. Prof. of Art, Tex. Woman's Univ., 1961-67; Vis. Prof. of Design, Schl. of Arch., Ohio Univ., 1967-68; Prof. of Art, Tex. Tech. Univ., 1968-71; Mgr., Ion Div., Am. Desk Mfg.

Co., Temple, Tex. Interior Designs: Tex. Woman's Univ.; Coll. of Nursing Dormitory; Coll. of Nursing Classroom; John A. Guinn Hall; Mary Gibbs Jones Hall, etc. Paintings exhibited: Beaumont Art Mus.; S.W. Am. Painting & Sculpture, Seattle World's Fair. Permanent Collects; City of L.A., etc. One-man exhib., Ball State Univ., 1962. 2-Man Exhib., Univ. of S. Calif., 1960. Address: 2114 S. 5th St., Apt. 18, Temple, TX 76501, U.S.A. 7, 125, 128.

ROSEN, David Moses, b. 23 July 1912. Chief Rabbi. Educ: Fac. of Law, Budapest, Rumania; Rabbinical studies. Appts: Rabbi, Syn. Reschit-Daat, Bucharest, 1940; Rabbi, Great Synagogue, Bucharest, 1945; Chief Rabbi of Rumania, 1948; Ed., Revista cultului moseic, Jewish fortnightly, 1956; Mbr., Rumanian Parliament, 1957; Pres., Fedn. of Jewish Communities in Rumania, 1964. Mbrships: Governing Coun., World Jewish Congress, Geneva, Switzerland; Pres., Int. Comm., House of the Diaspone, Tel Aviv, Israel; Bd. of Govs., Hebrew Univ., Jerusalem; Bd. of Dirs., Mem. Fndn. for Jewish Culture, N.Y., U.S.A.; Standing Comm., Conf. of European Rabbis, London, U.K.; V.P., Coun. of European Communities, Paris, France. Publs: In lumina Torei, 1970; The Paper Bridge, 1973. Hons: Star of Rumanian People's Repub.; Ordinul Muncii, Rumania. Address: 17 Maria Rosetti Str., Bucharest, Rumania.

ROSEN, (Rabbi) Jeremy, b. 11 Sept. 1942. Educ: Mir Yeshiva, Jerusalem, Israel; Pembroke Coll., Cambridge, U.K. Appts: Min., Hebrew Congregation, Bulawayo, Rhodesia, 1968; Min. of Giffnock & Newlands Hebrew Congregation, Glasgow, 1969-71; Hdmaster., Carmel Coll., Wallingford, Berks., 1971-. Address: c/o Carmel Coll., Wallingford, Oxfordshire, U.K.

ROSENBAUM, Madge M.S. (Mrs. Melvin Rosenbaum), b. 11 Aug. 1915. Librarian; Teacher; Book Review Columnist. Educ: B.A., Univ. of Calif.; Columbia Univ.; Univ. of Miami, Fla.; Univ. of Youngstown. Appts. incl: Tchr. & Libn., Youngstown, Ohio; Rschr. in Plastics, N.Y. & N.J.; Libn., Phoenix, Ariz.; Arts & Crafts Instr., Miami & Coral Gables, Fla.; Libn. & Lib. Cons., ibid; Book Reviewer & Columnist, Jewish Floridian; Free-lance Writer; TV & Radio Commercials. Mbrships. incl: Bd. Mbr., & Lib. Chmn., Cedar of Lebanon Hosp. Aux.; Regional Chmn., A.J.L.A.; Pres., Beta Omega Sigma Sorority; Ed., Yearbook & Weekly Newspaper Rayen Record, Youngstown, Ohio; Pres., Hist. Club, Spanish Club, Engl. Club, Youngstown, Ohio; Publicity Chmn., Braille Club, ibid. Publs. incl: Gourmet Recipe Cookbook; Party Cookie Cookbook; Tea Party Recipies; Stories for the Very Young; Childrens Poems; Arts, Crafts & Games for Children. Hons. incl: Cedars of Lebanon-Hosp. Award, 1970; Cert. from Heart Assn., 1965-68; Red Cross Braille Award, 1938, '42, '45. Address: 229 Cadima Ave., Coral Gables, FL 33134, U.S.A. 125.

ROSENBERG, Leonard H., b. 1 Dec. 1912. Company President. Educ: B.S.M.E., Carnegie Inst. of Technol., 1934; Grad., Air Force Navigation Schl.; Grad., Ctrl. Instrs. Schl., Courses in Philos., Loyola Coll.; Life Ins. Marketing, Southern Meth. Univ.; Courses in Ins. Mgmt., Univ. of Md. Appts: Ins. Salesman, Underwriter & Gen. Mgr., currently V.P., Strasco Ins. Agcy., Inc., 1935-; Pres. & Fndr., Chesapeake Life Ins. Co., 1956-; Pres., Chesapeake Fund, Inc. (mutual fund), 1968-; Mbr., Special Advsry. Bd., Suburban Trust Co., 1970-; Dir., Green Assocs. (Cons. Engrs.),

1960-; Bd. Mbr. & Trustee, Mid-Atlantic Real Estate Investment Trust, 1971-. Mbrships. incl: Pres., Nat. Assn. of Life Cos., 1968-70; Bd. of Dirs., ibid, 1965-; Cmmnr., Md. Pub. Broadcasting Commn., 1967-71; Chmn, ibid 1971-; Bd. of Dirs. & Bd. of Govs., Int. Ins. Seminars, 1970-; Nat. Advsry. Commn. on Flammable Fabrics, 1970-. Publs. incl: Development of Modern Merchandising in the Life Insurance Industry, 1972; Pros & Cons of "Adjusted Earnings" Method of Reporting Annual Financial Results, 1971. Recip. of hons. Address: Chesapeake Life Ins. Co., 527 St. Paul St., Balt., MD 21202, U.S.A. 6, 16, 27, 55.

ROSENBERGER, Homer Tope, b. 23 Mar. 1908. Historian; Personnel Training Consultant. Educ: B.Sc., Albright Coll., Reading, Pa., 1929; M.A., Cornell Univ., 1930; Ph.D., ibid, 1932. Appts. incl: Supvsr. of Trng., U.S. Bur. of Prisons, 1942-57; proposed & promoted The William Penn Memorial, Harrisburg, Pa., 1944-48; Chmn., U.S. Trng. Offs. Conf., 1949-50, & '55-57; Chief of Trng., U.S. Bur. Pub. Roads, 1957-65; Pres., Bur. of Rehab., Wash. D.C., 1958-61; Org. & Moderator, Rose Hill Sems., 1963-; Advsr. of dev. of admin. competence of govt. employees, Nigeria, 1963-64; Mbr. Advsry. Bd. of Review for Pa., Nat. Reg. of Historic Places, USA, 1969-; Mbr., Exec. Comm., Pa. Fed of Histl. Socs., 1969-; Chmn., Awards Comm., ibid, 1970-; Pres., Columbia Hist. Soc., Wash. D.C., 1968-; Chmn., Pa. State Bd. of Pvte. Corres. Schls.; Commnr., Pa. Histl. & Mus. Commn., 1972-. Mbrships: Hist. Comm., Cosmos Club, Eash. D.C.; Dir., Am. Peace Soc., 1960-; Pres., Pa. Histl. Assn., 1967-69. Publs: Testing Occupational Training & Experience, 1948; What Should We Expect of Education? 1956; Techniques for Getting Things Done, 7th ed., 1964; Letters from Africa, 1965; The Pennsylvania Germans, 1891-1965, 1966; Harriet Lane, 1969; Adventurs & Philosophy of a Pennsylvania Dutchman, 1971; Man & Modern Society; Philosophical Essays, 1972; The Philadelphia & Erie Railroad: Its Place in American Economic History, 1974; Mountain Folks: Fragments of Central Pennsylvania Lore, 1974. 225 articles. Recip., Hon. LL.D., Albright Coll., 1955; Cits., U.S. Trng. Offs. Conf., 1957, Pa. Histl. Junto, '57 & '67 & Bur. of Rehab., '68. Address: 2121 Massachusetts Ave., N.W., Wash. D.C. 20008, U.S.A. 2, 6, 7, 10, 13, 15, 30, 51.

ROSENBERGER, Stanley E., b. 2 Jan. 1923. Professor. Educ: B.S., Univ. of Fla., 1947; M.Agric., ibid, 1949, Ph.D., 1960; Purdue Univ., 1969. Appts: Asst. Prof., Vegetable Crops, Univ. of Fla., 1949-57; Assoc. Prof., ibid, 1957-62; Prof Agric. Econs., Food & Resource Econs. Dpet., Univ. of Fla., Gainesville, 1962-. Mbrships: Am. Agric. Econs. Assn.; Food Distribution Rsch. Soc.; Univ. Prof. for Acad. Order; Produce Marketing Assn.; Sec. Treas., Chapt. House Assn., Alpha Gamma Rho; Hon. Mbr., Fla. Seedsmen & Gdn. Supply Assn. Contbr. to profl. lit. Hons: Award of Appreciation, Okla. State Univ., 1963; Retail Grocers Assn. of Fla., 1963; Ldr., Party for Food Ind. Goodwill, People-to-People Mission, E. & W. Europe, 1966. Address: G120 McCarty Hall, Univ. of Florida, Gainesville, FL 32611, U.S.A.

ROSENQVIST, Ivan Thoralf Koss, b. 17 May 1916. Mineralogist; Petrologist. Educ: M.S., Univ. of Oslo, 1940; Dr. Philos., ibid, 1945; Vienna Univ. Appts: Mineral., Norwegian Hwy. Rsch. Lab., 1941-46; Hd., Materials Sect., Norwegian Defense Rsch. Inst., 1946-50; Sr. Lectr., Univ. of Bergen (Norway) Inst. of Geogl., 1950-52; Staff, Norwegian Geotech. Inst., 1952-61; on Fac., Univ. of Oslo., 1956-; Prof., ibid, 1956-; Chmn., Inst. of Geol. Mbrships. incl: Fellow, Norwegian Acads. of Sci. & of Tech. Sci.; Clay Minerals Soc.; Pres., Assn. Int. pour l'Etude des Argiles, 1960-66. Publs: Subsoil Corrosion of Steel, 1961; Geologien og Mennesket (Geology & Humanity), 1973; num. articles on geol., geotech. & chem. Rsch. on border of fields of phys., chem. & geol., dealing g esp. w. clays & clay minerals; has formulated theories for high sensitivity clays (quick clays). Recip. Fridtjof Nansen Reward, 1971. Address: Anton Schjødtsgt. 19, Oslo, Norway. 50.

ROSENSAFT, Melvin, b. 28 Jan. 1919. Business Executive. Educ: Cert., State Tchrs. Coll., Paterson, N.J., 1940; B.S., Rider Coll., 1942. Appts. incl: Gen. Mgr., Gt. Am. Plastics Co., Fitchburg, Mass., 1945-46; Comptroller, 1946-47; Works Mgr., 1947-48; Asst. to Pres., 1950-52; V.P. i/c Mfg., 1956-62; Exec. V.P., Gen. Mgr., 1962-71; Pres., 1971-; Pres., Artefactos Plasticos, Mexico City, 1948-49; Mgr., Plastics Div., Ideal Plastics Co., Hollis, N.Y., 1953-55; Exec., V.P., Irwin Corp., N.Y.C.; Fitchburg Realty Corp.; Factory St. Realty, Nashua, N.H. Mbrships: Chmn., Troop Comm., Boy Scouts Am.; Pres., Mbr. Bd., Trustee, Fitchburg Leominster Community Ctr.; Advsry. Comm., Mass. Regional Voc. Tech. Schl.; Bd. Dirs., Fitchburg Gen. Hosp.; V.P., Bd. Dirs., F.I.A. Credit Union. Address: 59 Crescent Rd., Leominster, MA 01453, U.S.A. 6, 16.

ROSENSHINE, Matthew, b. 25 May 1932. University Professor. Educ: A.B., Columbia Univ., 1952; M.A., Maths. Educ., ibid, 1953; M.S., Maths., Univ. of Ill., 1956; Ph.D., Ops. Rsch., SUNY at Buffalo, 1966. Appts: Aerodynamist, Bell Aircraft Corp., 1953-56 & Pt.time Instr., Stats., Univ. of Buffalo, 1953-55; Mathn., U.S. Army, 1956-58, & Pt.-time Instr., Univs. of Ala. & N.M. State, 1957-58; Prin. Mathn., Cornell Aeronautical Lab., Cornell Univ., 1958-68 & Pt.-time Lectr., Ops. Rsch., SUNY at Buffalo, 966-68; Assoc. Prof., Indl. Engrng., Pa. State Univ., 1968-. Mbrships: Ops. Rsch. Soc. of Am.; Sr. Mbr., Am. Inst. of Indl. Engrs.; Fellow, AAAS; Chmn., Pa. State Univ. Chapt. & Campus Activity Coord., Am. Soc. for Engrng. Educ.; Inst. of Mgt. Scis.; Am. Inst. for Decision Scis.; Mathl. Assn. of Am.; Phi Beta Kappa; Pi Mu Epsilon; Alpha Pi Mu; Sigma Xi. Contbr. to profl. jrnls. Hons: N.Y. State Regents Schlrship., 1949; Clifford Brewster Fellowship, 1957; Campus Activity Coord. of Yr., Zone I, & Nat. Runner-up, Am. Soc. for Engrng. Educ., 1973. Address: 207 Hammond Bldg., University Pk., PA 16802, U.S.A. 14.

ROSENSTEIN, Betty (Mrs. Allen B. Rosenstein) b. 29 June 1921. Educator. Educ: B.A., UCLA, 1943; M.A., ibid, 1952; Ed.D., 1967. Appts: Cons., Educl. Planning Profl. Schls., Nat. Univs. of Venexuela, 1965-72; Univ. of Med., 1970, Tchr., Spanish & Engl. to For. Born, UCLA, 1940's; Educl. Cons., External Degree Progs., Stanford Rsch. Inst., ibid, 1970-71; Unesco Cons., Educ. Planning, Venezuela; Instr., Adult Educ., UCLA Ext. Mbrships. incl: AEGLA; Ed.-in-Chief, Open Channels, Official publ. of AEGLA 1970-72; Pres., AWARE Int. Assn. for Women's Active Return to Educ.; Chmn., Palisodes Community Advsry. Coun. Sigma Delta Pi; Am. Educ. Rsch. Assn. Contbr. to educl. publs. Recip: Award Dr. B.R. for Servs. to Adult Educ., Adult Educrs. of Gtr. L.A., 1972; Minerva Award, Aware Int. Address: 314 S. Rockingham Ave., Los Angeles, CA 90049, U.S.A. 59.

ROSENTHAL, Alex, b. 16 Nov. 1913. Professor of Chemistry. Educ: B.Sc., Univ. of Alta., 1943; B.Ed., ibid, 1947; M.Sc., 1949; Ph.D., Ohio State Univ., 1952; Post-doct. wk., Univ. of Utah, 1953-54. Appts: High Schl. Tchr. & Prin. of Alta. Pub. Schls., 1938-46; Chem. Instr., Discharged Veterans Schl., Calgary, Alta., 1946-47; Prof. of Chem., Univ. of B.C., Vancouver, Canada, 1953-; Vis. Prof., Cambridge Univ., U.K., 1963-64. Mbrships: Sigma Xi; Phi Lambda Upsilon; Am. Chem. Soc.; Exec., Chem. Inst. of Canada, Vancouver; Ed., The Catalyzer; Coun., Schl. of Home Econs., Univ. of B.C.; Coun., Schl. of Nursing, ibid; Ed., Advsry. Bd., Jrnl. of Carbohydrates, Nucleosides & Nucleotides. Contbr. of over 80 papers to chem. int. sci. jrnls. Hons: Rsch. Fellowship, Ohio State Univ., 1950-51; Du Pont Fellowship in Chem., ibid, 1951-52; Fellow, Chem. Inst. of Canada. Address: Dept. of Chem., Univ. of B.C., Vancouver, B.C., Canada.

ROSENTHAL, Henry Moses, b. 9 Jan 1906. Educator. Educ: A.B., Columbia Unvi., 1925; Ordination, Rabbi, Jewish Theological Sem. of Am., 1929; Ph.D., Columbia Univ., 1940. Appts: Religious Dir., Dir. Adult Schl. of Jewish Studies, 92nd. St. Y.M.H.A. 1930-42; Dir., Hillel Fndn., Hunter Coll., 1942-45; Special Lectr., Systematic Theol., Jewish Theological Sem., 1944-46; Lectr., Cooper Union, 1940-48; Dept. of Philosophy, Hunter Coll., 1948-73, Prof. Emeritus, 1974; Vis. Prof. of Philosophy, Columbia Univ., 1962. Mbr., Phi Beta Kappa. Publs: On the Function of Religion in Culture, 1940; Foundations of Western Thought (co-author), 1962. Contbr., The Philosophy of George Santayana, 1941, & var. jrnls. Recip., John Simon Guggenheim Fellowship, 1947-48. Address: 65 E. 96th St., N.Y., NY 10028, U.S.A. 2, 6, 13, 55.

ROSENTHAL, Judah M., b. 21 Jan. 1904. Educator; Librarian. Educ: State Sem. for Jewish Tchrs., Warsaw, Poland, 1926; Friedrch-Wilhelm Univ., Berlin,1928-32; Hochschule fur die Wissenschaft des Judentums, Berlin, 1928-32; ordained Rabbi, ibid, 1938, Univ. of Leipzig, 1936-38; Ph.D., Dropsie Coll., Phila., Pa., U.S.A., 1942. Appts. incl: Prof. of Biblical Exegesis, Coll. for Jewish Studies, 1944-69; Libn., ibid; Assoc. Ctr. for Jewish-Christian Studies, Chgo. Theological Sem. & Coll. of Jewish Studies, 1966-69; Mbr. Edit. Bd., Ency. Judaica, Jerusalem, Israel, 1970-71. Mbrships: Fellow, Am. Acad. for Jewish Rsch., N.Y.; Alumni Assn., Dropsie Univ.; Soc. of Biblical Lit. & Exegesis; Am. Jewish Histl. Soc.; Histl. Soc. of Israel. Publs. incl: Hiwi Ha-Balkhi, 1949; Studies & Texts in Jewish History & LIterature, 2 vols., 1967; Ed., Perspectives in Jewish Learning, Vol. III, 1967; Ed., Meyer Waxman Jubilee Volume, 1967. Contbr. to periodicals & collective works in English, Hebrew & Yiddish. Hons: Moses B. Newman Award, Hebrew Acad. of N.Y., 1958. Address: Rehov Hameshoreret Rachel 10, Bet Hakerem, Jerusalem, Israel. 55.

ROSENTHAL, Lawrence Michael, b. 2 Jan. 1935. Investment Banker; Real Estate Developer. Educ: B.S., Wharton Schl., Univ. of Pa.; Harvard Bus. Schl., 1956-57. Appts: Chmn. & Chief Exec. Off., L.M. Rosenthal & Co., Inc.; Pres. & Chief Exec. Off., L.M. Rosenthal Properties, Inc., & The Lenox Fund; Dir., Arnav Inds., Inc. Eldon Inds., Inc., Masters, Inc., Security Supvsn. Corp., Police Athletic League, Am. Coun. for Nationalities Serv., Brotherhood in Action, Inc.; Trustee, The Lenox Schl., The L.M. Rosenthal Fndn. Address: 666 Fifth Ave., N.Y., NY 10019, U.S.A. 2.

ROSENTHALIS, Moshe, b. 18 Nov. 1922. Painter. Educ: M.A., Univ. of Vilnius, Lithuania (U.S.S.R.), 1950. Appts: Tchr., Wizo H.S. of Art, 1958-, Midrash Lemozim Tchrs. Coll., 1964-; Ldr., Study Grps., Univ. of Tel-Aviv, 1969-71, Univ. of Bar-Han, 1968-71; Tchr., Art Acad. 'Bezalel', 1972-73. Represented in the collects. of govt. mus., U.S.S.R. & Helena Rubinstein Mus., Tel-Aviv. Hons: Red Star, U.S.S.R., 1943; Victory Medal, U.S.S.R., 1945; Letter of Merit, U.S.S.R., 1953; Histadrut Prize, Israel, 1966. Address: 15 Fichman Str., Ramat-Aviv, Tel-Aviv 69027, Israel. 55.

ROSENZWEIG, Norman, b. 28 Feb. 1924. Psychiatrist. Educ: Univ. Coll.; N.Y. Univ., 1941-44; M.B., Chgo. Med. Schl., 1947; M.D., ibid, 1948; M.S., Mich. Univ., 1953. Appts: Sr. Clin. Instr.-Lectr., Dept. Psych., Mich. Univ. Med. Schl., Ann Arbor, 1952-63; Chmn., Dept. Psych., Sinai Hosp., Detroit, Mich.; Asst.-Prof., Dept. Psych., Wayne State Univ., Schl. Med., Detroit, 1961; Assoc. Clin. Prof., Dept. Psych., Mich. State Univ., Coll. Human Med., Lansing. Mbrships. incl: Fellow, Coun. on Int. Affairs, 1970-; Chmn., ibid, 1973-; Reference Comm., 1973-; Int. Affairs Survey Team, 1973; Arrangements Comm., Annual Meeting, Detroit, Mich., 1974; Am. Psych. Assn.; Fellow, Am. Coll. of Psych.; AMA; AAUP; AAAS; Pres. Elect., 1974; num. comms. inclng. Chmn., Comm. on Awards & Resolutions, 1973- & Comm. for Planning Scientific Progs., 1973-74; Mich. Psych. Soc.; Pan Am. Med. Assn.; British Soc. of Clin. Psychs.; V.Chmn., Sect. on Psych., Mich. State Med. Soc., 1972-73; N.Y. Acad. of Scis. Publs: Community Mental Health Programs in England: An American View, 1974; contbr. of articles to profl. publs. Hons. incl: Physn's. Recognition Award, AMA, 1972; Gold Award, 127th Annual Meeting, Am. Psych. Assn., Detroit, 1974. Address: c/o Sinai Hosp. of Detroit, 6767 W. Outer Dr., Detroit, MI 48235, U.S.A.

ROSITZKY, Simon, b. 31 Mar. 1905. Merchant. Educ: B.S., Univ. of Mo., 1926. Appts: V.P., Mercantile Jobbing Co.; Pres., ibid; V.P., United Dept. Stores; Pres., ibid. Mbrships: Pres. & Chmn. of Bd., Am. Humanics; Pres., Pony Express Coun., & Exec. Comm., Mo. Ctrl. Region, Boy Scouts of Am.; Pres., St. Joseph Audubon Soc.; Masonic Orders & Shrine; St. Joseph Country Club; St. Joseph Booster Club. Silver Beaver Award, 1944, Silver Antelope Award, 1956, Boy Scouts of Am.; Pro Deo et Juventute, Diocese of Kan. City, St. Joseph, 1968; Serv. to Mankind Award, Sertoma (Local & Regional), 1973; L.H.D., Mo. Valley Coll., 1972. Address: 104 Winston Pl., St. Joseph, MO 64506, U.S.A.

ROSKILL, Stephen Wentworth, b. 1 Aug. 1903. Historian. Educ: Royal Naval Colls. Osborne, Dartmouth & Greenwich, U.K. Appts. incl: Official Naval Histn., Cabinet Off., 1948-61; Lees Knowles Lectr., Cambridge Univ., 1961; Disting. Vis. Lectr., U.S. Naval Acad., Annapolis, 1965; Richmond Lectr., Cambridge Univ., 1967. Fellowships: Churchill Coll., Cambridge; British Acad.; Royal Histl. Soc. Mbr. & V.P., Navy Records Soc. Publs. inincl: A Merchant Fleet in War, 1962; The Art of Leadership, 1964; Naval Policy between the Wars, Vol. I 1968, Vol. II 1972, Vol. III 1974; Ed., Hawkey, Man of Secrets, Vol. I, Documents Relating to the Naval Air Service 1908-18, 1969. Hons. incl: M.A., Cambridge Univ.962; LL.D., ibid, 1971; C.B.E., 1971. Address: Frostlake Cottage, Malting Lane, Cambridge CB3 9HF, U.K. 1, 3.

ROSKOTHEN-SCHERZINGER, Alice (Mrs.), b. 9 Nov. 1902. Artist; Sculptor. Educ:

Old Acad. of Arts, Karlsruhe, Baden, Germany; Painting & Interior Arch., Phila. & N.Y., U.S.A.; Sculpture, Siegsdorf & Munich, Germany. Exhibs., 1931-73; Baden-Baden, Germany; Freiburg; Offenburg; Cologne; Stuttgart; Denzlingen; Int. Forum Burg Liebenzell; Bad Dürrheim (Black Forest). Mbrships: Friends of Modern Arts, Baden-Baden; GEDOCK (German-Austrian Lady-Artists), Freiburg, Baden; Fndr., Kulturkreis Denzlingen, ibid. Author of Alice Roskothen-Scherzinger, 1972. Address: D7737 Bad Dürrheim (Schwarswald) Breslauerstrasse, 7, Fed. Repub. of Germany.

ROSNER, M. Norton, b. 17 Aug. 1931. Business Executive. Educ: B.S., Univ. of Pa., 1953; M.B.A., Univ. of Mich., 1965. Appts. incl: Acct., Systems Analyst, Processing Specialist, Mgr. Overhd. Standards, R.C.A., Camden, N.J., 1953-62; Supvsr., Methods & Prog. Dev., & Internal Cons., Forward Model Planning Systems, Ford Motor Co., Dearborn, Mich., 1962-66; Asst. Controller, NACPG & V.P. & Dir. of Planning, NACPG, Singer Co., N.Y.C., 1966-70; Treas. & V.P. of Finance, Popular Sevs., Passaic, N.J., 1970-72; Dir., Financial Planning & Analysis, Xerox Corp., Stamford, Conn., 1972-. Mbrships. incl: Dir., Parcel Post Assn., 1970-71; Dir., Upper Saddle River Teen Ctr.; Am. Mgmt. Assn.; Planning Execs. Inst.; Systems & Procedures Assn. Contbr. to profl. jrnls. Address: 54 Pequot Ln., New Canaan, CT 06840, U.S.A. 6.

ROSQUETA-ROSALES, Lily M. (Mrs. Rodolfo Ch. V. Rosales), b. 3 Jan. 1932. Associate Professor; University Officer. Educ: B.Sc. in Ed., 1952; M.A., 1957; Ed.D., 1959. Appts: Engl. Instr., Univ. of Philippines, 1952-57; Res. Hall Dir., ibid, 1958; Sr. Guidance Counselor & Asst. Prof. of Guidance & Counseling, 1960-67; Off. i/c, Counseling & Testing Ctr., 1966-67; Assoc. Prof., Profl. Educ., 1968-; Off. i/c. Guidance Lab., 1970-. Mbrships: Fellow, Psychol. Assn. of Philippines; Assn. Int. de Psychologie Appliqué. Fndng. Mbr. & Dir., Philippine Guidance & Personnel Assn.; Am. Personnel & Guidance Assn.; Philippine Mental Hlth. Assn.; YMCA; Girl Scouts of Philippines. Publs: Ed., The Guidance Journal, 1972; num. articles in profl. jrnls. Address: 62 Roces Ave., U.P. Campus, Quezon City, D505, Philippines. 5, 138.

ROSS, Alan Strode Campbell, b. 1 Feb. 1907. University Professor. Educ: B.A., Balliol Coll., Oxford, U.K.; 1929. Appts: Asst. Lectr.-Lectr., Engl. Lang., Leeds Univ., 1929-40; For. Off., 1940-45; Lectr., in Engl. Lang., Birmingham Univ., 1946; Rdr., ibid, 1947; Prof., 1948; Prof. of Linguistics, 1951. Mbrships. incl: Corres. mbr.; Suomalaisugrilainen Seura; Philological Soc.; Liveryman, Worshipful Co. of Grocers; Viking Soc.; Engl. Place-name Soc. Publs. incl: Essentials of Anglo-Saxon grammar, 1948; Etymology, 1958; Essentials of German grammar, 1963; The Durham Ritual (co-author), 1969; How to pronouce it, 1970; Don't say it, 1973. Contbr. to jrnls. Hons: Schlrship. in Astronomy, Balliol Coll., Oxford, 1925; M.A., Oxon.; M.A., Birmingham. Address: c/o Lloyds Bank, Winslow, Buckingham, U.K. 1, 3, 34, 47.

ROSS, Angus, b. 19 July 1911. University Professor. Educ: M.A., Univ. of New Zealand; Ph.D., Cambridge, U.K. Appts: Lectr., Hist., Univ. of Otago, Dunedin, N.Z., 1936-56; Rdr., ibid, 1956-64; Prof., 1965-74; Dean, Fac. of Arts & Music, 1959-61; Temp. Vis. Lectr., Univ. of Cambridge, U.K., 1971. Mbrships. incl: N.Z. Univ. Grants Comm., 1967-74; Coun.,

Univ. of Otago, 1951-55; Fndn. Chmn., Otago Regional Comm., N.Z. Hist. Places Trust. Publs: 23 Battalion, 1959; New Zealand Aspirations in the Pacific in the 19th Century, 1964; Ed., New Zealand's Record in the Pacific Islands in the 20th Century, 1969; contbr. to books & jrnls. Hons. incl: Mil. Cross, 1943 & Bar, 1944; Aristion Andrias, Greek Order of Valour, 1944; Efficiency Decoration, N.Z. Army, 1957; Commonwealth Fellow, St. John's Coll., Cambridge, 1962; Smuts Fellow in Commonwealth Studies, Cambridge, 1970. Address: Hist. Dept., Univ. of Otago, Dunedin, New Zealand. 38.

ROSS, C. Howard, b. 6 July 1890. Retired Physician. Educ: A.B., Univ. of Mich., 1916; M.D., ibid, 1931. Appts: Village Schl. Master, 1909-1911; Instr., Bot., Univ. of Mich., 1913-16; H.S. Instr., Physiol. & Chem., Moline, Ill., & Sioux City, Iowa, 1916-17; Gen. Mgr., Union Malleable Iron Co., E. Moline, Ill., 1924-27; Instr., Internal Med., Univ. of Mich. Med. Schl., 1932-36; Med. Prac. (Geriatrics), 1932-69; Lectr., Med., Hist., Herbal Lure, Geriatrics, to present date; Lectr., Med. Ethics & Econs., Univ. of Mich. Med. Schl., 1955-66 '70; Served in WW, 1st Lt., San C., & Adjuntant, Base Hosp. 51, France. Mbrships: Advsry. Coun., Am. Med. Educ. Fndn.; Gov.'s Advsry. Comm., Whitehouse Conf. on Aging, 1971;; Fellow, Am. Med. Writers' Assn. & Nat. Bd. Mbr., 1966-68, '70-72; Pres., Mich. Acad. of Gen. Prac., 1959-60; Pres., Northern Tri-State Med. Assn., 1955-56; Nat. Bd. Mbr., Am. Geriatrics Soc., 1962-69; Theta Kappa Psi; Phi Kappa Phi; Alpha Omega Alpha. Author of 64 articles in profl. jrnls. Guest Ed., The New Physn., 1961. Recip. of Swanberg Disting. Serv. Award, 1967. Address: 1725 Glastonbury Rd., Ann Arbor, MI 48103, U.S.A. 8.

ROSS, Dorothy M. Business Executive. Educ: Grad., Bethesda Chevy Chase H.S., Md. Appts: Supvsr., Bata Shoe Factory, 1939-40; Civil Serv. Comm., Wash., D.C., 1940; Sec.-Clerk, Geo. F. Muth Co. Inc., 1941-47; Supvsr. Hotel, Motel Reservations Dept., Am. Automobile Assn., Wash., 1947-62; Exec. V.P., Gen. Mgr., Automotive Org. Team, Inc., 1963-; I/c. Hall of Fame Prog. & Disting. Serv. Citation progs., ibid, & Ed., newsletter. Hons: Disting. Women's Award, Northwood Inst., 1971; Atomotive Org. Team Disting. Serv. Citation, 1972; Num. awards, ch. activities. Address: 5300 Perrine Rd., Midland, MI 48640, U.S.A. 5.

ROSS, Mabel, b. 26 Dec. 1908. Physician. Educ: B.S., M.D., Univ of Iowa Med. Schl., Iowa City; M.P.H., Harvard Univ., Schl. of Pub. Hlth., Mass. Appts: Instr., Psych., John Hopkins Hosp., Balt., Md.; Dir., Outpatient Dept., Colo. Psychopath. Hosp., Denver; Dir., Guidance Ctr. of Buffalo, N.Y.; Asst. in Psych., Mill Hill Hosp., London, U.K.; Commissioned Off. of U.S. Pub. Hlth. Serv.; Prof., Hlth. Care Servs., Schl. of of Pub. Hlth., Univ. of Ill.; Prof., Dept. of Psych., Abraham Lincoln Schl. of Med., ibid; Asst. Surg. Gen., U.S. Pub. Hlth. Serv., 1971. Mbrships: Am. Psych. Assn.; Am. Pub. Hlth. Assn.; Am. Acad. of Child Psychs.; N.Y. Acad. of Med.; Grp. for Advmt. of Psych.; Pan-Am. Med. Assn. Co-author of You & Your Aging Parents & of var. articles in profl. jrnls. Recip. of Mental Hlth. Award, Am. Pub. Hlth. Assn., 1971. Address: c/o Schl. of Pub. Hlth., Univ. of Ill. at the Med. Ctr., P.O. Box 6998, Chicago, IL 60680, U.S.A. 5, 17, 112.

ROSS, Nathaniel, b. 11 June 1904. Physician; Psychiatrist; Psychoanalyst. Educ: A.B., Columbia Coll., 1924; Columbia Univ. Grad. Schl., 1925; Coll. Physns. & Surgs.,

Columbia Univ., 1929; N.Y. Psychoanalytic Inst. (Cert.), 1937-41. Appts: Instr., Psych., N.Y. Univ. Med. Schl., 1931-36; Asst. Clin. Prof., 1936, 41; Assoc. Clin. Prof., 1952, 55; Assoc. Clin. Prof., Psych., SUNY, 1955-60; Clin. Prof., Psych. 1960-; Trng. Analyst, Am. Psychoanalytic Assn., 1948-. Mbrships: Fellow, N.Y. Psychoanalytic Inst. & Soc., Am. Psych. Assn., Am. Psychoanalytic Assn., & Int. Psychoanalytical Assn., Royal Soc. of Med.; N.Y. Acad. of Med.; N.Y. Soc. Clin. Psych.; Med. Advsry. Bd. Hamptons Hosp.; Phi Beta Kappa; Alpha Omega Alpha. Co-ed., Author of 25 chapts., Annual Survey of Psychoanalysis, vols. 1-X. Assoc. Ed., Jrnl. of Am. Psychoanalytic Assn., 1952-72. Contbr. of articles to jrnls. Address: 830 Park Ave., N.Y., NY 10021, U.S.A. 6, 14, 17, 30, 55.

ROSS, Romaine Kay, b. 7 Oct. 1903. Barrister; Solicitor. Educ: Grad., Osgoode Hall Law Schl., Toronto, Canada, 1931; LL.B., Univ. of Toronto, 1937; LL.M., 1943. Appts: Legal Prac., St. Catharines, Ont., 1931-; K.C., 1947; Counsel, Judicial Comm., H.M. Privy Coun.; Submitted brief, Spec. Comm. of Senate of Canada on Human Rights & Fundamental Freedoms; Mayor, Port Dalhousie, 1949; Alderman St. Catharines City Coun., 1951-60. Mbrships: Past, Coun., Canadian Bar Assn.; Past Pres., Ont. Assn. Childrens Aid Socs.; Canadian Authors Assn.; St. Catharines Golf & Country Club; Port Dalhousie Yacht Club. Publs: Local Government in Ontario, 1949,'62; Regional Government in Ontario, 1970. Address: 18 South Dr., St. Catharines, Ont., Canada, 88.

ROSS, Shirley Walker, b. 21 Apr. 1923. Cosmetologist; Writer. Educ: Bus. Coll., Chgo.; Beauty Schl., Burlington, Iowa; Liberty Beauty Schl., Peoria, Ill. Appt: Pres., Lamoine Unit 25. Mbrships: Chmbr. of Comm.,; Repub. Women. Publs: Involvere; Spoon River Lore. Author, poetry & prose features. Contbr., newspapers & radio progs. Radio & TV appearances. Address: 1206 E. Jackson St., Macomb, IL 61455, U.S.A. 11, 120.

ROSS, Stanley, b. 18 Jan. 1914. Newspaper Editor; Author. Educ: B.S.S., CCNY; grad. courses, Univs. of Caracas & La Plata. Appts: Ed., Long Beach Line, 1940; Corres., S. Am., to N.Y. Times & Assoc. Press., 1941-44; Pres. & Gen. Mgr., Latin Am. Press Syndicate (inclng. 1 yr. in Off. of Strategic Servs), 1944-46; Ed. & Pres., daily El Caribe, Dominican Repub., 1947-48; Ed., Publr., Pres., The Star, Wilmington, Del.; Ed., The Amsterdam News, 1950-51, El Diario de Puerto Rico, 1952, & The S.W. Citizen, Lake Charles, La., 1953; Ed.-in-Chief & Assoc. Publr., El Diario (N.Y. daily), 1955-63; Ed. & Publr., El Tiempo, N.Y., 1964-69; Ed.-in-Chief & Gen. Mgr., The Bklyn. Eagle, 1963-64; Ed. & Publr., 'El-Mundo', 1969-73; Ed.-in-Chief, La Prensa (N.Y. daily); Exec. Ed., ABC de las Americas; currently Int. Ed., ABC, Madrid & N.Y.; Cons. to U.S. Congress & U.S. Dept. of Justice on Latin Am. Affairs, 1955-. Mbrships: Gov., Bklyn. Mus.; Manpower Coun., N.Y.C.; Masons; Overseas Press Club; Advtng. Club of N.Y. Publs: Sunlight on my Wings: Communism in Latin America; The War for Trade in Latin America; Axel Wenner-Gren; The Sphinx of Sweden; The Battle for Oil in Latin America. Hons: Orders of Ruben Dario (Nicaragua) & Miranda (Venezuela). Address: 230 E. 48th St., N.Y., NY 10017, U.S.A. 12.

ROSS, Terence William, b. 27 Sept. 1935. Architect. Educ: Grad., Univ. of Mich., 1958. Appts: V.P., Register, Ross & Brunet, Archts.; V.P., LUNA-Ross & Assocs., Archts. & Planners. Mbrships. incl: Pres., Santa Fe Chapt.,

N.M. Soc. of Archts.; Dir., N.M. Soc. of Archts.; Chmn., Jt. Exec. Comm., Colo. & N.M. Railroad Auths.; Vice Chmn., N.M. Railroad Auth.; Pres., Railroad Club of N.M.; Chmn., Narrow Gauge Railroad Preservation Soc.; etc. Publd. Track of the Cats. Hons: Hist. Preservation Award, N.M. Arts Commn., 1971; Outstanding Serv. Award, Santa Fe Press Club. Address: 1111 Barcelona Lane, Santa Fe, NM 87501, U.S.A. 9.

ROSSE, Allianora, E. (Mrs. Don Munson). Artist. Educ: Art Acad. of the Hague, Netherlands, 1942-46. Appts: Staff Illustrator, Flower Grower Mag. (later Home Garden), 1953-69; Illustrator, Ladies Home Jrnl., Life, Womens Day & House Beautiful. Exhibs: Garden Symposium, Williamsburg, Va.; Anheuser Busch Vistors Gall., Tampa, Fla. Mbrships: Soc. of Illustrators; Garden Writers Assn. Am.; Embroiderers Guild; Am. Horticultural Soc. Books illustrated incl: The Complete Book of Chrysanthemums; Contemporary Perennials; The Amaryllis Manual; The Best Day for Every Little Girl; A Sense of Seasons; Wild Flowers to Know & Grow; The Chrysanthemum Book; House Plants.; The Iris Book; Ency. of Gardening, 1969-72; The New York Times Book of House Plants; (forthcoming) Flowering Trees & Shrubs; Flower Embroidery. Address: Haverhill, NH, U.S.A. 5, 6, 132.

ROSSEELS, Daniel E.G., b. 22 June 1912. Advertising Consultant. Educ: Royal Atheneum, Antwerp, Belgium; Kennemer Lyceum, Haarlem, Holland; Chr. Lyceum, Zutphen, ibid. Appts: Dir., J. Walter Thompson Co., Antwerp, Belgium, until 1947; Advt. Mgr., Soc. d'Editions Périodiques S.A., ibid; Dir., Rosseels Reclame NV; Dir., Tchr., Advt. Schl., Antwerp, ibid., Mbrships: Int. Deleg., Advt. Club, Antwerp; Int. Advt. Assn.; Assn. Flemish Authors. Publs. incl: Blindeman; Halfwas; Windkracht 11; Buitenlandse vrienden (novels); Met de wherry op de Westerschelde; Mijn vriend Theo en zijn Griet; De Gele Trui; Teddy. Hons: A. Rotsaert Prize, Ligue Maritime belge, 1958-60; Lode Baekelmans Prize, Royal Acad. Flemish Lit., Belgium, 1958 (both lit. award); Kt., Order, Leopold II, 1958. Address: Multatuliplein 4, 2000, Antwerp, Belgium. 87.

ROSSMAN, Betty Jean, b. 6 Apr. 1931. Real Estate Broker; College Teacher. Educ: Grad., Real Estate Inst. Appts: Pres., Owner, Gateway Assocs., Inc. Realtors, Crystal Lake, Ill., Broker, 1967-; Tchr., Real Estate Fund & License Law, McHenry Co. Coll., 1971-. Mbrships: Dir., McHenry Co. Bd. of Realtors; Sec.-Treas., ibid, 1969-70, Pres., 1971; Sec. & Dir., McHenry Co. Educl. Fndn.; Nat. Assn. Realtors; State Educ. Comm. Mbr., Ill. Assn. Realtors. Hons: Family Living Queen Award, Fed. Jr. Woman's Club, 1966; Pres. Nixon Appreciation Award, 1971. Address: 305 Crest Dr., Cary, IL 60013, U.S.A. 5, 138.

ROSSOS, Nicos, b. 12 Dec. 1925. Economist. Educ: M.A., Trinity Coll., Cambridge Univ., U.K.; Grad., Schl. of Bus., Harvard Univ., U.S.A.; Appts: Exec. Dir., Family wine bus., Cyprus, 1949-64; Econ. Cons., 1965-70; Mng. Dir., food industry, 1970-; Mbrships. Incl: Advsry. Bd., Nat. & Grindlay's Bank Ltd., Cyprus, 1971-; Chmn., ibid, 1973-; Bd. of Dirs., Electy. Authority, ibid; Exec. Dir., Panagides Fndn.; Formerly Municipal Councillor, Limassol, 1969-71; Served in Cyprus Govt. Bds.; Cyprus Govt. Deleg., UN Symposium of Indl. Dev.; Ch. of Cyprus rep., World Conf. of Christian Youth, Oslo, Norway; Served as Chmn., Panagides Fndn. & Schl. for Retarded Fndn.; Sec.,

Limassol Schl. Comm. & Children's Holiday Camps Fndń. Publs: The External Economic Relations of Cyprus & num. studies & newspaper articles in field. Address: 10 Acad. St., P.O. Box 1160, Limassol, Cyprus. 43.

ROSTAGNI, Antonio, b. 14 July 1903. Professor. Educ: Dr., Turin Univ., Italy, 1925; Postdoct. Fellowships, K.W. Inst. für Phys. Chem., Berlin, Germany 1933; Cavendish Lab., Cambridge, U.K., 1934. Appts: Asst., Phys. Lab., Turin Univ., Italy, 1925-35; Prof., Phys., Messina Univ., 1935; Padua Univ., 1938-; Dir., Padua Sect., Istituto Nazionale di fisica nucleare, 1952-62; Dir., Rsch. Div., I.A.E.A., Vienna, Austria, 1958-59; Dean, Sci. Fac., Padua Univ., Italy, 1964-69; Mbr., Nuclear Energy Commn., 1965-72. Mbrships: Past Pres., Istituto Veneto di Sci., Lettere ed Arti; Accad. Nazionalde dei Lincei; Accad. Patavina di Sci., Lettere ed Arti; Accad. delle Sci. di Torino. Author: Papers on Optics, Geophys., Barkhausen-Kurz elec. oscillations, Ion & Atom Collisions, Nuclear Phys.; Textbooks on gen. Phys. Recip. Premio Feltrinelli Award, Accad. dei Lincei, 1956. Address: Istituto di Fisica G. Galilei, Via Marzolo 8, Padua, Italy. 56.

ROSTOCK, Palle, b. 13 Oct. 1915. Architect. Educ: self-taught, qualified mbr., Fedn. of Danish Archts., 1944-. Appts: Advsr. to Danish Bldg. Min., 1951-57; Mgr., Coop. Bldg. Ind., Ltd., 1964-. Mbrships: Chmn., Danish Assn. of Archts., 1954-73; Treas., Fedn. of Danish Archts., 1951-73. Works incl: 678 flats in Copenhagen Urban Plan; 1472 flats in Ishøj Plan (nr. Copenhagen); 1920 flats in Avedore Stn. City; 2000 flats in Lille Bierkolm Plan; sev. homes for elderly persons. Hons: Kt., 1973; 1st Prize, Bayer Contest for colourful environments. Address: KBI A/S NDR. Fasanvej 224, 2200 Copenhagen, Denmark. 43, 128.

ROSTON, Arnold, b. 29 June 1918. Educator; Advertising Consultant; Artist. Educ: C.C.N.Y., 1935-37; Nat. Acad. of Design, 1937-39; New Schl. for Soc. Rsch., 1939-40. Appts. incl: Asst. Art Dir., N.Y. Times, 1937-42; Instr., Cooper Union for Adv. of Sci & Art, 1946-53, Brooklyn Mus. Art Schl., & Pratt Inst. Grad. Schl., 1954-55, C.U.N.Y., 1972-73; Creative Dir. & Admin. Asst., MBS-RKO Teleradio Pictures, 1949-56; Pres., Roston & Company, 1958-. Mbrships. incl: Art Dirs. Club Inc., (Dir., Sec., Comm. Chmn.), Scholarship Fund, (Pres., Dir., Fndr.); Baker Hill Civic Assn., Gt. Neck, (Dir.). Art works in permanent collects. incl: Metropolitan Museum of Art, Lib. of Congress, The Vatican, Lib. of Windsor Castle, U.K. Exhibs. in num. galls. in N.Y. & N.J., etc. Book designer. Writer, art & advt. press. Recip., num. art & advt. awards. Address: 102 Station Rd., Gt. Neck NY 11023, U.S.A. 2, 6, 37, 40.

ROSTOW, Eugene V., b. 25 Aug. 1913. Lawyer; Economist. Educ: A.B., Yale Coll., 1933; King's Coll., Cambridge, 1933-34; LL.B., Yale Law Schl., 1937. Appts. incl: Law Prac., Cravath, Swaine & Moore, 1937-38; Yale Law. Fac., 1938-; Dept. of State, 1942-44; Univ. of Chgo., 1942. UN Econ. Commn. for Europe, 1949-50; Pitt Prof. & Fellow, King's Coll., Cambridge, 1959-60; Dean, Yale Law Schl., 1955-65; Undersec. of State, 1966-69; Eastman Prof. & Fellow, Balliol Coll., Oxford, 1970-71. Mbrships. incl: Advsry. Coun., Peace Corps, 1961; Trustee, Walter Meyer Inst. of Legal Rsch., 1958-65; Judicial Coun. of Conn., 1955-65; Am. Law Inst.; AAAS; Phi Beta Kappa; Alpha Delta Phi. Publs. incl: A National Policy for the Oil Industry, 1948; Planning for Freedom, 1959; The Sovereign Prerogative,

1962; Law, Power, & the Pursuit of Peace, 1968; Final Report, President's Task Force on National Communications Policy, 1968; Ed., Is Law Dead?, 1971; Peace in the Balance, the Future of American Foreign Policy, 1972. Hons. incl: LL.D., Cambridge, 1967; Kt., Legion of Hon., France, 1962; Grand Cross, Order of the Crown, Belgium, 1969. Address: Yale Law Schl., New Haven, CT 06520, U.S.A. 1, 2.

ROTELLA, Angelina Theresa. Banker. Educ: B.A., Rutgers Newark Coll. of Arts & Scis., 1952. Appts: Audit Clerk, 1st Bank & Trust Co., Perth Amboy, N.J., 1952-64, Asst. Auditor, 1964-65, Auditor, 1965-69; Asst. Auditor, Nat. State Bank, Perth Amboy, 1969-71; Asst. V.P., Nat. State Bank, Elizabeth, 1971-. Mbrships: Nat. Assn. of Bank Women; Am. Inst. of Banking; Rutgers Alumni Assn. Address: 365 Prospect St., Perth Amboy, NJ, U.S.A. 5.

ROTENSTREICH, Joshua, b. 27 Dec. 1910. Advocate. Educ: M.A., LL.D., Univ. of Jan Casimir, Lvov, Poland. Appts: Mbr., Law Coun., Israel; Former Lectr., law fac., H.S. of law & econ., Tel Aviv; Mbr., Judges Appt. Comm.; Pres., Press Coun., 1974-. Mbrships: Pres., Jewish Advocates Assn., Israel Bar; Chmn., Bar Coun.; Sev. govt. comms.; Rotary Club (governing body); Int. Bar Assn.; World Peace Thru' Law Ctr.; Hon. mbr., Jrnlsts. Assn. Publs: History of Arab National Movement, 1937; Articles in newspapers & legal jrnls. Recip., Israel Bar Award for servs. to legal prof., 1972. Address: 25 Ibn Guirol St., Tel Aviv, Israel. 55, 94.

ROTENSTREICH, Nathan, b. 1914. Professor of Philosophy, Educ: M.A., Hebrew Univ., Jerusalem, 1936, Ph.D., ibid, 1938. Appts. incl: Prin., Youth Aliyah Tchrs. Trng. Coll., 1944-51; Dean of Humanities, Hebrew Univ., 1957-61; Rector, ibid, 1963-69; Vis. Prof. of Philos., Grad. Ctr., CCNY, 1969-70; Vis. Fellow, Ctr. for the Study of Democratic Insts., 1971; Hd., Inst. of Philos., Hebrew Univ., 1972-. Mbrships: Int. Inst. of Philos.; Israel Acad. of Scis. & Humanities; Assoc., Ctr. for the Study of Democratic Insts. Publs. Incl: Between Past & Present - An Essay on History, 1958; Basic Problems of Marx's Philosophy, 1965; Tradition & Reality, 1972; Philosophy - The Concept & Its Manifestations, 1973. Recip., Israel Prize for Humanities, 1963. Address: The Hebrew Univ., Jerusalem, Israel.

ROTH, Andrew, b. 23 Apr. 1919. Writer. Educ: B.S.S., CCNY; M.A., Columbia Univ.; Univ. of Mich.; Harvard Univ. Appts. incl: For. Corres., The Nation, N.Y. & Star Weekly, Toronto, Canada, 1946-50; London Ed., Singapore Standard & France Observateur, 1950-60; Rsch. Ed., Parliamentary Profiles, 1958-72; Pol. Corres., Manchester Evening News, 1972-. Mbr. Phi Beta Kappa, 1939. Publs: Japan Strikes South; French Interests & Policies in the Far East; Dilemma in Japan; The Business Background of MPs; MP's Chart; General Election Forecast; Enoch Powell-Tory Tribune; Heath & the Heathmen; Can Parliament Decide? Address: 34 Somali Road, London NW2, U.K. 3.

ROTH, H. Peter Frederick, b. 11 Nov. 1942. Art Expert of the Far East. Educ: Sinol., Univ of Zürich, Switzerland. Appts: Proprietor & Dir., "Collection R" Ltd., Zürich, Int. Fine Art Antiques of the Far East & Europe; Councillor, Fndn. to Preserve Tibetan Sacred Art for Exile Tibet, S.E.T.S.E., Lenzburg. Mbrships: Pres., Chinese Art Club Int., 1964; Gesellschaft für Asienkunde; Rietburg Gesellschaft, Zürich;

Aarg. Kunstverein, Aarau; Asia Soc., N.Y., U.S.A.; Metropol. Mus. of Art, N.Y.; Cleveland Mus. of Art; Keramik-Freunde der Schweiz. Publs: Collection "R", 1966; Newspaper & mag. articles. Address: Bärenburg, CH-5600 Lenzburg, Switzerland. 133.

ROTHBERG, Joseph, b. 1909. Executive. Educ: MIT; Boston Univ. Appts: Sound Recording Cons., 1930-33; Rsch. Asst., Harvard Univ., 1932; Audio Visual Asst., Northeastern Radio, 1933-38; Newsreal Cameraman, Paramount News, 1935, Graphic Films, 1938-48, WOIX TV, 1956 & CBS TV 1950-58; War Corres., News—Reel Pool, W/RAF, 1943-44; Pres., Dekko Film Prodns. Inc., Dir., United Broadcasting Corp. & Pres., Ballantyne Radio Corp; Mgr. Ops., S.P.H.-O.I.D., Harvard Univ., 1971. Mbrships: Audio Engrng. Soc.; Bd. of Mgrs., Soc. of Motion Picture & TV Engrs., Broadcast Execs. Club; Delta Kappa. Address: 29 Harold St., Sharon, MA 02067, U.S.A.

ROTHENSTEIN, (Sir) John Knewstub Maurice, b. 11 July 1901. Writer; Director of Art Galleries; University Professor. Educ: M.A., Worcester Coll., Oxford; Ph.D., Univ. Coll., London. Appts: Asst. Prof., Art Hist., Univ. of Ky., U.S.A., 1927-28, Univ. of Pitts., 1929; Dir., City Art Gall., Leeds, U.K., 1932-34, Sheffield, 1933-38; Dir., The Tate Gall., London, 1938-64; Rector, Univ. of St. Andrews, 1964; Prof., Art Hist., Fordham Univ., N.Y., U.S.A., 1967-68, Agens Scott Coll., Ga., 1969-70; Disting, Prof., CUNY, 1971-72; Regents' Lectr., Univ. of Calif., 1973. Mbrships: Pres., Friends of the City Art Colls., 1973; Hon., Chelsea Arts; Athenaeum. Publs. incl: British Artists & the War, 1931; An Introduction to English Painting, 1934; Augustus John, 1944; Modern English Painters, 4 vols., 1952-74; The Tate Gallery, 1958; British Art since 1900, 1962. Hons: C.B.E. 1948; Kt., 1952; LL.D., New Brunswick, Canada, 1961, St. Andrews, 1962; Kt.-Cmdr., Order of the Aztec Eagle of Mexico, 1953; Fellow, Worcester Coll., Oxford, 1963. Address: Beauforest House, Newington, Dorchester-on-Thames, Oxford, OX9 8AG, U.K. 1, 19, 34, 43.

ROTHMEYER, Helmut Bruno, b. 28 Sept. 1911. Certified Public Accountant; Tax Lawyer. Educ: Grad., Commercial Acad., Prague, Czechoslovakia, 1930. Appts: Author, War Jrnl., Gen. Staff. German 7th Army, 1943-44; Sybdic, Union of Bavarian Mining Enterprises, Schwarzenbach, Germany, 1947-64; Tax Lawyer, 1951-; Cert. Pub. Acct., 1952-. Mbrships: Chmbr. of Cert. Pub. Accts., Dusseldorf; Chmbr. of Tax Lawyers, Nuremberg. Address: Nuremberg, Pilotystrasse 20, German Federal Repub. 43.

ROTHSCHILD, Richard C., b. 24 Mar. 1895. Writer; Lecturer; Public Relations Counsel. Educ: B.A., Yale Univ., 1916. Appts: Ensign, U.S. Naval Aviation, WW I; Bd. of Dirs., Parents Mag., 1928-46; Am. Jewish Comm. 1938-; Chmn., Survey Comm., ibid, 1939; Exec. Comm., Gen. Jewish Coun., 1939-40; Planner, Dir., campaign against anti-Semitism in in U.S., 1938-50; Propaganda Advsr. to Gov. Rockefeller, Coord., Inter-Am. Affairs, 1941-44. Publs: Paradoxy, the Destiny of Modern Thought, 1931; Reality & Illusion, 1934; Three Gods Give an Evening to Politics, 1936. Address: 1165 Park Ave., N.Y., NY 10028, U.S.A. 6, 55.

ROTHSCHILD, Ya'acov, b. 23 Dec. 1909. Graduate Library School Director. Educ: Goethe Univ., Frankfort; Univ. of Heidelberg; Grad. Lib. Schl., Hebrew Univ., Jerusalem;

D.phil. Appts: Tchr., var. Jewish secondary schls. Germany, 1934-38; Prin., Elem. Schl., Israel, 1940-48; Dpty. Chmn., Bd. of Educ., Jewish Displaced Persons Camps, Am. Occupation Zone, Germany, 1948-49; Educl. Supt., Dept. of Youth Aliyah, Israel Agcy., 1950-57; Sr. Libn., Jewish Nat. & Univ. Lib., Jerusalem, 1957-69; Dir., Grad. Lib. Schl., Hebrew Univ., Jerusalem, 1969-. Mbrships: Israel Lib. Assn.; Israel Soc. of Special Libs. & Info. Servs.; World Union of Jewish Studies. Jerusalem. Publs: 60 articles in profl. jrnls. Hons: Shohelman Prize, Grad. Lib. Schl., Hebrew Univ., 1958. Address: 14 Rehov Alfasi, Jerusalem 92303, Israel.

ROTHSTEIN, Samuel, b. 12 Jan. 1921. University Professor. Educ: B.A., Univ. of B.C., Canada, 1939; M.A., ibid, 1940; B.L.S., Univ. of Calif., U.S.A., 1947; Ph.D., Univ. of Ill., U.S.A., 1954. Appts. incl: Asst. Univ. Libn., Univ. of B.C., Can., 1954-57; Assoc. Univ. Libn., 1957-60; Act. Univ. Libn., 1961-62; Dir. & Prof., Schl. of Libnship., 1961-70; Prof. of Libnship., 1970-. Mbrships: Past Pres., B.C. Lib. Assn.; Can. Lib. Assn.; ALA; Pacific N.W. Lib. Assn., Past Pres.; Assn. of Am. Lib. Schls., Past Pres., Bibliographical Soc. of Can.; Can. Assn. of Lib. Schls. Publs: Monographs: The Development of Reference Services, 1955; Training Professional Reference Services, 1955; Training Professional Librarians for W. Canada,· 1957; As We Remember It, 1970 & 35 articles in jrnls. Address c/o Schl. of Libnship., Univ. of B.C., Vancouver 8, B.C., Canada. 2, 88.

ROUDYBUSH, Franklin, b. 17 Sept. 1906. U.S. Foreign Official. Educ: M.A., Ph.D.; attended sev. univs., inclng: Paris, France, Geo. Wash., U.S.A. Harvard, ibid. Appts: Dean of For. Serv. Schl., 1931-42 & '57-71; U.S. Govt. Serv., 1942-57; Dir. of Pan Am. Inst.; Ed. of Affairs, 1938-42; Prof. of Int. Econ. Rels. Southeastern Univ., U.S.A., 1938-45; w. For. Serv. Inst. of Dept. of State, Paris, France, Strasbourg, ibid & Coun. of Europe, 1948-54; Am. Embassy, Paris, France, Lahore, Pakistan & Dublin, Ireland. Mbrships. incl: Am. Soc. of Int. Law; Delta Phi Epsilon; Assns. des Amis du Salon d'Automne, Paris, France., & France-Amerique; ibid. Publs. incl: Diplomacy & Art; Why the Tragic Collapse of the British Empire; The Twentieth Centry; The Cultural Battle; Diplomatic Language; The French System of Education. Address: 15 Ave. du Président Wilson, Paris, 16e, France. 22.

ROUHANI, Fuad, b. 23 Oct. 1907. Lawyer. Educ: LL.B. & LL.M., London Univ.; Docteur (Admin. Int.), Paris Univ. Appts: Legal Advsr., Anglo-Iranian Oil Co.; Legal Dir.-Dpty. Chmn., Nat. Iranian Oil Co.; Sec.-Gen., The Org. of Petroleum Exporting Countries (OPEC); Advsr. to Prime Min.; Sec.-Gen., Regional Coop. for Dev. (w. status of Amb.); Legal Advsr., Ctrl. Bank of Iran. Mbrships: Sec., Philharmonic Soc. of Teheran. Publs: History of OPEC (in Engl.); History of the Nationalisation of Oil in Iran (in Persian); Transl. Plato's Republic into Persian, "Elahi-Nameh" (mystical work in verse) into French for UNESCO, C.G. Jung's Answer to Job & Psychology & Religion into Persian, & B. Croce's Brevario of Estetica into Persian. Hons: Order of the "Taj" (3rd), 1960; Commendatore (Al Merito della Repubblica Italiana), 1966. Address: 16 Khiaban Rasht, Teheran, Iran. 34.

ROUSE, Sharon Lynne, b. 4 Dec. 1945. Music Specialist; Vocalist. Educ: B.A., Columbia Coll., S.C., 1967; special courses, voice, chorus, opera workshop, Brevard Music Ctr., N.C., 1970-73. Appts. incl: Tchr., Engl. & Drama, Woodruff H.S., S.C., 1967-69; Music Specialist, Choral Dir., Spartanburg Co. Schl.

Dist. 6, S.C., 1969; Mbr., Spartanburg Symph. Chorus, Spartanburg Philharmonic; appearances, var. prods., Brevard Music Ctr., Spartanburg Little Theater, choral & solo performances, var. conventions, festivals. Mbrships. incl: 1st V.P., S.C. Soc. Colonial Dames XVII Century; Spartanburg Co. Coun.; AAUW; United Fund; S.C. Educ. & Spartanburg Co. Educ. Assns.; Roebuck PTA. Hons. incl: Dist. Winner, Metropol. Coun. Audition, 1968; 2nd Place, Grad. Div., Nat. Assn. Tchrs. of Singing, 1971. Address: 619 Norwood St., Spartanburg, SC 29302, U.S.A. 22, 60, 125.

ROUSSOPOULOS, Athanase, b. 1903. Former Minister of Public Works; Professor; Author. Educ: Civil Engr., Tech. Univ. of Athens; further studies & rsch. at for. Tech. Univs. Appts: Prof., Structural Engrng., Statics & Anti-seismol., Tech. Univ. of Athens, 1930-58; Tech. Dir., Min. of Hlth., 1937; Pres., Tech. Chmbr. of Greece, 1951-58; M.P., 1961-67; Min. of Pub. Works, 1965. Mbrships: Am. Soc. Civil Engrs.; Greek Sect., European Movement. Publs: Metallic Constructions, 1934, reprinted, 1947, 65; Construct & Rejoice, 1936, reprinted, 1966; Les chaines dans la theorie des Groupes, 1948, Applied Statics, 1949, reprinted, 1951; Anti-seismic Constructions, 1949, reprinted, 1956; Calcul des constructions hyperstatiques, 1958; Theory of Elastic Complexes, 1965; Collective Mind, 1966; Religion of Love & Construction, 1966; Productive Monetary System, reprinted, 1966; Theorie des Structures Elastiques, 1967; Homo Mathematicus Constructor, 1971. Hons: Gold Cross, King Geo. 1st; Gold Cross, Order of Phoenix. Address: 79, Vassilissis Sophias Ave., Athens 140, Greece. 43.

ROUTLEY, Stuart Waldemar Leslie, b. 5 Apr. 1897. Director. Educ: Gordon Tech. Schl., Geelong; S. Melbourne Tech. Schl. Appts: 40 yrs. Staff, Metropolitan Gas & Gas & Fuel Corp., Victoria. Mbrships. incl: Royal Victoria Hon. Justices Assn., 1950-; Chmn., Festival of Empire & Remembrance, Melbourne, 1950-61; Active Victoria Returned Soldiers League, 54 yrs. (former Commdr. & Sr. V.P., 8 yrs., Life Mbr., 1950-); Red Cross (Ctrl. & Dist. Citizen Appeal Comms., 1950-72); Dir., Lord Mayor's Childrens Camp Fund, 1956-; Hon. Life Gov., Austin Hosp., 1945, Royal Children's Hosp., 1947; Life Gov., Prince Henry's Hosp., Melbourne, 1959; Life, Seymour Racing Club, Vic., 1971; Trustee, Young Oakleigh Club, 1957-; Royal Melbourne Hosp., 1959. Hons. incl: Mil. Medal, 1917; O.B,E., 1959; J.P., 1950-. Address: 1512 Dandenong Rd., Oakleigh 3166, Vic., Australia.

ROUX, Ambroise Marie Casimir, b. 26 June 1921. Company Executive. Educ: École Polytechnique; École des Ponts & Chaussées; École Supérieure d'Électricité. Appts: Engr., Dept. of Civil. Engrng., France, 1944-51; Exec. Dir., Sec. of States, Ind. & Commerce, 1952-55; Sr. V.P., Compagnie Générale d'Electricité, Paris, 1955-63, Pres., 1963-, Chmn. of Bd., 1970-; Dir., Hon. Chmn., Pétrofigaz; Chmn. of Bd., Afnor, 1972-; CIT-ALCATEL, 1966-; Compagnie Electro-Financière, 1969-; Dir., var. cos., inclng. Bd. of Dirs., Cinémateque. Mbrships: Fedn. French Inds. Hons: Cmdr. Légion d'Honneur, Cmdr. Mérite Commercial, Off. Instruction Publique. Address: 17 place des Etats-Unis, 75116, Paris, France.

ROVELSTAD, Trygve A., b. 27 Sept. 1903. Sculptor. Educ: Art Inst. of Chgo.; Univ. of Wash., 1927; studies in France & U.K. Appts. incl: Asst., Lorado Taft, 1922 & Stage & Studio Asst., 1928-30; Asst. to Frederick Hibbard,

Chgo. & Fred Torrey, Chgo., 1923; Dir., Govt. Relief Proj., 1934; Artist Lithographer (later Heraldic Artist), U.S. Govt. 1944-46; Sculptor Instr., U.S. Army, Oxford, U.K., 1945; Dir.-Pres., Tryg's Sculpture, Summer Schl. Works of Art incl: 5 Medallions, Children Of The Races, Orthopedic Hosp., Seattle, Wash., 1927; Death Mask, Frank Knox, Sec. of U.S. Navy, U.S.A., 1944; Stratton Campaign Medal & Bronze Medallion, 1955; Lincoln Medal, Abraham Lincoln Assn., 1967; Pioneer Father & Pioneer Mother, heroic bronze heads, 1972; U.S. Bicentennial Medal, 1972. Mbrships. incl: Gov. & Pres., Assocd. I Will Sculptors of Chgo., Inc.; Dir., Pres., Pioneer Mem. Fndn. of Ill., Inc. & Pathfinder Inc.; Alumni Assn., Schl., Art Inst. of Chgo; Am. Artists Profl. League, N.Y.C. Recip. of num. prizes, hons. & awards for work.Address: 535 Ryerson Ave., Elgin, IL 60120, U.S.A. 8, 37, 105, 128, 131, 133.

ROWDEN, (Mrs.) Marjorie Cole, b. 4 Apr. 1924. Educator; Administrator. Educ: B.A., Agnes Scott Coll., U.S.A.; M.R.E., New Orleans Bapt. Sem.; Grad. studies, Univ. S. Miss.; Am. Bapt. Theol. Sem. Appts: Rep., S. Bapt. For. Mission Bd., Israel, 1951-57; Dir. Pub. Rels., Alumni Affairs & Asst. Prof. Relig. & Philos., Wm. Carey Coll., 1962-. Mbrships: Recording Sec., Bapt. Pub. Rels. Assn.; Corres. Sec., Hattiesburg Civic Arts Coun.; Alpha Delta Kappa; Pi Tau Chi; Assn. Bapt. Profs. Relig.; Am. Alumni Coun.; Coll. Pub. Rels. Assn. Miss. Publs: Three Davids, 1963; Flying Dragon, 1966 (2 children's books); num. articles & features, mainly in S. Bapt. mission publs.). Hons: 1st woman to receive Outstanding Alumnus of Yr. award, New Orleans Bapt. Theol. Sem., 1973; Outstanding Bus. Woman, Hattiesburg Bus. & Profl. Women's Assn., 1967; Outstanding Woman, Valeda Club, Hattiesburg Lit. Club, 1965; Citation, outstanding civic contbr., United Givers Fund. Address: 615 Woodbine Lane, Hattiesburg, MS 39401, U.S.A. 5, 125.

ROWE, David Nelson, b. 21 Oct. 1905. Professor of History & Political Science. Educ: A.B., Princeton Univ., 1927; A.M., Univ. of Southern Calif., 1930; Ph.D., Univ. of Chgo., 1935. Appts. incl: Asst. Instr., Dept. of Hist., Univ. of Southern Calif., 1929-31; Rsch. Asst. Soc. Sci., Univ. Chgo., 1931-33, Fellow in Hist., 1933-35; Lectr., Far Eastern Affairs, Princeton Univ., 1938-43; Dir., Asiatic Studies, Yale Univ., 1945-51, Dir., Study of Human Resources, 1951-54, Dir., Studies Int. Rels., 1958-60, 1965-67, Sr. Fac. Fellow, 1960-61, 1967-68, currently Prof. of Pol. Sci.; Lt.Col., USAR, 1949-59, Col., 1959-64; Lectr., Army War Coll., var. periods, 1952-67, Naval War Coll., var. periods, 1957-66, Inter-Am. Defense Coll., var. periods, 1963-68; Chmn., Nat. Coun. Schlrs., 1969-. Profl. papers & articles, var. jrnls. & publs. Recip., 2 Awards, Order of Brilliant Star, Repub. of China. Address: Sterling Library, Yale University, New Haven, CT 06520, U.S.A.

ROWEN, Ruth Halle, b. 5 Apr. 1918. Musicologist. Educ: B.A., Barnard Coll., 1939; M.A., Columbia Univ., 1941; Ph.D., ibid, 1948. Appts: Mgr., Educ. Dept., Carl Fischer, Inc., 1954-63; Assoc. Prof., Music, Chmn. Grad. Comm. in Music, CCNY, 1967-; Mbr., Doctoral Fac. in Music, CUNY, 1967-; Prof., CCNY, 1972. Mbrships: Am. Musicological Soc.; Musicianship Chmn., Nat. Fedn. of Music Clubs, 1962-; Young Artist Auditions, N.Y. Chmn., ibid, 1964-72; Nat. Comm., 1966-; A.S.C.A.P.; Phi Beta Kappa. Publs: Early Chamber Music, 1948; Hearing-Gateway to Music (co-author), 1959. Address: The

Majestic, 115 Central Park West, N.Y., NY 10023, U.S.A. 3, 5, 6, 30.

ROWLAND, Dorothy Esther, b. 25 Jan. 1914. Professor; Librarian. Educ: B.S., Univ. of Conn., 1937; M.S., Syracuse Univ., 1950; grad. work, Columbia Univ., Springfield Coll., Am. Int. Appts: Hd., Film & Recording Dept., Chief, Art & Music Room, Hartford Pub. Lib., 1937-50; Supvsr., Young Adults City Lib., Spfd., Mass., 1950-52; Prof. & Libn., Westfield State Coll., 1952-69, until retirement. Mbrships: Pi Lambda Sigma; Beta Phi Mu; Golden Chapt. 5, Eastern Star; King's Sons & Daughters; V.P. & Asst. Treas., Women's Fellowship; Bunker Hill Congregational Ch. Contbr., newspapers & lib. mags. Address: Pine Acres, 6 Terry Rd., Prospect, CT 06712, U.S.A. 5, 15, 42.

ROWLAND, Virgil K., b. 4 May 1909. Administrator; Educator. Appts. incl: Personnel Admin., Detroit Edison Co., Detroit, 1937-58; Asst. to Pres., 1958-64, Asst. Sec., Asst. Treas., 1958, Detroit Edison Co., N.Y.; Asst. to Chmn. of Bd., 1964; Now retd.; Cons. on Mgmt. to 38 govt. agencies, 1951-; Prof., Japan-Am. Inst. of Mgmt. Sci.; Lectr., Univ. of Hawaii. 1st Am. Mgmt. Assn. Fellow, Ldr. of More than 200 Mgmt. Seminars. Mbr., SAR. Publs. incl: Managerial performance, 1958; Managerial Performance Standards, 1960; Evaluating & Improving Managerial Performance, 1970; Inside Looking Out—The Story of a Cardiac Arrest by the Patient, 1974; more than 45 articles & papers publd. in profl.jrnls. in U.S. & Europe; composer of sacred anthem, & arranger of 2 other compositions publd. by Pro Art, 1950-51. Hons: LL.D., Ctrl. Mich. Univ., 1963. Address: 555 University Ave. 2400, Honolulu, HI 96814, U.S.A. 6, 16, 30.

ROWNEY, George Edward Penrose, b. 24 Dec. 1920. Teacher; Author. Educ: B.Sc., Dip.Ed., Univ. of Melbourne, Australia. Appts: Tchr., 1938-41; Served WWII; Staff, Melbourne Tchrs.' Coll., 1945-50; Tchr., Melbourne H.S., 1950-70; Dpty. Prin., Ashwood H.S., 1971-74; Lectr., Melbourne Metropol. Fire Brigade Schl., 1950-74. Mbrships: Victorian Royal Soc., 1952-74; Hon. Fellow, Instn. Fire Engrs., Melbourne; Australian Soc. Authors; Fly Dressers' Guild, U.K.; Ed., publr., writer, jrnl. "The Fly Fisher", Southern Fly Fishers, Australia. Publs: New General Science (w. Dr. A.V.G. James), 1953; Practical General Science Manual (w. R.W. Roberts), 1958; Pursuit of Science (w. D. Lugg), 1965. Address: 4 Riddle St., Bentleigh, Vic., Australia, 3204. 3.

ROWNTREE, H.L., b. 2 June 1914. Barrister & Solicitor. Educ: B.A., Univ. of Toronto; Osgoode Hall Law Schl. Appts: Called to Ont. Bar, 1945; Q.C., 1956; Elected to Ont. Legislature for York West, 1956; Min. of Transport, 1960; Min. of Labour, 1962; Min. of Financial & Commercial Affairs, 1966; Mbr., Ont. Treasury Bd., 1961-70; Dir., Skyline Hotels Ltd. Mbrships: Chmn., Bd. of Trustees, Ont. Sci. Ctr., 1970-72; Bd. of Queensway Gen. Hosp.; Kt. of Grace Mil. & Hospitaler, Order of St. Lazarus of Jerusalem; 33 deg. Scottish Rite Mason. Address: 39 Old Mill Rd., Apt. 904, Toronto 18, Ont., Canada.

ROXBEE COX, (Sir) Harold, see KINGS NORTON of Wotton Underwood, (The Lord).

ROY, Ardemis Serposs, b. 13 Jan. 1920. Accountant. Educ: Univ. of Pa., 1941; Univ. of Del.; St. Joseph's Coll. Appts: Schl. Bd. Dir. & V.P., Upper Merion Area Schl. Dist.; Bd. Dir. & Vice Chmn., Central Montgomery Co. Voc.-Tech. Schl.; Asst. to Treas., Vishay

Intertechnol. Inc., Malvern, Pa. Mbrships: Bd. Mbr., Emergency Aid of Pa.; Repub. Women of Pa.; Phila. Art Alliance; Pa. & Nat. Schl. Bd. Assns.; Am. Assn. of Schl. Admnstrs.; W Pk. Hosp. Auxiliary; Past Pres., ibid; Armenian Gen. Benevolent Union; Past Bd. Mbr., ibid, & Treas., Metropol. Chapt.; King of Prussia Players; Past Pres., ibid, V.P. & Treas. Address: 123 Gypsy Rd., Gulph Mills, King of Prussia, PA 19406, U.S.A. 57, 130.

ROY, Concetta Constance Cornelia Cornacchia, b. 10 Dec. 1906. Educational Administrator. Educ: B.S., Washington Sq. Coll. of N.Y. Univ., 1931; M.A., Tchrs. Coll. of Columbia Univ., 1932; M.S., Queen's Coll. of City Univ., 1958. Appts. incl: Office & Credit Mgr., N.Y., 1928-36; Tchr., Secretarial Studies, Bushwick & John Jay H. Schls., Brooklyn, 1936-42; Flushing H.S., N.Y.; Tchr., 1942-56; Voc. & Guidance Counselor, Grade Advsr. & Dean, 1944-56; Asst. Prin., 1956-72; Acting Prin., 1968-70. Mbrships: Exec. Bd., Sec., H.S. Tchrs. Assn. of N.Y.C., 1946-59; Pres., ibid, 1955-57; Exec. Bd., Sec., V.P., H.S. Asst. Prins. Assn., N.Y.C., 1957-69; Pres., ibid, 1966-68; Exec. Bd., Sec., Coun. Supvsrs. & Admins., N.Y.C., 1965-69; Treas., Retired Schl. Supvsrs. & Admins. of C.S.A., 1971-74; Co-Ldr., Fusion Pty., Dist. 23, Brooklyn; Life, Delta Pi Epsilon; Univ. Women of Am.; Liaison & Sec., Flushing H.S. P.T.A., 1944-72. Contbr. to: N.Y. Times; Daily News; World Telegram & Sun. Address: 209-01 82 Ave., Queens Village, N.Y., NY 11427, U.S.A. 5, 6, 129, 131, 138.

ROYSTER, Vermont Connecticut, b. 30 Apr. 1914. Journalist; Author. Appts: Wash. Corres., 1936-40, Chief Wash. Corres., 1946-49, Assoc. Ed., 1949-58, Ed.-in-Chief, 1958-, Wall Street Jrnl.; V.P., Dow Jones & Co., Inc., & Mbr., Exec. Comm., 1960-. Past Pres., Am. Soc. of Newspaper Eds. Publs: Journey through the Soviet Union, 1962; Main Street & Beyond (w. others), 1959; A Pride of Prejudices, 1967; articles in var. mags. Recip. of Pulitzer Prize, 1953. Address: 903 Arrowhead Rd., Chapel Hill, NC 27514, U.S.A. 1, 2, 6.

R.-PORRERO DE CHAVARI, Fernando, b. 22 Dec. 1917. Diplomat; Ambassador of Spain. Educ: LL.D., Univ. of Madrid. Appts: Prof., Int. Law, Univ. of Madrid; Diplomatic Serv., 1942-; Embassies of Spain in Brussels, Lisbon, Athens, Paris, Libya; Dir., European Pol. Affairs, For. Off.; Dir. Gen. Political Affairs; Spanish Ambassador, Athens, 1974. Hons. incl: Grand Croix du Mérite Civil, Spain; Ordre du Merite, Germany; Ordre de l'Etoile, Ethiopia; Ordre de Phenix, Greece; Ordre du Christ, Ordre de Bienfaisance, Ordre de St. Jaqued, Portugal; Cmdr., Charles III, Spain; Cmdr., Légion d'Honneur, France. Address: Embassy of Spain, Vassilissis Sofias 29, Athens, Greece.

RÜBEL, Eduard Carl Albrecht, b. 28 Feb. 1911. Judge. Educ: Law Studies, Zurich & Geneva, Switzerland, & Heidelberg, Germany; Doct., 1935; Solicitor's Patent, 1937. Appts: Substitute, Co. Ct. Horgen, 1937; V.P., ibid, 1947, Pres., 1958; Mbr., Canton Zurich's Superior Ct., 1961; Pres., Canton Zurich's Commercial Ct., 1973. Mbrships: Pres., Charity Org., 1946-50; Pres., Schl. Org., Oberrieden, 1950-56; Consistory Canton Zurich; Stubenhitzer der Ges.d. Schildner zum Schlneggen; Saffran Guild; Gelehrte Ges.; Swiss Jurists. Publs: Der kommunale Zweckverband nach Zürcher Rect, 1936; Kirchengestetz und Kirchenordnung der Zürcher Landeskirche, 1968. Address: Fachstrasse 41, CH-8942 Oberrieden, Switzerland.

RUBEN, Robert J., b. 2 Aug. 1933. Otorhinolaryngologist. Educ: A.B., Princeton Univ., 1955; M.D., Johns Hopkins Schl. of Med., 1959. Appts. incl: Prof. & Chmn., Dept. of Otolaryngol., Albert Einstein Coll. of Med., 1971-; Dir. of Serv., Lincoln Hosp., Hosp. of the Albert Einstein Coll. of Med. & Bronx Municipal Hosp. Ctr., 1971-; Attending in Surg., Montefiore Hosp. & Med. Ctr. & Morrisania Hosp., 1970-. Mbrships. incl: Am. Assn. of Anatomists; Acoustical Soc. of Am.; AAAS; AMA; Comm. on Otalaryngologic Pathol., Am. Acad. of Ophthalmol. & Otolaryngol., 1972-; Fellow, Am. Coll. of Surgs.; Fellow, Am. Laryngological, Rhinological & Otological Soc., Inc. (The Triological Soc.); Royal Soc. of Med., London; Soc. for ENT Advances in Children. Author of articles in med. jrnls. Hons. incl: Award for serv. in educl. progs., Am. Acad. of Ophthalmol. & Otolaryngol., 1972; Edmond Prince Fowler Mem. Award, 1973. Address: Dept. of Otorhinolaryngol., Rm. 3C37, Van Etten Hosp., Albert Einstein Coll. of Med., 1300 Morris Park Ave., Bronx, NY 10461, U.S.A.

RUBES, Jan, b. 6 June 1920. Opera Singer; Director; Writer. Educ: Conservatory & Acad. Music, Opera Dept., Prague Univ., Czechoslovakia. 80 operatic bass roles inclng. appearances w. Canadian Opera, & at Stratford Festival; N.Y.C. Ctr.; Ottawa Nat. Art Ctr.; Pitts.; Wash. D.C.; Chgo.; New Orleans. TV CBC Opera Prods.; Castle Zaremba series; own series Guess What. 10 yrs. radio prog., Songs of My People. Films incl: Forbidden Journey; The Incredible Journey. Musical comedies incl: South Pacific; The Sound of Music; The King & I; Man of La Mancha. Writer & creator of TV series, Guess What; & radio series, Songs of My People. Recip., Canadian Centennial Award, 1967. Address: 55 Sumner Hts. Dr., Willowdale, Ont., Canada.

RUBES, Susan Douglas, b. 13 Mar. 1925. Actress; Theatrical Producer. Educ: Barnard Univ. Fndr. Prod., Young People's Theatre, Canada, 1967-. Broadway leads incl: He Who Gets Slapped; Heart Song; Druid Circle. Hollywood films incl: Lost Boundaries; Bell Ami; Five. Mbrships: Chmn., Home & Schl. Assn., 1966-67; Bd. Mbr., Nat. Theatre Schl. of Canada, 1971-73; Caledon Ski Club; Mayfair Tennis Club. Recip., Donaldson Award, Best Broadway Performance, He Who Gets Slapped, 1965. Address: 55 Sumner Ht. Dr., Willowdale, Ont. Canada.

RUBIE, Cecil Edward Henning, b. 29 Mar. 1909. Director of Public Relations. Educ: M.A., Univ. of Sydney, Australia. Appts: Tchr., N.S.W. Dept. of Educ.; War Serv., 1941-45; Jrnlst, Provincial Press; Dir. of Pub. Rels., N.S.W. Dept. of Educ. Mbrships: Fellow, Pub. Rels. Inst. of Australia; Pres., Tchrs. Returned Serviceman's Sub-Br.; Pres., British Commonwealth Movement; Australian Coll. of Educ.; N.S.W. Tchrs. Fedn.; Australian Jrnlsts. Assn.; Univ. Club. Directed films: Music in Our Schools; School of the Air. Fndr. & Org., Annual Educ. Week in N.S.W., 1954-73. Org., Teach in the Sun, overseas tchr.-recruitment op. for N.S.W. pub. schls., 1970. Address: Public Relations Division, N.S.W. Dept. of Education, Sydney, Australia. 24.

RUBIN, Arthur H., b. 14 Aug. 1927. Educational Administrator. Educ: B.S., Schl. of Educ., N.Y. Univ., 1950; M.A., ibid., 1951. Appts. incl: Prog. Dir., Grad. Students Org., Schl. of Educ., N.Y. Univ., 1954-63; Acting Asst. Prin., & var. offs., Robert F. Wagner Jr. H.S., N.Y.C., 1958-63; Dir., Bur. of Pub.

Occasions, N.Y. Univ., 1963-. Mbrships: Many offs. in num. orgs., inclg. Eastern Bus. Tchrs. Assn.; Educ. Alumni Ass., N.Y. Univ.; Bus. Educ. Assn. of Metropolitan N.Y.; Kappa Phi Kappa; Alpha Delta Pi Securities Club Inc. Contbr. to sev. profl. jrnls. & publs. Hons: Delta Pi Epsilon, Alpha Chapt. Serv. Award, 1971; N.Y. Univ. Presidential Citation, 1971. Address: N.Y. Univ., Bur. of Pub. Occasions, 1 Washington Sq. Village, Suite 0-1, N.Y., NY 10012, U.S.A. 6, 131.

RUBIN, Berthold Freidrich Wilhelm Rudolf, b. 10 July 1911. Professor of History. Educ: Abitur, 1932; Dr.phil., Berlin, 1938; Dr.phil. habil., 1941. Appts: Dpty. Full Prof. of German, 1942; Prof., Vienna, Austria, 1943; Ed. for Osteuropa Inst., Munich, German Fed. Repub., 1952; Lectr., Erlangen, 1953; Prof., Univ. of Cologne, 1957, Full Prof., 1960; Dir., Inst. für Altertumskunde, Abteilung Byzantinistik. Mbrships: Deutsches Archaologisches Institut; Mitteldeutscher Kulturrat. Publs. incl: Theoderich und Iustinian, 1953; Prokopios von Kaisareia, 1954; Das Zeitalter Iustinians, 1960; essays, articles, var. scientific jrnls. & newspapers. Recip., Cross of Athos, 1960. Address: Hildburghauser Strasse 109, D 1000 Berlin 45, German Federal Republic. 43, 92.

RUBIN, Martin, b. 2 Nov. 1915. Biochemist. Educ: B.S., City Coll., N.Y., 1936; Ph.D., Columbia Univ., 1942. Appts. incl: Assoc. Prof. Clin. Pathol. & Biochem., Georgetown Univ., Wash. D.C., 1948-54; Dir. Clin. Chem., Georgetown Univ. Hosp., 1949-54; Assoc. Prof., Organic Chem., 1954-60; Assoc. Prof., Biochem., 1960-65; Dir., Clin. Chem., Georgetown Univ. Hosp., 1960-; Prof., Biochem., 1965-; Fac., Walter Reed Army Inst. for Rsch., Mil. Med. & Allied Scis., 1958-; Fac., Walter Reed Army Inst. of Dentistry, 1962-. Fellowships: Am. Assn. of Clin. Chems.; Hon., Assn. Clin. Biochems., U.K.; Hon., Polish Soc. of Clin. Diagnostics. Mbrships. incl: Dipl., Am. Bd. Clin. Chem.; Soc. for Rsch. in Ophthalmol.; Am. Arthritis Assn.; AMA; Am. Chem. Soc.; Sigma Xi. Author of many articles in field. Recip., Capitol Chems. Award, 1966. Address: Georgetown Med. Schl., 3800 Reservoir Rd., Wash., DC 20007, U.S.A.

RUBIN, Seymour J., b. 6 Apr. 1914. Lawyer; Professor; Government Official. Educ: B.A., Univ. of Mich., 1935; LL.B., Harvard Law Schl., 1938; LL.M., 1939. Appts. incl: Mbr., Presidential Mission to Bolivia, 1961;• Gen. Counsel, Agcy. for Int. Dev., 1962; Special Ambassador to Bolivia, 1962; U.S. Rep. to Dev. Assistance Comm., 1962-64; U.S. Rep., Spec. Comm., UN Security Coun., 1964; U.S. Rep. to UN Commn. on Int. Trade Law, 1968-70; Pres., Law, Am. Univ., 1972. Mbrships incl: Nat. Lawyers Club; Am. Law Inst.; Am. Bar Assn.; Am. Soc. Int. Law; Fed. Bar Assn. Publs: Private Foreign Investment; Legal & Economic Realities, 1956; The Conscience of the Rich Nations: The Development Assistance Committee & the Common Aid Effort, 1966; Ed. & Contbr., Foreign Development Lending - Legal Aspects, 1971; Contbr., The International Corporation, 1970; articles in legal jrnls. Recip., Grand Cross of Austria, 1966. Address: Wash. Coll. of Law, Am. Univ., Wash. DC, U.S.A. 2.

RUBINS, Jack L., b. 25 Feb. 1916. Psychiatrist; Psychoanalyst. Educ: B.Sc., CCNY, 1937; B.Med.Sc., Med. Fac. Univ. of Geneva, Switzerland, 1942; M.D., ibid, 1943; Cert. Psychoanalyst, Am. Inst. for Psychoanalysis, 1955. Appts: Staff Psych., Bkln. Jewish Hosp., 1948-50 & Treatment Clin. for Adolescents, Probation Div. N.Y.

Magistrates Ct., 1949-50; Adjunct Psych., Goldwater Hosp. & Hosp. for Jt. Diseases, 1948-52; Vis. Psych., Metropol. & Flower-Fifth Ave. Hosps., 1962-72; Cons. Psych., N.Y.C. Bd. of Educ., 1952-67; Attending Psychoanalyst, Karen Horney Clin., 1955-; Dir., Day Care Ctr., ibid, 1968-74; Dir., Mental Hlth. Clin., Flushing Hosp., 1974-; Assoc. Clin. Prof., Psych., N.Y. Med. Coll.; Trng., Supvsng. Analyst & Asst. Dean, Am. Inst. for Psychoanalysts. Mbrships. incl: Fellow, Am. Psych. Assn., Am. Acad. of Psychoanalysis, AAAS, Royal Soc. of Hlth., German Acad. for Psychoanalysis (also on Profl. Advsry. Bd.) & Am. & Int. Soc. for Soc. Psych.; Past Pres., Queen's Co. Psych. Soc. & Assn. for Advancement of Psychoanalysis. Contbr. chapts. to books & articles to sci. jrnls.; Ed., Developments in Horney Psychoanalysis, 1972. Address: 125 E. 87 St., N.Y., NY 10028, U.S.A. 6, 14, 17, 112.

RUBINSTEIN, Amnon, b. 5 Sept. 1931. Professor of Law. Educ: B.A., Hebrew Univ., Jerusalem; LL.M., ibid, 1956; Ph.D., London Schl. of Econs., U.K. Appts: Clerkship, Off. of the State Atty., Jerusalem, 1957-58; Tel Aviv Br., Fac. of Law, Hebrew Univ., Jerusalem, 1961-64; Lectr., ibid, 1964-68; Sr. Lectr., Fac. of Law, Tel Aviv Univ., 1968-70; Dean, ibid, 1969-; Assoc. Prof., 1970-. Mbrships: Pres., Int. Soc. for the Study of Comparative Pub. Law, Wash. D.C., U.S.A.; Institut de la View, Paris, France; Edit. Bd., Israel Yrbook. on Human Rights, Tel Aviv Univ.; Edit. Bd., Ha'aretz, Tel Aviv. Publs. incl: Jurisdiction & Illegality; The Constitutional Law of Israel, 2 edits.; The Enforcement of Morality in a Permissive Society, forthcoming; Num. articles in Hebrew & Engl. Address: 30 Alumim St., Ofeka, Tel Aviv, Israel.

RUBINSTEIN, Michael A., b. 28 Nov. 1911. Physician; Hematologist; Educator. Educ. incl: M.Sc., Univ. of Wilno, Poland, 1932; M.D., ibid, 1936; Postgrad. studies, Univs. of Strasbourg, Paris, Vienna & London. Appts. incl: Hematol. & Attng. Physn., Montefiore Hosp., N.Y.C., 1942-54; Fac. Mbr., Columbia Univ., 1945-54, N.Y. Med. Coll., 1948-54, Yeshiva Univ., 1940-, Loma Linda Univ. Schl. of Med., 1956-, UCLA, 1971-; Hematol. & Attng. Physn., Cedars of Lebanon Hosp. & Mt. Sinai Hosp., L.A., 1956-. Mbrships: Fellow, Am. Coll. of Physns., N.Y. Acad. of Med.; N.Y. Acad. of Sci.; AAAS; Am. Fedn. of Clin. Rsch.; Int. Soc. of Hematol. Contbr. to med. jrnls. Hons. incl: Hon. Cert. for 10 yrs. Fac. work, Schl. of Med., Loma Linda Univ., 1967. Address: 435 N. Bedford Dr., Beverley Hills, CA, U.S.A. 9, 14, 17.

RUBY, Maurice Léonce Louis Marie, b. 20 Apr. 1916. Public Relations Director. Educ: Dip., Schl. of Pol. Scis., & Schl. of Colonial Preparation, Paris, France; LL.D. Num. appts. incl: Insp., Min. of Indl. Prod., 1944; Juridical Advsr., French High Commn. in Austria, 1946; Admnstr., Cabinet of French High Commn. in Germany, 1949; Staff., Nat. Fedn. of Electronic Inds., 1956; Chief Clerk, ibid, 1958; Dir., Exterior Rels. & Documentation, 1963-; Ed. in Chief, Review of Elec. & Electronic Inds.; Sec. Gen., Assn. for the Promotion of Exports of Electronic Inds.; Sec. Gen., Int. Electronic Confs. Mbrships. incl: French Assn. of P.R.; Nat. Union of Press Attachés; Assn. of Drs. of Law; French Assn. of Publicity Dirs.; Radio Veterans; Int. Union of the Radioelec. Press. Author, La Nationalité Allemande des Origines á 1945, 1955. Recip., Kt., Order of Mil. Merit. Address: Fédération Nationale des Industries Electroniques, 16 Rue de Presles, 75740 Paris Cedex 15, France.

RUCKNO, Elizabeth Regina Caffrey, b. 22 July 1913. Accountant. Educ: Bus. Coll.

Married George Louis Ruckno 1943; Seven children. Appts. incl: Acct., Earle R. Herbert; Cert. Pub. Acct., 1931-43; Co-Fndr. & Sec., George L. Ruckno Inc. & Forty Fort Lumber Co., 1949-. Mbrships. incl: Pa. Home Builders Assn.; Nat. Assn. of Home Builders; Westmoreland Club; Wilkes-Barre, Pa.; N. Mountain Club; Pres., V.P. & Treas., Women's Serv. Club; Bd. Mbr., Cath. Youth Ctr.; Ladies of Charity; Mercy Hosp. Aux. Hons. incl. Cath. Youth Center, 1955. Address: Box 439, R.R. No. 3 Dallas, PA 18612, U.S.A.

RUDD-OTTLEY, (Mrs.) Shirley Hilma, b. 7 June 1931. Company President Behavioral Scientist & Professional Public Relations Practitioner. Educ: Bus. Studies & Econs., City of Westminster Coll., U.K.; Trng. Offs. Cert. in Tech. Educ., Bristol Univ.; Corporate P.R., N.Y., U.S.A.; Mgmt. Trng. & Behavioral Sci., Tex. Appts: Coord/Organizer, C'Wealth Tech. Trng. Wk., 1961; Mbr., Comm. to Plan Independence of Trinidad & Tobago, 1962; Acting Hd., Bus. Studies Dept., John S. Donaldson Tech. Inst., 1962; Tech. Advsr. on Bus. Studies to Min. of Educ. & Culture, Govt. of Trinidad & Tobago, 1963; Govt.'s Bus. Studies Rep. on UNESCO, 1964; Administrative Asst. to Trng. Dir., FedChem Ltd., 1964; P.R. Off., ibid, 1964-70; Currently Pres., Ldrship. Dev. Inst. Mbrships: P.R. Soc. of Am.; Placements Comm., Univ. of W. Indies; Nat. Trng. Bd., Prime Min's Off.; Ctrl. Comm. in Guidance, Min. of Educ. & Culture; Unified Chmbrs. of Ind. & Commerce. Author of profl. publs. Int. Woman of the Year 1973, Success Motivation Inst., Tex. Address: Leadership Development Inst., 76 Pembroke St., Port-of-Spain, Trinidad, W. Indies. 24.

RUDER, Doris Edith, b. 23 Mar. 1926. Educator; Consultant. Educ: B.S., Fenn Coll. (now Cleveland State Univ.), 1949; Western Reserve Univ., Cleveland, Ohio, 1953. Appts: Tchr., Cleveland Emergency Day Care Ctrs., 1944-46, Merrick House Nursery, 1946-49, Benjamin Franklin Schl., 1949-50; Nathaniel Hawthorne Schl., 1950-51; Artemus Ward Schl., 1951-56; Wm. Rainey Harper Schl., 1956-58 & Thom L. Johnson Schl., 1970- (all in Cleveland); Gardens Tchr. & Supvsr., Cleveland Schls., 1960-63; Cons., Cleveland P.S. Kindergartens, 1969-70. Mbrships: Delta Kappa Gamma; Chmn., Int. Affairs Comm., Ohio State, Assn. Childhood Educ. Int., 1971-; Cleveland Tchrs. Union. Publs: Pilgrim Church 100th Anniversary Book (compiler), 1959; Pre-school and Kindergarten Teacher Aides, 1966. Selector, Writer, Evaluator, Co-Prodr., Once Upon & Time & Here We Go 'Round the World, radio series, stn. WOBE. Hons: Martha Holden Jennings Fndn. Master Tchr. Award for Excellence, 1968. Address: 8306 Bauerdale Drive, Parma, OH 44129, U.S.A. 5, 138.

RUDNYCKYJ, Joroslav Boholan, b. 28 Nov. 1910. Professor & Head of Department. Educ: M.A., Univ. of L'vov, 1934; Ph.D., ibid, 1937. Appts: Asst. Prof. & Hd., Dept. of Slavic Studies, Univ. of Man., Winnepeg, Canada, 1949-51; Assoc. Prof. & Hd. of Dept., ibid, 1951-59; Full Prof. & Hd. of Dept., 1959-74. Mbrships: Royal Commn. on Bilingualism & Biculturalism, Ottawa, 1963-71; Pres., Canadain Linguistic Assn., 1958; Pres., Canadian Assn. of Slavists, 1958; Pres., Canadian Inst. of Onomastic Scis., 1970-72. Publs. incl: Travelogues, 6 vols., 1958-72; Manitoba Mosaic of Place Names, 1970. Hons. incl: Margaret McWilliams Medal, Winnipeg, 1971; Silver Medal, Univ. of Parana, Brazil, 1973. Address: Univ. of Man., Winnipeg, Canada.

RUDNYTSKY, Antin, b. 7 Feb. 1902. Composer; Conductor; Pianist; Professor; Critic.

Educ: Ph.D., Friedrich Wilhelm Univ., Berlin, 1926; Study w. Egon Petri, Artur Schnabel, piano; Franz Schreker, composition & Julius Pruwer, conducting; Master class, composition, w. Busoni. Num. appts. incl: Conductor, opera cos. & choruses, Ukrainian Nat. Symph. Orch., Lviv, Kharkiv & Kiev, 1920-34; Musical Dir., Cosmopolitan Stars of Opera, U.S.A., 1946-50; Kobzar Chorus, Phila., 1954-; Ukrainian Sinfonietta, 1954-; Prof., conservatories in Kjarkiv, Kiev, Lviv, 1927-35; St. Basil's Coll. & Sem., Conn., U.S.A., 1939-43; Fndr., Dir., Ocean Co. Schl. of Music, Toms River, N.J., 1943-; Fndr., Pres., Music & Concert Guild Inc., 1950-; Prof., Ind. Univ. Schl. of Music, 1963-69; Youngstown State Univ., Dana Schl. of Music, 1972-; Mbrships: Shevchenko Sci. Soc.; AAUP; Assn. of Ukranian Am. Univ. Profs.; Assoc. Mbr., Polish Inst. of Arts & Scis. Composer of operas, ballets, oratorio, cantatas, piano, chamber music, etc. Author, books on Ukrainian music, num. articles & criticisms. Hons. incl: 1st Prize, Int. Competition for Composers, Warsaw, 1937. Address: 1030 Lakehurst Rd., Rte. 37 W., Toms River, NJ 08753, U.S.A. 10.

RUDOLF, Anthony b. 6 Sept. 1942. Translator; Editor. Educ: B.A., Cambridge Univ. Mbr., Gen. Coun. Poetry Soc. Publs: Selected Poems of Yves Benefoy (trans.), 1968; The Manifold Circle (poems), 1971; Anthology of French Poetry, 1973. Hons: Runner-up Scott-Moncrieff Prize of Soc. of Authors for trans. of Yves Bonnefoy, 1969. Address: 1 Primme Gardens, London NW3 4UT, U.K. 3.

RUDOLPH, Arthur Louis Hugo, b. 9 Nov. 1906. Mechanical Engineer. Educ: B.S. in Mech. Eng., Coll. of Berlin, Germany, 1930. Appts. incl: Independent Inventor, Rocket Engine Patents, 1932; Lab. Chief, Chief Engr., Works Dir., German Rocket Ctr., Peenemuende (German Ordnance Dept.), Dev. of V2 Rocket, 1937; Tech. Dir., Rsch. & Dev. Div., Army Ballistic Missile Agcy., 1956; Project Dir., Pershing Weapon System, ibid, 1958; Dir., Rsch. & Dev. Directorate, 1960; Asst. Dir., System Engrng., Apollo Prog., NASA, 1961; Mgr., Saturn V Launch Vehicle Prog., Marshall Flight Ctr., NASA, 1963; Ret. from US Fed. Serv., 1969. Mbr., Bd. of Dirs., Huntsville Sect., AIAA, 1963-65; Nat. Chmn., Space Electronics Symposium, IEEE, 1963; Fleeos, AIAA, 1971. Hons. incl: D.Sc., Rollins Coll., Fla., 1959; Exceptional Civil Serv. Award, US Army, 1960; Exceptional Serv. Medal, Nat. Aeronautics & Space Admin., 1968 & DSM, NASA, 1969 (both for mgmt. of Saturn V Prog.). Address: 5962 Colorview Ct., San Jose, CA 95120, U.S.A. 2.

RUDOWSKI, Witold J., b. 17 July 1918. Professor of Surgery. Educ: Med. Fac., Warsaw Univ., Poland, 1936-39; Clandestine Med. Schl., ibid (during Nazi occupation), 1939-43; M.D., ibid, 1947. Appts: Dept. Neurosurg., Warsaw Univ., 1945-47; Cons. Surg., Dept. Surg., ibid, 1947-53; Marie Curie Cancer Inst., 1948-64; Dir. & Hd., Dept. Surg., Warsaw Inst. Haematol. & Blood Transfusion, 1964-; Vis. positions: Sr. Surg. Registrar, Hammersmith Hosp. Post-grad. Med. Schl., London, U.K., 1957-58; 3 months' Vis. Profships: to many Univ. Surg. Ctrs. in U.S.A., 1963; Vis. Sci., NIH, Bethesda, U.S.A., 1973. Mbr. sev. profl. orgs. Author publs. on pathophysiol of burns, haemorrhagic shock & fluid replacement, etc. & num. papers, book reviews & monographs in field. Hons: Elected 1st V.P., Int. Fedn. Surg. Colls. 1970; Hon. Fellowships: Am. Coll. Surgs., 1971, Royal Coll. Surgs., Edinburgh, 1972, W. African Coll. Surgs., 1973, Royal Coll. Surgs., England 1973 & Royal Coll. Phys. Surg., Canada, 1974; Hon.

Mbr., Polish Acad. Scis. Address: Aleja Armii Ludowej 17-1, 00-632 Warsaw, Poland.

RUELLAN, Andrée, b. 6 Apr. 1905. Artist. Educ: Schlrship. Student, Art Students League, N.Y., 1920-22; Maurice Sterne Schl., Rome, Italy, 1922-23; Acad. de la Grande Chaumiére, Paris, France; Acad. Suedoise, Paris, w. Per Krogh & Dufresne. Vis. Artist, Pa. State Univ., main summer session, 1957. Mbrships: Woodstock Artists Assn.; Phila. Watercolor Club; Art Students League of N.Y. Works incl: Murals for Sect. of Fine Arts in Post Offs., Emporia, Va., & Laurenceville, Ga.; One-Waman Exhibitions inclng. Kraushaar Gall., N.Y., 1947, 1952, 1956, 1963, Am. Acad. of Arts & Letters, 1945, Staten Island Mus., 1958, Newcomb Coll. (Tulane Univ.), drawings & prints, 1959; Retrospectives, Lehigh Univ., 1965, Storm King Art Ctr., 1966; Works in num. museams & pvte collects. Hons. incl: John Simon Guggenheim Fellowship, for creative work abroad, 1950-51; Drawing Award, Ball State Tchrs. Coll., 1958. Address: Shady, NY 12479, U.S.A.

RUETH, Marion Ursula. Librarian. Educ: M.Music, Cath. Univ. of Am., 1946; M.A.L.S., Fla. State Univ., 1962. Appts: Dir., Silver Studio of Music, Silver Spring, Md., 1944-50; Lib. Asst., St. Petersburg (Fla.) Pub. Lib., 1953-58; Music Specialist & Cataloguer, Fla. State Univ. Lib., 1958-62; Asst. Hd., Tech. Processes, McKeldin Lib., Univ. of Md., 1962-66; Hd. Libn., Hood Coll., Frederick, Md., 1966-. Mbrships: ALA; Md. Lib. Assn.; Beta Phi Mu; Pi Kappa Lambda. Publs: The Tallahassee Years of Ernst von Dohnanyi, 1962. Address: Willowbrook Cottage, Old Middletown Rd., Jefferson, MD 21755, U.S.A.

RUFSVOLD, Margaret Irene, b. 18 Aug. 1907. Educator; Librarian. Educ: A.B., Univ of Wis., Madison, 1929; M.A., George Peabody Coll., Nashville, Tenn., 1933. Appts. incl: Libn., Ctrl. H.S., Tulsa, Okla., 1929-32, Gulf Pk. Coll., Gulfport, Miss., 1933-37; Supvsr., Schl. Lib. Lab., & Instr., Tchrs. Coll., Columbia Univ., N.Y.C., 1937-38; Instr. in Lib. Sci., Ind. Univ., Bloomington, 1938-41, Asst. Prof., 1941-47, Assoc. Prof. & Dir., Div. Lib. Sci., 1947-59, Prof. & Dir., Div. Lib. Sci., 1959-72, Prof. Emeritus, Grad. Lib. Schl., 1973-; Ind. Univ. Cons. on Lib. Servs. to Thailand Min. of Educ., 1954-60; Mbr., Edit. Bd., Cadmus Books, E.M. Hale Publishing Co., 1954-72, Chmn., 1968-72. Mbr. & Past Off., profl. orgs. & sororities. Author, books, monographs, num. articles, profl. publs. Hons. incl. disting. serv. awards & L.H.D., Mundelein Coll., Chgo., 1969. Address: Indiana Univ., Library Building, Bloomington, IN 47401, U.S.A. 5.

RUGGERI, Rosario, b. 19 Aug. 1905. Doctor of Medicine & Surgery. Educ: Med. degree, Rome, Italy, 1929. Appts. incl: study of Children's Neuropsychiatry, specializing in Pediatrics, 1933, Milan Univ.'s Pediatric Clin. & Clin. for Nervous & Mental Diseases, 1930-35; Hd. Physn., Milan Provincial Psychiatric Hosp., 1935; Dir., Paolo Pini Psychiatric Hosp., Milan; Lectr., Pediatric Clin. & Nervous & Mental Disease Clin., Milan Univ., 1942-; Mbr. 1st Italian Cultural Mission to China, 1955 & publd. paper, Ancient & Mod. Med. in Today's China. Publs. incl: Il Cervello Dei Nostri Figli; Psicologia é destino Del Nostro Popolo, Fra Malati Di Mente; 2 monographs, Course & Issues Of Epidemic Encephalitis In Infancy, 1933 & Encephalography In Infancy, 1939; 2 papers describing previously unreported med. syndromes, A Peculiar Family Syndrome (Cortical Ambiyopia, Epilepsy, Vestibular Disorders, 1939 & A Complex Family

Syndrome; Hereditary Acoustic, Optical & Cerebrospinal Degeneration, 1940. Address: 10, Via Lorenzo di Credi, 20149 Milan, Italy. 43.

RUIZ, Aldelmo b. 12 June 1923. Engineer. Educ: B.S. 1949; M.S., 1950, Va. Polytechnic Inst. & State Univ., Blacksburg,; Indl. Coll. of the Armed Forces, Wash. D.C. 1971-72; Bus. & Mgmt. courses, Appts. incl; Design Engr., Army Dept. Engrng. Rsch. & Dev. Labs., Ft. Belvoir, Va. 1951-52; Proj. Engr., ibid, 1952-55; var. positions, Far E. Div., Okinawa, 1955-58; Owner, Cons. Engrng. Firm, Puerto Rico 1958-62; Dir., Water Supply & Environmtl. Sanitn. Dept., YAR, 1963-66; Dev. Off., Sana'a, Yemen, 1966-67; Cheif Engrng. Advsr., AID, Kabul, Afghanistan, 1967-68; Gen. Engrng. Off., ibid, 1968-71; Inter-regional Engnrg. Coord., AID/Wash., 1972; AID Affairs Off., Yemen, 1972-. Mbrships. incl; Fellow, Am. Soc. Civil Engrs.; Nat. Soc. Profl. Engrs. U.S. Commn. on Irrigation, Drainage & Flood Control. Publs: USAID Sanitary Engineering Program & other Activities in Yemen, 1965; articles in profl. jrnls. Recip. Disting. Honor Award, Agcy. for Int. Dev. Dept. of State Wash. D.C. 1966. Address: Sana'a (ID) Dept. of State Washington, DC 20521 U.S.A. 2, 26.

RUKIN, Michael Barnett, b. 11 Feb. 1941. Engineering Executive. Educ: Hunter Coll., 1957-59; B.E.E., C.C.N.Y., 1962 M.S.E.E., Northeastern Univ. 1967. Appts: Tech. Staff, Mitre Corp., 1962-64; Gen. Mgr., Datamatik Processing, Inc., 1964-66; Assoc. Dept. Hd., Mitre Corp., 1966-69; Pres., Analytical Systems Engrng. Corp., 1969-. Mbrships: Dir., Small Bus. Assn. of New England & Am. Assn. of Small Rsch. Cos.; Chelmsford Housing Authority (Vice Chmn., 1969); U.S. Jr. Chmbr. of Comm, Am. Soc. of Planning Officials; I.E.E.E.; Armed Forces Communications Electronics Assn.; Tau Beta Pi; Eta Kappa Nu; Wild Goose Assn.; Am. Radio Relay League. Contbr. to num. profl. publs. Recip. of Sandor Oesteriecher Prize, 1962 & Special Citation, Commonwealth of Mass., 1973. Address: 22 Footpath Rd., Chelmsford, MA 01824, U.S.A. 6. 46.

RULAND, Bernd, b. 21 Jan. 1914. Editor; Writer. Educ: Univs. of Cologne, Germany & Bonn. Appts: Ed., Ullstein-Verlag, Berlin, from 1936; Chief reporter, Die Welt; Chief Ed., var. jrnls. incl. Bunte Illustrierte, 1949-. Publs. incl: Deutsche Botschaft Moskau; Deutsche Botschaft Peking; Corps diplomatique; Krieg aug leisen Sohlen; Geschaft ohne Erbarmen; Wernher von Braun - Ein Leben fur die Raumfahrt; Das war Berlin; Bahnhof zu den Sternen; Mit jeder Sekunde reicher- Portrats der Milliardare; Vorsicht, Falschgeld; Die Augen Moskaus; Gefahrtinnen durch Himmel und Holle. Address: Winzerstr. 2, D 76 Offenburg-Fessenbach, German Fed. Repub. 92.

RULAU, Russell, b. 21 Sept. 1926. Editor. Educ: Univ. of Wis., 1946-48. Appts: served w. US Army, 1944-50 & USAF, 1950-62; Asst. Ed., Coin World Newspaper, 1962-74; Ed., World Coins Mag., 1964-74 & Numismatic Scrapbook Mag., 1968-74; Ed. Coord., How to Order For. Coins, 1965-74; Ed., World Coin News Newspaper, 1974-; Ed. Coord., Standard Catalog of World Coins, 1974-; World Ed., Numismatic News Newspapers. Mbrships Fellow, Royal Numismatic Soc., 1963; Ed., Token & Medal Soc., 1962-63; Sec., Numismatic Terms Standardization Comm., 1966-71, 73-; Am. Numismatic Soc. & Assn.; Can. Numismatic Assn.; S. African Numismatic Soc.; Mont. Hist. Soc.; Soc. Numismatica de Mexico; Gesellschaft fuer Int. Geldgeschichte.

Publs. incl: Modern World Mint Marks, 2nd ed., 1970; Spiel Marken (co-author), 1972; American Game Counters (co-author), 1972; Coin World Guide to Coins (co-author), 1974; Early Tokens of the Queen City, Cincinnati, 1974; sev. thousand articles in numismatics jrnls., 1958-. Hons. incl: appointed Mbr., US Assay Comm., by Pres. Nixon, 1973; Best Feature Writer Awards, Numismatic Lit. Guild, 1970, 71, 72, 73; Best Columnist Awards, ibid, 1970, 71; Silver Lit. Award, Token & Medal Soc., 1961-62. Address: Rte. 2, Iola, WI 54945, U.S.A. 8, 133.

RUMAGGI, Louis Jacob, b. 3 Dec. 1900. Retired Army Officer; Civil Engineer. Educ: B.S., U.S. Military Acad., 1922; B.S., Univ. of Calif., 1927. Appts. incl: 2nd Lt.Major-Gen., Corps. of Engrs., U.S. Army, 1922-59; C.O. of various Engrng. Units, 1941-44; Dpty. & Acting Chief Engr., Army Forces, S.W. Pacific, 1945-46; Engr., 8th Army, Korea, 1952-53; Dpty. Chief of Engrs., 1954-55; Chief of Staff, 6th Army, 1955-57; Div. Engr., U.S. Engrng. Div., N. Ctrl., 1957-59; Fellow, Am. Soc. of Civil Engrs. Mbrships: Soc. of Am. Military Engrs.; Newcomen Soc.; Rotary Int.; Mason; Sons of Am. Revolution. Hons: Legion of Merit, 1946 & '59; Commendation Ribbon, 1946; D.S.M., 1954; Repub. of Korea D.S.M., 1953. Address: 8639 Edgemere Rd., Apt. D., Dallas, TX 75225, U.S.A. 2, 7.

RUMFIELD, May Lola (Mrs. Roy Rumfield), b. 15 Jan. 1897. Artist; Dancer; Poet. Appts. incl: Profl. dancer; Dancing tchr.; Artist, Ed. & Mgr., Community newspaper, Tampa, Fla., U.S.A. Mbrships: Co-Chairperson & Area Chairperson, United Fund, Heart & Muscular Dystrophy; Publicity Chairperson, Calif. Art Assn., Longbeach; Music Club, ibid; Long Beach Poets Lyceum; Offs.' Wives Club, Macdill Airforce Base, Fla.; Tampa Chapt. Retired Offs.' Wives Club; Wells Wood Civic Club, Tampa; Pres., 5 yrs.; Hillsborough Co., Fla. Coun. of Civic Assns.; Audubon Soc.; St. Joseph's Hosp. Dev. Coun., Tampa. Publs: The Crown Anthology of Verse, 1937; The World's Fair Anthology of Verse, 1938; Poems pub. in local newspapers, Honolulu, Hawaii & Balboa, Pntngs. exhibited at num. exhibs., Long Beach & Tampa, Fla.; Written sev. songs. Hons: Hon. City Coun. Mbr., Tampa, 1970; Tampa City Citizen's Award, 1966; Pres., Tampa Civic Club, 1969-74; 30 Silver Loving Cups for Special Dancing, Calif., 1926-30. Address: 4909 Wishart Blvd., Tampa, FL 33603, U.S.A. 125.

RUMMERFIELD, (Revd. Dr., Bishop) Walter Glen, b. 14 Nov. 1911. Clergyman; Bishop; University President; Analyst; Editor. Educ: B.S., W. Tex. State Univ., Canyon, U.S.A., 1956; Sev. doctorates, Coll of Universal Truth, Chgo., Ill., 1955-58; Ph.D., City Temple Schl. of Relig., 1967; D.B.A., Calif. Christian Coll., 1973; D.S.T., City Temple Inst., 1973. Num appts. incl: Life Inst. Exec., 1937-49; USN, 1943-45; Broker, Estate Planner, & Pub. Rels. Cons., 1949-57; Min. & Pres., City Temple, L.A. Calif., 1958; Bishop, Western Region, Ecumenical Movement for World Peace, 1962; Pres., Sem. City Temple Schl. of Relig. Inst., 1966; Pres., Calif. Christian Coll. & Univ. Inst., L.A., 1971-. Mbrships. incl: Chmbr. of Comm., 1940-56; Am. Legion, 1945-53; Treas. & Pres., Lutheran Brotherhood, 1953-55; Psychiatric Club of Am.; Min. Assoc., Int. New Thought Alliance, 1949-60. Publs. incl: Psychology of Religion Applied to Everyday Living, 1960; Ed., Next to the Top; Contbns. to num. jrnls. Hons. incl: Purple Heart, USN, 1945; Noble, Khiva Temple, Shrine of N. Am., 1948. Address: 966 S. Arapahoe St., Los Angeles, CA 90006, U.S.A. 57, 130.

RUNCK, Roger John, b. 24 May 1912. Metallurgist. Educ: B.S., Chem. Engrng. Colo. Univ., 1943; M.S., Metallurgy, Stevens Inst. of Technol., 1947. Appts: Process Engr., Metal & Thermit Corp., 1943-47; Battelle Mem. Inst., 1947-73; Prin. Metallurgist, 1947-54; Asst. Chief, 1954-57; Mgr., Titanium Metallurgical Lab., 1957-58; Dir., Defense Metals Info. Ctr., 1958-69; Retd., 1973; Metallurgical Cons., 1973-. Mbrships: Am. Soc. for Metals; Am. Defense Preparedness Assn. Publs: Chapts in textbooks, encys. Hons: 2nd Nat. Prize, Am. Inst. of Chem. Engrng., 1943. Address: 705 Robinwood Ave., Columbus, OH 43213, U.S.A. 8, 14, 16.

RUNTON, Gloria Cecilia, Librarian. Educ: B.A., Univ. of Tampa, 1944; M.A., Fla. State Univ., 1959. Appts: Statn., Dist. Offs., Fla State Dept. of Pub. Welfare, 1944-54; Catalogue Libn., Univ. of Tampa Lib., 1954-69; Hd., Tech. Servs. Div., Merl Kelce Lib., ibid, 1969-: Cons., Cath. Info. Ctr., & Sev. parochial schls. Mbrships: Fla. Lib. Assn.; S.E. Lib. Assn.; Pi Delta Epsilon; Sigma Tau Delta; Treas., Delta Zeta; Bd. Mbr. & Libn.-Histn., Tampa Audubon Soc.; Rosary Crusaders; Westown Players Theatrical Assn.; Sun State Opera Assn.; Topic Chmn., Tampa Br., AAUW; Univ. of Tampa Women's Club. Address: 3416 Ohio Ave., Interbay Subdivision, Tampa, FL 33611, U.S.A. 5, 42, 125, 138.

RUNYON, Alice Louise Minnerly (Mrs.), b. 12 June 1902. Teacher; Musician; Researcher; Executive. Educ: B.S., 1943, M.A., 1947, N.Y. Univ.; Dip., Guilmant Organ Schl., 1940. Appts: Tchr., 1921-46; Asst. Dir., Philipse Castle Restoration, 1943-47; Headed rsch. for restoration of Sunnyside, Washington Irving's Home, 1945-47; Assoc. Dir., Philipse Castle & Sunnyside, 1947-51, Sleepy Hollow Restorations, Inc., 1951-55; Dir., Specialized Rsch., 1956-. Mbrships: N.Y. State Gov., Dpty. Gov. Gen., Sons & Daughters of the Pilgrims; N.Y. State Pres., V.P., Nat. Chmn. of Histl. Educ., Nat. Corres. Sec. Daughters of Fndrs. & Patriots of Am.; Nat. Pres., Treas., Registrar, Order of Ams. of Armorial Ancestry; N.Y. State Pres., Nat. Histn., Mbr., Nat. Exec. Bd., Recording Sec. of Nat. Offs. Club, 2nd V.P., Daughters of Colonial Wars; Colonial Dames of Am.; Descendants of Kts. of the Garter; Descendants of Wm. I, the Conqueror; Order of the Crown of Charlemagne in U.S.; Registrar & Coun., Huguenot Soc. of Am.; many others. Author of var. mag. articles. Address: P.O. Box 187, N. Tarrytown, NY 10591, U.S.A. 5, 6, 13, 15, 22, 132.

RUOPPOLO, Catello, b. 24 Nov. 1916. Painter; Sculptor; Designer. Educ: Acad. Fine Arts, Naples. Mbrships: Tiberino Dé Cinquecento Acad.; Latinitati Excolendae; Free World Int. Acad., U.S.A.; Legion d'oro. Publs: Il Fachiro; Venezia che muore; Omaggio agli sposi. Contbr. to var. art jrnls. Hons. incl: Silver Medal, Nat. Art Exhib., Castellammare di Stabia, 1934; Premio Terni, 1951; Premio Michetti, 1954; Premio Margutta, Rome; Premio Marguttissima, Citta d'Italia, Rome; Premio internazionale, Sorrento. Address: Via F. Petrarca 77, 80053 Castellammare di Stabia, (NA) Italy.

RUPP, William Anthony, b. 17 July 1931. College Professor. Educ: B.S., Ft. Hays State Coll., Kan.; M.S., Southern Ill. Univ.; Ed.D., Univ. of Northern Colo. Appts: Tchr., Coach, Osborne H.S., 1956-58; St. Mary of Plains Coll., Dodge City, 1958-59; Wayne State Coll., Neb., 1959-60; Colo. State Coll., 1960-64; Longmont H.S., Colo., 1964-66; Abbey Schl., Canon City, Colo., 1966-67; Aims Jr. Coll., Greeley,

1967-69; Chmn., Educ. Dept., Marymount Coll., Kan., 1969-. Mbrships. incl: Chapt. Pres., Phi Delta Kappa, 1971-72; Pres., Kan. Higher Educ. Assn., 1974-; Instrn. & Profl. Dev. Commn., 1973, Kan.-NEA. Contbr. to educ. publs. Recip. of hons. in educ. Address: Educ. Dept., Marymount Coll. of Educ., Salina, KS 67401, U.S.A. 15, 139, 141.

RUPPIN, Rafael, b. 13 Feb. 1919. Civil Servant. Educ: Hebrew Univ., Jerusalem; London Schl. Econs., London Univ., U.K. Appts: Dir., Mevoot Yam, Fisheries & Nautical H.S., 1950-61; 1st Israeli Ambassador, Tanganyika (Tanzania), 1961-63; Dir., Nautical Educ. Div., Min. Educ. & Culture, Jerusalem, 1964-71; Coord., Hebrew Educ. in Diaspora, ibid; Cons., Fisheries Educ., F.A.O.; F.A.O. Cons., Govts. of India, Kenya, Tanzania, Uganda, Malawi, Zambia & S. Korea, 1958-. Chmn., Bd. Govs., Mevoot Yam, Nautical H.S. Publs. incl: Sev. on Fisheries Trng. & Educ. in India, E. & Ctrl. Africa & Israel; The Administration of Fisheries Training and Educational Institutions - a basic paper; Anu Hem Veeretz Yisrael - a tchr.'s guide to the Arab-Israeli Conflict. 1971. Address: Off. Coord. Hebrew Educ. in Diaspora, Min. Educ. & Culture, Jerusalem 91000, Israel 55, 94.

RUSH, (Nixon) Orwin, b. 18 Aug. 1907. Librarian. Educ: A.B., Friends Univ., 1931; B.S., Columbia Univ., 1932; M.S., ibid, 1945. Appts. incl: Libn. & Assoc. Prof. of Bibliog., Clark Univ., 1945-47; Exec. Sec. of the Assn. of Coll. & Ref. Libns., Chgo., 1947-49; Dir., Univ. of Wyoming Lib., 1949-51; Prof. of Lib. Sci., ibid, 1955-58; Dir. of Libs., Fla. State Univ. & Prof. of Lib. Sci., 1958-73; Cons.-Libn., Amarillo Coll., Tex., 1973-. Mbrships incl: Pres., Me. & Mountain Plains Lib. Assns.; Treas., Assn. of Coll. & Ref. Libns.; Chmn., Bd. Dirs., Rocky Mountain Bibliographical Ctr. Publs. incl: The History of College Libraries in Maine, 1946; The Battle of Pensacola, 1966; Frederick Remington & Owen Wister: The Story of a Friendship, 1961; Mercer's Baditi of the Plains, 1961; Special Collections: What They Mean to Librarians, Professors & Collectors, 1973; List of Books for High School Libraries, 1958; Ed., var. books. Recip. var. hons. Address: The Library, Amarillo Coll., Amarillo, TX 79178, U.S.A. 2, 7, 15, 42.

RUSH, Wilma Anderson (Mrs.), b. 17 Dec. 1919. School Psychologist. Educ: B.Ed., Ill. State Normal Univ., 1941; M.S.Ed., Ill. State, 1960; Postgrad., Univ. of Mo., 1961, ISU & Nat. Coll. of Educ., 1962-73. Appts: Tchr., Pub. Schls., Farina, Ill., 1941, Shirley, Ill., 1945, Downs, Ill., 1947, Bloomington, Ill., 1949-52 & 1963-65, Farmer City, Ill., 1955-58, Danvers, Ill., 1958, McLean, Ill., 1959 & Tremont, Ill., 1960-63; Ptnr., An. Antique Shop, 1947-65, For. Car Serv., 1963-65, Enfin Kennels, 1958-65; Rsch. Libn., Biddle Advt., 1952-55; Guidance Counsellor, Colegio Am., Caracas, Venezuela, 1965-67; Counsellor, Normal Community H.S., Normal, Ill., 1967; Schl. Psychol., Villa Pk., Ill. Dist. 45, 1968-; Ext. Tchr., Nat. Coll. of Educ., 1969-; Owner, Omnifiques, etc., 1970-. Mbrships: Ill. Psychol. Assn.; NEA; Ill. Educ. Assn.; Soc. for the Study of Perception; W. Suburban Psychols. Address: 386 N. LaLonde, Lombard, IL 60148, U.S.A. 5, 8.

RUSHTON, Mary Fay. Psychologist-Counselor. Educ: B.A., Univ. of Tex. 1940; M.A. Tex. A & M Univ., 1964. Appts: Dept. of Anthropol., Univ. of Tex., 1940-42; Voc. Adjustment Coord., Mercedes, Tex., 1952-72; Psychologist-Coord., Rio Grande Rehab. Ind. Schl. Dist., 1972-74.

Mbrships: Tex. Psychological & State Tchrs, Assns.; Am. Assn. Mental Deficiency; Coun. for Exceptional Children; DAR; Colonial Dames of XVII Century; Nat. Soc. of Magna Carta Dames. Address: Box 687, Mission, TX 78572, U.S.A. 5, 138.

RUSKE, Walter Albert, b. 14 Sept. 1921. Government Official; Chemist. Educ: Goethe-Oberschule Berlin-Wilmersdorf, Germany, 1940; Dip., Humboldt-Univ., Berlin, 1952; Promotion, ibid, 1954 & Habilitation, 1958. Appts. incl: Asst., Humboldt Univ., Berlin, 1952-58; Univ. Tchr., Organic Chem. & Hist. of Chem., ibid, 1959-61; Scientific Advsr., Verlag Chemie, Weinheim/Bergstr., 1962-65; Govt. Official, Fed. Inst. for Materials Testing, Berlin, 1963-; Univ. Tchr., Hist. of Sci. & Technol., Tech. Univ., ibid, 1967-. Mbrships. incl: Soc. of German Chemists; Task Grp., Hist. of Chem.; Georg Agricola Soc.; Task Grp., Hist. of Sci. & Technol. in the 19th Century. Publs. incl: 100 Jahre Deutsche Chemische Gesellschaft, 1967; Ein Beitrag zur Technikgeschichte, 1971; Reichs- und preussische Landesanstalten in Berlin, 1973; Num. publs. on subjects of organic chem. & hist. of sci. Recip. Humboldt Medal, Humboldt Univ., 1960. Address: Ehrenbergstrasse 22 B, D-1000 Berlin 33, German Fed. Repub. 43.

RUSSELL, (Andy) Andrew George Alexander, b. 8 Dec. 1915. Nature Writer; Photographer; Lecturer. Appts: Youngest lic. guide in Alta., Canada, 1934, Guide, 1934-44; Owner, operator, wilderness fishing, hunting & nature tour serv., Alta., 1944-54; Organizer, Ldr., expeditions to Canadian Far North; Owner, cattle ranch; Writer, photographer, lecturer. Mbrships: Pres., Foothills Protective Assn.; Nat. & Int. Wildlife Assn.; Sierra Club; Authors Guild of Am. Publs: Grizzly Country; Trails of a Wilderness Wanderer; Horns in the High Country. Num. mag. articles, weekly newspaper column, weekly CBC radio broadcast, & TV appearances. Hons: Highest Canadian award for individual contribution to conservation & outdoor recreation, Nat./Provincial Pks. Assn., 1971. Address: P.O. Box 68, Waterton Lakes Pk., Alta., TOK 2MO, Canada.

RUSSELL, Dennis Charles, b. 4 Sept. 1927. Professor of Mathematics. Educ: B.Sc., Univ. of Sheffield, U.K., 1948; M.Sc., Univ. of London, 1952; Ph.D., 1958; D.Sc., 1972. Appts: Asst. Lectr., Northampton Coll. of Adv Technol., City Univ., London, 1948-52; Asst. Lectr., Northampton Coll. of Adv. Technol., Assoc. Prof., Mount Allison Univ., Sackville, N.B., Canada, 1960-62; Prof., Maths., York Univ., Toronto, 1962-; Chmn., Dept., 1962-69. Fellow, Inst. of Maths. & Applications. Mbrships: Coun., Canadian Math. Congress, 1967-71, 73-75; London Math. Soc.; Am. Math. Soc.; Math. Assn. Am.; Hon. Pres., Ont. Assn. Tchrs. of Maths., 1967-68. Contbr. to profl. publs. Hons. incl: Nat. Rsch. Coun. of Canada Sr. Rsch. Fellowship, 1968; Canada Coun. Leave Fellowship, 1969; Nuffield Fndn. Rsch. Travel Grant, 1973. Address: Dept. of Maths., York Univ., Downsview (Toronto), Ont., M3J 1P3 Canada. 8, 14, 88.

RUSSELL, Edna Bonn. Consultant in Gerontology. Educ: A.B., Stanford Univ., Calif.; Ed.D., Univ. of Northern Colo. Appts. incl: Mbr., Calif. Commn. on Aging, 1956-59, Chmn., 1959-73; Appt. by Pres. Johnson, Nat. Advsry. Coun. on Poverty, 1965-66; Appt. by Pres. Nixon, Presidential Task Force on Aging, 1969-70; Cons., Dept. of Hlth. Educ. & Welfare, U.S. Govt., 1972-73; Chmn., Nat. Comm. Geriatric Blindness, Am. Fndn. for

Blind, 1972-; Bd. Councilors, Gerontol. Ctr., Univ. of Southern Calif., 1972-; Nat. Advsry. Comm., Sr. Advocates Int., Wash. D.C., 1973-. Mbr. Comm. Mbr. & Off., var. profl. orgs. Active Lectr. & Conf. Participant. Var. profl. papers, articles & case studies. Recip., var. citations, commendations & awards for profl. activities. Address: 147 Patricia Dr., Atherton, CA 94025, U.S.A. 5, 138.

RUSSELL, George (Gordon), b. 15 July 1932. Artist. Educ: Pa. Acad. of Fine Arts, 1950-54; Pa. State Univ., 1950, 1951; Barnes Fndn., 1951-53. Artist represented by Durlacher Bros., 1956-67; currently represented by Larcada Gall. Fellow, Pa. Acad. of Fine Arts. Solo exhibs. incl: Durlacher Bros., N.Y.C., 1957, '59, '61, '63, '65, '67; Ft. Worth Art Ctr., Tex., 1962; Larcada Gall., N.Y.C., 1969, '71. Participant, exhibs. throughout U.S.A. & Europe. Work in var. pub. & pvte. collects. Hons: Ramborger Prize, 1952; Thouron Prize, 1953; Lewis S. Ware Mem. Traveling Schlrship., 1953. J. Henry Schiedt Mem. Traveling Schlrship., 1954; 1st Toppan Prize, Pa. Acad. Fine Arts; Louis Comfort Tiffany Prize, 1968. Address: 117 E. Caroline Ave., Altoona, PA 16602, U.S.A.

RUSSELL, (Rev.Dr.) Horace Orlando, b. 3 Nov. 1929. Minister of Religion. Educ: B.D. (Hons.), Calabar Theological Coll., Kingston, Jamaica, 1954; Ph.D., Regent's Park Coll., Oxford, 1972. Appts: Advsr. on Religious Affairs, Radio Jamaica, 1958-70; Lectr. in Ecclesiastical Hist. to Theological Colls., 1960-66; Sec., Youth Dept., Jamaica Baptist Union, 1960-64; Mbr. Executive Coun., ibid, 1960-70 & 1972-; Lectr. in Ecclesiastical Hist. & Dpty. Pres., United Theological Coll. of W.I., 1966-70; Pres., ibid, 1972-. Mbrships: Chap., Masonic Lodges (Univ.); World Assn. Christian Communication; Historical Assn. Address: United Theological Coll. of W. Indies, P.O. Box 136, Kingston 7, Jamaica, W. Indies.

RUSSELL, James Sargent, b. 22 Mar. 1903. Retired Admiral, U.S. Navy; Naval Aviator Educ: B.S., USN Acad., 1926; M.S., Aero Engrng., Calif. Tech., 1935. Appts: Midshipman 1922-Admiral 1958; Designated Naval Aviator, 1929; Cmdr., Patrol Squadron 42, Aleutian Islands & Chief of Staff to Cmdr. Fast Carrier Task Grp., Western Pacific, WWII; Chief, Bur. of Aeronautics, USN, 1955-57; Vice Chief, Naval Ops., 1958-61; Cmdr.-in-Chief, Allied Forces, Southern Europe, 1962-65; Cons., Boeing Co., 1965-: Dir., Alaska Airlines, 1965-70; Dir., Airtronics Inc., 1965-71; Dir., Tacoma, Wash., Chamb. of Comm.; Trustee, Oceanographic Inst., Wash. State. Mbrships incl: Fellow, AIAA; Navy League; Am. Ordnance Assn.; Var. Advsry Bds. to USN. Hons: Collier Trophy, 1956; Peruvian Cross of Naval Merit, 1961; Grand. Off., Order of Naval Merit, Brazil, 1961; Cmdr, Legion of Honour, France, 1962; Grand Cross, Royal Order of King George I, Greece, 1965; Grande Ufficiale del Ordine del Republica, Italy, 1965; num. U.S. Naval Hons. Address: 7734 Walnut Ave. S.W., Tacoma, WA 98498, U.S.A. 2, 9.

RUSSELL, Jeffrey Burton, b. 1 Aug. 1934. Educator; Writer. Educ: B.A., Univ. of Calif., Berkeley, 1955; M.A., ibid, 1957; Ph.D., Emory Univ., Ga., 1960. Appts: Jr. Fellow, Harvard Univ., 1961-62; Asst. Prof. of Hist., Univ. of Calif., Riverside, 1962-65; Assoc. Prof., ibid, 1965-69; Prof., 1969-; Assoc. Dean of Grad. Div., 1967-72. Mbrships: Medieval Acad. Am.; Phi Beta Kappa; Am. Histl. Assn.; Am. Soc. Ch. Hist.; Medieval Assn. of Pacific; Sierra Club. Publs: Dissent & Reform in the Early Middle Ages, 1965; Medieval Civilization, 1968; A

History of Medieval Christianity; Prophecy & Order, 1968; Religious Dissent in the Middle Ages, 1971; Witchcraft in the Middle Ages, 1972; articles & reviews in profl. jrnls. & anthologies. Address: Dept. of Hist., Univ. of Calif., Riverside, CA 92502, U.S.A. 13, 30.

RUSSELL, Lao. Author; Artist; Lecturer. Educ: Pvte. Appts: Fndr., Mng. Dir., Walter Russell Fndn. 1948-, Pres. 1949-, Univ. of Sci. & Philos., 1957; Creator, Shrine of Beauty, Swannanoa, Va., ctr. for Dr. W. Russell's works of art, & teachings w. Mrs. Russell, Sci. of Man & of the Cosmos.; Lectr., 1947-. Mbrships: Fndr., Man-Woman Equalization League, 1955, Int. Age of Character, Arts & Cultural Ctrs., & Character Clubs, 1966. Publs. incl: God Will Work With You but not For You (N.Y. Herald Tribune prizewinner) 1955; An Eternal Message of Light & Love, 1964; Love—1966; Why You Cannot Die, 1972; w. W. Russell, Scientific Answer to Human Relations, 1951; Atomic Suicide? 1957; The World Crisis—1958; The One-World Purpose, 1960; Sculptor of models w. W. Ressell. Address: Swannanoa Palace, Waynesboro, VA 22980, U.S.A. 2, 22, 34, 57, 128.

RUSSELL, Mary, b. 21 Feb. 1910. Clinical Social Worker. Educ: B.A., Coll. of Ozarks, 1932; M.A., Univ. of Chgo., Schl. of Soc. Serv. Admin., 1940; McCormick Sem., 1933; Univ. of Calif., 1951; Univ. of Ind., 1942. Appts: Rural Tchr., Madison Co., Ark., 1928; Case Worker, Cook Co. Welfare Dept., Chgo., 1934-35; Child Welfare Worker, Dept. of Pub. Welfare, Ill., 1935-40; Exec. Dir., Family Serv., Richmond, Ind., 1941-45; Pasadena, Calif. 1945-48; Bakersfield, Calif., 1948-55; Pvte. Prac., 1955 & currently; Volunteer Lectr., Earlam Coll. Soc. Sci., 1942-45. Mbrships. incl: Fellow, Soc. for Clin. Soc. Wkrs.; Nat. Assn. Soc. Wkrs.; Charter, Am. Assn. Soc. Wkrs., 1934 & currently; Altrusa Int. Pres., Bakersfield Club, 1956 & currently Pres., Dist 5.; Phi Kappa Delta; Am. Acad. of Human Servs., 1974-75. Contbr. to jrnls. in field. Address: 1928 17th St., Bakersfield, CA 93301, U.S.A. 59, 129, 138.

RUSSELL, Paul Farr, b. 12 Aug 1894. Physician; Public Health Official. Educ: A.B., Boston Univ., 1916; M.D., Cornell Univ. Med. Coll., 1921; Intern, Bellevue Hosp., N.Y.C., 1921-23; M.P.H., Harvard Schl. Pub. Hlth., 1929. Appts: Staff Mbr., Rockefeller Fndn., 1923-59; Straits Settlements Rural Sanitation Campaign, 1925-28; Malaria Studies, Philippines, 1929-34, India, 1934-42; Lt.Col.—Col., Med. Corps, U.S. Army, 1942-46; Mbr., Malaria Panel, WHO, 1947-, Cons., WHO, 1954-55; Vis. Prof., Harvard Schl. Pub. Hlth., 1961-63. Mbr. & Fellow., profl. orgs. Publs. incl: Health Through Knowledge & Habits (co-author), 1933; Man's Mastery of Malaria, 1957; Clinical Parasitology (co-author), 8th edit., 1970. Num. papers, med. jrnls. Hons. incl: U.S. Legion of Merit, 1945, Oak Leaf Cluster, 1946; Walter Reed Medal, 1945; Darling Medal & Prize, WHO, 1957; Collegium Disting. Alumni, Boston Univ., 1974. Address: N. Edgecomb, ME 04556, U.S.A. 2.

RUSSELL, Randolph B., b. 22 Nov. 1927. Business Executive. Appts: Mng. Dir., Lyric Theatres Ltd., 1952-64, Westindia Dev. Co. Ltd., 1964-; Chmn. & Mng. Dir., St. Vincent Agric. Credit & Loan Bank Ltd., 1965-; Chmn., St. Vincent Equitable Bldg. Assn.; Elected Rep., House of Assembly, 1972-. Mbrships: Chmn., Ctrl. Housing & Planning Auth., 1969-72; Kingstown Town Bd., 1967-73; Chmn., ibid, 1971-73. Address: P.O. Box 851, Kingstown, St. Vincent, West Indies. 136.

RUSSELL, Sandra Lorelei, b. 3 Mar. 1936. Graphics Designer; Photographer. Educ: B.A., Hofsma Coll., 1957; Grad. Schl. of Arts & Scis., N.Y. Univ., 1957-58; Cooper Union Art Schl., 1960-64. Appts. incl: Musician & singer, var. clubs, N.Y. area, 1950-60; Assoc. Ed., Mod. Plastics Ency., 1959-60; Free-lance Graphics Designer, Photographer, Writer, Ed. & Cons., 1964-; Sr. Copy Ed., New Book of Knowledge, 1964-66, Ency. Americana, 1966-67, & w. Am. Heritage Publishing Co. Inc., 1967-69; Graphics Designer & Writer, Dept. Pub. Affairs, N.Y.C. Econ. Dev. Admin., 1970-74; Sec., Mayor's Oceanographic Comm., 1971-74. Mbr. & Off., var. profl. orga. Contbr., var. encys. Paintings in var. grp. exhibs. Hons. incl: Wassuny Music Award, 1952; Hofsma Coll. Schlrship., 1953-57. Address: Sunset Beach, Waterport, NY 14571, U.S.A. 5, 6, 130, 132, 138.

RUSSO, Joseph Nicholas II, b. 28 Feb. 1919. Obstetrician & Gynaecologist. Educ: M.D.; Univ. of Vt. (med.), 1942-45; Hartford Hosp. (internship) 1945-46; res. at sev. hosps., 1946-53. Appts: Conn. State Police Surg., 1962-; Mbr., CMS Med. Advsry. Bd., 1968-; Asst. Clin. Prof., Univ. of Vt., Coll. of Med., 1968-; Cons. Obs.-Gyn., Newington Hosp., Inst. for Living, Johnson Mem. Hosp. & Litchfield Co. Hosp. Mbrships. incl: Pres., Univ. of Vt. Coll. of Med. Alumni Assn.; Trustee, Heublein Fndn.; AMA; Am. Coll. of Ob.-Gyn.; Conn. State Med. Soc.; Nat. Bd. of Med. Examiners; Am. Coll. of Surgs.; Int. coll. of Surgs.; Hartford Co. & Hartford Med. Socs. Contbr. of var. articles to profl. jrnls. Recip. of Alumni Medal of Honor, Trinity Coll., 1968. Address: 85 Jefferson St., Ste. 801, Hartford, CT 06106, U.S.A. 6, 17, 22, 54.

RUST, Velma Irene Miller (Mrs. Ronald S. Rust), b. 22 May 1914. Educationalist & Statistician. Educ: B.Sc., Univ. of Alta, Edmonton, Canada, 1934; B.Ed., ibid, 1944; M.Ed., 1947; Ph.d., Univ. of Ill., Urbana, U.S.A., 1959. Appts. incl: Asst. Prof., Math-Educ., Fac. of Educ., Univ. of Alta, 1952-56; Rschr., Dept. of Nat. Defence, Ottawa, Ont. 1960-62; Chief, Staff Trng., ibid, 1962-65; Statn. Aviation Stats. Ctr., Canadian Govt., 1965-67, Statn.-Economist-Rschr., Soc. Security Rsch. Div., Dept. of Nat. Hlth. & Welfare, 1967-. Mbrships. incl: Am. Stat. Assn.; Canadian Econs. Assn.; Kappa Delta Pi; Am. Soc. Quality Control; Am. Math. Assn.; Canadian Math. Cong.; Profl. Inst. Pub. Serv.; Pres., Ottawa Br., Univ. of Alta. Alumni Assn.; 1969-70. Nat. coun. of Tchrs. of Maths; Canadian Educ. Assn. Contbr. to profl. publs. Address: 811 Adams Ave., Ottawa, Canada, K1G 2Y1, 5, 6, 14, 130, 132.

RUTGERS, Katherine Phillips (Mrs. Frederick Rutgers). Dancer. Educ: studied ballet w. Vera Trefilova (Paris), Carl Raimund (Vienna) & Varga Troyanoff (Bucharest); mod. dance w. Ireis Barbura (Bucharest), Vincenzo Celli, Igor Schwezoff & Jean Yazvinsky (all N.Y.C.); Hawaiian dance w. Mme Huapala for 8 yrs. Appts: gave dance concerts in Bucharest, Roumania; has danced in U.S.A. for num. benefit concerts and for club. orgs.; specializes in Relig. interpretations & has danced in num. chs.; Dir., Dance Dept., Fed. Music Clubs. of Conn., 1965-66; Dance Therapist, St. Barnabus Hosp., N.Y.C., 1965-70; currently Chmn., Ethnological Dance Dept., & Bd. of Dirs., Bruce Mus., Greenwich, Conn. Mbrships: Sacred Dance Guild; Pres., Greenwich Travel Club, 1963-69 & Margaret F. Dole Contemporary Arts Club, 1969-73; Alliance Française; Nat. League Am. Pen Women; V.P., Greenwich Br., ibid; DAR; N.Y.C. Colonial Dames; etc. Has written num. booklets on dance & over 100 Rose Verses for choreographies compiled in anthol., A Back Ground of Roses; Article & lect. demonstration "Poetry & Sculpture in the Dance", 1974; Prog. for Retd. Tchrs. Assn. "Women of the Bible", 1974. Address: Pecksland Road, Greenwich, CN 06830, U.S.A. 34, 57, 138.

RUTHERFORD, Richard James, b. 14 Aug. 1903. Executive & Professional Engineer. Educ: B.S., Univ. of Ill. Appts. incl: V.P. & Gen. Mgr., Worcester Gas Light Co., Worcester, Mass. 1936-51, Pres., ibid, 1951-68; Chmn. of Bd., Riley Stoker Corp., Worcester, Exec. Cons., & Dir., Worcester Gas Light Co., Ptnr., Hall-Bud Assocs., 1968-; Bd. of Dirs., var. cos. inclng. The Riley Co., Commonwealth Gas Co., NEGEA Serv. Corp., Thos. Smith Corp. Mbrships. incl: Vice Chmn., Inst. of Gas Technol.; Past Pres., Am. Gas Assn., New England Gas Assn.; Coun. mbr., & Chmn., Utilization Commn., Int. Gas Union (36 countries); Chmn., commn. to negotiate rsch. agreement between Am. Gas Assn., British Gas Coun. & Gaz de France; U.S. Commn. to Russia to study natural gas & oil reserves, 1969. Recip. of hons. Address: 42 Berwick St., Worcester, MA 01602, U.S.A. 2.

RUTHERFORD, William Kenneth, b. 24 Sept. 1907. Educator. Educ: B.S. in Educ., N.E. Mo. State Tchrs. Coll., Kirksville, 1935; M.Ed., Univ. of Mo., Columbia, 1948. Appts: Tchr., Gaines Rural Schl., Randolph Co., Mo.,1929-34, Waters Rural Schl., Jacksonville, Randolph Co., Mo., 1934-36; H.S. Prin., Clifton Hill, 1936-37, Lemons Putnam Co., 1937-39, Mo.; Supt. of Schls., Lemons, 1939-42, Greencastle, Sullivan Co., 1942; Mil. Serv. w. 411th Regiment, 103rd Infantry Div., U.S. 7th Army, Campains in Rhineland & Ctrl. Europe, 1942-45; Tchr., Moberly, Mo., 1945-50; Elem Prin., Elem Supvsr., Fulton. 1950-51; Supvsng. Prin., Dir. of Guidance, Lexington, 1951-57; Prin., Elem. Schls., ibid, 1957-73. Mbrships. incl: NEA; Nat. Assn. & Mo. Dept. Elem. Schl. Prins.; Mo. State Tchrs. Assn., Phi Delta Kappa; Rotary; Former Deacon, Ctrl. Christian Ch., Moberly; Deaon, 1955-60, Elder, 1960., Chmn. Bd., 1964-66, 1st Christian Ch., Lexington; New England Hist. Geneal. Soc. State Histl. Soc. Mo. Publs: Genealogical History of the Halliburton Family, 1959, revised 1972; Genealogical History of the Rutherford Family, 1969; Genealogical History of Our Ancestors, 1970. Recip., prizes for books on geneal. hist., Heart of Am. Geneal. Soc. 1971, '72 & '73. Address: 2101 Forest Ave., Lexington, MO 64067, U.S.A. 8, 15, 70, 120, 128, 139.

RUTLEDGE, Arthur B., b. 30 Apr. 1911. Clergyman; Church Executive. Educ: B.A., Baylor Univ., U.S.A., 1936; Th.M., Southern Bapt. Theol. Sem., 1939; Th.D., Southwestern Bapt. Theol. Sem., 1944. Appts: Pastor, Tex., Ky. & Ind., inclng. 1st Bapt. Ch., Marshall, Tex., 1945-57; Sec., Stewardship & Direct Missions, Bapt. Gen. Conv., Tex., 1957-59; Dir. Divinity Missions, 1959-64; Exec. Comm. Bapt. World Alliance; Bapt. Jt. Comm. Pub. Affairs; N. Am. Bapt. Fellowship; Atlanta Power Squadron. Publs: Homes That Last, 1952; Mission to America, 1969. Monthly Column, Home Missions mag. Hons: D.D., E. Tex. Bapt. Coll., 1956; LL.D., Baylor Univ., 1967; Disting. Alumnus, Southwestern Bapt. Theol. Sem., 1968; Disting. Serv. Award, Christian Life Comm., Southern Bapt. Conv., 1973. Address: 1350 Spring St. N.W., Atlanta, GA 30309, U.S.A. 2, 7, 128.

RUTZEBECK, Hans Hjalmar, b. 17 Apr. 1889. Co-operative Specialist. Educ: Feilbergs

Pvte. Schl., Copenhagen. Appts. incl: Real Estate Broker, N. & S. Calif., 1928-; Organizer, People's Party, Calif., Ed., Yolo Independent, Calif., & Hutzebeck's Weekly, Sacramento, 1930-31; Advsr. & Counsellor, Fed. Emergency Relief Admin., Wash D.C., 1933-34; Gen. Mgr., L.A. Co. (Calif.) Co-operative Inds., 1935-37; Organizer & Mgr., Northside Tax Grp., S. Calif., 1941-; Bd. Dirs., Nat. Urban League, L.A. Unit, 1943-46; Candidate for 42nd Dist., State Assembly, Calif., 1960. Publs. incl: Ten Principles of Government, 1932; Hell's Paradise, 1946; The Wind Is Free, 1957; Bait, 1965; Concerned Americans, 1972. Contbr., mags. & newspapers. Recip., D. Litt (Hon.). Da Landas Univ., 1941. Address: 10538 Art St., Sunland, CA 91040, U.S.A.

RUYTINX, Jacques Henri Jean,b. 2 June 1924. Professor. Educ: Ph.D., Univ. of Brussels, 1957. Appts: Asst. in Philos., Univ. of Liege, 1959-61; Lectr., now Prof., Univ. of Brussels, 1961-. Mbrships: Pres., Belgian Philos. Soc., 1969-72; & Belgian Soc. of Logic & Philos of Sci., 1970-; Treas., Nat. Ctr. of Studies in Logic; Dir., Ctr., of Empirical Epistemol., Univ. of Brussels; Aristotelian Soc. Publs: La morale bantoue et le probleme de l'éducation morale au Congo, 1960, 2nd edn., 1969; La Problématique philosophique de l'Unité de la Science, 1962; A New Introduction to Moral Philosophy (in Dutch), 1971; articles in var. jrnls. Hons: Prize, Acad. of Scis., Letters & Arts, for La Morale bantoue. . . ., 1962; Off., Order of Leopold, 1966. Address: 5, rue des Taxandres, 1040 Brussels, Belgium.

RYALI, Rajagopal, b. 10 Mar. 1937. University Professor; Teaching & Research. Educ: M.A., Univ. of Madras, India, 1959; Post-grad. Dip. in Anthropol., ibid, 1966; A.M., Duke Univ., U.S.A., 1968; Ph.D., ibid, 1970. Appts. incl: Lang. & Lit. Tutor, Madras Christian Coll., Tambaram, 1959-61; Lang. & Lit. Lectr., Madras, 1961-66; Tchng. Asst. in Anthropol., Duke Univ., 1966-67; Instr. in Anthropol., ibid, 1970; Asst. Prof. of Modernization Processes & Anthropol., Univ. of Wis.-Green Bay, 1970-; Chmn. of Anthropol., ibid, 1973-. Mbrships: Fellow, Am. Anthropol. Assn., Chmn., session on Kinship, Annual Conf., Toronto, Canada, 1972; Assoc. in Current Anthropol., Chgo.; Green Bay Area Chmbr. of Comm., Career Counseling Comm.; Nat. Geographic, U.S.A. Publs. incl: Handbook on Translation, 1965; Amerindians Of The Great Lakes: A Prehistory, 1972; num. contbns. in books, encys. & profl. jrnls. Hons. incl: Maharajah of Bobili, GCIE, Gold Medal, Univ. of Madras, 1959. Address: Coll. of Community Scis., Univ. of Wis.-Green Bay, Green Bay, WI 54302, U.S.A. 130.

RYAN, Eugene Joseph, b. 28 Aug. 1923. Social Service Administrator. Educ: A.B., Harvard Univ., 1954. Appts: Dir., Div. of Institutions, Hosps. & Nursing Homes, Dept. of Pub. Welfare, Commonwealth of Mass. Mbrships: Marsalin Inst.; Am. Pub. Welfare Assn.; Trustee, Mass. Guild of Soc. Serv.; Comm., John Alden Carpenter Mem.; Churchill Club, London; Beacon Soc., Boston; Algonquin Club, Boston; Bay Club, Boston. Address: 151 Tremont St., Boston, MA 02111, U.S.A.

RYAN, Ione Jean Alohilani Rathburn, b. 18 Oct. 1926. Professor. Educ: Ed.B., Univ. of Hawaii, 1948; M.S., Univ. of Minn., 1950; Ed.D., Stanford Univ., 1960; Educl. Leadership Trng. Prog., Univ. of Hawaii/State Dept. of Educ., 1957-59. Appts. incl: Assoc. Prof., Prof., E. Carolina Univ., 1966-; Asst. Prof., Coll. of Educ. & Counselor, Univ. Counseling Ctr., Univ. of Hawaii, 1961-62; Advsr., Ford Fndn.

Tchr. Educ. Prog., ibid, 1961-65; Grad. Fac., Schl. of Pub. Hlth., 1964-65; Hons. Prog. Advsr., 1960-65; Asst. Rschr., Ford Fndn. Projs., 1963-65; Mbr., Bd. Dirs., REAL Crisis Intervention Ctr., 1974; Mbrships. incl: Phi Kappa Phi; Assn. for Humanistic Psychol., Phi Lambda Theta. Hons: Real Dean, Hawaii Univ., 1948; 1 of 1st 2 recips., Pub. Hlth. Schlrship., Honolulu Chmbr. of Comm., 1948; Outstanding Alumna, Kamehameha Schls., 1956. Address: Counseling Ctr., E. Carolina Univ., Wright Bldg., Room 207, Greenville, NC 27834, U.S.A. 78, 125.

RYAN, Robert Brennan, b. 25 May 1920. Attorney; Food Company Executive. Educ: Student, Loyola Univ., Chgo., Ill., 1939-41; J.D., LL.B. DePaul Univ., 1947. Appts: Internal Revenue Agent, U.S. Govt., Chgo., Ill., 1948-56, Special Agent, Northwestern Mutual Life Ins. Co., Evanston, ibid, 1956-63; Asst. Sec., Asst. Treas., McDonald's Corp., 1963-67; V.P., ibid, 1967-; Treas., 1973-. Mbrships: Served to 1st Lt., USAAF, 1941-45; Fed. Bar Assn.; Roman Cath. Address: 1531 Basswood Circle, Glenview, IL 60025, U.S.A. 8.

RYAN, T. Antoinette. Psychologist. Educ: A.B., Stanford Univ./Sacramento State Univ.; M.A., Sacramento State Univ.; Ph.D., Stanford Univ.; Univs. of Oslo & Geneva. Appts: Hd. Counselor, Sacramento City Coll., 1957-60; Dir. of Testing & Vets. Counselor, ibid, 1961-62; Counselor, 1962-63; Prof., Ore. State Univ., 1963-68; Dir., Rsch. Coord. Unit, ibid, 1965-68; Rsch. Prof., Univ. of Hawaii, 1968-. Mbrships. incl: Am. Educl. Rsch. Assn. (V.P., 1970-72); Fellow, Am. Psychol. Assn.; Presidential appointee to White House Conf. on Children, 1971. Publs. incl: Guidance & the Emerging Adolescents, 1970; Organization & Administration of Guidance, 1972. Recip. Nat. Award, APGA, 1966. Address: 1776 Univ. Ave., Honolulu, HI 96822, U.S.A. 2, 9, 5, 22, 14, 130, 141, 120, 78, 30

RYDER, (Sir) Don (Sydney Thomas Franklyn), b. 16 Sept. 1916. Businessman. Appts: Ed., Stock Exchange Gazette, 1950-60; Jt. Mng. Dir., Kelly Iliffe Holdings & Assocd. Iliffe Pres., 1960-61; Sole Mng. Dir., ibid, 1961-63; Dir., Int. Publishing Corp. Ltd., 1963-70; Mng. Dir., Reed Paper Group Ltd., 1963-68; Chmn. & Chief Exec., Reed Int. Ltd., 1968-; Dir., MEPC Ltd., 1972-; p/t mbr., British Gas Corp., 1973-. Mbrships: Mbr. of Coun., British Inst. of Mgmt., 1970-; Mbr. of Ct. & Coun., Cranfield Inst. of Technol., Bedford, 1970-; Pres., Nat. Materials Handling Ctr., 1970-; Mbr. of Coun., Industrial Soc., 1971-. Recip., Knight Bachelor, 1972. Address: Reed Int. Ltd., 82 Piccadilly, London W1A 1EJ, U.K. 1, 32, 34, 35, 41, 43, 128.

RYDER, Michael Lawson, b. 24 July 1927. Biologist. Educ: B.Sc., Leeds Univ., U.K., 1951; M.Sc., 1954; Ph.D., 1956. Appts: Wool Inds. Rsch. Assn., Leeds; Sr. Lectr., Univ. of New Engl., Australia; Prin. Sci. Officer, Animal Breeding Rsch. Org., Edinburgh, U.K.; Hon. Lectr., Edinburgh Univ. Fellow & Mbr., P.R. Comm., Inst. of Biol. Mbrships: Comm., Scottish Ctr., Int. PEN; Coun., Rare Breeds Survival & Trust. Publs: Wool Growth (co-auth.), 1968; Animal Bones in Archaeology, 1969; Hair, 1973; contbr. to mags. Address: ABRO Field Lab., Roslin, EH25 9PS, U.K. 47.

RYF, Robert Stanley, b. 12 Aug. 1918. Professor; Writer. Educ: A.B., Occidental Coll., 1939; M.A., ibid, 1953; Ph.D., Columbia Univ., 1956. Appts: Writer, CBS, 1945-48; Free-lance Writer, 1948-53; Instr.-Prof., Engl. &

Comparative Lit., Occidental Coll., 1956-63; Dean of Students, ibid, 1961-65; Dean of Fac., V.P. for Acad. Affairs, 1967-72; Prof. of Engl. & Comparative Lit. & Arthur G. Coons Prof., 1972-. Mbrships: Phi Beta Kappa; MLA; AAUP; Twilight Club of Pasadena. Publs: A New Approach to Joyce, 1962; Henry Green, 1967; Joseph Conrad, 1970. Recip. acad. hons. Address: c/o Dept. of Engl. & Comparative Lit., Occidental Coll., Los Angeles, CA 90041, U.S.A. 2, 13.

RYMOWICZ, Alicia, b. 22 Sept. 1907. Painter. Educ: Schl. of Fine Arts, Geneva, Switzerland; Inst. Royal Supèrieur des Beaux Arts, Antwerp, Belgium; Student at Prof. Isidore Opsomer's personal workshop, ibid. Pictures in pvte. collections in Antwerp, Brussels, Ghent, Ostend, Hasselt, Paris, N.Y., Geneva, etc. Picture in pvte. collection of Princess Paola of Belgium; also one at Bogota Mus., Columbia & at Schoten Town Hall, Antwerp. Winner of sev. student awards from var. countries. Address: J. van Rijswijcklaan 34, Antwerp, Belgium. 105.

RYNELL, (Hans Torsten) Alarik, b. 7 Mar. 1913. Professor of English. Educ: Fil.Dr., Lund Univ., Sweden, 1948. Appts: Docent, Lund Univ., 1948-52; Prof., Engl., Stockholm Univ., 1952-. Mbrships: Swedish Humanistic Rsch. Coun., 1960-66. Publs: The Rivalry of Scandinavian & Native Synonyms in Middle English, 1948; Parataxis & Hypotaxis as a Criterion of Syntax & Style, Especially in Old English Poetry, 1952. Hons: Kt. Cmdr., Royal Order of Northern Star, 1970; Mbr., Royal Swedish Acad. of Letters, Hist. & Antiquities. Address: Pyrolavägen 13, S-181 60 Lidingö, Sweden.

RYSDORP, Klaas, b. 27 Nov. 1911. University Professor. Educ: Study of Phys. Educ., Physiotherapeutics, Constitutional Law, Pedagogy, Amsterdam & Utrecht; Doctorate, Phys. Educ., Leuven, Belgium; Postdoctoral study, N.Y. Univ., U.S.A. Appts: Tchr., Phys. Educ. & Law, var. elem. & secondary schls.; Lector, Univ. of Indonesia, Bandung; City Schl. Insp., The Hague; Tchr., Royal Marine Inst.; Rector, Acad. of Phys. Educ., The Hague; Prof., Gymnol., Univ. of Utrecht. Mbrships: Pres., Int. Coun. on Hlth., Phys. Educ. & Recreation; Comité Int. de Fair Play; Mbr., Tripartite Comm. of int. orgs. of phys. educ. & sports; Comm. Mbr., Freizeit und Sport; Profl. Advsry. Bd., Int. Recreation Assn.; Pres., state bur. for higher phys. educ. exams; Pres., State comm.; Modernising Curric of Phys. Educ.; Pres., Edit. Staff, Physical Education (Dutch); Edit. Staff Mbr., Pedagogical Studies (Dutch). Publs: 14 books in Dutch, num. essays, papers & lectures. Hons: Mbr., Dutch Phys. Educ. Assn., 1962; Tat McKenzie Medal, Jamaica, 1971; Int. Recognition Award, U.S.A., 1973. Address: Laan van Meerdervoort 691, The Hague, The Netherlands. 43.

RYTI, (Karl Johan) Henrik, b. 29 Dec. 1916. Professor. Educ: Dipl. Ins., Helsinki Univ. of Technol., Finland, 1940; Dr. Technol., ibid, 1949. Appts: Dipl. Ins., Valmet Oy, 1944-56; Prof. Heat Engrng., Helsinki Univ. of Technol., 1956-. Mbrships: Finnish Acad. of Tech. Scis.; Ed., Acta Polytechnica Scandinavica, subseries Mech. Engrng. Publs: Articles in Tekniikan Käsikirja (Tech. Handbook), 7th & 8th edits., 1951, 1972. Address: The Helsinki Univ. of Technology, 02150 Otaniemi, Finland. 90.

RYTÖMAA, Tapio Jouko Eero, b. 22 Feb. 1932. Physician; Educator. Educ: B.Med., Univ. of Helsinki, Finland, 1955; Lic.Med., 1959; Dr.Med. Scis., 1960. Appts. incl: Rsch. Asst., 2nd Dept. Pathol., Univ. of Helsinki, 1959-61, 62-63; Rsch. Fellow, Hallonblad Fndn., ibid, 1967-70; Lectr., Exptl. Cell Rsch., 1967-; Rsch. Asst., State Med. Commn., 1963-64; Jr. Sci., ibid, 1964-67; Cons., Med., Inst. of Radiation Phys., 1970-. Mbrships. incl: European Study Grp. for Cell Proliferation; European Assn. for Cancer Rsch.; Bd., Nordic Soc. for Radiation Protection, 1971-; Int. Radiation Protection Assn.; Finnish Med. Assn. Publs: Control of Cellular Growth in Adult Organisms, 1967; approx. 60 articles & reviews. Address: Inst. of Radiation Phys., Box 268, 00101 Helsinki 10, Finland. 134.

S

SÄÄF-NORDEN, Georg H.A., b. 8 June 1912. Mechanical Engineer; Director. Educ: Tech. Univ., Vienna, Austria. Appts: Engr., J. Pintsch K.G. Expmtl. Dept., Berlin, Germany, 1937; German Air Force, 1939; Tech. Dept. of Ctrl. Orgs. Austrian Pulp & Paper Ind., Vienna, 1947; Prokurist Zellstoff-und Papierfabrik Frantschach AG, ibid, 1961; Dir., Natronpapierindustrie AG, 1962; Tech. Cons. for Ctrl. Orgs. Austrian Pulp & Paper Ind., & Mng. Dir., ÖZEPA, 1967-. Mbrships. incl: Tech. Assn. of the Pulp & Paper Ind., U.S.A.; Tech. Sect. of Canadian Pulp & Paper Ind.; Assn. tech. de l'Ind. Papetière, France; Associazione Tecnica Italiana Cellulosa Carta, Italy; Paper & Paperboard Makers Assn., Tech. Sect., U.K.; Indian Pulp & Paper Assn.; Österreichischer Ingenieur- u. Architekten-Verein Chmn. of Tech. Comm., Österreichischer Energie-Konsumenten-Verein; Chmn. of var. comms., Österreichisches Normungsinst.; Societá Dante Alighieri, Austria; VP, Techniker Cercle, Vienna; Chmn. of Jury for Austrian Packaging Award; Cons. to Zollbeirat of Min. of Finance & Min. of Commerce & Ind. Address: Gumpendorfer Strasse 6, A-1061 Vienna, Austria. 43.

SAAGE, Gustav, b. 15 Aug. 1910. Chartered Accountant; Tax Consultant; University Professor. Educ: Bank apprenticeship; Dr.rer.pol. Chartered Acct., Prof., Univ. of Göttingen. Publs: Die stillen Reserven im Rahmen der Abschlussprüfung, 1959; Die Prüfung der Geschäftsführung, 1965; Veränderte Grundlagen der Gewinnermittlung nach Handels—& Steuerrecht, in Der Betrieb, 1969; Die Reform der Rechnungslegung der GmbH, in Neue Betriebswirtschaft, 1970; Die Überwachung der Vorstandstätigkeit durch den Aufsichtsrat in der AG, in Handbuch des Aufsichtsrats, 1972; Prospektprüfungen, in Der Betrieb, 1973. Address: Marienstr. 92, 3 Hanover, German Fed. Repub. 43.

SABA, Elias Shukri, b. 10 July 1932. Economist; Politician. Educ: B.A., Am. Univ. of Beirut, 1954; M.A., ibid, 1956; B.Litt., Univ. of Oxford, U.K., 1958. Appts: Econ. Advsr. to Min. of Finance & Oil, Kuwait, & to Kuwait Fund for Arab Econ. Dev., 1961-62; Chmn., Dept. of Econs., & Assoc. Prof. of Econs., Am. Univ. of Beirut, 1963-69; Dpty. Prime Min. & Min. of Finance & Defence, Lebanon, 1970-72; Econ. & Financial Advsr. to Pres., Repub. of Lebanon, 1972-73. Author of The Foreign Exchange System of Lebanon & Syria (preface by Sir Roy Harrod), 1962. Address: P.O. Box 9500, Beirut, Lebanon. 34.

SABADIN, Gavino, b. 4 Sept. 1890. Lawyer. Educ: Law degree, Univ. of Padua, Italy. Mayor, Cittadella, Counselor, Padua Prov., 1914-20; Pres., Cath. Trade Unions & Coops., Padua Prov., 1920-25; Pres., Civil Hosp., Cittadella, 1951-65; Pres., Assoc. Hosps. & Nat. Bd. of Hosp's. Dirs.; Pres., Inst. Houses for Wkrs., Padua, 1956-74; Hon. Pres., Nat. Inst. Houses for Wkrs. Mbrships: Fndr., Brigade Damiano Chiesa, 1943; Sr., Liberation Comm., Venetian Region; Prefect of Padua; Sec., Venetian Region, Christian Democratic Party; Hd., D.C. Grp., Comm. of Padua Prov., 1951-64. Publs. incl: The Economic Depression in the Venetian Region, 1955; Armonies of the Creation & of the History, 1958; History as Past Present & Future, 1967; The Resistance—A Revolution Not Yet Finished, 1973. Hons. incl: Silver Medal; Gt. Officer, Italian Repub.; Golden Crown for 58 yrs. serv. as lawyer. Address: Via Borgo Padova 72, 35013 Cittadella, Italy. 43.

SABET-SHARGHI, Zabiholah, b. 23 Aug. 1939. Industrial Psychologist. Educ: B.S., M.A., Tehran Univ., Iran; M.A., Ph.D., Case Western Reserve Univ., Cleveland, Ohio, U.S.A. Mgmt. Rsch. Cons., Cleveland Transit System, 1968-70; Mgmt. Cons., Cleveland Indl. Workshops, 1970-; Chmn., Psychol. Dept. & Assoc. Prof., St. Francis Coll., Ft. Wayne, Ind. Mbrships: Am. Psychol. Assn.; Acad. Mgmt. Contbr., profl. jrnls. Address: St. Francis Coll., 2701 Spring St., Ft. Wayne, IN 46808, U.S.A.

SABIDO, Almeda Alice McClellen, b. 24 Sept. 1928. Psychiatric Social Work Administrator. Educ: B.S., Ind. Univ. of Pa., U.S.A., 1950; Master of Soc. Work, Univ. of Pitts., Pa., 1958. Appts: Staff Psychiatric Soc. Wkr., Staten Island Mental Hlth. Soc., N.Y., 1958-63; Supvsr. of Psychiatric Soc. Wkrs., ibid, 1963-66; Asst. Dir. of Psychiatric Soc. Work, 1967-69; Dir. of Psychiatric Soc. Work, 1969-. Mbrships: Nat. Assn. of Soc. Wkrs.; Acad. of Cert. Soc. Wkrs.; NAACP; Urban League; Staten Island League for Better Govt.; Nat. Coun. of Negro Women; Family & Child Care Div., Staten Island Community Chest & Coun.; Cert. Soc. Wkr., N.Y. State. Address: 142 Benedict Ave., Staten Island, NY 10314, U.S.A. 5, 6, 129, 132, 138.

SABINAS, Leona Clare (Mrs. Floyd Sabinas), b. 18 July 1914. Commercial-Industrial-Residential Real Estate Broker. Educ: Bay City Jr. Coll., 1933-34; Delta Coll., 1961; Residential Course, Nat. Inst. of Real Estate Brokers. Appts. incl: Co-owner & mgr., grocery dept., White Way Market, Bay City, Mich., 1937-53; Off. mgr.-sec., Aluminum Co., Bay City, 1953-62; Assoc. saleslady, Jack Kreekun, Realtor, Bay City, 1962-65; Commercial, indl. & residential Real Estate Broker & Realtor, Bay City, 1966-. Mbrships. incl: Sec., Bay Co. Bd. of Realtors, 1968; V.P., ibid, 1969; Pres., 1970; Dir., 1970-73; Dir., Mich. Real Estate Assn., 1970; Nat. Assn. of Realtors; Nat. Inst. of Real Estate Brokers; Women's Coun., Nat. Assn. of Realtors; Am. Assn. of Bus. Women; Local & Int. Zonta Club. Hons. incl: Realtor of the yr., Bay Co., 1970. Address: 2115 Midland Rd., Bay City, MI 48706, U.S.A. 5, 138.

SABINE, Cornelia (Mrs. Paul E. Sabine). Clinical Psychologist. Educ: B.A., M.A.; Colo. Coll., Colo. Springs; Stanford Univ. Appts. incl: Chief Psychol., Child Guidance Clin., 1960-70; Pvte. Prac., Clin. Psychol. 1970-. Mbrships: Fellow, Am. Orthopsych. Assn.; Profl. Mbr., Nat. Vocational Guidance Assn.; Am. Psychological Assn.; Delta Epsilon. Address: 20 W. Espanola, Colo. Springs, CO 80907, U.S.A. 14.

SABISTON, David C., Jr., b. 4 Oct. 1924. Educator; Surgeon. Educ: B.S., Univ. of N.C., 1943; M.D., Johns Hopkins Hosp., 1947. Appts. incl: Asst. Prof.—Prof. Surg., Johns Hopkins Med. Schl., 1955-64; Howard Hughes Investigator, ibid, 1955-60; Prof. Surg., Chmn., Dept. Surg., Duke Med. Schl., 1964-. Mbrships. incl: Vice Chmn., Bd. of Govs., Am. Coll. Surgs.; Soc. Univ. Surgs.; Soc. Vascular Surg.; Soc. Thoracic Surg.; Soc. Surg. Alimentary Tract; Soc. Thoracic Surg. Gt. Britain & Ireland. Publs. incl: Davis-Christopher Textbook of Surgery: The Biological Basis of Modern Surgical Practice (Ed.); Annals of Surgery (Ed.); Cardiovascular & Thoracic Surgery; Circulation. Recip. of Career Rsch. Award, NIH, 1962-64. Address: Dept. of Surg., Duke Univ. Med. Ctr., Durham, NC 27710, U.S.A.

SABLE, Martin Howard, b. 24 Sept. 1924. University Professor. Educ: A.B., Boston Univ.; M.A., ibid; Ph.D., Nat. Univ. of Mexico; M.L.S., Simmons Coll., Boston, Mass. Appts: Asst. Rsch. Prof., Latin Am. Ctr., Univ. of Calif., L.A., 1965-68; Assoc. Prof., Schl. of Lib. & Info. Sci., Univ. of Wis., Milwaukee, 1968-72; Prof., ibid, 1972-. Mbrships. incl: Hon., Lib. Assn. Colombia, 1962; AAUP; Latin Am. Studies Assn.; ALA; Fndr., Ed., Pacific Coast Coun. on Latin Am. Studies, 1964-68; Conf. on Latin Am. Hist.; Am. Assn. of Lib. Schls. Publs. incl: Master Directory for Latin America, 1965; Periodicals for Latin American Economic Development, 1965; A Guide to Latin American Studies, 2 vols., 1967; Communism in Latin America, 1968; A Bio-Bibliography of the Kennedy Family, 1969; Latin American Studies in the Non-Western World, 1970; Latin American Urbanization, 1971; International & Area Studies Librarianship; Case Studies, 1972. Hons: Fellowship, Nat. Univ. of Mexico, 1962; Vis. Prof., Hebrew Univ., Jerusalem, 1972-73. Address: 4831 N. Oakland Ave., Milwaukee, WI 53217, U.S.A. 8.

SABLIER, Edouard, b. 29 Feb. 1920. Radio & TV Commentator on Diplomatic Affairs. Educ: Law, Pol. Sci., Oriental Langs. Appts: For. Affairs Commentator, Ldr. Writer, Diplomatic Corres. w. Le Monde newspaper, 1945-62; V.P., French Diplomatic Press, 1962; Hd., French TV news & current affairs, 1963-69; currently Commentator on Diplomatic Affairs, French radio & TV (ORTF), & Lectr., Institut des Sciences Politiques. Mbrships: Société des Gens de Lettres; Presse Diplomatique Française; Club des Capucins. Publs: incl: De la Perse à l'Iran; De l'Oral à l'Atlantique; L'Islam. Hons: Legion d'Honneur, 1962; Order of Merit, 1967. Address: 8 Place des 4 frères Casadesus, Paris 18°, France. 91.

SABO, William Joseph, b. 4 Oct. 1938. Banker. Educ: B.S., Edinboro State Coll., Pa., 1960; Am. Inst. Banking, 1966-67; Columbia Univ. Schl. Commercial Banking, 1968. Appts: Commercial Loan Off., Pullman Bank & Trust Co., 1965-66; V.P., Commercial Banking, 1st Nat. Bank of Lockport, Ill., 1966-67, Exec. V.P. & Dir., 1967-68, Pres. & Dir., 1968-73, Pres., Chief Exec. Off., Dir., 1973-; Dir., Kinetic Systems Corp., 1971-, Dir.-Ptnr., Ark. Recreational Properties, 1972-, Dir., Ark. Leisure Homes, 1973. Mbrships. incl: Gov.'s Advsry. Coun., State of Ill., 1969; Advsr., Bd. Trustees, Lewis Univ., 1970-; Dir., YMCA, 1970-, Chmn., World Serv. Campaign, 1972-73; Old Oak Country Club; Dir., ibid, 1972. Edinboro State Coll., Dean's List, 1958, '59, '60. Address: c/o. 1st National Bank of Lockport, 800 S. State St., Lockport, IL 60441, U.S.A. 8, 117.

SABOURIN, Louis, b. 1 Dec. 1935. Professor of Political Science; Director of Institute for International Cooperation. Educ: B.A., Univ. of Ottawa, Ont., Canada; LL.L., ibid; Dip. in Int. Rels., Univ. of Paris, France; Dip. in Contemporary Lit., ibid; Ph.D., Columbia Univ., N.Y.C., U.S.A. Appts: Prof. of Pol. Sci., Univ. of Ottawa, 1958-64; Chmn., Dept. of Pol. Sci., ibid, 1964-65; Dean, Fac. of Soc. Sci., 1965-67; Fndg. Dir., Inst. for Int. Cooperation, Univ. of Ottawa, 1968-; Advsr. to Govt. of Canada & to Govt. of Quebec. Mbrships. incl: Pres., Canadian Soc. of Pol. Sci., 1966-67; Pres., Ottawa Chapt., Canadian Assn. of Int. Law, 1968-70; Pres., Canadian Assn. of African Studies, 1971-72; Pres., Int. Schol. Rels. Comm., Soc. Sci. Rsch. Coun., 1972-73; Canadian Bar Assn.; Quebec Bar Assn.; Canadian Inst. of Int. Affairs. Publs: Le

Système Politique du Canada: Institutions Fédérales et Québecoises, 1968; La Dualité Culturelle dans les Activités Internationales du Canada, 1970; Num. articles in jrnls., books, & ency. Address: 346 Rue Lévis, Hull, P.Q., Canada.

SACALLI, Avghi, Artist; Writer. Educ: Color & Design, Schl. of Aldo Galli, Zurich, Switzerland. Fiction Publs: L'Homme Azure; The Woman With The Black Spectacles; Who Am I? ; Poetry Colls: Visions; Confession; The Passer-by With The Sun; The Lost Adler; White Light; Without Compass. Exhibs. of paintings in Switzerland, Greece & Cyprus. Mbrships: Hon. Mbr., Acad. Int. de Lutèce; Nat. Soc. of Greek Authors; PEN. Address: Democritou 32, Athens, Greece.

SACCHETTI, James Vincent Joseph, b. 15 Nov. 1901. Surgeon; Hospital Administrator. Educ: A.B., Harvard Coll., 1923; M.D., Harvard Med. Schl., 1927. Appts. incl: Surg. Intern, Boston City Hosp., Mass., 1928-29; Res. Surg., E. Boston Relief Stn., 1929-35; Res. Surg., Haymarket Relief Stn., 1935-38; Instr. in Surg., Tufts Univ. Med. Schl., 1935-39; Med. Dir., L.I. Hosp., Boston Harbor, 1940-51; Med. Supt., William J. Seymour Hosp., Eloise, Mich., 1951-54; Asst. Supt., Wayne Co. Gen. Hosp., ibid, 1951-54; Asst. Supt., Boston City Hosp., 1954-64, Dpty. Supt. Surg. Servs., 1962-64, Acting Supt., & Acting Dir., Hosp. Dept., 1965-66; Dpty. Commnr., Dept. Hlth. & Hosps., 1971, Commnr., 1971-73; retirement, 1973. Mbr. & Off., num. profl. & civic orgs. Profl. papers & lectures. Hons. incl: Boston City Coun. Citation for 50 Yrs. Serv. to City, 1972; var. other awards & citations. Address: 457 Gallivan Blvd., Dorchester, MA 02124, U.S.A. 6, 130, 131.

SACHS, Arieh. Theatre Director; University Professor; Writer. Educ: B.A. (Hons.), Johns Hopkins Univ., U.S.A., 1954; M.A., ibid, 1955; Sorbonne, Paris, France, 1956; Cambridge Univ., U.K., 1958-60; Ph.D., Hebrew Univ., Israel, 1962. Appts: Infantry Off., Israel Army Reserve, 1950-65; Lectr., Engl. Dept., Hebrew Univ., Jerusalem, 1956-, Hd., Dept. of Theatre, 1971-. Mbr., Israel Arts Coun. Publs: Passionate Intelligence, Reason & Imagination in the Work of Samuel Johnson, 1967; Studies in the Drama (ed.), 1967; The English Grotesque, 1969; Ze Haya Yofi (poems), 1973. Plays prod: The Deluge, 1966; Alice in Wonderland, 1967; Aristophanes' Peace, 1968; Kol-Adam (Everyman), 1969; Euripides' Bacchae, 1971; Doctor Faustus, 1973. Recip., Woodrow Wilson Fellowship, 1956. Address: Dept. of Theatre, Hebrew University, Jerusalem, Israel. 94.

SACHS, Jan, b. 17 Aug. 1911. Physician; Psychiatrist. Educ: M.D., Med. Schl., Univ. of Copenhagen, 1937; Psychiatric Specialist, 1949. Appts: Jr. Psych., Herstedvester Detention Ctr., 1943-45, 1949-52, Sr. Psych., 1952-54; Chief Psych., Horsens Detention Ctr., 1954-73; Pvte. Prac., Psych., 1973-. Mbrships: Danish Psychiatric & Criminological Socs. Contbr., var. profl. publs., newspapers & jrnls. Address: Clarasvej 12, DK-8700 Horsens, Denmark. 43.

SACKETT, Floyd Ernest, b. 17 June 1934. Educator. Educ: B.A., McMurray Coll., Abilene, Tex., 1959; M.Ed., W. Tex. State Univ., Canyon, 1964; Tex. State Tchr., Admnstr. & Supt. Certs. Appts: Tchr., 8th grade Hist., Pampa Jr. H.S., 1959-65; Asst. Prin., Robert E. Lee Jr. H.S., ibid, 1965-69; Prin., Baker Elem. Schl., 1969-. Mbrships. incl: V.P., Elem. Sect., Panhandle Schl. Ldrs. Assn.; Pampa Chmbr. of Comm.; Chmn., City of Pampa Traffic Commn.; Am. Red Cross; Pres.,

V.P., Sec., Phi Delta Kappa; Life, NEA; Pres., Gray-Roberts Unit, Tex. State Tchrs. Assn.; Tex. Elem. Prins. & Supvsrs. Assn.; Dpty. Dist. Gov., Lions Int., 1971; Dist. Gov., 1972; Tex. State Mbrship. Chmn., 1973. Hons. incl: Lion of the Yr., Pampa Evening Lions Club, 1969; Educr. of the Yr., Phi Delta Kappa, 1973. Address: P.O. Box 1317, Pampa, TX 79065, U.S.A. 125.

SADEH, Dror, b. 25 Feb. 1932. Scientist. Educ: M.Sc., Hebrew Univ., 1956; D.Sc., Sorbonne, Paris, France, 1960. Appts: Mbr., Israel Atomic Energy Commn., 1957-65; Lectr., Haifa Technion, 1960-62; Rsch. Assoc., Univ. of Calif., U.S.A., 1965-66, Naval Rsch. Lab., Wash. D.C., 1966-68; Prof. of Astron., Tel-Aviv Univ., 1968-. Mbrships: AAAS; European & Israel Phys. Socs.; Am. Astronomical Soc. Initiated & supervised num. experiments in field of astronomy. Recip., Gravitational Award, 1969. Address: Department of Physics & Astronomy, Tel-Aviv University, Ramat Aviv, Tel-Aviv, Israel. 94.

SADLER, William Alan, Jr., b. 2 Mar. 1931. Educator; Author. Educ: B.A., Univ. of Mich., Ann Arbor, U.S.A., 1953; S.T.B., Gen. Theol. Sem., 1956; Th.M., Harvard Univ., 1957; Ph.D., ibid, 1962. Appts: Asst. Prof., Bishop's Univ., Lennoxville, P.Q., Canada, 1964-68; Assoc. Prof., Cultural Studies & Sociol., Bates Coll., Lewiston, Me., U.S.A., 1968-72; Prof., Sociol., & Hd., Interdisciplinary Studies, Bloomfield Coll., N.J., 1972-. Mbrship: Am. Sociological Assn. Publs: Master Sermons through the Ages, 1963; Existence & Love: A New Approach in Existential Phenomenology, 1969; Personality & Religion: The Role of Religion in Personality Development, 1970; Num. articles & reviews in profl. jrnls.; Papers read. Hons. incl: Frederick Sheldon Travelling Fellowship, Harvard Univ., 1958-59; Outstanding Educator of Am., 1973; Postdoctoral Fellowship, Soc. for Relig. in Higher Educ., 1973. Address: Bloomfield College, Bloomfield, NJ 07003, U.S.A. 6, 13, 139.

SADOWSKA, Krystyna, b. 2 July 1912. Artist. Educ: Acad. of Fine Arts, Warsaw, Poland; Central Schl. of Arts & Crafts, London, U.K.; Grande Chaumiere, Paris, France. Appts: Instr. & Lectr., Handcrafts Div., Govt. of N.S., Canada, 1949; Lectr. in Design, Ont. Coll. of Art, Toronto, 1953-59. Mbrships: Ont. Soc. of Artists, Canada; Int. Artists Assn., London, U.K.; Hampstead Artists Coun., London; Central Inst. of Arts & Design, London; Arts & Crafts Exhibition Soc., London; Sindicato dos Artistas Plasticos de Sao Paulo, Brasil; Polish Artists Assn. "Lad", Warsaw, Poland. Works incl: Sculpture for Ont. Govt., placed in Ont. House, London, U.K.; Sculpture for Ont. Gov. for Queen's Park; Sculpture for Univ. of Saskatoon, Canada; 4 Batiks for Winnipeg Airport for Govt. of Canada. Recip. of awards. Address: 561 Spadina Rd., Toronto 10, Ont., Canada.

SAFRAN, Alexandre, b. 12 Sept. 1910. Chief Rabbi of Geneva; Scholar; Philosopher. Educ: Jewish Theol. Sem. of Vienna; Phil. Dr., Philos. Fac., Univ. of Vienna. Appts: Former Chief Rabbi of Rumania & Mbr. of Rumanian Senate; Chief Rabbi of Geneva, Switzerland, 1948-; Lectr. on Jewish Thought, Univ. of Geneva; Pres., Underground Jewish Coun., Bucharest, WWII; Rep., Jewish World Orgs., European Off., Int. Comm., Red Cross High Commn. for Refugees, Geneva; Guest Prof., Bar-Ilan Univ., Ramat-Gan., Israel; Guest Lectr., Ecumenical Inst., Chateau de Bossey, Switz. Publs: Erziehung und Selbsterziehung, 1952; Les rapports spirituels entre l'Etat

d'Israël et la Diaspora, 1954; La Cabale, 1960, 2nd edn. 1972; La Conception juive de l'homme, 1964; Die Kabbala, 1966; Moussar vehevra beidan hamoderni, 1969; Nahmanide et les interrogations de notre temps, 1971; Le peuple de Dieu dans la tradition juive, ancienne et moderne, 1972; etc. Recip., L'esprit du Sabbat, 1973. Address: 11, rue Marignac, CH 1206, Geneva, Switzerland. 10, 55.

SAFRO, Paul, b. 29 May 1912. Certified Public Accountant. Educ: CCNY. Appts: Dir., Flushing Nat. Bank; Sr. Ptnr., Westheimer, Fine, Berger & Co., Certified Pub. Accts. Mbrships: N.Y. State Soc. of Certified Pub. Accts.; Am. Inst. of Certified Pub. Accts.; Trustee, Bnai Zion; Pres., Kfar Masada, Inc. (Youth Camp); Campaign Cabinet, United Jewish Appeal; Assembly of Jewish Agcy.; Coun., World Zionist Org.; Bd. mbr., Herzog World Acad.; Bd. mbr., Temple Bethel of Cedarhurst; Fndr., Eleanor Roosevelt Cancer Rsch. Inst. Author of 2 articles on acctng. & taxes, Your Tax Guide & Pay as You Go Tax Explained. Hons. incl: Guest of Hon. & Awards, Israel Bond & United Jewish Appeal. Address: 11 Copper Beech Lane, Lawrence, N.Y., NY 11516, U.S.A. 55, 94.

SAGGIORI, Renato, b. 28 Dec. 1939. Publisher; Autograph Dealer. Educ: Dr., Pol. & Soc. Sci., Padua Univ., Italy. Appts: Dir., Studio A. Mussato, Padua, 1963-73; Dir., Jrnl. Il Bo, 1964; Publr. & Dir., revue, L'Autographe, Meylan, France, 1973-; Dealer, Art, Autographs, Documents, old Books, Drawing, old Prints. Mbrships: Tribunato dell'Università di Padova, 1960-65; Coun., O.S.I.S.P., 1962-66; Assn., Fil Padovana, 1960; U.N.C.I. of Italian Coll., Rome, 1960; Assn. des Coll. Suisses d' Autographes, Basle, 1962; Manuscript Soc., Carbondale, U.S.A., 1969, etc. Publs: Catalogues of Studio A. Mussato; Revue l'Autographe; Contbr. many articles on art & histl. subjects in jrnls. & magazines. Hons: Sev. prizes as Autograph collector. Address: 51, Ave. de la Cartreuse, F-38240, Meylan (Isére), France. 133.

SAHINKAYA, Fatma Rezan, b. 30 Jan. 1924. Professor. Educ: Fac. Agric., Ankara Univ., Turkey, 1945; Fac. Lang., Hist. & Geography, Dept. Engl. Lang. & Lit., ibid, 1949; Ph.D., ibid, 1951; Post-grad. studies, Lincoln Grad. Schl., Neb. Univ., U.S.A., 2 yrs. Appts: Min. Agric. Tech. Schl. Agric., 1945-46, Dept. Animal Husbandry, Dept. Home Econs. & Dept. Fiber, Fac. Agric., Ankara Univ., Turkey, 1946-. Mbrships: Turkish Agric. Engrs. Assn.; Past Pres., Turkish Univ. Women's Assn.; Turkish Coun. of Women; Turkish Women's Assn.; Int. Fedn. Home Econs.; Turkish Assn. Early Childhood Educ. Publs. incl: Effects of War Upon Early Marriage, 1957; Emergence of Sex and Race Friendship Preferences; Different Aspects of Family Planning in Regard to Turkey, 1962; Child Mortality in the Hatay, 1962; Family Structure in the Middle Anatolian Villages, 1965; Family Happiness and Child Mortality in the Rural and Urban Areas in Hatay Region, 1970 (all jrnl. articles); Psycho-Social Aspects of Family (textbook), 1967. Address: Dept. Home Econs., Fac. Agric. Ankara Univ., Aydinlikevler, Ankara, Turkey.

SAIN, Charles H., b. 20 Jan. 1923. Consulting Engineer. Educ: B.C.E., Univ. of Fla., Gainesville, U.S.A., 1949. Appts. incl: Maths. Instr., Corps of Engrs., U.S. Army, 1944-46; Proj. Mgr., Moss-Thornton Co. Inc., Texarkana, Tex., 1949-52; Chief Engr., Moss-Thornton Co. Inc., Leeds, Ala., 1952-54; V.P. Engrng., ibid, 1954-60; Assoc., Charles H. Sain & Assocs., Birmingham, Ala., 1961-;

Lectr., Civil Engrng. Short Courses, Auburn Univ., Ala. Mbrships. incl: Am. Soc. of Civil Engrs.; Am. Soc. of Mil. Engrs.; Am. Soc. of Profl. Engrs.; Advsry. Bd., Ala. Highway Dept.; V.P. & Dir., Golf Ctr., Inc., Birmingham, 1958-; Toll Bridge Authority, Ala.; Am. Rd. Bldrs. Assn.; Dir., Ala. Rd. Bldrs. Assn., Inc.; Kappa Alpha; Gamma Lambda Sigma; Sigma Tau. Publs: Contbn. to Stardard Handbook for Civil Engineers, 1968; Articles in profl. mags. Recip., Mbrship., as Eminent Engr., Tau Beta Pi, 1971. Address: P.O. Box 5705, Birmingham, AL 35209. 6, 7, 16, 57, 132.

SAINE, Leonard Watson, b. 1 July 1894. Company Owner. Educ: Ga. Schl. of Technol.; LL.B., Atlanta Law Schl., 1916. Appts: Field Engr. & Supt. Pub. Wkrs., J.B. McCrary Co., 1916-17, '19-27; Chief Warrant, USNRF, 1917-18; Sales Mgr., Ctrl. Foundry Co., 1928-29; Gen. Sales Mgr., Universal Pipe & Dir., Ctrl. Foundry Co., 1930-33; Sales, McCrary Co., Walworth Co., Ctrl. Foundry Co., until 1938; Pres., Treas., Saine Co.; Owner, Leonard W. Saine Dealers. Mbrships: Beta Theta Pi; Mason; Fla. Engrng. Soc.; Nat. Soc. Profl. Engrs. Holder of patents. Address: 1555 W. Fairbanks Ave., Winter Park, FL U.S.A. 7, 16, 26.

SAINI, TejBhan Singh, b. 17 June 1921. Economist; Forester. Educ: B.A., Govt. Coll., Lyallpur, India, 1941; M.A., Forman Christian Coll., Lahore, 1943; D.D.R., Indian Forest Ranger Coll., Dehadun, 1945; D.Forestry, Duke Univ., Durham, N.C., U.S.A., 1958; Ph.D., New Schl. for Soc. Rsch., N.Y.C., 1972. Appts: Range Forest Off., Punjab, India, 1945-54; Lectr., New Schl. for Soc. Rsch., N.Y.C., U.S.A., 1960-61; Forest Econ., Food & Agric. Org., UN, Africa, Middle E. & Europe, 1962-65; Assoc. Prof. & Chmn., Dept. of Bus. & Econs., Bluffton Coll., Ohio, 1966-68; Prof. & Chmn., Dept. of Econs., Bloomsburg State Coll., Pa., 1968-. Mbrships incl: Am. Econ. Assn.; Econometric Soc.; Soc. Am. Foresters; Fndr. & Sec.-Treas., Eastern Econ. Assn.; Fndr., Mng. Ed., Eastern Economic Jrnl.; AAUP. Author of many publs. in field. Address: Dept. of Econs., Bloomsburg State Coll., Bloomsburg, PA 17815, U.S.A. 6, 14.

ST. AUBIN, Darrel Lee, b. 22 Feb. 1944. Director of United Ministries in Higher Education. Educ: B.A., Ill. Wesleyan Univ., 1966; M.Divinity, Garrett Theological Sem., 1969. Appts. incl: Asst. Pastor, 1st Meth. Ch., Pontiac, ill., 1962, Trinity Meth. Ch., Mt. Prospect, Ill, 1966; Wyo. Dir., Min. Staff, Mammoth Hot Springs, Yellowstone Nat. Pk., 1967; Pastor, El Portal Community Ch., Calif., 1968-69; Dir., Norse Campus Min., Miami, Okla., 1969-72; Dir., United Mins. in Higher Educ., Pitts., Kan., 1972.; Co-Fndr., V.P., Campus Child Care Ctr. Inc.; V.P., Help Now Inc.; Mbr., Advsry. Bd., Family Planning Prog. Mbrships. incl: Bd. of Dirs., Miami Jaycees & Rotary Club; V.P., Pitts. (Kan.) Ministerial Assn. Hons: Disting. Serv. Award for Miami, & Outstanding Citizen of Yr. Award, 1971. Address: 201 E. Williams, Pittsburg, KS 66762, U.S.A. 125.

ST. CYR, Carol R., b. 25 Dec. 1924. Professor of Education. Educ: B.S., Willimantic State Coll., Conn., 1946; M.A., Trinity Coll., Hartford, 1949; Ph.D., Univ. of Mich., Ann Arbor, 1955. Appts: Tchr., Conn., 1946-53; Rsch. Asst., Univ. of. Mich., 1953-55; Vis. Prof., Univ. of N.C., summer, 1955; Asst. Prof., Geo. Wash. Univ., 1955-60; Assoc. Prof., ibid, 1960-64; Prof., Educ., 1964-; Educ. Cons. Mbrships: Phi Delta Kappa; AAUP; AAUW; Assn. for Supvsn. & Curric. Dev.; Bd. of Dirs.,

Nat. Aerospace Educ. Assn., 1967-; Pres., ibid, 1972-74; A4; AAAS; Pi Lambda Theta; V.P., Fedn. Aeronautique Int. Address: Schl. of Educ. Geo. Wash. Univ., 2201 G. St., N.W., Wash. DC 20004, U.S.A. 5, 15, 22, 25.

ST. HILL, Irvine Chalmer McCarthy, b. 21 Jan. 1920. Librarian. Educ: B.A., Univ. of London, U.K.; B.L.S., Univ. of Toronto, Canada. Appts: Schl. Tchr., Primary Schls., 1940-43, Secondary Schl., 1943-59; Chief Libn., Pub. Lib., Bridgetown, Barbados, 1959-. Mbrships: Pres., Lib. Assn. of Barbados, 1968-70; Barbados Mus. & Hist!. Soc.; Past Mbr., Bd. Dirs., Caribbean Broadcasting Corp.; Dpty. Chmn., ibid, 1968-70. Publs: book reviews in BIM mag.; article in Ency. of Lib. & Info. Sci. Address: Pub. Lib., Coleridge St., Bridgetown 2, Barbados, W. Indies.

SAINT-LOU, Maurice (Count Dom Palatino De Kelidonia), b. 24 Oct. 1897. Artist. Educ: studied Violin, Paris Conservatory, France; studied painting, Beaux Arts, Nice, France; Hon. Ph.D. Appts. incl: Free-lance expressionist & portrait painter; Concert Violinist; Film Dir. & Prod., 1926-52; Film writer, 1948-50; Art Tchr., Mus. of Shreveport, La., U.S.A. Work included in worldwide exhibs. One-Man shows in France, Mexico & U.S.A. Paintings in many pub. collects. inclng. City Hall, Phila., Mexican Embassy, Wash., Beaumont Mus., Tex., Israel Mus. & Shreveport Mus. of Art, La., U.S.A. Mbrships. incl: Assn. des Auteurs des Films; Beaux Arts, Nice, France; Fine Arts & Educl. Inst., Wash., U.S.A.; Int. Am. Inst., Wash. DC; Hon. Advsr., Columbus Assn., U.S.A.; Hon. Mbr., Mexican Int. Acad.; Fellow & Hon. Life Mbr., Am. Int. Acad.; Hon. Prof., Humani, Humanist Inst., France. Hons. incl: Silver Medal, Japanese Red Cross, 1967; Gold Medal of Arts, Scis. & Letters, Paris, France, 1970; Nobility of Chevalier, Greek Order, 1970. Address: Ranchito Saint-Lou, 225 Mohawk Rd., Santa Barbara, CA 93109, U.S.A. 55.

SAINT-SMITH, J.C., b. 15 Apr. 1912. Engineer; Executive. Educ: B.E., Univ. of Qld., Australia. Appts: Exec. Engr., City Elec. Light Co. Ltd., Brisbane; Chief Engr. & Mgr., Wide Bay Burnett Regional Elec. Bd.; Mgr., The Townsville Regional Elec. Bd.; Gen. Mgr., Copper Refineries Pty. Ltd., Townsville; Gen. Mgr., Tech. Dev., M.I.M. Holdings Ltd., Brisbane; Served WW II. Mbrships: Fndn. Pres., Townsville Sr. Citizens Welfare Assn.; Coun. mbr., James Cook Univ. of N. Qld.; Past Pres., Maryborough Legacy Club; Past Pres., Townsville Legacy Club; Past Pres., Townsville Rotary Club; Johnsonian Club; Brisbane N. Rotary Club; Brisbane Club. Recip., C.B.E., 1968. Address: 33 Aston St., Toowong, Brisbane, Australia, 4066. 23.

SAJKOVIC, Vladimir, b. 25 Jan. 1912. College Professor. Educ: B.A., Russkoe Realnoe Uchilishche, Finland, 1932; Ceska Visoka Skola Technicka, Brno, Czechoslovakia, 1932-35; Univ. of Helsinki, Finland, 1935-37; M.A., Univ. of Pa., U.S.A.; 1949; Ph.D., ibid, 1953. Appts. incl: Instr. Assoc. Prof., Univ. of Pa. 1953-59; Vis. Instr., Bryn Mawr Coll., 1954-57; Asst. Prof.-Prof., Mt. Holyoke Coll., 1959-; Chmn., Dept. of Russian Lang. & Lit., ibid 1959-70. Mbrships: Am. Assn. Tchrs. of Slavic & E. European Langs; Am. Assn. Adv. Slavic Studies; Soc. of Sci. Study of Relig.; Fndg. Int. Dosteoysky Soc., 1971-; Assn. of Russian—Am. Schols. in U.S.A., 1973-. AAUP; Recip. of acad. hons. Address: Mount Holyoke Coll., Dept. of Russian Lang. & Lit., South Hadley, MA 01705, U.S.A. 2, 6, 13, 15.

SAKAOKA, Yasue, b. 12 Nov. 1933. Artist-Teacher. Educ: Aoyama Gakuin Univ., Tokyo, Japan, 1953; B.A., Reed Coll., Portland, Oregon, 1959; M.F.A., Univ. of Oregon, Eugene, 1973; Rinehart Inst. of Sculpture, Baltimore, Md., 1963-65. Appts: Instr., Univ. of Oregon Extension Div., Eugene, & Md. Inst. of Art Evening Schl., Baltimore; Asst. Prof. of Art, St. Paul's Coll., Lawrenceville, Va.; Vis. Lectr. to many profl. schls. & colls. Mbrships: Coll. Art Assn. of Am.; Nat. Art Educ. Assn.; Southeastern Coll. Art Conf.; Southern Assn. of Sculptors; Va. Art Educ. Assn.; Galerie Internationale, N.Y.; Delta Psi Omega, 1970-. Designer of stage sets; Exhibs. held in Va. & N.Y.C.; Sculptor of play-ground structures for S. Hill, Va. Works held in num. pvte. collections in U.S.A. Winner, Commn. Awards, Jr. Chmbr. of Comm., Albany, 1960; Parkside Gdns., Baltimore, Md., 1965; S.Hill, Va. Address: St. Paul's Coll., Lawrenceville, VA 23868, U.S.A. 105.

SALA, Florence Sarah, b. 7 Apr. 1905. Author. Educ: Hillyer Coll. Mbrships: Pioneer Valley Scripters Club; Poetry League Workshop; Conn. Trail Riders Assoc.; Springfield Ice Birds; Wethersfield Sport Club; Charter Oak Figure Skating Club. Author of novel, Heights & Depths. Poetry in Hartford Current, Hartford Times, New Haven Info., Wetherfield Post, West Hartford News, Vermont Horse & Bridle Trail Bulletin, Hoof Prints, Arizona. Recip., 1st Prize in poetry contest. Address: 398 Middletown Ave., Wethersfield, CT 06109, U.S.A. 11.

SALAMEH, Kamal Butros, b. 14 Nov. 1927. Pediatric Physician. Educ: B.A., Am. Univ. of Beirut, Lebanon, 1950; M.D., ibid, 1955; Res., Pediatrics, State Univ. of Iowa Hosps., Iowa City, U.S.A., 1964-66; Fellowship, Allergy, State Univ. of Iowa, 1966-67; Dipl., Pediatrics, Harvard Med. Schl., Boston, Mass., 1973; Dipl., Mental Retardation, ibid, 1973. Appts: Physn. i/c., Hosps. & Clins., Am. Tapline Co., Beirut, Lebanon, 1956-64; Staff Pediatrician, Caswell Ctr., N.C. Dept. of Mental Hlth., Kingston, U.S.A., 1967-; Clin. Instr., Pediatrics, Univ. of N.C., Chapel Hill, 1968-; Med. Staff Mbr., Lenior Mem. Hosp., Kingston.; Mbr., Edit. Bd., N.C. Jrnl. of Mental Hlth. Mbrships. incl: Dipl., Am. Bd. of Pediatrics, 1969; Fellow, Am. Acad. of Pediatrics, 1971; Fellow, Royal Soc. of Hlth., 1971; Dipl., Pan Am. Med. Assn.; N.C. Med. Soc.; Past Sec., Lenoir-Green-Jones Cos. Med. Soc., 1971-72. Contbn. to med. jrnl. Address: 112 Pecan Lane, Caswell Center, P.O. Box 909, Kinston, NC 28501, U.S.A. 17, 125.

SALAMONE, Gladys Lillian (Fisher), b. 28 Feb. 1921. Realist Painter in oils, water color & acrylics. Educ: self-taught profl. artist. Appts: painting & exhib. experience, over 30 yrs.; Art Tchr., over 7 yrs.; own studio & gall., Albuquerque, N.M. Mbrships: Am. Artists Profl. League; Smithsonian Instn. Assocs.; N.M. Art League; Nor Este Art Assn.: Albuquerque Art Ctr. Assn. Over 1000 paintings, pvte. collects., U.S.A. & abroad. Regular participant, competitive shows & exhibs.; 8 first places, 4 second places, 6 third places, 12 hon. mentions, 3 purchase awards. Address: 8301 Pickard Ave. N.E., Albuquerque, NM 87110, U.S.A. 37.

SALAN, Raoul (Albin Louis), b. 10 June 1899. General, French Army. Educ: Mil. Schl., St.-Cyr; Dip., Nat. Schl. of Mod. Oriental Langs. Appts. incl: Served as Volunteer, WW I; Volunteer, 17th Regiment Senegalese Tirailleurs, Levant, 1920; Wounded in combat, 1921; Lt., 1921; Capt., 1930; Lt. Col., 1941; Serv. in Indochina, Làos; Col., 1943; G3; Gén. de Brigade, cmdng. 14th Div. of Infantry, 1944; Gén. de corps d'armée & c.-in-C., Indochina, 1952-53; Mbr., Conseil supérieur de la Guerre, 1955; Insp. Gen. of Nat. Defense, 1959; Mil. Gov., Paris, 1959; Exile in Spain, 1960-61; Hd., Secret Army Org. (OAS), Algeria, 1961; Condemned to death, 1961; Arrested & sentenced to life imprisonment, 1962; Freed & pardoned during amnesty, 1968. Hon. Pres., Assn. des Combattants de l'Union Française. Author of memoirs, Fin d'un Empire, 4 vols., last vol. in preparation. Recip., many Franch & int. mil. hons. inclng. Grand Croix, Légion d'honneur, France, C.B.E., U.K. Address: 41 Blvd. Raspail, 75007 Paris, France. 34.

SALGO, Nicolas Miklos, b. 17 Aug. 1914. Aircraft Executive. Educ: LL.D., Pazmany Peter Univ., Budapest, Hungary. Appts: Ptnr. & Mgng. Dir., Salvaj & Cie., Geneva, 1940; Pres., Salvaj's N.Y. Affiliate Indeco Corp., Goal Credit Corp., 1948; Exec. V.P., Webb & Knapp, 1950; Nicholas Salgo & Co. Investment Banking, Corp. Acquisitions, 1959; Chmn., Putna Alegre Corp., 1960, & Bangor Punto Corp., 1964-73; currently Chmn., Piper Aircraft Corp. Mbrships: Past Chmn., Young Pres.'s Org., N.Y. Chapt.; Creek Club, Locust Valley, L.I.; Greenwich Country Club, Conn.; India House, N.Y.C.; Veteran, Swiss Alpine Club, Geneva; Mason de la Chasse, Paris, France. Contbr. to profl. publs. Address: 4 E. 72nd St., N.Y., NY 10021, U.S.A. 2, 22.

SALINAS, Baruj, b. 6 July 1935. Artist. Educ: B.Arch., Kent State Univ., 1957. Appts: Designer, Helmke & Allen, Archts., 1959-61; Chief Draftsman, Burger King Architectural Off., 1967-70. Mbrships. incl: Tex. Watercolor Soc., 1961-; Cuban Assn. of Plastic Arts in Fla.; Treas., ibid, 1961-63. Solo Exhibs. incl: Miami Beach Art Ctr., 1962; Galeria Centro Israelita, Mexico City, 1965; Galeria de Mexico, Montreal, Canada, 1967; Ft. Lauderdale Mus. of Art, Fla., 1969; Galerie Rene Borel, Deauville, France, 1971. Grp. Shows, U.S.A., Mexico, France, Guatemala, Venezuela, Cuba. Hons. incl: Purchase Prizes, 1963, 1964, 1965; 1st Prizes, Oil & Watercolor, Cintas Fdn. Exhib., 1965; Best Watercolor, 10th Annual Hortt. Exhib., 1968. Address: 2740 S.W. 92nd Ave., Miami, FL 33165, U.S.A. 37, 125.

SALINGER, Herman, b. 23 Dec. 1905. Professor; Writer; Translator; Poet. Educ: A.B., Princeton Univ., 1927; M.A., Stanford Univ., 1928; Ph.D., Yale Univ., 1937; Univ. of Berlin, Univ. of Cologne; Postdoct. study, Univ. of Wis. Appts. incl: Instr., German, Princeton Univ., 1932-35, Univ. of Wis., 1937-42, 1946; Asst. Prof., Univ. of Kan. City, 1946-47; Assoc. Prof.—Prof., Mod. Langs., Grinnell Coll., 1947-55; Prof., German, Duke Univ., 1955-; Chmn., Germanic Langs. & Lit., 1956-70, Chmn., Prog. in Comp. Lit., 1972-. Mbrships: Past Sec.-Treas., Int. Arthur Schnitzler Rsch. Assn.; MLA; S. Atlantic Mod. Lang. Assn., Am. Assn. of Tchrs. of German: Phi Beta Kappa. Publs. incl: Ed. & Translator, 20th-Century German Verse, 1952; Co-ed., The creative Vision, 1960; Author—Angel of Our Thirst: Poems, 1950-51; A Sigh Is the Sword: Poems, 1963; Poems Against Death, 1969. Poems in num. periodicals. Hons: Badge of Honor Poetry Prize, 1942; Roanoke-Chowan Poetry Prize, 1963; Fellow, Alexander von Humboldt Fndn., 1930-31, 1971. Address: 3444 Rugby Rd., Durham, NC 27707, U.S.A.

SALISBURY, Charles Victor. Consultant Gynaecological Surgeon. Educ: Sydney Univ., Australia & Royal Coll. of Surgs., Edinburgh,

U.K.; F.R.C.S.E., 1936; M.M.S.A., 1938; M.R.C.O.G., 1939; F.R.A.C.S., 1956. Appts: Res. Surg. Off., var. hosps. in U.K., 1928-39; Lt. Col. & Surg. Specialist, R.A.M.C., 1939-46; Hon. Cons. Gyn. Surg., St. Vincent's (1946), St. George's (1946) & Repatriation (1960) Hosps., Sydney; Lectr. & Examiner, Sydney Univ.; Res. Fellow, St. Paul's Coll., ibid. Mbrships: Past Pres., Southern Cross Gliding Club; Bathhurst Aero Club; Middle Harbour Yacht Club; Royal Sydney Golf Club. Publs: Fat Embolism in War Surgery, British Jrnl. of Surg., Vol.XXXI, no.124; Traumatic Rupture of Second Part of Duodenum, Lancet, 1944. Mentioned in Despatches, 1943, '44. Address: St. Paul's Coll., Sydney Univ., Newtown, Sydney, Australia 2042. 28.

SALISBURY, Frank Boyer, b. 8 Mar. 1926. Technical Representative in Plant Physiology. Educ: B.S., Univ. of Utah, Salt Lake City, 1951; M.A., ibid, 1952; Ph.D., Calif. Inst. of Technol., Pasadena, 1955. Appts. incl: Prof., Plant Physiol., & Plant Physiologist (Experiment Stn.), Colo. State Univ., Ft. Collins, 1961-66; Sr. Nat. Sci. Fndn. Post Doctoral Fellow, Tübingen, German Fed. Repub., & Innsbruck, Austria, 1962-63; Prof., Plant Sci., & Hd. of Dept., Utah State Univ., Logan, 1966-70; Prof. of Botany, ibid, 1968; Prof. of Plant Physiol., 1970; Tech. Rep. in Plant Physiol., Div. of Biomed & Environmental Rsch., U.S. Atomic Energy Commn., Germantown, Md. (on leave from Utah State Univ.), 1973. Mbrships: Aerial Phenomena Rsch. Org.; Fellow, AAAS; Am. Inst. of Biological Scis.; Am. Soc. of Plant Physiologists; Botanical Soc. of Am.; Ecological Soc. of Am.; Nat. Investigating Comm. for Aerial Phenomena; Phi Kappa Phi; Sigma Xi; Utah Acad. of Sci., Arts & Letters. Co-author of 3 textbooks in botany & 1 in plant physiol.; Author of 2 books in physiol. of plant reprod. (flowering). Address: 2020 Country Estates, (1255 East), N. Logan, UT 84321, U.S.A.

SALITERNIK, Zvi, b. 16 May 1897. Malariologist. Educ: M.Sc., Hebrew Univ., Jerusalem, 1936; Ph.D., ibid, 1945. Appts. incl: Pilot Field Experimental Rsch., Hadassa Med. Org., 1921-22; Chief Insp., Malaria Rsch. Unit, Min. of Hlth., 1923-28; Chief Insp. & ADvsr. Nesher, Gen. Sick Fund Org., Jewish Nat. Fund, Jewish Nat. Coun., Hadassa Med. Org. & Hebrew Univ., 1928-47; Dir., Antimalarial Sub-Dept., IDF (Capt.), 1948; Chief Malariologist, Dir., Antimalaria Div., Min. of Hlth., 1949-62; Med. Mission to Mali, 1961; Malaria & Schistosomiasis Advsr., Min. of Hlth. (Emeritus), 1962-. Mbrships: Israel Med. Assn.; Israel Entomological Assn.; Int. Microbiol. Assn. Publs. incl: Malaria In Israel (w. J. Shapiro), 1930; Survey Of Water Sources For Antimalaria Treatment (w. M. Yavor), 1954; Malaria & Its Eradication In Israel, 1963; num. contbns. in profl. jrnls. Hons: Prizes, Gen. Sick Fund Org., 1956, 1961; Israel Prize, Med. Scis. 1962. Address: Min. of Hlth., Jerusalem, Israel.

SALKEVER, Louis R., b. 1 Jan. 1914. Economist. Educ: B.A., Pa. Univ., Pitts., U.S.A.; M.A., Am. Univ.; Ph.D., Cornell Univ., N.Y. Appts: Econ., w. U.S. Govt., 1940-46; 1951-52; Asst. Prof.-Prof., Econs., SUNY, New Paltz, 1950-65; Econ., City of Phila., 1954-55; Prof. & Chmn., Econs. Dept., SUNY, Albany, 1965-72; Econ., N.Y. State Constitutional Conven., 1967; V.P., Rsch. & Dean, Grad. Studies, SUNY, Albany, 1972-. Mbrships: Nat. Panel Am. Arbitration Assn.; Nat. Commn. Consumer Econs. Am. Econ. Assn.; Am. Assn. Higher Educ; Indl. Rels. Rsch. Assn ; Exec. Bd., Eastern Econs. Assn. & Ed.-in-Chief Assn. Jrnl.; N.Y. State Econs. Assn.; àst Chmn., N.Y. State

Coun. Econ. Educ.; Bd. Dirs., Rsch. Fndn. SUNY; Pai Kappa Pai. Publs: Personal Income in Philadelphia, 1955; Sub-Saharan Africa (w. H. Flynn), 1963; Wage Structure Theory, 1964; African Economic Development (w. J. Upall), 1973; num. articles & reviews in profl. jrnls. Recip. L.H.D., Allen Univ., 1973. Address: 93 Jordan Blvd., Delmar, NY 12054, U.S.A. 2, 14, 30.

SALKIND, Alvin J., b. 12 June 1927. Corporative Vice President-Technology. Educ: Bachelor, Chem. Engrng., Pllytech. Inst., Brooklyn, N.Y., U.S.A., 1949; Master, Chem. Engrng., ibid, 1952; Doctor, Chem. Engrng., 1958. Appts. incl: Rsch. Assoc., Polytech. Inst., Brooklyn, 1956-58; ESB Inc., Yardley, Pa: Sr. Scientist, 1958-62; Sect. Ldr., l962-65; Hd., Electrochem. Lab., 1965-67; Rsch. Assoc., Exploratory Rsch., 1967-69; Mgr., Electromedical Products, 1969-71; Dir. of Technol., 1971-72; V.P.-Technol., 1972-; Adjunct Prof., Chem. Engrng., Polytech. Inst., Brooklyn, N.Y., 1960-70; Prof. of Boengrng., Dept. of Surg., Rutgers Med. Schl., New Brunswick, N.J., 1970-. Mbrships. incl: Chmn., N.Y. Sect., Electrochem. Soc., 1964, Exec. Comm., Battery Div., 1966-68, Chmn., Battery Div., 1970-; Assn. for Advancement of Med. Instrumentation; Acad.d. of Sci.; Sigma Xi; Phi Lambda Upsilon; Fellow, Am. Coll. of Cardiol. Publs: Alkaline Storage Batteries (w. S.U. Falk), 1969; Ed., Techniques of Electrochemistry (w. E. Yeager), 1971; Contbns. to profl. jrnls. Address: 37 Dempsey Ave., Princetoⱥ, NJ 08540, U.S.A. 6, 14.

SALLINEN, (Kaarlo Aarno) Kalevi, b. 10 Jan. 1915. Business Executive. Educ: M.A., Univ. of Helsinki, 1945. Appts: Rsch. Chemist, Central-laboratorium Ab., Helsinki, 1945-49; Tech. Mgr., Turun Asfalttitehdas Oy., Turku, 1949-52; Gen. Mng. Dir., Sul-Mu Oy., Porvoo, 1952-64; Dir., Kupittaan Savi Oy., Helsinki, 1964-67; Mng. Dir., K. Sallinen Ky., Helsinki, 1967-; Mng. Dir., Europhan Suomi Oy., (Unilever), Helsinki, 1970-. Mbrships: Rotary Club of Eira; Assns. Finnish Chem. & Geol.; Finnish Paper Engrs. Assn. Contbr., trade publs. Hons: VR 3, VR 4 w. spray of oak; VR 4 w. swords; War Mem. Decorations, 1939-40, 1941-45. Address: Pietarinkatu 5 A 4, 00140 Helsinki 14, Finland. 43, 90, 134.

SALMENSAARI, Lemmitty, b. 16 Jan. 1906. Professor. Educ: Dip. Ingenieur, 1929; Lic. of Technol., 1963. Appts: Cons. & Rsch. Engr., Puutalo Oy, Finland, 1947-55; Dir. of Gen. Dept., Municipal construction off., City of Helsinki, 1955-68; Prof. in construction econ., Univ. of Oulu, 1968-. Mbrships: Finnish Engrng. Soc.; Finnish Soc. Civil Engrs.; Finnish Soc. Municipal Engrs. Publs: Rakentamistalous (construction economy), 1970; Rakennuskoneiden talous (economy of construction machines), 1971. Recip., Finnish Cross of Liberty, VR 4, 1940, VR 3, 1943. Address: Kontiotie 5-7 E, SF—90530, Oulu, Finland. 43, 90, 134.

SALMI, Toivo Jalmari, b. 15 May 1917. Veterinarian; Food Hygienist. Educ: Grad., Veterinary Coll., Stockholm, 1947; Special Examination, Meat Insp., 1948, Food Hygiene, 1955; Scandinavian Coll. of Pub. Hlth., Göteborg, 1960; Coll. of Mil. Sci., 1966. Appts: Meat Insp. Veterinarian, Coop. Slaughterhouse, Pori, Finland, 1948-56; Veterinary Insp., Min. of Agric., 1956-61; Hd., Assn. of Milk Hygiene, 1961-71; Hd., Div. of Food Hygiene, Min. of Agric. & Forestry, 1971-. Mbrships: Finnish Deleg., Commn. of Milk Hygiene, Int. Dairy Fedn., 1963-; Permanent Comm., ibid, 1966-72; Sec., Finnish Veterinary Assn.,

1960-66; V.P., ibid, 1968-; Sec., Finnish Veterinary Med. Fndn., 1966-; Finnish Sect., Nordic Comm. on Food Analysis. Publs: Dictionary of Finnish Veterinary Biography (gen.ed.) 1963; contbr. to profl. jrnls. & Int. Ency. of Veterinary Med., 1966. Hons. incl: Kt. 1st Class of the Lion of Finland, 1967; Badge of Merit, Assn. of Reserve Offs., 1967. Address: Mechelininkatu 24 A 25, SF—00100 Helsinki 10, Finland. 43, 134.

SALOILA, Oiva Johannes, b. 24 June 1910. Director General of Posts & Telegraphs. Educ: Lower law Exam., Univ. of Helsinki, Finland, 1936; Higher law exam., ibid, 1943; Asst. judge, 1946; Postal & Telegraphic courses at General Post Off. Appts: Var. offs. at regional admin., 1928-36; General Direction, 1936-; Chief of Bur., ibid, 1946; Dir., Economic Div., 1948, Dir. Gen., 1962. Mbrships: Central Bd., Ajokki (Chassis plant), 1958- & Postal Savings Bank, 1960-; Chmn., Fndn. of Postal Mus., 1960-; Chmn., Bd. of Dirs., Televa Engine Plant, 1963- & Kokkola Telephones, 1963-; Bd. of Admin., Finnair, 1967-; Rotary Int. Author of var. articles in profl. publs. Hons. incl: Grant Kt., Order of the Falcon of Iceland, 1972; Cmdr., I Class, Order of the North Star of Sweden, 1972; Cmdr., Order of St. Olav of Norway, 1972. Address: Gen. Direction of Posts & Telegraphs, Mannerheimintie 11, SF-00100, Helsinki 10, Finland. 43. 134.

SALOMONSEN, Finn, b. 31 Jan. 1909. Associate Professor; Museum Keeper of Birds. Educ: Mag. Sci., Zool., 1932, Dr. Sci., 1939. Appts: Pol. Jrnlst., 1932-42; Asst., Danish Nature Conservancy, 1937-43; Asst., Zool. Mus., Copenhagen Univ., 1943; Keeper of Birds, ibid, 1958-; Assoc. Prof., Ornithol., 1960-; num. expeditions, Greenland 1925-73, Philippines 1951-52, Melanasia 1962. Mbrships: Hon., num. ornithol. unions, socs., assns.; Europe & U.S.A.; Corres. Mbr., Hungarian Inst. of Ornithol., Arctic Inst. of N. Am., etc.; Chmn., Club of Denmark, 1957-59; Pres., Danish Ornithol., Soc., 1959-71. Publs. incl: Aves of the Faroe Islands, 1935; Aaret og Flugene, 1940; The Atlantic Alcidae, 1944; The Birds of Greenland, 3 vols., 1950-51; Thee Arctic Year (w. Peter Freuchen), 1958 (Danish, Dutch, Norwegian, Swedish, Russian edits.); Notes on Flower Peckers, 1960-61; Karen Blixon og Euglene, 1964; Fuglene pa Gronland, 1967; Nordens Ynglefugle i Farver, 1968, 1973; 200 papers in periodicals. Hons: Grand Médaille, Soc. d'Acclimatation de France, 1930; Galathea Medal, 1955; Kt., Order of Dannebrog, 1970. Address: Zoological Mus., Universitetsparken 15, Copenhagen Ø, 2100 Denmark. 43, 134.

SALONI, Alfredo, b. 31 Dec. 1892. University Lecturer. Educ: Grad., Italian Lit. & Philos. Appts: Lectr., Pedagogy, Univ. of Bologna; Prof., Philos. & Pedagogy, in magisterial insts. Publs: G.F. Herbert. La Vita. La Svolgimento della dottrina pedagogica, 1937; Rousseau, 1949; Educazione Moderna, 1960; Educazione & Scuola in Aristide Gabelli, 1963; Il positivismo e Roberto Ardigò, 1969; Storia della pedagogia, 1969-74. Recip. Victory Kt., 1915-18. Address: Via delle Fonderie 7, 43100 Parma, Italy.

SALPETER, Eliahu A., b. 1 Nov. 1927. Journalist; Writer. Educ: Schl. of Jrnlsm., Univ. of Prague, Czechoslovakia; Fac. Soc. Scis., Hebrew Univ., Jerusalem, Israel. Appts: Reporter, Assoc. Press, Prague; Economic Corres., The Jerusalem Post, Israel; Economic Corres., Haaretz, Jerusalem; Wash. D.C. Corres., ibid; Israel Bur. Chief, Jewish Telegraphic Agcy., Jerusalem; Diplomatic Corres., Haartz,

ibid; Wash. D.C. Corres., Haaretz; Mng. Ed., Haaretz, Tel Aviv; Mbr. Edit. Bd., Haaretz, ibid. Mbrships: Israel Jrnlsts. Assn.; Nat. Press Club, Wash. D.C., U.S.A.; Int. Press. Inst., Zurich, Switzerland. Publ: Who Rules Israel (w. Y. Elizur), Hebrew & Engl. edits. 1973. Hons: Theodor Herzl Prize for Jrnlsm., 1972. Address: Haaretz, Zalman Schocken St., Tel Aviv, Israel. 94.

SALTER, John R., b. 16 Apr., 1898. Artist; Designer. B.F.A., Art Inst. of Chicago; M.A., Univ. of Iowa; M.F.A., ibid. Appts: Dir., Rockford Art. Assn., 1936-38; ibid, Berysee Gallery, Rockford Ill., 1936-38; Northern Ariz. Univ. Mbrships: Delta Phi Delta; Alpha Psi Omega; Blue Key. Works incl: A Comparison of Three Fertility Figures, Univ. of Iowa, 1954; also represented in pub. bldgs. & pvte. collections. Awarded plaque, Dist. Achievement in Liturgical Art., 1968; 1st Prize in Water Color, Nat. Am. Indian Art Exhib., 1973. Address: 811 N. Humphrey, Flagstaff AZ 86001, U.S.A. 9, 15, 37.

SALTINI, Lino, b. 29 Oct. 1908. Painter; Architect. Educ: Dip., Acad. of Fine Arts, Brera, Milan, Italy; Dip., Scuola Superiore di Arch. di Valle Giulia, Rome. Hon. Prof., Fine Arts, Nat. Univ., Canada. Mbrships. incl: Int. Am. Inst., Wash. D.C.; Int. Inst. of Arts & Letters, Geneva & Zurich, Switzerland; Unione Mondiale della Cultura, Rome, N.Y., etc.; Accad. Tiberina, Rome; Academician & Hon. Mbr., var. other Italian & for. cultural assns. Has held more than 100 grp. exhibs. in Italy & abroad. 14 one-man shows inclng. Milan, Rome, Como, Turin, Genoa, Paris, London (Woodstock Gall., 1966), etc. Work has been featured in Italian & int. jrnls. Recip., many art awards inclng. Premio Europa della Cultura delle Comunità Europee, Campidoglio, Rome, 1970, '71. Address: Studio, Via Luca Signorelli 12, C.A.P. 20154, Milan, Italy. 105, 133.

SALTZMAN, Charles Eskridge, b. 19 Sept. 1903. Investment Banker. Educ: B.S., U.S. Mil. Acad., 1925; B.A., M.A., Magdalen Coll., Oxford Univ., 1928 (Rhodes Scholar). Appts. incl: successively Asst. to Exec. V.P., Sec. & V.P., N.Y. Stock Exchange, 1935-49; on leave from N.Y. Stock Exchange, Lt. Col., Col. & Brig. Gen., U.S. Army, 1940-46, Asst. Sec. of State, 1947-49; Ptnr., Henry Sears & Co., 1949-56; on leave from Hrnry Sears & Co., Under Sec. of State for Admin., 1954-55; Gen. Ptnr., Goldman, Sachs & Co., 1956-73; Ltd. Ptnr., ibid, 1973-. Mbrships. incl: Nat. Pres., Engl. Speaking Union of the U.S., 1961-66; Hon. Dir., ibid; Century Assn., N.Y.; Pres., Univ. Club, N.Y., 1966-70; Soc. of the Cincinnati; Kappa Alpha. Hons. incl: Disting. Serv. Medal, U.S.A.; Legion of Merit, U.S.A.; O.B.E., U.K.; Croix de Guerre w. gold star, France; Cross of Merit w. swords, Poland; & c. Address: Goldman, Sachs & Co., 55 Broad St., N.Y., NY 10004, U.S.A.

SALTZMAN, Henry, b. 14 Mar. 1913. Art Dealer & Educator; Artist; Gallery Director. Educ: Independent studies w. Fred Hamilton, Ben Devine, Arthur Schweider, 1932-38. Appts: Artist-in-Residence, Bethune Cookman Coll., Adult Educ., Stetson Univ.; Dir., Mus. of the Blind; Dir., Henry Saltzman Schl. of Art; Dir., Saltzman's Galls. Mbr., Fla. Artists Grp., 1951-65. Paintings incl: The Peace Conference, Salon d'Hiver, Paris; King David Oratorio, for CBS TV; The Peace Makers, Stetson Univ. Mosaic, The Universal Christ, 1st Meth. Ch., Daytona Beach, Fla. Address: 133 Volusia Ave., Daytona Beach, FL 32014, U.S.A. 133.

SALUJA, Sundar Singh, b. 15 Apr. 1925. Professor of Mining Engineering; University Administrator. Educ: M.S., Ill., U.S.A.; Ph.D., Wis.; Specialist Course, Mining Engrng., Sheffield Univ., U.K. Appts: Mining Engr., mica mines, 1950-51; Asst. Mgr., coal mines, 1951-53, Mgr., 1953-57; Prof. of Coal Mining, Banaras Hindu Univ., 1957-66; Hd., Dept. of Mining, & Prin., Coll. of Mining & Metallurgy, ibid, 1966-68, Hd., Dept. of Mining, & Dean, Fac. of Engrng., 1968-70, Dir., Inst. of Technol., 1971-. Mbrships. incl: All India Coun. Tech. Educ.; Exec. Bd., Indian Schl. of Mines, Dhanbad. Articles & papers, profl. jrnls. & transactions. Hons. incl: Colombo Plan Fellowship, 1954; Nuffield Fndn. Travelling Fellowship, 1959; Invitation Lectr., Peoples Friendship Univ., Moscow, U.S.S.R., 1971. Address: Institute of Technology, Banaras Hindu University, Varanasi-5, India.

SALVADORI, Max, b. 16 June 1908. Professor. Educ: Lic. es Sci. Econ. et Soc., Geneva Univ., Switzerland, 1929; Dr. Sci. (Pol.), Rome Univ., Italy, 1930. Appts: Engaged anti-fascist activities, 1923-46; w. Inst. For. Trade, Rome, Italy, 1923-33; Farm Mgr., Njoro, Kenya, E. Africa, 1934-36; Privat-docent, Geneva Univ., Switzerland, 1937-39; Dept. Econs. & Sociol., St. Lawrence Univ., N.Y. U.S.A., 1939-41; Served to Lt. Col. Brit. Army, 1943-45; Div. Soc. Scis., Bennington Coll., Vt., ibid, 1945-62; Dept. Hist., Smith Coll., Northampton, Mass., 1949-73; Div. Soc. Scis., UNESCO, Paris, France, 1948-49; NATO Secretariat, ibid, 1952-53. Mbr. Special Forces Club, London, U.K. Publs. incl: Liberal Democracy, 1958; The Labour and the Wounds, 1958, The Economics of Freedom: American Capitalism Today, 1959; Prospettive Americane, 1960; Western Roots in Europe, 1961; Da Roosevelt a Kennedy, 1964; A Pictorial History of the Italian People, 1972; Breve Storia Della Resistenza Italiana, 1974; The Rise of Modern Communism, 1974. Hons: MC, 1945; DSO, 1945; D.Litt., 1959; Dwight W. Morrow Prof. Hist., 1964. Address: 36 Ward Ave., Northampton, MA, U.S.A. 2.

SALVE, Modesto C., b. 23 Aug. 1900. Corporation Executive; Importer & Exporter. Educ: Univ. of Hawaii, 1925-26; Kinji Kanasawa Real State Schl., 1956. Appts: Dairy Supt., Ahuimahu Stock Co., 1926-28; Teller & P.R. Off., Bishop Bank, then 1st Nat. Bank of Honolulu, 1928-45; Ins. Agt., U.S. Ins. Co., N.Y.C., 1940-47; Pres., U.S. Life Ins. Co., N.Y., 1942; Pres. & Chmn. of Bd., Philippine-Hawaiian Engrng. Co. Ltd., 1947-73. Mbrships. incl: Pres., Rizal Pioneers, 1934-38 & Filipino Coun. of Honolulu, 1940-46; Grand Master, Gran Oriente Filipino, 1930-40; Sec., Timarau Club, 1940-43; Pres., ibid, 1952-53; Hons. incl: Cert. of Serv., Rotary Club of Dumaguete City; Cert. of Appreciation, Ctrl. Br., YMCA. Address: 534 McNeill St., Honolulu, HI 96817, U.S.A.

SALZMAN, Barnett Seymour, b. 15 Feb. 1939. Psychiatrist. Educ: A.B., Hunter Coll., 1960; Rsch. Fellowship, Northeastern Univ., 1960; M.D., Univ. of Buffalo Schl. of Med., 1965; Internship, Good Samaritan Hosp., L.A., 1966; Res. Psych., Cedars-Sinai Med. Ctr., L.A., 1966-69; Clin. Assoc., S. Calif. Psychoanalytic Inst., 1968-73. Appts: Ldr., USN Chief of Psych., Eltoro Marine Air Stn., 1969-71; Chmn. & Dir., Laguna Beach Free Clin., 1970-71; Attending Physn., Westwood Hosp., L.A.; Attending Physn., Mem. Hosp. of Culver City; Cons., Sakya Ctr. for Tibetan Buddhism, Dehra Dun, India, Am. Indian Free Clin., Compton, Calif., Dept. of Hlth. Care Servs., L.A. & Drug

Rehab. Clin.,Provo, Utah. Mbrships: AMA; Am. Psych. Assn. Author of poetry & radio commentator. Recip., AMA Physn's Recognition Award, 1970-73. Address: 416 N. Bedford Dr., Beverly Hills, CA 90210, U.S.A. 57.

SAMARAS, Anastasios, b. 1 Apr. 1907. Physician; Hospital Director. Educ: Univ. of Athens, Greece & Paris, France; M.D. Appts. incl: Asst., Pathol. Sec., Univ. of Athens, 1927-30; Mil. Physn., 1930; Chief, Mil. Unit, Albanian Front, 1940; Chief, Dept. of Internal Med. & Cardiol., Veterans Hosp., Athens, 1942-73; Assoc. Prof., Med. Schl., Univ. of Athens, 1957. Mbrships. incl: Under Sec., Min. of Hlth., 1973; Pres., Panhellenic Med. Assn., 1971-73; Pres., Athens Med. Assn., 1968-71. Publs. incl: Repercussion de l'anoxemie sur le rein; Réanimation après arêt cardiaque par anoxie et électrocardiografie; Etude physiopathologique sur les exotoxines staphylococciques; Toxi-infection alimentaire massive provoquée par un porteur sain de Salmonella Blocкley, etc. Recip., num. hons. Address: 79 Vassilissis Sophias Ave., Athens T 140, Greece. 43.

SAMIMI, Reza, b. 1919. Portrait Artist. educ: Pvte study; studies at Acad. Julian, Paris, 1951. Appt: Prof. & Hd., art acad. in Teheran, Iran, 1952-60. Solo Exhibs: 6 Exhibs., Cannes, France, 1960-67; Gall. de Rohan, Paris, 1967; Whitgift Gall., Croydon, U.K., 1971; Ross Gall., London, 1973; Spillers Gall., Jacksonville, U.S.A. Portraits: Shah of Iran; Pres. Eisenhower; Princess Chams Pahlavi; Princess Soraya; Queen Farah; King Feisal of Iraq; King Saud of Arabia. 2 paintings w. Royal Portrait Soc., London, 1972-73. Address: Le Ténao, Blvd. du Ténao, Monte Carlo, Principality of Monaco.

SAMSAMI, Gholam-Ali. Diplomat; Lawyer. Educ: B.Sc., LL.B., Univ. of Teheran, Iran; D. en D., Dr.econ.pol., Univ. of Paris, France. Appts. incl: 1st Sec. of Legation, Rome, Italy, 1937-41; Premier Mbr., Legal Dept., Min. of For. Affairs, 1941-42; Premier Mbr., 2nd Pol. Dept., 1942; Dir., Nationality Bur., 1942-43; Legal Cons., 1943-44; Chief of Dept. for U.N.O. Affairs & Specialized Agcys., 1944-48; Counsellor & Chargé d'Affaires, Damascus, 1948-49; Chargé d'Affaires, Beirut, 1949; Chargé d'Affaires, Cairo, 1950; Counsellor of Embassy, Cairo, 1949-; Hd., Cultural Rels. Sect., Min. of For. Affairs, 1951-52; Min. Plen. to Afghanistan, 1952; Mbr., Supreme Pol. Coun., Min. of For. Affairs, 1956; Retd. 1958; Lawyer, 1st class, 1963-. Mbrships. incl: Pres., Freemantle Chmbr. of Comm.; 1st Freeman, City of Freemantle; Iranian Bar Assn. (Lawyers) Club. Author of United Nations & Specialised Agencies & of articles & reports on soc., econ. & cultural affairs. Hons: Order of Merit, Syria, 1950; Order of Homayoun, Iran, 1952. Address: 37 Kuye Ahar, Kooroshkalur Ave., Bissim, Kasr., Teheran, Iran. 1, 12.

SAMSON, Hugh Carey, b. 7 Feb. 1923. Public Relations Consultant. Educ: St. John's Schl., Leatherhead, Surrey, U.K. Appts. incl: Mil. Serv., to Capt., 1942-46; Jrnlst., Nottingham & Birmingham, 1946-48; News Ed., Westminster Press Newspaper Grp., London, 1949-51; Sr. P.R. Exec., Foote, Cone & Belding Ltd., U.K., 1952-56; Hd., Hugh Samson & Co., P.R. Consultancy, 1956-64; Jt. Mng. Dir., Noble & Samson, Ltd., 1964-. Mbrships: Fellow, Inst. P.R.; Press Club, London. Dir., Devopress Ltd., Compton Assocs. Ltd. Creator & script writer, TV film, Out of the Darkness. Author, Onslaught, mag. launching World Refugee Yr. in Gt. Britain,

1959. Address: 7 Montagu Mansions, London, W.1., U.K.

SAMUEL, (Archbishop Mar) Athanasius Yeshue, b. 25 Dec. 1907. Syrian Orthodox Archbishop of the U.S. & Canada. Educ: St. Mark's Syrian Orthodox Monastery Schl., Jerusalem; Coptic Theol. Coll., Cairo, Egypt, 1926-28. Appts: Professed as monk, 1926; Ordained priest, 1932; Father Superior, St. Mark's Syrian Orthodox Monastery, Jerusalem, 1933-46; Syrian Orthodox Archbishop of Jerusalem & Jordan, 1946-49; Syrian Orthodox Archbishop of the U.S. & Canada, 1949-; Major role in discovery, identification & dating of Dead Sea Scrolls, brought them to U.S. 1949 & lectured on them throughout U.S. Mbrships: Holy Synod of Syrian Orthodox Ch. of Antioch; World Coun. of Chs.; Nat. Coun. of Chs. of Christ in U.S.A. Publs: New Method Aramaic (Syriac) Readers, 4 vols., 1939-45; Treasure of Qumran: My Story of the Dead Sea Scrolls, 1966; Divine Liturgy of St. James, 1967. Gold Medal, H.M. Haile Selassie of Ethiopia, 1957; Gold cross & Papal Medallion, Pope Paul VI, 1971. Address: 293 Hamilton Pl., Hackensack, NJ 07601, U.S.A. 3, 131.

SAMUEL, Eva (Chava), b. 26 Nov. 1904. Painter & Ceramic Artist. Educ: Studied ceramic chem., Schl. for Applied Art, Stuttgart, Germany; studied painting w. C.E. Nyhoff, ceramics w. Will Lommert. Appts: Ceramic painter & sculptor, Margaretenhöhe ceramic workshop, Essen, 1926-27; Ceramic Painter, Hamelner Pottery, 1930; Set up workshop w. other ceramists, Palestine (later Israel), 1938; Own ceramic workshop, Rishen le Zion, Israel, 1948-. Mbrships: Israel Painters & Sculptors Assn.; Ceramic Artists Assn. of Israel. Exhibs: Sole & Grp. Shows in Mus. & Galls., Israel, Paris, France, N.Y.C., U.S.A., Brussels, Belgium, Milan Biennale & Faenza, Italy. Murals incl: Wkrs. Cultural Ctr., Rehovot; Bank, ibid; War Mem. Hall, Rishon le Zion. Works in permanent collects: Ceramic Mus., Faenxa, Italy; Munich Mus., Germany; Mus. Haarez, Tel-Aviv, Israel. Hons: Prizes for ceramic work & design, 1946, 1947, 1949; Mirzo Prize for Women, 1952. Address: 14 Menashe Habilin St. 17, Rishon le Zion, Israel. 55, 94, 133.

SAMUELS, Gertrude (Mrs.). Author; Journalist; Playwright. Educ: Geo. Wash. Univ.; Busch Conservatory of Music, Chgo. Appts: Staff, N.Y. Post, 1937-41; Staff, Newsweek, Time mags., 1941-43; Staff Writer, Photographer, N.Y. Times, 1943-71; Ed., N.Y. Times Sunday Mag., 1971-; Cons., UNICEF, 1948. Mbrships: Author's Guild; Dramatist's Guild; Drama Desk; Am. Newspaper Guild; UN Corres. Assn.; Actors Studio, N.Y.C. Publs: B-G, Fighter of Goliaths, 1961, 2nd edit retitled Ben-Gurion, 1974; The People vs. Baby, 1965; The Secret of Gonen, 1969; Run, Shelley, Runı 1974; Plays; The Corrupters, 1969; The Assignment, 1974; Judah the Maccabee & Me. Contbr. to num. periodicals. Hons: Geo. Polk Award, L.I. Univ., 1955; Overseas Press Club Citation, 1956; Page One Award, N.Y. Newspaper Guild, 1959, 65. Address: The New York Times, 229 W. 43rd St., N.Y., NY 10036, U.S.A. 5, 138.

SAMUELS, Harry, b. 18 Nov. 1893. Barrister. Educ: Wadham Coll., Oxford, U.K. Appts: Chmn., Islington & E. London Rent Tribunal, 1946-67; Gen. Ed., Knights Ind. Reports; Dpty. Chmn., var. Wages Couns. Mbr., Reform Club. Publs: Factory Law; Industrial Law; Trade Union Law; Law Relating to Shops; Industrial Injuries; Offices Shops & Railways Remises Act; collab., Redundancy Payments;

contbr. to Ency. Brit. & other works. Recip., O.B.E., 1958. Address: 5 Paper Buildings, Temple, London, E.C.4, U.K. 3, 30, 43.

SANBORN, Herbert J., b. 28 Oct. 1907. Exhibits Officer. Educ: Nat. Acad. of Design; Columbia Univ.; Univ. of Chgo. Appts: Dir., Davenport Municipal Art Gall., 1933-35; Dir. of Museums, Oglebay Park, Wheeling, W. Va., 1936-43; Exhibits Off., Lib. of Congress, Wash. D.C., 1946-. Mbrships: Artists Equity Assn., Inc.; Print Club of Phila.; Soc. of Wash. Printmakers; Inter-soc. Color Coun.; Am. Inst. of Graphic Arts. Publs: Hill Towns of Spain, 10 Lithographs, 1930; Modern Art Influences on Printing Design, 1956; Lithographs in collect. of Lib. of Congress, Nat. Collect. of Fine Arts, Hunterdon Co. Art Ctr., Clinton, N.J.; Exhibitions in num. museums & art galls. Recip., Pulitzer Travelling Fellowship, 1929. Address: 3541 Forest Dr., Alexandria, VA 22302, U.S.A. 7, 37.

SANCHEZ, Sonia B., b. 9 Sept. 1934. Associate Professor; Poet. Educ: B.A., Hunter Coll., 1955. Appts: Lectr., San Fran. State Coll., 1967-69, Univ. of Pitts., 1969-70; Asst. Prof., Rutgers Univ., 1970-71; Manhattanville Coll., 1971-73; Assoc. Prof., Amherst Coll., 1973-. Publs: Homecoming, 1969; We a BaddDDD People, 1970; It's a New Day, & 360 Degrees of Blackness Comin at You, 1971; A Blues Book for Blue Black Magical Women, Love Poems, The Adventures of Fathead, Smallhead & Squarehead, We be Word Sorcerers, 1973; A Sun Lady for all Seasons (recorded). Recip. of Hon. Doct., Wilberforce Univ., 1972 & P.E.N. Award for Writing. Address: 10 W. 135 St., Apt. 17S, N.Y., NY 10037, U.S.A.

SÁNCHEZ-TORRENTÓ, Eugenio, b. 15 June 1926. Psychologist; Professor; Writer. Educ: B.A., True Univ., Fla., 1967; Ed.D., Univ. of Havana, Cuba, 1954; Ph.D., Univ. 'Ignacio Agramonte', Camagüey, Cuba, 1957; M.A., Univ. of Miami, Fla., 1968; thesis approved for Dr. Mod Langs., Middlebury Coll., Vt., 1969. Appts: former Instr. of Spanish Studies, Barry Coll.,Miami, Fla.; former Public Info. Off., Cuban Refugee Prog.; former Minority Study Specialist (i/c Cuban affairs) in DHEW, Region III, Phila., Pa.; Instr. of Spanish Studies, Miami Dade Community Coll., Fla. Mbrships. incl: Fndr., Cervantes Coll., Phila., Pa.; Pres., Pan Am. Circle of Culture, Fla.; Sigma Delta Phi; Bd. Dirs., Ballet Concerto, Miami; Fndr., Hollywood & Young Coll., Fla. Publs: Child Psychology, 2 vols., 1959; Phonoanthology of the Spanish Literature, 10 Hi-Fi records, 1963; El Hombre de 'La Edad de Oro' está vivo, 1970; Francisco Manduley, 1969; A Modern Biography of Abraham Lincoln, 1972; Rocianante Gordo, poems, 1972; Fndr. & Ed., Prensa Hispana, 1973. Hons: Man of the Yr., Latin Am. Fraternal Assn., Miami, 1972. Address: 1927 S.W. 18 Court, Miami, FL 33145, U.S.A. 136.

SANCIPRIANO, Mario, b. 19 June 1916. Professor. Educ: degree in Educ., 1937; Ph.D., 1954. Appts: Prof. of Philos., Classical Schl., Italy, 1942; Prof. of Hist. of Philos., Arezzo Univ., ibid, 1970. Mbr., Acad. Petrarca di Lettere, Arti, Sci., Arezzo. Publs: Pedogogia dell'infante in "Trattato di Nipiologia," 1958; Il pensiero psicologico e morale di G.L. Vives, 1957; L'evoluzione ideale, Ferromenologia pura e teoria dell'evoluzione, 1961; Il logos di Husserl, Genealogia della logica e dinamica intenzionale, 1962; Il pensiero politico di Haller e Rosmini, 1968; Il Lamennais in Italia. Autorita e liberta nel pensiero filosofico-religioso del Risorgimento, 1974.

Recip., Int. prize, Nipiologia, Trieste, 1967. Address: Corso re Umberto 130, Torino, Italy.

SANDAUER, Arthur, b. 14 Dec. 1913. Writer; Professor. Educ: B.A., Lwow Univ., Poland, 1936; Ph.D., Cracow Univ., ibid, 1948. Appts: Habilitation Chr., Polish Lit., Warsaw Univ., 1963; Prof., Chr., Polish Lit., ibid, 1974. Mbrships: Soc. Polish Writers, 1944; Polish Sect., PEN Club, 1946. Publs: Narrative: Death of the Liberal, 1947; Notes of a Dead City, 1963; Critical Works: Poets of three generations, 1955; My Deviations, 1956; About the Unity of Content and Form, 1957; Without Reduced Tariff, 1959; Suicide of Mithridates, 1967; Lyrics and Logics, 1969; The Literary Bush, 1972; Translations of Ancient Greek & Contemporary Russian Lit.—Euripides, Ariphstophanes, Theocritus, Maiakovsky, Tschekhov, etc. Address: Karlowicza 20/m.1, Warsaw 02-552, Poland.

SANDBACH, Mary Warburton (Mrs. F. H. Sandbach), b. 25 Apr. 1901. Translator. Appts: Read the Norwegian Papers for Chatham House, 1939-40; Taught translation from Swedish, Norwegian, & Danish for the Bell Schl. of Langs. & other Lang. Schls. in Cambridge, 1956-66. Mbrships: Translator Assn. (Soc. of Authors), at present Mbr. of Exec. Comm.; Viking Soc. for Northern Research. Translations of: Strindberg, Inferno, 1962; From an Occult Diary, 1965; The Cloister, 1969; Getting Married (& ed.), 1972-73; Per Olaf Sundman, The Expedition, 1967; The Flight of the Eagle, 1970; Eyvind Johnson, Nu Var Det, 1914; Ingmar Fjell, Jack Fox Detective, 1968; Viola Wahlstedt, Aslak Where Are You? , 1971. Address: 2 Hedgerley Cl., Cambridge CB3 OEW, U.K. 30.

SANDBURG , Helga (Mrs. Geo. Crile, Jr.), b. 24 Nov. 1918. Writer. Educ: Mich. State Coll., 1939-40; Univ.of Chgo. Appts. Sec. to father, Carl Sandburg; Dairy Goat Breeder, 1944-51; Sec., Manuscript Div. & for Keeper of the Collections, Lib. of Congress, Wash D.C., 1952-56; Admin. Asst., Papers of Woodrow Wilson, Woodrow Wilson Fndn., N.Y.C., 1958-59. Mbrships: Author's Gild; Poetry Soc. of Am.; Am. Milk Goat Record Assn.; Nat. Nubian Club; Coun. Safe the Dunes; Am.-Luxembourg Soc. Publs. incl: The Wheel of Earth, 1958; Measure My Love, 1959; The Owl's Roost, 1962; Sweet Music, 1963; Blueberry, 1963; Gingerbread, 1964; The Unicorns, 1965; The Wizard's Child, 1967; Above and Below (w. Geo. Crile, Jr.), 1969; To a New Husband, 1970. Hons: Best Short Story, Va. Qtry. Review,19 59; 2nd Prize, Borestone Mtn. Poetry Award, 1962; 3rd Prize, Chgo. Tribune Poetry Award, 1970. Address: 2060 Kent Rd., Cleveland, OH 44106, U.S.A.

SANDERLIN, Owenita Harrah, b. 2 June 1916. Teacher; Writer. Educ: B.A., The Am. Univ., Wash. D.C., 1937; Grad. sutdy, Univ. of Maine, 1939-40, San Diego State Coll., 1969-70, Univ. of Calif., Santa Barbara, 1967; Calif. State Tchng. Credential. Appts: Puppeteer, Theodore Tiller Marionette Co., Wash. D.C., 1932-36; Engl. Instr., Univ. of Maine, 1941-42 & 1946-47; Tchr. & Coach, Speech & Drama, Creative Writing, Tennis, Acad. of Our Lady of Peace, San Diego, Calif., 1961-68; Cons. & Tchr., Gifted Progs., San Diego City Schls., 1971-73. Mbrships: Nat. Honor Soc.; Mortar Bd.; San Diego Tennis Patrons Assn.; Nat. Assn. for Gifted Children; Calif. Assn. for Gifted Children. Publs. incl: Johnny, 1968, paperback, 1969; Creative Teaching, 1971; Teaching Gifted Children, 1973; Many short stories, articles, verse, plays, in var. mags. & newspapers. Recip. of hons.

Address: 997 Vista Grande Rd., El Cajon, CA 92021, U.S.A. 30.

SANDERS, Faye Beverley (Mrs. John Hollis Martin), b. 6 Feb. 1934. Attorney. Educ: Ga. Southern Coll., Statesboro, U.S.A., 1952-54; Woodrow Wilson Coll. of Law, 1955-56; Admitted to Ga. Bar, 1956. Pvte. Prac. as Attorney, Statesboro, 1956-. Mbrships: Sec.-Treas., Bulloch Co. Bar Assn., 1956-72; Ogeechee Bar Assn.; Ga. Bar Assn.; V.P., Ga. Assn. of Women Lawyers, 1959-60; Statesboro Bus. & Profl. Women's Club; Statesboro-Bulloch Co. C. of C.; Zeta Tau Alpha. Address: 106 Chelsea Circle, Statesboro, GA 30458, U.S.A.

SANDERS, Jack Ernest, b. 30 Jan. 1931. Physician. Educ: Emory Univ., Atlanta, Ga.; Univ. of Md.; B.S.Pharm., Univ. of Fla., 1953; M.D., Univ. of Miami Coral Gables, 1957; Gen. Rotating Intern, Cook Co. Hosp., Chgo., III., 1957-58. Full time Staff Mbr., Campbelltown-Campbelltown-Graceville Hosp., 1964-. Mbrships: Phi Delta Chi, Univ. of Md., 1951; Alpha Epsilon Delta, Univ. of Fla., 1952; Phi Kappa Phi, ibid, 1953, Mason; Phi Chi, Univ. of Miami, 1954; Life Mbr., Century Club, Univ. of Miami, 1970; Mbr., Century Club, Univ. of Fla.; Official Bd., Meth. Ch. Recip. of acad. hons. Address: Winding Rd., Graceville, FL 32440, U.S.A. 125.

SANDKLEF, J. Albert, b. 13 May 1893. Museum Director. Educ: Ph.D., Univ. of Gottenburg, Sweden, 1950. Appts: Dir., Varberg's Mus., Varberg, 1921-61; Sec., Inst. for Rsch. of the Hist. of Culture of W. Sweden, 1940-. Mbrships: Royal Swedish Gustavus Adolphus Acad.; Hon. Mbr., ibid, 1964; Soc. Finno-Ougrienne, Helsinki, Finland; Int. Coun. of Mus.; Swedish Mus. Assn.; Assn. of Swedish Authors. Publs. incl: Äldre biskötsel i Sverige & Danmark, 1937; The Brocksten Fins, 1937; Brockstensmannen & hand olycksbröder, 1943; Singing Flails, 1949; Hallandsgärdar, 1953; August Bondeson, 1956; Lars Gathenhielms vittnesbörd (w. C-H. Hjortsjö), 1957; 1500-talets halländska tingböcker, 1959; Allmogesjöfart på Sveriges vstkust, 1575-1850, 1973. Hons: Prizes, Newspaper My Tid, 1961, Royal Gustavus Adolphus Acad., 1969, Assn. of Swedish Authors, 1970. Address: 432 00 Varberg, Sweden. 10.

SANDLIEN, Bertil, b. 30 Oct. 1920. Marine Engineer; Company Executive & Director. Educ: M.Sc., Tech. Univ. of Norway, Trondheim, Gothenburg Coll. of Navigation. Appts: Mgr., Seldens Ingeniorsbureau, 1949-51; Mgr., Ab. Gotaverken, 1951-52; Chief Engr., Aker Grp., 1953-59; V.P., ibid, 1962-63; Exec. V.P., 1964-; Mbr., Bd. of Dirs., Vif. Scandinavia, 1968-; Mbr., Bd. of Dirs., sev. Aker Grp. Cos., 1969-. Mbrships: Bd., Royal Norwegian Coun. for Sci. & Indl. Rsch., 1969; Bd., Abs Scandinavian Tech. Comm., 1970; Bd., Norske Veritas, 1971; Bd., Saga Petrochemi, 1973; N.E. Coast Inst. of Shipbuilders & Marine Engrs.; Inst. of Marine Engrng., U.K.; Norwegian Petroleum Soc. Address: C.N.R. Aamundsensu 5A, 1347 Hosle, Norway.

SANDON, Henry, b. 4 Aug. 1928. Museum Curator. Appts: Lay Clerk, Worcester Cathedral; Curator, Dyson Perrins Mus. & Worcester Royal Porcelain Co. Ltd. Mbrships: Vice Chmn.; Commemorative Collectors Soc.; Mbr., Comm. of Mgmt., Choir Benevolent Fund; English Ceramic Circle. Publs: Illustrated Guide to Worcester Porcelain 1751-1793; Royal Worcester Porcelain 1862 to Present Day; British Pottery & Porcelain for Pleasure &

Investment; Coffee Pots & Tea Pots; Flight & Barr. Address: Dyson Perrins Museum, Worcester, U.K.

SANDOZ, Marc, b. 24 Nov. 1904. Art Historian. Educ: Licence ès-lettres; Dip., Superior Schl. of Commerce, France; Dip., Ecole du Louvre; Docteur ès lettres. Appts. incl: Businessman before WW II; Curator, Museums of Poitiers, 1946-60. Mbrships: French Art Hist. Soc.; French Archaeol. Soc.; Assn. of Curators of French Pub. Collects.; French Alpine Club. Publs: Eloge d'André Derain, 1961; Eloge de Maurice Alsetin, 1962; Présence d'Albert Marquet, 1964; Théodore Chassérian (1819-1856) et le romantisme, 1974; num. art hist. articles in var. bulletins & jrnls. Address: 108 Rue du Ranelagh, Paris 16, France. 19.

SANDS, Ira Jay, b. 8 Oct. 1922. Lawyer; Investment Consultant. Educ: B.A., N.Y. Univ., 1941; J.D., Columbia Univ., 1944; admitted N.Y. State Bar, U.S. Circuit Ct. of Appeals & U.S. Dist. Ct., 1944, Supreme Ct. Bar, 1966. Appts: Law prac., N.Y.C., 1944-; Dir., Mgr., Ptnr., 1st Repub. Corp., 1957-; Bd. Chkn., ibid, 1958-; Sec., 1960-; Dir., Chmn., 1st Repub. Underwriter Inc., 1958-; Dir., Pres., Waltham Mgmt. Inc., 1959-; Ptnr. or Mng. Ptnr., numerous cos.; Chmn., Dir., sev. cos.; Chmn. Bd., Chmn. Exec. Comm., Sec., Dir., 1st Repub. Corp. Am., 1961-; Chmn. Exec. Comm., Sec., Dir., 1st Repub. Bldg. Corp., 1962-; Chmn., Tri-Mgmt. Co., 1957, Mat. Med. Inds. Inc., 1968-; Hlth. Insts. Leasing Corp., 1968-, Am. Med. Computer Corp., 1969-; Real Estate Bd.; Nat. Real Estate Club; N.Y. State & Nassau Bar Assns.; Fed. Bar Assn.; Bldg. Owners & Mgrs. Assn. Address: 701 7th Ave., New York, NY 10036, U.S.A.

SANDWICK, Harold John, b. 29 May 1924. Sales & Marketing Manager. Educ: B.E.E., Cornell Univ., 1950. Appts: Sales Engr., Brewer-Titchener Corp., 1950-57, Sales Mgr., 1957-70, Sales & Marketing Mgr., 1970-. Mbrships: Sr. Mbr., IEEE; Conference Internationale des Grands Reseaux Electriques; Am. Nat. Standards Inst.; Exec. & V oting Mbr., Hi Voltage Insulator Sect., Nat. Elec. Mfrs. Assn.; N.Y. Acad. of Scis. Address: 7 Westfield Pk., Cortland, NY 13045, U.S.A.

SANDYS, (Rt. Hon.) Duncan Edwin, b. 24 Jan. 1908. Member of Parliament. Educ: M.A., Magdalen Coll., Oxford, U.K. Appts. incl: Entered Diplomatic Serv., 1930; w. For. Off. & British Embassy, Berlin; M.P., Norwood Div., Lambeth, 1935-45, Streatham, 1950-; Pol. Columnist, Sunday Chronicle, 1937-39; Financial Sec., War Off., 1941-43; Parliamentary Sec., Min. of Supply, 1943-44; Min. of Works, 1944-45; Fndr., European Movement, 1947; Dir., Ashanti Goldfields Corp., 1947-51, 1966-72; Min. of Supply, 1951-54; Min., Housing & Local Govt., 1954-57; Min. of Defence, 1957-59; Min. of Aviation, 1959-60; Sec. of State for Commonsealth Rels., 1960-64; Sec. of State for Colonies, 1962-64; Chmn., Lonrho Ltd., 1972-; Ldr., British Delegn., Assemblies, Coun. of Europe & Western European Union, 1970-72; Pres., Fndr., Civic Trust, 1956-; Pres., Europa Nostra, 1969- (Chmn., Int. Organising Comm., European Archl. Heritage Yr.); Hon. Mbr., Royal Town Planning Inst., 1956-; Hon. Fellow, RIBA, 1968-. Hons: Grand Cross, Order of Merit, Italy, 1960; P.C., 1944; C.H., 1973. Address: 86 Vincent Sq., London SW1P 2PG, U.K. 1.

SANESI, Roberto, b. 18 Jan. 1930. Writer; Educator. Educ: Univ. of Urbino; Salzburg

Seminar of Am. Studies; Harvard Univ.; Univ. of Bari, Italy. Appts: Tchr., Elem. Schl.; Art Gall. Dir.; P;R. Dir.; Cultural Dir., CEntro Int. delle Arti e del Costume, Venice; Dir., Poetry Series, Guanda Publrs.; Prof. of Comp. Lit., Accademia di Brera, Milan. Publs: Il feroce equilibrio, 1957; Dylan Thomas, 1960; Oberon in catene, 1962; T.S. Eliot, 1965; Rapporto informativo, 1966 (Information Report, 1970); La rappresentazione per Enrico Quinto, 1967; L'improviso di Milano, 1969; La polvere e il giaguaro, 1972; Harrington Gardens Suite, 1973; The Graphic Works of Ceri Richards, 1973; num. anthols. of Engl. & Am. poetry w. Italian translations. Hons: Int. Byron Prize, 1960; Premio Cervia, 1961. Address: Via N. Machiavelli 10, Milan, Italy.

SANGSTER, William McCoy, b. 9 Dec. 1925. Educator. Educ: U.S. Naval Acad.; B.S.C.E., State Univ. of Iowa, 1947; M.S., ibid, 1948; Univ. of Mo.; Ph.D., State Univ. of Iowa, 1964. Appts: Asst Prof., Civil Engrng., Univ. of Mo., 1948-55; Assoc. Prof., ibid, 1955-61; Prof., 1961-67; Assoc. Dir., Engrng. Experiment Stn., 1963-67; Assoc. Dean, Coll. of Engrng., 1964-67; Dir. & Prof., Civil Engrng., Ga. Inst. of Technol., 1967-. Mbrships. incl: Fellow, Am. Soc. of Civil Engrs.; Pres.-elect, ibid, 1973-74; Chmn., Comm. on Nat. Meetings Policy & Prac., 1972-73; Comm. on Profl. Conduct, 1967-69; Nat. Dir., Dist. 14, 1965-67; Pres., Mid-Mo. Sect., 1961; Chmn., Region IV, Engrng. Educ. & Accreditation Comm., Engrs. Coun. for Profl. Dev., 1973-74; Chmn., Rels. w. Ind. Div., Am. Soc. for Engrng. Educ., 1972-73. Author of articles & papers in field. Hons. incl: Engr. of the Yr. in Educ., Metropol. Atlanta, 1974. Address: 4115 Candler Lake Ct., N.E., Atlanta, GA 30319, U.S.A. 2, 14, 15, 130.

SANGUINETI, Edoardo, b. 9 Dec. 1930. Professor, University of Salerno, Italy. Publs: Laborintus, 1956; Opus metricum, 1960; Interpretazione di Malebolge, 1961; Tre studi danteschi, 1961; Tra liberty e crepuscolarismo, 1961; Alberto Moravia, 1962; K. e altre cose, 1962; Capriccio italiano, 1963; Passaggio, 1963; Triperuno, 1964; Ideologia e linguaggio, 1965; Il realismo di Dante, 1968; Guido Gozzano, 1966; Il Giuoco dell'Oca, 1967; Teatro, 1969; Il giuoco del Stauricon, 1970; Storie naturali, 1971; Wirrwarr, 1972. Address: Via Napoli, 34-84100 Salerno, Italy.

SANKARAN, Ivatury Gowri, b. 21 Feb. 1922. University Lecturer. Educ: M.A., Madras Univ., India, 1943; LL.B., ibid, 1945; Grad. Dip. in Stats., 1949; M.B.A., Harvard Univ., 1954. Appts: Civilian Ordnance Off., Indian Army Ordnance Corp., 1945-46; Law Apprentice, 1947-48; w. father in Engrng. Bus., 1948-52; Purchase Off., Calico Mills, Ahmedabad, 1956-57; Lectr., Bus. Admin., Andhra Univ., 1957; Reader, Bus. Admin., ibid, 1958; Hd., Commerce Dept., 2nd campus at Guntur, Andhra Univ., 1967; Lectr., Bus. Admin., Univ. of Md., Eastern Shore, U.S.A, 1972-. Mbrships: Harvard Bus. Schl. Assn.; Am. Bus. Law Assn .; Acad. of Mgmt., U.S.A.; Couthern Mktng. Assn., U.S.A; Freemasonry of India. Address: Fac. Apts., Univ. of Md., Eastern Shore, Princess Anne, MD 21853, U.S.A. 125.

SANNUM, Per, b. 6 Nov. 1919. Public Relations Manager. Appts: Sec., Norwegian State Railways, 1955; Dept. Hd., Forenede Liv., 1956-61; Sales Mgr., ibid, 1962-64; P.R. Mngr., ibid, 1964-. Mbrships: Norwegian P.R. Soc. Address: Kronprins Olavs Alle 16, 7000 Trondheim, Norway.

SANO, Keiji, b. 30 June 1920. Professor of Neurosurgery. Educ: M.D., Fac. of Med., Univ. of Tokyo (then Imperial Univ. of Tokyo), 1945; D.M.S., ibid, 1951. Appts: Lectr. & Chief., Out-Patient Clin. (Neurosurg.), Univ. of Tokyo, 1956; Assoc. Prof., Neurosurg., Inst. of Brain Rsch., ibid, 1957; Prof. of Neurosurg. & Dir., Dept. of Neurosurg., 1962-. Mbrships: Pres., World Fedn. of Neurosurg. Socs., 1969-73; Hon. Pres. for Life, ibid, 1973-; Hon. Mgr., Soc. of Neurol. Surgs.; Corres., Am. Assn. Neurol. Surgs.; Ehrenmitglied der Deutschen Gesellschaft für Neurochirurgie; Pres., Japan Neurosurg. Soc., 1965; Pres., Asian & Australasian Soc. of Neurol. Surgs., 1967-71; Hon. Pres., ibid, 1971-. Contbr. num. articles to profl. publs. Address: 4-22-6 Den-en-chofu, Otaku, Tokyo, Japan.

SANTEE, Elsbeth E. (Mrs. Robert E. Santee), b. 3 June 1928. Assistant Professor of German. Educ: Degree, Glucker Coll., Stuttgart, W. Germany; Nat. Dip., Gymnastics & Phys. Therapy, 1950; B.S., Calif. State Coll., Pa., U.S.A., 1961; NDEA Schlrship., Albright Coll., Reading, Pa., summer, 1963; M.A., W. Va. Univ., Morgantown, 1968. Appts. incl: Tchr., Phys. Educ. & German, 1959-61; Tchr., 5th grade Arithmetic, Sci. & German, 1962-63; Tchr., N. Franklin Twp. Schl., 1963-65; Tchr., 7-9th grade German, Trinity-Joint Jr. H.S., 1965-66; Asst. Prof., German, Calif. State Coll., Pa., 1966-. Mbrships. incl: AATG; MLA; APSCUF; German Club Advsr.; AAUW; Hon. Mbr., Alpha Mu Gamma; Fac. & Senate, ibid, 1972-; V.P., Cal. St. Coll. Assn. of Women Fac.; Advsr. & Hon. Mbr., Kappa Delta Epsilon. Contbr. of articles to profl. jrnls. Address: P.O. Box 264, Richeyville, PA 15358, U.S.A. 57, 130, 138.

SANTI, Kathleen M. (Mrs. George C. Chappell), b. 8 Nov. 1941. Physician. Educ: B.S., Fla. Univ., U.S.A., 1963; Emory Schl. of Med., 1963-67; Intern-Res., Ob. & Gyn., St. Paul Hosp. Dallas, Tex., 1968-69. Pvte. prac., Palatka, Fla., 1970-. Mbrships: Sec. Treas., Putnam Mem. Hosp. Staff, 1970-74; Putnam Co. Med. Soc., 1970-73; Mem. Fla. Med. Assn.; Putnam Co. Chmbr. of Comm.; Pilot Club; Fla. Aca. Family Prac.; Palatka Jr. Women's Club. Address: 1401 S. Palm Ave., Palatka, FL 32077, U.S.A. 5.

SANTIAGO, Meléndez Efraín, b. 17 Feb. 1930. Businessman; Clergyman; Former Government Official. Educ: Defenders Theol. Sem., 1957-61; Ordained to Min., Meth. Ch., 1961; Psychol. Inst. of Puerto Rico, 1967-69. Appts. incl: Pastor, Wesleyan Meth. Ch., Puerto Rico, 1957-64; Pres., Wesleyan Conf., ibid, 1962-64; Pres., Safway Sales Co., 1959-63; Pres., Andamios Mfg. Inc., 1965-68; Coord. & Dir., Billy Graham Evangelistic Assn. in Latin Am., 1964-68; Sec. Servs. Dept. of Puerto Rico, 1969-72; V.P., Halco Sales Inc., 1973-; Pres., Andamios Mfg. Inc., 1973-. Mbrships. incl: Advsry. Comm., Columbia Univ.; Samaritan Fndn.; V.P., New Progressive Party of Puerto Rico; Exec. Bd., Boy Scouts of Am.; Nat. Coun. Family Rels.; Nat. Rehabilitation Assn. Hons. incl: Chapt. Award of Hon., Am. Nat. Red Cross, 1971; Youn g Mothers Coun. Award, 1971; Puerto Rico Dist. Exchange Clubs Awards, 1971 & 1972; Boss of the Yr., San Juan Chapt., Nat. Secs. Assn., 1972. Address: Box B, Carolina, PR 00630, Puerto Rico. 7.

SANTONASTASO, Guiseppe, b. 9 Feb. 1904. University Professor. Appts. incl: Prof. of Pol. Hist., Univ. of Bari, Italy, 1949-1967; Univ. of Naples, 1967-. Mbrships. incl: Corres. Mbr., Soc. Nat. di Sci., Lettere & Arti, Naples.

Publs. incl: Il socialismo francese, 1954; Il neoliberalismo di G. Mazzini, 1958, 2nd ed., 1972; Orientaciones actuales de las doctrinas politicas, 1962; Lineament di storia delle dottrine politiche, 1967, 2nd ed., 1972; Pensiero politico e azione sociale, 1967; E. Quinet e la religione della liberta, 1968; Studi di pensiero politicò, 1973. Recip. of Gold Medal of Merit, Pub. Instrn. Address: Piazza delle Medaglie d'Oro 20, Rome, Italy. 43.

SANTORINI, Paul E., b. 8 June 1893. Physicist & Engineer. Educ: Zurich Univ., Switzerland, Dr. Sc. phys. et math., Dipl.-Ing. Appts: Extraordinary Prof., Applied Phys., Athens Univ., Greece, 1935; Ordinary Prof., Phys. & Dir., Experl. Phys. Lab. II, Nat. Tech. Univ., ibid, 1946-64; Prof. emeritus, ibid, 1964. Mbrships. incl: Fellow, N.Y. Acad. Scis.; Royal Soc. Arts; many Inst. & learned Socs.; Hon. Pres., 7th Int. Philos. Congress, Nice, France; Deleg., over 50 int. sci. congresses. Author over 300 sci. publs. Discovered Elastic Inertia Effect in concrete mass under deformation, 1930; Built 1st centimetric wavelength radar in Greece, 1936-39; Invented & built 1st Proximity Fuse, 1936; Discovered natural & obtained artificial propagation of centimetric eletromagnetic waves beyond optical line of sight by Dispersion Effect on top of natural obstacles (S.-Effect), 1937; Holder, 2 Basic patents, Electronic Brain H, automatic guiding missiles type NIKE, 1942; Estab. lowest duration limit observable phys. phenomena in nature, 1958; etc. Recip. num. hons. Address: P.O. Box 49, Athens, Greece. 34, 43, 131.

SANTORO, Elissa J., b. 18 Oct. 1938. General Surgeon & Oncologist. Educ: A.B., Coll. of St. Elizabeth, Convent, N.J., U.S.A., 1960; M.D., Woman's Med. Coll. of Pa., 1965; Intern—Asst. Res. in Surg., Hosp., ibid, 1965-67; Sr. Asst. Res. in Surg.-Chief Surg. Res., St. Vincent's Hosp. & Med. Ctr., N.Y.C., 1968-70. Appts. incl: Instr. in Surg., & Assoc. Clin. Investigator for Ctrl. Oncol. Grp., N.Y. Med. Coll., 1970-72; Clin. Asst. Prof. of Surg., Coll. of Med. & Dentistry of N.J., Martland Hosp., Newark, 19730; Assoc. Attng. in Surg. & Oncol., Irvington Gen. Hosp. Mbrships. incl: Acad. of Med. of N.J.; AMA; Assn. of Am. Med. Colls.; Essex Co. Med. Soc.; Med. Soc. of N.J.; Assn. for Acad. Surg.; Am. Assn. of Cancer Educ.; N.Y. State Cancer Progs. Assn., Inc.; Am. Med. Women's Assn. Publs: Contbns. to surg. jrnls. & book. Recip., Physn. Recognition Award, AMA, 1969. Address: 987 Sanford Ave., Irvington, NJ 07111, U.S.A. 5.

SANTOS-JUNIOR, Joaquim Rodrigues dos, b. 21 May 1901. Professor. Educ: Licenciado, Natural Scis., Licenciado, Med. & Surg., Fac. of Med., Dr. of Natural Scis., Univ . of Oporto, Portugal. Appts: Asst., Zool. & Anthropol., Fac. of Scis., Univ. of Oporto. Mbrships. incl: Pres., Portuguese Soc. for Archaeol. & Ethnol.; Oporto; Pres., Portuguese Ornithol. Soc.; Int. Inst. of Anthropol., Paris; Ethnographic Soc., Paris. Publs. incl: Sociological Concept of Ethnography; About 200 other publd. works. Address: Inst. de Antropologia "Dr. Mendes Correia", Fac. de Ciências, Universidade, Porto, Portugal.

SAPENA PASTOR, Raul. Government Minister. Educ: Dr., Law & Soc. Scis., H.C. Dr., Brazil Univ. Appts: Currently—Min. For. Affairs, 1956-; Senator of Nation, 1973-78; Mbr., Permanent Ct. Arbitration, The Hague, Holland, 1954-; Rep., Paraguay, Inter-Am. Coun. Jurisprudence; Pres., Nat. Commn. Codification of Int. Law; Pres., Nat. Coun. For. Trade; Pres., Nat. Commn., La Plata Basin; Rep., Paraguay, Inter-Am. Econ. & Soc. Coun.,

Org. Am. States; Mbr., Inter-Am. Comm., Alliance for Progress; Pres., Qualifications & Discipline Tribunal, Min. For. Affairs; Dir., Diplomatic & Consular Acad.; Mbr., State's Coun., 1973-78; Prof., Pvte. Int. Law, Fac. Law & Soc. Scis.; Previously-Plenipotentiary Deleg. & Envoy Extraordinary on num. special missions to Govts.; Mbr., Supreme Ct. of Justice, Paraguay; Pres., Civil & Commercial Ct. of Appeals; Atty-Gen.; Judge, Civil Ct., 1st Instance; Judge, Criminal Ct., ibid; Hldr. num. prof-ships. Active num. legal & soc. orgs. Publs. incl. over 100 articles in profl. jrnl. Recip. num. hons. Address: Ave. Venezuela 157, Asunción, Paraguay, S. Am.

SAPIENZA, (Judge) Maurice, b. 10 Oct. 1915. Lawyer. Educ: A.B. Harvard Coll., 1937; J.D., Harvard Law Schl., 1940. Appts: Assoc., Arthur T. Vanderbilt, 1940-42; Office of Price Admin., 1942-45; Asst. U.S. Atty., Hawaii, 1945-48; Dpty. Atty. Gen., ibid, 1948-50; U.S. Judge, 3rd. Circuit Ct., Hawaii, 1950-55; Hawaii Senate Atty., 1959; Dept. Counsel, Gen. Elec., 1960-68; Div. Counsel, ibid, 1968-73; Mgr., Bus. Environment, Gen. Elec., 1973-. Mbr., Am. Bar Assn. Author, This Is V-J Day, 1945. Address: One Plastics Ave., Pittsfield, MA 01201, U.S.A. 6, 114.

SAPORI, Armando, b. 11 July 1892. University Professor. Educ: Grad., Law., Univ. Siena. Appts: State Archivist, Florence, 1921-32; Lectr., Hist., Econ. & Fon., Univ. of Ferrara, 1932-35, Econ. Hist., Milan, 1932-65, Pol. Hist., Florence, 1933-35, Econ. Hist., Univ. of Florence, 1935-62; Prin., Free Univ. of Commerce Luigi Bocconi, Milan, 1952-67; Town Councillor, Florence, 1946-51; Senator of 1st Repub. legislature, 1948-53. Mbrships. incl: Ital. Soc. for Int. Org.; European Soc. of Culture; Sci. Acad., Bologna; Int. Inst. Communications; Assn. Econ. Hist.; Serbian Acad. of Sci. & Lit.; Medieval Acad. of U.S.A.; Royal Hist. Soc. Publs. incl: Come uno storico vede gli uomini, 1966, 2nd. edit.m 1967; Libro giallo della compagina dei Covoni, 1970; Armando Sapori ricorda: Vol. I. Mondo finito, Vol. 2. Cose che capitano, 1971; La mercatura medievale, 1972. Hons. incl: Doct., Univ. Poitiers, 1950, Univ. Paris, 1960; Nat. Prize in Moral, Hist. & Philol. Sci., Nat. Acad. dei Lincei, 1953; Kt., Légion d'Honneur, 1958; High Off., Order of Ital. Repub., 1965; sev. gold medals & other awards. Address: Via Sabbatini 8, 20136 Milan, Italy.

SARAJAS, (Heikki Seppo) Samuli, b. 11 Apr. 1927. Professor. Educ: M.Sc., Univ. of Helsinki, 1951; M.D., ibid, 1961; Ph.D., 1965; Rsch. Fellow, Wenner-Gren Cardiovascular Rsch. Lab., Stockholm, Sweden, 1953-56; Establd. Investigator, Nat. Rsch. Coun. for Med. Scis., Finland, 1962-63 & 66. Appts: Asst.-Assoc. Prof., Inst. of Physiol., Univ. of Helsinki, 1958-72; Prof. of Physiol., Coll. of Vet. Med., Helsinki, 1972-. Mbrships: Bds., Finnish Physiol. Soc. & Coll. of Vet. Med.; Ed. Bd., Scand. J. Clin. Lab. Invest.; Hibernation Info. Exchange, Houston, Tex., U.S.A. Contbr. num. publs. on ctrl. nervous, endocrine, cardiovascular, haemostatic & metabolic responses during hibernation, hypothermia, exercise & other stress situations. Address: c/o Dept. of Physiol., Coll. of Vet. Med., Hämeentie 57, 00550 Helsinki 55, Finland. 50, 134.

SARAZIN, Gilles F., b. 23 May 1921. Engineer. Educ: Ecole Supérieure de Physique et de Chimie Industrielle, Univ. of Paris, France. Appts: Cons., Borg Warner Corp., Chgo., Ill., U.S.A.; Asst. Mgr., Constructions Mécaniques Chenard & Walcker, Gennevilliers,

France; Pres., Semiac, Vouziers, France. Mbrships: Rotary Int.; Past Pres., Club of Montfort l'Amaury. Holder, var. patents. Address: Château de Breuil, 78890 Garancières, France. 1.

SAREL, Shalom, b. 25 Oct. 1918. Professor; Research Director. Educ: M.Sc., Hebrew Univ. of Jerusalem, 1942; Ph.D., work done at Daniel Sieff Rsch. Inst. Rehovot, Palestine, degree conferred by Hebrew Univ. of Jerusalem, 1946; post-doct. work, w. M.S. Newman, Dept. of Chem., Ohio State Univ., 1952-54. Appts: Sci., Brit. War Supply Bd., Jerusalem, 1944-46; Instr., Organic CHem., Hebrew Univ. of Jerusalem, 1946-52; Sr. Lectr., Organic Chem., ibid, 1955; Hd., Dept. Pharmaceutical Chem., 1956-; Assoc. Prof., 1959-64; Prof., 1964-; Rsch. Assoc., Chem. Dept., Ohio State Univ., Columbus, U.S.A., 1952-54; Guest Rsch. Prof., Chem. Dept., Mich. State Univ., E. Lansing, 1965; Guest Sci., Eidgenossische Technische Hochschule, Zurich, & Dyson Perrins Lab., Oxford, UK, 1972. Mbrships. incl: Pres., Chem. Socs. of Israel, 1961-65; Chmn., Israel Medicinal Chem. Sect., 1971-; IUPAC Sect. on Medicinal Chem., 1973-. Publs: Identification & Characterization of Organic Compounds (in Hebrew), 1947; num. articles in profl. jrnls. Address: 36 Jabotinsky St., Jerusalem, Israel. 55, 94.

SARGENT, Genevieve (pen name for children's poetry & stories: Ginger). Engineering Technician; Free-lance Writer & Poet. Educ: Phoenix Coll. Ind. State Univ. Ext.; Ariz. State Univ.; Univ. of Calif.; Univ. of Santa Clara, Calif. Appts: Engrng. Techn., 8 yrs. Edships: The Sandcutters, 1971, '72, '73; Fndr. & 1st Ed., Silhouette, 1965-66; Edit. Asst., Drum, 1965. Mbrships. incl: Int. Poetry Soc., U.K. (Fellow, also U.S. Hon. Edit. Advsr., 1973-); World Poetry Soc. Intercontinental; Centro Studi e Scambi Int., Italy; Ariz. State Poetry Soc. (Ed., 1971, '72, '73; Nat. , '72, '73; Nat. Poetry Contest Chmn., 1970); Phoenix Poetry Soc. (Pres., 1971); Life, Int. Clover Poetry Assn.; Treas., Am. Poetry League; Am. Mosaic Fndn. for Creativity Educ.; Nat. Fedn. of State Poetry Socs.; Acad. of Am. Poets. Contbr. to num. jrnls. & anthols. inclng. Contact, 1967; Ballet on the Wind, 1969; Sing, Naked Spirit, 1970; Int. Poetry Soc. Anthol., 1973. Recip. num. prizes & awards. Address: P.O. Box 15092, Phoenix, AZ 85060, U.S.A. 11.

SARGENT, Gerald Ernest George, b. 15 June 1929. Geologist. Educ: Imperial Coll. of Sci., Kensington, London, U.K. Appts: Geologist, African Manganese Co., U.K., 1953-54; Geologist, British Titan Prods. Co., U.K., 1954-57; Geologist, Hunting Geol. & Geophysics Co., U.K., 1957-70; Prof., Econ. Geol., Univ. of Qld., Australia, 1970-. Fellowships: Inst. of Mining & Metallurgy, London; Geological Soc. of London; Royal Astronomical Soc., London. Mbr., Australian Inst. of Mining & Metallurgy. Author of papers in field. Contbr. to jrnls. inclng: Oceanology; Ultrasonics. Address: Qld. Univ., Dept. of Geol. & Mineral., St. Lucia, Brisbane, Qld., Australia.

SARGENT, Ralph M(illard), b. 10 May 1904. University Professor. Educ: B.A., Carleton Coll., 1925; Ph.D., Yale Univ., 1931. Appts: Asst. Prof. of Engl., Carleton Coll., 1931-34; Prof. of Engl., Knox Coll., 1937-41; F.B. Gunmere Prof. of Engl., Haverford Coll., 1941-71. Mbrships: M.L.A. of Am.; Past Pres. & Trustee, Highlands Biological Stn., 1940-; Nat. Coun., AAUP. 1956-59; Nat. Coun., Renaissance Soc. of Am.; Past Pres., Lit. Fellowship of Phila. & Phila. Botanical Club;

V.P. & Dir., Henry Fndn. for Botanical Rsch.; Botanical Soc. of Am.; Publs. Comm., Penna. Horticultural Soc. Publs: Life & Lyrics of Sir Edward Dyer; Books of the Renaissance; Co-ed, Pelican Complete Shakespeare; Ed., Peter Kalm's Travels into North America; Contbr. to learned jrnls. Address: 520 Panmure Rd., Haverford, PA 19041, U.S.A.

SARGIS, Samson George, b. 7 Nov. 1899. Consultant Geophysicist. Educ: Grad., Wittenberg H.S., Wis.; B.S., Univ. of Wis., 1925. Appts. incl: w. Madison, Slichter & Gauld, Cons. Engrs., Madison, 1925-30; Cons. Geophys., Salt Lake City, 1930-33; Design Engr., US Steel Corp., 1933-34; Coke Plant Engr., 1936; Test Engr., 1937; Ind. Engr., Geol., Utah Ops., 1938-41; Works Ind. Engr., Calif., 1941-42; Supt., Ind. Rels., ibid, 1942-43; Asst. Mgr., Ind. Rels., San Francisco, 1943; Asst. Supt., Mines, Utah, 1943-47; Supt., Raw Mats., Utah, 1948-53; Asst. Mgr., Exploration, San Francisco, 1953-64; Chief Geol., Western Dist., Provo, 1964-65; Retd., 1965; Cons. Geophys., San Francisco, 1965-. Mbrships: Engrs. Club, San Francisco; Soc. Exploration Geophysicists; Pres., Bay Area Geophys. Soc., San Francisco, 1967-68; Am. Inst. Mining, Metallurgy & Petrol. Engrs.; Soc. Mining Engrs.; Fellow, AAAS. Address: 11th-15th Ave., San Francisco, Calif. 94118, U.S.A.

SARIDIS, Eleftherios, b. 1907. Business Executive. Educ: Schl. of Commerce, Frères des Maristes, Athens, Greece. Fndr., Owner, Gen. Mgr., Saridis S.A., Furniture Mfrs. & Woodwork Enterprises. Mbrships. incl: Union Socs. Anonymes; Union Greek Industrialists; Interior Decorators & Designers Assn., London, U.K. Recip. Gold Cross, Royal Batralia of Phoenix, 1961. Address: 11 G. Frangoudi St., Syngros Ave., Athens 404, Greece. 34.

SARIOLA, Mauri Aukusti, b. 25 Nov. 1924. Author. Educ: Grad. in Law, Univ. of Helsinki, Finland. Appts: Tank Off., Finnish Army, 1944-45; Ed.-in-Chief, Police & Crome Sect., Helsingin Sanomat, 1955-66. Mbr., Lions, 1964. Author, 52 detective & other novels, published in Finland & 10 other countries. Engl. translations incl: The Helsinki Affair; The Torwick Affair; Broad is the Way. Hons: Prizes, Finnish Min. of Educ., 1966, 1969, 1972; Cross, Finnish Criminal Police Assn., 1967; Prix du Roman d'Aventures, Paris, 1969. Address: Laivurinkatu 35.C.51, 00150 Helsinki 15, Finland.

SARKAR, Anil Kumar, b. 1 Aug. 1912. Professor of Philosophy. Educ: M.A., Patna Univ., India, 1935; Ph.D., ibid, 1946; D.Litt., 1960. Appts: Prof. of Philos., Rajendra Coll., Patna Univ., 1940-44; Sr. Lectr., Univ. of Ceylon, 1944-60; Vis. Prof., Univ. of N.M., Alburquerque, U.S.A., 1964-65; Prof. of Philos., Calif. State Univ., Hayward, 1965-; Vis. Prof. & Rsch. Advsr., Calif. Inst. of Asian Studies, 1968-. Mbrships. incl: Speaker, Indian Philosophical Congress, 1955, Sect. Pres., 1956; Rep., Indian Sci. Congress, Ceylon Assn. of Sci., Colombo, Ceylon, 1956 & 1957; Am. Philosophical Assn. Publs. incl: An Outline of Whitehead's Philosophy, 1940; Moral Philosophy (A Study of Personality), 1943; The Changing Phases of Buddhist Thought, 1968; Whitehead's Four Principles—From West-East Perspectives, 1972; Num. papers & reviews in profl. jrnls. Hons. incl: Gold Medal, Patna Univ., 1935; Post-doctoral Rsch. Schlrship., Univ. of London, U.K., 1951-52 & 1958-59. Address: 818 Webster St., Hayward, CA 94544, U.S.A. 9, 13.

SARLES, Peter Mason, b. 29 May 1926. General Manager. Educ: Bachelor of Aeronautical Engrng., Rensselaer Polytech. Inst., Troy, N.Y., 1951; Master's in Ind. Mgmt., MIT, 1961. Appts: Engr. & Mfg. Exec. w. Westinghouse Elec. Corp., 1954-60; Staff Asst. to V.P. (Mfg.), ibid, Pitts. Pa., 1961; assigned Gen. Mgr., Westinghause Atomic Equipment Div., Cheswick, Pa., 1962; appointed Westinghouse V.P. (Mfg.), Pitts. Pa., 1969; Gen. Mgr., Westinghouse Gas Turbines Systems Div., 1972-. Mbrships: Soc. of Automotive Engrs.; AIAA; Chmbr. of Comm., Greater Pitts. Pa. Address: Westinghouse Electric Corp., Gas Turbine Systems Div., P.O. Box 9175, Philadephia, PA 19113, U.S.A.

SARÖKARI, Onni Vilhelm, b. 11 May 1918. Chief General Manager of Bank. Educ: LL.B., 1949. Appts: Chief Gen. Mgr., Ctrl. Bank of Finnish Savings Banks Ltd., Helsinki, 1967-; Bd. Mbr., Banque Nordeurope S.A., Luxemburg, Savings Banks Assn. in Finland, Keskinäinen Vakuutusyhtiö Sampo-Tarmo, Teollistamisrahasto, & Sponsor Oy; Chmn., Bd. of Dirs., Finnish Real Estaté Bank, & Savings Banks Pension Fund; Supvsry. Bd. Mbr., Interspar. Mbrships: Bd., Finnish Bankers Assn.; Bd., Helsinki Chmbr. of Comm.; Ctrl. Bank Comm., Int. Savings Banks Inst., Geneva, Switzerland; League of Finnish-Am. Socs., Helsinki. Hons: Order of the Cross of Liberty 4, 1942; Cmdr., Order of the Lion of Finland, 1968. Address: P.O. Box 400, SF-00101 Helsinki 10, Finland. 43.

SAROYAN, William, b. 31 Aug. 1908. Writer. Educ: Fresno H.S., Calif. Appts: V.P., Paramount Grape Distributing Co., Fresno, Calif., 1924; Br. Mgr., Postal Telegraph Off., San Francisco, Calif., 1928. Publs: The Daring Young Man on the Flying Trapeze, & other short stories, 1934; Places, 1974; 44 other books. Other works incl: The Time of Your Life (play), 1939; The Great American Goof (ballet), 1941; The Whole World Is a Joke and a Little Grocery Store (film), 1942; Hello Out There (opera), 1958. Hons. incl. The Hollywood Oscar, 1943. Address: Box 5052, Fresno, CA 93755, U.S.A.

SARRE, Hans J., b. 25 Mar. 1906. Professor of Medicine. Educ: Berlin; Kiel; Heidelberg; Freiburg; Grad., 1931. Appts: Fellow, Deutsche Forschungsgemeinschaft, Physiol. Inst., Univ. of Göttingen, 1932-34; Asst., ibid, 1934-38; Asst. Prof. of Internal Med., Med. Clin., Univ. of Frankfurt (Main), 1938-48; Prof. of Internal Med. & Chief of Dept., Univ. of Freiburg, 1948-. Mbrships. incl: German Soc. for Internal Med.; Pres., Soc. for Nephrol., 1961 & 72; Int. Soc. of Nephrol.; E.D.T.A.; Corres., Acad. Nacional de Buenos Aires; Hon. Mbr., S. German Soc. for Urol. Publs. incl: Nierenkrankheiten, 1957, 59, 67 & 74; Diät bei Erkrankungen der Niere und Harnwege, 8th edit., 1972; Hypertonie, 1969; Niere und Stoffwechselkrankheiten, 1973; Arterielle Hypertonie, 1971; contbr. to profl. jrnls. & anthols. Address: Medizin. Poliklinik der Univ., Herm. Herderstr. 6, D 78 Freiburg i. Br., German Fed. Repub. 92.

SASAKI, Kiyoshi, b. 4 Apr. 1916. Travel Executive. Appts: Clerk, Lihue Store, Hawaii, 1934-36; Off. Mgr., Nawiliwili Transportation Co. Ltd., 1936-48; Gen. Mgr., ibid, 1948-54; Owner-Mgr., Universal Tour & Travel Serv., 1954-; Pres., Kauai Corp. Inc., 1968-; Pres., Mgr., Universal Delivery Serv. Inc., 1970-. Mbrships: Bd. of Regents, Univ. of Hawaii, 1972-75; Am. Soc. of Travel Agts.; Dpty. Dist. Gov., Dist. 50, Lions Int., 1959-60; Air Pollution Control Comm.; Asst. Personnel &

Admin. Off., Kauai Civil Defense Agcy.; Past Pres: Kauai Jr. Chmbr. of Comm.; Kauai Dist. PTA; Kauai H.S. PTA; Lihue Schl. PTA; E. Kauai Lions Club; Lihue Bus. men's Assn.; Lihue Hongwanji Mission. Hons: Jaycees Disting. Serv. Award, 1947; Agt. of Yr., P & O Lines, 1966; Travel Agt. Award, United Air Lines, 1969. Address: 3175 Elua St., Lihue, Kuaik HI 96766, U.S.A. 78.

SASIDHORN, Nibondh, b. 3 Nov. 1931. Government Official; Political Scientist; Sociologist. Educ: A.B., Chulalongkorn Univ., Thailand; A.M., Int. Rels., Fletcher Schl. of Law & Diplomacy; A.M., Pub. Admin., & Ph.D., Ind. Univ., USA. Appts: 3rd—1st Grade Instr., Chulalongkorn Univ., 1954-61; Chief, Soc. Scis., Rsch. Div., Nat. Rsch. Coun., Thailand, 1962-65; Special Grade Dir., Planning & Rsch. Bur., Off. of Prime Min., 1963-69; Dean., Fac. of Soc. Scis., Chiengmai Univ., Thailand, 1967-73; Vis. Lectr., var. univs., USA, 1972-73; Univ. Prof., Pol. Advsr. attached to Off. of Prime Min., & Mbr., Legislative Coun., 1973-. Mbrships. incl: Soc. Chmn., Soc. Scis. Assn. of Thailand; PR Dir., Pol. Sci. Assn. of Thailand; Exec. Comm., Thai-Am. Assn.; Pres., Chiengmai Chapt., Int. Rotary Club, Cheingmai Girl's Schl. Tchr. & Parents Soc. & Pol. Sci. Alumni Assn. of Chulalongkorn Univ.; V.P., Chulalongkorn Alumni Assn. Contbr. num. articles to jrnls. Hons: Award for Best Student, H.M. King Bhumibhol, 1954; sev. fellowships & grants from US Govt.; invited by German, French & UK govts. to visit their countries, 1965, 67 & 74. Address: 212/6 Soi Rungrueng, Lad Prao Rd., Bangkok, Thailand.

SASLAW, Milton Sibley, b. 1 May 1911. Physician. Educ: B.S., N.Y. Univ., 1931; M.D., Bellevue Hosp Med. Coll., 1934; M.P.H., UCLA Schl. of Pub. Hlth, 1967; Certified by Am. Bd. Preventive Med., 1969. Appts: Prac. Internal Med. & Cardiol., 1937-51; Dir., Med. Rsch., Nat. Childrens Cardiac Hosp., 1951-64; Sr. Rsch. Sci., Grad. Schl., Univ. of Miami, 1964-69; Dir., Div. Rsch. & Epidem., Dade Co. Dept. Pub. Hlth., Fla., 1965-69; Dir., Dade Co. Dept. Pub. Hlth., 1969-; Clin. Prof., Dept. of Epidemiol. & Pub. Hlth., Univ. of Miami Schl. of Med., 1969. Fellowships: Am. Pub. Hlth. Assn.; Gov. for Fla., Am. Coll. Cardiol., 1959-62; Am. Coll. Chest Physns.; Am. Geriatric Soc., Epidemiol. Sect., Am. Heart Assn. Mbr., numerous local, state & nat. orgs. Author, approx. 90 sci. articles. Address: 1350 N.W. 14th St., Miami, FL 33125, U.S.A. 7, 14, 15, 17, 28, 81, 128.

SASNETT, Martena Tenney (Mrs. J. Randolf Sasnett), b. 2 May 1908. Author; International Education Researcher. Educ: Grad., Acad. of Speech & Arts, 1927; Geo. Wash. Univ., 1927-28; special studies, Odeon, Paris, France, 1928-29; Pasadena Inst. of Radio, 1944; Pasadena Playhouse TV Inst., 1954. Appts: For. Student Admissions Off., Univ. of Southern Calif., 1947-52; Coord. Int. Educ. Studies, Univ. of Calif., 1964-66; Assoc. Dir., Relig. in Educ. Fndn., 1969-; Assoc. Dir., Educ. Features, Int., 1974-. Mbrships: Am. Assn. of Collegiate Registrars & Admissions Offs.; Nat. Assn. of For. Student Affairs. Publs. incl: Financial Planning for Study in the United States: A Guide for Students from Other Countries, 1967; Educational Systems of Africa (co-author), 1966; Graduate Study in the United States, 1966; The Country Index: Interpretations for Use in the Evaluation of Foreign Secondary Academic Credentials, 1971; Ed., Foreign Students Look at the U.S., 1960; Contbr. to jrnls. Recip. sev. hons. inclng. Bradford Coll. achievement award, 1961.

Address: 2829 Miradero Drive, Santa Barbara, CA 93105, U.S.A. 5, 9, 138.

SASSY, Jean-Paul, b. 29 July 1931. Film producer; Writer. Educ: Lic. en Droit, Lic. de Philo, Aix & Paris, France. Appts: Asst. to var. French & for. films producers. Producer of La Peau et les Os; Prix Jean Vigo; (TV) Repos à Bacoli, L'Espion aux Yeux Vertes, Tête d'Horloge, Une Poignée de Mains. Author of Le Forcené (novel), in preparation. Recip. of num. T.V. awards. Address: 19 Route de la Reine, 92100 Boulogne s/S, France.

SATCHELL, Geoffrey Harold, b. 18 Apr. 1921. Professor of Zoology. Educ: B.Sc., Leicester Univ., 1942; Ph.D., Leeds Univ., 1944. Appts: Lectr., Univ. of Nottingham, 1944-48; Lectr., Univ. of Otago, N.Z., 1948-55; Lectr. Sr. Lectr., Physiol., Otago Med, Schl., 1955-62; Rdr., Zool., Univ. of Adelaide, Australia, 1962-65; Prof., Zool., Univ. of Sydney, 1965-71; Vis. Prof. , Univ. of Bristol, 1969; Prof., Zool., Univ. of Otago, N.Z., 1971-. Mbrships: Bd. of Control, CSIRO Jrnls. Comm.; Trustee, Australian Mus.; Bd. of Govs., McGlashan Coll., Dunedin; Treas., N.Z. Physiol. Soc.; Mbr., Exec. Comm., Gt. Barrier Reef Comm. Publs: Circulation in Fishes (monograph), 1971; Num. articles in sci. jrnls. Hons: Sir Jonathon North Schlrship. & Gold Medal, 1942. Address: 45 Every St., Andersons Bay, Dunedin, N.Z. 23, 128.

SATO, Eisaku, b. 27 May 1901. Member of House of Representatives, Japan. Educ: LL.B., Tokyo Imperial Univ., Japan. Appts: Vice Min. of Transportation, 1947-48; Chief Cabinet Sec., 1948-49; Min. of Postal Serv., 1951, of Telecommunications, 1951, of Posts & Telecommunications, 1951-52; Min. of Construction, 1952-53; Min. of Finance, 1958-60; Min. of Int. Trade & Ind., 1961-62; Min. of State, Div. of Sci. & Technol. Agcy., Chmn., Atomic Energy Commn. & i/c of Olympic Affairs, 1963-64; Prime Min., 1964-72. Mbrships: Pres., Japan Assn.; Pres., Pol. Fedn. of Japanese Minor Enterprises. Author of autobiography, Today is Tomorrow's Yesterday, 1964. Hons: LL.D., Columbia Univ., N.Y., U.S.A., 1967; Supreme Order of the Grand Cordon of tne Chrysanthemum, 1972. Address: 320th, 1st Bldg. of the Mbrs. of the House of Reps., 2-1, 2chome, Nagata-cho, Chiyoda-ku, Tokyo, Japan.

SATTER, Heinrich, b. 27 Sept. 1908. Writer; Journalist. Educ: Univs. of Vienna, Austria & Berlin, Germany. Appts: Ed., Ullstein Verlag, Berlin; Theater, film & literary critic; Author of biographies & novels. Mbr., Verband deutscher Schriftsteller. Publs: Angelica Catalani; Deutschland ohne Feigenblatt; Paul Ehrlich; Emil von Behring; Ida Orloff und Gerhart Hauptmann; Modell Nächstenliebe, Beispiel Bethel (w. foreword by W. German Chancellor Willy Brandt). Address: Hofmarkt 76, A 5602 Wagrain, Austria.

SAUER, Gordon Chenoweth, b. 14 Aug. 1921. Physician; Dermatologist. Appts. incl: Pvte. Prac., Kan. City, Mo. 1954-; Currently, Clin. Prof. of Med. & Hd. of Sect. of Dermatol., Univ. of Kan. Schl. of Med. Mbr., Am. Dermatol. Assn., etc. Publs. incl: Manual of Skin Diseases, 1959, 3rd. edit., 1973; Teen Skin, 1965. Contbr. of num. articles to profl. jrnls. Address: 6400 Prospect Ave., Kansas City, MO 64132, U.S.A. 2, 8, 14, 17, 22, 28, 54.

SAUL, Frank Philip, b. 31 Oct. 1930. Biomedical Anthropologist. Educ: A.B., Brooklyn Coll., 1952; A.M., Harvard Univ.,

1959; Ph.D., ibid, 1972. Appts: Asst. in Anthropol., Am. Mus. of Natural Hist., 1951-52; Phys. Anthropologist, Aero Med. Lab., USAF, 1953-58; Tchng. Fellow & Asst. in Anthropol., Harvard Univ., 1959-62; Instr.-Asst. Prof. of Anthropol., Pa. State Univ., 1962-69; Asst. Prof.-Assoc. Prof. of Anatomy, Med. Coll. of Ohio, 1969-. Mbrships. incl: Fellow, Am. Anthropological Assn.; Fellow, AAAS; Treas., Pan Am. Assn. of Anatomy; Int. Assn. of Human Biologists; Soc. for Med. Anthropol.; Int. Ergonomics Assn. Author of publs. in field. Address: Dept. of Anatomy, Med. Coll. of Ohio, P.O. Box 6190, Toledo, OH 43614, U.S.A. 8, 14.

SAULIEU, de la CHOMONERIE, (Vicomte) François de, b. 19 Feb. 1907. Journalist. Educ: Collège des Maristes, Riom (Puy de Dome) & Pontlevoy (Loir et Cher), France. Appts: Dir. Gen., Les Routiers, 1935-, "Guide des Relais Routiers"; Dir., Les Routiers British Isles & Commonwealth Ltd., 1972-; Pres., l'Union Internationale des Chauffeurs Routiers & Championnat Int. des Chauffeurs Routiers; Pres., Famille de la Route. Mbrships: Ordre des Cincinnati; Assn. d'entraide de la Noblesse Française; Conseil Supérieur des Transports; Commn. du Plan. Publs: Un Soir sur l'Euphrate, La Combe aux Loups (novels); Une Gentilhommière en Pays Brayaud (history); Histoire du Travail. Address: 24 Rue de Clichy, Paris 9, France.

SAUNAL, Robert, b. 2 Nov. 1920. Engineer; Business Executive. Educ: Polytech. Schl., Paris, France; Engr., Mining Corps. Appts. incl: Chief Engr., Mines, Madagascar, 1948, Dir., French Overseas Mining Bur., Cameroons, 1950, New Caledonia, 1954, Paris, 1957; Cons. Engr., Inst. of Iron Metallurgy Rsch., 1961-65; Engr., Naval Iron & Steel Works, Firminy & St.-Etienne, 1965-; Pres. Dir. Gen., Société de Moutiers, 1965, Admnstr., 1969-; Pres. Dir. Gen., Soc. of Mines of Anderny-Chevillon, 1966-; Dpty. Dir. Gen., Indl. & Commercial Soc. of Transport & Handling, 1966, Pres., 1969-; Mgr., Eurotainer Co., 1969-; V.P., Remafer Co., 1967-. Hons. incl: Off., Legion of Hon. Address: 12 Rue de la Rochefoucauld, Paris 9, France.

SAUNDERS, Basil, b. 12 Aug. 1925. Public Relations Officer. Educ: Wadham Coll., Oxford, U.K.; College de Tarascon, France. Appts: Hd. of P.R. Servs., The Wellcome Fndn. Ltd., London, 1963-; Assoc. Dir., Infoplan Ltd., London, 1958-63; P.R. Officer, British Inst. of Mgmt., 1955-58; Writer, General Electric Co., N.Y., 1952-53. Mbrships: former Mbr. of Coun., Inst. of Pub. Rels.; former Chmn., Mbrship. Comm., ibid. Publs: Crackle of Thorns (booklet of poems); short stories & articles in Brit. press. Recip., Fellowship, Inst. of Pub. Rels. Address: The Wellcome Fndn. Ltd., 183 Euston Rd., London NW1, U.K.

SAUNDERS, Donald Leslie, b. 28 Jan. 1935. Realtor. Educ: A.B., Brown Univ., Providence, R.I., 1957; Am. Inst. Real Estate Appraiser Courses; Inst. Real Estate Mgmt. Courses. Appts: Pres., Saunders & Assocs., Realtor; Licensed Real Estate Broker, Commonwealth of Mass., State of R.I.; Licensed Auctioneer. Mbrships: Past Dir. Gtr. Boston Real Estate Bd. (past mbr., exec. comm.); Mass. Assn. Real Estate Bds.; Nat. Assn. Real Estate Bds.; Inst. Real Estate Mgmt., Nat. Assn. Real Estate Bds.; Past Chmn. & Dir., Owner-Mbr. Advsry. Comm., Gtr. Boston Real Estate Bd.; Past V.P. & Dir., Rental Housing Assn., Gtr. Boston Real Estate Bd.; Mass. Bd. Real Estate Appraisers; Dir., Liberty Bank &

Trust Co., Boston, Mass.; Past Trustee, Brown Univ. Corp., Providence, R.I.; Commnr., Back Bay Archl. Commn., Boston, Mass. Address: 229 Newbury St., Boston, MA 02116, U.S.A.

SAUNDERS, (Miss) Marjorie, Inez. Public Relations Director. Educ: Southern Meth. Univ., Dallas, Tex.; LL.B., Jefferson Univ. Schl. of Law, Dallas; Grad., Dallas Acad. of Speech & Drama. Appts: Practised Civil Law, Dallas; Currently Dir., Pub. Rels., Baylor Univ. Med. Ctr., Dallas, Tex. Mbrships. incl: Dallas Bar Assn.; Am. Assn. of Blood Banks, Chgo., Ill.; Charter mbr., Am. Soc. for Hosp. Pub. Rels. Dirs., Am. Hosp. Assn., 1964-73; Bd. mbr., ibid, 1967-73; Pres., 1970-71; Pub. Rels. Comm., Am. Cancer Soc., Dallas Unit, 1962-68; Pub. Rels. Soc. of Am., 1967-73; Religious Pub. Rels. Coun., Inc., 1966-69; Nat. Assn. of Women Lawyers. Num. addresses given; Many papers publd. Hons. incl: Plaque award for outstanding achievement, Freedom's Fndn., 1973; Award of exceptional merit for total pub. rels. proj., Hons. competition, Bapt. Pub. Rels. Assn., 1973. Address: Baylor Univ. Med. Ctr., 3500 Gaston Ave., Dallas, TX 75246, U.S.A. 5, 7, 16, 24, 79, 128.

SAUTER, Hermann, b. 5 Jan. 1907. Librarian. Educ: Study of Mod. Langs., Univs. of Heidelberg, Paris, Exeter, Munich; Lib. Sci. trng., 1931-32; Dr. Diss., & Exam for Libnship., 1932. Appts: Dir., Municipal Libs., Munich, 1936-45; Dir., Palatinate State Lib., 1948-62; Dir., Univ. Lib., Mainz, 1962-72. Mbrships: Pres., Lib. Soc. of the Palatinate; Bd. Mbr., Gutenberg Soc., Mainz.; Soc. for Advancement of Sci., & Saarland Commn. for Hist. Publs: Author of books & essays in German & translator, Valery's 'Mon Faust.' Address: Zeisigweg 25, D 65 Mainz 21, German Fed. Repub.

SAUVY, Alfred, b. 31 Oct. 1898. Professor. Educ: Ecole Polytech., France, 1920. Appts: Dir., Inst. de Conjoncture; Dir., Inst. Nat. d'Etudes Démographiques (INED); Prof., Coll. de France, 1959-69; Mbr., Conseil Economique et Social, 1947-. Mbrships: Int. Statistical Inst.; Int. Union for Scientific Study of Population, etc. Publs: More than 30 works inclng. Théorie Générale de la Population; Malthus et les deux Marx; Les Limites de la Vie Humaine; Histoire économique de la France entre les deux guerres (III vols. have been publd.); La Montée des jeunes; La Révolte des jeunes; Mythologie de notre temps; Socialisme en liberté; De Paul Reynaud à Charles de Gaulle. Hons: Cmdr., Légion d'Honneur; Cmdr. d'Académia; Cmdr., Santé publique; Docts. from Univs. of Geneva, Burssels, Utrecht, Liege. Address: 76 Rue Lepic, Paris 18e, France. 34.

SAVAGE, Horace Christopher, b. 1 Aug. 1922. Educational Consultant; Radio Publicist; College Teacher. Educ: B.S., M.A., Schl. of Educ., N.Y. Univ.; advanced study, hist. educ., ibid; divinity studies, N.Y., Vanderbilt & Va. Union Univs. Appts. incl: Asst. Prof. Hist., Lane Coll., Jackson, Tenn., 1949-53; Assoc. Prof., Tenn. State Univ., Nashville, 1953-64; Pres., Tex. Coll., Tyler, 1964-67; Prof., Dean of Chapel, Lane Coll., 1967-71; Cons., Employee Rels., Bemis Co., Dir. Pub. Affairs, WTJS Radio Stn., Educl. Cons. & Pastor, CME Ch., 1971-. Mbrships: Fellow, The Philosophical Soc., London; Bd. Mbr., Jackson Br., Assn. for the Retarded, Salvation Army Day Care Ctr., Jackson, Tex. Assn. of Developing Colls.; Asst. Sec., Assn. Soc. Sci. Tchrs.; Mbr., AAAS, Royal Soc. of Hlth., U.K., Tenn. Histl. Soc. Author, The Life & Times of Bishop Isaac Lane, 1958. Contbr. to profl. & learned jrnls. Recip.,

Litt.D., Lane Coll., 1959. Address: Savage Assocs., 548 N. Cumberland St., Jackson, TN 38301, U.S.A. 7, 13.

SAVAGE, Warren Henry Jr., b. 15 Oct. 1938. Electronic Specialist. Educ: B.S., Thomas A. Edison Coll.; M.S., ibid. Appts: Secure Communications Specialist; Electronics Test Equipment Specialist; Electronics Rep., Atlantic Area, Metrol. Calibration Grp. Mbrships: Nat. Dir., Navy League of the U.S.; Nat. Dir., V.P., U.S. Naval Sea Cadet Corps. Publd. Electronic Test & Diagnostic Equipment Calibration & Repair Handbook. Address: 3732 Concord Dr., Suffolk, VA 23435, U.S.A.

SAVAS, Emanuel S. ("Steve"), b. 8 June 1931. Educator; Public Official. Educ: B.A., Univ. of Chgo., 1951; B.S., ibid, 1953; M.A., Columbia Univ., 1956; Ph.D., ibid, 1960. Appts: Control Systems Cons., IBM Corp., 1959-65; Mgr., Urban Systems, ibid, 1966-67; Dpty. City Admnstr., Off. of the Mayor, N.Y.C., 1967-69; 1st Dpty. City Admnstr., ibid (promoted by Mayor Lindsay), 1970-72; Prof.,Pub. Systems Mgmt., Grad. Schl. of Bus., Columbia Univ., N.Y.C., 1973-. Mbrships. incl: Assoc. Ed., Inst. of Mgmt. Scis.; Publs. Comm., Ops. Rsch. Soc. of Am.; AAAS; IEEE; Assn. for Computing Machinery; Urban & Regional Info. Systems Assn. Author of num. publs. in field. Hons. incl: Louis Brownlow Mem. Award, Am. Soc. for Pub. Admin., 1970; Am. Heritage Award, JKF Lib. for Minorities, 1972. Address: 608 Uris Hall, Grad. Schl. of Bus., Columbia Univ., N.Y., NY 10027, U.S.A. 6, 14, 30.

SAVCI, Mesut, b. 16 Oct. 1923. Professor of Ship Strength. Educ: M.Sc., Tech. Univ. of Istanbul, Turkey, 1948. Appts. incl: Mil. Serv., Navy Shipyard Golcuk & Taskizak, 1948; Asst., Dept. of Naval Arch., Tech. Univ. of Istanbul, 1950; Naval Archt., Bremerhaven, Germany, 1952; Asst., Tech. Univ. of Istanbul, 1953, Assoc. Prof., 1954, Prof. of Ship-Strength, 1963 & Dir., Shipbldg. Rsch. Inst., 1965; Shipbldg. Dept., Germanischer Lloyd, Hamburg, Germany, 1956. Mbr., Chmbr. of Turkish Naval Archts. & Marine Engrs. Publs. incl: Balikçi Gemilerinin Dizayni icin Yeni Yollar, 1956; Gemilerin Boyuna Mukavemeti, 1962; Gemilerde Levha Mukavemeti, 1962; Gemi Kirişleri Mukavemeti, 1967; Article in profl. jrnl. Address: Ataköy 2. Kisim H-4 No. 16 D.4, Istanbul, Turkey.

SAVEANU, Lascar, b. 21 May 1919. Professor. Educ: Licentiate in Law, Univ. of Bucharest, Rumania, 1941; Dr.rerum politicarum, Univ. of Innsbruck, Austria, 1949. Appts: Prof., Econs., Inst. Tecnológico del Sur, Bahía Blanca, Argentina, 1952-56 & Univ. of La Plata, 1956-58; Full Prof., Econs. & Econ. Hist., Univ. Nacional del Sur, Bahía Blanca, 1957-; Dir., Dept. of Econs., ibid, 1957-69; Dir., "Estudios Economicos", ed. by Inst. of Econs., 1962-70. Mbrships: Asociación Argentina de Economía Política (assoc. to Int. Econ. Assn.). Contbr. to profl. jrnls. Address: c/o Departamento de Economía, Universidad Nacional del Sur, Avenida Colón 80, Bahía Blanca, Argentina.

SAVIC-TICA, Tihomir, b. 3 Aug. 1927. Painter; Architect; Sculptor. Educ: Arch., Applied Arts Schls., Belgrade. One Man Exhibs: Belgrade, 1955, '62; Lausanne, 1967; N.Y., 1969. Grp. Exhibs: Monte Carlo, 1964; Perspective 68 Exhib., ibid, 1969; 4th. Grand Prix, Nice, 1968; 1st. Grand Prix de Festival. Cannes, 1968; 5th Grand Prix d'Ete, Nice, 1968; Exhib. of Contem. European Painters, N.Y., 1968; 5th Grand Prix de Noel, 1969; III Biennial Int., Merignac, 1971. Mbrships, incl:

Cmdr., Int. Arts Guild, Monte Carlo; Hon. mbr., Int. Acad. Tommaso Campanella. Hons. incl: Gold Medal, 5th. Grand Prix de Noel, 1969; Silver Medal, Int. Acad. Tommaso Campanella, Rome, 1970. Address: En Marin, Route du Golf, 1075 Chalet-a-Gobet, Switzerland. 105, 133.

SAVOY, Chyrl Lenore, b. 23 May 1944. Sculptor; Educator. Educ: B.A., La. State Univ., Baton Rouge, 1966; Sculpture & Drawing under Gallo & Berti, Acad. of Fine Arts, Florence, Italy, 1966-67; Dipl. di Profitto, Univ. Degli Studi di Firenze, 1967; M.F.A., Wayne State Univ., Detroit, Mich., U.S.A., 1970. Appts: Art Tchr., St. Martin's Schl., Detroit, Mich., 1969; Grad. Student Asst. in Sculpture, Wayne State Univ., Detroit, 1970; currently Asst. Prof., Fine Arts, La. State Univ., Shreveport. Works in Pub. Collects, incl: Herrod Jr. H.S. Lib., Abbeville, La.; Mamour H.S. Lib., Mamou, La.; Couvent St. Dominique de la Gloire de Dieu, Maison Mere des Dominicaines, Flavigny, France; Cath. Ch., S.A. Commns: Renovation & Redesigning of Chapel, Our Lady of the Bayous Convent, Abbeville, La., 1972; Sculpture, Our Lady Queen of All Saints, Ville Platte, La., 1972; Design for Sculpture of St. John the Baptist, Our Lady Star of the Sea, Cameron, La., 1973. Held One-Man Exhib., New Orleans Mus. of Art, La., 1972; in num. grp. exhibs. Hons. incl. Samuel Wiener Sculpture Award, 51st Regional Exhib., R.S. Barwell Mem. Gdn. & Art Ctr., Shreveport, La., 1973. Address: 1009 Poinciana Ave., Mamou, LA 70554, U.S.A. 37.

SAWYER, Dolores Jean Young, b. 16 Oct. 1938. Registered Nurse. Educ: B.S. in Nursing, Northwestern State Coll. (now Univ.), Natchitoches, La., U.S.A., 1960. Appts. incl: Hd. Nurse, Brooks Gen. Hosp., Atlanta, Tex., 1960-61; Hd. Nurse, O.B. Dept., Highland Hosp., Shreveport, La., 1961-63; Supvsr., O.B. Dept., ibid, 1963-64; Hd. Nurse or Charge Nurse, Med.-Surg. Units, Scott & White Hosp., Temple, Tex., 1967-72; Schl. Nurse, Temple Independent Schl. Dist., 1972-73; Asst. Instr., Scott & White Dept. of Nursing, Mary Hardin-Baylor Coll., Temple, 1973-74. Mbrships. incl: Am. Nurses Assn.; Continuing Educ. Recognition Prog. for R.N.'s in Tex.; Tex. State Tchrs. Assn.; Hlth. Sect. for Nurses, Tex. State Tchrs. Assn.; Past Chmn., Temple Piano Ensemble; Music Club of Temple; Past Pres., Better Homes & Gardens Club; Womens Soc. of Christian Serv. Presenter, sev. piano progs. Organist, pianist, & choir mbr., sev. chs. Address: 3702 Lancelot Lane, Temple, TX 76501, U.S.A. 125.

SAWYER, Henry Vernon, b. 23 Aug. 1918. Optometrist. Educ: Dr. of Optometry, Southern Coll. of Optometry, Memphis, Tenn., 1950; Postgrad. courses & seminars each yr. since graduation from coll. Mbrships: Past Pres., Dee Optometric Assn.; Past Pres., S.C. Optometric Assn.; Past Pres., Southern Coun. of Optometrists; Chmn., var. comms. in profl. assns.; Past Pres., Marion Lions Club; Past Cmdr.; Am. Legion Post 5; Past V.P., Chmbr. of Comm.; Past Pres., Jaycees; Dir. & Past Pres., Marion United Fund; Marion City Coun., 16 yrs.; Past mayor pro-tem; Past Co. Chmn., Nat. Fndn. for Infantile Paralysis. Hons: Community Serv. Awards, 1965-73; Young Man of the Yr., 1956. Address: P.O. Box 994, Marion, SC 29571, U.S.A.

SAWYERR, (Rev.) Harry Alphonso Ebun, b. 16 Oct. 1909. Clerk in Holy Orders; Principal. Educ: B.A., Univ. of Durham, U.K., 1933; M.A., St. John's Coll., Durham, 1936; M.Ed., ibid, 1940. Appts. incl: Tutor, Fourah

Bay Coll., 1933-41, Lectr., 1948-52, Chap., 1948-56, Sr. Lectr., 1952-62, Vice Prin., 1956-58 and 1964-68, Prof. of Theol. and Hd. of Dept., 1962-68, Prin., 1968-; Pro Vice-Chancellor, Univ. of Sierra Leone, 1968-70; Vice-Chancellor, ibid, 1970-72; Examining Chap. to the Bishop of Sierra Leone, 1948-; Canon, St. George's Cathedral, Freetown, 1961-; Sec., Theol. Advsr. Bd., Province of W. Africa, 1952-58. Mbrships. incl: Soc. of New Testament Studies; Int. Assn. of Missionary Socs.; Advsry. Bd., Ecumenical Studies, Lutterworth Pres, 1965-; Edit. Bd., Jrnl. of African Relig., 1966-; Comm. of Dirs., Theologia Africana. Publs. incl: The Springs of Mende Belief and Conduct (w. W.T. Harris), 1968; God: Ancestor or Creator?, 1970; Contbr. of var. articles to jrnls. Hons. incl: M.B.E., 1954; C.B.E., 1963; D.D., Univ. of Durham, U.K., 1970; Grand Cmdr., Order of the Star of Africa, Repub. of Liberia, 1971. Address: Fourah Bay Coll., Mount Aureol, Freetown, Sierra Leone, W. Africa. 1, 30, 135.

SAXOV, Svend Erik, b. 20 Mar. 1913. University Professor. Educ: Cand. mag., Copenhagen Univ., Denmark, 1937; Mag.sci., 1957. Appts: Jr. Geodesist, Geodetic Inst., Copenhagen, 1937; Sr. Geodesist, ibid, 1957; Prof., Univ. of Aarhus, 1964-; Chmn., Geol. Inst., 1966-71; Chmn., Nat. Sci. Fac. Grp., 1967-70; Dean, Fac. of Sci., 1968-69; Mbr., Consistory, 1966-70; Geophys. Cons., 1960-. Mbrships. incl: Pres., European Assn. of Exploration Geophys., 1965-66; Pres., Nordic Assn. for Applied Geophys., 1966-68; Coun., 1959-; Danish Geophys. Soc.; Coun., German Geophys. Soc., 1966-71; V.P., EDITERRA, 1969-72; Danish Geol. Soc.; Norwegian Geol. Soc. Hons: Kt., Order of Dannebrog, 1962; Medal of Defense Servs., 1963; 1st Class, Order of Dannebrog, 1973. Address: Elmevej 11, 8660 Skanderborg, Denmark. 134.

SAXTON, Donald Dean, b. 21 June 1917. Coal Company Executive. Educ: B.S., Mining Engrng., Univ. of Pitts., 1939. Appts. incl: Mine Engr., 1940-41-; Mgr., Gen. Supt., 1945-54; Hanna Coal Co. Div. Consol. Coal Co., Cadiz, Ohio; Served to Major, Artillery, AUS, 1941-45; Owner, Pres., Dir., Middleport Coal Co., Dover, Ohio, 1952-58; Pres., Germano Coal Co., Dover, Knight Coal Co. & Compton & Saxton Coal Co., Clarksburg, W. Va., 1955-60; V.P., Grafton Coal Co., Clarksburg, 1955-60; Owner., Pres., M & O Coal Co., Cleveland, 1961-68; Pres., Dir., Ella Coal Co., ibid, 1960-64; Owner, Pres., Saxton Coal Co., 1969-; Int. V.P., Peabody Coal Co., 1970-; Dir., cos. in Australia & Colombia, S. Am. Mbrships. incl: Am. Inst. Mining & Metallurgical Engrs.; Bd. of Dirs., Salem Coll., W. Va.; Meth. Ch. Bd., Clarksburg; Presby. Ch. Bd., Bay Village, Ohio; Republican; Mason; Elk; W. Va. Engrs. Soc.; Clarksburg Chmbr. of Comm.; Pi Kappa Alpha; Mo. Athletic Club. Address: Peabody Coal Co., 301 N. Memorial Dr., St. Louis, MO 63102, U.S.A. 16.

SAYGUN, Ahmed Adnan, b. 7 Sept. 1907. Composer & Musicologist. Musical Educ. at Izmir, Turkey & Schola cantorum, Paris, France. Appts: Prof., Music Tchrs. Coll., Ankara, Turkey, 1931-35; Conductor, Presidential Orch., 1935-36; Prof., Istanbul Conservatoire of Music, 1936-39; Musical Advsr., Peoples Houses for Adult Educ., 1939-50; Prof., Nat. Conservatoire of Music, Ankara, 1946-74; Mbr., Supreme Bd. Educ., Min. Educ., 1960-66. Past mbr. sev. musical orgs. Prin., Compositions: 4 Symphonies; Dictum for string orch.; 2 suites for orch.; A Forest Tale, choreographic suite for orch.; The Puppet (opera in 1 act); Kerem (opera in 3

acts); Köroglu (opera in 3 acts); 3 String Quartets; Violin Concerto; Piano Concerto; 10 Etudes for piano on Aksak Rhythms; 12 Preludes for piano on Aksak Rhythms; violin sonata, etc.; many books & conf. papers in field. Hons: Prix Inönü, 1948; Off. d'Acad., France, 1950; Stella della Soliderieta Italiana di la Classe, Italy, 1957. Address: Ulus Mahallesi, Bag app., 10 Levent I, Istanbul, Turkey.

SAYIGH, Adnan Abdul Rida, b. 30 Dec. 1922. Vice President, Research, Chemical Div., The Upjohn Company. Educ: B.S., Chem., Am. Univ. of Beirut, 1945; M.A., Columbia Univ., 1949; Ph.D.,Columbia Univ., 1952. Appts: Nat. Hlth. Fellowship, post doctoral work, Hickrill Chem. Rsch. Fndn., 1952; Assoc. Prof. of Chem., Coll. Arts & Scis., Baghdad, Iraq, 1954; Chem., The Carwin Co. now The Upjohn Co., 1956; Dir. of Rsch., The Upjohn Co., 1959; V.P., Rsch., Chem. Div., ibid, 1973. Mbrships: Am. & Brit. Chem. Socs.; Phi Lambda Upsilon; Sigma Xi. Num. patents & sci. publs. Address: Address: Donald S. Gilmore Rsch. Labs., The Upjohn Co., 410 Sackett Point Rd., North Haven, CT 06473, U.S.A.

SAYLER, Maurine Faulkner Bergland, b. 19 Jan. 1914. Business Executive; Free-lance Writer. Educ: B.S., M.A., Kan. State Coll., Ft. Hays. Appts: Assoc. Prof., Kan. State Coll., Hays, 1939-45, 1949-50; Owner & Pres., Campus Book Store, Inc., 1963-72; Pres., Walburn's Inc., 1967-69; Owner, Art 'n Such; Owner, Bygones, mail order antique bus. Mbrships. incl: Pres., P.E.O.; Pres., Meth. Women's Assn.; Pres., PTA City Coun.; Nat. Writers' Club of Am.; Kan. Authors' Club; Dir., Coll. Chapt., Delta Zeta Sorority; V.P., Ft. Hays Kan. State Alumni Assn. Contbr., articles, Hays Daily News, Kan. City Star & Times, Denver Post, Am. Mercury, CColliers Mag. Recip., 1st, 2nd, 3rd Prizes, & Hon. Mention, same contest, 6th Dist. Kan. Authors' Club. Address: 3 Elm Sq., Maryville, MO 64468, U.S.A. 5.

SAYRE, Harrison M., b. 21 May 1894. Editor; Publisher; Foundation Executive. Educ: B.A., Wesleyan Univ., Middletown, Conn., 1916. Appts: Debating Coach & Tchr., Middletown HS, 1914-17; Asst. in Philos., Wesleyan Univ., 1916-17; Ed., World News, 1923-32; Pres., Mng. Ed., Am. Educ. Press, Ind., Educl. Publng. Co., & Charles E. Merrill Co., 1938-52; Co-Fndr., Dir., Columbus Fndn., 1944-69; Mbr., Govng. Comm., ibid, 1944-. Mbrships: Pres., Nat. Coun. on Fndns., 1960-64 (Co-Fndr., ibid, 1949); pioneer in Ohio Regional Planning United Hosp. Bldg. efforts & Prs., Mid-Ohio Hlth. Planning Fedn., 1960-64; Phi Beta Kappa; Kit Kat Club; Univ. Club of Columbus; Rocky Fork Hunt & Country Club. Co-Fndr., My Weekly Reader, 1928, Modern Problem Books, 1932, & Unit Study Books, 1934. Publs: Ed., The Scroll (A. Adelaide Browne), 1970; Brown-Sayre Ancestry, 1971; Dynamic Democracy, Ohio Handbook for Civilian Mobilization; contbr. to var. educl. jrnls. Advsry. Ed., Ohio Histl. Soc. Hons: LL.D., Capital Univ., Ohio, 1954; recip. 1st Preston Davis Award for Disting. Citizenship, 1968; Chmbr. of Comm. Award, Columbus, Ohio, 1971; Citizen of Yr., Bexley, Ohio, 1972; recip. 1st Franklinton Award of Printing Trades of Ctrl. Ohio, 1974. Address: 485 S. Parkview Ave., Columbus, OH 43209, U.S.A. 2.

SAYRE, John Leslie, b. 28 Mar. 1924. Librarian. Educ: A.B., Phillips Univ., 1947; M.Div., Yale Univ., 1950; M.L.S., Univ. of Tex., Austin, 1963; Ph.D., 1973. Appts: Assoc. Min., Univ. Pl. Christian Ch., Enid, Okla., 1945-47; Campus Minister, First Christian Ch., Stillwater,

Okla., 1950-57; Campus Min., Univ. Christian Ch., Austin, Tex., 1957-62; Sem. Libn., Phillips Univ., Enid, Okla., 1962-; Dir., Univ. Libs., ibid, 1971-. Mbrships. incl: Am. Theol. Lib. Assn.; ALA; Okla. Lib. Assn.; Beta Phi Mu. Publs. incl: A Manual of Forms for Term Papers & Theses, 3rd edit., 1971; Index to Festschriften in Religion, 1971; An Illustrated Guide to the Anglo-American Cataloging Rules, 1971. Address: Box 2212, Univ. Stn., Enid, OK 73701, U.S.A. 7, 13, 15, 125, 128.

SCALLON, Frank John, b. 29 Aug. 1899. Louver Company Executive. Educ: Pub. Schls., Ridgefield, Conn., U.S.A. Pres., Midget Louver Co., Norwalk, Conn., 1948-. Patentee. Mbrships: Elk; Cath. Author of sev. booklets on ventilating problems. Address: 255 W. Rocks Rd., Norwalk, CT 06852, U.S.A. 6.

SCAMMELL, George Vance, b. 16 Aug. 1903. Company Director. Educ: B.Sc., Univ. of Sydney, Australia, 1925. Appts: Dir., F.H. Fauling & Co. Ltd., 1928-64; Mng. Dir., Monkseton Pty., Ltd. Num. mbrships. incl: Coun., Chmbr. of Mfrs. of N.S.W., 1962-64; Pres., Australian Assn. of Ethical Pharmaceutical Ind., 1955-59; Coun. & Exec., N.S.W. Div., Australian Red Cross Soc., 1941-, Nat. Coun., 1965-72, Dpty. Chmn., N.S.W. Div., 1967-72, V.P., 1972-73; Past Pres., Rotary Club of S. Sydney; Royal Zoological Soc. of N.S.W.; Linnean Soc. of N.S.W.; Australian Club, Sydney. Illustrator, The Orchids of New South Wales, 1943, originals at Nat. Herbarium, Royal Botanical Gdns., Sydney. Hons: Life Mbrship., Australian Red Cross Soc., 1964; Life Mbrship., Australian Pharmaceutical Mfrs. Assn., 1964. Address: 7 David St., Clifton Gardens, N.S.W. Australia 2088. 23.

SCAMMON, Richard M., b. 17 July 1915. Psephologist. Educ: B.A., Univ. of Minn., 1935; L.S.E., Univ. of London, U.K., 1935-36; M.A., Univ. of Mich., 1938. Appts: Radio Off., Univ. of Chgo., 1939-41; U.S. Army, & Mil. Govt., 1941-48; Chief., Div. of Rsch. for Western Europe, 1948-55; Dir., Elections Rsch. Ctr., Wash., D.C., 1955-; On leave, Dir. of Census, 1961-65. Mbr. var. profl. assns.; Chmn., U.S. Select Commn. on Western Hemisphere Immigration, 1967; Mbr., Org. of Am. States Mission to Dominican Repub., 1966; Mbr., Pres.' Commn. on Fed. Stats., 1970; Bd. of Trustees, Past Pres., Nat. Coun. on Pub. Polls; Mbr., U.S. Gelegn., UN Gen. Assembly, 1973. Publs: This U.S.A., 1965, The Real Majority, 1970 (both w. B. Wattenberg); America Votes (ed.), vols. 1-X, 1956-73; America at the Polls (ed.), 1965. Hons: Phi Beta Kappa Vis. Scholar, 1970-71. Address: 1619 Mass. Ave., NW, Washington, DC 20036, U.S.A. 2, 29, 34.

SCANTIMBURGO, Jaâo de, b. 31 Nov. 1915. Journalist; University Teacher. Educ: Ph.D., Superior Inst. of Philos., São Paulo, Brazil. Appts: Former Dir., Diarios Associados, Sao Paulo; Publr., Correio Paulistano, São Paulo; Pres., TV 9, São Paulo; Publr. & Ed., Diario do Comercio & Digesto Economico, São Paulo; Dir., Fac. of Communications, Univ. Fndn. Armando Alvares Penteado, São Paulo. Mbrships: Am. Cath. Philos. Assn., Wash. D.C.; Brazilian Inst. of Philos.; Brazilian Inst. of Soc. Law; Hist. & Geog. Inst. of Sao Paulo; Pen Club. Publs: Imanencia e transcendencia; O destino da America Latina; A crise da republica presidencial; A extensao humana; Tratado Geral do Brasil. Recip. Pen Club Prize. Address: 01332 Rua Prof. Picarolo 115–4°, Sao Paulo, Brazil. 2, 136.

SCARBOROUGH, Marion Elsi Nichols (Mrs.), b. 26 July 1915. Nutritionist; Educator.

Educ: A.S., Green Mtn. Jr. Coll., 1935; B.S., Kan. State Univ., 1937; Cert., Dietetics, Worcester Mem. Hosp., 1938; M.P.H., Harvard Univ., 1947. Appts: Tchng. & Admin. Dietitian, Newton Wellesley Hosp., 1938-41; Chief Dietitian, ibid, 1941-43; Chief Nutritionist, Diabetes Sect., USPHS, 1947-50; Regional Nutritionist, Fla. Bd. of Hlth., Jacksonville, 1950-52; Owner, Happy Acres Ranch, kindergarten & day camp, Jacksonville, 1953-; Tchng. Dietitian, pt.-time, St. Vincent's Hosp. & Brewster Meth. Hosp. Num. mbrships. incl: Var. comms., community child care progs., & home econs. educ., Jacksonville; Fellow, Am. Pub. Hlth. Assn.; Am., Fla., Jacksonville Dietetic Assns.; Past Pres., Chmn., Child Hlth. Comm., Fla. Assn. on Children under Six; Am. Camping Assn.; AAUW; Jacksonville Area Chambr. of Comm.; Charter Mbr., Past Pres., Duval Co. Children's Nursery Assn. Hons: Service Award, Community Planning Coun., Jacksonville, 1972; Address: Happy Acres Ranch, 7117 Crane Ave., Jacksonville, FL 32216, U.S.A. 5, 7.

SCARLATA, Gaetano Pio, b. 11 July 1904. Director of State Archives, Retired. Educ: Grad., Lit., Univ. of Palermo, 1926; Dipl., Paleography & Archivism, ibid, 1930. Appts: Dir., State Archives, Potenza, Salerno, l'Aquila, Reggio-Calabria, Agrigento, Sondrio, 1931-. Mbrships: Pres., Acad. Agrigentina of Sci., Lit. & Art, 1953-56; Ital. Philos. Soc., 1950-; Nat. Order of Authors & Writers, 1966; Int. Acad. Psychobiophysics, 1972; Teatina Acad. of Sci., 1967-; Lombard Coll., 1966. Publs. incl: Dio e l'individuo, 1949; Lineamenti di metalogica, 1951; Orientamenti pedagogici, 1952; Dalla selva all.Empireo—Studi danteschi, 1967; l'Archivio di Stato di Sondrio ed altre fonti storiche di Provincia, 1968. Hons: Columbus Prize for Philos. & Philol., 1950; Commendatore of Ital. Repub.; Gold Medal of Min. of Interior. Address: Via Mecenate 3, 20138 Milan, Italy.

SCERNO, J. Benedict, b. 25 Dec. 1936. Personnel-Industrial Relations Executive. Educ: B.S., N.Y. Univ., 1962. Appts., incl: V.P.-Gen. Mgr., Personnel Dir., Express Haulage Corp., N.Y.C., 1960-64; Asst. Dir. Indl. Rels., Tech. Material Corp., Mamaroneck, N.Y., 1964-66; Dir. Indl. Rels., Sel-Rex Corp., Div. Occidental Petroleum Corp., Nutley, N.J., 1968-72; Dir. Personnel, Hosp. for Jt. Diseases & Med. Ctr., N.Y.C., 1972-; Bd. Dirs., Saxon Morse Assocs., Monsey, N.Y. & Prospect House, E. Orange, N.J. Mbrships. incl: Am. Soc. Personnel Admin.; Pres., N.J. Chapt., ibid, 1969-71; Am. Soc. Trng. & Dev.; Int. Mgt. Assn.; V.P., Newark, N.J. Chapt., ibid, 1969-72; Am. Acad. Pol. & Soc. Scis.; Am. Mgmt. Assn., MENSA; Zeta Beta Tau; Mu Gamma Tau; Pi Sigma Epsilon. Contbr. to Jrnl., Personnel Admnstr., 1971. Address: Apt. A-32, 25 River Rd., Nutley, NJ 07110, U.S.A. 6.

SCHABACKER, Joan Flath, b. 20 Feb. 1930. Reading Specialist. Educ: A.B., M.A., Univ. of Hawaii. Appts: Classroom Tchr., 1958-68; Fndr., Owner, Dir., Tampa Reading Clin. & Day Schl., Fla., 1969-. Mbrships: Int. Reading Assn.; Fla. Reading Assn.; Assn. Children With Learning Disabilities; Kelta Kappa Gamma; Admin. Bd., Palma Ceia Meth. Ch. Tampa Reading Clin. & Day Schl. is 1 of only 50 in U.S.A. w. mbrship. in Nat. Assn. of Pvte. Schls. for Exceptional Children. Address: 2219 S. Occident St., Tampa, FL 33609, U.S.A. 125.

SCHABER, Lucille, b. 6 Apr. 1901. Real Estate Broker. Educ: Univ. of Cinn., Ohio; St. Xavier Coll., Cinn. Appts: Owner & Operator, own bus., 1926-26; Mgr., Hotel Sinton Coffee Shop, 8 yrs.; Real Estate Broker & operator, own Real Estate Off., Lucille Schaber, Inc., Realtors, 1944-. Mbrships. incl: Nat. Assn. of Realtors; Ky. State Bd. of Realtors; Profl. Bus. Women's Club; Pres., Campbell Women's Coun. of Realtors; Past Regional V.P., ibid; State of Ky. Gov., twice. Hons. incl: Woman Realtor of the Yr., Women's Coun. of Realtors, 1967; Realtor of the Yr., Campbell Co. Bd. of Realtors, 1968; Ky. Co.; Duchess of Paducah. Address: 221 S. Ft. Thomas Ave., Ft. Thomas, KY 41075, U.S.A. 138.

SCHACHT, Joy Critchett, b. 7 Feb. 1934. Journalist. Educ: B.A., Drake Univ., Des Moines, Iowa, 1959; Postgrad. study, Univ. of Northern Iowa, Cedar Falls, Iowa. Appts: Staff Mbr., Feature Writer on Women's Page, Des Moines Register & Tribune, 1955-58; Proofreader &Ed., Iowa State Univ. Press, Ames, 1960-62; Publs. Asst., Alumnus mag. writer & ed., Univ. Rels. Off., Univ. of Northern Iowa, Cedar Falls, Iowa, 1964-68. Mbrships. incl: Chapt. Advsr., I.S.U., Theta Sigma Phi (now Women in Communications Inc.); Pres., Chapt. EM, T.T.T. Soc., 1970-71; Sec., Cedar Falls Woman's Club, 1968-69; Treas., Sponsorship Chmn. & Sec., Waterloo-Cedar Falls Alumnae Chapt., Delta Zeta; Former Mbr., Press & Radio Club of Des Moines. Ed., Physical Education in the Elementary Schools & author of newspaper & mag. articles. Address: 1212 W. 7th St., Cedar Falls, IA 50613, U.S.A. 132.

SCHACHTEL, Hyman Judah, b. 24 May 1907. Rabbi. Educ: B.A., Univ. of Cinn., 1928; B.H., Hebrew Union Coll., 1931; D.D., ibid, 1958; Columbia Univ. Tchrs. Coll., 1933-37; Ed.D., Univ. of Houston, 1948; D.H.L., Southwestern Univ., 1955. Appts: Rabbi, Westend Synagogue, N.Y.C., 1931-43; Chief Rabbi, Temple Beth Israel, Houston, Tex., 1943-; Lect., Philos., Univ. of Houston, 1950-55; Lectr., Judaism, ibid, 1974-; Lect., Judaic Studies, St. Thomas Univ., 1970-74 & St. Mary's Sem. of Houston, 1972-. Mbrships. incl: Pres., Kallah of Tex. Rabbis, Southwest Ctrl. Conf. of Am. Rabbis, 1966-68, Houston Rabbinical Assn. & Harris Co. Mental Hlth., 1960-62; Tex. Philos. Soc.; Bd. of Dirs., Houston Symph.; Girl Scouts; Crime Commn.; etc. Publs: Real Enjoyment of Living; The Life You Want to Live; The Shadowed Valley; Aspects of Jewish Homiletics; The Challenge of Health; music for hymns, etc. Hons. incl: Kuhler Prize, 1928; Coronet Medal, St. Edwards Univ., Austin, Tex., 1964; Bonds for Israel Award, 1970; Composer of Hebrew Union Coll. Alma Mater Song Award, 1938. Address: 2527 Glenhaven, Houston, TX 77025, U.S.A. 2.

SCHADEN, Egon, b. 4 July 1913. Professor. Educ: Ph.B., Univ. of Sao Paulo, 1937;D.Sc., ibid, 1945. Appts: Asst. Prof. of Anthropol., Univ. of Sao Paulo, 1943-48; Prof., ibid, 1948-67; Prof. & Hd., Dept. of Anthropol., Univ. de los Andes, Bogota, 1968-69; Prof. of Anthropol. of Communication, Univ. of Sao Paulo, 1969-. Mbrships. incl: Fellow Royal Anthropol. Inst. of G.B. & Ireland, Soc. for Applied Anthropol.; Hon. Mbr., Anthropol. Assn., Wien; For. Fellow, Am. Anthropol. Assn. Publs. incl: Aculturação Indigena, 1965, '69; Homen, Sociedade Cultura no Brasil, 1972. Hons: Medal Sylvio Romero, 1958; Medal Marechal Candido Mariano da Silva Rondon, 1960. Address: Caixo Postal 5459, 01000 Sao Paulo, SP, Brazil. 136.

SCHADEN, Herbert Paul Friedrich, b. 27 June 1910. Engineer; Executive. Educ: Engrng.

Dip., Tech. Univ. of Vienna. Appts. incl: Design Engr., Wiener Lokomotivfabrik AG, Vienna-Floridsdorf, 1934-36; Engr.-Engrng. Mgr. & Asst. to Mgr. of Metallurgical Ops., Gutehoffnungshütte Oberhausen, 1936-45; Mil. Serv. & Prisoner of War, 1945-46; Ingenieurbüro Dipl. Ing. Poech, Vienna, 1946-50; w. Vereinigte Osterr. Eisen-und Stahlwerke AG, (since 1973 VÖEST-ALPINE AG), 1950-; Dir.ibid, 1959-; Exec. V.P., & Dpty. Gen. Mgr., 1967-. Mbrships. incl: AIME; AISE; Metals Soc.; Verein Deutscher Eisenhüttenleute; Verein Deutscher Ingenieure; Eisenhütte Osterreich. Hons: Goldenes Ehrenzeichen für Verdienste, Repub. of Austria, 1961; Grosses Ehrenzeichen für Verdienste, ibid, 1971; Grand Off., Brazilian Order of the Southern Cross, 1972. Address: VÖEST-ALPINE AG, Werksgelände, A-4010 Linz, Austria.

SCHAEFFER, Pierre, b. 14 Aug. 1910. General Telecommunications Engineer. Educ: Ecole Polytech., Paris, France. Appts: Responsible for the Radio at the Liberation of Paris; Fndr., Dir., SORAFOM (overseas radio & TV); Fndr., Dir., Rsch. Serv., ORTF. Publs: Traité des Objets Musicaux, 1966; Le Gardien de Volcan, 1969; Machines à Communiquer, 2 vols., 1970-72. Hons: Prix Sanite-Beuve for novel Le Gardien de Volcan, 1969. Address: Serv. de Rescherche, Centre Pierre Bourdan, 5 Ave. du Recteur Poincaré, 75016 Paris, France. 34.

SCHAERER, Charles J., b. 24 Nov. 1914. Civil Engineer. Educ: Coll., Geneva, Switzerland; Grad., Civil Engrng., Fed. Inst. of Technol., Zurich, 1938. Appts. incl: Scientific Asst., Rsch. Lab. for Hydraulics & Soil Mechanics, Fed. Inst. of Technol., Zurich, 1938-42; Projs. Engr., NOK, Baden, 1942-47; Engr., Solexperts S.A., Spain, 1948-57; Chief Engr., Soil Mechanics Div., Rsch. Labs. for Hydraulics & Soil Mechanics, Fed. Inst. of Technol., Zurich, 1957-; Lectr., Soil Mechanics, ibid, 1957-; Travelled to Spain, Congo, S.Am. as an Earth-Dam Expert. Mbrships. incl: Swiss Soc. of Soil Mechanics & Foundation Engrng.; Pres., ibid, 1962-65; Chmn., Redaer. Comm. Intern. Geotechn. lexicon, 2 Edit.; SIA Sect., Baden; Pres., Soc. of Mil. Technics, 1956-60; Road Prof. Assn.; Fed. Comm. for study of Civil Defense Problems. Var. publs. on soil mechanics & fndn.-engrng. problems. Address: Buchenweg 2, 8116 Wuerenlos/AG, Switzerland.

SCHAFER, Stephen, b. 15 Feb. 1911. University Professor. Educ: J.D., Univ. of Budapest, 1933; Prof. Agrégé, ibid, 1947. Appts: Univ. of Budapest until 1950; Lectr., Univ. of Md. Overseas Prog., 1958-61; Lectr., Polytech. Inst., London, 1959-61; Asst. Prof., Fla. State Univ., U.S.A., 1961-65; Assoc. Prof., Ohio Univ., 1965-66; Prof., Criminal Justice, Criminol. & Sociol., Northeastern Univ., Boston, 1966-; Vis. Prof., Tufts Univ., 1966-67; Vis. Prof., Boston Univ., 1967-. Mbrships. incl: Int. Soc. of Criminol.; Am. Soc. of Criminol.; Int. Assn. of Penal Law; Am. Sociol. Assn. Publs. incl: The Victim & His Criminal, 1968; Theories in Criminology, 1969; Juvenile Delinquency: An Introduction, 1970; The Political Criminal, 1974; 100 articles in var. langs. in profl. jrnls. Hons: Rsch. Grants—Home Off., U.K.; Nat. Inst. of Mental Hlth., U.S.; Ford Fndn., etc. Address: Coll. of Criminal Justice, Northeastern Univ., Boston, MA 02115, U.S.A. 6, 129, 131.

SCHAFER, Welter Erich, b. 16 Mar. 1901. Professor; Retired Theatrical Manager; Author. Educ: Univs. of Tübingen & Munich, Germany;

Landwirtschaftliche Univ., Hohenheim/Stuttgart. Appts: Tchr., Musikhochschule, Stuttgart, 1926; Dramatic Producer, Staatstheater, Stuttgart, 1928, & Nationaltheater, Mannheim, 1934; Chief Dramatic Producer, Staatstheater, Kassel, 1938-47; Theatrical Mgr., Württembergische Staatstheater, Stuttgart, 1949-72; Dir., Staatsoper, Vienna, 1962-63. Publs. incl: Dramas: Die Reise nach Paris, 1936; Die Verschwörung, 1949; Schwarzmann & die Magd, 1933; Hora Mortis, 1952; Radio Dramas: Malmgren, 1929; Die fünf Sekinden des Mahatma Gandhi, 1949; Biographies: Stuttgarter Staatsoper, 1972; Gespräche mit Cranko, 1974. Hons. incl: Grand cross of merit w. star, German Fed. Repub.; Off., Ordre arts et lettres, France. Address: Feuerreiterweg 32, D-7000 Stuttgart 70 (Sonnenberg), German Fed. Repub.

SCHALK, Adolph, b. 17 Jan. 1923. Journalist. Educ: St. Louis Preparatory Sem.; St. Louis Univ.; Notre Dame Univ., Roosevelt Univ., Chgo., & Marquette Univ., Milwaukee. Appts. incl: Co-fndr., Roman Cath. daily newspaper (since defunct), The Sun Herald, Kan. City, Mo., 1949; Ed.-in-chief, Today mag., 1952-55; Fndng. ed., The Bridge, Hamburg, German Fed. Repub., 1957-62; Free-lance author, 1962-. Mbrships: Authors GGuild; Authors League of Am.; Assn. de la Presse étrangère en Suisse. Publs. incl: The Germans; The Germans in America; Eyes on the Modern World (w. John Deedy). Contbr. to jrnls. Num. TV appearances. Recip., 1st Prize for outstanding religious reporting, Cath. Press Assn., U.S.A., 1949, 1954 & 1964. Address: Alte Land-Strasse 193, CH 8800 Thalwil, Switzerland.

SCHALLENBERGER, (Ernst) Horst, b. 14 Aug. 1925. Professor. Educ: Breslau Univ., Western Germany; Cologne Univ., ibid, Dr.Phil. Appts: Secondary Schl. Tchr.; Dpty Headmaster; Lectr.; Prof.; Snr. civil service, Min. of Educ.; Fndg. Vice-Chancellor, PH Siegerland; Dean, Fac. (sev. times); now Prof., Comprehensive Univ., Duisburg. Mbrships: Gesellschaft für Geistesgeschichte Comm.; Deutsche Vereinigung für Pol. Wissenschaft; Hist. Verband; Deutsches Inst. für Bildung Wissen; Edit. Bd. sev. jrnls.; Lions Club. Publs: The Wilhelmian Era and the Weimar Republic in Germany, 1964; Chief Ed., 3 series on educ.; hist. & Pol. Address: Am. Alten Hain 6, 5931 Netphen-Unglinghausen, German Fed. Repub. 43.

SCHANTZ, Viola Shelly, b. 22 June 1895. Mammalogist. Educ: Perkiomen Sem., 1911-13; Muhlenberg Coll. Appts: Tchr., Pub. Schls., Pa., 1913-18; Biol. Aide, Biol. Surveys, US Dept. Agric., 1918-29; Sr. Biol. Aide, ibid, 1929-44; Biologist, US Fish & Wildlife Serv., 1944-49; Systematic Zoologist, 1949-61; retd. Mbrships: Life Mbr., Treas., Am. Soc. Mammalogists, 1930-52; Past Matron, Order of Eastern Star, Chapt. of Chevy Chase, Md., 1934; Soroptimist Club; Woman's City Club, Wash. D.C. Publs: Co-author, Catalog of the Type Specimens of Mammals in the US National Museum including the Biological Surveys Collection, 1942; Index to Journal of Mammalogy, 1919-39, '45-49, '50-59. Recip. of Disting. Serv. Award, US Dept. of Interior, 1962. Address: 2475 Virginia Ave., N.W., Apt. 925, Wash. DC 20037, U.S.A. 14.

SCHARY, Dore, b. 31 Aug. 1905. Author; Playwright; Producer; Director; Executive. Appts. incl: Studio Hd., M.G.M. Studios, 1951-57; Self-employed Playwright, Theatre Dir. & Prod., 1957-71; Commnr., Cultural Affairs, City of N.Y., 1970-; Pres. & Chief Exec. Off., Theatre Vision Inc. & Schary Prods. Inc., 1971-. Mbr. num. profl. & civic orgs. Screenplays incl: Boys' Town; Battle of Gettysburg; Sunrise at Campobello; Storm in the West (w. Sinclair Lewis). Prod. and/or Exec. in Charge num. films inclng: Blackboard Jungle; Bad Day at Black Rock; American in Paris; Tea & Sympathy. Author & Prod. of Plays: Sunrise at Campobello; The Devil's Advocate; One by One. Author: Brightower. Dir.-Prod.: The Unsinkable Molly Brown; A Majority of One; The Zulu & the Zayda. Publs: Case History of a Movie: For Special Occasions. Contbr. to nat. mags. Hons: Num. profl. & civic Awards inclng. an Oscar, two Tony Awards & the Louis Marshall Award; L.H.D., Coll. of the Pacific, & Wilberforce Univ.; Dr. Fine Arts, Lincoln Coll. Address: 641 Lexington Ave., N.Y., NY 10022, U.S.A. 2.

SCHARY, Susan, b. 8 July 1936. Artist. Educ: B.F.A., Tyler Schl. of Fine Arts, Temple Univ., 1960; Postgrad. study, ibid; studies at Phila. Art Mus.; Samuel S. Fleisher Art Mem.; pvte. study under V. Shatolov. Appts: Art Instr., Harcum Jr. Coll. of Bryn Mawr, Pa., 1961-63; & Samuel S. Fleisher Art Mem., ibid, 1967; Art Coord., Westside Community Ctr., L.A., 1969. Mbr. of Artists' Equity Nat. Org. Seven solo exhibs.; commissions by var. instns. inclng. Temple Univ.; City Hall of Phila.; Ctrl. High Schl. of Phila.; Villanova Univ.; Thomas Paine Ctr., Phila. Hons: Gimble Awards, 1948-54; Gold Medal, 1954; Dean's Prize, Tyler Schl., 1959. Address: 672 S. Bronson Ave., L.A., CA 90005, U.S.A. 5, 37, 105.

SCHAUBEL, Howard James, b. 20 May 1916. Medical Doctor; Orthopaedic Surgeon. Educ: Assoc. in Sci., Grand Rapids Jr. Coll., 1936; B.A., Hope Coll., Holland, Mich., 1928; M.D., Mich. Med. Schl., 1942. Appts. incl: In Pvte. Prac., Grand Rapids, Mich., 1946-73; U.S. Army Med. Corps., 1953-54; Attending Cons. Orthop. Surg. to var. hosps. in area inclng: Chief Orthop. Surg., Saladin Shrine Crippled Childrens Ctr., 1947-73 & Chief, Orthop. Div., Ferguson Hosp., 1970-72; Prac., Orthop. Surg., Key West & Marathon Fla., 1970-; Sr. Attending Orthop. Surg., Fla. Keys Meml. Hosp., 1970-; Chief, Orthop. Div., ibid, 1973; Sr. Cons. Orthop. Surg., Fishermans Hosp., Marathon, 1970-. Chief, Orphoedic Div., ibid, 1973-. Fellow, Int. Coll. Surgs. Mbrships. incl: Exec. Bd., Latin-Am Congress of Phys. Med., 1955-58; Pres., Piedmont Orthop. Soc., 1963; Am. Bd. Orphopedic Surgs.; Eastern Orthopedic Assn.; Life, Southern Med. Assn.; AMA; Fla. Med. Assn.; Bd. of Govs., Camp Blodgett, United Fund of Mich. 1973, Pres. of Bd., 1973; Chmbrs. of Comm., Key West, 1971- & Lower Keys, 1969-; num. other profl. orgs. Contbr. many sci. papers to jrnls. Recip., sev. coll. hons. Address: Box 83 Big Pine Key, FL 33043, U.S.A. 7, 8, 10, 17, 36, 46, 54.

SCHAUDINISCHKY, Leo Herzl, b. 14 June 1905. Acoustician. Educ: Dipl. Ing., Technische Hochschule, Berlin-Charlottenburg, Germany, 1931. Appts. incl: Chief Engr., Palestine Rep. of Marconiphne Ltd., 1934-38; Pt.-time Instr., Radio-Electronics, Hebrew Tech., Haifa, Pt.-time Rschr., Fac. of Elec., Hebrew Inst. of Technol., Haifa, 1940-44; Hd., Spin Ltd., 1945-50; Hd., Dept. of Electronics, Hebrew Tech. H.S., Technion, Haifa, 1951-58; engagement w. fndn. & dev., Dept. for Applied Acoustics, Hebrew Inst. of Technol., 1959-64, Sr. Lectr., 1964-66, Assoc. Prof., 1966-70; Hd., Dept. Applied Acoustics, Fac. of Civil Engrng., Israel Inst. of Technol., Haifa, Technion City, 1971-. Mbr., var. profl. orgs. Publs: Law & Noise; Man, Noise & Building (in press). Holder, sev. patents. Address: Haifa, Neveh Shaanan, 31 Hatichon St., Israel. 94.

SCHAUMAN, (Georg August) Henrik, b. 7 Aug. 1916. Chief Librarian. Educ: M.A., 1943; Lic. in Pol. Hist., 1959. Appts: Asst. Libn., Helsinki Univ. Lib., 1943-50; Lib., Fac. of Pol. Sci., 1950-56; Dir., Lib. of the Finnish Parliament, 1956-. Mbrships: Chmn., Scandinavian Assn. of Rsch. Libns, 1963-66 & Finnish Assn. Rsch. Libs., 1966, 1968-69; Vice-Chmn., Finnish Lib. Assn., 1970-71. Publs: Finnish Historical Bibliography 1926-1950 (co-author), 1956; Finnish Historical Bibliography 1544-1900 (co-author), 1961. Hons: Cmdr., Order of North Star, 1971; Cmdr., Order of the Lion, 1972. Address: Fredsgatan 9 B 38, 00170 Helsinki 17, Finland.

SCHECHTER, Ruth Lisa, Poet; Poetry Therapist; Educator; Lecturer. Appts: Poet-in-Res., Mundelein Coll., Chgo.; Cons., Poetry Therapist, Odyssey House Rehab. Drug Abuse Agcy., N.Y.C. & Alfred Alder Mental Hygiene Clin.; Poetry Workshop Tchr., James Weldon Johnson Community Ctr., Harlem Adult Educ. Ctr., DeWitt Clinton H.S., Antioch Coll. Tutoring Prog., etc.; Lectr., num. univs.; Has read poetry in num. coffee houses & cafes. Mbr., var. profl. Socs. Publs: (books) Near The Wall Of Lion Shadows, 2nd ed., 1970; Movable Parts, 1970; Suddenly Thunder, 1972; Offshore, 1973; Anthology Of Gut Poetry (of ex-drug addicts), in prep.; Haiku/20; Poetry the Healer, 1973; Contbr. to num. anthols. & mags. Poetry recorded on L/P. 2-Act Play, Alan, Carlos, Theresa, appeared Off-Broadway, N.Y.C. Recip., Fellowship, The MacDowell Colony, 1963, '70, & N.Y. State Coun. Grants. Address: 9 Van Cortlandt Pl., Croton-on-Hudson, NY 10520, U.S.A. 11.

SCHECTMAN, Susan Mindelle, b. 24 Aug. 1940. Lawyer; Poet; Science Fiction Author. Educ: B.A., Cornell Univ.; J.D., Hastings Law Schl., San Fran., Calif. Appts: Psychol. Instr., Cornell Univ., 1962-63; Pub. Defender, San Fran. Hall of Justice, 1967-68; Legal Counsellor, San Bruno Co. Jail, Calif., 1969-70; Pvte. Law Prac., San Fran., 1971-73; Lectr., Criminal Law, Golden Gate Law Schl., ibid, 1974-. Mbrships: V.P. of Pub. Affairs, Calif. Bar. Assn., 1967-68; V.P., Sci. Fiction Writers of Am., 1969-70; San Fran. Lit. Soc.; San Fran. Mus. Soc. Publs: The Glass Onion, 1965; Evergreen, 1966; Pulsar; Eagle's Nest. Contbr. of stories to var. anthols., & of articles to profl. jrnls. Hons: Hugo Award, Sci. Fiction Writers' Convention, 1968; Nebula Award, ibid, 1969. Address: 3886 22nd St., San Francisco, CA 94119, U.S.A.

SCHEIBE, Fred Karl, b. 2 Dec. 1911. Professor of German Language & Literature. Educ: B.A., Clark Univ., 1938; M.A., Univ. of Pa., 1941; Ph.D., Univ. of Cinn., 1954. Appts: incl: Western Coll. for Women, Oxford, Ohio, 1947-51; Univ. of Mexico, 1951-52; Univ. of Cinn., Ohio, 1952-54; Brooklyn Coll., N.Y., 1954-55; Alderson-Broaddus Coll., W. Va., 1955-57; Thiel Coll., Pa., 1957-61; Emory & Henry Coll., Va., 1961-64; Hartwick Coll., N.Y., 1964-71; Shelton Coll., Fla., 1971-; MLA; Mbrships. incl: Atlantic MLA; Univ. Profs. for Acad. Order; Life Fellow, Int. Inst. of Life & Letters; Publs. incl: Rubinrot, 1944; Reflections, 1948; All, Erde und Mensch, 1950; Union of Fools, 1953; Walther von der Vogelweide-Troubadour of the Middle Ages, 1969. Contbr. to profl. publs. Recip. Gold Medal, Acad. Arts & Scis., Genoa, Italy, 1949. Address: 379 Harbor Dri., Cape Canaveral, FL 32920, U.S.A. 2, 6, 9, 11, 15, 22, 85, 128, 130, 131.

SCHEID, Francis James, b. 24 Sept. 1920. Professor of Maths. Educ: B.S., Boston Univ., 1942; M.A., ibid, 1943; Ph.D., MIT, 1948. Appts: Prof. of Maths., Boston Univ., 1948-; Chmn. of Dept., ibid, 1957-69; Cons. in astronautics, MIT, 1960-69; TV Lectr., WGBH-TV, Boston, 1960-69; Fulbright vis. lectr., Rangoon, Burma, 1961-62; Guest of Am. Univ., Beirut, Lebanon, 1962; Guest of Ecole Polytechnique, Lausanne, Switzerland, 1968-69. Mbrships: Soc. for Industrial & Applied Maths.; AAAS; Math. Assn. of Am.; Dir., Plymouth Yacht Club; Pres., Plymouth Country Club. Publs. incl: Numerical Analysis, 1966; Computer Science, 1968. Lects. on videotapes & articles in Golf Digest & math lit. Recip., Man of the Month Award, Golf Digest, 1971. Address: Boston Univ., 264 Bay State Rd., Boston, MA 02215, U.S.A. 2, 128.

SCHEID, Paul, b. 24 June 1908. Headmaster; Lecturer; Editor. Educ: Univs. of Frankfurt, Madrid & Greifswald; Ph.D. Appts: Headmaster, Pvte. Gesamtschule Anna Schmidt, Frankfurt; Lectr., Preprimary Educ., Europe, U.S.A., Africa & Asia; Ed., var. books on Montessori system. Mbrships: Pres., German Montesorri Assn.; Pres., Verband Deutscher Privatschulen; Pres., Int. Schls. Assn.; Pres., European Fedn. of Private Instruction; Rotary Int. Publs: Books in German; Report, Early Training for the Unknown, the Unexpected & the Possible; Film, Early Childhood Education in Practice. Hons: Deutsches Kreuz in Gold, 1944; Croix de Chevalier de l'Ordre du Combattant de l'Europe, 1968. Address: Schaferweg 10, D 6245 Rossert, German Fed. Repub. 43.

SCHEIN, Beatrice Weiss (Mrs. Bernard Schein), b. 21 May 1913. Librarian. Educ: B.A., Rutgers Univ., 1936; Postgrad. courses, Rutgers & Upsala for Tchrs. Cert., 1941; M.S., Columbia Univ., 1951. Appts: Lib. Asst., Newark Pub. Lib., 1936-38; Hd. of Work w. H.S. Students, ibid, 1938-44; Hd. of Teen Div., 1945-53; Rsch. Asst., Rutgers Univ. Grad. Schl. Lib. Serv., 1954; Pt.-time schl. libn. & edit. asst., Newark Schls., 1957-60; Libn., Vernon L. Davey Jr. H.S., E. Orange, N.J., 1960-. Mbrships: ALA (Coun., 1946-50, '51-53; Chmn., Young Adult Servs. Div., 1947-48; Advsry. Coun. to Boy Scouts of Am., 1965-71 & Chmn., 1966-67); N.J. Lib. Assn. (Chmn., Human Rels. Comm., 1951-52); Nat., N.J., Essex Co. & E. Orange Educ. Assns.; N.J. & Essex Co. Schl. Media Assns. Publs: Co-author, Public Library Plans for the Teen Age, 1948; Leisure-time Interests & Activities of Newark Youth, 1951; Contbr., ed., Open the Book, 1966; Contbr., articles to profl. lib. jrnls. Address: 405 Highland Ave., Newark, NJ 07104, U.S.A. 5.

SCHEIN, Martin Warren, b. 23 Dec. 1925. Biological Scientist; Educator. Educ: A.B., Univ. of Iowa, 1949; Sc.D., Johns Hopkins Univ., 1954. Appts. incl: Assoc. Animal Climatol., La. Agric. Experiment Stn., La. State Univ., 1952-55; Asst. Prof., Assoc. Prof., Prof. of Animal Behavior, Pa. State Univ., 1955-68; Commn., Undergrad. Educ. in Biol. Scis., 1962-64; Vice Chmn., ibid, 1964-65; Exec. Dir., 1965-68; Vis. Prof., Biol., Geo. Wash. Univ., 1965-68; Centennial Prof. of Biol. & Clin. Prof., Behavioral Med. & Psych., W. Va. Univ., 1968-. Mbrships. incl: Fellow, AAAS; active mbr., other profl. orgs. Ed. Bd., Animal Behavior, 1963-72; Educ. Ed., Bioscience, 1968-70. Contbr. to num profl. jrnls. Address: Dept. of Biol., W. Va. Univ., Morgantown, WV 26505, U.S.A. 6, 14, 15, 50.

SCHELKOFF, Russell Levoy, b. 30 June 1930. Veterinary Surgeon. Educ: B.S., Univ. of Neb., 1952; M.S., ibid, 1954; Ph.D., Iowa State Univ., 1958; D.V.M., ibid, 1958. Appts: Veterinarian Hall Vet. Clin., Elburn, Ill., 1958-59; Pvte. Prac., Sycamore, ibid, 1959-; Pres., Anderson-Schelkopf D.V.M. Ltd., 1970-, & Illini Farms Inc., Kingston, Ill., 1970-; Sec.-Treas., Cornhusker Agric. Assn. Inc., Schickley, Neb., 1969-, & Cornhusker Cattle Co. Inc., ibid, 1971-; Pres., Schelkopf Enterprises, 1972-. Mbrships: Phi Kappa Phi; Phi Zeta; Sigma Xi; Alpha Zeta; Gamma Sigma Delta; Alpha Gamma Rho. Contbr. of articles. Address: Rte. 64 East, Sycamore, IL 60178, U.S.A. 8.

SCHELLSTEDE, Eloise J. Rees (Mrs. John E. Schellstede), b. 11 Sept. 1918. Artist; Gallery Owner; Lecturer; Owner of Insurance Agency. Educ: B.A. Appts: Co-Owner then Owner, D.R. Rees & Co., gen. ins. agcy., 1939-; Owner, Eloise J. Schellstede Gall. of Fine Arts, Peoria in Tulsa, Okla., 1970-; Fndr., Green Country Schl. of Art, ibid; Promoter & Dir., Fine Art Shows, Poteau, Okla., Tulsa & Grand Lake. Mbrships. incl: Fndr., Dir. Pres., Green Country Art Assn.; Fndr., Green Country Art Fndn., Inc.; Gilcrease Mus.; Soroptimist; Tulsa Histl. Soc.; Okla. Mutual Ins. Assn.; Artists Equity Assn. Commns. incl: Mural for Sunnyside Bapt. Ch. of Broken Arrow, Okla.; Portrait, 'He Shall Be Called Sequoyah', Cherokee Nat. Mus., Okla; Mural for Sandusky Christian Ch., Tulsa; 9 portraits for Selco Corp.; 3 landscapes for Clint Miner collect. Publs: An Interpretation of the 23rd. Psalm; jrnl. & newspaper articles. Recip., hons. Address: 6254 S. Utica, Tulsa, OK 74135, U.S.A. 2, 7.

SCHEMBERGER, Ruth Marie Monke, b. 3 Nov. 1919. Farmer; Bank Cashier. Appts: Farmer, Regent, N.D., U.S.A., until 1960; Bookkeeper-Teller, Citizens State Bank of New England, N.D., 1960-69; Admin. Bookkeeper, Reports, & Asst. Cashier, ibid, 1969-70; Asst. Cashier & Security Off., Audits, 1970-73; Treas., New England Pub. Schl. Dist., 1971-74. Address: New England, ND 58647, U.S.A. 5, 138.

SCHENCK, Marcia Helen Merrifield (Mrs. John E. Schenck), b. 13 June 1921. Musician. Educ: B.A., Univ. of Chgo., 1942. Appts. incl: Accompanist, Tucson Boy's Chorus, Ariz., 1945-51; Dir. of Choir, Unitarian Ch., Tucson, 1956-70; Accompanist, Tucson Civic Chorus, 1955-58, 65-67, 69-71, Univ. of Ariz. Opera Workshop, 1958, Norma Bodanis Voice Studio, Tucson, 1967-68; Area Chmn., Cancer Fund, 1967-68. Mbrships. incl: Exec. positions, Women's Alliance, Unitarian Ch., Tucson, 1955-; Hospitality Chmn., UN Assn., Tucson,1967-68; Area Chmn., Cancer Fund, 1968-74; Area Capt., Heart Fund, 1968-74; Mbr., Bd. of Trustees of Unitarian-Universalist Ch. of Tucson, 1973-75. Has composed sev. songs & small piano works. Hons. incl: DAR Award for outstanding citizenship & schlrship., Hyde Park HS, Chgo., 1938; Silver Pin, Tucson Boy's Chorus, 1953, Unitarian Women's Alliance, 1967, & Unitarian Ch. Choir, 1970. Address: 4882 E. Scarlett St., Tucson, AZ 85711, U.S.A. 5, 9, 129, 130, 132.

SCHENK, André, b. 11 Dec. 1911. Silk-producing Station Director. Educ: Agricl. Engr., Nat. Agronomy Schl., Montpellier, France; Licencié ès Scis., Fac. of Scis., ibid; Bachelier, Law, Fac. of Law, ibid. Appts: Dir., Alès Silk-producing Stn., French Nat. Inst. of Agronomy Rsch.; Fndg. Sec. Gen., Int. Silk-producing Commn. Mbrships. incl: Nat. Corres., Agric. Acad.; Tech. Mbr., Alès Chmbr. of Comm.; Bd. of Dirs. & Commn. for Silk-naming, Int. Silk Assn.; Econ. Expansion Comm., Gard Region; Fndg. Pres., Olivier de Serres Fndn. Publs. incl: num. works on the prod. of silk; Le climat d'Alès; Le Plan Cévenol. Hons: War Cross; Mil. Medal; Off., Agricl. Merit; Off., Acad. Palms. Address: Stn. Séricicole, 30 Quai Boissier de Sauvages, Alès (Gard), France. 43.

SCHENKER, Eric, b. 24 Feb. 1931. Professor. Educ: B.B.A., CCNY, 1952; M.S., Univ. of Tenn., 1955; Ph.D., Univ. of Fla., 1957. Appts. incl: Asst. Prof., Econs., Mich. State Univ., 1957-59; Asst. Prof., Univ. of Wis., Milwaukee, 1959-62; Assoc. Prof., ibid, 1962-65; Prof., 1965-; Assoc. Dean, Coll. of Letters & Sci., 1963-69; Assoc. Dir., Ctr. for Gt. Lakes Studies, 1967-. Mbrships. incl: Chmn., Nat. Acad. of Sci. Port Requirement Panel, 1973-74; Gt. Lakes Pilotage Advsry. Bd., 1971-74; Chmn., Milwaukee Bd. of Harbor Commnrs., 1963-66; var. univs. comms. Publs. incl: The Port of Milwaukee: An Economic Review, 1967; var. tech. reports on Gt. Lakes transportation; Contbr. to num. profl. jrnls. Hons: Rsch. Grant, Dept. of Transportation, 1973-74; Grant as Proj. Coord., Sea Grant Proposal, 1972-75. Address: Univ. of Wis.-Milwaukee, Milwaukee, WI 53201, U.S.A.

SCHENKER, Henry H., b. 19 June 1926. Research Chemist. Educ: B.S., CCNY, 1949; Ph.D., Rutgers Univ., New Brunswick, N.J., 1953. Appts: U.S. Army, 1944-46; Tchng. Assoc., Rutgers Univ., 1950-51; Rsch. Fellow, ibid, 1951-52; Rsch. Chem., E.I.DuPont De Nemours & Co., 1952-56; Analytical Supvsr., ibid, 1956-61; Sr. Rsch. Chem., 1961-73. Mbrships: Am. Chem. Soc.; N.Y. Acad. of Sci.; Pres., Local Chapt., Sigma Xi; Sci. Rsch. Soc.; Pres., Green Acres Civic Assn.; Du Pont Country Club. Publs: Rsch. papers in Analytical Chem., 1953 & 1957. Holder, U.S. Patent, Multi-Step Stretching of Nylon Cords, 1957. Hons: Rsch. Fellowship, Rutgers Univ., 1951; Mbrship., N.Y. Acad. of Sci., 1963. Address: 1419 Bucknell Rd., Green Acres, Wilmington, DE 19803, U.S.A. 6, 14, 22, 57.

SCHEPPEGRELL, Ceril Solon, b. 29 July 1911. Dentist. Educ: La. State Univ., Baton Rouge; Tulane Univ., New Orleans; Loyola Univ. of the South, ibid. Appts: Intern, USPHS, 1939; Asst. Dental Surg., ibid, 1940; Passed Asst. Dental Surg., 1943; Dental Surg., 1945. Fellow, Royal Soc. Hlth. Mbrships. incl: New Orleans Dental Assn.; La. Dental Assn.; U.S. Dental Assn.; Pres., Cath. Alumni Assn., 1953-63; Pres., Exchange Club of New Orleans, 1960-61; Bd. Govs., Paul Morphy Chess Club, 1968-73; Chmn., Model Aviation Bd., New Orleans, 1958; Chmn., March of Dimes Comm., Exchange Club, 1957; Chmn., Crime Prevention Week, New Orleans, 1959. Named. Exchangite of the Yr., Exchange Club. New Orleans, 1958-59. Address: 609 Hibernia Bank Bldg., 812 Gravier St., New Orleans, LA 70112, U.S.A. 2, 7.

SCHER, Jordan Mayer, b. 24 Nov. 1924. Psychiatrist. Educ: B.S., Wesleyan Univ., 1945; M.D., Univ. of Md. Schl. of Med., 1949. Appts. incl: Pvte. Psych. Prac., Chgo., Ill., 1957-; Dir., Nat. Coun. on Drug Abuse; Methadone Maintenance Inst.; Vis., Prof., Div. of Addiction Scis., Dept. of Psych., Univ. of Miami, 1972-; Cons., Nat. Inst. of Mental Hlth. Nat. Drug Abuse Educ. & Trng. Ctr., Univ. of Miami, 1971-; Ed. & Fndr., Existential Psych., Drug Abuse Digest, Drug Abuse Newsletter. Mbrships. incl: Sec. & Fndr., Am. Ontoanalytic Assn.; Fellow, Am. Acad. Psychosomatic Med. Publs. incl: Theories of the Mind, 1963. Drug

Abuse in Industry: Growing Corporate Dilemma. Recip. num. hons. Address: 8 S. Mich. Ave., Suite 310, Chgo., IL 60603, U.S.A. 2, 8, 14, 17, 22, 54.

SCHERE, Richard Alan, b. 21 Jan. 1936. Educator. Educ: B.A., Brooklyn Coll., 1957; M.S., ibid, 1961; Ph.D., N.Y. Univ., 1969. Appts: Tchr., gifted & slow-learning children, pub. schls., N.Y.C., 1957-65; Sec.-Treas., Food Trading Corp., N.Y.C., 1966-; Lectr., Educl. Psychol. Brooklyn Coll., 1966-69; Asst. Prof., 1969; Dir., Tchr. Trng. for Mentally Retarded, 1969-; Chmn., Steering Comm., Mental Retardation Regional Prog., Brooklyn, 1969-71; Admnstr., Inst. for Study of Psychotherapies, 1972-; Admin. Dir., Kennedy Learning Clin., N.Y., 1973-. Mbrships: Am., Eastern & Brooklyn Psychological Assns.; Am. Educl. Rsch. Assn.; Am. Assn. Mental Deficiency.; Assn. Children w. Retarded Mental Dev. Publs: Stones for Goliath, a Book of Poems, 1961; Learning, Teaching & the New Technologies, 1969. Recip., Founder's Day Award, N.Y. Univ., 1970. Address: Dept. Educ., Brooklyn Coll., Brooklyn, NY 11210, U.S.A.

SCHERICH, Erwin Thomas, b. 6 Dec. 1918. Civil Engineer. Educ: B.Sc., Univ. of Neb.; M.Sc., Univ. of Colo. Appts: Civil Engr., U.S. Bur. Reclamation Engrng. & Rsch. Ctr., Denver, Colo.; mbr., U.S. Comm. on Large Dams. Mbrships: Grp. Chmn., Colo. Sect., Am. Soc. Civil Engrs.; Nat. Soc. Profl. Engrs.; Dir., & V.P., Jefferson Chapt., Profl. Engrs. Colo.; Denver Fed. Ctr. Profl. Engrs. Grp.; Pres., Wheat Ridge Chmbr. of Comm. Address: 3915 Balsam St., Wheat Ridge, CO 80033, U.S.A. 9.

SCHERMER, Hans, b. 26 Mar. 1916. Publisher. Educ: Univs. of Vienna, Austria and Hamburg, Germany, 1943-48. m. Ina Ottsen, 1947; Two children. Appts. incl: Treas., Adolf Borgfeldt, Lubeck, Germany, 1948-54; Editor, Erich Schmidt Verlag, Berlin/Bielefeld, 1954-58; Pres., Verlag Chemie GmbH, 1958., Physik Verlag GmbH, 1973-; Bd. Chmn., Volksbank Weinheim EG, 1971-. Mbrships. incl: Lions International; Verband Deutscher Zeitschriftenverleger VDZ; Bundesverband Deutscher Volks-u. Betriebswirte BDVB; Deutsche Gesselschaft für chemisches Apparatewesen DECHEMA. Publs. incl: Maschineneinsatz in der Betriebsbuchhaltung, 1957; Jahresabschlusstechnik, 1958; Chief Ed., Jrnl. fur modernes Management, RDO, 1955-72. Address: Kreutzerweg 6, D-694 Weinheim, German Fed. Repub.

SCHERRER-BYLUND, Paul, b. 18 Aug. 1900. Librarian. Educ: Univs. of Munich, Berlin, Glasgow; Ph.D., Munich Univ., 1927. Appts: Asst. Libn., Lib., Univ. of Basle, 1928, Libn, 1931; Chief Libn., 1947, Dir., 1953, Main Lib. of Swiss Fed. Inst. of Technol., Zürich; Dir., Ctrl. & Univ. Lib., Zürich, 1963; Retd., 1973. Mbrships: Past Pres., Swiss Soc. of Bibliophiles; Pres., Gottfried Keller Soc. Publs: 12 scholarly books, in German, 1929-72. Hons: Mbr., Swiss Soc. of Bibliophiles & Int. Assn. of Bibliophily; Mbr., Naturforschende Gesell., Zürich, 1972. Address: Beckhammer 32, CH-8057 Zürich, Switzerland. 34, 43, 103.

SCHERZER, Doris Brown. Violinst; Music Coach; Bakery Owner. Educ: Grad., Baldwin-Wallace Coll., 1937; Grad. study, Chgo. Musical Coll., Currently studying Baroque Violin. Appts: Violinist, Annual Bach Festival, Baldwin-Wallace Coll., 1930-38; Concert mistress, Coll. Orch., 1936-37; Violinist, Cleveland Philharmonic Orch., 1937-46; Concert mistress & Asst. Conductor,

Columbus Orchl. Soc., 1955-60; 1st Violin, Columbus Symph. Orch., 1956-68; 1st Violin on tour of Europe, Am. Community Symph. Orch., 1968. Mbrships: Mu Phi Epsilon; Delta Kappa Gamma; Music Educators Nat. Conf.; Am. String Tchrs. Assn. Address: 396 Mimring Rd., Columbus, OH 43202, U.S.A. 5, 8, 138.

SCHETLIN, Eleanor Margaret, b. 15 July 1920. University Dean for Students. Educ: B.A., Hunter Coll., CUNY, U.S.A., 1940; M.A., Columbia Univ., N.Y., 1942; Ed.D., ibid, 1967. Appts: Playground Dir., Dept. of Pks., N.Y.C., 1940-43; Libn., Metrop. Hosp. Schl. of Nursing, 1943-44; Dir., Recreation, ibid, 1944-48; Dir., Recreation & Guidance, 1948-59; Coord., Student Activities, Plattsburgh Coll., SUNY, 1959-63; Asst. Dean of Students, ibid, 1963-64; Asst. Prof., Coord., Student Personnel Servs., Off. of Dean of Students, Hunter Coll., CUNY, 1967-68; Asst. Dir., Student Personnel, Coll. of Pharmaceutical Scis., Columbia Univ., 1968-69; Dir., ibid, 1969-71; Assoc. Dean for Students, Hlth. Scis. Ctr., Stony Brook, SUNY, 1971-73; Asst. V.P. for Student Servs., ibid, 1973-. Mbrships. incl: NEA; Am. Assn. for Higher Educ.; Am. Personnel & Guidance Assn.; Kappa Delta Pi. Publs: Articles in profl. jrnls. Address: 20 Barberry Ln., Sea Cliff, NY 11579, U.S.A. 5, 6, 46, 132.

SCHETTINI, Franco, b. 20 June 1907. Architect; Monument Supervision Officer. Educ: Grad., Archt., Higher Schl. of Archt., Rome, 1933. Appts: Tech. Hd., Monument Supervision, Bari, 1935; Asst. Archt. of Monuments Service, ibid, 1938, Archt., 1940; Dir., Monument Serv., 1943; Calabria, 1953; Supt. of Monument Serv., Emilia, 1965. Author, many books on archt. subjects & contbr. to var. archtl. jrnls. Hons. incl: Kt. of Italian Crown, 1941; Kt., Order of S. Salvatore & S. Brigida, 1949; Kt. of Repub., 1953; Gold Medal, Bari, 1954; Grand Off., Italian Repub., 1957; Grand Off., Order of S. Gregorio Magno, 1959; Gold Medal, Imola, 1973. Address: Via Venezia 36, Bari, Italy.

SCHEUER, Lucile M. University Administrator. Educ: A.B., Mt. Holyoke Coll., S.Hadley, Mass., U.S.A., 1931; M.A., Columbia Univ., N.Y.C., 1934. Appts. incl: Dir., Speech & Dramatics, Tech. H.S., Scranton, Pa., 1931-38; Engl. & Speech Tchr., & Dean of Women, Keystone Jr. Coll., 1938-43; Dir., Women's Housing & Residence Hall, Northwestern Univ., Ill., 1944-48; Assoc. Dean of Students, DePauw Univ., Greencastle, Ind., 1948-60; Dean of Women, Temple Univ., Phila., Penn., 1960-70; Assoc. to V.P. for Student Affairs, ibid, 1970-. Mbrships. incl: Nat. Assn. of Women Deans & Counselors; Sev. offs., Bds., Ind. & Pa. Assns. of Women Deans & Counselors; V.P., Ind. State Div. Bd., AAUW, 1956-59, Pres., Phila. Br. Bd., 1962-64; Bd., Phila. Girls Club of Am.; Bd., Mid-City YWCA, Phila.; Hon. Mortar Bd., DePauw Chapt., Alpha Lamda Delta; Kappa Delta Pi; Pi Lamda Theta; Phi Delta Gamma. Address: Temple University, 1806 N. Park Mall, Philadelphia, PA 19122, U.S.A. 2.

SCHEUNERT, Gerhart (Otto), b. 11 Jan. 1906. Psychoanalyst; Psychiatrist. Educ: Studied med., Leipzig, Vienna & Berlin, 1925-30; Grad., med., Leipzig, 1930; Med. Assistantship; Studied neurol. & psych., Univ. Nervenklinik, Leipzig; Psychoanalytical trng., 1928-34. Appts: Specialist, neurol. & psych., Erfurt, 1936; Psychoanalytical Prac., W. Berlin, 1949; Lectr. & Educl. Analyst, Berlin Psychoanalytical Inst., 1950-59; Psychoanalytical Prac., Hamburg, 1959-; Lectr., Hamburg Psychoanalytical Inst. (Michael-Balint-Inst., 1972-), 1959-; Prof.,

Univ. of Hamburg, 1959-; Hon. Prof., ibid, 1972-. Mbrships. incl: Co-Fndr., Deutsche Psychoanalytische Vereinigung (br. of Int. Psychoanalytic Assn.), 1950; Bd. of Dirs., ibid, 1950-64 & 1966-70; Pres., 1956-64; Co-Fndr., Berlin Psychoanalytic Inst., 1950; Bd. of Dirs., Deutsche Gesellschaft für Psychotherapie und Tiefenpsychologie, 1955-66. Author of num. articles in jrnls. Address: Cranachstr. 87, D-2000 Hamburg 52, German Fed. Repub.

SCHEURER, Rudolf, b. 18 July 1931. Sculptor. Educ: Study in Basle, Linz, Paris; Study of Arch., travel in Egypt, India, Nepal, Siam, Japan. Mbrships: Fachverband bildenter, Künstler, Germany; Studi e Scambi, Rome; Int. Art Guild, Monaco. Sculpture in Bronze, stone, cast aluminium, pub., pvte. collects., France, U.K., Belgium, Switzerland, Sweden, Italy, Hungary, Austria, Germany, U.S.A.; Exhibs., London, Paris, Rome, Brussels, Hamburg, Zurich, Basel, Monte Carlo, etc.; Int. Art Fair, Basle & Düsseldorf, Berlin, 1972-74. Hons: Num. prizes for archtl. sculptures; Dipl.: Palme d'or des Beaux Arts, Monte Carlo; Accademia Int. Leonardo da Vinci; Biennale delle Regioni, Ancona. Address: Hüsingerstr. 35, 7852 Brombach/Lörrach, German Fed. Repub.

SCHIAVO, Giovanni Ermenegilgo, b. 28 May 1898. Author; Journalist; Editor. Educ: Johns Hopkins Univ., Balt., undergrad & postgrad., 1917-20; N.Y. Univ., 1928-29; Columbia Univ., 1929-31. Appts: Edit. Staff, Balt. & N.Y. newspapers; Financial Ed., La Domenica Illustrata, N.Y., 1921-22; Ed. & Publr., Il Corriere del Wis., Milwaukee, 1922-26; Mng. Ed., Atlantica Mag., 1929-31; Ed. & Publr., Vigo Review, N.Y., 1938-39. Publs. incl: The Italians in Chicago, 1928; The Italians in America Before the Civil War, 1934; Italian-American History, 2 vols., 1947-49; Philip Mazzei, 1951; American Guide to Italy, 1952-54; Antonio Meucci, Inventor of the Telephone, 1958; The Truth About the Mafia, 1962; Italian Dictionary for Travelers, 1963. Ed., Publr., Italian-American Who's Who, 1935-67. Contbr., Encyclopedia Americana, 1922-32. Recip., Hon. Fellowships, N.Y. & Columbia Univs. Address: 943 Driver Circle, El Paso, TX 79903, U.S.A. 43.

SCHIAVONE, James, b. 22 Jan. 1933. Educator. Educ: B.A., N.Y. Univ., 1955; M.A., ibid, 1956; Profl. Dip., Columbia Univ., 1957; Postgrad. studies, Univ. Degli Studi Di Roma, 1964-65. Appts: Reading Specialist in schls., 1955-66; Educl. Cons., G.S. Cook, Consultants, Ft. Lauderdale, Fla., 1966-68; Coord. of Reading Instrn., Monroe Co. Schl. Dist., Key West, Fla., 1968-70; Dir. of Basic Educ., CUNY, Regional Opportunity Ctrs., 1970-71; Asst. Prof., Developmental Skills & Coord. for Remediation, Borough of Manhattan Community Coll., CUNY, 1971-. Mbrships: Life Mbr., NEA; Int. Reading Assn.; Nat. Reading Conf., Inc.; Phi Delta Kappa; Profl. Staff Congress of CUNY; N.Y. State Assn. of Jr. Colls. Author of books & articles in field. Recip. of hons. Address: Borough of Manhattan Community Coll., CUNY, 134 West 51st St., N.Y., NY 10020, U.S.A. 6, 30, 57.

SCHIBY, Baruch, b. 15 May 1906. Journalist; Author. Educ: Greek & French Culture. Appts: Jrnlst., 1925-39, & after WWII until 1948; Ed., Delphica Tetradia, philological review, 1964-67. Mbrships: Past Pres., League of Letters & Arts of Northern Greece; Past Pres., Zionist Socs. of Thesseloniki. Publs: The Jews; Flegomeni Vatos; Hagada of Pessah; num. articles on Jews of Thessaloniki. Address: 9 Cleauthous, Thessaloniki, Greece.

SCHICK, Eduard, b. 23 Feb. 1906. Professor of Theology; Auxiliary Bishop. Educ: Phil.-Theol. Sem., Fulda, Germany; Univs. of Göttingen, Bonn & Würzburg; Dr.Theol., 1940; Tchrs. exam. Appts: Ordained Cath. priest, 1928; Chap., Hattenhof & Kassel, 1928-35; H.S. Headmaster, Grossauheim, 1936-38; Hd., priest sem., Fulda; Prof., New Testament Exegesis, Fulda, 1947; Fulda Cathedral, 1957; Hon. Bishop, Ardai, N. Africa, & Aux. Bishop, Fulda, 1962. Pres., Pontifical Commn. for New-Vulgate-Edition, Vatican City, Italy. Publs: Formgeschichte und Synoptikerexegese, 1940; Kommentar zur Apokalypse, 1952, 1968; Kommentar zum Johannesevangelium, 1956, 1965; Offenbarung und Geschichte, 1968; Die Apokalypse, in Geistliche Schriftlesung No. 23, 1971. Address: Domdechanei 4/6, D-6400 Fulda, German Fed. Repub.

SCHIEBER, David, b. 30 May 1938. Electrical Engineer. Educ: B.Sc., Technion, Israel Inst. of Technol., Haifa, 1960; M.Sc., ibid, 1962, D.Sc., 1965. Appts: Lectr., Technion, Israel Inst. of Technol., 1965, Sr. Lectr., 1966, Assoc. Prof., 1970-; Vis. Assoc. Prof., M.I.T., Cambridge, Mass., U.S.A., 1972-73. Sr. Mbr., I.E.E.E. Over 50 publs., elec. engrng., int. jrnls. Address: Faculty of Electrical Engineering, Technion, Haifa, Israel. 94.

SCHIEBER, Jacob, b. 9 July 1905. Lawyer; Company Executive. Educ: Grad., Law Fac., Czernovitz Univ. Appts: Legal prac., Czernovitz; Dir., Romis Ltd.; currently Dir., Univers Travel & Transportation Co. Ltd. Mbrships: Free Masons Order; Diners Club. Collaborator, publ. of school text book, tchng. of Hebrew, Bucharest, 1938. Hons: Haganah Badge; Decoration of the State fighters. Address: 118 Arlozoroff St., Tel Aviv, Israel. 55, 94.

SCHIEBER, Michael, b. 4 Nov. 1928. Materials Scientist; Engineer. Educ: Dip., Imperial Coll., London, 1963; Ph.D., Hebrew Univ./Weizmann Inst., 1962. Appts: Rsch. Assoc., Weizmann Inst., 1957-62; Rsch. Fellow, Imperial Coll., 1962-63; Rsch. Fellow, Harvard Univ., 1963-64; Rsch. Staff Mbr.; Nat. Magnet Laboratory, MIT, 1964-66; Assoc. Prof., Hebrew Univ. of Jerusalem, 1966-; Prin. Ed., Jrnl. of Crystal Growth, N. Holland-Elsevier, 1966-. Mbrships: Sec., Int. Org. of Crystal Growth, 1966-; Sigma Xi; Am. Phys. Soc.; Am. Electrochem. Soc. Publd. Experimental Magnetochemistry, 1967. Contbr. to profl. jrnls. Address: Hebrew Univ. of Jerusalem, Jerusalem, Israel.

SCHIFF, Frank William, b. 15 July 1921. Economist. Educ: A.B., Columbia Coll., N.Y., 1942; Grad. Studies, Econs., Columbia Univ., 1946-49. Appts: Instr. Economics., Columbia Coll., 1946-51; Rsch. Dept., Fed. Reserve Bank of N.Y., 1951-64; Asst. V.P.; ibid, 1963-64; Sr. Staff Economist (on leave from N.Y. Fed. Bank), Pres.'s Coun. for Economic Advsrs., 1964-68; Dpty. Undersec. for Monetary Affairs, U.S. Treasury Dept., 1968-69; V.P. & Chief Economist, Comm. for Economic Dev., 1969-. Mbrships: Pres., Nat. Economists Club & Nat. Economists Club Fndn.; Trustee, Fed. Stats. Users Conf.; Coun. on For. Rels.; Conf. of Bus. Economists; Am. Economic Assn; Phi Beta Kappa. Address: 1000 Conn. Ave. N.W., Washington, DC 20036. 7, 14.

SCHIFF, James, b. 1 Dec. 1941. Dentist. Educ: Grad., Univ. of Md., 1963; Grad., Dental Schl., ibid, 1966; Intern, Sinai Hosp., Balt., Md., 1967. Appts: Pres., Eastland Air Inc., airline charter, 1970-; Pres., E. Coast Land Co., 1971-; Pres., E.C.I., investment syndicate, 1972-; V.P., Schiff Milling Co., 1973-. Mbrships: Am. Dental Assn.; Eastern Shore Dental Soc.; Farm Bur.; V.P., Cambridge Profl. Bldg. Inc. Address: 8 Aurora St., Cambridge, MD 21613, U.S.A. 6.

SCHIFF, Saul Ben, b. 15 Apr. 1898. Shoe Company Executive. Appts: Dir., Shoe Corp. of Am., Columbus, Ohio, U.S.A., 1940-62; Pres. & Dir., A.S. Beck Shoe Corp., N.Y.C., 1947-68; Currently Pres. & Dir., Am. Israel Shoe Corp., N.Y.C. & Alma Shoe Co., Bat Yam, Israel; Dir., Allied Foods, Inc.; Dir., Bank Leumi Trust Co. Mbrships. incl: Chmn., Shoe Retail Div., Gtr. N.Y. Fund, 1958, & 1964-65; Chmn., Shoe Ind. Campaign, United Jewish Appeal, 1950-53; Chmn., Shoe Div., Nat. Fund for Med. Educ., 1961-62; Trustee, Jewish Home & Hosp. for Aged, 1951-72; Co-fndr., Albert Einstein Coll. of Med.; Sponsor, Herbert H. Lehman Inst. of Ethics; Bd. of Dirs., Am. Friends of Hebrew Inst.; U.S. Navy League; Econ. Club. Hons: Louis Marshall Award, Jewish Theological Sem. of Am., 1960; Mbrships., Soc. of Alumni of Hebrew Univ. of Jerusalem, Israel. Address: 60 Park Rd., Scarsdale, NY 10583, U.S.A. 2.

SCHIFFER, Irvine, b. 8 Feb. 1917. Physician; Psychoanalyst. Educ: M.D., Univ. of Toronto, 1941. Appts: Dir., Toronto Psychoanalytic Forum of the Humanities; Prof., Applied Psychoanalysis, Vic. Univ.; Rsch. Prof., Pol. Econ., Univ. of Toronto; Pres., Ont. Div., Inst. Assoc. Dir., Canadian Inst. of Psychoanalysis. Author, Charisma: A Psychoanalytic Look at Mass Society, 1973. Recip., African & Italian Stars, WW II. Address: 91 Gordon Rd., Willowdale, Ont., Canada.

SCHILBRED, Cornelius Severin Scheel, b. 13 Dec. 1906. College Principal. Educ: B.L., Univ. of Oslo, 1931; Commercial Schl., Oslo, 1932-37; Tchr., Wangs Commercial Schl., Oslo, 1937-38; Prin., ibid, 1938-53; Mgr., Soc. for Protection of Animals, 1949-60; Tchr., Municipal Commercial Schl. of Oslo, 1938-48, 1957-58; Prin.-Rektor, ibid, (now Frogner Municipal Commercial Schl.), 1958-. Mbrships. incl: Hon. Fellow & V.P., Soc. for Protection of Animals; Pres., Norwegian Soc. for Heraldry; Pres., Norwegian Genealogical Soc.; former Pres., Norwegian Soc. for Commercial Educ. Publs. incl: Brevik gjennom tidene I, 1946; Brevik i bilder, 1958; Slekten Wilhelmsen, 1970; Slekten Backer, 1972; Kjenn din slekt, 1973; edited sev. publs. Address: Holmenkollveien 29, Oslo 3, Norway. 43, 134.

SCHILLING, Edward George, b. 9 Nov. 1931. Statistician. Educ: B.A., Univ. of Buffalo, 1953; M.B.A., ibid, 1954; M.S., Rutgers Univ., 1962; Ph.D., ibid, 1967. Appts: Instr. in Stats., Univ. of Buffalo, 1957-59; Engr., Radio Corp. of Am., 1959-61; Tchng. Asst. in Stats., Rutgers Univ., 1961-62, Instr., 1964-67; Sr. Engr., Carborundum Co., 1962-64; Assoc. Prof., Rochester Inst. of Technol., 1967-69; Cons. Statistician, Lamp Div., Gen. Elec. Co., 1969-. Mbrships: Councillor, Chem. Div., Am. Soc. Quality Control, 1971-; Am. Statistical Assn.; Pres., Cleveland Chapt., ibid, 1973; Mbr., Comm. E-11, Am. Soc. for Testing & Mats., 1973-; Inst. of Math. Stats.; Am. Econ. Assn. Contbr., var. profl. publs. & jrnls. Hon. Fellow, Am. Soc. for Quality Control, 1973. Address: 1683 Rushton Rd., S. Euclid, OH 44121, U.S.A. 6.

SCHILPP, Paul Arthur, b. 6 Feb. 1897. Professor; Philosopher; Writer. Educ: B.A., Baldwin-Wallace Coll., Ohio, 1916; B.D., Garrett Theol. Sem., 1922; M.A., Northwestern Univ., 1922; Ph.D., Stanford Univ., 1936. Appts: Prof. of Psychol. & Relig. Educ., Coll. of Puget Sound, 1922-23; Prof. of Philos., Coll. of the Pacific, 1923-34; Assoc. Prof. to Prof. of Philos., Northwestern Univ., 1936-65; Prof. Emeritus, ibid, 1965-; Mbrships: Western Div. V.P., Am. Philos. Assn., 1957-58, Pres., ibid, 1958-59; Publs. incl: Human Nature and Progress, 1954; The Crisis in Science and Education, 1963. Ed. & Contbr. to num. publs. inclng: The Critique of War, 1969; Value and Valuation, 1971. Fndr., Ed. & Pres., Library of Living Philosophers (14 vols. to date). Hons: Hon. Lit.D., Baldwin-Wallace Coll.; Hon. L.H.D., Springfield Coll., Mass. 1963. Address: 9 Hillcrest Dr., Carbondale, IL 62901, U.S.A. 2, 13, 15, 30, 34, 51, 128, 141.

SCHIMELFENIG, Grace O'Malley, b. 9 Feb. 1931. Executive Secretary & Assistant Board Secretary. Educ: var. post grad. bus. courses. Appts: Exec. Sec., & former Bus. Mgr., Northeastern Pa. Educl. TV Assn., WVIA-TV/FM, Channel 44; Asst. Sec., Bd. of Dirs., ibid; Notary Pub. & Tax Cons. Mbrships. incl: Pres., Am. Women in Radio & TV, Northeastern Pa. Chapt.; Former Recording Sec., Mbrship. Chmn., Deleg. to Int. Convention, 1970, & Deleg. to Nat. Convention, 1971, ibid; Var. offs., Am. Bus. Women's Assn.; Diocesan Commn. on Ecumenism & Human Affairs, Diocese of Scranton, 1973; Immaculate Conception Ch. of Scranton. Recip., Woman of the Year award, Lackawanna Chapt., Am. Bus. Women's Assn., 1971. Address: 216 Lake Scranton Rd., Scranton, PA 18505, U.S.A.

SCHIÖTTZ-CHRISTENSEN, Alf Krabbe, b. 12 Feb. 1909. Editor-in-Chief; Managing Director. Educ: B.A., Univ. of Copenhagen, 1927; Litt. B., Columbia Univ., N.Y. Appts: Jrnlist., Seattle Times, Wash., 1931; Corres. from Geneva, Switzerland, to Danish Newspapers, 1932-33; Reporter, Editl. Staff, Aalborg Stiftstidende, 1933; Ed.-in-Chief & Mgng. Dir., ibid, 1940; Publr., 1950; Dir., Aalborg Stiftsbogtrykkeri (printing works), 1944. Mbrships: V.P., Danish Newspaper Publrs. Assn., 1959-71; Exec. Comm., Fedn. Int. of Newspaper Eds., 1961-; Bd., INCA-FIEJ Rsch. Assn., 1970- Past Pres., Aalborg Rotary & Aero Clubs; Past Pres., Aalborg Sect. of Norden, Assn. for Scandinavian Coöp. Hons: Order of Benignitate Humana, Findland, 1946; Order of Dannebrog, 1st Glass, Denmark, 1956; Order of Mérito Civil, - Cruz de Oficial, Spain, 1966; Order of Vasa, 1st Class, Sweden, 1969; Cmdr., Order of the Finnish Lion, 1972; Croix d'Officier, Legion of Honour, France, 1973. Address: P.O. Box 461, DK-9100 Aalborg, Denmark.

SCHJAASTAD, Dolores Fay, b. 26 Dec. 1920. Free-lance Writer. Educ: US Coast Guard Trng. Stn., Palm Beach, Fla.; B.S., Univ. of Tampa, Fla., 1949; Nashville Schl. of Soc. Work, Tenn.; Nat. Cath. Schl. of Soc. Serv., Cath. Univ. of Am., Wash. D.C. Appts. incl: Admnstr., Hillsborough Co. Welfare Dept., Tampa, Fla.; active duty w. armed forces, WWII; Chief Yeoman, US Coast Guard Reserve; Case Wkr., Family Serv. Assn., Tampa, Fla.; active duty w. armed forces, during & after Korean War; Lt., USNR; Free-lance Writer. Mbrships. incl: Life Mbr., Sigma Sigma Sigma; Chmn., Pub. Info. Comm. & Corres., 'Triangle, Tampa Alumnae Chapt.; Int. Mbr.-at-large, Beta Sigma Phi Retired Offs. Assn., Wash. D.C. Hons: Commendations, US Govt., 1957, Univ. of Tampa Alumni Assn., 1958, Pres. (Dr.) E.C. Nance, Univ. of Tampa, 1962; The Triangle Award, Sigma Sigma Sigma, 1972; Hon.

Mention, ibid, 1973. Address: 10014 Hyacinth Ave., Tampa, FL 33612, U.S.A. 125.

SCHLAIFER, Charles. Executive. Educ: Litt.D., John F. Kennedy Coll., Neb. Appts: Newspaper Reporter, Dir., Advt. & Publicity; Mng. Dir., Publix Theatres, Neb., Iowa; V.P., United Artists Theatres, San Fran., Calif.; Cons., Samuel Goldwyn, David Selznick, Walter Wanger, James Roosevelt, & Alexander Korda; V.P., 20th Century-Fox, Advt., P.R.; Pres., Charles Schlaifer & Co., Advt. Agcy., N.Y. & Calif. Mbrships. incl: Chmn., N.Y. State Facilities Dev. Corp.; Hon. Fellow, Am. Psych. Assn., Postgrad. Psych. Ctr., Am. Orthopsych. Assn., & Brit. Royal Soc.; Chmn., N.Y. State Hlth. & Mental Hygiene Facilities Corp.; Fndr., Co-Chmn., Nat. Hlth. Comm.; Fndng., Nat. Assn. for Mental Hlth.; Advsry. Coun. to Surg. Gen.; Cons. to Surg. Gen., USPHS; Sec.-Treas., US Jt. Commn., Mental Hlth. & Congressional Jt. Commn. Mental Hlth. for Children; Prof., New Schl., 1955-60. Publs. incl: Motion Pictures Association Advertising Code, 1948; Action for Mental Health, 1960. Hons: Wisdom Mag. Award, 1969; Karen Horney Soc. Conscience Award, 1972. Address: 150 E. 58th St., N.Y., NY 10022, U.S.A. 2, 6.

SCHLEEH, Hans, b. 9 Oct. 1928. Sculptor. Educ: Studies w. Richard Class, Germany, 1948-51; Studied, France, Italy, Switzerland & Germany, 1963-64. Exhibs. incl: Confrontation 65, Int. Exhib. Sculpture, 1965; 2nd Open Air Sculpture Exhib., Stratford, 1966; Canadian Sculpture, Expo 67, 1967; Presentation 70, Quebec Sculptors Assn., 1970; Panorama de la Sculpture au Quebec, Mus. Rodin, Paris, 1970-71; IV Exposition Int. de Sculpture Contemporaine, ibid, 1971. Mbrships: Quebec Sculptors Assn.; Sculptors Soc. Canada. Perm. Works in perm. collects. in Canada, U.S.A., Europe, Israel, inclng: Art Gall. of Winnipeg; Vancouver Art Gall.; Sarnia Art Gall.; St. Catherine's & Dist. Arts Coun.; Univ. of Sherbrooke; Tel Aviv Mus., Israel; Bloomfield Coll., London; Chmbr. of Trade, Düsseldorf, Germany. Address: 1040 Carson Ave., Dorval, P.Q., Canada. 37.

SCHLEGEL, Wolfgang (Fritz), b. 8 Sept. 1912. Professor. Educ: Tchrs. exams., 1934 & 1935; Dr., Tech. Univ., Braunschweig, Germany, 1937; Tchng. exams., 1938, 1940, 1954. Appts. incl: Secondary schl. tchr., 1954-56; Lectr., Pädagogische Akad., Kaiserslautern, 1958-62; Prof., Pädagogische Hoscschule, Kaiserslautern, 1962-69; Vice Chancellor, ibid, 1965-67; Prof., Erziehungswissenschaft-liche Hochschule, Rheinland-Pfalz, 1970-. Mbrships. incl: Pfälzische Gesellschaft zur Förderung der Wissenschaften; Sci. Advsr., Historischer Verein der Pfalz; Bd. of Dris. & mbr., sci. comm., Verein für Pfälzische Kirchengeschichte; Raabe Gesellschaft. Publs. incl: Handbuch für Geschichtsunterricht an Volks- & Realschulen, Vol. I, pt. 1, 1973, Vol. II, 1961, Vol. III, 1964, Vol. IV, 1964; Over 100 articles in jrnls. Hons. incl: Bronze Serv. Plaque, Historicher Verein der Pfalz, Arbeitsgemeinschaft Kaiserslautern, 1962. Address: Madenburgstr. 18. 6740 Landau i. d. Pfalz, German Fed. Repub. 43.

SCHLEIN, Irving, b. 18 Aug. 1905. Composer; Teacher. Educ: Ph.G., Brooklyn Coll. Pharmacy, 1927; Degree in Piano, N.Y. Coll. Music 1928, Inst. Musical Art, 1930; B.A., CCNY, 1936; grad. courses in music, Brooklyn Coll. & Manhattan Schl. of Music. Appts: Conductor, Broadway musicals, 1940-58; Lectr. & Tchr., Brooklyn Coll. & var. H.S., N.Y.C. Mbrships: Am. Soc. Composers,

Authors & Publrs.; Am. Fedn. Musicians; United Fedn. Tchrs. Compositions incl: Salammbo (opera based on novel of Flaubert); Symphonies 1 to 10 for full Orch.; Chamber works; Ode to the United Nations; Grand Central Station - a travesty; Essays for Orchestra; On A Summer's Day. Publs. incl: Dance Overture; Slave Songs of the United States; Recip., 1st Prize, B.M.I.-A.C.A. contest, 1947. Address: 650 Ocean Ave., Brooklyn, NY, 11226, U.S.A.

SCHLESIER, Raimund, b. 18 July 1910. Professor; Concert Pianist. Educ: Univs. of Freiburg, Munich & Berlin, Germany; Hochschule für Music, Berlin; Städtisches Konservatorium (Master Class), Berlin. Appts: Asst. to Artur Rother, Deutsches Opernhaus, 1938-48; Piano Tchr., Hochschule für Musik, 1948-; Hon. Prof., 1952-; Extraordinary Prof., 1962-; Full Prof., 1970. Mbrships: Artistic advsry. comm., V.D.M.K., & Deutscher Musikerzieher & Konzertierender Künstler; 1st Chmn., ibid, 1965-71; Elected Senator, Staatliche Hochschule für Musik & darstellende Kunst, Berlin-Charl. Performances in concert, on radio & on record. Address: Am Rathaus 43, 2954 Wiesmoor, German Fed. Repub. 43.

SCHLESINGER, Hugo, b. 5 May 1920. Author; Journalist; Economist. Educ: Courses in Admin., Cracov, Poland; Econ. & Commerce, Univ. of Florence; & in Jrnlsm., Communication, Sociol., PR, Community Leadership, Creativity. Appts: Dir. Supt., Soc. Brasiliera de Comedia; Dir., O Mundo em Noticias, ALFA, & RICLA, São Paulo. Mbrships. incl: Co-Pres., Jewish Christian Fraternity Coun.; Fndr., Inst. de Estudos, Pesquisas e Estatisticas; Former Pres., B'nai B'rith Publishing Soc.; Coord., Univ. no Lar; Brazilian Jornalist Assn.; Brazilian Soc. of Writers; PEN Club; Christian Acad. of Letters; Brazilian Acad. of Soc. Sci. & Politics. Publs. incl: Enciclopedia da Industria Brasileira; Enciclopedia de Administracão e Negocios; Dicionario de Vendas; Moderna Enciclopedia de Administração de Empresas. Prod. & Dir. of O Mar Sem Fim...; Eva; Parabens Gigantes da Copa; Menina de Sonhos de Mais, & about 30 documentary films. Recip. of num. mil. & civil awards & decorations. Address: Caixa Postal 5026, São Paulo, Brazil. 55.

SCHLEY, Norman Edward, b. 5 Oct. 1908. Certified Public Accountant. Educ: Grad., Carroll Coll.; Acctcy. courses, Univ. of Wis.; Study of law, Marquette Univ., 1937-39. Mbrships: Past Pres., Wis. Soc. of C.P.A.'s; Past. Pres., Milwaukee Chapt., Nat. Assns. of Accts.; Past Pres., Waukesha Kiwanis Club; Past Dist. Gov., Wis. Upper Mich. Dist., Kiwanis Int. Publs: Schley's Income Tax Guide - 15 Easy Steps to Prepare Your Income Tax Return, 1972; Num. articles in profl. jrnls. Address: Box 985, Waukesha, WI 53186, U.S.A.

SCHLICHTING, Catherine Fletcher (Nicholson), b. 18 Nov. 1923. Librarian. Educ: B.S., Univ. of Ala., 1944; M.L.S., Univ. of Chgo., 1950. Appts: Asst. Libn., Educ. Lib., Univ. of Ala., summers 1944-45; Libn., Sylacauga H.S., Ala., 1944-45; Hinsdale H.S., Ill., 1945-49; Asst. Libn., Ctr. for Children's Books, Univ. of Chgo., 1950-52; Ref. Libn., Beeghly Lib., Ohio Wesleyan Univ., Delaware, 1965-. Mbrships. incl: Ohio Wesleyan Univ. Woman's Club; Pres., ibid, 1969-70, Exec. Bd. 1969-72; AAUP; Chapt. Sec., ibid, 1967-68, Chmn., Fac. Status Comm., 1973-74. Del. Hist. Club; Treas., ibid, 1968-69, Pres., 1971-73. Publs: Beeghly Library Handbook; Bibliographic Research in English. Recip., Mellon Fndn. Grant, Ohio Wesleyan Univ.,

1972-73. Address: 414 N. Liberty St., Delaware, OH 43015, U.S.A. 5, 129, 138.

SCHLICK, Heinrich, b. 20 Nov. 1905. Managing Director. Educ: Dr.Jr. & Dr. Phil., Univs., of Karlsruhe & Heidelberg, Germany. Appts: Post, I.G. Farbenindustrie, Ludwigschafen-Oppau, & Hoechst; Post, Oberschlesische Hydrierwerke; Exec. Chmn., Chem. Ind. Assn. of Baden-Wurttemberg; Exec. Chmn., S.-W. German Plastics Ind. Assn.; Chmn., Fed. Assemblage Union of German Fotofinishers; Pres., Vereinigte Firmenpensionskasse. Mbrships. incl: Judge, Fed. German Ct. of Indl. Legislation; Pres., Dptys. of Landesversicherungsanstalt Baden; Deleg. to OECD; Pres., Deutsche Gesellschaft für Warenkunde & Technologie; Bundesinnenministerium; Bundesanstalt für Arbeit. Publs: Num. treatises & articles on commercial & indl. law, econ. & soc. policy, & histl. subjects. Recip., Grosses Bundesverdienstkreuz des Verdienstordens der Bundesrepublik Deutschland, 1973. Address: 68 Mannheim, Viktoriastrasse 8, German Fed. Repub. 43, 92.

SCHLOSS, Edith. Painter & Writer. Educ: Boston Schl. of Practical Arts; Art Students' League, N.Y. Appts: Edit. Assoc., Art News, 1954-62; Art Critic for Italy, Int. Herald Tribune, Paris, France, 1969-; Rome Corres., Art News, 1973-; Occasional Corres. for Village Voice, N.Y., M.S. mag., N.Y. & others. Mbr., Educl. Alliance, N.Y. 12 one-woman shows inclng. Am. Acad., Rome, Italy, 1971; Group shows in N.Y. & Italy; Color reproduction of oil painting in Art News, 1974; Contbr. to Assemblage by William C. Seitz, 1961, How To Make Collages by John Lynch, 1961, Collage by Harriet Janis & Rudy Blesh, 1961, The Artist's World by Fred W. McDarrah, 1961; Currently working w. Barbara Glasser on tech. handbook The Spirit & Technique of Watercolor; Author of articles in jrnls. Address: Via della Vetrina 18, 00186 Rome, Italy.

SCHLOSSER, Joseph Leo, b. 22 Aug. 1925. Architect. Educ: B.S., Ga. Inst. of Technol., 1954; B.Arch., 1954. Registered as Archt., States of Ga., 1961 & Fla., 1971. Mbr., Nat. Coun. of Archtl. Registration Bds., 1970. Mbrships. incl: Am. Inst. Archts.; Construction Specifications Inst.; Advsry. Comm. Drafting Dept., Brunswick Jr. Coll.; Brunswick Chmbr. of Comm.; Downtown Redev. Comm.; Dir., Sea Circus, Inc.; Pres., Glynn Co. Heart Assn., 1968-71; V.P., Kiwanis Club, Brunswick, Ga., 1973-; Dir., Brunswick Jaycees, 1958-60; Chmn., St. Francis Xavier Schl. Bd., 1964-66; Glynn Co. Bldg. Code Appeals Bd., 1966-70; St. Francis Xavier Parish Bd., 1964-68. Contbr. to var. jrnls. Hons: Citation for Community Serv., United Community Fund; Plaque for Serv. to Glynn Co. Heart Assn. Address: 1027 Lanier Blvd., Brunswick, GA 31520, U.S.A. 7.

SCHLUMBERGER, Robert F., b. 10 Mar. 1902. Wine Trade Executive; Owner of Vineyards & Wine Museum. Educ: Philos. & Law studies, Univ. of Vienna; Doctor rerum politicarum, 1927; Doctor juris, 1933. Appts: Mng. Dir., Jawornica Sparkling Wine Mfrs., Andrychow, Poland, 1927-36; Assoc., Franz Leibenfrost & Co., Vienna, Austria, 1928-52; Mbr., Bd. Dirs., August Schneider AG, 1928-44, Chief Owner & Mng. Dir., 1942-; Assoc. & Sole Owner, R. Schlumberger, sparkling wine mfr., 1952-; retirement from trade to mgmt., own vineyards & wine mus., Vöslau, 1973-. Mbrships. incl: Verein Altschotten; Verein für Landeskunde von Niederösterreich und Wien; Verein für Landeskunde der Stadt Wien; Heraldisch-Genealogische Gesellschaft Adler.

Contbr., var. publs. Address: 2540 Bad Vöslau, Florastrasse 19, Austria.

SCHMETTERER, Leopold, b. 8 Nov. 1919. Professor of Mathematics & Statistics. Educ: Dr.rer.nat., Univ. of Vienna, Austria, 1941. Appts. incl: Full Prof., Univ. of Hamburg, German Fed Repub., 1956-61; Rsch. Prof., Adolph C. & Mary Sprague Mille Inst. for Basic Rsch., Univ. of Calif., Berkeley, U.S.A., 1959; Full Prof., Maths., Univ. of Vienna, 1961-71; Vis. Prof., Cath Univ. of Am., Wash. D.C., 1962-63; Vis. Prof., Technion, Haifa, 1966-67; Assoc. Prof., Univ. de Clermont-Ferrand, 1967 & 1968-69; Full Prof., Statistics, & Hon. Prof., Maths., Univ. of Vienna, 1971-; Vis. Prof., Univ. of Bowling Green. Ohio, U.S.A., 1973. Mbrships. incl: Fellow, Inst. of Math. Statistics, 1961; Fellow, Am. Statistical Assn., 1973; Austrian Acad. of Scis.; Deutsche Akademie der Naturforscher Leopoldina; V.P., Int. Statistical Inst., 1967-71; Am. Math. Soc.; Deutsche Math. Verein; Ostereischische Math. Gesellschaft. Author of books & about 60 papers in field. Hons: Förderungspreis, Vienna, 1952, Dr.h.c., Univ. de Clermont-Ferrand, 1972. Address: Rennweg 45, 1030 Vienna, Austria. 43, 86.

SCHMID, Frédéric Charles, b. 1 Aug. 1892. University Professor; Institutional Administrator. Educ: Dr. of Med. Appts: House Physn.; Lectr.; Titular Prof.; currently Hon. Prof., Hon. Medecin-Commandant. Hon. Mbrships: Assn. int. des Pharmacologistes; Union Int. de Thérapeutique; Soc. Franc. Thérapeutique & Pharmacondynamie; Union Fédperative des Médecin de Réserve; Soc. d'Hydrologie de Paris; Ancien Président de la Soc. de Médecine de Strasbourg; Ancien Président du Club Universitaire. Publs. incl. books on Renal Physiol. & Pathol., Diabetes, Alkali-Reserve, Insulin, Morphine & other stupefactive drugs. Hons: Officer of the Legion of Honour; Officer of Palmes Academiques; Medal of Resistance; Cross of Combatants, 1914-18 & 1939-45; Cross of Voluntary Mil. Serv. Address: 16 Ave. du Général de Gaulle, 67000 Strasbourg, France.

SCHMID, Josef, b. 14 Feb. 1919. University Professor. Educ: Med. Fac., Univ. of Vienna, Austria. Appts: Asst. Prof., Univ. of Vienna; Specialist, Internal Med. Mbrships: Med. Soc., Vienna; Soc. Internal Med. of Vienna; Pres., Int. Soc. for Prospective Med. Publs: Die Blutgerinnung in Theorie & Praxis, 1951; Klinik & Therpie des Chron. Gelenksrheumatismus, 1954; Neuraltherapie, 1960; Approx. 200 publs. on blood coagulation, rheumatic diseases, neuraltherapy &, during the last 10 yrs., on computer med. Address: Walfischgasse 10, Vienna 1010, Austria.

SCHMIDEBERG, Melitta, b. 17 Jan. 1910. Psychiatrist; Criminologist. Educ: M.D., Friedrich Wilhelm Univ., Berlin, Germany. Appts: Trng. Analyst, Brit. Psychoanal. Soc., U.K., 1936-49; Physn., London Clin. of Psychoanal., 1933-49; Psych., Int. for Sci. Treatment of Delinquency, 1933-49; Co-Fndr. & Dir., Clin. Servs., N.Y. Chapt., Assn. for Psych. Treatment of Offenders, 1951; Prof., Psych., Adelphi Univ., N.Y., 1949-51; Ed., Int. Jrnl. of Offender Therapy & Comparative Criminol., 1967-. Fellowships: Fndr., Royal Coll. Psych.; Corres., Am. Psych. Assn.; Hon., Am. Sect., Int. Assn. Penal Law. Int. Pres., Assn. for Psych. Treatment of Offenders. Publs: Children in Need, 1948; Short Analytic Therapy, 1950; over 100 articles in field. Address: 199 Gloucester Place, London NW1 6BU, U.K. 5, 14, 15, 28, 138.

SCHMIDT, (Carl Oscar) Torsten Måtte, b. 5 Apr. 1909. Managing Director. Educ: LL.B. degree. Appts: Sect. Hd., Civil Defence Bd., Sweden, 1938-44; Mng. Dir., Stockholm Assn. of Retail Grocers, 1944-46; Mng. Dir., Swedish Booksellers' Assn., Swedish Stationers' Assn., & Swedish Music Dealers' Assn., 1947-74. Mbrships: Coun., Strindberg Soc., 1948-, Sec., 1954-60; Treas., Idun Soc., 1961-68; Coun., Bellmans Minne Soc.; Pres., Coun., Bellman Mus.; Sveriges Författarförbund & Publicistklubben; Sållskapet Club. Publs: Bockerna - Kultur till Bruttopris. 1963; Strindbergs Måleri, 1972; sev. articles & reviews. Hons: Gold Medal, Swedish Civil Defence Union, 1943; Medal, Finnish Civil Defence, 1943; Gold Medal, Swedish Retailers' Assn., 1958; Off., Order of Acad. Palms, 1965; Medal, Royal Patriotic Soc., 1973; Medal, Royal Swedish Pro Patria Soc., 1973. Address: Grev Turegatan 76 n.b., 114 38 Stockholm, Sweden.

SCHMIDT, Frederick Lee, b. 11 Dec. 1937. Artist; Painter. Educ: B.A., Colo. State Coll., Greeley; M.A., Univ. of Iowa; M.F.A., ibid. Appts: Asst. Prof. of Art, Northwestern Coll., Iowa, 1968-70, Western Carolina Univ., N.C., 1970-72, Va. Polytechnic Inst. & State Univ., Blacksburg, 1972-. Mbr., Nat. Coll. Art Assn. Paintings, Landscape, figure, imaginative, in acrylic & oils. Drawings, human figure, charcoal, pencil, pastels & crayon. Solo Exhibs. incl: Unity Coll., Me.; Marshfield Ctr., Univ. of Wis. Grp. Exhibs. incl: Kan. State Coll.; Western Carolina Univ.; Mint Mus. of Art, Charlotte, N.C.; Gall. of Contemporary Art, Winston-Salem, N.C. Hons. incl: Purchase Award, Roanoke Area Artists; Cash Prize, Lynchburg Arts Festival; grants & schlrships. Address: 410 Hampton Ct., Blacksburg, VA 24060, U.S.A. 37.

SCHMIDT, Gerhard Johann, b. 25 June 1902. University Professor. Educ: Univs. of Berlin, Munich, Freiburg, Germany; Univ. of N.Y.; Doct., Univ. of Berlin. Appts: Nat. Bureau of Statistics, Berlin, Germany; Ptnr., Isr. Schmidt Söhne, Berlin-Frankfurt; Instr., Bergen Jr. Coll., Teaneck, N.J., U.S.A.; Asst. Prof.-Prof. Emeritus, Fairleigh Dickinson Univ., Teaneck, N.J. Mbrships: Assoc. Academico, Academia Tiberina, Rome, Italy; Am. Coun. for Emigrés in the Professions; Am Economic Assn.; AAUP. Publs: Der Konstante Geldwert von Oreimius bis Knapp: an Introduction into the History, Theory & Administration of Money. Contbr. to var. mags. in 13 countries. Hons: Community Leader of America. Address: 212 W. 91st St., N.Y., NY 10024, U.S.A. 6, 14, 15, 28, 128, 130, 131.

SCHMIDT, Lowell H., b. 18 Aug. 1911. Lawyer. Educ: J.D., Univ. of S.D., 1933. Appts: Pvte. Prac., 1933-34; Atty., Standard Oil, 1943-53; States Atty., 1934-38; Mayor, City of Huron, S.D., 1965-69; Admnstr., Huron Clin., S.D., 1953-69; Commnr. of Rev., 1969-73, now ret. Mbrships: Pres., Sertoma Int., 1962-63; Delta Theta Phi; State Bar of S.D.; Republican Party. Publs: 'The Case for a Tax Court', S.D. Bar Jrnl.:'Freedom Why', Congressional Record & Vital Speeches, 1962. Recip. of Bronze Freedom Medal. Address: Rte. 1-Box 179A, Rimrock Rd., Rapid City, SD 57701, U.S.A. 8, 22.

SCHMIDT, Robert Oliver, Jr., b. 6 June 1918. Clergyman; Mission Director. Educ: Southwestern Coll., Winfield, Kan.; B.D., Bible Bapt. Sem., Ft. Worth, Tex., 1947; Master of Theol., ibid, 1953; Alliance Française, Paris. Appts. incl: Pastor, chs. in Tex., Kan. & Colo.; Tchr., European Bible Inst.; Prof. of Missions,

Bible Bapt. Sem., Arlington, Tex., 6 yrs.; Missionary, France, 7 yrs.; Dir. of Missions, World Bapt. Fellowship Mission Agcy., Arlington, Tex., 1962-; Ed., Reapers Report, Hons: D.D., Seminario Biblia Batista, Benevides, Para, Brazil, 1972, Bapt, Theol. Sem., Madrid, 1974. Address: P.O. Box 1345, Arlington, TX, U.S.A.

SCHMIDT, Roland, b. 12 Sept. 1917. Painter; Designer; Art Lecturer. Educ: Var. art courses. Appts. as commercial artist, free-lance graphic artist, painter, illustrator, interior decorator, restorer, art tchr., jrnlst., critic, lectr., etc. Mbrships: Berufsverband Bildender Künstler, Koblenz; Confedn. Int. des assoc. d'artistes, Brussels; Deutsch-italienische Künstlergemeinschaft, Turin; Rothenburger Künstlerbund e.V.; Hon. mbr., Accademia int., Rome; Kunstforum & Galerie Pavl, Garmisch-Partenk; Südpfälzische Kunstgilde e.V., Bad Bergzabern. Pvte. Publs: Ins Land Italia, 1952; An sonnigen Ufern, 1962; R. Schmidt überregional, 1967; R. Schmidt mit Jubiläen, 1970. Hons: Silver medal & dip. of hon., 1971; Gold medal & dip. of hon., 1972; Entered in golden book, 1972; Silver medal & dip. of Hon., 1973. Address: Schwegenheimer Weg 61a, 672 Speyer, German Fed. Repub. 19.

SCHMIDT, Werner, b. 18 Apr. 1896. Professor of Biology. Educ: Dr. phil., Königsberg Univ. Germany, 1924; Forest Coll., Eberswalde. Appts: Lectr., 1925; Prof. & Dir. of Inst. of forest seed & genetics rsch., Forest Coll., Eberswalde, 1926; Prof. (emeritus), Univ. of Hamburg & Fndr., Biol. diagnostic Inst., 1945-. Mbrships: A.A.A.S.; Biometric Soc.; Assn. of Applied Bot.; Int. Union of Forest rsch. Orgs. (Pres., Int. seed Commn., 1936). Publs. incl.: Forest Tree Seed, 1930; Early diagnosis in breeding work, issues of Der Zuchter (Ed.), 1957, '63; Design & analysis of data in Biological, Medical, Psychological & Economical Research, 1961; contbr. to num. profl. publs. Holder of patents in forest tree breeding. Recip. of Royal Rumanian Order of Cultural Merit, 1940. Address: 205 Hamburg 80, Glindersweg 72, German Fed. Repub. 43, 92.

SCHMIDTBOCHUM, Erich, b. 30 Nov. 1913. Sculptor. Educ: Sculptor Trainee; Arts & Crafts Schl., Dortmund, Germany. 3. yrs. practical work as cooperator. Mbrships: Fed. Creative Artists of Germany; Int. Cultural Ctr., Amsterdam, Netherlands. Studio & since 1974 open air mus. attached to home inclng. "!n the early morning", "Tragic of life", "Old miner", "Peer Gynt". Major works incl: Nathan der Weise, Lessing Haus, Wolfenbüttel; Miners Bundesknappschaft, Bochum; Der Hoffende Sanatorium Seesen; Miner Lengede; Versuchsschmelzer Edelstahlver, Düsseldorf; Super size relief, Fight with the Bison-Bull, Lebenstedt; Portrait of Duchess Victoria Luise. Recip., Matthias Claudius Medal, 1961. Address: Friedrich-Wilhelm Sr. 2 c, 334 Wolfenbüttel, German Fed Repub. 43, 133.

SCHMITH, Poul, b. 27 June 1916. Barrister. Educ: Grad., Univ. of Copenhagen, Denmark, 1940; Admitted to Bar, 1943. Appts: Legal Advsr., Counsel, Danish Govt. Depts., 1965; Barrister, Supreme Ct. of Denmark; Bd. Mbr., Kryolitselskabet Oresund A/S, 1965; Bd. Mbr., Nestlé Nordisk A/S, 1969, Chmn., 1972; Bd. Mbr., Det Classenske Fideicommis, 1970; Bd. Mbr., Nordisk Fjerfabrik A/S, 1971, Chmn. & bd. mbr., affiliated cos., 1972; Bd. Mbr., Dansk Naturgas A/S, 1971, Chmn., 1973; Bd. Mbr., Nordisk Mineselskab A/S & Arktisk Minekompagni A/S. 1973. Address:

Vimmelskaftet 47, 1161 Copenhagen K, Denmark. 43.

SCHMITHÜSEN, Gerhard Franz Josef, b. 30 Jan. 1909. Professor of Geography. Educ: Dr.Phil., Univ. of Bonn, Germany. Appts: Prof., Geography, Univ. of Saarland, Saarbrücken, 1962-; Dir., Geog. Inst., ibid; Ed.-in-chief, Biogeographica. Publs: Das Luxemburger Land, 1940; Allgemeine Vegetationsgeographie, 1959, 3rd edit. 1968; Geschichte der geographischen Wissenschaft, 1970. Address: Mecklenburgring 31, 66 Saarbrücken, German Fed. Repub. 43, 92.

SCHMITT, Charles Rudolph, b. 31 Mar. 1920. Chemist. Educ: B.S., Queens Coll., Flushing, N.Y., 1942; grad. studies, Univ. of Tenn., Knoxville. Appts: Supvsr., TNT Prod., Plum Brook Ordnance Wks., Sandusky, Ohio, 1942-43; Dev. Engr., K-25 Uranium Gaseous Diffusion Plant, Nuclear Div., Union Carbide Corp., Oak Ridge, Tenn., 1945-46; Dev. Chemist, Y-12 Plant, ibid, 1956-65, Sr. Rsch. Chemist, 1965-68, Dev. Specialist & Supvsr., 1968-. Mbrships. incl: Am. Chem. Soc.; Tenn. Acad. of Sci.; Nat. Soc. Profl. Engrs.; Nat. Assn. Corrosion Engrs. Over 200 scientific & tech. reports, Union Carbide Corp. & U.S. Atomic Energy Commn.; many tech. articles, U.S. & int. profl. jrnls. Awarded 12 U.S. Patents, assigned to Atomic Energy Commn. Hons. incl: Manhattan Dist. Special Award, U.S. War Dept., 1945; Indl. Rsch. Products Award, 1974. Address: 110 Montana Ave, Oak Ridge, TN 37830, U.S.A. 7, 125.

SCHMITT, Patricia Jean (Mrs. Nobert T. Schmitt), b. 15 Nov. 1940. Elementary Education. Educ: A.A., Auburn Community Coll., N.Y., 1960; B.S., State Univ. Coll. at Cortland, ibid, 1962; M.S. in Ed., Syracuse Univ., 1966. Appts: Elem. Team Tchr., Union Springs Ctrl. Schl. Dist., N.Y., 1962-67. Mbrships: Pres., 1962-69. Sec., 1971-73. Hon. Lifetime Trustee, Union Springs Ctrl. Schl. Alumni Assn.; Treas., 1968-70, Instant Aid Emergency Vehicle Serv.: Trust., 1962-67, Auburn Community Coll. Alumni Assn.; Nat. Vocational Guidance Assn.; Am. Personnel & Guidance Assn.; N.Y. State Personnel & Guidance Assn.; Co-ldr., Auburn Grp., LaLeChe League Int.; Trustee Hazard Pub. Lib., Poplar Ridge, N.Y., 1974-; Tchr., Sunday Schl., Our Lady of the Lake Ch., King Ferry; Moravia Car Club, 1969-73. Address: R.D., Aurora, NY 13026, U.S.A. 5, 129, 132.

SCHMITZ, Charles Edison, b. 18 July 1919. Clergyman. Educ: Wheaton Coll.; B.A., Wartburg Coll., 1940; B.D., Wartburg Theol. Sem., 1942; Mich. State Univ. Appts. incl: Home Mission Devr. & Parish Pastor, Am. Luth. Ch., 1942-65; Fndng. Pastor, 9 parishes inclng. Ascension Luth. Ch., L.A., 1942-48, Am. Evang. Luth., Phoenix, Ariz., etc.; Fndr. & Former Prin., Parochial Schls., L.A. & Phoenix; Dir., Intermtn. Missions (Ariz., N.M., Utah, Nev.), & Parish Pastor. Phoenix, Ariz., 1948-65; Staff Evangelist, Am. Luth. Ch., Mpls., Minn., 1965-73; Pastor, Peace Luth. Ch., Palm Bay, Fla., 1973-. Mbrships. incl: Dir., Parish Mission Bldr. Prog.; Former Chmn., Bd. Mbr., Ariz. Christian Cong., Christian Inst. Min., Camelback Girls Res., Ariz. Alcohol & Narcotics Edn. Assn., Phoenix Coun. of Chs. & Evang. Mins. Assn.; chmn., Nat. Luth. Soc. Welfare Conf., 1944-; etc. Co-Ed: The ABC's of Life. Ed: Body of Christ - Evangelism for the Seventies. Contbng. Ed: Good News mag., 1965-73. Hons. incl: Disting. Alumni Award, Wartburg Coll., 1959. Address: 301 S.E. Port Malabar Boulevard, Palm Bay, FL 32905, U.S.A. 7, 8.

SCHMITZ, T.J., b. 3 Oct. 1941. Executive Director. Educ: Grad., Univ. of Wis., Whitewater; Further study, Northwestern Univ., Univ. of Wis., Green Bay, Univ. of Northern Colo. & Univ. of Wis., Milwaukee. Int. HQ Staff, Tau Kappa Epsilon Int. Fraternity, 4 yrs.; Exec. Dir., ibid, 1973-. Mbrships. incl: Life mbr., NEA; Pres., Iola Scandinavia Educ. Assn., 1964-65, 1965-66; Exec. Comm., & Chmn., Constitution-Legislation Comm., Hamilton Educ. Assn., 1967-69; Dir., Indpls. Northwest Lions Club, 1972-73; Prog. Chmb., ibid, 1972-73; Sec., 1973-74; Deleg., Ind. Lions Conven., 1973; Republican Vice-Precinct Committeeman, 1972-73; Mayor's Speakers Task Force, 1971; Republican Candidate Selection Comm., 1972; Wayne Twp. Finance Chmn., 1970-72; Ops. Comm., Greater Indpls. Republican Finance Comm.; Dir., Eagle Creek GOP Club, Inc., 1973-74; Dir., Ind. Chapt., Am. Soc. for Trng. & Dev.; 1971; Am. Soc. of Assn. Execs. Hons. incl: Award of Excellence, presented by Mayor Richard Lugar, 1972; Outstanding Performance Award, Greater Indpls. Finance Comm., 1972. Address: 3502 N. Rybolt Ave., Indpls., IN 46222, U.S.A.

SCHMUCKER, Hannes, b. 6 Apr. 1899. Painter. Educ: Acad. of Arts, Munich, Germany. Mbrships. incl: Neue Muchner Kunstler Assn.; Seerose Munich; Int. Arts Guild, Monte Carlo; Juries of sev. exhibs. Paintings shown at exhibs. in Munich, Berlin, Bremen, Lindau, Frankfurt, Heilbrunn, Giessen, Marburg, & other German towns, Paris, France, & Belgrade, Yugoslavia. Represented in num. museums & collects., inclng. Munich, Hamburg, Konigsberg, Frankfurt. Main critical appreciation of his work: Der Maler Hannes Schmucker, by W. Romstoeck, 1967, & in Les Arts en Europe, Vol I, Collect. Art du XX Siécle, 1973. Address: 63 Giessen, Johannesberg 21, German Federal Repub.

SCHMULLER, Aaron, b. 27 May 1910. Company Director. Educ: CCNY. Appts. as small businessman & publisher, author, poet & translator; Currently Dir., Parthenon Publishing Co. Mbrships: Poetry Soc. of Am.; Am. Poetry League. Publs: Man in the Mirror; Moments of Meditation; Treblinka Grass; Crossing the Borderland; Legend of His Lyre; Tokens of Devotion; While Man Exists; Triumphalis; Co-ed., 2 anthols. of poetry, The Muse Anthology of Poetry, & The Singing Muse Anthology; Poems & groups of poems publd. in 140 mags., anthols. & newspapers. Publd. vols highly praised by competent critics inclng. Alfred Kreymborg, Alfred Dorn, Alice MacKenzie Swaim. Address: Parthenon Publishing Co., 9227 Kaufman Pl., Brooklyn, NY 11236, U.S.A. 2, 6, 11, 30.

SCHMUNK, Donald Fred, b. 9 Mar. 1937. Physicist. Educ: B.S., Portland State Coll., Oregon, U.S.A., 1959; M.S., Oregon State Univ., 1961; Postgrad., Univ. of Southern Calif., 1962; Univ. of Calif., L.A., 1967. Appts: Tech. Staff, Pacific Semiconductors Inc., Lawndale, Calif., L.A., 1967. Appts: Tech. Staff, Pacific Semiconductors Inc., Lawndale, Calif., 1961-64; Tech. Staff, TRW Systems, Redondo Beach, Calif., 1964-66; Mgr., Rsch., TRW Semiconductors, Lawndale, 1966-67; Grp. Sci., Supvsr., Solid State Materials Studies, Autonetics Div.-Mgr., Advanced Dev., Microelectronics Div., Rockwell North Am. & Int., Anaheim, Calif., 1967-. Mbrships: IEEE; Am. Vacuum Soc. (Tech. Chmn., Thin Film Sect., 1968, 1969); Orange Co. Amateur Astronomers Assn.; IEEE Computer Soc. Author many papers for symposia in field. Address: 3245 East Greenleaf Dr., Brea, CA 92621, U.S.A. 9, 57, 59, 69, 74, 131, 139.

SCHMUTZHART, Berthold, b. 17 Aug. 1928. Sculptor; Educator. Educ: Acad. Applied Arts, Vienna, Austria. Appts: Assoc. Prof. of Art, Corcoran Schl. of Art, Wash.D.C. Mbrships: Chapt. Pres., Artists Equity Assn., Wash.D.C.; Guild for Religious Arch., AIA; AAUP; Nat. Sci. Tchrs. Assn. Sculptures incl: 2 figures of Christ, St. James, Capitol Hill, Wash.D.C.; Steel Statue of Christ, St. Clements, Detroit, Mich.; Bacchus Fountain, Gall. of Mod. Art, Fredericksburg, Va. Sculptures, over 200 pvte. collects. Hons. incl: 1st Prize, Wash. Religious Arts Festival, 1960; 1st Prize, Southern Sculpture, Little Rock, Ark., 1965; Silver Medal, Audubon Soc., 1971. Address: 1011 E. Capitol St., Washington, DC 20003, U.S.A. 37.

SCHNACK, George Ferdinand, b. 17 June 1917. Physician; Psychiatrist. Educ: A.B., Stanford Univ., Calif., U.S.A., 1939; A.M., ibid, 1940; M.D., Schl. of Med., Johns Hopkins Univ., Balt., Md., 1951; Psychoanalytic Clin., Columbia Univ., N.Y.C., 1953-58. Appts. incl: Pvte. Prac., Adult & Child Psych., N.Y.C., 1955-59, Honolulu, 1960-; Psych. Cons., Peace Corps Trng. Proj., Hilo, Hawaii, 1962-, & Molokai, Hawaii, 1966-68; Lectr., Soc. Work, 1965-71; Clin. Prof., Pub. Hlth., Univ. of Hawai Med. Schl., 1966-; Clin. Assoc. Prof., Psych., ibid, 1968-. Mbrships. incl: Chmn., sev. comms., & Fellow, Am. Psych. Assn.; Fellow, Am. Coll. of Psychs.; Fellow, Australia & N.Z. Coll. of Psychs.; AMA; AAAS; Pres., Big Brothers of Hawaii, Inc., 1972-74; Pres., Palama Settlement, 1974-; Phi Beta Kappa. Recip., Big Brothers of Hawaii Award, 1971. Address: P.O.Box 5263, Honolulu, HI 96814, U.S.A. 9, 14, 17, 28, 78, 120, 131.

SCHNASE, Annemarie Charlotte Rischke (Mrs.), b. 1 May 1905. Antiquarian Bookseller & Publisher. Appts: Apprentice, Paul Gottschalk, Berlin, Germany, 1922-24; Antiquarian Bookseller, ibid, 1925-32; Owner of Co., Annemarie Schnase, Berlin-Spandau, 1950-56; Owner of Co., Annemarie Schnase, Scarsdale, N.Y., U.S.A., 1956-. Mbrships: Am. Musicolog. Soc.; Int. Musicolog. Soc.; Int. Assn. Music Libs.; Int. League of Antiquarian Booksellers; Antiquarian Booksellers Assn. of Am.; Verband Deutscher Antiquare e. V. Recip. of Bronze Medal, N.Y. Pub. Lib., 1961. Address: Scarsdale, NY 10583, U.S.A. 5.

SCHNEIDER, Betty Vance Humphreys (Mrs. Jerome C. Schneider), b. 3 Dec. 1927. Research Economist; Lecturer. Educ: A.B., Univ. of Calif. at Berkeley, 1949; Ph.D., London Univ., 1954. Appts: Rsch. Econ., Inst. of Indl. Rels., Univ. of Calif., Berkeley, 1954-; Lectr., Labour Econs., Mills Coll., Oakland, Calif., 1968-; Dir., Calif. Pub. Employee Rels. Rsch. & Publs. Prog., 1969-. Mbrships: Indl. Rels. Rsch. Assn.; Soc. of Profls. in Dispute Resolution; Phi Beta Kappa. Publs: Clerical Unions in the Civil Service, 1958; Num. articles in U.S., U.K. jrnls., monographs & book chapts; Ed., var. bulletins, & Labor & Management in Industrial Society by Clark Kerr, 1964. Hons: Kennard Prize in Jrnlsm., Univ. of Calif., 1949; Sigma Delta Chi Prize in Jrnlsm., 1949. Address: Inst. of Indl. Rels., Univ. of Calif. Berkeley, CA 94720, U.S.A. 3.

SCHNEIDER, Franz Josef Michael, b. 13 Dec. 1909. Lawyer. Educ: LL.D., Univ. of Vienna; Bar Exam., 1936. Appts: Lawyer, 1946-; Mbr., Examining Bd., Vienna Univ.; Mbr., Supreme Ct. for Disciplinary Matters of Lawyers & Lawyers' Assts.; Pres. of Bd., Europa Carton AG, Gazelle AG, Streumpfe und Waesche & Dr. August Serrat & Co. AG; on Bd. of Dirs., Neusiedler Wiener Wellpappe G.m.b.H., AESCA Chemisch-pharmazeutische Fabrik G.m.b.H. & Julius Meinl AG. Mbrships: Pres., Vienna Law Soc. & Austro-Brit. Soc.; V.P., Assn. for Comparative Law; Austrian Commn. of Jurists; Union Int. des Avocats; Int. Law Soc. Contbr. articles to legal periodicals & legal text books. Hons: O.B.E. Address: Stephansplatz 8A, A-1010 Vienna, Austria. 43, 86.

SCHNEIDER, George William, b. 4 Apr. 1916. Educator. Educ: B.S., Ohio State Univ., 1938; M.S., ibid, 1939; Ph.D., Rutgers Univ., 1950. Appts. incl: Asst. Prof., New Mexico State Univ., 1939-46; Asst. Prof., Rutgers Univ., 1946-50; Assoc. Prof. & Prof., N.C. State Univ., 1950-58; Prof. & Dept. Chmn., Univ. of Ky., 1958-60; Assoc. Dir., Coop. Univ. of Ky., 1960-69; Prof., Univ. of Ky., 1969-. Mbrships: Fellow, AAAS, 1972; Am. Soc. Horticultural Sci., Pomol. Chmn.; Am. Inst. Bioll. Sci.; Am. Pomoll. Soc.; Bot. Soc. Am.; Gamma Sigma Delta; Sigma Xi; Epsilon Sigma Phi. Publs. incl: Fruit Growing, 1960, Spanish translation, 1961. Address: Horticulture Dept., Univ. of Ky., Lexington, KY 40506, U.S.A. 2, 7, 14, 15, 125.

SCHNEIDER, Urs, b. 16 May 1939. Conductor. Educ: Dip., Zurich Conservatory & Acad. of Music, Switzerland, 1961. Appts: Fndr. & Conductor, Pro Musica Orch., 1955-63; Fndr., Ostschweizer Chmbr. Orch., 1962; Musical Dir., St. Moritz Summer Symph. Orch., 1964-66; Permanent Conductor, Camerata Suttgart, 1967-; Chief Conductor, Samerata Academica Salzburg, 1971-73; Artistic Dir., Musiksommer Weggis Festival & Kunstwochen Lenk Festival, Switzerland. Guest conductor, inclng. operas, radio concerts, & making records, over 50 major orchs, Europe, U.S.A., & S. Am. Hons: Kulturpreis, Town of St. Gallen, 1967; Master of Fine Arts Int., 1969. Address: Gatterstrasse 1B, 9010 St. Gallen, Switzerland.

SCHNEIDER, William George, b. 1 June 1915. Scientist. Educ: B.Sc., Sask., Canada, 1937; M.Sc., ibid, 1939; Ph.D., McGill, 1941. Appts: Rsch. Physicist, Woods Hole, Mass., 1943-46; Hd., Phys. Chem. Sect., Div. of Pure Chem., Nat. Rsch. Coun. of Canada, 1946; Dir., Div. of Pure Chem., ibid, 1963; V.P., (Sci.), 1965; Pres., 1967-. Fellowships: Chem. Inst. of Canada; Royal Soc. of Canada; Royal Soc. of London. Mbrships: Am. Chem. Soc.; Am. Phys. Soc. Co-author, High Resolution Nuclear Magnetic Resonance, 1959 & author of 120 sci. papers. Hons: Chem. Inst. of Canada Medal, 1961; Henry Marshall Tory Medal, Royal Soc. of Canada, 1969; Montreal Medal, Chem. Inst. of Canada, 1973. Address: Nat. Rsch. Coun. of Canada, Ottawa, Ont. K1A 0R6, Canada. 1, 34.

SCHNOHR, Edgar, b. 15 Aug. 1900. Surgeon. Educ: M.D., Univ. of Copenhagen, Denmark, 1927. Appts: Registrar & Cons. Surg., gynecol., obstetrical & radiol. depts., hosps., Copenhagen & the provinces; Study tours to var. for. hosps.; Chief Surg., Finnish camp hosp., Finnish-Russian war, 1939-40; Chief obstetrician; Rigshospitalets Maternity ward, Copenhagen, 1943; Chief Surg., surg. outpatient dept, Sundby Hosp., ibid; Cons., pvte. surg. clin., 1970-. Mbrships: Inst. Soc. Surg.; French Assn. Surg.; Danish Assn. Surg.; Northern Surg. Assn.; Danish Assn. Gyn. & Ob.; Danish Soc. Bio.; Southern & Western Swedish Socs. Gyn. & Ob.; La Confrerie des Chevaliers du Tastevin. Contbr. of num. articles to profl. jrnls. Hons. incl: Kt. of Dannebrog, 1958; Finnish Cross of Freedom, 1940. Address: Gothersgade 103, 1123 Copenhagen K, Denmark. 43.

SCHNURMANN, Erika. Librarian. Educ: A.M., Pembroke Coll., Brown Univ., R.I., 1937; M.L.S., Grad. Schl. of Lib. Sci., Columbia Univ., N.Y., 1947; Simmons Coll. Schl. of Publs., Boston, Mass., 1938. Appts. incl: Hd., P.R. & Order Dept., Paterson Pub. Lib., 1961-62; Dir.-Cons., Wayne Pub. Lib., 1960-64; Dir., Hawthorne Pub. Lib., 1966-68; Dir., Little Falls Pub. Lib., 1968-69; Dir., Kearny Pub. Lib., 1969-; Cons. to var. other N.J. Libs.; Assoc. Book Reviewer, Paterson Morning Call, 1955-57. Mbrships: Sec., Prog. Chmn., Coun. Serv. Clubs, 1960-62; V.P., Paterson Br., AAUW; Paterson Br., Nat. League Am. Pen Women; Past Pres., Bergen-Passaic Co. Lib. Club; Past Treas., N.J. Lib. Assn.; Charter Mbr., Lib. P.R. Coun.; ALA; Pres., Hudson Co. Lib. Assn., 1972-74; Arlington Women's Club; Past Pres., Passaic Co. Hlth. Educ. & Welfare Assn.; Bus. & Prof. Div., Little Falls Women's Club; W. Hudson-S. Bergen Chmbr. of Comm.; Chaucer Guild. Contbr. of articles to profl. jrnls. & papers. Winner, Preston Gurney Lit. Prize, Pembroke Coll., 1937. Address: 335 Sylvan St., Rutherford, NJ 07070, U.S.A. 5, 6, 22, 42, 57.

SCHOCK, William Wallace, b. 15 Aug. 1923. Physician (Pediatrics). Educ: Juniata Coll., Huntingdon, Pa., 1941-43; Temple Univ. Schl. of Med., 1947. Appts. incl: Pediatrician, Warren AFB Hosp.; Chief, Out Patients Serv., USAF, Cheyenne, Wyo., 1951-52; Local Pub. Hlth. Pediatrician; Pediatrician, J.C. Blair Meml. Hosp. Fellow, Royal Soc. of Hlth. Mbrships: Pres., Huntingdon Chapt., Am. Cancer Soc., 1955-57; Bd. Dirs., Local Chapt., Am. Heart Assn., 1955-62; Past Pres., Huntingdon Co. Med. Soc.; Wisdom Hall of Fame, 1970. Hons: Wisdom Award, 1970; Community Ldr. Award, 1969; Address: 213 Standing Stone Ave., Huntingdon, PA 16652, U.S.A. 57.

SCHODER, (Rev.) Raymond V., S.J., b. 1916. University Professor of Classical Literature & Archeology. Educ: Milford Br., Xavier Univ., Cinn.; W. Baden Coll., Ind. (br. of Loyola Univ.); A.B., 1938; M.A., Loyola Univ., Chgo., 1940; Ph.D., St. Louis Univ., 1944; S.T.L., W. Baden Pontifical Univ., 1948; Ordained priest, 1947. Appts. incl: Tchr., W. Baden Coll., 1950-59; Tchr., Colombiere Coll., Univ. of Detroit, 1959-60; Prof., Loyola Univ., Chgo., 1960-; Fulbright Prof., Greek Art & Archeol Univ. of Nijmegen, Netherlands, 1956-57; Vis. Prof., Am. Schl. of Classical Studies, Athens, Greece, 1961-62, Sophia Univ., Tokyo, Japan, 1964; Dir., summer courses of Vergilian Soc.; Cumae, Italy, 8 summers since 1953. Mbrships. incl: Mng. Comm., Am. Schl. of Classical Studies, Athens; Archaeological Inst. of Am.; Am. Philological Assn.; Vergilian Soc.; Former Pres., Ind. Soc., Archaeological Inst. of Am. Publs. incl: Masterpieces of Greek Art (color photos & text, translated into 8 European langs.); Ancient Greece From The Air (photos & text), 1974; Num. articles in classical, theological & literary jrnls. in U.S.A. & abroad. Address: Loyola Univ., 6525 N. Sheridan Rd., Chgo., IL 60626, U.S.A. 13.

SCHOENBERG, B. Mark, b. 17 Aug. 1928. Psychologist. Educ: B.A., Tex. Technol. Univ., U.S.A., 1951; M.A., Houston Univ., 1963; Univ. Tex.-Austin, 1964; Ed.D., Houston Univ., 1969. Appts: w. Pennsalt Chem. Corp., Phila., Pa., 1951-53; w. Tunnell Publs., Trade Jrnls., Houston, Tex., 1953-54; w. L.O.F. Glass Fibers Co., Plastics, ibid, 1954-56; Houston Independent Schl. Dist., ibid, 1956-64; Dept. Educ., Govt. Guam, Agana, Guam, 1964-65; Dir. Counseling, S. Tex. Coll., Houston, Tex., U.S.A., 1965-69; Dir., Counseling Ctr., Nflnd. Mem. Univ., St. John's, Nflnd.; Profl. Dir., St.

John's Community Counselling Ctr., Nfld., 1969-. Mbr. num. profl. assns. Author articles in jrnls: Sensitivity to Others, 1970; A Speed Reading Primer for the University Student, 1971; Personal Characteristics of the Successful Counselor, 1971; Sex Education: Its Place in the Curriculum, 1972; Cat of a Different Breed (An Encounter in Human Sexuality), 1974. Recip. V.P.'s Grant, 1974. Address: Nflnd. Mem. Univ., Elizabeth Ave., St. John's, Nflnd., Canada, 57.

SCHOLES, Olive. Teacher. Tchr., mainly of Poetry & French, Oldham, London & Coventry, U.K., Paris, France, 41 yrs. Mbrships: Sec., Oldham Poetry Soc.; Quill Club; Leader of Wireless Discussion Grps. on Poetry, Coventry Pub. Libs.; Poetry Adjudicator at Midland Eisteddfodau. Contbr. of poetry to Nash's, Chambers' Jrnl., The Queen, Empire Review, The Lady, The Field, Country Life, Christian Science Sentinel & Jrnl., etc. Address: Treblok, St. Mawes, Truro, Cornwall, U.K. 3, 138.

SCHOLLE, Donald Williams. Investor. Educ: Dartmouth Coll., Hanover, N.H., 1959. Mbrships: Dartmouth Coll. Club; Regency Club; Union League Club; Ch. Club; Metropolitan Club; Eastern Yacht Club, Boston, Mass. Address: 176 East 77th St., N.Y., NY 10021, U.S.A.

SCHONFIELD, Hugh Joseph, b. 17 May 1901. Author. Educ: Univ. of Glasgow. Mbrships: Int. P.E.N.; Soc. of Authors; Past Chmn., H.G. Wells Soc.; Old Pauline Club; World Coun., Men of the Trees. Publs. incl: The Authentic New Testament; The Passover Plot; The Incredible Christians; Secrets of the Dead Sea Scrolls; The Politics of God; The Suez Canal in Peace and War. Recip. Doct. of Sacred Lit.. 1955. Address: 35 Hyde Park Sq., London W2 2NW, U.K. 3, 43, 128.

SCHÖNHERR, Max, b. 23 Nov. 1903. Conductor; Composer; Musician. Educ: Graz Conservatory, Austria; Dr.phil., Vienna, ibid, 1973. Appts: Bass Violinist, Choirmaster, Conductor, Stadttheatre, Graz, Austria; Conductor, Marishca-Britsrien Vollesoper, Vienna, ibid; Conductor, State Orch., Austrian Radio & Johan Strauss Orch., 1931-. Mbr. Assn. Drama Writers & Composers. Creative Works: Compositions for orch., Austrian peasant dances, the stage, ballet, opera, 1957; Deutselmeissterkapelle, an operetta, Vienna, 1958; Bombenwalser, an operetta, München, Germany, 1967; Orchestral arrangements of works of Spanish composers, Lelias, Hellmer-Berger u.a. Hon. mbr., Johan Straus Socs., G. Britain, Vienna & Paris. Address: Schubertstrasse 10, 2500 Baden bei, Vienna, Austria.

SCHOOLER, Bertha T., b. 29 Dec., 1886. Realtor. Educ: Brigham Young Univ., 1909-10; Boise State Univ., 1958-59. Appts: Legal Sec., 1914-15; Ada Co. Recorders Off., 1915-19; Jrnl. Clerk, Idaho State Legislature, 1919-20; Asst. Off. Mgr., State Insurance Fund, 1920-22; Idaho State Bd. of Educ., 1923-24; State Highway Dept., 1925-27; Dist. Organizer for Nat. Delphian Soc., 1927-50; Real Estate Brokerage, self-employed, 1957-. Mbrships: incl: Idaho & Nat. Bd. of Realtors; Charter Mbr. & Pres., John Regan Unit, Boise; Dept. Sec., Dept. VP, Dept. Pres., Nat. Comm. Woman & all State Chmnships., Rehabilitation & Child Welfare, Americanism etc.; Altrusa Int.; Idaho State Fedn. Repub. Women; Pres., PR Chmn., Finance Chmn., Deleg. at Large, Ada Co. Club; Alpha Xi Delta; Chmn., Citizens Comm. in Dev. Boise Jr. Coll.; Am. Legion Aux. Hons: Award for Mbrship., Am. Legion Aux., 1927;

Victory Award, Nat. Fedn. Repub. Women, 1970. Address; 819 E.Bannock St., Boise, ID 83702, U.S.A. 130.

SCHOPPMEYER, Martin W., b. 15 Sept. 1929. Professor of Education. Educ: B.S., Fordham Univ., N.Y., U.S.A., 1950; M.Ed., Univ. of Fla., Gainesville., 1955; Ed.D., ibid, 1962. Appts: Tchr., Pub. Schl., Bevard Co., Fla., 1955-56; Tchr., Pub. Schls., Broward Co., Fla., 1956-59; Grad. Asst., Univ. of Fla., 1959-60; Instr., Coll. of Educ., ibid, 1960-62; Asst. Prof., 1962-63; Assoc. Prof., & Dir., Inst. for In-serv. Educ., Fla. Atlantic Univ., Boca Raton, 1963-65; Dir., Continuing Educ., ibid, 1965-67; Prof., Educ., 1965-68; Assoc. Prof., Educ. Admin., Univ. of Ark., Fayetteville, 1968-71; Prof., ibid, 1971-. Mbrships: Nat. Coun. on Educ. Profns. Dev., U.S. Off. of Educ., 1973-; Am. Assn. of Schl. Admnstrs.; Ark. Schl. Admnstrs. Assn.; Ark. Educl. Rsch. & Dev. Coun.; Phi Delta Kappa; Kappa Delta Pi; Phi Kappa Phi. Publs: Articles in profl. jrnls. Address: Coll. of Educ., GE 248, University of Arkansas, Fayetteville, AR 72701, U.S.A. 125, 141.

SCHOU, Helen Rée (Mrs. Holger Hoiriss Schou), b. 19 Apr. 1905. Sculptress. Educ: Studied w. Anne Marie Carl Nielsen, 1923-27; Royal Acad. of Art, Copenhagen, Denmark, 1928-33; Studied in Paris, Rome & Florence; Study tours to Morocco, Spain, etc. Mbrships. incl: Grants Comm. & Trustees of Eckersberg-Thorvaldsen Fndn., Denmark, 1959-; Art Soc. of Gentofte, 1960-; Acad. Coun., 1959-. Main works in bronze incl: Mother & Child, 1943 (Bellevue Pk. near beach); Jutland Mare w. Foal in the Field; Equestrian Statue of King Christian X, 1955 (Bispetorvet, Arhus, Jutland); The Jutland Stallion, 1969 (Randers, Jutland); Sev. portrait busts, inclng. C.L. David, Advocate of the Supreme Ct., 1939; Holger Gabrielsen, Actor, 1939 (The Royal Theatre & Theatre Mus., Copenhagen); E. Hauch, Prof., 1936 (The Nat. Hosp., Copenhagen). Hons: Kt. of the Dannebrog; The Agnes Lunn Prize, 1956. Address: Strandvejen 257, 2920 Charlottenlund, Denmark. 43, 134.

SCHOU, Mogens Abelin, b. 24 Nov. 1918. Professor; Research Director. Educ: Copenhagen Univ. Med. Schl., Denmark, 1944; Psych., Danish, Norwegian & Swedish Hosps.; Exptl. Biol., Copenhagen, N.Y. & Aarhus. Appts: Hd., Psychopharmacol. Rsch. Unit, Aarhus Univ. Psych. Inst., Denmark, 1956-; Assoc. Prof., Aarhus Univ., 1966-71; Prof., ibid, 1971-. Mbrships incl: Pres., Scandinavian Soc. for Biol. Psych., 1967-68; WHO Expert Grp. for Biochem. of Mental Disorders, 1968; Officer, Danish Psych. Assn.; Rsch. Comm., ibid, 1964-68; Panel, Int. Brain Rsch. Org., 1956-. Contbr. to publs. in field. Hons. incl: Alfred Benzon Prize, 1967; Ernst Carlsen Prize, 1968; Jt. Recip., 1st Prize, Anna Monika Stiftung, 1969 & Paul Martini Prize, Medizinisch Pharmaceuticsch Studienges. e. V. & Deutsche Ges. für Medizinische Dikumentation & Stat., 1969; Novo Prize, 1970. Address: Psychopharmacol. Rsch. Unit, Aarhus Univ. Psych. Inst., Statshopsitalet, 8240 Risskov, Denmark. 43.

SCHRATZ, Paul Richard, b. 1 Oct. 1915. Consultant; Writer. Educ: B.S., USN Acad., Annapolis, 1939; M.A., Boston Univ., Mass., 1961; Ph.D., Ohio State Univ., Columbus, 1966. Appts: Special Asst. to Dir., Politico-Mil. Policy Div., Off. of Chief of Naval Ops., 1951-54; Fac.(Acad. planning), Naval War Coll., 1959-61; Dept. of Defense & JCS Rep., U.S. Deleg., Disarmament Conf., Geneva,

Switzerland, 1963-64; Chief of Plans, Policy Planning Staff, Off. of Sec. of Defense/Int. Security Affairs, 1964-65; in Dept. of Political Affairs, Nat. War Coll., 1966-68; Dir., Int. Studies, Univ. of Mo., 1968-73; For. Affairs Specialist, Commn. on the Org. of the Govt. for Conduct of For. Policy, 1973-. Mbrships. incl: Int. Studies Assn.; V.P.; Am. Friends of Wilton Pk.; Adminstr., Wingspread Wilton Pk. Confs.; Life Mbr., USN Inst.; Mil. Ops. Rsch. Soc.; Arms Control Assn. Publs: History of the Naval War College, 1960; The Mediterranean & Southern Flank of NATO, 1969; Monthly Edit. Writer, Shipmate, 1946-; Contbr. to books & jrnls. Hons. incl: Mershon Fellow, Ohio State Univ., 1966; Wilton Pk. Fellowships, Steyning, Sussex, 1967 & 72. Address: c/o Commn. on the Org. of the Govt. for the Conduct of For. Policy, 2025 M St., N.W., Washington, DC 20506, U.S.A. 14.

SCHREIBER, Ann F. Executive Secretary & Administrative Assistant. Educ: Proviso H.S., Maywood, Ill. Appts: Sec. to Dir. of Engrng. Dept., Fred S. James & Co., Chgo., Ill., 1927-40; Passenger Dept. Asst. Agent, Santa Fe RR, ibid, 1940-44; Sec. to Assoc. Dir., Nat. Physns. Comm., 1944-49; Admnstry. Asst. to Congressman Edgar A. Jonas, Wash. D.C., 1950-54 & to Congressman John F. Baldwin of Calif., ibid, 1955-56; Exec. Sec. & Aide to Congressman Jerome R. Waldie of Calif., 1966-74; now ret. Mbrships: Congressional Staff Club; Calif. State Soc. Address: 8110 El Paseo Grande, La Jolla, CA 92037, U.S.A. 5, 57, 114.

SCHREIBER, Hermann, b. 4 May 1920. Writer. Educ: Dr. Phil., Univ. Vienna, Austria, 1944, thesis entitled Gerhart Hauptmann und das Irrationale. Appts: Ed., then Chief Ed., Geistiges Frankreich, weekly German/French mag., 1946-51; freelance writer & ed., 1951-. Mbrships: Austrian PEN-Club, Vienna; Soc. German Writers, Munich, Germany; Austrian Geographical Assn., Vienna. Author, Vanished Cities, Merchants, Pilgrims, Highwaymen; Teuton & Slave; The Oldest Profession; Paris, Biographie einer Weltstadt; Vom Experiment zum Erlfog; Schiffe und ihre Schicksale. Hons: Citation in Austrian State Prize; Named in Hons. List, German Youth Book Prize; nominated Prof. honoris causa thru' Austrian State Pres., 1968. Address: D-8000 Munich, Schleissheimerstrasse 274/VIII, German Fed. Repub. 3, 30.

SCHREITER, Johannes, b. 8 Mar. 1930. Artist; Graphic Artist. Educ: Werkkunstschule, Münster, German Fed. Repub., 1949-52; Hochschulinst. für Kunsterziehung & Univ. of Mainz, 1952-57; Hochschule für bildende Künste & Free Univ., W. Berlin, 1954. Appts: Dir., Abteilung Fläche, Staatliche Hochschule für Gestaltung, Bremen, 1960-63; Dir., free painting & graphic art dept., Staatliche Hochschule für bildende Künste, Frankfurt/Main, 1963-; Vice Chancellor, ibid, 1971-. Mbrships: Deutscher Künstlerbund, 1968-; Westdeutscher Künstlerbund, 1966-; Neue Darmstädter Sezession, 1968-; Co-Wkr., Kunst & Kirche, econ. jrnl. for art & arch., Linz/Danube, Marburg/Lahn, 1971-. Fndr. of technique, Brandcollage, 1958; Brandcollages & stained glass window designs publd. in num. books & art jrnls.; Num. pub. collects.; Glass window designs in contemporary & histl. bldgs., 1960-. Hons. incl: Title of Prof., Hessischer Kultusminister., 1967; Art Prize for exhibition of current European graphic art, Salzburg, 1974. Address: Rotkehlchenweg 7, D-607 Langen/Hessen, German Fed. Repub. 43, 92, 133.

SCHRIKKER, Anthony John, b. 9 May 1892. Diplomat. Educ: Univs. of Neuchatel & Amsterdam; Mil. trng.; Passed competitive exams. for consular serv., 1913 & 1915. Appts. incl: Consul Gen. & Commercial Counsellor, Düsseldorf, Germany, 1932-40, interned by Gestapo as hostage; Released to Switzerland, 1941, i/c of Dutch refugees; Consul Gen., British Zone, Hamburg, 1945-50; Min. Plenipotentiary & Emissary Extraordinary, Hd. of Diplomatic Mission, Ct. of Shah of Persia; Last mission of good will to the Far East, visiting authorities in India, Ceylon, Rangoon, Bangkok, Hongkong, Taiwan, Teheran, 1962. Mbrships. incl: Fndr. & Pres., Netherlands-Free China Fndn., 1961-67; V.P., Netherlands-Thailand Soc., 1961-67; V.P., Netherlands-Iran Soc., 1961-67; V.P., Netherlands-Irish Soc., 1961-67; Nederland in der Vreemde Soc.; Hon. Pres., var. Dutch socs. Author of num. publs. on econs. & pols. in jrnls. & newspapers. Hons. incl: Grand Cross, 1st Class, Order of Homayoun, Iran, 1954; Grand Cross, 1st Class, Order of the Brilliant Star, China. Address: "Petit Bellaria", Ave. de Sully 126, CH 1814 La Tour de Peilz, Switzerland. 12, 100.

SCHRIMPF, Hans Joachim, b. 28 Mar. 1927. University Professor. Educ: Studied at Univs. of Münster, Bonn & Sheffield, U.K., 1946-51; Dr.phil., Münster, German Fed. Repub., 1951; Inaugurated, Bonn, 1962. Appts: Lectr., Univ. of Bonn, 1962; Extraordinary Prof., Univ. of Münster, 1962-63; Full Prof. & Dir., German Inst., ibid; Fndr., Ruhr-Univ., Bochum; Dean, Philol. Fac., ibid, 1969-70; Vis. Prof., Univ. of Minn., U.S.A., 1964-65 & 1968-69, Japan, 1966; External Examiner, Chinese Univ. of Hong Kong, 1968-71. Mbrships: Assn. int. de langues et litt. germ.; Goethe-Gesellschaft, Weimar;, Bd. of D.i.r.s., Gerhart-Hauptmann-Gesellschaft, Berlin. Publs. incl: Lessing & Brecht. Von der Aufklärung auf dem Theater, 1965; Tragedy & Comedy in the Works of Heinrich von Kleist, 1966; Goethes Begriff der Weltliteratur, 1968 (also translated into Japanese); Karl Philipp Moritz: Andreas Hartknopf, 1968. Address: Askulapweg 5, 463 Bochum-Querenburg, German Fed. Repub. 43, 92.

SCHRÖDER, Hanning (Hans), b. 4 July 1896. Composer; Violist. Educ: Studied composition w. Julius Weismann & viola w. Gustav Havemann. Appts: Solo Violist, & Ldr., Chamber Music, Schauspielhaus Orch., Dusseldorf, Germany, 1924-25; Concert tours w. Havemann Quartet & Harlan Trio; First Violist w. sev. radio & film orchs. Mbrships: GEMA; German Sect., Int. Soc. for New Music; German Union of Composers & Musicilogist; Chamber Music Assn., Berlin; German Union of Music Teachers & Concert Artistes. Compositions incl: Klaviermusik 1950; 2 flute solo sonatas; Metronom 80 for solo violin; Divertimenti for wind instruments; String Quartet; Varianten for flute & orch.; Music for string orch.; Sev. song cycles; Cantatas & other choral music; Music for films. Recip., First Mention, Prince Rainier III of Monaco musical composition competition, 1964. Address: Quermatenweg 148, 1 Berlin 37, German Fed. Repub. 4.

SCHRÖDER, Hans Eggert, b. 13 Dec. 1905. Archive Director; Publisher's Reader; Teacher. Educ: Studied at Univs. of Hamburg & Berlin, Germany, 1925-31. Appts: Publishing works; Served WWII; Prisoner of war, Douglas, Isle of Man, U.K., 1941-46; Fndr. & Dir., camp schl., ibid; Publishing work, 1948-; Publisher's work, 1948-; Publisher's rdr.; Lectr.; Dir., Klages-Archiv, Schiller-Nationalmuseum, 1960-.

Mbrships: Deutsche Schillergesellschaft, 1957-; Bd. of Trustees, Ludwig Klages Stiftung, Zurich, 1959; Mng. Dir., Klages-Gesellschaft, Marbarch e.V., 1963-. Publs. incl: Ludwiges Klages—Die Geschichte seines Lebens, Vol. I, Die Jugend, 1966, Vol. II, 1, Das Werk, 1972, Vol. II, 2, forthcoming; Theodor Lessings autobiographische Schriften. Ein Kommentar, 1970; Schiller—Nietzsche—Klages. Abhandlungen & Aufsätze zur Geistesgeschichte der Gegenwart, 1974. Address: Kernestrasse 37, D 7142 Marbach, German Fed. Repub. 43.

SCHRØDER, Michael, b. 7 May 1918. Author; Scientist. Educ: B.Sc., Univ. of Copenhagen, Denmark, 1941; Dr. Phil., Hist. of Sci., & jus docendi, ibid, 1969. Appts: Asst. Ed., Danish State Radio, 1945; Sci. Ed., ibid, 1954; Chief, Adult Educ. Progs., ibid, 1965-73; Fndr. & Ed.-in-Chief, Vor Viden, Scandinavian sci. jrnl., 1949-53. Mbrships: Academician, Danish Acad. for Tech. Scis., 1973; Assn. of Danish Authors; Assn. of Danish Masters of Sci. & Arts; The Oersted Soc. for Propagation of Sci.; Danish Soc. for Hist., Lit. & Art. Publs. incl: Danish Butterflies & Moths, I-II, 1943-44; Calcul Eclair, Frer.ch ed. 1964, Danish, Swedish, Norwegian, Finnish & Icelandic eds. 1961-63; Better Smoking, U.K. ed. 1964, Danish & Finnish eds. 1963-65; The Oil Lamp in the Culture of the Western World, 1964; The Argand Burner: Its Origin & Development in France & England, 1969. Recip., Svend Bergsoe Fndn.'s Sci. Prize, 1964. Address: Sandbjerg Dale, 2950 Vedbaek, Denmark. 43, 134.

SCHRÖDER, (Wilhelm) (Otto) Emil, b. 2 Jan. 1896. Journalist; Writer. Educ: Friedrich-Wilhelm Univ., Berlin, Germany. Appts. incl: Ed., Spandauer Volksblatt, Berlin, 1925-33; Clandestine Corres., Reuters, Havas, & other int. news agcys., 1933-35; Inmate, Concentration Camp, 1935-36; Corres., Chgo. Tribune, & Mainichi Shimbun, Berlin, 1936-44; Ed. in Chief, Der Märker, Potsdam, 1945-46; Dpty. Ed. in Chief, Volksblatt, Berlin, 1946-61; Free-lance Jrnlst., Steinheim, Westphalia, 1962-; Publr. & Ed. in Chief, Stil & Sprache, 1962-. Mbrships: Arbeitsgemeinschaft Junger Publizisten e.V.; Hon. Chmn., Interessengemeinschaft Deutschsprachiger Autoren e.V. Publs. incl: Die Jagd nach der Minute, 1925; Das Flügelschiff, 1928; Spandau in der Hand, 1933; Die Brücke, 1946; Verschwörung gegen die Freiheit, 1966; Num. stories, essays, & poems in newspapers, jrnls., & anthols. Address: D-3282 Steinheim, Westphalia, Am. Silberberg 12, German Federal Repub. 43.

SCHROEDER, Leila Obier (Mrs. Martin C Schroeder), b. 11 July 1925. Teacher. Educ: B.A., Tulane Univ., 1946; M.A., La. State Univ., 1953; J.D., ibid, 1965. Appts: Exec Dir., Evangeline Area Guidance Ctr., 1955-57 Dir., Soc. Serv. Dept., E. La. State Hosp. 1957-60; Psych. Soc. Work Cons., 1960-61 Asst. Prof.-Assoc. Prof., Coll. of Bus. Admin. La. State Univ., Baton Rouge, 1968-74 Mbrships: La. State Bar. Assn.; Am. Bar Assn. Baton Rouge Bar Assn.; Judicature; Nat. Assn of Soc. Workers; Phi Kappa Phi. Contbr. o articles to profl. jrnls., inclng. Am. Jrnl. Psych. Soc. Casework. Address: 4336 Oxford Ave. Baton Rouge, LA 70808, U.S.A.

SCHROETER, Harry Francis, b. 8 Jun 1911. Corporate Executive. Educ: A.B. Princeton Univ., 1931; Grad., Advd. Mgmt Prog., Harvard Univ., 1950. Appts. incl: w DeCoppet & Doremus, N.Y.C., 1931-40; w Procter & Gamble Co., Cinn., Ohio, 1941-45 Nabisco Inc., N.Y.C., 1946-, V.P., Corporat

Marketing & Communications, 1962-, Shareholders Rep.-Europe, Brussels, Belgium, 1970-. Mbrships. incl: Bd. of Dirs., Advt. Rsch. Fndn., 1956-65 & Audit Bur. of Circulations, 1961-; Nat. Advt. Review Bd., 1971-; Steering Comm., 1973-; Assn. Nat. Advertisers, Chmn. of Bd., 1963; Princeton Club. Hons. incl: Advt. Man in Residence, Univ. of Ill., 1973. Address: 1 W. 72nd St., N.Y., NY 10023, U.S.A. 2.

SCHROETTER, Hilda Bloxton Noel (Mrs. Samuel T. Schroetter Jr.), b. 11 Oct. 1917. Editor; Writer; Educator. Educ: A.B., Randolph-Macon Woman's Coll., 1938; M.A., Univ. of Va., 1946. Appts: Tchr., Va. H.S.'s, 1938-45; Reporter, Herald Courier, Bristol, Va.-Tenn., 1946-47; Histn., Va. WW II Hist. Commn., 1947-50; Copy Chief, Radio Stn. WINA, 1952-54; Ed., Univ. of Va. 'Record', 1954-66; Instr., Engl., Jrnlsm. Va. Commonwealth Univ., 1966-; Reviewer, Richmond Times-Dispatch; Free-lance Ed. & Copy Ed.; Free-lance Pub. Speaker. Mbrships. incl: Va. Writers' Club; Poetry Soc. Va.; The Woman's Club; Bd. of Dirs., 1970-72, Ginter Pk. Woman's Club; Exec. Bd., Assocs. James Br. Cabell Lib. Publs: Bethune Center Nursery School, 1947; Forecasting the Weather (Ed.), 1969; Selector for sev. books; Contbr. to Chgo. Tribune & Richmond Times-Dispatch. Address: 100 West Franklin St. 300, Richmond, VA 23220, U.S.A. 5, 30, 132, 138.

SCHUCK, Marjorie Brackenridge Massey, b. 9 Oct. 1921. Publisher; Editor; Writer; Poet; Lecturer. Educ: Univ. of Minn., 1941-43; The New Schl., N.Y.C., 1948; N.Y. Univ., 1952, 1954-55. Appts: Co-fndr., co-ed., publr., int. poetry mag., Poetry Venture, 1968-69; Ed. & publr., ibid, 1969-; Co-ed., publr., The Poetry Venture Quarterly Essays, Vol. 1, Nos. 1-4, 1968-69, Vol. 2, Nos. 1-4, 1970-71; Fndr., owner & pres., Valkyrie Press., Inc., St. Petersburg, Fla., 1972-; Ed. & publr., poetry anthols., 1972-; Cons. in field. Mbrships. incl: Acad. of Am. Poets; Comm. of Small Mag. Eds. & Publrs.; Coordinating Coun. of Literary Mags.; St. Petersburg Chmbr. of Comm.; Pi Beta Phi; Planning Comm., V.P., Poetry Chmn., Lectr., Fla. Suncoast Writers' Confs. Corp. Publs. incl: Speeches & Writings for the Cause of Freedom, 1973; Contbr. to var. jrnls. & anthols. inclng. Selected Passages from Int. Authors, N.Y. Times. Num. lects., speeches, workshops, poetry readings & radio & TV appearances. Recip. of num. hons. Address: 8245 26th Ave. North, St. Petersburg, FL 33710, U.S.A. 5, 7, 11, 138.

SCHUETTINGER, Robert Lindsay, b. 12 Sept. 1936. Professor; Congressional Assistant. Educ: B.A., Queens Coll., 1959; M.A., Comm. on Soc. Thought, Univ. of Chgo., 1968; Ph.D. Candidate, ibid; Grad. Study, Columbia Univ. & Oxford Univ., U.K.; Mbr., Inner Temple, Inns of Ct. Appts: Asst. Prof., Grad. Inst. of Int. Rels., Cath. Univ. of Am., 1965-68; Vis. Lectr., St. Andrews Univ., U.K., 1968-70; Vis. Lectr., Labour Party Pol. Studies Ctr., Oxford Univ. Summer Schl., 1972; Asst. Prof., Lynchburg Coll., Va., 1970-73; Vis. Lectr., Pols., Davenport Coll., Yale Univ., 1974; Special Asst. to Congressman Steven Symms, U.S. House of Reps. Mbrships. incl: Nat. Bd. of Dirs., Univ. Profs. for Acad. Order, 1972. Publs: Ed., The Conservative Tradition in European Thought, 1970; Co-Author, Toward Liberty: Essays in Honor of Ludwig von Mises, 1971. Hons. incl: Phi Alpha Thata; var. Fellowships. Address: 2805 Olive St. N.W., Georgetown, Wash. DC 20007, U.S.A. 30.

SCHULE, Bernard Emmanuel, b. 22 July 1909. Composer. Educ: Conservatory & Univ.

Zurich, Switzerland; Studied under Nadia Boulanger, Alfred Cortot & Paul Dukas, Paris, France. Appts: Tchr., Ecole Normale de Musique, Paris, France, 1934-39; Organist, Basilique de Ste. Clotilde, ibid, 1938-45; Organist & Choirmaster, Brit. Embassy Ch., ibid, 1935-39; '45-60; Composer, Geneva, Switzerland, 1960-; Pt.-time Advsry. Councillor, Music, German-Swiss TV, Zurich, ibid, 1970-; Pres., Revue Musicale de Suisse Romande, 1973. Mbrships: Swiss Musicians Assn.; Swiss Soc. Authors & Eds. Creative Works: Eluminures for Organ, 1944; Introitus in ceremonium, for orch., 1958; Concerto for Double Bass w. strings & Percussion, 1969; Concerto for Piano, 1971; Passage au Zénith for clarinet & electronic music, 1972; Doppelglück der Töne, 2 poems of Goethe for choir & instruments, 1973; Concerto for Oboe, 1974; Srim Symphony for Children's orch., 1974; Dramaturgie des Fernsehtons, publ. for TV, 1970. Recip. hons. Address: II Rue Butini, 1202 Geneva, Switzerland.

SCHULSOHN, Samuel Joseph, b. 16 May 1902. Rabbi; Lawyer; Author. Educ: Univ. of Vienna, Austria; Dr.Phil., Univ. of Berlin, Germany, 1927; Licentiate in Law, Univ. of Czernowitz, Bukowina, 1932. Appts. incl: Rabbi, var. European communities, 1928-47, inclng. Nazi concentration camps, 1942-44; Rabbi, Beth Israel Congregation, Wash. Hts., N.Y., U.S.A., 1948-50, Jewish Friends Soc. & Bukowiner Congregation, N.Y., 1957-; Chap., Kingston Ave. Hosp., Brooklyn, 1951-56, Kings Co. Hosp. Ctr., Brooklyn, 1956-. Mbr. & Off., var. Rabbinical & welfare orgs. Author, History of Jews in Bukowina, 1744-1948. Contbr., Jewish Ency. & Juedisches Lexikon. Contbr., var. books & jrnls., Austria, Germany, Rumania & U.S.A. Hons. incl: Selection by E. European Rabbis to plead cases for Nazi victims before German Bundestag & Restitution Comm. of German Parliament, 1964 & 1968. Address: 2915 W. 5th St., Apt 6-H, Brooklyn 24, NY 11224, U.S.A. 6, 55.

SCHULTE, Rainer, b. 8 July 1937. Professor. Educ: Ph.D., Comp. Lit., Univ. of Mich.; Study in Europe, Mexico, S. Am.; Masterclass in piano, Music Acad., Darmstadt, Germany. Appts: Dir., Comp. Lit. Prog. & Translation Workshop, Ohio Univ., 1965-; Ed.-in-Chief, Mundus Artium, Jrnl. of Int. Lit. & Arts, 1967-. Publs: The Suicide at the Piano (poems), 1969; Sunburst: Third World Writing (co-ed.), 1974; Translations, contemporary German, French, Spanish-Am. poets in U.S., Canadian jrnls. Address: Dept. of English, Ohio Univ., Athens, OH 45701, U.S.A. 11, 30.

SCHULTHEIS, Edwin Milford, b. 15 Apr. 1928. Administrator; Educator. Educ: B.Sc., Hofstra Univ., 1950; M.B.A., N.Y. Univ., 1958; Ed.D., ibid, 1972. Appts: N.Y. Off. Mgr., Topton Rug Mfg. Co., N.Y.C., 1950-54; Mktng. Rep., Mobil Oil Co., N.Y.C., 1954-62; Coord. of Distributive Educ., N. Babylon Pub. Schls., N.Y., 1962-; Instr., Bus. Admin., SUNY, Farmingdale, N.Y., 1970-; Curric. Cons. & Test Writer, NY. State Educ. Dept., Albany, 1970-; Assoc. Dir., Curric. Studies, Syracuse Univ., N.Y., 1973-; Asst. Prof., Educ., N.Y. Univ., 1973-. Mbrships: Pres., Suffolk Co. Assn. of Distributive Educ. Tchrs.; Regional Ldr., Bd. of Govs., & Dist. Advsr., Distributive Educ. Clubs. of N.Y.; Nat. Assn. of Distributive Educ. Tchrs.; Suffolk Co., Nat. & Eastern Bus. Tchrs. Assn.; Kappa Delta Pi; Phi Delta Kappa; Work Experience Coords. Assn.; NEA; N.Y. State Tchrs. Assn.; Am. Security Coun. Publs: Modernization of Retail Petroleum Marketing, 1958; Retail Petroleum Marketing, 1972; The Content & Structure of Belief-Disbelief

Systems—Their Effects upon Administrative Perceptions of Vocational Education in the Public High Schools of Nassau & Suffolk Counties, New York, 1972. Hons: Cert. of Merit, Hoftstra Univ., 1971; Cert. of Award, Suffolk Co. Assn. of Distributive Educ. Tchrs., 1971, 72, 73; Outstanding Serv. Award, Distributive Educ. Clubs of N.Y., 1974. Address: 10 Brendan Ave., Massapequa Park, NY 11762, U.S.A. 6, 139, 141.

SCHULTZ, Fred B., 3 July 1920. Priest; Marriage Counselor; Psychiatric Social Worker. Educ: B.A., Wilkes Coll., Wilkes-Barre, Pa., 1950; M.Div., Schl. of Theol., Temple Univ., Phila., Pa., 1951; S.T.M., Dept. of Relig., ibid, 1962; M.A., Glassboro State Coll., N.J., 1971; Licensed Marriage Cnslr., 1973; N.J. Dept. of Educ. Cert.; Student Personnel Servs., Engl. & Soc. Studies. Ordained Deacon, Episcopal Ch., 1951; Priest, 1952. Appts. incl: Curate, St. Luke's Ch., Scranton, Pa., 1951-52; Rector, St. John's Ch., Salem, N.J., 1952-; Substitute Tchr., Salem Pub. H.S.; Psych. Soc. Worker, Salem Co. Drug Abuse Control Bd., 1970-. Mbrships. incl: Bd. of Dirs., Salem Adult Evening Schl.; Drug Cnslr., SALY AIDE; Bd., Christian Freedom Fndn.; Acad. of Relig. & Mental Hlth.; Life Mbr., Order of St. Luke the Physn.; Past Pres., Salem Ministerial Assn.; Am. Personnel & Guidance Assn.; Nat. Voc. Guidance Assn.; Am. Schl. Cnslrs. Assn.; Assn. of Soc. Workers; Am. Assn. Marriage & Family Cnslrs.; Nat. Alliance for Family Life, Inc. Hons. incl: Holder Bishop's Medal of Hon., 1962 & Bishop's Ring of Hon., 1971, Diocese of N.J.; Hon. Canon, Trinity Cathedral, Trenton, N.J., 1966. Address: 211 Ninth St., Salem, NJ 08079, U.S.A.

SCHULTZ, Theodore William, b. 30 Apr. 1902. Professor of Economics. Educ: B.S., S.D. State Coll., 1928; M.S., Univ. of Wis., 1928; Ph.D., ibid, 1930. Appts: Iowa State Coll., 1930-34; Prof. & Hd., Dept. of Econs. & Sociol., ibid, 1934-43; Univ. of Chgo., 1943-; Prof. & Chmn., Dept. of Econs., 1946-61; Chas. L. Hutchinson Disting. Serv. Prof., 1952-69; Chas. L. Hutchinson Disting. Serv. Prof. Emeritus, 1969-. Mbrships. incl: Pres., Am. Econs. Assn., 1960; Disting. Fellow, ibid, 1965; Nat. Acad. of Scis., 1974-; Fndng. Mbr., Nat. Acad. of Educ., 1965; Fellow, Am. Philos. Soc., 1962-. Publs. incl: The Economic Value of Education, 1963; Transforming Traditional Agriculture, 1964; Economic Crises in World Agriculture, 1965; Economic Growth & Agriculture, 1968; Investment in Human Capital, 1971; Human Capital, 1972. Hons. incl: Hon. LL.D., Grinnell Coll., 1949, Mich. State Univ., 1962, Univs. of Ill. & Wis., 1968; Hon. D.Sc., S.D. State Coll., 1959. Address: Dept. of Econs., Univ. of Chgo., Chicago, IL 60637, U.S.A. 2.

SCHULTZ, Zora Chandler (Mrs.), b. 12 July 1907. Educator; Administrator. Educ: B.S., S.W. Tex. State Univ., 1937; M.A., 1948. Appts: Tchr., Prairie Lea H.S., Weimar H.S., Victoria H.S., Luling I.S.D.; Supvr., Instrn., Ft. Bend Co. Schls., Dewitt Co. Schls., Coord., Lackland I.S.D.; Prin., ibid. Mbrships. incl: Pres., Lackland T.S.T.A.; Pres., San Antonio Br., Assn. for Childhood Educ.; V.P., Delta Kappa Gamma; Alpha Chi; Tex. Elem. Prins. & Supvrs. Contbr. to: Tex. Outlook & Tex. Assn. for Childhood Educ. Address: Box 502, Waelder, TX 78959, U.S.A. 5, 7, 15.

SCHULZ, Hans-Joachim, b. 3 Sept. 1913. Engineer; Company Director. Educ: Dip.Ing., Tech. Univ., Dresden, Germany, 1939; Dr.Ing., Tech. Univ., Braunschweig, 1958. Appts: Asst. to Prof. Dr. Beyer, Tech. Univ., Dresden;

Served WWII; Constructor, Fried. Krupp Maschinel & Stahlbau, Rheinhausen; Tech. Dir., construction firms Johann Völker, Gladbach, 1948-50, Heinrich Hagen KG, Duisburg, 1950-54; Tech. Mng. Dir., Fried. Krupp Universalbau, Essen, 1954-; Assoc. & Dir., Fa. Lenz Planen & Beraten GmbH, Essen; Assoc. & Chmn., Bd. of Dirs., Fa. Lenz Contract GmbH, Essen. Mbrships: Sworn Expert, Ind.- & Handelskammer, Essen; Deutscher Beton-Verein, Wiesbaden; Hafenbautechnische Gesellschaft; Deutsche Gesellschaft für Erd- & Grundbau. Publs. incl: Versuchs-Winterbau mit der Traglufthalle im Winter 63/64, 1964; Spannbeton-Druckbehälter in Mehrlagenbauweise für Kernkraftwerke, 1969. Address: Büssemstr. 23, D-4300 Essen-Steele, German Fed. Repub.

SCHULZ, Klaus-Peter, b. 2 Apr. 1915. Author; Physician. Educ: Trng. as jrnlst., local paper, Berlin, Germany, 1934-35; Dr.med., 1945. Appts. incl: Ed., Tagesspiegel, Chief Ed., Sozialdemokrat, Berlin, 1946-48; Asst., Nordwestendeutscher Rundfunk & Südwestfunk, 1948; Chief Commentator, Südwestfunk, 1949-55; Asst., var. radio stns., 1955-62; Dir., Berlin Studio, Deutsche Welle, Cologne, 1962-66; Accepted Fed. Govt. post, 1966. Mbrships. incl: Europa-Union, 1950-; Bd. of Dirs., Deutscher Rat der Europäischen Bewegung, 1967-; Beratende Versammlung des Europarats, 1966-73; German V.P., ibid, 1970-71; European Parliament, 1973-. Publs. incl: Die Gästebücher von Sesenheim, 1965; Auftakt zum Kaltum Krieg, 1965; Der Reichstag: Gestern—morgen, 1969; Ich warne, 1972. Recip., Prize for book Proletarier—Klassenkämpfer—Staatsbürger, Otto Wels-Gesellschaft, 1963. Address: Eichkampstr. 16, 1 Berlin 19, German Fed. Repub. 43.

SCHULZ, Michael Anthony, Jr., b. 17 Dec. 1934. Contractor; Engineer. Educ: B.S., La. State Univ.; U.S. Army Engr. Schl., & Cmd. & Gen. Staff Coll.; Indl. Coll. of Armed Forces. Appts: Estimator, Crawford Corp., 1956-67; Plant Mgr., Tidewood Corp., 1957-58; Engr., La. Concrete Products, 1959-61; Dept. Hd., Wilson P. Abraham, 1961-64; Construction Mgr., Otis F. Haymon, 1964-67; Sec.-Treas., Bedford Corp., 1967-. Mbrships: Am. Soc. Civil Engrs.; Sect. Hd., La. Engrng. Soc.; Soc. Am. Mil. Engrs.; Reserve Offs. Club; V.P., Sertoma Club of Baton Rouge; Magnolia Woods Club; Alpha Tau Omega. Address: 864 Albert Hart Dr., Baton Rouge, LA 70808, U.S.A. 7, 125.

SCHULZ, Mildred V. Librarian. Educ: B.A., Augustana Coll.; postgrad., Columbia Schl. of Lib. Serv., N.Y., 1944-45. Appts: Hd., Hist. Dept., E. Moline Elem. Schls.; Hd. Libn., E. Moline Pub. Lib., Ill., 1945-64; Ref. Libn., Ill. State Histl. Lib., Springfield, 1964-70, Hd. Libn., 1970-. Mbrships. incl: Woman's Club, E. Moline; Sec., ibid, 1962; Community Improvement, E. Moline; Chmn., ibid, 1963; Ill. Lib. Assn.; Sec., ibid 1968-69; ALA; Exec. Bd. Mbr., Hist. Sect., ibid, 1968-72; AAUW; Past Pres., Moline-Rock Island Br., ibid; Chmn., Am. Cancer Soc. Hons: Community Serv. Award, E. Moline Community Chest, 1961-63; Woman of Yr., Capital City Chapt., ABWA, Springfield, 1964. Address: Illinois State Historical Library, Old State Capitol, Springfield, IL 62706, U.S.A. 5.

SCHULZ, Paul, b. 31 Jan. 1911. Professor of Physical Electronics & Lighting Engineering. Educ: Univ. of Munich; Dr.phil., Univ. of Rostock, 1934; Dr.rer.nat.habil., Univ. of Bonn, 1943. Appts: Asst., Phys. Insts. of Univs. of Rostock & Bonn., 1934-37; Lab. Dir.,

Osram Study Grp. for Elec. Lighting, Berlin, 1937-46; Dir., Rsch. Inst. for Gas Discharge Phys., German Acad. of Sci., 1946-49; Prof., Univ. of Griefswald, 1948-49; Prof., Univ. of Karlsruhe, 1949-; Pres., (Rector) of Univ., 1963-65. Mbrships: Chmn., Comm. of Gas Discharges, German Phys. Soc., 1950-56; Pres., German Soc. of Illuminating Engrng., 1954-56; Am. Phys. Soc. Publs: Der Plasmazustand der Gasse, 1964; Elektronische Vorgänge in Gasen und Festkörpern, 1968, 2nd ed., 1974; about 80 publs. in jrnls. concerning broadening of spectral lines, light sources, high pressure elec. discharges in mercury, rare gases & gas mixtures, determination of electron & ion densities in gas plasmas by electron impact broadening of spectral lines & dev. of methods for determination of temperatures in high pressure discharges. Holder of num. patents. Inventor, High pressure xenon discharge lamp, 1943 & halogenid discharge lamp, 1949. Hons: Elenbass-Preis, Eindhoven, Netherlands, 1969. Address: c/o Univ. Karlsruhe, Kaiserstr., 12, 75 Karlsruhe, German Fed. Repub. 92.

SCHULZE, John, b. 7 June 1915. Professor of Art & Photography. Educ: B.S., Kan. State Tchrs. Coll.; M.F.A., Univ. of Iowa. Appts: on staff, Schl. of Art & Art Hist., Univ. of Iowa., 1948-; Rsch. Profship., photographing Mexico, 1968-69; Artist in Res., Washborn Univ., Topeka, Ks., 1972, Western Ky. W., Bowling Green, 1973, & State Coll., Genoseo, N.Y., 1973. Collects. of work in: Oakland Mus., Calif; Nihon Univ., Tokyo & MIT Hayden Gall.-Archives. One-man exhibs: Ill. Inst. of Technol., Chgo., 1971; Exposure Gall., NYC, 1973; Mid.-W. Invitational Walker Art Ctr., Mpls., Minn., 1973. In many grp. exhibs. inclng: Light Seven, Haydon Gall., MIT, 1968; Goduc Gall., San Fran., 1968; The Art of Photog., tour of S. Am. under auspices of US State Dept., 1967. Mbrships: Mbrships Chmn., Soc. Photog. Educ., 1966-70; Mid.-Am. Coll. Arts; Coll. Art Assn.; Judge, 9th Annual Film Festival, Calif., 1970. Address: 5 Forest Glen, Iowa City, IA 52240, U.S.A. 37.

SCHULZE, Wilhelm, b. 10 Dec. 1920. Professor of Veterinary Medicine. Educ: Veterinary Colls., Leipzig & Hanover, Germany. Appts: Veterinary Off., German Army; Asst.-Lectr.-Prof., Veterinary Med., Univ. of Leipzig; Dean, ibid, 1957-; Prof., Tierarztliche Hochschule, Hanover, 1957-; Rector & Prorector, ibid, 1965-69. Mbrships: V.P., Int. Veterinary Soc., 1967-69, Pres., 1969-72, Hon. Pres., 1972-; Royal Acad. of Med. of Belguim; Polish Veterinary Soc. Author, approx. 220 papers on diseases of animals. Address: D 3011 Bemerode/Hanover, Am Sandberge 10, German Federal Repub.

SCHUMACHER, Gebhard F.B., b. 13 June 1924. Physician; Obstetrician & Gynecologist. Educ: M.D., Univ. of Goettingen, W. Germany, 1951; Med. Schls., ibid & Univ. of Tuebingen, 1945-51; Intern, Med. Schl., Univ. of Tuebingen, 1951-52. Appts. incl: Res. Ob. & Gyn., 1954-59, Asst. Sci. Ob. & Gyn. & Biochem. Rsch., 1959-62; Asst. Prof., 1964-65, Dept. of Ob. & Gyn., Univ. of Tuebingen; Rsch. Assoc., Asst. Prof., Dept. of Ob. & Gyn., Univ. of Chgo., Ill., U.S.A., 1963-64; Assoc. Prof., Dept. of Ob. & Gyn., Asst. Prof., Dept. of Biochem., Albany Med. Coll., Union Univ., 1965-67; Currently, Prof. Ob. & Gyn., Chief, Sect. Reprod. Bio., Univ. of Chgo. Pritzker Schl. of Med., Chgo. Lying-in Hosp. Mbrships. incl: Fellow, Am. Coll. Obstetricians & Gynecologists, Inst. Med. Chgo. N.Y. Acad. Sci.; Am. Soc. Experimental Pathol. German Med. Soc., Chgo.; var. German Med. Socs. Author & Co-author, many publs. in field.

Address: Dept. of Ob. & Gyn., Univ. oт Chgo. Pritzker Schl. of Med., 5841 S. Maryland Ave., Chgo., IL 60637, U.S.A. 8, 14.

SCHURR, Hans, b. 6 Nov. 1902. Scholar; Antiquarian Bookseller. Appts: Antiquarian Bookseller w. K.F. Koehler's Antiques, Leipzig, Germany, 1922-41, latterly as Commercial Rep. & Hd. of Antiquarian Bookshop; Hd. Antiquarian Bookseller & Mgr., Univ. Bookshop, Strasbourg, 1941-45; Hd. Antiquarian Bookseller w. Weise's Hofbuchbdlg., Stuttgart, 1949-60; Self-employed, Stuttgart, 1960-72. Work featured in Borsenblatt für den Deutschen Buchhandel, 1967, '72. Address: Greutterstr. 15, 7000 Stuttgart 31 (Weilimdorf), German Fed. Repub. 105.

SCHÜTZ, Wilhelm Wolfgang, b. 14 Oct. 1911. Writer. Educ: Dr. Phil., Heidelberg. Appts. incl: London Corres., Neue Zürcher Zeitung, till 1951; Exec. Chmn., Coun. For An Indivisible Germany, till 1973; Writer & Ed., Politik & Kultur. Author of plays, Pol. essays & books on For. Policy. Plays incl: Der Fall Sokrates; Gebrauchsanweisung für einem Reichsverweser; Temerlan Der Grosse; Galopp Rechts. Pol. Essays incl: Reform Der Deutschland Politik; Deutschland— Memorandum. Address: D53 Bonn, Remigiusstr. 1, German Fed. Repub.

SCHWAGER, Virginia, S.P., b. 15 Nov. 1924. Religious Sister; Administrator. Educ: Mercy Coll., Detroit, Mich., 1941-43; B.S., Coll. of St. Teresa, Winona, Mo., 1943-45; Intern (dietetics), St. Mary's Hosp., Detroit, 1945; M.H.A. St. Louis Univ., Mo., 1955-57; Res. (hosp. admin.), St. Francis Hosp., Pitts., Pa., 1957. Appts. incl: Admnstrv. Hd., Dietary Dept., Providence Hosp., Seattle, Wash., 1948-55; Admnstr., ibid, 1961-72; Admnstrv. Asst., Mt. St. Vincent, Seattle, 1957; Asst. Admnstr., St. Vincent Hosp., Portland, Ore., 1958; Admnstr., Providence Hosp., Everett, 1958-61; Dr., Div. of Hlth. Affairs, U.S. Cath. Conf., Wash. D.C., 1972-. Mbrships: Comm., Am. Hosp. Assn. Commnr., Jt. Commn. on Accreditation of Hosps., 1973-; Hlth. Ins. Benefits Advsry. Coun., Soc. Security Admin., 1973-; former Pres., Assn. Western Hosps.; Regent, Wash. & Alaska, Am. Coll. Hosp. Admnstrs., 1970-72; Comm., Blue Cross Assn. Inc. Contbr. to profl. jrnls. Recip. num. hons. & awards. Address: c/o Div. of Hlth. Affairs, USCC, 1312 Massachusetts Ave., N.W., Wash. DC 20005, U.S.A.

SCHWARTZ, Barbara Wilner, b. 1 Mar. 1941. Lawyer. Educ: B.A., Univ. of Buffalo, N.Y., 1962; LL.B., Columbia Univ. Schl. of Law, 1965. Appts: Atty., Rosenman, Colin, Kaye, Petschek, Freund & Emil, N.Y.C., 1965-67; Atty., Dinsmore, Shohl, Coates & Deupree, Cinn., Ohio, 1967-; Cons., The Legal Rsch. Grp. Inc., Charlottesville, Va., 1970; Legal Ed., The Michie Co., ibid, 1970-71. Mbrships: Cinn. Bar Assn. (Sec. Taxation Sect.); Assn. of Bar of City of N.Y.; Am. Bar Assn.; Phi Beta Kappa; Cinn. Estate Planning Coun. Publs: Ed., Michie on Banks & Banking, Vols. 4 & 8, 1971; Ed. Columbia Law Review, 1963-65; Contbr. to profl. jrnls. Lectr., Tax. Insts. & Forums, var. States. Hons: Co-Winner, C.B. Beck Prize, 1962-63; J.M. Murphy Prize, 1964-65; Recip. var. Schlrships, 1962-65. Address: Dinsmore, Shohl, Coates & Deupree, 2100 Fountain Sq. Plz., 511 Walnut St., Cincinnati, OH 45202, U.S.A. 5, 138.

SCHWARTZ, Chaja, b. 8 Mar. 1912. Painter. Educ: Bezalel Schl. of Arts, Jerusalem; Study w. Paldi & Zaritsky; Study in Paris w.

Marcel Gromaire & Othon Friesz. One man exhibs. Israel; Tel-Aviv Mus., 1949; Tel-Aviv Mus., Jerusalem, 1961; Nagev. Mus., Beer-Sheva, 1966; Haifa Mus. of Mod. Art, 1969; One man exhibs. abroad: Paris, 1950, '64; London, 1953, '64; Rome, 1962; Group exhibs: Gall. Niveau, Paris, 1938; Venice Biennial, 1958; Jewish Painters of Paris Schl., Paris, 1959; Marseilles, 1964; In pvte., mus. collects., Israel & abroad. Hons: Dizengoff Prize, 1944, '49, '60. Address: 10 Mazal Dagim St., Old Jaffa, Israel.

SCHWARTZ, Eleanor Brantley (Mrs. David J. Schwartz), b. 1 Jan. 1937. University Professor. Educ: B.B.A., 1961, M.B.A., 1963, D.B.A., 1969, Ga. State Univ. Appts. incl: Deptl. Admin. Asst., & Sec., Mercer Univ., 1954-55; Admin. Sec., Statn., Fed. Govt., in Ga., Va. & Pa., 1955-58; Legal Admin. Asst., Atty. Gen.'s Off., 1959-61; Asst. Dean of Admissions, Ga. State Univ., 1961-66; Asst. Prof., ibid, 1966-70; Assoc. Prof., Bus. Admin. Cleveland State Univ., Ohio, 1970-; Cons., Ind. & Govt. Orgs., 1966-. Mbrships: Acad. of Int. Bus.; Am. Marketing Assn.; Am. Inst. of Decision Scis.; Cleveland Sales & Marketing Execs.; Bus. & Profl. Women's Club; recording Sec., Local Chapt., AAUW: Phi Chi Theta; Sigma Iota Epsilon; Beta Gamma Sigma. Publs: Articles in profl. jrnls., monographs & rsch. papers. Hons: Hon. Schlrship. Award, Mercer Univ., 1954; Crimson Key Achievement Recognition Award, 1961; Phi Chi Theta Schlrship. Award; Crimson Key Hon. Soc. Address: 895 Northboro Drive, Mayfield Village, OH, U.S.A. 5, 76, 132, 138.

SCHWARTZ, Elliott, S., b. 19 Jan. 1936. Composer; Author; Professor. Educ: A.B., Columbia Univ., 1957; M.A., 1958; Ed.D., 1962; composition studies w. var. tchrs. Appts. incl: Tchng. Asst., Columbia Univ., 1958-60; Instr., Univ. of Mass., 1960-64; Asst. Prof., Bowdoin Coll., 1964-70; Assoc. Prof., ibid, 1970-. Mbrships: Nat. Coun., Dir., Region I, Am. Soc. Univ. Composers; Am. Music Ctr.; Coll. Music Soc.; Am. Soc. Composers Authors & Publrs. Publs. incl: The Symphonies of Ralph Vaughan Williams; Contemporary Composers on Contemporary Music (co-ed); Electronic Music: A Listener's Guide. Compositions incl: Music for Orchestra; Island for orch.; Magic Music for piano & orch.; Texture for chmbr. orch.; Voyage & Eclipse II for large wind ensemble. Hons. incl: ASCAP Annual Awards, 1965-; Me. State Award in Arts & Humanities, 1970; Nat. Endowment for the Arts Composition Grant, 1974. Address: Dept. of Music, Bowdoin Coll., Brunswick, ME 04011, U.S.A. 6, 21, 30.

SCHWARTZ, Francis, b. 10 Mar. 1940. Composer; University Professor; Critic. Educ: B.S., Juilliard Schl. of Music., N.Y.C., 1961; M.A., 1962. Appts: Assoc. Prof., Music, Univ. of Puerto Rico, 1966-; Chmn., Dept. of Music, ibid, 1971-; Hd. Music Critic, San Juan Star, 1966-; Pres., Steering Comm., Puerto Rico Bi-Centennial Commn., 1973-; Co-Dir., Grupo Fluxus de Puerto Rico, 1968-. Mbrships: Bd. Dirs., Overseas Press Club of P.R.; Music Critics Assn. Am.; Inter-Am. Music Critics Assn.; Am. Soc. Univ. Composers; Coll. Music Soc. Compositions: Auschwitz, tape aromas, dancer, 1968; Plegaria, orch. & tape, 1972; I Protest, orch & tape, 1973; Geoflux, electronic ballet, 1974. Commns: Casals Fest. Org., 1973; Inst. of P.R. Culture, 1974. Address: Univ. of Puerto Rico, Box AL, Music Dept., Rio Piedras, Puerto Rico 00931.

SCHWARTZ, James P., b. 30 Oct. 1919. Real Estate Broker. Educ: Coll. of Commerce, New Haven, Conn. Appts. incl: Fndr. & Dir., Lafayette Bank & Trust Co.; Bd. of Assocs., Univ. of Bridgeport; J.P.; Zoning Bd. of Appeals, Easton Conn.; Writer & Photographer, 1940-47; Pres., Photo Co., 1947-70; Real Estate Broker, 1970-. Mbrships. incl: Masons; Conn. Assn. of Realtors; Nat. Assn. of Realtors; Bd. of Mgmt., Barnum Festival Soc.; Trustee, Optometric Vision Ctr. Contbng. Ed., Photographic Trade News. Recip. of Community Serv. Award, Sociol. Dept., Univ. of Conn., 1965. Address: 78 Blanchard Rd., Easton, CT 06612, U.S.A. 6, 16, 24.

SCHWARTZ, Jeanna (Mrs. O.Z. Moscovici), b. 23 Jan. 1921. Physician. Educ: Fac. of Natural Scis., Bucharest, Rumania, 1939-40; Schl. of Med. for Jewish Students, Abason, 1941-45; Med. Schl., Bucharest Univ., 1945-47; Doctor in Med. & Surg., ibid, 1948. Appts: Asst. Phys., Cantacuzino Hosp., Bucharest, 1948-49; Preparator, Asst., Instr., Lectr., Dept. of Virol., Med. Schl. & Postgrad. Med. Schl., Bucharest, & Sci. Collaborator, Chief Rsch. Fellow, Chief of Lab., Inst. of Inframicrobiol., Rumanian Acad., 1948-58; Instr., Lectr., Sr. Lectr., Fac. of Microbiol., Tel-Aviv, Israel, & Sr. Lectr., Med. Schl. & Fac. of Continuing Med. Educ., Dept. of Human Microbiol., Telaviv Univ., 1959-. Mbrships: Sec., Israel Soc. of Clin. Pathol.; Israel Soc. of Immunol.; Israel Soc. of Microbiol.; Israel Soc. of Allergol.; Assn. des Résidents Estrangers de l'Inst. Gustave-Roussy. Author of about 90 sci. publs. in the field of med. rsch.; contbr. to var. sci. jrnls. Winner, Award of Min. of Hlth., Rumania, 1956. Address: Dept. of Human Microbiol., Med. Schl., Tel-Aviv Univ., Ramat-Aviv, Israel. 94.

SCHWARTZ, Leonard Jules, b. 25 Nov. 1926. Psychologist. Educ. B.S.S., C.C.N.Y., 1949; M.S.S., ibid, 1950; Ph.D., N.Y. Univ., 1954; N.P.A.P., Psychoanalyst, 1956. Appts. incl: Cons., Leake & Watt Children's Home, 1959; Supvsr. of Psychotherapy, Post Doctoral Prog., Adelphi Univ., 1963; Cons., Yeshiva Inst. for Deaf & Hard of Hearing, 1966; Supvsr., Sensitivity Trng., Migrant Wkrs. Proj., Dowling Coll., 1967; Dir., Inst. for Sensitivity Trng. & Educ. Programming, 1968; Dir., Group Process Inst., currently. Mbrships. incl: N.Y. Soc. for Clin. Psychologists; N.Y. State Psychological Assn.; Am. Psychological Assn. Publs. incl: Therapeutic Acting Out (w. Roslyn Schwartz), in Psychotherapy, 1971; The Use of Encounter & Marathon Groups in Couples Therapy (w. Roslyn Schwartz), in The Neurosis of Our Time-Acting Out, 1973. Gives num. lects. & demonstrations. Address: 140 S. Windsor Ave., Brightwaters, NY 11718, U.S.A. 6, 14.

SCHWARTZ, Lita Linzer (Mrs. Melvin Jay Schwartz), b. 14 Jan. 1930. Psychologist. Educ: A.B., Vassar Coll., 1950; Ed.M., Temple Univ., 1956; Ph.D., Bryn Mawr Coll., 1964. Appts: Pt.-time Psychol., Psychol. Serv. Ctr., Phila., 1957-62; Lectr., Psychol., Temple Univ., 1959; Instr.-Assoc. Prof., Educl. Psychol., Pa. State Univ., 1961-. Mbrships: Am. Psychol. Assn.; Am. Educl. Rsch. Assn.; Coun. for Exceptional Children; Psi Chi; Pi Lambda Thete; AAUP; NEA. Publs: American Education: A Problem-Centered Approach, 1969, 2nd edit.; 1974; Educational Psychology: Focus on the Learner, 1972; Ed., Current Concerns in Educational Psychology, & contbr. of articles, reviews, to profl. jrnls. Hons: Humanitarian Award, N.Y. Philanthropic League, 1973. Address: 411 Lodges Lane, Elkins Pk., PA 19117, U.S.A. 2, 5, 6, 14, 132.

SCHWARTZ, Margaret June, b. 19 May 1923. Educator. Educ: B.A., Hiram Coll. Ohio, 1944; M.A. Syracuse Univ., N.Y., 1950; M.A.,

Columbia Univ. Appts. incl: Asst. Dean, Women, Meredith Coll., N.C., 1950-53; Counselor & Housemother, U.S. Army Schls., W. Germany, 1954-58; teaching & admin. posts, N.Y., Wash. D.C., Greece, Puerto Rico, 1958-68; Tchr., Adult Educ. Prog., White Plains, N.Y. 1969-71; Counselor, White Plains H.S., 1969-. Mbrships. incl: Nat. Assn. Women Deans & Counselors; World YWCA & YWCA, U.S.A.; Pi Lambda Theta; Int. Conven. Christian Chs., U.S.A. Writer of Melodies Afar (poetry), 1950. Address: 44 Scott Ave., Chautauqua, NY 14722, U.S.A. 5, 132.

SCHWARTZ, Modest Euphemia Ratkowski (Mrs. Edward Joseph Schwartz), b. 14 Dec. 1915. Librarian. Educ: B.A., Univ. of Calif., L.A., 1936; M.A., ibid, 1938; post-grad., Immaculate Heart Coll., L.A., 1958. Appts: Tchr., Alhambra H.S., Calif., 1938-58, Libn., 1958-72; Serv., WAC, 1943; Sec., Fremont Serv., 1959-; V.P., Moulding Supply Co., 1967-; Volunteer, Pasadena Cardio-Vascular Fndn., 1974-. Mbrships. incl: AAUW; NEA; CTA; Santa Teresita Hosp. Auxiliary; Women's Ambulance Auxiliary; Euterpe Opera Club; Republican Women's Club. Address: 385 S. Los Robles, Pasadena, CA 91101, U.S.A. 5, 138.

SCHWARTZ, Sheila. Professor. Educ: B.A., Adelphi Univ.; M.A., Tchrs. Coll., Columbia; Ed.D., N.Y. Univ. Appts: Coll. Prof., Hofstra Univ., City Coll., Hunter Coll., 1958-; Prof., New Paltz, 1963-. Mbrships: V.P., N.Y. State Engl. Coun., 1964-70; Pres., ibid, 1973-74; Dir., Nat. Coun. of Tchrs. of Engl., 1970-73; Pres., N.Y. State Comm. of Engl. Educators, 1964-70; Pres., Div. VI, Nat. Assn. for Humanities Educ., 1971-72. Publs: How People Lived in Ancient Greece & Rome, 1967; How People Live in Mexico, 1969; Teaching the Humanities, 1970; This Spaceship Earth, 1975; Introduction to Science Fiction, 1975; Women in Science Fiction, 1975, Over 60 articles in mags. Recip., Fellows Award, N.Y. State Engl. Coun., 1973. Address: 5 Spies Rd., New Paltz, NY 12561, U.S.A. 5, 13, 15, 30, 129, 130, 138, 140, 141.

SCHWARTZBERG, Ralph M., b. 16 June 1906. Attorney at Law. Educ: Univ. of Mich.; J.D., ibid. Appts: Law Clerk, Assoc., Ptnr. Currently Sr. Ptnr. w. Schwartzberg, Barnett & Schwartzberg, 1939-. Mbrships: Hon. Chancellor, Tau Epsilon Rho Int. Law Fraternity, 1953-; Chancellor, ibid, 1941-46; Pres., Tau Epsilon Rho Schlrship. Fndn., 1955-73; Life Mbr., Bd. of Dirs., Bd. of Jewish Educ.; Trustee, Coll. of Jewish Studies, 1948-69; Chmn., Int. Travel Comm., Am. Hotel & Motel Assn.; Univ. of Mich. Club; Covenant Club of Ill.; Twin Orchard Country Club. Recip. Tau Epsilon Rho Lifetime Serv. Award, 1972. Address: 11 S. La Salle St., Chicago, IL 60603, U.S.A. 8.

SCHWARZ, Charles Frederick, b. 15 Jan. 1913. Medical Practitioner; Lecturer; Author. Educ: Grad. in Arts, Sci. & Med., Univ. of Qld., Australia. Appts: Tchr., Qld. schls., Australia, 1934-43; Med. Practitioner, 1944-55; Pres., Christian Anti-Communism Crusade, 1953-. Publs: You Can Trust the Communists (to be Communists), 1959; The Three Faces of Revolution, 1972. Ed., Christian Anti-Communism Newsletter, 1953-. Address: 124 E. 1st St., Long Beach, CA 90801, U.S.A.

SCHWARZ, David, b. 9 Dec. 1928. Research Psychologist; Lecturer; Writer. Educ: Fil. lic. degree in educl. psych., 1971. Appts: Rsch. Fellow, Univ. of Stockholm, Sweden; Hd., Botkyrka Proj. (Adjustment & bilingualism among immigrants & their children in Sweden); Ed., Nordisk Minoritetsforsking; Participant in

confs. & seminars on inter-ethnic rels. Mbrships: Swedish Psychological Assn.; Swedish Union of Authors. Publs: Ed., Swedish Minorities, 1966; Swedish Immigration & Minority Policy 1945-68, 1971; Ed., Identity & Minority. Theory & Policy in Sweden Today, 1971; Can Immigrants be Swedes? A Study of Ethnic Identity & Stigma, 1973; Bibliography of Immigration & Ethnic Minority Research, 1973; Num. contbns. to jrnls. & newspapers. Address: University of Stockholm, Fack, S-104 05 Stockholm 50, Sweden. 134.

SCHWARZ, Helmut Julius, b. 20 Nov. 1915. Professor of Physics. Educ: M.S., Univ. of Cologne, German Fed. Repub., 1938; Ph.D., Univ. of Bonn 1940. Appts. incl: Asst. Prof., Univ. of Bonn, 1940-41; Prof. Applied Phys., Tech. Acad., German Air Force, Berlin-Gatow, 1941-44, Dir., Rsch. Inst. Phys. Electronics, 1944-45; Fndr. & Dir., Phys. Sci. Schl., Wuppertal, 1945-49; Prof., Universidade do Brasil, Rio de Janeiro, 1951-60; Cons. Physicist, United Aircraft Corp., 1960-63; Prof., Rensselaer Polytech. Inst., Hartford Grad. Ctr., 1963-; Cons., Ion Phys. Corp., Burlington, Mass., 1965-, Carson Labs., Bristol, Conn., 1965-. Mbr., profl. orgs. Over 60 profl. papers & reports. Hons. incl: NASA Technol. Award, 1970; NASA Invention Award, 1972. Address: Rensselaer Polytechnic Institute, 275 Windsor St., Hartford, CT 06120, U.S.A. 2, 6, 14, 34, 50.

SCHWARZ, Richard, b. 29 May 1910. University Professor. Educ: D.Phil., Univ. of Greifswald, Germany, 1934. Appts. incl: Lectr., Univ. of Würzburg, 1949-51; Prof., Philosophical-Theological Univ. of Bamberg, 1951-58; Prof., Univ. of Vienna, Austria, 1958-63; Prof., & Dir., Inst. of Educ. I, Univ. of Munich, Germany, 1963-. Mbrships. incl: German Educl. Sci. Soc.; Past Commnr., Inst. for Study of the German People; Austrian UNESCO Commn.; Past Chmn., Schl. Comm., Austrian Rectors' Conf. Publs. incl: Das Christusbild des Deutschen Mystikers Heinrich Seuse, 1934; Wissenschaft & Bildung, 1957; Humanismus & Humanität in der Modernen Welt, 1965; Ed., Universität & Moderne Welt, ein Internationales Symposion, 1962; Ed., Ein Internationales Symposion zum Selbstverständnis des Heutigen Menschen, 1967; Ed., Internationales Jahrbuch für Interdisziplinare Forschung, 1973-74; Contbns. to profl. jrnls. Address: Institut für Pädogogik I der Universität München, D-8 Munich 40, Leopoldstrasse 23/I, German Federal Repub.

SCHWARZ, Stefan S., b. 12 Dec. 1910. Engineer; Author; Journalist; Historian. Educ: Univ. of Prague, Czechoslovakia; Dipl. Engr., Deutsche Technische Hochschule. Appts. incl: In German Concentration camp, 1942-45; Ed. & Co-fndr., "Moment", Regensburg, & Collaborator on papers "Unser Weg" & "Unser Wort", Munich, 1945; Ed., "Renaissance", Zurich, Vienna, Berlin; Fndr. & Chmn., Israel Cong., Straubing, 1945-74; Co-Fndr., Regional Comm. for liberated Jews in Bavaria, Regensburg, 1945; Mng. Dir., Regional Comm., Israel Cong., Munich, Bavaria, currently. Mbrships: Exec. Bd. Regional Comm., Regensburg, & Coun. of Ctrl. Comm., Munich; Deleg. to Zionist & Jewish World Congresses, Jerusalem, Stockholm, Brussels & Geneva; Advsry. mbr., Akad. für Politische Bildung, Titzing; Film-Selbst-Kontrolle, Wiesbaden, 1974. Publs. incl: Thomas G. Masaryk, monograph, 1949; Die Juden in Bayern im Wandel der Zeiten, 1963; Sage nie, du gehst den letzten Weg, 1971; Synagoge in Floss/Obpf., 1972. Recip. of hons. Address: Gabelsbergerstr. 16, D-844 Straubing, German Fed. Repub. 55.

SCHWARZ-LIEBERMANN VON WAHLENDORF, H.A., b. 2 Aug. 1922. University Professor; former International Civil Servant. Educ: studied Law, Tübingen Univ.; Dr. of Law, 1950; British Coun. Schlrship., Sidney Sussex Coll., Cambridge Univ., U.K., 1950-51. Appts. incl: Rsch. Assoc., For. & Pvte. Law Max-Plank Inst. 1946-52; Hd. of Sect., Min. For. Affairs, Bonn, German Fed. Repub., 1952-53; Exec. Sec., For. Affairs, Christian-Democratic Parliamentary Pty., Bonn, 1954-57; Rep., German Fed. Govt., European Saar Commn., 1955-56; Asst. Dir., Pol. Affairs, NATO, 1957-60; Special Missions for German Fed. Govt., 1961; Hd., Div. for Higher Educ. & Rsch., Coun. of Europe, 1962-67; Assoc. Prof.-Prof.,. Law Schl., Rice Univ., 1967-74; Prof., Law Schl., Lyon Univ. (Jean Moulin), 1974-. Mbrships. incl: Int. Law Assn.; Am. Soc. of Int. Law; sev. European profl. assns. Publs. incl: Guardianship & Trust 1951; Majority Rule & Weighting of Votes, 1953; Structure & Function of Second Chambers, 1958; Fondements & Principes d'un Ordre Juridique Naissant, 1971; Nature des Choses & Logique du Droit, 1973; Executive Responsibility & Democratic Control, 1974. Address: 1 Ave. Liserb, Cimiez, F 06 Nice, France. 43, 91.

SCHWARZOTT, Wilhelm, b. 14 Dec. 1914. Concert Pianist; Professor. Educ: Royal Music Conservatory, Oslo, Norway; Vienna State Acad. & Vienna Univ., Austria. Appts: Dir. & Prof., Klaverakademiet, Oslo, 1950-55; Prof. & Hd., Piano Dept., Univ. of Denver, U.S.A., 1957-61; Prof. & Hd., Piano Dept., Calif. State Polytech. Univ., 1961-63; Fac., San Francisco Conservatory of Music, 1963-68; Lectr. in Music, Sonoma State Coll., Calif., 1971-; Lectr. in Music, Univ. of Calif. Ext., 1966-; Concert Pianist, Soloist, Chamber musician, Europe & U.S.A.; num. performances, Scandinavian Broadcasting Corp. & Am. Educ. TV. Mbrships. incl: Artists Soc., Norway; Pacific Music Soc.; Music Tchrs. Assn. of Calif.; Am. Coll. Musicians; F.I.B.A. Address: 444 Collingwood St., San Francisco, CA 94114, U.S.A. 57, 120, 131.

SCHWEITZ, Rütting Carsten, (paintings signed: C. Rütting. S 74), b. 13 Jan. 1929. Artist; Art Teacher. Educ: Art studies w. Jacob Meyer, Copenhgen, Denmark. Study tours: Iceland, 1947; France, 1953; Holland, 1954; Canada, U.S.A., 1956-60, 1964-5; Poland, 1968, 1973; Luxembourg, 1971, 1973. Exhibs: Contemporary Art Gall., Toronto, Canada, 1956, '58, '65, B.P. Art Soc., Den Frie Exhib., Helligaandshuset, Charlottenborg, Youth & Culture Ctr., Banks Gall., all in Copenhagen, 1969-73; Gall. Huuset, Aarhus, Denmark, 1970; Diekirch Mus., Luxembourg, 1972; Town Hall, Holte, Denmark, 1972, 1973; Maribo Mus., Denmark, 1973; Gdansk, Poland, 1974. Pub. Collects: Museo Mansion de Arte, Palma de Mallorca, Spain; Art Lib., Copenhagen; Town Hall, Holte, Denmark. Address: Slagelsegade 24, 2100 Copenhagen, Denmark.

SCHWEITZER, Jerome W., b. 28 Dec. 1908. Educator. Educ: A.B., Univ. of Ala., 1930; M.A., ibid, 1932; Ph.D., Johns Hopkins Univ., 1940; Nat. Univ. of Mexico, 1946. Appts: Instr. in Romance Langs., Univ. of Ala., 1930-35, Johns Hopkins Univ., 1935-40; Asst. Prof., Univ. of Ala., 1940-47; Assoc. Prof., ibid, 1947-51, Prof., 1951-. Mbrships: Los Comediantes; MLA; Am. Assn. of Tchrs. of Spanish & Portuguese; Phi Beta Kappa, 1929; Pres., Ala. Alpha, 1960-61. Publs: Georges de Scudéry's 'Almahide', 1939, 1973. Co-ed., Théatre de Tristan l'Hermite, 1974. Contbr. to anthols. & jrnls. Address: Drawer AJ, Univ. of Alabama, AL 35486, U.S.A. 13, 15, 30, 55.

SCHWEITZER, Thomas Fred. Educator. Educ: A.B., Columbia Coll., 1959; A.M., N.Y. Univ., 1962. Appts. incl: Sci. Tchr., Metropol. N.Y., 1962-66; Asst. to Chmn., Dept. of Biol. Scis., SUNY, Stony Brook, 1966-67; Sci. Tchr., Gt. Neck Pub. Schls., L.I., 1967-. Mbrships. incl: Life, Alpha Phi Omega; British Anti-Slavery Soc.; Int. Postcard Collectors Assn.; Nat. Sci. Tchrs. Assn.; Environmental Preservation Comm., Torrey Botanical Club, 1970-. Publs: Jt. Author, Ideas & Techniques for Seventh Grade General Science: A Guide for Teachers, 1964; Asst. Ed., Am. Biol. Tchr., 1966-69; Special Contbr., Mbr., Edit. Staff, ibid, 1970; Columnist, The Pages of History, Queens Co. Times, 1969-; var. articles. Hons. incl: U.S. Army Commendation Ribbon, 1953; N.Y. State Conspicuous Serv. Cross, 1955; Bronze Plaque, Int. Postcard Exhib., 1970; Postcard Collectors Hall of Fame, 1972. Address: 89-19 218th St., Queens Village, L.I., NY 11427, U.S.A. 30.

SCHWENZNER, Julius Erik, b. 5 Feb. 1908. Managing Director. Educ: Univs. of Bonn & Cologne, Germany; Madrid; Spain, 1927-33; Doct., Bonn Univ., 1934. Appts: Mng. Dir., GFM/Gesellschaft für Marktforschung mbH., Hamburg, Germany, 1945-; Lectr., Market Rsch., Hamburg Univ., 1958-67; Mbr., Direktorium, Chem. Works, Dr. Kurt Herberts & Co., Wuppertal-Barmen, 1958-67; Prof., Hamburg Univ., 1968-. Mbrships: Pres., Arbeitskreis Deutscher Marktforschungs-Inst. e.V., Bonn; Ubersee-Club Hamburg e.V., Hamburg. Publs. incl: Exportbetriebslehre (w. C. Kapferer), 1935; Zur Morphologie des Zentralspanischen Hochlandes, 1936; Der Brotmarkt in der Bundesrepublik Deutschland (w. H. Mosolff), 1954; Marktanalyse über Zucker (w. H. Mosolff), 1954; Das Beste und seine Leser—ein Versuch über Images, 1960. Address: GFM/Gesellschaft für Marktforschung mbH., Langelohstr. 134, D-2000, Hamburg 53, German Fed. Repub.

SCHWERDTFEGER, Peter, b. 23 Dec. 1935. Meteorologist. Educ: B.Sc., Melbourne Univ., Australia, 1957; M.Sc., ibid, 1959; Ph.D., McGill Univ., Montreal, Canada, 1962. Appts: Teaching Fellow, Phys., McGill Univ., Montreal, 1959-61; Lectr., Glaciol. & Meteorol., Univ. of Melbourne, Australia, 1962-65; Vis. Prof. Geophys., Univ. of Alaska, U.S.A., 1965-; Sr. Lectr., Meterol., Univ. of Melbourne, 1965-71; Vis. Prof., Meterol., Cologne, Germany, 1969; Prof. Meterol., Flinders Univ. of S.A., Australia, 1971-; Dir., Flinders Inst. for Atmospheric & Marine Scis., 1973-; Mbrships: Past Pres., Australian Nat. Antartic Rsch. Expedition Ski Club. Contbr. to learned jrnls. of over 30 publs. on glaciol., meterol. & environmental sci., 1961-. Hons: Alexander von Humboldt Fndn. Lecturing Fellow, 1969. Address: Institute for Atmospheric & Marine Sciences, Flinders University of S.A., Bedford Park, S.A., Australia 5042. 23.

SCHWERIN, Kurt, b. 17 Apr. 1902. Professor of Law; Librarian. Educ: Univ. of Breslau, Germany, 1934; M.S.Sc., New Schl. for Soc. Rsch., N.Y., 1940; B.S., L.S., Columbia Univ., 1944; Ph.D., ibid, 1955. Appts. incl: Hd., Cataloging Dept., Univ. of Va. Law Lib., 1946-48; Hd., For. & Int. Law Sects., Northwestern Univ. Law Lib., 1948-64; Asst. Libn., ibid, 1953-64; Libn., 1964-70, 1972-73, Assoc. Prof. of Law, 1958, Prof., 1963-70, Prof. Emeritus, 1970-. Mbrships. incl: Am. Assn. of Law Libs.; Bd. of Dirs., Int. Assn. of Law Libs., 1965-71; Pres., Chgo. Chapt., Am. For. Law Assn., 1963-68; Lib. Comm., Am. Soc. of Int. Law, 1962-; Pres., Chgo. Assn. of Law Libs., 1958-59; Bd. of Dirs., Leo Baeck

Inst., 1971-, Pres., Chgo. Chapt., 1958-. Publs: Classification for International Law & Relations, 1947, 3rd ed., 1969; Historia Judaica; Index to Vols. 1-20, 1938-58, 1961; International Law (w. W. L. Gould), 1968. Editl. Bd: Excerpts Criminologica, 1961-64; Jrnl. of Criminal Law, Criminol. & Police Sci., 1949-70. Comm. on Index to For. Legal Periodicals, 1960-. Hons. incl: Officer's Cross, Fed. Repub. of Germany, 1965. Address: Northwestern Univ. Schl. of Law, 357 E. Chgo. Ave., Chgo., IL 60611, U.S.A. 2, 8, 13, 15, 42, 46, 51.

SCHWIND, Martin Georg, b. 29 Oct. 1906. University Professor. Educ: Dr.'s degree, Geog. & Philos. Univ. of Leipzig, 1932; Rsch. expeditions to Japan, Sakhalin, Manchuria, 1934-39; Dr. phil.habil., Univ. of Leipzig, 1942. Appts: Tchr., German shcl., Tokyo; H.S.Prin. & Lectr., Geog., Tech. Univ., Danzig, 1942; Lt., German Army, WW II; Sci. Sec. Gen., Acad. for Urban & Country Plannig, Hanover, 1946-48; Mbr., Univ. Fndng. Commn., Bremen, 1948-50; Lectr., Geog., Tech. Univ., Hanover, 1951-61; H.S. Prin., Hanover, 1952-68, Dir., Friedrich Rauch Inst. for Soc. Scis., 1966-; Hon. Prof., Geog., Ruhr Univ. Bochum, 1967-. Mbrships: Friedrich Rauch Fndn.; Pres., Friedrich Rauch Inst. for Soc. Scis.; Acadamecian, China Acad., Taipei; Geog. Soc., Tokyo; German-Japanese Soc., Berlin. Publs: Books on geog., in German, 1939-74; Ed., publs. of Friedrich Rauch Inst., 1967-. Hons: Prof., Normal Univ., Taipei, 1957. Address: Grosse Heide 14, 3000 Hanover, German Fed. Repub.

SCHWINGE, Erich, b. 15 Jan. 1903. Professor of Law. Educ: Univs. of Jena, Munich & Berlin; J.D. Appts: Full Prof., Law, Univ. of Marburg, 1932-; Rector, ibid, 1954-55. Publs: Kommentar zum Militarshrafgesitzbuch, 1944; Grundlagun des Revisionsrechts, 1960; Der Kampf um die Schurngrichte bis zur Frankfurter Nationalversammlung, 1970; Der Furist und Sien Beinf (under pseudonum, Maximilian Facta), 1960; Berühmte Straffrozerol (12 vols.), 1962-74. Address: 27, von-Harnack-Str. 27, 355 Marburg (Lahn), German Fed. Repub.

SCIACCA, Michele Federico, b. 12 July 1908. University Professor. Educ: Grad., Philos., Univ. of Naples, Italy; Post-Grad. Studies, Univ. of Rome. Appts: Lectr., Hist. of Mediaeval & Mod. Philos., Univ. of Naples, 1935; Lectr., Ancient Philos., ibid, 1936-38; Lectr., Hist. of Philos., Univ. of Pavia, 1938-47; Lectr., Theoretical Philos., Univ. of Genoa, 1948-. Mbrships: Nat. Coun. of Rsch.; Nat. Acad. of Athens; Acad. of Sci., Lit. & Arts, Palermo; Pontariana Acad. of Naples; Acad. peloritana, Messina; Ligurian Acad. of Sci., Lit. & Art, Genoa; Acad. degli Agiati, Rovereto. Publs: L'interiorità oggettiva; L'Uomo, questo squilibrato; Alto ad essere; La Filosofia; La Filosofia morale di A. Rosmini; Morte e immortalità; Filosofia e Metafisica; La filosofia di Tommaso Reid; La libertà e il tempo; Platone; L'oscuramento dell'intelligenza; Antologia triadica e trinitaria; Figure e problemi del pensiero contemporaneo. Hons. incl: Hon. Degree, Univ. of Bordeaux, 1958, Univ. of Barcelona, 1972, Univ. El Salvador, Buenos Aires. Address: Casella Postale 1200, Genoa, Italy.

SCIONTI, Joseph Natale, b. 25 Sept. 1931. Historian. Educ: B.A., Suffolk Univ., 1960; M.A., Tufts Univ., 1961; Ph.D., Brown Univ., 1967. Appt: Assoc. Prof. of Hist., South-eastern Mass. Univ. Mbrships: New England Renaissance Conf. (Prog. Dir., 1973); Renaissance Soc. of Am.; Am. Hist. Assn.

Contbr. to Hist. Abstracts; Author of 23 biographical articles for Encyclopaedia of World Biography. Hons: Dankstipendium, German Fed. Repub., 1963; Leo M. Sullivan Tchr. of Year Award, Fac. Fedn. of Southeastern Mass. Univ., 1971. Address: Dept. of Hist., Southeastern Mass. Univ., Old Westport Rd., N. Dartmouth, MA 02747, U.S.A. 130, 13.

SCOFIELD, James Steve, b. 26 Sept. 1928. Librarian; Journalist. Educ: B.S., Univ. of Ill., 1954. Appts. incl: Administrative Asst., Hammond City Ct., 1956-60; Dir., Fla. Suncoast Publishers, St. Petersburg, Fla., 1960-62; Chief Libn., St. Petersburg Times & Evening Independent, 1962-; Lib. Cons., Lakeland, Fla., Ledger, 1967, Congressional Quarterly, Wash., 1969, Am. Press Inst., Reston, Va., 1973. Mbrships. incl: Int. Chmn., Newspaper Div., Special Libs. Assn., 1970-71; Publs. Ed., Automated Systems Comm. of Newspaper Libns., 1967-68; Supreme Gov., Order of Ahepa, int. Hellenic fraternity, 1966-68; Supreme Trustee, ibid, 1969-72; Archdiocesan Coun., Greek Orthodox Archdiocese of N. & S. Am., 1970-72. Author of publs. in field. Recip. of hons. Address: 6100 Sixth Ave. South, St. Petersburg, FL 33707, U.S.A. 2, 42, 125, 129.

SCOTESE, Peter Gabriel, b. 13 Mar. 1920. Corporation President. Educ: Grad., Wharton Schl. of Bus., Univ. of Pa., 1942, Advanced Mgt. Prog., Harvard Univ., 1960. Appts: Parachute Infantry Off., WW II; Salesman—V.P., Indian Head Mills, N.Y.C., 1947-63; Bd. Chmn., Milwaukee Boston Store, Div. of Federated Dept. Stores, 1963-69; V.P., Federated Dept. Stores, 1964-69; Pres., Springs Mills, Inc., N.Y.C., 1969-; Dir., Springs Mills, Inc., Bath Inds., Bell & Howell Co. Mbrships: Trustee, Fashion Inst. of N.Y.; Mus. of Mod. Art; Am. Fedn. of Art. Contbr. to num. profl. jrnls. Hons: Peter G. Scotese Day, Milwaukee, July 25, 1968; 1st Annual Community Serv. Award, Wis. Allied Construction Employers Assn., 1968; Alumni Award of Merit, Girard Coll. H.S., Phila., 1968. Address: Springs Mills, Inc., 104 W.40th St., N.Y., NY 10022, U.S.A. 2, 36.

SCOTFORD, Herbert Edward, b. 1 Jan. 1910. Newspaper Executive. Educ: Dip. of Commerce, Sydney Univ.; Fellow—Chartered Inst. of Secs., Australian Soc. of Accts., Australian Inst. of Mgmt. Appts: Sec., Associated Newspapers Ltd., 1954-58; Dir., ibid, 1956-58; Dir., Sungravure Pyt. Ltd., 1956-58; Chief Acct., John Fairfax Ltd., 1956-58; Mng. Dir., Mirror Newspapers Ltd., 1959-61; Sales Mgr., John Fairfax & Sons Ltd., 1961-71; Sec., Indl. Mgr. & Dir., John Fairfax Ltd. Grp., 1971-. Mbrships: Mbr., Corporate Trustees, Presby. Ch. of Australia in N.S.W.; Chmn., Schls. Commn, Presby. Ch.; Chmn., Scots Schl. Albury; Rotary Club, Sydney; Imperial Serv. Club., Sydney. Address: 33 Greengate Rd., Killara, N.S.W., Australia 2071. 23.

SCOTLAND, James, b. 8 Sept. 1917. Principal, Aberdeen College of Education. Educ: M.A., LL.B., & M.Ed., Univ. of Glasgow, U.K., 1934-40 & 1946-49. Appts: Lectr., in Hist., Jordanhill Coll. of Educ., Glasgow, 1949-50; Prin. Lectr. in Educ., ibid, 1950-61; Prin., Aberdeen Coll. of Educ., 1961-. Mbrships. incl: Vice-Chmn., Tchng. Coun. for Scotland, 1966-; Gov., Scottish Police Coll.; Police Advsry. Bd. for Scotland; Chmn., Scottish Community Drama Assn.; Sec., Standing Conf. on Studies in Educ. Publs: Modern Scotland (a History from 1707), 1955;

History of Scottish Education, 1969; Our Law, Scottish TV, 1956; Contbns. to books on educ.; 6 plays inclng. The Honours of Drumlie, Whisky Galore, & Wild Geese at Midnight; Num. one-act plays for stage, TV, & radio. Recip., Fellowship, Educl. Inst. of Scotland, 1973. Address: 67 Forest Rd., Aberdeen, AB2 4BJ, U.K. 30.

SCOTT, Ainsworth David, b. 27 Jan. 1912. Civil Engineer; Painter; Sculptor. Educ: B.Sc., McGill Univ. Canada, 1940; M.E.I.C., Canada; M.I.A.S., U.S.A. Appts: i/c Aerodrome Constrns., Montreal & B.C., 1940-44; Grp. Ldr., Engr., Canadair Ltd., 1944-48; Res. Engr., Univ. of W.I. 1949-53; Mng. Dir., A.D. Scott Ltd.; Olympia Residential Hotel Ltd.; Jamaica Razor Blade Co. Grp. Exhibs: Inst. of Ja., 1970, 71; Ja. Art Fest., 1970, 71; Contemp. Ja. Artists Assn. Gall., 1970, 71. Chmn., Contemp. Ja. Artists Assn. Works incl: (sculpture) In the Beginning; Man 10,000 A.D.; The Family; (painting) In the Beginning; Down to the Sea in Ships; Jonah. Hons: Musgrave Silver Medal, Inst. of Ja.; Hon. Mention, All Island Exhib., ibid, 1970; Cert. of Merit, Sculpture, Ja. Art Fest., 1970; 2nd Prize, ibid, 1971. Address: 19 Gordon Town Rd., Kingston 6, Jamaica, W. Indies.

SCOTT, Arthur Finley, b. 30 Nov. 1907. Lecturer; Author. Educ: B.A., Emmanuel Coll., Cambridge Univ., U.K., 1930; M.A., ibid, 1934. Appts: Sr. Engl. Master, Oakham Schl., 1930-33; Sr. Engl. Master, Taunton Schl., 1933-43; Hdmaster, Kettering Grammar Schl., 1943-51; Sr. Lectr., Borough Rd. Coll. of Educ., 1952-; Tchr., Univ. of London; Examiner in Engl., London Univ. Mbrships: Royal Soc. of Lit.; Soc. of Authors, 1960-; Life, Nat. Book League; Inst. of Educ., London Univ. Publs: incl: Poems for Pleasure, 3 vols., 1955; The Poets Craft, 1957; The Spoken Word, 1961-63; The Craft of Prose, 1963; Current Literary Terms, Dictionary of their Origin & Use, 1965; Vital Themes Today, 1967; New Horizons, 10 vols., (co-author), 1968-71; Every One a Witness, The Georgian Age, 1970; The Plantagenet Age, 1973; The Tudor Age, 1973; The Stuart Age, 1973; Who's Who in Chaucer, 1974. Address: 59 Syon Park Gdns., Osterley, Isleworth, Middx. U.K. 3, 30, 35, 131.

SCOTT, Catherine D., b. 21 June 1927. Librarian. Educ: A.B., Cath. Univ. Am., 1950; M.S.L.S., 1955. Appts: Asst. Libn., Export-Import Bank of Wash., 1950-55; Asst. Libn., Nat. Assn. of Home Bldrs., 1955-62; Chief Tech. Libn., Bellcomm Inc., A.T. & T. Co., 1962-72; Hd. Libn., Nat. Air & Space Mus. Lib., Smithsonian Intn., 1972-. Mbrships incl: Vice Chmn., Nat. Commn. of Libs. & Info Sci.; Pres., Spec. Libs. Assn., Wash. D.C., 1971-72; Sec., Aerospace Div., Nat. Spec. Libs. Assn., 1968-69; Chmn., Publicity Comm., Int. Fed. of Libs. Assn. Conf., 1974; Deleg. & Mbr., Platform Comm., Republican Nat. Comm., 1964, 68; Dir., League of Republican Women & Bd. Dirs., 1956-68; Exec. Sec., Women for Nixon Nat. Advsry. Coun., 1968; 1st V.P., Everett McKinley Dirksen Republican Forum, 1969-72; Bd. Visitors, Cath. Univ. of Am. Lib., 1974; Vice Chmn., Nat. Commn. on Libs. & Info. Sci., apptd. by Pres. Nixon, 1969-76. Address: Nat. Air & Space Museum Lib., Smithsonian Instn., Wash., DC 20560, U.S.A. 5, 114.

SCOTT, Franklin Daniel, b. 4 July 1901. Educator. Educ: Doane Coll.; Ill. Coll.; Ph.B., 1923, M.A., 1924, Univ. of Chgo.; M.A., 1929, Ph.D., 1932, Harvard Univ.; Univ. of Stockholm, 1930-31. Appts: H.S. Tchr.,

1921-25; Asst. Prof., Simpson Coll., 1925-28; Superior State Coll., 1932-35; Northwestern Univ., 1932-69; Emeritus Prof., 1969-; Vis. Prof., Univ. of Southern Calif., Stanford Univ. & Pomona Coll.; Curator, Nordic Collects., Honnold Lib., 1970-. Mbrships. incl: Past Pres., Swedish Pioneer Histl. Soc.; Chmn., num. comms., Am. Histl. Assn.; Past Pres., Lib. of Int. Rels., Chgo.; Am. Scandinavian Fndn.; Past Pres., Northwestern Chapt., AAUP. Publs. incl: Bernadotte & the Fall of Napoleon, 1935; American Experience of Swedish Students, 1956; World Migration in Modern Times, 1968; Peopling of America, 1972. Hons: North Star, Sweden, 1952; White Rose, Finland, 1967; LL.D., Ill. Coll., 1958, Doane Coll., 1964; Fil.Dr., Uppsala Univ., Sweden, 1970. Address: Honnold Lib., Claremont, CA 91711, U.S.A. 2, 13, 30.

SCOTT, George E., b. 9 Nov. 1924. Physician (psychiatrist & neurologist). Educ: B.A., Univ. of Colo., 1946; M.D., Schl. of Med., ibid, 1948. Appts. incl: Pvte. Prac., 1952-56, '59-62; '66-; Chief of Neurol, Colo. State Hosp., Pueblo, 1961-63; Staff Psych., Denver Gen. Hosp., 1964-65; Dir. of Hosp. Psych. Servs., ibid, 1965-68; Clin. Dir.; Northwest Mental Hlth. Clin., 1969-73, Emergency Psych. Servs., Denver Gen. Hosp., 1973-; Electroencephalographer, ibid, 1964-68, Mt. Airy Hosp., 1968-. Mbrships: AMA; Am. Psych. Assn.; Am. Acad. Neurol.; Am. Med. Electrographic Assn.; Am. Assn. Hist. of Med.; Alpha Epsilon Delta; Phi Delta Chi. Contbr. of articles to profl. jrnls. Address: Psych. Emergency Servs., Denver Gen. Hosp., W. 8th. & Cherokee Sts., Denver, CO 80204, U.S.A.

SCOTT, Harold W., b. 30 Sept. 1906. Geologist. Educ: B.S., Univ. of Ill., Urbana, U.S.A., 1929; M.S., ibid, 1931; Ph.D., Univ. of Chgo., Ill., 1934. Appts. incl: Asst. Prof., Dept. of Geol., Mont. Schl. of Mining, 1933-37; Asst. Prof.-Assoc. Prof., Dept. of Geol., Univ. of Ill., 1937-47; Prof., ibid, 1947-69; Prof. & Chmn., Dept. of Geol., Mich. State Univ., E. Lansing, 1969-; Cons. & Pres., Geological Servs., Inc., 1945-55; Dir., For. Ops., Hunt Int. Petroleum Corp., 1955-56; Pres., Fishook Gas Corp., 1961-67. Mbrships. incl: Fellow, Geological Soc. of Am.; Soc. of Econ. Paleontologist & Mineralogist; Paleontological Soc.; Am. Assn. Petroleum Geologists; Phi Kappa Phi; Sigma Xi; Pres., Champaign-Urbana, Kiwanis Club, 1958-. Publs: Lectures on Geology by John Walker, 1966; Part Q, Arthropoda, Treatise on Invertebrate Paleontology, 1961; Articles in profl. jrnls. Hons: Disting. Lectr., Am. Assn. of Petroleum Geologists, 1949; Award, Am. Learned Soc., 1962. Address: 613 W. Delaware St., Urbana, IL 61801, U.S.A. 2, 14.

SCOTT, James Victor, b. 25 Dec. 1930. Veterinarian. Educ: B.S., Univ. of Ill., 1952; B.S., ibid, 1957; M.S., 1957; D.V.M.U. of Ill., 1959; Postgrad., Columbia Univ., 1954-55 & CCNY, 1954-55. Appts: Rsch. Assoc., Univ. of Ill., 1956-61; Prac., Vet. Med., Philo, Ill., 1959-; Prac., Speciality Cons. in Bovine Reprod.; Rsch. Dir. & Cons. for Eureka Mineral Co., Inc., Congerville, 1970-; Owner & Dir., Triple S.Bull Stn. 1973. Mbrships: Am. Vet. Med. Assn.; Vet. Med. Assn.; AAAS; Sigma Xi; Gamma Sigma Delta; Phi Zeta; Mason 32. Publs: Fertility Results using illini Temerature Semen Diluent in Beef Cattle, Jrnl. of Am. Vet. Med. Assn., 1958; Evaluation of the Electroejaculation Technique & the Spermatozoa Thus obtained from Rats, Mice & Guinea Pigs, The Anatomical Record, 1959. Address: Univ. of I. Trail, Philo, IL 61864, U.S.A. 8.

SCOTT, Johnie Harold, b. 8 May 1946. Writer; Filmmaker; Poet. Educ: B.A., Stanford Univ., Palo Alto, Calif., 1970; M.A., ibid, 1973; Am. Film Inst., Beverly Hills, Calif., 1972-73. Appts. incl: Ed., The Grapevine, monthly newspaper publd. by Watts Hlth. Fndn., L.A., Calif.; Press Sec., Assemblyman Leon Ralph (Dem.—55th Calif. Assembly Dist.); Corres., Time Mag., San Fran. Bur. Time-Life Inc.; Community Arts Specialist, Nat. Endowment for Arts Expansion Arts Prog.; Corres., Newsweek Mag., San Fran. Bur.; Proj. Coordinator, Stanford-Nairobi Summer Film Proj., Nairobi, Calif.; Deleg. to White House Conf. "To Fulfill These Rights", Wash. DC, 1966; Testified before Senator Abraham Ribicoff's Senate Comm. on Urban Problems, 1967. Mbrships: Stanford Alumni Assn.; Harvard Club of L.A.; Alpha Phi Alpha Fraternity, Inc. Work in many books & mags. inclng. From The Ashes: Voices of Watts (ed. by B. Schulberg); The New Black Poetry (ed. by C. Major); We Speak As Liberators: Young Black Poets (ed. by Orde Coombs); Nommo (ed. by W. Robinson); A Rock Against the Wind: Black Love Poems (ed. by D. Randall). Hons. incl: Bank of Am. Liberal Arts Award, 1964; Emmy Nomination by Nat. Acad. of TV Arts & Scis. for work in NBC TV Experiments in TV Special, The Angry Voices of Watts, 1966. Address: 12746 Belhaven Ave., L.A., CA, U.S.A.

SCOTT, John-Paul, see FARQUHAR, Jesse Carlton, Jr.

SCOTT, Marian Dale (Mrs. F.R. Scott), b. 26 June 1906. Painter. Educ: Montréal Art Assn., 1917-20; Monument Nat., Montreal; École des Beaux Arts, Montréal, 1922-23; Slade Schl. of Art, U.K., 1926. Appts: Tchr., Painting, St. Georges Schl., Montréal, 1949 & Montréal Mus. of Fine Arts, 1950-51; One-Man Shows: Grace Horne Galls., Boston, Mass., U.S.A., 1939; Queen's Univ., Kingston, Ont., 1948; Dominion Gall., Montréal, 1954, 56 & 58; Laing Gall., Toronto, 1961; Galerie Camille Hérbert, Montréal, 1964; Galerie Libre, Montréal, 1966. Also in num. dual & grp. exhibs. Works in num. colls. inclng: Nat. Gall. of Canada; Bezalel Mus., Jerusalem; Thomas More Inst., Montréal; Toronto Dominon Bank Coll etc.; Commns. incl: Murals in McGill Univ. & Montréal Gen. Hosp. Mbrships: Royal Canadian Acad. of Arts; Quebec Soc. of Profl. Artists; Canadian Artists' Representation; Hons. incl: 1st Prize, Canadian Grp. of Painters Exhib., 1966. Address: 451 Clarke Ave., Montréal, P.Q. H3Y 3C5, Canada. 5, 19, 133.

SCOTT, Nancy Rose Phillippi (Mrs. Donald S. Scott), b. 1 Oct. 1931. Teacher. Educ: B.A., Radford Coll., Va., U.S.A. Appts: Tchr., George Wythe H.S., 1 yr.; Tchr., Ft. Chiswell H.S., 1 yr.; Tchr., Rural Retreat H.S., 3 yrs.; Tchr., Wytheville Elem. Schl., 1 yr.; Tchr., Wytheville Intermediate Schl., 7 yrs. Mbrships. incl: NEA; Va. Educ. Assn.; Wythe Co. Educ. Assn.; Wytheville Intermediate PTA; Pres., Wytheville Woman's Club, 2 yrs., Sec., 2 yrs.; Girl Scout Ldr.; Helen Trinkle Music Club; Chi Beta Phi. Recip., Outstanding Jr. Clubwoman, 1964-65. Address: 380 E. North St., Wytheville, Va., U.S.A. 125.

SCOTT, Norma Linn (Mrs.), b. 13 Oct. 1894. Educator. Educ: B.A., Univ. of Tex., Austin, 1943; M.A., ibid, 1949. Appts: Tchr., Tex. Pub. Schls., 1915-65; Prin., Mullin H.S. & Buffalo H.S., Tex.; Asst., Govt. Schl., Univ. of Tex. Summer Sessions. Mbrships. incl: Hon. Pres., Alpha Chapt., Austin, Tex., Alpha Epsilon Chapt., Palestine & Gamma Psi Chapt., Leon Co., Delta Kappa Gamma Soc.; Pres., Austin Classroom Tchrs.; Pres., Engl. Sect., Dist. X, T.S.T.A.; Pres., AAUW, Austin; Pres., K.C. Muse Chapt., United Daughters of the Confederacy; State Pres., ibid; Daughters of the Repub. of Tex.; Austin Ret. Tchrs. Assn.; Smithsonian Instn.; Red Cross; Tarrytown Bapt. Ch.; Heritage Soc. Contbr. to educ. jrnls. Recip. Kellogg Fndn. Schlrship., Univ. of Tex. Address: 3001 Beverly Rd., Austin, TX 78703, U.S.A. 5, 7.

SCOTT, Osborne Ernest, b. 5 Feb. 1916. Professor. Educ: B.S.Ed., Hampton Inst., 1938; B.D., Oberlin Grad. Schl. Theol., 1941; M.A., Columbia Univ., 1951. Appts: Asst. Dir., Oberlin Community Ctr., Ohio, 1939-40; Asst. to Pres., Hampton Inst., Va.; 1941; Asst. Div. Chap., Korea, 1953; Div. Chap., Europe, 1960-63; FAc., U.S. Army Chap. Schl., 1950-53, 1956-59, retd. 1964; Exec. V.P., Am. Leprosy Mission, Inc., 1964-69; Prof., Dept. Chmn., Urban & Ethnic Studies, CCNY, 1969-71, Prof., Dept. Black Studies, 1972; Sr. Assoc., Ldrship. Resources Inc.; Bd. Mbr., Ch. World Serv. Mbr., num. profl. orgs. Collaborated in dev. of trng. prog. in human rels., Metropol. Police Dept., Wash. D.C. Hons. incl: var. mil. hons.; Citation for rehab. work, V.P. of Korea, 1954; commissioned to make study of serv. projs. in S.E. Asia, Ch. World Serv. & Nat. Coun. of Chs., 1973. Address: 323 Egmont Ave., Mt. Vernon, NY 10553, U.S.A. 6.

SCOTT, Willard Philip, b. 8 Jan. 1909. Lawyer & Business Executive. Educ: Grad., Ohio State Univ.; Dean's Schol., Columbia Univ. Law Schl. Appts: Ptnr., Oliver & Donnally, N.Y.C., 1938-68; Dir.-V.-Chmn., Bd., Am. Potash & Chem. Corp., 1951-; V.P. & Gen. Counsel-Sr. V.P., Kerr-McGee Corp., 1968-; Dir., 1st Nat. Bank & Trust Co., Okla. City, Transocean Drilling Co., Marine Resources Ins. Co. Ltd., Kerr-McGee Chem. Corp., kerr-McGee Fndn. Inc., Bikita Minerals (Pvt.), Okla Symphony Soc. & Okla. Arts & Sci. Fndn. Mbrships. incl: Fellow, Am. Bar Fndn.; Chmn., Sect. Corp., Banking & Bus. Law, Am. Bar Assn.; Chmn., Comm. Corporate Laws, ibid; Mbr., House of Delegs., ibid; Patron, Int. Bar Assn.; Rsch. Fellow, Southwestern Legal Fndn.; Phi Beta Kappa; Phi Beta Kappa Assoc.; Phi Alpha Theta; Pi Sigma Alpha; Am. Law Inst.; N.Y. State Bar Assn.; Okla. Bar Assn.; Am. Judicature Soc. Author num. legal articles; Co-author, Model Business Corporation Act Annotated; Former Ed., The Business Lawyer. Address: Kerr-McGee Corp., P.O. Box 25861, Oklahoma City, OK 73125, U.S.A. 2, 7, 12, 16, 22.

SCOTT-ATKINSON, David J.M., b. 1 Jan. 1920. Public Relations Consultant. Educ: St. Paul's Schl., London, U.K. ; Weinsburg, Germany. Appts: Hd. of P.R., Control Commn., N. Rhine, Westphalia, Germany, 1946; P.R. Off., Conservative Central Off., London, U.K., 1947-52; Mng. Dir., P.R. Servs. Ltd., U.K., 1952-57; V.P., Pub. & Indl. Rels. Ltd., Toronto, Canada, 1957-62; Dir., Planning & Dev., Clairtone Sound Corp., Toronto, 1963; Ptnr., Hall P.R. Ltd., 1964-67; Sr. Ptnr., Scott-Atkinson, Viccari, Only, Int. Ltd., 1967-. Mbr. & Off., var. P.R. socs. Publs: May I Tell Him Who's Calling?, 1974; An Immigrant's Guide to Canada, 1974. Columnist & contbr., Marketing Mag., 1968-. Recip., Fellowship of Inst. P.R., 1969. Address: 740 Bexhill Rd., Mississauga, Ont., Canada. 24.

SCRAGG, Roy Frederick Rhodes, b. 19 Feb. 1924. Physician. Educ: M.B., B.S., Univ. of Adelaide, 1946; D.T.M.&H., Univ. of Sydney, 1950; M.D., Univ. of Adelaide, 1954;

Fellow, Australian Coll. of Med. Admnstrs., 1968. Appts: Med. Off., T.P.N.G., 1947-56; Dir. of Pub. Hlth., T.P.N.G., 1957-70; Fndn. Prof., Soc. & Preventive Med., Univ. of Papua New Guinea, 1970-. Mbrships: Local sec., Royal Soc. of Tropical Med. & Hygiene; Councillor & local sec., Australian & N.Z. Assn. for Advancement of Sci.; Councillor, Coll. of Med. Admnstrs. Publs: Monographs & articles in profl. jrnls. Hons: O.B.E., 1971. Address: P.O. Box 592, Port Moresby, T.P.N.G., Australia. 23.

SCRIVEN, Michael, b. 28 Mar. 1928. Philosopher. Educ: B.A., Hons. Schl. of Maths., Univ. of Melbourne, Australia, 1948; D.Phil., Oxford Univ., U.K., 1956. Appts: Instr. Dept. of Philos., Univ. of Minn., U.S.A., 1952-56; Rsch. Assoc., Minn. Ctr. for Philos. of Sci., 1953-56, Asst. Prof., Swarthmore Coll., 1956-60; Prof., Hist. & Philos. of Sci., Ind. Univ., 1960-66; Prof., Philos., Univ. of Calif., Berkeley, 1966-. Mbrships: Govng. Bd., Philos. of Sci. Assn.; Bd. of Scientific & Ethical Responsibility, Am. Psychol. Assn.; Comm. on Tchng. of Philos., Am. Philos. Assn. Publs: Primary Philosophy, 1966; Applied Logic: An Introduction to Scientific Method, 1966; Co-Author, w. A. Calvin, Psychology, 1961; contbr. to var. profl. jrnls. Hons: Essay Prize, British Jrnl. for Philos. of Sci., 1954; Disting. Vis. Schol., Educl. Testing Serv., Princeton, N.J., 1970; Fellow, Ctr. for Adv. Study in Behavioral Scis., Stanford, Calif., 1963; Alfred North Whitehead Fellowship for Adv. Study in Educ., Harvard, 1970-71; Disting. Vis. Schol., Ctr. for Adv. Study in Theoretical Psychol., Univ. of Alta., Canada, 1967, 1970. Address: 1384 Queens Rd., Berkeley, CA 94708, U.S.A. 2, 23.

SCUCCHI, Robie P., Jr., b. 10 Apr. 1944. Artist; Assistant Professor of Art. Educ: B.S.E., Ark. State Univ., 1967; M.F.A., Inst. Allende, San Miguel de Allende, Guanajuato, Mexico, 1971; Grad. study, Southern Ill. Univ., Edwardsville. Appts. incl: Art Instr., Northwest H.S., House Springs, Mo., 1967-71; Chmn. of Art & Dist. Fine Arts Curriculum Coordinator, ibid, 1970-71; Art Instr., Miss. State Univ., 1971-74; Asst. Prof. of Art, ibid, 1974-. Mbr. num. profl. assns. inclng. former Chapt. Pres., Kappa Pi, Advisor & Fndr., Miss. State Univ. Hon. Artists' Guild & former Pres., Jefferson Co. Dist. Educ. Assn. for Arts. Solo Exhibs. incl: Ursuline Acad., St. Louis, Mo., 1969; Notre Dame Coll., St. Louis, Mo., 1970; Univ. of Ark. at Little Rock, 1974. Represented in pvte. & Univ. collections. Recent Grp. Exhibs. incl: Am. Inst. of Archt.'s, Ark. Br., Travelling Art Exhib., Little Rock, Ark., 1972; Jackson Municipal Art Gall., Jackson, Miss., 1973; Birmingham Art Mus., Mbrship. Exhib., Birmingham, Ala., 1973; Miss. State Univ. Art Fac. Exhib., Jackson Municipal Art Gall., 1974. Recip. many awards inclng. Best in Show, St. Charles' 4th Annual Guild Exhib., Mo., 1969, Purchase Award, Ark. Br., Am. Inst. of Archts., Ark. Artists' Exhib., 1972 & Best in Show, 15th Annual N. Little Rock Art Exhib., Ark., 1973. Address: P.O. Box 5215, Miss. State Univ., MS 39762, U.S.A.

SCULLY, Francis Joseph, b. 12 June 1925. Publishing Executive. Educ: B.S., Bus. Admin., LaSalle Coll., Phila., 1949; Postgrad. Work, N.Y. Univ. Schl. of Bus., 1959. Appts: w. Kurnit, Geller Assocs., Advt., N.Y.C., 1962-64; V.P., Norman, Craig & Kummel, ibid, 1964-66; Dir., Advt. & Merchandising, Hertz Corp., 1966-69; Pres., Standard Reference Lib., Inc., 1969-71; Pres., Dir., Funk & Wagnalls, Inc., 1971; Dir., Dun Donnelley Pub. Co.; Served w. U.S. Army, WW II. Mbrships: Phila. Art Dirs.

Club; Am. Inst. Graphic Arts; N.Y. Athletic Club; Exec. Coun., Dun & Bradstreet Cos., Inc. Recip., Purple Heart, Combat Inf. Badge. Address: 53 E. 77th St., N.Y., NY 10021, U.S.A. 2, 6.

SCUTELLA, Saverio, b. 11 Aug. 1910. Painter; Writer. Educ: Art Schl. & Acad. of Fine Arts, Rome; Grad., classical lit., Univ. of Urbe. Mbr. of var. acads. Contbr. to var. art exhibs. Hons. incl: First Prize, Roman Coll., Rome, 1932; First Prize, Calabro-Siculi Exhib., Messina, 1957; First Prize, Nat. Painting Competition, Rome, 1967; First Prize, Arte pro Arte Competition, Terni, 1969; Gold Medal of Pres. of the Senate, 1963; Gold Medal, Costa Viola Poetry Competition, Rome, 1966; Gold Medal, Int. Exhib., Miami, 1965; Gold Medal, Passion of Christ Exhib., Burkhardt Gall., Rome, 1970. Address: Via Alessandro Poerio 136, Rome Italy.

SCUTT, Winifred, b. 15 May 1892. Artist; Writer; Evangelist. Educ: Mary Baldwin Sem., Stanton, Va.; Art Students' League, N.Y. 1st poetry, as child, 1907; 1st drawings, as student, Art Student's League, N.Y.; 1st portrait paintings, 1932; Fndr. & Pres., Ave. of Am. Art, Pasadena, Calif., for exhib. religious art, 1950. Mbrships. incl: Art Comm., Pen & Brush Club, N.Y.C.; Nat. League of Am. Pen Women; Nat. Soc. of Arts & Letters; Taos, N.M., Art Assn. Publs. incl: (self-illustrated) Tomorrow; The Children's Master; The Mystical Marriage of Christ; Is Your Death Inevitable? . Solo art exhibs. incl: Delphic Galls., N.Y.C., 1934; Sartor Gall., Dallas, Tex., 1943. Grp. exhibs. incl: Madouna Exhib., L.A., Calif., 1950; Ave. of Am. Art, Calif., Colo., Tex. Recip., var. art awards. Address: Acacia Inn 21, 811 E. Washington Blvd., Pasadena, CA 91104, U.S.A. 5, 9, 22, 37, 57, 74, 128, 129.

SEABORG, Glenn Theodore, b. 19 Apr. 1912. Chemist; Educator. Educ: A.B., Univ. of Calif., L.A., 1934; Ph.D., Univ. of Calif., Berkeley, 1937. Appts: Rsch. Assoc., Univ. of Calif., Berkeley, 1937-39, Instr., 1939-41, Asst. Prof., 1941-45, Prof., 1945-71, Univ. Chancellor, 1958-61, Univ. Prof., 1971-; Dir., Manhattan Prof., Univ. of Chgo. Metallurgical Lab., 1942-46; Dir., Nuclear Chem. Div., Lawrence Berkeley Lab., 1946-58, 1971-, Assoc. Dir., 1954-61, 1971-; Chmn., U.S. Atomic Energy Commn., 1961-71. Mbr., Fellow & Off., nat. & for. profl. orgs. Publs. incl: Elements of the Universe, 1958; Education & the Atom (co-author), 1964; Nuclear Milestones, 1972. Over 200 sci. papers & ency. articles. Co-discoverer, plutonium, & 8 other chem. elements. Hons. incl: Nobel Prize for Chem., 1951; Disting. Honor Award, U.S. State Dept., 1971; over 40 doctoral degrees. Address: Lawrence Berkeley Laboratory, University of California, Berkeley, CA 94720, U.S.A. 1, 2, 14, 34.

SEABURG, Alan Leslie, b. 28 Feb. 1932. Librarian. Educ: A.B., Tufts Univ., 1954; B.D., Crane Theological Schl., ibid, 1957; M.L.S., Simmons Coll., 1959; Grad. courses in relig., Boston Univ., 1957-58. Appts. incl: Bibliographer, Tufts Univ. Lib., 1959-65; Libn., Crane Theological Schl., Tufts Univ., 1957-65; Min., Charles St. Meeting House, Boston, Mass., 1965-68; Libn. & Archivist, Unitarian Universalist Assn., 1967-70; Curator of Manuscripts, Andover-Harvard Theological Lib., Harvard Divinity Schl., Harvard Univ., 1970-. Mbrships: Comm. on Histl. Schlrship., Unitarian Universalist Assn., 1961-; Dir., Universalist Histl. Soc., 1970-; Bd. of Dirs., Am. Mus. of Negro Hist., 1967-69; Dir., West End Ecumenical Min., 1968. Author of articles &

poetry in num. jrnls. Address: Andover-Harvard Theological Lib., 45 Francis Ave., Cambridge, MA 02138, U.S.A. 6.

SEADLER, Stephen Edward. Ideologist; Behavioral Scientist; Management Consultant. Appts. incl: Ed., AEC Digest, Congressional Record & Legal Rschr., U.S. Atomic Energy Commn., Wash., 1947-51; Electronic Engr., Cushing & Neville, Warner Inc., N.Y.C., 1951-54; Mktng. Rsch. Mgr., W.A. Scheaffer Pen Co., Ft. Madison, Iowa, 1959-65; Fndr., Int. Dynamics Corp., ibid, 1965; Pres., 1965-70; Fndr., Ideological Defense Ctr., Ft. Madison & N.Y.C., a tax-exempt corp. for dev. of Ideol. Defense Systems, 1968; Pres., 1968-; Dir., Behavioral Rsch. Survey Ctr., 1969-70; Pres., Uniconsult, 1973-, specializing in strategic planning, computerized mgmt. systems, advanced int. pol. econ. & conflict reduction. Mbrships. incl: Acad. of Pol. Sci.; Am. Sociol. Assn.; Am. State. Assn.; IEEE; Am. Phys. Soc.; Am. Mgmt. Assn.; Princeton Univ. Club; Mason, Scottish Rite 32nd degree; Shriner. Author of articles on radar, computers, neurophysiol., biochem., ideol. disarmament, soc. indicators. Creator, The DELTA Prog. for Prevention & Treatment of Violence. Address: 520 Fifth Ave., N.Y.; NY 10036, U.S.A. 8, 16.

SEAGA, Edward Philip George, b. 28 May 1930. Member of Parliament, Government of Jamaica; Financial Consultant. Educ: B.A., Harvard Univ., 1952; Sociol. Rschr., "Revival Cults" & "Dev. of Child", Inst. of Soc. & Econ. Rsch., Univ. of W. Indies, in Jamaica, 1952-55. Appts: Mbr. of Legis. Coun. (youngest in hist.), & Mbr. of Comm. which drafted Constitution of Jamaica, 1959-62; Sec., Jamaica Labour Party, 1960-62; M.P., 1962-; Min. of Dev. & Welfare (youngest Min. in hist.), resp. for Econ. Planning, Community Dev. & Cultural Dev. inclng. Nat. 5-yr. Plan, 1963-68, Comprehensive Community Dev. Prog. (100 village prog.), Nat. Vols. & Jamaica Festival, 1962-67; Min. of Finance, resp. for Finance, Econ. & Phys. Planning, Phys. & Cultural Dev., inclng. 20-yr. Nat. Phys. Dev. Plan, 1970-90, Comprehensive Fiscal Reform Prog. & Jamaicanization Prog. (of for. owned instns.), also Jamaican Gov. of World Bank, Gov., IMF, & Gov., Inter-Am. Dev. Bank, 1967072; Jamaican Gov., Caribbean Dev. Bank, 1971-72; Dir., Cons. Servs. Ltd., Kingston. Mbrships: Kingston Cricket Club; Patron, Nat. Dance Theatre Co.; Jamaica Gun Club. Publs: Parent Teacher Relationship in a Jamaican School, in Social & Economic Studies; Faith Healing in Jamaica, in Tomorrow Magazine; Revival Spirit Cults, in Jamaica Journal. Recip., Independence Medal, 1962. Address: P.O. Box 573, Kingston 10, Jamaica. 96, 109.

SEALTS, Merton Miller, Jr., b. 8 Dec. 1915. Professor of English. Educ: B.A., Coll. of Wooster, Ohio, 1937; Ph.D., Yale Univ., 1942. Appts: Instr., Engl., Univ. of Mo., 1941-42; Instr., Engl., Wellesley Coll., 1946-48; Asst. Prof., Engl., Lawrence Coll./Univ., 1948-51; Assoc. Prof., ibid, 1951-58; Prof., 1958-65; Prof., Univ. of Wis., Madison, 1965-. Mbrships: MLA; AAUP; Am. Studies Assn.; Phi Beta Kappa; Nat. Coun. Tchrs. of Engl. Publs. incl: Melville's Reading: A Check-List of Books Owned & Borrowed, 1966; Co-Ed., Emerson's Nature: Origin Growth Meaning, 1969; The Early Lives of Melville: Nineteenth-Century Biographical Sketches & their Authors, 1974. Hons. incl: Guggenheim Fellow, 1962-63; Edward & Rosa Uhrig Mem. Award for Excellent Tchng., 1964-65; Sr. Fellow, Nat. Endowment for the Humanities, 1975. Address: 4006 Mandan Crescent, Madison, WI 53711, U.S.A. 2, 13, 30.

SEALY, Desmond Hollinsworth, b. 24 Feb. 1924. Manpower Official, Labor Department. Educ: Manpower Official, Labor Department. Educ: B.A., Brooklyn Coll., 1959; M.A., Univ. of Chgo., 1960; Dip., Dale Carnegie Inst., 1966. Appts. incl: Dir., Equal Opportunity, Bur. of Works Progs., Manpower Admin., Labor Dept., Wash., 1966-67; Chief, Div. of Prog. & Budget Planning, Manpower Admin., ibid, 1967-68; Chief, Div. of Special Progs., 1968-69; Special Asst. to Dir., Off. Trng. & Employment Opportunities, Manpower Admin., 1969-. Mbrships. incl: Panelist, White House Conf. on Equal Opportunity & Conf. on Tech. Assistance, U.S. Equal Employment Opportunity Commn., 1965; Fellow, Nat. Urban League. Address: P.O. Box 4886, Wash., DC 20008, U.S.A.

SEALY, Theodore Eustace, b. 6 Nov. 1909. Journalist; Editor. Appts: w. editl. staff, Gleaner Co. Ltd., 1928; Co-ord. Ed., ibid, 1944; Assoc. Ed., 1946-51; Ed., Daily Gleaner & other newspaper publs. of the Gleaner Co. Ltd., 1951-. Mbrships. incl: Pres., Jamaica Press Assn., 1943-45, '50-53, '60-65; Co-org., All-Island Arts & Crafts Exhib., 1938; Fndr. & Org., The Sir Edward Denham Shield (Annual) Art Exhib. for Schls., 1938; Chmn., Jamaica Tercentenary Celebrations, 1955; Rep. W.I., N.Z. Conf. on Commonwealth Rels., 1959; Chmn., Jamaica Independence Celebrations, 1962; Fndr. & 1st. Chmn., Jamaican Coun. Int. Affairs. Hons: C.B.E., 1956; Jamaica Independence Medal, 1962; Musgrave Gold Medal, Inst. of Jamaica, 1966. Address: P.O. Box 40, Kingston, Jamaica, W. Indies.

SEAMAN, Robert LeRoy, b. 26 Mar. 1924. Corporation Executive. Educ: B.Mgmt.E., Rensselaer Polytech. Inst., 1950; S.M., Sloan Schl., MIT, 1968. Appts: Naval Aviator, W.W.II; Var. Analytical & Supvsry. Assignments, Ford Motor Co., 1950-55; Div. Controller, Curtiss-Wright Corp., 1956-58; Internal Mgmt. Cons., C.B.S., Inc., 1958-60; Asst. Controller, Financial Analysis & Mgmt. Info., 1960-67, Dir., Corporate Planning, 1968-69, V.P., 1969-; Raytheon Co., Lexington, Mass. Dir., Iowa Mfg. Co., Cedar Rapids, Iowa, 1972-. Mbrships: Trustee, Lexington Savings Bank; Sigma Xi; Tau Beta Pi; Financial Execs. Inst.; Rensselaer Soc. Engrs.; Epsilon Delta Sigma. Co-Author, STEPS, A Computer-Aided, On-Line, Planning & Analysis System. Address: 141 Spring St., Lexington, MA 02173, U.S.A. 16.

SEARLE, Ronald, b. 3 Mar. 1920. Artist. Educ: Cambridge Schl. of Art. Appts: Dir., Perpetua Books, London, 1951-61; Punch Table, 1956-; Contbr., New Yorker, 1966-. Fellow, Soc., Ind. Artists. Mbr., Alliance Graphique Ind. Artists. Publs. incl: Forty Drawings; Le Nouveau Ballet Anglais; Hurrah for St. Trinian's; The Female Approach; Back to the Slaughterhouse; Souls in Torment; The Rakes Progress; Merry England etc.; Which Way Did He Go; From Frozen North to Filty Lucre; Searle in the Sixties; Pardong M'sieur; Searle's Cats; Take One Toad; The Square Egg; Hellow—Where Did All the People Go; Secret Sketchbook; The Second Coming of Toulouse-Lautrec; The Addict; Co-author: The Terror of St. Trinian's; Down with Skool; How to be Topp; The Compleet Molesworth; Paris Sketchbook; Looking at London; The St. Trinian Story; The Big City; U.S.A. for Beginners; Russia for Beginners; The Great Fur Opera. Address: c/o Hope Leresche, 11 Jubilee Place, London SW3, U.K. 1, 2, 3, 30, 34, 43, 128.

SEARLES, Anna Hawley (Mrs. Herbert L. Searles), b. 8 Sept. 1898. Educator. Educ: State Univ. of Iowa, 1920-24; James Millikin Univ., 1929-30. Appts. incl: Asst., Student Counselor, State Univ. of Iowa, 1918-25, Instr., Dept. of Romance Langs., 1922-23, Literary Critic & Rsch. Assoc., Inst. Character Rsch., 1925-30; Chmn., Inst. Character Rsch., Schl. of Philosophy, Univ. of Southern Calif., 1930-37, Dir., Lit. Proj., 1937-43, Acad. Coord., Navy Coll. Trng. Prog., 1943-57, Acting Dir., Inst. of Character Rsch., 1943-46, Dir., 1946-. Mbr., Profl. & civic orgs. Publs. incl: The Road Series (Co-ed.), 1930; Living Through Biography Series (Co-ed.), 1936; The Searles Readers, Living Through Reading Series (Author & Ed.), 1950-51. Contbr., var. profl. jrnls. Hons: Dir., Palmer Fndn., 1943; admin. of Anna Hawley Searles Grant-in-Aid Schlrships. by Delta Kappa Gamma, var. dates. Address: 10381 Glenbarr Ave., Los Angeles, CA 90064, U.S.A. 5, 9, 141.

SEARLES, Stephen. Sculptor. Educ: Art Students League, N.Y.C.; Grand Central Art Schl., N.Y.C.; Fontainebleau, France, under Gelini Study under Jay Conaway, Monhegan Is., Me. Appts: Art Instr., Newark (N.J.) Schl. of Fine & Indl. Art; Tchr., summers, own studio, E. Gloucester, Mass.; Art Instr., Vesper George Schl. of Art, Boston, 1974; Capt., Educl. Div. U.S. Army, Tchr., Drawing & Sculpture, Biarritz, 1945-46; Lt.-Col., USAR (retd.). Mbrships: Nat. Sculpture Soc.; Am. Artists Profl. League; Guild of Boston Artists; Rockport Art Assn.; Am. Vets. Soc. of Artists; Copley Soc. of Boston; Allied Artists of Am. Sculpture: Num. portraits, bronze & stone, inclng. Am. artists Gordon Grant, James Montgomery Flagg, Howard Chandler Christie, Harvey Dunn; Designer of Copley Soc. Medal, Boston; Our Lady of Good Voyage, statue in Gloucester, Mass. Hons: Prizes, Montclair Mus. of Art, 1950, Salmagundi Club, N.Y.C., 1952; Springfield (Mass.) Mus., 1965; Rockport Art Assn., 1968. Address: Fenway Studios, 30 Ipswich St., Boston, MA 02215, U.S.A. 37.

SEARS, Jim M., b. 30 Sept. 1939. Retail Trading Executive. Educ: B.A., N. Tex. State Univ., 1962. Appts: Personnel Staff, Sears-Roebuck & Co., Dallas, Tex.; Personnel & Ops., Sanger-Harris, Dallas; Central Ops. Mgr., Joske's of Houston, Tex. Mbr. & Pres., Local Chapt., Theta Chi. Recip., Colley Mem. Award as Outstanding Grad., Theta Chi. Address: 10803 Idlebrook, Houston, TX 77070, U.S.A.

SEARS, Oretta Dianora (Mrs. Donald Albert Sears), b. 1 Feb. 1928. Attorney-At-Law. Educ: Liceo Michelangelo, Florence, Italy, 1946; B.A., Upsala Coll., E. Orange, N.J., U.S.A. 1960; J.D., Univ. of Calif., L.A., 1963. Appts. incl: Trial Atty., Lands & Natural Resources Div., Dept. of Justice, Wash. D.C., 1963-66; Lectr., Engl. & Law, Abdullahi Bayero Coll., Ahmadu Bello Univ., Kano, N. Nigeria, 1966-67; Pvte. Prac., Kellogg & George, Oakland, Calif., 1967; Dpty. Dist. Atty., Orange Co., Calif., 1968-; Municipal Ct. Trial Atty., 1968-69; Hd., Writs & Appeals Sect., 1970-. Mbrships. incl: Calif., Am. & Fed. Bar Assn.; Chmn., Comm. on Mines, Minerals & Natural Resources, 1965-66; Orange Co. Bar & Criminal Bar Assns.; The Coll. Engl. Assn.; Nat. Lawyers Club, D.C.; Assoc. Mbr., The Lotos Club, N.Y.C.; Admitted to Calif. Supreme Ct., U.S. Circuit Ct. of Appeals; U.S. Dist. Ct. of Appeals, U.S. Supreme Ct., U.S. Ct. of Claims. Num. articles in profl. jrnls. Hons. incl: Upsala Award; Mbr., N.J. Histo. Soc. Address: 700 Civic Ctr. Dr. W., Santa Ana, CA, U.S.A. 5.

SEAVER, George, b. 23 July 1890. Clergyman. Educ: M.A., Oxford Univ., U.K.,

1912; B.D., London Univ., 1925. Litt.D., Univ. of Dublin, Ireland, 1947. Ordained Southwark Diocese, 1925. Appts. incl: Tutor & Lectr., St. Aidan's Coll., 1933; Rector, Berrow & Pendock, Worcs., U.K., 1944; Bishop's Vicar, Kilkenny, Ireland, 1946; Rector, ibid, & Dean of Ossory, 1950-57; Canon, St. Patrick', Dublin, 1951-57. Mbrships. incl: Fellow, Royal Geog. Soc.; Fellow, Royal Soc. of Antiquaries, Ireland. Publs. incl: Sir Francis Younghusband, 1952; The Deep Church (Introduction), 1952; Icelandic Yesterdays, 1957; David Livingstone—His Life & Letters, 1957; Tales of Brother Douglas, 1960; John Allen Fitzgerland Gregg—Archbishop, 1953; Introduction to The Worst Journey in the World (intro. to new ed.), 1965; Richard Archer Houblon—A Memoir, 1966. Address: St. Ernan's, Donegal Town, Repub. of Ireland. 1, 3.

SEAY, Peggy Casey, b. 24 Aug. 1928. Real Estate Broker. Educ: Ga. Bapt. Hosp., Atlanta, 1947-50; Univ. of Ga., Atlanta, 1947-50; Ga. Inst. of Real Estate, 1966; Ga. Realtors Inst., Univ. of Ga., 1973. Appts: Hd. Nurse, Ga. Bapt. Newborn Nursery, 1962-63; Indl. Nurse, Rich's Dept. Store, 1963-64; Sales Rep., Bullard Realty, Atlanta, 1962-67; Owner, Broker, Seay Realty Co., Fayetteville, Ga., 1967-74. Mbrships. incl: Make Am. Better Chmn., Ga. Assn. of Realtors; Fayette Co. Indl. Authority; Charter mbr., Fayette Count Human Soc.; Fndr., Fayette Co. Realtors Bd., 1970; Served as Charter Pres., V.P., Treas. & Bd. of Dirs.m ibid; Charter Sec., Fayette Co. Bus. & Profl. Club, 1970; Sec. & Dir., Fayette Co. Chmbr. of Comm., 1972-74. Hons. incl: Award of recognition, Ga. Realtors Assn., 1971; Realtor of the Yr., Fayette Co., 1972. Address: Seay Realty Co., 520 N. Glynn St., Fayetteville, GA, U.S.A. 5, 125.

SEBAGEREKA, Samwiri Kato, b. 9 Oct. 1933. Company Director; Accountant. Educ: King's Coll., Budo, Uganda, 1946-56; Birmingham Polytech., U.K., 1958-60; Birmingham Univ., ibid, 1960-61. Appts: Acct., Uganda Govt., 1961-64; Acct.-Gen., E. African Community, 1965; Commnr.-Gen. Income Tax, ibid, 1965-69; Chmn., Mackenzie Dalgety Ltd., 1969-; Dir., Uganda Cement Ind., 1969-; Financial Dir., Export & Import Corp., 1970-72; Chmn., J.H. Minet Uganda Ltd., 1971-; Chmn., Sales & Serv. Ltd., 1971-; Chmn., Peoples Newspapers Ltd., 1971-; Chmn., Bus. Machines (U) Ltd., 1972-; Dir., Lint Marketing Bd., Uganda, 1973-. Mbrships: Chmn., Assn. Chartered Secs., Uganda; Patron, Makerere Univ. Commerce Students Assn.; Chmn., Nat. Comm. Commercial Educ.; V.P., Kampala Rotary Club; Treas., Ch. of Uganda Special Fund. Author articles on Problems of Taxation in Developing Countries, 1969; Commercial Education in Uganda, 1971. Recip. Uganda Govt. Medal for servs. to Commerce & Ind. Address: P.O. Box 2019, Kampala, Uganda, E. Africa. 135.

SEBASTIEN, G.S., b. 28 Mar. 1909. Painter; Sculptor. Self-taught. Mbr., Salon d'Automne et des Indépendants, Paris. Exhibs: Paris, Brussels, Milan, Rome, etc. Works in collects. incl: Bachir (London); La Source (Canada); La Venus Verte (Switzerland); Les Mendiants (N.Y.); Les Rois (Maeght Coll.); La Balance (Milan); La Pomme (San Francisco); Les Voix (Mexico); La Culture de l'Ame (Paris); Hons: Laureate, Blumenthal Fndn., 1936; Dips., Paris Int. Exhib., 1937; Silver Medal, Brussels, 1958; Gold Medal, Milan; Hon. Mbr., Acads. London & Rome, 1970; Gold Medal, Mérite Civique. Address: 7 Passage Ricaut, 75013 Paris, France. 105, 133.

SECHER, Bjorn. Author; Lecturer; Educator. Educ: Advanced study in Maths., Johannesburg Coll., Copenhagen, Denmark. Appts: Mil. Serv. w. Royal Danish Guard; Apprentice, Gapp's Inc., London, U.K.; Steamship Broker, Hamburg, Germany; Mgr., Hotal Scandia, Mallorca, Spain; Salesman, Pitney-Bowes, San Fran., Calif.; Pres., Nitfisk of Am., Greenville, S.C.; Dir., Sci. of Personal Achievement, Ft. Lauderdale, Fla.; currently Pres., Bjorn Secher Fndn. & Inst. for Profl. Dev. Originator of Progs: Personal Development Motivational & Self-Discovery Program; The Science of Achievement; You—In Steps to Success (LP album & cassetts). Author of books: Appointment with Success; Success is Luck—Ask Any Failure. Hons: num. nat. & local awards. Address: P.O. Box 1305, Evergreen CO 80439, U.S.A.

SECKLER, Max, b. 23 Sept. 1927. Professor. Educ: Philos. & theol. studies, Tübingen & Münich, Germany, Paris, France & Rome, Italy; Ordained Cath. priest. Appts: Parish work; Asst. to Prof. H. Fries, Munich; Lectr., Passau, 1964; Prof., Systematic Theol., Tübingen; Co-Ed., ThQ & TTS. Publs: Instinkt und Glaubenswille nach Thomas von Aquin, 1961; Das Heil in der Geschichte. Geschichtstheologisches Denken bei Thomas von Aquin, 1964; Theologie vor Gericht. Der Fall Wilhelm Koch—Ein Bericht, Tübingen, 1972; Hoffnungsversuche, 1972. Address: Sommerhalde 5, D-74 Tübingen 6, German Fed. Repub. 43.

SECORD, Lloyd Calvin, b. 28 Aug. 1923. Consulting Engineer. Educ: B.Sc., Queen's Univ., Kingston, Ont., Canada, 1945. Appts. incl: Chief Design Engr., A.V. Roe (Canada) Ltd., 1946-53; Assoc., Paul Dilworth & Co., 1953-56; Prin., (V.P.), Dilworth, Secord & Assocs. Ltd., 1956-58 & Dilworth, Secord, Meagher & Assocs. Ltd., 1958-. Mbrships. incl: Sci. Coun. of Canada; Dir., Canadian Nuclear Assn.; V.P., Pres., ibid, 1967-70; Fellow, Canadian Aeronautics & Space Inst.; Assn. Profl. Engrs. of Ont.; Engrng. Inst. Canada. Publs. incl: What's Ahead in Canada's Nuclear Future?, 1970; Co-author, In Orbit Servicing of Spacecraft, 1972. Holder of 8 patents. Recip., Gold Medal for highest standing in Mech. Engrng., 1945. Address: Dilworth, Secord, Meagher & Assocs. Ltd., 4195 Dundas St. W., Toronto, Ont. M8X 1Y4, Canada. 88.

SECREST, Daisy Howerton, (Mrs. Raymond M. Secrest), b. 9 May 1911. Home Economist. Educ: Elem. Tchrs. Cert., Ferrum Trng. Schl., Va.; 1929; Normal Profl. Cert., Radford Coll., Va., 1930; Coll. Profl. Cert., ibid, 1940; postgrad. work, Va. Polytechnic Inst., Univs. of Ark., Colo., & Ariz. Appts: Elem. Schl. Prin., Patrick Co., Va., 1930-32; Elem. Schl. Tchr., Charlotte Co., 1933-34; Elem. Schl. Prin., 1934-39; w. Va. Agricl. Ext. Serv., 1940-59; Dietician, Chesepeake & Ohio Railway Hosp., 1959-61; w. Ohio Coop. Serv., 1961-71, until retirement; return to tchng., elem. schl., Drakes Br., Va., 1973-. Mbrships. incl: Va. Home Econs. Assn., var. comms.; Dist. Pres., Va. Home Demonstration Agts. Assn.; NEA. Hons. incl: Nat. Award for Disting. Serv. in Ext. Serv., 1969; 1st Hon. Citizen, Carroll Co., Ohio, 1969. Address: 310 W. Sycamore St., Chase City, VA 23924, U.S.A.

SECREST, Vivian Virginia (Mrs. Robert M. Secrest), b. 8 May 1917. Librarian. Educ: B.S., Ball State Univ., 1943; M.L.S., Tex. Woman's Univ., 1960. Appts: Tchr., Gov. I.P. Gray H.S., Portland, Ind., 1944-45; Tchr., Denver high schls., 1957-58; Catalogue Libn., Olin Lib., Wash. Univ., St. Louis, 1961-68; Hd.,

Cataloguing Div., ibid, 1968-70; Dir., Art & Arch. Lib., Steinberg Hall, Wash. Univ., 1970-. Mbrships: ALA; CAA; Directory Comm., ARLIS/NA; ARLIS/KM. Address: Art & Arch. Lib., Washington Univ., St. Louis, MO 63130, U.S.A. 5.

SEDYCH, Andrei, b. 14 Aug. 1902. Newspaper Editor & Executive. Educ: Schl. of Pol. Scis., Paris, France, 1925. Appts: Parliamentary Corres., Poslednie Novosti, of P.N. Milioukoff, Paris, 1924-40; City Ed., Novoye Russkoye Clovo, N.Y.C., U.S.A., 1942-67, Mng. Ed., 1967-73, Ed.-in-Chief & Pres., 1973-. Mbrships. incl: Pres., Russian Literary Fndn.; Chmn., Exec. Comm., Am. European Friends of ORT; Central Bd. Mbr., World ORT Union; Exec. Comm. Mbr., Am. ORT Fedn. Publs: This Land of Israel, 1968; 15 books, hist., essays, short stories, reminiscence, in Russian. Recip., Man of the Yr. Award, Am. ORT Fedn., 1968. Address: Novoye Russkoye Slovo, 243 W. 56th St., N.Y., NY 10019, U.S.A.

SEEBINGER, Fred Louis, b. 13 June 1918. Engineering Company Executive. Educ: B.S., Brooklyn Poly. Inst., 1940; Postgrad., R.C.A. Inst., 1942. Appts: served USNR, 1945; Engr., Int. Projector Corp., N.Y.C.; Sr. Engr., Sperry Gyroscope, Lake Success, N.Y.; now Chief Engr., Atlas Sound, Parsippany, N.J. Mbrships: IEEE (Sr.); Audio Engrng. Soc. (Charter); Acoustical Soc. Contbr., articles on sound, to: Sound Communication; Factory; Insurance New; Elec. Cons. Patentee, 1st Electronic Depth Sounder & 4 other patents on sound equip. Address: 115-25 Tower Hill Ln., Kinnelon, NJ 07405, U.S.A. 6.

SEEGER, Walther Hans Paul, b. 19 May 1932. Manufacturers' Representative & Consultant. Educ: Commercial Schl., Germany, 1950-53. Appts: Trng. in commerce, wholesale, ind., banking, ins., import & export, as Asst., Rhine-Ruhr Dist. & Hamburg; Dept. Mgr., Africa; Asst. to Mng. Dir., Singapore, 1960-63; Mng. own bus. as Mfrs.' Rep. & Indl. Cons., 1963-. Mbrships: Jr. Chambr. of Comm., Singapore (Comm. Chmn. & Dir.); Dir. & Chmn., P.R., Lions' Club, Tanglin, Singapore; China (Art) Soc; Singapore Acad. of Arts; Singapore Art Soc.; Japan Club; Intercontinental Biographical Assn.; Senator, Jr. Chmbr. Int. Author of market reports for BDA. Hons. incl: Dip., Singapore Acad. of Arts. Address: 16-D, 4th Floor, Block B, First Mansion, Meyer Rd., Jalan Daliah, Singapore, 15, 131.

SEEGMILLER, Ben Lorin, b. 27 Sept. 1940. Mining Engineer. Educ: B.S., Geological & Mining Engrng., Univ. of Utah, Salt Lake City, U.S.A., 1964; M.S., ibid, 1966; Ph.D., 1969. Appts: Rsch. Asst., Rock Mech., Univ. of Utah, 1964-69; Tchng. Asst., Mining, ibid, 1967-69; Mining Rsch. Engr., Corp. Mining Rsch. Dept., The Anaconda Co., Salt Lake City, 1969-71; Sr. Mining Rsch. Engr., ibid, 1971-72; Chief Rock Mech. Engr., Primary Metals Div., Anaconda Co., Tucson Ariz., 1972-74; Pres., Seegmiller Assocs., Tucson, 1974-. Registered Profl. Engr: Ariz., Idaho, Mont., Nev., N.M., & Utah. Mbrships: Int. Soc. of Rock Mech.; Am. Inst. of Mining, Metallurgical & Petroleum Engrs.; Canadian Inst. of Mining & Metallurgy; Nat. Soc. of Profl. Engrs.; Ariz. Soc. of Profl. Engrs. Contbr., articles in profl. jrnls. & handbooks. Holder, 2 U.S. patents. Address: 8117, E. Baker Dr., Tucson, AZ 85710, U.S.A. 9.

SEELEY, John Ronald, b. 21 Feb. 1913. Educator; Social Scientist. Educ: A.B., Univ. of

Chgo., 1942; Postgrad., 1945-46. Appts. incl: Fac. Mbr., Univ. of Toronto, 1948-64; Prof., York Univ., 1960-63; Chmn., Dept. of Sociol., ibid, 1962-63; Dean & Dir. of Prog., Ctr. for Study of Democratic Instns., 1966-69; Prof. of Critical Studies, Cal. Inst. for the Arts, 1970-72; Rsch. Sociol., UCLA Neuropsych. Inst., 1972-. Mbrships. incl: Phi Beta Kappa, Chgo, 1942; Sci. Assoc., Acad. of Psychoanalysis; Fellow, AAAS; Am. Acad. of Pol. & Soc. Sci; Fellow, Am. Assn. for Humanistic Psychol. Publs. incl: The Pulhems Dictionary, A Manual for Military Manpower Classification, 1944; The Americanization of the Unconscious, 1967. Contbr. to profl. jrnls. Address: 666 Hampden Place, Pacific Palisades, CA 90272, U.S.A. 2, 14, 50, 88, 128, 131, 140.

SEELMANN-EGGEBERT, Ulrich, b. 5 June 1919. Author. Educ: Studied Romance Langs., art hist. & musicol. Appts: Theatre & Art Critic, National Zeitung, Basle, Switzerland; Jt. Theatre Critic & Theatre News Ed., Neue Zürcher Zeitung, Zurich. Mbrships: PEN, Ctr. of German-speaking Writers Abroad, London; Int. Schutzverband deutschsprachiger Schriftsteller, Zurich; Assn. de la Presse Etrangère en Suisse, Bern; Soc. d'histoire du theatre, Paris, France; Schweizerische Gesellschaft für Theaterkultur, Bern; Basle Sect., Int. Soc. for Contemporary Music; Verein für das Jüdische Museum der Schweiz, Basle. Publs: Käthe Kollwitz—Der Mensch, das Werk, der Geist, 1947; Christliche Dichter der Gegenwart, 1955; Theaterstadt Stuttgart 1912-1962, 1962; Maria von Ostfelden und das Theater unserer Zeit, 1974; Translations of Eugène Ionesco, Arthur Adamov & Michel de Ghelderode into German. Hons: Reuchlin Medal, Pforzheim, 1955; Medaille de la Exposition Universelle, Brussels, Belgium, 1958. Address: 5 Burgstrasse, CH-4125 Riehen (Basle), Switzerland. 43.

SEELYE, Edward Eggleston, b. 8 Feb. 1924. Psychiatrist. Educ: B.A., Columbia Coll., Columbia Univ., N.Y.C.; M.D., Albany Med. Coll., N.Y. Appts: Res. Physn., Psych., Grasslands Hosp., Valhalla, N.Y., 1957-58 & N.Y. Hosp.-Westchester, White Plains, 1958-59; Staff Psych., N.Y. Hosp.-Westchester Div., 1960-; Asst. Prof., Psych., Cornell Univ. Med. Coll., 1965-. Mbrships: AMA; Am. Psych. Assn.; Assn. for Advancement of Psychotherapy; Assn. for Rsch. in Nervous & Mental Diseases; Am. Med. Soc. on Alchoholism; AAAS; Royal Soc. of Hlth. Contbr. chapts. to books & articles to profl. jrnls. Address: 21 Bloomingdale Road, White Plains, NY 10605, U.S.A. 17

SEERING, Ruth, b. 19 Jan. 1923. Writer; Journalist. Educ: Studied hist. & archaeol., Univs. of Berlin, Prague & Innsbruck. Appts: Lectr. in further educ.; Free-lance reporter & author (aviation, natural sci., geog., interviews); Female co-pilot, supersonic flights, F-100, USAF, 1960, Phantom II, USAF, 1968, Lightning, British Royal Air Force, 1969; Participator, R.A.F. survival trngs. (jungle, ocean, ice, desert), 1970-71. Mbrships: Rep., German War Graves Commn., North Rhine-Westphalia; Hon. mbr., Mach Buster's Club, N. Am. Aviation, 1960, The 1000 Miles per hour Club, Royal Air Force, 1970. Publs. incl: Mein tödliches Risiko, 1973; König Faisal—Koran & Öl, 1974; Exhibition, World Press Photo, The Hague, Netherlands, 1963, '64, '66. Address: Rheinuferstr. 52, D-404 Neuss, German Fed. Repub.

SEGAL, Mendel, b. 8 June 1914. Printing Executive. Educ: Emory Univ., 1931-33.

Appts: Pres., Printing Inds., Atlanta; Chmn. of Bd., Printing Inds., Am.; Pres., Union Employers Sect., ibid. Mbrships. incl: Pi Sigma Epsilon; Alpha Epsilon Pi; Masons; Standard Club; Pres., Metro Atlanta Mental Hlth. Assn.; Pres., Gate City Lodge B'nai B'rith; Chmn., Fulton Co. Mental Hlth. Advsry. Comm.; Pres., Community Friendship, Inc. Publs: How to Sell Printing Creatively; How to Develop Your Personal Selling Power; Sales Management for Small Medium Sized Businesses; How to Sell More Profitable Printing. Hons: Man of the Yr. Award, Atlanta Club of Printing House Craftsmen, 1959; Atlanta Advt. Club Silver Award, 1961. Address: c/o Stein Printing Co., 2161 Monroe Dr., N.E., Atlanta, GA 30324, U.S.A. 7, 16, 55.

SEGAL, Ronald Michael, b. 14 July 1933. Author; Editor. Educ: B.A., Univ. of Cape Town, S. Africa, 1951; B.A., Trinity Coll., Cambridge, U.K., 1953; Univ. of Va., U.S.A., 1955. Appts: Publr. & Ed., Africa South & Africa South in Exile, 1956-61; Gen. Ed., Penguin African Lib., 1961-. Mbrships. incl: Gov., Int. Conf. on Econ. Sanctions Against S. Africa, London, 1964; Gov., Int. Conf. on S.W. Africa, Oxford, 1966; Hon. Sec., S. African Freedom Assn., 1961-61. Publs. incl: The Crisis of India, 1965; The Race War, 1966; Ed., South West Africa; Travesty of Trust, 1967; America's Receding Future, 1968; The Struggle Against History, 1971; Whose Jerusalem: The Conflicts of Israel, 1973; The New Crash, 1974. Hons. incl: Banned by S. African Govt., 1959; Vis. Fellow, Ctr. for Study of Democratic Instns., Santa Barbara, Calif., 1973. Address: The Old Manor House, Manor Rd., Walton-on-Thames, Surrey, U.K.

SEGALL, Alice P., b. 17 Oct. 1899. Artist. Educ: B.A., Ohio Wesleyan Univ., 1922; M.A., Columbia Univ. Tchrs. Coll.; Further study, Ind. Univ., Fort Wayne Art Schl., State Univ. Coll., Famous Artists Schl., Old Mill Art Schl. Appts: Dir., Phys. Educ. for Girls, YWCA, Wheeling, W. Va., 1922-25; Fort Wayne, Ind., 1925-37; Asst. Prof., Phys. & Hlth. Educ. for Women, Ohio Wesleyan Univ., 1937-39; Dir., Phys. Educ. for Girls, Newton, N.J., 1946-53; Proprietor, Alice's Gift Ct. & Gall., 1953-60. Mbrships: Sec. & Fndng. Mbr., Clinton Co. Artists Assn.; Histn., All Communities Arts, Brooklyn, N.Y.; Artists Equity Assn. of N.Y. One man exhibs: Brooklyn Pub. Lib., 1971; Atlantic Liberty Savings & Loan Assn. Gall., 1973; Major exhibs: Société de l'Ecole Francais, Paris; Brooklyn Mus.; Nantucket Gallery; Intercontinental Gall. Hons: Hon. Mention, Parkchester Outdoor Show, 1969. Address: 1620 Ocean Ave., Apt. 4F, Brooklyn, NY 11230, U.S.A. 133.

SEGGELKE, Herbert. Author; Director. Educ: Studies in Munich, German Fed. Repub. & Paris, France. Appts: Holder of var. positions as Photographer; Referent of Arts; Film Dir. & Author of educational films, films on art, & expmtl. films; Publicist & Critic for newspapers; TV Author & Dir.; Speaker, Prod. & Author, Radio Munich, 1945. Mbr., Assn. Int. des Documentaristes. Films incl: Strich-Punkt-Ballett, 1943; Immortal Circus (w. Grock), 1952; One Melody—Four Painters (w. J. Cocteau), 1956; Thousand Little Letters, 1957; A la Loupe, 1961; The Great Garden, 1963; Nightmare, 1968; Concert in G-major by Beethoven, 1967; Heinrich Heine, 1972. Winner of about 40 nat. & int. prizes. Address: Uerdingerstr. 26/1, D4 Düsseldorf, German Fed. Repub. 43.

SEGOVIA Y MUÑOZ, (Fr.) Augusto, b. 7 Apr. 1902. Jesuit Priest; Educator; Librarian.

Educ: Humanities & Philos., Granada, Spain, 1925-27; Theol., Oñna Burgos, Spain, & Marnefee, Belgium, 1930-33; Theol., Univ. of Bonn, Germany, 1935; D.S.T., Louvain Univ., Belgium. Appts. incl: Tchr., Latin, Greek & Hebrew, Granada, & Puerto de Sta. Maria, Cadiz, Spain, 1924-25; Dir. of Studies, Theol. Fac., Granada, 1950-54; Rector, ibid, 1951-53; Hd. Libn., 1959-74. Publs. incl: Espiritualidad Patrística, 1944; Num. articles in Spanish & other jrnls; Contbns. to encys. Address: Facultad Teológica, Ap. 32, Granada, Spain.

SÉGUIN, Paul Henri, b. 12 May 1925. Company Director. Educ: Lic. en droit, Univ. of Paris. Appts: Asst. to Dir.-Dir. Gen. Adj., Babbitless S.A., Paris; Admnstr.-deleg., Babbitless Co. (Great Britain) Ltd.; Pres.-Dir. Gen., Fonderies et Ateliers de Corbeil-Essonnes; Pres., Nova S.P.A., Milan, Italy; Admnstr., Babbitless S. Africa (Pty.) Ltd.; Pres., Syndicat National des Industries M.T.P.S.; Admnstr. & Bd. Mbr., Fedn. des Industries Mécaniques. Mbrships: Automobile Club of France; Cercle Interallié; R.A.C., London; R.A.F.; M.C.C.; Rye Golf Club. Hons. Légion d'Honneur; Ordre National du Mérite, France; C.B.E., Britain. Address: c/o Babbitless, 9 Rue Boissy d'Anglas, 75008, Paris, France. 43, 91.

SEGURA, Pearl Mary, b. 12 June 1909. Librarian; Educator. Educ: B.A., Univ. of Southwestern La., 1930; B.S. in L.S., La. State Univ., 1941. Appts: Tchr.-Libn., Maurice H.S., La., 1933-41; Asst. Circulation Libn., Stephens Mem. Lib., Univ. of Southwestern La., 1941-44; Acting Ref. Libn., 1944-46; Ref. Libn., 1946-62; Libn., Jefferson Caffery La. Room, 1962-; Assoc. Prof. of Lib. Sci., 1953-. Mbrships. incl: ALA; Southwestern, La. & Special Lib. Assns.; La. Tchrs. Assn.; AAUW; Assn. Coll. & Ref. Libs.; Nat. Trust for Hist. Preservation; 1st Vice Regent, Galvez Chapt., DAR, 1968-71, 74-; La. State Poetry Soc.; La. Folklore Soc. Publs: Acadians in Fact & Fiction: A Classified Bibliography, 1955; Introduction to Perrin's Southwest Louisiana, 1971 edn; various articles. Address: 140 S. Magnolia St., Lafayette, LA 70501, U.S.A. 5, 7, 42.

SEIDEL, Gladys Louise (Mrs. Allen J. Seidel, Sr.), b. 26 Jan. 1931. Civic Worker. Educ: 1 yr. at Evansville Univ.; currently nursing student, Community Coll., Henderson, Ky. Mbrships: Pres., Henderson Altrusa Club, 1969-74; V.P., 1971-72, Chmn., Band Uniforms, Henderson Co. HS Band.; Chmn., many fund-raising progs.; Chmn., Dir. of Music, Henderson Ctrl. Park; Vol. Soc. Worker; Bd. of Advsrs., Christian Coll. of Colo.; Immanuel Bapt. Temple. Hons: Hon. Degree, Colo. Christian Coll., 1973; Cert. of Appreciation for outstanding & dedicated serv. to City of Henderson, Ky., 1973. Address: 1224 S. Main St., P.O. Box 802, Henderson, KY 42420, U.S.A. 5.

SEIDL, Florian, b. 30 Apr. 1893. Author. Mbrships: Hd., Authors Grp., Die Gegenwart, Munich, West Germany; Hd., German Authors' Assn., Dramatic sect.; Pres., Hölderlin-Gesellschaft; Hd., Schriftstellerkreis, Seerose, Munich; Deutscher Schriftstellerverband; Accad. Int., Pontzen, Naples, Italy; Acad. Int., Lutèce, Paris, France. Publs. incl: Stage plays: Ein Spiel der Liebe; Der verlorene Sohn; Na also; Junge Note; Heilige Heimat; Der Meister und der Dekan. Radio plays: Scherzo; Denn was man einer Frau verbietet. Novels: In der Hütte; Der Weg der Eva Brugger Der Bau; Ein Leben verrauscht; Nebuürgen; Drei Menschen; Das harte Ja; Die Fahrt in der Sommer; Welt neben dir. Poetry:

50 poems. Hons: Max-Rheinhardt-Preis, Deutschen Theaters, Berlin, 1930; Hörspielpreis, Bayerischen Rundfunks, 1932; Albertus-Magnus-Medaille der Stadt, Regensburg, 1952; Nordgaukunstpreis, 1954; Kulturpreis Ostbayern, 1962; Ehrenpreis, Schwabinger Kunstpreise, 1972; Medaille d'or, best German Poetry, Lutèce, Acad., Paris, France, 1972; Coupe de Lutèce, best int. poetry, 1972, ibid. Address: Bismarckstr. 1, D 8000 Munich 40, German Fed. Repub. 43, 92.

SEIDLER, Grzegorz Leopold, b. 18 Sept. 1913. Educator. Educ: Ph.D., Jagielloniam Univ., Poland, 1938; Additional study at Univ. of Vienna, Austria & Oxford Univ., U.K. Appts: Lectr. in Hist. of Philos., Jagiellonian Univ., Cracow, Poland, 1945-50; Prof., Philos. of Law, Marie Curie-Sklodowska Univ., Lublin, ibid, 1950-; Ed.-in-chief, Univ. Jrnl., ibid, 1955-; Rector, V.-Chancellor, 1959-69, '71-; Dir., Polish Cultural Inst., London, U.K., 1969-71. Publs. iricl: Myśl Polityczna Czasów Nowozytnych, 1972; Sociale Ideen in Byzanz, 1960; Emergence of the Eastern World, 1968. Recip. of Hon. D., Marie Curie, Sklodowska Univ., 1970. Address: Lublin, ul. Rektora H. Raabego 7m. 17, Poland. 30.

SEILER, George C., b. 30 Sept. 1934. Dentist. Educ: B.A., Ctrl. Wash. State Univ., Ellensburg, U.S.A., 1956; D.D.S., Creighton Univ., Omaha, Neb., 1965. Appts: Capt., Dental Corps, U.S. Army, 1966-69; Staff Dentist, VA Hosp., White River Junction, Vt., 1969-70; Chief, Dental Serv., ibid, 1970; Chief, Dental Serv., ibid, 1970-; Clin. Asst. in Restorative Dentistry, Harvard Schl. of Dental Med., 1971-. Mbrships: Am. Dental Assn.; Am. Assn. of Hosp. Dentists; Vt. Dental Soc.; Grafton Sullivan Dental Soc. Address: South St., Enfield, NH 03748, U.S.A. 6.

SEITELBERGER, Franz, b. 14 Dec. 1916. Professor. Educ: Fac. Med., Vienna Univ., Austria, 1935-40; M.D., ibid, 1940; Trng. in Neurol & Psych., Bad Ischl, Vienna, 1945-50; Specialist study, Neurol. & Psych., 1950; Asst., Neurol. Inst., Vienna Univ., 1951; Vis. Sci., Max-Planck-Inst. Brain Rsch., Giessen, 1952-53; Vis. Sci., NINDB, NIH Bethesda, Md., U.S.A., 1960. Appts: Docent-Prof., Neurol., Neuroanatomy & Neuropathol., Vienna Univ., Austria, 1954-59; Dir., Neurol. Inst.-Prof., Neurol., Vienna Univ., 1959-70; Dir., Brain Rsch. Inst. Osterreichische Akad. der Wissenschaften, 1970-. Mbrships: Österreichische Akad. der Wissenschaften; Max Planck Gesellschaft zur Förderung der Wissenschaften; Deutsche Akad. der Naturforscher Leopoldina; IBRO; Soc. Française de Neurol.; Brit. Neuropathol. Soc.; Am. Neurol. Assn.; Am. Assn. Neuropathols.; Soc. Neuropathol. Italiana; Gesellschaft Österreichischer Nervenärzte und Psychiater. Author num. rsch. papers in field & over 230 articles in handbooks & sci. jrnls. Address: Vorstand des Neurologischen Insts. der Univ. Wien, Scharzspanierstrasse 17, 1090 Vienna, Austria. 50, 86.

SEITTELMAN, Estelle M. b. 13 Mar. 1927. Educator. Educ: B.A., Hunter Coll.; M.A., Grad. Fac. of Philos., Columbia Univ.; Advanced study, Tchrs. Coll., ibid; Special Trng., Am. Mgmt. Assn. Appts: Tchr., 1948-59; Asst. Prin., P.S. 59 Bronx, 1959-68; Lectr., Engl., Bronx Community Coll., 1963-67; Acting Prin., P.S. 59 Bronx, 1961-62, '66-67; Adjunct Asst. Prof., Instrnl. Internship. Prog., Fordham Schl. of Educ., 1970, '72; Prin., Alfred E. Smith Elem. Schl., 1968-. Mbrships. incl: Treas., V.P., Dist. 3, Coun. of Supvsry.

Assns., 1970-; Exec. Bd., N.Y.C. Elem. Schl. Prins. Assn., 1973-; Advsry. Policy & Planning Comm., Apprentice Tchr. Prog., Fordham Univ., 1973-; Nat. Assn. Elem. Schl. Prins.; Nat. Coun. Admin. Women in Educ.; Phi Beta Kappa; Sigma Tau Delta. Contbng. Ed., Alfred E. Smith Newsletter. Hons: Dist. Serv. Award for Outstanding Community Serv. & Ldrship, 1970; Dist. Rep. to N.Y. State Invitational Inst. Guidance for the '70's, 1970. Address: Alfred E. Smith Schl., 163 W. 97 St., N.Y., NY 10025, U.S.A. 5, 6.

SEITZ, Helmuth, b. 18 Sept. 1899. Retired Manufacturer. Educ: Tradesman's Dip., Univ. of Cologne; Dr.rer.pol. Appts: Mng. Dir., later Chmn., Bd. of Dirs., Seitz-Werke, Kreuznach; Mng. Dir., Seitz-Automaten GmbH, Kreuznach. Mbrships: Casino Gesellschaft & Ruderverein Krueznach; Free Mason, Kreuznach Lodge. Address: Am Tannenwäldchen 6, Bad Kreuznach, German Fed. Repub.

SEITZ, Mildred Ann (Mrs. Albert Blazier Seitz, Jr.), b. 21 June 1900. Retired Lumber Executive. Educ: Ohio State Univ., U.S.A., 1918-20; A.M., Berlin Univ., Germany, 1947; Bucharest Univ., Romania. Appts: Sec.-Treas., D & S Lumber & Tie Co., 1929-49; Pres. & Owner, ibid, 1949-61; Corporate Mbr., Ry-Tie Assn.; Mbr., For. Affairs Comm., ibid; Mbr., Comm. on Resolutions, ibid. Mbrships: Vol. Asst., Child Reclamation & Food Prog., Bucharest, Romania, 1946; Child Relief Prog., Salonika, Greece; Past Pres., Watch Washington; Use of Modern Looms, Ventiane, Laos, 1958-60; Descendants Kts. of Garter; Plantagenet Soc.; Order of Washington; Colonial Order of the Crown; Ams. of Royal Descent; Nat. Soc. Magna Charta Dames; DAR; League Am. Pen Women. Author articles on Laos, Greece & Romania. Recip. Commendation, for estab. Teen Canteen for Am., from Gen. Ryan, Berlin, Germany, 1947. Address: 2613 Grv. St., Sarasota, FL 33579, U.S.A. 57, 132, 138.

SEKELY, Steve, b. 25 Feb. 1899. Motion Picture Director & Writer. Educ: Coll., Hungary. Appts: Newspaperman; Writer; For. Corres.; Motion Picture Dir. & Prod.-Dir.; TV Dir. & Prof.-Dir. Mbrships. incl: Acad. Motion Pictures Arts & Scis.; TV Acad. of Arts & Scis. Publs. & Films: One-act plays & short stories, prod. in sev. countries; Incl. in book, Best One-Act Plays; Dir. of 60 feature films, inclng. one for Rank Org., The Day of the Triffids; About 44 TV films, mostly shown on BBC, inclng. Orient Express, New York Confidential, etc. Address: P.O. Box 1685, Palm Springs, CA 92262, U.S.A. 9, 72, 75, 122.

SELBERG, Arne Brigt Bru, b. 11 Aug. 1910. Professor, Speciality—Steel Bridges & Structures. Educ: C.E., 1934, Dr. Techn., 1946, Norwegian Inst. of Technol., Univ. of Trondheim. Appts: var. posts as Chief Engr. in Norway Pub. Road Admin., 1935-49; Chief Engr., Bridge Construction, 1946-49; Dir., Bridge Bldg. Sect., Norwegian Pub. Road Admin., 1958-59; Prof., Norwegian Inst. of Technol. (Trondheim Univ. since 1969), 1949-; Rector, ibid, 1963-69. Mbr., NTVA; Pres., ibid, 1971-. Publs: over 60 treatises & books, related to bridge bldg. or steel structures.Cmdr., Order St. Olav. Address: Univ. of Trondheim, Norwegian Inst. of Technol., Div. of Steel Structures, 7034 Trondheim-NTH, Norway. 43.

SELBST, George, b. 21 Feb. 1917. Music Teacher. Educ: Master's Degree in Music Theory; Julliard Schl. of Music; N.Y. Coll.; Manhattan Schl. of Music; Hebrew Union Coll. Appts. incl: Music Prog. Dir., Suffolk Co., Bd.

of Coop. Educ. Servs.; Conductor & Dir., Islip Community Symphony Orch.; Tchr., Islip Public High Schl. Mbrships: Kts. of Pythias; Chmbr. Music Assn. Works incl: Organ Preludes; Violin Concerto in G Minor; Yizkor Service for Solo, Chorus and Symphony Orchestra. Address: 96C Enfield Court, Ridge, NY 11961, U.S.A. 130.

SELBY, Cora H.E. Norwood, b. 15 July 1920. Teacher. Educ: B.S., Del. State Coll. 1940; M.Ed., Univ. of Del., Newark, 1959; grad. work, Morgan State Coll., Balt., Md., & Temple Univ., Phila., Pa. Appts: Elem. Tchr. 25 yrs.; Reading Tchr., 1 yr.; Primary Special Educ. Tchr., 1 yr.; Local Advsr., Headstart Follow Through Prog., 5 yrs.; Tchr. of ABE, 7 yrs.; Youth Counselor. Mbrships. incl: NEA; Bd. Pensions Mbr., Legislative Comm. Mbr., DSEA; Pres., V.P., LEA; Pres., SCEA; Pres., DSTA, Sussex Co.; Lay Speaker, Lay Deleg. for N.E. Jurisdictional Conf., Lay Deleg. for Peninsula Annual Conf., UM Ch.; Pres, PTA; Sec., DC PTA; Ldrship. Chmn., DCPT; Pres., MUF. Hons. incl: Del. State Coll. Alumni Award, 1969; Ford Fndn. Travel Grant, 1969; Laurel Schl. Dist. PTA Award, 1971. Address: R.2 Box 343, Laurel, DE 19956, U.S.A. 130.

SELBY, John Millin, b. 9 May 1905. Retired Army Officer, Lecturer, Writer. Educ: M.A., Univ. of Cambridge, U.K., 1935. Appts: Off., British Army, 1924-28 & 1940-47; Schlmaster, 1929-40; Lectr., Royal Mil. Acad., Sandhurst, 1947-72. Mbr., Soc. for Army Histl. Rsch. Publs: The Second World War, 1967, Greek edit., 1973; Stories of Famous Sieges, 1967; Stonewall Jackson, 1968; The Paper Dragon, 1968; The Boer War, 1969; The Thin Red Line, 1970; The Iron Brigade, 1971; The United States Cavalry, 1972; A Short History of South Africa, 1973; 5 other books. Recip., Territorial Decoration, 1947. Address: Waverley Cottage, 23 Waverley Dr., Camberley, Surrey GU15 2DP, U.K. 30, 131.

SELDEN, Kurt, b. 27 May 1906. Electrical Engineer & Administrator. Educ: Dipl. Elec. Engrng., Tech.Dr., Tech. Univ., of Munich; Dipl. Engr., Doktor der technischen Wissenschaften. Appts: Elec. Engr., Siemens-Schuckertwerke AG, Vienna, Austria, & Berlin, Germany, 1930-37; Chief Elec. Engr., finally Tech. Dir., Nordwestdeursche Kraftwerke AG, Hamburg, Germany, 1937-47; Mgr., Assn. Austrian Elec. Works (Power Cos.), Vienna, Austria, 1947-72; Cons. Engr., ibid, after retirement, 1972-. Mbrships: incl: Directing Comms., Int. Union for Electroheat, Paris, France, Österreichische Lichtteschnische Arbeitsgemeinschaft, Vienna, Austria, & Österreichisches Kuratorium für Landtechnik, Vienna; Österreichischer Alpenverein, Sektion Salzburg. Papers & articles, prod. & distribution, elec. energy, var. jrnls., Austria & Belgium. Recip., Goldenes Ehrenzeichen für Verdienste um die Republic Österreich, 1971. Address: Fürstenallee 12g, A-5020 Salzburg, Austria. 43, 86.

SELENIUS, Clas-Olof, b. 28 Sept. 1922. Docent; University Lecturer. Educ: Helsingfors Univ.; Univs. of Göttingen, Copenhagen, Würzburg, Uppsala & Cambridge. Appts. incl: Sr. Tchr., Ekenäs Lyceum, 1949-60; Helsingfors Tchr. Trng. H.S., 1960-66; Docent in Maths., Abo Acad., 1963-; Univ. Lectr., Uppsala Univ., 1966-; Lectr., ibid, 1968-; Ed., Nordisk matem. tidskrift for Finland, 1966; ibid for Sweden, 1969-. Mbrships. incl: V.P., Swedish Peoples Party, Nyland Province, Finland, 1958-69; Town Coun., 1957-60; Pres., Soc. for Swedish Finlanders, Uppsala, 1972-. Contbr. to profl. jrnls. Hons: Badge of Merit, Swedish Peoples

Party, Finland, 1967; 1st Prize, F.R.I.S. Nat. Poetry Competition, 1971, 1972. Address: Dagermansgatan 8, 75428 Uppsala, Sweden. 134.

SELIGER, Martin (Menachem), b. 5 Sept. 1914. Professor. Educ: M.A. Studies, Hebrew Univ., Jerusalem, Israel, 1936-40; Rsch. work, Inst. Histl. Rsch., London Univ., 1951-53; Ph.D., Jerusalem, 1955. Appts: Tchr.-Headmaster, Grammar Schl.; Prin., Tchrs. Trng. Coll.; Lectr., Tel-Aviv Univ., Israel; Lectr.-Prof., Hebrew Univ., Jerusalem, 1956; Hd., Dept. Pol. Sci., 1963-67; Simon Sr. Rsch. Fellow, Manchester Univ., U.K., 1967-68; Vis. Fellow, Ctr. Int. Studies, Schl. Econs., London Univ., U.K., 1970. Mbrships: Bd., Israeli Pol. Sci. Assn.; Coun. Int. Pol. Sci. Assn.; Exec. Comm., 1970-73, 1974-. Author num. publs. inclng: The Foundations of European Policy in the Near East, 1941; The Liberal Politics of John Locke, 1968; Idealogy and Politics, 1974; The Marxist Conception of Ideology—A Critical Essay, 1974 & num. articles in Hebrew, German & Engl. on pol. ideas of liberal French histns. of the Restoration, Locke's pol. theory, Marcuse & the concept & nature of ideology etc. Address: Dept. Pol. Sci., Hebrew Univ. of Jerusalem, Jerusalem, Israel.

SELIGMAN, Bernard, b. 25 Aug. 1898. Medical Doctor. Educ: M.D., Bellevue Hosp. Med. Coll., N.Y. Univ., 1920; Intern, Jewish Hosp. of Brooklyn, 1920-23; Res., Bedford Hills TB Sanitarium, 1926; Res., Montefieore Hosp., 1927-28; Postgrad. study, Vienna, Berlin. Appts. incl: Med. Staff, Jewish Hosp., 1928-; Attending, 1956-69, Cons., 1969-; Cons., Kings Co. Hosp., 1968-; Tchr., L.I. Med. Coll., 1935-39, 1948-50; Postgrad. Courses, Endocrinol., Jewish Hosp., 1939-62; Dipl., Internal Med., 1939. Num. mbrships. incl: AMA; Fellow, Am. Coll. of Physns.; Int. Soc. for Internal Med.; N.Y. Acad. of Scis.; Am. Heart Assn.; Fellow, Royal Soc. for Promotion of Hlth.; Bd. of Dirs., Prospect Park Jewish Ctr.; N.Y. Physns. Art Club; Am. Physns. Art Assn.; Bd. of Achievement, Boy Scouts of Am. Contbr. to num. jrnls.; Lectr., radio speaker; Book reviewer. Hons: Var. art awards, sculpture, oils, enamel, watercolor, Am. Physns. Art Assn., N.Y. Physns. Art Club, 1966-. Address: 163 Ocean Ave., Brooklyn, NY 11225, U.S.A. 6, 55, 64.

SELIGSON, Thomas Stephan, b. 16 Jan. 1946. Writer. Educ: Grad., Phillips Acad., Andover, Mass, 1964; B.A., Columbia Univ., N.Y.C., 1968; Grad. work in educ., N.Y. Univ. & Hunter Coll., N.Y.C. Appts. incl: Tchr., Pub. Schls., N.Y.C., 1968-70; Assoc. Ed., Defiance review, 1970-72. Mbrships. incl: Co-Chmn., Humanitas, 1966-68; Treas., Benefit Comm. for the People's Coalition for Peace & Justice, 1971. Publs. incl: The High School Revolutionaries, 1970; To be Young in Babylon, 1971; Contbr. of articles, stories, reviews to: N.Y. Times, Look, Penthouse, etc. Address: c/o Betty Anne Clarke, International Famous Agcy., Inc., 1301 Ave. of the Americas, N.Y., NY 10019, U.S.A. 30.

SELKIRK, (Lord) George Nigel Douglas Hamilton, b. 4 Jan. 1906. Educ: M.A., Balliol Coll., Oxford, U.K; LL.B., Univ. of Edinburgh. Appts. incl: Serv. to Grp. Capt., Auxiliary Air Force, 1932-45; Mbr., Edinburgh Town Coun., 1935-40; Scottish Rep. Peer, 1945-63; Lord-in-Waiting to H.M. King George VI, 1951-52, to H.M. Queen Elizabeth II, 1952-53; Serv. in successive Govts., 1951-59, inclng. Chancellor of Duchy of Lancaster, 1955-57, First Lord of Admiralty, 1957-59; U.K. Commnr. for Singapore & Commnr. Gen. for

S.E. Asia, 1959-63; U.K. Coun. Rep., SEATO, 1960-63. Mbrships. incl: Freeman of Hamilton; Pres., Ski Fedn. of G.B., 1965-69; Pres., Bldg. Socs. Assn., 1965; Pres., Royal Ctrl. Asian Soc.; Pres. Anglo-Swiss Soc. Hons. incl: P.C., 1955; G.C.M.G., 1959; G.B.E., 1963; Air Force Cross; Q.C. (Scotland), 1959. Address: 60 Eaton Place, London SW1, U.K. 1.

SELLERS, Florence Elizabeth, b. 4 Aug. 1913. College Professor of Library Science. Educ: B.S., Trenton State Coll., 1935; M.A., Univ. of Pa., 1940; B.S., Drexel Inst. of Technol. (now Drexel Univ.), 1944; Var. other grad. courses. Appts: H.S. Libn., Woodbury, N.J., 1935-44; Circulation Libn., Glassboro State Coll., 1944-58, 1960-62; Ref. Libn., ibid, 1958-60; Acquisitions Libn., 1962-66; Educ. Libn., 1968-69; Asst. Dept. Chmn., 1962-69; Mbr., Lib. Educ. Dept. & Dept. Grad. Prog. Advsr., 1969-; Dept. Acad. Advisement Coord.; Asst. Prof., 1954-60; Assoc. Prof., 1960-; Summer positions in coll., pub., co. & special libs. Mbrships. incl: Glassboro State Coll. Fac. Assn., 1953-54; Sec., ibid, 1973-74; NEA; Kappa Delta Pi; Alpha Beta Alpha. Reviewer of children's books for School Library Journal. Recip., Kate Stout Schlrship., 1935. Address: 39 High St., Woodbury, NJ 08096, U.S.A. 5.

SELLHEIM, (Carl Gerhardt) Rudolf, b. 15 Jan. 1928. Professor. Educ: Univ. of Halle/Saale & Frankfurt/Main, 1946-53; Dr.phil., Univ. Frankfurt/Main, 1953; Habilitation, Univ. Bonn/Rh., 1957. Appts. incl: Full Prof., Semitic Langs. & Islamic Studies & Dir., Oriental Sem., Univ. Frankfurt/Main, 1958-; Dean. Philos. Fac., ibid, 1961-62; Vis. Prof., UCLA, 1966. Mbrships: Fellow, Royal Acad. Barcelona, German Archaeol. Inst., Wissenschaftliche Gesellschaft, Egyptian Acad. & Arabic Acad.; Pres., Int. Soc. for Oriental Rsch., Istanbul, 1968-; German Oriental Soc., Mainz; Union Européenne d'Arabistants et Islamisants, Paris. Publs: Die klassisch-arabischen Sprichwörtersammlungen, 1954 (arabic trans., 1971); Gelehrte und Gelehrsamkeit im Reiche der Chalifen, 1962 (arabic trans., 1972); Die Gelehrtenbiographien des Abu 'Ubaid al-Marzubani, I, 1964 (reprinted, 1968); Der zweite Bürgerdreig im Islam, 1970 (arabic trans., 1974); Arabische Handschriften, Marterialien zur arabischen Literaturgeschichte, I, 1974; Ed. & contbr. to other publs. in German, English, French, Arabic & Persian. Address: Bross-Str. 5, D 6 Frankfurt/Main 90, German Fed. Repub. 43.

SELLICK, Phyllis Doreen, (Mrs. Cyril Smith), b. 16 June 1911. Concert Pianist. Educ: Glenarm Coll., Ilford, U.K.; Royal Acad. of Music, London; Am. Conservatoire, Fontainbleau, France. Appts: Prof. of Pianoforte, Royal Coll. of Music, London, U.K., 1964-. Mbrships: Fellow of Royal Acad. of Music; Royal Coll. of Music; Incorp. Soc. of Musicians; Hon. Mbr., Soroptimist Club of Richmond-on-Thames. Publs: Duet for Three Hands with Cyril Smith. Hons: Blakiston Mem. Prize. Address: 33 Fife Rd., London S.W. 14, U.K. 1, 21, 34.

SELVAGE, Ian Charles, b. 29 July 1926. Company Managing Director. Appts: Dir., Ira L. & A.C. Berk Pty. Ltd., 1960-; Mng. Dir., Ira Berk (Qld.)Pty. Ltd., 1963-; Dir., Ira L. & A.C. Berk (Holdings) Ltd., 1968-. Mbrships: Inst. of Dirs. in Australia; Pres., Chmbrs. of Automotive Inds. of Qld., 1966-68; Pres., Fed. Chmbr. of Automotive Inds., 1967; Rotary Club of Hamilton, Qld.; Tattersalls Club; United Servs. Club; Pres., Sherwood Dists. Australian Football Club. Address: 38 Tweedale St., Graceville, Qld., Australia 4075, 23.

SELWYN, Donald, b. 31 Jan. 1936. Rehabilitation Engineer. Educ: Univ. of Wis. Appts. incl: Proposal Engr., Advanced Design Grp., Curtiss-Wright Corp., Paterson, N.J, 1960-64; Cons., Bio-med. & Rehab. Engrg., N.Y.C., 1960-67; Cons., N.Y. State Off., Voc. Rehab., 1964-; Cons., Pres.'s Comm. on Employment of the Handicapped, 1966-; Exec.-Tech. Dir., Nat. Inst. for Rehab. Engrg., Prompton Lakes, N.J., 1967-. Mbrships. incl: Inst. of Elect. & Electronics Engrs.; Chmn., Engrg. Mgmt. Grp., N.Y. Chapt., ibid, 1966; Soc. Tech. Writers & Publrs., N.Y. Acad. of Scis., Nat. Rehab. Assn.; Am. Acad. of Cons.; Bd. of Trustees, Nat. Inst. Rehab. Engrg.; Pres., ibid, 1967-. Publs.: Human Factors in Medicine & Rehabilitation, 1966; num. articles in profl. & gen. mags. Hons. incl: Humanitarian Award, U.S. Congress, 1972; Kt. of Malta, 1973. Address: 238 Poplar Ave., Pompton Lakes, NJ 07442, U.S.A. 6.

SEMINARA, Robert, b. 1 Oct. 1929. Dentist. Educ: B.S., L.I. Univ., 1953; D.D.S., N.Y. Univ., 1957; Postgrad. study, Orthodontics, N.Y. Univ., 1961-65. Appts: Intern. Oral Surg., Coney Island Hosp., 1957; Pvte. Prac., Brooklyn, 1958-66; Instr., Dept. Endodontics, N.Y.U., 1959-61; Specializing in Orthodontics, Brooklyn & Staten Island, 1966-; Co-Chief, Dept. of Orthodontics, Cabrini Med. Hlth. Ctr.; Attending Orthodontist, Staten Island Hosp.; Chie Cons. Orthodontics, St. Michael's Home for Children. Mbrships: Am. Assn. Orthodontists; Northeastern Assn. Orthodontists; 2nd Dist. Dental Soc.; Treas., Richmond Co. & Italian Dental Soc., 1973; Past Pres., Catholic Dental Soc. & S. Shore Study Club of Staten Island; Oral Hlth. Comm. of N.Y. Author, Team Approach to Multi-Phasic Problems involving Supernumerary Teeth, N.Y. State Dental Jrnl., 1973. Recip., Schwartzburg Award (Biol.), 1953. Address: 511 Tysens Ln., Staten Island, N.Y., NY 10306, U.S.A. 6.

SEMONES, Jo Ann, b. 28 Oct. 1945. Journalist. Educ: B.A., Schl. of Fine Arts & Profl. Studies, Calif. State Univ., Northridge, U.S.A., 1968; Cert., Special Progs. in Communication Skills, U.S. Dept. of Agric., Wash. D.C., 1972; M.S. in progress, Grad. Prog. in P.R., Am. Univ., ibid. Appts: Writer, Rutledge, Inc., N. Hollywood, Calif., 1968-69; Reporter & Photographer, San Fernando Valley Sun, ibid, 1969-70; Press Sec., Congressman, 22nd Dist. of Calif., House of Reps., Wash. D.C., 1970-71; Writer, Educl. Rsch. Assocs., Inc., ibid, 1971-72; Pub. Info. Specialist, Off. of Pub. Info. AA/Congressional & Pub. Affairs, U.S. Small Bus. Admin., 1971-. Mbrships: Newsletter Ed., Calif. State Univ. Alumni Assn.; Valley Press Club; AAUW; Nat. Ballet Soc.; United European Am. Club; Nat. Women's Pol. Caucus; Theta Sigma Phi. Hons: Cert. of Merit, N.E. Valley Regional Med. Prog., 1969; Award of Merit, Valley Press Club, 1969; Cert. of Appreciation, USN Recruiting Serv., 1970. Address: 16354 Tupper St., Sepulveda, CA 91343, U.S.A. 22.

SEMPERE, Eusebio, b. 3 Apr. 1923. Painter; Sculptor. Educ: Schl. of Fine Arts of San Carlos, Valencia. 1941-47; further studies, Paris, France. Appt: Co-designer, Open Air Sculpture Pk., Madrid, 1970. Mbr., Grupo Parpallo, Valencia, 1960. Paintings & Sculptures in Collects. inclng: Mus. of Mod. Art, N.Y.C., U.S.A.; Fogg Mus. of Harvard Univ.; Brooklyn Mus., N.Y.; Aschenbach Fndn. for Graphic Arts, San Francisco, Calif.; Balt. Mus., Md.; Mus. of Mod. Art, Atlanta, Ga.; Mus. of Mod. Art, Santiago, Chile; Mus. of Mod. Art, Rio de Janeiro, Brazil; Museums of Mod. Art, Bilbao, Portugal, & Barcelona, Spain; Museums

of Contemporary Art, Madrid & Seville, Spain; Mus. of Valencia; Mus of Hamburg, German Fed. Repub.; British Mus., London, U.K. Hons. incl: Ford Fndn. Grant, 1960; Juan March Grant, 1965. Address: José Marañón 10, Madrid 10, Spain.

STEMPIO, Cesare, b. 18 Aug. 1902. Professor of Plant Pathology. Educ: Agric. Scis. Degree; Ph.D. Appts: Asst. Prof., Inst. of Plant Pathol., Univ. of Perugia, 1930-46, Prof., & Chmn., Inst. of Plant Pathol., 1946-. Mbrships: Societa Fitopatologica Mediterranea; Am. Phytopathological Soc., 1948-58. Address: Istituto di Patologia vegetale, Facoltà di Agraria, Borgo XX Giugno, Perugia, Italy. 43.

SEMPRINI, Giovanni, b. 20 Nov. 1893. Professor of Historial & Philosophical Sciences. Educ: Univ. of Bologna. Appts: Lectr., Sanskrit, Univ. of Genoa; Dir., Rovigo Acad.; Lectr., Pol. & Naval Hist., Univ. of Genoa, 1934-65. Mbrships: Mazzinian Inst., Philos. Circle of Genoa; Risorgimental Hist. Inst.; Nat. Ctr. of Napoleonic Studies; Italian Ctr. for the Progress of Social Sci.; Tiberina Acad.; Dei Cinquecento Acad.; Legion d'Oro. Works incl: Giovanni Pico della Mirandola, 1921; I platonici italiani, 1926; L.B. Alberti, 1927; Melchiorre Gioia e la sua dottrina politica, 1934; Il pensiero di M. Delfico, 1935; La filosofia di Pico della Mirandola, 1936; La liberta come ascesa a Dio, 1940; La civilta dell'Umanesimo nell'Utopia di T. More, 1940. Contbr. to var. jrnls. Hons: Victor Emmanuel prize, Univ. of Bologna, 1920; Gold Medal, Rimini, 1952; Gold Medal of the Pres. of the Repub. of Italy, 1963; Kt. of Repub., 1964. Address: Salita Sup. S. Tecla 29, Genoa, 16132 Italy.

SEN, Sudhir, b. 29 Dec. 1906. Economist. Educ: B.A., Calcutta Univ., India, 1928; B.Sc., London Schl. of Econs., U.K., 1931; Ph.D., Univ. of Bonn, Germany, 1933. Appts. incl: Var. posts, Govt. of India & Provincial Govt. of Bengal to 1947; Gen. Mgr., Damodar Valley Corp., India, 1948-54, Gt. Eastern Shipping Co., Bombay, 1954-56; (U.N.), Dir. Prog. Div., Tech. Assistance Bd., N.Y., U.S.A., 1956-61, Res. Rep. & Dir. Special Fund Progs., Ghana, 1961-62, Dpty. Admnstr., Temporary Exec. Authority, W. New Guinea/W. Irian, 1962-63, Rep. Dev. Progs., Belgrade, Yugoslavia, 1963-66; Vis. Prof. Sociol., Brown Univ., R.I., U.S.A., 1967-68. Mbrships: Soc. for Int. Dev.; Assn. of Former Int. Civil Servants. Publs. incl: United Nations in Economic Development - Need for a New Strategy, 1970; A Richer Harvest - New Horizons for Developing Countries, & Reaping the Green Revolution - Food & Jobs for All, in preparation; num. reports & articles. Address: 210 E. 47th. St., Apt. 10 C, N.Y., NY 10017, U.S.A.

SENDREY, Albert Richard, b. 26 Dec. 1924. Music Composer; Conductor; Pianist. Educ: Univ. of Southern Calif., L.A.; Leipzig Conservatory, Germany; Ecole Normale, Paris, France; Trinity Coll. of Music, London, U.K. Composer-arranger for MGM Studios, 1946-60, orchestrated many Broadway Shows (Peter Pan, New Faces & Others), over 100 films, inclng. The Yearling, American In Paris, Great Caruso, Guys & Dolls, High Society, Opposite Sex, Raintree County, Three Musketeers, also scenarios & screenplays, inclng. L'Infidele, libretto of father's opera, Night of the Tiger (The Lanza Story), The Kingston Kaper, Quit While You're Ahead. Mbrships: Am. Soc. of Authors, Composers & Publishers; Composers & Lyricists Guild of Am.; Acad. of Motion Pictures Arts & Scis.; Am. Soc. of Music Arrangers. Compositions incl: 3 Symphonies; Grande Chaconne for Piano; String Quartets 1,

2, & 3; Cello Sonata (Hungarian Divertimento); Piano Sonata. Recip. of hons. Address: 1377 Miller Place, L.A., CA 90069, U.S.A. 1, 9.

SENEHI, David, b. 10 Dec. 1931. Publisher. Educ: Grad., Cheshire Acad., Conn., 1951; B.A., Ohio Wesleyan Univ., 1955; Postgrad., paper chem., Syracuse Univ. Appts: Publisher, Ctrl. New Yorker Mag.; Bd. of Dirs., Ferdows Shoe Factories Inc. (Iran). Mbrships: Bd. Dirs., World Affairs Coun.; Syracuse Press Club. Address: 3633 Fenner Rd., Cazenovia, NY 13035, U.S.A. 6.

SENFF, Ernst, b. 26 Jan. 1905. Conductor; Choral Director. Educ: Studied piano & cello; Conductor's trng. w. Prof. Ehrenberg, Cologne, 1926. Appts: Engagements in Lübeck, 1929-33; Staatstheater, Danzig, 1933-35; Conductor & 1st Choir Master, Volksoper, Berlin, 1935-45; 1st Choir Master & occasional conductor of concerts & opera, Städtische Oper, Berlin, 1945-61; Dir., Opera Choir Schl., Hochschule für Musik, Berlin, 1960-71; Currently Fndr. & Dir., Kammerchor Ernst Senff; Concerts & recordings in SFB/WDR; Philharmonic concerts. Hons: Title of Prof., 1968; Silver & gold medals, Genossenschaft Deutscher Bühnenangehöriger. Address: Irmgardstr. 12, 1 Berlin 37, German Fed. Repub. 92.

SENO, Satimaru, b. 10 Mar. 1915. Professor. Educ: Kyoto Univ. Schl. Med., Japan, 1936-40. Appts: Asst. Pathol., Kyoto Univ., Japan, 1940-46; Prof. Pathol., Mie Prefectural Med. Coll., 1947-54; Prof. Pathol.-Dean, Okayama Univ. Med. Schl., 1955-73. Mbrships: Pres., Japan Soc. Cell Biol., 1970-73; V.P., Int. Fed. Cell Biol.; Chmn., Prog. Comm. 16th Int. Congress of Hematol.. Exec. Comm. Japan Soc. Hematol.; Advsry. Bd. Japan Soc. Pathol.; N.Y. Acad. Sci.; Int. Soc. Hematol. Publs: Structure of reticulocytes and the Mechanism of denucleation of erythroid cell., 1958, '68; Electron microscopy of frozed-dried cells, 1960; Relation between structure and function of mitochondria in Intracellular Membrane Structure, 1965. Recip. Testimonum, Swiss Soc. Haematol., 1959. Address: Dept. Pathol., Okayama Univ. Med. Schl., 2-5-1 Shikata-cho, Okayama, 700, Japan.

SEO, Stanley T., b. 5 Mar. 1928. Chemist. Educ: B.S., Univ. of Hawaii, Honolulu, 1950; M.S., ibid, 1952. Appts: Rsch. Chem., U.S. Dept. of Agric., Agric. Rsch. Serv., Entomol. Rsch. Div., Hawaii Fruit Fly Investigations, Honolulu, 1955-70. Mbrships: Am. Chem. Soc.; AAAS; Entomological Soc. of Am.; Am. Radio Relay League; Honolulu Amateur Radio Club. Address: Hawaii Fruit Fly Investigations, P.O. Box 2280, Honolulu, HI 96804, U.S.A. 57.

SEPESHY, L. Zoltan, b. 24 Feb. 1898. Artist; Educator. Educ: M.F.A., Acad. of Fine Arts & Art Educ., Budapest; Further study, Vienna, Paris, Germany, Italy, U.S.A., Canada, Mexico, Near East. Appts: Cranbrook Acad. of Art, Bloomfield Hills, Mich., U.S.A., 1931-67; Dir., 1947-59; Pres., 1959-66; Prof. Emeritus & Cons., 1967-. Mbrships: Nat. Acad. of Design; Nat. Inst. of Arts & Letters; Phila. Watercolor Club; Nat. Soc. of Mural Painters; Scarab Club, Detroit; Midtown Galls., N.Y.C.; Mbr., Comm. on Accreditation, N. Ctrl. Assn. of Colls. & Secondary Schls., 1965-68. Paintings, drawings, in 34 U.S., for. museums; 36 one man exhibs.; Jury Mbr., nat. & Western Hemisphere exhibs.; Murals in var. pub. bldgs., U.S.A.; Author, Tempera Painting, 1946. Hons: 26 dips., medals, prizes, grants, 1924-55. Address: 787 Harmon. Birmingham, MI 48009, U.S.A. 2, 10, 37.

SERAPHIM, Juliane, b. 13 Apr. 1934. Painter; Designer; Engraver. Educ: St. Fernando Acad., Madrid, Spain; Acad. of Fine Arts, Florence, Italy. Appts: Sec., UNRWA, 1953-58; Free-lance Painter, 1958-. Mbrships. incl: Lebanese Musical Youth; Lebanese Assn. of Painters & Sculptors; Congress for Cultural Freedom; Dar el Fan. One-man shows: Int. Gall., Florence, Italy, 1959; Lalicorne Gall., Beyrouth, Lebanon, 1961; Garzouzi Gall., ibid, 1964; L'Orient Gall., 1965 & 1967; Cassia Gall., 1969; Amadis Gall. & Goya Ctr., Madrid, Spain, 1963; Antiquaire Gall., Beyrouth, 1973. Num. grp. exhibs. incl: Nicolas Sursock Mus., Beyrouth, 1961; London, U.K., 1967; Motte Gall., Paris, 1968; Smithsonian Mus., Wash. D.C., U.S.A., 1969; Nat. Mus., Tokyo, Japan, 1973. Hons. incl: Silver Medal, Town of Viareggio, Italy, for painting acquired by mus., 1959; Gold Medal, City of Tome, 1971; Address: Imm. Khawaja-Suidan No. 9. Parc Tabet-Sin-El-Fil (Beirut,) Lebanon. 97.

SERFATY, (Hon.) Abraham William, b. 3 Oct. 1910. Architect; Chartered Engineer. Appts: City Councillor, 1951-54; Mbr., House of Assembly, 1954-; Chmn., Civil Defence Comm., 1958-63; Mbr. for Med. Servs., 1959-64; Min. for Tourism, 1964-69; Min. for Tourism, Trade & Econ. Dev., 1972-. J.P. Hons: Ordinary Off., O.B.E., 1958. Address: 66 Main St., P.O. Box 63, Gibraltar.

SERGEYEV, Konstantin Mikhailovitch, b. 20 Feb. 1910. Ballet Dancer; Choreographer. Educ: Leningrad Schl. of Choreography., U.S.S.R. Appts. incl: Soloist, Premier Dancer, Choreographer, State Kirov Acad. Opera & Ballet Theatre, Leningrad, 1930-62; Artistic Dir., ibid, 1951-55, '60-70; Artistic Dir., aganova Schl. Choreography, 1973; danced all the prin. parts of the male classical repertoire, notably those of Albrecht & Siegfried; created prin. parts in num. modern Soviet ballets; Choreographer, Co-Dir. & Co-Scenarist, films of Sleeping Beauty & Swan Lake. Mbr., Bd., All Russian Theatre Soc. (Hd., Ballet Sect.). Author of var. articles. Hons. incl: Order of the Red Banner, 1940; State Prize for gt. achievements in the promotion of ballet art, 1946; People's Artist of the U.S.S.R., 1957; Order of Lenin, 1970. Address: Kirovsky Prospect 2 Fl. 33, Leningrad P 101, U.S.S.R.

SERGOTT, Kathleen York (Mrs. Conrad A. Sergott), b. 25 June 1917. Librarian. Educ: A.B., Suffolk Univ., 1955; Postgrad., Boston Univ., 1956-57; M.S., Simmons Coll., 1960; Postgrad., ibid, 1964. Appts: Asst. Libn., Blue Hill Pub. Lib., Me.; Bibliotherapist, State of Conn.; Bibliother., Mass. Gen. Hosp., Boston; Libn., Boston Univ. Schl. of Nursing, Mass. Bay Community Coll., Swampscott Pub. Lib.; Rsch. Libn., David L. Babson & Co., Boston. Mbrships: ALA; Mass. & New England Lib. Assns.; Gtr. Boston Book Review Assn.; Bus. & Profl. Women's Club; V.P., Past Pres., currently Pres., N. Shore M.S. Club; Poetry Soc. of N.H. Publs: 'Through the Pages', 1965-; An Old Ghost: On the Job Training, 1968; Courses, Courses, Who's Got the Courses, 1970; We Need to Write Poetry, Poetry Soc. of N.H.; Ed., N. Shore M.S. Club News Letter; Poetry Society of New Hampshire Newsletter, 1975. Recip., Lit. Prize, Suffolk Univ., 1955. Address: 5 Oceanside Terrace, Swampscott, MA 01907, U.S.A. 5, 6, 42, 132.

SERNAGLIA, Rino, b. 1 Mar. 1936. Painter. Educ: Inst. of Art, Venice. Appts: Scene Painter, RAI & TV, Milan, 1960-65. One man exhibs., Italy & abroad. Hons: 1st Prize S. Fedele, Milan, 1965; 1st Prize, Cesare da Sesto, 1966. Address: Via Broletto 41, Milan, Italy.

SERSTOCK, Doris Shay (Mrs. Ellsworth I. Serstock), b. 13 June 1926. Microbiologist; Mycologist. Educ: B.A., Augustana Coll., 1947; Univ. of Minn., 1966-67; Duke Univ., 1969; Communicable Disease Ctr., Atlanta, Ga., 1972. Appts: Rsch. Bacteriol., Univ. of Minn., 1952-53; Clin. Bacteriol., Dr. Lufkin's Lab., 1954-55; Chief Technol., St. Paul's Regional Blood Ctr. Am. Red. Cross, 1959-65; Microbiol., Veterans' Hosp., Mpls., 1968-; Instr. in Lab. Med., Coll. of Med. Scis., Univ. of Minn., 1970-. Mbrships. incl: Sec., Richfield Planning Comm., 1965-71; Am. Assn. Blood Banks.; Minn. Assn. Blood Banks; Intercontinental Biog. Assn. Contbr. to sci. & gardening jrnls. Address: 7201 Portland Ave. South, Minneapolis, MN 55423, U.S.A. 5, 8, 22, 57, 68, 120.

SERVOLINI, Luigi, b. 1 Mar. 1906. Painter; Xylographer; Writer; Historian; Art Critic. Educ: Grad., Letters, Univ. of Pisa; Dipl., Carrara Fine Arts Acad.; Postgrad. studies in Mediaeval & Mod. Art & Greek/Latin Diplomatic Paleog. Appts: Prof., Techniques of Xylog. & Lithog., R' Istituto del Libro, Urbino, 1930-39; Hd. Libn., Univ. of Urbino, 1933-39; Dir., Artistic & Cultural Inst., ibid, 1939-53; Dir., State Archives Dept., ibid, 1940-47; Lectr., Hist. of Art, Berchet Schl., Milan, 1952-57 & Niccolini Schl., Leghorn, 1958-65; Dir. Gen., Rizzoli Inst. of Graphic Art, Milan, 1952-58; Hdmaster. Portoferraio, 1965-66, Piombino, 1966-69, Rome, 1969-72, Cecina, 1972-; Prof., Univ. of Pisa, 1958-61 & 1968-71. Mbrships: Acad. of Art of Design, Florence; Fellow, Royal Soc. of Art, London, U.K.; Sec. Gen., Italian Etchers Soc. Publs. incl: 30 books on art. Contbr. to var. jrnls. Hon: Grand Off. of Italian Repub., 1972. Address: Piazza della Liberta 33, 57023, Cecina, Italy.

SETÄLÄ, Kai Martin Edvard, b. 13 Sept. 1913. Physician; University Professor. Educ: M.D., 1941; Qualified, roentgen diagnostics & Therapy, 1946; Qualified, radiotherapy of cancer, 1949. Appts: Assoc. Prof., Radiotherapy, 1948; Ord. Prof., Pathol., Univ. of Helsinki, Finland, 1953-; Chief Dept. of Pathol., ibid, 1953-; Prof., Radiotherapy, 1968; Prof., Pathol., Univ. of Copenhagen, Denmark, 1961. Mbrships. incl: Finnish Assn. of Disables Soldiers; Mbr. & assoc. of many sci. assns.; Participant in num. sci. congresses & meetings. Author of approx. 200 sci. publs. in the field of cancer rsch. Hons: sev. war medals & crosses, 1939-45; Cmdr., Order of the Finnish Lion, 1962. Address: Uudenkaupungintie 8 B 10, SF 00350 Helsinki 35, Finland.

SETÄLÄ, Vilho Suonio, b. 4 April 1892. Writer; Encylopaedist. Educ: M.Sc., Univ. of Helsinki. Appts: Editorial staff, Finnish Ency.; 1925; Prin. Ed., Polyglot Tech. Dict., 1932-40; Tchr. of Theory of Photography, Ctrl. Inst. of Indl. Art, Helsinki, Finland, 1935-39; Free-lance author of text-books etc. in Esperanto; Dir., Esperanto Inst., Finland. Mbrships. Kalevala Soc.; Fenno-ugrical Soc.; Fédération Int. de l'Art Photographique, Berne, Switzerland; Assn. of Sci. & Informative Authors in Finland; Esperanto Acad., Paris, France; Universala Esperanto-Asocio, Rotterdam (Comm., 1921-63); Finnish Esperanto Assn. (former Sec., Pres., Hon. Pres.). Publs: Dynamics of the Finnish language, 1972; Fortoj de l'vivo; text-books, dictionaries, workbooks in Esperanto; three books on photographic art; sev. handyman's books; schl. textbooks of phys. & chem.; contbr. to Int. Dictionary of Photography & Cinematography. Photographys published in album Umpuja; 3 exhibs. of photographs. Designer of Depth of field scale for miniature

cameras, 1927. Hons. incl: State Hon. Prize for Art Photography, & Doctor philos. hon. causa, Univ. of Helsinki, 1973. Winner of medals & prizes in var. photographic exhibs. Address: Espernatotie 4, SF-02220 Iirislahti, Finland. 43, 90.

SETHNA, Minocher Jehangirji, b. 1 Nov. 1911. Barrister-at-Law; Advocate; Professor. Educ: Ph.D., Bombay Univ.; Barrister-at-Law, Middle Temple, London. Appts: Prof., Law, Govt. Law Coll., Bombay, 1952-60; Rdr., Jurisprudence & Roman Law, Post Grad. Fac. of Law, Bombay Univ., 1960-69; Prof., Law, ibid, 1969-. Mbrships: Royal Econ. Soc., London; Hon. Soc. of Middle Temple; Advocate, High Ct. of Judicature, Bombay; Past Pres., Indian Schl. of Synthetic Jurisprudence. Num. publs. incl: Essentials of Ideal Law-Making, 1968; Indian Company Law, 7th edit., 1969; Society & the Criminal, 3rd edit., 1971; Art of Living, 1972; Contbr. to books & jrnls. Hons: Pedroza Prize, Wilson Coll., Bombay Univ., 1929. Address: Sethna House, 251 Tardeo Rd., Bombay 7, India. 1, 30.

SETTLE, Glen Allen, b. 28 Sept. 1911. Mining Company Executive. Educ: Tex. A & I, 1929-30; Ripon Coll., Wis., 1931-32; Fresno State Coll., 1933-34. Appts: Ptnr., A.V. Dist. Co., 1933-42; Asst. Mgr., Burton Mines, 1948-56; Mgr., Burton Bros. Inc., 1956-71; Pres. & Mgr., Burton Tour Co., 1958-71; Mbrships: Calif. State Landmarks Comm., 1966-72; Chmn., 1971-72. Pres., Kern Antelope Hist. Soc. 1960-63; Dir., 1960-71; Chmn. Landmarks Comm., Calif. Conf. of Hist. Socs., 1970-71. Publs: Tropico the Rich Red Hill; Here Roamed the Antelope; Bears, Borax & Gold; Along the Rails from Lancaster to Mojave; Various articles in mags. & newspapers. Hons. incl: LA Co. Award of Merit; Resolution Award, 1967. Address: Rt. 1, Box 98 c/o Tropico Mine, Rosamond, CA 93560, U.S.A. 9.

SEUNARINE, James Forbes, b. 18 Oct. 1921. Christian Minister. Educ: B.A., Victoria Coll., Toronto, 1947; B.D., Dip. Theol., Emmanuel Coll., Toronto, 1950; ordained, 1950; Th.M., Princeton, N.J., 1959; doct. studies prog., Princeton, N.J., 1968-70; Rsch. Yr., India, 1970-71. Appts: Pastor, Knox Presby. Ch., Couva, Trinidad, 1950-55 & Morton Mem. Ch., Guaico, ibid, 1956-58; Prin., St. Andrew's Theol. Coll. of W. Indies, Kingston, Jamaica, 1966-68; Pastor, United Presby. Ch., Wharton, N.J., 1971-73; Assoc. Sec., Div. of World Outreach, United Ch. of Canada, Toronto, 1974-; Moderator, Synod, Presby. Ch., Trinidad; Moderator, Caribbean Assembly of Reformed Chs., 1965-67. Mbrships. incl: Y's Mens Club, Kingston, Jamaica; Dist. Clergy Assn.; Am. Acad. of Relig.; Soc. for Scientific Study of Relig. (& affiliates). Publs. incl: The Desire of All Nations, (article) Trinidad Presby.; Ed., New Forms of Ministry, (report), 1967. Address: Div. of World Outreach, United Church of Canada, 85 St. Clair Ave. E., Toronto 7, Ont., Canada.

SEURAT, Silvère, b. 20 June 1918. Company Executive. Educ: Engr. Grad., École Polytech. France, 1940; Naval Engr., École d'Application Génie Maritime, 1939-40; École Nat. des Scis. & Techniques Nucléaires, Saclay. Appts. incl: Naval Engr., French Navy, N. Africa, 1939-48; Hd., Construction for Bône Power Stn., Asst. Hd., 'Serv. Ctrl. des Etudes & Projets Thermiques' & Asst. Dir. to 'Prod. Thermique', Electricité de France, 1948-58; Fndr., Chmn. & Mng. Dir., Euréquip (Mgmt. Cons.'), 1961-; Pres., Mgmt. Sect., Syntec (Nat.

Assn. of Engrng. & Cons. firms), 1973. Mbrships: Club Eropéen pour la Coopération des Entreprises; Cercle de l'Opinion; Club Alpin Français; Club Gault-Millau. Lectr. & author of num. articles in profl. jrnls. on engrng. & mgmt., trng. & ind., ind. & ecology & directs book series, Languages of Action. Hons. incl: Croix de Guerre, 1939-45; Chevalier de la Legion d'Honneur, 1956. Address: Soc. Eurequip, 19 Rue Yves du Manoir, 92420 Vaucresson, France. 1.

SEVER, Shmuel, b. 16 Jan. 1933. Librarian; Educator. Educ: B.A., Hebrew Univ., Jerusalem, Israel, 1956; Grad. Dip., Lib. Scis., 1957; M.A., Chgo. Univ., U.S.A., 1968; Currently studying for Ph.D., ibid. Appts: Serials Cataloguer-Reference Libn., Jewish Nat. Univ. Lib., Jerusalem, Israel, 1954-59; Hd. Libn., Israel Atomic Energy Commn., Nahal-Soreq, 1959-61; Dir., Libs., Nat. Univ. Inst. Agric., Rehovot, 1961-67; Exec. Sec., Lectr., Grad. Lib. Schl., Hebrew Univ., Jerusalem, 1968-69; Counselor, Pub. Libs., Min. Educ. & Culture, Israel, 1966-; Lib. Dir.-Assoc. Prof., Lib. Scis., Schl. Lib. Studies, Haifa Univ., Israel, 1969-. Mbr. sev. profl. orgs. publs. incl: Survey of the Libraries of the Israel Defense Forces, 1958; Some Social Aspects of Israeli Libraries, 1968; Automation in Libraries, 1969; The Libraries of Scandinavia, 1969; Survey on the Flow of Science Information in Israel's University Libraries, 1970; Organizing a University Library: The Haifa University Library, 1970. Recip. Ruth Cohen Mem. Lib. Sci. Grant, 1970. Address: Oren St. 24, Haifa, Israel.

SEVERANCE, Jay Lavin, Jr., b. 9 Apr. 1939. Real Estate Investor. Educ: B.A., Hanover Coll., Ind., U.S.A; M.B.A., Cinn. Univ., Ohio. Appts: Pub. Rels. Dir., Howey Acad., Howey in the Hills, Fla., 1965-66; Pub. Rels. Assoc., Ketchum, Inc., Pitts., Pa., 1966-69; Ptnr., McLeod/Severance, Pub. Rels., Jacksonville, Fla., 1969-73; Real Estate Investor, Jacksonville, Fla., 1973-. Mbrships. incl: Pres., Young Repubs., Duval Co.; Past V.P, Corporate Sec., Jacksonville Jaycees; Past Pres., Exec. Assn., Jacksonville; Sigma Chi; Jacksonville Sigma Chi Alumni Club; Barnett Lodge Free & Accepted Masons; Am. Legion, Arlington Post; Duval Co. Repub. Men's Club; Repub. Exec. Comm., Duval Co.; Fla. Fedn. Young Repubs. Exec. Comm.; Credentials Comm.; Gator Bowl Assn.; Fla. Pub. Rels Assn.; Delta Sigma Pi; Alpha Phi Gamma. Hons. incl: US Young Repubs. Hardcharger Award, 1974; Top 5 Young Repubs., Fla. State, 1974; Outstanding Mbrship. Recruiter, Fla. Young Repubs., 1974; Community Chmn., Watchdog, TV Prog., 1974; Man of Month Award, Jacksonville Jaycees, 1973. Address: 902 Blackstone Bldg., 233 E. Bay St., Jacksonville, FL 32202, U.S.A. 125.

SEVERIN, Wendell Harold, b. 7 May 1914. Secretary-Treasurer of cattle club. Educ: Graduated from 3 serv. schls., U.S. Army. appts: Showcattle Herdsman & Breeding Farm Wkr., 1933-41 & '46; Pvte. to Capt., Army of U.S., 1941-46; Fieldman, Red Poll Cattle Club of Am., 1947-53; Livestock Photographer & Sales Mgr., 1954-57; Sec.-Treas., RPCC of Am., 1957-; Trustee, The Red Poll Endowment Fund, 1964-. Mbrships: Red Poll Cattle Club of Am.; Neb. Red Poll Breeders Assn.; Neb. Thoroughbred Breeders Assn.; Past Dir., Nat. Soc. Livestock Record Assns.; A.F. & A.M. ('Bluelodge' only); Assoc. Mbr., Assn. of Agricl. Coll. Eds.; Farmer, breeder at Red Poll Cattle & Thoroughbred Horses, 1965-. Ed., Red Poll News, 1957-, & Red Poll Newsletter, 1971-. Author of num. promotional articles concerning Red Poll Cattle. Address: 3275 Holdrege St., Lincoln, NB 68503, U.S.A. 8, 16, 120.

SEYDELL, Mildred (Mrs Max Seydel). Writer; Author; Publisher. Educ: Lucy Cobb Inst., Athens, Ga., U.S.A. Sorbonne, Paris, France. Appts: Journalist; For. Corres.; Publr. of Seydell Quarterly, Silent Singing by Suzanne Keener, Essays Wise & Otherwise by Lamar Rutherford Lipscomb, Poetry Profile of Belgium; Advsry. Bd., Sunshine Mag.; Advsr., Fellowship in Prayer. Hon. Mbrships: Beta Sigma Phi; Peony Gdn. Club; Atlanta Br., Ladies Mem. Assn.; Bd. of Dirs., A.G. Thodes Home; Friends of Lib. Emory Univ. Mbr., Atlanta Br., Nat. League Pen Women & United Daughters of Confederacy. Publs: Secret Fathers; Chins Up; Then I Saw North Caroline; Poetry Profile of Belgium; Come Along to Belgium. Hons: Knighted by Baudouin, King of Belgian, 1972; Chevalier de l'Ordre de Leopold, Belgium for work in spreading Belgian culture, 1973. Address: Scott Rd., Rt. 2 Roswell, GA 30075, U.S.A. 2, 5, 7, 125.

SEYERSTED, Finn, b. 29 Dec. 1915. Professor of Law. Educ: Law Degree, Univ. of Oslo, Norway, 1941. Appts. incl: Dpty. Judge. Norwegian Min. of Justice, 1943-45; Sec., Norwegian Permanent Delegn. to U.N., 1946-49; Sec., 1st Pol. Div., Min. for For. Affairs, 1949-50; Sec., Legal Div., ibid, 1951-53; Chief, Legal Div., 1955-60; Mbr., UNESCO Mission to Indonesia, Philippines & Laos, 1953-54; Norwegian Deleg., Geneva Conf. on the Law of the Sea, 1958, Gen. Assembly of U.N., 1959, & other int. confs.; Dir., Legal Div., Int. Atomic Energy Agcy., Vienna, Austria, 1960-65; Norwegian Consul Gen., Mpls., Minn., U.S.A., 1967-68; Norwegian Ambassador, Argentina, Paraguay, & Uruguay, 1968-73; Prof., Law Univ. of Oslo, 1974-. Mbrship: Assoc., Inst. of Int. Law. Publs: United Nations Forces in the Law of Peace & War, 1966; Die Internationale Atomenergie-Organization - ihre Rechtlichen Aufgaben & Funktionen, 1966; Articles & papers in legal & pol. Jrnls. Recip., Dr. Juris, Univ. of Oslo, 1966. Address: Universitetet, Karl Johans gt. 47, Oslo 1, Norway.

SEYMOUR, Alan, b. 6 June 1927. Author. Appts: Writer, Australian Broadcasting Commn.; Dir., Sydney Opera Grp.; Playwright, Novelist, Critic, TV Writer, 1954-. Publs: Plays - Swamp Creatures, 1957, Donny Johnson, 1960; The One Day of the Year, 1960; The Wind from the Plain, 1973; Oh Grave Thy Victory, 1973; The Shattering, 1974; Novels - The One Day of the Year, 1967; The Coming Self-Destruction of the United States of America, 1969; Stories, articles, criticisms, Australian, U.K. & U.S. periodicals. Hons: Finalist, Observer Play Competition, 1957; Jt. Winner, Australian Jrnlsts.' Club Play Competition, 1961. Address: c/o Laurence Fitch Esq., Film Rights Ltd., 113 Wardour St., London W.1, U.K. 23.

SEYMOUR, James Walter, b. 6 Aug., 1919. Businessman. Appts: Foreman, Heron's Rest Estate, Southampton, Bermuda; Owner/Mgr., Walter J. Seymour Bookings & Rental Agt., Hamilton; Fndr., Pres. & Chmn., now Hon. Pres., Provident Investment & Holdings Co. Ltd.; Dir., Provident Bank. Mbrships: Berkeley Educ. Soc., Trustee & Finance Bd.; African Meth. Episc. Ch.; Alpha Enterprise (Chap.); Bermudans for Reconciliation Org. Recip. of church & community awards. Address: Burnaby St., P.O. Box 1830, Hamilton 5, Bermuda. 109.

SEYMOUR, William Kean, b. 27 Sept. 1887. Bank Manager (Retired); Author; Poet. Educ: King's Coll., London, U.K., 1912-14. Appts: Mgr., Midland Bank, Ltd., Chelsea, London, 1928-47; Retd., 1947; Hon. Treas., PEN, Engl. Ctr., 1932-37; V.P., The Poetry Soc., 1947-; Mbr., Gen. Coun., 1948-64, Chmn., Gen. Coun., 1961-64, ibid; Pres., 1960-73, Hon. Life Pres., 1973-, Guildford Ctr. of Poetry Soc.; Chmn., W. Country Writers' Assn., 1973. Mbrships: Fellow, Royal Soc. of Lit., 1947-; Soc. of Authors; Lib. & Art Comm., Nat. Liberal Club, 1965-; Fndr.-Fellow, Int. Poetry Soc.; V.P. for G.B., United Poets Laureate Int., Philippines, 1970. Publs. incl: (Poetry) The Street of Dreams, 1914; To Verhaeren; 23 Poems, 1917; Swords & Flutes, 1919; Caesar Remembers, 1929; Time Stands, 1935; Collected Poems, 1946; Burns into English, 1954; (Verse-play) The First Childermas, 1959; (parodies) A Jackdaw In Georgia, 1925; Parrot Pie, 1927; Chinese Crackers, 1938; (Criticism) Jonathan Swift: The Enigma of a Genius, 1967; Co-ed., The Pattern of Poetry, 1963; Happy Christmas, 1969; Ed., A Miscellany of Poetry, 1919; Ditto, 1920-22; The Cats of Rome, 1970; Contbr. to Daily News, Daily Herald, Outposts, John O'London's, Mercury, Observer, New Age, To-day, Poetry Review, Contemporary Review, Sunday Times, Good Housekeeping, Country Life, The Sackbut, Pall Mall Mag., GK's Weekly, N.Y. Times, The Scotsman, Decachord, Week-End Review, Wheels, Shorter Lyrics, Best Poems Series, Treasury of Living Poets, & other jrnls. & anthols. in U.K., U.S.A. & Canada. Hons: Philippines Pres. Gold Medal for Poetry as Disting. Anglo-Irish Poet, 1968; D.Litt., Free Univ. of Asia, Karachi, 1968. Address: White Cottage, Old Alresford, Hants., U.K. 1, 3, 11.

SHACHTER, Haim, b. 13 Mar. 1911. Educator; Author; Editor. Educ: Queens Univ., Belfast; London Univ.; Hebrew Univ., Jerusalem. Appts: Ed. Staff, Palestine Post; Sr. Engl. Master, Hebrew Coll., Jerusalem; Lectr., Schl. of Higher Studies, Jerusalem; Examiner, Israel Min. of Educ.; Ed. Publs., Info. Dept., Jewish Agcy.; Ed.-in-Chief Press Serv., World Zionist Org. Publs: The Universal Hebrew-English Dictionary; The New English-Hebrew Dictionary; A History of English Literature (Hebrew); num. textbooks used in Israeli schls.; Contbr. to World Jewish Press. Recip. Ot Aleh, decoration for Fighters for the State. Address: 5 David Marcus St., Jerusalem, Israel. 55, 94.

SHACKLETON, Robert, b. 25 Nov. 1919. University Librarian. Educ: M.A., D.Litt., Oriel Coll., Oxford Univ., U.K. Appts: Fellow, Brasenose Coll., Oxford Univ., 1946-; Libn.-Professl. Fellow, 1948-; Lectr.-Bodley's Libn., 1949-; Vis. Prof., Wis. Univ., U.S.A., 1968. Mbrships: V.P., Int. Soc. for Eighteenth-Century Studies; Int. Comp. Lit. Assn. (Pres. 1964-67); Assn. Int. de Bibliophilie; Australasian & Pacific Soc. for Eighteenth-Century Studies; Athenaeum, London, U.K.; Nat. Lib. Club, ibid; Grolier, N.Y., U.S.A. Publs. incl: Fontenelle, Entretiens sur la pluralité des mondes, 1955; Montesquieu, a critical biography, 1961; num. articles in reviews & lit. jrnls. Hons: Hon. Dr., Bordeaux Univ., France; Hon.Litt.D., Dublin Univ., Repub. of Ireland; Hon. Fellow, Oriel Coll., Oxford Univ., U.K.; Hon. Professl. Fellow, Univ. Coll., Wales; Assoc. Fellow, Silliman Coll., Yale Univ., U.S.A.; Fellow, British Acad.; Fellow, Soc. of Antiquaries; Fellow, Royal Soc. of Lit.; For. Hon. Mbr., Am. Acad. of Arts & Scis.; Corres. Mbr., Bordeaux Acad., France. Address: Bodleian Lib., Oxford OX1 3BG, U.K. 1.

SHACKLOCK, Constance (Mrs. Eric Mitchell), b. 16 Apr. 1913. Opera & Concert Singer. Educ: Lic., Royal Acad. of Music, London. Appts: w. Int. Ballet in A Masque, Milton's Comus; appeared w. Royal Opera, Covent Gdn.; Fellow & Prof. of Singin, Royal Acad. of Music. Recip. O.B.E., 1970. Address: East Dorincourt, Kingston Vale, London SW 15 3RN, U.K. 4, 21.

SHAFFER, Dale Eugene, b. 17 Apr. 1929. Library Consultant; Library Director. Educ: B.S., Kent State Univ., Kent, Ohio, 1955; M.A.L.S., ibid, 1960; M.A., Ohio State Univ., Columbus, 1956. Appts. incl: Trng. Specialist, Ohio State Employment Serv., Columbus, 1962-63; Hd. Libn. & Hd., Lib. Sci. Dept., Glenville State Coll., W. Va., 1963-65; Lib. Dir., Ocean Co. Coll., Toms River, N.J., 1965-67; Lib. Dir., Capital Univ., Columbus, Ohio, 1968-71; Lib. Dir., Assoc. Prof., Univ. of Pitts., Johnstown, Pa., 1972-73; Lib. Cons., own consulting & pub. bus., Salem, Ohio, 1973-. Mbrships. incl: ALA; Soc. for the Advancement of Mgmt.; Ohio Bus. Tchrs. Assn.; Delta Sigma Pi. Copyrighted books incl: Library Resources for Nurses, 1973; Library Job Descriptions, 1973; Creativity for Librarians, 1973. Contbr. to profl. jrnls. Address: 437 Jennings Ave., Salem OH 44460, U.S.A. 2, 8, 22, 30, 42, 129, 130, 131.

SHAFI, Mohammad, b. 1 Aug. 1924. Professor of Geography. Educ: B.A., Allahabad Univ., India; M.A., Aligarh Muslim Univ.; Ph.D., Univ. of London, U.K. Appts: Lectr., Geog., Aligarh Muslim Univ., 1948-51; Sr. Lectr., ibid, 1951-56; Rdr., 1957-62; Prof. & Hd., Geog. Dept., 1962-; Sr. Prof., 1967-; Pro-Vice-Chancellor, 1971; Dir., Acad. Prog., 1972-. Mbrships. incl: Pres., Aligarh Geog. Soc.; Am. Geog. Soc.; Edit. Bd., Geog. Sect., Hungarian Acad. of Scis.; Working Grp., Nat. Commn. of Indian Agric.; Chief Ed., Geographer, Jrnl. of Aligarh Geog. Soc. Publs: Land Utilization in Eastern Uttar Pradesh; Num. papers at confs. & contbns. to books & profl. jrnls. Recip., Medal in recognition of Pioneer Work on Land Use, Univ. of Liege, Belgium, 1967. Address: Dept. of Geography, Aligarh Muslim University, Aligarh, India.

SHAFRAN, (Rabbi) David, b. 8 Jan. 1915. Rabbi; Educator. Educ: B.A. in Humanities; Dr. Pedagogy; Dip. of Rabbi. Appts: Rabbi, The Holy Unification Synagogue, Bucharest, Rumania, 1940-48, '54-58; Gen. Sec., Rabbinical Ctr. of Bucharest, 1955-56; Dir., Relig. Tchr.'s Sem., Jerusalem, Israel, 1959-60; Corres., Radio Free Europe, Israel, 1960-65; Chief Reporter, "Menora" (publd. monthly), 1959-; Tchr., Aianot Sem. & Second. Schl., Israel, 1960-. Mbrships: Gt. Masonic Lodge, Rumania & Hashachar Masonic Lodge, Israel. Publs: about 29 works, 9 in Rumania, the rest in Israel, inclng: Quo Vadis Germany?, 1960; The Art of Reading, 1971; Reminiscences, 1972; Gog & Magog (novel), 1973; Ideal Women in Judaism, 1974; Jubileum, at My Sixties, 1970. Hons: Decoration, Defense Dept. of Israel for Zionist Activity in the Diaspora. Address: 2 Gordon St., Kyriat Yovel, Jerusalem, Israel. 55, 94.

SHAH, Idries, b. 16 June 1924. Author; Philosopher. Appts. incl: Dir. of Studies, Inst. For. Cultural Rsch., London, U.K., 1966-. Publs. incl: Wisdom of the Idiots; Caravan of Dreams; The Sufis; Special Problems in the Study of Sufi Ideas; Destination Mecca; Exploits of Nasrudin; The Subtleties of the Inimitable Mulla Nasrudin; The Book of the Book; Reflections; Learning How to Learn; The Elephant in the Dark; Thinkers of the East;

Textos Sufis; The Secret Lore of Magic; The Magic Monastery; Lo Que un Pajaro Deberia Parecer. Fellowships: Royal Soc. of Arts; Royal Commonwealth Soc. Mbrships. incl: Soc. of Authors; PEN; Life, Brit. Assn. Advancement of Sci.; Royal Humane Soc.; Folklore Soc.; Gov., Royal Hosp. & Home for Incurables; The Club of Roman (German Peace Fndn. Award, 1973). Activities featured in num. publs. Hons. incl: Dermis Probe, Outstanding Film of the Year, London & N.Y. Film Festivals, 1965; The Way of the Sufi, & Reflections, Outstanding Books of the Year, BBC, 1968; Paradise of Song, Classic Story Choice, Nova, 1970; The Magic Monastery, Book of the Year, The Observer, 1972; 6 1st Prizes (int. Lit. Awards), UNESCO Int. Book Year, 1972; Int. Community Serv. Award, 1973. Address: Langton House, Langton Green, Nr. Tunbridge Wells, Kent TN3 OJD, U.K. 3, 13, 30, 58, 131.

SHAH, Krishna Bhogilal, b. 10 May 1938. Writer; Director. Educ: LL.M., Yale Univ., 1958; M.A., Iowa Univ., 1960. Dir., TV shows, Love American Style, Iron Side, Questor, 1973. Writer, Dir., Co-Prod., Rivals (film), 1972. Plays: Adaptor & Dir., King of the Dark Chamber, R. Tagore, 1961; Co-Auth., Sponono, 1964. Mbrships: Sec., Dirs. Guild Am., 1973-75; Writers Guild Am.; Dramatists Guild. Hons: 201-203, Best Picture of Yr., Photographic Soc. Am., 1965; Cine Golden Award; Our Gang, Official U.S. Entry, Locarno Film Fest. Address: c/o Int. Famous Agcy., 9255 Sunset Blvd., Los Angeles, CA 90069, U.S.A.

SHAHANE, Vasant Anant, b. 18 Dec. 1923. Professor; College Principal. Educ: B.A., Univ. of Bombay, 1944; LL.B., ibid, 1946; M.A., 1947; Ph.D., Univ. of Leeds, U.K., 1958. Appts: Lectr., Reader, now Prof., Engl., Osmania Univ., Hyderabad, India, 1947-; Prin., Univ. Coll. of Arts, ibid, 1973-; Vis. Prof., Wisc. Univ., U.S.A., 1967-68 & Wayne State Univ., Detroit, 1970-71. Mbrships: Sec., 17th Session All India Engl. Univ. Tchrs. Conf., Hyderabad 1966 & Gen. Sec., 1967; MLA; Indian PEN; Poetry Soc. (London) Hyderabad Ctr.; Editl. Bd., Indian Jrnl. of Am. Studies. Publs: E.M. Forster-A Reassessment, 1962; Perspectives on E.M. Forster's A Passage to India, 1968; Khushwant Singh, 1972; Notes on Walt Whitman's Leaves of Grass, 1972; Rudyard Kipling-Activist & Artist, 1973; articles in profl. jrnls. Recip. Fulbright Grant, 1966. Address: University Coll. of Arts of Osmania Univ., Hyderabad-7, Andhra Pradesh, India 500007, 30.

SHAHAR, David, b. 17 June 1926. Writer. Educ: Hebrew Univ., Jerusalem. Appts: Lectr., Contemp. Hebrew Lit., Nat. Inst. of Oriental Langs. & Civilizations, Univ. of Paris, 1972. Mbrships: Chmn., Assn. Hebrew Writers in Israel, 1972; Ctrl. Comm., Israeli PEN; Assoc., French PEN Ctr. Publs. (in Hebrew): The Moon of Honey & Gold (novel), 1959; The Palace of Broken Vessels (novel), 1969; Voyage to Ur of the Chaldees (novel), 1971; The Death of the Little God (stories), 1970; The Pope's Moustache (stories), 1971. Transls: in French, La Colombe et la Lune, 1971; in Engl., News from Jerusalem (stories), 1974. Hons: Prime Min.'s Award for Lit., 1969; Agnon Prize, City of Jerusalem, 1973. Address: 17, Hovevey Zion St., Talbieh, Jerusalem, Israel. 55, 94.

SHAIN, Richard Arthur, b. 18 Mar. 1948. Psychologist. Educ: B.A., Queens Coll., Flushing, N.Y., 1970; M.A., Temple Univ., Phila., Pa., 1972; Ph.D. candidate, ibid., 1972-. Appts. incl: Tchr.-Coord., Special Educ. H.S. Work-study Prog., Mt. Vernon Pub. Schls.,

N.Y., 1970; Rsch. Asst., Tchng. Asst. & Programming Cons., Dept. of Psychol., Temple Univ., 1970-71; Admin. Asst., Developmental Rsch. Lab., ibid., 1971-73; Tchng.Asst.-Instr., Dept. of Psychol., ibid., 1973-74. Mbrships. incl: Am. Psychol. Assn.; Soc. for the Rsch. of Child Dev.; Jean Piaget Soc.; Coun. for Exceptional Children; Psi Chi. Publs. incl: Poems in num. jrnls. & anthols. Hons. incl: Masonic Award, 1967, Student Serv. Award, Senate Key, 1969, Queens Coll., Flushing, N.Y.; World Poet Award, World Poetry Soc., 1970. Address: 1300 W. Columbia Ave., Philadelphia, PA 19122, U.S.A. 11, 46, 57, 129.

SHALDON, Stanley, b. 8 Nov. 1931. Physician. Educ: Sorbonne, Paris, France; B.Sc., Queen's Coll., Cambridge, 1952; M.D., ibid, 1961; Middlesex Hosp. Med. Schl. Appts: Lectr. in Med., Dept. of Med., Royal Free Med. Schl., London Univ., 1960-65; Cons. Physns., Royal Free Hosp., 1965-66; Med. Dir., Nat. Kidney Ctr., London, 1966-. Mbrships: European Soc. of Clin. Investigation; Coun. of European Dialysis & Transplant Assn.; Med. Rsch. Soc.; Renal Assn.; Fellow, Royal Soc. of Med.; Am. Soc. for Artificial Internal Organs; Int. Soc. & Congress of Nephrol.; Advsry. Working Pty. on Chronic Dialysis to the Min. of Hlth., 1965-66. Contbr. chapts. & articles to profl. publs. Ed. Symposium on Acute Renal Failure, 1964. Hons. incl: John Murray Schlrship. & Gold Medal in Theoretical & Practical Med. & Hetley Clin. Prize in Med., Surg. & Obstetrics, both 1955; Raymond Horton-Smith Prize for Best M.D. thesis, Univ. of Cambridge, 1961; Legg Award for publd. work, Royal Free Hosp. Med. Schl., 1962. Address: 5 Chessington Ave., Finchley, London N3, U.K. 50.

SHALLCROSS, Virginia (Mrs. Preston Shallcross), b. 7 Nov. 1910. Farmer. Educ: Md. Inst., Balt.; Peabody Inst., Balt.; Univ. of Md., Coll. Pk.; Studio of Acting, N.Y.C.; N.Y. State Inst. of Agric., Farmingdale; Int. Corres. Schl., Scranton, Pa. Mbrships: Minervian Soc.; Children of Am. Revolution; Am. Assn. of Retd. Persons; Repub.; Citizens Volunteer Fire Co.; United Burmese Cat Fanciers, Inc.; Nat. Detectives & Special Police Assn.; Mbr. & Asst. Sunday Schl. Tchr., Adult Class of Prospect United Meth. Ch., New Pk., Pa.; Charter Mbr., Am. Fed. of Police; Deleg.-at-Large, 3rd World Police Congress, 1972. Recip. of Cert. of Achievement, Women's Land Army, WWII. Address: Heavenly Acres, New Park, PA 17352, U.S.A.

SHALOWITZ, Erwin Emmanuel, b. 13 Feb. 1924. Civil Engineer. Educ: Navy Off. Trng. Prog., Univ. of Pa. & Univ. of Notre Dame, 1944-45; B.C.E., Geo. Wash. Univ., Wash., D.C., 1947; Grad., Soil Mechs., Cath. Univ., ibid, 1950-51; M.A. in Pub. Admin., Am. Univ., ibid, 1954. Appts: Engrng. Off. on destroyer, USN, 1944-46; Engr.-i/c, Construction Site, Klemitt Engrng. Co., N.Y.C., 1947; Sanitary Engr., Cons. Firm, Whitman, Requardt & Assocs., Balt., Md., 1947-48; Chief Structural Rsch. Engr., Proj. Off. & Tech. Advsr., Atomic Tests, Hd., Defense Rsch. Sect., Mbr., Navy's Special Weapons Effects Test Planning Grp., Navy Dept., 1948-59; Supvsry. Gen. Engr., Special Asst. i/c Protective Construction Progs., Proj. Mgr. for Bldg. Systems, Lectr., Engrng. Rsch. & Mgmt. Systems, Chief, Rsch. Br., Mbr. of Interagcy. Comm., Housing Rsch. & Bldg. Technol. sponsored by Exec. Off. of Pres., Chief, Mgmt. Info., Chief, Contracting Procedures (Construction Procurement Policy), Gen. Servs. Admin., 1959-. Mbrships: Fellow, Am. Soc. Civil Engrs.; Sigma Tau; Pi Sigma

Alpha; Soc. for Advment. of Mgmt.; Soc. of Am. Mil. Engrs.; Past, Am. Acad. Pol. & Soc. Sci. Contbr. of articles to tech. & profl. jrnls. Recip., Gen. Servs. Admin. Commendable Serv. Award, 1968. Address: 5603 Huntington Parkway, Bethesda, MD 20014, U.S.A. 7, 125, 130.

SHAMIR, Moshe, b. 7 Dec. 1923. Company President. Educ: Civil Engr. Appts: Gen. Mng. Dir., Sugat-Sugar Works, Ltd., 1958-72; Pres., Vishay Israel Ltd., Tel-Aviv, V.P., Vishay Intertechnol., Inc., Malver, Pa., U.S.A., 1972-; Dir. & Mbr. of Exec. Comms., Clal-Israel Investment Co. Ltd., Assia-Chem. Labs. Ltd., Zori-Pharm. & Chem. Inds. Ltd., Teva-Middle E. Pharm. & Chem. Works Ltd. & Sugar-Sugar Works Ltd. Mbrships: Mgrs. Assn. of Israel; Israel Mgmt. Ctr.; Israel Export Inst.; Assn. of Engrs. & Archts. of Israel; O.R.T. Israel; Bd. of Govs., Technion-Israel Inst. of Technol. Address: c/o Vishay Israel Ltd., 3 Ha'Ahim Mislavita St., Tel-Aviv, Israel. 94.

SHANDRICK, Albert Joseph, b. 22 Jan. 1920. Clergyman-scientist. Educ: B.S., Colo. Coll., 1942; M.Th., Chgo. Luth. Schl. Theol., 1948; M.R.E., Iliff Schl., 1951; Prof.'s Degree in Phys., Univ. of Calif. at Berkeley. Appts: Rsch. Physicist, U.S. Navy Ordnance Lab., & Univ. of Calif., 1942-45; Seminarian, 1945-48; Asst. Pastor, St. Mark's Luth. Ch., San Francisco, Calif., 1948-50; Mission Developer, Redding, Calif., 1950-51; Grad. Wkr., 1951-52; Fac. Mbr., Ctrl. Luth. Theological Sem., Fremont, Neb., 1952-61; Pastor, Zion Luth. Ch., Trinidad, Colo., 1961-. Mbrships. incl: Am. Assn. Theological Sems.; Rotary Int.; var. literary & ch. related orgs. Author, num. articles, religious publs. Recip., var. citations, inclng. Am. Assn. Theological Sems., 1965. Address: 613 Prospect, Trinidad, CO 81082, U.S.A. 9. 60, 120, 130, 131.

SHANE, Harold D., b. 22 Jan. 1936. Mathematician. Educ: S.B., MIT, 1957; M.S., Courant Inst., N.Y. Univ., 1962; Ph.D., ibid, 1968. Appts: Engr., Electric Div., Daystrom Inc., Poughkeepsie, N.Y., 1958-61; Instr. of Maths., The Cooper Union, N.Y.C., 1962-68; Asst. Prof.-Assoc. Prof., Maths., Baruch Coll., CUNY, 1968-; Chmn., Dept. of Maths., ibid, 1971-. Mbrships. incl: Math. Assn. of Am.; Exec. Coun., N.Y. Metropolitan Chapt., ibid; Inst. of Math. Statistics; N.Y. Acad. of Sci.; A AUP. Publs: Finite Mathematics: an Integrated Approach, 1974; articles in profl. jrnls. Hons: Nova Scotia Rsch. Fndn. Grant, 1956-57. Address: Dept. of Mathematics, Baruch College of CUNY, 17 Lexington Ave., N.Y., NY 10010, U.S.A. 6.

SHANKER, Albert, b. 14 Sept. 1928. Union Leader; Teacher. Educ: Univ. of Ill.; grad. studies, Columbia Univ. Appts. incl: Assoc., Univ. Seminar on Labor, Columbia Univ.; Bd. Dirs., N.Y.C. Coun. of Econ. Educ.; Advsry. Coun. of Edward Corsi Labor-Mgmt. Rels. Inst. of Pace Coll.; Pres.'s Coun. of Schl. of Educ. at N.Y. Univ.; Pres., United Fedn. of Tchrs.; V.P., Am. Fedn. Labor-Congress of Industrial Orgs.; Executive V.P., N.Y. State United Tchrs.; Bd. of Dirs.; A. Philip Randolph Inst., United Housing Fndn.; United Fund of Gtr. N.Y.; Mbrships: V.P., Jewish Labor Comm.; Boy Scouts Labor Comm. Address: 260 Park Ave. S., N.Y., NY 10010, U.S.A.

SHANKMAN, Florence V. (Mrs.), b. 16 July 1912. College Professor; Author; Reading Consultant. Educ: B.S., Tchrs. Coll., Columbia Univ., 1934; M.A., ibid, 1959. Appts: Pub. Schl. tchr., all grades, tchng. for. born; substitute Tchr., all grades & subjects; Supvsr.,

of Instruction, N.Y. Univ, Reading Inst. & Tchr., sev. univs.; Prof., Curric. & Instruction, Temple Univ. Coll. of Educ., Phila., Pa., 1967-; Vis. Prof., Educ., Colo. State Coll., summer 1967; Coll. Holy Names, Oakland, Calif., summer, 1969. Mbrships. incl: Life Mbr., A.C.E.I.; Nat. Soc. for Study of Educ.; Am. Educ. Rsch. Assn.; Int. Reading Assn.; Nat. Coun. for Tchrs. of Engl.; Exec. Bd., Advsr., Nat. Register Prominent Ams. & Int. Notables; Life, Kappa Delta Pi; Pi Lambda Theta.; N.Y.C. Womens Press Club. Publs. incl: Reading Success with Young Children; Reading for Inner City Children; How to Teach Study Skills; Successful Practices in Remedial Reading; How to Teach Reference & Research Skills; Research Studies in Reading, 2 vols.; Reading About Reading Instruction; Readings in the Language Arts, 3 vols.; Film, We Discover the Encyclopedia; many profl. jrnl. articles. Address: Temple Univ. Coll. of Educ., Phila., PA 19122, U.S.A. 2, 5, 6, 13, 15, 126, 128, 130, 132, 141.

SHANNON, Betty Ziegler, b. 1 Aug. 1927. Marketing Research Director. Educ: B.A., Univ. of S.C., 1948; Marketing, Advt. courses, Emory Univ., Ga. State Coll. Appts: Nat. Field Dir., W.H. Long Marketing, 1960-62; Regional Supvsr., Nat. Marketing Studies, 1962-65; Dir., Shannon Marketing Rsch., 1962-. Mbrships: Sec., N.C. Chapt., Am. Marketing Assn.; Marketing Rsch. Assn.; Assn. of Pub. Opinion Rsch.; Am. Bus. Women's Assn.; Fine Arts Chmn., Women's Club, Greensboro, N.C.; Sec., Arthritis Fndn., 1972; Nat. Hon. Soc.; Sec., Delta Zeta; 1st woman mbr., Rsch. Comm., Greensboro Chmbr. of Comm. Address: 1103 Imperial House, Nashville, TN 37205, U.S.A. 57, 125.

SHANNON, Elsie June Arthur, b. 16 Apr. 1913. Schoolteacher; Poet. Educ: A.A., Tarleton State Univ., Stephenville, Tex., U.S.A., 1931; B.S., Daniel Baker Coll., Brownwood, Tex., 1936; M.S., Abilene Christian Coll., Tex., 1959. Appts: Tchr., Brown Co. Schls., 1932-59; Tchr., Stephenville H.S., 1959-. Mbrships. incl: Chmn., Tex. Jt. Engl. Comm. for Schl. & Coll.; Pres., Int. Poetry Rdrs. & Writers Assn.; Pres., Brown Co. Engl. Tchrs. Assn.; Pres., Stephenville Br., AAUW; Pres., Stephenville Br., Tex. Classroom Tchrs. Assn.; NEA; Chmn. of Arts, 1st Dist., Tex. Congress of Parents & Tchrs.; Educl. & Radio Chmn., 1st Dist., Tex. Fedn. of Women's Clubs; Pres. & other offs., Gamma Zeta Chapt., Delta Kappa Gamma. Publs: Language Arts Study Guide, 1958; A Study of Some of the Competencies of a High School English Teacher, 1959; Wake Up, America! 1968; Down-to-earth Philosophy, 1972; Four Voices of Happiness & Other Poems, 1974. Recip., sev. awards & guest lectureships. Address: Rt.4, Box 21, Stephenville, TX 76401, U.S.A. 125, 138.

SHANNON, Mary Coleen, b. 17 Oct. 1940 Social Worker. Educ: B.A., Tex. Christian Univ., 1962; M.S.W., Tulane Univ., 1965. Appts. incl: Casewkr., Homestead Child Placement Agcy., Ft. Worth, Tex., 1962-63, Family Serv. Assn., ibid, 1965-68; Inst., Schl. of Relig., 1st United Meth., 1968; Soc. Work Cons., Glenview Extended Care Ctr. 1969-70; Field Inst. Grad. Achl. of Soc. Work, Univ. of Tex., Austin, 1968-69; Cons., Volunteers of Am., St. Worth, 1968; Pub. Hlth Dept., 1969, Sisters of St. Mary of Namur, 1969; Vis. Lectr. Sociol. Dept., Univ. of Tex. at Arlington, 1970; Dir. of Profl. Servs., Family Serv. Travelers Aid Assn., Ft. Worth, 1968-70; Cons., Cath. Soc. Servs., ibid, 1971-72, Soc. Servs. Dept., St. Joseph Hosp., ibid, 1971-73; Asst. Prof., Grad.

Schl. of Soc. Work, Univ. of Tex Arlington, 1070-. Mbrships. incl: Var. past offs., Longhorn Cahpt., Nat. Assn. of Soc. Wkrs.; Acad. of Cert. Soc. Wkrs. Author of article in The Jrnl. of Suggestive Therapeutics, Vol. 1, No. 4, 1973. Address: 4725 Madella, Ft. Worth, TX 76117, U.S.A. 5, 7, 129, 132.

SHANNON, (Sister) Theresa Marie, b. 14 June 1919. Librarian. Educ: A.B., M.L.S., Villanova Univ., Pa.; courses, Syracuse Univ., N.Y., Wm. & Mary· Coll., Va. Appts: Tchr., elementary schls., Archdiocese of Phila., 1940-55; Libn., St. Hubert H.S., Phila., 1955-62, 1968-71, John W. Hallahan H.S., 1062-68, Walsingham Acad., Williamsburg, Va., 1971-; Mbr., Comms. for Black Lit. & Early Childhood Educ., State Dept. Educ., Harrisburg., Pa. Mbrships. incl: Cath. Lib. Assn., 1955-; Advsry. Bd., H.S. Sect., ibid, 1971-74; Pa. Lib. Assn., 1968-71; Va. Lib. Assn., 1971-.Past. Ed., Newsletter of Eastern Pa. Unit, Cath. Lib. Assn. Recip., Silver Life-Saving Cross, Girl Scouts of Am., circa 1933. Address: Walsingham Academy, P.O. Box 159, Jamestown Rd., Williamsburg, VA 23185, U.S.A. 5.

SHANQITI, Mohammad Al-Amin Mohammad Al-Kheder, b. 1905. Ambassador. Educ: Certs., Madina Monwwara & Al-Azhar Mosque, Cairo. Appts: Chief Judge, 1937; Min. of Educ. & Chief Judge, 1938; Min. of Justice & Chief Judge, 1939; Mbr. of Congress, 1951; Min. of Educ. & Chief Judge, 1955; Ambassador, Saudi Arabia, 1963-. Mbrships: Dpty. Dean, Diplomatic Corps; Islamic League, Mecca Mokarrama. Hons: Husein Ben Ali Necklace, Jordan; Nahda Decoration, 1st class, Jordan; Estiqlal Decoration, 1st class, Jordan; Kowkab (star), 1st class, Jordan; Ratidayn, 2nd class, Iraq; Estiqlal, 2nd class, Morocco. Address: Jordanian Embassy, P.O. Box 204, Jeddah, Saudi Arabia.

SHAPIRA, I., b. 1907. Teacher. Educ: Tchrs. Coll., Jerusalem; M.A., London Univ., U.K. Appts: Prin., Kiryat Motzkin Schl., 1933-44; Vice Prin., Reali Schl., Haifa, 1945-54, Prin., 1955-. Mbrships: Govt. Comm., Israeli Scouts Movement; Nat. Coun. for Culture & Art; Nat. Comm. for Educ.; Bd. of Govs., Univ. of Haifa. Publs: History of the Nations in Modern Times; From the Point of View of an Educator. Articles, educl. & other jrnls. Hons. Freeman of the City of Haifa. Address: 13 Zerubabel St., Mt. Carmel, Haifa, Israel.

SHAPIRA, Raphael, b. 16 June 1920. President of Yeshivot; Rabbi. Educ: studied w. Rabbi of Brisk, 1940-48. Appts: Pres., Yeshiva TIFERETH ISRAEL, Haifa, 1948-; Co-Fndr., TIFERETH HACARMEL, Mt. Carmel, Haifa, 1961; Hd., Coll. for Post-Grad., & HARHEI KALA. Mbrships: in num. pub. comms. inclng: Comm. for Observation of Sabbath; Comm. for Purification of Family; Comm. for Maintenance of Mikvoth (Ritual Baths). Publs: sev. books on Halacha & Hagadah in preparation. Address: Pewsner St., No. 37, Haifa, Israel.

SHAPIRO, Carol Sadie, b. 24 Sept. 1939. Plastic Surgeon. Educ: B.S., Univ. of Pitts., 1961; M.D., Med. Coll. of Pa., 1965; Intern, Phila Gen. Hosp., 1965-66; Res., Georgetown Univ. Hosp., 1966-72. Appts: Clin. Inst., Georgetown Univ. Hosp.; Staff Physn., ibid & Prince. William Hosp., Potomac Hosp., Morris Caffritz Hosp. Mbrships. incl: Cand. Mbr., Soc. of Plastic & Reconstructive Surgs.; Med. Soc. of Va.; AMA; Am. Coll. of Surgs. (Cand.); Alumni Assn., Med. Coll. of Pa.; Am. Med. Women's Assn.; Prince William Co. Med. Soc. Contbr. to

profl. jrnls. Hons: AMA Physn.'s Recognition Award, 1972. Address: Dumfries Med. Ctr., Dumfries, VA 22026, U.S.A. 5, 138.

SHAPIRO, Charlotte Heller, b. 30 June 1912. Educator. Educ: A.B., M.A., Ph.D., Pittsburgh Univ., Pa., U.S.A.; Postgrad. study, Chgo. & Temple Univs.; Exeter & London Univs., U.K.; Munich Univ., Germany & The Sorbonne, France. Appts: Soc. Wkr., Family Case Wkr., Jewish Family Welfare Assn., Pittsburgh; Supvsr., Allegheny Co. Bd. Assistance; Med. & Psych. Case Wkr. & Supvsr., Allegheny Gen. Hosp., Pittsburgh (all before 1948); Tchr., Girls' Advsr. & Activities Dir., Herron Hill Jr. H.S., 1948-57; Schl. Pychol., Elem., Secondary, Vocatl. & Special Educ. areas, 1957-60; Prin., Elem. & Jr. H.S., Pittsburgh, 1960-71; Demonstration Tchr., Pittsburgh Univ., 1962; Lectr., ibid, 1964; Currently Prin., Morningside Elem. Schl., Pitts. Pa. Mbrships. incl: Past Pres.; Pitts. Elem. Prins. Assn., Secondary Prins. Assn. & Coun. for Exceptional Children (Local chapt.); Past Pres., Pi Lambda Theta; N.E.A.; P.S.E.A; Alpha Epsilon Phi; V.-Prin., Rodef Shalom Temple Relig. Schl.; Past Worth Matron, Order of Eastern Star. Recip. George Washington Carver Award, 1972. Address: Chatham Ctr. Tower - 8A Pitts., PA 15219, U.S.A.

SHAPIRO, Harry, L., b. 19 Mar. 1902. Anthropologist. Educ: B.A., Harvard Univ., 1923; M.A., ibid, 1925; Ph.D., 1926. Appts. incl: Chmn., & Curator of Phys. Anthropol., Dept. of Anthropol., Am. Mus. of Natural Hist., 1942-70; Prof. of Anthropol., Columbia Univ., 1939-43; Adjunct Prof., ibid, 1943-; Vis. Prof., Univ. of Pitts., 1970. Mbrships. incl: Sec., Am. Assn. of Phys. Anthropol., 1935-39; V.P., ibid, 1941-42; Pres., Am. Ethnological Soc., 1942-43; Bd. of Dirs., Assn. on Am. Indian Affairs, 1947-55; Pres., Am. Anthropological Assn., 1948; Pres., Am., Am. Eugenics Soc., 1955-62; Comm. on Sci. & Pub. Policy, Nat. Acad. of Scis., 1962-65; Am. Acad. of Arts & Scis.; Hon. Fellow, Die Anthropologische Gesellschaft in Wien, 1964; Bd., Field Fndn., 1964. Publs. incl: Ed., Man, Culture & Society, 1956; The Jewish People: a bilogical history, 1960; Peking Man, 1974. Recip., Theodore Roosevelt Disting. Serv. Medal for pub. serv. in sci., 1964. Address: Dept. of Anthropol., Am. Mus. of Natural Hist., Central Park West at 79th St., N.Y. NY, 10024, U.S.A.

SHAPIRO, Leonard, b. 1 Feb. 1917. Political Economist; Executive; Newspaper Correspondent; Government Official. Appts. incl: USAF, retd. as Col., 1939-65; Dir., Int. Studies, Northrop Corp., 1965-69; Asst. Admnstr., Econ. Dev. Admin., Govt. of Puerto Rico, 1970-. Mbr., Bd. of Govs., Georgetown Univ., 1971-. Author of Soviet Treaty Series, 2 vols. Hons. incl: Hon. Pilot, French Air Force, 1962; Italian Air Force, 1964. Address: 860 Ashford Ave., Apt. 9A, Santurce, Puerto Rico 00907. 6, 7, 9, 14, 59, 69.

SHAPIRO, Solomon K., b. 23 Apr. 1914. Rabbi; Social Worker. Educ: B.A., Bklyn. Coll., 1941; M.A., Hunter Coll. Ordained Rabbi, Yavne Hebrew Theol. Sem., 1939. Appts: Rabbi, Temple Beth Israel, Stevens Pt., Wis., 1946-48, Temple Beth Israel, Salisbury, M.D., 1949-51 & Prin., Heb. Inst., S. Bklyn., 1952-; Former Dir., Yavne J Theol. Sem.; Social Worker w. Social Servs. Dept., N.Y.C. Mbrships: Trustee, Machon Marshal Inst. of Higher Jewish Learning, Jerusalem, Israel. Assistin in publication of the Otzan Ha-Shelloth

U-Teshevoth (Compendium Responsarum). Address: 718 E. 7th St., N.Y., NY 11218, U.S.A.

SHAPSHAK, René. Sculptor. Educ: Ecole des Beaux Arts, Paris; Ecole Julien, Paris; Ecole des Beaux Arts, Brussels; Tate, London, U.K.; Art Schl., Dalston, London. Appts. incl: Patron, Syndicate African Artists; Art Lectr., Donnel Lib., N.Y., Central Lib., City Art League, Pinakotheki, Athens, Greece, 1959-65; René Shapshak Modern Art Mus., attached to Philathea Ecumenical Sem., London, Ont., Canada. Mbrships. incl: Life Mbr., Int. Fine Arts Counc.; Hon. Life Mbr., Am. Int. Acad.; Order of St. John of Jerusalem; num. museums in many countries. Portraits & Sculptures incl: Pres. Harry S. Truman; Yehudi Menuhin; Gen. Charles De Gaulle; George Bernard Shaw. Collects. incl: Buckingham Palace, London; Pvte. Collect., H.M. Queen Elizabeth; Royal Collect., Denmark; Duchess of Kent, U.K.; Sir Ernest Oppenheimer Collect.; Baron de Rothchilde, Paris. Num. exhibitions in U.S.A. & O'seas. Var. commns. on bldgs. Recip. of many hons. Address: Hotel Chelsea, 222 West 23 St., N.Y., NY 10011, U.S.A. 6, 19, 37.

SHARENSON, Reuben Mordecai, b. 5 Feb. 1888. Dentist. Educ: CCNY, 1911; D.D.S., Coll. of Dental & Oral Surg., 1915. Appts: Rabbi, 1910; Tchr., Hebrew, Hebrew Orphan Asylum, N.Y.C., 1910-15; Clin. Demonstrator, Coll. of Dental & Oral Surg., N.Y.C., 1916-17; Pvte. Prac., Dentistry, N.Y.C., 1915-18, Roxbury, Mass., 1920-32, Brookling, Mass., 1932-; Served w. Dental Corps, U.S. Army, 1918-19. Mbrships: Zionist Org. of Am.; Regional V.P., ibid, 1968-; Educ. Chmn., ibid, 1969-; Am. Dental Assn.; Mass. & Gtr. Boston Dental Socs.; Hadassah. Address: 1812 Beacon St., Brookline, MA 02146, U.S.A. 6.

SHARIFF, Ismail, b. 5 Dec. 1938. Academic. Educ: B.A., Univ. of Mysore, 1958; M.A., ibid, 1960; Ph.D., Univ. of Wis., Madison, 1965. Appts: Sr. Stats. Asst., State of Mysore, India, 1960-61; Tchng. & Rsch. Asst., Grad. Schl., Univ. of Wis., Madison, 1961-65; Rsch. Assoc., U.S. Dept. of Agric., Wash. D.C., 1965-66; Asst. Prof., Univ. of Wis., 1967-69; Chmn., Dept. of Econs., Univ. of Wis., Green Bay, 1970-72; Assoc. Prof., ibid, 1973-. Mbrships. incl: Am. Econ. Assn.; Am. Assn. of Agric. Econs.; Population Ref. Bur.; Indian Econ. Assn.; Int. Assn. of Agric. Econs. Publs: The Development of Indian & American Agriculture, A Comparative Study, 1968; Cooperatives, A Handbook, 1972. Contbr. to profl. jrnls. & anthols. Recip. 1st Prize, Engl. Debate, Univ. of Mysore, 1958. Address: College of Community Sciences, Univ. of Wisconsin - Green Bay, WI 54302, U.S.A. 14, 130.

SHARMA, Jitendra Mohan, b. 9 Dec. 1938. Educator; Researcher; Administrator. Educ: B.A., Delhi Univ., India, 1956; Ph.D., Coll. of Comm., Lucknow Univ., ibid, 1971; M.B.A., Western Mich. Univ., U.S.A., 1966; M.A., Northern Mich. Univ., ibid, 1968; Ph.S., London, U.K., 1967. Appts. incl: Lt., Indian Army 1962-66; Asst. Exec. Off., Delhi Cloth & Gen. Mills, 1961-66; Asst. Prof. of Bus., Dept. of Comm., & Ind., Northern Mich. Univ., Marquette, U.S.A., 1966-71; Assoc. Prof. & Dir. HSIP, ibid, 1971-72; Assoc. Prof. of Bus., Grand Valley State Coll., Allendale, ibid, 1972-; Cons. to var. U.S. Depts. inclng. Mich. Dept. of Labor Safety Educ. & Trng. Div., N.Y. State Dept. of Civil Serv. & Peace Corps; 6 yrs. in sev. capacities as researcher inclng. USAF Rsch. Proj. GS RPG 1048, Econs. Dept., Howard Univ. & Marquette Chmbr. of Comm. Mbrships.

icnl: Fellow, Royal Soc. Arts: Fellow, Royal Philos. Soc.; AAUP; Acad. Mgmt; ASTD; Soc.Advmt. of Mgmt.; Soc. Personnel Admin.; Phi Sigma. Publs. incl: Dictionary of Jargons; Resolving Supervisory Middle Mgt. dilemma; The Art of Decision Avoidance, (all in 1972); sev. articles in var. profl. jrnls. Recip. of many awards. Address: Schl. of Bus. & Econs., Grand Valley State Coll., Allendale, MI 49401, U.S.A. 8, 117.

SHARMAT, Marjorie Weinman (Mrs. Mitchell Brenner Sharmat), b. 12 Nov. 1928. Writer. Eudc: Lasell Jr. Coll., 1946-47; Grad., Westbrook Jr. Coll. (now Westbrook Coll.), 1948. Appts: Mbr., Circulation Staff, Yale Univ. Lib. & Yale Law Lib., New Haven, Conn. Mbrships: Action on Smoking & Hlth.; PTA; Friends of the Irvington Lib. Publs. incl: Rex, 1967; Goodnight Andrew Goodnight Craig, 1969; Gladys Told Me to Meet Her Here, 1970; Getting Something on Maggie Marmelstein, 1971; A Hot Thirsty Day, 1971; 51 Sycamore Lane, 1971; A Visit with Rosalind, 1972; Nate the Great, 1972; Sophie & Gussie, 1973; Morris Brookside, a Dog, 1973. Hons. incl: Selected Children's Books of 1967, Lib. of Congress; Children's Books of the Yr., Child Study Assn. of Am., 1971; Saquoya List, 1973-74 & 74-75. Address: 51 Sycamore Lane, Irvington-on-Hudson, NY 10533, U.S.A. 5, 30, 138.

SHARP, Ernest Dee Whitt, b. 15 Nov. 1929. Businessman. Educ: Off Cand. Schl., Ext. Courtse Inst., Air Univ., Gunter AFB, Ala., 1964. Appts: Fndr., Owner & Mgr., Dee Whitt's Teen-Ctr., U.S.A., 1958. Owner & Mgr., Dee Whitt's Emergency Ambulance Serv. Mbrships: Cmdr., Civil Air Patrol; Capt. & Charter Mbr., ibid; Charter Mbr., Andrews Rescue Squad; Bd. of Dirs., ibid; Charter Mbr., Andrews Emergency Relief Org.; Chmn., Exec. Bd., ibid; V. Cmndr., Leslie Stillman Post 97, Am. Legion; Civil Defence Dir., Cherokee Co.; Local Bd. 20, Selective Serv. System of Cherokee Co.; Mbr., Cherokee Co. Chmbr. of Comm.; Cand., Cherokee Co. Bd. of Co. Commissioners; Notary Pub.; Democrat; Deacon, 1st Bapt. Ch., Andrews, N.C.; Tchr., Jr. Sunday Schl. Class, ibid; Ch. Choir, ibid. Hons: Cert. of Proficiency, Civil Air Patrol; Award, Cherokee Co. Un. Fund Inc., for outstanding Community Serv., 1971-72; Cert. of Hon., Am. Legion Dept. of N.C. Address: P.O. Box 907, Andrews, NC, U.S.A. 125.

SHARP, Ernest Leonard, b. 25 Mar. 1926. Social Worker. Educ: B.S., Miss. State Univ., 1950; M.S.W., Tulane Univ., 1962. Appts. incl: Casework Supvsr., Miss. State Dept. of Pub. Welfare, Meridan, 1954-61; Casewkr., Supvsr., Jefferson Co. Child Welfare Unit, Tex. State Dept. of Pub. Welfare, 1962-63; Dir., Lubbock City-Co. Child Welfare Unit, ibid, 1963-71; Chief Soc. Serv. Asst. Supt., Crockett State Schl. for Girls, 1971-; Field Inst., Worden Schl. of Soc. Serv., Our Lady of the Lake Coll., San Antonio, 1967-71; Casework Supvsr., Volunteers of Am., Shreveport, La., 1974-. Mbrships. incl: Alpha Tau Alpha; Coun. of Soc. Work Educ.; Tex. Soc. Welfare Assn.; Tex. Corrections Assn. Address: Villa Norte Apt # 1316, 1602 Barton Dr., Shreveport, LA 71107, U.S.A. 2.

SHARPE, Ruth Collier (Mrs. Richard Sharpe VI), b. 6 Aug. 1897. Writer; Poet. Publs: The Song of the Paramahamsa (poems), 1940; Tristam of Lyonesse (novel), 1949; When Falcon From the Wrist (poems), 1949. Poems included in: Poets on Parade, 1939; Poetry Digest, 1950; Mid-Century Anthology, 1950; Important American Poets and Songwriters,

Mbrships. incl: Pen & Brush, N.Y.C.; Intercontinental Biog. Soc.; Marquis Biog. Lib. Soc.; Int. Platform Assn. Hons. incl: Olcott Fnd. Award for The Song of the Paramahamsa, 1940; 1st Prize for poems in Important American Poets and Songwriters, 1948; Poets on Parade Prize for Tristram's Song and other poems, 1939; Poetry Digest Prize & Mid-Century Anthol. Prize for When Falcon From the Wrist, 1950. Address: El Morya, 956 W. Point Rd., Lake Oswego, OR 97034, U.S.A. 5, 9, 11, 22, 57.

SHARR, Francis Aubie, b. 1914. Librarian. Educ: Univ. Coll., London. Appts: Dpty. Co. Libn., Derbyshire, U.K., 1946-49; Dpty. City Libn., Manchester, 1949-53; State Libn., Western Australia, 1953-. Mbrships: Pres., Lib. Assn. of Australia, 1969-70; Fellow, ibid; Assoc., Royal Photographic Soc., London; Pres., W.A. Region, Royal Inst. of Pub. Admin., 1957-59; Vice Chmn., W.A., Nat. Trust of Australia, 1965-67. Address: 3 Francis St., Perth, W.A., Australia, 6000. 23, 128.

SHARTLE, C.L., b. 26 June 1903. Psychologist. Educ: A.B., Univ. of Northern Iowa, 1927; A.M., Columbia Univ., 1932; Ph.D., Ohio State Univ., 1933; Dipl. in Indl. Psychol., Am. Bd. of Examiners, 1946-. Appts. incl: Prof. Psychol., Ohio State Univ., 1944-68; Dir. Rsch., Human Resources Rsch. Inst., 1952-53; Chief, Psychol. & Soc. Sci. Div., Off. Sec. Defense, Pentagon, 1961-64; U.S. Mbr., Human Factors Grp., NATO, 1961-65; Prof. Emeritus, Psychol. & Admin. Sci., Ohio State Univ., 1968-; Cons., var. Agcys. in Manpower & Sooc. Sci. Rsch. Mbrships incl: Fellow, Am. Psychol. Assn. (Treas. 1947-57, Pres. Indl. Div. 1950); Soc. Sci. Rsch. Coun.; Phi Beta Kappa. Publs: Executive Performance & Leadership, 1957; Occupational Information, 1959; An Interaction Model for Administrative Decisions, 1971. Hons: Award for Meritorious Civiliam Serv., USAF, 1953; Centennial Achievement Award, Ohio State Univ., 1970. Address: 218 Leland Ave., Columbus, OH 43214, U.S.A. 2, 14, 50.

SHAVER, Jess Carman, b. 15 Oct. 1910. Educator. Educ: B.A., Northeastern State Coll., Tahlequach, Okla., 1934; M.Ed., Univ. of Okla., Norman, 1941; Ed.D., ibid, 1950. Appts. incl: Asst. Prof., Educ., Ark. State Tchrs. Coll., Conway, 1946-47; Acting Hd., Dept. of Educ., ibid, 1947-48; Assoc. Prof., 1950-53; Educl. Specialist, Extension Course Inst., Gunter AFB, Montgomery, Ala., 1953-57; Assoc. Prof., Educ., & Hd., Dept. of Educ. & Psychol., Dir., Tchr. Trng. & Placement, Georgetown Coll., Ky., 1957-59; Asst. Prof., Long Beach State Coll. (now Calif. State Univ., Long Beach), Calif., 1959-62; Asst. to Div. Chmn., ibid, 1961-67; Assoc. Prof., 1963-70; Prof., 1970-. Publs: Ed. & co-author, Adolescence: Quest for Relevance, Address: Calif. State Univ. at Long Beach, Long Beach, CA 90840, U.S.A. 14, 15, 59, 131, 141.

SHAVER, Paul Merl, b. 19 Apr. 1922. Educator. Educ: A.B., Syracuse Univ., 1942; M.S., ibid, 1947; Ph.D., 1967. Appts: Secondary Sci. Tchr., Corfu Ctrl. Schl., Corfu, N.Y., 1942-44; Secondary Sci. Tchr., Sodus Ctrl. Schl., Sodus, N.Y., 1947-60; Coll. Prof., State Univ. Coll. at Oswego, N.Y., 1960-. Mbrships: Nat. Sci. Tchrs. Assn.; NEA; N.Y. State Tchrs. Assn.; Nat. Assn. of Geol. Tchrs.; N.Y. Acad. of Sci.; AAAS; Am. Phys. Soc.; Sigma Pi Sigma; Sigma Zeta; Pres. & V.P., Sodus Rotary Club. Conbr. profl. publs. Recip. of Shell Merit Fellowship, 1956. Address: Swift St., Oswego, NY 13126, U.S.A. 6, 14, 28.

SHAW, Charles Thurstan, b. 27 June 1914. University Professor of Archeology. Educ: Sidney Sussex Coll., Cambridge Univ., B.A., M.A., Ph.D.; Inst. of Educ., London Univ. Appts: Curator, Achimota Coll. Anthropol. Mus., Gold Coast, 1937-45; Mbr., Cambridgeshire Educ. Comm., U.K., 1945-51; Tutor, Cambridge Inst. of Educ., 1951-62; Prof., Archeol., Univ. of Ibadan, Nigeria, 1963-74; Vis. Fellow, Clare Hall, Cambridge, 1973. Mbrships: Fellow, Sox. of Antiquaries; Fellow, Royal Anthropol. Inst.; V.P., Pan-african Cong. of Prehist. & Study of Quaternary. Publs. incl: Excavation at Dawn, Archeology & Nigeria, Africa & the Discovery of Man, Discovering Nigeria's Past; Conbr. to jrnls.; Fndr., Ed., W. African Archeol. Newsletter, & W. African Jrnl. of Archeol. Hons: Amaury Talbot Prize, Royal Anthropol. Inst., 1970; C.B.E., 1972; Onuna Ekwulu Ora of Igbo-Ubwu, 1973. Address: 37 Hawthorne Rd., Stapleford, Cambridge CB2 5DU, U.K. 1, 3.

SHAW, Elizábeth Christine Fox, b. 17 Oct. 1914. Educator, Counselor & Minister. Educ: B.S., Ohio State Univ., 1949-52; Grad. Schl., ibi. ibid., 1968-69; Univ. of Dayton, Ohio, 1971; Meth. Theological Schl., Ohio, 1971. Appts. incl: Cottage Wkr., State Bur. of Juvenile Rsch.; Schl. Tchr., Columbus Bd. of Educ.; Student Personell Asst., Ohio State Univ.; Organizer & Coord., Tutorial Serv. for Communication & Maths Dept., ibid.; wkr. for Meth. Ch. in Ohio. Mbrships. incl: W. Ohio Meth. Ch. Conf.; Ohio Bus. Tchrs. Assn.; Alpha Xi; Pi Omega Pi; Am. Nat. Theatre & Acad.; Columbia Scholastic Press Advisers' Assn. Hons: Good Neighbor, Coun. of Soc. Agencies, 1949; Human Rels. Scroll of Honor, Mu Iota Chapt., Omega Psi Phi, 1959; Mother of the Yr., Hilltop Kiwanais Club, 1967; Proclamation Mayor's Off. City of Columbus, 1967. Address: 47 Whitethorne Ave., Columbus, OH 43223, U.S.A. 57, 116.

SHAW, Frederick, b. 24 Sept. 1912. Research Administrator. Educ: B.A., C.C.N.Y., 1932; M.A., Columbia Univ., 1933; Ph.D., ibid, 1950; Postgrad. Studies, Oxford Univ., U.K., 1937; New Schl. Soc. Rshc., U.S.A., 1939-40; N.Y. Univ., 1939-40; '54-56; Cornell Univ., 1961. Appts: Soc. Studies Instr., N.Y.C. H.S., 1935-43; Chmn., Soc. Studies Dept., 1942-43; U.S. Army, 1943-46; Rsch. Assoc., Bur. Admin & Budgetary Rsch., 1953-64, '66-67; Inst., Thesis Advsr., City Coll., 1959-64; Vis. Asst. Prof., Pol. Sci., ibid, 1964-66; Special Examiner, N.Y.C. Dept. Personnel, 1965; Lectr. & Adjunct. Asst. Prof., Baruch Coll., 1966-72; Coord., Fed. Funded Progs. for Handicapped, Bd. Educ., 1967; Bur. Hd., Educl. Prog. Rsch., Bd. Educ., N.Y.C., 1967-. Mbrships. incl: Trustee, Payne Educl. Sociol. Fndn.; Rsch. Cons., Legislative Finance Unit, N.Y.C. Coun. & num. other Comms., Couns. & profl. assna. Publs. incl: The American City, 1953; History of the New York City Legislature, 1954; Urban Affairs, 1962; Economics in a Free Society, 1966. Address: 41 Henry St., Brooklyn, NY 11201, U.S.A. 6, 13, 14. 141.

SHAW, Grace Goodfriend (Mrs. Herbert Franklin Shaw). Editor. Educ: Bennington Co., 1938-39; Fordham Univ., 1970-. Appts: Reporter, Port Chester (N.Y.) Daily Item, 1942-45; Edit. Coord., World Scope Encylopedia, N.Y.C., 1946-50; Assoc. Ed., Clarence L. Barnhardt Inc., Bronxville, N.Y., 1950; Freelance writer & Ed., 1951-61; Sr. Ed., Coll. Dept., Bobbs-Merrill, 1961-62; Mng. Ed., ibid, 1963-65; Edit. Supvsr., World Publng. Co., N.Y.C., 1965-68; Mng. Ed., ibid, 1968-69, Sr. Ed., 1969; Mng. Ed., Peter H. Wyden Co.,

N.Y.C., 1969-70; Assoc. Ed., Dial Press, N.Y.C., 1971-72; Sr. Ed., ibid, 1972; Sr. Ed., David McKay Co., 1972-. Mbrships: Mbrship.Chmn., Nat. Assn. of Book Eds., 1967-68; Treas., ibid, 1968-69. Contbr. num. articles to ref. books. Address: 85 Lee Road, Scarsdale, NY 10583, U.S.A. 5, 132, 138.

SHAW, Helen Lilian (Hofmann), b. 20 Feb. 1913. Writer. Educ: B.A., Univ. of Canterbury., Christhurch. Appts: formerly tchr. & freelance writer; Oceanian Ed. for "Poet", 1971-72; Contbng. Ed., Ocarina, an Indian bi-monthly of poetry & aesthetics; currently ed., poet & short story writer. Mbrships: PEN N.Z. Ctr. (Int. PEN); Int. Poetry Soc.. World Poetry Soc. Intercontinental, 1967-73. Publs. incl: The Orange Tree & other stories, 1957; Out of Dark (poems), 1968; The Letters of D'Arcy Cresswell, 1971; The Girl of the Gods (poems), 1973; The Word & Flower (poems, in preparation). Contbns., anthols., poetry & prose. Hons. incl: Disting. Serv. Citations, World Poetry Soc., 1968, 1971; Litt.L.D., Int. Acad. Ldrship., Quezon Capitol City, 1968; World Poet Award, World Poetry Soc. (Intercontinental), 1972. Address: 42, Bassett Rd., Auckland 5, New Zealand.

SHAW, Marsden John, b. 29 Oct 1918. Electronics Company Executive. Educ: Univ. of Newark, 1938-40; Université de Besanccon, France, 1945; Schl. of Bus. Admin., Rutgers Univ., 1946-48. Appts: Tech. Sales Asst., N.J. Zinc Co., N.Y.C., 1940-42; Serv. in USAF, 1942-45; Purchasin Agt., Kay Elemetrics Corp., Pine Brook, N.J., 1948-. Mbr., Purchasing Agts. Assn. of N.Y. Address: 78S, Livingston Ave., Livingston, NJ 07039, U.S.A. 6.

SHAW, Mildred S. (Mrs. Warren C. Shaw). Consultant; Librarian. Educ: B.A., Ariz. State Univ.; Librarian Degree, Univ. of Ariz.; M.A., Claremond Grad. Schl. Appts: Tchr., Dysart Schl., Peoria, Ariz., 1939-43; Placentia, Calif., 1944-45; Pima Co. Schls. Libn., Tucson, Ariz., 1949-53; Asst. Cons., Duarte Unif. Schl. Dist., Calif., 1953-65, Dist. Libn., 1965-68, Audio Visual Coord., 1968-70, Instrnl. Servs. Cons., 1970-. Mbrships. incl: Sec., Int. Reading Assn.; AAUW; NEA; Calif. Art Educ. & Tchrs. Assns.; Calif. Assn. Schl. Libns.; Pres., Delta Kappa Gamma; Pi Lambda Theta. Co-author, Puppets for All Grades. Contbr., mags. inclng. Schl. Arts Mag., Arts & Activities Mag., Instr. Mag., Tchr. Mag. Recip., Masonic Lodges Cert. of Appreciation, Meritorious Civic Serv., 1971. Address: 1635 S. 3rd Ave., Arcadia, CA 91006, U.S.A. 5, 59, 120.

SHAW, Stanford Jay, b. 5 May 1930. Professor. Educ: B.A., Stanford Univ., Palo Alto, Calif., 1951; M.A., ibid, 1952; M.A., Princeton Univ., N.J., 1955; Ph.D., ibid, 1958; Schl. of Oriental & African Studies, Univ. of London, U.K., 1955; Univ. of Cairo, Egypt, 1955-56; Univ. of Istanbul, Turkey, 1956-57. Appts: Rsch. Fellow, Harvard Univ. Ctr. for Middle Eastern Studies, 1958-60; Asst. Prof., Turkish, Harvard Univ., 1960-65; Assoc. Prof., Turkish Lang. & Hist., ibid, 1965-68; Prof., Turkis & Near Eastern Hist., UCLA, 1968-; Ed. in Chief, Int. Jrnl. of Middle East Studies, 1967-; Vis. Prof., Hist., Univ. of Wash., summer 1970. Mbrships: Chmn., Publs. Comm., Middle East Studies Assn.; Royal Asiatic Soc., Int. Sco. for Oriental Rsch.; Am. Oriental Soc.; Am. Histl. Assn.; Middle East Inst.; AAUP. Author of books & articles in field. Hons. incl: Soc. Sci. Rsch. Coun. Fellowship, 1972; Rsch. Fellowship, Nat. Endowment for the Humanities, 1972-73. Address: Near Eastern Ctr., UCLA, L.A., CA 90024, U.S.A. 2, 9, 13.

SHAWCROSS, John T., b. 10 Feb. 1924. Teacher. Educ: A.B., Montclair State Univ. 1948; A.M., 1950, Ph.D., 1958, N.Y. Univ. Appts: Prof., Douglass Coll., Rutgers Univ., 1963067; Prof., Univ. of Wis., 1967-70; Disting. Prof., Staten Island Community Coll., 1970-; Grad. Ctr., CUNY, 1971-. Mbrships: Pres., Milton Soc. of Am; MLA; Sec., Past Mbr., Exec. Coun., Andiron Club of N.Y. Pubs: Language & Style in Milton; Myths & Motifs in Literature; Poetry & Its Conventions; Seventeenth-Century Poetry; Milton: The Critical Heritage, 2 vols.; Ed., The Complete Poetry of John Milton, The Complete Poetry of John Donne. Address: 20 Vernon Ter., Bloomfield, NJ 07003, U.S.A. 6, 13, 15.

SHAY, Arnold Leo, b. 16 Feb. 1922. Custom Tailor; Lecturer on WWII History. Mbrships: Past Nat. V.P., Soc. of Israel Philatelists; Past Regional Pres., ibid; Past Pre., Israel Numismatic Soc.; Trustee, Jewish Nat. Fund; Nat. Chmn., 70th anniversary, ibid; Exec. mbr., Jewish Community Rels. Coun.; Chmn., Mem. Comm., 6 Million Jewish Martyrs; Past Chmn., Allied Jewish Appeal; Fndr. mbr., Masonic Stamp Club, Phila.; Past Chmn., Israel 23, Israel 24, & Israel 25; Chartered mbr., other philatelic orgs. Author of articles in jrnls. inclng. Judaica Philatelic Jrnl., Israel Philatelist, Polonus Philatelic Soc. Bulletin, New Americans of Phila. Bulletin. Hons. incl: Gold Medal, Sepad, 1972; Gold Medal, Soc. of Israel Philatelists, 1972; Gold Medal, Polpex, 1973; Copernicus Medal, ibid, 1973; Vermeil Medal, Stampex, 1973. Address: 205 Haverford Rd., Wynnewood, PA 19151, U.S.A. 55.

SHEA, John Joseph, Jr., b. 4 Sept. 1924. Physician. Educ: B.S., Univ. of Notre Dame, Ind., U.S.A., 1945; Harvard Med. Schl., 1944-47 7 1948-49; Intern, Bellevue Hosp., N.Y.C., 1947-48; Mass. Eye & Ear Infirmary, Boston, 1949-50. Certificated: Am. Bd. of Otolaryngol., 1951; Am. Coll. of Surgs., 1955. Appts: Lt. Cdr., USNR; Const. in Otolaryngol., Surg. Gen., USN; Clin. Asst.,Dept. of Otolaryngol., Univ. of Tenn.; Cons., Kennedy VA Hosp., Memphis, Tenn.; Lectr., Nat. Naval Med. Ctr., 1973. Num. mbrships. incl: AMA; Tenn. Med. Assn.; Fndr., Memphis Fndn. of Otol., 1957; Fndr., Memphis Otologic Clin., 1959; Fndr., Memphis Eye & Ear Hosp., 1967; Southern Med. Assn.; Otosclerosis Study Club; Am. Otological Soc.; French Soc. of Otolarnygol.; Danish Soc. of Otolaryngol.; Royal Soc. of Med., U.K. Over 160 pubs. Hons. incl: Order of Southern Cross, Brazil, 1963; Award of Merit, Am. Acad of Ophthalmol., 1967. Address: 1060 Madison Ave., P.O. Box 4049, Memphis, TN 38104, U.S.A.

SHEARIN, Forrest Greene, b. 13 Mar. 1903. Association & Company Executive. Appts: Dir. & Treas., Mechanics Mutual Ins. Co. of Tenn.; Exec. Sec., State Coun., Jr. Order United Am. Mechanics; Controller & Treas., Children's Home, ibid; Gen. Mgr., State Coun. Ins. Dept.; Owner, Sec. & Treas., Colonial Foods, Inc.; Owner, Forrest G. Shearin Finance Bus.; Gen. Real Estate Bus.; Owner, operator, Forrest G. Shearin Ins. Agcy.; Pres. & Dir., Investment Enterprises; Sec. & Treas., Scotland Neck Bus. Bur.; Chmn., Halifax Dev. Commn.; Mbr. & Finance Off., City Coun. of Scotland Neck; Dir., Br. Bank & Trust Co.; Nat. Coun. Bd. of Trustees; Bd. of Control. Mbrships. incl: Nat. Coun., Jr. Order United Am. Mechanics; Nat. Treas., ibid; State Coun. Hons. incl: Mr. Jr. Order 1969, Wisdom Award of Hon., 1970. Address: 1109 Main St., Box 217, Scotland Neck, NC 27874, U.S.A. 7, 83.

SHECHTER, Moshe, b. 10 Apr. 1896. Physician. Educ: M.D., Univ. of Karkov, 1923; M.D., Univ. of Berlin, 1931. Ordained Rabbi, Rabbinical Sem., Kishinev, 1914. Appts: Asst., Charité Med. Clin., Univ. of Berlin, 1923-33; Rsch. Wjr., Biol. Dept., Kaiser Wilhelm Inst., Dahlem, Berlin, 1931-33; in pvte. med. prac., specializing in internal med. & metabolism, Palestine, 1933-; Chief Med. Advsr. at Israel Min. of Fin. on people disabled during Nazi regime, 1957-; Lectr., Endocrinol. for post-grad students. Mbrships: Ctrl. Comm & Sci. Coun. Israel Med. Assn.; Hlth. Coun. State of Israel; B'nai B'rith; ScottishRite; Masons. Contbr. to profl. jrnls. Co-Ed: Ha-Talmud ve-Chachmath Harefua & The Medical & Health Thesaurus. Address: 10 Modiliani St. Tel Aviv, Israel.

SHECHTERMAN, A., b 3 Dec. 1910. Civil Engineer; Company Director. Educ: Civil Engrng. degree, Royal Ghent Univ., Belgium, 1935. Appts: Co-fndr., Aviation Schl., Palestine, 1938; Mbr., Reps. Assembly, Palestine, 1939-43; Works Mgr., South Dead Sea Palestine Potash Ltd., 1943-46; Mbr., Municipal Coun., Tel-Aviv-Jaffa, 1955-65 & Hd., Pub. Works & Pub. Hlth. Depts.; Dpty. Mayor i/c Jaffa, 1957-59; Mbr. of Knesset & Chmn., Econs. Comm., 1969-73; Mbr., Knesset & Chmn., Educ. & Culture Comm., 1973-; Municipal Councillor, Tel-Aviv-Jaffa, 1973; Initiator, Old City of Jaffa Dev. Co., Mng. Dir., Netivot Dev. Co. Ltd.; Bd. of Dirs., Pioneer Concrete (Israel) Ltd. Mbrships: Co-fndr., Chmn., Fund for Advancement of Med. in Israel; Chmn., Inst. for Contemp. Soc. & Econ. Rsch. Ltd.; Chmn., Soc. of Friends of Theatre in Israel; Mbr., Ctrl. Comm. Revisionist Zionists, 1938-46. Address: 20 Dubnow St., Tel-Aviv, Israel.

SHEDD, Virgia Brocks, b. 22 June 1943. Librarian. Educ: B.S., Jackson State Coll., Miss; M.L.S., Atlanta Univ., Ga.; further studies, Fisk Univ., Nashville, Tenn., & Jackson State Coll. Appt: Asst. Libn., Tougaloo Coll. Miss., 1965-. Mbrships: Sec., Central Regional, Mis. Lib. Assn.; YWCA; Southeastern Lib. Assn.; Farish St. Bapt. Ch. Mng. Ed., Contbr., poems & articles, Close-Up Mag. Contbr., poetry, other publs. Recip., Miss Permanent Alumna Award, Class of'64 Jackson State Coll., 1964. Address: c/o Library, Tougaloo College, MS 39174, U.S.A. 76, 125.

SHEESE, Frederick George, b. 28 May 1913. Dentist. Educ: Predental, Gettysburg Coll., Pa; D.D.S., Temple Univ. Dental Schl., Phila., PA., 1937; Adv. Studies, Am. Acad. of Gen. Dentistry. Appts. incl: Dental intern., Reading Gen. Hosp., Pa., 1937; Assoc. Dentist, Hazleton, Pa., 1937-39; pvte. prac., Annville, Pa., 1946-; Dental Schl. examiner, State of Pa., 1950-65; Fndr., Free Dental Clin. for Underprivileged in Annville-Cleona Schls., Pa. Mbrships incl: Past Pres., Lebanon Co. & 4th Dist. Dental Assns., Pa; Am. Dental Assn.; Am. Acad. of Gen.Dentistry; Trustee, Annville Free Lib.; Mason (Shriner, 32nd degree); Hershey Dental Study Club; Annville Hlth.Coun. Address: 33 S. Whiteoak St., Annville, PA 17003, U.S.A. 6.

SHEFT, Casimir Richard, b. 15 Jan. 1920. Dentist. Educ: N.Y. Univ.; D.D.S., Univ. of Md. Dental Schl., 1944; Grad., Civilian Pilot Trng. Prog., Univ. of Newark, 1940; Postgrad. work, Tufts Dental Schl., 1956. Appts. incl: Supvsr., Dental Clin., Naval Trng. Stn., San Diego, 1945; Chief Dental Surg., Naval Operating Base, Saipan, M.I., 1946; Charity Dentist, Immaculate Conception Orphanage, Lodi, N.J., 1948-68. Mbrships. incl: Am.Dental Assn.; Psi Omega; Univ. of Md. Alumni Assn.; Int. Soc.

for Fluroide Rsch.; Dir., N.J. Coun. Opposing Forced Fluoridation; N.J. Conservative Union; Am. Profl. Prac. Assn.; Fellow, Royal Soc. of Hlth., U.K., 1973; Omicron Kappa Upsilon; Saddle River Bd. of Educ., 1964-68; V.P., ibid, 1968-70; Saddle River Youth Guidance Coun., 1965-70. Author of anti-fluoridation articles. Address: 15 Christopher Place, Saddle River, NJ 07458, U.S.A. 6.

SHEIN, Louis Julius, b. 22 Dec. 1914. Professor of Russian Literature. Educ:: B.A., Univ. of Dubuque, Iowa,U.S.A., 1942; M.A., Univ. of Toronto, Ont., Canada., 1943; B.D., Knox Coll., ibid, 1945; Ph.D., 1946. Appts: Lectr., Philos., Univ. of Toronto, 1944-46; Special Lectr., Philos. & Philos. of Relig., Carleton Univ., Ottawa, Ont., 1951-54; Lectr., Mod. Philos. & Hebrew, McMaster Univ., Hamilton, Ont., 1954-57; Org., Russian Dept., ibid, 1957; Chmn., Russian Dept., 1957-71; Prof., Russian Lit., 1968-; Mbrships: Canadian & Am. Assn. of Slavists; Canadian Philos. Assn.; Reviewing Comm., Canada Coun., 5 yrs. Publs: Reading in RussianPhilosophical Thought, 3 vols., 1968-74; Articles & reviews in learned jrnls. Recip., D.D., Knox Coll., 1974. Address: 150 Judith Crescent, Ancaster, Ont., L9G 1L5, Canada, 13.

SHEINMAN, Kannon, b. 23 Mar. 1889. Oral Surgeon, Retd. Educ: CCNY; Columbia Univ. Coll. of Dental & Oral Surg.; Postgrad. study, Univs. of Berlin, Vienna; D.D.S.; M.D. (H.O.); Dipl., Oral Surg. F.I.C.A.; Appts: Chief, Oral Surg. Clin., Lebanon Hosp., N.Y.C.; Tchr., Postgrad. Oral Surg., Allied Dental Coun. & 1st Dist. Dental Soc. Mbrships: Life Mbr., Am. Dental Assn.; Fndr., Northern Dental Soc.; N.Y. Inst. of Clin. Oral Pathol.; Fellow, Int. Coll. of Anesthetists; 1st Dist. Dental Soc. of N.Y.; N.Y. State Dental Soc. Publs: Articles on sci., pol. & philos. in num periodicals; Past Ed., Dental Outlook, Northern Dental Bulletin; Rsch. resulting in anesthetic 'Neuorolene'. Hons: Bronze Schlrship. Medal, 1908. Clarkson Cowl Gold Medal, 1910; Bronze Medal, Int. Coll. of Anesthetists, 1939. Address: 800 West Ave., Apt. 502, Miami Beach, FL 33139, U.S.A. 55.

SHELBY, Charles Edwin, b. 19 July 1925. Research Geneticist; Administrator. Educ: B.S., Univ. of Ky., 1948; M.S., ibid, 1949; Ph.D., Iowa State Univ., 1952. Appts: Rsch. Geneticist, US Range Livestock Experiment Br., ARS, USDA, Miles City Mont., 1952-55, & Beef Cattle Rsch. Br., ARS, USDA, Denver, Colo., 1955-59; Dir. & Investigations Ldr., REgional Swine Breeding Lab., ARS, USDA, Ames, Iowa, 1959-70; USDA Liason Off., ARS, USDA, Ky. State Univ., Frankfort, 1970-. Mbrships: Am. Soc. Animal Sci.; Genetic Soc. of Am.; Am. Genetic Assn.; Biometric Soc.; Am. Meat Sci. Assn.; AAUP; OPEDA; AIBS; AAAS; Sigma Xi; Alpha Zeta; SAR; Ky. Histl. Socl.; Filson Club; Pres., Ctrl. Ky. Geneal. Soc. Author or co-author of abour 70 sci. publs. Address: USDA Liaison Officer, Ky. State Univ., Frankfort, KY 40601, U.S.A. 7, 8, 14, 28, 125, 129, 139.

SHELDON-WILLIAMS, Inglis Patric, b. 30 Nov. 1908. Part Time Lecturer. Educ: Univ. Coll., 1926-29. Appts: School-master, 1929-41; British Council, 1946-68; p/t. Lectr, Univ. Coll., Dublin, 1969-. Publs: Part VI of the Cambrdge History of Later Greek & Early Mediaeval Philosphy, 1967; in collaboration, Iohannis Scotti Erizigonae Periphyseon, Liber Primus, Dublin, 1968; Liber Secundus, Dublin, 1971; contbns. to schol. jrnls. Address: 59 Staunton Rd., Headington, Oxford OX3 7TJ, U.K. 3.

SHELDRICK, Helen M., b. 28 Feb. 1903. Instructor of English & Journalism. Educ: B.A., Univ. of N.H., Durham, U.S.A., 1924; M.A., Boston Univ., Mass., 1930; M.A., Trinity Coll., Hartford, Conn., 1956. Appts. incl: Instr. of Engl., Maynard H.S., Mass., 1926-30; Instr. of Engl. & Jrnlsm., The Gilbert Schl., 1932-73; Publicity Reporter, Winsted, Conn., Defense Coun., Winsted Evening Citizen, WWII. Mbrships. incl: Pres., Conn. Scholastic Press, 1952-53; Pres., Women's Coll. Club of Litchfield Co., 1959-61; Chmn., Drama Comm., Conn. State Fend. of Women's Clubs, 1938-41; Litchfield Audobon Soc.; Delta Kappa Gamma. Publs: One Act Play Tournament Catalogue; Ed., Pioneer Women Teachers of Connecticut, 1967-1970; Ed., The Keynote; Num. contbns. to jrnls. Hons. incl: Newspaper Fnd. Fellowship, Univ. of Iowa, 1962; Hartford Times Schlrship., 1962; Waterbury Republican Schlrship., Univ. of R.I., 1963; Gold Key Award for Jrnlsm., Columbia Univ., 1967. Address: 126 Williams Ave., Winsted, CT 06098, U.S.A. 57.

SHELINE, Darrel Wayne, b. 14 May 1929. Food Store Executive. Appts: Fndr. & Pres., Advance, Inc., Belpre, Ohio, & Parkersburg, W.Va., U.S.A., 1964-; Fndr. & Pres., Darrel's, Inc., Parkersburg, W.Va., 1972-. Mbrships: Blennerhassett Histl. Soc.; Treas., Grand Ctrl. Mall Mershants Assn.; Bd. of Dirs., Sons & Daughters of Pioneer Rivermen; Admiral, Cherry River Navy of W.Va.; Benevolent Protective Order of Elks; Pres., Associated Grocers of Dennison, Ohio, 1970-71. Address: 513 33rd St., Vienna, WV 26105, U.S.A. 8, 57.

SHELL, William Henry, b. 22 Aug. 1910. Medical Social Worker. Educ: A.B., Morehouse Coll., Atlanta, Ga., U.S.A., 1933; A.M., Atlanta Univ., 1935. Appts. incl: Med. Soc. Wkr., VA, Tuskegee, Ala., 1949-50; Admin. Off., Off. of Admnstr., U.S. Dept. of Agric., 1950-53; Asst. Brooklyn & Manhattan Dir., Manhattan Community Appeal. 953054; Med. Soc. Wkr., N.Y.C. Dept. of Hosps., 1954-; Admin. Asst. to Min., Friendship Bapt. Ch., & Assoc. Exec. Dir., House of Friendship Community Ctr., 1959-63. Mbrships. incl: Fellow, Royal Soc. for Promotion of Hlth.; Chmn., Bd. of Christian Educ.; Cornerstone Bapt. Ch., Brooklyn, 1973; Am. Fedn. of State, Co. & Municipal Employees; Am. Nat. Red Cross; NAACP; Unity Democratic Club; Charter, Nat. Assn. Soc. Wkrs. Contbr., articles in mags. & newspapers. Address: 503 Decatur St., Brooklyn, NY 11233, U.S.A. 6, 57.

SHELLEY, Florence D., b. 21 Jan. 1921. Editor; Writer. Educ: A.B., Barnard Coll., 1940; M.S., Columbia Univ. Grad. Schl. Jrnlsm., 1941. Appts. incl: Greelance Ed. & Writer, 1946-; Edit. Educl. Cons., N.Y. State Citizens Commn. for Pub. Schls., Nat. Ctr. for Citizens in Educ., 1965-68; Edit. & Educl. Cons., E.F. Shelley & Co., Inc., 1967-; Resource Cons., N.Y. State Dept. Educ., 1967; Publr., Educ.-Trng. Market Report, 1970-73; Cons., Nat. Commn. on Resources for Youth, 1971-, Nat. Prog. for Educl. Ldrship., 1973-; Pub. Affairs Cons., Nat. Commn. for Citizens in Educ., 1973-.Mbrships incl:New Rochelle, N.Y., Coun. of PTAs (Pres. 1964-66); Advsry Bd., Community Action Prog.; Advsry Comm., New Rochelle Bd. of Educ.; Barnard Coll. Class of 1940 (Pres. 1965-70). Publs. incl: Community Tensions/Attacks on the Schools; ES '70 News, 1968, 1969; Leadership Role of Responsible School Officers. Address: 339 Oxford Rd., New Rochelle, NY 10804, U.S.A. 5, 6, 16.

SHELTON, Bessie Elizabeth. Librarian; Media & Research Specialist; Showbusiness Enterntainer Musician. Educ: Chgo. Conservatory of Music; Northwestern Univ.; Ind. Univ., B.A., W. Va. State Coll., 1958; M.S., N.Y. State Univ. Coll of Educ., 1960; Columbia Schl. of Broadcasting; Univ. of Va.; N. Am. Schl. of Travel; Nashville Schl. Songwriting. Appts. incl: Music Cons.; Lib./Media Specialist, Lynchburg Pub. Schls., 1966-; Rsch. Specialist, McCoy Film Prod., 1968-; Asst. Hd., Ctrl. Ref. Div., Queens Borough Pub. Lib., 1962-65. Mbrships. incl: Music Educators Nat. Conf.; Music City Songwriter's Assn.; NEA; Va. & Lynchb. Educ. Assns.; Int. Entertainers Guild; Sigma Delta Pi; Pi Delta Phi; Nat. Assn. Educ. Broadcasters. Author of Study Guide Bibliog. for Docum. Film, Azania, Int. Film Bur; Intercontinental Biographical Assn.; Life mbr.; Vocal Artists of Am.; Life Danae mbr., Clover; Int. Poetry Assn. Author composition in Clover Collect. of Verse, vol. 7. Recip. of various hons. Address: 1800 Bedford Ave., Apt. 12, Lynchburg, VA 24504, U.S.A. 42, 138.

SHENG, Ching Lai, b. 20 July 1919. University President. Educ: B.Sc., Chiao Tung Univ., Shanghai, China, 1941; Ph.D., Univ. of Edinburgh, U.K., 1948. Appts. incl: Assoc. Prof., Elec. Engrng. Dept., Nat Taiwan Univ., 1949-52; Prof., ibid, 1952054; Prof. & Hd., 1954-62; Adj. Prof., Chiao Tung Inst. of Electronics, 1958-60; Assoc. Prof., Univ. of Ottawa, Canada, 1962-66; Prof., ibid, 1966-73; Pres., Nat. Chiao Tung Univ., Hsinchu, Taiwan. Fellow, Instn. Elec. Engrs., U.K. Mbrships: Pres., Chinese Inst. Elec. Engrs., 1973-74; Sr. IEEE; Assn. Profl. Engrs., Ont. Publs: Fundamentals of Servomechanism, 1959; Power System Analysis, 1963; Thrshold Logic, 1969; Introduction to Switching logic, 1972. Hons: UNESCO Fellowship, 1953-54; Prize & Award for Outstanding Acad. Achievement, Sun Yat-Sen Cultural Fndn., 1972. Address: Nat. Chiao Tung Univ., 45 Po-ai St., Hsinchu, Taiwan, Repub. of China. 6. 14.

SHENKEN, Leon I, b. 6 Mar. 1927. Medical Practitioner; Psychiatrist. Educ: M.B. & Ch.B., Univ. of N.Z., 1949; Dip., Psychological Med., Royal Colls. of Surgs. & Physns. in Ireland, Dublin, 1953. Appts. incl: Med. Res., Mater Hosp., Auckland, & Waikato Hosp., Hamilton, N.Z., 1950-52; Sr. Med. Off., Professorial Psychiatric Unit, Glasgow, U.K., 1953; Pvte. Prac., Psych., Auckland, N.S., 1954-; Vis. Psychiatrist, Auckland Hosp Bd., 1964-; Lectr., Ethological Sociol., Auckland Univ., 1974. Mbrships. incl: Pres., Auckland Mental Hlth Assn., 1960; Selection Comm., Auckland Marriage Guidance Coun.; Assn. for Advancement of Psychotherapy, U.S.A.; Fellow, Australian & N.Z. Coll. of Psychs., 1971-. Publs: 12 rsch. papers in profl. jrnls. Address: Address: 72 Remuera Rd., Remuera, Auckland, 5, New Zealand.

SHENTON, Leonard Roy, b. 4 Feb. 1909. Scientist; Professor. Educ: B.Sc., Manchester Univ., 1932; Tchrs. Dip., ibid, 1936; Ph.D., Univ. of Edinburgh, 1940; D.Sc., ibid, 1960. Appts: Meteorol., (Fl. Lt.), RAF, 1939-45; Lectr., Sr. Lectr. then Reader, Fac. of Technol., Univ. of Manchester, 1948-62; Prof. of State., Univ. of Ga., Athens, U.S.A., 1964-. Mbrships: Fellow, Royal Statl. Soc. & Am. Statl. Assn.; Assoc. Ed., Jrnl. Am. Statl. Soc., 1972-; Int. Statl. Inst. Contbr. over 50 papers to statl. jrnls. Hon. Citizen of Tenn., 1965. Address: Office of Computing Activities, Boyd Graduate Studies Building, Athens, GA 30602, U.S.A.

SHENTON, Reginald, b. 10 Jan. 1900. Oil & Gas Lease Broker. Appts: w. Singer Mfg. Co., St. John, P.Q., 1911-15; Am. Locomotive Co., Montreal, 1915-17; Jackson Vitrified China Co., Falls Creek, Pa., 1917-23; Agt., Ins. Cos., 1923-39; Oil & Gas Broker, 1929-39; w. Phila. Navy Yard, 1939-40; Am. Locomotive Co., Schenectady, N.Y., 1940; Govt. Insp., Watervliet Arsenal, N.Y., 1940-45; Broker, Oil & Gas Royalties & Leases, Caspar, Wyo., 1945-47, Newcastle, Wyo., 1947-. Mbrships. incl: Newcastle City Coun., 1964-66; Pres., ibid, 1964-66, 1968-; Chmn., Newcastle 75th Anniversary Comm., 1964; Indl. Petroleum Assn.; Am. Petroleum Club, Denver; Newcastle Chmbr. of Comm.; Pres., ibid, 1965; Lay Rdr., Episc. Ch.; Chmn., United Fund, Weston Co., 1967. Address: P.O. Box 160, Newcastle, WY 82701, U.S.A. 9, 57, 120.

SHEPARD, Frederick Wells, b. 30 Apr. 1937; Teacher; Potter. Educ: B.A., M.A., M.F.A., 1963, Mich. State Univ. Appts: Prof., Ceramics, Murray State Univ., Ky. Mbrships: Past Chmn., Standards Comm., Ky. Guild of Artists & Craftsmen; Nat. Coun. for Educ. in Ceramic Arts. Exhibs: Over 50 regional, nat. & int. shows; Permanent collects: Mich. State Univ., Middle Tenn. State Univ., Ky. Arts Commn., Tenn. Arts Commn. Address: Rte. 6, Elm Grove Rd., Murray, KY 42071, U.S.A. 125.

SHEPHERD, Florence Mildred, b. 12 Jan. 1916. Missionary; Educator. Educ., A.B., Union Coll., 1937; Arbury Theol. Sem., 1937; M.A., Univ. of Ky., 1939; Kennedy Schl. of Missions, Conn., 1939; Ph.D., Geo. Peabody Coll. for Tchrs., Nashville, Tenn., 1949; Inst. of Biblical Theol., Lincoln Coll., Oxford Univ., 1958; L.H.D., Union Coll., 1966. Appts. incl: Prin., Lal Bagh Girls Intermediate Coll., Lucknow, India, 1950-52; Prin. & Mgr., Howard Plested Girls' H.S., 1952-57; Mgr., Howard Plested Girls' Intermed. Coll. & Meth. Elem. Schl., 1959-66; Instr., Engl., Sue Bennett Coll., London, Ky., 1968-; Chmn., Communications Div., ibid, 1971-. Mbrships. incl: Ky. Hist. Soc.; YWCA; Bd. of Govs., Isabella Thobren Coll., Lucknow. Office holder & active worker w. various confs. & toy exhibs. while in India. Author of articles & books inclng. English Written Usage In Selected High Schools In India & America, Vocabulary English As Second Language, Usage & Grammar English As Second Language. Hons. incl: Iota Sigma Nu Alumna Award, 1974. Address: Sue Bennett Coll., London, KY 40741, U.S.A. 130, 138.

SHEPHERD, Walter, b. 9 Nov. 1906. School Principal. Educ: B.D., Melbourne Coll. of Divinity, 1931; M.A., Melbourne Univ., 1934; Ed.B., ibid, 1939. Appts: Prin., Tubou Coll., Tonga, 1937-39; Sr. Maths. Master, King's Schl., Parramattu, N.S.W., 1950-51; Prin., Meth. Ladies Coll., Claremont, W.A., 1953-72; Chief Moderator, Maths., Perth, 1972. Mbrships: Claremont Rotary Club, 1958-, Pres., 1965; Australian Coll. of Educ. Author, 2 schl. textbooks, algebra. Recip., M.B.E., 1972. Address: 26 Ward Ave., Greenmount, Western Australia, 6056. 23.

SHEPP, George Richard, Sr., b. 17 Jan. 1912. Film Theatre Manager. Educ: Law Enforcement Course, Md. Univ. Appts: Chief of Police, Brentwood, Md.; Currently, City Mgr., Eastern Fed. Theatres. Mbrships: Charter & V.P., Lions Club; Elks Lodge; Fraternal Order of Police; V.P., Optimist Club; Motion Picture Pioneers. Hon. Lit. Col. & Aide de Camp to Gov. Jimmy Carter. Address: 4701 Flat Shoal Rds., Villa 56F, Union City, GA, U.S.A. 125.

SHEPPARD, (The Rt. Rev.) David Stuart, Bishop of Woolwich. Educ: Trinity Hall & Ridley Hall, Cambridge Univ. Appts: Curate, St. Mary's Islington, 1955-57; Warden, Mayflower Family Ctr., Cannin Town, 1957-69; Bishop of Woolwich, 1969-. Cricket: Cambridge Univ. Capt., 1952; Sussex Capt., 1953; England Captain, 1954. Author of Parson's Pitch, 1964. Hons: Exhib. in Classics, Trinity Hall, Cambridge, 1946. Address: 12 Asylum Rd., Peckham, London SE15, U.K.

SHEPPARD, Faith Tresidder, b. 4 June 1920. Landscape & Marine Painter. Educ: Royal Acad. Schl. of Painting, U.K.; Chelsea Schl. of Art; Byam Shaw Schl. of Art. Exhibs. incl: Royal Acad.; Paris Salon; Royal Glasgow Inst. of Fine Arts; Royal Soc. Marine Artists; Royal Soc. Portrait Painters; Royal Soc. Brit. Artists; Chelsea Art Soc.; Artists of Chelsea; Gall. San Marco, Rome; Palazzo Exposioni, Rome; Gall. Rene Borel, Deauville; Gal. Borel, 1973; Gal. de Rohan, Paris; 10th Grand Prix Int. de Painture de la Cote d'Azur, Cannes, 1974. Mbrships incl: Hon. Sec., Welwyn Garden City Art Club Jubilee Yr., 1970-71; Comm., St. Alban's Art Soc.; Royal Glasgow Inst. of the Fine Arts. Works incl: Kings Road, Chelsea; St. Jean Cap Ferrat, 1970; St. Columba's Pont St.; Bruges Pont du Cheval; Villefranche; Pastures Green. Hons. incl: Prix Int. de Peinture de la Cote d'Azur, 1972; Laureate Ier Gran Premio Roma, 1973; Laureate 9e Grand Prix de la Cote d'Azur, 1973. Address: 29 Digswell Rd., Welwyn Garden City, Herts., U.K. 19, 133.

SHEPPARD, Posy (Rose Jackson) Mrs. John W. Sheppard), b. 23 Aug. 1916. Social Worker. Appts. incl: Rep., League of Red Cross Socs. to UN, 1957-; Mbr., 1960-66; Vice-Chmn., 1962-66; Nat. Bd. of Govs., Am. Red Cross; Chmn., NGO Comm. on UNICEF, 1961-63; UNICEF, '71-73; Chmn., Exec. Comm., NGO-OPI Conf., 1963-65; Pres., NGO conf. of Consultative NGOs, UN, 1966-69; Chmn., NGO-UN Comm. on Field Rels., 1974-; Deleg., White House Conf. on For. Aspects of U.S. Nat. Security, 1962, on Int. Coop. Yr., 1966. Address: 535 Lake Ave., Greenwich, CT 06830, U.S.A. 2, 5, 6.

SHERFIELD, (Lord) Roger, b. 3 Feb. 1904. Diplomat; Company Chairman. Educ: B.A., Christchurch Coll., Oxford, U.K., 1925; Fellow, All Souls Coll., 1925. Appts: Barrister-at-Law, Inner Temple, 1927; H.M. For. Off., 1928-56; Ambassador, Wash. D.C., U.S.A., 1953-56; Jt. Permanent Sec. to Treasury, 1956-60; Chmn., U.K. Atomic Energy Authority, 1960-64; Dir., Times Publishing Co., 1964-67; Chmn., Indl. & Commercial Finance Corp. & Assocd. Cos., 1964-74. Chmn., Hill Samuel Group Ltd., 1966-70, A.C. Cossor Ltd., 1966-, Wells Fargo Ltd., 1972-, Finance for Ind. Ltd., 1973-, Finance Corp. for Ind. Ltd., 1973-; Chancellor, Univ. of Reading, 1970-; Chmn., Governing Body, Imperial Coll. of Sci. & Technol., 1963-; Chmn., Marshall Aid Commemoration Commn., 1966-73; Trustee, Kennedy Mem. Fund. Mbrships: Coun. mbr., Royal Albert Hall; Fellow, Winchester Coll.; Chmn., Charles Lindemann Fellowship Comm., 1971-; Chmn., The Ditchley Fndn., 1962-65; Pres., Parliamentary & Sci. Comm., 1969-73; Pres., British Standards Instn., 1970-73; Athenaeum; Middlesex Co. Cricket Club. Publs: The Social & Economic Consequences of Nuclear Energy (Ed.), 1972; Var. lects. & articles. Recip. of hons. Address: Sherfield Court, Basingstoke, Hants., U.K.

SHERIDAN, Harriet W. (Mrs. Edward P. Sheridan), b. 21 July 1925. Educator. Educ: A.B., Hunter Coll., U.S.A., 1944; M.A., Smith

Coll., 1945; Ph.D., Yale Univ., 1950. Appts: Instr., Engl., Hunter Coll., 1947-49; Asst.-Assoc. Prof., Engl. & Educ., Carleton Coll., 1953-67; Dir., Tchr., NDEA Inst. in Engl., 1965; '66; Prof., Carleton Coll., 1967-; Chmn. of Fac., 1971-73; Prof., Humanities, Andrew W. Mellon Fndn., Carleton Coll., 1974-; Chmn., Dept. of Engl., ibid, 1973-; Mbr., Gov.'s Advsry. Coun., Minn. Right-t o-Read Prog., 1972-; Chmn., Minn. Assn. Dept. Engl. Chmen., 1973-. Mbrships: Past Pres., Carleton Chapt., Phi Beta Kappa; Past Minn. Chmn. Achievement Awards Prog., M.L.A., N.C.T.E.; Advsry. Coun., M.C.T.E. Int. Reading Assn.. Orton Soc.; A.A.U.P. Author, Structure and Style: An Analytical Approach to Prose Writing, 1966 & Ed., Minn. Engl. Jrnl., 1968-73. Hons: Helen Gray Cone Fellowship, 1945-46; Marjorie Hope Nicholson Fellowship, 1945-46; Yale Univ. Fellowship, 1946-47; Louis W. & Maud Hill Family Fndn. Rsch. Grant, 1962-63. Address: Carleton Coll., Northfield, MN 55057. 5, 8.

SHERIDAN (Sister) M. Florianne, b. 27 Dec. 1908. Nurse; Director, School of Nursing. Educ: R.N., St. Anthony Hosp. Schl. of Nursing; B.S., Ind. State Tchrs. Coll., 1941; M.S., DePaul Univ., 1954. Joined Order of Sisters of St. Francis, 1944. Appts: Elem. Tchr., 1929-35; Nursing Schl. Instr., 1939-44; Dir., St. Margaret's Hosp. Schl. of Nursing, 1946-58; Dir., St. Elizabeth Hosp. Schl. of Nursing, Lafayette, Ind., 1958-. Num. mbrships. incl: Past Mbr., Bd. of Trustees, St. Francis Coll.; Past Pres., Ind. Conf., Cath. Schls. of Nursing; Bd. of Dirs., Vis. Nursing Serv.; Med. Lib. Assn.; Am. Nurses Assn.; Nat. Charter Mbr., Smithsonian Assocs.; Nat. League for Nursing; Past Pres. Ind. Cath. Hosp. Assn.; Nat. Securities Voters Advsry. Bd.; Am. Soc. Hlth. Assn. Address: St. Elizabeth Hosp. Schl. of Nursing, 1508 Tippecanoe St., Lafayette, IN 47904, U.S.A. 5, 8, 49, 120.

SHERIDAN, Vincent G., b. 15 Apr. 1921. Ecological Planner; Real Estate Analyst. Educ: B.Sc.(Bus.), B.Sc.(Civil Engrng.), Univ. of Colo.; extensive grad. studies. Appts. incl: USN, 1942-46, ISMR. 1046-51; Prin., Sheridan & Gally, Dailey-Sheridan Assocs," & Buck-Sheridan Assocs.; Appraiser for var. civic & commercial orgs. inclng. City of Kingston, Fed. Housing Admin., Savings & Loan of Kingston, State Bank of Albany; Real Estate Cons., N.Y. State Dept. of Pub. Works; Staff Mbr., Bur. of Claims, N.Y.C. Bd. Water Supply; Commnr. in Condemnation, Urban Renewal Chmn., Ecological Corp. of Am.; Cons., Ulster Co. Community Coll. Fac. Mbr. & Off., num. profl. assns., civic & fraternal orgs. Contbr. to Jrnl. of Appraisal Inst. of Canada. Hons. incl: Dr. Religious Humanities; Wisdom Award of Hon. Address: 305 Main St., Catskill, NY 12414, U.S.A. 6, 28, 130, 139.

SHERIFF, Noam, b. 7 Jan. 1935. Composer; Conductor. Educ: Herzlia Hebrew Coll., Hebrew Univ., Jerusalem, 1955-59; Hochschule für Musik, Berlin, 1959-62; pvte. music studies. Appts: Dpty. Conductor, Israel Army Symphony Orch., 1952-54; Fndr. & Musical Dir., Hebrew Univ. Symphony Orch., 1955-59; Prof. of orchestration & conducting, Music Acads. of Jerusalem & Tel-Aviv, Israel, 1965-67; Assoc. Musical Dir. & Res. Conductor, Israel Chmbr. Ensemble, 1972-; Musical Dir., Tel-Aviv's Tzavta Ctr. for Progressive Culture, 1973-. Mbr., Israel Nat. Coun. of Culture & Art. Compositions: Festival Prelude, 1957; Songs of Degrees, 1959; Ashrei, 1961; Music for Woodwinds, Trombone, Solo Piano & Bass, 1961; Destination 5, 1962: Sonata, 1962; Heptaprisms, Metamorphosis on a Galliard, &

Confession, 1965; Inventions, 1967; Two Epigrams, & Chaconne, 1968; Sonata for Chamber Orchestra, 1972; Cain & String Quartet, 1974. Composer of music for films, TV, plays, light & sound shows, 200 arrangements of songs for Broadcasting Serv. Hons: Winner of prizes awarded by Israel Philharmonic Orch., 1957-59. Address: 20, Mishmar Hagvul St., Afeka, Tel-Aviv, Israel.

SHERLOCK, Dulcie-Ann Steinhardt (Mrs.) b. 1 Nov. 1925. Civic Worker. Educ: Am. Womens Coll., Istanbul, Turkey; Univ. of London, U.K. Appts: Soc. Sec. to U.S. Ambassador, 6 yrs; Embassy Hostess, Turkey, Czechoslovakia & Canada. Mbrships. incl: Sec., Parents Assn., Sheridan Schl., Wash. D.C., U.S.A., 1969; 1st V.P., Womens Bd., All Saints Ch., Chevey Chase, Md., 1963-64; Pres., ibid, 1964-65; Chmn., St. Mary's Guild, 1969-72; Vestryman, 1971-74, 74-; Alternate Deleg. & Deleg., Diocesan Conventions, Episc. Ch., Wash. D.C., 1967-73; Convocation 3, 1967-73; V.P., Womens Bd., Episc Ch. Home, 1971-73; Pres., Womens Bd., 1974-; Bd. Govs., Episc. Ch. & Friendship Terrace inc., 1973-74; 1st V.P., ibid, 1974-; Florence Crittenden Home Circle, 1973-. Address: 5808 Connecticut Ave., Chevy Chase, MD 20015, U.S.A.

SHERMAN, (Edward) David, b. 15 Mar. 1908. Physician. Educ: M.D.C.M., Fac. of Med., McGill Univ., Montreal, 1932; Intern., Woman's Gen. Hosp., Montreal, 1931-33; Res., Mt. Sinai Hosp., N.Y.C., 1933-35; postgrad. studies, internal med., 4 wks. annually, Mt. Sinai Hosp., N.Y., 1937-42. Appts: Attending Staff, Montefiore Hosp., N.Y. Hosp.-Cornell Med. Ctr., Bellevue Hosp., 2nd (Cornell) Med. Div., N.Y.C., 1946-55, City of Sydney, St. Rita, Marine & Veterans' Hosps., Sydney, N.S., Can., 1935-46; V.P., Inst. of Gerontol., Univ. of Montreal, 1961-64; Assoc. Physn., Jewish Gen. Hosp., 1956-70; Assoc. Physn.-in-Chief, Maimonides Hosp. & Home for Aged, 1956-70; Lectr., Geriatrics, Univ. of Montreal, 1959-; Med. Dir., Sheltered Workshop, Jewish Vocational Serv., 1959-; Dir. of Rsch., Rehab. Inst. of Montreal, 1962-. Mbrships. incl: Fellow, Am. Geriatrics Soc., Royal Coll. Physns. of Canada, Am. Coll. of Physns. Royal Soc. of Arts, Royal Soc. of Med., Int. Coll. of Angiol., Gerontol. Soc. & Am. Coll. Preventive Med. Contbr. about 42 articles to sci. jrnls. in fields of internal med., geriatrics & rehab. Hons. incl: Rabbi Dr. Harry J. Stern Award for disting. serv. to community, Temple Emanu-El, Montreal, 1974. Address: 4330 Hampton Ave., Montreal, P.Q. H4A 2L2, Canada.

SHERMAN, Harold, b. 13 July 1898. Researcher in Extra Sensory Perception; Author. Educ: Univ. of Mich. Appts. incl: Newspaper Reporter, Marion Chronicle, Ind.; Free-lance Writer, sports stories & adventure novels, 2 plays on Broadway, N.Y.C., & broadcaster, Your Key to Happiness, Columbia Network series, 1924-41; Author, screen play, Adventures of Mark Twain, Hollywood, Calif., 1941; Fndr., Extra Sensory Perception Rsch. Assocs. Fndn., Little Rock, Ark. Publs. incl: Your Power to Heal; Wonder Healers of The Philippines; Adventures in Thinking; How to Make ESP Work for You; Thoughts Through Space (co-author); Your Key to Happiness; You Live After Death; Know Your Own Mind; The Harold Sherman ESP Manual. Also record & cassette series. Address: ESP Research Associates Foundation, 1650 Union National Plaza, Little Rock, AR 72201, U.S.A.

SHERMAN, Ingrid (Mrs. Morris Sherman, Dame, Lady of Grace, Divine Nobility), b. 25 June 1919. Counselor; Educator; Lecturer;

Author; Poet; Naturopath. Positions held: Pvte. Sec. to Jan Kiepura & Marta Eggerth, opera singers & film stars, 1958-62; Couns., Spiritual Psychol., Poetry Therapist, Peace of Mind Studio, 1962-; Subst. Tchr., For. Langs., Art, etc., Jr. & Sr. H.S., Yonkers, N.Y., 1963-; Fndr., Dir., Peace of Mind Studio; Fndr., Golden Rose Chapel, 1973-. Mbrships. incl: Field Rsch. Corres., World Field Rsch. Inc.; Fndr., Westchester Philo-Cultural Soc. Publs. incl: For Your Reading Pleasure; Natural Remidies for Better Health, 1970. Contbr. of over 400 poems to publs. all over world. Composer of 10 songs, 1972. Num. radio, TV appearances & lectures. Hons. incl: Hon. Poet Laureate; 1st Lady of Poetry Therapy; Dr. of Naturopathy & Ostenopathy; 6 hon. degrees; Baroness Ecclesiast of All Byelorussia & Miensk, 1973. Address: 102 Courter Ave., Yonkers, NY 10705, U.S.A. 5, 6, 11, 22, 30, 128.

SHERMAN, Lenore Walton, b. 11 May 1920. Artist. Appts: Conjurer, Ventriloquist & Comedienne, Theatres & Night Clubs, 1943-50; Free-lance painter, San Diego, Calif., U.S.A.; Tchr., Painting. Mbr., San Diego Art Inst. Oil paintings in num. Collects., U.S.A. & abroad. Hons: First Award for Oils, Landmarks Theme, Southern Calif. Exposition, 1970; Purchase Award, San Diego Art Inst. Annual Exhib., 1971; First Award in Landmarks, & 2nd Award in Still Life, Calif. Federated Women's Clubs Fine Arts Festival, 1971. Address: 6217 Winona Ave., San Diego, CA 92120, U.S.A. 37.

SHERMAN, Winnie Borne (Mrs. Lee D. Sherman), b. 10 Nov. 1902. Artist; Teacher; Lec turer. Educ: Tchrs. Coll., Columbia Univ.; Nat. Acad. of Design; Art Students League; B.F.A., Cooper Union Inst.; Licensed Tchr., Fine Arts, Higher Bd. of Educ., N.Y. Appts. incl: Fine Arts H.S., N.Y.C.; CCNY; Inst. for Retd. Profl., New Schl. Fellow, Royal Soc. of Arts. Mbrships: Am. Artists Profl. League; former Pres., Catharine Lorillard Wolfe Art Club; Nat. League Am. Pen Women, V.P., 1969-72, Recording Sec., N.Y. Br., 1974-76; Hon. Mbr., Kappa Pi; Assoc. Mbr., Am. Watercolor Soc. 5 one-man exhibs., N.Y.C. & N.Y. state. Grp. shows, N.Y.C. & nationally. Works represented in many pvte. & pub. collections inclng. Seton Hall Univ. Lib. & Okla. Art Inst. Contbr. to art publs. Recip. of sev. art awards. Address: 500 E. 77th St., Apt. 934, N.Y., NY 10021, U.S.A. 5, 6, 15, 57.

SHERRY, Raymond Henry, b. 3 Oct. 1924. Member of Parliament. Appts: Free-lance Actor-Writer-Broadcaster, 1947-; Actor, Royal Shakespeare Co., U.K., 1952-55; Broadcaster, Commentator, TV News Reader, Hobart, Tasmania, 1956-69; Parliamentarian, Fed. Mbr. for Franklin, Tas., 1969-. Mbrships. incl: Hobart Journalists' Club; Jt. Statutary Comm. on Broadcasting of Parliament, 1969-; House of Reps, Select Comm. on Wildlife Conservation, 1970-; Chmn., Govt. Arts & Media Comm.; Dpty. Ghmn., Govt. Transport, Civil Aviation & Primary Ind. Comm.; Australian Deleg., Commonwealth Parliamentary Assn. Cons., London, 1971; Exec. Mbr., Aust. Br., ibid, London, 1973. Address: Stratford House, Wellington St., Richmond, Tasmania, Australia 7025.

SHIDELER, Ross Odor, b. 4 Mar. 1922. Chemical Engineer & Executive. Educ: B.S., Perdu Univ.; Grad. work, Ind. Univ.; Music & theatrical work, Butler Univ.; For. langs., Univs. of Barcelona & Lisbon. Appts. incl: Owner, Beauty-Seal Plastics Co., 1950-52; Pres., U.S. Equipment Corp., 1952-67; Sales Dir., Sheraton Inns, 1967; Gen. Mgr., Manchester Hotel, 1968;

Asst. Mgr., Fairmont Hotels, 1969-. Mbrships. incl: Past Pres., Alpha Phi Omega; Sigma Nu; Catalyst Club; Am. Inst. of Chem. Engrs. Address: Box 2426 Station. A, Champaign, IL 61820, U.S.A. 12, 128.

SHIELDS, John Edgar, b. 8 May 1924. Editor; Author; Lecturer. Educ: A.B., Univ. of Md., 1950. Appts: Prodr.-Dir., CBS, Wash.D.C., 1946-49; Pvte. Sec., Editl. Asst. to Ambassador Wm. C. Bullitt, 1950; w. CIA. Wash., 1950-52; Exec., Asia Fndn., var. Far. E. countries, 1952-55; For. Corres., Author, Ed., var. media, 195 62; w. Congressional Digest Mag., 1962-; Ed., ibid, 1968-; Dir. to mining & aircraft corps. Mbrships: Sons of Am. Revolution; MENSA; Phi Kappa Phi; Sigma Alpha Epsilon; Alpha Phi Omega; Nat. Press Club, Wash. D.C.; var. for. corres.'s clubs, U.S.A. & abroad. Publd. a number of books & monographs on local hist., geneal., etc. incln A History of the Shields Family, 1968; East Tennessee Migrations-Factors & Families, 1969; The Scotch Irish in Augusta County, Virginia, 1971; Narratives of Westward Movement, 1973. Address: 19128 Roman Way, Gaithersburg, MD 20760, U.S.A. 7.

SHIELDS, (Sister) Mary Jean Ellen, b. 30 Apr. 1912. Librarian. Educ: B.A., Marquette Univ., Milwaukee, Wis., 1945; M.A., St. Louis, Mo., 1954; M.A. L.S., Rosary Coll., River Forest, Ill., 1962. Appts: Elem. Tchr., Wis., Ill., Iowa, Calif., 1933-54; Secondary Tchr., Wis. & Calif., 1954-69; Libn., Bellarmine Jefferson H.S., Burbank, Calif., 1962-72, Kan. City, Mo., 1966, Guadalupe Coll., Los Gatos, Calif., 1967, Notre Dame Univ., Ind., 1968, San Francisco, Calif., 1969, Burbank Pub. Lib., Calif., 1969-72, Don Bosco Tech. Inst. Lib., Rosemead, Calif., 1972-. Mbrships: Chmn., Southwest Unit Cath. Lib. Assn., 1969-71, Chmn., Coll. Sect., 1973-; ALA; Calif. Assn. Schl. Libns. Recip., Brotherhood Award, Burbank Interfaith Coun., 1969. Address: 130 S. Holliston Ave., Pasadena, CA 91106, U.S.A.

SHIELDS, Milford E., b. 29 Oct. 1898. Poet; Author; Retired Farmer; Motion Picture Projectionist. Appts: Poet Laureate of Colo., 1954-; 1st Poet Laureate, Int. Platform Assn., 1970. Mbrships: Exec. V.P., United Poets Laureate Int., 1963-; Guest Ed., World Poetry Day No. of Poet, 1970; Royal Order of Scotland; For. Assoc., Acad. Française de la Poesie; Past Pres., Am. Lit. Assn.; Pres. Emeritus, Poets of the Pacific Ing.; Life Fellow, FIAL; Hon. Mbr., Int. Acad. Jain Wisdom & Culture- Centro Studi e Scambi Int. Publs. incl: Colorado & Other Poems; Burning Weeds & Other Poems; Dirty Face; Static Land (prose); Engine 315; Poems of International Goodwill (5 vols.) Contbr. to num. publs. in U.S. & abroad. Hons. incl: Litt.D., Int. Acad. of Ldrship.; Ph.D., Free Univ. of Asia; LAS, Gt. China Arts Coll.; Hon. Worlds Poet Laureate of Peace w. Gold Medal & Laurel Wreath from Pres. Macapagal, 1965; Pres. Marcos Gold Medal for efforts on behalf of world peace, 1966; Bronze, Silver & Gold Medals, Silver Pen & Parchment, & Cețts., Centro Studi e Scambi; Humanist Award, AMORC, Rosicrucian, 1963; H.L.D., Coll. of St. Thomas; Poet Laureate of World Peace, 2nd. World Congress of Poets, 1973. Address: P.O. Box 1217, Durango, CO 81301, U.S.A.

SHIFFMAN, Melvin A., b. 23 Aug. 1931. Physician. Educ: B.S., Union Coll., 1953; Harvard Schl. of Dental Med., 1953-54; M.D., Northwestern Univ. Schl. of Med., 1957; Internship, L.A. Co. Gen. Hosp., 1957-58. Appts: Res., VA Hosp. (Gen. Surg.), 1960-64; Asst. Clin. Prof. of Surg., Univ. of Calif., Irvine.

Mbrships: Dipl., Am. Bd. of Surg., 1965; Fellow, Int. Coll. of Surgs., 1967 & Royal Soc. of Hlth.; Past Pres., Oncol. Soc. of Orange Co.; Soc. of Head & Neck Surgs., 1969; Pres., Orange Co. Unit, Am. Cancer Soc.; Soc. of Abdominal Surgs.; Orange Med. Assn.; Am. & Pan. Am. Med. Assns. Contbr. of articles to profl. jrnls. Address: 1076 E. First St., Tustin, CA 92680, U.S.A. 9.

SHINDELBOWER, Martha Elise, b. 6 Sept. 1923. School Teacher & Principal. Educ: B.A., Univ. of Ky., 1950; M.A., ibid, 1953: adv. work, Univ. of Ky., Lexington, & Northern Mich. Coll., Marquette. Appts: Serv. w. USN, 1944-46. Tchr., Ore. Coll. of Educ., Monmouth, 1950-51, Kenwick Schl., Lexington, Ky., 1951-54, Asst. Prin., 1957-62; Tchr., Yates Schl., Lexington, 1954-55, Dependent Schl., Bamberg, Germany, 1955-56, Sandia Base Mil. Schl., Albuquerque, N.M., U.S.A., 1956-67; Prin., Cardinal Valley Schl., Lexington, 1962-. Mbrships. incl: V.P., & Pres., Local Chapt., Kappa Delta Pi; V.P., Pres., Local Chapt., Music Chmn., State Chapt., Delta Kappa Gamma; Sec., Treas., Fayette Co. Educ. Assn.; Sec., Treas., Ctrl. Ky. Elem. Prins. Hons. incl: Ky. Col., 1967; Boy Scouts of Am. Cert. of Appreciation, 1967. Address: 632 Cardinal Ln., Lexington, KY 40503, U.S.A. 5, 125.

SHINE, Frances Louise, b. 8 Jan. 1927. Author; Educator. Educ: B.A., Radcliffe Coll., Cambridge, Mass., 1948; M.A., Cornell Univ., Ithaca, N.Y., 1952. Appts: Sec., Trustees Off., Boston Pub. Lib., 1948-50; Sec., Interdept. Comm. on Lit., Cornell Univ., Ithaca, N.Y., 1951-52; Sec., Hardy Hall Iddings & Grimes, Boston, 1952-53; Tchr., St. Monicas Schl., Montreal, Canada, 1953-54; Tchr., Gloucester Pub. Schls., Mass., U.S.A., 1954-56; Tchr., Framingham Pub. Schls., 1956-. Mbr., Mass. Audubon Soc. Publs: The Life Adjustment of Harry Blake, 1968; Johnny Noon, 1973; short stories; poetry. Recip., Nat. 5 Arts Award for short story, The Exile, 1952. Address: 17 Clark St., Framingham, MA 01701, U.S.A. 5.

SHINEDLING, Abraham I., b. 8 Sept. 1897. Rabbi; Historian; Editor; Author. Educ: B.A., Univ. of Cinn., 1919; M.A., Columbia Univ., 1928; Rabbi, Hebrew Union Coll., 1920. Appts: Rabbi, congregations in Mo., Tex., Ga., & N.C., 1920-26; Hosp., Prison & Instnl. Chaplain, Soc. Wkr., N.Y.C., Westchester Co., 1926-43; Rabbi, La., Ala. & W. Va., 1943-56; Staff Mbr., Am. Jewish Archives, Cinn., 1956-. Mbrships: V.P., B'nai B'rith Lodge 336, Albuquerque, N.M.; Congregation Albert, Albuquerque; Past V.P., Temple Albert Men's Club; Alumni Assns., Univs. of Cinn., Ga.; Ctrl. Conf. of Am. Rabbis; Hebrew Union Coll-Jewish Inst. of Relig. Alumni Assn. Publs. incl: History of the Los Alamos Jewish Center, 1958; West Virginia Jewry - Origins & History: 1850-1960, 3 vols., 1963; Translator,¬ History of the Jews by Ismar Elbogen (from the German), 1926; Var. family, personal biogs. Hons: D.D., Hebrew Union Coll., 1959. Address: 615 Aliso Drive S.E., Albuquerque, NM 87108, U.S.A. 9, 55, 63.

SHINEY, Margaret Louise, b. 27 Nov. 1926. Physician. Educ: A.B., Bryn Mawr Coll., 1948; M.D., Kansas Univ., U.S.A., 1954; Intern, St. Francis Hosp., Wichita, Kan.; Res. trng., Dayton, VA Hosp; Pa. Grad. Hosp.; Denver Gen Hosp., Colo., 1960-61. Appts: Pvte. prac., Wich., Kan., 1955-59; Staff Physn.-Chief/Dept. of Med., Mem. Hosp., Topeka, Kan., 1962-. Mbrships: Am. Med. Assn.; Kan. State Med. Soc.; Shawnee Co. Med. Soc.; Exec. Comm., med. staff, Mem. Hosp.; Bryn Mawr Coll.

Alumnae Assn.; Bryn Mawr Coll. Admissions Inf. Rep.; Am. Med. Women's Assn. Co-author The Significance of Pulmonary Coil Lesions, Kan. State Med. Jrnl., 1954. Recip. 7-Coll. Schlrship., 1944. Address: 1617 W. 26th St., Topeka, KS 66611, U.S.A. 5.

SHINGLETON, Royce Gordon, b. 25 Oct. 1935. Educator; History Professor. Educ: B.S., E. Carolina Univ., 1958; M.A., Appalachian State Univ., 1964; Ph.D., Fla. State Univ., 1971. Appts: Admnstrve. Asst., U.S. Army, W. Germany, 1958-60; Tchr., Dinwiddie H.S., Dinwiddie, Va., 1960-61, & Greene Ctrl. H.S., Snow Hill, N.C., 1961-63. Dean of Men, Lees-McRae Coll., Banner Elk, N.C., 1964-65; Hist. Instr., Ga. State Univ., Atlanta, 1968-. Mbrships: Am. Histl. & Southern Histl. Assns; Phi Alpha Theta; Pi Gamma Mu. Contbr. of articles to var. jrnls.; Ed., America in the Making, 1969., other work in progress. Address: D27-6851 Roswell Rd. NE, Atlanta, GA 30328, U.S.A. 7, 30.

SHINITZKY, Moshe I., b. 9 Sept. 1909. Insurance Broker; Industrial Executive. Educ: Yeshiva, Poland & Israel, & tech. coll., Israel. Appts. incl: Mfr., Hashemesh Perambulators, 1927-49; Major w. Hagana, serv. in War of Liberation, Sinai Campaign & Six Day War; Jt. Owner, Shinitzky & Co., agricultural machinery, & Israel Rep., B.S. Engrng. Co. Ltd., Galvano Tech. Ltd., 1949-57; Chmn., Ins. Assn. of Israel, & Kapat Tagmulim; Mbr., BPR & var. financial mgmts.; currently Mbr. Bd. Dirs., Kupat Am Bank of Israel Ltd., Kupat Am (Ins. Servs.) Ltd., Owner of Shinab Trust Investment & Ins. Serv. Ltd., Mbrships: Pres., Shar Zion B'nei B'rith, Tel Aviv; Israel Indl. & Commercial Club; Hon. Sec., Israel Ins. Brokers Assn.; Israel British Commonwealth Assn.; BIPAR. Address: 13 Berdischevsky St., Tel Aviv, Israel. 55.

SHINNERS, Stanley Marvin, b. 9 May 1933. Electronics Engineer & Educator. Educ: B.E.E., CCNY, 1954; M.S. in E.E., Columbia Univ., 1959. Appts: Proj. Engr., Polarad Electronics Corp., Queens, N.Y., 1956-57; & Consolidated Avionics Corp., Westbury, ibid, 1957-58; Sr. Rsch. Sect. Hd., Sperry Systems Mgmt. Div., Gt. Neck, 1958-; Adjunct Prof. of Elec. Engrng., Polytech. inst. of Bklyn., Farmingdale, 1959-, & The Cooper Union, N.Y., 1966-. Mbrships: Am. Soc. for Engrng. Educ.; N.Y. Soc. of Profl. Engrs.; Fellow, IEEE, 1973; Chmn. of L.I. Sect.'s Automatic Control Grp., ibid, 1968-69; Eta Kappa Nu; Tau Beta Pi. Publs: Modern Control System Theory & Application, 1972; Technique of System Engineering (Japanese trans., 1972), 1967; Control System Design, 1964. Address: 28 Sagamore Way N., Jericho, NY 11753, U.S.A. 6, 14, 16, 130, 131.

SHIPLEY, L. Earle, b. 1 Aug. 1916. Clergyman; Director of Public Relations. Educ: B.A., Linfield Coll.; M.A., Univ. of Pa.; B.D., Eastern Bapt. Sem. Appts: Pastor, Bapt. chs. in Ojai, L.A. & San Luis Obispo, Calif., 1941-55; Asst. to Pres., Linfield Coll., McMinnville, Ore., 1955-64; V.P., Berkeley Bapt. Divinity Schl., Calif., 1964-67; Dir. of Ch. & Community Rels., Am. Bapt. Homes of the W., Oakland, Calif., 1968-. Mbrships: Lions Club; Kiwanis Club; Am. Bapt. Mins. Coun.; Past Pres., Am. Bapt. Mins. of Southern Calif.; Past Pres., Life Mbr., P.R. Assn. of Am. Bapt. Conv.; Dev. Exec. Roundtable of San Fran. Contbr. to periodicals. Hons: D.D., Linfield Coll., 1966. Address: 5290 Broadway Ter., Apt. 302, Oakland, CA 94618, U.S.A. 9.

SHIPPER, Mildred Louise. Classroom Teacher. Educ: B.S., E. Tex. Univ., 1942; M.Ed., Univ. of Houston, 1951. Appts: Classroom Tchr., var. schls., & Brazosport Ind. Schl.; Past Pres., Mary Martha Bapt. Sunday Schl. Class., Freeport; Tex.; Histn., Alpha Delta Kappa, hon. soc. for women educators, 1970-74; Past Sergeant-at-Arms, Alpha Chapt., ibid; Histn., 16th Dist., Dept. of Tex. Veterans of For. Wars, 1973-74; Pres., Ladies Auxiliary No. 4341, Veterans of For. Wars, 1973-74. Mbrships. incl: Life Mbr., Tex. State Tchrs. Assn.; Tex. & Brazosport Classroom Tchrs. Assns.; NEA; Life Mbr., S.F. Austin PTA, 1968. Hons. incl: Presentation for 30 yrs. serv. as Brazosport tchr., 1973: Serv. on Schl. Textbook Comm., 1973-74; BEA Exec. Bd. Rep., Austin Elem., 1973-74. Address: 1606 W. 9th St., Freeport, TX 77541, U.S.A. 125.

SHIPPEY, Stanley Lawrason, b. 11 Dec. 1901. Clergyman. Educ: B.A., Eureka Coll., Ill., U.S.A., 1929; B.D., Lexington Theol. Sem., Ky., 1941. Ordained Clergyman, 1928. Appts: Min. of Christian Ds. of Christ, Newman, Ill., 1929-30, Maroa, Ill., 1930-32, Guelph, Ont., Canada, 1932-36, Winnipeg, Man., 1936-38, Sem., Ky., U.S.A., 1938-41, Brentwood, Pa., 1941-43, Valpariso, Ind., 1943-46, Kokomo, Ind., 1946-49 & Stow, Ohio, 1949-51; Salesman, Prentice Hall, 1952-55; Clergyman, Vanceburg, Ky., 1955-58, Georgetown, Ohio, 1958-61 & Kingston, Pa., 1961-62; Utd. Ch. of Christ Min., Springbrook, Pa., 1963-64 & Nuremburg, Pa., 1964-67. Mbrships. incl: Minl. Assn.; Pres., ibid, Guelph, Ont.,Canada, Valpariso, Ind., U.S.A. Vanceburg, Ky. & Georgetown, Ohio; Pres., Hort. Soc., Rodney, Ont., Canada; Sat Eve. Club, Valpariso, Ind.; Lions Int., Vanceburg, Ky.; Asst. Comm., ibid; Psi Alpha Lambda; Eureka Coll., Ill.; Laymen's Assn.; Susquehanna Assn., Pa.; Counselor & Dir., Utd. Christian Youth Mvmt.; Brown Co., ibid; Instnl. Rep., Boy Scouts Am., Kingston; Tchr. & Lectr., Young People's confs.; Speaker, Convens., Youth Rallies, H.S. Assemblies, Bus. Men's Clubs, Serv.Clubs, Men & Women's Clubs, Univ. Clubs. Radio appearances. Dial-A-Prayer & many Baccalaureate servs. Publs. incl: sev. articles in var. ch. publs. Hons. incl: 2 Citations for Pastoral Serv., Presidents Staff Prentice Hall, 1954-55; Assistance Comm. apptd. by Gov. of Ky., Lewis Co., 1957; Min.'s Pin, 1967. Address: 281 Ridout St., P.O. Box 165, Rodney, Ont., NOL 2C0, Canada, 2, 8, 57.

SHIPTON, Sidney Lawrence, b. 25 July 1930. Solicitor. Educ: LL.B., London Univ., 1951. Appts: Qualification as Solicitor, 1954; Pvte. Prac., 1955-; Gen. Sec., Zionist Fedn. of Gt. Britain & Ireland. Mbrships. incl: British Acad. Forensic Soc.; Medico Legal Soc.; Law Soc.; Royal Inst. Int. Affairs; Jewish Histl. Soc.; UN Assn. Publs: Towards a Practical Zionism; The Arab Refugee Problem, 2nd edit., 1971. Address: Rex House, 4/12 Regent St., London, SW1Y 4PG, U.K.

SHIRAEF, John Dragon II. Lecturer; Educator. Appts: Tchr., Detroit H.S's., Mich.; w. Detroit Times, 4 yrs.; Lectr., mostly on Russia, Mich., Ohio, Ind. schls. & clubs. Has given 4947 lectures, 1947-74. Mbr., Assn. of Lectr. Burs., Speakers, Statesmen, Actors & Educrs. Innovator, Compressed Method of Speech for use in H.S. lectrs. Travels: U.S.; Austria; Belgium; Canada; Czechslovakia; U.K.; Finland; France; Germany; Greece; Holland; Italy; Mexico; New Guinea; Norway; Poland; Russia; Sweden; Switzerland; Trieste; Turkey; Yugoslavia. Address: P.O. Box 451, Owosso, MI 48867, U.S.A. 57.

SHIRK, Frank Charles, b. 2 Apr. 1917. Librarian. Educ: B.A., Rutgers Univ., 1939; B.S.L.S., Drexel Univ., 1940. Appts. incl: Hd., Documents Dept., Rutgers Univ. Lib.; Documents Libn.-Hd., Engrng. Lib.-Assoc. Libn.-Acting Lib. Dir.-Lib. Dir., Va. Polytech. Inst., Blacksburg; Lib. Cons., State Coun. of Higher Educ. for Va.; Cataloger-Asst. Acquisitions Libn., Va. Polytech. & State Univ. Mbrships. incl: Pres., Va. Lib. Assn., 1965; Pres., Va. Chapt., Spec. Libs. Assn., 1968-69; Vice Chmn., Lib. Advsry. Comm., State Coun. of Higher Educ. for Va., 1968-70; AAUP. Publs: Guide to the Map Collection in the Carol M. Newman Library; Athletic Statistics of Virginia Polytechnic Institute 1872-1951; conthr. to profl. jrnls. Address: 111 Country Club Dr., S.E., Blacksburg, VA 24060, U.S.A. 2, 7, 15, 42, 46, 85, 128, 129, 130.

SHIRLEY, George Irving, b. 18 Apr. 1934. Singer (opera, concert, oratorio). Appearances incl: debut, Metropolitan Opera as ldng. tenor, 1961; Spoleto Festival, 1961; Santa Fe Opera, 1961; Teatro Colon, 1964; La Scala, 1965; Glyndebourne Festival, 1966; Royal Opera, Covent Gdn., 1967. Mbrships: Recording Sec., Am. Guild Musical Artists, 1963-73. Hons. incl: winner of Am. Opera Auditions, 1960; Metropolitan Opera Auditions, 1961; Disting. Alumni Award, Wayne St. Univ., 1967; Hon. Dr. Humanities, Wilberforce Univ., Ohio, 1967. Address: c/o Artists Int. Mgmt., 5 Regent's Park Rd., London NW1 7TL, U.K. 2.

SHNEOUR, Elie Alexis, b. 11 Dec. 1925. Research Neurologist; Educator; Administrator. Educ: B.A., Bard Coll., Columbia Univ., 1947; M.A., Univ. of Calif., Berkeley, 1955; Ph.D., Univ. of Calif., L.A., 1958. Appts. incl: Tchng. & Rsch. Asst., Univ. of Calif., 1953-58; Sr. Rsch. Fellow, Am. Heart Assn., 1958-62; Exec. Sec., Steering Comm. Mbr., Nat. Acad. Scis. Study Grp., 1962-65; Assoc. Prof. of Biol., Univ. of Utah, 1965-69; Vis. Rsch. Neurochem City of Hope Nat. Med. Ctr., 1969-71; Dir. of Rsch., Calbiochem, 1971-. Mbrships. incl: Life, AAAS; Am. Chem. Soc.; Am. Inst. Biological Scis.; N.Y. Acad. of Scis.; Am. Socs. Biolog. Chems. & Neurochem.; Int. Soc. for Neurochem.; Soc. for the Neuroscis.; IEEE; Soc. for Expmntl. Biol. & Med.; Sigma Xi; Phi Sigma. Author, The Malnourished Mind, (in preparation). Num. reports, reviews & articles in med. & scientific publs. Recip., Hon., Sc.D., Bard Coll., 1969. Address: 8492 Cliffridge Av., La Jolla, CA 92037, U.S.A. 2, 9, 128.

SHOCKLEY, Alonzo Hilton, Jr., b. 30 Sept. 1920. Education Administrator. Educ: Master's Degree, Mich. State Univ.; B.S., Delaware State Coll.; Advance Cert. in Admin./Supervision, N.Y. Univ.; Postgrad. work at N.Y. Univ.; Univ. of Delaware; Univ. of Maine; Boston Univ.; Univ. of Puerto Rico; Queens Coll.; Univ. of Bridgeport; Adelphi Univ. Appts. incl: Asst. Elem. Prin. (K-6) & Bldg. Prin. (4-6), Wyandanch, L.I., N.Y., 1962-64; Assoc. Admnstr., N.Y. Educ. Dept., Albany, N.Y., 1964-65; Educ. Coord., Nassau Co. Commn. of Econ. Opportunity, Garden City, L.I., N.Y., 1965-66; Dir., State & Fed. Progs., Freeport, ibid, 1966-. Mbrships. incl: Phi Delta Kappa; Kiwanis Club; Lions Club; L.I. Curric. Dirs. Assn.; Educ. Chmn., Ctrl. L.I. Br., NAACP; U.N. Assn. U.S.A. (U.N. Day Chmn. Suffolk Co.; Bd. of Dirs., Int. Sonnenberg Assn. of N.Y.); Educational Rsch. Assn. of N.Y. State; Fed. Legislative Comm., Am. Assn. for Schl. Admnstrs. Publs: Better Education Through Community Involvement in Freeport, New York 1969-70; That a Child May Reach In Freeport, New York (both w. R.S. Dunn). Address: 290 Fulton St., N. Babylon, L.I., NY 11703, U.S.A. 15, 130.

SHOE, Charles Ronald, b. 21 May 1933. Commercial Banker. Educ: Univ. of N.C., U.S.A. Appts. incl: Asst. Cashier, Citizens & Southern Nat. Bank, Columbia, S.C., 1961-67; Asst. V.P., ibid, 1968; V.P., City Exec. Off., & Mbr., Advsry. Bd. of Dirs., Citizens & Southern Nat. Bank, Sumter, S.C., 1969-. Num. mbrships. incl: Pres., Dir., & other Offs., Columbia Jaycees; State Chmn. & Treas., S.C. Jaycees; U.S. Jaycees & Jr. Chmber Int.; Chmn., Loan Comm., Bus. Dev. Corp. of S.C.; State Treas., S.C. Chapt., Nat. Multiple Sclerosis Soc.; Bd. of Dirs., Gtr. Columbia Chmbr. of Comm.; Bd. of Dirs., & Chmn., sev. comms., Gtr. Sumter Chmbr. of Comm.; Instr., Am. Inst. of Banking; S.C. Bankers Assn.; Sumter Area Tech. Educ. Commn. Originator, Jaycee Forum, TV discussion prog. Hons. incl: Cert. of Merit, U.S. Jaycees, 1968; J.C.I. Senator, 1971. Address: 5 Fern Court, Sumter, SC 29150, U.S.A. 117, 125.

SHOE, Thomas Eugene, b. 10 Dec. 1943. General Manager. Educ: B.S., Mars Hill Coll., 1962-66. Asst. Gen. Mgr.-Gen. Mgr., Pike's Drug Stores, Inc., 1966-. Mbrships: Dir., Chmn., Special Projs. & Past V.P., Concord Boys Club; Past Pres., Noon Optimist Club; Past Dir., 1st & 2nd V.P. & State Dir., Concord Jaycees; Bd. Mbr. & Past Co. Chmn. & Greater Peidmont Chapt. Chmn., March of Dimes; Fndr. & Chmn., Nat. Cabarrus 500 Festival; Pres. & Past Sec. & Treas., Tusk & Trunk Club; Pas Chmn. & V.-Chmn., Miss Cabarrus Co. Pageant; Cabarrus Co. Repub. Exec. Comm.; Cabarrus Co. Personnel Assn.; Dist. Boys Scout Coun. Advsry Comm.; Cabarrus Co. United Fund Advsry. Bd. Hons: Presidential Citation, Optimist Int., 1971; Disting. Pres., Local Optimist Club, 1970-71; Jaycees Awards: Spoke, 1967; Spark, 1969; '73; Key Man Awards, 1970-73; Jaycee of Yr., 1970; Comm. Chmn. of Yr., 1971-72; Proj. of Yr., 1972-73; DSA Young Man of Yr., 1971; Serv. Awards, March of Dimes, 1970, '71; Nominee, 5 Outstanding Young Men, N.C., 1971. Address: P.O. Box 3394, Concord, NC 28025, U.S.A. 117, 125.

SHOEMAKER, Benjamin H., III, b. 27 Aug. 1901. Investment Banker. Educ: Ph.B., Yale Univ., 1923; Haverford Coll.; Univ. of Pa. Appts. incl: Purser, Steamer Stanley, Barber Line, 1923-24; Clerk, Int. Mercantile Marine, N.Y., 1925; Sales Mgr., Benjitt Shoemaker Inc., 1926-29; Clark Printing House, 1930-32; Investment Banker, C.C. Collings & Co. Inc., 1932-, Phila. V.P., 1949, Bd. of Dirs., 1952- & Vice Chmn., 1971-. Mbrships. incl: Former Bd. Mbr., Colonial Soc. of Pa., Welcome Soc. of Pa., Mil. Order Loyal Legion; Pa. Chapt. Sons of the Revolution, Franklin Inst., Acad. of Natural Scis., Phila. Yale Club, Phila. Cricket Club, Erie Zool. Soc. Publs. iincl: Shoemaker Pioneers, 1955; author of num. mag. articles. Hons. incl: Ky. Col., 1966; Inventor of the game Shoemaker Solitaire, 1928; Ldr., Hunting Expedition across Rhodesia on foot, 1928-29. Address: 515 Locust Ave., Germantown, PA 19144, U.S.A.

SHOEMAKER, David P., b. 12 May 1910. Chemist; University Professor. Educ: B.A., Reed Coll., Portland, Ore., 1942; Ph.D., Calif. Inst. of Technol., 1947. Appts: Guggenheim Mem. Fellow, Inst. Theoretical Phys., Copenhagen, Denmark, 1947-48; Sr. Rsch. Fellow in Chem., Calif. Inst. of Technol., U.S.A., 1948-51; Asst. Prof.-Prof. of Chem., Mass. Inst. of Technol., 1951-70; U.S.A. Co-ed., Acta Crystallographica, 1964-69; Prof. & Chmn., Dept. of Chem., Ore. State Univ., Corvallis, 1970-. Mbrships. incl: Exec. Comm., Int. Union of Crystallography; Am.

Crystallographic Assn.; Pres., ibid, 1970; Am. Acad. Arts & Scis.; Sigma Xi; Phi Beta Kappa. Co-author, Experiments in Physical Chemistry, 1962, 3rd edit., 1974. Over 60 sci. papers, var. jrnls. & books. Address: Dept. of Chemistry, Oregon State Univ., Corvallis, OR 97331, U.S.A. 2, 14, 50.

SHOEMAKER, Lois Meier, b. 20 Oct. 1899. Biology Teacher; Author. Educ: A.B., Wellesley Coll., Mass., U.S.A., 1921; M.A. Tchrs. Coll., Columbia Univ., N.Y., 1924; Ph.D., Columbia Univ., 1930. Appts: Biol. Tchr., H.S., Framingham, Mass., 1921-23; Biol. Tchr., H.S., White Plains, N.Y., 1924-26; Prof. of Sci., N.J. State Tchrs. Coll., Trenton, 1929-59. Mbrships: Fellow, AAAS; Nat. Geog. Soc.; Nat. Assn. for Rsch. in Sci. Tchng.; Trenton Naturalist Club; Past Pres., Nat. Coun. for Supvsrs. of Elem. Sci.; Kappa Delta Pi. Pubsl: Natural Science Education in the German Elementary Schools, 1930; Essentials of Biology (w. W.H.D. Meier), 1931; Wonderworld of Science (w. Meister & Keirstead), 1943; Bulletins on N.J. wildlife. Hons. incl: Am.-German Exchange Fellowship, Frankfurt-am-Main, Germany, 1927-28; Sci. Educ. Recognition Award, 1967. Address: 515 Ewingville Rd., Trenton, NJ 08638, U.S.A. 5, 132.

SHONEKE, Frances Maudine Martin, b. 16 July 1916. High School Teacher. Educ: A.B., Limestone Coll,; grad. work, Univ. of Miami, Univ. of S.C. Appts: Elementary Tchr.; H.S. Tchr. & Libn.; Sponsor of French Club, Quill & Scroll; Sponsor of H.S. newspaper & literary mag.; Feature Ed., The Challenge, educl. publ. Mbrships: Publicity Chmn., Am. Legion Auxiliary; Organizer & Past Pres., PTA; Pres., Homemakers' Club; NEA; AATF; SCEA; SISPA; Chmn., March of Dimes; Pres.'s Coun., White House Conf. Comm.; Cowpens Garden Club; Order of Eastern Star; Kappa Delta Epsilon. Edit. comments & contbnrs., local hist. comments, poems, newspapers & jrnls. Cowpens H.S. Tchr. of Yr., 1967. Address: Box 391, Pacolet Rd., Cowpens, SC 29330, U.S.A. 125.

SHOOK, John Louis, b. 23 May 1908. Lawyer. Educ: LL.B., Southern Meth. Univ. Appts: Mbr., law firm, Smithdeal, Shook, Spence & Bowyer, Dallas, Tex., 1931-36; Smithdeal, Shook & Lefkowitz, 1937-40; Shook & Shook, 1940-55; Locke, Purnell, Boren, Laney & Neely, 1955-71; Own prac., 1972-; Underwriting Mbr., Lloyd's of London, 1973-; Dir., E. Dallas Bank; Dir., Repub. Fin. Servs. Inc. & subsidaries; Dir. & Sec., McIngvale Assocs. Gen. Agcy. Inc. & subsidiaries. Fellow, Am. Coll. Trial Lawyers. Mbrships. incl: Chmn., Bd., State Bar of Tex., 1964-65; Southwestern Legal Fndn.; Am. Bar Assn.; Dallas Bar Assn.; Dir., Int. Acad. Trial Lawyers, 1973-77; Int. Assn. Ins. Counsel; Fed. of Ins. Counsel; Am. Judicature Soc.; Delta Theta Phi; Delta Sigma Phi. Address: Park Towers, 3310 Fairmount, Apt. 5-D, Dallas, TX 75201, U.S.A. 2, 7, 113, 116, 125.

SHORROSH, Anis A., b. 6 Jan. 1933. International Baptist Evangelist. Educ: Dip., Clarke Mem. Coll., Newton, Miss.; B.A., Miss. Coll., Clinton, Miss.; M.Divinity, New Orelans Bapt. Theological Sem., New Orleans, La. Appts: Evangelistic Wkr. & Pastor, Jordan, 1959-63; Pastor, Jerusalem Bapt. Ch., Jerusalem, Jordan, 1964-66; World Evangelist, HQ Mobile, Ala., U.S.A., 1966-; Goodwill Ambassador for Mobile, Ala., around the world, 1969; Main Spkr. at Nagaland, India Bapt. Centenary celebration, instead of Dr. Billy Graham, 1972. Mbrships: Pres., Int. Club, Miss. Coll., Clinton, 1956; Official deleg., Jordan

Baptists, at Youth Congress, Beirut, Lebanon, 1963. Publs. incl: The Ultimate Reality, Basic Gospel Messages, 1971, reprinted 1973; The Fig Tree, The Second Coming & Israel Today, 1974. Documentary Films: Come with Me to the Holy Land; Come with Me to Jordan; Come with Me to India. Address: 3767 Airport Blvd., Mobile, AL 36608, U.S.A. 125.

SHORT, (Right Rev.) H.V.R., b. 24 Jan. 1914. Clerk in Holy Orders, Anglican Church of Canada. Educ: B.A., Univ. of Toronto; L.Th., B.D., Trinity Coll., Univ. of Toronto. Appts. incl: Deacon, 1943; Priest, 1944; Lectr. & Sr. Tutor, Trinity Coll., 1947-51; Rector, Holy Trinity, Cochrane, Ont., 1951-56; Examining Chap. to Bishop of Moosonee, Exec. Comm. of Diocese, Gen. Synod (1955-). Provincial Synod. & Rural Dean of Cochrane, 1951-56; Rector, St. Barnabas' Ch., St. Catharines, Ont., 1956-63; Examining Chap. & Rural Dean, Diocese of Niagara, 1956-63; Canon, Christ's Ch. Cathedral, Hamilton, Ont., 1962-63; Dean of Sask., 1963-70; Archdeacon of Prince Albert, 1966-70; Bishop of Sask., 1970-. Mbrships. incl: Chmn. of Bd., Prince Albert Regional Community Coll.; Senate, Univ. of Emmanuel Coll., Saskatoon, Sask.; Pres., Coun., Coll. of Emmanuel & St. Chad, Saskatoon. Hons. incl: Prize for best degree, Trinity Coll., Toronto, 1941; D.D. ibid, 1971. Address: Bishopsthorpe, 427 21st St. W., Prince Albert, S6V 4J5, Sask., Canada. 88.

SHORT, Robert Clyde, b. 3 Dec. 1925. Electrical Engineer. Educ: B.Sc., Univ. of Toronto, Ont., Canada, 1949. Appts. incl: Canadian Army, 1943-45; Ont. Dist. Mgr., Ferranti-Packard Elec. Co. Ltd., Toronto, 1952-60; Marketing Mgr. for Canada, Edwards of Canada Ltd., Owen Sound, Ont., 1960-63; Pres., ibid, 1963-64; Pres., Edwards Co., Inc., Norwalk, Conn. U.S.A., 1964-67; Fndr. & Pres., St. Lawrence Coll. of Applied Arts & Technol., Kingston, Ont., 1967-70; Pres., Canadian Cable TV Assn., Ottawa, Ont., 1970-. Num. mbrships. incl: Chmn., Tech. Study Grp. on Elec. Power Distribution in Ind., IEEE; Exec. Comm., Engrng. Inst. of Canada, 1951-53; Canadian Elec. Assn.; Assn. of Profl. Engrs., Ont.; Canadian Legion; Rideau Club, Ottawa; Dir., Canadian Club, Ottawa. Author, Take Charge of Your Career, 1970. Hons: Nesbitt Gold Medal, & R.A. Bryce Engrng. Schlrship., Univ. of Toronto Schls., 1943. Address: 60 Aleutian Rd., Ottawa, Ont., K2H 7C8, Canada. 16, 88.

SHOULBERG, Harry, b. 25 Oct. 1903. Artist. Educ: CCNY; Art Students League; John Reed Schl. Mbrships: Audubon Artists; Am. Soc. of Contemporary Artists; N.J. Soc. of Painters & Sculptors;Artists Equity. Permanent Collects: Metropol. Mus.; Balt. Mus.; San Fran Mus.; Carnegie Inst.; N.J. Mus.; Denver Mus.; Norfolk Mus. Hons. incl: Tanner Prize; Emily Lowe Award; Jane Peterson Prize; Grumbacher Award. Address: 567 Ave. of the Americas, N.Y., NY, U.S.A. 2, 6, 37, 55.

SHOUP, Carl Sumner, b. 26 Oct. 1902. Economist. Educ: A.B., Stanford Univ., Calif., U.S.A., 1924; Ph.D., Columbia Univ., N.Y.C., 1930. Appts: Prof., Econs., Columbia Univ., 1931-71; Dir., Twentieth Century Fund Survey of Taxation in U.S.A., 1935-37; Dir., Tax Missions to Japan, 1949-50, Venezuela, 1959-60, & Liberia, 1969; Dir., Int. Econ. Integration & Capital Tax Projs., Columbia Univ., 1962-65; Inter-Regional Advsr. on Tax Reform Planning, UN, 1971-74; Vis. Rsch. Prof., Dalhousie Univ., Halifax, N.S., Canada, 1974-75. Mbrships: Pres., Nat. Tax Assn., 1949-50; Pres., Int. Inst. of Pub. Finance, 1950-53; Am. Econ. Assn.; Fiscal & Financial

Comm., European Econ. Community; Pres.'s Commn. on Budget Concepts, 1967-68. Publs: The Sales Tax in France, 1930; Principles of National Income Analysis, 1947; Ricardo on Taxation, 1960; The Tax System of Brazil, 1965; Federal Estate & Gift Taxes, 1966; Public Finance, 1969. Hons: Doctoral Degree, Univ. of Strasbourg, France, 1967; Order of the Sacred Treasure, 2nd class, Emperor of Japan, 1968. Address: Sandwich, NH 03270, U.S.A. 2, 3, 14.

SHRAGAI, Eliyahu, b. 8 Jan. 1929. Teacher; Journalist; Economist. Educ: Tchrs' Trng Coll., Jerusalem, Israel; Univ. of Geneva, Switzerland. Appts: Tchr., Israel; Jrnlst., Israeli Knesset (Parliament); Ed., Toren; Dir., Press, Pub. Rels., & Publicity, Zim Israel Navigation Co. Ltd., Haifa. Mbrships: Israel Assn. of Grads. in Soc. Sci. & Humanities; Chmn., Israel Soc. of Eds. of Periodicals; Mgmt. Comm., Pub. Rels. Assn. of Israel; Int. Pub. Rels. Assn.; Israel Mgmt. Ctr.; Mgmt. Comm., Assn. d'Amitié Haifa-Anvers et Israël-Belgique, Haifa. Address: P.O. Box 1723, Haifa, Israel.

SHULKO, Patricia Lee (Mrs. Richard Shulko), b. 24 Sept. 1934. Dietitian & Professor. Educ: B.S., M.S., Mich. State Univ., U.S.A. Appts: Prog. Coord., Dairy Couns., Ga.; Instr., Distributive Nursing Med. Coll., Ga. Mbrships: Pi Beta Phi; Past Nat. Pres., Kappa Beta; Omnicron Nu; Am. Dietetic Assn.; Am. Home Econs. Assn.; Med. Coll. Ga. Fac. Club; Ga. Heart Assn.; Ga. Nutrition Coun. Address: 3126 Exeter Rd., Augusta, GA 30904, U.S.A. 76, 125.

SHULL, Charles William, b. 26 May 1904. College Professor; Political Scientist. Educ: B.A. Ohio Wesleyan, 1926; M.A., Ohio State Univ., 1927; Ph.D., ibid, 1929. Appts. incl: Instr., Univ. of Ky., 1929-30; Instr., Wayne State Univ., 1930-36; Asst. Prof., 1936-43; Assoc. Prof., 1943-50; Prof., 1950-69; Prof. Emeritus, 1969-. Mbrships: Am. Pol. Sci. Assn.; V.P., Midwest Pol. Sci. Assn., 1953; AAUP; Hansard Soc.; Nat. Pres., Pi Sigma Alpha, 1940-46. Publs. incl: Legislative Apportionment, 1943, '52, '62; Co-author, Introduction to Political Science, 1950; Your Government, 1951; American Legislatures, 1954. Fndr., Midwest Jrnl. Pol. Sci.; Mgng. Ed., ibid, 1957-60; Bd. of Eds., 1960-69; Book Review Ed., Soc. Sci., 1947-62. Address: 8900 E. Jefferson, Apt. 304, Detroit, MI 48214, U.S.A.

SHUMAN, Alan M., b. 12 Nov. 1929. Periodontist; Associate Professor. Educ: B.S., Univ. of Mass., 1951; D.M.D., Tufts Dental Schl., 1955; Cert. in Periodontol., Schl. of Grad. Study, Boston Univ., 1963. Appts: Staff Mbr., Univ. Hosp., 1968-; Staff Mbr., Beth Israel Hosp., 1968-; Asst. Prof.-Assoc. Prof., Boston Univ. Schl. of Grad. Dentistry, 1968-; Advsry. Coun., Blue Cross, Blue Shield, 1970-. Mbrships: Gtr. Boston Dental Soc. Exec. Bd., ibid, 1969-73; Brookline Dental Soc.; Treas. & Soc.; Exec. Bd., ibid, 1969-73; Brookline Dental Soc.; Treas. & Sec., ibid, 1972-73; Am. Dental Assn.; Am. Acad. Periodontol.; Metropol. Dental Soc.; Robert R. Andrews Hon. Soc.; Scribe, ibid, 1954-55; Alpha Omega; Pres., ibid, 1954-55. Contbr. to profl. jrnls. & publs. Guest Lectr., E. African Dental Soc., 1972. Lectr. num. State Soc. & Acad. meetings. Address: 111 Radcliffe Rd., Weston, MA 02193, U.S.A. 6.

SHUMIATCHER, Morris Cyril, b. 20 Sept. 1917. Lawyer. Educ: B.A., Univ. of Alta., Canada, 1940; LL.B., 1941; LL.M., Univ. of

Toronto, 1942; Dr. Juris, 1945. Appts. incl: Served w. RCAF, 1943-45; Law Off., Dept. of Atty.-Gen., Sask., Counsel to Cabinet of Province, Personal Advsr. & Asst. to Premier of Sask., 1945-49; Counsel for Sask., var. tax cases, labour litigation, & in pipeline hearings, 1945-49; Named King's Counsel, Sask., 1948; Gen. Prac. of Law, Sask., Alta., & B.C., 1949-; Lectr., guest speaker, var. orgs.; Has daily radio prog. on current affairs & TV prog. Mbrships. incl: Law Socs. of Provinces of Alta., B.C., & Sask.; Canadian Bar Assn.; Chmn., Civil Liberties Sect., ibid, 1971-74; Dir., Sask. Ctr. of Arts, 1969-73; Dir., Inst Int. Affairs. Publs. incl: Welfare, Hidden Backlash, 1971. Recip., var. profl. & acad. hons. Address: Haldane House, 2100 Scarth St., Regina, Sask., Canada.

SHUMWAY, Mary Louise, b. 21 Aug. 1926. Writer; Educator. Educ: A.B., Univ. of Chgo., 1957; M.A., San Fran. State Coll., 1965; Ph.D., Univ. of Denver, 1971. Appts: Instr., Engl., George Williams Coll., Chgo.; Instr., Coord. of Undergard. Studies & Dean of Women, Anthro. Coll., San Fran. Art Inst.; currently Prof. of Engl., Univ. of Wis., SP. Mbrships: AAUP; Assn. of Univ. of Wis., Facs.; Assoc. Fellow, Soc. for the Arts, Relig. & Contemporary Culture; Robert Frost Fellow in Poetry, Bread Loaf, 1969; MacDowell Fellow, The MacDowell Colony, 1973. Publs: Song of the Archer, and other poems, 1964; Headlands, 1972; poems in var. jrnls. Hons: Acad. of Am. Poets Prize, SFSC, 1965; Acad. of Am. Poets prize, DU, 1969. Address: Dept. of Engl., Univ. of Wis.-SP, Stevens Point, WI 54481, U.S.A. 5, 30, 138.

SHUNAMI, Shlomo, b. 4 Oct. 1897. Librarian; Teacher. Educ: Am. Lib. Schl., Paris, France. Appts: Libn., Jewish Nat. & Univ. Lib., 1921-61; Guest Libn., Hebrew Union Coll. Lib., Cincinnati, Ohio, 1929-30, & Harvard Univ. Lib., 1960-61; Chief Bibliographer, Encyclopaedia Judaica, 1967-69; Acting Libn., Judaic Lib., Yeshiva Univ., N.Y., 1970-71; Tchr., Grad. Lib. Schl., Hebrew Univ. Jerusalem, Israel, 1956-69. Mbrships: Chmn., Ruth Kahan Eber Fund for Librarianship; Lib. Terms Commiss., Hebrew Lang. Acad. Publs: Bibliography of Jewish Bibliographies, 1965; About Libraries & Librarianship, 1969. Winner, Israel Schapiro Award, Hebrew Univ., 1965. Address: 25 Alfasi St., Jerusalem, Israel. 55, 94.

SHUSTER, Carl N., b. 16 Feb. 1890. University Professor. Educ: B.S., Tchrs. Coll., 1915; M.S., 1918; Ph.D., Columbia Univ., 1940. Appts. incl: Hd., Maths. Dept., Orange H.S., N.J.; Hd., Math. Dept., N.J. State Coll., Trenton, 1929; Vis. Prof., Columbia Univ., Emeritus, 1956; Hd., Math. Dept., Tampa Univ.; Coll. of Adv. Sci.; Adirondack Southern Schl., Univ. of Fla., Gainsville. Mbrships. incl: Bd. Dirs., Assn. Math. of N.J., 20 yrs.; Pres., Assn. of Maths. Tchrs. of N.J.; Dir.-Comm. Chmn.-Pres., Nat. Coun. Tchrs. of Maths.; Am. Maths. Assn. Publs. incl: Field Work in Mathematics; Three sets of arithmetic books; Scribners Geometry; Functional Mathematics Series; num. papers in field. Holder of sev. patents. Hons: Columbia Scholastic Gold Key, 1938; Alumni Citation, Trenton Coll., 1942. Address: 2035 26A North, St. Petersburg, FL 33713, U.S.A. 2, 28.

SHUTTLEWORTH, Ronald Gordon, b. 1 Jan. 1913. Scientist; Diplomat. Educ: B.Sc., Rhodes Univ., Grahamstown, S. Africa, 1933; M.Sc., Univ. of Cape Town, 1938; Ph.D., ibid, 1941; Num. appts. incl: Lectr., Chem., Univ. of Cape Town, 1941-43; Chief Chem., Petersen Ltd., Cape Town, 1943-48; Tech. Mgr., Vitamin Oils Ltd., Cape Town, 1948-49; Hd., Liaison Div., Nat. Chem. Rsch. Lab., S. Africa Coun.

for Scientific & Indl. Rsch., Pretoria, 1950-52; Scientific Attache, S. African Embassy, Wash. D.C., U.S.A., 1953-59; Scientific Counsellor, ibid, 1960-; Hd., Indl. Rsch. & Dev. Div., S. African Coun. for Scientific & Indl. Rsch., Pretoria, 1960-64. Mbrships: Fellow, Royal Inst. of Chem., London, U.K; Cosmos Club, Wash. D.C., U.S.A. Publs: Rsch. papers in sci. jrnls. Recip., U.S. Antarctic Serv. Medal, 1974. Address: Silver Leaves, Rhodes Dr., Constantia, Cape Province, South Africa 7800. 2, 39.

SHWADRAN, Benjamin, b. 14 Sept. 1907. Historian; Political Scientist. Educ: B.A., M.A., Ph.D., Clark Univ., Worcester, Mass.; Rsch. Fellow, Hebrew Univ., Inst. of Jewish Studies, Jerusalem, 1925-27. Appts: Rsch. Assoc., E.S.C.O. Fndn., 1942-46; Lectr., Middle Eastern Studies, New Schl. for Soc. Rsch., 1942-57; Prof., Middle Eastern Studies, & Dir., Middle East Inst., Dropsie Univ., Phila., 1958-62; Prof., Middle Eastern Studies, Yeshiva Univ., 1963-66; Vis. Prof., Tel Aviv Univ., 1968-69; Prof., Pol. Sci., Hofstra Univ., 1970-. Mbrships: Pol. Sci. Assn.; Sec.-Treas., Coun. for Middle Eastern Affairs. Publs. incl: General Index Middle Eastern Affairs, 1968; The Middle East, Oil & the Great Powers, 1955, 3rd edit. 1973. Contbr., Former ed. Middle Eastern Affairs; contbr. to other profl. jrnls. Address: 8 Rehov Yaakov Cohen, Jerusalem, Israel. 55.

SHWAYDER, King David, b. 21 Aug. 1910. Business Executive. Educ: Univ. of Colo & Pa.; Appts: Credit Mgr., Denver Off., Samsonite Corp., 1930-34; Exec. V.P., ibid, 1960-61; Pres., 1961-; Asst. Gen. Mgr., Detroit Off., 1934-46; V.P. & Gen. Mgr., ibid, 1946-60. Mbrships. incl: Bd. Dirs., Beatrice Foods Co., United Bank of Denver, Pub. Serv. Co. of Colo.; Pizza Hut; Bd. Trustees, Univ. of Denver; Regional Co-Chmn., Nat. Conf. of Christians & Jews; Dir., Colo. Assn. of Commerce & Ind.; Boy Scouts Am.; Denver Advsry. Coun. & Nat. Coun.; Dir., United Negro Coll. Fund Inc.; Rotary Club, Denver. Recip., Nat. Brotherhood Award, Nat. Conf. Christians & Jews, 1973. Address: Samsonite Corp., 11200 E. 45th Ave., Denver, CO 80217, U.S.A. 2, 9, 139.

SIBIRZEFF, Toivo (L R.), b. 17 May 1923. Journalist; Public Relations Administrator; Industrial Executive. Appts. incl: Ed., var. Swedish newspapers, 1940-47; United Press, 1950; V.P. Pub. Affairs, Info. Bur. of Pvte. Enterprise in Sweden, 1955; Hd., P.R. Dept., Swedish Bankers Assn., 1956-69; Hd., P.R. & Info., Stockholm Enskilda Bank, 1959-70; V.P., Hd. of Pub. Affairs & Communications, Swedish Match Co., 1970-. Mbrships: Swedish P.R. Assn., Journalists' Union, Publicists' Club; Int. P.R. Assn. Publr., econ. & pol. subjects. Articles, for. pol. Address: Swedish Match Co., P.O. Box 16 100, S-103 22 Stockholm 16, Sweden. 24.

SIBLEY, Alden Kingsland, b. 3 Jan. 1911. Retired Major General; Business Executive. Educ: B.S., U.S. Mil. Acad., W. Pt., N.Y., U.S.A., 1933; B.A., Univ. of Oxford, U.K., 1936. Num. appts. incl: Col., War Dept. Gen. Staff, & Off. Sec. of Army, 1945-52; Chief Strategic Logistics Br., SHAPE-NATO, Paris, France, 1952-55; Dir. of Educ., Nat. War Coll. Fac., 1955-57; Brigadier Gen., Div. Engr., U.S. Army, New England, 1957-60; Maj. Gen., Dpty. Chief, U.S. Mil. Assistance Advsry Grp., Vietnam, 1960-61; Cmdng. Gen., U.S. Army Mobility Cmd., 1962-64; Dpty. Chie, Staff Logistics, U.S. Army, Europe, 1964-66; Cmdng. Gen., XI U.S. Army Corps, 1966-67; Dpty. Cmdng. Gen., 5th U.S. Army, 1967-68; Exec. Asst. to Bd. Chmn., & Chief Exec. Off., Champion Int. Corp., N.Y.C., 1968-. Num.

mbrships. incl: AAAS; Am. Soc. of Civil Engrs.; Past Nat. Dir., Soc. of Am. Mil. Engrs.; Am. Ordnance Assn.; Am. Mil. Inst.; Am. Security Coun.; SHAPE Offs. Assn.; Past Dir., World Affairs Coun., Boston, Mass.; Trustee, Coll. of Adv. Sci., Canaan, N.H.; Mass. Chapt., Sons of the Am. Revolution; Assn. of Am. Rhodes Schlrs.; Sigma Xi; Tau Beta Pi. Publs: Num. contbns. to mil. & other jrnls. Lectures delivered at sev. univs. & mil. colls. Hons. incl: O.B.E.; French Legion of Honor; Croix de Guerre w. Palm; Num. campaign medals & other Am. mil. decorations. Address: 775 Park Ave., N.Y., NY 10021, U.S.A. 2, 8, 14.

SIBLEY, D. Jacobi Jr., b. 5 Mar. 1913. Physician. (retd.). Educ: B.A., Univ. of Tex., 1933; M.D., Univ. of Tex. Schl. of Med., 1937. Appts: Med. Officer, AUS, 1940-48; Civilian Gen. Prac., Ft. Stockton, Tex., 1949-61; Postgrad. Student, Univ. of Tex. Postgrad. Schl. of Med., 1961-62; Special Rsch. Assoc., Clayton Fndn. Biochem. Inst., Univ. of Tex., 1962-65; Dir., Med. Rsch., Drugs Plastic Toxol. & Rsch. Schl. of Pharmacy, ibid, 1965-71. Mbrships. incl: AMA; Travis Co. Med. Soc.; Tex. Med. Assn.; Fndr., Charter Pres., Ft. Stockton Hist. Soc.; Southern Med. Assn.; Pres., Austin-Tex. Br., Engl. Speaking Union, 1967-68; Trustee, Austin Environmental Coun., Bd. of Advsrs., Environic Fndn. Int.; Bd. of Dirs., Am. Cancer Soc. for Tex., 1955-60; Life mbr., AAAS; Dir., Tex. Hist. Fndn., 1970; Tex. Acad. of Sci.; Alpha Epsilon Delta; Alpha Omega Alpha. Recip. of Bronze Star, 1945. Address: 2210 Windsor Rd., Austin, TX 78703, U.S.A. 7, 57, 128.

SICILIANO, Italo, b. 27 July 1895. University professor. Appts: Asst. Lectr., Univ. of Grenoble, 1920-1922; Prof., Italian Lit., Univ. of Budapest, 1922-23; Hd. of Cultural Affairs w. Hungary, 1922-1933; Prof., Univ. of Warsaw, 1933-35; Univ. of Paris, 1936-; Prof., French Lit., Univ. of Venice, 1936-70; Rector, Univ. of Venice, 1953-71. Mbrships: Pres., Ctr. of Culture & Civilization of the Cini Fndn.; Pres., Venice Biennial Art. Exhib.; Royal Belgian Acad.; Royal Acad., Barcelona; Venice Inst. of Sci. & Letters; Venice Acad.; Institut de France. Publs. incl: Lirici francesi del primo ottocento, 1945; Verlaine, 1946 & 1964; Molière, 1947; Corneille, 1950; Il romanticismo francese de Prévost ai nostri giorni, 1959; les chansons de geste et l'epopée, mythes, histoire, poèmes, 1968; Mes aventures postumes de François Villon, 1973. Hons. incl: Doct., Univs. of Paris & Grenoble; Kt., Grand Cross of the Italian Repub.; Légion d'honneur; Kt., Order of Arts & Letters; Gold Medal of Italian Culture; The Guizot Prize, French Acad.; Marzotto prize; Grand Prix du Rayonnement français, Académie Française, 1970; 'dei Lincie' Acad. prize for Hist. & Lit. Criticism, 1972; Montagne Prize, 1974-75. Address: Via S. Gregorio 335, Venice, Italy.

SIDELL, Frederick Russell, b. 27 July 1934. Physician. Educ: B.S., Marietta Coll., Ohio, 1956; M.D., N.Y. Univ., N.Y.C., 1960; Res., Internal Med., Cleveland Metropolitan Gen. Hosp., Cleveland, Ohio, 1961-64. Appts: w. U.S. Army, 1964-66; Chief, Clin. Investigation Br., Biomed. Lab., Edgewood Arsenal, Md., 1964-. Fellow, Royal Soc. of Hlth. Mbrships: AMA; Am. Soc. Pharmacol. & Experimtl. Therapeutics; Harford Co. Med. Assn.; Rsch. Soc. of Am. Author of approx. 40 sci. reports in Clinical Pharmacology. Address: 14 Brooks Rd., Bel Air, MD 21014, U.S.A. 125, 131.

SIDKY, Mohammad Osman, b. 12 Oct. 1914. Diplomat; Author; Poet. Educ: B.A., Kabul Univ., Afganistan, 1940; M.A., N.Y. Univ., U.S.A., 1952. Appts: Dir., Kabul Radio, 1940-44; Ed., Daily Newspaper, Anees, 1944-47; Mbr., UN Info. Off., 1948-59; Chief, Info. Off., Kabul Ctr., 1959-63; Dir., Info. Ctr., New Guinea, 1963-64; Dpty. Prem. Deleg. from Afganistan to UN, 1964-65; Min. of Info. & Culture, 1965-67; Sec.-Gen., Min. of For. Affairs, 1967-68; Afgan Ambassador to Turkey, 1968-70; Afgan Ambassador to China, 1970-73; Fac. of Law & Econs., Kabul Univ. Mbrships: Afgan Lit. Soc., 1938; Afgan Hist. Soc., 1939. Author of books, short stories, plays, poems, articles & translations. Recip., 1st Prize, Drama, 1939. Address: 1305 Dehboori, Kabul, Afghanistan.

SIEGEL, Benjamin M(orton), b. 26 Mar. 1916. Educator; Physicist. Educ: B.S., MIT, Cambridge, U.S.A., 1938; Ph.D., ibid, 1940. Appts. incl: Assoc. Sci., Weizmann Inst. of Sci., Rehovot, Israel, 1946-48; Assoc. Prof. of Applied & Engrng. Phys., Cornell Univ., Ithaca, N.Y., 1949-59; Prof., ibid, 1959-; Vis. Prof. of Experimental Phys., Hebrew Univ., Jerusalem, Israel, 1962-63; Vis. Fellow, Salk Inst. for Biol. Scis., La Jolla, Calif., 1970-71. Mbrships. incl: Dir., Electron Microscopy Soc. of Am., 1952-55, Pres., 1973; Am. Phys. Soc.; AAUP; Biophys. Soc.; Am. Jewish League for Israel; Am. Friends of the Hebrew Univ.; Sigma Alpha Mu; Sigma Xi. Publs: Modern Developments in Electron Microspcy, 1964; Ed., Electron Microsopy: Physical Aspects, 1974; Approx. 100 contbns. on electron microscopy to sci. jrnls. & encys. Address: Dept. of Applied & Engineering Physics, Clark Hall, Cornell Univ., Ithaca, NY 14850, U.S.A. 2, 6, 14.

SIEGEL, Herbert J., b. 7 May 1928. Business Executive. Educ: B.A., Lehigh Univ., Pa., 1950. Appts: V.P., Dir., Bev-Rich Products, Phila., 1955-56; V.P., Dir., Westley Inds., Cleveland, 1955-58; V.P., Dir., Phila. Ice Hockey Club, 1955-60; Bd. Chmn., Ft. Pitt Inds., Pitts., 1956-58, The Seeburg Corp., Chgo., 1958-60, Centlivre Brewing Corp., Ft. Wayne, 1959-61, & Gen. Artists Corp., N.Y., 1960-63; Pres., Gen. Artists Corp., 1960-65; Bd. of Dirs., Paramount Pictures Corp., N.Y., 1965-66, Chris-Craft Inds., Inc., 1967-; Bd. Chmn., Baldwin-Montrose Chem. Co., Inc., 1960, merged into Chris-Craft Inds., Inc., 1968; Bd. Chmn. & Pres., ibid, 1968-; Bd. of Dirs., Piper Aircraft Corp., 1971-. Address' Tower E., 190 E. 72nd St., N.Y., NY, U.S.A.

SIEGEL, Milton P., b. 23 July 1911. Foundation Official; Educator. Educ: Drake Univ. Appts: Dir., Fin. & Stats., Iowa Emerg. Relief Admin. & Treas., Iowa Rural Rehab. Admin., 1933-35; var. positions, last being Chief Fiscal Off., Farm Security Admin., U.S. Dept. of Agric., 1935-42; Asst. Treas., Dir. Off. for the Far East, UNRRA, 1944-45; w. Prodn. & Mktng. Admin., U.S. Dept. of Agric., 1945-47; Asst. Dir. Gen., WHO, Geneva, Switzerland, 1947-71; Chief Exec. Off., Fedn. of World Hlth. Fndns., ibid, 1973-; Pres., World Hlth., Fndn. of U.S.A.; Vis. Prof., Univ. of Mich., 1967; Cons., Univ. of N.C., 1970; Prof. of Int. Hlth., Univ. of Tex., Hlth. Sc. Ctr., Houston & Dir., S.-N. Ctr., 1971-. Mbrships: Am. Pub. Hlth. Assn.; AAAs; Am. Acad. of Political & Soc. Sci.; Soc. of Int. Dev. Publs: Mankind's Struggle for Survival in the 21st Century; num. reports & analyses for WHO. Recip. Sam Beber Award, 1960. Address: 1 Rue Viollier 1207, Geneva, Switzerland. 2, 9, 12, 34, 103.

SIEGMEISTER, Elie, b. 15 Jan. 1909. Composer. Educ: B.A., Columbia Univ.; Julliard Grad. Schl.; Pvte. study w. Wallingford Riegger, Nadia Boulanger. Appts: Instr., Brooklyn Coll.; Lectr., New Schl. for Soc. Rsch.; Dir., Am. Ballad Singers; Conductor, Pro Arte Symph.; Prof. of Music, Hofstra Univ., Composer-in-res., ibid. Mbrships: A.S.C.A.P.; Former V.P., Am. Music Ctr.; Chmn., Coun. of Creative Artists, Libs. & Museums; Am. Fedn. of Musicians.Compositions incl: Operas; Music for Braodway stage; Scores for films, TV & dance; Works for chorus, piano, solo instruments, band & over 100 songs; Chmbr. music inclng. 2 string quartets, 3 sonatas for violin & piano, & sextet for brass & percussion. Recip., 10 A.S.C.A.P. Awards, 1964-74. Address: 56 Fairview Ave., Great Neck, NY, U.S.A. 2, 4, 18.

SIGMON, Jackson M. Corporation President. Pres., Sigmon, Littner, Ross & Keenan, profl. corp. Mbrships: Pres., Northampton Co. Bar Assn., 1963; Original House of Delegs., Pa. Bar Assn., 1966-70; Bd. of Govs., ibid, 1971-74; Disciplinary Bd., Supreme Ct., 1973-; Pa. Soc.; Am. Bar Assn.; Am. Judicature Soc.; Defense Rsch. Inst.; Am. Trial Lawyers; Platform Comm., Republican Party, State of Pa. Address: 146 E. Broad St., Bethlehem, PA 18018, U.S.A. 2, 6.

SIGSTAD, John Stephen, b. 20 Oct. 1939. Archaeologist. Educ: B.A., Western State Coll. of Colo., Gunnison; M.A., Univ. of Colo., Boulder; Ph.D., Univ. of Mo., Columbia. Appts: Asst. Archaeologist, State Histl. Soc. of N.D., 1968; Asst. Prof. Anthropol., Univ. of S.D., 1969-73, Curator of Anthropol., W.H. Over Mus., 1969-; Commnr., S.D. Archaeological Commn., 1969-73; Dir., Archaeological Rsch. Ctr., S.D. & State Archaeologist, 1974-. Mbrships: Soc. Am. Archaeol.; Am. Anthropological Assn.; Archaeological Soc. of S.D.; Northwest Chapt., Iowa Archaeological Soc.; Wyo., Mont., & Minn. Archaeological Soc.; Sigma Xi. Articles & reports, co-ed., field notes. Hons: Grad. Fellowship, Nat. Inst. Mental Hlth., 1967; Nat. Sci. Fndn. Rsch. Trainee, 1969. Address: Archaeological Research Ctr., W.H. Over Museum, Univ. of S. Dakota, Vermillion, SD 57069, U.S.A.

SIGUION REYNA, Leonardo T., b. 18 Apr. 1921. Lawyer. Educ: Ateneo de Manila Univ., Philippines; LL.B., Univ. Sto. Tomas, ibid. Appts: Sr. Ptnr., Siguion Reyna, Montecillo & Ongsiako; Chmn., Bd., Philippine Match Co., Ltd.; Sandvik Philippines, Inc.; Centennial Trading Corp.; V.-Chmn., Bd., Warner Barnes & Co., Inc.; Dir., Philippine Airlines, Inc.; Goodyear Tyre & Rubber Co. of Philippines, Inc.; Scott Paper, ibid; Philippine Refining Co.; Standard (Philippines) Fruit Corp.; Int. Harvester MacLeod, Inc.; Rizal Commercial Banking Corp.; Dole (Philippines), Inc.; Richardson-Merrell (Philippines), Inc.; Deleg., Philippine Constitutional Conven., 1971. Mbrships: Rotary Club, Manila; Polo Club, ibid; Yacht Club, ibid; Philippine-Brit.Soc.; Casino Espanol de Manila. Recip. Order of White Elephant, Thailand. Address: 5th Floor, A. Soriano Bldg., Ayala Ave., Makati, Rizal, Philippines.

SIGURDSSON, Pórdur B., b. 9 July 1929. Electronic Data Processing Manager. Educ: Univ. of Iceland, 1949-52. Appts: Chief Acct. & Off. Mgr., Icelandic Agricl. Colonization & Land Off, 1948-71; Mng. Dir., Raftekjavezlunin Ltd., 1959-66; Maths. Tchr., Coll., Reykjavik, 1966-71; Electronic Data Processing Mgr., Agrick. Bank of Iceland, Reykjavik, 1972-; Mbr., Advsry. Bd., Datacentre of Icealndic Banks. Mbrships: Langholt Parish Coun., Reykjavik, 1970-; Exec. Comm., Reykjavik Football Club, 1951-54, 1955-59, & 1965-72. Publs: Ed., Icelandic translation of Int. Amateur Athletic Assn. Handbook, 1973; Articles on sport in newspapers & mags. Hons. incl: Icelandic Hammerthrowing Champion, 1950 & 1952-65, beating Icelandic record 12 times; Capt., Icelandic Nat. Athletic Team, 1955-60 & 1964; Sev. medals, Knattspyrnufélag Reykjavikur, 1961 & 1974, Athletic Union of Oceland, 1972, & Icelandic Sports Fedn., 1972. Address: c/o Búndarbanki Islands, Reykjavik, Iceland. 43.

SIGURDSSON, Sigurjón, b. 16 Aug. 1915. Commissioner of Police Educ: LL.B., Univ. of Iceland. Appts: Legal Advsr., Icelalandic Ins. Co., 1942-44; Dpty. Commnr. of Police, Reykjavik, 1944; Commnr., ibid, 1948; Chmn., Reykjavik Comm. of Pub. Hlth., 1947-70, Reykjavik Air Raid Precaution Comm., 1952-62, Special Traffic Law Comm., 1955- Nat. Traffic Coun., 1969-, Traffic Coun. ot Reykjavik, 1949-; Mbr., Nat. Civil Defence Coun., 1962-, Civil Defence Comm. of Reykjavik, 1962-. Mbrships: incl: life mbr., Int. Assn. Chiefs of Police; Assn. of Judges of Iceland; Assn. of Icelandic Lawyers. Hons. incl: Cmdr., Order of Icelandic Falcon; Cmdr., Order of Dannebrog, Denmark. Address: Police H.Q., Hverfisgata 115, Reykjavík, Iceland. 134.

SIHTOLA, Hannes, b. 3 July 1912. University Vice-President. Educ: M.Sc., Univ. of Helsinki, Finland, 1937; D.Sc., ibid, 1945. Appts: Rsch. Asst., Enso-Gutzeit Oy, 1937-40; Tchng. Asst., Univ. of Helsinki, 1940-51; Lectr,, Macromolecular Chem., ibid, 1952-; Hd., Dept. for Polymer (Cellusose) Cem., Finnish Pulp & Paper Rsch. Inst., 1947-; Asst. Dir., ibid, 1948-. Mbrships: incl: Gen. Sec. & Bd. Mbr., Finnish Acad. of Tech. Scis., 1967-; Finnish Paper Engrs. Assn.; Finnish Chem. Soc.; Tech. Assn. of Pulp & Paper Ind.; Am. Chem. Soc. Author, 100 sci. publs. Hons: Kt. 1st class, White Rose of Finland, 1967; Hon. Prof., 1973. Address: Finnish Pulp & Paper Research Institute, P.O. Box 136, 00101 Helsinki 10, Finland. 43, 50, 134.

SIKJOR, Soren, b. 25 Nov. 1904. Professor of Physics. Educ: Cand. mag., Univ. of Copenhagen, Denmark, 1929; Pedagogical Educ. studies, U.S.A., 1959, 1967. Appts: Master, The Metropol. Schl., Copenhagen, 1934; External Examiner in Physics, Univ. of Copenhagen, 1939; Hdmaster., Grammar Schl., Jutland, 1941, Copenhagen, 1948; Prof. of Physics, Royal Danish Schl. of Educl. Studies, 1960-72, retd. Mbrships: Pres., The Danish Soc. of Physics, 1958-60; O.E.E.C.'s Study Group in Physics, 1959; Pres., Groupe int. de recherche sur l'enseignement de la physique, 1969-72. Publs. incl: Elementer af Einsteins Relativitetsteori, 1938, 2nd edit. 1960; Pysik for Gymnasiet, I, II, III, (co-author), 1944, 6th edit. 1965; Klassisk mekanik med relativistisk afrunding, 1973. Contbr. to jrnls. Address: Harsdorffsvej 6A, 1874 Copenhagen V, Denmark.

SILBERSTEIN, Werner, b. 24 Nov. 1899. Physician. Educ: Studied Med., Univs. of Berlin & Freiburg, Germany. Appts. incl: Asst., Robert Koch Inst., Berlin, 1925-33; Bacteriologist, Hadassah Hosp., Jerusalem, 1933-38; Rsch. work, Microbiological Inst., Istanbul Univ., 1938-42; Dir., Govt. Ctrl. Labs. & Div. of Pub. Hlth. Labs., Min. of Hlth., Israel, 1948-64; Prof., Sci. Advsr., Robert Koch Inst., Berlin. Mbrships: Israel Microbiological Assn.; Union of Clin. Pathol., Israel. Publs: num. works on microbiological rsch. Hons: Calmette

Medal, 1963. Address: 5 Brenner St., Jerusalem, Israel.

SILBERT, Nathan Ernest, b. 6 Oct. 1908. Physician. Educ: Grad., Tufts Coll. Pre-med. Schl, 1928; A.B., Boston Coll., Mass., 1958; M.D., Coll. Physns. & Surgs., Kan. City Univ., 1933; Student, Harvard Univ. Schl. of Pub. Hlth, 1935-36; Special Student Harvard Coll., 1939-40; Clin. Fellow, Grad. Student. Dept of Dermatol., Mass. Gen. Hosp., 1951. Appts: Intern, Cambridge Relief Hosp., Mass. 1933-34; Gen. Prac., Med., Somerville, Mass., 1934-42; Served from Lt. - Major, U.S. Army, 1942-46; Specializing in allergic diseases, Lynn, ibid, 1946-; Allergy Serv., Out-patient Dept., Mass. Gen. Hosp., 1945-46; Dept. of Dermatol., Allgemeines Krankenhaus, Vienna, Austria, 1956; Cons. Allergist, Danvers State Hosp., Mass. U.S.A., Benjamin Stickney Cable Mem. Hosp., Ipswich, ibid, St. John's Hosp., Lowell, Saugus Gen. Hosp., Lynn Hosp.; Chief of Dept., Sr. Cons., Allergic Diseases, Lawrence Quigley Mem. Hosp. & Soldiers Home, Chelsea, Mass., St. Joseph's Hosp., Lowell. Mbrships: Mass. Dir., Myles Standish State Schl. for Mentally Defective Children; Pres. Nat. Allergy Seminar; Ambassador, Jewish Theol. of Am.; Bd. of Dirs., Allergy Fndn. of Am.; State Bd. of Registration of Nursing, Mass.; Dipl. Am. Bd. Clin. Immunol. & Allergy; Fellow, Am. Coll. Allergists, (V.P. 1973), Int. Assn. Allergol., Am. Coll. Chest Physns. (Chmn. Int. Comm. on Allergy, 5th Int. Congress Diseases Chest, Tokyo, Japan, 1958; Sec. Comm. on Allergol., 6th Int. Congress, Vienna, Austria, 1960); Am. Assn. for Clin Immunol. & Allergy; Past Pres., Assn. of Convalescent Homes & Hosps. for Asthmatic Children; Mass. Med. Soc.; Fellow, Am. Acad. Allergy; Am. Geriatric Soc.; Am. Med. Writers Assn.; New England Pediatric Soc.; Am. Thoracic Soc.; Harvard Club, Boston; Yorick Club, Lowell; Jewish Relig. (Dir. & V.P., temple, Pres., temple). Contbr. of articles in field. Recip. Zeugnis in Allergic Diseases, Univ. of Vienna, Austria, 1958, & Awards from Jewish Theol. Sem. 1971, '72. Address: Allergy Med. Assocs., Inc., 214, Ocean St., Lynn, MA 01902, U.S.A. 6.

SILER, Milton Kirpatrick, Jr., b. 28 Feb. 1933. Educator; Psychotherapist; Businessman. Educ: B.A., SUNY, Albany, N.Y., U.S.A., 1955; M.A., ibid 1956. Appts: Chmn., Soc. Studies Dept., Brentwood Pub. Schls., L.I., N.Y., 1960-; Psychotherapist, Pvte. Prac.; Owner, Mod. Times Bookshop; Ptnr., Kiku Art Imports. Cons. & Writer, Dept. for Continuing Educ., N.Y. State Dept. of Educ. Mbrships. incl: Am. Orthopsychiatric Assn., Inc.; Acad. of Human Serv. Scis.; Assn. for Humanistic Psychol.; Int. Soc. for Gen. Semantics; Bd. of Dirs., Brentwood Histl. Soc.; Formerly Bd. of Dirs., Brentwood Chmbr. of Comm.; Kappa Phi Kappa; Pi Gamma Mu. Publs: Column, "Depending on Education", Bay Shore Sentinel, Islip, L.I. Hons. incl: Order of Chevalier, Grand Coun. of the Order of Demolay; Americanism Award, Am. Legion, 1970. Address: 12 Brevoort Place, Brentwood, NY 11717, U.S.A. 6.

SILL, Webster Harrison, Jr., b. 4 Dec. 1916. Educator; Plant Pathologist. Educ: B.S., W. Va. Wesleyan Coll., 1939; M.S., Pa. State Coll., 1942; M.A., Boston Univ., 1947; Ph.D., Univ. of Wis., 1951. Appts: Rsch. Assoc., Univ. of Wis., 1951-52; Asst. Prof.-Prof., Bot. & Plant Pathol., Kan. State Coll., 1952-69; Chmn. & Prof., Dept. of Biol., Univ. of S.D., 1969-; Dir., Ctr. for Environmental Studies, ibid, 1972-; UN, FAO Agric. Off., Manila, Philippines, 1962-63; US/AID Advsr. for Rsch., APA Univ., Hyderabad, India, 1966-68. Mbrships: Nat.

Councillor, Am. Phytopathol. Soc., 1956-58; Regional Lectr., 1972-74, Local Chapt. Pres., 1973, Sigma Xi; Pres., Local Chapt., Phi Sigma, 1971; Gamma Alpha; Gamma Sigma Delta; Bot. Soc. of Am.; Rotary Int.; 4-H Club—All Star; Kan. State Pres. & Hon. Life Mbr., PTA. Publs: Sourcebook of Laboratory Exercises in Plant Pathology (co-author), 1962; about 125 sci. articles on plant pathol., virol., mycol., microbiol. & environmental biol. Hons. incl: Danforth Fellow, 1957; Lisle Fellow, 1937; Wis. Alumni Rsch. Fndn. Fellow, 1948-51; Nat. Sci. Fndn. Sr. Post-Doct. Fellow, 1972; Sr. Rsch. Fellow, E-W. Ctr., Univ. of Hawaii, 1974; Kan. Layman of Yr., 1957. Address: 515 N. Prentis, Vermillion, SD 57069, U.S.A. 2, 8, 14, 15.

SILLITOE, Alan b. 4 Mar. 1928. Writer Editorial Cons., W. H. Allen. Publrs. Mbr., Soc. Authors. Publs: Saturday Night and Sunday Morning, 1958; The Loneliness of the Long Distance Runner, 1959; The General, The Rats & other Poems, 1960; Key to the Door, 1961; The Ragman's Daugher, 1963; Road to Volgograd - Travel, 1964; The Death of William Posters, 1965; A Tree on Fire, 1967; Guzman Go Home, 1968; Love in the Environs of Voronezh (poems) 1968; All Citizens are Soldiers (play w. Ruth Fainlight), 1969; A Start in Life, 1970; Travels in Nihilon, 1971; Raw Material, 1972; Men, Women and Children, 1973. Hons: Prize, Authors Club for best first novel, 1958; Hawthornden Prize for Lit., 1960. Address: c/o. W. H. Allen, Publrs., 43, Essex St., London WC2 U.K.

SILLITOE, (Rev.) Hubert J., b. 15 Oct. 1886. Clerk in Holy Orders. Educ: Univ. of Durham, U.K., 1910-13. Appts: Curate, Putney, Surrey, 1914-17; Chap., Forces, B.E.F., France, 1917-19; Priest in Charge, St. Martin, Croydon, 1919-21; British Chap. of Java, Diocese of Singapore, 1921-24; Rector, St. Thomas, Brampron, Chesterfield, Derby, 1925-44; Rector, Hoggeston & Dunton, 1944-. Hon. Chap. to Forces, 1919. Mbrships: Pres., Soc. of King Charles the Martyr; Christs Hosp. Old Blues Club; Overseas; Park Place; St. James's St., London. Recip., Sci. Prize, Christ's Hosp., London, 1900. Address: The Rectory, Dunton, Buckingham, MK18 3LW.

SILLS, Arthur J., b. 19 Oct. 1917. Lawyer. Educ: B.A., Rutgers Univ., 1938; law degree, Harvard Univ., 1941. Appts. incl: Admitted N.J. Bar, 1941; Partner, Willentz, Goldman, Spitzer & Sills, 1950-62; Pub. rate counsel, N.J., 1958-61; Atty. Gen., N.J., 1962-70; Exec. Bd., Nat. Conf. Bail & Criminal Justice, 1964-; Chmn., State Law Enforcement Planning Agcy., Police Trng. Commn., 1962-70; Bd. of Govs., Hillel Commn., 1970-72; currently Sr. Partner Sills, Beck, Cummis, Radin & Tischman; Dir., City Title Ins. Co., Channel Cos., Inc., Packaging Products & Design Corp., Dev. Corp. of Am. Inc.; former & present mbr. & chmn., num. Govt. & State comms. Mbrships. incl: Am.,N.J., Middlesex Co., Perth Amboy Bar Assns.; Am. Judicature Soc.; Phi Beta Kappa; B'nai B'rith (past Pres.). Contbr. to profl. jrnls. Hons. incl: Docts., Rutgers Univ., 1966, Newark State Coll. 1967; Pope Paul VI Humanitarian Award, 1968. Address: 204 Dellwood Rd., Metuchen, NJ, U.S.A. 2, 6, 57.

SILLS, Beverly (Mrs. Peter B. Greenough), b. 25 May 1929. Operatic Soprano. Educ: Profl. Childrens Schl., N.Y.C.; pvte. study w. Estelle Liebling (voice), Paolo Gallico (piano) & Desire Defrere (stagecraft). Made opera debut as Frasquita, Carment, Phila. Civic Opera, 1946; has sung w. San Fran. Opera; N.Y.C. Opera; Teatro Colon, Buenos Aires; La Scala, Milan;

Teatro San Carlo, Naples; Royal Opera, Covent Gdn., U.K.; Deutsche Opera. Berlin; La Fenice, Venice, Italy; has played num. roles inclng. leads in N.Y.C. Opera's Donizetti cycle on British queens; gave special orchestral prog., Salle Pleyel, Paris, France, 1970;; has appeared w. many symph. orchs. Hons: D. Mus., Temple Univ., 1972; Edison Recording Award for Manon, 1972. Address: c/o Edgar Vincent Assocs., 156 E. 52nd St., New York, NY 10022, U.S.A. 2, 4, 21, 138.

SILVER, Francis, 5th, b. 4 Jan. 1916. Consulting Environmental Engineer; Land Surveyor. Educ: B.E., Johns Hopkins Univ., 1937; Seminar, Inst. Gen. Semantics, 1946. Appts: Engr., Heavy Chem. Mgt. & Engrng., Standard Lime & Stone Co., 1937-42; w. U.S. Army, 1942-46; w. John W. Bishop Co., 1947-50; Aircraft Engr., Fairchild & Boeing, 1951-57; Cons. Environmental Engr., 1958-; Land Surveyor, 1960-; Surveyor, Lands of Berkeley Co., W. Va., 1964-. Fellowships: Soc. for Clin. Ecol. (Fndng. Mbr. & Dir., ibid); Royal Soc. for Hlth. Mbrships. incl: Nat. Soc. Profl. Engrs.; Dipl., Am. Acad. Environmental Engrs.; Am. Pub. Hlth. Assn.; Am. Chem. Soc. Author of many sci. & tech. publs. Recip. of hons. Address: 501 S. Queen St., Martinsburg, WV 25401, U.S.A. 6, 12, 16, 28,

SILVER, Isidore, b. 16 Apr. 1934. Attorney; Law Professor; Writer. Educ: B.S., Univ. of Wis., 1955; J.D., N.Y. Univ., 1959; M.A., ibid, 1965. Appts: Lectr., Dept. of Econs., Hunter Coll., CUNY, 1961-66; Asst. Prof., Schl. of Bus. Admin., Univ. of Mass., 1966-68; Assoc. Prof., ibid, 1968-70; Assoc. Prof., Constitutional Law & Hist., John Jay Coll. of Criminal Justice, CUNY, 1970-73; Prof., ibid, 1973-. Mbrships: N.Y. Bar; Mass. Bar; U.S. Supreme Ct.; Exec. Comm., Nat. Emergency Civil Liberties Comm.; Fa. mbr., Nat. Humanities Fac. Publs: The Crime Control Establishment, 1974; Introduction & Afterword, The Challenge of Crime in A Free Society, 1968; Num. law review & popular mag. articles. Address: Dept. of Hist., John Jay Coll. of Criminal Justice, 445 W. 59th St., N.Y., NY 10019, U.S.A. 9.

SILVER, Melvin J., b. 12 Nov. 1903. Lawyer. Educ: Univ. of Minn.; William Mitchell Law Coll. Appts: Sr. ptnr. in law firm of Silver & Ryan; Special Asst. to Atty. Gen., 1944. Mbrships. incl: Am., Minn. & Ramsey Co. Bar Assns.; Bd. of Educ., 1950-52; Chmn., Univ. of Minn. Schlrship. Comm. for Dr. William Ginsberg Fndn., Edward Hoffman Fndn., Albert Shapira Fndn.; Chmn., Israel Bond Comm.; Past mbr., Exec. Comm., Minn. Jewish Coun.; V.P., St. Paul Jewish Coun.; St. Paul Community Chest Solicitation Comm. Hons: B'nai B'rith award for outstanding serv. to St. Paul community, 1951; Scroll of Hon. for serv., Bd. of Educ., 1952; Hon. award for servs., Supreme Lodge of B'nai B'rith, 1958; Hon. award, Wisdom Ency., 1969. Address: 2029 Upper St. Dennis Rd., St. Paul, MN 55116, U.S.A. 2, 16, 55, 94, 128.

SILVERBERG, Stuart O., b. 14 Oct. 1931. Obstetrician; Gynecologist. Educ: B.A., Univ. of Colo., 1952; M.D., 1955. Appts: Asst. Clin. Instr., SUNY, Donwstate, 1961-62; Formerly, Clin. Instr., Ob. Gyn., Univ. of Colo. Schl. of Med.; Asst. Clin. Prof., Ob. Gyn., ibid, 1972-. Fellow, Am. Coll. of Obs. Gyn. & Am. Coll. of Surgs. Mbrships: Dipl., Am. Bd. Obs. & Gyn.; Int. Fertility Assn.; Am. Fertility Soc.; AMA; Am. Assn. Gynecologic Laparoscopises; Flying Physns. Assn.; Aircraft Owners & Pilots Assn.

Address: 2140 E. 88th Ave., Denver, CO 80229, U.S.A. 14.

SILVESTER, Victor Marlborough. Musical Director. Educ: Trinity Coll. of Music, U.K. Broadcasts w. his orch. regularly for BBC Radio & TV, & on gramophone records, 1937- (contracted to E.M.I. & Pye Records). Mbrships: Pres., Lord's Taverners, 1972-73; Pres., Imperial Soc. of Tchrs. of Dancing, 1956-; Variety Club of Gt. Britain. Publs: Modern Ballroom Dancing; Theory of Ballroom Dancing; The Art of the Ballroom; Autobiography—Dancing is My Life. Composer of 196 musical pieces, many publd. Hons: Italian Bronze Medal for Mil. Valour, 1918; O.B.E., 1960; Winner, World's Dancing Championship & many other championships. Address: 19 Boydell Court, St. John's Wood Park, London N.W.8, U.K.

SILVING, Helen (Mrs. Paul K. Ryu), b. 8 Mar. 1906. Professor. Educ: Dr. Pol. Sci., Vienna Univ., Austria, 1929; J.U.D., ibid, 1936; LL.B., Columbia Univ. Law Schl., N.Y., U.S.A., 1944. Appts: Rsch. Asst., Harvard Univ., U.S.A., 1940-42; Assoc. Atty., w. law firm, Mudge, Stern, Williams & Tucker, N.Y., 1944-45; Atty., U.S. Dept. Justice, 1948-53; Rsch. Assoc., Harvard Law Schl., 1954-56; Prof., Law, Univ. Puerto Rico, U.S.A., 1956-; Vis. Lectr., Yale Law Schl., 1958-59; Fulbright Lectr., Seoul Nat. Univ., Korea, 1964; '67-68. Mbrships: Am. Bar Assn.; Trial Lawyers Assn.; World Peace Through Law; Am. Sect., Int. Criminal Law Assn. Int. Advsry. Comm. Comparative Criminal Law Proj., N.Y. Univ. Schl. of Law. Publs: Essays on Criminal Procedure, 1964; Constituent Elements of Crime, 1967; Essays on Mental Incapacity and Criminal Conduct, 1967; Sources of Law, 1968; Criminal Justice, 2 vols., 1971. Recip. Special Presidential Citation, Am. Soc. Criminol., 1971. Address: Univ. Puerto Rico Schl. of Law, Rio Piedras, PR 00931, U.S.A.

SIMIRIOTIS, Nicos, b. 11 Oct. 1911. Civil Engineer. Educ: Polytechnic Schl. of Athens, 1936. Appts: Chief Engr., reconstruction of Preveza & Leukas after earthquake, 1938; Chief Engr., Tech. Serv., Dist. of Epirus, 1940; Dist. of Attica, Athens, 1946; Retd., 1972. Mbrships: Past Sec. Gen.,Nat. Soc. of Greek Authors; Lit. Soc. Parnassos; V.P., Int. Arts Guild; Eart, Rhapsody in 15 Cantos, 1947-70; Alcyons (poetry), 1949; Stars, Rhapsody in 10 Cantos, 1972; Wings in the Night, 1973; Translations of Poe, Pound, Lorca, Lindsay & others; Exhibs. of oil paintings, sculpture, wood engravings. Hons: 1st Prize, Lit. Soc. Parnossos, 1946; 1st Prize, Acad. of Athens, 1972; Gold Medal, City of Athens, 1973. Address: Korinthias 9 St. (T 608), Athens, Greece. 43.

SIMMANG, Clifford Max, b. 14 Feb. 1912. Teacher; Administrator. Educ: B.S., 1936, M.S., 1938, Mech. Engrng., Texas A&M Univ.; Ph.D., Univ. of Tex., 1952. Appts: Petroleum Engr., Humble Oil Co., 1936-37; Instr.-Prof., Tex. A&M Univ., 1937-57; Hd., Dept. of Mech. Engrng., ibid, 1957-; Brig. Gen., U.S. Army, retd. 1966. Mbrships: Am. Soc. of Mech. Engrs.; Soc. of Am. Mil. Engrs.; Am. Ordnance Assn.; Am. Soc. of Engrng. Educators; Tau Beta Pi; Pi Tau Sigma; Sigma Xi. Publs: Problems in Thermodynamics (co-author); Solutions Manual, Problems in Thermodynamics (co-author), both in 6th edit. Hons: Bronze Star w. Cluster, 1945; Num. combat ribbons, 1943-46; Legion of Merit, 1966. Address: Mech. Engineering Dept., Texas A&M Univ., College Station, TX 77843, U.S.A. 2, 26, 113, 125.

SIMMEL, Johannes Mario, b. 7 Apr. 1924. Chemist; Script Writer; Journalist; Author. Educ: State, Tchrs. & Rsch. Insts. for Chem., Vienna, Austria. Appts. incl: Hd., Austrian Culture Dept., Viennese paper; Work for var. papers; Script Writer for film prods. in Austria & abroad; 1st Corres. & Writer, Quick; Free-lance writer, 1962-. Mbrships: Authors Guild, Inc., U.S.A.; Verein Deutscher Schriftsteller. Author of best-selling books, translated into 18 langs. w. world sales of 13 millions, dramatised & filmed; About 150 short stories, num. articles & serials; 3 books for children; 36 film scripts from own or other material. Hons. incl: Num. prizes for film scripts, 1952-62; Johannes Mario Simmel Collect., Univ. of Boston Mugar Mem. Lab., U.S.A. Address: Chateau Perigord II, Bloc E, 27e Etage, 6 Lacets St. Leon, Monte Carlo, Monaco. 3.

SIMMONS, David Roy, b. 6 Sept. 1930. Ethnologist. Educ: B.A., M.A., Auckland Univ.; Vic. Univ., Wellington; Auckland Tchrs. Coll.; Sorbonne, Paris; Dip., Celtic Studies, Univ. of Rennes. Appts: Asst. Keeper, Anthropol., Otago Mus., Dunedin, N.Z., 1962-64; Keeper, ibid, 1964-67; Ethnol., Auckland War Mem. Mus., 1968-74. Mbrships: Polynesian Soc.; Past V.P. & Coun. Mbr., N.Z. Archaeol. Assn.; Past Coun. Mbr., Linguistic Soc. of N.Z.; Past Coun. Mbr., Otago Br., Royal Soc. of N.Z.; Royal Soc. of N.Z. & Acukland Inst. & Mus.; Cons., Civic Trust of Auckland. Contbr. to num. jrnls. Address: Auckland Museum, Pvte. Bag, Auckland, N.Z.

SIMMONS, Rosemary, b. 8 Dec. 1940. Educator. Educ: Mus.B., Univ. of Southern Miss., 1962; Mus.M., ibid, 1971. Appts. incl: Music Supvsr., Picayune City Schls., 1962-69; Mbr., State Bd. of Execs., Piano Div., & Chmn., Dist. VIII, State Piano Div., 1962-69, Sec., State Bd. of Execs., 1968-69; Bd. of Reps., Miss. Music Educ. Assn., 1962-; Dir., Southern Div., Miss. Music Tchrs. Assn., 1962-72; Sec., Picayune Educ. Assn., 1962-69; Music Instr., Northwest Miss. Jr. Coll., Fac. Advsr. & Fac. Rep., Student Senate, 1972-. Mbrships. incl: AAUW; Music Educators Nat. Conf.; Miss. Music Educ. Assn.; Music Tchrs. Nat. Assn.; Miss. Educ. Assn.; Miss. Dept. Classroom Tchrs.; Tate Co. Chapt., Univ. Southern Miss. Alumni Assn.; Pres., ibid, 1973-74; Mu Phi Epsilon; Phi Kappa Phi. Address: P.O.Box 366, Northwest Mississippi Junior College, Senatobia, MS 38668, U.S.A. 76, 125.

SIMMONS, William I., b. 14 Feb. 1924. Orthodontist. Educ: D.D.S., Loyola Univ., New Orleans; Orthodontic Cert., Univ. of Pa., Phila. Appts: Prof., orthodontics, Univ. of Tex. Dental Schl., 1950; Pvte. Prac., 1951-. Mbrships: A.D.A.; V.P., 4th Dist. Dental Soc.; Am. Orthodontic Assn.; S.W. Orthodontic Assn. Address: 3019 Old Minden Rd., Bossier City, LA, U.S.A.

SIMON, Benjamin, b. 31 May 1903. Physician-Psychiatrist & Neurologist. Educ: A.B., Stanford Univ., Calif., 1925; A.M., 1927; M.D., Wash. Univ. Schl. of Med., 1931. Appts. incl: Cons., Psych., VA Hosp., Bedford, Mass., 1950-; Lectr., Harvard Univ. Dept. of Soc. Rels. & Dept. Psych., 1956-; Dir., Psych., Westborough State Hosp., 1960-73; Cons., Psych., ibid, 1973-; Asst. Clin. Prof., Psych., Tufts Univ. Schl. of Med., 1964-; Cons., Psych., Boston State Hosp., 1964-; Med. Cons., BDI, SSA, HEW, 1974. Fellowships: Am. Acad. Neurol.; Am. Assn. Mental Deliciency; AAAS; Am; Am. Grp. Psychotherapy Assn.; ANA; Life Fellow, Am. Psych. Assn.; Am. Acad. Psychoanal.; Fndng. Fellow, Am. Coll.

Psychoanalysts; Alpha Omea Alpha; Sigma Xi; Fellow Emeritus, Am. Coll. of Psychs.; many profl. orgs. Publs. incl: Toward Therapeutic Care, 1961, '70; Co-author, The Interrupted Journey, 1966; Crisis in Psychiatric Hospitalization, 1969; sev. other publs. Hons. incl: mil. decorations; Physns. Recognition Award, 1969-72. Address: 10 Hawthorne Place, Charles River Park, Boston, MA 02114, U.S.A. 6, 14, 17, 55, 112.

SIMON, Emanuel Ernst, b. 23 July 1898. Physician. Educ: Med. studies, Berlin, Munchen, Wuerzburg Univs., Germany; M.D., 1923; postgrad. studies, Scandinavia, U.K., S.Africa, U.S.A. Appts: Hd., Dept. Phys. Hygiene, Straus Hlth. Ctr., Jerusalem, 1929-36; Dir., Dept. of Phys. Educ., Jewish Com. Coun., 1939-53, & Min. Educ. & Culture, 1948-53; Hd., Dept. of Rehab., Med. Corps IDF, 1948-49; Med. Advsr., Min. Educ. & Culture, 1954-60; Sci. Sec., Rsch. Comm., Icspe-UNESCO, 1960-64, V.P., 1964-68, Hon. V.P., 1968-. Mbrships: incl: Fedn. Int. Medico-Sport, 1949-; Bd. Trustees, Wingate Inst., 1950-; Pres., Israel Sport-Med. Assn., 1954-60, Hon. Pres., 1960-. Publs. incl: The Foot (co-author), 1944; International Research in Sport & Physical Education (co-author), 1964. Num. articles, profl. & sci. jrnls. Hons. incl: Dov-Hos-Prize, Tel Aviv Municipality, 1968. Address: 40 Ruppin St., 63457 Tel-Aviv, Israel. 55, 94.

SIMON, Hazel Tippet Jones, b. 7 July 1905. Educator & Counselor. Educ: Tchng. Cert., Chgo. Normal Coll., Ill., U.S.A., 1925; B.A., Roosevelt Univ., Chgo., 1956; M.A. ibid, 1962; M.Ed., Chgo. State Univ., 1964. Appts: Tchr., Home Econs., Adult Evening Div., Chgo. Bd. of Educ., 1925-35; Elem. Tchr., Home Econs., 1927-32; Luncheon Mgr., & Supvsr., H.S. lunchrooms, 1932-39; H.S. Tchr., Home Econs., 1939-64; Ldr., Family Finance Sect., Planned Parenthood, 1954-55; Supvsr. of Voc. Educ., 1966-67; Assoc. Prof. of Educ., Roosevelt Univ., 1967-68. Mbrships: Franklin Honor Soc., Roosevelt Univ.; Counselor Contact; Pres., Volunteers for Geriatric Servs., Little Rock, Ark., 1969; Counselor, Adult Educ. Ctr., Dysart Ctr., El Mirage, Ariz., 1971-72; Volunteer, Sun City Lodge, Sr. Citizen Residence & Infirmary, 1971-; Chapt. Pres., Women's Soc. of Christian Serv., 1958-59 & 1972; Chapt. Pres., Delta Kappa Gamma, 1966-68. Author, An Experiment in Motivating Achieving & Underachieving Gifted Students. Address: 10018 Oak Ridge Drive, Sun City, AZ 85381, U.S.A. 5, 132.

SIMON, Joseph H., b. 11 Oct. 1913. Artist; Author; Editor. Educ: Attended Art Classes, Syracuse Univ., N.Y. Appts. incl: Art Dir. & Staff Cartoonist, Rochester Jrnl., Syracuse Herald, Syracuse Jrnl.; Ed., Fox Publs., Timely (Marvel) Publs., Harvey Publs., Crestwood Publs., Pyramid Books, Nat. Periodical Publs. (Warner Communications). Mbrships. incl: L.I. Olympic Comm. Rockefeller Team; Comm. to re-elect pres.; L.I. Care & Hope for Youth. Works incl: Creator of Capt. Am.; Boy Commandos & many comic book characters; Author of Adventure is my Career, U.S. Coast Guard, Look Who's Talking, A Funny Thing Happened on the Way to Tel-Aviv; Fndr., Sick Mag., Ed. Ensiklopedia. Recip. of var. hons. Address: 11 Arbutus Ln., Stony Brook, NY 11790, U.S.A. 2, 6.

SIMON, Paul Ludwig, b. 17 Apr. 1923. Industrial Executive. Educ: Tech. Acad., Budapest, Hungary; Univ. of Munich, Germany; Dip. in Engrng., Dip. in Nat. Econ. Appts. incl: Mbr., Central Lab., Siemens, Munich, 1948;

Sales Mgr., 1957; Dir., Deutsche Fernkabel-Gesellschaft, Berlin, Rastatt, 1962; Dir., Electromedica Siemens-Reinigerwerke, Erlangen, 1966; Mng. Dir., Mbr. Bd. of Dirs., Electromedica Espanola S.A., Madrid, Spain, 1967; Mbr., Mgmt., Rudolf A. Hartmann GmbH & Co., Berlin, Adam Schneider GmbH, E.F.G. Küster GmbH, 1968; Mng. Dir., Mbr., Bd. of Dirs., Burger Eisenwerke AG, Burg, 1970; Gen. Mgr., Buderus'sche Eisenwerke, Wetzlar; Chmn. of Mgmt., Senkingwerk GmbH KG, Hildesheim; Mbr. Supvsry. Bd., Roeder Grossküchentechnik GmbH, Darmstadt. Author, var. tech. publs. Address: Bergwiese 2, D-6348 Herborn, German Fed. Repub. 43, 92.

SIMONART, Albert, b. 29 Sept. 1916. Business Executive. Educ: Ing.-Chim.Ind.Agr., Univ. of Louvain, Belgium. Appts: Engr., Soc. Citrique Belge SA; Engr., Tirlemont Refinery; Admnstr., Tirlemont Elec. Co.; Commnr., Tirlemont Organic Products Co.; Admnstr., Distrelgas Co.; Advsr., Northern Belgium Elec. Co.; Admnstr., Soc. Citrique Belge. Publs. incl: Sur un moyen simple de conserver les pulpes de betteraves pendant leur transport, 1952; La Conservation du jus dense et son travail ultérieur, 1967; La microbiologie de la diffusion, 1969. Address: Saint Maartenstraat I, Vissenaken, 3307 Kumtich, Belgium.

SIMONDS, Rollin Head, b. 9 Jan. 1910. Educator. Educ: B.S., 1935, M.A., 1936, Ph.D., 1948, Northwestern Univ. Appts: Mich. State Univ.—Assoc. Prof., Mgmt.; Prof. & Chmn., Dept. of Mgmt. & Finance; Prof., Mgmt. Mbrships: Past Pres., Midwest Div. & Past Mbr., Bd. of Govs., Acad. of Mgmt.; Indl. Rels. Rsch. Assn.; Phi Beta Kappa; Phi Kappa Phi; Beta Gemma Sigma. Publs: Safety Management (co-author), 1956, 2nd edit., 1963; Human Resources Administration (co-author), 1970; Business Administration (co-author), 1963. Address: 410 Kedzie Drive, E. Lansing, MI 48823, U.S.A. 14, 16.

SIMONS, Charles Dewar, b. 26 Apr. 1903. Retired Educator. Educ: Princeton Univ., N.J., U.S.A. Num. mbrships. incl: Royal Soc. of Arts; Royal Philatelic Soc., London, U.K.; Royal Philatelic Soc. of Vic., Australia; Austria Philatelic Soc. of N.Y.; Cinderella Philatelic Soc.; Cancellation Club; British Interplanetary Soc.; Royal Schl. of Ch. Music; Nat. Audubon Soc.; E. African Wild Life Soc.; Smithsonian Soc., Wash. D.C.; Soc. for Ancient Monuments; British Mus. Soc.; Musicological Soc.; Heraldry Soc.; Int. Order of St. Luke; Loch Ness Bur. of Investigation; Shakespearean Authorship Soc.; Steamship Soc. of Am.; World Wildlife Fund; British Commonwealth Alliance in the Dominion of Canada; Metropol. Opera Guild. Address: Windrode House, Route 1, Box 638, Westerly, RI 02891, U.S.A. 6, 22, 57, 128, 130.

SIMONS, Netty (Mrs. Leon G. Simons). Composer. Educ: N.Y. Univ. Schl. Fine Arts, 1931-33, '34-47; Juilliard Grad. Schl. Music, 1933-34. Appts: Tchr., 3rd. St. Music Schl. Settlement, N.Y.C., 1928-33; pvte. music tchr., 1928-56; Producer, scriptwriter, radio broadcasts for Am. Composers Alliance, WNYC, N.Y.C., 1966-71; scriptwriter, prod., series of contemporary music, WUOM-WVGR, Univ. of Mich., Ann Arbor, 1971; Prod., Coord., Composers Concerts, Carnegie Recital Hall, 1960, '61; Music Chmn, Bd. Dirs., Rockland Fndn., Nyack, N.Y., 1959-61. Mbrships: Broadcast Music, Inc.; Am. Composers Alliance (bd. govs., 1972-74); Am. Music Ctr.; Composers in Performance (auspices, N.Y. State Coun. on Arts). Compositions incl: Illuminations in Space 12 (for viola & orch.), 1972; Trialogue 3 (chamber

music), 1973. Recip., recording/publ. award, Ford Fndn., 1971. Address: c/o Theodore Presser Co., 111 W. 57th St., N.Y., NY 10019, U.S.A. 5, 138.

SIMONSOHN, Shlomo, b. 30 Oct. 1923. Professor of History. Educ: M.A., Jerusalem, 1946; Ph.D., Univ. Coll., London, U.K., 1953. Appts: Prof. Hist., Tel Aviv Univ., 1955-, Chmn., Dept. Jewish Hist., 1957-, Dir., Univ Lib., 1959-64, Dir., Diaspora Rsch. Inst., 1968-, Dean, Schl. of Jewish Studies, 1970-72, Univ. Rector, 1972-; Vis. Prof., Yeshiva Univ., N.Y.C., 1965-66; Rotating Chmn., Comm. of Vice Chancellors & Prins. of Israel Univs., 1973-74. Mbrships: Fellow, Israel Histl. Soc.; Am. Acad. Jewish Rsch. Publs: Leo Modena, 1953; The Response of Leo Modena, 1956; Clipeus et Gladius, 1960; History of the Jews in the Duchy of Mantua, 2 vols., 1962-64. Ed., Diaspora Rsch. Inst. Publs. Textbooks, papers, articles, Medieval & Renaissance Jewish Hist. Recip., Ben Zvi Prize, 1964. Address: Tel Aviv University, Ramat Aviv, Israel. 94.

SIMOTAS, Panagiotis, b. 20 Mar. 1927. University Professor. Educ: Theol. & Hebrew studies, Athens, Jerusalem, Tübingen, Bonn, Louvain; D.Theol., 1959. Appts: Lectr., 1963; Ord. Prof., Old Testament, Univ. of Thessaloniki, Greece, 1970. Mbr. Deutscher Verein zur Erforschung Palästinas. Publs: The Boundaries of Ephraim & Manasse, 1959; Papyrus Bodmer IX, 1960; Nehemiah, 1960; The Book of Ruth, 1962; David & the Moabites, 1964; The Hebrew 'Deber' by Septuagint, 1964; A Brief Introduction on Biblical Hebrew & Archaeology, 1964; The Famine in the Old Testament, 1965; Sin by Hebrew Prophets, 1968; Judaism & Greek Orthodoxy, 1971; The World of the Old Testament, 1973; contbr. to learned publs. Address: Univ. of Thessaloniki, Greece.

SIMPKINS, Alyne Jordan Johnson, b. 6 Sept. 1908. Teacher (retd.). Educ: B.A., Queen's Coll., 1929; Univ. Extension Courses in Educ., 1946, '47, '48; For. Lang. Inst., Univ. of Ga., summer 1960. Appts. incl: Tchr., Engl. French & Latin, & Coach of Basketball & Drama, N. H.S., 1931-32; Tchr., Engl., Latin & French, Basketball Coach & Sr. Sponsor, Swansea H.S., 1932-33 & 1933-34; Tchr., Engl. Basketball Coach & Sr. Sponsor, Union H.S., Georgetown Co., 1934-35; Tchr., Engl., Latin, French & Maths., Winyah H.S., 1946-73. Mbrships: incl: Bus. & Profl. Women's Club; NEA; S.C. Educ. Assn.; Nat. Retd. Tchrs. Assn.; Georgetown Rice Mus.; Chmn., Liaison Comm., For. Lang. Inst., Univ. of Ga. Author of sev. articles in Chicora Coll. Mag. & of dramas, speeches & poems for num. events during tchng. career. Hons. incl: Star Tchr., Winyah H.S., 1972-73; Star Tchr., Georgetown Co., 1972-73. Address: 3 East Bay St., Georgetown, SC, U.S.A. 125.

SIMPKINS, Nathaniel Stone III, b. 16 Apr. 1921. Horticulturist; Executive. Educ: Columbia Univ., N.Y.C. Appts: Dist. Mgr., Bartlett Tree Experts, 1940-65; Exec. V.P., Horticultural Servs. Ltd., Bermuda, 1963-; Pres., Hort. Servs. (Bahamas) Ltd., 1965-. Mbrships. incl: Pres. Manchester Hist. Soc.; Sec., Treas., N. Shore Hort. Soc.; Exec. V.P., Cape Anne Symph.; RHADC, Bermuda; Sec., Treas., Bermuda Art Soc. Author of num. travel articles & theatre reviews. Recip. many prizes for hort. exhibs., 1943-59. Address: 908 E. 6th St., Stuart, FL 33494, U.S.A. 128.

SIMPSON, Dean, b. 20 Nov. 1917. Journalist. Educ: Coll. of the Pacific, Stockton, Calif., 1945-47; Calif. State Univ.,

Fresno, 1964-66. Appts: var. positions in brokerage houses, San Fran., 1935-41; Gen. Assignment Reporter, Stockton Record, Calif., 1943-47; Reporter, Newswriter, Radio Stn. KWG, Stockton, Calif., 1947-53; Gen. Assignment Reporter, Fresno Bee, Calif., 1953-59; Copy Ed., ibid., 1959-62; T.V. Ed.-columnist, 1962; Owner, Operator, Mid-Valley News Serv., Stockton, 1948-53. Mbrships: Pres., Fresno Press Club, 1954-55; Mbr. of Vestry, St. Columba's Episcopal Ch., Fresno, 1956-59, Jr. Warden, 1957, Sr. Warden, 1958. Contbr. of articles & photographs to var. mags. Address: Fresno Bee, 1551 Van Ness Ave., Fresno, CA 93721, U.S.A. 9.

SIMPSON, Edith Child, b. 9 Apr. 1905. University Professor. Educ: 1st Class Tchng. Cert., 1930; B.Sc., Univ. of Sask., 1932; M.Sc., Univ. of Wis., U.S.A., 1939; Ed.D., Columbia Univ., 1956. Appts: Tchr., pub. schls., 5 yrs.; Univ. of Sask., 1932-72: Home Econs. Ext. work, 1932-44; Asst. Prof., 1942-54; Dean of Women, 1944-50; Assoc. Prof., 1950-62; Prof., 1962-72; Dean, Coll. of Home Econs., 1965-72. Mbrships: Past Pres., Canadian Home Econs. Assn.; Canadian Dietetic Assn.; Am. Home Econs. Assn.; Am. Dietetic Assn.; Int. Fedn. of Home Econs. Publs: Home Economics in Canada, 1964. Hons: Fellow, Sask. Home Econs. Assn.; Life Mbrship., Sask. Dietetic Assn.; 1972 Branded Foods Award for outstanding achievement in dietetics; Edith Rowles Simpson Lectrship. est. 1972; Life Mbrship., Canadian Home Econs. Assn. Address: 1015 Osler St., Saskatoon, Sask. S7N 0T5, Canada.

SIMPSON, Eugene Thamon, b. 4 Apr. 1932. Educator; Musician. Educ: Mus.B., Howard Univ., Wash. D.C., 1951; Mus.B., Yale Univ., 1953; Mus.M., 1954; Ed.D.; Columbia Univ., 1956. Appts: incl: Vocal Music Tchr., N.Y.C. H.S's., 1956-68; Pvte. voice tchng. & coaching Carnegie Hall, 1964-68; Assoc. Prof., Chmn., Voice & Dir., Choral Activities, Va. State Coll., Petersburg, 1968-70; Prof. & Chmn., Dept. of Music, Bowie State Coll., Md., 1970-; Chmn., Div. of Humanities, ibid, 1972-; Asst. to the Provost, Johns Hopkins Univ., 1973-74. Acad. Admin. Fellow, Am. Coun. of Educ. Mbrships. incl: Music Educrs. Nat. Conf.; Md. Music Educrs. Assn.; Am. Choral Dirs. Assn.; Am. Guild of TV & Radio Artists; Screen Actors Guild. Author, A Study Analysis & Performance of the Schwanengesang of Franz Schubert, 1968. Composer, Hold On. Has made sev. recordings as conductor or soloist. Recip., acad. hons. Address: 1314 Paddock Lane, Bowie, MD 20716, U.S.A. 6, 46, 125, 131.

SIMPSON, Grace, b. 12 Nov. 1920. Research Archaeologist. Educ: Dip. in Prehistory, London Univ., 1948; D.Phil., Lady Margaret Hall, Oxford Univ., 1960. Appts: Rsch. Asst. in Archaeol., Durham Univ., 1950-54; Hon. Curator, Chesters Mus., Hadrian's Wall, 1950-72; Rsch. for Rheinisches Landesmuseum, Bonn, Germany, 1961-73; Philips Visitor, Haverford Coll., Pa., U.S.A., 1968-69. Mbrships: Fellow, Soc. of Antiquaries, 1958; Int. Rei Cretariae Romanae Fautores, 1958-. Publs: Central Gaulish Potters (co-author), 1958; Britons & the Roman Army, 1964; Novaesium: the Bronze & Iron Objects from the Excavations at Neuss, Limesforschungen, 1955-62 (forthcoming). Ed., 2nd edn., of Oswald & Pryce, An Introduction to the Study of Terra Sigillata, 1920. Contbns. & reviews to many jrnls. & excavation reports. Hons: Wates Fndn. Vis. Vellow in France for rsch. on Terra Sigillata, Brit.Acad., 1971-. Address: 52 Beechcroft Rd., Oxford 0X2 7AZ, U.K. 133.

SIMPSON, Gwen-Holly, b. 14 Jan. 1915. Educator. Educ: B.A., Coll. of St. Catherine, St. Paul, Minn., U.S.A.; M.A., Occidental Coll., L.A., Calif.; Ph.D., Univ. of London, U.K., 1971; Dipl. & D.Litt., Colo. Christian Coll., 1974. Appts. incl: Dir., Theatre Dept., San Diego Coll. for Women, Calif., 1956-58; Tchr., Pasadena City Schls., & Dir., Dept. of Theatre Arts & Assemblies, 1958-68; Instr., Modern Drama & Shakespeare, Int. Univ., 1971-72; Currently Cons., Dramatic Lit., Pasadena City Schls., Calif. Mbrships. incl: Chmn., Coll. of St. Catherine L.A. Co. Alumnae Chapt., 1940-52; State Dir., Nat. Thespian Soc., 1964-69; Nat. Collegiate Players Fraternity; Am. Theatre Assn.; Profl. Educators Grp., NEA; Pres., Pasadena Charter Chapt., Profl. Educators, 1974; Area Sec., Am. Inst. for For. Study. Publs: The Bridal Path, Low I Kneel, Drama Course, 1952; A Time For Love, 1956; Assignments in Drama, 1970; Articles & criticisms in jrnls. Author, dir., prod., & set designer, Enigma In the Mirror. Hons. incl: Flynn Fndn. Award for Cultural Dev. of Youth, 1953 & 1954; 5 nat. awards, Nat. Thespian Soc., 1962-68. Address: 1001 La Cadena, Arcadia, CA 91006, U.S.A. 5, 57.

SIMPSON, Minnie Elizabeth Miller (Mrs. K. K. Simpson), b. 31 Jan. 1903. Artist; Art Instructor. Educ: Studies w. Frederic Taubes, Donald Pierce, Elliot O'Hara, Jacob Getlar Smith. Art Instr., Tex., 26 yrs. w. classes sponsored by many art orgs. Exhibs: Centennial Mus., Corpus Christi, Tex., 1953; YMCA, 1953-54; Waco, 1953; Laredo, 1958; Austin, Sallas & Ft. Worth; Smithsonian Instn., Wash. D.C.; Int. Show, Int. Platform Assn., Wash. D.C., 1965, '67. Mbrships. incl: Pres., S. Tex. Traditional Art Assn., 1961-70; Nat. League Am. Pen Women; Corpus Christi Art Guild; Hon. Mbr., Bd., Rome, Centro E. Scambi Int. Recip., Silver Plaque in recognition of community servs. to City of Corpus Christi over period of 17 yrs., 1973. Address: 722 Drexel Dr., Corpus Christi, TX 78412, U.S.A. 5, 7, 132.

SIMPSON, Patricia Anne (Mrs. Henry Emerson Simpson), b. 27 Feb. 1935. Primary School Teacher. Educ: Wellington Tchrs. Trng. Coll., N.Z. Appts. (all in N.Z.): Primary Schl. Tchr., Masterton Ctrl., 1955-59; St. Patrick's Schl., 1961-68; Tchr., Jr. Special Class for Retarded Children, 1970-. Mbrships: N.Z. Rose Soc.; N.Z. Educl. Inst.; Royal Nat. Rose Soc. Publs: Children's nature books. Address: 13 Weka Place, Masterton, N.Z.

SIMRI, Uriel, b. 22 May 1925. Physical Educator. Educ: Dip., Phys. Educ. Tchrs. Coll., Tel-Aviv, Israel, 1945; B. Sc., CCNY, U.S.A., 1952; M.Sc., W. Va. Univ., ibid, 1965; Ed.D., ibid, 1966. Educ: Lectr., Phys. Educ. Tchrs. Coll., Wingate Inst., Israel, 1957-; Athletic Dir., Haile Selassie I Univ., Addis Ababa, Ethiopia, 1962-64; Dpty. Dir.-Dir., Dept. Instrl. Media, Wingate Inst., Israel, 1966-; Advsr., Malayasian Govt., 1969, '73. Mbrships: Pres., Soc. Hist. Phys. Educ. & Sports, Asia & Pacific Area, 1972-; V.P., Int. Comm. Phys. Fitness Rsch., 1972-. Author 27 books & over 200 articles inclng. Mi-va-ma besport (w.Israel Paz), 1959; From Athens to Rome (w. Nehemia Ben-Avvaham), 1960; The History of Physical Education and Sports (w. Raphael Panon), 1961; The Organization of Sport Events, 1960; 7th ed., '73; The History of Physical Education and Sports in Modern Israel, vols. I & II, 1970; The Religious and Magical Function of Ball Games in Various Cultures, 1967; Comparative Physical Educations and Sports (w. Bruce L. Bennett & Maxwell L. Howell), 1974. Address: Wingate Inst. for Phys. Educ. & Sport, Wingate P.O., Israel.

SIMS, Dean Stratton, b. 30 Sept. 1921. Public Relations Agency President. Educ: B.A., Univ. of Kan.; Grad. Work, Univs. of Colo. & Kans. City. Appts. incl: Reporter, The Kan. City Star, Hawk-Eye Gazette, Burlington, Iowa, & The Associated Press, 1945-48; Publicist, Kan. City Power & Light Co., 1948-51; Mgr., P.R., The Nat. Mgmt. Assn., 1951-57; Dir., P.R., APCL & K Inc., 1957-60; Mgr., P.R. Dept., Marathon Oil Co., 1960-65; Pres., P.R. Int. Ltd., 1965-; Chmn., Dean P.R. Ltd., London, 1973-. Mbrships. incl: The Tulsa Club; Nat. Press Club, Wash. D.C.; Deadline Club, N.Y.C.; Tulsa Press Club; Int. P.R. Assn.; P.R. Soc. of Am.; Sigma Delta Chi; Profl. Journalistic Soc. Address: 3479 S. Florence Pl., Tulsa, OK 74105, U.S.A.

SIMS, E. Ralph, Jr., b. 12 Oct. 1920. Consulting Industrial Engineer. Educ: B.Admin. Engrng., Coll. of Engrng., N.Y. Univ., 1947; Grad., Sperry Gyroscope Co. Apprentice Schl., 1943. Appts. incl: Corp. Materials Handling Engr., Asst. to V.P., Engrng. & Rsch., Anchor Hocking Glass Corp., Lancaster, Ohio, 1954-56; Dir. of Ind. Engrng., Assoc., Alden E. Stilson & Assocs., Ltd., Columbus, Ohio, 1956-58; Pres., E. Ralph Sims, Jr. & Assocs., Inc., Lancaster, Ohio, 1958-, Fairhill Dev. Corp., ibid, 1965-. Mbrships. incl: V.P., Assn. Mgmt. Cons.; Sr. Mbr., Am. Inst. Indl. Engrs., Am. Soc. Mech. Engrs., Brit. Inst. Mech. Engrs., Nat. Soc. Profl. Engrs., Am. Mgmt. Assn. Publs. incl: Euphonious Coding, 1967; Marketing Strategy & Economics, 1967; Planning & Managing Material Flow, 1968; Contemporary Comment in Retrospect, 1973. Contbng. Ed. of 3 Handbooks & Contbr. of over 40 articles to profl. jrnls. Address: 919 E. Fair Ave., Lancaster, OH 43130, U.S.A. 8, 16, 26.

SIMS, Ruth Carter (Mrs.). Educator; Counselor; Rancher. Educ: Secretarial Dip., 1943; Hunter Coll., N.Y.; Northwestern Univ., Cedar Falls, Iowa; A.B., Second Cert. Engl. & Soc. Studies, Marshall Univ.; M.Ed., Cert., Special Ed., Lang. & Learning Disabilities, Educl. Diagnostician, Cnslr., W. Tex. State Univ. Appts. incl: Tchr., Engl. & Lit., Logan Sr. HS, 1949-50; w. USAF, 1950-53, attended Offs. Trng. Schl., Counseling Schl & Recruiting Schl., discharged as 1st Lt.; Substitute Tchr., Happy HS, 1968-74; Owner-Operator of 2000 acre farm & ranch. Mbrships. incl: Am. Nat. Cow Belles; Tex. & Happy Cow Belles; Alpha Sigma Alpha; Beta Sigma Phi; Worthy Matron Elect, Order Eastern Star; PTA; Music Club of Happy. Hons: Grand Cross of Color, Int. Order of the Rainbow for Girls, 1967. Address: Box 457, Happy, TX 79042, U.S.A. 125.

SIMSON, Bevlyn Thall (Mrs. Theodore Richard Simson), b. 9 Oct. 1917. Artist; Painter; Printmaker. Educ: B.F.A., Ohio State Univ., U.S.A.; M.F.A., ibid. Many exhibs., incl. num. one-Artist exhibs. Mbrships: Phi Sigma Sigma; num. acad. & profl. assns. Creative Works: Edit. 20 original, handwritten poems & silkscreen prints—Prints and Poetry, Lib. of Congress & Rare Book Collect., Ohio State Univ., 1969; Art work in many collects., incl. Pres. Richard Nixon; Tyler Mus., Tex.; Wichita Mus. of Art, Kan; Kyoto City Univ. of Fine Arts, Japan; Columbus Gall. of Fine Arts; Meth. Theol. Schl., Ohio; Chase Manhattan Bank; Kresge Co. Collects.; I.B.M.; Bordens; Ohio Bell; Am. Bancorporation; 1st Investment Co. Hons: Art work chosen for Nat. Community Art Competition, U.S. Dept. of Housing & Urban Dev., Wash. D.C. 1973; Columbus Pntng. Awards, 1969, 1971; 8th Grand Prix Int. de Peinture de la Côte d'Azur, France & 23rd Grand Prix Int. de Peinture de Deauville, France, 1972, & sev. others. Address: 289

South Roosevelt Ave., Columbus, OH 43209, U.S.A. 5, 37.

SIMTEKPEATI, Michel Pablignou, b. 31 Dec. 1927. Professor; Diplomat; Sociologist; Economist. Educ: Tchr.'s Trng. Course, Atakpame, Togo, 1943-45; Inst. of Pol. Scis., Strasbourg, 1959-61; Fac. of Letters, Univ. of Strasbourg, 1961-64; Inst. Int., Univ. of Geneva (Cours de Vacance), 1960; Diplome de Sc. Pol.; Doct. Es-Lettres. Appts: Prof., French, Wash. Carver's Inst., Accra, 1948-52; Prof., Hist. & Geog., Luth. Trng. Inst., Harisburg, Liberia, 1953-56; Rsch. Off., African & Asian Affairs, State Dept., Monrovia, Liberia, 1965-66; Prof., Engl., Lycée de Munster, France, 1964-65; Hd. of Soc. Dept., O.A.U. Addis Ababa, 1966-67; Togo Amb. to Ghana & Nigeria, 1968-69. Mbrships: Grand Orient. Publs: Bases Historique de l'Economie Liberienne; Le peuple Kabrè et le Christianisme; Les Scarifications chez les Kabrè; Culture et Civilisation chez les Kabrè. Hons: Ordre du Mono, 1969. Address: Conseiller Technique, Ministère des Affaires Etrangères, Lome, Togo.

SINCLAIR, George, b. 5 Nov. 1912. Professional Electrical Engineer. Educ: B.Sc., Univ. of Alberta, Can., 1933; M.Sc., ibid, 1935; Ph.D., Ohio State Univ., U.S.A., 1946. Appts: Fndr., 1st Dir., Antenna Lab., Ohio State Univ. Columbus, 1942-47; Prof., Elec. Engrng., Univ. of Toronto, Can., 1947-; Orgr., then Chmn.-Chief Exec., Sinclair Radio Labs. Ltd., Concord, Ont., 1951-; Pres., Sinclair Radio Labs. Inc., Tonawanda, N.Y., U.S.A., 1960-. Mbrships. incl: Fellow, Royal Soc. of Can.; Fellow, IEEE; Dir.-at-large, ibid, 1960-62, 1964-66, 1969-70; Regional Dir., Canadian Region, 1974-76; Engrng. Inst. of Can.; Kiwanis Club of W. Toronto. Publs: 14 papers in profl. jrnls. Hons: Cert. of Appreciation, U.S. War & Navy Dept., 1948; Guggenheim Fellowship, 1958; D.Sc., Ohio State Univ., 1973. Address: Sinclair Radio Labs. Ltd., 122 Rayette Rd., Concord, Ont L4K 1B6, Canada.

SINCLAIR, Keith Val, b. 8 Nov. 1926. University Professor. Educ: M.A., Univ. of N.Z., 1949; Licence ès Lettres, Univ. of Paris, France, 1951; Docteur de l'Université, ibid, 1954; Ph.D., Oxford Univ. 1960; D.Litt., Victoria Univ. of Wellington, 1973. Appts. incl: Sr. Lectr. & Assoc. Prof., Univ. of Sydney, Australia, 1964-72; Vis. Prof., Northestern Univ., Chgo., U.S.A., 1971; Prof. Medieval French, Univ. of Conn., 1972-. Mbrships incl: Linguistic Soc., Paris; Australian Humanities Rsch. Coun. (Sec. 1965-69); Australia & N.Z. Assn. for Medieval Studies (Fndn. Sec. 1967-70); Fellow, Soc. of Antiquaries, London & Royal Geog. Soc. Publs. incl: Anglo-Norman in Last 20 Years, 1965; Descriptive Catalogue of Medieval MSS in Australia, 1969; Tristan de Nanteuil, Chanson de Geste inédite, 1971; var. Catalogues; num. articles in profl. jrnls. Hons. incl: Personnalité invitée, Govt. of France, 1971; Off. Ordre des Palmes Académiques, 1972. Address: Dept. of Romance Languages, Univ. of Connecticut, Storrs, CT 06268, U.S.A. 2, 3, 13, 23, 38.

SINCLAIR, Patricia Thompson, b. 21 May 1914. Editor. Educ: B.A., Dalhousie Univ., Halifax, N.S., Canada; B.S., Boston Univ., Mass., U.S.A.; M.A., Am. Univ., Wash. D.C. Appts: Tchr., Engl. & Latin, Mt. Royal Coll., Calgary, Alta., Canada, 1932-33; Sec. to Air Attaché British Embassy, Wash. D.C., U.S.A., 1935-42; Special Asst. to Min. for For. Affairs, For. Off., Seoul, Korea, 1950-51; Asst. Ed., Jrnl. of Tchr. Educ., Wash. D.C., U.S.A., 1962-73. Publs: Articles in profl. jrnls.; Compiler & Ed., 2 publs. on profl. accrediting.

Recip., Avery Prize, Dalhousie Univ., 1932. Address: Box 249, Route 5, Charlottesville, VA 22901, U.S.A. 5.

SINGER, Federico, b. 9 Oct. 1903. Doctor of Dentistry. Educ: Coll., Merano, Italy 1914-22; M.D., Univ. of Bologna, 1928; D.D.S., ibid, 1934. Appts. incl: Asst., Dental Schl., Univ. of Bologna, 1946-52; Dr., Dental Surg., Dental Schl., Univ. of Mainz, German Fed. Repub., 1953; Tchr. of Prosthodontics, Dental Schl., Univ. of Bologna; Dir., Dental Inst. of Merano. Mbrships. incl: Pres., Italian Dental Assn., Northern Italy; Pres., European Sect., Int. Coll. of Dentists; Mbr., 23 sci. dental & med. assns.; Corres. mbr., 4 dental socs.; Hon. mbr., 7 dental socs., For. Assoc. mbr., Acad. Dentaire Francaise. Author of 228 publs., all based on personal rsch. Hons. incl: Cross "pour le merite", 1st Class, Pres., German Fed. Repub., 1971; Cross of Hon., 1st Class, for sci. merits, Pres., Austrian Repub., 1973. Address: via Piave 8, I 39012 Merano, Italy.

SINGER, Irving, b. 1 Sept. 1924. Financial Executive. Educ: B.S.A., CCNY, 1948. Appts: Sr. Acct., Klein & Ziegler, Certified Pub. Accts., N.Y.C., 1948-54; Controller, Carr Systems, Inc., N.Y.C., 1954-55; Cons. to Law Firm & Builders re. acquisitions & tax loss corps., 1955-59; Sr. V.P. & Treas., Aetna Bus. Credit, Inc., successor to Amsterdam O'seas Corp., Hartford, Conn., 1959-. Mbrships: N.Y. State Soc. of Certified Pub. Accts.; Hartford Club; Financeman's Club. Address: 2 Northcliff Dr., W. Hartford, CT 06117, U.S.A. 6.

SINGER, Madelyn Hershfield (Mrs. Lee Singer). Associate Professor of Mathematics. Educ: B.A., Brooklyn Coll., 1942; M.A., Columbia Univ., 1946; Grad. study, Univ. of Va.; Doct. Cand., Va. Polytechnic Inst. & State Univ. Appts: Grad. Asst., Univ. of Tex., 1944; Jr. Engr.'s Asst., Civil Serv., USN, 1943; Maths., Sci. Tchr., Boro-Hall Acad., 1945-48; Maths. Tchr., Jefferson H.S., 1957-60, Patrick Henry H.S., 1961-69; Chmn., Maths. Dept. ibid, 1965-69; Asst. Prof., Maths., Va. Western Community Coll., 1969-72; Assoc. Prof., ibid, 1972-. Mbrships: Nat. Coun. of Tchrs. of Maths.; Maths. Assn. of Am.; Exec. Coun., Secondary Collegiate Maths., Va. Educ. Assn.; Nat. Coun. of Tchrs. of Sci.; Va. Community Coll. Comm., Curric. for Developmental Maths., 1970; Nat. Sci. Curric. Study, 1965-66; Chmn., Self-Study Educ. Standard, 1972-73. Publs: Community College Pre-Algebra Modules. Hons: Regent's Schol., Brooklyn Coll.; Dean's Schol., Columbia; Tchr. of Year, 1967, '68. Address: Va. Western Community Coll., Box 4195, Roanoke, VA 24015, U.S.A. 5, 7.

SINGH, Amarendra Narayan, b. 16 Aug. 1935. Physician. Educ: Grad., Sci., Bihar Univ., India, 1955; M.B.B.S., ibid, 1962; Postgrad. work, UK, 1962; Degrees obtained, UK & Canada; FRCP(C), MCRP, DPM, DTM & H, MRC PSYCH. (Lond.), FASCH, FIPA, FICPM. Appts: Sr. Psych., Prince Albert Saskatchewan, Canada, 1969-70; Med. Dir., NE Regional Mental Hosp., S. Porcupine, Ont., 1971-72; Dir., Psycho-Pharmacol. Unit., Hamilton Psych. Hosp., McMaster Univ. Dept. Psych., Ont., 1972-. Mbrships: Fellow, Int. Soc. Psychosomatic Med. & Indian Psychiatric Soc.; World Med. Assn.; World Psychiatric Assn.; Brit. Med. Assn.; Canadian Med. Assn.; Indian Med. Assn.; Canadian Psychiatric Assn.; Indian Psychiatric Soc. Author var. articles in profl. publs. Hons: Many merit awards, inclng. Morris Hallet Prize; Recip. var. Fellowships, inclng. Royal Coll. Canada. Address:

Psychopharmacol. Unit., Hamilton Psychiatric Hosp., Dept. Psychiatry, McMaster Univ., P.O. Box 585, Hamilton, Ont., Canada.

SINGH, (Bajwa) Fauja, b. 18 Sept. 1918. Professor of History. Educ: B.A., Khalsa Coll., Amritsar, India, 1941; M.A., Hist., S.N. Coll., Lahore, 1943; M.A., Econs., 1949. Appts. incl: Lectr., Hist., Khalsa Coll., Amritsar, 1946-51; Hd., Dept. of Hist., Shri Guru Teg Bahadur Khalsa Coll., Delhi, 1951-61; Rdr., Hist., Univ. of Delhi, 1961-67; Dir., Punjab Histl. Studies, & Prof. & Hd., Dept. of Hist., Punjabi Univ., Patiala, 1967-; Dean, Acad. Affairs, ibid, 1973-. Num. mbrships. incl: Bds. of Studies, Univs. of Delhi & Kurukshetra; Acad. Coun., Punjabi Univ., 1967-; Exec., Indian Hist. Congress; Local Sec., Punjab Hist. Conf.; Punjab Hist. Soc., Patiala; Indian Histl. Records Commn., Edit. Bd., Punjab Past & Present. Publs. incl: Military System of Sikhs (1799-1849), 1945; Kuka Movement, 1965; Travels of Guru Gobind Singh (atlas), 1968; Freedom Movement in the Punjab, 1972; Eminent Freedom Fighters of the Punjab, 1972. Recip., Ph.D., Univ. of Delhi, 1958; & other hons. Address: History Dept., Punjabi University, Patiala, India.

SINGH, Baljit, b. 1 Oct. 1929. University Professor. Educ: B.A., Agra Univ., India, 1951; M.A., Aligarh Univ., 1953; Dip. For. Affairs, 1953; Ph.D., Univ. of Md., Coll. Park, U.S.A., 1961. Appts. incl: Asst. Prof., Dept. of Pol. Sci., Wayne State Univ., Detroit, Mich., 1962-63; Asst. Prof., Dept. of Pol. Sci., Mich. State Univ., E. Lansing, 1961-62, 63-65; Assoc. Prof., ibid, 1965-71; Prof., 1971-; Asst. Dean, Coll. of Soc. Sci., 1967-. Mbrships: Life, Int. Studies Assn.; Midwest Conf. of Asian Affairs; Prog. Chmn., Mich. Acad. of Sci. Arts & Letters; Pi Sigma Alpha; Delta Phi Epsilon. Publs: Co-Auth., The Theory & Practice of Modern Guerrilla Warfare, 1971, Spanish edit., 1973; Indian Foreign Policy, 1974; contbr. to profl. jrnls. Recip., Fellowships & grants. Address: 2400 Tulane Drive, Lansing, MI 48912, U.S.A. 14, 30.

SINGH, Bhagwant, b. 23 July 1926. University Professor. Educ: B.A, Punjab, India, 1945; M.A, ibid, 1948; M.S., Cornell Univ., Ithaca, N.Y., U.S.A. 1957; C.F.E.A.E., Ohio Univ., Athens, 1958; Ph.D., Univ. of Md., College Park, 1962; Recip., Fellowships. Appts. inl: Asst., Assoc. Prof., Econs., Mem. Univ. of Nflnd., Canada, 1962-67; Canadian External Aid Prof., Econs., Univ. of W. Indies, Barbados, 1967-68; Guest Prof., Chr. Michelsen Inst., Norway, 1969-70; Prof. & Dir. Econ. Rsch., Inst. of Soc. & Econ. Rsch., Mem. Univ. of Nflnd, 1971; Colombo Plan Prof., Univ. Sains, Malaysia, 1972; Prof., Mem. Univ. of Nflnd., 1973-. Mbrships. incl: Am. & Canadian Econ. Assns.; Canadian Assn. of Univ. Tchrs.; Soc. for Int. Dev.; Canadian Assns., S. Asian & Latin Am. Studies. Author, articles & reports on econs. & agric. Address: Dept. of Economics, Memorial Univ. of Newfoundland, St. John's, Newfoundland, Canada. 14.

SINGH, (The Rt. Rev. Bishop) Garnish Benedictus, b. 2 Dec. 1927. Roman Catholic Bishop. Educ: Licentiate in Philos., Univ. of Propaganda, Rome, Italy; S.T.D., ibid. Appts: Parish Priest, Guyana (First Cath. priest of Indian origin in Guyana), 1959; Chancellor of Diocese, Georgetown, Guyana, 1968; Aux. Bishop of Georgetown & Vicar Gen., 1971; Bishop of Georgetown (First local Bishop of Guyana), 1972. Mbrships: Antilles Episcopal Conf.; Sec., ibid; Caribbean Conf. of Chs.; Guyana Coun. of Chs. Address: Bishop's House, 27 Brickdam, Georgetown, Guyana.

SINGH, Kirpal, b. 15 Oct. 1911. Consultant Psychiatrist. Educ: M.B., B.S., Madras; D.P.M., (U.K.); M.S., Harvard Univ., U.S.A. Appts: Kenya Med. Serv., 1933-39; Indian Med. Serv., & Army Med. Corps, 1941-68; Psych. Specialist, 1944-51, Psych. Advsr., 1952-66; Assoc. Prof., Hd. of Dept. Psych., Armed Forces Med. Coll., Poona, 1956-65; Mbr., WHO Expert Advsry. Bd. on Mental Hlth., 1961-66; Sr. Psych. Advsr., Armed Forces Med. Servs., Dpty. Dir. & Off. i/c., Directorate of Psychological Rsch., Min. of Defence, Govt. of India, 1966-68; Cons. Psych., State of Vic., Australia, 1968-72; Hon. Advsr., Armed Forces Med. Servs., India, 1973-; Hon. Cons., Employers' State Ins. Hosp., New Delhi, 1973-. Mbr., Fellow & Off., var. profl. orgs. Over 50 papers, Indian & int. med. jrnls. Recip., 1st Sandoz Award, Indian Psych. Soc., 1966. Address: T-38 Rajouri Garden, New Delhi 27, India. 93, 112.

SINHA, Rohini Pati, b. 3 July 1932. Educator. Educ: I.Sc., Patna Univ., India; B.A., Bihar Univ.; M.A., New Schl. for Soc. Rsch., N.Y., U.S.A., 1961; Ph.D., ibid, 1965. Appts: Tchng. Assoc., Columbia Univ., 1962-63; Instr., Econs., CUNY, 1964-65; Assoc. Prof., Muhlenberg Coll., Allentown, Pa., 1965-; Vis. Lectr., Hofstra Univ., L.I., N.Y., 1966-67. Mbrships: Am. Economic Assn.; AAAS; AAUP; Pa. Conf. of Economists; Indian Soc. of Labor Economists; V.P., Pharatiya Cultural Soc., Blakeslee, Pa. Publs. incl: Work or Not to Work: An Analysis of Differential Supply Elasticities of Labor, (dissertation), 1965; The Economics of Brain Drain, Manpower Jrnl., 1968; Manpower Crisis: the Problem of Educated Unemployment, (Seminar), 1969; Co-author, Indian Economic Problems, 1973. Recip., Moses Blitzer Schlrship., New Schl. for Soc. Rsch., 1960-61. Address: 2291 Nottingham Rd., Allentown, PA 18103, U.S.A.

SINK, John Davis, b. 19 Dec. 1934. Scientist. Educ: B.S., The Pa. State Univ., Univ. Park, Pa., 1956; M.S., ibid, 1960; Ph.D., 1962; Nat. Sci. Fndn. Postdoctoral Fellow, Univ. of Wis., Madison, Wis., 1964-65. Appts. incl: Assoc. Prof. of Meat Sci., Pa. State Univ., Univ. Park, Pa., 1966-72; Sr. Mbr., Grad. Fac., Dir., Meat Rsch. & Grad. Progs. & Chmn., Grad. Prog. Comm. in Food Sci., ibid, 1966-; Prof. of Meat Sci., 1972-. Mbrships. incl: Pres.-Elect, Am. Meat Sci. Assn., 1973; Nat. Councilor, Phi Tau Sigma, 1969; Bd. of Trustees, Pa. Air Nat. Guard Armory, 1968; Bd. of Dirs., Alpha Zeta Corp.; Sea Power Comm., Navy League of U.S., 1969; Meat & Meat Products Food Safety Comm., Am. Soc. of Animal Sci., 1973; Fellow, Am. Inst. of Chemists; Fellow, AAAS. Author of num. publs. in field. Recip. of hons. Address: 15 Meats Lab., Univ. Park, PA 16802, U.S.A. 6, 14, 28, 128, 129.

SIRENA, (Contessa Antonia Mastrocristino Fanara). Artist; Painter. Self-educated. Early career, singer in nightclubs & theatres, Europe & U.S.A. Early artistic career, creator new art form, marbelized painting. 1st studio & gall., E. Meadow, L.I., N.Y. 1st solo exhib., Rome, Italy, 1966. Other solo exhibs., Paris, Milan, Trieste, Rome, N.Y. Paintings purchased by: Museums of Mod. Art, Rome & Castello Sforzesco, Milan; Mus. Revoltella, Trieste; Mus. of State of Venice, Giulia; Museums of Bologna & Palermo. Pvte. collectors incl: Senator Edward J. Spino; Gina Lollobrigida; Frankie Lane; Frederico Fellini; Giuseppe Saragat. TV appearances U.S.A. & Europe. Hons. incl: Universal Gold Cup, Quadrenale, Rome; Gold Cup, Cultural Ctr., Naples; Medal of the Vatican; Silver Trophy, Comm. of Culture, Belgium; Grand Cross, Order of St.

Constantine; Amita Award, 1969. Address: 1724 Hempstead Tpke., E. Meadow, L.I., NY 11554, U.S.A. 37.

SIREVÅG, Tønnes, b. 21 Jan. 1909. Education Administrator. Educ: Dip. Educ., Oslo Univ., 1935; Cand. Philol., ibid, 1936. Appts: Asst. Master, secondary schls., 1936-53; Headmaster, secondary schls., 1953-54; Dir., State Coun. for Innovation in Schls., 1954-60; Dir., Gen. Educ. Dept., Min. of Educ., 1960-68; Highmaster, Cath. Schl. of Oslo; State Supt. Secondary Educ., & External Examinations of Adult Candidates, Oslo & Co. of Akershus. Coun. Mbr., Comm. Mbr., & Off., var. educl. authorities & orgs. Publs: The region of Jaeren emerging from self-sufficient economy, 1938; The Rise of Medieval Cities and of Laic Culture, 1943; Anglo-American Reader I, II, III (co-author), 1951; Ed. of series, Experimentation & Reform in Education, 1956-. Var. articles on educl. affairs. Address: Smestadhagan 7, Oslo 3, Norway. 43.

SIROL, Jean, b. 15 Feb. 1910. Professor of Law; French Embassy Counsellor. Educ: Doct., Legal Sci., Econs. & H'storic Dip., Free Schl. of Pol. Sci. Appts. incl: Cultural & Press Counsellor, French Embassy, Mexico, 1947; Hist. Prof., Econs., Politics & Soc. Sci., Mexican Univ., 1950; Full Prof., Fac., Toulouse, France; Full Prof., Fac. of Econs./Sci., U.N.A.M., Mexico; Ex-Univ. Prof., Ibero-americano, Mexico; Deleg., French Tourist Serv., Mexico, Unifrance Film, Mexico, & Tourist Serv. for Principality of Monaco. Mbrships: Hon. mbr., Mexican Cultural Inst., 1961; French Riding Club, Mexico; Mexican Pvte. Pilots Assn. Author of num. articles in jrnls. Hons. incl: Order of Legion of Hon., 1956; Kt. of arts & letters; Off., Cruzero del Sur, Brazil. Address: French Embassy, Havre No. 15, Mexico D.F., Mexico.

SISKIN, Milton, b. 14 May 1921. Dentist; Endodontist. Educ: B.A., D.D.S., Univ. of Tenn.; Intern, Walter G. Zoller Mem. Dental Clin., Billings Hosp., Univ. of Chgo.; Dipl., Am. Bd. Endodontics, Am. Bd. Oral Med. Appts. incl: Instr.-Prof., Coll. of Dentistry, Univ. of Tenn., 1947-; Chief, Div. of Oral Med. & Surg., ibid, 1955-58; Hd., Dept. of Oral Med., 1955-58; Lectr., Dept. of Gen. Anatomy & Embryol., 1954-; Lectr., Grad. Schl. of Orthodontics, 1954-; Cons., var. hosps., assns., state & nat. orgs. Fellowships: Am. Acad. Oral Pathol.; AAAS; Am. Assn. Endodontists; Am. Coll. Dentists; Int. Coll. Dentists. Mbrships. incl: num. committees; Am. Bd. Endodontics, 1963-69, 1971-; Am. Dental Assn.; Coun. on Fed. Dental Servs., ibid, 1971-; Am. Med. Writers' Assn.; Am. Inst. Oral Scis.; Omicron Kappa Upsilon; Alpha Omega. Publs: Ed., The Biology of the Human Dental Pulp, 1973; Asst. Ed., Jrnl. of Dental Med. Contbr. to var. dental publs. & nat. periodicals. Hons. incl: Tenn. Dental Assn. Fellowship Award, 1967; Wisdom Hall of Fame, 1972. Address: Univ. of Tenn., Coll. of Dentistry, 847 Monroe Ave., Memphis, TN 38163, U.S.A. 7, 14, 28, 57.

SISSON, Jacqueline Demorest (Mrs.), b. 3 July 1925. Librarian. Educ: B.A., Ohio State Univ., 1946. Appts: Lib. Asst., Columbus (Ohio) Pub. Lib., 1946-47; Lib. Asst., Circulation Dept., 1947-48, Fine Arts Lib., Ohio State Univ., 1948-59; Instr., 1963-69; Hd., Fine Arts Lib., & Asst. Prof., Lib. Admin., 1969-. Mbrships: ALA; Bd. of Dirs. & Past Chmn., Art Sect., Am. Coll. & Rsch. Libs.; Charter Mbr., Art Libs. Soc. of N.Am.; Coll. Art Assn.; Int. Ctr. for Medieval Art; Fndr., Coord., Art Rsch. Libs. of Ohio. Publs: Cooperative System of Ohio Art Libraries,

1969; Contbr. of articles, reviews, to profl. jrnls.; Lectr., coop. systems for art libs.; In progress, Index to Venturi's Storia dell'Arte Italiana. Hons: 4 grants to complete Venturi, Nat. Endowment for the Humanities. Address: 554 N. Selby Blvd., Worthington, OH 43085, U.S.A. 5, 138.

SISTIAGA, José Maria, b. 23 June 1927. Doctor in Chemical Sciences. Educ: Univ. of Madrid, Spain; Tech. Univ., Braunschweig, German Fed. Repub.; Univ. of Syracuse, U.S.A. Appts: Instituto de la Soldadura; Dir., Instituto de Metales no Férreos; Dir., Centro Nacional de Investigaciones Metalurgicas; Currently, Dir.-Gen., Indl. Promotion & Technol., Spanish Min. of Ind. Mbrships. incl: Consejo Superior de Investigaciones Cientificas; Am. Welding Soc.; Int. Iron & Steel Inst.; Am. Soc. for Metals; Iron & Steel Inst.; Welding Inst.; Verein Deutscher Eisenhüttenleute; Deutsche Gesellschaft für Metallkunde. Publs: Aleaciones de Aluminio y Magnesio, 1963; Tech. articles in jrnls. Hons. incl: Commendation w. Badge, Order of Alfonso X, The Wise, 1964; Scroll of Hon., Iron & Steel Inst., 1966. Address: Ministerio de Industria, Ayala 3, Madrid 1, Spain. 43.

SITTE, Hellmuth, b. 6 May 1928. University Professor. Educ: Dr.phil, Univ. of Innsbruck, Austria, 1956; Special trng. in Electron Microscopy & Kopler Micro Methods; Inaugurated, Univ. of Heidelberg, German Fed. Repub. Appts: Univ. Lectr., Heidelberg, 1962; Hd. of Dept., Univ. of Saarland, Homburg-Saar, 1963; Full Prof. & Dir., Inst. of Cytol., ibid, 1966; Vice-Chancellor, 1968-73. Mbrships. incl: German Soc. for Electron Microscopy; Gesellschaft für Nephrologie; Japanese Soc. for Electron Microscopy; Deutsche Gesellschaft für Naturforscher und Arzte; Rotary. Creative works incl: Development of the Reichert-Ultramicrotome Types OM-U-I, II & III, inclng. accessory instruments (w. C. Reichert); More than 30 patents relating to ultra microtomy; More than 30 publs. in sci. jrnls., handbooks & proceedings. Address: Listerstr. 3, D-665 Homburg-Saar, German Fed. Repub. 86.

SIUNG, Oswald Horace, b. 18 Aug. 1915. Medical Practitioner. Educ: B.Sc., Univ. of Edinburgh, 1941; M.B., Ch.B., ibid, 1941; D.P.H., 1943; Cert. for ascertainment of educl. subnormality, Univ. of London, 1948. Appts: House Surg., Halifax Royal Infirmary, Yorkshire, 1941; Asst. Med. Off. of Hlth., Whitehaven Borough, Cumberland, 1942; Bacteriol., Pub. Hlth. Lab., King's Coll., Newcastle-on-Tyne, 1943-48; Med. Off. of Hlth., Wallsend-on-Tyne, 1948-50; Co. Med. Off. of Hlth., Berbice, Guyana, 1950-52; Bacteriol., Gen. Hosp., Port of Spain, Trinidad, 1952-56; Co. Med. Off. of Hlth., Caroni, Trinidad, 1956-62; Specialist, Marariologist, Trinidad, 1962-; Prin. Med. Off. (Epidemiol.), Trinidad, 1967-. Mbrships. incl: Brit. Med. Assn.; Trinidad & Tobago Med. Assn.; Lectr., Royal Soc. for the Promotion of Hlth.; V.P., Soc. for the Care, Promotion & Application of the Environment of Trinidad & Tobago, 1970. Contbr. articles to med. jrnls. Address: 9 Coblentz Gardens, Port of Spain, Trinidad.

SIVAN, Gabriel A., b. 30 Aug. 1934. Author; Critic; Editor. Educ: B.A., Oriel Coll., Oxford, U.K., 1958; M.A., ibid, 1962; Univ. Coll., London, U.K., 1959-61; Ph.D., Hebrew Univ. of Jerusalem, Israel, 1974. Appts: Dir., European Off., Bar-Ilan Univ., Israel, 1961-66; Asst. Ed., Ency. Judaica, 1967-71; Lit. Critic, The Jerusalem Post, 1970-; Dpty. Ed., Ency. Judaica Year Book, 1974; Ed., Mizrachi World,

1974-. Mbrships: Chmn., Univs.' Zionist Coun. of Great Britain, 1959-60; Vice-Chmn., Inter-Univ. Jewish Fedn., 1960-61; Chmn., British Settlers' Assn., Jerusalem Br., 1968-69; Oxford Univ. Union; Oriel Soc.; Oxford Soc., Jerusalem Br. Publs: Three Lovers of Zion, 1970; Heine & Israel, 1971; The Bible & Civilization, 1973. Contbr. to var. jrnls., inclng: The Manchester Guardian, Jewish Chronicle, Jerusalem Post, & to Ency. Judaica, Hebrew Encyclopaedia. Address: 9 Habanai St., Bet Hakerem, Jerusalem, Israel. 55.

SIVEL, Wenceslas Joseph Henry, b. 22 Nov. 1901. Research Engineer; Physicist. Educ: Dr. Civil Engrng.; Dr. Rerum Nat. Appts. incl: Dir., Pool Construction Co., Inc., 1959-; Pres., Regina Press & Publishing Co., San Fran., 1959-; Designer & Supvsr., Dresden, Ill., Atomic Power Plant, & Chief Design Engr., San Fran. Bay Area Rapid Transit Study; Pres., & Dir., G.A. Eng. Soc., Inc. Mbrships: Am. Concrete Inst.; Am. Assn. Mil. Engrs.; German Engrng. Soc.; Am. Assn. Road Builders; Fellow, N.Y. Acad. Scis. Author of 41 vols. on sci. & var. tech. engrng. subjects. Hons: Off. d'Acad. Française w. palms. Address: 735 Geary St.-403, San Francisco 9, CA 94109, U.S.A. 2, 9, 16.

SIVIRSKY, Antal Lajos István, b. 14 Dec. 1909. University Assistant Professor; Interpreter; Novelist. Educ: Masters seminar, Breda & Amsterdam, Netherlands; Ph.D., Univ. of Debrecen, Hungary; Cand. scientiarum litteraturae, Acad. of Sci., Hungary. Appts: Dutch master, several grammar schls., Lyceum-Hohan de Witt, Scheveningen, Netherlands; Univ. Lectr., Utrecht, 1952; Asst. Prof. & mgr., Inst. for Hungarian lang. & lit., ibid, 1972-; Sworn translator, 1942. Mbrships. incl: Hon. mbr., Magyar Nyelvtudomanyi tarsasag (Hungarian Soc. of linguistics); Maatschappij der Nederlandse letterkunde (Soc. of Dutch lit.); PEN-ctr.; Gen. Chmn., Haagse Kunstkring (Artists Circle of The Hague), 1971-72. Author of publs. in Dutch & Hungarian. Address: Laan van Poot 163, Den Haag 2023, Holland. 43, 100.

SIZEMORE, Margaret Lee Davidson (Mrs.). Educator. Educ: A.B., Samford Univ.; M.A., ibid; Degrée Normal, Univ. of Paris, France; Grad. study, Western Reserve Univ.; Special Study in T.V., Univ. of Ala. Appts. incl: Lang. Dept., Samford Univ., 1947-; Dean of Women, ibid, 1950-70; Asst. to Pres. for Community Affairs, ibid, 1970-. Active Civic Worker & mbr. num. prof., civic & cultural socs. inclng.: Life Fellow, Royal Soc. of Arts; Phi Kappa Phi; Charter Mbr., Ala. Chapt., Kappa Kappa Iota; Pi Delta Phi; Alpha Lambda Delta; Exec. Comm., Nat., Gamma Beta Phi; Kappa Delta Epsilon; Beta Pi Theta; AAWU; Advsry. Bd., Ala. Historical Commn.; Ala. Constitution Commn.; U.S. Defense Advsry. Comm. on Women in the Servs.; State Pres. & former Birmingham Br. Pres., Nat. League Am. Pen Women. Publs. incl: The Amazing Marriage of Marie Eustis & Josef Hofmann (co-author); Columnist for Colonial Courier. Recip. num. Hons. inclng: State DAR Distinguished Award, 1965; Alumna-of-the-year, Samford Univ., 1971. Address: 3084 Sterling Rd., Birmingham, AL 35213, U.S.A. 5, 7, 13, 15, 30, 57, 125, 141.

SJÖBERG, Göran E., b. 15 Mar. 1934. Public Communications Director. Educ: M.A., Uppsala Univ., 1958. Appts: Secondary Schl. Tchr., 1958-59; Gen. Sec. of Educ., Swedish Nat. Union of Students, 1959-60; Chief Info. Off., Swedish Confederation of Profl. Assns., 1960-65; Sr. Cons., P.R., PR-Plan AB, 1966-68; Dir. of Pub. Communication, AGA, AB, 1968-72; Pub. Communications Dir., Swedish

Forest Ind., 1972-. Mbrships: Corres. Coun. Mbr., Int. P.R. Assn.; Past Chmn., Swedish P.R. Assn. Contbr. to periodicals, profl. jrnls. Address: Forest Industry House, Villagatan 1, S-114 32 Stockholm, Sweden.

SJÖBLAD, (Karl Erold) Knut, b. 9 Jan. 1912. International Furbroker. Educ: studies in int. bus., Sweden, 6 yrs. Appts: Dir., Grand Pälsmagasin, 1938-61; Dir., Grand Fur Ltd., 1961-68. Mbrships: Pres. of Hon., Kamratskapet, 1961- (Pres., 1952-55); Pres., Svenska Pensionärsförbundet, 1969-. Publs: Num. works on world peace contbd. to Swedish newspapers & mags. Through Svenska Pensionärsförbundet has distributed a proposal for world peace to ldng. statesmen all over world & received approbation from U.N. & num. Hds. of State. Address: Olof Skötkonungsgatan 2, 412 67 Gothenburg, Sweden. 43.

SJÖSTRAND, Bengt Håkan Wilhelm, b. 19 Aug. 1909. Professor. Educ: Teol-Kand., Univ. of Uppsala, Sweden, 1932; Fil.kand., 1935; Fil.lic., Educ., 1937, Fil.dr., 1942. Appts: Asst. Prof., Uppsala Univ., 1942; Prof., Educ. & Educl. Psychol., 1949-; Special Tchr. in Educ., Agricl. Coll., Uppsala, 1939-64; Tchr., var. schls., 1939-43. Mbrsbips. incl: Swedish Soc. of Psychol.; Chmn., ibid, 1952-54; Royal Swedish Acad. of Humanities; Soc. of Humanities, Uppsala; Bd. Chmn., Inst. for Psychotherapy, Stockholm. Publs. incl: History of Swedish Military Education until 1792, 1941; The Theory of Formal Training. History & Experimentation, 2 vols., 1945; History of Education, 4 vols., 1954-65; Education as an Academic Discipline, 1967; Freedom & Equality. Two Main Concepts in Swedish Education 'Thinking in the 60's, 1970; Freedom & Equality as fundamental education Principles in Western Democracy. From John Locke to Edmund Burke, 1973; contbr. to num. jrnls. Hons. incl: Cmdr., Order of the N. Star. Address: Gotavagen 5, S-752 36 Uppsala, Sweden. 43, 134.

SKÅRMAN, Bo, b. 19 Sept. 1908. Land Surveyor. Educ: K.T.H., Stockholm; Dip. in tech. cult. Appts: Formerly Dir., Dist. of Vättle, Gothenburg; Currently Dir., Dist. of Alingsås; M.P. Author of about 600 cultural articles, var. newspapers & publs. Hons: Cavalier, Order of Polar Star. Address: Mariedalsvägen 2, 441 00 Alingsås, Sweden..43.

SKARSTEN, Malvin Olai, b. 28 Sept. 1892. Educator; Administrator; Author. Educ: B.A., M.A., Univ. of Minn.; Ed.D., Univ. of Northern Colo. Appts: Tchr., Elem. & H.S., Minn., 6 yrs.; Schl. Supt., Minn., 2 yrs.; Fellowship in Schl. Admin., Univ. of Minn.; Dir., Student Tchng., & Fac. Mbr., Black Hills (S.D.) State Coll., 18 yrs.; Dir. of Admissions, Registrar, Dir. of Elem. Educ., Hd., Dept. of Educ., & Dir., Grad. Schk., Pacific Univ., 19 yrs. Mbrships: Phi Delta Kappa; Kappa Delta Pi. Publs: George Drouillard, Hunter & Interpreter for Lewis & Clark; The Least of These; Their Hearts Were Right; Contbr. to periodicals. Address: 3601 Reder St., Rapid City, SD 57701, U.S.A. 9.

SKAUG, Arne, b. 6 Nov. 1906. Economist; Diplomat. Educ: Econs. deg., Oslo Univ.; Grad. studies, London Schl. of Econs. & sev. U.S. univs. Appts: Norwegian Ctrl. Bur. of Stats., 1930-39; Rockefeller Fellowship to U.S., 1939-41; Norwegian Govt. Serv., N.Y.C., 1941-44; Commercial Counsellor, Norwegian Embassy, Wash., D.C., 1944-46; Dir.-Gen., Norwegian Ctrl. Bur. of States., 1946-48; Asst.

Sec. of State, For. Off., 1948-49; Hd., Norwegian OEEC Deleg., 1949; Permanent Rep. to NATO, 1952; Min. of Commerce & Shipping, 1955; Ambassador to Court of St. James & Ireland, 1962-68; Ambassador to Denmark, 1968-. Hons. incl: Kt. Grand Cross Royal Victorian Order, Royal Order St. Olav, Danneborg (Denmark), Northern Star (Sweden), Falcon (Iceland). Address: Royal Norwegian Embassy, Trondhjems Plads 4, DK-2100 Copenhagen Ø, Denmark. 12, 34.

SKEETE, Harold, Edward, b. 13 Dec. 1892. dec. 1972. Medical Practitioner. Educ: M.D.C.M., M.C.P. & S. (Quebec), McGill Univ., Montreal, Canada. Appts. incl: C.S.M., 6th Field Ambulance 2nd Div., C.E.F. (Canadian Expeditionary Force), France & Belgium, enlisted 1914; Lt., 9th Field Ambulance, C.E.F., Siberia; Major (M.O.), Barbados Regiment; Asst. Vis. Surg., Gen. Hosp.; Vis. Surg., ibid.; Dist. Surg., St. John Ambulance Brigade. Mbrships. incl: Barbados Yacht Club; Wanderers Cricket Club; Offs. Mess, Barbados Regiment; Lodge No. 253 ER; Rose Croix Chapter 143 PMWS 310 (32nd degrde). Hons. incl.; C. St. J.; O.B.E.; McGill Gold Medallist. Address: c/o Mrs. M. Packer, Warleigh, St. Peter, Barbados, W. Indies. 109, 136.

SKEHAN, Joseph Theodore, b. 13 July 1924. Diplomat; Economist; Educator; Writer. Educ: B.A., Syracuse Univ., 1947; Dip., Heidelberg Univ., Germany, 1950; Ph.D., Georgetown Univ., U.S.A., 1964. Appts. incl: Budget Analyst, Exec. Off. of U.S. Pres., 1948-49; Diplomat, U.S. State Dept., Consulates in Germany, 1951-57; Asst. Prof., Econs., U.S. Naval Acad., Annapolis, Md., U.S.A., 1964-65; Assoc. Prof., Seton Hall Univ., 1965-68; Assoc. Prof., Bloomsburg State Coll., 1969-. Mbrships: Exec. Bd., Nat. Assn. of Laity, 1970-; Pres., 1973-; Phi Beta Kappa; Pi Sigma Rho; Pres., Fac. Senate, Seton Hall Univ., 1967-68; AAUP; Nat. Coun., Nat. Pub. Educ. & Relig. Liberty, 1973-. Author of many papers on econs. & ch. reform & the Liturgy, 1970. Hons. incl: Fulbright Scholar, 1949-50; Hon. Mention, Nat. Sci. Fndn., Doct. Thesis, 1963-64. Address: 638 E. 3rd St., Bloomsburg, PA 17815, U.S.A. 6, 14, 15.

SKEMPTON, Alec Westley, b. 4 June 1914. Professor of Civil Engineering. Educ: Imperial Coll., Univ. of London, U.K., 1932-36. Appts: Sci. Off., Bldg. Rsch. Stn., 1936-46; Rdr. in Soil Mechanics, Imperial Coll., Univ. of London, 1946-55; Prof., ibid, 1955-57; Prof. of Civil Engrng., 1957-. Mbrships: Fellow, Royal Soc.; Fellow, Instn. of Civil Engrs.; Pres., Int. Soc. of Soil Mechanics & Fndn. Engrng., 1957-61. Author of num. papers in field. Hons: Ewing Medal, Instn. of Civil Engrs., 1968; D.Sc., Univ. of Durham, 1968; Lyell Medal, Geological Soc., 1972. Address: Imperial Coll., London SW7, U.K. 1.

SKEY, Lawrence Wilton, b. 29 Oct. 1911. Investment Counsellor. Educ: B.Comm., Univ. of Toronto; Royal Canadian Air Force Staff Coll., Armour Heights, Toronto. Appts. incl: Auditor, Clarkson, Gordon & Co., 1934-36; served RAF, 1939-44 & RCAF (Wing Cmdr.), 1944-46; Conservative M.P. for Trinity, Toronto, 1945-49; Dir., & Treas., Scudder Int. Investments Ltd.; Dir. & Mgr., Econ. Investment Trust Ltd.; Gen. Mgr. & Treas., Scudder, Stevens & Clark of Canada Ltd.; Pres. & Dir., York Assocs. Ltd.; V.P., Dir. & Treas., Canadian Scudder Investment Fund Ltd.; Dir., Metropolitan Trust Co. Mbrships: Chmn. Investment Comm., Canadian Red Cross Soc.; Gov., Canadian Corps of Commissionaires; Pensions Comm., Synod of Anglican Ch.; Pres.,

John Howard Soc. of Ont.; Sigma Chi. Hons: D.F.C.; Twice mentioned in despatches. Address: Dominion of Canada Gen. Ins. Bldg., 165 Univ. Ave., Toronto M5H 3B8, Ont., Canada. 88.

SKIDMORE, Donald E., b. 12 May 1920. Corporation Executive. Educ: Racine's Western Inst., 1937-41; Knapp Coll., 1946-48. Appts. incl: Bookkeeper and Acct., Ace Furnace and Steel Co., Tacoma, 1938-44; Acct., ibid, 1946-50; Ptnr. and Acct., Ctrl. Steel and Tank Co., Yakima, Wash., 1950-58, Sec.-Treas and Dir., 1958-66, V.P. and Dir., 1966-67, Pres. and Dir., 1967-. Mbrships. incl: Yakima Co. Manpower Advsry. Comm., 1966-; Wash. Soc. of Cert. Pub. Accts.; Sheet Metal and Air Conditioning Contractors Assn., Local Labor Advsr., 1959-6; V.P., Lions Club of Yakima; Northwest Coll. Assemblies of God, Kirkland, Wash. (Pres., Lay Coun., 1965-68, 1971); Coun., Evangel Coll., Springfield, Mo., 1960-; Stone Ch. Assembly of God, Yakima (Bd. Mbr., Sec., V.P.); Bd. of Dirs., Schl. Dist. No. 7, Yakima, 1965-; Sec., Exec. V.P., Yakima Chapt., Full Gospel Bus. Men's Fellowship Int.; Dir., Yakima Valley Youth for Christ, 1961-64. Address: 3402 Roosevelt Ave., Yakima, WA 98902, U.S.A. 9, 120, 131.

SKIFFINGTON, Mary I.A.L., b. 3 Sept. 1930. Librarian. Educ: Scottish Schl. of Librarianship; Currently External Undergrad., Queen's Univ., Canada. Appts: Interne Children's Libn., Toronto Pub. Libs., 1956-57; Children's Libn., N. Central Sask. Regional Lib., Prince Albert, Sask., 1958-63; Ref. Libn., Bermuda Lib., 1964-69; Hd. Libn., ibid, 1969-. Mbrships: Bermuda Nat. Trust; Bermuda Histl. Soc.; Bermuda Biological Stn. for Rsch. Address: Bermuda Lib., Hamilton 5-31, Bermuda.

SKILTON, John H. Clergyman. Educ: B.A., Univ. of Pa., 1927; M.A., 1928; Ph.D., 1961; M.Div., Westminster Theol. Sem., 1939. Appts: Tchrng. Asst., Engl., Univ. of Pa., 1927-32; Pastor, 2nd Parish Ch., Portland, Me., 1933-39; Instr., N.T., Westminster Theol. Sem., Phila., Pa., 1939-42; Asst. Prof., N.T., ibid, 1942-48; Assoc. Prof., 1949-62; Assoc. Dean, 1959-62; Dean of Students, 1962-63; Prof., N.T., Lang. & Lit., 1962-64; Chmn., Dept. of N.T., 1962-73; Prof., N.T., 1964-73. Mbrships. incl: Moderator, Gen. Assembly, Orthodox Presby. Ch., 1953; Phi Beta Kappa; Pi Mu Epsilon; Soc. of Biblical Lit.; Evangelical Theol. Soc.; Am. Acad. Relig. Publs. incl: Think on These Things: Bible Truths for Faith & Life, 1972; Contbr., The Infallible Work, 1946, 3rd edit., 1968; Ed. & Contbr., Scripture & Confession, 1973. Address: 930 W. Olney Ave., Philadelphia, PA 19141, U.S.A. 6, 13, 15, 30.

SKINA, Ansbert G., 18 Feb. 1910. International Industrial Utilities Executive. Educ: B.S.E.E., Univ. of Idaho, Moscow, Idaho, 1935; Completed series of Exec. Courses, Am. Mgmt. Assn. Appts. incl: Chmn., Bd. of Dirs., Mbr., Admin. Comm. & Chmn., Int. Comm., Commonwealth Servs., Inc.; Pres. & Chmn. of Advsry. Bd., Commonwealth Mgmt. Consultants; Pres. & Dir., Commonwealth Servs. Int., Inc.; V.P. & Dir., CSI Constructors, Inc.; V.P. & Dir., Transportation Consultants Int., Co.; Dir., Int. Gas & Power Engrs. Pty. Ltd., Australia. Mbrships. incl: IEEE; Engrng. Advsry. Coun., Dean of Engrng., Univ. od Idaho, Moscow, Idaho; Am. Inst. of Mech. Engrs.; Dir., Am. Inst. of Mgmt.; Am.-Arab Assn. of Commerce & Ind.; Pres., & Dir., U.S.-Arab Chmbr. of Comm., N.Y. Recip. of num. mil. & civilian hons. Address: 11 East 73rd St., N.Y., NY 10021, U.S.A. 6.

SKINNARD, F.W., b. 8 Mar. 1902. Literary Critic & Essayist. Educ: Plymouth Tech. Coll. & Schl. of Art, U.K.; Borough Rd. Trng. Coll.; Lincolns Inn. Appts: Tchr., Lectr., London Co. Coun., Willesden; Tutor, Cambridge Helsingor Lund Summer Courses; Assoc., Fac. of Soc. Sci., Reed Coll., Ore., U.S.A., 1937; M.P., Labour, for Harrow East, 1945-50; Registrar & External Dir. of Exams., Inst. of Optical Sci., 1951-59, 1962; Critic on Books & Bookmen, 1972-. Mbrships: Fed. Coun., Independent Labour Pty., 1935-40; Exec., Nat. Coun. of Schoolmasters, 1935-40; Exec., Colonial Bur. & Commonwealth Burs. of Fabian Soc., 1945-59; Imperial Advsry. Comm., Labour Pty., 1946-53. Publs: Logic in the Curriculum, 1937; Art & Craftiness, 1974; Contbr. to num. jrnls.; Co-ed., Education for Citizenship, 1939. Hons: Fellow, Inst. of Optical Sci., 1957. Address: 1 Oakfield Ave., Kenton, Harrow, Middlesex, HA3 8TH, U.K. 1, 41, 43.

SKOG, Hazel Kristine (Mrs.), b. 12 Apr. 1903. Certified Public Accountant. Educ: B.C.S., Kinman Bus. Univ., 1933. In prac. as Prin. Profl. Mbrships: Orgr., 1st Pres., Spokane Chapt. Am. Soc. of Women Accts., 1938; Sec., Treas., V.P., Pres., Spokane Chapt., Wash. Soc. C.P.A.'s, 1943-53; Nat. Pres., Am. Woman's Soc. of C.P.A.'s, 1944-45; Chmn., By-laws Comm., then Sec., Wash. Soc. C.P.A.'s, 1965-74; Am. Inst. C.P.A.'s. Mbr. many social & civic orgs. inclng: Treas., Prevocational Trng. Ctr. for Mentally Retarded, 1973-; Treas., on Bd., Spokane Co. Chapt. Wash. Assn. for Retarded Cits., 1973-; Pres., Spotlight on Youth Month Assn.; Gov.'s Comm. for Employment of the Handicapped, 1974-. Contbr. articles to profl. jrnls. Hons: Wash. State 1973 Woman of Achievement, Wash. State Bus. & Profl. Woman's Club. Address: 3118 E. 15th Ave., Spokane, WA 99203, U.S.A. 5, 16, 120, 128, 130, 132, 138.

SKOLNICK, Malcolm Harris, b. 11 Aug. 1935. Educator. Educ: B.S., Univ. of Utah, 1956; M.S., Cornell Univ., 1959; Ph.D., ibid, 1962. Appts. incl: Mbr., Schl. of Maths., Inst. Adv. Study, Princeton, N.J., 1963-64; Staff Sci., Elem. Sci. Study Educ. Dev. Ctr., Newton, & Prog. Coord., Peace Corps Trng. & Support Servs., 1965-67; Assoc. Prof. Phys., Pathol., & Hlth. Scis. Communication, Dir. Hlth. Scis. Communication, & other admin. posts, SUNY, Stony Brook, N.Y., 1967-71; Adjunct Assoc. in Physiol., Mt. Sinai Schl. Med., CUNY, N.Y.C., 1970-72; Dir. & Prof., Biomed. Communications, & Prof., Physiol., Univ. of Tex. Med. Schl., Houston, 1971-. Mbr., profl. orgs. & fraternities. Author & co-author, sci. papers, reports & book chapts. Recip., Ford Fndn. Schlrship, 1952. Address: Univ. of Texas Medical School, 6400 W. Cullen St., Texas Medical Ctr., Houston, TX 77025, U.S.A. 6, 7, 14.

SKORNIA, Harry Jay, b. 2 Apr. 1910. University Professor; Broadcasting Executive; Author. Educ: A.B., Mich. State Univ.; M.A., ibid; Ph.D., Univ. of Mich. Appts. incl: Dir. of Broadcasting, Chmn. of Dept., Ind. Univ., 1941-53; Chief of Radio for Austria, & Radio Attaché, U.S. Embassy, Vienna, 1951-53; Exec. Dir., Nat. Assn. Educl. Broadcasters, U.S.A., Chmn. & Mbr., var. nat. comms., 1953-60; Prof., Univ. of Ill., Chgo. Circle, 1953-; Mbr., edit., exec. & advsry. bds., var. mags. & broadcasting assns. Mbrships: Pres., var. exchange & rotary clubs; Pres., Bds. of Deacons, Presby. Chs. Publs. incl: Television & the News, 1968; Problems & Controversies in Radio & TV, 1968; some 400 articles & reviews, profl. jrnls. Recip., Pioneer-Laureate Award, Int. Broadcasting Soc., 1968. Address:

Univ. of Illinois, Box 4348, Chicago, IL 60680, U.S.A. 1, 2, 8, 15.

SKOULIKIDIS, N. Theodor, b. 2 Sept. 1925. Professor. Educ: Dipl., chem. engrng., Nat. Tech. Univ., Athens, Greece, 1948; Ph.D., ibid, 1950; Postdoct. fellowship, Inst. Phys. Chem., Munich Univ., Germany, 1952-54, '55, '56-58;. Appts: Asst., Inst. Phys. Chem., Nat. Tech. Univ., Athens, 1954; Lectr., ibid, 1955; Forschungsprivatdozent, Munich Univ., Germany, 1956-58; Assoc. Prof., phys. chem. & applied electrochem., Nat. Tech: Univ. of Athens, 1960; Prof., ibid, 1968-. Mbrships: Int. Comm. of Corrosion & Fouling; European Fed. Corrosion; Assn. Greek Chem. Engrs.; Assn. Greek Chems.; Tech. Chmbr. of Greece. Author, num. profl. publs. Hons: Gold Medal, Inst. of Valorisation of Greek raw materials, 1955; Gold Medal, Order of King George II, 1968; Taxiarch of King George II, 1971. Address: Lab. of Phys. Chem. & Applied Electrochem., Nat. Tech. Univ. of Athens, 42 Patission str., Athens 147, Greece.

SKUSZANKA-KRASOWSKA, (Mrs.) Krystyna, b. 24 July 1924. Stage Manager; Director. Educ: M.A., Magister Philos., Poznan Univ., Poland, 1949; Dip. Stage Mgmt., State High Theatrical Schl., Warsaw, ibid, 1953. Appts: Artistic Dir., State Theatre, Opole, Poland, 1953-55; Dir., People's Theatre, Nowa Huta, Cracow, ibid, 1955-63; Dir., Polish Theatre, Warsaw, 1963-64; Dir., Polish Theatre, Wroclaw, 1965-72; Dir., Slowacki Theatre, Cracow & Asst. Prof., Fac. Staging, State High Theatrical Schl., ibid, 1972-. Mbrships: Polish Theatre & Film Artists & Actors Assn.; Int. Theatre. Inst. Prin. Prods. Shakespeare: 12th Night; Measure for Measure; As You Like It; The Tempest; The Winter's Tale; Goldoni: The Servant of Two Masters; Princess Turandot; Calderon: Life is a Dream; Mickiewicz: Dziady; Slowacki: Balladyne; Lilla Weneda; A Silver Dream of Salomea; Fantazy; Kordian; Aeschylus: Orestes. Recip. sev. hons. inclng: The State Prize, 1953; The Theatre Critics' Prize, 1958; The Golden Cross of Merit, 1955. Address: Teatr im. J. Slowackiego, Plac SW. Ducha, Kraków, Poland.

SKWERES, Thomas Walter, b. 11 May 1929. Marketing Administrator. Educ: Wright City Coll., 1947-49; Northwestern Univ., 1949-55. Appts: Prod. Mgr., Reincke, Meyer & Finn, 1953-55; V.P. Account Exec., Hanson & Stevens, 1955-62; V.P. Sales, Ross & White Co., 1962-. Mbrships: Am. Mgmt. Assn.; Chmbr. of Comm. Address: 5613 Snowdrop Ln., Lisle, IL 60532, U.S.A. 8, 16.

SKYLLSTAD, Kjell Müller, b. 30 June 1928. Assistant Professor. Educ: B.A., U.S.A., 1950; M.A., 1952; Mag. art. Musicol. & Cand.philol., Oslo Univ., Norway, 1960. Appts: Asst. Prof., Inst. of Musicol., Oslo Univ., 1962-; Coun. Mbr., Inst. of Folk Music, ibid, 1971-; Music Critic, 1966-; Lectr., State Schl. of Opera, Oslo, & Philharmonic Soc. & Pedagogical Inst., 1966-68; Vis. Rsch. Fellow, Inst. of Evaluation Rsch., Graz, Austria, 1972-74. Mbrships: Comm. Mbr., Norwegian Vietnam Movement; Vice-Chmn., Norwegian Socialist Culture Wkrs. Assn., 1969-70; Chmn., Norwegian Sect., Int. Assn. for Contemporary Music, 1968-70; Chmn., Norwegian Musicological Assn., 1972-; Pres., Fartein Valen Soc., 1967-72. Publs: Critical Ed., Edv. Grieg: Piano Concerto & Two-Piano Works, Grieg Gesamtausgabe; Music Ed., Familieboken, 1972-. Mixed Media & Instrumental Theatre Works: Neo-Dada Cabaret, ABC Theatre Oslo, 1966; Abstraction I, Munch Mus., Oslo, 1967;

DadaScope, Homage à Bergen, Bergen Art Galleri, 1970. Hons. incl: Deutsche Akademische Austauschdienst Rsch. Grant, 1959-60; Nat. Humanistic Rsch. Coun. Rsch. Grant, 1972-74. Address: Inst. of Musicol., Chateau Neuf, Slemdalsveien 7, Oslo 3, Norway. 46, 134.

SLACK, Florence Kantor (Mrs. Melvin F. Slack) b. 4 Jan. 1922. Educator. Educ: B.A., Hunter Coll., 1960; M.S., ibid, 1962; Econs., CCNY; M.A., Psychol., New Schl. Soc. Rsch., 1972. Appts: Tchr., Drake Bus. Schl., N.Y.C., 1960-62; Roosevelt H.S., 1962; Ctrl. Commercial H.S., 1962; Eastern Dist. H.S., 1962-63; Walton H.S., Bronx, 1963-. Mbrships: F.I.B.A.; Pitman Tchrs. Assn.; News Letter Ed., Alpha Chap., Delta Pi Epsilon, 1963-67; Exec. Bd., Bus. Educ. Assn., 1970. Address: 9 Farrand Dr., Parsippany, NJ 07054, U.S.A. 5, 6, 22, 57, 138.

SLATER, Joseph Elliott, b. 17 Aug. 1922. President., Aspen Institute for Humanistic Studies. Educ: B.A. Univ. of Calif., Berkeley. Appts. incl: Prog. Off. i/c Int. Rels. Prog., The Ford Fndn, 1966-67; Assoc. Dir. Int. Affairs, ibid, 1957-60, '62-66; Pres., The Salk Inst., 1967-72, The Anderson Fndn., 1969-72; Pres., Aspen Inst. for Humanistic Studies, 1970-; Special Fellow, The Salk Insc.; Vis. Prof., Univ. of Colo.; Cons., Int. Affairs Prog., Ford Fndn. Mbrships. incl: Trustee & Exec. Comm., Aspen Inst. for Humanistic Studies, Salk Inst.; Trustee, Acad. for Educl. Dev., Soc. Sci. Fndn., World Affairs Coun., San Diego, Eisenhower Exchange Fellowships Prog.; Dir., Am. Coun. on Germany, Overseas Dev. Coun., The Design Ctr., U.N. Assn., U.S.A.; Advsry. Coun., U.S. Inst. Human Rights, Am. Univ. Schl. of Int. Serv. Address: 870 United Nations Plaza, Apt. 11G, N.Y., NY 10017, U.S.A.

SLATER, Kenneth Frederick, b. 27 Dec. 1917. Bookseller. Educ: St. Lukes Coll. Appts: Army Serv., 1940-54, Commissioned 1943, RARO, 1954. Mbrships: Vice Chmn., Ed., Brit. Sci. Fiction Assn.; Vice Chmn., Sec., Wisbech Riding Club; First Fandom. Publs: Ed., Operation Fantasy, 1947-53; Compiler & Ed., Brit. Sci. Fiction Book Index, 1955; Checklist of Sci. Fiction, Fantasy & Supernatural Stories available in paperback in Britain, 1966. Co-ed., Vector, Jrnl. of Brit. Sci. Fiction Assn., 1967-68. Book reviews, inclng. regular column in Nebula Science Fiction & Science Fantasy Review. Hons: 'Doc' Weir Award, Brit. Sci. Fiction Assn. Address: c/o F(M)L, 39 West St., Wisbech, Cambs. PE13 2LX, U.K.

SLATER, Van Edward, b. 14 June 1937. Artist; Teacher. Educ: B.A., Univ. of Calif, L.A., 1961; M.A., ibid, 1965. Appts: Art Instr., Santa Monica City Coll., Calif., 1965-66; Art Instr., Compton Coll., Calif., 1966-69, Prof. of Art, 1969-; Drawing Instr., L.A. City Coll., Calif., 1969-70; Cons., Albany State Coll., Ga., 1972. Mbrships: L.A. Art Assn., 1965-66; Art-W. Associated Inc.; Treas., ibid, 1968-70, Pres., 1970-72. Publs: Local Black Artists of Southern California (manual), 1969, 3rd edit., 1971; Black Artists of Southern California (manual), 1972. Sev. educl. films. Exhibs. incl: Oakland Mus., UCLA Art Gall., Compton Coll., L.A. City Hall Gall., Calif.; Carnegie Inst., Pitts., Pa. Work in pub. & pvte. collects. Hons: Watts Festival Purchase Award, 1971; Hale Woodruff Award, 1972. Address: P.O. Box 8997, Los Angeles, CA 90008, U.S.A. 59, 130, 131, 139.

SLAVIN, (Msgr.) William Michael, b. 17 Nov. 1907. Catholic Priest. Educ: La Salle Inst., 1925; A.B., Georgetown Univ., 1929; M.A., St.

Bonaventure Univ., 1930. Appts. incl: Res. Cath. Chap., Rensselaer Polytech. Inst., Troy, NY, 1936-41, '46-59; Chap., USN, 1942-46; Pastor, Our Lady of Victory Ch., Troy, 1959-. Mbrships. incl: Bd. Consultors, Diocese Albany; Pres., Bd. Trustees, Troy Pub. Liv.; La Salle Inst., Cath. Ctrl. HS, Rensselaer Co.; Am. Red Cross, Human Rights Comm., City of Troy, Family & Children's Serv.; Bd. Govs., Georgetown Univ., Wash. DC; Army & Navy Club; Troy Country Club; Lake Placid Club. Apptd. Papal Chamberlain by Pope John XXIII, 1959. Address: 55 N. Lake Ave., Troy, NY 12180, U.S.A.

SLAYTON, Ronald Alfred, b. 16 Dec. 1910. Artist; Writer; Teacher. Educ: Pratt Inst., Brooklyn, N.Y., 1931-34; Univ. of Vt., Burlington, 1935-36; B.S., Tchrs. Coll., Columbia Univ., 1945; Univ. of Tenn., Knoxville, 1946-48. Appts. incl: Crafts Specialist, Tenn. Agricl. Extension Serv., 1945-51; Assoc. Prof., Univ. of Tenn., 1945-51; Tchr., Fletcher Farm Craft Schl., 1959-70; Dir., ibid, 1959-60; Schl. Tchr., 1959-73; Community Coll. Tchng. Staff, 1973-74; Trustee & Curator, T.W. Wood Art Gall., 1968-. Mbrships: Pres., S.E. Wash. Co. Tchrs. Assn., 1958, Vt. Art Tchrs. Assn., 1965-66. Montpelier Theatre Guild, 1969-70; Bd., Unitarian Ch., 1964-66, Vt. Theatre Assn., 1966-67. Contbr. of articles to var. jrnls. Exhibs. of Paintings., Boston & New Engl. Recip., Award of Merit, Vt. Coun. Arts, 1971. Address: RFD 2, Montpelier, VT 05602, U.S.A. 6, 37.

SLEEPER, Samuel, b. 1 Mar. 1910. Educational Administrator. Educ: A.B., Clark Univ., 1930; M.A., Columbia Univ., 1931; Postgrad., Harvard Univ., 1933-39. Appts: Tchr., Worcester Pub. Schls., 1933-71; Dept. Hd., Soc. Studies, ibid, 1950-68; Coord., Soc. Studies Curric., 1968-; Tchr. Corps Coord., 1969-71; Owner, Fndr., Dir., Camp Wamsutta, Inc., Oxford, Mass., 1945-. Mbrships: Pres., Community Concert Assn., Worcester, 1968-70; Bd. of Dirs., Worcester Symph. Orch.; NEA; Am. Hist. Assn.; Nat. Coun. Soc. Studies; Am. Camping Assn.; Ctr. for Democratic Studies. Address: Camp Wamsutta, Oxford, MA 01540, U.S.A.

SLESINGER, Donald, b. 27 Dec. 1897, Retired Psychoanalyst. Educ: Columbia Coll., 1920; Harvard & Columbia Univs.; William Alanson White Inst. Appts: Asst. Prof., Law & Exec. Sec., Yale Instn. of Human Rels., 1928; Prof., Law & Dean Student Div. of Soc. Scis., 1930-36; Dir., Am. Film Ctr., 1938-46; Psychoanal., 1948-68. Past Pres., Assn. Psychoanal. Psychols. Address: North Pamet Rd., Truro, MA 02666, U.S.A. 2.

SLINKARD, Robert Jay, b. 15 Jan. 1926. State Government Administrator. Educ: Grad., Utterback-Brown Bus. Coll., Danville, Ill., U.S.A., 1948; Grad., Int. Accts. Soc., Chgo., Ill., 1950; A.A., Mesa Community Coll., Ariz., 1972. Appts: Mgmt. positions in ind., Ill., 1950-65; Purchasing Dir., Navajo Tribe, Window Roack, Ariz., 1965-69; Dir., Bus. Dev., Indian Dev. Dist., Phoenix, Ariz., 1969-71; Dir., Am. Schl. Table Mfg. Corp., Phoenix 1970-73; Exec. Dir., Bus. Dev. Prog., Navajo Community Coll., Many Farms, Ariz., 1971-73; Dir., Indian Am. Mercantile Corp., Chandler, Ariz., 1972-73; Dir., Admin. Servs., Dept. of Econ. Security, State of Ariz., 1973-; Pt.-time Jr. Coll. Instr., Ariz. State Prison, Florence, 1974. Mbrship: Int. Accts. Soc., Inc. Author, Arizona Indian Business Development Program, a Technical Assistance Project Report for U.S. Department of Commerce, 1971. Address: P.O.

Box 1467, Coolidge, AZ 85228, U.S.A. 9, 57, 139.

ŚLIWIŃSKI, Wincenty Piotr, b. 18 Jan. 1915. Painter; Graphic Artist; Poet; Constructor of Violins. Educ: Univ. & Engrng. Coll., Warsaw, Poland, 1936-39; Acad. of Fine Arts, Warsaw, 1936-39, 1948. Career: Investigated & collected Polish Folk Art, 1931-37; Archeological excavations for Mus. of Sci. Soc., Plock, & Univ. of Wilno, 1931-39; Construction of violins, restoration of instruments by old Italian masters, sci. investigations & experiments in violin construction, 1940-46; Active as painter & graphic artist, 1946-; Active as poet, painter & graphic artist, 1965-. Mbrships. incl: Deleg., Accademia Int. Leonardo da Vinci; Deleg., Comitato Int., Centro Studi e Scambi Int., Rome, Italy; Int. Arts Guild, Monte Carlo, Monaco; Union of Polish Plastic Artists, Warsaw; World Poetry Soc. Num. exhibs. in museums & art galls. in Poland, U.S.A., Australia, Italy, France, Canada, Denmark, German Fed. Repub., Spain, Monaco. Author of theoretical work, The Violin Mezzosopran & an Instrument Strengthening the Sound of the Violin, 1942; Developer of violin based on laws contrary to those used in Mezzosopran. Address: 4/78 Tatrzańska St., 00 742 Warsaw, Poland. 11, 43, 129, 132.

SLOAN, Addie Cannon. Teacher. Educ: A.B., Morris Brown Coll., Atlanta, Ga.; M.A., Atlanta Univ.; Further study at Ga. State Univ., Wayne Univ., Detroit, Mich., Savannah State Interdenominational Theological Ctr. Appts: Supply wk., Atlanta Pub. Schls., 1 yr.; Asst. Prin., Villa Rica Elem. Schl.; Asst. Prin., Pine St. Nursery Schl.; Currently Tchr., 5th grade, J.F. Beaver Elem. Schl., Fulton Co. Bd. of Educ. Mbrships. incl: Pres., Atlanta Dist. Missionary Dept., 8 yrs.; V.P., Local Missionary Dept.; Youth Counselor; Urban League; NEA; Nat. Coun. of Chs.; Ch. Women United. Organizer, 1st Character Bldg. Prog., Fulton Co. Schls., & Christian Youth Fellowship, Butler St. C.M.E. Ch.; Ed., J.F. Beaver Newsletter, J.F. Beaver Schl. Hons. incl: 4 trophies for outstanding wk. in YWCA Mbrship. Drive, 1964-74; Chosen by Butler St. Ch. for outstanding wk. in educ. & soc. reform, 1974. Address: 159 Whitefood Ave., N.E., Atlanta, GA 30307, U.S.A. 125.

SLOAN, Albert John Hicks II, b. 24 Sept. 1942. College Chaplain. Educ: A.B., Albany State Coll., Ga., U.S.A., 1965; Master of Divinity, Interdenominational Theological Ctr., 1969. Appts. incl: Dir., Youth Work, Christian Meth. Episcopal Ch., Atlanta, Ga., 1962-64; Ctr. Dir., City of Atlanta Recreational Dept., 1965-67; Counselor & Asst. Dir., Upward Bound, Ala. State Univ., Montgomery, 1969-71; Dean of Chapel, Miles Coll., Birmingham, Ala., 1971-. Mbrships. incl: Bd., Children's Hope Ctr., Montgomery; Bd., Montgomery Assn. for Retarded Children; Bd., Ala. Coun. on Human Rels.; NAACP; Ga. Coun. of Chs.; Nat. Pres., Christian Meth. Episcopal Ch.'s Youth, 1964-69; Nat. V.P., Sigma Rho Sigma; Chap., Alpha Phi Chapt., Omega Psi Phi. Hons. incl: Omega Man of the Yr., Chi Epsilon Chapt., Omega Psi Phi, 1965; Omega's Outstanding Achievement Award, Albany State Coll., 1971. Address: 5500 Avenue G, Fairfield, AL 35064, U.S.A. 125.

SLOAN, David Edward, b. 29 Mar. 1922. Business Executive. Educ: B.Comm., Univ. of Man., Winnipeg, Canada, 1942. Appts. incl: Serv. to Lt., Canadian Active Army, 1942-45; Treas., Canadian Pacific Ltd., Montreal, P.Q., 1947-; Dir., Canadian Pacific Securities Ltd.,

1965-, Treas. & Pres., 1969-; Dir., Fire Ins. Co. of Canada, 1974-. Mbrships: Pres. & Dir., Financial Execs. Inst., Montreal Chapt.; Dir., Financial Exevs. Inst. of Canada; Vice-Chmn., Consultative Comm., Sir George Williams Univ. Montreal; Canadian Chmbr. of Comm.; Fedn. of Financial Analysts; Nat. Assn. of Bus. Economists; Soc. of Investment Analysts, U.K.; Elder, Mt. Royal United Ch.; Royal Montreal Golf Club. Address: Canadian Pacific Ltd., Suite 247, Windsor Stn., Montreal, P.Q., H3C 3E4, Canada. 2.

SLOAN, Douglas A., b. 26 June 1920. Management Consultant. Educ: Carleton Coll., Ottawa, Ont., 1944-45; B.Sc., Queen's Univ., Kingston, Ont., 1949. Appts. incl: R.C.A.F. Ottawa, 1941-45; Miner, Buffalo Ankerite, & Noranda Mines, 1945-49; Supervisory Mgmt., Falconbridge Nickel Mines Ltd., 1950-56; Cons., Urwick, Currie, Toronto, 1956-; Mng. Ptnr. - Int., Urwick, Currie; Dir., Coopers & Lybrand Assocs. Ltd.; Pres., Personnel Appraisal Co. Ltd. Mbrships incl: Fellow, Past Pres. & Fndg. Mbr., Inst. of Mgmt. Cons. of Ont.; Past Pres., Inst. of Mgmt. Cons. of Canada; Assn. of Profl. Engrs. of Ont.; Canadian Inst. of Mining & Metallurgy; Chmn., C.I.M.M. Univ./Ind. Sub-Comm.; Am. Inst. Mining Engrs.; British Inst. of Mgmt.; Am. Inst. of Ind. Engrs. Contbr. of Num. articles, papers, to profl. jrnls. & confs. Recip. The Canadian Mining & Metallurgical Prize, 1950. Address: Urwick, Currie & Partners Ltd., 145 King St. W., Toronto, Ontario, M5H 1J8, Canada. 32, 88.

SLOAN, Henry S(iegmund), b. 27 Mar. 1926. Editor; Writer. Educ: B.A., San Francisco State Coll., 1950; M.A., N.Y. Univ., 1952; Grad. Study, Univ. of Calif., Berkeley 1953-55; Ph.D., N.Y. Univ., 1962. Appts: Optical Benchman, var. optical firms, 1942-44, 1946-53; Serv., U.S. Army, 1944-46; Soc. Case Wkr., L.A. Co. Bur. of Pub. Assistance, Calif., 1955-58; Var. Free-lance writing assignments, 1958-60; Assoc. Ed. & Writer, Current Biography, H.W. Wilson Co., N.Y.C., 1961-; Writer, Ency. Americana, 1965-68; Writer, Americana Annual, 1966-. Mbrships: Am. Histl. Assn.; Am. Acad. Pol. & Soc. Sci.; Phi Alpha Theta; Mensa; Sierra Club; Am. Youth Hostels (Hike Comm.). Publs: Num. articles in Current Biography, Ency. Americana, Americana Annual, World Authors. Contbr. to travel publs. Address: 210 W. 70th St., Apt. 504-A, N.Y., NY 10023, U.S.A. 6, 13, 55.

SLOLY, Michael Arthur Richard, b. 6 July 1937. Attorney-at-Law. Educ: Univ. Coll. of W. Indies, 1954-57; B.A., London, 1957; Articled to H.O.A. Dayes, Solicitor, 1957. Admitted Solicitor, Supreme Ct., Jamaica, 1961. Appts: Ptnr., Dayes & Sloly, 1961-65; Assoc., Manton & Hart, Solicitors, 1965-67; Ptnr., ibid, 1968-72; Ptnr., Lake, Nunes, Scholefield & Co., 1973-; Co. Dir.; Mbr., Advsry. Comm. to Min. of Home Affairs & Justice, 1972-. Mbrships: Exec. Comm., Jamaica Nat. Theatre Trust; Past Mbr., Exec. Comm., Howard League of Jamaica. Recip., Jamaica Govt. Exhib., 1954. Address: 72-76 Harbour St., Kingston, Jamaica, W. Indies. 109.

SLONE, Horace Evans, b. 28 Jan. 1906. Electronic Engineer; Educator. Educ: E.E., Syracuse Univ., N.Y., 1927; Postgrad. work, Cornell Univ., Ithaca, ibid, 1938, '39. Appts: Radio Engr., Gen. Elec. Co., Schenectady, N.Y., 1927-30; Chief Engr., Stn. WGH, Newport News, Va., 1931-37; Asst. Prof., Elec. Engrng., Clemson A & M Coll., S.C., 1937-39; Tchr., Tech. Electircity, Binghamton H.S., N.Y.. 1939-40; w. Fed. Communications

Commn., Phil. Pa. & Wash. D.C., 1940-71; Supvsry. Engr., Off. of Opinions & Reviews, 1949-57; Engrng. Asst. to Commnr., 1957-62; Mbr., Review Bd., 1962-71. Mbrships: Mason; Past Patron, Silver Spring, Md. Chapt., Order Eastern Star; Meth.; Ancient & Accepted Scottish Rite of Freemasonry, Southern Jurisdiction, U.S.A. Recip. of Outstanding Serv. Award, FCC, 1957. Address: 6005 Landon Ln., Bethesda, MD 20034, U.S.A.

SLOOK, Thomas Harrison. Professor of Mathematics. Educ: B.S., Temple Univ., Phila. Pa., U.S.A., 1943; M.A., Univ. of Pa., Phila., 1947. Appts: Mbr., Maths. Fac., Temple Univ., 1948-; Cons., U.S. Army Ordnance Dept., 1960-; Dir., Temple's Nat. Sci. Fndn. In-Serv. Inst. for Secondary Schl. Tchrs. of Maths. & Sci. Mbrships: Am. Maths. Soc.; Lecture Comm., Am. Maths. Assn.; Grad. Educ. Comm. for the State of Pa., 1965; Fndr., Zeta Chapt. at Temple. Pi Mu Epsilon; Capt. of Fleet 357, Int. Lightning Sailing Assn.; Red Dragon Canoe Club. Publs: Elementary Modern Mathematics (w. M.A. Wurster); Sev. contbns. to math. jrnls. Hons: Fellowship, Nat. Sci. Fndn., 1961-62; Citation, Newark Coll. of Engrng., 1970. Address: Route 38, Moorestown, NJ 08057, U.S.A. 6.

SLOWTER, Edward E., b. 1 Nov. 1912. Executive Administrator. Educ: B.Chem. Engrng., Ohio State Univ., 1934; M.S., 1935; Chem. Engr., 1939. Appts. incl: Rsch. Engr.-Asst. Supvsr., Battelle Mem. Inst., Columbus Ohio, 1936-42; Supvsr.-Bus. Mgr., ibid; V.P., 1957-; Sec., 1956-; Treas., 1963-. Mbrships incl: Soc. Profl. Engrs.; Bd. Electors, Sigma Xi, 1972-; Investment Comm., Am. Soc. Metals, 1971-. Author of tech. publs. Holder of 3 U.S. patents. Hons. incl: Commendation Ribbon, U.S. Army, 1944; Ohio Soc. Profl. Engrs. Citation, 1970; Cert. of Award for Outstanding Servs., Profl. Engrs. in Ind. & Nat. Soc. Profl. Engrs., 1970-71. Address: 505 King Ave., Columbus, OH 43201, U.S.A. 2, 14, 26.

SMALES, Helen Kinnear (Mrs. Clarence P. Smales), b. 18 June 1903. Minister of Religion; Stenographer; Poet. Educ: Otterbein Coll.; Holbrook Coll., Manchester, Ohio. Appts: Licensed preacher, 1926 or 27; Ordained Min., Assemblies of God, 1942; Asst. Libn., Orly AFB, France. Mbrships: Poets of the Pacific, 1960-62; V.P., Apollo Chapt., Calif. Fedn. of Chaparral Poets, 1970-72; Affiliated Mbr., Orpheus Chapt., ibid, 1973-; Mbrship. Chmn., Women's Soc. of Christian Serv., 1st United Meth. Ch., 1970-72. Contbr. poems to var. jrnls. & anthols., inclng: Verse for Today (Columbus, Ohio, Evening Dispatch), Davis Anthol. of Newspaper Verse, Stars & Stripes, Full Gospel Herald, Ch. of Christ Advocate, Pentecostal Evangel, Philo-Duncan Falls News & Religious Telescope. Hons. incl: 1st Prize, Free Verse Contest, Orpheus Chapt. Calif. Fedn. of Chaparral Poets, 1974; 2nd Prize, Apollo Chapt. Contest, ibid, 1973; 1st Hon. Mention, Apollo Contest, 1970 & 71. Address: 6002 Freckles Rd., Lakewood, CA 90713, U.S.A.

SMALL, Robert Van Dyke, b. 29 Nov. 1924. Professor of Psychology; Author. Educ: B.A., Morehouse Coll., Atlanta, Ga., M.A., Atlanta Univ., Ga.; Doctoral Trng. in Psychotherapy & Counseling, Rutgers Univ.; Hon. Doct., Psychol. & Metaphysics, Am. Bible Inst. Appts. incl: former Rsch. Asst. in Psychol. & Educ., Atlanta Univ.; former Cons. Psycholgst., & Counseling Psycholgst., Fed. Govt.; Asst. Prof. of Psychol. & Cons. Psycholgst., Mercer Co. Coll., Trenton, N.J.;

Cons. Psycholgst., pvte. & N.J. State Prison System.; Commnr. of Human Rights, Newark, N.J. Author & Lectr. in field of relig., psychcl. & psychic phenomena. Mbrships: N.Y. Psycholl. Cooperation; Assn. of Black Psycholgsts.; AAUP; Int. Rsch. Coun., Rose-Croix Univ., San Jose, Calif.; Mercer Coll. Speakers Bur. Publs: The Legal Slaughter of Peace; The Victims; Undercurrents; Confrontations With Hang-Ups. Hons. incl: Certs. from Lion's Club, Kiwanas Club, Rose-Croix Univ.; Award, Parapsychol. Club, Mercer Co. Coll.; Gold Plaque, Presby. Ch., Newark, N.J. Address: 680 Summer Ave., Apt. 8, Newark, NJ 07104, U.S.A.

SMALLACOMBE, Robert Joseph, b. 26 May 1933. Company Executive. Educ: B.S., Univ. of N.Y., 1960. Appts: Composing Room Foreman, Plattsburgh Press-Republican, 1953-60; Asst. Prod. Mgr., Dow Jones & Co., Wall St., Jrnl., 1960-64; Prod. Dir., Wash. Daily News, 1964-68; Pres., Milgo-Idab Corp., Miami, Fla., 1968-71 & Idab Am. Corp., E. Patterson, N.J., 1969-71. Pres., Tal-Star Computer Systems, Inc., Princeton Junction, ibid, 1971-. Mbrships: Arlington Co. Chmn., 1967 & 10th Congressional Dist. Rep., 1968. Young Repubns.; Sr. Mbr., Am. Inst. Indl. Engrs., 1968-; Am. Mgmt. Assn. Contbr. of articles to profl. jrnls. Hons: Certs. of Appreciation, Am. Newspapers Publrs. Assn., 1967, '68; Young Repubn. of Yr. in Va., 1968. Address: Tal-Star Computer Systems, Inc., P.O. Box T1000, Princeton Junction, NJ 08550, U.S.A. 16.

SMART, (Peter) Alastair (Marshall), b. 30 April 1922. University Professor. Educ: M.A., Univ. of Glasgow, U.K., 1942; Edinburgh Theological Coll., 1944-46; Edinburgh Coll. of Art, 1946-49; Inst. of Fine Arts, N.Y. & Columbia Univs., U.S.A., 1954-55. Appts. incl: Tutor in Hist. of Art, Depts. of Adult Educ. & Hist., Univ. of Hull, U.K., 1949-56; Hd., Dept. of Fine Art, Univ. of Nottingham, 1956-; Mbr., Inst. for Adv. Study, Princeton, 1966-67. Mbrships. incl: Fellow, Royal Soc. of Arts; Coun., Assn. Internationale de Critiques d'Art. Publs. incl: The Life & Art of Allan Ramsay, 1952; The Assisi Problem & the Art of Giotto, 1971; The Renaissance & Mannerism in Italy, 1972; The Renaissance & Mannerism outside Italy, 1972; contbr. of articles to art jrnls. Recip., Scottish P.E.N. Commendation, 1953; Commonwealth Fund Fellowship, N.Y., 1954-55. Address: Fothergill House, 7 Lenton Road, The Park, Nottingham, U.K. 19, 43.

SMEDLEY, Harold, b. 19 June 1920. Diplomatist. Educ: B.A., Pembroke Coll., Cambridge, 1946; M.A., ibid, 1948. Appts: entered Dominions Off. (later C'wlth. Rels. Off.), 1946; served in New Zealand, 1948-50, Southern Rhodesia, 1951-53 & India, 1957-60; Pvte. Sect. to Sec. of State on C'wlth. Rels., 1954-57; Brit. High Commnr., Ghana, 1964-67; Brit. Amb., Laos, 1968-70; Asst. Under Sec. of State, For. & C'wlth. Off., 1970-72; Sec. Gen., Commn. on Rhodesian Opinion, 1971-72; Brit. High Commn. in Sri Lanka (Ceylon) & Non-res. Amb. to Repub. of Maldives, 1973-. Mbrships: Athenaeum Club; United Oxford & Cambridge Univ. Club, London. Hons: M.B.E., 1946; C.M.G., 1965. Address: c/o For. & C'wlth. Off., London SW1A 2AH, U.K. 1.

SMEDS, Gunnar, b. 1 July 1923. Deputy Mayor. Educ: Dip. in Mining Engrng., Inst. of Technol., Finland, 1948. Appts: Dept. Mgr., Oy Rudus Ab, 1947-53; Mng. Dir., ibid, 1953-68; Dpty. Mayor, City of Helsinki, 1968-. Mbrships: Pres., Helsinki Golf Club; Sev. other clubs. Hons: Liberty Cross of Finland with oak leaves & sword, 1943; Cmdr., Order of the Lion of Finland, 1970. Address: City Hall, Helsinki 17, Finland. 43.

SMEE, Thelma Davis (Mrs.), b. 10 Dec. 1905. Retired Civil Servant. Educ: Ark. State Coll.; Jonesboro Bapt. Coll.; Jefferson Coll., St. Louis, Mo.; Tulane-Pensacola Univ. Ctr.; Quartermaster Schl., Ft. Lee, Va. Appts: Draftsman, U.S. Engr. Corps; Purchasing Agt., AUS; Asst. Inst. to Wing Cmdr., CAP, St. Louis, Mo.; w. U.S.A.F., WWII; 1st Sgt., WAC Grp., Army Security Agcy., Arlington Hall Stn., Va.; Transportation Agt. for U.S. Army, Ft. Chaffee, Ark.; retired from Civil Serv., 1968. Mbrships: Ark. Order of the Eastern Star Rep., N.B., Canada, 1969-72; White Shrine; Am. Red. Cross; OCD, 3 yrs.; Gray Lady USN Hosp., Oakland, Calif.; Sr. Off., Am. Legion Post No. 63, 22 yrs.; Sec.-Treas., Am. Legion Aux.; Chmn., Girls State Comm., 9 yrs.; Bd., Order of Rainbow, 11 yrs.; Mem. United Meth. Ch.; United Meth. Women; Wesleyan Serv. Guild. Hons: 1st Runner-up, Citizen of the Yr. Award, Chmbr. of Comm., 1970; Dist. Serv. Award, Civil Serv., 1968. Address: 614 W. Main, Ozark, AR 72949, U.S.A. 125.

SMILG-BENARIO, Michael, b. 16 Mar. 1895. Journalist; Author. Appts: Asst., Münchener Post; Ed., Münchener Neueste Nachrichten; Ed., Konfektionär, jrnl., Berlin; Asst., Kölnische Zeitung, Berliner Börsencourier, Berliner Tageblatt, Baseler National Zeitung, Switzerland, Prager Presse, Nieuwe Rotterdamsche Courant, Die Weltbühne, Argentinisches Tageblatt & others; Ed., Deutsche Freiheit, Pariser Tageblatt; Former Chief Ed., Semanario Israelita, Buenos Aires, Argentine. Publs: Ein Jahr im Dienste der Sowjetrepublik; Die Quintessenz des Bolschewismus; Von der Demokratie zur Diktatur; Der Zusammenbruch der Zarenmonarchie; Von Kerensky zu Lenin; Muerte y resurreccion de la democracia en Europa; La leyenda del crimen ritual. Address: Conde 1995, dep. 8, Buenos Aires, Argentina. 55.

SMIRK, (Sir) Frederick Horace, b. 12 Dec. 1902. Physician; Professor. Educ: M.B., Ch.B., Univ. of Manchester, U.K., 1925; M.D., 1927. Appts. incl: Beit Mem. Rsch. Fellow-Asst., Dept., Pharmacol. & Med., Univ. Coll., London, 1930-34; Prof., Pharm., Egyptian Univ., 1935-39; Prof., Med., Univ. of Otago, Dunedin, New Zealand, 1940-61; Rsch. Prof., Med., ibid, 1962-67; Dir., Wellcome Med. Rsch. Inst., 1962. Num. vis. professorships, lectrs. & conf. chmnships. Mbrships. incl: F.R.C.P., 1940; Hon. F.R.A.C.P., 1940; Coun., Med. Rsch. Coun., N.Z., 1944-60; V.P., Royal Australasian Coll. Phys., 1958-60. Publs: High Arterial Pressure, 1957; Contbr. of chapts. to med. books; 135 other publs., mainly concerning pathogenesis & treatment of high blood pressure & cardiac irregularities. Hons. incl: K.B.E., 1958; D.Sc., Hahnemann Coll., Phila., U.S.A., 1958. Address: 68 Cannington Rd., Maori Hill, Dunedin, New Zealand. 1, 43, 50.

SMITH, Arthur James Ralph, b. 7 Jan. 1926. Economist. Educ: B.A., McMaster Univ., Hamilton, Ont., Canada, 1947; M.A., Harvard Univ., 1949; Ph.D., 1955. Appts. incl: Canadian Econ., The Conf. Bd. in Canada, 1954-57; Pres., ibid, 1971-; Lectr., McGill Univ., 1955-56; Dir., Rsch. & Sec.-Treas., Pvte. Planning Assn. of Canada, 1957-63; Dir., Rsch., Canadian-Am. Comm., ibid, 1957-63; Sec., Canadian Trade Comm., 1960-63; Dir., Econ. Coun. of Canada, 1963-67; Chmn., ibid, 1967-71. Mbrships. incl: Sci. Coun. of Canada, 1967-71; Am. Econ.

Assn.; Canadian Econ. Assn.; AAAS; Agric. Econs. Rsch. Coun. of Canada, 1967-71; Advsry. Coun., Howe Rsch. Inst., 1973-; Bd. Dirs., IBM Canada Ltd., 1972-; Bd. Dirs., Bank of Nova Scotia, 1973-; Bd. Dirs., Interprovicial Steel & Pipe Co. Ltd., 1973-. Author of publs. in field. Hons: Dr., Univ. of Calgary, 1970; LL.D., McMaster Univ., 1971. Address: The Conf. Bd. in Canada, Suite 1800, 333 River Rd., Ottawa, Ont. K1L 8B9, Canada.

SMITH, Ashley Alexander, b. 25 Sept. 1929. Minister of Religion. Educ: Tchrs. Dip., Dept. of Educ., Jamaica, 1949; St. Colmes Theol. Coll., Jamaica, 1950-54; Dip. Theol., London, 1954; B.D., Lancaster Theol. Sem., 1961; Th.M., Princeton Theol. Sem., 1968. Appts. incl: Min., Rural Chs., Jamaica, 1954-60; Min., St. Johns United Ch., Kingston, 1963-; Chmn., Bd. of Educ., United Ch. of Jamaica & Grand Cayman, 1965-67; Moderator, ibid, 1960-72; Chmn., Bd. of Ch. Min., 1970; Chmn., Bd. of Govs., United Theol. Coll. of the W.I., 1972-; Pres., Jamaica Coun. of Chs., 1969-71; Mbr., Steering Comm., Caribbean Conf. Chs., 1971-; Chmn., Bd. of Theol. Educ., Caribbean Assembly of Reformed Chs., 1968-; Mbr., Task Force on Study of U.S.-Cuba Rels., United Presby. Ch., U.S.A., 1971-. Contbr. to relig. publs. Address: United Ch. of Jamaica & Grand Cayman, 24 Hagley Park Plaza, Kingston 10, Jamaica, W. Indies.

SMITH, Barney McCoy, Jr., b. 5 Apr. 1921. Professor of Accountancy; Cerified Public Accountant; Attorney-at-Law. Educ: B.B.A., Univ. of Tex., U.S.A., 1949; M.B.A., ibid, 1950; J.D., 1954. Appts: Pilot Off.-1st Lt., U.S.A.A.F., 1942-46; Instr., Acctcy., Lamar State Coll. of Technol., Beaumont, Tex., 1955-56; Assoc. Prof., Acctcy., Univ. of Houston, Tex., 1956-67; Prof., Acctcy., Western Ill. Univ., Macomb, 1967-. Mbrships: Tex. State Bar Assn.; Delta Sigma Pi; Phi Alpha Delta; Omicron Delta Epsilon; Beta Alpha Psi; Phi Eta Sigma. Publs: Highlights of the Texas Sales Tax Law, 1962; Understanding & Using the Federal Income Tax Law, 1966; Federal Income Taxation, 1971, 2nd edit. 1972. Recip., Outstanding Educator of Am., 1972. Address: Dept. of Accountancy & Information Science, Western Illinois University, Macomb, IL 61455, U.S.A.

SMITH, Bernard, b. 29 Aug. 1900. Consulting Engineer. Educ: Oxford Univ., U.K.; B.Eng. & M.Eng., Univ. of Liverpool. Appts. incl: City Mgr., Baytown, Tex.; Engr. Examiner, Pub. Wks. Admin., Ft. Worth; Dir., Rsch. & Personnel, City of Ft. Worth; Acting State Dir. & State Planning Engr., Pub. Wks. Reserve; Asst. Regional Rep. & Regional Econ., Nat. Housing Agcy., Dallas; Chief, San Fran. Bay Sect., U.S. Corps & Engrs., Calif.; State Engr., San Fran. Bay Conservation & Dev. Commn. Fellow, Am. Soc. Civil Engrs. Mbrships. incl: Am. Waterworks Assn.; Am. Econ. Assn.; Western Econ. Assn.; AAAS; Soc. of Evolutionary Econs.; Commonwealth Club of Calif. Publs. incl: Town Building; Sedimentation in the San Francisco Bay System; Population & Housing Goals; Art & Environment; Profl. reports & papers. Address: P.O. Box 663, Aptos, CA 95003, U.S.A. 7, 9, 14, 26, 28, 51, 128.

SMITH, Bettye L. Sebree (Mrs.), b. 25 Feb. 1926. Business Executive. Educ: Student, Brigham Young Univ., Provo, Utah, 1944-45; Links Schl. of Bus., Boise, Idaho, 1946; Nampa Bus. Coll., 1956; B.S., Alaska Meth. Univ., 1972. Appts. incl: Owner, Fairbanks Sectl. Schl., 1956-58; Anchorage Sectl. Schl., 1958-59; Pres., Alaska Bus. Coll., Inc.,

Anchorage, 1959-; Owner, City Employment Ctr., ibid, 1962-68; Western Girl Temps., 1962-68; Manpower, Inc. Bus. Servs., 1969-72; Alaska Employment Agcy., 1970-72; Franchise holder for: Speedwriting Shorthand, 1957-; Nancy Taylor Finishing Schl., 1960-; ITT Nat. Data Processing, 1968-; Taylor Airlines Careers, 1968-; Arctic Tech. Inds., Sec.-Treas., Mbrships: Gtr. Anchorage Chmbr. of Comm., Chmn., Educ. & Philos. Comm., 1972; Anchorage Businessmen's Assn.; Nat. Secs. Assn., Chapt. V.P., 1962, Seminar Chmn., 1961, '67, Chmn. Mgmt. Seminar, 1972-; Appt. by Mayor to Parking & Traffic Commn., 1974-; Credit Women Int.; Anchorage Borough Schl. Dist.; Citizens Advsry. Bd.; Bus. Educ. Comm. Recip. of Best Dressed Career Woman Award, Anchorage, 1972. Address: 328 E. Fourth Ave., Anchorage, AK 99501, U.S.A. 5, 9, 16, 120, 126, 130, 132, 138.

SMITH, Bruce Henry, b. 3 Aug. 1925. Chartered Accountant. Appts. incl: Sr. Ptnr. & Co-Fndr., B.O. Smith & Son., 1955; Chmn., Cemac Assoc. Ltd., 1956; Dir., Int. Footwear Inds. Ltd., 1965; Chmn., 1969; Dir., F.T. Wimble & Grp., 1965; Chmn., 1969; Chmn., Shepherd Mercantile Agcy. Pty. Ltd., 1969; Chmn., Hawley Credit Serv. Pty. Ltd., 1969; Chmn., Neville Jeffress Pty. Ltd., 1966; Chmn., R.M. Tyson Pty. Ltd., 1969; Chmn., Assoc. Bus. Cons. Pty. Ltd., 1972; Chmn., Transport Distributors Int. Pty Ltd., 1972; Chmn., Epstein & Co. Ltd., 1973; Dir., Pacific Mining Ltd., 1971; Dir., Tullabong Tin Ltd., 1973; Chmn., Proj. Dev. Corp. Ltd., 1966-69; Chmn., Tangible Securities Ltd., 1965-70; Chmn., Proj. Mining Corp. Ltd., 1968-69; Chmn., Vokes Aust. Pty. Ltd., 1965-71. Fellowships: Inst. of Chartered Accts.; Inst. of Mgmt.; Inst. of Credit Mgmt. Mbrships. incl: Commonwealth Soc.; UN Org. Address: c/o B.O. Smith & Son, 68 Pitt St., Sydney, Australia 2000. 12, 16, 23, 123, 128.

SMITH, C.E., b. 4 Jan. 1926. Librarian. Educ: B.A., Univ. of Sydney, Australia; F.L.A.A. Appts. incl: Libn., N.S.W. Educ. Dept., 1949-54; Shire Libn., Sutherland Shire Coun., 1954-56, 1958-61; Libn., N.S.W. Film Coun., 1957-58; City Libn., Newcastle City Coun., 1961-; Lectr.-in-Charge, Newcastle Lib. Schl., 1962-. Mbrships. incl: Lib. Assn. of Australia; Pres., N.S.W. Br., ibid, 1955-56, Sec., Special Libs. Sect., 1955, Pres., N.S.W. Ctrl. Coast Regional Grp., 1970-71, Cons., Fed. Govt. Aid for Pub. Libs., 1972-73, Mbr., Pub. Libs. Comm., 1973; Sec., Assn. of Local Govt. Libns., N.S.W., 1959-65 and Pres., 1965-; V.P., Newcastle and Hunter Dist. Histl. Soc., 1965-67 and Pres., 1968-; Trustee and Mus. Dir., Newcastle Local Hist. Mus. Trust, 1969-; Trustee, Lambton Mech. Inst., 1971; Comm. Mbr., Newcastle Maritime Mus. Soc., 1972-73. Publs: Dr. James Mitchell; Aspects of Public Library Administration: Jrnl. articles. Hons: Albert Mainerd Schlrship., 1968; Fellowship, Lib. Assn. of Australia, 1970. Address: Newcastle Public Library, P.O. Box 489G, Newcastle, N.S.W., Australia, 2300. 23, 128.

SMITH, Clagett G., b. Dec. 1930. Social Psychologist; University Professor. Educ: B.A., Univ. of Md., 1953; M.A., ibid, 1955; Ph.D., Univ. of Mich., 1961. Appts. incl: Study Dir., Survey Rsch. Ctr., Inst. for Soc. Rsch., Univ. of Mich., 1960-64; Assoc. Prof. Soc. Psychol., Ctr. for Advanced Study in Organization Sci., Univ. of Wis., 1964-68; Assoc. Prof. Sociol., Univ. of Wis.-Milwaukee, 1964-68; Prog. Dir., Rsch. Grant Nat. Inst. Mental Hlth., U.S. Pub. Hlth. Serv., 1966-71; Assoc. Prof., Dept. of Sociol. & Anthropol., Univ. of Notre Dame, Ind., 1968-. Mbrships. incl: Am. Psychological Assn.; Am.

Sociological Assn.; Am. Acad. Soc. & Pol. Scis.; Phi Kappa Phi; Psi Chi. Publs. incl: Conflict Resolution: Contributions of the Behavior Sciences, 1971; Mental Hospitals: a Study in Organizational Effectiveness,(at press); Tech. Reports. Contbr. to profl. jrnls. Address: Department of Sociol. & Anthropol., Univ. of Notre Dame, Notre Dame, IN 46556, U.S.A.

SMITH, Clarence Otto, b. 14 Jan. 1930. Executive. Educ: B.Sc., Fresno State Coll., U.S.A., M.B.A., Am. Univ., 1973; Postgrad. study, ibid, 1969, 1971. Appts: Auditor-Asst. Dir., U.S. Gen. Acctng. Off., 1958-; Mgmt. Intern Interviewer, U.S. Civil Serv. Commn.; Lectr., Am. Univ., 1974-. Mbrships: Inst. of Internal Auditors, 1974-; Soc. for Mgmt. Inf. Systems, 1970 (Sec.-Treas., Wash. DC Chapt.); Fed. Govt. Accts. Assn., 1961-; Mil. Ops. Rsch. Soc., 1973-; Am. Acctng. Assn., 1958-74; Off. many civic orgs., e.g. Civic Assns., PTA. Contbr. sev. articles & papers to profl. review & symposia. Hons: Winner, Tech. Writing Competition Northern Va. Chapt. Fed. Govt. Accts. Assn., 1969; Mbr., winning team, Nat. Rsch. Competition (Compendium on Auditing—Operational Mgmt. Performance Effectiveness), 1972; GAO Grp. Meritorius Serv. Award, 1964 & 1969; Letter of Special Recognition, U.S. Civil Serv. Commn., 1965; Letter of Appreciation, Chmn., Inter-Govtl. Rels. Sub-comm., U.S. House of Reps., 1967. Address: 6700 Hopewell Ave., Springfield, VA, 22151, U.S.A. 125.

SMITH, Cyril James, b. 11 Aug. 1909. Concert Pianist. Educ: Royal Coll. of Mus., London. Appts: Prof., Royal Coll. of Mus., 1934-40, 1957-. Hon. Mbr., Royal Soc. Musicians. Compositions: Duet for Three Hands. Hons: O.B.E., 1971; Hon.R.A.M., 1962; F.R.C.M., 1958. Address: 33 Fife Rd., London S.W.14 7EJ, U.K. 1, 21, 34, 128, 139.

SMITH, Denison Langley, b. 2 Feb. 1924. Librarian. Educ: Trinity Hall, Cambridge, U.K., 1942-43, 1946-48; Hons. degree, ibid. Appts: Royal Navy, 1943-46; Br. Libn., Gloucestershire Co. Lib.; Ref. Libn., Taunton Borough Lib.; Asst. Libn., Govt. Communications HQ; Libn., Oxford Polytechnic, 1958-. Mbrships: Fellow, Lib. Assn.; Former Ed., bulletin, "Colls. of Technol.", Further Educ. Sect., Lib. Assn.; Former mbr., Lib. Assn. Coun. & Nat., Univ. & Med. Libs. Comm. Publs: College Library Administration (co-author), 1965; How to find out in architecture & building, 1967; Articles in var. educl. & lib. jrnls.; Translation of Detail V from German. Recip., Exhibition to Trinity Hall, Cambridge, 1941. Address: Oxford Polytechnic, Headington, Oxford, OX3 0BF, U.K.

SMITH, Dodie (pen name: C.L. Anthony, until 1935), Dramatist; Novelist. Educ: Studied at Royal Acad. of Dramatic Art, U.K. Appts. incl: on stage, several yrs.; Buyer, Heal & Son, Tottenham Ct. Rd., London; gave up bus., 1931. Plays: Autumn Crocus; Service; Touch Wood; Call It A Day; Bonnet Over the Windmill; Dear Octopus; Lovers & Friends; Letter from Paris; I Capture the Castle. Plays produced at Lyric Theatre, Wyndham's Theatre, Theatre Royal Haymarket, Globe Theatre, New Theatre, Queen's Theatre, Plymouth Theatre (N.Y.), Aldwych Theatre. Novels: I Capture the Castle, 1949; The New Moon with the Old, 1963; The Town in Bloom, 1965; It Ends with Revelations, 1967; A Tale of Two Families, 1970. Children's Books: The Hundred & One Dalmatians, 1956; The Starlight Barking, 1967. Address: The Barretts, Finchingfield, Essex, U.K. 1, 18.

SMITH, Dolores Davidson, b. 4 June 1916. Real Estate Broker & Developer. Educ: Coll. & Grad. Profl. Courses. Appts: Sec., Engrng. Off., 1936-38; Developer Subdivision, 1953; currently owner, Davidson Realty, Ocean Springs, Miss. Mbrships: Organizing Regent, Biloxi Chapt., DAR; Past Pres., ibid; Sec., Ocean Springs City Planning Commn.; Pres., Jackson Co. Citizens Advsry Comm.; Dir., United Fund, Scouts. Articles, regional interest. Lectr., commentator, civic worker. Hons: Bus. & Profl. Outstanding Woman of Yr., 1970; var. awards & citations for civic activities. Address: 810 Iberville St., Ocean Springs, MS 39564, U.S.A. 5.

SMITH, Donald Vincent, b. 16 Dec. 1933. Author & Publisher. Educ: Univ. of Miami, Fla. Appts: Ed., Olivant Press, 1952-. Publs: New Poems 68, 1968; Odyssey 69; Vacationing in Contemporary Greece, 1969. Contbr. of Poems & Essays to num. lit. mags. Hons: Ed.'s Choice, Tulsa Poetry Quarterly, 1969; First Prize, Poetry, The Village Post, 1969; Guest of Hon., Mid-South Poetry Festival, 1971. Address: P.O. Drawer 1409, Homestead, FL 33030, U.S.A. 7, 30.

SMITH, Dwight L., b. 11 Apr. 1918. University Professor. Educ: A.B., Ind. Ctrl. Coll., 1940; A.M., Ind. Univ., 1941; Ph.D., 1949. Appts. incl: Instr., Ohio State Univ., 1949-53; Rsch. Histn., Ohio Hist. Soc., 1950-51; Asst. Prof., Miami Univ., Oxford, 1953-56; Asst. Prof., ibid, 1956-60; Prof., 1960-; Carnegie Vis. Asst. Prof., Columbia Univ., 1954-55; Vis. Prof., Ind. Univ., 1962-63. Mbrships. incl: Pres., Am. Indian Ethnohist. Conf., 1955-56; Western Hist. Assn.; Org. of Am. Histns.; Canadian Hist. Assn.; Am. Hist. Assn.; AAUP. Publs. incl: Western Life in the Stirrups, 1965; The Photographer & the River, 1967; John D. Young & the Colorado Gold Rush, 1969; (co-auth.) The American Political Process, 1972; America: History & Life, 1972. Recip., acad. awards. Address: Dept. of Hist., Miami Univ., Oxford, OH 45056, U.S.A. 8, 13, 15, 30, 51, 126.

SMITH, Earl Vern, b. 1 Feb. 1915. Engineer. Educ: Nat. Tech. Schls., 1934; Student, Indl. Arts, Univ. of Calif., L.A., 1944; Grad., Alexander Hamilton Ext. Workshop, Burbank, Calif., 1945. Appts. incl: Supvsr., Lockheed Aircraft Experimental Div., Burbank, 1940-47; Tooling & Fabrication Engr., Lear A.E.D., Inc., Santa Monica, 1953-57; Chief Tool Engr., Advd. Structures Co., Monrovia, 1958-62; Chief Engr., Tooling & Design, Metal Products Engrng., Inc., L.A., ibid, 1962-. Mbrships: Calif. Soc. Profl. Engrs. (CSPE/NSPE); Life Cert. Engr., Soc. Mfg. Engrs; Nat. Assn. Mfrs. Publs. on safety standards & mfg. in engrng.; Metal Fabrication: its Hazards & Satisfaction (to be released 1974); Newsletter Ed., CSPE/PEI. Hons. incl: Bronze Cert., Foreman's League for Educ. & Assn., 1945; Patentee in Field, 1952; Bicentennial Resources Honoree. Address: 2767 W. 1st St., 77, Santa Ana, CA 92703, U.S.A. 9, 57.

SMITH, Emily Myrtle, b. 29 Dec. 1900. Professional Registered Nurse; Flower, Portrait & Landscape Painter. Educ: Gen. Hosp. Schl. Nursing, Spartanburg, S.C. 1928; Peabody Coll. for Tchrs., Nashville Tenn., 1930; B.S., Columbia Univ., 1942, M.S., ibid 1949; studied painting, var. masters. Appts. incl: Sr. Asst. Nurse Off., to Nurse Dir., U.S. Dept. of Hlth., Educ. & Welfare, Pub. Hlth. Serv. Commissioned Offs. Corp, 1945-65, w. var assignments, inclng: Regional Nurse Cons., N.Y., 1954-58; Cons., Staff Educ. Fed.

Employee Hlth., 1958-60; Cons., Chronic Diseases & Gerontol., 1960-64; Pt.-time voluntary Art Tchr., 1965-. Mbrships. incl: Tenn. State Nurses Assn.; V.P., ibid, 1943-45; Am. Nurses Assn.; Nat. League for Nursing; Fellow, Am. Pub. Hlth. Assn. Publs: Reports on var. assignments; Contbr. to profl. jrnls. Sole & Grp. exhibs. of paintings. Hons. incl: Wallace Mem. Medal for Med. Nursing; Silver Plaque, Nat. Taiwan Univ., 1954; Nat. Defense & Veterans WWII Medals of Honor. Address: 642 Woodland St., Spartanburg, SC 29302, U.S.A. 5, 132, 138.

SMITH, Frederick E(screet), b. 4 April 1922. Novelist; Playwright. Educ: Malet Lambert H.S., U.K. Profl. author since 1952. Mbrships: Soc. of Authors. Publs: Of Masks & Minds, 1954; Laws Be Their Enemy, 1955; 633 Squadron, 1956; Lydia Trendennis, 1957; The Sin & the Sinners, 1958; The Grotto of Tiberius, 1962; The Devil Behind Me, 1962; The Storm Knight, 1966; A Killing for the Hawks, 1966; The Wider Sea of Love, 1969; Waterloo, 1970; The Tormented, 1974. Also 6 novels under pseudonym David Farrell, 80 short stories; Plays—The Glass Prison, A House Divided; Film credits—633 Squadron, The Devil Doll. Hons: Mark Twain Lit. Award, U.S., for A Killing for the Hawks, 1967. Address: 3 Hathaway Rd., Southbourne, Bournemouth, Hants., U.K. 3, 30, 34, 43, 128, 131.

SMITH, G.E. Kidder, b. 1 Oct. 1913. Architect; Author. Educ: A.B., Princeton Univ., 1935: M.F.A., ibid, 1938. Appts: Fellow, Am. Inst. of Archts.; Mbr., Soc. Architectural Histns.; Mbr., Coll. Art Assn. Mbrships. incl: Century Assn., N.Y.C.; Princeton Club, N.Y.C. Publs. incl: The New Churches of Europe; The New Architecture of Europe; Italy Builds; Brazil Builds (co-author). Exhibs., Mus. of Mod. Art, N.Y.C.; Am. Fedn. of Arts; Smithsonian Instn. Photographs in permanent collect., Mus. of Mod. Art. Hons. incl: Order of Southern Cross, Brazil, 1943; ENIT Gold Medal, Italian Govt., 1957; Gold Medal, Architectural Photography, A.I.A., 1964; E.M. Conover Award, 1965; var. fellowships & grants. Address: 163 E. 81st St., N.Y., NY 10028, U.S.A. 2, 6, 12, 30.

SMITH, George, b. 4 June 1919. Regius Professor of Surgery. Educ: Univs. of St. Andrews & Glasgow, U.K., Johns Hopkins, Case-Western & Columbia, N.Y., U.S.A.; Ch.M., St. Andrews, 1959; M.D., 1957; M.B., Ch.B., 1942; F.R.C.P.S., Glasgow, 1949; F.R.C.S., Edinburgh, 1949; F.A.C.S., 1958; F.C.C.P., 1963; F.Inst. Biol.; A.I.L. Appts. incl: Convenor, Postgrad. Med. Educ. Comm., Univ. of Aberdeen, 1968-72; Regius Prof. of Surg., ibid, 1962-; Chmn., North-Eastern Regional Postgrad. Med. Educ. Comm., 1972-; Dean, Fac. of Med., Univ. of Aberdeen, 1974-; Vis. Prof., & External Examiner, var. univs. Mbrships. incl: Fellow, Assn. of Surg., Gt. Britain & Ireland; Fellow, Royal Soc. of Med.; Scottish Soc. of Experimental Med.; British Surg. Rsch. Soc.; European Surg. Rsch. Soc.; British Cardiac Soc.; Int. Surg. Group; Sec. & Fndr. mbr., W. of Scotland Cardiac Soc. Author of books & articles on cardiovascular & respiratory topics. Recip. of hons. Address: 22 Rubislaw Den North, Aberdeen, AB2 4AN, U.K. 1, 128, 131.

SMITH, George P., b. 9 Sept. 1932. Consultant; Educator. Educ: B.A., Univ. of Calif., Riverside, 1961; Ph.D., Claremont Grad. Schl., 1964. Appts: Prin. Assoc., Norris & Gottfried, Consultants to Mgmt.; Ptnr., Consultants Circle (Consultants in Educ., Drug Abuse, Govt. Progs., Evaluation); Dir., Geo. P.

Smith Assocs., Consultants in Educ., Drug Abuse, Govt. Progs., Evaluation; Sr. Rsch. Assoc., Kirschner Assocs., Inc., Wash. D.C. & Nice, France. Mbrships. incl: Acad. of Soc. & Pol. Sci.; Am. Pol. Sci. Assn.; Law & Soc. Assn.; Am. Judicatore Soc.; Assn. for Legal Hist.; Acad. of Pol. Sci. Author of var. articles & reports. Recip. of hons. Address: Kirschner Assocs., Inc., 733-15th St., Suite 1137, Wash. DC 20005, U.S.A. 9.

SMITH, George Patrick Christopher ('Carter') II, b. 1 Sept. 1939. Attorney; Author; Educator. Educ: B.S., 1961; J.D., 1964, Ind. Univ., Bloomington, U.S.A.; Dip., Acad. de Droit Int., De La Haye, Palais De La Paix, The Netherlands, summer, 1965. Appts. incl: Tchng. Fellow, Ind. Univ. Schl. of Law, Bloomington, 1964-65; Limited Gen. Prac., Law, Ind., 1965-; Instr., Law, Mich. Univ., Ann Arbor, 1965-66; Legal Advsr., For. Claims Commn., U.S. State Dept., 1966; Asst. Dean, Asst. Prof., Law, Law Schl., N.Y. State Univ., 1967-69; Vis. Prof., Law, Geo. Wash. Univ. Schl. of Law, summer, 1968; Special Counsel Environmental Legislation to Gov., Ark., 1970-71; Special Counsel for Intergovtl. Rel., U.S. Environmental Protection Agcy., Wash. D.C., 1971-; Assoc. Prof., Law., Ark. Univ., Fayetteville, 1969-71; Dpty. Dir., Admin. Conf. of U.S., Wash. D.C., 1974-. Mbrships. incl: Am. & Ind. State Bar Assns.; Am. Judicature Soc.; Am. Law Inst.; World Wildlife Fund; Am. Soc. Int. Law; Selden Soc.; Soc. Legal Hist.; Scribes; Maritime Law Soc.; Fed. Bar Coun.; Sigma Alpha Epsilon; Phi Alpha Delta; Alpha Kappa Psi; Life, Ind. Univ. Fndn.; Cosmos Club; Nat. Lawyers Club. Publs. incl: Articles in fields of family law & population control, legal educ., Natural resources & ecol., jurisprudence & legal hist., etc. Address: 1400 S. Joyce St., Apt. C.-1607, Arlington, VA 22202, U.S.A. 7.

SMITH, George Winston, b. 10 June 1911. Educator; Author. Educ: A.B., Univ. of Ill., 1934; M.A., 1935; Ph.D., Univ. of Wis., 1939. Appts: Instr., Wash. & Lee Univ., 1938-40; Asst. Prof., Am. Univ., Wash. D.C., 1940-42; Assoc. Prof., 1942-45; Hd., Dept. Hist., 1940-45; Asst. Prof., Hist., Univ. of Ill., 1945-49; Univ. of N.M., Albuquerque, 1949-52; Assoc. Prof., 1952-59; Prof., 1959-. Mbrships. incl: Phi Beta Kappa; Phi Kappa Phi; Phi Alpha Theta; Pi Gamma Mu; Am. Hist. Assn.; Org. of Am. Histns. Publs. incl: Henry C. Carey & American Sectional Conflict, 1951; Co-author, The Unchosen, 1962; Medicines for the Union Army: The U.S. Laboratories During the Civil War, 1962; Co-author, Life in the North During the Civil War, 1966; Chronicles of the Gringos: The U.S. Army in the Mexican War. 1846-48, 1968. Address: Hist. Dept., Univ. of N.M., Albuquerque, NM 87106, U.S.A. 8, 9, 13, 51.

SMITH, Gordon Roysce, Jr., b. 7 Mar. 1924. Executive Director. Educ: Ala. Polytechnic Inst.; La. State Univ. Appts: Asst. Buyer, Book Dept., Davison's, Atlanta, Ga., 1949-57; Mgr., Book Dept., Yale Co-operative Corp., New Haven, Conn., 1957-71; Educl. Proj. Dir., Am. Booksellers Assn., N.Y.C., 1971-72; Exec. Dir., ibid, 1972-. Publs: Articles in profl. jrnls.; Weekly newspaper column; Prod.-Moderator, weekly show, The Opinionated Man, WNHC-TV, 1966-71; Writer-Narrator, daily radio book news, WELI, 1966-71; Co-ed., A Manual on Bookselling, 1974. Address: Am. Booksellers Assn., 800 2nd Ave., N.Y., NY 10017, U.S.A. 2, 6.

SMITH, Grace Kellogg. Writer. Educ: A.B., Smith Coll.; M.A., Univ. of Vt. Mbr., Authors' Guild of Am. Novels incl: A Keeper of the Door; The Mould; The House; The Silent Dawn;

The Two Lives of Edith Wharton: The Woman & Her Work; Arise & Go Now (in press). Weekly column, Provincetown Advocate. Short stories, articles & newspaper features. Wkr. for World Peace, Purified Politics. Address: 495 N. Lake St., Aurora, IL U.S.A. 2.

SMITH, Harold Harry, b. 8 Feb. 1913. Architect; Town Planner. Educ: Assoc. Archt., Sydney Rech. Coll., Australia, 1937; Cert., Town Planner, N.S.W., 1946; Registered Archt., ibid, 1937; Postgrad. study travel, Europe, U.S.A., Ctrl. Am., Far E., Latin Am. Appts: Design Archt., Commonwealth Works Dept., Sydney, 1940-46; Pvte. Prac., 1946; Town Planning Cons. to 4 municipal couns., Sydney area, 1949-61; Sr. Pt.-time Lectr., Archl. Design, N.S.W. Univ., Sydney Tech. Coll. & N.S.W. Inst. of Tech., 1946-72; Archl. Dip. Course Advsry. Comm., N.S.W. Dept. of Educ., 1962-73; currently Sr. Partner, Harold H. Smith & Jesse. Mbrships. incl: Fellow, Royal Aust. Inst. Archts., 1950-56; Coun., N.S.W. Chapt., ibid, 1963-64; Fellow, Royal Aust. Planning Inst.; Pres., N.S.W. Div., ibid, 1961-62; Councillor, 1951-64. Publs: Planning for the Community, 1945; Valid Architecture, 1971. Bldgs: Fairfield Town Hall & Civic Ctr.; Commonwealth Bank, N. Sydney & Canberra; Campbelltown Dev. for 50,000 people. Recip., 1st Prize, Nat. Homes Design Comp., 1944. Address: 66 Berry St., N. Sydney, N.S.W., Australia 2060. 23.

SMITH, Harold Neil, b. 21 Jan. 1907. Administrator. Educ: B.A., Tas. & Qld. Univs., Australia. Appts: Asst. Sec., Dept. of Co-ordinator Gen., Pub. Works, Qld.; Asst. Sec., Allied Works Coun.; Sec., The State Electricity Commn., Qld.; Commn. for Electricity Supply, Qld., 1950-72. Mbrships: V.P., Electricity Assn. of Aust.; Mbr. & Inter-State Dir., Fndn. for Aust. Lit. Studies, James Cook Univ., N. Qld.; Fellow, Aust. Inst. of Mgmt.; Life Fellow, Royal Inst. Pub. Admin.; Aust. & N.Z. Assn. for Advancement of Sci.; Fellowship, Aust. Writers; Life, Museum Soc. of Qld.; Life, Elec. Dev. Assn. of Qld.; Aust. Pioneers Club, Sydney. Publs: articles, monographs, papers, reports; verse in lit. jrnls. & anthols. Hons: Companion, Imperial Serv. Order, 1972; Companion, Instn. Elec. Engrs., London, 1970; Ford Mem. Prize, Poetry, Univ. of Qld., 1936. Address: Northcote, Longford, Tasmania, Australia 7301. 23.

SMITH, Helen (Mrs. R.A.A. Smith), b. 7 Mar. 1907. Language Teacher (ret.'d). Educ. A.B., Whitman Coll., 1927. Appts: Playground Leader, Seattle Pks., summers, 1925, '27, '28; Tchr., H.S., Roslyn, Wash., 1927-29, Grangeville, Idaho, 1929-30, Longview, Wash., 1930-46, '47-49, Ruston Acad., Havana, Cuba, 1946-47; Substitute Tchr., Cowlitz Co., Wash., 1950-70. Mbrships: Past Pres., Evergreen Area Girl Scout Coun.; Badoura Club, Daughters of Nile, Longview Garden Club, Martha Circle, Longview Community Ch.; For. Rels. Chmn., Longview Am. Legion Aux., 1957-74; Chmn., Cowlitz Co. Am. Red Cross, Jr. Div., 1954-58; Worthy Advsr., Job's Daughters, 1960-61. Publs: co-author, booklet, Spanish Teaching, 1944; jrnl. articles. Recip., Disting Serv. Award, Longview '23 Club, (City Fndrs. Club), 1968. Address: 1521 22nd Ave., Longview, WA 98632, U.S.A. 5, 138.

SMITH, Jack Darling, b. 25 Jan. 1920. Publisher. Educ: S. Ga. Coll., 1948-50; A.B., 1952, B.S., 1952, Valdosta State Coll.; B.D., Emory Univ., 1955; M.Div., ibid, 1972; LL.B., Blackstone Schl. of Law, 1970; J.D., 1971. Appts. incl: V.P., Gen. Mgr., Nat. P.R., Inc., Thomasville, Ga., 1946-48; Ordained to Min.,

Meth. Ch., 1952; Pastor, Ludowici, Ga., 1948-52, Stockbridge, ibid, 1952-55, Wadley 1st Ch., 1955-60, Sylvania, 1960-64, Dublin, Ga., 1964-68; V.P., P.R., Fulghum Inds., Inc., Wadley, 1968-73; Trustee, Ga. Magnolia Manor, Americus, 1965-72; Served w. USAAF, 1940-45; Publr. & Pres., Dixie Publs. & Arts Co., 1973; Mbr., Ga. Gov.'s Staff, 1966-68, '68-70, '70-73; Admiral, Ga. Navy, 1971-. Mbrships: Mason; Lion; Rotarian; Pres., Wadley Chmbr. of Comm., 1972-73. Publs: Up the Ladder, 1953; They Did It, 1954 Vacation Church School Digest, 1955; Titbits with a Golden Crust, 1959; Contbr. to Dixie Logger & Lumberman Mag., 1970-, Woodchuck, 1970-. Address: Box 703, Wadley, GA 30477, U.S.A. 7.

SMITH, James Ellis, b. 12 Dec. 1936. School Administrator. Educ: B.S. in Educ., Miss. Coll., Clinton; M.Ed., ibid. Appts: Tchr. of Engl., Pearl River Ctrl. H.S., Miss., 1959-60, Poplarville H.S., Miss., 1960-62; Prin., Savannah Elementary Schl., 1962-64, Nicholson Elementary Schl., 1965-68, Timberlawn Elementary Schl., 1968-69, all Miss.; Prin., Byram H.S., Miss., 1970-. Mbrships: Phi Delta Kappa; Miss. Educ. Assn.; Miss. Schl. Admnstrs. Assn.; Hinds Co. Educ. Assn. (Past-Pres.); Byram Lions Club; Past-Pres., Poplarville Educ. Assn., Picayune Educ. Assn., Capital Athletic Conf. Address: Route 5, Jackson, MS 39212, U.S.A. 125.

SMITH, James Henry, b. 24 Jan. 1908. Professor of Engineering (Retd.). Educ: E.E. & M.A., Univ. of Cinn., 1931; A.B. & B.S., Univ. of Ill., 1946; Ph.D., ibid, 1951. Appts. incl: Elec. Engr., Cinn. Gas & Elec. Co., Ohio, 1930-38; Prof., Elec. Engrng., Hd. Dept., Detroit Inst. Tech., 1938-39; Instr., Univ. of Ill., 1939-41; Cornell, 1942; Asst. Prof., 1942-47; Assoc. Prof., Univ. of Neb., 1947-51; Sr. Rsch. Phys., Sandia Corp., N.M., 1951-53; Mbr., Rsch. Staff, Los Alamos Sci. Lab., Calif., 1953-55; Assoc. Prof., Engrng., Fresno State Coll. (now Calif. State Univ., Fresno), 1955-61; Acting Chmn., ibid, 1961; Coord. in Elec. & Electronics Engrng., 1955-71; Dean, 1971-73; Num. summer positions in ind. & many other pt.-time tchng. activities; Pt.-time Cons. to var. Calif. firms. Active mbr., profl. socs. Author of profl. reports. Address: 847 E. Hedges Ave., Fresno, CA 93728, U.S.A. 9, 14.

SMITH, John Gettys, b. 24 Nov. 1932. Public Relations Executive. Educ: B.A., Univ. S. Carolina. Appts: Tchr., Hist. Art; Reporter, Bur. Chief, Rock Hill Evening Herald, S.C.; Dir., Pub. Rels., Sea Pines Plantation Co.; V.P., ibid; Pres., John Gettys Smith Assocs. Mbrships: Pres: S.C. Travel Coun., 1972-73 & Hilton Hd. Chmbr. of Comm., 1967; S.C. Pub. Rels. Soc; Pub. Rels. Soc. Am.; Oglethorpe Club, Savannah; Chatthan Club, ibid; S. Caroliniana Soc.; Hugenot Soc.; S.C. Histl. Soc. Contbr. to A.P. Stories; Am. Heritage Mag.; Golf Mag.; Golf Canada Mag.; Sandlapper Mag.; Travel & Leisure Mag.; sev. newspapers. Hons. incl: 1st Place Award, Resort Pub. Rels., Discover Am. Travel Org., 1967, '73; Order of The Corte (Coun. Regional Travel Execs.), for contrbns. to Travel in The South, 1973 & others. Address: 48 Beach Lagoon Rd., Sea Pines Plantation, Hilton Hd. Island, SC 29928, U.S.A. 7, 84.

SMITH, John Harold, b. 10 Sept. 1926. Marketing Director. Educ: Univ. of Mont., 1945. Appts: Purchasing Agt., Edcliff Instruments, 1956-61; Fairchild Controls, 1961-63; Realty Exec., Western Realty, 1963-65; Purchasing Agt., Newton Insert Co., 1965-67; Contract Admnstr., Circle Seal Corp.,

1967-72; Owner, J. Smith Enterprises, Thrifty Printing Co., J. Smith & Son, Three S Sales Co., 1948-73; Marketing Exec., Blackfield Hawaii Corp., 1973-. Mbrships: Int. Senator, Life Mbr., Jr. Chmbr. Int.; Life, Whittier Area Jaycees; Life, PTA; B.P.O.E.; Purchasing Agts. Assn. Hons: Outstanding State V.P. Address: 4825 Kahala Ave., Honolulu, HI 96816, U.S.A. 2, 9, 22, 57, 59,72, 74.

SMITH, Joseph Percy. Professor of English; Academic Vice President. Educ: B.A., M.A., Univ. of Sask., Canada; Ph.D., Univ. of Calif. at Berkeley. Appts: Instr., Univ. of Sask., 1945-46; Tchng. Asst., Univ. Fellow, Univ. of Calif., Berkeley, 1946-48; Asst., Assoc. Prof., Univ. of Sask., 1948-58; Prof., ibid, 1958-64; Exic. Sec., Canadian Assn. of Univ. Tchrs., Ottawa, 1964-69; Prof. & V.P. Acad., Univ. of Guelph, Ont., 1970-. Mbrships: Assn. of Canadian Univ. Tchrs. of Engl.; Hon. Life Mbr., Canadian Assn. of Univ. Tchrs.; Mbr., Edit. Bd., Canadian Soc. for Studies in Higher Educ.; Humanities Assn. of Canada. Publs: The Unrepentant Pilgrim, 1965; Contbr. to encys., books & profl. jrnls. Hons: Travelling Fellowship, Nuffield Fndn., London, 1969-70; D.Lit., Carleton Univ., 1970; Milner Mem. Award, Canadian Assn. of Univ. Tchrs., 1973. Address: Univ. of Guelph, Room 357, McLaughlin Lib., Guelph, Ont. Canada. 13, 88.

SMITH, Laura Lee Weisbrodt (Mrs. Ora Smith), b. 16 July 1903. Educ: B.S., Miami Univ., Oxford, Ohio, 1925; M.S., Iowa State Univ., Ames, 1927; Ph.D., Univ. of Calif., Berkeley, 1930. Appts. incl: Instr., Food Chem., Coll. of Home Econs., Cornell Univ., 1937-40; Adult Educ. Tchr., Nutrition, Ithaca Pub. Schls., 1942-46, 48-50; Nutrition Cons., Inter-Am. Inst. of Agric. Scis., Turrialba, Costa Rica, 1946-48; Asst. Prof., Food Chem.-Prof. Emeritus, Food Chem., Schl. of Hotel Admin., Cornell Univ., 1956-. Mbrships. incl: Am. Chem. Soc.; Inst. Food Technol.; N.Y. Acad. of Sci.; Nutrition Comm., Am. Red Cross; AAUW; Fellow, Am. Inst. of Chems., Inc., 1969-; Coun. on Hotel, Restaurant & Institutional Educ. Publs: Food Service Science, 1974; articles in profl. jrnls. Address: 1707 Slaterville Rd., Ithaca, NY 14850, U.S.A.

SMITH, Leslie Francis, b. 30 June 1901. Professor of History. Educ: Glasgow Univ., U.K., 1917-21; Brit. Schl., Rome, 1921-23; St. Catherine's Coll., Oxford, 1923-25; Columbia Univ., N.Y.C., U.S.A., 1928-36. Appts: Asst. to Prof., Humanities, Glasgow Univ., U.K., 1925-26; Lectr., Greek & Latin, Columbia Univ., U.S.A., 1929-36; Asst. Prof., Classics, Univ. of Me., 1938-47; Prof., Hist., Univ. of Okla., 1947-71. Mbrships. incl: Am. Hist. Assn.; Norwegian Hist. Assn.; V.P., Classical Assn. of New England, 1946. Publs. incl: (co-auth.) Thesaurus Linguae Litinae Epigraphicae, vol. II; Modern Norwegian Historiography; contbr. to schol. periodicals. Address: c/o Dept. of Hist., Univ. of Okla., Norman, OK 73069, U.S.A. 13.

SMITH, (Rev.) Lucretia Luttie, b. 28 Dec. 1909. Pastor. Appts: Pres., Ministers' Local Coun., Chgo., Ill., 1951-; Chap., Northern Dist., Club Women, 1971-. Mbrships: Beatrice Charmond Club; Chap., ibid, 1970-71; Satellite Civic & Culture Club; Chap., ibid, 1971-72. Recip., Seven Co. 100 Award, 1971. Address: 257 W. 48th Pl., Chicago, IL 60609, U.S.A. 8, 57.

SMITH, Lucy Faye Yoachum, b. 15 Aug. 1926. School Teacher. Educ: B.A., M.A., Eastern N.M. Univ., Portales; Grad. study, Tex. Tech. Univ., Lubbock. Appts: Sec., Roosevelt Co. Chmbr. of Comm., N.M., 1948-57;

Children's Shop Owner, 1958-59; Tchr., H.S., Gainesville, Ga., 1959-60; Grad. Asst. & pt.-time instr., Eastern N.M. Univ., 1961-64; H.S. Tchr., Muleshoe, Tex., 1965-. Mbrships. incl: NEA; Pres., Dist. XVII, Tex. State Tchrs. Assn., 1974-75; Pres., Muleshoe Local Unit, ibid; Tex. Classroom Tchrs. Assn.; Delta Kappa Gamma; Past Pres., Muleshoe Chapt., AAUW; Schlrship. Advsr., Eastern N.M. Univ. Chapt. (Theta Zeta), Chi Omega; Beta Sigma Phi; Kappa Kappa Iota. Hons: Beta Sigma Phi Girl of the Yr., 1964; Muleshoe H.S. Annual Decidation, 1971. Address: 1810 W. Ave. H., Muleshoe, TX 79347, U.S.A. 125.

SMITH, M. Estellie, b. 1 Dec. 1935. Professor of Anthropology. Educ: B.A., Univ. of Buffalo, 1962; M.A., SUNY, Buffalo, 1964; Ph.D., ibid, 1967. Appts: Pt.-time Instr., Dept. of Sociol., SUNY, Buffalo, 1962-63, Dept. of Anthropol., 1963-66; Asst. Prof., Dept. Anthropol., Fla. State Univ., Tallahassee, 1966-69, & Eastern N.M. Univ., Portales, 1969-70; Permanent Rsch. Assoc., Ft. Burgwin Rsch. Ctr., Taos, 1968-; Asst. Prof., Dept. Anthropol., Eastern N.M. Univ., 1969-70, Permanent Rsch. Prof., 1972-; Assoc. Prof., Dept. Anthropol., SUNY, Brockport, 1970-; Book Review Ed., Urban Anthropol., & Studies in European Soc., 1972-. Mbr., profl. orgs. Profl. papers, reports & reviews. Recip., var. acad. grants & hon. appts. Address: 51 E. Main St., Ontario, NY 14519, U.S.A. 5, 138.

SMITH, Malcolm Sommerville, b. 22 June 1933. Opera & Concert Singer. Educ: B. Mus.Ed., Oberlin Coll. Conservatory of Music, U.S.A., 1957; B.Mus.(Voice), ibid, 1960; M.A. Ed. Admin., Tchrs. Coll., Columbia Univ., N.Y., 1958; Doct. studies, Ind. Univ. Schl. Music, Bloomington, 1960-62. Appts: Music Tchr., Ramapo Regional H.S., Franklin Lakes, N.J., 1958-60; Soloist, Robert Shaw Choral, Cultural Exchange w. Russia, 1962; Lyric Opera, Chgo., Ill., Houston Symphony under Sir John Barbirolli, Cinn. Symphony, etc., 1963-64; Leading Bass w. N.Y.C. Opera, 1965-70; European Opera Debut, Spoleto Festival, 1968; Currently engaged at Deutsche Oper am Rhein, Düsseldorf, Germany & guesting w. Hamburg, Cologne & Vienna Operas as leading Basso; also w. San Fran. Opera; Concert appearances w. Boston, Mnpls., Ottawa Symphonies, etc. Mbr. Platform Club, U.S.A. Address: 22 Woodland Ave., Montvale, NJ 07645, U.S.A. 2.

SMITH, Marian Adams, b. 6 June 1928. Volunteer Administrator of Cultural Arts. Educ: B.F.A., Univ. of N.C., Greensboro, U.S.A., 1951. Appts: Art Tchr., Pub. Schl., Art Supvsr., Pub. Schl.; Admin. Dir., Southeastern Theatre Conf., Inc. Mbrships. incl: Pres., Southeastern Theatre Conf.; V.P., Theatre for Young People, Univ. of N.C., Greensboro; Bd. of Govs., Children's Theatre Assn.; Pres., N.C. Theatre Conf.; Regional Chmn., Am. Coll. Theatre Festival; Bd. of Dirs., Am. Theatre Assn.; Chmn., Bicentennial Festival, Children's Theatre Assn.; Pres., Greensboro Study Club. Recip., Community Arts Award, Altrusa Club, 1972. Address: 310 Irving Place, Greensboro, NC 27408, U.S.A. 5, 7, 138.

SMITH, (Mrs.) Mary (pseudonym, Mary Drewery), b. 9 May 1918. Author. Educ: Westfield Coll., Univ. of London. Appts: War serv. w. Min. of Works; Asst. Libn., Hulton Picture Lib.; J.P., S.W. London Commn. Area, 1966. Mbrships: Soc. of Authors; Vice Chmn., Croydon Writers' Circle. Publs: Guide & Observer, 1953; The Way to the Stars, First Star, 1954; Jungle Lore, 1957; Rebellion in the West, 1962; Devil in Print, 1963; The Silvester Wish, 1966; A Donkey Called Haryat, 1967; A

Candle for St. Georgios, 1969; Where Four Winds Meet, 1971; Window on My Heart, 1973; Richard Wurmbrand: The Man Who Came Back, 1974. Contbr., Southern I.T.V., Radio London, scouting publs. Composer, hymns & carols, var. collects. Address: 20 Furze Ln., Purley, Surrey CR2 3EG, U.K. 3, 30, 137.

SMITH, Milton Shumway, b. 2 Sept. 1912. College Professor & Administrator. Educ: B.A., Wesleyan Univ., Middletown, Conn., 1933; M.A., Harvard Univ., Cambridge, Mass., 1934; Grad., Yale Univ., New Haven, Conn., 1934-37; Ph.D., Fordham Univ., Bronx, N.Y., 1955; Grad., Univ. of Wash., Seattle, 1962. Appts. incl: Sec. to Coroner, Middlesex Co., Conn.; Asst. Prof., Engl., Trinity Coll., Hartford; Instr. & Asst. Prof., Engl., Hillyer Coll., Univ. of Hartford; Assoc. Prof., Engl., S.Eastern La. Univ., Hammond; Prof., Engl., Yankton Coll., S.D.; Dept. Chmn., ibid; Prof., Engl., Hd., Engl. Prog., Houston Bapt. Coll., Tex.; Prof., Engl., Hd., Engl. Prog., Chmn., Humanities Div., Va. Western Community Coll., Roanoke. Mbrships. incl: Advsry. Comm. for Va. & Regional Exec. Comm., Southeastern Conf. on Engl. in 2-yr. Coll., 1972-74; Int. Treas., Lambda Iota Tau; Sec.-Treas. for Tex., Am. Studies Assn.; Sec., Houston Coun., Tchrs. of Engl.; Newcomen Soc. of N. Am.; Scottish Rite Mason, Af & AM & Kazim Temple, AAONMS; MLA; NEA; Sec., Hillyer Coll., & Pres., Va. Western Comm. Coll., AAUP; Modern Humanities Rsch. Assn.; Coll. Engl. Assn. Co-author, A Checklist of the Correspondence of Edmund Burke, 1956. Cited as Outstanding Am. Tchr., 1971. Address: 1929 Greenwood Rd., S.W., Roanoke, VA 24105, U.S.A. 7, 13.

SMITH, Morton Howison, b. 11 Dec. 1923. Professor of Theology. Educ: B.A., Univ. of Mich.; B.D., Columbia Theol. Sem.; Th.M. & Th.D., Free Univ. of Amsterdam; Univ. of N.C.; Westminster Theol. Sem. Appts: 1st Lt., Pilot-Instr., USAF, 1943-45; Asst. to Registrar, Univ. of Mich., 1947-49; Prof. & Chmn., Dept. of Bible, Belhaven Coll., Jackson, Miss., 1954-63; Guest Lectr., Westminster Theol. Sem., Phila., 1963-64; Fndg. Prof., Prof. Systematic Theol., Reformed Theol. Sem., Jackson, Miss., 1964-. Mbrships: Evangelical Theol. Soc.; Sec., Presby. Reformation Soc. & Presby. Churchmen United; Bd. Dirs., Nat. Presby. & Reformed Fellowship & Presby. Jrnl.; Stated Clerk, Presbytery of Miss. Valley, Atlanta Convocation, etc. Publs: Studies in Southern Presbyterian Theology, 1962; How is the Gold Become Dim, 1973; Contbr. to: Interpreting God's Word Today, (chapt.), 1970; Baker's Dictionaries of Theology & Ethics; Ency. of Christianity, vols. I-IV. Hons: Fulbright Fellowship, 1958-59; Bd. of Christian Educ. Grant, 1959-60; study grant, Am. Assn. Theol. Schls., 1972. Address: Rt. 1, Box 517, Clinton, MS 39056, U.S.A. 13.

SMITH, Nila Banton. Author; Educator. Educ: B.A., Univ. of Chgo., Ill., 1928; M.A., Columbia Univ., N.Y., 1932; Ph.D., ibid, 1936. Appts: Tchr., Supvsr. of Reading, Detroit Pub. Schls., 1928-33; Hd., Dept. of Educ., Greensboro Coll., N.C., 1934-35, & Whittier Ind. Univ., 1937-39; Prof., Univ. of Southern Calif., 1939-49; Prof. & Dir. of Reading Inst., N.Y. Univ., 1949-63; Disting. Prof., Glassboro State Coll., N.J., 1963-67, & currently, Univ. of Southern Calif. Mbrships. incl: Past Pres., Chmn. of sev. commns., Int. Reading Assn.; Chmn. of Comm., Nat. Coun. Rsch. in Engl.; Phi Beta Kappa, 1928; Phi Lambda Theta, 1929; Kappa Delta Pi, 1932; Hon., Delta Phi Upsilon, 1935; State Pres., Delta Kappa Gamma, 1937. Publs. incl: Learning to Read series, 1945, revised, 1974; Reading Instruction

for Today's Children, 1963, revised, 1974; Be a Better Reader Series Foundations A, B, & C, 1968; approx. 200 articles in profl. jrnls. Recip. Disting. Serv. Award, LA Reading Assn., 1965. Address: 800 W. First St., Los Angeles, CA 90012, U.S.A. 5, 9, 132, 141.

SMITH, Ora, b. 13 Apr. 1900. University Professor. Educ: B.S., Univ. of Ill.; M.S., Iowa State Univ.; Ph.D., Univ. of Calif. Appts. incl: Asst. Prof., Cornell Univ., N.Y., 1930-38; Prof., ibid, 1938-67; Emeritus, 1967-; Dir., Rsch., Potato Chip Inst. Int., 1949-; Prof., Inter-Am. Inst. of Agric. Scis., Costa Rica, 1946-47. Fellow, AAAS. Mbrships incl: Pres., Potato Assn. Am.; European Assn. for Potato Rsch.; Canadian Inst. for Food Sci. & Technol.; Sigma Xi; Alpha Zeta; AAUP; N.Y. Acad. Scis. Publs. incl: Potato Processing; Potatoes: Production Storing Processing; over 450 sci. & popular articles. Address: East Roberts Hall, Cornell Univ., Ithaca, NY 14850, U.S.A.

SMITH, Oce Worthington, Jr. Realtor; Businessman; Administrative Officer. Educ: Fairmont State Coll., W. Va.; W. Va. Univ., Morgantown. Appts. incl: Real Estate Appraiser & P.R. Aide, W. Va. State Tax Commn., 5 yrs; Aide, Clerk, & Admin. Hd., W. Va State Legislature, many yrs.; currently Sgt.-at-Arms, W. Va. House of delegs; active in local & state pol.; licensed realtor & real estate appraiser, also mortgage loans & ins. Mbrships. incl: Nat. Assn. Realtors; W. Va. Assn. Realtors; Bd. Dirs., Marion Co. Chambr. of Comm.; V.P., Marion Co. Histl. Soc.; Fairmont State Coll. Alumni Soc.; Alpha Psi Omega. Sev. articles on State & Nat. Govt. ldrs. Address: Room 700, 1st Nat. Bank Bldg., Fairmont, WV 26554, U.S.A. 6, 125.

SMITH, Ralph Blair, b. 12 Mar. 1914. University Physical Plant Administrator. Educ: B.S., Univ. of Neb., Lincoln, 1941. Appts. incl: Landscape Engr., Neb. Highway Dept., 1946; Dir. of Bldgs. & Grounds, Neb. Wesleyan Univ., Lincoln, 1946-53; Supt. of Bldgs. & Grounds, Adams State Coll., Alamosa, Colo., 1953-56; Supt. of Bldgs. & Grounds & Dir. of Safety, Drew Univ., Madison, N.J., 1956-63; Supt. of Construction & Dir. of Safety, ibid, 1963-66; Dir of Phys. Plant, 1966-. Mbrships. incl: Trustee, Admnstv. Bd., & Chmn., Property Comm., United Meth. Ch., Madison, N.J.; Dir., Past Pres. Treas., Eastern Region Assn. of Phys. Plant Admnstrs. of Univs. & Colls.; Past 10-yr. Pres., Madison Community Christmas Comm. Hons. incl: Scoutmasters Key (Boy Scouts), 1955; Madison, N.J. Jaycees Disting. Serv. Award, 1970. Address: 6 Campus Dr., Madison, NJ 07940, U.S.A.

SMITH, Ray Winfield, b. 4 June 1897. Lecturer & Writer in Fields of Archaeology & Technology. Educ: B.S., Dartmouth Coll., N.H., 1918; Courses in Classical & Colloquial Arabic & Hist. of Islamic Art, Am. Univ., Cairo, Egypt, 1963-64. Appts. incl: Positions at Dir. level w. Am. Oil Interests, U.S.A., Belgium, Netherlands & Germany, 1919-36; Pres., Export-Import Co., U.S.A., 1936-41; Mil. & Civilian Serv. w. U.S. Govt., 1941-54; (in W. Germany, 1951-54); Supvsr., Marshall Plan, Berlin, 1951-52; U.S. Commnr., Mil. Security Bd., 1952-54; Dir., Am. Rsch. Ctr., Egypt, 1963-65; Dir., Akhenaten Temple Proj., ibid, 1966-72; U.S. Attache, Olympic Games, Amsterdam, Netherlands, 1928; Hon. Chmn., Exhib., The Art of Glass, Houston Mus. of Art, 1970; Rsch. Assoc., Univ. Mus., Phila., 1964-; Bd. of Visitors, Mus. of Fine Arts, Boston, 1956-64; Cons., Brookhaven Nat. Lab., 1955-; Bd. of Ed. Review, Jrnl. of Glass Studies, 1956-; Has delivered more than 100 lectures.

Mbrships: Archaeoloigcal Inst. of Am. (Trustee, 1957-66, Chmn., Comm. on Ancient Glass, 1955-68); Chmn., Int. Comm. on Ancient Glass, 1948-68; Coun., AAAS; Fellow, Deutsches Archäslogisches Institut. Publs. incl: Glass from the Ancient World, 1957; Contbr., articles, History Revealed in Ancient Glass, 1964, Computer Helps Scholars Recreate an Egyptian Temple, 1970, Nat. Geographic Mag.; Contbr., articles, A Glass Bowl with the Judgment of Paris (w. Gisela M. A. Richter), Burlington Mag., 1953, Significance of Roman Glass, Bulletin, Metropolitan Mus. of Art, Use of Electronic Computers in Archaeology, Bulletin de l'Institut d'Egypte, 1968-69, New Finds of Ancient Glass in North Africa, Ars Orientalis, 1957, Technological Reseach on Ancient Glass, Archaeology, 1958, Analytical Study of Glass in Archaeology, Science in Archaeology, 1969. Pvte. Collector of Ancient Glass. Hons. incl: Holder, Purple Heart & Legion of Merit, 1918 & 1946; Key to City of Newark, N.J., 1951; 1st Award, Am. Inst. of Arch., Wash. D.C., 1962; L.H.D., Dartmouth Coll., 1958. Address: P.O. Box 43, Dublin, NH 03444, U.S.A. 2, 6, 37, 105, 133.

SMITH, Rita (I.) b. 9 Dec. 1923. Newspaper Editor. Educ: B.A. (Cum Laude), D'Youville Coll., Buffalo, N.Y. Appts: Reporter, Courier Express Daily, Buffalo, N.Y., 1944-67, Asst. Women's Ed., 1967-69, Women's Ed., 1969-; also currently Travel Lectr., community grps., chs., schls. Mbrships: Niagara Frontier Chapt., Am. Newspaper Guild; WNY Chapt., Nat. League of Am. Pen Women; D'Youville Coll. Alumnae Assn. Regular by-line, w. Courier Express, Buffalo, on stories, features, travel articles. Recip., 1st Prizes, Buffalo Chapt., Nat. Newspaper Guild Annual Competitions. Address: 2 Osgood Ave., W.'Seneca, NY 14224, U.S.A. 5.

SMITH, Robert G., b. 16 Oct. 1913. Professor; Author; Consultant on Special Purpose Governments. Appts. incl: Instr. in Hist., Drew Univ., 1940-44; Chief Army Med. Hist., US Army, China, 1945-46; Chmn., Dept. Pol. Sci., 1946-; Dir., inst. For. Rsch. on Govt., 1964-; Adjunct Prof., Pol. Sci., Hunter Coll., 1965-67; Vis. Prof., Pub. Admin., Grad. Schl. Pub. Admin., NY Univ., 1966-67; Cons. on Pub. Auths., NYC, 1965-68; to Nat. Assn. of Cos., 1964-; Pfeiffer Prof. Pol. Sci., Drew Univ., 1971-. Active Mbr. of profl. socs. Publs. incl: Public Authorities, Special Districs & Local Government, 1964; Public Authorities in Urban Areas, 1969; Ad Hov Governments: Special Public Authorities in Britain & the United States, 1974; Chapts. in profl. books & articles in profl. jrnls. Address: 5 Wyndehurst Dr., Madison, NJ 07940, U.S.A. 6, 14, 15, 50.

SMITH, Robert Houston, b. 25 Apr. 1907. Baptist Clergyman. Educ: B.A., La. Coll., 1929; Th.M., New Orleans Theol. Sem., 1934; Th.D., ibid, 1940. Appts: Tchr., Grimes Bluff Schl., 1926-27; Asst. Prin., LaFargue HS, 1929-30; Min., 1st Bapt. Ch., Bossier City, La., 1941-45; 1st Bapt. Ch., Arkadelphia, Ark., 1945-46, & 1st Bapt.C h., Pineville, La., 1946-72; Pres., La. Bapt. Convention, 1956-57 & Bd., Rapides Gen. Hosp., 1954-56; Mbr. Home Mission Bd., Atlanta, Ga., 1959-67. Mbrships: La. Hist. Soc.; Masons: Rotary Int.; Pi Kappa Delta; Alpha Phi; Omicron Delta Kappa; Ed. Advsry. Staff, Broadman Commentary, Nashville Tenn. Contbr. to syndicated newspaper column, Bible Words to Live By & var. other publs. Hons: Plaque for Serv. as Pres., La. Bapt. Convention, 1957; Cert. of Recognition for Serv. Rendered to Home Mission Bd., Southern Bapt. Convention, 1967. Address: P.O. Box 1370, Pineville, LA 71360, U.S.A. 7, 125.

SMITH, Robert S., b. 28 May 1929. Physician. Educ: B.S., Randolph-Macon Coll., Ashland, Va., 1951; M.D., Med. Coll. of Va., Richmond, 1956; Dipl., Am. Bd. Family Prac., 1970. Appts: Pvte. Prac., Family Med., Dinwiddie, Va., 1958-69; Emergency Room Physn., Petersburg Gen. Hosp., Va., 1969-73. Mbrships. incl: Charter Fellow, Am. Acad. of Family Physns.; V.P., Va. Acad. of Family Prac., 1973-74; Hon. Coun., Med. Coll. Va., 1952-55; AMA; Am. Coll. Emergency Physns.; Am. Med. Pol. Action Comm.; Alpha Sigma Chi; V.P., ibid, 1955; Chi Beta Phi; Omicron Delta Kappa. Recip., Most Outstanding Sr. Citizen Award, Dinwiddie Co Ruritan Clubs, 1964. Address: Rte. 1, Box 16, Dinwiddie, VA 23841, U.S.A. 7, 17, 116.

SMITH, Roger Davis, b. 21 May 1923. Lawyer. Educ: S.B., MIT, 1948; LL.B., Yale Law Schl., 1953. Appts: Assoc., Carter, Ledyard & Milburn, N.Y.C., 1953-66; Ptnr., Jackson Nash Brophy Barringer & Brooks, 1966-; Trustee, Profl. Childrens Schl., 1968-; Pres., ibid, 1973; Mbrships: Am. Bar Assn.; N.Y. State Bar Assn.; Assn. of Bar of N.Y.C.; Yale Club; Sigma Alpha Epsilon; Phi Alpha Delta. Address: 330 Madison Ave., N.Y., NY 10017, U.S.A. 6.

SMITH, Russell Lynn Jr., b. 25 Dec. 1919. Consulting Civil & Sanitary Engineer. Educ: Stanford Univ., Calif. 1938-41; B.A., Univ. of Hawaii, 1948. Appts: Jr. Eng., H.A.R. Austin, 1947-53; Design Engr., H.A.R. Austin & Assocs., Ltd., 1953-57; V.P., ibid, 1957-59; V.P., Austin, Smith & Assoc., Inc., 1959-; Cons. on Water Supplies, Territory of Guam, 1967-; Master planner of Water & Sewerage Systems, Govt. of Am. Samoa, 1963; Cons., Water Supplies, Territory Am. Samoa, 1963; '72; Con. & Master planner of Water & Sewerage Systems, Trust Territory of Pacific Isls. 1966-; Lectr., Univ. of Hawaii. Lect., Mo. Univ., Rolla, U.S.A., 1973. Mbrships. incl: V.-Cmndr., Hawaiian Dept., Am. Legion, 1958; Dir., 1971-72,Cons. Engrs. Coun. U.S.A; Int. Comm., 1971; Cons. Engrs. Coun. (U.S.A.) Int. Comm., 1971-; U.S. Rep. to Fedn. Int. des Ingenieurs-Conseils & Liaison to Asian Dev. Bank, 1971-72; Pres., 1970, Cons. Engrs. Coun., Hawaii; Western U.S., Rep. on Comm. on Local Sects., Am. Soc. of Civil Engrs., 1972-77; Pres., 1961, Hawaii Sect.; Pres., 1967, Water Pollution Control Assn.; Dir., Soc. of Am. Mil. Engrs., Hawaii, 1963 & Engrng. Assn. of Hawaii, 1956-57. Publs: Water Pollution in Pearl Harbor—Steps to Reverse the Present Trend, 1964; Hawaii Gives Leis to New Tertiary Waste Plant, 1973. Hons. incl. Cons. Engrs. Coun. of Hawaii Award for Masterplanning Water & Sewerage Systems for Trust Territory of Pacific Isls. 1972.; Excellence Award, Tertiary Wastewater Treatment Design, Cons. Engrs. Coun., Hawaii, 1971; Air Medal w. Oak Leaf Cluster, 1946. Address: Ste. 900, 745 Fort St., Mall, Honolulu, HI 96813, U.S.A. 2, 9, 78, 139.

SMITH, S. Strother III, b. 1 Aug. 1941. Attorney-At-Law. Educ: Va. Mil. Inst., 1959 & '60; B.A., Univ. of Richmond, 1963; B.C.L., Marshall-Wythe Schl. of Law, Coll. of William & Mary, 1966; J.D., ibid, 1967; Grad. Law Schl., Univ. of Va., 1966-67. Appts. incl: Law Clerk, Hirschler & Fleischer, Attys., 1964-66; Legislative Asst., S.S. Smith Jr., Mbr. Va. House of Delegs., 1963; Ptnr., More & Smith, Attys.-At-Law, 1967-69; Pres., Smith, Robinson & Vinyard, Attys.-At-Law Inc., Abingdon, Va., 1973-; Pres., Smith, Venable & Assocs., Attys.-At-Law Inc., Richmond, Va., 1974; Dir., Legislative Counsel: Compensation Dept. Dist. 28, United Mine Workers of Am.,

1969-. Mbrships. Incl: Wash. Co., Buchanan Co., Wise Co., Va. State & Am. Bar Assns.; Vice Chmn., Legal Counsel Young Republican Fedn. of Va., 1960-64, '73; Vestry, St. Thomas Episc Ch., 1969-72; Local & State Dir.; Abingdon Jay Cees, 1967-68. Publs. incl: Black Lung, 1972 & '73; Poems, Sketches & Articles in Mags. & Reviews. Hons. incl: Omicron Delta Kappa Nat. Ldrship. Soc., 1963; Key Man Award, Abingdon Jay Cees, 1968. Address: Smith, Venable & Assoc., Attys.-At-Law, Inc., 422 E. Main St., Richmond, VA 23219, U.S.A. 46, 125.

SMITH, Shirley Dorn, b. 28 May 1903. Administrative Public Relations Executive. Educ: Allegheny Coll., Pa. Appts. incl: Newspaper Cons., 1938-40; Advt. Exec., Jamestown Post Jrnl., N.Y., 1940-41; Dir. of P.R., Am. Aviation Co., 1941-45; Owner, Shirley D. Smith & Assocs., P.R., 1945-57; Exec. Dir., P.R. Soc. of Am., Inc., 1957-61; Cons. on Mbrship, Advt. Fed. of Am., 1964-66; V.P., Hank Meyer Assocs., 1967-68; Asst. to the Pres., Sterling Movies, 1968-70; Asst. to the Pres., Association-Sterling Films, div. of Macmillan Incorp., 1970-. Mbrships incl: Dist. V.P., 1955, Nat. Sec., 1956, Exec. Dir., 1957-61, P.R. Soc. of Am.; Dir., Int. Affil. of Advt. Clubs, 1942-43; Sec., Shelby Co. Chapt., Soc. for Crippled Children, 1948-55; Fndr., Memphis Better Bus. Bureau, 1948. Author of over 100 articles on P.R. & Advt., appearing in leading U.S. mags. Guest Lectr. at sev. univs.; num. speeches on P.R. Hons. incl: Cit., Mid-South Chapt., P.R. Soc. of Am., 1953; Accredited by the P.R. Soc. of Am., 1965. Address: 4 Peter Cooper Rd., 11F, N.Y., NY 10010, U.S.A. 2, 24.

SMITH, Susan J., b. 1 Dec. 1942. Art Dealer. Educ: Wash. Univ., St. Louis, Mo., 1960; Kansas City Jr. Coll., Mo., 1961-62; B.F.A., Kansas City Art Inst., ibid, 1966; Postgrad. work, Univ. of Calif. at Davis, 1966. Appts: Ptnr. in East of the Sun, San Francisco, Calif., 1967-73; Ptnr. & Curator, West of the Moon, ibid, 1971-. Recognized Collector of Am. Indian Art, historic quilts, & other Americana, & folk costume & toys. Exhibs: Toys, San Francisco Art Inst. Gall., Calif., 1970; Am. Indian Art, William Rockhill Nelson Gall. of Art, Kansas City, Miss., & Changing Faces, M.H. de Young Mus., San Francisco, Calif., 1972. Address: West of the Moon Gall., 3464 Sacramento St., San Francisco, CA 94118, U.S.A. 5, 138.

SMITH, T. Lynn, b. 11 Nov. 1903. Professor of Sociology. Educ: B.S., Brigham Young Univ., 1928; M.A., 1929, Ph.D., 1932, Univ. of Minn. Appts: Asst., Assoc. Prof., Prof. & Hd., Depts. of Sociol. & Rural Sociol., La. State Univ., 1931-47; Prof., Hd., Dept. of Sociol. & Anthropol., & Dir., Inst. of Brazilian Studies, Vanderbilt Univ., 1947-49; Prof., Sociol., 1949-59, & Grad. Rsch. Prof., Sociol., 1959-, Univ. of Fla. Mbrships: Am. Sociol. Assn.; Past Pres., Rural Sociol. Soc.; Population Assn. of Am.; Int. Population Union; Sociol. Rsch. Assn.; Inter-Am. Statl. Inst.; Int. Inst. of Sociol. Num. publs. incl: The Sociology of Rural Life, 1940, 3rd edit., 1953; Brazil: People & Institutions, 1946, 4th edit., 1972; Agrarian Reform in Latin America, 1965; Principals of Inductive Rural Sociology (w. P.E. Zopf, Jr.), 1970. Hons: Order of Southern Cross, Brazil, 1951; Dr. h.c., Univ. of Brazil, 1946, Univ. of São Paulo, 1951; Guggenheim Fellowships, 1951, 1954-59. Address: 632 S.W. 27th Ct., Gainesville, FL 32601. 2, 14.

SMITH, Thomas Brown, b. 3 Dec. 1915. Professor of Law. Educ: M.A., B.C.L., D.C.L.,

Christ Ch., Oxford Univ.; LL.D., Edinburgh Univ. Appts: Barrister-at-Law, 1938; Advocate of Scottish Bar, 1947; Q.C., 1956; Prof., Scots Law, Aberdeen Univ., 1949-58, Edinburgh Univ., 1968-73; Prof., Civil Law, Edinburgh Univ., 1958-68; Commn., Scottish Law Commn., 1973-; Vis. Prof., Harvard Law Schl., Tulane, Cape Town, & Witwatersrand Univs. Mbrships: Fellow, Brit. Acad.; Pres., Soc. Pub. Tchrs. of Law, 1972; Hon. For. Mbr., Am. Acad. Arts & Scis.; Naval & Mil. Clubs, London; New Club, Edinburgh. Publs: Doctrines of Judicial Precedent in Scots Law, 1952; Scotland-The Development of its Laws & Constitution, 1955; British Justice—The Scottish Contribution, 1961; Studies Critical & Comparative, 1962; A Short Commentary on the Laws of Scotland, 1962; articles in legal jrnls., encyclopaedias, etc., Hons: LL.D., Cape Town Univ., 1959 & Aberdeen Univ., 1969. Address: 11 India St., Edinburgh EH3 6HA, U.K. 1, 3, 35.

SMITH, Virginia Dodd (Mrs. Haven), b. 30 June 1912. Lecturer; Agricultural Leader. Educ: B.A., Univ. of Neb. 1934. Mbrships. incl: Nat. Pres., Am. Country Life Assn., 1951-53; USDA Home Econs. Rsch. Advsry. Comm., 1956-60; Bd. Dirs., Am. Farm. Bur. Fed.; Dpty. Pres., Assoc. Country Women of the World, 1962-68; V.P., Nat. Farm Film Fndn.; Chmn., Am. Farm Bur. Women's Comms.; AAUW; Bd. Govs., Agric. Hall of Fame; Bus. & Profl. Women; U.S. Govt. Advsry Comm., Rural Educ. & Small Schls. 1970-74 & U.S. Dept. of Commerce, Census on Agricl. Stats, 1972-74; lectured before educl., med. & agric. grps. in 50 States & sev. for countries. Goodwill Ambassador, Switzerland, 1951. Rep., Assoc. Country Women of the World on tour of Latin-Am. countries, 1963. '68; DAR Recip. many hons inclng: Int, Serv. Award. Midwest Conf. of World Affairs, 1971 Neb. Woman of Achievement, Bus. & Profl. women, 1970, 4-H Alumni Award, Iowa State Univ., 1973; Nat. 4-H Alumni Award, 1974. Address: Box 643, Chappell, NB 69129, U.S.A. 2, 5, 8, 120.

SMITH, Walter Delos, b. 7 June 1936. Certified Public Accountant; Financial Executive. Educ: B.S., Acctng., Walton Schl. of Commerce, U.S.A. Appts: Sr. Acct., Frazer Torbet, 1960-66; Asst. Controller, The Rath Packing Co., Waterloo, Iowa, 1966-68; Sec., Treas., & Controller, DeLeuw, Cather Int., 1968-72; Controller & Treas., DeLeuw, Cather & Co., N.Y.C., 1968-72; V.P.,Controller, & Treas., Genimar, Inc., & Dur-o-Wal Grp. of Cos., 1972-73; Corporate Controller, Mohawk Data Scis., 1973-. Mbrships. incl: Chmn., Off. Pracs. Comm. & Uniform Cost Acctng. Comm., Cons. Engrs. Coun. of the U.S.; Newcomen Soc. of N. Am.; Ill. Soc. of CPA's; Kiwanis Int.; Toastmasters Int. Contbr. to book, Uniform Cost Accounting. Address: 10 Rollingwood Ave., New Hartford, NY 13413, U.S.A. 8, 57.

SMITH, Warren Allen, b. 27 Oct. 1921. Corporation President; Educator. Educ: B.A., Univ. of Northern Iowa; M.A., Columbia Univ., N.Y. Appts: Chmn., Dept. of Engl., Bentley Schl., N.Y.C., 1949-54 & New Canaan H.S., Conn., 1954-; Pres. & Chmn. of Bd., Variety Sound Corp., N.Y.C., 1961- & Taursa Fund, 1970-71; Dir., Mensa Investment Club, 1967-; Mbrships: Mensa; Am. Unitarian Assn.; Brit. Humanist Assn.; Pres., Humanist Book Club, 1957-62; Book Review Ed., The Humanist (U.S.A.), 1953-58. Contbr. to Lib. Jrnl; Syndicated Columnist, Manhattan Chessboard, to Caribbean Newspapers. Hons: Guest, Govt. of Dominica, Independence Day, 1969. Address: Ste. 856, 130 W. 42nd St., N.Y., NY 10036, U.S.A. 6, 16, 128.

1970-; Dir., Mensa Investment Club, 1967-; Chmn., ibid, 1967-70. Mbrships: Mensa; Am. Unitarian Assn.; Brit. Humanist Assn.; Pres., Humanist Book Club, 1957-62; Book Review Ed., The Humanist (U.S.A.), 1953-58. Contbr. to Lib. Jrnl; Syndicated Columnist, Manhattan Chessboard, to Caribbean Newspapers. Hons: Guest, Govt. of Dominica, Independence Day, 1969. Address: Ste. 856, 130 W. 42nd St., N.Y., NY 10036, U.S.A. 6, 16, 128.

SMITH, Wendell Ross, b. 4 Mar. 1911. Academic Dean; Professor. Educ: B.Sc., Univ. of Iowa, 1932; M.A., ibid, 1935; Ph.D., 1941. Appts: Fac. Mbr.-Dept. Hd., Coll. of Commerce, Univ. of Iowa, 1934-54; Ptnr.-V.P., Alderson & Sessions, 1954-59; Dir., Marketing Rsch.-V.P., Staff, Marketing Dev., RCA, N.Y., 1959-62; Pres., Marketing Sci. Inst.-Prof., Univ. of Pa., 1962-68; Dean, Schl. of Bus. Admin., Univ. of Mass., 1968-. Mbrships: Dir., Am. Marketing Assn., 1952-53; Nat. V.P., 1956-57; Nat. Pres, 1958-59; Order of Artus; Chmn., Nat. Marketing Advsry. Comm. to Sec. of Commerce, 1966-69; Beta Gamma Sigma; Pi Gamma Mu; Nassau Club, Princeton, N.J. Publs: (co-author) Public Utility Economics. Contbr. to profl. publs. Hons: Alpha Kappa Psi Award, 1956; Distribution Hall of Fame, 1962. Address: Schl. of Bus. Admin., Univ. of Mass., Amherst, MA 01002, U.S.A. 2, 128.

SMITH, Wilbur Stevenson, b. 6 Sept. 1911. Consulting Engineer. Educ: B.S., Univ. of S.C., Columbia, U.S.A., 1932; M.S., ibid, 1933. Appts. incl: Dir., Traffic Engrng. Dept., S.C. Hwy. Dept., 1933-43; Transport Cons., Off. of Civil Defense, & Coord., Traffic Studies, FBI, 1943-46; Fac. Mbr. & Assoc. Dir., Bur. of Hwy. Traffic, Yale Univ., 1943-68; Pres., Wilbur Smith & Assocs., Columbia, S.C. 7 Sev. br. offs., 1952-72; Pres. & Bd. Chmn., ibid, 1972-. Num. mbrships incl: Bd. Chmn., Eno. Fndn. for Transportation, Inc.; Nat. Acad. of Engrng.; V.P., Southern Dist., Am. Rd. Bldrs.' Assn.; Bd. of Dirs., S.C. Safety Coun.; Inst. for Transportation, Am. Pub. Works. Assn.; Am. Inst. of Cons. Engrs.; Phi Beta Kappa; Tau Beta Pi. Publs: State-City Relationships in Highway Affairs (w. Hebden) 1950; Traffic Engineering (w. Matson & Hurd), 1955; Num. tech. papers & Bulletins. Hons. incl: LL.D., Univ. of S.C., 1963; Engr. of the Yr., S.C. Soc. of Profl. Engrs., 1964. Address: Wilbur Smith & Assocs., P.O. Box 92, Columbia, SC 29202, U.S.A. 2, 6, 7, 16.

SMITH, William Arthur, b. 19 Apr. 1918. Artist. Educ: M.A., Univ. of Toledo, Ohio, U.S.A.; Ecole des Beaux Arts, Paris, France; Academie de la Grande Chaumière, Paris. Appts: Mbr., Exec. Comm., Int. Assn. of Art. 1963-69; Pres., U.S.A., Nat. Comm., Int. Assn. of Art, A.I.A.P., 1969-; Pres., Int. Assn. of Art (UNESCO), 1973-. Mbrships: Coun., Nat. Acad. of Design, 1953-56; Pres., Am. Watercolor Soc., 1956-57; Dutch Treat Club; Tile Club; Phila. Water Color Club. Painted Mural, Maryland House, 1968. Num hons. incl: Silver Medal & Prize, Am. Watercolor Soc., 1948, 52 & 73; Nat. Acad. Award, 1949 & 51; Obrig Prize for Oil Painting, 1953; Am. Artists Group Prize for Lithography, Soc. of Am. Graphic Artists, 1954; Stuart Watercolor Prize, 1954; Knobloch Prize, 1956; Award for Lithography, Contemporary Arts of U.S., 1956; Gold Medal & Grand Prize, Am. Watercolor Soc., 1957 & 65. Address: Windy Bush Rd., Pineville, Bucks Co., PA 18946, U.S.A. 2, 6, 19.

SMITH, William Reece, Jr., b. 19 Sept. 1925. Lawyer. Educ: B.S., Univ. of S.C., U.S.A., 1946; J.D., Univ. of Fla., 1949; Rhodes Schol., Oxford Univ., 1949-52. Appts: Pres.,

Hillsborough Co. (Fla.) Bar Assn., 1963; Sec. Am. Bar Assn., 1967-71; Pres., Fla. Bar Fndn., 1971-72; Sec. Am. Bar Endowment, 1972-; Pres., Fla. Bar, 1972-73; Pres., Fla. Legal Servs., Inc., 1973-. Mbrships: Pres., Tampa Philharmonic Assn. & Fla. Gulf Coast Symph.; Fellow - Am. Coll. of Trial Lawyers, Int. Acad. of Trial Lawyers, Int. Soc. of Barristers, Am. Bar Fndn.; Am. Law Inst.; Sec., Fla. Rhodes Schol. Selection Comm. Hons: Outstanding Young Man of Tampa, Tampa Jaycess, 1960; Award for Disting. Serv., Fla. Jaycees, 1965; LL.D., Univ. of S. Fla., 1973. Address: POB 3239, Tampa, FL 33601, U.S.A. 2, 12, 16, 128.

SMITH, Wray Cameron, b. 27 Mar. 1922. Clergyman. Educ: D.D., Wittenberg Univ., 1968; M.Div., Hamma Schl. of Theol., 1973. Appts. incl: Pres., Ohio Luther League, 1943-45; Mbr., Chmn., Acting Dir., Christian Educ., Ohio Synod, Luth. Ch. of Am., 1945-68; Fndr., Pastor, Holy Trinity Luth. Ch., Mansfield, 1948-; Fndr., Bd. of Dirs., Bldg. Chmn., Good Shepherd Home for Aged, Ashland, 1956-; Pres., Luth. Pastors' Assn., Mansfield; Mbr., Exec. Bd., Ohio Synod, 1968-; Dean, Lectr., Summer Schls., ibid, 1963-; Dir., Radio Broadcasting, Luth. Pastors' Assn. Mbrships: Pres., Exchange Club of Mansfield; Chmn., Sheriff's Advsry. Commn.; Am. Security Coun. 1976 Bi-Centennial Comm.; Mansfield. Publs. incl: Jesus Interprets the Ten Commandments. Also author & prod. of dramas inclng: That Same Night, 1965; The Promise Was Not Vain. Named Exchangite of the Yr., 1973-74. Address: Box 3504, 1020 Laurelwood Rd., Mansfield, OH 44907, U.S.A. 8, 57, 128, 130, 131.

SMOKE, Stephen D., b. 16 Oct. 1919. Public Relations Consultant. Educ: B.A., Lehigh Univ., 1941; Further study, Pa. State Univ., Cornell, Temple Univs., La Salle Coll. Appts: Sr. Acct. Supvsr., Hill & Knowlton, Inc., 1949-57; Sr. V.P., Gaynor & Ducas, Inc., 1957-60; Pres., 1960- Stephen D. Smoke Copr., Communications Satellite Corp., Int. Telecommunications Satellite Consortium, Am. Metal Climax, Inc. Mbrships: Newcomen Soc. of N. Am.; P.R. Sooc., of Am. & Charter Mbr., Counselor's Sect. Publs: Judgement, 1965-66; Contbr. to periodicals; Ed., The U.S.A. in the World Economy, 1966. Address: Stephen D. Smoke Corp., 4749, MacArthur Blvd., Washington, DC 20007, U.S.A. 7, 24.

SMOOT, Joe Ashley, b. 10 Apr. 1916. Osteopathic Physician & Surgeon. Educ: A.B., Phillips Univ., Enid, Okla., U.S.A., 1936; D.O., Kan. City Coll. of Osteopathy & Surg., 1941. Appts: Intern, Lakeside Hosp., Kan. City, Mo., 1941-42; Res., ibid, 1942-43; Preceptor, Okla. Osteopathic Hosp., Tulsa, 1945-47; Gen. Prac., Osteopathic Physn. & Surg., Tulsa, 1943-; Chief of Staff, Okla. Osteopathic Hosp., 1962-63; State Chmn., Osteopathic Medicare & Med. Review Bd., 1968-; Mbr., Admissions Comm., Okla. Coll. of Osteopathic Med. & Surg., Tulsa; Lectr. at seminars & profl. meetings. Mbrships. incl: Pres., Okla. Osteopathic Assn., 1967-68, Legislative Comm., 1970-; Am. Osteopathic Assn.; Pres., Tulsa Dist. Osteopathic Soc.; Tulsa Area Christian Mission Bd., 1946-51; Exec. Comm., Tulsa Council of Chs., 1945-52; Bd. & Exec. Comm., Okla. Christian Home, 1954-62; Pres., Optimist Club of Tulsa, 1951; Dir., Nat. Equity Life Ins. Co., 1967-72; Pres., SGH Bldg. Corp., 1962-. Publs: Articles in profl. jrnls. Address: 1936 S. Harvard Ave., Tulsa, OK 74112, U.S.A. 7.

SMYTH, Charles Phelps, b. 10 Feb. 1895. Chemist. Educ: A.B., 1916, A.M., 1917, Princeton Univ.; Ph.D., Harvard Univ., 1921.

Appts: 1st Lt., Chem. Warfare Serv., U.S. Army, 1918; Inst.—Prof., Chem., Princeton Univ., 1920-58; Lt. Cmdr., USNR, 1937-41; Chem., Atomic Bomb Proj., 1943-45; Expert Cons., OSRD, U.S. Army, European Theater of Ops., 1945; David B. Jones Prof., 1958-63; Prof. Emeritus, 1963-; Sr. Rsch. Chem., 1963-68; Liaison Sci., Off. Naval Rsch., London, 1969-70; Cons., 1963-69, 1971-. Mbrships: Fellow, Am. Phys. Soc.; Nat. Acad. of Scis.; Am. Chem. Soc.; Am. Philos. Soc.; Chem. Soc., Royal Instn., London; Sigma Xi; Alpha Chi Sigma; Phi Beta Kappa. Publs: Dielectric Constant & Molecular Structuture, 1931; Dielectric Behavior & Structure, 1955; Past Assoc Ed., Jrnl. Chem. Physics; Contbr., 300 papers to profl. jrnls. Hons: Nichols Medal, Am. Chem. Soc., 1954; Medal of Freedom; Certs. of Appreciation, War Dept., U.S. State Dept.; Hon. Chmn., Gordon Conf. on Dielectrics, 1970. Address: 245 Prospect Ave., Princeton, NJ 08540, U.S.A.

SMYTH, (Brig. The Rt. Hon. Sir) John (George), (Jackie Smyth), b. 24 Oct. 1893. Retired Army Officer; Politician; Author. Appts. incl: Entered army, 1912; Serv. WWI; Disting career in campaigns & Expeditions inclng. Egypt & Far East, 1915-35; Brevet Major-Col., 1928-36; Instr., Staff Coll., Camberley, U.K., 1931-34; Comdt. 45th Rattray Sikhs, 1936-39; Comdr. 127 Infantry Brigade in ops. in France & Belgium, WWII; Acting Major Gen., 1941; Comd. 17th Div. in Burma at time of Japanese invasion; retired 1942; Hon. Brig., 1943; Mil. Corres. nat. newspapers, 1943-46; Lawn Tennis Corres., 1946-57; Author, Wimbledon Prog. articles, 1947-; Comptroller or Gov. num. schls. or hosps., 1948-62; Conservative M.P., 1950-66; Parliamentary Sec.-Jt. Parliamentary Sec., Min. of Pensions (& Nat. Ins) 1951-55. Mbrships. incl: 1st Chmn., Life Pres., Victoria Cross Assn.; Pres., S. London Br., Burma Star Assn.; Past V.P. & Pres., Disting. Conduct Medal League; V.P., Dunkirk Veterans Assn.; Int. Lawn Tennis Club of G.V. Publs: num. books on war, defence, lawn tennis etc; children's books; playwright. Num. hons. incl: Sev. mentions in despatches; V.C., 1915; M.C., 1920; created 1st Baronet, 1955; Privy Councillor, 1962. Address: 807 Nelson House, Dolphin Square, London SW1V 3PA, U.K. 1.

SMYTHIES, John Raymond, b. 30 Nov. 1922. Physician. Educ: Christ's Coll. Cambridge, U.K., 1942; Univ. Coll. Hosp., London, 1942-45. Appts. incl: Sci., Lab. of Neurophysiol., Worcester Fndn., 1958-59; Sr. Lectr., Univ. of Edinburgh, 1961-68; Rdr., Psych., ibid, 1968-73; Cons. Psych., Royal Edinburgh Hosp. & Royal Infirmary, 1968-73; Charles Barney Ireland Prof., Psych. & Biochem., Univ. of Ala., Birmingham, U.S.A., 1973-. Fellowships: Royal Soc. Med.; Royal Coll. Psych. Mbrships incl: Cons., WHO, 1962-68; Pres., Int. Soc. Psychoneuroendocrinol., 1971-74.; Am. Soc. Pharmacol. & Exptl. Therapeutics. Publs. incl: Analysis of Perception, 1956; The Neurological Foundations of Psychiatry, 1966; Amines & Schizophrenia, 1967; Beyond Reductionism, 1969; Brain Mechanisms & Behavior, 1970. Address: Neurosci, Prog., U.A.B. Med. Ctr., Birmingham, AL 35294, U.S.A.

SNAPIRI, Nachum, b. 9 July 1911. Certified Internal Auditor. Educ: Hebrew Univ., Jerusalem, 1930-34. Appts: Internal Auditor, Nat. Labour Org., Nat. Sick Fund in Israel; Mbr., Supreme Control Comm., Nat. Labour Org., 1930-; Treas., Internal Auditors, Israel, 1968-. Mbrships: Chmn., Cert. Acct. & Income Tax Advsrs. Assn., Israel; Heruth Pol.

Movement; Vaad Kehila, Jerusalem; World Comm. of Jews from Wilno; Ctrl. Comm., Brit Rishonim. Conbr. to profl. jrnls. Address: Rambam 57, Rehavia, Jerusalem, Israel.

SNELL, John Raymond, b. 9 Dec. 1912. Consulting Engineer. Educ: B.E., Vanderbilt Univ., U.S.A., 1934; M.S., Ill. Univ., 1936; D.S., Harvard Univ., 1939. Appts: Inst., Hangchow Univ., 1934-35; Water Supply Engr., Obres Publicas, Venezuela, 1939-41; w. Metcalf Eddy, Foy Spafford Thorndyke, Stone Webster, 1941-43; Army Corps Engrs., 1st Serv. Cmnd., 1943-45; US Pub. Hlth. Serv. China Theatre, 1945-46; Pres., Engrng. Serv. Inc., Melrose, Mass., 1947-50; Lectr. Sanitary Engrng., MIT, 1948-50; Prof. & Hd., Civil & Sanitary Engrng. Dept., Mich. State Univ., 1951-55; Pres., John R. Snell Sngrs. Inc., Cons., 1955-; Special Cons., WHO, AID & sev. for. govts; Fndr. & Chmn., Bd. Op. Bootstrap Inc. Mbrships: Tau Beta Pi; Chi Epsilon; sev. profl. assns. Publs. incl: Profl. jrnl. articles—New and Unique Solutions to Solid Wast Problems, 1970; New and Unique Low Cost Ways of Stabilizing Liquid and Solid Organic Waste, 1970; Dredging Restores Dying Inland Lakes— World Dredging and Marine Construction, 1973; Contbr., Evironmental Engineering Handbook, 1974. Recip. hon. Address: 221 W. Saginaw St., Lansing, MI 48933, U.S.A.

SNELL, Marvis Virginia Reeder, b. 1 Jan. 1924. Rancher; Music Teacher. Educ: B.S., Aubern Univ., 1944; Music studies, Manatee Jr. Coll. Appts: Owner & Operator, Reeder Ranch & Dairy Inc., & Reeder Farms Inc.; Pvte. Piano Tchr.; Class Tchr., Dir. Children's Choirs, Gillette 1st Bapt. Ch., 17 yrs. Mbrships: V.P., Aubern Univ. Home Econs. Club & Debate Coun.: Manatee Co. Piano Tchrs. Assn.; Past Pres., ibid, 2 yrs., Past Treas., 5 yrs.; Pres. & 1st V.P., Bradenton Beethoven Music Club; Manatee Co. Histl. Soc.; Past Mbr.; Am. Dietic Assn., Bradenton Jr. Woman's Club, PTA; Tau Kappa Alpha. Author, Going to Church. Address: R.F.D.1, Box 316, Palmetto, FL, U.S.A. 125.

SNELLGROVE, Harold Sinclair. b. 18 May 1913. University Professor. Educ: B.A., Duke Univ., 1936; M:A., ibid, 1940; Ph.D., Univ . of N.M., 1948. Appts: Instr., Gulf Coast Mil. Acad., 1936-41; U.S. Army, 1942-46; Instr., Univ. of N.M., 1946-47; Instr. thru' to Hd. of Dept., Hist., Miss. State Univ., 1947-. Mbrships: Am. Hist. Assn.; Medieval Acad. of Am.; Sigma Delta Pi; Pi Delta Phi; Alpha Psi Omega; Omicron Delta Kappa; Phi Kappa Phi; & many others. Publs: The Lusignans in England, 1247-58, '1951; Contbr. of articles to Speculum, The American Historical Review & others. Recip. of Miss. State Univ. Alumni Award, 1970. Address: Drawer H., Mississippi State Coll., MS 39762, U.S.A. 2, 13, 22, 128.

SNELLINGS, Eleanor Craig, b. 3 Nov. 1926. Educator. Educ: B.A., Univ. of N.C., 1947; M.A., ibid, 1950; Ph.D., Duke Univ., 1957. Appts: Instr., Univ. of Ark., Fayetteville, 1949-50; Instr., Univ. of N.C., Greensboro, 1950-56; Rsch. Assoc., Fed. Rsch. Bank of Richmond, Va., 1956-58; Assoc. economist-economist, ibid, 1959-60; Adj. fac., Va. Commonwealth Univ., Richmond, 1962-68; Assoc. Prof., econs. ibid, 1968-. Mbrships: Am. Econ. Assn.; Southern Econ. Assn.; Southern Finance Assn.; Phi Theta Kappa; Chi Delta Phi; Sigma Pi Alpha. Address: 4607 King William Rd., Richmond, VA 23225, U.S.A. 5, 14, 125.

SNODGRASS, Carl Ray, b. 13 Mar. 1937. Banker. Educ: Cert., Clinch Valley Coll., Univ. of Va., Wise, U.S.A.; 1957; Va.-Md. Schl. of

Bank Mgmt., Univ. of Va., 1963-66. Appts: Var. posts, First Nat. Bank, Wise, Va., 1957-63; Cashier, ibid, 1963-69; Asst. V.P., Wise Co. Nat. Bank (successor to First Nat. Bank), 1969-71; V.P., ibid, 1971-72; Exec. V.P., & Dir., 1972-; Mayor, Town of Wise. Mbrships: Pres., Wise Kiwanis Club; Pres., Wise Elem.-Primary PTA; Treas. & Trustee, Hoge Lodge #8, AF & AM; Past Pres., Wise-Lee-Scott Bankers Assn.; Past Pres., Clinch Valley Alumni Assn.; Chapt. & Commandery Masonic orgs.; Kazim Temple Shriner. Hons: Outstanding Young Man, Norton-Wise Jaycees, 1971; Kiwanian of the Yr. Award, Wise Kiwanis Club, 1971. Address: P.O. Box 611, Wise, VA 24293, U.S.A. 125.

SNOOK, John McClure, b. 31 May 1917. Company President. Appts. incl: Instr. of Hist., Fine Arts & Sci., Ohio State Univ., Columbus, Ohio, 1936-43; Capt.-Mgr., Ohio State Gymnastic Tram, 1938-39; 7 yrs. Col., engaged in communications betterment experimentation, mil. ROTC, 1936-38, Special Servs., 1938-42; Pres., Gulf Telephone Co. Mbrships. incl: former Pres., Kiwanis, Lions, Hunt Club; Chmn., Baldwin Co. Sesquincentennial; Mbr., Hon. Staff Gov., 1967; Hon. Lt. Col., Ala. State Trooper; Life Mbr., Nat. Rifle Assn.; Am. Ordinance Assn.; S. Baldwin Chmbr. of Comm.; Ohio State Alumni Assn.; Ala. Independent Telephone Assn.; Telephone Pioneers; active in Hist.; Pageants in Delaware Co., Ohio & Baldwing Co., Ala.; Chmn., Ceremony, Ala. State Fox Hunt Assn., 1954-56; Asst. Parade Chmn., Annual S. Baldwin Christmas Parade & Pty., 1969-73; Hon. Rep., City of Foley, carrying greetings to City of Dunedin, Fla. Highland Games, 1972-73; Pres., Friends of Lib. Assn., 1973-74; Pres., Baldwin Co. Histl. Soc., 1974-76; Asst. Civil Defense Dir., Baldwin Co., 1974 & supporter of Scout work. Hons. incl: Citizen of Yr. Award, Gulf Shores, 1956-57. Address: Gulf Telephone Co., Drawer 670, Foley, AL 36535, U.S.A.

SNOW, P.A., b. 7 Aug. 1915. Administrator. Educ: M.A., Christ's Coll., Cambridge, U.K. Appts: Magistrate, Provincial Commnr., Asst. Col. Sec., Chmn., Civil Serv. State Bd., Govt. of Fiji & Western Pacific, 1938-52; Bursar, Rugby Schl., U.K., 1952; Examiner, Pacific Subjects, Oxford & Cambridge Univs., 1955. Fellow, Royal Anthropol. Inst., G.B. & N. Ireland. Mbrships incl: Chmn., Pub. Schl. Bursars Assn., G.B. & Commonwealth, 1962-65; V.P., Fiji Soc.; Perm. Rep., Fiji, Int. Cricket Conf.; Hon., Marylebone Crecket Club, 1973. Publs. incl: Cricket in the Fiji Islands, 1948; Rock Carvings on Pacific Archipelagoes, 1950; Stories of the South Seas, 1967; Bibliography of Fiji Tonga & Rotuma, 1969; contbr. to books & jrnls. Hons. incl: For. Specialist Award for report on U.S. schls. & univs., U.S. Govt., 1964; J.P., Co. of Warwicks., 1967. Address: The Bursary, Rugby Schl., Rugby, Warwicks., U.K. 3, 30 35, 41, 128, 129, 139.

SNOW, Vernon Fred, b. 25 Nov. 1924. Professor: Foundation Officer. Educ: B.A., Wheaton Coll., Ill., 1948; M.A., Univ. of Chgo., 1949; Ph.D., Univ. of Wis., 1953. Appts: Inst., Univ. of Ore., 1953-56, Asst. Prof., 1957-60; Vis. Lectr., Univ. of Wis., 1959-57; Asst. Prof., Univ. of Mont., 1960-61; Assoc. Prof., ibid, 1962-66; Prof., Engl. Hist., Univ. of Neb., 1966-; V.P., Snow Fndn., 1967-. Mbrships: Royal Histl. Soc.; AAUP; Am. Histl. Assn.; V.P., Conf. of British Studies, 1972-74; Legal Histl Soc.; Lincoln Univ. Club. Publs. incl: The Noble Rebel: the Life & Times of Robert Devereux, third Earl of Essex, 1970; Contbr. to num. profl. junls. Hons. incl: Fellow, Royal Histl. Soc., 1969; recip., num. rsch. & travel

awards. Address: Dept. of Hist., Univ. of Neb., Lincoln, NB 68508, U.S.A.

SNYDER, Bill Burlin, b. 8 July 1931. Elementary School Principal. Educ: A. B., M.A., Ldrship. Cert. in Schl. Admin. Appts: Tchr., one room schls., Pulaski Co., Ky., 2 yrs.; Jr. H.S., 1 yr.; Jr. H.S. (emotionally disturbed), Middletown, Ohio, 4 yrs.; Guidance Dir. & Counselor, H.S., Quincy, Mich., 1 yr.; Prin., Frazee Elem. Schl., Connersville, Ind., 1966-72; Prin., Harding Elem. & Jr. H.S., Steubenville, Ohio, 1972-73; Prin., Madison Elem. Schl., Licking Valley Pub. Schls., Newark, Ohio, 1973-. Mbrships: Nat. Assn. Elem. Schl. Prins.; OEA & Ohio Assn. Elem. Schl. Prins.; NEA; Nominating Bd., Dist. 10 Ind. Elem. Prins. Assn. Author of the Dictionary as a Textbook in the Elementary School (article). Address: Route 2, Nashport, OH 43830, U.S.A. 57, 120, 130, 131.

SNYDER, Ellsworth J., b. 13 May 1931. Pianist; Educator. Educ: studies w. Ralph Zerkle, Springfield Ohio, Robert Goldsand, N.Y.C., Rudolf Firkusny, Aspen, Colo., & Alice Ehlers, Univ. cf Southern Calif.; B.M., M.M., pupil of Jeno Takacs, Conservatory of Music, Cinn., Ohio; Ph.D., Univ. of Wis., Madison. Appts: Tchr., E. Tenn. State Coll., Newcomb Coll. (Tulane Univ.) & Beloit Coll.; currently Tchr., Milton Coll., Ws. Recordings: 20th century piano music, Advance Records; Polish Radio, Warsaw; Nat. Radio, Iceland; appeared on TV & recorded for Radio Free Europe w. Jeno Takacs. Live Performances: Recitals, Brussels, Amserdam, London, Madrid, Florence & Ctrl. Am.; Soloist w. symph. orch., Ohio, Tenn., La., Iowa & Wis. Mbrships: Charter, Int. Webern Soc.; Phi Kappa Lambda. Hons: Wanda & Chalmers Clifton Prize, 1954. Address: 247 Langdon St., Apt. 6, Madison, WI 53703, U.S.A.

SNYDER, Gladys Reid (Mrs. Hugh A. Snyder), b. 12 Apr. 1918. Pension Consultant. Educ: Utah State Univ.; Life Off. Mgmt. Assn. courses. Appts: Sec. & Off. Mgr., Walter C. Green & Assocs., Cons. Actuaries, Salt Lake City, 1960-65; Prin., Chmn. & Pres., Income Investment Plans, Securities broker-dealer, ibid, 1968-72; Pension Cons., Income Trust Plan Assocs., 1965-; Registered Prin., Lincoln Equities Corp., Lincoln, Neb., 1973-. Mbrships: Registered Prin., Nat. Assn. Securities Dealers; Sec.-Treas., Utah Home Off. Underwriters Assn., 1962-64; Utah Life Underwriters Assn.; Pres., Salt Lake Lady Lions, 1973-74; Kappa Kappa Gamma Mothers' Club; Salt Lake Coun. Women; Daughters of Utah Pioneers. Address: 2790 E. 3000 S., Salt Lake City, UT 84109, U.S.A. 5,138.

SNYDER, Jane Peters, b. 23 July 1925. Public Relations Officer. Educ: Geo. Wash. Univ.; Columbia Univ. Appts: Newspaper reporter, 1952-60; P.R. Asst., E, Orange Gen. Hosp., N.J., 1962-63; P.R., Asst., United Hosps. of Newark, N.J., 1963-64; Dir. Community Rels., Georgetown Univ. Hosp., Wash. D.C., 1966-68; Dir. P.R., Metrop. Wash. Regional Med. Prog. & Med. Counc. of Nat. Capital Area, 1968-70; Dir. P..., Wash. Hosp. Ctr., 1970-. Mbrships: Dir., Am. Soc. Hosp. P.R.; Treas., Acad. Hosp P.R. Recip., MacEachern Awards for excellence in hosp. P.R. Address: 5235 Elliot Rd., Wash., DC 20016, U.S.A. 5, 24.

SNYDER, John Joseph, b. 30 June 1908. Optometrist. Educ: A.B., UCLA, 1931; Special Student, ibid, 1931-32; Postgrad., Univ. of Colo., summers 1936, 1938, 1940 & 1941; Postgrad., Univ. of Southern Calif., 1945-46, 1947; B.S., L.A. Coll. of Optometry, 1948;

O.D., ibid, 1949. Appts: Tchr., Grade Schls., La Plata Co., Colo., 1927-28; Supt., Pub. Schls., Marvel, Colo., 1933-34; Tchr., Biol., Physics, Chem., Durango H.S., Colo., 1934-41; Practising Optometrist, L.A., 1952-72, Torranee, Calif., 1972-. Mbrships: Past Pres., Past Sec., The Exchange Club of S. L.A.; Past mbr., Bd. of Dirs., Francia Boys Club, L.A.; Intercontintal Biographical Assn., 1972-73. Address: 735 Luring Dr., Glendale, CA 91206, U.S.A. 9, 51, 129, 130, 131.

SNYDER, Joseph H. b. 24 Sept. 1920. Communicator. Educ: Cornell Univ., 1941-42; Triple Cities Coll., 1945-47. Appts: Fndr., Youth Enterprise Awards, Yeal, 1971, Young Enterpreneurs of Am., 1972; Chmn., Joe Snyder & Co. Ltd.; Fndr. & Pres., Color Corp. of Am.; Co-fndr., Fine Arts in Photography; Serv. to Capt., HQ ATSC, USAF, Wright Field, Dayton, Ohio, WW II. Mbrships. incl: P.R. Soc. of Am., 1973; Counselors Sect., ibid; Nat. Investor Rels. Inst. Patentee, color reproduction. Address: 155 W. 68th St., N.Y., NY 10023, U.S.A. 2.

SNYDER, Melvin Harold, b. 1 Jan. 1912. Clergyman; Church Administrator. Educ: Frankfort Pilgrim Coll., 1927-31; D.D., Eastern Pilgrim Coll., 1960. Appts. incl: Dist. Supt., Southern Ind. Dist., Ind. Pilgrim Holiness Ch., Terre Haute & Bedford, 1948-58; Asst. Gen. Supt., Pilgrim Holiness Ch., Indpls., 1954-58; Gen. Supt., 1958-68; Gen. Supt., Wesleyan Ch., Marion, 1968-; Chmn., Polity Comm., Wesleyan Meth. & Pilgrim Holiness Chs., 1962-68; Co-Chmn., Wesleyan & Free Meth. Chs. Comm. on Merger, 1970-; Chmn., Wesleyan World Fellowship, 1972-; Pres., Trustees, Frankfort Pilgrim Coll., 1947-58; Wesleyan Ch. Corp., 1969-72; Houghton N.Y. Coll., 1970-72; Pres., Pilgrim Holiness Ch. Corp., 1966-68. Mbrships: Comm. of Chaps., Nat. Assn. of Evangelicals, 1964-68; Bd. Admin., 1966-; Treas., Bd. of Admin., Christian Holiness Assn., 1964-69. Composer of hymns. Contbr. to periodicals Recip., Alumni Award, Franford Pilgrim Coll., 1951. Address: 5604 S. Scott Rd., Marion, IN 46952, U.S.A. 2, 8.

SNYDER, Robert Martin, b. 6 Sept. 1912. Agriculturist; Government Administrator; Consultant. Educ: W.Va. Univ., B.S., Princeton Univ., Harvard Univ., USN, 1944. Appts. incl: Chief Agriculturist, Agric. Advsr. to Govt. of Pakistan, U.S. Mission, Karachi, 1952-55; Dir., USOM & Counselor, Embassy for Int. Coop., Kabul, Afganistan, 1955-59; Dir., U.S. AID to E. Africa, Nairobi, Kenya, 1959-61; Food & Agric. Off., Ivory Coast, Upper Volta, Niger, Dahomey, Abidjan, 1961-63; AID Affairs Off., Zomba, Malawi, 1964-68; Evaluations Off., Rsch. & Instnl. Grants Staff, War on Hunger, AID, 1968-69; Food & Agric. Off., USAID, Amman, Jordan, 1969-70; Planning Advsr., Min. Nat. Resources, Nigeria, 1970-72; Currently, Cons., U.S. & Int. orgs. Mbrships. incl: Soc. for Int. Dev.; Acad. Pol. & Soc. Sci.; For. Serv. Assn.; W.Va. Univ. Alumni; W.Va. 4-H Club Fndn.; Nat. Trust for Historic Preservation. Recip. of 35 yr. Pin for Serv. in U.S. Govt. & U.S.G. State Dept. Plaque for 35 yrs. serv. & dedication to U.S. Govt. Address: Lahmansville, WV 26731, U.S.A. 2, 6, 22, 57, 131.

SOARES MARTINEZ, Pedro Mario, b. 21 Nov. 1925. Professor of Finance & Fiscal Law. Educ: Doctorate, Econs. & Pol. Scis., Univ. of Lisbon, Portugal, 1953. Appts: Portuguese Diplomatic Serv., 1948-54; Lawyer, 1954-; Econ. Advsr., 1954-; Prof. of Finance & Fiscal Law, Univ. of Lisbon, 1953-; Mbr., High House

of Portuguese Parliament, 1960-68; Min. of Hlth. & Pub. Assistance, 1962-63. Mbrships. incl: Lisbon Acad. of Scis.; Geographical Soc.; Int. Inst. of Pub. Finance. Publs: 12 books inclng. Hierarquia de Valores e Ordem Social, 1965, Manual de Economia Politica, 2nd edit., 1973. Address: Rua de Sao Bento 26, Lisbon, Portugal. 43.

SOBERMAN, Daniel Allan, b. 19 Oct. 1929. Professor of Law; Lawyer. Educ: B.A., Dalhousie Univ., Halifax, N.S., Canada, 1950; LL.B., ibid, 1952; LL.M., Harvard Univ., Cambridge, Mass., U.S.A., 1955; Mbrship., N.S. Bar, 1952; Mbrship., Ont. Bar, 1955. Appts: Instr., Fac. of Law, Dalhousie Univ., 1955-56; Asst. Prof., ibid, 1956-57; Asst. Prof.—Assoc. Prof. of Law, Queen's Univ., Kingston, Ont., 1957-65; Prof. of Law, ibid, 1965-; Assoc. Dean, 1967-68; Dean, 1968-. Mbrships: Pres., Soc. Sci. Rsch. Coun. of Canada, 1971-73; Past Sec.-Treas., V.P., & Pres., Assn. of Canadian Law Tchrs.; Canadian Bar Assn.; Nat. Exec., World Univ. Serv. of Canada, 1961-63. Publs: The Law & Business Administration in Canada (w. J.E. Smyth), 1968; Chapt. in Studies in Canadian Company Law, 1967; Articles in jrnls.; Tchng. material for students. Hons: Sr. Postgrad. Rsch. Fellowship, Edinburgh Univ., 1963-64; Leave Fellowship, Canada Coun., 1973-74. Address: Fac. of Law, Queen's University, Kingston, Ont., Canada. 88.

SOBOCINSKI, Boleslaw, b. 22 June 1906. Educator; Logician. Educ: Ph.M., Warsaw Univ., Poland, 1930, Ph.D., ibid, 1937. Appts: Ed., Polish Quarterly Philosophical Review, 1932-39; Sr. Asst., Philos. of Maths., Privat Dozent, Logic, Warsaw Univ., Poland, 1934-46; Extraordinary Prof., Logic, Łódź Univ., ibid, 1946; Mbr. Polis Sci. Inst., Brussels, Belgium, 1946-49; Sci. Rschr. on Logical Designs, Computer Ind., St. Paul, Minn., U.S.A., 1949-56; Fac., Univ. Notre Dame, Ind., 1956-; Prof., ibid, 1960-; Prof. Polish Univ. Abroad, London, U.K., 1962; Fndng. Ed., Jrnl. Formal Logic, 1960-. Mbrships' Fellow, Polish Soc. Arts & Scis. Abroad, London, U.K.; Assn. Symbolic·Logic; Polish Inst. Arts & Scis., Am.; Am. Philos. Assn.; Am. Cath. Philos. Assn. Author about 100 papers in Polish & for. profl. jrnls. Address: 2405 Club Dr., S. Bend, IN 46615, U.S.A. 2.

SOBOYEJO, Olujimi Akanbi, b. 23 Aug. 1921. Physician. Educ: M.B., Ch.B., Med. Schl., Birmingham Univ., U.K., 1950; T.D.D., Univ. of Wales, Cardiff, 1955; D.P.H., R.C.P.S., F.M.C.P.H., Royal Inst. of Pub. Hlth. & Hygiene, London, 1970. Appts: House Surg., Birmingham Gen. Hosp., 1951; House Phsyn.-Snr. House Off., Walsall Gen. Hosp., 1951-52; Med. Off.-Special Grade Med. Off., Lagos Gen. Hosp., Nigeria, 1952-62; Specialist-Snr. Specialist, Fed. T.B. Serv., Lagos, 1961-68; Permanent Sec., Min. of Hlth., Lagos State, 1968-; Assoc. Lectr., Med., Lagos Univ. Mbrships: British Tuberculosis Assn., Nigeria Med. Coun. (Treas.); Dpty. Int. Commnr., Boy Scouts; Exec. Comm., YMCA, Island Club; Yoruba Tennis Club; Ikoyi Club. Contbr. article & paper on T.B., med. jrnl. & conf. Address: 4 Second Ave., Ikoyi, Lagos,' Nigeria, West Africa. 135.

SOCHACKI, Alexander Walter Stephen, b. 14 Apr. 1929. Dentist. Educ: B.S., Muhlenberg Coll., 1952; D.D.S., Temple Dental Schl., 1957. Appts: Chemist, Lucas Paint Co., Gibbsboro, N.J., 1952-53; Lt.Cmdr., Dental Corps, U.S.N., 1957-59; Pvte. Prac., Medford Lakes, N.J., 1959-71; Pvte. Prac. w. Ptnr. Stanley J. Zaleski, Cherry Hill, N.J., 1971-. Mbrships. incl: Assn.

Mil. Surgs.; Am. Dental Assn.; Southern Dental Soc.; N.J. Dental Soc.; Dir., Reward Bldg. & Loan Assn., Candu, N.J., 1958-60; Alpha Tau Omega; Xi Psi Phi; 32° Shriner. Address: Christopher Mill Rd., Medford, NJ 08055, U.S.A. 6.

SOCHAVA, Victor B., b. 20 June 1905. Scientist; Geographer; Geobotanist. Educ: Grad., Leningrad Agric. Inst., U.S.S.R.; Rsch. Asst., Botanical Mus., U.S.S.R. Acad. Sci., 1926-29; Dr., Biol. Scis. Appts: Acad. Sci. Instns., 1926-; Komarov Botanical Inst., Leningrad, 30 yrs.; Hd., Lab. of Geography & Cartography of vegetation, 1950-65; Lectr.-Prof., Leningrad Univ., 1938-50; Dir., Inst. Geography of Siberia & Far East (Irkutsk), 1959-; Chmn., Siberian Sect. & Mbr., Presidium, ibid, U.S.S.R. Acad. Sci. Mbrships. incl: Chmn., Bur. Siberian Orgs., U.S.S.R. Geographical Soc.; Chmn., Commn. on Thematical Maps, Int. Cartographic Assn., 1968-72; Acting mbr., Commn. Applied Geography, Int. Geographical Union, 1964-72. Author about 400 publs. inclng: The new geographical service in Siberia, 1972; Classification of vegetation as a hierarchy of dynamic systems, 1972. Hons. incl: Komarov Award, works on cartography of vegetation, U.S.S.R. Acad. Sci., 1950; Pierre Ferma Medal, Toulouse, France, 1960. Address: Inst. Geography of Siberia & Far East, Kievskaja I, Irkutsk 664003, U.S.S.R.

SODEN, James Arthur, b. 20 Oct. 1922. Lawyer; Company Director. Educ: McGill Univ., Montreal, Canada. Appts. incl: Mbr., Wainwright Elder Laidley Leslie Chipman & Bourgeois; Mbr., Phillips Bloomfield Vineberg & Goodman; Dir. & Pres., Tristar Devs. Inc. (U.S.A.); Trisud Corp. Inc.; Triton Shopping Ctrs. Ltd.; Trizec Corp.; Webb & Knapp (Canada) Ltd., Dir. & Chmn. Bd., Ctrl. Park Lodges of Canada Ltd.; Canadian Inst. of Pub. Real Estate Cos.; Granite Holdings of Canada Ltd.; Place Bonaventure Inc.; Scarborough Shopping Ctr. Ltd. Mbrships. incl: Dir., Canadian Inst. Pub. Real Estate Cos.; Hon. Life, York Finch Gen. Hosp.; Dir., St. Marys Hosp. Address: Trizec Corp. Ltd., 8th Floor, 5 Place Ville Marie, Montreal, P.Q., H3B 2G6 Canada.

SÖDERBERG, Sten V., b. 26 Aug. 1908. Author; Journalist. Educ: Studied in Stockholm, Sweden, & London, U.K. Appts: Dagens Nyketer, 1928-33; Goteborgs Handelstidning, 1933-36; Nya Dagligt Allekaura, 1936-44; Sci. ed., Mag. Industria, 1946-71; Ed., Katolsk Kyrkotidning, 1958-62. Mbrships: Bd., Swedish Union of Authors, 1965-; PEN Club; Bd., Mus. of Sci. & Technol.; Bd., Swedish Authors Fndn., 1966-70; Co-fndr., Sci. Youth of Sweden, 1962. Publs. incl: 2 books of poetry, 1934, 1939; 6 novels, 1938-51; 3 books of essays, 1958, 1959, 1960; 4 books of popular sci.; 4 works of biography; 5 works on Swedish inds. inclng. History of Technology, 1974, in Finnish & other langs.; 3 books for the young; 400 translations & 700 TV & radio progs. Hons. incl: Prize, Authors Fndn., 1969; Pub. schlrship., 1970-75. Address: Atterbomsvagen 32, 112 58 Stockholm, Sweden. 134

SOLBRAA-BAY, Juliane Marie (Andvord), b. 30 Dec. 1901. Editor (retd.); Free-lance Journalist; Author. Educ: Coll., 1920; Studied Nutrition, U.S.A. & Oslo, Norway; Many courses. Appts: Women's Page, Nordisk Tidende, N.Y., 1928-32; Free-lance Jrnlst. & regular page in Urd, women's mag., 1932-40; Lectr. on nutrition, Ed., Husmorbladet, jrnl. of Norwegian Housewives Union, 1948-66; Weekly page, Alle Kvinner, women's mag. & free-lance

jrnlst., especially in Drammens Tidende, 1969-. Mbrships: Var. offs., Norwegian Housewives Union; Food Comm., 1954-; State Coun. of Nutrition, 1962-70; State Coun. of Children's Books, 1954-62; Hon. mbr., Assn. of Authors of Juvenile Lit., 1963. Publs. incl: 3 children's books; 14 books on nutrition, inclng. Be Slender & Healthy, 5 edits. 1933-69 (translated into Swedish & Finnish); 50 Years History of the Nordic Housewives Union, 1970. Recip., H.M. King Olav's Gold Medal of Merit, 1965. Address: Tord Pedersensgt. 34, 3000 Drammen, Norway. 134.

SOLLAZZI, Lucio, b. 30 Apr. 1925. Artist. Educ: Brera Acad. Works incl. Relitti sulla laguna. Hons. incl: Amadeo Modigliani prize, Florence; Badrutt's prize, St. Moritz, Switzerland; Contea prize, Bormio; Il Vicolo Int. prize, Alessandria. Address: Casella Postale 8, 27100, Pavia, Italy. 19.

SOLLERS-RIEDEL, Helen (Mrs.), b. 29 Sept. 1911. Medical Entomologist. Educ: B.S., James Ormond Wilson Tchrs. Coll. Appts: U.S. Dept. of Agric., Bur. of Entomol. & Plant Quarantine, 1937-; Jr. Entomol., 1943-47; Asst. Entomol., 1947-53; Entomol., Plant Pest Control Div., 1953-71; Rsch. on mosquitoes, Nat. Inst. of Hlth. Grant, 1971-. Mbrships. incl: Past Pres., Entomol. Soc. of Wash.; Hon. Mbr., Indian Soc. for Malaria & Other Communicable Diseases; Past Dir., Exec. Comm., Trop. Med. Assn. of Wash.; Fellow, Royal Soc. of Tropical Med. & Hygiene, London; Entomol. Socs. of Am., Ga., Canada, Australia, Egypt; Am. Mosquito Control Assn. Publs: Contbr. to profl. jrnls. Hons: Meritorious Serv. Award, Am. Mosquito Control Assn., 1974. Address: P.O. Box 19009, Washington, DC 20036, U.S.A. 5, 6, 7, 14.

SOLOH, (Dato) Wan Ibrahim Bin Wan, b. 24 Sept. 1905. Justice of the Peace; Civil Servant. Educ: Malay Coll., Kuala Kangsar, Malaysia. Appts. incl: Registrar, Coop. Socs., Kedah; Sr. Asst. State Sec., ibid; Chmn., Town Coun., Alor Star; ret., 1960-; Past Mbr., Pub. Serv. Commn., State of Kedah; Mbr., State Pardons Bd.; Mng. Dir., Sharikat Perusahaan Utara Malaya Bhd.; Justice of the Peace, 1968-. Mbrships. incl: State Relig. Coun.; Standing Comm., State Awards & Decoration; Chmn., Bd. of Mgmt., Kedah State Mus.; Pres., Kedah Hist. Soc.; Bd. of Dirs., Tchrs. Provident Fund Bd., Malaysia. Contbr. to Kedah Hist. Mag. Hons: made Dato Seri Amar di-Raja by His Royal Highness the Sultan of Kedah; Hon. Order, Crown of Kedah, ibid. Address: 62A Jalan Telok Wan. Jah., Alor Star, Malaysia.

SOLOMON, Donald William, b. 6 Feb. 1941. Research Mathematician; Educator. Educ: B.S., A.B., Wayne State Univ., Detroit, Mich., 1961; M.S., M.A., ibid, 1963; Ph.D., 1966. Appts: Sec. Schl. Tchr., Detroit Pub. Schls., 1961-63; Instr., Wayne State Univ., 1966; Asst. Prof., Univ. of Wis., Milwaukee, 1966-70; Assoc. Prof., ibid, 1970-. Prin. Investigator, Grants, Nat. Sci. Fndn., 1967-69, '70-71 & Wis. Grad. Rsch. Grants, 1967, '69. Mbrships: Am. Math. Soc.; Nat. Rifle Assn.; London Math. Soc.; Soc. for Indl. & Applied Maths.; Am. Assn. for Advmt. of Sci.; Math. Assn. of Am.; Am. Contract Bridge League. Publs: Functions of a Real Variable (text); articles in math. jrnls. Recip. of Wis. Grad. Schl. Rsch. Grant, 1973. Address: Dept. of Maths., Univ. of Wis.-Milwaukee, Milwaukee, WI 53201, U.S.A. 8, 14, 28, 141.

SOLOMON, Goody L. (Mrs. Theodore A. Braun), b. 1 June 1929. Journalist. Educ: B.A., Brooklyn Coll., 1950; N.Y. Univ., 1955. Appts.

incl: Edit. Cons., Pres's. Consumer Advsry. Coun.; Exec. Ed., Off. for Consumer Servs., U.S. Dept. of Hlth. Educ. & Welfare, 1972; Consumer Educ. Dir., N.Y. State Consumer Protection Bd., 1973. Mbrships. incl: Am. Newspaper Womens Club; Nat. Fed. of Bus. & Profl. Women; Nat. Fed. Press Women; Va. Citizens Consumer Coun.; Consumers Union, Am. Coun. of Consumer Interests. Publs: The Radical Consumers Handbook, 1972; var. booklets, articles & reports on consumer matters. Address: 1712 Taylor St., N.W., Washington, DC 20011, U.S.A. 5.

SOLOMON, Ruth Freeman (Mrs. Joseph C. Solomon), b. 21 Apr. 1908. Novelist. Educ: Syracuse Univ., U.S.A., 1929. Mbrships: Delta Sigma Rho; Phi Kappa Phi; Phi Beta Kappa; Commonwealth Club; Am. Women Int. Understanding; Civilian Advsry. Bd., 6th Army. Publs: The Candlesticks and The Cross; The Eagle and The Dove; The Ultimate Triumph. Address: 34 25th Ave., San Fran., CA 94121, U.S.A.

SOLOMON, Samuel, b. 20 Sept. 1904. Indian Civil Service Officer, Retd. Educ: M.A. (Cantab), King's Coll., Cambridge. Appts: Asst. Magistrate, Indian Civil Serv., then Subdivisional Off., Dist. Judge, Sessions Judge, Dist. Off., Dir. of Dev., Additional Sec. to Govt.; retirement from Indian Civil Serv., 1947; subsequently lit. & pol. activities in U.K.; Liberal Party Parliamentary Candidate for Hornsey, Gen. Elections, 1959, 1964. Life Mbr., Nat. Liberal Club, London. Publs. inclng. translations of plays: Poems from East & West, 1927; The Saint & Satan, 1930; The Dying Rajput & other Poems, 1937; Winning the Peace, 1943; The Arch of Titus, & other Poems, 1945; The Complete Plays of Jean Racine, 1967; Franz Grillpaizer—Plays on Classic Themes, 1968; Pierre Corneille—7 Plays, 1969. Address: c/o National & Grindlay's Bank, 13 St. James's Sq., London, S.W. 1, U.K. 3.

SOLOMON, Vita Petrosky (Mrs. Charles M. Solomon) b. 16 Dec. 1916. Artist; Educator. Educ: Dip., Moore Inst Art., 1937; B.F.A., Tyler Schl. Fine Arts, Temple Univ., 1958; B.S.Ed., ibid, 1958; M.F.A., 1960. Tchr., Art & Art Hist., Cheltenham H.S., Pa., Solo Exhibs. incl: four, Phila. Art Alliance, 1953-58; three, Red Door Gall., 1959-61; Newman Gall., 1964. Grp. shows incl: Nat. Acad. Design, N.Y.; Detroit Inst. Art; Phila. Mus. Art; Allied Artists Am., N.Y.; Metropolitan Mus., N.Y.; Royal Inst., Royal Acad. Arts, United Soc. Artists & Fed. Brit. Artists, London, U.K. Represented in permanent collects. Nat. Portrait Gall., Smithsonian Instn., Wash. D.C. Mbrships. incl: Am. Water Color Soc. NEA; Allied Artists Am. Recip. num. art awards inclng. Audubon Artists, Nat. Acad. of Design, N.Y., 1960; Silver Medal Paris Salon, 1966. Address: 112 Glenview Ave., Wyncote, PA 19095, U.S.A. 5, 6.

SOLTANOFF, Walter, b. 21 Dec. 1914. Endodontist; Dental Educator. Educ: B.S., Univ. of Md., 1936; D.D.S., Univ. of Pa., 1940. Appts. incl: Staff Mbr., Mountainside Hosp., Montclair, N.J., 1946-; Dir., Dental Dept., ibid, 1973; Lectr., Grad. Endodontics, Einstein Med. Ctr., 1960-62; Instr., N.J. Coll. of Med. & Dentistry, 1960-62; Asst. Prof., ibid, 1962-67; Assoc. Prof., 1967-. Fellowships: Am. Coll. Dentists; Am. Assn. Endodontists. Mbrships. incl: Dipl., Am. Bd. Endodontists; Am. Dental Assn.; Am. Acad. Oral Med.; Fed. Dentaire Int.; Acad. of Med. of N.J.; Fac. Appt., Omicron Kappa Upsilon; Newark Dental Club. Contbr. to dental publs. Address: 20 Trinity Place, Montclair, NJ 07042, U.S.A. 6, 28.

SOLTES, Avraham. Clergyman-Executive. Educ: B.S.S., CCNY, U.S.A., 1937; M.A., Columbia Univ., N.Y.C., 1938; Rabbi, & M.Hebrew Litt., Jewish Inst. of Relig., N.Y., 1942; D.Hebrew Litt., Hebrew Union Coll., 1967. Appts. incl: Chap. to Jewish Students, Cornell Univ., Ithaca, N.Y., 1943-45; Dir., Hillel Fndn., McGill Univ., Montreal, P.Q., Canada, 1945-46; Assoc. Rabbi, Temple Sharey Tefile, E. Orange, N.J., U.S.A., 1949-64; Rabbi, Temple Emanuel of Gt. Neck, 1964-69; V.P., Community Affairs, Glen Alden Corp., 1969-74. Mbrships: Chmn., Nat. Jewish Music Coun., 1964-70; Chancellor, Am. Coll. in Jerusalem, 1971-72; Chmn., Int. Jewish Music Lib., Lincoln Ctr., N.Y.C., 1970-. Publs: Invocation; Haggadah for Young Children; Jewish Holidays; Off the Willows; Jewish Idnetity. Hons. incl: Robert E. Sherwood Award, 1956; Titular Cruz Eloy Alfaro, 1962; Kavod Award of Cantors Assembly, 1971. Address: 711 Fifth Ave., N.Y., NY 10022, U.S.A. 55.

SOLVEY, Joseph, b. 16 Apr. 1910. Aeronautical Engineer. Educ: Dip. Phys., Lithuanian Univ., Kaunas, Lithuania, 1930; M.M.E., Univ. of Melbourne, Australia, 1947. Appts: Techn., Lithuanian Air Force, 1933-37; Insp., Trade Schl., 1937-38; Design Engr., Commonwealth Aircraft Corp., Melbourne, 1940-47; Prin. Rsch. Sci., Aeronautical Rsch. Labs., Melbourne, 1947-. Mbrships. incl: Fellow, Royal Aeronautical Soc., London, U.K., Chmn., Melbourne Br., 1967; Assoc. Fellow, AIAA.; Past Pres., Zionist Fedn. of Australia & N.Z.; Exec. Coun. of Australian Jewry; Past Pres., State Zionist Coun. of Vic.; Past Pres., Victorian Zionist Org.; Victorian Jewish Bd. of Dptys.; Sec., Fed. Keren Hayesod, Australia; Exec. Bialik Coll.; Fndn. Chmn., Bialik Hebrew Schl. Publs: 50 profl. papers, some classified; Contbns. to Australian Jewish News. Address: Fl.2, 29A Hampden Rd., Armadale, Victoria, Australia 3143. 23, 55.

SOLYMOSSY, Alfred Austin, b. 29 Dec. 1913. Senior Medical Officer. Educ: Univ. of Budapest Med. Schl., Hungary, 1932-38; M.D., ibid, 1942; M.Chirurg., 1945; M.P.H., 1954. Appts: Gen. Med. Prac., 1942-; Dist. Med. Off., Budapest, 1951-54; Dir., Min. of Hlth., Hungary, 1954-56; Rotating Intern, Lebanon Hosp., Bronx, N.Y., U.S.A., 1960; Gen. Practitioner, Raleigh-Boone Clin., W. Va., 1966-69; Sr. Med. Off., U.S. Dept. of H.E.W., 1969-. Mbrships: Fellow, Royal Soc. of Hlth., U.K.; AAAS; Sci. Rsch. Soc. of Am.; Nat. Aeronautic Assn.; Nat. Geog. Soc.; Hungarian Reformed Ch. of Am. Hons: Fire Cross, WWII, 1944; Medal of Hon., for disaster servs., 1954. Address: 12916 Twinbrook Pkwy., Rockville, MD 20851, U.S.A. 6.

SOLYOM, Janos, b. 26 Oct. 1938. Concert Pianist. Educ: Studied under Profs. Gisella Béres, Arnold Székely, Kornel Zempleni, Béla Bártok Conservatory, Hungary & Prof. Lajos Hernádi, Franz Liszt Acad. of Music; Pvte. studies w. Ilona Kabos, London, U.K., Nadia Boulanger & Magda Tagliaferro, Paris, France. Appts: Debut, Sweden, 1959; num. appearances on Swedish & for. radio & TV; Regular tours in most European countries & has also appeared in U.S.A., Canada, Israel & S. Am.; Recordings made for EMI, CBS & Caprice (Swedish). Address: Wivalliusgatan 11, 112 60 Stockholm, Sweden. 4.

SOLZBACHER, William Aloysius, b. 1 Feb. 1907. Linguist; Sociologist; Government Official. Educ: Ph.D., Univ. of Cologne, Germany, 1931. Appts. incl: Asst. Prof., Hist.

& Pol. Sci., Coll. of Mt. St. Vincent, N.Y.C., U.S.A., 1950-51; Chief, Prog. Schedule Sec., Voice of Am., 1951-53; Chief, Monitoring Staff, ibid, 1954-67; Policy Application Officer, Latin Am. & Africa, 1967-; Educ. Dir., Study Tours, Affiliated Schls. & Seminars fir Int. Study & Trng., 1953-54. Mbrships. incl: Pres., Esperanto Assn. of N. Am., 1948-53; Chmn., Int. Commn. on Esperanto & Sociol., 1949-; Ling. Soc. Am.; MLA; Am. Assn. for Adv. of Slavic Studies; Polynesian Soc.; Am. Sociol. Assn.; Int. Sociol. Assn.; Am. Hist. Soc. Publs: Walther Rathenau als Socialphilosoph, 1933; Pie XI Contre Les Idoles, 1939; Co-Auth., Esperanto: The World Interlanguage, 1948, 3rd edit., 1966; Say it in Esperanto, 1957. Address: 6030 Broad St., Wash. DC 20016, U.S.A. 2, 7, 13, 14, 28, 49, 128.

SOMERALL, James Bentley, b. 19 Dec. 1917. Company President & Chief Executive. Appts: V.P. & Gen. Mgr., Coca-Cola in R.I., U.S.A., 1945-49; V.P., Pepsi-Cola in N.Y.C., 1953-55; Co-owner, Pres., & Gen. Mgr., Pepsi-Cola Franchise, Cinn., Ohio, 1955-63; Pres. & Chief Exec. Off., 18 Pepsi-Cola Metropol. bottling cos., 1963-65; Pres., Chmn., & Chief Exec. Off., Pepsi-Cola Co., 1965-71; Chmn. & Chief Exec. Off., Am. Pepsi-Cola Bottlers, Inc., 1971-73; Dir. & Exec. Comm. Chmn., Iroquois Brands Ltd., 1970-; Pres. & Chief Exec. Off., Champale, Inc., 1973-. Mbrships. incl: Nat. Chmn., Univ. of Ala. Commerce Execs.' Soc.; Bd. of Visitors, Schl. of Commerce & Bus. Admin., Univ. of Ala.; Past Pres., Assn. for the Blind in Cinn. Hons: LL.D., Univ. of Ala., 1971; Num. awards in food & beverage ind. Address: 30 Sutton Place, New York, NY 10022, U.S.A. 2.

SOMERVILLE, James Hugh Miller, b. 10 Nov. 1922. Journalist. Educ: Royal Naval Coll., Dartmouth. Appts: Served in RN, 1940-47; Invalided from RN, 1949; Assoc. Ed., Yachtsman Mag., 1949-58, Ed., 1958-65; Yachting Corres., Sunday Times, 1954-; Contbr., var. publs., U.K. & U.S. Mbrships: Inst. of Jrnlsts.; Assoc., Royal Inst. of Naval Archts.; Royal Cork Yacht Club; Royal Motor Yacht Club; Royal Forth Yacht Club; Past Comm. Mbr., Royal Thames Yacht Club; Past Sec., Imperial Poona Yacht Club. Yacht & Dinghy Racing; Yacht Racing Rules Simplified. Hons: D.S.C., 1945. Address: 1b, Elm Place, London S.W. 7, U.K. 3, 127.

SOMMER, Otto, b. 6 June 1902. University Professor. Educ: Univs. of Hohenheim & Freiburg, Germany; Dipl. Agric.; Dr.Agric.sc. Appts: Special educ. in husbandry; Sci. Asst., Univ. of Inst.; Tchr., Agricl. Schl.; Dir., husbandry org.; Univ. Prof., Göttingen & Hohenheim; Dir., Nat. Inst. for Husbandry, Bavaria; Prof., Univ. of Münster. Mbrships: Deutsche Landes Gesellschaft; Deutsche Gesellschaft für Züchtungskunde; Verband der Diplomlandwirte. Author of Rinderzucht, 2 edits. Address: Hohenbachernstr. 13, 805 Freising-Vöttling Obb., German Fed. Repub.

SOMMERFELT, Aimée D., b. 2 Apr. 1892. Author. Educ: Sworn Translator of French, 1918. Mbrships: Nat. Evaluation Bd. on Films for Norway, 1941-43, 1945-62; Pres., Union of Juvenile Authors, 1957-65; Dpty. mbr., The Literary Bd., Norwegian Union of Authors; Bd. mbr., Norwegian Bd. on Books for Young People; PEN. Publs. incl: Veien til Agra, 1959 (translated into 28 langs.); Den Hvite Bungalowen, 1962; Pablo og de Andre, 1964; Den Farlige Natten, 1971 (translated into Engl. & German); Three short stories from developing countries, 1972-73; Veien til Ingensteder, 1973-74. Hons. incl: Norwegian State Prizes for

Den Hvite Bungalowen, 1962, Pablo og de Andre, 1964; Hon. Prize, N.Y. Herald Tribune for Pablo og de Andre, 1966; 1st Prize, competition arranged by Damm's Publishing House & Allers mag. for Den Farlige Natten. Address: Johan Castbergsvei 9, Oslo 6, Norway.

SOMMERS, Waldo, b. 27 May 1908. Educator. Educ: A.B., Heidelberg Coll., 1927; Grad. study, Northwestern Univ., 1927 & Columbia Univ., 1931-32; M.A., Yale Univ., 1934; Ph.D., ibid, 1948. Appts. incl: Div. Chief, Asst. Regional Dir., Assoc. Regional Dir., etc., U.S. Civil Serv., 1939-59; Asst. Prof., Sociol., Maxwell Grad. Schl. of Citizenship & Pub. Affairs, Syracuse Univ., 1946-48; Vis. Prof. & Acting Chmn., Sociol., Ohio Wesleyan Univ., 1949-50; Prof., Pub. Admin., George Wash. Univ., 1959-; Cons., Brookings Inst., 1963-64. Fellow, Am. Sociol. Assn. Mbrships. incl: Am. Soc. Pub. Admin.; AAUP; Int. Personnel Mgmt. Assn. Author of Reorganizing Federal Personnel Management, 1945-60. Books Ed., Personnel Administration, 1962-65. Address: Hall of Government, The George Washington Univ., Wash., DC 20006, U.S.A. 6, 14, 125.

SONESSA, John Anthony. Educational Administrator. Educ: Temple Univ., Phila., Pa., 1946-47; B.S., St. Joseph's Coll., 1959; M.A., Trenton State Coll., N.J., 1970; Postgrad., Univ. of Pa., 1959-60 & Columbia Univ., summer 1969. Appts: Tchr., mentally retarded & emotionally disturbed children, The Woods Schls. & Residential Treatment Ctr., Langhorne, Pa., 1963-66; Educl. supvsr., ibid, 1966-67; Prin., 1968-69; Asst. Dir., Educ. & Trng., 1969-70; Acting Dir., Educ. & Trng., 1970-71; Prog. coord., Montgomery Co. Mental Retardation Ctr., King of Prussia, Pa., 1971-72; Educl. Cons., 1972-, to Pa. State Univ., Inst. for the Study of Human Dev., Ctr. for Human Servs. Dev., Univ. Park, Pa. Mbrships. incl: Chmn., Legislative Comm., Coun. for Exceptional Children, 1969; Am. Assn. Mental Deficiency. Author of publs. in field. Address: 4423 Sherwood Rd., Phila., PA 19131, U.S.A. 6.

SONIN, Eileen, b. 26 Nov. 1917. Author; Lecturer; TV & Radio Personality. Educ: Ginner-Moore & Royal Albert Hall Schls. of Drama & Speech Trng.,U.K. 1st appts. as actress in London; TV, Canada, 1957-; Lectr. & Writer on parapsychol. & kindred subjects. Mbrships: British Soc. of Psychical Rsch. Publs: Ghosts I Have Known, 1972; Especially Ghosts, 1973; More Canadian Ghosts, 1974; The Palace That Jan Built, 1970; Assorted children's stories & books. Address: 1302 Ambleside Dr., Lorne Park, Mississauga, Ont., Canada. 57.

SONNEMANN, Nell Battle Booker (Mrs.), b. 19 Aug. 1918. Artist; Assoc. Professor. Educ: A.B., Univ. of N.C. at Chapel Hill, 1938; M.A., ibid, 1940; under George Grosz & Raphael Soyer, Art Students League, N.Y.C., 1940-42; N.Y. State Ceramics Coll., Alfred Univ., N.Y., 1954-55; M.F.A., Cath. Univ. of Am., Wash. D.C., 1959. Appts: Freelance Artist, 1942-; Instr. Assoc. Prof., Cath. Univ. of Am., 1959-; Pub. Lectr., Wash. D.C. area, 1959-; Spec. Rschr. & Guest of Staff, Schl. of Textile Design, Royal Coll. of Art, London, U.K. Mbrships. incl: Phi Beta Kappa; Alpha Kappa Gamma. Illustrations for: Jane Eyre, Charlotte Bronte, 1946; Wuthering Heights, Emily Bronte, 1947; The Scarlet Letter, Nathaniel Hawthorne, 1947; Baby Book, N.Y.C. Hlth. Dept., 1947; var. contbns. of articles & book reviews to publs. One-Man Exhibs. incl: Univ. of South, Sewanee, Tenn., 1972; Univ. of N.C. at Chapel Hill, 1970. Grp. Nat. Atlanta, Ga., 1972; Geo. Wash. Univ. Nat. Exhib. of Arts of the Needê. Wash. D.C., 1971; Nat. Interfaith Conf. on Relig. & Arch., Mpls., Minn., 1973; Athenaeum Mus., Alexandria, Va., 1973; Corning Mus., Corning, N.Y., 1973. Num. Prizes incl: 31st Naf. Conf. on Relig. Arch., 1970; N.C.State Annual Art Exhib., 1953, '59. Address: 4807 Cumberland Ave., Chevy Chase, MD 20015, U.S.A. 5, 7, 22, 83, 125, 129, 130, 132, 138.

SONNEMANN, Ulrich, b. 3 Feb. 1912. Author; University Teacher. Educ: Univs. Berlin, Freiburg, Frankfurt, Germany; Vienna, Austria & Basle, Switzerland, 1930-35; Ph.D., Basle Univ., 1935. Appts: Clin. Psych., VA, U.S.A, 1946-49; Assoc. Prof., Psych., News Schl. Soc. Rsch., NY, 1949-51; Free lance writer, 1952-69; Docent, Hochschule für Fernsehen und Film, Munich, Germany, 1969-; Vis. Prof., Bremen Univ., 1971-. Mbrships: PEN, Fed. Repub. Germany; Humanistische Union. Publs. incl: Existence and Therapy. An Introduction to Phenomenological Psychology and Existential Anlaysis, 1954; Das Land der unbegrenzten Unzumutbarkeiten, 1963; Die Einübung des Ungehorsams in Deutschland, 1964; Die Dickichte und die Zeichen. A Novel, 1964; 2nd ed., '66; Institutionalismus und studentische Opposition. Thesen zur Ausbreitung des Ungehorsams in Deutschland, 1968; Negative Anthropologie. Vorstudien zur Sabotage des Schicksals, 1969; Der Bundesdeutsche Dreyfus-Skandal. Rechtsbruch und Denkverzicht in der zehn Jahre alten Justizsache Brühne-Ferbach, 1970. Recip. Ludwig Thoma Medal, City of Munich, 1969. Address: Am Jagdweg 1, 8000 Munich 90, German Fed. Repub. 43.

SONNICHSEN, Blendena Lylien, b. 10 Aug. 1905. Professional Organist; Entertainer; Writer. Educ: Am. Conservatory of Music., Chgo., Ill.; Calif. Valley Coll., San Bernardino. Appts: Theater Organist; Ch. Organist; Entertainer, nigh clubs throughout U.S.A.; KITO Radio, NCO Clubs. Mrbships: Charter Mbr., Alpha Psi Chapt., Phi Lambda Chi; Assoc. Mbr., Casa Ninos Children's Home Soc.; City of Hope; Pres., San Bernardino Chapt. 434, 1969, 1970; Women's Club; Newcomers Club. Articles & stories, narcotics & drugs, var. mags. inclng. Grit; Hearthstone; Padre; Exchangite; Sunday Digest; Sunshine Mag.; Signs of the Times; Listen Mag.; Alert; Home & Health; Independent Press-Telegram; Narcotics Education Inc. Hon. Citizen, Father Flannigan's Boys Town, 1964. Address: 16516 Bothell Way N.E., Seattle, WA 98155, U.S.A.

SONTAG, Frederick H., b. 29 Apr. 1924. Public Affairs & Research Consultant. Educ: A.B., Colby Coll., 1946; Grad. student, Columbia Univ., 1947-48. Appts. incl: Special Cons. to the Right Rev. Albert A. Chambers, Bishiop of the Episc. Diocese of Springfield, Ill., 1947-; Dir. of PR, Bus. Week mag., NYC, 1951-55; Special Cons., US Sec. of Labour, Wash. D.C., 1954-61, Pres.'s Comm. on Govt. Employment Policy, Wash. D.C., 1955-60, Civic Serv. Inc., St. Louis, Mo. & Wash. D.C., 1957-; Monsanto Co., St. Louis, Mo., 1962-, Bd. of Soc. Concerns, United Meth. Ch., Wash. D.C., 1965-71; Co-Dir.-Dir., Study of Am. Pol. Parties, S. Orange, N.J. & Cambridge, Mass., 1969-; Analyst-Commentator, Maine Pub. Broadcasting Network, 1973-. Mbrships. incl: Am. Pol. Sci. Assn.; PR Soc. of Am.; Bd. of Dirs., Am. Assn. of Pol. Cons.; Overseas Press Club of Am.; Phi Delta Theta; Phi Gamma Mu; Ed. Advsry. Bd., Electoral Studies Yrbook., Waterville, Me. Publs: Co-author, Parties, the RealOpportunity for Effective Citizen Politics, 1972; contbr. to N.Y. Times, LA Times, Am. Ch. News, The Witness, The Living Ch. &

Scroll. Hons: Cert. of Achievement, Am. PR Assn., 1952 & 54; Silver Anvil Award, ibid, 1953. Address: 764 Scotland Rd., Suite 45, S. Orange, NJ 07079, U.S.A. 2, 6.

SOO, Charles H. Business Executive & Consultant. Educ: M.B.A., Univ. of Chgo., Ill.; other univs. Appts: Pres., Chgo. Int.; Commnr. of Ill. Econ. Dev. Commn.; Dir., Econ. Dev. Admin., Mont.; Dir., Chgo. Econ. Dev. Mbrships. incl: Advsry. Chmn., future Bus. Ldrs. Am.; Chmn., 18th Dist., Community-Police Coun.; Prog. Chmn., Chgo. Press Club; Trustee, Ctrl. Ch. Chgo.; Bd. of Dirs., num. bus. & civic orgs.; Chgo. Assn. Commerce & Ind.; Execs. Club Chgo.; Nat. Writers Club. Publs. incl. What I Think of America. Hons. incl: Chgo.'s Ten Outstanding Young Men; Man of Yr., City of Hope; Award for Outstanding Serv. to State, Ill. Econ. Dev. Commnr. Address: 162 N. State St., Chgo., IL 60601, U.S.A. 16.

SOPER, Robert L., b. 10 Aug. 1921. Manufacturing Executive. Educ: Grad., Army Cmd. & Gen. Staff Schl., 1945; B.A., Univ. of Mich., Ann Arbor, U.S.A., 1946; M.B.A., Harvard Bus. Schl., Mass., 1948. Appts: Asst. Credit Mgr., Black & Decker Mfg. Co., Towson, Md., 1948; Mgr., Data Processing, ibid., 1949; Off. Mgr., Calif. Pellet Mill Co., San. Fran., 1950-60; Treas., ibid, 1960-71; Exec. V.P., 1971-74; Pres., 1974-; Dir., El Morro Inds.; Dir., Calif. Pellet Mill Co., Dir., Calif. Pellet Mill Europe Ltd. Mbrships: Calif. & San Fran.Chmbrs. of Comm.; Financial Execs. Inst.; Soc. for Int. Dev.; World Affairs Coun.; Commonwealth Club Calif.; Bankers Club. Hons: Air Medal, 1943; Disting. Flying Cross, 1944. Address: 2264 Hyde, San Francisco, CA 94109, U.S.A. 9.

SOPOROWSKI, Joseph James, Jr., b. 4 May 1929. Educator. Educ: A.B., Rutgers Univ., 1951; M.B.A., ibid, 1956; Ed.D. candidate. Appts. incl: var. posts, finally asst. to Sec. & Treas., Chevron Oil Co., Perth Amboy, N.J., 1953-63; var. posts w. City of Perth Amboy, finally Dir., Bur. of Air Pollution Control & Dpty. Mayor, 1962-66; Full Prof., Specialist in Environmental Scis., Rutgers Univ., 1966-. Mbrships. incl: Nat. V.P., Exec. Comm., Air Pollution Control Assn.; N.J. Acad. of Sci.; Hlth. Offls. Air Pollution Coun. of N.J.; Bd. of Dirs., Middlesex Co. Mental Hlth. Assn. & Nat. Coun. on Noise Abatement; Pres., Acad. of Ind. Environmental Scis. Contbr. to profl. publs. Hons. incl: Air Pollution Control Assn. C.A.W. Blue Ribbon Award for Educ. Activity, 1967 & 68. Address: c/o Dept. of Environmental Scis., Rutgers Univ., P.O. Box 231, New Brunswick, NJ 08903, U.S.A. 6, 130.

SORENSON, Carl Woodrow Whilhelm, b. 27 July 1917. Agricultural Editor. Educ: B.S., S.D. State Univ., Brookings, 1941; Tchng. Fellow & Grad. Student, Iowa State Univ., Ames, 1941-42; Post-grad. Communications Schl., U.S. Naval Acad., Anpls., Md., 1943. Appts: Communications Off., USNR, 1942-46; Info. Dir. & Ed., S.D. Farm Bur., 1946-47; Agricl. Extension Ed.,S.D. State Univ., 1947-53; Assoc. Ed., Am. Hereford Jrnl., 1953-58; Info. Off., S.W. Region, U.S. Dept. of Agric., 1958-; Info. Advsr. in Agric. & Home Econs., Min. of Agric., Eastern Region, Nigeria, 1966-67 (on leave from Univ. of S.D.). Mbrships: Sigma Delta Chi; Am. Assn. of Agricl. Coll. Eds.; Nat. Assn. of Farm Broadcasters; Am. Lutheran Ch.; Dallas Agricl. Club. Publs: Ed., S.D. Bur. Farming, 1946-47; Ed.,S.D. Weed Manual, 1949; Co-author, The Missouri River Development Plan, 1952; Assoc. Ed., The Am. Hereford Jrnl., 1953-58; Num.

articles. Hons. incl: Superior Serv. Award, U.S. Dept. of Agric., 1971. Address: Vikingland, U.S.A., 837 Evergreen Hill Rd., Dallas, TX 75208, U.S.A. 125.

SOTA MAC MAHON, Patricio de la, b. 1 July 1930, Economist. Educ: B.A., Cornell Univ., U.S.A., 1954. Appts: Asst. Gen. Mgr., Soc. Franco-Expanola de Alambres Cables y T.A., 1957-58; Gen Mgr., ibid, 1958-71; Exec. Pres., 1971-; Exec. Pres., Forjas y Alambres del Cadugua S.A.; Chmn., Bd., Distribuidora de Alambres y Cables S.A.; Sec. of Bd., Soc. Anonima de Trefileria y Derivados. Mbrships: Real Club do Golf de Neguri; Real Club de Jolaseta; Athletic Club de Bilbao; Biarritz Olmpique. Address: Soc. Franco-Espanola de Alambres, Cables y Transportes Aereos S.A., Apartado 67, Bilbao, Spain. 43.

SOTO-RAMOS, Julio, b. 20 Apr. 1903. Writer; Poet. Appts: U.S. Customs Patrol Insp.; Prohibition Agent, Bur. of Prohibitation; Investigator, Alcohol Tax Unit; U.S. Storekeeper-guager; U.S. Army Off., Puerto Rico & Trinidad, WWII; Insp., Alcohol & Tobacco Tax Div., U.S. Internal Revenue Serv., ret.'d, 1963. Mbrships. incl: Academician, Int. Pontzen Acad. for Letters, Scis. & Arts, Naples, Italy; Ret.'d Offs. Assn., Wash., D.C.; Hon. Mbr., Delta Phi Delta, Coamo, Puerto Rico, Argentine Cultural Comm. Publs. incl: Essays: Bocetos Biograficos Puertorriquenos, 1973; Yo Soy Yo y Mi Verdad, 1973; Cumbre y Remanso, 1963; Panorama Literario y Periodistico de Puerto Rico, 1955, '63; Poems: : Trapecio, 1955; Soledades en Sol, 1952; Relicario Azul, 1933; Cortina de Suenos, 1923. Hons. incl: Municipal Admin. Plaque, Coama, 1973; Medal of Merit, Int. Assn. Lions Clubs, 1973. Address: 429 Salvador Brau, Floral Park, Hato Rey, PR 00917, U.S.A. 136.

SOTTUNG, George K. Artist. Educ: Chgo. Acad. Fine Art; DePaul Univ.; grad., Art Inst. Chgo.; Brooklyn Mus. Art. Appts: Chief Staff Artist, Chgo. Tribune (covered opening of St. Lawrence Seaway, 1958, w. series of watercolour paintings & text); NACAL Artist on assignment for U.S. Navy (painted series of paintings entitled The Phasing Out of the Seaplanes, U.S. Naval Air Stn., San Diego,Calif., 1967, The Wounded Returning from Vietnam, 1968 etc. Mbrships. incl: Am. Watercolor Soc.; Soc. of Illustrators, N.Y. Paintings incl: Fishermen, 1971; Old Car, 1972; Still Point, 1172; Woodspurge, 1973. Author, Illustrator, The Art of Portrait Painting, in The Art of Acrylic Painting, 1969. Hons. incl: J.W. Goff Mem. Award, Ringwood Manor Assn. of Arts, 1966; Berkshire Mus. Watercolor Award, Pittsfield, Mass., 1973. Address: 96 Aspen Ledges Rd., Ridgefield, CT 06877, U.S.A. 6.

SOUCY, W. Roland, b. 6 May 1925. Professional Engineer; Environmental Developer. Educ: B.Engrng., Rensselaer Polytechnic Inst., Troy, N.Y., 1945; M.Engrng., ibid, 1948; postgrad work, 1949. Appts: Structural Engr., Bell Aircraft Corp., Buffalo, N.Y., 1945; Instr., Rensselaer Polytechnic Inst., Troy, N.Y., 1945-49; Proj. Engr., State of N.Y. Exec. Dept. Off. of Gen. Servs., Albany, N.Y., 1949-. Mbrships: Nat. & N.Y. State Socs. of Profl. Engrs.; Smithsonian Assocs. (Smithsonian Instn.); Monarch & Albany Country Clubs. Engrng. designs incl. Empire State Plaza Proj. in Albany, multi-award winning 100 million gallon-per-day Riverfront Pumping Stn. & Treatment Plant, serving N.Y. State. Holder of a U.S. Patent. Address: 8 Maple Ln. N., Loudonville, NY 12211, U.S.A. 57, 129, 130, 139.

SOUHAMI, Gérard, b. 30 May 1928. Company Executive. Educ: Ecole de Commerce & Am. Schl. of Paris, France. Appts: Mng. Dir., Chmn. of Bd., J. Walter Thompson S.A.; Vice Pres., J. Walter Thompson Co., U.S.A.; Counsellor for Info. & Tourism, Monaco Govt.; Advsr., Commerce Extérieur de la France. Mbrships: Assn. France-Etats Unis, Dir.; Am. Chmbr. of Comm.; Blood Donors Assn. of Corrèze, Pres. on Hon.; Grandes Causes Nat., Dir.; Histl. Socs., Passy & Auteuil-Corrèze; Yacht Club of Monaco; Polo de Paris. Publs: Impressions sur, 1970; writer of articles for papers & magazines. Hons: Kt. of Order of Belgian Crown; Off., Order of Leopold; Silver Medal for civic servs. Address: 17 Ave. Matignon, 75008 Paris, France.

SOURIAU, Manon, b. 2 July 1924. Dancer; Educator; Administrator; Editor. Educ: Lic.ès Lettres, Sorbonne, Paris France, 1942; M.A., Columbia Tchrs. Coll., U.S.A., 1972. Appts. incl: Dancer, Merry-go-Rounders, 1952-56; Dir., ibid, 1958-61, 62-63; Dancer, Marion Scott Co., Hebraica, 1957-58; Solo Concerts, Robert Coll., Istanbul, Turkey, 1961-62; Fndr., Kew Gardens Schl. of Creative Dance, 1962-72; Prof., Dance, Lycèe Francais de N.Y., 1965; Ed., Am. Dance Guild, Newsletter, 1963-66, 70-; Bus. Mgr., Dance Scope, 1964-68; Gen. Mgr., ibid, 1970-; Exec. Dir., Am. Dance Guild, 1972-. Mbrships incl: ADG Rep., Am. Coun. of Arts in Educ., 1969; Bd. Dirs., Dance Notation Bur., 1968-69; Bd. Dirs., Comm. on Rsch. in Dance, 1971-74. Author of publs. on dance. Address: 124-16 84th Rd., Kew Gardens, NY 11415, U.S.A. 6.

SOUSA e HOLSTEIN MANOEL, Diogo (Count of Atalaya, Marquis of Tancos), b. 26 Nov. 1930. Farm and Company Administrator. Educ: Grad., Inst. Superior de Ciências Econs. & Financieras, Lisbon. Appts: Sec., Admin. of Inst. Pasteur de Lisboa; Sec., Min. of Educ., Portugal; Insp. Gen., Banco Totta, Acores; Gen. Mgr., farming estate; Admnstr., Sadomar Co. & Modern Office Co.; Pres., Gen. Meeting, Soc. Comercial Orey & Antunes, Sarl; Mbr., Investigation Comm., Bank of Portugal. Mbr., Turf Club, Lisbon. Recip. Oficial da Instrucaõ Púbica, Portugal. Address: Travessa do Abarracamento de Peniche, 9, Lisbon 2, Portugal. 43.

SOUSER, Roslyn Coskery (Mrs. Kenneth Souser) Jr.), b. 27 Mar. 1939. Plastic Surgeon. Educ: A.B., Duke Univ., 1961; Univ. of Munich, 1959-60; M.D., Woman's Med. Coll. of Pa., 1966. Appts. incl: Asst. Plastic Surg., Out-Patient Clin., Bryn Mawr Hosp., Pa.; Instr. in Surg., Thos. Jefferson Univ. Schl. of Med., Phila., Pa.; Cons. in Plastic Surg., N. Penn Hosp., Lansdale, Pa. Mbrships. incl: Montgomery Co. Med. Soc., 1973; Pa. State Med. Soc. 1973; Fellow, AMA, 1973; Am, Med. Women's Assn., 1973; Int. Med. Women's Assn., 1973; Cand. Mbr., Am. Coll. of Surgs. Contbr. articles to med. jrnls. Recip. 2nd Prize, Robert H. Ivy Residents Conf. Paper, 'Gunshot Wounds of the Hand', 1973. Address: Bryn Mawr Med. Bldg., Suite 110, Bryn Mawr, PA 19010, U.S.A. 5, 138.

SOUTHBY, Robert, b. 16 Nov. 1897. Consultant. Paediatrician. Educ: B.S., M.B., 1921, M.D., 1923, Univ. of Melbourne, Australia; Mbr., 1938, Fellow, 1948, Royal Australasian Coll. of Physns. Appts: Lectr., Paediatrics, Univ. of Melbourne; Sr. Physn., Royal Children's Hosp., 1958-; Currently Hon. Cons. Physn., ibid & cons. Paediatrician, Dept. of Hlth., Vic. Mbrships: Standing Comm. of Convocation, Univ. of Melbourne; Vic. Br.

Coun., B.M.A., 1943-73; Pres., ibid, 1950; Hon. Life, Paediatric Soc. of Vic., Aust. Paediatric Assn. & Vic. Coun. Soc. Serv.; Coun., Med. Defence Assn. of Vic., 27 yrs.; Dpty. Pres., Aust. Coun. Soc. Serv.; Advsry. Coun., Hosp. & Charities Commn.; Med. Servs. Comm., Aust. Red Cross Soc.; Pres., Medico-Clerical Soc. of Vic., 1955-73; Med. Bd. of Vic. Monographs: Pink Disease, 1950; Achlorhydria in Children, 1950. Contbr. to: Med. Jrnl. of Aust., 1922-62. Hons: O. St. J., 1967; Fellow, Aust. Med. Assn., 1966 & Aust. Coll. Speech Therapists, 1950. Address: Flat 31 Hotham Gdns., 61a Haines St., N. Melbourne, Vic., Australia 3051. 23.

SOUTHGATE, Donald George, b. 31 Oct. 1924. University Teacher; Historian. Educ: Univ. Coll., Exeter, U.K. 1941-44; B.A., London, 1944; Inst. of Hist. Rsch., 1944-45; Christ Ch., Oxford, 1945-47; D.Phil., Oxford Univ., 1949. Appts: Asst. Lectr., 1947, Lectr., 1950, Univ. Coll., Exeter; Sr. Lectr., Rhodes Univ., Grahamstown, S. Africa, 1951-53; Lectr., 1956, Sr. Lectr., Univ. of St. Andrews, Scotland (Queen's Coll., Dundee), U.K., 1965; Sr. Lectr., Rdr., 1968, Ct. Mbr., 1972, Univ. of Dundee. Fellow, Royal Hist. Soc. Pubs: The Passing of the Whigs 1932-86, 1962; 'The Most English Minister' . . . Palmerston, 1966. Ed., The Conservative Leadership 1832-1932, 1974; Contbr. to profl. publs. Recip. of var. schlrships. Address: 40 Camphill Rd. Broughty Ferry, Dundee, U.K. 3.

SOWA, Rose, b. 22 Sept. 1914. Educator. Educ: B.S., State Coll., Slippery Rock, Pa., 1937; Ed.M., Univ. of Pitts., Pitts., Pa., 1942. Appts. incl: Tchr., Pub. Schls., Arnold, Pa., 1937-43; Engr. Asst., Wright Aeronautical Corp., Cinn., Ohio. 1944-45; Instr., Women's Hlth. & Phys. Educ., State Coll., Dickinson, N. Dakota, 1946-47; Instr., Phys. Educ., Univ. of Oregon, Eugene, Ore., 1946-47; Secondary Tchr., Miami Pub. Schls., Miami, Fla., 1947-50; & Dir., Miami Edison Cadet Corp., 1 yr. & Activities Dir., Vocational Schl., 1 yr.; Secondary Tchr., Phys. Educ. & Gen. Sci., Deptendent Schls., Tokyo, Japan, 1950-54 & planned & directed Int. Play Day w. 6 Am. & Japanese Schls.; Secondary Tchr., Phys. Educ., Biol. & Gen. Sci., Am. Dependent Schls., Stuttgart & Wiesbaden, Germany, 1954-59; Secondary Tchr., Phys. Educ. & Biol., & organized Int. Play Day w. 9 Am. & Filipino Schls., Am. Dependent Schls., 1959-66; Educ. Off., U.S. Army, Korea, 1965-66; Dir., Gen. Educ. Dev. Prog., Madigan Gen. Hosp. (Army), Tacoma, Wash., 1966-71; Staff Advsr., Transition Prog., H.Q. U.S. Army, Okinawa, 1971-. Mbrships: Am. Personnel & Guidance Assn.; Nat. Vocational Guidance Assn.; Nat. Employment Counselors Assn.; Am. Fedn. of Govt. Employees; Fed. Employed Women. Hons. incl: Cert. of Achievement as Educ. Off., Sept. 1968, Outstanding Performance Rating w. Sustained Superior Award as Educ. Off., June 1968 & Outstanding Performance Rating as Educ. Off., Nov. 1970, Madigan Gen. Hosp. (Army), Tacoma, Wash. Address: Educ. Br., P.O. Box 546, Hq. USARBCO, APO San Francisco 96331, U.S.A. 5, 132.

SOWDEN, Lewis, b. 24 Mar. 1905. Writer; Journalist. Educ: M.A., Univ. of the Witwatersrand, Johannesburg, S.A., 1928. Appts: joined staff of Rand Daily Mail, Johannesburg, 1927; Lit. Ed., ibid, 1935-; Dramatic Critic & Asst. Ed., 1945-66; Staff Ed., Encyclopaedia Judaica, Jerusalem, 1966-71; For. Corres., S.A. morning newspapers, 1968-.

Mbrships: V.P., S.A. PEN Ctr., 1960-63; Sigma Delta Chi, U.S.A., 1962-. Publs:(plays) The Fugitives, 1934; The Man in Checks, 1935; Red Rand, 1937; The Gold Earth, 1944; Ramses the Rich, 1957; The Kimberley Train, 1958; (politics) The South African Union, 1945; (poems) The Charmed Fabric, 1943; Poems with Flute, 1955; Poems from the Bible, 1960; The Jaffa Road, in prep.; (novels) The Man Who was Emperor, 1947; The Lady of Coventry, 1949; The King of High Street, 1950; Tomorrow's Comet, 1951; Family Cromer, 1952; The Crooked Bluegum, 1955; Kop of Gold, 1956; (biog.) Both Sides of the Mask, 1964; (memoirs) The Land of Afternoon. Address: 12 Shamai St., Jerusalem, 94631, Israel. 3, 12, 39, 139.

SOWDER, Anna L. Retired Government Official; Poet. Educ: Geo. Wash. Univ., D.C., U.S.A.; Benjamin Franklin Univ.; Grad. Schl., Dept. of Agric., Wash. D.C. Appts: Bur. of Immigration & Naturalization Serv., Dept. of Labor, U.S. Govt., Wash. D.C., 1924-40; Dept. of Justice, 1940-64; Fed. Grand Jury, Criminal Ct., D.C., 1969-71. Mbrships: Bd., Profl. Writers Club of D.C.; Past Regent, Margaret Whetten Chapt., D.C., DAR., & past holder of many other offices, Margaret Whetten Chapt.; Pt.-time Docent, DAR Mus. Publs: Poems in sev. mags. & anthols. Hons: Silver Honor Roll, Margaret Whetten Chapt., DAR; First Prize, Poetry Contest, Profl. Writers Club, 1973. Address: Trees, 4320 Klingle St. N.W., Wesley Hts., Washington, DC 20016, U.S.A. 22, 132, 138.

SOWOOLU, Sorinolu Olatunde, b. 11 Aug. 1929. Archivist. Educ: B.A., Univ. Coll., Ibadan, 1953; Postgrad. Cert. of Educ., Univ. of London, 1956; B.A., 1957. Appts: Grad. Tchr., Bapt. Acad., 1953-59; Archivist, 1959-62; Sr. Archivist, 1962-64; Prin. Archivist, 1964-67; Dir., Nat. Archives of Nigeria, 1967-. Mbrships: Sec. Nat. Archives Comm.; Comm. on Archival Dev., Int. Coun. on Archives; Int. Advsry. Comm. on Documentation, Lib. & Archives, UNESCO; Histl. Soc. of Nigeria; Bapt. Acad. Old Boys Assn. Address: Nat. Archives, P.M.B. 4, Univ. Post Off., Ibadan, Nigeria.

SOYARS, Crystine Yates (Mrs. Aubrey F. Soyars). Teacher. Educ: B.S., Geo. Peabody Coll. for Tchrs., Nashville, Tenn., 1935; M.A., ibid, 1955; A.B., Trevecca Nazarene Coll., Nashville, 1965. Appts: Elem. Schl. Tchr., Nashville City Schls., 1929-61; Alumni Off., Sec., Off. Ed. of alumni publ. & Liaison between Admin. & Alumni, Trevecca Nazarene Coll., 1965-. Mbrships. incl: Life Mbr. & Fac. Rep., NEA; Life Mbr. & Rep. Assembly, Tenn. Educ. Assn.; Life Mbr., Sec., Chap., Alpha Delta Kappa Int.; Life Mbr., Nazarene World Missionary Soc.; V.P., Sec., Publicity, Ed. of Dist, Bulletin, local, dist. & regional level, ibid; local, state & Nat. Assn. of Retired Tchrs. Contbr. poems and/or articles to Schl. Arts Mag., The Tenn. Tchr., The Other Sheep & The Upper Room. Hymn publd. in Glory Chimes, No. 2. Hons: Tchr. of the Yr., Ch. of the Nazarene, 1962; Plaque, Pres.'s Club, Trevecca Nazarene Coll., 1970; Pres.'s Silver Dollar Award, ibid, 1971, 72 & 73; Cert. of Recognition, Nashville City Tchrs. Assn., 1961, Pres. of U.S., 1941; Cert. of Recognition & Gold Serv. Pin, Am. Red Cross, 1946; Meritorious Serv. Award, US Off. of Price Admin., 1942. Address: 3600 Dartmouth Lane, Nashville, TN 37215, U.S.A. 125.

SOYINKA, Wole, b. 13 July, 1934. Author. Educ: Govt. Coll., Ibadan, Nigeria; B.A., Univ. of Leeds, U.K., 1957. Appts: Play Rdr., Royal

Ct. Theatre, London, 1958-59; Rsch. Fellow In Drama, Dept. of Engl., Univ. of Ibadan, Nigeria. 1960-61; Lectr. in Engl., Univ. of Ife, 1962-63; Sr. Lectr., Dept. of Engl., Univ. of Lagos, 1967-69; Dir., Schl. of Drama, Univ. of Ibadan, 1969-72; Prof. in Drama, Dept. of Engl., Univ. of Ife, 1972-. Mbrships: London Poetry Secretariat. Publs. incl: The Interpreters, 1965; Idanre, 1967; A Shuttle in the Crypt, 1972; The Man Died: prison notes, 1972; Season of Anomy, 1973; & plays inclng: The Lion & The Jewel; The Swamp Dwellers; A Dance of the Forests; The Road; Before the Blackout; Kongi's Harvest; Madmen & Specialists. Hons: Negro Arts Festival Drama Award, 1966; John Whiting Award for Drama, London, 1966; Jock Campbell/New Statesman Lit. Award, 1968; D. Litt., Univ. of Leeds, 1973. Address: Dept. of English, University of Ife, Ilf-Ife, Nigeria.

SPACU, Petru George, b. 6 June 1906. Professor of Chemistry. Educ: Grad., Univ. of Cluj, 1929; Dr. in chem., ibid, 1932; special studies, Paris & Munich, 1934-37. Appts. incl: Asst., 1929, Hd. of Univ. Lab. for Inorganic & Analytical Chem., 1932, Univ. of Cluj; Prof. of Inorganic Chem., 1937, Pro-Dean, Chem. Tech. Fac., 1944, Dean, Chem. Ind. Fac., 1951, Polytech. Schl., Bucharest; Prof. of Inorganic Chem., Univ. of Bucharest, 1955; Vice-Rector, ibid; 1966-69. Mbrships: Acad. of the Socialist Repub. of Romania, 1963-; Corres. Mbr., Akademie der Wissenschaften, Göttingen, 1970-; Comm., Inorganic Chem. Div.,IUPAC, 1967-71. Contbr. approx. 300 works to profl. jrnls. Hons: Order of Labour, Socialist Repub. of Romania, 1964; Star of the Socialist Repub. of Romania, 1966; Order of Sci. Merit, ibid, 1967. Address: Str. Corbeni 30, Bucharest 13, Romania. 34.

SPALDING, Henry A., b. 20 Mar. 1899. Engineer. Engaged in engrng. practice, 1924-. Mbrships: A.I.M.E. (Legion of Hon.); A.S.C.E.; Past Pres. & Hon., K.S.P.E.; C.E.C.; Dir., Nat. Rifle Assn. Am. Publs: Co-Author, Engineers Vest Pocket Book; Valuation of Mineral Properties; var. papers in field. Recip., Water Conservation Award, Nat. Wildlife Fed., Sears Roebuck, 1968. Address: 1028 Connecticut Ave., Suite 509-A, Washington, DC 20036, U.S.A.

SPANGLER, Anna Barbara, b. 1 Mar. 1891. Educator; Life Insurance Executive. Educ: Valley City Tchrs. Coll., N.D. Appts: Tchr., Pub. Schls., N.D., 1910-23; Field Rep., Royal Neighbors of Am. (Ins. Coop.), 1925-32; State Supvsr., ibid, Colo., Wyo., Utah, 1932-41; Nat. Bd. of Auditors, ibid, 1941-50; Nat. Bd. of Dirs., 1950-54; Supreme Oracle (Pres.), 1954-73. Mbrships: Pres., Pres. Sect., Nat. Fraternal Congress of Am., 1964-; Bus. & Profl. Women's Club. Address: Blackhawk Hotel, Apt. 710, Danenport, IA 52801, U.S.A. 5, 57, 138.

SPANGLER, Daisy Kirchoff, (Mrs. Francis R. Spangler), b. 27 Jan. 1013. Associate Professor. Educ: B.S., Millersville State Coll., 1963; M.Ed., 1966, D.Ed., 1972, Pa. State Univ. Appts: (all in Pa.): Rural Schl. Tchr., Lancaster Co., 1933-42; Elem. Tchr., 1942-51; Elem. Prin., Manheim Ctrl. Schl. Dist., 1952-66; Assoc. Prof., Educ., Millersville State Coll., 1968-. Mbrships: Advsr., Beta Omicron Chapt., Pi Lambda Theta; 1st V.P., Delta Kappa Gamma; Nat., Pa. Couns. of Soc. Studies; NEA; Pa. Educ. Assn.; Am. Educl. Rsch. Assn.; Pres., Lancaster City & Co. Prins.' Assn. Contbr. to The Instructor Mag. Hons: Dean's List. Address: Rte. 1, Box 840, Manheim, PA 17545, U.S.A. 5, 138, 141.

SPARKS, Othel N., Jr., B. 29 Apr. 1931. Postal Worker. Educ: law courses, LaSalle Univ., 1960. Appts: w. U.S. Postal Serv. Mbrships: Chmn., Bd. of Dirs., Richmond Community Action Prog. & Dept. Recreation & Parks, City of Richmond; Va. State Bd. of Housing; Bd. of Dirs., Rubicon Drug Prog.; Policy Bd., Model Cities Prog.; Tech. Advsry. Comm., Richmond ARCA Manpower Trng. Prog.; Advsry. Bd., Church Hill Sr. Citizens Prog.; Cnslr., Boy Scouts of Am.; Pres., 4 terms, Eastview Civic Assn.; Astoria Benefit Club. Hons: Citizenship Awards, Alpha Phi Alpha, Phi Beta Sigma, Sr. Citizens Prog., Rubicon Drug Prog., E. End Civic League. Address: 2404 Redwood Ave., Richmond, VA 23223, U.S.A. 125.

SPAZIANI, Maria Luisa, b. 7 Dec. 1924. University Professor; Writer. Educ: Liceo Classico, Univ. of Turin; Schlrship., The Sorbonne, Paris, France, 1953, '54; Int. Seminar, Harvard Univ., Boston, U.S.A., 1955. Appts: Responsible for TV & Radio Servs., 1957-; Prof., German Lit., Messina Univ., 1964-66, French Lit., 1966-, & at Univ. of Palermo, 1973-; Acvsr. to many publishing houses. Mbrships. incl: PEN Club; Soroptimist Club; Associazione Internazionale Critici Letterari; Sindicato Scrittori. Publs. incl: Le acque del Sabato, 1954; Primavera a Parigi, 1954; Luna Limbarda, 1959; Charles d'Orleans, 1969; Ronsard fra gli astri della Pleiade, 1972. Hons. incl: Premio Viareggio, 1950; Premio Siena, 1955; Int. Byron Award, 1960; Premio Firenze, 1962; Premio Trieste, 1970. Address: Via del Babuino 68, Rome 00187, Italy. 11, 95.

SPEAIGHT, Robert William, b. 14 Jan. 1904. Author; Actor; Lecturer. Educ: M.A., Oxford Univ. Profl. engagements incl: original Becket in T.S. Eliot's Murder in the Cathedral, 1935; original Hibbery in Journey's End., 1929; Shakespeare roles at Old Vic., 1931-32. Mbrships: V.P., Royal Soc. of Lit.; Pres., Virgil Soc., 1957-59; Pres., Edinburgh Sir Walter Scott Club, 1971-72. Publs: The Lost Hero; The Angel in the Mist; The Unbroken Heart; Acting: Thomas Becket; George Eliot; William Poelin the Elizabethan Revival; Hilaire Belloc; William Rothenstein; Nature in Shakespearian Tragedy; The Christian Theatre; Ronald Know the Writer; The Property Basket, etc. Hons: C.B.E., 1958; Off. of Legion d'Honneur, 1969. Address: Campion House, Benenden, Kent., U.K. 1, 3, 18.

SPEAR, Adolph Flatauer, b. 29 Apr. 1917. Financial Executive. Educ: A.B., Oglethorpe Univ., 1939; Advanced courses, Naval Supply, Harvard Grad. Schl. of Bus. Admin., 1943; Certified Pub. Acct. Appts: Auditor, Ernst & Ernst, Certified Pub. Accts., Atlanta, Ga., 1939-43, 1945-46; Supply Off. (Ensign to Lt.), USNR, Pacific Theater of Ops., WWII; Auditor, Am.-Standard, N.Y.C., 1947-52; Sec., Treas. & Dir., Gen. Plywood Corp., Louisville, Ky., 1953-62; Pres. & Dir., Adolph F. Spear & Co., Inc., 1963-; Dir., Int. Resources Corp., Am. Bus. Brokers, Inc., Certified Realty, Inc., Corporate Enterprises, Inc. Mbrships: Am. Inst. of Certified Pub. Accts.; Ky. Soc. of Certified Pub. Accts.; Ga. Soc. of Certified Pub. Accts.; Fndg. mbr., Southern Inst. of Mgmt.; Hon. Order of Ky. Cols.; Hon. Order of Confederate Cols. of Ky.; Admirals Club; Le Club Int.; Blue Key Nat. Hon. Fraternity, 1939. Pamphlet Publs: Financing Small Business; Business & Public Opinion. Recip., Key to the City of Louisville, KY., 1969. Address: 3021 N.E. 42nd St., Ft. Lauderdale, FL 33308, U.S.A. 7, 16, 22, 125.

SPECHT, Raymond Edwin, b. 1 June 1918. Associate Professor of Geography; University Planner, University of Wisconsin. Educ: B.S., Univ. of Wis., Oshkosh, 1940; M.A., Clark Univ., Worcester, Mass., 1947; Studies at Northwestern Univ., 1957 & McGill Univ., Montreal, P.Q., Canada. Appts. incl: 1st Lt., Jr. Mil. Acad., Chgo.; Tchr. & Coach, Oconto Falls Wis. H.S.; Tchr. & Coach, Wis. Rapids H.S.; Univ. Planner & Assoc. Prof., Geog. Dept., Univ. of Wis., Stevens Pt.; Planning Commnr., City of Stevens Pt.; Redev. Commnr., ibid; Dir., Admnstr. & Tchr., Semester Abroad, England, 1972. Mbrships. incl: Assn. of Am. Geographers; Soc. Coll. & Univ. Planners; Assn. of Wis. Planners; Mbr. & Past Pres., Wis. Coun. for Geographic Educ.; Railway & Locomotive Histl. Soc. of Am. Publs. incl: Story of the Green Bay & Western (w. E. Specht), 1966; History of the Milwaukee & Northern & Milwaukee Lake Shore & Western, 1969; num. pamphlets on railroads & mining. Hons. incl: Carnegie Arctic Fellowship, McGill Univ., 1954; Num. photogrpahy one man shows & awards. Address: 2008 W. River Dr., Stevens Point, WI 54481, U.S.A.

SPECTOR, Walter Graham, b. 20 Dec. 1924. Pathologist. Educ: Queen's Coll., Cambridge; Univ. Coll. Hosp. Med. Schl. Appts: Prof., Path., St. Bartholomew's Hosp., Med. Coll., Univ. of London; Cons. Path., ibid. Mbrships: Sec., Brit. Mem. Fellowships for Med. Rsch.; Coun., Imperial Cancer Rsch. Fund; Sci. Adv. Comm., Brit. Empire Cancer Campaign; Treas., Path. Soc. of G.B. & Ireland. Author of numerous sci. papers on path. topics. Address: Dept. of Path., St. Bartholomew's Hosp., W. Smithfield, London, E.C.1, U.K. 1, 50.

SPEIR, Alvie Nadine (McDougal) (Mrs. Bill Leo Speir), b. 29 Oct. 1922. District Court Clerk. Educ: H.S., 1941; Beauty Operator & Instr. License, Linda Schl. of Charm, 1942; Machinist & Tool Maker, Marine Schl., 1943. Appts: Beauty Operator, Albuquerque, N.M., 1942-43; Machine & Tool Maker, Consolidated Vultee Aircraft, San Diego, Calif., 1943-45; Clerk-Typist & Bookkeeper, Luna Co. Abstract & Title Ins. C., Deming, N.M., 1946-49; worked ranch & farm w. husband, 1948-; Substitute Tchr., Art Instr., Luna Co. Schls., N.M., 1950-58; Dpty. Co. Clerk & Dist. Ct. Clerk, Deming, 1958-63; Dist. Ct. Clerk, 6th Judicial Dist., Deming, 1963-. Mbrships. incl: Assn. of Dist. Ct. Clerks; Am. Quarter Horse Assn.; PTA; Bus. & Profl. Womens Club; Blackrange Artists Assn.; Beta Sigma Phi. Recip., ribbons for Quarter Horses shown at fairs, Deming, N.M., 1952-70. Address: Route 1, Box 145, Deming, NM 88030, U.S.A. 55, 138.

SPEIRS, Doris Louise Huestis (Mrs. J. Murray Speirs), b. 27 Oct. 1894. Artist; Author. Educ: Univ. of Toronto, 1914-16; Univ. of Ill., U.S.A., 1940-41. Mbrships. incl: Toronto Jr. Field Naturalists; Past Pres., ibid; Dir., Fedn. of Ont. Naturalists; Fndng. Mbr., Margaret Nice Ornithological Club. Solo Exhibs. of Paintings incl: Jerrold Morris Gall., Toronto, 1970; Robert McLaughlin Gall., Oshawa, 1971. Pub. Collects. incl: Nat. Gall. of Canada; Art Gall. of Toronto. Work in pvte. collects., Canada, Finland, Channel Isles, U.S.A. Publs. incl: Life History of Lincoln's Sparrow, 1968; Exercise for Psyche (poems, 1922-72), 1974; poems, essays, translations, var. publs. Recip., Dip. of Philos., 1974. Address: Cobble Hill, 1815 Altona Rd., Pickering, Ont., Canada, L1V 1M6. 5, 6, 8, 132, 133, 138.

SPELLER, Cyril Alfred, b. 4 Sept. 1919. Journalist. Appts: J.P., Co. Borough of Bournemouth, 1959; Juvenile Ct. Magistrate; Wessex Corres., London Jewish Chronicle. Mbrships: Guild of Jewish Jrnlists; World Fed. of Jewish Jrnlists; P.R.O., Bournemouth Coun. of Christians & Jews; Press Officer, Bournemouth & Dist. Fabian Soc.; Press Officer, Bournemouth Labour Party; Sec., Bournemouth Jewish Blind Aid Soc.; Past Gen. Sec., Nat. Soc. for Prevention of Venereal Disease. Address: 5 Earls Court, 9 Gervis Rd., Bournemouth BH1 3ED, U.K.

SPELTS, Richard Errett Jr., b. 1 Jan. 1919. Business Executive. Educ: B.S., Univ. of Neb., 1941; A.B., Hastings Coll., Neb., 1948. Appts: Chmn. of Bd., 1st Nat. Bank of Grand Island; Chmn. of Bd., Bankshares of Neb., Inc., Grand Isle.; Exec. V.P., & Dir., Spelts of Neb., Inc., ibid; Off. & Dir., Spelts-Schultz Lumber Co. of Grand Isle., Mid-Am. Co., ibid, Spelts Lumber Co. of Kearny, Spelts-Swanson Implement Co., Kearny, Spelts-Scheiding Lumber Co. of O'Neill & Spelts Lumber Co. of Valentine; Sr. V. Pres. & Dir., Investors Growth Inds., Inc., Mpls., Minn.; Dir. of many other cos. Mbrships: Chmn., Golden Age Village (Hall Co. Housing Auth.); Pres., Gtr. Grand Isle. Dev. Corp.; Dir., Grand Isle. Indl. Fndn., Neb. Assn. of Comm. & Ind., etc. etc. Recip. of many awards. Address: 304 First National Bank Bldg., Grand Island, NB 68801, U.S.A. 8, 16, 22, 128, 131.

SPENCE, Allan William, b. 4 Aug. 1900. Consultant Physician. Educ: Gonville & Caius Coll., Cambridge Univ.; St. Bartholomew's Hosp. Med. Coll.; B.A., 1922; M.A., B.Chir., 1926; M.B., 1927; M.D., Cambridge, 1931; M.R.C.P., 1928; F.R.C.P., London, 1937. Appts. incl: Rsch. Fellow, w. Dr. David Marine, N.Y., 1931-32; Asst. Dir., Med. Unit, 1936-37, Physn., 1937-65, Hon., 1965-. St. Bartholomew's Hosp; Physn., King George Hosp., Ilford, 1938-67, Hon., 1967-; Lieut.-Col., RAMC, 1942-45; Cons., Endocrinol., H.M. Army at Home, 1954-65; Mbr., Med. & Agric. Rsch. Coun. Advsry. Comm. on Iodine Deficiency & Thyroid Disease, 1933-39; Med. Rsch. Advsry. Comm. on Hormones, 1937-41. Contbr. to profl. jrnls. Hons: Brackenbury Schlrship. in Med., 1926; Lawrence Rsch. Schlrship., 1929, & Gold Medal, 1930; Cattlin Rsch. Fellowship, 1938, St. Bartholomew's; Rockefeller Travelling Fellowship, 1931-32. Address: Oak Spinney, Liphook Rd., Lindford, Bordon, Hants. GU35 OPN, U.K. 1, 3.

SPENCE, Janet Blake Conley (Mrs. Alexander P. Spence), b. 17 Aug. 1915. Civic Volunteer Worker. Educ: Vassar Coll., Poughkeepsie, N.Y.; Cert., Katharine Gibbs Secretarial Schl., N.Y., 1936; Pvte. studies in drawing, painting, piano & voice. Activities incl: Co-Chmn. & Chmn., series of dances, Darien Assembly, 1953-56; Co-Chmn. & Chmn., re-org., Dobbs Alumnae Assn., Southern Conn., 1959-63; Comm. work, var. projs., Vassar; Club, Fairfield Co., Conn., 1949-73; Chmn., i/c of planting & maintenance of sects. of town, Garden Club, Wilton, Conn., 1962-65; Collector & Chmn., neighborhood div., United Fund of Wilton, Inc., 1961-64; Bd., Corres. & Recording Sec., Pub. Hlth. Nursing Assn. of Wilton, Inc., 1962-67; Coun. Rep., Vassar Coll., Class 1937, 1973-78. Other mbrships. incl: Wash. Valley Community Assn.; Woman's Home Econs. Club, Wash. Valley; Nat. Trust for Historic Preservation. Address: Hilltop, Washington Valley Rd., Morristown, NJ 07960, U.S.A. 5, 129, 138.

SPENCER, Jean Marie Morgan, b. 3 Mar. 1927. Geologist; Scientific Editor. Educ: B.S., Baylor Univ., Waco, Tex., U.S.A., 1961; M.S., ibid, 1964. Appts: Ed., Baylor Geological Studies Bulletin, 1966-; Rsch. Assoc., Dept. of Geol., Baylor Univ., 1966-68; Instr., ibid, 1968-71; Asst. Prof., 1971-. Mbrships: Fellow, Tex. Acad. of Sci., V.P., Earth Scis., 1972; Ed., Tex. Sect., Nat. Assn. of Geol. Tchrs., 1971, Sec.-Treas, 1972, V.P., 1973, Pres., 1974; Assn. of Earth Sci. Eds.; Soc. for Environmental Geochemistry & Hlth.; AAAS; Animal Protection Inst. of Am.; Baylor Geological Soc.; Alpha Chi. Publs: Contbns. to profl. jrnls.; Co-Ed., Environmental Phosphorus Handbook, 1973. Address: Dept. of Geology, Baylor University, Waco, TX 76710, U.S.A. 5, 138.

SPENCER, Thomas, III, b. 25 June 1939. Educator; Mathematician. Educ: B.S., 1964, M.S., 1969, Newark Coll. Engrng.; M.S., Stevens Inst. Technol., 1967; post-grad. work, ibid, 1967-. Appts. incl: Asst. to Elec. Engr., Triangle Conduit & Cable Co., New Brunswick, N.J., 1961-62; Instr., Dept. of Math., Newark Coll., Engrng., 1964-68; Asst. Prof., Dept. of Math., Trenton State Coll., 1968-; Indl. Cons., Western Elec. Corp., Princeton, N.J., Nametre Inc., Edison, N.J., etc. Mbrships: Am. Math. Soc.; Inst. Maths. & Its Applications; Soc. Indl. & Applied Maths.; Math. Assn.; Math. Assn. Am.; Royal Astronomical Soc. of Canada; Sigma Xi; Tau Beta Pi; Eta Kappa Nu; Theta Chi. Contbr. to var. profl. jrnls. Recip., 5th Prize, Metropolitan Student Coun., IEEE, 1964. Address: R.D. 1, Box 425A, Bergen Ave., Princeton, NJ 08540, U.S.A. 6.

SPERANZA, Francesco, b. 19 Oct. 1902. Artist. Educ: Lic. Artistico, Brera's Acad., Milan. Appts: Art Tchr., Guglielmo Marconi H.S., Milan. Mbrships: Acad. dei Cinquecento; Acad. Tiberina, Rome. Exhibs: 3 biennials, Venice; Nat. Quadrennial of Art, Rome; Shows in Milan, Turin, Genoa, Mantua, Bergamo, Brescia, Naples, Florence, Rome, Bari, etc.; Int. shows, Sao Paulo, Brazil, Sydney, Australia, Basle, Switzerland. Hons: Num. prizes, int. & nat. exhibs.; Gold Medal-Pres. of Italian Repub., Pres. of Senate, Chmbr. of Deputies, City of Milan, City of Bitonto; Cavaliere della Repub. Italiana. Address: 13 via Gran Sasso d'Italia, Milan, Italy.

SPERRY, Margaret, Author. Educ: B.A., Univ. of Wis., Madison; Jrnlsm., Columbia Univ.; P.R., N.Y. Univ. Appts: Reporter, Columnist, Brooklyn Daily Eagle; Feature Writer, Courier-Jrnl., Lousiville, Ky.; Writer, Off. of War Info., 1943-44. Mbrships: Phi Beta Kappa; Kappa Alpha Theta; Authors Guild, N.Y.; Prog. Dir., Guild of St. Birgitta, Darien, Conn. Publs: The Golden Wind (w. T. Ohta); Sunway; Porttait of Eden; The Magician's Cloak; The Hen That Saved The World; Scandinavian Stories; Who Can Tell; Painted Houses; The Golden Seeds; Brides of Darkness; Dream Harvest; also var. plays & poems. Address: c/o Crane, Russak & Co. Inc., 52 Vanderbilt Ave., N.Y., NY 10017, U.S.A.

SPICER, Erik John, b. 9 Apr. 1926. Librarian; Administrator. Educ: B.A., Vic. Coll., Univ. of Toronto, Canada, 1948; B.L.S., Lib. Schl., ibid, 1949; Schl. of Grad. Study, ibid; M.A.L.S., Lib. Schl., Univ. of Mich., U.S.A., 1959. Appts. incl: Dpty. Libn., Ottawa Pub. Lib., 1954-60; Parliamentary Libn., Ottawa, 1960-; Nat. Lib. Advsry. Coun. (ex-officio), 1960-69; Nat. Lib. Advsry Bd. (ex-officio), 1970-; Canadian Corres., Inter-Parliamentary Union's Int. Ctr. for Parliamentary Documentation, Geneva, Switzerland, 1966-; Trustee Ottawa Pub. Lib.

Bd., 1970-73. Mbrships. incl: Parliamentary & Administrative Libs. Sect., Int. Fedn. of Lib. Assns., The Hague, Netherlands; Ont., Canadian, Am. & British Lib. Assns.; Inst. of Pub. Admin. of Canada; Canadian & Int. Pol. Sci. Assns.; Royal Canadian Mil. Inst.; Beta Phi Mu; Phi Kappa Phi. Contbr. to num. profl. publs. Hons: Canada Coun. Fellowship, 1959; Canadian Forces Decoration, 1962; Centennial Medal, 1967. Address: Library of Parliament, Parliament Bldgs., Ottawa, Ont., K1A OA9, Canada. 2, 6, 88, 139.

SPIEGEL, John P., b. 17 Mar. 1911. Psychiatrist; Psychiatric Research Administrator. Educ: B.A., Dartmouth Coll., 1934; M.D., Northwestern Univ. Schl. of Med., 1938; Grad., Chgo Inst. for Psychoanalysis, 1949. Appts: Assoc. Dir., Inst. Psychiatric & Psychosomatic Rsch. & Trng., Michael Reese Hosp., 1951-54; Lectr., Dept. Soc. Rels., Harvard Univ., Cambridge, Mass., 1953-66, Rsch. Assoc., Lab. Soc. Rels., 1954-66, Assoc. Clin. Prof. of Psych., Harvard Med. Schl., 1957-66; Asst. Psych., Children's Med. Ctr., Boston, Mass., 1954-66; Dir., Lemberg Ctr. for Study of Violence, Brandeis Univ., Waltham, Mass., 1966-73, Soc. Psych., Heller Schl. for Soc. Welfare, Brandeis Univ., 1966-. Mbr. & Comm. Mbr., profl. orgs. Publs. (co-author) incl: War Neuroses, 1945; Men Under Stress, 1945; Messages of the Body (in press). Recip., Special Award for Contbn. to Psychol., 1974. Address: Ford Hall, Room 229, Brandeis University, Waltham, MA 02154, U.S.A.

SPIEGEL, Siegmund, b. 13 Nov. 1919. Architect; Professional Planner. Educ: CCNY, 1939-40; Columbia Univ., N.Y., 1945-50. Appts: Draftsman, Mayer & Whittlesey, Archts., N.Y.C., 1941-47; Archt. & Off. Mgr., ibid, 1947-55; Pvte. Prac., Arch., E. Meadow, N.Y., 1955-; Fellow, Acad. of Marketing Sci., L.I. Univ., Greenvale, N.Y., 1972. Mbrships: Am. Inst. Archts.; N.Y. State Assn. Archts.; Dir., L.I. Chapt., AIA; Assoc., Nat. Assn. of Home Bldrs.; L.I. Bldrs. Inst.; Assoc. Advsry. Coun., ibid. Author of articles in field. Hons: Grand Prize for instnl. bldgs (for Syosset Hosp.), L.I. Assn., 1963; Grand Prize, Human Resources Schl., 1966; Grand Prize, Stony Brook Profl. Bldg., 1966; Beautification Award, Town of Hempstead, N.Y., 1969; Arch. Award, Harbor Club Apts., 1970. Address: 2035 Hempstead Turnpike, E. Meadow, NY 11554, U.S.A. 6.

SPIEGEL, Walter F., b. 7 Nov. 1922. Consulting Engineer. Educ: Cert., summer course, Sorbonne, 1945; B.S.M.E., 1948; M.S., 1957, Univ. of Pa., U.S.A. Appts: Staff Engr., Charles S. Leopold, Inc., Consulting Engrs., Phila., 1948-61; Prin./Pres., Walter F. Spiegel, Inc., Jenkintown, Pa., 1963-. Mbrships: Past Pres., Am. Soc. of Heating, Refrigerating & Air Conditioning Engrs.; Am. Consulting Engrs. Coun.; Nat. Soc. of Prolf. Engrs.; Am. Technion Soc.; Tau Beta Pi; Sigma Tau. Publs: Mechanical & Electrical System Design for Protective Shelters; Rsch. papers, articles in profl. jrnls. Address: 321 York Rd., Jenkintown, PA 19046, U.S.A. 6.

SPIEGELMAN, Sol, b. 14 Dec. 1914. Molecular Geneticist. Educ: Undergrad. Study, CCNY, 1933-35, 1938-39; Grad. Study, Columbia Univ., 1940-42; Ph.D., Wash. Univ., St. Louis, Mo., 1944. Appts: Lectr. in Phys., Wash. Univ., 1942-44; Lectr. in Applied Maths. ibid, 1943-44; Instr. in Bacteriol., Schl. of Med., ibid, 1945-46; Asst. Prof. in Bacteriol., ibid, 1946-48; Special Fellow, U.S. Pub. Hlth. Serv., Univ. of Minn., 1948-49; Prof. of Microbiol., Univ. of Ill., 1949-69; Mbr., Ctr. for

Advd. Study, ibid, 1964-69; Dir., Inst. of Cancer Rsch. & Prof. of Human Genetics & Dev., Coll. of Physns. & Surgs., Columbia Univ., 1969-. Mbrships. incl: Am. Soc. for Microbiol.; Soc. of Am. Naturalists; Soc. of Gen. Physiologists.; Brit. Soc. for Gen. Microbiol.; Am. Soc. of Biol. Chemists; Genetics Soc. of Am.; Phi Beta Kappa; Sigma Xi; Tau Pi Epsilon; Phi Kappa Phi; Nat. Acad. of Scis.; Fellow, Am. Acad. Arts & Scis.; Nat. Cancer Advsry Bd. Author & Co-Author of num. articles in profl. jrnls. Hons. incl: Bertner Fndn. Award in Cancer Rsch., 1968; Townsend Harris Medal, Alumni Citn., CCNY, 1972; Papanicolaou Award for Cancer Rsch., Papanicolaou Cancer Rsch. Inst., Miami, Fla., 1973; Marrs McLean Lectr., Baylor Coll. Med., 1974; S. Steven Brodie Mem. Lect., Jewish Mem. Hosp., N.Y.C., 1974; Docts. of Sci., sev. univs. Address: Inst. of Cancer Research, 99 Ft. Washington Ave., New York, NY 10032, U.S.A. 2, 8, 28.

SPILHAUS, Margaret Whiting (Mrs. Ludolph Spilhaus), b. 29 Sept. 1889. Author. Educ: Univ. of Cape Town, S. Africa. Mbr., Int. PEN Club. Publs: The First South Africans; The Background of Geography; The Land They Left (1820 Settlers); Trees of the Cape Peninsula; South Africa in the Making; Company's Men; The Limber Elf; Under a Bright Sky; Doorstep Baby; (for children) South African Nursery Rhymes; Series of decorative maps. Address: 205 Grosvenor Sq., College Rd., Rondebosch, Cape, S. Africa. 3.

SPILIOTOPOULOS, Stathis (Efstathios), b. 30 Dec. 1903. Retired Journalist. Educ: Law Schl., Athens Univ., Greece; Columbia Univ., N.Y., U.S.A. Appts: w. Nat. Bank of Greece, 1919-53; Secretariat & Sec. of Bd., ibid, 1951-53; For. Corres., Acropolis newspaper, N.Y. 1947-48; Drama Critic, ibid, 1949-62; Critic, Alpha Mag., 1967-68; Critic, Nea Estia Mag., 1972-73. Mbrships incl: V.P., Soc. of Greek Playwrights; Ctrl. Lectr. Comm., State Theatres Org. of Greece; Bd., Union of Greek Drama Critics. Publs. incl: In the Land of the Fjords, 1935; The History of the National Bank of Greece, 1949; Dance & Drama in Pharaoh's Land & in the Land of Promise, 1963; The Theatre as I Lived it. 1965; The Book of My Little Friend, 1967; The Boy with the Candle, 1969; var. translations. Hons. incl: Gold Cross of King George, 1st Order; Gold Cross of the Hellenic Red Cross. Address: 15 Ioustinianou St., Athens, 707, Greece. 43.

SPINA, Alfred Eugene, b. 24 Jan. 1932. Food Processing Executive. Educ: A.A. Modesto Jr. Coll., 1952; A.B. Coll. of the Pacific, 1954. Appts: Tchr., Elem. Grades Lammersville Schl., Tracy, Calif., 1955-56. Personnel Mgr. Turlock Coop. Growers, Modesto, 1957-63; Personnel Mgr., Tri Valley Growers, San Fran., 1963-64; Dir., Ind. Rels., ibid, 1964-68, V.P., 1968-; Sr. V.P. Admin., 1973; Cons., Mgmt. Rsch. Assocs., San Fran., 1970-. Mbrships: Dir., Calif. Processors, Inc.; Altenate Dir., Canners League of Calif; Dir., Modesto Chmbr. of Comm.; V.P. & Pres., Stanislaus Co. Personnel Mgmt. Soc. Address: Tri Valley Growers, 100 California St., San Fran., CA 94106, U.S.A. 9.

SPINK, Edna H. Sanderson (Mrs.), b. 8 June 1892. Musician; Poet. Educ: Univ. Schl. of Music, Ann Arbor, Mich; Pvte. tuition. Appts. incl: Ch. Organist; Soloist; Choir Dir.; Music Tchr.; Theater Organist & Accompanist. Mbrships: Astara, 5th degree mbr.; Ruby Focus of Magnificent Consummation; Temple of Cosmic Radiation. Author of num. poems & songs. Poems publd. in THe Muse, 1944; Poetry

House, Poetry Program, 1945; Exposition Press, 1946; etc. Songs incl: The Old Water Wheel; How Can I Tell? Address: 5447 S. Magnolia Ave., Whittier, CA 90601, U.S.A.

SPINKS, William Herschel, b. 20 Apr. 1917. Public School Suprintendent. Educ: B.S., E. Tex. Univ.; Masters Degree, Tex. A.I. Univ. Appts. Serv., 5 yrs., WWII: Schl. Supt., McAllen, Tex., 1946-. Mbrships: Local Tchrs. Assn.; Dist. Tchrs. Assn.; Tex. State Tchrs. Assn.; Nat. Tchrs. Assn.; Tex. Educators Assn.; Nat. Educators Assn.; Tex. & Nat. Prins. Hons: Named as Outstanding in field of educ. in South U.S.A., 1972. Address: Rt. 2 Box 1675, McAllen, TX 78501, U.S.A. 57, 125.

SPIRÉA, Andrei, b. 21 Jan. 1932. Composer. Educ: Acad. of Music, Bucharest. Appts: Tchr., clarinet & chamber music, Israel Kibbutzim, 1962-; Instr., Dept. of Theoretical Studies, Tel-Aviv Univ., 1968-70; I/c 2 kibbutz music studios. Mbrships: Israeli Composers League; ACUM. Compositions incl: 2 symphonies; 4 concerti, for oboe, viola, violin, piano & orch.; Chamber music; Var. piano, voice, string compositions. Address: 29 Brandeis St., Tel-Aviv, Israel. 94.

SPITTLER, Betty Jane Jones (Mrs.), b. 12 Nov. 1922. Motel Manager. Educ: Universal Motel Schl., Miami, Fla. Appts: Mgr. & Buyer, Terrace Inn & Restaurant, Terre Haute, Ind., 1964; Mgr., Hickory Manor, Crystal Lake, Ill., 1965; Mgr. & Buyer, St. Mary's Motel, Evansville, Ind., 1965-72, Donna Ct. Motel, ibid, 1972-. Mbrships: Evansville Chmbr. of Comm. (tourist comm.); Lutheran Ch. Coun., 1962-65; Lutheran Parish Bd., 1951-65; Sunday Schl. Supt., 1950-65. Address: Donna Ct. Motel, 2416 Highway 41 N., Evansville, IN 47727, U.S.A. 5, 138.

SPITZ, Barbara S. (Mrs. Lawrence S. Spitz), b. 8 Jan. 1926. Artist; Printmaker. Educ: A.B. Pembroke Coll., Brown Univ., 1947; Rhode Is. Schl. of Design; Art Inst. of Chgo. Held One-Man shows, Benjamin Gails, 1971 & 72; Workshop Gall. of Letterio Calapai, 1971; R.S.T. Gall., 1974. Grp. Exhibs: Wadsworth Atheneum; Silvermine Guild of Artists; State Univ. of Potsdam N.Y.; Soc. of Am. Graphic Artists; Speed Art Mus.; Smithsonian Instn.; Lib. of Congress. Gall. Affiliations incl: Benjamin Gall.; Art Rental & Sales-Art Inst. of Chgo.; Margo Leavin, L.A.; Lumley Cazalet Ltd., London; Elca London, Montreal; Kunsthaus Bühler, Stuttgart. Mbrships: Artists Equity Assn.; Arts Club of chgo.; Renaissance Soc., Univ. of Chgo.; Chgo. Soc. of Artists; Print Club of Phila.; Boston Printmakers. Has publd. about 59 eds. of intaglio prints, 1965-. Hons. incl: Childe Hassam Purchase Award, Am. Acad. of Arts & Letts., 1973; Purchase Awards from Okla. Art Ctr., 1972, Boston Printmakers, 1971 & 72, Dulin Gall. of Art, 1973 & DeCorva Mus., 1971 & 72. Address: 150 Indian Tree Dr., Highland Pk., IL 60035, U.S.A. 5, 37, 105.

SPITZ, Hans, b. 19 Nov. 1911. Company Director. Educ: B.Com., Vienna, Austria; Dr. Econ., Florence, Italy; AASA, Melbourne, Australia. Appts: Dir. Or Jt. Mng. Dir., Prompt Builders' Supply Pty. Ltd., Caspi Pty Ltd., Alparex Pty. Ltd., Jertex Pty. Ltd., Caspi Nominees Pty. Ltd. Australian deleg., Int. Multiple Sclerosis Congress, Brussels 1972, Barcelona 1973. Mbrships: Multiple Sclerosis Soc. of Vic.; Pres., ibid, 1971-; B'Nai B'Rith; Int. Coun., ibid, 1962-68, Pres., Australia-N.Z. Dist 21, 1964-67, Int. V.P. (Wash.), 1965-68; Dir., Australian Jewish Welfare Soc., 1963-65. Author var.

articles in jrnls. & brochures. Address: 29 Longview Rd., N. Balwyn, Vic., Australia, 3104. 23, 55, 128.

SPITZER, Lyman, Jr., b. 26 June 1914. Astronomer. Educ: A.B. Yale Univ., U.S.A., 1935; Henry Fellow, Cambridge Univ., U.K., 1935-36; M.A., Princeton Univ., N.J., U.S.A., 1937; Ph.D., ibid, 1938. Appts: Instr., Phys. & Astron., Yale Univ., 1939-42; Sci., Special Studies Grp.-Dir., Sonar Analysis grp., Columbia Univ. Div. War Rsch., 1942-46; Assoc. Prof. Astrophys., Yale Univ., 1946-47; Prof., Astron., Chmn., Dept. Astrophys. Scis. & Dir., Princeton Univ. Observ., 1947-; Charles A. Young Prof. Astron., 1952-; Dir., Proj. Matterhorn, 1953-61; Chmn., Exec. Comm., Princeton Univ. Plasma Phys. Lab. (formerly Proj. Matterhorn), 1961-66; Chmn., Univ. Rsch. Bd., 1967-72. Mbrships: Past Pres., Am. Astron. Soc.; Nat. Acad. Scis.; Am. Philos. Soc.; Am. Acad. Arts & Scis.; Am. Phys. Soc.; Royal Astron. Soc., U.K.; Am. Alpine Club. Author books & contbr. articles to profl jrnls. in field. Hons: Dr. Sc., Yale Univ., 1958; Case Inst. Technol., 1961; LL.D., Toledo Univ., 1963; Rittenhouse Medal, Franklin Inst., 1957; Bruce Gold Medal, Astron. Soc. of Pacific, 1973; Henry Draper Medal, Nat. Acad. Scis., 1974. Address: Princeton Univ. Observ., Peyton Hall, Princeton, NJ 08540. 1, 14.

SPOERRI, Theodor H., b. 7 Apr. 1924. Psychiatrist. Educ: M.D.; Ph.D., Psych.; Med. & Psychol. Studies, Zurich, Basle, Tübingen & Bern, Switzerland. Appts. incl: Asst. Psych., Univ. Clin., Waldau-Bern; Chief Physn., Münsingen Hosp.; Vice-Dir., Univ. Clin., Waldau; Dir., Psych., Univ. Polyclin., Bern, 1966-. Mbrships. incl: Swiss Psych. Assn.; Int. Soc. of Art & Psychopathol. Publs. incl: Genie und Krankheit 1952; Georg Trakl, 1954; Nekrophilie, 1959; Komp. d. Psychiatrie, 5th ed., 1969; Sprachphänomene und Psychose, 1964; Ekstase, 1968; Publr., Confinia psychiatrica & Psychotherapy & Psychosomatics; Bibliotheca Psychiatrica. Address: Hügelweg 2, Bern, Switzerland. 43, 103.

SPONG, Jon Curtis, b. 5 Dec. 1933. Concert Organist; Composer; Accompanist; Educator. Educ: B.M.E., Drake Univ., 1956; M.M., 1958; Pvte. Study, N.Y.C. Appts: Acting Dir., Choral Activities, Wash. State Univ., Pullman, 1959-60; Asst. Dir., Choral Activities, Drake Univ., Des Moines, Iowa, 1961-66; Artist, Tchr., Univ. of Mo., Kan. City, 1966-69; Artist Tchr., Angelo State Univ., Tex., 1970-71; Concert Accompanist for Sherrill Milnos, Baritone of Met. Opera Assn. Played num. recitals in U.S., Korea, Okinawa, Hong Kong, Vietnam, Philippines & Guam. Mbrships. incl: Omicron Delta Kappa; Pi Kappa Lambda; Am. Guild Organists; Organ Hist. Soc.; Nat. Assn. Organ Tchrs. Fellow, Intercontinental Biog. Assn., 1970. Publs: Our American Heritage, two vols, 1967; Scenes from the Life of Christ, Early American Compositions for Organ & Three Pieces by Early American Composers, 1968; Christmas Pastorals for the Organ, 1970; In Joyous Praise, Eight Organ Gems from the Past, Organ Rarities, Vol. I, 1971. Address: First United Meth. Ch., 10th & Pleasant, Des Moines, 50309, U.S.A. 8

SPONGBERG-HOLMBERG, Viola. Musician; Lecturer; Author. Educ: B.A., Hunter Coll., CUNY, U.S.A.; M.A., Columbia Univ., N.Y.; Mus.D., N.Y. Coll. of Music; Ph.D., N.Y. Univ. Appts: Debut as Concert Violinist at age of ten; Later appeared as Pianist, Organist & Composer; Prima Donna (Soprano), Opera Cos.,

U.S.A. & Europe; Lectr., num. colls. & univs., U.S.A., Canada, & Europe; Cons., Philos. & Music, Funk & Wagnalls Co., N.Y.C., for 4 yrs.; Dir. of Music, Augustana L.C., Jackson Hts., N.Y., 1963-. Mbrships: Am. Security Coun.; Am. Philosophical Assn.; Bd. of Dirs., N.Y. Univ. Alumnae; Bd. of Dirs., Percy Grainger Lib. Soc.; Am. Guild of Musical Artists; Am. Fedn. of TV & Radio Artists; Pres., N.Y. Chapt., Swedish Cultural Soc. Publs: The Philosophy of Erik Gustaf Geijer; Articles on philos. & musicol. in The New International Year Book; Contbns. to philosophical jrnls. Hons. incl: Presidential Citation for meritorious serv. in hosps., fund rallies, & special progs., Treasury Dept.; Gen., Blue Star Brigade, after WW II. Address: P.O. Box No. 177, Thornwood, NY 10594, U.S.A. 4, 6, 10, 13, 15, 111.

SPORN, Philip, b. 25 Nov. 1896. Consultant on energy & electric energy. Educ: E.E., Columbia Univ. Schl. of Engrng., 1917. Appts. incl: Protection Engr., Am. Elec. Power Co. (formerly Am. Gas & Elec. Co.), 1920; Chief Elec. Engr., ibid, 1927; Chief Engr., 1933; V.P., 1934; Exec. V.P., 1945; Pres., 1947-61; Chmn., System Dev. Comm., 1961-67; Dir., 1943-69; Cons., 1961-71; Pres. & Dir., Ohio Valley Elec. Corp. & Ind.-Ky. Elec. Corp., 1952-67; Vis. Prof., Cornell Coll. of Engrng., 1963-64, MIT, 1970-71. Mbrships. incl: Nat. Acad. of Scis.; Nat. Acad. of Engrng.; Fellow & Hon. mbr.; Am. Soc. of Mech. Engrs., IEEE; Fellow, AAAS, Am. Nuclear Soc., Am. Soc. of Civil Engrs.; Hon. Fellow, Instn. of Mech. Engrs. Publs. incl: Heat Pumps (w. Ambrose & Baumeister); The Integrated Power System; Energy: Its Production, Conversion & Use in the Service of Man. Hons. incl: Prometheus Award, 1967; Faraday Medal Medal, 1969; 13 hon. degrees. Address: 320 E. 72 St., N.Y., NY 10021, U.S.A. 2, 14, 26, 34, 56.

SPRAOS, John, b. 4 Nov. 1926. Economist; University Teacher. Educ: Univ. of Edinburgh, 1946-50; M.A., ibid, 1950; Postgrad., Univ. of Manchester, 1950-53. Appts: Rsch. Fellow, Univ. of Sheffield, 1953-57; Lectr., Pol. Econ., Univ. Coll., Univ. of London, 1957-64; Reader, ibid, 1964-65; Prof., 1965-. Mbrships: Chmn., Greek Comm. against Dictatorship, 1967-; Ed.Bd., Review of Econ. Studies, 1955-65; Exec. Comm., Assoc. of Univ. Tchrs. of Econ., 1966-. Publs: The Decline of the Cinema: An Economist's Report, 1962; papers in Economic Journal, Quarterly Journal of Economics, Review of Economic Studies, Economica, Manchester School, Metroeconomica, Yorkshire Bulletin. Address: Univ. Coll., London, Gower St., London, W.C.1, U.K. 50.

SPRAY, Paul, b. 9 Apr. 1921. Orthopedic Surgeon. Educ: B.S., Univ. of Pitts., 1942; M.D., Geo. Wash. Univ., 1944; M.S., Univ. of Minn., 1950; Appts: Orthopedic Surg. in Pvte. Prac., Oak Ridge, Tenn., 1950-; Vis. Staff, Oak Ridge Hosp.; Cons., ORINS Med. Div.; Cons., Chamberlain Mem. Hosp., Rockwood; LaFollette Community Hosp.; Courtesy Staff, E. Tenn. Bapt. & Univ. of Tenn. Hosps., Knoxville; Vis. Assoc. Prof., Orphopedic Surgs., Univ. of Nairobi, Kenya, 1973. Fellowships: Int. Coll. Surgs.; Am. Coll. Surgs. Bd., Sec., Orthopedies Overseas Div., CARE-MEDICO; Participant in overseas projects of Medico-Care in Jordan, 1959, Nigeria, 1962 & '65, Algeria, 1963 & Afghanistan, 1970; Volunteer Physn. to S. Vietnam, AMA prog., 1967; Past Chmn., Tenn. Div., U.N. Assn. of U.S.A.; Bd. Mbr. & Exec. Comm. & Chmn. Supply & Fin. Comm.; Medico Advsry. Bd. for CARE-MEDICO. & Nat. Bd., Med. Examiners.; Am. Acad. Orthopedic Surgs.; Int. Coll. Trop. Med.; AMA; SICOT; Past Chmn., Tenn. Div., UN Assn. Am.

Fracture Assn; Lions Club. Author of sev. articles in med. jrnls. Hons. incl: AMA Cert. of Humanitarian Serv. & Sertoma Serv. to Mankind Award, 1967; Lions Club Humanitarian Award, 1968. Volunteer Phys. to Vietnam, 1972 (AMA). Address: Oak Ridge Orthopedic Clin., Oak Ridge, TN 37830, U.S.A. 7, 17, 54, 125.

SPREITHER, Franz Ludwig Alfred August Rudolf Heinrich Siegfried, b. 19 Aug. 1912. Lecturer. Educ: Studied, Amsterdam, Netherlands. Special Prac., Constance & Urach-Schanz. Publs: Psychologie & Lebenserfolg?, 3rd edit. 1957; Verwirklichen, Aufriss einer Realisations-Psychologie, 1958; Spitzenkräfte-Vandemekum I, 1961, II, 1962; Schöpferisch-Bewältigende Hochform, 4th edit. 1963; Verwirklichende Kern-Zentrierung, 2nd edit. 1959; Signale aus Uns Selbst, Aufriss einer Persönlichkeits-Okonomik, 1968; Der Königliche Weg (Manual), 19th edit. 1973 (Info. Lit.); Suprarationales, Berichte zur Erschliessung der Kreativität, 1971- (as occasion demands) (Info. Lit.). Address: P.O.Box 5050, D-775 Konstanz 12, German Fed. Repub.

SPRINGOLO, Agostino, b. 1 Mar. 1886. Painter. Educ: Studies under Laurenti, Venice; under von Habermann, Acad. of Fine Arts, Munich. Works incl: La casetta rossa; Ragazza in viola; Autunno suburbano; Paesaggio di Fonte; Anselmo; Franciulla; Tramonto d'inverno; Estate. Hons. incl: Gold Medal, Paris Exhib., 1937; Soppelsa Prize, Venice, 1942; Umanità Prize, Milan, 1949; Marzotto Prize, 1954, '55; Asolanno Prize, 1957; Bagutta Prize, 1958; Vergani Sportono Prize, 1963; Bergamo Prize, 1959; Gold Florin, 1967; Gold Medal, Padua, 1969; Kt. of Order of Merit of Repub. Address: Via Montello 6, 31100, Treviso, Italy. 43.

SPROUL, Robert Charles, b. 13 Feb. 1939. Theologian. Educ: B.A., Westminster Coll., Pa.; B.D., Pitts. Theological Sem.; Doct., Free Univ. of Amsterdam. Appts. incl: Asst. Prof., Biblical & Theological Studies, Gordon Coll., Wenham, Mass., 1966-68; Asst. Prof., Philosophical Theol., Conwell Schl. of Theol., Phila., Pa., 1968-69; Min. of Theol., College Hill United Presby. Ch., Cinn., Ohio, 1969-71; Staff Theologian, Ligonier Valley Study Ctr., Pa., 1971-; Vis. Prof. of Apologetics, Gordon-Conwell Theological Sem., 1971-; Lectr., num. Colls. & Confs. inclng. Harvard Christian Fellowship. Mbrship: Eta Sigma Phi. Publs. incl: The Symbol; The Psychology of Atheism (in preparation). Contbr. to: Ency. of Christianity; jrnls. & periodicals. Hons: Philosophy Prize, Westminster Coll., New Wilmington, Pa., 1961. Address: R.D., Stahlstown, PA 15687, U.S.A. 6.

SPURLING, Arthur Dudley, b. 9 Nov. 1913. Barrister & Attorney. Educ: M.A., Trinity Coll., Oxford Univ.; Bermuda Scholar, 1930-33; Rhodes Scholar, 1933-36; called to English Bar, 1937, Bermuda Bar, 1938. Appts: Barrister & Attorney, Sr. Ptnr., Appleby Spurling & Kempe, Hamilton, Bermuda; Chmn., Law Reform Comm., 1969-; Speaker, House of Assembly, 1972-; Justice of the Peace. Mbrships: Royal Bermuda Yacht Club; Royal Hamilton Amateur Dinght Club; St. David's Co. Cricket Club, Bermuda; Pres., Bermuda Hist. Soc. Awarded C.B.E. Address: c/o Appleby, Spurling & Kempe, Reid House, Church St., Hamilton, Bermuda. 109.

SPURLOCK, Jack Marion, b. 16 Aug. 1930. Research Consultant, Biomedical Engineering. Educ: B.Ch.E., Univ. of Fla., 1952; M.S.Ch.E., Ga. Inst. Technol., 1958; Ph.D., 1961. Appts. incl: Rsch. Assoc., Ga. Inst. Technol., 1955-58; Instr., ibid, 1958-61; Asst. Prof., 1961-62; Mgr., Aerosci. Rsch. Dept., Martin Marietta Corp., Orlando, Fla., 1962-64; Dir., Engrng. Rsch. Dept., Atlantic Rsch. Corp., Alexandria, Va., 1964-69; Exec. V.P., Hlth. & Safety Rsch. Inst., Springfield, 1969-71; Sr. Rsch. Sci., Versar Inc., 1969-71; Pvte. Cons. to ind., univs. & govtl. agcies. in biomed., chem., environmental & systems engrng. & rsch. mgmt., 1971-. Fellowships: Am. Inst. Chems.; Royal Soc. Hlth.; Assoc. Fellow, Am. Inst. Aeronaut & Astronaut, & Aerospace Med. Assn. (V.P. Elect, Biomed. Scis. & Engrng. Br.); Mbr. var. profl. socs. inclng. Chmn., Comm., Soc. of Automotive Engrs. Jt. Author, Research & Development Management & Author sev. sci. papers. Patentee. Address: 6144 Roxbury Ave., Springfield, VA 22152, U.S.A. 7, 14, 125.

SPURR, Rita (Mrs. Leonard D. Spurr). Writer; Poet; Lecturer. Educ: B.A., Univ. of Manchester. Appts: Dept. Dir., Czech Refugee Trust; Editorian Info. Serv., UNRRA; Lectr. & Orgr., Educ. & Drama, H.M. Forces; holds Editl. Posns. w. publng. houses & jrnls.; Festivals Adjudicator. Mbrships. incl: Poetry Soc. of Gt. Britain; Hon. Poetry Advsr., Writers' Guild; Lancs. Authors' Assn.; Chmn., Camden Poetry Grp.; Fndn. Fellow, Int. Poetry Soc. Publd: Footprint in Snow, 1954. Contbr. poems to anthols. & jrnls. in U.K., U.S.A., Canada, Australia & N.Z. Hons. incl: Diurna actu award, Manifold, 1966. Address: Flat 4, 7 Netherhall Gdns., Hampstead, London NW3 5RW, U.K. 11, 137, 138.

SPUT, Murray, b. 25 Apr. 1923. Architect. Educ: Cert. Arch. Drawing & Building Construction, Pratt Inst., Brooklyn, N.Y.; B.Arch., Columbia Univ., N.Y.C., 1958. Appts. incl: Draftsman, C. B. Meyers Archs., N.Y.C., 1951-54; Job Captain, Skidmore Owings & Merrill, Archs., 1954-62; Project Arch., Gruzen & Ptnrs. & Predecessor Firm, 1962-66; Sr Assoc., ibid, 1966-68; Assoc. Ptnr., i/c of Hosps. & Health Facilities, 1968-. Mbrships. incl: Tech. Comm., Am. Inst. of Archs. N.Y. Chapt.; Hosp. & Health Facilities, ibid; N.Y. Soc. of Archs.; Pratt Architectural Club. Address: 1821 Glenn Lane, Merrick, NY 11566, U.S.A. 6.

SPYRIDAKIS, Constantinos, b. 21 May 1903. Educationist. Educ: Classical Philol., Athens Univ.; Classical Philol. & Ancient Hist., Univ. of Berlin, Germany. Appts. incl: Tchr., Secondary Educ., Pancyprian Gymnasium, Nicosia, Cyprus, 1923-31, 1934-35; Asst. Dir., ibid, 1935-36; Dir., ibid, 1936-60; Pres., Greek Bd. of Educ., Cyprus; Pres., Greek Communual Chmbr., Cyprus, 1960-65; Min. of Educ., Cyprus, 1965-70. Mbrships. incl: Pres., Soc. of Cypriot Studies, Nicosia, 1936-; Pres., Greek Intellectual Soc., Cyprus, 1947-; Pres., Assn. of Greek Philologists, Cyprus, 1962-74; Corres. Mbr., Acad. of Athens & many other assns. in Greece. Publs. incl: Evagoras T, King of Salamis Cyprus (German & Greek); Kings of Cyprus (Greek); Brief History Of Cyprus (Greek, English, Arabic). Hons. incl: Gold Medal, Goethe Inst., Munich, Germany; Gold Medal, Ch. of Cyprus. Address: St. Helena St. 8B, Nicosia, Cyprus.

SSEBUNNYA-KASULE, Robert Bellerman, 31 Dec. 1942. Company Executive. Educ: Dip. in Jrnlsm., Univ. of Nairobi/I.P.I. Zurich; Dip. in Marketing & P.R., Makerere Univ., Kampala, Uganda; Dip. in Export Marketing, Helsinki Schl. of Econs. & Bus.Admin., Finland. Appts: Asst. P.R. & Marketing Off., Madhvani Grp.,

1965, P.R., Marketing & Advt. Mgr., 1970; Acting Gen. Mgr., Mulux Ltd., bulb factory, 1972, & Gen. Mgr., 1972; Exec. Dir., Mulux & Mulbox, cardboard factory; Alternating Exec. Dir., Textiles Div., Uganda Dev. Corp., 1973; Mng. Dir., Mfg. Stationers Ltd., 1974; Councillor & Chmn., Pub. Hlth. Comm., Jinja Municipal Coun.; Sec. & Acting Pres., Jinja Chmbr. of Comm. & Ind.; Treas., Jt. Advsry. Welfare Coun. Mbrships: Chmn., Uganda YMCA Personnel Coun.; Treas., Rotary Club. Address: P.O. Box 22358, Nairobi, Kenya. 135.

STAAB, Heinz A., b. 26 Mar. 1926. Professor of Chemistry; Institute Director. Educ: Dipl. Chem., Tübingen Univ., 1952; Dr. rer. nat., 1954, Dr.med., 1959, Heidelberg Univ. Appts: Rsch. Assoc., Max Planck Inst. for Med. Rsch., 1954-59; Asst. Prof., 1959, Assoc. Prof., 1961, Dept. of Chem., Univ. of Heidelberg; Prof., Organic Chem. & Dir., Inst. of Organic Chem., 1962-; Dean, Fac. of Sci., 1968; V.P., Univ. of Heidelberg, 1969. Mbrships: Max Planck Soc.; Acad. of Sci., Heidelberg, & Sec., Div. of Maths. & Sci.; German Chem. Soc.; Am. Chem. Soc.; Chem. Soc., London. Publs: 150 sci. papers; Ed., var. profl. jrnls. Address: Schloss-Wolfsbrunnenweg 43, 69 Heidelberg, German Fed. Repub. 43, 50, 92.

STAATS, Elmer Boyd, b. 6 June 1914. Public Administrator. Educ: B.A., McPherson Coll., Kan., 1935; M.A., Univ. of Kan., Lawrence, 1936; Ph.D., Univ. of Minn., Mpls., 1939. Appts. incl: Staff, Asst. to Dir., Asst. Dir., Exec. Asst. Dir., Dpty. Dir., Bur. of the Budget, 1939-53; Asst. Dir. & Dpty. Dir., ibid, 1958-66; Rsch. Dir., Marshall Field & Co., Chgo., 1953; Exec. Officer, Ops. Coord. Bd., Nat. Security Coun., 1954-58; Comptroller Gen. of the U.S., 1966-. Mbrships. incl: Bd. Govs., Int. Org. of Supreme Audit Instns., 1969-; Bd. Dirs., Am. Acad. Pol. & Soc. Sci., 1966-; Am. Soc. Pub. Admin.; Am. Pol. Sci. Assn.; Nat. Planning Assn.; Fed. Govt. Accts. Assn.; Phi Beta Kappa; Pi Sigma Alpha; Beta Alpha Psi; Alpha Kappa Psi. Publs: Personnel Standards in the Special Security Program, 1939; articles in profl. jrnls. Recip., sev. awards. Address: 5011 Overlook Rd., N.W., Washington, DC 20016, U.S.A. 2, 14, 114, 128, 130.

STABELL, Waldemar Christian, b. 3 Jan. 1913. Painter. Educ: Studied art at the Anglo-French Art Ctr., London, U.K., Brighton Coll. of Art, State Acad., Oslo & Royal Acad., Copenhagen, Denmark. m. Margit Baugsto; Two Children. Mbrships. incl: Fndr. & Bd. Mbr., Voss Summer Schl. of Fine Arts, Voss, Norway; Chmn., Bergen Arts Soc., Norway, 1969-. Creative Works incl: One Man Exhibs., Bergens Kunstforening, 1938, '53, '63, Gall. Per Oslo, 1953, Oslo Kunstforening, 1965, St. George's Gall., London, U.K., 1947-50; Gall. Bernheim-Jeune, Paris, France, 1948; Archer Gall., London U.K., 1952, N.Y. Vision Ctr. Gall., London, 1964; Grp. Exhibs. incl. Spring Exhib. of Mod. Paintings, St. George's Gall., London, 1949; Portrait of the Artist, ibid, 1950, Artists of Fame & Promise, Leicester Gall., 1952-61; Sev. permanent collects.; Contbr. to The Norseman, London, Bergens Tidende, Morgenavisen, Bergen, Aftenposten, Morgenbladet, Kunst og Kultur, Oslo. Address: Sydneskleven 31, 5000 Bergen, Norway. 19, 133.

STACEY, Nicholas Anthony Howard, b. 5 Dec. 1920. Economist. Educ: Birmingham Univ., U.K., 1938-41; London Univ., 1942-43; Fellow, Chartered Inst. of Secs., 1970. Appts: Ldr. Writer, Fin. Times, 1944-45; Asst. Sec., i/c

Parliamentary Bus. & Rsch.; Ed., Jrnl. of Acctcy., Assn. of Cert. & Corp. Accts., 1946-51; Vis. Schlr., Columbia Univ., 1951-53; Econ. & Mktng. Advsr., GEC, 1954-62; Fndr.-Mng. Dir., Chesham Amalgamations & Investments, 1962. Mbr., Reform Club, London. Publs: English Accountancy 1900-1954: A Study in Social & Economic History, 1954; The Changing Pattern of Distribution, 1958; Industrial Market Research: Management & Technique, 1963; Mergers in Modern Business, 1966. Hons: Sr. Smith-Mundt Rsch. Fellow, u.S. Govt., 1951-53; Fulbright Travelling Fellow, 1951-53. Address: 36 Chesham Place, London, SW1X 8HE, U.K. 3.

STACEY, Tom, b. 11 Jan. 1930. Publisher; Author. Educ: Worcester Coll., Oxford, 1950-51. Appts: Staff Writer, Picture Post, 1952-53, (London) Daily Express "Explorer", 1954, Montreal Star, 1955-56; Diplomatic Corresp., Daily Express, 1956-60; Chief Roving Corresp., Sunday Times, 1960-65; Columnist (London) Evening Standard, 1965-68; Ed., Corresps. World Wide, 1968-, Chambers' Ency. Yearbook, 1969-; Mng. Dir., Tom Stacey Ltd., 1969-. Mbrships. incl: Royal Inst. Int. Affairs; Royal Geog. Soc.; White's Club. Publs. incl: Immigration & Enoch Powell, 1971; Today's World, 1968. Hons: Llewelyn Rhys Mem. Prize, 1953; Granada Award (as for. corresp.), 1960. Address: 128 Kensington Church St., London W8, U.K. 3, 30.

STACK, George Joseph, b. 8 Nov. 1931. University Professor. Educ: B.A., Pace Univ., N.Y.C., 1960; M.A., Pa. State Univ., 1962; Ph.D., ibid, 1964. Appts. incl: Instr. in Humanities, Pa. State Univ., 1962; Instr.-Asst. Prof. in Philos., C.W. Post Coll. of L.I. Univ., 1963-67; Asst.-Assoc. Prof. of Philos., SUNY at Brockport, 1967-70; Prof. of Philos., Chmn., Dept. of Philos., ibid, 1970-. Mbrships. incl: Am. Philos. Assn.; Delta Tau Kappa; Edit. Advsr., Folia-Humanistica, Barcelona, Spain; Advsr., Ctr. for Philosophic Exchange, Brockport Coll. Publs. incl: Berkeley's Analysis of Perception, 1970, reprinted 1972; contbr. of 77 philosoph. essays & 73 reviews to profl. jrnsl. Hons: Nat. Defense Educ. Act Grad. Fellowship, 1960-63; Nat. Endowment for Humanities Summer Fellowship, 1969; SUNY Rsch. Fellowship, 1970. Address: Philosophy Dept., SUNY at Brockport, NY 14420, U.S.A. 2, 13, 15, 30.

STACKHOUSE, Ella Bernice, b. 5 Apr.1909. Consultant in Urban Home Economics. Educ: B.S., Lincoln Univ., Jefferson City, Mo.; M.S., Cornell Univ., Ithaca, N.Y.; Ph.D., Colo. Christian Coll., Evergreen; Additional study, var. colls. Appts. incl: Home Economist, Univ. of Mo., 1958-62; Urban Extension Home Economist, ibid, 1962-70; W. Central Dist. Dir. on Home Agt., State Org.; Cons., Urban Home Econs., Environmental Rsch. & Dev. Fndn., 1971-74. Mbrships. incl: Nat. Am. Home Econs. Assn.; Hon. Life mbr., Nat. Am. Extension Home Economists; Alpha Tau Epsilon Sigma Phi; Kan. City Consumer Assn.; Bd. mbr. & news reporter, Mo. Assn. for Soc. Welfare. Publs. incl: Fun in the Kitchen with Commodity Food, 1963; Quick Tips on Food Stamp Management for Good Nutrition, A Shopper's Guide, forthcoming. Recip. of num. hons. Address: 5240 Cypress, Kan. City, MO 64130, U.S.A. 5.

STACKHOUSE, Roy David. Real Estate Developer & Investor. Appts: Engaged in gen. construction, mortgage financing, 1936-; Pres., Gen. Mgr., Stackhouse Corp., Titusville, Fla. Mbrships: Comm. 100, Titusville; Pres., N. Brevard Dev. Commn.; Organizing Pres., ibid,

1969; Past V.P., Chmbr. of Comm.; Past V.P., Kiwanis Int.; Past Chmn., Bd. of Trustees, 1st United Methodists. Recip., Man of the Yr. award, Titusville Chmbr. of Comm., 1965. Address: P.O. Box 2110, Titusville, FL 32780, U.S.A. 2, 7, 125.

STACKPOLE, Edouard Alexandre, b. 7 Dec. 1903. Historian; Museum Director. Appts: Assoc. Ed., The Inquirer & Mirror, Nantucket, Mass., U.S.A., 1932-52 & 1966-71; Curator, Marine Histl. Assn., Mystic Seaport, Conn., 1953-66; Pres., The Coffin Schl., 1967-; Dir., Peter Foulger Mus., Nantucket, 1971-. Mbrships: Sec., The Winter Club, 1940-49; Cornet, Sons of the Revolution, 1941-42; Pres., Nantucket Histl. Assn., 1938-52 & 1966-71, Histn., 1971-; Royal Soc. of Arts, London, U.K. Publs: Smugglers' Luck, 1931; Privateer Ahoy, 1937; Rambling Through the Streets & Lanes of Nantucket, 1946, 4th edit. 1970; Scrimshaw at Mystic Seaport, 1956; The Story of Yankee Whaling, 1960; Whales & Destiny, 1971; Nantucket in Color, 1974; 13 other books; Num. contbns. to mags & newspapers. Recip., M.A., Yale Univ., 1964. Address: The Peter Foulger Museum, Nantucket, MA 02554, U.S.A. 6.

STAFFORD, (Brigadier General) Thomas P., b 17 Sept. 1930. NASA Astronaut. Educ: B.S., U.S. Naval Acad., 1952. Appts: Commnd. in U.S.A.F. after graduation; Chief, Performance Br., U.S.A.F. Aerospace Rsch. Pilot Schl., Edwards; Instr., flight test trng. & specialized acad. subjs., ibid; Selected as astronaut, NASA, 1962; Backup pilot, Gemini 3 flight; Co-astronaut w. cmd. pilot Walter M. Schirra, Gemini 6 flight, 1965; Cmd. pilot, Gemini 9 mission, 1966; Backup Cmdr., Apollo 7; Spacecraft Cmdr., Apollo 10, 1969; Chief, Astronaut Off., 1969-71; Dpty. Dir., Flight Crew Ops., 1971-74; Currently involved in preparations for role as cmdr., U.S. flight crew, for Apollo-Soyuz Test Proj. mission, scheduled for launch 1975. Mbrships: Fellow, Am. Astronautical Soc.; Soc. of Experimental Test Pilots; Explorers Club; Hon. Life mbr., Am. Fedn. of Radio & TV Artists. Co-author, Pilot's Handbook for Performance Flight Testing & Aerodynamics Handbook for Performance Flight Testing. Hons. incl: Disting. Serv. Medal, NASA; 2 Exceptional Serv. Medals, ibid; Cert. of Commendation, J.S.C., 1970. Recip., hon. degrees, several univs. Address: NASA, Lyndon B. Johnson Space Ctr., Houston, TX, U.S.A.

STAGGERS, Harley O., b. 3 Aug. 1907. Congressman. Educ: A.B., Emory & Henry Coll., Emory, Va., 1931; Grad. work, Duke Univ. Appts. incl: Sheriff, Mineral Co.; 1937-41; W. Va. State Dir., Off. of War Info.; Navigator, Atlantic & Pacific Theaters, U.S. Naval Air Corps., WWII; Mineral Co. Dir., Rent Control; Elected to 81st Congress, 1948, & subsequent Congresses; Served as Mbr., House Post Off. & Civil Serv. Comm., Chmn., Subcomm. on Census & Govt. Stats. & Mbr., House Comm. on Veterans' Affairs; Asst. Whip, U.S. House of Reps., 1955-; Chmn., House Interstate & For. Commerce Comm., 1966-. Mbrships. incl: Am. Legion; V.F.W.; AMVETS; Disabled Am. Veterans; W. Va. Farm Bur.; Keyser-Mineral Co. Chmbr. of Comm.; Past Pres., W. Va. State Moose Assn.; Former Dist. Gov., W. Va. Lions Clubs. Hons: LL.D., Emory & Henry Coll., Emory, Va., Davis & Elkins Coll., W. Va., W. Va. Univ., Morgantown, & W. Va. Wesleyan Coll., Buckhannon. Address: Congress of the U.S., House of Reps., Wash. DC 20515, U.S.A.

STAHL, Frank L., b. 29 Jan. 1920. Structural Engineer. Educ: B.S., Zurich Tech. Coll., Switzerland, 1946. Appts: Draftsman, Amman & Whitney, N.Y.C., U.S.A., 1946; Designer, ibid; Structural Engr.; Proj. Engr.; Assoc. i/c. contract specification, mats. rsch., & cost estimating dept. Mbrships: Fellow, Am. Soc. of Civil Engrs.; Chmn., Subcomm. for Steel Reinforcement, Am. Soc. for Testing & Mats.; Exec. Comm., Rsch. Coun. on Riveted & Bolted Structural Joints, Engrng. Fndn.; Am. Inst. of Steel Construction. Fabricator & Constructor, Verrazano-Narrows Bridge. Contbr., articles on quality control in construction, to sev. mags. Recip., Thomas Fich Rowland Prize, Am. Soc. of Civil Engrs., 1967. Address: 209-11 28th Rd., Bayside, NY 11360, U.S.A. 6.

STAHR, Elvis J(acob), Jr., b. 9 Mar. 1916. Conservationist; Lawyer; Educator. Educ: A.B., Univ. of Ky., 1936; B.A., Oxford Univ., U.K., 1938; B.C.L., 1939; M.A., 1943; Dip., Chinese Lang., Yale Univ., 1943. Appts. incl: Lawyer, Mudge Stern Williams & Tucker, N.Y., 1939-47; Assoc. Prof., Law, Univ. of Ky., 1947; Prof., ibid, 1948-56; Dean, 1948-56; Provost, 1954-56; Vice Chancellor, Univ. of Pitts., 1957-58; Pres., W. Va. Univ., 1958-61; Sec. of the Army, Wash. D.C., 1961-62; Pres., Ind. Univ., 1962-68; Pres., Nat. Audubon Soc., 1968-; Mbr., Aviation Advsry. Commn., U.S., 1970-73; Mbr., U.S. Deleg., U.N. Conf. Human Environment, Stockholm, Sweden, 1972; Mbr., Jt. U.S.-U.S.S.R. Comm. Cooperation Protection Environment, 1973. Mbrships. incl: Phi Beta Kappa; Assn. of Am. Rhodes Scholars Co-Author, Economics of Pollution, 1971; Nat. Chmn., USO, Inc., 1973-; Trustee, Sigma Chi Fndn., 1973-; Bd. Dirs., Am. Cancer Soc.; Regional Plan Assn.; Comm. Econ. Dev. Contbr. to var. publs. Hons. incl: 23 hon. degrees; Bronze Star Medal, 1944; Oak Leaf Cluster, 1945; Order of Grand Cross of Peru, 1962; Centennial Medal & Alumni Hall of Fame, Ky. Univ., 1965; Sesquicentennial Medal, Mich. Univ., 1967; Disting. Civilian Serv. Medal, U.S. Dept. of Army, 1971. Address: Martin Dale, Greenwich, CT 06830, U.S.A. 2, 6, 10, 12, 13, 34.

STAKMAN, Elvin Charles, b. 17 May 1885. Plant Pathologist. Educ: B.A., Univ. of Minn., 1906; M.A., ibid, 1910; Ph.D., 1913. Appts: Mbr. fac., Univ. of Minn., 1909-53; Prof. of Plant Pathol., 1918-53; Hd., Sect. of Plant Pathol., 1913-40; Hd., Div. of Plant Pathol. & Botany, 1940-53; Currently Prof. Emeritus; Pathologist, i/c barberry eradication campaign, U.S. Dept. Agric., 1918; Pathologist, agt., ibid, 1919-55; Collaborator, 1955-; Cons., Rockefeller Fndn., 1941-. Mbrships. incl: Pres., AAAS, 1949; Nat. Acad. Sci.; Am. Philos. Soc.; Pres., Am. Phytopath. Soc., 1922; Am. Acad. Arts & Sci.; Hist. Sci. Soc.; Bot. Soc. Am.; Hon. mbr., Am. Coll. Allergists. Publs: Principles of Plant Pathology (w. J.G. Harrar), 1957; Campaigns against Hunger (co-author), 1967; Num. bulletins, articles in profl. jrnls. Hons. incl: Curz de Boyaca, Colombia, 1964; Cosmos Club Award (1st), 1964; Award of Distinction (1st), Am. Phytopath. Soc., 1967. Address: Inst. of Agric., Univ. of Minn., St. Paul, MN 55101, U.S.A. 2, 14.

STALEY, Thomas F., b. 13 Aug. 1935. Professor of Education. Educ: B.A., B.S., Regis Coll., 1957; M.A., Univ. of Tulsa, Okla., 1958; Ph.D., Univ. of Pitts., Pa., 1962. Appts. incl: Asst. Prof., Rollins Coll., Winter Pk., Fla., Vis. Prof., Univ. of Pitts., Summer 1962-67; Asst. Prof., Univ. of Tulsa, 1962-67; Assoc. Prof., ibid, 1967-69; Prof. of Engl. & Dean, Grad. Schl., ibid, 1969-. Mbrships. incl: AAUP; MLA;

S.-Ctrl. MLA; Chmn., Comp. Lit. Sect., ibid, 1965-66; Chmn., Anglo-Irish Sect., 1970-71; James Joyce Fndn; Chmn., Mbrship. Comm., Midwest Assn. of Grad. Schls., 1973-74. Publs. incl: James Joyce Today (Ed.), 1966, translated into Italian, 1973; James Joyce's Portrait of the Artist, 1968; Italo Svevo: Essays on his Work (Ed.), 1969; Approaches to Ulysses: Ten Essays (w. B. Benstock), 1970; Contbr. to schol. jrnls. Hons. incl: Fulbright Rsch. Prof., Trieste, Italy, 1966-67; Danforth Assoc., 1962-66. Address: Graduate School, University of. Tulsa, 600 S. College, Tulsa, OK 74104, U.S.A. 2, 13.

STALLARD, Jacklyn Joyce (Mrs. Roger Stallard). Elementary School Teacher. Educ: Radford State Tchrs. Coll.; B.A., Emory & Henry Coll., 1970. Appts: Lorain Co. schls., Ohio, 1959-61; Tazewell Co. schls., Va., 1968-74. Num. mbrships. incl: Past Pres., Tazewell Co. PTA Coun.; Past Pres., Jewel Ridge PTA; Intermediate Woman's Club; Ldr., Brownie & Cub Scouts; Ft. Witten Square Dance Club; Fellowship Class; Fidelis Grp.; Past Mbr., Nat. Beta Soc. & Beta Club. Hons: Emily Post Award, 1952; Address: Box 175, Richlands, VA 24641, U.S.A. 2, 125, 138.

STALLINGS, James Henry, b. 20 Sept. 1892. Principal Research Specialist, Soil Conservation Service, U.S. Dept. of Agriculture. Educ: B.S., Tex. A & M Univ., 1914; M.S., ibid, 1917; Ph.D., la. State Univ., 1926. Appts. incl: Regional Dir. Soil Conservation Serv., U.S. Dept. Agric., N.C., 1934-37; Org., Flood Control Prog., ibid, Wash. D.C., 1937-41; Mbr., War Food Admin., Staff, Wash., D.C., 1942-44; Prin. Rsch. Specialist, Soil Conservation Serv., 1945-59. Mbrships. incl: N.Y. Acad. Sci.; AAAS; Am. Soc. Agronomy; Soil Sci. Soc. Am.; Sigma Xi; Chmn., Agricl. Comm., Int. Rotary Club, Shreveport, La., 1929-33. Publs: Soil Science, 1957; Soil Use & Improvement, 1957; jrnl. articles; Soil Sci. Ed., Biol. Abstracts, 1952, 3rd. Edit.; Webster's Int. Dict., 1968. Address: 5146 Neb. Ave. N.W., Wash., DC 20008, U.S.A. 2, 7, 14, 130.

STALLMAN, Robert Wooster, b. 27 Sept. 1911. Emeritus Pressor. Educ: B.A., Univ. of Wis., 1933; M.A., 1939; Ph.D., 1942. Appts. incl: Lectr., Katharine Gibbs Schl. of Boston, 1944-46; Asst. Prof., Univ. of Kan., 1946-49; Assoc. Prof., Univ. of Conn., Storrs, 1949-52; Prof., ibid, 1952-74; Emeritus, 1974-; Univ. of Strasbourg, France, 1958-59; Camargo Fellow, Cassis, 1974-75. Mbrships. incl: MLA; Coll. Engl. Assn.; Hon., Phi Beta Kappa. Ed./Co-Ed.: The War Dispatches of Stephen Crane, 1964; The New York City Sketches of Stephen Crane, 1866; The Sullivan Country Tales & Sketches of Stephen Crane, 1968; The Stephen Crane Reader, 1972. Author: The Houses that James Built, 1961; Stephen Crane: A Biography, 1968, 73; Stephen Crane: A Critical Bibliography, 1972; num. articles. Recip., sev. acad. awards. Address: 1 Westwood Rd., Storrs, CT 06268, U.S.A. 2, 3, 6, 13, 15, 30.

STAMM, Elisabeth, b. 14 Aug. 1890. Painter; Graphic Artist. Educ: Studies w. Alcide Le Beau; Art Schls., Berne, Switzerland, 1906, & Geneva, 1907-10. Mbrships: Pres., Bernese Sect., Swiss Soc. of Women Painters, Sculptors & Artisans, 1937-54; Sec., SAFFA Art Exhib., Berne, 1914; Pres., SAFFA Art Exhib., Zurich, 1958; Lyceum Club. Oil-paintings & lithographs acquired by Swiss Govt. Recip., Silver Medal, City of Paris, for collaboration at Int. Exhib. of Women Artists, 1958. Address: Quartierweg 21, 3074 Muri/Bern, Switzerland. 105.

STANCZYKOWSKI, Casimir G., b. 25 Jan. 1929. Business executive. Educ: Sir George

Williams Univ. (Bus. Schl.), 1949; McGill Univ. (Commerce), 1957. Appts. incl: served WWII, Polish Underground Army; Prod., Canada's first continental lang. broadcasts; w. CHLP, 1950-57; CJMS, 1957-58; CHRS, 1957-62; CFCF, 1962; Pres., 1959-72, Gen. Mgr., Chmn. of Bd., 1972-, & Gen. Mgr., Chateau Broadcasting Co. Ltd., (CFMB); Pres., C.G. Stanczykowski & Assocs. Ltd., & Amalgamated Broadcasting Systems Ltd. Mbrships. incl: Pres., 1968-72, Hon. Pres, 1972-, Canadian Citizenship Fedn.; First V.P., Montreal Citizenship Coun.. 1969-71; Broadcast Exec. Soc.; Canadian Assn. of Broadcasters; Montreal Mus. of Fine Arts; U.N. Assn., Canada; Int. Ctr. of Winnipeg; Canadian Inst. of Int. Affairs. Hons. incl: LL.D., Sir George Williams Univ., 1972; Mbr., Order of Canada, 1973; Howard Caine Mem. Award, 973; num. awards for war serv. & from soc. and profl. orgs. Address: CFMB Radio, 2015 Drummond St:, 8th floor, Montreal, P.Q. H3G 1W8, Canada. 88.

STANETZKY, Jan, b. 22 Oct. 1901. Physician; Specialist in Microbiology. Educ: M.D., Breslau, Poland; Ph.D., Lemberg; D.M.D., Poznan. Appts: Prof., HS, Pol., 1929-39; Lectr., For. Langs., to Offs. of Red Army, 1939-41; Prof., Inst. Food Ind., 1944-45; Hd., Inst. Pub. Hlth., Breslau, 1953-57; Hd., Bacteriol. Dept., Govt. Hosp., Israel, 1957-. Mbrships: Israel Med. & Microbiol. Assns. Publs: The Prayer of Grass, 1926; The Book of Songs, 1928. Profl. papers, biochem., bacteriol., immunol., microbiol. Hons: Sci. Studies Grant, Israel Min. of Hlth., 1967; WHO Grants, 1969, 1971. Address: 11 Bney Moshe St., Tel Aviv 62 308, Israel. 55, 94.

STANG, Gunvor (Mrs.), b. 9 May 1903. Educator; Civic Worker. Educ: Tchrs. Exam., 1923; Oslo Univ., Norway, 1924-26. Appts: Tchr., Faginborg Schl., Oslo, 1923-24, 26-27; Sec., 1934-40; Cons., Hüsmorbladet, organ of Norwegian Housewives Union, 1948-66; Mbr., State Supvsry. Coun. for Labour concerned w. domestic serv., 1948-69; Mbr., Working Comm. for Housewives Holidays, 1952-53; Housewives Holiday Comm, State Holiday Coun., 1953-61; Mbr., Comm. for the Revision of Interim Laws on Working Conditions for Domestic Servants, 1954-60. Mbrships: Hon., Norwegian Housewives Union, 1965; Soroptimist Int.; Drammen Club; Norden Assn. for Nordic Coop. Author of newspaper articles on soc. questions. Recip., King Olav V Gold Medal for Merit, 1964. Address: Wilhelmsgate 10 A, Oslo 1, Norway.

STANGE, Hans O.H., b. 13 Nov. 1903. Professor of Sinology. Educ: Univ. of Goettingen; Dr. phil. 1934, Dr. phil. habil., 1939, Univ. of Berlin. Appts: Asst., Univ. of Berlin, 1933; Lectr., ibid, 1939; Dir.,Sinol. Seminar, Univ. of Goettingen, 1939; Prof., Sinol., ibid, 1953. Mbrships: German Oriental Soc. Publs: Author, co-author, books; Translator from the Chinese. Ed. w. Rüdenberg, German/Chinese Dictionary, 1963. Hons: 1st Prize, German Acad., Munich, 1939. Address: Konigsberger Str. 6, D-3406 Bovenden, German Fed. Repub.

STANKARD, Francis X., b. 13 Jan. 1932. Banker. Educ: Coll. of Holy Cross, 1953; Fellow, Brookings Instn., Wash., D.C., 1967; Harvard Sr. Mgrs. Prog., Switzerland, 1973. Appts: Asst. Treas., Chase Manhattan Bank, 1959-62; Asst. V.P., ibid, 1962-64; V.P., 1964-70; Sr. V.P., 1970-; Dir., Chase Manhattan Int. Banking Corp., All States Commercial Bills Ltd.; Dir. & V.P., Chase Manhattan Overseas Banking Corp.; Dir., Chase Manhattan Overseas Corp., Chase Manhattan Investment Corp.,

Thailand Ltd., Far East Am. Coun.; Am. Australian Assn.; Managed Deposits Ltd.; Alliance Holdings: Afghanistan Bank; Commercial Bank of Dubai; Japan Soc., Inc. Hons: One of Outstanding Young Men of Am., 1966. Address: 10 Autumn Lane, Middletown, NJ 07748, U.S.A.

STANLEY, C. Maxwell, b. 16 June 1904. Consulting Engineer. Educ: B.S., Univ. of Iowa, 1926; M.S., ibid, 1930. Appts. incl: Ptnr., Stanley Engrng. Co., 1939-61; Pres., 1961-66; Pres., Stanley Cons., Inc., 1966-71; Chmn., Bd., 1971-; Pres., Stanley Cons., Ltd., Liberia, 1959-; Mng. Dir., Stanley Cons., Ltd., Nigeria, 1960-67; Dir., 1967-; Chmn. Bd., Hon Inds., Inc. & Prime-Mover Co. Mbrships. incl: Am. Soc. Civil Engrs.; IEEE; Am. Soc. Mech. Engrs.; Am. Inst. Cons. Engrs.; Nat. Soc. Prof. Engrs.; Am. Water Works Assn.; Nat. Planning Assn.; Chmn., Confs on UN of the Next Decade, 1965-; Pres., Univ. of Iowa Fndn., 1971- (Dir., 1966-71); Chmn., Stategy for Peace Confs., 1962-; Chmn., World Assn. World Feds., 1958-65. Publs: Waging Peace, 1956; The Consulting Engineer, 1961; over 50 profl. articles. Hons. incl: Dr. Humane Letters, Iowa Wesleyan Coll., 1961; Award, Nat. Soc. Profl. Engrs., 1965; D. Humanities, Univ. of Manila, 1970. Address: Stanley Bldg., Muscatine, IA 52761, U.S.A. 2, 8, 12, 16, 26, 116, 123.

STANTON, Jack G.B., b. 31 Aug. 1919. Baptist Minister. Educ: Wm. Jewel Coll., Liberty, Mo.; B.A., Shurtleff Coll., Alton, Ill.; B.D., Ctrl. Bapt. Theol. Sem., Kan. City, Kan.; Th.D., Luther Rice Theol. Sem., Jacksonville, Fla. Appts: Pastor; Dir. of Evangelism, Kan. Convention of Southern Bapts.; Dir. of Evangelism, Colo. Bapt. Gen. Convention, territory inclng. Colo., Wyo., N. & S. Dakota & Western Neb.; Assoc. Dir., Div. of Evangelism of Home Mission Bd. of Southern Bapt. Convention i/c of Personal Evangelism; Dir., Mass Evangelism, Div. of Evangelical Home Mission Bd., Southern Bapt. Convention. Publs: Co-Author, Southern Baptist Handbook on Evangelism; Training Materials for WIN Lay Evangelism Schools; Training Materials for TELL Lay Evangelism Leadership Training Schools; How to Have a Full & Meaningful Life; articles in Southern Bapt. mags., jrnls. & curric. materials. Address: 1350 Spring St. N.W., Atlanta, GA 30309, U.S.A. 125.

STANTON, Jeanne Frances, b. 22 Jan. 1920. Attorney. Educ: B.A., Univ. of Cinn.; J.D., Salmon P. Chase Coll. of Law, 1968. Appts: Legal Asst., Proctor & Gamble, Cinn., 1952-54; Hd., Adv. Servs., Trade Practices Dept., Legal Div., ibid, 1954-; Mgr., Advtng. Servs., 1973-. Mbrships. incl: Int. Copyright Comm., Patent, Trademark & Copyright Law, Am. Bar Assn.; AAAS; Cinn. Law Lib.; Chmn., Uniform State Laws Comm., Ohio State Bar Assn.; Life, Vicksburg & Warren Co. Hist. Soc.; Cinn. Hist. Soc.; Benefactors Club, Salmon P.; Int. Oceanog. Fndn.; Chmn., Comm. Preservation of Hist. Documents, & Centennial Planning Comm., Cinn. Bar Assn. Off. Commentator, Australasia Bus. & Law Symposium, Auckland Univ., New Zealand, 1968. Author, "Cincinnati Lawyers in Business" in the Law in Southwestern Ohio (book). Address: 2302 E. Hill Ave., Cinn., OH 45208, U.S.A. 5, 8, 132.

STANTON, Royal Waltz, b. 23 Oct. 1916. Choral Director; Music Educator. Educ: B.E., UCLA, 1939; M.A., 1946. Appts. incl: Chmn., Music Dept., Long Beach City Coll., Calif., 1950-61; Dir., L.A. Bach Fest., 1959-60; Chmn., Fine Arts Div., Foothill Coll., Los Altos, 1961-67; Chmn., Fine Arts Div., De

Anza Coll., Cupertino, 1967-72; Fndr.-Dir., Schola Cantorum, ibid, 1964-; Dir., Choral Orgs., ibid, 1972-. Mbrships. incl: ASCAP; Am. Musicol. Soc.; Music Educrs. Nat. Conf.; NEA; Am. Choral Dirs. Assn.; Am. Choral Fndn. Publs: The Dynamic Choral Conductor, 1971; Steps to Singing for Voice Classes, 1971; 80 compositions & choral arrangements. Recip., ASCAP Educl. Award, 1969, 70, 71, 72. Address: 22301 Havenhurst Drive, Los Altos, CA 94022, U.S.A. 30.

STAPP, Christopher Dennison, b. 12 Dec. 1943. Corporate Executive. Educ: B.S., Woodbury Coll., L.A., Calif., 1970; postgrad. work, ibid. Appts: Exec. Trng. Prog., var. posts to Asst. Sales Mgr., Air-Vent Aluminium Awning Co., Chino, Calif., 1962-66, Credit Mgr. & Asst. to Pres., 1968-71, Gen. Mgr. Northern Calif. Ops., V.P., & Sec. to Bd. of Dirs., 1971-; Mil. Serv., Intelligence Sect., U.S. Army Corps of Engrs., German Fed. Repub., 1966-68. Mbr., profl. assns. & schol. fraternities. Recip., U.S. Army medals & Citation w. Cert. Address: 3381 Pinewood Ct., Hayward, CA 94542, U.S.A.

STAPPER, Margaret Bray (Mrs. Bruno Stapper), b. 26 Feb. 1915. Assistant Professor. Educ: B.S., N. Tex. State Univ., 1935; M.S., ibid, 1945; N.Y. Univ., 1949, 53; Tex. Woman's Univ., 1954; Univ. of Tex., Austin. Appts: Asst. Prof., Hlth. & Phys. Educ. Mbrships. incl: Chmn., Tex. Div. of Girls & Women's Sports & Southern Dist., ibid.; Pres., Dist. Chmn., Tex. Assn. Hlth., Phys. Educ. & Recreation; V.P., Delta Kappa Gamma; Tex. Congress of Parents & Tchrs.; Delta Psi Kappa; State Pres. for Driver Safety & Educ., 1956. Has acted at TV tchr. on video-taped shows. Created Driver Educ. Courses for Edgewood Schl. Dist. Publs: Cross Word Puzzle, Soccer Rules; articles in sports jrnls. Hons: Hon. Award, TAHPER; Hon. Award, Region XX, Tex. State Tchrs. Assn.; 1973. Address: 319 Cloverleaf, San Antonio, TX 78209, U.S.A. 5, 7, 130, 138.

STARASOLER, Stanley, b. 13 Dec. 1921. Dentist. Educ; A.B., Wash. Sq. Coll., N.Y. Univ., 1944; D.D.S., Schl. of Dentistry, Univ. of Pitts., 1948; D.M.D., Schl. of Dental Med., ibid, 1970. Appts: Intern, Oral Surg. & Gen. Anesthesia, Greenpoint Hosp., Dept. of Hosp., NYC, 1948-49; Clin. Asst., Oral Surg. Dept., Greenpoint Hosp., 1950-60; Asst., ibid & Unit of Mt. Sinai Hosp., 1960-65; Sect. Chief, Oral Surg. Dept., Greenpoint Hosp. Unit of Brooklyn Jewish Hosp. & Med. Ctr., 1965-. Fellowships: Am. Soc. for Adv. of Gen Anesthesia in Dentistry, 1948; Int. Acad. of Anesthesiol., 1949; Royal Soc. of Hlth., London, 1973. Mbrships: AAAS; N.Y. Acad. Scis.; N.Y. Univ. Varsity Club; Am. Dental Assn.; N.Y. State Dental Soc.; Pan. Am. Med. Soc.; Pan Am. Odontological Assn.; Fed. Dentaire Int.; Pres., Jt. Dental Staffs, Greenpoint Hosp. & Jewish Hosp. of Brooklyn & Med. Ctr., 1968.; Century Club, Pitts. Univ. Contbr. to dentistry jrnls. Address: 8656 Woodhaven Blvd., Woodhaven, NY 11421, U.S.A. 6, 14, 57.

STARE, Dayle Horst, b. 24 Oct. 1942. Mathematician. Educ: A.B., Lebanon Valley Coll., Annville, Pa., 1964; M.A., Pa. State Univ., 1966; Univ. of Minn., 1968, Rutgers Univ., 1969, Courant Inst., N.Y. Univ., 1970. Appts. incl: Instr. of Maths., Susquehanna Univ., Selinsgrove, Pa., 1966-68; Asst. Prof. of Maths., Lebanon Valley Coll., Annville, 1968-72; Mathn., Provident Mutual Life Ins. Co. of Am., Phila., 1972-. Mbrships: Pi Mu Epsilon; Phi Theta Kappa; Math. Assn. of Am.; Free & Accepted Masons; Ancient Accepted Scottish

Rite Body. Contbr. to: Wide Band Recording of the Electrocardiogram & Coronary Heart Disease, (article) Am. Heart Jrnl.; Computor Progs. of Mid. Atlantic Educ. & Rsch. Ctr., 1971. Hons: Boy Scout, Order of Arrow, 1955; Nat. Sci. Fndn. Grant, Univ. of Minn., Rutgers Univ., & Courant Inst. Address: 410 Village Ln., Broomall, PA 19008, U.S.A. 6.

STARK, Claude Alan, b. 27 Apr. 1935. International Financier, Educ: B.A. (cum laude) Clark Univ.; M.B.A., Babson Coll.; B.D., (cum laude), Harvard Univ.; Ph.D., Boston Univ. Appts: Security Analyst, Nat. Shawmut Bank of Boston; Sr. Security Analyst, Fidelity Fund, Boston; Loan Officer, Export Import Bank of the U.S.; Economic Coun., U.S. Senate, Select Comm. on Small Business; Pres., Sodesmir, The Development Co. in the Congo, Kinshasa, Congo; Dir., Branden Press, Boston; Wallace Patriots Club, 1972; Min., Unitarian-Universalist Ch. Mbrships: Bankers Club of Am.; Trustee, Inst. for Expmtl. Psych., Phil.; Am. Chmbr. of Comm. in France; Mbr., Coun. for Latin Am.; Mbr. Fellow, President's Coun., AIM; Boston & Wash. Security Analysts Soc.; Chart. Fin. Analyst; Fed City Club (Wash. D.C.); Harvard Club (Boston); Down Town Club (ibid). Hons. incl: Certificate of Merit, U.S. Senate, 1967; Chief, Province of Kongo Ctrl.. Rep. of Zaire. 1969: Hon. Lt. Col.. Ala. State Militia, 1971. Address: Cape Cod, MA 02670, U.S.A. 7, 16, 22, 69.

STARK, Franklin Culver, b. 16 Apr. 1915. Lawyer. Educ: A.B., Dakota Wesleyan Univ., 1937; J.D., Northwestern Univ., 1940; LL.D., 1959. Appts: Admission Ill. Bar, 1940, Calif. Bar, 1946; Assoc., Sidney, McPherson, Austin & Burgess, Chgo., 1940-41, Fitzgerald, Abbott & Beardsley, Oakland, Calif., 1946-47; Sr. Mbr. firm, Stark, Stewart, Simon & Sparrowe, & Predecessors, Oakland, 1947-; Lectr., Univ. Calif. Schl. of Bus., 1946-66; Pres., Oakland Coun. of Chs., 1954-56; Bd. Dirs., Dakota Wesleyan Univ.; Chmn., Bd. Trustees, Calif.—Nev. Meth. Homes. Mbrships. incl: Am., Calif., Alameda Co. Bar Assns.; Am. Trial Lawyers Assn.; Phi Kappa Phi; Pi Kappa Delta; Phi Alpha Delta. Alumnus of Yr. for Notable Achievement, Dakota Wesleyan Univ., 1966. Address: 333 Wayne Ave., Oakland, CA 94606, U.S.A.

STARK, (Dame) Freya Madeline, D.B.E., b. 31 Jan. 1893. Explorer & Writer. Educ: Schl. of Oriental Studies, London Univ. Appts: joined Min. of Info., 1939, sent to Aden, 1939, Cairo, 1950, Baghdad, 1941, USA & Canada, 1944. Publs: The Valley of the Assassins, 1934; The Southern Gates of Arabia, 1936; Baghdad Sketches, 1937; Seen in the Hadramaut, 1938; A Winter in Arabia, 1936; Letters from Syria, 1942; East is West, 1945; Perseus in the Wind, 1948; Traveller's Prelude, 1950; Beyond Euphrates, 1951; The Coast of Incense, 1953; Ionia: A Quest, 1954; The Lycian Shore, 1956; Alexander's Path, 1958; Riding to the Tigris, 1959; Dust in the Lion's Paw, 1961; The Journey's Echo, 1963; Rome on the Euphrates, 1966; The Zodiac Arch, 1968; Space Time & Movement in Landscape, 1969; The Minaret of Djam, 1970; Turkey (w. F. Roiter), 1970. Hons: LL.D., Glasgow Univ., 1952; D.Litt., Durham Univ., 1970; Fndrs. Medal, Royal Geog. Soc., Sir Percy Sykes Medal, Royal Ctl. Asian Soc., Burton Medal, Royal Asiatic Soc., Mungo Park Medal, R. Scottish Geog. Soc. Address: Asolo, Treviso, Italy.

STARK, Jesse Donald, b. 3 Dec. 1899. Physician; Radiologist. Educ: A.B., Cornell Univ., 1921; M.D., Jefferson Med. Coll., 1925. Appts: Staff, Polyclin. Hosp., N.Y.C., 1934-35,

Metropol. Hosp., 1935-39; Cons. Roentgenologist, Ft. Jay, N.Y., 1935-41; Vis. Roentgenologist, Gouverneur Hosp., N.Y.C., 1939-41, Chief Roentgenologist, 1946-61; Attng. Cons. Roentgenologist, VA Hosp., Bronx, 1946-47; Instr., Radiol., N.Y. Univ Coll. Med., 1935-49, Asst. Clin. Prof., 1953-64, Attng. Radiologist, Clin., 1935-41; Asst. Clin. Prof., Radiol., N.Y. Univ.-Bellevue Post Grad. Med. Schl., 1950-53; Exec. Dir., X-Ray Dept., Bird S. coler Hosp., 1961-64; Roentgenologist, ibid, 1964-71; Dir., X-Ray Dept., Prospect Hosp., Bronx, 1968-; Chief, X-Ray Serv. & Instr., U.S. Mil. Acad., W. Pt., 1941-46. Mbr., num. profl. orgs. Hons. incl: num. mil. hons.; num. Fellowships & awards from for. nations inclng. French Legion of Hon. Address: 1082 Park Ave., N.Y., NY 10028, U.S.A. 6.

STARKE, Catherine Juanita, b. 5 April 1913. Professor of English. Educ: B.A., Hunter Coll., N.Y., 1936; M.A., Columbia Univ., 1937; Ed.D., Tchrs. Coll., ibid, 1963. Appts: St. Paul's Coll., Lawrenceville, Va. 1938-46; Morgan State Coll., Baltimore, Md., 1947-56; Jersey City State Coll., N.J., 1957-. Mbrships: Pi Lambda Theta; Kappa Delta Pi; Ctr. for the Study of Democratic Instns.; U.N.O; MLA; Publs. incl: Black Portraiture in American Fiction: Stock Characters, Archetypes, & Individuals, 1971. Address: Dept. of English, Jersey City State College, Jersey City, NJ 07305, U.S.A.

STARKMAN, Ernest S., b. 8 Oct. 1919. Corporation Executive. Educ: B.S. M.E., Univ. of Calif., 1942; M.S., ibid, 1945. Appts: Instr., Mech. Engrng., Univ. of Calif., 1943-44; Rsch. Engr., Shell Dev., 1944-50; Asst. Prof., Mech. Engrng., Univ. of Calif., Berkeley, 1950-54; Assoc. Prof., Aeronautical Engrng., ibid, 1954-60; Prof., Mech. Engrng., 1960-71; Chmn., Thermal Systems Div., 1964-69; Asst. V.P. Statewide Univ., 1970-71; Emeritus Prof., 1971-; V.P., Environmental Activities Staff, Gen. Motors Corp., 1971-. Mbrships: Dir., SAE, 1962-65; Fellow, ASME; Dir., Combustion Inst., 1964-; Inst. of Mech. Engrs.; Tau Beta Pi; Pi Tau Sigma; Sigma Xi; AAAS. Author of approx. 100 publs. in field of thermo-dynamics, combustion & internal combustion engines. Hons: Horning Mem. Award, SAE, 1960; Colwell Award, ibid, 1968. Address: Environmental Activities Staff, Gen. Motors Tech. Ctr., Warren, MI 48090, U.S.A. 2, 14.

STAROBINSKI, Jean, b. 17 Nov. 1920. University Professor. Educ: Docteur ès lettres, Geneva Univ., Switzerland, 1958; Docteur en médecine, ibid, 1960. Appts: Residency, Geneva Hosp., 1948-53; Asst. Prof., Johns Hopkins Univ., Balt., Md., U.S.A., 1954-56; Prof. of French Lit., Faculté des Lettres, Univ. of Geneva, Switzefland, 1958-. Mbrships: Pres., Soc. Jean-Jacques Rousseau, Geneva; Pres., Rencontres Internationales de Genève; Socio straniero, Accademia Nazionale dei Lincei, Rome. Publs: Montesquieu, 1954; Jean-Jacques Rousseau: la transparence & l'obstacle, 1957, 2nd edit. 1971; L'oeil Vivant, 1961; L'invention de la Liberté, 1964; Portrait de l'artiste en Saltimbanque, 1970; La relation critique, 1970; Les mots sous les mots, 1971; Les emblèmes de la raison, 1973. Hons: Prix Amiel, Geneva, 1957; Prix Rambert, Lausanne, 1965; Prix de la Recherche Littéraire, Paris, 1971; Grand Prix de Littérature française hors de France, Acad. royale, Belgium, 1972; Prix Pirre-de-Régnier, Acad. Française, Paris, 1973; Doct., Univ. of Lille, France, 1973. Address: 12 Rue de Candolle, 1205 Geneva, Switzerland. 43, 103.

STARR, Edward Caryl, b. 9 Jan. 1911. Librarian. Educ: A.B., Colgate Univ., 1933; B.S., Columbia Univ. Schl. of Lib. Serv., 1939; B.D., Colgate-Rochester Divinity Schl., 1940; Ordained Bapt. min. Appts: Curator, Samuel Colgate Baptist Histl. Collect., Colgate Univ., 1935-48; Libn., Crozer Theol. Sem., 1948-54; Curator, Am. Bapt. Histl. Soc., 1948-55; Curator, combined Samuel Colgate Bapt. Histl. Collect. & Am. Baptist Histl. Soc., Colgate-Rochester Divinity Schl., 1955-. Also Exec. Dir., Dept. of Archives & Hist., Am. Bapt. Conv.; Archivist, Colgate-Rochester Divinity Schl.; Archivist, Am. Bapt. Conv., 1961-. Mbrships: Am. Soc. of Ch. Hist.; Am. Archivists; Am. Assn. of Theol. Libns.; Phi Beta Kappa. Publs: Compiler, A Baptist Bibliography, 1947-, vol. 20 in preparation. Also articles in periodicals. Address: Am. Baptist Historical Soc., 1106 S. Goodman St., Rochester, NY 14620, U.S.A.

STASSINOPOULOS, Michel, b. 27 June 1903. Chief Justice; Emeritus Professor; Academician. Educ: Dr., Fac. of Law, Univ. of Athens. Appts: Lectr., Admnstv. Law, Athens Univ., 1937; Prof., Admnstv. Law, HS of Pol. Scis., Athens, 1939-68; Dean., ibid, 1951-58; State Councillor, 1943; V.P. of State Coun., 1963; Pres. (Chief Justice), 1966; Min. of the Press., 1952 & 58; Min. of Labour, 1952; Pol. Advsr. to Dodecanese Govt., 1947. Mbrships: Chmn., Comm. for Civil Servants Code, 1948; Chmn., Hellenic Broadcasting Inst., 1953; Chmn., Nat. Opera Admin. Bd., 1953-64; Acad. of Athens, 1968; Fndr., Hellenic Admin. Law Review, 1957. Publs: The States' Civil Responsibility, 1949; Poems, 1949; The Land of the Blue Lakes, 1949; Administrative Acts Law, 1950; Civil Servants Law, 1951; Traité des actes administratifs, 1954; Harmonia (poems), 1956; Principles of Administrative Law, 1957; Historical Studies of the Greek Monarchy, 1960, 68; Administrative Disputes Laws, 1964; Principles of Public Finances, 1966; The First Steps of the Greek University, 1970; The Thought & The Life (essays), 1970; Two Great Figures of the 4th Century, 1972; The Lentil Pottage & the Law of the Wolwers (essays), 1973; Our Company (novel), 1973. Hons: Order King George I, 1960; Order of Phoenix, 1st Class, 1965; Silver Medal, Town of Athens, 1958. Address: Taygetou St., 7, (Psicicon), Athens, Greece. 34, 43.

STATHAM, Francis West, b. 25 June 1916. Chartered Engineer. Educ: Sydney Tech. Coll.; Grad. in Engrng., 1938; Session 25, Aust. Admin. Staff Coll., Mt. Eliza, Vic., 1966. Appts: Engr., British Tobacco Co., Sydney, N.S.W.; served in Middle E. & Pacific, Royal Aust. Elec. & Mech. Engrs.; discharged 1945, rank Lt. Col.; Design Engr.-Chief Engr., Brit. Tobacco Co. Ltd., 1946-49; Works Mgr., Standard Steel Pty. Ltd. Grp., 1950-52; Asst. Dir. Gen., Commonwealth Dept. of Works, 1953-65; Dir. of Works, W. Aust., ibid, 1965-. Mbrships. incl: Fellow, Instn. of Engrs. & Aust. Inst. of Mgmt.; Councillor, W. Aust. Br., Royal Commonwealth Soc. Hons: O.B.E., Mil. Div., 1946; Efficiency Decoration. Address: 32 Tyrell St., Nedlands, W.A., Australia 6009. 23.

STATHIS, Eleytherios C., b. 6 Aug. 1903. Professor of Chemistry. Educ: B.Sc. & D.Sc., Athens Univ.; Greek Ramsay Fellow, 1937; Univ. & Imperal Colls., London, U.K.; Univ. of Minn., U.S.A. Appts: Instr., Chem., Univ. of Athens., 1939; Extraordinary Prof. of Inorganic Chem., ibid, 1953; Prof. of Inorganic Chem., 1959-. Mbrships: Fellow, AAAS; Greek Chem. Soc.; Chem. Soc., England; Am. Chem. Soc.; Ill.State Acad. of Sci. Contbr., num. publs. in field. Hons: Cmmdr., Order of Phoenix,

Athens, 1961; Médaille Vermeil, Paris, France, 1967. Address: 9. Didotou St., Athens (144), Greece.

STATOM, Jodellano Johnson, b. 27 Jan. 1933. Professor of Education. Educ: B.S., Miner Tchrs. Coll., (Magna Cum Laude), 1954; M.Ed., A.G.S., Univ. of Md., 1968; Ed.D., ibid, 1972. Appts: Tchr., Powell Elem. Schl., Wash.D.C., 1954-55, Burgundy Farm Country Day Schl., Alexandria, Va., 1955-62; Tchr. of socially maladjusted, Glaydin Schl., Leesburg, Va., 1962-63, Tchr. educable mental retards, Buchanan Elem. Schl., Wash. D.C., 1963-66; Mbr., Bd. Dirs., Burgundy Farm Schl., 1966-68, Glaydin Schl., 1968-; Dir., Prog. Content Enrichment & Campcraft Activities, Beauvoir Nat. Cathedral Elem. Schl., Wash.D.C., 1968-69; Asst. Prof. of Educ., D.C. Tchrs. Coll., 1968-72; Asst. Prof. of Curriculum, Univ. of Md., 1972-. Mbr. & Off., profl. orgs. & fraternities. Hons. incl: Experienced Tchr. Fellowship, 1966-68; PACT Fellowship, 1970-72. Address: 227 Jefferson St., Washington, DC 20011, U.S.A. 125.

STAUB, Robert Andre, b. 2 Apr. 1934. Board Chairman & Chief Executive Officer. Educ: B.B.A., Univ. of Miami, Coral Gables, Fla., 1956. Appts: Personnel Mgr., Ford Motor Co., 1956-60; Dir. of Personnel, Allstate Ins. Co., 1960-61; Bd. Chmn. & Chief Exec., Staub, Warmbold & Assocs. Int., Inc., 1962-. Mbrships. incl: Dir., Assn. of Exec. Recruiting Consultants; Inst. of Elec. & Electronics Engrs.; Am. Mgmt. Assn.; N.Y. Athletic Club; Jockev Club; Royal Cercle Gaulois, Lambda Chi Alpha. Address: Staub, Warmbold & Assocs. Int., Inc., 919 3rd Ave., N.Y., NY 10022, U.S.A. 2, 6, 22.

STAUDACHER, Hans, b. 14 Jan. 1923. Artist. Educ: Arnold Clementschisch Inst., Klagenfurt, Austria. Mbrships: Wiener-Secession; Forum Stadtpark, Graz; Kärntner Kunstverein, Klagenfurt. One-man shows incl: Biennale, Venice, 1956; Galerie Koepcke, Copenhagen, Denmark, & Galerie Le Soleil dans la Tete, Paris, France, 1960; Osterreichisches Museum für angewandte Kunst, Vienna, 1970; Modern-Art Galerie, Vienna, & Galerie Basilisk, Vienna, 1971; Galerie Schottenring, Vienna, 1972; Group shows incl: Junge Kunst aus Kärnten, Venio, Netherland, 1970; Ausstellung "Bilder", Secession, Vienna, 1970; Royal Acad., London, U.K., Wiener Secession & Biennale, Florence, 1971; Parzer-Kontakte 1972, Schloss Parz, 00, 1972; Poetry pictures, action pictures, happenings, multi-visual exhibitions, ironical TV pictures etc. Hons: Prize, Vienna; Prize, Biennale, Tokyo, Japan, 1965; Purchase prize, Premio Marzotto; Josef Hoffman Hon., Viener Secession. Address: Pressgasse 7/24, 1040 Vienna, Austria.

STAUFFER, Mary Ruth Schuh (Mrs. Floyd Randall Stauffer), b. 26 Aug. 1917. Physician. Educ: B.S., Capital Univ., Bexley, Ohio, 1939; M.D., Ohio State Univ. Med. Schl., Columbus, 1943; M.S., 1943. Appts: Intern, Cleveland City Hosp., 1943; Res., Franklin Roosevelt Hosp., Bremerton, Wash., 1944; Res., Sacred Heart Hosp., Pensalcola, Fla., 1948, 49; Chmn., Perinatal Mortality Comm., L.A. Co., Calif., 1969; Chief of Staff, Downey Community Hosp., 1971, 72. Mbrships: Alpha Omega Alpha; Sigma Xi; AMA; Calif. Med. Assn.; L.A. Co. Med. Assn.; Quota; Treas., Downey-Guadalajara Sister City Assn., 1974. Recip., Cariol. Award, 1943. Address: 11411 Brookshire Ave., Downey, CA 90241, U.S.A.

STAVIS, Barrie, b. 16 June 1906. Writer. Educ: Columbia Univ., N.Y.C., 1924-27.

Appts: For. Corres. in Europe, 1937-38; w. Rignal Corps, U.S. Army, 1942-45; Free-lance Jrnlst., 1945-50; Co-Fndr. & Mbr., Bd. of Dirs., New Stages, N.Y.C., 1947-50, & U.S. Inst. Theatre Technol., 1961-64, 1969-; Conductor of seminars in playwriting, var. univs., 8-10 yrs., inclng. Univ. of Wis., Milwaukee, 1968, Brigham Young Univ., 1972; Vis. Fellow, Inst. Arts & Humanistic Studies, Pa. State Univ., 1971. Mbr., profl. orgs. Original Play Prods. incl: In These Times, N.Y.C., 1932, The Sun & I, 1933, Lamp at Midnight, 1947; Joe Hill (opera, w. music by Alan Bush), Berlin, 1970. Publs. incl: Home, Sweet Homeı (novel), 1949; John Brown: The Sword & the Word (hist.), 1970; var. stories, essays & articles in jrnls. Recip., profl. awards. Address: 70 E. 96th St., N.Y.C., NY 10028, U.S.A. 30, 44.

STAVRIDIS, Stavros, b. 14 Nov. 1914. Physician. Educ: Study at Univs. of Athens, Vienna. Appts: Specialist, children's diseases, pvte. clin., Serres, Greece, 1942-; Mayor, Town of Serres, 1959-63; Pres., Serres Municipal Bd., 1965-67. Num. mbrships: Athens & N.Greece-Thessalonika Brs., Greek Assn. of Pediatrics; Pres., Omilos Orpheus Org., Serres, 1967-68; Pres., Physiolatrikos Syllogos, 1951-. Hons: War Silver Cross w. Swords, 1941; Martial Cross of Bravery, 1941; Commemorade Medal of Emmanouil Pappas, Serres, 1962. Address: Venizelou St. N.2, Serres, Greece.

STEARNS, Peter Nathaniel, b. 3 Mar. 1936. Historian. Educ: A.B., Harvard Univ., 1957; A.M., ibid, 1959; Ph.D., ibid, 1963. Appts: Instr.-Assoc. Prof., Univ. of Chgo., 1962-68; Prof., Rutgers Univ., New Brunswick, N.J., 1968-; Chmn., Dept. of Hist., ibid, 1969-. Mbrship: Managing Ed., Jrnl. of Soc. Hist. Publs: European Society in Upheaval, 1967; Priest & Revolutionary; Lamennais, 1967; Modern Europe, 1789-1914, 1969; Century for Debate, 1969; Revolutionary Syndicalism & French Labor, 1971; Workers & Protest, 1971; Impact of Industrial Revolution, 1972; European Experience since 1815, 1972; Other Side of Western Civilization, 1973; Essays in Labor History, 1973; 1848: The Revolutionary Tide, 1973; num. articles & reviews. Hons incl: Korem Prize, Soc. for French Historical Studies, 1965; Newcomen Special Award, Bus. Hist. Review, 1966; J.S. Guggenheim Mem. Fndn. Fellowship, 1973. Address: Dept. of History, Rutgers University, New Brunswick, NJ 08903, U.S.A. 1, 8, 13.

STEARNS, Walter V., b. 25 Oct. 1903. Engineer. Educ: A.B., A.M., Harvard, 1924, 1925. Appts. incl: Mech. Engr., Process Engr., Chief of Lubricating Oil Div., Arthur G. McKee & Co.; Overall Proj. Mgr., Salamanca Lubricating Oil Proj., Caltex Yokohama Proj., H.K. Ferguson Co.; Chief, Petrol Engrng. Hydrocarbon Rsch., Sci. Design Co.; Process & Engrng. Designer, Goodyear Butsyn & Tufsyn Plants, Crawford & Russell; Engr. Design, The Stilling Co.; V.P., Tech. Enterprises Inc.; V.P., Engrng., Parsons, Bromfield & Redniss, Engrng. Cons. Past Mbr., var. profl. assns. Holder, var. patents for processes for petroleum & lubricating oil processes, vitamin recoveries & saline water. Author, Thermodynamic Properties of Propane. Contbr. to var. publs. Address: 33 Prospect St., White Plains, NY 10605, U.S.A.

STEARS, Thelma Alford (Mrs.), b. 17 Mar. 1902. Librarian. Educ: Coll. of Music & fine Arts, Indpls., Ind., 1921-22; Ind. Summer Schl. for Libns., 1924. Appts: Libn., 1924-35; Hd. Libn., Carnegie Pub. Lib. Dist., Fortville, Ind., ibid. Mbrships: ALA; Ind. Lib. Assn.; Small Lib. Grp. of Ind. Libns; Trustee, United Meth.

Ch.; Educ. Bd., United Meth. Ch.; Old Trails Chapt., DAR; 55 Mbr., Fortville 1st United Meth. Ch.; Trustee, Gravel Lawn Cemetery Bd., Fortville; Charter, Psi Iota Xi; Charter, United Meth. Women. Address: Carnegie Pub. Lib. Dist., 115 N. Main St., Fortville, IN 46040, U.S.A. 5.

STEBBINS, Arthur Pierre, b. 17 July 1912. Physician; Psychiatrist. Educ: B.S., Univ. of Vt., Burlington, 1936; M.D., 1939. Appts. incl: Pvte. Prac., Psych., Bangor, Me., 1944-56; Owner & Operator, Russell Hosp., Brewer, 1950-56; Pvte. Prac., Portland, 1956; Staff, Mercy Hosp., 1956; Clin Dir., Baldpate Inc., Georgetown, Mass., 1963; Clin. Dir., Westwood Lodge Inc., 1964; Clin. Dir., Bournewood Hosp., Brookline, 1965; Med. Dir., ibid, 1966-73; Psych., VA Hosp., Salem, Va., 1973. Fellowships: Am. Geriatrics Assn.; Acad. of Psychosomatic Med.; Mass. Med. Soc. Mbrships incl: Life Mbr., Am. Psych. Assn. & New England Soc. of Psych.; Me. Med. Assn.; AMA. Author of papers in field. Recip., Award for contbn. to psych., 1960. Address: 5920 Flamingo Drive, S.W., Roanoke, VA 24018, U.S.A. 6, 112.

STECHER, Hans B., b. 16 June 1923. Business Executive. Educ: Queens Royal Coll., Trinidad. Appts: Fndr. & Owner, Stecher's, one of leading Jewelry & Gift Shop Chains of Southern Caribbean, w. Brs. in Barbados & St. Vincent, late 1940s-; Trinidad & Tobago Tourist Bd., 3 terms, 1958-70; Mbr., Stamp Advsry. Comm.; Mbr., City Coun. Tourism Comm.; Advsr., Govt.'s Fiscal Review Comm.; num. other Comms. Mbrships: Port of Spain Rotary Club, Trinidad (Past-Dir.); Chmn., Travel & Tourism Sect., Trinidad & Tobago Chmbr. of Comm. & Ind. Publs: Studies on Tourist Ind. inclng. proposal for Token-Duty-Plan. Designer of Interiors. Hon. Consul Designate for Austria. Address: 62 Independence Square, Port of Spain, Trinidad, W. Indies.

STEED, Gitel, b. 3 May 1914. Anthropologist. Educ: B.A., N.Y. Univ.; Ph.D., Columbia Univ. Appts. incl: Lectr., Hunter Coll., 1945 & 1947; Staff Cons., Rsch. in Contemporary Culture Proj., China, 1947; Dir., Rsch. in Contemporary India Field Proj., 1949-52; Dir., Rsch. in Contemporary India, 1952-62; Assoc. Prof., Hofstra Univ., 1963-73. Mbrships: Am. Anthropological Assn.; Assn. for Asian Studies; Soc. for Applied Anthropol.; Asia Soc. Contbr. to Village India, 1955, Women in India, 1973 & Main Currents in India Sociology, 1974. Hons: Summer Grant, Field work among Blackfeet Indians, 1939; Fellowship, Columbia Univ., 1939-42; Rsch. Grant to India, ibid, 1949-57; Travel Grant to India, Wenner-Gren Fndn., 1970; Rsch. Grant, Hofstra Univ., 1971. Address: 455 West 21 St., N.Y., NY 10011, U.S.A. 14.

STEEL, Robert B., b. 15 Feb. 1931. Company Executive. Educ: B.A., Furman Univ., Greenville, S.C., 1952; M.A., Fla. State Univ., Talahassee, Fla., 1956. Appts: Engr.-Writer, later Dir., Audio Visual Trng. for Convair-Astronautics (div. of General Dynamics Corp), San Diego, Calif., 1956-60; Gen. Mgr., Miles-Samuelson Inc., San Diego, 1960-61; Sales Engr., UNIVAC Div. of Sperry Rand Corp, San Diego, 1961-63; Marketing Proposal Mgr., Litton Data Systems, LA., Calif., 1964; Dir., Advt. & P.R., Informatics Inc., L.A., Calif., 1964-. Mbrships: Publicity Chmn., First US-Japan Computer Conf., Tokyo, 1972; Assn. for Computing Machinery (received outstanding serv. award to chapt.), 1970. Producer of tech. films for IBM Corp, N.Y., Nat. Aeronautical &

Space Admin., & U.S.A.F. Address: 10907 Etiwanda Ave., Northridge, CA 91324, U.S.A. 16.

STEELE, Charles William, b. 1 Dec. 1905. Physician. Educ: A.B., Univ. of Mo., 1927; M.A., ibid, 1929; M.D., Harvard Med. Schl., 1931. Appts. incl: Intern, under Frank B. Mallory M.D., Boston City Hosp., 1931-32; Res. in Med., Ctrl. Me. Gen. Hosp., Lewiston, 1933-36; Pvte. Prac., Internal Med., Lewiston & Auburn, Me., 1936-; served WW II, 1942-46; Cardiol., Sr. Attng. Physn., Ctrl. Me. Gen. Hosp., 1938-71; Cons., Int. Med., V.A. Ctr. Hosp., Togus, Me., 1947-; Cons., U.S. Armed Forces, Manpower Div. of U.S. Pub. Hlth. Serv., Soc. Security Admin. New England, Rehabilitation Serv. Me.; var. hosps. Mbrships. incl: Pres., Me. Heart Assn., Me. Soc. Int. Med., Androscoggin Co. Med. Soc.; Fellow, Am. Coll. Physns.; AMA; Am. & Int. Socs. Int. Med.; Am. Heart Assn.; Am. Diabetic Assn.; Armed Forces Assn; Phi Beta Kappa; Sigma Xi; Alpha Omega Alpha. Author, 35 scientific papers, sev. concerning atomic & hydrogen bombs & biol. warfare. Hons: Freedom Fndn. Geo. Wash. Award, 1952; Robbins Award, 1964; Pfizer Award, 1960; Disting. Physns. Award, AMA, 1971. Meritorious Serv. Citation, Am. Soc. of Int. Med., 1972. Address: 472 Main St., Lewiston, ME 04240, U.S.A. 6.

STEELE, Horace Claude, b. 15 Jan. 1930. Geologist. Educ: B.S., Tex. Tech. Univ., U.S.A., 1950. Appts: Coord., Reserves, Corpus Christi Area, Exxon, U.S.A., 1961-66; Coord., whole Exxon Co., 1966-. Mbrships: Am. Assn. of Petroleum Geols.; A.A.I.M.E.; Houston Geol. Soc., Tex.; Gulf Coast Geol. Soc.; Reserves Comm., Am. Gas Assn.; Reserves Comm., Am. Petroleum Inst.; Mem. Drv. United Meth. Ch., Houston. Hons: 5-Yr. Serv. Award, Am. Petroleum Inst., 1972; 5-Yr. Serv. Award, Am. Gas Assn., 1973; Nominated for Boss of the Yr., Secs.' Club, Houston, 1974. Address: 13511 Barryknoll, Houston, TX 77024, U.S.A. 125.

STEEN, Peter, b. 22 Jan. 1936. Actor; Playwright. Educ: Univ. of Copenhagen, 1955-56; Actors' Schl., Royal Theatre, Copenhagen, 1960-63. Appts: Actor, Royal Theatre, Copenhagen, 1963; Stage Dir., 3 prods., Royal Theatre, 1968, '70, '74; Mbr., Danish Film Coun., 1968-72. Mbrships: Danish Actors, Playwrights & Film Wkrs. Assns.; Assn. Danish Theatre Hist. Author of plays: The More We Are Together (Theatre Royal, Copenhagen), 1970; From Five Until Seven (Danish TV), 1970; A Husband (Danish TV), 1974. Num. leading roles at Royal Theatre, & in films, TV & radio. Recip., grants, Polly Sander, 1965, Fr. Schybert, 1967, Poul Reumert, 1969. Cl. Pontoppidan, 1970, Knutzon-Ziegler, 1974. Address: Pileallé 17, 2840 Holte, Denmark.

STEENSBERG, Axel, b. 1 June 1906. Professor Emeritus. Educ: cand. magisteri, Copenhagen, Denmark, 1937; Dr.phil., 1943. Appts. incl: Lectr. on cultural hist., Univ. of Copenhagen, 1954-59; Prof. of material folk culture, ibid, 1959-70; Prof. Emeritus, 1970-; Hd., Bd. of histl. & archaeol. experiment ctr., Lejre, 1964-70; Cons. for UNESCO, 1970-71. Mbrships. incl: Pres., Assn. Int. des Mus. d'agric., 1971-74; Gustavus Adolphus Acad., Stockholm; Finnish Acad.; Royal Danish Acad. Scis. & Letters. Publs. incl: Danish Peasant Furniture, 1949, '73; A History of the Danish Village during 6000 years, 1973. Recip., hons. Address: Royal Danish Acad.'s Commn. for Rsch. on Hist. of Agricl. Implements & Field Structures, Nat. Mus., Brede, Denmark 2800.

STEENSEN, Niels Rasmus, b. 13 Oct. 1904. Consulting Engineer. Educ: M.Sc., Royal Tech. Univ. of Copenhagen, 1927. Appts. incl: w. Emprezas Electricas Brasileiras S.A. Rio de Janiero, 1929-31; planning new univ. w. Prof. E. Suenson, Concurrently Asst. Tchr., reinforced concrete constrns., Royal Tech. Univ., Copenhagen, 1931-34; Contractor P.W. Hoest, 1934-35; Ptnr., Steensen & Varming, 1933-73, J. Varming & S. Mulcahy, Dublin, 1946-69, Steensen, Varming, Mulcahy & Ptnrs., London, 1957-69 & Edinburgh, 1960-69; Cons., Steensen & Varming, Copenhagen, London, Sydney, Edinburgh, 1974-; Mbr. cons. grp. "Danconsult", 1956; Mbr. grp. Spain-Denmark-Switzerland, SDS, Basel, 1956-60. Prin. works incl: Nield Bohr's Inst., Copenhagen & Risö; Atomic Ctr., Risö; European Space Technol. Ctr., Noordwijk, Netherland. Mbrships: Pres., Comm. for Stability of Bldgs., 1968-69 & Perm. Comm. for Concrete Constrns., 1967-, both Danish Soc. Civil Engrs.; Instn. Structural Engrs., London; Pres., Danish Concrete Assn., 1961-63; Controller, planning for NATO's H.Q., Paris, 1955-59; Royal Soc. of Hlth., London. Address: Tokkeköbgaard, Kettinge, Stumpedyssevej 37, DK 2970, Hörsholm, Denmark. 43.

STEERS, James Alfred, b. 8 Aug. 1899. Professor Emeritus of Geography. Educ: St. Catherine's Coll., Cambridge, U.K. Appts: Schoolmaster, Framlingham Coll., 1921-22; Departmental Demonstrator, Geog., Cambridge, 1922-26; Univ. Demonstrator, ibid, 1926-27; Univ. Lectr., ibid, 1927-49; Prof. of Geog., ibid, 1949-66; Fellow, St. Catharine's Coll., 1925; Dean, Tutor, Pres., ibid. Mbrships: V.P., Coun., Royal Geog. Soc., 1959-63, 1967-72; Hon. V.P., ibid, 1972-; Pres., Inst. of British Geographers, 1956; Pres., Geog. Assn., 1959; Pres., British Assn., Sect. E., 1954; Pres., Norfolk & Norwich Naturalists Soc., 1940-41. Publs. incl: Introduction to the Study of Map Projections, 1926; The Unstable Earth, 1932; The Coastline of England & Wales, 1946; The Sea Coast, 1953; Scolt Head Island, ed., 1934; The English Coast & the Coast of Wales, 1966; Coasts & Beaches, 1969; The Coast of Scotland, 1973; various articles in profl. jrnls. Hons. incl: Victoria Medal, Royal Geog. Soc., 1960; Gold Medal, Royal Scottish Geog. Soc., 1969; LL.D., Aberdeen, 1971; CBE, 1973. Address: c/o St. Catharine's Coll., Cambridge CB2 1RI, U.K. 1.

STEERS, Philip L., Jr., b. 8 Mar. 1917. Government Official; Certified Public Accountant. Educ: B.S., N.Y. Univ., 1938; Univ. of Vienna, Austria, 1950-51; var. mil. studies. Appts. incl: Serv. Lt.-Lt.-Col., U.S. Army, 1941-47; Mil. Govt. Off., Germany, France, Italy, 1944-47; Chief Auditor, Dept. of Army, HQ U.S. Forces in Austria, 1948-49; Asst. Comptroller, Economic Cooperation Admin., Austria, 1949-50; Controller, Mutual Security Agcy., ibid, 1950-53; w. Panama Canal Co., Balboa Hts., Canal Zone as Chief, Acctng. Systems Staff 1953-54, Dpty. Comptroller 1954-55, Comptroller 1955-66, 1967-; Asst. to Pres., William R. Staats, Inc., N.Y.C., 1966-67. Mbrships incl: Certified Pub. Acct., States of N.Y., Calif., Ill.; Am. Inst. Certified Pub. Accts.; N.Y. & Calif. Assns. Certified Pub. Accts.; Fed. Govt. Accts. Assn. (Past-Pres. Canal Zone Chapt.); World of Life Fellowship, Inc. Address: Panama Canal Company, Balboa Heights, Canal Zone. 2, 128.

STEFANELLI, John Robert, Sr., b. 23 Sept. 1938. Educator. Educ: B.S., Ball State Univ., Muncie, Ind., U.S.A., 1958; M.A., Roosevelt Univ., Chgo., Ill., 1964. Appts: Tchr., sev. elem. & high schls., Gary, Ind.,

1958-67; Asst. Prin., Beckman Jr. H.S., ibid, 1967-69; Asst. Prin., W. Side Sr. H.S., 1969-72; Prin., Horace Mann. H.S., 1972-; Dir. & Co-owner, Mother Goose Nursery Schl. & Kindergarten, 1964-; Guest Lectr., Ind. Univ., 1965-72. Mbrships. incl: NEA.; Ind. State Tchrs. Assn.; Am. Fedn. of Tchrs.; Ball State Alumni Assn.; Roosevelt Univ. Alumni Assn.; Nat. Assn. of Secondary Schl. Prins.; Gary Soc. Studies Coun.; Sigma Tau Gamma. Publs: Contbns. to profl. mags. & local newspapers. Recip., Award as First Outstanding Young Educator, & financial schlrship., Gary Jaycees, 1964. Address: 845 W. 35th Ave., Gary, Ind., U.S.A.

STEFFEE, Helga E.A., b. 14 May 1922. Manager of Arlington Towers, Reno, Nevada. Appts. incl: Min., Wayside Chapel, Medford, Ore., U.S.A., 1946-56; Correspondent Medford Mail Tribune, 1954-58; Mgr., Squaw Lakes Resort, Jacksonville, Ore., 1958-61; Mgr., Nev. Credit Rating Bur., Reno, 1962-64; Account Exec. & Chief Copywriter, KOLO Radio, Reno, 1964-65; Exec. Dir., Carson City Nugget, Nev., 1965-72; Mgr., Arlington Towers, Reno, 1972-. Mbrships: V.P., Credit Women's Breakfast Club, Reno, 1962-64; Dir., Chmbr. of Comm., Carson City, 1967-72; Publicity Dir., Bus. & Profl. Women's Club, 1966-67. Publs: Rural Reflections, newspaper column; Contbns. to Good News, religious jrnl. Address: Arlington Towers, 100 N. Arlington Ave., Reno, NV 89501, U.S.A. 5.

STEFFEN, Johann Wolfgang Eberhard, b. 28 Apr. 1923. Composer. Educ: Staatliche Hochschule für Musik, Berlin, 1949-54; Free Univ., Berlin. Appts. as free-lance composer, 1947-, & Choir & Orch. Conductor, 1947-59. Mbrships: Chmn., Berlin Sec., Deutscher Komponistenverbank; Dir., Studio Neue Musik, VDMK, Berlin; Berliner Kulturrat; Jury mbr., Music Sect., Deutscher Akademischer Austauschdienst; Bd. of Dirs., AMPHION, Gesellschaft für Förderung von Kunst & Wissenschaft; Music comm., V.P., Berliner Sängerbund; Int. Gesellschaft für Neue Musik; G.E.M.A.; Dramatiker Union. Composer of 55 publd. works for stage, orch., choir, chmbr. orch., piano & voice inclng: Aus dem Lebensbuch eines Tänzers (ballet), 1955; Violin concerto, 1966; Polychromie for piano & orch., 1971; Erfahrungen (Ingeborg Drewitz) for choir, 6 voices & instruments, 1973; Triplum 72 for percussion, flute & piano, 1972; Les Spirales pour piano, 1969; Gertrud-Kolmar-Trilogie for soprano & chmbr. ensemble, 1968. Hons. incl: Johann Wenzel Stamitz Prize, German Fed. Repub., 1972. Address: Hundekehlestr. 29, 1 Berlin 33 (West), German Fed. Repub.

STEGALL, Alma L., b. 19 Jan. 1911. Educator. Educ: A.B., Miss; Ind. Coll., Holly Springs, 1931; Ed.M., Atlanta Univ., Ga., 1945; Ed.D., Ind. Univ., Bloomington, 1949. Appts. incl: Supvsr., Instrn., Lowndes Co., Ga., 1935-44; Instr. & Tchr., Demonstration Schl., Fort Valley Coll., 1938-42; Instr., Dir., Student Tchng., Prin., Campus Lab. Schl., Albany State Coll., Ga. 1944-45; Cons., State Dept. of Educ., 1947; Prof., Educ. & Hd., Dept. of Educ., Savannah State Coll., 1947-50; Prof., Educ., Va. State Coll., Petersburg, 1950-. Mbrships incl: NEA; Va. Educ. Assn.; Int. Reading Assn.; S. Atlantic Philos. Soc.; Nat. Coun. Tchrs. of Engl.; Nat. Soc. for the Study of Educ.; Assn. for Higher Educ.; AAUP; Pi Lambda Theta; Alpha Kappa Delta; Kappa Delta Pi. Contbr. to publs. in field & reports. Address: Box 325 Va. State Coll., Petersburg, VA 23803, U.S.A. 5, 125.

STEGNER, Dorothy Carnes, b. 10 Apr. 1932. Real Estate Broker. Educ: Real Estate Courses, Ball State Univ., Muncie, Ind. Appts: With Cooper Realty, New Castle, Ind., 1961-; Property Mgr., ibid, 1962-72; Sales Mgr., 1965-. Mbrships. incl: Shawnee Nation, United Remnant Band; Deleg., Nat. Congress of Am. Indians; Corporate mbr., Am. Indian Histl. Soc.; Assoc., Smithsonian Inst., Wash. D.C.; Sec.-Treas., Henry Co. Realtors Bd., 1969-71. Author of several Indian articles in New Castle Courier-Times & The Indnpls. Star. Address: Cooper Realty, 1203 Race St., New Castle, IN 47362, U.S.A. 5.

STEIGER, Washington Selden, b. 25 Jan. 1912. Insurance Executive; Engineer; Educator. Educ: B.Sc., Brown Univ., Providence, R.I., 1934; B.Sc., Ohio State Univ., Columbus, 1945; M.A., ibid, 1947; Ph.D., 1954. Appts. incl: Chmn., Engrng. Dept., Univ. of Bridgeport, Conn., 1947-48; Fac. Pension Rep., Ohio State Univ., 1949-50; Educl. Dir., A & H Underwriters, 1950-57; Field Dir., ibid, 1958-59; V.P., Protection House Corp., 1960-61; Gen. Agt., Europe, Am. Life Ins. Co., 1962-65; Ind. Financial Cons., 1966-. Mbrships. incl: Resolutions Chmn., Engl. Speaking Union; Past Cmdr., Disabled Am. Veterans; Deleg., Am. Legion; Am. Soc. for Engrng. Educ. Contbr. to jrnls. Hons. incl: Pres.'s Award, 1956; Brown Univ. Alumni Award, 1973. Address: 4135 Pamona Ave., Coconut Grove, Miami, FL 33133, U.S.A. 15, 22, 128.

STEIL, Gesina Schurmann (Mrs. Chas. M. Steil), b. 14 Sept. 1892. Banker. Educ: Fremont Coll., Neb. Appts: Book-keeper, 1st. Nat. Bank, Scribner, 1912; Asst. Cashier, ibid, 1913-62; Cashier-Dir., 1962; Liquidating Agent, Nat. Banking Dept., Wash., D.C., 1963; V.P., Scribner Bank, Neb., 1963-72. Mbrships: Dodge Co. Histl. Soc. (Treas., 1953-57); Lutheran Sunday Schl. (Supt., 1928-61). Address P.O.Box 433, Scribner, NB 68057, U.S.A. 5, 8.

STEIMAN, Leon Arie. Psychiatrist. Educ: M.D., German Univ., Prague,.Czechoslovakia, 1937; N.Y. Psych. Inst., U.S.A., 1955-58. Appts. Res., Med. Ctr., Prague, Czech., 1937-39; Med. Dir. & Cons. Internist, Displaced Persons Hosp. & Forest Hills Gen. Hosp., N.Y.C., U.S.A., 1951-55; Sr. Supvsng. Psych., Hudson River State Hosp., Poughkeepsie, 1955-66; Chief, Res. Servs., Astor Home for Emotionally Disturbed Children, Rhinebeck, 1958-; Cons. Psych., Rhinebeck Country Schl. for Mentally Retarded Children, 1959-; Profl. Advsr., Fndn. for Day Hosp. & Pilot Projs., 1958-61; Family Ct. Psych., Dutchess Co. Family Ct., 1966-; Pvte. Prac., 1960-. Mbrships: AMA; Am. Psych. Assn. Contbr. to profl. publs. Address: 3 Scenic Drive, Hyde Park, NY 12538, U.S.A. 112.

STEIN, Arthur Philip, b. 26 Aug. 1908. Designer; Stylist. Appts: Ctrl. Buyer Rudolph Karstadt A.G., Hamburg & Berlin, Germany, 1929-33; Prod. Mgr., Stylist & Designer of Fashion Belts, R. & H. Bucholtz, Berlin, 1933-36; Owner, A. & E. Stein Shanghai, China, 1938-47; Stylist & Designer, Nash, Inc., Jersey City, N.J., U.S.A., 1947-53; Designer & Patternmaker, Hagerstown Leather Goods Co., Hagerstown, Md., 1953-; Owner, Stein Originals, Hagerstown. Mbrships. incl: Master Degree, Craftsmen Guild, Shanghai; Fndr. & 1st Pres., Bd. of Dirs., German-Am. Social Club, Gemuetlichkeit Inc.; Ed., Thomas Wilde Lodge, Oddfellows; Chmn. for Int. Rels., Kiwanis Int., Hagerstown; Collectors Club of N.Y. Creative wks: Paintings; Sculptures; Leathercraft; Jewelry; Recip., 2 Citations for Bravery & Heroism, Japanese Govt., & Govt. of Repub. of

China, 1943. Address: 1070 View St., Hagerstown, MD 21740, U.S.A. 6.

STEIN, Lester M., b. 4 Feb. 1930. Architect. Appts: Proj. Archt., var. schls. & bank bldgs.; Inst., Archtl. & Construction Curriculum, Pa. State Univ. Mbrships: Sec., Eastern Pa. Chapt., Am. Inst. Archts., V.P., 1968, '69; Pres., 1970. Address: 3205 Lord Byron Dr., Bethlehem, PA 18017, U.S.A.

STEIN, Peter Gonville, b. 29 May 1926. Professor of Law. Educ: M.A., LL.B., Gonville & Caius Coll., Cambridge, U.K.; Univ. of Pavia, 1951-52; Ph.D., Aberdeen, 1955; Admitted as Solicitor, Supreme Ct., 1951. Appts: Asst. Lectr., Nottingham Univ., 1952-53; Lectr., Aberdeen Univ., 1953-56; Prof., Jurisprudence, ibid, 1956-68; Vis. Prof. of Law, Va. & Colo., U.S.A., 1965-66; Regius Prof. of Civil Law, & Fellow, Queens' Coll., Univ. of Cambridge, 1968-; Justice of the Peace, Cambridge City, 1970-. Mbr., Univ. Grants Comm. Publs: Fault in the Formation of Contract in Roman Law & Scots Law, 1958; Regulae Iuris: from juristic rules to legal maxims, 1966. Address: Queens' Coll., Cambridge, U.K. 1, 43, 128.

STEINBERG, Gunther Theodore, b. 28 Nov. 1912. Corporation Executive. Educ: B.A., Univ. of Northern Iowa, 1936; M.B.A., Univ. of Chgo., 1938; postgrad. studies, 1938-41. Appts: Teaching Asst., Univ. of Chgo., 1938-40, Inst. (Econs.) 1942-44; Personnel Statn., Western Elec. Co., Chgo., 1941-45; Statl. Economist-Asst. Dir., Mgmt. Inf. Systems, Western Elec. Co., N.Y., 1945-. Mbrships: Am. Mgmt. Assn.; Econometric Soc.; Am. Statl. & Econ. Assns.; Assn. of Bus. Economists; Downtown Economists Luncheon Grp. Contbr. to Western Elec. publs., 1952-72. Address: 10 Kevin Rd., Scotch Plains, NJ 07076, U.S.A. 6, 14.

STEINBERG, Joseph L., b. 6 Oct. 1928. Attorney. Educ: B.A., Brooklyn Coll., Brooklyn, N.Y., 1950; LL.B., Columbia Law Schl., N.Y.C., 1953. Appts: Individual prac., 1955-58; Sr. Ptnr., Kleinman, O'Neill, Steinberg & Lapuk, 1958-; Adjutant Fac., Univ. of Hartford, 1968-; Moderator, Weekly newsprog. "Fourth Estate", Conn. Pub. TV; Anchorman, State Election returns-State nominating convention State Legislative Sessions. Mbrships. incl: Pres., Ararat Lodge 13, B'nai B'rith, 1955-57; Co-Chmn., Conn. Valley Anti-Defamation League, 1959; Pres., Fndr., Greater Hartford Forum, 1959-69; Dir., Family Servs. Soc. of Hartford, 1962-72. Publs: Mortgage your way to wealth (The Principles of Supplemental Real Estate Financing), 1967; Real Estate Sales Contracts, 1970; "Campers' Favorite Campgrounds", Vol. I, 1974. Address: 99 Pratt St., Hartford, CT 06103, U.S.A. 6, 30.

STEINBRENNER, Arthur Henry, b. 23 July 1917. Professor. Educ: B.A., Columbia Coll., 1940; M.A., Tchrs. Coll., Columbia Univ., 1941; Ph.D., Columbia Univ., 1955. Appts: Tchr., maths. & sci., Graham-Eckes Schl., Palm Beach, Fla., 1941-46; Prin., ibid, 1944-46; Asst., tchng. maths., Tchrs. Coll., Columbia Univ., 1946-48; Asst. Prof., maths., U.S. Naval Acad., 1948-53; Prof., secondary educ. & maths., Univ. of Ariz., Tucson, 1953-. Mbrships: Math. Assn. of Am.; Nat. Coun. of Tchrs. of Maths.; Schl. Sci. & Maths. Assn., Inc.; Ariz. Assn. of Tchrs. of Maths.; Phi Delta Kappa; Pi Mu Epsilon. Author of publs. in field. Hons: Fulbright Lectureship, Univ. of Western Australia, 1963; Creative Tchng. Award, Univ. of Ariz. Fndn., 1971. Address: Dept. of Maths., Univ. of Ariz., Tucson, AZ 85721, U.S.A.

STEINER, George, b. 23 Apr. 1929. Writer;

Scholar. Educ: B.es Lettres et Philosophie, Paris, France; B.A., Univ. of Chgo., U.S.A.; M.A., Harvard; D.Phil., Oxford, U.K. Appts: Edit. Staff, Economist, London; Inst. of Adv. Study, Princeton, N.J., U.S.A.; Fellow, Dir., Engl. Studies, Churchill Coll., Cambridge, U.K.; Extraordinary Fellow, ibid. Fellow, Royal Soc. of Lit. Publs: Tolstoy or Dostoyevsky, 1958; The Death of Tragedy, 1960; Anno Domini: Three Stories, 1964; Language & Silence, 1967; In Bluebeard's Castle: Notes Toward the Redefinition of Culture, 1971; Extraterritorial: Papers on Literature & the Language Revolution, 1971; The Sporting Scene: The White Knights of Reykjavik, 1973. Hons. incl: Bell Prize, Am. Lit., Harvard; Rhodes Schlrship., Balliol Coll., Oxford; Chancellor's Engl. Essay Prize, ibid; O.Henry Short Story Prize, 1958; Fulbright Professorship; Guggenheim Fellowship; Zabel Award, Nat. Inst. of Arts & Letters, U.S.A.; Cortina Ulisse Prize, Address: Churchill Coll., Cambridge, U.K. 1, 34.

STEINER, Roger Jacob, b. 27 Mar. 1924. University Professor. Educ: A.B., Franklin & Marshall Coll.; M.Div., Union Theol. Sem.; M.A. & Ph.D., Univ. of Pa. Appts. incl: Clergyman, Meth. Ch., 1945-61; Lectr., Univ. of Bordeaux, France, 1961-63; Assoc. Prof., French, Univ. of Del., U.S.A., 1963-. Mbrships. incl: Phi Beta Kappa; MLA; Am. Assn. Tchr. of French; Am. Assn. Tchrs. of Spanish & Portuguese. Publs: Two Centuries of Spanish & English Bilingual Lexicography 1590-1800, 1970; The New College French & English Dictionary, 1972; var. articles and reviews. Address: Dept. of Langs. & Lit., Univ. of Del., Newark, DE 19711, U.S.A. 13, 30.

STEINHART, Dean R., b. 6 May 1930. School Administrator. Educ: B.S., Kutztown State Coll.; M.S., Pa. State Univ.; Nat. Sci. Fndn. Fellow, Geol., Franklin & Marshall Coll.; Temple Univ. Appts: Sci. Tchr., 1957-65; Chmn., Sci. Dept., 1959-65; H.S. Prin., 1965-71; Dir., Secondary Educ. Mbrships: Rotary Int.; Nat. Assn. of Secondary Schl. Prins.; Phi Delta Kappa; Nat. Sci. Tchrs. Assn.; Elizabethtown (Pa.) Chmbr. of Comm.; Boy Scouts of Am. Contbr. to jrnls. Hons: Nat. Sci. Fndn. Fellow, 1959, '60, '61, '62, '63; Outstanding Citizen, Elizabethtown Bus. & Profl. Women's Club, 1965. Address: R.D. 2, Box 229, Mount Joy, PA 17552, U.S.A. 130.

STEINMANN, Martin, Jr., b. 3 Mar. 1915. Professor of English. Educ: B.A., Univ. of Minn., 1937; M.A., ibid, 1946; Ph.D., 1954. Appts: Instr.-Prof., Univ. of Minn., 1946-60; Prof. of Engl., ibid, 1960-; Dir., Minn. Ctr. for Advanced Studies in Lang., Style & Literary Theory, 1972-; Vis. Prof., Columbia Univ., summer 1967. Mbrships: AAUP; Am. Soc. for Aesthetics; Lectological Assn.; Linguistic Soc. of Am.; MLA. Publs. incl: Ed. (w. Robert C. Rathburn), From Jane Austen to Joseph Conrad, 1958, 1967; Ed. (w. Robert C. Rathburn), 75 Prose Pieces, 1961, 1967; Ed. (w. Gerald Willen), Literature for Writing, 1962, 1967, 1970; Ed., New Rhetorics, 1967; Num. articles, notes, reviews, etc. in jrnls. Hons. incl: Grants, Univ. of Minn., 1964, 1967, 1973, Putnam D. Macmillan Fund & Rockefeller Fndn., 1964. Address: 1627 W. 26th St., Mnpls., MN 55405, U.S.A. 13, 131.

STELLA, Frank D., b. 21 Jan 1919. Business Executive. Educ: Coll. of Comm. & Finance, Univ. of Detroit. Appts. incl: currently Pres., F.D. Stella Products Co.; Mbr., Advsry. Bd., & past Pres., Nat. Commercial Refrigerator Sales Assn.; past Mbr., Bd. of Dirs., Pres., 1967-68; Detroit Alumni Assn.; Chmn. of

Exec. Comm., Presidents' Cabinet, Univ. of Detroit; Chmn., Income Tax Bd. of Review, City of Detroit, Exec. Bd. of Advsrs., Mt. Carmel Mercy Hosp. & Med. Ctr.; Mbr., Bd. of Trustees, Univ. of Detroit, & Maryglade Coll.; Past Pres., Alpha Kappa Psi; Mbr., Bd. of Dirs., Peoples Fed. Savings, Detroit; Food Serv. Exec. Assn. Address: 7000 Fenkell Ave., Detroit, MI 48238, U.S.A. 16, 130.

STELLINGWERFF, Johannes, b. 5 Dec. 1924. Librarian. Educ: Civil Engr., Tech. Univ., Delft, Holland, 1952; Dr., ibid, 1959. Appts: Deptl. Hd., local govt., Eindhoven, Holland, 1952-57; Hd. Libn., Tech. Univ., ibid, 1957-60; Hd. Libn., Free Univ., Amsterdam, 1960-. Publs: Werkelÿlheid en grondmotief by Vincent Willem van Gogh, 1959; 2nd ed., '63; Oorsprorg en toekomst van de creatieve mens, 1965; 2nd ed., '66; De hermetische schilderkunst van Diana Vandenberg, 1969; La peinture hermetique de Diana Vandenberg, 1970; Inleiding tot de universiteit, 1971; De koers van de Vrije Universiteit, 1971; De M.H. Bos-bibliotheek van de Vrije Universiteit, 1971. Address: 80 Haagbenklaan, Amstelveen, Netherlands.

STELZER, Irwin M., b. 22 May 1932. Economist. Educ: B.A., N.Y. Univ., 1951; M.A., 1952; Ph.D., Cornell Univ., 1954. Appts. incl: Econ., W.J. Levy Inc., 1955-56; Lectr., N.Y. Univ., 1955-56; Rschr., Brookings Instn., 1956-57; Lectr., CCNY, 1957-58; Sr. Cons., V.P., Boni Watkins Jason & Co. Inc., N.Y.C., 1956-61; Pres., Nat. Econ. Rsch. Assocs. Inc., 1961-. Mbrships. incl: Phi Beta Kappa; Bd. Dirs., U.S. Nat. Comm., World Energy Conf.; Cornell Univ. Coun.; Am. Econ. Assn.; Am. Stat. Assn.; Nat. Assn. Bus. Econs. Publs: Selected Antitrust Cases: Landmark Decisions; articles & reviews & profl. jrnls.; Econs. Ed., Antitrust Bull. Hons: Goldwin Smith Fellowship, Cornell Univ., 1952; Univ. Fellowship, ibid, 1953; Pres., Emerson Schl., 1970-71. Address: Nat. Econ. Rsch. Assocs. Inc., 80 Broad St., N.Y. NY 10004, U.S.A. 2, 6, 14, 16, 30.

STEMBRIDGE, John Madison, b. 17 Aug. 1937. Businessman; Mayor. Educ: B.A., Bob Jones Univ., Greenville, S.C., U.S.A., 1960; Postgrad., Southwestern Bapt. Theol. Sem., Ft. Worth, Tex. Appts: Sec.-Treas., Edison Furniture of N. Miami, Inc., Fla.; V.P., Stembridge Realty, Inc.; Pres., Stembridge, Inc.; Mayor, City of N. Miami. Mbrships. incl: U.S. Conf. of Mayors' Comms.; Community Dev. Comm.; Am. Revolution Bicentennial Comm.; Fndr. & Dir., Gtr. Miami Inspirational Concert Series; Host, Inspirational Chapel Hour Radio Prog., 1961-; Bd. of Dirs., Fndn. for Emotionally Disturbed Children; Bd. of Trustees, Third Century, U.S.A.; Chmn., Congregation, Bethany Evangelical Covenant Ch.; Fla. Furniture Dealers Assn.; N. Dade Bus. & Profl. Club; Kts. of Pythias; Soc. of the Arts. Author, num. sermons & papers on theol., doctrinal, & missionary subjects. Hons. incl: True Gentleman Award, Sigma Alpha Epsilon, 1956; Elected State Senator; Nominated for Gov. Address: 545 N.E. 125 St., North Miami, FL 33161, U.S.A. 125.

STEMPLE, Joseph, b. 13 Sept. 1908. Steel Company Executive. Appts: Pres., Mulberry St. Corp., Newark, N.J., 1956-63; V.P., Cap Screw & Nut Co., ibid, 1956-63; Pres., Elizabeth Bolt & Nut Mfg. Corp., Elizabeth, N.J., 1960-; Pres., Stemple Corp., ibid, 1968-. Address: 49 Melrose Ave., N. Arlington, NJ, U.S.A. 6.

STENBÄCK, Guy, b. 27 July 1924. General Manager. Educ: Grad., Swedish Commercial

Univ., 1950. Appts: Asst. Mgr., Oy Alftan Ab, Helsinki, Finland, 1947-58; Bd. Mbr., ibid, 1958-60; Mng. Dir. & Gen. Mgr., 1966-; Bd. Chmn., Oy Edalf Ab, 1971-; Mng. Dir. & Gen. Mgr., Oy Elektro-Diesel Ab, 1971-; Mng. Dir. & Gen. Mgr., Oy Elektro-Diesel Ab, 1972-; Bd. Chmn., Oy Wickström Motors Ab, 1969-; Controller, Nordiska Foreningsbanken Ab, 1966-; Bd. Chmn., Alppilan Tehdastalo Oy, 1968-. Mbrships: Finlands Dieselförbund; Vientiyhdistys r.y.; Finlands Motorbåtsklubb; Pentalon Moderne; Helsingfors Simsällskap. Address: Oy Alftan Ab, P.O. Box 5, 00521 Helsinki 52, Finland.

STENHOUSE, Douglas Simms, b. 16 June 1932. Architect & Planner. Educ: A.B., Princeton Univ., N.J., 1954; B.Arch., Univ. of Pa., Phila., 1957; M.Arch., Cath. Univ. Am., Wash. D.C., 1970; M.City & Regional Planning, 1971. Appts. incl: Job. Capt. & Designer, Faulkner Kingsburg & Stenhouse, Wash. D.C., 1958-63; Prin., Douglas S. Stenhouse, 1964-69; Arch. & Asst. to Dir., Tech. Servs. Div., HAA, U.S. Dept. of HUD, 1969-70; Arch., Operation Breakthrough, Off. of Asst. Sec. for Rsch. & Technol., ibid, 1970-72; Urban Planner, Div. of Site & Land Planning, 1972; Chief Arch. & Planner, Community Technol. Corp., Subsidiary of TRW Inc., Redondo Beach, Calif., 1972-. Mbrships. incl: Am. Inst. Archs.; Soc. Am. Mil. Engrs.; Nat. Assn. Housing & Redev. Officials; Am. Soc. Planning Officials. Contbr. to publs. in field. Hons: Nat. Student Award, Am. Inst. Planners, 1971; Spec. Achievement Award, U.S. Dept. Housing & Urban Dev., 1972. Address: 20329 Roslin Ave., Torrance, CA 90503, U.S.A. 7, 117, 125, 130.

STENSTROM, Åke Johannes, b. 3 Jan. 1925. Company Director. Educ: B.Sc. (Econ.), 1954; M.Sc. (Econ.), 1958; Chartered Acct., 1961. Appts: Sev. posts, retail trade, 1939-45 & 1948-49; Auditor, Suomen Osuuskauppojen Keskuskunta, Turku, Finland, 1949-51; Auditor, Suomen Osuuskauppojen Keskuskunta, Helsinki, 1954-59; Chief, Audlt Dept., ibid, 1960-62; Mng. Dir., Varuboden Coop. Retail Soc., Helsinki, 1962-72; Material Mgmt. Dir., & Mbr., Bd. of Dirs., Suomen Osuuskauppojen Keskuskunta, Helsinki, 1972-. Address: Pihlajatie 37 A 11, Helsinki 27, Finland. 43.

STENSTRÖM, Rasmus, b. 7 Oct. 1920. Physician & Docent. Educ: Cand. med., 1942; Lic. med., 1947; Specialist in radiol., 1951; Med. dr., 1968. Appts. incl: Fellow in X-ray diagnosis, Karolinska Sjukhuset, Stockholm, Sweden, 1946-47; Res., Maria Hosp. Helsinki, Finland, 1948-49; Res., X-ray Dept., Helsinki Univ. Hosp., 1949-51; Radiologist, Aurora Hosp., Helsinki, 1952-56; Hd., X-ray Dept., ibid, 1956-; Docent in X-ray Diagnosis, Helsinki Univ., 1969-. Mbrships: Radiological Soc. of Finland; European Soc. of Paediatric Radiol., Paris, France; Royal Soc. of Med., London, U.K.; Finnish Soc. of Physns.; Swedish Club, Helsinki. Publs. incl: Arthrography of the Knee Joint in Children: X-ray Anatomy, Diagnosis & the Use of Multiple Discriminant Analysis, 1968; num. contbns. to profl. jrnls. Hons: Combat medals, Winter War & WWII. Address: Gumböle, 02810 Långängen, Finland. 134.

STENSTRÖM, Thure Oscar, b. 12 Apr. 1927. Professor. Educ: B.A., Uppsala Univ., Sweden, 1950, M.A., 1951, Ph.D., 1961. Appts: Lectr., Asst. Prof., Acting Prof., Literary Hist., Uppsala Univ., 1961-68; Vis. Prof., Comp. Lit. & Scandinavian Studies, Harvard Univ., U.S.A., 1968-69; Prof. Regius & Ordinarius, Lit., Uppsala Univ., 1971-. Mbr., Soc. Litterarum Humaniorum Regiae

Upsaliensis, 1973. Publs. incl: Berättartekniska studier i Pär Lagerkvists, Lars Gyllenstens och Cora Sandels prosa, 1964; Existentialismen. Studier i dess idétradition och litterära yttringar, 1966; Jean-Paul Sartre's First Play, 1967; Robert Lowell's Falling Asleep over the Aeneid, 1971; Gammal och ny Hamsun-forskning, 1973. Recip., Karl & Betty Warburg Prize for Literary Rsch., Royal Acad. of Letters, Hist. & Antiquities, Stockholm, 1968. Address: Uppsala Univ., Dept. of Lit., Villavägen 7, 752 36 Uppsala, Sweden.

STEPAKOV, Vladimir Ilich, b. 13 June 1912. Soviet Diplomat. Educ: Grad., Communist Higher Learning Inst., 1935; Cand. Econ. Scis., Moscow State Lenin Pedagogical Inst., 1952; D.Hist. Scis., Communist Party Soviet Union Acad. Social Scis., 1957. Appts: Dept. Hd., Admin., MGB, Moscow region, 1952-53; Dept. Hd., Sec., 2nd Sec., MGK, 1957-61; Ctrl. Inspection Comm., 1961-66; Dept. Hd., Ctrl. Comm., 1965-70; Chief Ed., Izvestia, 1964-65; Ambassador Extraord. & Plenipotentiary to Yugoslavia, Belgrade, 1971-. Address: Embassy of U.S.S.R., 32 Deligradska St., Belgrade, Yugoslavia.

STEPHEN, (Sir) Alastair Edward, b. 27 May 1901. Solicitor. Educ: B.A., St. Paul's Coll., Univ. of Sydney. Appts: Solicitor, Supreme Ct., N.S.W., 1926-; Ptnr., Stephen Jaques & Stephen, 1926-; Dir.-Chmn., Royal Prince Alfred Hosp., Sydney, 1944-; Pres., Australian Hosp. Assn., 1969-71; Dir., Coal & Allied Industries Ltd., United Ins. Co. Ltd., & other cos. Mbrships: Union Club, Sydney; Australian Club, Sydney; Royal Sydney Golf Club; Australian Jockey Club. Recip., Knighthood, 1973. Address: 60 Fairfax Rd., Bellevue Hill, N.S.W., Australia 2023.

STEPHEN, Mae (Mrs.). Sociologist. Educ: A.B., Univ. of N.C., 1940; Grad. work at other univs. Appts. incl: Personnel Techn., Dept. of Army, 1942-44, '47-48; Soc. Sci. Analyst, Nat. Inst. of Mental Hlth., Dept. of Hlth., Educ. & Welfare, Bethesda, Md., 1959-61; Pub. Hlth. Analyst, 1966-67; Prog. Analyst, Nat. Inst. of Child Hlth. & Human Dev., 1967-70; Currently, Sociologist, Urban & Soc. Systems Div., Stanford Rsch. Inst., Menlo Pk., Calif. Mbrships' Am. Sociol. Assn.; Pacific Sociol. Assn.; AAAS; Am. Educ. Rsch. Assn.; Alpha Kappa Delta. Publs. incl: Co-author, Methodology of Educational Futurology (Engl. & French Eds.), 1971 & The Most Critical Problems Facing America Today, 1971; Career Education: Limitations & Possibilities, 1971; Early Childhood Education: Perspectives on the Federal & Office of Education Roles, 1972; contbr., Revisiting Early Childhood Education. Recip. of Superior Serv. Award, Dept. of Hlth., Educ. & Welfare, 1967. Address: Stanford Rsch. Inst., 333 Ravenswood Rd., Menlo Park, CA 94025, U.S.A. 5, 9.

STEPHENS, Frank Douglas, b. 10 Oct. 1913. Physician; Surgeon. Educ: Trinity Coll., Univ. of Melbourne, Australia. Appts. incl: Rsch. Surg., Royal Children's Hosp., Melbourne, 1950-57; Dir., Dept. of Surg. Rsch., ibid, 1957-; Hon. Paediatric Surg., Royal Womens Hosp., 1953-; Clin. Surg. Tchr., Univ. of Melbourne, 1950; Exec. Chmn., Royal Childrens Hosp. Rsch. Fndn., 1972. Hon. Fellowships: Am. Acad. Paediatrics; Argentinian/Brazil Soc. Paediatric Surgs. Mbrships. incl: Chmn., Paediatric Surg. Sect., Royal Australasian Coll. of Surgs.; Aust. Med. Assn.; Aust. Paediatric Assn.; Urol. Soc. Australasia. Publs: Congenital Malformations of the Rectum Anus & Genito-urinary Tracts, 1963; Anorectal Malformations in Children,

1971; contbr. to books & med. jrnls. Hons. incl: D.S.O., WWII, 1942; Triennial Rsch. Medal, Brit. Med. Assn., 1962. Address: 44 Cromwell Rd., South Yarra, Vic., Australia 3141. 23.

STEPHENS, Mae Bullington, b. 16 Feb. 1911. Classroom Teacher. Educ: Univ. of Ark., Fayetteville, 2½ yrs.; B.S., Jacksonville Univ., Ala. Appts: Elem. Tchr. & H.S. Basketball Coach; Elem. Tchr., Ark., 6 yrs.; Tchr., Etowah H.S., Attalla, Ala., 2 yrs.; Tchr., Alma Hinson Jr. H.S., 11 yrs.; currently tchng. elem. levels; Chmn., Soc. Studies Comm. & Lang. Arts Comm. Mbrships: Pres., Attalla Tchrs. Assn., Ala. Educ. Assn.; Sec., PTA; NEA; 2nd V.P., Alpha Iota Chapt., Delta Kappa Gamma; Charter Mbr., Attalla Garden Club; Pres., ibid, 1 yr.; Attalla Study Club. Contbr. of article, Hesitant to Change, Ala. Schl. Jrnl., 1963. Recip., Alma Hinson Jr. PTA Yr. Book Dedication, 1967-68. Address: Route 1, Box 322, Attalla, AL 35954, U.S.A.

STEPHENSON, Bette Mildred, (Mrs. G.A. Pengelly), b. 31 July 1924. Physician. Educ: M.D., Fac. of Med., Univ. of Toronto, Canada, 1946. Appts: Pvte prac., Willowdale, Ont., 1948-; Med. Staff, Womens Coll. Hosp., 1949-; Chief, Dept. of Gen. Prac. & Dir., Out Patients' Dept., ibid, 1953-64; Med. Staff, North York Gen. Hosp., 1967-; Clin. Tchr., Dept. of Family Med., Univ. of Toronto, 1968-. Mbrships. incl: Standards Coun. of Canada; Bd. of Dirs., Ont. Med. Fndn.; Canadian Med. Assn.; Pres.-elect, ibid, 1973-74; Bd. of Dirs., ibid, 1968-76; Chmn., Bd. of Dirs., ibid, 1972-73; Exec. Comm., ibid, 1972-76; Ont. Med. Assn.; Bd. of Dirs., ibid, 1964-71; Chmn., Bd. of Dirs., ibid, 1968-69; Pres., ibid, 1970-71; Coll. of Family Physns. of Canada; Hon. Fellow, ibid, 1968. Contbr. to profl. jrnls. Hons: Centennial Medal, Govt. of Canada, 1967; Woman of the Yr. Award, B'nai B'rith Coun. of Women, 1973. Address: 20 McKee Ave., Willowdale, Ont., M2N 4B8, Canada 5, 138.

STEPHENSON, Ian, b. 11 Jan. 1934. Painter. Educ: B.A. Durham; King Edward VII Schl. of art, King's Coll., Univ. of Durham, Newcastle-upon-Tyne, U.K., 1951-56; Tutorial Student, ibid, 1957-58. Appts. incl: Studio Demonstrator, King Edward VII Schl. of Art, King's Coll., Univ. of Durham, 1957-58; Vis. Lectr., The Polytechnic Schl. of Art., London, 1959-62; Vis. Painter, Chelsea Schl. of Art, London, 1959-66; Dir., Fndn. Studies, Dept. of Fine Art, Univ. of Newcastle-upon-Tyne, 1966-70; Dir., Higher Dip. Studies in Painting, Chelsea Schl. of Art, London, 1970-. Mbrships. incl: Visual Arts Panel, Northern Arts Assn., Newcastle-upon-Tyne, 1967-70; Fine Art Panel, Nat. Coun. for Dips. in Art & Design, London, 1972-; Permanent Comm., New Contemporaries Assn., London, 1973-. Exhibs. incl: British Painting in The Sixties, Whitechapel Art Gall., London, 1963; Junge Generation Grossbritannien, Akademie der Kunste, Berlin, Germany, 1968; Retrospective Exhib., Laing Art Gall., Newcastle-upon-Tyne, 1970; La Peinture Anglaise Aujourd'hui, Musee d'Art Moderne, Paris, France, 1973. Works represented in num. pub. collects. Hons. incl: Marzotto Selection Prize, European Community Contemporary Painting Exhib., Valdagno, Italy, 1964; Num. Schlrships. Address: 4 Elm Park Gdns., London SW10 9PA, U.K. 19, 133.

STERCHO, Peter George, b. 14 Apr. 1919. Professor of Economics. Educ: Ph.D., Ukrainian Grad. Schl. of Econs., Munich, W. Germany; Ph.D., Univ. of Notre Dame, U.S.A., 1959. Appts: Asst. Prof.-Assoc. Prof.,

Econ. & Pol. Sci., St. Vincent Coll., Latrobe, Pa., 1955-63; Assoc. Prof. of Econs., Drexel Inst. of Technol., Phila., Pa., 1963-69; Prof., Drexel Univ., Phila., 1969-. Mbr. & Off., var. acad. & scientific orgs. Publs: The Carpatho-Ukrainian Republic, 1965; Diplomacy of Double Morality, 1971; Ukraine & the European Turmoil, 1917-1919 (co-author), 2 vols., 1973. Monographs: Slovak-Ukrainian Relations, 1938-39, 1965; Soviet Concept of National Self-Determination, 1973. Num. articles. Address: 340 Meeting House Lane, Narberth, PA 19072, U.S.A.

STERGIOPOULOS, Constantin, b. 23 Dec. 1907. Philologist; Historian. Educ: A.M., Univ. of Athens, Greece; Practical Schl. of Higher Studies, Paris, France. Appts: Tchr., H.S., Yannina, Greece, 1929; Dir. H.S.'s, Viannos, Crete, 1939; Yannina, 1943; Kephisia, 1945, & 6th H.S., Athens, 1948; Prefect, Phtiotis, 1962; Prefect, Xanthi, 1963. Mbrships: Parnassos Literary Soc.; Histl. & Ethnological Assn. of Greece; Greek Geographical Assn. Publs: Remarks on the Modern Historical Geography of Epirus, 1937; Ancient Aetolia, 1939; Greek Finance in the 6th Century B.C. (in French), 1949; The Responsibles for War in Ancient Times, 1952; Political Parties in Ancient Athens, 3 vols., 1952-64; The Mixed Epirotical Army in the Deliverance of Epirus (October-November 1912), 1968; The Siege of Arta in November 1821, 1972. Address: Od. Crissis 15, Athens 808, Greece.

STERIOTIS, Peter, b. 13 Mar. 1914. Professor of Mathematics & Physical Sciences. Educ: Grad., Maths. & Phys. Scis., Univ. of Athens. Appts: Asst., Univ. of Athens, 1946; Lectr., Financial & Ins. Maths., 1955; Prof. of Math. Econ., 1961; Under Sec. of Agric., 1963-64; Min. of Commerce, 1964; Min. of Finance, 1966-67; Rector, Higher Schl. of Econs. & Commercial Scis., Athens, 1966, 1969-. Mbrships. incl: Greek & Italian Math. Soc.; Greek & Am. Statistical Soc.; Int. Inst. of Stats. Author, profl. papers & articles. Hons. incl: Cmdr., Royal Order of Phoenix; Cmdr., Orthodox Patriarchates; War & Resistance Medals. Address: 116 Patissiou St., Athens, Greece.

STERLING, Noel, b. 28 Mar. 1903. Editor; Writer. Educ: Univ. of Calif.; Univ. of Paris, France; Columbia Univ. Appts: Writer, Reporter, Sub-Ed., Newspapers in San Francisco, Chgo., N.Y.C., 1921-31; Paris Edit. Chgo. Tribune, Paris, France, 1931-34; Managing Ed., N.Y. Journal American, 1937-42; Lt-Cmdr., USNR, 1942-45. Liaison. Off., French Navy. 1943-44; Managing Ed. & Exec. Ed., Baltimore News American, 1956-70; Columnist, Hearst Newspapers & Edit. Cons., 1970-. Mbrships: Dramatists Guild (Authors League of Am.); Soc. of Profl. Jrnlsts., Sigma Delta Chi; Kt. Templar. Publs. incl: I Killed Stalin, 1951; Few Die Well, 1953; To Paris With Love, 1954; Hydra Head, 1955; Storm over Paris, 1955; Run For Your Life, 1958; Prelude to Murder, 1959; We Who Survived, 1959; Empire of Evil, 1960; num. film scripts & plays. Hons: Croix de Guerre & Silver Star, 1944; num. Combat Medals. Address: Apdo. Postal 357, San Miguel de Allende, Gto., Mexico. 2, 3.

STERN, Clarence A. Educator; Historian; Political Scientist. Educ: A.B., E. Mich. Univ., 1934; M.A., Wayne State Univ., Mich., 1938; Ph.D., Univ. of Neb., Lincoln, 1958. Appts: Tchr., Hist. & Soc. Sci., Mich. Pub. Schls., 1934-42, 1954-55; serv. w. USAAF, European Theatre of Ops., 1942-46; Asst. Prof., Coll. of Engrng., Lawrence Inst. of Technol., 1946-50; Assoc. Prof., Hist. & Pol. Sci., Wayne State Coll., 1958-65; Assoc. Prof., Hist., Univ. of Wis., Oshkosh, 1965-; Distributor, C.A. Stern Publs., 1962-. Mbrships. incl: var. offs., AAUP; ACLU; WCLU Comm. on Acad. Freedom, 1973-; AHA; Coun., Wis. Educ. Assn. Publs. incl: Republican Heyday: Republicanism through the McKinley Years, 1962, 1969; Golden Republicanism: The Crusade for Hard Money, 1964, 70; Protectionist Republicanism: Republican Tariff Policy in the McKinley Period, 1971. Address: Dept. of Hist., Univ. of Wis., Oshkosh, WI 54901, U.S.A. 8, 13, 14, 30, 120, 128, 129, 130, 131, 139.

STERN, Friedel. Cartoonist; Artist; Journalist; Graphic Designer; Lecturer. Educ: Schl. of Arts & Crafts, Leipzig; Bezalel Acad. of Art & Design, Jerusalem; Study in Paris. Lectr., Drawing, Bezalel Acad., 1961—. Mbrships: Israel Painters & Sculptors Assn.; Int. Assn. of Art, Paris; Graphic Designers Assn. of Israel; Icograda, London. Publs: Illuminated Atlas; In Short, Israel; 10 Israeli Postage Stamps. Contbr. to var. newspapers & periodicals, Israel & Europe. Illustrations for children's books. One-man exhib., Tel-Aviv, 1971; Sev. grp. shows. Radio & TV appearances. Hons: Palma di Bronza, Int. Cartoon Exhib., Bordighera, Italy, 1961; 2nd Prize, 1968, 5th Prize, 1969, Int. Cartoon Exhibs., Montreal. Address: 8 Yehoash St., Tel-Aviv, Israel. 94, 138.

STERN, (Rev. Dr.) Harry Joshua, b. 24 Apr. 1897. Rabbi. Educ: B.A., Univ. of Cinn., Ohio, 1920; B.H.L., Hebrew Union Coll., 1919; Rabbi, 1922. Appts: Rabbi, Temple Israel, Uniontown, Pa., 1922-27; Rabbi, Temple Emanu-El, Westmont, Montreal, Canada, 1927-72; Rabbi Emeritus, ibid, 1972-. Mbrships. incl: Am. Acad. Pol. & Soc. Sci.; Biblical Soc. Canada; Canadian Coun. Reform Rabbis; 1st Pres., Bd. Jewish Mins. of Gtr. Montreal; Fdr., Inst. on Judaism for Christian Clergy & Educrs. Publs. incl: The Jewish Spirit Triumphant, 1944; Martyrdom & Miracle, 1950; Pilgrimage to Israel, 1951; Entrusted with Spiritual Leadership, 1961; One World or No World, 1973; num. essays & sermons. Hons. incl: LL.D., McGill Univ., 1938; D.D., Hebrew Union Coll., 1947; D.Litt., Coll. of Steubenville, 1970; B'nai B'rith Humanitarian Award, 1968; Legion of Hon., Kiwanis Int., 1973. Address: 4100 Sherbrooke St., W., Montreal, P.Q. H3Z 1A5, Canada. 88.

STERN, James Andrew, b. 26 Dec. 1904. Author. Educ: R.M.C., Sandhurst, U.K. Fellow, Royal Soc. of Literature, 1953. Publs: The Heartless Land; Something Wrong; The Man Who Was Loved; The Hidden Damage; The Stories of James Stern. Hons: Nat. Inst. of Arts & Letters Grant, 1949; British Arts Coun. Award, 1966. Address: Hatch Manor, Tisbury, Wiltshire, U.K.

STERN, Pavao, b. 17 Mar. 1913. Professor of Pharmacology. Educ: Grad., Med. Fac., Zagreb, 1936; specialized studies in Pharmacol., Vienna & Amsterdam, 1937-38. Appts: Chief, Pharmacol. Inst. of pharmaceutical factory Pliva, 1939-45; Lectr., Pharmacol., Zagreb., 1945; Full Prof., Pharmacol., Med. Fac., Sarajevo, 1948-. Mbrships: active, Acad. of Scis. & Arts, Bosnia & Herzegovina; Corres., N.Y. Acad. of Scis., German French & N.Y. Allergol. Socs., European Allergol. Acad., Int. Psychopharmacol. Soc. (CIMP), Royal Soc. of Med. (London), Academia Medica Lombarda, European Toxicol. Soc., & Int. Bd., Int. Fedn. for Multiple Sclerosis Rsch. Rsch. interests incl: neuro & psychopharmacol., particularly w. diseases of Corpus Striatum & w. pharmacol. of "Substance P"; Pathophysiol. of Botulinus toxine & of Latrodectus Tredecimguttatus spider toxine; formerly interested in histamine & inflammation & now studying role of histamine in ctrl. nervous system. Hons: July 27 Award, Repub. of Bosnia & Herzegovina, 1960; Purkinj Medal, Czech. Soc. of Med., 1963. Address: c/o Dept. of Pharmacol., Med. Fac., 71001 Sarajevo, Yugoslavia.

STERNBERG, Herbert B., b. 20 May 1917. Mechanical & Systems Engineer. Educ: Columbia Univ., N.Y.C., U.S.A. Appts: Civil Servant, U.S. Army Engr., 1939-47; Combat Serv., 1940-44; Pvte. Cons. Serv., 1947-58; Pres., Auto Forte Systems, Inc., 1958-68; Pres., Automated Reference Corp., N.Y.C., 1968-. Holder, 4 U.S. patents, & Canadian, British & Italian patents. Address: 116 Central Park S., N.Y., NY 10019, U.S.A.

STERNBERG, Mary Jo, b. 17 Mar. 1928. Merchant; Artist. Educ: B.F.A., Tulane Univ., 1950. Appts: Sales Staff, Hardy Dabbs Interiors, Gulfport, 1950-52; Sales Dept. Mgr., Buyer, Northrops, 1952-55; Proprietor, Purple Lantern, Gulfport, 1955-, Br., Biloxi, 1972-. Mbrships: St. John's Cath. Ch., (Choir, 1942-73, Parish Coun., 1970); Bd. of Mgrs., Gift & Decorative Assn.; Gulfport Chmbr. of Comm. (V.P. 1970-73); Gulfport Little Theatre (past Chmn., Vice Chmn., Sec. Treas., Bd. of Trustees, 1971-72); Nat. Fedn. Ind. Bus.; Gulfport Merchants, (Exec. Comm., 1970). Recip. of Display Award, Gift & Decorative Accessories Mag., 1969, Nat. Awards of Merit, Color, Display, Lighting, 1967 & 1971. Address: 1640 E. Beach, Gulfport, MS 39501, U.S.A. 5.

STERNE, Richard Stephen, b. 9 May 1921. Sociologist. Educ: B.A., Swarthmore Coll., 1942; Duke Univ., 1948; Ph.D., Univ. of Pa., 1962. Appts: Rsch. Asst., Pa. Comm. on Penal Affairs, Phila., 1946; Rsch. Asst. & Instr., Tufts Coll., Mass., 1948-49; Instr., Northeastern Univ., Boston, 1949-50; Rsch. Cons., Mass. Comm. for Mid-Century White House Conf. on Children & Youth, Boston, 1950; Dir., Budgeting, R.I. Community Chests, Providence, 1951-55; Dir., Rsch. & Budgeting, Del. Valley United Fund, Trenton, N.J., 1955-60; Dir. of Rsch., Soc. Serv. Coun. of Gtr. Trenton, 1960-62; Dir., Rsch., Welfare Planning Coun., Dade Co., Fla., 1962-68; Adjunct Assoc. Prof., Univ. of Miami, 1962-68; Dir., Soc. Rsch., Citizens Planning Coun., Rochester, N.Y., 1968-73; Assoc. Prof., Urban Studies & Sociol., Univ. of Akron, Ohio, 1973-. Publs: Delinquent Conduct & Broken Homes, 1962; Contbr. to var. books & jrnls. Hon: Pi Gamma Mu, 1956. Address: Dept. of Urban Studies, Univ. of Akron, Akron, OH 44325, U.S.A. 6, 14, 30, 139.

STEURT, Marjorie Rankin, b. 8 Oct. 1888. Educationalist; Author. Educ: B.A., Mt. Holyoke Coll., 1911; M.A., Tchrs. Coll., Columbia Univ., 1928; Ph.D., ibid, 1929. Appts: Tchr. & H.S. Supvsr., China, Hd. of Engl. Dept., Ceeloo Univ., Hd. of Experimental Dept., Nankai Univ., Summer Tchr., Govt. Normal Schl., 1912-33; Hd., Psychol. Dept., Monmouth Jr. Coll., N.J., U.S.A., 1935-37; Psychologist, Hawthorne Schl. System, N.J., 1937-39; Operator of Experimental Airplane Engines, Write Aeronautical Co., WW II; Substitute Tchr., Hamet H.S., Calif., 1950-56; Cons. Psychologist, Hemet, & Tchr. Creative Writing, Adult Educ. Classes, 1965-69. Mbrships. incl: Pres., Int. Assn. of Univ. Women, 1932-; AAUW; Phi Beta Kappa. Publs. incl: Broken Bits of Old China, 1973. Address: P.O. Box 72, Hemet, CA 92343, U.S.A. 5.

STEVENS, Elisabeth Goss, b. 11 Aug. 1929. Writer. Educ: B.A., Wellesley Coll., 1951; M.A., Columbia Univ., 1956. Appts: Tchr., Engl. Composition & Lit., Upsala Coll., Fairleigh Dickinson Univ., & Staten Island Community Coll., 1958-63; Edit. Assoc., Art News mag., & free-lance writer, 1964; Art Critic & Reporter, The Wash. Post, 1965-66; free-lance writer, fiction & non-fiction, 1966-. Mbrships: Authors' League; Coll. Art Assn.; Sigma Delta Chi. Contbr., Wall St. Jrnl., 1969-73, var. newspapers & mags. Recip., Art Critics' Fellowship Award, Nat. Endowment for the Arts, 1973-74. Address: 289 Carter Rd., RD 2, Princeton, NJ 08540, U.S.A. 5, 133.

STEVENS, George Roy, b. 18 June 1892. Military & Business Historian; Author. Educ: B.A., Univ. of Alta., 1915. Appts. incl: Serv. w. Canadian Army, 1915-19; Canadian Govt. Trade Commr., Cuba, Jamaica, S. Africa, Peru, Australia; 1921-35; Cos. Dir., Johannesburg, 1935-39; P.R. Off., Int. Tea Bd., London, U.K., 1940-47; Lt.Col., Indian Army P.R. Liaison Off., on loan from Int. Tea Bd., 1942-46; retired Int. Tea Bd. & returned Canada as Mil. & Bus. Histn., 1947. Mbr., United Servs. Club, 1922-. Publs. incl: English Harvest, 1935; The Tiger Kills, 1943; Ogilvie in Canada, 1951; A City Goes to War, 1964; Canadian National Railways, 1973. Over 100 short stories in mags. & jrnls., Canada, U.K., U.S.A., S. Africa. Hons: O.B.E., 1946; LL.D., D. Litt., Univ. of Alta., 1964. Address: 144 Strathearn Ave., Montreal W., H4X-1X9, Canada.

STEVENS, Jocelyn Edward Greville, b. 14 Feb. 1932. Newspaper Executive. Educ: Trinity Coll., Cambridge Univ., U.K. Appts: Chmn., Mng. Dir., Stevens Press Limited, & Ed., Queen Magazine, 1957-68; Personal Asst., to Chmn., Beaverbrook Newspapers Ltd., 1968; Mng. Dir., Evening Standard Co. Limited, 1969-72; Mng. Dir., Daily Express, 1972-. Address: Daily Express, 121 Fleet St., London EC4A 2NJ, U.K. 1, 12, 32.

STEVENS, Leslie Clark b. 19 Feb. 1895. Naval Officer; Retired Vice Admiral. Educ: A.B., Neb. Wesleyan Coll., 1913; Grad., U.S. Naval Acad., 1918; M.S., MIT, 1922. Appts. incl: Queenstown Destroyer Forces, WW I; Naval Aviator, 1924; i/c Carrier Installation, Bur. of Aeronautics, 1926-30; Asst. Naval Attaché, Am. Embassy, London, 1934-37; Advsr., London Disarmament Conf., 1936; on staff Cmdr. Aircraft, forward area in Pacific, WW II; Asst. Chief, Bur. Aeronautics, Rsch. & Dev., Wash. D.C., 1946-47; Naval Attaché & Naval Air attaché, Moscow, 1947-49; w. Jt. Chiefs of Staff, Wash. D.C., 1949-51; Ret. as Vice Admiral, USN, 1951. Mbrships. incl: Chmn., Am. Comm. for Liberation from Bolshevism, N.Y.C., 1951-52; Inst. of Aero Scis.; Am. Anthropol. Assn.; Archaeol. Inst.; Explorers Club; N.Y. Yacht Club, N.Y.C.; PEN; Army-Navy Club, Wash. D.C.; Army-Navy Country Club, Wash. D.C. Publs: Russian Assignment (U.K. title, Life in Russia); contbr. to U.S. Naval Inst. jrnl., Atlantic Monthly, Life mag. & Readers Digest. Hons: CBE; Legion of Merit, U.S.A.; Bronze Star, U.S.A.; Commendation Ribbon, ibid; Plaque Commemorating 1st 44 Offs. selected by Sec. of Navy for Naval Aeronautical Engrng. Duty. Address: Annapolis, MD, U.S.A.

STEVENS, Ramona Katherine (Mrs. William R. Stevens), b. 30 Mar. 1933. Public Relations Advisor. Educ: Grad., Van Sant's Bus. Coll., Omaha; Coll. Ext. Courses, Nat. Delphian Soc., 14 yrs. Appts. incl: Radio & TV Script Writer, Handy-Andy Supermarkets, Inc.; Ed.,

Handy-Andy Herald; Exec. Sec., Handy-Andy, Inc.; P.R. Advsr., Community Realty, Inc. Mbrships. incl: San Antonio Coun. of Pres.', Pres., 1970-72, 1st, 3rd & 4th V.P., Recording Sec.; San Antonio Coun. of Delphian Chapts., V.P., 1964, Pres., 1965; San Antonio Club Women of Today, V.P.; United Way of San Antonio, Bd. Mbr.; Tex. Fedn. of Women's Clubs, Bd. Mbr.; San Antonio Women's Fedn., Inc., Bd. Mbr.; San Antonio Conservation Soc.; Nat. Assn. of Parliamentarian; Inner Wheel, San Antonio Rotary; Concordia Luth. Ch., San Antonio, Chmn., Women's Evangelism Comm., Treas., Adult Bible Class. Hons. incl: Outstanding Serv. Award, San Antonio Club Women of Today, 1964-74; Nat. Award of Merit, Nat. Delphian Soc., 1965; Outstanding Serv. Award, San Antonio Women's Fend., 1967, 1968; Outstanding Ldrship., San Antonio Coun. of Pres.', 1971, 1972; Outstanding Ldrship., United Way of San Antonio, 1971, 1972; San Antonio Outstanding Club Woman, 1970 Express-News Contest; San Antonio Outstanding Civic Ldrship. Award, 1973; "Matrix Headliner" Sponsored by Women In Communication (formerly Theta Sigma Phi). Address: 622, Wyndale Drive, San Antonio, TX 78209, U.S.A. 57, 125.

STEVENSON, Hugh Lee, b. 27 Nov. 1924. Phonograph Recording Executive; Writer. Appts: Serv., USAAF, 1943-46; Owner, Stevensons Ins. Agcy., Richlands, Va., 1947-53; Mgr., Rubestons Furniture Co., Elkton, Md., 1953-58; Ptnr., A & R Blue Hen Record Co., Harrington, Del., 1956-; Ptnr. & Mgr., Stevensons Furniture Co., Elkton, 1958-64; Owner, Hugh Lee Stevenson Music, 1960; Pres., Three Star Record Co., Newark, Del., 1963; Pres., Reprize Records, 1967; Agt.-Mgr., musicians, Three Star Prods., Elkton, 1968-; Pres., Jude Gospel Records. Mbrships: Am. Soc. Composers, Authors & Publrs.; Hist. Soc.; Sons of Confederate Veterans; Civil War Round Table; Mason. Publs: num. musical compositions & Poems. Address: Todd Estates, Newark, DE 19711, U.S.A. 6.

STEVNING, Donald A., b. 26 Jan. 1907. Citrus Ranch & Packing Plant Owner & President. Educ: B.S., U.S. Mil. Acad., 1929. Appts: Owner, Coachella Ranches, Indio, Calif., 1946-; Gen. Mgr., L.V.W. Brown Estate, Riverside, Calif., 1946-; Fndr. & Pres., Stevning Citrus, Inc., Coachella, Calif., 1963-; Dir., Sunkist Growers, Inc, Calif. Chmbr. of Comm., Co. River Assn., & Calif. Date Growers Assn. Mbrships: Calif. Club, L.A., Calif.; Newport Harbor Yacht Club, Newport Beach, Calif.; Thunderbird Country Club, Palm Springs, Calif.; La Quinta Country Club, Calif. Awarded Legion of Merit, USAAF, 1945. Address: P.O. Box 1028, Coachella, CA 92236, U.S.A. 9, 16.

STEWARD, (Sir) William Arthur, b. 20 Apr. 1901. Restaurateur; Politician; Farmer. Appts: MP for W. Woolwich (Conservative), 1950-59; Chmn., Kitchen Comm., House of Commons, 1951-59; Mbr., London Co. Coun., 1949-52. Mbrships: Master, Worshipful Co. of Distillers, 1964-65; Carlton Club; Royal Thames Yacht Club; Nat. Sporting Club. Hons: Kt. Bachelor, England, 1955; Kt., Order of St. Lazarus of Jerusalem, 1972. Address: Palazzo Marnisi, Marsaxlokk, Malta. I.

STEWART, David Francis, b. 14 Dec. 1925. Chemical Engineer; Plant Manager; Vice President of Manufacturing. Educ: B.S., Chem. Engrng., Ohio State Univ., Columbus. Appts: Chemist, Ohio Dept. of Hlth. Water Pollution Control, 1949-51; Prod. Foreman, Marketing & Sales, Tech. Serv. Rep., Koppers Co., Pitts., Pa., 1951-59; Plant Mgr., V.P., Mfg., Sweetheart

Plastics, Wilmington, Mass., 1959-. Mbrships: Alpha Lodge, A. F. & A. M., Framingham, Mass. Holds U.S. patent. Address: 23 Hillview Rd., N. Reading, MA 01864, U.S.A. 6.

STEWART, Dwight Davies, b. 22 Apr. 1907. Rancher; Horse Breeder, Trainer & Exhibitor; Writer; Lecturer. Educ: Ariz. State Coll. Appts: Trainer, Show Horses; Approved Judge, AQHA & AHSA; Instr., Equitation; Writer & Lectr. on Horses. Mbrships. incl: Past Pres., Calif. Cutting Horse Assn.; Life mbr., ibid; Past Pres., Ariz. Profl. Horse Trainer's Assn.; Life mbr., ibid, 1968; Dir., Nev. Quarter Horse Assn.; Dir., Lone Star Quarter Horse Assn., currently; Am. Quarter Horse Assn.; Am. Horse Shows, Inc.; Nev. State Horseman; Am. Horse Coun.; Masonic Lodge, Tujunga, Calif.; S.W. Cattlemen's Assn. Publs. incl: Western Quitation, Horsemanship & Showmanship, 1973; Articles in var. jrnls. Address: P.O. Box, 2415, Huntridge Stn., Las Vegas, NV 89104, U.S.A.

STEWART, Fred Mustard, b. 17 Sept. 1932. Novelist; Screenwriter. Educ: B.A. (Hist.) Princeton Univ., N.J., 1954. Publs. (novels): The Mephisto Waltz, 1968, (made into a film), translated into 13 langs; The Methuselah Enzyme, 1970, tranlated into French, German, Italian, Dutch, Spanish, Japanese; Lady Darlington, 1971, tranlated into French; The Manning, 1973. Mbrships: P.E.N. Club; Author's League of Am.; Writers' Guild of America (East); Dramatists' Guild. Address: Muller Road, Kent, CT 06757, U.S.A.

STEWART, Hal D., b. 7 Mar. 1899. Author; Theatrical Manager. Appts: 2nd Lt., Lt., Royal Field Artillery, 1917; Dir., Henry J. Stewart & Bro., 1921-37; Actor & Stage Mgr., Scottish Nat. Players, 1928-37; Stage Mgr., Howard & Wyndham Repertory Co., 1938; Prod., Colchester Repertory Co., 1938-39; w. Royal Artillery in rank of Maj., City of Glasgow Field Reg., 1939-45; Stage Dir., W. End, London, 1945-55; Gen. Mgr., Players Theatre Ventures, 1955-. Mbrships: PEN; Players Theatre Club; Arts Theatre Club. Author of num. profl. publs. Hons: Territorial Decoration, 1939; Mentioned in Despatches, 1944; Netherlands Bronze Lion, 1945. Address: 12 Goodwin's Ct., London WC2N 4LL, U.K. 3, 30, 43, 128, 131.

STEWART, Harris Bates, Jr., b. 19 Sept. 1922. Oceanographer. Educ: A.B., Princeton Univ., 1948; M.S., Scripps Instn. Oceanog., Univ. of Calif., 1952; Ph.D., ibid, 1956. Appts: Chief Oceanog., U.S. Coast & Geodetic Survey, 1957-65; Dpty. Asst. Dir., ibid, 1962-65; Dir., Atlantic Oceanog. & Meteorol. Labs., Environmental Sci. Servs. Admin. 1965-70; Dir., Atlantic Oceanog. & Meteorol. Labs., Nat. Oceanic & Atmospheric Admin., 1970-. Mbrships. incl: Chmn., Fla. Commn. Marine Scis. & Technol.; Pres., Zool. Soc. Fla.; V.P., Econ. Soc. S. Fla.; Fellow, Geol. Soc. Am. Publs: The Global Sea, 1963; Deep Challenge, 1966; The Id of the Squid, 1970. Recip., two awards, U.S. Dept. of Commerce, 1960, 1965. Address: NOAA, Atlantic Oceanographic & Meteorological Lab., 15 Bickenbacker Causeway, Virginia Key, FL 33149, U.S.A. 2, 14, 50.

STEWART, Jeannie Calder, b. 19 Nov. 1913. Psychologist. Educ: A.B., Brown Univ., Providence, R.I., U.S.A., 1945; A.M., Univ. of Calif., 1945. Appts: Investigator, Jackson Lab., Me., Summer, 1946; Rsch. Asst., ibid, 1945; Instr., Vassar Coll., Poughkeepsie, N.Y., 1946-49; Rsch. Asst., Brown Univ., 1953-56; Rsch. Staff, Pembroke Coll., 1954-61; Rsch. Staff, Boston Univ., Mass., 1966-70; Rsch.

Advsr., Garland Jr. Coll., Boston, 1965-66 & 1970-71; W. House in the Pines Schl., 1971-72; Expediting Dept., Stone & Webster Engrng. Corp., Boston, 1973-74. Mbrships. incl: Am. Psychol. Assn.; AAAS; Eastern Psychol. Assn.; R.I. Psychol. Assn.; Nominating Comm., Boston Br., AAUW; Engl. Speaking Union; Deleg., 19th Int. Congress Psychol., U.K., 1969. Publs: Lack of Correlation between Dominance & Leadership (w. J.P. Scott), 1947; Extinction of Success Aspiration (w. A.Gilinsky). Address: 5 Concord Ave., Apt. 32, Cambridge, MA 02138, U.S.A. 138.

STEWART, Lawrence H., b. 5 Oct. 1922. University Professor. Educ: B.S., Western Carolina Univ., 1943; M.A. & Ed. D., Tchrs. Coll., Columbia Univ., 1947-50. Appts: Asst. Prof., Educl. Psychol., George Peabody Coll. for Tchrs., Nashville, Tenn., 1950-54; Asst. Prof.-Prof., Educ. (Counseling Psychol.), Univ. of Calif., Berkely, 1954-; Vis. Prof., Educ., Univ. of Ore., Eugene, summer 1960; Vis. Prof., Psychol., Univ. of Hawaii, summer 1962, & N.C. State Univ., Raleigh, summer 1963. Mbrships: Fellow, Am. Psychological Assn.; Am. Personnel & Guidance Assn.; Nat. Vocational Guidance Assn.; Am. Personnel & Guidance Assn.; Nat. Vocational Guidance Assn.; Am. Educl. Rsch. Assn.; AAAS; Int. Assn. for Educl. & Vocational Guidance. Author of over 60 articles & monographs dealing w. measurement, manpower dev. & guidance fields; Co-author of The Counselor & Society (w. C. Warnath), 1965. Hons: Disting. Alumni, Western Carolina Univ., 1960; Fulbright Fellowship, Univ. of Reading, U.K., 1968-69. Address: Schl. of Educ., Univ. of Calif., Berkeley, CA 94720, U.S.A. 14, 131.

STEWART, Ora Pate (Mrs. Robert W.), b. 23 Aug. 1910. Writer; Lecturer; Composer; Poet. Appts. incl: w. Nat. Artist & Lectr. Serv., 1953-; Lectr., numerous coll. forums; Pres., Hollywood Branch, Nat. League of Am. Pen Women; Historian, Calif.-Utah Women's Club; Mbr. of Bd., Ettie Lee Homes for Boys, Inc.; State Pres., Mutual Improvement Assoc., 1967-68; Poetry Soc. of Am., 1946-; World Poetry Soc., 1969. Publs. incl: Pages From the Book of Eve; I Talk About My Children; Gleanings; Brown Leaves Turning; West Wind Song; Mopey the Mop; Tender Apples; A Ladder in the Sky; Buttermilk and Bran; God Planted A Tree; Branches Over the Wall; Treasures Unearthed; Dear Land of Home; A Letter to My Son; A Letter to My Daughter; We Believe; This World of Wisdom From Where I Stood; How Beautiful Upon the Mountains; Heroes in Gold; The Brightness of Hope; Golden Promise. Composer of songs, including 'To A Child'. Numerous awards for writing including Nat. First Place award for short story, 'The Tramp', 1968. Address: 11282 Anabel Ave., Garden Grove, CA 92640, U.S.A. 5, 9, 11, 22, 59.

STEWART, P. Brian, b. 7 Aug. 1922. Physician. Educ: M.B.B.S., Middlesex Hosp., London, 1950; M.R.C.P., London, 1953. Appts: House Physn., Middlesex, Brompton Hosps., London, 1950-52; Gen. Prac., Barnstaple, Devon, 1952-54; Rsch. Assoc., Nat. Rsch. Coun. of Canada, & Dept. of Physion., McGill Univ., Montreal, 1957-; Asst. Prof. of Med., McGill Univ., 1957-; Asst. Physn., Royal Vic. Hosp., Montreal, 1957-; Med. Dir., Geigy Canada Ltd., 1957-62; Rsch. Dir., Pharma-Rsch. Canada Ltd., 1962-. Mbrships: Am. Physiol. Soc.; Canadian Soc. of Immunol.; Am. Assn.; Immunologists; Canadian Pharmacological Soc.; Canadian Med. Assn.; Brit. Med. Assn.; Transplantation Soc. Contbr.

to profl. jrnls. Hons: D.F.C., 1944. Address: Pharma-Research Canada Ltd., 250, Hymus Blvd., Pointe Claire, P.Q. H9R 1G8. Canada.

STEWART, Peggy Lou, b. 7 Dec. 1936. Biologist. Educ: A.B., E. Carolina Coll., 1957; M.A., Univ. of Kan., 1950; Fellowship in Zool., ibid, 1956-60. Appts: Spectroscopist, Chemstrand Rsch. Ctr., 1961-63; Rsch. Asst., Analytical Hlth. Phys., Univ. of Tenn., 1963-65, Rsch. Assoc., 1965-69; Pres., Stewart Labs. Inc., 1968-; Mbrships: Soc. of Applied Spectroscopy; Hlth. Phys. Soc.; N.Y. Acad. Scis.; Water Pollution Control Fedn.; Knoxville Exec. Club; Chi Beta Pi; Phi Sigma; Sigma Xi. Profl. papers, var. publs. Address: c/o. Stewart Laboratories Inc., 820 Tulip Ave., Knoxville, TN 37921, U.S.A.

STEYN, Douw Gerbrand, b. 7 Mar. 1898. Emeritus Professor of Pharmacology. Educ: B.Sc., Univ. of Stellenbosch, S. Africa, 1919; Veterinary Schl., Univ. of Utrecht, Netherland, 1920-21; Veterinary Schl., Univ. of Vienna, Austria, 1922-24; Dr.Med.Vet., Univ. of Pretoria, 1925; Dr.Med.Vet. (Pharmacol.), ibid, 1934. Hd., Sect. of Toxicol. & Pharmacol., Veterinary Rsch. Instn., Orderstepoort (Pretoris) & Prof., Pharmacol. & Toxicol., Univ. of Pretoria, 1925-46; Prof. of Pharmacol., Med. Fac., Univ. of Pretoria, 1946-63; Positions at var. rsch. instns., govt. comms. & commns. of enquiry. Mbr., var. assns. Author of over 200 articles in med., veterinary, botanical, chem. jrnls. & of 4 books. Hons. incl: Sr. Capt. Scott Medal, S. African Biological Soc.; Dom Steyn Symposium, S. African Chem. Soc. Address: 456 Sappers Contour, Lynnwood, Pretoria, Repub. of S. Africa.

STICE, Janice Lorraine (Mrs.A.I. Stice), b. 1 May 1899. Teacher of Piano. Educ: William Woods Coll. for Women; Student of E. R. Kroeger, St. Louis, E. Robert Schmitz, Paris & San Fran. Appts: Pvte. Tchr., piano, St. Louis, Mo., 1938-53, Ozark, Mo., 1954-. Mbrships: Past Pres., mbr., Piano Tchrs. Round Table, St. Louis; Adjudicator, Nat. Guild of Piano Tchrs., Austin, Tex., 15 yrs.; Piano Tchrs. Forum, St. Louis; Springfield Music Club; Mo. State Music Tchrs. Assn.; Nat. Music Tchrs. Assn.; Charter Mbr., Phi Theta Kappa. Address: 711 E. McCracken Rd., Ozark, MO 65721, U.S.A. 120.

STIEGLITZ, William Irving, b. 7 June 1911. Engineering Consultant. Educ: B.S., Aero. Engrng., MIT, 1932. Appts. incl: Chief Tech. Engr., Ctrl. Aircraft Corp., Keyport, N.J., 1938-41; Chief, Aerodyn. & Flight Testing, Fleetwings Div., Kaiser Corp., Bristol, Pa., 1941-44; Spl. Lectr., Aerodynamics, Princeton Univ., 1942-43; Design Engr. to Mgr., Design Safety & Reliability Div., Repub. Aviation Corp., Farmingdale, N.Y., 1944-64; Mbr., sev. advsry. bodies for aviation, 1951-58; Adjunct Prof. of Phys., C.W. Post Coll., 1956-59; Ptnr., William I. Stieglitz Assocs., Huntington, N.Y., 1964-; Vis. Lectr., Nat. Aircraft Accident Investigation Schl., 1965; Cons., sev. Fed. & State Aviation & Vehicle bodies. Mbrships. incl: AIAA; Royal Aeronaut. Soc.; Soc. of Automotive Engrs.; System Safety Soc. (Chmn., N.E. Chapt., 1971-72); V.P., N.Y. Chapt., 1971-72, '72-73, Soc. of Air Safety Investigators. Contbr. to profl. publs. Author of "Automobile Accident Reconstruction" in Products Liability, 1972. Address: Nine Howard Dr., Huntington, NY 11743, U.S.A. 6, 26.

STIER, William Frederick, Jr., b. 22 Feb. 1943. Professor & administrator. Educ: B.A.,

St. Ambrose Coll., Davenport, Iowa, 1965; Masters degree, Temple Univ., Phila., Pa., 1966; Doct., Univ. of S.D., 1972. Appts. incl: Chmn., Hlth., Phys. Educ., Recreation & Athletics & Varsity Basketball Coach, Briar Cliff Coll., Sioux City, Iowa, 1968-71; Dir., Intercollegiate Athletics, Shepherd State Coll., Shepherdstown, W. Va., 1972-73; Chmn., Hlth., Phys. Educ., Recreation & Athletics & Varsity Basketball Coach, St. Mary's Coll., Winona, Minn., 1973-. Mbrships. incl: Am. Assn. for Hlth., Phys. Educ. & Recreation; Nat. Assn. for Intercollegiate Athletics; NEA; Am. Red Cross; Nat. Assn. of Collegiate Dirs. of Athletics. Author of num. articles in jrnls. Recip., Outstanding Phys. Educ. Major Award, St. Ambrose Coll., 1964-65. Address: P.O. Box 915, Winona, MN 55987, U.S.A.

STIERNSTEDT, (Baron) W. Gordon, b. 10 June 1885. Former Maaging Director. Educ: Dr.Phil.; Kand.Juris. Appts: Mng. Dir., Stockholm Chmbr. of Comm., Sweden; Sec., Swedish Bd. Trade. Author sev. books on commercial, geneal. & histl. subjects etc. Recip. Hon. degree, Dr. Phil., Uppsala Univ., Sweden & sev. Swedish & for. decorations. Address: Levenstams Vag 40, S-12385, Farsta - Stockholm, Sweden 43.

STIFTER, Herbert Josef Gustav, b. 25 Oct. 1897. Author. Educ: Ph.D., Univ. of Graz, Austria, 1922. Appts: Ed., Tyrol, periodical, Innsbruck, 1924; Ed., Bergland, monthly jrnls., Innsbruck & Vienna, 1926; w. Philips Works, Eindhoven, Netherlands, 1940; Hon. Vice Consul for Austria, 1947; Lectr., Netherlands Coll. For. Serv., 1947-49; Hon. Consul for Austria in N.-Brabant & Limburg, Netherlands, 1951; var. activities in jrnlsm. Mbr., int. profl. orgs. Publs: Menschenland; Grenzenlos; Der unzahmbare Vogel; Iffinger (co-author); Lict aus Assisi; W.N. Prachensky, ein Malerleben. Co-author, monographies. Contbr., anthols. Translator, sev. books, from Dutch & French into German. Hons. incl: Silver Medal for Bravery, 1917; Signum laudis, 1918; Goldenes Ehrenzeichen für Verdienste um die Republik Osterreich, 1961. Address: Goorstraat 1, Eindhoven, Netherlands. 43, 86, 100.

STIGEN, Anfinn, b, 22 Oct. 1923. Professor of Philosophy. Educ: M.A., Univ. of Chgo., 1953; Mag.art. & Cand.philol., Univ. of Oslo, Norway, 1954; Studies at Sorbonne, Paris, France, & Oxford, U.K. Appts: Univ. Lectr., Univ. of Oslo, 1956-61; Asst. Prof., Univ. of Aarhus, Denmark, 1961-65; Assoc. Prof., Univ. of Oslo, Norway, 1965-72; Chmn., Coun. of Examen philosophicum, ibid, 1971-; Asst. Dean of Humanities, ibid, 1970-72. Publs: The theory of universals in Aristotle, Leibniz & Locke, 1953; Ideas in philosophies & histories, 1954; Betydning og mening, handling og ytring, 1967; The structure of Aristotle's thought, 1966; Aristoteles, 1964; Wittgenstein, 1967; Filosofiske tekster, Vol. 1.2, 1958; Gud i moderne filosofi, 1968; Generasjoner i norsk filosofi, 1973; Arbeid og menneskeverd, 1973; (translations) Plato's Apology, Gorgias, Crito, Phaido, & Symposion; Aristotle's Nicomachean Ethics; Contbr. of articles to var. profl. jrnls. Hons. incl: Smith-Mundt-Fulbright Schlrship., 1951-52; Univ. Fellow, Univ. of Chgo., 1952-53; Boursier, French Govt., 1956-57; British Coun. Schl., 1958-59. Address: Inst. of Philos., Univ. of Oslo, Blindern, Oslo 3, Norway. 134;

STIGLICH, Nicholas M., b. 2 July 1918. Consulting Professional Engineer. Educ: B.M.E., Brooklyn Polytec. Inst.; Nuclear Engrng., Stevens Inst.; Bus. Admin., Alexander Hamilton Inst.; M.Engrng.Mgmt., Brooklyn Polytech. Inst. Appts: Ptnr. & Supvsr., George G. Sharp Co., 1940-64; Cons. Engr. & Pres., Eness Rsch. & Dev. Corp., 1964-. Mbrships: Nat. Soc. Profl. Engrs.; Soc. Naval Archts. & Marine Engrs.; Int. Material Mgmt. Soc.; Am. Mgmt. Assn.; Marine Technol. Soc.; Instrument Soc. of Am.; Int. Cargo Handling Co-Ordination Assn. Holder of 2 U.S. Patents. Author of profl. papers. Address: 75 Carver Ave., Westwood, NJ 07675, U.S.A. 16.

STIKEMAN, Harry Heward, b. 8 July 1913. Barrister; Legal Editor; Writer. Educ: B.A., B.C.L., McGill Univ., Canada; D.S., Univ. of Dijon, France. Appts: Sr. Ptnr., Stikeman, Elliott, Tamaki, Mercier & Robb, Montreal, Stikeman, Elliott, Robarts & Bowman, Toronto; Ed.-in-Chief, Richard De Boo Ltd., Toronto; Former Asst. Depty. Min., Revenue, Ottawa. Mbrships. incl: Bar. P.Q.; Law Soc.; Upper Canada; Canadian Tax Fndn.; The Mt. Royal Club, Montreal. Publs: Stikeman Income Tax Act; Canada Tax Service; Canada Tax Cases; Canada Tax Manual; Canada Tax Letter. Address: 1155 Dorchester Blvd. W., Montreal H3B 3V2, P.Q., Canada. 38.

STILES, Lindley J., b. 1 July 1913. Professor of Education. Educ: A.B., 1935, M.A., 1939, Ed.D., 1945, Univ. of Colo. Appts: Prin., Northside Jr. H.S., Boulder, 1939-41; Dir., Instrn., Boulder Pub. Schls., 1941-43; Prin., Sr. H.S., Boulder, 1943-45; Dir., Student Tchng., Univ. of Ill., 1946-47; Assoc. Prof. & Dir., Grad. Studies in Educ., Ohio State Univ., 1947-49; Dean. Schl. of Educ., Univ. of Va., 1949-55, & Univ. of Wis., 1955-56; Prof., Educ. for Inter-disciplinary Studies, Northwestern Univ., 1966-. Mbrships. incl: Past Pres., Nat. Soc. of Coll. Tchrs. of Educ.; Past Mbr., Exec. Comm., John Dewey Soc.; Past Pres., Aerospace Educ. Fndn.; AAAS; Am. Acad. of Soc. & Pol. Sci.; AAUP; NEA; Am. Assn. for Higher Educ. Publs. incl: Supervision as Guidance (co-author), 1946; Moods & Moments (poems), 1955; The Scholar Teacher, 1966; The Present State of Neglect, 1967. Hons. incl: D.Litt. Rider Coll.; LL.D., McKendree Coll.; Hoyt S. Vandenberg Trophy, Air Force Assn., 1962. Address: 1211 Pleasant Rd., Glenview, IL 60025, U.S.A. 2, 8, 14, 15, 30, 120, 126, 128, 141.

STILL, Rex. G., b. 14 Apr. 1904. Retired Civil Engineer. Educ: Purdue Univ., 1927. Appts: w. Wash. State Dept. of Hwys., Olympia, 1927-35; Proj. Engr., ibid, 1935-39; Asst. Dist. Maintenance Engr. & Safety Engr., 1939-41; Dist. Traffic Engr., 1941-48; Asst. State Traffic Engr., 1948-51; State Traffic Engr., 1951-68. Mbrships: Am. Assn. of State Hwy. Officials; Hwy. Rsch. Bd.; Inst. of Traffic Engrs.; Mason; Elks. Hons: Award of Merit in Traffic Engrng., N.W. Trucking Assn., 1950; 1st Place Award, Outstanding Performance in Traffic Engrng., Nat. Safety Coun., 1950-65; Award of Merit, Wash. State Patrol, 1968. Address: Rt. 7, Box 588-A, Olympia, WA 98506, U.S.A. 9, 120

STILLWAGON, Drucilla Jane, b. 12 Nov. 1929. Teacher; Writer; Poetess; Hypnotist. Educ: B.S., Ball State Tchrs. Coll., Muncie, Ind., 1951; M.A., 1957; Ph.D., Purdue Univ., La Fayette. Appts: Speech & Hearing Therapist, Cerebral Palsy Clin., ind. Univ. Med. Ctr., Indpls.; Tchr., Engl., Speech & Drama & Drama Dir., Muncie Community Schls., Southside H.S. & Ctrl. H.S.; Hd., Speech & Drama Dept. & Drama Dir., Polk-Lincoln-Johnson Community Schls., St. Joseph Co.; Currently, Tchr., Engl., Creative Writing & Drama, Crown Point, H.S. Mbrships. incl: NEA; Ind. Speech Assn.; Ind. State Tchrs.

Assn.; Int. Thespian Soc.; Theta Alpha Phi. Author of poems & articles in var. publs. Recip., Purdue Univ. Schlrship for Grad. Studies, 1965. Address: Crown Point H.S., 401 W. Joliet St., Crown Point, IN, U.S.A. 57, 130.

STILLWELL, Ray, b. 10 Aug. 1910. Librarian. Educ: B.A., Univ. of Calif. at L.A., 1927-29; Cert. in Libnship., Schl. of Libnship., Univ. of Calif., Berkeley, 1929-30; M.S., Schl. of Lib. Serv., Columbia Univ., N.Y.C., 1943. Appts incl: Asst. libn., Securities & Exchange Commn., Wash., D.C., 1925-42 & Phila., Pa., 1942-43; Hd. Cataloger, UN Relief & Rehab. Admin., 1944; Asst. Attaché (Dir. of Lib. Servs.), U.S. Info. Serv. Lib., Am. Embassy, Lisbon, Portugal, 1950-52; Supvsr., Engrng. Lib., Temco Aircraft Corp., Dallas, Tex., 1955-56; Libn., U.S. Army Lang. Trng. Facility, Ft. Hood, Tex., 1958-63; Libn., Tech. Lib., U.S. Navy Fleet Computer Programming Ctr., Pacific, San Diego, Calif., 1964-69. Mbr., San Diego Historical Soc. Hons: First Prize, Post-War Planning Contest, Lubbock Evening Jnl., Tex., 1943; Outstanding Performance Rating, Dept. of Army, 1963. Address: 570 Tarento Drive, San Diego, CA 92106, U.S.A. 9, 42, 57, 59, 132.

STINDL, Erwin, b. 28 Nov. 1925. Publishing Manager. Educ: Acad. of Govt. Admin. & Econs. Appts: Chief-Ed., Deutsche Tagespost, 1956-; Publng. Mgr., ibid, 1969-. Mbrships: Zentraler Familienrat; Treas., Deutsches Aussstzigen- Hilfswerk E.V.; Bund Katholischer Unternehmer. Publs: num. books 7 articles on socio-political topics. Hons: Homayoun Order of Iran; Komtur des Ordens des Hl. Silvester; Goldene Ehrennadel des Volksbundes Deutsche Kriegsgräberfürsorge. Address: 3, Schönleinstr., D-78 Würzburg, German Fed. Repub. 92.

STINNETT, Nick, Jr., b. 27 Sept. 1942. Associate Professor of Family Relations & Child Development. Educ: B.A., Univ. of Ga., Athens, U.S.A., 1963; M.S., Fla. State Univ., Tallahassee, 1965; Ph.D., ibid, 1967. Appts: Asst. Prof., Dept. of Family Rels. & Child Dev., Okla. State Univ., Stillwater, 1967-69; Assoc. Prof., ibid, 1970-; Pres., Okla. Coun. on Family Rels., 1970-72; Chmn., Community White House Conf. on Aging, 1971. Mbrships: Nat. Coun. on Family Rels.; Am. Home Econs. Assn.; Omicron Nu; Phi Upsilon Omicron. Publs: Weekly column on family rels., sev. newspaper, Okla., Tex., & Kan., 1970-72; Ed., Readings in Family Relationships, 1970; Ed., Home Economics Research Abstracts, Family Relations & Child Devlopment, 3 vols., 1970, 71, & 72; Contbns. (some w. co-authors) to profl. jrnls. Address: Dept. of Family Relations & Child Development, Oklahoma State University, Stillwater, OK 74074, U.S.A. 125.

STIRRAT, James Hill, b. 17 Sept. 1913. Physician-Pathologist. Educ: B.Sc., Glasgow Univ., U.K., 1935; M.B., Ch.B., ibid, 1938; M.D., 1945; F.R.C., Founder Fellowship, Coll. of Pathols., U.K., 1963; Cert. in Pathol., Univ. of Alta., Canada, 1964; F.C.A.P., Coll. of Am. Pathols., 1964. Appts. incl: Dir., Dept. of Lab. Med., Misericoridis Hosp., Edmonton, Alta., Canada, 1963073, Bacteriologist, Dept. of Lab. Med., & Chmn., Infection Control Comm., 1973-; Asst. Prof. of Pathol., Univ. of Alta., 1963-; Advsr., Schl. of Med. Lab. Technol., Northern Alta. Inst. of Technol., 1963-73.; Cons., Bacteriol. & Pathol., var. hosps.; Chmn., Edit. Bd., Alta. Med. Bulletin, 1957-60. Mbrships. incl: Sec.-Treas., Alta. Soc. of Pathols., 1964-66; The Fac. Club, Univ. of Alta., Edmonton; The Sir Winston Churchill

Soc.; Canadian Soc. Forensic Med.; Sci. Assn. of Univ. of Alta.; Past Pres. & V.P., Collip Rsch. Club, ibid; Past Ed. & Asst. Ed., Alta. Med. Jrnl., Canadian Med. Assn., Alta. Div.; sev. comms., Misericordia Hosp. Author/Co-author of essays, edits., case reports, etc. in med. jrnls. Address: 601 Valleyview Manor, 12207 Jasper Ave., Edmonton, Alta. T5N 3K2, Canada, 9, 14.

STIRRAT, William Albert, b. 5 Nov. 1919. Electronic Engineer. Educ: Triuna Arts of Theatre Schl., 1936; Saratoga Eastman Schl. of Bus., 1936-37; B.S., Rensleaer Polytech. Inst., 1942; Grad. Student, Rensselaer Polytech. Inst., 1949-50; Grad. Student, Rutgers Univ., 1951-58; Grad. Student, Fairleigh Dickinson Univ., 1971. Appts: Student Engr., Gen. Elec. Co., 1942-43; Rsch. Asst., Rensselaer Polytech. Inst., Troy, N.Y., 1941-42 & '49-50; Instr. in Phys., Clarkson Coll. of Technol., Potsdam, N.Y., 1947-49; Electrn. Engr., U.S. Army Electrn. Command, Ft. Monmouth, N.J., 1950-. Mbrships. incl: Sr. Mbr., IEEE; Assoc. Ed., IEEE G-EMC Trans.; Assoc. Ed., IEEE N.J. Coast Sect. G-EMC; formber mbr., Am. Phys. Soc. & Inst. of Environmental Scis.; Nat. Geographic Soc.; formerly, Instnl. Rep. & Publicist, Cub Pack 158, Monmouth Coun., Boy Scouts of Am., Now Histn. of PR, Battleground Dist., ibid. Publs: approx. 10 sci. papers in jrnls.; Report on the Seminar Cruise (mag. article w. photographs), 1973; Photographs in var. mags. w. regular publ. in Scouting Trail; Unchained Melody (lyricist), 1955-; sev. songs under pseudonyms; publ. of picture stories under own by-line in local newspapers; limited. publn. of PRISONER OF WAR a song suite of words, mus. & arrangement concerning POW'S in Vietnam. Address: 218 Overbrook Dr., Freehold Twp., NJ 07728, U.S.A. 6, 57, 131.

STIVENS, Dallas George, b. 31 Dec. 1911. Author. Educ: Barker Coll., Hornsby, NSW, Australia. Appts: Australian Army Educ. Serv., 1943-44; Dept. Info., 1944-50; Press Officer, Australia House, London, UK, 1949-50. Mbrships: Fndn. Pres., Australian Broadcasting Commn., 1968-72; Chmn., Lit. Comm., Capt. Cook Bicenetnary Celebration, 1969-70. Publs: The Tramp & Other Stories, 1936; The Courtship of Uncle Henry, 1946; Jimmy Brockett, 1951; The Gambling Ghost & Other Tales, 1953; Ironbark Bell, 1955; The Wide Arch, 1958; Three Persons Make a Tiger, 1968; Selected Stories, 1936-68, 1970; A Horse of Air, 1970. Recip. lit. hons. Address: 5 Middle Harbour Rd., Lindfield, NSW, Australia 2070. 23, 30.

STOCK, Frances Patricia, b. 31 July 1937. Educator. Educ: B.S., Univ. of Ore., Eugene, U.S.A., 1959; M.S., ibid, 1965. Appts: Tchr., Phys. Educ., Thomas Downey H.S., Modesto, Calif., 1959-61; Chmn., Girls Phys. Educ. Dept., Coalinga Jt. Union H.S. Dist., 1961-65; Assoc. Supvsr. II, Dept. of Phys. Activities, Univ. of Calif., Santa Barbara, 1965-. Mbrships. incl: Treas., Tri-Cos. Chapt., Calif. Assn. of Hlth., Phys. Educ. & Recreation, 1966-69; Chmn., Bylaws Comm., & mbr., Exec. Bd., Western Soc. for Phys. Educ. of Coll. Women, 1969-72 & 1974-76; Chmn., Bylaws Comm., & mbr., Exec Bd., Nat. Assn. for Phys. Educ. of Coll. Women, 1972-73; Am. Assn. of Hlth. Phys. Educ. & Recreation; AAUP. Publs: Personal Safety & Defense for Women, 1968; Curriculum Design for Physical Activities; Num. newspaper articles on defense for women. Author, educl. film, Nobody's Victim, 1973. Address: 8002 Dept. of Physical Activities, University of Calif., Santa Barbara, CA 93106, U.S.A. 5, 129, 132, 138.

STOCKLMEIR, Louis Emil, b. 28 Oct. 1892. Consulting Civil Engineer. Educ: A.B., Leland Stanford Jr. Univ., 1916. Appts. incl: Res. Construction Engr., Dry Docks & Harbor, 1916-17; Structural & Hydraulic Engr., Pub. Pvte. Fire Defences; Municipal Pvte. Water Supply & Distribution Requirement, 1920-24; Engr.-Advsr., sev. ins. cos., 1924-32; Gen. Engrng. Off., 1932-72. Mbrships incl: Life, Am. Soc. Civil Engrs.; Life, San Fran. Sect.; Engrs. Club, San Fran.; Soc. Ins. Brokers; Commnr., Santa Clara Co. Histl. & Heritage Commn. Author of sev. tech. papers & reports. Hòns. incl: Victory Medal & Battle Star, WW I; Senate of State of Calif. Commendation Award; Cupertino Hist. Soc. Appreciation Award; Resolution No. 901, Commendation by Assembly of State of Calif., 1974. Address: 22120 Stevens Creek Blvd., Cupertino, CA 95014, U.S.A. 9, 57, 130, 131.

STOCKTON, Jack Edwin, b. 7 July 1931. Educational Administrator. Educ: B.S., Ctrl. Mo. State Univ., Warrensburg 1960; M.S., Univ. of Fla., 1961; Doctoral Cand., Va. Polytech. Inst. & State Univ. Appts: Grad. Asst., Univ. of Fla., 1960-61; Tchr., Coach, St. Lucie Pub. Schls., Ft. Pierce, Fla., 1961-64; Prof. Coach, Palm Beach Jr. Coll., 1964-66; Supvsr. Tchr. in Elem. Phys. Educ., Palm Beach Pub. Schls., 1966-68; Dir. of Continuing Educ., Va. Community Coll. System, S.W. Va., Community Coll., 1968-. Mbrships: Am. Mgmt. Assn.; Scottish Rite; 32 deg., Shrine Kazine Temple, R. Roanoke, Va.; Masonic Lodge, Warrensburg, Mo.; Phi Kappa Phi; Adult Educ. Assn. of USA; Treas., Adult Educ. Assn. of Va.; Nat. Coun. on Community Servs.; Nat. Assn. of Community Schl. Dirs.; Am. Assn. of Adult Admnstrs. Publs: Virginia Plans for Mine Manpower Training, 1971; sev. fed. grant applications; papers on field. Hons. incl: Pres.'s Club, Tazewell Co. Country Club & 4 1st prizes in golf tournaments; Meritorious Award, Outstanding Continuing Educ., Community Serv. Prog., Va. Community Coll. System, 1969, 70, 71 & 72. Address: 416 Suffolk Ave., Richlands, VA 24641, U.S.A. 125.

STOCKTON, Rodney M., b. 3 Feb. 1913. Business Executive. Educ: Asbury Coll., Wilmore, Ky., 1930-33. Appts: Ind. Sales Engr., Sylvania Indl. Corp., Chgo., 1937-41; Sales Engr., L. Sonneborn & Sons, Chgo., 1941-47; Pres., Fndr., Chmn. of the Bd., Aloe Creme Labs., Inc., Fla, 1953-. Mbrships. incl: Ft. Lauderdale Univ. Advsry. Bd. of 100; Aerospace Medical Assn.; Fla. & Ft. Lauderdale Chmbrs. of Comm.; Fellow of Pres.'s Coun., Am. Inst. of Mgmt; Nat. Advsry. Coun. Bd.; Am. Security Coun. Hons. incl: sev. awards for pub. serv. Address: 4120 N. E. 25th Ave., Ft. Lauderdale, FL 33308, U.S.A. 7, 57, 125, 128, 130, 131.

STODDART, David Ross, b. 15 Nov. 1937. University Lecturer. Educ: St. John's Coll., Cambridge, 1956-59; Ph.D., Cambridge Univ., 1964. Appts: Univ. Demonstrator, Cambridge, 1962-67; Univ. Lectr., ibid, 1967-; Fellow, Churchill Coll., ibid, 1966-; Sci. Coord., Royal Soc. Aldabra Rsch. Prog., 1968-. Publs: Regional Variation In Indian Ocean Coral Reefs (w. C.M. Yonge), 1971. Hons: Darwin Lectr., British Assn., 1972; Mrs. Patrick Ness Award, Royal Geog. Soc., 1965; Medallist, Inst. Océanographique, 1973. Address: Dept. of Geog., Downing Place, Cambridge, U.K.

STOESSEL, Carole Jean (Mrs. Alexander W. Zvonar), b. 14 July 1936 Physician; Pianist. Educ. incls: Student, Piano, w. Raymond Lewenthal, N.Y.; A.B. Magna cum laudi, A.B. Catawba Coll., Salisbury, N.C., 1959; M.D.,

Bowman Gray Schl. of Med. of Wake Forest Univ., Winston-Salem, N.C., 1963; Lic. to prac. med., N.C. State Bd. of Med. Examiners, 1964. Appts: Intern Pathol., Columbia-Presby. Med. Ctr., N.Y.C., 1963-64; Res. Fellow, Dept. of Microbiol., ibid, 1964-65; Physn. w. Rowan Co. Chapt. Am. Red Cross Bloodmobile Unit, N.C., 1972-; Concert pianist, 1950-59; '71-; Var. TV & radio appearances, 1950-55; Dealer in antique dolls, 1967-. Mbrships: As child, active in Children of Am. Revolution; Charter Mbr., Historic Salisbury Fndn., Inc., Salisbury, N.C.; Special Advsry. Comm., Bd. of Trustees, ibid. Contbr. to profl. jrnls. Hons. incl: Reynolds Schlr., Nancy Lybrook Lasater Award, Bowman Gray Schl. of Med., Winston-Salem, N.C., 1959-63. Address: 329 S. Fulton St., Salisbury, NC 28144, U.S.A. 5, 138.

STOIANOVICH, Traian, b. 20 July 1921. Historian. Educ: B.A., Univ. of Rochester, 1942; M.A., N.Y. Univ., 1949; Doctorat de l'Université, Univ. de Paris, France, 1952. Appts: Instr., N.Y. Univ., 1952-55; Instr., Rutgers Univ., 1955-57. Asst. Prof.-Assoc. Prof., 1957-67, Prof., 1967-; Vis. Asst. Prof., Univ. of Calif. at Berkeley, 1960, Stanford Univ., 1960-61, Vis. Assoc. Prof., N.Y. Univ., 1963, 1966-67 Vis. Prof., Sir George Williams Univ., Montreal, Canada, 1969. Am. Mbr., Econ. & Soc. Hist. Comm., Assn. Int. d'Etudes du Sud-est Europeen, 1967-72. Author, A Study in Balkan Civilization, 1967. Articles, var. profl. jrnls. & learned publs., Am. & for. Hons: Fulbright Fellowship, 1958-59; Rutgers Fellowship, 1965-66. Address: History Dept., Rutgers University, New Brunswick, NJ 08903, U.S.A. 6, 13, 139.

STOLPE, Elsa Viola, b. 29 Mar. 1913. Artist. Educ: Kyrkerud H.S., Sweden. Appts: Tchr., Art, Göteburg schls. Mbr., human rights orgs., UNESCO, var. art assns. Exhibs. of painting, graphic arts, sculpture, ceramics, Europe & U.S., inclng: World Exposition, Brussels, 1966-67; UNESCO; Monte Carlo, 1967, Var. Exhibs., Scandinavia, 1968; Finland, Iceland, Denmark, Belgium, Italy, Spain, 1969; Joan Miro Premi, U.S.A., 1970; Mod. Art Mus., Barcelona; Univ. of Utah; Guggenheim Mus., N.Y.C.; One man exib., Denmark, 1969-70, Buchanan, Liberia, 1970-71, Gall. Mouffe, Paris, & Mus. of Mod. Art., N.Y.C.; Contbr. of articles to periodicals. Num. hons. incl: Griffe Escoda, Palma, Barcelona, Valencia; Hons. at Brussels Exposition & Monte Carlo; Ancona Gold Medal & Dip., 1968; Italian State Gold Medal; European Critics Gold Medal; Given workroom in Göteburg by city. Address: Box 11, S 6702Y, Klassbol, Sweden. 1, 2, 131, 133.

STOLPEN, Beulah Harris (Mrs. A. Anton Stolpen). Author-Inventor; Publishing Company Executive. Educ: Hunter Coll.; Vassar Summer Inst. Appts: Designer of Children's Clothing: Buyer-Merchandise Mgr., Infants', Children's Wear & Toys; Pres., The Rolling Reader Publng. Co., Westport, Conn., 1958-; Author-Inventor of Reading Progs. for Scott, Foresman & Co.; Cons., Nat. Reading Ctr., Wash. D.C., Migrant Prog., Univ. of N.Y., & 'The Magic Door' Children's TV, Wash. D.C.; Speaker at univs., clubs, schls. & tchng. confs. Mbrships: Fndng. Bd., United Cerebral Palsy, & Fndr., Riverdale Chapt., ibid; Int. Reading Assn.; Nat. Coun. Tchrs. of Engl. Publs. (reading games & progs.): Johnny CAN Read; The Rolling Reader; The Rolling Phonics; Geome-Tricks; Sum-Antics; The Linguistic Blocks Series; The New Linguistic Blocks Series; The First, Second & Third Rolling Readers; The Rolling Phonics-Vowels; The Rolling Phonics-Consonants. Holder of US & Can. Patents for innovative methods of tchng.

reading & math. Address: 282 N. Ave., Westport, CT 06880, U.S.A. 5, 141.

STOLPIN, Dorothy Florence Mitchell (Mrs. William Stolpin), b. 12 June 1917. Educ. incl: Pharmaceutical Apprentice, Hurley Hosp., 1935-36; Dip. Assoc. Scis., Flint Jr. Coll., 1938; Elem. Tchrs. Cert. (Music), Wash. Univ., St. Louis, Mo., 1938; Wisc. Coll. of Music, (pt.-time & full time) 1949-53; Dip. in Acctng., Baker Bus. Univ. 1956; Dale Carnegie Class No. 186 (Effective Speaking, Human Rels. & Ldrship. Trng.), 1958; Work of the Stock Exchange & Brokerage Off. Procedures, 1957; Cert., Brokerage Ops. Dept. Procedures, 1969; Cert., Fundamentals of Investment Banking, 1962; B.A., Univ. of Mich. (Flint Br), 1967; Cert., Mgmt. Prog., Gen. Motors Inst. (1st woman to complete pt-time prog.), 1972; Int. Graphoanalysis Soc. gen. course, 1972; studies at Berlitz Schl. of Langs., Detroit, Mich., 1972; currently enrolled in Gen. Mgmt. Skills course; completed Commodities Futures course, 1974. Appts: Pvte. Piano Tchr., for 15 yrs.; w. Fahnestock & Co., Flint Br. (Stock Brokers), 1956-, currently Registered Rep.; Owner, Resort Property. Mbrships. incl: Pres.'s Club, Univ. of Mich.; Comm. of One Thousand, Mich. State Univ.; Mailing Chmn., 1961-68, Bd. Mbr. at Large, 1973 & '74 seasons, Flint Community Players; Treas., 1961, Bd. of Dirs., 1965-66, Zonta Int.; Am. Mgmt. Assn.; League of Women Voters; Var. State & Nat. orgs.; Am. Anthropol. Assn.; Life, Pi Mu; Sigma Chi Lambda (HS); Women Stockbrokers' Assn., Inc.; Hon. Fellow, Harry B. Truman Lib. Inst.; Flint Coll. Cultural Dev. Assn.; Fndrs. Soc., Flint Inst. of Arts.; Flint Br., AAUW; Genesee Co. Histl. Mus. Soc.; Charter, MPAA; Gtr. Flint Arts Coun., Inc.; Life Fellow, Intercontinental Biog. Assn.; Mich. Chapt., Int. Graphoanalysis Soc.; Life, Permanent Endowment Fund, Mich. Alumni Assn.; Histl. Soc. of Mich.; Chapt. & Charter Mbr., Alumni Bus. Soc. of Flint Coll., Univ. of Mich.; Life Alpha Chi Omega Alumni Club; Sponser, Things Theatrical, 1969-70; Active (Piano), St. Cecilia Soc., Flint, Mich.; Postal Commemorative Soc. Hons: 2nd Award for Best Scholastic Record, Mgmt. Prog., Gen. Motors Inst. Address: 140 E. Carpenter Rd., Flint, MI 48505, U.S.A. 5, 8, 16, 22, 57, 128, 129, 132, 133, 138.

STOLTZFUS, Ben Frank, b. 15 Sept. 1927. Professor of French Literature & Humanities; Writer. Educ: B.A., Amherst Coll., Mass., U.S.A., 1949; M.A., Middlebury Coll., Vt., 1954; Ph.D., Univ. of Wis., 1959. Appts: Instr., French, Smith Coll., Northampton, Mass., 1958-60; Prof., French Lit. & Humanities, Univ. of Calif., Riverside, 1960-; Vice Chmn., Div. of Humanities, ibid, 1962-63; Chmn., Interdisciplinary Studies in the Humanities, 1972-75. Mbrships: MLA; Assn. des Amis D'André Gide. Publs. incl: Alain Robbe-Grillet & the New French Novel, 1964; Georges Chennevière et l'Unanisme, 1965; The Eye of the Needle (novel), 1967; Guide's Eagles, 1969; Black Lazarus (novel), 1972; Poems, reviews, & articles in num. jrnls.; Contbns. to books. Hons. incl: Humanities Inst. Awards, Univ. of Calif., 1972. Address: Dept. of French & Italian, University of California, Riverside, CA 92502, U.S.A. 13, 30, 139.

STOLZ, Alan J., b. 7 May 1931. Executive-Owner, Children's Summer Camps; Real Estate Co. Officer. Educ: A.B., Wabash Coll., Ind., U.S.A., 1953; Postgrad., Columbia Univ., N.Y.C., & N.Y. Univ. Appts: Mbr., Bd. of Dirs., New England, N.Y., & Pvte. Summer Camping Assns., since mid-1960's; Pres., N.H. Camp Dirs. Assn., 1970-; Nat. Sec., Nat. Camping Educ. Comm., 1971-; P.R. Dir., N.Y.

Camping Assn., 1972-; Nat. Bd. of Dirs., & Nat. Legislative Dir., Am. Camping Assn., 1973-; Standards Insp. & Lectr. on Safety & Programing in Youth Camping. Mbrships. incl: Past Pres., Wel Met Camps Assn.; Boy Scouts of Am.; Advsr. & Bd. Mbr., Camp Am., London U.K. Publs: Num. articles & parental guidance mats. in jrnls., press, radio, & TV. Hons: L.H.D.; Sev. awards for youth work, Boy Scouts of Am. & other agcys.; Sev. acad. awards in jrnlsm. & govt. Address: Five Lockwood Circle, Westport, CT 06880, U.S.A. 6.

STOLZENBURG, Mabel Elizabeth Lawson (Mrs. Harold Lester Stolzenburg), b. 15 Mar. 1908. Teacher. Educ: B.S. in Educ., Miami Univ., Oxford, Ohio, 1956; M.Ed., Ohio State Univ., Columbus, Ohio, 1969. Appts: Tchr., Murdock Schl., 1927-28, Springboro Schl., 1928-30, 1945-47, Dayton Schl., 1931-33, Franklin, Ohio, 1948-51, Middletown, Ohio, 1952-74; Resource Tchr. for the visually handicapped, 1966-74; Fndr., Vision Ctr. for Middletown Schls., 1971. Mbrships: Middletown Tchrs. Assn.; Ohio Educ. Assn.; NEA; Local Pres., State Sec., Assn. for Childhood Educ. Int., 1967-; Nat. Soc. for the Prevention of Blindness; Coun. for Exceptional Children; Am. Fndn. for the Blind. Address: 600 Beachler Rd., Carlisle, OH 45005, U.S.A. 5.

STONE, Arthur William, b. 15 Mar. 1907. College Professor; Theatre Director. Educ: B.A., Hiram Coll., 1933; M.A., Western Reserve Univ., 1937; Tchrs. Coll., Columbia Univ.; State Univ. of Iowa; Ph.D. course work completed, La. State Univ. Appts: Coll. student & Profl. Actor, 1925-39; Tech. Dir. & Instr. in Stage Scenery & Lighting, Duquesne Univ., 1939-41; Pvte. - Major, US Army Air Corps, 1941-46; Assoc. Prof. of Speech & Dir. of Theatre, La. Tech. Univ. (formerly La. Polytech. Inst.), 1947-. Mbrships: Theta Alpha Pi; Nat. Collegiate Players; Theatres of La., Inc.; S.W. Theatre Conf.; Am. Theatre Assn.; Omicron Delta Kappa; Tau Kappa Epsilon; Circus Fans Assn. of Am.; Episc. Ch. Address: 304 E. Colorado Ave., Ruston, LA 71270, U.S.A.

STONE, Edward, b. 25 May 1905. Lawyer; Financial Consultant; Economist; Retired Major. Educ: A.B., Columbia Univ., N.Y.C., 1935; LL.B., ibid, 1927; A.M., 1931; LL.M., N.Y. Univ., 1953. Appts: Admitted to N.Y. Bar, 1927; Dir., Indl. ops., N.A.M., N.Y.C., 1945-49; Atty. & Financial Cons., Inst. Life Ins., N.Y.C., 1949-54; Chief Economist & Mgr., Corp. Planning, Republic Aviation Corp., Farmingdale, L.I., 1959-65; Sr. Ptnr., Stone & Moore, Acquisition Specialists, 1961-68; Mbr., Fac., Columbia Univ., N.Y.C., Johns Hopkins Univ., Am. Bankers Assn., Grad. Schl. of Banking Rutgers Univ., Am. Inst. of Banking, 1961-72. Mbrships. incl: Am. Econ. Assn.; Econ. Club of N.Y.; N.Y. Soc. of Security Analysts; Pres., Long-Range Planners, 1965-. Publs. incl: Anti-Depression Legislation; Contemporary Legislative & Banking Problems. Address: 160 Riverside Dr., N.Y., NY 10024, U.S.A. 6, 14, 16.

STONE, Frank Fairbanks, b. 26 Feb. 1909. Educator; College Professor. Educ: Grad., New England Conservatory of Music, Boston, Mass., 1931; B.A., Hiram Coll., Ohio, 1933; M.A., Hartford Schl. of Religious Educ., Hartford Sem. Fndn., Conn., 1940; M.Div., Union Theoligical Sem., N.Y., 1944; Special Student, Gen. Theological Sem., N.Y. 1943-44; S.T.M., Hartford Theological Sem., 1945; Th.D., ibid, 1950; Post- Doctoral work, La. Polytechnic Univ., 1959-60. Appts. incl: Asst. to Dean of Admin.. Hartford Sem. Fndn., Conn., 1947-59;

Bethel Coll., McKenzie, Tenn., 1960-63; Prof., Philos. & Relig., & Chmn., Dept. of Philos. & Relig., Schl. of the Ozarks, 1963-. Mbrships. incl: Am. Acad. of Relig.; Soc. for Sci. Study of Relig.; Religious Educ. Assn.; AAUP; Ctr. for the Study of Democratic Instns. Author of 2 unpubld. books & drama reviews. Recip. of hons. Address: The Schl. of the Ozarks, P.O. Box 4, Point Lookout, MO 65726, U.S.A. 130.

STONE, Jessica Justine, b. 15 Dec. 1915. Real Estate Promoter. Appts: Pres., Stone Realty; Exec. Sec. & Hd., Publicity, Walton Hills Chmbr. of Comm. Comm. Mbr., Walton Hills Chmbr. of Comm. Address: 18205 Fern Ln., Walton Hills, OH 44146, U.S.A.

STOPPANI, Andrés O.M., b. 19 Aug. 1915. Professor. Educ: M.D., Univ. of Buenos Aires, 1941; Dr. Chem., ibid, 1945; Ph.D., Univ. of Cambridge, U.K, 1951; Brit. Coun. Schlr., trng. in enzyme biochem. w. Profs. M. Dixon & D. Keilin, ibid, 1945-47; postgrad. rsch. work in phyiol. & biochem. w. Profs. B.A. Houssay & V. Deulofeu, 1940-45; Rschr., w. Prof. M. Clavin, Radiation Lab., Univ. of Calif., 1954. Appts: Prof., Biochem., Univ. of La Plata, Argentina, 1947-48 & Schl. of Med., Univ. of Buenos Aires, 1949-55; Full-time Prof. & Dir., Inst. of Biochem., Schl. of Med., ibid, 1955-; Dir., Dept. of Physiol. Scis., ibid; Mbr., Bd. of Dirs., Nat. Rsch. Coun. of Argentina, 1963-65. Mbrships: Past Pres., Argentine Assn. for Advancement of Sci.; Fellow, AAAS; Biochem. Soc.; Soc. for Gen. Microbiol.; Soc. for exptl. Biol.; N.Y. Acad. of Scis.; Am. Chem. Soc.; Am. Soc. for Biol. Chem.; Past Pres., Argentine Soc. for Biochem. Rsch.; Mbr., Inst. of Biol., GB, 1951; Mbr., Nat. Acad. of Scis., Argentina, 1965; Mbr., Nat. Acad. of Cordoba, Argentina, 1972. Contbr. over 100 rsch. papers to profl. jrnls. Hons: Acad. awards; Weissman Prize, Nat. Rsch. Coun. of Argentina, 1962; Campomar Prize, Campomar Fndn. for Biochem., Rsch., 1970. Address: Viamonte 2295, 5°piso, Buenos Aires, Argentina. 34.

STORER, Morris Brewster, b. 14 Nov. 1904. Educator; Professor, Educ: B.S., Dartmouth Coll., 1926; M.A., Univ. of Chgo., 1929; M.A., 1932, Ph.D., Philos., 1937, Harvard Univ. Appts: Instr., Philos., Univ. of Pitts., 1927-28; Lafayette Coll., 1929-30, Dartmouth Coll., 1932-35; w. Prog. Study & Discussion Div., U.S. Dept. of Agric., Wash. D.C., 1936-46; Dean of Instrn., Mt. Vernon Jr. Coll., ibid, 1946-47; Prof., Humanities, Univ. of Fla., 1947-73 Prof. Emeritus, 1973-. Mbrships. incl: Am. & Fla. Philosophical Assns.; AAUP; Unitarian Universalist Fellowship, Gainesville, Fla. (Chmn., 1945-46); Pres., Santa Fe Telephone Co., REA Coop., 1950-52; Vice Chmn., Gainsville Humanist Soc., 1974; Am. Fedn. Tchrs. (Sec., local chapt., 1971-72); Melrose Civic Club (Pres., 1948-49). Publs: Public Affairs Discussion Guides, U.S. Dept. of Agric.; Toward a Theory of Moral Debt, etc., in Inquiry. Address: Swan Lake, P.O. Box 148, Melrose, FL 32666, U.S.A. 2, 7, 13, 130.

STORMS, Everek Richard, b. 19 Oct. 1914. Editor; Author. Educ: B.A., McMaster Univ., Hamilton, Canada, M.A., Winona Lake Theol. Schl., Ind., U.S.A. Appts: Tchr., Ont., Canada, 1933-58; Prof., Ch. Hist. & Missions, Emmanuel Bible Coll., Ont., 1949-55; Schl. Admnstr., Kitchener, Ont., 1958-73. Mbrships: Gideons Int., Canada, 1946-; Pres., Kitchener Camp, 2 yrs., Chap., 11 yrs.; Fndr. & 1st Pres., Christian Writers of Canada, 1954; Charter mbr., Canadian Coll. of Tchrs., 1958; Publs. Bd., Missionary Ch., 1952-. Publs: Ed., Gospel Banner, 1951-69; Assoc. Ed., Emphasis on Faith and Living, 1969-73; Ed., Emphasis,

1974-; Author: Germs That Are Different, 1944; What God Hath Wrought, 1948; History of the United Missionary Church, 1958; Contbr. to Encyclopedia Canadiana, 1957. Hons: LL.D., Bethel Coll. Ind., U.S.A., 1974; F.I.B.A., London, 1974. Address: 336 Dumfries Ave., Kitchener, Ont., Canada NZH 2G1. 8, 57, 130.

STORRER, William Allin, b. 22 Mar. 1936. Educator. Educ: Albion Coll., Mich., 1954-56; A.B., Harvard Coll., 1959; M.F.A., Boston Univ., 1962; Ph.D., Ohio Univ., 1968. Appts: Instr., Theatre & Speech, Lectr., Opera, Hofstra Univ., Hempstead, N.Y., 1963-66; Asst. Prof., Theatre, Univ. of Toledo, Ohio, 1968-69; Assoc. Prof., Theatre, Speech, Film & Photography, Southampton Coll., L.I. Univ., N.Y. 1969-73; Asst. Prof., Cinema Studies & Still Photography, Schl. of Communications, Ithaca Coll., N.Y., 1973-. Mbrships: Fndr., A Soc. of Integrated Arts; Am. Theatre Assn.; Soc. of Archtl. Histns.; Speech Communications Assn.; Univ. Film Assn.; Nat. Freelance Photographers Assn.; Coll. Art Assn. of Am. Creative Works: The Architecture of Frank Lloyd Wright, a complete catalog, 1974; Stage Dir., 1 musical, 1 operetta, 1 opera, 21 plays, 1961-73; Articles in The Jewish Advocate; Reviews of opera, Opera News; Articles, Opera Mag. Hons. incl: Dean Earl Siegfred Award for Acad. Excellence, Ohio Univ., 1968; Hons. in Directing, Schl. of Fine & Applied Arts, Boston Univ., 1962. Address: Schl. of Communications, Dillingham Ctr. for the Performing Arts, Ithaca Coll., Ithaca, NY 14850, U.S.A. 6, 8, 13.

STORSTEIN, Ole, b. 16 July 1909. Professor of Medicine. Educ: M.D., Oslo Univ., 1936; Ph.D., Bergen Univ., 1953; Rsch. Fellow, Yale Univ., U.S.A., 1957-58. Appts: Asst. Prof., Bergen Univ., 1950-52; Hd. Physn., Stokmarknes Co. Hosp., 1952-54, Bodê Co. Hosp., 1954-59; Assoc. Prof. of Cardiol., Oslo Univ., 1959-63, Prof. of Med., 1963-; Mbr., Edit. Bd., Am. Heart Jrnl., 1965-70, Goriatrics, 1966-; Acta medica scandinivica, 1966-. Mbrships: Corres. Mbr., British Cardiac Soc., 1965; Pres., Norwegian Socs. of Internal Med., & Cardiol., 1969-71. Publs. incl: Klinisk Cardiologi, 1969; Hjerte-karsykdommer, 1970; Nar hjertet svikter, 1972; Digitalis (Ed.), 1973. Hons: Medla Gio.nate Medici, Verona, Italy, 1963; Medal, Univ. of Helsinki, Finland, 1965. Address: University Hospital, Rikshospitalet, Oslo 1, Norway. 50.

STOTT, (The Hon.) Tom Cleave, b. 6 June 1899. Member of Parliament; Administrator. Educ: Norwood Primary Schl., Australia; Privately tutored in Econs. & Secretarial Responsibilites. Appts. incl: Gen. Sec. & Co-Fndr., Australian Wheatgrowers Fedn., 1930-69; Gen. Sec., S.A. Wheat & Woolgrowers Assn., 1927-1933; Gen. Sec., United Farmers & Graziers of S.A., 1945-1969; Rep., Australian Nat. Farmers Union at Int. Fedn. of Agric. Prods., Sweden, 1950; Mbr., Australian Delegn., Int. Wheat Conf., Wash. D.C., U.S.A., 1953 & Geneva, Switzerland, 1956; Speaker, S.A. Parliament, 1962-1965 & 1968-70. Mbrships. incl: Pres., S.A. Race Horse Owners Assn., Australia, 1960-69; J.P., 1930-73; Justices Assn., 1930-73. Co-Archt. in creating the Australian Wheat Stabilisation Plan. Hons. incl: C.B.E., 1954; Life Mbr., United Farmers & Graziers Assn., 1973; Won the Tattersalls Cup & Trophy, 1960. Address: 20 McGlasson Ave., Glenelg N., S.A., Australia, 5045.

STOVER, Herman Dinsmore, b. 14 Nov. 1918. Business Administrator. Educ: Grad.,

Northeastern Bus. Coll., 1938; Cert. in Pub. Admin., Univ. of Me., 1967. Appts. Incl: Cryptographer, U.S. Army Air Corps., WWII; Purchasing Agt., Baker Refrigeration Mfg. Corp., S. Windham, Me., 1947-53; Admnstr., Me. State Liquor Commn. (State Govt.), Augusta, Me., 1953-68; V.P., Admin., Distilled Spirits Coun. of U.S., Wash. DC, 1968-. Mbrships: former Presiding Off., Masonic Lodge, Scottish Rite Bodies & Eastern Star, all Augusta, Maine; V.P., Maine State Soc., Wash. DC; Nat. Press Club, Wash. DC. Publs. incl: num. articles & position papers; Creator, Artist & Writer comic strip 'Penguin Pete', 1930's & proposes to revive it on retirement from Bus. career. Address: 8525 Milford Ct., Springfield, VA 22152, U.S.A. 2.

STOWE, Thomas Canterbury, Doctor of Dental Surgery. Educ: B.S., Wilberforce Univ., Ohio; D.D.S., Meharry Med. Coll. Dental Schl., Nashville, Tenn.; Intern, Forsyth Dental Infirmary, Harvard Grad. Dental Schl., & N. Eastern Univ., Boston. Mbr., Bermuda Govt. Dental Bd. of Examiners, 1949-59; Chmn., ibid, 1960-71; Mbr., Dental Staff, King Edward VIIth Mem. Hosp., Bermuda. Mbrships: Treas., Phi Kappa Delta, Wilberforce, Ohio., 1931; Ewell Neal Dental Soc., Meharry Med. Coll., 1936; Am. Dental Assn., 1937-39; Bermuda Dental Assn.; Chmn., Matilda Smith Williams Home for Aged; Chmn., Keep Bermuda Beautiful; Grand Lodge of Ireland; Hamilton Bermuda Rotary Club; Bermuda Nat. Trust; Sr. Trustee, St. Paul Meth. Ch.; Alpha Phi Alpha; Appeals Comm., Bd. of Educ.; Bermuda Rental Control Panel. Num. Hons. incl: MBE, 1970; J.P., 1971. Address: 'Swanstowe', Pembroke W. 545, Bermuda. 109.

STRACHAN, John George, b. 23 May 1910. Administrator; Lecturer; Author; Program Consultant in Alchohol Studies. Educ: Univ. of Dayton, Ohio, 1927-28; St. John's Coll., Brooklyn, N.Y., 1928-32; Pace & Pace Inst., N.Y. 1932-33; Rutgers Schl. on Alcohol Studies, Conn., 1950. Appts. incl: USAF, 1941-45; Planning & Systems Dir., Fed. Refrigerator Mfg. Co., Milwaukee, Wis., 1945-47; Exec. Dir., Milwaukee Info. & Referral Ctr., 1947-53; Org., Wis. Coun. on Alcoholism & Wis. State Bur. on Alcoholism, 1945-54; Off. & Bd. Mbr., ibid, 1947-65; Exec. Coun., Dept. of Atty. Gen., Province of Alta., Canada, 1965-69; Cons., Alcoholism, ibid, 1969-. Mbrships. incl: Alcohol & Drug Problem Assn. of N. Am.; Citizens Comm. on Alcoholism; Sec. & Org., Canadian Coun. of Alcoholism, 1954-62; Nat. Coun. of Alcoholism, Inc.; Alta. Br., Canadian Authors Assn.; Fellow, Royal Soc. of Arts. U.K. Publs. incl: Alcoholism: Treatable Illness, Practival Alcoholism Programming; Fndr. & Ed., Progress (alcoholism jrnl.) Recip., LL.D., Univ. of Alta., Edmonton, 1973, & other hons. Address: Box 2266, Sidney, B.C., V8L 3S8, Canda. 8.

STRAETER, (Mrs.) Jane, b. 12 Sept. 1919. Public Relations. Educ: Columbia Univ., N.Y., U.S.A. 1960. Appts: Nat. Sales Trnr., Sendley Jewelers; Campaign Org., Muscular Dystrophy Assn.; Prog. Dir., Am. Cancer Soc.; Pub. Rels. Dir., Goodwill Inds.; Dir., Educ. & Cultural Affairs, Y.M.C.A.; Prog. Dir., Mayor's Coun. on Youth; Dir., Pub. Rels., St. Mary's Hlth. Ctr. Mbrships: Pres., Hosp. Pub. Rels. Dirs., St. Louis; V.P., Community Serv. Pub. Rels. Dirs., ibid, V.P., Indl. Press Assn.; Bd. Mbr., Metropol. St. Louis Press Club; Am. Hosp. Assn. P.R. Soc. Hons: United Fund Publs. Award, 1969; 1st Place Award, Interpretative Pub. Rels. Prog., Am. Hosp. Assn., 1970; 1st Place, best non-profit publ., St. Louis Advt. Women's Flair, 1971-72; 1st Place Awards,

complete internal Pub. Rels. Prog., Mid-West Hosp. Assn., 1971, '72 & '73; MacEachern Nat. Award, Hosp. Publs., 1971, '72 & '73. Address: 6420 Clayton Rd., St. Louis, MO 63074, U.S.A. 5, 24.

STRAIN, Grace, b. 19 Feb. 1905. Welfare Worker. Educ: Univ. of Pitts., Pa.; Univ. of Mich., Ann Arbor; Civil Defense Schl. of Soc. Work, Richmond, Va.; Soc. Work Supvsr., W. Va. Univ., Morgantown. Appts: Soc. Wkr., Supvsr. & Dir., Kanawha Co. Relief Admin., Va., 1932-51; Supvsr., Div. of Soc. Servs., W. Va. Dept. of Welfare, 1961; Dir., Food Stamp Prog., ibid, until 1972; Exec. Dir., Transportation Remuneration Incentive Prog., 1974-. Mbrships. incl: Bd. Dirs., Mbrship. Chmn., Southwest Region & Co-Chmn., Nat. Mbrship. Comm., Am. Pub. Welfare Assn.; Bd. Dirs., W. Va. Soc. for Blind; Nat. Assn. of Food Distribution; Am. Assn. of Retired Persons. Hons. incl: Ky. Col., 1965; Cert of Appreciation, U.S. Dept. of Agric., 1972; Cert. of Hon., Div. of Voc. Rehab., 1973. Address: 955 Mathews Ave., Charleston, WV 25304, U.S.A.

STRALEY, H.W., III, b. 12 May 1906. Geologist; Geophysicist; Mining Engineer. Educ: B.S., Concord Coll., Athens, W. Va., 1925; Ph.D., Univ. of N.C., Chapel Hill, 1938; Ph.D., Univ. of Chgo., 1939. Appts. incl: Mineral Specialist, For. Econ. Admin., Wash. D.C., 1941-46, Int. Bank for Reconstruction & Dev., Wash. D.C., 1947-48; Vis. Assoc. Prof., Okla. Univ., 1948-49; Prof., Ga. Inst. of Technol., Atlanta, 1949-66; Vis. Geol. Prof., Morehead State Univ., Morehead, Ky., 1968-70; Seismicity Cons., Dames & Moore, Atlanta, Ga., 1966-. Mbrships. incl: Am. Assn. of Petroleum Geols.; Am. Geophys. Union; Am. Inst. of Mining Engrs.; Fellow, Geol. Soc. of Am.; Life Mbr., Ga. Geol. Soc. Contbr. num. articles to profl. jrnls. Recip. Sigma Xi Lectrships., Morehead State Univ., 1969. Address: 5910 Riverwood Dr., nw, Atlanta, GA 30328, U.S.A. 2, 14, 26, 28.

STRAND, Kenneth Albert, b. 18 Sept. 1927. University Professpr. Educ: B.A., Emmanuel Missionary Coll., 1952; M.A., Univ. of Mich., 1955; Ph.D., ibid, 1958. Appts: Pastor, Mich. Conf. of SDA, 1952-59; Assoc. Prof. of Religion, Emmanuel Missionary Coll., 1959-62; Assoc. Prof. of Ch. Hist., Andrews Univ. Sem., 1962-66; Prof. of Ch. Hist., ibid, 1966-; Dir. of M.A. Prog. in Religion, Andrews Univ. Grad. Schl., 1967-; Assoc. Ed., Andrews Univ. Sem. Studies, 1968-74; Ed., Andrews Univ. Sem. Studies, 1974-. Mbrships: Am. Hist. Assn.; Soc. of Biblical Lit.; Am. Soc. for Reformation Rsch.; AAUP.; Phi Beta Kappa. Publs: some 20 books inclng: German Bibles Before Luther, 1966; Early Low-German Bibles, 1967; Brief Introduction to the Ancient Near East, 1969; Essays on the Northern Renaissance (ed.), 1968; Essays on Luther Renaissance (ed.), 1969; Woodcuts to the Apocalypse in Dürer's Time (compiler), 1968; contbr. to many schol. jrnls. Address: 129 N. George, Berrien Springs, MI 49103, U.S.A. 8, 13, 15, 30, 120.

STRANG, Peter MacDonald, b. 20 Feb. 1896. Textile Research Consultant. Educ: B.S., Engrng. Admin., MIT, 1918; Further studies, ibid & Lowell Textile Inst. Appts: Supvsr., Installation Punch Card Mat. Control System, Hog I. Shipbldg. Co., 1918-1919; Asst. Mgr., Loom-Reed & Harness Co., Small Bearing Plant, Mgr., Cotton Farm, S.C., 1920-27; Sr. Cotton Technologist, U.S. Dept. of Agric. 1927-33; Organizer, Cotton Proj., Div. of Indl. Coopn., MIT, 1933-41; Off., USNR, Res. Naval Insp.,

Ordnance, Navy Working Mbr., War Prod. Bd. Army-Navy Bombsight Ball Bearing Comm., 1942-45; Retd. Cmdr., USNR; Rsch. Assoc., Inst. Textile Technol., 1946-48; Rsch. Cons. Whitin Machine Works, Whitinsville, Mass., 1948-60; Textile Rsch. Cons., 1960-. Mbrships. incl: N.Y. Acad. Sci.; U.S. Retd. Offs. Assn.; Textile Inst., Manchester, U.K.; Am. Assn. for Textile Technol.; Mass. Horticultural Soc.; Am. Rose Soc.; Int. Textile Assn., Switzerland; Acad. Pol. Sci., Columbia Univ. AAAS; Mason. Contbr., articles in textile publs. Patentee in field. Address: 31 Laurel Dr., Needham, MA 02192, U.S.A. 6, 14, 139.

STRASBURGER, Kurt W., b. 11 July 1918. Managing Director. Appts: V.P., F.L. Strasburger Co., Sassmannshausen, 1945-50; Pres., Walf Tools Co., N.Y., U.S.A., 1950-55; Pres., Am. Garden Supply Co., N.Y.C. & Trans-Atlantic Commerce Serv., Oyster Bay, N.Y., 1952-55; Exec. V.P., Scobalitwerk, Andernach, German Fed. Repub., 1956-; Mng. Dir., Kornel Wagner GmbH, Andernach, & Ferd. Wil. Wagner, Andernach, 1973-. Mbrships: German-Am. Chmbr. of Comm., N.Y.C.; Soc. of Plastics Ind., N.Y.C.; Pres., Scobalit Int., Nuerensdorf-Zurich, Switzerland; Past Pres., Lions Int., Club Neuwied. Contbr. to profl. jrnls. Address: Kirchberg 34, D-547 Andernach, German Fed. Repub. 43, 92.

STRASSER, Arnold, b. 8 Oct. 1932. Economist. Educ. B.S., N.Y. Univ., 1957; Postgrad. studies, ibid. 1957-61. Appts. incl: Sr. Econ., Office Rsch. & Stats., N.Y. State Div. of Employment, 1958-63; Dir., Compensation Structure Studies, 1963-67, Wage Trend & Construction Compensation Projs., 1967-69, Annual Earnings & Employee Benefit Projs., 1969-72, U.S. Bur. of Labor Stats.; Dpty. Chief Econ. & Dir., Div. of Case Econs. & Policy, U.S. Cost of Living Coun., 1973-. Mbrships: Am. Econ. Assn.; Indl. Rels. Rsch. Assn. Contbr. of articles, reports & reviews to profl. jrnls. & orgs. Address: 106 Julian Court, Greenbelt, MD 20770, U.S.A. 6.

STRASSER, William Carl, b. 4 Feb. 1930. College President. Educ: B.A., Univ. of Md., 1952; M.A., ibid, 1954; Ph.D., ibid, 1961; Carnegie Postdoct. Fellow, Coll. Admin., Univ. of Mich., 1961-62. Appts: Rsch. Asst., U.S. Off. of Educ., Wash. D.C., 1959-60; Specialist, Educl. Info., Bd. of Educ., Balt. Co., Md., 1960-61; Asst. Dean, Asst. Prof., Schl. of Educ., SUNY, Buffalo, 1962-64; Asst. Exec. Sec., Western N.Y. Schl. Study Coun., Schl. of Educ., ibid, 1962-64; Specialist, Educl. Admin., U.S. Off. of Educ., Wash. D.C., 1964-65; Asst. Dir., Personnel, Montgomery Co. Pub. Schls., Rockville, Md., 1965-66; Exec. Dean, Takoma Pk. Campus, Montgomery Jr. Coll., Md., 1966-; Acting Pres., ibid, 1966-67; Pres., ibid, 1967-69; Pres., Montgomery Community Coll., Md., 1969-. Mbrships. incl: Chmn., Fndg. Mbr., Steering Comm. for Formation, Nat. Coun. of Chief Exec. Admnstrs. of Community & Jr. Colls., 1972-73; Exec. Comm., ibid, 1973-74; Chmn., Commn. on Instrn., & Comm. on Improvement of Instrn., Am. Assn. of Jr. Colls.; Exec. Comm. Jr. Coll. Coun., Middle Atlantic States; Pres., V.P., ibid, 1971-72; Fndr., Organizer, Potomac Coun. of Community Coll. Pres's. Publs. incl: Co-Author, Dual Enrollment in Public & Nonpublic Schools, 1965; A Summer Odyssey, 6 poems, 1972; Contbr. to num. profl. jrnls. Hons. incl: Phi Kappa Phi; Omicron Delta Kappa; Pi Delta Epsilon; Phi Eta Sigma; Phi Delta Kappa; Deleg., UNESCO Conf. on Africa, 1961; Alumni Citation, Coll. of Educ., Univ. of Md., 1952; Recip., Danforth Fndn. Grant. Address: 19557 Brassie Rd., Gaithersburg, MD 20760, U.S.A. 2, 6.

STRATOS, Andrew (Andreas) N., b. 17 July 1905. Lawyer; Politician, retired. Educ: Univs. of Iena, Berlin, Paris & Athens. Appts. incl: Nominated Lawyer, Athens, 1928; Promoted to Ct. of Appeal, 1933 & Supreme Ct. of Appeal, Athens, 1938; Elected Mbr. of Parliament, Greece, 1932, '33, '35, '46, '50, '51, '52, '58, '61; Min. of Labour, 1946, 1954-55; Min. & Gov. Gen. of Northern Greece, 1952-54; Min. of Soc. Welfare, 1958-62; Retired from Politics, 1963. Chief of Hellenic Delegation, ILO Confs., Montreal, 1946, Geneva, 1955 & at Confs. of High Commissary of UNO for refugees, Geneva, 1959, 1960, 1961; Mbr. Hellenic Delegation in UNO during 11th Session, 1956-57 & Supplementary Chief of Hellenic Delegation at 12th Session, 1957; V.P., Conf. in Stockholm, 1949. Mbrships. incl: Bd. Mbr., Hellenic Comm., Int. Assn. of Byzantine Studies; Mng. Dir., Ionic Ins. Co.; Club of Athens; Tennis Club. Publs. incl: Byzantium During The VII Century, Vol. 1, 1965, Vol. II, 1966, Vol. III, 1969, Vol. IV, 1972 (1st 2 vols. condensed & translated into English 1969, English edit. Vol. III, 1972, English edit. Vol. IV, in prep); num. articles in field of hist., pol., econ. & soc. affairs. many speeches at various confs., UN & in ILO. Hons. incl: num. Greek Decorations & 2 Gt. Cordons of For. States; Hist. Prize, Acad. of Athens, 1970. Address: 10 Skoufa Str., Athens, Greece. 43.

STRAUB, Nellie Cora Perry. Retired Merchant. Educ: Coll. of Comm., Univ. of Ill., Urbana. Personal Details: b. Mapleton, Peoria, Ill., d. of Will N. & Mattie M. Perry of Hume, Ill. Appts: Travelers' Aid, Broad St. Railroad Stn., Phila., Pa., 1922. Mbrships: DAR; United Nations; Levis Faculty Ctr., Univ. of Ill., Urbana. Address: Box 410 - Ilikai Apts., 1777 Ala Moana, Waikiki, Honolulu Oahu, HI 96815, U.S.A.

STRAUSS, Alma Caroline Browder (Mrs. Harvey Strauss). Theatre Director; Producer. Educ: B.F.A., Wesleyan Coll., Macon, Ga.; post-grad work, Univ. of Ga., Athens, & F.A.U., Boca Raton, Fla. Appts. incl: Radio Commentator, own 15-min. show, WAPG, & Recreation Supvsr., drama for children, DeSoto Co. Schl. Bd., Arcadia, Fla., 1958; Speech & Drama Instr., Palmetto H.S., Fla., 1959; TV Studio Traffic Coord., Slide Libn. & Asst. on Children's TV show, WDBO-TV, Orlando, Fla., 1959-60; Asst., Grad. Schl., Univ. of Ga., Athens., 1960-61; Dir., Tobay Players, Plainview, N.Y., & Pequa Players, Massepequa, N.Y., 1964; Dir., Surfside Players, Cocoa Beach, Fla., 1967-68; Dir., Coastal Players, 1968; Hd., Surfside Schl. of Theatre, Surfside Players, 1968-69; Dir., Puppetry & Drama, N.P. Beach Rec. Dept., Fla., 1970-74. Mbrships: Bd. of Govs., Surfside Players; Sec., N. Co. Democratic Club, P.B. Co.; M.A.D., N. Palm Beach, Fla.; League of Women Voters; Comm., Planning Action Dev. for Cultural Affairs; Alpha Psi Omega; Am. Theatre Assn.; Beta Sigma Phi; NOW; Dade Fed. Sav. Club. Address: 6641 Emeral Lake Dr., Miramar, FL 33023, U.S.A. 5, 7.

STRAUSS, Dorothy B. Psychologist; Marital & Sex Therapist; Educator. Educ: B.A., CUNY; M.A., Ph.D., N.Y. Univ. Appts: Prof., Grad. Psychol., N.J. State Colls.; Instr., Univ. of Pa. Schl. of Med., Dept. of Psych., Div. of Family Study; Pvte. Prac., Marital & Sex Therapy; Rschr., Phychoendocrinol., Phila. Gen. Hosp. Mbrships: Am. Psychol. Assn.; Am. Assn. of Marriage & Family Cnslrs.; Eastern Acad. of Sex Therapy; N.J. Psychol. Assn.; Soc. for Clin. & Expmtl. Hypnosis; Kappa Delta Pi; Pi Lambda Theta; N.J. Gerontol. Soc. Author of num. articles in profl. jrnls. Address: 1700 Ditmas Ave., Bklyn., NY 11226, U.S.A. 5, 6, 14.

STRAUSS, Leo H., b. 11 Oct. 1911. Corporate Executive. Educ: Univ. of Calif. Ext. Courses, 1936-39; var. mgmt. courses, 1951-71. Appts. incl: Var. Exec. positions Am. Building Maintenance Inds., San Francisco, 1933-60; Fndr., Pres. & Dir., Building Servs. Corp., ibid, 1960-61; VP & Cons., Allied Maintenance Co., N.Y., 1961-68; L.H. Strauss & Assocs., Financial Cons., Honolulu, Hawaii, 1964-68; Exec. V.P. & Dir., 1968-69, Pres. & Chief Exec. Off. 1970-71, Ross Medical Corp., Ross, Calif., & Dir. Ross Subsidiaries; Dir., Hosp. Corp. of Am., (Bd. of Govs., 1972-), Sr. V.P. & Dir. HCA-West, & Dir., HCA West Subsidiaries, 1971-; Pres. & Dir., Valdrin Holding Corp., Medland Dev. Co., Bus. Profl. Servs. Inc., 1972; Pres. & Dir., Gen. Mgmt. Servs. Corp., 1973; Dir., Sinco Oil Inc., 1973. Mbrships. incl: Soc. Am. Mil. Engrs.; Am. Security Coun.; Am. Coun. Independent Labs., Inc.; num other profl. & civic orgs. Address: 15 Bret Harte Rd., San Rafael, CA 94901, U.S.A.

STRAUSS, Richard Louis, b. 25 Jan. 1909. International Agricultural Consultant & Project Director. Educ: Cheam Schl.; Malvern Coll.; Royal Agricl. Coll., Cirencester, U.K. Appts: Dir., then Mng. Dir., B. M. & J. Strauss Ltd., 1928-39; Served R.H.A., WW II, 1939-45; Land Reclamation, U.K., 1947-51; i/c. pilot scheme to reclaim Kafue Flats (potential 450,000 acres), Zambia, 1954-58; Study in Soil Erosion, 1959-60; Gen. Mgr., Tryall Estates, Jamaica, 1960-66; Introduced terracing, close planting, soil sterilisation, high fertilisation, mixed cropping w. proper crop rotation, Jamaica; Int. Agricl. Cons. specialising in integrated self help agro indl. projs. w. emphasis on labour intensive work combined w. appropriate technol. & new forms of ptnrship. between govts. of developing countries & multinational corps. based on mutual understanding. Mbrships: Veteran Mbr., HAC; Life Gov., Royal Agricl. Coll. of U.K.; S.I.D.; FAO/ICP; Gov., Jamaica Schl. of Agric.; Cons., Jamaica Agric. Soc.; Liguanea Club. Contbr. of num. articles on agric., marketing, prod., & processing to var. jrnls. inclng. Rhodesia; Bulaway Chronicle; Northern News; Rhodesia Herald; Rhodesian Farmer; Rhodesian, Ctrl. African Annual; Daily Gleaner; Farmers Weekly, etc. Num. Radio & TV speeches & farm lectures. Address: Liguanea Club Cottage, Kingston 5, Jamaica, W. Indies. 109.

STRAZZABOSCO, Luigi, b. 22 Feb. 1895. Sculptor. Educ: Scuola d'Arte 'Pietro Selvatico', Padua; Istituto Superiore d'Arte-Venezia (Studio Prof. Carlo Lorenzetti). Represented in permanent collects. at Mus. of Mod. Art, Venice, Padua Civic Mus., Alessandria Civic Mus., Noto Civic Mus., FAO-UNESCO Bldg. (Rome), & Quirinale Palace (Rome). Represented in pvte. collects. in Padua, Venice, Rome, Trieste, Fiume, London, New York, Spain, Portugal & Switzerland. Num. commnd. works inclng: Crucifix & Hunger, Gregorianum, Padua, 1965; Sculptures in the Bishop's Chapel, Duomo di Portogruaro, 1966; Relief, Univ. of Padua Bldg.; Crucifix & Figures, Temple of Peace, Padua; Side Altars, ibid; num. portraits. Exhib. at num. int. shows, inclng: 7 Biennale, Venice; Mostra Int., Madrid; Mostra Int. di Vitoria, Spain. Hons: Kt. of the Republic; Kt. of Vittorio Veneto; Civil Decoration for Valour; Acad.-Gentium 'Pro Pace'. Address: Via Montenero 10, 35100 Padua, Italy.

STRECKER, Heinrich, b. 13 Sept. 1922. Professor. Educ: Ludwig-Maximilians-Univ., Munich, 1941-47; Dipl.Math., 1947; Dr.rer.nat., 1949; Privatdozent der Statistik, 1955. Appts: Mbr., Sci. Staff, Bavarian Off. of Stats., Munich, 1948-57; Prof., Stats. & Maths. for Econs., Mannheim Univ., German Fed. Repub., 1957-59, & Tuebingen Univ., 1959-. Mbrships: Fellow, Royal Statl. Soc.; Int. Statl. Soc., 1967-; German & Am. Statl. Assns.; Inst. of Math. Stats.; Econometric Soc.; Deutsche Mathematikervereinigung. Hons: Off., Order of Leopold II, Belgium. Address: c/o Univ. Tuebingen, D-74 Tuebingen, Im Rotbad 40, German Fed. Repub.

STREET, Harry, b. 17 June 1919. Professor of English Law. Educ: LL.B., Manchester Univ., 1938; LL.M., 1948; Ph.D., 1951; Solicitor, 1940. Appts. incl: Lectr., Law, Manchester Univ., 1948-51; Sr. Lectr., Law, ibid, 1951-52; Prof., Pub. Law & Common Law, 1956-60; Prof., Engl. Law, 1960-; Prof., Law, Nottingham Univ., 1952-56. Mbrships: Chmn., Comm. on Racial Discrimination, 1967; Commn. on Constitution FBA, 1968. Publs: A Comparative Study of Governmental Liability, 1953; Law of Torts, 5th ed., 1972; Law of Damages, 1961; Freedom the Individual & the Law, 3rd ed., 1972; (co-author) Principles of Administrative Law, 5th ed., 1973; Law Relating to Nuclear Energy, 1966; Road Accidents, 1968; Justice in the Welfare State, 1968; num. articles in law jrnls. Address: Fac. of Law, The University, Manchester M13 9PL, U.K. 1.

STREETEN, Paul Patrick, b. 18 July, 1917. Educator. Educ: M.A., Univ. of Aberdeen, U.K.; B.A. & M.A., Oxford Univ. Appts: Fellow, Balliol Coll., Oxford, 1948-66; Dpty. Dir. Gen., Economic Planning Staff, Min. of O'Seas Dev., 1964-66; Fellow & Acting Dir., Inst. of Dev. Studies, & Prof. of Economics, Univ. of Sussex, 1966-68; Warden, Queen Elizabeth House, Oxford, & Dir., Inst. of Commonwealth Studies, ibid., 1968-. Mbrships. incl: Chmn., U.K. Chapt., Soc. for Int. Dev.; Royal Economic Soc.; Am. Economic Soc.; Dir., Commonwealth Dev. Corp., 1967-73; Vice-chmn., Soc. Scis. Comm., U.K. Nat. Commn. of UNESCO. Publs. incl: Value in Social Theory, (Ed.); Economic Integration; Commonwealth Policy in a Global Context, (Co-Ed.); Aid to Africa; The Frontiers of Development Studies; Trade Strategies for Development (Ed.). Address: 21 St. Giles, Oxford OX1 3LA, U.K. 1, 139.

STREETER, William Joseph, b. 14 Nov. 1938. Company President. Educ: B.S., Photographic Scis., Rochester Inst. of Technol., N.Y., 1960; M.B.A., Marketing, N.Y. Univ. 1971. Appts: Photographic Engr., GAF Corp., 1960-64; Int. Sales Engr., ibid, 1964-66; Tech. Serv. Mgr., Chemco Photoproducts Co., Glen Cove, N.Y., 1966-71; Pres., Dalco, Inc., Soestduinen, Netherlands, 1971-. Mbrships: Am. Soc. for Quality Control; Tech. Assn. for the Graphic Arts; Soc. of Photographic Scis. & Engrs.; Amateur Fencers League of Am.; Fed. Internationale d'Escrime. Contbr. to profl. jrnls. in field. Hons: Outstanding Young Man of Am., 1971; Outstanding Alumni Award, Rochester Inst. of Technol., 1972. Address: Sparrenlaan 1, Soest, Netherlands. 43, 117.

STREHLOW, Theodor George Henry, b. 6 June 1908. University Professor. Educ: M.A., Univ. of Adelaide, Australia. Appts: Linguistic Reschr., Aust. Nat. Rsch. Coun., 1932-36; C'wealth Patrol Off., N.Y., 1936-42; Rsch. Fellow, Aust. Linguistics & Lectr., Engl. Lit., Univ. of Adelaide, 1946-49; Rdr., Aust. Lings., ibid, 1954; Prof., 1970-73; Emeritus, 1974; Mbrships. incl: Aust. Humanities Rsch. Coun., 1956; Fndn. Mbr. Aust. Inst. Aboriginal Studies, 1964-73; For. Corres., Royal Swedish Acad. Letters, Hist. & Antiquities, 1964; Fndn. Mbr., Aust. Soc. Classical Studies, 1966; Fndn. Fellow, Aust. Acad. Humanities, 1969. Permitted by Ctrl. Aust. tribal elders to film secret ceremonial cycles & to record some 8,000 secret verses. Publs. incl: Aranda Phonetics and Grammar, 1944; Aranda Traditions, 1947; 2nd ed., '68; Journey to Horseshoe Bend, 1969; Songs of Central Australia, 1971; contbr. num. articles to sci. publs. Recip. Wickhardt Award for Aust. Lit., 1970. Address: 30 Da Costa Ave., Prospect, S.A. Australia, 5082. 23, 128.

STRICKLAND, Alice D. (Mrs. Clarence A. Strickland), b. 21 May 1919. Executive. Educ: Grad. Dipl., Am. Savings & Loan Inst., Chgo., Ill.; Manatee Jr. Coll., Bradenton, Fla., 1966-68. Appts: Bookkeeper-Ins. Clerk, Arcadia Gen. Hosp., Fla., 1948-52; Asst. Bookkeeper, ibid, 1952-56; Teller, 1st Fed. Savings & Loan of Manatee Co., Bradenton, 1957-59; Asst. to Hd. Teller, ibid, 1959-60; Asst. to Controller, 1960-61; Controller & Treas., Manatee Fed. Savings & Loan Assn., Bradenton, 1961-72; V.P. & Treas., ibid, 1972-. Mbrships: Sec., 1966, & Mbr. Bd. of Govs., 1967, Sarasota-Manatee Chapt., Am. Savings & Loan Inst.; Beta Sigma Phi; Supt., Young Peoples Dept. 1959-61; Tchr., Adult Dept., 1962-72 & Tchr., Jr. Dept., 1972-, 1st Baptist Ch.; Zonta Club of Bradenton. Contbr. articles to Controllers Soc. publs. Hons: Boss of Yr., Credit Women of Manatee Co., 1964; Award for Tchng. Classes, Sarasota-Manatee Chapt., Am. Savings & Loan Inst., 1968-72. Address: 4903 26th Ave. W., Bradenton, FL 33505, U.S.A. 5.

STRICKLAND, Freeman Roland George, b. 19 July 1921. Company Director. Appts: Chmn., Customs Agts. Sect., Melbourne Chmbr. of Comm., 1958-63; Pres., Customs Agts. Inst. of Australia, 1964-70; Dir., Scottish Union & Nat. Ins. Co., 1965-72, Chmn., 1972-; Dir., Norwich Union Life Ins. Soc., 1971-; Mbr., Export Dev. Coun., 1966-70; Exec. Mbr., 1971-72; Dir., Universal Transport & Terminals Ltd., 1968-; Mng. Dir., H. Halford Pty. Ltd., 1954-. Mbrships. incl: Coun. Exec., Melbourne Ch. of England Grammar Schl., 1967-; V.P., Confedn. of Asian Chmbrs. of Comm. & Ind., 1970-72; Sr. V.P., ibid, 1972-; Dir., United Employee Benefit Soc., 1971-73; Pres., Melbourne Chmbr. of Comm., 1971-73; V.P., Fedn. Chmbrs. of Comm. of Commonwealth, 1972-; Dpty. Pres., Australian Chmbr. of Comm., 1972-; V.P., Customs Agts. Fedn. Australia, 1972-. Address: 232 Kooyong Rd., Toorak, Vic., Australia 3142. 23.

STRICKLAND, (Hon.) Mabel Edeline Carmela Ethel, b. 8 Jan. 1899. Journalist; Politician; Poultry Farmer. Appts. incl: Asst. Sec., Constitutional Party, Malta, 1921-45; Mbr., Legislative Assembly, 1950-53, 62-65; Ed., Times of Malta, 1935-50; Ed., Sunday Times of Malta, 1935-56; Mng. Dir., Allied Malta Newspapers Ltd., 1940-55; Chmn., ibid, 1950-55; Dir., 1966-; Dir., Progress Press co. Ltd., 1957-61, 66-71; Chmn., Xara Palace Hotel Co. Ltd., 1949-61; Dir., 1966-. Mbrships incl: Commonwealth Press Union; Int. Press Inst.; Commonwealth Parliamentary Assn. Publs: A Collection of Essays on Malta, 1955; Maltese Constitutional & Economic Issues 1955-59. Hons. incl: O.B.E., 1944; Cmdr., Order of St. John of Jerusalem, 1969; Astor Award, 1971. Address: Times of Malta, P.O. Box 328, Valetta, Malta. 1, 34, 41.

STRICKLER, Earl Taft, b. 27 Nov. 1908. Antiquarian Horologist; Banker; Corporation Executive; Editor. Dipl., Horological Inst. of Am. Appts. incl: Bd., Mng. Dir., Sec.-Asst. Treas., Fellow, Nat. Assn. Watch & Clock Collectors Inc.; Sec.-Treas., Jeanne G. Parkhurst Fund Fndn. Inc.; Acting Treas., Bowman Tech. Schl.; V.P., Dir., Home Bldg. & Loan Assn.; Dir., Am. Mus. Clocks & Watches & Manor Hts. Mus.; Fndr., Curator, Columbia Mus.; Dir., Columbia Hosp. Corp.; Advsry. Bd., Asst. Sec., Am. Bank & Trust Co. of Pa.; Advsry. Bd., Am. Diversified Corp., Selected Investments Corp. Mbrships. incl: Dir., Admin. Mgmt. Soc.; Horol. Inst. of Am.; Am. Watchmaker's Inst.; Newcomen Soc. in N. Am.; Am. Inst. of Mgmt.; Antiquarian Horol. Soc.; Pres., Columbia Canoe Club; V.P., Rotary; Corp. Fellow, Royal Soc. of Arts; Fellow, Brit. Horol. Inst., Intercontinental Biog. Assn., Ancient Monuments Soc. Hons. incl: Ky. Coll., 1963, '66; Miss. Col., 1972; Dpty. Sherriff, Dallas; Master Watchmaker (AWI); Mbr., Japanese Soc. of Chronometry; Wisdom Soc. Award of Hon.; San Fernando Valley Engr's. Coun. 1974 Engrng. Award; Soc. of Mfg. Engrs. 1974 Disting. Contributions Award. Address: P.O. Box 33, Columbia, PA 17512, U.S.A. 2, 6, 12, 16, 22, 57, 128, 133.

STRIGL, Richard Adolf Anton, b. 1 Jan 1926. Professor of Canon Law. Educ: studied Philos. & Theol., 1946-51; studied Canon Law, Lic.jur.can., Dr. jur. can., habil., Univ. of Munich, 1955-62. Ordained, 1951. Appts: Chap., Munich, 1951-55; Prof., Canon Law, Freising & Munich, 1963-69; Full Prof., Canon Law, Univ. of Salzburg, 1970-; Dir., St. Joseph's Orphanage, Munich, 1957-; V.P., Consistory & Metrop. Tribunal, Munich, 1963-72. Mbrships: Görres-Gesellschaft; Austrian Soc. for Canon Law; V.P., St. Joseph's Assn., Munich. Contbr. num. articles to jrnls. Address: Dreifaltigkeitsgasse 14, A-5024 Salzburg, Austria.

STRINGER, Paula L. (Mrs.), b. 9 Oct. 1924. Realtor. Educ: Southern Meth. Univ., 1942-43. Appts: Assoc., Stewart Smith, Realtor, Houston, Tex., 1954-56; Co-owner, Suburban Realtors, 1958-60; Owner, Paula Stringer Realtors, 1960-. Mbrships: Chmn., Woman's Coun., Dallas Real Estate Bd.; Nat. Assn. Real Estate Brokers; Nat. Inst. of Real Estate Brokers; Int. Traders Assn.; Tex. Real Estate Assn., Dallas Home Builders Assn.; Advsry. Bd., League of Women Voters; Kappa Alpha Mothers; Delta Delta Delta Mothers; Canyon Creek Country Club; Tanglewood Country Club; Hurricane Creek Country Club; Hollow Bend Polo & Hunt Club; Sponsor, Richardson Symph. Orch. Address: 7235 Foxworth, Dallas, TX 75240, U.S.A.

STRINGFIELD, Hezz, Jr., b. 4 Oct. 1921. Professional Manager. Educ: Grad. Bus. Admin., Draughon Coll., 1939; Univ. of Tenn. Appts: Bus. Mgr. & Dir. of Fiscal Affairs, E.I. DuPont DeNemours, Inc., Clinton Labs., 1941-43; Monsanto Chem. Co., 1943-45; Univ. of Chgo., 1945-48; Union Carbide Corp., ORNL, 1948-; Headed US Aid Delegation to Middle East for Ctrl. Treaty Org., 1964; Dir., FBF, Inc. Mbrships: Int. Pres. & Bd. Chmn., Soc. for Advancement of Mgmt.; Bd., Coun. for Int. Progress In Mgmt., 1963-68; Bd. & Pres., Fndn. for Mgmt. Educ., 1963-69; local civic & profl. clubs. Contbr. of articles in profl. jrnls. & mags. on mgmt. techniques & educ. Awarded profl. mgrs. citation, 1968, Int. Award, 1966, Clyde Carpenter Award, 1968, all from Soc. for Advancement of Mgmt.-Am. Mgmt. Assn. Address: 5000 Trent Lane, Knoxville, TN 37922, U.S.A. 2, 7, 16, 57, 116, 125, 128.

STROH, Oscar S., b. 20 Jan. 1914. Steel Importer. Educ: LL.D., Univ. of Vienna, Austria. Appts: Traffic Mgr., Sopic Corp., N.Y.C., U.S.A., 1940-48; Pres., Standard Int. Corp., N.Y., 1948-72; Officer., B.S. Livingston & Co. Mbrships: Past Dir., Am. Inst. of Imported Steel, N.Y.C.; Hospitality Comm., UN; Steel Wire Assn. Contbr., music critical essays to a N.Y. newspaper. Address: 3050 Fairfield Ave., N.Y., NY 10463, U.S.A. 6.

STROJNY, Mariano, b. 20 Nov. 1906. Prelate of The Catholic Church; Canon; Sculptor. Educ: Studied med., Univ. of Poznan, Poland; Philos. & theol., Univ. of Cracow; Canon law & civil law, Pontificia Univ. Lateranense, Rome, Italy; Dr. in Canon Law, 1935; Fine Arts, Castello Rotaio Studio. Appts. incl: Ordained priest, 1931; Rector, Pont. Polish Inst. Eccl., Rome, 1949-58; Comm., Sacred Cong. of the Sacraments, 1940-70; Cons., ibid, 1967-; Comm. & Cons., Sacred Cong. for the Eastern Ch., 1943-73; Judge, Trib. of Appeal of the Vicariate, Rome, 1954-. Mbrships. incl: Coun., Sacred Cong. for the Propagation of the Faith, 1951-71; Proc., Sacred Cong. of Rites for the Causes of beatification & canonization of Saints, 1953-; Prelate Referendary, Sup. Trib. of the Apost. Signatura. Publs: Die rechtlich-diplomatische Stellung der Päpstlichen Gesandten an die Mongolen unter Innocenze IV, 1939; Sculptures in Polish Mus. of Am., Chgo., Ill., U.S.A. & in num. pvte. collects. in U.S.A. Hons. incl: Cross w. Star, Polonia Restituta, 1966; Premio Internazionale "Arte pro Arte (Silver Cup), Rome, 1972. Address: Casella Postale 9019, Rome 00165, Italy. 43.

STROKE, George Wilhelm, b. 29 July 1924. Educator; Physicist; Biophysist; Government Consultant. Educ: B.Sc., Univ. of Montpellier, France, 1942; Ing.Dipl., Optics, Inst. of Optics, Univ. of Paris, 1949; Ph.D., Sorbonne, 1960. Appts: Rsch. Staff, Defense Rsch. Staff, MIT, U.S.A., 1952-63; Lectr. Elec. Engrng., ibid, 1960-63; Asst. Rsch. Prof., Physics, Boston Univ., 1956-57; Prof., Elec. Engrng. & Hd., Electro-Optical Scis. Lab., Univ. of Mich., 1963-67; Prof., Elec. Engrng. & Med. Biophysics, & Dir., Electro-Optical Scis. Lab., SUNY, Stony Brook, 1967-; Vis. Prof., Med. Biophysics, Harvard Med. Schl., 1970-73; Cons., NASA, Nat. Sci. Fndn., Am. Cancer Soc., etc. Mbrships. incl: Past Pres., N.Y. Sect., & Fellow, Optical Soc. of Am.; Fellow, Am. Phys. Soc.; Fndng. Mbr., Biomed. Engrng. Soc. Publs: An Introduction to Coherent Optics & Holography, 1966; Over 100 sci. articles, book chapts.; Originator, num. methods of holography & of optical computing; Patent holder. Hons: NATO Rsch. Fellow, 1959-60; Summa cum laude Dr. ès., Sorbonne, 1960; Allan Gordon Mem. Award, Soc. of Photo-Optical Instrument Engrs., 1971; Advsr., Japanese Min. of Int. Trade & Ind., 1971. Address: SUNY, Stony Brook, NY 11790, U.S.A. 2, 14, 28.

STROM, Ingrid Mathilda, b. 8 Dec. 1912. Educator. Educ: B.Ed., Univ. of Minn. at Duluth, 1935; M.A., Univ. of Minn., Mpls., 1944; Ph.D., ibid, 1955. Appts. incl: Instr. & Critic Tchr., 1944-53; Hd., Engl. Dept., Univ. H.S., Ind. Univ., 1946-53; Asst. Dir., Student Tchng., ibid, 1953-55; Asst. Prof., Educ. & Asst. Dir., Student Tchng., 1955-61; Assoc. Prof. Educ. & Asst. Dir., Student Tchng., 1961-. Mbrships: Nat. Advsry. Bd. of Lit. Cavalcade (schol. mag.), 1952-54; Nat. Advsry. Textbook Commn. of USAFI, 1949-50; Pub. Rels. Rep. of Ind. Coun. of Tchrs. of Engl., 1944-57; Engl. Standards Comm., State of Ind., Ind. Coun. of Tchrs. of Engl., 1957-; Chmn. of

Nominating Comm., NCTE, 1958-59; Assoc. Chmn., Comm. on Utilization of Tchr. Time, Comm. to review Resource Unites & Curric. Bulletins; Rsch. Comm., NCTE; Chmn., Rsch. Comm., Assn. for Student Tchng., 1960-62; Pres., Engl. Sect., Ind. State Tchrs. Assn., 1949-50; NEA; AST; NCTE; AAUW; AAUP; Nat. League of Am. Pen Women, etc. Publs. incl: Implications of Research in Grammar & Usage for Teaching Writing, 1960; The Role of Literature in the Core Curriculum, 1958; The Teaching Load of Teachers of English in Indiana, 1956. Address: Schl. of Educ., Rm. 338, Ind. Univ., Bloomington, IN 47401, U.S.A. 5, 8, 15, 22, 30, 132, 141.

STRÖMBÄCK, Dag Alvar, b. 13 Aug. 1900. Professor. Educ: Cand. Phil., Uppsala Univ., Sweden, 1921; Lic. Phil., ibid, 1926 & 1929; Ph.D., ibid, 1935. Appts. incl: Vis. Prof. Scandinavian Langs., Univ. of Chgo., U.S.A., 1937-38; Prof., ibid, 1938-39; Dir., Inst. for Dialect & Folklore Rsch., Uppsala, Sweden, 1940-67; Prof., Nordic & Comparative Folklore, Univ. of Uppsala, 1948-67; Emeritus Prof., ibid, 1967-. Mbrships. incl: Royal Gustav Adolf's Acad., Uppsala; Pres., ibid, 1957-65; Royal Acad. of Letters, Hist. & Antiquities, Stockholm; Pres., ibid, 1965-; Norwegian, Danish & Finnish Acads. Sci.; Royal Irish Acad. Publs. incl: Lex Uplandiae, 1960; Co-Author, European Folk Ballads, 1967; Folklore & Philology: Selected Papers, 1970. Ed., ARV Jrnl. of Scandinavian Folklore, 1952-. Hons: LL.D., Aberdeen Univ., U.K., 1958; Ph.D., Reykjavik, Iceland, 1961; D.Litt., Dublin, Repub. of Ireland, 1967; Cmdr., Order of the Lion, Finland, 1966; Royal Prize, Swedish Acad., 1969; Kt. Cmdr., Order of the Northern Star, 1971. Address: P.O. Box 10005, 75010 Uppsala, Sweden. 134.

STRÖMHOLM, Stig Fredrik, b. 16 Sept. 1931. Professor of Jurisprudence. Educ: B.A., 1952, LL.B., 1957, Uppsala Univ.; Dip., Comparative Legal Studies, Cambridge Univ., 1959; LL.D., Munich Univ., 1964; LL.D., Uppsala Univ., 1966. Appts: Clerk, Southern Dist. Ct. of Upland, 1958-60; Admitted as Jr. Judge, Stockholm Ct. of Appeal, 1961; Sec., Mbr., Legislative Comms., 1960-71, & deleg., diplomatic confs. & int. comms.; Mbr., Comm. of Experts on Human Rights, Coun. of Europe, 1970-73. Also Lectr., Comparative Law, 1966, Prof. of Jurisprudence, 1969-, Uppsala Univ.; Capt., Royal Armoured Corps Reserve, 1969. Mbrships: Royal Acad. of Scis. Uppsala; Sällskapet, Stockholm. Publs: 12 books, Swedish, French, Engl., inclng: Torts in the Conflict of Laws, 1961; Legal Values in Modern Sweden (co-author), 1964; Right of Privacy & Rights of the Personality, 1967. Also articles in Swedish & for. law reviews, periodicals. Hons: Kt., Royal Swedish Order of the Polar Star. Address: Norra Rudbecksgatan 5, S-752 36 Uppsala, Sweden. 43.

STROMNES, Martin, b. 20 Apr. 1900. Professor. Educ: Tchr. Cert. Tromsö Tchr. Trng. Coll., Norway, 1922; Tchr. Dip., Norwegian State Coll. of Educ., 1929; Ed.D., Stanford Univ., U.S.A., 1958. Appts: Elem. Schl. tchr., Norway, 1922-37; Tchr., Student Tchng., Volda Coll., 1937-48; Asst. Prof., Methods of Tchng., Norwegian State Coll. of Educ., 1949; Prof., Educ., ibid, 1967; Served as UNESCO expert in field of curric. revision & educl. planning, Repub. of China, 1961-62 & '64. Mbrships: Chmn., var. tchr. socs., 1932-37, '38-40, '47-50; Pres., Int. Assn. of Educators for World Peace, 1970; Publs. incl: World Education for Peace, 1959; Our Schools & International Understanding, 1961; Theory of Moral Education, 1968; A Critical Curriculum

Analysis, 1971. Winner of 1st Prize for essay (publs. as Our Schools & International Understanding, 1961), Norwegian UN Assn. & Norwegian Nat. Commn. for UNESCO on peace Educ., 1960. Address: Sorli Terrasse 48, 1473 Skarer, Norway. 134.

STROUD, Charles Warren, b. 8 Aug. 1935. Public Relations & Communications Director. Educ: Northwestern Univ., Ill., U.S.A. Appts. incl: Promotion Supvsr., NBC, Chgo., Ill., 1958-59; Client Serv. Dir., WGN, Inc., Chgo., 1959-62; Mgr., Pub. Rels. & Advt., WLS, Inc., Chgo., 1962-64; Community Rels. Dir., St. Joseph Hosp., Joliet, Ill., 1965-69; Mgr., Promotion, Kaiser Broadcasting Corp., Detroit, Mich., 1969-70; Dir., Pub. Rels. & Dev., Ctrl. DuPage Hosp., Winfield, Ill., 1970-. Mbrships: Am. Soc. of Hosp. Pub. Rels.; Acad. of Hosp. Pub. Rels.; Broadcast Promotion Assn.; Bd., Ill. Mental Hlth. Soc., 1966-69; Engl.-Speaking Union, 1958-65; Bd. Advsr., Lib. of Int. Rels., Chgo., 1958-65; V.P., Advsry. Bd. of Alvernia Manor, Lemont, Ill. Address: 207 Freeport Dr., Bloomingdale, IL 60108, U.S.A. 24.

STROUD, Etta J. (Mrs. James L. Platter), b. 22 May 1907. Missionary; Notary Public. Educ: Grad., Grace Bible Inst., 1973; Grad., Schl. of Instrn. of Interdenominational Nat. Ch. Ushers Assn. Appts: formerly w. U.S.N. Ordinance Plant, Baldwin, L.I., N.Y.; ending 12 yrs. as Notary Pub. for Cwlth. of Pa. Has sung w. many choirs & was soloist on own radio prog. Began Broadcasting, 1956; was 1st female relig. commentator & only Negro disc jockey, WCOJ radio; had produced & directed many shows. Mbrships. incl: Christian Missionary Worker, sent by Tabernacle Bapt. Ch., Coatesville, Pa.; Vol. Worker, Salvation Army Servicemen's Ctr., Harlem; State Fedn. Negro Women's Clubs, Inc.; Mary Tent No. 25 Lodge of Coatesville; NAACP; YWCA; Am. Assn. Retired Persons; Community Fellow Circle; 60 plus Club, Coatesville. Recip. num. hons. inclng: Mayor of Coatesville declared 7 Apr. 1973, Etta J. Stroud Day; Awards from Coatesville Hosps. for vol. servs., 1973. Address: P.O. Box 803, Coatesville, PA 19320, U.S.A.

STROUP, Herbert. Professor of Sociology. Educ: B.D., Union Theological Sem., N.Y.C.; Ph.D., Grad. Fac. Pol. & Soc. Sci., New Schl. for Soc. Rsch., N.Y.C. Appts. incl: Currently Prof. of Sociol., Brooklyn Coll., CUNY; Mbr., Bd. of Trustees, Ripon Coll.; Chmn., Dept. Higher Educ., Nat. Coun. of Chs., & Div. of Hlth. & Welfare, United Ch. of Christ; Mbr. Prog. Bd., Div. Overseas Mins., Nat. Coun. Chs.; Florence Hammersley Walker Lectr., Chgo. Theological Sem.; Mbr., Edit. Bd., Jrnl. of Contemporary Psychotherapy; Hd., var. study teams in soc. welfare, visiting many countries, Middle E., Asia, Africa & Europe, var. occasions. Publs. incl: Bureaucracy in Higher Education, 1966; Four Religions of Asia, 1968; The Future of the Family, 1969; Like a Great River: An Introduction to Hinduism, 1972; Founders of the Living Religions, 1974. Address: 171 Fairlawn Ave., W. Hempstead, NY 11552, U.S.A. 2.

STRUTZ, Gloria Marie, b. 5 Apr. 1933. Thoracic & Cardiovascular Surgeon & Physician. Educ: B.S., Univ. of Mich., Ann Arbor, U.S.A., 1954; M.D., Woman's Med. Coll. of Pa., 1964; Intern, Physn. & Surg., Riverside Meth. Hosp., Columbus, Ohio, 1964-65. Appts. incl: Med. Technologist, Mt. Clemens, Mich, 1956-59; Pt.-time Med. Technologist, Eastern Pa. Psychiatric Inst., Phila., 1961-64; Res. Surg., Henry Ford Hosp., Detroit, Mich., 1965-69; Res. Surg., Thoracic & Cardiovascular

Surg., Univ. of Iowa Hosps., Iowa City, 1969-71; Instr. & Assoc., Dept. of Gen. Surg., ibid, 1969-71; Emergency Room Physn. w. E.R. Doctor, P.C., Mt. Clemens, 1972-. Mbrships. incl: AMA; Mich. State Med. Soc.; Candidate Grp., Am. Coll. of Surgs.; Roy D. McClure Surg. Soc.; Am. Med. Women's Assn.; Detroit Surg. Assn.; Mt. Clemens Community Concert Assn.; Gamma Delta. Author, article in profl. jrnls. Recip., Regents-Alumni Schlrships. to Univ. of Mich., 1950-53. Address: 28123-23 Mile Rd., Colonial Country Club Apartments No. 87, New Baltimore, MI 48047, U.S.A. 5, 138

STUART, Frances Crook (Mrs. Thomas B. Stuart), b. 7 June 1919. Librarian. Educ: B.A., Univ. of S.C., 1936-40; B.S.L.S., Geo. Peabody Coll. for Tchrs., 1943; M.L.S., ibid, 1971. Appts: Tchr.-Libn., Calhoun Falls, S.C., 1940-41; Circulation Libn., S. Carolina Lib., Univ. of S.C., 1941-45; Asst. Libn.-Libn., Carnegie Pub. Lib., Sumter, S.C., 1946-51; Dept. Libn., Post Lib., Ft. Jackson, S.C., 1951-53; Asst. Libn., Atlas Chem. Inds., Wilmington, Dela., 1954; Hosp. Libn., Ft. Jackson, S.C., 1956; Cataloger, State Lib. Bd., Columbia, S.C., 1957-66; Dir. of Lib. Servs., Midlands Tech. Educ. Ctr., Columbia, 1966-; on Evaluation Teams, Southern Assn. of Colls. & Schls., 1969-74; participant in special workshop for revising & improving standards, ibid; Cons. to Libns. beginning in Tech. Libs., 1967-73; Tchr., Cataloging & Classification course, Columbia Coll. Lib. Sci. Schl. Mbrships: S.C. & Southeastern Lib. Assns.; ALA; S.C. Tech. Educ. Ctr.; Libns. Assn.; S.C. State Employees Assn.; Beta Phi Mu. Address: 3546 Greenleaf Rd., Columbia, SC 29206, U.S.A. 5.

STUART, (Vivian), Alex, b. 2 Jan. 1914. Author (also as Barbara Allen). Publs. incl: The Beloved Little Admiral; biog. of Ad. Sir H. Keppel, 1967; The Valiant Sailors, 1967; The Brave Captains (as Vivian Stuart), 1968; There But for Fortune, Random Island, 1966-67; Strangers When We Meet (as Alex Stuart); Captain Hazard, R.N. 1969; The Swan River Sailors; many romantic novels under var. names, Samaritans Hospital, & The Scottish Soldier, etc.; also hist. novels, Like Victors Like Lords, etc. V.P. & Co-Fndr., Romantic Novelists' Assn.; V.P., Assn. of Yorkshire Bookmen; Pres., ibid, 1968; Chmn., Writers's Summer Schl., 1965-67; Comm. Mbr., ibid, 1968-69; Tutor, Practical Writing, WEA, 1968-69 & York Further Educ. Ctr. Mbrships. incl: Soc. of Authors; Inst. of Jrnlsts.; Soc. for Nautical Rsch.; Soc. for Individual Freedom. Address: Hop Grove Farm Cottage, 461 Malton Rd., York YO3 9TH, U.K. 3.

STUBER, Helen Hill (Mrs. Stanley I. Stuber), b. 31 Mar. 1904. Churchwoman. Educ: A.B., Bates Coll., 1925. Appts: Pres., Womens Bapt. Mission Soc., N.J., 1953-56; Bd. Mgrs., N.J. Bapt. Conv., 1953-56; Deleg., Bapt. World Alliance, London, U.K., 1955; V.P., Missions, Mo. Bapt. Womens Fellowship, 1956-59; Gen. Coun., Am. Bapt. Conv., 1957-59; Comm. rels. w. other relig. bodies, 1957-59; Commn. on Mln., 1959-63; Commn., Rural Advance, 1960-63; Pres., Am. Bapt. Women, 1959-63; Bd. Mgrs., United Ch. Women, 1959-63; Advsry. Coun., Am. Bible Soc., 1960-63; Womens Planning Comm., Int. Christian Univ., Tokyo, 1956-; Deleg., Bapt. World Alliance, Rio de Janeiro, 1960; Deleg., Assembly Nat. Coun. Chs., San Fran., 1960; Chmn., Prayer Fellowship Team, United Ch. Women, Hong Kong, 1961; Deleg., White House Conf. on Aging, 1961; Pres., Ch. Women United, Ridgewood, N.J., 1968-70. Contbr. to relig. publs. Hons: D.H.L., Bates Coll., 1962; Award,

Bergen Co. Coun. of Chs. for ecumenical serv., 1972. Address: 74 Burma Rd., Wyckoff, NJ 07481, U.S.A. 2, 5.

STUBER, Stanley Irving, b. 24 Aug. 1903. Clergyman; Author; Ecumenical Leader. Educ: A.B., Bates Coll., Lewiston, Me., 1926; B.D., Rochester Theol. Sem., N.Y., 1928; Th.M., Colgate-Rochester Divinity Schl., Rochester, 1929; D.D., Keuka Coll., Keuka Pk., N.Y., 1946. Appts. incl: Gen. Sec., Japan Int. Christian Univ. Fndn., 1950-56; Gen. Sec., Coun. of Chs., Greater Kansas City, Mo., 1956-60; Exec. Dir., Mo. Coun. of Chs., 1961-64; Dir., Assn. Press, N.Y.C., 1964-69; Ecumenical Min., Bergen Co. Coun. of Chs., 1969-; Pres., N.J. Div., UN Assn., 1972-73; Pres., N.J. Coun. of Orgs., 1972-74. Mbrships: Pres., Rotary Club, Clifton Springs, N.Y.; Coll. Club, Bates Coll.; Bd., Religion in Am. Life; Relig. PR Coun. Inc. Publs. incl: The Living Water; Treasury of the Christian Faith; How Protestants Differ from Roman Catholics; Who We Are. Hons. incl: Award, UN Assn., 1968; Award, UN Wk. Chmn., Gov. of N.J. Address: 74 Burma Rd., Wyckoff, NJ 07481, U.S.A. 2, 3, 6, 8.

STUDLEY, V.C., b. 11 Nov. 1907. Banking Executive Retired. Educ: Educ. in Engrng. w. special courses in Pol. & Econ. Geog., Acctng., Int. Bus. & Langs., U.S.A. & U.K. Appts. incl: Ind., U.S.A. & Abroad, 1933-63; Int. Banking until retirement; Chmn., Gtr. Kan. City For. Trade Zone Inc.; Dir. of firms in U.K., Canada, & U.S.A.; Hon. British Consul for Mo. & Kan., Kan. City. Mbrships. incl: Kappa Sigma; Int. Trade Club, Kan. City; Walker Club; Waterbury Club; Arbroath Tennis Club; River Tennis Club; Milwaukee Club; Royal Tay Yacht Club. Publs. incl: Contbr. of num. papers on int. monetary matters, trade, econs. & multi-nat. cos.; Fndr., Int. Bus. course at a mid-western coll.; Cons. to colls., banks, city, state & nat. govts. Hons. incl: Fellow, Inst. of Dirs., Gt. Britain; Chmn., Regional Export Expansion Coun.; UN Special Serv. Award; Women's Chmbr. of Comm. Award; Coun. for Dev. & Ind.; Trustee for two U.S. Philanthropic Orgs. Address: 4550 Warwick Blvd., Kansas City, MO 64111, U.S.A. 2, 8.

STULTUS, Dyalma Augusto, b. 31 Oct. 1901. Painter; Sculptor; Designer. Educ: Acad. Fine Arts, Venice. Appts: Prof., Figure Drawing, Art Schl. & Fine Arts Acad., Florence. Mbrships: Latinitati Excolendae Acad., Rome; Tiberina Acad., Rome; Del Cinquecento Acad., Rome; Universale G. Marconi Acad., Rome; Theatine Acad. of Sci. & Art, Pescara. Works located in galls. & pvte. collects in Rome, Latina, Udine, Gorizia, Trieste, Vicenza, etc. Hons. incl: Premio Pippo Faggioli, 1965. Address: Vle. M. Fanti 207, 50137 Florence, Italy.

STUMMVOLL, Josef Leopold, b. 19 Aug. 1902. Librarian. Educ: Sc.D., M.Sc., Tech. Univ. of Vienna; Ph.D., Univ. of Leipzig; studies, Kiel Univ. Appts. incl: Rsch. Libn. & Dir., Reading Dept., Deutsche Bucherei, Leipzig, 1925-33; Dir., Lectr., & Organizer, Lib. of Coll. of Agric. & Veterinary Med., Ankara, Turkey, 1933-37; Rsch. Libn., Dpty. Dir. of Lib. of Patent Off., Berlin, Germany, 1939-45; non-combatant war serv., 1943-45, & prisoner-of-war, 1945; Libn., Austrian Nat. Lib., 1946, & Dpty. Dir.-Gen., 1946, Dir.-Gen., 1949-67; on leave as Dir., UN Lib., N.Y., U.S.A., 1959-63. Mbr. & Off., var. profl. orgs. Publs. incl: Biblos, Austrian Period (Ed.), 1952-; Biblos-Schriften (Ed.), 78 vols., 1953-; Codices Selecti (Ed.), 40 vols., 1960-; ed. & author, var. other books; num. articles,

libnship., documentation, etc. Recip., var. merit awards. Address: Flamminggasse 36, A 2500 Baden, Austria. 2, 34, 43, 86.

STUMP, John Lee, b. 29 Aug. 1946. Educator; Chiropractic Student. Educ: B.S., Univ. of Md.; grad. work, Univs. of Fla. & Iowa; currently cand. for D.C. degree, Palmer Coll. of Chiropractic & M.D., Univ. of Iowa. Appts: HS Biol. & Soc. Studies Tchr., Salisbury, Md., 1970; HS Hlth. & Phys. Educ. Tchr., Athletic Dir., Football, Basketball & Track Coach, John Carroll HS, Ft. Pierce, Fla., 1971-72; Coll. Instr., Med. & Sci. Terminol., Palmer Coll., 1973. Mbrships: Alpha Kappa Mu; Beta Kappa Xi; Md. Bi-Racial Comm.; V.P., Md. Student Senate; Nippon Shorinji Kempo Fedn.; I.C.A.; YMCA; A.A.H.P.E.R.; U.S.C.A. Publs: Health of the Ghetto Child; The Genetic Key to Life; Laxatives & Myths (unpubld.). Hons: S. Fla. Coach. of the Yr., 1972. Address: 1105 W. 10th St., Davenport, IA 52803, U.S.A. 125.

STUMPF, Lowell Clinton, b. 8 Dec. 1917. Artist; Designer. Educ: Grad., Chgo. Acad. of Fine Arts, 1938; art schls., U.K. & France, 1943-45. Appts: Staff Artist, Int. Harvester Co., Chgo., U.S.A., 1939-42; w. Nugent-Graham Studios, ibid, 1945-47; Free-lance artist, designer, 1947-. Mbrships: Artists Guild Chgo.; Gideons Int.; Evangelical Luths. in Mission. Illustrations: Compton's Pictured Ency., 1957-; World Book Yr. Books, 1964, 65; World Book Ency; Sci. Yr., 1968, 69, 71; Childcraft Annual, 1969, 71; Childcraft Lib., 1972. Art Ed., Concordia Torch, 1966-. Address: 203 N. Wabash Ave., Chgo., IL 60601, U.S.A. 8, 120, 131, 133.

STUNZI, H., b. 9 Jan. 1920. University Professor. Educ: Univ. of Zurich, Switzerland; Veterinary H.S., Stockholm, Sweden; Veterinary Coll., Cornell Univ., Ithaca, U.S.A. Professor & Hd., Dept. of Veterinary Pathol., Univ. of Zurich. Mbrships. incl: Pres., World Assn. of Veterinary Pathologists; Europäische Arbeitsgemeinschaft der Veterinär-Pathologen; Deutsche Gesellschaft für Pathologie; Schweizerische Gesellschaft für Pathologie. Publs: Co-author, International Encyclopedia for Veterinary Medicine; Co-author, Cohrs-Jaffé-Meessen: Pathologie der Laboratoriumstiere, 1958; Lehrbuch der Pathophysiologie der Haustiere (w. Spörri), 1969; Ed., Handbuch der speziellen pathologischen Anatomie der Haustiere, 8 vols.; Co-ed., Lehrbuch der allgemeinen Pathologie, 6th edit., 1972. Recip., Doct., Univ. of Munich, German Fed. Repub. Address: Veterinär-Pathologisches Institut der Univ. Zurich, Winterthurerstr. 260, CH 8057 Zurich, Switzerland. 103.

STURDEVANT, William Desmond, b. 3 July 1922. Artist; Educator; Writer. Educ: B.S.E., Drake Univ., Iowa, 1945; M.S.E., ibid, 1947. Appts. incl: Supvsr. of Art, Joliet Pub. Schls., Ill., 1955-59; Asst. Prof. of Art, Calif. Western Univ., San Diego, 1959-61; Artist, Pvte. Profl. Studio, ibid, 1961-65; Asst. Prof. of Art Educ., Bemidji State Coll., Minn., 1965-67; Art Instr., Des Moines Tech. H.S., Iowa, 1968-. Mbrships. incl: Soc. Am. Graphic Artists; Boston Printmakers; Nat. Woodcarvers; Izaak Walton League; Evaluator, N. Ctrl. Assn. of Colls. & Sec. Schls., Iowa Div.; Charter Assoc., Parapsychol. Assn.; Am. & Fed. Mineralol. Socs. Contbr. of articles to profl. jrnls. One Man Exhibs: Mex. Inst. of N. Am. Cultural Rels., DF, 1958; Am. Graphic Artists Int. Exchange Exhib., Isetan Gall., Tokyo, 1967. Permanent Exhib. in Dehn Mem. Print Collection of N.Y. Lib., 1972. Recip. of Lady

Black Purchase Prize. Address: 616 S.W. Rose St., Des Moines, IA 50315, U.S.A. 120, 128.

STURLUSON, Ragnar V(aldimar), b. 29 July 1909. Foreman. Appts. incl: Work in factory, Reykjavik, Iceland, 1946-49; Daylabourer & fisherman, 1949-57; Labourer on city performances, 1957-; Foreman on city performances, 1965-. Mbrships. incl: Fndr., Ungmennafelag Bardstrendinga (assn. of the youth of Bardaströnd), 1930; Life mbr., Bunadarfelag Islands (assn. for agric. of Iceland), 1940; Idja (soc. for workers in factories), 1947; Esperantistafelagid "Aurora" (soc. for Iceland Esperantists), 1947; Sjomannafelag reykjavikur (soc. of fishermen in Reykjavik), 1950; Fndr., Landssambands islenzkra Graenlandsahugamanna (confedn. of icelandic interests in Greenland, 1957; Sec., Comm., ibid; Verkstjorafelag Reykjavikur (soc. of foreman in Reykjavik), 1965; Soc. Felag Nyjalssinna, 1967. Author of articles in newspapers & jrnls. Address: Snorrabraut 42, Reykjavik, Iceland. 43.

STURM, Ephraim H., b. 5 May 1924. Organization Executive. Educ: B.A., Brooklyn Coll., 1944; M.A., Columbia Univ., 1946. Appts: Asst. Prin., Yeshiva of Brighton Beach, 1947-48; Registrar, Young Israel Inst. for Adult Jewish Studies, 1948-50; Ed., Young Israel Viewpoint, 1950-52; Asst. Dir., Nat. Coun. of Young Israel, 1952-54; Assoc. Dir., ibid, 1954-59, Nat. Dir., 1958-; Guest Lectr., N.Y. Univ., 1957-; Lectr., Yeshiva Univ., 1962-. Mbrships. incl: Bd. of Dirs., Nat. Assn. of Hebrew Day Schls. PTA-, Rabbinical Alliance, 1954-; Sec., Coun. of Young Israel Rabbis, 1950-; Bd. of License, Jewish Educ. Comm., 1956-; Exec. Bd., Mesivta Talmudical Acad., 1955-; Rabbinical Coun. of Am.; Phi Delta Kappa. Co-author, The Sanctity of the Synagogue, 1959. Hons. incl: Hon. Award, State of Israel Bonds, 1958; Plaque, Pace Coll., 1959, Young Israel of 5th Ave., 1971, City of L.A., 1973. Address: National Council of Young Israel, 3 W. 16th St., N.Y., NY 10011, U.S.A. 6, 55, 94, 130.

STÜRZL, Erwin Anton, b. 15 Feb. 1920. University Professor. Educ: Mag.phil. Tchrs. Cert, Engl. & Latin, for grammar schls., 1948; Ph.D., Vienna Univ., Austria, 1949. Appts. incl: Instr., Higher Trng. & Rsch. Inst. for Graphic Arts, Vienna, 1948-64; Univ. Lectr., Engl. Lang. & Lit., Vienna Univ., 1964; Prof. & Hd., Engl. Dept., Salzburg Univ., 1964; Hd., Dept. of Phys. Educ., ibid, 1965; Dean, Philosophical Fac., 1969; Ed., Moderne Sprachen, 1960-70; Ed., Contact, Jrnl. of Fedn. Int. des Profs. de Langues Vivantes, 1963-68. Mbrships. incl: Sec.-Gen., Fedn. Int. des Profs. de Langues Vivantes, 1962-65; Pres., Austro-German Soc. of Salzburg, 1971-; Sec., Austrian MLA, 1961-65; Pres., ibid, 1965-70; Int. Assn. of Univ. Profs. of Engl. Author of books & num. articles in field. Recip. of hons. Address: Institut für englische Sprache & Literatur, Univ. of Salzburg, Akademiestr. 24, 5020 Salzburg, Austria. 43.

STUTSCHEWSKY, Joachim (Jehojachin), b. 7 Feb. 1891. Cellist; Composer; Writer. Educ: Mus. Schl., Cherson, Ukraine; Grad. Leipzig Conservatorie, 1912. Appts. incl: Performer & Tchr., Zürich, Switzerland, 1914-24; Performer (Mbr. Vienna String Quartet), Tchr., Newspaper Columnist, Vienna, Austria, 1924-38; In Israel 1938-; Insp. Music Dept., Jewish Agcy., 1938-48. Mbrships: League of Composers, Israel; Israeli Royalties Soc.; MILO (Artists' Club). Publs. incl: The Art of Playing the Violincello, 6 vols.; Studies for a New Technique of Violincello Playing, 3 vols.; The Art of Studying: New Collection of Studies for Violincello, 4 vols.; Musical Folklore of E. European Jewry, 1959; Klezmorim, (Jewish Folk Musicians), 1959; Der Wilner Balebesl, 1968; Author & subject of num. newspaper articles. Compositions: Num. Orch., Chamber music, cantatas & instrumental works, inclng. Israel, symphonic suite, 1964; Songs for Children, Jewish songs, collects. fold songs. Final style developed from European & Folk phases. Hons. incl: Engel Prize, Tel-Aviv Municipality, 1951, 1959, 1966; MILO Artists' Club prize, 1958; Piatigorsky Prize, Violicello Soc., N.Y., U.S.A., 1963; Israel Philharmonic Orch. Prize, 1973. Address: Bodenheimer St., 37, 62008, Tel-Aviv, Israel. 21.

STUTZ, Geraldine. Fashion Executive. Educ: B.A., Mundelein Coll., Chgo., Ill., 1945. Appts: Assoc. fashion ed., Glamour mag., 1947-52; Fashion & Promotion Dir., I. Miller & Sons, Co., N.Y.C., 1953-54; V.P., Gen. Mgr., ibid, 1954-57; Pres., Henri Bendel, Inc., 1957. Mbrships: Dir., Reality House; Dir., Phoenix Theatre; Past Dir., Carnegie Hall, City Ctr.; N.Y. Urban Design Coun.; Kappa Gamma Pi. Hons: Best Dressed Hall of Fame; Tobe Award, for Creative Merchandising, 1964; Ambassador Award, 1970; Best Coiffed Am. Women Award, 1959; Spirit of Achievement Award. Address: Henri Bendel, Inc., 10 West 57 St., N.Y., NY 10019, U.S.A.

STYLE, Colin Thomas Elliot, b. 3 Aug. 1937. Marketing & Market Research Manager. Educ: Rhodes Univ., Grahamstown. Appts: Exec. Off., Labour Rsch. & Stats., Rhodesian Govt., 1960-63; Mkt. Rsch. Off., Lever Bros. (Rhodesia) (Pvt) Ltd., 1963-67; Mktng. & Mkt. Rsch. Mgr., Commercial TV (Pvt.) Ltd., 1968-. Mbrships: Rhodesia Ctr., P.E.N. Int.; Chmn., Poetry Soc. of Rhodesia, 1972, 74; Chmn., Ed. Comm., Rhodesian Poetry (biennial review), 1972 & 74. Poems publd. in anthols. & periodicals inclng: Poetry in Rhodesia- 75 Years (ed. D.E. Finn), 1968; Rhodesian Poets (L.P. Gramophone record), 1968; Beneath a Rhodesian Sky (ed. D.Ê. Finn), 1972; The Contemp. Review, UK; Cornhill Mag., UK; Outposts, UK; Stand, UK; The Christian Sci. Monitor, USA; Swanee Review, USA; Dalhousie Review, Can.; The Wascana Review, Can.; Poetry Australia; Contrast, R.S.A.; New Coin, R.S.A.; New Nation, R.S.A.; Standpunte, R.S.A. Poems broadcast on BBC African Serv. & SABC Engl. Serv. Co-Ed. CHIRMO, Lit. jrnl. (ceased publ., 1970). Co-Prod. w. wife O-lan, Rhodesian Poets, L.P. record of readings of poems in Shona, Engl. & Ndebele. Ed. Cons., Contemporary Poets of Engl. Lang. Recip. Rhodian Poetry Prize. 1956. Address: P.O. Box A 294, Avondale, Salisbury, Rhodesia. 11, 139.

STYLIANOS, A. Mousis, b. 28 Oct. 1898. Journalist. Educ: Grad., Schl. of Law, Athens Univ., Greece. Appts: Jrnlst., sev. Greek newspapers, 1916-69; Corres., Greek-lang. newspapers of N.Y., U.S.A. & Alexandria, Egypt; Pol. Ed., to Vima newspaper, Athens, 40 yrs. Mbrships: Bd. of Dirs., Union of Athens Dailies Jrnlsts.; Past Chmn., Pensioners Fund Bd. of Greek Jrnlsts. Publs: Num. articles, editorials, pol. comments, news stories, & features, in sev. Greek newspapers. Recip., Gold Medal for Jrnlsm., 1966. Address: 6 Sakellaridis St., Athens (TT 815), Greece.

SUAREZ GOMEZ, Julián-Mario, b. 19 Jan. 1906. Editor. Educ: Bachillerator, Piano, Harmony & Composition; Music Studies, 1918-30. Appts: 1st performance of his symphonic works, Phil. Orch. of Madrid, 1926; Dir., (choral soc.) Orfeón Santa Cecilia, 1930; Obtained place of prof., music, Coll. for

Orphans of Post Off. Wkrs., 1930; Fndr., Ed., Ediciones Hispania Music Eds., 1938-. Mbr., Gen. Soc. of Spanish Authors. Compositions: Danza Betica (piano); Evocaciones Versallescas (symph. orch.); Evocacion Asturiana (orch.); Ecos de Andalucia (orch.). Hons: 1st Prize for Piano, 1925; 1st Prize for Harmony, 1925; Extraordinary Prize for Composition, 1925. Address: Ediciones Hispania, Avenida de José Antonio 31, Madrid 13, Spain.

SUBBIAH, Bommireddi, b. 13 Jan. 1917. Professor of Political Science. Educ: B.A., CD Coll., India; M.P.A., N.Y. Univ., U.S.A.; Ph.D., ibid. Appts: Asst. Sec., Andhra State Govt., India, 1952-65; Prof., Pol. Sci., W. Va., U.S.A., 1965-. Mbrships: AAUP; Am. Soc. of Pub. Admin; Am. Mgmt. Assn.; Am. Pol. Sci. Assn.; Smithsonian Instn.; Int. Biographical Assn., U.K. Publs: The Tragedy of a Papal Decree, 1970; The Population Crisis, 1972; Toward a New System of Criminal Justice for Modern America (in preparation). Recip., Disting. Merit Cert., N.Y. Univ., 1965. Address: 417 Circle Dr., Hurricane, WV, U.S.A. 6, 14, 30, 125, 130, 131.

SUCHENWIRTH, Richard Mathias August, b. 1 Nov. 1927. Neurologist. Educ: M.D., Univ. of Munich, German Fed. Repub., 1950. Appts: Scientific Asst., Univs. of Munich, Freiburg, Kiel, 1952-62; Hd. Physn., Med. Acad., Lubeck, 1962-66; Univ. Lectr., Lubeck & Erlangen, 1965-72; Univ. Prof., Univ. of Erlangen, 1972; Hd. Physn., Neurol. Clin., ibid, 1967-70; Med. Supt., Neurol. Clin., Tchng. Hosp., Kassel, 1970. Mbrships. incl: Deutsche Gesellschaft für Neurologie; Soc. Int. pour Psychopathol. d'Expression. Publs: About 100 studies in neurol. & other med. jrnls.; Co-author, 10 books; Author, Abbau der graphischen Leistung Thieme, 1967. Address: Moenchebergstr. 41, D 3500 Kassel, German Fed. Repub. 50.

SUCCAR, Toufic, b. 29 Nov. 1925. Musician; Composer. Educ: Dip., Harmony, Counterpoint, Fugue, & Composition, Higher Nat. Conservatoire of Music, Paris, France, 1952. Appts: Prof., Nat. Conservatoire of Music, Beyrouth, Lebanon, 1953-; Dir., ibid, 1964-69; Rep. of Lebanon at sev. int. music festivals & congresses. Compositions incl: Requiem; Suites; "Cedars" symph.; Choral, ballet, chamber, & instrumental music. Author, Cent Exercises de Solfège, 1969. Address: c/o M. Khoury, B.P. 5018, Beirut, Lebanon.

SUGAR, Peter Charles, b. 21 Nov. 1932. Architect. Educ: B.A. (Hons.) Arch., London Univ., U.K., 1955; M.Arch., MIT, Mass., U.S.A., 1960. Appts. incl: Archt. w. A.G.Porri & Ptnrs., London, U.K., 1958; Yorke, Rosenbert & Mardall, ibid, 1960-61; Sir Robert Matthew, Johnson-Marshall & Ptnrs., ibid, 1961-62; Designer sev. schls. & chs., & Job Chapt., Ptnr. 1965-, James Assocs., Indpls. Ind., U.S.A., 1962-67; Assoc., Eduardo Catalano, Cambridge, Mass., 1968-, Job Capt., Gaystate W. Hotel, Springfield, Mass., 1971, & Greensboro/Guilford Co. Govtl. Ctr., N.C., 1973. Mbrships: Royal Inst. of British Archts.; Am. Inst. of Archts. Hons. incl: Herbert Batsford Prize, 1951; Sir Andrew Taylor Prize, 1954; Royal Inst. of British Archts. Donaldson Medal, 1955; Commonwealth Fund (Harkness) Fellow in U.S.A. 1958-60. Address: Short Hill Rd., Todd Pond, Lincoln, MA 01773, U.S.A. 6, 82.

SUGARMAN, Robert Reuben, b. 17 June 1898. Lawyer; Emeritus Professor of Law. Educ: B.A., CCNY, 1920; LL.B., Bklyn. Law Schl., St. Lawrence Univ., 1926; J.S.D., ibid,

1927. Appts: Asst. Mgr., Law Dept., Title Guarantee Trust Co., N.Y., 1923-27; Mbr., Comm. on Character & Fitness, Appellate Div., Supreme Ct., 2nd Judicial Dept., 1958-; Prof. of Law, Bklyn. Law Schl., St. Lawrence Univ., 1927-74; Emeritus Prof., ibid, 1973; Arbitrator, Civil Ct., NYC, 1929-. Mbrships: Chancellor, Philonomic Coun., Hon. Soc., Bklyn. Law Schl., 1935-; Fndr., Fac. Advsr., City Coll. Club., ibid, 1930-; Co. Cmdr., Am. Legion, King's Co., 1951-52; Bklyn., N.Y. State & Am. Bar Assns.; Profl. Assns. of Lawyers of N.Y., Conn. & N.J.; Iota Theta; Kappa. Publs: Sugarman on Partnership (in 4th ed.); Sugarman's Cases on Agency & Partnership; Supplement to Sugarman's Cases on Agency & Partnership; revised 4th ed. of Richardson on Evidence, 1931; contbr. num. articles to legal jrnls. Hons. incl: LL.D., Bklyn. Law Schl., 1972. Address: 441 Ocean Ave., Brooklyn, NY 11226, U.S.A. 6, 55.

SUGHRUE, Kathryn Eileen (Mrs. Herbert Sughrue), b. 2 May 1914. Home Economist. Educ: B.S., Kan. State Univ., 1936; Kan. State Tchrs. Coll.; M.S., Colo. State Univ . Appts. (all in Kan. State Univ.): Home Econs. Tchr., 4 yrs.; Ext. Home Economist, 1937-41; Dist. Supvsr., Ext. Home Econs., 1961-67; Assoc. State Ldr., Home Econs., 1967-69; Advsr., Andra Pradesh Univ., Hyderabad, India, 1968; State Ldr., Home Econs. Ext., N.D. State Univ.; Pub. speaker, num. nat., state, local events. Mbrships: Past State Pres., Kan. Ext. Home Econs. Assn.; Past State Pres., Epsilon Sigma Phi; Life Mbr., India Home Econs. Assn.; Kan. Coun. of Pres.; Dist. Pres., Home Econs. Assn.; Advsr. & Off., Nat. & Kan. Assns. of Ext. Home Econs. Advsrs. Publs: Num. booklets, bulletins. Hons: Beauty Queen, Kan. State Univ., 1936; Schlrship., Nat. Epsilon Sigma Phi; Senator for Kan. State Univ.; Outstanding Mother Award, 1964. Address: 810 Central, Dodge City, KS U.S.A.

SUHONEN, Onni, b. 5 Feb. 1903. Violinist; Teacher. Educ: Grad., Viipuri Music Inst., Finland, 1924; Music Acad., Budapest, Hungary; Dip., Master Class of Jenö Hubay, 1924-25. Appts: Tchr., Viipurin Music Inst., 1929-39; Sibelius Acad., 1943-; Instr., 1950-; Mbr., 1st Violin, Helsinki City Symph. Orch., 1943-66. Mbr., Soc. of Friends of Chmbr. Music. Given concerts in Finland, Budapest & Paris. Hons: Hon. title of Prof., 1972; Wihuri Hon. Award, 1972; Martin Wegelius Medal, 1973. Address: Pohjois-Rautatienkatu 9, Helsinki 10, Finland. 90.

SUITS, Chauncey Guy, b. 12 Mar. 1905. Research Scientist; Research Director. Educ: B.A., Univ. of Wis., 1927; Sc.D., Eidgen. Tech. Univ., Zurich, Switzerland, 1929. Appts: Physicist, U.S. Forest Prods. Lab., Madison, Wis., 1929-30; Rsch. Physicist, Gen. Elec. Rsch. Lab., 1930-40; Asst. to Dir., ibid, 1940-45; V.P. & Dir. of Rsch., 1945-65; Cons., Indl. Rsch. Mgmt., 1965-. Mbrships. incl: Vice Chmn., N.Y. State Sci. Tech. Fndn., 1965-; Nat. Defense Rsch. Comm., 1942-46; Mbr., Div. 14, Chief, Div. 15, ibid; Dir., Am. Inst. Physics, 1961-64; Nat. Acad. Scis.; Fndg. mbr., Nat. Acad. Engrng.; Am. Philosophical Soc.; Fellow, Am. Phys. Soc.; Fellow, IEEE. Author of over 80 sci. rsch. papers & over 50 publd. reports concerning mgmt. aspects of indl. sci. rsch.; Holder of 79 U.S. patents. Hons. incl: Adv. of Rsch. Medal, Am. Soc. for Metals, 1966; Hon. degrees, Union Coll., Hamilton Coll., Drexel Inst., Marquette Univ., Rensselaer Poly. Inst. Address: Crosswinds, Pilot Knob, NY 12844, U.S.A.

SULLENBERGER, Ara Broocks Cox (Mrs. Hal. J. Sullenberger), b. 3 Jan. 1933. Educ: B.A. Tex. Tech. Univ., 1955; M.A., ibid, 1958; grad. studies, Univ. of Tex., Austin, E. Tex. State Univ., Tex. Christian Univ., N. Tex. State Univ. Appts: Maths. Tchr., Tom S. Lubbock H.S., Lubbock, Tex., 1955-56; Instr., Maths., Tex. Tech. Univ., Lubbock, 1956-63; Grad. Fellow, Tex. Christian Univ., Ft. Worth, 1963-64; Chmn., Math. Dept., Ft. Worth Country Day Schl., 1964-67; Instr., Maths., Tarrant Co. Jr. Coll., Ft. Worth, 1967-70, Asst. Prof., 1970-. Mbrships. incl: Math. Assn. of Am.; Nat. Coun., Tchrs. of Maths.; AAUP; Tex. Jr. Coll. Tchrs. Assn.; Jr. League Ft. Worth. Inc., 1954-, Bus. Mgr., 1966-73; Phi Beta Phi. Recip., Outstanding Tchr. Maths. Award, Gen. Dynamics, Ft. Worth, 1966. Address: 600 Eastwood, Fort Worth, TX 76107, U.S.A. 5, 138.

SULLENS, Idelle DePere, b. 28 June 1921. College Teacher. Educ: A.B., Stanford Univ., U.S.A., 1943; M.A., Wash. Univ., Seattle, 1954; Ph.D., Stanford Univ., 1959. Appts: Commerce, 1939-41; Supply Corps, USN, 1943-49, 1950-54 (now Cmndr. (SC) USNR-Retired); Tchng: Stanford Univ., 1956-57; Monterey Peninsula Coll., 1958- (Chmn., Dept. of Engl., 1968-69). Mbrships. incl: AAUA, NCTE, MLA, EETS, CTS. Publs. incl: Principles of Grammar, 1966; The Inquiring Reader (w. Edith Karas & Raymond Fabrizio) 1967, 2nd ed., '74; The Inquiring Reader: Essays, 1969; Basic Research Procedures, 1971; The Whole Idea Catalog: College Writing Projects, 1971. Hons: Nat. Endowment for the Humanities Fellowship, 1974-75 (to support completion of The Works of Robert Mannyng of Brunne, 1303-1338). Address: P.O. Box 4418, Carmel, CA 93921, U.S.A. 5, 13, 30, 138.

SULLINS, Judith Jones, b. 4 Aug. 1943. Musician. Educ: B.A., Tenn. Wesleyan Coll., 1964. Appts: Ch. Organist, 1959-; Pvte. Music Tchr., 1965-71. Mbrships. incl: Am. Optometric Assn. Aux., 1965-; Tenn. Optometric Assn., 1965, Educl. Chmn., 1972-73, Pres., 1974-; Jaycettes, 1965-67; Nat. Fedn. Music Clubs, 1966-, Corres. Sec., 1970, V.P., 1971, Pres., 1972; Nat. Music Tchrs. Assn., 1966-, Sec. for Albany, Ga., 1967-69; Off.'s Wives Club, Naval Air Stn., Albany, 1967-69, Activities Chmn., 1967-68; NAS Ladies Golf Assn., 1967-69, Sec., 1967-68; Am. Guild of Organists, 1968-; United Meth. Women, 1970-; Bd. of Dirs., Contact Inc., Telephone Crisis Ctr.; Sec., ibid, 1972-. Address: P.O. Box 666, Athens, TN 37303, U.S.A. 76, 125.

SULLINS, Robert Michael, b. 31 Aug. 1926. Artist; Teacher. Educ: B.A., Univ. of Wyo, 1950; M.A., 1958; M.F.A., Univ. of Gunaj. Appts: Dpty. Sheriff, Carbon Co., Wyo, 1950-54; Supvr., Art, pub. schls., Rawlins, 1954-59; Artist, Tchr., SUNY, Oswego, N.Y., 1960-; Currently, Prof. One man exhibs: Janson Gall., N.Y.C.; Aspect-Aegis Gall.; Pickwick Gall., Greenwich, Conn.; Johnson State Coll., Vt.; Univ. of Fla., Gainsville; SUNY, Oswego. Participant in over 200 grp. exhibs. Mbrships. incl: Coll. Art Assn.; Phi Kappa Phi; Vets for For. Wars. Perm. collects. incl: Civic Ctr., Scottsdale, Ariz.; Univ. of Wyo, Laramie; SUNY; Art Mus., Las Vegas; Dulin Gall., Knoxville, Tenn.; Norfolk Mus. of Art, Va. Hons. incl: SUNY Grant in Aid, 1971; SUNY Rsch. Grant, Kinetic Art, 1972. Address: Dept. of Art, State Univ. of N.Y., Oswego, NY 13126, U.S.A. 37, 133.

SULLINS, William David, Jr., b. 3 Aug. 1942. Doctor of Optometry. Educ: B.Sc., Southern Coll. of Optometry, 1962; Dr. of Optometry, ibid, 1965; Fellow, Am. Acad. of Optometry, 1973. Appts: Entered pvte. prac. of optometry, 1965; Optometry Off., USN, 1967; Re-entered pvte. prac., 1970-; Lectr. Optometry Off., USNR, 1971-. Mbrships: Am. Optometric Assn.; Southern Coun. of Optometrists; V.P., Tenn. State Optometric Assn.; Past Pres., E. Tenn. Optometric Soc.; Am. Acad. of Optometry; Tenn. Acad. of Optometry; Past V.P., Jaycees; Bd. of Dirs., YMCA; Pres., Armed Forces Optometric Soc.; Optometric Extension Prog.; Am. Optometric Fndn.; Kiwanis; Tenn. Vision Servs. Coll. Aide de Camp, Gov.'s Staff, State of Tenn., 1974. Address: P.O. Box 666, Athens, TN 37303, U.S.A. 117, 125.

SULLIVAN, D. George, b. 6 Feb. 1906. Investment Consultant; Trustee. Educ: A.B., Harvard Coll., 1927; M.B.A., Harvard Grad. Schl. of Bus. Admin., 1929. Appts: incl: Dir., Fidelity Mgmt. & Rsch. (Bermuda) Ltd.; Trustee, The Boston Five Cents Savings Bank & Mass. Life Fund; Retd. Pres. & Dir., Fidelity Grp. of Funds; V.P., Fidelity Mgmt. & Rsch. Co.; Dir., Fidelity Mgmt. Rsch. Investment Mgmt. Serv. Inc., FMR Serv. Corp., The Crosby Corp. & Crosby Plans Corp.; V.P. & Dir., Pacific N.W. Mgmt. & Rsch. Co., Seattle, Wash.; Pres. & Dir., Equity Fund, Inc. & Equity Western Fund Inc.; V.P., Treas. & Dir., Mass. Life Co., 1937-54; Chmn., Bd. of Govs., Investment Co. Inst., 1964-66. Mbrships. incl: Boston Soc. of Security Analysts; Am. Finance Assn.; Dir., Engl. Speaking Union; Beacon Soc.; Charitable Irish Soc.; Clover Club; Braeburn Country Club; Eastward Ho Country Club. Address: 35 Congress St., Boston, MA 02109, U.S.A. 2, 6, 32.

SULLIVAN, John Patrick, b. 13 July 1930. Professor. Educ: B.A., St. John's Coll., Cambridge Univ., 1953; M.A., ibid, 1957; B.A., Oxford, 1954; M.A., ibid, 1957. Appts: Classical Tchr., Clare & Magdalene Colls., Cambridge, 1953; Fellow & Tutor, Classics, Oxford, 1956-62; Dean, Lincoln Coll., 1960-61; Vis. Prof., Classics, Univ. of Tex., 1961-62; Assoc. Prof.-Prof., Classics, ibid, 1962-69; Chmn., Dept. of Classics, 1963-65; Fac. Professor, SUNY at Buffalo, 1969-; Acting Assoc. Provost, Fac. of Arts & Letters, ibid, 1970-71; Provost, ibid, 1972-. Mbrships: Dir., Am. Philol. Assn., 1971-73; Ed., Arion, 1961-69; Contbng. Ed., The Tex. Observer, 1969-; Ed., Arethusa, 1971-74; Advsry. Bd., Tex. Studies in Lang. & Lit., 1965-; Bd. of Advsrs., Orpheus (Italy), 1969-. Publs. The Satyricon of Petronius-A Literary Study, 1968; Penguin Critical Anthologies-Ezra Pound, 1970; Contbr. to many schlrly. reviews. Hons. incl: John Stewart of Rannoch Schlrship. in Greek & Latin, 1953; Gregg Bury, Burney Prizes in Philos. of Relig., 1953, 54; Redditt Award for Ezra Pound & Sextus Propertius, 1965. Address: Fac. of Arts & Letters, SUNY at Buffalo-Old Fac. Club, 3435 Main St., Buffalo, NY 14214, U.S.A. 2, 3, 139.

SULLIVAN, Margaret Rita, b. 17 Oct. 1912. Librarian. Educ: B.S., M.Ed., Boston Univ.; Bristol Community Coll.; Bridgewater Coll. Appts: Hostess, Women's Prog., WALE; Fall River Summer. Rec. Supvsr.; Tchr., Sr. H.S. Engl.; Libn., Case H.S., Swansea, Mass. Mbrships: Chmn., Rec. Bd. of Model Cities; Mass., New Engl. & Cape Cod Libns. Assns.; AAUW; Sec., Fall River Pk. Bd.; Sec., Swansea Tchrs. Club; Mass. Tchrs. Assn.; Boston Univ. Alumni Assn.; Sec., Pi Lambda Theta; Cath. Women's Club; Holy Name Women's Guild;

Women's Bd. of Union Hosp.; Coll. Club; Friends of Lib.; 1923 Club; Altar & Rosary Soc. Publs: Ed., The Beacon, Boston Univ.; wrote commercials & radio scrips, WALE. Address: 860 President Ave., Fall River, MA 02720, U.S.A. 5.

SULLIVAN, Mary W. (Mrs.), b. 2 Sept. 1917. Legal Secretary; Legal Assistant. Educ: John B. Stetson Univ.; Ctrl. Fla. Coll.; Ctrl. Fla. Community Coll. Appts: Sec. to Wm. M. Cobb, Atty. at Law, Daytona Beach, Fla., 1937-41; Sec. to Chief of Staff, 7th Naval Dist., Key W. & Miami, Fla., WW II; Legal Sec. & Asst. to Frank R. Greene, Atty. at Law, Ocala, Fla., 1948-68, & to Judge Wm. T. Swigert, Ocala, Calif., 1968-. Mbrships: V.P., Pres. & Gov., Nat., Fla. & Marion Co. Legal Secs. Assn.; Bus. & Profl. Womens Assn.; League of Women Voters; Grace Episc. Ch. Address: 820 N.E. 11th Ave., Ocala, FL, U.S.A. 125.

SULTAN, Stanley, b. 17 July 1928. University Professor; Author. Educ: A.B., Cornell Univ., 1949; M.A., Boston Univ., 1950; Ph.D., Yale Univ., 1955. Appts: Ed., Nat. Lexicographic Co., N.Y., 1952-55; Instr., Engl., Smith Coll., 1955-59; Asst. Prof.-Prof. Engl., Clark Univ., 1959-. Publs. incl: The Argument of Ulysses, 1965; The Playboy of the Western World, 1970; Lit. Essays on John Heywood, Synge, Joyce, Faulkner. Recip. of hons. Address: Dept. of Engl., Clark Univ., Worcester, MA 01610, U.S.A. 13.

SULZER, Alexander Jackson, b. 13 Feb. 1922. Immunoparasitologist; Microbiologist. Educ: B.A., Hardin-Simmons Univ., Abilene, Tex., 1949; M.S., Emery Univ., Atlanta, Ga., 1960; Ph.D., 1962. Appts: Currently, Rsch. Microbiol., U.S. DHEW, PHS Ctr. for Disease Control., Atlanta, Ga.; Hon. Prof., Univ. Peruana Cayetano Heredia, Lima, Peru, 1973. Fellowships: Royal Soc. of Trop. Med. & Hygiene; Atomic Energy Commn., Vanderbilt Univ., 1950-51; Communicable Disease Ctr., Emory Univ., 1959-60; Nat. Inst. Hlth., ibid, 1960-62. Mbrships: Rsch. Soc. Am.; Am. Soc. Parasitol.; Am. Soc. Trop. Med. & Hygiene; Nat. Geog. Soc.; Am. Mus. Nat. Hist. Author of many sci. publs. Address: Parasitol. Div., Parasite Serol. Br., Immunofluorescence Lab., CDC, 1600 Clifton Rd., Atlanta, GA 30333, U.S.A. 7, 14.

SUMERLIN, William Tileston, b. 29 Mar. 1917. Electrical Engineer. Educ: A.B., Stanford Univ., 1937; Electrical Engr., ibid, 1939; Registered Profl. Engr., N.Y., 1947-. Appts: Design Engr., Hollywood Transformer Co., 1939-41; Proj. Engr. Radio Div., Hughes Aircraft Co., 1941-45; Hd., Electronic Dev., Guided Missiles Div., Fairchild Engine & Airplane Corp., 1945-51; Guided Missiles Cons. & Mgr., Reliability Engrng., Philco Corp., 1951-62; Mgr., Engrng. Reliability, McDonnell Aircraft Co., McDonnell Douglas Corp., 1962-; Cons., U.S. Dept. of Defense, 1955-73. Mbrships: Fellow, Inst. Electrical & Electronics Engrs. (Dir., 1968-69); Assoc. Fellow, Am. Inst. Aeronautics & Astronautics; Am. Statl. Assn.; Inst. Math. Stats. Ed., Reliability of Military Electronic Equipment, 1957. Author of profl. papers. Address: P.O. Box 181, Hazelwood, MO 63042 U.S.A. 8, 14, 16, 26.

SUMMERFIELD, (Sir) John Crampton, b. 20 Sept. 1920. Barrister. Educ: Gray's Inn, London; Called to Bar, 1949; Q.C., Bermuda, 1963. Appts: Capt., Royal Signal Corps, 1939-46; Crown Counsel, Tanganyika, 1949. Legal Draftsman, 1953; Dpty. Legal Sec., E.A. High Commn., 1958; Mbr., Exec. Coun. & Legislative Coun., Bermuda, 1962-68; Atty.

Gen., Bermuda, 1962; Chief Justice, Bermuda, 1972. Mbrships: Naval & Mil. Club, London; Royal Bermuda Yacht Club; Royal Hamilton Amateur Dinghy Club, Bermuda. Publs: Preparation of Revised Laws of Bermuda, 1963, '71 edits. Hons: O.B.E., 1961; C.B.E., 1966; Kt., 1973. Address: Supreme Ct., Bermuda. 1, 35.

SUMMERLIN, William Joseph, b. 14 Aug. 1921. Artist; Teacher; Lecturer; Writer. Educ: B.A., Commercial Art & Pathological Drawing; Graphic Art Cert., Indian River H.S. Appts: Tchr., Anatomy, Village Gall., Va. Beach, Va.; Tchr., Anatomy, Immlers Gall., Chesapeake, Va.; Dir. & Fndr., Young Artist Guild, Va. Beach, Va. Mbrships: Past Pres., Chesapeake Art Guild, Va.; Chesapeake Bay Art Assn., Norfolk, Va.; Va. Beach Arts Ctr.; Profl. Artist Forum, E. Coast; Charter mbr., Guadacanal Campaign Veterans Assn.; Disabled Am. Veterans, Va. Beach One-man shows: Village Gall., Tidewater, 1969; DeCor House; Churchland; Green Run Club House; Pvte. collects. in U.S.A., Netherlands, Belgium & Canada; Group graphic exhibitions; Writer of art column, Chesapeake Post. Hons: num. prizes for drawings & sculpture; var. mil. medals. Address: Route 2, Box 2226, Va. Beach, VA 23456, U.S.A. 125.

SUMMERS, Dirk Wayne. Producer; Director; Writer. Educ: B.A., Univ. of Ill.; M.F.A., CCNY; Hon. Doct., Univ. of S. Calif. Appts: Dir., N.Y. Stage Soc., 1951-53; Pres., Roslyn Records Inc., 1954-60, & DIBA Prods. Inc., 1960-68; Dir., Drury Lane Theatre, Chgo. Ill., 1965-70; Pres., United Prods. Ltd., 1970-. Mbrships: Writers Guild of Am.; Dirs. Guild of Am.; Nat. Acad. of TV Arts & Scis.; Phi Kappa; Int. Assn. of Film & TV Prods.; Nat. Assn. of Film & TV Prods.; UN Assn. Author, Dir. & Prod. of Survival of Spaceship Earth; Author of Heroes & Other Losers; Make Love Not War etc. Dir. of num. TV prods., motion pictures & stage plays. Prod. of num. films, TV & stage prods. inclng: Beyond Tomorrow; Mission Battangas (co-prod.); Night Music; The Great Sex War; A Deeper Darkness. Hons: EMMY Award, Nat. Acad. of TV Arts & Scis., 1972; N.Y. Stage Soc. Award for Outstanding Achievements, 1952; Order of Merit, Cuban Govt., 1958; For. Press Club Award, 1972. Address: 3921 Deervale Drive, Sherman Oaks, CA 91403, U.S.A.

SUMMERS, George Vernon, b. 21 Apr. 1929. Librarian; Teacher. Educ: B.A., Columbia Union Coll., 1951; M.S.L.S., Drexel Univ., 1963; Univ. of Md.; Ph.D., Lib. Sci., Univ. of Southern Calif., 1973. Appts: Libn., Tchr., Mt. Pisgah Acad., N.C., 1951-52; Lib. Asst., Univ. of Md., 1952-53; Prin., Pitts. Jr. Acad., 1953-55; Libn., Tchr., Blue Mtn. Acad., 1955-64; Hlth. Scis. Libn., Loma Linda Univ., Calif., 1964-67; Dir. of Libs., ibid, 1968-; Lectr., Schl. of Hlth., & Schl. of Lib. Sci., ibid, 1973-. Mbrships: ALA; Med. Lib. Assn.; AAUP; Am. Soc. for Info. Sci.; Calif. Lib. Assn.; Am. Soc. for Hist. of Med.; Beta Phi Mu. Publs: Library Science Syllabus, 1963; Contbr. to profl. jrnls. Hons: Lib. Sci. Fellowship, Univ. of Southern Calif., 1969-72; Med. Lib. Assn. Certification Grade III. Address: Univ. Libs., Loma Linda Univ., Loma Linda, CA 92354, U.S.A. 9, 15, 42.

SUMMERS, Malcolm Macgregor, b. 24 Dec. 1924. Commissioner. Educ: B.Comm., Univ. of Qld., Australia. Appts: Serv. WWII; Dir., Tariff Br., Dept. of Trade & Industry, Australia, 1960; Dpty. Sec. ibid, 1967-69; Dir., Australian Dept. of Transport, 1969-73; Commnr., Maritime Ind. Commn. of Inquiry, 1973-. Address: c/o

Maritime Industry Commission of Inquiry, P.O. Box 547, Canberra City, A.C.T., Australia, 2602. 23, 128.

SUMMERSELL, Charles G., b. 25 Feb. 1908. Professor of History. Educ: A.B., Univ. of Ala., 1929; M.A., ibid, 1930; Ph.D., Vanderbilt Univ., 1940. Appts: Instr., Hist., Univ. of Ala., 1935-40; Asst. Prof., ibid, 1940-46, Assoc. Prof., 1946-47, Prof., 1947-, Chmn., Dept. of Hist., 1954-70. Mbrships: Pres., Ala. Histl. Assn., 1955-56; Pres., Ala. Chapt., Phi Beta Kappa, 1953-54; Phi Alpha Theta; Org. of Am. Histns.; Southern Histl. Assn.; Am. Histl. Assn.; Am. Assn. of State Local Hist. Publs: Alabama Past & Future (co-author), 1941, 2nd edit., 1950; Historical Foundations of Mobile, 1949; Exploring Alabama (co-author), 1957, 2nd edit., 1961; Alabama History for Schools, 1957, 5th edit., 1970; Mobile: History of a Seaport Town, 1957; History Film Strips of Alabama (co-author), 1961; Florida (co-author), 1963; Texas (co-author), 1965; The Cruise of C.S.S. Sumter, 1965; Ohio, 1967; California, 1970; Illinois, 1971; The Journal of George Townley Fullam: Boarding Officer of the Confederate Sea Raider Alabama (ed., w. introduction by Charles G. Summersell), 1973. Address: 1411 Caplewood Dr., Tuscaloosa, AL 35401, U.S.A. 2, 7, 12, 13, 15, 51.

SUMMERSETT, Kenneth George, b. 9 Mar. 1922. Social Work Executive. Educ: B.S., Univ. of Mich., 1948; M.A., Northern Mich. Univ., 1964; M.S.W., Wayne State Univ., 1951. Appts. incl: w. Newberry State Hosp., Mich., 1954-; Dir., Soc. Serv. Dept., ibid, 1954-66; Dir., Cons. Soc. Servs., 1966-; Lectr., Lake Superior State Coll., 1968-. Mbrships. incl: Grad. & Undergrad. Ext. Fac., Northern Mich. Univ., 1962-; Acad. Cert. Soc. Wkrs., Psych. & Med. Sects.; Mich. Chapt. Am. So. Grp. Psychotherapy & Psychodrama; Mich. Dept. Mental Hlth., Marquette Child Guid. Clin., 1950-52; V.P., Comprehensive Hlth. Planning Bd., Upper Peninsula of Mich.; V.P., 1972-73, Nat. Assn. Soc. Wkrs.; Pres., Chmn., Upper Peninsula of Mich. Br., 1957-59 & '63-64; Bd. Dirs., Upper Peninsula Mental Hlth. Interchange, 1970-72. Author of Chapt. X "Child Guidance" Textbook "Social Services in the School", 1955; Stat. Tables on In-Patients, 1962. Address: Newberry State Hosp., Newberry, MI 49868, U.S.A. 8, 120, 128, 131.

SUMPTER, Betty Cuthbertson (Mrs. John A. Sumpter), b. 1 Apr. 1920. Teacher. Educ: A.B., William Jewell Coll., Liberty, Mo., U.S.A.; Postgrad., Univ. of Mo.; Inst. of Fndn. for Am. Christian Educ., San Fran., Calif.; Maryville State Tchrs. Coll., Mo. Appts: Sec., U.S.N. Preflight Schl., William Jewell Coll., WWII; Sec., Offs. of Recorder, Co. Clerk, & Co. Atty., Clay Co. Cthouse.; Tchr., Ridgeview Jr. H.S., Liberty; Tchr., Liberty Sr. H.S. Mbrships. incl: Pres., Liberty Br., AAUW, 1974-; NEA; Mo. Tchrs. Assn.; Liberty Community Tchrs. Assn.; PTA; Nat. Forensic League; Pres. & Charter Mbr., Liberty Harmony Homemakers; 2nd Bapt. Ch., Liberty; Chmn., Schl. & Community Day, Clay Co. Sesquicentennial, 1972; Phi Epsilon; Zeta Tau Alpha; Delta Kappa Gamma. Recip., DAR Medal for Citizenship, 1938. Address: 1037 Lindenwood Ln., Liberty, MO 64068, U.S.A. 8.

SUNDAHL, Craig Oscar, b. 2 Mar. 1935. Dentist. Educ: B.A., N.Y. Univ., 1957; D.D.S., ibid, 1961. Appts: Attng. Dentist, New Rochelle Hosp. Med. Ctr., N.Y. Mbrships: Ninth Dist. Dental Soc. of N.Y. State; Mbrship. Comm., ibid; Ethics Comm., ibid; Necrol.

Comm., ibid; Dental Hlth. Comm., ibid; New Rochelle Dental Forum (Pres., 1968-69); New Rochelle Suburban Dental Soc.; Meth. Ch.; Lions Club; Univ. Club, New Rochelle; Chmbr. of Comm., ibid. Hons: N.Y. State Schlrship. for Dental & Med. Educ., 1957. Address: 26 Country Rd., Marmaroneck, NY 10543, U.S.A. 6.

SUNDARAVADIVELU, Neyyadupakkam Duraiswamy, b. 15 Oct. 1912. University Vice-Chancellor. Educ: M.A. & Lic., Tchng., Madras Univ., India. Appts: Asst. Panchayat Off., 1935-40; Insp., Madras Educl. Subordinate Serv., 1940-42; Insp., Madras Educl. Serv., 1942-54; Dir., Pub. Instrn., Tamil Nadu, India & Commnr., Govt. Exams., ibid, 1954-65; Dir., Pub. Libs., ibid, 1954-69; Dir., Higher Educ., ibid, 1965-66; Jt. Educl. Advsr., Govt. India, Min. Educ., New Delhi, 1966-68; Chief Educl. Advsr. & Additional Sec., Govt. Tamil Nadu Educ. Dept., Dir. Collegiate Educ., 1968-69; V.-Chancellor, Madras Univ., Tamil Nadu. Mbrships. incl: Nat. Coun. Educl. Rsch. & Trng., New Delhi; Past Mbr., Nat. Commn., UNESCC; Nat. Coun. Rural Higher Educ.; Pres., Madras Comm. World Univ. Serv.; Chmn., Southern Langs. Book Trust; V.P., Indian Adult Educ. Assn.; V.P., Indian Nat. Comm., World Univ. Serv.; Pres., Indo-Soviet Cultural Soc., Tamil Nadu. Author 27 books in Tamil. Recip. Padma Shri Award, Pres., India, 1961. Address: 90-C Shenoynagar, Madras-30, India. 1.

SUNDQVIST, Alfons (Immanuel), b. 2 Oct. 1909. Principal Emeritus. Educ: Sacr.min.kand, Univ. of Helsinki, Finland, 1937; Teol.cand., Abo Akad., 1951; Magister Philos., 1959; Teol. lic., 1961; M.A. & D.Theol., Berkeley Bapt. Divinity Schl., Calif., U.S.A., 1951. Appts: Min., Bapt. Chs., Malax, Karis, Helsinki, Larsmo & Vasa, 1930-45; Prin., Free Christian Folk H.S., Veikars, 1945-62; Prin., Swedish Ostrobotnia Folk H.S. & Acad., Yttermark, 1962-72; Retd., 1972. Mbrships. incl: Bd., Swedish Folk H.S. Assn. of Finland, 1946-71; Pres., 1952-67; V.P., Folk H.S. Assn. of Finland, 1952-67; Nordic Folk H.S. Coun., 1953-67. Publs. incl: De vandrade den vägen, 1946; Fria kristliga folkhögskolan tio ar, 1955; Maria Ekqvist och baptisternas vardagsskola i Forsby Pedersöre 1873-1883, 1965; Baptisternas predikantseminarium 50 ar, 1974. Hons: incl: Order of Cross of Liberty, 1944; Order of the Lion of Finland, 1962; Hon. Schl. Councillor, 1973. Address: Ulriksvägen 12, SF 65610 Smedsby, Finland. 43, 90.

SUNDSTROM, Harold Walter, b. 26 Jan. 1929. Public Relations Consultant; Publisher. Educ: B.A., Mich. State Univ., 1952; M.A., ibid, 1954. Appts. incl: Assoc. Dir., Mich. Citizenship Clearing House, 1954-55; For. Serv. Info. Off., U.S. Info. Agency, Wash., Am. Embassies, Tokyo, Jakarta, Seoul, 1955-61; P.R. Counsel, Author, Scottsdale, Ariz., 1961-62; Sr. P.R. Assoc., Eli Lilly & Co., Indpls., 1962-66; P.R. Dir., People to People Int., Kans. City, Mo., 1966-67; V.P., Scandinavian Comm., Copenhagen, Denmark, 1967-68; Govt. & Pub. Info. Rep., N.Ctrl. States, Automobile Mfrs. Assn., Kan. City, 1968-69; P.R. Counsel, Cons., Speech Writer, U.S. C-in-C., Pacific, Hawaii, 1969-73; Publsr. & Ed., Hawaiian Dog Review, Alaskan Dog Review, Lhasa Apso Review, 1973-; Breeder, Halamar Collies, 1970-. Mbrships. incl: Pres., Hawaii Chapt., P.R. Soc. of Am., 1973; Pres., Collie Club of Hawaii, 1972-73. Publs. incl: The American West in Prose, Poetry & Pictures, 1956; Garuda: Introducing Indonesia, 1962; Faces of Asia: Korea, 1965; Messengers of Modern Technology, 1959-60; Progress 1959-60, Economic & Technical Assistance

Cooperation, Rep. of Korea & U.S.A. Recip. var. hons. Address: 1076 Kamahele St., Kailua, HI 96734, U.S.A. 9, 24.

SUNTER, Faruk A., b. 30 Aug. 1909. Economist. Educ: Grad., Dept. of Econs. & Commerce, Fac. of Law, Univ. of Lausanne, Switzerland. Appts. incl: Cons. to sev. Am. & European firms, 1930-; Min. of Economy & Commerce, Turkish Export Promotion Off., 1930-33; V.P., For. Trade Dept., ibid, 1933-36; 1st Dir., Dept. of Standardization, ibid, 1936-47; Gen. Dir., Cooperative Orgs., ibid, 1947-48; Fndr. & Chief Ed., Yeni Istanbul (daily newspaper), 1948-50; Under Sec., Min. of Economy & Commerce, 1950-52; Fndr. & 1st Gen. Sec., Union of Chmbrs. & Ind. of Turkey, 1952-55; Fndr., elected 1st. Pres. & Pres., Turkish Standards Instn., 1954-72; Pres., Int. Org. for Standardization (ISO), 1968-70; Re-elected Pres., Turkish Standards Instn., 1974. Chief Ed., sev. Turkish newspapers inclng. Istanbul Ekspres & Haynak & of Standard Mag. & Turkish Economic Jrnl. Mbrships. incl: Pres., Disciplinary Comm., Galatasaray Club. Publs. incl: 4 vol. textbook on Merchandising Technol.; Chmn., grp. which prepared book on Standardization in Turkey & Turkish Standards Instn. Hons. incl: Hon. Press Card, Gen. Directorate of Press Off., 1967; Chevalier de la Légion d'Honneur of France, 1971. Address: Güven Sokak No. 26, Kavaklidere, Ankara, Turkey. 43.

SUOMALAINEN, Heikki, b. 26 Jan. 1917. Professor of Biochemistry; Industrialist. Educ: M.Sc., in Biochem., Univ. of Helsinki, Finland, 1942; M.Sc. in Microbiol., ibid, 1945; D.Sc., 1948. Appts. incl: Chief, Biochem. Dept., Finnish State Alcohol Monopoly, 1943-51; Hd., Rsch. Labs., ibid, 1951-58; Mgr., Rajamaki Factories, 1955-58; Mbr., Bd. of Dirs., & Dir. of Indl. Prod. & Chem. Rsch., 1958-; Dpty. Gen. Mgr. of the Monopoly, 1972-; Asst. Prof. of Microbiol., Univ. of Helsinki, 1949-; Asst. Prof. of Biochem. & Food Chem., Helsinki Univ. of Technol., 1958-; Pres., Finnish Yeast Prods. Corp., 1959-; Finnish Ed., Acta Chemica Scandinavica, 1968-73. Num. mbrships. incl: Chmn., Finnish Chem. Soc., 1959-60 & 1969-70; Vice-Chmn., Fedn. of Finnish Chem. Ind., 1966-; Bd. Chmn., Assn. of Finnish Chem. Soc., 1970-; Int. Union of Pure & Applied Chem.; Bd., Finnish Acad. of Tech. Scis., 1973-. Publs: Approx 250 reports on biological chem. in int. jrnls. & reviews. Hons: Medal of Liberty, 1941; Cmdr., Order of Lion of Finland, 1963; Gedd Medal, Finnish Chem. Soc., 1965; Professor honoris causa, 1969. Address: Alko, Box 350, SF-00101 Helsinki 10, Finland. 43, 90, 134.

SUPEK, Ivan, b. 8 Apr. 1915. University Professor. Educ: Zagreb, Zürich, Leipzig & Cambridge. Appts: Prof.-Full Prof., Fac. of Nat. Scis., 1946-74; Dir., Ruder Boskovic Inst., 1950-57; Chief Ed., Encyclopedia Moderna, 1966-. Mbrships: Yugoslav Acad. of Scis. & Arts, 1958-; Pres., Inst. for the Philos. of Sci. & Peace, 1966-. Publs. incl: Teorijska Fizika i struktura materije (Theoretical Physics & the Structure of Matter), 1949-74; Spoznaja (Cognition), 1971; Opstati usprkos (Survival Against Odds), 1971; Teorija spoznaje (Theory of Knowledge), 1974. Dramas & novels incl: Izlet u nebo (An Excursion into the Skies), 1959; Na atomskim vulkanima (On Atomic Volcanoes), 1959; Proces stoljeca (The Trial of the Century), 1963; Heretic (novel), 1965, (play), 1969; Dramas, 1971; Extraordinarius, 1974. Address: Rubetićeva 10, 41000 Zagreb, Yugoslavia.

SUROYA, Antonius, b. 23 Sept. 1915. Medical Doctor (Physician). Educ: Medical H.S., Jakarta, 1936-45; Post-grad. study in Hosp. Mgmt., Univ. of Nijmegen, Netherlands, 1964-65. Appts. incl: Army Dr. (TNI), E. Java Army Div. 'Ronggo Lawe'', Cepu, 1945-49; Army Dr., Medan & Padang, Sumatera, 1950-53; Dr., Ctrl. Mil. Hosp., Jakarta, 1953-56; Dr., Mil. Hosp., Magelang; Hd., Mil. Hosp., Semarang, 1960-66; Rector Magnificus, Katholic Univ. Atma Jaya, Semarang; Rector Magnificus, Diponegoro State Univ., Semarang, 1966-; Brigadier Gen., Army, retired, 1969. Mbrships: Indonesian Med. Assn. (IDI). Hons. incl: Guerilla Warfare Merits, 1945-1949. Address: jl. Pandanaran no. 124, Semarang, Indonesia.

SURYONO, b. 28 Nov. 1928. Engineer; Project Manager. Educ: M.Sc., Civil Engrng., Bandung Inst. of Technol., 1954; For. Student (on Grad. Student Fellowship), Summer Project, MIT, U.S.A., 1954. Appts: Sr. Official (Hd. of Rural Electricity & Water Power Dept.), State Electricity Corp., 1955-61; Gen. Mgr.,Brantas River Multipurpose Dev. Project (1st comprehensive basin-wider water resource undertaking in Indonesia), 1961-; Dean & Lectr. on River Basin Dev., Fac. of Engrng., Brawijaya State Univ., Malang, 1963-. Mbrships: Chmn., Malang Region Br., Indonesian Inst. of Engrs. Author of working papers & background papers for seminars, meetings, etc. Hons: Award for Educ., Dedication & Sci., for special servs. & motivation in engrng., Min. of Educ. & Culture, 1972; Award for sincerity in 16 yrs. serv. in Power Dev., & Certificate of Appreciation for outstanding servs. in engrng. w. gt. impact on accomplishment of 1st 5 yr. plan, both from Min. of Pub. Works & Elec. Power, 1972. Address: Jalan Tampomas 4, Malang, Indonesia

SÜSSENBERGER, Erich, b. 13 Feb. 1911. Meteorologist. Educ: A.M., Univ. of Frankfurt, German Fed. Repub., 1935; Dr.'s Degree, ibid, 1935. Appts: Meteorologist, Marineobseratorium, Wilhelmshaven, 1935-45. Meteorologisches Amt für Nort-West-deutschland, Hamburg, 1948-52; Dpty. Hd. & Hd. of Sect. Watterdienst, Bundesverkehraministarium, Bonn, 1952-66; Pres., Deutscher Wetterdienst, 1966-; Permanent Rep., Fed. Repub. of Germany, to World Meteorological Org., 1966-; Exec. Comm. Mbr., World Meteorological Org., 1967-; Chmn., Interim Coun., European Ctr. for Medium-Range Weather Forecasting, 1973-. Contbr., papers & articles, var. profl. publs. Address: Deutscher Wetterdienst, Frankfurter Str. 135, D 6050 Offenbach (Main), German Federal Republic. 92.

SUSSMAN, Harold Irwin, b. 4 Nov. 1938. Periodontist. Educ: B.S., CCNY, 1959; D.D.S., Columbia Dental Schl., 1964; M.S.D., Dental Schl., N.Y. Univ., 1968. Appts: Lt., Dental Corps., U.S.N.R., 1964-66; Instr., N.Y.C. Community Coll., 1967; Asst. Clin. Prof., Dental Coll., N.Y. Univ., 1968-73; Staff Mbr., Mt. Sinai Hosp., N.Y.C., 1970-73; Pvte. Prac. in Periodontics, N.Y.C., 1968-. Mbrships: Am. Assn. of Periodontists; Rsch. Scis. of Am.; Am. Dental Assn.; First Dist. Dental Soc. Publs: 10 articles in profl. jrnls. Hons: Caduceus Soc., 1957; Student Table Clinic Award, 1963; Dental Educator of the Yr. Award, Grad. Students in Periodontics, N.Y. Univ. Dental Schl., 1973. Address: 4 Washington Sq. Village, New York, NY 10012, U.S.A. 6.

SUTHERLAND, (Sir) Gordon (Brims Black McIvor), b. 8 Apr. 1907. Scientist; Master, Emmanuel College, Cambridge, U.K. Educ:

M.A., B.Sc., St. Andrews Univ.; Ph.D., Sc.D., Cambridge Univ. Appts: Fellow & Lectr., Pembroke Coll., Cambridge, 1935-49; Prof. of Phys., Univ. of Mich., U.S.A. 1949-56; Reilly Lectr., Univ. of Notre Dame, 1954-55; Dir., Nat. Dir. Phys. Lab., U.K., 1956-64; Master, Emmanuel Coll., Cambridge, 1964-. Mbrships: V.P., Royal Soc., 1961-63; Int. Org. for Pure & Applied Biophys., 1961-64; Int. Comm. on Data for Sci. & Technol., 1968-; V.P., Int. Union of Pure & Applied Phys., 1963-69; Pres., Inst. of Phys. & the Phys. Soc., 1964-66; Trustee, Nat. Gall., 1971-; Hon., Am. Acad. Arts & Scis., 1968. Publs: about 150 scientific papers & articles on spectroscopy & molecular structure & on sci. & educl. policy. Hons: Kt., 1960; Fellow, Royal Soc., 1949; LL.D., St. Andrews, 1958; D.Sc., Strathclyde, 1966; Fellow, Pembroke Coll., 1959; var. schol. awards & fellowships inclng. Guggenheim Fellow, 1956; Glazebrook Prize & Medal, Inst. of Physics, 1972. Address: The Master's Lodge, Emmanuel Coll., Cambridge, U.K. 1, 34.

SUTHERLAND, Malcolm Graham, Jr., b. 7 June 1919. Welfare Supervisor. Educ: Marshall Univ.; Logan Jr. Coll.; Grad., U.S.A.A.F. Tech. Trng. Cmd., Radio Schl., Scott Field, Ill., 1942; Yale Univ., U.S.A.F., Gen. Communications, 1943. Appts: Water Plant Mgr., Pure Water Co., Logan, W. Va.; U.S.A.A.F., 1941-46; Instr., AAFTTS Radio Operator & Mechanic, Scott Field, Ill. & Sioux Falls, S.D.; AACS Detachment Cmdr., Acting Air Base Cmdr., San Marcellano Air Base, Luzon, Philippines; Owner, Operator, Grocery Store & Restaurant, 1946-48; Salesman, Logan Grocery Co., 1948-59; Salesman, N.Y. Life Ins. Co., 1960-61; Soc. Wkr., W. Va. Dept. of Welfare, 1962-65; Field Rep., ibid, 1965-72; Supvsr., ibid, 1972- Mbrships: Masons; Moose; Am. Pub. Welfare Assn.; W. Va. Welfare Conf. Inc.; past Post Cmdr., Dallas Cook Post, Veterans of For. Wars; Past Treas., Matewan Rotary Club & Magnolia Fair, Inc.; Nat. Advsry. Bd., Am. Security Coun.; Logan Co. Coun. for the Arts; V.P., Wheatley. Enterprise, inc. Hons: Special Assignments in planning & dev. of Food Stamp Prog. & Transportation Remuneration Incentive Prog. (Trip); Mbr., Gov's. Conf. on Aging; Cmdr. of Yr., Veterans of For. Wars, 1958-59; Outstanding Mbr., ibid, 1960; Commnr's. Task Force, ibid, 1973; Philippines Liberation Medal, 1945; Underwriters Award, N.Y. Life Ins. Co., 1960; Am. Defence Medal; Victory Medal; Good Conduct Medal. Address: 92 Buskirk Addition, Logan, WV 25601, U.S.A. 6.

SUTLEY, Melvin Lockett, b. 13 Mar. 1892. Hospital Administrator. Educ: A.B., Univ. of Colo., Boulder, U.S.A., 1913; LL.B., ibid, 1917. Appts: Instr., Saguache Co. H.S., Colo., 1914-15; Hokkaido Univ., Japan, 1919-22; Supt., St. Luke's Int. Hosp., Tokyo, Japan, 1922-25; Asst. Supt., Pa. Hosp., Phila., U.S.A., 1926-27; Admnstr., Delaware Co. Hosp., Drexel Hill, Pa., 1927-41; Admnstr., Wills Eye Hosp., Phila., 1941-61. Mbrships: incl: Fellow & Past Pres., Am. Coll. of Hosp. Admnstrs.; Past Pres., Pa. Hosp. Assn.; Past Pres., Phila. Hosp. Assn.; Past Pres., Delaware Valley Hosp. Purchasing Serv.; Phila. Writers Club; Rotary Club. Publs: Articles on hosps. in various mags. Recip., Special Prize, as Originator & Pres., Delaware Valley Purchasing Serv. Address: 5649 Upland Way, Philadelphia, PA 19131, U.S.A.

SUTORIUS, Edward Phillip, b. 1 Sept. 1916. Consultant/Producer, Exhibitions & Advertising. Educ: B.A., Wittenberg Univ., Ohio, 1938; grad. studies, Hamma Divinity Schl., 1938-39 & Western Reserve Univ., 1940. Appts: Show Mgr., Gen. Elec. Co., 1943-46;

Prod. Mgr., Ivel Corp., N.Y.C., 1946-50; V.P. & Gen. Mgr., Gardner Display Co., Chgo., 1950-57; Sr. V.P., Three Dimensions Corp., 1957-63; Pres., Fair Mgmt., 1962-67; V.P., Assoc. Display Servs., Premier Design Int. of Chgo., 1967-71; Pres., Sutorius Grp., Denver, 1972-. Mbrships. incl: Exhibit Designers & Prods. Assn. (V.P., 1959, Pres., 1960-61); Execs. Club, Reception Comm.; Chgo. Assn. of Commerce & Ind., Chmn., Trade Show & P.R. Comms.; Am. Inst. of Mgmt.; Am. Red Cross, P.R. Comm. Publs: Industrial Marketing; International Executive; Sales Meetings; Printers Ink. Recip. of hons. Address: Pinewood Springs, Lyons, CO 80540, U.S.A. 8, 57, 128, 130, 131.

SUTTMAN, Paul R., b. 16 July 1933. Artist; Sculptor. Educ: B.F.A., Univ. of N.M., 1956; M.F.A., Cranbrook Acad. of Art, Bloomfield Hills, Mich., 1958. Appts: Architectural Designer, Stanley & Wright, Am. Inst. of Archts., 1957-58; Prof. of Art, Univ. of Mich., 1958-62; Artist-in-Residence, Dartmough Coll., Hanover, N.J., 1973. Fellow, Am. Acad. in Rome. Solo Exhibs: Donald Morris Gall., Detroit, 1959, '62, '65, '67, '69; Terry Dintenfas Gall., N.Y.C., 1962, '64, '65, '67, '69, '71, '73; Mus. of Art, Dartmouth Coll., 1973. Grp. Exhibs: San Francisco Mus. of Art, 1958; Guggenheim Mus., N.Y.C., 1962; Rodin Mus., Paris, France, 1968, '69, '70. Hons. incl: 1st Prize in Sculpture, Salzburg Int. Kokoschka Schl. of Vision, 1960; Fulbright Fellowship, 1963; Prix de Rome, Am. Acad. in Rome Fellowship, 1956, '66, '67. Address: Via delle Mantellate 15/A, Rome, 00165, Italy.

SUTTNER, (Sven Oscar) Georg, b. 26 July 1922. Artist. Educ: Valand Schl. of Art, Gothenburg, 1943; Acad. of Arts, Copenhagen, 1948-50; Study w. Fernand Leger, Paris, 1950-52. Appts: Prof., Free Acad., Stockholm, 1956-58; Pres., Stockholm Dist., Swedish Artists' trade union, 1965-67, & Pres., for all of Sweden, 1970-72; Vice Headmaster, Prof., & Hd., French Sect., Gerlesborgsskolan, Stockholm, 1953-. Mbrships: Art Club, Stockholm, Gothenburg; Soc. for Swedish Artists, Stockholm; Dalslands' Art & Lit. Club. Exhibs: Stockholm, Gothenburg, Uppsala, Lund, Oslo, Paris, Marseille, Toulon, Nimes, N.Y., San Fran., Amsterdam, etc.; Permanent collects., Swedish Nat. Mus. & co., community collects.; 'The Old Town in Stockholm' named polyrealistic masterpiece, 1964. Hons: Num. schlrships. inclng: Work schlrship., 1966, Merit Schlrship., 1972, City of Stockholm; Travel Schlrship., French Govt., 1971; Work Schlrships., State of Sweden 1973, '74. Address: Hastholmsvagen 8^{VI} 116 44 Stockholm, Sweden. 43.

SUTTON, Glenn W., b. 25 July 1904. Foreign Trade Consultant. Educ: B.S., Ind. Univ., Bloomington, U.S.A., 1926; A.M., ibid, 1927; Ph.D., Ohio State Univ., Columbus, 1938. Appts: Rsch. Asst.-Ed., Ind. Bus. Review, Ind. Univ., 1925-27; Ed., Idaho Econ. Review-Instr., Econs., Univ. of Idaho, 1927-29; Prof., Finance-Chmn., Finance Div.-Ed., Ga. Bus. Review-Dir., Grad. Div., Coll. of Bus. Admin., Univ. of Ga., Athens, 1929-54; Regional & Nat. Dir., Bur. of Labor Stats., U.S. Dept. of Labor, 1936-41; Line Off.-Capt., USN, 1942-64; Mbr., Vice Chmn.-Chmn., U.S. Tariff Commn., 1954-72. Mbrships: Rotary; Cosmos Club, Wash. D.C.; Beta Gamma Sigma. Contbr. to Govt. publs. Recip., Disting. Fac. Award, Coll. of Bus. Admin., Univ. of Ga., 1973. Address: 208 Southern Mutual Bldg., Athens, GA 30601, U.S.A. 2, 7, 12, 13, 14, 15, 16, 51, 114, 128.

SUTTON, James Owen, Sr., b. 24 May 1933. Minister; Educational Administrator. Educ. incl: Jr. Acctng. Dipl., Draughon's Bus. Coll., Amarillo, Tex., 1952; Grad., Ctrl. Bible Coll., Springfield, Mo., 1955; B.Sc., Eastern Mich. Univ., Ypsilanti, 1967; M.A., ibid, 1969. Ordained Min., Mich. Dist. Coun., assemblies of God., 1960. Appts. incl: Tchr., 6th grade for 4 yrs., Montrose Community Schls., Mich.; Elem. Prin., Albee Elem. Schl., Chesaning Union Schls., Mich., 1968-; Asst. Pastor, Trinity Assembly of God, Columbus, Ohio, 1956; Pastor, Flushing, Mich., 1957-60; Pastor, Chelsea, Mich.; Pastor, Bethel Temple, Longmont, Colo., 1962-64; Min. of Music, 1st Assembly of God, Saginaw, Mich., 1968-; has given pvte. voice & piano lessons & dir. choirs & orchs. Mbrships. incl: num. posts in ch. orgs. inclng. Dist. Music. Dir., Mich. Dist., 1973- & Tchr., Full Gospel Bus. Men's Fellowship. Int., Tri-Cities Chapt., 1973-; NEA; Mich. Educ. Assn.; Mich. Assn. Elem. Schl. Prins. Address: 14515 East Street Road, Montrose, MI 48457, U.S.A. 130.

SUTTON, Kenneth Coleridge Turvey, b. 9 Feb. 1926. Professor. Educ: B.A., LL.B., LL.M., Univ. of N.Z.; Ph.D., Univ. of Melbourne, Australia. Appts: Barrister, Auckland, N.Z., 1956-60; Sr. Lectr. in Law, A.N.U., 1960-63, Sydney, 1963-67; Assoc. Prof., Sydney, 1968; Prof. of Law, Univ. of Qld., 1968-; Dean Fac. of Law, ibid, 1969-70; Academic Mbr., N.S.W. Law Reform Commn., 1973-; Councillor, Australia-Japan Trade Law Fndn., 1973-; Exec. Mbr., Australian Univs. Law Schls. Assn., 1969-70; Mbr., Legal Educ. Comm., Qld. Law Soc., 1970-72, Editl. Bd., Bus. Law Review, 1973-. Mbrships. incl: Univ. of Qld. Club; Australian Inst. Int. Affairs. Publs. incl: Law of Sale of Goods in Australia & New Zealand, 1967, '74; Consideration Reconsidered, 1974; The Pattern of Law Reform in Australia, 1970. Recip. of num. Schlrships. & Rsch. grants. Address: N.S.W. Law Reform Commn., Goodsell Bldg., Chifley Sq., Sydney, N.S.W., Australia 2000. 23.

SUTTON, Leonard V. B., b. 21 Dec. 1914. International Lawyer. Educ: B.A., Colo. Coll.; J.D., Schl. of Law, Univ. of Denver. Appts: Pvte. Prac., 1941-42; U.S. Army, 1942-46; Pvte. Prac., 1946-56; Justice, Colo. Supreme Ct., 1956-68; Chief Justice, ibid, 1960 & 66; Chmn., For. Claims Settlement Commn., 1968-69; Pvte. Prac., 1969-. Mbrships. incl: Rotary; Cosmos Club, Wash. D.C.; Sugar Club, NYC; Am. Chmbr. of Comm., Mexico; Int. Comm., US Chmbr. of Comm.; Hon. Trustee, Inst. of Int. Educ.; Hon. Mbr., Consular Law Soc.; Phi Delta Phi; Am., Colo., D.C., Int., & Inter-Am. Bar Assns.; Am. Arbitration Assn.; Mexican Acad. of Int. Law; Past Pres., Wash. For. Law Soc. Contbr. articles to legal jrnls. Address: 800 Western Federal Savings Bldg., Denver, CO 80202, U.S.A. 2, 9, 114, 128.

SUVANTO, (Kai) Kalevi, b. 12 Mar. 1918. Insurance Company Executive. Educ: Finnish Mil. Acad., 1943; M.A. Degree, 1948. Appts: Artillery Off.; Field Chief; Marketing Mgr.; Asst. Mgr.; Mgr.; Alternate Bd. Mbr., Vastuu Reinsurance Co. Mbrships: Bd. Mbr., Finnish House Property Owners' Assn., 1960-, V.P. of Bd., 1972-, Assn. V.P., 1974-; Bd. Mbr., Ins. Cos. Marketing Mgrs. Assn., 1960-, Pres., 1972-; V.P., Finnish Reserve Offs. Southwestern Dist., 1969-; V.P., Finnish Fedn., of Rifle Clubs, 1971-; Mbr. of Delegation, Support of Finnish Nat. Defence, 1971-. Recip., Order of the Finnish Cross of Freedom, 3rd & 4th Class. Address: Uudenmaankatu 11 C, SF-20500 Turku 50, Finland. 43.

SUYAMA, Yoshio, b. 16 Nov. 1920. Professor. Educ: Grad., Dept. of Zool., Fac. of Sci., Tokyo Univ., 1949. Appts: Asst.-Prof., Biochem., Fac. of Agric., Meiji Univ., 1949-; Dean., ibid, 1966-68; Dean., Fac. of Agric., 1970-72, 72-74; Mbr. of Bd. of Trustees, 1972-. Mbrships: Japanese Biochem. Soc.; Agric. Chem. Soc. of Japan; Zool. Soc. of Japan. Address: Meiji Univ., Ikuta Campus, Fac. of Agric., 5158, Ikuta, Tama-Ku, Kawasaki City, 214. Japan.

SUZMAN, Janet (Mrs. Trevor Nunn). Actress. Educ: B.A., Univ. of the Witwatersrand, S. Africa; London Acad. Music & Dramatic Art, U.K. Assoc. Artist, Royal Shakespeare Co. Stage roles incl: Portia; Joan la Pucelle; Katharina; Rosalind; Beatrice; Lavinia; Cleopatra; Hester, Hello & Goodbye; Berinthia, The Relapse. TV plays incl: St. Joan; Hedda Gabler; Lady Macbeth; Masha, The Three Sisters; Viola; Florence Nightingale. Films incl: A Day in the Death of Joe Egg; Nicholas & Alexandra;, Drabble. Mbrships: Coun., London Acad. Music & Dramatic Art; Coun. Working Grp. Hons: Acad. Award nomination, Best Actress, Nicholas & Alexandra, 1971; N.Y. Critics Circle nomination, Best Actress, Joe Egg, 1972. Address: c/o Wm. Morris Agcy., 4 Savile Row, London, W1, U.K. 18, 138.

SUZUKI, Jiro, b. 17 May 1916. Professor. Educ: Fac. Lit., Waseda Univ., Japan, 1942. Appts: Rsch. Fellow, Japanese Assn. Ethnol., 1942-43; Asst., Inst. Ethnol., Min. Educ., 1943-45; Asst. Prof., Sociol., Waseda Univ., 1947-51; Assoc. Prof.-Prof., Soc. Anthropol., Tokyo Metropol. Univ., 1952-; Rsch. Assoc., Anthropol., Ill. Univ., USA, 1957-59. Mbrships: Pres. Nat. League Acad. Assn. Japanese Outcasts; Pres., Acad. Assn. Japanese Outcasts, Tokyo; Bd. Mbr., Inst. Japanese Outcasts; Japanese Ethnol. Soc.; Japanese Soc. Sociol. Publs. incl: Translations into Japanese: Ideologie und Utopie, by Karl Mannheim, 1929; Prejudice: Japanese Americans; Symbol of Racial Intolerance, by Carey William, 1944; The Human Meaning of the Social Sciences, by Daniel Lerner, 1959; Protest and Prejudice; A Study of Belief in the Black Community, 1967; Author: Social Organization of the Primitive People, 1949; Sociological Study of Urban and Rural Community, 1956; Black Americans, 1957; Present Situation of the Outcast Problem in Japan, 1963. Address: 2-14-27-401, Mure, Mitaka City, Tokyo-to, Japan.

SVEDA, Michael, b. 3 Feb. 1912. Scientist; Chemist; Research & management counsel. Educ: B.S., Univ. of Toledo, Ohio, 1933; Ph.D., Univ. of Ill., 1939. Appts. incl: var. positions in rsch., sales & product mgmt., du Pont Co., Cleveland, Ohio & Wilmington, Del., 1939-54; Mgmt. counsel, Wilmington, 1955-59; Admnstr. of grants in rsch., educ. & sci. reporting, Nat. Sci. Fndn., 1960-61; Corporate Assoc. Dir., Rsch., FMC Corp., N.Y.C., 1962-64; Rsch. & Mgmt. Cons., Greenwich & Stamford, Conn., 1965-. Mbrships. incl: Am. Chem. Soc.; AAAS; Sigma Xi; Phi Kappa Phi. Discoverer of cyclamates sweetening agents; devised new way to tale off human fat, 1971. Hons. incl. Outstanding Alumnus Award, Univ. of Toledo, Ohio, 1954. Address: P.O. Box 3086, Stamford, CT 06905, U.S.A. 2, 6, 14, 29, 50.

SVENDSEN, Arnljot Stromme, b. 5 Dec. 1921. Professor. Educ: cand. oecon., Univ. of Oslo, 1936; Schlrship., Norwegian Schl. of Econ. & Bus. Admin., 1947-55. Appts. incl: Assoc. Prof. of Econ., Norwegian Schl. of Econ. & Bus. Admin., 1956-65; Prof. of Maritime Econ., ibid, 1966-; Dir. Inst. for Econ., 1957-67; Dir., Inst. for Shipping Rsch., 1958-;

Exec. Comm., City Coun., Bergen, 1956-67; Dpty Chmn., Bd., Bergens Sporvei, 1960-63; Chmn. of Bd., Bergen Theater, 1960-, Scientific Bd., Inst. for Transport Econs., Oslo, 1968-, Norwegian Theater League, 1969-. Mbrships. incl: Chmn., Bergen Assn. for Econs., 1957-66; Sci. Soc. of Bergen. Publs. incl: Norsk industri og fremtiden, 1972; Union 1873-1973, 1973.; Scandinavian Cooperation Around the World, 1973. Kt., 1st Class, Order of St. Olav, 1973. Address: Norges Handelshoyskole, Skipsfartsokonomisk Institutt, Helleveien 30, 5000 Bergen, Norway. 134.

SVILOKOS, Nikola, b. 25 Oct. 1931. Mathematician; Systems Analyst. Educ: B.Sc., Loyola Coll., Montreal, Can., 1953; A.M., Harvard Univ., Cambridge, Mass., USA, 1959; num. short courses in Engrng., Security Analysis, IBM, etc., 1964-74. Appts: Math. Engr., Canadair Ltd. (sub. Gen. Dynamics Corp.), Montreal, Can., 1956-58; Rsch. Mathn., Dow Chem. Co., Williamsburg, Va., USA, 1958-59; Ops. Rsch. Analyst, Bankers Trust Co., NYC, 1961-63; Applied Mathn., Allied Chem. Co., NYC, 1963-65; System Analyst, N.Y. Stock Exchange, Pres., Evening Math., Inc., 1965-. Mbrships: Am. Math. Soc.; N.Y. Acad. of Scis.; Harvard Grad. Soc. of Study & Rsch.; Math. Assn. of Am. Author of rsch. works in aerodynamics (flutter), thermodynamics (de-icing), econometrics & econ. maths., color theory, system designs, standards & Boolean econ. analysis techniques, many of which are still confidential. Hons: Sophomore Class Prize, 1950; Rsch. Fellowship, McGill Univ., Montreal, 1958. Address: 1060 Park Ave., N.Y., NY 10028, U.S.A. 14.

SVORONOS, Dionyssiou Nicolas, b. 9 Apr. 1921. Manufacturer; Industrial Executive. Educ: Grad., Mech. Elec. Engr., Tech. Univ. of Athens, 1950. Appts: Dir., Viossol S.A., Athens, United Tube Mills IBS, S.A.; Mbr., Bd. of Dirs., Hellenic Indl. Dev. Bank S.A., Hellenic Investment Co. S.A., Lavreotiki S.A., Archimedes S.A., Union S.A., Société Hellénique de Construction Automobiles S.A. Mbr., Athenian Club. Recip., Golden Cross of King George I. Address: United Tube Mills I.B.S., S.A., 16 Eleft. Venizelou Ave., Kallithea, Athens, Greece.

SWAHN, Jan-Öjvind, b. 15 May 1925. Writer; Publisher. Educ: Ph.D., Univ. of Lund, Sweden, 1955. Appts: Free-lance, Swedish Broadcast Corp., 1949-; Libn., Univ. of Lund, 1951-56; Asst. Prof., Folklore, ibid, 1956-. Mbrships: New Soc. of Letters, Lund; Am. Folklore Soc. Num. publs. incl: The Tale of Cupid & Psyche, 1955; Svenska Folksagor, 1959; I Glädje och Sorg, 1963; Fionns Äventyr, 1963; Jubelfest, 1963; Lyckeoborg, 1964; Häxor, Tomtar, Jättar och Huldror, 1964; Ronneby Blodbad, 1965; Europeiska Folksagor, 1965; God Jul, 1966; Snöbollar, 1967; Vin, Kyssar och Soppa, 1968; Man Tager Vad Man Haver, 1970. Address: Persikovägen 23, 22355 Lund, Sweden. 43.

SWAIM, John Franklin, b. 24 Dec. 1935. Medical Doctor; Farm Owner & Manager; Corporation President. Educ: B.S., Ind. Univ., 1960; M.D., ibid, 1963; Intern, Travis Air Force Base Hosp., Calif. 1964. Appts. incl: Farm Owner & Co.-Mgr. 1966-; Cmndng. Off., 559th Med. Serv. Flight, USAF, An' Xuyen Province, Vietnam, 1966-67; Pvte. Prac. of Med., Rockville, Ind., 1967-; Owner, Dir., Parke Clin. ibid, 1969-; Asst. Med. Dir., Newport Army Ammunition Plant, Ind., 1972-; Med. Dir., Rockville Trng. Ctr., 1971-; Pres., Parke Investments Co., 1971-; Fndr., Dir., Kingman

Community Hlth. Ctr., Ind., 1971-; Owner, Med. Off., Clinton, Ind., 1972-; Pres., Parke—Vermillion Co. Med. Soc., 1972-; Pres., Vermillion Co. Hosp. Med. Staff, 1971-72; Bd. of Dirs., Katherine Hamilton Mental Hlth. Ctr., Terre Haute, Ind., 1972-; Owner, Dir., Cayuga Community Hlth. Ctr., 1974-; Parke Co. Coroner, 1974-. Mbrships. incl: AMA; Pres, 5th Dist. Chapt., Ind. Acad. of Family Prac.; Country Club, Terre Haute; Terre Haute Acad. of Med.; Am. Thoracic Soc. Recip., Bronze Star, USAF, Vietnam, 1967. Address: P.O. Box 185, Anderson St., Rockville, IN 47872, U.S.A. 8.

SWAIN, Alice Marie McNeely (Mrs. Robert A. Swain), b. 3 Feb. 1924. Teacher. Educ: B.S., Langston Univ.; M.Ed., Univ. of Okla.; Reading Specialist Cert., ibid. Appts: Tchr., Elem. Pub. Schl. System, Okla. City, 1950-70; Reading Specialist, Northeast H.S., Okla. City, 1970-73; Asst. Prof., Educ. & Coord. of Reading, Langston Univ., Okla., 1973-. Owner, Pres., Prod., together Charm & Modeling Schl., Fashion Prods., Hal Jackson's Miss U.S. Teen Review. Num. mbrships. incl: Past Chmn., Bd. of Dirs., Youth Servs. Dir., SW Region, Nat. P.R. Chmn., Sigma Gamma Rho Sorority, Inc.; Past Sec., V.P., Nat. Pan-Hellenic Coun., Inc.; Am. Parliamentarians Assn.; Smithsonian Instn.; Educ. Assn. for Higher Educ. Publs: Clice's Short Seven, 1975. Hons: SW Regional Sigma of Year Plaque; One of nation's 10 Outstanding Sigma Women; Sigma of Year, Local Sigma chapt., 1970; Schlrship., Mod. Maths. & Livingtext Book series, Univ. of Okla. Address: 3016 Norcrest Dr., Okla. City. OK 73111, U.S.A. 5.

SWALLOW, Norman, b. 17 Feb. 1921. Television Writer; Producer & Director. Educ: B.A.(Hons.), Keble Coll., Oxford, 1942. Appts: Mil. Serv., 1942-46; Radio Features Prod., BBC, 1946-50, TV Documentary Writer & Prod., 1950-57, Asst. Hd. of Films for TV. 1957-60, Asst. Ed. of current affairs TV series Panorama, 1960-63, Exec. Prod. of TV series Omnibus, 1968-71, Hd. of TV Arts Features, 1971-; Free-lance Writer, Prod. & Dir. of TV documentaries in U.K., 1963-68. Fellow, Guild of TV Prods. Mbr., var. profl. orgs. Author: Factual Television, 1965; some 40 radio & 50 TV scripts. Num. articles, var. jrnls. inclng. New Stateman, Spectator, Listener, Sight & Sound, Times Educl. Supplement, Music & Musicians. Hons. incl: Prix Italia, 1965; 1st Prize, Leipzig Film Festival, 1966; Soc. of Film & TV Arts Award for Omnibus series, 1973. Address: 36 Crooms Hill, London, S.E.10, U.K. 3.

SWAN, George S., b. 9 Aug. 1914. Independent Oil Operator. Educ: Univ. of Md.; Univ. of Va.; John Hopkins Univ. Appts: Asst. Off. Mgr., Plant Cashier, Chevrolet Motor Co., 1932-36; Oil Scout, Tex.-Jersey Oil Corp., Tyler, Tex., 1937-39; Independent Oil Prod., Saginaw, Mich., 1939-. Mbrships: Past mbr., Bd. of Dirs., Saginaw Div., A.R.C.; Bd. of Dirs., Cancer Soc.; Dir., Mich. Oil & Gas Assn.; Pub. Info. Comm., Independent Petroleum Assn.; Pi Kappa Alpha; Past Sr. Warden, Vestryman, Episc. Ch.; Past Pres., Saginaw Club & Saginaw Kiwanis; Detroit Club; Otsego Ski Club, Gaylord, Mich. Address: Cottage Grove, Rte. 1, Roscommon, MI 48653, U.S.A.

SWAN, Henry, II, b. 27 May 1913. Physician. Educ: A.B., Williams Coll., Mass., 1935; M.D., Harvard Med. Schl., 1939. Appts. incl: Asst.-Assoc.-Prof., Surg., Univ. of Colo. Med. Schl., 1946-50; Prof. & Hd., Dept. Surg., ibid, 1950-61; Clin. Prof., 1961-; Prof., Surg., Rsch., 1963-; Staff, Colo. Gen. Hosp.; Cons. Surg., Fitzsimons Gen. Hosp. & Denver VA

Hosp. Mbrships incl: Int. Cardiovascular Soc.; Sci. Coun., Int. Soc. of Surg.; Am. Heart Assn.; Am. Surg. Assn.; Am. Coll. Surgs.; AAAS; Phi Beta Kappa; Alpha Omega Alpha. Author of aprox. 240 sci. publs. Hons. incl: AMA Hektoen Gold Medal for Original Rsch., 1955; D.Sc., Williams Coll., 1959; num. Univ. & Acad. awards. . Address: 6700 W. Lakeridge Rd., Lakewood, CO 80227, U.S.A. 2, 9, 17, 50, 60, 120, 128.

SWANN, (Sir) Michael Meredith, b. 1 Mar. 1920. Broadcasting Executive. Educ: Gonville & Caius Coll., Cambridge, U.K. Appts: Demonstrator, Cambridge Univ., 1946-52; Prof., Edinburgh Univ., 1952-65; Prin. Vice-Chancellor, ibid, 1965-73; Chmn., Govs., BBC. Fellowships: Royal Soc.; Royal Soc. Edinburgh; Inst. Biol.; Hon., Royal Colls. Physns. & Surgs. Author of papers in sci. jrnls. Hons: Degrees, Leicester & York Univs.; Kt. Bach., 1972. Address: Broadcasting House, London, W.1, U.K. 1, 34.

SWANN, Thomas Burnett, b. 11 Oct. 1928. Professor of English; Author. Educ: B.A., Duke Univ., 1950; M.A., Univ. of Tenn., 1955; Ph.D., Univ. of Fla., 1960. Appts: Tchr., Fla. Southern Coll., Fla. Atlantic Univ., Wesleyan Coll., Macon, Ga. Mbrships: Sci. Fiction Writers of Am.; Phi Beta Kappa. Novels: Day of the Minotaur; Wolfwinter; The Goat without Horns; How Are the Mightly Fallen; The Not-World. Poetry Collects: Driftwood; Wombate & Moondust; Alas, in Lilliput. Other Publs: The Classical World of H.D.; Wonder & Whimsy: The Fantastic World of Christina Rossetti; A.A. Milne; Ernest Dowson; The Urgirt Runner: Charles Sorley, Poet of World War I; I Like Bears. Recip., Phoenix Award, 1973. Address: Box 232, Winter Haven, FL, U.S.A. 7.

SWANSON, Fern Rose (Mrs. Walter E. Swanson), b. 5 July 1900. Educator (Retired). Educ: B.S. & M.S., St. Cloud State Coll., Minn. Appts: Asst. Prin., Eyota, Minn., 1920-21; Tchr., Jr. H.S., Appleton, Minn., 1921-22, Harmony, Minn., 1922-23, Augusta, Wise, 1923-24; Asst. Prin., South Haven, Minn., 1927-41, 1943-51; Tchr., Prin., Silver Creek, Minn., 1941-43; Tchr. Prin. & Elem. Prin., Annandale, Minn., 1951-67; Reading Tchr., Belgrade, Minn., 1967-71. Mbrships: Delta Kappa Gamma, Pres., Upsilon Chapt., 1970-; Jr. V.P., Dept. of Minn., Ladies of GAR; DAR: Minn. Reading Assn.; Charter Mbr. & Former Dir., Ctrl. Minn. Reading Coun.; Int. Reading Assm.; Nat. Coun. of Tchrs. of Engl.; Minn. Educ. Assn.; NEA; Silver Leaf Rebekah Lodge, Past Noble Grand & Musician; Minn. Histl. Assn.; Charter Mbr., Minn. Elem. Schl. Prins. 25 Yr. Club, 1967. Contbr. to Delta Kappa Gamma publs. Hons. incl: 50 Yr. Jewel, Silver Leaf, Rebeka Lodge, 1970, 50 Yr. Jewel, Royal Neighbours of Am., 1973. Address: 541 Fairhaven Ave., South Haven, MN 55382, U.S.A. 5, 8, 15, 70, 120, 126, 132.

SWANSON, George Damian, b. 25 Dec. 1939. Teacher; Educational Administrator. Educ: B.A., Jersey City State Coll.; postgrad work, ibid, & Seton Hall Univ. Appts: Acting Dir. of Educ., Children's Residential Ctr., Denville, N.J., & Counsellor, N.J. Boystown, 1963-72; Soc. Studies & Lang. Arts Tchr., Children's Residential Ctr., 1970-71, 1972, Dir., Counselling Staff, N.J. Boystown, 1973-; Asst. Supt., N.J. Boystown, Kearny, 1973-; Liaison Chmn., Mt. Olive Charter Study Commn., 1970; Mbr., Mt. Olive Indl. Commn., 1974. Mbrships: Mt. Olive Rep. Club; Pres., ibid, 1970; J.J. Educ. Assn.; Kts. of Columbus; VASA Order of Am.; Loyal Orders of Moose &

Elks. Contbr., Star Jrnl., Ledgewood, N.J., & Mt. Olive Drumbeat. Address: 7. S Hillside Dr., Budd Lake, NJ, U.S.A. 130.

SWANSON, T.B., b. 5 Oct. 1910. Executive. Educ: M.Sc., Adelaide Univ., Australia. Appts. incl: Lectr., Adelaide Univ., 1938-39; Lectr., i/c Chem. Dept., New Engl. Univ., 1939-45; var. exec. positions, ICI (Aust.) Ltd., 1945-55; Dir., ibid, 1955-64; Mng. Dir., 1964-68; Dpty. Chmn., 1968-71; Chmn., Aust. Commn. of Adv. Educ., 1971-. Fellowships: Fed. Pres., Royal Aust. Chem. Inst.; Chem. Soc. London. Mbrships: Royal Soc. N.S.W.; Melbourne Club; Aust. Club, Melbourne; Univ. Club, Sydney. Contbr. to sci. jrnls. Recip., Leighton Medal, Royal Aust. Chem. Inst., 1972. Address: P.O. Box 364, S. Yarra, Vic. Australia 3141.

SWANSTROM, Selma Elvira, b. 18 Aug. 1897. Teacher, Retd.; Counsellor. Educ: B.E., Univ. of Wis., 1928; M.S., Univ. of S. Calif. at LA., 1939; Work toward Ph.D., ibid, 1940-41; Int. Schl., Univ. of Geneva, Switzerland, 1958. Appts. (all in Wis.): Tchr., Rural Schl., Poplar, 1915-16; State Graded Schl., S. Range, 1917; Jr. H.S., Rhineland & Superior, 1918-42; Sr. H.S., Superior, 1942-63. Num. mbrships. incl: YWCA; Life Mbr., N. Wis. Educ. Assn., Superior Mem. Hosp. Aux., Douglas Co. Histl. Soc., Friends of Life; Nat., State, Local Retd. Tchrs. Assns.; Nat. Travel Club; Pres., Wis. Coun. for Geog. Educ.; People to People Int.; Douglas Co. Assn. for Retarded Children; World Federalists; League of Women Voters. Fndr., 1st boys' band in U.S., 1923-26; Pioneer developer of schl. guidance plans. Hons: Leading Superior Citizen Award, 1974; Hon. Life Mbr., N. Wis. Lake Superior Educ. Assn. Address: 1220½ N. 16th Superior, WI 54880, U.S.A. 130.

SWANTON, E.W., b. 11 Feb. 1907. Cricket Correspondent & Author. Appts: Evening Standard Sporting Corres., 1927-39; Illustrated Sporting & Dramatic News Corres. & BBC Commentator, 1934-39; Cricket Corres., Daily Telegraph; Ed. of The Cricketer. Mbrships: MCC; Bath Club; Royal St. George's Golf Club, Sandwich. Publs: A History of Cricket, 1938, 46, 48, 62; Denis Compton, A Cricket Sketch, 1948; Elusive Victory, 1951; The Ashes in Suspense, 1963; Cricket & the Clock, 1952; West Indian Adventure, 1954; Victory in Australia, 1954/5; The Test Matches of 1956; Report for South Africa, 1957; West Indies Revisited, 1960; The Ashes in Suspense, 1963; Cricket from all Angles, 1968; Sort of a Cricket Person, 1972; Gen.Ed., World of Cricket, 1966. Recip., O.B.E., 1965. Address: Delf House, Sandwich, Kent, U.K.

SWARTHOUT, Herbert Marion, b. 29 Aug. 1900. Life Insurance—Estate Planning. Educ: Neb. Univ., 1920-21; Wash. Univ., 1922; Grad., Am. Coll. of Life Underwriters, 1942. Appts. incl: Rep., Mutual Benefit Life Ins. Co., Newark, 1947-; Exec. Dir., Uniformed Services Benefit Assn., 1959-; Pres., Herrick Financial Servs., Inc., 1964-. Mbrships. incl: YMCA, Sponsor, activities; Pres. & Gen. Chmn., Heart of Am. Mem. Torch Ceremony, 1963-64; Neb. Univ. Alumni Assn., former Pres., K.C. Chapt.; Life Underwriters Assn., Kan. City; Life & qualifying, Million Dollar Round Table; Nat. Assn. of Life Underwriters; Am. Soc. Chartered Life Underwriters; Sons of the Revolution, Pres., Kan. City, 1956 & Mo. Soc., 1958-59; Sons of the Am. Revolution; Assn. of U.S. Army, Liaison Chmn.; Kan. City Art Inst.; Country Club Christian Ch., Deacon; Mason (Kt. Templer, Shriner, Royal Order of Jesters); Advt. & Sales Execs. Club. Address: 1221

Baltimore—Suite 912, Kansas City, MO 64105, U.S.A. 2, 8.

SWEARINGEN, Annette Wildman (Mrs. Dick Swearingen), b. 21 May 1897. Teacher; Minister; Counselor; Writer. Educ: Kan. City Univ.; Unity Schl. of Christianity, Unity Village, Lee's Summit, Mo., 1925-47. Appts. incl: Instr. in Adult Educ., Youth Counselor, Leader in Jr. Ch., Bible Schl., Tchr. in Sunday Schl., Unity Temple on the Plaza, Kan. City, 1948-63; Min. & Co-Fndr., Unity Northeast Ch., ibid, 1963-67; Min. of Educ., Unity Valley Ch., Hemet, Calif., 1967-68. Mbrships. incl: Unity Ministerial Assn., hon. mbr., Int. Mark Twain Soc.; Nat. League Am. Pen Women; Nat. Fed. Press Women Inc. Publs. incl: Moments of Mood (poetry), 1952; Of Heart & Home (poetry), 1956. Address: 25124 N. Yale St., Hemet CA 92343, U.S.A. 11, 132, 138.

SWEET, Cody. Specialist in nonverbal communications. Educ: B.S., M.A., Ph.D., Northwestern Univ.; Post-doct. rsch., Harvard Univ., Bureau for Movement Rsch., N.Y. Appts: Cons., num. nat. & int. accounts on visual aspects of communication; 'Miss Kleenex' for Kimberly-Clark, num. Radio/TV progs.; Theatre Directing Assignments. Mbrships: Bd. Dirs., Nat. Speakers' Assn.; Sales & Marketing Execs. Int.; Am. Marketing Assn.; Am. Anthropological Assn.; Dance Notation Bureau of N.Y.; Comm. on Rsch. in Dance. Publs: World Beyond Worlds (book); Dr. Body Talk Speaks (cassette tape series); Dr. Body Talk (radio show); A Woman's Place is in her Body (book, in preparation). Newspaper interviews incl: Chgo. Sun Times; Atlanta Jrnl.; Houston Post. Hons: Spotlighted Speaker, World Meeting Planners Congress & Exposition. Address: Nonverbal Communications Inc., The World Beyond Words, 606 Locust Rd., Suite 101, Wilmette, IL 60091, U.S.A. 57.

SWEET, Dee McDaniel, b. 3 June 1913. Camp Director; Teacher; Antiques Shop Owner. Educ: Butler Univ., Ind., U.S.A. Appts: Designer, L.S. Ayers & Co., Indpls.; Owner, Acorn Farm Camp, Carmel, Ind., 1934-; Owner, Acorn Farm Antiques Shop; Lectr., Antiques, Ind.-Purdue Univ. Mbrships: Children's Mus. Guild; Am. Camping Assn.; V.P., Am. Women in Radio & TV; Ind. Histl. Soc.; Am. Assn. of Appraisers; Ind. Mus. Soc. Publs: 'Try It', books; 'Try It' articles in newspapers & other mag. articles. Address: R.R. 1, Box 810, Carmel, IN 46032, U.S.A. 5, 82.

SWEET, Herbert A., b. 17 Nov. 1908. Camp Director; Teacher; Antiques Shop Owner. Educ: B.S., Butler Univ., Ind., U.S.A., 1932. Appts: Asst. Headmaster, Orchard Country Day Schl.; Owner, Acorn Farm, Inc., 1938-; Lectr., Antiques, Ind.-Purdue Univ.; Owner, Acorn Farm Antiques Shop. Mbrships: Past Pres., Am. Camping Assn.; Ind. Histl. Soc.; Ind. Mus. Soc.; Indpls. Lit. Club; Ind. Soc. of Pioneers; Nat. Audubon Soc.; Ind. Audubon Soc.; Boy Scouts of Am. Publs: 'Try It' books; 'Try It' articles in newspapers & other mag. articles: Drawings for state pk. books. Address: R.R. 1, Box 810, Carmel, IN 46032, U.S.A. 82.

SWEET, William Herbert, b. 13 Feb. 1910. Neurosurgeon. Educ: S.B., Wash. Univ., Seattle, 1930; B.Sc., Magdalen Coll., Oxford Univ., U.K., 1934; M.D., Harvard Med. Schl., Boston, Mass., U.S.A., 1936; D.Sc., Magdalen Coll., Oxford Univ., U.K., 1957. Appts: Num. Neurosurg. appts. in Am. & U.K., 1936-57; Vis. Neurosurg.-Chief, Neurosurg. Serv., Mass. Gen. Hosp., 1957-; Prof., Surg., Mass. Gen. Hosp., Harvard Med. Schl., 1965-. Mbr. num. Am. & for. profl. assns. Publs: Pain: Its Mechanisms

and Neurosurgical Control (w. J.C. White), 1955; Pain and the Neurosurgeon: a Forty Year Experience (w. J.C. White), 1969; 250 chapts. & articles on Neurosurg. Hons: Phi Beta Kappa, 1930; Rhodes Schol., 1932-34; Alpha Omega Alpha, 1936; H.M. Medal for Serv. in Cause of Freedom, 1945; Rhodes Rsch. Fellow, Nat. Hosp. for Nervous Diseases, London, U.K., 1939; Commonwealth Fund Fellow, Harvard Med. Schl., 1940-41. Address: Mass. Gen. Hosp., Boston, MA 02114, U.S.A. 14, 17, 36, 50, 56, 139.

SWIFT, Barbara Buckman (Mrs. Douglas H. Swift), b. 10 Oct. 1937. Librarian. Educ: B.S., Univ. of S.D., Vermillion, 1972. Appts. incl: Tchr., Bonners Ferry, Idaho, 1958-60; Pt.-Time Libn., Deadwood H.S., S.D., 1960-61; Children's Libn., Casa Verdugo Br., Glendale Pub. Lib., Calif., 1963-65; H.S. Libn., Inland Lakes Schl., Indian River, Mich., 1968-69; Libn., Am. Bibliographical Ctr., Clio Press, Santa Barbara, Calif., 1969-73. Mbrships. incl: Sec., Spearfish Jaycettes, S.D., 1961-62; Pres., 1962-63; Lutheran Lib. Tech. Advsr., 1971; Organizer, Lib., Ch. Day Schl., 1965-68. Address: 618 Andamar Way, Goleta, CA 93017, U.S.A. 5.

SWINTON, W.E., b. 30 Sept. 1900. Educator. B.Sc., Ph.D., D.Sc., Univ. of Glasgow, U.K. Appts: Dept. of Geo./Palaeontol., British Mus. (Natural Hist.), London, U.K., 1924-61; Lt. Cmndr., RNVR, 1939-45; Hd. of Life Scis., Royal Ont. Mus., Toronto, Canada, 1961-63; Dir. of Royal Ont. Mus., 1963-66; Prof., Toronto Univ., 1963-68; Vis. Prof., Waterloo Univ., Ont., Canada, 1974-. Mbrships. incl: Sr. Fellow, Massey Coll., Univ. of Toronto; Fellow of Royal Soc. of Edinburgh & of Royal Anthropol., Geol., Royal Geog., Linnean & Zool. Socs. in London; Fellow, Royal Soc. of Arts; Bd. of Govs., Ont. Sci. Ctr., Toronto; Hons: Trustee, Royal Ont. Mus., ibid, Bd., Toronto Zool. Soc.; Past Pres., Hist. of Sci. Soc., ibid; N.Y. Acad. of Sci.; Hon. Fellow, Acad. of Med., Toronto & Rochester Mus. of Arts & Scis., N.Y., 1965; Hon. Admiral, Neb., 1959; Publs: The Dinosaurs, 1924 & '70; Corridor of Life; Wonderful World of Prehistoric Animals; Digging for Dinosaurs; Fossil Amphibians & Reptiles (6 edits.); Fossil Birds (3 edits.); Dinosaurs (5 edits.) Address: Massey Coll., 4 Devonshire Pl., Toronto 5, Ont., Canada. 6, 47, 50.

SWOBODA, Henry. Conductor. Educ: Ph.D., Prague Univ.; Prague Music Conservatory; M.A., Harvard Univ. Appts: Conductor, Prague Opera House, Opera House, Dusseldorf; Conductor & Prog. Organizer, Prague Broadcasting Stn.; Conductor, Concert Hall recording co., U.S.A.; Music Dir., Westminster recording co., ibid; Lectr., Harvard Univ. & Cond., Harvard-Radcliffe Orch.; Vis. Prof., Dir. of Orch. & Opera Workshop, Univ. of Tex. Appearances incl: RIAS Orch., Berlin; Statradiofonien, Copenhagen; Philharmonia Orch., BBC, London; Symph. of the Air, N.Y. Author, The American Symphony Orchestra, 1967; Orquesta Sinfonica del Gran Teatro Liceo, Barcelona, Spain; Orquesta Sinfonica del Radio del Estado, Buenos Aires, Argentine; Orchestre de la Suisse Romande, Geneva, Switzerland; Orquesta Nacional, Mexico City, Mexico; Vienna Symph. Orch., Austria. Recip., Grand Prix du Disque, Paris, 1950. Address: 11855 1st St. E., Treasure Island, FL 33706, U.S.A. 4, 6.

SWYRYDENKO, Walter, b. 12 Oct. 1942. Artist; Educator. Educ: B.S., Kent State Univ., Ohio; M.A., ibid. Appts: Instr., Kent State Univ.; Art Supvsr., Nordonie Hills Bd. of Educ.;

Instr., Cooper Schl. of Art; Chmn., Art Dept., Lincoln Jr.-Sr. H.S., Cleveland, Ohio. Mbr., Calif. Nat. Watercolor Soc. Solo exhibs. incl: Ahde Artzt Gallery, N.Y.; Akron Art Inst., Ohio; Cooper Schl. of Art, Cleveland; Kent State Univ.; Massillion Mus., Ohio; Univ. of Windsor, Canada; Gallery Yonge, Toronto; Symbol Gallery of Arts, Albuquerque, N.M. Over 100 grp. & juried exhibs. Hons. incl: Painting & Purchase Award, Massillion Mus., 1967-68, 1971; Silver Medal for Painting, N.Y. Int. Art Show, 1970; Grand Finalist, 7th Grand Prix Internationale de Peinture de la Cote d'Azur, Cannes, France, 1971. Address: P.O. Box 09092, Cleveland, OH 44109, U.S.A. 8, 117, 130, 133.

SYDLER, Jean-Pierre, b. 30 June 1921. Librarian. Educ: Dr.math., Swiss Fed. Inst. of Technol. Appts: Asst., Geom.; Libn., Documentalist; Dir., Lib., Swiss Fed. Inst. of Technol. Publs: Papers on polyhedra. Hons: Gold Medal, Danish Acad. of Scis. Address: ETH-BIBL, Rämist. 101, CH-8401 Zurich, Switzerland.

SYETTA, Phyllis Scher (Mrs. Ely Syetta), b. 8 May 1928. Administrator. Educ: Music Degree, 3rd St. Settlement Schl., 1943; B.A., Brooklyn Coll., 1946; NY Univ. Grad. Schl. Bus. Admin., 1964. Appts: Dir., Community Org., Jewish Assn. Serv. to Aged; Exec. Dir., Nat. Women's League Conservative Judaism; Rsch. Assoc., Jewish Occupational Coun.; Mgmt. Rschr. & Writer, Nat. Indl. Conf. Bd. Mbrships: Fndr., 42nd Assembly Dist., Reform Democratic Party; Nat. Bd. Mbr., Am. Jewish Comm.; Am. Jewish Congress; VP, Marine Pk. Jewish Ctr. Creative Works: Author articles on Labor-Mgmt., Management Record; Worked on Govt. Proj., Follow-Up Counseling, 1969; Ed., PTA Bulletin. Recip. testimonials & gen. awards for work as civic ldr. Address: 2036 E. 35 St., Brooklyn, N.Y., NY 11234, U.S.A.

SYKES, Christopher Hugh, b. 17 Nov. 1907. Writer. Educ: Oxford Univ., U.K.; Sorbonne, Paris, France. Appts: Hon. Attaché to HM Embassy, Berlin, 1928-29, HM Legation, Tehran, 1930-31, '41-43; Special Corresp., Daily Mail, 1946; Dpty. Controller, 3rd. Prog., BBC, 1948; Features Dept., ibid, 1949-68. Mbrships: Fellow, Royal Soc. Lit., Royal Geog. Soc.; Lit. Soc.; London Lib. Comm., 1965-. Publs. incl: Character & Situation, 1949; Two Studies in Virtue, 1953; A Song of A Shirt, 1953; Dates & Parties, 1955; Orde Wingate, 1959; Cross Roads to Israel, 1965; Troubled Loyalty: a Biography of Adam von Trott, 1968. Recip., Croix de Guerre. Address: Swyre House, Swyre, nr. Dorchester, Dorset, U.K. 1.

SYKES, Edward Irving. Professor. Educ: B.A., Queensland Univ., Australia, 1930; LL.B., Melbourne Univ., ibid, 1936; LL.M., ibid, 1938; LL.D., ibid. Appts: Barrister-Solicitor, Queensland, 1939-45; Barrister, Pt.-time Lectr.-Dean, Fac. Law, Queensland Univ., 1945-67; Prof., Pub. Law, Melbourne Univ., 1967-. Mbrships: Past Pres., Indl. Rels. Soc., Queensland; Ind. Rels. soc., Vic.; Indl. Rels. Soc., Australia; num. Queensland & Melbourne Univs. assns. & clubs. Publs. incl: Law of Securities in Australia, 1962; 2nd ed., '73; Cases and Materials on Private International Law, 1962; 2nd ed., '69; Australian Conflict of Laws (Textbook), 1972; Australian Labor Law (w. H.J. Glasbeek), 1972; num. articles in periodicals. Hons: Carnegie Travelling Grant, 1954; Fulbright Travel Grant, 1954. Address: Law Schl., Melbourne Univ., Parkvilie, Vic., Australia, 3052.

SYMES, (Major Gen.) George William, b. 12 Jan. 1896. Retired Major General, British Army. Educ: Army Staff Coll., Camberley, U.K., 1930-31. Appts. incl: D/Cmdr., Special Force, India, 1943-44; D/Cmdr., L. of C. Command, 21st Army Group, 1944; Cmdr., L. of C., S.E.A.C., 1944-46; Cmdr., S.W. Dist., Taunton, 1946-48; Cmdr., 43rd Wessex Div. T.B., 1947-48; Retd., 1949; Col., The York & Lancaster Regiment, 1946-48; Fndr., Nat. Trust of S. Australia, 1954-55; Pvte. Sec. to Gov., S. Australia, 1956-64; V.P., Nat. Trust of S. Australia, 1965-; Dir., Santos Ltd., 1955-; Hon. Col., 10th Battalion C.M.F., 1958-60. Mbrships. incl: United Serv. & Royal Aero Club; Royal Geographical Soc. of Australia; Pres., S. Australia Br., ibid, 1954-57. Contbr. to jrnls. Recip. of hons. Address: 81 Esplanade, Tennyson, S.A., Australia, 5022. 1, 23.

SYMOENS, Jean-Jacques A., b. 21 Mar. 1927. University Professor. Educ: Bachelor in Philos. & Scis., Univ. of Lille, 1945; Lie. in Chem. Scis., Univ. of Brussels, Belgium, 1948; Ph.D. in Bot. Scis., ibid, 1955. Appts. incl: Asst., Free Univ. of Brussels, 1948-55; Prof. of Botany, Univ. Nat. du Zaire, Lubumbashi, 1956-72; Prof. of Botany, Free Univ. of Brussels, 1970-; Prof. of Biol., Univ. of Mons, 1973-. Mbrships. incl: Royal Acad. of Overseas Scis., Brussels, 1964-; Int. Acad. of Fishery Scis., Rome, 1970-. Author of over 80 books & papers inclng. Acquisitions Récentes En Limnologie, 1950-51, Le Lac Tanganika, 1956, Les Eaux Douces De L'Ardenne & Des Régions Voisines, 1957; Contribution A La Flore Algale De L'Ardenne & Des Régions Voisines, 1960. La Minéralisation Des Eaux Naturelles Du Bassin Du Lac Bangweolo & Du Luapula, 1968. Hons: Crepin Prize, Royal Botanical Soc. of Belgium, 1959; Ordre Du Mérite Civique, Repub. of Zaire, 1968. Address: Rue St.-Quentin 69, B-1040 Brussels, Belgium. 43, 87.

SYNNERGREN, Stig Gustaf Eugen. b. 25 Feb. 1915. General, & Supreme Commander, Swedish Armed Forces. Educ: Off.'s Commn., 1939. Appts: Col. & Cmdr., 21st Infantry Regiment, 1962; Major Gen. & Chief, Swedish Army Staff, 1963; C.-in-C., 5th Mil. Cmd., 1966; Lt. Gen. & Chief, Swedish Defence Staff, 1967; Gen. & Supreme Cmdr., Swedish Armed Forces, 1970. Mbrships: Royal Swedish Acad. of Mil. Scis.; Hon. Mbr., Royal Swedish Soc. of Naval Scis.; Swedish Touring Club. Address: Överbefälhavaren, 100 45 Stockholm 90, Sweden.

SYRKIN, Simon, b. 20 Apr. 1906. Engineer. Educ: Dipl.-Eng., Polytech., Hanover, Germany. Appts: Dist. Eng., Palestine Jewish Colonization Assn., Baron Rothschild Fndn., 1927-29; Dist. Eng., S., Jewish Nat. Fund, 1929-32; own off., Cons. Engr., Water Supply, Irrigation Sewerage, 1932-39, 1945-48 & 56-; w. Brit Army, holding rank of Maj., 1939-45; w. Israel Army of Defence, Dpty. Adjutant-Gen., rank of Lt. Col., 1948-51; Mil. Attaché to Western Europe, France, Italy, Belgium, Holland, Switz., rank of Col., 1955-56. Mbrships: Acad. of Sci., N.Y., U.S.A.; Civil Engrs. Assn., U.S.A.; Assoc., Engrs. & Archts. of Israel; Past Pres., Assn. of Water Engrs. of Israel. Address: 8, Shalagstr., Tel-Aviv, Israel.

SYVERTSEN, Jan Helge, b. 6 Oct. 1941. Economist; Public Relations Officer. Educ: Mktng. Schl. of Oslo, Norway. Appts: Jrnlist.; Asst. Advt. Mgr., A/S John Petersen, Kloverhuset; Mgr., P.R. Dept. & Mktng. Asst. A/S, ibid; P.R. Cons., The Info. Serv. Bur., Norwegian Weekly Press; Gen. Mgr., Direct

Mktng. Grp. Mbrships: Int. P.R. Assn.; Norwegian P.R. Assn.; Mktng. Assn. of Oslo; Sales Mgmt. Club of Oslo; Interallied Reserve Offs. Assn.; Norwegian Reserve Offs. Assn. Author, Corporate Identity & Public Relations in a wider perspective (monograph), 1972. Address: Vestbygaten 38B 2000 Lilleström, Norway.

SZABO-PELSOCZI, Miklos, b. 10 June 1924. Economist. Educ: Univ. of Agrictural Scis., Budapest, Hungary, 1942-46; M.A., Grad. Inst. Int. Studies, Univ.'of Geneva, Switzerland, 1950; M.A., Yale Univ. Grad. Schl., 1954. Appts: V.P., Czarnikow-Rionda Co., N.Y.C., 1954-63; Int. Economist, Bur. of Economic Affairs, U.S. Dept. of State, Wash. D.C., 1963-65; V.P., Czarnikow-Rionda Co., N.Y.C. & Managing Dir., Rionda, de Pass, Ltd., London, U.K., 1966-70; Cons. to Int. Bank for Reconstruction & Dev., 1970-72; Dir. of Rsch., Continental Grain Co./ContiCommodity Servs., 1972-. Mbrships: Am. Economic Assn.; Yale Club, N.Y.C.; Inst. of Dirs., London, U.K.; The Am. Club, ibid. Address: Continental Grain Company/CCS, Two Broadway, N.Y., NY 10004, U.S.A. 6.

SZAPIRO, Shlomo, b. 19 Apr. 1927. Chemist. Educ: Master of Techn Scis., Lodz, Poland, 1952; Master of Philos., Univ. of Lodz, 1952; Ph.D., Feinberg Grad. Schl., Weizmann Inst. of Sci., Rehovoth, Israel, 1966. Appts: Rsch. Asst. Inst. of Technol, Lodz, 1951-57; Rsch. Jr., Weizmann Inst. of Sci., Rehovoth, Israel, 1957-67; Rsch. Assoc., Soreq Nuclear Rsch. Ctr., Yavne, 1968-. Mbr., Israel Assn. of Growth of Crystals & Thin Films. Author, var. profl. papers, Isobaric liquid-vapour equilibrium, Polymer Sci., separation of mixtures by distillation, phys. properties of heavy oxygen. Recip., Polish Chem. Soc. Prize, 1956. Address: Solid State Physics. Dept., Soreq Nuclear Research Center, Yavne, Israel. 44.

SZEGHO, Emeric, b. 10 Sept. 1907. University Professor. Educ: Lic. Law, Univ. Cernauti, Rumania, 1938; Dip., Atty. at Law, Rumanian Bar Assn., Bucharest, 1941; J.D., Univ. of Cluj., 1947. Appts: Mbr., Bar Assn., Timisoara, Banat, 1938; Atty. at Law, Juricons., Timisoara, Sibiu, 1941-60; Prof., Alliance Coll., Cambridge Springs, Pa., U.S.A., 1966-. Mbrships: AAUP; Nat. Advsry. Bd., Am. Security Coun., 1972-73; Nat. Bd. of Sponsors, Inst. for Am. Strategy, 1972-73. Preparing Crime & Punishment, The Problem of Crime for publn. Address: 215 Ross Ave., Cambridge Springs, PA 16403, U.S.A. 54, 57, 130, 131, 139.

SZELL, George, b. 7 June 1897. Musical Director; Conductor. Educ: State Acad. of Music, Vienna, Austria. Appts. incl: 1st pub. concert as child prodigy, age 11; 1st appearance as conductor, Vienna Symph. Orch., age 16; Conductorial Staff, Berlin State Opera, Germany, 1914-16; Chief Conductor, ibid & Berlin Broadcasting Co. Symph. Orch., 1924-29; Gen. Musical Dir., German Opera House, Prague, Czechoslovakie & Prof., Acad. Music & Dramatic Arts, 1929; Conducting engagements, U.S.A. & U.K., 1930-37; N.Y. Debut, NBC Symph. Orch., 1941; Regular Conductor, Metropolitan Opera, 1942-46; Musical Dir., Cleveland Orch., 1946. Compositions incl: Variations for Orchestra; Symph. in B Major; Lyric Overture; chmbr. works. Hons. incl: C.B.E., 1963; Austrian Order 1st Class for Art & Sci., 1965; Cmdr., Order of the Lion, Finland, 1966; Officer, Legion of Honour, France, 1969. Address: Severance Hall, 11001 Euclid Ave., Cleveland, OH 44106, U.S.A. 8.

SZÉNÁSSY, István Lajos, b. 15 Feb. 1937. Museum Director; Art Historian; Archaeologist. Educ: Drs., Art Hist. & Archaeol., Univ. of Amsterdam, Netherlands, 1967. Appts: Asst., Inst. of Art Hist., Univ. of Amsterdam, 1965-68; Dir., Bonnefantenmuseum/Mus. for Art & Antiquities, Instn. Province Limburg, Maastricht, 1968-. Mbrships. incl: Bd. mbr., Royal Dutch Antiquity Soc., The Hague, 1970; Netherlands Mus. Assn./Netherlands Nat. Comm., I.C.O.M., 1972; Comm. of Cultural Affairs, Netherlands-Luxemburg, 1973; Fndr. mbr., Soc. Int. of Art Exhibition Ldrs. Meeting, Berlin, 1973 (called I.K.T., Berlin); Assn. of Art Histns. of Netherlands. Publs. incl: Catalogue Exhibition G. Rietveld, archt., Amsterdam-London, 1971-72; Bonnefantenmuseum, 1972; Articles in Jrnls. Hon: Off., Ordre Grand-Ducal de la Couronne de Chêne de Luxembourg, 1974. Address: Voederruwe 8, NL 5002, Maastricht, Netherlands. 133.

SZENDI, Balazs, b. 14 May 1904. Professor of Obstetrics & Gynaecology; Urologist. Educ: State Univ. of Med., Debrecen, Hungary, 1924-30; postgrad. studies, Univ. of Debrecen, 1925-30 & 1930-41, Univ. Frauenklinik, Charitée Clin. & Univ. of Berlin, Germany, Univ. of London, U.K., 1938. Appts: Asst. Prof. Ob. & Gyn. Clin., Univ. of Debrecen; Dir. in Chief, Midwifery Schl., Miskolc, & Cou. Hosp. of Lilienfeld, Austria; Hd., Gyn., Cou. Hosps., Szikszó & Gyula. Fellowships: Hungarian Coll. of Ob. & Gyn.; Hungarian Coll. of Urol. Contbr. to num. jrnls. in field. Recip., Widder Ignacz Medal, Royal Hungarian Med. Soc., 1936. Address: Arpád str. 28/b, 5700 Gyula, Hungary.

SZILARD, Claire, b. 31 Mar. 1921. Painter. Educ: studied w. Galle & A. Bernath, Free Acad., Budapest, 1940-44; at Ecole des Beaux-Artes, Geneva, Switz., 1948; study tour in Italy, studied "fresco-buono" w. Prof. T. Orselli, Acad. of Fine Arts, Ravenna, 1955. Opened own Studio & Permanent Exhib., Old Jaffa, 1967. Has participated in num. grp. shows, Israel & abroad, 1943-. Has had 13 one-man shows inclng: Artists-House of Israel's Painters & Sculptors Assn., Tel-Aviv, 1970; Mod. Art Mus., Eilat, 1971; Artists-House Jerusalem, 1971; Gall. for Old-Jaffa Artists, 1972. Works in pvte. collects., Israel, Switz., France, Italy, UK & USA, & civic collects, Budapest, Zurich, Ramat-Gan (Israel), Tel-Aviv (Israel) & Eilat (Israel). Has executed stained glass windows for public bldgs., synagogues, & pvte. houses, 1957-; inclng: Histl. Mus.; Tel-Aviv; Ctrl. Synagogue, Pardes Hannah; "Shivat-Zion"-Gt. Synagogue, Tel-Aviv; Glass Wall, Citrus Mktng. Bd.'s House, Tel-Aviv. Mbrships: Israel Painters & Sculptor's Assn. Hons: Nordau Prize, 1969. Address: Mazal-Dagim St., 11, Old-Jaffa (68036), Israel.

SZILVASY, Frank Albert, b. 30 Dec. 1912. Architect. Educ: B.S., Univ. of Ill., Champaign, 1937. Appts: Designer, N.Y. Ctrl. R.R., 1946-50, Vern Alden Co., 1950-54; Job Capt., Loebl Schlossman Bennett & Dart, Archts., 1955-56; Chief Archt., Vern Alden Co. Engrs., 1957-62; Specification Writer, Loebl Schlossman Bennett & Dart, 1963-69; Archt., Nelson Ostrom Baskin & Berman, Engrs., 1970-. Mbrships: Ill. Soc. Archts.; Construction Specification Inst.; Am. Railway Engrng. Assn.; Nat. Geog. Soc. Address: P.O. Box 6864, Chgo., IL 60680, U.S.A. 8, 57.

SZONDI, Leopold, b. 11 Mar. 1893. Psychologist; Psychotherapist; Fate Analyst. Educ: Dr.med. Appts: Prof. & Dir., Rsch. Lab. for Psychopathol. & H. für Heilpäd., Budapest,

Hungary, 1927-41; Prof., Univ. of Zurich, Switzerland, 1962-63. Mbrships: Hon. Pres., Schweizerische Arbeitsgemeinschaft für Experiment, Triebdiagnostik & Schicksalpsychologie, 1946; Schweizerische Gesellschaft der Schicksalsanslyt. Therapie, 1961; Int. Rsch. Soc. for Fate Psychol., 1958; Hon. mbr., Schweizerische Gesellschaft für Psychiatrie. Publs. incl: Triebdiagnostik (also in French, Engl., Japanese, Spanish, Italian), 1947, 3rd edit. 1973; Freiheit & Zwang im Schicksal des Einzelnen, 1968; Kain, Gestalten des Bösen, 1968; Moses, Antwort auf Kain, 1973; Articles in books & jrnls. Hons: Dr.h.c. psychologiae educationisque scientiarum, Löwen; Saenger Prize, Ungarische Arzte Gesellschaft, 1926. Address: Stiftung Szondi Inst., Krählbühlstr. 30, 8044 Zurich, Switzerland.

SZOVERFFY, Joseph, b. 19 June 1920. University Professor. Educ: B.A., St. Emeric Coll., Budapest, Hungary, 1939; Ph.D., State Univ., Budapest, ibid, 1943; Dr. Phil. Habil., Medieval Studies & Comp. Folklore, Fribourg Univ., Switzerland, 1950. Appts. incl: Asst. & Sr. Asst. Prof., Budapest Univ., 1943-48; Archivist & Rsch., Libn., Irish Folklore Commn., Dublin, 1952-57; Asst. Prof., Univ. of Alta., Canada, 1959-62; Assoc. Prof., Yale Univ., 1962-65; Prof., Boston Coll., 1965-70; Prof., Dir. Grad. Studies, Chmn. Comp. Lit. & Medieval Studies, SUNY, Albany, N.Y., 1970-. Mbrships. incl: Yale Fac. Club; Exec. Coun., Am. Folklore Soc.; MLA of Am.; Co.-Chmn., Bibliographic Comm., Comp. Lit. VII, ibid, 1969-; Schlr's Lib. Selection Comm., 1971-73. Author num. books & contbrns. academic

publs. Address: Dept. Comp. & World Lit., Edith O. Wallach Humanities Bldg., SUNY at Albany, 1400 Wash. Ave., Albany, NY 12222, U.S.A. 6, 13, 15.

SZÜCS, Erno Béla, b. 19 Aug. 1932. Museum Collector, Reaserch Worker. Educ: Grad., Secondary Schl. Appts: Tech. Tchr., Hungary; Tech. Ldr., Flour Mill, Vac., Hungary; Collector, Researcher, own pvte. mus. Mbrships: Magyar Régészeti, Müvészettörténéti és Éremtani Tarsulat; Budapest Eremgyüjtok Egyesülete. Exhibs: Vac, 1964, '67; Perocsény, 1968. Address: 2621 Veroce, Arpad ut 73, Hungary. 105, 133.

SZYRYNSKI, Victor, b. 10 Oct. 1913. University Professor; Neurologist; Psychiatrist. Educ. incl: M.D., 1938; Ph.D., 1949; L.M.C.C., 1949; F.R.C.P. (C), 1954; Appts. incl: Assoc. Prof.-Prof., Univ. of Ottawa, 1948-60; Assoc. Prof. Neurol., Prof. Psych. & Psychotherapy, Univ. of N.D., Grand Forks, 1961-64; Prof. & Hd., Dept. Psych., Ottawa Gen. Hosp., 1964-70; Prof. of Psych., Prof. Psychotherapy, & Prof., Dept. of Criminol., Univ. of Ottawa, 1972-; Vis. Prof. & Dir., Ctr. of Pastoral Psych., St. Paul Univ., Ottawa, 1972-. Dipl. d'Etudes Française, Univ. of Poitier, 1972. 8 Fellowships med. orgs., Canada, U.S.A., U.K. Mbr. var. med. orgs., Canada, U.S.A. 4 books, 50 papers in neurol., psych. & psychol. Assoc. Ed., Psychosomatics (N.Y.), 1961. Hons. incl: Polish Cross of Merit w. Swords, 1945; Gold Medallist, Acad. Psychosomatic Med., 1959; Kt. of Order of Holy Sepulchre, 1968. Address: 33 Cedar Rd., Ottawa, Ont. K1J 6L6, Canada. 15, 54.

T

TAARNHOJ, Knud Palle, b. 26 Aug. 1918. Physician. Educ: Soro Academi, 1934-37; Med. Schl., Univ. of Copenhagen, Denmark, 1937-45; Neurosurg, Trng., Univ. Hosp., Copenhagen, 1946-53; Danish Med. Licence, 1945; Ohio Med. Licence, U.S.A., 1955; Specialized in Neurosurg., 1953. Appts: Staff Mbr., Neurosurg., Cleveland Clin., Ohio, 1955-60; Chief, Neurosurg., Copenhagen Co. Hosp., Denmark, 1960-. Mbrships: Scandinavian Neurosurg. Soc.; Danish Neurosurg. Org.; Pres., ibid, 1965-72; Cong. of Neurological Surgs.; British Neurosurg. Soc.; Am. Assn. of Neurological Surgs.; AMA; Royal Danish Aeroclub; Ch. Coun. Author, num. publs. on trigeminal neuralgia, intracranial pressure, Parkinsonnisme, Hyperhidrosis, shot gun wound of hd., etc. Developed new surg. treatment of Trigeminal Neuralgia, Decompression of the posterior root of the Trigeminal nerve, 1951. Address: Bakken 11, 2600 Glostrup, Denmark. 134.

TABANERA, Rafael Cesar, b. 24 Oct. 1904. Lawyer. Educ: Fac. of Law & Soc. Scis.,Capital Fed., Argentina. Appts. incl: Counsel, Poor & Missing Persons, Mendoza, 1926-28; Advsr., Supt. Gen. of Irrigation, 1925; Chief, Legal Dept., Dept. of Irrigation, 1925-26; Dpty., Mendoza Legislature, 1934-37; Vice Gov., Province of Mendoza, 1946-49; Conven. Pres., 1948-49; Min., Govt. of Santa Fe., 1955. Mbrships: Pres., Coll. of Lawyers of Mendoza & Assn. of Lawyers, 1922-25; Sec., Gen. Confederation of Profls.; Pres., Jockey Club, Mendoza. Publs. incl: Sinopsis de Derecho Civil Argentino, 3 vols., 1923-24; Dictamenes Sobre Cuestiones Municipales, 1944. Hons: Oficial de la Orden al Merite de la Repub. de Chile; Comendador, Orden Al Merite Civil, Spain, 1950. Address: Hipolite Irigoyen 296, ler piso, Dpte. 1, Godoy Cruz, Province of Mendoza, Argentina.

TABENKEN, Samuel, b. 1 May 1906. Business Executive. Educ: Portland Univ., 1924-26. Appts: Pres., H. Tabenken Co. Inc., Bangor & Caribou, Me., 1933; Treas., Tablease Inc., Bangor, 1955; Bd. Chmn., Kennebec Trading Co. Inc.; Financial Cons., Camp Pinecrest for Girls, Naples, Me., 1954-59. Mbrships: Me. Beer Wholesalers Assn. (Pres., 1953-55); Dir., Nat. Beer Wholesalers Assn., 1955-65; Me. Trucking Assn.; Assocd. Inds. of Me.; Me. Bd. Dirs., Small Bus. Admin.; Bd. Chmn. & Treas., Wine Int., San Fran., Calif.; Bangor Chmbr. of Comm.; Mason; Penobscot Valley Country Club, Orono, Me.; Patron of Fine Arts, Univ. of Me., ibid; Patron, Bangor Symph. Orch. Address: 187 Clyde Rd., Bangor, ME 04401, U.S.A. 6.

TABLER, D-Jane A.P. Musician; Educator. Educ: Mus.B., New England Conservatory of Music, Boston, Mass.; Mus.M., Cath. Univ. of Am., Wash. D.C.; grad. work, Fontainebléau, France, 1961. Appts: Music Instr., Coll. Misericordia, Dallas, Pa.; Pub. Schls. Music Instr., Kingston, Pa., Montgomery, Md.; Prince George, Md. Mbrships: AAUW; Wilkes-Borre Musicians Union Local 140; var. educl. orgs.; Sigma Alpha Iota. Hons. incl: Music Schlrships., New England Conservatory & Cath. Univ. Address: 3700 Kenilworth Dr., Chevy Chase, MD 20015, U.S.A. 57, 125, 130, 132, 138.

TABOGA MORA, Cornelia (Mrs.), Artist; Theatre Director; Art & Theatre Writer & Critic. Educ: Theatre Schl. Appts: Art, Theatre, Music, Cinema & Book Critic, Patavium, Le Venezie, Viviamo, L'Avvenire d'Italia & Il Veneto; Mbr. of Org. Comm. & Hd. of Press Off., Int. Biennale of Bronzetto (small bronze sculptures); Fndr., Teatro Sperimentale & Ora Teatro 70, 1954 & new form of theatre, L'Antologia; researched & reconstructed XII & XIII century relig. mystery plays w. original music. Theatrical presentations incl: Teatro E Musica del 500; Teatro Goldoniano; Teatro Dell'800; Teatro Guiapponese; Teatro Americano; Strindberg; Maeterlink; Claudel. Exhibs. incl: Venice Biennale, 1956; All Biennale Trivenete, 1953-; All Biennale Arte Sacra-Bologna; Milan; Parma; Naples; Japan; Int. Exhib. of Relig. Art, Padua. Mbrships: Dir. Comm., Soroptimist Club, Padua; Sec., Union of Cath. Artists of Italy. Hons: var. art awards. Address: Via S. Pietro 133, 35100 Padua, Italy.

TABOR, David, b. 23 Oct. 1913. Physicist. Educ: B.Sc., London, U.K., 1934; Ph.D., Cambridge, 1939; Sc.D., ibid, 1956. Appts: Div. of Tribophys., SCIRO, Australia, 1940-46; Lectr., Univ. of Cambridge, U.K., 1961, Rdr., 1964, Prof., Phys., 1973; Hd., Phys. & Chem. of Solids Grp., Cavendish Lab., ibid. Fellowships: Royal Soc., 1963; Gonville & Caius Coll., Cambridge, 1957; Inst. of Phys. Publs: The Hardness of Metals, 1951; Gases, Liquids & Solids, 1969; Co-Author, Friction & Lubrication, 1967; Friction-an Introduction to Tribology, 1973; Friction & Lubrication of Solids, Part I, 1950, Part II, 1963. Hons: Wilson Award, Am. Soc. for Metals, 1969; Inaugural Tribol. Gold Medal, Instn. of Mech. Engrs., 1972. Address: Phys. & Chem. of Solids, Cavendish Lab., Cambridge, U.K. 1.

TABORI, Paul, b. 8 May 1908. Author; Educator. Educ: Ph.D., Kaiser Wilhelm Univ., Berlin, Germany, 1930; Dr. of Econ. & Pol. Sci. Peter Pazmany Univ., Budapest, Hungary, 1932. Appts. incl: BBC European Sect. Broadcaster, 1941-50; Vis. Prof., Fairleigh Dickinson, N.J., U.S.A., 1966; Rsch. Fellow, Hoover Instn., Stanford, 1971. Mbr. of var. profl. assns. Publs. incl: Non-fiction: Harry Price; Alexander Korda; The Anatomy of Exile; The Natural Science of Stupidity; The Art of Folly; Crime & the Occult; The Borley Ghosts; Fiction: Hazard Island; Song of the Scorpions; They Came to London; Lily Dale; Solo; The Talking Tree; The Plague of Sanity. Hons. incl: Award of Brit. Writers Guild, 1964; Award of Int. Writers Guild, 1967. Address: 14 Stafford Terr., London W.8, 3, 58.

TADLOCK, Frances Ayers (Mrs. William R. Tadlock), b. 2 May 1926. Educator. Educ: B.S., Winthrop Coll., Rock Hill, S.C., U.S.A., 1946. Appts: Tchr., Home Econs., Simpsonville Pub. Schl., 1946-48; Tchr., Home Econs., Paris H.S., 1948-57; Tchr., Tanglewood Elem. Schl., 1965-70; Tchr., W.Greenville Elem. Schl., 1970-71; Tchr., Ellen Woodside Elem. Schl., 1971-74. Mbrships: State V.P., Assn. for Childhood Educ.; NEA; S.C. Educ. Assn.; Greenville Co. Educ. Assn.; Int. Reading Assn.; PTA; Delta Kappa Gamma. Address: 20 Westbrook Lane, Greenville, SC 29605, U.S.A. 5, 130, 138.

TADLOCK, Lila Clementa Swindell (Mrs. William Lawton Tadlock), b. 13 Jan. 1903. School Teacher (Retired). Educ: B.S., E. Tex. State Univ.; M.S. & Advd. Studies, ibid; Cert., Famous Writers Schl., Westport, Conn. Appts: Tchr., small schls., Fannin Co., until 1941; Supt., Ravenna; Sci. Tchr., Bells H.S. & N. Fannin H.S.; Maths. Tchr., Sober HS., 1946; Engl. Tchr., Lannius; Prin., Windom Primary Schl., 1955-68; Retd., 1969. Mbrships. incl: Poetry Soc. of Tex., 1946-; V.P., Fannin Co. Tchrs., 1954-63; V.P., Bonham Women's Club,

1973-74; Nat. Retd. Tchrs. Club; 1st Presby. Ch. Publs: Four songs, It Was Too Late, Forever Yours, To the Class of Twenty One, Angels Unaware; Poems, Love Lives Here, May April March, Sittin Thar, Poetry Soc. of Tex. Recip. of poetry awards. Address: Box 334, Bonham, TX 75418, U.S.A. 11, 57, 128.

TAE, Wan-Son, b. 20 Jan. 1915. Politician. Educ: Grad., Coll. of Law, Seoul Nat. Univ., Korea, 1936. Appts: Congressman, 2nd Nat. Assembly, 1950 & 5th Nat. Assembly, 1960; Min., Min. of Reconstrn., 1961, & Min. of Commerce & Ind., 1961; Councillor, Econ. & Sci. Advsry. Comm. to Pres., 1970; Pres., Dai Han Coal Corp., 1970; Min., Min. of Constnr., 1971; Dpty. Prime Min. & Min. of Econ. Planning Bd., 1972-. Publs: Electric Utilities in the United States, 1959; The Economic Development of Korea, 1973. Hons: The Grand Cordon of the Order, Govt. of Repub. of China, 1973. Address: Off. of Dpty. Prime Min. & Min. of Econ. Planning Bd., Seoul, Korea.

TAFT, Ronald, b. 3 June 1920. University Professor. Educ: B.A., Univ. of Melbourne, Australia, 1939; M.A., Columbia Univ., U.S.A., 1941; Ph.D., Univ. of Calif., Berkeley, 1950. Appts: Sr. Lectr., Rdr. in Psychol., Univ. of Western Australia, 1951-65; Rdr. in Psychol., Univ. of Melbourne, 1966-68; Prof., Soc. Psychol., Educ. Fac., Monash Univ., 1968-. Mbrships: Fellow, Acad. of Soc. Scis. in Australia; Fellow, & former Pres., Australian Psychological Soc.; Sociological Assn. of Australia & N.Z.; Int. Assn. of Applied Psychol.; Int. Assn. of Cross-Cultural Psychol.; Am. Educl. Rsch. Assn.; Soc. for the Psychological Study of Soc. Issues; For. Affiliate, Am. Psychological Assn.; Monash Univ. Club. Publs. incl: Attitudes & Social Conditions, 1970; Jews in Australian Society, 1973. Address: Fac. of Educ., Monash Univ., Clayton, Vic., Australia, 3168. 23, 55, 128.

TAIT, George Edward, b. 19 July 1910. Professor of Education. Educ: B.A., Univ. of Western Ont., Canada; B.Pedagogy, Univ. of Toronto; Ed.D., ibid. Appts: Elem. Tchr., London, Ont., 1931-41; Dir., Anglo-Am. Schl., Bogota, Colombia, 1941-44; Insp. of Pub. Schls., Ont., 1944-50; Chmn., Dept. of Elem. Educ., Univ. of Toronto, 1950-73, retd.; Prof. Emeritus, ibid, 1973. Mbrships. incl: Pres., Toronto Br., Canadian Authors Assn., 1954; Life mbr., Ont. Schl. Insps.' Assn.; Canadian Assn., Profs. of Educ.; Canadian Educ. Assn. Publs. incl: The World Was Wide, 1954; The Upward Trail, 1956; Fair Domain, 1960; One Dominion, 1962; revised edit. 1973; The Eagle & The Snake, 1968; The Unknown People, 1974. Recip. of hons. Address: 105 Golfdale Rd., Toronto, M4N 2B8, Canada. 88, 141.

TAKACH, Eileen Therese (Butkus), b. 26 Sept. 1946. Research Mathematician. Educ: B.S., Marian Coll., Indpls., Ind., U.S.A., 1968; Postgrad., Purdue Univ., Lafayette, Ind. & Ind. Univ., Indpls., 1970-71. Appt: Rsch. Mathn., Naval Avionics Facility, Indpls., 1968-. Mbrships: Math. Assn. of Am.; Applied Rsch. Investment Club. Author, Rsch. reports on aerodynamic simulations & math. modelling for a digital computer. Address: 8220 Crousore Rd., Indianapolis, IN 46219, U.S.A. 5, 138.

TAKAGI, Kentaro, b. 17 Mar. 1910. University Professor & Administrator. Educ: Grad., Schl. of Med., Kyushu Univ., 1934. Appts: Assoc. Prof., Schl. of Med., Niigata Univ., 1939, Prof., 1945; Prof., Schl. of Med., Nagoya Univ., 1956, Acting Dean, 1969, Univ. Pres., 1972-. Mbrships: Physiological Soc. of Japan; Japan Socs. of Med. Electronics &

Biological Engrng., Ergonomics, Autonomic Nervous System, Chest Diseases; Japanese Coll. of Angiol.; Japan Acupuncture & Moxibustion Soc.; Soc. for Oriental Med. in Japan. Publs. incl: Physiology, 1960; Introduction to Physiology, 1964; Handbook of Physiology, 1972; New Physiology, 1974. Hons: Asahi Prize for Incentive to Sci., 1960; Chunichi Culture Prize, 1967. Address: Nagoya City University, Kawasumi, Mizuhocho, Mizuho-ku,Nagoya 467, Japan.

TAKINO, Masuichi, b. 14 Apr. 1905. Physician. Educ: M.D., Kyoto Univ., Japan. Appts: Lectr., Kyoto Univ., 1939-40; Dir., Dainippon Zoki Inst. for Med. Rsch., 1941-61, Nippon Zoki Inst. for Constitutional Diseases, 1962-; Permanent Advsr., Nippon Zoki Pharm. Co. Ltd., 1968-; Ed., Alergia, 1973-. Mbrships: Japan Soc. of Autonomic Nervous System, Constitution, Endocrinol. & Angiocardiol., Counselor; Japan Soc. of Allergol. (Hon., 1970-); Fellow, Am. Coll. of Physns.; Int. Soc. of Biometeorol.; Int. Assn. of Allergol. Publs: A New Direction in the Asthma Treatment, 1948 (in English, 1952); Allergy & Asthma; contbr. to profl. publs. Holder of patents for rsch. methods. Recip. of Prize of Meritorious Serv. from Japan Soc. of Allergy, 1970. Address: Nippon Zoki Inst. for Constitutional Diseases, Heiwa Bldg., 10 Nichome, Hiranomachi, Higashi-ku, Osaka, Japan. 50, 129.

TAKSERMAN-KROZER, Rachel, b. 31 Dec. 1921. Professor Physics. Educ: M.Sc., Fac. Theoretical Phys., Univ. of Tschkent, USSR, 1947; D.Sc., Inst. Gen. Chem., Warsaw, Poland, 1961; Docent, Tech. Univ. of Lodz, Poland. Appts: Asst., Sr. Asst., Tech. Univ., Taschkent, USSR, 1947-48; Sr. Asst., Lectr., Univs. of Leningrad & Petrosavodsk, 1948-59; Sr. Rsch. Fellow, Inst. of Gen. Chem., Warsaw, Poland, 1959-66; Docent (Ass. Prof.), Inst. of Fundamental Problems, Warsaw, 1966-68; Prof., Technion, Inst. of Technol., Israel, 1968-. Mbr., Polish Chem. & Phys. Scientific Socs., 1959-68. Contbr., chapt., book, The Structure of Macromolecules in Solutions, 1968. Contbr., papers & articles, sci. jrnls. & publs. Hons: Sci. Awards, Polish Chem. Soc., 1963, Inst. of Gen. Chem., Poland, 1964. Address: Technion City, Dept. of Mechanics, Haifa, Israel.

TAL, Miriam (Mrs.), b. 29 June 1910. Art Critic; Writer; Translator & Interpreter. Educ: Univ. studies, Berlin & Jerusalem; Cert. of Proficiency in Engl., Cambridge, 1937. Appts: Art Critic, daily Hebrew newspapers Haboker, Hayom, Lamerhav, Yedioth Aharanoth, in Israel; Sr. Staff Mbr., Jewish Nat. Fund; Past Mbr., Advsry. Comm. on Plastic Arts, Min. of Educ., Israel. Mbrships: Int. Assn. of Art Critics; Mbr., num. juries & selection comms. Publs: 16 art books, 14 in Hebrew & Engl. edits., inclng: Jerusalem, work of Yossi Stern,1956; 6 Safed Artists, 1960; Drawings, Itszhak Yamin, 1966; Aharan Kahana, Drawings & Biography, 1971; Author, 1 novel, 1938, 1 vol. of poetry, 1964, & num. critiques & essays, Israel, German, French & Engl. periodicals; Contbr. to Larousse Ency. of Contemporary Art & others; Translator, Gerard de Nerval, Rimbaud, etc. Hons: French decoration for contribution to French culture, 1962. Address: Hazanowitz St. No. 5, Jerusalem, Israel. 55.

TALARI, (Holger) Erkki (Konstantin), b. 8 Mar. 1907. Painter; Graphic Artist. Num. solo exhibs. held since 1943 in Finland & abroad, inclng. oils, woodcuts, etchings & drawings. Overseas exhibs: Gothenburg, Sweden, 1946; Zurich, Switzerland, 1952; Solje, Maribor, 1963, & Skopje, 1964, Yugoslavia; Ancona,

Italy, 1969; Biarritz & Paris, France, 1973. Participated in exhibs. throughout Europe, India, U.S.A. Illustrator of book Kanteletar. Mbrships: Painters', Graphics & Drawing Socs. of Finland. Hons. incl: Special Medals, Galleria Europa Arte 1968; Ancona; Co-Recipient of Award, Italy, 1969, Finland, 1970. Address: Siilitie 13 P 560, 00800 Helsinki 80, Finland.

TÂLAT-ERBEN, M., b. 6 Sept. 1917. Physical Chemist. Educ: B.S., Fac. of Sci., Univ. of Istanbul, Turkey, 1944; Ph.D., Tech. Univ., Istanbul, 1949; Nat. Rsch. Coun. of Canada Postdoct. Fellow in High Polymet Chem., Ottawa, Canada, 1952-54; Schl. of Nuclear Sci. & Engrng., Argonne Nat. Lab., U.S.A., 1955-56; Res. Rsch. Assoc., Fission Chem., ibid, 1956-57. Appts: Lectr., Chair of Phys. Chem., Fac. of Chem. Engrng., Tech. Univ., Istanbul, 1957-62; Prof., Phys. Chem., ibid, 1962; Chmn., Dept. of Phys. Chem., 1973; Hd., Fundamental Process Chem. Sect., European Co. for the Chem. Processing of Irradiated Fuels (EUROCHEMIC), Belgium, 1959-61; Bd. of Dirs., ibid, 1966-72; Hd., Chem. Dept., Cekmece Nuclear Rsch. Ctr., Istanbul, 1961-72; Edit. Bd., Chimica Acta Turcica. Mbrships: Fellow, Inst. of Physics, London, U.K., 1965; Nat. Geographic Soc., U.S.A., 1970. Author of about 40 papers on original work in field. Hons: Sci. Prize, Sci. & Tech. Rsch. Coun. of Turkey, 1966; Cert. of Merit, Am. Chem. Soc., Chem. Abstracts Serv., 1972. Address: Kimya Fakültesi. Teknik Universite, Tesvikiye, Istanbul, Turkey. 56.

TALBERT, Marijo Lee (Mrs. Charlie Joe Talbert), b. 7 Nov. 1929. Educator. Educ: B.A., Blue Mt. Coll., 1950; M.Ed., Univ. of Southern Miss., 1961; D.Ed., Fla. St. Christian Coll., 1972. Appts: Tchr., Phila H.S., Miss., 1950-; Tchr., Claiborne Elem., New Orleans, La., 1953-; Tchr., Northside Elem. Schl., Bogalusa, 1959-. Mbrships. incl: Sec., La. Tchrs. Assn.; Assn. Classroom Tchrs.; Assn. Tchr. Educ.; Nat. Reading Coun.; Rotary Aux.; Am. Legion Aux.; Theta Gamma Chapt., Kappa Delta Phi; Alpha Psi Omega; Beta Sigma Phi; Bogalusa Garden Guild; Latin Club; Mill Town Players; Mtn. Masqueraders; ARC; Marine Officers Wives Club, New Orleans; 1st Bapt. Ch.; Pearl River Chmbr. of Comm. Aux. Hons: Key to City of Bogalusa; Key to the City of New Orleans. Address: 826 Mississippi Ave., Bogalusa, LA 70427, U.S.A. 125.

TALKINGTON, Perry Clement, b. 28 Aug. 1909. Physician. Educ: Howard Coll., Birmingham, Ala., 1926-27; Baylor Univ., Waco, Tex., 1927-29; M.D., Baylor Univ. Coll. of Med., Dallas, Tex., 1934. Appts. incl: Staff, Timberlawn Sanitarium, 1938-; Pres., ibid, 1949-65; Psych.-in-Chief & Chmn. of Bd., 1949-68; Sr. Cons. in Psych., 1968-; Attending Staff, Baylor Hosp., Baylor Univ. Med. Ctr., Dallas, Tex., 1938-; Chief-of-Staff, Psych., ibid, 1955-69; Clin. Prof. of Psych., Univ. of Tex., Southwestern Med. Schl., 1969-; Pvte. Prac. of Psych., 1938-. Mbrships. incl: AMA; Pres., Am. Psych. Assn.; Pres., Nat. Assn. of Pvte. Psych. Hosps.; Pres., Soc. of Med. Consultants to Armed Forces; Pres., Inst. for Advancement of Mental Hlth. Admin. Contbr. to num. med. jrnls. Address: 4645 Samuell Blvd., Dallas, TX 75228, U.S.A. 2, 7, 17, 112.

TALMI, Igal, b. 31 Jan. 1925. Professor of Physics. Educ: M.Sc., Hebrew Univ. of Jerusalem, 1947; Dr.Sc.Nat., Swiss Fed. Inst. of Technol., Zurich, 1952. Appts: Vis. Fellow, Princeton Univ., U.S.A., 1952-54; Vis. Assoc. Prof., ibid, 1956-57; Vis. Prof., 1961-62 & 1966-67; Weizmann Inst. of Sci., Rehovot, Israel, 1954-; Prof. of Physics, ibid, 1958-; Hd.,

Dept. of Nuclear Physics, 1967-; Dean, Fac. of Physics, 1970-. Mbrships: Israel Phys. Soc.; Fellow, Am. Phys. Soc.; Israel Acad. of Scis. & Humanities. Publs: Nuclear Shell Theory (w. A. de-Shalit), 1963; Num. publs. in theoretical nuclear physics in sci. jrnls. & proceedings of confs. Hons: Weizmann Prize, 1962; Israel Prize, 1965; Rothschild Prize, 1972. Address: The Weizmann Inst. of Sci., Rehovot, Israel. 50.

TAMBOURAS, Alexander, b. 2 July 1912. Company Executive. Educ: Athens Univ. Law Schl., Greece. Appts. incl: Co-Fndr. & Asst. Mgr., Aspis-Pronia Ins. Co., 1945; Mgr., ibid, 1956; Gen. Mgr., 1965; Pres., 1969; Co-Fndr., w. INA Corp., Interam. Life Ins. Co.; Fndr., Tambouras Org. Co. Inc., 1962 (holding co. of Tambouras Org. Grp.); currently Chmn. of Bd., Pres. & Chief Exec. Off., Tambouras Org. Inc. Mbrships. incl: Chmn., Ins. Inst., Athens, 1963; Helenic Ins. Assn.; Chmn., Assn. of Reps. of Ins. Cos. operating in Greece, 1962-66, '67-68; Rep. of Greece, Int. Ins. Congress, Berlin, European Econ. Community's Permanent Comm. of Insurers, European Ins. Comm.; V.P., Greece, Soc. of Int. Dev.; Bd. Dirs., Int. Ins. Seminars; Bd. Electors, Ins. Hall of Fame. Publs. incl: The Inside Story of the Greek Insurance Market, 1962; Greek Insurance Overshadowed by a De Facto Bank-Imposed Monopoly, 1968. Address: 4 Othonos St., Athens 118, Greece. 43.

TAMBURINE, Jean, b. 20 Feb. 1930. Artist; Designer; Author. Educ: Traphagen, N.Y., 1948-49; Art Students' League, N.Y., 1948-50. Appts: Designer, Norcross Inc., N.Y.C., 1948-50; Freelance Painter, Sculptor, Author, Illustrator, Book Designer, 1950-; Designer, Rust Craft, Dedham, Mass., 1955-57. Mbrships. incl: Authors' Guild; Women's Nat. Book. Assn.; Allied Artists of Am. Author, Designer & Illustrator of Publs: Almost Big Enough, 1963; I Think I Will Go to the Hospital, 1965; How Now, Brown Cow, 1967. Illustrator, num. other books. Portrait, landscape, still-life painting & sculpture commns. Recip., var. painting prizes. Address: The Bertolli Studio, 73 Reynolds Dr., Meriden, CT, U.S.A. 5, 6, 57.

TAMMINEN, Kalevi Reino, b. 5 Apr. 1928. Professor. Educ: Dr.Phil., 1967; Dr.Theol., 1967. Appts: Lectr., Tchrs. Trng. Coll., Savonlinna, 1952-54 & Tchrs. Coll., Helsinki, 1961-62; Sec., Pedagogical Matters, Luth. Ch. of Finland; Asst. in Practical Theol., Univ. of Helsinki, 1958-68; Lectr. in Pedagogy, ibid, 1967-70; Prof. of Relig. Educ. (Pedagogy of Relig.), 1970-. Mbrships: Chmn., Union, of Christian Tchrs. in Finland. Publs: Kansakoulun uskonnonopetus vuosisadan vaihteen murroksessa, 1967; Kansakoulun uskonnon opetussuunnitlema vuosina 1912-39, 1967. Address: c/o Univ. of Helsinki, Inst. of Practical Theology, Neitsytpolku 1 b, SF-00140 Helsinki 14, Finland. 43, 134.

TAN Kok-Seng, b. 6 Apr. 1939. Author. Publs: Son of Singapore, The Autobiography of a Coolie, 1972; Man of Malaysia, 1974. Address: 684-F Commonwealth Dr., Singapore, 3.

TAN, Liat, University Professor. Educ: B.Sc., Univ. of Amsterdam, Netherlands, 1953; M.Sc., Univ. of Munster, Germany, 1955; D.Sc., Univ. of Freiburg, 1958. Appts. incl: Rsch. Sci., Union Chimique Belge, Brussels, Belgium, 1960-62; Rsch. Assoc., Laval Univ., Quebec, Canada, 1962-63; Patent Examiner, Govt. of Canada, Ottawa, 1963-66; Rsch. Assoc., Instr., Univ. of Tex. Med. Fac., Galveston, U.S.A., 1966-67; Asst. Prof., Univ. of Sherbrooke Med.

Fac., Canada, 1967-70; Assoc. Prof., ibid. 1970-. Mbrships. incl: N.Y. Acad. Scis.; Sigma Xi; Canadian Biochem. Soc.; Belgian Chem. Soc.; AAAS. Author of sci. publs. Hons. incl: Nat. Rsch. of Canada Postdoc. Fellowships, 1962-63; Robert A. Welch Fellow, 1966-67. Address: Dept. of Biochem., Univ. of Sherbrooke, Fac. of Med., Sherbrooke, P.Q., Canada. 6, 14.

TANASE, Alexandru, b. 16 Nov. 1923. Professor of Philosophy. Educ: B.A., Univ. of Jassy, Rumania, 1950; Ph.D., Univ. of Bucharest, 1962; Doctor Docent, ibid, 1971. Appts: Instr., Univ. of Jassy, 1950-53; Hd., Rsch. Dept., Inst. of Philos., Rumanian Acad., 1955; Assoc. Prof., Schl. of Soc. & Pol. Scis. "Stefan Gheorghiu", 1957-58; Chmn., Dept. of Philos., Conservatoire "Ciprian Proumbescu", 1968; Counsellor, Rumanian Nat. Coun. of Sci. Rsch., 1966; Sec. for Soc. Scis. & Humanities, Rumanian Nat. Comm., UNESCO, 1971; Dir., Inst. of Philos., Bucharest, 1971. Mbrships: Rumanian Acad. of Soc. & Pol. Scis., 1970; Int. Humanist & Ethical Union, 1966; V.P., Rumanian Nat. Comm.-for Philos., 1972; Exec. Coun., Rumanian Assn. for Pol. Scis., 1970. Publs. incl: Cultura si religie, 1973; Culture-civilization-humanisme, 1974; Cultura si umanism, 1974. Hons: Vasile Conta Prize, Rumanian Acad., 1964; Order of Sci. Merit, 3rd degree, 1966. Address: Inst. of Philos., 6 Bd. Ilie Pintilie, Bucharest, Romania.

TANGRI, Shanti S., b. 1 Feb. 1928. Professor of Economics. Educ: B.Sc. & M.A., Punjab Univ., India, 1947 & '49; Ph.D., Univ. of Calif., U.S.A., 1961. Appts. incl: Lectr., E. Punjab Univ. Coll., 1950-53; Assoc. then Lectr., Univ. of Calif., U.S.A., 1957-60; Asst. Prof., Southern Meth. Univ., 1961-63; Rsch. Assoc., Univ. of Mich., 1964-70; Assoc. Prof., Wayne State Univ., 1963-70. Mbrships: S. Asia Regional Council, 1969-72; Assn. for Asian Studies. Publs: Hamare Ganv, 1950; Command versus Demand: Systems for Economic Growth (ed.), 1967; Co-ed. (w. H.P. Gray), Capital Accumulation & Economic Development, 1967 & Population or Progress: Development Dilemma, 1970; Contbr., profl. publs. Recip., educ. fellowships. Address: Livingston Coll., Rutgers Univ., New Brunswick, NJ 08903, U.S.A.

TANGUMA, Ramon Hector, b. 22 Mar. 1939. Educational Administrator. Educ: B.A., N. Tex. State Univ., Denton, U.S.A., 1960; M.A., Tex. A. & I. Univ., Kingsville, 1970. Appts. incl: Engl. & Speech Tchr., Secondary Schl., Benavides, Tex., 1960-66; Engl. Speech & Drama Tchr., Secondary Schl., San Diego, Tex., 1966-69; Speech & Hearing Therapist, Elem. Schl., ibid, 1969-70; Instr. (Educ.), Tex. A. & I. Univ., Kingville, 1971-72; Title VII ESEA Bilingual Prog. Dir., San Diego Independent Schl. Dist., 1972-73; Grad. Ldrship. Trng. Prog. Coord., Dept. of Educl. Admin., Univ. of Tex. at Austin, 1973-74. Mbrships. incl: NEA; Pres., Benavides Local Unit, Tex. State Tchrs. Assn., 1963, Pres., San Diego Local Unit, 1967; Tex. Assn. of Bilingual Educ.; Tex. Assn. of Mexican-Am. Educators; V.P., San Diego Local Unit, PTA, 1968; Phi Delta Kappa. Author, The Relationship Between the Affective & the Cognitive Domain in English & Spanish. Recip., Residential Yr. Fellowship, Univ. of Tex. at Austin, 1970-71. Address: 409 S. Perez St., San Diego, TX 78384, U.S.A. 57.

TANKSLEY, M. Hollis, b. 22 Mar. 1937. Physician. Educ: B.A., Piedmont Coll., Demorest, Ga., 1962; D.O., Coll. of Osteopathic Med. & Surg., 1968; Rotating Internship., Dr.'s Hosp., Tucker, Ga., 1968-69;

Inst. of Comprehensive Med., LA, Calif., 1972. Appts: Elected Mbr., Union Co. Schl. Bd., 1970-; Licensed by written bd., Ga., Fla., Mo., N.C.; Past Chief of Staff, Union Gen. Hosp.; Chief of Staff, Blairsville Gen. Hosp.; Chmn., Bd. of Dirs., ibid; F.A.A. Med. Examiner; Past Mbr., Bd. of Hlth. of Union Co. Mbrships: Am. Osteopathic Assn.; Ga. & N. Ga. Osteopathic Med. Assns.; Coll. of Gen. Practitioners; Dipl., Nat. Bd. of Examiners; Civil Air Patrol; Wing Med. Examiner, State of Ga.; Union Co. Lions Club. Hons: Grad. Magna Cum Laude, Piedmont Coll., 1962; Special Awards for exceptional contbns., Med. Schl., 1. Psych., 2, Harrison Alcoholic & Drug Abuse Ctr. & 3. Biochem. Address: Hospital St., Blairsville, GA 30512, U.S.A. 46, 125.

TANNER, Leon George, b. 10 Sept., 1906. Barrister. Educ: LL.B., Univ. of Sydney, 1928; LL.M., ibid, 1971. Appts: called to Bar of New S. Wales, 1934; Metropolitan Crown Prosecutor, 1954; Dpty. Sr. Crown Prosecutor, 1969; Sr. Crown Prosecutor, New S. Wales, 1973. Mbrships: New S. Wales Bar Assn.; Aust. Acad. of Forensic Scis. Recip. appointment as Queen's Counsel, 1969. Address: Crown Prosecutor's Chambers, P.O. Box 579, Darlinghurst, Australia, N.S.W. 2010. 23.

TANOUS, Helene. b. 22 Oct. 1939. Physician. Educ: B.A., Marymount Coll., Tarrytown, N.Y., 1961; Postgrad., Univ. of Tex., Austin, 1961-63; M.D., Univ. of Tex. Med. Schl., Galveston, 1967. Appts: Intern, Univ. of Southern Calif., Schl. of Med., 1967-68; Res., Radiol., ibid, 1969-71; Instr., Diagnostic Radiol., 1971-72; Pvte. Prac., L.A., 1972-73; Asst. Prof., Diagnostic Radiol., Baylor Coll. of Med., Houston, Tex., 1973-; Dir., Med. Student Elective, Diagnostic Radiol., Ben Taub Hosp. Mbrships: Am. Med. Womens Assn.; Deleg., Int. Meeting, Paris, France, 1972; Student Am. Med. Assn.; Dipl., Am. Bd., Radiol. in Diagnostic Radiol., 1972. Address: Radiol. Dept., Baylor Coll. Med., Houston, TX 77025, U.S.A. 5, 138.

TANYOL, Cahit, b. 1914. Professor of Sociology. Educ: Grad., Inst. of Educ., Ankara, Turkey, 1935; Grad, Fac. of Human Scis., Istanbul Univ., 1944; Doctorate, Sociol., ibid, 1948. Appts: Coll. Tchr., Yozgat, 1936-37, Corum, 1937-38, Izmir, 1938-40, Istanbul, 1940-44; Asst., Istanbul Univ., 1944-50; Assoc. Prof., ibid, 1950-60; Prof., 1960-; Dir., Sociological Inst. Mbrships: Sociological Soc.; Turkish-Engl. Cultural Assn.; Soc. for the Diffusion of Liberal Ideas. Publs. incl: Art & Morality; Social Morality; Epopee of the Foundation of the Ottoman Empire & Constantinople's Conquest; Dialogue on Sociological Questions; Contbns. to newspapers & scientific jrnls. Address: Sociological Institute, Istanbul University, Istanbul, Turkey.

TANYOLAC, Necmettin, b. 10 Sept. 1918. Educator; Electrical Engineer. Educ: B.S.E.E., Robert Coll., Istanbul, 1943; M.S.E.E., Purdue Univ., 1945; Ph.D., ibid, 1949. Appts: Dir.,Org. Mech. & Chem. Inds. Inc., Ankara, 1950-53; 1st Sec. Gen., Turkish Standard Inst., 1953-55; 1st Sec. Gen. & Acting Pres., Middle E. Tech. Univ., Ankara, 1955-57; Prof., Dept. of Elec. Engrng. & Dir. of Rsch. Ctr., Robert Coll., Istanbul, 1957-71; Prof. in Elec. Engrng. & Chmn., Bd. of Dirs of Rsch. Ctr., Boğaziçi Univ., Istanbul, 1971-. Mbrships: incl: Sci. Comm., Min. of Defense; Fndr., Bd. Mbr., Turkish Mgmt. Inst.; Bd., Turkish Standard Inst.; N.Y. Acad. of Sci.; Bio-med. Engrng. Assn.; AAUP; Turkish Cancer Assn. Contbr. to profl. jrnls. Hons. incl: Disting. Serv. Award, M.K.E., 1954; Rsch. Grant & Award, NATO,

1965; NATO Award, 1966. Address: Boğaziçi University, Istanbul, Turkey. 43, 104.

TANZER, Abraham Herman, b. 13 Oct. 1935. Rabbi; Rector. Educ: Rabbinical Dip., Rabbinical Coll., Telshe, Wickliffe, Ohio, U.S.A.; Post-Grad. Schl., Telshe, Kolal P.6. Schl. Appts: Lectr., Hebrew Acad. of Cleveland, U.S.A.; currently Rector, Rosh Yeshiva, Yeshiva Coll. of S. Africa, incorporating Solomon L. Brunner Rabbinical Acad., Yeshiva Coll. Boys' H.S., Yeshiva Nursery Schl., Menora Girls' H.S., Primary Schls., & Nursery Schl.; Rabbi, Glenhazel Area Hebrew Congregation. Mbrships: Chmn., Hanhala (Mgmt.) Yeshiva Coll. Schls.; Exec. Comm. Mbr., Rabbinical Assn. of S. Africa; Exec. Comm. Mbr., Mizrachi Org., S. Africa. Address: P.O. Box 6098, Johannesburg, Repub. of S. Africa. 55.

TANZER, Charles, b. 4 Dec. 1912. Science Educator. Educ: B.S., L.I. Univ., 1933; M.S., N.Y. Univ., 1936; Ph.D., ibid, 1941; Additional studies at Columbia Univ. & Univ. of Vt. Appts: Tchr. of Sci., N.Y.C. High Schls., 1936-49; Chmn., Sci. Dept., Seward Park H.S., 1949-56; Prin., Jr. High Schls., N.Y.C., 1957-65; Coord., Scis., & Prof. of Educ., Hunter Coll., 1965-73; Adjunct Prof., Columbia, N.Y., & Educl. Cons., L.I. Univs., 1946-. Mbrships. incl: Former Chmn., Biol. Chairmen's Assn.; N.Y.C. Br., Am. Soc. for Microbiol.; Nat. Assn. of Biol. Tchrs. Author of publs. in field. Hons. incl: Meritorious Serv. Award, Am. Cancer Soc., 1973. Address: 600 W. 218th St., N.Y., NY 10034, U.S.A. 6, 14, 141.

TAPFER, Siegfried, b. 9 July 1900. Gynaecologist. Educ: Dr.med., Med. Univ., Innsbruck, Austria, 1924. Appts: Pathological Inst., Univ. of Vienna, 1925; Ops. student, Surg. Clin., Leipzig, 1926; Volunteer Physn., Univ. Women's Clin., Innsbruck, 1927; Asst., Women's Clin., Erfurt, 1928-29; Asst., Univ. Women's Clin., Innsbruck, 1929; Lectr. in ob. & gyn., 1938; Prof., 1943; Bd. of Dirs., Univ. Women's Clin., Innsbruck, 1944; Dean, Med. Fac., Innsbruck, 1955-56; Vice Chancellor, Univ. of Innsbruck, 1960-61. Mbrships: Hon. mbr., Osterreichische Gesellschaft für Geburtshilfe & Gynaekologie, 1971; Hon. mbr., Deutsche Gesellschaft für Gynaekologie, 1972. Publs. incl: Technische Vorteile bei den typischen gynaekologischen Operationen, 3 edits., translated into Engl. & Spanish; Contbr. to Biologie & Pathologie des Weibes, by Seitz-Amreich. Hons: Chevalier, Ordre de la Santé Publique, France, 1950; Grand silver medal of hon. for servs. to Repub. of Austria, 1968. Address: Kaiser Josephstr. 15, Innsbruck, Austria.

TAPLIN, Walter, b. 4 Aug. 1910. Journalist. Educ: Univ. of Southampton, 1930-33; The Queen's Coll., Oxford Univ., 1933-36. Appts: Tutor-Org. for Adult Educ., W. Hampshire & E. Dorset, 1936-38; Asst. Ed., The Economist, London, 1938-40; Ministry of Food, 1940-42; Office of War Cabinet, Ctrl. Statl. Off., 1942-45; Asst. Ed., The Spectator, 1946-53; Ed., ibid, 1953-55; Sr. Econ., Iron & Steel Bd., 1955-57; Rsch. Fellow, L.S.E., 1957-61; Ed., Accountancy, 1961-71; Ed., Accoutning & Business Research, 1971-. Publs: Advertising: A New Approach, 1960; Origin of Television Advertising, 1961; (w. J.C. Carr) History of the British Steel Industry, 1962. Address: Kent Hatch Lodge, Crockham Hill, Edenbridge, Kent, U.K. 1, 3, 139.

TAPP, Gerald LaVaughn, b. 9 Aug. 1925. Corporation Executive. Educ: Memphis Schl. of Comm. & Jackson State Coll. Appts. incl: Pres., Millbranch Corp., Memphis, Tenn., 1965-; Pres., Apt. Devs., Inc., Jackson, ibid, 1965-; V.P., Golden Chain Motels, Inc., Memphis, 1965-; current; Pres. & Chmn. of Bd. of Jackson Fast Foods, Inc., 1967-; Pres. & Chmn. of Bd. of J's Enterprisee Inc., 1967-; Pres. & Chmn. of Bd. of J's Steakhouses, Inc., 1967-; Mbr. of Bd. & Sec.-Treas., Springbrook Lake Estates, Inc., 1972-; Pres. of Trailer Travel, Inc., 1972-. Mbrships: Advsry. Bd., Salvation Army, Jackson, 1963; Bd. of Dirs., Nat. Assn. of Home Bldrs. of U.S., 1967-70; Pres. of Area Homebldrs., 1970. Address: 2267 Humboldt Hwy., Jackson, TN 38301, U.S.A.

TAPPÉ, A. Anthony, b. 12 Aug. 1928. Architect; Town Planner. Educ: B.S.Arch., Univ. of Va. Charlottesville, 1952; M.Arch., M.C.P., MIT, 1958. Appts. inc. Planner & Archt., Archts. Collab., Cambridge, Mass., 1958-61; Instr., Dept. of City Planning, MIT, ibid, 1959-60; Ptnr., Huygens & Tappe Inc., Boston, 1962-; Archtl. Cons., Bur. of Lib. Extension, Commonwealth of Mass., 1966-. Mbrships. incl: Am. Inst. Archts.; Boston Soc. Archts.; Am. Inst. Planners; Am. Soc. Planning Officials; ALA; V.P. & Regional Dir., Guild for Relig. Archth. Works incl: Relig. Facilities Ctr., Columbia, Md., 1971; N.H. Coll., Manchester, 1971; Franklin Park Zoo, Boston, 1973. Author, Guide to Planning a Library Building, 1967. Hons. incl: Brookline Bldg. Commn., 1971; Back Bay Archtl. Commn., 1973. Address: Huygens & Tappé Inc., 462 Boylston St., Boston, MA 02116, U.S.A. 2, 6.

TAPSELL, Robert Frederick, b. 3 Aug. 1936. University Administrator. B.A., Univ. of London, 1963. Appts: Admnstr., Univs. of Manchester, 1964-66, E. Anglia, 1966-69, Essex, 1969-74, Murdoch, W.A., Australia, 1974-. Publs: The Year of the Horsetails, 1967; The Unholy Pilgrim, 1968; Shadow of Wings, 1972. Address: c/o Murdoch Univ., W.A., Australia 6153. 3.

TARANTOLA, Charlsie Lovell Bradshaw, b. 16 Aug. 1920. Secondary Science Teacher. Educ: B.S., Smith Hughes N. Tex. State Tchrs. Coll., Dention, 1945; M.S. Va. Polytechnic Inst. & State Univ., Blacksburg, 1974. Appts. incl: Muenster Pub. Schl., Tex., 1941-43; Breakenridge Independent Schl., Tex., 1945; Sasebo, Japan, Am. Dependent Schl., 1947-49; Glenhausen Pub. Schl., Germany, 1951-54; Pemberton Pub. Schls., N.J., 1954; Va. elem. schls., Ft. Myer & Oakridge, 1957-72; Thomas Jefferson Jr. H.S., Arlington, Va., 1972-. Mbrships. incl: K-12 Sci. Comm.; Outdoor Educ. Assn.; 1st V.P., Alpha Delta Soc.; Publicity Chmn., Iota State, Delta Kappa Gamma Soc.; var. local comms. for tchrs. Hons. incl: Human Resource Award, Lib. of Human Resources Am. Bicentennial Rsch. Inst., 1973. Address: 515 N. Longfellow St., Arlington, VA 22203, U.S.A. 5, 7, 15, 132.

TARBELL, D(ean) Stanley, b. 19 Oct. 1913. Professor of Chemistry. Educ: A.B., Harvard Univ., Cambridge, Mass., 1934; A.M., ibid, 1935; Ph.D., 1937. Appts: Asst., Radcliffe Coll., Cambridge, Mass., 1936-37; Postdoctoral Fellow, Univ. of Ill., 1937-38; Mbr., Chem. Fac., Univ. of Rochester, N.Y., from Instr. to Dept. Chmn. & Houghton Prof., 1938-67; Disting. Prof., Chem., Vanderbilt Univ., Nashville, Tenn., 1967-; R.C. Fuson Lectr., Univ. of Nev., 1972. Mbrships: Am. Chem. Soc.; Chem. Soc. of London; Hist. of Sci. Soc.; Nat. Acad. of Scis.; Am. Acad. of Arts & Scis. Publs: About 200 rsch. papers, structural & theoretical organic chem., & hist. of chem. Recip., C.H. Herty Medal, 1973. Address: Dept.

of Chemistry, Vanderbilt University, Nashville, TN 37215, U.S.A. 2, 14, 34.

TARBOX, Frederick Charles, Jr., b. 11 May 1942. Computer Company Executive. Educ: B.S., Case Inst. of Technol., 1964; Ohio State Univ., 1964-65; N.C. State Univ., 1967. Appts: Owner, Upper Arlington Lawn Serv., Columbus, Ohio, 1951-60; Engr., Columbus & S. Ohio Elec. Co., 1960-65; Plant Engr., Carolina Power & Light Co., 1965-67; Pres., Hydra Computer Corp., Raleigh, N.C., 1967-. Mbrships: Am. Soc. Mech. Engrs.; Alpha Phi Epsilon. Address: 300 Cedar Crest Ct., Raleigh, NC 27609, U.S.A. 7.

TARHAN, Münip, b. 25 Aug. 1927. Notary Public; Doctor in Law. Educ: Law Fac., Univ. of Ankara, 1946-50; Dr. in Law, Paris Univ. Schl. of Law, France, 1955; further studies, Inst. of Int. Jurisprudence. Appts. incl: Dpty. Commercial Attaché, Turkish Embassy, Paris, 1954-55; Reserve Off., Turkish armed forces, Ankara, 1955; Pvte. Law Prac., Istanbul, 1958; Advsr., Repub. of Turkey Agricultural Bank, 1958; Dept. Chief, P.R. & Tourism Dept., Chmbr. of Comm., Istanbul, 1962; 6th Notary Pub., & Mbr., Provincial Tourism Comm. & Standing Commn., Istanbul, 1962; currently engaged, notorial affairs. Mbr., profl. & soc. orgs. Publs: Legal Status of Foreigners in Turkey, 1955; Working Security at Industrial Plants, 1960; The Economic Policy of Tourism Industry, 1964. Contbr., sci. & rsch. articles, profl. publs. Address: Istanbul Altinci Noteri, Sirkeci Büyük Postahane karsisi Vlora Han, Istanbul, Turkey.

TARKOVSKY, Andrei Arsenievitch, b. 4 Apr. 1932. Director & Screen Writer. Educ: Middle Musical Schl.; Middle Art Schl.; All-Union State Inst. of Cinematography (Direction Dept.). Appts. incl: Worker & Collector, Geological Expedition, Siberia, 1952-54; Dir., Mosfilm Studio, 1961-. Mbrships. incl: Trade Union Workers of Culture; Film-Maker's Assn. (Direction). Productions incl: The Road-Roller & The Violin (Dir. & Screen Writer), 1961; Ivan's Childhood (Dir.), 1962; Andrei Rubler, 2 parts (Dir. & Co-Screen Writer), 1966/71; Solaris, 2 parts (Dir. & Co-Screen Writer), 1972; The Mirror (Dir. & Co-Screen Writer), 1974. Recip. of many major film prizes at int. Film Festivals & Hon. title, One Disting. in Art, 1974. Address: Orlovo-Davidovsky 2/5 ap. 108, Moscow 1-41, U.S.S.R.

TARLATZIS, B. Constantine, b. 5 April 1909. Professor. Educ: D.V.M., Brussels, Belgium. Appts: Jr. Veterinary Off., Dept. of Trikala, Thessaly, 1936; Chief, Lab. of Biol. Prods., Veterinary Bacteriol. Inst., Min. of Agric., Athens, 1943; Asst. Prof., Athens Coll. of Agric., 1951; Professor, 1965, Vice-Rector, 1970-. Mbrships: Pres., Hellenic Veterinary Med. Soc.; Hellenic Soc. of Eugenics; Hellenic Soc. for Rsch. & Prevention of Pollution; Hellenic Soc. for Protection of Nature; Royal Yacht Club of Greece; Hellenic Touring & Automobile Club. Publs: Over 50 papers in Greek, U.S., French & Belgian jrnls; 3 manuals on comparative anat. comparative physiol. & hygiene of domestic animals, 1974. Hons: War Medal 1940-41; Silver Cross, Royal Order of Phoenix. w. Sabres; Golden Cross, Royal Order of Phoenix. Address: Ergotimou St. 17, Athens, 516, Greece. 43.

TARLO, Hyman, b. 17 Sept. 1921. Professor of Law. Educ: LL.B., M.A., Univ. of Dublin; Solicitor, Ireland; Barrister & Solicitor, Vic. & Australia. Appts: Solicitor, pvte. prac., Dublin, 1945-56; Lectr., Inc. Law Soc. of

Ireland, 1951-56; Sr. Lectr., Canberra Univ. Coll., Australia, 1957-60; Sr. Lectr., Australian Nat. Univ., 1960-64; Sub-Dean, Fac. of Law, ibid, 1960-62; Rdr., ibid, 1964-65; Prof., Univ. of Qld., 1966-; Dean, Fac. of Law, ibid, 1967-69. Mbrships: Exec. Comm., Commonwealth Legal Educ. Assn., London; Past Pres., Australasian Univ. Law Schls. Assn.; Soc. of Pub. Tchrs. of Law. Publs: A.C.T. Company Law, 1959; Lswyers in the Making, 1967. Also contbr. to profl. jrnls. Hons: Fndn. Schol., Trinity Coll., Univ. of Dublin, 1942; 1st Class Moderatorship, ibid, 1943; Findlater Schol., Inc. Law. Soc. of Ireland, 1945; Travel Fellowship, Carnegie Corp. of N.Y., 1963. Address: Law School, Univ. of Qld., St. Lucia, Brisbane, Qld., Australia 4067. 23, 128.

TARNOKY, András Lászió, b. 14 Sept. 1920. Clinical Biochemist. Educ: Minta Schl. Budapest; Univs. of Manchester & London, U.K.; Ph.D., F.R.I.C., F.R.C. Path. Appts: Rsch. Asst., Postgrad. Med. Schl., Hammersmith Hosp., London, 1945; Biochemist, Grp. Lab., Mile End Hosp., London, 1948-51; Biochemist, Royal Berkshire Hosp., Reading, 1951-. Mbrships: Past Sec., Assn. of Clin. Biochems.; Biochemic. Soc.; Royal Coll. of Pathologists; Royal Inst. of Chem.; Assn. of Clin. Pathologists. Publs: Clinical Biochemical Methods, 1958; Contbr. to books & sci. jrnls. Address: Royal Berkshire Hosp., Reading RG1 5AN, U.K. 3.

TARNOPOLSKY, Walter S., b. 1 Aug. 1932. Professor of Law. Educ: B.A., Univ. of Sask., 1953, LL.B., 1957; A.M., Columbia Univ., 1955; LL.M., Univ. of London, U.K., 1962. Appts: Coll. of Law, Univ. of Sask., 1959-60, 1963-67; Fac. of Common Law, Univ. of Ottawa, 1962-63; Osgoode Hall Law Schl., York Univ., 1967-68, Acad. V.P., 1972, Prof., 1972-; Prof., Dean of Law, Univ. of Windsor, 1968-72. Mbrships: Sask. Bar, 1960; Law Soc. of Upper Canada, 1970. Publs: The Canadian Bill of Rights, 1966; Contbr. of articles on civil liberties & human rights to var. jrnls. Hons: Newton W. Rowell Fellowship, 1960-62; UN Human Rights Fellow, India & Malaysia, 1970. Address: Osgoode Hall Law Schl., York Univ., 4700 Keele St., Downsview, Ont. M3J 2R5, Canada. 3.

TARRAGONA COROMINA, Enrique, b. 21 Aug. 1950. Business Manager; Lawyer. Educ: Grad. in Law & Econs.,Univ. of Barcelona. Appts: Asst. Mgr.-V.P., Galerias Tarragona S.A., Balaguer (Lerida). Mbrships: Lyon's; Joven Camara de Comercio; Club Dirigentes de Marketing. Publs: Posibilidades comerciales de la region catalana; La empresa multinacional y su influencia en España. Hons: Premio Extraordinario de Licenciatura en Leyes, Fac. de Derecho de Barcelona., 1971-72. Address: Sepulveda, 150, Barcelona-11, Spain. 102.

TARTOUE, Cassie Eugenia, b. 9 June 1931. Writer; Secretary; Art Lecturer. Secretarial appts. with: Prof. of Agric.; Panhandle A. & M. Coll., Alva, Okla.; Wolfe Advt. Agcy,. Utterback Printing Co.; Okla. League for the Blind; Standard Life & Accident Ins. Agcy.; Hartford Ins. Co. Lectr. on husband's work as portrait painter. Mbrships: Idaho Poets & Writers Guild; Okla. Writers Assn.; Cath. Poetry Soc. of Am. Publs. incl: Palette & Palate (cook book); Poems of Nostalgia & Hope; Fields of Harvest; An Embroidery of Words; These Things of Beauty; Poetic Ponderings; One Small Candle; Silver Etchings; Gypsy Shadows; Souvenir; & other books of poetry; Stories, poems & articles in sev. jrnls. & mags. Hons: Critics & Judges Award, for poem, Bringing the Cattle Home, 1967; First place Award, by readers' vote, 1967; Angel Hour Award, for Brotherhood & Peace, 1968. Address: Apt. 311, Hotel Moscow, Moscow, ID 83843, U.S.A. 57.

TARWATER, Ella Floyd, b. 3 Dec. 1894. School Teacher (retd.). Educ: B.S., Univ. of Tenn., Knoxville, 1956. Appts: Tchr., Elem. Schls., Sevier Co., Tenn., 1915-20; Prin., Elem. Schls., ibid, 1920-23; Prin., Shiloh Elem. Schl., Sevier Co., 1942; Employee, Alcoa Aluminum Co., Alcoa, Tenn., 1943-46; Prin. & Tchr., Whites, Knights & Zion Hill Elem. Schls., Sevier Co. Tenn., 1946-58; Tchr., hist. geog. & maths., Sevier Co. H.S., Sevierville, Tenn., 1958-65. Mbrships: Pleasant Hill United Meth. Ch., Sevierville, Tenn., 1906-; Adult & Children's Class Tchr., Class Sec., V.B.S. Tchr., mbr. W.S.C.S., W.M.U. & Administrative Bd. of Ch., ibid; Regent, Spencer Clack Chapt., DAR, 2 yrs.; Tenn. Educ. Assn.; E. Tenn. Educ. Assn.; Am. Hemerocallis Soc.; Whites Home Demonstration Club, Sevierville, Tenn. Hons. incl: Letter of Congratulations from Gov. Frank G. Clement, Tenn., for tchng. in Sevier Co. during a 50 yr. period, 1915-65. Address: Route 5, Sevierville, TN 37862, U.S.A. 125.

TARZIAN, Mary Mangigian. Business Executive; Publisher. Educ: B.S., M.A., Ph.D., Univ. of Pa., 1927, '29, '34. Appts. incl: Co-Fndr., Sec./Treas., V.P., Sarkes Tarzian Enterprises, Bloomington, Ind., 1944-; Sarkes Tarzian Divs., U.S.A., Mexico, Taiwan, India; Mfrs. for Gen. Electric, RCA, Zenith, Magnavox; Radio & TV Stns.; Newspapers incl. Bloomington Courier-Tribune, Martinsville Gazette. Mbrships. incl: Fndr. & Bd. Mbr., Eisenhower Mem. Schlrship. Fndn.; Ind. Mfrs. Assn.; Am. Newspaper Publrs. Assn.; Nat. Assn. Broadcasters; Kappa, Kappa, Gamma; Phi Beta Kappa; Kappa, Kappa, Kappa. Features & edits., Courier-Tribune, Banner-Graphic & other newspapers. Hons. incl: LL.D., Tri-State Coll., Angola, Ind., 1971; Disting. Serv. Award, Int. Who's Who in Community Serv., 1972. Address: 515 Kessler Blvd. W. Dr., Indpls., IN 46208, U.S.A. 2, 8, 57, 123, 132, 138.

TASSIOS, Theodossios P., b. 22 Jan. 1930. Civil Engineer; Professor. Educ: Dip., Civil Eng., 1953, Dr.Eng., 1959, Nat. Tech. Univ., Athens; Study in Paris, 1953-54. Appts: Cons., NATO naval works, Greece, 1956-58; Dir., Bridge Design Off., 1959-62; Gen. Dir., Hellenic Fndn. Co., 1963-64; Prof., Structural Mechanics, Nat. Tech. Univ., Athens, 1965-69; Prof., Reinforced Concrete, ibid, 1969-. Mbrships. incl: Pres., Permanent Conf. of Engrs. of S.E. Europe; Nat. Deleg., European Comm. of Concrete; Brit. Concrete Soc.; Am. Concrete Soc.; Hellenic Humanistic Soc. Publs: Over 60 sci. papers & books in French, Engl., Italian & Greek. Hons: Cross, Royal Order of George 1st, Greece, 1965. Address: Nat. Tech. Univ., 42 Patission St., Athens 147, Greece. 43.

TASZYCKI, Witold, b. 20 June 1898. University Professor. Educ: Ph.D., Jagellonian Univ., Cracow, Poland, 1922; Venia legendi, ibid, 1925. Appts: Asst. Prof., Slavonic Lings., Stefan Batory Univ., Wilno, 1929; Assoc. Prof., Jan Kazimierz Univ., Lwow, 1929-36; Prof., Univ. of Lwow, 1936-41; Prof., Polish Lings & Onomastics, Jagellonian Univ., Cracow, 1946-68; Dir., Dept. of Polish Lang., ibid, 1951-68. Mbrships: Corres., Polish Acad. of Learning; Corres., Polish Acad. of Scis.; Int. Comm. of Onomastics, Louvain; Hon., Polish Ling. Soc. Publs. incl: Papers & Studies on Polish Language, 5 vols., 1958-73; Dictionary of Older Polish Personal Names, 3 vols. Hons: Cmdrs. Cross, Polonia Restituta, 1954; Banner of Labour, 1st class, 1962; Medal, Comm. of

Nat. Educ., 1971. Address: ul Retoryka 20, Krakow, Poland.

TATA, Ray, b. 22 Feb. 1926. Educator. Educ: B.S., Conn. Ctrl. Coll.; M.A., Columbia Tchrs. Coll., N.Y.C.; Cert. of adv. studies in admin., Fairfield Univ. Appts: Instr. of math., Wilton Jr. H.S., Conn., Staples H.S., Westport, ibid; Dir., Westport Pub. Adult Educ., ibid; Dir. of Adult Educ. & Summer Schl. Studies; currently Prin. of Continuing Educ., Adult Educ. & Summer Schl. Mbrships: Rotary Club (chmn. of progs.; chmn. of fellowship comm.); Nat. Assn. for pub. continuing & adult educ.; past pres., Conn. Assn. for pub. continuing & adult educ.; NEA; Conn. Educ. Assn.; Westport Educ. Assm.; Nat. Assn. Secondary Schl. Prins.; Past Pres., Wilton Educ. Assn. Author, Jrnl. article. Address: 7 Pleasant Valley Lane, Westport, CT 06880, U.S.A. 15.

TATE, Evelyn Austin, b. 13 June 1913. Chartered Land Surveyor. Educ: Articled to Mssrs. Abraham, Henriques & Joy, 1932-35; Commissioned Land Surveyor, 1935; Higher Surveying Course, Univ. of Toronto, Canada, 1946-47; Fellow, Royal Inst. Chartered Surveyors, 1960. Appts: Staff Surveyor, Survey Dept., Jamaica, 1939; Sr. Surveyor, ibid, 1950; Asst. Dir. Surveys, Jamaica, 1955; Dpty. Dir. Surveys, ibid, 1963; Dir. of Surveys, 1968; Liaison Off. between Survey Dept., Jamaica & Inter-Am. Geodetic Survey, 1952-72. Mbrships: Chmn., Advsry. Comm. on Trng. of Land Surveyors, 1972; Chmn.. Land Surveyors Bd.; Advsry. Planning Comm., Min. of Mining & Natural Resources, Govt. of Jamaica, 1972; Pl. Names Comm., 1972. Author, paper on role of survey dept. in community. Recip., sev. hons. Address: 6 Montclair Dr., P.O. Box 78, Kingston 6, Jamaica, W. Indies.

TATE, James, b. 8 Apr. 1914. Artist. Educ: Ctrl. Schl. Arts & Crafts, London, U.K., 1946-48. Appts: Proprietor, Tate Studios, James Tate Agcy.; Dir., The City Gents Ld. Property Co. Mbrships: Assoc. Mbr., Royal Soc. Miniature Painters, Sculptors & Gravers, Soc. des Artistes Français; Int. Assn.Art. Faintings incl: Paris Salon (Madonna & Child; Les Petits Pauvres; Orange Pickers; La Vieille Dame); Monte Carlo (Bathers in a Mountain Stream, Gala); Middle E. Tour (Water Wells of the Desert Lands); Contemporary Painters U.K. Tour (Regeneration); London Galls. (Jamboree, Morning Post; The Visitors; The Bathers, Sky Fragment; City of Mosques; A Man & his Dog; Off-watch Gossip; Reflection; Baby Sparrow; Desert City; The Jospeh Conrad; Young Barbary Ape; Canadian Red Squirrel; Destruction of Sodom); also num. works in provincial galls. Hons. incl: Laureat, 8th Grand Prix de Peinture, Cote d'Azur, Nice, France, 1972. Address: Willow House, Ealing Green, London W5 5EN, U.K. 19, 133.

TATHAM, (Mrs.) Julie Campbell, b. 1 June 1908. Christian Science Practitioner; Author. Appts. incl: Asst. Soc. Ed., N.Y. Evening Post; Owner, literary agcy. Publs: The Mongrel of Merryway Farm; The World Book of Dogs; To Nick from Jan; Cherry Ames, Nurse, series of books; Num. articles & short stories in mags.; Religious articles in Christian Sci. jrnls. Address: 130 E. 39th St., N.Y., NY 10016, U.S.A.

TATOMIR, Nicolae, b. 2 Feb. 1914. Writer; University Professor & Administrator. Educ: Fac. of Law, Iassy, 1932-36; Dr. in Law, Univ. of Iassy, 1947. Appts: Admission to Rumanian Bar, 1938; Judge, 1939-48; Prof. of Law, Univ. of Iassy, 1948-, Dean, Fac. of Law, 1952-; Dir. of "New Iassy", review, 1952-. Mbrships: Int.

Assn. Law, The Hague, Netherlands; Pres., Assn. Int. Law, Iassy; Writers Union of Socialist Repub. of Romania; Acad. Soc. & Pol. Scis. Publs. incl: poetry collects., Black Swans, 1936, Carmen Terrestre, 1968, My Book of Clay, 1972; The Manuscript from Marrakech (novel), 1972; Criminality in Literature, 1973; Poems, 1974; translations of Baudelaire & Laforgue. Hons. incl: Ordre de travail 3rd class, 1960; Poetry Prize, Writers Assn., 1968. Address: 14 Palade, Iassy, Romania.

TATT, Lee Kum, b. 23 Mar. 1927. Scientist; Administrator. Educ: B.Sc., Univ. of Malaya, Singapore, 1951; B.Sc. Hons. (Chem.), ibid, 1952; Ph.D., 1955. Appts: Govt. Chem., Singapore, 1954-61; Sr. Clin. Biochem., Min. of Hlth., Singapore, 1962-68; Chmn., Sci. Coun. of Singapore, 1967-; Dpty. Dir., i/c Tech. & Consultancy Servs., Econ. Dev. Bd., 1969-71; Exec. Chmn., Singapore Inst. of Standards & Ind. Rsch., 1969-; Pt.-time Lectr., Univ. of Singapore, 1959-67; Supvsr. of Postgrad. Students, ibid, 1962-71; Exec. Chmn., Engrng. Inds. Dev. Agcy., Singapore, 1970-71; Dir., Fed. Chem. Inds., Singapore, 1968-73; Chmn., Dyno Inds. (S) Pte. Ltd., Singapore, 1973-; Bd. of Govs., Singapore Polytech. Mbrships: Chmn., Singapore Sect.,1961-63, & Fellow, Royal Inst. of Chem.; Singapore Nat. Inst. of Chem.; Fndg. Mbr., Singapore Nat. Acad. of Scis.; Chem. Inst. Can.;Chmn., Standards Coun., Singapore, 1969-. Contbr. of articles on chem. analyses, enzymol., clin. biochem. & ind. rsch. mgmt. to profl. jrnls. Hons: Pub. Admin. Star, 1967, Pub. Admin. Gold Medal, 1973, Singapore Govt.; UN Fellow, 1956-58; US Ldrship. Grantee, 1971. Address: Singapore Inst. of Standards & Ind. Rsch., 179 River Valley Rd., Singapore 6, Repub. of Singapore. 98.

TATTA, Joseph, b. 24 Dec. 1933. School Master. Educ: B.A., Eastern Coll., St. Davids, Pa., 1955; M.A., Univ. of Penn., Phila., 1957; Tchrs. Coll., Temple Univ., Phila., Ap., 1958; Wm. Coe Fellowship to Eastern Coll., St. Davids, Pa., 1959. Appts: Hist. & Lang. Tchr., Haverford Schl., 1958-; Coord., Am. Histl. Film Ctr., 1959-; Main Line Schl. Night Instr., 1960-; Counselor, Haverford Schl. Day Camp, 1968-73. Mbrships: Ed.-in-Chief, Coll. Newspaper, 1953-55; Newman Club, 1951-53; Phi Sigma Kappa; Philos. Club, 1951-55; Lit. Soc., 1954-55; Sports Ed., Coll. Yrbook., 1955; Coll. Student Govt. Rep., 1954-55; Chmn., Coll. Alumni Assn. Bd. of Dirs., 1966-69. Publs: Soviet Justice & Judicial System 1936-56, 1957. Hons. incl: City of Youngstown Serv. Award, 1951; Coll. Alumnus of Yr., 1971. Address: c/o The Haverford School, Lancaster Ave., Haverford, PA 19041, U.S.A. 117, 130.

TAUBE, Herman, b. 2 Feb. 1918. Author; Public Relations Consultant. Appts: Medic & Hosp. Admnstr., Polish Army, Russia & Germnay, WWII; Mbr., Jewish Histl. Commn., Regional Comm. of Liberated Jews in Gross-Hessen, 1946-47; Newswriter, Jewish Daily Forward, Balt., Md., U.S.A., 1947-50; Pvte. Prac., Pub. Rels. & Publicity Servs., Balt., 1950-. Mbrships. incl: Fndr. & Pres., Md. Comm. for New Americans; Co-Fndr., Jewish Cultural Comm., Jewish Community Ctr.; Bd. of Dirs., Hebrew Immigrant Aid Soc.; Dir., Histadrut in Md.; Fndr., Histadrut Coun. of Gtr. Wash.; Wash. Area Dir., Metropol. Div., United Jewish Appeal; Fndr., Club Shalom. Publs: The Unforgotten, 1948; Remember, 1958; Empty Pews, 1959; The Last Train; The Refugees of Red Village; Num. contbns. to Jewish jrnls. & newspapers. Recip., Nat. Achievements Award, Nat. Comm. Labor Israel of Histadrut. Address: 4105 Bel Pre Rd., Rockville, MD 20853. U.S.A. 55.

TAUCHNER, Maximilian, b. 7 May 1917. Lawyer; Journalist. Educ: Magister Juris, Univs. of Cracow & Lvov, Poland, 1940; J.D., Univs. of Munich & Graz, 1957. Appts: Solicitor & Jrnlst., Chief Ed., newspaper Opinia, Poland, until 1950; Solicitor for Restitution Claims, Munich, 1951-; Jrnlist. & Corres., var. newspapers abroad. Mbrships: Chmn., Zionistische Organisation Deutschlands; Chmn., Jüdische Nationalfonds in Deutschland; Chmn., Independent Liberal Zionist Party in Europe; Bd. of Dirs., var. orgs. in Germany. Author of hundreds of publd. articles in newspapers & jrnls. all over the world. 55.

TAVORA, Virgilio (Moraes Fernandes), b. 29 Sept. 1919. Senator & Colonel of Brazilian Army. Educ: Mil. Coll. of Fortaleza; Engrng. course, Mil. Coll. of Realengo & Acutalization course, Superior War Coll., 1953; Hon.Dr., Admin. Coll., Philos. Fac., Fed. Univ. of Ceara. Appts. incl: Fed. Dpty. during 3 legislatures; Traffic & Works Min., 1st Parliamentary Cabinet of Repub.; Rep. of Nat. Democratic Union (UDN); Gov., State of Ceara, 1963-66; V.P., Finance Commn. & Mbr. of Econ., Budget & Nat. Security Commns.; V. Ldr., Govt. in Senate; Sev. positions, Exec. Commn., ARENA (Govt. Pty.). Participated in Nuclear Energy Congresses & Interparliamentary Conf., Rome. Mbrships. incl: Superior War Assn.; Engrng. Club; Ideal Club; Nautic Athletic of Ceara; Congress Club. Publs. incl: Tarron Military Bridges (studies); Northeast's Developing Project; Brazilian Development (1964-1973). Hons. incl: Citizen of many cities of State of Ceara & of Parnaiba, State of Piaui; num. medals inclng. Duque de Caxias, Good Servs., Marechal Hermes (2 golden stars), Peacemaker, Agricl. Merit, Tamandare, "Patriarca", Dandido Rondon, Rio Branco (Grand Official) & Mil. Value. Address: SQS 309 - Bloco C- Apt. 604, 70000 Brasilia, Brazil. 34.

TAYEAU, Francis, b. 24 Nov. 1913. Professor of Medical Biochemistry. Educ: D.Sc., 1939, M.D., 1944, Univs. of Lille & Bordeaux, France. Appts. incl: Asst. Prof., Fac. of Med. & Pharmacy, Univ. of Bordeaux, 1946-50; Lectr., & Prof., without Chair, ibid, 1950; Prof., Med. Biochem., 1950-; Assessor, 1955-61; Dean, 1961-69; Hon. Dean, 1969-. Mbrships: Nat. Acad. of Med.; Past Pres., Nat. Acad. of Scis., Letters & Arts, of Bordeaux; Nat. Corres., Nat. Acad. of Pharmacy. Publs: 278 contbns. to sci. jrnls. & books. Hons. incl: Ph.D., Univ. of Teheran, Iran; Hon. Prof., Nat. San Marcos Univ., Lima, Peru; Grand Cross, Order of St. Sepulcre, 1965; Cmdr., Nat. Order of Senegal, 1965; Off., Nat. Order of Merit; Off., Order of Sepas, Iran, 1966; Off., Scientific Merit, 1967; Off., Legion of Hon., 1968; Cmdr., Nat. Order of Ivory Coast, 1969; Off., Order of the Cedar, Lebanon, 1970. Address: 95 Cours Balguerie-Stuttenberg, 33300 Bordeaux, France. 43, 91.

TAYLOR, Aline Mackenzie. Professor of English Literature. Educ: Ph.D., Bryn Mawr Coll., 1943; Postdoctoral study, var. libs. Appts: Instr. in Engl., Newcomb Coll., Tulane Univ., 1938; Asst. Prof., ibid, 1943; Assoc. Prof., 1949; Prof., 1956; Prof., Coll. of Arts & Scis., Tulane Univ., 1967-. Mbrships: Soc. for Theatre Rsch., London, U.K.; U.S. Int. Sec., Amici Thomae Mori, Anger, France, 1963-73; Sponsor, Soc. for the Preservation of the B.C.P., Vanderbilt Univ.; AAUW. Publs. incl: The Patrimony of James Quin: The Legend & the Facts, in Tulane Studies in Engl., 1958; Dryden's "Enchanted Isle" & Shadwell's "Dominion", in Studies in Philol., 1967. Hons: John Simon Guggenheim Fellowship, 1952; Folger Shakespeare Lib. Fellow, 1963, '65, '67. Address: Dept. of Engl., Coll. of Arts & Scis.,

Tulane Univ., New Orleans, LA 70118, U.S.A. 13, 125.

TAYLOR, Carrie Lee Smith. Radiologic Technologist. Educ: Provident Hosp. Schl. Radiologic Technol., Chgo., Ill., USA, 1946-47. Appts: w. City of Chgo. Bd. Hlth. & Municipal TB Sanitarium, Stock Yards, Kenwood M.T.S. Mercy, M.T.S. Provident Clins., 1948-59; Sr. Radiologic Technologist i/c, Grand Crossing Clin. & Chest Hosp., Cook Co. Hosp., Chgo.. Ill.; Currently w. LA Co. Univ. Southern Calif. Med. Ctr. Acute Unit, Pediatric Pavilion & Psych. Units. Mbrships: Am. Soc. Radiologic Technols.; Am. Registry Radiologic Technols. Author profl. jrnl. article, Useful Magnified Distortion in Apical and Sub-Apical Lesions, 1950; Contbr. Radiographic Exhibit, Am. Soc. Radiologic Technols. Conven., 1949, '50. Awarded 1st Grade, 2 Civil Serv. Exams., Radiologic Technols., City of Chgo. & State of Ill., 1950. Address: 3974 Hillcrest Dr., L.A., CA 90008, U.S.A. 5, 120, 130, 138.

TAYLOR, Charles Alfred, b. 14 Aug. 1922. Professor of Physics. Educ: B.Sc., Queen Mary Coll., Univ. of London, U.K., 1942; Ph.D., Univ. of Manchester Inst. of Sci. & Technol., 1951; D.Sc., 1959. Appts: Admiralty Signals Est., 1942-46; Rsch. Dept., Metro-Vickers Elec. Co., 1946-48; Univ. of Manchester Inst. of Sci. & Technol., 1948-65; Prof. & Hd. Dept. of Phys., Univ. Coll., Cardiff, 1965-. Fellow & V.P., for Educ., Inst. of Phys. Chmn., Tchng. Commn., Int. Union of Crytallography. Publs: Fourier Transforms & X-Ray Diffraction (co-auth.), 1959; Optical Transforms (co-auth.), 1964; The Physics of Musical Sounds, 1965; Sounds of Music, 1974. Address: Dept. of Physics, Univ. Coll., P.O. Box 78, Cardiff, CF1 1XI, U.K. 21.

TAYLOR, Edith Lent (Mrs.), b. 15 Dec. 1913. Educator; Writer. Educ: B.A., Swarthmore Coll.; Columbia & Syracuse Univs.; Univ. of Buffalo. Appts: Vis. Tchr., Newton, Mass. Schls., 1941-42; Engl. Tchr., Garland Jr. Coll., 1945-46; Instr., Univ. of Buffalo, 1946-51; Chmn., Engl. Dept., Dean of Students, Buffalo Sem., 1951-74; Rdr., Educl. Testing Serv., 1955-60; Evaluator, Atlantic States Sec., Coll. & Sec. Schl. Accreditation Bd., 1970. Past Mbrships: N.Y. State Coun. for Tchrs.; Assn. for Coll. Advsrs. Author, The Serpent Under It, 1973. Contbr., Mystery Writers of Am. Anthol., 1974. Address: S-6154 Hunters Creek Rd., South Wales, NY 14139, U.S.A.

TAYLOR, (Rev.) Edwin Llewellyn, b. 3 May 1924. Methodist Minister. Educ: B.D., Univ. of London, U.K. Appts. incl: Meth. Min., Kingstown, St. Vincent, Jamaica, W.I., 1950-51, Tunapuna, Trinidad, ibid, 1951-52, Andros & Windward Mission, Bahamas, 1952-57, Wesley Meth. Ch., Nassau, 1958-67, St. Michael's Meth. Ch., ibid, 1964-67; Sec., Bahamas Dist., 1962-64, Provincial Synod, Meth. Ch., W.I., 1962-67, Conf. of Meth. Ch. in Caribbean & Ams., 1967-70; currently Chmn., Dist. & Gen. Supt., Meth. Ch. in Bahamas, 1970-. Mbrships. incl: Ctrl. Comm., World Coun. Chs., 1968- (comm., div. of World Mission & Evangelism, 1968-); World Meth. Coun., 1966-; V.P., Bahamas Christian Coun., 1972-. Co-Ed., The Constitution & Discipline of the Methodist Church in the Caribbean & the Americas, 1967. Address: Turton House, Windsor Ave., P.O. Box N. 3702, Nassau, Bahamas. 109; 136.

TAYLOR, Elizabeth, b. 27 Feb. 1932. Actress. Films incl: Lassie Come Home, 1942; National Velvet, 1944; Little Women, 1948;

Father of the Bride, 1950; A Place in the Sun, 1950; Ivanhoe, 1951; Beau Brummell, 1954; Raintree County, 1957; Suddenly Last Summer, 1959; Butterfield 8, 1960; Cleopatra, 1963; The VIPs, 1963; The Sandpiper, 1965; Who's Afraid of Virginia Woolf 1966; The Taming of the Shrew, 1967; The Comedians, 1968; Reflections in a Golden Eye, 1968; Secret Ceremony, 1968; The Only Game in Town, 1970. Book, Elizabeth Taylor, published 1966. Recip., Acad. Awards, Butterfield 8 & Who's Afraid of Virginia Woolf. Address: c/o John Springer Associates, 667 Madison Ave., N.Y., NY 10021, U.S.A. 1, 138.

TAYLOR, Ella Louise (Richards) (Mrs. Howarth Taylor), b. 2 Apr. 1925. Corporation Executive; Chemist; Teacher. Educ: B.S., Wheaton Coll., Ill., 1947; Ph.D., Univ. of Ill., 1952. Appts: Tchng. Asst., Wheaton Coll., 1944-47; Chem., Celanese Corp. of Am., Cumberland, Md., 1947-48; Tchng. Asst., Univ. of Ill., 1948-52; Tchr., Hickory Ridge H.S., 1952-53; Sec.-Treas., Taylor Seed Farms, Inc., 1958-; Sec.-Treas., Taylor Seed Processing Plant, Inc., 1958-; Sec.-Treas., Hickory Ridge Farm Supply, Inc., 1962-. Mbrships: Sigma Xi; Sigma Delta Epsilon; Past V.P. & Pres., Ill. Chapt., Iota Sigma Pi; Sigma Pi Sigma. Named Ark. Farm Family of Yr., 1969. Address: R 1, Hickory Ridge, AR 72347, U.S.A. 5, 7, 14, 16, 129, 132, 138.

TAYLOR, Ellen Borden Broadhurst (Mrs. Marvin E. Taylor), b. 18 Jan. 1913. Homemaker; Volunteer Worker. Positions. incl: Mbr., St. Paul's Episcopal Ch., Smithfield, N.C., Life mbr., Nat. Soc. of Colonial Dames of Am., 2578, & Garden Club of N.C., Inc.; Mbr., Action Comm. for the Environment, Nat. Coun. of State Garden Clubs, Inc.; Life mbr., ibid; Regional Roadside Dev. Chmn., S. Atlantic Region; N.C. Gov's Advsry. Comm. on Beautification, 1971-73; Charter mbr. & former Pres., Smithfield Garden Club; Mbr., N.C. Soc. of Co. & Local Histns.; Mbr., Nat. Trust for Historic Preservation; Fndg. mbr., Friends of John F. Dennedy Ctr. for the Performing Arts, Wash. D.C.; Mbr., Bd. of Govs., Elizabethan Garden, Manteo, N.C., 1964-74; Bd. of Dirs., Keep N.C. Beautiful, Inc., 1973-77. Hons: Master Judge of Flower Shows Cert., Nat. Coun. of State Garden Clubs, Inc.; Nat. Accredited Rose Judge, Am. Rose Soc. (selected to judge rose arrangement div., Am. Rose Soc. Nat. Conven., 1973). Address: 616 Hancock St., Smithfield, NC 27577, U.S.A.

TAYLOR, Gerry Mailand, b. 7 July 1913. Libarian. Educ: Farmington State Tchrs. Coll., Me., 1931-32; B.A., 1951, M.A., 1952, Baylor Univ.; M.L.S., Univ. of Tex., 1955. Appts: Served w. U.S. Army, 1940-45; Grad. Lib. Asst., Baylor Univ., 1951-52; Revisor, Grad. Schl. of Lib. Sci., Univ. of Tex., 1953-54; Sr. Lib. Clerk, Law Schl. Lib., ibid, 1954-55; Asst. Libn., Tex. Agricl. & Indl. Coll., 1955-56; Assoc. Libn., Sam Houston State Univ., 1956-66; Lib. Bldg. Cons., City of Huntsville, Tex., 1965-66; Hd. Libn., Ark. State Univ., 1966-. Mbrships: Pres., Ark. State Univ. Chapt., Phi Deleta Kappa; Pres., N.E. Ark. Shrine Club; V.P., N.E. Ark. Schlmasters. Club; ALA; Ark. Lib. Assn., & Pres. of its Coll. & Univ. Div.; Alpha Chi; Phi Beta Mu; Psi Chi; Ark. Coun. on Lib. Educ.; Bapt.; Deacon; all Masonic bodies & 32° Mason & Shriner. Guest ed., vol. 1, issue 1 of Computerized Acquisitions Systems Series; Contbr. to nat. lib. jrnls. e.g., Lib. Resources & Tech. Servs., Coll. & Rsch. Libs., S.Eastern Libn. Recip., Waterman Prize for schol. excellence, 1930. Address: P.O. Box 1017, State Univ., AR 72467, U.S.A. 7, 42, 125.

TAYLOR, Harold McCarter, b. 7 May 1907. University Teacher. Educ: M.Sc., Univ. of Otago, New Zealand, 1928; M.A., Ph.D., Clare Coll., Cambridge, U.K., 1933. Appts: Univ. Lectr., Maths., Cambridge, 1933-45; Served in WWII; Treas., Univ. of Cambridge, 1945-53; Sec.-Gen. of Facs., ibid, 1953-56; Vice-Chancellor, Univ. of Keele, 1961-67; Rede Lectr., Univ. of Cambridge, 1966. Publs: Anglo-Saxon Architecture, 1965; Why Should We Study the Anglo-Saxons, 1966. Hons: CBE, 1955; TD, 1945; Smith Prize, Univ. of Cambridge, 1932; LL.D., ibid, 1966; Hitchcock Medal, Soc. of Archtl. Histns., 1966. Address: 192 Huntingdon Rd., Cambridge CB3 OLB, U.K. 1, 34.

TAYLOR, (Rev.) Ira Moulton, b. 31 Dec. 1921. Minister of Religion. Educ: Caribbean Wesleyan Coll., Jamaica., W.I.; Pelman Inst., U.K.; La Salle Ext. Univ., U.S.A. Appts: Pastor, St. John's Antigua Wesleyan Ch.; Pastor, Trinidad Wesleyan Ch., San Fernando; Evangelist for the Ch. in Caribbean, U.K. & U.S.A.; Supt., Wesleyan Ch., U.S. Virgin Isles; Dist. Pastor, Oakwood Wesleyan Ch., Toronto, Canada; Asst. Supt., Central Canada Conf. of Wesleyan Ch., Canada. Mbrships: Am. Geographic Soc.; Am. Rose Soc.; Antigua Art Soc. Address: 8 Kirkland Blvd., Toronto, Ont., M6A 1E6, Canada. 136.

TAYLOR, Jean Landon, b. 24 Feb. 1902. Retired Professor of Journalism & Photography. Educ: A.B., Western Mich. Univ., Kalamazoo, 1928; A.M., Columbia Univ., N.Y.C., 1940. Appts. incl: Hd., Dept. of Engl., Morgan Pk. Mil. Acad., Chgo., Ill., 1929-45; Dir., Publs. & Photography, Compton Coll., Calif., 1945-67; Cons. in Educ., Claremont Coll., 1962. Mbrships. incl: Bd. of Dirs., V.P., Pres., Southern Sect., Calif. Tchrs. Assn.; Deleg. to Gov.'s & White House Confs. on Educ.; Pres., S.Bay Chapt., Phi Delta Kappa; Nat. Pres., Beta Phi Gamma. Publs: Articles in educl. jrnls. Hons. incl: Gold Key Award, Columbia Univ., 1957; Official Citation, Calif. State Senate, 1967. Address: 4917 Rockbluff Dr., Rolling Hills Estates, CA 90274, U.S.A. 13, 129.

TAYLOR, Jesse Frederick, b. 8 Apr. 1936. Educator. Educ: B.A., Ariz. State Univ., Tempe, U.S.A. 1952; M.A., ibid, 1956; Cand., Ed.D., Counseling Psych., Heed Univ., Fla. Appts: Tech. Instr., USAF, 1952-54; Educ. Advsr. & Instr., Engl., USAF, Japan, 1954-56; Chmn., Humanities Div., Assoc. Prof., Engl. Humanities; Inst., Engl., Dept., Prairie View A & M Coll., 1957-59; Tchng. Asst., Engl. Dept., Ariz. State Univ., Tempe, 1959-60; Instr., Glendale Community Coll., Phoenix, Ariz., 1965-66; Assoc. Prof., Engl. Dept., Lakehead Univ., Thunderbay, Ont., Canada, 1967-68; Dir., Inst. Afro-Am. & Comp. Cultures, Lectr., Cons., Instr., Afro-Am. Culture, 1970; Co-Chmn., Assoc. Prof., Black Studies Dept., 1969-70; Lectr. (Pt.-time), Afro-Am. Lit., Engl. Dept., Univ. Coll., Tulane Univ., 1971-; Dir., Rehab. Prog., Pub. Offenders, New Orleans Area. Mbrships: Fellow, Royal Inst. Anthropol.; Congress Black Profls. in Higher Educ., Austin, Tex.; Coven. Nat. Cath. Conf. Interracial Justice, 1971; Cons., 'Blackness', Paine Coll., EPDA Prog. in Engl., 1971; Contbng. & Advsry. Bd., The Black Scholar (jrnl.); Book Reviews. Address: 3140 New Orleans St., New Orleans, LA 70122, U.S.A. 57.

TAYLOR, John Paul, b. 24 June 1918. Publisher, Editor, Managing Director. Educ: B.S., Purdue Univ., 1939. Appts: Asst.-Assoc. Ed., Ind. & Power Mag., 1939-42; Pres., John Paul Taylor Co., 1942-; Exec. Dir: Indl.

Marketing Assocs., Inc., 1947-; Materials Marketing Assocs., Inc., 1963; Profl. Manufacturers' Agts., Inc., 1968-; CORMAC, Inc., 1971-; Parmar, Inc., 1971-74; Mass Merchandising Distributors' Assn., Inc., 1972-; Co-Fndr. & Sec.-Treas., Probsting, Taylor, Inc., 1948-55; Sec.-Treas., Work-at-Ease Chair Co., 1948-61; Owner, Runyan/Taylor Advt., 1961-; Pres., Parmar, Inc., 1974-. Mbrships: Pres., Econ. Club, South-western Mich.; Past Pres., Ft. Miami Heritage Soc.; Pres., Bd. Trustees, St. Joseph Pub. Lib.; Instrument Soc. Am.; Am. Soc. Mech. Engrs.; Tau Beta Pi; Sigma Delta Chi; Pi Tau Sigma; Acacia; Rotary. Contbr. articles to Ency. of Management; Handbook of Modern Marketing; Tech. & Marketing Mags. Recip. Liberty Bell Award, Young Lawyers Sect., State Bar, Mich., 1962. Address: P.O. Box 43, St. Joseph, MI 49085, U.S.A. 8.

TAYLOR, Joye Wilhelmina, b. 15 Oct. 1899. School Teacher. Educ: private. Appts: apprenticed millinery trade, 1913; started own experimental schl., 1918; Maori schl., 1921; Sister at residential nursery, Newtown, 1946; sub-matron, Orient Hostel, 1947; Producer of plays for schls. & children's grps. Mbrships: Sec., Hataitai discussion grp., WEA, 1936-40; Pres., Wadestown Br., Brit. & For. Bible Soc.; Exec. Mbr., Eng. Speaking Union; Victoria League; Nat. Historic Places Trust. Publs. incl: Verses for Children; Flashes from Childhood & Adventures in Education; Henry Head of Niue Island. Recip., various awards. Address: Meolody Cottage, 156 Barnard St., Highland Pk., Wellington 1, New Zealand. 38.

TAYLOR, Katharine Whiteside (Mrs.), b. 24 Dec. 1897. Educator; Psychologist; Lecturer; Author. Educ: M.A., Columbia Univ., 1936; Ed.D., ibid, 1937; C.G. Jung Inst., Zurich, 1962, 63, 65 & 72. Appts. incl: Chief, Div. of Educ., Wis. Dept. of Mental Hygiene, 1938-39; Cons., Seattle Pub. Schls., 1941-46; Coord., Long Beach City Coll., 1948-51; Supvsr. in Parent Educ., Balt. Pub. Schls., 1951-62; Lectr., Univ. of Calif. Ext., 1967-; Lectr. for UNESCO; Fullbright Lectr., N.Z. Univs., 1964. Mbrships. incl: Ed., 1958-63, Hon. Ed., 1964-, The Parent Coop.; Hon. Life Mbr., Parent Coop. Preschools Int.; V.P. & Life Mbr., Am. Coun. on Family Rels.; Life Mbr., Am. Educ. Assm. & Am. Psychol. Assn.; Phi Beta Kappa; Pres., Theta Sigma Phi; Kappa Delta Pi. Publs. Incl: Do Adolescents Need Parents?, 1938; Getting Along with Parents, 1952; Parent Cooperative Nursery Schools, 1954; Parents & Children Learn Together, 1967; Contbr. to, US Yr. Book of Educ., 1958 & num. jrnls. Hons. incl: name given to Whiteside Taylor Ctr. for Coop. Educ., Montreal, 1968; Int. Award, Parent Coop. Preschools Int., 1972. Address: 1591 Shrader St., San Francisco, CA 94117, U.S.A. 5, 15.

TAYLOR, Kenneth Robert, b. 17 Mar. 1906. Physician. Surgeon. Educ: Grad., Southern Ill. State Univ., 1928; M.B., Chgo. Med. Schl., 1938; M.D., 1939; Postgrad., Ill. Post Grad. Med. Schl.; Intern, W.Side Hosp., Cook Co. Hosp., Chgo., 1938-40. Appts. Incl: Owner, Operator, N. Ave. Hosp., Chgo., 1936-58; Chief Surg., 1939-58; Chief Surg., Riverview Amusement Park, 1940-57; Capt., U.S. Army, 1943-46; Operator, Gen. Surg., Jackson Hosp., Olney, 1949-53; Attending Staff, Am. Hosp., Chgo., 1960-.; Cons., Forensic Med., 1940-; Pres., Taylor Oil & Minerals Corp., 1958-. Mbrships: AMA; Ill., Chgo. Med. Soc.; Assn. of Mil. Surgs. of U.S.; Am. Soc. of Abdominal Surgs.; Lions Int.; Ky. Col.; Med. Parents Loyalty Fund Comm., Duke Univ.; Fund Raiser, Southern Ill. Univ. Address: 1009 Jackson Ave., River Forest, IL 60305, U.S.A. 8, 10, 22, 120, 128.

TAYLOR, Max Tourner, b. 2 Oct. 1928. Surgeon-General, Thoracic & Cardiovascular. Educ: B.A., Andrews Univ., 1950; M.D., Loma Linda Univ., 1955; Surg. Trng., Marien Co. Gen. Hosp., Indpls., Ind. Appts: Recovery Surg., Proj. Mercury, NASA, 1960-62; Chief Thoracic Surg., Martin Army Hosp., 1960-62, Tempe Community Hosp., 1963-, & St. Luke's Hosp., Phoenix, 1968-; Pres.-Surg. Clins. of Ariz., Ltd., 1968-. Mbrships: Dipl., Am. Bd. of Surg.; Fellow, Am. Coll. of Surgs. & Am. Coll. of Chest Physns.; Southwestern Surg. Congress; Pan-Pacific Surg. Assn; Phoenix Surg. Soc.; Pan-Am. Med. Assn.; AMA; Ariz. Med. Assn.; Maricopa Co. Med. Soc. Contbr. of articles to med. jrnls. Address: 525 N. 18th St., Ste. 8, Phoenix, AZ 85006, U.S.A. 9, 131.

TAYLOR, Maxime, b. 11 Sept. 1908. Medical Social Worker; Legislative Advocate. Educ: B.S., Univ. of N.C., 1929; 2 yr. course in med. soc. work, Delehanty Inst. for Soc. Studies, 1930-32; N.Y. Univ. Grad. Schl. courses, 1936-37; Am. Inst. of Mgmt., 1938. Appts. incl: Registry, L.A., 1940-46; Established A-1 Nurses Registry, San Fran., 1947; Off. opened, 1953; Registered in 1950 as Legislative Advocate for Nursing Problems & Nurses Registries, 1951-; Legislatively active in raising standards within Nursing Referral Servs., 1951-. Mbrships. incl: Charter mbr., Calif. Employment Assn., 1953-; State Chmn. & Dir., New Nurses Registry Sect., C.E.A., 1961-63; Co-Trustee, C.E.A. Schlrship. Comm. Fund, 1963-; World Med. Assn., U.S. Comm., Inc.; Western & Calif. Hosp. Assns.; Nat. Employment Assn.; Calif. Chapt., Am. Bus. Women's Assn.; Am. Inst. of Mgmt. Author & Ed., A-1 Reporter over 14 yrs w. circulation of over 15,000 per month. Address: Profl. Nurses Bur., 6430 Sunset Blvd., L.A., CA 90028, U.S.A.

TAYLOR, Morris Fenton, b. 21 Oct. 1915. Teacher. Educ: B.A., Univ. of Colo., 1939; M.A., Cornell Univ., 1940. Appts: Prof., Hist., Trinidad State Jr. Coll., 1941-; Served in WWII, 1941-42; Fulbright Exchange Tchr., Bromley, Kent, U.K., 1960-61; Vis. Prof., Univ. of Denver, summer, 1966. Mbrships: Western Histl. Assn.; Org. of Am. Histns.; State Histl. Soc., Colo.; N.M. Histl. Soc.; Hon. Pres., Trinidad Histl. Soc.; Past State Pres., Colo. Archaeol. Soc. & Colo. Fedn. Tchrs.; Regional V.P., State Histl. Soc. Colo.; Inst. of Gt. Plains. Publs: Pioneers of the Picketwire, 1964; Trinidad, Colorado Territory, 1966; First Mail West: Stage Lines on the Santa Fe Trail, 1971; contbr. to var. profl. jrnls. Hons. incl: L.H.D., Univ. of Colo., 1969. Address: Trinidad State Jr. Coll., Trinidad, CO 81082, U.S.A. 9, 30, 60.

TAYLOR, Paul Schuster, b. 9 June 1895. Economics Professor. Educ: A.B., Univ. of Wis., 1917; M.A., Univ. of Calif., 1920; Ph.D., ibid, 1922. Appts: Univ. of Calif. Economics Fac., 1922-; Dept. Chmn., ibid, 1952-56; Chmn., Inst. of Int. Studies, 1956-62; Emeritus, 1962-; Vis. Prof., Univ. of Alexandria, UAR, 1962-63; Cons., Nat. Commn. on Law Observation & Enforcemant, 1930-31; Regional Labor Advsr., Resettlement Admin., 1935-36; Cons., Soc. Security Bd., 1936-41; Cons., Interior Dept., 1943-52; Cons., Export-Import Bank, 1952; Cons., U.S. Agcy. for Int. Dev., var. yrs. 1955-68; Cons., UN, 1960 & 1063; Cons., Stanford Rsch. Inst., 1967; Rsch. Dir., Calif. Labor Fedn., 1970. Mbrships: Cosmos Club, Wash. D.C.; Fac. Club, Berkeley; Phi Beta Kappa; Chi Phi; Author of books. Recip., Hon. LL.D., Univ. of Calif., 1965. Address: 1163 Euclid Ave., Berkeley, CA 94708, U.S.A. 2, 34, 128.

TAYLOR, Russel Reid, b. 9 Sept. 1917. Business Executive. B. Comm., Univ. of Toronto, Canada, 1938. Appts. incl: Servd. Royal Canadian Navy, WWII; V.P., Annis Furs Inc., 1951-57; Pres., ibid, 1957-61; Pres., Russel Taylor Inc., Div. of Consolidated Foods Corp., 1961-73; Chmn., ibid, 1973-; Assoc. Prof., Schl. of Bus., Fairleigh Dickinson Univ., 1970-. Mbrships. incl: Bd. Dirs., Mamaroneck (N.Y.) chapt. A.R.C., 1957-60; Chmn., Coat & Suit Ind. Div. Am. Cancer Soc., 1971. Trustee, Delta Upsilon Fraternity; Royal Canadian Navy Offs.' Club, Toronto; Union League Club, N.Y.; Publs: The Fur Industry, 1948; How to Buy a Fur Coat, 1951. Address: 71 Byram Shore Rd., Byram, CT 10573, U.S.A. 6, 16.

TAYLOR, Sam W., b. 8 Aug. 1935. Attorney at Law. Educ: B.S., Univ. of Ala., 1956; LL.B., ibid, 1958; LL.M., N.Y. Univ., 1959. Appts: admitted to prac., 1958; Asst. to Dist. Atty., Mobile, 1958; Law Clerk, U.S. Dist. Judge, 1959; Law Clerk, Chief Justice, Supreme Ct. of Ala., 1959-60; Capt., Judge Advocate Gen.'s Corps, 1962-64; Pvte. Prac., Montgomery, Ala., 1965-. Mbrships: House of Reps., State of Ala., 1970-74; Vice Chmn., Montgomery Delegation; Vice Chmn., Ins. Comm.; Fndr. & Exec. Trustee, WORK, Inc.; Am., Fed., Ala., Montgomery Co. Bar Assns.; State Dir., Ala. Wildlife Fedn.; Former Pres., Toastmasters Club; Area Gov., Toastmasters Int.; Mason; Shriner; Pi Kappa Alpha. Hons: Montgomery Toastmaster of Yr., 1970-71; Ala. Ins. Code named Timmons-Taylor-Lybrand Ins. Code Act. Address: 2429 Woodley Rd., Montgomery, AL 36111, U.S.A. 114, 125.

TAYLOR, Theophilus Mills, b. 22 June 1909. Ordained Minister; Church Executive; Seminary Professor. Educ: B.Arch., Univ. of Pa., 1935; B.Th., Pitts. Theological Sem., 1941; D.D., Muskingum Coll., 1944; Ph.D., Yale Univ., 1956. Appts: Pastor, Barnet Ctr. United Presby. Ch., 1941-43; Prof., Pitts. Theol. Sem., 1943-62; Moderator, Gen. Assembly, United Presby. Ch., U.S.A., 1958-59; Sec., Gen. Coun., ibid, 1962-72; Pres., Presby. Historical Soc., 1964-73; Pres., Relig. in Am. Life, 1971-73. Mbrships: Am. Oriental Soc.; Archaeol. Inst. of Am.; Soc. of Biblical Lit. & Exegesis Studiorum Novi Testamenti Societos. Author of Survey of Theological Education in Overseas Seminaries, 1962. Contbr. chapts. to sev. publs. Address: Old Tabor House, Topsham, VT 05076, U.S.A. 2, 6, 13, 128.

TAYLOR, Vera C., b. 4 June 1924. Professor; Educational Psychologist. Educ: B.S., 1946, M.S., 1949, Iowa State Univ.; Ph.D., Educl. Psychol., Univ. of Southern Calif., 1970. Appts: Pub. Schl. Tchr., 4 yrs.; Iowa State Univ. Ext., 1955-58; Instr., Dept. Chmn., Coll. of Sequoias, 1958-65; Prof., Child Dev. & Early Childhood, Calif. State Univ., Fresno. 1965-. Vis. Prof., Univ. of Alta., Canada, 1961; Univ. of Southern Calif., summer, 1968, '69. Mbrships: Past Calif. State Pres., Past Ctrl. Calif. Pres., Nat. Assn. for Educ. of Young Children; Past Pres., Ctrl. Calif., Am. Home Econs. Assn.; U.S. Nat. Comm. on Early Childhood Educ.; Am. Assn. for Higher Educ.; Soc. for Rsch. in Child Dev.; Phi Kappa Phi; Omicron Nu; Kappa Delta Pi; Delta Phi Upsilon. Publs: Evaluation of Three Kindergarten Models, 1970; Ed., Readings in Child Development, 1969. Hons: Lavern Noyes Schlrships., 1943-46; Disting. Serv. to Early Childhood Educ., 1973. Address: 205 N. Crest, Madera, CA 93637, U.S.A. 5, 9, 129, 132, 138.

TAYLOR, Walter Harold, b. 2 Dec. 1905. Civil Engineer. Educ: Royal Melbourne Inst. of

Technol., Australia, 1921-25; Trinity Coll., Univ. of Melbourne, 1928-31; B.C.E., 1931; M.C.E., 1937; Dips. in Civil Engrng., 1928, Municipal Engrng., 1928, Admin., 1932, Bus. Admin., 1947. Appts. incl: Rsch. & Consultative Engr., in connection w. 30,000 projs., Div. of Bldg. Rsch., CSIRO, Melbourne, 1945-70; Tech. Serv. Dir., John Connell & Assocs., Cons. Engrs., 1971-; Post-tertiary Educationist, Seminar Convener & External Studies Mgr., qualification courses on Concrete Technol. & Prac., Insts. of Advanced Educ., 1945-; Study Mission & Colloquia Deleg. to Japan, Canada, U.S.A. & Mexico, 1965-73. Mbrships. incl: Fellow & Past Br. Chmn., Instn. of Civil Engrs., U.K., 1939-; Fellow, Instn. of Engrs., Australia, 1932-; Hon. Fellow, ibid, 1971-; Australian Inst. of Mgmt., 1944-; Comm. mbr., Standards Assn., Australia, 1945; Life mbr., Engl.-speaking Union. Author of about 100 tech. & topical publs. Recip. of hons. Address: 19 Lawson St., Hawthorn E., Vic., Australia, 3123. 23, 128, 139.

TAZIEFF, Haroun, b. 11 May 1914. Volcanologist. Author. Educ: Degree, Agricl. Engrng., State Fac. of Agronomy, Gembloux, Belgium, 1938; Degree, Geological Engrng., Univ. of Liege, 1944. Appts. incl: Rsch. Off., Nat. Ctr. of Scientific Rsch., Paris, France, 1969-72; Rsch. Dir., ibid, 1972-; Hd., Volcanol. Serv., Earth Phys. Inst., Paris; Chmn., Scientific Coun., Int. Inst. of Volcanol., Rome, Italy; Lectr., Volcanol., sev. univs.; Expert for UNESCO, Chile, 1961, Costa Rica, 1964, Indonesia, 1964-65, & Iceland, 1973. Mbrships. incl: Geological Soc. of France; Mineralogical Soc., Manchester, U.K.; Explorers Club, N.Y.C., U.S.A. Publs. incl: Cratères en Feu; Les Volcans; Quand la Terre Tremble; Les Volcans & la Dérive des Continents; 5 other books; Num. contbns. to sci. jrnls. & encys. Dir., sev. films inclng. Les Rendez-vous du Diable, & Le Volcan Interdit. Hons. incl: Pellman Prize, 1959; Robert Flaherty Prize, 1966; Gold Medal, Royal Geographical Soc., 1970. Address: 15 Quai de Bourbon, 75004, Paris, France.

TCHETCHIK, Alexander, b. 21 Aug. 1895. Professor. Educ: Dip., Elec. Engr., Univ. of Lausanne, Switzerland, 1915-19. Appts: Mgr. & Chief Engr., Israel Elec. Corp., Northern Dist., 1920-57; Assoc. Prof., Technion, Israel Inst. of Technol., Haifa, 1926-68. Mbrships: F.I.E.E., U.K.; F.Illum. E.S., U.K.; M.A.F.E., France; M. AI &I, Italy; Pres., Assn. Engrng. & Arch., Israel, 1963-65; V.P., Int. Comm. on Illumination, 1963-71; Hon. Chmn., Israel Nat. Comm., World Energy Conf.; Chmn., Nat. Illumination Comm., Israel. Publs: Fundamentals of Lighting Engineering, Part One, 1971; articles & reports in field. Address: 5 Yitzhak Ave., Mt. Carmel, Haifa, Israel. 94.

TEAGUE, Elizabeth Camp, b. 21 Feb. 1926. Librarian. Educ: A.A., Brevard Coll., N.C; Ext. Courses, Fla. State Univ., Tallahassee; Var. Courses, Fla. Jr. Coll., Jacksonville, 1968-72; Univ. of N. Fla., ibid. Appts: Hd. Libn., Effie R. Russell Community Lib., Jacksonville Beach, Fla., 1953-57; Libn., Jacksonville Pub. Lib. System, Fla., 1957-. Mbrships: Sec.-Treas., Exec. Bd., Women's Ctr. for Reproductive Hlth., Jacksonville. Chmn., Advsry Comm., Jacksonville Clergy Consultation Serv., Inc.; Coord., Abortion Task Force, Jacksonville Nat. Org. for Women; Negotiator & Shop Steward, Profl. Chapt., Jacksonville Pub. Employees Local 1048; Rep., Jacksonville Pub. Employees Union Local 1048, AFSCME, AFL-CIO, Jacksonville Coalition of Equal Rights Amendment. Hons: Carol Downer Annual Award for Servs. to Women's Hlth., Jacksonville. Women's Movement, 1974. Address: 612 4th Ave. N., Jacksonville Beach, FL 32050, U.S.A. 125.

TEAL, Valentine Moline (Val), b. 14 Feb. 1903. Free-lance writer. Educ: B.A., Univ. of Minn. Publs: It Was Not What I Expected; The Little Woman Wanted Noise; Angel Child; Short stories in Ladies Home Jrnl., Saturday Evening Post, Good Housekeeping, Woman's Home Companion, The Am. Mag., Woman's Day, etc.; Children's stories in Child Life & other children's mags.; Many stories for children & adults resold to rdrs. & anthols. & republd. in for. mags. & books; Category of adult writings, primarily humor; With Sirens Blowing, play for adults; Grandmother's Magic Clock, play for children. Address: 5620 Western Ave., Omaha, NB 68132, U.S.A. 140.

TEDDLIE, Stella Maye Harwell, b. 21 Oct. 1907. Educator; Tour Escort; Writer. Educ: B.A., Univ. of Wyo., Laramie. Appts: Binding Libn., Dallas Pub. Lib., Tex., 1936-42; Asst. Libn., Univ. of Wyo., 1943-45; Mgr., Preston Ctr. Travel Serv., 1956-58; Mgr., Dallas Travel Serv., 1958-61; Classroom Tchr., Jr. H.S., Dallas Independent Schl., 1961-74. Mbrships: Int. Sorority for Women Tchrs., 1955-; Transportation Chmn., ibid, 1957-69; NEA; Tex. State Tchrs. Assn.; Tex. & Dallas Classroom Tchrs. Assns.; Alpha Delta Kappa; State Histn., ibid, 1972-74. Author, Practical Handicrafts for Librarians, 1940. Hons: Assembly Awards, Univ. of Wyo., 1943, 1944, 1945; Ph.D., Hamilton State Univ., Tucson, Ariz., 1973. Address: 2718 Overcrest St., Dallas, TX 75211, U.S.A. 5, 7, 125, 132.

TEFS, Rudolf, b. 9 Nov. 1905. Banker. Educ: H.S. of Econs., Berlin, Germany. Appts: w. Min. of Econ s., Bonn., W. Germany; w. For. Office, ibid; Germany Embassy, Cairo, Egypt; Dresdner Bank A.G., Frankfurt am Main, W. Germany. Mbrships: Pres., Turkish-German Chmbr. of Comm.; Pres., Orient Inst., Frankfurt; Vorstand, German-Iranian Chmbr. of Comm. Hons: Hon. Citizen, State of Ariz., U.S.A.; var. for. decorations. Address: Rösslerstr. N 2, 62 Wiesbaden, German Fed. Repub.

TEH, Hoon-Heng, b. 10 Jan. 1934. Professor. Educ: B.Sc., Nanyang Univ., Singapore, Malaysia, 1960; M.Sc., Queen's Univ., Belfast, N. Ireland, 1961; Ph.D., ibid, 1962. Appts: Queen's Univ., Belfast, 1962-63; Nanyang Univ., Singapore, Malaysia, 1963-64; Queen's Univ., Kingston, Ont., Canada, 1964-65; Univ. Malaya, 1965-66; Prof.-Dean, Coll. of Grad. Studeis, Nanyang Univ., Singapore, 1966-. Mbrships: V.P. & Pres.-elect, S.E. Asia Math. Soc.,1973-; Pres., Math. Soc., Nanyang Univ., 1958-59; V.P., FES, Singapore, 1971. Author, num. papers in math. bulletins, incl: Construction of Orders in Abelian Groups, 1961; A Note on L-groups, 1962; The Chromatic Number of Product Graphs, 1965; On the Decomposition of a Partial Ordering of an Abelian Group, 1960; Some Fundamental Concepts and Theorems of Generalized Algebraic Systems, 1961; On Ideal Coverings of a Set and some Directed Product of Groups, 1962; A Note on Hasse Diagrams, 1962; on 3-valued Sentential Calculus, 1963; Fundamentals of Group Graphs, 1969. Address: Coll. Grad. Studies, Nanyang Univ., Singapore-22, Malaysia. 98.

TEICH, Ralph Donald, b. 24 May 1925. Businessman. Educ: B.S., Northwestern Univ., Evanston, Ill., 1949. Appts: Mgr., Contract Sales Div., Curt Teich & Co. Inc., 1957; Mgr., Sales, Europe, Middle East, & Africa, ibid,

1960; Dir., Curt Teich Fndn., 1960; Various trusteeships. Mbrships. incl: Life, Art Inst. Chgo., 1968; Life, Field Mus. Natural Hist., 1969; Dir., Am. Friends of Austria 1965-72; Execs. Club., Chgo.; V.P., Lake Forest Property Owners Assn., 1970; Deacon, Lutheran Ch. of Holy Spirit, 1966-73; V.P., ibid, 1967-73; V.P., Ill. Bd. Govs., Mid Am. Ballet Assn., 1971; Inter State Bd. Govs., ibid, 1972; Life Mbr., Chgo. Histl. Soc.; Univ. Club, Chgo.; Waukegan Yacht & Swedish Glee Clubs; Power Squadron, U.S. Coast Guard Aux.; Engl. Speaking Union; Bd. Dirs., Chgo. Ballet, 1974. Address: Few Acres, 700 S. Ridge Rd., Lake Forest, IL 60045, U.S.A. 8, 16, 22, 57.

TEICHMANN, Horst (Oskar Paul Hans), b. 12 Jan. 1904. University Professor; Postal Director. Educ: Tech. Univ., Dresden, Germanyy, 1923-27; Dip.Ing., 1927; Dr.Ing., 1929. Appts. incl: Prof., theoretical physics, Univ. of Heidelberg, 1943-45; Lectr., applied physics, Univ. of Würzburg, 1948-53; Hon. Prof., ibid, 1953-; Deutsche Bundespost, Würzburg, 1945-49, Nürnberg, 1949-69; Promotion ot Postal Dir., retd. 1969. Mbrships: Deutsche Physikalische Gesellschaft; physikalisch-Medizinische Gesellschaft, Würzburg; Chmn., local sect., N. Bavaria, Verband Deutscher Elektrotechniker, 1955-59; Bd. of Dirs., Deutsche Gesellschaft für Dokumentation, 1967-69; Chmn., Hauptausschuss für Dokumentation in der Elektro-Technik, ibid, 1963-73. Author of over 100 publs. in field. Address: Mittl. Dallenbergweg 45, D 8700 Würzburg, German Fed. Repub. 43.

TEICHOLZ, Bruce B., b. 20 Feb. 1914. Real Estate & Insurance Executive. Educ: Acad. Econ. & Bus., Lwow, Poland, 1932-35; Univ. of Florence Schl. of Econ., Italy, 1950-51; CCNY, U.S.A., 1959-61. Gen. Ptnr., Bldg. & Real Estate Dev. Mbrships: Democratic Club, N.Y.C.; Sutton Tennis Club, ibid; Matterhorn Ski Club; Community Life (charity & philanthropic assn.). Author of articles for Jewish Press. Hons: Chief Cmdr., Bricha in Europe; Golden Book, Jewish Nat. Fund, 1946, '51; Man of Yr., O.R.T., 1967; Citation Award, B'nai B'rith, 1965, '66; Medal (OT Hagana), Govt. of Israel, 1968; Letters of Recognition, Int. Comm. for Jewish Refugees & Inmates from Concentration Camps, 1951; Am. Jt. Distribution Comm., 1950, Repub. of Austria, Int. Min., 1950, Polish Ctrl. Comm., Budapest, 1946, etc. Address: 410 E. 57th St., N.Y., NY 10022, U.S.A. 6.

TEIGEN, Dorothy Marie Russell (Mrs. Ferdinand A. Teigen) Writer; Public Relations Consultant. Educ: B.A., Hunter Coll., N.Y.C.; Postgrad. work, Columbia Univ., N.Y.C., Sorbonne, Paris, France. Appts. incl: Former P.R. Dir., Women's Div., Am. Soc. for British War Relief (later Aldrich Comm.), N.Y.C., & Am. Red Cross War Fund, N.Y.C.; Former info. specialist, feature & mag. writer, Off. of Coord. of Inter-Am. Affairs; Info. specialist, writer, U.S. Dept. of State, Wash. D.C.; P.R. Cons., Nat. Women's Party, Pilot Club Int. & others, Wash. D.C.; Chief of News Bur., Mgr., Press Rels., P.R. Cons., Investors Diversified Servs., Inc., Mnpls., Minn., 1953-69; Currently, free-lance writer, P.R. Cons. Mbrships. incl: Am. Newspaper Women's Club, HQ Wash. D.C.; Charter mbr., Minn. Press Club. Publs: Carol of Roumania, Playboy of the Balkans; Edit. work on special publs. such as The Trumpeter; Num. articles in nat. publs. & abroad. Recip., War Serv. Cert., Off. of Coord. of Inter-Am. Affairs, 1946. Address: 1767 Humboldt Ave. S., Mnpls., MN 55403, U.S.A. 5, 138.

TEISSEYRE, Roman Marian, b. 11 Apr. 1929. Geophysicist. Educ: Wroclaw Univ., 1947-49; M.Sc. Warsaw Univ., 1952; Ph.D., 1959. Appts: Asst., Dept. Geophys.-Dept. Theoretical Phys., Warsaw Univ., Poland, 1950-53; Hd., Seismol. Div., Inst. Geophys., Polish Acad. Scis., 1953-61; Dpty. Dir.-Dir., ibid, 1961-72; Dpty. Dir., ibid, 1972-; Chmn., Geophys. Comm., Polish Acad. Scis., 1972-; Ed.. Publs. of Inst. Geophys., ibid; Chief, Geophys. Expedition to D.R. Vietnam, 1957-60. Mbrships: VP, European Seismol. Comm.; Exec. Comm., Int. Assn. Seismol. & Phys. Earth's Interior; Corres., Polish Acad. Scis. Publs. incl: The Diffraction on a Conducting Wedge. The General Solution for Dipole Field, 1955; Non-Local Models of Seismic Foci, 1956; Dynamic and Time Relations of the Dislocation Theory of Earthquakes. Dislocation Field Dynamics as an Approach to the Physics of Earthquake Processes, 1968; Dislocational Representation of Thermal Stresses, 1969; Crack Formation and Energy Release Caused by the Concentration of Dislocations along Fault Planes, 1970. Recip. hons. Address: Inst. Geophys., Polish Acad. Scis., ul. Pasteura 3, 00-973, Warsaw, P.O. Box 155, Poland.

TEITELBAUM, Harry Allen, b. 7 Oct. 1907. Psychiatrist; Neurologist. Educ: Columbia Univ., NY, 1925-26; B.S., Univ. of Md., 1929; M.D., Univ. of Md. Med. Schl. & Grad. Schl., 1935; Ph.D., ibid, 1936. Appts. incl: Pvte. Pract., Psych. & Neurol, 1940-; w. Epilepsy Clin., The Johns Hopkins Hosp., 1941-47; Rsch. in conditional reflexes, Pavlovian Lab., Johns Hopkins Med. Schl., 1946-70; Dipl., Am. Bd. of Psych. & Neurol., 1947; Vis. Active Staff, Seton Psych. Inst., 1949-; Hd., Div. of Neuropsych., ibid, 1948-65; Hd. Div. of Neurol., ibid & Sinai Hosp., Balt., Md., 1948; Assoc. Prof. of Neurol., Univ. of Md. Med. Schl., 1952-; Asst. Prof. of Psych., Johns Hopkins Med. Schl., 1962-; various positions as med. advsr. & cons. Mbrships. incl: Am. Assn. Anatomy, 1930-40; AMA; Fellow, Am. Psych. Assn.; Fellow, AAAS; Pavlovian Soc., etc. Author of num. papers & contbr. to books in field. Address: 200 W Cold Spring Lane, Baltimore, MD 21210, U.S.A. 6, 14, 28, 55, 125.

TELEMAQUE, Harold Milton, b. 20 Aug. 1910. Schools Supervisor (Retired). Educ: Govt. Tchrs'. Coll., Trinidad; London Univ, U.K.; Hampshire Educ. Authority; Nat. Educ. Fndn. of England & Wales. Appts: Prin., Fyzabad Secondary Schl., Trinidad, 1941-53; Insp. of Schls., Schls. Aupvsr., Trinidad, 1953-69; Sec., Anglican Schls. Bd. Educ. Mbrships: Pres., Lit. League of Trinidad & Tobage, 1948-50; Anglican Diocesan Coun.; Pres., Anglican Tchrs. Assn.; Chmn., Sr. Citizens Home Comm.; Past Pres., Lions Club of St. Patrick. Publs: Burnt Bush (Poems); Scarlet (Poems); Primary Geography for the Caribbean; General Progress Papers for the Caribbean, Books I & II, Hons. incl: Nat. Golden Award for Disting. Servs. to Educ.; Humanist Award for Unselfish Serv. to Humanity. Address: Bungalow II (Bel Air), No. 22 Rd., Fyzabad, Trinidad, W.I.

TELL, Bjorn, b. 23 Sept. 1918. Library Administrator. Educ: Ph.D., Stockholm Univ.; M.B.A., Stockholm Schl. of Econs. Appts: Hd. Libn., Stockholm Schl. of Econs., 1952-59; UNESCO Expert, Scientific Documentation, Venezuela, 1958, 1974, India 1963, Yugoslavia, 1973; Mgr., Documentation Dept., AB Atomenergi, 1959-63; Cons. to IAEA, 1962-63, ESRO, 1965-, Nat. Lib. of Australia, 1973; Hd. Libn., Royal Inst. Technol., Stockholm,

1963-73; Mbr., OECD Info. Policy Grp., 1965-; Dir. of Libs., Lund Univ., 1973-; Mbr., UNESCO/UNISIST Steering Comm., 1973-; Mbr., Swedish UNESCO Coun., SINFDOK, Rsch. Lib. Coun. Mbr., Sweidish Soc. Documentation; Dhmn., ibid, 1960-60. Ed., Scandinavian Documentation Jrnl., 1960-. Articles, papers & lects., documentation & scientific info. Address: Lund Univ. Library, S 221 03 Lund. Sweden. 43.

TEMIR, Ahmet, b. 14 Nov. 1912. Professor. Educ: Ph.D., Berlin, Germany,1 943. Appts. incl: Asst., Directorate Gen. of Mus., Ankara, Turkey, 1947-52; Lectr., Turkish, Univ. of Hamburg, Germany, 1952-54; Asst. Lectr., Fac. of Letters, Univ. of Ankara, 1955; Prof. of Turkology & Mongolistics, ibid, 1962. Mbrships: Inst. for study of Turkish Culture, Ankara (Fndr. & Dir., 1961-); Int. Soc. Oriental Rsch., Frankfurt, W. Germany; Soc. Uralo-Altaica, Hamburg, ibid; Soc. Finno-Ougrienne, Helsinki, Finland; Bund der deutschen Fernschachfreunde, Hamburg; Chess Club of Andara (Fndr. & Pres., 1968-); Temporary Pres., 16th. meeting, Permanent Int. Altaistic Conf., Ankara, 1973. Publs. incl: Die arabisch-mongolische Stiftungsurkunde von 1272, 1960; Mogollarin Gizli Tarihi, 1948. Address: P.K. 14, Cankaya, Ankara, Turkey. 43.

TENDLER, Moshe David, b. 7 Aug. 1926. Rabbi; Professor of Talmudic Law; Professor of Biology. Educ: B.A., N.Y. Unvi., 1943; M.A., ibid, 1947; Ph.D., Columbia Univ., 1957; Rabbi Isaac Elchanan Theological Sem. of Yeshiva Unvi., N.Y. 1949. Appts. incl: Prof. of Talmud, Rabbi Isaac Elehanan Thological Sem. of Yeshiva univ., 1969-; Prof. & Chmn., Biol. Dept., Yeshiva Unvi., 1966-; Rabbi, Community Synagogue of Monsey, 1967-; Rsch. Fellow in Oncol. & Prof. of Microbiol., Kingsbrook Jewish Med. Ctr., Brooklyn, N.Y., 1963-; Dir., Nat. Sci. Fndn. Inst. for Gifted Secondary Schl. St1; Exec. Bd. Inst. of Sci. & Halacha, Jerusalem, Israel, 1972-. Mbrships. incl: Pres., Assn. of Orthodox Jewish Scis., 1970-72; Chmn. of Bd., ibid, 1972-; Chmn., Med. Ethics Task Force, Fedn. of Jewish Philanthropies, 1969-74; Kashruth Advsry. Bd., U.S. Dept. of Agric., 1964-.Publs: Coll. Textbook of Biology, 1969; Pardes Rimonim, 1969; Compendium of Jewish Medical Ethics, 1969. Discoverer of Anthramycin. Winner, Man of the Year, Nat. Coun. of Young Israel, 1963. Address: 4 Cloverdale Lane, Monsey, NY 10952, U.S.A. 2.

TEN EYCK, Catryna, b. 30 June 1931. Artist; Author. Educ: Smith Coll., Northampton, Mass., 1949-51; Art Students League, N.Y.C., 1971-72; Parsons Schl. of Design, N.Y.C., 1974. Mbrships: Print Club of Phila., Pa.; Southern Vt. Art Assn.; Cooperstown Art Assn., N.Y.; Munson-Proctor Art Inst., Utica, N.Y. Works: Author of Enjoying the Southwest, 1973; Paintings & Prints of New England Trees & Views of the Southwest. One-Woman show, New Schl. for Soc. Rsch., N.Y., 1973; Represented in collects. of major museums. Hons: 1st Prize, Springfield Art Assn., Mass., 1971; Nat. Juried Exhibitions, 1972. Address: P.O. Box 353, Salisbury, CT 06068, U.S.A. 37.

TEN HOOR, Elvie, b. 23 Oct. 1900. Artist; Lecturer; Author. Educ: Art Inst., Chgo.; Inst. de Allende, San Miguel, Mexico; Acad. N.D. Des Champs, Paris, France. Appts: Art Tchr., Village Artists, Chgo. Heights, Ill., U.S.A. & pvte. studio. Mbrships: Alumni Sigma Kappa Chapt. Beta, (pres. 1964-66); Renaissance Soc.; Artists Equity; Art Inst. Sales & Rental Gall.;

Arts Club of Chgo. Publs: Collage & Found Art, 1963, Collage & Assemblage, 1974 (both w. D. Meilach); work appears in sev. books & mags. Solo exhibs., Munster, Ind., Rubino Galls. Chgo. (1973). Other exhibs., Chgo., N.Y., Mich. & Paris, France. Paintings in pub. & pvte. collects. in U.S.A. & Canada. Recip. of outstanding prize for oil, Dunes Art Fndn. of Ind., 1958. Address: 6740 Oglesby Ave., Chgo., IL 60649, U.S.A.

TENNANT, Harry LaRenze, b. 17 Aug. 1909. Editor; Writer. Educ: B.A.J., State Univ. of Iowa, 1933; Postgrad. work, Univ. of Calif., Berkeley, 1936. Appts. incl: Writer, U.P.I., Omaha, Neb. & Phila., Pa., 1940; Corres., Chicago-N.Y. Jrnls. of Commerce, 1945-50; Edit. Dir., Interavia Publ., Geneva, 1955-68; Ed., Watson Publs., 1952-; Ed., Biomedical News, 1971-. Mbrships. incl: Nat. Press Club; Nat. Space Club; White House Correspondents Assn.; State Dept. Correspondents; Assn. Aviation & Space Writers Assn.; Nat. Space Writers Assn. Contbr. of articles to sev. mags. & jrnls. & to Funk & Wagnalls Yearbook. Recip. of Pioneer Space Writers Award, 1968. Address: Nat. Press Bldg., Wash. D.C. 20004, U.S.A. 7, 16,

TENNBERG, Bo Johan Gustaf, b. 14 Mar. 1919. Judge. Educ: Grad., Swedish Co-educational Schl. of Vasa, 1939; LL.B., Univ. of Helsinki, 1949; Vicehärad-shövding/varatuomari, 1951. Appts: Court dits. off., 1949; Ct. of Appeal, Vasa, 1951; Judge, Ct. Dist. of Taivalkoski, 1960, Pedersöre, 1962; Sr. Judge, Ct. of Appeal, Vasa, 1974. Mbrships: Bd. Mbr., Life Mbr., Soc. Heraldica Scandinavia; Bd. Mbr., & The Riders' Assn. of Finland; Chmn., Riding club of Jakobstad; Life Mbr.-Nordenskiöld-Samfundet i Finland, Sportsfishermens Assn. of Finland; Heraldry Soc. of Finland; Heraldry Soc. (G.B.); Heraldischer Verein Zum Kleeblatt. Conbr. to heraldic publs. Hons: Kt., Order of Freedom of Finland IV Class, 1944; Cmdr., Order of the Lion of Finland, 1971. Address: Vasa, Finland. 43.

TENNYSON, Jean, b. 15 Sept. 1905. Singer, Educ: profl. studies w. Cattone in Italy, Madame Gilly & Mary Garden in Paris, Florence Easton in N.Y. Appts. incl: Operatic debut, Mimi in La Boheme, La Fenice Theater, Venice, Italy, 1930; w. San Carlo Opera Co., Canada & U.S.A., 2 seasons; w. Chgo. Civic Opera Co., 1934-35, 1935, '36, '38; at Salzburg Festival w. Vienna Symph., 1935; European tour, leading opera houses, inclng. Prague, Budapest, Vienna, Bucharest, Belgrade, Sofia, 1935; w. San Francisco Opera Co., U.S.A., 1936-37; featured in Gt. Moments in Music prog., CBS, 1942; Exec. Vice Chmn., Stadium Concerts, N.Y.C., 1942-46; Pres., Jean Tennyson Fndn.; Bd. Mbr., N.Y.C. Opera; Patron, Philharmonic Symph. Soc., N.Y. Hons. incl: Stella della Solidarieta Italiana, Italy; St. Olaf Medal, Norway. Address: 21 E. 62nd St., N.Y., NY 10021, U.S.A. 2, 5, 6, 52.

TENTORI, Tullio, b. 11 Apr. 1920. University Professor. Educ: Elementary Degree to Laurea, Univ. of Rome, Italy; 3 Libera Docenza, ibid. Appts. incl: Curator, Americanistic Div., Nat. Prehistoric & Ethnographic Mus. L. Piogorini, Rome, 1946; Asst. Prof., Univ. of Rome; Estab. Nat. Mus. of Folk Arts & Traditions, Rome, 1956; Dir., ibid, 1956-72, Hon. Curator, 1972-; Prof., Am. Indigenous Civilizations & Cultural Anthropol., Univ. of Rome, 1961-72; Dir., Inst. of Cultural Anthropol., Univ. of Trento, Italy, 1972; Dean, Dept. of Human Scis., ibid. Mbrships. incl: Int. Soc. Scis. Coun. of UNESCO, Paris, France,

Italian Nat. Commn. of UNESCO, Rome, Italy; Ctr. Naz. Difesa e Prevenzionne Sociale, Milan, Italy. Publs. incl: Main anthropol. writings in Scritti Antropologici, Vol. 1-4, 1970-72; Main writings in Americanistics in Scritti Americanistici, 1968. Address: Via A. Nibby 5 a, 00161 Rome, Italy. 43.

TEODORU, Constantin Valeriu, b. 14 Feb. 1915. Physician; Scientist; Educator. Educ: M.D., Bucharest Univ., Rumania, 1939. Appts. incl: Assoc. Prof., Physiol., Bucharest, 1940-48; Attng. Physn., Bucharest Pub. Hosps., 1942-48; Mbr., Advsry. Comm., & Hd., Med. Depts., Am. Red Cross, & Nat. Cath. Welfare Conf. Bucharest, 1946-48; Chief, Rsch. Lab., Roussel, France, 1949-52; Rsch. Asst.-Rsch. Assoc., Dept. of Microbiol., Mt. Sinai Hosp., N.Y.C., U.S.A., 1952-57; Hd., Applied Physiol., Isaac Albert Rsch. Inst., Jewish Chronic Disease Hosp., Brooklyn, N.Y., 1957-64; Clin. Asst. Prof.-Assoc. Prof., Med., Downstate Med. Ctr., SUNY, 1961-71; Mbr., Vis. Staff, Kings Co. Hosp. Ctr., 1961-; Attng. Physn., Dept. of Med., & Chief, Long Term Med. Care, Kingsbrook Med. Ctr., 1964-71; Vis. Physn. & Assoc. Dir. of Med., N.Y. Univ. Med. Ctr., Goldwater Mem. Hosp., 1972-. Num. mbrships. incl: AAAS; Fellow, Am. Coll. of Physns.; N.Y. Acad. of Med.; Harvey Soc. Publs. incl: 61 original rsch. papers. Hons. incl: Medal, Rumanian Red Cross, 1946; Ribbon Bar, Am. Red Cross, 1947. Address: 34-23 86th St., Jackson Heights, NY 11372, U.S.A. 6, 14, 28, 50, 131.

TERAI, Kiyoshi, b. 6 Jan. 1927. Naval Architect; Engineer. Educ: Grad., Dept. Naval Arch., Fac. Engrng., Osaka Univ., Japan, 1951; Postgrad. study, Tech. Rsch. Inst. Transportation Min., 1953-54; Ecole Supérieure de Soudage Autogéne, Paris, France, 1958-59; Dr. Engrng., 1962. Appts: Mgr., Shipbuilding Dept., Kobe Shipyard, Kawasaki Heavy Inds. Ltd., 1964-69; Mgr., Welding Rsch. Labs., Khi, 1969-; Vis. Lectr: Nagoya Univ., 1968-; Osaka Univ., 1970-72; Tohoku Univ., Sendai, 1972-; Tokyo Univ., 1973-; Dir., Japan Welding Soc., 1974-. Mbrships: Am. Welding Soc.; Brit. Welding Inst.; Soc. des Ingenieurs Soudeurs; Ashiya Co., Takarazuka Golf & Sanda Golf Clubs. Creative Works: Theoretical Rsch., Initiation Brittle Fracture in Welded Structures; Dev. of 1-side Automatic Welding; Automation of Welding; Rsch. Application Electron Beam Welding for Prod. Large Structures; Author 5 publs. in field. Hons. incl: Tanaka Mem. Prize, Japan Welding Soc., 1968; Prize, Soc. Naval Archs. Japan, 1968; Okichi Mem. Award 1967. Address: Kawasaki Heavy Inds. Ltd., Kobe, Japan.

TERCEIRA, Maurice Eugene, b. 17 Oct. 1933. Architect. Educ: Cert. in Engrng., Mt. Allison Univ., Canada; B.Arch., N.S. Tech. Coll. Appts: Prin., Maurice Terceira, Archts.; Mbr., Archts. Registration Coun. of Bermuda & of Advsry. Archtl. Panel. Mbrships: 1st V.P. Hamilton Lions Club; Royal Hamilton Amateur Dinghy, Riddell's Bay Golf & Country, Pomander Gate Tennis Clubs; Trustee, Emmanuel Meth. Ch. Address: Airlie House, Ch. St., Hamilton, Bermuda.

ter HAAR, Jaap (Jacob Everard), b. 25 Mar. 1922. Writer. Educ: Univ. studies, interrupted by WWII. Appts: Mbr., Underground Forces, WWII; Marine Corres., Royal Netherlands Marines, 1945-47; Hd., Transcription Serv., Radio Nederland, 1947-55; Fulltime Writer, 1955-. Mbrships: Invited mbr., De Muiderkring; Pres., group of Children's Authors, Dutch Writers Assn. Publs. incl: The History of the Low Lands (4 vols.); The History of America; The History of Russia; The History of the Roman Empire; The History of the French Revolution; Napoleon; King Arthur (Novel); Great Stories from the Dark Ages; Boris (Novel); Many books for children inclng. Saskia & Jeroen Series. Hosn. incl: Bijenkorf Award; Rotterdam Youth Award (twice). Address: Eikenlaan 57, Hilversum, The Netherlands.

TERRACE, Ralph, b. 31 Jan. 1920. Dentist; Educator. Educ: Villanova Univ., Pa., 1938-40; D.D.S., Schl. of Dentristry, Univ. of Pa., 1943. Appts: Asst. Prof., Operative Dept., Fairleigh Dickinson Univ. Schl. of Dentistry, 1957; Acting Chmn., ibid, 1958; Assoc. Prof., 1959; Chmn., Operative Dept., 1961; Prof., Operative Dentistry, 1967. Mbrships: Fellow, Am. Coll. of Dentists; Fellow, N.Y. Acad. of Dentistry; Exec. Comm., Am. Assn. of Dental Schls.,1 1972-; Omicron Kappa Upsilon; Am. Acad. of Gold Foil Operators; N.J. & Am. Soc. of Dentistry for Children; Am. Acad. of Oral Med.; Northern N.J. Chapt., Xi Psi Phi Dental Fraternity; Essex Co. Dental Soc.; N.J. State Dental Assn.; Am. Dental Assn. Address: 149 Old Short Hills Rd., Short Hills, NJ 07078, U.S.A. 6.

TERREL, Charles Lynn, b. 19 Apr. 1904 Financial Consultant. Educ: B.A., Ohio State Univ., 1928; M.B.A., Harvard Bus. Schl., 1932 Appts: incl: Econ. & Indl. Analyst, U.S. Senate's Temp Nat. Econ. Comm., 1938-41 Chief Mission Off., Allied Combined Chiefs of Staff, Exec. Off. to Pres., Wash., D.C. & Chmn. N. African Econ. Bd., Algiers, 1943; Pres. Continental Investment Corp. & Exec. Dir., Mgmt. Serv. Co., Dayton, Ohio, 1944-48; Exec. Dir., For. Trade Admin. of Greek Govt., Athens, 1948-51; Dept. Chief, U.S. AID Mission to China, Taipei, Formosa, 1951-53; Pres., Int. Cons., Inc., San Diego, Calif., 1952-60; Chief, Indl. Dev. Div., U.S. Agcy. for Int. Dev., Lagos, Nigeria, 1960-63; Dir., Dev. Serv. Inst. & Cons., Nat. Investment Bank, Accra, Ghana, 1963-68; Pres., Int. Cons. Investment Co., Ltd., Nassau, Bahamas & Int. Dev. Cons., Inc., Wash., D.C., 1965-74; Financl. Advsr., Korea Dev. Finance Corp., Seoul 1968-74; Korea Investment & Finance Corp., 1972-74;Advsr., Jorea Capital Corp., ibid, 1973-74; Advsr., Ind. Dev. Bank, Saigon, S. Vietnam, 1973-74. Mbrships. incl: Soc. Advancement Mgmt. (Pres., San Diego, 1958-59, Nat. Dir., 1959-60); Royal Astatic Soc. (V.P., Korea Br., 1971-72); Rotary Club, Seoul, (Dir. Chmn., Int. Rels. Comm. 1972-73). Decorated by late King Paul of Greece w. Order of Battalion of Geo. 1, 1951. Address: Suite 500 1629 K St., N.W., Washington, DC 20006, U.S.A.

TERZIAN, Shohig Sherry. Psychiatric Librarian & Communication Specialist. Educ: A.B.(cum laude), Radcliffe Coll., Harvard Univ., 1937; M.S., Grad. Schl. Lib. Serv., Columbia Univ., 1942; grad. courses, Columbia Univ. & Univ. of Calif., L.A. Appts. incl: 1st Libn., Neurological Inst., Columbia-Presby. Med. Ctr., N.Y.C., 1940-41; Picture Ed. & Rsch. Asst., var. U.S. Govt. Dept. Offs., N.Y.C., 1943-46; Rsch. Libn., Time Inc., N.Y.C., 1947-48; Libn. i/c. Bus. & Recreation Libs., Western Home Off., Prudential Ins. Co. of Am., L.A., Calif., 1948-61; Libn., Profl. Staff & Patients' Libs., Neuropsychiatric Inst., UCLA Ctr., L.A., 1961-; var. cons. & advsry. appts., profl. & acad. orgs. Mbr. & Off., var. profl. orgs. Contbr., var. publs. & num. profl. jrnls. Recip., Citation for Radcliffe hons. thesis, Harvard Dept. Engl. Address: Neuropsychiatric Inst. UCLA Ctr. for Hlth. Sciences, Los Angeles, CA 90024, U.S.A. 5, 9, 42, 51, 130, 138.

TESAURO, Guiseppe, b. 21 June 1928. University Rector. Educ: Dr., Med. & Surg. Appts: Prof. Ob. & Gyn., Unvi. of Sassari, Italy, 1935-36; Univ. of Messina, 1936-42; Univ. of Naples, 1943-; Rector, ibid, 1959-. Expert Ob. & Gyn., WHO, 1958-. Mbrships. incl: Pres., Int. Fertility Assn. 1962-66; Pres., Int. Fedn. Gyn. & Ob. Pres., Societa Italiana di Ostetricia e Gimecologia, 1959-61. Publs: Trattato di Semeiotica e Diagnostica Ginecologica, 1963; Trattato Italiano di Ginecologia, Vol.6, 1970. Hons. incl: Gold Medal for Pub. Instrn. in Schl. Cultures & Arts; Gold Medal for merit in Pub. Hlth. Address: 51 Via S. Brigida, 80133 Napoli, Italy. 34, 43, 131.

TESCHL, Leopold, b. 14 Oct. 1911. Architect. Educ: Royal Danish Acad. of Fine Arts, 1938. Appts: Independent Archt., 1942-; Royal Surveyor, N. Jutland, 1953. Mbrships: Soc. of Acad. Archts.; Soc. of Danish Archts.; Archt. Sect., Soc. of Artists; Rotary Club, Frederikshavn. Archt. of churches; Reconstruction of Roman-Danish village ch., Mus. of Hjerl Hede; Restoration of Danish medieval churches; Organs in sev. churches; Schools, pub. bldgs., etc. Hons: Arch. Prize, Municipality of Aalborg, 1962, '63; Kt. of Daneborg 1st deg. Address: Søndergade 21². 9900 Frederickshavn, Denmark. 43.

TESORO, George Alfred, b. 6 Feb. 1904. Attorney. Educ: J.D., Univ. of Rome, Italy, 1925; Dr. Pol. Sci., ibid, 1929; Ph.D., 1930; Law Schl., Geo. Wash. Univ., U.S.A., 1946-47. Appts. incl: Corp. Lawyer, Tax Expert, Rome, Italy, 1927-38; Inst., Lectr., Univ. of Rome, 1930-35; Assoc. Prof., Univ. of Bari, 1935-38; Fndr., Ed., Rivista Italiana di Diritto Finanziario, 1937-38; News Ed., Italian Announcer, Radio Stn. WOV, N.Y.C., U.S.A., 1941-42; Adj. Prof., Am. Univ., 1942-55; Economist, Dpty. Econ. Advsr., Econ. Advsr., Div. Econ. Dev. & Off., Counselor, U.S. Mision, Geneva, Switzerland, 1956-65; Counsel, firm Cox, Langford & Brown, U.S.A. 1965-69, Coudert Bros., Wash. D.C., 1969-. Mbr., profl. orgs. Author, sev. books. Cmdr., Italian Order Merito della Repubblica. Address: Coudert Brothers, 1 Farragut Sq. S., Washington, DC 20006, U.S.A. 2.

TEZLA, Albert, b. 13 Dec. 1915. Professor, Educ: B.A., Univ. of Chgo., 1941, M.A., 1947, Ph.D., 1952. Appts: Instr., Engl. Lit., Ind. Univ. Ext. Div., S. Bend, 1946-48; Prof., Engl. Univ. of Minn., Duluth, 1949-; Vis. Prof., Hungarian Lit., Columbia Univ., 1966. Mbrships: Mod. Lang. Assn.; AAUP. Publs: An Introductory Bibliography to the Study of Hungarian Literature, 1964; Hungarian Authors: a Bibliographical Handbook, 1970; Translator, Ferenc Santa's 'God in the Wagon', New Hungarian Qtly.; Contbr. to book, East Central Europe: a Guide to Basic Publications, 1969. Hons. incl: Fac.-Staff Award, Student Assn., Univ. of Minn., Duluth, 1957; Fulbright Rsch. Fellow, Vienna, 1959-60; Commemorative Medal, Inst. of Culbural Rels., Budapest, Hungary, 1970. Address: Dept. of Engl., Univ. of Minn., Duluth, MN 55804, U.S.A. 13, 30.

THALBEN-BALL, George. Musician. Educ: Royal Coll. of Music, London. Appts: Organist, The Temple Ch., London, 1923; Prof., Royal Coll. of Music, 1923; Examiner, Royal Coll. of Organists, 1923 & Royal Schls. of Music, 1923; Curator-Organist, The Royal Albert Hall, 1930; Music Advsr, B.B.C., 1948; Univ. & Civic Organist, Birmingham, 1948. Mbrships: Pres., Inc. Soc. of Musicians, 1939, London Soc. of Organists, 1935, Royal Coll. of Organists, 1948 & num. other music socs.; Publd. sev.

compositions. Hons. incl: D.Mus. w. Gold Medal, Birmingham, 1972; C.B.E., 1967; Master of Bench, Inner Temple London. Address: c/o Inner Temple, London, EC4, U.K. 1, 4, 21,

THALHAMMER, Erwin, b. 11 July 1916. Director, Austrian State Theatre Administration. Educ: Univ. of Graz. Appts: Jr. Judge & Admnstrve. Off., Murau, Styria, 1947-50; Dir., dept. of mus., monuments & acads., Govt. Dept. of Educ., Austria, 1951; Dir., Austrian State Theatre Admin., 1965-69. Mbrships: V.P., Osterr. Burgenverein; Rotary Club, N.W. Vienna. Hons: Grosses Ehrenzeichen für Verdienste um die Repub. Osterreich; Silbernes Ehrenzeichen für Verdienste um die Repub. Osterreich; KmtK d norw St00. Address: Bundesdenkmalamt, Hofburg, Säulenstiege, A 1010, Vienna, Austria.

THATCHER, Hugh Knox, Jr., b. 16 May 1910. Physician & Surgeon. Educ: A.B., Butler Univ.; M.D., Ind. Univ. Med. Schl.; Intern & Surg. Res., Indpls. City Hosp. Appts: on staff, Meth., St. Vincents & Winona Meml. Hosps.; Chmn., Gen. Prac. Dept., Meth. Hosp., 1954; V.P. of Staff., ibid, 1972-73; Chmn., Ind. State Hosp. Licensing Coun., 1972-73; Pres., Staff Meth. Hosp., Indpls., Ind., 1974-. Mbrships: Past-Pres. Marion Co. Med. Soc. (On Coun., 1951-53, Bd. of Dirs., 1965-66); Treas., & Exec. Comm., Ind. State Med. Assn., 1972-73; Ind. State Gov.'s Commn. on Aging, 1956-57; AMA; Masons; Deacon, then Elder, Presby. Ch.; Pres., Tech. H.S. Alumni Assn., 1936. Address: 4548 M. Coll. Avenue, Indianapolis, IN 46205, U.S.A. 8, 82.

THAU, Avshalom, b. 18 June 1916. Architect. Educ: B.Sc., Fac. of Arch. & Town Planning, Technion-I.I.T., Haifa, 1939; Dipl., Ingineer-Archt., ibid, 1941. Appts: Tech. Dept., Solel-Boneh Ltd., Israel, 1941-48; Off. Cmdng. Bldg. & Construction Units, Israel Defence Army-Air Force, 1949-52; Off. i/c. Planning Dept., Off. Cmdg. Bldg. & Construction Units, Israel Defence Army Engrs. Corps, 1952-57; Lectr., Fac. of Arch. & Town Planning, Technion-IIT, Haifa, 1953066, Sr. Lectr., 1966-72, Assoc. Prof., 1972-; Pvte. Prac. in Arch., Haifa, 1957-. Mbrships: Assn. Engrs. & Archts. in Israel; Mbr., var. Govt. & Profl. comms. Contbr., articles profl. jrnls. Address: 1I4 Hanassi Ave., Haifa, Israel. 55, 94.

THEBERGE, Sévère, b. 15 Sept. 1915. Industrialist. Educ: St. Charles Sem., P.Q., Canada. Appts: Pres., Maibec Inds. Inc.; Maibec Logging Inc.; Maibec Lumber Inc.; Verbois Inc. Mbrships: Dir., P.Q. Forestry Assn.; P.Q. Forest Inds. Assn.; Mktng. Comm.; Nat. Am. Wholesaler Lumber Assn.; Forest Prods. Rsch. Soc.; Am. Pulpwood Assn.; N.E. Manpower & Trng. Comm., ibid; Am. Mgmt. Assn.; Me. Forest Prods. Coun.; Canadian Pulp & Paper Assn.; Bd. of Trade, Quebec Dist.; Garrisson Club. Address: Maibec Inds. Inc., 915 ouest, boul. St. Cyrille, Quebec, P.Q., G1S 1T8, Canada.

THEDE, Marion Draughon, (Mrs. Fred Thede), b. 11 Nov. 1903. Musician; Writer; Lecturer. Educ: Mus.B., Univ. of Okla.; Tchng. Cert., Chgo. Musical Coll. Appts. incl: Radio prog., Voice of Am., for twenty yrs.; H.S. Tchr., Engl., Spanish, Orch., 1929-34; Violinist & Violist, Okla. City Symph. Orch., 1937-67 & w. Tulsa Philharmonic Orch., 1965-71; Travelling instumental Tchr., Okla. Pub. Schls., 1952-70; Pvte. Studio w. husband, 1960-; Free Lance Writer on Folk Music subjects; Writer, Real West Mag.; Performances as violinist, violist, hardingfele, & fiddle in all fields of music bus.; Nat. Folk Festival Performances. Mbrships. incl: Fndr., Okla. Folk Coun., 1967 & Okla. State Fiddler's Assn., 1971; Folk Archivist, Okla., Fedn. of Music Clubs, 1964- & Folk Cons., 1972-73; Nat. Chmn., Folk Archives & Folk Music, Nat. Fedn. of Music Clubs, 1968-72; Nat. Bd. of Advsrs., Nat. Folk Festival, 1952-70; Acad. of Am. Educators. Author of the Fiddle Book, 1967. Address: 1824 N.W. 23rd St., Oklahoma City, OK 73106, U.S.A. 2, 30.

THELEN, Albert Vigoleis, b. 28 Sept. 1903. Author; Translator. Educ: Prussian coll. for textile ind., Krefeld; Univs. of Cologne & Münster. Appts: Sci. Asst., Pressa, Cologne, 1927-28; Chicken farmer & tech. advsr., Süchteln, 1928-31; Contbr. (under pseudonym Leopold Fabrizius), Het Vaderland, the Hague, 1933-40; Lit. Advsr., fndg. of Editiones Corona Paramaribo, Amsterdam/Paramaribo, 1947-49. Mbr. of var. socs. & acads. Publs. incl: Schloss Pascoaes, 1942; Die Insel des zweiten Gesichts, 1953, 8th edit. 1967, dtv edit., 1970. (Dutch & French translations forthcoming); Vigolotria, 1954; Der Tragelaph, 1955; Der Schwarze Herr Bahssetup, 1956; Runenmund, 1963; Glis-Glis, 1967; Ed. & translator of works by Teixeira de Pascoaes in Dutch & German; Articles in jrnls. Hons. incl: Fontane Prize, Berlin, 1954; Dr. hum C. und Ritter des Jungen Lichts der Acad. Equitans Dulcensis, 1973. Address: Chemin Ysabelle de Montolieu 179 5, Lausanne-Vennes, Switzerland. 43.

THEODORE, Frederick Harold, b. 4 Apr. 1908. Physician (Ophthalmologist), Educ: A.B., Columbia 1927; M.D., ibid, 1931; Internship & Residency in Ophthalmol., Mt. Sinai Hosp., N.Y.C., 1931-36. Appts. incl: former Attng. Opthalmic Surg., Mt. Sinai Hosp., N.Y.C.; former Attng. Ophthalmic Surg., Manhattan Eye, Ear & Throat Hosp., N.Y.C.; Assoc. Clin. Prof. Ophthalmol., N.Y. Univ., 1950-73; Clin. Prof. Ophthalmol., Mt. Sinai Schl. of Med., 1966-73; Cons. Ophthalmic Surg., Mt. Sinai Hosp., 1970-; Clin. Prof. Emiritus, Mt. Sinai Schl. of Med., 1973-; former Assoc. Ed., AMA Archives Ophthalmol.; Assoc. Ed., Eye, Ear, Nose & Throat Monthly & Pediatric Ophthalmol. Responsible for U.S.A. Law on Sterility of Eye Drops, 1953 & for sev. initial descriptions of new diseases. Mbrships. incl: Chmn., Sect. on Ophthalmol., N.Y. Acad. of Med.; Pres., N.Y. Soc. for Clin. Ophthalmol.; Pres., Manhattan Ophthalmological Soc.; AMA. Publs: Sr. author, Ocular Allergy; Ed., Complications After Cataract Surgery; contbns. in num. sci. books & author num. sci. papers. Hons. incl: Jacobi Medallion for Contributions to Med., Asscd. Alumni, Mt. Sinai Hosp., N.Y.C., 1973. Address: 625 Park Ave., N.Y., NY 10021, U.S.A. 55.

THEODORESCU, Radu Amza Serban, b. 12 Apr. 1933. Professor of Mathematics. Educ: B.Sc., M.Sc., Univ. of Bucharest, Rumania, 1954, D.Sc., 1967; Ph.D., Acad. of Romania, 1958. Appts: Asst. Prof.-Assoc. Prof., Sect. Hd. & Sci. Sec., Inst. of Maths., Acad. of Romania, 1954-64; Prof., Hd. of Dept., Ctr. of Math. Stats. ibid, 1964-68; Prof., Univ. of Bucharest, 1968-69; Prof., Laval Univ., Quebec, Canada, 1969-; Mbrships. incl: Canadian Math. Congress; Am. & German Math. Socs.; Am. Soc. for Quality Control; Int. Statsl. Inst.; Econometric & Biometric Socs. Publs: Processes with Complete Connections (w. G. Ciucu) 1960; Mathematical Information Theory, 1968 & Uncertainty & Information, 1971 (w. S. Guiasu); Random Processes & Learning (w. M. Iosifescu) 1969; Concentration Functions (w. W. Hengartner) 1973; contbr. to profl.

publs. Recip. of G. Lazar prize, Acad. of Romania, 1960. Address: 2276 Chemin Ste-Foy, Apt. 300, Ste-Foy, Quebec, G1V 1S7. Canada. 2, 6.

THEPSITHAR, Somphorn, b. 3 Nov. 1925. Government Official. Educ: Bach. Acctcy.; Bach. of Law; Master, Bus. Admin. Appts: Special Grade Econ., Dept. For. Trade, Min. Commerce; Dpty. Under-Sec. State for Commerce; Dir-Gen., Dept. Bus. Econs., Min. Commerce; Mbr. Nat. Legislative Assembly. Mbrships: Pres., Nat. Coun. Young Buddhists Assn.; VP & Chmn., Exec. Comm., Nat. Coun. Soc. Welfare. Author many publs. on econs., trade & Buddhism. Address: Dept. Bus. Econs., Min. Commerce, Bangkok, Thailand.

THERAIOS, Demetrios (Kutsoyannopulos), B. 28 Sept. 1932. Professor of Philosophy. Educ: Dip., Law, Athens Univ., 1954; Ph.D., Univ. of Freiburg i. Br., German Fed. Repub., 1959; Dip., Classical Philol., Athens Univ., Greece, 1961. Appts: Extraordinary Prof., Athens Univ., 1966, Ordinary Prof., 1969, 2nd-1st Vice Rector, 1970-73; Under Sec. of Educ., 1968. Dir. Gen. for Greeks Abroad, 1967; Mbrships: Sec. Gen., Greek Philosophical Soc.; Admin. Comm., Greek Humanistic Soc.; Greek Philological Soc.; Cambridge Philological Soc. Publs. in Greek incl: Hermeneutics of Logos, 1962; Theory of the 1st Principles, 1965. Author, var. papers in german. Recip., Cross of St. Marc 2nd Class, H.E. The Patriarch of Alexandreia. Address: Phokylidou Str. 6, Athens, Greece.

THERIOT-THERIEAU, Francis R., b. 2 May 1916. Medical Scientist; Clinical Psychologist; Nuclear Physicist. Educ: LL.B., Northeastern Univ., Boston, Mass., 1935; Md.Sc. & Ph.D., Georg August Univ. Gottingen, Germany, 1939; D.Sc., Kaiiser Wilhelm Inst. of Chem., 1939; Bus. Admin. & Econs., Georg August Univ., Gottingen, Germany. Appts. incl: Clin. Psychologist, administered psychological tests to German High Command, 1939; Liaison Off., Exec. Off. of Pres. Roosevelt assigned to Atomic Fission Prog., U.S.A. 1940-45; Rsch. Scientist, assigned by Pres. Truman to U.F.O.s, 1947-48; Clin. Psychologist, Sec. of Defense, 1948-49; Med. Rsch. Scientist, Marine Bio., Oceanography, Cardiol., Arthritis, White Caps, N.Y. Mbrships. incl: Hon. Fellow, Royal Acad., London , England; Guest Fellow, Phi Kappa Phi, Sigma Xi, Tau Beta Pi, Am. Assn. of Emeriti. Publs. incl: Num. profl. reports; Communication with Space Travelers: Artificial Hearts; Cancer-Cause, Effect, Treatment, & Elimination; Pregnancy and Cancer Compared. Hons. incl: Merit Award, Pres. Truman, 1946; J.D., War Trials. Address: P.O. Box 105, Stuyvesant, NY 12173, U.S.A. 6.

THERNEAU, Mary Ann (Ricky) (Mrs. Donald R. Therneau), b. 27 Nov. 1943. Piano Teacher; Social Service Director. Educ: A.A., Kilgore Coll., T.C.U.; B.A., Stephen F. Austin State Univ.; grad. work, S.F.A. Appts: Soc. Serv. Dir., Kilgore Nursing Ctr.; Piano Tchr.; Organist in Chs.; Display Advtng., Kilgore News Herald; Tchr., S.F.A. Mbrships: Pres. of PTA for 2 yrs., Parliamentarian for 1 yr. & V.P. for 1 yr.; Neighborhood Chmn., Girl Scouts for 2 yrs.; Pres. Epsilon Omega Chapt., Phi Sigma Alpha; Phi Theta Kappa. Address: Box 66, Kilgore, TX 75662, U.S.A. 125.

THEVENET, René, b. 5 May 1926. Film Producer. Educ: Lyons & Paris Univs. Appts: Jrnlst., 1947-50; Prod., Approx. 50 long features inclng: Serie Noire, 1954; The Twilight Girls, 1956; Sins of Youth, 1958; The Killing Game, 1966; You Only Love Once, 1967; Le

Temoin, 1969; Springtime, 1970; Le Sourire Vertical, 1972; Pres., Gen. Mgr., TV Cinema Co., 1972-. Mbrships: Past V.P., French Prods. Motion Picture Assn.; Rotary Int. Hons: Chevalier de l'Ordre des Arts & Lettres. Address: 79, Champs-Elysees, 75008, Paris, France. 43, 91.

THÉVENOT, Jean, b. 11 July 1916. Journalist; Radio and Television Writer and Producer. Educ: Bachelier, Licencié en Droit; Docteur ès-Scis. Sociales & Politiques. Appts. incl: Journalistic activities, Paris Radio Stn., 1936-38; Sub-Ed., Petit Radio, 1938; Prin. Ed., Paris-Mondial State Radio, 1939-40; Dir., Radio-Jeunesse, Nat. Radio, Vichy, 1941; Participated in liberation of the Radio & acted as Sec. Gen., Radiodiffusion, Aug. 1944; Dpty. Dir., Variety Serv., French Radiodiffusion, 1945-46; Author, Prod., Announcer, Promoter, Radio & TV Progs., France & abroad, 1946-; Promoter, var. pub. demonstrations of amateur sound recordings. Mbrships. incl: Hon. Pres., World Union of French Voices, & Int. Schol. Ctr. of Sound Corres.; Pres., Nat. Syndicate of Radio Prods.; V.P., Soc. of Writers for Cinema & TV; Terminol. Commn., ORTF. Publs. incl: L'âge de la Télévision et l'avenir de la Radio, 1946; TV (w. Jean Queval), 1957. Num. recordings. Hons. incl: Edouard Belin Prize for Radio & TV, 1961. Address: 9 Blvd. Julien Potin, 92200 Neuilly-sur-Seine, France.

THIÉBAULT, André Arthur Alfred, b. 24 Dec. 1918. Bridges & Highways Engineer. Educ: Ecole Polytechnique, Paris, 1938; Ecole Nationale des Ponts et Chaussées, Paris, 1945. Appts: Bridges & Hwys. Engr., Lyons, France, 1947; Chief Eng., Bridges & Hwys., Paris, 1959; Dir., l'Ecole Nationale des Ponts et Chaussées, Paris, 1967; Ingénieur Général des Ponts et Chaussées, 1969; Mbr., Gen. Coun. Bridges & Hwys., 1973. Mbrships: Pres., French Comm. Int. Assn. Rd. Congresses; Bd. Mbr., Société Nationale des Chemins de Fer Francais. Var. articles, profl. trng. & educ. Hons. incl: Off., Legion of Honour, 1966; Kt. of Acad. Palms, 1970; Off., Nat. Order of Ivory Coast, 1972; Cmdr., Order of Merit, 1973. Address: 33 Ave. Croulebarbe, F-75013 Paris, France. 91.

THIMANN, Kenneth Vivian, b. 5 Aug. 1904. Biologist. Educ: B.Sc., Royal Coll. of Sci., Imperial Coll., 1924; Assoc., Royal Coll. of Sci., 1924; Ph.D., 1928; Postdoct. Fellowship w. Profs. Pregl & Emich, Graz, 1928. Appts. incl: Instr., Bacteriol. & Biochem., Calif. Inst. of Technol., Pasadena, U.S.A., 1930-35; Asst. Prof. of Biol., Harvard Univ., 1935-39; Tutor in Biol., ibid, 1936-42; Assoc. Prof., Plant Physiol., 1939-46; Prof. of Biol., 1946-61; Higgins Prof. of Biol., 1961-65; Prof. of Biol. & Provost of Crown Coll., Univ. of Calif., Santa Cruz, 1965-. Mbrships. incl: Councillor, U.S. Nat. Acad. of Scis., 1968-71; For. mbr., Royal Soc., 1969-; Councillor, U.S. Philosophical Soc., 1972-; Pres., Am. Inst. of Biological Scis., 1965; Pres., Botanical Soc. of Am., 1960; Am. Acad. of Arts & Scis.; Dir., AAAS, 1968-71. Publs. incl: The Life of Bateria, 1955, 2nd edit. 1963, German translation 1964; The Natural Plant Hormone, 1972. Recip. of hons. Address: Thimann Labs., Univ. of Calif., Santa Cruz, CA 95064, U.S.A. 1, 2, 14, 34, 50, 128.

THIND, Khushdarshan Singh, b. 17 Aug. 1932. Medical Microbiologist; Scientist. Educ: Punjab Univ., India; Master's & Doct., Univ. of Pa., & Thomas Jefferson Univ., Phila., U.S.A. Appts: Fac., Jefferson Med. Coll., Thomas Jefferson Univ.; responsible for establng. lab. servs. in rural areas. Punjab; Mgr., Nat. Communicable Diseases Control Prog., Punjab;

Dir., State Pub. Hlth. & Malaria Labs., ibid; Hd., Hygiene & Vaccine Inst., ibid; Mbr., Sr. Civil Serv. Mbrships: Am. Soc. Microbio.; Am. Assn. Immunologists; Indian Assn. Microbiols.; Indian Assn. Pollution Control; Freemasons; Rotary Club. Author, num. articles & rsch. publs. in fields of immunol. & infectious diseases. Recip., num. hons. Address: No. 21, Sector 11-A, Chandigarh-11, Punjab, India.

THINET, Marcel, b. 19 Feb. 1907. General Building Contractor. Appts. incl: Admnstr., Entreprise Marcel Thinet, 1930-, Soc. des Grands Travaux of Africa & Menuiserie Marcel Thinet; Gen. Mng. Dir., Soc. Thinet et Cie, 1965- & Soc. des Sablières et Gravières du Forez; Fndr. & Hon. Pres., Assn. of Bldg. & Civil Engrng. Contractors of the Loire; Mayor, Talaudière, Loire. Mbrships: Rotary Club, Saint-Etienne; Yacht Club, France. Hons: Chevalier de la Légion d'Honneur; Chevalier du Mérite Soc.; Gold Medal, for Physical Educ. & Sports; Off. de l'Ordre Nat. de la Côte d'Ivoire. Address: Entreprise Thinet & Cie, 5 Ave. du Maréchal Juin, 92100 Boulogne, France. 91.

THIRKELL, Lancelot George, b. 9 Jan. 1921. Executive, BBC. Educ: Magdelan Coll., Oxford Univ. Appts: 3rd Sec., Western Dept., For. Off., 1946; 3rd Sec., British Legation, Budapest, Hungary, 1947; 2nd Sec., Eastern Dept., For. Off., 1948; Report Writer, BBC Monitoring Serv., 1950; Asst., BBC Appoints. Dept., 1950; Asst., BBC Staff Admin., 1955; Hd. of BBC Secretariat, 1961; Controller, Staff Trng. & Appts., BBC, 1964; Chief Asst. to Mng. Dir., External Servs., BBC. Also Councillor, Royal Borough of Kensington & Chelsea, 1959-62; Chmn., Notting Hill Adventure Playground, 1964-; European Advsry. Coun. of Salzburg Seminar in Am. Studies, 1969-. Publs: Russian Food for Pleasure, 1953; A Garden Full of Weeds, 1962. Address: 31 Lansdowne Rd., London W11 2LQ, U.K. 1, 131.

THODAY, John Marion, B. 30 Aug. 1916. Geneticist. Educ: B.Sc., Univ. Coll. of N. Wales, Bangor, U.K.; Ph.D., Trinity Coll., Cambridge; Sc.D., ibid, 1965. Appts: Cytologist, Mt. Vernon Hosp., Northwood, Middlesex, 1946-47; Lectr., then Hd. of Dept., Genetics, Sheffield Univ., 1947-59; Arthur Balfour Prof. of Genetics, Univ. of Cambridge, 1959-. Mbrships: Fellow, Royal Soc., 1964; Genetical Soc.; Eugenics Soc.; Fellow, Emmanual Coll., Cambridge. Publs: num. papers on experimental population genetics esp. in Heredity. Address: Dept. of Genetics, Milton Rd., Cambridge, CB4 1XH, U.K. 1.

THODY, Philip Malcolm Waller, b. 21 Mar. 1928. University Professor. Educ: King's Coll., London Univ., 1948-51; M.A., Univ. of London, 1953. Appts: Lecteur anglais, Univ. of Paris, 1953-54; Temp. Asst. Lectr., Univ. of Birmingham, U.K., 1954-55; Asst. Lectr., Lectr., Queen's Univ., Belfast, 1956-65; Prof., French Lit., Univ. of Leeds, 1965-; Chmn., French Dept., ibid, 1968-72; Chmn., Bd. of Facs. of Arts, Econ. & Soc. Studies & Law, ibid, 1972-. Also Vis. Prof., Univ. of Western Ont., Canada, 1963-64; Berkeley Summer Schl., Calif., U.S.A., 1964; Harvard Summer Schl., Mass., 1968. Publs: Albert Camus, A Study of His Work, 1957; Jean-Paul Sartre, A Literary & Political Study, 1960; Albert Camus, 1913-1960, 1961; Jean Genet, A Study of His Novels & Plays, 1968; Jean Anouilh, 1968; Four Cases of Literary Censorship, 1968; Laclos: Les Liaisons dangerereuses, 1970; Jean-Paul Sartre, A Bibliographical Introduction, 1971; Aldous Huxley, A Bibliographical Introduction, 1973. Address:

Dept. of French, Univ. of Leeds, Leeds LS2 9JT, U.K.

THOM, James Theophilus, b. 27 Apr. 1916. Associate Professor of Education. Educ: Primary Tchrs. Trng. Coll., Guyana, 1938-40; B.A., Univ. of London, J.K., 1951; M.A. (Ed.), ibid, 1961; Ph.D., 1969. Appts. incl: Tchr., sev. schls., Guyana, 1938-48; Master, Montserrat Govt. Secondary Schl., Georgetown, 1948-53; Prin., Valley Secondary Schl., Anguilla, British W. Indies, 1953-57; Dist. Educ. Off., Min. of Educ., Guyana, 1957-65; Dpty. Chief Educ. Off., ibid, 1965-70; Assoc. Prof., Educ., Bowie State Coll., Md., U.S.A., 1971-. Mbrships. incl: Chmn., Anguilla Br., St. Kitts-Nevis-Anguilla Tchrs. & Civil Serv. Assns., 1954-56; Chmn., Sr. Profl. Sect., Guyana Civil Serv. Assn., 1964-70; AAUP; Md. Assn. of Higher Educ.; Exec., Guyana Red Cross Soc., 1967-70. Recip., Guyana Independence Medal for Long & Meritorious Serv. in Educ., 1969. Address: 12504 Millstream Drive, Bowie, MD 10715, U.S.A. 136, 141.

THOM, William Cumming, b. 6 July 1898. Minister, Church of Scotland, U.K. Educ: Univs. of Aberdeen, Glasgow & Columbia, N.Y., U.S.A.; M.A., B.D., Ph.D., Aberdeen; S.T.M., Union Sem., N.Y., U.S.a. Appts: Ch. of Scotland Min., Carnoustie, Glasgow & Edinburgh; Prin. & Prof., St. Andrew's Coll., Univ. of Sydney, Australia; Presby. Ch., Haberfield, Sydney; Retd. 1968; Moderator, N.S.w. Assembly, Australia, 1955-56. Recip., D.D., Aberdeen. Address: 25 Wongoola Close, O'Connor, Canberra, A.C.T., Australia.

THOMAS, Alois, b. 18 Jan. 1896. Professor. Educ: Theol. Fac., Trier & Innsbruck. Appts: Vicar, W. Germany, 1920; Archivist & Diocesan Chancellor, Trier, 1936; Synodical Judge, 1941. Univ. Lectr., Sem. of Trier, 1946; Fac. of Theol., ibid, 1952; Assoc. Prof., ibid, 1957; Prof. Emeritus, 1966. Mbrships: Gesellschaft fur rheinische Geschichtskunde; Gesellschaft fur mittelrheinische Kirchengeschichte (V.P.); Gesellschaft fur saarlandische Geschichte & Volkskunde; Inst. Grandducal de Luxemburg. Publs. incl: Die Darstellung Christi in der Kelter, 1936; Handbuch des Bistums Trier, 1938, '52; Der Weltklerus der Diözese Trier, 1941; Wilhelm Arnold Günther, 1957; Neue Bauten im Bistum Trier, 1967. Hons. incl: Papal Prelate; Order Cavaliers, Holy Sepulchre. Address: Domfreihof 2, 55 Trier, German Fed. Repub. 43.

THOMAS, Anthony Frederick Leighton, b. 28 Apr. 1927. Musician; Company Director. Educ: New Coll., Oxford, U.K., 1948-51. Appts: Extra-Mural Lectr. in Music, Univ. Coll., Swansea, 1964-; Libn., Welsh Nat. Opera Co., 1966-71; Sec., The Guild for the Promotion of Welsh Music, 1965-68; Ed., Welsh Music, 1968-73; Choirmaster & Organist, All Saints' Ch., Llanelli, 1971-. Mbrships: The Royal Musical Assn.; Ch. Music Soc.; Humn Soc. of Gt. Britain & N. Ireland; Hon. Life mbr., Llanelli Organists' Assn.; V.P., Llanelli Conservative Assn. Publs: Arrangements of Welsh Folk Songs; Articles in jrnls. & newspapers inclng. The Times, The Oxford Times, The Music Review, The Musical Times, Musical Opinion, Welsh Music, The Anglo-Welsh Review, Radio Times, Composer, Mosaic, Western Mail. Address: "Glyneithin", Burry Port, Carmarthenshire, U.K. 4.

THOMAS, Carol J. (Mrs. Charles R. Thomas), b. 29 Aug. 1923. City Planner. Educ: Vassar Coll., 1941-43; Boston Univ., 1943, '49; A.B., Syracuse Univ., 1948; M.A., Univ. of Conn., 1950; Post Grad., MIT, 1950-51. Appts:

Freelance Community Planner, working w. Arthur Comey et al, 1950-58; Ptnr., Sonthoff & Thomas, Community Planners, 1958-61; Pres., & Treas., Thomas Assocs., 1961-69; Dir., Thomas Assocs. Div., Universal Engrng. Corp., 1969-; Vis. Lectr., Grad. Curric. in Community Planning & Urban Dev., Univ. of R.I., 1964-66, Asst. Prof., 1966-72, Adjunct Prof., 1972, Dir. of Summer Inst., 1969; Lectr., Urban Planning, Boston State Coll. 1971-. Mbrships: Pres., New England Chapt., Am. Inst. of Planners, 1966-68, V.P., 1965-66, Treas., 1963-65, Mbr. of Jury Awards, 1968-71, Mbr. of Bd. of Examiners, 1968-; Dir.-at-large, Mass. Fedn. of Planning Bds., 1959-62, 1972-; Am. Soc. of Planning Officials; Mass. Conf. of Planning Dirs. Contbr. of articles & reports to profl. jrnls. Address: 100 Boylston St., Boston, MA 02116, U.S.A. 5, 6, 16, 132,

THOMAS, Clarice A. Educator. Educ: B.S., Morgan State Coll., Balt., Md.; M.A., N.Y. Univ. Appts: Elem. Schl. Tchr., Virgin Islands, 1924-35; Elem, Schl. Prin., 1935-. Mbrships: Organist & Choir Dir., Treas., Sec., Women's Fellowship, Bethany Moravian Ch.; Am. Red Cross; Community Chest; Girl Scouts Am.; Bus. & Profl. Women's Club; League of Women Voters Club. Recip., Disting. Serv. Award, V.I. Dept. of Educ., 1971. Address: P.O. Box 15, Cruz Bay, St. John, VI 00830, U.S.A. 136.

THOMAS, Daniel H., b. 6 Dec. 1904. Professor of History. Educ: A.B., Univ. of Ala., 1925; M.A., 1929; Ph.D., Univ. of Pa., 1934. Appts: Tchr., pub. & pvte. schls., Ala., 5 yrs.; Fac., Dept. of Hist., Butler Univ., 1930-31; Univ. of Ala., 1935-36; Temple Univ., 1938-40; Prof., Hist., Univ. of R.I., 1940-74; Vis. Prof., Univs. of Pa. & Ala. & Emory Univ. Mbrships: Chmn., Fndng. Comm. & Pres., New Engl. Hist. Assn.; Phi Alpha Theta; Pres., New Engl. Hist. Tchrs. Assn.; Am. Hist. Assn.; Phi Beta Kappa; Phi Kappa Phi. Contbr., Diplomacy in an Age of Nationalism, 1970 & Good Reading, 1945-60. Co-Ed., Guide to Diplomatic Archives of Western Europe, 1975. Author of articles in profl. jrnls. Hons: Univ. of Pa. Harrison Post-Doct. Fellow; C.R.B. Fellow; Fulbright Rsch. Fellow; Officer, Order of Leopold II, Belgium. Address: 12 Briar Lane, Kingston, RI 02881, U.S.A. 13, 30.

THOMAS, Della Pauline (Mrs. J.E. Thomas), b. 27 Mar. 1913. Librarian; Consultant. Educ: Grad., Wis. State Coll. of Superior, 1935; Grad., Lib. Schl., Univ. of Wis.,1942. Appts. incl: Cons. & Bibliographer, Scott, Foresman Co. (Publrs.), Chgo., 1945-56; Hd. Educ. Area & Asst. Prof. Lib. Sci., Okla. State Univ. Lib., 1957-65; Hd., Curriculum Mats. Lab. & Assoc. Prof., ibid, 1965-69; Dir., Int. Studytours, Children's Lit., 1967-74; Cons., H.W. Wilson Publrs., 1968-. Mbrships: ALA (Num. Comms. inclng. Newbery-Caldecott, 1970, CSD Int. Rels. 1968-75, Chmn., ibid 1969-74); Okla. Lib. Assn. (Pres. 1964-65); SW Lib. Assn. (Pt.-time Exec. Sec. 1969-72); Beta Phi Mu. Publs: Practical Projects for the School Library; Third Book of Junior Authors; Fourth Book of Junior Authors; Your Library Resources (Media Kit); Contbr. to profl. jrnls. & newspapers. Hons: Disting. Serv. Award, Okla. Lib. Assn., 1969. Address: 217 N. Stallard, Stillwater, OK 74074, U.S.A. 5, 7, 42.

THOMAS, George Isaiah, b. 16 June 1915. Educational Administrator, Writer & Researcher. Educ: B.A., Ctrl. Conn. State Coll., 1937; M.A., Tchrs. Coll., Columbia Univ., 1940; Ph.D., ibid, 1951. Appts. incl: Tchr., Colebrook, Clinton & Hartford, Conn., 9 yrs.; Prin., R.J. Kinsella Schl., Hartford, 2 yrs.; Ridge Rd. Schl., N. Haven, '4 yrs.; Prof. of

Educ., Univ. State Coll. of New Paltz, 3? yrs., Dir., Lab. Schl., ibid, 3 yrs.; Supt. of Schls., Morris Twp., N.J., 2? yrs., N. Arlington, N.J., 5? yrs.; Cons., State Educ. Dept., Div. of Rsch. 7 yrs. Mbr., profl. orgs. Publs. incl: Individualizing Instruction in the Elementary Schools (co-author); Guiding the Gifted Child (co-author); Administrator's Guide to the All Year School; num. articles, nat. & state jrnls., & reports, State Educ. Dept., N.Y. Recip., book club awards. Address: 80 Montrose Dr., Elsmere, NY 12054, U.S.A.

THOMAS, Grace Fern, b. 23 Sept. 1897. Physician; Psychiatrist; Minister. Educ: B.S., Univ. of Neb., 1924; M.A. (Biochem), Creighton Univ., Omaha, Neb., 1926; M.D., Univ. of Southern Calif. Schl. of Med., 1935; M.A. (Relig.), ibid, 1968; postgrad. studies; Dipl., Am. Bd. Psych. & Neurol., 1953. Ordained Min., Meth. Ch., 1968. Appts. incl: Capt., Med. Corps., Army of U.S., 1944-46. Chief, Psych. Educ., Porterville State Hosp., Calif., 1965-66; Dir., Tuolumne Co. Med. Hlth. Servs., Sonora, Calif., 1966-70; Pvte. Prac., Psych., Turlock Calif., 1970-73 & Modesto, Calif., 1973-; Psych.-Cons., Stanislaus Co. Mental Hlth. Dept., Modesto, 1972-73; Alienist, Stanislaus Co. Superior Ct., Modesto, 1972-; Staff Mbr., Emanuel Hosp., Turlock, 1970-; Doctors Hosp. & Scenic Gen. Hosp., Modesto, 1973-, Modesto City Hosp. & Mem. Hosp., 1974-. Mbrships. incl: AMA; Calif. Med. Assn.; Ctrl. Calif., Am. & Stanislaus Co. Psych. Socs.; Am. Med. Women's Assn.; Insts. of Relig. & Hlth. Publs: Collaborative Psychotherapy by Psychiatrist & Clergy in Problems of Guilt & Suffering, 1968. Address: 1900 N. Denair Ave., Turlock, CA 95380, U.S.A. 5, 9, 17, 132.

THOMAS, Graham Stuart, b. 3 Apr. 1909. Horticulturist. Educ: Cambridge Univ. Botanic Garden, U.K. Appts: Six Hills Nursery, Herts., 1930; Foreman-Mgr., T. Hilling & Co. Ltd., Cobham, Surrey, 1931; Mgr., Sunningdale Nurseries, Surrey, 1956; Assoc. Dir., ibid, 1968-71; Gardens Advsr., Nat. Trust, 1955-74; Gardens Cons., ibid, 1974-. Felkowships: Judge, Royal Horticultural Soc.; Northern Horticultural Soc. Mbrships: Brit. Pteridol. Soc.; Coun., Royal Nat. Rose Soc.; Comm., Garden Hist. Soc. Publs. incl: Shrubs Roses of Today, 1962; Climbing Roses Old & New, 1965; Plants for Ground Dover, 1970; Ed., Book of Garden Ornament, 1974. Hons: Veitch Mem. Medal, Royal Horticultural Soc., 1966; Victoria Medal of Hon., 1968. Address: Briar Cottage, Fairfield Lane, West End, Woking, Surrey, U.K. 3.

THOMAS, (Rev.) John David, b 24 June 1928. Priest; Superintendent of Schools. Educ: B.A., Boston Coll., Mass., 1950; S.T.B., Gregorian Univ., Rome, Italy, 1953; S.T.L., ibid, 1955; M.A., Assumption Coll., Worcester, Mass., U.S.A., 1962. Ordained Roman Cath. Priest, N. Am. Coll., Rome, Italy. Appts: Ft. Diocese of Worcester, 1956-57, Tchr. of Theol., St. Vincent Hosp. Schl. of Nursing, ibid; Secondary Schl. Tchr. of Classics, 1957-61; Headmaster, St. Peter C.C. H.S., 1961-66; Asst. Supt for Diocesan Schls. (Elem. & Secondary), 1961-66; Asst. Supt. for Diocesan Schls. (Elem. & Secondary), 1961-66; Supt. of Diocesan Schls., 1966-. Mbrships. incl: Nat. Cath. Educl. Assn.; New Engl. Regional Chmn. & Nat. Exec. Comm., Dept. of Chief Admnstrs.; Bd. of Dirs., New Engl. Cath. Educ. Ctr. (Boston Coll.); Educl. Dev. Commn. for Commonwealth Mass. Contbr. to reports for Mass. Advsry. Coun., 1971 & Bd. of Educ., 1971. Recip. of Pro Deo et Juventute Award for outstanding contbn. to youth, 1967. Address: Diocese of Worcester-Chancery Bldg., Dept. of Educ.-Schl.

Div., 49 Elm St., Worcester MA 01609, U.S.A. 49.

THOMAS, Keith Vivian, b. 2 Jan. 1933. University Teacher. Educ: Balliol Coll., Oxford Univ., B.A., 1955; M.A., 1959. Appts: Fellow, All Souls Coll., Oxford Univ., 1955-57; Fellow, Tutor in Mod. Hist., St. John's Coll., ibid, 1957-. Also Vis. Prof., La. State Univ., La., U.S.A., 1970. Mbrships: Fellow, Joint Lit. Dir., Royal Historical Soc.; Publs: Religion & the Decline of Magic, 1971; Also contbr. of chapts. to books & author, articles, reviews in periodicals; Edit. Bd., Past & Present, 1968-. Hons: 1st Class Hons., Mod. Hist., Oxford Univ.; Wolfson Lit. Award for Hist., 1972. Address: St. John's Coll., Oxford Univ., Oxford OX1 3JP, U.K.

THOMAS, Lionel (Arthur John), b. 3 Apr. 1915. Associate Professor. Educ: John Russel Schl. of Fine Arts, Toronto, Ont., Canada, 1933-35; Ont. Coll. of Art, 1936-37; Hans Hoffman Schl. of Fine Art, Provincetown, Mass., 1947; Calif. Schl. of Fine Art, San Fran., 1949. Appts. incl: Instr., Schl. of Arth., Univ. of B.C., 1950-59; Asst. Prof., ibid, 1959-64; Assoc. Prof., Dept. of Fine Arts, 1964-. One man exhibs: Vancouver Art Gall., 1942, 48; Fine Arts Gall., Univ. of B.C., 1947, 48, 51. Grp. exhibs. incl: Sao Paulo Biennial, 1954; Caracas, Venezuela, 1954; Seattle Art Mus., 1954; Univ. of Calif., San Fran., 1960; Corvallis State Univ., 1963; Zan Art Gall., Victoria, B.C., 1973. Mbrships. incl: B.C. Soc. Artlsts; Canadian Grp. of Painters; Royal Canadian Acad. Arts. Works incl: murals, bronze bas relief, fountains, etc. Perm. collects. incl: Nat. Gall. of Canada, Ottawa; Art Gall. of Ont.; Vancouver Art Gall. Recip., award, Pacific N.W. Artists Exhib., Seattle, 1952. Address: Univ. of B.C., Dept. of Fine Arts, 2075 Wesbrook Place, Vancouver, B.C., V6T 1W5, Canada.

THOMAS, Llewellyn Hilleth, b. 21 Oct. 1903. Physicist. Educ: Trinity Coll., Cambridge Univ., U.K., 1921-29; B.A., 1924; M.A., 1928; Ph.D., 1927; D.Sc., 1965; Univ. Inst. for Theoretical Phys., Copenhagen, 1925-26. Appts. incl: Fellow, Trinity Coll., Cambridge Univ., 1926-30; Asst. Prof. of Phys., Ohio State Univ., 1929-30; Assoc. Prof., ibid, 1930-36; Prof., ibid, 1936-46; Mbr. of Sr. Staff, Watson Scientific Rsch. Labs., Columbia Univ., 1946-68; Prof. of Phys., Columbia Univ., 1950-68; Emeritus Prof., 1968-; Vis. Prof. of Phys., N.C. State Univ. at Raleigh, 1968-. Mbrships: Nat. Acad. of Scis.; AAUP; Am. Phys. Soc.; Phi Beta Kappa; Sigma Xi; Royal Astronomical Soc.; Cambridge Philosophical Soc.; British Assn. for Advancement of Sci.; AAAS. Author of num. articles in scientific jrnls. Hons: Smith Prize, 1924. Address: Dept. of Phys., N.C. State Univ. at Raleigh, Raleigh, NC, U.S.A. 1, 14, 47, 50, 128.

THOMAS, Margaret Darley, b. 7 Jan. 1899. Business Executive. Educ: Grad., Ga. Normal Coll. & Bus. Inst. Appts: Pvte. Sec., lawyer's off., 7 yrs.; Assoc., Fairfax Tractor & Implement Co. (John Deere), husband's firm; Pres., ibid, at husband's death, 1961, until retirement, 1973. Mbr. & off., var. ch. orgs. Honoured by Bapt. Ch. observance of Margaret Darley Thomas Day, 27 May, 1973. Address: Fairfax, SC 29827, U.S.A. 125.

THOMAS, Mary Lou, b. 27 Apr. 1927. Office Manager; Secretary. Educ: Sul Ross State Tchr. Coll., Alpine, Tex.; S.W. Tex. Jr. Coll., Uvalde, Tex.; var. bus. courses, Tex. Christian Univ. & Univ. of Tex., Austin. Appts: Owner-Operator, Romper House Childcare, Santa Fe, N.M.; Asst. Admnstr., Carrizo Springs

Nursing Home, Tex.; Mgr.-Sec., Dimmit Co. Chmbr. of Comm., Carrizo Springs; Co. Off. Clerk, Farmers Home Admin., U.S. Dept. of Agric.; currently Staff, Nursing Home Mgmt. Co. Inc., San Antonio, Tex. Mbrships. incl: Pres. & Charter Mbr., Carrizo Springs Bus. & Profl. Womens Club; Charter Mbr., Carrizo Springs Nursing Home Auxiliary. Contbr., weekly news column, Carrizo Springs Javelin. Recip., Tex. Mgrs. & Secs. Assn. of Chmbr. of Comm. Schlrship. Award, 1968. Address: 706 Finale Ct., San Antonio, TX 78216, U.S.A. 57, 138.

THOMAS, Minna Lee (Mrs. Charles Curtis Thomas). Writer; Artist; Song Composer. Appts: Newspaper Columnist; Edit. Writer; Poetess; Song Composer. Mbrships: Eastern White Shrine of Jerusalem; Celebrities Club, Hollywood; Pliades Club, L.A., Calif.; Nat., State & local chapts., Nat. Grange, a farm org.; Centro Studi e Scambi Int., Rome, Italy; Chmbr. of Comm., Chappral of Riverside; Nat. League of Am. Pen Women. Publs. incl: Your America & Mine (poem); Golden Dream Land (song); Beautiful Riverside (poem); Light of Home (poem); "Sunshine Corner", a poetry column for Antelope Valley Press; num. poems & songs in newspapers & jrnls. Address: 8570 Cypress Ave., Riverside, CA 92503, U.S.A.

THOMAS, Peter Edward, b. 4 Nov. 1936. General Insurance Underwriter. Educ: Temple Univ., Phila., Pa., U.S.A., 1963-64; Assoc., Chartered Ins. Inst., London, U.K. Appts: Motor Mgr., Ins. Co. of Jamaica, W. Indies, 1966; Accident Supt., Jamaica Hd. Off., Nat. Employers Mutual, 1967; Br. Mgr., Nat. Employers Mutual, Grand Cayman & Montego Bay, 1969; Asst. Mgr., Motor Owners Mutual Ins. Assn. Ltd., Kingston, 1970; Mgr., ibid, 1972; Exec. Dir., 1973; Dir., Caribbean Holidays Ltd., 1973; Dir., P.E.M. Ltd., 1973. Mbrships: Chmn., Jamaica Amateur Operatic Soc., 1970, Stage Mgr., 1969-73; Chmn., Youth Educ. & Community Dev. Comm., Lions Club, 1972-73; Comm., Ins. Inst. of Jamaica, 1972-73; Jamaica Expoeters Assn.; Inst. of Dirs.; Jamaica Inst. of Mgmt. Address: c/o Motor Owners Mutual Insurance Association Ltd., 16A Half Way Tree Rd., Kingston 5, Jamaica, W. Indies.

THOMAS, Wayne Elvin, b. 16 Feb. 1928. Lawyer. Educ: B.A., W. Tex. State Univ., 1947; LL.B., Univ. of Tex., 1951. Appts: Admitted to Tex. Bar, 1951; Supreme Ct. of U.S., 1959; Tax Ct., U.S., 1967; Ptnr., Thomas & Burdett, Hereford, Tex., 1951-. Fellow, Am. Coif Probate Coun., Tex. Bar Fndn. Mbrships incl: Grievance Comm., Tex. State Bar, 1972-; Am. Bar Assn.; Am. Judicature Soc.; Chmn., United Fund, 1963-64; Chmn., Ind. Dev. Comm., 1967-68 Dir., Deaf Smith Gen. Hosp., 1954-67; Pres., 1957; Chmn., Coord. Bd., Tex. Coll. & Univ. Systems, 1969-; Deaf Smith Co. Chmbr. of Comm.; Delta Theta Phi. Address: 116 S. 25 Mile Ave., Hereford, TX 79045, U.S.A. 7.

THOMEIER, Siegfried, b. 19 Dec. 1937. Scientist; Educator. Educ: Dipl.-Math., Frankfurt, Germany, 1962; Dr.Phil.Nat., Johann-Wolfgang-Goethe-Univ., ibid, 1965. Appts: Scientific Asst., Frankfurt Univ., 1963-65; Lektor, Amanuensis, Matematisk Inst., Aarhus, Denmark, 1965-68; Prof., Maths., Mem. Univ., St. John's, Nfld., Canada, 1968-. Mbrships: Deutsche Mathematiker-Vereinigung; London Math. Soc.; Wiskundig Genootschap van Belgie; Soc. Math. de Belgique; Am. Math. Soc.; Dansk Matematisk Foreningen; Canadian Math. Cong.; Math. Assn. Am. Publs: Ed., Topology & its Applications, 1974; Reviewer,

Zentralblatt fur Mathematik, 1967-; contbr. of articles to var. profl. jrnls. Hons. incl: Rsch. Grants, Nat. Rsch. Coun., Canada, 1969-. Address: 13 Exmouth St., St. John's, Nfld., A1B 2E1, Canada. 6.

THOMPSON, Andrew W., b. 14 Nov. 1924. Senator; Company Executive. Educ: Univ. of Toronto; B.A., Univ. of Queens; M.S.W., Univ. of B.C. Appts: Atty. Gen.'s Dept., B.C., 1949-51; Dept. of Citizenship & Immigration, Canada, 1951-57; Spec. Asst., Hon. L.B. Pearson, 1957-59; Ont. Legis., 1959, re-elected 1963; Senator, 1967; Chmn., Canadian Foods, Ltd.; Dir., Deltan, Delzotto Enterprises. Mbrships: Canadian Folk Arts Coun. (Chmn.); Canadian Ethnic Press Club (Hon.); Canadian Commonwealth Parliament Assn. (Exec. Comm.); N.A.T.O. Assn.; World Federalist Parliament Assn.; Rideau Club, Ottawa; Nat. Club, Toronto. Address: 12 Ava Cres., Toronto, Canada. 88.

THOMPSON, Bernice Joyce, (Mrs. H. Thurlow Thomson), b. 25 Aug. 1923. Physiotherapist; Specialist in Respiratory Diseases. Educ: Otago Univ., N.Z.; N.Z. Schl. of Physiotherapy, Dunedin. Appts: Physiotherapist i/c, Gray River Hosp., N.Z., 1944-45; Friends Ambulance Unit, North Honan, Inst. of Hosp. Technol., Hankow, 1945; Physiotherapist, St. John's Hosp., Lewisham, London, 1948; Trng. in Thoracic Physiotherapy, Sully Hosp., Wales, 1949-50; Pvte. prac., Christchurch, N.Z., 1959-. Mbrships: Past V.P., N.Z. Soc. of Physiotherapists; Chartered Soc. of Physiotherapy, G.B.; Past Sec., South Is. Br., Physiotherapy Pvte. Prac. Soc., N.Z. Publs: Asthma & Your Child, 1963, 4th edit., 1972; Better Breathing, 1967, 3rd edit., 1973; Films—Asthma & Your Child, Attack on Asthma, Asthma & Bronchitis. Hons: N.Z. Deleg., World Conf. of Physiotherapy, Melbourne, 1967; World Cong. of Rehab., Sydney, 1972. Address: 73a Hackthorne St., Christchurch 2, N.Z.

THOMPSON, Bryant Forrest, b. 10 Jan. 1933. Church Musician; Church Financier. Educ: B.A., Univ. of Ky., Lexington, U.S.A.; Postgrad., Southern Bapt. Sem., Louisville, Ky. Ordained to Gospel Min., 1957. Appts. incl: Dir. of Ch. Music, var. chs., Ky., Ind., & Fla., 19 years.; Music Dir. & Staff Announcer, WEKY Radio, Lexington, 2 yrs.; Music Dir., Univ. of Ky. Broadcasting Servs., 2 yrs.; Exec. Dir., & Mgr., WVCF & WWQS Christian Broadcasting Stns., United Communications Mission, 1966-70; P/T Min. of Music, Dover Shores Bapt. Ch., Orlando, Fla., 1968-; Ch. Prog. Dir., & State Dir. for Fla., Fidelity Plan, Inc., Atlanta, Ga., 1972-73; V.P., Heritage Institutional Securities, Inc., Orlando, 1974-. Mbrships: Active Civitan, 1967-, Pres., 1970-71; Sec., Southeastern Chapt., Nat. Religious Broadcasters, 1968; Phi Mu Alpha. Hons: Outstanding Young Broadcaster of 1954, Ky. Broadcasting Assn.; Man of the Yr. Award, Psi Alpha Chi Chapt., Tri-Hi-Y (YMCA), 1972. Address: 2305 Buckminster Circle, Orlando, FL 32803, U.S.A. 125.

THOMPSON, Charles Benjamin, Jr., b. 22 Oct. 1917. Civil Engineer. Educ: B.S., Univ. of N.M., Albuquerque, U.S.A., 1940; M.S., Univ. of Iowa, Ames, 1948. Appts. incl: Jr. Assoc., Chief Insp. of Ordnance Mats., War Dept., St. Louis Ordnance Plant, 1941-43; Ordnance Engr., Ind. Specialist, Ind. Engr., Tech. Ed., War Dept. Off., Chief of Ordnance, Wash. D.C., 1943-46; Asst. Prof., Civil Engrng., Univ. of N.M., 1948-51; Engr., N.M. Interstate Stream Commn., Santa Fe, 1951-53; Chief, Tech. Div.,

N.M. State Engrng. Off., ibid, 1953-58; Civil Engr., Litchfield Whiting Browne Assoc., Bangkok, Thailand, 1958-59; Hydraulic Engr., U.S. Study Comm., Houston, Tex., 1959-61; Water Resources Engr., U.S. State Dept., Agcy. Int. Dev., Wash. D.C., 1961-. Profl. Engr. in 11 States. Mbrships: Am. Soc. of Civil Engrs.; Int. Assn. of Irrigation & Drainage; Int. Assn. for Hydraulic Rsch.; Am. Water Works Assn.; Am. Ordnance Assn.; Nat. Soc. of Profl. Engrs.; Int. Comm. on Large Dams; Int. Water Supply Assn.; Am. Legion; Sigma Tau; Cni Epsilon. Author, num. reports, manuals & tech. papers. Address: 5705 Indian Ct., Alexandria, VA 22303, U.S.A. 7, 16, 26, 63.

THOMPSON, Edward Ian, b. 25 Feb. 1931. Musician; Potter; Librarian. Educ: M.A., Mus. B, Univ. of Glasgow, Appts: Libn.- Sr. Libn., Lectr., Royal Scottish Acad. of Music & Drama, 1956-74; Lectr., Music, Extra Mural Dept., Glasgow Univ., 1957-74. Mbrships: Int. Assn. of Music Libns.; Inc. Soc. of Musicians; Assoc., Royal Coll of Organists; Scottish Mountaineering Club; Swiss Alpine Club; Royal Musical Assn.; Assoc., Craftsmen Potters Assn.; Hon. Past Pres. & Past Pres., Jr. Mountaineering Club of Scotland. Publs: Early English Church Music, Vol. 7 Robert Ramsey, English Church Music, 1967; Vol. 19 & 20 (in preparation). Address: The Library, Royal Scottish Acad. of Music & Drama, 58 St. George's Place, Glasgow, G2 1BS, U.K. 4.

THOMPSON, Fred Edgar, b. 28 Dec. 1909. Teacher; Accountant. Educ: B.A.E., Univ. of Miss., 1936; M.B.A., ibid, 1951. Appts: Bookkeeper, Copiah-Lincoln Jr. Coll., Wesson, Miss., 1933-35; Asst. Fin. Sec., Univ. of Miss., Oxford, Miss., 1941-43; w. Armed Servs., Psychol. Testing, 1943-45; Bus. Mgr., Copia-Lincoln Jr. Col., 1945-47; Tchr. & Chmn., Div. of Bus., ibid, 1947-. Mbrships: Phi Delta Kappa; Chmn., of Sect., Jr. Coll. Bus. Assn., Miss. Educ. Assn.; Nat. Bus. Educ. Assn.; Past Master, Masonic Lodge; Past Cmdr., Am. Legion Drane Prine Post 317; Forty & Eight; Sec., Lion's Club; Chmn., Admin. Bd. & Fin. Comm., Ch. Schl. Tchr., Meth. Ch. Address: Noble Dr., P.O. Box 321, Brookhaven, MS 39601, U.S.A. 125.

THOMPSON, George Alfred, Jr., b. 21 Feb. 1909. Medical Entomologist. Educ: B.S., R.I. State Coll., 1932; M.S., ibid, 1934. Appts: Asst. State Entomologist, R.I. State Dept. of Agric., 1932-38; Entomologist, U.S. Dept. of Agric., 1938-42; USPHS, Malaria Control in War Area, Ga., 1942-44; Jamaica, W.I., 1944-46; Entomologist, Malaria Control in War Area, San Juan, Puerto Rico, 1946-47; Vector Control Rsch., 1948-51; Med. Entomologist, Communicable Disease Ctr., Okla. & Tex., 1951-53; Dir., Jefferson Co. (Tex.) Mosquito Control Dist., 1953-. Mbrships: Scientific Rsch. Soc. Am.; Am. Registry Cert. Entomologists; Entomological Soc. of Am.; Am. Mosquito Control Assn. Num. contbns. to Mosquito News & other profl. publs. Recip., Army Commendation Medal, 1946. Address: 2313 Ave. B., Nederland, TX 77627, U.S.A. 7.

THOMPSON, Harlan H. (pseudonym, Stephen Holt), b. 25 Dec. 1894. Writer; Rancher. Educ: Univ. Southern Calif. Mbrships: Pres., Int. P.E.N., L.A., 1958-59; Calif. Writers Guild Bd., 1953-. Publs. (under pseudonym Stephen Holt): Wild Palomino; Prairie Colt; Phantom Roan; The Whistling Stallion; Ranch Beyond the Mountains; Stormy; We Were there with the California Forty - Niners; We Were there with the California Rancheros. Publs. (under Harlan Thompson): Star Roan; Spook the Mustang Outcast Stallion of Hawaii; Silent

Running. Hons: Gold Medal, Boys Clubs of Am., 1947; Silver Medal, Commonwealth Club of San Fran., 1956. Address: 136 Monarch Bay S. Laguna, CA 92677, U.S.A.

THOMPSON, Kenneth W(infred), b. 29 Aug. 1921. Foundation Executive. Educ: A.B., Augustana Coll., Sioux Falls, S.D., 1943; M.A., Univ. of Chgo., 1948; Ph.D., 1950. Appts. Incl: Cons., Int. Rels., Rockefeller Fndn., 1953-55; Asst. Dir. for Soc. Scis., ibid, 1955-57; Assoc. Dir. for Soc. Scis., 1957-60; Dir. for Soc. Scis., 1960-61; V.P., 1961-73; Dir., Higher Educ. for Dev., Int. Coun. for Educ. Dev., 1974-. Fellow, Am. Acad. of Arts & Scis. Mbrships. incl: Am. Pol. Sci. Assn.; Coun. on For. Affairs; Bd. Trustees, Coun. on Relig. & Int. Affairs; Bd. Govs., Inst. of Current World Affairs; Phi Beta Kappa; Sigma Nu. Publs. incl: Political Realism & the Crisis of World Politics, 1960; American Diplomacy & Emergent Patterns, 1962; The Moral Issue in Statecraft, 1966; Foreign Assistance: A View from the Private Sector, 1972. Recip., 5 hon. degrees. Address: ICED, 680 5th Ave., New York, NY 10019, U.S.A. 2, 6, 128.

THOMPSON, (The Hon.) L.H.S., b. 15 Oct. 1923. Deputy Premier & Minister of Education, Victorian Government, Australia. Educ: B.A., Univ. of Melbourne, Australia, 1950; Parliamentary Sec. to Cabinet, 1956-58; Asst. Chief Sec. & Asst. Atty. Gen., 1958-61; Min. of Housing & Forests, 1961-67; Min. of Aboriginal Welfare, 1965-67; Dpty. Ldr. of Govt. in Legislative Coun., 1962-70; Min. of Educ., 1967-; Elected to Legislative Assembly, Vic., 1970; Dpty. Premier & Ldr. of Legislative Assembly, 1972-. Mbrships. incl: Pres., Vic. Br., Royal Life Saving Soc., 1970-; State Govt. Rep., Univ. of Melbourne Coun., 1955-59; Australian Coll. of Educ. Publs: Victorian Housing Today & Tomorrow, 1965; Looking Ahead in Education, 1969. Hons: 1st Place Hist. of Educ., Univ. of Melbourne, 1951; Victorian Father of the Yr. Award, 1970. Address: 19 Allenby Ave., Glen Iris, Vic., Australia 3146. 23, 34.

THOMPSON, Lois Adele, b. 21 Apr. 1925. Dean of Women; Professor of Business. Educ: B.S., Okla. Coll. of Liberal Arts, Chickasha, U.S.A., 1946; Master of Commercial Educ., Univ. of Okla., Norman, 1951; Ed.D., ibid, 1961. Appts. incl: Asst. Prof., Bus., & Dir., Audio-Visual Ctr., Okla. Coll. of Liberal Arts, 1949-60; Asst. Prof., Bus., Kan. State Coll. of Pittsburg, 1960-62; Assoc. Prof., Bus., Southern Ore. Coll., Ashland, 1962-66; Dean of Women, & Prof., Bus., Coll. of Southern Idaho, Twin Falls, 1966-. Mbrships. incl: Okla., Ore., Mountain-Plains, Western, Nat., & United, Bus. Educ. Assns.; Dept. of A-V Instrn., NEA; Nat. Women Deans & Counselors Assn.; Delta Pi Epsilon. Publs. incl: Ed., Roses Along Your Pathway; Articles in bus. educ. jrnls. Address: Box 1238, College of Southern Idaho, Twin Falls, ID 83301, U.S.A. 132, 138.

THOMPSON, Malcolm F., b. 2 Sept. 1921. Electronic Engineer. Educ: B.S., Ga. Tech. Coll., 1943; M.S., ibid, 1947. Appts: Capt., U.S. Army, 1943-46; Instr., MIT, 1947-49; Mbr., Tech. Staff, Autonetics, 1949-70; Dir. of Rsch., 5RC Div., Moxon, Inc., 1970-73; Engrng. Specialist, Northrop Aircraft Div., 1973-. Mbrships: Sr., IEEE; AOA; NRA; Nat. Geographic Soc. Publs: Magnetic Puse Generators Practical Design Limitations (jt. author), 1957; Radar Optic Techniques for Rocket & Missile Scoring, Machine Screening of EEG's, 1968. Patents: Magnetic Amplifier, 1958; Current Limiting Reactor, 1958; Tape

Transport, 1965; Artillery Fire Control System, 1967; Tape Drive, 1968; Extendable Package for Electronic Assemblies, 1970. Address: 1602 Indus St., Santa Ana, CA 92797, U.S.A. 50.

THOMPSON, Marietta Eileen (Mrs. Lloyd Thompson), b. 28 May 1920. Educator. Educ: Awarded Bursary for Refresher Course in Maths. Tchng., Inst. of Educ., Univ. of Southampton, U.K., 1960-61. Appts: Asst. Mistress, 1937-65, Acting Headmistress, 1966-67, Girls' H.S., W. Indies; Dpty. Headmistress, Basseterre H.S., 1967-71; Educ. Off., St. Kitts., 1971-. Mbrships: Pres., Girls' Brigade Coun., 1966-69; Rep., Educ. Comm., Epworth Jr. Schl., 1973-. Address: P.O. Box 76, St. Kitts, W. Indies, 136.

THOMPSON, Marilou Bonham, b. 24 Jan. 1936. Writer. Educ: B.A. (magna cum laude), Univ. of Tenn., 1957; grad., Famous Writers' Schl., 1966. Appts: Tchr., French & Engl., Bartlett H.S., 1957-60; Translator, Cotton Trade Jrnl., 1958; Soc. Liason Off., U.S. Air Force Base, Laon, France, 1964-67; & Tchr., French, Dir., Mid-S. Poetry Festival, U.S.A., 1973. Mbrships. incl: Sec., Memphis Br., Nat. League of Am. Penwomen; Poetry Soc. of Tenn.; Tenn. Press & Authors' Club; Admin. Coun., Alliance francaise; V.P., Memphis Ballet Guild. Contbr. short stories, poetry, articles, var. mags. & jrnls., inclng. Famous Writers' Mag., The Christian Home, Old Hickory Review, Tenn. Voices, Explore, Accent, Hi Times, Christian Action, Youth Leader. Hons. incl: Jesse Hill Ford Poetry Award, 1972; var. profl. prizes, for fiction & non-fiction. Address: 35 Belleair Dr., Memphis, TN 38104, U.S.A. 76, 125.

THOMPSON, Martin L., b. 18 Jan. 1921. Library Educator. Educ: B.S., Clarion State Coll., 1953; M.Ed., Pa. State Univ., 1960; M.L.S., Univ. of Pitts., 1967. Appts: Libn., Redbank Valley Area Schls., 1953-54; Dir. of Libs., Philipsburg-Osceola Area Schls., 1954-59; Chmn., Lib. Dept., Slippery Rock State Coll., 1959-65; Dir., Lib. Sci. Dept., Ibid, 1960-. Mbrships: Pa. Lib. Assn.; NEA; Pa. State Educ. Assn.; Am. Legion; Butler Co. Learning Resources Assn.; Beta Phi Mu; Alpha Beta Alpha; Pa. Assn. Higher Educ.; Assn. Pa. Coll. & Univ. Fac.; Pa. Schl. Libns. Assn. Publs: The Role of the Library in Guidance Services; The Psychology of Adolescent Behavior. Recip., U.S. Navy Commendation, WWII. Address: Dept. Lib. Sci., Slippery Rock State Coll., Slippery Rock, PA 16057, U.S.A. 6, 15, 42.

THOMPSON, Paul Anton Heron, b. 24 June 1913. Company Manager. Educ: Coop. Inst., St. Francis Xavier Univ., N.S., Canada, 1947; Pub. & Bus. Admin., Univ. of W. Indies (Ext. Admin. Staff Coll., U.K.), 1958. Appts. incl: 2nd Class Clerk-Acting Prin. Assessor of Income Tax, Income Tax Dept., Jamaica Civil Serv., 1942-53; Asst. Registrar & Acting Registrar Coop. Socs., Coop. Dept., ibid, 1953-59; Justice of Peace, Kingston, Jamaica, 1957; Mgmt. Off., Asst. Dir. Housing & Prin. Asst. Sec., Min. of Housing, Jamaica, 1959-69; Chmn. & Managing Dir., Mutual Housing Servs. Ltd., 1969-; Pres., Sodality Credit Union Ltd.; Fndr. & Pres., G.S.B. Clerks Coop. Credit Union Ltd. Mbrships. incl: Prefect, Cath. Young Men's Sodality; Pres., Jamaica Coop. Credit Union League. Publs: Consuming Dialogue (pamphlet 1947; articles in local press. Hons: UN Fellow in Agricultural & Coop. Credit, FAO, 1955-56. Address: 48 Sandhurst Cres., Kingston 6, Jamaica, W. Indies.

THOMPSON, Ray, b. 21 Aug. 1924. Company Director. Appts: Mng. Dir., CPV Italiana S.p.A., Milan, Italy 1952; Chmn., ibid, & European Dir., Colman Prentis & Varley Ltd., London, 1962; Pres., Ray Thompson Assocs. S.r.l., Milan, 1969; holder of var. other directorships in advt., marketing & PR cos. in Europe. Mbrships: Dir., British Chmbr. of Comm. for Italy; Fellow, Inst. of Practitioners in Advt.; Distribution Comm., Int. Chmbr. of Comm. Contbr. of articles to var. newspapers & mags. Speeches made at var. int. confs. Address: Corso Venezia, 2a, 20121 Milan, Italy. 43.

THOMPSON, Robert Allan, b. 10 June 1937. Administrator; Engineer. Educ: B.S.E.E., Case Western Reserve Univ., 1958; Postgrad., Cleveland State Univ. Appts: Rsch. Engr., 1958-63, Dir., 1964-65, Sohio Satellite Tracking Stn.; Maths. Instr., Cleveladn Bd. of Educ., 1958-63; Dir., Warrensville Hts. Planetarium & Space Sci. Prog., 1964-65; Sci. Dir., Cleveland Bd. of Educ. Supplementary Ctr., 1965-66; Dir., James A. Lovell Regional Space Ctr., 1967-73. Mbrships. incl: Chmn., Wis. Sect., AIAA, 1969; State of Wis. Aerospace Educ. Comm., 1968-70; Mbrship. Chmn., Cleveland Sect., IEEE, 1965; Fellow, Brit. Interplanetary Soc.; Exec. Comm., Cleveland Astronomical Soc., 1966; Chmn., Kiwanis Cir. K, Cleveland, 1965 & Key Club Chmn., Milwaukee, 1969, Author of publs. in space sci. & Contbr. to Ency. of Aviation & Space Science, 1968. Hons: Top Ten Young Men Finalist, Cleveland Jr. Chmbr. of Comm., 1961; Advsr.'s Award, Kiwanis Key Club, 1961. Address: 2650 Lakeview Ave., 4001, Chicago, IL 60614 U.S.A. 8, 22, 128.

THOMPSON, Roland M., b. 10 Sept. 1910. Highway Engineer Retired. Educ: Grad., Balt. Polytechnic Inst. of Tech.; Special Courses in Design & Mgmt., Univ. of Md.; Registered Profl. Eng. & Profl. Land Surveyor, Md. Appts: Asst. Location Engr., Md. State Hwy. Admin. Off., 1952-54; Admmn. Location Engr., ibid, 1954-63; Chief Bur. Location & Surveys, 1963-73; Asst. Chief Engr., Design, 1973-. Mbrships: Md. Classified Employees Assn.; Assn. Hwy. Offls. of N. Atlantic States. Hons: Am. Assn. of State Hwy. Offs. 25 yr. award for Meritorious Serv. to Public, 1964; State of Med., 40 yr. Award for Meritorious Serv. to Public, 1969. Address: 3102 Ramblewood Road, Ellicott City, MD 21043, U.S.A. 6.

THOMPSON, (William) Godfrey, b. 28 June 1921. Librarian. Appts: Chartered Libn., Coventry City Libs.; Dpty, Borough Libn., Chatham; Dpty, City Libn., Kingston-upon-Hull; Dpty, City Libn., Manchester; City Libn., Leeds: Guildhall Libn., Dir. of Libs. & Art Galls., City of London (currently). Mbrships: Hon. Treas., Lib. Assn.; Mbr. of Coun., ASLIB; Gov., St. Bridge Fndn.; Hon. Libn., Company of Clockmakers; Hon. Libn., Company of Gardeners; First Hon. Sec., Int. Assn. of Metropolitan City Libraries; Press Club. Publs: London for Everyman, Ed., 1969; Encyclopaedia of London, Ed., 1970; London's Statues, 1971; Planning & Design of Library Buildings, 1973. Address: Guildhall Lib., London EC2P 2EJ, U.K. 1, 19.

THOMSEN, Per, b. 17 Aug. 1905. Editor. Educ: Handelsgymnas Bergen (Coll. of Commerce), 1925. Appts: Journalist, Stavanger Aftenblad, 1926-41; Dpty. Ed., ibid, 1945-55; Ed. in chief, 1955-73; Contbng. ed. & Pres. of bd. of co., 1973-. Mbrships: Chmn., Stavanger Press Assn., 1950-54; Bd. mbr., Norwegian Press Assn., 1954-62; Chmn., Stavanger Tourist

Assn., 1950-55; Hon. mbr., ibid; Hon. mbr., Norwegian Tourist Assn. Publs: Pa Tomannsfot, 1932; Hypp alle mine hester, 1935; MED kikkert pa maven, 1935; Tomannsbu, 1938; Translation of Three in Norway, by Lees & Clutterbuck, into Norwegian, 1935, latest edit. 1973; Selection of newspaper articles, Kan hende med Torden (Maybe with thunder), 1973. Hons: World Press Achievement Award, on behalf of Stavanger Aftenblad. Am. Newspaper Publishers Assn. Fndn., 1970; Royal Order of St. Olav, 1973. Address: Gauselvaagen 76, 4032 Gausel, Norway.

THOMSON, Garry, b. 13 Sept. 1925. Government Official. Educ: B.A., Magdalene Coll., Cambridge, U.K., 1951; M.A. Appts: Rsch. Chemist, Nat. Gall., London, 1955-60; Sci. Advsr. to Trustees & Hd., Sci. Dept., ibid, 1960-. Mbrships: Fellow & Coun. mbr., Int. inst. for Conservation of Historic & Artistic Works; Hon. Ed., Studies in Conservation, jrnl. of Int. Inst. for Conservation of Historic & Artistic Works, 1959-67; Coor. on Lighting, Int. Coun. of Museums; Athenaeum. Publs: Ed., Recent Advances in Conservation, 1963; Ed., Museum Climatology. Address: Nat. Gall., Trafalgar Square, London, WC2N 5DN, U.K. 1, 43.

THORARINSSON, Hjalti, b. 23 Mar. 1920. Professor. Educ: grad., Med. Schl., Univ. of Iceland, 1948; Univ. Hosp., Reykjavik, ibid, 1949-52; Univ. of Wis. Med. Schl., Univ. Hosp., Madison, U.S.A., 1952-54. Appts: Cons. Surg., Univ. Hosp., Reykjavik, 1955-59; Asst. Surg. in Chief, ibid, 1959-62; Surg. in Chief & Assoc. Prof. of Thoracic Surg., 1962-72; Prof. of Surg., Surg. in Chief, Surg. Dept., 1972. Mbrships: Fellow, Icelandic Surg. Assn. (chmn., 1964), Am. Coll. Chest Physns.; Scandinavian Assn. for Gen. Surg.; Scandinavian Assn. for Thoracic & Cardiovascular Surg.; Fellow, Int. Fedn. Surg. Colls.; European Assn. for Cancer Rsch.; Anglia (Engl.-Icelandic Soc.); Icelandic Am. Soc.; Lions Club Reykjavik; Reykjavik Golf Club. Contbr. of articles to profl. jrnls. Address: Laugarasvegur 36, Reykjavik, Iceland. 43.

THORBJÖRNSSON, Sigurbjörn, b. 18 Nov. 1921. Tax Official. Educ: B.B.A., w. distinction; Commercial Schl. of Iceland, Reykjavík, 1942; Univ. of Minn., U.S.A., 1946. Appts. incl: Auditor, Off. Tax Commnr., Reykjavík, 1942-43; Dpty., ibid, 1947-51; Chief Acct., Flugfelag Islands, Reykjavík, 1952-62; Mbr., Inter-Parliamentary Comm., Tax Legislation, 1952-54; Mbr., Municipal Tax Bd. of Reykjavík, 1957-62; Chmn., Bd. of Tax Appeals, 1962-72, Tax Penalties Comm., 1965-72; Dir., Internal Revenue, 1962-; Mbr., Govt. Comm. Tax Legislation, 1969-71. Mbrships. incl: Lions Club Baldur, Reykjavík; Sec., ibid, 1953-54, Chmn., 1955-56; Boy Scouts of Reykjavík. Articles, taxation, newspapers & jrnls. Cmdr., Order of Lion of Finland, 1972. Address: Skúlagata 57, Reykjavík, Iceland. 43.

THORELL, Bo, b. 26 Mar. 1921. Professor of Pathology; M.D. Educ: M.D., Karolinska Institutet, Stockholm, 1947. Appts: Karolinska Institutet–Rsch. Asst., 1941-48; Prof., Cell Rsch., 1948-51; Assoc. Prof., Pathol., 1951-62; Prof., Pathol., & Dept. Chmn., 1962-. Also Vis. Prof., Biophysics, Univ. of Calif. at Berkeley, U.S.A., 1955, '62, '69. Mbrships: Int. Soc. of Hematol.; Int. Soc. of Cell. Biol.; Int. Acad. of Pathol.; N.Y. Acad. of Scis., etc. Publs. incl. 200 papers, monographs. Hons: Fellow, N.Y. Acad. of Scis., 1952; Fellow, Papinicoulau Cancer Inst., Miami, 1970; D.V.M. h.c., Stockholm Univ., 1970. Address: Dept. of Pathology, Karolinska sjukhuset, 10401 Stockholm 60, Sweden. 43.

THORLACIUS, Magnus, b. 19 Nov. 1905. Solicitor. Educ: Grad., Law, Reykjavik Univ., Iceland. Appts: Solicitor to Supreme Ct. of Iceland; Hon. Legal Advsr. to French Embassy, Reykjavik. Mbr. & Past Chmn., Icelandic Bar Assn. Address: 19 Hafnarstraeti, Reykjavik, P.O. Box 752, Iceland. 43.

THORMUNDSSON, Jónatan, b. 19 Dec. 1937. Professor of Law. Educ: Cand. Jus., Univ. of Iceland, 1964; Postgrad. studies, Univ. of Calif., Berkeley, U.S.A., 1965-66 & in Denmark & Norway, 1967. Appts: Dpty. State Prosecutor Iceland, 1964-70; Prof. of Law, Univ. of Iceland, 1970-; Dean, Fac. of Law, ibid, 1972-; Acting Rector, 1972-73. Mbrships: Vice-Chmn., Assn. of Icelandic Lawyers; Chmn., Icelandic Assn. of Criminalists. Publs: Opinbert Réttarfar I, 1971; Ed., Vidurlög Vid Afbrotum, 1971; Contbns. to law jrnls. Address: Háskóli Islands, Reykjavík, Iceland. 134.

THORN, Niels Anker, b. 1 Aug. 1924. Professor of Physiology. Educ: M.D., Univ. of Copenhagen, Denmark, 1951. Appts: Fellow, Rockefeller Inst. for Med. Rsch., N.Y., 1953-56; Asst. Prof., Univ. of Copenhagen, 1956; Assoc. Prof., ibid, 1959; Prof. & Chmn,. Inst. of Med. Physiol., ibid, 1967; Cons., Royal Dental Schl., 1960-66. Mbrships: Sec. Gen., Scandinavian Physiological Soc., 1973-; Chmn., Danish Biological Soc., 1972-74; Harvey Soc.; Soc. for Experimental Biol. & Med.; British Biochem. Soc. Publs. incl: Advances Metabolic Disorders, Vol. IV (co-author), 1970; Transport Mechanisms in Epithelia (w. H.H. Ussing), 1973; secretory Mechanisms of Exocrine Glands (w. O.H. Petersen), 1974. Hons: Alfred Benzon Prize, 1959; Thorvald Madsen Prize, 1967. Address: Inst. of Med. Physiol., Univ. of Copenhagen, 71 Raadmandsgade, DK-2200 Copenhagen N., Denmark. 43, 50.

THORNE, John Thomas, b. 17 Apr. 1926. Instrumentation Specialist. Educ. incls: Tex. Coll. of Mines, El Paso, 1944-45; Le Tourneau Tech., Longview, Tex., 1949-50; Lamar Coll., Beaumont, 1952-53; Nat. Radio Inst., Wash. D.C., 1965; Tchr. Trng., Univ. of Tex., Austin, 1963-66; Indl. Educ., Lee Coll., Baytown, 1964-65, & Univ. of Houston, 1967-68. Appts. incl: U.S. Army & AF, 1946-49, '50-53; Instrument Techn., Tex. City Refining Inc., 1953-63; Instr., Lee Coll., Baytown, 1963-66; Dept. Hd., San Jacinto Coll., Pasadena, 1966-68; Regional Systems Sales Mgr., Robertshaw Controls Co., Houston, 1968-70; Independent Cons., 1970-72; Mgr. of Trng., Tex-A-Mation Engrng. 1971-72; Instrument Designer & Job Boss, S.I.P., Inc., Houston, 1972-73; Instrument Engr., Tellepsen Petro-Chem. Construction Co., ibid, 1973-. Mbrships. incl: Instrument Soc. of Am.; Am. Soc. of Engrng. Techns.; Master Mason. Hons. incl: Sev. awards. Address: 2118 Flynn Dr. Pasadena, TX 77502, U.S.A. 7, 125, 130.

THORNES, R. Douglas, b. 15 Aug. 1926. Physician. Educ: B.A., Dublin Univ., Repub. Ireland, 1949; M.B., B.Ch., B.A.O., ibid, 1951; M.A., ibid, 1952; Ob. Fellowship, Harvard Med. Schl., USA, 1954; B.M., Uppsala Univ., Sweden, 1957; M.D., Dublin Univ., Repub. Ireland, 1958; Ph.D., ibid, 1962. Appts: House Surg. & House Physn., Royal City of Dublin Hosp., 1951-52; Immunol., Karolinska Inst. & Uppsala Univ., Sweden, 1952-53; Ob., Rotunda Hosp., Dublin, Repub. Ireland, 1953-54; Obstet. Immun., Harvard Med. Schl., USA, 1954-56; Anaesthetist & Radiotherap., Eskilstuna, Sweden, 1956-57; Gynaecol., Eskilstuna & Uppsala, Sweden, 1957-59;

Pathol., Trinity Coll. & St. Luke's Hosp., Dublin, Repub. Ireland, 1959-62; Lectr., Expl. Med., Trinity Coll., ibid, 1962-65; Vis. Lectr., Pathol., Johns Hopkins Hosp., Balt., Md., USA, 1965-72; Rdr., Dept. Med., Royal Coll. Surgs., Ireland, 1965-69; Prof. & Chmn., Dept. Expl. Med., ibid, 1969-. Mbr. num. profl. orgs. Author profl. jrnl. articles, inclng. The Use of the Proteolytic Enzyme Brinase to Produce Autocytotoxicity in Patients with Acute Leukaemia and its possible role in Immunotherapy, 1972. Address: Dept. Expl. Med., Royal Coll. Surgs., Ireland, St. Stephen's Green, Dublin 2, Repub. Ireland.

THORNTON, Bob M., b. 24 Apr. 1932. University Professor. Educ: B.S., Auburn Univ., Ala., 1959; M.S., ibid, 1960; Ed.D., Duke Univ., Durham, N.C., 1965. Appts. incl: Instr., Duke Univ., Durham, N.C., 1965; Vis. Assoc. Prof., Educ., Jacksonville Univ., Fla., 1965; Chmn. & Prof., Psychol., Valdosta State Coll., Ga., 1965-67; Prof., Educ., Univ. of W. Fla., 1967-; Var. Cons. appts. Mbrships. incl: British Psychological Soc.; NEA; Am. Psychological Assn.; Nat. Coun. for the Soc. Studies; AAUP; Assn. for Supvsn. & Curric. Dev.; Psi Chi; Kappa Delta Pi; Phi Delta Kappa. Author of The Psychology of the Individual, 1972. Contbr. to jrnls. Address: 129 Eufaula St., Gulf Breeze, FL 32561, U.S.A. 7, 125.

THORNTON, Robert Wheeler, b. 24 Dec. 1922. Structural Engineer. Educ: B.S., Univ. of Conn., Storrs, U.S.A., 1950. Appts: Draftsman, Ebasco Servs., N.Y.C., 1950-51; Estimator, H.J. High, Orlando, Fla., 1951-52; Structural Designer, Westcott & Mapes, New Haven, Conn., 1952-53; Estimator, Gellatly Construction Co., Bridgeport, Conn., 1953-56; Sec.-Gen. Mgr., The Thornton Co., Trumbull, Conn., 1956-62; Pvte. Prac. as Cons. Engr., Strafford, Vt., 1963-70; Pres., Thornton, Inc., Boothbay Harbor, Me., 1968-. Mbrships. incl: 32 Degree, Past Master, Vt. & Conn. Masons; Chmn., Strafford Athletic Assn., 1965-67; Fndr., Sprucewold Beach Club; Cons. Engrs. Coun.; Am. Hotel & Motel Assn.; New England Innkeepers Assn.; Boothbay Harbor Region Chmbr. of Comm. Address: Plainfield, NH 03781, U.S.A. 6.

THORPE, William Homan, b. 1 Apr. 1902. Emeritus Professor of Animal Ethology. Educ: Jesus Coll., Cambridge; M.A., Ph.D., Sc.D., ibid. Appts: Fellow, Sr. Tutor, Jesus Coll., Cambridge; Prather Lectr. in Bio., Harvard Univ., U.S.A.; Vis. Prof., Univ. of Calif.; Ridell Lectr., Durham Univ.; Fremantle Lectr., Balliol Coll., Oxford, U.K.; Gifford Lectr., St. Andrew's Univ.; Dir., Sub-Dept. of Animal Behaviour, Cambridge Univ. Mbrships. incl: Pres., Assn. for Study of Animal Behaviour, 1948-52, Soc. of British Entomol., 1951-53, British Ornithologists' Union, 1955-60; Chmn., British Sect., Int. Coun. for Bird Preservation, 1959-; Pres., Sect. D., British Assn., 1956. Publs: Learning & Instinct in Animals, 2nd Edit., 1963; Current Problems in Animal Behaviour, co-author, 2nd edit., 1963; Bird Song: The Biology of Vocal Communication & Expression in Birds, 1961; Biology & the Nature of Man, 1962; Science, Man & Morals, 1965; Duetting & Antiphonal Song in Birds, 1972; Animal Nature and Human Nature, 1974; contbr. to various jrnls. Hon., Fellow. Royal Soc., 1951. Address: Jesus Coll., Cambridge CB5 8BL, U.K. 1, 34.

THORS, R. Thor, b. 15 June 1919. Managing Director. Educ: Commercial Coll., Iceland; Postgrad. studies in U.K., Germany & U.S.A. Appts: Mng. Dir., Kveldulfur Ltd.; Bd. of Dirs., Iceland Steamship Co., Flugfelag Islands (Icelandair), & Icelandic Fish Meal Producers; Mng. Dir., Hannes Thorsteinsson & Co., Ltd. Mbrships: Pres., Rotary Club Seltjarnarnes; Var. local sci. socs. & sports clubs; Cultural Comm., Seltjarnarnes; Corps Consulaire of Iceland. Hons: Consul Gen. of Italy in Iceland; Cmdr., Stella della Solidarieta Italiana. Address: Hamar, Seltjarnarnes, Reykjavik, Iceland. 43.

THORSEN, Harald, b. 7 Sept. 1905. Headmaster. Educ: Cand. mag., 1934; M.A., 1938. Appts: Master, Munchs Boarding Schl. Norway, 1930-32; Master, Otto Mindes Boarding Schl., 1932-37; Sr. Master, Mandal Grammar Schl., 1937-48; Headmaster, Levanger Grammar Schl., 1948-53, Elverum Grammar Schl., 1953-63, Arendal Grammar Schl., 1963-73. Mbrships: Chmn., Nordic Assn. (Foreningen Norden); also chmn. of some comms., etc. Publs: Dr. Georg Fasting, 1941; Many articles in var. newspapers, & articles on For. Policy & Security problems in Etudes Atlantiques, 1967. Lectr., Denmark, Norway & Sweden. Address: 3144 Veierland, Norway. 134.

THORSTEINSSON, Bogi I., b. 2 Aug. 1918. Chief Air Traffic Controller, Keflavik International Airport, Iceland. Educ: Grad., Post & Telegraph Radio Offs. Schl., 1941; Air Traffic Control, Reykjavik, Iceland, 1946-47; Air Traffic Control & Radar Control, Atlanta, Ga., U.S.A., 1950-51. Appts: Radio Off., S/T Belgaum, 1941-42, Iceland Steamship Co., 1943-46; Radio Off. & Trng., ATC, Civil Aviation Admin., Reykjavik, 1946; Air Traffic Control Off., Reykjavik Airport, 1948; Chief Air traffic control Off., Keflavik Int. Airport, 1951-. Mbrships. incl: Fndr. & Chmn., IKF Sports Club, 1951-60; Pres., Icelandic Basketball Assn., 1961-69; Icelandic Olympic Comm., 1966-; Njardvik Lions Club. Sports Reporter, Morgunbladid, 1954-70. Hons. incl: Gold Emblem, Icelandic Basketball Assn., 1969, Icelandic Sports Club Union, 1969. Address: P.O. Box 75, Keflavik Int. Airport, Iceland. 43.

THRASHER, Craig Lee, b. 10 Apr. 1941. College Professor; Author. Educ: B.S., U.S. Naval Acad., Annapolis, Md.; M.B.A., SUNY, Buffalo. Appts: Officer, USN, 1959-67; Dir., Undergrad. Progs., Schl. of Mgmt., SUNY, Buffalo, 1967-70; Dir., Dev., ibid, 1970; Dir., Resource Mgmt. & Systems, 1971; Assoc. Prof. & Dept. Chmn., Erie Community Coll., 1971-. Mbrships incl: Soc. of Naval Arch. & Marine Engrns.; USN Inst.; Chapt. Pres., USN Acad. Alumni Assn., 1968-70. Contbr. to profl. publs. Address: Erie Community Coll., 1309 Main St., Buffalo, NY 14209, U.S.A.

THRASHER, Emma Reid (Mrs. Harold Morgan Thrasher), b. 8 Nov. 1921. City Extension Agent. Educ: B.S., Child Dev., Home Econs., Pa. State Univ., 1944; Wm. & Mary Coll., 1955 & 58; Univ. of Va., 1957; Va. Polytech. Inst. & State Univ., 1962. Appts: Tchr., Friends Community Schl., W. Chester, Pa., 1944-45 & Chesapeake, Va. Pub. Schls., 1951-53, 1955-61; Ext. Agt., Ext. Div. of V.P.I. & S.U. Coop. Ext. Serv., 1961-; Spvsr., 4-H Prog., 1970; Saleswoman & Unit Mgr., Tupperware Home Parties Inc., 1953-56. Mbrships. incl: Official Bd., Oak Grove Meth. Ch., 1972; Nat. & Va. Assns. of Ext. 4-H Agts. (var. offs.); Nat. & Va. Assns. Ext. Home Economists; Nat. & Va. Home Economics Assns.; Va. Ext. Serv. Assn.; Bd. of Dirs., 4-H Camp Farrar Inc. Hons: Disting. Serv. Award, Nat. Assn. Ext. Home Economists, 1973; Unit Citation Award, Va. Chapt., Epsilon Sigma Phi; Hon. Mbr., Va. Chapt. 4-H All Stars. Address:

Agric. Dept., 300 Cedar Rd., Chesapeake, VA 23320, U.S.A.

THRASHER, Warren Atticus, b. 8 Feb. 1914. University Professor; U.S. Army Officer (retired). Educ: B.S., M.B.A., Ph.D., Univ. of Ga.; Armed Forces Staff Coll.; Command & Gen. Staff Coll.; var. schls. of U.S. Armed Forces. Appts: Int. Bus. Machines Corp.; U.S. Army Off., 1st Armored Div., 1st & 44th Infantry Divs., 25th & 26th Repub. of Korea Divs.; Advsr., Imperial Iranian Gendarmerie; w. var. Staff Offs., at Pentagon; Aide-de-Camp to Gen. Mark W. Clark, N. Africa & Italy; Prof. of Mil. Sci., Marion Inst. & Univ. of Ga.; retirement from U.S. Army as Col., 1967; Prof. of Mgmt., Univ. of Ga. Mbr., profl. orgs., soc. clubs & fraternities. Author, monograph, The Battle of Salerno, & mil. hist. textbook for Infantry Schl. Recip., mil., nat., & for. medals & hons. Address: Dept. of Management, College of Business Administration, Univ. of Georgia, Athens, GA 30601, U.S.A. 125.

THUM, Marcella Laura. Librarian; Writer. Educ: B.A., Wash. Univ., St. Louis, Mo.; M.L.S., Univ. of Calif., Berkeley, Calif. Appts: Worked for U.S. Govt. (Civil Serv.) as Pub. Rels. Writer, Okinawa, Writer, Histl. Div., Heidelberg & Karlsruhe, German Fed. Repub., Libn., Scott Field, Ill., Libn., USAF, Korea, & Libn., Schofield Barracks & Hickam Air Force Base, Hawaii, 1949-60; Libn., Affton Sr. H.S., Mo., 1962-67; Reference Libn., Meramec Community Coll., Kirkwood, Mo., 1968-. Mbrships: Pres., St. Louis Writer's Guild; V.P., Mo. Writers Guild; Mo. Lib. Assn. Publs. incl: Mystery at Crane's Landing; Treasure of Crazy Quilt Farm; Anne of the Sandwich Islands; Librarian with wings; Young Reader's Guide to Black America. Recip. of hons. Address: 6716 Smiley Ave., St. Louis, MO 63139, U.S.A. 5, 30.

THUMAN, Bertha Margaret Petronella Mitchell (Mrs.), b. 16 Apr. 1905. Secretary; Writer; Artist. Educ: Lincoln Bus. Coll., 2 yrs.; Trinity Tchrs. Coll., 2 yrs. Appts: Ins. Agent; Acting City Clerk & Mayor, City of Scottsbluff; Libn., Schedule Surg., Fund Drive Mgr., St. Mary Hosp., Scottsbluff; Sec., Neb. State Employment Serv.; Off. Mgr., Neb. State Dept. of Hlth. Lab., Scottsbluff; Sec., Retail Credit Co., Hastings, Neb. Mbrships. incl: Camp Fire Girl; Teenage Girl Rep., Trinity M.E. Ch.; Bus. & Profl. Women's Club; Forum Club; Platte Valley Oratorio Soc.; Pres., United Commercial Club; Comm., Hastings Christian Women's Club; Am. Red Cross 1st Aid; St. Mark's Pro-Cathedral Episc. Ch., Hastings; sang in choirs, 40 yrs. Recip. Cert., Meritorious Serv., Neb. State Dept. of Hlth., 1970. Address: 723 N. Burlington, Apt. 206, Hastings, NB 68901, U.S.A. 120, 138.

THUMM, Walter, b. 14 Jan. 1921. Physicist. Educ: B.A. & B.Ed., Univ. of B.C., Canada; B.Sc., Sir George Williams Univ.; M.A.T., Colo. Coll. Appts. incl: Lectr., Phys., Canadian Servs. Colls., 1953-60; Instr., Sci. Educ., Univ. of Vic., B.C., 1960-64; Hd., Dept. of Phys., B.C. Inst. of, Technol., Burnaby, B.C., 1964-68; Prof., Phys. Educ. & Lectr. in Radiol., Queen's Univ., Kingston, Ont., 1968-; Vis. Prof. Physics, Austin Peay State Univ., Clarksville, Tenn., 1971. Mbrships. incl: Chmn., Phys. Educ. Div., Canadian Assn. of Physicists, 1969-70; Am. Assn. Phys. Tchrs.; Chmn., Nat. Comm. for Phys. in Insts. of Technol., Canada, 1965-67; Med. & Biol. Div., Canadian Assn. Physicists; Advsry. Comm., Eastern Ont. Schl. X-Ray Technol. Publs. incl: (co-author) The Physics of Medical Radiography, 1968; Physics: A Modern Approach, 1970; College Physics, 1971; Physics in Medicine, 1972; Physics for College Students (co-author), 1974. Author of various tech. papers. Some TV progs. on sci., 1962, '66. Recip., Lt. Gov's. Medal in Maths. & Physics, Sir George Williams Univ., Montreal, P.Q., 1958. Address: Duncan McArthur Hall, Queen's Univ., Kingston, Ont., Canada. 141.

THÜMMEL, Hans Gunther, b. 1 May 1921. Attorney-at-Law. Educ: Tech. Univ., Stuttgart, Germany; Referendar, Univ. of Tübingen, 1950; J.D., ibid, 1952; Assessor, 1954; Univ. of Va. Law Schl., U.S.A. Appts: Assoc., Stuttgart law firm, 1954-58; Ptnr., ibid, 1959-66; Sr. Ptnr., law firm Thümmel, Schütze, Bodendorf & Oldenburg, currently; Mng. Dir., Hannoversche Allgemeine Zeitung, 1959-63; Dir., Deutsche Simplex Time Recorder GmbH, Stuttgart/Zell, Römer-Wingard-Sicherheitsgurte GmbH, Stuttgart; Dpty. Dir., Stuttgarter Zeitungsverlag GmbH, 1970-. Mbrships. incl: Stuttgart Lawyers Assn.; German Bar Assn.; Int. Bar Assn.; Deutsche Vereinigung für gewerblichen Rechtsschutz & Urheberrecht; Am. Chmbr. of Comm. in Germany. Author of Franchising & Antitrust Law in West Germany, 1970. Address: Landhausstrasse 90, 7000 Stuttgart 1, German Fed. Repub.

THUNBERG, (Rev.) Lars Anders, b. 9 July 1928. Educator; Minister. Educ: B.A., Uppsala Univ., Sweden, 1950; B.D., 1953; Th.D., 1965; Studies in Switzerland, 1953-54, Paris, 1954-55. Appts: Tchr., New Testament Exegesis, Uppsala, Sweden, 1958-70; Sec., Swedish Ecumenical Coun., 1965-70; Dir., Nordic Ecumenical Inst., Sigtuna, 1966-; Lectr., Dogmatics, Uppsala, 1970-. Mbrships: Assn. of Swedish Writer; Nathan Soderblom Soc. Publs: Welfare State & Christian View of Man, 1956; World Ecumenism, 1961; Microcosm & Mediator. The Theological Anthopology of Maximus the Confessor, 1965; Co-Author, The Power to be Human, 1972; var. collects. of poetry; num. articles on theological & literary subjects. Address: Nordiska ekumeniska institutet, Box 68, S-190 30 Sigtuna, Sweden. 134.

THURSTON, Flora Mildred, b. 5 Apr. 1906. Educator. Educ: Ed.B., Nat. Coll. Educ., Evanston, Ill., 1929; M.A. Columbia Univ., N.Y.C., 1939; postgrad., Univ. of Pa., Ind. & Chgo. Univs. Appts. incl: Tchr., pub. schls., E. Chgo., Ind., 1929-30, Kindergarten 1st Grade, Hartford, Conn., 1930-34, Dalton Schl., N.Y.C., 1934-39; Fac. Mbr., W. Chester State Tchrs. Coll., Pa., 1939-43, Ind. Univ., Bloomington, 1943-47; Tchr. & Prin., Lab. Schls., Univ. of Chgo., 1947-63; Assoc. Prof. Educ., Roosevelt Univ., Chgo., 1963-68. Anderson Coll., Ind., 1968-72. Mbrships. incl: Bd. Dirs., Am. Bapt. Assembly, 1945-; Nat. & Ind. Assns. Educ. Young Children; Anderson Fine Arts Ctr.; NAACP; Psi Iota Xi. Publs., tchng. methods, young children. Hons. incl: Dr. of Pedagogy, Franklin Coll., 1955; Outstanding Alumni Award, 1973. Address: 623 Maplewood Ave., Anderson, IN 46012, U.S.A. 5, 8, 130.

THWAITE, Ann Barbara, (Mrs. Anthony Thwaite), b. 4 Oct. 1932. Writer. Educ: M.A., St. Hilda's Coll., Oxford Univ., 1959. Appts: one-time Lectr. at Tokyo Women's Univ. Mbrships: Comm. Mbr., Children's Writers Grp.; Soc. Authors. Publs: The Young Travelling Tooth; The Camelthorn Papers; The Only Treasure; The Pen-Driving Machine, a biography of Frances Hodgson Burnett; Ed. Allsorts. Address: The Mill House, Low Tharston, Norfolk, NOR 7OW U.K.

THWAITE, Anthony Simon, b. 23 June 1930. Writer & Editor. Educ: Oxford Univ.

Appts: Vis. Lectr. in Engl. Lit., Tokyo Univ., 1955-57; BBC Producer (Radio), 1957-62; Lit.Ed., The Listener, 1962-65; Asst. Prof. of Engl., Univ. of Libya, 1965-67; Lit.Ed., New Statesman, 1968-72; Co-Ed., Encounter, 1973-. Mbrships: Soc. Authors; Engl. Ceramic Circle; Soc. for Post-Medieval Archaeol.; Soc. for Libyan Studies. Publs: Home Truths, 1957; Contemporary English Poetry, 1959; The Owl in the Tree, 1963; Co-ed., Penguin Book of Japanese Verse, 1964; The Stones of Emptiness, 1967; Japan in Colour, 1967; The Deserts of Hesperides, 1969; Penguin Modern Poets 18, 1970; Inscriptions, 1973; The English Poets, (co-ed.), 1973; Poetry Today, 1973; New Confessions, 1974. Recip., Richard Hillary Prize, 1968. Address: The Mill House, Tharston, Norfolk NOR 7OW, U.K. 3.

THWAITES, Bryan, b. 6 Dec. 1923. University Professor. Educ: M.A., Clare Coll., Cambridge; Ph.D., London. Appts: Sci. Off., Nat. Phys. Lab., 1944-47; Lectr., Imperial Coll., London, 1947-51; Asst. Master, Winchester Coll., 1951-59; Prof. of Theoretical Mechs., Southampton Univ., 1959-66; Dir., Schl. Maths. Proj., 1961-; Prin., Westfield Coll., Univ. of London, 1966-; Gresham Prof. of Geom., City Univ., 1969. Mbrships: US Educl. Commn., 1966-; Acad. Advsry. Comms., Univ. of Bath & Open Univ.; Chmn., Ch. of Engl. Colls. of Educ., 1969-71; J.P., Winchester City Bench, 1963-66; Chmn., Northwick Pk. Hosp. Mgmt. Comm., 1970-74, Brent & Harrow Area Hlth. Auth., 1974-; Pres., Inst. of Maths. & Its Applications, 1966-67; F.I.M.A.; Athenaeum Club, London. Publs: Incompressible Aerodynamics, 1960; On Teaching Mathematics, 1961; contbr. num. articles to sci. jrnls. Address: The Old House, Westfield Coll., Kidderpore Ave., London NW3 7ST, U.K. 1, 128.

TIBBETTS, Keith Parker, Jr., b. 27 June 1947. Managing Director; Insurance Agent. Educ: H.S. Diploma, Bob Jones Academy, Greenville, S.C. Married Alesia Valetta Tibbetts, 1970. Appts. incl: Airline Agent, Cayman Brac, 1964-69; Insurance Agent, 1968-; Managing Director, own businesses, 1970-. Mbrships. incl: Former Treasurer & Director, Rotary Club of Grand Cayman; Cayman Islands Chamber of Commerce; International Traders. Address: P.O. Box 516, Grand Cayman, Cayman Islands, West Indies. 109.

TIBERGHIEN, Albert, b. 11 Jan. 1915. Tax Advisor; Professor of Tax Law. Educ: Dr. juris; Lic. notariat; Lic. sc. admin. Appts: Pres., Confederation of Tax Advisors, EEC; Pres., Nat. Fedn. of Tax Advisors, Belgium; Pres., Fiscle Hogeschool, Brussels. Mbrships: Pres., Flemish Econ. Coun. (VEV), Brussels. Publs: Manuel des Impôts sur les revenus; Manuel de droit fiscal, 3rd ed. Address: Blvd. Brand Whitlock 66, B 1200 Brussels, Belgium.

TICHOVSKIS, Heronims, b. 22 Sept. 1907. Professor ot Modern Languages. Educ: M.A., Univ. of Latvia, 1933; Ph.D., Univ. of Bonn, German Fed. Repub., 1949; Postgrad. studies, Univ. of Toronto Canada, 1958-60. Appts. incl: Asst. Dir. of Latvian Schls. in Riga & Germany, Latvian Min. of Educ., 1939-46; Advsr., Tchng. of Mod. Langs., Canadian Dept. of Educ., Ont., 1954-60; Chmn., Latvian Press Soc. in Canada, 1954-60; Instr., Univ. of Conn., 1960-61, Asst. Prof., 1962-67; Literary Advsr. & Lectr., Cult. Fndn. of Am.-Latvian Assn., 1965-71; Assoc. Prof.-Prof., N.C. Agric. & Tech. State Univ., 1970-. Mbr., var. profl. orgs. Publs. incl: Ten Years of the Latvian Exile, 1954; Ave Maria Anthology (ed.), 1958. Contbr., European jrnls. & collects. Hons. incl: Latvian Cultural Fndn.

Awards, 1935, 1940; Bishop Joseph Rancaus Mem. Fndn. Award, 1973. Address: P.O.Box 21024, Greensboro, NC, U.S.A. 6, 13, 15, 125.

TIDWELL, Oscar Cromwell, Jr., b. 15 June 1914. Dentist. Educ: B.A., Vanderbilt Univ., 1936; D.D.S., Coll. of Dentistry., Univ. of Tenn., 1940; Dental Intern, Knoxville Gen. Hosp., 1941. Appts: Gen. Prac. of Dentistry; Dental Staff, Jr. League Crippled Children's Hosp., 1946-70; Dental Mbr., Midsouth Regional Med. Prog. Mbrships: Pres., Nashville Dental Soc., 1955; Pres. Tenn. Dental Assn., 1974; Coun., Am. Dental Assn., 1965-67 & '72-; Advsr. Comm. to Selective Serv. System in Tenn.; Assn. of Mil. Surgs.; AAAS; Pierre Fauchard Acad.; Fellow, Am. Coll. of Dentists & Royal Soc. of Hlth.; Fedn. Dentaire Int.; Alpha Tau Omega; Psi Omega; Bachelor Club of Nashville; Belle Meade Country Club; Kiwanis; Tenn. & Nat. Hist. Soc.; Civic Bds.; Nashville Songwriters Assn. Contbr. articles to profl. jrnls. Recip. Tenn. Dental Assn. Fellowship Award for Outstanding Serv., 1972. Address: 512 Midstate Med. Ctr., Nashville, TN 37203, U.S.A. 7

TIDWELL, Robert Earl, b. 21 July 1883. Educator. Educ: B.S., 1905, LL.D., 1927, Univ. of Ala.; Courses at Univ. of Chgo. & Harvard Univ.; M.A., Columbia Univ., 1925; Supt.'s Dip., 1925; LL.D., Birmingham-Southern Coll., 1923. Appts. incl: Prin., Ensley H.S., Birmingham, Ala., 1906-12; Supt., Tenn. Coal & Iron R.R. Co, Schls., U.S. Steel, Southern Br., 1913-17; Dir. of Tchr. Trng., 1918-27, Asst. State Supt. of Educ., 1920-27, State Dept. of Educ.; State Supt. of Educ., Ala., 1972-31; Dean.; Univ. Ext., Univ. of Ala., 1930-54; Asst. to Pres. of Stilman Coll., Tuscaloosa, Ala., 1954-64; Educl. Cons. to Min. of Educ., Baghdad, Iraq, 1957. Mbrships. incl: Phi Beta Kappa; Phi Delta Kappa; Kappa Delta Pi; Phi Kappa Phi; Kappa Sigma; NEA; Ala. Educ. Assn. Publs. incl: Teacher Training in Alabama, 1930; Study of Latin American in the Elementary Schools of Alabama, 1938; Curriculum Development in the Rural Schools of Alabama, 1940; A Program of Plant Development for the Teacher Training Institutions of Alabama, 1929; Adult Education in a Free Society, 1955; Some Observations on Educational Needs of Iraq, 1957; Biographies of the Pastors of the First Baptist Church, Tuscaloosa, Ala., 1818-1968; Articles in num. educl. mags. Hons. incl: Plaque, Julium M. Knolte Award, Nat. Univ. Ext. Assn., 1968; Plaque Stillman Coll. Fac. & Staff, 1964; Tidwell Hall, Univ. of Ala., named in his hon., 1954. Address: 1602 Alaca Pl., Tuscaeosa, AL 35401, U.S.A., 2, 7, 10, 15, 130, 141.

TIEDTKE, John Meyer, b. 15 Sept. 1907. Educator; College Administrator; Farm & Grove Manager. Educ: Grad., Dartmouth Coll., Hanover, N.H., U.S.A., 1930; Amos Tuck Schl. of Bus. Admin., 1931. Appts. incl: Instr., Rollins Coll., Winter Pk., Fla., 1936-40; Prof., Bus. Admin., ibid, 1946-49; Treas. & Bus. Mgr., 1948; V.P., 1951; Dean of Grad. Progs., 1960-65; Financial V.P., 1969; Dir., Orlando Fed. Savings & Loan; Dir., Sugar Cane Growers Coop. of Fla.; Dir., Fla. Fruit & Vegetable Assn.; Dir., Water Users Assn. of Fla.; Dir., Fla. Farm Bur. Fedn. Sugar Comm.; Supvsr., Diston Island Drainage Dist. Mbrships. incl: Pres., Bach Festival Soc., Winter Pk., Fla.; Dir., Fla. Symph. Orch.; Past mbr., Bd. of Mgmt., YMCA; Past mbr. & Sec., Gov.'s Fla. Sugar Comm.; Bd. of Trustees, Rollins Coll. Co-inventor, Sugar cane loading machine used throughout Fla. Hons: Rollins Decoration of Honor, 1949; C.H.I.E.F. Award, Independent Colls. & Univs.,

1972; First Gov.'s Award for the Arts, 1973. Address: Rollins College, Winter Park, FL 32789, U.S.A. 7.

TIERNEY, Patrick Lennox. College Dean; Professor. Educ: Ed.B., Univ. of Calif., L.A., 1936; M.A., Columbia Univ., N.Y.C., 1944; Grad. Seizan I, Sogetsu-Ryu, Tokyo, Japan, 1952. Appts: Off., 1946-71; Chmn., 1958-71; Arts Fac., Pasadena City Coll., Calif., Arts Supvsr., Far E. Cmd., Tokyo, Japan, 1949-52; Lectr., Oriental Arts & Culture, Univ. of Calif. Ext., L.A. & San Diego, 1952-71; Arts Supvsr., European Cmd., Heidelberg, Germany, 1954-56; Assoc. Dean Coll. of Fine Arts & Prof. Hist. Oriental Art, Univ. of Utah, Salt Lake City, 1971-; Mbrships. incl: U.S. Commn., U.S. Pavillion, Expo '70, Osaka, Japan, 1961; Dir., Mus. Div., Pacificulture Fndn., Pasadena, Calif., 1961-70; Acad. TV Arts & Scis., 1967-; Dir., Japan-Am. Soc., Southern Calif., 1972-; Bd. of Dirs., Salt Lake Art Ctr., Utah, 1972-. Publs: Japan, 1956; Zen & Japanese Gardens, 1969 & The Japanese Garden, 1970 (both Book & film Series); History of World Art (in preparation); articles on Oriental Culture; contbr., Chanoyu Quarterly. Hons: "Emmy" Acad. of TV Arts & Scis., 1967; Christopher Award, Best Educl. Film Series, 1969; Citation, Bd. of Trustees, Pasadena City Coll., 1971. Address: Coll. of Fine Arts, Art & Arch. Ctr. 204, Univ. of Utah, Salt Lake City, UT 84112, U.S.A. 9.

TIFFANY, Marguerite. Artist; Lecturer; Weaver. Educ: B.S., Syracuse Univ., 1922; M.A., Columbia Univ., 1930; Postgrad. study, Columbia, N.Y. Univ., Parsons Art Schl., Fawcett Art Schl., var. painting courses. Appts: Tchr., N.Y. schls., 1914-20; Supvsr., Art, W. Orange, N.J., 1920-27; Tchr., Montclair, N.J., 1927-29; Prof., Hd., Art Dept., Wm. Paterson Coll., N.J., 1929-56; Art Dept., Fairleigh Dickinson Univ., 1956-64; Tchr., summer schls. & exts., 1925-53. Num. mbrships. incl: Pres., N.J. Br., Nat. League of Am. Pen Women; Pres., Century Theatre Club of N.Y.C.; Pres., Montclair Mus. Art Tchrs.; Pres., Associated Hand Weavers, N.J. & Pa.; Pres., Chi Omega, N.Y.C.; Pres., local art assns. Publs: Articles in newspapers; Booklets; Exhibs. of painting, Me., N.J., N.Y., Ore. & Alaska; Work in pvte. collects. in 18 states; Weaving exhibs., Associated Hand Weavers, 1967, '70, '72. Hons: Citation for contribution to Art Educ., 1950; Kappa Delta Pi, Pi Lambda Theta, Columbia Univ., 1929. Address: 330 E. 33 St., Paterson, NJ 07504, U.S.A. 5, 6, 15, 22, 37, 128.

TIKKANEN, Matti Haakon, b. 28 Nov. 1915. Professor of Process Metallurgy. Educ: Dipl. Eng., 1938; D.Sc., 1949. Appts: Metallurgist State Airplane Works, Tampera, 1940-45; Chief Metallurgist, Suomi Foundry, Helsinki, 1945-46; Lab. Chief, Powder Metallurgy Dept., Husquarna Arms Factory, Sweden, 1946-49; Prof. Metallurgy, Helsinki Univ. of Technol., Otaniemi, 1949-; Hd. Metallurgical Dept., State Rsch. Ctr., Helsinki, 1949-60. Mbrships: AIME; ACS; APMI (U.S.A.); Metallografförbundet, Sweden. Author, Corrosion & Its Prevention, 1961. About 100 other scientific publs. Recip., Tech. Rsch. Fnd. Nat. Hon. Award, 1969. Address: Helsinki Univ. of Technol., Dept. of Metallurgy, 02150 Otaniemi, Finland.

TILDEN, Lorraine Frederick (Mrs. Wesley R. Tilden), b. 16 May 1912. Educator. Educ: A.A., Ill. State Univ.; B.A., Univ. of Calif., L.A.; M.A., Claremont Grad. Schl. UCLA; Univ. of Redlands; Univ., of Guanajuato, Mexico. Appts. incl: various coll. tchng. positions, 1950-65; at Scripps Coll., UCLA, Claremont Men's Coll., La Verne Coll., Upland Coll.; Assoc. Prof., Humanities Spanish & Engl. Lit., 1962-65; formerly Asst. to Mng. Ed., Nat. Printer Jrnlist. & Asst. to Spec. Edits. Ed., Ill. State Jrnl.; Tchr., World Mythol., Glendora H.S., Calif.. 1967-75. Mbrships: Classical Assn. of Western States; State Arts Chmn., AAUW; Pres., Town Affiliation Assn. of Claremont; Sigma Delta Pi; Pi Lambda Theta; Claremont Grad. Schl. Alumni Coun., 1973-75. Publs. incl: num. dramatic, music & lit. reviews in mags. & newspapers, e.g., Atlantic & Hispania; author of Modernism in the Poetry of Jose Asuncion Silva, 1954. Recip. of civic hons. Address: 351 Oakdale Dr., Claremont, CA 91711, U.S.A. 5, 9, 11, 13, 15, 57, 59.

TILGHMAN, Donald Matthews, b. 11 June 1936. Oral Surgeon. Educ: B.S., Univ. of Md. Coll., 1958; D.D.S., Schl. of Dentistry, ibid, 1961; Internship, Johns Hopkins Hosp., 1961-62; Res., ibid, 1962-63; Grad., Schl. of Med., Univ. of Pa., 1963-64; Res., Univ. of Mich. Hosp., 1964-65; Postgrad., Student-Orthodontics, Univ. of Md., 1972-. Appts. incl: Asst. Prof., Oral Surg., Schl. of Dentistry, Univ. of Md., Balt., 1968-; Active Staff, Div. of Oral Surg., Univ. of Md. Hosp., 1968-; Dir., Out-Patient Dental Servs., ibid, 1969-; Active Staff, Dental Serv., Johns Hopkins Hosp., 1971-; Cons., Balt. City Hosps., 1968-; Provident Hosp., Balt., 1969-; Mercy Hosp., Balt., 1969-; VA Hosp., Balt., 1969-; & Children's Hosp., 1971-. Mbrships. incl: Am. Dental Assn.; Am. Soc. of Oral Surg.; Pan Am. Med. Assn.; Am. Cancer Soc. Author of articles & tapes in field. Recip., Cancer Award, Md. Div., Am. Cancer Soc., 1971. Address: Dept. of Oral Surg., Univ. of Md. Schl. of Dentistry, 666 W. Baltimore St., Balt., MD 21201, U.S.A. 2.

TILLANDER, Oy, b. 19 Mar. 1909. Jeweller. Educ: Fellow, Gemmological Assn., U.K., 1935; Certified Gemologist, U.S.A., 1937; Master Goldsmith, 1949; Diamond Grading exam., U.S.A., 1957. Mng. Dir., Oy Tillander Ab, mfg. & retail jewellers, 1939-74. Mbrships: Bd., Jeweller's Assn. of Finland, 1945-58; V.P., ibid, 1958-59; Hon. mbr., 1972; Charter Pres., Gemmological Soc. of Finland, 1960-; Charter Pres., Scandinavian Diamond Nomenclature Comm., 1971-; Past Club Pres., Dist. Gov. etc., Rotary Int.; "Sea Bears" commodore, Finnish Cruising Assn., 1961-69; Pres., Scandinavian Diamond Inst., 1971. Author of publs. in field. Hons. incl: Jeweller by appt. to H.M. the King of Sweden, 1952-; Cmdr., Order of the Lion of Finland, 1971; Hon. Consul Gen. of Indonesia, 1961-. Address: Tulppatie 24, 00810 Helsinki 81, Finland. 134.

TILLEY, Eugene D., b. 22 Sept. 1913. Retired Farm Manager & Owner. Appts: Farm Owner & Mgr.; Served 20 Air Arm USAF, WW II; Ch. Schl. Dir. & Sec.-Treas., 10 yrs.; Deacon, Reorg. Ch., Jesus Christ of Latter Day Saints; Free-Lance Writer, Poet & Speaker-Humorist. Mbrships: Ark. Poets Round Table, Ark.; Authors, Composers & Artists, Creative Writers Soc. Creative Works: The Minutes of the Years, 1972; Pamphlets: One Dozen Poems; Big Shot Farmer; The Deer Slayer; The Dyke Walker; Harvest Moan; et al, 1965-72; Recordings: Tears on White Carnations & Moon Madness, 1965; Regular contbr., World of Poetry radio prog., 1973-74; Work pub. by Anthology Am. Poetry; Poetry Parade; Poetry Pageant; Voices Int.; The Daily Oklahoman; Memphis Commercial Appeal; Fort Smith Southwest Times Record; The Ark. Farmer; The Saints Herald; Saline Co. News; Southern Standard; Hot Springs News; Wynne Progress; Salem Headlight; Contbr. regular poetry column, The Modern News, 1964-74. Recip. sev. hons.

Address: Rte. 1, Box 5, Fisher, AR 72429, U.S.A. 11, 125.

TILLINGHAST, Pardon E. College Professor. Educ: A.B., Bronw Univ., 1942; M.A., Harvard Univ., 1947; Ph.D., 1952. Appts: Instr., Hist., Middlebury Coll., Vt., 1947-52; Asst. Prof., ibid, 1952-58; Assoc. Prof., 1958-64; Prof., 1964-. Mbrships: Am. Hist. Assn.; Medieval Acad. Am.; Renaissance Soc. Am.; Guild of Scholars; Phi Beta Kappa. Publs: Approaches to History, 1962; The Specious Past, 1972; contbr. to profl. publs. Hons: Danforth Assoc., 1954-58; Fulbright Exchange tchr., 1956-57. Address: 6 Adirondack View, Middlebury, VT 05753, U.S.A. 2, 13.

TIMASHEFF, Nicholas S., b. 22 Nov. 1886. Professor of Law; Author; Journalist. Educ: B.A., Emperor Alexander Coll., St. Petersburg, Russia, 1908; Mag. of Law, Petrograd Univ., Russia, 1914; LL.D., ibid, 1916. Appts. incl: Asst. Prof.-Assoc. Prof., & Dean, St. Petersburg Polytech. Inst., 1915-21; Prof., Prague Univ., Czechoslovakia, 1923-27; Prof., Slavic Inst., Sorbonne, & Franco-Russian Inst., Asst. Ed.-in-Chief, Russian Daily Renaissance, Paris, France, 1927-36; Vis. Prof., Harvard Univ., U.S.A., 1936-40; Prof., Grad. Schl., Fordham Univ., 1940-57, Prof. Emeritus, 1957-; Prof., Grad. Inst. Soviet Studies, Middlebury Coll., 1958-62. Emeritus Fellow, Hon. Mbr., Am. & Russian acad., histl., theological Socs. Author num. books. Recip., H.H.D., Wyndham Univ., 1964. Address: 39 Pkwy. E., Mt. Vernon, NY 10552, U.S.A. 2, 6, 36.

TIMBERG, Sigmund, b. 5 Mar. 1911. Lawyer. Educ: M.A., Columbia Univ., 1930; LL.B., Law Schl., ibid, 1933. Appts: Sr. Atty., Off. of Solicitor, Dept. of Agric., Wash., D.C., 1933-38; Sr. Atty., Securities & Exchange Commn., 1938-42; Chief, Indl. Org. Div., Bd. of Economic Warfare & For. Economic Admin., 1942-44; Special Asst. to Atty. Gen., & Chief, Judgements & Judgement Enforcement Sect., Antitrust Div., Dept. of Justice, 1944-52; Sec., UN Ad Hoc Comm. on Restrictive Bus. Pracs., 1952-54; Pvte. prac., 1954-. Mbrships: Chmn., Int. Trade Comm., Antitrust Div., Am. Bar Assn.; Pres., Wash. For. Law Soc.; Trustee, Copyright Soc. of Am.; Am. Law Inst.; Am. Patent Law Assn.; Int. Law Assn.; N.Y.C., N.Y. State, D.C., Fed. & Int. Bar Assns.; Am. Econ. Assn.; Am. For. Law Assn. Publs: Num. articles, monographs. Address: 815 15th St. N.W., Washington, DC 20005, U.S.A. 2, 12.

TIMBERLAKE, Lora Dell (Mrs. Marlin C. Timberlake), b. 26 June 1934. Teacher/Librarian. Educ: B.A., Southern Univ., 1954; M.L.S., La. State Univ., 1969. Appts. incl: Tchr./Libn., Wash. Parish H.S., Franklinton, La., 1954-55; Tchr./Libn., Phoenix H.S., Carlisel, La., 1956-62; Tchr., Herndon H.S., Belcher, La., 1962-63; Tchr./Libn., Walnut Hill H.S., 1963-. Mbrships: Caddo Libns. Org., Sec., 1965-67; Volunteer Ldr., 4-H Club, 1970-; Modisette Award Sub-Comm., Chmn., 1970-71; Caddo Educ. Assn., Bldg. Rep., 1970-72; Home Econs. Advsry. Coun., 1971-; La. Educ. Assn.; NEA; Am. Int. Charolais Assn.; Kappa Delta Pi; Beta Phi Mu. Hons: Modisette Award, La. Lib. Assn., 1969; Educator of the Yr., Caddo Educ. Assn., & Shreveport Times, 1969. Address: Route 6, Box 659, Dawson Rd., Shreveport, LA 71109, U.S.A. 5, 7, 138.

TIMBS, Maurice C., b. 14 July 1917. Secretary, Australian Department of Services & Property. Educ: B.Economics; Assoc., Australian Inst. of Accts.; Fellow, Australian Inst. of Mgmt.; Fellow, Royal Australian Inst. of Pub. Admin. Appts: 1st Asst. Sec., Prime Min.'s Dept., 1956-60; Exec. Commnr., Australian Atomic Energy Commn., 1960-73; Alternate Gov. for Australia, Int. Atomic Energy Agcy., Vienna, Austria, 1962-73; Sec., Dept. of Servs. & Property, 1973-; Dir., N.S.W. Inst. for Deaf & Blind Children. Mbrships. incl: Elanora Country Club; Am. Nat. Club; Royal Sydney Yacht Squadron; Athenaeum Club; Royal Agricultural Soc., Sydney; Australian Elizabethan Theatre Trust; Australian Opera Co. Address: Dept. of Services & Property, C.A.G.A. House, Akuna St., Canberra City, A.C.T., Australia 2601.

TIMMAS, Osvald, b. 17 Sept. 1919. Artist; Painter in Watercolor, Acrylics, Oils. Educ: Univ. of Tartu, Estonia, 1940-44; Studio Schls., Tartu & Tallinn, w. Nicholas Kummits & Gunther Reindorff. Var. independent commns., Art Cons. & Advsr., 1965-. Mbrships: Royal Canadian Acad. Arts; Am. Watercolor Soc.; V.P., Ont. Soc. of Artists; Canadian Soc. Painters in Water Colour; Dir., ibid, 1966-69. Watercolors in Collects inclng: London Art Mus., Canada; Art Gall. of Hamilton, Ont.; Canton Art Inst., Ohio, U.S.A.; Erindale Coll., Univ. of Toronto; Erie Art Ctr., Pa., U.S.A. Hons. incl: John Ernst Award, 1967; Audubon Artists Awards, 1967, 1968; Coutts-Hallmark Co. Awards, 1969, 1970; John Labatt Ltd. Award, 1971; Best Watercolor Award, Ont. Soc. Artists, 1974. Address: 776 Marlee Ave., Toronto 19, Ont. M6B 3J9, Canada. 37.

TIMMEL, Roland Gustav, b. 1 Mar. 1902. Dental & Maxillary Surgeon. Educ: Studied at Vienna & Graz Univs., Austria, & also in Berlin, Germany; Dr. medicinae universae. Appts: Dental & maxillary prac., Vienna; Major (Physn.), front line, wounded, later Dir., Red Cross Hosp., WW II. Mbrships. since 1945 incl: Pres., Freiheitlicher Akademikerverband für Wien, Niederösterreich & das Burgenland; Pres., Notrings für Südtirol; V.P., Union für Südtirol; Pres Orientinstitut; Bd. mbr., Gesellschaft zur Förderung der Landesverteidigung; Disciplinary Comm., Bd. of Dirs. & Welfare Fund, Arztekammer, Vienna; Chmn., Advsry. Bd., Volkstreuer Verbände Osterreichs; Hon. mbr., Gesellschaft für Freie Publizistik, Deutscheskulturwerk Europäischen Geistes; Hon. mbr. & Hon. Pres., Freiheitlicher Akademikerverband für Wien, Niederösterreich & das Burgenland. Author of var. med., pol. & histl. publs. Recip. of hons. Address: Geusaugasse 12, A-1030 Vienna, Austria.

TIMMERMANS, John Jay, b. 22 Nov. 1936. Oral & Maxillo Facial Surgeon. Educ: Augustana Coll., 1954-57; D.D.S., State Univ., Iowa, 1961; M.S., N.Y. Univ., 1970. Appts: Pvte. prac., oral surg., N.Y.C., 1969-; Attending oral surg., Lenox Hill Hosp., S.I. Hosp., Roosevelt Hosp., 1969-; Asst. Prof., Oral Surg., N.Y. Univ., 1969-; Cons., USCG Dental Clin., Govs. Island, N.Y., 1969-; Mbr., Courtesy Staff, Richmond Mem. Hosp., S.I., N.Y., 1969-; Served to Cmdr., USPHS, 1961-69. Mbrships: Diplomate, Am. Bd. Oral Surg.; Am. Dental Assn.; Am. Soc. Oral Surgs.; Am. Assn. Dental Schls.; Fellow, Am. Dental Soc. of Anesthesiol.; Assn. Mil. Surgs.; Flying Dentists Assn.; N.Y. State Soc. Oral Surgs.; N.Y. Inst. Clin. Oral Pathol.; N.Y. Acad. of Dentistry; 1st Dist. Dental Soc.; Delta Sigma Delta; Rotary Club. Author (Gerard L. Courtade) Pins in Restoration Dentistry, 1971. Address: 875 Fifth Ave., N.Y., NY 10021, U.S.A.

TIMMINS, William Frederick. Painter of Landscapes & Portraits. Educ: Am. Acad. of Art, Chgo.; Art Students League, N.Y.C.; Grand Central Art Schl., N.Y.C. Mbrships: Soc. of

Illustrators, N.Y.; Westport Artists, Inc.; Providence Art Club, R.I.; Soc. of Western Artists; Carmel Art Assn. One-man shows: Cochrane Gall., Darien, Conn., 1963; Perry House Gall., Monterey, Calif., 1967 & 1973. Works: Contbr. of illustrations to Cosmopolitan Mag., Colliers, Family Circle, Macleans, Boy Scout Handbook, Rand McNally Books, Western Publishers Books. Address: P.O. Box 5685, Carmel, CA 93921, U.S.A. 6, 37.

TING, Er Yi, b. 3 June 1919. Physician; Educator; Researcher. Educ: Nat. Defense Med. Coll., China, 1948. Appts. incl: Intern, Res., Attending Physn., Nat. Defense Med. Ctr., Shanghai & Taipei, China, 1949-54; Res., Bronx Municipal Hosp. Ctr., N.Y.C., U.S.A., 1954-56; Rsch. Fellow, Univ. of Buffalo & State Univ. Downstate Med. Ctr., N.Y., 1956-59; Instr., Albert Einstein Coll. of Med., N.Y., 1959-63; Asst. Prof., N.Y. Med. Coll., N.Y.C., 1963-; Dir., Pulmonary Function Rsch. Lab. ibid, & Metropol. Hosp., N.Y.C., 1963-; Assoc. Attending Physn., ibid, 1963-. Mbrships: Am. Physiol. Soc.; Am. Thoracic Soc.; Am. Fedn. Clin. Rsch.; Int. Union of Physiol.; AAAS; Am. Coll. Chest Physns.; AMA; Med. Soc. of State of N.Y. Address: Pulmonary Function Rsch. Laboratory, N.Y. Med. Coll.-Metropol. Hosp. Ctr., 1901 1st Ave., N.Y., NY 10029, U.S.A. 57.

TING, (Rev.) Simon, b. 19 Jan. 1925. Professor; Clergyman; Guidance Counsellor. Educ: Bapt. Bible Sem., Manila, 1941; Th.B., Union Theol. Sem., Manila, 1944; A.A., Coll. of Liberal Arts, Arellano Univ., Manila, 1946; A.B., Philos., Cornell Coll., Iowa, U.S.A., 1948; M.A., Philos. or Relig., Oberlin Coll., 1950; D.Phil., Mansfield Coll., Oxford Univ., U.K., 1958; M.Div., Divinity Schl., Vanderbilt Univ., U.S.A., 1973. Appts: Admnstr. of Gen. Affairs, Instr., Anglo-Chinese Schl., 1945-47; Instr., Psychol. & Philos., Coll. of Arts, 1950-55; Prof., Philos., Coll. of Arts & Scis., 1958-; Dir., Inst. of Chinese Culture, Philippine Christian Coll., Manila; Guidance Supvsr., Instr. Chinese Hist. & Lit., Hope Christian H.S., 1950-55, 1958-. Mbrships, incl: Commn. on Christian Lit. & Educ., Nat. Coun. of Christian Chs. in Philippines; Dir., Philosophical Assn. of Philippines. Publs. incl: Selected Short Stories from Chinese Classical Literature, 1946; Mysticism of Chuang Tzu, 1958. Hons. incl: Commendation, Nat. Coun. for Chinese Cultural Renaissance, 1968; Citation of Merit, Dept. of Educ., Repub. of Philippines, 1971. Address: Philippine Christian Coll., P.O. Box 907, Manila, Philippines. 11.

TINKLE, Maybelle, b. 20 Dec. 1909. Educator. Educ: B.S., Tex. Wesleyan Coll., 1931; M.Ed., The Univ. of Tex., 1932; N.Tex. Schl. of Law, 1936-37; Univs. of Colo. & Wis., 1937, '38; D.Ed., Univ. of Mich., 1955. Appts: Co-owner, M.B. Tinkle Dept. Store, Ft. Worth, Tex., 1932-38; Asst. Prof. of Phys. Educ., Tex. Wesleyan Coll., 1937-46; Acting Registrar, ibid, summer 1942; Counsellor, var Camps, summers '42, '43-49 & '56-57; Assoc. Prof. of Phys. Educ., Tex. Christian Univ., 1946-. Mbrships. incl: Am., Southern & Tex. of Hlth., Phys. Educ. Recreation; Ft. Worth Women's Phys. Educ. Assn.; Nat. & Southern Assns. of Phys. Educ. for Coll. Women; Pres., Ft. Worth Br., 1959-61, AAUW; Pres., Altrusa Club of Ft. Worth Inc.; Delta Kappa Gamma; Alpha Chi; Delta Delta Pi; Pi Lambda Theta; Sponsor, Selta Psi Kappa. Publs: A Survey of Health & Physical Education Programs in Public Secondary Schools of Texas, 1955; articles in jrnls. Address: 4900 Staples, Ft. Worth, TX 76133, U.S.A. 5, 132.

TINSLEY, James Robinson, b. 15 Feb. 1944. Educator. Educ: A.B., Centenary Coll. of La., 1966; A.M., E. Tex. State Univ., 1967; Grad. study, Univ. of Ala. Appts: Grad. Asst., E. Tex. State Univ., 1967; Instr. in Hist., Wm. Carey Coll., 1967-68, Morehead State Univ., 1968-71; Asst. Prof. of Hist., ibid, 1971-. Mbrships. incl: Southern Hist. Assn.; Am. Hist. Assn.; Mennoite Hist. Assn.; Past & Present Soc.; Royal Australian Hist. Soc.; Ala. Hist. Soc.; Phi Alpha Theta; Pi Gamma Mu; Gamma Theta Upsilon; Tau Kappa Epsilon; &c. Publs: America's Reaction to Great Britain's Entry into World War II, 1967. Hons. incl: Ky. Col.; Ky. Admiral; Kt. of St. John of Jerusalem; Hon. Citizen, Boys Town. Address: P.O. Box 767-M.S.U., Morehead, KY 40351, U.S.A. 125, 129, 130, 131, 139.

TINSLEY, Mary-Stella Markides, b. 20 Nov. 1948. Reacher. Educ: B.A., Morehead State Univ., 1970; M.Higher Educ., ibid, 1972; M.A., 1974; Also studied at Univ. of Ala.; Rsch. travel to U.K. & Europe. Appts: Tchr.'s Aide, Duquesne, Pa., summer 1967; Lib. Searcher, Morehead State Univ., Ky., 1972; Hist. Tutor, ibid, 1973-74. Mbrshi̧ps. incl: Phi Alpha Theta; Sec., Pi Gamma Mu, 1971-72; Kappa Delta Pi; AAUP; Women's Caucus, Am. Histl. Assn.; Southern Histl. Assn.; Ky. Histl. Assn. Hons: Newman Ldrship. Award, 1969; Ky. Col., 1971; Outstanding Grad. mbr., Kappa Delta Pi. Address: 128 A Carey Ave., Morehead, KY 40351, U.S.A. 125.

TIPTON, (The Rev.) Ervin Charles, b. 26 Sept. 1900. Clergyman; Church Architect; Poet. Educ: A.B. Neb. Wesleyan Univ., Lincoln, U.S.A., 1934; S.T.B., Schl. of Theol., Boston Univ., Mass., 1939; Master of Divinity, ibid, 1973; Ordained Min., United Meth. Ch.; Deacon, 1933; Elder, 1935. Appts: Min. for 39 yrs., Chs. in Neb., Mass., & Calif.; Staff Mbr. for 9 yrs., Nat. Missions of the Meth. Ch., Ch. Extension Sect., Dept. of Ch. Arch. Mbrships: Nat. Psychol. Assn.; Chap., Sons of the Am. Revolution, 1973. Designer, 36 chs. in U.S.A., Japan, & Puerto Rico. Woodcarvings on 3 ch. altars. Publs: Gleanings from Old-World Flower Fields; Voices from the Holy Land; Take Five; To Worlds Just Dreams Away; Devotions by Candle Light; The Family of Tipton, 1974; Poems & articles in newspapers, books, & jrnls. Commnd, Ky. Col., 1972. Address: 25 Sunset Way, San Rafael, CA 94901, U.S.A. 116.

TISDALE, Barbara, b. 24 Dec. 1913. Librarian. Educ: A.B., Radcliffe Coll., 1935; Postgrad. work, ibid, 1942-43; B.S. in L.S., Syracuse Univ., 1940; Postgrad. work, Queens Coll., 1958-65; M.A., N.Y. Univ., 1971. Univ. of Milan, Rome Italy, 1970. Appts: Asst. Catalogue Dept., Harvard Univ. Lib., 1936-39; Libn., var. schls., Mass., 1940-42; Asst. Libn., Cataloguer, Northeastern Univ. Lib., Boston, 1942-43; Libn., HS, Bristol, Conn., 1943-45; Rec. & Circulation Asst., Bus. Dept., Columbia Univ., Lib., N.Y.C., 1945-46; Extension Libn., Great Neck Lib., N.Y., 1946-50; Libn., Lakeville Br., 1951-. Mbrships. incl: ALA; Nassau Co. Lib. Assn.; Recording Sec., Art Comm., Gt. Neck Lib., 1970-; League of Women Voters; Great Neck Nat. Trust for Hist. Preservation.; Prog. Chmn., Bus. & Profl. Women, Women's Guild, Community Ch., Gt. Neck, 1973-; Chmn., Comm. Community Servs., Gt. Neck Lib. Staff Assn., 1973. Address: 475 Great Neck Rd., Great Neck, NY 11021, U.S.A. 5, 6, 22, 132.

TITIUS, Ruth (Lätitia Dorothea), b. 9 May 1922. Painter & Designer; Secretary Correspondent. Educ: Univs. of Hamburg & Heidelburg, 1949. Appts: Admin. posts, var.

commercial & indl. offs., diplomatic missions. Mbrships: Deutsch-Französische Gesellschaft CLUNY, Hamburg; Hamburger Kunstverein; Int. Arts Guild, Monte Carlo, 1965-69; Accademia Campanella. Author, Essays & contbrns., women's mags., inclng. Madame. Paintings reproduced in Repertorium Artis & Concours de la Palme d'Or Catalogue, Monte Carlo. Grp. Exhibs. incl: Stuttgart-Bernhausen; Monte Carlo, Monaco; Lyon, France. Recip., Gold Medal, Accademia Campanella, Rome, Italy, 1972. Address: Otterhaken 9, 2102 Hamburg 93, German Fed. Repub.

TITMUSS, Richard M., b. 16 Oct. 1907. University Professor. Appts. incl: Ind. & commercial experience, 1922-42; Official Histn., Cabinet Officer, U.K., 1942-48; Dpty. Dir., Soc. Med. Rsch. Union, 1948-50; Prof., Soc. Admin., London Schl. of Econs. & Pol. Scis., 1950-. Fellow, Brit. Acad. Mbrships. incl: Dpty. Chmn., Supplementary Benefits Commn.; Nat. Ins. Advsry. Comm.; Rsch. Study Grp., Planning Comm., Int. Soc. Security Assn.; Med. & Sci. Advsry. Panel, Family Planning Assn. Publs. incl: Essays on the Welfare State, 1957, 63; Income Distribution & Social Change: A Study in Criticism, 1962; Commitment to Welfare, 1968; The Gift Relationship: From Human Blood to Social Policy, 1971; num. chapts., intros., forwards, articles, etc. Hons. incl: Cmdr., Order of the Dannesbrog, Denmark, 1965; C.B.E., 1966; LL.D., Univ. of Chgo., 1970; D.Tech., Brunel Univ., 1972. Address: London Schl. of Econs. & Pol. Sci., Houghton St., London, WC2A 2AE, U.K. 3.

TIUSANEN, Timo, b. 13 Apr. 1936. Theatre Administrator & Scholar. Educ: M.A., Comp. Lit., Engl., Psychol., 1959; L.Lett., 1965. Ph.D., 1968, Univ. of Helsinki, Finland; Grad. studies, Yale Univ., U.S.A., 1963-64. Appts: Literary Critic, daily Helsingin Sanomat, Finland, 1958-63; Instr. Drama, 1964-67, Acting Asst. Prof., 1967-68, Docent, Theatre Rsch., 1969-, Univ. of Helsinki; Vis. Stage Dir., Helsinki City Theatre, 1963-68; Gen. Dir., 1970-74; Asst. Mgr., Finnish Nat. Theatre, 1969; Rsch. Schlr., Finnish Acad. of Arts & Scis., 1974-. Mbrships: Pres., Finnish PEN Club, 1967-68; Bd., Finnish Union of Theatre Mgrs., 1968-74; Bd., Scandinavian Union of Theatre Mgrs. (Nordiska Teaterledarradet), 1970-74. Publs: Tapa puhua (A Way of Speaking), 1963; O'Neill's Scenic Images, 1968; Teatterimme hahmottuu (Our Theatre Finds its Shape), 1969. Hons: Vaaskivi Medal for a Literary or Theatre Critic, 1962; Art Medal, daily Lansi-Suomi, 1963. Address: Vironkatu 4 C 19, 00170 Helsinki, Finland. 90, 134.

TOBIAS, Phillip Vallentine, b. 14 Oct. 1925. Professor; Anatomist; Anthropologist. Educ: Univ. of Witwatersrand, Johannesburg, S. Africa; Emmanuel Coll., Cambridge Univ., U.K.; B.Sc., 1946; M.B.B.Ch., 1951; Ph.D., 1953; D.Sc., 1967. Appts: Lectr., Univ. of Witwatersrand, Johannesburg, 1951-52; Sr. Lectr., ibid, 1953-58; Prof. & Hd., Dept. of Anatomy, 1959-; Vis. Prof., phys. anthropol., Cambridge Univ., U.K., 1964; Examiner, Coll. of Surgs., S. Africa. Mbrships. incl: Fellow, Royal Soc of S. Africa (Pres., 1970-72); Fellow, Royal Anthropol. Inst. of G.B. & Ireland, Linnean Soc. of London; Pres., S. African Archaeol. Soc., 1964-65. Publs. incl: Man's Past & Future, 1969; The Brain in Hominid Evolution, 1971. Hons. incl: S. Africa Medal, 1967; Sr. Capt. Scott Medal, 1973. Address: Dept. of Anatomy, Med. Schl., Hosp. St., Johannesburg, 2001, S. Africa. 30, 34, 39, 131.

TOBIN, Frances Mae, b. 26 Feb. 1941. Health Educator. Educ: B.S., Bklyn. Coll., N.Y.; M.S., Univ. of Ill., Urbana; Ed.D., Columbia Univ., Tchrs. Coll., ibid. Appts: Asst. Prof. of Hlth. Educ., Herbert H. Lehman Coll., Bronx, N.Y., 1964-. Mbrships: Am. Pub. Hlth. Assn.; Chmn., Coll. Hlth. Sect., Eastern Dist. Assn. for Hlth., Phys. Educ. & Recreation. Author 2 profl. jrnl. articles, A Suggested Drug Abuse Education Program for Freshman Women Students Attending An Urban College, 1973; A Realistic View of Drug Abuse 1973. Address: 87-50 204 St., Hollis, NY 11423, U.S.A. 5, 132.

TOBIN, Margaret Mary, b. 11 Oct. 1928. Librarian. Educ: B.A., Marywood Coll., 1950; M.Ed., Duquesne Univ., 1958; postgrad. study, Pa. State Univ., 1962. Appts: Instr., St. Francis Coll., Loretto, Pa., 1958-62; Assoc. Prof., ibid, 1963-; Libn., 1950-62; Assoc. Libn., 1962-. Mbrships: Cons. Barnesboro Pub. Lib. 160, Pa.; AAUP; Am., Pa., Cath. Lib. Assns.; Bus. & Profl. Womens Club. Publs: co-author, Bibliographic & Library Manual, 1953, rev. edit., 1962; profl. articles. Address: Pius XII Mem. Lib., St. Francis Coll., Loretto, PA 15940, U.S.A.

TOBOLOWSKY, Jack Lehman, b. 16 Jan. 1917. Business Executive. Educ: Univ. of Tex., U.S.A. Appts: Sr. Engr., Western Elec. Co.; Pres., Midlo Textile Co.; Pres., Wolf Textile Co. Address: 5909 Waggoner Drive, Dallas, TX 75230, U.S.A. 7.

TODD, Cyrus Edwin, b. 23 Jan. 1911. University Professor. Educ: B.S., W. Tex. State Univ., Canyon, Tex., 1935; M.S., N. Tex. State Univ., Denton, Tex., 1954; Ed.D., ibid, 1963. Appts. incl: Tchr. & Admin., Elem. Pub. Schls., Fifteen yrs.; H.S. Admin., Five Yrs.; Univ. Tchr. & Admin., Eleven Yrs.; Chmn., Dept. of Educ.; Dir., Secondary Educ.; Counselor, Elem. & Secondary Tchr. Progs. Mbrships. incl: Charter Pres., Phi Delta Kappa, Epsilon Alpha Chapt.; Chmn., Univ. Senate; Trustee & Bd. Mbr., First Bapt. Ch.; Exec. Comm., State Assn. of Coll. Tchrs. & Southern Assn. Regional; Dir., Southern Assn. Evaluation Team; Nat. Educ. Assn.; Nat. Prin. Assn.; Sec., Javelina Kiwanis Club, Kingsville, Tex. Author of A Study of Supervisory Practices in Certain States as Compared to those in Texas. Address: 237 Pasadena Drive, Kingsville. TX 78363, U.S.A.

TODD, Erwin Murray, b. 2 Oct. 1894. Banker. Educ: D.Sc., Monmouth Coll. Appts: Am. Cyanamid Co., 1916-20; Phillips & Avery, attys., N.Y., 1920-45; Tax Cons., E. M. Todd & Co., N.Y.C., 1945-55; Ocean Co. Nat. Bank, Point Pleasant, N.J., 1962-; Dir., ibid, 1962-. Mbrships: V.P., Monmouth Coun., Boy Scouts Am., 1955- (chmn., bd. trustees, 1960-; chmn., long range planning, 1960-); N.E. Region Exec. Comm., Boy Scouts Am.; Treas., Monmouth Med. Ctr., 1957- (bd. dirs.); Trustee Pingry Schl.; Trustee, Bd. Dirs., Monmouth Coll.; Mason; Deal Golf Club, N.J.; Navesink Golf Club, Red Bank, ibid; Kenwood Golf Club, Cinn., Ohio; Lakewood Golf Club; Pass-a-Grille Yacht Club, Fla.; Downtown Athletic Club, N.Y.C.; Union League, ibid; Advt. Club. Recip., Silver Beaver & Silver Antelope awards, Boy Scouts of Am. Address: 862 Holmdel Rd., Holmdel, NJ 07733, U.S.A.

TODD, Lee Barnhardt, b. 13 Mar. 1905. Physician. Educ: B.S., Coll. of Wm. & Mary, 1927; M.D., Med. Coll. of Va., 1932; Internship, ibid, 1932-34. Appts: Gen. Prac. of Med., Quinwood, W.Va., 1934-43 & 51-; Major, Med. Corp., AUS, 1943-46; Dir., Hlth. Dept.,

Newport Mews, Va., 1946-51; Mbrships: Past Pres., Grbr. Med. Assn.; W.Va. Med. Assn.; Assn. of Am. Physns. & Surgs.; Smithsonian Assocs.; Pres's. Coun. of Coll. of Wm. & Mary; AMA; PIKA; ODK; AOA; AAPS; Chi Beta Phi; Theta Chi Delta; W. Va. Chapt. Am. Acad. of Ped.; Mason 32; Am. Thoracic Soc.; Shriner; W. Va. Heart Assn.; Nat. Rehab. Assn.; Am. Heart Assn. Address: Quinwood, WV 25981, U.S.A. 6, 22, 57, 125, 128, 130, 131.

TODD, Lionel Milton, b. 27 Feb. 1930. Architect. Educ: Sydney Tech. Coll., Australia. Appts: Design Archt., Commonwealth Indl. Gases Ltd.; Jr. Ptnr., Spencer Hanson & Ptnrs.; Sr. Ptnr., Hanson Todd & Ptnrs.; Dir., Hanson & Todd Pty. Ltd.; Lectr., Arch. Final Yr., Univ. of N.S.W. Mbrships: Fellow, Royal Australian Inst. of Archts.; Past Pres., St. George Bowling Club; Deleg., Royal N.S.W. Bowling Assn.; Australian Golf Club; N. Sydney Club; Masonic Club; Georges River Sailing Club; Rolls Royce Owners Club. Buildings: Elec. & Mech. Engrng. Schls., Univ. of N.S.W.; Passenger Servs. Bldg., Admin. Bldg., & Flight Catering Bldg., Qantas Mascot; Sydney Opera House Stage III. Address: c/o Hanson & Todd Pty. Ltd., 225 Miller St., N. Sydney, N.S.W., Australia 2060.

TODD, Vivian Edmiston. Educational Consultant. Educ: B.S., Univ. of Idaho, Moscow, U.S.A.; M.S., ibid; Ph.D., Univ. of Chgo., Ill. Appts. incl: Demonstration Tchr., Wash. State Univ., Pullman; Rsch. Assoc., Tchrs. Coll., Columbia Univ., N.Y.C.; Cons., Tchr. Educ. & Child Dev., Assn. of Colls. & Univs. of N.Y. State; Cons., Nat. Commn. on Tchr. Educ.; Assoc. Educl. Supvsr., N.Y. State Dept. of Educ.; Curriculum Specialist, GHQ, Supreme Cmd. of Allied Powers; Self-employed Cons. Mbrships: Assn. for Childhood Educ. Int.; Nat. Assn. for the Educ. of Young Children; Am. Educl. Rsch. Assn.; NEA; Sigma Xi; Pi Lambda Theta; Kappa Delta Pi. Publs. incl: The Kindergarten Teacher; Elementary Teacher's Guide to Working with Parents, 1969; The Years Before School, 1970; The Aide in Early Childhood Education, 1973. Recip., Dr. of Pedagogy, Univ. of Idaho, 1973. Address: 1873 Stearnlee Ave., Long Beach, CA 90815, U.S.A.

TODESCHINI, Marco, b. 25 Apr. 1899. Scientist. Educ: Grad. in Engrng., Polytechnic of Turin; post-grad. studies in Phys. & Biol. Appts: Prof., Engrng., S.T.G.M., 1936; Prof., Thermodynamics, Bergamo Tech. Inst., 1950-65. Mbrships. incl: Am. Int. Acad. of N.Y.; Tiberina Acad., Rome; Nat. Coun. of Sci. Rsch., Haiti; St. Etienne Acad., France; Valence Acad., France; Bergamo Sci. Acad.; Agrigenta Acad. of Sci.; Pythagorian Soc. of N.Y.; World Inst. of Geophys. Rsch., Brussels; Astron. Soc. of France; Int. Ctr. of Biol. Rsch., Geneva; Italian Sci. & Metaphys. Assn., Milan; Itlain Phys. Soc., Milan; Maths. Circle, Palermo; Inst. of Am. Culture, Tolosa; Int. Acad. of Pantzen, Naples; Radian Sci. Soc., Catania; Pres., Int. Acad. of Psychobiophys., Bergamo; Teatina Acad.; Assisi Acad.; Italian Engrng. & Communications Assn. Publs: The theory of appearances; The psychobiophysics; What is the key of the Universe? ; Decisive Experiments in Modern Physics; Unification of Matter and its fields of forces; Universal Science. Hons: Kt. & High Off. of Crown of Italy; Kt. of the Order of Merit of the Italian Repub.; Star & Cross of Am. Int. Acad. of N.Y.; War cross; Inter-allied victory medal; Gold cross for Long Service; A.N.G.E.T. Gold medal. Address: Via Fra Damiano 20, 24100 Bergamo, Italy. 43.

TOEPLITZ, Jerzy, b. 24 Nov. 1909. Film Critic; Historian; Professor of Film History. Educ: Master in Law, Warsaw Univ., 1933; Ph.D., 1957. Appts: Sec.-Gen., Polish Film (State enterprise), 1945, Dir., For. Dept., 1946, Asst. Dir.-Gen., 1947; Dir., Polish Film Schl., Lodz, 1949-52, Rector, 1957-68; Hd., Film Dept., Inst. Art, Polish Acad. Sci., 1949-72, Dir., Inst. Art, 1961-68; Vis. Prof., La Trobe Univ., Melbourne, Australia, 1972-73; Fndn. Dir., Film & TV Schl., Sydney, 1973-. Mbr. & Off., film & TV orgs. Publs. incl: History of Cinematographic Art, Vols. 1-5, 1955-71; Film & TV in U.S.A., 1964; 25 Years of Film in Post-War Poland, 1969; New American Film, 1973, Engl. edit., Hollywood & After, 1974. Recip., Special Publ. Award, Assn. of Polish Film Makers. Address: Film & TV School, P.O. Box 245, Chatswood, N.S.W., Australia, 2067.

TOFT, Olav Andersen, b. 10 Sept. 1926. Electrical Company Executive. Educ: M.Sc., Tech. H.S., Graz, Austria. Appts: Owner/Managing Dir., Electroconsult, Bergen; Dir., Norsk Skjemaforlag, Bergen, Gula Tidend, Bergen & Aasane Trade Schl., Nyborg. Mbrships: Norwagian Assn. Engrs.; Tech. Soc. for Shipbuildirg, Hamburg; Austrian Soc. Electrotechnics, Vienna. Author, articles in field. Address: Tertnesvn. 14, 5084 Tertnes, Bergen, Norway.

TOGAWA, Naosuke, b. 25 Feb. 1917. Educator; Film Critic. Educ: B.A., Tokyo Imperial Univ., Japan, 1941. Appts: Edit. Staff, Eiga Hyoron, Tokyo, Japan, 1939-41; w. Nat. Bd. Info., 1941-45; Reporter, Jiji Press, Tokyo, 1945-58; Edit. staff, Kinema Jumpo, ibid, 1946-57; Prof., Film, Nihon Univ., 1958-; Dean, Coll. Arts, ibid, 1969-72. Mbrships: Dir., Japan Film Lib. Coun.; Japan Film Pen Club; Film Selection Comm., Nat. Bd. Culture, Min. Educ., 1947-; Jury, Film Festival, Asia, 1964-68; Jury, Int. Film Festival, Vancouver, Canada, 1966, Cracow, Poland, 1972 & Cannes, France, 1972. Recip. Audio-Visual Educ. Contrbn. Award, 1972. Address: 3-1633 Ikebukuro, Toshima-ku, Tokyo 171, Japan.

TOHARI, Edward, b. 11 Jan. 1910. Real Estate Investor & Importer. Educ: Grad., Law Schl., Univ. of Cracow, Poland, 1933; B.Econ. London Schl. of Econs., U.K.; Degree in pol. sci., Univ. of Geneva, Switzerland. Appts: Youngest mbr., Financial & Econ. Sect., League of Nations, 1930; Practising Atty. at time when Nazis. overran Poland; Active in Polish Underground & emissary to London, 1943; Jr. Ptnr., London merchant shippers firm, Harlow & Jones Ltd., 1948; Pioneer of bus. from Continental Europe to People's Repub. oc China, 1950-53; Moved to U.S.A., becoming active in real estate & ins., 1956; Organizer of Gulf & Eastern Trading Corp. for trade w. People's Repub. of China, 1971. Mbrships: Charter mbr. & 1st Sec., Lions Club, Cape Coral, Fla.; Chmn., Finance Comm. for Incorp. of Cape Coral. Publs. incl: Handbook on Civil Law Procedure in Poland (co-author); History of the First Polish Armored Division. Recip. of hons. Address: P.O. Box 2242, Ft. Myers, FL 33902, U.S.A. 125.

TOIVONEN, Leo Paavali Jalmari, b. 24 Dec. 1915. General Manager. Educ: M.Sc., Helsinki Univ., Finland, 1944; Postgrad., 1945, 46. Appts: Engr., Post & Telegraph Admin., 1939-49; Lectr., Radio Technics, Helsinki Tech. Univ., 1946-50; Lectr., Telephone Technics, ibid, 1946-47; Gen. Mgr., Nat. Assn. Pvte. Telephone Cos., 1949-. Mbrships. incl: Rotary Club; Helsinki Exchange Club; Engrng. Soc. Finland. Author of num. articles in jrnls. Ed. in Chief, Puhelin. Hons. incl: Cross of Liberty, 4th Class, 1942; Kt., 1st Class, Order of the White Rose of Finland, 1966; Gold Badge of Merit,

Nat. Assn. Pvte. Telephone Cos., 1971. Address: Nat. Assn. Pvte. Telephone Cos., Fredrikinkatu 61, 00100 Helsinki 10, Finland. 43, 90, 134.

TOLLEY, William Pearson, b. 13 Sept. 1900. University Professor. Educ: A.B., Syracuse Univ., 1922; M.A., ibid, 1924; B.D., Drew Univ., 1925; M.A., Columbia Univ., 1929; Ph.D., ibid, 1930. Appts: Asst. to the Pres., Drew Univ., 1925; Dean, ibid, 1928-31; Pres., Allegheny Coll., 1931-42; Chancellor & Pres., Syracuse Univ., 1942-69; Chmn. of Bd., Mohawk Airlines, 1970-72. Mbrships. incl: V.P., Japan Christian Univ. Fndn.; Pres., Century Club, Syracuse; Pres., Univ. Senate, United Meth. Ch.; Pres., Fndn. for Christian Higher Educ. Publs: The Idea of God in The Philosophy of St. Augustine; Alumni Record, Drew Theological Seminary; Preface to Philosophy; The Transcendent Aim. Hons. incl: Chevalier, Legion d'Honneur; 35 degrees, U.S. & for. univs. Address: 107 Windsor Place, Syracuse, NY 13210, U.S.A. 2, 6, 32.

TOLONEN, Jouko Paavo Kalervo, b. 2 Nov. 1912. Professor of Musicology; Composer; Pianist. Educ: Pvte. studies in piano, composition & conducting, 1919-39; Studied Musicol., Philos., Psychol., Aesthetics & Sociol., Helsinki Univ.; M.A., 1939; PH.Lic., 1964; Ph.D., 1969. Appts. incl: Adjoint Hd., Music Dept., Finnish Broadcasting Co., 1941-46; Hd., Music Dept., ibid, 1946-55; Gen. Dir., Finnish Nat. Opera, 1956-60; Tchr. of Choir Technics, Klemetti Inst., 1955-56; Tchr., Theory & Comp., Sibelius Acad. of Music, 1960-66; Conductor of Lappeenranta Orch. & Chmbr. Choir, 1960-66; Instr. of Musicol., Turku Univ., 1966; Hd., Music Sect., ibid, 1970; Prof. of Musicol., ibid, 1972-; Jurist, many music competitions. Active Mbr. sev. profl. orgs. inclng. Bd. Mbr., Finnish Sect., JSCM (State Comm. for Music). Author of sev. books, num. articles in jrnls. & newspapers & given many Radio broadcasts. Compositions incl: Symphony in 1 Movement, 3 Arabesques, Andante & Rondo Alla Burla, Suites for Orch.; Cantata Profana (Notku Nuori Neitsykainen); Cantata Psalmodica (Ylistäkää Jumalaa); works for Choir, Solo instruments & song. Hons. incl: Cmdr. of Finnish Lion; Cmdr. of Stella Della Solidarieta d'Italia. Address: Tuhkimontie 2.A.4, 00820—Helsinki—82, Finland. 21, 43, 90.

TOLPO, Carl, b. 22 Dec. 1901. Fine Art Painter & Sculptor. Educ: Univ. of Chgo., Ill.; Art Inst. of Chgo., Ill. Mbrships: Former All-Ill. Soc. of the Fine Arts; Former mbr., Am. Artists Profl. League. Works: Heroic Lincoln Hd. Bronze, 42 inches high, Lincoln Mus., Wash. D.C.; 33 half life size Lincoln Hd. Bronzes, var. collects. inclng. U.S. Senate Ldr. Off., Lib. of Congress, Ill. State Histl. Lib.; 14 official portraits, Ill. State Capitol; Num. pvte. commns., paintings & sculpture; Recently completed painting, 8½ x 15 feet, of Yellowstone Grand Canyon from Tolpo Point; Currently working on Heroic Hd. & Heroic Standing Sculpture of late Hon. U.S. Senator Everett McKinley Dirksen, commnd. by State of Ill. for Ill. Capitol, Peking, Ill. & Wash. D.C. Recip., Hon. mention, Abraham Lincoln Portrait Prize, 1959. Address: Sky Ridge Rd., Rt. 2, Stockton, IL 61085, U.S.A. 8, 37.

TOLPO, Lily, b. 13 Sept. 1917. Fine Art Painter; Sculptor. Educ: Chgo. Acad. Fine Art, 1934-39; also violin studies, Sherwood Music Schl. & pvte. tchrs. Profl. debut in solo exhib., All-Ill. Soc. of Fine Art, Chgo., 1941. Introduction of original technique, Biographical Portrait Painting, in solo exhib., Freeport C.C.,

1973. Mbrships: Charter Mbr., Heritage League N.W. Ill.; Xi Zeta Lambda Chapt., Beta Sigma Phi. Sculptures incl: Law & Justice, symbolic structure, chandelier in Rotunda, Waukegan Co. Bldg.; Inspiration of Youth, Thomas Jr. H.S., Arlington Hts., Ill. Biographical Portrait Paintings incl: Dr. Norman N. Watson, Supt. Schls., Glenbrook, Ill.; Maurice L. McClanathan, Retired Pres., Econ. Fire & Casualty Co.; Mrs. Pat Nixon, 1st Lady of U.S.A. Address: Sky Ridge Road, Route 2, Box 180A, Stockton, IL 61085, U.S.A. 5, 37.

TOLSON, John Jarvis III, b. 22 Oct. 1915. Retired Lt. Gen., U.S. Army; Member of State Governor's Cabinet. Educ: Univ. of N.C., 1932-33; U.S. Mil. Acad., 1937; U.S.A. Army Parachute Schl., 1941; British Staff Coll., 1951; U.S. Army War Coll., 1953, Aviation Schl., 1957; Univ. of Pitts., 1960. Appts. incl: Chief, Mil. Assistance Advsry. Grp., Addis Ababa, Ethiopia, 1961-63; Dir. of Army Aviation, Off. of the Asst. Chief of Staff for Force Dev., Dept. of the Army, Wash. D.C., 1963-65; Cmdg. Gen., U.S. Army Aviation Ctr. & Cmdt., U.S. Army Aviation Schl., Ft. Rucker, Ala., 1965-67; Cmdg. Gen., 1st Air Cavalry Div., Vietnam, 1967-68, XVIII Airborne Corps & Ft. Bragg, N.C., 1968-71; Dpty. Cmdg. Gen., U.S. Continental Army Cmd., Ft. Monroe, Va., 1971-73; Sec. of Mil. & Veterans' Affairs, N.C., 1973-. Mbrships. incl: V.P., Assn. of the U.S. Army, 1971; Army Aviation Assn. of Am.; Am. Helicopter Soc.; Am. Legion; Disabled Am. Veterans. Author of Vietnam Studies, Air Mobility 1961-71, 1974. Recip. of num. mil. & civilian hons. Address: 116 W. Jones St., Raleigh, NC 27611, U.S.A.

TOMBLESON, Esmé Irene (Mrs. Thomas William John Tombleson) b. 1 Aug. 1917. Member of Parliament. Appts: War Serv., Women's Auxilliary Signalling Corps, Sydney, Austalia; Mbr., Monte Carlo Ballet Co., Sydney visit, 1939; Sec., Man Power Advt. Comm., N.S.W., 1942-47; Sec., Hd., Commonwealth Employment Serv., 1947-50; Elected Nat. M.P., Gisborne, New Zealand, 1960-; Mbr., Parliamentary Select Comm. into Fishing Ind., 1962, '69; Chmn., Maori Affairs & Island Territories Comms., 1970. Mbrships: M.I.S.T.D.; Women & Children's Rep., New Zealand Road Safety Coun., 1963; Winston Churchill Mem. Trust Bd., 1966; Co—opted Exec. Mbr., New Zealand Multiple Sclerosis Soc., 1964; V.P., 1970-; Ldr., New Zealand Deleg., Inter-Parliamentary Union Conf., Ottawa, Canada, 1965. Contbr. of articles on soc. & pol. affairs. Recip., U.S.A. Int. Visitor Grant, 1970. Address: Burnage Rakauroa, R.D. Matawai, Gisborne, New Zealand. 23, 38.

TOMEO, Betty Jane, b. 21 June 1929. Purchasing Agent. Educ: B.A., U. Cal. at L.A., 1951. Appts: w. Revell Inc., Venice, Calif, 1953-; Purchasing Agent, ibid, 1966-. Address: 3482 Meier St., Mar Vista, CA 90066, U.S.A. 5.

TOMKINS, Oliver Stratford, b. 9 June 1908. Clerk in Holy Orders; Bishop of Bristol. Educ: Christ's Coll., Cambridge; Westcott House, ibid; M.A. Appts: Asst. Gen. Sec., Student Christian Movement, 1933-40; Ed., Student Movement Mag., 1937-40; Deacon, 1935; Priest, 1936; Vicar, Holy Trinity, Millhouses, Sheffield, 1940-45; Assoc. Gen. Sec., World Coun. of Chs. & Sec. of its Commn. on Faith & Order, 1945-52; Warden, Lincoln Theological Coll. (Scholae Cancellarii), & Canon & Prebend, Lincoln Cathedral, 1953-59; Bishop of Bristol, 1959-. Mbrships: Ctrl. Comm., World Coun. of Chs., 1968; Athenaeum. Publs: The Wholeness of the

Church, 1949; The Church in the purpose of God, 1950; Ed. & Contbr., The Universal Church in God's Design, 1948; Intercommunion, 1951; Ed., Faith & Order (Lund Conf. Report), 1953; Life of E.S. Woods, Bishop of Lichfield, 1957; A Time for Unity, 1964; Guarded by Faith, 1971. Recip., D.D., Edinburgh Univ., 1953. Address: Bishop's House, Clifton Hill, Bristol, BS8 1BW, U.K. 1.

TOMLINSON, William West, b. 28 Nov. 1893. Educator. Educ: A.B., Swarthmore Coll. 1917. Appts: various positions in ind., 1923-37; Educ. Pub. Info. Serv., 1937-42; Sec., Temple Univ., 1942-44; V.P., ibid, 1944-; Innovator, Anatomy of Freedom, CBS radio series. Mbrships: Phi Beta Kappa; Am. Acad. Pol. & Soc. Sci.; Am. Acad. Pol. Sci.; Engl.-Speaking Union; Life, Bd. of Trustees, Temple Univ.; Bd. of Mgrs., Swarthmore Coll., 1944-48; 1st People-to-People Comm. on Educ.; Chmn., Projs. Comm., ibid; Advsry. Bd., Am. Coll. Admissions Ctr.; Dir., World Affairs Coun. of Phila.; Bd. of Trustees, Eastern Pa. Psych. Inst.; former Pres., Phila. Tuberculosis & Hlth. Assn. Publs: Time Out to Live; The Flickering Torch; There is No End; num. articles on world affairs & people. Hons: 2 nat. citations for CBS radio series; Russell H. Conwell Disting. Serv. Award, Temple Univ.; 3 Geo. Wash. Hon. Medals, Freedoms Fndn.; 5 hon. doctorates. Address: Temple Univ., Broad St. & Montgomery Ave., Phila., PA 19122, U.S.A. 2, 6, 15, 46.

TOMPKINS, Dorothy Campbell, b. 9 July 1908. Bibliographer; Editor. Educ: B.A., Univ. of Calif., Berkeley, 1929; M.A., ibid, 1937. Rsch. Asst. (Bibliographer), Sr. Rsch. Techn., Asst. Pub. Admin. Analyst & Pub. Admin. Analyst (Ed. & Bibliographer), Inst. of Governmental Studies (formerly Bur. of Pub. Admin.), Univ. of Calif., Berkeley, 1927-74. Mbrships: Am. Soc. of Indexers; Mus. Soc. of San Fran. Publs. incl: The Prison & the Prisoner, 1972; Local Public Schools: How to Pay for Them?, 1972; Power from the Earth: Geothermal Power, 1972; Strip Mining for Coal, 1973; Court Organization & Administration: a Bibliography, 1973; Furlough From Prison, 1973; Selection of the Vice President, 1974. Recip., Joseph Andrews Bibliographical award, Am. Assn. of Law Libs., 1971-72. Address: 909 Regal Rd., Berkeley, CA 94708, U.S.A. 5, 14, 132.

TOMPKINS, E. Berkeley, b. 26 Jan. 1935. Historian Educ: B.A. (Magna Cum Laude), Yale Univ., 1957; M.A., ibid, 1960; Ph.D., Univ. of Pa., 1963. Appts: Dir., Pa. Maritime Mus., 1961; Mbr., Hist. Dept. Stanford Univ., 1963-68, Dean, Summer Session, 1963-68, Archivist & Sr. Staff Mbr., Hoover Instn., 1968-69, Sr. Fellow, Hoover Instn., 1969-71; Dir., Div. Histl. & Cultural Affairs, State of Del., 1971-73; Exec. Dir., Nat. Histl. Publs. Commn., 1973-. Mbr., var. profl. orgs. Publs: Anti-Imperialism in the United States, 1970; Peaceful Change in Modern Society, 1971; The United Nations in Perspective, 1972. Num. essays, reviews, var. jrnls. Hons. incl: Carnegie Award, 1961; George Lieb Harrison Fellowship, 1962; Williamsburg Fellowship, 1963. Address: National Historical Publications Commission, National Archives Building, Washington, DC 20408, U.S.A. 9, 13, 30, 59, 131, 139.

TOMKINSON, Constance see WEEKS, (Lady) Constance Avard.

TOMS, Alvin Lee, b. 9 Oct. 1932. Banker. Educ: Grad., Schl. of Consumer Banking, Univ. of Va. Appts: Bookkeeper; Teller; Hd. Teller; Asst. Mgr.; Asst. Cahsier & Mgr.; Asst. V.P. &

Mgr; Bd. Dirs., Greenwood Chem. Co. Mbrships: Chmn., Albermarle Co. Welfare Bd.; Chmn., Finance Comm., Crozet Meth. Ch.; Life Mbr., Crozet Fire Co.; Crozet Lions Club; Elks Lodge; Va. Coun. on Soc. Welfare; Nelson Co. Chmbr. of Comm. Address: P.O. Box 128, Crozet, VA 22932, U.S.A.

TONE, Belle Louise Shamblin (Mrs. Van A. Tone), b. 16 July 1922. Executive Secretary; Real Estate Salesman. Educ: Bus. Coll. & some coll. courses. Appts: Exec. Sec., Jr. League of Chattanooga, 1955-, & Chattanooga Cotton Ball Assn., 1965-; Licensed Real Estate Salesman (State of Tenn.), managing personal real estate of 16 units. Mbrships: Prog. Chmn., Xi Rho Chapt., Beta Sigma Phi; Sec., Debbie Fox Fndn. for Treatment of Craniofacial Deformities; Eastern Star; Kappa Sigma Mothers' Club, Univ. of Chattanooga; 1st Bapt. Ch. of Chattanooga. Address: 208 W. Leawood Ave., Chattanooga, TN 37415, U.S.A. 125.

TONKIN, Viola Englehardt (Mrs. Charles Tonkin), b. 6 Jan. 1905. Teacher. Educ: B.S., Oakland City Coll. Ind., U.S.A., 1932; M.S., Ind. Univ., Bloomington, 1938. Appts: Tchr., 1938-70; Dir., Flagler Co. Pvte. Schl., 1970-. Mbrships: AAUW; Nat. Tchrs.' Assn.; Bus. & Profl. Women; Fla. Educ. Assn. Address: P.O. Box 722, Flagler Beach, FL 32036, U.S.A. 125.

TONNA-BARTHET, Gaston, b. 17 Nov. 1905. Retired University Lecturer. Educ: Alliance Française, Paris. Appts. incl: French Examiner, H.M. Forces Exams, 1928-40 & local G.C.E. & B.A., Univs. London & Cambridge, 1928; Fndr., Dir., Barthet's Lab. & Observ., 1921 & Malta Cultural Inst., 1949-; Lectr., French Lit. & Civilization, Royal Univ. of Malta, 1945-66; Ed., Academically Speaking (Rediffusion), 1959-63; Supvsr., Evening Ctrs., Educ. Dept., Malta Govt., 1961-66. Mbrships: Sovereign Order, St. John of Jerusalem; Bailiff, Grand Prior of Malta. Publs: La Chanson de Roland, 1934; Méditations Sentimentales (poem), 1944; Poètes et Prosateurs, 1946; Contes et Récits du Moyen Age, 1950; History of the Order of St. John, 1964; Maltese Poets of the XX Century, 1968; The Grand Masters of the Sovereign Order of St. John of Jerusalem, 1973; Biography Of the Grand Masters of the Order of St. John, 1974; pamphlets in Maltese. Hons. incl: OBE, 1959; Kt. Grand Off., White Eagle of Yugoslavia (King Peter), 1969. Address: 5/3, Sceberras Square, Floriana, Malta. 9, 99, 128, 131.

TONSON, Albert Ernest, b. 18 June 1917. Publisher & Company Director. Educ: Druleigh Coll.; ext. courses, Auckland Univ. Appts: Naval Serv., RNVR, RN, RNZN, RNZNVR, 1939-46; commencement in bus., 1946, currently Govng.-Dir., Paramount Enterprises Ltd., incorporating Tonson Publishing House, Auckland; Mbr., Papatoetoe Borough Coun., 1959-62, Urban Fire Authority, 1959-62, City Coun., 1965-68; Life Mbr., Papatoetoe sub-ctr. N.Z. Red Cross Soc., Pres. & Patron, 1960-62; Mbr., N.Z. Historic Places Trust & Auckland Regional Comm., 1962-69. Fellowships: Royal Geographical Soc., 1963-; Royal Soc. of Arts, 1970-. Mbr., lit. & heraldry orgs. Publs: Our First Hundred Years (co-author & ed.); Old Manukau. Contbr. articles on heraldry, jrnls. inclng. The N.Z. Armorist, The Coat of Arms. Address: 19 Pah Rd., Papatoetoe, Auckland, New Zealand.

TOOMEY, (Right Rev. Monsignor) Kevin Michael, b. 11 May 1921. Catholic Priest. Educ: De La Salle Coll.; Malvern & Corpus Christi Theological Coll., Werribee. Appts: Clerk, Dept. Trade & Customs, 1938-45; Nat. Exec., Young

Christian Wkrs' Movement, 1943-44; Ordained Priest, 1952; Asst. Priest, Brunswick, Vic., 1953-54; Nat. Chap., Young Christian Wkrs' Movement, 1955-63; Rep., ibid, Rome, Italy, 1957, Rio de Janeiro, 1961; Admnstr., Parish of Ivanhoe, 1963-68; Parish Priest, St. Peter's Parish, Clayton, Vic., 1968-72; Chap., Young Offenders' Group, Pentridge Gaol, Melbourne, 1964-68; Dir., Pastoral Renewal, 40th Int. Eucharistic Congress, Melbourne, 1971-73; Parish Priest, Holy Redeemer, Surrey Hills, Melbourne, 1972. Mbr., V.F.L. Park, Waverley, Melbourne. Hons: Prelate of Hon. of His Holiness Pope Paul VI, 1973; O.B.E., 1973. Address: Holy Redeemer Parish, 4 Barton St., Surrey Hills, Vic., Australia, 3127. 23.

TOOTHAKER, Ronald Wayne, b. 4 Nov. 1940. Educational Administrator. Educ: B.S., Ark. Polytechnic Coll., 1965; M.Ed., Univ. of Ark., 1969; Ed.D., ibid, 1974. Appts: Asst. Dean of Men, Ark. Polytechnic Coll.; Instr. Phys. Educ., Asst. Athletic Coach, ibid; Asst. Prof., Phys. Educ. Mbrships: Am. Football Coaches Assn.; Am. Assn. of Hlth., Phys. Educ. & Recreation; Blue Key Nat. Hon. Soc.; Phi Delta Kappa; Sigma Phi Epsilon; Lions Club. Address: P.O. Box 1293, Ark. Tech. Coll., Russellville, AR 72801, U.S.A. 46, 117, 125.

TOOTHMAN, Glenn R. Jr., b. 9 Aug. 1920. Lawyer. Educ: A.B. Hampden Sydney Coll., 1942; LL.D., Wash.-Lee Univ., 1948. Appts: Gen. Prac. of Law, Waynesburg, Green Co., Pa., 1950-66; Dist. Atty., Greene Co., 1956-64; Pres. Judge, Common Pleas Ct., 13th Judicial Dist., Greene Co., 1966-; Instr., Constitutional Law, Bus. Law & Govt., Waynesburg Coll. Mbrships: Past Pres., Greene Co. Bar Assn.; Green Co. TB Hlth. Soc.; Waynesburg Rotary Club; V.P., Green Co. Historic Soc.; Greene Co. Acad. of Art. Hons: Omicron Delta Kappa, Hampden-Sydney, 1942; Wisdom Award of Hon., Wisdom Soc., 1970. Address: 114 W. Wayne St., Waynesburg, PA 12370, U.S.A. 6, 131.

TOPKINS, Katharine (Mrs. Richard M. Topkins), b. 22 July 1927. Writer. Educ: B.S., Columbia Univ., 1949; M.A., Claremont Grad. Schl., 1951. Novels: All the Tea in China; Kotch; Passing 60 (co-author); II Boom (w. Richard Topkins), 1974; short stories. Address: P.O. Box 198, Ross, CA 94957, U.S.A. 2, 5, 30.

TOPKINS, Richard M., b. 26 Aug. 1925. Advertiser; Writer. Educ: B.Sc., McGill Univ., 1946; M.A., Univ. of Southern Calif., 1955. Advertiser, Hoefer, Dieterich & Brown, San Fran. Novels in collaboration w. Katharine Topkins: Passing Go, 1968; II Boom, 1974. Address: Box 198, Ross, CA 94957, U.S.A.

TOPOLSKI, Jerzy, b. 20 Sept. 1928. Historian. Educ: M.P.E., Poznan Univ., Poland, 1950; Ph.D., Torun Univ., ibid, 1951. Appts: Asst. Prof., 1956; Prof., Poznan Univ.; Polish Acad. Scis., 1961-68; Prof., Poznan Univ., 1968-69; V.-Dir., Inst. Hist., Poznan Univ., 1969-; Disting. Vis. Prof., Calif. State Univ., 1972-73. Mbrships: V.P., Polish Histl. Assn.; Polish Acad. Scis.; Comm. Int. Assn. Econ. Hist. Publs. incl: Rural Economy of Archbishopric of Gniezno, 1958; Development of Capitalism in Europe, 14th-17th Centuries, 1965; History of Western Poland (Ed. & Co-author), 1969; World Without History, 1972; Western Poland throughout the Centuries, 1973. Hons: Sci. Award, City of Poznan; Min. Higher Educ. Awards, 1964, '67, '73; Polityka Jrnl. Histl. Award, 1969; Miesiecznik Literacki Monthly Award, 1973; State Sci. Award, Methodology of History,

1970. Address: 26/2 Pamiatkowa, Poznan, Poland.

TOPPIN, Alexandra (Alyx) Hope Johnston. Antique Dealer & Collector. Educ: Munich Univ., Germany. Owner & Dir., The Antique Shop, Victoria, B.C., Canada, 1965-. Mbrships: Art Gall. of Gtr. Victoria, Ways & Means Comm., 1971; Past V.P., Ice-Breakers Club, Victoria. One-man exhib. of personal antique collection, Spencer Castle, Victoria, 1964. Address: 3877 Cadboro Bar Rd., Victoria, B.C. V8N 4G3, Canada. 5, 133.

TOPPING, Seymour, b. 11 Dec. 1921. Newspaperman. Educ: B.J., Schl. of Jrnlsm., Univ. of Mo., 1943; Also studied at Coll. of Chinese Studies, Peking, 6 months. Appts: Covered Civil Wars in China, w. INS, 1946-47; w. A.P., 1948-59; Corres., Berlin, German Fed. Repub., 1957-59; Mbr. Staff, N.Y. Times, 1959; Chief Corres., Moscow, U.S.S.R., 1960-63; S.E. Asia, 1963-66; For. Ed., 1966-69; Asst. Mng. Ed., 1960-. Mbrships: Coun. on For. Rels., Century Assn., Asia Soc.; Bd. of Dirs., N.Y. Quarterly; Corporate mbr., Inst. Current World Affairs; Nat. Comm., U.S.-China Rels., Inc. Author of Journey between Two Chinas, 1972. Recip., Disting. Serv. Award, Univ. of Mo. Schl. of Jrnlsm., 1968. Address: The N.Y. Times, 229 West 43rd St., N.Y., NY 10036, U.S.A.

TORAL PEÑARANDA, Maria Teresa, b. 20 May 1911. Doctor of Chemical Science; Etcher. Educ: Dr. Chem. Sci., Univ. of Madrid, Spain; Nat. Inst. of Phys. & Chem., Rockefeller Fndn., Madrid; Taller de la Ciudadela, Nat. Inst. Fine Arts, Mexico D.F., Mexico. Appts: Asst. Prof., Univ. of Madrid; Nat. Inst. Phys. & Chem., Rockefeller Fndn., Madrid; Prof. Phys. Chem., Fac. of Chem., Universidad Nacional Autónoma de México, Mexico City, Mexico. Mbrships: Salón de la Plástica Mexicana, Mexico City; Pratt Ctr. for Contemporary Printmaking, N.Y.C., U.S.A. Contbns., phys. chem. rsch., var. publs., Austria, France, U.K. Over 400 profl. etchings. Recip., Julio Guzman Award, Rockefeller Fndn., 1935. Address: Avenida Mexico 167-H, Mexico 11 D.F., Mexico. 37.

TORF, Jane Hamilton (Mrs Al Torf), b. 29 Aug. 1916. Antique Dealer; Lecturer on Antiques. Educ: Acad. of Fine Arts, Chgo., III., U.S.A. Appts: Saleslady, Marshall Field, Chgo., 1935-40; Owner, Hamilton House Antiques, Glendora, Calif., 1951-; Lectr., Various Clubs, 1960-65. Mbrships: V.P., Prog. Chmn., & Show Chmn., Southern Calif. Antique Dealers Assn.; Antiquarian Soc. of Southern Calif.; L.A. Co. Mus.; Glendora Chmbr. of Comm.; Glendora Womans Club; Chmn., Parsonage Comm., Meth. Ch. Author, lectures on A Thing of Beauty is a Joy Forever, & The Past is your Future. Exhibs. of antiques: Santa Monica, Calif.; Hollywood Paladium, Calif.; San Fran., Calif.; Pasadena Civic Assn., Calif. Address: Hamilton House Antiques, 1030 E. Alosta Ave., Glendora, CA 91740, U.S.A. 5, 133.

TORMA, Toivo Topi, b. 11 May. 1916. Company President. Educ: M.A., Univ. of Turku, Finland, 1939; Reserve Offs. Schl., 1940; Advt. Dip., Marketing Inst., 1941; Courses in Nat. Defense, Mil. Acad., Helsinki, 1966, '72; Fellow, Int. Inst. of Licensed Accts. U.K., 1971. Appts: Lectr., Marketing Inst., 1945-50; Mgr., Oy Gustav Paulig, 1952-62; Pres., Topitorma Marketing, 1963-. Num. mbrships: incl: Pres. of Bd., Marketing Inst.; Chmn., Helsinki Dist., Assn. of Reserve Off.; Past Mbr., Praesidium, Scandinavian Marketing Fedn.; Sales & Marketing Execs. Int., U.S.A.; Int. Advt. Assn., U.S.A.; Pres.' Assn., U.S.A.;

Assn. Belgo-Hispanica, Brussels; Rotary Club Kamppi, Helsinki; Finnish-Am. Club 32, Helsinki; Cmdr., Hospitaliter Orden in Finland. Publs: Books on marketing, battle hist., WWII, & gastronomy, in Finnish: Ed., Reservilainen. Num. hons. incl: Mbr., Finnish Assn. of Sales & Advt., Finnish Assn. of Advt. Cons., German-Jordan Soc., Hannover; Kt. 1st Class, Order of Lion of Finland; Cmdr. 1st Class, Order of Merit, Arab Repub. of Egypt; Golden Badge of Merit, Nat. Assn. of Reserve Offs., Finland; Golden Badge of Merit, Free Enterprise Org. of Finland. Address: Topeliuksenkatu 3bA, 00260 Helsinki 26, Finland. 43, 134.

TORNATORE, Connie Crimi (Mrs. James Joseph Tornatore), b. 12 Feb. 1927. Library Media Specialist; Teacher. Educ: B.S., Syracuse Univ. Schl. of Educ.; M.S.L.S., Schl. of Lib. Sci., ibid, 1972. Appts: Exec. Sec. to V.P., Oneida, Ltd., 1944-55; & to Treas., Syracuse Univ., 1958-59; Tchr., Canastota Ctrl. Schl. Dist., 1965-69; Libn.-Tchr., ibid, 1969-. Mbrships. incl: Beta Phi Mu; A.L.A.; Mbrship. Comm., Ctrl. N.Y. Libns. Assn.; Syracuse Univ. Schl. of Lib. Sci. Alumni Assn.; Syracuse Univ. Charter Mbr. of Univ. Coll. Alumni Assn.; Nat. Educ. Assn. Author, Elvis the Educated Elf, 1965, & of children's poetry booklets 1965-72; Poetry publd. in weekly newspaper. Hons: NDEA Schlrship. Award, 1964; Am. Newspaper Publishers Assn.'s Newspaper in the Classroom Schlrship. Award, 1966; Lions Club Educational Comm. Cert. of Merit. Address: 216 Prospect St., Canastota, NY 13032, U.S.A. 5, 138.

TÖRNUDD, Elin Maria, b. 22 Apr. 1924. Library Director. Educ: M.Sc., Helsinki Univ. of Technol., 1950; M.S., Lib. Sci., Carnegie Inst. of Technol., 1953. Appts: Libn., Finnish Ctrl. Chem. Assn., 1949-53; Hd., Info. Serv., ibid, 1954-56; Sec. Gen., Scandinavian Coun. Coun. for Applied Rsch., 1956-68; Dir. of Lib., Helsinki Univ. of Technol., 1968-. Mbrships. incl: Chmn., Finnish Coun. on Sci. Info. & Finnish Rsch. Lib. Assn.; Vice Chmn., Finnish Coun. of Sci. Info. & Rsch. Libs.; Bd., Finnish Assn. for Documentation; Vice Chmn., Finnish UNESCO Commn. Publs: Scandinavian Research Guide, 3rd ed., 1971; num. papers in sci. jrnls. Address: Helsinki Univ. of Technol. Lib., SF 02150 Otaniemi, Finland.

TÖRNVALL, Kurt Robert, b. 27 Sept. 1909. Director of Music; Organist; Cantor. Educ: Elem. Tchng., 1933; Dir. of Music, 1934; Ordained, Ch. of Sweden; V.D.M., 1968; Dr.Phil. (Fil. lic.), 1972. Appts: Organist, Conductor, Carl Johans Ch., Gothenburg, Sweden; Prof., Instrumental Music, Royal Tchrs.' Coll., Gothenburg. Mbrships: Rotary Int.; Int. Order of Odd Fellows; Order of Free Masons of Sweden; Society Svenska Män; Midwestern Orders & Medals Soc. (Chgo.); Heraldic Soc. of W. Sweden; Soc. of History; Soc. Gnistan, Gothenburg; Orden Militar del SS.Salvador & Santa Brigida de Suecia, Italien; Societas Intellectualis Seniorum, Gothenburg. Music publs: Ordinarium Missae Sancta Birgitta, 1973; Romances, cantatas, songs & hymns for choirs, piano, organ compositions. Hons. incl: Off. (clerical order), Royal Order of Vasa; Gold Medal, 1st class, Royal Patriotic Soc.; Gt. Gold Medal, Royal Soc. Pro Patria; Gold Medal, org. of Parishes of Ch. of Sweden. Address: Jakobsdalgatan 30, 412 68 Gothenburg, Sweden. 43.

TORP, Olaf Chr., b. 30 Oct. 1924. Librarian. Appts: Journalist, Trondheim, Norway, 1945-47; Asst. Libn., Lib. of Parliament, Oslo, Norway, 1949-51; Dpty.

Libn., ibid, 1951-58; Hd. Libn., 1959-; Lectr. in Pol. & Ref. Works, Norwegian Schl. of Libnship., 1964-. Publs: Stortinget 1958-61, 1958; Stortinget 1961/62-64/65, 1962; Stortinget 1965/66-68/70, 1966; Stortinget hosten 1969- varen 1973, 1970, revised edit. 1972; Stortinget høsten 1973-våren 1977, 1974. Address: Stortingsbiblioteket, Stortinget, Oslo 1, Norway. 134.

TORRES, John, Jr., b. 7 Mar. 1939. Sculptor; Art Educator, Administrator. Educ: New Schl. for Soc. Rsch., N.Y.C.; Art Students League; B.F.A., Rhode Island Schl. of Design, 1972; Apprentice under Arnold Prints, William Zorack. Appts: Instr., Henry St. Settlement, N.Y.C., 1963; Proj. Dir., Ford Fndn., 1968; Asst. to Coll. Dean, R.I. Schl. of Design, 1969; Asst. to Pres., ibid, 1971; Dean, Developing Coll. Prog., Inst. of Am. Indian Arts, 1973-; Special Cons., Nat. Endowment for the Arts, State Arts Couns. of R.I. & Alaska. Mbrships: McDowell Colony; Art Students League; Salmagundi Club, N.Y.C. Sculptor, over 200 stone carvings. Hons. incl: Fellowships to McDowell Colony, 1965, '66, '67, '70, '71, '72; Ford Fndn., Bd. of Control Schlrships., Art Students League. Address: Inst. of Am. Indian Arts, Cerrillos Rd., Santa Fe, NM 87501, U.S.A. 37.

TORRES, Ramón, b. 26 Jan. 1896, d. 20 Dec. 1973. Violinist. Educ: Conservatory of Music, Barcelona, 1915. Appts: Pablo Casals Symph. Orch., 1920s; Violinist in U.S. orchs., inclng: Roxy Theatre Orch., Radio City Music Hall, China Doll Night Club, Rainbow Room, El Chico's, Chateau Madrid, Meyer Davis' Orch. Mbrships: Local 802, AFM, N.Y.C. Address: c/o Helen D. Costello, 20 Tonnelle Ave., Apt. 3A, Jersey City, NJ 07306, U.S.A.

TORRES-OLIVER, Luis J., b. 16 Apr. 1921. Physician; Surgeon. Educ: B.S., Univ. of Puerto Rico, 1941; M.D., Hahnemann Med. Coll., Phila., Pa., 1944; Postgrad. studies in surg., Montreal Gen. Hosp., Canada, Columbia Univ., N.Y., U.S.A., Cook's Co. Hosp., Chgo., Cornell Med. Ctr., N.Y. Appts: Med. Dir. & Hd., Dept. of Surg., Hosp. de la Concepcion, San German, P.R., 1947-; Former Mbr., P.R. Bd. of Med. Examiners, 1960-64; Mbr., Bd. of Dirs., Banco Economias, 1962-72; V.P., Municipal Coun. of San German, 1972-. Mbrships. incl: Fellow, Int. Coll. of Surgs.; P.R. Med. Assn.; Western Med. Assn. (Former Pres.); P.R. Hosp. Assn. (Former Pres.); P.R. Assn. of Hosp. Admnstrs.; Am. Assn. Abdominal Surgs. Author of sci. papers & Cuatricentenario de San German (Hist. of Colonization & Fndn. of San German). Hons: Medal Pro Ecclesia et Pontifice, Pope John XXIII, 1960; Mbr., Order of Kts., Equestrian Order of Holy Sepulchre of Jerusalem, Kt. Cmdr., Pope Paul VI, 1967; Gold Medal, 400th Anniversary of Fndn. of San German, Govt. of P.R., 1971. Address: Box 105, San German, Puerto Rico 00753, 136.

TORREY, Rubye P. University Professor of Chemistry. Educ: B.Sc., 1946, M.Sc., 1948, Ph.D., 1968, Syracuse Univ., N.Y., Appts: Instr. & Rsch. Assoc., Tenn. State Univ., 1948-57; Asst. Prof.-Prof., ibid 1957-72; Asst. Lectr., Syracuse Univ., 1963-68; Prof., Univ. of Tenn.-Nashville, 1969-70; Prof., Tenn. .State Univ., 1972-; Rsch. Fellow, U.S. Atomic Comm., 1970-; Rsch. Collaborator, Brookhaven Nat. Lab., 1970-73. Mbrships: Sigma Xi; Am. Chem. Soc; A.A.A.S.; Beta Kappa Chi; Alpha Kappa Mu; A.A.U.W.; Alpha Kappa Alpha. Contbr. to profl. jrnls. on rsch. in polarographic diffusion coefficients, radiolysis & high pressure mass spectrometry. Recip., Atomic Energy Rsch. Grant, 1970. Address: Tenn. State Univ.,

Campus P.O. Box 526, Nashville, TN 37203, U.S.A. 14, 57, 130.

TORY, Avraham, b. 10 Dec. 1909. Lawyer; Notary. Educ: Fac. of Law, Univ. of Lithuania, Kaunas, 1933; Law Lic., Israel, 1952; Notary Lic., 1962. Appts. incl: Sec.-Gen., Palestine Delg. to Italy, clandestine org. for illegal immigration to Palestine, 1945-47; Pvte. Clerk, Tel-Aviv, Israel, 1948-52; Lawyer, 1952-; Notary, 1962-. Mbrships incl: Ctrl. Comm., Zionist Org., Lithuania, 1932-41; Deleg., World Zionist Congress, 1939-72; World Zionist Ct., 1955-64; Exec., Int. Assn. Jewish Lawyers & Jurists; Coun., Israel-Italy Friendship League; Hon. Sec. Gen., Maccabi World Movement, 1952-68; Hon. Legal Advsr., Lithuanian Jews Mutual Relief Fund; Exec., Indep. Liberal Party. Publs. incl: The Escape from the IX Fort, 1958; Zionist Lithuania, 1971. Recip., ALE, Israeli Min. of Defence, 1969. Address: 17 Neardea St., Tel-Aviv, Israel. 94.

TOSIA, Malamud (Mrs.), Sculptor. Educ: trnd. in music, ballet, hand crafts & sev. langs.; Masters in Plastic Arts., studying w. sev. prominent Mexican artists inclng. Francisco Goitia, painter, Ignacio Asunsolo & Luis Ortiz Monasterio, Sculptors, Acad. de San Carlos; studies at tor. museums. Appts: sometime Counselor in art at pvte. schls. & Judge in art competitions; Tchr. of sculpture to chosen students. Mbrships: Salon de la Plastica Mexicana (Mex. Inst. of Fine Arts); Offl. Sculptor, Mex. Acad. of Med. & Med. Socs.; Hon., Tommaso Campanella Int. Acad. of Letters, Arts & Scis., Rome, Italy. Works reproduced in var. mags. & periodicals, Mexico & abroad. Wind (sculpture) purchased & made "emblem" of Mus. of Contemporary Art, Morelia, Mich. Mexico. Sculpted 2 monumental figs. for Mexico City. Hons: Dip., Mex. Soc. of Gynecol. & Obstetrics., 1963; 1st, Hon. Mention, Nat. Sculpture Biennial, 1964; 1st Prizes, Mex. Inst. of Art Contemp. Sculpture Salon, Chihuahua, 1964 & 65. Address: Hamburgo 319-A, México 6, D.F. 105, 133.

TOSTENRUD, Donald Boyd, b. 24 Mar. 1925. Banker. Educ: B.B.A., Univ. of Minn., 1948; Schl. of Banking, Rutgers Univ., 1957. Appts: Nat. Bank Examiner, U.S. Treasury Dept., Mnpls., 1948-57; V.P., 1st Nat. Bank of Black Hills, S.D., 1957-59; A.V.P., Commercial Loans, The Ariz. Bank, Phoenix, 1959-61; V.P., Loan Supvsr., ibid, 1962; V.P., Southern Area Supvsr., Tucson, 1963-64; Sr. V.P., Southern Area Supvsr., ibid, 1965-66; E.V.P., Earning Assets Div., Phoenix, 1967-68; Sr. E.V.P., ibid, 1969-70; Pres., 1971-. Mbrships: Am. Bankers Assn.; Pres., Ariz. Bankers Assn., 1974; Nat. Dir., Robert Morris Assocs., 1973-76; State Banking Chmn., Treasury Dept., U.S. Savings Bond Div., 1973 & 1974; Bd. of Trustees, Mus. of Northern Ariz.; Governing Bd., Western Art Assocs., Phoenix Art Mus. Address: The Ariz. Bank, P.O. Box 2511, Phoenix, AZ 85002, U.S.A. 2.

TOTEN, John Ernest, b. 4 May 1918. Economist. Educ: B.A., Univ. of Western Ont., Canada, 1948. Appts: Bank of Montreal, London, Ont., 1935; Royal Canadian Engrs., Canadian Army, WWII.; Sec. to Pres., Bank of Montreal, London, Ont., 1951; Br. Mgr., Bank of Montreal, Montreal, P.Q., 1953; Asst. Mgr., Bank of Montreal, Hamilton, Ont., 1956; Asst. Supt., Western Credit Dept., Hd. Off., Bank of Montreal, Montreal, 1958; Assoc. Econ. Advsr., ibid, 1959; Econ. Advsr., 1961; V.P., Planning, 1966; V.P., Planning & Econs., 1969-. Mbrships: Int. Conf. of Commercial Bank Econs.; Montreal Econs. Assn.; Canadian Bus. & Ind. Advsry. Comm. to the Org. for Econ.

Cooperation & Dev.; Univ. Club, Montreal. Author, The Service Industries, 1955. Recip., Gold Medal, Univ. of Western Ont., 1948. Address: Bank of Montreal, Head Office, 129 St. James St. W., Montreal, P.Q., H2Y 1L6, Canada. 32, 88.

TOUCHBERRY, John W., b. 16 Jan. 1930. Minister. Educ: B.A., Furman Univ., 1951; M.Div., Louisville Theol. Sem., 1955; Cert. Clin. Trng., Schl. of Pastoral Care, Winston Salem, N.C.; further studies, Yale Univ., Union Univ., Inst. for Advanced Pastoral Trng. Appts: Pastor, Ebenezer Bapt. Ch., Cordova, S.C., Westside Chapel, Gainesville, Fla. & Faith United Ch. of Christ, Clearwater, Fla.; Chaplain, Men's Christian Coop. Union of Fla., Gainesville; Sr. Min., St. John's United Ch. of Christ, Lansdale, Pa. Mbrships: Chmn. of Charity Project, Rotary Club; Pres., Human Rels. Coun. of Pervellas Co.; Chmn., Christian Educ. Dept. of Fla. Conf.; Sec., Fla. Commn. on United Mins. in Higher Educ.; Pres., Bd. of Dirs., Sr. Citizens Retirement Facility; Chmn., Mayor's Community Rels. Bd., Clearwater, 1971; Chmn., World Serv. Comm., YMCA, Lansdale. Contbr. articles to A.D. Mag. Hons: Cert. of Appreciation, 1971, Humanitarian of Yr., 1972, Hon. Citizen, 1972, Clearwater, Fla. Address: 230 S. Valley Forge Rd., Landsale, PA 19446, U.S.A. 125.

TOUCHE, Armand Paul, b. 27 June 1899. Consul General. Appts: Hd. of Dept., Min.(H.), Paris, France; Consul Gen., ibid, 1936-. Mbrships: Pres., Acad. of Courtesy & Pub. Welfare; Pres., Artists' Automobile Club; Pres., Edit. Com., Common Market Review of Commerce & Ind., & Western & Eastern Europe; Pres., Int. Acad. of Scientific & Artistic Rsch.; Admin. Coun., French Publicity Savings Fund; French Exhibs. Com.; Pres., The Int. Exporter; Past 1st V.P., Nat. Commercial & Indl. Union, Fedn. of Trades Union Coms.; 1st V.P. & Treas. Gen., France-Baltic Assn.; Coun., French Overseas Commerce, 1933-42; Pol. Economy Soc.; Stats. Soc. of Paris; Past Pres., C.I.D.A.L.C.; PEN Club; Var. admin. offs., sev. nat. & int. exhibs. Author, Traité de Législation & de Finances, 1931. Num. hons. incl: Chevalier, Legion of Hon., 1952; Silver-gilt Medal, Town of Paris, 1967; Chevalier, Order of Soc. Merit; Cmdr., Order of St. Lazare of Jerusalem. Address: 96 Boulevard M. Barrès, 92 Neuilly-sur-Seine, France.

TOUMAZIS, A. Panayiotis, b. 24 Sept. 1912. Civil Engineer; Company Director. Educ: M.Sc. Eng., Nat. Metsovion Polytech. (Tech. Univ.), Athens. Appts: Famagusta Municipal Engr., until 1950; Pvte. Prac. as Cons., 1937-; Fndr. & Dir. of Cos., 1950-; Mbr., House of Reps., 1960-70; Min. of Natural Resources & Agric., 1970-72. Mbrships: Cyprus Chmbr. of Comm.; Pres., Famagusta Dev. Assn., Cyprus Archts. & Civil Engrs. Registration Coun., & Famagusta Fedn. of Trade & Ind.; Civil Engrs. & Archts. Assn. Coun. Address: 5, Edisson St., P.O. Box 99, Famagusta, Cyprus.

TOUNTAS, Constantine, b. 14 Apr. 1917. Surgeon; University Professor. Educ: Grad., Univ. of Athens Med. Schl., Greece, 1940; Postgrad. trng., Evangelismos, King Paul's & Brompton Hosps., London, U.K. Appts: Assoc. Prof., 1st Surg. Clin., Univ. of Athens Med. Schl., 1952; Hd., Surg. Dept., Piraeus State Gen. Hosp., 1955; Prof. of Surg., Univ. of Thessaloniki Med. Schl., 1955; Dean, Fac. of Med., Thessaloniki Univ., 1967; Prof. & Hd., 2nd Surg. Clin., Med. Schl., Univ. of Athens, 1968; Dean, Fac. of Med., ibid, 1969; Chancellor, 1970-72; Pres., 1972-73; V.P., Superior Hlth. Coun. of Greece. Mbrships. incl:

Soc. Int. de Chirurgie; Soc. Int. de Chirurgie Cardio Vasculaire; Collegium Int. Chirurgiae Dijestivae. Author of num. publs. in field. Recip. of hons. Address: 8 Academias St., Athens, Greece. 43.

TOUPS, Don St. Cyr, b. 13 June 1933. Artist. Educ: B.Art Educ., Schl. of Art Inst., Chgo., 1960; M.Art Educ., Art Inst., Loyola Univ. & Chgo. Tchrs. Coll., 1963. Appts. incl: Art Tchr., John Marshall H.S., 1961-; Chmn., Art Dept., ibid, 1965-; Art Inst., Fenger Coll., 1965, 66; Art Instr., Roosevelt Univ., Chgo., 1973-74; Area Art Cons., Chgo. Bd. of Educ., 1970. Exhibs. incl: Invitational, Nat. Decorative Arts & Ceramics Exhib., Wichita, Kan., 1968; Ill. State Mus., Springfield, 1968; Edward Sherbeyn Gall., Chgo., 1969; Push Expo Exhib., 1972; One Man Show, 414 Art Gall., 1973; Pan Am. Univ. Art Gall., Edinburg, Tex., 1974; Hyde Park Art Ctr., Chgo., 1974. Mbrships. incl: Nat. Art Educ. Assn.; Nat. Craftsmens Soc.; Nat. Harp Soc.; Mus. of Nat. Hist., N.Y. Address: 401 E. 32nd St., Chgo., IL 60616, U.S.A.

TOUTORSKY, Basil Peter D., b. 10 Jan. 1896. Pianist; Director & Owner, Toutorsky Academy of Music. Educ: various pvte. tutors; Grad., Novotcherkask Musical Coll., 1913; LL.B., Imperial Lycee; LL.M., Univ. of Moscow, 1916; B.A., Moscow Cons. of Music, 1916. Appts: served as Naval Officer, WW I; Dir., Fndr. Tchr., Toutorsky Studio-Salon, L.A., Calif., U.S.A.; Org., Mus. Lectures; Adj., contests for various orgs.; Org., Benefit Performances; Hd., Piano Dept., Chevy Chase Coll., Md., 1943-50. Concert Tours: U.S.A., Europe, Canada Mexico. Publs: num. articles & compositions on Russian music. Hons. incl: Dr. of Mus., Am. Int. Acad., 1937; Dip. de Médaille d'Or, Compagnie Théâtrale Philantropique, France; Grand Prix Humanitaire de Belgique; Chevalier de Grand Croix. Address: Toutorsky Acad. of Music, 1720-16th St., N.W., Wash. DC 20009, U.S.A. 69..

TOWNE, William Chester, b. 20 May 1943. Educator. Educ: B.S.Ed., Bridgewater State Coll., Mass., 1965; M.Ed., ibid, 1973; Postgrad. Work, Univ. of Nevada, Pa. State Univ., Bridgewater State Coll. Appts: Tchr. of Educable Retarded, Old Rochester Regional Schl., Mass., 1965-66; Tchr. of Trainable Retarded, Clark Co. Schl., Nevada, 1966-67; Tchr. of Educationally Handicapped, Clark Co. Pub. Schl., ibid, 1967-70; Tchr. of Trainable Retarded, Bucks Co. Intermediate Schl. Unit 22, Pa., 1970-; Cons., Hd. Start, Instrl. TV; Co-Prod., film, Pub. Schl. Activities for the Retarded, 1968. Mbrships. incl: Kappa Delta Pi; NEA; Pa. Educ. Assn.; Am. Assn. on Mental Deficiency; Coun. for Exceptional Children. Hons: Outstanding Young Educator Award, 1968; White House Fellow Nominee, 1969; Disting. Serv. Award, Outstanding Young Man of Yr., 1970; Elected Mbr., Royal Soc. Preservation of Hlth., 1974. Address: 349C Willowbrook Dr., Norristown, PA 19401, U.S.A. 2, 6, 57, 120, 130, 139.

TOWNLEY, Finos J., b. 26 Aug. 1902. Company Executive. Educ: Grad., North Western Univ. Appts. incl: Nat. Sales Mgr., Swift & Co.; V.P., Sales & Dir., ibid; Asst. to Pres., Murray Biscuit Co., Augusta, Ga.; Bd. Dir. & Chmn., Bd., Nova Sales Inc., Lakeland, Fla. & Inland Distributing Inc., Lakeland, Fla. Mbrships: Bd. Dir., Grocery Mfg. Assn., Am. Meat Inst. & Nat. Sales Execs.; former Pres., Nat. Assn. Food Rsch.; Lincolnshire Country Club; V.P., Lone Palm Golf Club. Hons. incl: Mayor, Lone Palm, Fla. Address: 540 Lone Palm Drive, Lakeland, FL 33801, U.S.A. 1, 125.

TOWNSEND, David R., Jr., b. 14 Apr. 1943. Salesman. Educ: SUNY, Morrisville; N.Y. State Police Acad. Appts: Policeman, City of Rome; Trooper, N.Y. State Police; Salesman, Don Davidson Chevrolet Inc.; Gen. Mgr., Copper City Chiefs Profl. Hockey Team; Treas., Northeastern U.S. Hockey League. Mbrships: Past V.P., Rome Jaycees; Rome Community Theatre; Amateur Hockey Assn., U.S.; Rome Moose Lodge; Past Pres., Northern N.Y. Meth. Coun. Hons. incl: Commendation, City of Rome; Award, Int. Hockey Comp.; num. awards, U.S. Jaycees. Address: 8411 Dawn Dr., Rome, NY 13440, U.S.A.

TOWNSEND, Elsie Doig, b. 15 Oct. 1908. Teacher. Educ: B.S., Ctrl. Mo. State Univ.; M.S., Mont. State Univ., 1960. Appts: Tchr., rural schls., 6 yrs., H.S., 20 yrs.; Tchr., Engl., Coll., 12 yrs. Mbrships: AAUP (sec., local chapt., 1968-70); Nat. Coun. Tchrs. of Engl.; CCCC; Delta Kappa Gamma. Publs: None to give away; Always the Frontier; If You Would Learn, Go Teach; num. jrnl. articles. Address: 3141 Santa Fe, Independence, MO, U.S.A. 30, 138.

TOWNSEND, Julia (Judy) Annice Garner, b. 11 Nov. 1935. Newspaper Associate Editor & Columnist. Educ: Bethel Coll., McKenzie, Tenn. Appts: w. Parsons Printing Corp., 1956 as Bookkeeper, Soc. Ed., & Advt. Mgr., Parsons News Leader; Purchased firm w. husband, 1963, and became V.P. & Sec. Treas., Printing firm, & Assoc. Ed., News Leader. Mbrships. incl: Nat. Edit. Assn.; Tenn. Press Assn. (Centennial Comm. 1968-69, Advt. Comm.); Order of the Eastern Star (Past Matron & other offs.); Decatur Co. Bus. & Profl. Women's Club (Pres. 1973-74); V.F.W. Ladies Aux. (State PR Chmn.); Past Girl Scout & Girl Scout Ldr.; Tennessee Beautiful Inc.; Tenn. Fedn. Democratic Women; Ctrl. Ch. of Chris. Prominent in Fund-raising activities. Publs: Short stories under pen name Jaye Garend. Hons. incl: State Advt. Award, Tenn. Press Assn., 1958; Plaque for 4-H Work, 1968; Decatur Co. Woman of Yr., 1970; Democratic Women's Spot-Lite Award, 1974; num. awards for Bowling. Address: P.O. Box 339, Parsons, TN 38363, U.S.A. 57, 125.

TOWNSEND, Lewis Franklin, Jr., b. 17 Nov. 1922. Periodontist; Educator; Retired Colonel U.S.A.F. Educ: Pre-med., Emory Univ., 1940-43; D.D.S., Schl. of Dentistry, ibid 1946; M.S., Tufts Schl. of Dental Med., 1956; Res. in Periodontics, Wilford Hall Med. Ctr., Tex., 1958-59. Appts. incl: Mil. career, 1947-69; Chmn., Dept., of Periodontics, Wilford Hall Med. Ctr., Tex., 1966-69; Assoc. Prof., w. title Coord., Grad. Periodontics, Emory Univ. Dental Schl., 1969-; Staff Periodontist, Atlanta Hops., Ga., 1970-; Cons., VA Hosp., Atlanta, Ga., 1973-; Cons., Ga. Retardation Ctr., Atlanta, Ga., 1972-. Mbrships. incl: Fellow, Am. Coll. of Dentists, 1968; Diplomate, Am. Bd. of Periodontics, 1965; Am. Acad. of Periodontics; Am. Dental Assn.; Air Force Assn.; Retd. Offs. Assn. Recip., "A" rating in Periodontics, Surg. Gen., U.S.A.F., 1969. Address: Emory Univ. Schl. of Dentistry, 1462 Clifton Rd. N.E., Atlanta, GA 30322, U.S.A. 7, 113, 131.

TOYOMURA, Dennis Takeshi, b. 6 July 1926. Architect. Educ: B.S., Chgo. Tech. Coll., 1949; Postgrad., Univ. of Ill. Ext., 1950, 1953-54, Ill. Inst. Technol., 1954-55, Univ. of Hawaii, 1966-67. Registered Profl. Archt., State of Ill. & Hawaii. Appts: Designer, Draftsman,

James M. Turner, Hammond, Ind., Wimberly & Cook, Honolulu, 1952, Gregg & Briggs, Chgo., 1952-54; Archt., Holabird, Root & Burgee, 1954-55; Pvte. Prac., 1954, 1962-; Loebl, Schlossman & Bennett, 1955-62; Archtl. Cons., Honolulu Redev. Agcy., Kapahulu Dist., City of Honolulu, 1967-71; Fallout Shelter Analyst, Dept. of Defense; Dir., Sec., Maiko of Hawaii, Inc., 1972; Real Estate Broker, Ill.; Dir., Pacific Canal of Hawaii, Inc., 1972 & Hawaii Chapt. Am. Inst. Archts., 1973. Mbrships. incl: Del. Commnr., State Assembly, Synod of Ill. Presby. Ch., 1958; AIA; Am. Concrete Inst.; Acad. Pol. Sci. Chgo. Nat. Hist. Mus.; Chgo. Art Inst.; Construction Specifications Inst.; Coun. Educl. Facility Planners, Int.; Ill. Assn. of Profession; Bldg. Rsch. Inst./Bldg. Rsch. Advsry Bd. of Nat. Acad. Scis.; Honolulu Acad. Arts; AAAS; Am. Soc. Testing & Mats.; Kappa Sigma Kappa; Elder & Trustee, Presby. Ch. Address: 1370 Kapiolani Blvd., Suite 201, Honolulu, HI 96814, U.S.A. 9, 16, 22, 128.

TRACHTENBERG, Stephen Joel, b. 14 Dec. 1937. College Dean. Appts: B.A., Columbia Univ., 1959; J.D., Yale Univ., 1962; M.P.A., Harvard Univ., 1966. Appts. incl: Atty., N.Y. Off., U.S. Atomic Energy Commn., 1962-65; Tutor, Law, Harvard Univ., 1965-66; Special Asst. to U.S. Commnr. of Educ., Lectr., Educ., Trinity Coll., 1966-68; Assoc. Dean, Coll. of Liberal Arts, Boston Univ., 969-73; Interim Dean, Coll. of Liberal Arts, Assoc. Prof., Pol. Sci., Boston Univ., & Assoc. in Educ., Harvard Univ., 1973-. Mbrships: State Dir., Mass. Educl. Seminar, Boston Univ.; Bd. of Dirs., Exec. H.S. Internship Prog.; Task Force on Proprietary Educ., Mass.; Mayor's Comm. on Urban Univ., Boston; Citizen's Comm., Mass. Mental Hlth. Assn.; Metropol. Boston Hillel Advsry. Coun.; Gov.'s Task Force on Open Univ., Mass.; N.Y. State Bar Assn. Contbr. to books, jrnls. Hons: One of Boston's 10 Outstanding Young Men, Jr. Chmbr. of Comm., 1970; Winston Churchill Fellowship; Wilton Park Fellowship. Address: Dean's Off., Boston Univ., 725 Commonwealth Ave., Boston, MA 02215, U.S.A.

TRACY, Michael Alec, b. 22 Oct. 1932. Economist; International Civil Servant. Educ: B.A., 1955, M.A., 1960, Pembroke Coll., Cambridge Univ. Appts: Rsch. Asst., UN Econ. Commn. for Europe, Geneva, 1955-57; Rsch. Asst., Pol. & Econ. Planning, London, 1958-60; Mbr., Hd., Agricl. Policies Div., OECD, Paris, 1960-73; Vis. Prof., Kyoto Univ., Japan, 1972; Dir. in Coun. Secretariat, European Communities, Brussels, 1973-. Mbrships: Int. Assn. of Agricl. Economists; U.K. Agricl. Econs. Soc. Publs: Agriculture in Western Europe—Crisis & Adaptation since 1880, 1964; Japanese Agriculture at the Crossroads, 1972; Contbr. to var. jrnls. Address: Council of the European Communities, 170 rue de la Loi, 1040 Brussels, Belgium.

TRACY, Neil, b. 31 Aug. 1905. Educator. Educ: B.A., Bishops Univ., Lennoxville, P.Q., 1928; M.A., ibid, 1929. Appts: Field Sec., Canadian Nat. Inst. for the Blind, 1941-67; Assoc. Prof., Univ. of Sherbrooke, 1963-74. Mbrships: Sherbrooke Lions Club; Pres., Boy Scouts Assn. of Sherbrooke, 934 & 38. Publs: The Rain it Raineth, 1938; Shapes of Clay, 1967; Voice LINE, 1970; Collected Works, in preparation. Hons: Scout Order of Merit. Address: 46 Deacon Ave., Lennoxville, P.Q. J0B 1Z0, Canada. 11, 57.

TRACY, Pauline Aloise Souers (Mrs. J. Richard Tracy), b. 20 Nov. 1914. Educator; Poet; Author. Educ: B.Ed., Eastern Ill. Univ.; grad. art courses, ibid & Univ. of Mo.; course in

Engrng. Drawing, Purdue Univ.; workshops & writing confs., Ill., N.C. & N.M. Appts: Tchr., Wiley Brick Elem. Schl., 1937-38 & Tracy Elem. Schl., 1938-46. Mbrships: Nat. League Am. Pen Women (Egypt Br.); Ill. Pen Women; Ill. Woman's Press Assn.; Nat. Fed. of Press. Women; Am. Poetry League; Hon. Life Mbr., Am. Poets Fellowship Soc.; Charter, Ill. State Poetry Soc.; New World Poets Club; The Pensters (Ala.); Major Poets Chapt.; Nat. Ret. Tchrs. Assn.; Corres. Sec. & V.P., Chap. AJ, P.E.O. Sisterhood; Eastern Ill. Alumni Assn. Publs. (books of poetry): His Handiwork, 1954; Memory Is a Poety, 1964; The Silken Web, 1965; A Merry Heart, 1966; In Two or Three Tomorrows, 1968; All Flesh Is Grass, 1971; Beyond the Edge, 1973. Address: 447 Chestnut St., Bridgeport, IL 62417, U.S.A. 5, 8, 11, 120, 125, 128, 130, 132, 138.

TRAGER, Bernard H., b. 18 July 1906. Lawyer. Educ: LL.B., N.Y. Univ., 1928. Appts: Admitted to Conn. Bar, 1929; Sr. Ptnr., Firm, Trager, Kleban Trager, 1965-. Mbrships: Pres., Conn. Conf. of Soc. Work, 1948-49; Chmn., Nat. Community Rels. Advsry. Coun., 1953-57; Algonquin, Birchwood Country, N.Y. Univ. & Nat. Lawyers Clubs; Chmn., Conn. Bd. of Pardons, 1959-73; Pres., Bridgeport Bar Assn., 1959-61; Pres., Conn. Bar Assn., 1964-65; Trustee, Univ. of Bridgeport, 1973-; Trustee, People's Savings Bank, Bridgeport, 1964-; House of Delegs., Am. Bar Assn., 1964-66; Dir., Conn. Attys. Title Guaranty Fund, Inc., 1965-; Financial Advsry. Commn., City of Bridgeport, 1966-; Trustee, Bridgeport Area Fndn., Inc., 1968-; Dir., Bridgeport Hosp., 1970-. Contbr. of articles to Conn. Bar Jrnl. Address: 1305 Post Rd., Fairfield, CT 06430, U.S.A.

TRAGER, Eugene P., b. 2 Nov. 1933. Psychiatrist. Educ: B.S., Univ. of Ill., 1954; Rsch. in Physiol., ibid, 1954-55; M.D., Coll. of Med., ibid, 1959. Appts: Clin. Instr., Upstate Med. Ctr., SUNY, Syracuse, 1963-65; Pvte. Prac., Des Plaines, Ill., 1966-; Clin. Asst. Prof., Coll. of Med., Univ. of Ill., 1968-70; Attng. Staff, Forest Hosp., Des Plaines & Northwest Community Hosp., Arlington Heights, Ill. Mbrships: Phi Beta Kappa; Am. Psychiatric Assn.; Am. Med. Assn. Publs. incl: Bureaucracy & Community Mental Health, in Bulletin of Northwest Community Hosp. Assn., 1971. Address: 3609 Davis St., Skokie, IL 60076, U.S.A. 112.

TRAGER, Gerry A. (Mrs. Lee Trager), b. 2 May 1920. Furniture Desigern. Appts: Asst. Mgr., Radio & Music Dept., R.H. Macy Co.; Profl. Singer, 1940-46; Sec. & Treas., Park City Fixture Co., 1946; Treas., Custom Hall Inc., 1951-. Mbrships. incl: Pres., United Jewish Coun., Gtr. Bridgeport, Conn., 1969-71; Nat. Chmn., Wills & Bequests, Am. Technion Soc., 1973; Chmn. of the Bd., Israeli Schlrship. Prog., Univ. of Bridgeport, 1973; Chmn., Women's Div., United Jewish Appeal; Life Mbr., Park City Hosp. Aux.; Life Mbr., Exec. Bd. Mbr., Jewish Home for the Elderly, Fairfield Co. Hons. incl: State of Israel Award, 1971; Testimonial & Award, Fed. Women's Clubs, 1967; Testimonial, Newington Childrens Home & Hosp., 1953. Address: 188 Skytop Dr., Fairfield, CT 06604, U.S.A. 55.

TRAILL, Paul Gerard, b. 28 Jan. 1941. Solicitor. Educ: LL.B., Sydney Univ., Australia, 1962; LL.M., ibid, 1967. Appts: Solicitor, mbr. of firm of Messrs. Gaden, Bowen & Stewart, Sydney & New Guinea; Dir., David Jones Finance Ltd., 1973. Mbrships: Hon. Sec., Law Coun. of Australia, 1970-; Exec. Mbr., Australian Soc. of Legal Philos., 1967-; V.P., ibid, 1971; Pres., 1972-73; Councillor, St.

Thomas More Soc., 1967-; Royal Automobile Club of Australia, Sydney. Author, Laymen in the Administration of Law, 1970. Address: 86 Pitt St., Sydney, Australia 2000.

TRAIN, Oswald, b. 8 June 1915. Bookseller & Publisher. Appts: Foreman, Cabinet-making company for over 25 yrs.; Ptnr., The Prime Press, publrs., 1946-53; Bookseller, late 1950s-; Publr., Science, Fantasy, Mystery & Detective Fiction, 1968-., Mbrships: Fndr.-Mbr., Phila. Sci. Fiction Soc., 1935- (Past Pres., V.P., Sec. Treas.); Assoc., Mystery Writers of Am.; Past Mbr., Hydra Club, N.Y.C. Encouraged early efforts of num. well-known Sci. Fiction authors during yrs. as publr. Address: 1129 W. Wingohocking St., Philadelphia, PA 19140, U.S.A.

TRAINER, Robert Browning, b. 15 May 1918. Attorney-at-Law. Educ: Grad., Harvard Univ., Mass., 1938; Harvard Law Schl., 1941. Appts: Atty., White & Case; V.P., Jos. Schlitz Brewing Co.; Dir., First Wis. Nat. Bank; Dir., First Wis. Trust Co.; Dir., First Wis. Bankshares Corp. Mbrships: incl: Bd. of Dirs., Milwaukee Blood Ctr., Pres., 1962-73; Coun., Med. Ctr. of Southeastern Wis.; Bd. of Dirs., Columbia Hosp., V.P., 1972-; Pres., Milwaukee Div., Am. Cancer Soc., 1963-65, Bd. Chmn., 1965-71; Trustee, Village of River Hills, 1959-72; Bd. of Dirs., Metropol. Milwaukee Assn. of Commerce; Bd. of Trustees, Milwaukee Downer Coll., 1951-64; Milwaukee Bar Assn.; Wis. Bar Assn.; Navy League of the U.S.; Master Brewers Assn.; Univ. Club of Milwaukee; Wis. Zoological Soc. Address: 31182 W. Thompson Lane, Hartland, WI 53029, U.S.A. 8, 120.

TRAMONTE, Michael Robert, b. 19 Oct. 1934. School Psychologist. Educ: A.B. (Cum Laude), A. & S. Coll., Boston, 1960; M.Ed., State Coll., Boston, 1963; postgrad., Boston Coll. Grad. Schl., & State Colls., Salem & Boston. Appts: Tchr., Roberts Jr. H.S., Medford, Mass., 1961-68. Instr. Psych. & Educ., Anna Maria Coll., Paxton, Mass., 1968-69; Schl. Psychologist, Lowell Pub. Schls., Mass., 1970-; Instr. in Psychol., Evening Div. of Mass. Bay Community Coll., 1972-73; active pub. speaker. Mbrships: Medford Mental Hlth. Assn.; Recording Sec., ibid, 1961-62, Assn. Advsr., 1967, 1969, Educ. Comm. Mbr., 1968; Medford Chapt., Gtr. Boston Assn. Retarded Children; Recording Sec., ibid, 1967-68, Pres. & Chmn., 1969-70. Recip., citations for servs. in mental hlth. activities. Address: 33 Grape St., Woburn, MA 01801, U.S.A. 130.

TRANIÉ, André Pierre, b. 27 Sept. 1911. Business Executive. Educ: Ecole Polytechnique, Paris; Institut des Hautes Etudes de Défense Nationale, Paris. Appts: Serv., French Army, until 1947, now Hon. Col.; Mgr., Simca, 1948-49; Mgr. & Gen. Sec., Panhard, 1949-65; Chmn., Dir., Compagnie Francaise de Prospection Sismique, 1965-69; Prin. Advsr., Houillières de Lorraine, 1965-69; Chmn. & Mng. Dir., Techniques Electriques Jarret, 1967-; Chmn., BTE, 1971-; Chmn., Centre International de Recherches pour l'environnement et les loisirs, 1972-. Mbrships. incl: Association des Auditeurs de l'Institut des Hautes Etudes de défense Nationale; Pres., ibid, 1961-66, now Hon. Pres.; Comm. Mbr., Assn. Anc. élèves de Polytechnique. Tech. & literary articles, newspapers & jrnls. Hons. incl: Officier, Legion d'Honneur; Croix de Guerre. Address: 144 Blvd. Suchet, 75016 Paris, France. 43, 91.

TRANSEAU, Leon Wayne, b. 14 Nov. 1935. Government & Company Executive; Educator. Educ: B.I.E., Ga. Inst. of Technol.,

1959; M.B.A., Univ. of Del., 1963; Ph.D., Am. Univ., 1968. Appts: Planning & Controls Engr., Int. Latex Corp., Dover, Del., 1959-63; Rsch. Engr., Ops Rsch. Inc., Md., 1963-64; Proj. Dir., Tech. Staff, Rsch. Analysis Corp., Va., 1965-68; Mgr., Ops. Rsch., Control Data Corp., Wash. D.C., 1968-69; Asst. & Assoc. Prof., Geo. Wash. Univ., 1968-70; V.P., Synergistic Cybernetics, Va., 1969-71; Pres. Deltran Corp., Md., 1971-73; Cons., Chief, Mgmt. Inf. & Control Div., Price Commn., Wash. D.C., 1972-; Div. Chief, U.S. Dept. of Justice & Lectr., Univ. of Md., 1973-. Mbrships: Inst. of Mgmt. Sci.; A.A.A.S. Author of various studies & reports. Speaker at nat. confs. Address: 7105 Old Gate Rd., Rockville, MD 20852, U.S.A. 6, 14.

TRANTER, Nigel, b. 23 Nov. 1909. Novelist; Author. Mbrships. incl: Chmn., Nat. Forth Rd. Bridge Comm., 1953-57, Nat. Book League, Scottish Comm., 1955- & St. Andrew Soc. of E.Lothian, 1966-; Past-Chmn., Soc. of Authors (Scotland); Past-Pres., Scottish PEN Club; Pres., E. Lothian Liberal Assn., 1960-. Publd. 54 adult novels ncing: Robert the Bruce trilogy; The Young Montrose; Montrose: Captain General; many children novels; also The Fortified House in Scotland (5 vols.); The Queen's Scotland (2 vols.); Portrait of the Border Country; Land of the Scots. Hons: Chevalier, Order of St. Lazarus of Jerusalem, 1961; M.A., Univ. of Edinburgh, 1971. Address: Quarry House, Aberlady, East Lothian, U.K. 1, 3,

TRATTNER, Walter I., b. 26 July 1936. University Professor. Educ: B.A., Williams Coll., 1958; M.A.T., Harvard Univ., 1959; M.S., Univ. of Wis., 1961; Ph.D., ibid, 1964. Appts: Asst. Prof., N. Ill. Univ., 1963-65; Asst. Prof., Univ. of Wis., 1965-67; Assoc. Prof., ibid, 1967-71; Prof., 1971-. Mbrships: incl: Past V.Chmn. & Current Chmn., Soc. Welfare Hist.G rp.; Am. Hist. Assn.; Org. of Am. Histns.; Am. Studies Assn.; Nat. Conf. on Soc. Welfare. Publs: Homer Folks: Pioneer in Social Welfare, 1968; Crusade for the Children: A History of the National Child Labor Committee and Child Labor Reform in America, 1970. Contbr. to profl. jrnls. Address: Dept. of Hist., Univ. of Wisconsin, 704 Bolton Hall, Milwaukee, WI 53201, U.S.A. 13.

TRAUGER, Donald B., b. 29 June 1920. Educ: A.B., Neb. Wesleyan Univ., U.S.A., 1942; Postgrad. study, Columbia Univ., NY, 1942-46; Tenn. Univ., 1946-49; Appts: Columbia Univ.-Union Carbide Corp., Manhattan Dist. Proj., 1942-46; w. Union Carbide Corp., Oak Ridge Gaseous Diffusion Plant, 1946-54; Oak Ridge Nat. Lab.—nuclear fuel irradiation & Dir., Gas-Cooled Reactor Prog., Assoc. Dir., Rector & Engrng., Scis., 1954-. Mbrships: V.P., Tenn. Sect., Am. Nuclear Soc.; ANS Planning Comm., ibid; Sigma Xi; Sigma Pi Sigma; Past V.-Chmn., Oak Ridge Bd. Educ.; Bd. Trustees, Holston Conf. Colls.; Oak Ridge Bd. Educ.; Bd. Trustees, Holston Conf. Colls.; Oak Ridge Hosp.; Am. Phys. Soc.; AAAS; Tenn. Acad. Sci. Author papers publd. in: ANS Transactions; ASME Transactions; Euratom Conf. PrProceedings; Nuclear Sci. & Engrng.; Symposium on Isotope Separation, 1957; Review of Sci. Instruments etc. Hons: Neb. Wesleyan Univ. Alumni Achievement Award, 1962; Fellow, Am. Nuclear Soc.; D.Sc., Neb. Wesleyan Univ., 1974. Address: Oak Ridge Nat. Lab., P.O. Box X, Oak Ridge, TN 37830, U.S.A. 2, 14.

TRAVAGLIA, Carlo, b. 21 Apr. 1918. Painter. Educ: Art Dip., Acad. of Art (Studio Prof. B. Saetti), Venice, Italy. Appts: Art

Master, Inst. of Magistr., Rovigo, 1939; Art Master, Art Inst. P. Selvatico, Padua, 1940; Acad. of Art, Venice, 1941-44; Hd., Art Dept., Inst. of Educ., Padua, 1944-72. Pres. & Mbr., num. Nat. Art Selection Comms. Mbr: Assn. of Painters & Sculptors, Padua. Major Works: Frescoes, Univ. of Padua; Parish Ch. Mestrino, Vicenza & Parish Ch. of Sacred Family, Padua; Altar Piece, Ch. Paleullo, Stra, Venice; Stations of the Cross, Ch. Lioni, Avellino. Permanent Coll. of Works, Villa Belgioioso. Has exhibited at 5 Solo & 50 Grp. Exhibs. Hons: Bevilacqua La Masa Award, Venice, 1947; 1st Nat. Art Tchng. Award, Rome, 1948; Premio Bergamo, 1949; Permanent Coll., Milan, 1950; 1st Prize, Art Festival, Monselice, 1951; Gold Medal, Nat. Prize S. Margherita Ligure, 1972. Address: Via. A. Gabelli 66, 35100, Padua, Italy. 133.

TRAVERS, Maurice, b. 18 Mar. 1919. Data Processing Consulting Engineer. Educ: Ecole Speciale Mil., St. Cyr., France; Fac. des Lettres, Lyon. Appts: French Air Force, Royal Air Force, 1939-47; Marketing Mgr., Compagnie des Machines Bull, 1954-67; Compagnie Int. pour l'Informatique, 1967-68; Dir., Soc. Traitement Automatique de Donnees (STAD), 1969-74; Admnstr., ibid, 1972; Data Processing, Ordina, 1970. Mbrships: Pres., Assn. Francaise des Informaticiens; Soc. de Statistique, Paris; Grand Carré, St. Cyr; V.P., Assn. Informatique et Gestion. Author of French data processing publs. Mbrships: Croix de Guerre, WWII, 1944; Médaille de la Résistance, 1944; King's Medal for Courage, 1945; chevalier, Legion of Hon., 1948. Address: 11 Rue de la Vistule, Paris, 75013, France 1.

TRAVERS, Richard Lawrence, b. 16 Sept. 1906. Barrister-at-Law. Educ: Lancing Coll.; Inns of Court; Ecole Normale de Musique, Paris. Appts: Called to Bar, 1940; 2nd Lt., Intelligence Corps, 1940; Legal Advsr., Brit. Motor Trade Assn., 1956-63. Mbrships: Worshipful Co. of Plaisterers, City of London; Army & Navy Club; Monday Club. Publs: Husband & Wife in English Law, 1956; Contbr. to periodicals. Hons: Kt. of Grace & Devotion, Sovereign Order of Malta, 1962 (resigned 1970). Address: 5c Artillery Mansions, Westminster, London SW1H 0HZ, U.K.

TRAVIESO, Carlos R., b. 27 Feb. 1901. Doctor of Medical Sciences; Surgeon; University Professor. Degrees: Bachelor, Biological Sciences; Bachelor, Philos. & Letters; Dr., Med. Scis. Appts: Prof., Pathological Surg.; Hd., Clin. Surg.; Prof., Clin. Surg.; Prof., Surg. Technique. Mbrships. incl: Nat. Acad. of Med., Venezuela; Hist. of Med. Soc.; Venezuelan Surg. Soc.; Int. Surg. Soc.; Int. Coll. of Surgs.; Royal Acad. of Med. of Belgium; Paris Acad. of Surg.; Fellow, retired status, Am. Coll. of Surgs. Publs. icl: Cirugia (w. F.C. Jahn), 1930; Estudios de Cirugia Clinica y Operatoria, 1937; Urgencias de Cirugia, 1940; Discursos Academicos, 1940; Homenaje a los Maestros de la Cirugia Venezolana, 1962; Articles in profl. jrnls. Hons. incl: Grand Cordon, Order of the Liberator, Venezuela; Grand Cordon, Andres Bello Order, Venezuela; Order of the Crown of Belgium; Grand Cordon of the Sun of Peru; Ruben Dario Order, Nicaragua. Address: Academia Nacional de Medicina, Palacio de las Academias, Bolsa a San Francisco, Caracas 101, Venezuela.

TRAYLOR, Idris Rhea, Jr., b. 4 Feb. 1935. University Professor; Administrator. Educ: B.A., Univ. of Tex., Austin, 1957; M.A., ibid, 1959; Ph.D., Duke Univ., 1965; Sorbonne, Paris, France; Univ. of Vienna, Austria. Appts: Asst. Prof. of Hist., Tex. Tech. Univ., 1965-67;

Asst. Prof. of Hist. & Dpty. Dir., Int. Ctr. for Arid & Semi-Arid Land Studies, Tex. Tech. Univ., 1967-68; Asst. Prof. of Hist., Dpty. Dir., Arts & Humanities, Chmn. of the Bd. of Dpty. Dirs., ibid, 1968-69; Assoc. Prof. of Hist., Dpty. Dir. for Acad. Affairs & Chmn. of the Projs. Bd., ibid, 1971-72; Dpty. Dir., ICASALS, Inc., 1969-72. Fellow, Middle East Studies Assn. of N. Am. Mbrships incl: Bd. of Trustees, W. Tex. Mus. Assn., 1969-73; Am. For. Serv. Assn.; Active mbr. of num. socs. Publs: Proceedings of the Third Symposium on Arid Lands (co-ed.); ICASALS Newsletter (ed.), 1967-; (co-ed.) Art & Environment in Native America, 1973. Hons. incl: Fulbright Fellow, Univ. of Vienna, Austria; Spencer A. Wells Fndn. Fac. Award, 1969-; Gold Key of Hon., Delta Phi Epsilon, 1971; Kt. Cmdr's Accolade, Kappa Alpha Order, 1972; Man of Yr., contbns. Tex. Tech. Univ., 1974; Most outstanding Fac. Mbr., ibid, 1974; various awards for tchng., for outstanding serv. in field of int. rels., etc. Address: Int. Ctr. for Arid & Semi-Arid Land Studies, Tex. Tech. Univ., Lubbock, TX 79409, U.S.A. 13, 14.

TREASE, Robert Geoffrey, b. 11 Aug. 1909. Author. Educ: Queen's Coll., Oxford. Mbrships: Chmn., Comm. of Mgmt., Soc. of Authors, 1972-73; Fellow of P.E.N. Publd. num. books for young readers beginning w. Bows Against the Barons, 1934; recent titles incl: The Italian Story, 1963; This is Your Century, 1965; The Grand Tour, 1967; Nottingham, a Biography, 1970; The Condottieri, 1970; A Whiff of Burnt Boats, an Early Autobiography, 1971; Samuel Pepys & His World, 1972. Recip. N.Y. Herald Tribune Award for This is Your Century, 1966. Address: The Croft, Colwall, Malvern, Worcs. WR13 6EZ, U.K. 1, 3.

TREES, Clyde Beverly, b. 4 Mar. 1909. Orthopedic Surgeon. Educ: A.B., Kan. Univ., 1929; M.D., Harvard Univ., Mass., 1933; Intern: Western Pa. Hosp., Pitts., 1933-34; Union Mem. Hosp., Balt., Md., 1933-35; X-Ray Serv., 1935-37; Orthopedic Serv., Boston City Hosp., Mass.; Res., Fellow Carnegie III. Steel Co., 1937-39; Res., Scottish Rite Hosp. for Crippled Children, Dallas, Tex., 1942-43. Appts: Chief Orthopedic Serv., Ft. McClellan Stn. Hosp., Anniston, Ala., 1945-46; St. Ptnr. in Orthopedic Firm, Trees, Joyce, Kroll, Hobbs, Payne & Thurston; Staff, Santa Fe- Mem. Hosp., Topeka, Kan.; Stormont-Vail Hosp., ibid; St. Francis Hosp.; Cons: Menninger Fndn.; Capper Crippled Children Fndn.; Kan. Crippled Children Commn.; Topeka State Hosp. Mbrships. incl: Dipl., Am. Bd. Orthopedic Surg.; Am. Acad. Orthopedics; Am. Coll. Surgs.; Fndr. Mbr., Mid Ctrl. States Orthopedic Soc.; AMA; Kan. Orthopedic Soc.; Southwestern Surg. Congress. Address: Med. Arts Bldg., 10th & Horne, Topeka, KS, U.S.A. 8,

TREGER, Charles, b. 13 May 1935. Concert Violinst. Educ: Violin studies w. var. tchrs. Appts: Prof., Violin, Hd., String Dept., Univ. of Iowa, 1961-70; Vis. Artist-Prof., New Engl. Conservatory of Music, 1971-72; Vis. Artist-Prof., Hartt Schl. of Music, Hartford, Conn., 1971-74; Artist in Res., Aspen Music Fest., 1971-73. Appeared in over 3,000 concerts throughout the world. Annual world tours w. leading orchs.; TV, radio & recordings. Performed before Queen Elizabeth & Presidents Kennedy & Johnson. Hons: 1st Prize, Wieniawski Int. Violin Competition, Poland, 1962; Wieniawski Gold Medal, 1964; D.F.A., Lawrence Univ., Wis., 1973. Address: Herbert Barrett Mgmt. Inc., 1860 Broadway, N.Y., NY 10023, U.S.A. 2.

TREJOS, Charlotte (Carlota) M. (Mrs. Jose M. Trejos), b. 5 July 1920. Educator; Writer; Lecturer. Educ: Calif. Credentialled Tchr., Creative Writing & Pub. Speaking. Appts: Free-lance Writer, mags. & newspapers; Elem. Schl. Tchr., Hawthorne Christian Schls., Calif.; Engl. Tchr., El Colegio Anglo-Am., Cochabamba, Bolivia; Remedial Tchr., Harbor City Christian Schls., Calif., U.S.A. Mbrships: Pres., Apollo, Long Beach Chapt., Calif. Fed. Chaparral Poets; World Poetry Soc. Intercontinental; Int. Comm., Centro Studi e Scambi Int. Publs: Variegated Verse; sev. articles poems. Hons. incl: Award of Appreciation for Devotional Lectrs., Harbor City Schls., 1972; Cert. for Disting. Contbns. to Poetry, Am. Poets Fellowship Soc., Ill., 1973. Address: 22503 Meyler St., 33, Torrance, CA 90502, U.S.A. 57.

TRELFORD, John D., b. 7 Feb. 1931. Professor of Obstetrics & Gynaecology. Educ: M.D., Univ. of Toronto, Canada; Attended other univs., U.K., Austria, Italy. Currently Assoc. Prof., Ob. & Gyn., Univ. of Calif., Davis, Calif., U.S.A. Mbrships: F.R.C.S.; M.R.C.O.G.; Am. Cancer Soc.; Soc. Obstrns. & Gynaecologists of Canada. Contbr. to profl. jrnls., inclng. Univ. of Toronto Med. Jrnl., Canadian Med. Assn. Jrnl., Am. Jrnl. of Ob. & Gyn., Med. Times, Ob. & Gyn., Jrnl. of Med., Jrnl. of Cancer. Address: 3420 Lakeview Dr., El Macero, CA 95618, U.S.A. 22,

TRENERY, Frank E., b. 8 Feb. 1921. Educator; Librarian. Educ: Bradley Univ., Peoria, Ill.; B.Gen. Ed., Univ. of Neb., Omaha; M.A., Rosary Coll. Grad. Schl. Lib. Sci., River Forest, Ill. Grad. work, DePaul Univ., Chgo.; will receive M.Ed., Loyola Univ., 1973. Appts. incl: Documents Libn. & Instr., Univ. of Neb., 1966-67; Documents Libn., N. Eastern Ill. Univ., Chgo., 1967-69; Instr., Multi-Media Prog., ibid, 1970-72; Asst. Librí., Divine Word Coll., Dubuque, Iowa, 1969-70; Currently Dir., Pompano Beach Lib., Fla. Mbrships: Sec.-Treas., Lib. Educ. Div., Cath. Lib. Assn.; Formerly, Exec. Bd., Chmn., Mbrship. Comm., Northern Ill. Unit, ibid; Ed., NIUCLA Newsletter, 1969-71; AAUP; Coun. on Lib. Technol.; Ill., Fla. & Neb. Lib. Assns.; Charter mbr. & Chmn., Nominating & Prog. Comms., Pompano Beach Histl. Soc.; V.P.-Pres. elect, Broward Co. Lib. Assn.; Phi Alpha Theta. Address: Pompano Beach Lib., Pompano Beach, FL 33061, U.S.A. 42.

TRENNT, Evelyn Ladene, b. 28 Jan. 1920. Educator. Educ: B.A., Univ. of Omaha, Neb., 1942; M.A., Univ. of Ill., Urbana, 1946. Appts: Maths. Tchr., Gaza, Iowa H.S., 1942-43 & Walnut Iowa H.S., 1943-45; Instr. of Maths., Springfield Jr. Coll., Ill., 1946-53; Tchr. of Maths., Milwaukee-Downer Sem., Wis., 1953-55; Assoc. Prof. of Maths., Monticello Coll., Godfrey, Ill., 1955-71; Prof. of Maths., Lewis & Clark Community Coll., ibid, 1971-. Mbrships: Judge in Maths. Div. of Annual State Sci. Exposition of Ill. Jr. Acad. of Sci., 1958-; Bd. Mbr., 1960-61, Ill. Coun. of Tchrs. of Maths.; Nat. Coun. of Tchrs. of Maths.; Math. Assn. of Am.; AAUP; Alton Bus. & Profl. Women; Pi Mu Epsilon; Sigma Pi Phi. Recip. of Award for Disting. Serv. to Monticello Coll., 1965. Address: 1012 Richard Dr., Godfrey, IL 62035, U.S.A. 5, 8, 120, 130, 132.

TRENT, Ray, b. 27 Jan. 1916. Insurance. Owner, Tex. Ins. & Real Estate Agcy., 30 yrs. Mbrships: Fndr. & Pres., S. Plains Gospel Music Assn.; Sec., Yoakum Co. Bowling Assn.; Dist. Finance Chmn., Gov. George C. Wallace; Masonic Lodge. Creative Works: Songwriter &

Musician; Copyrighted Country Gosepl Songs. Recip. Congress of Freedom Liberty Award, 1969. Address: P.O. Box 162, Denver City, TX 79323, U.S.A. 125.

TRESHAN, Allan, b. 11 Dec. 1915. Newspaper Man. Educ: Bachelor of Soc. Sci., CCNY, 1943. Appts: Assoc. Ed., First to Final club publ., Proofreaders Club of N.Y., 1957-58, Club Pres., 1958-60, 1961-, Chmn., Exec. Comm., & Chmn., Prog., Publicity & Mbrship. Comms., var. intervals; Mbr., Z39 Comm., Subcomm. on Proofreading, Am. Standards Assn., 1962-. Mbrships: Corres. Sec., Class of '43 Alumni Assn. of CCNY, 1953-; Int. & N.Y. Typographical Unions, 1947-; Treas., Citizens Comm. for Educ. of Gifted Child, 1962-66; Pres., YM-YWHA of Gtr. Flushing, 1970-72, Financial Sec., 1972-. Address: New York Times, Co., 229 W. 43rd St. (4th Floor), N.Y., NY 10036, U.S.A. 6, 130.

TRETCHIKOFF, Vladimir, b. 13 Dec. 1913. Artist. Appts: Propaganda Artist, Brit. Min. of Info., Malaya, WWII; Now settled in S. Africa. Mbr., S. Africa Assn. of Arts, Cape Town. One man exhibs: 43 between 1933-73; Nat. Exhib. Tour, U.S.A., 1953; Nat. Tour, Canada, 1954, 65; London, 1962; S. Africa, 3 Nat. tours, 1948-70; Birmingham & Manchester, U.K., 1972; Edinburgh Int. Fest., 1973. Exhibs. have drawn record attendance in U.S.A., Canada, U.K. & S. Africa (total attendance of all exhibs., 2,450,000). Subject of 5 books publd. U.S.A., Canada, S. Africa, Europe & U.K.: Tretchikoff Art, R. Buncher; Tretchifoff Colour Prints, L. Richfield; Tretchikoff Native Studies, ibid; Art of Tretchikoff, H. Timmins. Autobiog., Pigeon's Luck, Collins, U.K. Num. lithogs. & prints reprod. all over world. Recip., Medal, Gall. of Sci. & Art, 1939, N.Y. Address: 'Tretchis', Norwich Dr., Claremont, Cape Town, Rep. of S. Africa. 39, 133.

TREUTING, Waldo Louis, b. 28 Apr. 1911. Physician; Educator. Educ: B.S., Tulane Univ., 1930; M.D., ibid, 1934; M.P.H., Johns Hopkins, 1939; Cert., Fndr.'s Group, Am. Bd. of Preventive Med., 1950. Appts. incl: Prof., Pub. Hlth. Admin., Tulane Univ. Schl. of Med., 1948-58; Acting Chmn., Dept. of Tropical Med. & Pub. Hlth., ibid, 1953-58; Prof. & Hd., Dept. of Pub. Hlth. Prac., Grad. Schl. of Pub. Hlth., Univ. of Pitts., 1958-; Dir., Allegheny Co. Hlth. Dept., Pitts., Pa., 1967-69; Chmn. of Bd., Comprehensive Hlth. Planning Assn. of W. Pa., 1969-71; Cons., WHO, Egypt, 1953, Venezuela, 1960. Mbrships. incl: Fellow, Am. Coll. of Preventive Med.; Treas., ibid, 1954; Bd. of Regents, 1955-58; Fellow, Am. Pub. Hlth. Assn.; Am. Med. Soc.; Fellow, Pa. Pub. Hlth. Assn.; Pres., ibid, 1964-65; Nat. Pres., Delta Omega, 1960-61. Authr of articles in med. books & jrnls. Recip. of hons. Address: 231A Parran Hall, Grad. Schl. of Pub. Hlth., Univ. of Pitts., Pitts., PA 15261, U.S.A. 2, 14, 54.

TREVIÑO, Tapia José Guadalupe, b. 21 Aug. 1889. Catholic Priest; Manager of Mag. "La Cruz". Educ: Inst. Cientifico del Sagrado Corazon de Jesus & Sem. Conciliar, Morelia, Mich. Publs. incl: La Eucaristia, 9th ed.; Madre, 5th ed.; La Mujer, 3rd ed.; (Biography) Antonio Plancarte y Labastida, 2nd ed.; El Cielo; Espiritu y Vida; Heroismo Critiano; La Direccion Espiritual; Luz en la Senda; (Biography) San Gabriel de la Dolorosa; El Sacrificio de Jesus; El Misterio de la Soledad; La Sencillez; Confianza; La Soledad de Maria; (Biography) Una Azucena Ensangrentada; Los Elegidos, 2nd ed.; many others. Address: Apartado 1580, Mexico 1, D.F.

TREXLER, Laura M., b. 26 May 1913. Educator. Educ: Dip., State Tchrs. Coll., W. Chester, Pa., 1931; B.S., Temple Univ., Phila., 1940; M.Ed., ibid, 1943; Grad. Study, ibid & Tchrs. Coll., Columbia Univ. Appts. incl: Tchr., Pottstown Jr. H.S., Pa., 1942-43, 1949-50; U.S.N., 1943-47; Jr.-Sr. H.S. Prin., Hatfield Jt. Consolidated Jr.-Sr. H.S., Pa., 1951-55; Dir., Guidance, Northern Valley Regional H.S., Demarest, N.J., 1955-64; Asst. Instr., Montclair State Coll. Grad. Schl., N.J., 1958-60; Dist.Dir., Pupil Personnel Servs., Northern Valley Regional H.S., 1964-66; Educ. Prog. Specialist, U.S. Off. of Educ., Wash. D.C., 1966-. Mbrships. incl: NEA; Am. Personnel & Guidance Assn.; Exec. Comm., Northern Valley Br., AAUW, 1956-59. Recip. of Hons. Address: 732 9th St. S.E., Wash. DC 20003, U.S.A. 5, 15.

TREXLER, Virginia Ruth Hamilton, b. 9 June 1928. Dentist. Educ: B.A., Cedar Crest Coll., Allentown, Pa., U.S.A., 1951; D.D.S., Schl. of Dentistry, Univ. of Pa., Phila., 1954. Appt: Priv. Prac., Cons. Dentistry, in assn. w. Dr. E.E. Hamilton, Allentown, 1954-. Mbrships: Pres., Cryer Soc., Univ. of Pa., 1953-54; Charter Mbr., Univ. of Pa. Women's Dental Soc.; Int. Assn. of Anesthesiol.; AAUW; Bd., League of Women Voters, 1972-73; Allentown Woman's Club. Contbr., (w. E.E. Hamilton), papers in profl. jrnls. Recip., Cert. of Merit, for disting. writing in the sci. of anesthesiol., Int. Jrnl. of Anesthesia, 1957. Address: Stone Creek Rd., R.D.2, Huntingdon, PA 16652, U.S.A. 5, 138.

TREZZA, Alphonse F., b. 27 Dec. 1920. Librarian. Educ: B.S., Univ. of Pa., 1948; Lib. Cert., Grad. Schl. of Lib. Sci., ibid, 1949; M.S., 1950. Appts. incl: Lectr., Grad. Schl. of Lib. Sci., Drexel Inst. of Technol., 1951-60; Instr., Dept. of Lib. Sci., Villanova Univ., 1956-60; Hd., Circulation Dept., Univ. of Pa. Lib., 1950-56; Exec. Sec., Cath. Lib. Assn. & Ed., Cath. Lib. World, Villanova, Pa., 1956-60; Assn. Exec. Dir., ALA & Exec. Sec., ALA-LAD, 1960-68; Assoc. Exec. Dir. for Administrative servs., ALA, 1968-69. Mbrships. incl: Pres., Chgo. Lib. Club, 1969-70; Chmn., Bd. of Mgrs., Ill. Lib. Materials Processing, 1963-69; Ill. State Lib. Advsry. Coun., 1963-69; Chmn., Leg.-Lib. Dev. Comm., Ill. Lib. Assn., 1963-69; Coun., ALA, 1971-. Co-author of Parish Library Manual, 1956. Ed. of publs. in field. Recip. of hons. Address: Ill. State Lib., 209 Centennial Bldg., Springfield, IL 62756, U.S.A.

TRHLÍK, Otakar, b. 19 Jan. 1922. Conductor. Educ: Conservatory & Acad. of Music, Prague, Czechoslovakia, 1945-48; D.Musicol., Univ. of Brno, 1953. Appts: Conductor, State Opera Ostrava, 1948-52; Conductor, Radio Symph. Orch., Brno, 1952-56; Conductor, State Philharmonic, Brno, 1956-62; Chief Conductor, Radio Symph. Orch., Bratislava, 1962-68; Chief Conductor, Janacek Philharmonic Ostrava, 1968. Mbr., Union of Czech. Composers & Interpretors. Recip., Master of Merit, Min. of Culture. Address: Hlávkova 6, 602 00 Brno, Czechoslovakia.

TRIADIS, Demetrius Nicolas, b. 11 Nov. 1928. Chemical Engineer. Educ: Chem. Engr., Nat. Tech. Univ., Athens, 1952; M.Sc., MIT, 1954. Appts: Rsch. Engr., Int. Nickel Co., Bayonne, N.J., 1954-56; Process Engr., Hydrocarbon Rsch. Inc., N.Y., 1957-59; Project Engr., Lumus Co., Paris, The Hague, 1957-61; Gen. Mgr., Pfizer Hallas S.A., subsidiary of Pfizer Int. Inc., N.Y., 1962-72; Area Mgr. for Southern Europe & Middle E., Cooper Laboratories Inc., 1972-73; Gen. Mgr., ITT World Directories (Greece), 1973-. Mbrships: Am. Chem. Soc.; Nat. Assn. of Corrosion Engrs.; Sigma Xi; Tech. Chmbr. of Greece; Hellenic Am. Chmbr. of Comm.; Royal Yacht Club, Piraeus. Contbr. to profl. jrnls. Recip. Chrysoverges Prize, 1952. Address: ITT Hellas S.A.I., 24 Syngrou Ave., Athens 403, Greece. 43.

TRIANO, Anthony Thomas, b. 25 Aug. 1928. Artist; Educator. Educ: Newark Schl. of Fine Art, 1946-50; Apprenticeship w. sculptor Rueben Nakian & painter Samuel Brecher. Appts. incl: Instr., many schls., orgs. & mus., 1950-74; Dir., Triano Schl. of Fine Art, E. Orange, N.J., 1960-64; Prof. of Art & Artist-in-Residence, Seton Hall Univ., ibid, 1970; U.S. Govt. Art Surveyor and Cons., 1972; Bd. of Dirs., Kennedy Art Collect., Seton Hall Univ., 1973; Dir., Seton Hall Art Workshop-Gall., Inc., Arlington, N.J., 1973. Mbrships. inlc: BSA, Order of the Arrow, 1942; Moderator & Lifetime Brother, Phi Beta Gamma Frat., 1971. Publs. incl: Illuminations of James Joyce 'Portrait of The Artist As A Young Man', 1954; Illustrations of Voltaire's 'Candide', 1955; Visit to the Wizard, 1971; Wedding of Aquarius, 1971; Bruges Madonna And Child, 1973; Many exhibs. & paintings in all mediums. Hons. incl: Artist of the Yr., Morris Cablevision, N.J., 1972; Num. first awards and purchase awards. Address: Triano Studio, 586 Devon St., Kearny, NJ 07032, U.S.A. 6, 37, 133.

TRIANTAPHYLLOPOULOS, John, b. 7 Sept. 1921. University Professor. Educ: LL.D., Fac. of Law, Univ. of Athens, Greece, 1957; postgrad. studies, Univs. of Heidelberg & Munich. Appts. incl: Lectr. in Hist. of Greek Law, Fac. of Law, Univ. of Athens, 1960; Commissioned Lectr. in Hist. of Greek & Roman Law, ibid, 1962; Extraordinary Prof. in Hist. of Greek & Roman Law, ibid, 1966; Ordinary Prof. in Hist. of Greek & Roman Law, ibid, 1969; Sec. Gen. to Min. of Educ., 1964; Min. of Justice, 1968. Mbrships. incl: Archaeological Soc. of Athens, Mbr., Admin. Coun.; Soc. of Hellenic Studies, London, U.K.; Soc. of Roman Studies, London; Assn. d'Etude Grecque, Paris, France; Soc. d'Etude Latine, Paris; Assn. Int. d'Epigraphie Latine, Paris; Soc. of Greek & Latin Epigraphy, U.K.; Soc. Int. de Papyrologues, Brussels; Fndn. Egyptologique "Reine Elizabeth", Burssels. Author of many publs. in sev. langs. & also produced paintings. Hons: Prize, Acad. of Athens "Chrysa epe Adamantios Korais", 1939, 1945; Docoration, Commendator nell 'Ordine al Merito della Repubblica Italiana, 1970. Address: 22 Anagnostopoulos St., Athens 136, Greece. 43.

TRIBOULET, Raymond, b. 3 Oct. 1906. Politician. Educ: Mil. Acad. St. Cyr, France. Appts. incl: Farmer, 1928-39; Infantry Lt., French Army, 1939-41; Resistance Fighter, 1941-44; First Sub-prefect for Liberated Communes, Bayeux, 1944-46; Dpty. for Calvados, French Nat. Assembly, 1946-58; Min., War Veterans, 1955 & 1959-62; Dpty. for Bessin, Nat. Assembly, 1958-; Min., Cooperation, 1962-66; Mbr., European Parliament, Strasbourg, 1967-68; Pres., French Com. for Paneuropean Union, 1973-. Mbrships. incl: Socialist Republican Party; Fndr. & Past Pres., European Federalist Grp.; Fndr. & Pres., Bayeux Preservation Com.; Pres., European Confedn. of War Veterans; Pres., Nat. Assn. of Volunteer Resistance Fighters; Combattant Authors Assn.; Men of Letters Soc. Publs. incl: Les Billets du Négus, 1939; Sans Dessus Dessous, 1951; Halte au Massacre. Num. hons. incl: Croix de Guerre, 1940; Resistance Medal; O.B.E.; Off., Mil. Legion of Hon., 1974.

Address: 119 Rue Brancas, 92310 Sèvres, France.

TRICART, Jean Léon François, b. 16 Sept. 1920. Professor & International Consultant. Educ: Sorbonne, Paris & Bordeaux, France—Lic., 1942; Dip. d'Etudes Supérieures, 1942; Agrégation, 1943; Doctorat d'Etat, 1948. Appts: Army serv., 1939-40; Tchr., Prytanée Mil., 1943-45; Asst., Sorbonne, Paris, France, 1945-48; i/c Course, L'Ecole Supérieure des Scis. Géographiques, 1946-51; i/c Course, Master of Confs., Prof., Strasbourg Univ. & currently Prof., Louis-Pasteur Univ., Strasbourg, 1945-; Collaborator-Prin. Collaborator, Géol. Map Serv., 1947-; V.-Dean & Mbr., Coun., Louis-Pasteur Univ., 1967-70; Sci. Cons., IRAT, 1972-; Cons., UNESCO & var. orgs. Publs: Traité de Céomorphologie (w. A. Cailleux); Principes et Méthodes de la Géomorphologie; Ecographie et Aménagement intégré du milieu naturel (w. J. Kilian); over 420 sci. & tech. publs. Hons: Prix Bastian, Acad. des Scis, 1943; Grandes Médailles des Univs. de Liège et de Gand; Médaille Dumont de la Soc. Géol. de Belgique. Address: Ctr. de Géographie Appliquée, Univ. Louls-Pasteur, 43 R. Goethe, 67,000 Strasbourg, France. 43, 91.

TRICE, Jeannette Marie, b. 8 Oct. 1922. Teacher. Educ: B.A., St. Louis Univ.; Our Lady of Victory, Ft. Worth & Incarnate Word Coll., San Antonio, Tex. Appts: Tchr. for 31 yrs. in Tex. & Calif.; Asst. Dir., Headstart prog., N. Tex., 1973. Mbrships: Tex. State Tchrs. Assn.; Tex. & Nat. P.T.A.s. Recip., Outstanding Elem. Tchrs. of Am. award, 1972. Address: 400 N. 40th. St., Waco, TX 76710, U.S.A. 57, 125.

TRICKETT, Joyce, b. 21 Nov. 1915. Recitalist; Teacher; Writer; Artist. Educ: H.S., Australia, & pvte. study. Appts: Tchr., Speech, Drama, Singing Voice Prod., pvte. schls., Moss Vale & Sydney, Australia, 1958-. Supporter & Donator, num. Charities. Mbrships: Musical Assn. of N.S.W. Publs. incl: Songs—The Wooden Madonna, Song to a Queen, Wattle Gold, Bridge Blues; Books—The Light Shines, 1962; Pool of Quiet, 1963; Bless This House, 3rd edit., 1970; Stage presentation, An Australian Vision, 1972; Var. exhibs. of work in oil pastels. Hons: N.S.W. Musical Assn. Award, 1963; A.B.C.8s "Search for a Song" Prize, 1964; 2nd Prize, "Search for an Australian Musical", 1965. Address: Quibree, 23 Lavender Crescent, N. Sydney, Australia 2060.

TRIEM, Eve, b. 2 Nov. 1902. Poet; Lecturer; Director of Poetry Workshops. Educ: Univ. of Calif., Berkeley, U.S.A. Appts: Tchr., sev. schls., Wash.; Rdr., own poems; Lectr., poetry; Dir., poetry workshops, Seattle, Wash., 1961-. Mbrships: Poetry Soc. of Am.; Prog. Chmn., Wash. Herb Soc.; Chmn., Comm. for Visiting the Sick & the Aged, Episcopal Ch. Publs: Parade of Doves, 1946; Poems, 1965; Heliodora: Translations from the Greek Anthology, 1967; E.E. Cummings, 1969; Selected Poems, 1974; Poems in num. mags. & anthols. Hons. incl: Charlotte Arthur Award (twice), 1940; Award, Nat. Inst. of Arts & Letters, 1966; Prize, Hart Crane & Alice Crane Mem. Fund, 1971. Address: 911 Alder St., Apt. 790, Seattle, WA, U.S.A. 11.

TRIFFIN, Robert, b. 5 Oct. 1911. Professor of Economics. Educ: Bachelor of Philos. & Letters, Univ. of Louvain, 1931; LL.D., ibid, 1934; Lic. in Econs., ibid, 1935; Ph.D., Econs., Harvard Univ., 1939. Appts. incl: Chief, Latin Am. Sect., Fed. Reserve Bd., 1942-46; Chief, Exchange Control Div., Int. Monetary Fund, 1946-48; Dir., European Off., ibid, 1948-49; Special Advsr., European Recovery Admin., 1949-51; U.S. Alternate Rep., European Payments Union, 1950-51; Pelatiah Perit Prof. of Pol. & Soc. Sci., Yale Univ., 1958-67; Frederick William Beinecke Prof. of Econs., ibid, 1967-; Master, Berkeley Coll., ibid, 1970. Also Cons., European Communities & others, 1951-. Publs. incl: Europe & the Money Muddle, 1957; Gold & the Dollar Crisis, 1960; The World Money Maze, 1966; Our International Monetary System, 1968; The Fate of the Pound, 1969. Also contbr. to jrnls. in Europe, Asia, Latin Am., U.S. Hons. incl: Wells Prize in Econs., 1938; Cmdr., Orden del Merito, Paraguay, 1944; Couverneur Emile Cornez Prize, Univ. of Louvain, 1969; Dr. h.c., ibid, 1970; Cmdr., Ordre de la Couronne, Belgium, 1973. Address: 403A Yale Stn., New Haven, CT 06520, U.S.A. 2, 14, 34, 131.

TRIGGIANI, Domenico, b. 12 Sept. 1929. Writer; Poet; Publicist; Critic; Dramatist. Publs. incl: Inchiesta sulla gioventu Bruciata; Storia delle riviste letterarie d'oggi; Zoo letterario; Processo alla gioventu; Guida storica, artistica e turistica illustrata della Provincia di Bari; Il Patto Atlantico; Vecchio e nuovo Sud; Alle soglie del caos; Dizionario degli scrittori; Piccola antologia francese; Diario artistico—culturale; Mezzogiorno in cammino; Poesie scelte. Hons. incl: Cultural Prize, Prime Min.; Educ. Min. Prize, 1962 & '64; Gold medal, jrnlsm.; Gold medal, Die Cinquecento Acad.; Bracco Prize Medal; Beardelli Lit. Competition Trophy; Silver Laurel, Int. Poetry Competition; Voci d'Italia Gold medal; Silver medal, City of Salerno Prize, Kt., Italian Repub. Address: Via Guilio Petroni 37, 70124, Bari, Italy.

TRIGUEIROS, Luis Forjaz, b. 15 Apr. 1915. Author; Director of Companies. Educ: Dr. (h.c.), Cath. Univ., Porto Alegro, Brazil. Appts. incl: Lit. Critic, var. mags., newspapers, radio & TV, 1936-; Ed., Lisbon newspaper, 1946-53; Adminstr., Portuguese Airways, 1954; Currently, Dir., Portuguese Airways, Bertrand Ltd. & Heywards Assocs. Mbrships. incl: Acad. Scis. Lisbon; Brazilian Acad. Letters; Coimbra Inst.; Geography Soc. Lisbon; Int. Assn. Lit. Critics. Publs. incl: Boa noite, Pai (short stories), 1950; Sombra do Tempo, 1950; Campos Elisios, 1956; Perspectivas I, 1960 & II, 1969 (essays); Ventos e Mares, 1967; Monólogo em Efeso, 1972. Hons. incl: El Soldel Peru, 1949; Leopold II, Belgium, 1950; Légion d'Honneur, France, 1951; Santiago da Espeda, Portugal, 1971. Address: Rua Imprensa a Estrelia 191, Lisbon, Portugal. 43.

TRIMBLE, Vance Henry, b. 6 July 1913. Editor. Appts: Newspaper cub reporter, working on 25 newspapers, Okla. & Tex.; City Ed. & Mng. Ed., The Houston Press, Tex., 1939-55; Transferred by Scripps-Howard Newspapers to Nat. Bur., Wash. D.C., as news ed. Mbrships: Trustee, Scripps-Howard Fndn.; Am. Soc. of Newspaper Eds.; Nat. Press Club, Wash. D.C.; Twice judge, Pulitzer Prize competition; Queen City Chapt., Sigma Delta Chi; Houston Press Club, Tex.; Dir., Goodwill Inds. & Sr. Citizens Ctr., Covington, Ky. Author of The Uncertain Miracle, 1974. Hons: Pulitzer Prize, for nat. reporting, 1960; Raymond Clapper award, 1960; Sigma Delta Chi award, 1960. Address: 1013 Sunset Ave., Kenton Hills, Covington, KY 41011, U.S.A. 2.

TRIPLETT, Bill, b. I0 Feb. 1935. Real Estate Broker; Developer; Builder. Educ: Univ. Minn. Appts: V.P., Harrison Jewelry Co., 1955-6I; Real Estate Salesman, 1961-69; Pres., Triplett Realty Co., Vinton, Va., 1969-, Meadowood, Eden, N.C., 1972-; Ptnr., Cascade

Dev., Bedford Co., Va., 1972-. Merships. incl: Past Grand Master, I.O.O.F. of Va., 1965; Ed. Dir., Vinton Chmbr. of Comm., (Pres., 1974); Trustee, Mt. Dale Lodge 49, Roanoke, Va.; U.S. Chmbr. of Comm.; Chmn., Am. Party in Va.; Nat. Ctrl. Comm., Am. Party; Soc. of Real Estate Appraisers; Am. Forestry Assn.; B.B.B. of Roanoke Valley; Roanoke Merchants Assn. Author of sev. publd. poems. Hons. incl: Royal Purple Degree Ring, I.O.O.F., Copenhagen, Denmark, 1970; Liberty Award, Congress of Freedom, 1973. Address: P.O. Box I, Vinton, VA 24179, U.S.A.

TRIPPS, Manfred Wolfram, b. 9 Sept. 1925. Professor of Art History & Art Education; Artist. Educ: Tech. Univ., Berlin, Germany, 1943-45; Nat. Acad. Fine Arts, Stuttgart, 1947-49; Ph.D., Univ. of Heidelberg, 1967. Appts. incl: Dir., Leopold Hoesch Mus., City of Duren & regional Mus., Duren, 1968-71; Dir., Adult Educ. Schl., ibid, 1968-71; Lectr., Acad. of Color, Stuttgart-Feuerbach, 1971; Art Educator, N. Württemberg, 1971; Prof., 1971—, Mbr., Exec. Comm. 1972-73, Dean, Dept. V & Mbr. of Senate, 1973—, Tchrs. Trng. Coll., Ludwigsburg. Mbrships incl: Soc. German Art Histns.; num. cultural & histl. bodies. Publs. incl: Hans Multscher: Seine Ulmer Schaffenszeit 1427-67, 1969; Duren, Diekulturelle Entwicklung der Stadt, 1971. Organizer num. Exhibs., 1966—. Major Works incl. Landscapes, Sculptures, Metal Work. Hons: Exhibited, German Book Exhib., Belgium 1970; Recip. mil. hons. Address: D—71 Heilbronn-Bockingen, Konradweg 10-12, Germany. 43, 92, 133.

TRITICO' Frank Edward, b. 1 Aug. 1930. Educator; Administrator. Educ: B.A., Univ. of St. Thomas; M.Ed., Univ. of Houston; Grad. studies, Univ. of Va. & Columbia Univ. Appts. incl: Hist. Instr., 1960-67; Cons., Dept. of Educ., 1967-71; Dir. of Instruction, 1971-. Mbrships. incl: Sovereign Colonial Soc. of Ams. of Royal Descent; Soc. of Descendants of Kts. of Most Noble Order of the Garter; Baronal Order of Magna Charta; Gen. Soc. of Colonial Wars, Gov., Tex. Soc.; Nat. Soc., Sons of the Am. Revolution, Chapt. Pres.; Soc. of Descendants of War of 1812; Sons of Repub. of Tex., Pres. Gen.; Kts. of Order of San Jacinto, Kt. Cmdr.; Hon. Mbr., Daughters of Repub. of Tex.; Sons of Confederate Veterans, Cmdr., Tex. Div.; Pres., Educ. Assn. Publs: weekly newspaper column, History Cornered. Histn.-Designer, The Clock of Texas. Hons. incl: Award, Freedoms Fndn. at Valley Forge, 1970; Gov.'s Disting. Serv. Award, Tex. Historical Commn., annually, 1965-74. Address: 11931 Kimberley Ln., Houston, TX 77024, U.S.A. 130.

TROEDSSON, Tryggve Bengt Johan, b. 14 May 1923. Professor. Educ: Phil. cand., 1948; Dr. phil., 1950; D.Sc., 1955. Appts:Geol. Dept., Univ. of Lund, Sweden, 1946-49; Asst. Prof., Royal Coll. of Forestry, Stockholm, 1949-55; Docent, ibid, 1955-57; Prof. & Hd., Dept. of Forest Soils, 1957— Hd., Dept. of Plant Ecol. & Forest Soils, 1971-. Mbrships: Collegium, Royal Swedish Acad. of Argic. & Forestry; Swedish Nat. Comm. for Geol.; Past Pres., Swedish Soc. of Soil Sci.; Mbr., Coun. for Forestry & Agric. Rsch. Publs: The Hydrology of Forest Soils, 1965; The Importance of Soil Properties in Modern Planning, 1972; Books in Swedish, total of 70 sci. publs. Hons: Pole & Star, 1961. Address: Dept. of Forest Soils, Royal Coll. of Forestry, Uppsala 7, Sweden.

TROFIMENKOFF, Susan Mann (Mrs. Nicholas N. Trofimenkoff), b. 10 Feb. 1941.

Associate Professpr of History. Educ: B.A. Univ. of Toronto, 1963; M.A., Univ. of Western Ont., 1965; Ph.D., Univ. Laval, 1970. Appts: Lectr. in Engl., Toyo Eiwa Jogakuin, Tokyo, 1963-64; Chargée d'enseignement sr., Univ. of Montreal, 1966-70; Asst. Prof. of Hist., Univ. of Calgary, 1970-72, Univ. of Ottawa, 1972-74; Assoc. Prof. of Hist., ibid, 1974-. Mbrships: Can. Histl. Assn.; Coun., ibid, 1971-74. Publs: Variations on a Nationalist Theme, Abbé Groulx & Henri Bourassa in the 1920's. 1970; Abbé Groulx, 1973; Action Françcaise, Nationalism in French Canada in the 1920's, 1975. Hons. incl: 4 undergrad., 2 grad. awards; Can. Coun. Doct. Fellowship, 1968-69, 69-70. Address: Hist. Dept., Univ. of Ottawa, Ottawa, Ont., Canada. 13.

TROLL, John H., b. 20 April 1919. Physicist. Educ: B.A., M.A., Harvard Univ.; Ph.D., Columbia Univ. Appts: V.P., Avion Instrument, Paramus, N.J., 1950-54; V.P., Electronics Corp., Cambridge, Mass., 1954-59; Cons., N.Y.C., 1959-64; Pres., Dir., Pyrotel, Inc., 1964- 66, Ovitron Corp., 1966-69, Ecological Resources, N.Y.C., 1969-71, Ecopower Systems, N.Y.C., 1971-. Mbrship: Sr. Mbr., IEEE. Holder, 14 U.S. patents. Address: 17 Cedar Rd. E., Katonah, NY 10536, U.S.A. 6, 16.

TROLLOPE-CAGLE, Vivian Jewel (Mrs.). Teletype Operator & Reciptionist (Retired), U.S. Civil Service. Offs. held in Poetry Socs.: Nev. (State) Poetry Soc. (Charter Mbr., Bd. of Dirs., 1st Sec.-Treas.); Am. Rep., Poetry Soc. Australia, 1969; Judge, Nat. Contests, Am. Poetry League, 1968-69; N.W. Rep., Int. Poets' Shrine, Hollywood, Calif., 1969-72; Rep., Las Vegas, Nev., Centro Studi e Scambi Int., Rome, 1969. Mbrships: Life, Poetry Soc. Am.; Fndr., Acad. Am. Poets United Poets Laureate Int.; Utah State & Tex. Poetry Socs.; Clark Co. Humane Soc., Las Vegas, Griggsville Wild Bird Soc., Ill.; Am. Assn. Retd. Persons; Las Vegas Art League; Southern Nev. Mus. Publs: approx. 400 poems in mags., newspapers, jrnls. & anthols., U.S.A., Australia, India, etc. Recip., many hons. & awards for poetry. Address: : 4211 W. Baxter Pl., Las Vegas, NV 89107, U.S.A. 11, 140,

TROMBLEY, Joyce Gendzwill, b. 8 Aug. 1927. Physician (Health Officer). Educ: B.A., Univ. of Mich., Ann Arbor, 1949; M.D., ibid, 1952; M.P.H., 1961. Appts: Hlth. Off., Med. Dir., Dickinson-Iron Dist. Hlth. Dept., Stambaugh, Mich., 1959-. Mbrships: AMA; Mich. Med. Soc.; Am. Pub. Hlth. Assn.; Dickinson-Iron Dist. Med. Soc.; Am. Schl. Hlth. Assn.; Phi Beta Kappa; Phi Kappa Phi; Delta Omega. Address: 130 Third St., Stambaugh, MI 49964, U.S.A. 5, 8, 130,

TRONE, Curvin J. Jr., b. 15 May 1921. Business Executive. Educ: A.B., Brown Univ., 1948; M.A., Harvard Univ., 1949; Univ. of Mich. Law Schl., 1950. Appts. incl: Whirlpool Corp., 1953-63, Asst. to Pres., Ops. Controller; Pres. of subsidiary, S.A. Royal Corp., Paris, France, 1962-63; Corp. Dir. of Financial Planning & Control, Hunt Foods & Inds., Inc., 1964-67; V.P. Finance & Chief Financial Off., Allis-Chalmers Corp., 1967-71; Grp. V.P. Consumer Prods., Dir.: Allis-Chalmers Power Systems, Inc., Allis-Chalmers France; A.-C. U.K.; A.-C. Australia; A.-C. Italy; Pres., A.-C. Credit Corp., 1969-70; Pres., A.-C. Int. Finance Corp. Exec. V.P. & Dir., Penn-Pacific Corp., Dir.; Trustee, Westgate-Calif. Corp.; Dir., Air Calif. The Sidaris Co.; Azcor, Inc., 1971-. Mbrships. incl: Financial Execs. Inst.; Phoenix Soc. Financial Analysts; Nat. Assn. Accts. Sr. Mbr., Am. Inst. Indl. Engrs. Awards incl:

Citation of Merit, Disabled Am. Veterans, 1971. Address: 1010 2nd Ave., Suite 1200, San Diego, CA 92101.

TROSKY, Helene Roth (Mrs.) Artist; Lecturer; Writer; Teacher. Educ: New Schl. for Soc. Rsch., N.Y., 1944-50; B.A., Manhattanville Coll., 1964; Postgrad., 1964-68. Appts: Tchr., Printmaking, Westchester Art Workshop, 1968 & '69; Art Cons., Westchester Lib. System; 1967-; Exec. Dir., Westchester Art Soc., 1969-; Art Dir., Westchester Music & Art Camp, 1966, '67, '71, '72; Instr., Printmaking, Manhattanville Coll., 1971 & '72; Lectr., Brandeis Univ. Women, 1965-; Columnist, "Muse Roundup", Harrison Indep., Yonkers Record, Greenburgh Record, Indep. Herald of Westchester, 1960-. Mbrships: Pres., White Plains Outdoor Festival; Dir., Mamaroneck Artists Guild; Former Pres., Dir., Purchase Community Chest; Yonkers Art Assn.; Former Pres., Dir., Purchase Community House; Pres., 1962, '63, '67, Bd., Chmn., '64-65, Westchester Art Soc.; other nat. & state orgs. Works included in many pvte. & pub. collects., e.g., Hudson River Mus. & Staten Island Mus. Awards incl: Nat. Acad. for NAWA Exhib.; 1st Prize, N. Westchester Juried Exhib. Address: Yarmouth Rd., Purchase, NY 10577, U.S.A. 5, 37.

TROTT, James Edwin, b. 9 Feb. 1911. Sales Engineer; Teacher. Educ: Canadian Inst. (heating & engrng.); Am. Standard Schl. (plumbing), Princeton, N.J.; Cert. of Proficiency & Merit, Gould's Factory Schl., 1958. Appts. incl: New England Coke & Wood Co. 1930; Heating Engr., York Shipley Corp., 1936-39, Colonial Supply Co.; Heating & Sales Engr., Johnson Supply Co.; i/c Am. Standard Showroom, ibid, 1970-; Instr., heating, Southern Me. Vocational Inst., S. Portland, 1973-. Mbrships. incl: Co-Fndr., Me. Poetry Week (Legislation), 1957; Me. Poetry Week Comm., 1950-; Clerk of Judges, Me. Poetry Week. Contbr. of articles & photos. to profl. jrnls. Address: Blueberry Hill, Freeport, ME 04032, U.S.A. 131.

TROTT, Rosemary Clifford (Mrs. James E. Trott), b. 8 Mar. 1914. Author; Poet; Freelance Writer; Lecturer. Educ: Gray's Bus. Coll., Portland, Me.; Bates Coll., Lewiston; Gorham State Coll.; Univ. of Me.; Columbia Schl. of Jrnlsm. Appts. incl: Staff Corres., Dealerscope Mag., 1969-72; Columnist, Freeport Post, 1972-; Radio Copywriter, WPOR & WLOB; Tchr., Poetry, Portland YMCA, Me. Mbrships. incl: Nat. League of Am. Pen Women; Me. Poetry Day Assn.; Me. State Writers' Conf. Publs: Sea Mist & Balsam; Maine Christmas; Path of Roses; By Wind & Water; From One Bright Spark (ed.) Contbr. articles & poems to jrnls & anthologies. Recip. of poetry prizes since 1928, inclng: Hon. Poet Laureate of Nature, United Poets Laureate Int., 1966. Address: Blueberry Hill, Freeport, ME 04032, U.S.A. 5, 6, 11, 22, 128, 130, 132.

TROUT, Maurice Elmore, b. 17 Sept. 1917. Diplomat. Educ: B.A., Hillsdale Coll., Mich., 1939; M.A., St. Louis Univ., Mo., 1948; Ph.D., ibid, 1960. Appts: w. U.S. For. Serv., 1950-; Attache, Am. Embassy, Paris, France, 1950-52; 2nd Sec. & Consul, Am. Embassy, Vienna, Austria, 1952-55, London, U.K., 1955-59, Vientane, Laos, 1959-61; Off. of Exec. Dir., Bur. of Far Eastern Affairs, Dept. of State, Wash. D.C., U.S.A., 1961-65; Consul, Am. Consulate Gen., Munich, Germany, 1965-69; 1st Sec. & Consul, Am. Embassy, Bangkok, Thailand, 1969-72; Dpty. Off. Dir., Bur. of Politico-Mil. Affairs, Dept. of State, Wash.D.C.,

U.S.A., 1972-. Mbr., profl. orgs. & var. clubs. Recip., Achievement Award in Diplomacy & Int. Affairs, Hillsdale Coll., Mich., 1962. Address: 6203 Hardy Dr., McLean, VA 22101, U.S.A. 2, 22, 128.

TROUT, Virgil R., b. 29 July 1927. Minister & Lecturer. Educ: Dr. of Laws, Pepperdine Univ., L.A., Calif.; Cameron State Coll.; Southwestern State; Univ. of Tex.; Spartan Schl. of Aeronautics, Tulsa, Okla.; Coast Navigation Schl., Santa Barbara; La Salle Univ.; Univ. of Tex.; awarded Doct. in Christian Philos., Brantridge Forest Schl., Sussex, U.K. Appts: Instr., USAF; Min., Ch. of Christ & Chap., Veterans' Hosp., Dallas; Counselor, Fed. Correctional Inst., Dallas Co.; Chap., Univ. of New Mexico, Albuquerque; Guest Instr., Chair of Bible, Tex. Tech., Lubbock; Vis. Min., Fed. Reformatory, El Reno, Okla.; currently Min., Mayfair Ch. of Christ, Okla. City. Mbrships. incl: Exec. Dir., Int. Fndn. Relig.-Sci.-Rsch.; Chmn., Speaker's Bur., Okla Christian Coll.; Chmn., Ethics Commn., State of Okla.; AAAS; Soc. for Sci. Study of Relig.; Vis. Inst. of G.B.; Acad. of Relig. & Mental Hlth.; Air Force Assn.; Lions Int. Presented over 300 lecture series. Speaking assignments in 43 states & 8 nations. Recognition from 3 states for work w. youth. Address: Box 12734, Oklahoma City, OK 73112, U.S.A. 28, 125, 130, 139.

TROUTWINE, Charlotte W. (Mrs.) b. 27 Nov. 1906. Educator; Psychologist. Educ: B.S., Simmons Coll., 1927; M.A., Northeastern Univ., 1966. Appts. incl: Exec. Sec., Pres., Hygrade-Sylvania, 1927-28; var. posts, Harvard Med. Schls. & Med. Socs., 1928; Exec. Dir., Postgrad. Med. Inst., Boston, Mass., 1951-57; Mgr., Postgrad. Info. Servs., Lederle Labs., Am. Cynanamid Co., Pearl River, N.Y., 1957-61; Exec. Sec., Postgrad. Med. Educ., Hahnemann Med. Coll. & Exec. Dir., Mary Bailey Inst., Phila., Pa., 1961-; Guidance Counselor & Instr., Pyschol., Holliston H.S., Mass., 1965-66; Falmouth Schls., 1966-. Licensed & Certified Schl. Psychol., 1969. Mbrships. incl: Mass. Schl. Psychol. Assn.; Mass. Psychol. Assn.; Emeritus, Am. Assn. Med. Soc. Execs.; Am. Personnel & Guidance Assn.; Life, Nat. Educators Assn., Mass. Tchrs. Assn.; & Nat. Schl. Counselors Assn.; Mass. Assn. Women Deans & Counselors; AAUW.; Life, Soc. of Mayflower Descendants. Contbr. to profl. jrnls. Address: 10 Waterside Dr., North Falmouth, MA 02556, U.S.A. 5, 6, 57.

TROVIK, Olav Meidell, b. 10 Dec. 1920. University Director. Educ: Grad. in Law, Univ. of Oslo, 1949. Appts: Tchr. & Schl. Insp., Oslo, 1940-48; Admitted to Norwegian Bar, 1949; Sec. to Min. of Justice, 1949; Sec., Facs. Univ. of Oslo, 1949-54; Sec., Univ. of Oslo, 1954-62; Dir., ibid, 1962-. Mbrships. incl: Gen. Sec., Norwegian Conf., Rectors of Univs. & Colls.; Comm. for Higher Educ. & Rsch., Council of Europe; Coun. Mbr., UNESCO Ctr. for Higher Educ. in Europe; Bd. Mbr., Oslo Univ. Press, & Student Assn. Publs: Univ. of Oslo Yearbook, 1954-; Statues of University 1957; Contbr. to jrnls., encys. Hons: Norwegian Royal Gold Medal Merits, 1961; Kt. 1st Class, Order of St. Olav, 1970; Cmdr., Order of Merit, German Fed. Repub., 1970. Address: Director's Office, Univ. of Oslo, Blindern, Oslo 3, Norway. 43.

TROYER, Thomas F., b. 5 Jan. 1910. Realtor. Educ: B.S. in Ed., Kent State Univ., Ohio, 1933; Inst. of Children's Lit., 1971. Appts: Tchr., Ohio Pub. Schls., 1928-43; Design Engr., automotive engines, 1944-57; Realtor, 1958-. Mbrships: Rotary Int., Stow, Ohio Chapt., Dir., 1967-69, Pres., 1972-73; Akron, Ohio Area Chmbr. of Comm., Stow,

Ohio Chmbr. of Comm., Dir., 1967-69, Pres., 1970-71; Nat. Birdwatching Soc.; Izaak Walton League of Am.; Men's Gdn. Club of Am.; Am. Forestry Assn. Publs: The Allegheny Hermit; For the Birds; Strange Goings-on In the Bird World; In Retrospect (articles); 2 poems in anthol., Lyrics of Love, A Treasury of Romantic Poetry, 1972; Labor of Love. Hons: Nominee, Ohio Realtor of Yr., 1966; Writer's Digest Article Award, 1972; Poetry Award, Int. Clover Poetry Assn., 1974. Address: 4174 Kent Rd., Stow, OH 44224, U.S.A. 16, 57, 128.

TRUCKELL, Alfred Edgar, b. 14 Feb. 1919. Museum Curator. Educ: Dumfries Acad., U.K.; Muss. Assn. Dip. Course. Appts: Clerk, Dumfries Town Coun., 1937; Pt.-time Clerk, Burgh Mus., Dumfries, 1947; Full-time appt., ibid, 1948. Mbrships. incl: Soc. Antiquaries of Scotland; Dumfries & Galloway Nat. Hist. & Antiquarian Soc.; Curator, ibid, 1948-, Ed. & Co-Ed., Soc.'s Transactions, 1953-; Soc. for Mediaeval Studies; Pres., Scottish Grp., Coun. British Archaeol.; Prehistoric Soc. Author, num. Mus. leaflets. Contbr., Transactions of Dumfries & Galloway Nat. Hist. & Antiquarian Soc., Galloway News, Dumfries & Galloway Standard. Hons: Fellowship, Museums Assn., 1956; M.A., Edinburgh Univ., 1962; M.B.E., 1970. Address: Burgh Mus., Corberry Hill, Dumfries, DG2 7SW, U.K. 133.

TRUDEAU, Yves, b. 3 Dec. 1930. Sculptor. Educ: Coll. Marie Mediatrice, Montreal, P.Q., Canada; Ecole des Beaux Arts, Montreal; Advanced study in anatomy drawing w. Jean Lang, S.J., in ceramic w. Gaetan Beaudin. Tchr., Ecole des Beaux Arts, Montreal, 1967, & Tchr., sculpture, Univ. of Quebec, Montreal, 1969. Mbrships: Nat. V.P., Canadian Conf. of the Arts; Fndg. Pres., Quebec Sculptors Assn.; Pres. in Off., ibid, 1960-66, 1968; V.P., 1969-72, resigned; Assn. Int. des Arts Plastiques, UNESCO; Assoc., Int. Mus. Coun. Exhibitions in Canada, France, Italy, Sweden, Belgium & U.S.A.; Participator, sculpture symposia, Yugoslavia, Canada & Czechoslovakia; Canadian Rep., 4th Biennale, Paris, 1965, 3rd Biennale of Contemporary Sculpture, Musee Rodin, France, 1966, 1st Biennale of Small Sculpture, Budapest, Hungary, 1971; Sev. large pub. sculptures; Work in pvte. collects. & in museums. Recip. of hons. Address: 5429 Ave. Durocher, Montreal, P.Q., Canada.

TRUE, Henry Alfonso (Dave), Jr., b. 12 June 1915. Oil Producer; Drilling Contractor; Rancher. Educ: B.S., Montana State Coll., 1937. Appts. incl: Ptnr., True Drilling Co., 1951-, True Oil Co., 1951-; Pres., Toolpushers Supply Co., 1954-, Belle Fourche Pipeline Co., 1957-, Camp Creek Gas Co., 1964-, Reserve Oil Purchasing Co., 1973-; Owner, True Ranches, 1957-, Camp Creek Gas Co., 1964-, Black Hills Oil Mktrs. Inc., 1973-; Owner, True Ranches, 1957-; Dir., 1st Nat. Bank of Casper, 1962-. Mbrships. incl: Dir., Am. Assn. of Oilwell Drilling Contractors, 1950-; Bd. Dirs., Am. Petroleum Inst., 1960-; Exec. Comm., ibid, 1970-; Ky. Col.; Sigma Chi. Hons. incl: Disting Serv. Award, Tex. Mid-Continent Oil & Gas Assn., 1971; Annual Indl. Award, Wyo. Assn. of Realtors, 1965. Address: P.O. Box 2360, Casper, WY 82601, U.S.A. 128.

TRUE, Jean Durland (Mrs. H.A. True). Oil Producer; Business Executive. Appts. incl: Ptnr., True Drilling Co., Casper, Wyo., 1951-, True Oil Co., 1951-; Dir., Geo. Mancini Feed Lots Inc., Brighton, Colo., 1964-72, Black Hills Oil Marketers Inc., Casper, Wyo., 1964-, Camp Creek Gas Co., Casper, 1968-, Reserve Oil Purchasing Co., Casper, 1970-72; Treas., True Serv. Co., Casper, 1954-70, Toolpushers Supply Co., 1954-, White Stallion Ranch Inc., Tucson, Ariz., 1965-. Mbrships. incl: Exec. Bd. of Trustees, 1966-, V.P. of Exec. Bd., 1973-, Gottsche Rehab. Ctr., Thermopolis Wyo.; Nat. Fedn. of Repub. Women's Clubs; Petroleum Women's Club; Alpha Gamma Delta; St. Mark's Episc. Ch.; Nat. Deleg., Repub. Conven., 1972; Ft. Casper Commn., Casper, Wyo., 1973-. Address: 6000 S. Poplar St., Casper, WY 82601, U.S.A.

TRUESDELL, Clifford Ambrose III, b. 18 Feb. 1919. Author. Educ: B.S., Calif. Inst. of Technol., 1941; M.S., ibid, 1942; Ph.D., Princeton Univ., 1943. Appts. incl: Radiation Lab., MIT, 1944-46; Chief, Theoretical Mechs. Subdiv., USN Ordnance Lab., Md., 1946-48; Lectr. to Assoc. Prof. of Maths., Univ. of Md., 1946-50; USN Rsch. Lab., Wash. D.C.; Hd., Theoretical Mechs. Sect., 1948-51, Cons., 1951-55; Prof. of Maths., Ind. Univ., 1950-61; Maths. Rsch. Ctr., U.S. Army, Univ. of Wis., 1958; Fndr.-Ed., Jrnl. of Rational Mechs. & Analysis, 1952-56, Archive for Rational Mechs. & Analysis, 1957-, Archive for Hist. of Exact Scis., 1961-; Cons., U.S. Nat. Bur. Standards, 1959-62; Prof. of Rational Mechs., Johns Hopkins Univ., 1961-. Mbrships. incl: Co-Fndr., Past Sec. & Chmn., Soc. for Natural Philos.; Soc. Onorario dell'Accad. Nazionale di Sci., Lettere ed Arti, Modena. Publs. incl: The Kinetics of Vorticity, 1954; The Rational Mechanics of Elastic or Flexible Bodies, 1638-1788, 1960; The Non-Linear Field Theories of Mechanics (co-author), 1965; The Elements of Continuum Mechanics, 1966; Essays in the History of Mechanics, 1968; Rational Thermodynamics, 1969; Introduction to Rational Elasticity, 1973; many rsch. papers. Hons. incl: Dott. ing. h.c., Politecnico di Milano, 1965; Gold Medal & Int. Prize, Accad. di Sci. di Torino, 1967. Address: Il Palazzetto, 4007 Greenway, Balt., MD 21218, U.S.A. 14.

TRUGLIO, Mario Thomas, b. 26 May 1942. Musician; Educator. Educ: Dip., Juilliard Schl., 1964; Mus.B., 1965; Mus.M., 1966; M.S., Hofstra Univ., 1969. Appts. incl: Vis. Prof. of Music, Conservetory De Musique, Quebec, Canada, 1966; Tchr., music special educ. for mentally retarded, Nassau Co. Bd. of Co-op. Educl. Servs., Wantagh, N.Y., 1966-70; Dir., music & performing arts, Jericho, N.Y., 1971; Prog. Admnstr., Cultural Arts Ctr., Wantagh, N.Y., 1973. Mbrships. incl: Nat. Coun. Christians & Jews; Am. Assn. on Mental Deficiency; Coun. for Exceptional Children; A.S.C.A.P.; A.F.T.R.A.; Am. Acad. TV Arts & Scis.; Am. Fedn. of Musicians. Compositions incl: Symphonic Variations, 1962; Music for the Retarded, 1970; Music Syllabus for Exceptional Children, 1971; Tone Poem in A minor; Consolation in C major. Recip. of hons. Address: BOCES Cultural Arts Ctr., 2850 N. Jerusalem Rd., Wantagh, NY 11793, U.S.A. 6.

TRUHER, (Sister) Mary Terese, O.S.F., School Librarian. Educ: B.A., Immaculate Heart Coll., Hollywood, 1960; M.S.L.S., Catherine Spalding Coll., 1964. Appts. incl: Religious, Order of St. Francis, 1932-65; Tchr., Child Care Schl. Admin., 1932-61; Tchr., St. Judes H.S., Havre, Mont., 1961-62; Ref. Libn., Santa Clara Pub. Lib., 1965; Asst. Archivist, Santa Clara Univ., 1965-66; Libn., Document Rsch., Am. Standard Advanced Technol. Div., Aerospace Instrumentation for Gemini Flights Prog., 1966-67; Applied Technol., ITEK, 1967; Libn., Woodside Priory Schl., Calif., 1968-. Mbrships. incl: AAUW; ALA; Calif. Lib. Assn. Address: 1060 Noel Drive, Menlo Park, CA 94025, U.S.A. 5, 138.

TRUJILLO, Jose M., b. 16 Dec. 1925. Pathologist. Educ: B.S., Inst. Nacional, Panama City, Panama, 1944; M.D., Med. Schl., Nat. Univ. of Buenos Aires, Argentina, 1956; Rotating Intern, St. Joseph Hosp., Kan. City, Mo., U.S.A., 1957-58, Res., Pathol. Dept., 1958-60; Fellow, Experimental Pathol. Dept., City of Hope Med. Ctr., Duarte, Calif., 1960-61; Sr. Fellow in Pathol., Univ. of Tex. M.D. Anderson Hosp. & Tumor Inst., Houston, 1962-63. Appts. incl: Asst.-Assoc. Pathologist, Asst.-Assoc. Prof., Dept. of Pathol., Univ. of Tex. M.D. Anderson Hosp. & Tumor Inst., Houston, 1963-69; Assoc. Pathologist & Assoc. Prof., Dept. of Clin. Chem. & Lab. Med., ibid, 1969-73, Asst. Hd., Dept. of Clin. Chem. & Lab. Med., 1970-73, Chief, Sect. of Cytogenetics-Immunol.-Ultra-structure, 1970-, Hd. of Dept., Pathologist, & Prof., 1973-. Mbr., profl. orgs. recip., var. hon. appts. Address: Dept. of Clin. Chem. & Lab. Med., The Univ. of Tex. System Cancer Ctr., M.D. Anderson Hospital & Tumor Institute, 6723 Bertner Ave., Houston, TX 77025, U.S.A.

TRUNK, Isaiah E., b. 21 July 1905. Historian. Educ: M.A., Humanities, Univ. of Warsaw, Poland; Dr. of Jewish Lit., Jewish Tchrs. Sem., N.Y., U.S.A. Appts. incl: Tchr., Jewish H.Ss., Poland; Mbr., Edit. Staff, Jewish Histl. Inst., Warsaw, Poland, 1946-50; Rsch. Asst. & Archivist, YIVO Inst. for Jewish Rsch.; Prof., Hist., Max Winveich YIVO Ctr. for Advd. Jewish Studies, Hebrew Union Coll. & Inst. of Jewish Relig., N.Y. Mbrships. incl: Union of Jewish Studies, Cambridge, Mass.; Histl. Soc. of Israel, Jerusalem; World Union of Jewish Studies, Jerusalem, Israel. Publs. incl: A Jewish Community in Poland At The End of The 18th Century, 1934; Studies in Jewish History in Poland, 1963; The Lodz Ghetto: A Historical and Sociological Study, 1962; The Jewish Councils in Eastern Europe Under Nazi Occupation, 1972; Num. essays in histl. periodicals. Hons. incl: Cert. of Hon. & The Don Jolson Award, Jewish Book Coun. of Am., 1967; The Nat. Book Award, 1973. Address: YIVO Inst. for Jewish Rsch., 1048 Fifth Ave., N.Y., NY 10028, U.S.A.

TRUTTER, John T., b. 18 Apr. 1920. Communications Executive. Educ: B.A., Ill. Univ., U.S.A., 1942; Postgrad. study, Northwestern & Chgo. Univs. Appts. incl: Lt. Col., Chief, Personnel Servs., US Forces, India, Burma, 1943-46; V.P., Operator Servs., Ill. Bell Telephone Co.; Gen. Mgr., ibid. Mbrships. incl: many civic, bus. & profl. orgs.; Dir., State Nat. Bank, Evanston; Pres., Hull House Assn.; Pres., Regional Bd., Nat. Conf. Christians & Jews; Fndr., Past Pres., Sangamon Co. Histl. Soc.; Exec. Comm. & Trustee, Ill. Children's Home & Aid Soc.; Past Exec. V.P., Int. Visitors Ctr. Chgo.; Past Pres., 1st Ward Assn., Evanston; Exec. Comm. & Trustee, United Cerebral Palsy, Chgo.; Trustee, Ill. Univ. YMCA; Exec. Coun., Boy Scouts; Evanston City Zoning Bd., 1967-68; Alpha Sigma Phi; Phi Delta Phi. Publs: Co-author, Handling Barriers in Communications, 1957; num. articles in profl. jrnls. & Rotarian Mag. feature. Recip. Legion of Merit, US Mil. Forces, 1945. Address: Room 28A, 225 W. Randolph St., Chgo., IL 60606, U.S.A. 16.

TRÜTZSCHLER, Heinz. Performing Artist in Residence. Educ: Conservatory of Music, Berlin, Germany; Cert. of Maturity, Paulsen Coll., Berlin; Master Study under Kulenkampff & Frederick Bolt, Berlin; Concert Master, 1944; Composition studies under Frederick Bolt. Became US Citizen, 1966. Appts: Violinist & Composer; 1st pub. appearance at age of 12; num. recitals for Allied troops in Europe; num. pub. appearances; Performing Artist in Res., Spelman Coll.; Dir. & Conductor, Chmbr. Orch., Atlanta Univ. Ctr., 1967-; Recording Artist, NRC & World Wide Records Int.; Prod. Dir. of Classical Series. Mbrships: AAUP; Pi Kappa Lambda. Compositions incl: (Violin & Piano) Mariae Love Song; Mariae Waltz; Spring Day in Atlanta; Capricious Waltz; Felicity; Longing; The Blue Ridge; Violin Solo Sonatas; Sonata Americana; Chmbr. Music & Songs. Contbr. of articles to Music Jrnl. Address: 710 Peachtree St., Atlanta, GA 30308, U.S.A. 57, 125, 131, 139.

TRYON, Charles Philip, b. 4 May 1938. Watershed Scientist. Educ: B.S., Purdue Univ., W. Lafayette, Ind., 1959; M.S., 1961; Univs. of Minn. & Co. Appts: Dist. Forester, U.S. Forest Serv., Ironton, Ohio, 1961-62; Watershed Forester, Bedford, Ind., 1962-64; Asst. Dist. Ranger, Cadillac, Mich., 1964-65; Watershed Sci., Rolla, Mo., 1966-74. Mbrships: Citizens United to Restore the Environment Inc.; Alpha Tau Omega; Xi Sigma Pi. Contbr. to profl. jrnls. Hons: Jaycees Disting. Serv. Award, Rolla, Mo., 1972; Mo. Jaycees Outstanding Young Men of Mo. Award, 1972; Am. Motors Corp. Conservation Award, 1974. Address: 1 Johnson St., Rolla, MO 65401, U.S.A. 117.

TRYON, Sharon E. Stratton, b. 26 Dec. 1937. Speech Therapist. Educ: B.S., Ind. State Univ., Terre Haute, 1958. Appts: Recreational Therapy Aide, 1958; Tchr. of Mentally Retarded, Ferndale, Mich., 1958-59, Indpls., Ind., 1959-61; Speech Therapist, Mo. Div. Hlth., 1966-; Substitute Tchr., Rolla Pub. Schls., Mo., 1966-; Mbr., U.S. Jaycee Environmental Advsry. Staff; Co.-Dir., Rolla Recycling Ctr. for UCRE; Vice Chmn., Rolla Housing Authority; Chmn., Rolla Mo. Commn. on Human Rights; Mbr., Phelps Co. Ext. Advsry. Coun. on Environmental Affairs; Sec., Phelps Co. Home Hlth. Agcy. Advsry. Bd. Mbrships. incl: Treas., Gardeners of Ozark Hills; Former Mbr., AAUW; Bulletin Ed. & Community Problems Chmn., ibid, 1967-73. Recip. Nomination as Outstanding Young Woman of Rolla & State of Mo., 1972. Address: 1 Johnson-Laird, Rolla, MO 65401, U.S.A. 76, 130.

TRYPANIS, Constantine Athanasius, b. 22 Jan. 1909. University Professor. Educ: Univs. of Athens, Berlin & Munich; D.Phil., Athens; M.A. (Oxon); D.Lit. (Oxon). Appts: Lectr., Classics, Univ. of Athens, 1939-47; Prof., Medieval & Mod. Greek Lit. & Lang., Oxford Univ., 1947-67; Prof., Classics, Univ. of Chgo., 1967- Mbrships: Emeritus Fellow, Exeter Coll., Oxford Univ.; Fellow, Royal Soc. of Lit.; Corres. Mbr., Inst. of Balkan Studies, Thessalonika; Corres. Mbr., Acad. of Athens; Medieval Acad. of Am. Num. publs. incl: Alexandrian Poetry, 1943; Callimachus, 1956; Fourteen Early Byzantine Cantica, 1970; Stones of Troy, 1956 (poetry); Pompeian Dog (poetry), 1965; Contbr. to encys. & num. lit. jrnls. Hons: Koraes Prize, Acad. of Athens, 1936; Heineman Award, Royal Soc. of Lit., 1959; Stones of Troy, & Pompeian Dog, choices of Poetry Soc. Address: 5825 S. Dorchester Ave., Chicago, IL 60637, U.S.A. 1, 2, 3, 34, 131.

TRZEBIATOWSKI, Wlodzimierz, b. 25 Feb. 1906. Professor. Educ: Ing-chim., Inst. of Technol., Lvov, 1929; Dr.Sc., ibid, 1931; Dr.habil., 1935; Prof., Inorg. Chem., Univ. Lvov, 1938. Appts: Asst. & Lectr., Chem., Inst. of Technol., Lvov, 1929-38; Dir., Inst. Inorg. Chem., Univ. of Lvov, 1938-45; Dir., Inst. Inorg. Chem., Univ. & Inst. of Technol., Wroclaw, 1945-61; Dir., Inst. Low Temperature

& Structure Rsch., Polish Acad. of Scis., Wroclaw, 1968-. Mbrships: Pres., Polish Chem. Soc., 1953-54; Polish Phys. Soc.; Chem. Soc.; Am. Chem. Soc.; For. Mbr., Czech. Acad. of Scis., 1973 & German Acad. of Scis. (German Dem. Repub.), 1974; V.P., 1969-71, Pres., 1972-, Polish Acad. of Scis. Publs: Inorganic Chemistry (in Polish & German, 4 eds.); The Structure of Metals, 1953; X-Ray Structural Analysis (w. K. Lukaszewics, 1960. Hons: Dr. h.c., Univ. of Wroclaw, 1970; State Prize in Chem., 1955; Cmdr., Cross Polonia Restituta, 1960; Order of Banner of Labour I Class, 1964 & '70. Address: 20, ul. Gierymskich, Wroclaw 12, Poland. 34.

TSAI, Hsiao-Hsia (Hobbs), b. 15 Dec. 1929. Artist. Educ: B.A., Nat. Coll. of Arts, China; M.F.A., Okla. Univ., Norman, U.S.A.; Advanced rsch., Univ. of Okla. Owner, Hsiao-Hsia Tsai's Gall of Fine Art, Corpus Christi, Tex. Mbrships. incl: El Modjel; Kappa Pi; Nat. Assn. of Women Artists, N.Y., 1965; Sume-E Soc. of Am., N.Y.; Int. Art Guild, Paris, France, 1973. 149 group shows; 97 one-man shows; Exhibs. in many countries inclng. U.S.A., China, India, Mexico, Monaco, Canada, France, U.K., Italy, Spain, Portugal, U.S.S.R. Author of 2 articles on art; Illustrator of books. Hons. incl: Silver Medal, Dip. de'Hoxnent in Int. Art Guild, Palme Dor des Beaux Arts, 1970; Award, 84th Annual Exhib. Nat. Assn. of Women Artists, Nat. Acad. Galls., N.Y., 1973; Int. Competition Exhib., Cannes, France, 1973. Address: 1437 Casa Verde Dr., UL 3-3074, Corpus Christi, TX 78411, U.S.A. 5, 133.

TSAMRIYON, Tsemah M., b. 9 Nov. 1919. Teacher; Lecturer; Writer. Educ: Schl. of Law & Econ., Tel-Aviv; Schl. of Philos. & Theol., Regensburgh, Germany; Ph.D., Munich Univ., 1951. Appts: Ed. of Unser Welt, 1948-51; Tchr., Galilee Secondary Schl., Tiberias, Israel, 1951-60; Dir., ibid, 1953-60; First Dir., Haifa Municipal Secondary Schl. 'A', 1960-63; Dir., State Hebrew Tchrs. Coll., Haifa, 1963-; Lectr., Haifa Univ., 1966-69; Lectr., Israel Inst. of Technol., 1970-. Mbrships: Youth Movement of Jewish State Party, Haifa; Jewish Brigade Comm.; United Zionist Revisionists, Germany & rest of Europe; Chmn., Tchrs. Movement for the Nat. Fund, Tiberias & Jordan Valley & mbr. of its Council in Israel; Chmn., Jury Comm. of Rupin Prize of Haifa Municipality; Chmn., Ctrl. Comm. of Dirs. of Tchrs. Colls. in Israel; Bible Rsch. Comm., Haifa; var. other comms. Publs: Wegweiser, 1949; Haitonut Shel Sheerit Hapleta Begermaniya, 1970; Torat Hachibur (co-author), 1964; author of var. pamphlets on Old Testament & Hebrew hist.; ed. of var. papers & books; contbr. to num. profl. jrnls. Address: 14 Nahalal St., Haifa, Israel. 55.

TSATSAS, George, b. 16 Mar. 1912. Professor of Pharmaceutical Chemistry. Educ: Grad. Pharm., Univ. of Athens; Dr. Phys. Scis., Fac. of Scis., Univ. of Paris; D.Pharm., Schl. of Pharm., Paris. Appts: Fellowship, for studies in France, Univ. of Athens, 1926-40; Fellowship, C.N.R.S., France, 1944-45; Rsch. Asst., ibid, 1945-47; Chief of Rsch., 1947-55; Hd. of Rsch., 1955-57; Fellowship for rsch., in Zurich C.N.R.S., 1953; Fellowship., Battelle Mem. Inst., Polytech. of Zurich, 1953-54; Assoc. Prof., Pharmaceutical Chem., Univ. of Athens., 1950; Full Prof., ibid, 1957-. Mbrships: Acad. of Athens; Corres., French Acad. of Pharm. & Nat. Acad. of Med., & Acad. of Pharm. of Barcelona; Sec., Supreme Hlth. Coun.; Pres., Supreme Chem. Coun., 1968-; Comm. of Narcotics Sec., Supreme Hlth. Coun.; Pres., Supreme Chem. Coun., 1968-; Comm. of Narcotics, Min. of Soc. Servs.; Int.

Pharmaceutical Fedn. (F.P. Sec., Supreme Hlth. Coun.; Pres., Supreme Chem. Coun., 1968-; Comm. of Narcotics, Min. of Soc. Servs.; Int. Pharmaceutical Fedn. (F.I.P.); Pres., Greek Pharmaceutical Soc.; Chem. Soc. of Brit.; Am. Chem. Soc. Publs: Pharmaceutical Chem., 2 vols., in Greek; about 90 works on organic chem. & chemotherapy. Hons: Off., Order of Merit for Rsch. & Invention, France; Laureat, Fac. of Pharm., Paris (Thesis Prize, 1947); A. Dam ergis Award, Acad. of Athens, 1952; Laureat, Chem. Soc. of France (LeBel Prize, 1954); Laureat, Nat. Acad. of Med. (Jansen Prize, 1955); Award of the Empirikion Inst., 1969. Address: Vassilissis Sofias 121, Athens, 602, Greece.

TSATSOS, Constantine, b. 1 July 1899. Emeritus Professor. Educ: Univ. of Athens, Greece; Univ. of Heidelberg. Germany; Paris, France. Appts. incl: Prof., Philos. of Law, 1932-41; M.P. for Athens, Greece, 1946-50. 61-67; Min. of Educ., 1949; Under Sec. of State for Econ. Coord., 1950-51; Min. to Prime Min., 1956-61; Min. of Soc. Welfare, 1962-63; Min. of Justice, 1967; Mbr., Acad. of Athens, 1961-; Past Pres., ibid. Mbrships: Chmn., Greek Soc. of Philos. of Law Chmn., Greek Soc. of Philos. Publs. incl: The Problem of Interpreting the Law, 1932; Greece on the March, 1953; Aesthetics; Politics, The Social Philosophy of the Ancient Greeks; Essays on Legal Philosophy; Aphorisms & Thoughts, 4 vols. Hons. incl: Kt. Cmdr., Greek Order of George I; Kt. Cmdr., Royal Order of Phoenix. Address: 9 Kydathineon St., Athens 119, Greece.

TSCHUDY, William. Electrical, Mechanical & Research Engineer. Educ: E.E., M.E., Fed. Tech. Univ., Zurich, Switzerland, 1908; D.Sc., ibid, 1912. Appts. incl: Rsch. Engr., Asst. Prof. Elec. & Phys. Labs., Elec. & Mech. Designer, var orgs., Germany, Switzerland & U.S.A., 1908-19; Pvte. Rsch., N.Y. & Switzerland, 1919-23; Cons., Construction & Rsch. Engr., L.A. & San Francisco, Calif., U.S.A., 1925-41; Gardena, Calif., 1947-55; w. Calif, Ship-building Corp., Terminal Island, 1942-46; Test Engr., Todd Pacific Shipyards Inc., San Pedro, Calif., 1946-47; Gen. Engr., Dist. Pub. Works Off., U.S. Navy, San Diego, Calif., 1955-60; Pvte. Rsch., 1960-. Mbr. & Fellow, profl. orgs. Contrb., tech. publs. Holder of patents, U.S.A., U.K., France, Germany, Switzerland. Address: 2800 Quebec St. N.W., Apt. 514, Washington, DC 20008, U.S.A. 14, 26, 28, 57, 131.

TSELLOS, Epaminondas, b. 4 July 1898. Bank & Company Executive. Educ: Mil. Cadets Schl., 1915-18; Artillery Schl., Army Automotive Transport Schl. Appts: Off., Greek Army, 1918-34, called again into serv. for war of 1940, retd. w. rank of Col.; Sec. Gen., Greek United Party, 1935-50; Dir. Gen., Greek Nat. Radical Union, 1956; Dir. Gen., Greek Telecommunications Org., 1957-64; Bd. of Dirs., Bank of Greece, 1971-; Pres. & Dir., cos. of "Viohalco"group, 1971-; Min., Greek Govt. in Exile, Cairo, 1932-43; Min. of Commerce, 1967-70. Publs: From the Middle Class to the Uniting Society; Greece's Contribution to the Allied Victory; The Approaching End of the Lie; Var. articles in newspapers etc. Hons: Grand Cmdr., Order of Georges I; Cmdr., Order of the Phoenix (2 awards); Medal for Valor (twice); Mil. Cross, Class "A"; Disting. Serv. Medal; Cross of Merit; Allied War Medal, 1918; Nat. Resistance Medal, 1941-44. Address: Viohalco S.A., 115 Kifissias Ave., Athens 606, Greece.

TSIGRIS, (Right Rev.) Ignatios, b. 13 Feb. 1911. Minister of Greek Orthodox Church;

Bishop of Arta. Educ: Divinity Schl. of Athens Univ.; Ordination as Bishop, 1958. Appts. incl: Preacher, Diocese of Attikis & Megaridos, 1942-58; Priest & Preacher, Nat. Army of Greece, 1951-55; Bishop, Diocese of Arta, 1958-; Locum Tenens, Diocese of Aitolias & Acarnanias, 1961-65; Mbr., Holy Synod of Greek Orthodox Ch., 1964-. Active Fndr., Mbr. & Off., var. religious, community & welfare orgs. & instns. Responsible for num. soc., educl. & charitable activities, especially in connection with youth, the aged & the poor. Hons. incl: Gold Medal of City of Megara, Attikis; Cross of Michaelmass, Order of George A, 1961; Cross of Archangels Michael & Gabriel, Order of Phoenix, 1964. Address: Sacred Metropolis of Arta, Greece.

TSO, Raymond Hosteen, b. 14 Oct. 1934. Human Resources Development Specialist. Educ: A.A. Degree, Phoenix Coll., Ariz. Appts. incl: Med. Soc. Wkr., Shiprock Indian Hospital., N.M., 1961-62; Soc. Security Field Wkr., Navajo Tribe, Shiprock, 1963-67; Asst. Dir., Pub. Servs. Div., Navajo Tribe, Window Rock, Ariz., 1967-69, Dir., 1969-71; currently Human Resources Dev. Specialist, Admin. Off., Shiprock Indian Hosp. & Kayenta Hosp. Mbrships: 4 Corners Frontier Rodeo Assn. of Teecnospos, Ariz.; Pres. ibid. 1965-69; Past Mbr., Window Rock Lions Club, ZIA & Hawk Flying Clubs, Farmington, N.M. Hons. incl: Col. Aide-de-Camp & Mbr. of Staff of Gov., State of N.M., 1964; Cert. for Improvement of Communication & Rels. w. Pub., 1972. Address: P.O. Box 1041, Shiprock , NM 87420, U.S.A.

TSUJIMURA, Lillie Yuriko, b. 30 May 1923. Hotel Administrator. Educ: Special Hotel Seminars, Cornell Univ. Appts: Cashier & Room Serv. Mgr., Moana Hotel Dining Room, 1948-49; Reservations Mgr., Surfrider Hotel, 1949-52; Reservations & Front Off. Mgr., Waikiki Biltmore Hotel, 1952-57; Reservations & Sales Mgr., Island Holidays Resorts Hotel Chain, 1957-63; Grp. Sales & Reservations Mgr., Ilikai Hotel, 1963-67; Admin. Asst., Ambassador Hotel, 1967-68, Pagoda Hotel/Terrace & Pacific Beach Hotel, 1970-. Mbrships: Bd. Dirs., Hawaii Hotel Assn., Hotel Sales Mgmt. Assn. Int.; Hawaii Visitors Br.: Bd. Dirs., H.T. Hayashi Enterprises Ltd.; Japanese Chmbr. of Comm.; Gov.'s Commn. on Manpower & Full Employment; Gov.'s Advsry. Coun. on Voc. & Tech. Educ; Mayor's Comm. on Status of Women: Precinct V.P., Democratic Party of Hawaii. Address: 760 Hao St., Honolulu, HI 96821, U.S.A. 5.

TSUZUKI, Yojiro, b. 13 May 1903. Educator; Chemist. Educ: Tokyo Imperial Univ., Japan. 1926; Dr. Sci., 1939. Appts: Prof., Musashi Higher Schl., 1930-42; 1st Higher Schl., 1942-45; Tech. of Sci. Nat. Chem. Lab. Ind., Tokyo, Japan, 1946-50; Prof., Sci. Univ., ibid, 1950-. Mbrships: Chem. Socs: Japan, Germany & Am.; Hist. Sci. Soc., Japan. Publs: Polymer chem: starch, 1928; 1st synth. resin unsaturated acids, 1935; Sterochem: elucid. optical anomaly hydroxy-acids by ORD & IR analysis, 1936-57; taste, sense & chem. structure, esp. sugars, 1946-74; Histl. studies, Japanese organic chemists, 1955-70; Sugars. 1954; History of Chemistry, Its Idea and Technology, 1966; Origin of Technical Terms used in Chemistry, 1974; The Course of a Chemist, 1974. Address: 71 Yakuoji, Shinjuku-ku, Tokyo 162, Japan.

TUCAZINSKY, Nissan Aaron, b. 1922. Rabbi. Educ: Etz-Hayim Talmud Torah & Yeshivah. Appts: Dean & Gen. Dir., Etz-Hayim Torah Ctr., Israel. Mbrships: Amateurs of

Astron. Soc., Jerusalem; Pres., United Charity, Jerusalem. Publs: Compiler, Grand Annual Calendar for Rules & Practices Relating to Israel & the Diaspora (started by late father); expanded & annotated 3rd ed. of father's Bridge of Life (3 vols.); completed from manuscript & annotated father's The Holy City & the Temple (5 parts in 3 vols.); The Land & Its Boundaries (according to Biblical sources); prepared from old manuscript, annotated & explained, Paraphrase on Sanctification of the Month worked out by the author of 'Tosphoth Yom-Tow' & based on Malmonides. Address: P.O. Box 300, Jerusalem, Israel.

TUCK, Miriam Lyons. Professor of Health Education, Educ: R.N., Cumberland Hosp. Schl. of Nursing, Bklyn., N.Y., 1945; P.H.N. Cert., Univ. of Calif., Berkeley, 1947; B.S., N.Y. Univ., 1954; M.A., Tchrs. Coll., Columbia Univ., 1956; Ed.D., ibid, 1961. Appts. incl:Assoc. Prof.-Prof., Hlth. Educ., Chmn., Undergrad. Major Div., Hlth. Educ., Initiator & Dir., Community Hlth.-Schl. of Community Servs. & Pub. Affai·s, Univ. of Ore., Eugene, 1962-68; Organizer, Coord., Community Hlth. Coun. & Dir., Community Self-Study, Lane Co., Ore., 1963-68; Assoc. Prof.-Coord. of Hlth. Educ, Organizer-Coord. of Hlth. Educ. Prog., Project Dir. of Intensive Tchr. Preparation Prog. & of Multi-Media Resource Materials, Herbert H. Lehman Coll., CCNY, 1968-71; Prof.-Coord. of Hlth. Educ., Chmn. Grad. Comm., Tex. Woman's Univ., Denton, 1971-72; Prof. of Educ., Dir. of Hlth. Educ., & Organizer of Grad. & Undergrad. Progs. in Hlth. Sci., Russell Sage Coll., N.Y., 1972-73; Chmn., Hlth. Educ. Dept., ibid, 1973-. Mbrships: incl: Fellow, Am. Pub. Hlth. Assn., Am. Schl. Hlth. Assn., Int. Union of Hlth. Educs., Soc. of Pub. Hlth. Educators, Royal Soc. of Pub. Hlth. (GB), & N.Y. Acad. of Scis. Publs: Health Sciences (jt. author), 1961; Training Manual for School Nurse-Teachers (co- author), 1970; (co-author), 1970; Consumer Health (co-author), 1972; num. articles in profl. jrnls., etc. Recip. sev. citations for work. Address: c/o Russell Sage Coll., 140 New Scotland Ave., Albany, NY 12208, U.S.A. 5, 6, 132.

TUCK, Raphael, b. 5 Apr. 1910. Barrister; Member of Parliament. Educ: B.Sc., London Schl. Econs., 1936; M.A., Trinity Hall, Cambridge, 1939; LL.M., Harvard Univ., U.S.A., 1940; Called to Bar, U.K., 1951. Appts: Staff, British Embassy, Wash. D.C., 1940-41; Lectr.-Prof. Law, Univ. of Sask., Saskatoon, Canada, 1941-45; Constitutional Advsr. to Premier of Man., 1943; Special Rsch., Dept. of Labour, Ottawa, 1944; Prof., Pol. Sci., McGill Univ., Montreal, 1945; Prof., Pol. Sci., Tulane Univ., New Orleans L.A., U.S.A., 1947-49; M.P., Watford Herts, U.K., 1964-. Mbrships incl: V.P., Watford Soc. for Mentally Handicapped Children; V.P., Herts. Soc.; V.P., Watford Operatic Soc. Contbr. to profl. publs. Address: 10 King's Bench Walk, Temple, London, E.C.4, U.K.

TUCKER, Emma S. (Mrs. Francis Carlile Tucker), b. 19 June 1916. Lecturer; Social Worker. Educ: B.S., Geo. Wms. Coll., 1941; Far Eastern Lang. Dept., Columbia Univ., 1942. Appts. incl: Asst., Physiol. Dept., Geo. Wms. Coll., 1939-41; Women's Recreational Dir., Coll. Camp, Lake Geneva, Wis., 1939-41; Volunteer Soc. Worker, Girl Scouts of Am. for 40 yr. & Sr. Ldr., ibid, 1958-; World Travel Lectr., 1970-. Mbrships. incl: Ill. State Med. Aux & Steph. Co. Med. Soc. Woman's Aux., 1958-; State & Co. Hist. Soc. of Ill., 1958-; Am. Field Serv., 1966-; Chmn., Am. Mothers Comm., Inc., State of Ill., 1973-; Nat. Art Comm., Am. Mothers Comm., Inc., 1974;

Chmn., III. State Conven., Kings Daughter's, 1974 & Pres., Kings Daughters City Union, 1974 & Deleg. to Int. Kings Daughters Conven., N.B., Canada, 1974; Bd. Salvation Army, 1971-; YWCA Sustaining Mbrships., 1950-; Deleg. to N. at Conven., Evangelic Free Ch., 1972; Co.-Chmn., Comm. to Preserve the Gt. Western III. Nature Trail & Trustee, Jane Addamsland Park Fndn., 1973-; Kappa Delta Pi, 1941. Hons: Disting. Serv. Award Thanks Badge, Girl Scouts, 1969; Mother of Yr. Award, III. State, Am. Mothers Comm., Inc., 1970; Disting. Alumnus Award, Geo. Wms. Coll., 1970; Disting. Citizenship Award, BPO Elks, 1970. Address: 861 W. Stephenson St., Freeport, IL 61032, U.S.A. 57, 129, 130.

TUCKER, James Warnock, b. 30 Nov. 1914. Physicist. Educ: Univ. of Va., 1932-35; B.S., Va. Polytechnic Inst., 1940; Pa. State Univ., 1940-42; Ohio State Univ., 1946-47; Md. Univ., 1948-52. Appts: Instr., Pa. State Univ.; Radio Engr., storm & lightning rsch., Wright Field, Ohio; Rsch. Physicist, optics, gen. physics & laser physics rsch., Naval Rsch. Lab., Wash. D.C. Mbrships: IEEE; Optical Soc. of Am.; Rsch. Soc. of Am. Recip., Decoration for Exceptional Civilian Serv., 1946. Address: 6112 Beachway Dr., Falls Church, VA 22041, U.S.A. 7, 14.

TUCKER, Martin, b. 8 Feb. 1928. Writer; Professor; Editor. Educ: B.A., N.Y. Univ., 1949; M.A., Univ. of Ariz., Tucson, 1954; Ph.D., N.Y. Univ., 1963. Appts: Bureau Chief, N.M. Newspapers, 1955-56; Newswriter, Associated Press, Huntington, W. Va., 1954-55; Assoc. Ed., Quick Frozen Foods mag., 1950; Co. Chmn., Int. Writers Conf., L.I. Univ., 1965; Prof. of Engl., L.I. Univ., Brooklyn, 1968-; Ed., Confrontation Mag., 1969-; Cons. Ed., Belles-Lettres in Engl., Johnson Reprint Corp., 1969-; Ed., PEN Newsletter (Am. PEN), 1972-. Mbrships. incl: Fellow, African Studies Assn., Official Am. Del. to PEN Int. Congress, 1967. Publs: Africa in Modern Literature, 1967; Ed., The Critical Temper, 1970, 3 vols.; Ed., Moulton's Library of Literary Criticism, 1968, 4 vols.; articles, verse & fiction in var. jrnls., newspapers, etc. Recip. var. hons. Address: 35 High St., Armonk, NY 10504, U.S.A. 6, 30.

TUCKER, Walter O, b. 1 Dec. 1924. Life Insurance Field Underwriter. Educ: SUNY, Cortland; Chartered Life Underwriter Deg., Am. Coll., Life Underwriters, 1961. Appts: Underwriter, 1955-; Mbr., Cortland Life Underwriters Assn., 1956-; V.P., ibid, 1963-64; Pres., 1964-65 & 71-72; Bd. of Dirs., 1966-68 & 71-; Regional Legislative Chmn., Regional V.P., N.Y. State Life Underwriters Assn., 1965-68; Trustee Pension Plans, Spencel Mkt., Inc., 1970-; Skyline Elec. Supply Co., Inc., 1972- & Q. & S. Dining, Inc., 1973; Co-Trustee, Estate Trust, 1971-; Mbr., Profls. Serv. Corp., Physns. Planning Serv. Corp., 1973-; Chmn., Bd. of Dirs., Ames of Ithaca, Inc., 1974-; Bd. of Dirs., Compagni Constrn. Co., Inc., 1974-. Mbrships. incl: Home Life Pres. Coun., 1967-68 & 71-73; Million Dollar Round Table, 1967, 68, 71 & 73; Cortland Jr. Chmbr. of Comm.; B.P.O. Elks. Holds copyrights on animated statuettes. Recip. profl. awards. Address: 47 Fairview Dr., R.D. 3, Cortland, NY 13045, U.S.A. 130.

TUCKER, William Joseph, b. 19 Nov. 1896. Author; Journalist; Scientist; Publisher. Educ: Am. Inst. of Applied Psychol. Appts: Ed., 'Sci. & Astrol'; Astrol. Ed., The Mod. Mystic; Columnist to Sunday Dispatch (pen-name Scorpio & to Heim und Welt; T.A. in Min. of Supply (Bofors Sect.); Freelance Jrnist. & Sci. Rscher; Publr. (proprietor of Pythagorean Publs.) Fellow, Brit. Interplanetary Soc., 1966;

Mbrships: Soc. of Authors; Translators' Assn.; Brit. Astronom. Soc. Publs. incl: The 'How' of the Human Mind; The How, What & Why of Astrology; Astrology for Everyman; The Principles of Scientific Astrology; Astrology & the Abnormal Mind; Physics & Astrology', Genetics & Astrology; Astronomy for Students of Astrology; The Foundations of Astrology; Your Stars of Destiny; Astrology & Your Family Tree; Harmony of the Spheres; It is in the Stars; The Fixed Stars & your Horoscope; Autobiography of an Astrologer; Investigating & Coordinating the Psyche; Man & His Destiny. Hons. incl: D.Sc., 1937; Ph.D., 1937. Address: 45 Penshurst Ave., Sidcup, Kent, DZ15 9EZ. U.K. 4, 47.

TUCKERMAN, Charles S., b. 2 Oct. 1922. Professor. Educ: A.B., Harvard Coll., 1948; M.A., Harvard Univ., 1949; Ph.D., ibid, 1958. Appts: Serv. w. Army of U.S., 1942-45; Translator sci. lib. U.S. Patent Off., Wash., 1959; Asst. Prof. of German & Germanics, Tulane Univ., New Orleans, 1960-62; Asst. Prof. of French & Linguistics, Rensselaer Polytechnic Inst., Troy, N.Y., 1962-. Mbr., Linguistic Soc. of Am. Author of article on Jabberwocky, Explicator, 1972. Address: RD2, Averill Park, NY 12018, U.S.A. 6, 13.

TUFTS, John Marshall, b. 1 Sept. 1914. Professor of English. Educ: Ed.D., Columbia Univ., U.S.A; M.A., ibid; B.S., Hamilton Coll. Appts: Pub. High Schl. Tchr., 1938-41; Lt., USNR, 1941-45; High Schl. Tchr., 1946-48; Grad. Study, 1948-51; Fac. Mbr., Western Conn. State Coll., 1951-. Mbrships: Advsry. Coun. to Bd. of Trustees, Conn. State Colls.; Past Pres., WCSC Fac. Assn., Brookfield Improvement Soc.; Exec. Bd. of State Fac. Assn.; AAUP; NEA; CEA; CSEA; NCTE; CCCC; Theta Delta Chi; Hon. Sec., Phi Delta Kappa, 1968. Publs: Reading Improvement in the English Program at Danbury State Teachers College; various stories, essays & poems; Teacher Education Quarterly (former editor). Hons. incl: USN Commendation Medal for Valor, 1944. Address: Rt. 25, Brookfield Ctr., CT 06805, U.S.A. 13.

TUGAULT, Jean Henri, b. 2 July 1909. Documentalist; Leisure Activities Organiser. Educ: Engr., Ecole Centrale des Arts & Manufactures; Dip., Adv. Studies, Econs. & Pub. Law; State Dip., Chartered Acct.; Auditor, Ct. of Appeals, Paris. Appts. incl: Chartered Acct., 1942-64; Auditor, then Trustee, Registered cos., 1942-72; var. mandates & missions, France & abroad; Rep., Gen. Confedn. of Agric., Nat. Commn. on Interprofl. Acctcy. Plan, 1947; Min. of Agric. Rep., European Commn. to formulate European Agricl. Acctcy. Plan, Rome, 1947; Mbr., Nat. Jury, Chartered Accts. Exams., 1949-58; Prof., Acctcy. Inst., Nat. Conservatory of Arts & Trades, 1950-51; Creator, course on agricl. cost price calculation, ibid. Mbrships: Fndr., Les Amis des Sagathèques (cupboard of tales), meetings for telling stories & just talking, 1968; Pres., ibid, 1972-. Address: 154 Rue de Vaugirard, 75015 Paris, France. 43, 91.

TUGGLE, H. Cherry, b. 9 Dec. 1942. Real Estate Developer; Company President. Educ: Grad., Emory Univ. Grad. Schl. Bus. Admin., Atlanta, Ga., 1965. Appts: Pres., Tuggle Enterprises, 1963-, Massey Jr. Coll., Atlanta, Ga., 1970-71; Bd. Chmn., Vinyloy Products, Inc., Stone Mountain, Ga., 1971-; Chmn., Tuggle Fndn. Inc., Atlanta, 1967-; V.P., Mews Dev. Corp., 1973-; Pres., Inter-Urban Enterprises Ltd., 1974-. Mbrships: Ga. Real Estate Commn.; Atlanta Real Estate Bd. Address: Tuggle Enterprises, P.O. Box 2076, Atlanta, GA 30301, U.S.A. 7.

TUITA, b. 29 Aug. 1920. Civil Servant. Educ: Wesley Coll., Auckland, N.Z. Appts: 2nd Ltd., Tongan Army, 1942; Clerk, Supreme Ct., Tonga, 1942, Registrar, 1945, 1953; Asst. Sec., Prime Min.'s Off., Tonga, 1953; Gov. of Vava'u, 1956; Min. of Lands & Survey, Min. of Hlth., 1966; Dpty. Prime Min. of Tonga, 1972. Mbrships: Hon. Mbr., Nuku'Alofa Club, Nuku'Alofa Yacht & Motor Boat Club; Life Mbr., Tonga & Helepeku Clubs. Noble of the Realm, at death of father, 1972. Address: Mahinafekite, Nuku'Alofa, Tonga Islands.

TULIN, Stephen Wise, b. 30 Oct. 1928. Lawyer. Educ: B.A., Oberlin Coll., 1949; LL.B., Yale Univ., 1954. Appts: Law Clerk, U.S. Dist. Ct., Southern Dist., N.Y., 1954-55; Admitted N.Y. Bar, 1955; U.S. Dist. Ct., Southern Dist., 1956; U.S. Ct. of Appeals, 2nd Circuit, 1957; Assoc., Paul Weiss, Rifkind & Garrison, N.Y.C., 1956-61; Ptnr., Polier, Tulin & Clark, N.Y.C., 1961-. Mbrships: Bd. of Dirs., Am. Technion Soc.; Bd. of Dirs., Palestine Endowment Fund, & Bloomingdale House of Music; Sec., Bd. of Dirs., Shirley & Sophie Cohen Fndn.; Sec., Tappanz Fndn.; Sec., Kenworthy-Swift Fndn.; Order of Coif; Phi Beta Kappa. Address: 16 Walnut Ave., Larchmont, NY 10538, U.S.A. 2, 6.

TULK, Alfred James, b. 3 Oct. 1899. Artist; Painter. Educ: B.F.A., Yale Univ., 1923; M.F.A., Univ. Guanajuato, Mexico, 1962. Appts: Asst. to Ezra Winter, Mural Artist, N.Y.C., 1924, J. Monroe Hewlett, 1925; Dir., Mural Dept., Rambusch Decorating Co., N.Y.C., 1926-44; Instr., Art Dept., Pub. Schl. System, Stamford, Conn., 1939-42, N. Haven, Conn., 1964-60. Mbrships: Nat. Soc. Mural Painters, N.Y.C.; Mbr. Emeritus, N. Haven Art Guild, Conn. Mural works incl: Culver Mil. Acad., Ind.; State Univ., Edinboro, Pa.; St. Ignatius Ch., Chgo. Var. stained glass & mosaic works. 45 paintings for U.S. Armed Servs., WW II. Many solo exhibs. inclng. Art Mus., Hollywood, Fla., Birmingham, Ala., Architectural League of N.Y. Hons. incl: Oil Painting Prize, Greenwich Soc. of Artists, Conn., 1936; Patriotic Serv. Award, U.S. War Dept., WW II. Address: 210 Upper State St., N. Haven, CT 06473, U.S.A. 6, 19.

TUNDO, M. Piero, b. 29 Nov. 1893. Writer, Publicist. Educ: Dr., Soc. Sci.; Dr., Cosmopsychobiophys., Trieste Univ., Italy. Mbrships: Grand Master, Universal Masonry, Scottish Rite; Prima Linea Comm.; Pub. Opinion Movement. Publs: La via maestra della pace; Chi era Auro Principe; L'Universo e l'Uomo; I segreti della massoneria; Al di là delle Tenebre; Si vis pacem...; Non è vero che le Pace è una Utopia; Per la pace generale e la fratellanza universale; Fasti e Nefasti delle Scienze. Hons. incl: Kt., Grand Cross, Star of Peace; Grand. Off., Crown of Italy; Grand Off., Mil. Imperial Constantinian Order, St. George the Martyr; Kt. & Consul, Sovereign Mil. Order, Kts. of Colombo; Kt., Ordo Supremos Militaris Templi Hierosolimitani; Kt., Brotherhood of Pegasus; Off., Génie Francais. Address: Corso Umberto 1, N.13, Brindisi, Italy, 1.

TUNSTALL, Velma (Mrs. Earl A. Tunstall), b. 11 Aug. 1914. Poet. Mbrships: Calif. State Poetry Soc.; Calif. Fedn. of Chaparral Poets; Nat. Fedn. of State Poetry Socs., Inc. Publs: Shadows on My Soul (book of love poems); num. contbns. to anthols., papers & mags. Has sold works for TV & radio prodn. Hons: Hall of Fame in W. Plains, Mo. (home town); Beaudoin Gemstone Award, Nat. Fedn. of State Poetry Socs., 1973. Address: 928 Third Place, Upland, CA 91786, U.S.A. 5, 11, 57.

TUNSTILL, Garland Albert, b. 16 Nov. 1901. Lawyer; Government Relations Consultant. Self-employed. One of 43 Dirs. in 17 Countries of Western Hemisphere of Movimento Pro Federación Americana, Buenos Aires, Argentina. Author of Govt. Reports. Address: 3613 Audubon Place, Apt. B, Houston, TX 77006, U.S.A. 7, 16, 22.

TUOHY, William, b. 1 Oct. 1926. Journalist. Educ: B.A., Northwestern Univ. Appts: Reporter-Night City Ed., San Fran. Chronicle, 1952-58; Writer, Ed. & Corres., Newsweek mag., 1959-66; Saigon Bur. Chief, LA Times, 1966-68; Beirut Bur. Chief, ibid, 1968-71; Rome Bur. Chief, 1971-. Mbrships: Overseas Press Club of Am.; Stampa Estera, Rome. Hons: Headliners Award, 1965; Pulitzer Prize for Int. Reporting, 1969; Best For. Reporting Award, Overseas Press Club, 1970. Address: Los Angeles Times; 51 Piazza di Spagna, Rome, Italy.

TUPPER, Robert Ingersoll, b. 2 May 1921. Real Estate Developer. Educ: Univ. of N.C., 1942-43. Appts: Serv. WWII w. U.S.N.R., Metal Engr.; Pres., Hebron Dev. Corp.; Real Estate Developer, Builder, Sales Commercial & Residential. Mbrships: Dir., Hebron Lions Club; Past Pres., E. Ctrl. Bd. of Realtors; Selectman, Town of Otisfield, Me.; Pres., Men's Fellowship, Hebron Congregational Ch.; Dir., State of Conn. Bd. of Realtors. Address: P.O. Box 52, Main St., Hebron, CT 06248, U.S.A. 6.

TURK, William Luther, b. 10 May 1929. Superintendent of Schools. Educ: B.S. in Ed., S.W. Mo. State Univ., 1952; M.S. in Ed., Univ. of Mo., Columbia, 1960. Appts: Tchr., Mt. Vernon H.S., Mo., 1953-62; H.S. Prin., Greenfield H.S., ibid, 1962-65; Supt. of Schls., Greenfield R-IV Schls., 1965-. Mbrships: Past Pres., 1st V.P. & 2nd. V.P., S.W. Mo. Tchrs. Assn.; Mo. & Am. Assns. of Schl. Admnstrs.; Phi Delta Kappa; Exec. Bd. Ozark Area, Boy Scouts of Am.; Kappa Alpha Order; Past Chmn., Mo. 7th Congressional Dist. Young Democs.; Presby. Ch.; Mo. State Tchrs. Assn.; Participant, Am. Assn. of Schl. Admnstrs. Int. Field Study Mission to Soviet Union, 1973; Deleg., NEA Conven., 1969., Mo. Dept. of Educ. Guide for Jrnlsm., 1965; 1st Nat. Conf. of Compensatory Educ., Wash. D.C., 1968; Bd. Regents, S.W. Mo. State Univ., 1973; Mo. Coun. on Higher Pub. Educ., 1973-. Author of articles in: News Notes Wall St. Jrnl. Newspaper Fund, Inc., 1967; Schl. & Community, 1967; Taylor Talk, 1969; Mo. Guidance & Counseling Bulletin, 1968. Address: R. Rte. 2-Box 135, Mt. Vernon, MO 65712, U.S.A. 8.

TURKAY, Osman (Mustafa), b. 16 Mar. 1927. Journalist; Writer. Educ: Regent St. Polytech., London, U.K.; Univ. of London. Appts. incl: Ed. & Ldr. Writer, Bozleurt; Mbr., Cyprus Turkish Consultative Assembly, 1959-61; Freelance Jrnlist, Ed., Vatan, 1969-73; Sec.-Gen., Cyprus Turkish Assn., London; Ed., Turkish-Engl. Mag., Toplumun Sesi. Fndr. Fellow, Int. Poetry Soc. Mbrships. incl: Int. PEN; Poetry Soc., London; Nat. Union of Jrnlists; Int. Commn., Centro Studi e Scambi Int. Publs: Septet, 1959; Somnambulist, 1969; Waking to the Light with Beethoven, 1970; Travelling the Universal Dream, 1971; The Doomsday Observations, 1974; translator, T.S. Eliot, etc. Somnambulist chosen as one of best book of poems, Int. (Turkish) PEN. Address: 22 Ave. Mansions, Finchley Rd., London, N.W.3, U.K. 11.

TÜRKER, Rüstü Kâzim, b. 1 May 1928. Professor of Pharmacology. Educ: Fac. of Med.,

Istanbul Univ., Turkey, 1952; Grad. Trng., Dept. of Pharmacol. & Clin. Therapeutics, 1956. Appts: Chief Res., Dept. of Pharmacol., Istanbul Univ., 1956-61; Assoc. Prof., ibid, 1961-63; Assoc. Prof., Dept. of Pharmacol., Ankara Univ., 1963-64; Prof., ibid, 1967-70, '72-; Rsch. Fellow, Rsch. Div., Cleveland Clin. Fndn., U.S.A., 1964-66; Full Staff, ibid, 1970-72. Mbrships: AAAS; Am. Soc. for Pharmacol. & Exptl. Therapeutics; Int. Soc. for Hypertension; Nat. Geo. Soc.; Turkish Pharmacol. Soc.; Turkish Physiol. Soc. Contbr. to books & jrnls. Named, Disting. Sci. in Med. Scis., Turkish Sci. & Tech. Rsch. Assn., 1973. Address: Dept. of Pharmacol., Fac. of Med., Univ. of Ankara, Sihhiye, Ankara, Turkey.

TURKOW, Jonas, b. 15 Feb. 1898. Theatre Director; Author; Translater. Educ: H.S.; Theatrical Seminars, Poland & Austria. Appts. incl: Theatre Dir., Cracow, 1926-27, Warsaw, 1929-30, 1938-39, Vilna, 1932-33, Danzig, 1937-38; Dir., Yiddish Drama & Hebrew Theatrical Schls., Vilna, 1933-34; Sect. Hd., Jewish orgs., Warsaw Ghetto, 1939-42; Dir., Jewish Auditions, State Radio, Poland, 1944-45; Dir., Pkwy. Theatre, N.Y.C., U.S.A., 1952, Roosevelt Theatre, 1954; Researcher & Archivist, Yivo Inst. Jewish Rsch., N.Y.C., 1954-66. Mbr., var. Jewish & profl. orgs. Author, num. books in Hebrew, Yiddish, Spanish, Polish, French & Engl. Yiddish translations, German, Russian & Polish plays. Hons: Decoration for Pre-State Servs., Israel, 1968; Israeli Medal for Nazi resistance; var. literary awards. Address: 5 Rehov Uziel, P.O. Box 1050, Bat-Yam, Israel. 55, 94.

TURKOW, Marc, b. 28 Apr. 1904. Journalist. Appts: Ed. staff, Der Moment, Warsaw, Poland, corres., League of Nations, Geneva; Fndr. Ed., Dos Poilishe Yiddeńtum, Biblioteca Popular Judia; Rep., World Jewish Congress, 1954-, Sec. Gen., Latin Am. br. 1959-. Mbrships: Hon. Pres., Fedn. Polish Jews in Argentina, S. Am. Fedn. of Jewish students. Publs: (Yiddish) Roosevelts Amerike, 1937; Oif Yiddishe Felder, 1938; Malka Owsiana derseilt, 1946; Die letzte fun a groisen dor, 1954; (Polish) Zydzi y Mechesi, 1930; Gadnsk na Wukjanie, 1932; rewolucja Amerikanska, 1937; (Spanish) Janusz Korczak, 1937. Address: Aguero 1775, Buenos Aires, Argentina. 55.

TROJAK, Therese Anne, b. 17 Nov. 1929. Bank Officer; Teller & Bookkeeper. Educ: Phillips H.S., Wis., 1947; Chgo. Schl. Nursing Corres. Course, 1950-51; N. Central Tech. Inst. Adult Educ., 1971, 1972, 1974. Appts: Clerk & Bookkeeper, State Bank of Phillips, Wis., 1950-53, Teller & Bookkeeper, 1953-55, 1961-70, Asst. Cashier, 1970-; Snowmobile Safety Instr., Wis. Dept. Natural Resources, 1972-. Mbrships. incl: Sec., Ladies Drum & Bugle Corps, 1951-53; Treas., Lugerville PTA, 1962-63, Pres., 1963-65, 1968-70, Sec.-Treas., 1970-; Treas., S. Price Co. Am. Red Cross, 1966-68; Chmn., Price Co. Friendship Campaign for Retarded Children, 1972; V.P., Women's Softball League, Mgr., Softball Team, 1973. Recip., Wis. Am. Red Cross Achievement Award, 1973. Address: Luger Rte., Box 174, Phillips, WI 54555, U.S.A. 5.

TURNBULL, Alan Ewart, b. 3 June 1927. Journalist; Company Director. Educ: Maidstone Grammar Schl., U.K.; London Schl. of Econs. Appts. incl: Lt., Army; News Ed., Contract Jrnl., 1948; Dpty. Orgr., Pub. Works Exhib.; Ed., 4 Municipal Publs., 1951-54; Feature Writer, Hultons Press, 1954-57; Dir., Sidney Barton Ltd., 1957-61; Mng. Dir., The Int. News Serv. Ltd., 1961-. Mbrships. incl: Inst. of Marketing; Inst. of P.R.; Press Advsr., Exec.

Assn. of Gt. Britian; Press Club; Market Rsch. Inst. Publs. incl: How to Drive, 1958. Address: Hillside, Lubbock Rd., Chislehurst, Kent. U.K.

TURNELL, (George) Martin, b. 23 Mar. 1908. Solicitor; Writer. Educ: M.A., Corpus Christi Coll., Cambridge, U.K., 1930; Sorbonne, France, 1930-31. Appts: Publrs. Asst., Sheed & Ward, 1932-34; Asst., Prog. Contracts Dept., BBC, 1939-45; Asst. Hd., ibid, 1945-59; Hd., 1959-69. Fellow, Royal Soc. Lit. Mbrships: MCC; Soc. Authors; Brit. Film Inst.; Inst. of Contemp. Arts; Inst. Français du Royaume-Uni. Publs. incl: The Novel in France, 1950; Baudelaire: A Study of his Poetry, 1953; Jacques Rivière, 1953; The Art of French Fiction, 1959; Modern Literature & Christian Faith, 1961; Graham Green: A Critical Essay, 1967; Jean Racine: Dramatist, 1972. Translator, var. books from French. Address: 37 Smith St., London, SW 3 4EP, U.K. 3, 30.

TURNER, Amos, b. 18 Feb. 1926. Electrical Engineer. Educ: B.S.E.E., Inst of Technol., Munich, 1949; M.S.E.E., Ill. Inst. of Technol., Chgo., 1955. Appts: Chief Elec. Engr., Meissner Engrs., Chgo., 1959-62; V.P.-Treas., HST Mgmt. Inc., Hoyer-Schlesinger-Turner Inc., Chgo., 1962-. Mbrships: Chmn., Ind. Comm., Chgo. Sect., Am. Inst. of Elec. Engrs.; Tau Beta Pi; Eta Kappa Nu; Nat. Soc. of Profl. Engrs.; IEEE; Am. Inst. of Steel Engrs. Contbr. paper, 'Cement Plant Lighting', Cement Ind. Conf., Am. inst. of Elec. Engrs., St. Louis, Mo., 1962. Recip. Award of Merit for Lighting Excellence, 1968. Address: 300 W. Adams St. - Room 630, Chgo., IL 60606, U.S.A. 2, 8.

TURNER, Bessye Tobias, b. 10 Oct. 1917. Educator; Poet. Appts. incl: Asst. Prof. Engl. & Dir., Dramatics, Alcorn A & M Coll., 1955-62; Asst. Prof., Engl. & Speech, Southern Univ., 1962-63; Asst. Prof., Engl. Speech, Tex. Southern Univ., 1964; Asst. Prof., Engl. & Speech, Miss. Valley State Coll., Itta Bena, 1968-. Mbrships: Int. Poetry Soc.; The N.Y. Poetry Forum; IBA; Hon. Mbr., Ctr. Studi e Scambi Int., Italy; Speech Communication Assn.; Nat. Histl. Soc., 1973; United Meth. Women, 1973-. Participant, Int. Exhib. Art & Poetry, La Librae, Florence, Italy, 1971. Publs. incl: Just One Day of Positives; So Misty Are My Eyes For You; La Librae: an Anthology of Poetry for Living, 1969; Bouquet of Poems, 1971; Quaderni Di Poesia—Peace & Love, "Bouquets of Poetry" one poem, 1973 & "Justice Must Incorporate Mercy", Albo d'oro 1973—XV Anniversario, Rome, Italy. Participant, Poetry Display - Peace & Love, Int. Exhib. Art & Poetry, Rome, 1972. Address: 829 Wall St., McComb, MS 39648, U.S.A. 5, 7, 11, 13, 125, 128, 132, 138.

TURNER, Carlton Edgar, b. 13 Sept. 1940. Professor of Organic Chemistry; University Administrator. Educ: B.S., Univ. of Southern Miss., Hattiesburg, 1966; M.S., ibid, 1968; Ph.D., 1970. Appts: Rsch. Chemist, Miss. Rsch. & Dev. Ctr., Jackson, 1968-70; Postdoctoral Rsch. Assoc., Marihuana Proj., Dept. of Pharmacology, Schl. of Pharmacy, Univ. of Miss., 1970-71, 1971-72, Assoc. Dir., Rsch. Inst. of Pharmaceutical Scis., Schl. of Pharmacy, 1973-. Mbrships. incl: AAAS: Am. Chem. Soc.; Soc. of Econ. Botany; Am. Soc. Pharmacognosy; Assn. Farmaceutica Mexicana, A.C.; Kappa Psi; Rho Chi; Sigma Xi. Profl. papers & reports. Contbr., var. jrnls. & publs., mainly Jrnl. of Pharmaceutical Sci. Recip., var. hon. Fellowships & appts. Address: Research Inst. of Pharmaceutical Sciences, School of Pharmacy, Univ. of Mississippi, University, MS 38677, U.S.A. 14, 125.

TURNER, Dennis Edgar, b. 29 Oct. 1926. Managing Director. Educ: B.Sc.Econ., London Schl. of Economics, U.K., 1948. Appts: Managing Dir., Peter Jones Dept. Store, London, 1962-67; Indl. Advsr., Dept. of Economic Affairs, H.M. Govt., U.K., 1967-69; Gen. Mgr., Retailing, Waltons, Australia, 1969-71; Managing Dir., Lamson Inds., ibid, 1972-. Mbr: Beaumaris Yacht Club. Hon: 1st Nat. Serviceman to receive RAF Sword of Honour, 1948. Address: 26 Gladstone St., Sandringham, Vic., Australia 3191. 23.

TURNER, Ed, b. 25 Sept. 1935. Journalist. Educ: B.A., Univ. of Okla., 1957. Appts: Prod.-Dir., documentary films, Univ. of Okla.; Pol. Reporter, KWTV, Okla. City; Newcaster, ibid; Press Sec., Bud Wilkinson U.S. Senate Campaign (Republican-Okla.); News Dir., WTTG, Wash. D.C.; V.P., News & Pub. Affairs, Metromedia Inc.; V.P., News, U.P. Int. TV News; Exec. Prod., Evans-Novak (syndicated columnist) Report, Jack Anderson Report & num. news specials. Mbrships: Phi Gamma Delta; Nat. Press Club; Radio TV News Dirs. Assn. Hons: Best Educational Documentary, Cannes Film Festival; Sigma Delta Chi award for best reporting, 1962; 4 U.P. Int. Awards for best reporting; 6 Emmies for news progs. or specials, Wash. D.C.; Ohio State Award for best 1 hour news special. Address 321 W. 44, N.Y.C., NY, U.S.A. 16, 65.

TURNER, Elizabeth Esta Lane (Mrs. Earl Turner), b. 15 Apr. 1900. Teacher; Cashier Typist. Educ: Okla. Univ., Ctrl. Tchr.'s Coll., Edmond, Okla. & Okla. City Univ.; Power Machine Ops. Course, Franklin Vocational Schl. Appts. incl: Schl. Tchr., Norman, Okla.; Tube Room Cashier, Miami & N.Y.; Owner w. husband, Ice Cream Stn. & Store, Antlers & store, Boggy Bridge, Atoka Co.; Clerk-Typist, Phila. Navy Yard, 1942-46 & Tinker Field AF Base, Okla City, Okla., 1950; Piano & Accordian Tchr. & presented progs. over 2 local radio stns. Mbrships. incl: Order of Eastern Star, 1950- holding many major offices inclng. Worthy Matron & Grand Comm. Mbr.; Rugged Cross Shrine, White Shrine of Jerusalem, 1951- holding major offices inclng. Noble Grand, Savannah Rebekah Lodge; Hemerocallis Soc. Address: R 3 Box 84 - McAlister, OK, U.S.A.

TURNER, (Henry) Arlin, b. 25 Nov. 1909. Professor; Editor. Educ: B.A., W. Tex. State Univ., 1927; M.A., Univ. of Tex., 1930; Ph.D., ibid, 1934. Appts. incl: Instr., Univ. of Tex., 1934-36; Instr.-Prof., La. State Univ., 1936-53; Prof., Duke Univ., 1953; Chmn., Dept. of Engl., ibid, 1958-64; Ed., Am. Lit., 1969-; Mgng. Ed., ibid, 1954-63; Vis. Prof., Canada, 1951, India, 1964; Fulbright Lectr., Australia, 1952, U.K., 1966-67. Mbrships. incl: MLA of Am.; Edit. Bd., S. Atlantic Quarterly, 1956-; Nat. Coun. Tchrs. Engl.; Coll. Engl. Assn.; Soc. Am. Histns. Phi Beta Kappa. Publs: Nathaniel Hawthorne: An Introduction & Interpretation, 1961; Mark Twain & George W. Cable: The Record of Literary Friendship, 1960; George W. Cable, A Biography, 1956, 68; Hawthorne as Editor, 1941, 71. Hons. incl: Guggenheim Rsch. Award, 1969. Address: Dept. of English, Duke Univ., Durham, NC 27708, U.S.A. 2, 7, 13, 30.

TURNER, Herbert Keith, b. 23 Apr. 1910. Mining Consultant; Company Director. Educ: Broken Hill Tech. Coll., Australia. Appts. incl: Jr., Underground Off., Zinc Corp., Broken Hill, 1929-35; Mining Engr., Société Chimique du Chrome, New Caledonia, 1936-37; Field Engr., Wellington Alluvials, N.S.W., 1938; Asst. Mgr., Ronpibon Tin, Thailand, 1939-41; Mgr., Dorset Tin, & Dir.-Cons., Endurance Tin, Tas., 1946-60; Dir., Aberfoyle Holdings, Aberfoyle

Tin, Ardlethan Tin, Greenbushes Tin, & Paringa Mining & Exploration Ltd., 1960-69; Dir. & Cons., Quest Mining & Exploration Ltd., Melbourne, Vic.; Dir. & Cons., Murchison Ctrl. Mines Ltd., Melbourne; Dir., Amber Gold Ltd., Melbourne; Dir., Minefields Exploration N.L., Melbourne; Dir., Colortone Holdings Ltd., Melbourne; Dir., Consolidated Exploration N.L., Melbourne; Dir., Austral Mining Ltd., Adelaide, S.A.; Dir., Southern Cross Mineral Exploration Ltd., Auckland, N.Z. Mbrships. incl: Australian Inst. of Mining & Metallurgy; Co. Dirs. Assn. of Australia. Address: 2nd Floor, 100 Collins St., Melbourne, Vic., Australia 3000. 23.

TURNER, Mary Louise, b. 13 Oct. 1925. Librarian; Psychologist. Educ: A.B., Univ. of Mo., Columbia, 1967; M.A., ibid, 1968. Appts: Bookeeper/Lib. Asst., Little Dixie Regional Lib., Moberly, Mo., 1959-62; Lib. Asst., Univ. of Mo., Columbia, 1962-67; Cons., Instnl. Lib. Servs., Mo. State Lib., 1968-69; Libn. Mo. State Trng. Schl. for Boys, Boonville, 1969-71; Libn., Parkway Schl. Dist., Chesterfield, Mo., 1971-73; Ref. Libn. Meramec Community Coll., summer, 1972; Hd. Libn., El Paso Community Coll., Tex., 1973-. Mbrships: Beta Phi Mu; ALA; Tex. & Border Regional Lib. Assns.; El Paso Community Coll. Jt. Fac.-Senate; AAUW; Pres., Mo. State Lib. Staff Assn., 1969; Mo. Assn. Schl. Libns.; Deleg., Mo. State Tchrs. Assn., 1972-73; Chmn., Bibliotherapy Comm., Am. Hosp. & Inst. Lib. Assoc., 1971. Hons. incl: Mo. State Lib. Schlrship, 1967; Cert. of Recog. for volunteer work, Mid-Mo. Mental Hlth. Assn., Columbia, Mo., 1968. Address: 299 King's Point Drive, Apt. 103, El Paso, TX 79912, U.S.A. 5, 138.

TURNER, Mina Teada Bogle (Mrs. Veno W. Turner), b. 29 Nov. 1901. Teacher of Piano, Voice, Speech; Painter; Poet. Educ: Music Study under Grace Switzer, Paul Bentley, Sherwood Music Schl., Edward Hearn, Alfred Richter, Grady Barnes, Navarro Coll.; Art under Mrs. Louis Durst, Art Publn. Soc. Appts: Tchr., Music, Piano, Vocal, Song Speech; Former Owner, Ladies' Tailor Shop; Owner, Turner Music Schl. Mbrships: Pres., Corsicana (Tex.) Music Tchrs. Assn.; Past Chmn., Nat. Guild of Piano Tchrs.; Past 2nd V.P., Nevin Fedn. Music Club; Dir., Bd. Mbr., Women's Club House, Corsicana; Fndr., Myrtle S. Dockrum Mem. Schlrship. Fndn., in Piano, Navarro Coll.; Mem. Hosp. Aux.; Candidate for Mayor, Corsicana. Compositions: 4-pt. harmony 'Hymnals', piano solos, lyrics; Num. poems; Paintings, inclng. baptistry mural; Needlework art. Hons: Gold Seal Certs., Music Tchrs. Nat. Assn., Am. Coll. of Musicians, Sherwood Music Schl., Tchrs. of Applied Music, State Dept. of Educ., Tex. Educ. Agcy.; Hon. Mention, The Old Chisholm Trail, oil painting. Address: 1321 N. Beaton, Corsicana TX 75110, U.S.A. 125.

TURNER, Sally B. (Mrs.) Bank Director; Homemaker. Appts. incl: Automobile Dept., State Capitol Frankfort, Ky., 1925-26; Libn., Johnson Co. Lib., 1940-41; Coal, Oil & Real Estate, 1959-; Dir., 1st Nat. Bank, 1963-. Mbrships: Pres., Ladies Div. & other offs., Paintsville Country Club, 1949-60; Trustee, Mayo Meth. Ch., 1959-67, 1968-70, Pres. & other offs., Wesleyan Serv. Guild of Ch.; Admimstrative Ch. Bd., 1959-; Am. Red Cross (Grey Lady); Treas., Johnson Co. Histl. Soc., 1963-; Pastoral Rels. Comm., 1963-; Parsonage Comm., 1963-. Hons: Paintsville Country Club Golf Champion, 1930, 1944; Cert. of Appreciation, Am. Red Cross. Address: P.O. Box 726, Paintsville, KY 41240, U.S.A. 5, 138.

TURNER, Stanley, b. 16 May 1933. Administrator. Educ: B.S., St. Paul's Coll.,

Lawrenceville, Va., U.S.A.; M.A., Hampton Inst., Hampton, ibid; Postgrad. work, Va. Univ., Charlottesville; Va. State Coll., Petersburg, ibid; Old Dominion Univ., Norfolk, ibid; Va. Polytech. Inst., Blacksburg, (working towards Ed.D.), ibid. Appts: Tchr., Sussex Co. Schl. Bd., Va.; Tchr. & Civil Defense Coord., Isle of Wight Co., ibid; Supvsr., Voctnl. Educ., Va. Schl., Hampton, ibid; Dir., Voctnl. Educ., ibid. Mbrships: Am. Personnel & Guid. Assn.; Am. Assn. Schl. Admin.; Nat. Schl. Pub. Rels Assn.; Am. Instrs. for Deaf; Cooperative Area Man Power Planning System & Man Power Planning Staff; Nat. Assn. Cos.; Isle of Wight Co. Org. Better Pub. Schls.; Notaries Pub. Assn.; Va. Coun. Human Rights; NAACP; Isle of Wight Co. Bd. Zoning Appeals; Charter Mbr., Nat. Assn. Trade & Indl. Educ.; Omega Psi Phi; Treas., Chiloh Bapt. Ch., Windsor, Va. Hons: Award, Patriotic Servs., Dept. of Treasury; Man of Yr., Progressive Men's Org., Isle of Wight Co., 1971. Address: Va. Schl. at Hampton, 700 Shell Rd., Hampton, VA 23661, U.S.A. 125.

TURNER, Telcine Eureka, b. 3 Dec. 1943. Teacher. Educ: B.A., Univ. of the W.I., Jamaica, 1969; Dipl. Educ., ibid, 1970; M.A., Northwestern Univ., Evanston, Ill., U.S.A., 1973. Appts: Asst. Tchr., pub. schls., Bahamas, 1965-66, Baillou Hill H.S., ibid, 1970-71, Bahamas; Tchrs. Coll., 1971-72; Hd. of Engl. Dept., Bahamas Tchrs. Coll., 1973-. Mbrships: Riding Club, Univ. of W.I., 1969-70; V.P., The Bahama Drama Circle, 1971-72; Sec., P.T.A., Baillou Hill H.S., 1970-71; Northwestern Univ. Alumni Assn. Author of num. jrnl. articles. Address: P.O. Box N 4380, Nassau, N.P., Bahamas, W. Indies.

TURNER, Walter Leroy, b. 29 Mar. 1924. Teacher; Supervisor. Educ: B.S., Roosevelt Univ., Chgo., Ill., 1949; M.A., N.Y. Univ., 1953; Further study, var. colls. Appts. incl: Rsch. Chemist, Harvard Univ. Med. Schl., Boston, 1950-51; Schl. Soc. Wkr., Hillsborough Co. Pub. Schls., 1951-53; Dean of Boys, Carver Jr. H.S., ibid, 1955-56; Guidance Counselor, H.W. Blake H.S., 1956-63; Administrative Dean, ibid, 1963-69; Supvsr. of Re-Educ., 1969-. Mbrships. incl: Sec., Mbrship. Chmn., Phi Delta Kappa; Tampa Urban League; Am. Assn. of Behavior Therapy; Hillsborough Admnstrs. & Supvsrs. Assn.; Sec., Landmark Lodge 93, Masons; Institution Rep., Boy Scouts of Am. Author of articles in jrnls. Hons. incl: Award, Citizens Alert, 1970; Award for outstanding servs., Tampa Model Cities Work Ctr., 1973. Address: 2207 N. Grady Ave., Tampa, FL 33607, U.S.A.

TURNEY, Alfred Walter, b. 6 Aug. 1916. College Professor; Retired Military Officer. Educ: B.A., M.A., & Ph.D., Univ. of N.M., Albuquerque, U.S.A., 1969. Appts: Soldier, U.S. Army, 1938-41; Off., U.S. Army, 1941-63, retired as Lt. Col.; Assoc. Prof., Mod. Hist., Southwestern Okla. State Coll., Weatherford, 1967-. Mbrships: Retired Offs. Assn., Wash. D.C.; NEA; Southern Histl. Assn.; Rocky Mtn. Soc. Scis. Assn.; Okla. Assn. of Coll. Hist. Profs.; Phi Alpha Theta. Author, Disaster at Moscow, 1970. Hons. incl: Bronze Star, 1945; Am. Medal, European Medal, Pacific Medal, & WWII Victory Medal, 1946; Korean War Medal, 1955; Repub. of Korea Citation, 1955; U.S. Army Commendation Medal, 1963. Address: 1529 Pine Ave., Weatherford, OK 73096, U.S.A.

TURSI, Peter Budd, b. 4 Mar. 1919. Corporation Executive; Metallurgist. Educ: B.S., Temple Univ.; Drexel Inst. of Technol. Appts: Metallurgist, 1949-52, Chief Metallurgist, 1952-62, Asst. Works Mgr.,

1962-66, Works Mgr., 1966-70, V.P. & Gen. Mgr., 1970-, Riverside Metals Corp. Mbrships: Am. Soc. for Metals; Am. Inst. of Mining & Metals Engrng.; Educ. Comm. for Metallurgy, Temple Univ.; Riverside Rotary Club (Pres.); Bd. of Educ. (Pres.); Episcopal Ch. Contbr. to profl. publs. Address: Riverside Metals Corp., Riverside, NJ 08075, U.S.A. 1.

TURTON, Reginald John, b. 6 Mar. 1932. Public Administrator. Educ: B.Sc., Birmingham Univ., U.K., 1953; Ph.D., ibid, 1956. Appts: Hd., Computer Servs. Group, Blackburn Aircraft Ltd., U.K., 1956-62; Prin. Programmer, Dept. of Defence, Australia, 1964-65; Asst. Sec., ibid, 1965-71; 1st Asst. Sec. (E.D.P.), 1971-. Mbrships: Sec.-Treas., 2nd Div. Offs. Assn., 1969-72; Australian Computer Soc.; Royal Inst. of Pub. Admin.; United Serv. Instn., Australia; Canberra Club, Australia; Fellow, Australian Computer Soc., 1969. Address: Dept. of Defence, Canberra, A.C.T., Australia 2601. 23.

TUSHINGHAM, Rita, b. 14 Mar. 1942. Actress. Stage appearances incl: The Changeling, The Kitchen, 1961; A Midsummer Night's Dream, Twelfth Night, The Knack, 1962; The Giveaway, 1969; Lorna & Ted, 1970; Mistress of Novices, 1972. Film appearances incl: A Taste of Honey, 1960; Girl with Green Eyes, 1963; Dr. Zhivago, 1965; The Trap, 1966; Diamonds for Breakfast, 1968; The Bed-Sitting Room, 1970; Straight on Till Morning, 1971; The Situation, 1972; Instant Coffee, 1973. Awards incl: Silver Heart, as Most Promising Newcomer, Variety Club, 1961; Best Actress, Cannes Film Festival, France, 1962; Best Actress, N.Y. Film Critics, 1963; Silver Heart, as Best Actress, 1964. Mexico Silver Goddess, as Best For. Actress, 1965. Address: ALS Mgmt. Ltd., 67 Brook St., London W1., U.K. 1, 138.

TUTHILL, Arthur H., b. 27 Mar. 1919. Metallurgical Engineer. Educ: B.Chem.Engrng., Univ. of Va., 1940; M.Sc., Metallurgy, Carnegie Inst. of Technol., 1946. Appts: Lt. Cmdr., USNR, 1941-46; Supt., Equipment Inspn. Dept. Esso Standard Oil (N.J.), 1948-50; Mats. Cons., E.I. du Pont, 1950-54; Pres., Valco Engrng. Inc., Baton Rouge, La., 1954-59; Int. Nickel Co., 1959-, Mgr., Marine Marketing, 1964-72, Proj. Grp. Mgr., Commercial Dev., 1972-. Mbrships: Marine Tech. Soc.; Soc. of Naval Archts. & Marine Engrs. Am. Soc. for Metals; Nat. Assn. of Corrosion Engrs.; Tau Beta Pi. Publs: Articles in profl. jrnls. & tech. papers. Hons: Raven Soc. Address: 3 Chapel Lane, Riverside, CT 06878, U.S.A.

TUTIN, Dorothy (Mrs. Derek Waring), b. 8 Apr. 1931. Actress. Educ: Royal Acad. of Dramatic Art. Parts incl: Rose, The Living Room; Katherine, Henry V; Sally Bowles, I am a Camera; St. Joan, The Lark; Catherine, The Gates of Summer; Hedwig, The Wild Duck; Viola, Twelfth Night; Juliet, Romeo & Juliet; Ophelia, Hamlet, Russia, 1958; Dolly, Once More with Feeling, 1959; Portia, Viola, Cressida, Stratford upon Avon, 1960; Juliet, Desdemona, ibid, 1961; Sister Jeanne, The Devils, 1961, 62; Vanya, Cherry Orchard, 1961; Cressida, Prioress, The Devils, Edinburgh, 1962; Polly Peachum, Beggars Opera, 1963; The Hollow Crown, N.Y.; Queen Victoria, Portrait of a Queen, 1965; Rosalind, As You Like It, Stratford, 1967, L.A., 1968; Portrait of a Queen, N.Y., 1968; Play on Love, 1970; Old Times, 1971; Peter Pan, 1971, 72; What Every Woman Knows, 1973. Films: The Beggars Opera; The Importance of Being Ernest; A Tale of Two Cities; Cromwell; Savage Messiah. Hons: Evening Standard Award for Best Actress,

1960; C.B.E., 1967; Variety Club of G.B. Film Actress Award, 1972. Address: c/o Peter Browne Management, 185 Oxford St., London, W.1., U.K. 1.

TUTOROW, Norman Eugene, b. 23 July 1934. Historian; Businessman. Educ: Dips., Naval Electronics Schl., 1953 & Marine Corps Radar Schl., 1954; A.B., San Diego State Coll.; 1958; M.A., Philos., Stanford Univ., 1960 Ph.D., ibid, 1968; M.A., Hist., San Jose State Coll., 1965; Dip., Anthony Real Estate Schl., San Jose, 1972; Grad., Realtors Inst., 1974; Real Estate Cert. Inst., 1974; further non-deg. work at these and many other instns. Appts. incl: Electronics Instr., Marine Corps. Radar Schl., San Diego, 1952-55; Environmental Techn. & Sr. Electronics Techn., Ctrl. Rsch. Div., Varian Assocs., Palo Alto., 1959-63; Instr., var. topics, W. Valley & Foothill Jr. Colls. & San Jose State Coll., 1964-67; Prof., Hist., Univ. of Santa Clara, 1967-69; Chief, Archives Br., L.A. Fed. Records Ctr., 1969-70; Cons., Nat. Archives & Records Ctr., San Fran., 1970; Fndr. & Pres., Peninsula Editl. Assoc., Sunnyvale, 1970-71; Owner-Broker, Golden State Realty, 1972-74; Tchr., Real Estate Econs., Foothill Coll., Real Estate Finance & Real Estate Prins., W. Valley Coll.; Anthony's Real Estate Schl., 1973-. Mbrships. incl: Alpha Mu Gamma; Phi Alpha Theta; Phi Kappa Phi; Judge Am. Hist. Symposia, 1968, 1969; Am. & Calif., Hist. Socs.; Org. of Am. Histns.; Westerns; Sunnyvale & San Jose Bds. of Realtors; Calif. Real Estate Assn. Publs: California—An Illustrated History (co-author), 1968; Leland Stanford—Man of Many Careers, 1971; pamphlets & articles in jrnls. Address: 233 W. Edith Ave., Los Altos, CA 94022, U.S.A.

TUTTLE, Lee Foy, b. 21 Jan. 1905. General Secretary, World Methodist Council. Educ: A.B., Duke Univ., 1927; B.D., Yale Divinity Schl., 1934; D.D., Elon Coll., 1955. Appts: Admitted to Western N.C. Conf., 1929; 1st Ch., Thomasville, N.C., 1939-44; Ctrl. Ch., Asheville, N.C., 1944-49; 1st Ch., Charlotte, N.C., 1949-56; Supt., Winston-Salem Dist., 1956-61. Mbrships: Rotary Clubs, Thomasville, Asheville, Winston-Salem & Waynesville, N.C.; Past Int. Pres., Lambda Chi Alpha. Publs: Name Dropping, By An Expert; Ed., "World Parish" (official publ. of World Meth. Coun.), proceedings of the Twelfth World Methodist Conference, num. brochures & pamphlets; Co-Ed., Proceedings of the Eleventh World Methodist Conference; Contbng. Ed., Encyclopedia of World Methodism. Recip. John Wesley Ecumenical Awards, Old St. Geo.'s Ch., Phila., 1968. Address: P.O. Box 518, Lake Junaluska, NC 28745, U.S.A. 2, 116.

TUTTLE, William McCullough, Jr., b. 7 Oct. 1937. Professor of History. Educ: B.A., Denison Univ., 1959; M.A., Univ. of Wis., 1964, Ph.D., 1967. Appts: Histn., Educl. Testing Serv., 1965-67; Asst. Prof.-Assoc. Prof., Univ. of Kan., 1967-; Sr. Fellow, Southern & Negro Hist., Johns Hopkins Univ., 1969-70; Rsch. Fellow, Charles Warren Ctr., Studies in Am. Hist., Harvard Univ., & Younger Humanist Fellow, Nat. Endowment for Humanities, 1972-73. Mbrships: Soc. & Org. of Am. Histns.; Am. & Southern Histl. Assns.; Assn., Study of Afro-Am. Life & Hist; Phi Alpha Theta; Phi Gamma Delta; Omicron Delta Kappa (Hon.). Publs: Race Riot, 1970; W.E.B. Du Bois; Great Life Observed, 1973; contbr. to profl. jrnls. Hons: Awards of Merit, Ill. State Histl. Soc., 1971, Am. Assn. State & Local Hist. 1972. Address: Dept. of Hist., Univ. of Kan., Lawrence, KS 66045, U.S.A. 8, 13, 30.

TUUKKANEN, Kalervo, b. 14 Oct. 1909. Composer; Conductor. Educ: Violin studies, 1914-1930; Comp. & theory studies under individual tutors; M.A., Helsinki Univ., 1933. Appts. incl: 1st Violin, sev. amateur, student & profl. orchs., 1920-35; Conductor, student, amateur & profl. orchs. & choirs, 1930-; Music Tchr., Viipuri Inst. of Music, 1935-38, Helsinki H.S. for Girls, 1938-67, Helsinki Soc. Univ., 1947-49, Helsinki Univ., 1947-48, 1955-56 & Sibelius Acad., 1971-; Vis. Prof., Chung Chi Coll., Chinese Univ. of Hong Kong, 1967-69. Conductor at many Concerts of own comps. played by Orchs. inclng. Viipuri Orch., Helsinki City Orch., Hong Kong Philharmonic Orch. Orchl. & Choral Conductor at many Finnish nat. music festivals. Musical Comps. incl: Symphs., Symphonic poems, Suites, Instrumental orchl. works, vocal music & incidental music for plays. Publs. incl: biography, Leevi Madetoja, 1947; travel book in prep.; num. articles in Music Critic. Mbrships: incl: State Music Commn., 1954-56, State Film Prize Comm., 1961-64 & State Art Comm., 1962-65; Fndr., Sec. & Bd. Mbr., Soc. of Finnish Composers, 1945-54. Recip of num. grants. Address: Apollonkatu 13 D 31, 00100 Helsinki 10, Finland. 10, 43.

TUXEN, S.L., b. 8 Aug. 1908. Keeper of Entomological Department. Educ: D.Sc., Univ. of Copenhagen, Denmark, 1933; Ph.D., ibid, 1944. Appts: Curator, Dept. of Insects, Zoological Mus., Copenhagen, 1933-58; Keeper, ibid, 1958-; Acting Dir., Zoological Mus., 1968. Mbrships. incl: Bd., Danish Entomological Soc., 1930-72, Pres., 1960-72; Permanent Comm., Int. Congresses of Entomol., 1951-72, Pres., 1964-72; Entomologiska Föreningen i Helsingfors; Accademia Nazionale Italiana di Entomologia; Entomological Soc. of U.S.S.R. Publs. incl: The Diptera of Iceland, 1952; The Hot Springs of Iceland & their Animal Communities, 1964; Et Sted ved Amazonas, 1972; Ed., Taxonomist's Glossary of Genitalia in Insects, 1956, 2nd edit. 1970; Rsch. papers. Address: Universitetets Zoologiske Museum, Universitetsparken 15, 2100 Copenhagen Ø, Denmark. 43, 50.

TUYPENS, Henry J-M., b. 21 Dec. 1894. Pharmacist; General Manager of Pharmaceutical Labs. Educ: B.Nat.Scis., Univ. of Louvain, 1913-14; Pharm.Scis., ibid, 1919, 20 & 21; Pharm. of Fac. of Pharm., 1921. B.Nat.Scis., Univ. of Utrecht, Netherlands, 1914-15. Appts: 4th title-holder, Tuypens Pharm., 1929-37; Gen. Mgr., Pres. of Bd., Tuypens Labs., Sint-Niklaas, 1937-; Gen. Mgr., Pres. of Bd., T.V.R. Ltd., Sint-Niklaas, 1967-. Mbrships: Fndng. Mbr., Rotary Club of Sint-Niklaas; Fedn. of Chem. Inds.; Assn. Gen. de l'Ind. du Mèdicament; 'Assn. Européenne des Spécialités Grand Public. Hons: Croix du Feu; Belgian War Cross w. palms; French War Cross w. bronze star; Chevalier de l'ordre de la Couronne, 1949; Médaille civile de Première Classe, Min. of Nat. Defence; Chevalier de l'Ordre de Léopold, 1959; Lauréat du Travail, Décoration d'argent, Ind. Chimique, Classe-Direction générale des enterprises; Off., Ordre Leopold II, Min. of Econ. Affairs, 1972. Address: H. Sakramentstraat 1, 1700 Sint-Niklaas, Belgium.

TVETERÅS, Harald Ludvig, b. 15 Oct. 1904. Director of Libraries. Educ: Cand.philol., 1932; Dr.philos., 1966. Appts: Hd. Libn., Royal Univ. Lib., Oslo, Norway; Chief Libn., ibid, 1953; Chief Libn., UNESCO Lib., Paris, France, 1947-48; Riksbibliotekar (Dir. of Norwegian Rsch. & Special Libs.), 1969-. Mbrships: Chmn., Norwegian Nat. Commn. for UNESCO, 1952-67; Vice Chmn., ibid, 1967-73; Chmn., Nordic Fedn. of Rsch. Libns., 1956-63;

Bd. Chmn., European Translations Ctr., Delft Netherlands, 1961-66; Chmn., Sect. of Nat. & Univ. Libs., Int. Fedn. of Lib. Assns., 1966-69; Chmn., Norwegian State Lib. Schl., 1955-63. Publs: History of the Norwegian Book Trade, Vols. I-II, 1950-64; Ed., Humaniora Norvegica, The Year's Work in Norwegian Humanities, 1954-62. Hons: Kt., 1st Class Order of St. Olav, Norway, 1967; Cmdr., Italian Repub.; Kt., 1st Class, Order of Danneborg, Denmark; Cmdr., Order of the Falcon, Iceland. Address: Riksbibliotektjenesten, Drammensvn. 42, Oslo 2, Norway. 43, 133.

TWEEDY, Sara C. (Mrs. Harvey F. Tweedy), b. 10 Nov. 1917. Private Piano Teacher. Educ; Cert., Cox Coll.; Piano & Organ w. C.W. Dieckmann; Agnes Scott Coll. Appts: w. Personnel Dept., S. Ctrl. Bell Telegraph & Telephone Co., Atlanta, Ga.; Kindergarten Music. Dir., Decatur, Ga.; Pvte. Piano Classes, Decatur, & Jackson, Miss.; Asst. Organist, Decatur Bapt. Ch.; Dir. of Children's Choirs, Decatur, Jackson & Nashville, Tenn. Mbrships. incl: Pres., Miss. Fedn. Music Clubs, Willana Buck Chapt. of Past Presidents Assembly, MacDowell Music Club, Camenae Literary Club; Life Mbr., Nat. Fedn. Music Clubs; Nat. Advsry. Coun. Brevard Music Ctr.; Nat. Guild Piano Tchrs. Hons. incl: S. Ctrl. Bell Telegraph & Telephone Co. donation of Sara Tweedy Piano Schlrship., 1973. Address: 5216 Meadow Oaks Park Dr., Jackson, MS 39211, U.S.A. 125.

TWIGGS, Leo Franklin. College Professor. Educ: B.A., Claflin Coll., 1956; Art Inst. of Chgo., 1960; M.A., N.Y. Univ., 1964; Ed.D., Univ. of Ga. Appts: Art Instr., Lincoln H.S., Sumter, S.C., 1958-64; Asst. Prof., S.C. State Coll., Orangeburg, 1964-69; Assoc. Prof., ibid, 1970-72; Prof. of Art & Dir., Art Prog. & Whitaker Gall., 1972-. Mbrships: Coll. Art Assn.; V.P., Guild of S.C. Artists, 1973; Nat. Art Educ. Assn.; Nat. Conf. of Artists; S.C. Art Collect. Comm.; State Advsry. Comm. on Film; Special Advsr., S.C. Arts Commn., 1972-73; S.C. State Mus. Commn., 1973-. Publs: Paintings on cover of Crisis Mag. & Instructor Mag.; Articles in jrnls. Hons. incl: Smith Mason Gall. Award of Distinction, Wash. D.C., 1971; 1st Prize, Painting, Black Art Expressions, Ill. State Univ., Normal, 1973. Address: P.O. Box 1691, S.C. State Coll., Orangeburg, SC, U.S.A. 37, 117, 125.

TWIRBUTT, Josef, b. 18 Jan. 1930. Architect; Artist. Educ: M.Arch. Mbrships: Int. Arts Guild, Monte Carlo, Monaco; Centro Studi E Scambi Int., Rome, Italy; Hon. Mbr., Int. Acad., ibid; U.S. Fine Arts Registry. One man exhibs: Grand Ctrl. Moderns Gall., N.Y., 1965, '66. Pub. Colls: Mus. of Modern Art, Mex. City, Mex.; Mus. of Modern Art, Phoenix, Ariz.; Andrew D. White Mus. of Art Coll., N.Y.C.; N.Y. Univ. Art Coll., ibid; Int. Arts Guild Art Coll., Monte Carlo, Monaco; Mus. of Modern Art, N.Y.C. Exhibs. incl: La Boetie Gall., N.Y., 1970; Eklektra '70, Int. Art Show, ibid, 1970; Joan Miro Fndn. Int. Art Show, Barcelona, Spain, 1970; Benson Gall., L.I., N.Y., 1972. Hons: Silver Medal, Int. Acad. Tomasso Campanella, Rome, Italy, 1970; Gold Medal, ibid, 1972. Address: 33 Ivy Close, Forest Hills, NY 11375, U.S.A. 133.

TWISLETON-WYKEHAM-FIENNES, Richard Nathaniel, b. 26 Nov. 1909. Biologist; Veterinary Surgeon; Author. Educ: B.A., M.A. (Cantab.), Magdalene Coll., Cambridge; Royal Veterinary Coll., Edinburgh. Appts: Veterinary Off., Uganda; Veterinary Rsch. Off., Uganda; Sr. Veterinary Rsch. Off., Kabete, Kenya, & Dean, Makerere Veterinary Schl.; Sr. Lectr., Veterinary Sci., Univ. of Gold Coast;

Pathologist, Zoological Soc., London, U.K.; Hd. Dept. of Pathol., Nuffield Inst. Comp. Med., Zoological Soc. of London. Mbrships: Sec. & Past Pres., Comp. Med. Sect., Royal Soc. Med.; Pres., Primate Soc. of Gt. Britain. Publs. incl: Some Recent Developments in Comparative Medicine (Ed.), 1966; Biology of Nutrition (Ed.); Pathology of Simian Primates (Ed.), 2 vols. Address: The Old Manor, Dalham, Newmarket, Suffolk, U.K.

TWOREK, Stanisław-Zygmunt, b. 2 May 1932. Historian. Educ: M.A., Maria Curie-Skłodowska Univ., Lublin, Poland, 1955; doct. dissertation, 1961; docent exam., 1967. Appts: Dean, Fac. Humanities, Maria Curie-Skłodowska Univ., Lublin, Poland, 1970-; Hd., Cultural Hist. Dept., Inst. Hist., ibid, 1972-. Mbrships: Polish Histl. Assn.; Lublin Sci. Soc.; Polish Assn. Histns. Relig. Publs: The Antitrinitarian Church in Lublin and its Role in the Antitrinitarian Movement in Poland in 16th & 17th Centuries; Cultural and Educational Activities of the Calvinists in the Małopolska Province, 16th-18th Centuries; 56 papers, 21 monographs & sev. reviews. Hons; Min. Higher Educ. Award, 1967; Golden Order of Merit, 1969; French Embassy Rsch. Fellowship. Address: Sowinski St. 8, 20-040 Lublin, Poland.

TWOREK, Wandy, b. 25 June 1913. Musician. Educ: w. Max Schlüter & Erling Bloch, Royal Conservatory of Music, Copenhagen. Appts: Debut as profl. Classical Violinist, 1923; Leader of variety band & popular violinist, age 15; gave 1st European performance of Bartok's Solo Violin Sonata, Copenhagan, 1943; returned classical repertoire, 1944, w. performance of Brahms Violin Concerto w. Tivoli Gardens Symph. Orch., Copenhagen; has since made solo performances thru'out world, inclng. appearances on TV & in films; Cons. for Choir, Gladsaxe Music Schl., Copenhagen. Publs: Violin instrn. course w. text & records. Hons. incl: Peder Moller Prize, 1945; Swedish Theatre Medal, 1950. Address: Estate "Akjaer" Moshusevej, Sdr. Stenderup, 6092 Varmark Jylland, Denmark.

TWUM-BARIMA, Kankam, b. 28 Dec. 1918. Agriculturist. Educ: B.A., Trinity Coll., Cambridge Univ., U.K., 1946; Postgrad. Dip. in Agric., ibid, 1947; Special course in agricl. econs., 1948; Dip. in Tropical Agric., Imperial Coll. of Tropical Agric., Trinidad, 1949; M.A., Cantab., 1953. Appts. incl: Hd., Schl. of Agric., Dean, Fac. of Agric., Pro Vice-Chancellor, Acting Vice-Chancellor, Univ. of Sci. & Technol., Kumasi, 1955-68; Commnr. for Agric. & Forestry, 1969; Mbr., FAO Advsry. Comm. on Sociological Problems of Agricl. Dev., 1967-70; Exec. Bd., UNESCO, 1970-76; Chmn., Ghana Cocoa Marketing Bd., 1970-72; Dir., Inst. of Statistical, Soc. & Econ. Rsch., Univ. of Ghana, Legon, 1972. Mbrships. incl: Life mbr., Cambridge Union Soc.; Fndn. Fellow & mbr., Governing Coun., 2 terms, Ghana Acad. of Scis. Recip., Grand Medal for Serv. to the nation, 1969. Address: Inst. of Statistical, Soc. & Econ. Rsch., P.O. Box 74, Univ. of Ghana, Legon, Ghana.

TWYMAN, James Elliott, b. 7 Aug. 1935. Educator. Educ: B.A., Northwestern Univ., 1957; M.A., ibid, 1960; Cert., Inst. of African Studies, 1970. Appts: Probation Off./Soc. Wkr., Family Ct. of Cook Co., Chgo., Ill., 1960-61; served to 1st Lt., AUS, Med. Serv. Corps, 1961-64; Asst. Ed., The World Book Ency., Field Enterprises Educl. Corp., Chgo., 1965-66; Area Studies Ed., ibid, 1966-68;

Instr., Soc. Scis., St. Xavier Coll., 1968-70; Asst. Prof., Soc. Scis., ibid, 1970-; Lectr., Anthropol., Loyola Univ., 1969-73; Dir., Chicago; 20th Century Man & The City Symposium, (Treas., 1973-74). Publs. incl: (genealogy) Robert Henry Davis & Mary Ann Law Davis; John Barefoot Descendant; Descendants of John C. Weeks & Lena Boyett Weeks. Articles in Ch. monthly paper & book reviews. Address: 1033-F Ont. St., Oak Pk., IL 60302, U.S.A. 5, 7, 8, 22, 57, 125, 130.

TYLER, Cyril, b. 26 Jan. 1911. University Professor. Educ: Univ. of Leeds, 1929-35. Appts: Lectr. in Agricl. Chem., R.A.C., Cirencester, 1935-39; Lectr., Univ. of Reading, 1939-47, Prof. of Agricl. Chem., 1947-58, Prof. of Physiol. & Biochem., 1958-, Dean, Fac. of Agric., 1959-62, Univ. Dpty. Vice-Chancellor, 1968-. Fellow, Royal Inst. of Chem. Publs: Organic Chemistry for Students of Agriculture, 1946; Avian Eggshells, 1964; num. papers, poultry metabolism & egg shells, var. sci. jrnls. Address: Dept. of Physiology & Biochemistry, The University, Whiteknights, Reading RG6 2AJ, U.K.

TYLER, (Mrs) Evelyn Sills, b. 16 Oct. 1919. Educator. Educ: B.S., E. Carolina Coll. (now Univ.), Greenville, N.C., U.S.A., 1956. Appts: Tchr., Cecil Elem. Schl., Lexington, N.C., 1956-57; Tchr., Grimes Elem. Schl., Lexington, 1957-61; Tchr., McIver Elem. Schl., Greensboro, N.C., 1961-69; Pres., N.C. Assn. of Classroom Tchrs., Raleigh, N.C., 1969-71; Tchr., Jonesboro Elem. Schl., Greensboro, 1971-. Mbrships: Chmn., Policies Comm., N.C. State Bd. of Educ; Bd. of Dirs., & Chmn., Prog. Comm., Learning Inst. of N.C.; NEA; Bd. of Dirs., N.C. Assn. of Educators; N.C. Assn. of Classroom Tchrs.; Assn. for Childhood Educ. Int.; PTA; Alpha Delta Kappa; Kappa Delta Pi. Author, pamphlets about work of Assn. of Classroom Tchrs. Composer, Song for Jonesboro Elem Schl. Glee Club, 1972. Hons: Num. awards, N.C. Assn. of Classroom Tchrs., 1969-73; Ben L. Smith Tchr. of the Yr. Award, Jaycees of Greensboro, 1972. Address: 407 Mimosa Drive, Greensboro, NC 27403, U.S.A. 5, 7.

TYLER, Jack Maurice, b. 11 Nov. 1938. Librarian. Educ: Univ. of Utah, 1956-58; B.S.,

Brigham Young Univ., 1963; M.L.S., Univ. of Pitts., 1964. Appts: Dir., Instructional Resources, Florissant Campus, Jr. Coll. Dist. of St. Louis, 1964; Ref. Libn., Knowledge availability Systems Ctr., Univ. of Pitts., 1965; Dir. of Extension, Utah State Lib. Commn., 1965-68; Wyo. State Libn., Wyo. State Lib., 1968-69; Dir. of Libs., Del. State Div. of Libs., 1969-73; City Libn., Berkeley, Calif., 1973-. Mbrships: Berkeley Breakfast Club; ALA; Calif. Lib. Assn. Publs: A Measure of Success (contbng. author), 1969; Delaware Planning for Statewide Library Development, 1972. Recip. of hons. Address: 733 The Alameda, Berkeley, CA 94707, U.S.A. 2, 6, 9.

TYNER, Max R., b. 21 Nov. 1925. Educ: Ind. Univ. Ext.; Special courses, Mich. State Coll., Univ. of Okla. & Univ. of Houston. Mbrships: Mason, Scottish Rite, Commandery, Shrine; Elks; McAllen Real Estate Bd.; McAllen Chmbr. of Comm.; McAllen Ins. Bd.; Nat. Free-lance Photographers Assn.; Nat. Writers Club; Am. Legion. Author of relig. publs. Hons: Citizen, Guadalajara, Jal., Mexico, 1963; Citizen, Jalapa, Vera Cruz, Mexico, 1964; Outstanding Man of Yr. & Outstanding Mbr. of Kokomo. Ind. Jaycees, 1956. Address: P.O. Box 3568, McAllen, TX 78501, U.S.A. 57, 125, 130, 131.

TZALLAS, Niove (Mrs. Neocosmos Tzallas), b. 26 Jan. 1938. Painter. Educ: Grad., Athens Schl. Fine Arts, Greece, 1958; Ctrl. Schl. Arts & Crafts, London, UK, 1959-61; Atelier André Lhote, Paris, France, 1958-59. One-man exhibs: Grande Hotel, Paris, France, 1962; Gal. Margutiana, Rome, Italy, 1963; Gall. Royal Soc. Painters, London, UK, 1964; Gal. du Damier, Paris, France, 1968; Gal. de l'Univ., Paris, 1969, '72; Mus. of Arts, Le Havre, 1971; Floating exhibs. on bd. SS Pegassos & SS Semiramis, 1966, Olympia, 1967; Participated 84th & 85th annual exhibs., Salon des Independents, Grand Palais des Champs Elysees, 1973, '74; Grand Prix Int. de la Baie des Anges, Nice & Grand Prix Int. de la Mediterranée, Gal. Riviera, Nice, France, 1974. Rep. permanent collects., Mus. Mod. Art, Haifa, Israel & Nat. Bank of Greece, Athens. Address: 13 Pericleous Stavrou St., Psyhiko, Athens, Greece.

U

UDELL, William N., b. 4 Sept. 1921. Broadcaster; Yacht Broker. Educ: Duke Univ.; Ind. Univ.; Mich. State Univ. Appts. incl: Neblett Radio Prods., Chgo., 1947; Prog. Dir., WLOL, Mpls., 1948; Publr., Lakeview News, 1949; Pres., Northern Ind. Broadcasters, Inc., Oprs. WIMS & WKAM, Pres., Great Lakes Marine, Inc. & Treas., Marine Bldg. Corp., 1950-. Mbrships: Broadcast Pioneers; Ind. Broadcasters Assn.; Mich. City Yacht Club; Gt. Lakes Cruising Club; Everglades Yacht Club. Address: c/o WIMS, Old Chgo. Rd. Mich. City, IN 46360, U.S.A. 8.

UDICK, Robert E., b. 27 May 1922. Newspaper Executive. Educ: B.A., Colo. Coll. Appts: Staff Corres., Rocky Mtn. News, Denver, 1947-49, United Press, Denver & Santa Fe, 1950-51; War Corres., Korea, 1951-53; Mgr., U.P.I. Hong Kong & Manila Burs., Mgr., S.E. Asia, Singapore; Ed., Publr., Bangkok—1967; currently Publr. Pacific Daily News, Agana, Guam. Mbrships: Civilian Advsry Bd., 8th. Air Force; Navy League, Pres. Guam Coun.; Regent, Univ. of Guam; Pres., Guam Stock Exchange & For. Corres. Assn., Thailand; Phi Delta Theta; Rotary. Address: P.O. Box DN, Agana, Guam 96910.

UDWIN, Saul, b. 6 Feb. 1922. Consulting Engineer. Educ: B.Sc., Univ. of Witwatersrand, S. Africa, 1948. Appts: Chief Agent, Sir Alfred McAlpine & Son, N. & S. Rhodesia, 1950-51; Pvte. Prac., Sr. Ptnr., Udwin & Vrettos & Ptnrs. & assoc. soc., United Technologists (G.B.) Ltd., United Technologists Zambia, Tersive Ltd., Malawi, 1952-. Mbrships: Inst. Dir.; Mazoe Sailing Club; country mbr., Wanderers Club, Johannesburg; past vice chmn., Wingate Club, Salisbury; Mbr., Fed. Parliamnt, 1957-63; F.ASCE.; F.(S.A.)I.C.E.; F.(RHOD)I.E. Address: P.O. Box 329, Lusaka, Zambia.

UEMATSU, Tadashi, b. 21 Jan. 1906. Professor; Barrister. Educ: Grad., Nihon Univ., 1929, Tohoku Imperial Univ., 1935; Bungaku-Hakushi (Ph.D.), 1962. Appts: Lectr., Philos. & Psychol., Nihon Univ., 1927; Pub. Prosecutor, 1936; Judge, 1940; Asst. Prof., Criminal Law, Taipei Imperial Univ.; Prof., ibid, 1944; Judge, Tokyo Ct. of Appeal, 1945; Pub. Prosecutor, ibid, 1946; Prof., Criminal Law, Hitotsubashi Univ., 1950; Prof. Emeritus, ibid, 1969; Prof., Meijigakuin Univ. & Barrister, 1969. Mbrships. incl: Chmn., 3rd Drafting Comm. for New Penal Code; Pres., Drafting Sect. of New Juvenile Code, Legis. Coun.; Commn., Correction & Rehab. Coun.; Commn., Japanese Lang. Coun.; Dir., Japanese Assns. of Criminol. & Med. Law; Dir., Int. Acad. of Forensic Psychol. Publs: Race & Criminality, 1947; Treatises on Criminal Law, 1947; Psychology of Criminal Behaviour, 1951; Outline of Criminal Law, 2 vols., 1952, rev. ed., 1970; An Introduction to Japanese Criminal Law, 2 vols., 1956, rev. ed., 1974; Reliability of Testimony, 1957; Some Aspects of Forensic Psychology, 1958; Psychology of Testimony, 1964; Essays on Criminal Law, 2 vols., 1966; Society & Criminal Law, 2 vols., 1968; Reflections on Law, 1972; Inside & Outside Law, 1974. Hons: Shiju-Hosho (Purple Prize), 1971. Address: 1-13-21 Nishiogi-kita, Suginami-ku, Tokyo, Japan.

UHLIG, Franklin R., Jr., b. 15 June 1927. Editor. Educ: B.A., Kenyon Coll., 1951. Appts: Reporter, Fairchild Publs., 1952-54; Asst. Ed., Funk & Wagnalls, 1955-57; Ed., Our Navy mag., 1957-60; Ed., Book Dept., U.S. Naval Inst., 1960-61; Ed., Naval Review, 1961-; Sr. Ed., U.S. Naval Inst., 1969-. Mbrships: U.S. Naval Inst.; Naval Acad. Sailing Squadron. Publs: Num. articles, reviews, commentaries. Hons: Alfred Thayer Mahan Award for Lit. Achievement, Navy League of U.S. Address: U.S. Naval Inst., Annapolis, MD 21402, U.S.A. 6.

UHRICH, Helen B., b. 13 Jan. 1908. Librarian. Educ: A.B., Albright Coll., 1929; B.S., Drexel Univ. Grad. Schl. Lib. Sci., 1930; postgrad. studies, N.Y. Theological Sem., Columbia Univ. Schl. Lib. Ser., Yale Divinity Schl., 1931-46. Appts. incl: Cataloguer-Libn., Biblical Sem. in N.Y., 1931-36; Hd. Cataloguer, Hartford Sem. Fndn., Conn., 1936-37; Cataloguer-Asst. Admin. Libn., Yale Divinity Lib., 1937-. Mbrships. incl: Pres., Am. Theol. Lib. Assn., 1956-57; AAUW, until 1965; Pi Gamma Mu; Sigma Tau Delta; Tau Kappa Alpha. Co-Ed: Index to Religious Periodical Lit., Volumes 3 & 5, 1963-64. Num. reports & articles in var. publs. Recip. of Albright Coll. Alumni Citation, 1953. Address: 216 Bishop St., New Haven, CT 06511, U.S.A. 6, 42.

UHRMAN, Celia, b. 14 May 1927. Educator; Artist; Poet; Writer. Educ: B.A., Brooklyn Coll., 1948; M.A., ibid, 1953; Tchrs. Coll., Columbia Univ., 1961; Admin. & Supvsn. course, CUNY, 1966; Bklyn. Mus. Art Schl., 1956-57. Appts: Tchr., N.Y. City Schl. System, 1948-; Self-employed Artist & Writer, 1958-; Tchr., special art classes, Lefferts Jr. H.S. One-Man Shows: Lefferts Jr. H.S. In many grp. shows inclng: Smithsonian Inst.; Carnegie Endowment Int. Ctr., N.Y.; Bklyn Mus.; Springfield Mus. of Fine Arts, Mass.; Palacio de la Virreina, Spain; Premi Int. Dibuix-Joan Miro, Barcelona, Spain; Premier Salon Int. Charlerio, Belgium; IPA Art Show, Wash. D.C.; Mus. of Ovar, Portugal; Luxembourg Cultural Authorities Exhib.; Palme D'Or Beaux-Arts Exhib., Monaco, Monte-Carlo; Perspective, '68, ibid. Rep. in many perm. collections. Mbrships: Cmdr., Int. Arts Guilds; Hon. U.S. Rep., Int. Exec. Comm. Centro Studi e Scambi Int.; Rep.-at-Large, World Poetry Soc., Intercontinental; Life, Bklyn. Coll. Alumni Assn.; United Fedn. of Tchrs. Publs: Poetic Ponderances, 1969; A Pause for Poetry & Poetic Love Fancies, both 1970; A Pause for Poetry for Children, 1973; Diary of a Harassed Teacher (forthcoming; poems mags., anthols., jrnls., etc. Recip. many awards inclng: Silver & Gold Medals, C.S.S.I.; Geo. Wash. Medal of Hon., Freedoms Fndn., 1964; Order of Gandhi Award of Hon., 1972; Ph.D., Acad. of Philos., 1973; D.Litt., World Acad. of Lang. & lit., 1973. Address: 1655 Flatbush Ave., Apt. C2010, Brooklyn, NY 11210, U.S.A. 11, 57, 105, 133.

UHRMAN, Esther, b. 7 July 1921. Artist; Writer; Public Servant. Educ: Traphagen Schl. of FAshion, 1955; A.A., N.Y. City Community Coll., 1974; Seminars, N.Y. City Dept. of Soc. Serv. Schl. & N.Y. State Personnel Admin., 1973. Appts: Self-employed Artist & Writer, 1954-; on staff, Trade Publs. & Off-Beat Advt., 1954-59; N.Y. State Employee 1959-72; w. N.Y.C. Dept. of Soc. Serv., 1972-. Exhib. w. sister Celia in shows sponsored by New London & Bklyn. Chmbr of Comm. Grp. shows incl: Smithsonian Inst.; Carnegie Endowment Int. Ctr., N.Y.; IPA Art Show, Wash. D.C.; Mus. of Ovar, Portugal; Luxembourg Cultural Exhib.; Springfield Mus of Fine Arts, Mass; Palacio de la Virreina, Spain; Premi Int. Dibuix-Jean Miro, Spain; Premier Salon Int., Belgium; Palme D'Or Beaux-Arts, Monaco; Perspective 68 Monaco; Traphagen Schl. of Fashion; USPO Civil War Centennial. Mbrships: Cmdr. Int. arts Guild; N.Y. Community Coll. Alumni Assn.; Hon.

U.S.A. Vice-Rep., Int. Exec. Comm., Centro Studie Scambi Int. Publs: Gypsy Logic, 1970; Mocking Ghost, 1972; items in anthols., jrnls., mags., etc. hons. incl: Silver Medal (Olympic) Designs for Verso Mexico, 1968; Cert. for Stamp Designs, 1968 Olympics; 5 Merit Awards, N.Y. State, 1964-66; N.Y. State Brotherhood Award, 1969; Hon. Mention, Palme d'Or, 1971; Golden Windmill Radio Drama Contest Award, 1971. Address: 1655 Flatbush Ave., Apt. C2010, Brooklyn, NY 11210, U.S.A. 11, 57, 105, 133.

UKEJE, Bennett Onyerisara, b. 22 Apr. 1927. University Professor; Educational Administrator. Educ: B.S. (Hons.), Ohio Univ., Athens, U.S.A., 1952; M.S., ibid, 1953; M.A., Tchrs. Coll., Columbia Univ., 1955; Ed.D., ibid, 1955. Appts: Prin., New Bethel Coll., Onitsha, Nigeria, 1957-61; Lectr., Univ. of Nigeria, Nsukka, 1961-64, Sr. Lectr., 1964-66. Assoc. Prof. of Educ., 1966, Hd., Dept. of Educ., 1966-72, Dean, Fac. of Educ., 1970-73; Prof. of Educ., & Dir., CUDIMAC, 1971-73; Provost, Alvan Ikoku Coll. of Educ., Owerri, 1974-. Mbr., & Off., var. profl. orgs. & comms. Publs. incl: Education of Social Reconstruction, 1966; Entebbe Primary Mathematics Series (co-author), Books 2-5; var. papers, & contbns., profl. publs. Hons. incl. African-Am. Inst. Educl. Travel Grant, 1972. Address: Alvan Ikoku College of Education, P.M.B. 1033, Owerri, E. Central State, Nigeria.

ÜLKEN, Hilmi Ziya, b. 3 Oct. 1901. University Professor. Educ: Fac. of Pol. Scis., 1921; Fac. of Art, 1923, 1933; Rsch. in Staatsbybliothek, Berlin, Germany, 1933. Appts: Assoc. Prof., Fac. of Art, 1934, Prof., 1941, Chmn. of Fac., 1957; w. Tech. Univ., 1944-48; Chmn. of Philos., Divine Fac., Ankara, 1957-73; retirement, 1973; Hon. Prof. of Philos., 1973-74. Mbrships. incl: Int. Sociological Assn., 1950; Int. Inst. of Sociol., 1950; Pres., Turkish Sociological Assn.; Nat. Comm., UNESCO; Société des Études des Réfugiés. Publs. incl: Incomplete Man, 1932; The Talk with Satan, 1933; Battle of Iznik (poetry), 1923; The Conquest of the Fatherland (poetry), 1949. Hons. incl: Mbrship., Acad. Human Rights, 1957; Diploma, Int. Inst. Sociol., 1959. Address: Harbiye, Cumhuriyet Cad., 361/11 Safir apart., Istanbul, Turkey.

ÜLKÜTASIR, M. Sakir, b. 15 Oct. 1894. Folklorist; Writer. Educ: Fac. of Art, Istanbul Univ., Turkey. Appts: Tchr., Maras H.S., 1915-18; Writer, 1920-30, 64-; Cons., Turkish Lang. Assoc. est. by Ataturk, 1930-64. Mbrships: Turkish Club; Folk Club; Turkish Assn.; Turkish Folk & Ethnographical Club; Ancient Ruins Club of Sirop. Author of over 1500 publs. inclng 15 books on Turkish culture. contbr. to Islamic-Turkish Ency. Address: Namik Kemal Mahallesi, 3 Cad. No 3/3, Yenisehir, Ankara, Turkey.

ULLMANN, Stephen, b. 13 June 1914. University Professor. Educ: Ph.D., 1936, Dip. Ed., 1937, Univ. of Budapest, Hungary; D.Litt., Glasgow Univ., U.K., 1949; M.A., Oxford Univ., 1968. Appts: Lectr., Sr. Lectr., Romance Philol. & Gen. Linguistics, Univ. of Glasgow, 1946-53; Prof., French Lang. & Romance Philol., Univ. of Leeds, 1953-68; Prof., Romance Langs., Oxford Univ., & Fellow, Trinity Coll., 1968. Also Vis. Prof., Univ. of Toronto, Canada, 1964, '66; Univ. of Mich., U.S.A., 1965; Australian Nat. Univ., 1974. Mbrships: Pres., Philolog. Soc.; Past Pres., MLA; Coun. Mbr., Société de Linguistique Romane. Publs. incl: Precis de semantique française, 2nd edit., 1959; Style in the French Novel, 2nd

edit., 1964; The Image in the Modern French Novel, 2nd edit., 1963; Semantics, An Introduction to the Science of Meaning, 1962; Language & Style, 1964; Meaning & Style, 1973; Hons: Fellow, Inst. of Linguistics, 1968; Diamond Jubilee Medal, ibid, 1972. Address: Trinity Coll., Oxford Univ., Oxford, U.K. 1.

ULLMANN, Walter, b. 29 Nov. 1910. University Professor. Educ: Univs. of Vienna, Innsbruck, Munich & Cambridge. Appts. incl: Fellow, Trinity Coll., Cambridge, U.K.; Univ. Lectr., Medieval Hist., Cambridge, 1949-57; Rdr., Medieval Ecclesiatical Instns., ibid, 1957-65; Prof., 1965-72; Maitland Mem. Lectr., 1947-48; Birkbeck Lectr., 1968-69. Fellowships: Royal Hist. Soc.; Brit. Acad. Pres., Ecclesiastical Hist. Soc. Publs. incl: Principles of Government & Politics in the Middle Ages, 1961, 3rd edit., 1974; History of the Political Ideas in the Middle Ages, 1965; The Individual & Society in the Middle Ages, 1967; A Short History of the Papacy in the Middle ages, 1972, 74; Papst und König, 1966; The Future of Medieval History, 1973; num. articles. Hons: Dr.rer.pol.h.c.; Jubilee Medal for disting. servs., Univ. of Innsbruck. Address: Trinity Coll., Cambridge, CB2 1TQ, U.K. 1, 3.

ULLMEN, Mary Agnes, b. 4 June 1912. Real Estate & Insurance Broker. Educ: B.A., Rosary Coll., River Forest, Ill., 1934. Appts: Tchr., Morton, Ill., H.S., 1934-35, Trinity H.S., River Forest, ibid, 1935-36, Niles Grammar Schl., 1937-40; Sec., Lyon & Healy, Chgo., 1937-40, Schieff, Dahlstream & Harding, 1940-45, John E. Colnon & Co., 1945-55; Assoc. Broker, Fager Homes, Maywood & Elmhurst, 1955-65; Pvte. Prac., Real Estate & Ins., Oak Pk., 1955-65; Owner Broker, Ullmen Real Estate, Glen Ellyn, 1965-. Mbrships: Fndr., Dir., Sec., Treas., The Ellyn Corp., Custom Homes, 1967; Bd., Asst. Chmn., 14th. Congressional Dist. Democratic Party, 1965-66; Fndr., Mgr., Friends of St. Francis Animal Shelter, 1967; Alumnae Bd., Rosary Coll., 1945-50; DuPage Bd., Realtors; Nat. Assn. Real Estate Bds.; Ill. Brokers. Address: 485 Forest Ave., Glen Ellyn, IL 60137, U.S.A. 5.

ULLOM, Madeline Marie, b. 1 Jan. 1911. Nurse. Educ: Thomas Jefferson Univ. Hosp., 1937; B.S.N. Educ., Incarnate Word Coll., 1949; M.S.N. Educ., Cath. Univ. Am., 1953; Univ. of Pitts., 1950; Univ. of Tex., 1959. Appts: Staff Nurse; Hd., Supvsr.; Asst. Chief Nurse; Chief Nursing Serv.; Educ. Coord.; Dir., Clin. Techn. Course, 1937-64; 2nd Lt. to Lt.-Col., U.S. Army, 1938-64; served, Philippines, 1940-45 & Germany, 1951-53. Mbrships. incl: Am. Acad. Pol. & Soc. Sci.; AAAS; Soc. Archtl. Histns.; Pres., El Paso League for Nursing, 1951-60; Dir., Dist. 8, Tex. Bus. & Profl. Women's Club, Tex., 1960; Pres., Tucson Unit Women's Overseas Serv. League, 1969-70; Tucson Br., AAUW; Rep., Tucson Coun. on Aging, 1968-71; Chmn., Practical Nursing Coun., Colo. League for Nurses, 1962-64.; Am. Nurses Assn.; Nat. League for Nurses.; Pi Gamma Mu; Sigma Theta Tau. Hons. incl: Presidential Unit Citations; Bronze Star; Commendation Medals. Address: 2901 E. Waverly, Tucson, AZ 85716, U.S.A. 5, 9, 22, 28, 57, 120.

ULLRICH-ZUCKERMAN, B. (Mrs. Murray G. Zuckerman). Painter; Photographer; Clinical Social Worker. Educ: B.A., Northwestern Univ., Evanston, Ill.; B.F.A., Art Inst. of Chgo.; Postgrad. Work in Sculpture & Lithography, ibid; M.A., Univ. of Chgo.; Photographic study w. Edward Weston; Postgrad. Study, Univ. of Calif., Berkeley. Appts. incl: Pvte. instrn. in art & photography; Psychiatric Caseworker &

Supvsr., United Charities of Chgo., 1949-53 & Lake Co. Mental Hlth. Clin. of Gary, Ind., 1955-57. Mbrships. incl: Common Cause; Pub. Citizen; Artists' Equity Assn., Sec., 1955-56; San Fran. Women Artists; Friends of Photography; Nat. Assn. of Soc. Wkrs.; Acad. of Cert. Soc. Wkrs. Works incl: One-Man Shows in San Fran. Mus. of Art, G Place Gall., Wash. D.C., Humanist House, San Fran.; many grp. shows & exhibs. Hons. incl: Print Prize, Laguna Beach Mus., 1938; Newspaper Photographic Awards inclng. Grand Prize, Chgo. Daily News & Hon. Award, Nat. Salon, 1959. Address: 2254 42nd Ave., San Francisco, CA 94116, U.S.A. 37, 120, 133.

UMBERGER, Katrina Alda, b. 4 July 1905. Librarian. Educ: Dip., Marion Jr. Coll., 1925; B.Sc., Univ. of Va., 1938; M.A. & M.S., Appalachian Univ., Boone, N.C., 1960. Appts. incl: Tchr., Smyth Co., 1925; Tchr., Konnarock Trng. Schl. for Mountain Girls, 1926-36; Prin., ibid, 1938-45; Libn., Smyth Co., 1945-72. Mbrships. incl: Nat. & State Educ. Assns.; Nat., State & Dist. Lib. Assns., Chmn., Dist. Lib. Assn., 1970-71; Sec., Smyth Co. Assn. for Retarded Children, 1969; Sec., Marion Choral Soc., 1969; Sec., Friends of the Lib., 1973; Sec., Book & Study Club, 1974. Author of short stories & pamphlets in connection with work at Konnarock Trng. Schl. Hons. incl: Alumnae of the Yr., Marion Jr. Coll., 1963; Life Mbr., Parent Tchrs. Assn., 1970. Address: Box 165, Marion, VA 24354, U.S.A. 5, 125.

UMEZAWA, Sumio, b. 22 Nov. 1909. Educator; Institute Director. Educ: Dept. of Chem., Fac. of Sci., Hokkaido Imperial Univ., Japan, 1930-33; Grad. course, ibid, 1933-35; Ph.D;. 1942. Appts: Assoc. Prof., Dept. of Chem., Hokkaido Imperial Univ., 1940-42; Assoc. Prof., Fujiwara Inst. of Technol., Tokyo, 1942-44; Dean of Fac., Keio Univ., Yokohamo., 1964-69; Prof., Dept. of Applied Chem., Fac. of Engrng., ibid,1944-; Expert Mbr., Sci. & Technol. Coun. (Cabinet), 1967-70; Dir., Inst. of Microbial Chem., 1958-. Mbrships: V.P., Microbial Chem. Rsch. Fndn., 1971-; Pres., Soc. of Synthetic Organic Chem., 1964; V.P., Chem. Soc. of Japan, 1965-66; Councilor, Japan Antibiotics Rsch. Assn., 1952 & Soc. of Polymer Chem., Japan, 1968; Am. Chem. Soc. Author of papers on chem. Hons: Chem. Soc. of Japan Award, 1964; Fukuzawa Prize Keiogijuku, 1963 Address: Dept. of Applied Chem., Fac. of Engrng., Keio Univ., Hiyoshi 832, Yokohama, Japan.

UNDERWOOD, Benjamin Hayes, b. 10 Mar. 1942. Hospital Administrator. Educ: Grad., Ga. Mil. Coll., 1962; B.B.A., Univ. of Ga.; courses in Hosp. Admin., Ga. State Univ. Appts: Asst. Admin., Northside Manor Hosp., Atlanta, Ga., 1965-67; Admin., Metropol. Psychiatric Ctr., ibid, 1967-. Mbr., Bd. Dirs., Exec. Comm., Family Learning Ctrs. Inc., Atlanta, Ga.; Mbr., Bd. Dirs., Medic Corp., Ata., Ga. Mbrships: Assn. of Mental Hlth. Admins.; Hosp. Finance Mgmt. Assn.; Am. Socs. for Hosp. P.R. Dirs. & Hosp. Purchasing Agents; Ga; Hosp. Assn.; Atlanta Chmbr. of Comm; Chattahoochee Plantation Club; Phi Delta Theta. Recip. Boss of Yr. Award, Tara Chapt., Am. Bus. Womens Assn., 1973; Nominated Am. Acad. Med. Admnstrs., 1974. Address: c/o Metropolitan Psychiatric Center, 811 Juniper St., N.E., Atlanta, GA 30308, U.S.A. 7, 125.

UNDERWOOD, Evelyn Notman (Mrs. Harold B. Underwood), b. 20 Feb. 1898. Artist; Art Techer, retired. Educ: Grad. Art Ed., Pratt Inst.; Grad. Landscape Painting, Berkshire Summer Schl. of Art, 1920; studied, State Univ. Coll., Buffalo, N.Y. State Univ. of Buffalo, N.Y. & in Greece, Mexico & U.K. Appts. incl: Art Tchr., Buffalo Pub. Schls., 14 yrs.; Jr. Educ. Dept., Buffalo Mus. of Sci., 1950-51; Arcade Ctrl. Schl., N.Y., 1963-64; Lectr. on world travels. Exhibd. in num. shows inclng. One-man Exhibs., in Buffalo, N.Y. & Muscat, Oman, S.E. Arabia & 3 man show, Lynn Kottler Galls., N.Y.C., 1973. Work included in num. pub. & pvte. collects. inclng. Veterans Hosp., Buffalo, N.Y. & Roswell Park Mem. Inst., Buffalo. Mbrships. incl: Nat. League of Am. Pen Women, Art Chmn., 1966-68, NLOAPW Deleg., Assocd. Art Orgs. of World, N.Y., Resource Chmn., 1972-74; sev. local Art Socs. Hons. incl: Nat. League of Am. Pen Women, Regional Shows, 1st Prize, N.Y.C.; Paul Lindsay Sample Mem. Award, Chautauqua's 16th Nat. Show, 1973. Address: 362 Linden Ave., E. Aurora, NY 14052, U.S.A. 37, 57, 132, 138.

UNDERWOOD, Horace Grant, b. 11 Oct. 1917. Educational Missionary. Educ: B.A., Hamilton Coll., Clinton, N.Y., U.S.A., 1939; M.A., Grad. Schl. of Educ., N.Y. Univ., 1955; adv. study, ibid, 1955, 1961-62. Appts: Instr. of Engl., Chosun Christian Coll (now Yonsei Univ.), 1940-41; serv. w. U.S. Navy, 1941-46, 1950-53; Registrar, Seoul Nat. Univ., for U.S. Mil. Govt. in Korea, 1946-47; Asst.Prof.-Prof. of Educ., Yonsei Univ., 1947-50, 1955-, Dir., Ctrl. Lib., 1966-, Dir., Int. Div., 1968-. Mbrships: Coun. Mbr., Korea Br., Royal Asiatic Soc.; Past Pres., ibid; Seoul Rotary Club; Past V.P., ibid. Profl. articles, newspapers. Hons. incl: Freedom Medal, U.S. Govt., Legion of Merit, Bronze Star, Commendation Ribbon, U.S. Navy, 1950; Order of Civilian Merit, Repub. of Korea, 1973; sev. degrees, Korean univs. Address: Yonsei University, Seoul, Korea.

UNDERWOOD, Peter, b. 16 May 1923. Author. Worked at J.M. Dent & Sons Ltd. (Publrs.), 1939-72, ending as Prod. Mgr. Lectured at London, Cambridge, Oxford, Sussex & Birmingham Univs. Cons. & Advsr. to BBC, ITV etc. Mbrships: The Ghost Club (Pres. since 1960); Unitarian Soc. for Psychical Studies (V.P., 1969-); Constitutional Club (Hon. Libn., 1968-72); Savage Club (Hon. Libn., 1973-); Soc. for Psychical Rsch.; British Film Inst.; Folklore Soc.; Dracula Soc.; Soc. of Authors; Int. P.E.N. Publs: A Gazetter of British Ghosts, 1971, 2nd ed. '73; Into the Occult, 1972 (translated into Italian & Dutch); Horror Man—The Life of Boris Karloff, 1972; Gazetteer of Scottish & Irish Ghosts, 1973; A Host of Hauntings, 1973; The Ghosts of Borley, 1973; Haunted London, 1973; Gazetteer of Scottish Ghosts, 1974; Contbr. to Everyan's Encyclopaedia, num. magazines, periodicals etc.; Radio & TV broadcaster. Address: 86 St. James's St., London, S.W. 1., U.K. 3.

UNGER, Abraham Alfred, b. 20 June 1906. Industrialist. Educ: Deg. in Metallurgy, Univ. of Vienna. Appts: Owner, Dir., Dental-Sahav A. Unger Ltd., Tel Aviv. Mbrships: Fndr., Pres., Dental Gold Mgrs. & Importers Assn., Israel; Bne-Brith; Masonic Lodge; Commercial & Indl. Club; Chmbr. of Comm.; Past Mbr., Zionist Org., Austria & Dir., Palestine Off., Vienna. Address: 21 Chen Blvd., Tel Aviv, Israel. 55, 94.

UNWIN, David Storr (David Severn), b. 3 Dec. 1918. Author. Educ: Abbotsholme Schl., Derbyshire, U.K. Mbrships: Int. P.E.N.; Authors' Soc. Publs: The Governor's Wife, 1954; A View of the Heath, 1956; Children's books, as David Severn: Dream Gold, 1948; Drumbeats!, 1953; The Future Took Us, 1956; Foxy-boy, 1959; The Girl in the Grove, 1974;

& many others. Hons: Author's Club First Novel Award, for The Governor's Wife, 1956. Address: St. Michael's, Helions Bumpstead, Haverhill, Suffolk, U.K. 1.

UNWIN, Rayner S., b. 23 Dec. 1925. Publisher. Educ: M.A., Trinity Coll., Oxford; M.A., Harvard Univ., U.S.A. Appts: Mbr., Coun. of Publrs. Assn., 1965, Treas., 1969, Pres., 1971-73, V.P., 1973-75; Chmn., George Allen & Unwin Ltd., 1968; Dir., Dillon's Univ. Bookshop, London, 1969, Australasian Publishing Co., Australia, 1969; Chmn., George Allen & Unwin (India) Ltd., 1970; Chmn., Blackie & Son (India) Ltd., 1970. Mbr., Garrick Club. Publs: The Rural Muse, 1954; The Defeat of John Hawkins, 1960. Address: c/o George Allen & Unwin Ltd., 40 Museum St., London WC1A 1LU, U.K.

UPPMAN, Ragnar Emanuel, b. 12 Mar. 1929. Professor; Architect. Educ: B.Sc., Tech. Coll., Norrköping, Sweden, 1949; M.Sc., Royal Inst. Technol., Stockholm, 1955. Appts: ARcht., Planner, Chief of Div., KF Archl. & Engrng. Cons., STockholm, 1954-58; Mgr. & Cons., A4 Archl. Cons. Ltd., ibid, 1958-63, 69-; Prof. & Dean, Fac. of Arch., Royal Inst. of Technol., 1963-69; Chmn., Bd. of Cons., Scan Plan Coord. Ltd., Copenhagen, Denmark, 1971-. Mbrships: Past Chmn., Assn. Swedish Cons. Archts.; Past Sec., Assn. of Swedish Archts. Works incl: housing projs.; dept. stores; offices; govt. bldgs.; urban planning; air terminal planning; dev. studies in prefab. housing, ind. bldg. & low cost bldg. in developing countries. Contbr. to profl. publs. Hons: Order of the North Star; prizes in approx. 10 archl. competitions. Address: A4 Archl. Cons. Ltd., Box 1218, S-111 82 Stockholm, Sweden. 43.

UPSHAW, Jefferson Davis, Jr., b. 19 July 1929. Physician. Educ: B.S., Univ. of Ala., 1950; M.D., Schl. of Med., Johns Hopkins Univ., 1954. Appts: Intern-Chief Res. in Med., Johns Hopkins Hosp., 1954-61; Assoc. Clin. Prof. Med., Coll. of Med., Univ. of Tenn.; Dir. Intern Trng., Chief, Div. of Hematol., Active Staff Mbr., Bapt. Mem. Hosp; Cons. Staff, Meth. Hosp. & St. Joseph's Hosp. Mbrships. incl: Fellow, Royal Soc. Hlth.; Fellow, Am. Coll. Physns.; Am. Soc. Hematol.; AMA; Coun. Mbr., Memphis Acad. Internal Med; Southern Med. Assn.; Tenn. State Med. Assn.; Johns Hopkins Med. & Surg. Assn.; Phi Beta Kappa; Phi Eta Sigma; Alpha Epsilon Delta; Omicron Delta Kappa; Pres., Sigma Chi Fraternity. Recip., Daniel Baker Mem. Award, 1961. Address: 929 Madison, Suite 1002, Memphis, TN 38104, U.S.A. 7.

URBINATI, (Sister) Anna, b. 25 Aug. 1925. Special Education Teacher; Elementary Teacher. Educ: B.S., Our Lady of the Lake Coll., San Antonio, Tex., 1962; M.Ed., N.E. La. Univ., Monroe, 1972. Appts. incl: Entered the Cong. of the Sisters of Our Lady of Sorrows, Rimini, Italy, 1943; Tchr., Parochial Schls., Diocese of Alexandria, 1952-63; Mistress of Novices, Superior & Directress, St. Mary Trng. Schl. for Retarded Children, Clarks, La., U.S.A., 1963-71; Tchr., Parochial Schl., Monreauville, La., 1971-73; Prin. & Tchr., Christ the King Schl., Bossier City, La., 1972-74. Mbrships. incl: AAMD; N.E. La. Univ. Alumni Assn. Recip. of Cert. of Appreciation, La. Assn. for Retarded Children, 1970. Address: Christ the King School, 1000 Ogilvie St., Bossier City, LA 71010, U.S.A. 57, 125.

URI Alpert, b. 10 May 1909. Labour Council Official. Educ: Yeshiva & Hebrew Univs., Jerusalem. Appts: Hagana Comm., Jerusalem; Brit. Army, 1942-46; Mbr., Exec., Histadruth.; Ctrl. Comm., Labour Party; Mng. Bd., Shikun Hordim, Martachin, Trade Union Depr. Mbrships: Mng. Bd., Otzar Hahayal, Phiharmonic Orch., Israel Nat. Opera. Contbr. to prof. jrnls. Hons: War Awards—Africa Star, Army, Europa Star, 2nd WW Star; Hagana Star, Independence War Star. Address: 5 Brener St., Brenerhouse, Tel Aviv, Israel.

URIEL, (Miss) Gila, b. 23 Jan. 1913. Administrator. Educ: Grad., Herzlia Coll., Tel-Aviv, Israel; Schl. of Law & Econs., Tel-Aviv; London Schl. of Econs., U.K.; Courses in London, Oxford, Cambridge, Swansea; U.N.P.A. Fellow in Pub. Admin. & Human Rehationship, U.K., 1953. Appts: Dir., Mayor's Parlour, Tel-Aviv, 1932-53; Dir., Org. & Trng. Dept., Tel-Aviv, 1953-72; Advsr., Improvement of Municipal Serv., 1973-; Chief Instr. & Dir. of Studies, Inst. of Pub. Admin. in Israel, 1946-56; Co-ed., Haminhal Quarterly, Tel-Aviv, 1950-60; Mbr., edit. bd., Org. & Admin., City & Region, Jerusalem. Mbrships: Fellow, R.I.P.A., London, U.K.; Int. Inst. of Admin. Scis., Brussels, Belgium. Publs. incl: The Father of the City (Hebrew), 1972; Mother's Day, 1973. Recip., Poetry Review Competition Prize, London, 1959. Address: 9 Prague Str., Tel-Aviv, Israel.

URQUHART, Alastair Hugh, b. 3 Nov. 1919. Stock Broker. Appts: Mbr., Sydney Stock Exchange, Ltd., 1949-; Vice-Chmn., ibid, 1956, 58 & 59; Chmn., 1959-66; Pres., Australian Assoc. Stock Exchanges, 1959 & 64-66; V.P., ibid, 1960-63; Sr. Ptnr., Mullens & Co.; Mbr., Dev. Corp. of N.S.W., 1966-; Chmn., Swedex Clothing Pty. Ltd., Oswalds Bonded & Free Stores Pty. Ltd.; Dir., Pan-Australian Investments Inc., Chubb's Australian Co. Ltd., N.S.W. Permanent Bldg. Soc. Ltd. Mbrships. incl: Exec. Coun., Australian Red Cross Soc. (N.S.W.) Div., 1959-; Sydney Chmbr. of Comm., 1959-; Nat. Pres. & Fellow, Securities Inst. of Australia; Trustee, Sydney Opera House Trust; Coun. (V.P., 1968, '69 & '70), Civic Reform Assn. of Sydney, Ltd.; Dir. N.S.W. Div. & Hon. Nat. Treas., Nat. Heart Fndn.; Comm. nst. Dirs. in Australia, N.S.W. Div.; Coun. Nat. Roads & Motorists Assn.; Advsry. Bd. of Salvation Army; Australian Soc. Security Analysts; var. soc. clubs. Recip., C.B.E., 1967. Address: c/o Mullens & Co., G.P.O. Box 394, Sydney, N.S.W., Australia 2001. 12, 23, 34.

URQUHART, John Rankin, b. 29 May 1921. Business Executive. Educ: Emmanuel Coll., Cambridge, U.K.; M.A., Cambridge Univ. Appts: Marketing & Sales Mgmt., Cadbury Bros. Ltd., U.K., 1948-57; Marketing & Sales Mgr., Cadbury Fry Pty. Ltd., S. Africa, 1957-67; Dir., ibid, 1960-; Marketing Dir., Cadbury Fry Pascall Australia Ltd., 1967-70; Mng. Dir., ibid, 1970-71; Jt. Mng. Dir., & Chmn., Cadbury Div., Eadbury Schweppes Australia Ltd., 1971-. Mbrships: Past Pres., Confectionery Mfrs. of Australia Ltd.; Exec. Comm., Grocery Mfrs. of Australia Ltd.; Fellow, Inst. of Dirs. in Australia; Fellow, Inst. of Sales & Marketing. Recip., Sr. Schlr., Emmanuel Coll., Cambridge, 1948. Address: Cadbury Schweppes Australia Ltd., 323-351 Canterbury Rd., Ringwood, Vic., Australia 3134.

URRY, Dan Wesley, b. 14 Sept. 1935. Molecular Biophysicist. Educ: B.A., Univ. of Utah, 1960; Ph.D., ibid, 1964; Harvard Corp. Fellow, 1964-65. Appts: Vis. Investigator, Chemical Biodynamics Lab., Univ. of Calif., Berkeley, 1965-66; Assoc. Mbr., Inst. for Biomedical Rsch., AMA, 1965-69; Mbr., ibid, 1969-70; Editl. Bd. of Rsch./Dev. Mag., 1969-;

Professorial Lectr., Univ. of Chicago, Dept. of Biochemistry, 1967-70; Prof. of Biochemistry, Univ. of Ala. in Birmingham, 1970-; Dir., Div. of Molecular Biophysics of the Lab. of Molecular Biol., ibid, 1970-72; Dir., Lab. of Molecular Biophysics, 1972-; Editl. Bd., Biochimica et Biophysica Acta, 1972-. Mbrships. incl: Am. Soc. Biolog. Chemists; Am. Chem. Soc.; AAAS. Publs: Spectroscopic Approaches to Biomolecular Conformation, 1970; over 100 contbns. to sci. jrnls. Hons. incl: Univ. of Utah Sigma Xi Award, 1963. Address: Univ. of Ala. in Birmingham, Univ. Stn., Birmingham, AL 35294, U.S.A. 7, 8, 14, 125, 131.

URSILLO, Margaret Cecelia, b. 18 Feb. 1920. Writer; Housewife. Educ: Creative Writing, Spanish, Pub. Speaking, Personality Dev., Typing, Northern Valley Regional H.S. evening courses. Mbrships. incl: Montorsorri Soc.; Am. Poetry League; World Poetry Soc. Intercontinental. Contbr. to: Prairie Poet Anthology, 1965; Am. Poetry League, 1971; Poet, 1970; Yrbook. of Mod. Poetry, 1972. Address: 84 Franklin St., Haworth, NJ, U.S.A. 11.

URSO di RAYNERI, (Baron) James, b. 12 Mar. 1932. Editor (Heraldry); Printer; Writer of Genealogical Works. Appts: Printer, 1960-; Ed., Italian List of the Nobility (Albo Nazionale) & International List of the Nobility, 1973-. Mbrships: Heraldry Soc., London; Tiberina Acad.; Yacht Club of Alassio. Address: Via Andrea Verga, 4, Milan, 20144, Italy.

USHER, Elizabeth Reuter (Mrs. Harry T. Usher). Librarian. Educ: Dip., Concordia Tchrs. Coll.; B.S., Univ. of Neb.; B.S.L.S., Univ. of Ill., 1944. Appts. incl: Libn., Cranbrook Acad. Arts, Bloomfield Hills, Mich., 1945-48; Catalog & Ref. Libn., Met. Mus. Art, N.Y., 1948-53, Hd. Cataloguer & Ref. Lib., 1953-54, Asst. Libn., 1954-61, Chief, Art Ref. Lib., 1961-68, Chief Libn., 1968-; Lib. Advsry. Comm. Mbr., Coun. of Higher Educl. Instns. in N.Y.C., 1958-64; Cons. on Lib. Matters, Nat. ssn. Retarded Children Inc., 1960, Mus. of Am. Folk Art, 1970; Bd. of Trustees, N.Y. Metropol. Ref. Rsch. Lib. Agcy., 1968-. Mbrships. incl: num offs. held, Mem. Spl. Libs. Assn.; Chmn., Libns. Sect., Coll. Art Assn., 1972-73; Am. Assn. Museums; N.Y. Lib. Club. Contbr. to profl. publs. Recip. of hons. Address: Fifth Ave., 82nd St., New York City, NY 10028, U.S.A. 2, 5, 42.

USINGER, Fritz, b. 5 Mar. 1895. Author. Educ: Studied at Univs. of Munich, 1913-14, Heidelberg, 1914, Giessen, 1915, 1918-21; Dr. phil., 1921. Appts: Served WWI; Tchr., Darmstadt, Mainz, Bingen, Offenbach a. Main & Bad Nauheim, until 1949; Free-lance author, Friedberg/Hessen, 1949-. Mbrships: V.P., Darmstadt, Deutsche Akad. für Sprache & Dichtung, 15 yrs.; Akad. der Wissenschaften & der Literatur, Mainz; Corres. mbr., Acad. Goetheana, Sao Paulo, Brazil; PEN, German Fed. Repub. Publs. incl: Notizbuch, 1966; Tellurium, 1966; Hessen im Farbbild, 1966; Gottfried Benn & die Medizin, 1967; Hans Schiebelhuth, 1967; Canopus, 1968; Das unwahrscheinliche Glück, 1969; Dichtung als Information, 1970; Der Sinn & das Sinnlose, 1970; Die Verwandlungen, 1971; Haus aus Kubus & Kugel, 1971; Der Planet, 1972. Hons. incl: Goethe Plaque, Hessen, 1960; Plaque of Hon., Landkreis Friedberg/Hessen & Kreisstadt Friedberg/Hessen, 1970. Address: Burg 28, 636 Friedberg/Hessen, German Fed. Repub.

USRY, Milton F., b. 31 Aug. 1931. Regents Professor of Accounting. Educ: B.B.A., Baylor Univ., U.S.A., 1952; M.B.A., Houston Univ., 1959; Ph.D., Tex. Univ., 1964. w. Shell Chem. Co., 1955-59; w. Houston Univ., 1959-61; w. Okla. State Univ., 1961-. Mbrships: Am. Acctng. Assn.; Am. Inst. CPAs; Beta Gamma Sigma; Beta Alpha Psi; Delta Sigma Pi. Publs: Cons. Ed., Cost Accounting: Planning and Control, 4th ed., 1967; 5th ed., '72; Capital-Expenditure Planning and Control, 1944; Author articles 13 var. periodicals. Recip. Price Waterhouse & Co. Doct. Dissertation Grant, 1963. Address: Dept. Acctng., Okla. State Univ., Stillwater, OK 74074, U.S.A. 2, 7, 14, 119, 139.

USTAD, Eric, b. 6 Jan. 1936. Company Executive. Computer Consultant. Educ: B.Com. course, Sir Geo. Williams Univ; Profl. Cert., Data Processing, 1962. Appts. incl: Marketing Specialist, Moore Bus. Forms, 1962-67; Co-fndr., Dir., M.I.C.R. Systems Ltd., 1964-69, Key Punch Ctr. 1965-69 & Systogram Ltd. 1968; Fndr., Pres., Maric Bus. Forms & Systems Design Ltd. 1967-69; Dir., Fastforms Ltd., 1967-69, Sir George Williams Univ., 1968-69, PRA Data Mgmt. Resources Ltd. (Exec. V.P.), Page Raymond & Assocs. Ltd., 1971-72, Computer Fndn. Organizing Comm. 1972-73; Int. V.P., Data Processing Mgmt. Assn., 1970-73; Gen. Chmn., 1972 N.Y. Int. Data Processing Conf. & Bus. Exposition 1971-72; Western Reg. Mgr., Computel Systems Ltd., Ont. Mbrships. incl: Montreal Bd. of Trade; Data Processing Mgmt. Assn. (Chmn. Certn. Coun.); Inst. for Certn. of Computer Profls. (Dir.). Contbr. to profl. publs. Address: 55 Babcombe Drive, Thornhill, Ont., Canada. 88.

UTTER, Charles Wilbar, b. 6 Dec. 1917. Journalist; Editor. Educ: Univ. of Vt., 1937-40. Appts: w. Westerly Sun, R.I., 1945-; Ed., ibid, 1955-; Co-Publr., 1967-; Treas., Utter Co., 1955-. Mbrships. incl: Moderator, Westerly Fire Dist., 1956-; Dir., Westerly & Pawcatuck Community Fund, 1957-; R.I. Chmn., New Engl. Coun.; Am. Newspaper Publrs. Assn.; N.E. Daily Newspaper Publrs. Assn.; N.E. Soc. Newspaper Eds.; Dir., Westerly Chmbr. of Comm., 1945-62; Pres., R.I. Press Assn., 1971-; New Engl. Assoc., Presss News Execs. Assn.; Nominating Comm., 1965-; Inter-Am. Press Assn.; Nat. Press. Photographers Assn.; R.I. News Photographers Assn. Hons: Disting. Flying Cross; Air Medal w. 4 Oak Leaf Clusters. Address: The Westerly Sun, 56 Main St., Westerly, RI 02891, U.S.A. 6.

UTTER, John E., b. 13 Mar. 1905. Banker, Diplomat, Retd.; Private Secretary to Dutchess of Windsor. Educ: B.A., Harvard Univ., 1925. Appts: Prof., French, Choate Schl., 1925-27; Off., 1st Nat. Bank in Paris, 1929-40; For. Serv. Off., 1941-55; Peace Conf., Paris; Am. Rep., 4-Power Commn. to former Italian colonies; UN Deleg.; Dir. African Affa rs, Wash., D.C., 1952-55; Pvte. Sec. to Duke & Duchess of Windsor, 1962-72, & to Duchess of Windsor, 1972-. Mbrships: Harvard Club, N.Y.C.; Metropol. Club, Wash., D.C.; Autombile Club, Paris. Hons: Off., Legion of Hon., Order of Merit, U.S.A.; Cmdr., Star of Ethiopia; C.V.O., 1972. Address: 16 Quai de Béthune, 75004 Paris, France. 43.

UYEO, Shojiro, b. 20 Sept. 1909. University Professor. Educ: Grad., Tokyo Imperial Univ., 1932; Ph.D., ibid, 1937. Appts: Asst., Tokyo Imperial Univ., 1937-39; Instr., then Asst. Prof., Kyoto Univ., 1939-51; Prof., 1960-, Dean, Fac. of Pharmaceutical Scis., 1964-68, 1970-72; Prof., Osaka Univ., 1951-60, Dean, Fac. of Pharmaceutical Scis., 1959-60; Prof., Mukogawa Women's Univ., 1973-.

Mbrships: Sci. Coun. of Japan, 1963-72; Fellow, Chem. Soc., London, U.K.; Am., Swiss & Japanese Chem. Socs.; Pharmaceutical Soc. of Japan; Pres., ibid, 1969. Num. publs., organic chem. Hons: Pharmaceutical Soc. of Japan Award, 1956; Japan Acad. Prize, 1970. Address: Yanaginobamba Rokkakusagaru, Nakagyo-ku, Kyoto 604, Japan. 50.

UYSAL, Ahmet Edip, b. 26 Mar. 1922. Professor of English. Educ: Fac. of Letters, Univ. of Ankara, Turkey, 1941-44; Univ. of St. Andrews, U.K., 1944-45; M.A., Univ. of Aberdeen, 1948; Ph.D., Fac. of Letters, Univ. of Ankara, Turkey, 1952. Appts: Asst., Engl. Dept., Fac. of Letters, Ankara Univ., 1948-56; Assoc. Prof., ibid, 1957-65; Full Prof., 1965, 1968-; Vis. Prof., Englisches Seminar, Univ. of Cologne, German Fed. Repub., 1963-64; Vis. Prof., Tex. Tech. Univ., Lubbock, Tex., U.S.A., 1966-68. Mbr., Exec. Comm., & Treas., Turco-British Assn. Publs: Concept of Time in English Literature, 1966; Street Cries in Turkey, in Jrnl. of Am. Folklore, 1968; Co-ed., Tales Alive in Turkey, 1966; Co-ed., The Book of Dede Korkut: A Turkish Epic, 1972. Address: Ingilizce Bölümü, Dil ve Tarih-Coğrafya Fakültesi, Ankara, Turkey.

UZODINMA, John Eze, b. 26 July 1929. Professor of Biology. Educ: B.A., Grinnell Coll., Iowa, 1954; M.S., Univ. of Iowa, 1956; Ph.D., ibid. Appts: Bacteriologist, State Hygienic Labs., Iowa City, 1957-58; St. Microbiologist, Broadlawn Co. Hosp., Des Moines, Iowa, 1958-61; Prof., Jackson State Univ., Miss., 1964-, Prof. & Hed., Dept. of Biol., 1967-; Dir., Summer Inst. in Biol. for Secondary Schl. Tchrs., 1968-73; Cons. to Nat. Sci. Fndn., 1974. Mbrships. incl: Am. Soc. Microbiol.; AAUP; AAAS; Am. Soc. Clin. Pathologists; Am. Inst. Biological Scis; Southeastern Assn. Allied Hlth. Advsrs.; Miss. Acad. of Scis.; Fellow, Royal Soc. of Tropical Med. & Hygiene, London, U.K.; Sigma Xi, 1956; Beta Beta Beta, 1968. Recip., Tchr. of Yr. Award, Jackson State Univ., 1972. Address: Dept. of Biology, Jackson State University, Jackson, MS 39209, U.S.A. 14, 125.

UZOMA, Reuben Ibekwe, b. 1915. Educational Administrator. Educ: B.S. (Hons), London Univ., U.K., 1943; Dip. in Educ., ibid, 1947. Appts: Prin., Awka Coll. Practising Schl., 1939-43, Okrika Grammar Schl., Rivers State, 1944-46; Supvsr. of Schls., Delta Diocese, 1948-51; Min. of Educ., Eastern Region, Nigeria, 1952-53; Educ. Sec. & Supvsr., Niger Delta Diocese, 1954-62; Educ. Sec., Owerri Diocese, 1963-67; Chmn., Divl. Schl. Bd., Nkwerre Div., 1971-. Fellow, Royal Geographical Soc. Hons: Life Mbr., Ch. Missionary Soc., 1958; O.B.E., 1961; Order of Fed. Repub. of Nigeria (O.F.R.), 1965. Address: P.O. Box 9, Nkwerre via Orlu, E.C. State, Nigeria.

V

VAALAS, Pauli Oskar Gunnar, b. 12 Oct. 1906. Managing Director, Helsinki Deaconess Institution. Educ: M.Sc. Theol., Helsinki Univ., Finland, 1930. Appts: Finnish Pastor, Alta., Canada, 1930-31; Gen. Sec., YMCA, Turku, Finland, 1932-34; Mgr. & Ed. of Publishing, Finnish Mission Soc., 1934-57; Appointed Dean, 1955; Managing Dir., Helsinki Deaconess Instn., 1957-71. Mbrships: Chmn. or Bd. Mbr., num. Finnish Socs. & Assns. connected w. Ch. of Finland, Soc. & Deaconal Instns.; Bd., World Fedn. of Deaconess Assocs., 1961-72. Publs: Ed. (Finnish) Mission News, 1938-57; Ed., Deacony (Finnish), 1960-73; num. missionary, deaconal & hymnolog. publs. & articles. Hons: Cross of Freedom, 3rd & 4th Classes; White Rose of Finland. Address: Hiidenkiukaantie 3 E, 00340 Helsinki 34, Finland. 90.

VACHON, (Msgr.) Louis-Albert, b. 4 Feb. 1912. Professor. Educ: B.A., Laval Univ., Pq., Canada, 1934; D.Ph., ibid, 1947; D.Th., St. Thomas Aquinas, Rome, Italy, 1949. Appts: Ordained priest, 1938; Prof., Philos.-Theol., Laval Univ., Pq., Canada, 1941-55; Superior-Superior-Gen., Grand Séminaire de Pq., 1955-; V.-Rector-Rector, Laval Univ., 1959-72; Protonotary Apostolic, 1963. Mbr. num. profl. assns. Publs: Espérance et Presomption, 1958; Vérité et Liberté, 1962; Unité de l'Université, 1962; Mémorial, 1963; Communauté universitaire, 1963; Apostolat de l'Universitaire catholique, 1963; Progrès de l'université et consentement populaire, 1964; Responsabilité collective des universitaires, 1964; Les humanités adjourd'hui, 1966; Excellence et loyauté des universitaires, 1969. Hons: Univ. Degrees: Montreal, McGill & Vic., 1964; Guelph, 1966; Moncton, 1967; Bishop's, Queen's & Strasbourg, 1968; Notre Dame, Ind., U.S.A., 1971; Carleton, 1972; Hon. Fellow, Royal Coll. Physns. & Surgs., Canada, 1972; Companion, Order of Canada, 1969; Centennial Medal, 1967. Address: Univ. Laval, PQ, G1K 7P4, Canada. 2, 6, 88.

VADER, Usha Shankarrao. Principal. Educ: Art Master. G.D. Art, Directorate of Art, M.S. Bombay; Embroidery Dipl., Tech. Educ. Bd., Bombay. Appts: Painting Lectr., Grihini-Maha Vidyalaya Kolhapur, Bombay; Lectr., Dalvis Art Inst., Kolhapur, for past 15 yrs.; Prin., ibid, 1964-; gives lectrs. & seminars on var. subjects. Mbrships: Bombay Art Soc.; Dalvis Art Educ. Soc., Kalhapur; Shantedevi Gaikwad Shikashan Sanstha, Kolhapur; Rajaram Art Soc., Kolhapur; Fedn. of Arts, Bombay. Works incl: Budha Nirvan; Damayanti; Sea-Shore; Shivanji. Has exhibited paintings in Goa & Delhi. Address: c/o Dalvis Art Inst., Parmar Bldng., Laxmipuri, Kolhapur, Maharash-Tra, India.

VADI, Ramesh Lalbhai, b. 23 July 1931. Surgeon. Educ: M.B.B.S., Gujarat Univ., 1955; M.S. Part I, ibid, 1957; M.S. Part II, 1959. Appts. incl: Lectr., Anatomy, B.J. Med. Coll., Ahmedabad, 1957-60, Sr. Lectr. Embryol., 1960-61, Asst. Prof. of Surg., 1963-64; Dpty. Surg. & Sr. Lectr., Paediatric Surg., M.P. Shah Med. Coll. & Irwin Grp of Hosps., Jamnagar, 1961-63; Asst. Hon. Prof. of Surg., V.S. Hosp. & K.M. Schl. of Postgrad. Med. & Rsch., Ahmedabad, 1965-69, Hon. Assoc. Prof. of Surg., 1969-72, Hon. Additional Prof., 1972-; Cons. Surg., Himabhai Inst., Ahmedabad; Vis. Hon. Surg., H.K. Patal Hosp., Jadar, Gujarat, & Chanchalban Diagnostic Ctr., Ahmedabad; Dean, Fac. of Med., Gujarat Univ., 1970-71. Mbrs., instnl. orgs., comms. & couns. Author, profl. papers. Address: Himabhai Institute,

Opp. C.T.O., Bhadra, Ahmedabad-380001, Gujerat, India.

VAFOPOULOS, George Thomas, b. 6 Sept. 1903. Retired Librarian; Writer. Educ: Athens Univ., Greece. Appts: Sec., City Coun., Thessaloniki, Greece, 1932-39; City Libn., ibid, 1939-63. Mbrships: Sec., Govng. Bd., State Theatre, N. Greece, Thessaloniki; Assn. Greek Writers; Soc. Macedonian Studies, Thessaloniki; Brit. Lib. Assn. Publs. incl: Poetry: The Roses of Myrtale, 1931; Offering, 1938; The Offering and Songs of Resurrection, 1948; The Floor and Other Poems, 1951; The Vast Night and the Window, 1959; Death Songs and Satires, 1966; The Poeticals, 1970; Poetic Drama: Esther, 1934; Prose: Pages of Autobiography, Vols. I-IV, 1970-74; Vol. I: The Passion, 1903-35; Vol. II, The Resurrection, 1935-51; Vol. III Travels and Intervals, A, 1951-67; Vol. IV, Travels and Intervals, B, 1967-73; Translations of selections of poetry in num. anthols.; Contbr. essays, etc., var. Greek newspapers & periodicals, esp. Nea Estia, Athens. Recip. sev. hons., inclng. Medal, City of Thessaloniki, 1963; 1st Greek State Prize, Poetry, 1966. Address: 17 Kennedy Ave., Thessaloniki, Greece.

VAGTS, Detlev Frederick, b. 13 Feb. 1929. Professor fo Law. Educ: A.B., Harvard Univ., 1948; LL.B., ibid, 1951. Appts: Cahill, Gordon & Reindel, N.Y.C., 1951-53, '56-59; 1st Lt., USAF, 1953-56; Asst. Prof., Harvard Law Schl., 1959-62; Prof., ibid, 1962-. Mbrships: Dir., Am. For. Law Assn.; Chmn., Comm. on the Jt. J.D.-M.B.A. Prog., Harvard Law & Bus. Schls.; Bd. of Visitors, Univ. of Indiana Law Schl. Publs: Basic Corporation Law, 1973; Transnational Legal Problems (w. Prof. H.J. Steiner), 1968. Address: Harvard Law Schl., Cambridge, MA 02138, U.S.A.

VAGUE, Jean Marie, b. 25 Nov. 1911. Professor. Educ: Baccalaureat, Cath. Coll., Aix en Provence, France, 1928; M.D., Marseilles Univ., 1935. Appts. incl: Med. Prac., specialising in endocrinology, Marseilles, 1943-; Assoc. Prof., Marseilles Univ., 1946-57; Prof., Clin. endocrinol., 1957-; Dir., Ctr. Alimentary Hygiene & Prophylaxis nutrition diseases Nat. Rys. Mediterranean region, 1958-; Expert, chronic degenerative diseases (diabetes), WHO, 1962-. Mbrships. incl: Endocrine Soc., U.S.; Acad. de Méd.; Am. Diabetes Assn. Publs. incl: La différenciation sexuelle humaine, 1953, Le Conseiller du Diabétique, 1971. Hons. incl: Off., Legion of Hon.; Laureat, l'Acad. Française, 1943, l'Acad. de Med., 1937, '54. Address: Clinique Endocrinologique, Hôpital de la Timone, F13005 Marseille, France.

VAILLANCOURT, Pauline Mariette, b. 19 Apr. 1925. Associate Professor of Library Science. Educ: D.L.S., M.S.L.S., Columbia Univ. Schl. Lib. Serv.; B.S. St. John's Univ. Appts: Cons., United Hosp. Fund, 1955; Queensboro TB & Hlth. Assoc., 1952, '54; Chief Libn., Kings Park State Hosp., N.Y., 1959-60; Chief Libn., Mem. Sloan-Kettering Cancer Ctr., 1960-68; Ind. Lib. Cons., 1968-; Pt.-time Lectr., Queen's Coll., N.Y., 1968-69; Adj. Assoc. Prof., L.I. Univ., 1969; Assoc. Prof., SUNY at Albany, 1970-. Mbrships: ALA, Special Libs. Assn.; Med. Lib. Assn.; N.Y. Acad. Scis.; AAAS; Assn. Am. Lib. Schls.; Am. Chem. Soc.; Assn. Computing Machinery; Am. Soc. Info. Sci. Publs. incl: Bibliographical Control of the Literature of Ocology, 1800-1960, 1969; Contbr. of articles & reviews to profl. publs. Address: State Univ. of N.Y., School of Library & Info. Sci., 1400 Washington Ave., Albany, NY 12222, U.S.A. 5, 6, 130, 138.

VAINIO, (Simo) Veikko, b. 1 Apr. 1915. Chief General Manager, Osuuskunta Metsäliitto. Educ: master of law; M.Sc.; chartered acct. Appts: Lawyer & personnel mgr., Outokumpu Oy, Pori, Finland; lawyer & off. mgr., Suomen Maanviljelijäin Kauppa Oy, Tampere; V.P., Osuuskunta Metsäliitto, Helsinki; Chief Gen. Mgr., Raision Tehtaat Oy, Raisio; Chief Gen. Mgr., Osuuskunta Metsäliitto, Helsinki, 1973. Hon. title Vuorineuvos 1971. Address: Osuuskunta Metsäliitto, P.O. Box 186, SF-00101 Helsinki 10, Finland. 134,

VAINIO, Valde Anton, b. 4 Jan. 1901. Industrial & Commercial Executive. Educ: M.B.A., M.Sc. Appts: Mgr., Oy Voimavaunu Ab, automobile distributors; Mgr., Commercial Sect., Finnish Indl. Assn.; Mng. Dir., Hämeenlinnan Verkatehdas Oy., & Oy Turun Verkatehdas Ab., woollen ind.; Chmn., Bd. of Dirs., Silo Oy., hosiery & knitting mill; Hon. Consul of Belgium in W. Finland. Mbrships. incl: Pres., Assn. of Bus. Men, Turku; V.P., Turku Chmbr. of Comm.; V.P., Woollen Indl. Assn.; City Coun. Mbr., Hämeenlinnan; Admin. Bd. Mrb., Commercial H.Ss., Helsinki & Turku. Hons: 9 Finnish decorations, 1 Belgian decoration. Address: Silo Oy., 20521 Turku 52, Box 39, Finland.

VAIZEY, John, b. 1 Oct. 1929. Economist. Educ: Queen's Coll., Cambridge, U.K.; M.A. Cantab; M.A., Oxon.; D.Tech., Brunel. Appts: Fellow, St. Catharine's Coll., Cambridge Univ., 1953-56; Lectr., Oxford Univ., 1956-60; Dir. of Rsch. Unit, Univ. of London, 1960-62; Fellow & Tutor, Worcester Coll., Oxford Univ., 1962-66; Prof., Econs., & Hd. of Dept., Brunel Univ., Uxbridge, Middlesex, 1966-. Mbrships: Garrick Club; French Club; Royal Econ. Soc. Publs. incl: Scenes from Institutional Life; Social Democracy; Capitalism; Political Economy of Education; The Economics of Education; Education for Tomorrow; Education in the Modern World; The Economics of Research & Technology (w. K. Norris). Hons: Scholar of Queen's Coll.; Gladstone Mem. Prizeman, Cambridge Univ., 1954; Cmdr. of El Sabio (Alfonso XI), Spain, 1970. Address: 24 Heathfield Terrace, London, W4 4JE, U.K. 1, 2.

VAKIL, Rustom Jal, b. 17 July 1911. Consultant Cardiologist. Educ: M.B.B.S. (Lond.), 1934; M.D. (Lond.), 1937; D.T.M. & H. (London.), 1938. Appts: Hon. Cons. Physn. & i/c Cardiol. Dept., King Edward Mem. Hosp., 1941-58; Lectr. in Med., G. S. Med. Coll., 1941-58; Hon. Physn., Gov. of Bombay, 1950-65; Hon. Asst. Physn., Sir. J.J. Grp. of Hosps. & Lectr. in Med., Grant Med. Coll.; Hon. Physn., Bombay Hosp., 1960; Hon. Cons. Cardiol., Bhatia Gen. Hosp., Nanavaty Hosp., King Edward Mem. Hosp. Mbrships. incl: Past Pres., Cardiol. Soc. of India; Fellow, Royal Soc. Hlth., Royal Coll. Physns.; Royal Soc. Med. Publs. incl: Clinical Diagnosis—A Textbook of Physical Signs & Symptoms; Diagnosis & Management of Medical Emergencies. Recip., num. hons. Address: Standard Bldg., 346 Dr. D. Nawroji Rd., Bombay 1 (BR), India. 2

VALAORAS, Vasilios G., b. Nov. 1902. Professor of Hygiene & Epidemiology. Educ: M.D., Med. Schl., Univ. of Athens, 1926; Master Pub. Hlth., Schl. of Hygiene, Athens, 1930; Dr.P.H., John Hopkins Univ., Balt., U.S.A., 1936; post-grad. studies, Paris, London, & U.S.A. Appts. incl: Lectr., Athens Schl. Hygiene, 1936-47; Pub. Hlth. Specialist & Demographer, UN, N.Y., 1947-61; Prof., Univ. of Athens, 1961-68; Pres., Dentistry Schl., ibid,

1964-66; Med. Commn., World Coun. of Chs., Geneva, 1968-70; Chmn., UN Expert Comm., N.Y., 1971. Mbrships. incl: Med. Assn. of Athens; Pres., ibid, 1966-68; Int. Statl. Inst.; Royal Soc. Hlth., London Am. Pub. Hlth. Assn., Wash. D.C. Publs. incl: Village Hygiene, 1945, 2nd edit., 1947; Human Hygiene, 1962, 2nd edit., 1967. Contbr., var. scientific publs. Address: Asklepiou 14, Athens 144, Greece. 43.

VALAVAARA, (Frans Kaino) Veikko, b. 27 Sept. 1911. Executive Vice President. Educ: M.A., Univ. of Turku, Finland, 1935. Appts: Prin., Civic Inst. of Korkeakoski, 1937-38; Cashier of Turku, 1939-44; Personnel Mgr., Huhtamäki-yhtymä Oy, 1944-48; Mbr., Bd. of Dirs., ibid, 1948-; Prod. Mgr., 1957-58; Exec. V.P., 1958-; Mgr., Hellas Chocolate Plant, 1948-57. Mbrships. incl: Chmn., Econ. Bd., Unvi. of Turku; Admin. Bd., Finnish Food Inds. Fedn.; Admin. Bd., Turku Chmbr. of Comm., Chmn., Traffic Comm.; Rotary Club. Hons: Cross of Liberty 4th class w. sword, 1940; Cross of Liberty 4th class w. oak leaves, 1942; Cross of Liberty 3rd class, 1943; Kt., 1st class, Order of the White Rose of Finland, 1961; Indl. Councillor, 1967; Major, 1968; Cmdr., Order of the Lion of Finland, 1972. Address: Linnankatu 21 B, SF-20360 Turku 36, Finland. 43.

VALENCIK, May Virginia Kunz, b. 25 Mar. 1909. Librarian. Educ: A.B., Rutgers Univ., 1931; Postgrad. study, Cornell Univ., Univ. of Chgo., New Schl. for Soc. Rsch., Columbia Univ. Grad. Lib. Schl. Appts: Lib. Asst., Passaic, (N.J.) Pub. Lib., 1931-36; Sr. Ref. Asst., Utica (N.Y.) Pub. Lib., 1936-41; State Supvsr., Ky. Lib. Proj., 1941-42; Hd. Libn., Allentown (Pa.) Free Lib., 1942-63; Dir., White Plains (N.Y.) Pub. Lib., 1963-. Num. mbrships. incl: Mbr., Pres. Eisenhower's Comm. on Traffic Safety, 1955-57; Nat. Women's Advsry. Comm. to Fed. Civil Defense Admins., 1955-57; Int. Pres., Quota Int., 1955-57; Trustee, N.Y. Metropol. Ref. & Rsch. Lib. Agcy.; Past Pres., Pa. Lib. Assn.; Past Mbr., Coun., ALA; N.Y. Lib. Assn.; Exec. Bd., Westchester Lib. Assn.; Smithsonian Instn.; Wildlife Fedn. Contbr. to profl. jrnls. Hons: LL.D., Cedar Crest Coll., 1952; Life Mbr., Quota Int., Inc.; Mbr., Quota Club of Allentown, Pa. Address: 10 Nosband Ave., White Plains, NY 10645, U.S.A. 5, 6, 15, 42, 126, 138.

VALENT, Henry, b. 21 July 1915. Lawyer. Educ: A.B., Cornell Univ., 1936; LL.B., Cornell Law Schl., 1938. Appts: Gen. prac. of law, 1938-41, '46-; Owner, Finger Lake Broadcasting Co., (WFLR, Dundee, N.Y.); Ptnr., Glenfield & Baxter Dairies; Pres., Watkins Glen Grand Prix Corp., 1963-. Mbrships. incl: Dir. & Sec., Hi-Speed Checkweigher Co., Inc.; Dir., Glen Nat. Bank & Trust Co.; Dir., Schuyler Hosp. Inc., 1960-; Sec., Watkins Glen Youth Ctr., 1962-; Trustee, Glen Springs Acad.; Am., N.Y. State & Schuyler Co. Bar Assns.; Nat. Pres., Improved Order of Red Men; Co. Cmdr., Am. Legion; Rotarian; Veterans of For. Wars; Chmbr. of Comm.; Subcomm. on Grievances, N.Y. State Bar Assn., 1971. Author of First Ten Years of Road Racing at Watkins Glen. Recip. of hons. Address: Old Corning Rd., Watkins Glen, NY 14891, U.S.A. 6, 16.

VALENTIN, Hartmut Hans Burchard, b. 8 Jan. 1923. University Professor of Geography. Educ: Dr.phil., Free Univ. of Berlin, German Fed. Repub., 1949; Inaugurated for geog., ibid, 1955. Appts: Sci. asst., Inst. for Geomorphol. & Cartography, German Acad. of Scis., Berlin,

1947-48, & Dept. of Geog., Free Univ. of Berlin, 1948-55; British Coun. rsch. schlr., Univ. of Cambridge, U.K., 1951-53; Lectr., Free Univ. of Berlin, 1955-61; Vis. Fellow, Australian Nat. Univ., Canberra, 1958-59; Sr. Lectr., Free Univ. of Berlin, 1961-62; Prof. & Hd., Dept. of Geog., Tech. Univ., Berlin, 1962-. Mbrships. incl: V.P., Geographical Soc. of Berlin, 1963-; Royal Geographical Soc., London, 1951-; Corres. mbr., Subcommn. on Shorelines of Northwestern Europe & Int. Assn. for Quaternary Rsch., 1969-. Author of publs. in field. Hon: Prof., Free Univ. of Berlin, 1963. Address: 53 Paulsenstrasse, D-1 Berlin 41, German Fed. Repub. 43.

VALES VILLAMARIN, Francisco, b. 7 May 1891. Academy Secretary. Educ: Magisterio de Ensenanza Primaria, Normal Schl., Santiago de Compostela. Appts. incl: Prof., Los Castros Nat. Schl., 1918-61; Official Newswriter, City of Betanzos; Sec., Real Acad. Gallega, La Coruña. Mbrships. incl: Provincial Commn. of Histl. & Artistic Monuments; Treas., Royal Acad. of Fine Arts of Our Lady of the Rosary, La Coruña. Publs. incl: El sepulcro de Andrade o Bôo, 1949; Contribución a la historia de Betanzos. El retablo mayor de Santa María del Azogue, 1951; El santuario de los Remedios de Betanzos, 1968; La sepultura de Juan Nunes Pardo, padre del mariscal Pardo de Cela, 1974. Hons. incl: Cmdr., Civil Order of Alfonso X el Sabio; Medal, City of Betanzos. Address: Ramón y Cajal 5, 2°, La Coruña, Spain. 43.

VALLE, Carlos, b. 5 Feb. 1911. Lawyer. Educ: Grad., Juridical Scis., Law Fac. of the Classic Univ. of Lisbon. Appts: Mbr. of the Regional Coun. of the Lawyers Order, 6 yrs.; Delegate to the Gen. Meetings, ibid, in representation of the Oporto Jurisdiction. Mbrships: Pres., Bd. Dirs., Associaçao dos Jornalistas e Homens de Letras do Porto, 7 yrs.; Automóvel Club, Portugal; Pres., Gen. Meeting, Sociedade Portuguesa de Numismática; Sociedade da Independência de Portugal; Assoc., Liga dos Combatentes; Hon. Assoc., Circulo Mercantil de Vigo, Spain. Publs: Fumarada; Páginas Acidas; Jogos Florais; Escritos e Ditos (1 vol.); Tradiçoes do Casamento e Superstiçoes Populares; Baile do José do Egipto (auto popular); O Castelo de Gaia e a Lenda do Rei Ramiro; Relicário de Cantigas, 1 vol. (Cancioneiro); sundry reprints of 'Revista de Etnografia' (Oporto). Hons: Cruz de Benemerência de Cruz Vermelha Portuguesa; Comenda do Mérito Civil da Espanha; Medalha de ouro do Vilanovense Futebol Clube. Address: Rua do Cabo Borges, 278, Vila Nova de Gaia, Portugal. 43.

VALLENTIN du CHEYLARD, Raymond, b. 2 Apr. 1907. Lawyer. Educ: Fac. of Law, Grenoble, France; Doct. in Law. Appts: Lawyer, Montélimar Bar, 1931-; Pres., Order of Laywers, 1945-47, 1956-58; Municipal Councillor, Montélimar. Mbrships. incl: Past Pres., Acad. Delphinale & Rotary Club of Montélimar; Hon. Pres., Masque de Fer (Iron Mask) & Rhodania; Fndg. Pres., Soc. for the Protection of Ancient Monuments of Drôme; Hon. Pres., Drôme Acad. of Letters, Scis. & Arts. Publs. incl: Les Saints Lieux de Provence; Cartulaire de Montélimar, 1974; num. brochures & works on Cardinal Maury, Foch, & Clemenceau. Hons: Off., Acad. Palms; Chevalier, Arts & Letters; Cmdr., Order of Civil Merit of Spain. Address: 13 Rue Bouverie, 26200 Montélimar, France.

VALLINKOSKI, Jorma Väinö, b. 14 Aug. 1915. Chief Librarian. Educ: Phil. cand., 1939; Dr. phil., 1948. Appts: ˙Libn., Chief of Finnish Dept., Univ. Lib. of Helsinki, Finland, 1949-56;

Chief Libn., ibid, 1956-. Mbrships: V.P., Finnish Rsch. Libs., 1957-72. Publs: The History of the University Library at Turku, 1, 1640-1722, 1948; L'Italia nella letteratura finlandese 1640-1953, 1955; Bibliographie historique finlandaise 1926-1950, 1-2, 1955-56, & 1544-1900, 1961; Die Dissertationen der alten Universität Turku (Academia Aboënsis) 1642-1828, 1-2, 1962-69. Hons: Cmdr., Order of Lion of Finland; Cmdr., Order of the Pole Star; Silver Medal of Italian Culture. Address: Pihlajatie 52, 00270 Helsinki 27, Finland.

VALLIS, Valentine Thomas, b. 1 Aug. 1916. Lecturer. Educ: Univ. of Qld., Australia; Birkbeck Coll., London, U.K. Appts: Clerk, Town Coun. Off., Gladstone, 1933-41; War Serv., New Guinea, 1941-45; Lectr., Philos., Univ. of Qld., Aust., 1950; Engl. Dept., ibid, 1965; Rdr., Engl., 1974. Publs: (poetry) Songs of the East Coast, 1947; Dark Wind Blowing, 1961; contbr. to jrnls. & anthols. Recip., 2 prizes, Univ. of Qld. Address: c/o Dept. of Engl., Univ. of Qld., St. Lucia, Qld. 4067, Australia.

VALORE, Evelyn Grace Hunt (Mrs. Abram Valore, Jr.), b. 8 Feb. 1937. Librarian/ Teacher. Educ: B.A., Southern Univ., 1957; M.S., Univ. of Wis., 1962; further studies at Univs. in La. Appts. incl: Libn., George W. Carver H.S., 1957-64; Libn., Valencia H.S., 1964-67; Educ. Div. Libn., Grambling Coll., Summer, 1966; Libn., Capt. Shreve H.S., 1967-. Mbrships: NEA; ALA; Am. Assn. of Schl. Libns.; La. Educ. Assn.; La. Lib. Assn.; Caddo Educ. Assn.; Pres., Caddo Libns. Org.; Kappa Delta Pi; YWCA; NAACP; Silhouettes of Kappa, V.P., Shreveport Chapt.; Anti-Basileus, Grammateus, Dean of Pledgees, Hodegoes, Parliamentarian, Alpha Kappa Alpha Sorority, Inc. Publs. incl: articles in La. Educ. Assn. Jrnl. Address: 125 Fondren Circle, Shreveport, LA 71103, U.S.A. 5.

VALPOLA, (Kustaa) Veli, b. 24 Apr. 1922. Lexicographer. Educ: mag.philos., Univ. of Helsinki, Finland, 1947; Dr.philos., ibid, 1955. Ed.-in-Chief, Finnish Encyclopaedias, 1959-. Mbrships: Soc. for Finnish Lit.; Soc. pour l'étude de la langue maternelle; Finnish Mathematical Soc.; Assn. for Symbolic Logic. Address: Metsätie 12-14, SF-02240 Frisans, Finland. 90, 134.

VALZELLI, Luigi, b. 16 June 1927. Physician; Bio-Medical Scientist. Educ: M.D., Univ. of Milan, 1951; specialization, Cardiol., Univ. of Pavia, 1956. Appts: Asst., Neuropsych. Ward, Milan Main Gen. Hosp., 1954-56; Asst. Prof., Inst. of Pharmacol., Univ. of Milan, 1958; Chief., Sect. of Neuropsychopharmacol., Inst. of Pharmacol. Rsch. "Mario Negri", 1963-; Prof., Psychopharmacol., Univ. of Milan, 1968-; Adjunct Prof. of Psychol., Queens Coll., CUNY, U.S.A., 1971-. Mbrships: Collegium Int. Neuropsychopharmacologicum N.Y. Acad. of Scis.; Int. Soc. for Rsch. on Agression; Soc. of Biol. Psych.; Int. Soc. for Biochem. Pharmacol.; Fndng. Mbr., European Sleep Rsch. Soc. Publs. incl: Elementi di Psicofarmacologia Sperimentale e Clinica, 1970; Psychopharmacology—An Introduction to Experimental & Clinical Principles, 1973; about 140 sci. papers on neurochem., neuropharmacol., biol. psych. & behavioral scis. in int. jrnls. Address: Viale Romagna 74, 20133 Milan, Italy. 43.

VAN, Tan Tran, b. 24 June 1930. University Professor. Educ: Doctorat du 3e Cycle en Mathematiques Appliquees, Toulouse Univ., France; Doctorat d'Etat (Mathematiques), Paris Univ., France. Appts:

Dean, Fac. of Pedagogy, Univ. of Saigon, 1963-, Univ. Vice-Rector, 1970-; Mbr., Govng. Bd., Regional Ctr. of Sci. & Maths., 1970-; Mbr., Pacific Sci. Coun, 1971-. Contbr., acad. & educl. publs. Address: Faculty of Pedagogy of Saigon, 221 Công-Hòa St., Saigon, S. Vietnam.

VAN AALTEN, Jacques, b. 12 Apr. 1907. Artist-Painter. Educ: Grad., Nat. Acad. of Design, NYC, 1926-30; Art Students League of N.Y., 1932-34; Grande Chaumiere, Paris, France, 1955; Tulane Univ., New Orleans, La., 1970-71. Appts: Instr., Nassau Conservatory of Art, Rockville Ctr., L.I., 1940; van Aalten Studio Schl., Detroit, Mich., 1944-47. One-man shows: Gall. Circle, New Orleans, 1960; Le Petit Theatre du Vieux Carre, ibid, 1961; Delray Playhouse, Fla., 1963; Galerie van Aalten, Palm Beach, Fla., 1963-64; Rockport Art Assn., Mass., 1965. In num. grp. shows. Works incl: Fresco Mural, Straubenmuller Textile HS, N.Y.C., 1938-39; num. portraits inclng. one of Pope Pius XII, in perm. collect. of Vatican Mus., Rome, Italy. Paintings in num. pvte. collects. & sev. pub. collects. Mbrships: Life, Rockport Art Assn. & Art Students League of N.Y.; Nat. Soc. Mural Painters, NYC, 1940-41; Isaac Delgado Mus. of Art Assn., New Orleans. Hons. incl: Silver Pontifical Medal, Pope Pius XII, 1956; Suydam Medal, 1930. Address: 1500 Bay Rd., Apt. 527—N. Bldg., Miami Beach, FL 33139, U.S.A. 2, 7, 37.

VAN ARKEL, Hubertus, b. 14 Jan. 1913. Mining Engineer; Management Consultant. Educ: M.Sc., Tech. Univ. of Delft, Netherlands. Appts. incl: Sev. posts, Billiton Co., Dutch Guiana, Celebes, & Banka, Sumatra, 1939-51; Off., Motorised Artillery, WWII; Plant Mgr., Alcoa, Moengo Wks., Dutch Guiana, 1952-54; Tech. Sec. to Mng. Dir., Naarden Chem. Wks., 1956-61; V.P., Chem. & Process Div., Berenschot Mgmt. Cons., 1964-68; Sec.-Gen. & Dir., Bur. of Int. Contact for Mgmt. Educ., 1970-71; Co-fndr. & Sec.-Gen., European Fndn. for Mgmt. Dev., 1972-73; Owner-Exec., Management-Spreekuur, 1974. Mbrships. incl: Am. Inst. of Mining, Metallurgical & Petroleum Engrs, Soc. of Mining Engrs.; Deutsche Mgmt. Gesellschaft. Publs: Translations into Dutch of 2 books on bus. mgmt.; Article in jrnl.; Paper given at 36th World Congress of Chem. Address: Nieuwe Bussummerweg 34, Huizen, NH, Netherlands. 12, 43.

VAN BAREN, Ferdinand Alexander, b. 26 June 1905. Professor of Soil Science; Museum Administrator. Educ: M.Sc., Agricl. Univ., Wageningen, Netherlands, 1933; Dr.Sc., ibid, 1934; Appts. incl: Sci. Off., Soils Dept., Agricl. Univ., 1933-37; Sci. Off., Soil Rsch. Inst., Bogor, Indonesia, 1937-41, Dir., 1945-48; Pt.-time Prof., Fac. of Agric., Univ. of Indonesia, Bogor, 1940-42, Full Prof., & Dean of Fac., 1948-50; Dir., Soils Dept., Royal Tropical Inst., Amsterdam, Netherlands, 1950-66; Dir., Int. Soil Mus., Utrecht, 1962-; Prof., State Univ., Utrecht, 1966-, Dean, Fac. of Geol. & Geophys., 1966-72; Soils Advsr., Royal Tropical Inst., Amsterdam, 1966-; Cons., for. cons. engrs., U.K. & U.S.A., 1966-. Mbrships. incl: Sec.-Gen., Int. Soc. Soil Sci., 1950-; Pres., Royal Geographic Soc., 1956-66; Egyptian Soc. Soil Sci., 1960; For. Mbr., Acad. of Agric. Scis., U.S.S.R., 1970. Address: Soils Dept., State Univ., Oude Kamp 9-11, Utrecht, Netherlands. 43.

VANCE, Bruce, b. 23 June 1931. Educational Consultant. Educ: B.A., M.A., M.Ed., Univ. of Toronto, 1953-74. Appts: Fiction Ed., New Liberty Mag., Toronto, 1953-54; Master, Lower Schl., Ridley Coll., St. Catharines, Ont., 1954-55; Tchr., 1956-63;

Asst. Hd. Engl., Jarvis Collegiate, Toronto, 1963; Hd. of Engl., Monarch Pk. Secondary Schl., Toronto, 1964-67; Co-ordinating Cons., Lang. Study Ctr., Toronto Bd. Educ., 1967-. Ed. var. anthologies, series & books adapted for schls., inclng: Narrative & Thythm, An Introduction to Poetry, 1964; Description, Narration, Exposition, 1969; Short Plays for Reading & Acting, 1970; Being Born & Growing Older, 1971; In & Out of Love, 1971. Address: The Lang. Study Ctr., Toronto Bd. of Educ., 155 Coll. St., Toronto 2B, Ont., Canada. 30.

VAN DE BOGART, Willard George, b. 29 Dec. 1939. Artist. Educ: B.B.A., Ohio Univ. Athens, 1965; McGill Univ., Montreal, Canada, 1969; Nat. Film Bd. of Canada, Montreal, Quebec Rsch. Inst., 1969; M.F.A., Calif. Inst. of the Arts, Valencia, 1971. Appts. incl: Instr., Allegheny Community Coll., Pittsburgh, Pa., 1968-69, Ivy Schl. of Profl. Art, ibid, 1969-70, Calif. Inst. of the Arts, Valencia, 1970-71, Univ. of Pittsburgh, Pa., 1971-73; The Comm. for the Future, Inc., Wash., D.C., 1972-74; Prof. of Media Ecol., Jersey City State Coll., N.J., 1973-74. Mbrships: Bio-Feedback Rsch. Soc., Univ. of Colo. Med. Ctr., Denver; Expmts. in Art & Technol., N.Y. & L.A.; Wide Screen Assn., London, U.K.; Am. Film Inst., Wash., D.C.; Fndr., Pittsburgh Independent Film-Makers Assn., 1969; Inst. of Noetic Scis. Contbr. of articles to var. Mags. Works exhibited in var. Am. Galls., 1970-73. Hons: Andrew W. Mellon Award, Educational & Charitable Trust Fund, 1969; Robert Flaherty Int. Film Sem. Schlrship. Award & Calif. Inst. of the Arts Schlrship. Award, 1970. Address: The Comm. for the Future, Inc., Int. H.Q. & New Worlds Trng. & Educ. Ctr., 2325 Porter St., N.W., Wash. DC 20008, U.S.A. 37.

VAN DEMAN, Dorothy Denny, b. 12 Aug. 1909. Professor; Author; Counselor; Speaker. Educ: B.A., Whittier Coll., Calif., 1931; M.A., Claremont Coll., 1934; UCLA; Northwestern Univ.; Univ. of Calif., Santa Barbara. Appts. incl: Instr., Santa Barbara State Coll., 1040-44; Fac., Univ. of Calif., Santa Barbara, 1944-64; Prof. Emeritus, 1964-; Writer, Lectr., Counselor, 1966-. Mbrships. incl: Assn. for Childhood Educ. Int.; Assn. for Supvsn. & Curric. Dev.; Delta Kappa Gamma; Delta Phi Epsilon; Calif. State Employees Assn. Jt. Author: Foundations of Learning in Childhood Education, 1963; Basic Learning in the Language Arts, 1965; Counseling with Parents, 1954; Say It & Play It, 1951; Through Faith the Victory, 1967. Address: P.O. Drawer JJ, Santa Barbara, CA 93102, U.S.A. 130, 138.

VANDEPLASSCHE, Marcel, b. 16 Feb. 1914. Professor. Educ: Classic humanities, 1933; Dr. Veterinarius, 1939; post-grad. studies in Vienna, Hannover, Utrecht, & U.S.A. Appts: Asst., Fac. of Vet. Med., Ghent, 1940; Prof., Dept. of Reproduction & Obstetrics, ibid, 1941; Vis. Prof., Fac. Vet. Med., Cairo, 1957 & Ont. Vet. Coll., Guelph, Can., 1969. Mbrships: Pres., Comm. for Control of Sterility, Fac. of Vet. Med., Ghent; Standing Comm., Int. Congress Animal Reprod. & A.I.; Consultative Comm., Agric. in Nat. Belgian F.A.P.; Expert Panel on Vet. Educ., F.A.O.-WHO; Corres., Soc. Ital. Zootec. Publs: books on artificial insemination, 1947, bovine caesarean section, 1953 & Vibrio fetus infection, 1963; collab. on Advances in Veterinary Science, 1957, International Encyclopaedia of Veterinary Medicine, 1st ed. 1966, Large Animal Surgery, 1974 & The Veterinary Annual, 1974; contbr. articles to jrnls. in field. Hons: Dr. h.c., Vet. Schl., Hannover, 1963; Belgian-Mullie-Prize, 1963; Dr. h.c., Fac. Vet. Med., Univ. of

Utrecht, 1971; Pesian-Medaile, BRNO, 1969. Address: c/o Fac. Vet. Med., Casinoplein, 24, B-9000, Ghent, Belgium. 87.

VANDERBILT, Amy (Mrs. Curtis B. Kellar). Author, Journalist, Syndicated Daily Columnist on Etiquette for United Features Synd. Educ: Inst. Heubi, Lausanne, Switz.; Packer Coll. Inst., Bklyn.; Schl. of Journalism, N.Y.U., 1926-28. Publs. & Features incl: Amy Vanderbilt's Everyday Etiquette, 1945; Amy Vanderbilt's Complete Book of Etiquette, 1952; TV Artist Etiquette Program, It's Good Taste, 1954-60; Radio Program, The Right Thing To Do, 1960-62; Amy Vanderbilt's Complete Cookbook, 1961; Amy Vanderbilt's New Complete Book of Etiquette, 1963; monthly page, McCall's, 1963-64; Columnist, Ladies' Home Jrnl., 1964-; United Feature Syndicate, 1954-68; now w. Los Angeles Times Sync., 1968-; Dir., Amy Vanderbilt Success Prog. for Women, 1963-. Ed., monthly brochures; contbr. to newspapers, nat. mags. & World Book Ency. Mbrships. incl: Bd. of Dirs., Nat. Assn. Mental Hlth., 1966; Bd. Mbr., N.Y. Acad. of Scis. Women's Aux.; Chmn., Bd. of Trustees, Richmondtown Hist. Restoration Soc.; Author's Guild INc. & Author's Leaaue of Am. Address: 438 E. 87th St., New York, NY 10028, U.S.A. 2, 5, 6,

VANDERBILT, Gloria (Mrs. Wyatt E. Cooper), b. 20 Feb., 1924. 10 One-woman Shows of paintings & collages, N.Y.C., Wash. D.C., Dallas, Tex., Houston, Tex., Southampton, & Palm Beach, 1953-68. Publs. incl: Love Poems, 1953; also short stories & book reviews for periodicals & jrnls. Recip. Sylvania Award for Disting. Achievement in Creative TV Tech., Outstanding Comedy Prog. Art Carney Show, 1959. Address: 45 E. 67th St., New York, NY 10021, U.S.A.

VAN DER KUYP, Edwin, b. 23 Oct. 1913. Physician; Educator. Educ: Physn., Med. Schl., Surinam, 1938; M.P.H., Johns Hopkins Univ., U.S.A., 1948; Doctorandus, Univ. of Amsterdam, Neths., 1949; Physn., ibid, 1950; Dr.Med. (Diss.), 1950; Dip. Trop. Med. & Hygiene, 1951; Specialist, Soc. Med., 1966. Appts. incl: Dir., Bur. of Pub. Hlth., Surinam, 1951-73; Lectr., Surinam Med. Schl., 1951-69; Dir., ibid, 1954-55; Lectr., Schl. for Nurses, 1951-; Lectr., Trng. Coll. for Tchrs., 1952-; Prof., Environmental Hlth., Leyden State Univ., Neths., 1968; Prof., Pub. Hlth. & Soc. Med., Univ. of Surinam, 1971-; Dean, Fac. of Med., ibid, 1969-71. Mbrships. incl: Pres., Surinam Red Cross; Past Treas. & Chmn., Med. Soc.; Chmn., Fndn. Sci. Inst.; Soc. Sci. Wkrs. Author of num. publs. in field & Ed., Surinam Ency. Hons. incl: 20 yrs. Serv. Medal & Golden Cross of Merit, Neths. Red Cross, 1969; Kt. Officer, Order of Orange Nassau, 1968; Silver Boerhaave Badge, State Univ. of Leyden, 1969. Address: Medisch Wetenschappelijk Inst., Kernkampweg 3, Paramaribo, Surinam, S.Am., 136.

VANDERLIP, Arthur Nelson, b. 7 July 1901. Professional Engineer; Educator; Consulting Engineer. Educ: Sibley Schl. of Mech. Engrng., Cornell Univ., Ithaca, N.Y., 1920-22; C.E., ibid, 1927; M.C.E., 1928; McMullen rsch. fellow, 1927-32. Appts. incl: Asst. Prof., Civil Engrng., Univ. of Conn. Storrs, 1938; Assoc. Prof.-Prof., involved in war oriented inds. in Conn., ibid, 194-47; Civil & Hydraulic Engr., & later Cons. Engr., F.W. Scheidenhelm Assoc., N.Y.C., 1947-50; Cons. to Am. Elec. Power Serv. Corp., N.Y.C., 1959-; Cons., N.J. Zinco Co.; Cons., Gwin Engrs., Inc., Altoona, Pa. Mbrships. incl: Am. Soc. of Civil Engrs.; Am. Concrete Inst.; Am. Inst. of Cons. Engrs.; Am. Soc. for Testing & Materials; Assn.

of Asphalt Paving Technologists; Am. Geophus. Union. Author of bulletins & papers in field. Address: 1569 Storrs Rd., Storrs, CT 06268, U.S.A. 6, 14, 26, 36.

VAN DERPOOL, James Grote, b. 21 July 1903. Architectural Historian; Historic Preservationist; Administrator. Educ: B.Arch., MIT, 1927; M.F.A., Harvard Univ., 1939. Appts: Fndr., Study of Arch. Hist., Rensselaer Polytech. Inst., 1933; Prof., Hist. of Arch., Univ. of Ill., 1934-46; Hd., Dept. of Art, ibid; Prof., Acting Dean, Assoc. Dean, Schl. of Arch., Columbia Univ., 1946-60; Fndng. & Exec. Dir., Landmarks Preservation Commn., N.Y., 1960-65; Nat. Co-chmn., Venice Comm., U.S.A. Fellowships: Benjamin Franklin & Life, Royal Soc. of Arts; Hon., Am. Inst. of Archs. Mbrships. incl: Nat. Dir., Int. Fund for Monuments; A Fndr., Past Pres., Dir. & Advsry. Bd., Soc. of Arch. Histns.; Hon., Phi Beta Kappa; Century Assn. of N.Y.; Trustee, Holland Soc.; Edit. Bd. Mbr., St. Nicholas Soc.; Grolier Club, N.Y. Contbr. to encys. & schol. jrnls. Recip., George McAneny Medal for Hist. Preservation. Address: Ocean Towers, 201 Ocean Ave., Santa Monica, CA 90402, U.S.A. 2.

VANDERPOOL, Ward Melvin, b. 20 Jan. 1915. Management & Marketing Consultant. Educ: M.A. & M.E.E., Tulane Univ., New Orleans, La., U.S.A. Appts: V.P., Sales, Van Lang Brokerage Co., 1934-38; Mgr., Agricl. Div., Dayton Rubber Co., 1938-48; Pres., Veemac Co., 1948-; Pres., Zipout, Inc., 1948-; Bd. Chmn., 1959-; Pres., Wife Saver Products, 1948-; Bd. Chmn., Atlas Chem. Int., 1959-; Bd. Chmn., Global Enterprises Ltd., 1959-. Mbrships. incl: Marlin Club; Dolphin Club; Dir., Am. Heart Assn.; Dir., Ctrl. Amateur Athletic Union; Advsry. Bd., Nat. Security Coun.; Dir. at large, Sales & Marketing Execs. Int.; Past Pres., Am. Mgmt. Inst.; Dir., Int. Acad. of Aquatic Art. Hons: Army Ordnance Engrng. Award, 1945; Marketing Ma of the Yr., 1956; Outstanding Pres., Sales & Marketing Execs. Int., 1956; Outstanding Master of Ceremonies, Int. Amateur Athletic Assn., 1971. Address: Box 1972, Cedar Rapids, IA 52406, U.S.A. 7, 8, 128.

VANDERPOOL, Wynant Davis, Jr., b. 12 Apr. 1914. Architect. Educ: A.B., Princeton Univ., 1936; M.F.A., 1940. Appts: Designer, Offs. of J.H. & W.C. Ely, Archts., Newark, N.J., 1940-42; Skidmore Owings & Merrill, N.Y.C., 1946; Designer & Admin., Faulkner Stenhouse Fryer & Faulkner, Wash. D.C., 1965-68; Ptnr., Faulkner Fryer & Vanderpool, ibid, 1968-; Mbr., Bd. of Archtl. Cons., Georgetown Commn. of Fine Arts. Mbrships: Sr. Warden. St. Johns Ch., Lafayette Sq., Wash. D.C., 1973; V.P., Holland Soc. of N.Y., 1972-73; Trustee, ibid, 1974; Trustee, Fndn. fo; the Preservation of Historic Georgetown, 1971-; Pres., Hist. Georgetown Inc., 1971-; Am. Inst. of Archts.; Century Assn., N.Y.; Metropol. Club, Wash.; Mid-Ocean Club, Tuckerstown, Bermuda. Works incl: Perinatal Clin., Nat. Instn. of Hlth., Bethesda, Md., 1973; Am. Univ. Master Plan, 1974; St. Johns Ch. Columbarium, Wash. D.C., 1974. Address: P.O. Box 2220, Washington, DC 20013, U.S.A. 7.

VANDER SCHEER, Gary M., b. 6 Nov. 1933. Factory Worker & Poet. Educ: course in creative writing. Mbrships: Christian Reformed Ch., S. Grandville, Mich.; Former mbr., Lib. Bd., Grandville. Publs: Antique Gem (poem) in Writer's Notes & Quotes, 1961; Hush now Wind; Breathe not a Whisper, (book of poems) 1968; Puzzled Wonder (poem in the Banner, Jan. 1971. Address: 4152, Pineview S.W., Grandville, MI 49418, U.S.A.

VAN DER VOORT, Amanda Venelia. Artist. Educ: Nat. Acad. Schl. of Design, N.Y.C., U.S.A., 1945-48 & 1950-56; Columbia Univ., N.Y.C., & N.Y. Univ., 1949-51. Num. mbrships. incl: DAR; Fellow, Nat. Acad. of Design; Fellow, Royal Soc. of Arts; Nat. Bd. of Dirs., Am. Artists Profl. League; Publicity Chmn., Pen & Brush Club, N.Y.C., 1964-65, Bd. of Dirs., 1967-70, V.P., 1970-; Bd. of Dirs., Hudson Valley Art Assn., 1966-, Awards Chmn., 1968-72, Recording Sec., 1969-72; Acad. Artists Assn.; Nat. Arts Club; Art Chmn., Bridgeport Chapt., Nat. League of Am. Pen Women; Bd. of Dirs., Catharine Lorillard Wolfe Art Club, N.Y., 1960-70, Publicity Chmn., 1961-65. Solo exhibs: Am. Artists Profl. League, Jackson Heights, L.I., 1952; Bruce Mus., Greenwich, Conn., 1969. Num. other exhibs, oils & watercolours, incl: Art Ctr., Ogunquit, Me., 1959; Frederic Thompson Fndn., Poughkeepsie, N.Y., 1966; Contemporary Arts Club, Greenwich, 1966; Art Soc. of Old Greenwich, 1970; Conn. State Fedn. of Womens Clubs, 1972. Recip., num. prizes & awards. Address: 17 Stonehedge Drive S., Greenwich, CT 06830, U.S.A. 2, 5, 6, 37, 70, 138.

VAN DER VYVER, Johan David, b. 21 Feb. 1934. Professor of Law. Educ: B.Comm., 1954; LL.B., 1956; Hons. B.A., 1965; LL.D., 1973. Appts: Lectr. in Law, Potchefstroom Univ. for Christian Higher Educ., 1958; Sr. lectr., ibid, 1962; Prof., 1970; Dean, Fac. of Law, 1972; Advocate of Supreme Ct. of S. Africa, 1962. Mbrships: Bd. for Recognition of Law Exams.; Ed. Bd., Jrnl. for Contemp. Roman-Dutch Law; Soc. Hugo de Groot. Publs: Inleiding tot die Regswetenskap (w. F.J. van Zyl), 1972; Die juridiese Funksir van Staat en Kerk-n Kritiese analise van die beginsel van Soewereiniteit in eie Kring, 1972; Menseregte, 1974. Address: 13 Postma St., Potchefstroom, S. Africa.

VAN DER WOUDE, Adam Simon, b. 16 Oct. 1927. Professor of Old Testament & Intertestamental Literature. Educ: D.D., State Univ. of Groningen, Netherlands, 1957. Appts: Asst., Old Testament Studies, Groningen Univ., 1954-57; Min., Dutch Reformed Ch., Noordlaren, Groningen, 1957-60; Prof., State Univ. of Groningen, 1960-. Mbrships: Soc. of Old Testament Study in the Netherlands; Hon. mbr., Soc. of Old Testament Study in S. Africa; Pres., Poor-Relief Bd., Dutch Reformed Ch., Parish Groningen. Publs. incl: Bÿbelcommentaren en bÿbelse verhalen, 1958; Le Targum de Job de la grotte XI de Qumran (w. J.P.M. van der Ploeg), 1971; Many articles in jrnls., contbns. to handbooks etc. in field of Old Testament Study & Ancient Near Eastern Lit. & Religions. Recip., D.D., Evangelisch Theologische Fakultät, Munich, 1972. Address: Domela Nieuwenhuislaan 57, Groningen, Netherlands. 100.

VAN DEVENTER, William Carlstead, b. 22 Oct. 1908. University Professor. Educ: B.A., Central Meth. Coll., Fayette, Mo., 1930; M.A., 1932, Ph.D., 1935, Univ. of Ill.; Post-Doctoral work, Tchrs. Coll., Columbia Univ., 1945 Appts: Grad. Asst., Zool., Univ. of Ill., 1930-34; Biologist, Monroe Co. Pks., Rochester, N.Y., 1934-35; Prof., Biol., St. Viator Coll., Bourbonnais, Ill., 1935-38; Prof., Stephens Coll., Columbia, Mo., 1938-53; Prof., Western Mich. Univ., 1953-; Hd. of Biol. Dept., ibid, 1953-63. Mbrships. incl: AAAS; Nat. Assn. Rsch. in Sci. Tchng.; Pres., ibid, 1957; Ecological Soc. of Am.; Nat. Sci. Tchrs. Assn.; Mich. Sci. Tchrs. Assn.; Exec. Bd. Mbr., ibid, 1963-. Num. articles in var. sci. publs. Address:

3629 Canterbury Ave., Kalamazoo, MI 49007, U.S.A. 2, 14, 15.

VAN DUSEN, Austin Keeler, b. 16 Feb. 1925. Architect; Government Official. Educ: B.S., Arch., Kan. State Univ., 1950. Appts: Draftsman, Gen. Petroleum Corp., Seattle, 1950-52; w. John Graham & Co., Archts., ibid, 1952-53; Facilities Engr., Boeing Airplane Co., 1953-64; Plans Examiner, King Co. Bldg. Dept., 1964-67; Dir. of Bldg., ibid, 1967-70; Chief Insp., Factory-Built Housing, Wash., 1970-; Ptnr., Austin K., Van Dusen, A.I.A. & Assocs., Seattle, 1965-73; Prin., Austin K. Van Dusen, A.I.A., Seattle, 1973-. Mbrships: Chapt. Pres., N.W. Wash., 1968, '70 & Rsch. Comm., Int. Conf. Bldg. Offs., 1968-; Codes & Stds. Comm., 1972-, & Corp. Mbr., 1968-, Am. Inst. Archts.; Asst. Coun. Commnr., Boy Scouts Am., 1966-68; Soc. Am. Registered Archts., 1968-; Soc. Am. Mil. Engrs.; Disabled Am. Veterans; Benevolent & Protective Order Elks; Fire Safety Task Force, A.I.A., 1974-. Author, var. papers, biblical doctrine. Profl. contbns., mags. Hons: Mil. Order of Purple Heart, 1944; Silver Beaver, Boy Scouts Am., 1964; Vigil, Order of Arrow, 1965. Address: 3549 N.E. 165th St., Seattle, WA 98155, U.S.A. 2.

VANDYGRIFF, Torance Olen, b. 6 Sept. 1941. Educator. Educ: B.A., Baylor Univ.; M.Ed., E. Tex. State Univ. Appts: Tchr., Coach, George Peabody Elem., 1963-66; Tchr. & Coach, Greiner Jr. High, 1966-68; Tchr. & Coach, David W. Carter H.S., 1968-70; Admin. Intern, O.W. Holmes Jr. H.S., 1970-71; Asst. Prin., ibid, 1971-72; Prin., John F. Peeler Schl., 1972-73; Prin., T.G. Terry Elem. Schl., 1973-74. Mbrships. incl: Local, State & Nat. PTA; Dallas Schl. Admnstrs, Assn.; Tex. State Tchrs. Assn.; Tex. Elem. Prins. & Supvsrs. Assn.; Nat. Assn. Elem. Schl. Prins. Phi Delta Kappa; Bd. Dirs., Pal Cliff YMCA, 1974-76; Bd. Dirs., Dallas Co. Red Cross Youth Prog. Hons. incl: Classroom Tchrs. of Dallas T.S.T.A. Human Rels. Award, 1973; Elected to Quorum 50, Oak Cliff Chmbr. of Comm., 1974. Address: 2838 Cain Blvd., Dallas, TX 75211, U.S.A. 117, 125.

VAN DYKE, Gene, b. 5 Nov. 1926. Independent Oil & Gas Producer. Educ: Univ. of Ill., 1946; Okla. State Univ., 1947; B.S., Geol. Engrng., Univ. of Okla., 1950. Appts: Geol., Kerr-McGee Oil Co., Okla. City, 1950; Chief Geol., S.D. Johnson, Wichita Falls, Tex., 1950-51; Pvte. Prac. Geol., Independent Oil Opr., ibid, 1951-58; Ptnr., Van Dyke & Mejlaender, Independent Oil & Gas Prods., Houston; 1958-62; Pres., Van Dyke Oil Co., ibid, 1962-. Mbrships: USAAC, WW II; Houston Club; Petroleum Club; Univ. Club; Athletic Club; Racquet Club (all in Houston); Am. Petroleum Inst.; Am. Assn. of Petroleum Geols.; Independent Petroleum Prods. Assn. of Am.; Houston & New Orleans Geol. Socs. Author of Index of Geological Articles on South Louisiana. Address: 400 Southwest Tower, Houston, TX 77002, U.S.A.

VAN DYKE, Willard Ames, b. 5 Dec. 1906. Motion Picture Director & Educator. Educ: Univ. of Calif. Appts: Photographer, PWA Art Proj., San Francisco, Calif., 1934; Film Dir., OWI, 1942-45; Pres., N.Y. Film Coun., 1947; Pres., Van Dyke Prods., 1958-65; Pres., Int. Film Seminars, 1965-71; Dir., Dept. of Film, The Mus. of Modern Art, N.Y.C., 1965-74; Prof. of Theatre Arts, SUNY, 1972-. Mbrships: Screen Dirs. Guild; Pres., ibid, 1960-62; Co-Fndr., Grp. f64, 1933; Century Assn.; Coffee House Club. Photographic exhibs: DeYoung Mus., 1932; San Diego Mus., 1933; Penn State Univ., 1970; Budapest, Hungary,

1974. Documentary films incl: The City; Valleytown; Rice. TV Programs incl: High Adventure, 1958; 20th Century, 1963-65; 21st Century, 1968. Address: 505 West End Ave., N.Y., NY 10024, U.S.A. 2, 6, 133.

VAN EMDE BOAS, Conraad, b. 17 June 1904. Psychiatrist; Sexologist. Educ: Med. Study, Univ. of Leiden, Netherlands, 1921-32. Appts: Chmn., Med. Dept., Dutch Soc. fo;Sexual Reform, 1946-55; V.P., Int. Planned Parenthood Fed., 1952-70; Pres., Regio Europe, Africa, Nr. East, ibid, 1958-64; Chmn., Dutch Soc. for Med. Sexol., 1955-; Mbr., Int. Coun. Grp. Psychotheraphy, 1956-73; Exec. Mbr., ibid, 1973-. Fellow, Soc. for the Sci. Study of Sex. Mbrships. incl: German Psychoanal. Soc.; Hon., Am. Assn. or Grp. Psychotherapy; Soc. Europeenne de Culture. Publs. incl: Shakespeare's Sonnets & Their Connection with Travesty Double Plays, 1951; Abortus Provocatus, 1952; Obscenity & Pornography, 1966; Essays in Eroticism; Medicine & Morality: The Doctor in the Shadow of Taboos; The Doctor & the Sexual Revolution, 1973; num. articles. Address: Stadionweg 80, Amsterdam, Netherlands. 43.

VAN EMDEN, A., b. 22 Oct. 1909. Director-General of Netherlands Red Cross. Educ: Univ., Rotterdam. Appts: Ptnr., van Emden & Co., Bankers, 1933; joined Netherlands Red Cross, 1945; Dir., ibid, 1948; Dir.-Gen., 1962-. Holder of hon. offs. in num. grps. inclng: Treas., Int. Soc. Serv., Dutch Br.; Dpty. Gov., League of Red Cross Socs., Geneva; Sec., Nat. Bd., Disaster Fund; Bd. of Film Censors; Sec., Bd. of Netherlands Burn Ctr. Fndn.; Bd. of Netherland War Graves Fndn.; Sec., Gen. Dutch Lottery Fndn. Mbrships: de Witte Soc., The Hague; Hermes Soc., Rotterdam; Soc. for Cultural Coop., The Hague. Hons. incl: Kt., Order of de Nederlandse Leeuw; Off., Order of Oranje Nassau; Govtl. Medal of Netherlands Red Cross; Cmdr., Order of Crown of Belgium, Royal Order of Phoenix of Greece, Order of Pole Star of Sweden, Order of Crown of Thailand & Order of Merit of Italian Repub.; Cmdr. 1st Class, Order of Merit of Austrian Repub.; Golden Tilanus Medal, Royal Netherlands Soc. of 1st Aid. Address: R.J. SchimmelpenninckIaan 8, The Hague, Netherlands. 43, 100.

VAN GENECHTEN, Jean-Baptiste (Jules), b. 7 Aug. 1902. Painter & Lithographer. Appts. incl: Post, Belgian Min. of Pub. Wks., 1920-39; Hd., Tech. Exhibs. Sect., Belgian Off. of Info. & Documentation, London, U.K., 1942-45; Exhib. Org., INBEL, Brussels, Belgium, & N.Y.C., U.S.A., 1945-47. Mbrships: Royal Assn. of Profl. Belgian Artists; Fndr., 1929, & Pres., Royal Grp. of Arts & Crafts. Publs: Impasses et Vieux Coins de Bruxelles, 15 lithographs, 1938; Visages de Grande-Bretagne, 30 lithographs, 1949; Mon Anderlecht, 25 lithographs, 1952; Bruxelles et Son Charme, 16 lithographs, 1957; La Côte Belge, 20 lithographs, 1958. One-man shows, aquarelles & lithographs, Anderlecht, Belgium, 1953, 1955 & 1958. Hons: Gold Medal, Order of the Crown, 1947; Kt., Order of Leopold II, 1948; Kt., Order of the Crown, 1955; Bronze Medal, European Coun. of Art & Esthetics, 1968; Schiblio-Mousson Prize, Salon des Arts en Europe, 1970; Bronze Medal, Royal Assn. of Profl. Belgian Artists, 1971. Address: 71 Rue de Veeweyde, Anderlecht, Belgium. 105.

VanGILDER, Marvin L., b. 24 Sept. 1926. Newspaperman; Historian; Musician. Educ: Mus.B., Drury Coll., Springfield, Mo., 1948; tchng. certs. Appts: Supvsr. of Music, var. pub. schls., Mo., 1948-54; News Dir. & Sports Ed.,

Radio Stn. KDMO, Carthage, ibid, 1956-60; var. offs., Carthage Press, 1960-70; Histn., Edl. & Relig. Writer, 1970-; Dir., VanGilder Music Studio, Carthage, 1968-70. Mbrships. incl: U.S. Civil Defence Advsry. Coun., 1970-73; Am. Assn. for State & Locl. Hist., 1972-; State Histl. Soc. of Mo., 1953; Jasper Co. Histl. Soc., 1960-; (Pres., 1968-73); Carthage Lions Club, 1966-; at var. times Pastor of Chs. in Mo. Publs: The Story of Barton County, Missouri s Cradle of Fame, 1972; also articles and verse in periodicals & newspapers. Hons. incl: Edgel Oratorical Prize, 1947; Hoover Award for Outstanding Musicianship, 1948; Mo. Press Assn. Best Edit. Award, 1964; Drury Coll. Disting. Alumni Serv. Award, 1971. Address: 527 S. Main St., Carthage, MO 64836, U.S.A. 8, 57, 120,

VAN HAEGERNDOREN, Maurits, b. 23 Aug. 1903. Senator. Educ: Dr. Mod. Hist., Univ. of Louvain, 1925. Appts: Archivist of the Realm, 1928-68; Prof., Hist., pt.-time, Higher Inst. Adminstry. Scis., Brussels, 1948-73; Senator, Flemish Nat. Pty., Volksunie, 1968-. Mbrships: Chief-Commnr., Flemish Scout Assn., 1933-50; Int. Commnr., Belgian Scouts; Fndr. & Pres., "Folk H.S." (Stichting L. de Raet), 1950-68; Royal Soc. of Lit., Leiden. Publs. incl: num. archival works; Verkennersieven (in 3 pts.), 1938-40, 2nd ed.; 1945; De Vlaamse Beweginy Nu en Moryen (in 2 pts.), 1962; Nationalisme en Federalisme, 1971. Hons: Cmdr., Royal Order Leopold I; Zilveren Anjer, Fndn. Prince Bernard of the Netherlands. Address: Guido Gezellelaan 63, 3030 Heverlee, Belgium. 43.

van IERLAND, Johnny, b. 26 Dec. 1934. Airline Catering Manager. Educ: Mgmt. Course, Dutch Antillean Airlines, Curacao, 1969; Mgmt. & Staff Course, KLM, Netherlands, 1970. Appts. incl: Steward, KLM Royal Dutch Airlines, 1961-70; Commercial Rep., ALM Dutch Antillean Airlines, 1970; Asst. Chief Cabin Personnel, ibid, 1970-; Asst. Catering Mgr., 1972-; Mbr., Catering Servs., 1972-. Mbrships. incl: Neths. Antilles P.R. Assn., 1966-71; Dir., 1971-72; Pres., 1973; Soc. Econ. Coun., Neths. Antilles, 1966-68; Dpty. Sec., 1968-69; Dpty. Pres., 1969-70; Int. P R. Assn., 1970-; Bd., Fed. of Interam. Assns. of P.R. Officers, 1972-; Deputized Mbr., Antilliaanse Reisvereniging, 1970-; P.R. Dir., Indian Neths. Antilles Assn., 1973; Attended IV All India P.R. Conf., Bombay, 1974. Recip., sev. certs. of appreciation. Address: Fokkerweg 7, Curacao, Netherlands Antilles. 136.

VAN JOLE, Marcel, b. 7 Sept. 1916. University Professor; College President. Educ: B.A., M.A., M.S., Ph.D. Maths. & M.A. in Art Hist., Brussels Univ., Belgium. Appts. incl: Prof. of Maths., Royal Atheneum, Hoboken; Nat. High Inst. of Arch. & Town Planning, Antwerp; Prof. of Aesthetics, Nat. High Inst. of Fine Arts, Royal Acad., Antwerp; Prof. of Aesthetics, SUNY, U.S.A.; Dir. of European Prog., ibid; Pres., Tchr.'s Coll., Dir., Schl. of Soc. Promotion, Antwerp. Mbrships: Belgian Intelligence Serv., WWII; Corres. Mbr., Acad. d'Hist., Paris; Pres., Alliance Francaise, Anvers; V.P., org. of all Alliances Francaises of Belgium; Pres. of Hon., Alumni, Antwerp Atheneums; Co.-Fndr. & Bd. Mbr., Philharmonic Soc. & Int. Schl.; Bd. Mbr., Assn. Int. des Critiques d'art; ABCA, Belgian Assn. of Art Critics—Mbr. of the Press, accredited at UN & OTAN; ABA Am. Belgian Assn. Author of many publs. Hons: Off. d'Acad., 1955; Chevalier dans l'Ordre Léopold, 1959; Off. dans l'Ordre des Palmes Académiques, 1966; Off. dans l'Ordre Léopold II, 1968; Chevalier de la Légion l'Honneur, 1969; 1st Prize Hors Concours, Diano Marina

(Italy) for Album, Pol Mara, as most Beautiful Publ. of 1974; Special Award, Diano Marina, for Leherb Au Miroir d'Orphée. Address: Simonslei 34, B 2130 Brasschaat, Belgium. 43, 87.

VAN KATWIJK, Paul, b. 7 Dec. 1885. Pianist; Conductor; Composer. Educ: Royal Conservatory of Music, The Hague, Netherlands, 1899-1904; Stern Conservatory, Berlin, Germany; Imperial Acad. of Music, Vienna, Austria. Appts. incl: Hd., Piano Dept., Drake Univ., & Conductor, Des Moines Symph. Orch., Iowa, U.S.A., 1914-18; Dean of Music, & Hd., Piano Dept., Southern Meth. Univ., Dallas, Tex., 1919-49; Conductor, Dallas Symph. Orch., 1925-36; Conductor, Dallas Oratorio Soc., Dallas Municipal Chorus, Dallas Male Chorus, & Dallas Civic Opera. Mbrships. incl: Pres., Dallas Music Tchrs. Assn.; Tex. Music Tchrs. Assn.; Tex. Composers Guild; Phi Mu Alpha; Iota Kappa Lambda. Solo Pianist w. Houston, St. Louis, Mpls., & New Orleans Symph. Orchs. Piano recitals given, num. U.S. cities. Accompanist to Cesar Thomson, num. European cities. Compositions incl: Hollandia Suite; Other works for orch.; Piano pieces; 2-Piano transcriptions; Sons. Hons. incl: Doctorate, Drake Univ., 1931; Sigma Alpha Iota Award for servs. to music in Dallas, 1959; Cert. of Merit, Concertgebouw Orch. of Amsterdam, 1961. Address: 4610 Wildwood Rd., Dallas, TX 75209, U.S.A. 2, 4, 7, 10.

VANKERKHOFF, Harry Peihl, b. 23 Aug. 1908. Professional Engineer. Educ: Chgo. Tech. Coll. Appts: Contractor, Supt. of Construction, J.B. Mobley, Augusta, Ga., 1930-38, Structural Engr., 1938-49; Pres., Peihl Corp., N. Augusta, S.C., 1949-; Harry Peihl Vanderkhoff, F. ASCE, P.E., Bldg. Design, Inspection & Analysis, 1968-; Registered Profl. Engr., 27 States & D.C. Mbrships: Ga. Soc. Profl. Engrs.; Past State Dir., ibid; Nat. Soc. Profl. Efrs.; Fellow, Am. Soc. Civil Engrs.; Past Br. Pres., ibid; Am. Weldin Soc.; Am. Concrete Inst. Address: P.O. Box 550, Augusta, GA 30903, U.S.A.

VAN KREVELEN, Dick Arnold, b. 9 Aug. 1909. Child Neuropsychiatrist; Ex-Lecturer in Child Psychiatry; Educ: Univs. of Utrecht, Leiden & Vienna; Dr.'s degree, Univ. of Leiden, 1946. Appts: Dpty. Chief, Sect. Mental Hygiene, Royal Army Med. Corps; Chief, Child Psych. Sect., Pub. Hlth. Dept., Roterdam; Med. Dir., Child Psych. Hosp. "Curium", Oegstgeest; Dir., Fndn. Med.-Psychological Children's Hosp.; Lectr., Univ. of Leiden; Chief, Child Psych. Sect., Pub. Hlth. Dept., Haarlem, Netherlands; Ed.-in-Chief, Acta Paedopsychiatrica, 1963-. Mbrships: Pres., Int. Assn. Child Psych. & Allied Professions; V.P., Union of European Paedopsychs.; Bd. mbr., sev. soc. instns., inclng. Pro Juventute Rotterdam; Hon. mbr., var. socs.; Corres. mbr., Czechoslovak Med. Soc. "J.E. Purkyne"; Deutsche Vereinigung für Jugendpsych.; Schweiz. Gesellschaft Kinderpsych. Author of about 250 publs. in Dutch, French, German, Engl. Italian, Portuguese, Spanish, Arabic. Address: Scheveningseweg 3, The Hague, Netherlands. 43, 50, 100.

VAN KREVELEN, Dirk Willem, b. 8 Nov. 1914. Executive. Educ: M.Sc., Univ. of Leyden, 1938; D.Sc., Univ. of Delft, 1939. Appts: Rsch. Asst., Unvi. of Delft, 1937-39; pt.-time Prof., ibid, 1952-; Rsch. Chem., Dutch State Mines, 1940-47; Dir. of Rsch., ibid, 1948-59; V.P. (Rsch.), AKU N.V., 1959-69; V.P., Akzo N.V., 1969-; Pres., Akzo Rsch. & Engrng. bv, 1969-. Mbrships: Royal Inst. Engrs. (Dutch); Royal Chem. Soc. (Dutch); Am. Inst. Chem. Engrs.; Am. Chem. Soc.; Fellow, Inst. of Fuel. Publs:

Induced Pyrolysis of Methane (in Dutch), 1939; Gas Purification (w. H.A.J. Pieters), 1946; Coal Science (w. J. Schuyer), 1957; Coal-Typology, Chemistry, Physics, Constitution, 1961; Properties of Polymers, 1972; num. sci. publs. in int. jrnls. Hons: Coal Sci. Medal, 1954; Medaille de l'Univ. de Liège, 1954; Ph.D., Univ. of Darmstadt, 1966. Address: Bakenbergseweg 85, Arnhem, The Netherlands. 43, 100.

VAN LANDINGHAM, Leander Shelton, Jr., b. 15 July 1925. Patent Lawyer. Educ: B.S., Univ. of N.C., 1948; M.A., ibid, 1949; J.D., Georgetown Univ., 1955. Appts: Patent Advsr., Dept. of Navy, Wash. D.C., 1953-55; admitted to D.C. Bar, 1955; Pvte. Prac., Cons., Patent, Trademark & Copyright Law, Chem. Patent Matters, Wash., 1955-. Mbrships: Am. Chem. Soc.; Sci. Assn.; Fed., Am. & D.C. Bar Assns.; Am. Patent Law Assn.; Am. Judicature Soc.; Sigma Xi; Phi Alpha Delta. Address: 10726 Stanmore Dr., Potomac Falls, Potomac, MD 20854, U.S.A. 16.

VAN LANSCHOT, Willem Charles Jean Marie, b. 30 June 1914. Banker. Educ: Royal Mil. Acad., Breda, Holland, 1935-38; Leiden Univ., ibid, 1940-42. Appts: Cmdng. Off., Netherlands Army—Ret'g. as Col., 1935-49; w. NV Philips Gloeillampenfabrieken, elec. mfg. co., Eindhoven, Holland—1st Sec., Gen. Serv.-Mng. Dir., N. Africa & Middle East, 1949-66; Ptnr., F. van Lanschot Bankers, 's Hertogenbosch, Holland, 1966-; Dir: Indl. Turnkey Internat. NV, The Hague, ibid; de Lage Landen printing/publrs., Amsterdam, ibid; Zuid-Nederlandsche-Drukkerij, printing/publrs., 's Hertogenbosch; Radio Nederland Wereldomroep; Mbr. Com. For. Trade. Mbrships. incl: Bd. Dirs., Dutch War Graves Assn. & Internat. Assn. Legal Order; Past Pres., World Vets. Fedn., Dutch Ass. Mil. War Victims & Netherlands Arab Circle. Contbr. articles on war vets. affairs, dev. aid, Middle East to publs. in field. Hons. incl: Cmdr., Mil. Order of William; Kt., Order of Dutch Lion; Legion of Honour, France; Order, Gregorius the Gt.; Order of Merit, Italy; Order of Merit, U.A.R. Address: 9 Leeuweriklaan, Eindhoven, Netherlands.

VAN LECKWYCK, William Peter Edward Joseph, b. 16 Nov. 1902. Geologist; Professor. Educ: Univ. of Liege, Belgium, 1921-26. Appts: Geol. Investigator & mapper, Morocco, Greece, Bulgaria, Finland, Italy, France, Luxembourg, Belgium, 1930-38; Coal miner for Tunisian Govt., 1939-40; Investigator, mineral deposits, Belgium, 1941-46; Dir., Belgian Nat. Rsch. Stn. for Geol. of Coal-bearing Strata, 1946-67; Sec.-gen., Int. Union of Geol. Scis., 1964-70; Prof., geol. & stratigraphical palaeontology, Univ. of Louvain, 1964-73. Mbrships. incl: Royal Acad., Belgium; Geol. Soc. of France. Contbr. of articles to profl. jrnls. Recip., num. hons. Address: Mechelse Steenweg 206, B-2000 Antwerp, Belgium.

VAN METER, Clifford W., b. 15 Apr. 1937. Police Officer; Educator. Educ: B.S., Schl. of Police Admin., Mich. State Univ., 1959; M.A., Western Ill. Univ., 1969; Ph.D. Cand. in Higher Educ., Southern Ill. Univ. Appts: Clerk, FBI; Patrolman, Mich. Police Dept.; Lt., Mil. Police Corp, U.S. Army; Personnel Asst., St. Louis, Mo., Police Dept.; Asst. Dir. of Trng.; Dir. of Safety & Security, Western Ill. Univ.; Chmn., Dept. of Law Enforcement Admin., ibid. Mbrships: Int. Assn. of Chiefs of Police; Trng. Comm., Ill. Assn. of Chiefs of Police; V.P., Ill. Law Enforcement Educ. Assn.; Past Pres., Mid St. Louis Co. Jr. Chmbr. of Comm. Publs: Proj. Dir. for 5 rsch. publs. in Ill.; Case Study in Police Administration & Criminal Investigation,

1974. Address: Dept. of Law Enforcement Administration, Western Ill. Univ., Macomb, IL 61455, U.S.A.

VAN METER, Ruth Frances, b. 6 Feb. 1911. Social Group Worker; YWCA Consultant. Educ: B.A., Asbury Coll., Wilmore, Ky.; Grad. Study, Schl. of Soc. Work, Univ. of Southern Calif., L.A., & Near & Middle East Inst., Columbia Univ. Appts. incl: Exec. Dir., YWCAs in Vallejo, Calif., Ogden, Utah, & Berkeley, Calif., 1944-54; Fulbright Tchng. Fellow, Schl. of Soc. Work, Athens, Greece, 1954-56; Dir., Girls Serv. Ctr., YWCA, Istanbul, Turkey, 1956-62; Dir., Fernhurst YWCA, Honolulu, Hawaii, 1962-63; Cons. & Advsr., YWCAs in Mexico, S. Am., Iran, India, Pakistan, Ethiopia & Ceylon, 1964-. Mbrships. incl: Nat. Assn. Soc. Wkrs.; Am. Acad. Pol. & Soc. Sci.; YWCA, Portland, Ore.; Acad. Certified Soc. Wkrs. Publs: Normas y Procedimientos Relacionados con El Personal de la Asociación Cristiana Femenina, 1968; Organización de la Asociación Cristiana Femenina, 1970; articles in YWCA mag. Hon: Recognition for Work on U.S.O. Comm. & U.S.O. Club, Istanbul, Turkey, 1961. Address: 3217 S.W. Ridge Drive, Portland, OR 97219, U.S.A. 5.

VANN, Elizabeth Chapman Denny (Mrs. E.E. Vann), b. 7 Jan. 1884. Teacher; Author; Genealogist. Educ: B.A., Vanderbilt Univ., Nashville, Tenn., 1904; M.A., ibid, 1905. Appts: Tchr., Agnes Scott Coll., Decatur, Ga., 1906-07; Colegio Mineiro, Juiz de Fora, Brazil, 1911-14; Pvte. Schl., N.Y.C., 1914; Pvte. Schl., Palo Alto, Calif., 1915-16; Pvte. Schl., Providence, R.I., 1916-17; Postal Censorship Off., N.Y.C., 1917-18; Works Progress Admin., State Off., Newark, N.J., 1935-41; Rsch. Genealogist. Mbrships. incl: Phi Beta Kappa; Delta Delta; Bd. Dirs., Int. YWCA, Rio de Janeiro, Brazil, 1918-20; DAR. Publs: Denny Geheaology, 3 vols. (w. sister), 1944, '57, '61; Virginia's First German Colony (booklet), 1961. Has been furnishing histl. records of Vanderbilt Univ. in the 19th C. to authors of the forthcoming 'Centennial History of Vanderbilt Uni.', 5 yrs. Address: c/o Collins Denny White, Ross. Bldg., 8th & Main, Richmond, VA, U.S.A.

VANN, Rochelle, b. 27 Oct. 1918. Educator. Educ: B.S., Elizabeth City State Univ., N.C.; M.A., Columbia Univ., N.Y.C.; Geo. Wash. Univ., Wash. D.C.; A & T State Univ., Greensboro, N.C.; Howard Univ. Appts: Tchr., C.S. Brown H.S., Winton N.C.; Counselor, Basic Educ. & Enrichment, Elizabeth City State Univ.; Inst.,'Soc. Sci., ibid. Mbrships: Pres., Hertford Co. Tchrs. Assn.; Chap., ibid; Pres., Chowan Sunday Schl. Convention, Hertford Co.; White Lilly Lodge, Elks; Mason; Chmn., Dean, Bd., 1st Bapt. Ch., Winton. Maned, Disting. Tchr. of the Yr., Elizabeth City State Univ. Address: Box 173, Elizabeth City State Univ., Winton, NC, 27986, U.S.A. 125.

VAN NORMAN, Royce Wayland, b. 9 Dec. 1928. Educator. Educ: B.S., Jones Ormond Wilson Tchrs. Coll., Wash., DC, 1950; M.A., The Cath. Univ. of Am., Wash., DC, 1953; Ph.D., Johns Hopkins Univ., Balt., Md., 1966. Appts: Secondary Schl. Tchr., 10 yrs.; Supvsr., Intern Tchrs. for Johns Hopkins Univ., 5 yrs.; Mbr., Grad. Fac. of Educ., Towson State Coll., Balt., Md., 1967-; Dir., Profl. Progs., ibid 1969-. Mbrships: Phi Delta Kappa; Kappa Delta Pi; AERA; NSSE; AESA; Cons. State-wide planning in higher educ. & state int. study comm. mbr. Contbr. of articles to sev. profl. publs. Address: Education Dept., Towson State Coll., Baltimore, MD 21204, U.S.A. 46.

VAN NOSTRAND, Morris Abbott, b. 24 Nov. 1911. Publisher; Literary Representative. Educ: B.A., Amherst Coll., 1934. Appts: Mbr., Samuel French, Inc., N.Y., 1934-; Pres., ibid, 1952-; Pres., Samuel French (Canada) Ltd., 1952-; Pres., Walter H. Baker Co., Boston, Mass., 1953-; Pres., Hugo & Luigi-Samuel French Music Publs., Inc., 1964-; Dir., ASPRO, Canton, Ohio; Pres. & Trustee, French & Polyclin. Med. Schl. & Hlth. Ctr., N.Y.C. Mbrships. incl: V.P., Forest Hills Garden Assn.; Dir., New Dramatists Comm.; Dir., Travelers Aid Soc.; Trustee, Lincoln Savings Bank, Brooklyn, N.Y.; Trustee, Kew Forest Schl.; Dir., Friends of Amherst Lib.; Chi Phi; Lambs, N.Y.C. Address: 25 West 45 St., N.Y., NY 10036, U.S.A. 44.

VAN PELT, Edgard Charles, b. 1 May 1910. Business Executive. Educ: Licensee, Comm. & Financial Scis., Inst. Supérieur de Comm., 1931. Appts: Mng. Dir., Comptoir de Warrantage Industriel & Commerciel S.A., Antwerp, 1937; Chief, Finance Sect., Belgian Econ. Mission, London, 1945-46; Pres., Belgian Assn. of Exporters & Importers; V.P., Belgian Serv. for Export Trade; Dir., Ets. Cigrang Freres N.V.; Dir., S.A. Cagetra; Dir., Belgo-Indian Chmbr. of Comm. & Ind.; Mbr., Belgian Shipper's Coun.; Bd. Mbr., Profl. Union of Comm. & Shipping Offs.; V.P., World Trade Ctr. of Belgium N.V. Mbrshis: Pres., Rotary Club, Antwerpen-Pak;Pres., Delphi Assn.; Bd. Mbr., Am.-Belgian Assn. Hons: Kt. of the Crown; Laureate of Labour (1st class). Address: Lysenstraat 10, B-2600, Berchem, Belgium.

VAN RIPER, Paul P., b. 29 July 1916. Educator. Educ: A.B., DePauw Univ., 1938; Ph.D., Univ. of Chgo., 1947; Grad., U.S. Army Command & Gen. Staff Coll., 1960. Appts. incl: Chief, Mil. Servs. Sect., Off. of the Army Comptroller, Dept. of the Army, 1951-52; Assoc. Prof. & Prof., Pub. Admin., Grad. Schl. of Bus. & Pub. Admin., Cornell Univ., 1952-70; Prof. & Hd., Dept. of Pol. Sci., Tex. A & M Univ., 1970-; Acting Dean, Cornell Univ., 1961; Lt. Col., QMC-USAR. Mbrships. incl: Nat. Gen. Sec., Beta Theta Pi, 1963-65; Phi Beta Kappa; Phi Kappa Phi; Sigma Delta Chi; Exec. Comm., Civil Serv. Reform Assn. of N.Y., 1960-64; Histl. Advsry. Comm., Nat. Aeronautics & Space Admin., 1964-66; Nat. Advsry. Coun., Am. Soc. for Pub. Admin., 1957-60; Edit. Cons., Pub. Personnel Review, 1959-; Cooperating mbr., Int. City Mgmt. Assn. & Am. Pol. Sci. Assn. Author of books in field. Recip., Alumni citation, DePauw Univ., 1966. Address: 712 E. 30th St., Bryan, TX 77801, U.S.A. 2, 14, 15, 30.

VAN ROSSEM, Rudolf Harold., b. 19 Mar. 1924. Graphic Artist. Educ: Riksmus. Schl. of Art, Amsterdam. Appts: Instr. of Graphic Art, Gt. Yarmouth Coll. of Art, U.K., Tilburg Acad. of Fine Arts, Netherlands; represented in pub. collections in Holland, U.S.A., France, Poland, N.Z., Italy, Yugoslavia & Nigeria. Mbrships: Hon. Mbr. Accademia Fiorentina del Arte e del Disegni, 1966; Fedn. of Plastic Arts, Netherlands; Soc. of Woodengravers, London. Hons: Master of Fine Art Int., N.Y., 1970; Gold Medal, Biennale, Perugia, Italy, 1973; Prize for Graphic Art, Biennale Gorizia, Italy, 1964, Biennale Malbork, Poland, 1965. Address: Burg. Vonk de Bothstr. 54, Tilburg, Netherlands. 133,

VAN SLYKE, Marian Wasley. Musician. Educ: B.Mus., Eastman Schl. of Music. Appts: Tchr., Pawling Schl. for Boys, & Organist, Choir Dir., Meth. Ch., 1937-41; Pvte. Tchr., Piano & Organ, 1942-46; Organist, Choir Dir., 1st Presby. Ch., Newport, R.I., 1948-63, & Off.

Cand. Schl., Newport; Min. of Music, 1st Bapt. Ch., Fall River, Mass., 1965-73; Music Dir., Trinity Ch., Newport, 1973-. Num. mbrships. incl: Sigma Alpha Iota; Am. Guild of Organists; Am. Choral Dirs. Assn.; New England Guild of Handbell Ringers; AAUW; Bd. Mbr., Civic Music Assn.; R.I. DAR; Newport Preservation Soc. Hons: Award of Merit, DAR, 1956; Appreciation Award, Gen. Commn. of Chaps. & Armed Forces Personnel, 1961; Letters of Appreciation, Plaque, U.S. Marines & Mayor of Newport, 1972. Address: 11 Sherri Lane, Middletown, RI 02840, U.S.A. 130.

van SOEST, Henri, b. 20 Nov. 1919. Solicitor. Educ: LL.D., Univ. of Liege, Belgium; Masters degree; Notary Public. Appts: Legal Officer, real estate co., 1942-45; Tchr., 1943-47; Solicitor, Notary Public, 1947-65; Pres. & Dir., Bank, Ins. & Montgage Cos., 1966-73; Judge, Ct. of Commerce, Brussels, 1971-74; Notory Public, Brussels, 1974-. Mbrships: Past Gov., Dist. 112 & Vice Chmn., Int. Bd. of Govs. Exec. Coun., Lions Int.; sev. profl. assns. Author of legal publs. Hons: Gold Medal, City of Hasselt, Prize of Excellence, Belgian Govt., 1937; Silver Medal, 2nd class, Belgian Red Cross, Bronze Medal, of Nat. Thankfulness, 1945; Agric. Badge 2nd Class, 1966. Address: Rue de Châtelain 25, 1050 Brussels, Belgium. 43, 87.

VAN TIEM, Florentine Stewart (Mrs. Richard L. Van Tiem). Business Executive. Educ: B.A., Wayne State Univ.; grad. work in bus. admin. & psych. Appts: Copy Writer, Account Exec., Wolf Jickling Dow & Conkey, Inc.; Exec. V.P., Ruse & Ruban, Inc., 1954-56; Pres., Specialty Bankers, 1956-68; Pres., Hilltop Farm Prods., 1968-; Pres., I.H.M., Inc., 1973-; Gen. Ptnr., St. Lucia Investment Corp., Ltd., 1972-; Owner, FDD Farms & Trng. Stables, Davie, Fla. & Victoria Farms, Ft. Lauderdale. Mbrships: Fndr., Youth for Am.; Dir., Hillcrest Labs., F.I.C.C., Louise K. Buell Schlrship. & Award Fndn., Grace Hosp., Nat. Enrichment Assn., Soc. for the Performing Arts, Ctrl. Dist. Bus. Assn. & Project Hope. Hons: Crusade for Freedom Award; Nat. Woman of Yr.; Viscountess. Address: Hilltop Farms, 1779 Brocker Rd., Metamora, MI 48455, U.S.A. 5, 8, 16, 22.

VAN VLACK, Melva Bullington (Mrs. William C. Van Vlack), b. 3 Apr. 1909. County Extension Agent. Educ: B.S.H.E., Univ. of Ark., Fayetteville, Ark., 1932; M.S., ibid, 1966. Appts. incl: Home Econs. Instr., Ark. H.S. Prairie Grv., 1932-33; Elem. Tchr., Liberty Schl., Tulsa Co., Okla., 1933-34; Home Demonstration Agent, Agricl. Ext. Serv., Univ. of Ark. & USDA, Magnolia, Ark., Columbia Co., 1934-36; Home Dem. Agent, Hope Ark., Hempstead Co., 1936-39; Home Dem. Agent, Pine Bluff, Ark., Jefferson Co., 1939-47; Home Econs. Instr., Jr. H.S., Attalla, Ala., 1949-57; Ext. Home Economist-Co. Ext. Agent, Home Econs. Ldr., Ft. Smith, Ark., Sebastian Co., 1957-. Mbrships. incl: Bus. & Profl. Womens' Clubs; Local, State & Nat. Tchrs.' Assn., Attalla, Ala., Pres., local Assn.; Ark. Ext. Home Econs. Assn., NW Counselor, Constitution & Bi-Laws Comm.; Bd. Mbr., YWCA 6 yrs.; Epsilon Sigma Phi & Gamma Sigma Delta. Publs: stories & newspaper articles in field of Home Econs. Hons. incl: Achievement Award, N. Sebastien Co. Coun., Ext. Homemakers Clubs, 1973. Address: 11 Salome—Hillcrest, Ft. Smith, AR 72901, U.S.A. 5, 138.

VAN VOORTHUYSEN, Jan, b. 9 Sept. 1911. Musicologist. Educ: Leyden Univ.; Netherlands; Royal Conservatory, The Hague. Appts: Début as musicologist & soloist, 1935; Début as jrnlst. & radio soloist, 1937; Collaborator, clandestine press, 1940-45; Music Ed., daily paper "Het Parool", 1945; Music Ed., daily paper "Haagsche Courant", 1947-72; Musicological lects. & broadcasting series, 1949-; Guest Critic to Louisville Times, Ky., & Dallas Morning News, Dallas, Tex., U.S.A., 1958-59; Collaborator, "Algemene Muziekencyclopedie", Ghent, Belgium, "Grote Winkler Prins Encyclopedie", Amsterdam, "Grote Nederlandse Larousse Encyclopedie", Hasselt, Belgium, 1959-. Mbr., Netherlands Jrnlst. Soc. Publs: Subjective & Objective Elements in Art (essay), 1934; Speaking with Two Mouths (novel), 1943; 70 Poems; 8000 reviews & 7000 articles in monthly & daily papers, etc.; Frank van Borselen (play for broadcasting), 1950. Hons: Kt., Order of Acad. Palms, France, 1967; Kt., Order of Crown of Belgium, 1968. Address: Resedastraat 18, The Hague 2024, The Netherlands. 43.

VAN WAGTENDONK, Willem Johan, b. 10 Apr. 1910. Professor of Biochemistry. Educ: B.A., Rijks Univ., Utrecht, Netherlands, 1931; M.A., ibid, 1934; Ph.D., 1937. Appts. incl: Rsch. Assoc., Stanford Univ., Calif., U.S.A., 1939-41; Asst. Prof., Biochem., Ore. State Univ., 1941-44; Assoc. Prof., ibid, 1944-46; Assoc. Prof., Ind. Univ., 1946-60; Chief, Basic Rsch., V.A. Hosp., Miami, Fla., 1960-71, Talladega Coll., Ala., 1971-; Exchange Fellow, Nat. Acad. Sci., U.S., w. Polska Akademia Nauk, Nenski Inst., Warsaw, Poland, 1973. Fellowships: AAAS; N.Y. Acad. Sci.; Am. Inst. of Chems. Mbrships: Am. Soc. Biol. Chem.; Biochem. Soc., U.K.; Soc. Gen. Microbiol., ibid; Soc. of Protozool.; Edit. Bd., Jrnl., ibid. Author & Co-author of 110 papers. Holder of U.S. Patent. Address: Dept. of Biol., Talladega Coll., Talladega, AL 35160, U.S.A. 14, 131.

VAN WINKLE, Bonnie Dodson (Mrs. LeRoy Van Winkle), b. 26 Aug. 1920. Company President. Appts: Sales Asst., Radio Stn. WWDC, 1945-50; V.P. & Treas.-Pres., Wm. D. Murdock Advt. Agcy. Inc., 1962-. Mbrships: Pres. & Sec., Soroptimist Club, Alexandria, Va.; Treas., Bd. mbr., Am. Women in Radio & TV, Wash. DC; Sec., Bus. & Profl. Women's Club—l'Enfant Chapt.; Advt. Club, Metropol. Wash. Recip. Bus. Woman of Yr. Award, Bus. & Profl. Women's Club, Wash. DC, 1973. Address: 5421 Powhatan Rd., Riverdale, MD 20840, U.S.A.

VAN WOLF, Henry, b. 14 Apr. 1898. Sculptor. Educ: Munich Art & Art Craft Schl., w. Germany, 1912-16; Sculpture & Bronze Technique studies w. Ferdinand von Miller, Munich, Germany, 1919-22, '23-26. Appts: Free-lance Sculptor & Owner of pvte. studio; Tchr. for N.Y. Bd. of Educ., Studio in Bklyn., N.Y., 1937-39 & Tchr., Studio, Van Nuys, Calif., 1950-54. Fellow, Am. Inst. of Fine Arts. Mbrships: Fndr. & Past Pres., San Fernando Valley Profl. Artists' Guild—now Valley Artists Guild; Nat. Sculpture Soc.; Dir., Coun. of Traditional Artists Socs.; Fedn. Int. de la Medaille, Paris, France. Works incl: 3 times life-size bust of Albert Einstein, Albert Einstein Med. Ctr., Phila., Pa.; life-size Polar Bear, bronze; Statue of Indian, Van Nuys Mall, Calif.; Bust of Mayor Yorty; Sculptured Grp., Peace on Earth; Statue of Ben Hogan, Golf House, N.Y.C., 1955; Bronze doors for St. Nicholas Episc. Ch., Encino, Calif., 1956-57. Recip. of 40 top awards inclng. 7 gold medals. Address: 5417 Hazeltine Ave., Van Nuys, CA 91401, U.S.A. 9, 37, 59, 128.

VAN YOUNG, Oscar, b. 15 Apr. 1906. Artist; Teacher. Educ: Art Acad., Odessa, Russia; B.A., M.A., Calif. State Univ., L.A.

Appts: Pvte. Tchr., 1940-; L.A. State Univ., 1961-63; Pasadena City Coll., 1959-73. One-man shows: 10 Chgo. Painters, Art Inst. of Chgo.; L.A. Co. Mus.; San Fran. Mus. of Art; Pasadena Art Mus.; Santa Barbara Mus.; Cowie Galls., L.A., 5 times 1953-71. Exhib. incl: Am. Paintings, Chgo. Art Inst.; Ency. Brittanica Collect.; Nat. Acad., N.Y.; Va. Mus. Biennial; Calif. Palace of the Legion of Hon., San Fran.; Corcoran Biennial, Wash. D.C.; Int. Water Colors, Art Inst. of Chgo.; World's Fair, San Fran.; Int. Lithography, Art Inst. of Chgo. Collects. incl: L.A. Co. Mus.; Chaffey Coll., Ont., Canada; Tel Aviv Art Mus., Israel. Hons. incl: Bartels Prize, Art Inst. of Chgo.; Purchase Award, City of Chgo., Int. Exhib. of Lithography, Art Inst. of Chgo. Address: 2293 Panorama Terr., L.A., CA 90039, U.S.A. 9, 37, 59.

VANZANDT, Dorothy Perkins, b. 4 Sept. 1913. Food & Nutrition Specialist. Educ: B.S., Pa. State Univ., 1935; Tchng. Cert., Univ. of Md., 1956; M.S., Tex. Woman's Univ., 1967; Ph.D., ibid, 1969. Appts. incl: Home Econs. Tchr., Hepburnville H.S., Lycoming Co., Pa., 1943-44; 5th Grade Tchr., Pimmit Hills Elem. Schl., Fairfax Co., Va., 1956-57; Substitute Tchr., pub. schls., LaGrange, Ill., 1958-59; Home Econs. Tchr., Gurrie Central Jr. H.S., LaGrange, 1959-66; Assoc. Prof., Foods & Nutrition Specialist, Md. Cooperative Extension Serv., Univ. of Md., Coll. Park, 1969-. Mbrships: Legislative Chmn., Md. Dietetic Assn., 1971-73; Nominee for Pres., ibid, 1974; Am. Dietetic Assn.; Chmn., Foods & Nutrition Sect., Md. Home Econs. Assn.; Am. Home Econs. Assn.; Omicron Nu; Iota Sigma Phi; Epsilon Sigma Phi; Kappa Kappa Gamma; AAUW. Address: Md. Cooperative Extension Serv., Room 1210, Symons Hall, Univ. of Md., College Park, MD 20742, U.S.A. 5.

VARDAKOS, Gr. Sotirios. Economist; Finance Counsellor; Chief Accountant; Company Director. Educ: H.S. of Econs. & Commerce Scis., Athens. Appts: Chief Econ., Greek Cotton Org., 1933; Counsellor of Commerce, Greek Embassy, Czechoslovakia, 1946; Gen. Sec., Panhellenic Soc. Sci. Acctcy., 1956; Fndr. Mbr., Costing Inst., 1965; Prof., Greek Ctr. of Prod., 1965; Introductory Mbr., State Establd. Comm. to draw up unified acctcy. plan in Greece; Mbr., State Comm. for re-examination of rules for pub. acctcy., w. special regard to decimal codified articulation of budget expenses & receipts; Currently, Financier, Econ., Counsellor, Chief Acct., Eriomar Co. Ltd., & B. Maragopoulos Co. Ltd. Mbrships: Assn. Ancient Students of H.S. of Econs. & Commerce Scis., Athens; Panhellenic Soc. Sci. of Acctng. (P.E.L.E.) Publs: Our Monetary System in the 20th Century, 1934; Accountancy of Loans, Existing Theories, 1936; Balance of Accounts, Theory & Applications, 1937; Amortizations in Economy & Accountancy, 1937; Accommodation Accounts in General Accountancy, 1939; The Accountancy of Liquidations & Amalgamations, 1943; Plan of Accountancy, 1957; Amortization as Element of the Cost in Exploitation, 1966; var. econs. articles in profl. publs. Address: 2 Ave. Sygrou T.T. 403, Athens, Greece.

VARGA, Ferenc, b. 29 May 1906. Sculptor. Educ: Karoly Fine Arts Acad., Budapest, Hungary, 1924; further educ., Academi Hungarica, Rome, Italy, and in Florence. Appts: Asst. to Prof., Karoly Acad., Budapest, 1928; Schlrship. Study, Rome & Florence, Italy, 1937; Rsch. Assoc., Pazmany-Peter Univ., Budapest, Hungary, 1941; currently operating own studio, Delray Beach, Fla., U.S.A.

Mbrships. incl: Nat. Art Soc. of Budapest; Nat. Sculpture Soc. of N.Y.; Hungarian Arts Club, Detroit. Commissioned Works incl: War Mem., Piszke, Hungary, 1935; War Mem., Kiskunfelegyhaza, Hungary, 1941; New Creations, for Grotto Ch. of Cistercial Order, 1947. Commissioned works in Canadian & Am. cities inclng. Toronto, Montreal, Ottawa, New York, Wash. D.C., Mpls., Pitts, St. Louis. Hons. incl: 1st Prize for Szatmar War Mem. Hungary, 1942; Louise Bennett Prize, Nat. Sculptor Soc. of N.Y., 1960. Address: 296 N.E. 6th Ave., Delray Beach, FL 33444, U.S.A.

VARGAS, Manuel, b. 23 Nov. 1924. Lawyer. Educ: Law Studies, Univ. of Chile, Santiago, 1942-46; LL.B., ibid, 1950; Southern Meth. Univ., Dallas, Tex., U.S.A., 1958-59; M.C.L., ibid, 1960. Appts: Law Clerk, Supreme Ct. of Chile, 1948-51; Lawyer, Andes Copper Mining Co., 1953-61; Lawyer, Chile Exploration Co., 1961-66; Chief Lawyer, ibid, 1966-71; Asst. V.P., 1971-72; Chilean Counsel, The Anaconda Co., 1972-. Mbrships: Union Club, Santiago, Chile; Chilean Bar Assn., Santiago; Am. Soc. of Int. Law, Wash. D.C., U.S.A.; Inter-Am. Bar Assn., Wash. D.C. Author, La Sociedad Anonima en el Derecho Anglo-Norte Americanc, 1964. Hons: Premio Jose Gabriel Ocampo, Univ. of Chile, 1948; Premio Jose Clemente Fabres, Chilean Bar Assn., 1951. Address: Casilla 83-D, Santiago, Chile. 136.

VARGAS, Rudolph, b. 20 Apr. 1904. Sculptor. Educ: San Carlos Acad. of Fine Arts, Mexico City. Appts: Film cos., sculpture & model work; commercial cos., original works of art & display works. Mbrships: San Diego Chmbr. of Comm.; Christmas Community Ctr. Sculptures: Madonna in Engl. Rosewood, Vatican Mus., Rome, Italy; large collect., life size figures & panels in wood, Santa Teresita Hosp., Duarte, Calif.; religious figures in wood, var. chs. Portraits in bronze, prominent persons. Recip., Large Art Works Award, City of Ontario, Calif. Address: 3661 Whittier Blvd., L.A., CA 90023, U.S.A. 9.

VARNER, Charleen LaVerne McClanahan (Mrs. Robert Bernard Varner), b. 28 Aug. 1931. Educator; Administrator; Nutritionist; Consultant. Educ: B.S., Kan. State Coll. of Pitts., 1953; M.S., Univ. of Ark., 1958; Ph.D., Tex. Woman's Univ., 1966. Instr., Home Econs., Kan. State Coll., 1959-63; Pt-time Lectr., Rsch. Asst., Coll. of Household Arts & Scis., Tex. Woman's Univ., 1963-66; Assoc. Prof., Home Econs., Ctrl. Mo. State Univ., 1966-70; Prof., Hd., Home Econs., Dept., Kan. State Tchrs. Coll., 1970-73; Prof., Chmn., Home Econs. Dept., Benedictine Coll., Kan., 1973-. Mbrships: Am. Home Econs. Assn.; Am. Dietetics Assn.; Phi Upsilon Omicron; Local chapt., Sigma Xi. Contbr. to profl. jrnls. Hons: Grant, NASA Rsch. Ctr. for Human Nutrition, 1964-66; Coll. Beauty Queen, 1952, '53. Address: Main P.O. Box 1009, Tope-Ka, KS 66601, U.S.A. 5, 8, 138.

VARNEY, Robert N(athan), b. 7 Nov. 1910. Physicist; Retired Commander U.S.N.R. Educ: A.B., Univ. of Calif., Berkeley, 1931; M.A., ibid, 1932; Ph.D., 1935. Appts. incl: Asst. Prof.-Assoc. Prof., Physics, Wash. Univ., St. Louis, Mo., 1938-48; Prof., ibid, 1948-64; Sr. mbr., rsch. lab., & Sr. Sci. Cons., Lockheed Missiles & Space Co., Palo Alto, Calif., 1964-; Nat. Sci. Fndn. Sr. Postdoctoral Fellow, Dept. of Electronics, Royal Inst. of Technol., Stockholm, Sweden, 1958-59; Fulbright Lectr., Univ. of Innsbruck, Austria, 1971-72. Mbrships: Fellow, Am. Phys. Soc.; Fellow, AAAS; Am. Geophys. Soc.; Am. Assn. of

Physics Tchrs.; Phi Beta Kappa; Sigma Xi; Omicron Delta Kappa; Tau Beta Pi; Pi Mu Epsilon. Author of 3 instructional books in introductory physics, chapts. in review books & tech. articles. Address: D/52-14; B/202, Lockheed Palo Alto Rsch. Lab., 3251 Hanover St., Palo Alto, CA 94304, U.S.A. 2, 50, 128.

VASILACH, Serge, b. 26 July 1904. Mathematician; Educator; Engineer. Educ: Bach. of Phys. Scis., Bach. of Math. Scis., D.E.S., Math. Phys. & Calculus of Probabilities, Univ. of Paris, France, 1927-30; Dr. ès Sciences, Math. Scis., Univ. of Rennes, 1966. Appts. incl: Rsch. Asst., Univ. of Paris, 1928-35; Dir., Rsch. Laboratoire d'Electricité, Paris, 1939-43. Rsch. Asst., Univ. of Bucharest, 1944-50; Rsch. Dir., Math. Inst. of Acad. of Rumanian Socialist Repub., 1950-65; Prof., Dept. of Maths., Univ. Laval, Quebec, Canada, 1966-. Mbrships: Am. Math. Soc.; Soc. Math. de France; Canadian Math. Congress. Author num. papers in pure & applied maths. Hons: Work Merit Order, Acad. Rumanian Socialist Repub.; Annual Grant, Nat. Rsch. Coun. of Canada, 1966-. Address: Laval Univ., Dept. of Maths., Quebec G1K 7P4, Canada. 2, 6.

VASILIU, Emanuel, b. 7 Sept. 1929. University Professor. Educ: Grad., Univ. of Bucharest, Rumania, 1952; D.Philol. Scis., 1957; Dr. Docent, 1969. Appts: Asst.-Lectr.-Assoc. Prof., Dept. of Rumanian Lang. & Lit., Univ. of Bucharest; Prof., ibid, 1970-. Mbrships: Ling. Soc. Am.; Int. Phonetic Assn.; Comm., Rumanian Soc. for Romance Lings.; Comm., Rumanian Ling. Soc. Publs: Phonology of Rumanian, 1965; Historical Phonology of Dacoromanian Dialects, 1968; Elements of Semantics of Nuetral Languages, 1970; Outline of a Semantic Theory of Kernel Sectences, 1972; The Tranformational Syntax of Rumanian, 1972. Address: Intrarea Lucaci 3, Bucharest IV, Rumania.

VASQUEZ, Antonio Ouano, b. 13 June 1943. Public Relations Executive. Educ: B.A., Ateneo de Manila Univ., 1966; M.B.A., Ateneo Grad. Schl. of Bus. Appts: Pub. Rels. Account Exec., Ace Compton Advt., Inc., 1963-64; Accounts Mgr., Communications Counsellors, Inc., 1964-65; V.P., Philconsultants Assocs., Inc., 1965-66; Exec. Asst. & Ed. of Publs. San Miguel Corp., 1966-69; Pub. Affairs Dir., 1st Nat. Bank, 1969-73; V.P., Corp. Affairs Grp., Philippine Commercial & Ind. Bank, 1973-; Lectr., Pub. Rels. & Ind. Communications, Ateneo de Manila Univ., 1971-; Lectr., Pub. Rels in Banking, Philippine Inst. of Banking, 1972-73. Mbrships. incl: Assoc., P.R. Soc. of Am.; Int. Assn. of Bus. Communicators; Chmn. of Bd., Philippine Coun. of Ind. Communicators, 1974. Publs: Job Attitudes & the Employee Publication, 1968; Philippines & You (Folio Dir.), 1973; PCI Bank Moneyshop Concept, 1973. Hons. incl: Lone Achievement Award, Philippine Coun. of Ind. Communicators, 1972; Anvil Award for Pub. Rels. Prog. Involving Special Audiences, PRSP, 1972. Address: c/o Philippine Commercial & Ind. Bank, Corporate Affairs Grp., P.O. Box 2958, Manila, Philippines. 24.

VASSALLO, Giovanni M., b. 4 Aug. 1906. Writer; Cultural Consultant. Educ: Econ. & classical studies. Appts: Personnel Mgr., Olivetti Spa; Commercial Mgr., Osram—Edison Clerici, & later Pagot Film; Dir., Centro Culturale Pirelli, Milan, Italy. Mbrships: Italian Ordine Nazionale Autori e Scrittori; Svenska Institutet i Rom. Publs: Preludi; L'Orciolo di Rame; Il Sogno di Duccio; La Congiura di Sangry; Storia Della Repubblica di San Marino; Gli Animali di Khorsabad; Works in anthols.; Articles in encys.

& mags.; Author of proj. of Int. Youth Mag. submitted to UNESCO Int. Educ. Bur. Hons: Golden Laurel for Poetry, Orvieto Prize; Special mention for narrative works at Orvieto Prize, Collodi Prize & others. Address: Viale Campania 31, 20133 Milan, Italy. 43, 95.

VASSILIOU, Spiros, b. 1902. Painter. Educ: Schl. of Fine Arts, Athens, Greece, 1921-27. Appts: Art Prof., Papestietos Schl. of Decoration, 1929-33; Prof., Scenography, Dramatic Schl., Nat. Theatre, Athens, 1940-47; Art Dir., Doxiedis Schl. of Decoration, 1956-62. Mbrships: Techni Grp.; Stathmi. One-man shows: Stretizopoulou Gall., 1929; Sev. Greek towns, 1952-66; Paris, France, London, U.K., Basle & Zurich, Switzerland, & Nicosia, Cyprus, 1966-74. Participant, num. exhibs. inclng: Exhibs. of the Four, Athens, Volos, & Thessaloniki, 1926-27; Studio Gall., Athens, 1932-33; 19th Venice Biennale, Italy, 1934; Inst. of Arts, Detroit, Mich., U.S.A., 1955; Venice Biennale, 1964. Designer, sets for 80 plays & films, 1929-73. Publs. incl: Ships of Galaxidi; Children's Drawings; Greek Merchant Ships; Lights & Shadows. Illustrator, num. books. Hons: Award, Acad. of Athens, for frescoes for St. Denis of the Areopagus, 1930; Guggenheim Award, 1960. Address: 5 Webster St., Athens 402, Greece.

VATIKIOTIS, Panayiotis J., b. 5 Feb. 1928. Professor. Educ: B.A., Am. Univ., Cairo, Egypt, 1948; Ph.D., John Hopkins Univ., U.S.A., 1954. Appts: Instr., Soc. Scis., Am. Univ., Cairo, Egypt, 1948-49; Fellow & Instr., Arabic, Johns Hopkins Univ., 1951-53; Instr.-Prof., Govt., Ind. Univ., U.S.A., 1953-65; Prof., Pol., London Univ., U.K., 1965-; Vis. Professorships: Johns Hopkins Univ. Schl. Adv. Int. Studies, U.S.A., summer, 1957; Mich. Univ., summer 1960; Calif., Univ., LA, 4 mths., 1969; Vis. Prof. & Sr. Fellow, Humanities, Princeton Univ., NJ, 1973-74; Chmn., Prof., Near Eastern Studies, Ind. Univ., 1959-65; Chmn., Ctr. ME Studies, Schl. Oriental & African Studies, London Univ., U.K., 1966-69; Mbr., Edit. Bd., ME Studies. Publs. incl: The Egyptian Army in Politics, 1961; The Modern History of Egypt, 1969; The Fatimid Theory of the State, 1957; Politics and the Military in Jordan, 1967; Conflict in the Middle East, 1971; Ed., Egypt since the Revolution, 1966; Revolution in the Middle East and other case studies, 1972. Recip. Guggenheim Fellowship, 1961-62. Address: London Univ. Schl. Oriental & African Studies, Malet St., London WC1E 7HP, U.K.

VAUDRIN, (William Hartfield) Bill, b. 31 May 1943. Writer; Educator; Commercial Fisherman. Educ: Baccalaureate cum laude, Alaska Meth. Univ., 1966; M.F.A., Ore. Univ., 1968. Appts: Pt.-time Instr., Engl., Ore. Univ., 1967-68; Instr., Engl., Anchorage Community Coll., 1968-70; Dir., Community Liaison, Alaska State-operated Schl. System & Alasks Fedn. Natives, 1971-73; Exec. Dir., Alaska State Commn. Human Rights, 1973-74. Mbrships: Chmn., Bd. Alaska Fedn. Natives Educ., Alaska Student Higher Educ. Servs.; Chmn., Cook iInlet Native Assn. Educ.; Nat. Indian Educ. Assn.; Nat. Assn. Univ. Profs.; Phi Alpha Theta; MALA. Publs: The Amigook, the Eiukna and the Voncha, 1963; There Used to be a World, 1965; And Still the Rain, 1969; The Sea & I, 1969; Mannerly Moon, 1969 (all jrnl. articles); Tanaina Tales from Alaska, 1969; Native/Non-Native Communications: Creating a Two-Way Flow, 1973. Address: Pedro Bay, AK 99647, U.S.A. 9, 30.

VAUGHN, Bill Edward, b. 28 May 1933. College Professor. Educ: B.A., Bethany

Nazarene Coll.; M.A., Ph.D., Speech Communication, Univ. of Kan.; M.Div., Nazarene Theol. Sem. Appts: Ordained Elder, Ch. of Nazarene, 1957; Pastor, ibid, 1955-68; Speech Communication Tchng. Asst., Rsch. Asst., Univ. of Kan., 1966-68; Prof., Chmn., Dept. of Speech Communication, Bethany Nazarene Coll., 1968-; Chmn., Div. of Lang. Lit. & Speech, ibid, 1969-. Mbrships: Speech Communication Assn. of Am.; Ctrl. States, Okla. Speech Assns.; Kiwanis Int.; Sponsor, Circle K Int.; Pi Delta Lambda. Address: 2805 Windsor Blvd., Okla. City, OK 73127, U.S.A. 125, 130, 131.

VAUGHN, Gerald Franklin, b. 8 Aug. 1938. Community Development Educator. Educ: B.S., Univ. of Md., 1960; M.S., Univ. of Del., 1962; Postgrad. work, ibid & Tex. A & M Univ. Appts: Agricl. Economist, Urban Impact Investigations, U.S. Dept. of Agric. (Econ. Rsch. Serv.), 1960-63; Extension Resource Dev. Specialist, Tex. A & M Univ., 1963-64; Planner, Md. State Planning Dept., 1964-66; Extension Coord., Community & Resource Dev., Univ. of Del., 1967-. Mbrships: Community Dev. Soc.; Am. Soc. for Pub. Admin.; Am. Soc. of Planning Officials; Epsilon Sigma Phi; Mbr. or Advsr., num. bds. & comms., inclng. Chmn., Del. Coun. on Indl. Financing. Author of num. monographs & articles on community dev. & of biographies of Wm. M. Stone (Episcopal bishop) & Ray Whitley (entertainer). Address: 2 Pagoda Lane, Newark, DE 19711, U.S.A. 6, 14, 130, 131, 141.

VAUGHT, Jack Thomas, b. 16 June 1908. Management Consultant; Banker. Educ: Am. Inst. of Banking; Grad. Schl. of Banking, Rutgers Univ., 1949. Appts: Transit Clerk-Transit Mgr., Operations off.-Sr. V.P. & Cashier, 1st. Nat. Bank of Ft. Worth, Tex, 1926-73; Mgmt. Cons., J.T. Vaught & Assocs. Mbrships: Am. Inst. of Banking; Bank Admin. Inst.; Adminstrve. Mgmt. Soc. & Ft. Worth Personnel & Indl. Rels. Soc. (Past Pres.); Am. Soc. of Indl. Security; Julian Feild Masonic Lodge 908 (Past Master); Moslah Temple Shrine (Treas. 1970-71); Tarrant Co. Civil Defense; Chmbr. of Comm.; Postal Customers. Coun. (Chmn., 1967-73); Meth. Ch. Recip. of P.B.X. Club award, 1967. Address: 1301 1st. Nat. Bank Bldg., Ft. Worth, TX 76102, U.S.A. 2, 125.

VAUPEL, (Rev.) Orval Herbert, b. 24 Apr. 1907. Baptist Minister. Educ: S. Ill. Univ.; Hannibal LaGrange Bible Coll.; courses in ext. work. Appts: Pastor, Chs., 1951-54; Pioneer Missionary, Mo., 1954; Pastor, Ill. Chs., 1955-. Address: 710 N. 6th St., Carmi, IL 62821, U.S.A. 120.

VAURS, Roger, b. 26 Aug. 1920. Diplomat; French Ambassador to Turkey. Educ: Licence, Law, Dip., Adv. Studies, Pub. Law & Pol. Econs., Fac. of Law, Paris; Pol. Sci. Schl., Paris; Nat. Admin. Schl. Appts: For. Serv., 1944-; Mbr., Pvte. Secretariat, For. Min., 1947-48; Mbr., Econ. Div., Min. of For. Affairs, & Permanent Deleg., OEEC, 1948-52; Dir., Press Info. Serv., French Embassy, N.Y., 1952-56; Dir., Press Info. Serv., Min. of For. Affairs, Spokesman of For. Min., 1966-69; Exec. Asst. to Prime Min., Couve de Murville, 1969, & Chaban-Delmas, 1969-72; Ambassador to Turkey, 1973-; French Deleg. to UN General Assmblies, var. For. Mins.' Confs., inclng. Summit Conf., Geneva, 1955. Mbrship: Golf Club of La Boulie. Hons: Off., Legion of Hon.; Off., Nat. Order of Merit. Address: 70 Paris Caddesi, Ankara, Turkey. 43, 91.

VAVARETOS, Georgios, b. 1 July 1902 (d. 17 Aug. 1973). Lawyer; Author; Journalist. Educ: Grad., Schl. of Law, Athens Univ., Greece. Appts: Law prac., Supreme Ct. of Greece; Ed.-in-Chief, Ethnos, Ellas, Athinaiki, & Proodos newspapers; V.P. & Bd. Mbr., Union of Athens Dailies Journalists. Mbrships: Athens Bar Assn.; Athens Epizotic Soc. Publs. (in Greek) incl: Automobile Law, 1932; Modern Civil Laws, 1934; Confiscations—Bids, 1936, 2nd edit. 1938; The Civil Code, 1950, 6th edit. 1972; The Constitution of Greece, 1952, 5th edit. 1969; Code of Penal Procedure (Analysis), 1954, 5th edit. 1972; Penal Code (Analysis), 1956, 5th edit. 1972; Num. contbns. to encys. & dictionaries. Address: Alkis Vavaretos, Griva 16, Filothei, Athens, Greece.

VAVOUSKOS, Constantin, b. 18 Nov. 1921. Professor of Civil Law; Educ: LL.D., Univ. of Paris, France; Univ. of Salonika, Greece; Acad. of Int. Law, The Hague, Netherlands. Appts: Lawyer, Ct. of Thessalonika, Greece, 1955; Asst. Prof., Civil Law, Univ. of Salonika, 1957; Prof. Extraordinary, ibid, 1964; Full Prof., Civil Law, 1969; Juridical Counselor, 1972. Mbrships: Admin. Coun., Soc. for Macedonian Studies of Thessalonika; Coun., Balkan Studies Ctr. of Thessalonika; Coun., Byzantine Ctr. of Studies of Thessalonika. Num. publs. incl: Manuel du Droit Civil; Manuel du Droit Ecclesiastique; Manuel du Droit des Biens; Church & State in Modern Greece; L'Evolution de la Legislation sur la Filiation Naturelle; De l'Inscription de l'Hypothèque Judiciaire Provisoire dans le Droit Hellenique; Greek Macedonian Struggle for Freedom. Hons. incl: Gold Cross of Kts. of Patrirchate of Jerusalem, 1966; Archon Megas Dikaiophylax, Patriarchate of Constantinople, 1973. Address: Boulevard J. Kennedy 73, Thessalonika, Greece. 43.

VAZQUEZ, Juan Julian, b. 2 Jan. 1929. Physician; Psychiatrist. Educ: Dip. Univ. of Madrid Med. Schl., Spain, 1967. Appts. incl: Pvte. Prac, in Psych., Madrid, Spain, 1962-65; Res. in Psych., Ill. State Psych. Inst., U.S.A., 1965-68; Asst. Dir., Out-Patient Dept., ibid, 1965-67; Cons., 1970-71; Staff Psych., Dyslexia Inst., Chgo., 1967-; Asst. Prof., Clin. Psych., Abraham Lincoln Schl. of Med., 1967-; Pvte. Prac., Chgo., Ill., 1968-70; Dir. of Psykch. Educ., Mercy Hosp., ibid, 1972; Sr. Attendant, 1968-; Staff Psych., St. Francis Hosp., Evanston, Ill. Mbrships. incl: AMA; Am. Psych. Assn.; Fellow, Royal Soc. of Hlth.; AAAS; Chgo. Med. Soc.; Ill. State Med. Assn. Contbr. of articles, monographs & papers on psych. subjects. Address: 233 E. Erie Ave., Suite 1005, Chicago, IL 60611, U.S.A. 17, 120.

VEATCH, Prudence Melvina, b. 28 Aug. 1906. Retired Educator. Educ: B.A. Wellesley Coll., 1929; M.A., Yale Univ., 1931; courses, Univ. of Buffalo. Appts: Tchr. of Sec. Schl. Engl., Buffalo Bd. of Educ., 1933-70. Mbrships. incl: Ed. of Column in Sunday Courier Express, 1936-42 & Pres., 1943-44, Buffalo Poetry Soc.; Pres., Tri-L. Class, Ctrl. Park United Meth. Ch., 1971-73; Western N.Y. Br., Nat. League A., Pen Women; Buffalo Br., AAUW; Pi Lambda Theta, Buffalo & Erie Co. Hist. Soc.; Prog. Chmn., Thursday Book Club, 1972-74; Grads, Assn. of Buffalo Sem.; Buffalo Wellesley Club; Deleg., H.S. Tchr. Assn., Buffalo, 1941-43 & Buffalo Tchrs. Fedn., 1960-66. Contbr. articles to var. mags., profl. jrnls. etc. Hons: Prizes in Poetry, Buffalo Sem., 1921 & 25; var. Pen Women, etc. awards from var. lit contests. Address: 157 Huntington Ave., Buffalo, NY 14214, U.S.A.

VEITEL, Jenny Frieda, b. 21 Apr. 1909. Hosiery Manufacturer; Registered Nurse. Educ:

Grad., Hornell Bus. Schl.; Grad., Buffalo City Hosp., 1931. Appts: Sec., Dr. Carl Schwan, 1926-28; Rigistered nurse, pvte. duty, self-employed, Hornell, N.Y., Cornwall on Hudson, Cornwall, N.Y., & Buffalo, N.Y., 1931-42; Pvte. Sec. to father, Franz W. Veitel, Veitel Hosiery Mill, 1942-46; Mgr., Veitel Hosiery Co., 1946-50; Exec. Ptnr., Veitel Hosiery Mill, 1950-; Travelling Saleslady, ibid, 1950-62. Mbrships: Warder, Martha & Esther, Order of the Eastern Star, 1942-50; N.Y. State Nurses Assn.; Buffalo City Hosp. Alumni Assn., 1931-42. Discoverer of cause of sickness in astronauts through her own sickness caused by fumes from malassembled cars. Address: 28 W. Main St., Le Roy NY 14482, U.S.A. 5, 138.

VEIARDO, Joseph Thomas, b. 27 Jan. 1923. Educator; Scientist. Educ: A.B., Colo. State Coll. Educ., Greeley, 1948; S.M., Miami Univ., Osford, Ohio, 1949; Ph.D., Harvard Univ., 1952. Appts. incl: Rsch. Assoc. Surg., Harvard Med. Schl., 1954-55; Asst. Prof., Anat. & Endocrinol., Yale Univ. Schl. of Med., 1955-61; Prof. & Chmn., Dept. Anat., N.Y. Med. Coll., 1961-62; Dir., Inst. for Study of Human Reproduction, Cleveland, Hd., Div. of Rsch., St. Ann Hosp. & Prof., Biol. & Endocrinol., John Carrol Univ., 1962-67; Prof. & Chmn., Dept. of Anat., Strich Schl. of Med., 1967-. Fellowships: Gerontol. Soc.; AAAS. Mbrships. incl: Am. Assn. Anats.; Physiol. Soc.; Soc. Zools.; Soc. Exptl. Biol. & Med.; Pres., Midwest Assn. Anats., 1973-74. Contbr. & Ed., publs. in field. Address: 2160 S. 1st Ave., Maywood, IL 60153, U.S.A. 8, 14, 28, 50, 128.

VELÁZQUEZ, Maria del Carmen, b. 3 Feb. 1912. Historian; Writer. Educ: Qualified as Primary Schl. Tchr., Escuela Nacional de Maestros, Mexico; Dr. in Hist., Univ. Nacional Autónoma, Mexico; B.A., Mt. Holyoke Coll., Mass. Appts. incl: Spanish Asst. Tchr., Mt. Holyoke Coll., Mass.; Lectr. in the Hist. of Mexico & Am., Mexico City Coll.; Lectr. in Am. Hist., Univ. Nacional Autónoma, Mexico; Hd., Ctr. of Histl. Studies, El Colegio de México. Publs. incl: El Estado de Guerra en Nueva España 1760-1808, 1950; Colotlán—Doble Frontera contra los Bárbaros, 1961; La España de Carlos III, Según Informes de los Embajadores Austriacos, 1963; Hispanoamerica en el siglo XX, 1965; Los Mexicanos—Síntesis de Su Historia, 1970; contbr. articles to num. profl. jrnls. Address: Coahuila 188, Mexico 7 D.F., Mexico.

VELIOTIS, Panagiotis Takis, b. 11 Aug. 1926. Shipbuilding Company Executive. Educ: B.A., St. Paul Coll., Greece; engrng. degree, Royal Naval Acad., ibid; Postgrad. studies, Nat. Univ., Athens. Appts: Engr., E.G. Veliotis shipowners; Engrng. Draftsman, Davie Shipbuilding Ltd., P.Q., Canada, 1953; Supt., Gen. Engrng. Div., ibid, 1954; Mgr., Gen. Engrng. Div., 1955-59; Asst. Gen. Mgr., Construction, 1959-62; Dir. Gen. Mgr., 1962-72; Pres. Gen. Mgr., Dir., 1972; V.P., Gen. Dynamics Corp., St. Louis, Mo., U.S.A., 1973; Pres., Gen. Mgr., Quincy Shipbldg. Div., ibid, Mass., 1973. Mbrships: Am. Comm., Lloyds Register Shipping; Am. Bur. Shipping; Soc. Naval Archts. & Marine Engrs.; Shipbldrs. Coun. of Am.; P.Q. Garrison; P.Q. Yacht Club. Address: Gen. Dynamics, Quincy Shipbuilding Div., 97 E. Howard St., Quincy, MA 02169, U.S.A. 6, 88.

VELLA HABER, (Baron) Kelinu, b. 1 Oct. 1913. Author; Broadcaster; Journalist; Retired Civil Servant. Educ: Langs. & Philos., St. Mark's Coll. Appts: Mgr., Victory Kitchens, 1940; Prof., Maltese Gozo Lyceum & Gozo Sem., 1941-43; Insp.-Info. Off., Agric., 1943-58; Sr.

Info. Off., Info. & Publy. Sect., 1958-73; Ed., Qawsalla lit. monthly & agric. bi-monthly paper, 1958-73. Mbrships: Fndr. & Int. Grand Prior, Langue of Malta OSJ; Fndr., Nat. Farmers' Union, Gozo; Assn. Fishermen, Gozo; Socs. Diffusion Maltese Lang., Gozo; Maltese Lang. Movement; Grand Bailiff Hereditary Grand Cross OSJ; Grand Collar Order St. Agatha. Publs: The National Sanctuary of Qala and the Hermit of Mosta, 1938; 2nd ed., '46; Poultry Secrets, 1946, 2nd ed., '73; The Calendar of Flowers, 1958; 2nd ed., '58; 3rd ed., '74; The Calendar of Vegetables and Herbs, 1959; 2nd ed., '59; 3rd ed., '74; Home-making of Wines, 1961; Gardening Secrets, 1965. Hons: Baronetage, 1966; Marquisate, Royal House Aragon, 1969; Collar Order Royal Crown of Balearics; Caballero de la Real Orden de Jaime I de Aragon. Address: 66 Stuart St., Gzira, Malta. 99, 131.

VELLAY, Pierre, b. 15 Feb. 1919. Physician; Gynaecologist. Educ: M.D.; Dips., Med. Jurisprudence, Neuropsych., & Hydrol. Appts: Asst. to D·. F. Lamaze, Pierre Rouques Hlth. Ctr., France, 1947-57; Maternity Cons., Rothschild Hosp., Paris, 1958-. Mbrships. incl: French Gyn. Soc.; French Psychosomatic Soc.; French Anatomy-Pathol. Soc.; Nat. Soc. for the Study of Sterility; V.P., French Obstetrical Psychoprophylaxis Soc.; Sec. Gen., Int. Obstetrical Psychoprophylaxis Soc., 1959-; Gyn. & Obs. Socs. of Cuba, Colombia, Uruguay, Chile, Venezuela, & Spain; Hon. Pres., Am. Psychoprophylaxis Soc.; Int. Childbirth Educ. Assn., U.S.A. Publs: Dèveloppement Sexuel & Maternité; Témoignages sur l'Accouchement sans Douleur; La Vie Sexuelle de la Femme; La Vie Sexuelle du Couple; Le Vécu de l'Avortement. Maker, num. educl. films. Hons. incl: Croix de Guerre with Star, 1939-45; Resistance Medal; Chevalier, Nat. Order of Merit. Address: 31 Rue Saint-Guillaume, 75-Paris 7e., France.

VENCOVSKY, Eugen, b. 9 Apr. 1908. Professor. Educ: Med. Fac., Charles Univ., Prague. Appts: Assoc. Prof. of Psych., Charles Univ. Prague; Dir., Psych. Univ. Clin., Pilsen; Vice-Dean, Med. Fac., Pilsen; Chief, edit. bd., "Czechoslovak Psych". Mbrships: Comm., World Psych. Assn.; Pres., Czechoslovak Psych. Soc.; Hon. Mbr., Czechoslovak Med. Assn., Yugoslav Psych. Assn., German Democratic Repub. Psych. Soc.; Corresp. Mbr., German Fed Repub. Psych. Soc., Swiss Psych. Soc.; Hon. mbr., Polish, Hungarian & Bulgarian Psych. Socs., 1973; Soc. Médico-psychologique; Royal Soc. Med. Publs. incl: History of Czech Psychiatry; Paraphrenia. (monographs); History of World Psychiatry; Textbook of Psychiatry; Masked Depressions. Hons. incl: Czechoslovak State Order J.E. Purkinje, 1968; Polish State Order Polonia Restituta, 1969; Medal, Charles Univ., Prague, 1970; Medal, Wroclaw Univ., 1971. Address: Dukelská 69, Pilsen, Czechoslovakia.

VENKAYYA, Vipperla B., b. 16 May 1931. Aerospace Engineer. Educ: B.Sc., Andhra Univ., India; B.Tech. (Hons.), Indian Inst. Technol., 1956; M.S., Mo. Univ., U.S.A., 1959; Ph.D., Ill. Univ., 1962. Appts: Asst. Engr., Designs, Damodar Valley Corp., Calcutta, India, 1956-57; Bridge Design Engr., C'wealth, of Pa., Harriesburg, Pa., U.S.A., 1958-59; Asst. Prof., Schl. Engrng., SUNY, Buffalo, 1962-67; Aerospace Engr., Air Force Flight Dynamics Lab., Wright Patterson Air Force Base, Ohio, 1967-. Mbrships: Am. Inst. Aeronautics & Astronautics; Am. Soc. Civil Engrs.; Task Comm., Automated Analysis & Design; ASCE Electronic Computation Comm. Author sev. Papers on Structural Optimization. Recip. Gen.

Foulois Hon. Mention Award, Air Force Flight Dynamics Lab., 1969, '71. Address: AFFDL-FBR, Wright Patterson AFB, OH 45433, U.S.A. 14.

VENNEMA, A., b. 11 Aug. 1932. Doctor of Medicine. Educ: B.A., Western Reserve Univ., Cleveland, Ohio, U.S.A., 1958; M.D.C.M., McGill Univ., Montreal, Canada, 1962; M.P.H.-Tropical Med., Tulane Univ., New Orleans, La., U.S.A., 1969. Appts: Team Capt., Care-Medico, Quang-Ngai, Provincial Hosp., S. Vietnam, 1964-65; Tech. Advsr. to Govt. of S. Vietnam under Canadian Colombo Plan, ibid, 1965-66; Dir. of Canadian Med. Assistance to S. Vietnam, ibid, inclng: dev. of provincial tuberculosis prog., trng. personnel, designing & building T.B. Clinic, 1966-68; Lectr., Div. of Community Med., Univ. of Dar Es Salaam, 1970-72; Rsch. related to Tanzania, Dept. of Demography, London Schl. of Hygiene, U.K. Publs. incl: The Harvest of Death (co-author); contbr. to profl. jrnls.; Hons. incl: Order of Merit, Govt. of S. Vietnam, 1965; Order of Canada, 1966. Address: 2120 Wellington Ave., Burlington, Ont., Canada.

VENTURI, Denise Scott Brown (Mrs. Robert Venturi), b. 3 Oct. 1931. Architect; Planner. Educ: Univ. of Witwatersrand, Johannesburg, S. Africa, 1948-51; A.A. Dip., Archtl. Assn., London, England, 1952-55; M.C.P. & M.Arch., Univ. of Pa., Phila., U.S.A., 1958-60, 1965. Appts. incl: Instr. & Asst. Prof., Univ. of Pa. Schl. of Fine Arts, 1960-65; Assoc. Prof., UCLA Schl. of Arch. & Urban Planning, 1965-68; Joined Venturi & Rauch, Archts. & Planners, Phila., Pa., 1967 & Ptnr., 1969; Vis. Prof., Yale Univ. Schl. of Art & Arch., 1967-70; Vis. Comm., MIT Schl. of Arch. & Planning, 1973-. Mbrships. incl: Assoc., Royal Inst. of British Archts.; Archtl. Assn., London, U.K.; Alliance of Women in Arch., N.Y., U.S.A. Publs. incl: Learning From Las Vegas (w. S. Izenour), 1972; Num. publs. in profl. jrnls.; Exhibs. at Phila. Art Alliance, 1968 & '73; Whitney Mus., N.Y., 1971. Hons. incl: Gold Medal, Am. Inst. of Archts., 1972; Var. prizes in competitions. Address: 333 S. 16th St., Philadelphia, PA 19102, U.S.A. 5, 30, 138.

VERDON, Joseph M., b. 4 July 1941. Engineer. Educ: B.S., Webb Inst. of Naval Arch., 1963; M.S., Univ. of Notre Dame, 1965; Ph.D., 1967. Appts: Rsch. Engr., United Aircraft Rsch. Labs., E. Hartford, Conn., 1967-68; Rsch. Engr., ibid, 1972-; Asst. Prof., Mech. Engrng., Univ. of Conn., Storrs, 1968-72; Cons., Pratt & Whitney Aircraft Co., E. Hartford, 1970-71. Mbrships: Am. Soc. Mech. Engrs.; AIAA; Soc. Ind. & Applied Maths.; Am. Soc. Engrng. Educ.; Sigma Xi. Author of tech. publs. Hons; Schmitt Fellowship, Univ. of Notre Dame, 1963; NASA Predoct. Traineeship, ibid, 1965; NASA-Am. Soc. Engrng. Educ. Summer Fac. Fellowship, Langley Rsch. Ctr., 1971, 72. Address: Sherry Circle, Tolland, CT 06084, U.S.A. 6, 14.

VERHEYLEZOON, Pol Jean Aimé, b. 23 Feb. 1940. Decorative Arts Teacher. Educ: Atelier Iris, Paris, France, 1956. Appts: Show-window decorator & shop installations, 1963-72; Tchr., Municipal Acad. of Design, Maldegem, Belgium, 1963-; Tchr., Applied Arts, Municipal Secondary Inst. of Fine Arts, Ghent, 1973-; Interior Designer & Decorator, 1970-. Mbrships. incl: Fndr., Xeno Art Group; Assn. of the Mus. of Fine Arts; Youth & Music; Youth & Plastic Arts; Sincfala Art Group, Netherlands. Work in many pub. & pvte. collects. Hons: 1st Prize, Sofina, Brussels, 1956; 3rd Prize, Beatrys, Eeklo, 1957; Hon. mentions

at exhibs. of paintings at Olivetti, 1958, St. Niklaas, 1971, & Waregem, 1971. Address: Aardenburgkalseide 336, 9990 Maldegem, Belgium.

VERNEZOBRE, Ernest Francisco, b. 4 Dec. 1927. Physician. Educ: B.S., Inst. of Secondary Educ., Havana, Cuba, 1945; D.Med. & Surg., Univ. of Havana, 1952. Appts. incl: Rotating Intern, Univ. Hosp. Havana, 1953-54; Res., Ob. & Gyn., 1955-57; Cons., Gyn., TB Hosp., Las Villas, Cuba, 1957-59; Med. Dir., St. Emily Hosp., Havana, 1959-60; Staff Physn., San Antonio TB Hosp., U.S.A., 1963-64; Family Prac., Med., Midland, Tex., 1966-; Mbr. of Staff, Midland, Mem., Parkview Hosps., Midland; Chief, Staff, Parkview Hosp., 1971; Chief, Med., 1972 & '73. Mbrships. incl: Dip., Am. Bd. Family Prac.; Am., Pan Am., Southern, Tex. Med. Assns.; Fellow, Am. Acad. Angiol., Am. Acad. Family Prac.; Am. & Tex. Acads. of Gen. Prac.; Am. Acad. Geriatrics; AMA; Am. & Tex. Thoracic Socs.; Am. & Tex. Diabetes Assns.; Pan Am. Cancer Soc.; Tex. Heart Assn.; Midland Co. Med. Soc. Decorated Off., Charles J. Finlay Nat. Merit Order, Cuba. Address: 1802 W. Wall St., Midland, TX 79701, U.S.A. 7, 17.

VERNICE, (Sister) Mary Makovic. Professor; Administrator; Academic Dean. Educ: B.S., St. John Coll., 1938; M.A., St. Louis, Univ., 1942; Ph.D., Case-Western Reserve Univ., 1968; Mbr., Sisters of Notre Dame. Appts: Tchr., Ohio, Calif., Tenn., 1930-40; Asst. Prof., Educ., Grad. Schl. of Arts & Scis., Cath. Univ. of Am., 1943-57; Prin., Notre Dame Acad., L.A., 1958-63; Supvsr., 11 secondary schls. of Sisters of Notre Dame, Ohio & Va., 1963-66; Prof., Educ., & Dean, Acad. Affairs, Notre Dame Coll., Cleveland, Ohio, 1966-. Mbrships. incl: Diocesan Schl. Bd., Cleveland; Am. Assn. of Higher Educ.; Am. Conf. of Acad. Deans.; Am. Educ. Rsch. Assn.; Sec. & Chmn., Midwest Region, Nat. Cath. Educ. Assn.; Pi Delta Phi; Phi Alpha Theta; Int. Hon. Soc. in Hist. Publs. incl: Geography Workbook for North American Neighbors, 1952; Teachers' Manual for American Neighbors, 1952; Contbr. to educl. jrnls. & author 20 book reviews. Hons. incl: 2 Ph.D. Schlrships. Fordham Univ., 1957, '58; Assistantship & Schlrship. for Ph.D., St. Louis Univ., 1943; Fed. Rsch. Grant, 1968. Address: Notre Dame Coll., 4545 College Rd., Cleveland, OH 44121, U.S.A. 5, 138, 141.

VERNON, Walter N., b. 24 Mar. 1907. Minister. Editor. Educ: B.A., Southern Meth. Univ., Dallas, Tex., 1926; B.D., 1931; M.A., 1934. Appts: Pastor, Dallas, 1927-38; Ed., Youth, Ch. Schl. Publs., Meth. Ch., 1938-44; Admin. Assoc., Gen. Bd. Educ., Meth. Ch., 1944-72; Sec., Curric. Comm., 1952-72; Sec., TV Radio & Film Comm., 1948-64; Sec. Treas. Meth. Conf. on Christian Educ., 1957-69. Mbrships: Sigma Delta Chi; Tau Kappa Alpha; Tex. Hist. Soc.; Okla. Hist. Soc.; Ark. Hist. Soc.; Tenn. Hist. Soc. Publs. incl: Methodist Profile, 1959; Methodism Moves Across North Texas, 1967; United Methodist Profile, 1968; William Stevenson Riding Preacher, 1969; Forever Building: The Life & Ministry of Paul E. Martin, 1973. Recip., Hon. D. Litt., W. Va. Wesleyan Coll., 1963. Address: 4013 Dorcas Dr., Nashville, TN 37215, U.S.A. 7, 116.

VERRET. (Baron) Alexandre C., b. 5 June 1914. Attorney at Law; Diplomat; Teacher. Educ: B.A., B.S., St. Louis de Gonzague Inst., Port au Prince, Haiti, 1934; LL.M., Fac. of Law, Port au Prince, 1942; Music courses. Appts: Prof. of Maths., Coll. Polymathique, Port au Prince, 1936; Co-Dir., Jrnl. Latribune,

Port au Prince, 1938; Prof. of Soc. Scis., Lycée Petion, Port au Prince, 1946; Prof. of Latin & Lit., Lycée Toussaint Louverture, Port au Prince, 1950; Attaché of Embassy, 1958; 2nd Sec., ibid, 1959; Consul Gen. & 1st Sec., 1960; Min. Counselor to Un, 1972; Ambassador of Haiti, Dpty. Permanent Rep. to UN, N.Y.C., U.S.A., 1973; Rep. of Haiti to UN Gen. Assembly, 1960-74. Mbrships: Inter-Am. Bar Assn., 1965; Cercle d'Or, N.Y., 1965; Am. Soc. of Int. Law, 1968. Author of poetry & articles publd. in newspapers in Haiti; Composer of music. Address: Mission Permanente d'Haiti auprès des Nations Unies, 801 2nd Ave., N.Y., NY 10017, U.S.A. 34.

VERROCCHIO, Vacre, b. 17 Oct. 1929. Sculptor; Painter; Engraver; Artist in Ceramics & Metals. Educ: studies in art, philos., tech., crafts. Mbrships: Accad. dei 500, Italy; Accad. Tiberina; Free Int. Acad.; Temple of Arts Acad.; Accad. Tetradramma; Unione della Legion d'Oro; Prop. Onor., Cavaliere della Repub. Italiana; num. Italian & for. acads. Work featured in num. art publs. Has held 25 one-man exhibs. in Italy & abroad. Works represented in pvte. & pub. collections, Italy, Germany, France, Austria, U.K., Finland, Venezuela, Ethiopia, U.S.A. & in permanent exhibs. in Mus. of Mod. Art, Legnano, Gall. d'Arte Verrocchio, Pescara. Hons. incl: Dip. & Gold Medal, Florence, 1963; Silver Medal, Exhib. of Graphics, Osimo, 1968; Premio Marc'Aurelio award for artistic merit, by Italian State, 1974; many others. Address: Via Fratelli Bandiera 15, 65100 Pescara, Italy. 105, 133.

VERT, Richard Frederick, b. 17 June 1939. Educator. Educ: B.S., High Pt. Coll.; M.Ed., Univ. of Md.; D.Ed., Geo. Wash. Univ. Appts: Tchr., Guilford Co., N.C., 1960, Montgomery Co., Md., 1961-; Chmn., Dept. of Phys. Educ., Montgomery Co., 1965-, Pres., Jr. High Athletic Bd., 1969, 1971, Supt., Advsry. Comm., 1973. Mbrships: Am. Assn. of Community-Jr. Colls.; NEA; Md. State & Montgomery Co. Educl. Assns.; Montgomery Co. Educl. & Coaches Assns.; Rock Creek Civic Assn.; Meth. Men of Francis Asbury Ch.; Wood Investment; Former Pres., Newport Investment; Phi Delta Kappa. Author, monograph, Physical Education Boys Like. Hons: Jr. High Basketball Coach of Yr., 1972; Md. Assn. of Phys. Hlth. Award, 1973; Outstanding Tchr. in State, Educ. & Recreation. Address: 14203 Parkvale Rd., Rockville, MD 20853, U.S.A. 125.

VERTEFEUILLE, Albert B., b. 2 Sept. 1933. Elementary School Principal. Educ: B.S., Eastern Conn. State Coll.; M.A., Univ. of Conn.; 6th yr. Profl. Dip., ibid. Appts: Tchr., Lebanon Elem. Schl., 2 yrs.; Tchr., Augsburg Elem. Schl., Germany, 1 yr.; Tchr., Eastford Elem. Schl., 2 yrs.; Prin., Union Elem. Schl., 1 yr.; Prin., Lebanon Elem. Schl., 8 yrs.; Guest Lectr., Eastern Conn. State Coll. & Univ. of Conn. Mbrships. incl: Nat. Conf. Discussion Ldr., Nat. Assn. of Lelm. Prins., 1970-72; Dir., Assn. of Conn. Elem. Schl. Prins., 1967-69; 2nd V.P., ibid, 1969-70; Pres.-elect, 1970-71; Pres., 1971-72; Chmn., Conn. Fall Conf., 1970; Chmn., Windham-Willimantic Democratic Town Comm., 1070-72; Pres., Eastern Conn. State Coll. Alumni Assn., 1970-71; Rep., Northeast Regional Prins. Coun., 1970-72; Cons., Am. Educ. Publs.; Phi Delta Kappa. Recip., Award for Outstanding Serv., Conn. Elem. Prins., 1972. Address: Old South Windham Rd., S. Windham, CT 06266, U.S.A. 114.

VERZYL, Kenneth H., b. 18 Sept. 1922. Mayor; Artist; Art Gallery Director. Educ: Grad., N.Y. State Inst. Agric., 1942. Appts: Mayor, Village of Asharoken; L.I., N.Y.; Artist;

Dir., Verzyl Art Gall., Northport, N.Y.; Bldr.; Union Labour Contractor; Construction Supt. Mbrships: Mason; Am. Fedn; Arts, N.Y.C.; Hechscher Mus., Huntington, N.Y.; Guild Hall, Easthampton, ibid; Suffold Co. Village Officials Assn.; N.Y. State Conf. Mayors. One Man Exhibs: Mus. of Confedaracy, Richmond, Va.; Nicholas Roerich Mus., N.Y.C; Berkshire Mus., Pittsfield, Mass.; Northport Lib., N.Y.; Syosset Pub. Lib., ibid; Performing Arts Fdnd. Gall., Huntington Stn., Grp. Exhibs: Guild Hall Mus., Easthampton, N.Y.; Parrish Art Mus., Southampton, ibid; Firehouse Gall., Nassau Community Coll., Garden City, N.Y. Address: 25 Bevin Rd., Asharoken, Northport, NY 11768, U.S.A.

VETESSY, George B., b. 22 May 1923. Composer. Educ: Degree, Theory & Composition, Franz Liszt Acad. of Music, Budapest, Hungary. Appts. incl: Tchr., Music Hist. & Appreciation, Rákóczi Schl., Budapest, 1954-55; Free Lance Composer, Budapest, 1955-. Vienna, Autsria, 1957-61 & N.Y., U.S.A., 1961-67; Arranging Staff, Big 3 Music Corp. (Metro-Goldwyn-Mayer), N.Y., 1967-71; Free Lance Composer & Music Dir., var. Choral Socs., N.Y., 1971-. Mbrships: Assn. of Authors, Composers & Music Publrs., Vienna; Am. Music Ctr., N.Y.; Am. Fedn. of Musicians, Local 802, N.Y. Compositons. incl: Merry Overture for Orchestra; Serenade for Strings: Suite No. 1 for Orchestra; Concerto for Piano & Orchestra; Festival for Contemporary Band Music. Hons: Franz Liszt Award, Budapes; Bela Bartok Prize, Acad. of Mus., ibid, 1949. Address' 43-19 39th Place, Apt. 33, Sunnyside, NY 11104, U.S.A.

VETTORI, Vittorio, b. 24 Dec. 1920. Writer; Teacher. Educ: M.A., Univ. of Florence, Italy, 1946. Appts: Ed., Studi Gentiliani, Pisa, 1951-55; Ed., Biblioteca dell'Ussero, Pisa, 1959-; i/c of bibliographical work in newspaper Il Telegrafo, Leghorn, 1963-; Ed., Nuovi Studi Gentiliani, Rome, 1966-67; Ed., Revisione, Rome, 1972-; i/c of bibliographical work, Agenzia Stampa Cattolica Associata, Rome, 1972-. Mbrships: Pres., Academia Pisana Dell'Arte, Pisa; Fndr., Societa Gentiliana di Studi Umanistici, Rome; Sec., Associazione Amici della Rassegna di cultura e vita scolastica, Rome; Vice Sec., Sindacato Libero Scrittori Italiani, Rome. Publs. incl: B. Croce e il rinnovamenta della cultura nell'Italia del Novecento, 3 vols., 1970, 2nd edit. 1973; E questi visi che prima non c'erano?, 1973; L'amico del Machia, 1973. Hons. incl: 4 times Premio della Cultura della Presidenza del Consiglio dei Ministri, 1962, '64, '66, '73. Address: Via Masaccio 199, 50132 Florence, Italy.

VIALOUX, Henry Richardson Augustus, b. 23 June 1897. Barrister; Solicitor; Notary Public. Educ: Auckland, New Zealand. Appts: w. New Zealand Justice Dept., 1915; Pvte. Prac., Law, 1929; Ptnr. w. R.N. Vialoux, 1955; Inspector, Dist. of Auckland, Under Mental Hlth. Act. 1953-74 Mbrships: Past Pres., Coun., Auckland Law Soc.; Past V.P., Per Coun., New Zealand Law Soc.; Auckland Club; Northern Club; Past Dpty. Grand Master, New Zealand Freemasons; Past 1st Grand Prin., Royal Arch Masons, New Zealand. Author of sev. papers on Masonic Hist. Address: P.O. Box 6026, Auckland, New Zealand. 38, MCL.

VICK, John Edward, b. 10 Mar. 1939. Executive. Educ: B.S., Auburn Univ., U.S.A., 1962. Appts: V.P.-Dir., Dixon Lumber Co.; Gen. Mgr., Dixon Plywood; Dir., Andalusia Broadcasting Corporation; Export Advsry. Comm., Am. Plywood Assn.; Owner & Mgr., John Vick & Co. (Farming Op.). Mbrships:

Past-Pres., Andalusia Lions Club; Past-Pres., Covington Co. Cattlemen; Past-Trustee, Ala. Sheriff's Boys Ranch; Past-Dir., Andalusia Chmbr. of Comm.; Past-Pres., Andalusia United Meth. Men; Ala. Cattlemen's Assn.; Am. Nat. Cattlemen's Assn.; Ala. Forestry Assn.; Am. Forestry Assn.; Forest Farmers' Assn.; Forest Products Rsch. Soc.; USN Inst.; Ala.-Guatamala Friends of the Alliance for Progress; U.S. Chmbr. of Comm.; Pi Kappa Phi. Address: 511 Chapman St., P.O. Box 41, Andalusia, AL 36420, U.S.A. 117, 125.

VICKERS, William Ward, b. 21 June 1923. Geophysicist. Educ: B.A., M.A., UCLA; Ph.D., McGill Univ. Appts: Officer, U.S. Marine Corps., 1943-48; Master, world voyage, Barkentine 'California', 1949-53; Prin. Investigator, Continental Ice Accumulation Proj., Antarctica, 1957-61; Inst. Rsch. & Dev., Tech. Ops. Inc., EG & G Inc. & the Mitre Corp., 1961-; Tech. Dirs. Coun., Mt. Wash. Observatory, 1971-. Fellow & V.P., New Engl. Chapt., Explorers Club, 1973. Mbrships: Pres., New Engl. c Chapt., Am. Meteorol. Soc., 1972; Am. Geophys, Union. Author of tech. publs. Hons: Fullbright Scholship, Norak Polar Inst., 1955; Carnegie Scholship, McGill Univ., 1958-59. Address: Indian Hill, Prides Crossing, MA 01965, U.S.A. 6, 14, 28.

VIEIRA, Clibas, b. 27 Dec. 1927. University Professor; Agronomist. Educ: Grad. in Agric., Univ. of Viçosa, Brazil, 1952; M.Sc., Univ. of Calif., U.S.A., 1958; Dr. Agr. Sci., Univ. of Viçosa, Brazil, 1961. Appts: Drawing Tchr., Viçosa Jr. H.S., 1951-52; w. Am. Int. Assn. for Econ. & Soc. Dev., Brazil, 1953-54; Asst. Prof. of Agron., Univ. of Viçosa, 1955-62; Prof., ibid, 1962-; Dean, Grad. Schl., 1965-69; 'Pesquisador-conferencista', Nat. Rsch. Coun. 1968-; Dir., Nat. Bean Proj., EMBRAPA, 1972-; Hd., Tech.-Sci. Dept., Brazilian Enterprise for Agricl. Rsch. (EMBRAPA), 1974-. Mbrships: Counsellor, Brazilian Soc. for the Progress of Sci., 1965-69; Latin-Am. Assn. of Plant Scis.; Brazilian Soc. of Genetics; Bean Improvement Coop. Publs: (book) The Common Bean—Culture, Diseases & Breeding, 1967; author or co-author of some 70 rsch. papers principally on beans & soybeans. Address: Universidade Federal de Vicosa, 36.570, Vicosa, MG, Brazil. 136.

VIEIRA, Henrique Bandeira, b. 19 Apr. 1936. Petroleum Engineer; Petroleum Company Director & General Manager. Educ: M.S., Stanford Univ., Calif., U.S.A., 1960. Appts: Asst., Geol. & Mineralogy, Higher Tech. Instn., Lisbon, Portugal, 1957-58; Petroleum Engr., Petrangol, Angola, 1961-63; Asst. tp Pres., Am. Petrofina Exploration Co., U.S.A., 1964-65; Asst. to Gen. Mgr., Exploration-Prod., Petrofina, Belgium, 1965-66; Asst. to Gen. Mgr., Petrangol, Angola, 1967-68; Gen. Mgr., ibid, 1968-73; Dir. & Gen. Mgr., 1973-. Mbrships: Ordem dos Engenheiros, Portugal; Soc. of Petroleum Engrs. of AIME; Am. Assn. of Petroleum Geologists; Lions Club, Luanda, Angola. Publs: Breve História de Pewquisa do Petróleo em Angola, 1970; As Necessidades Energéticas Mundiais na Década de Setenta, 1972. Address: c/o Companhia de Petróleos de Angola (Petrangol), Caixa Postal 1320, Luanda, Angola (Portuguese W. Africa).

VIERTEL, George Joseph, b. 10 June 1912. Attorney at Law; Consulting Engineer. Educ: B.S.C.E., Coll. of Engrng., N.Y. Univ., 1934; Dep., Int. Accts. Soc., Chgo., Ill., 1950; LL.B., La Salle Ext. Univ., 1952; J.D. (Hon.), Berna Dean Univ., Las Vegas, Nev., 1973; Th.D., ibid, 1974; various trng. courses. Appts. incl: Engr. & Cons. Engr., 1934-; Atty. & Counselor at Law, 1954-; Admitted to the Va. & Dist. of Columbia Bars & the following Cts:- Supreme Ct. of Appeals, Va.; Supreme Ct. of U.S.A.; U.S. Ct. of Appeals, 4th, 7th 9th, & Dist. of Columbia Circuits; U.S. Dist. Ct., E. Dist., Va. & Dist. of Hawaii; Dist. of Columbia; Tax Ct. of U.S.A.; U.S. Ct. of Claims; Superior Ct. of Dist. of Columbis. Fellowships: Coun. of Law & Sci., Int. Acad. Law & Sci.; Am. Soc. Civil Engrs. (Pres., ibid, 1965-67); Property Consultants Soc., U.K.; Int. Consular Acad. Mbr., num. profl. orgs. inclng. Nat. Panel of Arbitrators, Am. Arbitration Assn. Author of publs. in field. Address: Suite 702 Law Bldg., 147 Granby St., Norfolk, VA 23510, & W935, 1011 Arlington Blvd., Arlington, VA 22209, U.S.A. 7, 16, 26, 85, 125.

VIETS, (Rev.) Wallace Trowbridge, b. 26 Nov. 1919. Clergyman. Educ: B.A., Yale Univ., 1941; B.D. (now M.D.), ibid, 1944; M.S.T., Hartford Sem. Fndn., 1950; Additional grad. study at Union Theological Sem., Boston Univ. Schl. of Theol. & Inst. for Advanced Pastoral Studies. Appts: Pastor, Meth. Chs., E. Northport & Commack, N.Y., & Chap., Pilgrim State Hosp., 1943-45; Pastor, Emanuel Meth. Ch., W. Hartford, Conn., 1945-50, Calvary Meth. Ch., Albany, N.Y., 1950-57, Christ Ch., Meth., Glens Falls, N.Y., 1957-60, 1st Meth. Ch., New Haven, Conn., 1960-66; Lectr., Pastoral Theol. & Meth. Hist., Yale Univ. Divinity Schl., 1960-66; Pastor, United Meth. Ch., Huntington, N.Y., 1966-73; Dist. Supt., Conn. W. Dist., N.Y. Conf., ibid, 1973-. Mbrships. incl: Bd. of Dirs., Yale Alumni Fund; Fund Chmn., Yale Divinity Schl. Alumni Coun.; Fellow, Timothy Dwight Coll., Yale, 1961-; Past Pres., Huntington Club, Rotary Int. Author of 3 books & num. mag. articles. Recip., D.D., Shorter Coll. & Jackson Theological Sem., 1972. Address: 791 Newfield Ave., Stamford, CT 06905, U.S.A. 3, 6, 116.

VIGDERHOUSE, Mildred Anne. Director of Public Relations. Educ: B.A., George Wash. Univ., Wash., D.C. Appts: Dir., Radio/TV, Ruder & Finn Inc., 1958-63; Owner, Vigderhouse & Assocs., 1963-66; Special Asst. P.R. & Pub. Affairs to Pres., Gulf Am. Corp., 1966-69; Dir. of P.R., ITT Community Dev. Corp., N.Y.C., 1970-. Mbr., P.R. Soc. of Am. Address: ITT Community Development Corp., 430 Park Ave. N.Y., NY 10028, U.S.A. 5, 6.

VIKAINEN, Inkeri, b. 1914. Professor. Educ: M.A., 1943; Ph.D., 1955. Appts: Lectr., Tchrs.' Colls. Jyväskylä & Turku, 1946-59; Lectr., Univ. of Turku, 1956-59; Prof. of Educ., ibid, 1959-. Mbrships: Finnish Acad. of Scis. & Letters; Int. Assn. for Advancement of Educl. Rsch.; Am. Educl. Rsch. Assn.; Finnish Soc. for Educl. Rsch. Publs: Sentence Sense, 1955; Synopsie und Didaktik, 1959; Adolescents & Educators, 1971; Secondary School Economics, 1971 & 73; textbooks for reading & grammar. Holder of patents for learning materials for different schl. subjects. Hons: Medal of Liberty, 1941 & 43; Cmdr., Mark of the Finnish Lion, 1969. Address: Mustainveljestenkuja 3, 20100 Turku 10, Finland. 43.

VIKSTEN, Hans (Olof), b. 10 July 1926. Artist; Author. Educ: Gerlesborg Schl. of Art, Stockholm, Sweden, 1958-60; Royal Acad. of Art Schl., ibid, 1960-65. 20 solo exhibs., w. accompanying commentary & music by artist, in Sweden, N.Y.C., New Delhi (India), Oslo (Norway) & Paris (France), 1964-74; participation in 50 grp. exhibs., Sweden, Denmark, Norway, N.Y.C., Paris, Tokyo & Kyoto (Japan), 1968-74. Commissioned works incl: Tele-visions (mural), Swedish Nat. Telephone Corp., 1969; The Radar Eye (painting) for ITT, N.Y.C., 1968; The Magic Owl (tapestry), IBM Scandinavian Educ. Ctr., Lidingö, Sweden, 1973. Works in museums in Sweden, Amsterdam, N.Y.C. Films: Ten to One (the artist at work), 1970, Visions of the Present, (based on details in Hans Viksten's paintings depicting life from birth to the grave), 1973. Viksten acts & participates mixing talk, poetry & music in addition to paintings in both films. Publs: (poetry) Life & Death, 1966; Count Down, 1968. Mbrships: Org. of Swedish Artists; Swedish Union of Authors. Hons. incl: City of Stockholm Award, 1960; H.R.H. Gustaf Adolf VI Fund for Swedish Culture, 1969; Swedish Govt. Schlrship., 1969, '70; Swedish Film inst. Award, 1971. Address: Tegnérgatan 6, 113 58 Stockholm, Sweden. 134.

VILENSKA, Esther (Mrs. Zvi Breitstein), b. 8 June 1918. Teacher. Educ: Hebrew Univ., Jerusalem; B.A., Jerusalem Univ.; Study toward M.A., Mod. Hist., ibid. Appts: Mbr., Israel Communist Party Ctrl. Comm. & Politburo, 1944-73; Mbr., Israel Aseifat Hanifeharim, 1944-47; 1st Chief Ed., daily Communist newspaper Kol-Haam, 1947-51; Communist Mbr., 2nd, 3rd & 5th Knessets; Deleg., var. Communist congs., U.S.A., Hungary, Czechoslovakia, France; Deleg., world gathering of 81 Communist parties, Moscow, 1960; Deleg., Int. Congs. of Women, Moscow, Helsinki; Delg., World Congs. of Peace Movement, Stockholm, Berlin, & World Peace Coun., Budapest, 1971. Mbrships: Exec. Comm., Gen. Fedn. of Labour; Nat. Comm. & Secretariat, Israeli Communist Opposition; Mbr. of Coun., World Peace Movement; Mbr., Secretariat, Israel Movement for Peace & Security; Israeli Presidium, Israeli Peace Movement. Publs: Lines to the Road of Israel to Socialism, 1968; The Great Peasants' Insurrection in Germany 1525, 1971; The Socialist International & the Formation of the Comintern 1974; Ed., var. collects.; Author, booklets, articles. Address: Kirjat-Shalom, Dik St. 6, Tel-Aviv, Israel. 94.

VILENTCHUK, Lydia (Mrs.), b. 7 Apr. 1907. Civil Engineer; Information Scientist. Educ: Dipl.Ing., Tech. Univ., Berlin-Charlottenburg, Germany, 1930; London Univ. Coll., U.K. Appts. incl: Hd., Tech. Lib. & Info. Serv., Assn. Engrs. & Archts., Israel, 1946-68; Pt.-time Cons., ibid, 1961-68; Lectr., Grad. Lib. Schl., Hebrew Univ. of Jerusalem, 1956-69; Curric. Cons. & Lectr., Technion, Israel Inst. of Technol., Ext. Div., 1958-; Hd., Div. Documentation, Trng. & Publs., Nat. Ctr. of Sci. & Tech. Info., 1961-68; Hd., Div. Trng. & Publs., ibid, 1968-. Mbrships. incl: Assn. Engrs. & Archts., Israel; Chmn., Israel Soc. Special Libs. & Info. Ctrs., 1966-; Examiner, Exam. Comm., Israel Lib. Assn., 1965; Chmn., 1974-. Contbr. to publs. in field. Hons. incl: War Medal, U.K., 1939-45; Ot Ha-Hitnadvut, Israel, 1939-45; Itur Lohame Ha-Medina. Address: Nat. Ctr. of Sci. & Technol. Info., P.O.B. 20125, Tel-Aviv, Israel. 55, 94.

VILJANTI, Arvo Kunto, b. 24 Aug. 1900. Professor. Educ: Matriculation, Finland, 1920; Fil.kand. (B.A.), 1922; Lic. & Phil.Dr., 1935. Appts. incl: Fndr. & Mng. Dir., Union of Finland Proper Province, 1927-68; Quastor, Turku Univ., 1928-30; Sec., ibid, 1935-36; Tchr., Hist., Nat. Econ. & Soc. Studies, Upper Stage, Turku Classical Secondary Schl., 1941-44; Fndr. & Mng. Dir., Kustannus Oy Aura Publrs., 1943, '46-47; Docent, Finnish Hist., Turku Univ., 1943-70; Acting Prof., Gen. Hist., ibid, 1943; Acknowledged qualified to off. of Prof., Finnish Hist., 1957-. Mbrships. incl: Rsch., Porthan's Soc., 1940-; Rsch., Finnish Histl. Soc., 1946-; Finnish Soc. of

Heraldry; Soc. of Tchrs. & Officials at Turku Univ. (Sec., 1951-64); Turku Histl. Soc. (Sec., 1932-44, V.Chmn., 1945-50, Chmn., 1958-63, Hon. Chmn., 1974); Govt. of Finnish Tourist Assn., 1940-56; Flag Expert for the Independence Assn., 1927-46 & Initiator of the Finnish Flag Day, celebrated on Midsummer Day, 1927-. Publs. incl: Our Blue Cross Flag, 1927; Finland Proper as a Tourist Region, 1930; Finland's First Bookseller, 1946; The Russian War of Gustav Vasa 1554-1557 I-II, 1957. Hons: Liberty Medal, 1st Class, 1940; Ensign, 1940; Gold Medal, Finnish Tourist Assn., 1960. Address: Puolalankatu 4 B, Turku 10, Finland. 134.

VILLA, Juan Francisco, b. 23 Sept. 1941. Professor of Chemistry. Educ: B.S., Univ. of Miami, Coral Gables, Fla., 1965; M.S., ibid, 1967; Ph.D., 1969; Post-doct., Univ. of N.C., Chapel Hill, 1969-71. Appts: Grad. Tchng. Asst., Univ. of Miami, Coral Gables, Fla., 1965-69; Post-doctoral Rsch. Assoc., Univ. of N.C., Chapel Hill, 1969-71; Asst. Prof.-Assoc. Prof., Lehman Coll., CUNY, 1971-. Mbrships: Exec. Comm., Lehman Coll. Club, Soc. of Sigma Xi, 1972-; Am. Chem. Soc.; The Chem. Soc.; N.Y. Acad. of Scis.; Am. Inst. of Chemists; AAAS. Author of papers & articles in jrnls. inclng. Inorganic Chem., Spectroscopic Letters, Inorganic Chim. Acta, Jrnl. of Am. Chem. Soc., Chem. Phys. Letters. Hons: Petroleum Rsch. Fund rsch. grant, 1971; G.N. Shuster Fellowship, 1972. Address: Chem. Dept., H.H. Lehman Coll. of CUNY, Bedford Park Blvd. West, Bronx, NY 10468, U.S.A. 14, 125.

VILLALOBOS, Heber Dario, b. 15 Sept. 1930. Medical Doctor. Educ: M.D., Univ. of Zulia, 1954; postgrad. courses, Univs. of Pa. & Miami, U.S.A., 1963-65; 1st Int. Course, Org. Cons. Servs. in Genetics, OMS, Italy, 1972. Appts: Prof., Fac. of Med., Univ. of Zulia, 1954-, Chmn., Lab. Dept., Univ. Hosp., 1962, Coord. of Postgrad. Course in Clin. Pathol. for Med. Drs., 1968, Dean, Fac. of Med., 1969, Chmn., Med. Genetics Unit, Univ. Hosp., 1972. Mbrships: Zulia State Acad. Med.; Venezuelan Assn. fo·' Advancement of Scis.; Zulian Med. Assn. Author & co-author, med. & sci. papers. Contbr., profl. publs. Hons. incl: Zulian Med. Assn. Prize, 1960, 1972; Zulia State Acad. of Med. Prize, 1962; Venezuelan Med. Fedn. Prize, 1973; Venezuelan Pub. Instrn. Medal, 2nd Class, 1974. Address: Calle 68 No. 13-11, Maracaibo, Venezuela.

VILLALON-GALDAMES, Alberto, b. 1 Feb. 1920. Lawyer; Librarian. Educ: Law degree, Univ. of Chile, 1945; B.A.L.S., 1948, M.A.L.S., 1949, Ph.D.L.S., 1959, Univ. of Mich., U.S.A. Appts. incl: Law prac., 1944-47, 1954-57, Santiago; Dir., Lib. Fac. of Med., Univ. of Chile, 1951-56; Prof., Dept. of Lib. Sci. & Documentation, Fac. of Philos. & Letters, ibid, 1952-; Dir., 1959-69, 1972-73; Sec.Gen., UNESCO Nat. Commn., 1954-57; UNESCO Expert in Libnship., 4 missions to Colombia, 1962-63; Dir. of Libs., State Tech. Univ., Santiago, 1970-71; Dir., Libs., Univ. of Concepcion, 1971-72. Mbrships: Phi Kappa Phi; Sigma Delta Pi; Beta Phi Mu; Int. Fedn. for Documentation; Lawyers Soc., Chile; Counselor, Libns. Assn. Publs: Num. books in Spanish, some Engl., French edits., inclng: An Introduction to Latin American Juridical Bibliography, 1959. Hons: Hon. Citizen of New Delhi, India, 1956. Address: Dept. of Lib. Sci. & Documentation, Fac. of Philos. & Letters, Univ. of Chile, Santiago, Chile.

VILLARES, Enrique J., b. 3 Jan. 1922. Chemist; Toxicologist. Educ: B.Sc., Univ. of

Puerto Rico, 1943; Master of Pub. Hlth., Univ. of N.C., 1955; Doct.cand., Univ. of Puerto Rico. Appts, incl: Chem., var. Govt. Agcys.; Ind. Hygenist, Chief Occupational Diseases Hazards Control Div., Bur. of Work Accident Prevention, Labour Dept., 1955-63; Schl. of Pub. Hlth., Univ. of Puerto Rico, 1963-; Asst. Prof. of Environmental Hlth.; Acting Dir., Dept. of Environmental Hlth., 1966-67 & 72-73; Dir., Univ. of Puetro Rico Study Grp., Europe, 1969-70; Proj. Dir., Community Studies on Pesticides, 1967-69; Co-investigator, Chronic Effects of Pesticides Residues Proj., 1973-. Mbrships. incl: Dipl., Am. Acad. Cert. Sanitarians; Am. Ind. Hygiene Assn.; Royal Soc. of Hlth.; Pres., Puerto Rico Chapt., Am. Conf. Govtl. Ind. Hygienists; AAAS; Am. Chem. Soc.; Air Pollution Control Assn.; Nat. Environmental Hlth. Assn.; Treas., 1961-62, Sec., 1962-63, Puerto Rico Coll. of Chems.; Bd. of Dirs., Puerto Rico Accident Prevention Coun., 1969-71 & 74-; V.P., 1962-63, Pres., 1963-65, Alumni Assn., Univ. of Puerto Rico. Contbr. articles to profl. jrnls. Address: Schl. of Pub. Hlth., Med. Sci. Campus, G.P.O. Box 5067, San Juan, Puerto Rico 00936. 125.

VILLAR Palasi, Jose Luis, b. 30 Sept. 1922. Legal Adviser, Spanish Council of State. Educ: Master,Law, Master Arts, Valencia Univ., Spain; Dr., Law, Madrid Univ., ibid. Appts: Legal Advsr., Spanish Coun. State; Prof., Fac. Law, Madrid Univ. Mbrships: Chmn., Inst. Admin. Law; Int. Law Assn.; Royal Acad. Law, Spain; Royal Acad. Fine Arts, Sevilla; Int. Assn. Admin. Scis. Publs: Administración y Planificación; Tratado de Derecho Administrative; Contratos Administrativos; Bases para una Politíca Educativa; Curso de Derecho Administrativo; Derecho Administrativo. Hons. incl: Gt. Crosses: Mérito Civil; Alfonso X; San Raimundo de Peñafort; Isabel la Católica; Carlos III; Mérito Militar; Crown Order, Thailand; Pub. Educ., Portugal; Independence, Guinea; Order of Nil, Rau; Order Merit Fine Arts, France. Address: Av. Ahonés, 11 (Parque Conde de Orgas), Madrid, 33, Spain. 43.

VILLASEÑOR, Eduardo, b. 13 Sept. 1896. Economist; Banker. Educ: Colegio de San Nicolas de Hidalgo, Univ. of Michoacan, Mexico; Fac. of Law & Soc. Sci. & of Philos. & Letters, Univ. of Mexico; London Schl. of Econs., U.K. Appts. incl: Sec., Nat. Econ. Coun., 1932-34; Consul Gen., N.Y., U.S.A., 1935; Pres., Nat. Agricl. Bank, 1936-37; Undersec., Finance & Pub. Credit, 1938-40; Dir. Gen., Bank of Mexico, 1940-46; Pres., Banco del Atlantico, 1950-65; Pres., Banco de la Cuidad de Mexico, 1966-71; Ambassador at large, several missions. Mbrships: Club de Banqueros; Mexico City Country Club. Publs. incl: La farce et la mort au Mexique (essay), 1957; Los recuerdos y los dias (poems) 1960; Memorias-Testimonio, 1974. Recip., Cmdr., Legion of Hon., France, 1956. Address: Reyna 39, San Angel, Mexico 20, D.F. 34.

VILLE, Jean André, b. 24 June 1910. Mathematician. Educ: Univ. of Paris, France. Appts: Tchr., Special Maths., Clemenceau H.S., Nantes; Instr., Fac. of Sci., Univ. of Poitiers; Engr.-Chief Engr.-Dir., Alsation Mechanical Construction Co.; Currently Prof., Math.Econs., Univ. of Paris VI, & Nat. Inst. of Nuclear Scis. & Tech. Mbrships: Int. Stats. Inst.; Statistical Soc. of Paris. Author, Théorie des Martingales & Théorie du Collectif (Calcul des Probabilités & Théorie des Jeux). Hons: Monthion Prize for Stats.; Off., Acad. Palms. Address: La Boulaye à Langdon, 41320 Mennetou sur Cher, France. 43, 91.

VILLEGAS, Antonio de Jesus, b. 9 Feb. 1928. City Mayor; Attorney. Appts. incl: Legal Officer, Malacanang, Philippines; Aide, Commnr. of Customs; V.Chmn., Pres. Complaints & Action Comm.; V.Mayor, City of Manila, 1959-62; Mayor, ibid, 1962-. Mbrships. incl: Exec. Sec., Anti-Communist League of Philippines; Sec.-Gen., Progressive Party of Philippines. Contbr. of feature articles & legal briefs in local & internat. jrnls. Address: City Hall, Manila, Philippines.

VIMBLIS, Miltiades, b. 8 May 1894. Retired General. Educ: Mil.Acad. of Greece; Greek Army Staff Coll.; French Army Staff Coll., Paris. Appts: Lt., Arty., 1916 & during WWI; in expedition at Asia Minor as Captain; Col. in WWII; Brigade Cmdr., 1946-47; Div. Cmdr., & Corp. Cmdr., 1947; Lt. Gen., & Cmdr., Mil. Acad., 1948; Vice-Chief of Hellenic Army Gen. Staff., 1948-49; Ret., 1949. Mbrships: V.P. & Pres., Assn. for Liberation of Northern Epirous. Publs: The Future War, 1949; Important Subjects on National Defense, 1950; Critical Points Around the World, 1951; articles in Greek Army Mil. Review. Recip. sev. Greek & For. Mil. Decorations. Address: 21st April Ave. No. 54, Papagou, Athens, Greece. 43

VINCENT, Tom J., b. 8 Apr. 1930. Artist; Painter; Muralist; Teacher; Lecturer. Educ: Univ. of Mo., U.S.A.; B.F.A. & M.F.A., Kansas City Art Inst., Mo. Appts: Stage Setter, Theatre, Opera, United Scenic Artists of Am., N.Y., 1951-58; Self-employed Artist, 1958-. Mbrships: United Scenic Artists of Am.; Am. Watercolor Soc.; Bd. of Acquisition, Montclair Art Mus., N.J.; Bd. of Dirs., The Whole Theatre Co. One-man Exhibs: Highgate Gall., 1958, 62, 64, 68, 70; Nessler Gall., N.Y., 1962; Seton Hall Univ., N.J., 1967; Cernuschi Gall., Paris, France, 1972 & 73; Caravan de France Galls., N.Y., 1973. Other exhibs. incl: Nelson Gall. of Art, Kansas City, 1950-51; Mus. of Mod. Art, 1956; Am. Watercolor Soc., 1959-66; Pa. Acad., 1962-63; Steuben Glass Designs, 1962-70. Paintings in Springfield Mus. of Fine Arts, Kansas City Art Inst., Patteron State Tchrs. Coll., Milwaukee Art Ctr., Atlanta Mus., Ctrl. Iowa Art Assn., & Montclair Art Mus. Address: 172 Gates Ave., Montclair, NJ 07042, U.S.A. 19, 37.

VINCK, François, b. 5 Sept. 1906. Government Official. Educ: Econs. & commerce. Appts. incl: Insp.-Gen., Dept. of Nat. Equipment, Belgian Govt., 1946; Dir.-Gen. for Fuel & Power, ibid, 1949; Dir.-Gen., High Authority, European Coal & Steel Community, 1952-67; Dir.-Gen., Soc. Affairs, Commn. of European Communities, 1968; Hon. Chef de Cabinet & Hon. Dir.-Gen., ibid; Prof., Coll. of Europe-Bruges, 1971. Mbrships: Acting Chmn., Paul Finet Fndn.; Chmn., Belgian Sect., Assn. of Former Officials, European Communities; Sci. Bd., European Inst. for Soc. Action at Marcinelle; Exec. Comm., European Movement. Author of var. publs. Hons. incl: Cmdr., Order of Leopold, Belgium, 1966; Grand Officer, Italian Repub., 1971; Médaille d'argent du Mérite Européen, 1972. Address: Ave. du Frêne 48, 1020 Brussels, Belgium. 43, 87.

VINICCHAYAKUL, Serm, b. 2 June 1908. Politician; Jurist; Economist. Educ: Barrister at Law, Thailand; Dr.en Droit, Paris, France; Dip. d'Etudes Supérieures de Droit Privé et d'Economie Politique, Univ. of Paris. Appts: Sec.-Gen., Juridical Coun., 1946; Gov., Bank of Thailand, 1946-47 & 1954-54; Gov. for Thailand in Bd. of Govs. of I.B.R.D. & IFC, 1952-59 & 1965-73; Prof., Civil Law, Thamasat Univ., 1938-; Chmn., Exec. Comm., Nat. Econ.

Dev. Bd., 1971-; Min. of Finance 1965-73. Mbr., Bar Assn. of Thailand. Hons: Kt. Grand Cordon, Most Noble Order, Crown of Thailand; Kt. Grand Cordon, Most Exalted Order of the White Elephant Kt.; Grand Cross (1st class), Most Illustrious Order of Chula Chom Klao; LL.D., Thamasat Univ. Address: 159 Soi Asoke Suknumvit Rd., Bangkok, Thailand.

VINTON, Eleanor W., b. 25 July 1899. Retired Nurse-Companion, Bookstore Employee. Educ: Concord Bus. Coll. Mbrships: Pres., Stratford Shakespeare Club, Concord, N.J., 1968-70; Publicity Chmn., Women's Club of Concord; Histn., Music Club of Concord; Charter mbr., Poetry Soc. of N.H. Publs: Sounding Piquant Verses, 1940 (now out of print); Contbr. to H.H. Profiles, Yankee, Ladies Home Jrnl., Spur, Town & Country, Chgo. Daily News, N.Y. Sun, N.Y. Herald Tribune, Christian Sci. Monitor, Sunburst Anthol., Dragonfly, A Quarterly of Haiku Highlights & others. Hons. incl: Prizes, N.H. Poetry Soc. Sonnet for Redheads, 1967, Broad Cove (Tanka), 1971, Literary Question, 1972, Limerick, 1972, Lines w. a Theme of Finality, 1972; Appointed Poet Laureate of N.H. by Gov. Walter Peterson, 1972. Address: 8 Humphrey St., Concord, NH 03301, U.S.A.

VIPONT, Elfrida (Mrs. R. Percy Foulds), b. 3 July 1902. Author. Publs. incl: Arnold Rowntree; A Life: The Spring of the Year; The High Way; The Secret of orra; More About Dowbiggins; Bless This Day; Henry Purcell & His Times; Ackworth School; Changes at Dowbiggins; Flowering Spring; The Story of Christianity in Britain; What about Religion; The Bridge; Search for a Song; A Faith to Live By; Some Christian Festivals; Stevie; Larry Lopkins; Rescue for Mittens; The Offcomers; Weaver of Dreams; Terror by Night; Children of the Mayflower; The China Dog; The Secret Passage; A Child of the Chapel Royal; The Pavilion; Michael & the Dogs; Towards a High Attic; The Elephant & the Bad Baby. Mbrships incl: PEN; Soc. of Authors; Assoc. Countrywomen of the World; recip., Carnegie Medal, 1950. Address: Green Garth, Yealand Conyers, Nr. Carnforth, Lancs., U.K. 3,

VIRTA, Nikolay E., b. 19 Dec. 1906. Writer; playwright; film scriptwriter. Mbr., Writers Union, U.S.S.R. 1937-. Author of 3 trilogies, 5 novels, 9 plays, 3 films. Hons: Lenin's Order, 1939; Govt. Prizes, 1940, 1942, 1949, 1951; War Medal for Battle of Stalingrad, WWII. Address: Writers Union, 52 Vorovsky St., Moscow, U.S.S.R.

VIRTANEN, Heikki, b. 28 Dec. 1930. Managing Director. Educ: M.A., Univ. of Econs., Helsinki. Appts: Mng. Dir., Roobertin Kello Oy, N.S. Montin Oy, & Kellotuote Oy. Mbrships: Pres., Watch & Jewelry Wholesalers' Assn.; Bd. of Commnrs., Finnish Wholesalers' Assn.; Co. Comms. Address: c/o Kellotuote Oy, I. Roobertink. 14 A, 00120 Helsinki 12, Finland. 43.

VIRTUE, Constance (Mrs. Clark W. Virtue), b. 6 Jan. 1905. Musician; Composer. Educ: Mus.B., Coll.-Conservatory of Music, Univ. of Cinn., 1927; Am. Conservatory, Chgo., 1932-33; S.M.M., Union Theological Sem., N.Y., 1945; individual tuition in piano, organ & comp. Appts. incl: Pvte. Tchr., piano, organ, theory; Organist-Dir., Mt. Auburn Presby. Ch., Cinn., 1927, St. Luke's Evangl. Luth. Ch., N.Y., 1945, Mission Hills Congl. Ch., San Diego, 1955-57 & 1st Unitarian Ch., San Diego, 1960-65; Organ Instr., Convent of the Sacred Heart, El Cajon, 1960-68; Instr., Grossmont Coll., 1961-63; Pianist for local artists concerts;

toured w. opera prog. for Alaska Music Trails, 1968; Live Music & Lecture courses, Univ. of Calif. Ext., San Diego, 1969-70, 1972; Originator, 1933, of Virtue Notagraph. (7-line semitone staff notation); Ed. & Pres., Virtue NotaGraph Edits. Composer of music dramas, anthems, instrumental works & songs. Mbrships. incl: Am. Guild of Organists; Mu Phi Epsilon. Music Educators' Nat. Conf.; Music Tchrs.' Assn. of Calif. Publs: Design For A Modern Notation, 1945; Virtue NotaGraph Manual, 1974; NotaGraph Sampler. Hons. incl: sev. comp. & music awards; MOE Rsch. Award, 1938. Address: 4940 Beaumont Drive, LaMesa, CA 92041, U.S.A. 5, 138.

VISAPÄÄ, Niilo Karl Robert, b. 27 May 1904. Counsellor of Schools; Principal. Educ: M.Div., 1926; M.A., 1928. Appts: Sr. Tchr., Sec. Schl. Tchrs. Trng. Coll., Finland, 1929-36, 46-68; Prin., ibid, 1968-71; Mng. Dir., Voluntary Blood Donors Corps., 1939-45; Mng. Dir., Mannerheim League for War Orphans, 1944-46. Mbrships. incl: V.P., Int. Bd. on Books for Young People, 1968-70; Pres., 1970-; Chief Scout of Finland, 1933-48; Hon., Relig. Tchrs. Assn., 1970; Pres., Helsinki Rotary Club; Gov. Nominee, Rotary Dist. 142, 1974-75. Co-Ed., Bookbird. Author of var. articles. Hons. incl: Cross of Liberty, 4th class, 1941; Kt., 1st class, Order of the Lion, 1953; Kt., 1st class, Order of the Falcon, Iceland, 1939; Kt., 1st class, Order of Vasa, Sweden, 1950. Address: Puistokatu 3 C 47, 00140 Helsinki, Finland. 90. 134,

VISINE, François (Emile Joseph), b. 24 Sept. 1922. International Legal Adviser. Educ: Baccalauréat, Lycée Henri Poincaré, Nancy, 1943; Dr. in Law, Faculté de Droit, Nancy, 1949; Dr. in Econs., ibid, 1952; further studies, Inst. d'Etudes Politiques, Paris. Appts. incl: w. Bur. Universitaire de Statistiques, 1950-51; Lectr. in Econs., Faculté de Droit de Paris, 1950-56, Ecole Nationale des Impôts, 1955-56; Sr. Off., Int. Staff at NATO, 1951-58; Legal Advsr., Maintenance & Supply Agcy., NATO, 1959-. Mbrships: Fndng. Pres., Mérite Européen; Mouvement Européen; Société d'Economie Politique; Scoiété des auteurs et compositeurs de musique. Publs. incl: L'Economie Franâise face au Marché Commun, 1959; ABC de l'Europe, 5 Tomes, 8 Vols., 1967-72. Recip. of hons. Address: 60 Rue Chardon Lagache, 75016, Paris, France.

VISSER, Audrae Eugenie, b. 3 June 1919. Teacher. Educ: B.S., S.D. State Univ., 1948; M.A., Univ. of Denver, Colo., 1954. Appts: Tchr., Elem. Schls., Moody Co. & Hot Springs, S.D., 1939-45, H.S., Elkton, DeSmet, Pierre, ibid, 1948-53, Am. Village Schl., Nagoya, Japan, 1954-55; Libn., S.D. State Univ., 1955-56; Tchr., H.S., Elkton, Pierre, Flandreau, S.D., Windom, Minn., 1956-71. Mbrships. incl: S.D. State Poetry Soc. (co-pres., 1967; bd., 1972-75; recording sec., 1974-; regional v.p., 1960's); Bus. & Profl. Women's Club; AAUW; life mbr., S.D. & Nat. Educ. Assns. Publs: Rustic Roads (poetry), 1961; Poems for Brother Donald, 1974; Adeline M. Jenney, a Woman of Faith (biog.), 1974; poems in anthols. Hons. incl: Doct., Coll. of Heraldry, Barcelona, 1971, Great China Arts Coll., World Univ., Hong Kong, 1972; Sev. poetry awards. Address: Elkton, SD 57026, U.S.A. 11.

VITALE, Simone Joseph, b. 19 Mar. 1908. Educator; Librarian; Lecturer. Educ: Ph.D., Pontifical Univ. Pius XI, Molfetta, Italy; M.L.S., Univ. of So. Calif., L.A., U.S.A.1960; Grad. studies, ibid, 1960-69; M.A., State Univ., L.A. 1972. Appts: Tchr., Latin & Hist., Sem. Coll. of Monreale, Palermo, Italy, 1933-35 & 1938-40;

Chancellor, Archidiocese of Monreale, ibid, 1935-40; Eccles min. in Italy & U.S.A., 1940-58; Libn., State Univ., L.A., Calif., 1959-62; Tchr., & Dir. of Libs., Baldwin Pk. Dist., 1962-67; Tchr. & Libn., Rio Hondo Coll., Whittier, 1967-74; Pt.-time Hist. Tchr., ibid; Fndr. w. wife, Montessori-Vita Schl., W. Hollywood, Calif., 1970; Supvsr. & Owner w. wife, Penfield Schls., Glendale, Calif., 1973-. Mbrships: Calif. Tchrs. & Community Colls. Philos. Rsch. Soc.; Beta Phi Mu, 1961; Phi Delta Kappa, 1963. Publs: Humanizing the Divine: A Guide to Successful & Happy Living, forthcoming. Articles in jrnls. Address: 918 E. Tujunga Ave., Burbank, CA 91501, U.S.A.

VITESTAM, (Nils) Gösta, b. 2 Mar. 1921. Professor. Educ: Ph.Cand., 1947; Ph.Mag., 1953; Ph.Lic., 1957; Ph.D., 1960; participant sev. Int. Congresses of Arabic & Islamic Studies. Appts: Asst. Master, State Sec. Schl., Trelleborg, 1954-57; Docent of Semitic Lang., 1960-64; Ad interim commnd. Prof., Oriental Langs., Univ. of Lund, 1964-68; Full Prof. of Semitic Langs., ibid, 1968-. Mbrships: Vetenskapssocieteten i Lund; Kungl. Humanistiska Vetenskapssamfundet i Lund; Insp., S.-Scanian Nation of Lund. Publs: Kitab ar-radd ala l-ghamiya, 1960; La grande lettre d'Evagre le Pontique à Mélanie l'ANCienne, 1964; Kitab tabaqat al-fuqaha as-safi iya, 1964; trans. Swedish, 1967; Kanz al-muluk fi kaifiyyat as-suluk, 1970. Recip. Kt., Order of North Star, 1969. Address: c/o Dept. of Semitic Languages, University of Lund, Tunavägen 39 F, 223 63 Lund, Sweden.

VITORITTO, Elvira Lanza. Retired Educator & Social Worker. Educ: Certs., Carrol Robbins Trng. Schl., State of N.J. & Rider Coll. Mbrships. incl: Nat. Retd. Tchrs. Assn.; Am. Assn. of Retd. persons; N.J. Educ. Assn.; Am. Poetry League; Am. Mus. of Natural Hist.; Int. Writer's Fellowship: Am. Poets Fellowship Soc.; World Poetry Day Assn.; United Poets Laureate Int., Manilla, Philippine Islands; World Poetry Soc. Intercontinental; Eastern Ct., Poetry Soc. of London & World Poets Resource Ctr.; Amateur Press Assn., United Press Assn. Publs. incl: Gentle On The Wind, 1969; Dropping Pebbles in The Pond, 1969; Mediterranean Mood, 1970; Boulevard & Backstreet, 1971; Another Dawn - Another Flowering, 1973; Substance & Dreams, 1972. Hons. incl: Poet Laureate, United Amateur Press Assn., 1972-73; E.J. Murfey Mem. Award, 1972, 1973; Book Award, Am. Poet Fellowship Soc. Anthol., 1972; 1st place tied, Poem of The Yr. Award, Inky Trails, 1972. Address: P.O. Box 116, W. Trenton, NJ 08628, U.S.A. 5, 11, 57, 140.

VIVONA, Nicolo, b. 12 June 1907. Headmaster; Poet. Educ: Grad., Litt., Univ. of Palermo, 1930. Appts: Tchr. at var. schls. in Lucera, Castellamare del Golfo, La Spezia, Subiaco, Latina, Lido, Rome; Italian Alpine Club, Rome; Inst. of Linguistic & Philol. Studies, Palermo; Sicilian Acad. of Litt. & Arts, Palermo; Universal Assn. of writers & poets for peace; Free Union of writers, Rome, Publs: Adolescenza poesia; Vento Solare; Lungo un secolo; Ascensore lunare; Lampiride; Francesco Vivona, Poeta; Ars Dictandi; Res Gestae; Antiqua Humanitas; Omar Khayyam; Vertigini. Hons: Hig Off. of Mil. Order of Italian Repub; Prize of the Presidency of the Coun. of Mins., 1965 & 1970; Gold medal of Eternal City; gold medal of A.I.P.G. Address: Liceo Classico Statale 'Francesco Vivona', Piazza Francesco Vivona, EUR 00144, Rome, Italy.

VLOCK, Laurel Fox. Television producer; Author. Educ: B.A., Cornell Univ., Ithaca, N.Y.; M.A., Queen College. Appts. incl: Prod., Moderator, Radio & TV series, W.Y.B.C.-F.M., W.T.N.H.- T.V., W.T.I.C.-T.V.; Free-lance film maker, prod., moderator & rschr. Mbrships: The Authors Guild; U.J.A., Nat. Speakers Bur. Publs. incl: Contraband of War (co-author), 1970; Prod.-dir., documentary & feature films. Hons. incl: Woman of the Year Award, Anti-Defamation League, 1969; Chris Award, Columbus Film Festival, 1970; Nat. First Prize, T.V. Progs., Coun. of Jewish Welfare Funds & Feds., 1973. Address: 101 Ansonia Rd., Woodbridge, Conn. 06525, U.S.A.

VOELLER, Gert W., b. 5 July 1929. Medical Doctor, Neurologist & Psychiatrist. Educ: Grad., Univ. of Würzburg, Germany, 1956; Postgrad., Univ. Clin. of Goettingen. Appt: Med. Dir., Queen Elena Hosp., Kassel. Mbrships: German Neurological Soc.; German Soc. for Psychiatric & Nerve Therapeutics; Int. Soc. for Rehabilitation Med.; European Soc. for Stereotactic & Functional Neurosurgery; Sec., European Rsch. Grp. on Parkinson's Disease. Publs: 28 papers on rehabilitation of extrapyramidal motor disturbances & biochem. studies of the nervous system. Address: D-35 Kassel-Harleshausen, Klinikstr. 16, German Fed. Repub. 43.

VOGELMAN, Joseph Herbert, b. 18 Aug. 1920. Engineer-Scientist. Educ: B.S., CCNY, 1940; M.B.A., ibid, 1942; M.E.E., Polytechnic Inst. of Brooklyn, N.Y., 1948; Dr.E.E., ibid, 1957. Appts. incl: w. Rome Air Dev. Ctr., N.Y. as Chief Sci., Gen. Engrng. 1951-52, Chief, Electronic Warfare Lab. 1952-55, Dir. Communications, 1955-59; V.P. & Dir., Capehart Corp., 1959-64; w. Chromalloy Am. Corp. as Dir. Electronics 1964-67, Gen. Mgr. Pocket Fone Div. 1965-67, V.P. 1967-73; V.P. & Dir., Cro-Med. Bionics Corp., 1968-73; Vice-Chmn. Bd. & Sr. V.P., Laser Link Corp., 1968-73; Dir., Theatre-Vision Inc., 1971-73; Cons. 1964-72, Dir. & Chief Sci., 1973-, Orentreich Fndn. for Advancement of Sci.; Pres., Vogelman Dev. Co., 1973-. Holder of over 55 Patents. Mbrships incl: Fellow, AAAS & IEEE; Sigma Xi; Eta Kappa Nu; Profl. Engr., States of N.Y. & N.J. Publs: Over 100 contbns. to tech. jrnls., encys. & books. Hons: Outstanding Performance Award, USAF, 1957. Address: 48 Green Drive, Roslyn, NY 11576, U.S.A. 6, 28, 131.

VOGELSANG, Thomas Martin, b. 1 Aug. 1896. Professor. Educ: M.D., Oslo, Norway, 1922. Appts. incl: Dir., leader of microbio. sect., Gades Inst., Bergen, Norway, 1936-66; Prof. oj med. microbio., Univ. of Bergen, 1948-66; Chmn., Med. Soc., Bergen, 1939-40; Norwegian Fndn. for sci. & the humanities, 1949-1956; (vice chmn., 1953-56); Jt. Panel, Norwegian Sci. counc., 1954-56; Pres., 10th. Scandinavian Congresses of pathol. & microbio., Bergan, 1952; V.P., Scandinavian Congresses of pathol. & microbio., Aarhus, 1955, Goteborg, 1959, Abo, 1961; Dir., Broegelmann's rsch. lab., Bergen, 1957-70, Norwegian ctr. for staphylococcaphage typing, 1959-67; Chmn., Scandinavian staphylococcal symposium, Bergen, 1961. Mbrships. incl: Soc. for gen. microbio.; London; Sci. Soc., Bergen. Contbr. of 200 articles to profl. jrnls. Off., 1st. class, Norwegian St. Olav Order, 1966. Address: Havna Allé 15, Oslo 3, Norway. 43.

VOICU, Ion (Ion Voicou), b. 8 Oct. 1925. Violinist; Conductor; Professor; Composer. Educ: Royal Acad. of Music, Bucharest; Tchaikowsky Conservatory, Moscow; studied violin w. Geo. Enacovici & Geo. Enescu, Bucharest, Abram Ilici Jampolski & David Oistrach, Moscow, harmony w. Ion Chirescu,

Bucharest, harmony & counterpoint w. Müller, Moscow, chamber music w. Mihail, Bucharest. Appts: Soloist & Mbr., Radio Symph. Orch., 1940-45; Soloist, Geo. Enescu Bucharest Philharmonic, 1946-73; Soloist & Gen. Dir., ibid, 1973-; Soloist & Conductor, The Bucharest Orch., 1969-; Fndr., summer boarding schl. for gifted violinists, Prahova Valley. Mbrships: Permanent Mbr., Int. Rumanian Inst. for Cultural Rels. & Nat. Concours for Young Soloists; High Coun. of Arts; V.P., Tchaikowsky Int. Competition, Moscow; Jury, Bach Int. Competition, Leipzig & Flesch Int. Competition, London. Publs: On David Oistrach, 1956; Oistrach is Music in Itself, 1956; Unforgettable Impressions of China, 1955. Num. recordings, radio & TV broadcasts, lectures, recitals & concert performances. Hons. incl: 1st Prize, Nat. Enescu-Menuhin Comp., 1946; Double 1st Prize, Int. Comp. of Youth & Students, 1953; Highest Title in Rumania, People's Artist, 1964; Medal of 20th Anniversary of Liberation, 1964; Order of Work, 1966; Eugene Ysaÿe Medal, Brussels, 1967; Order of Cultural Merit, 1st class, 1968. Address: Allée Ioanid 4, Bucharest, Rumania. 4, 21.

VOIGHT, Robert Guy, b. 26 Mar. 1921. Associate Professor of English. Educ: B.A., John Brown Univ.; M.A., Univ. of Ark.; Ph.D., ibid; additional grad. study, Univ. of Tulsa. Appts: Asst. Prof. of Engl.; V.P. for Student Affairs, Oral Roberts Univ.; Assoc. Prof. of Engl., ibid. Mbrships: Phi Beta Kappa; Phi Delta Kappa; MLA; Am. Acad. of Pol. & Soc. Sci.; Coll. Engl. Assn.; Nat. Coun. of the Tchrs. of Engl.; Int. Transactional Analysis Assn. Address: Oral Roberts Univ., 7777 S. Lewis Ave., Tulsa, OK 74135, U.S.A. 125.

VOISINE, Valida Dolores (Sister Mary Emma, RSM), b. 13 June 1914. Religious; Teacher; Librarian; Instructor; Technologist. Educ: Notre Dame Univ., U.S.A.; B.A., Mercy Coll., Detroit, Mich.; West Mich. Univ.; Mich. Univ.; Wane State Univ.; M.A., Aquinas Coll. & Detroit Univ. Appts: Entered R.S.M., Cinn., Ohio, 1931; Tchr., Mich. parochial schls.; Prin., 5 yrs.; Libn.; Media Ctr. Org., Designer, Dir., H.S.; Cons., Libs., AV Ctrs. & Relig. Ctrs.; Demonstrator & Lectr., AV Sessions, Mercy Coll. Courses & MUCLA Conven.; Tchr. Trner., Mercy Coll.; Area Publcty. Chmn., MUCLA; Area Chmn., Cath. Book Week Activities; Comm. Chmn., Mercy Community Lib. Mbrships: ALA; CLA; Chmn.-Sec., MUCLA; Mich. State Curric. Planning Comm.; Jt. Lib. Dev. Comm. Creative Works incl: Co-author, The Instructional Materials Center, 1965; Poems in nat. anthol.; Designer num. educl. tools; Hons. incl: NCLA Cath. Book Fair Award; 1st place, AV Prod. Exhibit, Mich. Univ. Address: 29000 11 Mich. Rd., Farmington Hill, MI 48024, U.S.A. 5.

VOKES, Christopher R. b. 13 Apr. 1904. Major General, Canadian Army, retired. Educ: Grad., Royal Military Coll., Kingston, Ont., 1925; B.Sc., McGill Univ., Montreal, P.Q., 1927; Grad., Staff Coll., Camberley, U.K., 1935. Appts: Cmdr., 2nd Canadian Infantry Brigade, 1942-43; Gen. Off. Cmdng., 1st Canadian Infantry Div., 1943-44, 4th Canadian Armed Div., 1944-45, Canadian Army Occupation Force, Germany, 1945-46, Ctrl. Command Canadian Army, 1946-51, W. Command Canadian Army, 1951-59; Retired, 1960. Mbr., R.M.C. Club of Canada. Hons: D.S.O., 1943; C.B.E., 1944; C.B., 1945; Off. Legion of Hon., France, 1944; Commendatore Order of Italy, 1945; Greek War Cross. Address: 40 First St., Oakville, Ont. L6J 3R3, Canada. 1, 41.

VOLINI-GRUIA, Clara (Mrs. Abraham Gruia), b. 16 Nov. 1922. Ballerina; Teacher of Classical & Character Dancing. Educ: Liceum & Ballet Schl. Appts. incl: Barasheum Theatre, Rumania, 1942-45; Sawoy Theatre, Rumania, 1946-47; Soloist Dancer w. Opera of Bucharest playing solo parts in Swan Lake, Aida, Carmen, Lakmé, Nut Cracker Suite, Coppelia, etc., 1947-65; Appeared in solo & grp. Dance Evenings in Rumania, Russia, Germany & Bulgaria; Choreographed works for Rumanian TV & also gave TV dancing performances; Tchr. of Character Dancing, Choreography Schl., Bucharest, 1947-66; Solo Dancer w. Israelian Opera, Tel Aviv, Israel w. parts in Coppelia, Carmen, Strauss & Offenbach Evening etc., 1966-70; Made appearances on Israli TV; Tchr., Miriam Kaufmann Studio, Pettach-Tikro & Rulish Acad., Jerusalem for Character Dance. Choreographs own dancing & designs & makes own costumes. Author of poems in Rumanian lang. publd. in Israel. Hons. incl: 2 Prizes for comps. from Min. of Educ., Rumania. Address: Reh Mahanaim 9/3, Neve-Salem, Tel Aviv, Israel. 94.

VOLLMER, William Elwell, b. 25 Sept. 1906. Banker. Educ: Am. Inst. of Banking, 1922-28; Hons. Grad., Wharton Evening Schl., Finance, Univ. of Pa., 1934; Stonier Grad. Schl. of Banking, Rutgers Univ., 1942-44; Mgmt. course, Am. Mgmt. Assn., 1954-55. Appts. incl: Asst. V.P., SKF Inds., Inc., 1944-52; Treas., Asst. Sec., ibid, 1952-55; V.P., Liberty Real Estate Bank & Trust Co., Phila., 1955-64; V'P., The Fidelity Bank, Phila., 1964-67; Sr. V.P., ibid, 1967-71; Cons., 1971-73; Pres. & Dir., Neshaminy Valley Bank, Cornwells Heights, Pa., 1973-; Dir., var. cos. inclng. Continental-Wirt Electronics Corp., Warminster, Pa., MDC Corp., Cherry Hill, N.J., Milk Ind. Mgmt. Corp., Doylestown, PA.; Trustee, Fidelity Bond & Mortgage Investors, Phila., Pa. Mbrships. incl: Dir., Northeast Phila. Chmbr. of Comm.; Past Pres., Credit Mgmt. Assn. of Del. Valley; Past Chmn., Indl. Credit Club; Past mbr., comm. on govt. expenditures, U.S. Chmbr. of Comm.; 50 Yr. Club, Pa. Bankers Assn.; Past mbr., Bd. of Dirs. & Exec. Comm., Jr. Achievement, Inc. Author of The Wool Industry & Its Financing, 1944. Recip. of hons. Address: 1305 Washington Lane, Rydal, PA 19046, U.S.A. 2, 6, 128, 129, 130, 140.

VOLPE, Edmond L., b. 16 Nov. 1922. Educator. Educ: A.B., Univ. of Mich., 1943; M.A., 1947, Ph.D., 1954, Columbia Univ. Appts: Instr., Engl., N.Y. Univ., 1949-54; Instr., Asst., Assoc Prof., Full Prof., 1954-74 & Chmn., Dept. of Engl., 1964-70, CCNY; Pres., Richmond Coll., CUNY, 1974-. Mbrships: MLA; Past Mbr., Exec. Comm., Assn. of Depts. of Engl.; Bd. of Dirs., Coll. Engl. Assn.; AAUP; Pres., Andiron Club of N.Y. Publs: A Reader's Guide to William Faulkner, 1964; 15 texts & anthols.; Num. articles in profl. jrnls. Hons: Fulbright Professorship, France. 1960-61. Address: Richmond Coll., Staten Is., NY 10301, U.S.A. 2, 6, 13.

VOLTI, Antoniucci, b. 1 Jan. 1915. Sculptor. Educ: Nat. Schl. of Decorative Arts, Nice, France, 1928-32; Nat. Schl. of Fine Arts, Paris, 1932-36. Appts: Prof., Sculpture, Nat. Schl. of Applied Arts, Paris. Individual Expostiions incl: Maison de la Pensée Française, 1952; Palais de la Méditerranée, 1953; Musée d'Antibes, 1973, etc. Mbrships: V.P., Salon d'Automne; Fndg. Mbr., Salon Jeune Sculpture, Human Forms Salon, & Comparison Salon. Works incl: Sculpture decoration, Charles de Gaulle Airport, Boissy; over 50 monuments; Minèrve, Niort; Mélancolie, Cachan; Flore, Orléans, etc. Hons. incl: Prix de Rome,

Sculpture, 1936; Chevalier, Legion of Hon.; Off., Order of Arts & Letters. Address: 15 Rue du Moulin de la Vierge, Paris 14, France.

VON BERTALANFFY, Ludwig, b. 19 Sept. 1901. Faculty Professor. Educ: Univ. of Innsbruck, Austria; Ph.D., Univ. of Vienna, 1926. Appts. incl: Prof., Dir., Biological Rsch. Dept., Univ. of Ottawa, Canada, 1948-54; Dir., Biol. Rsch., Mt. Sinai Hosp., & Vis. Prof. Physiol., Univ. of Southern Calif., Los Angeles, Calif., U.S.A., 1955-58; Sloan Vis. Prof., The Menninger Fndn., Topeka, Ka., 1958-60; Prof., Theoretical Biol. (Emeritus), Univ. of Alberta, Edmonton, Canada, 1961-68; currently, Fac. Prof., Univ. of N.Y. at Buffalo, U.S.A. M'brships incl: Fndr. & V.Pres., Soc. for Gen. Systems Rsch., 1956-60; Fellow, Int. Acad. of Cytol. Author of approx. 270 publs., inclng., 15 books, publd. in Engl., German, French, Spanish, Japanese; Main works incl. Problems of Life, 1949, '52, '61; Robots, Men & Minds, 1967; General System Theory, 1968. Hons. incl: Deutsche Akad. der Naturforscher, 1968; Hon. Fellow, Am. Psych. Assoc., 1967; Gold Medal, Posta Hist. Soc. of Am., 1963. Address: Ctr. for Theoretical Biol., State Univ. of N.Y. at Buffalo, 4248 Ridge Lea Rd., Amherst, NY 14226, U.S.A. 2, 8, 14, 28, 43, 86, 122.

von BIBRA, Adele Patricia Cecelia Stephanie, b. 31 Jan. 1924. Geographer; Analyst; Lecturer. Educ: B.A., Univ. of Calif., L.A., 1948; B.S., Sierra States Univ., 1957. Appts. incl: Sec. Treas., Whitehouse, Inc., 1953-60, Stanodel, Inc., Las Vegas, 1961-75; Assoc., Sr. Housing Cons., L.A., 1960-61; Pres., Allison-Bibra, Inc., Corona del Mar, Calif., 1965-68; Tchr., Soc. Studies & Home Econs., Newport Mesa Unified Schl. Dist., 1966-69; Vice Pres., Platinotipia y Galvanoplastia S.A., Mexico, 1968-70; Pres., Liner-Bibra, Inc., Calif., 1968-; Ops. Mgr., Jesup & Lamont, 1971-72; Sr. Exec. Off., Monarch Mgmt. Ltd., 1973-. Mbrships: Assn. of Am. Geographers; World Affairs Couns., L.A. & Orange Co.; Navy League, U.S.; Fine Arts Assn., Newport Beach; Desert Sun Alumni Assn., Idyllwild. Address: 900 Sea Lane # 117, Corona del Mar, CA 92625, U.S.A.

Von BRAUN, Wernher, b. 23 Mar. 1912. Rocket & Space Scientist. Appts. incl: Rocket Dev. Engr., German Ordance Dept., 1932-37; Tech. Dir., Army Experimental Station Peenemuende, 1937-45; Project Dir., U.S. Army Ordnance Corps., Ft. Bliss, Tex., U.S.A., 1945-50; Tech. Dir., Guided Missile Dev. Group, Redstone Arsenal, 1950-52; Chief, Guided Missile Dev. Div., 1952-56; Dir., Dev. Operation Div., Army Ballistic Missile Agcy., 1956-60; Dir., G. C. Marshall Space Flight Ctr., NASA, 1960-. Mbrships. incl: Internat. Acad. Astronautics; Fellow, Am. Inst. Aeronaut. & Astronaut.; Fellow, Am. Astronaut. Soc. Co-author of the following: Across the Space Frontier, 1952; Conquest of the Moon, 1953; Exploration of Mars, 1956; Start in den Weltraum, 1958; Careers in Astronautics & Rocketry, 1962; History of Rocketry & Space Travel, 1966. Author, The Mars Project, 1953; First Men to the Moon, 1960; Space Frontier, 1967. Address: Marshall Space Flight Ctr., NASA, Huntsville, AL 35812, U.S.A.

von BRENTANI, Mario, b. 5 Mar. 1908. Publisher; Writer; Painter; Editor. Educ: B.Sc., Univ. of Frankfurt on Main, 1931. Appts: Newspaper Publisher; Painter of the Canadian Arctic; Fndr. & Ed -in-Chief, weekly newspapers, Montrealer Nachrichten, & Ihre Brigitte, 1954-. Mbrships. incl: Mgng. Pres., Germancanadian Soc. in Montreal, 1953-55; Fndr. of European Settlement, "Homeland Village", in Montreal. Publs. incl: Die Hessische Truhe, 1951; Canada, das Land von Uber Morgen, 1954. Exhibs. incl: Acad. of Fine Arts, Vienna, 1970 & '72; Mus. of Fine Arts, City of Rostock, Germany, GDR, 1973. Hons. incl: Order of the Peace, 1972 & Golden Medal of Merit, 1969, GDR Govt. Address: 3458 Marlowe Ave., Montreal 260, Quebec, Canada. 128, 92,

von BRENTANO, Margherita, b. 9 Sept. 1922. Professor of Philosophy. Educ: Studied at Univs. of Berlin & Freiburg/Baden; Ph.D., Freiburg, 1947; Inaugurated, Berlin, 1971. Appts: Ed., "Rencontre Das Treffen", 1947-49; Dir., Educl. Prog., Südwestfunk (Southwestern Radio), 1950-55; Asst., Wissenschaftlicher Rat, 1960; Prof., Free Univ., Berlin, 1971; V.P., ibid, 1970-72. Mbrships: Deutsche Gesellschaft für Philosophie; Bd. mbr., Bund Demokratischer Wissenschaftler; Pres., Heinrich Heine Stiftung für Philosophie & Kritische Wissenschaft. Publs. incl: Bürgerlicher & faschistischer Antisemitismus, 1967; Zum Problem der "Ersten Philosophie" bei Aristoteles, in Wirklichkeit & Reflexion, 1973; Sev. essays on philosophical & pol. theory. Address: Heydenstr. 15, 1 Berlin 33, German Fed. Repub.

VON CASTELBERG, Guido, b. 6 Sept. 1927. Layer. Educ: Dr.Econs., LL.D.,Univs. of Zurich & Paris; Admitted to bar, 1955. Appts: Dpty. Mbr., Ct. of Cassation, Canton of Zurich, Switzerland, 1965-70; Mbr., ibid, 1970-; Chmn., Bd. of Dirs., Pfizer AG, Zurich, 1959-, Ring-Chemie AG, Zurich, 1961-, Lecipharma AG, Zurich, 1971-; Vice Chmn., Bd. of Dirs., Kredietbank (Suisse) S.A., Geneva, 1970-; Mbr., Bd. of Dirs.,Emhart Zurich SA, 1959-, Johnson Waz AG, Weiningen, 1960-, Teldec Int. AG, Zug, 1971-, TED Bildplatten Aktiengesellschaft AEG-Telefunken, Teldec, Zug, 1971-. Mbrships: Bd. mbr., Tonhalle Gesellschaft, Zurich, 1959-; Pres., Music Commn., ibid, 1968-; Zurich Bar Assn.; Swiss Lawyers Assn. Publs: Politik des billigen Geldes in der Schweiz, 1951; Der Geldwert Als Rechtsproblem, 1953; Var. essays on constitutional law. Address: Rämistrasse 25, CH-8001 Zurich, Switzerland.

VON DER GRÜN, Max, b. 25 May 1926. Author. Educ: Commercial schl. Appts: Prisoner of war, U.S.A., 3 yrs.; Builder, 3 yrs.; Miner, 1951-63; Free-lance author, 1964-. Mbrships: PEN, German Fed. Repub.; Group 61; Deutscher Schriftstellerverband. Publs: Männer in zweifacher Nacht, 1962; Irrlicht & Feuer, 1963; Zwei Briefe an Pospischiel, 1968; Stellenweise Glatteis, 1973; Menschen in Deutschland, 1973; TV plays: Feierabend, 1968, Schichtwechsel, 1968; Aufstiegschancen, 1970; Films: Irrlicht & Feuer, 1965; Zwei Briefe an Pospischiel, 1970; Stellenweise Glatteis, 1975. Address: Am Gulloh 97, 46 Dortmund-Brechten, German Fed. Repub.

VON DEWITZ, Arden, b. 7 Mar. 1915. Artist. Educ: Soro Acad., Denmark, 1927; Stickney Art Schl., Pasadena, Calif., U.S.A., 1930; Otis Art Inst., L.A., Calif., 1935. Appts: Prof. of Painting, Laguna Beach Schl. of Art, 1964; Prof. of Anatomy, Life Drawing & Painting, Marymount Coll., Palos Verdes Estates, Calif., 1964-65; Prof. of Painting & Drawing, L.A. Bd. of Educ., Calif., 1974. Mbrships: Pres., Am. Inst. Fine Arts, Beverley Hills, Calif, 1965, United Nat. Assn. Artists & Sculptors, 1973. Solo Exhibs. incl: Sydney & Melbourne, Australia, 1968; Auckland, N.Z., 1970; L.A. City Hall Rotunda, Calif., U.S.A., 1970; Papeete, Tahiti, 1970; 19th All City Outdoor Festival, Barnsdall, U.S.A., 1971.

Hons. incl: Painters & Sculptors Club Award, L.A., 1961; 1st Purchase Award, Sacramento State Fair, 1964; Coun. of Traditional Artist Socs. Award, 1967. Address: 5132 White Oak Ave., Encino, CA 91316, U.S.A.

von ERFFA, Helmut Hartmann, 1 Mar. 1900. Art Teacher; Historian. Educ: A.B., Harvard Univ., 1931; M.A., ibid, 1933; M.F.A., Princeton Univ., 1938. Appts. incl: Tutor, Harvard Univ., 1931-33; Tchng. Asst., ibid, 1932-33; Lectr., Bryn Mawr Coll., 1935-36; Instr., Northwestern Univ., 1938-43; Asst. Prof. & Acting Chmn., Art Dept., Swarthmore Coll., 1943-46; Chmn., Asst. Prof., Assoc. Prof. & Prof., Dept. of Art, Rutgers Unig., 1946-64; Guest Prof., Univ. of N.M., 1964-66. Mbrships. incl: N.J. Art Ctr., 1946-66; Bd. Mbr.,V.P. & Chmn. for Lectures, Am. Oriental Soc.; Coll. Art Assn.; Mus. of Mod. Art; Am. Archaeol. Soc. Works incl: Drawing of Mark Tobey in Seattle Art Mus.; Desl, drawing at Rutgers Univ. Mus. of Art; Many priv. Collects. Author of articles in jrnls. Book reviews. Recip. of Harvard Univ. Sheldon Fellowship, 1933-34. Address: 38 Juniper Ln., Piscataway, NJ 08854, U.S.A. 2, 6, 13, 37, 57, 129, 133.

VON GUNTEN,Roger, b. 29 Mar. 1933. Painter. Educ: Study of Drawing, Painting, Kunsdtgewerbeschule, Zurich; Metal Engraving, Univ. Ibero-Am., Mexico City. Appts: Tchr., Drawing, Univ. Ibero-Am., 1963-64; Tchr., Metal Engraving, Mexico City Coll., 1964. Mbrship: Fndng. Mbr., Salon Independiente, Mexico, Mexico, 1968-70. Works incl. paintings, drawings, metal engraving; Mural, Mexican Pavilion, Expo '70, Osaka; 3 Stage Designs, Mexico City. Hons: 1st Prize, Painting, II Festival Pictórico de Acapulco, 1964. Address: Avenido Hidalgo Nte. 63, Tacámbaro, Michoacan, Mexico.

von HANDEL, Paul F., b. 30 Jan. 1901. Physicist; Electronics Engineer. Educ: B.S., Inst. of Technol., Munich, Bavaria, 1921; M.S., ibid, 1923; Ph.D., Tech. Univ., Berlin., 1931. Appts: Assoc. Prof., Univ. of Berlin., 1937; Full Prof., ibid, 1939; Dir., Inst. for Electronics & Physics, German Inst. for Aeronautical Rsch., 1936; V.P., Bd. II, German Comm., for Sci. Radio Rsch., 1936; Pres., Berman Bd. of Aeronautical Radio-Navigation, 1940; Dir., Ferdin & Braun Inst. & V.P., Nat. Bd. of High Frequency Rsch., 1942; Tech. Dir., Koerting Radio Corp., Bavaria, 1953; Chief Rsch. Div., Airforce Missile Dev. Ctr., Holloman, N.M., U.S.A., 1953; Sr. Sci., Inst., for Defense Analyses, Wash. D.C., 1959; Ret., 1966-. Mbrships: N.Y. Acad. of Scis.; Assoc. Fellow, Am. Inst. of Aeronautics & Astronautics; Sr., IEEE, ret., 1966; o. Mitglied der Deutschen Akademie der Lu ftfahrt Forschung, 1937-45. Contbr. 60 publs. to sci. jrnls. & books. Recip. Lilienthal Prize for Aeronautical Rsch., 1944. Address: Fischerndorf I, A-8992 Altaussee Austria, 2, 14, 28.

von HILSHEIMER, George Edwin III, b. 15 Aug. 1934. Clinical Ethologist. Educ: B.A., Univ. of Miami, Fla., 1955; Gad. Study Univs. of Miami, Chgo., Md. & Wash. Univ.; B.D., Free Religious Assn., 1957; Rsch. Fellow, Humanistic Psychol. Inst., Assn. for Humanistic Psychol. Appts. incl: Min. of Educ., All Souls Ch., Chgo., 1956; Dir. of Educ., St. Louis Ethical Soc., 1957; Agt., Mil. Intelligence, U.S. Jt. Intelligence Agcy., 1957-59; Grp. Counsellor, Am. Humanist Assn., 1959-60; Min., St. Lucie Ch., Ft. Pierce, Fla., 1961-62; Exec. Dir., Lincoln Park Child Care Ctr., 1961-62; Hdmaster, Summerlane Schl., North Branch, N.Y., 1963-64 & Green Valley Schl., Orange City, Fla., 1964-69; Clin. Dir., Korczak

Mem. Med. Clin., ibid, 1973-. Mbrships. incl: Fndg. Fellow, Int. Coll. of Psychosomatic Med.; Fellow, Acad. of Psychosomatic Med.; Assoc. Fellow, Soc. for Clin. Ecol.; Phi Kappa Phi; A.A.A.S. Publs. incl: How to Live With Your Special Child, 1970; Understanding The Problem Child, 1974; Ed., Human Learning & Proceedomgs; Num. profl. papers. Cons., Pres. Kennedy's Comm. for Nat. Voluntary Servs., Migratory Labor & Juvenile Delinquency & Youth Crime, 1962. Address: P.O. Box 606, Orange City, FL 32763, U.S.A. 7, 125.

von JULIN, Jacob Albert Carl Gustaf, b. 23 July 1906. Company Chairman. Educ: Univs. of Helsinki, Finland & Cambridge, U.K. Appts: Asst. Dir., Finncell, 1938-42; Mng. Dir., Kaukas Co., 1942-67; Chmn., ibid, 1951-; Chmn., Finncell, 1962-; Chmn., Fiskars Co., 1947-; V. Chmn., Nordiska Foreningsbanken, 1961-73, Chmn., 1973-. Hons: Mining Councillor, 1950; Dr. Sc., Econ., 1970; Commdr., 1st class, White Rose of Finland; Finnish Lion; Swedish Order of Vasa; Egyptian Order of Nile; Commdr. Norwegian Order of Olav; Off., French Legion of Honour; Comrndr., French Order of Mérite Nationale, 1972. Address: 4 Union Street, Helsinki, Finland. 123.

VON KEMPSKI RAKOSZYN, Jürgen Herbert Alexander, b. 20 May 1910. University Professor. Educ: Univs. of Freiburg im Breisgau & Berlin, Germany; Dr.phil., Univ. of Frankfurt/Main, 1951. Appts: Referee for Int. Law, Deutsches Inst. für Aussenpolitische Forschung, 1939-45; Prof., math. logic, Tech. Univ., Hanover, 1954-58; Prof., soc. sci. logic, Univ. of Münster; Hon. Prof., legal & soc. philos., ibid, 1961-; Hon. Prof., philos., Ruhr Univ., Bochum, 1973-; Prof., politics & math. soc. theory, Univ. of Münster, 1971-. Mbrships: PEN, German Fed. Repub.; Deutsche Vereinigung für mathematische Logik & Grundlagenforschung. Publs. incl: Brechungen. Kritische Studien zur Philosophie der Gegenwart, 1964; Recht & Politik. Studien zur Einheit der Sozialwissenschaft, 1965; Ed., Archiv für Philosophie, 1947-64; Ed. Archiv für mathematische Logik & Grundlagenforschung, 1950-. Address: Lange Str. 32, D 3492 Brakel-Hembsen, German Fed. Repub. 43, 92.

von MAUCHENHEIM, Egon. Director of Public Relations. Educ: Gymnasium Grad., Munich, Germany; Bus. Econ., Univ. of Mich., U.S.A. Appts: Pvte. Prac., Bus. Analyst, N.Y.C., & assoc. of Nat. Indl. Conf. Bd. Inc., N.Y.C., U.S.A., 1952-60;Lester B. Knight & Assocs. Inc., Chgo., Ill., & Mng. Dir., Knight GmbH, Dusseldorf, Germany, 1960-63; Mgt. Exec., Fried. Krupp, Essen, Germany, 1963-67; Dir. of P.R., PA Mgt. Conss. GmbH., Frankfurt/Main, Germany, 1968-. Publs: Financial Management of Pension Trusts; Financial Management of Public Relations. Num. articles, U.S. bus. & ind., var. Am. & German publs. For. Trade Rels. broadcasts for U.S. Dept. of State. Address: Mendelssohnstrasse 53, Frankfurt/Main 6, German Fed. Repub. 43.

von NUSSBAUMER, Aliyah Wolfgard-Margot, b. 11 May 1925. Research Librarian. Educ: Bach. degree, Goethe Lyceum, Erfurt, Germany, 1943; Goethe Univ., ibid, 1943-45; B.S., Lib. Sci., Sorbonne, Paris, France, 1947; M.S., Pol. Sci., ibid, 1949; Ph.D., Nat. Sci., Univ. of Hamburg, Germany, 1957. Appts: Chief of Protocol to H.M. King Faisal 2nd of Iraq, Baghdad, 1949-58; Base Libn. & Recreation Ldr., USAF Base, Sidi Slimane, Morocco, 1959-62; Serial & Exchange Libn., Centenary Coll., Shreveport, La., U.S.A, 1963-65; Rsch. Libn. & i/c Rsch. Lib., Dresser Inds., Inc., Houston, Tex., 1966-. Mbrships: Am. Petroleum Inst.; Am. Special Lib. Assn.;

ALA; Advsry. Coun., Sci. & Info. Ctr., Southern Meth. Univ.; Smithsonian Instn.; Nat. Fertilizer Solutions Assn.; Nat. Owner Handler Assn. of Am.; Metropol. Houston Chapt., ibid; Houston Obedience Trng. Club; Weimaraner Clubs of Am. & Germany; Pres., German-Am. Club; V.P. & Life Mbr., World Islamic Community (HQ Berlin, Germany); Am. Cat Assn.; Am. Cat Fancier Assn. Publs: articles, weekly column & feature articles, Moroccan Flier & Author's Spotlit, periodically during 1961-62. Hons: D.Theol., Univ. of Hamburg, Germany, & thru' World Islamic Community (because of relig. work & travel to Mecca), 1957; sev. Awards w. Mgmt. of Cambridge, 1968. Address: 11110 Hazen Rd., Houston, TX 77072, U.S.A. 125, 138.

von PUTTKAMER, Jesco Karl Eugen, b. 20 Feb. 1919. German Ambassador to Israel. Educ: War Schl. for Career Offs.; Schl. of Jrnlsm., Germany. Appts: Off., German Army, POW, Russia, 5 yrs.; Jrnlst., leading German newspapers, 22 yrs., Radio & TV Commentator; For. Serv., 1971-; Ambassador to Israel, 1971-. Mbrship: Rotary Club. Contbr. to periodicals. Hons: Bundesverdienstkreuz & other war decorations. Address: POB 16038, Deutsche Botschaft, Tel-Aviv, Israel. 34.

von REUTER, Florizel, b. 21 Jan. 1890. Concert Violinist; Composer; Conductor; Author. Educ: Violin study w. Max Bendix, Chgo., 1896-99, Emile Sauret, London, 1899-1900, Cesar Thomson, Brussels, 1900; Dip. de virtuosité, inclng. music theory & piano, Conservatory of Geneva, 1901. Appts: Dir., Music Acad., Zurich, 1915; Dir., master class for violin, Vienna State Music Acad., 1932-33; Dir., master class, Klindworth-Scharwenka Conservatory, Berlin; Over 2000 concerts in Europe; Concertmaster, Waukesha, (Wis.) Symph.; Tchr. Mbr. music, psychich rsch., socs. Composer of num. compositions, inclng. one opera, Postmeister Wyrin, performed Berlin, 1947; Completed last unfinished untitled work of Max Reger; Author num. editions of violin compositions; Books incl: Psychical Experiences of a Musician, The Consoling Angel, both w. introductions by Arthur Conan Doyle; A History of Violin Music; The Psychology of Bowing; Great People I Have Known; Twilight of the Gods (novel); Maiden Worlds Unconquered (short stories). Hons. incl: Decorated by Sultan Abdul Hamid of Turkey, King Ferdinand of Bulgaria; Received "von" from Emporer Wilhelm, Germany, 1904; Title of Prof., Austrian Govt., 1932. Address: 517 Madison St., Waukesha, WI 53186, U.S.A.

VON REZNICEK, Felicitas Jutta, b. 18 Jan. 1904. Writer. Appts: Freelance writer, German, Swiss & British papers; & for King Features, U.S.A., 1939-40; Corres., Observer & for Basler Nationalzeitung; Writer, 1956-. Mbrships. incl: Writers Assn. of Ctrl. Switz.; Fndr., Rendez-vous Hautes Montagnes; currently Pres., ibid. Publs. incl: 16 books, mostly novels, & Gegen den Strom (biog. of E.N. von Reznicek); Von der Krinoline zum sechsten Grad (hist. of women's climing); num. articles for newspapers & jrnls. Address: Kantonsstr., CH 6390 Engelberg, Switzerland. 43.

von RINTELEN, Fritz-Joachim, b. 16 May 1898. Professor of Philosophy, Psychology & Education. Educ: Dr.phil., Munich, 1924. Appts: Asst. Prof., Univ. of Munich, 1928; Prof., Univs. of Bonn, 1933, & Munich., 1936; Co-Fndr., Univ. of Mainz, 1946; Vis. Prof., Cordoba, Argentina, 1949, L.A., U.S.A, 1959, Nihon Univ., Tokyo, 1972 & Chgo., U.S.A, 1973;Co-Ed., var. periodicals. Mbrships: Int.

Inst. of Philos., Paris; Acad. of Philos., Louvain; V.P., Int. Inst. of European Studies, Bolzano, Italy; Hon. Mbr., Ac. Goetheana & Inst. of Philos., Sao Paulo, Brazil; Philos. Socs., Monterrey, Mexico, & Genoa, Italy. publs. incl: Aufstieg im Geiste. Von Dionysos zu Apollo, 1948, 71; Der Rang des Geistes (Goethe), 1950, Brazilian ed., 1953; Endlichkeit als Spiegel der Gegenwart, 1951, 60, Italian ed., 1974; Beyond Existentialism, 1961; European Man., 1961; Contemporary German Philosophy, 1969, '73, Japanese ed., 1972; Values in European Thought, 1972; Das Tragische in der griechischen Geisteschaltung, 1972; articles in var. langs. Hon Doctorates: Santiago, Chile, 1950, Lima, Peru, 1951, Cordoba, Argentina, 1965. Address: Salvatorstrasse 1, 65 Mainz, German Fed. Repub.

Von ROSEN, Bjorn, b. 25 Oct. 1905. Artist; Author. Educ: Studied etching, Royal Acad. of Arts, Stockholm, Sweden; Further art studies, France, Italy, Germany & U.K. Appts: Columnist, Svenska Dagbladet, 1941-45; Book Reviewer, Bonnier's Literary Mag., 1940's. 1-man shows: Paintings & etchings, Stockholm, 1933, '48, '56, '70, Gothenburg, 1950, Linkoping, 1959, & Nykoping, 1968; Sculpture & paintings, Stockholm, 1971. Represented in var. museums inclng. Nat. Mus., Stockholm, Musee Galliera, Paris, & Ulster Mus., Belfast, U.K. Mbrships. incl: 1st Hon. Mbr., Swedish Elk Hound Club; Swedish Kennel Club. Publs. incl: (Poetry) Den leende faunen, 1927; Tjäderklockan, 1941; Grå fagel, 1960; (Prose) Gröna Kammarn, 1940; Axel Fridell, 1951; Minnen från vidden, 1973. Address: Majliden, 150 10 Gnesta, Sweden. 134.

von SANDOR, (Count of Sandorfalva), Robert, b. 16 Apr. 1929. Dean. Educ: Univ. of Stockholm, Sweden, & Univ. of Buffalo, U.S.A.; Dr. of Optometry; Ph.D. in Anthropol. Appts: Mng. Dir., Optical Info. Coun.; Dean, Coll. of Opthalmic Opticians; Japanese Expert, Swedish Ethnographical Mus. Mbrships: Pres., European Fedn. of Japanese Fencing (Kendo); V.P., Int. Fedn. of Japanese Fencing; Pres., Swedish Budo Fedn. (Kendo); Treas., European Fedn. cf Japanese Archery (Kyudo); Am. Acad. of Optometry; Am. Soc. of Optics. Publs. incl: The Way of the Samurai to Zen—Budo; The Way of Gentleness—Judo; The Way of the Universe—Aikido; The Way of the Sword—Kendo; The Way of the Blow—Kyudo; Textbook in Ophthalmic Optics. Recip. of hons. Address: Klippuddsvagen 13, S-181 62 Lidingo, Sweden. 24. 43.

VON SPAKOVSKY, Anatol, b. 27 Feb. 1895. University Professor (Emeritus). Educ: Univ., Moscow, Russia, 1914-15; Ph.D., Univ. of Ljubljana, Yugoslavia, 1925; Degree Prof., 1927; Univ. of Nancy, France, 1926. Appts incl: Prof., Philos., World Univ. Serv., Munich, W. Germany, 1950-51; Prof., Sociol., Russian, German, Jacksonville State Univ., Ala., U.S.A., 1957-65; Prof., Philos., Sociol. & French, Miles Coll., B'ham, 1968-69; Prof., Humanities & Sociol., Athens Coll., 1965-68, '69-70; Prof., Russian, Univ. of Ala., Huntsville, 1971-. Mbrships incl: Brit. Royal Inst. of Philos.; Gen. Soc. Philos., Germany; Nat. Histl. Soc.; FIBA; AAUP; AAAS; Edit. Bd., Int. Jrnl. of Contemporary Sociol.; Hon. Life, Delta Tau Kappa. Publs incl: Parallelism of Dynamical Development of Self & Culture; Thoughts; Perspectives of Culture in General & Western Europe in Particular; Analytical Structure of Human Consciousness; Physical Dynamism & its Moulding of the World; On the Roads of Life & Thought (poems); Freedom, Determinism, Indeterminism. Address: 1002C

Hampshire Dr., S.E., Huntsville, AL 35803, U.S.A. 7, 11, 14, 22, 128, 139,

VON WIREN, Vera. College Professor. Educ: B.A., Brooklyn Coll., 1958; M.A., Columbia Univ., 1961; Ph.D., N.Y. Univ., 1964. Appts. incl: Lectr., Queens Coll., 1962-64; Instr., City Coll., CUNY, 1964-67, Asst. Prof., 1967-73, Assoc. Prof., 1973-. Mbrships. incl: MLA Textbook Evaluation Comm. of Polish; Am. Assn. for Adv. of Slavic Studies & Fed. Int. Des Langue et Lit. Mod.; Polish Acad. of Arts & Scis.; Assn. Int. pour la Recherche et la Diffusion des Méthodes Audio Visuelles et Structure Globales. Publs. incl: Seven Russian Novel Masterpieces (Co-ed.), 1967; Pered voskhodom solntsa (Co-ed.), 1967; Before the Sunrise (Ed.), 1973; Articles in profl. jrnls. Hons. incl: Tuitions Schlrships., Columbia Univ., 1958 & N.Y. Univ., 1961-62; Rsch. Grant, N.Y. Univ., 1962; Num. Post-Doctoral Grants. Address: 3 Northfield Rd., Glen Cove, NY 11542, U.S.A. 13.

VON ZWEIGBERGK, Ulf, b. 27 Mar. 1926. Artist; Actor. Educ: Univ., Stockholm; Art studies, Otte Sköld & Bo Von Zweigbergk. Art Exhibs. incl: Stockholm, 1951, 1970, 1971; Paris, 1971, 1972; Biarritz, 1971, 1972; N.Y., 1962; London, 1973. Mbrships: Nat. Comm. of Art (KRO); Circle of Art, Bd. Mbr.; Collectors Assn., Nordstjörnen; Active Mbr., Gall. Mouffe, Paris; Hist. of Culture in Lund (Mus.). Contbr. to publs. Hons: Dip. D'Honneur, 1970, 1971. Address: Bellmansgatan 8¹, S-117 20 Stockholm, Sweden. 43.

VOS, Marianne Cramer (Mrs. Robert Vos), b. 22 Feb. 1927. Professor. Educ: Freie Univ., Berlin, Germany; Inst. de Touraine, Univ. de Poiters, France; M.A., Phila., Penna., U.S.A. 1962; Ph.D., Dept. Comparative & For. Lit., Rochester Univ., U.S.A., 1970. Appts: Tchr., Rider Coll., E. Bapt. Coll., Rochester & Ala. State Univs.; Prof., Romance Philol.; French Lit.; Mod. For. Langs; Currently, Hd., For. Lang. Area, Ala. State Univ., Montgomery, U.S.A. Mbrships: MLAA; Deleg., Nat. Conf., Am. Assn. Tchrs. French; S. Atlantic MLA; Soc. Rencesvals; AAUP; Women Schlrs. Am.; Sec., Friends, Asu Lib.; Alliance Française; Ex-Advsry. Bd. Mbr., S. Conf., For. Lang. Tchng.; Assn. Dept. Chrmn. For. Lang.; Am. Friends' Serv. Comm. Publs. inco: From Foreknowledge to True Knowledge: The Ascendancy of Bramimunde in La Chanson de Roland, 1974; Portraiture de la Haute Royauté du Charlemagne Epique, 1974. Hons: Prize, Novella, Germany; Haney Fellowship, Pa. Univ., Phila., U.S.A.; 3-yr. Doct. Fellowship, Rochester Univ., NY, U.S.A. Address: Box 168, Ala. State Unvi., Montgomery, AL 36101, U.S.A.

VOSS, E. Theodor, b. 25 Dec. 1928. Associate Professor of German. Educ: D.Phil., Univ. of Bonn, Germany, 1958. Appts: Staff Mbr., Schiller-Nat. Mus., Marbach, Germany, 1958-59; Ed., scholarly books on German lit.; Co-ed., Sammlung Metzier, 1959-65; Asst. Prof., German Lit., Univ. of Wis. Madison, 1965-67; Mbr., Editl. Bd., Monatshefte, Univ. of Wis. Press, 1966-67; Assoc. Prof., German Lit., Univ. of Minn., Mpls., 1967-69; Assoc. Prof., German Lit., Columbia Univ., N.Y., 1969-; Mbr., Edit. Bd., Germanic Review, 1970-. Publs: Erzahlprobleme des Briefromans, 1960; Edit. of: Johann Jakob Engel, 1965; Johann Heinrich Voss, 1968; Salomon Gessner, 1973; reviews in Germanistik & The Germanic Review. Address: Dept. of Germanic Lang. & Lit., Columbia Univ., 311 Hamilton Hall, N.Y., NY 10027, U.S.A. 13.

VOSS, Karl, b. 16 May 1907. Institute Director. Educ: Univ. of Kiel; Ph.D., Berlin Univ. Appts: Dir., European Schl., Luxembourg, & Goethe- Inst., Luxembourg. Publs: Englisch in der Tasche, 1969-64; Wege der französischen Literatur, 1965; Redeusarten der französischen Sprache, 1966; Redeusarten der englischen Sprache, 1967; Reiseführer für Literaturfreunde, Bd. I, 1971; Reseführer für Literaturfreunde Bd. II, 1974; Ed., L'Allemagne jugée par la France, 1957-67, Paul Bildt-Ein Schausprieler in seinen Verwandlingen, 1963, & Parliamentary Government in England, 1964-66. Hons: Chevalier des Palmes Academiques, France, 1962; Off., Order of Merit of Repub. of Italy, 1967; Gross Verdienstkreuz des Verdienstordenz der Bundes-republik Deutschland, 1971; Cmdr., Order of Merit, Grand Duchy of Luxembourg. Address: 24, rue Frantz Clement, Luxembourg.

VOULODIMOS, Anastassios, b. 23 May 1904. Professor of Mathematics. Educ: Univ. of Athens. Appts: Fndr., 1933, Arhimides Tech. Colls., Prin., 1933-67; Mbr. of Parliament, 5 times, 1951-63; Chmn., Coun. of Piraeus, 1950-53, Mbrships: Past Gen. Sec., Pvte Employees Assn.; Past Pres., Tchrs. & Lectrs. Assn.; Soc. of Mathns. of Greece; Astron. Socs. of Greece, France; Soc. of Intellectuals, Greece. Publs. incl: Effect of Comets & Sun Spots on Organic Beings, 1926; Retrograde Movement of Planets & Satellites, 1927; Studies in Antisolaire Lumiere, 1928; Textbooks on Geom., Algebra, Trig.; Publr., Nea Skepsi mag. Address: od. Charilaou Trikoupi 42, Piraeus, Greece. 43.

VOYENNE, Bernard, b. 12 Aug. 1920. Journalist. Educ: Litcencié ès-lettres, Aix-en-Provence, France, 1942. Appts: Sub-Ed., Ce soir, 1944, Terre des Hommes, 1945, Combat, 1946; Dir., Re vue de la Pensée française, 1948; Lectr., Ctr. for Formation of Jrnsts., 1948; Prof., ibid, 1957. Mbrships: French Pol. Sci. Assn.; French Sociol. Soc.; Assn. of European Jrnlsts.; French Commn. for UNESCO; Pres., Terminol. Sect., Int. Assn. of Studies & Rsch. on Info. Publs. incl: Mais où sont les révolutionnaires?, 1946; Honneur des Hommes, 1946; Histoire de l'idée européenne, 2nd ed., 1964; Guide bibliographique de la Presse, 1958; La Presse dans la société contemporaine, 4th ed., 1971; Le Droit à l'Information, 1970. Address: Centre de formation des journalistes, 29/33 rue de Louvre, 75002 Paris, France.

VOZZO, Hilario, b. 21 Apr. 1912. Sculptor. Works exhibited in num. salons throughout Argentina. Monuments incl: Gabino Ezeiza, Plaza de los Mataderos, Buenos Aires; Ruben Daria, Schl. No. 1, Dist. 14, Buenos Aires; El infante Argentino, Nat. Mil. Coll.; Soldado, Cmdr. in Chief, Argentinian Army. Works represented in num. mus. collects. inclng. Santa Rosa, La Pampa; la Plata, Buenos Aires; Villa Maria, Cordoba; Vicente Lopez, Buenos Aires; Rosario, Santa Fe.; San Miguel de Tucuman; Mercedes, San Luis. Hons. incl: 3rd Nat. Prize, 1943; Acquisition Prize, Min. of Housing, 1946; 1st Prize, Nat. Salon, 1950; Grand Prize of Hon., Salon of Rosario, 1958; Unique Prize for Sesquicentennial Medallion of Argentinian Independence, Min. of Interior, 1966; Winner, Contest for bust of Ernesto Sabate, Buenos Aires, 1972. Address: Ave. La Plata 2678, Buenos Aires, Argentina.

VRUTICKY, Josef Vlach, b. 24 Jan. 1897. Composer; Conductor; Writer; Teacher. Educ: Studied, piano, organ, conducting & pedagogics, Conservatory, Prague, 1914-16,

1918-21 & Mastery Composition Schl. in Dr. Jos. B. Foerster's Class, 1921-24. Appts. incl: Prague, 1922-24 & Dubrovnik, Yogoslavia, 1925-29; Lectr. in Music, Theological Fac., Dubrovnik, 1938-41 & Prague, 1958-63; Conductor, Philharmonic Soc., Dubrovnik Ragusa, & Choirmstr., Choral Soc. 'Dubrava', Dubrovnik, 1925-46; Prof., Acad. of Music, Dubrovnik, 1944-46; Chief, Orch. Symphonique à Marianské Lźné, Czechoslovakia, 1946-48. Composer of orchl. compositons, works for solo voices, choirs & orch., 150 comps. for mixed male, female & childrens choir, Chmbr. music, comps. for piano & stage works inclng. Ballet & Opera. Publs. incl: many essays, articles, poems & a collection of Slavonic Folk Songs. Hons. incl: Medla, PEN Clubs, 1934; Off. d'Acad., Paris, 1935; Chevalier de l'Etoile d'Ethiopie, 1935; Medal, Gundulić de la Ville de Dubrovnik, 1936; Off. d l'Ordre du St. Sava, 1938. Address: Rue Gottwaldova 700, 413 01 Roudnice n. L., Czechoslovakia.

VUCKOVICH, Dragomir Michael, b. 27 Oct. 1927. Neurological Physician. Educ: M.D., Univ. of Birmingham, U.K., 1953; Dip. Mbr., Royal Coll. of Surgs., & Licentiate, Royal Coll. of Physns., London, 1954; Dipl., Am. Bd. of Pediatrics, 1964, Am. Bd. of Psych & Neurol., 1971, & Pan Am. Med. Assn. in Psych. & Neurol., 1973. Appts. incl: Res., Neurol., Psych., V.A. Rsch. & Wesley Mem. Hosps., Chgo., U.S.A., 1958-60; Fellow, Neurol., 1960, Res., Pediatrics, 1961, Children's Mem., Northwestern Univ.; Neurologist, Columbus Hosp., 1962; Asst. Prof., Northwestern Univ. Med. Schl., 1968; Cons., Rockford Mental Hlth. Zone, Ill., 1967; Hd. of Neurol., Columbus-Cuneo Med. Ctr., 1970; Assoc. Clin. Prof., Neurol. & Pediatrics, Loyola Univ. Hosp., Maywood, Ill., 1970-. Mbrships incl: Fellow, Am. Acad. Pediatrics, 1964; AMA; BMA; Am. Acad. of Neurology. Contbr. of num. articles & papers to profl. jrnla. & confs. in sev. countries. Address: 104 S. Michigan Ave., Chicago, IL 60603, U.S.A. 130.

VYSE, Harold Griffin, b. 22 Oct. 1915. Physician. Educ: St. Thomas's Hosps., London Univ., U.K., 1933-38; D.P.H., 1946; Cert. of Venereol., 1946. Appts: Clin. Asst., Dept. of Ob. & Venereol., St. Thomas's Hosp., 1939; Asst. Med. Officer, Royal Arsenal, Woolwich, 1939; RAF, 1939-46; Pvte. Med. Prac., Jamaica, 1946-; R.M.O., 3rd Bn (N.R.), Jamaica Regiment, 1962-73. Mbrships. incl: Aerospace Med. Assn., U.S.; Med. Assn. Jamaica; Grabham Soc.; Dist. Surg.-Div. Surg.-Commnr., St. John Ambulance Brigade, 1952-66; Life V.P., Jamaica Legion B.C.E.L.; Chmn., Jamaica Br., RAF Benevolent Fund, 1949-. Hons: O.B.E., 1956; Officer, Order of St. John of Jerusalem, 1960; Order of Hipolito Unanué, Peru, 1970; Jamaica Medla of Hon., 1971. Address: c/o Reynolds Jamaica Mines, Lydford PO, St. Ann, Jamaica, WI.

W

WABER, James Thomas, b. 8 Apr. 1920. Professor. Educ: B.S. & M.S. in Chem. Engrng., & Ph.D. in Metallurgy, Ill. Inst. of Technol., Chicago, Ill.; Nat. Sci. Fndn. Sr. Fellow, Univ. of B'ham, 1960-61. Appts: Asst. Prof. Chem., Ill. Inst. of Technol., 1946-47; Staff Mbr. Los Alamos Sci. Lab., 1947-66; Prof. of Mat. Sci., Northwestern Univ., Evanston, Ill., 1967-. Mbrships: Exec. Comm. Chmn., Inst. of Metals Div. of the Metallurgical Soc., 1971-74; Chmn., Nuclear Metallurgy Comm., 1969-72; Chmn., Comm. on Alloy Phases, 1971-75; Hume-Rothery Award Comm., 1973-77; Fellow, Am. Phys. Soc., 1974. Publs: Ed. w. P.A. Beck, Magnetism in Alloys, 1972; Co-Ed., Electronic Structure of Metals & Alloys. Hons: Recip., Turner Book Prize for Young Authors, 1947; Willis Rodney Whitney Medal, Nat. Assn. of Corr. Engrs., 1963; Profl. Achievement Award, Alumni Assn., Ill. Inst. Technol., 1967. Address: Technological Inst., Northwestern Univ., Evanston, IL 60201, U.S.A.

WACHENHAUSER, Arie, b. 12 June 1917. Painter. Educ: Applied Art Schl., Warsaw, 1939; Painting Tchrs. Acad., Tel-Aviv, Israel, 1951. Exhibd. in num. shows inclng. Gen. Exhibs., Israeli Painters & Sculptors's Assn., 1943-. Exhibs. incl: Nat. Exhib., Posnan, Poland, 1930; Exhib. of Kibbutz Artists 1940/43; Decade Exhib., Ramatgan, Israel, 1958; Mus. of Mod. Art, Haifa, Israel, 1970; Museé Marmootan, Acad. Des Beaux Arts, Concours Pour Le Prix De Portrait-Paul Louis Neiler, 1971. One Man Shows incl: Youth Grp., Borochow Quarter, Israel, 1941; Katz Gall., tel-Aviv, 1945-54; Ctematzky Gall., Tel-Aviv, 1962-63; Senta's Taft Ctr., Sydney Australia, 1964; Ryna Gall., Jerusalem, Israel, 1965; Murray Greenfield Gall., N.Y., 1965; Chagal House, Haifa, Israel, 1968; Israel Gall., Amsterdam, Netherlands, 1968; Gall. Wisegaard, Groningen, 1968; Mus. Bat-Yam (Municipal Mus.), Israel, 1971. Mbrships: Israeli Painters & Sculptors' Assn.; Milo, (Artists & Authors Club), Tle-Aviv, Israel. Address: 45 Reines Str., Tel-Aviv, Israel. 94.

WACKENHUT, Ruth J. Executive. Appts: Sec., Special Agt. Investigators, Inc., Special Agts. Security Guards, Inc., Security Servs. Corp., Miami, 1954-58; Sec., The Wackenhut Corp., 1958-; Dir., Wackenhut Servs., Inc., 1960-; Dir., Pan Am. Bank of Coral Gables, Inc., 1973-. Mbr., Ocean Reef Club, Key Largo, Fla. Address: 3280 Ponce de Leon Blvd., Coral Gables, FL 33134, U.S.A. 2, 5, 7, 16, 125, 138.

WACKETT, (Sir) Lawrence James, b. 2 Jan. 1896. Retired Soldier & Aeronautical Engineer. Educ: Royal Mil. Coll., Duntroon, Australia; B.S., Melbourne Univ., 1923. Appts: Profl. Soldier, Australian Flying Corps, 1913-19; Wing Cmdr., Royal Australian Air Force, 1919-29; Mgr. & Dir., Commonwealth Aircraft Corp., Melbourne, 1936-61; Hon. Cons., Royal North Shore Hosp. Mbrships: Fellow, Royal Aeronautical Soc.; Fellow, Inst. of Prod. Engrs.; Am. Soc. of Automobile Engrs.; Commodore, Beaumaris Motor Yacht Squadron, 9 yrs.; Life mbr., ibid. Designer of 8 original aircraft & also of racing hydroplanes; Pioneer of Aeronautical Engrng. & Aircraft Construction in Australia. Hons. incl: D.S.C., 1918; Air Force Cross, 1919; Kt. Bach., 1954; Finlay Nat. Award for Prod. Engrng., 1969. Address: 55 Fidden's Wharf Rd., Killara, Sydney, Australia, 2071.

WACKS, Virgil Quinton, b. 1 May 1906. Film Producer. Educ: Bluefield Coll., 1928-30; Photography degree, N.Y. Inst. of Photography, 1933. Appts: Served WWII Owner, Virgil Q.

Wacks Agcy., producer TV shows, special film features for TV & theatres, Pennington Gap, Va., 1960-; Owner, operator, Lee Co. Agricl. Fair, Pennington Gap, 1945-63, Lee Block Plant, Inc., 1945-72; V.P., Southwestern Va. R.R. Co., 1972-, Knoxville Sox Baseball Club, 1972-. Mbrships. incl: Nat. Chmn., promoter, Nat. Press Day Celebration, Cumberland Gap Nat. Hist. Park, 1970-; Bd. of Dirs., Lee Co. Community Action Org., Lonesome Pine Dev. Corp., Lee indl. Commn.; Pres., Lee Co. Chmbr. of Comm., 1970-72; Exec. Dir., ibid, 1970-72; Post Cmdr., Am. Legion, 1955. Producer of films; Producer, promoter, Earl Hobson Smith Outdoor Dramas, inclng. Trail of Lonesome Pine, Valley Forge, Old Smokey; Host, 30 minute weekly TV travel show, WKPT-TV; Author of articles on snake-handling religious cult in St. Charles, Va. for nat. mags., 1940. Hons. incl: Ky. Col.; Nat. Man of Yr. Cert. of Hon., State of Ky. Veterans of For. Wars, Booneville, Ky., 1973. Address: P.O. Box 218, Pennington Gap, VA 24277, U.S.A. 2, 7, 125.

WADA, Kamekichi, b. 24 Mar. 1906. Company President. Educ: Dip.Engr., Tokyo Imperial Univ., 1929; Dr.Engrng., ibid, 1952. Appts: Dir., Rsch. Inst., Yawata Iron & Steel Co. Ltd., 1956; Mng. Dir., Yawata Iron & Steel Co. Ltd., 1962; Exec. V.P., Kurosaki Yogyo Co Ltd., 1963; Pres., Kurosaki Yogyo Co. Ltd., 1967. Mbrships: Sci. Coun. of Japan, 1955-64; Int. Lions Club, 1959-; Fed. Econ. Org. of Japan, 1967. Publs: Pig Iron Making. Recip., Shiju Decoration, Japan 1968. Address: Kurosaki Yogyo Co. Ltd., 1 Higashihama, Yahata Nishi, Kitakyushu 806, Japan.

WADDELL, (Sister) Mary, I.H.M., b. 9 Jan. 1931. Psychotherapist; Professor. Educ: R.N., Mem. Hosp., Winston Salem, N.C., 1951; B.S., Marywood Coll., Scranton, Pa., 1956; M.A.Ed., e. Carolina Univ., Greenville, N.C., 1969; Cert. in Admin., ibid, 1970; Ph.D., Univ. of Sarasota, Fla., 1973. Appts: Nurse, Supvsr., St. Joseph's Hosp., Carbondale, Pa., 1956-58; Elem. Thcr., Dundalk, Md., 1958- 60, & All SS. Schl., Masontown, Pa., 1963-65; Geriatric Nurse, Marion Convent, Scranton, Pa., 1960-63; Pastoral, Prison & Schl. Snslr., Lang. Arts Coord., St. Paul's Elem. Schl., New Bern, N.C., 1965-69; Dir. of Guidance Servs. & Coord., Lang. Arts Prog., John XXIII Expmtl. Schl., Balt., Md., 1969-70; Dir., Guidance Servs., Innaculata HS, NYC, 1970-71; Coord. of Project HELP (Human Experiences in the Learning Process), Schl. of Educ., E. Carolina Univ., 1971-72; Cnslr., Psychol., Marywood Coll. Counseling Ctr., & Prof.. of Cnslr. Educ., 1973-74. Mbrships: Pres., Eta Chi Chapt., Kappa Delta Pi; Bd. of Trustees, Univ. of Sarasota; Am. Personnel & Guidance Assn. Publs: Human Perspectives in Educational Research (co-author), 1973; Curriculum Plan for Black Studies, in Diocese of Raleigh Educational News. Hons: Hugo E. Miller Mem. Schlrship., 1967-69; Merit Schlrship., Univ. of Sarasota, 1971-73. Address: Box 864, Marywood Coll., Scranton, PA 18509, U.S.A. 125.

WADDELL, Mina Jean Gillespie (Mrs. Stanford C. Waddell), b. 15 Dec. 1916. Librarian. Educ: B.A., Wichita State Unvi., 1934; M.S., Kan. State Tchrs. Coll., 1965. Appts: Ref. Libn., Wichita State Univ., 1965-69; Hd., Ref. Dept., ibid, 1969-. Mbrships: ALA; AAUP; Apha Chi Omega; Phi Kappa Phi; Sweet Adelines, Inc. Address: 1444 Salina, Wichita, KS 67203, U.S.A. 5, 15.

WADDY, Willanna Ruth Gilliam (Mrs.), b. 7 Jan. 1909. Artist & Editor. Educ: Univ. of

Minn. 1928-3-; Famous Artist' Home Study Course. 1965; Otis Art Inst., L.A., Calif., 1966. Fndr. & 1st Pres. of Art West Assocd. Inc., L.A., 1962; Dir., Print Proj., ibid, 1973-74. Corres. Sec., Fedn. of Black Hist. & Arts Inc., 1970. Co-ed. of Black artists on Art, vols. 1 & 11, 1969-71. Hons: Cert., Nat. Assn. of Coll. Women, L.A. Br. in Observance of Nat Day, 1963; Angeles Mesa Ctr. YWCA, 1964; Cert. of Merit, Nat. Counf. of Artists, 1968; Award, Art West Assocd., Inc., 1972. Address: 1543 S. Western Ave., L.A., CA 90006, U.S.A. 9.

WADE, Donald Zahn, b. 26 July 1910. Banker. Educ: Cert., Columbia Inst. of Commerce; Am. Inst. of Banking. Appts. incl: Bank Examiner, Commonwealth of Pa.; Pres. & Chief Exec. Officer, Bank of Matamoras, Pa. Mbrships: Past Pres., Pa. Bankers Assn.; Exec. Coun., Am. Bankers Assn.; Pa. Dir., Independent Bankers Assn.; Exec. Comm., Econ. Dev. Coun., N.E. Pa.; Ind. Dev. Coun., Pa.; Comprehensive Planning Comm., Tocks Island Regional Advsry. Coun; Chmn. Finance Comm., St. Francis Hosp., Port Jervis, N.Y.; Bd. of Dirs., Pike Co. Chamber of Commerce; Mason; Shrine. Recip. of USN Unit Citation, 1945 & Award, Community Ldrs. of Am. Address: 710 Delaware Dr., Matamoras, PA 18336, U.S.A. 2, 6, 16, 139,

WADE, Eugene Michael, Jr., b. 4 Apr. 1914. Realtor. Educ: LL.B., Univ. of Memphis Law Schl.; Memphis State Univ.; Univ. of Tenn., Memphis. Appts. incl: Farm Equipment Mfr.; Exec. & Instr., Aircraft Factory, WWII; Real Estate Bus., 1950-; Broker & Realtor, Eugene M.Wade Jr. Realty Co., 1969-; Mbrships: Legis. Comms., Tenn. Assn. of Realtors & Memphis Bd. of Realtors; Nat. Assn. of Real Estate Bds.; Memphis & Shelby Co. Planning Commn., 1964-69; Vice Chmn.; ibid; US Congress Liaison, ibid, 1965-69; 4th Degree Mbr., Ktd. of Columbus; Roman Cath. Ch. Address: 756 S. Willet St., Memphis, TN 38104, U.S.A.

WADE, Lennis Preston, b. 30 June 1933. Professional Engineer. Educ: B.S., Va. Polytechnic Inst. & State Univ., Blacksburg, Va., 1955. Appts: Staff Engr., Assoc., Ptnr., V.P., Wiley & Wilson, Lynchburg, Va., 1958-; Mbrships: Va. Soc. Profl. Engrs.; Pres., ibid, 1970-71; Nat. Soc. Profl. Engrs.; Va. Assn. of Professions; Alumni Assn., Va. Polytechnic Inst. & State Univ.; Pres., Lynchburg Chapt., ibid, 1966-67; Tau Beta Pi; Chi Epsilon; Omicron Delta Kappa; Pershing Rifles Club; Cotillion Club. Hons. incl: Award of Societas Cincinnatorum Instituta, 1955; Disting. Serv. Award, Va. Soc. Profl. Engrs., 1971. Address: Wiley & Wilson, Inc., 2310 Langhorne Rd., Lynchburg, VA 24501, U.S.A. 7.

WADE, Neville Edward Henry, b. 5 Feb. 1945. Public Relations Manager. Educ: Coventry Tech. Coll.; Coventry Coll. of Art. Appts: P.R. Asst., Coventry Corp.; Press Off., Coventry Climax Engines Ltd.; P.R. Mgr., Lansing Bagnall Ltd. Mbrships: Inst. of P.R.; Inst. of Jrnlsts.; Brit. Direct Mail Advt. Assn.; Assoc., Brit. Assn. of Indl. Eds.; Hon. P.R. Off., Brit. Jr. Chmbrs. of Comm.; & Past Pres., Winchester Jr. Chmbr. Contbr. to Brit., European profl. jrnls. Address: Lansing Bagnall, Basingstoke, Hants. RG21 2XJ, U.K. 24.

WADE, Pauline L. (Mrs.) b. 26 Aug. 1910. Educator; Home Economist. Educ: Auburn Univ., Ala.; Grad. studies, Southern Union Coll., Wadley, Ala., & Univ. of Amherst, Mass.; framingham Coll., Mass. Appts. incl: Tchr., Vocational Home Economics, Wadley, Ala.; Tchr., Gen. Home Economics, Mt. Hope, Ala.; Home Serv. Advsr., Birmingham Housing Quthority; Tchr., H.S., Arlington, Mass.; Pres. & Gen. Salesman of own co. (w. husband), Wade's Maid Products, Maynard, Mass.; Home Economist, Birmingham Elec. Co., Birmingham Ala. Mbrships. incl: Am. Home Economics Assn.; Nat. Tchrs. Assn.; Mass. Tchrs. Assn.; Arlington Zonta; Past mbr., AAUW; Phi Kappa Sigma; Alpha Phi Epsilon. Recip., Citation for tchng. nutrition for adults, Pres. Truman, WWII. Address: P.O. Box 926, Marlin Rd., S. Harwich, Mass., Cape Cod, U.S.A.

WADE, Robert, b. 6 Jan. 1943. Artist; Educator. Educ: B.F.A., Univ. of Tex., Austin, 1965; M.A., Univ. of Calif., Berkeley, 1966. Appts: Instr., Art. McLennan Coll., Waco, 1966-70; Artist in Res., Northwood Inst., Cedar Hill, 1970-72; Dir., Northwood Exptl. Art Inst., Dallas, 1972-73; Asst. Prof., Art., N. tex. State Univ., Denton, 1973-. One man exhibs: Kelley Gall., Dallas, 1970, 71; Smither Gall., ibid, 1972; D Kornblee Gall., N.Y., 1971, 74. Grp. exhibs: Whitney Mus. Biennial, N.Y., 1969, 73; Options, Cinn. Mus. of Contemp. Art, 1973; Tyler Mus., Tex., 1973; Univ. of St. Thomas, Houston, 1973; Painting & Sculpture Today, Indpls. Mus. of Art, 1972; South-Southwest, Ft. Worth Mus., 1970; S. Tex. Sweet Funk, St. Edwards Univ., Austin, 1970. Hons: Nat. Endowment for the Arts Grant, 1973; N. Tex. State Univ. Rsch. Grant, 1973, 74. Address: 812 Haynes, Denton, TX 76201, U.S.A. 37.

WADE, Rosalind Herschel (Mrs. William Kean Symour), b. 9 Sept. 1909. Author; Journalist; Lecturer. Ed., Contemporary Review (incorporating The Fortnightly), U.K., 1970-. Mbrships: PEN (Comm., 1934-37); W. Country Writers' Assn. (Comm., 1953-64); Soc. of Women Writers & Jrnlsts. (Past V. Chmn.; Chmn., 1962-64; V.Pres., 1963-); The Poetry Soc. (Gen. Coun., 1962-65); Guildford & W. Surrey Br., ibid (Chmn., 1969-72). Publs: (Novels) Children, Be Happy, 1931; Kept Man, 1933; Pity the Child, 1934; Shadow Thy Dream, 1934; A Fawn in a Field, 1935; Men Ask for Beauty, 1936; Treasure in Heaven, 1937; Fairweather Faith, 1940; The Man of Promise 1941; Bracelet for Julia, 1942; Pride of the Family, 1943; Present Ending, 1946; As the Narcissus, 1946; The Widows, 1948; The Raft, 1950; The Falling Leaves, 1951; Alys at Endon, 1953; The Silly Dove, 1953; Cassandra Calls, 1954; Come Fill the Cup, 1955; Morning Break, 1956; Mrs. Jamison's Daughter, 1957; The Grain Will Grow, 1959; The Will of Heaven, 1960; A Small Shower, 1961; The Ramerson Case, 1962; New Pasture, 1964; The Vanished Days, 1966; Ladders, 1968; The Umbrella, 1970; The Golden Bowl, 1970; Mrs. Medlend's Private World, 1973; Happy Christmas, 1968; Contemporary Review, Poetry Review, Books & Bookmen, Cornish Review, etc. Hons: Prizes, Soc. of Women Writers & Jrnlsts. Address: White Cottage, Old Alresford, Hants., U.K. 1, 3, 11, 137.

WADE, Samuel David, b. 6 Dec. 1949. Microbiologist. Educ: B.S., Colo. State Univ., Ft. Collins, Colo. Appts: Rsch. Staff, Millipore Corp., Acton, Mass., 1971-; Bacteriologist, Norwood Hosp., Mass., 1971; Bd.Mbr., Maynard Bd. of Hlth., Mass., 1973-; Mbr., Maynard Hlth. Planning Coun., 1973-; Mbr., Task Force for Emergency Med. Servs., 1973-; Mbr., Gtr. Boston Hlth. Planning coun., 1973-. Mbrships: N.Y. Acad. of Sci.; Mbrships. Asst., Am. Pub. Hlth. Assn.; New England Br., Am. Assn. for Lab. Animal Sci.; Northeast Br., Am. Soc. for Microbiol.; Mass. Public Hlth. Assn.; Delta Upsilon. Address: P.O. Box 131, Maynard, MA 01754, U.S.A.

WADE, William Irl, Jr., b. 20 Sept. 1938. Physician. Educ: Little Rock Jr. Coll., Ark., 1956-59; Schl. of Med., Univ. of Ark., 1950-63; M.D.; Intern, Charity Hosp., New Orleans,1963-64; Res., USPHS Hosp., San FFrancisco, 1964-66. Appts: Lt. Cmdr., Chief, Outpatient Dept., San Fran., 1965; Surg. Cons., Highland, Alameda, Oakland, Calif., 1965; Family Physn., Little Rock, 1966-; Charter Mbr., Am. Acad. Emergency Room Physns., 1972-; Assoc. Prof., Family Prac., Med. Schl., Univ. of Ark., 1971-73. Mbrships incl: State Bd., Ed., State Paper, State Cancer Soc. Chmn., Profl. & Lay Educ., 1974; Rep., Am. Acad. ofFamily Prac.; Bd., Prog. Chmn., State Breast Exam. & Educ. Chmn., Ark. Acad. of Family Prac.; Pres., Rural Educ. Prog., Med. Schl., Univ. of Ark.; Soc. of Tchrs. Pres., Pulaski Co. Gen. Prac. Soc.; Jr. Chmbr. of Comm.; Sunday Schl. Tchr., St. Marks's Episc. Ch. Author of publs. in field. Winner of schol. awards. Address: 424 North Univ., Little Rock, AR 72205, U.S.A. 7.

WADE, William Raymond, b. 28 Oct. 1943. Professor of Mathematics. Educ: B.A. 1965, M.A. 1966, Ph.D. 1968, Univ. of Calif. Appts: Asst. Prof.-Assoc. Prof. Maths., Univ. of Tenn., 1968-; Cons., Oak Ridge Nat. Lab., Tenn., 1969-. Mbrships: Am. Math. Soc.; Math. Assn. of Am.; Sigma Xi; Pi Mu Epsilon. Publs: Papers incl: Sets of Divergence for the Group 2, San Francisco Meeting, Am. Math. Soc., Jan. 1974; Fast Walsh Transforms, series of Lectures at Oak Rodge Nat. Lab.; Contbr. to profl. jrnls. Address: 820 Ponder Rd., Knoxville, TN 37919, U.S.A. 125.

WADSWORTH, Dorothea Martin (Mrs. Eugene P. Wadsworth), b. 27 May 1917. Motel Owner & Manager. Educ: Oceana H.S.; Bible study, Back to the Bible Inst.; Bus. courses. Appts: Former owner, Wadsworth Super Market; Owner, Va. Reel Motor Lodge & C. & W. Realty Co., Chesapeake, Va. Mbrships: Past Pres., Pilot Club of Chesapeake; Past Gov., Dist II, & Dir., Exec. Bd. Mbr., Pilot Int.; Past Pres., Women's Div., Chesapeake Chmbr. of Comm.; Charter Mbr., Chesapeake Friends of Music, Chesapeake Friends of Lib., Chesapeake Beautification Coun., Tidewater Toastmistress Club; Steering Comm., Chesapeake Gen. Hosp. Fund Raising; Tidewater Assembly Family Life Comm.; Bd. of Dirs., Chesapeake Humane Soc. Hons: Hon. citizenship, var. cities. Address: 568 Kempsville Rd., Chesapeake, VA 23320, U.S.A. 125.

WADSWORTH, Gerald J., b. 19 May 1918. Machinery Company Executive. Educ: Grad., Gen. Motors Tech. Inst., 1940; Postgrad., Mich. State Coll., 1943. Appts: Tool Room Foreman, A.C. Spark Plug, 1941; Tool Maker, Indl. Metal Prod., Lansing, Mich., 1942-51; Foreman, ibid, 1951-52; Supt., 1952-68; Proposal Engr., 1968-69; Chief Sales Engr., 1969-; Adv. Planning Engr., 1969-. Mbrships: U.S. Army, 1944-46; Am. Bowling Congress; Am. Mus. Natural Hist.; Inl. Exec. Club; Republican; Presby.; Elk. Address: 2810 Delta River Dr., Lansing, MI 48906, U.S.A. 8,

WADSWORTH, Kevin Warren, b. 22 May 1948. U.S. Government Official. Educ: A.A., Valencia Jr. Coll., Orlando, Fla., 1969; B.A. Communication, Fla. Technological Univ., Orlando, 1971. Appts: Dist. Chmn., Fla. Student Congress, 1970; Attorney Gen., Fla. Technological Univ. Student Govt., 1970; Dir., P.R., ibid, 1971; Dir., P.R., Tau Kappa Epsilon Fraternity, 1971; Comm. of 20, Fla. Technological Univ., 1971; Res. Advsr., Fla. Technological Univ.; Campaign Mgr., Rep. Harvey W. Matthews; Chap. Servs. Dir., Tau

Kappa Epsilon Int. Fraterntiy; Exec. Asst., U.S. Senator Edward J. Gurney, R-Fla. Mbrships. incl: Dir., Tallahassee Jaycees; Tau Kappa Epsilon Int.; Regional Off., ibid; Delta Beta Pi; Fndng. Treas., ibid, 1968. Publs: Circuit Breakers (at press); Political column, Fla. Technological Univ. newspaper Future, 1970-71. Hons. incl: Jaycee of the Month, July 1973. Address: P.O. Box 5774, Tallahassee, FL 32301, U.S.A. 57, 117.

WAGENFUEHR, (Karl W.) Rolf, b. 5 Nov. 1905. University Professor. Educ: Studied econs. & statistics, Jena, Geneva & Kiel; Dr.rer.pol., Jena, 1928; Professorship, Heidelberg, 1957. Appts: Institut für Konjunkturforschung, Berlin, 1928-44; Statistical Off. of the British Zone, Minden, 1946-49; Wirtschaftwissenschaftliches Inst. der Gewerkschaften, Cologne, 1952-58; Dir. Gen., Statistical Off. of the E.E.C., Brussels, Luxemburg, 1958-66; Dir., Inst. für Int. vergleichende Wirtschafts- & Sozialstatistik, Univ. of Heidelberg, 1966-. Mbrships: Int. Statistical Inst.; Int. Assn. for Rsch. in Income & Wealth. Publs. incl Statistica in Europa, 1967; Wirtschafts- und Sozialstatistik, Band I, 1970, Band II, 1973. Recip. of hons. Address: Humboldtstrasse 10, D 69 Heidelberg, German Fed. Repub. 43.

WAGNER, Anabel Lee Ratcliff (Mrs.), b. 6 Sept. 1933. Physician; Anesthesiologist. Educ: B.A., Ind. Univ., 1955; M.D., 1959; Dipl., Am. Bd. of Anesthesiol., 1965. Appts: Intern, Meth. Hosp., Indpls., 1960; Res., Anesthesiol., Ind. Univ. Med. Ctr., 1961-62; Pt. Time Instr., ibid, 1963-; Tchng. Staff, VA Hosp., Indpls., 1962-63; Pvte. Prac., Lafayette, 1963-; Courtesy Staff, Purdue Univ. Hosp., W. Lafayette, 1970-. Fellow, Am. Coll. of Anesthesia. Mbrships. incl: Am. Soc. Anesthesiol.; Int. Rsch. Soc. (Anesthesia); Pan Am. Surg. Assn.; Phi Beta Kappa; Sigma Alpha Iota; Delta Phi Epsilon; Alpha Epsilon Delta; Kappa Kappa Kappa Address: 1834 Summit Drive, W. Lafayette, IN 47906, U.S.A.

WAGNER, Ann Capetillo, b. 19 Sept. 1926. Company President; Shop Manager. Educ: Grad., Garner Secretarial Coll., New Orleans, La. Appts: Prin., Nat. Assn. of Securities Dealers, C.H. Wagner & Co., Inc; Pres., Yankee Mortgage & Realty Co.; Mgr., Wellesley Inn Gift Shop; Columnist, Wellesley Townsman. Mbrships: Order Eastern Star; Christian Women's Assn. Address: P.O. Box 184, 2 Denton Rd., Wellesley, MA 02181, U.S.A. 5.

WAGNER, Charles Abraham, b. 10 Mar. 1901. Poet, Journalist, Historian. B.A., Columbia Coll.; Nieman Fellow, Harvard Univ.; M.A., Columbia Univ. Appts. incl: Book reviewer, art critic, N.Y. Daily Mirror, 1933-63; Ed.-in-Chief, Sunday Mirror mag., 1943-63; Exec. Sec., Poetry Soc. of America and Ed., PSA Bulletin, 1963-. Mbr., English Speaking Union, N.Y.C. Publs. incl: Poems of the Soil & Sea; Nearer the Bone; New Poems; Ed., Prize Poems; Harvard: Four Centuries & Freedoms. Numerous articles pub. in N.Y. Mirror, N.Y. Times. Poems pub. in N.Y. Times, Coronet, Christian Sci. Monitor, Chicago Tribune, N.Y. Herald Tribune, Poetry, Voices, Poetry Review etc. Hons. incl: 1st Prize in Poetry, Poetry Mag. of Chicago, 1930; 1st Prize, Edwin Markham Award, 1932; 1st Prize, Poetry Soc. of Am. Award, 1971. Address: Poetry Soc. of Am., 15 Gramercy Pk., New York, NY 10003, U.S.A. 2, 3, 6, 12.

WAGNER, Elaine Marie (Mrs. Darrell G. Wagner), b. 8 Mar. 1939. Librarian. Educ: B.A., Coll. of St. Catherine. Appts: Young Adult

Libn., St. Paul Pub. Lib., 1961-63; Coord., Br. Childrens Servs., ibid, 1963-64; Supvsr. of Publs. Off., 1964-65; Supvsr. of Community Rels., 1965-67; Supvsr. of Publs. Off., 1967-. Mbr., Delta Phi Lambda. Author, A Case of Bottled Murder, 1973. Address: 2152 St. Clair Ave., St. Paul, MN 55105, U.S.A. 5.

WAGNER, Elizabeth Marie (Smith) Hutchins, Librarian. Educ: B.S., Duke Univ., 1941; M.A. in L.S., Univ. of Mich., 1956. Appts: Asst. Libn., Young & Rubicam, Inc., 1956-64; Lib. Dir., Fremont Pub. Lib., 1964-67; Dir. of Lib. Servs., Young & Rubicam, Inc., 1967-71. Mbrships: Past Chmn., Advt. Div., Special Libs. Assn.; Past Dist. IV Chmn., Mich. Lib. Assn.; Past Dir., Lib. P.R. Coun.; N.J. Lib. Assn.; Chmn., Lit. Dept., Woman's Club of Cranbury, N.J.; Libn., Cranbury Histl. & Preservation Soc., Inc.; Phi Beta Kappa; Delta Phi Phi Kappa Phi. Publs: Freshman Advisory Handbook, Woman's Coll., Duke Univ., 1940. Hons: Grad. Magna Cum Laude, Duke Univ., 1941. Address: N. Main St., R.D.2, Cranbury, NJ 08512, U.S.A. 5, 6, 42.

WAGNER, Francis Stephen, b. 28 Feb. 1911. Historian; Librarian; Educator. Educ: HS Tchrs. Diploma, Univ. of Szeged, Hungary, 1935; Coll. Tchr. Diploma (Apponyi Coll.), ibid, 1935-37; Ph.D., 1940. Appts: Instr., Dept. of Hist., Univ. of Szeged, 1935-38; Prof. of Hist., Slavic & Hungarian Langs. & Lits., Budapest State Coll., 1938-45; Dir., Nat. Courses for Slovak Tchrs., Léva-Budapest, 1939-44; Slavic Specialist, & Hd., Czech. Sect., Min. of For. Affairs, Budapest, 1945-46; Hungarian Consul Gen., Bratislava, Czech., 1946-48; Dir., Hungarian Variety Hour (Radio), Bridgeport, Conn., & N.Y.C., U.S.A., 1949-53; Libn., Subject Cataloguer, Lib. of Congress, Wash. D.C., 1953-. Mbrships: Am. Histl. Assn.; Wash. Philos. Club; Am. Studies Assn.; Civil War Round Table of D.C.; Hleicon Soc., Toronto, Can. Publs: 9 monographs. inclng: Széchenyi & the Nationality Problem in the Habsburg Empire, 1960; The Hungarian Revolution in Perspective, 1967; Toward a New Central Europe, 1970; contbr. to Survival & the Bomb, Methods of Civil Defense; over 220 articles in profl. jrnls. & mags. Address: 4610 Franklin St., Kensington, MD 20795, U.S.A. 7, 13, 42, 57, 122, 125, 130, 131.

WAGNER, Helmut Eberhard Karl, b. 15 Mar. 1925. Company President. Fndr. in 1948 of Rehau Plastiks Grp. by progressive dev. of one of world's most important plastics factories; currently Pres. Mbrships: Beirat Bayerische Versicherungsbank AG; Beirat Dresdner Bank. Address: Chalet Castra Avarerum, CH 3780 Gstaad, Switzerland. 43, 92.

WAGNER, John Philip, b. 29 July 1943. Artist. Educ: B.A., Phila. Coll. of Art, Pa., U.S.A., 1965; M.F.A., Rinehart Schl. of Sculpture, Md. Inst. Coll. of Art, Balt., 1968. Appts: Fellow, Rinehart Schl. of Sculpture, 1965-67; Artist-in-Residence, Las Vegas, N.M., 1969-70. Publs: Flights, 1974; Black Range Tales, 2 vols.; Drawings in, Wipe Your Face, You Just Swallowed My Soul, by H. Prather, 1974. One-man shows: Jamison Galls., Santa Fe, N.M., 1970, 71, 72 & 73; Jamison Galls., Houston, Tex., 1974. Permanent Exhib: Okla. City Art Mus. Address: Route 1, Box 295-A, Santa Fe, NM 87501, U.S.A.

WAHLEN, Friedrich Traugott, b. 10 Apr. 1899. Educ: Dip., agr.ing., Swiss Fed. Inst. of Technol., Zurich. Appts. incl: Dir., Swiss Agric. Experiment Stn., Zurich, 1929; Deleg. for Switzerland to num. int. congresses; Commnr.,

War Food Prod., WWII; Mbr., Coun. of States (Senate), Canton of Zurich, 1942-49; Prof., Agronomy, Swiss Fed. Inst. of Technol., Zurich, 1943-49; Dir., Agric. Div., FAO, UN, Rome, Italy, 1949-57; Dpty. Dir. Gen., ibid, 1957-58; Elected to Swiss Fed. Coun., i/c successively of Dept. of Justice & Police, Dept. of Pub. Econ. & Political Dept. (For. Affairs); Pres., Swiss Confederation, 1961, retd. 1965; Pres., Commn. for the Total Revision of Swiss Fed. Constitution, 1967-. Mbrships: For. mbr., Royal Acad. of Sweden, 1946; For. mbr., Acad. of Bordeaux, France, 1967. Author of Wahlen Plan aiming at self-sufficiency in food supplies for war yrs. Hons. incl: Dr.iur.utr., Univ. of Basle, 1968; Dr.sc.techn., Swiss Fed. Inst. of Technol., Zurich, 1971. Address: Humboldtstrasse 39, Berne, Switzerland.

WAHLGREN, Christer (Fredrick Olof), b. 16 Oct. 1900. Army Officer; Publisher. Educ: Studies, 1918 & Univ. of Commerce, 1935-37. Appts: (Mil.) Commnd., 1920, Lieut., 1925, Capt., 1935, Major, 1943; Mng. Dir., Sydsvenska Dagbladets AB, 1937-67, Pres., Bd. of Dirs., from 1940; Chief Ed., Sydsvenska Dagbladet Snällposten, 1946-67; Pres.; Bd. of Dirs., Kvällspostens AB, from 1947. Mbrships: Rotary Club of Malmö, Sweden; Int. Press Inst.; Malmö Nat. Univ. Lund (Hon.). Author of På skilda fronter—upplevelser som officer och tidningsman (memoirs), 1970. Hons. incl: Kt., Spanish Mil. Order of the White Cross, 1929, Finnish Order of White Rose, 1942, Swedish Order of Sword, 1951; Cmdr., Danish Order of Dannebrog, 1967, Swedish Order of Vasa, 1972; Cmdr., Icelandic Order of the Falcon. Address: Sydsvenska Dagbladet, Box 145, S-201 21 Malmö, Sweden, 43, 134.

WAHLGREN, Olof G. Ch:son, b. 21 Sept. 1927. Chief Editor; Managing Director. Educ: B.A., 1951; M.A., 1954; Ph.D., 1957. Appts. incl: Jrnlst., Sydsvenska Dagbladet, Sweden, 1953-56, Dpty. Hd., Feature Dept., 1956-57, Paris Corres., 1957-61; Dpty. Chief Ed., 1961-67, Dpty. Mng. Dir., 1963-67, Chief Ed. & Mng. Dir., 1967-; Mng. Dir., Kvallsposten, 1963-. Mbrships. incl: Pres., S. Sweden Div., Swedish Div., Swedish Newspaper Assn., 1967-; Chmn., Swedish Nat. Comm., Int. Press Inst., 1972-; Bd. of Dirs., Sydsvenska Dagbladet & Kvallsposten, 1949-; Rotary Club, Malmo-Kirseberg, Sweden; Travellers Club, ibid. Publs. incl: Motsols genom Frankrike, 1962. Hons. incl: Kt., French Legion of Hon., 1968; Off., Italian Order of Merit, 1969; Cmdr., Finnish Order of the Lion, 1971; Kt., Danish Order of the Dannebrog, 1972; Cmdr., Icelandic Order of the Falcon. Address: Sydsvenska Dagbladet, Box 145, S-201 21 Malmö 1, Sweden. 134.

WAHREN, Karl Heinz, b. 28 Apr. 1933. Composer. Educ: Dip., Hochschule für Musik, Berlin, 1961; Pvte. study w. Josef Rufer in Berlin & w. Karl Amadeus Hartmann in Munich, 1961-63. Free-lance Composer. Major Compositions incl: Sonatine für Klavier, premiered Berlin, 1959; Frétillement, premd. Berlin, 1966; Sequenzen 1966, premd. Berlin, 1966; Wechselspiele, premd., Budapest, 1967; für Flöte u. 12 Instrumente, premd., Berlin Festival, 1967; L'art pour l'art, premd., Witten, 1968; 2 Klavierkonzert, premd. Berlin Festival, 1968; Konzert für klarinette u. Orchester (1968); Du sollst nicht töten, premd., Berlin Festival, 1969; Schallplatte Pelca "Frieden-Peace", 1970; Application for Organ, premd., Berlin, 1970; Increase, premd. Kassel, 1971; Die Wirbelsäulen Flöte (Homage à Maja Kowskij), premd., Berlin, 1972; Passioni, premd. Berlin, 1973; Dionysos meets Apollo, premd. Berlin, 1974; Vergangenes, 1974.

Mbrships: Gruppe Neue Musik Berlin; JGNM. Hons. incl: German Rome Prize (Villa Massimo), 1969/70. Address: Jenaer Str. 12, 1 Berlin 31, Germany. 21.

WAIDE, Peggy Ann Sullivan (Mrs. Harry D. Waide), b. 11 Dec. 1936. Realtor Associate. Educ: Western Ky. Univ.; Completed sev. Real Estate courses & Grad. (Courses I & II), Realtors Inst., Ky. Assn. of Realtors, Lexington, Ky., 1973. Appts. incl: Realtor Assoc., Charles Ashby Real Estate, Madisonville, Ky. Mbrships. incl: Ky. Assn. of Realtors, Sec., Class of '75; Publicity Chmn., Madisonville-Hopkins Co. Bd. of Realtors; Nat. Assn. of Realtors; Nat. Inst. of Real Estate Brokers; active Mbr., 1st United Meth. Ch., Madisonville, Mbr., United Meth. Women & Tchr., Sunday Schl. Nursery Dept.; actively connected w. Girl Scouting movement, organizing Troop 139, 1969- & helping w. many activities inclng. Madisonvilles' Newspaper Recycling Effort w. aid of all local area troops; formed Hoe-Hummers Garden Club for girls (jointly assocd. w. Pennyroyal Girl Scout Coun. & Garden Club Intermediate of Ky., Inc.), 1972 & helped w. many of their achievements inclng. installation of Mini-Park, Hopkins Co. Hosp., 1972; Jr. Garden Club State Chmn., 1973-75 for Garden Club of Ky., Inc. & Life Mbr., ibid, 1974-; Instrumental in org. Greenfields Garden Club, 1st Pres., 1971 & active current Mbr.; V.P., Madisonville Garden Club Coun., 1972-74; Earlybird Homemakers Club, Treas., 1971 & current V.P. & Mbrship. Chmn.; former Lectr. for Weight-Watchers of Kentuckiana, Inc. Recip. many awards from Gardening & Scouting Grps. inclng. Special Appreciation Award & Presentation Prog. (Silver Engraved Bowl) for Outstanding Serv. to Greenfields Garden Club, 1974. Address: 973 Skyline Drive, Madisonville, KY 42431, U.S.A. 76, 125.

WAIN, John Barrington, b. 14 Mar. 1925. Author. Educ: Oxford Univ. Appts: Fereday Fellow, St. John's Coll., Oxford, 1946-49; Lectr., Engl. Lit., Univ. of Reading, 1947-55; Churchill Vis. Prof., Univ. of Bristol, 1967; Vis. Prof., Univ. Experimentale de Vincennes, Paris, France, 1969; 1st Fellow in Creative Arts, Brasenose Coll., Oxford, 1971-72. Publs. incl: Hurry on Down, 1953; Living in the Present, 1955; The Contenders, 1958; A Travelling Woman, 1959; Nuncle & other stories, 1960; The Young Visitors, 1965; The Smaller Sky, 1967; A Winter in the Hills, 1970; The Life Guard & Other Stories, 1971; (poetry) A Word Carved on a Sill, 1956; Weep Before God, 1961; Wildtrack, 1965; Letters to Five Artists, 1969; (criticism) Preliminary Essays, 1957; Essays on Literature & Ideas, 1963; The Living World of Shakespeare, 1964; (autobiography) Sprightly Running, 1962. Address: c/o Macmillan & Co. Ltd. Little Essex St, London WC2, U.K. 1.

WAINWRIGHT, Gordon Ray, b. 14 Apr. 1937. Teacher. Educ: B.A., Nottingham Univ., 1958; Cert.Ed., Hull Univ., 1959; Reading for B.Ed., Sunderland Polytechnic, 1974. Appts: Tchr., Engl., Manvers Schl., Nottingham, 1959-61; Asst. Lectr., Liberal Studies, Coll. of Technol., Hull, 1961-65; Lectr., Engl. & Gen. Studies, Hebburn Tech. Coll., 1965-68; Hd., Dept. of Engl. & Liberal Studies, Wearside Coll., Sunderland, 1968-. Mbrships: Assoc. Mbr., Brit. Inst. of Mgmt.; Fellow, Royal Soc. of Arts; Soc. of Authors; Assn. for Liberal Educ.; Soc. for Acad. Gaming & Simulation in Educ. & Trng. Publs: Efficiency in Reading, 1965; Towards Efficiency in Reading, 1968; Rapid Reading Made Simple, 1972; Contbr. to num. periodicals. Address: 22 Hawes Court, Seaburn Dene, Sunderland SR6 8NU, U.K. 3.

WAINWRIGHT, Mary Lee Sellers (Mrs.), b. 24 Apr. 1913. Singer; Musician; Composer; Educator; Student of the Bible. Educ: studied Music, Stetson Univ., Deland, Fla.; Ldrship. Trng. Schl., Deland, Fla. Appts. incl: on Action Comm. to Pres. & Am. Security Coun., Wash. D.C.; Instr. for Democracy, U.S. Govt. (all levels); Music Therapist, S. Fla. State Hosp., Hollywood, 10 yrs.; rsch. for U.S. Govt. Mbrships: Am. Soc. of Composers, Authors & Publrs.; Nat. Fedn. of Music Clubs; World of Music; Chmn. for Fla., Int. Rels., U.N. Am. Music Legis.; Pres., Royal Poinciaia Dist., Fla. Fedn. of Music Clubs & Hollywood Music Club; Music Chmn., 1st Bapt. Ch. & Hollywood Woman's Club; Hon. Mbr., Pres., Lib. Am. Christian Coll.; active in Comm. to Help Restore the U.S. Constitution; Musicians Club of Am.; Trustee, White House of the Confederacy. Publs: The Master Key; Florida the Sunshine State. Songs incl: The Master Key; Wake Up America; The March of Faith; The Masquerade Is Over; Let the Bells of Freedom Ring; It's the Truth; When You Are Near; Good News for All Nations; God Is Love; I Want to Live Like Jesus; Wake Up World (world premiere, Miami, Feb. 4, 1974). Hons. incl: Oscar for Wake Up Am., Acad. of Motion Pictures Arts & Scis., 1960; ASCAP Award; Award for 18 annual yrs. in Parade of Am. Music Concerts; Stars, Double Blue & Double Gold Ribbons, Nat. Fedn. of Music Clubs; Hons. from City of Hollywood, S. Fla. State Hosp.; Honor Roll, Nat. Police Offs. Hall of Fame; Songwriters Hall of Fame. Address: 1519 Dewey St., Hollywood, FL 33020, U.S.A. 5, 57, 128, 138.

WAISSENBERGER, Robert, b. 16 Aug. 1926. Museum Director. Educ: Dr.phil., Univ. of Vienna, Austria. Appts: Cons., fine arts, Kulturamt, Vienna; Dir., Vienna town museums. Publs: Wien & die Kunst in unserem Jahrhundert, 1965; Buchkunst aus Wien, 1966; Arnulf Neuwirth, monography, 1967; Die Wiener Secession, 1971; Hagenbund— Geschichte der Wiener Künstlervereinigung (Mitteilungen der Osterreichischen Galerie), 1972; Num. articles on Viennese art & cultural hist. Address: Semmelweisgasse 49, A 1210 Vienna, Austria. 43.

WAKEMAN, Geoffrey, b. 18 Aug. 1926. Librarian. Educ: Keble Coll., Oxford, U.K. Appts: Travelling Libn., Herts.; Tutor Libn., Alsager Coll. of Educ.; Tutor, Libn., Glasgow Coll. of Building; Sr. Lectr., Loughborough Schl. of Librarianship. Publs: Typographia naturalis, 1967; Aspects of Victorian Lithography, 1970; XIX Century Illustration: Some Methods Used in English Books, 1970; English Hand Made Papers Suitable for Bookwork, 1972; Victorian Book Illustration: The Technical Revolution, 1973; contbr. to var. jrnls. Address: 28 Pantain Rd., Loughborough, Leicestershire, U.K. 30.

WAKIM, Salim Y., b. 28 Feb. 1931. Author. Educ: Studied Law, French Univ. of Beirut; Special courses on hist. in Europe. Appts: Collaborator, Beirut daily (Engl.) & Assaman daily (Arabic), & many other leading newspapers & mags., 1960-61; Assigned task of interviewing Kings & Hds. of State, 1958-68; Owner-Dir., Afro-Asian Publs., 1959-72; Nominee for Parliament (Independent Democrat), 1st constituency of Beirut, 1968 & 1972; Cons. & Intermediary in int. bus., 1972-. Mbrships: Int. League for the Rights of Man, N.Y.; PEN Club, Beirut. Publs. incl: History of Communism in the Middle East, 1971; The Permanent Struggle between Nationalism & Internationalism, 1971; An Empire on Horseback (The Mongols), 1973; On Lebanese

Heritage, 4 vols., 1974; Islamology & Arab Literature (essays), 1974; La Femme, ses Droits et ses Libertés, 1974. Recip., Cmdr., St. Peter's Cross, Paris, France, 1965. Address: Achrafieh, Zahar St., Victor Khouri Bldg., Beirut, Lebanon. 97.

WALBESSER, Henry Herman, Jr., b. 9 May 1935. Educator. Educ: B. S., SUNY at Buffalo, 1958; M.A., Univ. of Md., 1960; Ph.D., ibid, 1965. Appts. incl: Dir. of Evaluation, AAAS, Wash., D.C., 1962-68; Dir., Univ. of Md. Maths. Proj., 1968-73; Dir., Bur. of Educl. Rsch. & Field Servs., Univ. of Md., 1972-73; Prof., Asst. Dean i/c Grad. Studies & Rsch., ibid, 1973-. Mbrships: Fellow, Am. Math. Soc.; AAUP; Am. Educl. Rsch. Assn.; Nat. Coun. of Tchrs. of Maths.; Nat. Assn. for Rsch. in Sci. Tchng. Publs. incl: An Evaluation Model, 1968; Constructing Behavioral Objectives, 1969; Games & Algorithms (co-author), 1971; How to Meet Accountability (w. J. Marvin Cook), 1973. Hons. incl: B.S., 1958; Fulbright-Hays Fellow, Uruguay, S. Am., 1968, 1969; Disting. Achievement Award, Educl. Press Assn. of Am., 1973. Address: College of Education, Univ. of Maryland, College Park, MD 20742, U.S.A. 2, 6, 141.

WALCOTT, Clyde Leopold, b. 17 Jan. 1926. Personnel Officer. Educ: Harrison Coll., Barbados. Appts: Soc. Welfare Advsr., Guyana Sugar Prods. Assn., 1957-70; Indl. Welfare Off., Bookers Sugar Estates, 1970; Personnel Off., Barbados Shipping & Trading Co., 1970-. Mbrships: Sr. V.P., Barbados Cricket Assn.; Chmn., Barbados Nat. Sports Coun. Publs: Island Cricketers. Hons: O.B.E., 1965; Golden Arrow of Achievement, A.A., 1969; Life Mbr., M.C.C. Address: Wildey Heights, St. Michael, Barbados.

WALD, Arnoldo, b. 28 June 1932. Lawyer; Professor of Law; Bank Director. Educ: LL.B., LL.D., Nat. Law Schl., Brazilian Univ., 1949-55; Specialisation in Com. Commercial Law, Inst. de Droit Comparé, Paris, France. Appts: Corp. Lawyer, Rio de Janeiro, Sao Baulo & Brazilia, 1953-; Pvte. Lectr., Civil Law, 1956; Atty., State of Guanabara, 1963-; Gen. Atty., 1965-67; Full Prof., Pvte. Law, 1966-; Mbr., Fedl. Bur., Brazilian Bar Assn., 1964-; Assoc. Prof., Paris Law Schl., 1970; Vis. Prof., U.S.A. & France; Consulting Lawyer, multinational corps. & govt. agcies; Rep. of Brazil, int. legal meetings & congs., Paris, Munich & Buenos Aires; V.P., Banco Intercontinental de Investimentos, Brazil. Mbrships: Soc. Int. de Droit Comparé, Paris, France; nst. de Derecho Comparado de Mex.; Academic Paulista de Direito; Gen. Sec.,Brazilian Comm. of Comp. Law of UNESCO; Inst. dos Advogados Brasileiros (Gen. Sec., 1965-67); Pres., Brazilian Br., Assn. Henri Capitant pour la Culture Juridique. Publs: Author, co-author, 5 books on law & econs. in Portuguese; Contbr. num. articles in field. Hons: Medal Henri Capitant, 1953; Astolfo Rezende do Instituto dos Advogados Prize, 1954; Medal of High Distinction of Mil. Ct., 1966; Medal of Sociedade Brasileira de Direito Aeronautico, 1964. Address: Avenida Rio Branco, 123-18° andar, Rio de Janeiro, Brazil.

WALDBOTT, George Lee, b. 14 Jan. 1898. Physician. Educ: M.D., Univ. of Heidelberg, Germany, 1921; Intern, Jewish Hosp., Frankfort, 1922-23 & Henry Ford Hosp., Detroit, Mich., U.S.A., 1923-24. Appts. incl: Fndr. & former Chief, allergy clinics in 4 Detroit hosps.; Emeritus Physn. in Allergy, Harper Hosp.; Honorary Physn., Hutzel Hosp., Detroit. Mbrships. incl: Co-fndr. & former Pres., Mich. Allergy Soc.; Fndr. & Sec., Int.

Soc. for Flouride Rsch. & Ed. of jrnl. Flouride; AMA; Fellow; Acad. of Allergy, Am. Coll. Chest Physns. & Am. Coll. of Allerglsts; Alr Pollution Control Assn. Publs: Contact Dermatitis, 1953; Health Effects of Environmental Pollutants, 1973; about 250 rsch. papers, articles. Hons: 1st Prize for Exhib., Occupational Allergy, European Acad. of Allergy, The Hague, Netherlands, 1958; 1st Prize, CUTIS 6th Annual Manuscript Contest, 1970. Address: 28411 Hoover Rd., Warren, MI 48093, U.S.A. 130.

WALDEN, Amelia Elizabeth, Author; Novelist. Appts. incl: Off-Broadway Dir. & Actress, 1939-46; Tchr., Drama & Theatre Arts, to 1946; Contbr. to newspapers & mags., to 1946. Publs: 3 plays produced off Broadway; almost 50 novels inclng. The Spy Who Talked Tóo Much, 1968; Walk in a Tall Shadow, 1968; A Spycase Built for Two; The Case of the Diamond Eye, 1969; What Happened to Candy Carmichael, 1970; Valerie Valentine is Missing, 1971; Stay to Win, 1971; Play Ball, McGill! , 1972; Where Was Everyone When Sabrina Screamed? , 1973; Go, Phillips, Go! , 1974; Pioneer, Young Adult novel. The Walden Collection., estab. by Schl. of Lib. Sci., Case Western Reserve Univ., 1971. Address: 89 N. Compo Rd., Westport, CT 06880, U.S.A. 2, 5, 6, 30, 128, 138.

WALDHOUR, Elizabeth Ardelle (Mrs.), b. 15 Mar. 1918. Educator. Educ: A.B., Univ. of Ga., 1940; M.A., Univ. of Miami, 1957; Columbia Univ. Appts: Tchr., Engl., Savannah H.S., Ga., 1940-46; Instr., Univ. of Ga., Athens, 1946-47; Instr., Armstrong Coll., Savannah, 1955-57; Asst. Prof., Engl., Univ. of Miami, Fla., 1958-; w. Bouhan Lawrence Williams & Levy, 1948-52; WTOC-TV, 1953; Merrill Lynch Pierce Fenner & Smith, 1954-55. Mbrships. incl: Nat. Coun. Tchrs. of Engl.; S. Atlantic MLA; Hist. Assn. of S. Fla.; AAUP; MLA; Gamma Sigma Sigma; Alpha Lambda Delta; Univ. of Miami Womens Club. Compositions: Farewell Song; A Ticket to Dreamland; Swords & Roses Waltz. Author of poems & short stories. Address: 341 Fluvia Ave., Coral Gables, FL 33134, U.S.A. 125.

WALDIE, D., b. 20 Apr. 1930. Engineer. Educ: B. Eng., Univ. of Qld., Brisbane, Australia; B.Econ., ibid. Appts: Mgr., Townsville Regional Elec. Bd., Qld., 1969-70; Dpty. Commnr. for Elec. Supply (Engrng.), 1970-. Mbrships: Inst. of Engrs. (Australia); Inst. of Elec. Engrs.; Fellow, Australian Inst. of Mgmt.; Fellow, Royal Inst. of Pub. Admin. Publs: Sev. tech. papers on elec. dev. Address: State Electricity Commission of Queensland, G.P.O. Box 10, Brisbane,.Qld., Australia 4001. 23.

WALDINGER, Herbert Francis, b. 23 Nov. 1921. Dentist. Educ: Univ. of Ala., 1939-42; D.D.S., Univ. of Pitts. Schl. of Dental Med., 1945; Postgrad., N.Y. Univ. Schl. of Dentistry, 1955-56. Appts. incl: Prac. of dentistry, specializing in oral rehab., Flushing, N.Y., 1949-; Asst. Clin. Prof., N.Y. Univ. Schl. of Dentistry, N.Y.C., 1958-59; Bd. of Dirs., Queens Child Guidance Ctrs., 1960-66; Pres., Flushing-Queens Clild Guidance Ctr., 1964-66; Co-Chmn., Queens Div., United Jewish Appeal, 1962-63; Served to Capt., U.S.A.F., 1951-53. Mbrships. incl: Acad. Gen. Dentistry; Am. Dental Assn.; Med. Dental Plan Specialists; N.Y. Univ. Oral Rehab. Assn.; Alpha Omega; Discussion Ldr., Great Books Fndn., 1959-64. Recip., Nat. Cancer Fndn. Award, 1960. Address: 3 Ballantine Lane Kings Point, NY 11024, U.S.A. 6.

WALDMANN, Edward B., b. 6 Feb. 1926. Physician. Educ: B.S.M., Creighton Univ., Neb., 1946; M.D., Schl. of Med., ibid, 1948; M.S., Grad. Schl. ibid,1950; Res. in Psych., St. Bernard's Hosp., Council Bluffs, Iowa, 1950; Student Naval Flight Surg. Schl. of Aviation Med., USN. Pensacola, Fla., 1950-1951; Postgrad. Schl., Univ. of Minn, Mayo Fndn., 1952-55. Appts: incl: Asst. in Med., Schl. of Med., Creighton Univ., 1950-56; Grp. Prac., Internal Med., Med. Assocs. of Phoenix, Ariz. 1959-68; Currently Dir., Outpatient Servs., St. Joseph's Hosp. & Med. Ctrl. ibid. Vis. Staff, Good Samaritan & John C. Lincoln Hosps., 1969-, St. Luke's Hosp. & Med. Ctr., 1959-; Attng. Physn., Gen. Med. & Nephrol St. Joseph's Mercy Clin., Phoenix, 1959-. Mbrships. incl: Bd. of Dirs., Maricopa Heart Assn., 1962-63, 1971-; AMA; Maricopa Co. Med. Soc.; Ariz. State Med. Assn.; Life Phi Rho Sigma; Sigma Xi; Fellow, Am. Coll. Physns., Am. Coll. Chest Physns. & Coll. of Clin. Pharmacol.; Dipl., Nat. Bd. Med. Examiners, Am. Bd. Internal Med.; many others. Author & co-author, articles in profl. jrnls. Address: St. Josephs' Hosp. & Med. Ctr., P.O. Box 2071, Phoenix, AZ 85001, U.S.A. 9, 126.

WALDREP, (Rev.) Andrew Jackson (Jack), b. 30 Aug. 1916. Methodist Minister. Educ: Young Harris Coll., 1934-36; Emory Univ., 1936-38; Candler Schl. of Theol., 1938-41; Univ. of Wis., 1945-48. Appts. incl: Paster, Dillard-Rabun Gap, Ga. Community Ch. & Tchr., Rabun Gap Schls.; Paster, Albany Community Meth. Ch., Albany Wis.; Prof., Young Harris Coll.; Pastor Dir., Towns-Union Co. Coop. Min.; Dir., The Lord's Acre Plan, Home Off., Asheville, N.C., 1957-. Mbrships. incl: Rural Sociol. Soc. of Am.; Trustee, Hinton Rural Life Ctr., Hayesville; Past Pres., V.P. & Sec., N.C. Kiwanis Club; N.Ga. Meth. Annual Conf.; Western N.C. Meth. Conf.; Chap., Dist. Soil and Water Conservation Dist.; Int. Speakers Bur.; Eta Sigma Phi; Alpha Kappa Delta. Author of sev. articles in ch. publs. Hons. incl: Rural Min. of the Yr., 1951; Nat. Merrit Award, Soil & Water Conservation Serv., 1972. Address: Rt. l, Box 139, Horse Shoe, NC 28742, U.S.A. 2, 7, 125.

WALDSTEIN, Wilhelm, b. 9 Nov. 1897. Author; Composer. Educ: D.Phil., 1920. Appts: Secondary Schl. Tchr., 1921-38; Pvte. Tchr., 1938-45; Min. of Educ., 1946; Hd. of Fine Arts Dept., ibid, 1952-62; Tchr., Acad. of Music, Vienna, Austria, 1962-64; Councillor, Min. of Educ., 1962-72. Mbrships. incl: Bd. of Austrian P.E.N.; Pres., Osterreichlscher Schriftstellerveerband, 1965-72; Hon. Pres., ibid, 1972-; Bd., Osterreichische Gesellschaft für zeitgenössische Musik; Weinheber Gesellschaft; Franz Schmidt-Gemeinde. Publs. incl: Lied eines Menschen, 1937; Die goldene Blume, 1948; Pole der Menschheit, 1949; KKunst und Ethos, 1954; Waage des Lebens, 1956; Frühe Schatten, 1963; Erscheinung und Zeichen, 1964; Hans Gal, 1965; Brennspiegel, 1966; Herbstpastorale, 1967; Zwischenreich, 1968; Das gerettete Erbe, 1970; Bild und Widerbild, 1972. Composter of song cycles, chamber music, orchestral music & choral works. Hons. incl: Grosses Ehrenzeichen der Rep. Osterreich, 1959; Ehrenring des Bundesministeriums für Unterricht, 1962; Ehrenkreuz für Wissenschaft und Kunst, 1. Klasse, 1967; Kulturpreis des Landes Niederösterreich, 1967; Grosses Ehrenzeichen des Landes Niederösterreich, 1973. Address: Alserstrasse 69, A 1080 Vienna, Austria.

WALFORD, Lionel A., b. 29 May 1905. Marine Biologist. Educ: A.B., Stanford Univ., Calif., U.S.A., 1929; M.A., Harvard Univ., Cambridge, Mass., 1932; Ph.D., ibid, 1935. Appts: Aquatic Biologist, Calif. Fish & Game Commn., 1926-31; U.S. Bur. of Fisheries, 1936-; Dir.,Wash Biological Lab., 1958-60; Dir., Sandy Hook Marine Labe., 1960-71; Sr. Biologist, 1971-. Mbrships: Explorers Club; Fellow, AAAS; Hon. Fellow, Am. Geographical Soc.; Hon. Fellow, Atlantic Estuarine Soc. Publs: Game Fishes of the Pacific Coast from Alaska to the Equator, 1937; Living Resources of the Sea, 1958. Hons: D.Sc., Hartwick Coll., Oneonta, N.Y., 1962; D.Sc., Monmouth Coll., Ill., 1969; Disting. Serv. Award, U.S. Dept. of the Interior, 1969. Address: Sandy Hook Marine Laboratory, Highlands, NJ 07716, U.S.A.

WALGRAVE, Jan-Baptist Joseph (Father Henry), b. 30 Apr. 1911. Professor. Educ: S.Theol. lector, Collegium sancti Thomae Aquinatis O.P., 1930-38; S. Theol. Dr., Univ. of Louvain, 1938-42; S. Theol. Magister, Rome, 1954. Appts: Prof., Fundamental Theol., Collegium sancti Thomae Aquinatis O.P., 1942-68; Regent, ibid, 1958-64; Prof., Philos.,Vlaamse Katholieke Hogeschool, Antwerp, 1950-66; Rector, ibid, 1960-62; Prof., Theol. Hoger Inst. voor Godsdienstwetenschappen, Univ. of Louvain, 1957-67; Prof., Fundamental Theol., Fac., ibid, 1969. Mbrships: on num. Edit. Bds; Int. Acad. of Relig. Scis; Belgian Soc. of Logic & Philos. of Sci. Publs. incl: Newman 1960; Op menselijke grondslag, 1951; Newman vandaag, 1957; Person & Society, Belgian edit., 1960, English, 1965, French, 1968; Op de Grondslag van het Woord, 1965, French, edit. 1967, Spanish, 1970; Heil, Geloof en Openbaring, 1968, French edit., 1970; Unfolding Revelation, 1972. Hons: Award for Newman the Theologian, Koninklijke Vlaamse Acad., 1944; Vijfjaarlijkse Prijs voor het Essay uitgeloofd door de Provincie West-Vlaandersen, for book on Ortega y Gasset, 1957; Off., Order of Leopold, 1963. Address: Ravenstraat 112 B-3000 Louvain, Belgium. 43.

WALHOUT, John R., b. 5 Mar. 1925. Company Vice-President, Treasurer, Educ: B.S., Ferris State Coll., U.S.A.; LL.B., La Salle Ext. Univ. Appts: C.P.A.-Maihofer, Moore-De Long, 1945-56; Now V.P.-Treas., Challenge Stamping & Porcelain Co.; Puffer-Hubbard Refrigerator Div.; Pres., Aetna Plumbing Inds., Inc.; Treas., Metal-Wood Corp. Mbrships: Am. Inst. of Cert. Pub. Accts.; Mich. Assn. of Cert. Pub. Accts.; Financial Execs. Inst.; Spring Lane Country Club; Grand Haven Rotary; Econ. Club. Detroit, Mich. Mayor, City of Grand Haven, Mich., 1971-. Address: 1505 Pine Ridge Drv., Grand Haven, MI 49417, U.S.A. 8, 16, 130.

WALKER, Annita Louise Curry (Mrs.) b. 28 Mar. 1941. Research Chemist; Real Estate Sales person. Educ: B.S. Fla. A. & M. Univ.; Howard Univ., Wash. D.C.; Univ. of Miami, LaSalle Ext. Univ., 1973-74. Appts: Rsch. Chem. Dept. of the Treasury, U.S. Govt. & Dept. of Hlth., Educ. & Welfare; currently writing a book. Mbrships: Am. Chem. Soc.; Delta Sigma Theta; Sec., Epsilon Tau Lambda, 1973-75; Sec., Treas., Nat. Fedn. of Fed. Employees, Am. Fedn. of Govt. Employees; Whitmauer Collector's Guild; Longine's Symphonette Soc. Publs: co-author, 6 scientific rsch. papers in Jrnl. of Official Analytical Chemists, Jrnl. of Agriculture Food Chemistry & Bulletin of Environmental Contamination, Hons: White & Gold Hon. Soc.; Plaque, Community Ldrs. of Am., 1970; Schlrship., Most Well-rounded Student, 1960; Medal, Class Valedictorian, 1959; Medallion, Am. Legion Schl. Award, 1959; Miss Univ. High, 1958-59; Student Coun. Pres., 1958-59; Cert. 1st Prize, Writing Contest,

1959; Medals, Maths. & Sci. Awards, 1959; Bausche & Lomb Hon. Sci. Award, 1959; 1st Prize, Home Improvement Award, 1959; Miss Sophomore, 1960-61; Chem. Perserverance Award, 1963. Address: 5825 S. W. 62nd Terr., Miami, FL 33143, U.S.A. 46, 57, 130, 138.

WALKER, Audrey Jackson. Teacher. Educ: B.S. (cum laude), Hampton Inst., 1943; M.A., ibid, 1951. Appts: Instr., Biol. Dept., Hampton Inst., Rsch. Asst., P.R. Dept., ibid, Admin. Sec., Off. of Dean of Men.; Mbr., Gov.'s Cornmn. on Status of Women in Va., 1970-73. Mbrships: Pres., Va. State Fedn. of Club Women Inc.: Past Pres., Hampton City Fedn. of Club Women, Hampton Women's Serv. League, Inc.; Va. Women's Pol. Caucus. Author of a drama & short stories. Creator: an Easter pageant, Then Came Another Mary; histl. pageant, Who Is Your Neighbor. Hons. incl: Bronze Plaque for Dedicated Servs., Va. State Fedn. of Club Women: certs. of appreciation for community servs. Address: 1101 Aberdeen Rd., Hampton, VA 23666, U.S.A. 125.

WALKER, Bessie Griffith (Mrs.), b. 16 July 1929. Educator. Educ: B.S., Madison Coll., 1951; M.Ed., Radford Coll., 1964; Univ. of Va. & Radford Coll., 1966-70. Appts: Tchr., Pulaski H.S., Va., 1951-55; Tchr., Pocahontas H.S., Va., 1955-66 & 67-71; Prin., ibid, 1971-72; Tchr. & Asst. Prin., 1972-74; Asst. Supvsr. of Engl., State Dept. of Educ., Va., 1966-67. Mbrships: Delta Kappa Gamma; Kappa Delta Pi; Nat. Coun. Tchrs. of Engl; Va. Assn. of Tchrs. of Engl.; NEA; Va. & Tazewell Co. Educ. Assns.; Nat. Assn. Humanities Educ: AAUW; Bd. of Dir., Historic Pocahontas, Inc.; Bd. of Stewards, 1st United Meth. Ch.; Sigma Sigma Sigma. Publs: Incl. Award Cert., Soc. of Outstanding Am. H.S. Students, 1972-73. Address: P.O. Box 491, 43 E. Water St., Pocahontas, VA 24635, U.S.A. 57, 125.

WALKER, Charles Joseph, b. 2 May 1913. Assistant Postmaster. Educ: LaSalle Ext. Univ., 1931-32; Postal Serv. Courses; "Opto" Postal Trng., Univ. of Okla., Norman; Civil Defense Mgmt., Battle Creek, Mich. Appts: Foreman of Mails, 1961; Supt. of Mails, 1963; Asst. Postmaster, 1973-; Civil Defense Dir., Miami Co., Ind., & City of Peru, Ind., 1959-; Chmn., Selective Serv. Bd., ret. 1974 after 20 yrs. serv. Mbrships: Sec.-Treas., 1970-74, Asst. V.P., 1974-, Region IV, US Civil Defense Coun.; Pres., Ind. Civil Defense Dirs. Assn., 1969-70; 5th Dist. V.P., Nat. Assn. Postal Supvsrs., 1967; 1st V.P., Miami Co. Histl. Soc., 1973-; Cmdr., Post 14, 1952, Vice Cmdr., 5th Dist., 1956, Am. Legion; Chef de Guerre, Forty & Eight Voiture 1014, 1956; Pres., Peru YMCA Rocks & Minerals Club, 1974; Pres., Lambda Chapt., Phi Delta Kappa, 1952; F. & A. Mason; Scottish Rite; Shriner; B.P.O. Elks; Miami Co. Geneal. Soc.; Nat. Histl. Soc.; Smithsonian Assoc.; Mississinewa Country Club. Ed. & Bus. Mgr., The Indiana Civil Defender Magazine, 1971-72. Hons: Man of the Yr., Peru Daily Tribune, 1961; Prof. Neal Merrit Award, to outstanding mbr., Peru YMCA Rocks & Minerals Club, 1970. Address: Dir., Miami Co. Civil Defense, Room 102, Court House, Peru, IN 46970, U.S.A. 120.

WALKER, Clareta, b. 11 July 1907. Home Economics Educator. Educ: B.Ed. (Home Econs.), Iowa State Univ., Ames, 1932; post-grad work, Columbia Univ., N.Y., 1939; M.Sc., Univ. of Ill., 1947. Appts: Tchr., Home Econs., Amboy Township H.S., 1933-35; Ext. Advsr. Macoupin Co., Ill., 1935-42; Ill. Rural Youth Ext. Specialist, 1942-57; State Comm., Int. Four-H Exchange, 1948-; Family Life Ext. Specialist, Univ. of Ill., Urbana, Coop. Ext.

Serv. & U.S. Dept. of Agric., 1957-. Mbrships: Am. & Ill. Home Econs. Assns.; Nat. & Ill. Couns. on Family Rels.; Am. & Ill. Assns. of Univ. Profs; Nat. & Ill. Bus. & Profl. Women; Epsilon Sigma Phi; Gamma Sigma Delta; Phi Sigma; Alpha Gamma Delta. Recip. 25 yr. Service Award, Int. Four-H Youth Exchange Alumni Assn. Address: 612 West Iowa St., Urbana, IL 61801, U.S.A. 5.

WALKER, David Maxwell, b. 9 Apr. 1920. University Professor. Educ: M.A., Univ. of Glasgow, U.K., 1946; LL.B., ibid, 1948; Ph.D., Univ. of Edinburgh, 1952; LL.D., ibid, 1960; LL.B., Univ. of London, 1957; LL.D., ibid, 1968; Advocate, Scottish Bar, 1948; Barrister-at-Law, Middle Temple, 1957. Appts: Served WWII; Prac., Scottish Bar, 1948-53; Prof., Jurisprudence, Univ. of Glasgow, 1954-58; Regius Prof., Law, ibid, 1958-; Dean, Fac. of Law, 1956-59; Dir., Scottish Univs. Law Inst., 1974-. Mbrships: Stair Soc.; Scottish Hist. Soc.; Soc. of Pub. Tchrs. of Law; Fellow, Soc. of Antiquaries in Scotland. Publs: incl: Law of Prescription & Limitation in Scotland, 1973; Law of Civil Remedies in Scotland, 1974; Contbr. to collaborative works & legal jrnls. Hons. incl: Queen's Counsel, Scotland, 1958; LL.D., Edinburgh, 1974. Address: Dept. of Pvte. Law, Univ. of Glasgow, Glasgow, G12 8QQ, Scotland, U.K. 1, 41.

WALKER, Estellene Paxton, b. 13 Sept. 1911. Librarian. Educ: B.A., Univ. of Tenn., 1933; B.S., Emory Univ., Atlanta, Ga., 1935. Appts: Hd., Co. Dept., Lawson McGhee Lib., Knoxville, Tenn., 1935-41; Post Libn., Ft. Jackson, S.C., 1941-45; Materials-Supply Libn., Army Special Serv., European Theater, 1945-46; Dir., S.C. State Lib. Bd., Columbia, 1946-69; Libn., S.C. State Lib., Columbia, 1969-. Mbrships: Phi Kappa Phi; ALA; Southeastern Lib. Assn.; Pres., S.C. Lib. Assn., 1973-75; Chmn., Southeastern States Cooperative Lib. Survey, 1973-75; Pres., Am. Assn. of State Libs., 1967; S.C. Soc. Defenders of Wildlife; Am. Humane Assn. Author of articles in profl. jrnls. Address: S.C. State Lib., 1500 Senate St., P.O. Box 11469, Columbia, SC 29211, U.S.A. 2, 7.

WALKER, Eunice A. (Mrs.). Writer. Educ: A.B., Univ. of Ark.; Geo. Wash. Univ. Reporter & Feature Writer, The Monett (Mo.) Times & The Kansas City Star. Mbrships: House of Reps. Comm. on Sci. & Astronautics; Nat. Trust for Historic Preservation; Charter Mbr., Nat. Histl. Soc.; Nat. League Am. Pen Women; City Tavern Assn.; Capital Presswomen, Capital Chapt., Nat. Fed. of Press Women, Inc.; Huguenot Soc.; Intercontinental Biographical Assn.; Hereditary Register of U.S.A. Lambda Tau; Kappa Delta Pi; Mortar Bd. Publs: (Woodrow Wilson) Arms Control Dimension in our National Security; Mission of the Arms Control & Disarmament Agency; Physiological & Psychological Aspects of Man In Space. Recip. of Best Feature Story Prize, Nat. League Am. Pen Women, 1954. Address: 205 James Thurber Ct., Falls Church, VA 22046, U.S.A. 5, 57, 125, 132, 138.

WALKER, Harry G(ranville), b. 10 Jan. 1902. Entomologist. Educ: A.B., S.W. Coll., 1925; M.Sc., Kan. State Univ., 1926; Ph.D., Ohio State Univ., 1930. Appts. incl: Entomol., Va. Truck Experiment Stn., Norfolk, 1931-45; Grp. Ldr., Agric. Chems., Penn Salt Chem. Co., Phila., 1945-56; Plant Protection Specialist, Food & Agric. Org., UN, Rome, Italy, 1956-62 & Nicosia, Cyprus, 1962-66; Entomol., L.A. State & Co. Arboretum, Arcadia, Calif., U.S.A., 1966-72. Fellow, AAAS. Mbrships. incl: Past

Pres., Am. Entomol. Soc.; Past Chmn. Eastern Br., Entomol. Soc. Am.; Entomol. Soc. Wash.; Kan. Entomol. Soc.; Phi Kappa Phi; Gamma Sigma Delta; Gamma Alpha; Sigma Xi; Life, Entomol. Club of S. Calif.; Charter, Weed Soc. Am. Author of num. bulls., sci. papers & popular articles. Address: 610 Rose Marie Drive, Arcadia, CA 91006, U.S.A. 9, 14, 120.

WALKER, Iain Charles, b. 13 Jan. 1938. Archaeologist. Educ: M.A., Univ. of Edinburgh, U.K., 1961; Ph.D., Univ. of Bath, 1969. Appts. incl: Staff Archaeologist, Fortress of Louisbourg Restoration, Nova Scotia, 1962-66; Staff Archaeologist, Nat. Historic Sites Serv., Ottawa, 1966-70; Hd., Artefact Rsch., ibid, 1970-. Mbrships. incl: Soc. for Post-Medieval Archaeol.; Fellow, Soc. of Antiquaries of Scotland; Fellow, Royal Soc. of Antiquaries of Ireland; Coun. for N.E. Histl. Archaeol., Exec. Bd. Mbr., 1970-; Bristol & Gloucestershire Archaeoll. Soc.; Bristol Archaeoll. Rsch. Grp.; Bristol Indl. Archaeol. Soc.; Bristol Record Soc.; Ontario Archaeoll. Soc. Author of over 60 articles in profl. jrnls. of independent publs. dealing w. prehist. of NE Scotland, post-medieval & indl. British archaeol., histl. archaeol. in N. Am. & W. Africa & theory in histl. archaeol. Hons: Chalmers-Jervise Prizewinner, Soc. of Antiquaries of Scotland, 1965; Canada Coun. Doctl. Fellowship, 1967. Address: Dept. of Indian & Northern Affairs, Nat. & Historic Sites Br., 123 Kent St., Ottawa, K1A OH4 Canada. 6.

WALKER, (Sir) James G., b. 7 May 1913. Grazier. Appts: Owner, Cumberland Santa Gertrudis Stud, Longreach, Wakefield Merino Sheep Property, Issford, & Camden Park Sheep & Cattle Property, Longreach; Shire Chmn., Longreach Shire Coun., 1957; Councillor, ibid, 1954-; Chmn., Central Western Regional Elec., 1966-; Dpty. Chmn., Local Authorities of Qld., 1967-; Dpty. Pres., Santa-Gertrudis Assn. of Australia; Dpty. Chmn., Longreach Pastoral Coll.; Dir., Longreach Printing Co. Mbrships. incl: Sr. Clerk, Presby. Ch., Longreach; Past Pres., Longreach Rotary Club; Past Pres., Trustee & Life mbr., Longreach Club; Past Asst. Grand Master, Qld. Masonic Lodge; Qld. Club; Patron, Longreach Agricl. Show Soc. Hons: M.B.E., 1965; Kt. Bach., 1971. Address: Lambeth, Longreach, Australia, 4730.

WALKER, James Murray, b. 2 June 1924. Anthropologist; Clergyman. Educ: A.B., Mercer Univ., 1951; B.D., New Orleans Bapt. Theol. Sem., 1954; Th.D., ibid, 1960; Tulane Univ., 1960-61; Emory Univ., 1963; N.Y. Univ. in Jerusalem, Israel, 1965; Univ. of Colo., 1966; Univ. of Ky., 1967-70. Appts: Instr., Meteorol., USAF Tech. Schls., 1946-47; Lic. Bapt. Min., 1950; Ordained, 1953; Tutor, Relig., Union Bapt. Theol. Sem., 1954-55; Mbr., Ed. Staff, Times Picayune Publng. Co., 1955-61; Fellow, Archaeol., New Orleans Bapt. Theol. Sem. 1957-59; var. pastoral positions, 1959-; Asst. Prof., Hist. & Relig., Cumberland Coll., Ky. & Chmn., Educ. Comm., Whitley Co. Dev. Coun., 1961-63; Assoc. Prof., Relig. & Soc. Sci., Cumberland Coll., Ky., 1963-66; Asst. Prof., Anthropol. & Sociol., Eastern Ky. Univ., 1966-69; Assoc. Prof., Anthropol., ibid, 1969-. Mbrships. incl: Am. Anthropol. Assn.; Am. Ethnol. Soc.; Soc. for Am. Archaeol.; Archaeol. Inst. of Am.; Evangelical Theol. Soc. Publs: The Biblical & Historical Background of the Rise of the Zoroastrian Religion, 1960; History of Anthropology at Eastern Kentucky University, 1970; articles on linguistic rsch. in profl. jrnls. Hons. incl: Nat. Sci. Fndn. Grant for Anthropol. Inst., Univ. of Colo., 1966; Ky. Col., 1970. Address: 37 Lakeshore Dr., Deacon Hills, Richmond, KY 40475, U.S.A. 7, 15.

WALKER, John Alexander, b. 10 June 1922. Company Executive. Educ: Muhlenburg Coll., 1 yr. & Univ. of Penn., 2 yrs.; Grad., Northwestern Univ., 1944; Ensign, Navy, ROTC Prog., 1944. Appts. incl: Dist. Mgr., Hotpoint Distributing Div., Gen. Elec. Co., 1946-58; Lowe's Co., Inc., 1958-, Exec. V.P.; Dir., Lowe's Cos., Inc., Lowe's Profit-Sharing Plant & Trust, Lowe's Charitable & Trust Fndn. & Wilkes Dev. Corp.; former Chmn., N. Wilkesboro Housing Authority (HUD) & Wilkes Co. Planning Commn.; Dir., N.C. Home Builders Assn.; Dir., Brad Ragan, Inc.; Trustee, Northwestern Financial Investors. Mbrships. incl: Dir., Wilkes YMCA; Chmn., Bd. Deacons, N. Wilkesboro Presby. Ch.; Chmn., Elk's Club House Comm.; Mason; Shrine; Phi Kappa Sigma; Bus. Advsry. Coun. of Appalachian State Univ.; Republican Nat. Finance Comm.; former Pres., Oakwoods Country Club; Blowing Rock Country Club; Roaring Gap Club; Capitol Hill Club; Boca Raton Club; Charlotte City Club. Author of sev. publd. articles in field of bus. Hons. incl: Candidate for Lt. Gov. of N.C., 1972; Pres.' Award for Excellence & Distribution, Gen. Elec. Co.; N.C. Home Builders Assn. Award; N.C. Realtors Award; Wilkes Co. Man of Yr.; Financial Analysts Fedn. Award; "Salute to the Pres." Dinner Award, 1972. Address: 104 Coffey St., N. Wilkesboro, NC 28659, U.S.A. 2, 11, 22, 114, 125.

WALKER, Lucille Hill, (Mrs. Julius Waring), b. 2 Feb. 1900. Lecturer on Subjects of Interest to Women. Educ: A.B., Tex. Woman's Univ.; postgrad. courses, Tex. Technological Univ. Appts: Ed., Tex. Clubwoman, 1949-54; Lectr., Beta Delphian Club of Plainview, Tex., 9 yrs., Woman's Club of Plainview, 2 yrs., Book Club of Dimmitt, 6 yrs.; Music Dir., Presby. Ch., Plainview, 15 yrs.; Tchr., H.S. Sci., Chem. & Phys., Memphis, Tex., 4 yrs. Mbrships. incl: Chmn., Austin Bd. of Trustee, & Pres., Tex. Fedn. Women's Clubs; Pres., Knife & Fork Club, Plainview; Hale Co. Chmn., Democratic Party; Pres., Hale Co. Histl. Soc. Contbr., Lubbock Avalanche Jrnl., Gen. Fedn. of Women's Clubs Mag. Hons. incl: Citizen-of-Yr. for Plainview, 1960; Awards from U.S. Treasury Dept., Tex. Histl. Commn. Address: 704 W. 11th St., Plainview, TX 79072, U.S.A. 79, 114, 125.

WALKER, Ralph Spence, b. 25 May 1904. University Professor. Educ: M.A., Aberdeen Univ., 1928; B.A., 1931, M.A., 1934, Cambridge Univ. Appts: Sr. Engl. Master, Derby Schl., 1931-34; Lectr., Engl. Lang., Aberdeen Univ., 1936-44; Lectr., Engl. Lit., ibid, 1944-49; Sr. Lectr., 1949-55; Molson Prof. of Engl., McGill Univ., Montreal, 1955-70; Chmn., Dept. of Engl., ibid, 1955-66; Pt.-time Supvsr., St. Catharine's Coll., Cambridge, 1970-73; Lectr. on Shakespeare, Beaver Coll., U.S.A., London Prog., 1973-. Mbrships: Past Chmn., Assn. of Univ. Tchrs. of Scotland; Past Nat. Exec. Comm. Mbr., Assn. of Univ. Tchrs. of G.B.; Scottish Nat. Trust; English Speaking Union; Int. Assn. of Univ. Profs. of Engl. Publs. incl: Ed.-James Beattie's Diary, 1733, 1947; James Beattie's Daybook, 1773-98, 1948; James Boswell's Correspondence with John Johnston of Grange, 1966. Hons: Mbrs.' Prizewinner, Cambridge, 1931; Hon. Schol. St. Catharine's Coll., ibid; Emeritus Prof., McGill Univ., Montreal. Address: Peaveley House, Haslingfield, Cambridge CB3 7JE, U.K. 88, 128, 139.

WALKER, Robert Smith, b. 23 Dec. 1942. Legislative Assistant to U.S. Congressman. Educ: B.S., Educ., Millersville State Coll., 1964; M.A., Pol. Sci., Univ. of Del., 1968. Appts:

Tchr., Penn Manor Sr. H.S., Pa., 1964-67; Pa. Nat. Guard, 1967-73; Legislative Asst. to Congressman Edwin D. Eshleman, 1969-. Also Staff Coord. for Labor, Citizens for Nixon/Agnew, 1968; Press Room Dir., Repub. Nat. Conven., 1972; Inaugural Ball Dir., Presidential Inaugural Comm., 1972. Mbrships. incl: Past Pres., Repub. Communications Assn.; Young Repubs. of Lancaster Co.; Treas., & Exec. Comm., Bull Elephants. Publs: Contbr. to periodicals. Hons: Pa. State Winner, Voice of Democracy Contest, 1958, '60; Pres.' Cert., Pa. Jaycees, 1966; Freedoms Fndn. Award, 1973. Address: 6065 Parkridge Drive, E. Petersburg, PA 17502, U.S.A. 57, 114, 117.

WALKER, Sidney Harris, b. 14 Aug. 1925. Dentist. Educ: B.S., Hampton Inst., 1950; D.D.S., Howard Univ., 1958. Appts: Intern, Guggenheim Dental Clin., N.Y.C., 1953-59; Pvte. Prac. Dental Surg., 1959-73. Mbrships. incl: NAACP; Urban League; YMCA; Metropol. Police Boys Club; Robert T. Freeman Dental Soc.; Nat. Dental Soc.; Hu-Dent, 1958; Omega Psi Phi; Am. Legion; Southern Md. Dental Soc.; Md. State Dental Soc.; Am. Dental Assn.; Sr. Deacon, Marshal, Master of ceremonies, Sr. Warden, Past Master, Harmony Lodge 22; Jones Mem. Meth. Ch.; Kiwanis Int. Club; Grand Insp. Gen. 33, United Supreme Coun. Address: 826 Fairoak Ave., W. Hyattsville, MD 20782, U.S.A.

WALKER-MACRAN, Hugh Stewart Douglas, b. 1 Apr. 1929. School President. Appts: Sec., Am. Theatre of Paris, France, 1950-51; Co-Fndr., English Schl. of Paris (w. Mary J. Cosyn), 1954; Admnstr., ibid, 1966-73; Pres. Dir. Gen., 1973. Hon. mbr., Basset Hound Club de France, 1971. Other activities; Small parts in films w. Boris Vian; Small parts in Michel Audiard's "La Veuve en Or" & Clement's "La Maison sous les Arbres"; Organised Son et Lumière at Alexander Dumas' Chateau, Monte Cristo, 1969 & 1970. Address: 38 quai de l'Ecluse, 78290 Croissy-sur-Seine, France.

WALKER, William George, b. 2 Sept. 1928. University Professor & Dean. Educ: B.A., Univ. of Sydney, Australia, 1951; M.A., 1955; Ph.D., Univ. of Ill., U.S.A., 1958. Appts. incl: Lectr., Educ., Armidale Tchrs. Coll.; Sr. Lectr.-Assoc. Prof.-Prof., Educ., Univ. of New Engl. Mbrships. incl: Coun., Aust. Coll. Educ., Armidale Coll. of Adv. Educ.; Phi Delta Kappa; World Educ. Fellowship. Publs. incl: Headmasters for Better Schools; The Principal at Work; Theory & Practice in Educational Administration; Educational Administration; International Perspectives; School, College & University; Explorations in Educational Administration; A Glossary of Educational Terms: Usage in Five English Speaking Countries. Address: Univ. of New Engl., Armidale, N.S.W. 2351, Australia. 23.

WALL, Byron Emerson, b. 19 Apr. 1943. Composer; Teacher. Educ: Tulane Univ., U.S.A., 1961-65; St. John's Coll., Annapolis, 1965-66; Hope Coll., Vienna, 1966; B.S., Drew Univ., 1968; Univ. of Ill., 1968; Univ. of Toronto, Canada, 1971-; Piano student of Ellsworth Snyder; Bio-Energetic Analysis & trng. w. Kenneth R. Allen. Appts: Pres., Rochdale Coll., Toronto, Canada, 1968-69; V.P. & Treas., House of Anansi Press Ltd., Toronto, 1970-71; Pres., Thales Holding Co. Ltd., Toronto, 1969-; Tchng. Fellow, Univ. of Toronto, 1972-. Mbrships: Math. Assn. of Am.; Inst. for the Hist. & Philos. of Sci. & Technol., Toronto; Coun. of Schl. of Grad. Studies, Univ. of Toronto; U.S. Chess Fedn.; Corres. Chess League of Am.; Fellowship of Reconciliation. Compositions incl: Manual for Draft-Age

Immigrants to Canada; Sonata for Organ; 4 Little Piano Pieces. Recip., George Sidney Brett Mem. Fellowship, 1972. Address: Inst. for the Hist. & Philos. of Sci. & Technol., Univ. of Toronto, Toronto M5S 1AI Canada. 6.

WALL, Isabell Louise (Wood), b. 26 Oct. 1909. Public School Teacher & Clergywoman. Educ: Appalachian State Tchrs. Coll., Boone, N.C., 1928-33; Draughn's Bus. Coll. W.S., N.C., 1944-45; Kee Coll., Cleveland, Tenn., 1950-51; High Point Coll., N.C., 1958-60. Appts. incl: Pub. Schl. Tchr., Surry, Randolph & Davie Cos., N.C.; Prin. of Elem., 2 yrs., Hd., Jr. H.S., Ariz.; Tchr., Miracle Valley Bible Coll., ibid; var. commercial posts; preaching missions abroad. Mbrships: Fndr. & Pres., Int. Miracle Fellowship, 15 yrs.; past-mbr., P.R. Bd., Davie Co., N.C. Publs: Kaleidoscopic Poetry & Songs; Spiritual Steps; My Trip to the Grandfather Mountain; song, "Mother"; articles on relig. subjects; poems; contbr. to anthols., Poetry of the Americias, 1973 & Clover Collection of Verse, 1974. Address: 3231 High Point Rd., Winston-Salem P.O. Box 4622, NC 27107, U.S.A. 57.

WALLACE, Carolynn Reid (Mrs.), b. 26 June 1942. University Professor. Educ: B.A., Fisk Univ., Nashville, Tenn., U.S.A., 1964; M.A., Adelphi Univ., Garden City, N.Y., 1965; Ph.D., Geo. Wash. Univ., Wash. D.C., 1974. Appts: Instr., Talladega Coll., Ala., 1965-66; Instr., Howard Univ., Wash. D.C., 967-68; Asst. Prof., Bowie State Coll., Md., 1968-70; Adjunct Prof., Howard Univ., 1970-71; Asst. Prof., Grinnell Coll., Iowa, 1972-73; Fulbright Prof., Univ. of Guyana, Georgetown, 1973-74. Mbrship: Pres., Basielus, Pi Chapt., Alpha Kappa Alpha. Publs: The Letters of Charles Chesnutt: 1923 Spingarn Winner; Symbolism in Ralph Ellison's Invisible Man; Silhouettes in Black & White (play); Introduction to book of poetry, Black Chicago. Poetry readings given to univ. & community audiences, U.S.A., S. Am., & Caribbean. Hons: Rockefeller Schlr., 1960-64; Alternate John Hay Whitney Fellow, 1964-65; Ford Schlr., 1970-71; D.Litt., Hamilton State Univ., Tuscon, Ariz., 1973; Fulbright Schlr., 1973-74. Address: 506 S. Boundary St., Williamsburg, VA 23183, U.S.A. 5, 138.

WALLACE, Catherine Therese, b. 10 Mar. 1917. Educator. Educ: B.A., Dalhousie Univ., Halifax, Canada, 1939; M.A., Ph.D., St. John's Univ., N.Y. 1945, '52. Appts: Tchr., jr. & sr. H.S., N.Y. & Mass., 1939-53; Prin., Notre Dame H.S., Vancouver, B.C., 1959-65; Prof. Engl.-Pres., Mt. St. Vincent Univ., 959-. Mbrships. incl: Pres. & Dir., Assn. Univs. & Colls. Canada; Bd. Dirs., Serv. for Admission to Coll. & Univ.; Assn. Commonwealth Univs.; Coun. & Exec., ibid, 1972; Trustee, Inst. Rsch. on Pub. Policy. Hons: LL.D., St. Thomas Univ., 1969; D.C.L., Univ. of King's Coll., 1971; LL.D., Mt. Allison Univ., 1971; Medal of Serv., Order of Canada, 1972; LL.D., Univ. of N.B., 1973. Address: Apt. 528, 200 Willett St., Halifax, N.S., Canada. 2, 138.

WALLACE, David Russell, b. 27 June 1913. Public Health Dentist. Educ: B.S., Allegheny Coll., Meadville, Pa., 1935; M.A., Ohio State Univ., Columbus, 1939; D.D.S., Univ. of Pitts., Pa., 1943; M. Pub. Hlth. Admin., Univ. of N.C., Chapel Hill, 1958. Appts. incl: Dir. of Dental Hlth., Va. State Dept. of Hlth., 1954-59; Lectr., Med. Coll. of Va., 1954-59; Dir., Dental Hlth., N.J. Dept. of Hlth., 1959-68; Prof., Pub. Hlth., Seton Hall Coll. of Med. & Dentistry, 1959-68; Lectr., Pub. Hlth., Fairleigh Dickinson Univ., N.J., 1959-68; Dir. Dental Hlth., Pa. Dept. of Hlth., 968-; Asst. to Dir., Gov.'s Hlth. Servs.,

Commonwealth of Pa., 1972-; Legislative Liaison, Pa. Dept. of Hlth., 1972-; Sr. Dental Surg., U.S. Pub. Hlth. Serv. Mbrships. incl: Am. Dental Assn.; Pres., Assn. State & Territorial Dental Dirs.; Pres., Am. Assn. Pub. Hlth. Dentists. Co-Author, APHA Manual for Public Health Dentists (in preparation); Contbr. to profl. jrnls. Address: Division of Dental Health, Pennsylvania State Dept. of Health, Harrisburg, PA 17120, U.S.A. 6.

WALLACE, Gladys B. (Mrs.), b. 5 June 1923. Librarian. Educ: B.S., Oglethorpe Univ., Atlanta, Ga., U.S.A., 1961; M.L.S., Emory Univ., Atlanta, 1966; Postgrad., Univ. of Ga., Athens, 1970-71. Appts: Libn., Pub. elem. schls., Atlanta, 1954-66; Hd. Libn., Northside H.S., Atlanta, 1966-. Mbrships: ALA; Ga. Lib. Assn.; Southeastern Lib. Assn.; Metropol. Atlanta Lib. Assn.; Bd. of Dirs., Nat. Alumni Assn. of Oglethorpe Univ.; Women's Assn.; Atlanta Symph. Orch. Recip., Nat. Defense Educ. Act grants, 1963 & 1965. Address: 275 Collier Rd., N.W., Apt. 15, Atlanta, GA 30309, U.S.A. 5, 138.

WALLACE, Glenn Walker. Civic Worker. Educ: Grad., Mission Schl., Boston; Piano w. Carlo Buonamici, Boston. Mbrships: Fndr., Past Pres., Utah Symph.; Fndr., Pres., Ballet West; Fndr., Civic Music Assn.; Hon. mbr., Altrusa Int.; Boston Sewing Circle, 1916; Jr. League of Boston & Salt Lake; Phi Beta Kappa, 1973. Hons: Grand Cross, Elaine Knightly Order St. Brigitte, 1967; Woman of Yr., Lake Coun. of Women Hall of Fame, 1968; Only citizen to receive Gold State seal pin from Gov., 1972; Venerable Order, St. John of Jerusalem, 1972; Woman of Yr. Award for cultural achievement, AAUW.; H.H.D., Westminster Coll., 1968, Coll. of Eastern Utah, 1973. Address: 2520 Walker Lane, Salt Lake City, UT 84117, U.S.A. 2, 5, 9, 125, 132, 138.

WALLACE, Harold Lew, b. 9 Nov. 1932. College Professor. Educ: A.B., Ind. Univ., Bloomington, Ind., 1961; M.A., 1964; Ph.D., 1970. Appts. incl: Tchr., Hist. & Engl., Moorseville H.S., Ind., 1961-63; Tchng. Asst., Ind. Univ., 1963-64; Ind. Univ. Fellowship, 1964-65; Asst.-Assoc. Prof., Hist., Murray State Univ., Ky., 1965-71; Prof., Hist. & Chmn., Soc. Sci. Dept., Northern Ky. State Coll., Highland Heights, 1971-. Mbrships. incl: Edit. Bd., Univ. Press of Ky.; Chmn., Publs. Comm., Northern Ky. State Coll.; Ky. Hist. & Bicentennial Celebration Comm.; Am. Hist. Assn.; Org. Am. Histns.; Alpha Epsilon Delta; Phi Alpha Theta. Publs: The Crisis in Coal, 1975; Truman & the Politics of Upset; contbr. to mags. & jrnls. Cons., Narrator, The Next Crisis (documentary film), 1973. Recip., var. grants & fellowships. Address: Soc. Sci. Dept., Northern Ky. State Coll., Highland Heights, KY 41076, U.S.A. 13, 125.

WALLACE, Helen. Instructor & Lecturer, The Art of T'ai Chi Ch'uan. Educ: Univ. of Calif., 1955; Univ. of San Francisco, 1957. Appts: Pvte. Prac.; Fndr. & Dir. of T'ai Chi Ch'uan Exalted Hour; Originator of T'ai Chi Fans. Mbr. of Int. Assn. of Educators for World Peace. Author of T'ai Chi Ch'uan: Yang/Yin and Heaven. Guest on sev. TV & radio programs. Address: P.O. Box 5542, San Francisco, CA 94101, U.S.A. 57.

WALLACE, Irving, b. 19 Mar. 1916. Author. Educ: Williams Inst., Berkeley, Calif. Publs: The Fabulous Originals, 1956; The Square Pegs, 1958; The Fabulous Showman, 1960; The Chapman Report, 1961; The Sins of Philip Fleming, 1962; The Twenty-Seventh Wife, 1962; The Prize, 1963; The Three Sirens,

1964; The Man, 1965; The Sunday Gentleman, 1966; The Plot, 1967; The Writing of One Novel, 1969; The Seven Minutes, 1969; The Nympho & Other Maniacs, 1971; The Word, 1972. Contbr. to Ency. Britannica, Colliers Ency.; Am. Oxford Ency. Mbrships. incl: The Soc. of Authors, London; Authors League of Am., N.Y.; Writers Guild of Am., Los Angeles; The Manuscript Soc. Carbondale, Ill. Hons: George Washington Carver Inst. Award, 1964; Commonwealth Club of Calif., literary award, 1964; Bestsellers Inst. Paperback of the Yr. award, 1965. Address: c/o Paul Gitlin, Counselor at Law, Ernst, Cane, Berner & Gitlin, 5 West 45th St., N.Y., NY 10036, U.S.A. 1, 2, 3, 30, 128, 130.

WALLACE, Katie Dolly Cross. School Teacher & Principal. Educ: B.S., Jackson State Coll., 1949; M.S., Ind. Univ., Bloomington, 1954; further studies, Knoxville Coll., Tenn. Appts: Asst. Prin. & Tchr., Bobo, Miss., 1939-42; Prin. & Tchr., Crowder, Miss., 1942-43; Tchr., Tutwiler, Miss., 1943-44, Ruleville, 1945-46; Prin. & Tchr., Rome, Miss., 1946-49; Tchr., Myrtle Hall H.S., Clarksdale, Miss., 1949, Girls' P.E. Inst., 1949-51; Tchr., P.E. Inst., 1951-62; Prin., Myrtle Hall Elem. Schl., 1951-. Mbrships. incl: Fndr. & Organizer, Bus. & Profl. Club, Clarksdale; Nat. Tchrs. Assn.; Nat. Elem. Schls. Prins. Assn.; Am. Assn. on Mental Deficiency. Author, poetry & composer of songs. Recip., Am. Nat. Red Cross Certs. for Outstanding Fund Efforts, 1964, '65, '66. Address: 1202 6th St., Clarksdale, MS 38614, U.S.A. 5, 15, 57, 125.

WALLACE, Leon Harry, b. 24 Jan. 1904. Attorney; Law Teacher. Educ: Univ. of Ill., 1921-23; A.B., Ind. Univ., 1925; J.D., ibid, 1933. Appts. incl: Ptnr., Wallace, Randel & Wallace, Attys., Ind., 1933-45; Assoc. Prof., Law, Ind. Univ., 1945-47; Prof., ibid, 1947-51; Dean & Prof., 1951-66; Charles McGuffey Hepburn Prof., 1966-; Cons., State of Ind., Ind.-Ky. Boundary, 1966-; Gov.'s Rep., Int. Constitution Revision Comm., 1967-69; Special Hearing Off., U.S. Dept. of Justice, 1965-68; Special Master, U.S. Dist. Ct., No. Dist. Ind., 1969-72. Mbrships: Am. Bar. Assn. (Chmn., Local Govt. Law Sect., 1964-65); Ind. State Bar. Assn. (House of Delegs., 1957-71); Sec.-Treas., Ind. Bar Fndn., 1960-; Treas., Ind. Co. Legal Educ. Forum, 1966-; Phi Delta Phi (Pres., 1949-51); Phi Beta Kappa; Order of Coif; Am. Law Inst.; Am. Acad. of Pol. Sci.; Am. Acad. of Pol. & Soc. Scis.; Inst. of Judicial Admin. Contbr. to law jrnls. Address: 939 S. High St., Bloomington, IN 47401, U.S.A. 2, 8, 13, 15, 69, 108, 120, 128.

WALLACE, Sarah Leslie, b. 28 Oct. 1914. Librarian. Educ: A.B., Coll. of St. Catherine, 1935; B.S., ibid, 1936. Appts. incl: Asst., Ref. Dept., Mnpls. Pub. Lib., 1936-42; Publicity Asst., ibid, 1942-45; Administrative Asst., 1945-54; Administrative Asst., i/c of P.R. & Rsch., 1954-58; P.R. Off., 1958-63; Instr., Lib. P.R. & Pub. Lib. Admin., Coll. of St. Catherine, 1944-60; Publs. Off., Lib. of Congress, 1963-; Edit., Quarterly Jrnl. of Lib. of Congress. Mbrships: Mbrship. Chmn., ALA, 1962-63; Chmn., P.R. Sect., Lib. Admin. Div., ibid, 1964-65; Chmn., Adult Servs. Div., Special Promotion Comm., 1961-62; Chmn., Lib. Publs. Round Table, 1960-61. Publs. incl: CoCo-author & illustrator, Patrons Are People; Author & illustrator, Promotion Ideas for Small Public Libraries. Recip. of hons. Address: 8705 Jones Mill Rd., Wash. DC 20015, U.S.A. 5.

WALLACH, Jehuda L., b. 12 Mar. 1921. Professor. Educ: B.A., Hebrew Univ., Jerusalem, 1962; D.Phil., Oxford Univ.,

1962-65. Appts: Mbr., Perm. Staff of Haganah (Jewish underground army), 1945-; 2nd. i/c infantry battalion, outbreak of War of Independence, 1947; Major & battalion cmdr., 1948; Col. & brigade cmdr., 1949; var. appts. w. rank of Col., 1949-65; Ret. as Col. (Res.), 1965; Sr. Lectr., Mil. Hist., Tel-Aviv Univ., 1965; Assoc. Prof., ibid, 1972; Rsch. Fellow, Inst. of German Hist., Tel-Aviv Univ. 1971-; Dpty. Dir., ibid, 1972. Mbrships: Israel Soc. for For. Policy; Int. Tagung der Historiker der Arbeiterbewegung; participant, Arbeitskreis für Wehrforschung, Germany. Publs: Das Dogma der Vernichtungsschlacht, Die Lehren von Clausewitz und Schlieffen und ihre Wirkung in zwie Weltkriegen, 1967, 2nd edit, 1970; Die Kriegslehren von Friedrich Engels, 1968; Carta's Atlas of Palestine from Zionism to Statehood, 1972 (in Hebrew, Engl. edit. in preparation); Kriegstheorien, Ihre Entwicklung im 19 und 20., 1972 (also in Hebrew edit.); articles in profl. periodicals & encys. Address: 27, Ben-Zvi Ave., 52 247 Ramat Gan, Israel. 94.

WALLER, Ivar, b. 11 June 1898. Professor. Educ: Dr. Sci., Univ. of Uppsala, 1925. Appts: Lectr., later Prof., Math. Physics & Mechanics, Univ. of Uppsala, 1925-64; Prof., Emeritus, ibid, 1964-; Mbr., Swedish Atomic Comm. & Coun. of Atomic Rsch., 1947-65; Mbr., Bd. of Swedish Atomic Energy Co., 1947-69; Cons., ibid, 1964-; Deleg. to Cern, Geneva, 1952-65. Mbrships: Royal Swedish Acad. of Sci., Stockholm; Nobel Comm. for Physics, ibid, 1945-71; Regia Soc., Upsaliensis; Royal Physiog. Soc., Lund; Det Norske Videnskapsakademie, Oslo. Contbr. papers on sci. subjects. Hons: Dr. Hon. Causa, Univ. of Seiden, 1965; Cmdr. 1st Class, Order Northern Star, 1967. Address: Trädgårdsgatan 10, S-752 20 Uppsala, Sweden. 34, 43, 50, 134.

WALLER, John Henry, b. 8 May 1923. Diplomat. Educ: B.A., Univ. of Mich., 1946. Appts: Vice Consul, U.S. Embassy, Teheran, Iran, 1946-49, Meshed, Iran, 1949-50; Attache, U.S. Embassy, Teheran, 1950-53; For. Affairs Off., Dept. of Defense, 1953-55; Attache, U.S. Embassy, New Delhi, India, 1955-59; Staff Planning Off., U.S. Army, Wash. D.C., 1959-60; 2nd Sec., U.S. Embassy, Khartoum, Sudan, 1960-62; Pol. Analyst, U.S.Dept. of State, 1962-68; 1st Sec. & Special Asst. to the Ambassador, Am. Embassy, New Delhi, India, 1968-72; For. Affairs Off., Dept. of State, U.S.A., 1972-. Mbrships: Cosmos Club, Wash. D. C.; Oriental Club, London, U.K.; Dipolmatic & Consular Offs., Retd., Wash. D.C. Address: c/o Dept. of State, For. Serv. Mail Room, Wash. DC, U.S.A. 2.

WALLERSTEIN, Harry, b. 11 Dec. 1906. Physician. Educ: A.B., Geo. Wash. Univ., 1927; M.D., Med. Schl., ibid, 1930. Appts. incl: Assoc. Pathologist-Dir. Rsch., Jewish Mem. Hosp., 1937-; Dir. Blood Bank, 1956-, Vis. Pathologist, 1958-, Bronx Municipal Hosp. Ctr; Cons. Hematol., Morrisanie City Hosp., 1948-, Fordham City Hosp., 1951-, St. Elizabeth's Hosp., 1954-, St. Clare's Hosp. & Med. Cr., 1970-. Lectr. Pathol., 1956-, Vis. Asst. Prof. Pathol., 1959-; Albert Einstein Coll. of Med. Fellowships: N.Y. Acad. Med.; N.Y. Acad. Scis.; Fndr., Int. Soc. Hematol.; Am. Soc. Clin. Pathol.; AMA. Mbrships. incl: Am. Assn. Blood Banks; Am. Soc. Hematol.; AAAS. Author & co-author num. med. papers. Hons. incl: 1st Award for Sci. Rsch., Med. Soc., State of N.Y., 1964. Address: 720 Gratman Ave., Mt. Vernon, N.Y., NY 10552, U.S.A.

WALLOWER, Lucille, b. 27 July 1910. Author-Illustrator. Librarain. Educ: Pa. Sus.

Schl. of Art; Traphagan Schl. of Fashion, N.Y. Appts: Schl. Libn., Harrisburg Pub. Lib., 1943-44; Asst. Children's Libn., ibid, 1944-46; Dir., Harrisburg Art Assn. Studio, 1943-48; Fashion Artist, Pomeroy's Inc., Harrisburg, Pa., 1946-49 & Bowman's Inc., 1949-52; Children's Libn., Abington Lib. Soc., Jenkintown, 1959-70; Libn., ibid, 1970-. Publs: A Conch Shell for Molly, 1940; Chooky, 1942; The Roll of Drums, 1945; Your Pennsylvania, 1953; Old Satan, 1955; Indians of Pennsylvania, 1956; The Hippety Hopper, 1957; The Morning Star, 1957; All About Pennsylvania, 1958; They Came to Pennsylvania, 1960; The Lost Prince, 1963; Yours State, 1963; Pennsylvania ABC, 1964; My Book About Abraham Lincoln., 1967; New Pennsylvania Primer, 1969; William Penn, 1968; Colonial Pennsylvania, 1969; The Pennsylvania Dutch, 1971; Introduction to Pennsylvania, 1974. Address: 828 Greenwood Ave., Jenkintown, PA 19046, U.S.A. 5, 130, 138.

WALSH, Helena Teresa. Teacher; Librarian. Educ: B.Ed., St. Joseph Tchrs. Coll., Montreal, Canada, 1967; B.A., Loyola Coll., Montreal, 1967; M.L.S., Cath. Univ., Wash. D.C., U.S.A., 1972; Currently enrolled in Blackstone Schl. of Law. Appts: Tchr., Elem. Schl., Montreal, 1961-63; Tchr., Secondary Schl., Montreal, 1963-67; Pub. Libn., Woodbridge, Va., 1968; Tchr., Libn., Secondary Schl., Prince George's Co., Md., 1968-; Pt.-time Administrative Asst. & Law Clerk, Law Off., Wash. D.C., 1970-. Mbrships: Prince George's Co. Educators Assn.; Md. Tchrs. Assn.; NEA; Cath. Univ. Schl. of Lib. Sci. Alumni. Hons: Schlrship., Bd. of Educ., P.Q., Canada, 1967; Ed.D., Hamilton State Univ., Ariz., 1973. Address: 3114 Wisconsin Ave. N.W., Apt. 202, Wash. DC 20016, U.S.A. 5.

WALSH, James P., b. 7 Mar. 1910. Insurance Consultant. Educ: Com. E., Univ. of Cinn., 1933; U.S. Army Comman & Gen. Staff Coll.; Armed Forces Indl. Coll. Appts: Chief, Ohio Div. of Minimum Wage, Columbus, 1939-42; Col., U.S. Army, 1942-46; Asst. Sec.-Treas., Union Label Trades Dept. AFL, Wash. D.C., 1946-53; V.P., Pension & Grp. Cons., Inc., Cinn., 1953-. Mbrships: incl: Pres., Cinn. Club, 1973; Bd. of Dirs., Univ. of Cinn.; Nat. Fndn. Hlth., Welfare & Pension Plans, Inc.; Soc. for Advmt. Mgmt. Commn., Judicial & Congl. Salaries, 1954. Hons. incl: Legion of Merit, 1970; Disting. Alumnus Award, Univ. of Cinn., 1969; Named Ky. Col., 1959; Ky. Admiral, 1967; Benefactor, City of Cinn., 1968; St. Xavier H.S. Insignis Award, 1974. Address: 6 E 4th St., Rm. 900, Cinn., OH 45202, U.S.A. 2, 8, 16.

WALSH, Joseph James, b. 21 Dec. 1915. Company Director. Educ: Dublin, London Colls. of Technol. Appts: Mng. Ed., Munster Express, 1943; Gov. Dir., Newspaper & Printing Publishing Co. Mbrships. incl: Exec., Provincial Newspapers Assn.; Chmn., Waterford region, Publicity Club of Ireland; Nat. Coun. Mbr., Executive, Irish Master Printers' Assn.; Life Master, Holy Ghost Hosp., Waterford; Pres., Old Waterford (Histl.) Soc.; Pres., Iverk Farming Soc.; Chmn., Tramore Dev. & Tourist Assn.; Mil. Hist. Soc.; Georgian Soc. Publs: An Olympic Odyssey; Across the World for Sport; History of the Tithe War; Ed., contbr., Jrnl. of Old Waterford Soc.; Author, num. articles. Hons: Hon. Col., 69th Regiment, U.S. Army; Peace Commnr., 1949. Address: Cliff Grange, Tramore, Co. Waterford, Repub. of Ireland.

WALSH, Ylia Puig (Mrs. Paul E. Walsh), b. 13 Aug. 1916. Humanities Instructor. Educ: B.S., Univ. of N.C., Greensboro, 1938; M.A.

Appalachian State Univ., Boone, N.C., 1967. Appts: Instr., Spanish & Engl., Frank L. Ashley H.S., Gastonia, N.C., 1948-52, '54-64; Spanish Instr., Coll. Ctr., Univ. of N.C., 1946-47; Nat. Defense Educ. Act, Lang. Inst., Appalachian State Univ., Boone, 1961-64, Furman Univ., 1965-66; Spanish Instr., Gaston Coll. Gastonia, 1964-68; Humanities Instr., Gen. Studies Dept., ibid, 1968-. Mbrships. incl: var. past offs., N.C. Educ. Assn.; NEA; N.C. Assn. of Educators; Am. Assn. for Tchrs. of Spanish & Portuguese; S. Atlantic MLA: AAUW; Sigma Delta Pi; Delta Kappa Gamma; Pilot Club Int. Contbr. to Hispania, 1966, '68. Chosen to make demonstration film for N.C. Educl. TV Broadcast. Hons: Outstanding Tchr. of Week, Gastonia, N.C., 1968; Hon. Mention, Terry Sanford Award, 1969. Address: Gen. Studies Dept., Gaston Coll., Gastonia, NC, 18052 U.S.A. 15, 125, 126, 132.

WALTER, Charles Lee, b. 23 Nov. 1934. Company Executive; Store Owner. Educ: Student, Ferris Inst., Big Rapids, Mic., 1959-60. Appts: w. Coca-Cola Bottling Co. of Pontiac, Mich., 1960; Warehouse Foreman, ibid, 1968-69; Treas., 1969-; Dlr., 1971-; Stockholder, 1972; Owner, Charles L. Walter's Sporting Goods, Pontiac, Mich. Mbrships: Fndr., Pres., Int. Radio Patrol of Pontiac, Mich., 1969-; Croton Conservation Club, Mich.; Chtr., Franklin Mint Collectors Soc. Address: Coca-Cola Bottling Co. of Pontiac, 1130 Wide Track Dr. West, P.O. Box 268, Pontiac, MI 48056, U.S.A. 8, 16.

WALTER, Paul D(aniel), Educator & Psychologist. Educ: A.B., B.S. in Ed., Marion Coll., Ind.; A.M., Ind. Univ., Bloomington, Ph.D., Univ. of Pitts., Pa. Appts. incl: Tchr., Secondary Schs., 1940-43; D.E.M.L., U.S. Army, 1943-46; Trng. Off., V.A., 1946-50; Voc. Counselor & Lectr., Univ. of Pitts. Pa., 1950-57; Asst. to Dean, Schl. of Bus. Admin., ibid, 1957-61; V.P., Acad. Affairs, Waynesburg Coll., Pa., 1961-63; Acad. Dean, Univ. of Pitts. at Johnstown, 1963-71; Prof. Psychol. & Counselor, ibid, 1971-. Mbrships. incl: Sec., Fin. Comm., Bd. of Dirs., Quincy U.M. Home, 1960-; D.W.I. Counterattack, 1973-; Advsry. Bd., Goodwill Inds. of Cambria Co., 1973-; Exec. Comm., Bd. of Dirs., Arbutus Pk. Manor, Johnstown, Pa., 1966-; Trustee, Otterbein Coll., Ohi, 1961-70; Bd. of Mgmt., Pitts. YMCA, 1963-71; Am. Psychol. Assn., 1954-; Psi Chi; Beta Gamma Sigma; Phi Eta Sigma; Phi Theta Kappa; Druids; Alpha Kappa Psi; Alpha Phi Omega; AAAS; V.P., Mt. Pleasant Histl. Soc. Publs: Handbook of Classification & Assignment, U.S. Army (5th Corps Area), 1946; Contbr. of articles to periodicals. Recip., Disting. Serv. Award, Bus. Admin. Cabinet, Univ. of Pitts., Pa., 1960. Address: 844 Sunnehanna Drive, Johnstown, PA 15905, U.S.A. 6, 14, 15, 28, 108, 112.

WALTER, William Grey, b. 19 Feb. 1910. Physiologist. Educ: Kings Coll., Univ. of Cambridge, U.K., 1928-35. Appts: Rockefeller Fellow, Maudsley Hosp., London, U.K., 1935-39; Hd. of Physiol. Dept., Burden Inst., Bristol, U.K., 1939-45; Rsch. Dir., ibid, 1945-70; Sci. Cons., 1970-. Mbrships: Physiol. Soc.; Fellow, Inst. of Biol.; Fndr., Electroencephalographic Soc.; Int. Brain Rsch. Org.; Engl. Speaking Union; Hon. Mbr. of 8 For. Socs. Publs: The Living Brain, 1953; Further Outlook, 1956; The Curve of the Snow-flake. Contbr. of over 600 papers to var. sci. jrnls. Writer of poetry. Hons: Ambrose Fleming Premium, I.E.E., 1943; M.D., Univ. of Aix-Marseille, France, 1949. Address: Burden Neurological Inst., Stoke Lane, Stapleton, Bristol BS16 1QT, U.K.

WALTERS, (The Hon. Mr. Justice) George Henry, b. 23 Dec. 1914. Judge of Supreme Court of S.A., Australia. Educ: LL.B., Univ. of Adelaide, 1936. Appts: Capt., Australia Army Med. Corps, 1941-46; Major, Australia Army Legal Corps, 1965-71; Admitted as Practitioner, Supreme Ct. of S.A., 1936; Barrister, Solicitor, 1936-50; Special Magistrate, Suburban & Co. Cts. Dept., S.A., 1950-57; Acting Dpty. Master, Dpty. Master, Supreme Ct. of S.A., 1954-61; Master, ibid, 1961-65; District Registrar, High Ct. of Australia, 1961-65; Lectr., Law Schl., Univ. of Adelaide, 1961-66; Judge, Supreme Ct. of S.A., 1966-. Mbrships: Fac. of Law, Univ. of Adelaide, 1961-; Hon. Col., Australia Army Legal Corps, 1971-; Adelaide Club; Naval, Mil. & Air Force Club, Adelaide; Commonwealth Club of Adelaide (Pres., 1972-73). Address: Supreme Court, Victoria Sq., Adelaide, S.A., Australia 5000.

WALTERS, (Herman) Wayne, b. 19 Oct. 1938. Teacher. Educ: B.A., Shorter Coll., Rome, Ga., 1960; NDEA For. Lang. Inst., Univ. of Ga., 1960; M.A., Univ. of Ala., Tuscaloosa, 1963; A.B.D. (all course work & comprehensive exams taken for Ph.D.), ibid, 1965-66. Appts: Tchr., Pepperell HS, Lindale, Ga., 1960-61; Instr., Mobile Coll., Mobile, Ala., 1963-64, Ga. Southern Coll., Statesboro, 1964-65, Auburn Univ., Auburn, Ala., 1966-69; Asst. Prof., Ga. Coll., Milledgeville, 1969-. Mbrships: Sec., Phi Delta Tau, 1957-60; Phi Beta Kappa, 1960; Sigma Delta Pi; 1962-; AAUP, 1968-; MLA, 1965-; Am. Assn. of Tchrs. of Spanish & Portuguese, 1965-. Author of var. articles on 17th century French & Spanish dramatists; 1st novel in progress. Hons: 1st Hon. Grad. (Valedictorian), Rome HS, 1956; 3 yr. NDEA Title IV Fellowship, Univ. of Ala., 1961. Address: P.O. Box 1093, Milledgeville, GA 31061, U.S.A. 117, 125.

WALTERS, Margaret Artman (Mrs.); b. 27 Aug. 1910. Social Worker; Writer. Educ: Ph.B., Schl. of Soc. Serv. Admin., Univ. of Chgo., 1938-41; M.A., ibid; Soc. Wkr., Ch. Fedn. Boys Ct. Serv., ibid, 1943-47; Soc. Wkr., Hines Hosp., V.A., 1948-50; Instr., Dept. of Psych., Coll. of Med., Univ. of Ill., 1953-54; Casework Supvsr., 1955-58, Asst. Dir., 1959-61, Mental Hlth. Clin., Cook Co. Hosp.; Dir. of Soc. Serv., Mental Hlth. Div., Chgo. Bd. of Hlth, 1961-66; Coord. of Trng. & Mental Hlth. Educ., ibid, 1967-70; Ed. of Newsletter, Ill. Acad. of Criminol., 1972-. Mbrships. incl: Fellow, Am. Orthopsychiatric Assn. (Chmn., P.R. Comm., 1960); Nat. Assn. Soc. Wkrs. (V. Chmn., Chgo. Chapt., 1962, Bd. of Dirs. & Chmn., P.R. Comm., 1972-73); Acad. Cert. Soc. Wkrs.; var. offs., Ill. Acad. of Criminol.; Int. Coun. on Soc. Welfare; Int. Assn. for Suicide Prevention; World Fedn. for mental Hlth.; AAAS; Fedn. Am. Scis.; Pres., Retired City Employees' Club; Advsry. Coun., Nutrition Proj., Mayor's Off., for Sr. Citizens; Bd. Dirs., Midway, Chgo. Chapt., Am. Assn. Retired Persons. Phi Beta Kappa. Author of articles in periodicals. Address: 5732 Harper Ave., Chicago, IL 60637, U.S.A. 5, 8.

WALTERS, Maxine Bernice Oyler (Mrs. Robert Willis Walters), b. 4 June 1921. Educator. Educ: B.S. in Ed., Ohio State Univ., 1943; M.A., ibid, 1952. Appts: Secondary Tchr., Pickaway Co., Ohio, 1943-45, Ashville, Ohio, 1945-46, Pigua, Ohio, 1946-47; Elem. Tchr., Cleveland, Ohio, 1947-49, Columbus, Ohio, 1949-52; Elem. Schl. Prin., 1952-. Mbrships. incl: Pres., Nu Chapt., Pi Lambda Theta, 1952; Past Matron, Order of Eastern Star; Life Mbr., NEA, Nat. Dept. of Elem. Schl. Prins., Ohio Educ. Assn., Pi Lambda Theta, Ohio PTA, Ohio State Univ. Alumni Assn.;

Columbus Admin. Assn.; Ohio Assn. of Elem. Schl. Prins.; Columbus Elem. Prins. Assn. Address: 12 S. High St., Mt. Sterling, OH 43143, U.S.A. 5, 8, 22, 129, 130.

WALTERS, Walter H., b. 19 Dec. 1917. Educator; Administrator. Educ: B.S., Troy State Univ., Ala., 1939; M.F.A., Western Reserve Univ., Cleveland, Ohio, 1949; Ph.D., ibid, 1950. Appts. incl: Grad. Asst., Univ. of Wis., 1946-48; Instr.-Dean, Coll. Arts & Arch., Pa. State Univ., 1950-; Dir., Univ. Arts Servs., 1973-. Mbrships. incl: Chmn., Int. Coun. Fine Arts Deans, 1973; Pres., U.S. Inst. Theatre Technol.; Regional Rep., Alliance for Arts Educ. Co-author of Attending the Theatre. Hons. incl: Citation in Recognition of Disting. Contbns. to the Advancement of Educ., Commonwealth of Pa., 1972; Fellow, Am. Theatre Assn., 1973. Address: 111 Arts Bldg., Univ. Park, PA 16802, U.S.A. 2, 6, 13, 128, 141.

WALTERS O'NEILL, Malcolm, b. 17 Oct. 1921. Architect. Educ: B. Arch., Rensselaer Polytech. Inst., Troy, N.Y., 1950; Trans. Schl., Ft. Eustis, Va., 1953; Schl. of the Ams., St. Gulick, Canal Zone, 1968, 70. Appts: Archt., Henry Klumb, FAIA, 1950-59; Est. firm, Malcolm Walters, AIA, 1959-; Ops. & Trng. Officer, 246th Trans. Bn., 1964-69; Exed. Officer, ibid, 1969-70; Cmdrng. Officer, 448th Engr. Bn. (Const.), 1971-73; Pres., Walters Bros. & Assocs., 1963-. Mbrships. incl: Dir., Am. Inst. Archts., 1970-73; Puerto Rico Inst. Archts.; Interam. Planning Soc.; Bd., Aspira of Am. Inc., 1970-71; Treas. of Bd., Aspirs of P.R. Inc., 1971-73; Pres., Kiwanis Coun. of P.R. & Virgin Islands, 1973-. Works incl: O'Neal Bldg., St. Thomas, Virgin Islands, 1969; H.S., Aguada, P.R., 1972; Voc. Rehab. Unit, Guaynabo, P.R., 1973. Recip., army awards. Address: P.O. Box 8087, Santurce, Puerto Rico 00910, U.S.A.

WALTMAN, Tilia Shmelkin, b. 19 Apr. 1896. Doctor of Dental Surgery. Educ: Warsaw Schl. of Dentistry, Poland, 1915; D.D.S., Columbia Univ., 1925; Cert. Preventive Dentistry, Vienna, Austria, 1928. Appts: Pvte. Prac., Lenin, Russia, 1915-20; Dental Asst., N.Y.C., 1921-24; Pvte. Prac., N.Y.C., 1925-29; Lectr. & Specialist, Gum Disease & Preventive Dentistry, 1929-. Mbrships. incl: Organizer, Fund for Russian Authors, Artists, & Scis. & Exile, N.Y.C., & Russian Dental Soc., N.Y.C.; Organizer & Treas., Soc. of Women of Lenin, Russia, in Am.; Org. for Rehab. in Trade; Fedn. Jewish Philanthropics. Recip., Cert. of Hon., 1st Lady of Lenin, Russia, 1960. Lectures & courses preventive dentistry for dental socs., N.Y.C. Clins. Address: 41 W. 83rd St., N.Y., NY 10024, U.S.A. 6.

WALTON, Bryce, b. 31 May 1918. Author. Educ: L.A. State Coll., Calif. Appts: Sailor, migrant farmer, gold miner & other roving jobs, 1938-41; Combat Corres., USN & Marine Corp, S. Pacific, 1942-45; Freelance Fiction Writer, 1945-; Instr., short story writing, Ann Elwood Coll., L.A., 1946-47; Mbr: Mystery Writers of Am. Publs: Novels: Sons of the Ocean Deeps, 1952; The Long Night, 1952; Cave of Danger, 1967; Harpoon Gunner, 1969; Hurricane Reef, 1971; Fire Trail, 1974. Contbr. of num. short stories to mags. & anthols. Author of Sci. Fiction & Mystery TV scripts. Hons: Citation from Admiral Nimitz, WWII, for coverage of Iwo Jima & Okinawa battles; Hitchcock Best Short Story of Yr. Award, 1961; Story included in Best Detective Stories of Yr., Dutton, 1961. Address: Gargoyle Studios, 8935 Wonderland Ave., Hollywood, CA 90046, U.S.A. 30.

WALTON, DeWitt Talmage, Jr., b. 25 May 1937. Dentist. Educ: B.S., D.D.S., Howard Univ., 1960-61. Appts: U.S. Army Dental Corps, 1961-63; Reserve, ibid, 1963-69; Gen. Prac., 1963-. Mbrships: Am. Dental Assn.; Ga. Dental Assn.; Nat. Dental Assn.; Asst. Sec., Ga. Dental Soc.; Am. Soc. Dentistry for Children; Acad. Gen. Dentistry; Am. Endotontic Soc.; AAAS; Fedn. Dentaire Int.; NAACP; Nat. Rehab. Assn.; Local Co-Chmn. & State Bd. Dirs., Ga. Coun. on Human Rels., 1963; Bibb Co. Bd. Educ., 1969; Vice Basilens, Lambda Phi Chapt., Omega Psi Phi. Hons: 1st Negros on Bibb Co. Bd. of Educ., 1969. Man of Yr. Award, Lambda Phi Chapt., Omega Psi Phi, 1969; Citizen of Yr. Award, ibid, 1971. Address: 591 Cotton Ave., Macon, GA 31201, U.S.A. 7, 117, 125.

WALTON, Richard John, b. 24 May 1928. Writer. Educ: A.B., Brown Univ., 1951; Sc.M., Columbia Univ. Grad. Schl. of Jrnlism., 1954. Appts: Chief Announcer, News Ed., WIGF, Providence, R.I., 1952-53; Reporter, Providence Jrnl., 1954-55; Reporter, N.Y. World Telegram & Sun, 1955-59; Prod., Announcer, Report to Africa, Voice of Am., 1959-62; Prin., UN Corres., ibid, 1962-67; Self-Employed, 1967-. Mbrships: PEN; Authors Guild; Am. Hist. Assn. Acad. of Pol. Sci. Publs. incl: The Remnants of Power: The Tragic Last Years of Adlai Stevenson, 1968; Cold War & Counter-Revolution: The Foreign Policy of John F. Kenney, 1972; (for young adults) The United State of Latin America, 1972; Canada & the U.S.A., 1972; Congress & American Foreign Policy, 1972; The United States & the Far East, 1974. Address: 24 Cornelia St., New York, NY 10014, U.S.A.

WAMBSGANSS, Leon George. Journalist. Educ: Arlington Bapt. Schls. Coll.; B.D., Bible Bapt. Sem., Arlington, Tex.; Dipl. del Idioma Español, Univ. de Barcelona, Spain; Int. Schls., Ft. Lauderdale, Fla.; Titulo de Profesor del Espagñol, Inst. Naciónal de Idiomas; Ph.D., Bapt. Theol. Sem., Madrid, Spain; M.A.Th., Seminario Biblico Batista, Benevides, Para, Brazil. Appts: European Dir., World Bapt. Fellowship; Corres. for Readers Report Index; Dir., Rupert Neve recording co., Nuevo Acento S.A.; Pres., World Broadcasting Fndn. (Radio Div.). Mbrships: Asociacion Española De Prensa Y Publicaciones (Evangelical Press Club); Spanish Official Defense Commn. on Relig. Affairs; Evangelical Radio & TV Commn. Soc. Publs: The Death of Pompeii; What John Saw from the Island (In the Light of the Bible); Madrid Story; Spain Through the Eyes of a Protestant; Para El Que Pregunta; Momentos de Melodia. Hons: Torch Speaking Award, 1963; IFMA Essay Award, 1967; AEPPE Honor for Best Script, 1970; BTS Hon. D.D., 1974; HOPE Youth Retreat Cert., 1974. Address: 2821 Blackwood Dr., Arlington, TX 76013, U.S.A.

WANAMAKER, Robert Joseph, b. 24 Nov. 1924. Advertising Executive. Educ: Northwestern Univ., Evanston, Ill., 1946-50. Appts: Sr. V.P.-Creative Dir.; Mbr., Exec. Comm.-Dir. of Corp., Clinton E. Frank Inc., Chgo., 1962-72; Sr. V.P. & Creative Dir., Grey Advtng., 1972-. Mbrships: Chgo. Athletic Club; Oak Park Country Club. Contbr. to newspapers & trade jrnls. Address: 1005 Bonnie Brae, River Forest. IL 60305, U.S.A. 2, 22.

WANG, Chih-Chun, b. 9 Oct. 1932. Scientist. Educ: B.Sc., Chem. Engrng., Nat. Taiwan Univ., China; M.Sc., Kan. State Univ., U.S.A.; Ph.D., Phys. Chem., Colo. State Univ.; Post-doct. work, Univ. of Kan. Appts: Mbr., Tech. Staff, 1963-68, Rsch. Ldr., 1968-73, Fellow, Tech. Staff, 1973-, RCA Labs., David

Sarnoff Rsch. Ctr., Princeton, N.J. Mbrships: Am. Chem. Soc.; Electrochem. Soc.; Am. Vacuum Soc.; Sigma Xi; Sigma Pi Sigma; Phi Lambda Upsilon. Contbr. of 30 tech. publs. in leading Am. & int. jrnls; 5 US patents granted. Recip, Outstanding tech. achievement awards, RCA, 1966, '68, '71; mbrship. in nat. chem., phys., & sci. rsch. hon. socs. Address: 41 Maple . Stream Rd., E. Windsor, NJ 08520, U.S.A. 6, 14.

WANG, Frances Y.L.Dzo, b. 3 July 1918. Curator; Librarian. Educ: M.A., Soc. Work, Univ. of Chgo., 1950; M.A., Sociol., Univ. of Wash., Seattle; M.A., Libnship., 1958. Appts. incl: Rsch. Asst., Dept. of Sociol., Univ. of Wash., Seattle, 1953-55; Rsch. Assoc., Far Eastern & Russian Studies, ibid, 1955-56; Asst. Libn., Far Eastern Lib., 1956-69; Curator-Libn., Admin., Claremont Colls., Honnold Lib., Asian Studies Collect., 1969-. Mbrships. incl: Chmn., Southern Calif. Asian Libs. Org., 1971-; Subcomm. on Comm. on E. Asian Libs., L.C. Classification, 1973-; ALA; Am. Sociol. Assn.; Assn. for Asian Studies; Alpha Kappa Delta; Beta Phi Mu. Author of publs. in field. Address: Asian Studies Collection, Honnold Lib., Claremont Colls., Claremont, CA 91711, U.S.A.

WANG, Jaw-Kai, b. 4 Mar. 1932. Professor; Agricultural Engineer. Educ: B.S., Nat. Taiwan Univ., China, 1953; M.S., Mich. State Univ.,, E. Lansing, U.S.A., 1956; Ph.D., ibid, 1958. Appts: Asst. Prof., Agric. Engrng., Univ. of Hawaii, 1959-64; Assoc. Prof. & Chmn., Agric. Engrng. Dept., ibid, 1964-68; Prof. & Chmn., 1968-; Cons., Int. Rice Rsch. Inst., U.S. Army, Taiwan Sugar Co. Mbrships: Am. Soc. Agric. Engrs., (chmn., grad. instrn. comm., 1970-72); Soil Dynamics; Food Engrng.; Sigma Xi; Inst. of Food Technols.; Pi Mu Epsilon; Hawaii Sugar Technols. Contbr. of articles to profl. jrnls. Address: Agric. Engrng. Dept., Univ. of Hawaii, Honolulu, HI 96822, U.S.A. 2, 9, 14, 28, 78, 130, 131.

WANG, Joseph Shou-Jen, b. 17 Dec. 1933. Professor. Educ: B.S., Nat. Taiwan Univ., 1957; B.D., Asbury Theol. Sem., U.S.A., 1963; Th.M., Princeton Theol. Sem., 1964; Ph.D., Emory Univ., 1970. Asst. Prof., New Testament, Asbury Theol. Sem., 1970. Mbrships: Soc. of Biblical Lit.; Evangelical Theol. Soc.; Wesleyan Theol. Soc.; Theta Phi. Contbr. to: The Asbury Seminarian; Ambassadors. Recip., Highest Acad. Achievement Award in field of Biblical Lit., Asbury Theol. Sem., 1963. Address: Asbury Theol. Sem., Wilmore, KY 40390, U.S.A. 13, 125.

WANG, Jui Hsin, b. 16 Mar. 1921. Educator. Educ: B.Sc., Nat. Southwest Assocd. Univ., Kunming, China, 1945; Ph.D., Wash. Univ., St. Louis, Mo., U.S.A., 1949. Appts: Postdoctoral Fellow in radiochem., Wash. Univ., 1949-51; Mbr. of Yale fac., 1951-72; Prof. of Chem., ibid, 1960-62; Eugene Higgins Prof., 1962-64; Eugene Higgins Prof. of Chem. & Molecular Biophysics, 1964-72; Einstein Prof., SUNY, Buffalo, 1972-; Mbr., Biophysics & Biophys. Chem. Study Sect., Nat. Insts. of Hlth., 1965-69. Mbrships. incl: Am. Chem. Soc.; Fellow, AAAS; Chem. Soc., London, U.K.; Royal Instn. of Chem.; Biophys. Soc.; Am. Soc. of Biological Chemists; Am. Soc. for Photobiol.; Am. Acad. of Arts & Scis. Author of articles on molecular structure & biological function. Hons. incl: Guggenheim Fellow, 1960-61, 1972; Joseph W. Kennedy Mem. Lectr., Wash. Univ., 1972. Address: Bioenergetics Lab., Acheson Hall, SUNY, Buffalo, NY 14214, U.S.A. 2, 14, 28, 50.

WANG, Ling, b. 23 Dec. 1918. Historian of Science. Educ: B.A., Nat. Ctrl. Univ., China; M.A., Ph.D., Trinity Coll., Cambridge. Appts: Jr. Rsch. Fellow, Inst. of Hist. & Philol., Academia Sinica, 1941-44; Assoc. Fellow, Nat. Acad. of Sci., ibid, 1955-57; Sr. Lectr., Nat. Fu-tan Univ., 1944-45; Assoc. Prof., ibid, 1945-46; Collaborator w. J. Needham, Cambridge Univ., 1946-57; Vis. Lectr., ibid, 1953; w. Canberra Univ. Coll., Melbourne Univ., Aust., 1957-59; Sr. Lectr., Univ. Coll., Aust. Nat. Univ., Canberra, 1960-61; Assoc. Prof., ibid, 1961-63; Vis. Prof. of Chinese Lit., Cornell Univ., U.S.A., 1965-66; Vis. Prof. of Chinese Classics, Wis. Univ., 1965-66; Professorial Fellow, Inst. of Advanced Studies. Aust. Nat. Univ., 1963-. Mbrships: Commn. for Hist. of the Soc. Rels. of Sci., Int. Union for Hist. of Sci., Int. Union for Hist. of Sci., 1948-56; Corres., Int. Acad. of Hist. of Sci., Paris, 1964-. Publs: Collaborator w. Dr. J. Needham, Science & Civilisation in China, Vols. I-IV, 1954-71; Heavenly Clockwork (w. Dr. J. Needham), 1960; A Study on the Chiu Chang Suan Shu, 1962. Address: c/o Dept. of Far Eastern Hist., Inst. of Advanced Studies, Aust. Nat. Univ., Canberra, Australia. 23, 34.

WAN IBRAHIM BIN WAH SOLOH, (Dato' Seri Amar di-Raja), b. 24 Sept. 1905. Retired Civil Servant. Educ: Klang & Malay Coll., Kuala Kangsar, Perak, Malaysia. Appts: Registrar, Coop. Socs., Kedah Civil Serv.; Asst. State Sec.; Chmn., Town Coun., Alor Star; Retd. 1960; Sec., Treas., K.C.S. Coop. Thrift & Investment Soc.; Mng. Dir., Sharikat Perusahaan Utra Malaya Ltd. Mbrships. incl: Past Mbr., Kedah Pub. Serv. Comm.; State Religious Coun.; State Pardons Bd.; Standing Comm. Awards & Decoration; Chmn., State Mus. Bd.; Tchrs. Provident Fund, Malaysia; Pres., Kedah Histl. Soc.; Pub. Lib. Bd.; Chmn., Bd. of Govs., S.A.S. Secondary & Primary Schls.; Bd. of Govs., Sharifah Rodzoah Secondary Schl.; Past Pres., Kedah Club, Alor Star & Rotary Club. Hons: J.P., 1968; Hon. Order of Crown of Kedah; Conferred w. Datoship. Address: Kedah State Mus., Bakar Bata, Alor Star, Malaysia.

WARBURTON, Ralph, b. 5 Sept. 1935. Architect; City Planner; Engineer; Educ: B.Arch., MIT, 1958; M.Arch., Yale Univ., 1959; M.C.P., 1960. Appts. incl: Chief Planning & Assoc., Skidmore, Owings & Merrill, Chgo., 1962-66; Spec. Asst. for Urban Design, U.S. Dept. H.U.D., Wash. D.C., 1967-72; V.P., Ferendino, Grafton, Spillis, Candela, Coral Gables, Fla., 1972-; Assoc. Dean, Chmn. & Prof., Arch., Univ. of Miami, 1972-. Mbrships. incl: Am. Inst. Archs.; Am. Inst. Planner; Am. Soc. of Civil Engrs.; Cosmos Club, Wash. D.C.; Tau Beta Pi. Publs. incl: Man Made America, 1963, '66; Ed., New Concepts in Urban Transportation Systems, 1968; Ed., 1968 H.U.D. Awards for Design Excellence; Ed., Housing Systems Proposals for Operation Breakthrough, 1970; Ed., Docus on Furniture, 1971; 4th & 5th Biennial H.U.D. Awards for Design Excellence, 1971, '73; Urban Development in Iran, 1971; H.U.D. National Community Arts Program, 1973. Recip. of hons. Address: 6910 Veronese, Coral Gables, FL 33146, U.S.A. 7.

WARD, Allen Wayne, b. 31 Aug. 1933. Professional Engineer; Consultant. Educ: B.Sc., Mech. Engrng., Clemson Univ., S.C.; M.Sc., Gen. Engrng.-Metallurgy, Univ. of Ala., Tuscaloosa. Profl. Engr. in Mech. & Metallurical Engrng. (Nat.); Cert. Mfg. Engr., nat. standing. Appts: Profl. Engr.; Cons. in Mfng., Metallurgy & Mgmt.; has given var. lectrs. in U.S.A. on quality control, mgmt. & casting prodn.

techniques. Mbrships: Elder & Deacon, Presby. Ch. of U.S.A.; Nat. Soc. Prof. Engrs.; V.P., Okla. Soc. Profl. Engrs.; Nat. Chmn., Tech. Coun. Casting, Molding & Metallurgical Div., Soc. of Mfg. Engrs.; Pres., Ind. Mgmt. Club; Pres., Mid-S. Roundtable (IMC); State Dir., Profl. Engrs.; Dir., YMCA; Chmn., Aviation Comm., Stillwater (Okla.) Chmbr. of Comm. Contbr. articles to trade jrnls. on quality, engrng. & mgmt. Hons: Awards of Merit as Pres., Ind. Mgmt. Club, 1965 & Mid-S. Roundtable, 1966; var. profl. awards. Address: 3123 Fox Ledge Lane, Stillwater, OK 74074, U.S.A. 7, 125.

WARD, Christian George, b. 3 July 1914. Physician & Surgeon. Educ: B.A., N.Y. Univ., Wash. Sq. Coll., 1938; M.D., ibid, Coll. of Med., 1941. Appts: Staff Phys., Yankton State Hosp., S.D., 1941-42; Intern, N.J. City Hosp., Neward, 1942; Lt. to Capt. Major, U.S. Army Med. Corps, 1942-46; Intern Wilmington Gen. Hosp., Del., 1946-47; Rotating Res., Meth. Hosp., Peoria, III., 1947-48; Hosp. Staff Appts., St. Francis Hosp. & Freeport Mem. Hosp., III., Northwestern III. Gen. Hosp., Galena: Gen. Prac. of Med., Warren, 1948-; Warren Town Physn., 1973-. Mbrships: AMA; III. State Med. Assn.; Pres., 1952-55, Jo Daviess Co. Med. Soc.; Pres., 1952-55, Jo Daviess Co. Bd. of Hlth.; Pres., 1949-59, Jo Daviess Co. Tb. Assn.; Am. Acad. of Gen. Prac.; Warren Schl. Bd., 1954-60 (Pres., 1957-58); Ancient Free & Accepted Masons; Shrine; Lions Club; Warren Chmbr. of Comm. Contbr. of articles to profl. jrnls. Address: Warren, IL 61087, U.S.A. 8.

WARD, Connie Eugene, b. 19 July 1934. Clergyman. Educ: B.A., N.E. La. Univ., Monroe, 1956; B.D.D., New Orleans Bapt. Theol. Sem., La., 1959; M.Div., ibid, 1972; Dr.Min., 1974. Appts: Pastor, Holmesville Bapt. Ch., Downsville, La., 1953-54, Providence Bapt. Ch., Point, 1954-59, New Chapel Hill Bapt. Ch., W. Monroe, 1959-61, 1st Bapt. Ch., Delhi, La., 1961-67, 1st Bapt. Ch., Long Beach, Miss., 1967-68, 1st Bapt. Ch., Marshall, Tex., 1968-. Mbrships: Past Pres., Marshall Mental Hlth. Assn. & Harrison Co. Coun. on Alcohol Educ.; Bd. of Trustees, E. Tex. Bapt. Coll., Marshall; Pres., Tex. Alumni of New Orleans Bapt. Theol. Sem.; Comm. on Nominations for Mbrs. of Bds. of Trustees of Instns. of Bapt. Gen. Convention of Tex. Has done extensive work in expmtl. rsch. on in-depth Bible tchng. within context of local ch. Address: 511 W. Burleson St., Marshall, TX 75670, U.S.A.

WARD, (The Hon.) Hector Roy, b. 9 Dec. 1923. Journalist; Member of Parliament. Educ: Melbourne Tchrs. Coll., Australia; Univ. of Melbourne. Appts: Schl. Tchr., 1941-46; Ed., Tchr., Jrnl., 1956-59; Dpty. Sec., Victorian Tchrs. Union, 1959-70; Mayor, City of Mordialloc, 1964-65; Justice of the Peace, 1964; Legislative Coun., Victorian Parliament, 1970-. Mbrships. incl: Parliamentary Chmn., Select Comm. enquiring i to Osteopathy, Chiropractic, Naturopathy & Homeopathy, 1973-74; Chmn., Vic. Div., Red Cross Appeals; Chmn., Dev. Bd., McClelland Regional Art Gall.; Treas., Southern Histl. Assn.; Pres., Mordialloc Arts Festival Coun.; Life Gov., Victorian Civil Ambulance, 1965; Life Gov., Mordialloc-Cheltenham Hosp., 1965. Recip., Commendation for servs. to City of Morcialloc, 1970. Address: 10 Hillside Grove, Frankston, Vic., Australia 3199. 1.

WARD, James W., b. 27 Oct. 1904. Professor of Anatomy. Educ: B.A., 1929, M.A., 1932, Univ. of Ala.; M.S., Miss. State Univ., 1931; M.S., Univ. of Minn., 1945; Ph.D., Anat., Univ. of Miss. Schl. of Med., 1950. Appts. incl:

Instr., Asst. Prof., Zool. & Entomol., Miss. State Univ., 1929-32, 1933-36; Grad. Instr., Zool., Univ. of Minn., 1936-38; Assoc. Prof., Zool. & Entomol. Miss. State Univ., 1938-47; Civilian Hd., Dept. of Med. Aid, USAAF Trng. Schl., ibid, 1941-43; Assoc. Prof., Prof., Anat., Schl. of Med., ibid, 1947-70; Prof., Chmn., Dept. of Anat., Schl. of Med., Univ. of S. Fla., 1970-73; Prof., Anat., ibid, 1973-. Mbrships. incl: Am. Assn. of Anatomists; Am. Assn. of Parasitologists; Past Pres., Miss. Acad. of Scis.; Phi Sigma; Beta Beta Beta; Sigma Xi; Advsry. Comm., Gulf Coast Rsch. Lab.; State of Fla. Anatomical Bd.; Fla. Acad. of Scis.; Pan Am. Assn. of Anatomists. Creative works incl. papers, compositions, paintings. Hons: Commonwealth Schlrship., Pratt Dignostic Hosp. & Tufts Med. Coll., 1943. Address: Dept. of Anatomy, Coll. of Medicine, Univ. of S. Fla., Tampa, FL 33620, U.S.A. 14.

WARD, John William, b. 21 Dec. 1922. President of Amherst College. Educ: A.B., Harvard Coll., 1947; M.A., Univ. of Minn., 1950; Ph.D., ibid, 1953. Appts. incl: Instr., Engl., Princeton Univ., 1952-54; Asst. Prof., Engl., ibid, 1954-56, Assoc. Prof., Hist., 1956-64; Prof., Hist., Amherst Coll., 1964-; Pres., ibid, 1971-. Mbrships. incl: Am. Histl. Assn.; Miss. Valley Histl. Assn.; Am. Studies Assn. Publs. incl: Andrew Jackson: Symbol for an Age, 1955; Red, White & Blue: Men, Books, and Ideas in American Culture, 1969; The Nature and Tendency of Free Institutions (Ed.), 1968; Documents in American Civilization (Ed. w. Prof. Hennig Cohen); Articles in Profl. Jrnls. & Mags. Hons. incl: ACLS Fellowship, 1951-52; Guggenheim Fellow, 1956-57 & 1967-68; Fellow, Ctr. for Adv. Study in Behavioral Scis., 1963-64; Fulbright Lectr., U.K., 1967-68. Address: Amherst Coll., Amherst, MA, U.S.A.

WARD, Lew O., b. 24 July 1930. Oil Industry Executive. Educ: B.S., Okla. Univ. Appts: Dist. Engr., Delhi Taylor Oil Corp., Tulsa, 1955-56; Ptnr., Ward-Gungoll Oil Investments, 1956-71; Owner, L.O. Ward Oil Ops., 1963-71; Chmn., Indl. Dev. Comm.; Dir., Chmbr. of Comm., Okla. Independent Petroleum Assn., 1972, Community Bank & Trust Co. of Enid, 1974, Rotary Independent Petroleum Assn. of Am., Pulse Mag. Mbrships: Pres., Am. Bus. Club, 1960, Falcon Toastmasters, 1966; Chmn., Garfield Co. Republican Party, 1967-69; Dir., Metropol. Dinner Club, Okla. Pol. Action Comm., 1972; Alpha Tau Omega; Shriner. Address: P.O. Box 1187, Enid, OK 73701, U.S.A.

WARD, Mary Beatrice. Director of Guidance; School Psychologist. Educ: B.S. in Ed., Boston Univ., Mass., 1945; M.Ed., ibid, 1949; Cert. Schl. Psychologist, 1968; Musical Trng. w. Isadore Philipp, France, Mme. Avis Bliven Charbonnel, John S. Matthews, T. Tertius Noble, Nicolas Slonimsky, U.S.A. Appts. incl: Fndr. & Dir., Greystone Community Chorus, 1923-28, Fidelio Choral Soc., 1934-68; Instr., Music, Abbott Acad., Andover, Mass., 1930-32; Hd., Music Dept., N. Providence H.S., 1939-72; Choir Dir., Organist, Ch. of Master, Mathewson St. Meth. Ch., 1st Ch. Christ. Sci., Providence, R.I., 1935-72; Asst. Dir., (Settlement) Fed. Hill House Schl. of Music, 1932-57; Fndr. & Dir., One Worlders, 1952-72; Dir. of Guidance, N. Providence Schls., 1949-74; Schl. Psychol., Special Educ., 1968-74. Mbrships. incl: Pi Lambda Theta; R.I. State Pres., Delta Kappa Gamma, 1961-65, Music Dir., 1966-68; Bd. of Trustees, Union Free Lib., N. Providence, 1962-74; Dir., One Worlders, 1952-74. Author of songs & articles. Hons. incl: Woman of the Year, N. Providence

Bus. & Profl. Women, 1963; R.I. State Recreation Award for 20 yrs. of Serv. to Youth of Community, 1946-66; John Fitzgerald Kennedy Award to Educator & Community Leader, R.I. Coll. Alumni, 1973. Address: 112 Waterman Ave., N. Providence, RI, U.S.A. 5.

WARD, (Rev.) Peter Garnet, b. 23 June, 1928. Church of England Minister; Musician. Educ: Royal Acad. of Music, London, U.K., 1947-50; Reading Univ., 1950-51; Ridley Hall, Cambridge, 1959-61; G.R.S.M. (London), L.R.A.M., Dip. Ed. Appts: Dir. of Music, Cathedral Choir Schl., Oxford, Prenton Secondary Schl., Birkenhead; Asst. Curate, Maghull Parish Ch., Lancashire; Chap. & Dir. of Music, Kenya H.S., Nairobi, 1964-73. Mbrships: Royal Overseas League; Incorp. Soc. of Musicians; Past Pres., Kenya Ch. Music Soc. Author of Worship the King, servs. for schls. Address: St. Michaels, Parrock Lane, Hartfield, Sussex, U.K. 4.

WARD, Philip, b. 10 Feb. 1938. Library Planning Consultant. Educ: Univ. per gli Stranieri, Perugia, Italy; Univ., Coimbra, Portugal; Middle E. Ctr. for Arab Studies, Shemlam, Lebanon. Appts: Coord., lib. Servs., Oasis Oil Co. of Libya, based in Tripoli, 1963-71; UNESCO Cons. in Lib. Servs., Arab Repub. of Egypt, based in Cairo, 1973; UNESCO Expert in lib. Planning & Admin., Repub. of Indonesia, based in Jakarat, 1973-74. Mbrships: F.R.S.; Fndng. Sec., 1956, & for 7 yrs. Ed. of The Pvte. Lib., Pvte. Libs. Assn.; Assoc. of Lib. Assn. Publs. incl: Loakrime, (poem), 1967; Seldom Rains, (poems), 1967; Ambigamus of The Logic Box, 1967; Poems for Participants, 1968; At the Best of Times, 1968; A Musical Breakfast (play), 1968; Touring Libya-The Eastern Provinces, 1969; A Lizard & Other Distractions (stories), 1969; Maps on the Ceiling (poems), 1970; Garrity & other Plays, 1970; Spanish Literary Appreciation, 1970; Sabratha, 1970; Touring Lebanon, Cyprus, Iran (3 vols.), 1971; Come With Me to Ireland, 1972; A House on Fire, New Poems, 1973; The Aeolian Islands, 1974; Banghot—Portrait of a City & The Oxford Companion to Spanish Literature, forthcoming. Hons: Guinness Poetry Award. Address: c/o The Oleander Press, 28 Parkfield Cres., Harrow HA2 6JZ, U.K. 3, 30.

WARD, Ritchie R(unyan), b. 6 Apr. 1906. Writer. Educ: B.S., Univ. of Calif., Berkeley, 1927; M.J., 1966. Appts: Chem., Hawaiian Sugar Planter Assn., Honolulu, 1929-34; Chem., Mgr., Tech. Info., Shell Dev. Co., Emeryville, Calif., 1934-62; Free-lance Writer, 1962-. Mbrships: Alpha Chi Sigma; Sigma Delta Chi. Publs: Practical Technical Writing, 1968; The Living Clocks, 1971; Into the Ocean World, 1974; contbr. to mags. Address: 93 El Toyonal Rd., Orinda, CA 94563, U.S.A.

WARDEN, Margaret Smith (Mrs. Robert D. Warden), b. 18 July 1917. Civic Leader; Library Trustee. Appts. incl: Libn., Gt. Falls Tribune, Gt. Falls, Mont., 1935-42; Civilian Hd. Publs. Index. Sect. for Bur. of Aeronautics & Dpty. Chief Naval Ops. (Air) & Ed., Publs. Index going to 10,000 ships & stns., 1942-44; Ed. for proposed Navy-wide catalogue of publs. in off. of Sec. of Navy, James Forrestal, 1944-46. Mbr. num. civic assns. & holds off. in· many. Mbrships. incl: Am. Lib. Assn., 1957-; ALA, Am. Lib. Trustees Assn., 1957-; Mont. Lib. Assn., 1957-, Pres., 1973-74; Gt. Falls Pub. Lib. Trustee, 1957- & Chmn. Bd., 1963-; Pacific Northwest Lib. Assn., 1965-; Mont. Constitutional Conven. Deleg. & Pub. Info. Off., 1971-73; Mont. Comm. for the Humanities, 1973-; Mont. State Advsry. Coun. on Libs., 1973-74; Ratification Coun. for Equal Rights Amendment to U.S. Constitution, Mont., 1973-74; V. Chmn., Mont. State Lib. Commn., 1973-76. Publs: Montana Libraries, 1962-70. Hons. incl: Logo Pin Award, Nat. Commn. on Libs. & Infol. Sci., Seattle, 1974. Address: 208 3rd Ave. N., Gt. Falls, MT 59401, U.S.A. 5, 138.

WARDLE, Thomas Edward, b. 18 Aug. 1912. Company Director. Educ: Perth Boys Schl., Australia. Lord Mayor of Perth, 1967-72. Hons: Kt. Bach., 1970; Commenditore, Repub. of Italy, 1970; LL.D.,Univ. of W. Australia, 1973. Address: 3 Kent St., Bicton, W.A., Australia.

WARE, Eunice Letitia, b. 29 June 1895. Educator. Educ: B.A., 1916, M.A., 1928, Ph.D., 1936, Univ. of Tex. Appts: incl: Tchr., Longview, H.S., Tex.; Coll. of Marshall; Sr. H.S., Austin; Stephen F. Austin State Tchrs. Coll., Nacogdoches; E. Tex. Bapt. Coll., Marshall; Le Tourneau Coll., Longview, Mbrships: Magna Carta Dames: Daughters of Am. Colonies; Am.'s of Royal Descent; DAR; Daughters of Repub. of Tex.; Plantagenet Soc.; Descendents of Knights of Order of Garter; Colonial Order of Crown; Histn., United Daughters of Confederacy; Longview Woman's Forum; Longview Fine Arts Club; Longview Music Club; Longview Chmbr. of Comm.; S.-Ctrl. MLA. Address: 205 Isgren Dr., Longview, TX 75601, U.S.A. 22, 57, 128.

WARE, Mary Ann, b. 12 Mar. 1945. Home Economist. Educ: B.S., Univ. of Neb., 1967; M.S., ibid. Appts: Tchr.-Dir., Home Living Ctr. for Handicapped, Bklyn. Bur. of Community Serv., 1968-70; Dir., Rehab. Homemaking Project, W. Va. Univ., 1970-72; State Trng. Off., Hd. Start, Handicapped Children & Mgmt., 1972-. Mbrships: Rehab. Comm., Am. Home Econs. Assn., 1970-73; Nat. Assn. for Educ. of Young Children; Nat. Rehab. Assn.; Am. Assn. Workers for the Blind. Contbr. articles to jrnls. in field. Address: 704 Allen Hall, W. Va. Univ., Morgantown, WV 26506, U.S.A.

WARE, Naomi Cale, b. 4 Jan. 1899. University Professor. Educ: B.A., Univ. of Tex.; M.A., ibid. Appts: Asst., Hist. Dept., Univ. of Tex.; Prof.-Hd. Hist. & Pol. Sci. Dept. Hannibal La Grange Coll.; Prof.-Hd. of Hist. & Pol. Sci., Kidd-Key Coll.; Examiner, Cert of Title Sect.; Motor Vehicle Div., Tex State Hwy. Dept. Mbrships: Magna Carta Dames; Ams. of Royal Descent; Plantagenet Soc.; Order of the Crown; Descendants of the Kts. of the Garter; DAR; Daughters of Am. Colonists: United Daughters of the Confederacy; Daughters of Repub. of Tex.; Longview Fine Arts Club; Longview Woman's Forum; Longview Music Club; Pi Sigma Alpha, 1928. Address: 205 Isgren Dr., Longview, TX 75601, U.S.A. 22, 128.

WARFIELD, John Ogle, Jr. b. 3 Apr. 1900. Surgeon. Educ: A.B. St. John's Coll., Annapolis, 1919; M.A., ibid, 1922; M.D. Univ. of Md., Baltimore, 1922. Appts: Pvte. Surg. Prac., Wash. D.C., 1926-60; Staff Surg., Bionetics Rsch. Lab., Kensington, Md. 1965-69; Med. Prog. Dir., Community Hlth. Serv., Wash. D.C. 1969-; Mbrships. incl: Fndr., Sec. Pres., Med. Arts Soc., 1930, Wash. Acad. Surg 1933; Pres., Pan-Am. Med. Soc., 1958; Life Mbr., Med. Soc. of D.C., Am. Coll. of Surgs; Fndr., Huguenot Soc. in Md.; Military Order of the Crusades; Cosmos Club & many community & civic orgs. Contbr. of med. sci. articles to profl. jrnls. Hons. incl: Vicennial Medal, Georgetown Univ. Med. Schl., 1951; Alumni Award of Merit, St. John's Coll., 1960; Grant of Armorial Bearings, Am. Coll. of Arms, 1968. Address:

3544 Williamsburg Lane, N.W. WA D.C. 20008, U.S.A. 130, 131.

WARGA, Helen Alberta, b. 7 Mar. 1915. Social Worker; Salesman in Real Estate; Freelance Writer; Poet. Educ: B.A., Univ of Wash. Seattle, 1946; M.S.W. Univ. of Pitts., Pa., 1960. Appts: incl: W. Area Dir., YWCA of Pitts, Pa., 1955-58; Exec. Dir., Kensington Br., YWCA of Phila., ibid, 1960-63; Assoc. Metropol. Exec. Dir., & USO Coord., ibid, 1963-66; Exec. Dir., YWCA of Omaha, Neb., 1966-71; Real Estate Salesman, Riverside Lakes, Inc., A Recreational Subdiv., 1972-. Mbrships. incl; 1st Presby. Ch. of Phila.; former Trustee, McKees Rocks, Pa. Presby. Ch.; former Sun. School Ldr. & Christian Endeavor Off., 1st Presby. Ch. Plattsmouth, Neb.; Nat. Assn. Soc. Wkrs.; Acad. Cert. Soc. Wkrs.; YWCA; AAUW, Omaha Chapt.; Pres., Soroptimist Club of Omaha, 1971-72, '72-73; former V.P., Prog. Chmn. Chmn. Finance Comm.; KOIL Radio Community Advsry. Bd., 1969, '70; Steering Comm., "Anytown Nebraska", 1970-71; Middle Atlantic Area YWCA Exec. Dirs.' Roundtable, 1960, '66. Author of poems in many mags. Address: 120 N. 11th St., Plattsmouth, NB 68048, U.S.A. 5, 132.

WARING, (Sister) Mary Grace, b. 12 May 1897. Research Professor. Educ: A.B., Creighton Univ., Omaha, Neb., 1921; M.S., Kan. State Univ., 1926; Ph.D., Cath. Univ. of Am., 1931. Mbr., Congregation of the Sisters of St. Joseph, 1914. Appts: w. Nazareth Acad., Concordia, Kan., 1917-22; Chmn., Dept. of Chem., Marymount Coll., Salina, Kan., 1922-66; Chem. Rsch. Prof., ibid, 1966-. Mbrships: Am. Chem. Soc.; Nat. Sci. Tchrs. Assn. Presented a paper "Men & Women of the Priestley Centennial, at 1st Priestley Bicentennial, Wilkes-Barre, Pa., 26 Apr. 1974, 100 yrs. after her 2nd cousin W. Geo. Waring reported the Priestley Centennial, Northumberland, Pa., 31 July, 1874. Recip. Rsch. Grants from Kan. Heart Assn., Am. Cancer Soc. & Int. Union of Operating Engrs. Address: c/o Marymount Coll. of Kan., Salina, KS 67401, U.S.A. 14, 120, 138.

WARKE, William Benton, b. 27 May 1926. Realtor; Executive. Educ: Grad., Univ. of B.C., Vancouver, Canada; R.I. (B.C.), Profl. Div., Real Estate Inst. of B.C.; Fellow, Cert. F.R.I., Canadian Inst. of Realtors. Appts: Journeyman to Supt., Construction Ind., 1945-52; Columbia Pictures Ltd., 1953-56; Real Estate Dept. Crown Trust Co., 1957-59; Pres., Warke Agcys. Ltd., Pres., Llonarke Investment Co. Ltd., Pres., R.W. Timber Corp., Seattle, Wash., U.S.A., Pres., Templar Holdings Ltd., V.P., R.M. Timber Ltd., V.P., Pacific Projs. Ltd., V.P., Minerias Andes Corp. Ltd., Dir., Unidrug Systems Ltd., Dir., Four-Way Investments Ltd., 1959-. Mbrships: Real Estate Bd. of Greater Vancouver; Indl.-Comml.-Investment Div., ibid; Canadian Assn. of Real Estate Bds.; Int. Real Estate Fedn.; Terminal City Club; Hollyburn Country Club; Gizeh Shrine Temple, A.A.O.N.M.S. Address: Ste. 320, 355 Burrard St., Vancouver, B.C., V6C 2G8, Canada. 9.

WARLICH, Otto, b. 27 July 1902. Speech Educator & Recitor. Educ: Acad. for Church & Schl. Music, Berlin; Coll. of Music, ibid; Univ. of Berlin. Appts: Concert Violinist, Music Tchr. & Lectr. at Pub. Colls.; Actor & speaker at chamber evenings, 1930-; Asst. in Voice & Speech Educ., Univ. of Berlin, 1932; Prof. of Speech Educ., State Coll. for Music & Arts, Berlin, 1945-67; Tchr., Max Reinhardt Theater Coll., ibid, 1953-61. Mbrships: German Comm. for Speech & Speech Educ., 1932-33 & 1952-64; Assn. of German Stage Personnel,

1945-. Author of Innovative Formation of the Unconditionally Natural Act of Speech by means of Conscious Combination of the Musical Elements of Speech with the Logic of Sentence Development & the Transparency of the Psychological Background. Address: 19 Gervinusstrasse, 1 Berlin 12, German Fed. Repub. 43.

WARMING, Paul Victor, b. 4 Dec. 1913. The Heraldic Counsellor of the Danish State. Educ: M.L., Univ. of Copenhagen, Denmark, 1939. Appts: Civil Servant (Dpty. Hd. of Sect.), Govt. Admin.; The Heraldic Counsellor of the Danish State, 1954-. Mbrships: Dano-Belgian Soc. (Exec. Comm.); Royal Danish Yacht Club. Designer: Amendment to Royal Danish Coats of Arms, 1972; var. Heraldic Emblems of Danish Armed Forces; Coats of Arms, var. Danish Municipalities. Heraldic Rsch. work for Danish & other States. Hons: Kt., Order of Dannebrog; Kt., Order of the Crown, Belgium; Kt., Order of Leopold II, ibid. Address: Bredgade 4, DK 1260 Copenhagen K, Denmark; Office: c/o Ministry of the Interior, Christiansborg Slotsplads 1, DK 1218 Copenhagen K, Denmark. 43.

WARMING-LARSEN, Aage, b. 12 July 1912. Clinic President; Chief Physician. Educ: M.D., Univ. of Copenhagen, Denmark, 1941; Ph.D., 1947. Appts. incl: Rsch. Fellow, Children's Hosp., Boston, at Dr. Gambles Lab., Harvard Med. Schl., U.S.A., 1950; Sr. Res., Univ. Hosp., Copenhagen, 1951-53; Chief Asst. Physn., Med. Ward, ibid, 1953; chief, Lab. of Metabolism & Nutrition (inclng. out-patient clin.), Copenhagen Municipal Hosp., 1953-56; Pres., Clin. in Internal Med. (metabolism & gastro-intestinal diseases), Clin. Lab. & Rsch. Lab., 1956-; Mbr., Bd. of Examiners in Metabolism & Dietetics, Univ. Schl. of Dentistry, 1947-59. Publs. incl: Warming-Larsen. Nutrition & physiology in gastro-intestinal & gall bladder diseases, 1973; Alcoholic?, forthcoming; 67 var. publs. concerning liver & gallbladder diseases, sodium & potassium balances, liver biopsy, metabolism. Recip., WHO Fellowship, 1950. Address: Nørrevold 68, 1358 K, Copenhagen, Denmark

WARMOUTH, James Ernest, b. 5 May 1946. Doctor of Medicine. Educ: A.B., Univ. of Austria, 1969; M.D., Med. Univ. of S.C., U.S.A., 1973. Appts: Res. in Pediatrics, Med. Univ. Hosp. of S.C., 1973-74; Lt., U.S.N.R. Treas., V.P., O.D.K. Address: 71 B East Bay St., Charleston, SC 29401, U.S.A. 46, 125.

WARNER, Boyd, Jr. (Indian name: Blackhair), b. 26 May 1937. Painter; Decorator. Educ: Cert., painting, decorating & paperhanging, Phoenix, Ariz., 1961. Profl. painter & artist. Exhibitions: Daniel Frishman Gall. of Art, Osterville, Mass., Mrs. Tee Fleming, El Ares & Co., Indpls., Ind., & Gall. 3, Phoenix, Ariz. Hons: 2nd & 3rd in Fine Arts, Window Rock, Ariz., 1967; 2nd Award, Ariz. State Fair, 1966; 3rd Premium, ibid, 1970; Elkus Mem. Award, Peyote Symbol (Merit), Intertribal Ceremonial Gallup, N.M., 1971; Hon. Mention, Heard Mus. Guild, 1971; 2nd Award, 1st Place (Mixed Media), Gallup Intertribal Ceremonial, Gallup, N.M., 1972; 3rd, watercolor, Tanner's All Indians Arts & Crafts Show, 1973; 2nd & 3rd Award, mixed media, ibid, 1974; Hon. Mention, Scottsdale Nat. Indian Arts & Crafts Show, 1974. Address: 606 N. 4th St., Apt. 1, Phoenix AZ 85004, U.S.A. 37.

WARNER, Francis, b. 21 Oct. 1937. Poet; Playwright. Educ: London Coll. of Music; Music Schlrship., St. Catharine's Coll.,

Cambridge, 1956-59. Appts: Supvsr., St. Catharine's Coll., 1959-65; Fellow & Tutor, Engl. Lit. & Univ. Lectr., St. Peter's Coll., Oxford. Publs: (Poetry) Perennia, 1962; Early Poems, 1964; Experimental Sonnets, 1965; Madrigal, 1967; The Poetry of Francis Warner, 1970; Maquettes (trilogy of one-act plays), 1972; Lying Figures, 1972; Meeting Ends, 1974; Rep. in Garland (anthol.), 1968. Hons: Messing Int. Award for Lit., 1972. Address: c/o St. Peter's Coll., Oxford, U.K.

WARNER, Francis James, b. 3 Oct. 1897. Physician; Neuropathologist. Educ: B.A. Univ. of Iowa; M.A., Univ. of Mich., 1925; M.D., Loyola Univ. Med. Schl, 1919. Appts: Lectr. in Neuro-Anatomy, Univ. of Utah, 1946-48; Instr. in Neurol., Temple Univ., Med. Schl., 1957-. Mbrships. Fellow, Royal Soc. of Med., London, U.K.; Fellow, Zool. Soc., London; Am. Psych. Assn.; Am. Assn. of Neuropathols.; Am. Assn. Anatomists; Am. Soc. Zools. Author of num. papers on comp. Neuro-Anatomy & neuropathol. Dipl., Am. Bd. Pathol. 1952. Address: P. O Box 523, Philadelphia, 5, PA U.S.A. 22.

WARNER, Geoffrey John, (pseudonym, Geoffrey Johns), b. 9 Mar. 1923. Antique Dealer; Author. Educ: Salisbury Schl. of Art. Appts: Self-employed antique dealer & gall. proprietor, 1961-; Mng. Dir. & Dir., var. cos., 1973-; Schl. Gov., & Vice Chmn., Educ. Trust. Mbrships: Salisbury & S. Wiltshire Mus.; Salisbury Chmbr. of Comm. Publs.: Any Advance, 1961; What Am I Bid, 1962; Enjoy Collecting Antiques. Antique exhibs: Civic Hall, Salisbury, 1970; currently, Joiners' Hall, ibid. Address: The Joiners' Hall, St. Ann St., Salisbury, Wiltshire, U.K. 3, 30, 133, 137, 139.

WARNER, James McNeil, b. 26 July 1925. Teacher. Educ: B.Sc., Central State Univ.; Univ of Md. Appts: Asst. Tchr., Ord Rd. Schl.; Asst. Tchr., Central Schl.; Dpty. Prin., Prospect Secondary Schl. for Boys; Hd., Jr. Schl.,Boys; Hd., Jr. Schl., Churchill Schl.; Prin., Robert Crawford Schl. Mbrships: Chmn., United Bermuda Party; Dir., Christian Educ., Bermuda Conf. of A.M.E. Ch.; Min. of Music, Bethel A.M.E. Ch.; Past Pres., Socratic Literary Club; Kiwanis Int. Club; Alpha Phi Omega. Address: Sousa Estate, Devonshire, Bermuda.

WARNOCK, Geoffrey James, b. 16 Aug. 1923. Academic. Educ: New Coll., Oxford, U.K., 1945-48; Fellow, Magdalen Coll., Oxford, 1949. Appts: Fellow & Tutor, Brasenose Coll., Oxford, 1950-53; Fellow & Tutor, Magdalen Coll., Oxford, 1953-71; Emeritus Fellow, ibid, 1972; Prin., Hertford Coll., Oxford, 1971-; Hon. Fellow, New Coll., Oxford, 1973. Mbr., Aristotelian Soc. Publs: Berkeley, 1953; English Philosophy since 1900, 1958; Contemporary Moral Philosophy, 1967; The Object of Morality, 1971. Address: Hertford Coll., Oxford, OX1 3BW, U.K. 1, 34.

WARR, (The Ven. Archdeacon) Arthur Edward, b. 24 July 1902. Clerk in Holy Orders. Educ: Th.L., Australian Coll. of Theol., 1927; Deacon, 1927; Priest, 1928. Appts. incl: Rector, sev. parishes in N.S.W., 1934-69; Bishop in Coun. Mbr., 1938-65; Archdeacon of Kempsey, 1946-47, Clarence, 1947-49, South, 1965-69; Archdeacon Emeritus, 1969-; Chap., Grafton Gaol, 1947-65; Chap., Dept. of Immigration, 194-50 & 1965; Corporate Trustee, Diocese of Grafton, 1947-65. Mbrships. incl: Gen. & Provincial Synod, N.S.W. & Australia; Royal Empire Soc., 1934-69; Pres., Rotary Club, Kempsey, 1944; Fndr. & Sec., St. Thomas Ch. Restoration Appeal, 1966-. Publs: The Consecration of

Christ Church Cathedral, Grafton, N.S.W., 1959; The Church of S. Thomas 1824-. Hons: J.P., N.S.W., 1936; Preacher at St. Martin-in-the-Fields, Australia Day, 1950; Coronation Medal, 1953. Address: 9 Owen St., Port Macquarie, N.S.W., Australia 2444. 23.

WARREN, Dave, b. 12 Apr. 1932. Educator. Educ: B.A., 1955; M.A., 1962; Ph.D. (in progress). Appts. incl: Tchr., Taft Jr. H.S., Albuquerque N.M., 1957-58; Instr., USAF Reserve Officer's Trng. Courses in Ldrship. & Mgmt., USAF Reserve Trng. Ctr., ibid, 1958-59; Instr., Dept. of Hist., Okla. State Univ., Stillwater, 1964-66; Asst. Prof., Dept. of Hist., Univ. of Neb., Lincoln, 1966-68; Mbr., Latin Am. Studies Inst., ibid, 1966-68; Dir., Curric. & Instrn., Inst. Am. Indian Arts, Santa Fe, N.M., 1968-71; Dir., Div. Rsch. & Cultural Studies Dev., Bur. of Indian Affairs, ibid, 1971-. Mbrships. incl: Advsry. Bd., Ctr. for Studies of Am. West., Univ. of Utah, 1969-; Bd. Trustee, Am. Indian Schrlship. Inc., 1970-71; Cons., Lib. Servs. to the Disadvantaged, ALA, 1972-. Author of publs. in field. Recip., sev. fellowships & grants. Address: Rsch. & Cultural Studies Dev. Ctr., Inst. of Am. Indian Arts, Sante Fe, NM 87501, U.S.A.

WARREN, Harry Verney, b. 27 Aug. 1904. Geological Engineer. Educ: B.A., Univ. of B.C., Canada, 1926; B.A.Sc., 1927; B.Sc., Oxford Univ., U.K., 1928; D.Phil., 1929. Appts. incl: Lectr., Dept. of Geol. & Geog., Univ. of B.C., Canada, 1932-36; Asst. Prof., ibid, 1936-40; Assoc. Prof., 1940-45; Prof., 1945-73; Hon. Prof., 1973-; Tech. Advsr., Geochem., Kennco Explorations, 1951-71; Tech. Advsr., Placer Dev., 1973-. Fellowships: F.R.S.C.; F.G.S.A. Mbrships. incl: M.Inst.M.M.; A.I.M.E.; C.I.M.M.; Soc. Econ. Geols.; Minerol. Soc. Canada. Author of num. publs. in field. Hons. incl: Disting. Lectr., C.I.M.M., 1971-72; Officer, Order of Canada, 1972. Address: Dept. of Geological Scis., Univ. of B.C., Vancouver 8, B.C., Canada. 14, 88.

WARREN, Pamela S., b. 31 Dec. 1940. Librarian. Educ: B.A., Neb. Wesleyan Univ., 1962; M.A., Univ. of Ill., 1963. Appts: Admnstrve. Asst., Trails Regional Lib., Warrensburg, Mo., 1963-66; Dir., Rolling Hills Consolidated Lib., St. Joseph, Mo., 1966-. Mbrships: Mo. Lib. Assn. (pres.-elect, 1973-74; sec.; chmn., pub. lib. div.; jr. mbrs. round table chmn.; treas., pub. lib. div.); Comm. Chmn., V.p.'s; Bus. & Profl. Women (pres.; 1st & 2nd. V.p.; comm. chmn.); Altrusa Int. (pres.; 1st v.p.; corresp. sec.); Womens Div., Chmbr. of Comm. (1st V.p.); Delta Kappa Gamma; Beta Sigma Phi; Alpha Gamma Delta; DAR; AAUW; Alpha Mu Lambda; Alpha Lambda Delta. Outstanding Young Women, St. Joseph Mo. JC's, 1971. Address: 1211 Carol Dr., St. Joseph, MO 64506, U.S.A. 5, 76, 120, 130, 132, 138.

WARRICK, Carrie Repass (Mrs. L.M. Warrick), b. 17 July 1903. Teacher; Pianist; Organist. Educ: B. Mus, Grad. work, Cinn. Conservatory of Music. Appts: Pianist; Organist; w. Tchrs. Div., Am. Coll. of Music. Mbrships. incl: Delta Omicron; Delta Kappa Gamma; Nat. Maier Music Assn.; Fac. Mbr., Judge, Nat. Guild of Piano Tchrs.; Organist Guild; State Chmn., Tenn. Festival; Judge, Nat. Fedn. of Music Clubs. Hons: Piano Guild's Hall of Fame. Address: Limestone Rte. 2, TN 37681, U.S.A. 125.

WARSHAWSKY, Albert, b. 2 Oct. 1935. Certified Public Accountant. Educ: B.B.A., Univ. of Mich., 1957; M.B.A., ibid, 1958. Currently CPA, Price Waterhouse & Co., N.Y.C.

Mbrships: Am. Inst. CPA's; N.Y. State Soc. CPA's; Beta Alpha Psi; Univ. of Mich. Alumni Club. Address: 200 E. 78th. St., N.Y., NY 10021, U.S.A. 6.

WARTOFSKY, Marx William, b. 5 Aug. 1928. Professor of Philosophy. Educ: B.A., Columbia Coll., N.Y.C., 1948; A.M., Grad. Fac. of Philos., Columbia Univ., 1949; Ph.D., ibid, 1952. Appts. incl: Asst. Prof.-Assoc. Prof., Boston Univ. Coll. of Liberal Arts, 1960-67; Prof., ibid, 1967; Chmn., Dept. of Philos., 1967-73; Vis. Prof., Dept. of Philos., Brandeis Univ., 1966-67, Univ. of Calgary, 1968. Mbrships: Sec.-Treas., Eastern Div., Am. Philosophical Assn., 1967-70; Bd. of Offs., ibid, 1967-70; Nat. Coun. Rep., Dist. X (New England), AAUP, 1970-73; Nominee, Nat. Pres., ibid, 1973; Metaphys. Soc.; Am. Soc. for Aesthetics; British Soc. for Aesthetics; Philos. of Sci. Assn.; Study Group for the Unity of Knowledge. Publs. incl: Conceptual Foundations of Scientific Thought, 1968; The Philosophy of Ludwig Feuerbach, forthcoming; Articles in jrnls. Recip. of hons. Address: Dept. of Philos., Boston Univ., 232 Bay State Rd., Boston, MA 02215, U.S.A. 2, 13.

WASE, Arthur W., b. 16 Nov. 1919. Professor; Biomedical Research. Educ: A.B., Columbia Univ., 1941; Ph.D., Rutgers Univ., 1951. Appts: Asst. Prof., Biol. Chem., Hahnemann Med. Coll., Pa., 1951-56; Fulbright Prof., Univ. of Bruxelles & Inst. Burdet, 1956-57; Assoc. Prof., Hahnemann Med. Coll., 1957-68; Prof., ibid, 1968-. Also Manager, Biol. Rsch., Colgate Rsch. Ctr., 1961-63. Mbrships: Am. Cancer Soc.; N.J. Acad. of Sci.; AAAS; Am. Heart Assn. Publs: Num. papers, U.S. & for. jrnls. Hons: Fulbright Prof., 1956-57; Medal of Honor, Univ. of Bruxelles, 1957; Citation, Inst. Burdet, 1957; Rsch. Fellow, Merck Inst. of Therapeutic Rsch., 1963-; Prof., Univ. del Cauca, Colombia, 1965-. Address: Hahnemann Medical Coll., Philadelphia, PA, U.S.A.

WASHINGTON, (Lt. Gen.) G. Toe, b. 15 Apr. 1928. Soldier. Educ: Bus. Coll., Gold Coast (now Ghana), 1948; Offs. Basic course, Liberia, 1955; Quartermaster Schl., Ft. Lee, Va., U.S.A., 1956; Libn. For. Serv. Schl., 1960; Logistics Mgmt. Schl., Ft. Lee, Va., 1961; Dip., U.S. Army Cmd. & Gen. Staff Coll., Ft. Leavenworth, Kan., 1964. Appts. incl: Personnel Off., Off. of Adjutant Gen., 1953-56; Quartermaster, Armed Forces of Liberia, 1956-59; Asst. Chief of Staff, G-4 (Logistics), 1959-64; Asst. Chief of Staff, G-1 (Personnel) & Adjutant Gen., Armed Forces of Liberia, 1965; Chief of Staff, ibid, 1965-70; Advsr. to Pres. on Mil. Affairs, 1970. Mbrships. incl: Ancient Egyptian Arabic Order Nobles of the Mystic Shrine; Consistory 32; Master - Mason. Hons. incl: Long Serv. Medal, 1968; Kt. Grand Band, Humane Order of African Redemption; For. Decorations, Mauritania, Togo, Tunisia, Cameroons & Ctrl. African Repub. Address: Min. of Educ., Monrovia, Liberia. 135.

WASHINGTON, James Winston, Jr. Painter; Sculptor. Educ: Amit Co. Trng. Schl., Miss.; Nat. Landscape Inst.; Study of painting under Mark Tobey. Appts: Sec., Seattle (Wash.) Chapt., Artists Equity, 1949-53; Pres., 1960-62; Mbr., Governing Coun., ibid, State of Wash., 1959-60; State Art Commnr., 1961-66. Mbrships: Grand Insp. Gen., 33 degree, & Mbr., United Supreme Coun. of Masons: Bd. of Dirs., Centrum Fndn. Inc. Contbr. to periodicals. Hons: Purchase Prize, Sculpture, San Fran. Mus., 1956, Oakland Mus., 1957; Hon. Prize, Sculpture, Seattle, 1958; 2nd Prize, Sculpture, Seattle World's Fair, 1962; Gov.'s Sculpture

Award, Wash. State, 1970; Special Gov.'s Award, 1973; James W. Washington, Jr. Day, proclaimed by Mayor of Seattle, May 20, 1973; Salute to James W. Washington, Jr., Benefit Guild, Seattle, 1973. Address: 1816-26th Ave., Seattle, WA 98122, U.S.A. 2, 37, 133.

WASICKI, Adam C., b. 24 Dec. 1912. Artist; Art Restorer. Educ: B.F.A., Hartford Art Schl., Univ. of Hartford, Conn., 1952; studied (painting) art & art restoration, Paris, Warsaw, Berlin & Florence, 1935-37. Appts: former Dir. of own art schl.; Owner & Operator, own art Studio, Wasicki Art Ctr. Mbrships: Conn. Acad. of Fine Arts, Hartford; Essex Art Assn., Conn. Works incl: Murals, St. Mary's Ch., Middletown, Conn.; Painting of Main St., Middletown for the Farmers & Mechanics Savings Bank; Pink Roses; Rock Landing Rd., Haddam Neck, Conn.; portraits of friends. Has restored following paintings: a small Rembrandt; 'The Two Sisters' by John Singer Sargent; a Gilbert Stuart portrait of Geo. Washington; paintings that hang in the Olin Lib. at Wesleyan Univ.; var. other 16th & 17th century paintings. Hons. incl: Special Award for Achievement in Graphic Art & Thesis Painting, Hartford Art Schl., Univ. of Hartford, 1952. Address: Wasicki Art Ctr., 681 Saybrook Rd., Middletown, CT 06457, U.S.A. 105, 133.

WASILE, J. Elyse, b. 27 May 1920. Artist. Educ: Univ. of Calif., L.A., U.S.A. Mbrships: Int. Inst. of Conservation of Historic & Artistic Works; Bahamas Histl. Soc. Works incl: Murals, Widner Estate, Palm Beach, Fla., 1961; Murals, Palm Beach Int. Airport, 1960; Murals, Nassau Beach Hotels, Bahamas, 1961; Full definitive stamp issue (15 stamps), Post Off. Dept., Bahamas, 1971. Author, The Commonwealth Stamp Catalogue. Recip., Blue Ribbon, S. Fla. Exposition, 1960. Address: Nassau Art Gallery, Box N-1334, Nassau, Bahamas, W. Indies. 37.

WASS DE CZEGE, (Count) Albert (known as Albert Wass), b. 8 Jan. 1908. Poet; Author; University Professor. Educ: M.A., M.S., Reformed Collegium, Kolozsvar, Univ. of Debrecen, Hungary. Appts: Dept. of For. Langs., Univ. of Fla., U.S.A.; Script writer, Radio Free Europe; Pres., Danubian Press. Mbrships: Transylvanian Helicon; Zs. Kemény Literary Soc.; Kisfaludy Soc.; Fndr. & Pres., Am. Hungarian Literary Guild; Pres. Körösi-Csoma Soc.; Turan Soc.; Arpad Acad. Publs: 24 novels (many translated); 2 vols. short stories, 3 vols. poems; Contbr. sev. hundred articles to Hungarian publs. Hons: Baumgarten Award, Hungary, 1938; Klebelsperg Prize, Hungary, 1941; Arpad Acad. Award, U.S.A., 1968. Address: Astor Park, FL 32002, U.S.A.

WASSÉN, (Sven) Henry, b. 24 Aug. 1908. Professor. Educ: FL, Gothenburg Univ., 1936. Appts: Curator & Hd., Dept. of Am. Coll., Acting Dir., Dir., Gothenburg Ethnog. Mus., 1930-73; Ret., 1973; w. British Mus., Dept. of Ethnog., 1958-59. Mbrships. incl: Travellers' Club, Göteborg, 1935-; Sociedad Sueco-Hispano-Americana, Göteborg; Trustee, Med.-Hist. Soc., Göteborg. Publs: Facta ur Klubbens Acts, 1954; num. sci. publs. in jrnls. Hons: Kt. Cmdr., El Sol del Perú, 1947; Cmdr., Vasco Núñez de Balboa, Panama, 1958; Official, Orden de Boyacá, Colombia, 1966; Kt., Royal Order of Wasa, 1967; Loubat Prize, Royal Swedish Acad. Antiquities & Hist., 1967; Prof., h.c., 1972; Silver Plaquette, Göteborg Mus., 1973. Address: Skånegatan 21, S-412 51 Göteborg, Sweden.

WASSERMAN, Jack, b. 20 Feb. 1913. Attorney. Educ: B.A., CCNY, 1932; J.D.,

Harvard Law Schl., 1935. Appts: Past Mbr., Bd. of Immigration Appeals, U.S. Dept. of Justice; Prac. Law Inst. Lectr. on How the Practitioner Defends Deportation Cases; Counsel, num. Supreme Ct. & Ct. of Appeals immigration & deportation cases; Immigration Practitioner, 25 yrs. Mbrships: Dir. & Past Pres., Assn. of Immigration & Nationality Lawyers; Coun., Admin. Law Sec., Am. Bar Assn., 1970-73. Publs: Immigration Law & Practice, 1973; num. articles; Wash. Ed., Immigration Bar Bull. Address: 1707 H. St., N.W., Washington, DC 20006, U.S.A. 7, 16

WASSERMAN, Max Judd, b. 24 June 1895. Economist. Educ: A.B., Cornell Univ., .1918; A.M., Univ. of Ill., 1921; Doct. in Econs., Univ. of Lyons, France, 1925. Appts: Asst. Prof. of Econs., Univ. of Ill., U.S.A., 1925-34; Econ. Sect. Chief & Dir. of sev. fed. agcys. in U.S., 1934-65; Prof. of Econs., Univ. of Ky., 1959-65; Vis. Lectr., Econs., Ky. State Univ., 1965-; cons. Economist, 1965-. Mbrships: Phi Beta Kappa, 1918-; Zeta Beta Tau, 1914-; Am. Econ. Assn., 1920-; Rep. U.S. at sev. int. confs. in Europe & U.S. & Mbr. of Del., ibid. Publs: L'Oeuvre de le Fédéral Trade Commission, 1925; co-author of Modern International Economics, International Finance, The Common Market & American Business, The Balance of Payments; Contbr. of over 50 articles to bus. & profl. jrnls. Address: 1104 Fontaine Rd., Lexington, KY 40502, U.S.A. 6, 7, 13, 14, 16, 55, 131.

WASSERMAN, Paul. Professor; Librarian. Educ: B.B.A., CCNY, 1948; M.S.L.S., Columbia Univ., 1949; M.S., ibid, 1950; Ph.D., Univ. of Mich., 1960; Post-doct. Schlr., Data Processing & Info. Retrieval, Ctr. for Documentation & Communications Rsch., Western Reserve Univ., 1963-64. Appts: Asst. to Bus. Libn.-Chief, Sci. & Ind. Div., Bklyn. Pub. Lib., 1949-53; Asst. Prof.-Prof., Libn., Grad. Schl. of Bus. & Pub. Admin., Cornell Univ., 1953-65; Vis. Prof., Dept. of Lib. Sci., Univ. of Mich., summers, 1960, '63, '64; Lect. (pt.-time), Schl. of Lib. Sci., Western Reserve Univ., 1963-64; Dean, Schl. of Lib. & Info. Servs., Univ. of Md., 1965-70; Prof., ibid, 1970-. Mbrships. incl: AAUP; ALA; Soc. for Info. Sci.; Md. Lib. Assn.; Special Libs. Assn. Publs. incl: Decision Making—An Annotated Bibliography (w. Silander), 1958, Supplement, 1958-63, 1964; The Librarian & the Machine, 1965; A Study of the Executive in Library & Information Activity (w. Bundy), 1970; The New Librarianship—A Challenge for Change, 1972; num. articles in profl. jrnls.; Ed., Co-Ed. or Mng. Ed. of many profl. publs.; Project Dir. of many rsch. projects. Address: c/o Schl. of Lib. & Info. Servs., Univ. of Md., Coll. Park, MD 20742, U.S.A.

WASTAL, Patrick Henry, b. 8 Mar. 1932. Business Executive. Educ: Hon. Ph.D. in Bus. Admin., Hamilton State Univ. Appts. incl: V.P., Continental Packaging Inc., L.A., 1955-64; Pres., Sands Supply Corp., Glendale, 1965-66; Pres., Ph.H. Wastal & Assocs., Glendale, 1966-; Pres., LAD Sales & Serv., Los Alamitos, 1968-; Pres., Opti-Man Products, Los Alamitos, 1970-; Pres., The Profls., Anaheim, 1970-. Mbrships. incl: Mfr.'s Agents Nat. Assn.; Soc. Indl. Packaging & Handling Engrs.; Am. Ordnance Assn. Life Mbr.; Instrument Soc. of Am.; U.S. Coast Guard Aux.; U.S. Power Squadron; Los Alamitos Chmbr. of Comm.; Substaining Patron, Huntington Hartford Theatre Assn.; Old Ranch Tennis Club; Hollywood Turf Club; Santa Anita Turf Club; Del Mar Turf Club; Am. Yachting Assn.; Am. Power Boat Assn.; Horseman's Protective Benevolant Assn.; Acad. of Magical Arts. Patentee in field Plastic Products. Owner/Breeder Thoroughbred Race Horses. Author technical books. Address: P.O. Box 2064, Glendale, CA, U.S.A. 9, 16, 57, 120.

WATANABE, Takeo, b. 23 June 1907. University President; Educator. Educ: B.S., Geol. Inst. Fac. of Sci., Univ. of Tokyo, Japan, 1931; Dr. Sci., Univ. of Tokyo, 1943. Appts: Asst., Hokkaido Univ., 1931; Asst. Prof., ibid, 1936; Prof., 1942; Prof. of Geol., Univ. of Tokyo, 1944; Dean, Fac. of Sci., ibid, 1963; Prof. Emeritus, 1968; Prof., Nagoya Univ., 1968; Pres., Akita Univ., 1971. Mbrships: Pres., Int. Assn. on Genesis of Ore Deposits; 1st V.P., Int. Mineralog. Assn.; Gen. Comm., Int. Coun. of Sci. Unions; Japan Acad.; Hon., Soc. Francais de Mineralog. et Cristallographic; For., Geol. Soc. of London. Publs: Study of Mineral Deposits; Study of Minerals. Japan Acad. Prize, 1966. Address: Akita Univ., 1-1 Tebata Gakuencho, Akita City, Japan.

WATERHOUSE, Keith Spencer, b. 6 Feb. 1929. Writer; Journalist. Educ: Osmondthorpe Council Schl., Leeds. Appts: Columnist, Daily Mirror, 1970-. Mbrship: PEN. Publs: Novels—There Is a Happy Land, 1957; Billy Liar, 1959; Jubb, 1963; The Bucket Shop, 1968; Passing of the Third Floor Buck, 1974; Plays (all w. W. Hall)—Billy Liar, 1960; Celebration, 1961; England Our England, 1962; All things Bright & Beautiful, 1962; Children's Day, 1969; The Card (musical), 1973; Saturday, Sunday Monday (adaptation), 1973; Films (all w. W. Hall)—Whistle Down the Wind; A Kind of Loving; Billy Liar; Man in the Middle; West Eleven; Lock Up Your Daughters, etc. Address: 70 St. Paul St., London N.1, U.K. 1, 2, 3, 18, 30.

WATERMAN, John F(ranklin), b. 5 Dec. 1936. City Official. Educ: B.S., Univ. of Rochester, N.Y., 1964. Appts: Served w. USMCR, 1954-57; Real Estate Mgr., N.Y.C. Dept. Real Estate, 1965-66; Asst. Mgmt. Analyst, N.Y.C. Transit Authority, 1966-70; Prog. Rsch. Analyst, N.Y.C. Off. of Mayor, Budget Bur., 1970-. Mbrships: Transportation Comm., City Club of N.Y., 1972-; Transportation Comm., Citizens Union of Gtr. N.Y., 1971-; Dir., Comm. for Better Transit, 1971-; V.P., 1972-; Treas., Bur. of Budget Benevolent Assn., 1973-; Bd. of Dirs., Civil Serv. Merit Coun., 1973-; Am. Econ. Assn.; Union Int. des Transports Publics. Address: 1715 Ave. H, Brooklyn, NY 11230, U.S.A. 6.

WATERMAN, Paul, b. 3 July 1903. Retired Farmer. Educ: Cazenovia Sem., Cazenovia, N.Y.; Cornell Univ., Ithaca, N.Y. Mbrships: Haiku Soc. of Am., N.Y.C.; Western World Haiku Soc., Portland, Ore. Publs: 5 books; Boy For a Blonde; Cabin For Two; Love To The Town; Mad Land of Limerick; Those Brats From Limerick; Five Lines To Limerick; Wee Wings; Brief Candles; Whimsys; Lanternes. Hons: 1st Prize, 1970, & Hon. Mention, 1973, for Haiku Writing, Modern Haiku; Gift Award, Dragonfly, 1973. Address: Magnolia Hotel, Starke, FL 32091, U.S.A.

WATERS, Betty Hale (Mrs.), b. 21 Dec. 1927. Educator. Educ: B.Mus., Converse Coll., Spartanburg, S.C., 1949; M.Ed., 1968, Ed.S. 1971. Ga. State Univ., Atlanta; Ed.D., Univ. of Ga., Athens, 1973. Appts. incl: 1st Grade & Specific Learning Disabilities Tchr., Dekalb Co. Schls., 13 yrs.; In-Serv. Lectr., Maths. & Rdng., 2 yrs., Supvsng. Tchr., Grade Level Chmn., 8 yrs., Mbr., Curric. & Instrn. Comms., Dekalb Co. Schls.; Conven. Lectr.; Guest Lectr., Ga. State Univ., 1969, '70; Coll. Supvsr. of Student Tchrs., Grad. Asst., Univ. of Ga., Athens, 1971-; Dir., Learning Disabilities Prog., Newton

Co. Schls., Ga., 1973-74. Mbrships. incl: Delta Kappa Gamma; Kappa Delta Epsilon; NEA; AAUP; Coun. for Exceptional Children; Assn. for Children w. Learning Disabilities; Ga. Educ. Assn.; Assn. for Tchr. Educators; Treas., 1966-68, V.P., 1969-71, Pres., 1974-76, State of Ga. Assns. for Childhood Educ.; Admin. Bd., Tuckson United Meth. Ch., 1973-75; Soloist, var. chs. Hons. incl: schol. awards; Freedom Fndn. Tchrs. Medal, 1965; Tchr. of Yr. Award, Dogwood Chapt., Coun. for Exceptional Children, 1970; Bronze Plaque for Community Contbn., Clairmont Civitan Club, Decatur, Ga., 1970. Address: Rte. 1, Box 492, Piedmont Rd., Hull, GA 30646, U.S.A. 5, 7, 57, 125, 132, 138.

WATERS, Raymond P., b. 27 Jan. 1931. Public Relations Manager. Educ: B.A., Hofstra Coll., 1960. Appts: Jrnlst., USN, 1950-54; Ed., Levittown Press, N.Y., 1954-55; Advt. Asst., Allied Chem. Corp., N.Y.C., 1955-56; P.R. Account Exec., Mgr., Dir., V.P. & Mgr., N.Y. off., & Mbr., Bd. of Dirs., Walther Assocs., 1956-64; Eastern Ed., Industrial Marketing mag., 1964-66; Account Exec., Basford Inc., 1966-68; P.R. Mgr., M.W. Kellogg Co., Div. of Pullman Inc., Houston, Tex., 1968-. Mbrships: Past Pres., Kappa Chapt., Alpha Sigma Lambda; Pi Delta Epsilon; Past V.P., N.Y. Chapt., Assn. of Indl. Advertisers; Houston Chmbr. of Comm.; Publicity Club of N.Y. Address: 8834 Winningham Lane, Houston, TX 77055, U.S.A. 7, 24.

WATKINS, (Mrs.) Lottie. Real Estate & Property Manager. Appts: Sec., Alexander-Calloway Realty Co., Atlanta, Ga., U.S.A., 1945-54; Teller-Clerk, Mutual Fed. Savings & Loan Assn., 1954-60; Owner & Pres., Lottie Watkins Enterprises, Atlanta, 1960-. Num. mbrships. incl: Pres., Atlanta Chapt., Negro Bus. & Profl. Women's Club, 1963; Asst. Sec., Atlanta Bus. League; Sec., Southeastern Region, Nat. Negro Bus. & Profl. Women's Club; Co-Chmn., Bus. Div., Community Chest, 1955 & 1959; Exec. Comm., Sr. Citizens Servs.; Co-Chmn., NAACP Mbrship. Drive, 3 yrs., Exec. Comm., Bd. of Dirs.; Chmn., Prog. Comm. for Nat. Conven, NAACP, 1962; Chmn., Fund Drive, Am. Cancer Soc., 3 yrs.; Exec. Comm., Fulton Co. Democratic Party; Exec. Comm., 5th Congressional Dist., State of Ga., 1963; Atlanta Summit Ldrship. Conf.; League of Women Voters; Bd. of Dirs., Citizens Trust Bank. Hons. incl: Woman of the Yr. in Citizenship & Bronze Woman of the Yr., Iota Lambda Sorority, 1962; C.L. Harper Award, NAACP, 1969. Address: 1065 Gordon St., S.W., Atlanta, GA 30310, U.S.A. 5, 125, 129, 132.

WATKINS, Lowry, b. 23 Jan. 1897. Realtor. Past Dir., Louisville Real Estate Bd. Mbrships. incl: Masters of Foxhounds Assn.; Past V.P., US Equestrian Team; Nat. Steeplechase & Hunt Assn.; Royal Dublin Soc.; Past V.P., Peterborough Hound Show Assn., U.K.; Kentucky Histl. Soc.; Filson Club, Louisville. Author of Design & Construction of a Modern Stable & articles on hunting, etc. Hon. Admiral, Goose Greek. Address: 917 Bucida Rd., Delray Beach, FL 33444, U.S.A.

WATLER, (Hon.) Desmond Vere, b. 10 Oct. 1914. Civil Servant, B.W.I. Appts: Civil Service, B.W.I., 1937-; Collector of Customs; Postmaster; Competent Authority; Comptroller of Treasury, Customs & P.O.; Treasurer; Dpty. Adminstr.; Chief Sec., Grand Cayman, Cayman Islands, 1973. Mbrship: Rotary Club. Hons: O.B.E., 1966; Justice of the Peace. Address: c/o Governor's Office, Grand Cayman, Br. W. Indies.

WATLINGTON, John Bioren, b. 21 Nov. 1917. Public Transportation Director. Educ: B.A., Univ. of Pa., Phila., 1942. Appts: Bus Supvsr., Pub. Transportation Dept., Bermuda, 1946; Dpty. Dir., ibid, 1950; Dir., Pub. Transportation, 1965-. Mbrships: Past Pres., Hamilton Rotary Club, Bermuda; Bermuda Tech. Soc. Address: Dept. of Pub. Transportation, P.O. Box 443, Hamilton, Bermuda.

WATSON, Donna Rae, b. 25 July 1946. Teacher. Educ: B.S., Ouachitá Bapt. Univ., 1968; M.Ed., State Coll. of Ark., 1973. Appts: Home Econs. Tchr., St. Charles Schl. System, Ark., 1968-72; Jr. H.S. Sci. Tchr., N. Little Rock Schl. System, 1972-; Cheerleader Sponsor, 1972-73. Mbrships: Gamma Phi, 1964-; Student NEA, 1964-68; Am. Home Econs. Assn., 1968-72; Ark. Educ. Assn., 1968-; Classroom Tchrs. Assn., 1972-; F.H.A. Advsr., 1968-72; Home Econs. Advsry. Coun., 1971-72; Ark. Co. Family Living Comm., 1971-72; Pianist, Christmas Prog. Dir., Vacation Bible Schl. Tchr., Bapt. Ch. Hon: Outstanding Student in Home Econs., 1968. Address: 1300 Northwick Ct., Little Rock, AR 72207, U.S.A. 76, 125.

WATSON, George Albert, b. 4 Mar. 1905. Pathologist. Educ: A.B., Univ. of Calif., 1926. Appts. incl: Pathol., French Hosp., San Fran., 1945-, & Hahnemann Hosp., ibid, 1945-65; Polyclin. Hosp., 1965; Cons., Path., Weimar, Calif. Jt. Sanitarium, 1948, & Golden Gate Hosp., San Fran., 1950; Pathol., Garden Hosp., ibid, 1959. Mbrships. incl: Dip., Am. Bd. of Pathols.; Am. Soc. Clin. Pathols.; Soc. Nuclear Med.; Calif Soc. Pathols.; Am., San Fran. & Calif. Med. Assns.; Fellowships: Am. Geriatrics Soc.; Fndg., Coll. Am. Pathols. Address: 135 Belvedere Ave., Belvedere, CA 94920, U.S.A. 9, 10, 14, 17, 59.

WATSON, Irvine Armstrong, b. 31 Mar. 1914. University Professor. Educ: UNiv. of Sydney, Australia; Univ. of Minn., U.S.A. Appts: Lectr. in Agric., Sr. Lectr., Agric., Assoc. Prof., Genetics & Plant Breeding, Prof. of Agric Botany (Plant Breeding), Dean of Fac. of Agric., 1966-67, Acting Dean, 1968, Univ. of Sydney, Australia. Mbrships: Fellow, Australian Inst. of Agric. Sci., 1964; Am. Phytopathol. Soc.; Am. Crop Sci. Soc.; Linnean Soc. of N.S.W.; For., Soviet Acad. of Aci., 1972. Contbr. to sci. jrnls. Hons. incl: Farrer Mem. Medal, 1958; E.C. Stakman Medal, 1966. Address: Dept. Agric. Botany, Univ. of Sydney, Sydney, 2006. N.S.W., U.S.A. 23.

WATSON, (James) KIngston, b. 1st Sept. 1908. Appts. incl: Sub-Ed., The Star, Melbourne, Australia, 1933-36; Sub.-Ed., The Herald, 1936-37; Sub-Ed., Daily Telegraph, Sydney, 1938; War Corres., SHAEF, 1943-45; Estab. Paris Office, Australian Consolidated Press, 1945-46; Reported Paris Peace Conf. & Trial of Petain, 1946-47; Dpty. News-Ed., Daily Telegraph, Sydney, Australia, 1948; Ed., ibid, 1953-70; Ed., Sunday Telegraph, 1971-72; Ed., merged Sunday Telegraph/Sunday Australian, 1972-74 (retd.); TCN9 Sydney Meet The Press TV Panel, 1957-63; Producer & Panellist, Meet The Press (new series), 1971-; Australian Deleg., C'wlth. Press Union quinquennial confs., India-Pakistan, 1961, W. Indies, 1965; Ldr., U.K. & Mediterranean, 1970. Mbrships: Jrnlsts. Club, Sydney; Royal Automobile Club, London. Address: 1 Madeline St., Hunter's Hill, N.S.W., Australia 2110. 12, 23, 131.

WATSON, Kim Miner Morris. Director of Public Relations. Educ: A.A., Coll. of San

Mateo. Appts: Dept. Sales Mgr., The Emporium, 1956-59; Admin. Asst., Exec. Sec., MIT, 1960-66; Dir. of P.R., Brookline Savings Bank, Brookline, Mass., 1966-. Mbrships: Bd. of Dirs., Publicity Club of Boston; Publicity Chmn., Savings Bank Women of Mass.; Soc. of Mayflower Descendants; DAR; Int. Inst. of Boston. Contbr. to profl. jrnl. Address: 160 Washington St., Brookline, MA 02174, U.S.A. 5, 24, 138.

WATSON, Sidney John, b. 31 Mar. 1920. Author; Farmer; Colonel (ret.). Educ: B.A., M.A., Magdalen Coll., Oxford, Univ., U.K.; Brit. Army Staff Coll., Camberley; U.S. Army Staff Coll., Ft. Leavenworth. Appts: Mil. Attaché, Brit. Embassy, Tehran, 1960-64; Trustee, Dulverton Trust, London. Mbrships: Gov., Royal Agric. Soc. of Engl.; Pres., Clonmel Histl. Soc. Publs: Locomotives of Great Southern Railways of Ireland, 1937; Carnot, 1954; By Command of the Emperor, 1957; Bianconi, King of the Irish Roads, 1963; Between the Flags, 1969; The Cottage Countess, 1974. Hons: George Knight Clowes Mem. Prize, 1952; M.B.E. (Mil. Div.), 1953; Order of Homayun, Iran, 1960. Address: Ballingarrane, Clonmel, Co. Tipperary, Eire. 3.

WATSON, W. Marvin, b. 6 June 1924. Petroleum Company Executive. Educ: B.B.A., Baylor Univ., 1949; M.A., ibid, 1950. Appts: Exec. Asst. to Pres. Lone Star Steel, 1956-65; Special Asst. to Pres. Lyndon Baines Johnson, 1965-68; Postmaster Gen. of U.S., 1968-69; Pres., Occidental Int. Corp., 1969-; Exec. V.P. for Corporate Affairs, Occidental Petroleum Corp., 1972-. Mbrships: Tex. State Soc.; Univ. Club; Int. Club; Congressional Country Club. Hons: H.H.D., Ouachita Univ., 1968; LL.D., Hardin-Simmons Univ., 1972. Address: Suite 1201, 1717 Pennsylvania Ave., N.W., Wash. DC 20006, U.S.A.

WATT, Francis Edward (Frank), b. 19 Aug. 1923. Building Contractor. Educ: Kingston Tech. Schl., Jamaica. Appts: Managing Dir., Watt, McDermott & Co., Ltd.; Dir., Jamaica Nat. Building Soc.; Managing Dir., Frank Watt & Ptnrs., Ltd.; Justice of the Peace, 1965-. Mbrships: Fellow, Inst. of Dirs.; Free Mason; Fairfield Golf & Tennis Club; Paraides Park Club; Gov., Ironshore Golf & Country Club. Address: Salt Spring Rd., P.O. Box 223, Montego Bay (1), Jamaica, West Indies. 96, 109, 136.

WATT, George Coulter, b. 9 Feb. 1915. Accountant. Appts. incl: Assoc., Main & Co., Pitts., 1937-42; U.S.N.R. (to Lt.-Cmdr.), 1942-46; Ptnr., Price Waterhouse & Co., N.Y.C., 1946-. Mbrships: Acctng. Prins., Bd. of Am. Inst. of CPA's, 1968-73. Contbr. of articles to The Business Lawyer; The N.Y. CPA; The Jrnl. of Acctncy., etc. Address: Price Waterhouse & Co., 1251 Ave. of The Americas, N.Y., NY 10020, U.S.A.

WATTERSON, Bruce Carter, b. 26 Oct. 1939. Dentist. Educ: B.A., Univ. of Richmond, 1963; Grad. Schl., ibid, 1963; Grad. Schl., ibid, 1963-64; D.D.S., Med. Coll. of Va., 1968. Appts: Honorarium, Pub. Hlth. Dept., 1969-72. Mbrships: Am. Dental Assn.; Va. Dental Assn.; Va.-Tidewater Dental Soc.; Va. Beach Dental Soc.; Tidewater Dental Study Club; V.P., Witchduck Civic League, 1973; Beta Beta Beta, 1963. Address: 4060 Richardson Rd., Virginia Beach, VA 23455, U.S.A. 7.

WATTS, Ernest Alfred, b. 21 Apr. 1893. Chartered Builder. Educ: Building Dip., Int. Correspondence Schl., London, U.K. Appts: Dir., Melbourne Builders Lime & Cement Co.

Pty. Ltd., Vic., Australia, 1937-58; Dir., Australian Alliance Assurance Co., 1944-51; Governing Dir., Mecho Constructions Pty. Ltd. (Civil Engrs.), 1951-; Managing Dir. & Chmn., E.A. Watts Pty. Ltd. & Collingwood Timber Joinery & Trading Co. Pty. Ltd., 1953-65; Mng. Dir., Wet Mix & Precast Concrete Pty. Ltd., 1954-59; Governing Dir., Mecho Plant Hire Pty. Ltd., 1973-; Life Gov., Royal Victorian Inst. for Blind, & var. Hosps., Vic. Mbrships. incl: Australian Inst. Chartered Master Builders; Building Ind. Congress; Chmbr. of Mfrs.; Co. Dirs. Assn. of Australia; Master Builders Assn. of Vic. (Pres., 1937-38). Hons. incl: Bronze Medal for Serv. to Ind., Australian Inst. of Master Builders 1957; Home Study Man of Yr., Int. Corres. Schl., 1965. Address: 377 The Boulevard, E. Ivanhoe, Melbourne, Vic., Australia. 3079. 23, 123, 128.

WATTS, Frederick Ormond, b. 13 Aug. 1913. Chartered Builder. Educ: Collingwood Tech. Coll.; Stott's Bus. Coll.; Int. Corres. Schl. Appts. incl: Ptnr., E.A. Watts (Bldrs.), 1939-53, Dir., E.A. Watts Pty. Ltd., 1953-64, Jr. Mng. Dir., 1966, Chmn. & Mng. Dir., 1970-73, Chmn., 1973-; Dir., Collingwood Timber Joinery & Trading Co. Pty. Ltd., 1940-64, Mng. Dir., 1964-71, Dir., 1971-; Dir., Australian Alliance Assurance Co., 1951-69, Chmn., 1969-; Dir., Wetmix & Precast Concrete Co. Pty. Ltd., 1954-59, Melbourne Builders' Lime & Cement Co. Ltd., 1959-71, Dpty. Chmn., 1971-74; Jt. Mng. Dir., E.A. Watts Holdings Ltd., 1964-66, Mng. Dir., 1966-73, Chmn., 1973-; Chmn. & Mng. Dir., Compac Ltd., 1969-73, Chmn., 1973-. Mbrships. incl: Inst. of Dirs. in Australia; Royal Commonwealth Soc. Recip., C.B.E., 1972. Address: 17 Outlook Dr., Eaglemont, Vic., Australia 3084. 23, 128, 139.

WATTS, H. M., b. 22 Oct. 1920. Physicist. Educ: B.S., Univ. of Mo., 1942; Ph.D., Johns Hopkins Univ., 1952. Appts. incl: Rsch. Assoc. Prof., Johns Hopkins Univ., 1947-52; Dir. of Engrng., Bendix Communications Div., Balt., 1952-57; Martin-Orlando, Fla., 1957-60; Independent Cons., Pa. & Md., 1967-72; Sr. Sci., System Planning Corp., Arlington, Va., 1973-. Mbrships: N.Y. Acad. of Sci.; Am. Phys. Soc.; I.E.E.E.; A.A.A.S.; Sigma Xi; Tau Beta Pi; Eta Kappa Nu; M.E.N.S.A. Contbr. to num. sci. publs. Recip., Dist. Serv. Award, 1945. Address: 4302 Roberts Ave., Annandale, VA 22003, U.S.A. 6, 14, 26.

WAY, (Sister) Agnes Clare, b. 31 Dec. 1897. Teacher; Researcher. Educ: B.A., Our Lady of the Lake Coll., 1919; M.A., Cath. Univ. of Am., 1924; Ph.D., ibid, 1927. Appts: Mbr., Religious Congregation of the Sisters of Divine Providence; St. Cecilia H.S., Broussard, La., 1920-21; Our Lady of the Lake Grammar Schl., 1921-22; Our Lady of the Lake H.S., 1924-25; Instr., Our Lady of the Lake Coll., 1922-23; Prof., ibid, 1927-69; Prof. Emeritus, 1969-; Prof., Univ. of N.H., 1965. Mbrships: Classical Assn. of the Mid West & South; Mediaeval Acad. of Am.; Renaissance Soc. of Am.; Archaeological Inst. of Am. Author & translator of publs. in field. Hons: Grant from Am. Phil. Soc. for microfilm, 1954; Grant for 5 months' lib. rsch. in Europe, 1972. Address: Our Lady of the Lake Coll., 411 S.W. 24th St., San Antonio, TX 78285, U.S.A. 13.

WEATHERALL, Miles, b. 14 Oct. 1920. Pharmacologist. Educ: B.A., B.Sc., 1941, B.M., 1943, M.A., 1945, Oxford Univ.; D.M., 1951, D.Sc., 1966; F.I. Biol., 1968; Hon. M.P.S., 1970. Appts: Rsch. Work, Lectr., Pharmacol., Edinburgh Univ., 1945-48; Sr. Lectr. i/c Dept. of Pharmacol., London Hosp. Med. Coll., 1949, Rdr., 1953, Prof., 1958-67, Univ. of London;

Hd., Therapeutic Rsch. Div., Wellcome Rsch. Labs., Beckenham, Kent, 1967-74; Dir. of Estab., ibid, 1974-. Mbrships: Past Sec., Brit. Pharmacol. Soc.; Physiol. Soc.; Fellow, Coun. Mbr., Royal Soc. of Med.; Chmn. of Coun., Chelsea Coll., Univ. of London; Past Comm. Mbr., Biometric Soc.; Past Mbr., Biochem. Soc. Publs: Scientific Method, 1968; Statistics for Medical & Other Biological Students (co-author), 1952; Num. articles in profl. jrnls. Address: Wellcome Rsch. Labs., Langley Court, Beckenham, Kent, U.K.

WEATHERS, Bailey Graham, Jr., b. 12 Apr. 1932. Physician; Artist. Educ: Wake Forest Univ., 1953; Southern Bapt. Theol. Sem., 1953-56; Va. Commonwealth Univ. Med. Schl., Richmond, 1956-60. One Man Exhibs. incl: Elks Club, N. Wilkesboro, N.C., 1967; Gaston Co. Lib., 1969, 70; Gastonia, 1968. Grp. Exhibs. incl: Gaston Art Guild, 1968, 69, 70, 71; Gall. of Contemp. Art, Winston Salem, 1967, 68, 71; N.C. Mus. of Art, Raleigh, 1970; Durham Art Guild, 1971; Carson McKenna Galls., Charlotte, 1971, 72; N.C. Schl. of Pub. Hlth, Chapel Hill, 1973; Bashful's Ltd., Davidson, N.C., 1973, '74; McDonald's Art Galls., Charlotte, N.C., Hilton Hd. Island, S.C., 1974; Dock St. Gall., Wilmington, N.C., 1974. Work represented in perm. collections. Mbrship. incl: AMA; Fellow, Am. Acad. of Family Physns.; Royal Soc. of Hlth., G.B.; Int. Assn. of Applied Psychol.; Assn. of Humanistic Psychol.; N.C. Med. Soc.; N.C. Acad. of Family Physns.; N.C. Chapt., Am. Cancer Soc. Recip., 1st Place Award, Gaston Art Guild Exhib., 1974. Address: 222 S. Main St., Stanley, NC 28164, U.S.A. 2, 7, 125.

WEAVER, Barbara Frances, (Mrs.) b. 29 Aug. 1927. Library Administrator. Educ: B.A., Radcliffe Coll., 1949; M.L.S., Univ. of R.I. Grad. Schl. of Lib. Sci., 1968. Appts: Hd., Libn., Thompson Pub. Lib., Conn., 1961-69; Asst. Dir., Conn. State Lib. Serv. Ctr., Willimantic, 1969-72; Acting Dir., 1972-73; Regional Admnstr., Ctrl. Mass, Regional Lib. System, Worcester, 1973-. Mbrships: Legislative Comm., Mass. Lib. Assn., 1973-74; Chmn., Continuing Educ. Comm., Conn. Lib. Assn., 1971-73; Exec. Bd.; Chmn., Continuing Educ. Comm., New Engl. Lib. Assn., 1970-75. Recip., F.J. Barnard Schlrship, 1965. Address: P.O. Box 295, Thompson, CT 06277, U.S.A.

WEAVER, Barry Roland, b. 1 Nov. 1933. Resource Analyst; Conservationist. Educ: B.A., Ark. Univ., Fayetteville, U.S.A., 1955; Univ. NC, Chapel Hill, 1956-57. Appts: Exec. Dir., Human Engrng. Lab., Tulsa, Okla, 1958-64; Trustee & Asst. Treas., Johnson O'Connor Rsch. Fndn. Inc., 1959-63; Sr. Test Admnstr., ibid, N.Y.., 1965; Trustee & Asst. Treas., Human Engrng. Lab., Ont., Canada, 1959-64; Trustee, Fundacion de Investigaciones, Johnson O'Connor Fndn., Mexico DF, 1962-65; Resource Analyst, Off. Emergency Preparedness, Exec. Off., Pres., Wash. DC, 1965-70; Servs. Coord., Econ. Opportunity Agcy., Fayetteville, Ark., 1973-. Mbrships: Phi Alpha Theta; Dir., Soc. Environmental Stabilization; Coun. Rep., Sierra Club, 1969-70; Wilderness Soc. Publs: Princeton University Aptitude Differences, 1963; Roman Catholic Colleges and Universities, 1963; Rsch. thesis, Am. Hist. Survey, 1964; var. articles. Recip. Hon. Citizen, Little Rock, & Key to City Award, 1963. Address: Eagle's Rest, Rt.2, Springdale, AR 72764, U.S.A. 7.

WEAVER, (Rev.) R. Donald, b. 25 Mar. 1926. Clergyman; Educator. Educ: Univ. of Kan., 1944; B.S.C., St. Louis Univ., 1949; M.Div., Garrett Theological Sem., 1952; Univ.

of Chgo., 1951-53; Union Theological Sem., 1960; Scarritt Coll., 1973-74. Appts. incl: Pastor, Ind. Harbor United Meth. Ch., E. Chgo., Ind., 1958-73; Pastor, 1st United Meth. Ch., Hobart, Ind., 1973-; Lectr. in Theol., St. Joseph's Calumet Coll., E. Chgo., Ind., 1967-. Mbrships. incl: Chmn., Planning Div., Lake Area United Way, 1973; Pres., ibid, 1974; Am. Soc. of Ch. Hist.; Assn. for the Sociol. of Relig.; Hymn Soc. of Am.; Insts. of Relig. & Hlth.; Religious Educ. Assn. for the U.S. & Canada; Religious Rsch. Assn.; Soc. for the Sci. Study of Relig.; AAUP; Advsry. Coun., John Wesley Corp. Hons: Theol. Prize, Garrett Theological Sem., 1952; Community Ldrship. Award, Twin City Community Servs., 1971. Address: 654 E. Fourth St., Hobart, IN 46342, U.S.A. 82, 116, 131.

WEBB, Anne Holliday, b. 29 June 1892. Museum Executive; Writer; Research Officer. Educ: B.L., Baylor Univ., Waco, Tex.; Dip., Dana Hall, Wellesley, Mass.; B.A., Wellesley Coll., Mass.; Special courses, Harvard Univ. & New Schl. for Soc. Rsch., N.Y. Appts. incl: Asst. Ed., Bulletin of Mus. of Fine Arts, & publicity sec., Mus. of Fine Arts, Boston, Mass., 1927-31; Supvsr., Div. of Mus. Extension, ibid, 1931-41; 1st Dir. & Curator, Ft. Worth Children's Mus., Tex., 1948-55; Exec. Dir., Tex. Fine Arts Assn. & Laguna Gloria Art Gall., Austin, Tex., 1955-59; Organizer & Dir., community art proj., which became basic educl. prog. of Ark. Art Ctr., 1962; Dir. of rsch., Longyear Fndn., 1962-73; Ed., Longyear Quarterly News, 1962-73; Cons., ibid, 1973-. Mbrships. incl: Archaeological Inst. of Am.; Am. Oriental Soc.; Japan Soc. Author of num. articles in jrnls. inclng. Am. Mag. of Art, Art & Archaeol., Int. Studio. Recip. of hons. Address: 101 Monmouth St., Brookline, MA 02146, U.S.A. 5, 62.

WEBB, Bernice Elaine (Larson). University Professor. Educ: A.B., Univ. of Kan., 1956; M.A., ibid, 1957; Ph.D., 1961; Rsch. work, Univ. of Aberdeen, U.K., 1959-60 Appts. incl: Asst. Prof., Engl., Univ. of Southwestern La., Lafayette, 1961-67; Assoc. Prof., ibid, 1967-; Dir., grad. seminars, N.D.E.A. Inst. in Intellectual & Cultural Hist. of the U.S., summer 1966; Vis. Assoc. Prof., Creative Writing & Contemporary Lit., World Campus Afloat (round-the-world shipboard div. of int. studies, Chapman Coll., Orange, Calif.), 1972. Mbrships. incl: La. State Ed., AAUW, 1967-71; State Corres. Sec., Ed., La. State Poetry Soc., 1970-; Publicity Chmn., S.W. Br., ibid, 1970-; Sec.-Treas., S.W. La. Assn., Phi Beta Kappa, 1965-71; Pi Delta Phi; MLA, 1973-; S. Central Coll. Engl. Assn., 1971-. Publs. incl: The Basketball Man, 1973; Over 120 poems in jrnls. & newspapers; About 45 articles in jrnls. & newspapers; 3 short stories in jrnls. Recip. of hons. Address: 159 Whittington Dr., Lafayette, LA 70501, U.S.A. 5, 7, 11, 13, 15, 125, 132, 138.

WEBB, Charles, b. 9 June 1939. Novelist. Educ: Midland Schl., 1953-57; Williams Coll., 1957-61. Publs: The Graduate (novel), 1963; Love, Roger (novel), 1967; The Marriage of a Young Stockbroker (novel), 1969; Orphans & Other Children (novellas), 1974. Address: Box 182, Hastings-on-Hudson, NY 10706, U.S.A. 1.

WEBB, Ernest Packard, b. 30 Aug. 1907. Artist & Engraver. Educ: Fed. Art Schl., Mnpls., Minn.; I.C.S., Pa.; Alexander Hamilton Inst., N.Y. Appts: Artist, Parkersburg Engraving Co., 1929, Huntington Engraving Co., 1930; Profl. Art Studio, 1931-40; U.S. Army Air Force, 1941-45; Sec.-Treas., Roanoke Engraving Co., 1948; V.P., Roanoke Engraving

& Roanoke Offset Plants, 1962; Pres., W & H Corp., 1968. Mbrships: Richmond & Va. State Chmbrs. of Comm.; Richmond Indl. Club; Int. Craftsmens Club; Willow Oaks Country Club; Westwood Racquet Club. Address: 2000 Riverside Dr., Apt. 14F, Richmond, VA 23225, U.S.A. 57, 125.

WEBB, Greta Darlene, b. 19 Dec. 1929. Educator; Cattle Breeder. Educ: B.S., Southwest Mo. State Coll.; M.Ed., Univ. of Mo. Appts: Elem. Tchr., Mtn. Grove, Mo., 1959-69; Elem. Counsellor, ibid, 1969-. Mbrships: Am. Personnel & Guidance Assn.; Am. Schl. Counsellors Assn.; Nat. Vocational Guidance Assn.; Mo. Guidance Assn.; Mo.-Ozark Personnel & Guidance Assn.; Mo. State Tchrs. Assn.; Sec. & Treas., Mtn. Grove Community Tchrs. Assn.; Pres., Mtn. Grove Assn. for Childhood Educ.; Pres., Omicron Chapt., Delta Kappa Gamma, Mo.; Assn. for Mental Hlth.; State Pres., Ladies Aux. of Mo. Polled Hereford Assn.; Ch. of Christ. Address: Competition, MO 65448, U.S.A. 5, 126, 132.

WEBB, Jerry Edward, b. 3 Dec. 1946. Educator. Educ: B.A., Elon Coll., 1969; M.S., Longwood Coll., 1973; Postgrad. study, Coll. of Wm. & Mary. Appts: Tchr., Brunswick Co. H.S., Va., 1969-70; Prin., ibid, 1970-71; Prin., West End Elem. Schl., Victoria, Va., 1971-73; Gen. Supvsr., Lunenburg Co. Schl. Bd., Victoria, 1973-. Mbrships: Pi Gamma Mu; Tau Kappa Epsilon; Alpha Pi Delta. Publs: Ed., The Chalkboard. Hons: Advsry. Comm. on Tchr. Educ., Longwood Coll., 1973. Address: Rte. 6, Box 89, Farmville, VA 23901, U.S.A. 125.

WEBB, John Cother, b. 29 Dec. 1914. Electronic Powder Metallurgist. Educ: B.A., Oxford Univ., 1938; B.S., N.Y. Univ., 1942; B.A. Bus. Mgt., Columbia Univ., 1944. Appts: V.P., Ferro-Cart Corp. Am., 1941-44; Dir., Sales Maguire Industries, 1944-46; Chmn. of Bd., Magnetic Core Corp.; Pres., Electro Met. Prod.; John C. Webb & Assocs.; Pres., Fritzal Corp., Ft. Pierce, Fla.; V.P., Electronic Perfeccion Mexico D.F. Mbrships. incl: Ossining Chmbr. of Comm.; Past Pres., ibid; Metal Powder Industry Assn.; Past Pres., ibid; Lions Club; Past Pres., ibid; Ft. Lauderdale Coun. of 100. Publs: The New Rubaiyat & Other Verse. 3 times recip., Personality of the S., 1971-73. Address: 2782 N.E. 5th St., Pompano Beach, FL 33062, U.S.A.

WEBB, Martyn Jack, b. 28 Sept. 1925. Professor of Geography. Educ: Balliol Coll., Oxford, U.K., 1943-44 & 1947-50. Appts: Sr. Rsch. Off., Dept. of Econs., Univ. of Hull, 1951-53; Demonstrator, Schl. of Geog., Univ. of Oxford, 1953-55; Tutor, Balliol, Worcester & Wadham Colls., ibid, 1953-63; Lectr., 1955-63; Sr. mbr., Linacre Coll., 1962-63; Fndn. Prof., Univ. of Western Australia, 1964-; Guest Prof., Univ. of Heidelberg, German Fed. Repub., 1967; Vis. Prof., Carleton Univ., Ottawa, Canada, 1972. Mbrships. incl: Inst. of British Geographers; Inst. of Australian Geographers; Royal Geographical Soc.; Councillor, Australian & N.Z. Assn. for Advancement of Sci.; Nat. Comm. for Geog., Australian Acad. of Sci. Author of articles & working papers in field. Recip., Leverhulme award, 1958. Address: Dept. of Geog., Univ. of Western Australia, Nedlands, W.A., Australia, 6009. 23.

WEBB, Mary Lou (Mrs. David Webb), b. 1 July 1938. Newspaperwoman. Educ: B.S., Univ. of Southern Miss., Hattiesburg. Appts: Reporter-Feature Writer, Magee Courier, Miss.; Corres., Jackson Daily News, Miss.; Managing Ed., Tylertown Times, Miss.; Currently Assoc. Ed., Franklin Advocate, Meadville, Miss. &

Wilk-Amite Record, Gloster, Miss. Mbrships: Pres., Miss. Press Women; Pres., Franklin Womans Club; Nat. Fedn. Press Women (Corres. Sec. & Protocol Chmn.); Former Organiser of Choir, First Bapt. Ch., Bude. Hons: Over 50 Writing & Editing Awards, Miss. Press Women, 1962-72; Award for Interview, Nat. Fedn. Press Women, 1972. Address: c/o Franklin Advocate, Meadville, MS 39653, U.S.A. 76, 125.

WEBER, George Russell, b. 29 Dec. 1911. Microbiologist. Educ: B.S., Univ. of Mo., 1935; Ph.D., Iowa State Univ. (formerly Iowa State Coll.), 1940; Special evening student, Geo. Wash. Univ., 1944-45, Univ. of Cinn., 1948-49. Appts. incl: Bacteriologist, U.S. Pub. Hlth. Serv., 1946; Sr. Asst. Scientist, ibid, 1947; Scientist, 1949; Chief, Sanitizing Agts. Unit, 1949-53; Rsch. Microbiologist, Nat. Distillers & Chem. Crop, 1953; currently Sr. Rsch. Biochemist; Lectr., Biol., Univ. of Cinn. Evening Coll., 1969-70. Mbrships. incl: Reserve Offs. Assn. of U.S.; Chapt. Pres., Cinn., ibid, 1966-67; Fellow, Am. Pub. Hlth. Assn.; Fellow, Royal Soc. of Hlth., London, U.K.; Am. Soc. for Microbiol.; AAAS; Am. Inst. Biol. Sci.; Inst. of Food Technologists; Rsch. Soc. of Am.; Retd. Offs. Assn. of U.S. Recip., War Dept. Citation for control of food poisoning & infection, 1946. Address: 1525 Burney Lane, Cinn., OH 45230, U.S.A. 8, 14, 131.

WEBER, Harry Franklin. Educator; Management Specialist; Lecturer. Educ: A.B., B.S., Goshen Coll., Ind.; M.A., Bluffton Coll., Ohio; LL.M., Hamilton Coll. of Law, Chgo.; Ph.D., Hartford Fndn. Univ., Conn.; Rsch. work, var. univs.; Computer Systems workshops, 1958-; Trained & certified as instr. for Dale Carnegie & Elmer Wheeler Courses. Appts: Hd. & Prof., Dept. of Pre-Soc. Work, Albright Coll., Reading, Pa.; Dean of Men & Dir. of Guidance, Pa. State Coll., Lock Haven; Mgr., Clinton Co. Farm Labor Off., Pa.; Civilian Trng. Admnstr., Army Signal Corps, Pentagon, Wash. D.C.; Mgmt. Specialist, U.S. Fed. Govt.; Coord., Computer Systems, ibid; Educ. & Trng. Specialist, Fed. Civil Defense Admin.; Special Cons., Piper Aircraft Corp. Mbrships. incl: Sec., Pa. State Commn. on Consumer Educ.; Chmn., Pentagon Comm. on Trng. & Educ.; V.P., Nat. Aerospace Educl. Mem. Ctr., Coll. Park Airport, Md.; Life Mbr., Am. Mgmt. Assn.; NEA; Am. Sociological Assn. Author of publs. in field; developed curric. for Civil Defense Schl. & Wash. Inst. of (Mgmt.) Engrng. Address: 5401 Carolina Pl. N.W., Wash. DC 20016, U.S.A.

WEBER, Hulda, b. 2 June 1909. Author; Poet. Educ: Nat. Acad. of Design; New Schl. of Soc. Rsch., 1940-41. Mbrships: Poetry Soc. of Am.; Int. Poets' Shrine; Advsry. Bd., Marquis Biographical Lib. Soc.; Daughter of Mark Twain, 1970; Fndr. Mbr., Int. Poetry Soc.; Authors Guild Inc.; Authors League of Am., 1973. Poetry Anthols. incl: Blue River Anthol., 1959; Cavalcade of Poetry Anthol.—Best Poems, 1963; Melody of the Muse—Best Contemp. Poetry, 1964; Golden Harvest Anthol., 1967—Best Contemp. Poetry. Contbr. of over 100 poems to jrnls., mags. & radio inclng: Poetry Digest; Flatbush Mag.; We Do It Together Mag.; Blue River Poetry Mag.; American Bard—the Experimentalist Page; Personal Poetry—David Ross Radio Broadcast Stn. WBHL-AM, NBC-WLNA, WBUX, WNAK, WEFG, WHMC, etc.; The Villager; Wisconsin Poetry Mag; The Explorer; Vespers: Lutheran Companion; Scymitar & Song. Author of num. children's short stories inclng: Wizzie Stories (3); Juan and the Prize; Why is this Night Different; The Synagogue of Yousef; Jose and Sea Mamma; We do it Together. Num. hons. incl: 2nd Award, The American Bard Mag.,

1961, Bettie Payne Wells Award—American Bard, 1972, Int. Poetry Soc., 1st Anthol., 1973-74. Address: 915 W.End Ave., Apt. 5D, N.Y., NY 10025, U.S.A. 2, 5, 6, 34, 37, 55, 57, 64, 68, 105, 128, 129, 130, 132, 133, 138.

WEBER, Richard (Dick) A., 23 Dec. 1929. Professional Bowler. Appts: Proprietor, Dick Weber Lanes, Florissant, Mo. & Dick Weber Nu Bowl Lanes, Mt. Vernon, III. Mbrships: Pres., 1969 & 70, Sec., Exec. Bd., Bd. of Govs., Profl. Bowlers Assn.; Mbrship. Comm., Bowling Proprietors of Am.; Rotary Club; Elks; Hon. Mbr., Boy Scouts of Am.; Bd. of Dirs., Jr. Archway Bowling Assn. Publs: The Young Sportsman's Library (series); The Champions' Guide to Bowling (series); Sport Magazine Library; contbr. instructional series to Am. Bowling Congress Jr. Monthly Mag. & "Bowling Tips" to LA Times Syndicate. Hons: Hall of Fame, Am. Bowling Congress, 1970, Profl. Bowlers Assn., 1974, St. Louis Bowling Assn., 1960, Indpls. Bowling Assn., 1971; Bowler of the Yr., Writers Assn. of Am., 1963, 65. Address: 1305 Arlington Dr., Florissant, MO 63033, U.S.A. 2.

WEBKES, (Sister) Lillian, b. 6 June 1896. Teacher; Librarian. Educ: Ph.B., De Paul Univ., 1938, M.A., 1944; Cert. Libn., Cardinal Stretch Coll., 1959; Cert. Audio Visual Dir., 1951. Appts: Schl. Sisters of St. Francis, 1914; Tchr., Sacred Heart Schl., Peoria, III., 1916-23; St. John Monroeville, Ind., 1923-30; Prin., Sacred Heart Allenton, Wis., 1930-34; St. Nicholas Schl., Chgo., 1934-40; St. Ludger Schl. Greighton, Neb., 1940-45; Prin., St. John H.S., Rubicon, Wis., 1945-50, St. John, Petersburg, 1950-59; Libn. & Audio Visual Dir., 1959-69; St. Benedict H.S.; Lib. Cons. & Tutor, spec. educ., 1970-74. Mbrships: III. Lib. Assn.; Libns. of Chicagoland; ALA; Telecare Red Cross; Apostolate of Handicapped. Contbr. to Catholic Digest. Recip. of hons. Address: 2222 W. Byron St., Chgo., IL 60618, U.S.A. 5, 138.

WEBSTER, Burnice Hoyle, b. 3 Mar. 1910. Physician; Thoracologist. Educ: B.A., Vanderbilt Univ., 1936; M.S., Med. Schl., ibid, 1940; Th.D., 1969-70; D.Sc., Holy Trinity Coll., 1971. Appts. incl: V.P., Protestant Hosp., 1944; Pres., ibid, 1945-; Pres., Bapt. Hosp., 1950; Fndr. Mbr., Nashville Cancer Soc.; Dir., Nashville Chest Clin.; Active Staff, St. Thomas, Bapt., Nashville Gen. Hosps., Westside Hosp., Nashville Tumor Clin.; Cons. & Assoc. in Med., Vanderbilt Univ. Fellowships: Geriatric Soc.; Gerontol. Soc.; Royal Soc. of Hlth.; Am. Coll. of Chest Physns.; Spanish Speaking Physns.; Am. Coll. Angiol.; Int. Angiol.; Am. Acad. of Med. Dir., Med. Selective Serv., Tenn. Mbrships. incl: Pres., Middle East Tenn. Chapt., Arthritis Fndn., Muscular Dystrophy Soc.; Tenn., Southern Med. Assns.; Tenn. & Am. Thoracic Socs.; Phi Beta Kappa; Kts. Hospitaller Order of St. John of Jerusalem Delta Phi Alpha; Alpha Omega Alpha. Contbr. of 50 articles to profl. jrnls. Hons. incl: Silver Stethoscope, Award, Bapt. Hosp., 1971; Kt., Order of Constantine; D.D., Fla. Rsch. Inst., 1973; Kt. of the Sacred Cup; Fellow, Wisdom Soc. Address: 420 Mid-State Med. Ctr., Nashville, TN 37203, U.S.A. 7, 14, 22, 28, 131.

WEBSTER, Harvey Curtis, b. 6 Nov. 1906. English Professor; Writer. Educ: A.B., Oberlin Coll., 1927; M.A., ibid 1929; Ph.D., Univ. of Mich., 1935. Appts. incl: Asst. Prof., Univ. of Louisville, Ky., 1936-47; Assoc. Prof., ibid, 1948-50; Prof., 1951-70; Prof. Emeritus, 1972-; Vis. Prof., Univ. of Chgo., 1947-48; Fulbright Prof., Univ. of Durham, U.K., 1950-51, Univ. of Leeds, 1962-63; Vis. Prof., Univ. of Mont., 1965-66. Mbrships. incl: Pres., Ams. for

Democratic Action, Louisville, 1944-45; Pres., Am. Fedn. of Tchrs., Ky., 1944-45, 1949; Pres., Univ. of Louisville, AAUP, 1949-50; Co-Chmn., W. End Community Coun., Louisville, 1966-67; MLA; Am. Coun. of Tchrs. of Engl. Publs. incl: On A Darkling Plain: A Study of the Art & Thought of Thomas Hardy, 1947, re-issued w. new introduction 1964; After the Trauma: Representative British Novelists Since 1920, 1970; Selector (w. introduction), Selected Poems by Hortense Flexner, 1974; About 1000 articles & reviews, 1932-74. Recip. of hons. Address: 950 S. 47th St., Louisville, KY 40211, U.S.A. 7, 15.

WEBSTER, Hugh Colin, b. 24 Oct. 1905. Physicist. Educ: B.Sc., Univ. of Tas., Australia, 1926; D.Sc., ibid, 1941; M.Sc., Univ. of Melbourne, Vic., 1928; Ph.D., Univ. of Cambridge, U.K., 1932. Appts. incl: Lectr. in Biophys., Univ. of Qld., Australia, 1937-40; Rsch. Off. to Prin. Rsch. Off., CSIR, 1940-45; Lectr. to Assoc. Prof. in Radiation Phys., Univ. of Qld., 1945-49; Prof. of Phys., ibid, 1949-70; Sci. Counsellor, Australian Embassy, Wash., U.S.A., 1970-72; Mbr., (Australian) Radio Rsch. Bd., 1949-70 Chmn., ibid, 1964-70. Mbrships. incl: Hon. Fellow, Australian Inst. of Phys., 1971-; Fellow: Pres., Australian Br., Inst. of Phys., 1958-59; Instn. of Elec. Engrs., 1964-; Pres., Sect. A, Australian & New Zealand Assn. for Advancement of Sci. 1959; Inst. of Nuclear Engrs., U.K.; Life, IEEE, N.Y. Publs: Co-author, Medical & Biological Physics, 1968; articles in profl. jrnls. Recip. of C.M.G., 1959. Address: 12 Tarcoola St., St. Lucia, Qld. 4067, Australia. 1, 23, 34, 128.

WEBSTER, Philip Jonathan, b. 23 Jan. 1939. Corporation Executive. Educ: Cornell Univ., 1956-58; A.B., Boston Univ., 1963. Appts. incl: Pub. Info. Specialist, U.S. Army, U.S.A. & Europe, 1958-61; Account Exec., Newsome & Co. Inc., Boston, Mass., U.S.A., 1961-65; V.P., ibid, 1965-67, Admin. V.P. & Dir., 1967-68; Dir., Corp. Communications, Damon Corp., Needham, Mass., 1968-71; V.P., Corp. Communications, ibid, 1971-. Mbrships. incl: V.P., Int. Inst. of Boston, 1968-; Boston Univ. Pub. Affairs Comm., 1970-; Bus./Ind. Advsry. Comm., Boston Mus. of Sci., 1970-; Nat. Investor Rels. Inst., 1970-, & Chmn., Boston Chapt., 1972-73; Bd. of Govs., Handel & Haydn Soc. of Boston, 1968-71; V.P., Gtr. Boston Jr. Chmbr. of Comm., 1965-66, & Dir, 1964-65; P.R. Soc. of Am., 1967-; Alpha Tau Omega, 1958-; Cornell Club of Boston, 1973-. Num. articles on bus., histl. & musical subjs. in many publs. Hons. incl: Freedoms Fndn. Hon. Medal, 1961; Bell Ringer Award, 1970; Financial World Merit Award, 1971, '72, '73; P.R. News Gold Key Award, 1971. Address: Damon Corp., 115 Fourth Ave., Needham Hts., MA 02194, U.S.A. 24.

WECHTER, Vivienne Thaul. Artist; Educator. Educ: Currently Ph.D. Cand., Union Grad. Schl. Artist in Res., Prof., Creative Arts & Chmn., Acquisitions & Exhib., Fordham Univ., N.Y.C., 1964-. Mbrships. incl: Alpha Mu Gamma; AAUP; Am. Soc. Contemp. Artists; Bd. Dirs., Red. of Mod. Painters & Sculptors. Perm. Collects. incl: Mus. of Fine Arts, Houston, Tex.; Corcoran Gall., Wash. D.C.; Rose Mus., Brandies Univ.; Jewish Mus., N.Y.C.; Riverside Mus.; Mus. of Fine Arts, Phoenix, Ariz.; Mus. of Fine Arts, Ft. Worth; Mus. of Art, Berkeley, Calif.; N.Y. Univ. Mus. Collect. Publs: A View from the Ark; var. poems & essays. Address: 4525 Henry Hudson Parkway, Riverdale, NY 10471, U.S.A. 5, 6, 37.

WECKERT, Hans-Kurt, b. 26 Sept. 1920. Company Managing Director. Educ: Studied pol. econs. Appts: Mng. Dir., Schimmelpfeng GmbH, Frankfurt/Main, & C. Regenhardt GmbH, Berlin & Hamburg; Mbr., administrative bd., Inden-og Udenrigs Kreditvaern A/S, Copenhagen, Schimmelpfeng Skandinavien A/S, Copenhagen. Mbrships: Bd. of Dirs., & Treas., Deutsche Kriminologische Gesellschaft e.V., Frankfurt; Kriminologische Gesellschaft e.V., Frankfurt; Deleg., Beccaria-Medaille der Deutschen. Address: Die Steinwiesen 15, 638 Bad Homburg v.d.H., German Fed. Repub.

WEDDING, Erling Solheim, b. 29 May 1908. Physician; Pathologist. Appts. incl: Res. in Pathol., St. John's Hosp., Brooklyn, N.Y., 1941-42; Res., Internal Med., SUNY, Kings Co. Hosp., Brooklyn, 1946-48; Clin. Asst., Int. Med. ibid, 1948-55; Clin. Asst. Prof. of Pathol., 1956-61; Attending in Pathol., Dir. of Pathol. & Clin. Labs., Lutheran Med. Ctr., Brooklyn, 1948-59; Asst. Med. Examiner, N.Y.C., 1955-61; Pathol. & Dir., Clin. Labs., War Mem. Hosp., Sault Ste. Marie, Mich., 1962-; mbr., Pathol. Dept., Plummer Mem. Pub. Hosp., Sault Ste. Marie, Ont., Canada, 1968; mbr., Dept. of Nuclear Med., ibid, 1970; Cons., 507th USAF Hosp., Kincheloe AB., Mich., 1962-. Active mbr. of prof. & local socs. Author of sev. published med. papers. Recip. commendation on publ. of paper, A.U.S., 1946. Address: 203 Hudson Dr., Sault Ste. Marie, MI 49783, U.S.A.

WEDGWOOD, (Dame) Cicely Veronica, b. 20 July, 1910. Author; Historian. Appts. incl: Rsch. Asst., Royal Inst. of Internat. Affairs, 1939-41; Literary Adviser, Jonathan Cape, Ltd., 1941-44; Lit. Ed., Time & Tide, 1944-54; Special Lectr. in Hist., Univ. Coll., London, 1953-69; Trustee, Nat. Gall., 1962-69. Publs. incl: The Thirty Years War, 1939; William The Silent, 1944; Velvet Studies, 1946; The Last of the Radicals, 1947; Richelieu and the French Monarchy, 1949; Montrose, 1952; The King's Peace, 1955; The King's Trial, 1964. Recip., C.B.E., 1956, D.B.E., 1968. Address: c/o Collins, Publishers, 14 St. James's Place, London, S.W.1, U.K. 1, 34.

WEEKS, (Lady) Constance Avard, (pen-name, Constance Tomkinson), b. 22 June 1915. Author. Educ: Grad., The Neighbourhood Playhouse Dram. Schl., N.Y.C. Appts: Dancer & Actress in U.S.A. & Europe, 1936-39; Temporary Civil Servant in British Min. of Supply, N.Y.C., 1940-44; Sec., Royal Ballet, London, U.K., 1946-48; Sec. to Dir. of Old Vic Theatre, London, 1949-52. Mbrships: Canadian Women's Club; S. of England Airedale Club. Publs: Les Girls, 1956; African Follies, 1959; What a Performance!, 1962; Dancing Attendance, 1965. Address: 8 The Grove, Highgate Village, London, N.6, U.K. 3, 5, 88.

WEEMS, J. Eddie, b. 13 Nov. 1896. Minister; University Professor; Track Coach. Educ: A.B., Tex. Christian Univ., 1922; M.A., ibid, 1923. Appts: Min., Evangelist Ch. of Christ, 1923-; Engl. Tchr., Track Coach, pub. schls., Ft. Worth, Tex., 1923-25; Assoc. Prof., Dean of Men, Track Coach, Abilene Christian Coll., 1925-37; Pepperdine Univ., L.A., Calif., 1937-42; Engl. Tchr., Univ. of Tex., Track Coach, Austin H.S., 1942-45; Assoc. Prof., Track Coach, Tex. Christian Univ., 1955-63; Evangelist, Ch. of Christ, 1923-. Hon. Asst. Referee, Drake Relays, Des Moines, Iowa, 1949. Address: 1903 N. 7, Temple, TX 76501, U.S.A. 7, 125.

WEES, Wilfred Rusk, b. 24 Nov. 1899. Educator. Educ: B.A., Univ. of Alta., Canada, 1923; M.A., ibid, 1925; M.Ed., 1928; Ph.D., Univ. of Toronto, 1935. Appts. incl: Tchr., Elem. & Sec. Schls., Sask. & Alta & Camrose

Normal Schl., Alta., 1916-33; Ed.-in-Chief, Toronto Educl. Book Co., 1935-41; Dir. of Trng., Dept. of Veterans Affairs, Ottawa, 1945-46; V.P., & Gen. Mgr., Schl. Book Div., W.J. Gage Ltd., 1946-68; Assoc. Prof., Ont. Inst. for Studies in Educ., 1968-. Mbr. of num. profl. orgs. inclng: Hon. Pres., Ont. Assn. for Continuing Educ.: Pres., Ont. Assn. for Curric. Dev.; Dir., World Coun. for Curric. & Instrn.; Pres., Canadian Book Publrs. Assn. & Canadian Textbook Publrs. Inst. Publs: The Way Ahead: For the School; For Teacher & Child, 1967; Nobody Can Teach Anyone Anything, 1971. Address: Oise, 252 Bloor St. W., Toronto, Ont. M5S 1V6, Canada. 2, 15, 16, 88.

WEGELIUS, Ruth Alice Margaretha, b. 21 Jan. 1915. Physician; Paediatrician. Educ: M.D., 1943, Dr.med.sci., 1948, qualified paediatrician, 1951, Univ. of Helsinki, Finland; Fellow in Pediatrics, Univ. of Colo. Schl. of Med., Denver, U.S.A., 1948-49. Appts: Tchr., Pediatrics, Children's Hosp., Univ. of Helsinki, 1952; Acting Hd., Pediatric Dept., Maria Hosp., Helsinki, 1954-56; Lectr. in Pediatrics, Univ. of Helsinki, 1956-; Asst. to Chief, Pediatric Dept., Aurora Hosp., Helsinki, 1956-67; Hd., Pediatric Dept., ibid, 1967-. Mbrships. incl: Finnish Med. Soc.; Bd., Finnish Pediatric Assn., 1951-55, 1964-67; Gen. Sec., Scandinavian Assn. for Clin. Chem. & Physiol., 1950; Exec. Bd. of Counsellors, Int. Soc. of Haematol., 1968-72; Bd. of Counsellors, European & African Div., ibid, 1970-72; Life mbr., Nuclear Haematol., Instn. of Nuclear Engrs., Med. Sect. Author of about 55 med. publs. inclng. a monograph. Hons. incl: Cross of Liberty, IV Class, w. Red Cross; Prizes for med. papers. Address: Observatoriegatan 4 A 12, SF 00140 Helsingfors 14, Finland. 43, 90, 134.

WEGNER, Hans J., b. 2 Apr., 1914. Architect. Educ: Inst. Technol., 1936; Copenhagen Art Schl., Denmark, 1936-38. Appts: Own drawing office, Aarhus, Jutland, 1943-46; Tchr., Furniture Design, Copenhagen Art Schl.; w. Palle Suenson, 1946-48; Own drawing office, 1948-; Supervised & arranged exhibs. Danish Art & Handicraft, 1949-52. Mbr. Soc. of Art, Aarhus, Jutland, 1944-. Creative Works: Designed furniture for UNESCO HQ, Paris, France, 1958; Samples of work at Mus. Decorative Art, Copenhagen; Röhsska Mus., Göteborg, Sweden; Mus. Mod. Art, N.Y., U.S.A.; Nat. Gall., Melbourne, Australia; Nordenfjeldske Mus., Trondheim, Norway; Mus. Decorative Art, Oslo, ibid; Nat. Mus., Stockholm, Sweden; Metropol. Mus. Art, N.Y., U.S.A.; 1-man exhibs. at Zürich, Switzerland, 1958; Georg Jensen Mus., N.Y., U.S.A. 1959, '65; Röhsska Mus., Göteborg, Sweden, 1967; Rep. at Danish Pavilion, World's Fair, N.Y., U.S.A., 1965. Hons. incl: 24 Awards, Furniture, Cabinetmakers Assn. exhibs., 1938-; Cabinetmakers Annual Prize, 1965; Citation of Merit, Am. Inst. Interior Designers, 1968. Address: Tinglevvej 17, 2820 Gentofte, Denmark.

WEGOREK, Wladyslaw, b. 16 Feb. 1918. Entomologist. Educ: Acad. of Agric., Warsaw; Univ. of M. Curie-Sklodowska, Lublin. Appts: Hd., Dept. of Entomol., Inst. of Agric., Pulawy, 1945-54; Prof. of Entomol., Acad. of Agric., Warsaw, 1951-54; Hd., Dept. of Entomol., Acad. of Agric., Poznan, 1954-68; Rector, ibid, 1959-65; Dir., Plant Protection Inst., Poznan, 1956-. Mbrships: Vice-Chmn., Poznan Br. of Polish Acad. of Scis.; Vice-Chmn., Plant Protection Comm., Polish Acad. of Scis., Warsaw; Hd., Poznan Br., Polish Entomol. Soc.; Polish Zool. Soc.; Copernicus Soc. of Polish Naturalists; Dir., Coord. Comm., Plant Protection for Comecon countries; 6 sci.

comms. of other Agric. Insts. Publd. about 170 sci. papers & books on biol., ecol. & methods of insect pest control in Polish, Engl., German & Russian. Hons: Golden Cross of Merit, 1958; Commandoria of Polonia Restituta, 1964; Medal of 1000-yrs. existance of Polish State, 1966; num. profl. prizes. Address: Inst. of Plant Protection, Miczurina 20, 60-318 Poznan, Poland.

WEHMER, Carl, b. 9 Jan. 1903. University Librarian. Educ: Dr.phil., Univ. of Berlin, Germany, 1932. Appts: Collaborator, Gen. Catalogue of Incunabula, Berlin, 1925-40; Univ. Lib., Frankfurt/Main, 1949-53; Dir., Univ. Lib., Heidelberg, 1953-65. Mbr., Heidelberger Akademie der Wissenschaften. Publs. incl: Leonhard Wagner. Proba centum scripturarum. Facsimile mit Begleittext, 1963; Deutsche Buchdrucker des 15. Jahrhunderts, 1971. Hons: Prof., Heidelberg; Festschrift, on his 60th birthday, Bibliotheca docet. Festgabe für Carl Wehmer, 1963. Address: Im Hosend 10, D 6901 Dossenheim bei Heidelberg, German Fed. Repub.

WEHR, Wesley Conrad, b. 17 Apr. 1929. Artist. Educ: B.A. & M.A., Univ. of Wash., Seattle, U.S.A. Appts: Archival & Collects. Cons., Archives of N.W. Art, Henry Art Gall., Art Mus., Univ. of Wash.; Volunteer Asst., Paleobotanical Collects., Burite Mem. Mus., ibid. Mbrships: Art Gall. of Gtr. Victoria, B.C., Canada; Archival Donor, Archives of Am. Art, Smithsonian Instn., Wash. D.C. Paintings in num. pub. collects. & exhibs. inclng: Municipal Gall. of Mod. Art, Dublin, Ireland; Brooklyn Mus., N.Y.; Balt. Mus. of Art, Md.; Mpls. Inst. of Art., Minn.; Long Beach Mus. of Art, Calif.; Wichita Mus. of Art, Kan.; Carpenter Art Galls., Dartmouth Coll., Hanover, N.H.; Expo 70, Osaka, Japan; Francine Seders Gall., Seattle, 1967 & 1973; Humboldt Galls., San Fran., Calif., 1969, 1972 & 1974; Shepherd Gall, N.Y.C., 1973. Address: Henry Gallery, University of Washington Art Museum, University of Washington, Seattle, WA 98105, U.S.A. 37.

WEIDEN, Paul Ludwig, b. 28 Jan. 1908. Lawyer. Educ: LL.D., Univ. of Frankfurt, Germany, 1931; M.L., U.K., 1936. Appts: Chief Legal Sect., Liberated Areas Br., Bd. Econ. Warfare, U.S.A., 1943-44; Admitted to bar, U.K., 1936, Ore., 1938, D.C., 1943, N.Y., 1947, & Germany, 1960; Law Prac., Portland, Ore., 1938-42; w. Weiden, Grosswell & Gunnigle (name changed to Weiden & Gunnigle, 1960), N.Y.C., 1947-; Mbr., Zucker Weiden & Shapiro; Atty.; SEC, 1944-45; Chmn., dirs., var. European & Am. corps.; Chmn., Steinberg & Vorsaenger Corp., Wilag Corp. (Wiesbaden) Ltd., & Int. Mortgage Corp., N.Y.C.; Dir., Brema Mineral Oil Corp., Vienna, Austria. Contbr. to var. European & Am. legal publs. Address: 920 Park Ave., N.Y., NY 10028, U.S.A. 6.

WEIDLEIN, Johann, b. 25 Oct. 1905. Retired Higher Studies Director. Educ: Studied, Univ. of Budapest, Hungary, 1926-30. Appts: Tchr., evang. Gymnasium, Szarvas, 1930-40; Dir., Jakob-Bleyer-Gymnasium, Budapest, 1940-45; Dir. of studies, Gymnasium, Schorndorf/Württemberg, German Fed. Repub., 1946-69. Mbrships: Ungarische Sprachwissenschaftliche Gesellschaft, Budapest, 1936-45; Südostdeutsche hist. Kommn., Munich, 1964-. Publs. incl: Deutsche Schuld in Ungarn?, 1966; Die Schwäbische Türkei. Beiträge, 1967; Schuld des Volksbundes an der Vertreibung, 1967; Jüdisches & deutsches Schicksal in Ungarn unter dem gleichen Unstern, 1969; Num. articles in jrnls. Hons:

Donauschwäbischer Kulturpreis, 1959; Ungarndeutscher Kulturpreis, 1972. Address: Mönchsbrückenweg 16, 706 Schorndorf/Württemberg, German Fed. Repub. 43.

WEIDMANN, Silvio, b. 7 Apr. 1921. Professor of Physiology. Educ: M.D., Univ. of Berne, Switzerland, 1947; Rsch. Fellow, Dept. of Physiol., Univ. of Uppsala, Sweden, 1947/48; Physiological Lab., Cambridge Univ., U.K., 1948/50. Appts: Lectr. in Physiol., Univ. of Berne, 1953-58; Vis. Prof., Downstate Med. Schl., N.Y. Univ., Brooklyn, 1954-55; Assoc. Prof., Univ. of Berne, 1958-68; Chmn., Dept. of Physiol., ibid, 1968-. Mbrships: Swiss Physiological Soc.; Pres., ibid, 1968-71; Rektor, Univ. of Berne, 1974-75. Contbr., Jrnl. of Physiol., London, 1951-70. Hons: Theodor Kecher Prize, Univ. of Berne, 1956; Premio Viganello, Lugano, 1962. Address: Dept. of Physiol., Univ. of Berne, Buehlplatz 5, 301L Berne, Switzerland. 43, 103.

WEIGAND, Hans Martin Ferdinand, b. 15 Apr. 1909. Chemist. Educ: Studied at Univs. of Frankfurt/Main, Giessen & Freiburg/Breisgau, Germany; Dr.phil. nat., Univ. of Freiburg/Breisgau, 1935. Appts: Asst., Chem. Inst., Univ. of Freiburg, 1935-36; Chief of lab., Univ. Clin., ibid, 1936-37; Rsch. Chemist, Deutsche Rhodiaceta AG, Freiburg, 1937-39, & Süddeutsche Zwllwolle AG, Kelheim/Donau, 1940-44; Served WWII; Rsch. Chemist, August Luhn & Co., Wuppertal 1948-51; Supt., Dir. acetate textile, Deutsche Rhodiaceta AG, Freiburg, 1952-70; Retd., 1971; Aux. tchr., var. secondary schls., 1972-. Mbrships. incl: Bd. mbr. Deutsch-französischer Club, Radolfzell; Former Bd. mbr., Freiburg, Deutsche Chemische Gesellschaft; Fndr. & former hd., Upper Rhine Sect., Freiburg, Deutsche Orchideen-Gesellschaft. Author of publs. in field. Address: Schorenstr. 1, D 7761 Iznang, Lake Constance, German Fed. Repub.

WEIGEL, Christoph Karl Friedrich, (Fritz), b. 19 July 1926. University Associate Professor of Inorganic Chemistry & Radiochemistry. Educ: B.S., Göttingen, 1950; M.S., Mainz, 1954; Ph.D., ibid, 1956: post-doctorate studies, Munich, 1957-65. Appts: Post-doctoral student, Lawrence Berkeley Lab., 1956-57; Sci. Asst., Univ. of Munich, 1957-65; Lectr., ibid, 1962, Instr. Inorganic Chem. & Radiochem., 1965, Assoc. Prof. of Chem., 1971-; Regional Ed., Inorganic & Nuclear Chem. Letters, 1966. Mbrships: Am. Chem. Soc.; Am. Nuclear Soc.; var. German scientific orgs. Nu. scientific papers. Address: Titurelstr. 7/II, 8000 Munich 81, German Fed. Repub. 43.

WEIL, Herman, b. 15 Dec. 1905. University Professor: Associate Dean. Educ: Ph.D., Univ. of Marburg, Germany, 1928. Appts. incl: Prof., Neb. Ctrl. Coll., 1939-40; Prof., Chmn., Phys. Scis., Milwaukee Schl. of Engrng., 1940-43; Prof., Psychol., Hd., Dept. of Educ. & Psychol., Milwaukee State Tchrs. Coll., 1944-56; Prof., Chmn., Dept. of Psychol., Univ. of Wis., Milwaukee, 1955-61; Dir., Hons. Prog. for Superior Students, Coll. of Letters & Sci., ibid., 1960-; Assoc. Dean, ibid, 1967-. Mbrships. incl: Pres., Univ. of Wis., Milwaukee Chapt., AAUP, 1959-60; Pres., Milwaukee Co. Psychol. Assn., 1961-62; Wis. Psych. Assn., 1962-63. Publs. incl: Chapt., Milwaukee Makes Instructional Change, 1950; contbr. to psychol. jrnls. esp. on psychol. of prejudice. Address: 2027 E. Lake Bluff Blvd., Milwaukee, WI 53211, U.S.A. 2, 8, 14, 15, 55.

WEIL, Max Harry, b. 9 Feb. 1927. Physician; Professor. Educ: A.B., Univ. of

Mich., Ann Arbor, 1948; M.D., State Univ. of N.Y. Coll. of Med., N.Y.C., 1952; Ph.D., Univ. of Minn. Grad. Schl., Mpls., 1957. Appts. incl: Dir., Univ. of Southern Calif. Shock Rsch. Unit, 1961-; Cons. Physn., Cedars-Sinai Med. Ctr. & Temple & Midway Hosp., L.A., 1965-; Clin. Prof. of Med., Schl. of Med., Univ. of Southern Calif., 1971-; Clin. Prof. of Biomed. Engrng., Schl. of Engrng., ibid, 1972-. Mbrships. incl: Fellow, Am. Coll. Cardiol., Am. Coll. Physns., Am. Heart Assn.; Bd. Dirs., L.A. Co. Heart Assn.; Chmn., Co. of L.A. Bd. Supvsrs., Comm. on Emergency Med. Care (Pres., 1968-73); Soc. of Critical Care Med. (Pres., ibid, 1970-72). Address: 1300 N. Vermont Ave., L.A., CA 90027, U.S.A. 9, 14, 17, 28.

WEILER, Dorothy Esser (Mrs. Henry C. Weiler), b. 21 Feb. 1914. Librarian. Educ: B.A., Wash. State Univ., 1935; Grad. Degree. in Libnship., Univ. of Wash. Grad. Lib. Schl., 1936. Appts. incl: Asst. Br. Libn., Tacoma Pub. Lib., Wash., 1936-37; Tchr.-Libn., Roosevelt Schl. Dist. 66, Phoenix, Ariz., 1956-59; Ext. Libn., Ariz. State Dept. of Admin., Div. of Lib., Archives & Pub. Records, 1959-67; Dir., Tempe Pub. Lib., Tempe, Ariz., 1967-; Assoc. Prof., Ariz. State Univ., Dept. of Lib. Sci., Coll. of Educ., Spring Semester, 1968. Mbrships. incl: Ariz. State Lib. Assn., Pres. Elect, 1972-73, Pres., 1973-74, Pres., Pub. Lib. Div., Sec. & various Chmnships.; Southwest Lib. Assn., Exec. Bd., 1972-74; Am. Lib. Assn., Recruitment Chmn., Mbrship. Chmn.; Am. Bus. Women's Assn. Publs: Ed., Roadrunner (Ariz. Lib. Ext. Serv. publn.); Originator & Ed., Timbling Tumbleweed (publd. by Ariz. Lib. Ext. Serv.). Contbr. to Ency. Americana. Hons: Silver Book Award, Lib. Binding Inst., 1963; Libn. of the Yr. Award, Ariz. State Lib. Assn. 1971. Address: P.O. Box 26018, Tempe, AZ 85282, U.S.A. 1, 5, 9, 42, 132.

WEILERSTEIN, Sadie Rose (Mrs. B. Reuben Weilerstein), b. 28 July 1894. Author, Children's Books. Educ: B.A., Univ. of Rochester. Appts: Tchr., Engl., Rochester Schl. of the Deaf, 1917-20. Mbrships: Mbr., Nat. Bd., Nat. Women's League, United Synagogue of Am.; Advsry. Coun., Jewish Book Coun. of Am.; Hadassah; Mizrachi Women; Women's Bnai Brith; Ort; Technion; N.J. Audubon Soc. Publs: 12 Books, inclng: What Danny Did, 1928; What the Moon Brought, 1944; Our Baby, 1950; Ten & a Kid, 1961, 2nd edit., 1973; Jewish Heroes, 2 vols.; Contbr. to num. anthols. Hons. incl: Juvenile Award, Jewish Book Coun. of Am., 1956; Juvenile Lit. Award, 1962; Yovel Award, Nat. Women's League, United Synagogue of Am., 1966. Address: 129 S. Virginia Ave., Apt. 1313, Atlantic City, NJ 08401, U.S.A. 5, 55, 138, 141.

WEINBAUM, Eleanor Perlstein, Estate Manager; Real Estate Owner; Author. Educ: Short Story & Poetry Writing Classes under leading poets & writers, Benjamin Schl., N.Y.; Clement Wood & Boulder Univ. Appts: Executrix, Mamie Gordon Perlstein Trust; Ptnr., 23rd St. Shopping Ctr.; Owner of other real estate. Mbrships. incl: Fellow, Intercontinental Biographical Assn.; Am. Poets Fellowship Soc.; United Poets Laureate Int.; Poetry Soc. of Tex.; Am. Poetry League; Charter mbr., League of Women Voters; World Poetry Soc.; Life mbr., Big Thicket Assn.; Bd., Sabibe Oaks Home for Aged. Publs. incl: Jest for You, 1954; Shalom, America, 1970. Assisted in establishing· literary mag. Pulse & donated Eleanor Poetry Room, Lamar Univ. Hons. incl: M.H.D., Int. Acad., 1970; Disting. Serv. Citation, World Poetry Soc., 1970; Dr., Human Letters., Free Univ. (Asia), 1973.

Address: 203-A Gilbert Bldg., Beaumont, TX 77701, U.S.A. 11, 128, 132.

WEINHOLTZ, Yehuda S., b. 5 Feb. 1917. Metalurgical Technologist. Educ: Tech. H.S., Warsaw, Poland, 1934-36. Appts: Asst. Chief Engr., Locomotive Dept., Brest-Litoust, U.S.S.R., 1939-41; Underground Movement, German Occupied Territory, 1942-44; Chief Insp., 'Ort' vocational schls., U.S. Occupied Sector, Germany, 1945-49; Tech. Advsr., Metal Wkrs. Union, Israel, 1949-74. Mbrships: Exec., Nat. Metal Wkrs. Union, Israel; Sec., Electronics & Elec. Wkrs. Union, Israel; Ed., 'Basadlna U'bamiphal', technological Hebrew monthly. Author of var. publs. on safety & indl. hlth. matters & on metal processing. Address: 4 Yehezkel St., Ramat-chen, Israel. 55.

WEININGER, Freed, b. 29 July 1915. Poet; Painter; Psychiatric Social Worker. Educ: Master in Soc. Work, Wayne State Univ., Schl. of Soc. Work Appts: Prin. & Tchr., Workmen's Circle Schl., Bridgeport, Conn., 1952-56; Cultural Art Dir., Jewish Community Ctr., ibid, & Prog. Asst., Jewish Community Ctr., Detroit, Mich., 1956-58; Sr. Psych. Soc. Wkr., Psych. Clin., Buffalo, N.Y., 1963-66, & Jewish Family Serv., ibid, & Student Supvsr., Univ. of Buffalo, Schl. of Soc. Work, 1966-68; Psych. Soc. Wkr., Kfar Tikva, Village for Mentally Retarded, Tivon, Israel, 1969-71, & Oranim Child-Guidance Clin., Tivon, Israel, 1971-. Mbrships: Sec., Yiddish PEN, 1948-50; Nat. Assn. of Soc. Wkrs.; Acad. of Certified Soc. Wkrs., U.S.A. & Israel. Publs. incl: A Pastuch in New York, 1951; Baim Prut, La Plata un Yarden, 1966; In Groyssn Droyssn, 1974. Solo exhibs. held at Lyceum, Havana, Cuba, 1946; Ward Eggleston Galls., 1948; Anna L. Werbe Galls., Detroit, 1960; Sisti Galls., Buffalo, 1965. Grp. exhibs. at Jewish Artists Exhib., Jewish Mus., N.Y., 1948 & 1950; Detroit Inst. of Art, 1960; Albright Knox Mus., Buffalo, 1964, 1966, etc. Winner of Bimko Poetry Award, Congress for Jewish Culture, N.Y., 1967. Address: 50 Keren Kayemet, Tivon, Israel. 6, 55, 94.

WEINLANDER, Albertina Abrams (Mrs. Max M. Weinlander), b. 21 July 1919. College Professor. Educ: B.S., Ctrl. Mich. Univ., 1942; M.A., Univ. of Mich., 1947; Ph.D., 1955. Appts. incl: Instr.-Asst. Prof., Educ. & Integrated Studies, Miami Univ., Oxford, Ohio, 1948-55; Lectr., Extension Serv., 195-56; Asst. Prof.-Prof., Wittenberg Univ., 1956-. Mbrships incl: NEA; AAAS; Ohio Educ. Assn.; Nat. Aerospace Educ. Coun.; Assn. of Learning Disabilities; AAUP; Pi Lambda Theta; Kappa Delta Pi. Publs: Your Child in a Scientific World, 1959; How to Prepare for the National Teachers Examination, 1968, 70; Education in the Elementary School, 1970. Recip., Fellowship Grant, Econ. Educ. Conf., 1954. Address: 290 Ridge Mall, Springfield, OH 45504, U.S.A. 5, 8, 14, 15.

WEINMANN, Eric, b. 29 July 1913. Lawyer. Educ: Dipl. oec. Handels-Hochschule, Berlin, Germany, 1935; M.A., Columbia Univ., 1947; J.D., 1957. LL.M., Georgetown Univ., Law Ctr., Wash. DC, 1944-46. Assoc. Counsel, Legal & Monetary Affairs Subcomm., Comm. of Govt. Ops., U.S. House of Reps., 1958-59; Atty., U.S. Securities & Exchange Commn., 1960-63; w. U.S. Small Bus. Admin., 1963-; currently Chief Counsel for Investment. Mbrships. incl: Metropolitan Club, Wash. DC; Nat. Lawyers Club; City Tavern Assn. Contbr. to legal jrnls. Recip. Meritorious Serv. Award, U.S. Small Bus. Admin., 1972. Address: 1620 30th St., N.W., Washington, DC 20007, U.S.A.

WEINROTH, Ralph, b. 24 Apr. 1914. Psychologist. Educ: A.B., Washington Coll., Chesterton, Md.; M.Ed., & Ed.D., Temple Univ., Phila., Pa. Appts: Guidance Counselor, Pennsauken, N.J. Bd. of Educ., Pennsauken H.S., 1955-62; Voc. Psychologist, Voc. Rsch. Inst., Phila. Pa., 1962-63; w. N.Y. State Dept. of Mental Hygiene Unit at Elmira Reception Ctr., N.Y. as Sr. Clin. Psychologist, 1963-66, Assoc. Psychologist, 1966-69, Prin. Psychologist, 1969-; Special Lectr. in Psychol., Elmira Coll., 1964-. Mbrships: N.Y. State Psychologists in Pub. Serv.; B'nai B'rith, Elmira Chapt. (Exec. Bd. 1965-, Pres. 1967-68); Jewish Community Ctr. (Bd. of Dirs. 1973-); Big Flats Lodge, F. & A.M.; Ancient Accepted Scottish Rite, Valley of Corning, N.Y.; Kalurah Temple, Binghamton, N.Y. Address: 519 W. Water St., Elmira, NY 14905, U.S.A.

WEINSTEIN, George, b. 20 Mar. 1924. Certified Public Accountant; Trustee. Educ: B.S., Univ. of Ill; M.B.A., N.Y. Univ.; further studies, Law Schls., Univ. of Ill., N.Y. Univ. Appts: Lectureships w. Int. Assn. of Accts., & as Exec.-in-Residence at Univ. of Ill. Mbrships. incl: Nat. Treas., Tau Delta Phi; Delta Sigma Pi; N.Y. State Soc. of Certified Pub. Accts.; Am. Inst. of Certified Pub. Accts.; Club Pres., Univ. of Ill.; Westmoreland Club; Ambassadors Club. Address: 1 Lincoln Plaza, N.Y., U.S.A.

WEINSTEIN, Pál, b. 5 Sept. 1906. Professor of Ophthalmology. Educ: Med. dip., Budapest, Hungary, 1930; Dip. of Ophthalmol., ibid, 1936; D.Sc., 1960; Prof., 1962. Appts: Asst., Eye Clin., Budapest, 1930-36; Asst., Eye Dept., Polyclin., 1936-39; Chief, Eye Dept., Med. Postgrad. Schl., Budapest, 1939-. Mbrships: Ophthalmological Soc., U.K., 1959-; Deleg., French Ophthalmol. Soc., 1959-; Hon. mbr., Mexican Ophthalmol. Soc., 1966-; Corres. mbr., German Democratic Repub. Ophthalmol. Soc., 1969-. Publs: Glaucoma, Pathology & Therapy, 1953; Mechanische & neurovaskuläre Probleme des Glaukoms, 1963; Ophthalmologische Differentialdiagnose bei Gehirntumoren, 1972; 200 contbns. to profl. jrnls. in var. langs. Address: V. Balassi Bálint ucca 9-11, 1055 Budapest, Hungary. 55.

WEINSTEIN, Sidney M., b. 30 Jan. 1917. Executive. Educ: B.A., Harvard Coll., 1939; M.S., N.Y. Univ., 1943; Ph.D., ibid, 1951. Appts: Dir. of Rsch., Apex Chem. Co., 1944-52; Pres., Chem-Plex Co., Inc., 1952-57; V.P., Tanatex Chem. Corp., 1957-70; Pres., Tanatex Chem. Co., Div. of Sybron Corp., 1970-. Mbrships: Am.-Chem. Soc.; Am. Assn. of Textile Chems. & Colorists; Harvard Club of N.Y.; Essex Club; Sigma Xi; Phi Lambda Upsilon; Fellow, Am. Inst. of Chems., 1969. Worked on Rsch. & Dev. of Chem. Products for Dyeing & Finishing of Textiles Made of Var. Synthetic Fibres & their Blends, patented 1963. Address: 48 Rock Spring Rd., W. Orange, NJ 07052, U.S.A. 6, 14, 16.

WEINTRAUB, Daniel Ralph, b. 23 Apr. 1939. Health Planning Specialist. Educ: B.A., N.Y. Univ., 1959; D.D.S., Schl. of Dental & Oral Surg., Columbia Univ., 1963, Cert. in Pub. Hlth., of Wash., 1963. Appts: Volunteer Ldr., Coord., U.S. Peace Corps, Bolivia, 1964-65; Rural Community Dev. Advsr., Dominican Repub., 1966-68; Population & Pub. Hlth. Advsr., U.S. Accy. for Int. Dev., ibid, 1968-69; Assoc. Planning Dir., Ctr. for Family Planning Prog. Dev., Planned Parenthood Fedn., 1969-; Cons., U.S. Dept. Hlth., Educ., & Welfare, 1971-74; Cons., Nat. Ctr. Hlth. Stats., 1973. Mbrships. incl: Fed. Stats. Users' Conf.; population Assn. Am.; Kts. of Pythias. Author &

contbr. num. papers family planning progs. Recip., Cert. of Hon., Govt. of Dominican Repub., 1969. Address: 44 Amethyst St., Elmont, NY 11003, U.S.A. 6.

WEIR, (Brig.-Gen.) James Buchanan, b. 10 Apr. 1906. Stock Broker. Appts: Ptnr., Oswald & Drinkwater, Canada, 1928-63; Served w. Canadian Forces o'seas, 1939-45; Chmn., Canadian Stock Exchange, 1950-52; Chmn., Montreal Stock Exchange, 1952-57; Dir., Home Oil Co., 1950-72; Chmn., Oswald Drinkwater & Graham Ltd., 1963-. Mbrships: Mount Royal Club, Montreal, Quebec; Whitlock Golf & Country Club, Hudson, Quebec. Hons: E.D., 1943; O.B.E., 1944. Address: Choisy, R.R. No. 1, Hudson, Quebec, JOP 1HO, Canada. 12.

WEIS, Paul, b. 19 Mar. 1907. Lawyer. Educ: J.D., Univ. of Vienna, Austria; Ph.D., Univ. of London, U.K. Appts: Legal Advsr., Int. Refugee Org., Geneva, Switzerland, 1947-51, Off. of U.N. High Commnr. for Refugees, ibid, 1951-61; Dir., Legal Div., ibid, 1961-67; Special Advsr., 1967-71; Lectr., Zurich Univ., 1972-. Mbrships: Int. Law Assn. (ASYLUM comm.); Am. Soc. Int. Law; V.P., Int. Lawyers Club, Geneva; Commonwealth Assn., ibid. Publs: Nationality & Statelessness in International Law, 1956; Statelessness as a Legal-Political Problem (co-author) & Protection against Group Defamation (World Jewish Congress booklets), 1944; Refugees & the Law (World Peace Through Law Ctr. booklet), 1973; articles in field. Hons: Golden Nansen Ring, 1970; Hon. Award, Pres., German Fed. Repub., 1971; Civil Defence Medal, U.K., 1945. Address: 1 rue du Vidollet, CH-1202, Geneva, Switzerland. 43, 55.

WEISFOGEL, Jerry, b. 27 May 1928. Psychiatrist. Educ: B.S., City Coll. of N.Y., 1952; M.A., ibid, 1953; M.D., N.Y. Med. Coll., 1957. Appts: Chief Psych., Adult In-Patient Treatment Serv., Kings Co. Psych. Hosp., 1962-63 & Adult In-Patient Psychotherapy Serv., ibid, 1965-67; Dir., Emergency Treatment Serv., Kings Co. Psych. Hosp., 1967-68; Cons. in Psych., Northport, VA Hosp., 1968-; Clin. Asst. Prof. of Psych., SUNY, Downstate Med. Ctr., 1968-69; Asst. Prof. of Psych., ibid, 1969-70; Asst. Clin. Prof. of Psych., Mt. Sinai Schl. of Med., 1970-. Mbrships. incl: Am. Psych. Assn.; Chmn., Sci. Prog. Comm., Co-Chmn., Continuing Educ. Comm., Bklyn. Psych. Soc.; AMA Sec.-Treas., Schilder Soc. for Psychotherapy & Psychopath., 1970-, Pres. & Treas., 1974-; Exec. Coun. Mbr., Brooklyn Psychiatric Soc., 1973-74; Fellow, Am. Acad. of Pyschosomatic Med. Contbr., articles, psych. jrnls. Contbng. Abstract Ed., Psychosomatics, jrnl. of Am. Acad. of Psychosomatic Med. Address: 7 E. 85th St., N.Y., NY 10028, U.S.A. 17.

WEISMANN, Donald L., b. 12 Oct. 1914. University Professor; Artist; Writer. Educ: B.S., Ph.M., Univ. of Wis.; Ph.D., Ohio State Univ. Appts: Asst. Prof., Ill. State Univ., 1940-42, 46-48; Asst. Prof., Wayne State Univ., Detroit Mich., 1949-51; Prof. of Art & Chmn., Dept. of Art, Univ. of Ky., 1951-54 & Univ. of Tex., 1954-58; Prof. of Art., ibid, 1958-63; Univ. Prof. in the Arts, 1963-; Dir. of Comp. Studies, 1967-69. Mbrships: Kappa Delta Pi; Presidential Appt. Nat. Coun. on the Arts. Wash. D.C., 1966-72; Study Grp. on Unity of Knowledge, Univ. of Calif., 1967-; Nat. Humanities Fac. Publs. incl: Some Folks Went West, 1960; Jelly Was the Word, 1965; Language and Visual Form: The Personal Record of a Dual Creative Process, 1968; The Visual Arts as Human Experience, 1970; contbr. articles to lit. & educ. jrnls. Oil paintings reproduced in nat.

mags. Writer, Prod. & Dir., 2 films, Terlingua, 1971 & Station X, 1974. Recip. num. prizes for paintings & writings. Address: 405 Buckeye Trail, Austin, TX 78746, U.S.A. 7, 13, 15, 30, 37, 113, 125, 133, 140.

WEISS, G. Christian, b. 19 Nov. 1910. Clergyman; Missionary; Radio Minister. Educ: Grad., Kan. Bible Inst. & Bethel Theol. Sem. Appts: Pastor, 1st Bapt. Ch., Grove City, Minn.; Missionary to Morocco; Dir., Gospel Missionary Union; Dir., Back to the Bible Missionary Agcy.; Broadcaster, Voice of Missions. Mbrships: F.R.G.S.; Int. Mark Twain Soc. Publs. incl: The Perfect Will of God; On Being a Real Christian; The Man Everybody Should Know; Insights into Bible Times & Customs; God & the Nations; Man's Need, God's Plan, Our Mission; Our Guide the Bible; Involved or Uninvolved. The Contest of the Ages; Wring-Way Jonah. Recip., D.D., John Brown Univ., 1958. Address: 728 Eastridge Dr., Lincoln, NE 68510, U.S.A. 8, 128.

WEISS, Paul, b. 19 May 1901. Professor of Philosophy. Educ: B.S.S., CCNY, U.S.A., 1927; M.A., Harvard Univ., 1928; Ph.D., ibid, 1929. Appts. incl: Tutor, Bryn Mawr Coll., Pa., 1931-33; Assoc. Prof., ibid, 1933-40; Prof., 1940-46; Chmn., Dept. of Philos., 1944-46; Prof., Yale Univ., 1946-62; Sterling Prof. of Philos., ibid, 1962-69; Heffer Prof. of Philos., Cath. Univ. of Am., Wash. D.C., 1969-; Vis. Disting. Prof. or Vis. Lctr., num. Am. Univs. Mbrships. incl: Fndr., Metaphysical Soc. of Am., Pres., 1951-52; Pres., Am. Philosophical Assn., 1966; Fndr. & First Pres., C. A. Pierce Soc.; Fndr., Soc. for Schol. Rsch. in Sport; Fndr. & First Pres., Philosophical Soc. for Study of Sport, 1972; Bd. of Govs., Hebrew Univ., Jerusalem, Israel. Publs: 20 books inclng. Right & Wrong, Religion & Art, & Philosophy in Process (6 vols.); Ed., Judaism; Over 300 contbns. to var. jrnls. Hons. incl: L.H.D., Grinnell Coll., Iowa; L.H.D., Pace Coll., Brooklyn, N.Y.; L.H.D., Bellarmine-Ursuline Coll., Louisville, Ky. Address: 2000 N. St., N.W. Washington, DC 20036, U.S.A.

WEISS, Samuel A., b. 13 May 1923. Psychologist; Psychoanalyst. Educ: B.A., Yeshiva Univ., 1944; M.A., N.Y. Univ., 1948; Ph.D., ibid, 1957. Appts: Yeshiva Univ., Pvte Prac., 1955-; Assoc. Rsch. Sci., N.Y. Univ. Coll. of Engrng. & Med. Ctr., 1956-59; Assoc. Proj. Dir., N.Y. Univ., 1959-67; Rsch. Sci., ibid, 1960-68; Asst. Prof., 1960-61; Assoc. Prof., Psychol. Cons., 1961-71. Mbrships: Professorial Mbr., Assn. for Applied Psychoanalysis; Fellow, Am. Psychol. Assn.; Fellow, AAAS. Publs: A Psychological Battery for Predicting Success in Prosthetic Rehabilitation, 1971; author of articles on prevention of suicide in var. profl. jrnls. Address: 7 Park Ave., N.Y., NY 10016, U.S.A. 6, 14, 28.

WEITTING, June Arlene, b. 1 June 1922. Librarian. Educ: B.A., Western Mich. Univ., 1944; M.A., Wheaton Coll., 1949; M.L.S., Western Mich. Univ., 1966. Appts: Instr., Latin, Wheaton Coll., 1944-50; Instr., Latin & Engl., Wheaton Acad., 1945-64; Ref. Libn., Wheaton Coll., 1964-69; Acting Libn., ibid, 1969-71; Dir. of Lib., 1971-. Mbrships: ALA; Ill. Lib. Assn.; Ill. Regional Lib. Coun.; Sec., Libras, 1969-71. Ed., Libras Periodical Directory, 1969-. Address: 406 E. Madison, Wheaton, IL 60187, U.S.A.

WEITZ, Martin M., b. 2 Aug. 1909. Rabbi; Professor; Author. Educ: Colo. State Coll., Greeley, 1925-27; A.B., Univ. of Cinn., 1932; Rabbi, Hebrew Union Coll., Cinn., Ohio, 1934; Denver Univ., Colo., summer 1930; Harvard

Chap. Schl., 1943. Appts. incl: Rabbi, Temple B'nai Jeshurun, Des Moines, Iowa, 1946-48; Prof., Drake Univ., Des Moines, 1947-48; Rabbi, House of Israel, Hot Springs, Ark., 1948-51; Rabbi, Beth Israel Temple, Atlantic City, & Prof., Rutgers Univ., Camden, N.J., 1951-63; Rabbi, N. Shore Synagogue, Syosset, L.I., 1963-66; Prof., Lincoln Univ., Oxford, Pa., 1967-73; Rabbi, Temple of Israel, Wilmington, N.C., 1974-. Mbrships: Fndr., Atlantic City Nat. Conf. of Christians & Jews: Fndr., Atlantic Community Coll., Mays Landing; N.J.; Ed. & Trustee, Int. Rotary Club, Oxford, Pa.; Res. Lectr., Jewish Chautauqua Soc.; Dpty. Nat. Chap., Jewish War Veterans of U.S. Author of books, 15 booklets & mags. & over 200 articles for jrnls. Hons. incl: D.H.L., Colo. Northern Univ., Greeley. Colo., 1963; D.D., Lincoln Univ., Oxford, Pa., 1967. Address: 1220 Columbus Circle, Apt. C, Wilmington, NC 28401, U.S.A. 2, 30, 55, 128.

WEITZENHOFFER, Aaron Mac, Jr., b. 30 Oct. 1939. Art Dealer. Educ: B.F.A. Univ. of Okla., 1961. Appts.: Dir., David B. Findlay Galls., 1965-68; currently Pres., Gimpel & Weitzenhoffer Ltd., N.Y.C.; Dir., Seminole Mfg. Co., Columbus, Miss.; Mbr., Vis. Comm., Univ. of Okla. Mbrships: Art Dealers Assn. of Am.; Yale Club; Delta Kappa Epsilon. Address: 1040 Madison Ave., N.Y., NY 10021, U.S.A. 6, 37.

WEITZMANN, Kurt, b. 7 Mar. 1904. Professor Emeritus of Art & Archaeology; Museum Consultative Curator. Educ: Univs. of Munster, Wurzburg, Vienna & Berlin, 1923-29; Ph.D., Univ. of Berlin, 1929; Hon. degrees, Univ. of Heidelberg, 1967 & Univ. of Chgo., 1968. Appts. incl: Stipend, German Archaeoll. Inst., Greece, 1932; Archaeoll. Inst., Berlin, 1932-34; Permanent Mbr., Inst. of Advanced Study, Princeton, 1935-72; Assoc. Prof., Art & Archaeol., Princeton, 1945-50; Prof., Art & Archaeol., ibid, 1950-72; Vis. Lectr., Yale Univ., 1954-55; Vis Prof., Univ. of Alexandria, Egypt, 1960; Guest Prof., Univ. Bonn, 1962; Vis. Prof., Dumbarton Oaks, Wash. DC, 1972-73; Consultative Curator, Metropolitan Mus. of Art, N.Y.C., 1973-; Hon. Trustee, ibid. Mbr. many int. profl. socs. inclng. Am. Philosophical Soc., British Acad. (Corres.), Acad. of Scis., Heidelberg (Corres.), Acad. of Scis., Gottingen (Corres.) & Fellow, Mediaval Acad. of Am. Author many books in profl. field inclng. The Joshua Roll: A Work Of The Macedonian Renaissance, 1948, Greek Mythology In Byzantine Art, 1951, Ancient Book Illumination, 1959, A Treasury Of Icons (co-author), 1967 & The Monastery Of Saint Catherine At Mount Sinai: The Church & Fortress of Justinian (w. G. Forsyth), 1973. Hons. incl: Prix Gustave Schlumberger, Acad. des Inscriptions & Belles-Lettres, Paris, 1969; Haskins Medal, Mediaeval Acad. of Am., 1974. Address: 30 Nassau St., Princeton, NJ 08540, U.S.A. 2, 30, 34, 37.

WELCH, Robert, b. 1 Dec. 1899. Publisher; Organization Executive. Educ: A.B., Univ. of N.C., 1916; studies 2 yrs. at U.S. Naval Acad. & Harvard Law Schl. Appts: In candy mfg. bus., 1922-56, resigned all bus. connections to devote life to opposing the advance of Communism; Fndr., John Birch Soc., 1958; Pres., ibid, currently; Pres., Robert Welch, Inc., publishers, 1956-; Pres., Western Islands, publishers, 1961-. Mbrships. incl: O.P.A. Advsry. Comm. for candy mfg. ind., WWII; Bd. of Dirs., United Prison Assn., 1945-53; Treas., ibid, 1949; Bd. of Dirs., Nat. Assn. of Mfrs., 1951-57; Exec. Comm., ibid, 1953, '54, '57; Chmn., Educl. Advsry. Comm., 1953-54;

Regional V.P., 1955-57; Harvard Club of Boston; Harvard Club of N.Y.C. Publs. incl: The Politician, 1963; The New Americanism, 1966; The Romance of Education, 1973; Ed., Am. Opinion, 1958-; At first exclusive author, since 1959, now ed., monthly Bulletin, John Birch Soc. Recip., Candy Ind. Man. of Yr. Awar, 1947. Address: 395 Concord Ave., Belmont, MA 02178, U.S.A. 2.

WELD, (Rev. Dr.) Hiram Chester, b. 18 Feb. 1912. Educator; Clergyman; Realtor. Educ: A.B., Simpson Coll., Iowa; A.M., S.T.B., Ph.D., Boston Univ.; Adv. Study, Harvard Univ., Oxford Univ., U.K., & Heidelberg Univ., Germany; G.R.I., Ohio State Univ. Real Estate Inst. & Ohio Assn. of Real Estate Bds. m. Mary Elizabeth Williams, 1936, 2 s. Wayne Robert & Devereaux Chester. Appts: Prof., Philos. & Psychol., Baker Univ., Baldwin, Kan., 1940-44; Min., Elm Pk. Meth. Ch., Scranton, Pa., 1944-51, N. Meth. Ch., Indpls., Ind., 1951-59, Bexley United Meth. Ch., Columbus, Ohio, 1959-71; Fellow, Va. Theol. Sem., Alexandria, 1967-68; Vis. Fellow, Ohio State Univ., 1971; Chap., Riverside Meth. Hosp. & Columbus State Hosp. Psych. Facility, 1971-72; Realtor, Indian Hills Realty Co., 1972-; Fac. Mbr., Park Coll., Kan. City, & Columbus Tech. Inst. Mbrships. incl: W. Ohio Annual Conf., United Meth. Ch.; Am. & Ohio Philosophical Assns.; 32nd Degree Mason; Am. Assn. of Clin. Pastoral Educ.; Columbus Bd. of Realtors; Ohio Assn. of Real Estate Bds.; Nat. Inst. of Real Estate Brokers, Nat. Assn. of Realtors; Athletic Club, Columbus; Appalachian Mtn. Club; Acad. of Ohio Real Estate Instrs.; Am. Div., Bd. of Dirs., Ewha Woman's Univ., Seoul, Korea. Publs: Chapt. in Handbook of Church Management, 1958; On the Work of the Ministry in University Communities, 1962; num. articles in profl. jrnls. Hons: D.D., Simpson Coll., 1949; Hon. Life Mbr., Ohio Pastors Convocation, 1967. Address: 364 N. Ardmore Rd., Columbus, OH 43209, U.S.A. 116.

WELDON, Kevin Ernest, b. 14 Dec. 1933. Managing Director. Educ: Apprentice, Colour Etching, Art & Photographics, 1949-54; Grad., Schl. of Mgmt., Sydney, Australia, 1966. Appts: Qld. Mgr., Grenville Publishing Co., Australia, 1956-59; Sydney Gen. Sales Mgr., ibid, 1959-62; Gen. Mgr., ibid, 1962-68; Managing Dir. to establish Hamlyn grp. in Australia, 1968-; Dir., num. cos. inclng. Reed Consolidated Inds. & IPC Books Ltd; Fndr., Family Cos., Nodlew & Gwinganna. Mbrships incl: Fellow, Inst. of Dirs; Australian Inst. of Mgmt.; Past Pres., Pacific Surf Club, Qld.; Deleg.-Asst. Sec. Registrar, Gov. Body, Nat. Coun. of Surf Life Saving; Pres., World Surf Life Saving Movement; Wine & Food Soc., N.S.W.; Royal Prince Alfred Yatch Club. Address: 46 Bradleys Head Rd., Mosman, N.S.W., Australia 2088. 23.

WELLING, Alvin C., b. 18 Oct. 1910. Major General, Corps of Engineers, U.S. Army (Retired). Educ: B.S., U.S. Mil. Acad., West Point; M.S., Mass. Inst. of Technol.; Grad., Nat. War Coll., Wash. D.C. Appts: Chief Engr., & G-4 India-Burma Theater, WWII; Engr. Commnr. D.C., by appt. of Pres. Eisenhower; Cmdng. Gen., U.S. Army Corps of Engrs. Ballistic Construction Off.; Dpty. Cmdr., USAF Ballistic Systems Div; Div. Engr., U.S. Army Corps of Engrs., S. Atlantic Div.; V.P., Rsch. & Engrng., Wyandotte Chems. Corp., Mich.; V.P. Govt. Rels., BASF Wyandotte Corp., Wash. D.C. Mbrships: Am. Soc. Civil Engrs.; Am. Inst. Chem. Engrs.; Am. Sect., Soc. of Chem. Ind.; & Permanent Int. Assn. of Navigation Congresses; Soc. Am. Mil. Engrs. Hons: 3 Legion of Merit,

U.S. Army, 1943, '44, '46; Disting. Serv. Medals, USAF, 1962, U.S. Army, 1965. Address: BASF Wyandotte Corp., Suite 516, 1620 Eye St., N.W., Washington, DC 20006, U.S.A.

WELLS, Ben(jamin) H(arris), b. 11 June 1906. Beverage Company Executive. Educ: A.B., Univ. of Mich., Ann Arbor, U.S.A., 1929; M.A., ibid, 1931. Appts: Tchr., Eng. Lang. & Lit., John Burroughs Schl., St. Louis Co., Mo., 1929-31 & 1933-38; Critic Tchr., Schl. of Educ., Univ. of Mich., 1931-33; Post, The Seven-Up Co., St. Louis, Mo., 1938-64; Pres. & Chief Exec. Off., ibid, 1965-. Mbrships. incl: Pres., St. Louis Symph. Soc., 1970-; Chmn., Consumers Rsch. Inst., 1970-73; Bd. of Dirs., Grocery Mfrs. of Am.; St. Louis Chmbr. of Comm.; Civic Progress; Area Coun., Boy Scouts of Am.; Mississippi River Festival; St. Louis Art Mus Commn.; Trustee, John Burroughs Schl., 1954-61; Phi Beta Kappa; Sigma Chi. Hons: Man of the Yr., Am. Mgmt. Assn., St. Louis, 1973; Significant Sig, Sigma Chi, 1973. Address: 35 Westmoreland Place, St. Louis, MO 63108, U.S.A. 2, 8.

WELLS, Herman B., b. 7 June 1902. Educational Administrator. Educ: B.S., Ind. Univ., 1924; A.M., ibid, 1927; Grad. study, Univ. of Wis. Appts. incl: Pres., Ind. Univ., 1937-62; Chancellor, ibid, 1962-; Interim Pres., 1968; Chmn., Bd., Ind. Univ. Fndn., 1937-62, '69-72; Pres., ibid, 1962-69; Chmn., Bd., 1963-70, & Trustee, Educ. & World Affairs, 1963-71. Mbrships. incl: Past Pres., Div. of Higher Educ., NEA; ibid, Ind. Acad. of Scis.; State Univs. Assn.; Nat. Assn. of State Univs.; V.P. Int. Assn. of Univs., 1955-60; Am. Philos. Soc.; Benjamin Franklin Fellow, Royal Soc. Arts, London; Hon. Fellow, Am. Coll. Dentists; Mbr., sev. U.N. & Pres. Comms. Recip. of many hons. Address: Office of Univ. Chancellor, Owen Hall, Ind. Univ., Bloomington, IN 47401, U.S.A. 8.

WELLS, Katharine Abbot, b. 17 July 1906. Educator; Community Organizer; Lecturer; Author. Educ: A.B., Mt. Holyoke Coll., 1928; Ed.M., Harvard Univ. Grad. Schl. of Educ., 1932; M.S., Boston Univ. Grad. Schl. of Soc. Work, 1949. Appts. incl: Assoc. & acting Nat. Dir., Episc. Ch. Agcy. acting in U.S., Africa & Asia, 1937-40; Wkr., War Related Programs, USO, 1940-46; Sec., Ft. Dix Community Serv., 1940; Chmn., Speaker's Bur., New England USO Regional Office, 1941; Author of Report on Rehabil. Programs for ex-servicemen & women; Wkr., Int. Insts. of Boston & Jersey City, 1947-50; Organizer, Voc., Educ. & Soc. Rehabil. Progs. for civilian psychiatric casualties of the war, e.g., Brooklyn State Hosp., 1951-72; currently Cons., Community Mental Hlth. Progs., Mass.; Sec., Newburyport Coun. of Chs., 1973-; Mbrships. incl: Voting Rep., World Fed. for Mental Hlth.; Del. & Comm., Int. Fed. Univ. Women; Conf. Del., Int. Conf. on Soc. Welfare; Nat. Coun. Women of U.S.; Bd. & various positons. Am. Grp. Psychotherapy Assn.; many positions, AAUW; Nat Comm. on Mental Hlth. Educ. Nat. Assn. Soc. Wkrs.; Am. Soc. Pub. Admin., UNA; Nat. Audubon Soc. & active on comms. etc. in many other orgs. Publs: The Psychology of Beauty, 1963; Presented paper at 25th Anniversary Congress World Fedn. for Mental Hlth., Australia, 1973; contbr. of articles in field. Recip of various hons. Address: 38 Plummer Ave., Newburyport, MA 01950, U.S.A. 57, 129, 130, 132, 138.

WELLS, Martin, b. 1925. University Lecturer. Educ: M.A., Sc.D., Trinity coll.,

Cambridge Univ. Appts: Asst., Stazione Zool., Naples, 1953-56; Fellow, Trinity Coll., Cambridge, 1956; Univ. Demonstrator, Lectr., Dept. of Zool., Cambridge, 1960-; Fellow, Tutor & Dir. of Studies, Churchill Coll., ibid. Mbrships: Soc. for Experimental Biol.; Cambridge Philos. Soc.; Brit. Subaqua Club. Publs: Brain & Behaviour in Cephalopods, 1962; You, Me & the Animal World, 1965; Lower Animals, 1968; Contbr. to profl. jrnls. Address: The Bury, Home End, Fulbourn, Cambs., U.K. 3.

WELLS, Peter Frederick. University Teacher. Educ: Univs. of Wales & Geneva; Sorbonne; M.A.; Dip.Ed.; D.Phil. Appts: Asst., Chair of Eng., Univ. of Geneva; Sr. Lectr., Mod. Lang. Methodol., Auckland; Hd. of French., Waikato Univ., N.Z.; Hd. of Lang. Studies, ibid; Dir., Inst. of Mod. Langs., James Cook Univ. of N. Qld., Townsville, Aust. Publs: Kakikata-The Japanese Writing System; Let's Learn Japanese; Let's Learn French; Let's Teach French; Let's Read French; articles on mod. French poetry (esp. Appollinaire) & on lang. methodol. in learned jrnls. Landscape & surrealist painter, work publd. in La Revue moderne, Paris, 1948-. Address: Dir., IML, James Cook Univ., Univ. P.O., Queensland, Australia 4811.

WELPER, Francis Eugene, b. 4 July 1919. Educator. Educ: B.S., Eastern Mich. Univ.; M.A., ibid; Postgrad. work, Univ. of Southern Calif., Lehigh Univ., Pa. & Wayne State Univ., Mich. Appts: Aircraft Instr., Briggs Mfg. Co., Detroit, Mich.; Liaison Engr. in Aircraft Work, ibid; Tchr., Maths., Britton-Macon Schl.; Asst. Prof., Eastern Mich. Univ., Ypsilant; Coord. of Tech. Servs., ibid; Tchr., Maths., Pittsford Schl. Mbrships: Phi Delta Kappa; Kappa Delta Pi; NEA; Mich. Educ. Assn.; Congl. Ch; Past-master, Masonic Lodge. Conducted ext. rsch. & expmtation. in tchng. by TV & var. tchng. machine techs. at Eastern Mich. Univ. Address: 772 Beecher Rd., Osseo, MI 49266, U.S.A. 8

WELSFORD, Enid Elder Hancock, b. 26 Feb. 1892. Writer & Teacher (retd.). Educ: Univ. Coll., London, U.K., 1909-11; B.A., Newnham Coll., Cambridge, 1914; Marion Kennedy Student ibid, 1915-16; M.A. Appts: Rsch. Fellow, Newnham Coll., 1918-21; Probationary Lectr., Fac. of Engl., Cambridge Univ., 1926-28; Univ. Lectr., ibid, 1928-59; Lectr., Newnham Coll., 1927; Lectr. & Dir. of Studies in Engl., ibid,, 1929-52; Dir. of Studies in Archaeol. & Anthropol., 1939-52, in Moral Sci., 1941-52; Hon. Life Fellow, 1967. Mbrships. incl: Co-Fndr., Past Pres. & Life mbr., Cambridge Women's Rsch. Club; Comm., Christian Frontier Coun. & S.C.M., 1950-59; Ch. of England. Publs. incl: The Fool, His Social & Literary History, 1935; Salisbury Plain, A Study in the Development of Wordsworth's Mind & Art, 1966; Spenser, Fowre Hymnes Epithalamion, A Study of Edmund Spenser's Doctrine of Love, 1967. Hons. incl: Rose Mary Crawstay Prize for Engl. Lit., British Acad., 1967. Address: 7 Grange Rd., Cambridge, CB3 9AS, U.K.

WELSH, Harry Lambert, b. 23 Mar. 1910. Professor Physics. Educ: Univ. of Toronto, Canada, 1926-31, 33-36; Univ. of Göttingen, Germany, 1931-33. Appts: Demonstrator, Physics, Univ. of Toronto, Canada 1935-42; Asst. Prof., ibid, 1942-48; Assoc. Prof., 1948-54; Prof., 1954-; Chmn., Dept. of Physics, 1962-68. Fellowships: Royal Soc. Canada; Royal Soc. London; Am. Phys. Soc. Mbrships: Pres., Canadian Assn. Physicists, 1973; Soc. Française de la Physique. Author of many papers & review in field. Hons: Medal, Canadian

Assn. Phys. 1961; Tory Medal, Royal Soc. Canada, 1963; D.Sc., Univ. of Windsor, 1964; Mem. Univ., St. Johns, Nfld., 1968; Officer, Order of Canada, 1972. Address: 8 Tally Lane, Willowdale, Ont., M2K 1V4, Canada.

WELSH, Helen C., b. 20 June 1907. Librarian. Educ: A.B., Coll. of St. Rose, Albany N.Y., U.S.A.; M.A., SUNY, Albany; B.S., Schl. of Lib. Serv., Columbia Univ., N.Y.C.; M.S., ibid. Appts: Page- Clerk- Asst. Libn., N.Y. State Lib., Albany 1925-32; Libn., Philip Schuyler H.S., Albany, 1932-55; Libn., N. H.S., Valley Stream, N.Y., 1955-59; Hd. Libn., Seaford, N.Y., 1959-66; Dir. of Schl. Libs., ibid, 1966-. Mbrships. incl: ALA; Pres., Schl. Lib. Sect., N.Y. Lib. Assn., 1955-56; Prog. Chmn., Nassau-Suffolk Schl. Lib. Assn., 1958; Pres., Albany Unit, Cath. Lib. Assn., 1950-54; Sec., Metropol. Motion Picture Club of N.Y., 1959-62, Bd. of Dirs., 1959-66; Ed., 1960-63; Fellow, Soc. of Am. Cinematographers; Assoc., Photographic Soc. of Am.; Assoc., Amateur Cinema League. Motion Pictures: The Gilt-edged Diploma; A Look at Your Schools; Ireland Is... Contbr., book & film revies in amateur & Profl. film mags. Recip., Disting. Achievement Award, Coll. of St. Rose Alumni Assn., 1971. Address: 315 Atlantic Ave., E. Rockaway, NY 11518, U.S.A. 5, 6, 42.

WELSH, John Beresford Jr., b. 16 Feb. 1940. Legal Consultant; Lawyer Educ: B.A., Univ. of Wash., 1962; LL.B., Schl. of Law, ibid, 1965. Appts: Staff Counsel, Jt. Comm. on Govtl. Coop., 1965-66; Asst. Atty. Gen., Wash. 1966-67; Atty.-at-Law, (Staff Counsel, Pub. Hlth. & Pub. Asst. Comm., Labor Comm., Pub. Employees Collective Bargaining Comm., Agric. Comm. & Comm. on State Instns. & Youth Dev.), Legis. Coun., 1967-73; Sr. Counsel (Atty. to Speaker of House, Staff Counsel, House Comm. on Soc. & Hlth. Servs., & Coord., Model Staff Grant, Citizen's Conf. on State Legis. on dev. of hlth. care policy), House of Reps., State of Wash., 1973-. Legal Cons., Gov.'s Planning Comm. on Voc. Rehab., 1968 & Gov.'s Comm. on Youth Involvement, 1969, Mbrships: Wash. State & Am. Bar Assns.; Govt. Lawyers Assn. of Wash.; Am. Judicature Soc.; Life Soc. des Amis du Musee de l'Armee, Paris; Engl. Speaking Union, Seattle. Publs: Rehabilitation in Washington, Programs Provided by State Agencies, 1968; papers & reports for comms. Address: Legislative Coun., Legislative Bldg., Olympia, WA 98504, U.S.A. 9.

WEMBI (Rev. Dr.) Shungu, b. 11 Mar. 1917. Former Bishop & Pastor, United Methodist Church. Appts. incl: Pastor, Matapa Tunda, 1939-43; on trial C. Zaire Conf., 1942; Prof., O.T. & N.T., Wembo Nyama Bible Schl., 1949-54; D. Supt., Embo Nyama Dist., 1954-60; Dir., Bible Schl., & Pastor, Lodja, 1960-64; Bishop, Zaire area, 1964-68; re-elected, 1968-72; Legal Rep. Publs. incl: New Testament Otetela Bible Concordance (trans. & compiler); How To Pray; Temperance; History of Christian Church. Hon. Dr. of Divinity, Ashbury Seminary. Address: B.P. 940, Kananga, Rep. of Zaire. 116.

WEN, Henry L., b. 2 Feb. 1917. Registered Professional Engineer. Educ: A.B., St. John's Univ., Shangai, China; B.M.E., Cath. Univ. of Am., Wash. D.C.; M.A., Ind. Univ., Bloomington; M.P.A., Harvard Univ.; M.S.M.E., Newark Coll. of Engrng., N.J.; Ph.D., Ind. Univ. Appts. incl: Pres., Kiu Foong Enamelware Mgrs., Hong Kong; Tech. Expert, Min. of Agric. & Labor, Taiwan; Design Serv. Engr., Curtiss Wright Corp., Wood Ridge, N.J., U.S.A.; Prin. Engr. i/c. Stirling Cycle Engine Dev.,

Fairchild-Hiller Corp., Bay Shore, N.Y.; Mgr., Adv. Mfg. Technol., Singer Co., Kearfott Aerospace Div., Little Falls, N.J. Mbrships: AIAA: Am. Soc. of M.E.'s; N.J. Soc. of Profl. Engrs.; Nat. Soc. of Profl. Engrs. Author, Comparative Study of Theoretical & Experimental Stress Analyses of Sub-Scale Rocket Motor Cases. Recip., Incentive Awards, Curtiss Wright Corp., 1964 & 1965. Address: Imperial Apts., 390 Prospect Ave., Hackensack, NJ 07601, U.S.A. 6, 28.

WENDELBURG, Norma Ruth, Musican; Educator. Educ: B.M., Bethany Coll., Lindsborg, Kan., 1943; M.M., Univ. of Mich., Ann Arbor, Mich., 1947; M.M., Eastman Schl. of Music, Univ. of Rochester, N.Y., 1951; Ph.D., ibid, 1969; Grad. study, Mozarteum, Salzburg, Austria & Acad. of Music, Vienna, Austria. Appts. incl: Instr. in Piano & Music Educ., Wayne State Coll., Neb., 1947-50; Asst. Prof. (Hd.) Music Educ. & Piano, Bethany Coll., Lindsborg, Kan., 1952-53; Asst. Prof. of Piano, Univ. of Northern Iowa, Cedar Falls, Iowa, 1956-58; Asst. Prof. Theory, Comp. & Piano & Chmn., Grad. Comm., Hardin-Simmons Univ., Abilene, Tex., 1958-66; Fndr. & Chmn., Annual Contemporary Music Festival, ibid; Assoc. Prof. (Hd.) Theory & Comp., Southwest Tex. State Univ., 1969-71; Assoc. Prof. of Music, tchng. Piano (Hd. Dept.) Theory & Comp., Dallas Bapt. Coll., Tex., 1971-. Mbrships: MacDowell Colonists; Am. Soc. of Composers, Authors & Publrs.; Am. Soc. of Univ. Composers; Sigma Alpha Iota; Am. Music Ctr.; Music Tchrs. Nat. Conf. Comps. incl. orchl., chmbr. choral, vocal & piano solos & works for organ & percussion. Hons. incl: sev. musical Schlrships. & Fellowships. Address: Music Dept., Dallas Bapt. Coll., P.O. Box 21206, Dallas, TX 75211, U.S.A. 5, 8, 129.

WENIGER, Sidney N. Real Estate Financier; Mortgage Banker. Educ: B.C.E., Cooper Union Inst. of Technol., 1941; M.M.E., Polytechnic Inst. of Brooklyn, 1949. Registered Profl. Engr., N.Y. & N.J. Appts: Chief Exec. Off., var. real estate dev. corps., N.Y. & Fla., 1949-61; Pres., sev. investor owned pub. water & sewer utility cos., 1954-67; V.P., Kirkeby-Natus Corp., N.Y.C., 1962-65; V.P., Standard Financial Corp., N.Y.C., 1965-67; Owner, Pres., Sidney N. Weniger Orgs., 1967-; Pres., Gen. Resources Assocs. Inc., 1967-; Pres., Gen. Resources Ltd., 1972-; Dir., New Hwy. Water Works Co., Inc., Mineola, N.Y. Mbrships: Int. Coun. of Shopping Ctrs.; Nat. Assn. of Real Estate Investment Trusts; Mortgage Bankers Assn. of N.Y.; Nat. Soc. of Profl. Engrs.; Assn. of Navy Civil Engr. Corps Offs. Address: 68 Nancy Blvd., Merrick, NY 11566, U.S.A. 6.

WENO, Joachim W., b. 10 Dec. 1927. Cultural Officer. Educ: Univs. of Leipzig, Berlin, Cologne, 1946-51; Ph.D. Appts: Ed., Filmblaetter, Berlin, 1952-55; P.R. Mgr., Gloria-Film, Berlin, 1955-57; Ed., Berliner Zeitung, Berlin, 1957-58; Dir., German Cultural Inst., Bagdad, 1960-65; Dir., German Cultural Enst., Boston, U.S.A., 1965-69; Sec., Head Office, Goethe-Inst., Munich, 1969-. Publs: Lili Palmer (biog.), 1957; num. newspaper articles. Address: Graf Alban Str. 1, D 811 Murnau, German Fed. Repub. 92

WENTWORTH, Michael Justin, b. 15 June 1938. Museum Director; Art Historian; Painter. Educ: The Cranbrook Schl., Bloomfield Hills, Mich., 1956; B.S., Univ. of Mich., 1961; M.F.A., ibid, 1963; M.A., Harvard Univ., 1966. Appts. incl: Asst. Dir. & Curator of Prints, Smith Coll. Mus. of Art, Northampton, Mass., 1968-69; Acting Dir., ibid, 1969-70; Asst. Dir., Rose Art Mus., Brandeis Univ., Waltham, Mass.,

1970; Dir., ibid, 1970-. Mbrships. incl: Former Trustee, Master Inst. of the Riverside Mus., N.Y.; Am. Assn. of Muss.; Tau Sigma Delta; Phi Kappa Phi. Publs. inel: 19th & 20th Century Paintings from the Collection of the Smith College Museum of Art (w. M. Fabian & C. Chetham), 1970; Contbr. to var. exhibs. inclng. Painterly Realism, Am. Fedn. of Arts, N.Y., 1970. Address: Rose Art Mus., Brandeis Univ., Waltham, MA 02154, U.S.A. 133.

WENZE, Ira H., b. 10 Dec. 1932. Physician. Educ: B.S., Morehouse Coll., 1954; M.S., Univ. of Mich., 1958; M.D., Meharry Med. Coll., 1967; Internal Med., Menorah Med. Ctr., 1967-69. Appts: Instr., Biol., & Acting Chmn. of Biol., Fla. A.& M. Univ., 1958-63; Practicing Physn., Ft. Lauderdale, Fla. Mbrships: AMA; Alpha Phi Alpha; Beta Kappa Chi; Pres., N.W. Br., Ft. Lauderdale, Mbr. Bd. of Dirs., Brownard Co., YMCA; Bd. of Jr. Achievement, Brownard Co.; Nat. Cont. Comm., Meharry Alumni Assn. Address: P.O. Box 9523, 1433 N.W. 6th St., Ft. Lauderdale, FL 33311, U.S.A. 2, 7.

WENZL, Erwin, b. 2 Aug. 1921. Head of Local Government. Educ: LL.D., Univ. of Innsbruck, Austria, 1947. Appts: Sec., Reiffeisenverband, Austria, 1947-51; Party Sec., Osterreichische Volkspartei, local govt., Upper Austria, 1952-68; Mbr. of Austrian Parliament, 1955; Advsr. on roads & bldgs., Central Govt., 1955; Area rep., 1966; Area Chmn., Osterreichische Volkspartei, Upper Austria, 1968; Local Govt. Hd., Upper Austria, 1971-. Mbr., Lions Club; Hon. Senator, Hochschule für Sozial-und Wirtschaftswissenschaften, 1969. Address: Klosterstr. 7, A 4020 Linz, Austria.

WERA, Anne Regina, b. 1 June 1936. Educator. Educ: B.A., Viterbo Coll., LaCrosse, Wis., 1958; M.M., MacPhail Coll., Univ. of Minn., Mnpls., 1962; M.M.Ed., Univ. of Iowa, Iowa City & Postgrad., 1965-70; Ph.D. Candidate; M.A.Admn. Ed., Loras Coll., Dubuque, Iowa, 1972; Dr.Ed., Nat. Univ. of Grad. Studies, Dallas, Tex., 1974. Appts. incl: Hd. Organist, St. Joseph's Cathedral, 1954-63; Keyboard Instr., ibid, 1954-74; Supvsr. of Student Tchng., Univ. of Iowa, 1963-64; Acting Bd., Music Educ. Dept., Univ. of Nev., Reno, 1964-65; Asst. Prof., Musical Educ. & Keyboard, Univ. of Wis., Whitewater & River Falls, 1966-67; Instrumental Music Specialist, Dubuque, Iowa, 1968-74; Instr. of Keyboard, Loras Coll., Dubuque; Electronic Lab. Keyboard Coord., own bus., Dubuque. Mbrships. incl: Past Regional Dir., N.A.G.O.; Hd., C.U.R.A.; AAUP; Musical Educ. Nat. Conf.; Nat. Organists Guild; Music Tchrs. Nat. Assn. Address: 229 Ash St., Onalaska, WI 54650, U.S.A. 5, 129, 132.

WERCHICK, Arne, b. 20 Apr. 1940. Attorney at Law. Educ: A.B., Univ. of Calif., Berkeley, 1961; LL.B., J.D., Boalt Hall Schl. of Law, ibid, 1964. Appts: Ptnr., law firm of Werchick & Werchick, San Fran., Calif., 1965-; Asst. Prof. of Law, Hastings Coll. of Law, Univ. of Calif., ibid, 1971-; Asst. Ed., Calif. Trial Lawyers Jrnl., 1970-. Mbrships: U.S. Supreme Ct., 1968-; Calif. Supreme Ct., 1965-; V.P., United Nations Assn. of San Fran., 1969-70; Fellow, Int. Acad. of Law & Sci.; Life, East African Wild Life Soc. & Sierra Club; Am. Bar Assn.; State Bar of Calif.; Bar. Assn. of San Fran: Chmn., Ins. Negligence & Compensation Law Sect., 1971; Med.-Legal Liaison Comm., 1970; Lawyers Club of San Fran.; Calif. & Am. Trial Lawyers Assns.; Am. Judicature Soc. Contbr. of articles & a book review to profl.

jrnls. Address: 215 Market St., Ste. 1500, San Francisco, CA 94105, U.S.A. 9.

WERLEY, Harriet H., b. 12 Oct. 1914. Nurse; Psychologist. Educ: B.S., Univ. of Calif., Berkeley, 1948; M.A., Tchrs. Coll., Columbia Univ., 1951; Ph.D., Univ. of Utah, Salt Lake City, 1969. Appts. incl: Chief, Dept. of Nursing Rsch. & Cons., Dept. of Atomic Casualties, Walter Reed Army Inst. of Rsch., 1955-62; Chief Nurse, U.S. 8th Army, Korea, 1962-63; NIH Rsch. Fellow, Univ. of Utah, 1964-69; Dir., Ctr. for Hlth. Rsch., Wayne State Univ., 1969-73; Assoc. for Rsch., Coll. of Nursing, Univ. of Ill. at the Med. Ctr., Chgo., 1974-. Mbrships. incl: AAAS; Am. Nurses Assn.; Am. Psychol. Assn.; Am. Pub. Hlth. Assn.; Phi Lambda Theta; Sigma Theta Tau. Ed., Report on Nursing Research Conference. Contbr. to publs. in field. Hons. incl: Army Commendation Medal, 1964; U.S. Legion of Merit, 1970. Address: Assoc. Dean for Rsch., Coll. of Nursing, Univ. of Ill. at the Med. Ctr., Chicago, IL 60612, U.S.A. 5, 28.

WERN, Paulyne Dierlam (Mrs. Charles L. Wern), b. 1 Jan. 1926. Executive Secretary. Educ: Cert. Profl. Sec. Appts: Sec. to Purchasing Agt., Union Carbide Corp., Tex. City, U.S.A., 1947-54; Admin. Sec. to Chmn., Dept. Pathol., Tex. Univ. Med. Br., Galveston, 1958-62; Exec. Sec., Marketing Mgr., Falstaff Brewing Corp., Galveston, 1962-. Mbrships: Past Pres., Tex-La. Div., Nat. Secs. Assn. (Int.); Galveston Co. Chapt., NSA. Hon: Paulyne Wern Schlrship. to deserving student, Metropol. Bus. Coll. Address: 4316 Caduceus, Galveston, TX 77550, U.S.A. 125.

WERNER, Lambert Gustaf Roland Napoleon, b. 18 Nov. 1900. Artist. Educ: Paris & Berlin. Exponent, abstract painting. Mbrships: KRO (Nat. Org. Artists, Sweden); Ring Bergischer Kuenstler, Wuppertal; Roter Reiter, Munich. Solo exhibs. incl: Stockholm; Gothenburg; Malmo; Oslo; Berlin; Amsterdam; Brussels; Paris; Basle; Lucerne; Florence; Milan; Venice; Rome; N.Y.C. Works in num. galls. & collects. inclng: Swedish State Collect.; Nat. Mus., & Mus. Mod. Art, Stockholm; Cities of Stockholm & Gothenburg Collects.; Mus. of Gothenburg; Musée National d'Art Moderne, & Institut Tessin, Paris; French State Collect.; Nat. Mus., W. Berlin. Recip., Swedish State Nat. Gall. Award, 1967. Address: 11 Uggleviksgatan, 114 27 Stockholm., Sweden.

WERNER, Linda Gould, b. 17 Apr. 1944. Public Relations Specialist. Educ: B.A., Univ. of Vt. Appts. incl: Assoc. Ed., G.P. Putnam's Sons, 1966-67; Publicity Dir., Dell Publng. Co., 1967-68; Dir., Advt., Publicity & Promotion, New Am. Lib., 1968-71; V.P., Environmental Concepts Products Co., Inc., 1971-73; Ptnr., Werner Gold & Assocs., 1973-. Mbrships: Publrs. Publicity Assn.; Publrs. Advt. Club. Address: 780 Chestnut Street, # 5 San Fran., CA 94133, U.S.A. 132, 138.

WERNER, Pierre, b. 29 Dec. 1913. Prime Minister of Luxembourg. Educ: Dr. in Law, Fac. of Law, Univ. of Paris, France, 1938; Dip., Independent Schl. of Pol. Scis., Paris. Appts: Lawyer, 1938; w. Secretariat, Banque Générale de Luxembourg, until 1944; worked w. Underground, WWII; Commnr., Bank Control, 1945; Counsellor of the Govt., 1949; Min. of Finance, 1953; Min. of Finance & Min. of Armed Forces, 1954; Prime Min. of Luxembourg & Min. of Finance, 1959; Re-elected Prime Min., 1964; Min. of For. Affairs, Justice & Treasury, 1964-67; Prime Min., in. of Treasury & Civil Serv., 1967-68; Prime Min. & Min. of Finance, 1969-. Mbrships:

Past Pres., Luxembourg Cath. Univ. Students: Past V.P., Pax Romana; Chmn., special study grp. i/c. of working out plan for creating econ. & monetary union for EEC, 1970. Hons. incl: Gold Medal of Robert Schuman, 1971; num. awards from for. countries. Address: Rond-Point Robert-Schuman, Luxembourg, Luxembourg.

WERREMEYER, Benjamin E., b. 28 June 1928. Industrial Designer. Educ: B.F.A., Art Inst. of Chgo.; Grad. work, Educ., Ill. Inst. of Technol. Appts: Sr. Designer, H. P. Glass Assocs., until 1970; Sr. Designer, L. C. Jackson Assocs., 1971-; Pres., Good Idea, Inc. Mbrships: Fndg. Dir., Ind. Designers Soc. of Am., 1965; Regional V.P., ibid, 1967-68, '69-70; Nat. Dir., 1971; Nat. Sec., Ind. Designers Inst., 1964; Chmn., Chgo. Chapt., ibid; Art Inst. Alumni Assn. Author of U.S. Trade publs. Recip. of minor Trade Certs. Address: 880 Lake Shore Dr., Chicago, IL 60611, U.S.A. 8.

WERT, Charles Allen, b. 31 Dec. 1919. Educator. Educ: B.A., Morningside Coll., Iowa, 1941; M.S., Iowa Univ., 1943; Ph.D., ibid, 1948. Appts: Staff, Radiation Lab.,MIT, 1943-45; Asst., Iowa Univ., 1946-48; Instr., Inst. for Study of Metals, Chgo., Ill., 1948-50; Assoc. Prof., Univ. of Ill., Urbana-Champaign, 1950-56; Rsch. Prof., ibid, 1956-58; Prof., 1958-; Cons. to Ind. Mbrships: Fellow, Am. Phys. Soc.; AIME; ASM; AAAS; Sigma Xi; Metallurgy, Ceramics & Mats. Sci. in U.S. Contbr. of articles to Profl. jrnls. Cons. Ed., McGraw Hill Book Co. Recip. of Stanley H. Pierce Award, 1970. Named one of ten outstanding tchrs. in Univ., 1963. Address: Dept. of Metallurgy & Mining Engrng., Univ. of Ill., Urbana, IL 61801, U.S.A. 2, 14.

WERTIME, Rudolf M., b. 25 May 1912. Lawyer. Educ: A.B., Haverford Coll., 1932; LL.B., Dickinson Schl. of Law, 1935. Appts. incl: Admitted to Bar, 1936; Law. prac., Chambersburg, Pa., 1936-; Greencastle, 1939-; Pvte.-1st Lt., U.S. Army, 1943-36, 1st Lt.-Capt., U.S. Army Reserve, 1946-54; Solicitor, Chambersburg Schl. Dist., 1940-65, Greencastle-Antrim Schl. Dist., 1965-, Tuscarora Schl. Dist., 1971-; Dist. Atty., Franklin Co., Pa., 1948-56. Mbrships: Pres., Franklin Co. Bar. Assn., 1969-72; Mbr., House of Delegs., Pa. Bar Assn.; Dir., Chambersburg Community Cancer Assn.; Past Dist. Chmn., Conococheague Dist. Boy Scouts of Am.; Dir., Pres., Franklin Co. Unit, Am. Cancer Soc.; Life Mbr., Presby. Ch.; Elder, Presby. Ch. of Falling Spring, & Past Supt. Hons: J.D., Dickinson Schl. of Law, 1968. Address: 207 Leitersburg Rd., Greencastle, PA 17225, U.S.A. 6.

WERTLAKE, Paul Terence, b. 7 Sept. 1933. Director of Pathology Laboratories. Educ: B.A., Columbia Union Coll., Md., 1955; M.S., 1958, M.D., 1960, Loma Linda Univ., Calif.; Res. Trng., Nat. Insts. Hlth., Bethesda, Md., Anatomic Pathol., Nat. Cancer Inst., 1960-63, Clin. Pathol., Clin. Ctr., 1963-65. Appts. incl: Mil. Serv. as Lt. Cmdr., U.S. Pub. Hlth. Serv., Nat. Insts. Hlth., Bethesda, 1960-65; Asst. Clin. Prof., Dept. of Pathol., Univ. of S. Calif. Med. Schl., 1965-70, Columbia, Coll. of Physns. & Surgs., N.Y., 1972-, Coll. of Med. & Dentistry of N.J., 1972-; Pvte. Prac. Pathol., L.A., Calif. 1965-70; Currently Chmn., Dept. of Pathol. & Dir. Clin. Pathol. Labs., St. Barnabas Med. Ctr., Livingston, N.J. w. var. responsibilities, inclng. Dir., Schls. of Med. Technol. & Cert. Lab. Assts. & of Med. Technol. Retrng. Prof., 1970-; Pres., Applied Bioscience, Paterson, N.J., 1970-; also.Chmn. or Mbr. num. hosp. comms. & med. orgs. inclng. Cons., Chest (Jrnl), 1970-, Exec. Comm., N.J. Soc. of Pathol., 1972-, Sec., Sect.

of Clin. Pathol., Med. Soc. of N.J., 1972-. Mbrships. incl: AMA; AAAS; Calif. Med. Assn.; Coll. of Am. Pathologists; Am. Soc. of Clin. Pathologists; Am. Soc. of Cytol.; Calif. Soc. of Pathol.; Am. Assn. of Blood Banks. Contbr. of over 50 papers, presentations & exhibs. in field. Recip. of awards. Address: 332 Lupine Way, Short Hills, NJ 07078, U.S.A. 46, 120, 131.

WERTMAN, William Henry, b. 31 Dec. 1937. Mathematician. Educ: A.B., Gettysburg Coll., Pa., 1960; M.S., Lehigh Univ., Bethlehem, Pa., 1962. Appts: Mathematician, U.S.N. Ordnance Lab., White Oak, Silver Spring, Md., 1962-; Lectr., Maths., pt.-time Fac. Mbr., Montgomery Coll., Rockville, Md., 1968-73; Adjunct Prof., ibid, 1973-. Mbrships: Am. Math. Soc.; Soc. for Indl. & Applied Maths.; Phi Beta Kappa. Hons: Baum Mathematical Prize, Gettysburg Coll., Pa., 1958. Address: 10705 Lombardy Rd., Silver Spring, MD 20901, U.S.A. 6.

WERTZ, Marcus Emmons, Jr., b. 29 Dec. 1917. Company Senior Vice President. Educ: B.S., Lehigh Univ., Bethlehem, Pa., 1939; Psychol. & Indl. Engrng., ibid, 1946; USN Colls., 1940-41; Gen. Mgmt., Univ. of Pa., Pa. State Univ.; Labor Rels., Rutgers Univ., N.Y. Univ. Appts. incl: USNR, 1940-41; Dir., Indl. Rels., Asst. to Exec. V.P., Lehigh Structural Steel Co., Allentown, Pa., 1957-60; Prod. Mgr., Gen. Mgr., Gulf States Tube Co., Rosenberg, Tex., 1961-66; Cons., Houston, 1967-68; Plant Mgr., Rheem Superior Div., Rheem Mfg. Co., Pearland, Tex., 1969-70; Contract Mgr., Administrative V.P., Sr. V.P., Bethlehem Fabricators, Inc., Bethlehem, Pa., 1970-. Mbrships. incl: Assn. of Iron & Steel Engrs.; Am. Welding Soc.; Newcomen Soc.; Beta Theta Pi. Recip. of hons. Address: 14B Willowbrook Dr., RD7 Bethlehem, PA 18015, U.S.A. 6.

WESBERRY, James Pickett, b. 16 Apr. 1906. Baptist Minister. Educ: A.B., Mercer Univ., Macon, Ga., 1929; M.A., ibid, 1930; B.D., Andover Newton Theological Schl., Mass., 1931; S.T.M., ibid, 1934; further studies at sev. Univs. & Sems.; Hon. LL.D., D.D., L.H.D. & Litt.D. Appts. incl: Trustee, Mercer Univ., 1944-49, 1954-56, 1972-74; Prof., Atlanta Ext. Mercer Univ., 1944-53; former Pres. & V.P., Ga. Bapt. Conven. & off. holder sev. comms.; Chmn., Radio & TV Comm., Atlanta Coun. of Chs., 1959-71, Moderating This Is Your town, W A G A - T V , 1 9 6 1 - 7 1 ; Trustee, Truett-McConnell Coll., 1960-65, Asst. Sec., 1970, Rec. Sec., 1971-; Sec., Exec. Comm., 1971-; World Preaching Missions, USAF, 1960-71; Trustee, Atlanta Bapt. Coll., 1964-72; Apptd. Mbr., Fulton Co. Draft, Bd. 62, 1971; Mbr., Advsry. Comm., Mercer Schl. of Pharm. & Atlanta Mercer Univ., 1972-74. Mbrships. incl: Chmn., State Lit. Commn., 1953-74; Alpha Chi Omega; Nat. Pres., 1949-50; Blue Key Nat. Hon. Frat. Publs. incl: Evangelistic Sermons, 1973; Does Anybody Care, 1974; num. contbns. in Theological books, jrnls. & newspapers & Columnist, sev. publs. Hons. incl: Man of the S. & elected to South's Hall of Fame for the Living,, Dixie Bus. Mag., 1972. Address: 1715 Merton Rd., N.E., Atlanta, GA 30306, U.S.A. 2, 125.

WESENICK, Ermine Gilmour (Mrs.), b. 1890. Artist; Writer. Educ: Fed. Art Schl., Mpls., Minn., 1920. Has done 506 pictures, 3 of which are in African collects., & is working on 2 orders; has designed (illustrations w. poems, quotes, epigrams, etc.) boxes of stationary & notes, book marks, etc.; makes Wedding & Bride Books w. padded satin binding & hand-painted decoration. Mbrships: Kan. Authors Club, for 23 yrs.; Chaparral Poets; Former Mbr., United Amateur Press. Publs: Against the Wind (poetry); another book of poems in progress; Contbr. poems to Kan. Authors Club Annual & Kan. Kernels-Chapparral Poets Mag., & poems & comments to ULMAS; writes brief comments on var. current topics which are used as fillers by Humbolt Union. Collector of vases. Address: 908 Bridge St., Humboldt, KS 66748, U.S.A. 120.

WESKER, Arnold, b. 24 May 1932. Playwright; Director. Educ: London Schl. of Film Technique. Began stage work w. amateur grp., The Queery Players, 1945. Made debut as playwright w. Chicken Soup With Barley, Belgarde Theatre, Coventry, moving to The Royal Court, 1958; premiered in U.S.A. w. Roots, Mayfair Theatre, N.Y., 1961; other plays produced incl: The Kitchen, 1959 (film version, 1961); I'm Talking About Jerusalem, 1960; Chips With Everything, 1962; The Nottingham Captain, 1962; Their Very Own & Gold City, 1965; The Four Seasons, 1965; The Friends, 1970; The Old Ones, 1972 (premieres of last 3 plays directed by author). Has written for TV (inclng. Menace, B.B.C., 1963) & radio (inclng. The Stockholm Dairy, read for Swedish radio by author, 1970). Publs. incl: Fears of Fragmentation (essays), 1970; Six Sundays in January (a miscellany), 1971; edns. of most of the plays; articles, poems & short stories in jrnls. & anthols. Address: 27 Bishop's Rd., London N6, U.K.

WESSLER, Max Alden, b. 16 Jan. 1931. Professor of Mechanical Engineering. Educ: B.S.M.E., Bradley Univ., 1952; M.S.M.E., Univ. of Southern Calif., L.A., 1954; Ph.D., Purdue Univ., 1966. Appts: Tech. Staff, Hughes Aircraft, Calif., 1952-54; Rsch. & Dev. Staff, 1st Lt., U.S.A.F., B-58 Weapons System Proj. Off., AFB Ohio, 1954-56; Asst. Prof., 1956-60, Assoc. Prof., 1962-64, Bradley Univ.; Tech. Staff, Hughes Rsch. Lab., 1960-62; Rsch. Asst., Purdue Univ., Grad. Schl., 1964-66; Assoc. Prof., Prof., Chmn., Dept. of Mechanical Engrng., Bradley Univ., 1966-. Mbrships: Chmn., Engrng. Activity Comm., & Mbr., other comms., Soc. of Automotive Engrs.; Am. Soc. for Engrng. Educ.; Combustion Inst.; Bd. of Dirs., Ctrl. Ill. Dist. Luth Ch., Mo. Synod; Bd. of Dirs., Luth. Ctrl. Schl. Assn. of Peoria; Omicron Delta Kappa; Sigma Tau; Pi Tau Sigma. Hons: One of 6 Outstanding Grads., Bradley Univ., 1952; Hughes M.Sc. Fellowship, 1952-54; Nat. Sci. Fndn. Fac. Fellowship, 1964-66; Ralph R. Teetor Award, Soc. of Automotive Engrs., 1969. Address: 923 N. Maplewood Ave., Peoria, IL 61606, U.S.A. 8, 14, 15.

WEST, Carolyn Veronica, b. 7 June 1928. Writer; Artist. Educ: B.S., H.E. & Jrnlsm., Syracuse Univ., 1950; Attended Grad. Schl., ibid. Appts: Advt. Copywriter, Marketing Div., Crouse-Hinds Co., Syracuse, N.Y., 1953; Asst. to Advt. Mgr., ibid, 1957; Advt. & Promotion Specialist, ibid, 1967; Communication Mgr., Employe & Community Rels. Div., 1968-73; V.P., Press Rels., ibid, 1973-. Mbrships: Syracuse Press Club; Theta Sigma Phi; Omicron Nu; Phi Mu; Republican Citizens' Comm.; Off., Dir., Chmn., Cons., num. orgs. 1-Woman Art Exhibits of flower collages, 1972-. Address: 1365 Oak St., Syracuse, NY 13203, U.S.A. 5, 6, 57, 132.

WEST, Donald James, b. 9 June. 1924. Reader in Clinical Criminology. Educ: Liverpool Univ.; Maudsley Hosp.; M.D. Liverpool; Ph.D., Cambridge. Appts: Sr. Registrar, Forensic Psych. Unit., Maudsley Hosp.; Asst. Dir. of Rsch., Lectr., Rdr., Inst. of

Criminol., Cambridge Univ., 1960-. Mbrships: Fellow, Darwin Coll., Cambridge; Ed. Comm., Brit. Jrnl. of Psych., & Mbr., Royal Coll. of Psychs.; Brit. Acad. of Forensic Scis.; V.P., Past Pres., Soc. for Psychical Rsch. Publs: Psychical Research Today, 1962; The Young Offender, 1967; Homosexuality, 1968; The Habitual Prisoner, 1963; Murder Followed by Suicide, 1965; Who Becomes Delinquent? 1973. Hons: William McDougall Award for Disting. Work in Parapsychol. (jointly w. G.W. Fish). Address: Inst. of Criminol., 7 West Rd., Cambridge CB3 9DT, U.K.

WEST, Doris Ewers (Mrs. William G.), b. 29 May 1913. Educator. Educ: B.S., Longwood Coll., 1932; Yale Divinity Sch., 1937-40. Appts: Tchr., pub. schls., Lynchburg 1934-38; pvte. schls., New Haven, 1938-40. Mbrships: Chap., Kosmos Women's Club, Chattanooga, 1957-58; Chmn., Parliamentarian Brainerd Gdn. Club, ibid, 1955-57, state chap., 1956-57; Dir. worship, State Bd. Tenn. Christian Women's Fellowship, 1958-59; United Christian Missionary Soc., Indpls., 1956, 63; Fraternal deleg., Int. Conven. Christian Chs. of Christ, U.K., 1957; accredited vis. 3rd. Assembly World Coun. Chs., India, 1961. Address: 203 Hillcrest Ave., Chattanooga, TN 37411, U.S.A.

WEST, Louis Jolyon, b. 6 Oct. 1924. Physician. Educ: B.S., 1946, M.B., 1948. M.D., 1949, Univ. of Minn.; Med. Intern, Univ. of Minn. Hosp., 1948-49; Res., Psych., Cornell Univ. Med. Ctr.-N.Y. Hosp., 1949-52. Appts: Chief, Psych. Serv., Lackland AFB (Major, U.S.A.F.-MC), 1952-56; Prof. & Chmn., Dept. of Psych., Neurol. & Behavioral Scis., Univ. of Okla. Sch. of Med., 1954-69; Prof. & Chmn., Dept. of Psych., Univ. of Calif. Schl. of Med., L.A., 1969-; Dir., Neuropsych. Inst. & Psych.-in-Chief, hosps. & clins. ibid. Mbrships. incl: Fellow, Mbr., Bd. of Trustees, Am. Psych. Assn.; Charter Fellow, Am. Coll. of Neuropsychopharmacol.; Fellow, Am. Coll. of Psychs.; Am. Psychosomatic Soc.; V.P., Pavlovian Soc.; Alpha Omega Alpha; Past Pres., Southern Profs. of Psych. Publs: Num. papers in profl. jrnls., monographs, articles in encys. Hons. incl: Okla. Nominee, 1 of 10 Most Outstanding Young Men in Am., U.S. Jaycees, 1959; Sommer Mem. Lectr., Ore., 1968; Fellow, Ctr. for Advanced Study in Behavioral Scis., Stanford, 1966-68; Disting. Profl. Serv. Citation, Okla. State Psychol. Assn., 1969. Address: 760 Westwood Plaza, Los Angeles, CA 90024, U.S.A. 2, 14, 17, 50, 112.

WEST, Richard Vincent, b. 26 Nov. 1934.Museum Director. Educ: B.A., Univ. of Calif., Sta. Barbara; Acad. of Fine Arts, Vienna, Austria; M.A., Hist. of Art, Univ. of Calif. Berkeley, 1965. Appts: Curatorial intern, Cleveland Mus. of Art, 1965-66, Albright-Knox Art Gall., Buffalo, N.Y., 1966-67; Curator, 1967-69, Dir., 1969-72, Bowdoin Coll. Mus. of Art; Dir., E.B. Crocker Art Gall., 1973-. Publs. incl: Language of the Print (w. Donald Karshan), 1968; Exhib. catalogues. Hons: Ford Fellow, 1965-67; Smithsonian Fellow, 1971. Address: c/o E.B. Crocker Art Gallery, 216 0 St., Sacramento, CA 95814, U.S.A.

WEST, Stanley LeRoy, b. 15 Jan. 1912. University Librarian; Professor. Educ: A.B., Univ. of Calif., 1933; LL.B., Univ. of Fla., 1938; B.S., Columbia Univ., 1942; J.D., Univ. of Fla., 1968. Appts: Libn. posts, Univs. of Fla., Pitts. & Columbia, 1938-46; Dir., Libs., & Hd., Dept., Lib. Sci., Univ. of Fla., 1946-67; Prof., Univ. of Hawaii, 1967-68; Libn. & Prof., ibid, 1968-. Mbrships. incl: ALA; Latin Am. Studies Assn.; Pres., Fla. Lib. Assn., 1950; Chmn., Assn. of Rsch. Libs., Farmington Plan

Comm. for Latin Am., 1959-67. Contbr., profl. publs. Recip. Fulbright Lectureship, 1957. Address: Hamilton Lib., Univ. of Hawaii, 2550 The Mall, Honolulu, HI 96822, U.S.A.

WEST, Virginia South, b. 22 Aug. 1920. Businesswoman. Educ: B.S., Auburn Univ., Ala., 1941; E . Courses, ibid, 1972, '73; Mgt. Trng. Inst., Univ. of Ga., 1967; Dev. Prog. for Housing, Planning & Renewal, ibid, 1969. Appts: Proj. Auditor, Coosa River Valley Housing Authority, 1941; Sec.-Acct., Housing Authority, ity of Childersburg & Sylacauga Housing Authority, 1943; Housing Mgr., 1943, Exec. Dir., 1949-. Sylacauga Housing Authority. Mbrships. incl: Dir., Past Sec., Talladega Chapt., Ala. Soc. for Crippled Children & Adults; Dir., Chmn., of Comms., Sylacauga Beautification Coun .; Dir., Treas., Talladega-Clay-Randolph Area Community Action Comm., Inc.; Task Force, E. Ala. Planning & Dev. Commn. Areawide Proj. on Aging: Ch. of Christ; Sunday Schl. Tchr., ibid, many yrs.; Charter, sev. past offs., Sylacauga Br., AAUW; many past offs., Bus. & Profl. Women's Club ; Sylacauga Gdn. Club; Charter, Treas., 1972-73, 1973-74. Sylacauga Pilot Club; Nat. Housing Conf.; Housing V.P., Bd. of Govs., Exec. Comm., Nat. Assn. Housing & Redev. Officials; num. offs., S.Eastern Regional Coun., ibid. Hons. incl: Award, Sylacauga Pk. & Recreation Bd., 1966; Personal Dev. Award, Ala. Fedn. Bus. & Profl. Women's Clubs, 1971-72. Address: P.O. Box 539, Sylacauga, AL 35150, U.S.A. 5, 7, 80, 125, 128, 129, 132.

WEST, William Garrett, b. 25 Mar. 1913. Clergyman; Educator; Author. B.A., Lynchburg Coll., 1937; B.D., S.T.M., Ph.D., Yale Univ., 1940, '44, '49. Appts: Ordained Min. Christian Ch., 1937; Min., Melrose Ave. Christian Ch., Melford, Conn., 1937-46; Old Stone Ch., E. Haven, Conn., 1940-48; Civilian Chap., 429 Air Base, New Haven, 1942-45; 1st Christian Ch., Chattanooga, Tenn., 1948-; Pub. Speaking & Homiletics, Fac. Vanderbilt Univ. Schl. Relig., 1948-53, Univ. of Chattanooga, 1966-68, Univ. of Tenn., at Chattanooga, 1968-; Chap., Chattanooga Police Assn., 1950-58; Religious News Reporter, radio stn. WDEF, 1950. Mbrships. incl: Gen. Chmn., Chattanooga Roundtable Nat. Conf. Christians & Jews, 1954-62; Deleg. Chs. of Christ in Gt. Britain, 1957; 3rd Assembly World Coun. Chs., N. Delhi, India, 1961; V.P., Chattanooga Psychiatric Clin. Author, Barton Warren Stone, 1954. Address: 203 Hillcrest Ave., Chattanooga, TN 37411, U.S.A. 7.

WESTALL, William Gladstone, b. 14 July 1904. Civil Engineer. Educ: B.S., C.E., Geo. Wash. Univ., 1934; Grad., Engr. Schl., Ft. Belvoir, Va., 1941. Appts: 2nd Lt., U.S. Army Corps of Engrs., 1926; transferred as Major, USAF, 1949; retd. as Lt.Col., 1955; Admin. Engr., Paving Bur., Portland Cement Assn., 1955-66; Quality Control Engr., H.B. Zachry, San Antonio, Tex., 1967-68; Cons. Engr., Largo, Fla., 1968-. Mbrships: Fellow, Am. Soc. Civil Engrs.; Assoc. Mbr., Highway Rsch. Bd., Nat. Acad. Arts & Scis. Contbr. McGraw-Hill Handbook of Heavy Construction, 1971. About 50 contbns. tech. jrnls. inclng. Civil Engrng., Hwy. Rsch. Bd. Record. Recip., Army Commendation Medal, 1944. Address: 1700 S. Indian Rocks Rd., Largo, FL 33540, U.S.A. 7.

WESTBURY, John Burnet, b. 7 May 1933. Educator. Educ: Wofford Coll., 1951-53; B.S., Univ. of S.C., 1955; M.Ed., Univ. of Ga.; Summer work, Birmingham-Southern & St. Cloud State Colls., Cornell, Mich. State & Clemson Univs., Univ. of San Fran. & The

Citadel. Appts: Tchr., Maths., Andres Pub. Schls., 1955-57, N. Charleston H.S., 1959-60, Walterboro Jr. H.S., 1960-64 & 65-69 & St. Geo. H.S., 1969-. Mbrships: Phi Delta Kappa; V.P. for Sr. H.S. Tchrs., Assn. of S.C. Maths. Tchrs.; S.C. Math. Coun.; NCTM; SCEA; NEA; MAA; Fibonacci Assn.; Antiques Soc. of S. Inc. Recip. 7 Nat. Sci. Fndn. grants, 1961-71; Shell Merit Fellowship, 1967; 2 S.C. Commn. on Higher Educ. Grants, 1972 & '73. Address: 423 N. Parler Ave., St. George, SC 29477, U.S.A. 57, 125, 129, 130, 131.

WESTERHOLM, Nils (Erik), b. 7 Dec. 1912. Physician; Dentist. Educ: Cand.Odont., Univ. of Helsinki, Finland, 1935; Lic.Odont., ibid, 1938; Cand.Med., 1944; Lic.Med., 1947; Dr.Med. & Surg., 1953. Appts. incl: Communal Med. Off., Sibbo, 1948-60; Chmn., Bd. of Hlth., ibid, 1949-60; Physn. i/c., Söderkulla Hälsohem, 1959-61; Asst. Tchr., Dept. of Dental Surg., Inst. of Dentistry, Univ. of Helsinki, 1961-70; Asst. Ed., Odontologiska Tidskrift, 1964-69; Asst. Ed., Kvartetten, 1966-; Radio Doctor, 1966-72; Asst. Tchr., & Hd., Dept. of Periodontics, Univ. of Helsinki, 1967-72; Permanent Extraordinary Prof. of Periodontics, 1970-71; Tchr., Schl. for Dental Nurses, 1973; Asst. Ed., Liv och Spänst, 1973-. Mbrships. incl: Sec., Odontological Soc. of Finland, 1945-48, Vice Chmn., 1948-50, Chmn., 1950-54, Chmn., Continuation Studies Comm., 1950-65; Chmn., Finnish Sect., Scandinavian Dental Assn., 1968-; Pres., Scandinavian Soc. of Oral Surgs., 1966-67. Author or co-author, num. contbns. to profl. jrnls. Num. hons. incl: Order of Merit, Finnish Red Cross, 1955; Kt., 1st class, White Rose of Finland. Address: Skarpskyttegatan 3.B., 00130 Helsingfors 13, Finland.

WESTMORELAND, Marvin Lee, b. 27 Jan. 1907. Certified Public Accountant. Educ: Int. Accts. Soc. Inc., Chgo., Ill., U.S.A. CPA Degree, 1948. Appts: Acct., City Charlotte, NC, 1929-38; City Mgr., City Greenville, 1939; Asst. Admnstr., Charlotte Mem. Hosp., 1940; Sr. Acct., 1940-51; Self-employed CPA Practitioner, 1951-73. Mbr. sev. soc. orgs. Address: 5501 Wedgewood Dr., Charlotte, NC 28210, U.S.A. 83, 125.

WESTPHAL, William Harold, b. 16 June 1905. Certified Public Accountant. Educ: Ctrl. Night Schl., Atlanta, Ga. & var. corres. schls.; LL.B., Wilmington Law Schl., 1939; Certified Pub. Acct. certs., Ga., N.C. & Va. Appts: Internal Revenue Agt. (Income tax examiner, U.S. Internal Revenue Serv., 1935-39; Specialist, Staff, A.M. Pullen & Co., Certified Pub. Accts., 1939-43; Ptnr., ibid, 1943-71; Cons. & Retd. Ptnr., 1971-. Mbrships. incl: Former Coun. mbr., Am. Inst. of Certified Pub. Accts.; Former Vice-Chmn., Trial Bd., ibid; Past Pres., N.C. Assn. of Certified Pub. Accts.; Life mbr., ibid, 1973; Past Pres., now V.P., N.C. Symph. Soc. Contbr. to books & author of articles in Jrnl. of Acctcy. & other profl. mags. Recip., Medal for highest proficiency, Va. Certified Pub. Acct. exam., 1941. Address: 115 E. Avondale Dr., Greensboro, NC 27403, U.S.A. 2, 7, 16, 128, 139.

WEYAND, Alexander M., b. 10 Jan. 1892. U.S. Army Officer (Retd.); Sports Historian; Free-lance Writer. Educ: B.S., U.S. Mil. Acad., West Point, N.Y.; The Infantry Schl., Ft. Benning, Ga. Appts: 2nd Lt. to Col., U.S. Army. Mbrships. incl: Kts. of Columbus; Holy Name Soc.; Assn. of Grads., West Point; Touchdown Club, N.Y.; N.Y. Olympians; Mil. Order of World Wars. Publs. incl: American Football: Its History and Development; The Olympic Pageant; The Saga of American Football; The Cavalcade of Basketball; Football Immortals; The Lacrosse Story (w. M.R. Roberts); mag. and newspaper articles on mil. or sport subjects. Hons. incl: The Edgerson Sabre, West Point, 1916; Medal, Helms Athletic Fndn., 1955 and 1962. Address: 11 Tangle Ln., Wantagh, NY 11793, U.S.A. 6, 30.

WEYAND, Najla Evelyne, b. 11 Feb. 1942. Assistant District Attorney. Educ: Am. Schls., Paris, France & Monterrey Coll. Preparatory, Mex.; B.A., Univ. of Tex., Austin; Eurocentro, Florence, Italy; J.D., S. Tex. Coll. of Law, Houston. Appts: Asst. Dist. Atty., State Prosecutor in criminal offenses. Mbrships: Nat. & Tex. Dist. Attys. Assns.; Am., Tex. & Houston Bar Assns.; Iota Tau Tau; Pres., Pi Delta Phi, 1962. Hons: Scholastic Recog., Univ. of Tex., 1961, 62. Address: Criminal Ct. House Bldg., 301 San Jacinto, Houston, TX 77002, U.S.A.

WEYL, Nathaniel, b. 20 July 1910. Writer. Educ: B.Sc., Columbia Coll.; London Schl. of Econs., U.K. Appts: Econ., Agric. Adjustment Admin., 1933-34; Econ., Bd. of Govs., Fed. Reserve System, 1940-41; Econ. & Exec., Bd. of Econ. Warfare, 1941-43; Econ., Dept. of Commerce, 1945-47. Life Fellow, Int. Inst. of Arts & Letters. Mbrships: Southeastern Vice Chmn., Am. Mensa; Past Pres., Current Chmn., Bd., Int. Fndn. for Gifted Children; Phi Beta Kappa; Cmdr., Order of St. Lazarus. Publs. incl: Red Star Over Cuba, 1961; The Negro in American Civilization, 1961; The Jew in American Politics, 1970; Traitors End: The Rise & Fall of the Communist Movement in Southern Africa, 1970; Co-Auth., American Statesmen on Slavery on the Negro, 1971. Recip., Bronze Star. Address: 4201 S. Ocean Blvd., Delray Beach, FL 33444, U.S.A. 7, 13.

WEYMANN-WEYHE, Walter, b. 27 Feb. 1914. Programme Editor. Educ: Study of Philos., Hist., German & Engl. Lit., & Philol. at Univs. of Wurzburg, Munster & Leipzig; Dr.Phil.; State Exam. for Advd. Tchng. Profn. Appts. incl: Chief Ed., Frankfurter Hefte, 1947-49; Prog. Ed., N. German Broadcasting Serv., 1950-; Lehrbeauftragter for Philos., Univ. of Bermen, 1969-. Mbr., Paulus-Gesellschaft. Author of num. philosophical & theological essays. Address: D-2904 Sandkrug i.O., Barneführerholz-Weg 18, German Fed. Repub. 43, 92.

WEYRICH, Paul M., b. 7 Oct. 1942. Journalist. Educ: Univ. of Wis., 1962. Appts: News Dir., WAXO Radio Stn., Kenosha, Wis., 1962-63; City Hall Reporter, Milwaukee Sentinel, Wis., 1963-64; Pol. Reporter, CBS, Milwaukee, 1964-65; News Dir., KOXI, Denver, Colo., 1966; Asst. to U.S. Senator Gordon Allott, 1967-72; Asst. to U.S. Senator Carl Curtis, 1973; Pres., Heritage Fndn., 1973-. Mbrships: Nat. Bd., Caths. United for the Faith, N.Y.; V.P., Holy Transfiguration Greek Cath. Ch., Wash.; Elec. Railroaders Assn., N.Y.; V.P., Conservative Club of Capitol Hill, Wash. Wash. Ed., Transport Central, Chgo., Ill., weekly jrnl. Hons. incl: Common Coun. Milwaukee Award, 1964; TV Documentary Award, 1964; U.S. Senate Commendation, 1971. Address: 7053 Lanier Pl., Annandale, VA 22003, U.S.A.

WHALAN, Douglas John, b. 5 Feb. 1929. Professor of Law; Barrister. Educ: LL.B., Univ. of Otago, 1952; LL.M., ibid, 1955; Ph.D., 1969; Barrister (1951) & Solicitor (1950), Supreme Ct. of N.Z. Appts: Ptnr., Family Cattle & Sheep Stn., 1949-; Ptnr., Firm Barristers & Solicitors, 1952-58; Sr. Lectr. in Law, Univ. of Auckland, 1958-65; Warden, ibid, 1960-65; Fellow, Rsch. Schl. of Soc. Scis.,

Aust. Nat. Univ., 1966; Sr. Fellow, ibid, 1967; Prof. of Law, Univ. of Qld., 1967-73, & Aust. Nat. Univ., 1974-. Mbrships: Atty.-Gen.'s Comm. on Land Titles, 1967-70; Special Cons. to Papua & New Guinea Govt. on Land Registration, 1970-71; Fndn. Chmn., Aboriginal Legal Aid Serv. of Qld., 1971; Assoc. Mbr., Aust. Computer Soc., 1971; Social Implications Comm., ibid, 1971-; Human Environment Standing Comm. of UN Assn. of Aust., Qld. Div., 1972-74; Chmn., Aust. Fed. Govt.'s Comm. of Inquiry into Protection of Privacy, 1973-; A.C.T. Law Reform Commn., 1974-; External Cons., Univ. of Papua & New Guinea, 1972-. Publs: Law of Trusts & Trustees (3rd ed.), 1966; The Law & Computers, 1969; The New Zealand Torrens System Centennial Essays, 1971; about 40 articles in learned jrnls. Hons: Law Soc. Prize, 1948, '49, '50; Butterworth Prize, 1950. Address: c/o Fac. of Law, Aust. Nat. Univ., Box 4, P.O., Canberra, A.C.T., Australia. 23, 128, 139.

WHALEN, George J., b. 2 Sept. 1939. Writer. Educ: B.A., Hofstra Univ., 1965; Engrng. Studies, Polytechnic Inst. of Brooklyn. Appts: Sci. Writer, Safe Flight Instrument Corp., North Castle, N.Y., 1966-70; Dir. of Publs., Electronics for Med., Inc., White Plains, N.Y., 1970-. Mbrships: Soc. of Tech. Writers & Publishers; IEEE; Soc. of Automotive Engrs.; Nat. Assn. of Home Workshop Writers. Publs. w. Rudolf F. Graf: Automotive Electronics, 1970; The Manual of Car Electronics, 1971; 25 Solid-State Projects, 1972; Solid-State Ignition, 1974; How It Works Illustrated, 1974. Holder of several U.S. Patents. Address: 59 Lambert Lane, New Rochelle, NY 10804, U.S.A. 6, 13.

WHALEN, Lucille, b. 26 July 1925. Educator. Educ: B.A., Immaculate Heart Coll., L.A., 1949; M.L.S., Cath. Univ. Am., Wash. D.C., 1955; D.L.S. Columbia Univ., N.Y.C., 1965. Appts: Mbr., Immaculate Heart of Mary Community, 1943-69; Tchr., L.A. & Long Beach, Calif., 1945-52; Ref. Libn., Immaculate Heart Coll., 1954-58; Dean, Schl. of Lib. Sci., ibid, 1958-60, 65-70; Assoc. Dean, Schl. of Lib. & Info. Sci., SUNY, 1971-. Mbrships: ALA; Student Rels. Officer, Special Lib. Assn.; Pres., Lib. Educrs. Sect., N.Y. Lib. Assn.; Am. Soc. Info. Sci. Author of publs. in field. Address: 51-4 Woodlake Rd., Albany, NY 12203, U.S.A. 5, 6, 42.

WHALLEY, George, b. 25 July 1915. University Professor; Poet. Educ: B.A., Bishop's Univ., Canada, 1935, M.A., 1948; B.A., Oriel Coll., Oxford, U.K., 1939, M.A., 1945; Ph.D., King's Coll., London, 1950. Appts. incl: Schoolmaster, Rothesay Collegiate Schl., 1935-36, 1939-40; Lectr., Engl., Bishop's Univ., 1945-48; Served in WWII, 1940-45; Asst. Prof.-Prof., Queen's Univ., Kingston, Canada, 1950-; Hd., Engl. Dept., ibid, 1962-67; James Cappon Prof. of Engl., ibid. Mbrships: Pres., Assn. of Canadian Univ. Tchrs. of Engl., 1958-59; Pres., Kingston Symph. Assn., 1963-70; Fellow, Royal Soc. of Canada & Royal Soc. of Lit. Publs: No Man an Island, 1948; Poetic Process, 1953; Coleridge & Sara Hutchinson, 1955; The Legend of John Hornby, 1962; Ed., A Place of Liberty, 1964; num. essays, articles & broadcasts. Recip. of hons. Address: Dept. of Engl., Queen's Univ., Kingston, Ont., Canada. 88.

WHEATLEY, Dennis Yates, b. 8 Jan. 1897. Novelist. Appts. incl: Entered wine bus., 1914; Served in City of London Brigade, 1914, 36th Ulster Div., 1917; sold wine bus., 1931; Recommissioned RAFVR, 1941; Wing Cmdr., Sir Winston Churchill's staff. Mbrships: Pres.,

Old Comrades Assn. of 1914 War; Liveryman, Vintners Co., 1918; Fellow, Royal Soc. of Lit., Royal Soc. of Arts; Liveryman, Distillers Co., 1922; Pres., New Forest Agricl. Show, 1968. Publs. incl: The Forbidden Territory; The Devil Rides Out; The Eunuch of Stamboul; Contraband; Uncharted Seas; The Quest of Julian Day; Sixty Days to Live; Faked Passports; V for Vengeance; The Man Who Missed the War; Come into my Parlour; The Launching of Roger Brook; The Shadow of Tyburn Tree; The Haunting of Toby Jugg; The Rising Storm; The Seven Ages of Justerini; The Second Seal; The Man Who Killed the King; Star of III Omen; The Prisoner in the Mask; Traitors' Gate; The Satanist; A Vendetta in Spain; Mayhem in Greece; The Sultan's Daughter; Bill for the Use of a Body; They Used Dark Forces; Dangerous Inheritance; The White Witch of the South Seas; Evil in a Mask; Gateway to Hell; The Irish Witch. Address: 60 Cadogan Sq., London S.W.1, U.K. 1.

WHEELBARGER, Johnny J., b. 15 Feb. 1937. Educator. Educ: A.B., Bethany Nazarene Coll., Okla., U.S.A., 1963; M.Ed., Univ. of Va., Charlottesville, 1967; Ed.D., ibid, 1970. Appts: Min., Va. Dist., Ch. of the Nazarene, 1963-67; Tchr., Va. Pub. Schls., 1964-68; Instr., Ext. Div., Univ. of Va., 1969-70; Asst. Prof. of Educ. & Media Dir., Eastern Nazarene Coll., Quincy, Mass., 1970-71; Assoc. Prof. of Educ., Trevecca Nazarene Coll., Nashville, Tenn., 1971-; Dir. of Learning Resources, ibid, 1972-. Mbrships. incl: Assn. for Educl. Communications & Technol.; ALA; NEA; Tenn. Educ. Assn.; Tenn. Audiovisual Assn.; Tenn. Lib. Assn.; Assn. of Tchr. Educators; Kappa Delta Pi. Publs: Various edit. & other writings. Address: 210 Perlen Drive, Nashville, TN 37206, U.S.A.

WHEELDON, John Murray, b. 9 Aug. 1929. Barrister & Solicitor; Senator. Educ: B.A., Univ. of W.A., Australia. Appts: Pvte. prac., Law, Perth, W.A. until 1964; Senator, 1965-; Chmn., Parliamentary Jt. Comm. on For. Affairs & Defence, 1973-. Mbrships: W.A. State Exec., Australian Labor Party, 1952-; Past State V.P., ibid. Author of articles in var. Labor & Socialist publs. Address: Commonwealth Parliament Offices, 191 St. George's Ter., Perth, W.A., Australia 6000. 23.

WHEELEN, Thomas, L., b. 30 May 1935. Educator; Consultant. Educ: B.S., B.A., Boston Coll., 1957; M.B.A., Babson Coll., 1961; D.Bus. Admin., Geo. Wash. Univ., 1969. Appts. incl: Lt. (SC), USNR, Supply Corps, 1957-60; Mfg. Trng. Prog., Gen. Elec. Co., 1961-64; Systems Programmer, ibid, 1964-65; Univ. Tchng. Fellow, Geo. Wash. Univ., 1965-68; Lectr., Bus. Admin., ibid, 1966-68; Asst. Prof., Mgmt. Univ. of Va., McIntire Schl. of Commerce, 1968-71; Assoc. Prof., ibid, 1971-74, Prof., 1974-; Cons., FBI Acad., 1970-; Pres., Va. Mgmt. Dev. Assn., 1971-. Mbrships. incl: Beta Gamma Sigma; Acad. of Mgmt.; Am. Mgmt. Assn.; Southern Case Rsch. Assn. Co-Ed., Development in Management Information Systems, 1973. Contbr. to profl. jrnls. Address: 1706 Old Forge Rd., Charlottesville, VA 22901, U.S.A. 7.

WHEELER, Arline Zilpha Frank (Mrs. Dock Wheeler), b. 16 July 1908. Educator; Businesswoman. Educ: B.S., S.W. State Coll., Springfield, Mo., 1948; M.S., Univ. of Kan., Lawrence, Kan., 1954; Dip. of Advanced Study in Vocational Counselor Educ., Univ. of Ark., Fayetteville, Ark., 1964. Appts. incl: Tchr., Pub. Schls., Ozark Co., Mo., 1936-42; Tchr. Soc. Studies, H.S., Gainesville, Mo., 1942-48 & H.S., Bur. of Indian Affairs, Haskell Inst., Lawrence, Kan., 1948-53; Tchr. Advsr., Student Indian

Schl., Nev., 1953-54 & Steamboat Boarding Schl., Ganado, Ariz., 1954-55; Prin., Klagetoh Community Boarding Schl., Ganado, Ariz., 1955-57; Tchr. Advsr., Cheyenne River Boarding Schl., Cheyenne, Agcy, S. Dakota, 1957-60; Prin. Tchr., Dilcon Trailer Schl. & Coal Mine Mesa Trailer Schl., 1960-62; Dept. Hd. Guidance, Tuba City, Ariz., 1962-63; Counselor, Haskell Indian Jr. Coll. (Formerly Haskell Inst.), 1963-72; retired from Bur. of Indian Affairs & owner cattle bus., 1971-. Mbrships. incl: Am. Personnel & Guidance Assn. Publs: poem in Int. Clover Poetry Assn. publn., 1973. Hons. incl: Superior Serv. Award, Fed. Bur. of Indian Affairs, 1972. Address: R. Route 2, Rogers, AR 72756, U.S.A. 5, 7, 57, 125, 129, 132, 138.

WHEELER, Hugh Callingham, b. 19 Mar. 1912. Playwright; Novelist. Educ: Univ. of London. Publs: The Crippled Muse, 1952; Mystery novels—17 as Patrick Quentin, 5 as Q. Patrick (w. R. Wilson Webb), 8 as Jonathan Stagge (w. R. Wilson Webb). Plays: Big Fish, Little Fish, 1961; Look, We've Come Through, 1961; We have Always Lived in the Castle, 1966; Irene, 1973; A Little Night Music (w. Steven Sondheim), 1973; Candide (w. Leonard Bernstein), 1974. Films: Something for Everyone, 1969; Cabaret, 1972; Travels with My Aunt, 1973. Hons: Edgar Allen Poe Award, 1962, '73; Antoinette Perry Award, 1973; Drama Critics Circle Award, Drama Desk Award, Screen Writers Guild Award, 1973. Address: Twin Hills Farm, Monterey, MA 01245, U.S.A. 2, 3, 128.

WHEELER, Lillian Arnett (Mrs. Everly M. Wheeler), b. 14 Aug. 1938. Vocational Education Teacher. Educ: B.S., Morehead State Univ., USA, 1964; M.A., ibid, 1968; Postgrad. work, E. Ky. Univ. Appts: w. Morgan Co. Bd. Educ. (Elem.), W. Liberty, Ky., 1958-59; Johnson Co. Bd. Educ. (Elem.), Paintsville, ibid, 1959-66; Special Educ., ibid, 1966-71; Morehead State Univ., Ky. (Special), summer, 1970; Johnson Co. Bd. Educ., summer, 1965; Ky. Dept. Child Welfare, 1971-73; Dir.-Supvsr., Proj. Bootstrap (rsch. proj.); Mayo State Vocatl.-Tech. Schl. (Consumer Educ.), Paintsville, Ky., 1973-. Mbrships: Past Pres., VP, Scrapbook Chmn., Recording Sec., Pubcty. Chmn., Alpha Omega Chapt., Beta Sigma Phi; Past Sec., Jaycettes; Past 1st VP, 3rd VP, Pubcty. Chmn., Recording Sec., Pressbook Chmn., Chmn., Pub. Affairs Comm., Paintsville Jr. Woman's Club; Past Sec., Mountain Mental Hlth.; Past VP, Women's Bowling League. Hons. incl: Schlrship., Morehead State Univ., 1956-57; Fed. Traineeship, Adv. Study Special Educ., Morehead State Univ., 1966-68. Address: 1030 1/2 8th St., Paintsville, KY 41240, USA. 76, 125.

WHEELER, Phillip Rood, b. 23 Apr. 1906. Engineer. Educ: B.S. in Elec. Engrng., Univ. of Vt., 1928; Masters in Engrng. Admin., Geo. Wash. Univ., 1957. Appts: Examiner, U.S. Patent Off., 1928-29; Aero Engr., Nat. Bur. of Standards, 1929-33; Rsch. & Dev., Bur. of Ordnance & Bur. of Weapons, Dept. of Navy, 1933-65. Mbrships: Common Cause; Ralph Nader's Public Citizen; New England Coalition on Nuclear Pollution; Past Chmn., Wash. D.C. Chapt., Soc. of Automotive Engrs.; Past Nat. Pres., Armed Forces Writers League; Va. Coun. on Soc. Welfare; Nat. Soc. for Autistic Children. Publs. incl: China—Action Needed Now! 1959, 2nd edit., 1964; To Kill Is Not Enough, 1960; The Friendly American, 1963; American Business & the Cold War, 1967. Holder of 22 patents (6 jt.). Recip of sev. awards for profl. servs. & books. Address: 209

W. Pine St., Alexandria, VA 22305, U.S.A. 26, 131.

WHEELWRIGHT, Edward Lawrence, b. 19 Aug. 1921. Political Economist. Educ: M.A., Univ. of St. Andrews, Scotland, 1949. Appts: Asst. Lectr., Univ. of Bristol, 1949-52; Lectr.-Assoc. Prof., Univ. of Sydney, 1952-; Rockefeller Fellow in Soc. Sci., Harvard Univ., 1958; Vis. Fellow, Australian Nat. Univ., 1962; Vis. Prof., Di Tella Inst., Buenos Aires, 1964 & 66, Acad. of Sci., Moscow, 1966, Acad. Sinica, Peking, 1966-67, Univ. of Chile, Santiago, 1970-71; Cons. to the UN, Malaysia, 1971-72. Mbrships: Fellow, Senate, Univ. of Sydney, 1969-74. Publs: Ownership & Control of Australian Industry, 1957; Industrialization in Malaysia, 1965; Ed., Higher Education in Australia, 1965; The Highest Bidder (w. Brian Fitzpatrick), 1965; Anatomy of Australian Manufacturing Industry (w. Judith Miskelly), 1967; The Chinese Road to Socialism (w. Bruce McFarlane, 1970; Radical Political Economy, 1974; contbr. num. articles to var. jrnls. Recip. Disting. Flying Cross, 1943. Address: Dept. of Econs., univ. of Sydney, Sydney, N.S.W. Australia 2006, 131.

WHELPTON, Barbara Fanny (Mrs. Eric Whelpton), b. 4 Feb. 1910. Painter; Writer. Educ: Slade Schl. of Fine Arts, London. Appts: Lectr., Arts Coun., 1947-49; Broadcaster on Art for BBC, Canadian BC & Far Eastern Serv.; TV, BBC & Southern. Mbrships: Arts Theatre Club; Soc. of Authors. Publs: Window on Greece; Paris Triumphant; Rome Resplendent; London Majestic; Unknown Ireland; Unknown Austria (in 3 vols.); Painters' Paris; Painters' Provence; Painters' Ven ice; Painters' Florence; Art Appreciation Made Simple; contbs. to Nat. Press. Translations from French. Exhibs. of painting in London, Sussex, Suffolk, Kent. Works in South Africa House & in pvte. colls. in Britain, U.S.A., Australia. Illustrations for Nat. Press & Large number of publishers in Britain & France inclng. whole series of Holiday Guides. Recip., Silver Medal for Servs. to Austrian Tourism, 1970. Address: West Watch, Traders' Passage, Rye, Sussex TN31 7EX, U.K. 3.

WHELPTON, George Eric, b. 21 Mar. 1894. Author. Educ: B.A., Hertford Coll., Oxford Univ. Appts: Capt., 4th Royal Berkshire Regt.; Ed., Italian Mail, 1922-26; Hd. of Modern Studies, King's Coll. Schl. Mbrships: Soc. of Authors; The Savage Club. Publs: Paris Today; The Book of Dublin; The Balearics; Dalmatia; Summer at San Marino; Springtime at St. Hilaire; Calabria; Florence & Tuscany; Venice & North Eastern Italy; Medieval Europe; The Austrians How They Live & Work; contbr. to London, New York & Paris Press; broadcasts in English, French, German & Italians (17 networks). Hons: Kt. of the Order of Merit, Italy, 1956. Address: West Watch, Traders' Passage, Rye, Sussex TN31 7EX, U.K. 3.

WHIPPLE, Blaine, b. 22 Feb. 1930. Real Estate Company Executive. Educ: B.A., Univ. of Minn., 1956; M.S., Univ. of Ore., 1959. Appts. incl: Dir., Randall Construction Co. Inc. & Tolovana Dev. Co. Inc.; Pres., Whipple Dev. Corp.; Democratic Nominee for U.S. House of Reps., Ore. 1st Congressional Dist., 1962, '64; Chmn., Prog. Comm. Wash. City Pub. Affairs Forum & Wash. Co. Intermediate Educ. Dist., 1967-; Ore. Deleg. to Democratic Nat. Conven., 1968; Chmn., Ore. Delegation, ibid, 1972; Chmn., Ore. McCarthy for Pres. Comm., 1968 & Ore. McGovern for Pres. Comm., 1972; Ore. Democratic Nat. Comm. man, 1968-72, reelected, 1972; Democratic Nominee, Ore. State Senate, Dist. 3, 1974; Dir., Ore. State Homebuilders Assn., 1972; Ore. Mbr., U.S.

Small Bus. Admin., 1967-68; Pres., West Tualatin View Elem. Schl. PTA, 1968-69; Pres., Multifamily Housing Coun. of Portland; Exec. Comm. Mbr., Homebldrs. Assn. of Portland; Mbr., Willamette Valley Chapt., Sigma Delta Chi (profl. jrnlsm. frat.); Regional Ed., The Real Estate News Observer. Address: 8455 S.W. Brookridge, Portland, OR 97202, U.S.A. 9, 16, 120.

WHIPPLE, Fred Lawrence, b. 5 Nov. 1906. Astronomer. Educ: A.B., Univ. of Calif. at Berkeley, 1927; Ph.D., ibid, L.A., 1931. Appts: Instr.-Prof., Harvard Univ., 1931-56; Dir., Smithsonian Instn. Astrophys. Observatory, 1955-73; Phillips Prof. of Astronomy, Harvard, 1968-; Sr. Sci., Smithsonian Instn., 1973-. Mbrships. incl: Nat. Acad. of Sci.; Am. Acad. of Arts & Scis.; Am. Philos. Soc.; Assoc., Royal Astron. Soc., London; Int. Astron. Union; Am. Astron. Soc. Publs: Earth, Moon & Planets, 1942, rev. edits., 1963, 1968. Num. sci. papers in profl. jrnls. Hons. incl: Donohue Medals, for discovery of 6 new comets; Disting. Fed. Civilian Serv. Award, 1963; NASA Pub. Serv. Award, 1969; Kepler Medal, AAAS, 1971; Nat. Civil Serv. League's Career Serv. Award, 1972; Henry Medal, Smithsonian Instn., 1973. Address: 60 Garden St., Cambridge, MA 02138, U.S.A. 1, 2, 3, 14, 34.

WHITAKER, Benjamin Charles George, b. 15 Sept. 1934. Writer. Educ: New Coll., Oxford, U.K. Appts: Practised as Barrister, 1959-67; Extra-Mural Lectr. in Law, London Univ., 1963-64; Labour M.P. for Hampstead, 1966-70; Parliamentary Sec. for O'seas Dev., 1969-70; Dir., Minority Rights Group, 1971-. Publs: The Police, 1964; Ed., A Radical Future, 1967; Crime & Society, 1967; Parties for People, 1970; Ed., The Fourth World, 1972; The Foundations, 1974; Articles in Times Literary Supplement, New Statesman, The Times, The Listener, New Society, etc.; Over 100 broadcasts. Address: 13 Elsworthy Rd., London N.W. 3, U.K. 1.

WHITBURN, Joel Carver, b. 29 Nov. 1939. Researcher; Writer; Publisher. Educ: Elmhurst Coll., Ill.; Univ. of Wis., Milwaukee. Appts: Office Mgr., Carnation Co., Menomonee Falls, Wis.; Salesman, RCA Records, Milwaukee; Pres., Record Rsch., publng. co. Publs: Record Research 1955-1969; Top Country & Western Records, 1949-71; Top Rhythm & Blues (Soul) Records, 1949-71; Top Pop Records 1940-55; (forthcoming) Top LPs 1945-72; Classical Jazz; Easy Listening; Who's Who of Pop Music. Address: Record Rsch., P.O. Box 82, Menomonee Falls, WI 53051, U.S.A.

WHITCOMB, Hale Christy, b. 16 Aug. 1907. Professor; Author; Management Consultant; Certified Public Accountant; Financial Executive. Educ: B.A., Yale Univ., 1929; C.L.U., Am. Coll. of Life Underwriters, 1937; Cert. in Mgmt., 1938; Cert. in Ind. Mgmt., Univ. of Toledo Coll. of Engrng., 1944; CPA, Univ. of Ill. 1949; M.B.A., Northwestern Univ., 1949; D.B.A., Ga. State Univ., 1965. Appts. incl: Comptroller's Staff, Owens-Corning Fiberglas Corp., Toledo, Ohio, 1942-44; Mgmt. Cons., 1944-51; Controller, Murray Corp. of Am., Scranton, Pa., 1951-52; CPA-Mgmt. Cons., 1952-58; Rsch. Assoc. in Acctng., Northwestern Univ., 1958-59; Assoc. Prof., Econs., Univ. of Evansville, 1959-62; Regents' Fellow, Ga. State Univ., 1962-64; Assoc. Prof., Acctng., Purdue Univ., 1964-66; Prof., Finance, Miss. State Univ., 1966-69; Prof. of Quantitative Scis. (Acctng., Finance, Analytic Methods), Duquesne Univ., 1969-72, & Univ. of Wis., Whitewater, 1972-. Mbrships: Am. Acctng., Econ. & Finance Assns.; Am. Inst. of

CPAs; Financial Execs. Inst.; Financial Mgmt. Assn.; Delta Kappa Epsilon; Delta Mu Delta; Alpha Kappa Psi. Publs: Standard Costs for Valuing Inventories, 1949; Cases in Business Administration, 1959; Dow Theory Economic Forecasts (microfilm), 1965; articles in profl. jrnls. Address: 1037 W. Shaw Ct., Apt. 26, Whitewater, WI 53190, U.S.A. 8, 14, 30.

WHITCOMB, Kay (Aka Kathryn N. Keith), b. 20 May 1921. Artist; Craftsman. Educ: RI Schl. of Design; Cambridge Schl. of Art; Enameling Apprenticeship, U.S. Marine Corps. Women's Reserve, Cleveland, Ohio. Appts. incl: Bd., S. Calif. Designer Craftsmen, L.A., 1962-63; Treas., Women's Comm., La Jolla Civic Orch., 1962-63; Pres., ibid, 1963-64; Bd., San Diego Art Guild, Publicity Chmn., 1963-65, 1970; Juror, Calif. State Fair, Sacramento, S. Calif. Expo, 1965, 1970, 1972; Publicity, Corres. Sec., Allied Craftsmen, 1966-67; Pres., San Diego Art Guild (Artist Mbrs., San Diego's Mus.: Fine Arts Gall.), 1968-69; Artist in Residence, Crahait Emailleries, Belgium, 8 mnths. during 1970-72; V.P., Allied Craftsmen, 1972-73. Mbrships. incl: Laguna Beach Mus.; ACC; Soc. of Arts & Crafts, Boston; World Craft Coun. Lectured & exhibd. throughout U.S.A., Europe & Japan. One Man Exhibs. incl: Whistler Mus., Lowell, Mass., 1948; La Jolla Art Assn., 1958, 1960; Positano, Italy, 1961; Galeria del Sol. Santa Barbara, Calif., 971; Am. Lib., Brussels, Belgium, 1972; Esther Lewittes Design Gall., L.A., 1973. Hons. incl: U.S.A. representation, Int. Kunsthandwerk, Exhib., Stuttgart, German Fed. Repub., 1969; sev. Art Awards & Schlrships. Address: 1631 Mimulus Way, La Jolla, CA 92037, U.S.A.

WHITCOMB, Philip Wright, b. 24 Nov. 1891. Writer. Educ: B.A., M.A., Wadham Coll., Oxford Univ., U.K.; B.A., D.Litt., Washburn Univ., Topeka, Kan., U.S.A. Appts: European Corres. successively for Harpers Weekly, Boston Evening Transcript, Baltimore Sun; Assoc. Press Corres. for Occupied France (twice interned by Germany), 1940-41; Special Economic Corres., Christian Science Monitor, 1947-. Mbrships. incl: Oxford Soc.; Wadham Soc.; United Oxford & Cambridge Univ. Club, London, U.K.; Cercle Interalliee, Paris, France; O'seas Press Club, N.Y.C.; Kappa Sigma; Bd. of Trustees, Am. Coll. in Paris; Bd. of Dirs., Am. Ctr. for Students & Artists, ibid, Am. Chmbr. of Comm., France. Publs: Ed., Translator, Contbr., France During the German Occupation 1940-44, 3 vols., 1958; When You Come to France to Live, 1969; 75 Years in the Franco-American Economy, 1970. Hons. incl: O'seas Press Club Award for Economic Reporting, 1970; Disting Serv. Award, Am. Chmbr. of Comm., Germany, 1971. Address: 24 Rue de Surene, 75008 Paris, France. 43.

WHITE, Burton L., b. 27 June 1929. Educator. Educ: B.S., Tufts Univ., 1949; B.A., 1956, M.A., 1957, Boston Univ.; Ph.D., Psychol., Brandeis Univ. 1960. Appts. incl: U.S. Army, 1951-53; Tschng., Rsch. Asst., Brandeis Univ., 1957-60; Lectr., ibid, 1961; Lectr., Northeastern Univ., 1961; Lectr. Tufts Univ., 1962-65; Rsch. Assoc., MIT, 1963-65; Rsch. Assoc., Lectr., 1965-69, & Chmn., Psychol. Area, 1966-68, Harvard Grad. Schl. of Educ.; Assoc. Prof., ibid, 1969-72; Rsch. Assoc., Sr. Rsch. Assoc. & Lectr., ibid, 1972-; Proj. Dir., Prin. Investigator, var. rsch. projs. in early educ., etc. Hons. incl: F.F.R.P. Grant, 1961-63; Nat. Inst. of Mental Hlth. Grant, 1963-67; Var. Carnegie Corp. rsch. grants. Publs: Experience & Envirornment: Major Influences on the Development of the Young Child (co-author) vol. I, 1973; Num. reports, articles in profl.

jrnls.; Mbr., Edit. Bd., Child Development, 1966-71. Address: Harvard Univ. Grad. Schl. of Educ., Roy E. Larsen Hall, Appian Way, Cambridge, MA 02138, U.S.A.

WHITE, Charles. Painter. Educ: Sutton & Cheam Schl. of Art, 1943-45; Newport Coll. of Art, 1944; Kingston-upon-Thames Schl. of Art, 1946; Slade Schl. of Painting, London Univ., 1949. Appts: Tchr., Newport Coll. of Art, Swansea Coll. of Art, 1951-72; Hd., Art Dept., United World Coll., 1962-72; var. pt.-time posts inclng. Margam Coll. of Further Educ., Lectr. in Art, Extr-Mural Dept., Univ. of Wales & W.E.A., art therapist, mental hosps. & special schls. Mbrships: Comm. Mbr., S. Wales Grp.; Fndr. Mbr., Young Contemporaries, & European Grp.; Life Fellow, Royal Soc. of Arts; Fellow, Free Painters & Sculptors; Soc. Graphic Artists. Paintings in Royal & pvte. collects., & pub. collects. U.K., Europe & U.S.A. Recip., Slade Prize for Painting, 1949. Address: Ashgrove Studio, Llantwit Major, Glamorgan, S.Wales, U.K. 19.

WHITE, Charles Alexander, b. 3 Sept. 1899. Company Executive. Educ: Univ. of N.C., 1916-18. Appts: Ins. Adjuster, N.J. Fidelity & Plate Glass Ins. Co., N.Y.C., 1919-23; Assoc., Thomas A. dison, Inc., E. Orange, N.J., 1924-25, Hassell-Dupree Co., Realtors, Miami, Fla., 1925-26; Owner, Charles A. White, Broker, 1927-29; Ptnr., Mgr.-Buyer, White's Stores, Inc., Greenville, N.C., 1930; Currently, Pres., ibid, Treas., Carolina Mills Fabrics, Inc. Mbrships. incl: Cmdr., Civil Defense, Greenville, 1942-55; Chmn., Pitt Co. Chapt., N.C. Symph. Soc., 1947-50; Advsry. Bd., E. Carolina Univ. Summer Theatre, 1964-68, Artists Series, ibid, 1967-73; Bd. of Advsrs., Redev. Commn. for Ctrl. Bus. Dist., Greenville; Pres., Pitt Co. Histl. Soc., 1968-70; Bd. of Dirs., N.C. Merchants Assn., 1966-; Dit., 1966-74; V.P., Pitt Co. United Fund, 1966-67; Greenville Music Club, 20 yrs. (Pres., 1949); Episc.; Dir., Greenville Chmbr. of Comm. & Merchants Assn., 1964; Greenville Merchants Assn. (Pres., 1952, Dir., 1950-60); Chmbr. of Comm., (Pres., 1952, Dir., 1950-60); Chmbr. of Comm., (Pres., 1960, Dir., 1957-63). Address: 601-607 Dickinson Ave., Greenville, NC 27834, U.S.A. 7, 16.

WHITE, (Mrs.) Claude Porter, b. 30 Apr. 1907. Musician; Composer; Poet. Educ: B.A., Southwestern Univ., Georgetown, Tex.; Schl. of Music, Northwestern Univ., Evanston, Ill.; var. special studies. Appts: Concert soloist; Supvsr.; pub. schl. music; Choir dir.; Voice tchr.; Composer; Ed., Publr., Tex. Opera News, quarterly jrnl. Mbrships. incl: Am. Music Ctr., N.Y.C.; Life Mbr., Tex. & Nat. Fedn. of Music Clubs; State Chmn. for Opera, Tex. Fedn. of Music Clubs; Fndr. Mbr., Int. Poetry Soc., Derbyshire, U.K. Publs. incl: Fruits of My Spirit; Beauty for Ashes; Three Moods & Observations; Kinship. Operatic libretti. Composer, ballet, instrumental & choral works, songs. Recip., var. prizes & awards, music & poetry. Address: 1945 Bowie Dr., Corsicana, TX 75110, U.S.A. 11.

WHITE, (Sir) Ernest (Keith), b. 14 Aug. 1892. Company Director. Appts. incl: Serv. WWI as Capt. 4th Battalion AIF in Egypt & France; Chmn., R.J. White & Co. (Sydney) Pty. Ltd., 1935-; Fndr. & 1st Pres. (1943) Liberal Democratic Party of Australia, forerunner of present Liberal Party; apptd. to Provisional State & Fed. Coun., 1943. Mbrships: Fndr. & V.P., (1st Fed. Pres. 1936), Australian American Assn., now nation-wide; Tattersalls Club; Australian Golf Club; Australian Jockey Club; American Club. Author of pol. articles. Hons: Mentioned in Despatches, M.C., 1914-18;

O.B.E.; C.B.E., 1967; Kt., 1969. Address: Baden House, Kurraba Point, Neutral Bay, Sydney, Australia 2089. 23.

WHITE, Harry Crawford, b. 10 Apr. 1929. Life Insurance Representative. Educ: studied Banking & Trust Dept. Work at var. N.Y.C. schls. inclng: Tax. Insts. of N.Y. Univ.; courses, Mfrs. Hanover Trust Co., N.Y.C. Appts: Trust Off. i/c of Estate Planning, Wheeling Dollar Savings & Trust Co., W. Va. & Rep., Equitable Life Assurance Soc. of U.S.A. Mbrships: Ft. Henry Club, Wheeling; Past Dean, Wheeling Chapt., Am. Guild of Organists; Past Pres., Wheeling Symph. Soc.; Chmn., var. comms., Oglebay Inst.; Past Organist & Choirmaster, St. Mark's Lutheran Ch., Wheeling; Pension Originator & Advsr. for Pension (Nat.), Am. Guild of Organists; Fund Raiser, var. local orgs. Address: 73 Mt. Lebanon Dr., Wheeling, WV, U.S.A. 125.

WHITE, Ian McKibbin, b. 10 May 1929. Museum Director. Educ: B.A., Harvard Univ., Cambridge, Mass., 1951; Grad. Schl. of Design, ibid, 1951-52; Indl. design, UCLA, 1957-58. Appts: Administrative Asst. & Designer, Brooklyn Botanic Garden, Brooklyn, N.Y., 1959-60; Brooklyn Mus. of Art, 1961-67; Asst. Dir., ibid, 1964; Assoc. Dir., Calif. Palace of Legion of Hon., San Fran., 1967; Dir., ibid, 1968; Dir., Fine Arts Museums of San Fran. (M.H. de Young Mem. Mus. & Calif. Palace of Legion of Hon.), 1970-. Mbrships. incl: Mus. Advsry. Panel, Nat. Endowment for the Arts, 1973; Int. Coun. of Museums, 1972; Coun., Am. Assn. of Museums, 1970; Am. Assn. of Mus. Dirs., 1970; Trustee, Am. Fedn. of Arts, 1972. Designer, Peary-McMillan Arctic Mus., Peary-McMillan Arctic Mus., Bowdoin Coll., Brunswick, Maine, 1967; Contbr. to jrnls. Recip., Silver Medal for excellence in oil painting, The Cate Schl., 1947. Address: Calif. Palace of the Legion of Hon., Lincoln Park, San Fran., CA 94121, U.S.A. 2, 59.

WHITE, Irma Lenore Reed (Mrs. Wilford L. White), b. 4 Mar. 1897. Educator; Writer; Public Information Specialist. Educ: A.B., Univ. of Colo., 1919; A.M., Radcliffe Coll., 1926. Appts: Engl. Instr., Univ. of Colo., 1922-24; Report Writing Instr., Grad. Schl. Bus. Admin., Harvard Univ., 1925-28; Asst. Hd., Field Sect. & Ed., "Rationed Foods Letter", Off. of Price Admin., 1943-47; Pub. Info. Specialist, Bur. of the Census, 1958-71; Ed. & Coord. of Census Articles for "Commerce Today", 1970-71; i/c Press Room, Cost of Living Coun., 1971-. Mbrships: Am. Newspaper Women's Club; Nat. League Am. Pen Women; Chi Omega; P.E.O. Contbr. of articles to var. jrnls. Hons. incl: Cert. for Outstanding Serv., Cost of Living Coun., 1972, '73; Wash. Area Pan-Hellenic Award, 1973. Address: Apt. 331, 4000 Mass. Avenue N.W., Wash., DC 20016, U.S.A. 5, 138.

WHITE, Jack Hammons, b. 17 Feb. 1942. University Instructor of English. Educ: Southwestern Univ., Georgetown, Tex., 1960-62; B.A., E. Tex. State Univ., 1965, M.A., 1967; Tex. Tech. Univ. Appts: Grad. Tchg. Asst., E. Tex. State Univ., 1965-67; Instr., Mississippi State Univ., 1967-71, Tex. Tech. Univ., 1971-. Mbrships: Pres., Sigma Tau Delta, Grad. English Soc., Pi Kappa Alpha Alumni Assn.; Pi Kappa Alpha Mem. Fndn.; M.L.A.; S. Ctrl. Mod. Lang. Assn. & Renaissance Conf.; Lubbock Symphony, Club & Humane Soc. Address: 244 Plantation House, 2400 44th St., Lubbock, TX 79413, U.S.A. 117, 125.

WHITE, James Michael, b. 19 Nov. 1924. Lawyer. Educ: Adelaide Univ. Law Schl.,

Australia, 1946-50. Appts: Served WWII; Practising barrister & solicitor, as Ptnr., Kelly Travers O'Loughlin & White, Adelaide, S. Australia, 1950-70; Lectr., Adelaide Law Schl., 3 yrs.; Co-examiner, Jurisprudence, ibid, 2 yrs.; Co-examiner, Contracts, 2 yrs.; Dist. Ct. Judge, 1970-; Bankruptcy Ct. Judge, 1971-; Credit Tribunal Chmn., 1973-. Mbrships: Law Soc., 1950-70; Law Coun., 1967-70; Stock Exchange Club; Adelaide Univ. Fac. of Law. Contbr. of papers to Australian Law Jrnl., S. Australian Legal Profession, Adelaide Univ. Law Review. Recip. of awards, Adelaide Univ. Law Schl. Address: 16 Giles St., Toorak Gardens, S.A., Australia, 5065. 23.

WHITE, Louise Welk, b. 14 Jan. 1895. Teacher; Writer; Poet. Educ: A.B., Univ. of Denver, Colo., U.S.A. Appts: Tchr., 1915-19 & 1937-41; Writer & Ed., Engrng. Dept., Convair, 1943-45; Writer & Ed., Underwater Sound, Navy Electronics Lab., 1945-48; Writer & Ed., Convair, 1953-58. Mbrships: Nat. League of Am. Pen Women; V.P., San Diego Poets' Assn., 1971, Pres., 1972-74; Calif. Fedn. of Chaparral Poets; Pres., San Diego Browning Soc., 1959-60 & 1963-64; Fellow, Int. Poetry Soc.; Fndg. Mbr., Epsilon Chapt., Durango, Colo., Delta Kappa Gamma. Publs: World Poetry Day; The Poetry Hour; California Anthology; Blue Nose Rambler; Contbr. to newspapers & jrnls. Address: 4598 Edgeware Rd., San Diego, CA 92116, U.S.A. 11.

WHITE, Margarette Paulyne Morgan (Mrs.), b. 11 Sept. 1934. Journalism Educator. Educ: B.A., Morris Brown Coll., Atlanta, Ga., U.S.A.; Cert., Jrnlsm., Univ. of Toledo, Ohio; Cert., Jrnlsm., Univ. of Tenn. Appts. incl: Instr., Eng., Jrnlsm, & Drama, Trinity H.S., 1957-66; Specialist Staff Tchr., Communications Skills, Atlanta Pub. Schls., 1967-68; Instr., Jrnlsm., Mass Media, & Communications Skills, Charles L. Harper H.S., 1969-; Youth Ed. & Columnist, The Atlanta Inquirer, 1971-. Num. mbrships. incl: Pres., Jrnlsm. Club, Morris Brown Coll., 1954-57; Fndr. & Charter Pres., Sparklers Community Serv. Club 1960-64; Youth Advsry. Comm., Nat. Assn. of Bus. & Profl. Women's Clubs; Publicity Comm., Nat. Assn. of Negro Bus. & Profl. Women's Club, 1973-; Publicity Comm., Atlanta Chapt., AAUW; Pres., Ga. Assn. of Jrnlsm. Dirs., 1968-73; First black mbr., Atlanta & Ga. Chapts., Theta Sigma Phi. Author, A Human Relations Approach Handbook, 1968. Hons. incl: Outstanding Serv. Award, Ga. Assn. of Jrnlsm. Dirs., 1973; Breaking New Ground Award, Atlanta Alumnae Chapt., Delta Sigma Theta, 1974. Address: 1689 W. Lake Court, N.W., Atlanta, GA 30314, U.S.A. 76, 125, 130.

WHITE, Mary. Potter & Ceramic Artist; Calligrapher. Educ: Schl. of Arts & Crafts, Newport, Mon., U.K.; L.C.C. Hammersmith Schl. of Arts & Crafts, London; Goldsmiths Coll. of Art, London Univ. Appts: Art Tchr., var. Grammar Schls., Wales; Pt.-time Art Lectr., Swansea Coll. of Art; Ceramics Instr., Atlantic Coll., St. Donats Castle, Glam. Mbrships: Soc. of Scribes & Illuminators; British Crafts Ctr.; Craftsman Potters Assn. of Great Britain, Ltd.; South Wales Potters (Exhib. Off.). Exhibs. of Pottery & Ceramics incl: Hereford Mus. & Art Gall.; Lefor-Openo Gall., St.-Cloud, Paris, France; Welsh Arts Coun., Cardiff; Welsh Exhibs., Design Ctr., & C.P.A., London; Mignon Gall., Bath; Rye Art Gall. Sussex. Commonwealth Art Gall., Commonwealth Inst., London. Exhib. of Calligraphy: 2000 Yrs. of Calligraphy, Balt., U:S.A. 1965. Hons: Percy Smith Mem. Prize for Lettering, Royal Soc. of Arts, 1950. Address: Ashgrove Studio, Llantwit Major, Glamorgan, U.K.

WHITE, Robert (Winthrop), b. 19 Sept. 1921. Sculptor. Educ: R.I. Schl. of Design, Providence, 1938-42. Appts: Instr., painting & drawing, Suffolk Mus., Stony Brook, N.Y., 1948-50; Instr., life drawing, Parsons Schl. of Design, N.Y.C., 1950-52; Instr., archtl. ornamentation, ibid, 1955-56; Assoc. Prof., Art, SUNY, Stony Brook, 1962-; Sculptor in Res., Am. Acad., Rome, 1968, 69. Major commns. incl: Fountains for Griselda Cunningham, White Post, Va. & Mr. & Mrs. Amyas Ames, Matha's Vinyard, Mass.; St. Anthony of Padua, for St. Anthony of Padua Auditorium, E. Northport, N.Y.; 3 figures for St. Michael's R.C. Ch., Bedford, Mass.; also portraits, medals, illustrns., stained glass windows, etc. Works in Brooklyn Mus., N.y.C.; Springfield Mus., Mass.; R.I. Schl. of Design Mus., Providence; num. pvte collects. Mbrships: Fellow, Am. Acad. in Rome; Pres., Soc. of Fellows of Am. Acad. in Rome, 1963-64. Hons. incl: Sculpture Prize, Laurell Gall., N.Y.C., 1948. Address: Moriches Rd., St. James, NY 11780, U.S.A.

WHITE, Rodney Francis, b. 26 Sept. 1922. Professor of Sociology. Educ: B.A., Univ. of Toronto, Canada, 1943, B.A.Sc., 1968, M.Comm., 1949; Ph.D., Univ. of Chgo., U.S.A., 1964. Appts: Lectr., Sociol., Univ. of Sask., 1950-52; Asst. to Dir. Ind. Rels., A.V. Roe (Canada) Ltd., 1952-54; Assoc. Prof. & Prog. Dir., Sloan Inst. of Hosp. Admin., Cornell Univ., 1957-69; Prof. & Chmn., Dept. of Sociol., Trent Univ., 1969-. Mbrships: Exec. Comm., Soc. Sci. Rsch. Coun. Canada; Chmn., Rsch. Policy Sub-Comm., Canadian Soc. & Anthropol. Assn.; Fellow, Am. Sociol. Assn. Publs: Hospital Administration, 1962; Administering Health Systems & The Professional Woman, 1971; contbr. to num. profl. publs. Address: 634 Weller St., Peterborough, Ont., Canada. K95 4W9 14.

WHITE, Ruth Bennett (Mrs. Cal Milton White), b. 18 Aug. 1906. Nutritionist. Educ: B.A., Okla. Bapt. Univ., 1928; M.S., Univ. of Iowa, 1930; postgrad. studies, Cornell & Columbia Univs. Appts. incl; Lectr., Foods & nutrition, Ankara, Turkey, 1960-61, Nigeria, 1962-64; Mbr., Fed. Commn. on Rev. of Home Econ. Curric., Lagos, Nigeria, 1963-64; Lectr., profl. & educl. grps., 1934-; Tchr. nutrition & foods in Home Econ., N.Y.C. Pub. Schls, 1955-58; Fort Lee Pub. Schls., 1959-60; Mbr., Lake Placid Conf., Am. Assn. of Home Econs., 1973. Mbrships. incl: Pi Lambda Theta; Pi Kappa Delta; local, State of Calif., & Am. Home Econ. Assns., Int. Fed. Home Econ. Publs. incl. Food & Your Future, 1972; You & Your Food, 3rd edit., 1971. Hons. incl: Woman of Achievement Awards, City of San Diego, 1973, & San Diego Dist., Calif. Home Econs. Assn., 1973. Address: 5811 Beaumont Ave., La Jolla, CA 92037, U.S.A. 59, 132, 138.

WHITE, Ruth S., b. 1 Sept. 1925. Composer; Record Company Executive. Educ: B.F.A. (Piano), B.F.A. (Composition), M.F.A., Carnegie Mellon Univ. Appts. incl: Supvsr., Univ. of Calif. Lab. Schl., 1951-59; Pres., Rhythmns Prods. Records, 1955-; V.P., Cheviot Corp, 1961-; Film Prod. Mbrships. incl: Am. Soc. of Composers, Authors & Publrs.; Am. Fedn. of Musicians; Bd. of Govs., Nat. Acad. for Recording Arts & Scis.; Nat. Assn. Am. Composers & Conductors; Audio Engrng. Soc.; Electronic Music Assn.; Nat. V.P., Recording Acad. Inst. for Trng. & Creative Dev.; LA Bd. of Govs., Nat. Trustee, Recording Acad. Compositions incl: 7 Trumps from the Tarot Cards; Pinions; The Flowers of Evil; Short Circuits. Films incl: Garden of Delights. Recip. of Atlanta Film Festival Award for computer animated film, 'Steel', 1971. Address: Whitney Bldg., Box 34485, L.A., CA 90034, U.S.A. 9, 120, 132.

WHITEAKER, Stanley Cyril, b. 24 Nov. 1918. Accountant, Educ: Evening Student, Rockhurst Univ., 1955-58. Appts: Sgt., USNR, 1943-45; Acct., Mo. Pub. Serv. Commn., 1942-51; Utility Cons., 1951-58; Ptnr., Troupe Kehoe, Whiteaker & Kent, C.P.A., offs., in Kan. City, Kan. & Mo., 1958-; Cons., Kan. Corp. Commn., Mo. Pub. Serv. Commn., Nat. Energy Bd., (Canada) & major inds. in midw. on natural gas usage, also USAF; Dir., Tele Serve, Inc., T.K.W. Supply Co., Inc., Westboro Bldrs., Inc., Bichelmeyer Meat Co., Interstate Investments Inc. Mbrships. incl: Treas., Bd., Exec. Coun., Gtr. Kan. City Coun. on Alcoholism; Acctng. Comm., Fe Power Commn.; Chmbr. of Comm.; Kan. State Bd. Acctcy.; Am. Inst. & Kan. Soc. C.P.A.; Nat. Assn. Pub. Accts.; Kansas City Club; Milburn Golf & Co. Club; Co. Club, Mo. Author, articles on utility rate making. Address: 2900, Power & Light Bldg., Kan. City, MO 64105, U.S.A. 8, 16, 57.

WHITEFORD, Emma May Brittin (Mrs). Educator; Dietitian. Educ: B.S., N.D. State Univ., 1938; Dip. in Dietetics, Pa. Hosp., Phila, 1939; M.S., Univ. of Ill, 1951; Ed.D., ibid, 1955. Appts. incl: Admnstve. dietitian, York Hosp., Pa., 1939-40; Acting Chmn. Home Econs Dept. III, Wesleyan Univ., 1949-50; Instr., Home Econs. Educ., Univ. of Ill, 1953-55; Dir., Schl. of Home Econs., Univ., of Cinn, Ohio, 1959-66; Prof, Home Econs, Educ., Univ. of Minn, Mpls, 1967-. Chmn. of Dept., ibid, 1967-71. Mbrships. incl; Am. Home Econs Assn.; Am. Dietetic Assn.; Chmn. Tchr. Educ. & Profl. Advancement Comm.; Minn. Voc. Assn. Bd. of Trustees, Am. Tech. Educ. Assn.; Am. Soc. for Advancement of Sci.; AAUP; Omicron Nu.; Pi Lambda Theta; Kappa Delta Pi; Delta Kappa Gamma. Contbr. of articles to profl. jrnls. & to the Minn. Rsch. Coordng. Unit. Address: 740 River Drive, Apt. 12-C, St. Paul, MN 55116, U.S.A. 5, 8, 15, 141.

WHITEHEAD, Geoffrey Michael, b. 31 July 1921. Lecturer. Educ: Wymondham Tchr. Trng. Coll., U.K.; Commerce Degree Bur., London Univ. Appts. in primary schls., 15 yrs., secondary schls., 6 yrs. & tech. coll., 8 yrs. Mbrships: Soc. of Authors, London; Assn. of Tchrs. in Tech. Instns. Publs: Book-Keeping Made Simple; Commerce Made Simple; Economics Made Simple; Office Practice Made Simple; Success in Principles of Accounting & Answer Book; Success in Book-Keeping for the Small Business; History of Money. Address: 15 Camside, Cambridge, U.K. 3.

WHITEHEAD, Paxton, b. 17 Oct. 1937. Actor; Director. Educ: Webber-Douglas Drama Schl., 1955-57. m. Patricia Gage, 1971, 1 step-d., Heather. Theatrical Experience: Profl. Debut, Devonshire Pk. Theatre, Eastbourne, 1956; Repertory Cos. & tours, U.K., inclng. Royal Shakespeare Co., Stratford-on-Avon, 1957-60; N.Y. Debut, Gallows Humour, 1961; Broadway—Beyond the Fringe, C.P. Snow's The Affair, One Way Pendulum, Candida, The Brass Butterfly, A Dolls House; & Festival & Regional Theatres U.S.A. & Canada. Artistic Dir., Shaw Festival, Niagara-on-the-Lake, Canada, 1967-; Artistic Dir., Playhouse Theatre Ctr. of B.C., 1971-73. Mbr., The Players, N.Y. Plays: Translator, adapted w. S. Grossmann, The Chemmy Circle, 1st produced 1968, Barrymore Theatre, N.Y.C., 1973; There's One in Every Marriage, 1st produced 1971, Nat. Theatre of Canada & Royale Theatre, N.Y., 1972.

Address: c/o Shaw Festival, Box 774, Niagara on the Lake, Ont., Canada. 88.

WHITEHILL, Jules Leonard, b. 7 Mar. 1912. Surgeon; Medical Educator. Educ: B.Sc., CCNY, 1931; M.D., N.Y. Univ. Coll. of Med., 1935; Internship, Residency in Surg., Rsch. Fellow in Surg., Mt. Sinai Hosp., N.Y.C., 1935-42. Appts. incl: Staff, Mt. Sinai, Sydenham, Harem Hosps., N.Y.C., 1939-48; Med. Off., U.S. Army, 1st Major, 1942-46; Chief of Surg., Ctrl. Manhattan Med. Grp., N.Y.C., 1946-48; Pvte. Surg. Prac., Tucson, Ariz., 1948-63; Attng. Staff, St. Mary, St. Josephs, Tucson Med. Ctr. Hosps. & Pima Co. Hosp. (Chief of Surg.); Med. Dir., Mt. Sinai Hosp., Chgo. & Assoc. Dean, Chgo. Med. Schl., 1963-68; Prof. of Surg., Chgo. Med. Schl., 1963-73; Chmn., Dept. of Surg., ibid, 1968-70; Prof. Emeritus, 1973-; Cons. to Strategic Air Command, USAF, 1966-72, Col., USAF, retired; Vis. Prof. of Surg., Zagreb Univ., Yugoslavia. Active Mbr. num. profl. & acad. socs. inclng: Fellow, Int. Coll. of Surgs.; Co-Chmn., Bd. of Regents & Mbr., Int. Bd. of Govs., ibid; Phi Beta Kappa, 1931 Alpha Omega Alpha, 1935 & Sigma Xi, 1967. Author many publs. in field of Surg. w. original rsch. in fields of Electromagnetic Measurement of Blood Flow; Prevention of Keloids w. Cortico-Steriod Hormones & Automatic Anastomosis Device (The Whitehill Clamp). Hons. incl: Achievement Award, Surg. Gen. of USAF, 1967; Jules Leonard Whitehill Profship. in Surg. established at Schl. of Med., N.Y. Univ., 1973. Address: 1716 El Camino Del Teatro, La Jolla, CA 92037, U.S.A. 2, 14, 17.

WHITELOCK, Dorothy, b. 11 Nov. 1901. Professor (retd.). Educ: Newnham Coll., Cambridge, U.K. Appts: Lectr., later Fellow, Tutor & Vice Prin., St. Hilda's Coll., Oxford, 1930-57; Elrington & Bosworth Prof. of Anglo-Saxon, Univ. of Cambridge, 1957-69. Mbrships: Pres., Engl. Place-Name Soc., 1967-; Chmn., British Acad. Sylloge of Coins of the British Isles Comm., 1967-; Pres., Viking Soc., 1939-41; Fellow, British Acad., Soc. of Antiquaries, & Royal Histl. Soc.; Corres. Fellow, Mediaeval Acad. of Am., 1958; Assoc., Koninklijke Acad. voor Wetenschappen, Letteren en Schone Kunsten van Belgie, 1972. Publs. incl: Anglo-Saxon Wills; Sermo Lupi ad Anglos; The Beginnings of English Society; The Audience of Beowulf; English Historical Documents c. 500-1042; The Anglo-Saxon Chronicle: A Revised Translation (w. D.C. Douglas & S.I. Tucker). Hons. incl: C.B.E., 1964; Litt.D., Univ. of Leeds, 1971. Address: 30 Thornton Close, Cambridge, CB3 0NG, U.K. 1, 3.

WHITESCARVER, Edward Augustus, b. 31 May 1914. Educator; School Administrator. Educ: A.B., W. Va. Wesleyan Coll., 1935; M.A., W. Va. Univ., 1940. Appts: Grad. Asst., Coll. of Educ., W. Va. Univ.; Tchr., Engl., French & World Hist., Flemington H.S., 22 yrs.; Asst. Prin., Grafton Sr. H.S., 7 yrs.; Prin., ibid, 8 yrs.; Served in U.S. Army, WWII. Mbrships: Dir., Tygart Valley Dev. Assn., Inc., Rural Area Dev. Corp., & City-Co. Planning Commn.; Bd. of Govs., Educators Investors Ins. Co.; Americaniam Off., Am. Legion; Dir., Past Pres., Grafton Kiwanis Club; Dist. Chmn. Am. Legion Oratorial Contest; Gospel Four Quartet; Grafton Lodge 15, A.F. & A.M.; Deacon, Ch. Schl. Supt., Beulah Bapt. Ch.; NEA; Nat. Assn. of Secondary Schl. Prins.; W. Va. Educ. Assn.; W. Va. Secondary Schl. Prins. Commn.; Taylor Co. Educ. Assn. Publs: A Call to Arms, Veterans Day Address; And Gladly Teach; articles on local hist. Hons: Kappa Delta Pi, 1940; Veterans of For. Wars Patriotism Award,

1968; Chosen to deliver Veterans Day Address, Nat. Cemetery, 1970. Address: Rte. 2, Box 73, Grafton, WV 26354, U.S.A. 5, 125.

WHITFIELD, (Rev.), George Joshua Newbold, b. 2 June 1909. Educationalist. Educ: M.A., A.K.C., King's Coll., London Univ.; Bishop's Coll., Cheshunt. Appts: Headmaster, Tavistock Grammar Schl., Stockport Schl., Hampton Grammar Schl.; Sec. of Educ., Gen. Synod. C. of E. Mbrships: Past Pres., Headmasters' Assn. & Mbr., Headmasters' Conf. Publs: An Introduction to Drama; God & Man in the Old Testament; Philosophy & Religion; Ed.-Teaching Poetry; Poetry in the Sixth Form. Contbr. to Brit. Jrnl. of Educl. Studies. Hons: Barry Prizeman in Divinity, 1929. Address: Hampton House, 31 Foxholes Hill, Exmouth, Devon EX8 2DQ, U.K. 1, 3, 139.

WHITFIELD-FOX, Vallie Jo (Mrs. Robert Edward Whitfield), b. 18 Mar. 1922. Community Service Aide; Contractor; Broker. Educ: Belmost Coll.; Univ. of Tenn.; Rutgers Univ.; Diablo Valley Coll.; A.A., Holy Name Coll., 1962. Appts: Chem. Techn., Shell Dev. Co., Emeryville, Calif., 1943-45; Community Serv. Aide, Contractor, Calif. Human Resources Dev., Contra Costa Co., 1951-; Contractor, Broker, Real Estate Dev. & Sales, 1965, 1968-; Owner, Operator, Whitfield Farm, Contra Costa Co., 1952-62. Mbrships. incl: Christian Women Assn.; League of Women Voters; Girl Scouts of Am.; Boy Scouts of Am.; Past Mbr., Bd. of Dirs., Concord Hosp. Assn.; Calif. Hist. Soc.; Am. Assn. for State & Local Hist.; Geneal. Club of Am.; Life, PTA; Contra Costa Bd. of Realtors; Calif. Real Estate Assn. Publs. incl: Whitfield History & Genealogy of Tennessee, 1964; Life of Vallie Jo Whitfield, 1969; Newspapers on Whitfield Family, 1971. Hons: Boy, Girl Scouts of Am. awards. Address: Whitfield Court, Pleasant Hill, CA 94523, U.S.A. 5.

WHITING, James Allen, b. 21 Sept. 1922. Physician; General Surgeon. Educ: Univ. of Ala., 1942-43; Univ. of Va., 1945-46; Med. Coll. of Ala., 1946-47; Intern, City Hosp., Mobile, Ala., 1947-48; Res. in Surg., St. Vincent's Hosp., Toledo, Ohio, 1948-51; Fellow in Surg., Wallace Fndn., Spartanburg, S.C., 1951-53. Appts: Dir., Suburban Med. Corp.; Med. Staff, Suburban Hosp.; Pres. of Staff, ibid, 1966; Staff Dr.'s Hosp., Mobile Infirmary, Providence Hosp., Mobile Gen. Hosp.; Pres., Capa Records, Audiomaster Recording Studios, Medico Music Co.; V.P., Law Publishing Co., Saraland, Ala.; Prin. Stock Holder or Owner, sev. cos. Mbrships. incl: Assoc., Nat. Acad. of Recording Arts & Scis. & Country Music; AMA; Southern Med. Am. Coll. of Surgs.; Dipl., Am. Bd. of Surg. Author of sev. med. publs.; Composer of num. recorded country & western, popular songs. Address: P.O. Box 5777, Saraland, AL 36571, U.S.A. 7, 125.

WHITING, Oliver K., b. 28 May 1899. Lecturer; Journalist; Broadcaster; Instructor. Instr., Communications, 20 yrs.; Sponsor, Courses in Human Rels. & Effective Speaking, 14 yrs.; Free-lance jrnlst., The N.Y. Times, Herald Tribune, Saturday Review, Ladies' Home Jrnl., etc. Frequent contbr. Travel Talks, BBC. Mbrships: Fellow, R.S.A.; Engl. Speaking Union; Nat. Liberal Club, London, U.K.; Westchester Histl. Soc. Creative Works: Designed Map of the World United, a pictorial hist. of Communications & Paths to permanent Peace, distributed by UN & Carnegie Endowment for Peace; Map of Tariff Barrier of Europe, as published in Banking Credit and the

Crisis by J.W. Kempster; Introduced to U.S.A. Gardens of Fragrance for the blind, estab. in areas throughout U.S.A. & raised $125,000 for garden in Ctrl. Pk., N.Y. Shared w. Richard Dimbleby the Broadcast of visit of King George VI & Queen Elizabeth to N.Y. in 1937 & the hon. of repeating the broadcast of the Queen's visit to N.Y. in 1957. Address: The Lake House, Glenwolde Pk., Tarrytown, NY 10591, U.S.A.

WHITING, (Mrs.) Virginia Hearn, b. 31 July 1924. Certified Medical Assistant; Registered Medical Secretary. Educ: A.B., Averett Coll., Fredericksburg, Va., U.S.A., 1943; Schl. of Nursing, Univ. of Va., Charlottesville, 1943-45; B.A., Univ. of S. Ala., Mobile, 1973. Appts: Med. Asst., Admin. & Clin., to doctors, Toledo, Ohio, 1950-52, & Mobile, Ala., 1960-62; Med. & Admin. Asst., Internist Assocs., P.A., Mobile, 1963-71; Med. Asst., Admin. & Clin., to doctor, Mobile, 1971-. Mbrships. incl: Nat. Histl. Soc.; Treas., Mobile Chapt., Am. Assn. of Med. Assts., 1973-74, V.P., 1974-75, Deleg. to State Conven., 1973; Ed., Newsletter, Evening Student Coun., Univ. of S. Ala., Sec., 1971-74; Grad. Senator, Student Govt. Assn., Univ. of S. Ala., 1973-74; Nat. Rehab. Assn.; Ala. Rehab. Assn.; Beta Phi Kappa; Delta Tau Kappa; Phi Theta. Address: 958 Carlyle Way W., # 557, Mobile, AL 36609, U.S.A. 125.

WHITLOCK, Luder Gradick, Jr., Presbyterian Minister. Educ: B.A., Univ. of Fla., Gainesville, Fla., 1962; B.D., Westminster Theological Sem., Phila., Pa., 1966; D.Min., Vanderbilt Univ., Nashville, Tenn., 1974. Appts. incl: Tchr., Fed. prog. to rehabilitate Cuban refugees, Miami, Fla., 1962-63; Pastor, Sharon Orthodox Presby. Ch., Hialeah, Fla., 1966-69; Mbr. Denominational Comm. on Ministerial Trng., 1967-; Pastor, W. Hills Presby. Ch., Harriman, Tenn., 1969-; Mbr. Denomtl. Comm. on Home Missions & Ch. Ext., 1971-; Mbr. Trustee, Bd. Trustees, Westminster Theological Sem., 1973-; Mbr. Trustee, Bd. Trustee, Covenant Coll., Chattanooga, Tenn., 1973-; Dir., Southland Bible Conf., 1967, 1968, 1969, 1974. Mbrships. incl: Harriman Rotary Club, Pres., Mbr. Bd. Dirs., 1971-; Roane Co. United Fund, Bd. Dirs., 1971-72. Publs: contbns. in rel. jrnls.; Assoc. Ed., History Of Roane County. Hons. incl: Fraternal Deleg. of Orthodox Presby. Ch., Reformed Presby. Ch. Evangelical Synod, 1971. Address: W. Hills Presby. Ch., P.O. Box 26, Harriman, TN 37748, U.S.A. 125.

WHITLOW, Etholene R. (Mrs. Homer P. Whitlow), b. 6 Aug. 1910. Teacher. Educ: Ferrum Trng. Schl. (High), 1927; Radford Coll., 1928-29; Univ. of Va.; Wm. & Mary Coll. Appts: Tchr., Franklin Co., 1928-34, 1948-56; Prin., Snow Creek Elementary Schl., ibid, 1956-65; Tchr., 1965-71; Dir., Audio-Visual Ctr. for Franklin Co. Schls., 1971-. Mbrships: Bethlehem United Meth. Ch., Sydnorsville, Va.; Pres., United Meth. Women; Franklin Co. Artists Guild; Former Mbr., Va. Educ. Assn. & Nat. Educ. Assn.; Mental Hlth. Assn. of Franklin Co. Local exhibs. of oil paintings. Address: Rt. 2 Box 92, Rocky Mt., VA 24151, U.S.A. 5, 7, 85, 125, 132.

WHITLOW, Tyrel Eugene, b. 31 Aug. 1940. Art Instructor. Educ: B.S.E., Ark State Univ.; M.F.A., Instituto Allende, Mexico. Appts: Art Instr., Ill. Valley Community Coll., Oglesby, Ill. Mbrships: Am. Fedn. of Tchrs.; Rockford (Ill.) Art Assn.; Soc. of Art Histns. Exhibs: Mid-South Exhib., Brooks Mem. Art Gall., Memphis, Tenn., 1968; Monroe Annual, Masur Art Mus., Monroe, La., 1968; Contemporary Southern Art Exhib., Memphis, 1968; Delta

Annual, Ark. Art Ctr., Little Rock, 1968; Northern Ill. Univ., Nat. Print & Drawing Exhib., 1970; Ill. State Fair, 1970; Butler Inst. of Am. Art, Youngstown, Ohio, 1973. Hons: Top Award, Contemporary Southern Art Exhib.; Purchase Award, Ark. Arts Festival; Watercolor Award, Ark. State Watercolor Exhib. Address: Ill. Valley Community Coll., R.R.1, Oglesby, IL, U.S.A. 37.

WHITMAN, Agnes C., (Peggy), b. 9 Feb. 1907. Educator; Special Education Administrator. Educ: B.S., M.A., Glassboro State Coll. Appts: Special Class Tchr., Maple Shade, Millville & Franklinville Schls., N.J., 1956-64; Coord. Special Ed. Classes, Oakrest Regional H.S., Mays Landing, N.J., 1964-65; Sprvsr., Special Educ. Tchng. Interns, Temple Univ., Phila., Pa.; Dir. Educ. & Trng., Phila. Assn. Retarded Children; Educl. Coord. & Prog. Specialist, Dept. Pub. Welfare Off. Mental Retardation, Eastern Pa. & Southeastern Region. Mbrships. incl: Coun. for Exceptional Children; Past Pres., Cumberland-Cape May Ct. House, ibid; NEA; AAUP; Fellow, Am. Assn. on Mental Deficiency. Contbr., Secondary School Principals' Handbook, 1961. Recip., Nat. Sci. Fndn. Grant. Address: E. Weymouth Rd., R.D.1, Vineland, NJ 08360, U.S.A.

WHITMAN, Ainsley Abbott, b. 22 Sept. 1912. Librarian. Educ: A.B., San José State Coll., Calif., 1935; B.S. in L.S., La. State Univ., Baton Rouge, 1936. Appts: Libn., Coll. of Agric., Univ. of Ga., 1949-50, Willamette Univ. Salem, Ore., 1950-55, Central State Coll., Edmond, Okla., 1955-57; Asst. Libn., Jacksonville State Coll., Ala., 1957-62; Libn., Univ. of N.C., Asheville, 1962-. Mbrships: Pres., Ore. Lib. Assn.; V.P., Ark. Lib. Assn.; ALA; Southeastern Lib. Assn.; AUUP. Address: Univ. of N.C. at Asheville, Asheville, NC 28804, U.S.A.

WHITNEY, Ralph Royal Jr., b. 10 Dec. 1934. Financial Intermediary. Educ: B.A., Univ. of Rochester, 1957; M.B.A., ibid, 1973. Appts: Pres., Wadsworth Mfg. Assoc. Inc., 1964-68, & Warren Components Corp., 1968-70; Partner, Hammond Kennedy & Co., 1970-; Dir., Regency Electronics, Inc. Mbr., Lotos Club, N.Y.C. Address: 7099 Frank Long Rd., Rd 2 Jamesville, NY 10017, U.S.A. 6.

WHITSEL, Richard H., b. 23 Feb. 1931. Biologist; Entomologsit. Educ: B.A., Univ. of Calif., Berkeley, 1954; M.A., San Jose State Coll., Calif., 1962. Appts: Seasonal Naturalist, National Park Service, 1957-58; Sr. Rsch. Biologist, San Mateo Co. Mosquito Abatement Dist., Burlingame, Calif., 1959-72; Environ. Specialist, Calif. Reg. Water Quality Control Bd., Oakland, Calif., 1972-. Mbrships: Entomol. Soc. of Am.; Entomol. Soc. of Wash.; Am. Mosquito control Assn.; Midwest Bentholigical Soc.; Calif. Alumni Assn. Publs: A New distribution record & an aincidence of mermithid nematode parasitism for Leptoconops kerteszi Kieffer (Diptera Ceratopogonidae), Mosquito News; co-author of many articles in field to profl. jrnls. Address: 1459 San Marcos Drive, San Jose, CA 95132, U.S.A. 9, MCL.

WHITSON (Warren, Peter Whitson), b. 7 Sept. 1941. Mail Artist; Teacher. Educ: B.A., Univ. of N.H., Durham, U.S.A., 1963; M.A. & M.F.A., Univ. of Iowa, Iowa City, 1967. Appts: Tchng. Asst., Univ. of Iowa, 1965-67; Art Instr., Eastern Mont. Coll., Billings, 1967-69; Asst. Prof., Art, ibid, 1969-; Co-Pres., Western Dakota Junk Co., Billings, 1969-; Owner, Lost Lady Mining Co., 1970-; Owner, Al's Ham-'n'-Egger & Body Shop, 1971-; Owner, Art's Famous Schl., 1972-; Owner, Famous Lost Car Detective Agcy., 1973-. Mbrship: Co-Pres., United Sluj Wkrs. of Am. One-man shows: Univ. of Iowa, 1965 & 1966. Other Exhibs of Wks. incl: All Iowa Show, Des Moines, 1967; 13th Annual N.D. Art Exhib., 1969; Accordian Post Card Show, Mombacus Art Ctr., Accord, N.Y., 1973; U.S. Mail, Univ. of Me., Augusta, 1973. Drawings & Poems in sev. jrnls. Address: The Western Dakota Junk Co., 315 S. 34th St., Billings, MT 59101, U.S.A. 37.

WHITTINGHAM, Charles Arthur, b. 11 Feb. 1930. Publisher. Educ: Grad., Loyola Acad., U.S.A.; B.Sc., Loyola Univ., Chgo., 1951. Appts: Serv. USNR 1952-56; Publr.'s rep. McCall Corp., 1956-59; Time Inc: Publr.'s rep. Chgo., 1959-61 & N.Y.C., 1961-65, Fortune Mag.; Mgr., W. Coast Ops., San. Fran., 1965-69; Asst. to Publr., 1970, Asst. Publr., Fortune Mag., 1971-. Mbrships. incl: Univ. Clubs, San. Fran. & N.Y.C.; Belvedere Tennis Club; Mount Kisco Country Club. Recip., Athletics award (track), Loyola Univ. Address: 11 Woodmill Rd., Chappaqua, NY 10514, U.S.A. 6.

WHITTINGHAM, Charles Percival, b. 7 Sept. 1922. Scientist. Educ: St. John's Coll., Cambridge; Frank Smart Rsch. Student, Bot. Schl., Cambridge. Appts: Postdoct. Rsch. Fellow, Univ. of Ill., U.S.A., 1949-50; Rsch., Bot. Schl. Cambridge, 1950-52; Sr. Rsch. Asst., ibid, 1952-53, 1954-57; Vis. Lectr. & Rsch. Assoc., Bot. Dept., Univ. of Minn., U.S.A., 1953-54; Asst. Dir. of Rsch. in Bot., Cambridge Univ., 1957-58; Prof., Bot., Queen Mary Coll., London Univ., 1958-64; Prof., Imperial Coll., ibid, 1964-71; Dean, Royal Coll. of Sci., ibid, 1968-71; Hd., Bot. Dept., Rothamsted Experimental Stn., Harpenden, Herts., 1971-. Publs: The Chemistry of Plant Processes, 1964; Mechanisms of Photosynthesis. 1974. Address: Rothamsted Experimental Stn., Harpenden, Herts. AL5 2JQ, U.K.

WHITTINGTON, Charles Edward, b. 21 Apr. 1922. Business Executive. Educ: Univ. of Okla. Electronic Schl. Appts: Journeyman Electrician; Seabees, USN; Master Electrician; Co-owner, Whittington Washateria, Borger, Tex.; Pres. & Owner, C & M Furniture Mart, Borger; Pres. & Owner, Sand Motel & Restaurant, Borger; Real Estate Owner. Mbrships: Bapt. Ch.; Elks; Pres., Torch Club of Borger. Works incl: Builder of bldg. housing C & M Furniture Mart; Builder (w. help) of bldg. housing Sands Motel; Designer & builder of 52 ft. houseboat; Designer & builder of 30 ft. motor home. Address: 100 Tansy St., Meadow Lark Addition, Borger, TX 79007, U.S.A.

WHITTLE, Peter, b. 27 Feb. 1927. University Professor. Educ: B.Sc., Victoria Univ. Coll., Wellington, N.Z., 1948; M.Sc., ibid, 1949; Ph.D., Univ. of Uppsala, Sweden, 1951. Appts: Lectr., Univ. of Uppsala, 1951-53; N.Z. D.S.I.R. (rising to S.P.S.O.), 1953-59; Lectr. in Maths., Univ. of Cambridge, 1959-61; Prof., Math. Stats., Univ. of Manchester, 1961-67; Churchill Prof., Maths. of Operational Rsch., Univ. of Cambridge, 1967-. Mbrships: Fellow, Churchill Coll., Cambridge, 1967-; Int. Statistical Inst.; Royal Statistical Soc.; Inst. of Math. Stats. Publs: Hypothesis Testing in Time Series Analysis, 1951; Prediction & Regulation, 1963; Probability, 1970; Optimisation under Constraints, 1971; Some 60 sci. papers. Hons: Rsch. Medal, Assn. of N.Z. Sci. Wkrs., 1954; Guy Medal in Silver, Royal Statistical Soc., 1966. Address: Statistical Lab., Univ. of

Cambridge, 16 Mill Lane, Cambridge, CB2 1SB, U.K. 1, 128.

WHONSBON-ASTON (The Venerable) Charles William, b. 10 May 1899. Archdeacon Emeritus. Educ: Moore Theol. Coll., Sydney, Australia; Aust. Coll. of Theol.; Th.L., 1927. Appts. incl: Chap., Western Samoa, 1943-58; Archdeacon, Fiji & Vicar of Levuka, 1958-64; 1st Archdeacon of Polynesia, Suva, 1963; Dpty. Vicar Gen., 1965; Archdeacon Emeritus, 1967; Hon. Canon, Holy Trinity Cath., 1967; Canon, ibid, 1973. Life Fellow, Royal Commonwealth Soc. Mbrships. incl: Dist. Commnr., Boy Scouts, Fiji; Scout Coun., Fiji, 1964-74; S. Pacific Anglican Conf., 1957, 60; Coun., Pacific Theol. Coll., 1968-69. Publs. incl: Levuka Days, 1936; Polynesia Patchwork, 1948; Challenge in Polynesia, 1956; The Moon & Polynesia, 1961, 62; Pacific Irishman, 1971. Recip., O.B.E., 1972. Address: Unit 4, Gibbs Court, Nuffield Village, Castle Hill, N.S.W. Australia 2154.

WHYBREW, Evelyn Roberts, b. 10 Nov. 1918. Assistant Professor of Education; Director of Learning Laboratory. Educ: B.S., SUNY, Oneonta, N.Y.; M.S., Memphis State Univ., Tenn. Appts: Classroom Tchr., Gilbertsville, N.Y., Madison Co., Tenn., Jackson City Schls., Lambuth Coll. Mbrships: Pres., W. Tenn. Coun., Int. Reading Assn.; Former Pres., Jackson Br., AAUW; Pres., Theta Chapt., Delta Kappa Gamma; Kappa Delta Pi; NEA; Former mbr., Legislative Comm., Tenn. Educ. Assn. Address: 1270 Hollywood Dr., Jackson, TN 38301, U.S.A. 125.

WHYTE, Raymond A., b. 3 Aug. 1923. Artist. Educ: Univ. of Toronto, Canada; Art Students League, N.Y., & in Venice, Paris & Madrid, 7 yrs. Served WWII. Life Mbr., Art Students League, N.Y.C. Works incl: Mural, R.M. Stewart, Austral Oil Co., Houston, Tex.; Triptych, Dr. Gerald B. Kara, N.Y.C.; Memorabilia, Orson Bean, Vivian Vance, Isidore Becker, H. Bulova Henshel, N.Y., Bernard G. Cantor, Beverly Hills., Calif., & Malcolm Forbes, N.Y.C.; Triptych, Dr. Richard Hamilton, N.Y.C. One-man shows: De Saisset Art Mus., Santa Clara, Calif., 1967; Crocker Art Mus., Sacramento, Calif., 1967; Janet Nessler Gall., N.Y.C., 1961-63; E. Kuhlik Gall., N.Y.C., 1972; Galerie De Tours, San Fran., 1962-74; Mus. Collects: De Beers Mus., S. Africa; Crocker Art Mus., Sacramento, Calif.; Santa Clara Mus., Calif. Hons: Art Students League Schlrship., 1941; Purchase Award, Art Students League, 1950. Address: 30 Fayson Lakes Rd., Kinnelon, NJ 07405, U.S.A. 37.

WHYTE, Thomas J., b. 31 Dec. 1932. Lawyer. Educ: B.A. Jrnlsm., Ohio State Univ., 1954; LL.B., W. Va. Univ. Coll. of Law, 1960. Appts: Law Clerk, U.S. Dist. Ct., 1960; Atty. & Ptnr., Furbee, Hardesty, Critchfield & Whyte, Fairmont, W. Va., 1960-67 (& retains connection w. successor firm Furbee, Amos, Webb & Critchfield); Gen. Counsel 1969-70, V.P. 1970-72, Exec. V.P. 1972-, Consolidated Coal Co., Pitts., Pa. Mbrships. incl: Chmn. of Bd., W. Va. Coal Assn.; Dir., W. Va. Rsch. League, Western Pa. Coal Operators Assn., Inc., Keystone Bituminous Coal Assn.; Am. Bar Assn.; W. Va. State Bar; W. Va. Bar. Assn.; Pa. Bar Assn.; Phi Delta Phi; Duquesne Club, Pitts., Pa.; Downtown Club, ibid. Publs: Ed.-in-Chief, W. Va. Law Review, 1960. Hons: Outstanding Grad. of Class Award, Phi Delta Phi, 1960; Order of the Coif, 1960; Patrick D. Koontz Award, 1960; W. Va. Law Schl. Assn. Award, 1960. Address: 3300 One Oliver Plz., Pittsburgh, PA 15222, U.S.A.

WIACKLEY, Mildred L., b. 2 Nov. 1946. Playwright & Student. Educ: N.Y.C. Community Coll.; Univ. of Minn. Mbr., Am. Killifish Assn. Plays: Somebody Stoled the Garbage, 1964; Time on our Hands, 1964; Fly Trap Melody, 1965; Renouncement, 1965; Braker's Reef, 1966; The Turtle Walk, 1967; Dream Cantatas, 1968; Afghanistan: It's a Dog's Life (in preparation). Author, Sisters of the Moneyman (poems), 1972. Contbr. to: Ante; Dasein; Eikon; Graffitti; Kauri; New Orlando Poetry Anthol. Vol. III, etc. Address: P.O. Box 82, Peter Stuyvesant Stn., N.Y., NY 10009, U.S.A. 57.

WIBAIL, Amé-Henri, b. 5 Feb. 1908. University Professor. Educ: Mining Civil Engr.; Licencié, Econ. Scis.; Chem. Engr. Appts: Hon. Dir. Gen., Min. of Econ. Affairs; Hon. Prin. Pvte. Sec., var. mins.; Hon. Lt., Artillery Reserve. Mbrships: Pres., Royal Archaeol. Club, Enghien; Corres. Mbr., Royal Commn. of Monuments & Sites. Author, num. articles on econ. & statl. subjs. Hons: Grand Off., Order of the Crown, 1972; Cmdr., Order of Leopold, 1965; 1st Class Civic Cross, 1969; Commemorative War Medal w. crossed swords, 1946; Commemorative Medal, Reign of King Albert, 1964; Mil. Veteran Medal, 1969; Cmdr., Order of Merit, Italian Repub., 1954; Cmdr., Grand Ducal Order, Crown of Oak, 1954; Cmdr., Order of Orange-Nassau, Netherlands, 1958. Address: Rue d'Hoves 110-112, B-1390 Enghien, Belgium. 43, 87.

WICKENDEN, Barbara Lyddon Horner (Mrs. Herbert Russell Wickenden), b. 7 May 1925. Educational Consultant. Educ: B.S., Purdue Univ.; M.S., Univ. of Akron. Appts: Treas., ESTI, 1955-65; V.P., Invlux Corp., 1957-64; Pres., The Learning Ctr., Inc., 1965-; Cons., Encyclopaedia Britannica Corp., 1970-, Singer Soc. for Visual Educ., 1973-74, & Portage Co. Schls., 1973-. Mbrships: Int. Reading Assn.; Assn. for Supvsn. & Curric. Dev.; Assn. Second. Schl. Prins.; NEA. Ohio Educ. Assn.; Delta Gamma; Pi Lambda Theta; Delta Kappa Gamma. Publs: over 2000 books, films, filmstrips, tapes & educl. activities for Encylopaedia Britannica Corp.; 18 levels of Holt, Rinehart & Winston's Basic Reading Prog.; Logos, Primary Reading Program; Threshold for Reading; Ecology & Family Crossword Puzzles; Word Perception; Spelling Stumpers; Word Activities; Reading Mathematics; Preschool Patterns. Hons: D.D., Universal Life Ch. Address: The Learning Ctr. Inc., 3727 Darrow Rd., Stow, OH 44224, U.S.A. 5.

WICKRAMASINGHE, Nalin Chandra, b. 20 Jan. 1939. Professor of Applied Mathematics & Astronomy. Educ: B.Sc., Univ. of Ceylon; M.A., Ph.D., & Sc.D., Univ. of Cambridge, U.K. Appts: Fellow & Tutor, Jesus Coll., Univ. of Cambridge, 1963-72; Prof. & Hd. of Dept., Applied Maths. & Astron., Univ. Coll., Cardiff, 1973-. Mbrship: Fellow, Royal Astronomical Soc. Publs: Interstellar Grains, 1967; Light Scattering Functions with Applications in Astronomy, 1973; Over 100 papers in scientific jrnls. Recip., Powell Prize for Engl. Verse, Trinity Coll., Univ. of Cambridge, 1962. Address: Dept. of Applied Mathematics & Astronomy, University College, P.O. Box 78, Cardiff CF1 1XL, U.K.

WIDDOES, Lawrence Lewis, b. 15 Sept. 1932. Composer; Music Teacher. Educ: B.S., Juilliard Schl. of Music, N.Y.C., U.S.A., 1960; M.Sc., ibid, 1966. Appts: Instr., Composition, Pre-Coll. Div., Juilliard Schl. of Music; Instr., Fac. of Ext. Div., ibid, 1965-; Instr., Regular Div. Fac., 1972-. Mbrships: ASCAP; Am. Music

Ctr. Compositions incl: (orch.) 2 Symphs., 1957 & 1963; Nocturne for Strings, 1958; Journey, 1969-70; (chamber music) Tamarix, 1961; Sonatina, Flute & Piano, 1965; One Thousand Paper Cranes, 1966-72; From a Time of Snow, 1971; Acanthus, 1972; Moments Here, 1972; (choral) Pied Beauty, 1961-72; Sanctus, 1972; (song) Love Song, 1972; (piano) Five Pieces from New London, 1959. Recordings: One Thousand Paper Cranes; Morning Music. Hons. incl: Elizabeth Sprogue Coolidge Chamber Music Award, 1960, & Soc. for Publn. of Am. Music Award, 1965, both for Sonatina, Flute & Piano. Address: The Juilliard School, Lincoln Center Plaza, N.Y., NY 10023, U.S.A. 130.

WIDEGREN, K. Ragnar, b. 21 Nov. 1917. Civil Engineer; Managing Director of Professional Association. Educ: Mil. Coll. for Offs. of Reserve, 1940; Royal Inst. of Technol., Stockholm, 1946. Appts: Housing Investigator, City of Stockholm, 1944; Assn. for Water Regulation of Rivers, 1946; Municipal Insp., Bldgs., Stockholm, 1947-48; Int. Siporex AB, 1949-52; Cons. Engr., Gösta Lundin AB, 1952-53; Mng. Dir., Swedish Assn. of Civil Engrs., 1953-60; Major, Corps of Royal Engrs. Reserve, 1967; Mng. Dir., Swedish Assn. of Cons. Engrs., 1960-; Mng. Dir., Assn. of Cons. Firms, 1965-. Mbrships: Swedish Liberal Pty. & Past Chmn., Exec. Comm. in Stockholm; Mbr., sev. Bds., City of Stockholm. Contbr. to profl. jrnls. Address: Rastvägen 13, 16151 Bromma, Sweden. 43.

WIDEN, Rolf Villehad, b. 29 June 1920. Managing Director. Educ: LL.B., 1946; Barrister-at-Law, 1948. Appts: Sec., Finnish Employers' Conf., 1949; Hd., Soc. Dept., ibid, 1955; Cnslr., Finnish Metal Trades Employers' Assn., 1957; Juridicial Dir., ibid, 1961; Mng. Dir., 1962-. Contbr. articles to econ. press. Hons: Cross of Liberty 1st Class, for war-time efforts; Kt. 1st Class, White Rose of Finland; Cmdr., Lion of Finland. Address: Finnish Metal Trades Employers' Assn., Eteläranta 10, 00130 Helsinki 13, Finland.

WIDMAN, Alfred Bernard, b. 25 June 1921. Lawyer. Educ: Natal Univ., S. Africa; Practising Atty. Appts: Chief Whip, United Party, Transvaal Provincial Coun.; Mayor, Johannesburg, 1971-72. Mbrships: Chmn., Museums Man & Sci.; Vice-Chmn., S. African Nat. Coun. on Alcoholism & Drug Dependence; Chmn., Noise Abatement Control Comm.; Transvaal Municipal Exec. Writer, profl. papers. Address: P.O. Box 1744, Johannesburg, S. Africa. 39, 55.

WIENER, Robert Alvin, b. 1 June 1918. Certified Public Accountant. Educ: B.S., N.Y. Univ., 1938. Appts: Pub. Acct., 1937-71; V.P., Controller, Seeburg Inds., 1973; Asst. Prof., Acctng., Pace Univ.; Lectr., Bernard Baruch Coll., & Grad. Schl., N.Y. Univ. Mbrships: Pi Lamda Phi; Collectors Club; The Lambs. Address: 20 Waterside Plaza, N.Y., NY 10010, U.S.A. 6.

WIENER, Solomon, b. 5 Mar. 1915. City Official. Educ: B.S., Cornell Univ., 1936; M.P.A., N.Y. Univ., 1946. Appts: Examining Asst., N.Y.C. Dept. of Personnel, 1937-42; Civil Serv. Examiner, ibid, 1946-55; Asst. Div. Chief, 1955-59; Div. Chief, 1959-67; Asst. Dir., Exams., 1967-70; Dir., Exams., 1970-72; Asst. Personnel Dir. for Exam., 1972-; Tchr., Wash. Irving Evening Adult Schl., 1949-60; Tchr. in Charge, 1960-67. Mbrships: incl: Int. Personnel Mgmt. Assn.; Am. Soc. for Pub. Admin.; Profl. Assn. of Pub. Officials, N.Y.C. Publs. incl: A Handy Book of Commonly Used American Idioms, 1958; A Handy Guide to Irregular Verbs & the Use & Formation of Tenses, 1959; Questions & Answers on American Citizenship, 1960; Business Letter Writing, 1969; num. articles in profl. jrnls. Hons. incl: Battle Participation Star, Mandated Islands Campaign, 1944; Bronze Star Medal, 1945. Address: 523 E. 14 St., N.Y., NY 10009, U.S.A. 6, 30.

WIENER, Theodore, b. 28 Sept. 1918. Librarian. Educ: B.A., Univ. of Cinn., 1940; M.H.L., Rabbi, Hebrew Union Coll., Cinn., 1943; Grad. courses, Columbia Univ., N.Y. Appts. incl: Rabbi, Beth Israel Congregation, Corsicana, Tex., 1947-48; Staff, Hebrew Union Coll. Lib., Cinn., 1950-64; Supvsr., Hebraic Lang. Unit, Descriptive Cataloging Div., Lib. of Congress, Wash. D.C. 1964-; Catologer of Judaica, Subject Catloging Div., Lib. of Congress, 1967-. Mbrships: V.P., Port Arthur Day Nursery, 1946-47; V.P., Assn. of Jewish Libs., 1970-72; now ex-officio mbr., Coun., ibid; Dir., Coun. of Nat. Lib. Assns., 1970-; Dir., Govt. Dir., United Jewish Appeal of Greater Wash., 1966-; Central Conf. of Am. Rabbis; B'nai B'rith. Author of publs. in field. Recip., Claude G. Montefiore Prize, for essay in Jewish theol., Hebrew Union Coll., 1941. Address: 1701 N. Kent St., Arlington, VA 22209, U.S.A. 55.

WIESENBAUGH, Joseph M. Jr., b. 19 Oct. 1939. Oral Surgeon. Educ: D.D.S., Baltimore Coll. Dental Surg., Univ. of Md., 1963; M.S., Univ. of Pacific, San Francisco, 1970. Appts. incl: Capt., USAF, 3½ yrs., inclng. 2½ yrs. var. offs., Dental Clin., Ankara, Turkey; Pt.-time Pvte. Prac., Oral Surg., Vallejo & Richmond, Calif., 1969-70; Pvte. Prac., Oral Surg., Hagerstown, Md., 1970-; Mbrships. incl: Wash. Co. Dental Soc.; (P.R. Comm. Chmn., 1971, Sec., 1971-72); Md. State Dental Assn.; Am. Dental Assn.; Bd. Dirs., Am. Cancer Soc., Wash. Co. (Pres., 1973); Middle Atlantic & Md. State Socs. Oral Surgs.; Hlth Planning Coun. Appalachia, Md. (Bd. Dirs., 1972-74); Omicron Kappa Upsilon. Num. lectures, profl. papers & reports. Recip., Upjohn Rsch. Grants, 1967-70 & profl. awards. Address: 103 Overhill Dr., Spring Valley, Hagerstown, MD 21740, U.S.A. 6.

WIEST, Paul Herbert Otto, b. 14 Sept. 1904. University Professor. Educ: Tech. Univ., Stuttgart, 1924-26; Dip. Ing., Tech. Univ., Berlin, 1929. Appts: Asst., Tech. Univ., Stuttgart, 1929-34; with Robert Bosch GmbH, Stuttgart, 1935-63; Dir., metallurgic div., ibid, 1946-63; Prof., raw material technol., Tech. Univ., Berlin, 1963-; Dir., rsch. inst. ibid. Mbrships: Verein Deutscher Ingenieure, 1927-; Deutsche Gesellschaft für Metallkunde, 1937-; Verein Deutscher Eisenhüttenleute, 1947-; Arbeitsgemeinschaft Wärmebehandlung & Werkstofftechnik, Bremen, 1952-; Hon. mbr., ibid, 1964. Author of num. publs. in field & co-ed., vol. 3, Atlas zur Wärmebehandlung der Stähle, 1973. Address: Walter Giesekingstr. 27, 62 Wiesbaden, German Fed. Repub. 43.

WIGGINS, Marvin E., b. 25 Mar. 1941. Librarian. Educ: A.S., Weber State Coll., 1962; B.S., Sociol., Brigham Young Univ., 1965; M.L.S., Rutgers Univ., 1967. Appts: Brigham Young Univ., 1967-; Asst. Gen. Ref. Libn., 1967; Gen. Ref. Libn., 1967-; Hd. of Rsch. Servs., 1970-. Mbrships: Chmn., Coll. & Univ. Sect., Utah Lib. Assn.; Chmn., Lib. & Info. Scis. Div., Utah Acad. of Scis.; Phi Kappa Phi; Neighborhood Chmn., Rock Canyon Neighborhood, Provo City, Utah. Publs: Using the Library: The Card Catalog, (co-author), 1971; Contbr. to profl. jrnls. & books. Address:

370 Harold B. Lee Lib., Brigham Young Univ., Provo, UT 84601, U.S.A.

WIGGINTON, Ellen Offutt (Mrs. Samuel T. Wigginton), b. 11 Aug. 1917. Cosmologist. Educ: Fla. Mem. Coll. & Ky. State Univ.; extensive study in field of Cosmotol. Mbrships. incl: Co-Organizer, Ky. Poor People's Coalition, 1969, served as Co-Chmn. for 1 yr., Chmn., 1 yr. & apptd. Exec. Dir., 1971; Apptd. by Judge Robert Stevens to Merger Commn., Lexington & Fayette Co. & served as Chmn., Hlth. & Welfare; Mbr., State Commn. of Aging; KWA, Lexington-Fayette Co. Serv. Coun.; Chmn., Bd. Trustees, Hunter Fndn. for Hlth. Care; Nat. Beauty Culture League, Inc.; Ky. Human Resources Citizen Coun.; Ky. Congress of Cosmotol.; former Dir. of Artists & Models Bur., KCC; Mbr., Beautician Unit No. 1 Lexington; V.P. & Bus. Mgr. on Advsry. Comm. to Urban League; NAACP; Nat. Assn. of Community Dev.; Agcy. Cons. for Coll. of Soc. Profns. to Univ. of Ky. Assn. of Community Action. Hons. incl: Ky. Col., 1970; Ambassador of Good Will, Louisville & Jefferson Co., 1971; Community Serv. Award, Lexington & Frankfort Links, Inc., 1972; Outstanding Community Award, Urban League, 1973; 20 yr. Plaque & 25 yr. pin for Outstanding Contbn. in field of Cosmotol., Ky. Congress of Cosmotol.; Silver Cup for contbn. to Fayette Co. Commn. for Merger Govt. Address: 425 Oak St., Lexington, KY 40508, U.S.A. 125, 130, 138.

WIGGS, Henry Ross, b. 28 Dec. 1895. Architect. Educ: McGill Univ., Montreal, 1915-17, 1919-20; B.A., Mass. Inst. of Technol., Boston, 1922. Appts. incl: Serv. WWI; Archt. w. var cos., N.Y. & Montreal, 1922-32; Prin., own gen. prac. Arch., 1933; Fndr. Ptnr., Wiggs, Lawton & Walker, Archts., 1954; Wiggs & Lawton, Archts., 1962; Retd. active prac., 1966. Mbrships. incl: P.Q. Assn. Archts., Ont.; Coun. Mbr., ibid, 1938-52, Pres., 1951-52; Assn. Archts.; Royal Archtl. Inst. of Canada; Assoc. & Fellow, Royal Inst. British Archts., London, U.K.; Fellow, Royal Archtl. Inst. Canada. Commns. incl. chs. & schls. Montreal; Govt., pub., indl., & commercial bldgs P.Q., Ont., N.B., N.S. Profl. watercolours in pvte. collects., Montreal, Ottawa, San Francisco & N.Y. Recip., 5 Awards of 1st & wnd Prizes, Tourist Bur. & Dept. Agric., P.Q., 1942. Address: 239 Kensington Ave., Westmount, P.Q., H3Z 2H1, Canada.

WIGHTMAN, Peter, b. 2 June 1933. Librarian. Educ: Leeds Lib. Schl. Appts: Ref. Libn., Huddersfield, 1955-58; Regional Libn., Cornwall, 1958-59; Borough Libn. & Curator, Colne, Lancs., 1959-. Mbrships: Past Sec., Borough of Colne Welfare Fun; Sec., Colne Arts Coun. Publs: Whalley to Wycoller, 1963; Pennine Panorama, 1968; Wills of Colne, 1973; Colne & Its Times, 1974; John Harrison 1868-1929, 1974. Address: 33 Priestfield Ave., Colne BB8 9QJ, Lancs., U.K.

WIJDEVELD, Hendricus Theodorus, b. 4 Oct. 1885. Architect. Educ: Arch. off., Jacque van Straaten, Amsterdam, Netherlands, & Dr. P.J.H. Cuypers; Studied works of Morris & Ruskin, U.K.; Worked at offs. of John Groll & John Belcher, London; Studied at Lambeth Schl. of Art, & British Mus., London; Worked w. archt. Cordonnier, Lille & Paris, France. Appts. incl: Built blocks of working-class flats, country-houses, shops; Fndr., Int. Art Mag. "Wendingen"; Introduced new typography into Netherlands; Stage archt., designing setting & costumes; Organized Int. Theatre Exhibition, Amsterdam & London, 1921-22; Started H.S. for Arch. & Decor. Arts, Elckerlyc; Archt., s.s.

Nieuw Amsterdam, Holland-Am.-Line, & Dutch pavilion, world exhibition, Paris, 1937, 1947-51; Vis. Prof., Univs., U.S.A. Mbrships: Hon. mbrs., Soc. Kunst aan het Volk; Hon. V.P., Fac. of Arts, London. One-man exhibition, Amsterdam, 1953. Author of publs. in field. Recip. of hons. Address: de Laivessestraat 14, Amsterdam, Netherlands. 43.

WIJSENBEEK, Henricus, b. 28 May 1916. Psychiatrist; Educator. Educ: Med. Schl., State Univ. of Leiden, Holland; Res., Psych. & Neurol., State Univ. of Utrecht, Holland; Univ. of Minnesota, U.S.A.; Personal Psychoanalysis w. Prof. M. Wulff, Tel Aviv, Israel; M.D., Ph.D. Appts. incl: Dir. & Psych-in-Chief, Gehah Psychiatric Hosp.; Chmn. Psych., Sackler Schl. of Med., Assoc. Prof. Psych., Tel Aviv Univ.; Cons. Psych., Beilinson Med. Ctr. Pres., Israel Psych. Assn.; Chmn. Bd. of Dirs., William S. Schwartz Inst. for Psychiatric Treatment & Rsch.; Mbr., Dist. Psych. Commn. of Min. Hlth. Mbrships: Int. Coll. Psychosomatic Med.; var. med. socs. Contbr., var. med. & psychiatric books, jrnls., publs. Recip., Histedruth Rsch. Award, 1966. Address: Ofakim St. 13, Afeka, Tel Aviv, Israel, 55, 94.

WIKING-JOHNSSON, Uno, b. 10 Oct. 1914. Industrial Executive. Educ: Grad. in Metallurgy, Royal Tech. Univ. of Stockholm, 1942. Appts: Engr., blast & open-hearth furnaces, Boxholms AB, 1942-44, Tech. Dir., 1944-53, Pres. (U.S.A.), Mng. Dir. (U.K.), 1954-67; Pres. (U.S.A.), Mng. Dir. (U.K.), Hallstahammars AB, 1967-. Bd. Mbr., Swedish Iron Masters Assn. Hon. Kt. of Swedish Order of Vasa. Address: Åsby Hergård, 73400, Hallstahammar, Sweden. 43.

WIKTOR, Jackiewicz, b. 19 Mar. 1932. Architect. Educ: Dipl.Ing.Arch., 1954; Mgr. Arch., 1956; Dr.T.S., 1964. Appts: Asst., Dept. of Arch., Tech. Fac., Wroclaw, 1956-58; Sr. Asst., ibid, 1959-64; Adjunct, Inst. of Arch. & Urbanism, Gliwice, 1965-68; Lectr., ibid, 1968-; Designer, Project Hd., Serbian Nat. Theatre, Novy Sad, 1972-74. Mbrships: O.I.S.T.T.; I.T.I.; S.A.R.P. (Nat. Org. of Archts.). Prin. works incl: Theatre, Lask, 1968; Philharmonic Hall, Wroclaw, 1968; 2 auditoriums, Gliwice, 1967; Club, Szczawno, 1972; Tech. Inst. of Cool, Wroclaw, 1964; Tech. Inst. of Machines, Gliwice, 1958. Publs: The Multidirectional Auditoriums, 1963; The Simultanius Auditorium, 1970. Hons: 1st Prize, Ch. Project, Czestochowa, 1958, Flexybilly Hall Project, Szczecin, 1958, Nat. Serbian Theatre Project, Novy Sad, 1961, & Theatre Project, Ladek Zdroj, 1968; 3rd Prize, Project of Wroclaw City, 1965; 4th Prize, Opera & Ballet Theatre Project, Katowice, 1959; 1000 Yrs. Medal, Poland, 1965; Wroclaw Medal, 1968. Address: Dereniowa 18, 53008-Wroclaw, Poland.

WILBORN, Ethel B., b. 30 Aug. 1913. Realtor. Appts. incl: Home bldr., Contractor, Cheaha Acres Jo-Dell Sub-Div., Oxford, Ala., 1957-; Developer, Scenic Heights Sub-Div., Oxford, 1965-; V.P., Jarey Inc.; Sec.-treas., Tirobia, Inc.; V.P., Dutch Village. Mbrships. incl: Anniston Real Estate Bd.; Nat. Inst. Real Estate Bds.; 1st Bapt. Ch.; Hon. Lt.-Col., State of Ala. Address: P.O. Box 1707, Anniston, AL 36201, U.S.A. 5, 125.

WILBRANDT, Hans, b. 4 Jan. 1903. University Professor. Educ: Dr.agr., Berlin, 1930. Appts: Agricl. Expert, 1928-34; Expert & Advsry. Off., Turkish Govt., 1934-40; Pvte. Advsry. & Commercial Agt., 1940-52; Agric. Econ., Inst. for World Econ., Kiel, 1953-57; Mbr., Comm. for the Coord. of Rsch. Insts.,

1956; FAO Advsr., Royal Govt. of Afghanistan, 1957-59; Prof. of Overseas Agric., & Dir. of Inst., Berlin, 1959; Prof., Gottingen & Dir., Inst. of Overseas Agric. & Ctr. for the Study of Tropical & Subtropical Agric., 1963-70; Expert for Nat. & Int. Instns. (BMZ, SATEC, FAO, Asian Dev. Bank); Co-ed., Blätter für landwirtschaftliche Marktforschung & Zeitschrfit für Ausländische Landwirtschaft. Mbrships. incl: Bd. Mbr., Sci. Comm. of BMZ, German-Turkish Soc. & sev. sci. socs. Contbr. articles on econ., soc., agric., ind. & nutritional problems to agric. jrnls. & FAO publs. Hons. incl: Cert. of Merit, Govt. of Turkey, 1973; Dr. h.c., Univ. of Berlin, 1973. Address: Inst. for Overseas Agric., 34 Göttingen, Büsgenweg 2, German Fed. Repub.

WILBUR, Richard Purdy, b. 1 Mar. 1921. Writer; Teacher. Educ: B.A., Amherst Coll., 1942; M.A., Harvard, 1947. Appts: Jr. Fellow, Soc. of Fellows, Harvard, 1947-50; Asst. Prof., Engl., ibid, 1950-54; Assoc. Prof., Engl., Wellesley Coll., 1955-57; Prof., Engl., Wesleyan Univ., 1957-. Mbrships. incl: Am. Acad. of Arts & Letters, 1973; Nat. Inst. of Arts & Letters; Am. Acad. of Arts & Sci.; Acad. of Am. Poets. Publs. incl: Walking to Sleep, New Poems & Translations, 1969; School for Wives, 1971; Opposites, 1973. Address: Dodwells Rd., Cummington, MA 01026, U.S.A.

WILCHEK, Meir, b. 17 Oct. 1935. Biochemist. Educ: B.Sc., Bar-Ilan Univ., Israel, 1960; Ph.D., Weizmann Inst. of Sci., Rehovot, 1965. m. Esther Edlis; Three Children. Appts. incl: Chief Chemist, Yeda Co., 1960-62; Rsch. Assoc., NIH, Bethesda, Md., U.S.A., 1965-67; Sr. Sci., Biophys. Dept., The Weizmann Inst. of Sci., Rehovot, Israel, 1968-70; Assoc. Prof., ibid, 1970-; Vis. Prof., Bar-Ilan Univ., 1970-71. Mbrships. incl: Am. Chem. Soc.; Israel Chem. & Biochem. Soc. Publd. many rsch. papers in protein chem. related to affinities in biol. systems and fine structure of aromatic amino acids. Recip., The Marc R. Gutwirth Prof. of Molecular Bio. Chair, 1973. Address: Dept. of Biophys., The Weizmann Inst. of Sci., Rehovot, Israel.

WILCKO, Michael P., b. 26 Oct. 1921. Private Investor. Educ: B.S., Geneva Coll. Appts: Supt., Ellwood Forge Co., 1951-64; Pres. & Bd. Chmn., Bay City Forge Co., 1964-70; Private Investor, 1970-. Mbrships: Kahkwa Country Club; Erie Club; Maennerchor Club; Eire Yacht Club. Address: 1106 Southview Dr., Erie, PA 16509, U.S.A.

WILCOCK, John, b. 4 Aug. 1927. Editor; Author; Publisher. Educ: Rishworth Schl., Halifax, N.B. Appts: Reporter, Sheffield Telegraph, Daily Mail, Daily Mirror, UPI Toronto; Asst. Ed., Pageant, N.Y.C.; Co-fndr., & Columnist, The Village Voice, N.Y.C.; Asst. Travel Ed., N.Y. Times, 1957-60; Ed., East Village Other; Ed. L.A. Free Press, 1967; Ed., Publr., Other Scenes & Nomad; Co-ed. Annual Witches Almanac, 1970-. Publs: The Village Square, collected columns, 1957; The Autobiography & Sex Life of Andy Warhol (author & publr.); 7 travel books, inclng. Mexico on $5 a Day, Japan on $10 a Day, India on $10 a Day. Address: BCM-NOMAD, London WC1V 6XX, U.K.

WILCOX, Beatrice Shurly (Mrs.), b. 6 Feb. 1909. Secretary. Appts: Prin. Sec., Young & Rubican Inc., Detroit, Mich., 1½ yrs.; Advtng. Sec., Giffels & Rossetti, ibid. Mbrships: Jr. League of Detroit, 40 yrs.; Tau Beta, 50 yrs. Recip., marble plaque from Gov. Nelson Rockefeller of N.Y. & Pres. Richard Nixon for volunteer servs. to re-elect the Pres., 1972.

Address: Villa du Lac Apts., 525 Villa Lane, St. Clair Shores, MI 48080, U.S.A. 130.

WILCOX, Eleanor Larmour Reindollar (Mrs. George C. Wilcox, Jr.), b. 23 Feb. 1915. Artist; Writer. Educ: Dip., Md. Inst. of Fine & Applied Arts; Study toward M.F.A.; Courses at McCoy Coll., Johns Hopkins Univ., Loyola Coll., Community Coll. of Balt. Appts: Exhibs. Asst., Enoch Pratt Free Lib., 1937-41; Staff Artist, Assoc. Curator, Am. Ethnol., Lectr. & Film Libn., Md. Acad. of Sci., 1941-46; Assoc., Wilcox & Wilcox, Indl. Illustrators & Museums Unlimited, 1946-; Libn., Receptionist, Sec., Alumni Ed., etc., Park Schl. of Balt., 1954-67. Mbrships: Sec., Dorchester Community Assn.; Mtn. Club of Md.; Nat. Geographic Soc.; Smithsonian Instn. Publs: The Cornhusk Doll, 1956; Mr. Sims' Argosy, 1958; Contbr. to periodicals; Ed., News Letter of Archeol. Soc. of Md. Hons: Libn.'s Award, for Cornhusk Doll, 1955. Address: 4006 Liberty Heights Ave., Baltimore, MD 21207, U.S.A. 5, 128.

WILDER, Frederica W., b. 23 July 1909. Educator. Educ: B.A., Univ. of Ariz., Tucson; M.A., Tchrs. Coll., Columbia Univ., N.Y.C.; Grad. Work at Univ. of Calif., Univ. of S.C., Univ. of Ill., Univ. of Ariz., Stanford Univ. & Columbia Univ. Appts. incl: Elem. Classroom Tchr., Douglas Pub. Schls., 1929-37; Jr. H.S. Tchr., Tucson Pub. Schls., 1937-43 & 1946-50; Off., U.S. Marine Corps Women's Reserve, H.Q. Marine Corps, Wash. D.C., 1943-46; Elem. Schl. Prin., Tucson Pub. Schls., 1950-65, Asst. Supt. for Elem. Educ., 1965-73 & for Educl. Progs., K-12, 1973-. Mbrships. incl: Past Pres., Altrusa Club, Tucson, Ariz.; Comp. & Int. Educ. Soc.; Am. Assn. of School Admin.; Assn. for Supervision & Curric. Dev.; Nat. Assn. of Elem. Schl. Prins.; Ariz. Assn. of Elem. Schl. Admin., Past Pres., Nat. Educ. Assn.; Ariz. Educ. Assn.; Pi Beta Phi Alumnae Club. Valedictorian of Sr. Class, Douglas H.S., 1925. Address: 4417 La Jolla Circle, Tucson, AZ 85711, U.S.A. 5.

WILDER, Thomas Clinton, Jr., b. 14 July 1930. Funeral Director. Educ: Grad., Cinn. Coll. of Mortuary Sci., Ohio, 1955; Dept. of Ophthalmol., Univ. of Fla., 1971, 1974. Embalmer License, 1956 & Funeral Dir. License, 1957, State of Fla. Appts. incl: Self-employed Funeral Dir. Mbrships: Pi Sigma Eta, Chap., 1955; New Smyrna Beach Rainbow for Girls Advsry. Bd., 1971-; New Smyrna Beach Chmbr. of Comm., Pres., 1965-66, Pres. Elect, 1974; New Smyrna Beach Lions Club, Pres., 1970-71, 1971-72; Am. Red Cross, Volusia Co. Chapt., Bd. Dirs., 1962-69; Chmn., Red Cross Blood Bank, 1962-69; Salvation Army, New Smyrna Beach Unit, Treas., 1968-70, Dir., 1968-; Vis. Nurse Assn., Charter Mbr., Dir. & Treas., 1966-; United Fund Drive Chmn., 1969; 1st Meth. Ch., Chmn., Official Bd., 1966; Fla. Funeral Dirs. Assn., Legislative Comm., 1973; New Smyrna Lodge 149, Free & Accepted Masons; Bahia Shrine Temple, New Smyrna Chapt. 3, Order of Eastern Star. Hons. incl: State of Fla. Gov.'s Award for Outstanding Accomplishments in Tourism Promotion, 1965. Address: P.O. Box 819, New Smyrna Beach, FL 32069, U.S.A. 125.

WILENSKY, Alvin, b. 3 Nov. 1921. Certified Public Accountant. Educ: B.A., Pa. State Univ., U.S.A., 1943. Appts. incl: Bombardier-Navigator, 1st Lt., USAF, 1943-45; Sr. Acct., Alberts, Kahn & Levess, N.Y.C., 1945-48; Pvte. Prac., Scranton, Pa., 1948-72; Acctng. Instr., Keystone Jr. Coll., 1950-51; Cons., Leidigh & Bisbano, Scranton, 1973-; Comptroller, Cedar Lane Bowling Stadium, Inc., 1959-68; V.P., Finance, Cenvill Communities, Inc., W. Palm Beach, Fla., 1973-;

Pres., Gerald Data Ctr., Inc., Palm Beach, Fla., 1973-. Mbrships. incl: Am. Inst. of Cert. Pub. Accts.; Sev. comms., Pa. Inst. of Cert. Pub. Accts.; Chmn., Bd. of Trustees, Ins. Trust; Past Treas. & Dir., Glen Oak Country Club; Past Pres., Keystone Jr. Coll. Alumni Assn.; Past Financial Sec. & Dir., Temple Israel, Scranton; Mayor's Tax Study Comm., Scranton; Past Cmdr., Post 165, Jewish War Veterans. Hons. incl: Air Medal with 5 Oak Leaf Clusters, USAF, 1944-45; Cert. of Outstanding Serv., Jewish War Veterans of U.S.A., 1960; Devoted Serv. Award, Boy Scouts of Am., 1967. Address: 1723 Consulate Pl., W. Palm Beach, FL 33401, U.S.A. 6.

WILES, Lucile (A), b. 16 Oct. 1914. Kindergarten Teacher. Educ: B.S. in Ed., Omaha Univ., 1962; M.S. in Ed., Univ. of Neb. at Omaha, 1969. Appts: Rural Schl. Tchr., 6th & 7th Grades; Kindergarten Tchr., last 16 yrs. in Omaha. Mbrships: Pianist, Liberty United Meth. Ch. & 'Janice's Dance Studio, Plattsmouth, Neb.; Past Pres., Gamma Chapt. & Neb. State Pres., Alpha Delta Kappa; Neb. State Treas. & Past. Pres. of Pi Conclave, Kappa Kappa Iota; Corres. Sec. of Nu, Phi Delta Gamma; ACEI, Classroom Tchrs.; NSEA; NEA; OEA; Metro. Reading Coun; State Life Mbr., PTA. Address: Rte. 2, Plattsmouth, NB 68048, U.S.A. 57, 120, 130, MCL.

WILEY, Autrey Neil. Teacher; Administrator; Researcher; Writer. Educ: B.A., Tex. Woman's Univ., 1922; M.A., Columbia Univ., 1924; Sumer courses, var. univs.; Ph.D., Univ. of Tex., Austin, 1931; Post-doctoral fellowship in Humanities, Am. Coun. of Learned Socs., 1932-33. Appts: Instr., Engl., Tex. Woman's Univ., 1922-23; Asst. Prof., ibid, 1924-31; Assoc. Prof., 1931-39; Prof., 1939-71; Chmn. of Dept., 1948-71; Dean, Coll. of Arts & Scis., 1960-71; Retd., 1971. Mbrships. incl: Jt. Ed., Am. Newsletter, Modern Humanities Rsch. Assn., 1965-71; Chmn., Engl. VII, Sect. on 18th century, MLA of Am., 1952; Pres., Conf. of Coll. Tchrs. of Engl., 1951-52; Hon. mbr., ibid, 1972; Fellowship Awards Comm., AAUW, 1944-49. Publs. incl: Handbook for Directors of NDEA Institutes (co-author), 1966; Preparation & Certification of Teachers of English: A Bibliography 1950-56 (NCTE) w. annual supplements in Coll. Engl. to 1966; Articles in jrnls. Recip. of hons. Address: 110 W. College Ave., Denton, TX 76201, U.S.A. 2, 5, 7, 11, 13, 79, 125, 128.

WILFORD, Walton Terry, b. 27 Sept. 1937. Economist. Educ: B.B.A., Southern Meth. Univ., 1958; Ph.D., ibid, 1964. Appts: Asst. Prof., Econs., Univ. of Ga., 1962-63, Univ. of Idaho, 1963-65; Asst. Econ. Advsr. to Bolivia, U.S. Dept. of State, Agcy. for Int. Dev., 1966; Econ. Advsr. & Hd., Econs. Sect., A.I.D., LaPaz, Bolivia, & Advsr. to Bolivian Tax Reform Commn., 1966; Monetary-Fiscal Advsr., Agcy. for Int. Dev. Regional Off. for Central Am. & Panama, Guatemala City, 1967; Assoc. Prof. & Coord., Grad. Studies, La. State Univ., New Orleans, 1968-72; Prof., Econs. & Finance, ibid, 1970-; Chmn., Dept. of Econs. & Finance, 1972-. Mbrships. incl: Am. Econ. Assn.; Southern Econ. Assn.; Financial Mgmt. Assn.; Omicron Delta Epsilon. Author of articles in field. Recip. of hons. Address: Dept. of Econs. & Finance, Univ. of New Orleans, New Orleans, LA, 70122, U.S.A. 7, 14.

WILHELMSEN, Hans Richard, b. 27 Mar. 1929. Plastic, reconstructive & hand surgeon. Educ: D.D.S., Schl. of Dentistry, Univ. of Md., 1955; M.D., ibid, 1959; Internship, Mercy Hosp., Balt., Md., 1959-60; Gen. surg. res., Univ. of Md., Balt., 1960-63; Plastic surg. res.,

Univ. of Pitts., Pa., 1963-65. Appts: Asst. Prof. in Surg., Univ. Hosp.; Cons., State of Md., Div. of Crippled Childrens Servs., w. regular clins. in Anpls., Salisbury & Frederick; Cons., ibid, Chronic Hosp. Div., Montebello State Hosp. Paraplegic Rehab. Prog.; Chmn., Cleft Palate Evaluation Ctr., James Lawrence Kernan Hosp. Mbrships. incl: Fellow, Am. Coll. of Surgs., 1968; Dipl., Am. Bd. of Plastic Surg., 1967; Am. Soc. of Maxillofaxial Surgs.; Am. Soc. for Aesthetic Plastic Surg.; Am. Soc. of Plastic & Reconstructive Surgs.; Am. Cleft Palate Assn.; Am. Soc. for Surg. of the Hand; AMA; Am. Dental Assn. Address: St. Joseph Profl. Bldg., 7401 Osler Dr., Balt., MD 21204, U.S.A.

WILKE, Irene M., (née Snyder), b. 13 Nov. 1911. Executive Director—Housing. Educ: Kearney State Coll., Neb. Appts: Tchr., York Co., Neb.; Exec. Dir., Ravenna Housing, Neb. Mbrships: Neb., Fed. Woman's Club; Past-Sec., ibid; Crafts Chmn., ibid; Past-Pres., Dist. 6, ibid; Sec., G.I. Unit of Parliamentarians; Am. Legion Aux.; Dorcas Soc.; Past-Pres., Girl Scout Coun.; Girl Scout Ldr., 20 yrs.; Advsr., Youth Coun., for 18 yrs.; Sunday Schl. Tchr.; Fed. Garden Club; Sec., Bowling Assn.; Coach, Jr. Bowlers. Hons: Girl Scout Thanks Badge, 1960; Aksarben Good Neighbor, 1968. Address: 313 Buell Ave., Ravenna, NB 68869, U.S.A.

WILKERSON, John P., b. 7 Nov. 1918. Lawyer. Educ: Yale Univ. (ATCS), Engrng.; LL.B., Coll. of Law, Stetson Univ.; Univ. of Ga. Appts: Capt., USAF, Engrng.; Pvte. Prac., Law, 1949-; Municipal Judge, Eustis, Fla.; Atty., Tavares. Mbrships: Dir., Stetson Lawyers Assn., Stetson Coll. of Law, St. Pete, Fla; Nat. Bd. Dirs., Am. Security Coun.; Pres., Lake-Sumter Bar Assn.; Fla., State of Ga., 5th Judicial Circuit & Am. Bar Assns.; Past Pres., Eustis Rotary Club; Shrine, Elks Club; Mason; Judge Advocate, Am. Legion; York Rite; Fndng. Mbr., Nat. Hist. Soc. Address: Suite 2, Profl. Bldg., Eustis, FL 32726, U.S.A. 7, 57, 131.

WILKINS, Henry, III, b. 4 Jan. 1930. Associate Professor of Political Science. Educ: B.A., Agric., Mech. & Normal Coll., 1957; Univ. of Ark., Fayetteville, 1958; M.A., Atlanta Univ., Ga., 1962; Univ. of Pitts., 1966. Appts: Asst. Prof., Pol. Sci., Agric. Mech. & Normal Coll., 1959-66, Urban Affairs, Univ. of Pitts., 1966-67; Dir., Coop. Coll. Dev. Prog., N.Y.C.; Assoc. Prof., Pol. Sci. & Dir., Dev., Univ. of Ark., Pine Bluff, 1968-; Elected Ark. State Rep., Dist. 54, 1972-. Mbrships: Am. Pol. Sci. Assn.; Int. Benevolent Protective Order of Elks of World; Omega Psi Phi. Publs: Some Aspects of the Cold War, 1945-50, 1963; rsch. papers. Hons. incl: Pol. Achievement Award. Address: 303 N. Maple St., Pine Bluff, AR 71601, U.S.A. 114, 125.

WILKINS, William Richard, b. 3 Nov. 1933. Bonded Tax Consultant-Accountant. Educ: Univ. of Okla., 1951; LaSalle Ext. Univ., 1952-53; A.A., Columbia Basin Coll., 1959. Appts: w. USAF, 1951-55; Payroll Analyst, G.E. Co., 1955-58; self employed Bonded Tax Cons. & Acct., League of Am.; Professional Poets; World Poets; Modern Poets; United Poets; Fellow, IBA; V.F.W. Chmbr. of Comm. Publs: A Whisper in the Wind, 1962; Something Personal, 1974; publd. over 200 times during 1969-73 in var. poetry mags. & anthols. Recip. Korean Serv. Medal & UN Serv. Medal. Address: 331 W. Bonneville, Pasco, WA 99301, U.S.A. 139.

WILKINSON, E.J., b. 1 Mar. 1920. Chartered Engineer. Educ: Univ. H.S., Melbourne, Australia; Melbourne Tech. Coll.

Appts: Sr. Airways Engr., Dept. of Civil Aviation; Divisional Engr., Australian P.O. HQ; Sectional Engr., ibid; Asst. Dir. Gen. (Radio); Dir. of Tech. Servs., Australian Broadcasting Control Bd., Melbourne. Mbrships: Kelvin Club, Melbourne; Victorian Football League; Australia Japan Soc.; Rostrum Club. Contbr. to: Proceedings of the Instn. of Radio & Electronics Engrs., Australia; Jrnl. of Instn. of Engrs., Australia; Telecommunication Jrnl. of Australia; Australian Telecommunication Rsch. Address: Australian Broadcasting Control Bd., 570 Bourke St., Melbourne, Vic., Australia 3000.

WILKINSON, Nana Miriam. Realtor. Appts. incl: Sec., Pres.' Off., Depauw Univ., Greencastle, Ind., 1935-37; Exec. Sec., V.P., Beach & Arthur Paper Co. of Ind., Pa. & N.Y.C., 1937-45; Realtor, Henry B. Trachy Real Estate Agcy., Franklin, N.H., 1970-. Mbrships. incl: Life Mbr., Nat. Coun. State Gdn. Clubs, Inc., Parliamentarian, New England Region, 1965-67; Bd. Dirs., 1967-69, Treas., New Engld. Regional Symposium & Chmn., New Engld. Regional Youth Activities, 1969-71, New Engld. Region Nominating Comm. Mbr., 1971-73; V. Chmn., Conven., Nat. Coun. State Gdn. Clubs, Inc., 1973-74; held sev. offs., N.H. Fedn. of Gdn. Clubs, Inc.; Repubn. Rep., N.H. State Legislature (Gen. Ct.) Dist. 3, Belknap Co., 1970-72; mbr. sev. State Govt. Comms. & Commns.; former mbr. Bd. Trustees, Chmn., Music Comm., Tilton Congl. Ch., 1971-: Nat. Assn. of Women Legislators, 1970-; Nat. Assn. & N.H. Assn. Real Estate Bds., 1972-; Lakes Region Assn. & Nat. Inst. of Real Estate Brokers, 1972-, Women's Coun., NIREB, 1972-. Hons: Presl. Citation & Order of Purple Finch (Outstanding Woman of the Yr.), N.H. Fedn. of Garden Clubs, 1970. Address: Calef Hill Rd., Tilton, NH 03276, U.S.A. 5, 114, 132, 138.

WILLARD, Isabel Sims (Mrs. William Grant Willard, Jr.), b. 29 Dec. 1910. Oil Company Director. Educ: B.A., Converse Coll., 1932; Courses I-V, Nat. Coun. (of State Gdn. Clubs) Judging Schls., 1948, '49 & '50. Appts: Dir., Willard Oil Co., 1953-; Mbr., Exec. Comm., ibid, 1967-71; Dir. i/c of beautification, recreation & hlth., 1969-. Mbrships. incl: Chmn., Travellers Aid Volunteers, 43-50, Travellers Aid Bd., 1945-50, Advsry. Comm., Travellers Aid, 1965-70; V.P., 1959-60, 67-68, Sec., 1961-62, Georgia Cleveland Home for Aged Ladies; Music Fndn. Bd., 1959-66; Task Force, Bicentennial Celebration, Appalachian Coun. of Govts., 1974-81; Pres., Gdn. Study Club, 1949-50, & Reviewers Book Club, 1935-36 & 45-46; Nat. Accredited Mbr., Judges Club of S.C., 1957-67; Nat. Soc. & State Bd., 1959-70, Colonial Dames of Am.; Regent from S.C., Bd. of Regents, Gunston Hall, Lorton, Va., 1966-79; Thursday Study Club, 1957-; Ikebana Int., 1960-65; Spartanburg Country Club; Piedmont Club of Spartanburg. Winner of awards for flower arrangement. Address: Box 3000 Spartanburg, SC 29302, U.S.A. 5.

WILLAUER, William Richard, b. 14 Jan. 1894. Company Executive; Designer. Educ: Wofford Coll., Spartanburg, S.C. Appts: Gen. Mgr., Quality Ice Cream Co., Spartanburg, 1913-24; Pres., Marathon Mills Inc., Wis., 1924-28; Design Engr., Willauer Paper Box Co., Spartanburg, 1928-34, Pres. & Owner, 1935-53; Admnstr., Ruth Orvin Christian Schl. Inc., 1970-72. Mbrships: Nat. Assn. of Manufacturers; Masonic Order (Shriner), Elder, Presby. Ch.; Int. Assn. Musical Instrument Collectors; Bd., Colony of Mercy & Grace Homes, Boone N.C., Southern Presby. Jrnl.,

Weaverville. Address: P.O. Box 622, Sullivan's Island, SC 29482, U.S.A.

WILLEE, Albert William, b. 8 Mar. 1916. Educator; Researcher. Educ: B.A., Dip. Phys. Ed., London, U.K.; B.Ed., Melbourne, Australia; Ph.D., M.S., Ore., U.S.A. Appts. incl: Asst. Master, King Edward VI, Nuneaton, 1939-40; w. Royal Navy, 1940-46; Lt. Cmdr., RANR, 1950-63; Lectr., London Univ., U.K., 1947-50; Melbourne Univ., Australia, 1950-; Dir., Phys. Educ., ibid, 1963-. Mbrships. incl: Exec. Comm., Int. Coun. Hlth., Phys. Educ. & Recreation, 1964-; V.P., Int. Fedn. of Phys. Educ. & Recreation, 1971; Phys. Educ. Assn., G.B. & N. Ireland; Coun., Exec. Comm., Nat. Fitness Coun., Vic., 1965-; Life, Australian Phys. Educ. Assn.; Corres. Fellow, Am. Acad. of Phys. Educ.; Chmn., Vic. Br., Ergonomics Soc. of Australia & N.Z. Inc. Publs. incl: Playground Games for Secondary Boys (co-author), 1954; Small Apparatus for Primary School Physical Education, 1955; Dynamic Football—A Guide to Fitness, 1967; Ed., Australian Jrnl. of Phys. Educ., 1954-62, 1965-; Contbr. to Victorian Year Book Centenary Edition, 1973. Recip., Offs. Volunteer Reserve Decoration, 1962. Address: 24 Belgravia Ave., Box Hill N., Vic., Australia 3129. 23.

WILLIAMS, Albert W., b. 25 July 1902. Insurance Company Executive. Appts: Fndr., 1928; Sec. until 1938, Pres., 1938-62, Unity Mutual Life Ins. Co., Ill.; Co. consolidated w. N.C. Mutual Life Ins. Co., Durham, 1962; Chmn., Bd. of Dirs., N.C. Mutual Life Ins. Co., 1965-; One of Organizers & Mbr., Bd. of Dirs., Ill. Fed. Savings & Loan Assn., 1936-; Currently Pres., ibid, Pres., Funeral Dir., Unity Funeral Parlors, Inc. Mbrships: Chicagoans (Pres., 1967-68); Scufflers; Original 40 Club; Nomads; Past, Chgo. Civil Serv. Commn.; Chgo. Assn. Commerce & Ind.; Bd. of Dirs. Chgo. Urban League; var. past offs., YMCA; Sigma Pi Phi; St. Edmund's Episc. Ch. (Pres., Men's Club, 1971-72). Hons incl: LL.D., Allen Univ., 1958; Man of Yr. Award, Original 40 Club, Chgo., 1962; Disting. Serv. Award, Jt. Negro Appeal, 1971; Citation, U.S. Treasury Dept., W.W.II. Address: 4114 S. Michigan Ave., Chgo., IL 60653, U.S.A. 8.

WILLIAMS, Anita T.J.L., b. 5 Jan. 1896. Civic Worker. Educ: B.S., A.M., Vanderbilt Univ. Appts: Chmn., Steering Comm., State Legislative Coun. of Tenn. Women; State Pres., Tenn. League of Women Voters, 1925-29; Hon. Life Regent, DAR, 1934-. Mbrships. incl: Fellow, Inst. of Am. Geneal.; Nat. League of Am. Pen Women (var. offs., inclng. State Pres., Tenn., 1954-56, '72-74; Nat. Registra., 1974-76); Tenn. Fedn. Woman's Clubs (var. offs. inclng. State V.P., 1968-70; State Fine Arts Dept., 1974-76); Centennial Club of Nashville; NSDAR; NSUSD. 1812; Hon. Life Pres., Tenn. Women's Press & Authors, 1969-; Advsry. Bd., Poetry Soc. of Tenn., 1972-; Outlook Nashville, 1965-75; Delta Delta Delta; Chi Delta Phi. Publs. incl: Contbr. of material to Compendium of Am. Genealogy, 1935-38; Ed., var. genealogical volumes, 1973. Recip. of Citation for Outstanding Contbns. to Am. Community, Am. Honorarium, 1966; 2 Citations, Nat. League Am. Pen Women, 1974. Address: 746 Benton Ave., Nashville, TN 37204, U.S.A. 2, 5, 22, 57.

WILLIAMS, Bert, b. 19 Aug. 1930. Writer. Appts: Elem. Schl. Tchr. & Libn., Scarborough, Ont., educl. system, 21 yrs. Mbrship: Fndng. Ed., R III, Jrnl. of Richard III Soc. of Canada. Publs: Food for the Eagle, 1970; Master of Ravenspur, 1970; The Rocky Mountain Monster, 1972; Num. articles in histl., educl.

jrnls.; Humor, poetry, TV writing & performing. Address: Muirhead Rd., Apt. 504, Willowdale, Ont., Canada.

WILLIAMS, Celia Ann. Writer; Traveller; Lecturer. Educ: B.A., Southwestern Mo. State Univ.; Grad. work, Tufts Univ., Univ. of Mo., Univ. of Mich. & Univ. of Wash.; Studies in Italy, U.K., Germany, Switzerland, France, Greece, Asia Minor & N. Africa. Tchr. of Latin, secondary schls., Mo., 27 yrs. Mbrships: Nat. League of Am. Pen Women, Inc.; Archaeological Inst. of Am. Author of papers publd. in Classical Jrnl. & Engl. Jrnl.; Lectr. on tchng. of Latin at confs. Lects. in cassettes illustrated w. slides incl: The Historical Background & influence of the cult of Apollo Worship; Nero—The Singing Emperor; Artemis—Goddess of the Moon. Lects. illustrated w. slides incl: Unusual Gardens; Historical Bridges; Gateways & Doorways. Address: Mar-Bar Springs, Route 2, Box 88, Republic, MO 65738, U.S.A. 57.

WILLIAMS, Charles Ashley, b. 8 Nov. 1929. Minister; Educator. Educ: Georgetown Coll.; B.D., Th.M. & Th.D., Luther Rice Sem. Appts: Pastor, Oakland Bapt. Ch., Sparta, Ky.; Toomsboro Bapt. Ch., Ga.; Venetia Terrace, Bapt. Ch., Jacksonville, Fla.; Wingate Rd. Bapt. Ch., Jacksonville; Dean, Guided Studies, Ext. Studies & of Sem., Luther Rice Sem. Publs: John's Three Love Letters; Moonlighting Ministers; Look Out, Brother. Address: 1050 Hendricks Ave., Jacksonville, FL 32207, U.S.A. 125.

WILLIAMS, Charles Edward, b. 16 June 1935. Educator. Educ: B.S., Winston-Salem State Univ.; M.A., Seton Hall Univ.; F.A.Ed.D., ADM Supvsn.; Prof. Dip., Newark State Coll. Appts: Tchr., Newark Pub. Schls., N.J.; Coord.-Supvsr., Piscataway Township Pub. Schls., N.J.; Dir., Pupil Personnel Servs., Orange Pub. Schls., N.J.; Asst. Supt., Jersey City Pub. Schls., N.J. Mbrships: Phi Delta Kappa; Nat. & N.J. Assns. of Pupil Personnel Servs.; N.J. Educators of the Mentally Retarded; Coun. for Exceptional Children; N.J. Assn. for Schl. Psychols. Publs. incl: Curriculum Outlines—Trainable Mentally Retarded, Educable Mentally Retarded, Neurologically Impaired &, Emotionally Disturbed; P.D.T. Colors 4+ System for Neurologically Impaired Children (co-author); Kingergarten Screening Procedure for Urban Children. Hons: Outstanding Young Educator of Yr., N.J. Jaycees, 1969; Bamberger's Names in the News Portrait Gall. Address: 28 Clark St., Iselin, NJ 08830, U.S.A.

WILLIAMS, Coleridge A., b. 19 Aug. 1923. Barrister-at-Law. Educ: B.A., Morgans State Coll., Balt., Md., U.S.A.; Utter Barrister, Grays Inn, London, U.K., 1958. Appts: Formerly, V.P., Union Printery Ltd., Mbr. of Law Reform Comm. & Chmn., Archts. Appeals Comm.; Acting magistrate, Justice of the Peace, Acting Registrar of the Supreme Ct., 1969. Mbrships: Progressive Group; Comm. for Universal Adult Suffrage; Pub. Info. Off., Bermuda Democratic Pty.; Bermuda Bar Assn.; Pres., Kiwanis Club, Hamilton, 1972-73. Recip., Cert. & medal of hon., 1971. Address: P.O. Box 1155, Hamilton 5, Bermuda.

WILLIAMS, Donald Birtall, b. 14 Oct. 1920. Agricultural College Director. Educ: Univ. of Sydney, 1938-41; B.Sc.Agr., ibid; B.Comm., Univ. of Melbourne; Univ. of Ill., U.S.A., 1948-51; Ph.D., ibid. Appts: w. Bur. of Agricl. Econs., 1951-57; Off.-i/c, Agricl. Rsch. Liaison CSIRO, 1957-63; Vis. Prof., Agricl. Econs., Dir., Agricl. Ext., Univ. of Melbourne,

1964-70; w. Dept. Primary Ind., Canberra, 1972-74; Dir., Roseworthy Agricl. Coll., 1974-. Mbrships: Fellow, Aust. Inst. of Agricl. Sci. Publs: Fifty Years of Farm Management (w. H.C.M. Case), 1957; Agricultural Extension, 1968; other books & papers in sci. jrnls. relating to Agric. & Agricl. Econs. Hons; Ph.D. Thesis Award, Am. Farm Econs. Assn., 1950. Address: Roseworthy Agricl. Coll., Roseworthy, S.A., Australia 5371. 23.

WILLIAMS, Donald Dean, b. 23 Sept. 1930. Former Teacher; Antique Dealer in Fine Glass. Educ: B.S. in Educ., Mo. State Univ.; M.A. in Admin., ibid. Appts: Teacher, 1949-64. Address: 2753 North Court, Ottumwa, IA 52501, U.S.A.

WILLIAMS, Elizabeth Janes (Mrs. M.M.L. Williams), b. 21 May 1908. Artist; Art Teacher; Poet. Educ: B.A., B.F.A., Univ. of Mo.; M.A., Univ. of Okla.; 3 dips., Fontainbelau Schl. of Fine Arts, France; Slade Schl. of Art, London. Appts: Asst., Art Dept., La. State Univ., Okla. Univ.; Tchr., Okla. City Univ. Mbrships: Delta Delta Delta; Delta Phi Delta; AAUW; Okla. Artists; Poetry Soc. of Okla.; Ars Poetica of Neb.; Nat. Fedn. of State Poetry Socs. Exhibs: One man shows incl: Paris; Art Ctr., Okla. City, 1955; Edmond Lib., Okla., 1970. Works also exhibd. at: N.Y. Nat. Acad. of Design; Nouveau Art Salon, Paris; Assn. of Okla. Artists. Mural: Peekskill H.S., N.Y., French House, Univ. of La., Okla. State Histl. Bldg. Poetry: Poetry mags. & anthols. Recip., sev. award for paintings & poetry. Address: 10018 N. Western Ave., Oklahoma City, OK 73114, U.S.A. 11, 37.

WILLIAMS, Ernest Going, b. 24 Sept. 1915. Executive Vice President. Educ: B.S., Univ. of Ala., 1938. Appts. incl: Asst. to Treas., Univ. of Ala., 1938-42, 1945-48; USN, 1942-45, retired as Lt.; Treas., Univ. of Ala., 1948-56; V.P., Dir., 1st Nat. Bank of Tuscaloosa, Ala., 1956-58; V.P., Treas., Gulf States Paper Corp., Tuscaloosa, Ala., 1958-62; Exec. V.P., ibid, 1962-65; V.Chmn., Exec. Staff, ibid, 1965-. Mbrships: former Pres., Assocd. Inds. of Ala.; former Pres., Gtr. Tuscaloosa Chmbr. of Comm.; former Pres., Jaycees of Tuscaloosa; former Pres., Tuscaloosa Co. YMCA former Pres., Univ. Club, Inc., Tuscaloosa; former Pres., Tuscaloosa Exchange Club; former Pres., United Fund of Tuscaloosa Co.; former Chmn., Bd. Dirs., Tuscaloosa Co. Chapt., Am. Red Cross; Newcomen Soc. of N. Am.; Univ. Club, Jacksonville, Fla.; River Club, Jacksonville; Dir. & Mbr., Indian Hills Country Club, Tuscaloosa; Dir. & Mbr., N. River Yacht Club, Tuscaloosa; former Nat. Off., Kappa Alpha Order; Omicron Delta Kappa. Hons: Citizen of Yr., Tuscaloosa Co., 1973. Address: Gulf States Paper Corp., P.O. Box 3199, Tuscaloosa, AL 35401, U.S.A.

WILLIAMS, Eugene F., b. 22 Apr. 1919. Clergyman; Professor. Educ: B.A., Johnson Bible Coll., Kimberlin Hts., Tenn., 1942; B.A., Hardin-Simmons Univ., Abilene, Tex., 1965; M.A., ibid, 1967; Ph.D., Tex. Christian Univ., Ft. Worth, Tex., 1972. Appts: Min., Bethesda Christian Ch., Ohio, 1942-45; Chap., USAF, retd. Lt. Col., 1945-66; Min., Eastland Christian Ch., Tex., 1966-72; Asst. Prof., Hist., Mackinac Coll., Mackinac Island, Mich., 1972-73; Min., Bridgeport Community Ch., Mich., 1973-. Mbrships: F & AM Lodge, Hazen 251, Bethesda, Ohio; Eastland Chapt. 280, Tex., Order of Eastern Star; Scottish Rite, Albany, Ga.; Retd. Offs.' Assn. Recip. of mil. awards. Address: 3815 State St., Bridgeport, MI 48722, U.S.A.

WILLIAMS, Evan James, b. 13 Apr. 1917. Statistician. Educ: B.Com., Univ. of Tasmania, Australia, 1938; D.Sc., Univ. of Melbourne, 1954. Appts: Res. Off.-Prin. Res. Off., Div. of Math. Statistics, CSIRO, Melbourne, 1940-56; Prof., Statistics, Univ. of N.C., Raleigh, N.C., U.S.A., 1956-58; Sr. Prin. Res. Off., CSIRO, Canberra, Australia, 1960-63; Prof., Univ. of Melbourne, 1964-. Mbrships. incl: Int. Statistical Inst., 1954-; Fellow, Inst. of Math. Statistics, 1956-; Royal Statistical Soc., 1950-. Author of Regression Analysis, 1959. Address: Univ. of Melbourne, Parkville, Vic., Australia, 3052. 23.

WILLIAMS, Frederick D., b. 13 May 1918. Historian. Educ: B.A., Middlebury Coll., Vt., U.S.A., 1947; M.A., Univ. of Conn., Storrs, 1948; Ph.D., Ind. Univ., Bloomington, 1953. Appts: Instr., Wayne State Univ., Detroit, Mich., 1950-54; Asst. Prof. of Hist., Mich. State Univ., E. Lansing, 1954-60; Assoc. Prof., ibid, 1960-68; Prof., 1968-. Mbrships: Am. Histl. Assn.; Org. of Am. Histns.; Mich. Civil War Centennial Commn., 1960-66; Army Advsry. Panel on ROTC Affairs, 1970-; Phi Alpha Theta. Publs: Michigan Soldiers in the Civil War, 1960; Ed., The Wild Life of the Army: Civil War Letters of James A. Garfield, 1964; Co-Ed., The Diary of James A. Garfield, Vols. I-III, 1967-73; Articles & reviews in schol. jrnls; Contbns. to ency. Gave Clarence M. Burton Mem. Lecture, 1960. Address: Dept. of History, Michigan State University, East Lansing, MI 48824, U.S.A. 13.

WILLIAMS, G.A., b. 11 Sept. 1937. Physician. Educ: St. John Cass Coll., London, U.K., 1957-58; St. Mary's Hosp. Med. Schl., Univ. of London, 1958-63; LRCP; MRCS, 1963; M.B., B.S., London, 1963; F.M.C., P.H., Nigeria; M.P.H., Johns Hopkins Univ. Schl. of Hygiene & Pub. Hlth., 1966. Appts: Med. Officer of Hlth., Lagos, Nigeria, 1970-; Assoc. Lectr., Coll. of Med., Univ. of Lagos; Pt. Time Lectr., Dept. of Preventive & Soc. Med., Univ. of Ibadan. Mbrships: Island Club; Ikoyi Club. Contbr. to profl. & other jrnls. Address: Pub. Hlth. Dept., Lagos City Coun., City Hall, Cath. Mission St., Lagos, Nigeria.

WILLIAMS, George Doyne, b. 18 July 1935. Cardiovascular Surgery; Associate Professor of Surgery. Educ: B.A., Hendrix Coll., 1957; M.D. & B.S., Univ. Med. Ctr., 1961; Straight Med. Internship, Duke Univ., Durham, N.C., 1961-62; Gen. Surg. Residency, Univ. Med. Ctr., Little Rock, Ark., 1962-66; Thoracic Surg. Res., ibid, 1968-69. Appts. incl: Res.-Instr. in Surg., Univ. Med. Ctr., Little Rock, Ark., 1965-66; Asst. Prof. of Surg., ibid, 1970; Assoc. Prof. of Surg., ibid, 1972-. Mbrships: Soc. of Univ. Surgs.; Am. Coll. of Surgs.; Soc. of Vascular Surg.; Int. Cardiovascular Soc.; Am. Coll. of Cardiol.; Alpha Omega Alpha, Univ. of Ark. Med. Ctr., 1961; Alpha Epsilon Delta Premedical Hon. Soc., Hendrix Coll., 1954. Author of scientific papers & num. contbns. in med. jrnls. Hons. incl: Buchannan Acad. Key, Univ. of Ark. Med. Ctr., Little Rock, Ark., 1960, 1961; Bronze Star Medal, Meritorious Serv., Repub. of Vietnam, 1967. Address: Dept. of Surg., Univ. Med. Ctr., Little Rock, AR 72201, U.S.A. 117, 125.

WILLIAMS, George Howard, b. 12 Feb. 1918. University President. Educ: A.B., Hofstra Univ., 1939; J.D., N.Y. Univ. Law Schl., 1946; Inst. for Advanced Legal Studies, Univ. of London, U.K., 1959. Appts: Admitted to N.Y. Bar, 1946; Instr. & Prof. of Law, N.Y. Univ. Law Schl., 1948-62; V.P. for Univ. Dev., N.Y. Univ., 1962-66; Exec. V.P. for Planning & Dev.,

ibid, 1966-68; Pres., The American Univ., Wash. D.C., 1968-. Mbrships: Trustee, Fed. City Coun., 1968-; Am. Pol. Sci. Assn.; Am. Bar Assn.; Bd. of Dirs., Nat. Ctr. for Educ. in Pol., 1948-58. Publs: Co-author, Report on Liberal Adult Education (special report to Ford Fndn.); Improving Law Students Understanding of Professional Responsibility, in N.Y. State Bar Bulletin, 1960. Hons: Legion of Merit, Silver Star, U.S. Army, WWII; LL.D. Degrees, Hofstra Univ. & N.Y. Univ., 1969. Address: Office of the President, The American Univ., Washington, DC 20016, U.S.A. 2.

WILLIAMS, George Oga, b. 28 Jan. 1945. Teacher. Educ: B.S., Tougaloo Coll., Tougaloo, Miss., 1966; M.S., Univ. of Miss., Miss., 1968; 30 hrs. beyond M.S., ibid. Appts. incl: Tutor NSF, Univ. of Miss., Summer, 1971; Instr. of Zool. & Gen. Biol., Coahoma Jr. Coll., Clarksdale, Miss., 1968-71; Instr., Univ. of Miss., Spring & Fall Semesters, 1972; Instr. Unified Sci. 558, Fall, 1973; Instr., Biol. & Zool., Anatomy & Physiol., Hinds Jr. Coll., Raymond, Miss.; Advsr. to Black Student Assn.; Mbr., Admissions Commn.; Ptnr., S.O. Williams & Sons, Carthage, Miss., Williams Brothers, Carthage—Jackson, Miss.; Mbr., Bd. Dirs., Colman, Inc., Jackson, Miss.; Agent, Nat. Old Line & United Am. Ins. Cos. Mbrships: AAUP; NEA; Nat. Sci. Tchr.'s Assn.; Nat. Jr. Coll. Fac. Assn.; Miss. Tchr.'s Assn.; Miss. Sci. Tchr.'s Assn.; Miss. Acad. of Scis.; 3rd Dist. Tchr.'s Assn.; Coahoma Co. Tchr.'s Assn.; Hinds Jr. Coll. Educ. Assn.; Alpha Phi Alpha Frat., Chapt. Pres. & purchasing Life Mbrship.; Leake Co. Better Voter's League; Gallilee Missionary Bapt. Ch., 4 yrs. Sunday Schl. Supt. & Tchr. & Asst. Dist. Supt.; K. & P. Watter Assn., Bd. Dirs.; Hon. Mbr., Leake Co. Sheriff's Dept., 1972. Hons. incl: Alpha Phi Alpha Man of Yr. (Miss.), 1974. Address: Route 3, Box 83, Carthage, MS 39051, U.S.A. 117, 125.

WILLIAMS, Giula, b. 6 Dec. 1896. Pianist; Music Educator. Educ: Dip., piano theory, 1926; Grad., Chgo. Musical Coll., 1929; Studied w. Alexander Raab (piano), Percy Grainger (piano), Lillian Powers (piano & pedagogy), & others inclng. Dr. Herbert Witherspoon (voice & appreciation), Dr. William Madison (counterpoint, composition). Appts: Tchr., The Southern Ind. Inst., 1923-26 & 1933-36; Tchr., Thorsby Inst., 1926-28; Tchr., Chgo. Musical Coll., summer schls., 1926-30; Pvte. studio, 33 yrs.; Tchr., Birmingham City Schls., Ala.; Youth Concerts, Southern States. Mbrships: Fac. mbr., Am. Coll. of Musicians; Nat. mbrship. Comm. & Adjudicator, ibid; Chmn., Ala. State Comm. for Certification of Pvte. Music Piano Tchrs., 2 yrs. Compositions incl: Carol Spiritual (sung in Wash. D.C. Cathedral & other chs.); Reflections (piano); The Legend of Sleepy Hollow; Chaconne in A Minor; Menuet in G; March (Happy Hours) in B; The Mischevous Elf. Hons: Alexander Raab Schlrship., 1927; Percy Grainger Schlrship. (Master Classes), 1928. Address: 1914 4th Ave. N., Birmingham, AL 35203, U.S.A.

WILLIAMS, Glanville Llewelyn, b. 15 Feb. 1911. Univeristy Professor. Educ: Univ. Coll. of Wales, Aberystwyth, U.K.; St. John's Coll., Cambridge; LL.D. (Cantab.), 1946. Appts. incl: Rdr. in Engl. Law & successively Prof. of Pub. Law & Quain Prof. of Jurisprudence, Univ. of London, 1945-55; 1st Walter E. Meyer Vis. Rsch. Prof., N.Y. Univ., U.S.A., 1959-60; Charles Inglis Thompson Guest Prof., Univ. of Colo., 1965; Fellow, Jesus Coll., Cambridge, U.K., 1955-; Rdr. in Engl. Law, Univ. of Cambridge, 1957-65; Prof., 1966-; Special Cons. for Am. Law Inst.'s Model Penal Code, 1956-58; Mbr., Criminal Law Revision Comm.,

1959-, Law Commn.'s Working Party on Codification of Criminal Law, 1967-, & Butler Comm. on Mentally Abnormal Offenders, 1972-. Mbrships: Fellow, British Acad.; Fellow, Eugenics Soc.; Pres., Abortion Law Reform Assn. Publs. incl: The Proof of Guilt, 3rd edit. 1963; The Sanctity of Life & the Criminal Law, Am. edit. 1956, Engl. edit. 1958; The Mental Element in Crime, 1965. Hons. incl: Q.C., 1968; LL.D., Univ. of Wales, 1974. Address: Jesus Coll., Cambridge, CB5 8BL, U.K. 1, 3.

WILLIAMS, Jac Lewis, b. 20 July 1918. University Professor. Educ: Univ. Coll. of Wales. Appts: Schl. Tchr., 1942-44; Tech. Coll. Lectr., 1944-45; Tchr. Trng. Coll. Lectr., 1945-56; Advsry. Off., Fac. of Educ., Univ. Coll. of Wales, 1956-60; Prof. of Educ., Dean, Fac. of Educ., ibid, 1961-. Publs: Straeon & Meirw, 1947; Trioedd, 1973; Contbr. to Welsh lang. jrnls.; Radio, TV progs. in Wales; Ed. & Contbr. var. Welsh textbooks, dictionaries. Address: Quebec, Llanbadarn, Aberystwyth, U.K. 3.

WILLIAMS, James H., Jr., b. 4 Apr. 1941. Professor. Educ: S.B., MIT, 1967; S.M., ibid, 1968; Ph.D., Trinity Coll., Cambridge, U.K., 1970. Appts: Sr. Design Engr., Newport News, Va., 1968; Asst. Prof., Mech. Engrng., MIT, 1970-74; Assoc. Prof., ibid, 1974-. Contbr. papers & reports to publs. in field. Hons: du Pont Asst. Prof., 1972-73; Esther & Harold E. Edgerton Asst. Prof., 1973-75; Everett Moore Baker Award, 1973; Ralph R. Teetor Award, 1974; Charles F. Baily Bronze (1961), Silver (1962) & Gold (1963) Medals. Address: Room 3-358, MIT, Dept. of Mech. Engrng., 77 Massachusetts Ave., Cambridge, MA 02139, U.S.A. 130.

WILLIAMS, John Barry, b. 19 May 1928. Dentist. Educ: B.A., Univ. of Tex., 1948; D.D.S., Baylor Dental Coll., 1951. Appts: USAF, 1952-54; Gen. Prac., 1954-. Mbrships: Am. Acad. Operative Dentistry; Soc. Oral Physiol. & Occlusion; Am. Soc. Preventive Dentistry; Am. Dental Assn.; Tex. Dental Assn.; V.P., Austin Dist. Dental Soc., 1965. Address: 17 Medical Arts Sq., Austin, TX 78705, U.S.A. 7.

WILLIAMS, John D. Minister; Educator; Counseling Psychologist. Educ: B.S., Tuskegee Inst., 1946; M.A., N.Y. Univ., 1947; B.Th., Ohio Christian Coll., 1969; Dip., Moody Bible Inst., 1965; Ph.D., Ohio Christian/Southeastern Univ., S.C., 1973; Doct., Coll. of Divine Metaphysics, Ind., 1972; Doctoral Educ., Ky. Christian Univ., 1971; Law Trng. completed by Law Schl./Clerkship. Appts. incl: Tchr., Dept. Chmn., Guidance Counselor, Bur. of Special Educ., Bur. of Educ. Vocational Guidance, Bd. of Educ., N.Y.C., 1951-73; P.R. Coord., Sit. 23, Brooklyn, N.Y.; Guidance Counselor, Aux. Servs. for High Schls., Bd. of Educ., N.Y.C., 1971-72; Dir., Family Counseling Servs., pvte. agcy., N.Y., 1972-; Cons., Hd. Start Prog., United Meth. Ch. City Soc., N.Y.C. Mbrships. incl: Civil Liberties Union; Am. Personnel & Guidance Assn.; N.Y. State Personnel & Guidance Assn.; Life mbr., Alpha Psi Omega; Nat. Chap.'s Assn.; Hon. Fellow, Acad. of Police Sci., 1972. Composer of Music; Author of Poems. Hons. incl: H.H.D., Southeastern Univ., Greenville, S.C., 1973, London Inst. for Applied Rsch., 1973. Address: Family Counseling Servs., 133-140 133rd St., S. Ozone Pk., NY 11420, U.S.A. 125, 130.

WILLIAMS, John Egerton, b. 27 Apr. 1916. Medical Specialist. Educ: Sheffield Univ., U.K.; M.R.C.S., L.R.C.P., London, 1940; Fellow, Fac. of the Royal Australian Coll. of Surgs.,

1956. Appts: Served WWII; Vis. Specialist Anaesthetist, Repatriation Dept., Australia, 1949-55; Asst. Hon. Anaesthetist, Royal Melbourne Hosp., 1949-53; Vis. Specialist, Eye & Ear Hosp., 1950; Vis. Specialist Anaesthetist, Alfred Hosp., 1951; Full-time, Repatriation Dept., 1955-64; Cons., Repatriation Commn. (Anaesthesia), 1964-. Mbrships: Australian Soc. of Anaesthetists; Australian Med. Assn.; Naval & Mil. Club; Royal Melbourne Golf Club. Contbr. of articles to med. jrnls. inclng. Med. Jrnl. of Australia, Jrnl. of the Oto-Laryngological Soc. of Australia. Address: Dept. of Anaesthetics, Repatriation Dept., Gen. Hosp., Heidelberg, Melbourne, Australia, 3077.

WILLIAMS, John P., b. 25 July 1919. Industrial Relations Director. Educ: B.S., Univ. of Mich., Ann Arbor, U.S.A., 1951. Appts: Employment Mgr., King-Seeley Thermos Co., Ann Arbor, Mich., 1950-53; Asst. Personnel Mgr., ibid, 1953-56; Labor Rels. Mgr., 1956-58; Indl. Rels. Mgr., 1958-63; Corporate Indl. Rels. & Personnel Mgr., Butler Mfg. Co., Kansas City, Mo., 1963-66; Dir., Indl. Rels., Mueller Brass Co., Port Huron, Mich., 1966-69; V.P., Indl. Rels., ibid, 1969-. Mbrships. incl: Am. Soc. of Personnel Admins.; Indl. Rels. Rsch. Assn. of Detroit; Pres., Ann Arbor Mfrs. Assn., 1961; Vice Chmn., Labor Advsry. Comm., Copper Dev. Assn., 1973; Bd. of Dirs., Ann Arbor Family Servs., 1956-57; Deleg., Republican State Conven., 1961; Chmn., Indl. Div., Ann Arbor United Fund, 1954. Publs: Num. articles in profl. jrnls. Speaker, var. mgmt. assns. & grps. Address: 2212 Brandywin Lane, Port Huron, MI 48060, U.S.A. 8, 16.

WILLIAMS, Merton Yarwood, b. 21 June 1883. Geologist. Educ: B.Sc., Queens Univ., Kingston, Ont., Canada, 1909; Ph.D., Yale Univ., Conn., 1912. Appts: Tchr., Pub. Schls., Ont., 1903-05; Mbr., Geol. Serv. of Canada, summers, 1905, '09, '21-24; Full Time Mbr., ibid, 1911-20; Fac., Univ. of B.C., 1921-50; Currently, Hon. Prof. Fellowships: 2nd V.P., Geol. Soc. Am., 1946; Hon. Life Mbr., 1958; Charter, Canadian Geog. Soc., 1929. Mbrships: Pres., Royal Soc. Canada, 1960-61; Life, Canadian Inst. Mining & Metallurgy; Hon. Life., Profl. Engrs. B.C. Author of num. publs. in field. Address: 2376 W. 5th Ave., Vancouver, B.C., Canada.

WILLIAMS, Mervyn Oliver, b. 17 Feb. 1929. Naval Officer. Educ: Trng. w. Royal Navy, U.K., 1963-64; In-Serv. Trng., Custom & Excise Law, Navigation, Engl. Law. Appts: Customs Off., H.M. Customs, 1948; 1st Class, 1960; Sr. Customs Off., Grade II, 1960; Transfered to Defence Force, 1962; 1st Lt., H.M.T.S. Trinity; Lt. Cmdr., 1966; Sr. Off. Afloat, 1969; Gen. Staff Off. II to Brig. Gen. Serette, 1970; Exec. Off., Trinidad & Tobago Coast Guard, 1970; Acted in-Cmd. of Coast Guard, 1971-72. Mbrships. incl: V.P., Trinidad Yachting Assn.; Asst. Sec. & Permanent Rep. for Yachting, Trinidad Olympic Assn. Hons. incl: Medal of Merit, Order of Trinity for Defence; num. trophies, cups & medals for competitive yachting; Represented country in yachting in num. int. competitions inclng. Commonwealth Games & Pan Am. Games. Address: Trinidad & Tobago Coast Guard, Staubles Bay, Trinidad, W. Indies. 109.

WILLIAMS, Patricia Parker, b. 27 Jan. 1922. Radio Station Owner; Composer; Pianist. Educ: Univ. of Miss. Appts: Society Ed., Jackson Daily News, Miss., 1943; Women's Dir., Radio Stn. WNNT, Warsaw, Va. & Commentator, daily radio show "Chat with Pat", 1952-60; Pres.-Owner, 1961. Mbrships: Am. Women Radio & TV (Dir., Va. Chap.,

1962-66); Nat. Soc. Arts & Letters (Wash. Chap. Music Chmn.); Nat. Assn. for Am. Conductors & Composers; Wash. Club; Kenwood Country Club; Kenwood Garden Club; Indian Creek Country Club; Windmill Point Yacht Club; Chesapeake Club, Irvington, Va.; Nat. Press Club; Friday Morning Music Club; Nat. Symphony Women's Comm. Compositions: Rhapsody of Youth; Maid of Cotton; Lucky X. Address: 6211 Garnett Dr., Kenwood, Chevy Chase, MD 20015, U.S.A. 5, 7, 85, 125, 132.

WILLIAMS, Peter Frederick, b. 22 Oct. 1922. Orthopaedic Surgeon. Educ: M.B., B.S., Melbourne Univ., Australia, 1946; Fellowship, Royal Coll. Surgs., 1951 & Royal Australasian Coll. Surgs., 1953. Appts. incl: Cons. Orthopaedic Surg., Royal Australian Navy, 1960-; Chief Orthopaedic Surg., Royal Children's Hosp., Melbourne, 1962-; Cons. Orthopaedic Surg., Royal Women's Hosp., 1963-; Cons. Orthopaedic Surg., Mercy Maternity Hosp., 1971-. Mbrships: Censor in Chief, Aust. Orthopaedic Assn., 1966-73; Mbr. Ct. of Examiners, Royal Aust. Coll. Surgs., 1964-74; Fellow, British Orthopaedic Assn.; Corres. Mbr., Am. Orthopaedic Assn. Author of var. publs. in orthopaedic jrnls. Recip. Betts Mem. Medal, Aust. Orthopaedic Assn., 1973. Address: 7 Gawith Ct., Toorak, Melbourne, Australia. 23.

WILLIAMS, Raymond Henry, b. 31 Aug. 1921. University Reader in Drama. Educ: Trinity Coll., Cambridge Univ., U.K.; D.Litt., Cambridge Univ., 1969; Hon. Doct., Open Univ., U.K., 1974. Appts. incl: Adult Educ. Tutor for Oxford Univ. Delegacy for Extra-Mural Studies; Fellow, Jesus Coll. & Rdr. in Drama, Cambridge Univ. Publs. incl: Drama In Performance, 1954; Culture & Society 1780-1950, 1958; Border Country, 1960; The Long Revolution, 1961; Communications, 1962; Second Generation, 1964; Drama From Ibsen To Brecht, 1964; Modern Tragedy, 1966; Public Inquiry, 1967; May Day Manifesto (Ed.), 1968; The English Novel From Dickens To Lawrence, 1970; Orwell, 1971; A Letter From The Country, 1971; The Country & The City, 1973. Address: Jesus Coll., Cambridge Univ., Cambridge, U.K.

WILLIAMS, Roger, Jr., b. 19 Feb. 1920. Chemical Engineering Economist. Educ: A.B., Amherst Coll.; MIT. Appts. incl: w. Ammonia Dept., E.I. Dupont de Nemours, 1941-46; Rsch. Staff Asst., ibid, 1946-48; w. McGraw-Hill Publsng. Co., 1948-50; Fndr., Chmn. of Bd., Roger Williams Tech. & Econ. Serv., Inc., 1950-. Mbrships. incl: Am. Chem. Soc.; Am. Chem. Mkt. Rsch. Assns.; Soc. of Chem. Ind.; Fellow, Am. Inst. Chem. Engrs. & AAAS; Soc. of Plastics Ind.; Soc. de Chimie Ind.; Am. Phys. Soc.; Pres., 1970-72, Assn. of Cons. Chems. & Chem. Engrs.; Phi Gamma Delta; Chems. Club, N.Y.; Am. Club, London; Pres., 1971-72, Int. Trade Dev. Assn., Pa.; Dir., Chemurgic Coun.; Pres., Buckingham Taxpayers Assn.; Buckingham Twp. Planning Commn., 1970-72, V.Chmn., 1970-72, Chmn., Water & Sewer Commn. Publs: Technical Market Research—A Bird's Eye View; The Petrochemical Industry—Markets & Economics (collaborating author). Address: P.O. Box 426, Princeton, NJ 08540, U.S.A. 6, 12, 14, 16, 32, 68, 123.

WILLIAMS, Sarah Joyce Dayvault, b. 31 Mar. 1936. Educator; Reading Clinician. Educ: A.B., Lenoir Rhyne Coll., N.C., U.S.A.; M.A., Appalachian State Univ. Boone, N.C.; Postgrad., Emory Univ., Atlanta, Ga., & Univ. of N.C., Charlotte. Appts: Classroom Tchr. for 16 yrs. Num. mbrships. incl: Past V.P. & Past Sec., N.C. Assn. of Educators; Past Sec., Classroom Assn. of Tchrs.; NEA; Past Pres. & Past Treas., Piedmont Tri-Co. Coun., Int. Reading Assn., Chmn., Nominations & Hospitality; Exec. Bd., N.C. Coun., Int. Reading Assn.; Benton Heights, Monroe Middle Schl., & Monroe H.S. PTA's; N.C. Symph. Orch. Soc.; Past Pres., Wadesboro Jr. Woman's Club; Exec. Bd., Monroe-Union Co. Speech & Hearing Clin.; Union Co. Mental Hlth. Soc.; Beta Club, 1950-54. Publs: Articles in newspapers. Hons. incl: For God & Country Award, 1953; Arion Award for Music, 1954. Address: Hillsdale, Route 7, Box 72, Monroe, NC 28110, U.S.A. 125.

WILLIAMS, Shirley C., b. 22 Aug. 1930. Sculptor. Educ: Art Students League, N.Y.C.; Frank Reilly Schl. of Art, N.Y.C.; Craft Students League, N.Y.C.; John C. Campbell Folk Art Schl., N.C. Mbrships: Fellow, Am. Artists Profl. League; Int. Wood Collectors Soc.; Nat. Wood Carvers Assn.; Am. Forestry Assn.; Northeastern Loggers Assn.; DAR. Exhibs. incl: Catharine Lorillard Wolfe Art Club; Vt. Lumberjack Roundup; Int. Wood Collectors Exhib.; Am. Artists Profl. League Grand Nat.; Work in pub. collects., Northeastern Loggers Exhib. Hall, Old. Forge, N.Y., etc. Contbr. to profl. jrnls. Hons: Hon. Mention, Am. Artists Profl. League, 1972. Address: Box 43, Lake Rd., Rockland Lake, NY 10989, U.S.A.

WILLIAMS, Thelma Mundaugh. Associate Professor. Educ: M.A., Tchrs. Coll., Columbia Univ., N.Y.C., 1946; Ed.D., Yeshiva Univ., N.Y.C., 1963; Grad. Schl., ibid, 1970. Appts. incl: Asst. Supt. of Children's Instns. of N.Y.C., Dept. of Soc. Servs., N.Y.C., 1962-65; Sr. Staff Assoc., Ctr. for Urban Educ., Fed. Rsch. Lab., N.Y., 1966-70; Assoc. Prof., Dept. of Soc. Sci., Educ., Sociol. & Urban Educ., Queensborough Community Coll., CUNY, Bayside, N.Y., 1970-73; Assoc. Prof., Acad. Dev. Div., Educ., Medgar Evers Coll., CUNY, Brooklyn, N.Y., 1973-. Mbrships. incl: Int. Congress, Sociedad Interamericana De Psicologia; Acting V.P. & Resource Cons., Panama City, Panama, 1971, Montevideo, Uruguay, S. America, 1969, Mexico City, D.F., 1967; Mbr. at Large, Greater N.Y. Early Childhood Educ. Coun.; Org. Mondiale pour l'Educ. Prescolaire; Bd. mbr., N.Y. Conf. of United Meth. Ch., Hlth. & Welfare Mins.; Nat. Comm. for the Day Care of Children, N.Y.C.; Centro Cultural Int., Mexico D.F.; Kappa Delta Pi. Author of books & booklets in field. Address: 302 W. 12th St., N.Y., NY 10014, U.S.A. 15, 130, 138.

WILLIAMS, Thomas Earl, b. 21 Oct. 1924. Lawyer. Educ: LL.B., Baylor Univ., 1954, J.D., 1969. Appts: Asst. Criminal Dist. Atty., Collin Co., 1957-59; Asst. Dist. Atty., Dallas Co., 1959-60 & 1964-65; Criminal Dist. Atty., 1960-64; Co. Atty., Henderson Co., 1966; pvte. prac. & City Atty., 1967-. Mbrships: State Bar of Tex.; Henderson Co Bar Assn.; Am. Bar Assn.; Am. Judicature Soc. Address: 900 Ward Lane,, Athens, TX 75751, U.S.A.

WILLIAMS, Vira Kennedy, b. 24 July 1928. Civil Service Commission President. Educ: B.S., Bennett Coll., N.C., 1949; Cert., Boston Univ. Schl. of Med. Technol., 1952; Grad., Schl. of Chem., Howard Univ., Wash. D.C., 1955; M.S., Univ. of Southern Calif., 1961; Calif. Tchng. Credential, 1961. Appts: Med. Technologist, Free Hosp. for Women, Brookline, Mass., 1952-53; Rsch. Asst., Howard Univ. Schl. of Med., 1953-55; Med. Technologist, Guadalupe Clin., San Diego, Calif. 1955-56; Tchr., L.A. pub. schls., 1959-60; Substitute Tchr., San Diego, Calif., 1960-62; Pres., San Diego Civil

Serv. Commn. Mbrships. incl: Trustee, Children's Hlth. Ctr.; Bd. mbr., Salvation Army Door of Hope; Women's Aux., San Diego Med. Soc.; Med. Careers Dir., ibid, 1968-70. Hons. incl: San Diego Woman of Elegance, Salvation Army Aux., 1971; Mbr. of month, Women's Aux., San Diego Med. Soc., 1971. Address: 5740 Daffodil Lane, San Diego, CA 92120, U.S.A. 5.

WILLIAMS, Walter Henry, b. 11 Aug. 1920. Painter; Printmaker; Sculptor. Educ: Brooklyn Mus. Art Schl., 1951-55. Appts: Artist in Res., Fisk Univ., 1968-69; Tchr., Ceramics, evening schl., Copenhagen, Denmark. Mbrship: Terry Ditenfass Gall., N.Y.C. Exhibs: 5 Whitney Mus. Annuals, 1953-63; Int. Watercolor Biennial, Brooklyn Mus., 1963; Corner, Copenhagen, 1963; Pa. Acad. Annual, 1966; 147th Annual, Nat. Acad. of Design, 1972; Kunstindustrimuseet, Copenhagen, 1973. Hons: John Hay Whitney Fndn. Fellowship, 1955; Nat. Inst. of Arts & Letters Grant, 1960; Adolph & Clara Obrig Prize, Nat. Acad. of Design, 1972. Address: Hospitalsvej 4, Copenhagen F2000, Denmark. 37.

WILLIAMS, Warner, b. 23 Apr. 1903. Sculptor; Designer; Lecturer, Educ: Berea Coll., 2½yrs.; S.S., Butler Univ., 1924; Herron Art Inst., 3 yrs.; B.F.A., Art Inst., Chgo. Free-lance sculptor & designer in Chgo., 15 yrs., executing commns. in bronze, marble & other media, memorials, personal portraiture in sculpture; Lect. tour of 100 colls. & clubs, giving demonstrations for convocations, 1935; Artist in Res., Culver Educl. Fndn., 1941-69. Mbr., Nat. Sculpture Soc., Hoosier Salon. Works incl: Murals, Ceramic Bldg., World's Fair, Chgo., 1933; B.B. Culver & E.R. Culver busts & basreliefs, Culver Educl. Fndn.; Maimonides Mem., Univ. of Ill. Schl. of Pharmacy, Univ. of S.D. & Beth-el Hosp., Brooklyn, N.Y.; 3 archbishops, bas-reliefs for Nat. Polish Cath. Ch.; Helen Keller bas-relief, 30 U.S. Schls. for the Blind. Hons. incl: Daughters of Ind. Prize, 1939; Municipal Art League Prize, 1941; Spaulding Prize, 1942. Address: Geodesic Dome Studio, Culver, IN 46511, U.S.A. 8, 37.

WILLIAMS, William James. Educator & Civic Worker. Educ: B.A., Morehouse Coll., 1952; M.P.A., N.Y. Univ. Schl. of Pub. Admin., 1954; Dr. P.A., Univ. of Southern Calif., Schl. of Pub. Admin., 1966. Appts. incl: Assoc. Dir. & Acting Dir., Schl. of Pub. Admin. Ctr., Univ. of Southern Calif., 1955-57; Admnstrv. Advsr., N.Y. State Commn. on Govtl. Ops. of N.Y.C., 1959-60; Rsch., Civil Serv. Unions of Calif., 1960-61; Cons., Calif. State Legislature, 1961-62 & Off. of Econ. Opportunity Panel, Inst. Soc. Sci., San Fran. State Coll., 1966; Congressional Field Dir., U.S. Congress, 1962-66; Dpty. Staff Dir., Equal Employment Opportunity Commn., 1967; Dir., Western Prog., U.S. Commn. Civil Rights, 1967-68. Mbrships. incl: Am. Soc. Pub. Admin.; Int. Soc. Gen. Semantics; Inst. Gen. Semantics; Pres., USC Chapt., 1972, AAUP; Exec. Dir., Negro Pol. Action Assn. of Calif., 1964-66. Publs. incl: Contemporary Papers on Social Change & the Administrative Process; General Semantics & the Social Sciences, 1971; The Outsiders, 1972; Uncommon Sense & Dimensional Awareness, 1972; Collective Bargaining & General Semantics Epistomology. Recip. of many awards. Address: 211 S. Lafayette Pk. Pl., No. 205, Los Angeles, CA 900057, U.S.A. 9.

WILLIAMS, Winton· H., b. 14 Feb. 1920. Civil Engineer. Educ: B.C.E., Univ. of Fla., 1958; Grad., Command & Gen. Staff Coll., Fort Leverworth, Ks, 1963; Logistician, Assoc.

Logistics Exec. Dev. Course, Army Logistics Mgmt. Ctr., Ft. Lee, Va., 1972. Appts. incl: Civil Engr., Hwy., Air Fields & Missile Base Design Engr., U.S. Army Corps of Engrs., 1960-65; Chief, Master Planning & Layout, Jacksonville Dist. Office, ibid, 1965-70; Chief, Master Planning & Real Estate Div., Off. of Engr., U.S. Army Forces, Southern Cmd., Panama Canal Zone, 1970-; Nat. Dir., Univ. of Tampa, U.S.A., 1968-; Col., U.S. Army Corps of Engrs. Reserve, 1970-. Mbrships. incl: Am. Soc. Civil Engrs.; Nat. Soc. Profl. Engrs.; Pres., Dept. of the Canal Zone, Reserve Offs. Assn. of U.S.A, 1974-75; V.P., 1972-73, Pres., 1973-74, Ft. Clayton Riding Club; 1st V.P., Leo A. McIntyre Chapt., Dept. of Canal Zone, Reserve Offs. Assn. of U.S.A., 1972; Gamboa Golf & Country Club; Balboa Gun Club; Soc. Am. Mil. Engrs.; Comm. Chmn., Riverside Lions Club, 1962-70; Boy Scout Comm. Hons. incl: Breast Order of Yun Hi, Repub. of China, 1946; Presidential Citation, Repub. of Korea, 1950. Address: P.O. Box 771, Curundu, Canal Zone, Panama, 7, 16, 22, 68, 69, 81, 125.

WILLIAMS, Wirt Alfred Jr., b. 21 Aug. 1921. University Professor; Writer. Educ: B.A., Delta Coll.; M.A., La. State Univ.; Ph.D., Univ. of Iowa, 1953. Appts. incl: Staff Mbr., New Orleans Item, 1946-49; Instr., Engl., Univ. of Iowa, 1952-53; Asst. Prof.-Assoc. Prof.-Prof., Engl., Calif. State Univ., L.A., 1953-. Mbrships: Philol. Assn. of Pacific Coast; Authors League Am.; Kappa Alpha. Publs: The Enemy, 1951; Love in a Windy Space, 1957; Ada Dallas, 1959; A Passage of Hawks, 1963; The Trojans, 1966; The Far Side, 1972; The Tragic Art of Ernest Hemingway (in progess), Nominated for Pulitzer Prize for The Enemy, Ada Dallas & The Far Side. Address: Dept. of Engl., Calif. State Univ. at L.A., 5151 State Univ. Dr., Los Angeles, CA 90032, U.S.A. 9, 13, 30.

WILLIAMSON, Betty Jayne Hughes (Mrs. Joseph R. Williamson), b. 29 May 1941. Systems Design Consultant; Administrative Dietitian. Educ: B.S., Mich. State Univ., E. Lansing, Mich., 1963; Dietetic Internship & Certification w. Am. Dietetic Assn., Duke Univ. Med. Ctr., Durham, N.C., 1963-64; Certified as Registered Dietitian, Am. Dietetic Assn., 1968. Appts. incl: Therapeutic Dietitian, Lankenau Hosp., Phila., Pa., 1964-65; Asst. Chief Dietitian, ibid, 1965-66; Chief Dietitian, ibid, 1966-68; Admin. Dietitian, Hahnemann Med. Coll. & Hosp., Phila., Pa., 1968-72; Assoc., Facilities Planning, E.F. Johnson Co., Inc., Phila., Pa., 1972-; Food Serv. Cons., Community Mem. Hosp., Westgrove, Pa. & Larchwood Schl., Phila., Pa. Mbrships: Am. Dietetic Assn.; Pa. Dietetic Assn.; Phila. Dietetic Assn.; Dietitians in Bus.; Pi Beta Phi. Publs: sect. in Cyclopedia of Medicine, Surgery, Specialties, 1974; contbns. in Jrnl. Am. Dietic Assn., Hosp. & Nursing Home Food Mgmt. & Mod. Hosp. Address: 274 Iven Ave., Apartment 3-B, St. Davids, PA 19087, U.S.A. 5, 138.

WILLIAMSON, William Harvey, b. 31 Oct. 1908. Artist; Designer. Educ: Chouinard Art Inst.; Art Ctr. Schl., L.A., Calif; individual tuition in painting & sculpture. Traveled & painted in Europe, U.S.A. & the Caribbean. Appts. incl: Backgrounds, costumes & set dev. work, 20 Century Fox & Universal Pictures, Hollywood; Color Cons. archtl. interiors; WWII propaganda posters, mural panels & water colors. Air Corps., Douglas Aircraft Corp., 1942-45. Paintings, water colors & drawings in many pub. & pvte. collects. in Europe, U.S.A. & Hawaiian Islands inclng. Harrison Mem. Lib., Carmel, Calif., Oakland Art Mus., Calif. & Ackenbach Fndn., San Fran. Exhibd. in num. int. Grp. shows inclng. Nat. Soc. of Mural

Painters Show, Archtl. League of N.Y., 1956, 1961, Calif. Palace of Legion of Honor Mus., San Fran., 1963, 1964, Int. Art Fair, Basle, Switzerland, 1972 & exhib. of 5 Artists who paint horses, Gall. Arte de Colleccionistas, Hotel Maria Isabel, Mexico City, 1973. One Man Exhibs. incl: Gall. Iris, Paris, France, 1966; Gall. Costa., Palma de Mallorca, 1964, 1967; Myron Oliver Gall., Monterey, Calif.; Carmel Art Assn. Galls. Mbrships: Life Fellow, Int. Inst. of Arts & Letters, Switzerland; Nat. Soc. of Mural Painters, N.Y.C.; Archtl. League of N.Y.; Int. Assn. of Plastic Arts, UNESCO. Address: Hotels St. James & D'Albany, 211 Rue St. Honoré, 75001 Paris, France. 9, 37, 131, 133, 139.

WILLIFORD, William Bailey, b. 12 July 1921. Publisher; Author. Educ: Univ. of Firenze, Italy, 1945; Univ. of Ga., U.S.A., 1949; Univ. of Wis., 1960; Univ. of Tenn. Appts. incl: Major, AFUS (Ret.); P.R. Exec. w. var. corps. & govt. agcys., 1949-68; Organizer, own publng. bus., 1968; Currently, Pres., Cherokee Publng. Co. Mbrships. incl: Phi Delta Theta; Episc. Ch. of The Good Shepherd; Bd. of Councillors, Oxford Coll., Emory Univ.; Mbr. & former Chmn. Bd. Trustees, Newton Co. Hist. Soc.; Mbr. & former Trustee, Atlanta Hist. Soc.; former Trustee, Hist. Columbus Fndn., Inc.; Ga. Hist. Soc.; Ga. Trust for Historic Preservation. Hon. Ky. Col. Publs: Americus Through The Years; Peachtree Street, Atlanta; The Glory of Covington; Williford & Allied Families. Address: P.O. Box 1081, Covington, GA 30209, U.S.A. 22.

WILLING, Martha Cryer Kent (Mrs.), b. 8 Feb. 1920. Writer; Biologist. Educ: B.A., Bryn Mawr Coll., 1943; M.A., Univ. of Wash., 1965; MIT, 1973. Appts: Tchng. Asst., Bryn Mawr Coll. Biol. Grad. Schl.; Rsch. Asst., Univ. of Wash.; Tech. Ed., Oceanog., ibid; Clin. Asst., Dr. George Denniston, family planning & educ.; Treas., Population Dynamics. Mbrships: Sigma Xi; Alumnae Socs. Author, Beyond Conception: Our Childrens Children, 1971. Co-Prod. & Dir., films: Beyond Conception; Vasectomy Technique. Address: 3829 Aurora Ave., N., Seattle, WA 98103, U.S.A. 30.

WILLIS, Arthur James, b. 16 Jan. 1895. Chartered Quantity Surveyor; Geneologist. Educ: Exeter Coll., Oxford, 1914. Appts: Pvte. Prac. from 1924, later w. ptnrs. in the firm of Arthur J. Willis & Thompson. Mbrships: Royal Instn. of Chartered Surveyors; Hon. Fellow, Inst. of Quantity Surveyors; Fellow, Soc. of Geneols. Publs. incl: Geneology for Beginners; Introducing Geneology; To Be a Surveyor; Elements of Quantity Surveying (w. Christopher J. Willis); More Advanced Quantity Surveying (w. C.J. Willis); Practice & Procedure for the Quantity Surveyor (w. C.J. Willis); Specification Writing for Architects & Surveyors (w. C.J. Willis); The Architect in Practice (w. W.N.B. George & C.J. Willis); ed. of num. pub. records of histl. interest. Address: 8 Oriel Mt., Oriel Rd., Sheffield S10 3TF, U.K. 3.

WILLIS, Clayton. Writer; Consultant; Lecturer. Educ: B.A., Geo. Wash. Univ., 1957; Sorbonne, Paris; Univ. of Oslo; Univ. of Conn.; Grad., N.Y. Inst. Finance, 1966; Grad., Assn. Commodities Exchange Firms Inc., N.Y.C., 1966. Appts. incl: Staff Writer, Newsweek Mag., 1961-62; Announcer, Commentator, WAVA Radio., Wash., D.C., & World Radio News Network, Houston, Tex., 1963-64; Press Off., UN Secretariat, N.Y.C., 1965-66; Reporter, Critic, N.Y. Amsterdam News, 1967-68; Cons., Ford Fndn., 1968-69; Dir., Pub. Affairs, U.S. Equal Employment Opportunity Comm., 1969-70 & Nat. Coun. on Indian Opportunity, 1970-72; Cons., Community Rels. Serv., U.S. Dept. Justice, & Dir., Pub. Affairs & Congressional Rels., Pres.'s Nat. Commn. on Fire Prevention & Control, 1971-73; Dir., Pub. Affairs. Fedl. Off. Petroleum Allocation, 1973-74; Owner, The Mountain Eagle Newspaper, Durango, Colo., 1972-73; Lectr., Schl. Bus. & Pub. Mgmt., Fedl. City Coll., Wash., D.C., 1973-; Owner, Willis News Serv., ibid, 1974-; Contbr. to U.S., British & for. publs. Mbrships: Overseas Press Club; Sigma Delta Chi. Recip. of hons. Address: 8 Pomander Walk NW., Washington DC 20007, U.S.A.

WILLIS, Sharon Ozell, b. 11 June 1938. Librarian; Teacher. Educ: B.S., Southern Ill. Univ., 1960; M.S., Univ. of Ill., 1963. Appts: Tchr.-Libn., Columbia, Ill., 1960-61; Tchr., Mahomet, Ill., 1961-62; Libn. & Instr., Univ. of Wis., 1962-64; Cataloguer & Instr., Okla. State Univ., 1964-66; Libn. & Instr., Univ. of Mo., 1966-67; Instr., ibid, 1967-. Mbrships: Pres., Mo. Assn. of Schl. Libns.; Mbr., Legislative Comm., Am. Assn of Schl. Libns.; Am. Lib. Assn.; Assn. of Am. Lib. Schls.; Mo. Lib. Assn.; Mo. State Tchrs. Assn.; Mo. Assn. of Educl. Communication & Technol.; Delta Kappa Gamma; Advsr., Epsilon Beta; N.E. Mo. Libn.'s Assn. Publs: The Elementary School Library; Contbr. to Teamwork Techniques for Media Services, & Learning Resources Guide; Ed., Co-ed., Mo. Assn. of Schl. Libns. Newsletter, Univ. of Mo. Lib. Staff Newsletter, 1968-73. Address: 606 Westridge Dr., Columbia, MO 65201, U.S.A. 5, 30.

WILLMANN, Dean Elton, b. 1 Dec. 1932. Insurance Company Executive. Educ: B.S., Univ. of Ill., 1955. Appts: w. IBM, 1958-69; Acctng. Machine Mgr., Cinn., 1963-64; Mktng. Mgr., 1965-67; w. Corp. Govt. Info. Staff, Wash., 1968-69; V.P. Mgr., Mktng. Ops., Access Corp., Cinn., 1970-; Served w. U.S. Army, 1956-57; Mbrships: Assn. Computing Machinery; Sales & Mktng. Execs. (1st V.P., 1967); Lutheran. Address: 311 Pike St., Cinn., OH 45202, U.S.A. 8.

WILLOCKS, Robert Max, 1 Oct. 1924. Librarian. Educ: B.A., Maryville Coll., 1949; B.D., Golden Gate Bapt. Theol. Sem., 1951; Th.M., ibid, 1962; M.A., Peabody Coll., 1962. Appts. incl: Pastor, Calif., 1950-56; Missionary, Southern Bapt. For. Mission Bd., Taejon, Korea, 1956-65 Prof., Ch. Hist., Korea Bapt. Sem., 1957-65, Acting Pres., 1958-59, Libn., 1959-65; Dir., Korean Bapt. Press, 1959-61; Cons., Choong Chung Nam Province Lib. Assn., Korea, 1962-65; Vice Chmn., Korea Bapt. Mission, 1962-64; Chmn. of Trustees, Wallace Mem. Bapt. Hosp., Pusan, Korea, 1964-65; Assoc. Dir., Lib., Heidelberg Coll., Tiffin, Ohio, U.S.A., 1965-67; Lib. Dir., Columbia Coll., Columbia, S.C., 1967-70; Asst. Dir. of Libs., Syracuse Univ., N.Y., 1970-. Mbrships. incl: ALA; L.A.R.C.; Telefacsimile Communications Comm., ALA; Chmn., Tech. Servs. Comm., Five Associated Univ. Libs. Publs. incl: Thus it is Written (Ed.), 1963; The Progress of Worldwide Missions (Ed.), 1965; Periodical Holdings of the South Carolina Private College Libraries, 1969. Address: 308 Dewitt St., Syracuse, NY 13203, U.S.A. 2, 6, 9, 42.

WILLOUGHBY, Clarice Maud (Mrs.). Writer. Educ: Pub. schl., corres. schl., Australia. Mbrships: Royal Commonwealth Soc., Australia; Int. PEN; Soc. of Women Writers, Australia. N.S.W. Leagues Club, Sydney. Publs: Novels, short stories, poetry; Pictures & figurines in sea shell art for commercial sale. Hons: LL.B., London Univ., 1966; Grand Dame Sovereign Order of Alfred the Great, London,

1968. Address: Box 441, P.O., Manly, N.S.W., Australia, 2095.

WILLOUGHBY, Robert Hanley, b. 30 June 1927. Magazine Photographer. Educ: Cinema Dept., Univ. of Southern Calif., L.A., U.S.A. Prod., edit. photographs for num. Am. & European publs. inclng. Life, Vogue, Harper's Bazaar, Cosmopolitan, Saturday Evening Post, Sunday Times Mag., Queen, Paris Match, Stern, Oggi. Wkr., num. maj. motion pictures inclng. A Star is Born, Can Can, My Fair Lady, Who's Afraid of Virginia Woolf?, A Man for All Seasons, The Graduate, Goodbye Mr Chips, Catch 22. Mbrships: L.A. Co. Art Mus.; L.A. Ethnic Arts Coun.; Soc. of Photographers in Communication, N.Y.C. Exhibs. of photographs at num. Am. & European shows & collections, inglng. Permanent Collection, Mus. of Mod. Art, N.Y.C. Hons: Silver Medal, Welt-Fotoausstellung, Berlin, Germany, 1967; Silver & Gold Medals, 1971 Welt-Fotoausstellung, Berlin, 1972; Medaille Awards, Mantes-la-Jolie, France, 1970 & 1971. Address: Coolmaine Castle, Kilbrittain, Co. Cork, Ireland.

WILLOUGHBY, Winston C., b. 21 July 1907. Dentist. Educ: Howard Univ. Dental Schl., 1933. Appts. incl: D.C. Hlth. Dept. Schl. Clins., 1938-44; Staff Mbr., Grp. Hlth., 1949-50; Licensed to prac. dentistry in Ohio, Wash., D.C., N.Y. Fellowships: Int. Coll. Dentists; Royal Soc. Hlth. Mbrships. incl: Exec. Bd., D.C. Dental Soc.; Am. Déntal Assn.; Charter, Int. Assn. Anestheols.; Charter, Int. Acad. Orthodontists; Fed. Dentaire Int.; Chi Lamda Kappa; Alpha Phi Alpha; Charter, Am. Soc. Dentistry for Children; Smithsonian Inst.; AAAS; Wash. Performing Arts Soc.; UN Assn.; Hon., Cedars Home for Children. Composer, song, Keep Me In Your Heart, 1971. Recip., sev. awards, letters of appreciation, commendations, etc. Address: 4857 Colorado Ave., N.W., Washington, DC 20011, U.S.A. 7, 22, 125, 128, 129, 131.

WILLS, Lowell Edgar, b. 5 June 1925. Chemical Engineer. Educ: Ch.E., Univ. of Cinn., 1948; Radiation Technol., Northwestern Univ., 1957. Appts: Pilot Plant Supvsr., Vulcan copper & Supply Co., 1948-49; Engr., Rsch. & Dev., Gt. Lakes Carbon Corp., 1949-52; Process Engr., 1952-57; Sect. Hd., 1957-63; Ops. Mgr., Consumer Prods. Div., 1963-68; Asst. Gen. Mgr., 1968-. Mbrships: Am. Chem. Soc.; Am. Soc. Testing & Mats. (Chmn., Sub-Comm., 1971-72); AAAS; Inst. Briquetting & Agglomeration; Am. Inst. Mgmt.; Treas. & Exec. Comm., Charcoal Briquet Inst., 1969-70; Nat. Soc. Profl. Engrs.; Treas., Lambda Chi Alpha, 1946-48. Co-author of Coking Petroleum Residue, 1957. Patentee in field. Address: 333 N. Michigan Ave., Ste. 1600, Chgo., IL 60601, U.S.A. 8.

WILLSEY, Thelma Wilkin, b. 29 Jan. 1907. Real Estate Broker. Appts: Tchr., Pub. Schls., Greenwood, Mo., U.S.A., 3 yrs.; Record Clerk, Sears Roebuck, Kansas City, Mo.; 1929-32; Off. Sec., Purchasing Dept., Pritchard & Co., Kansas City, 1945; Real Estate Sales, 1948; Real Estate Broker, Willsey Realty Co., Blue Springs, Mo., 1961-. Mbrships: Eastern Jackson Co. Bd. of Dirs., 1967-, currently Treas.; Pres., Blue Springs Chmbr. of Comm., 1962, Treas., 1963-65; V.P., Womens Coun. of Realtors of Eastern Jackson Co., 1971-72; Past Deaconess, Blue Springs Christian Ch.; Ivy Leaf Chapt. No. 215, Pleasant Hill, Mo.; 1927-; Worthy Matron, 1936, held all elective offs.; Past Bd. Dir., Pilot Int., Blue Springs. Address: 80-D Lake Tapawingo, Box 232, Blue Springs, MO 64015, U.S.A. 5.

WILLSON, Mabel Parkes. Private Secretary. Educ: Grad., Hartford Pub. H.S. Appts: Sec. to V.P. of Travelers Ins. Co., Hartford, Conn., 1909-11; Secretarial post, Air Transport Cmd., Wash. D.C., 1941-43; Ct. & Convention Reporter, San Francisco, Calif., 1943; Staff Mbr., San Francisco Convention & Visitors Bur. Address: 900 Chestnut St., Apt. 604, San Francisco, CA 94109, U.S.A.

WILLSON, Richard Eugene, b. 1 Jan. 1933. Librarian. Educ: B.A., Bowling Green State Univ., Ohio, 1954; M.S. in L.S., 1957. Appts: Publicity Asst., Cuyahoga Co., Ohio, Pub. Lib., 1955-57; Art & Music Libn., ibid, 1957-58; Humanities Libn., Lib., Kent State Univ., 1958-63; Hd. Libn., Amos Mem. Pub. Lib., Sidney, 1963-67; Dir., Lorain Pub. Lib., 1967-. Mbrships: ALA; Ohio Lib. Assn. (Mbrship. Chmn., 1969-70); Nat. Soc. SAR; Tau Kappa Epsilon; John Bowne Histl. House Soc.; Masonic Lodge. Publs: English Benedictine Monastic Libraries During the Middle Ages, 1957; Contbn. on the Willson Family, 1672-1959, to Ency. Americana. Address: 4328 Edgewood Drive, Lorain, OH 44053, U.S.A. 8, 15, 42.

WILMOTT, Peter, b. 18 Sept. 1923. Sociologist. Educ: Ruskin Coll., Oxford Univ.; B.Sc., London Univ., 1959. Appts: Rsch. Asst., Labour Pty.,Transport House, 1949-54; Rsch. Off., Inst. of Community Studies, 1954-60; Dpty. Dir., ibid, 1960-64; Co-dir., ibid, 1964-; Vis. Prof., Ecole Pratique des Hautes Etudes, Univ. of Paris, 1972; Vis. Prof., Schl. of Environmental Studies, Univ. Coll., London, 1972-. Mbrships: Lee Working Men's Club, Lee Green, London; Brit. Sociol. Assn.; Assn. of Univ Tchrs. Publs. incl: Family & Kinship in East London (w. M. Young), 1957; Family & Class in a London Suburb (w. M. Young), 1960; Evolution of a Community, 1963; Adolescent Boys of East London, 1966; Contbr. to books. Address: Inst. of Community Studies, 18 Victoria Park Sq., London, E.2, U.K.

WILNER, Marie. Painter. Educ: B.A., Hunter Coll, CUNY, U.S.A. Mbrships. incl: Life Fellow, Royal Soc. of Art; Nat. Assn. of Women Artists; Artists Equity; Am. Artists Profl. League; League of Present Day Artists; Acad. of Sci., Letters & Arts, Milan, Italy; Kappa Pi. Num. one-man shows incl: Raymond Duncan Galls., Paris, France, 1961, 63, 65, 67, 68, & 69; Evansville Mus., Ind., 1964; Pietrantio Gall., N.Y., 1966, 68, & 69; LaSalle Coll., Phila, Pa., 1966, 67, & 68; Bohmann's Gall., Stockholm, Sweden, 1968. Paintings in num. collects. & exhibs. inclng: Bridgeport Mus. of Art, Conn.; Bat Yam Mus., Israel; Angouléme Mus., France; Mus. of Art, Buenos Aires, Argentina; Salon des Indépendants, Paris, France; Palais des Beaux-Arts, Rome, Italy; Staten Island Mus., N.Y. Num. hons. incl: Gold Medal, Am. Artists Profl. League; Bronze Medal, 3rd Biennale Internationli, Ancona, Italy, 1968; Chevalier 4th Grade, Mérite Belgo-Hispanique Promotion Reine Fabiola, 1973. Address: 77 Seventh Ave., N.Y., NY 10011, U.S.A. 2, 6, 37, 105.

WILSON, (Sir) Archibald Duncan, b. 12 Aug. 1911. Diplomat; Academic. Educ: Balliol Coll., Oxford Univ. Appts: Chargé d'Affaires, China, 1957-59; Ambassador to Yugoslavia, 1964-68; Russia, 1968-71; Master, Corpus Christi Coll., Cambridge Univ., 1971-. Mbrships: Hon. Mbr., Am. Acad. of Pol. Sci.; Royal Commonwealth Soc. Publs: Life & Times of Vuk Stefanović Karadzić, 1970. Hons: G.C.M.G., 1971. Address: Corpus Christi Coll., Cambridge Univ., Cambridge, U.K. 1, 34.

WILSON, Charles Randall, b. 9 Aug. 1918. University Professor; Minister. Educ: A.B., Northwesten State, 1943; M.A., Syracuse Univ., 1952; B.D., Asbury Theol. Sem., 1948; Ph.D., Venderbilt Univ., 1959. Appts: Prof., Bible & Theol., Miltonvale Wesleyan Coll.; Chmn., Dept. Theol., ibid; Prof., Bible & Theol., Houghton Coll.; Prof., Philos. & Relig. & Currently Hd., Dept. Relig., Taylor Univ. Mbrships: Soc. of Biblical Lit. & Exegesis; AAUP; Wesleyan Theol. Soc. Co-Ed., Boundless Horizons, 1960. Contbr., The Wesleyan Bible Commentary, 1967; Baker's Dictionary of Christian Ethics, 1973. Address: Taylor Univ., Upland, IN 46989, U.S.A. 13.

WILSON, Charles Hartley, b. 4 July 1904. Solicitor. Appts: Mbr., firm Tully & Wilson, Solicitors, Brisbane, Australia; Dir. Weedmans Ltd., Elphinstones Ltd., Ocean Resources N.L.; formerly B.C. 2 Australian A/tk Regt. & 2/6th. Australian Fd. Regt.; C.O. 11 Australian Fd. Regt., 13 Australian Fd. Regt. & 57 Australian AA Regt.; 1940-45; C.O. 11 Fd. Regt., C.R.A. Northern Cmd. & Cmd. 5 AGRA, 1948-56 (Brigadier, 1953). Pres., Qld. Law Soc., 1966-68. Address: c/o Tully & Wilson, Solicitors, Box 320, G.P.O , Brisbane, Qld., Australia 4001.

WILSON, Elizabeth A. Galley (Mrs. A.E. Wilson), b. 26 Sept. 1911. Teacher. Educ: B.A., Tex. Christian Univ., 1948; Th.B., Southwestern Assemblies of God Coll., 1949; M.A., Tex. Christian Univ., 1955; Studied at Coll. of Chinese Studies, Peking, China & Baguio, Philippines, 1939-41. Appts. incl: Missionary to China & Baguio, Philippines; Tchr., Bethel Bible Inst., Baguio; Prisoner of Japanese, 1941-45; Hd., Missions Dept., Southwestern Assemblies of God Coll., 1948-54; Tchr., Southwestern Assemblies of God Coll., 1956-57 & Hd., Soc. Sci. Dept., 1963-. Mbrships. incl: A.A.U.W.; Delta Kappa Gamma; A.A.U.P.; Org. of Am. Histns.; Southwestern Soc. Sci. Assn.; Southern Histl. Assn.; Faith & Hist.; Tex. Histl. Assn.; Ellis Co. Histl. Assn. Publs. incl: Making Many Rich; A History of the Assemblies of God in Africa; Sev. articles in ch. papers. Hons. incl: Dir., Am. Heritage Prog., 1970-; Asiatic-Pacific Ribbon, WWII. Address: 121 Vanderbilt Lane, Waxahachie, TX 75165, U.S.A. 125.

WILSON, Homer M., b. 3 Oct. 1934. Electrical Engineer. Educ: B.A., Rice Univ., Houston, Tex, 1959; B.S.E.E., ibid, 1960; Loughborough Coll., U.K., 1955-56. Appts: Electronic Design Engr., Hamner Electronics, 1 yr.; Tech. Mgr., Palmer Phys. Labs., Princeton Univ., 1 yr.; Elec. Engr., Nuclear Lab., Phys. Dept., Rice Univ., 1 yr.; V.P., Tech. Enterprises Corp., 4 yrs.; Pres., H.M. Wilson Co., 1965-. Mbrships: IEEE; Tex. Soc. Profl. Engrs.; Instrument Soc. of Am.; Nat. Assn. Corrosion Engrs.; Aircraft Owners & Pilots Assn. Holder of 19 U.S. Patents (5 in Well Logging Systems, 14 in elec. coalescence & associated equipment). Address: 11501 Chimney Rock, Houston, TX 77035, U.S.A. 7, 113, 125, 139.

WILSON, John D. b. 13 Feb. 1913. Banker; Economist. Educ: B.A., Univ. of Colo., 1935; M.A., Tufts Univ., 1937; M.A., Harvard Univ., 1940. Appts: Instr., Econs., Harvard Univ., 1937-40; Ed., Survey of Current Bus., U.S. Dept. of Commerce, 1940-42; Lt. j.g., USNR, assigned to Off. of Strategic Servs., 1942-46; Ed. & Publisher, McGraw-Hill Publishing Co., 1946-50; V.P., Inst. of Int. Educ., 1951-53; Chase Manhattan Bank, 1953-; currently Sr. V.P. i/c of Econs. Group & Chmn., Chase Econometric Assocs., Inc. Mbrships: Trustee, Inst. of Int. Educ.; Chmn., Econ. Policy Comm., U.S. Coun. of Int. Chmbr. of Comm.; Dir., United Neighborhold Houses, N.Y.C.; Coun. on For. Rels.; Planning Coun., Am. Mgmt. Assn.; Former Dir., ibid; Phi Beta Kappa, 1935; Harvard Club, N.Y.C. Author of num. articles in financial, bus. & econ. publs. Recip., Commendation Ribbon, U.S. Army, 1946, USN, 1946. Address: c/o The Chase Manhattan Bank, N.A., 1 Chase Manhattan Plaza, N.Y., NY 10015, U.S.A. 2.

WILSON, Leonard Richard, b. 23 July 1906. Educator; Geologist. Educ: Superior State Tchr.'s Coll., 1926; Univ. of Leeds, U.K., 1928-29; Ph.B., Univ. of Wis., U.S.A., 1930; Ph.M., 1932; Ph.D., 1935; Melhaupt Fellow, Ohio State Univ., 1939-40. Appts. incl: Rsch. Assoc., Wis. Geological & Natural Hist. Survey, 1931-35; Instr. Prof. of Geol., Coe Coll., 1934-46; Prof. & Hd., Dept. of Geol. & Mineral., Univ. of Mass., 1946-56; Ldr., Am. Geographical Soc. Greenland Ice Cap Expedition, 1953; Prof. of Geol., N.Y. Univ., 1956-57; Rsch. Assoc., Am. Mus. of Nat. Hist., 1956-; Geologist IV Okla. Geological Survey, 1957; Prof. of Gaol., Univ. of Okla., 1957-61; Rsch. Prof. of Geol., 1962-68; George Lynn Cross Rsch. Prof. of Geol & Geophys., 1967-; Adjunct Prof. of Geol., Tulsa Univ., 1969-; Curator of Micropaleontology & Paleobotany, Stoval Mus., Univ. of Okla., 1971-; Cons. to Petroleum cos., N. & S. Am., Europe, Africa, India & Australia. Active Mbr., many profl. orgs. inclng. Hon. Mbr., Phi Beta Kappa, 1972. Author of technical articles, monographs & books in profl. field. Hons. incl: Kt. of Order of Mark Twain, 1972; VIth Gunnar Erdtman Int. Medal for Palynol., 1973. Address: Schl. of Geol. & Geophys., Univ. of Okla., Norman, OK 73069, U.S.A. 2, 7,`14.

WILSON, Lorelle Borden (Mrs.), b. 6 Feb. 1912. Educator. Educ: B.S., Tenn. Technol. Univ. Appts: Elem. Schl. Tchr. for 33 yrs. Appts: Past Pres., Past Sec., Bus. & Profl. Women's Club; Pres., Alpha Delta Kappa; Worthy Matron, Eastern Star; Past Pres., Past Sec., Putnam Co. Classroom Tchrs.; Tenn. Educl. Assn.; NEA Hons: Woman of Achievement, 1968; Tenn. Merit Mother, 1971. Address: 6 W. Jackson, Cookeville, TN 38501, U.S.A. 125.

WILSON, Louie Cecil, b. 22 Mar. 1937. Surgeon. Educ: B.S., Univ. of Ala., 1959; M.D., Tulane Univ. Schl. of Med., New Orleans, La., 1963; Rotating Intern, Charity Hosp., ibid, 1963-64; Res., then Chief Res., Gen. Surg., Charity & Oschsner Fndn. Hosps., New Orleans, 1964-68; Res., Cardiothoracic Surg., Southwestern Med. Schl., Parkland Hosp., Dallas, Tex.; Baylor Univ. Med. Ctr., ibid; V.A. Hosp., ibid, 1968-69; Chief Res., Cardiothoracic Surg., N.C. Memorial Hosp., Chapel Hill, 1969-70. Appts: Pt.-time Instr., Cardiothoracic Surg., Univ. of N.C., Schl. of Med., 1969-70; Instr. of Surg., ibid, 1970-71; Asst. Prof., Dept. of Surg., Mobile Gen. Hosp., Univ. of S. Ala. Med. Schl., Mobile, Ala., 1970-; Thoracic Surg., Gravely Sanatorium, Chapel Hill, N.C., 1970-71; Thoracic & Cardiovascular Surg., Univ. of N.C. Memorial Hosp., Chapel Hill, 1970-71; Surg. Cons., N.C. TB Sanatorium System & Watts Hosp., Durham, 1970-71; Surg. Cons., or Courtesy Staff, sev. Ala. hosps. Mbrships. incl: Alpha Omicron Pi; Gamma Sigma Epsilon; AMA; Assoc. for Academic Surg.; Am. Thoracic Soc.; Am. Bd. of Surg.; Am. Bd. of Thoracic Surg.; Fellow, Am. Coll. of Cardiol., Am. Coll. of Chest Physns. & Am. Coll. of Surgs. Publs: Co-author, Valvar Regurgitation in Acute Infective Endocarditis: Early Replacement, 1970 & Coronary Artery Lacerations: An Analysis of 22 Patients, 1969.

Address: 1729 Springhill Ave., Mobile, AL 36604, U.S.A. 125.

WILSON, Mary Ellenor Mize (Mrs. Ezra Wilson), b. 3 May 1895. Conservationist; Mother & Housewife. Noted for her work in preserving the scenic & wild qualities of the Chattooga River & its environs & for planting flowers along the interstate 85 U.S. Highway 441 interchange in Banks Co. Subject of articles in: Classic Scene, June 1973; The Jackson Herald, Atlanta Constitution & Atlanta Journal, Dec. 1973; The Georgia Translator, Jan. 1974; & many other publs. Address: P.O. Box 1776, Homer, GA 30547, U.S.A. 125.

WILSON, Pearl Cleveland, b. 16 Dec. 1882. Teacher. Educ: A.B., Vassar, 1904; A.M. Columbia Univ., 1905; Ph.D., ibid, 1917. Appts: Lectr., Music, N.Y. Bd of Educ., 1908-18; Lectr., Greek & Latin, Hunter Coll., 1925-30; Asst. Prof., ibid, 1930-36; Assoc. Prof., 1936-52; Prof., 1952-53; Emeritus Prof., 1953-. Mbrships: Mng. Comm., Am. Schl. of Classical Studies, Athens, 1938-; Special Ed., Classical Lit. & Mythol. for Merit Students Ency., 1967; Pres., Phi Beta Kappa Alumnae, N.Y.; Pres., N.Y. Classical Club; Metropolitan Opera Guild; Citizens Union. Publs: Wagner's Dramas & Greek Tragedy, Sunt Lacrimae Rerum, a Latin play adapted from Virgil's Aeneid, Classics of Greek Poetry & Prose (a recording in ancient Greek); Librettists & Dir. for Opera, King Harald, 1967. Address: 600 W. 116 St., N.Y., N.Y., U.S.A. 6, 13, 15, 64, 138.

WILSON, Reginald Yelverton, b. 6 Aug. 1910. General Secretary, Liberal & Country League, South Australian Division, Liberal Party of Australia. Educ: Muirden Coll., Adelaide, Australia. Appts: assocd. w. sheep ind.; Exec. Off., Royal Automobile Assn. of S.A., 1937-40, '46-52; Commnd. in Australian Imperial Force, 1940; Capt., ibid, 1946; Gen. Sec., Liberal & Country Leagues, S.A. Div., Liberal Party of Australia, 1952-. Mbrships: past mbr., naval & mil. club; Freemason; var. sporting clubs. Author of newspaper articles. Address: 23 Hillcrest Dr., Eden Hills, S.A. 5050, Australia.

WILSON, Sodonia Mae (Mrs. James Wilson Jr.). Director of Special Programs & Services. Educ: A.A., City Coll., San Fran., 1961; B.A., Nursing, San Fran. State Univ., 1963; M.A., ibid, 1965. Appts: Nurse, French Hosp., 1956-57, Ft. Milay Hosp., 1957-62; Cnslr., Youth Guidance Ctr., 1965-66; Probation Off., ibid, 1966; Hd. Start Analyst, 1966-67; Supvsr., Soc. Servs. Dept., San Fran. Redev. Agcy. at Hunters Pt., Coord., Coll. Cnslng. Prog., 1969-72; Cnslr., Contra Costa Coll., 1972-73; Dir. of Special Progs. & Servs., ibid, 1973-. Mbrships: Calif. Personnel & Guidance Assn.; Jack & Gill of Am. Inc.; Calif. Tchrs. Assn.; San Fran. State Univ. Alumni Assn.; Am. Black Psychol. Assn. Publs: Evaluation of the Special Counseling Program, 1972. Recip. Cert. for Outstanding Serv., Cultural Ctr., Contra Costa Community Coll. Address: 540 Darien Way, San Francisco, CA 94127, U.S.A. 9.

WILTSE, James Cornelius, Jr., b. 16 Mar. 1926. Engineering Management. Educ: B.E.E., Rensselaer Polytech. Inst., 1947; M.E.E., ibid, 1952. Dr. Eng., Johns Hopkins Univ., 1959. Appts: incl: Prin. Sci., Lab. Chief, Martin Marietta Corp, Orlando, Fla., 1964-68; Mgr., electromagnetics dept., ibid, 1968-70; Mgr. lasers & optics, 1970-72; Mgr., electro-optics & microwaves, 1972-73; Prin. Engr., 1973-; Dir., Rsch. & Technol., 1973-. Mbrships. incl: Fellow, IEEE; AAAS; Bay Hill Country Club,

Orlando; Sigma Xi; Tau Beta Pi; Eta Kappa Nu. Contbr. to profl. publs. Hons: incl: Engr. of Yr., IEEE, Orlando Sect., 1968, Martin Marietta Corp., Orlando Div., 1970. Address: 8731 Bay Hill Blvd., Orlando, FL 32811, U.S.A. 7, 14.

WILTZ, John Edward, b. 21 Aug. 1930. Historian; University Professor. Educ: A.B., Univ. of Ky., 1954; M.A., ibid, 1955; Ph.D., 1959. Appts: Lectr. in Hist., 1958-59, Instr., 1959-62, Asst. Prof., 1962-65, Assoc. Prof., 1965-, Ind. Univ.; Vis. Lectr., Univ. of the W. Indies (Jamaica), 1965-66; Guest Prof., Hamburg Univ., German Fed. Repub., 1970-71. Mbrships: Am. Histl. Assn.; Org. of Am. Histns. Publs: In Search of Peace - The Senate Munitions Inquiry 1934-36, 1963; The Teaching of American History in High School (w. others), 1964; From Isolation to War, 1939-1941, 1968; The Search for Identity, 1972. Hons. incl: Fulbright-Hays Award, 1965-66 & 70-71. Address: Dept. of Hist., Ind. Univ., Bloomington, IN, U.S.A.

WIMMER, Glen Elbert, b. 16 Feb. 1903. Professional Engineer; Management Consultant. Educ: B.S., Iowa State Univ., 1925; M.S., 1933 & M.B.A., 1935; Northwestern Univ. Appts. incl: Engr., Checker, Lee Engrng. Co., 1942-43; Hd., Design & Dev. Dept., Cummins Perforator Co.,Chgo, Ill, 1943-45; Instr., Cost Analysis, evenings, Ill. Inst. of Technol, 1946-47; Staff. Engr., Chmn. of Design & Dev., Tammen & Denison Inc., 1945-58; Engr. ., Barnes & Reinecke Inc., 1958-60; Dev. Engr., B.H. Bunn Co. 1960-61; Engr., Barnes & Reinecke Inc., 1961-69; Engr., Alpha Servs. Inc., 1969-70. Mbrships: incl: Ill. Soc. of Profl. Engrs.; Iowa State & Northwestern Univs. Alumni Assns.; Nat. Soc. of Profl. Engrs.; Am. Defense Preparedness Assn. Soc. of Automotive Engrs.; Am. Soc. Mfg. Engrs.; Delta Chi; Dir., Ill. Engrng. Coun., 1958-68. Patentee. Recip. of sev. awards. Address: 3839-48 Vista Campana S., Oceanside, CA 92054, U.S.A. 22, 26, 28, 57, 68, 74, 120, 128, 130, 131.

WINCHESTER, Clarence F., b. 14 Oct. 1901. Chemist, Nutritionist. Educ: B.S., Univ. of Calif, Berkeley, 1924; M.S., ibid, 1935; Ph.D., Univ. of Mo, Columbia, 1939. Appts. incl: Educator, L.A., Palo Verde & Fresno, Calif, 1924-31; Rsch. Sci; Univ. of N.H., 1931-32; Univ. of Calif, Davis, 1932-37; Univ. of Mo., 1937-47; 1st Lt. to Capt. U.S. Army, 1942-47; Assoc. Chem. & Assoc. Prof, Univ. of Fla., 1947-49; Rsch. Sci., USDA, Beltsville, 1949-57, '59-61; Livestock Advsr., U.S. Overseas Mission to Ceylon AID, 1957-59; Animal Nutritionist U.S. Fish & Wild Life Serv., 1961-65; Lectr., Howard Univ., Wash.D.C. 1966-. Mbrships; incl; Fellow, AAAS & Am. Inst. of Chems.; Am. Soc. of Animal Sci.; Am. Inst. of Nutrition; AAUP. Contbr. of Articles to sci. jrnls. Address: 2124 Sudbury Pl, N.W. Wash. D.C. 20012, U.S.A. 6, 13, 22, 28, 41.

WINCKLER, Paul Albert, b. 17 May 1926. Professor of Library Science. Educ: B.A., St. John's Univ., 1948; M.L.S., Pratt Inst., 1950; Pub. Libns. Profl. Cert., SUNY, 1951; M.A., N.Y. Univ., 1953; Ph.D., ibid, 1968. Appts. incl: Libn., Brooklyn Pub. Lib., N.Y., 1950-51; Libn. & Asst. Prof., St. John's Univ., 1951-56; Lib. Dir., Bryant Lib., Roslyn, N.Y., 1956-60; Libn. & Asst. Prof., Suffolk Co. Community Coll., N.Y. 1960-62; Assoc. Prof. Lib. Sci., Palmer Grad. Lib. Schl., L.I. Univ., 1962-68; Prof. Lib. Educators Sect., N.Y. Lib. Assn.; Ed. Chmn., PLA Report publd. by CW Post Lib. Assn.; Alumni Fed. of N.Y. Univ. Publs: Bibliographies; contbns. to profl. jrnls. &

books. Address: 49 Hammond Rd., Glen Cove, L.I., NY 11542, U.S.A. 6, 15.

WINGARD, Raymond Randolph, b. 6 Nov. 1930. Corporate Executive. Educ: Southern Meth. Univ., Dallas, Tex.; Birmingham Southern Coll., Ala.; Brookings Inst., Wash. D.C.; Harvard Univ. Advanced Mgmt. Prog. Appts: U.S. Army, 1950-51; Operating & Sales Staff, Area Mgr., Koppers Co. Inc., Montgomery, Ala., 1951-60, 1962-63, Area Mgr., Kan. City, Mo., 1960-61, Asst. V.P., & Div. Mgr. of Railroad Dept., Chgo., Ill., & Pitts., Pa., 1963-: Agcy. Mgr., Ala. Farm Bur., Andalusta, 1961-62. Mbrships: incl: Independence Sub. Improvement League; Pres., ibid, 1959-60; R-1 Schl. Dist. (Mo.) Advsry Coun.; Pres., ibid, 1960; Dist. 58 (Ill.) Bd. of Educ.; Dir., ibid, 1969-71; Railway Tie Assn. of Am.; V.P., ibid, 1973-74; Am. Wood Preservers Assn. Hon. Charter Mbr., YMCA, Downers Grove, Ill., 1970. Address: Koppers Co. Inc., 700 Koppers Bldg., Pittsburgh, PA 15219, U.S.A. 2, 6.

WINGATE, Isabel B., b. 12 Oct. 1901. Professor Emeritus. Educ: A.B., Radcliffe Coll., 1923; M.S., N.Y. Univ., 1925; Ph.D., Yeshiva Univ., 1961. Appts: Assoc. Prof.-Prof. of Retailing, 1947-66; Prof. of Retail Mgmt., 1966-68; Prof. Emeritus, 1968-; Lectr., Textiles, N.Y. Univ. Schl. of Continuing Educ., 1968-. Mbrships. incl: N.Y. Univ. Senate (first woman), 1948-52; Chmn., Interfaith Coun., N.Y. Univ.; Sec., Comm. on Campus Work, YMCA of Gtr. N.Y.; Bd.Dirs., N.Y. Univ. Christian Fndn.; Am. Assn. of Textile Chemists & Colorists. Publs. incl: Visual Program in Six Parts: Textiles from Source to Consumer. Hons. incl: N.Y. Univ. Schl. of Educ. Award, 1968. Address: 202 Tisch Hall, N.Y. Univ., 40 W. 4th St., N.Y., NY 10003, U.S.A. 5, 138.

WINGATE, Robert Bray, b. 21 Sept. 1925. Rare Books Librarian; Free-lance Medical Illustrator. Educ: A.B., Lebanon Valley, 1948; M.A., Johns Hopkins, 1951; M.S., Drexel, 1960; D.Sc., 1971. Appts: Med. Illustrator, Walter Reed Army Hosp., Wash. D.C., 1954-56, Ophthalmological Fndn., Inc., N.Y.C., 1956-60, Freelance, 1960-; Chief, Rare Books & Special Collects., State Lib. of Pa., 1965-. Mbrships: AAAS; Affiliate, Royal Soc. of Med., London, U.K.; Pa. Acad. of Sci.; Bibliographical Soc. of Am.; Life Fellow, Royal Soc. of Arts, London; Beta Beta Beta; Beta Phi Mu. Illustrator of books inclng. Atlas of Strabismus, 1967, 2nd edit. 1973, Atlas of Ophthalmic Surgery, 1970; Surg. Illustrations in num. med. jrnls. Address: 136 Shell St., Harrisburg, PA 17109, U.S.A. 6, 28, 42, 139.

WINGFIELD, Josephine Bennington (Mrs. Joseph E. Wingfield), b. 12 Jan. 1915. Librarian. Educ: A.B., Randolph-Macon Woman's Coll., 1934; Va. Commercial Coll. Appts: Jones Mem. Lib., Lynchburg, Va., 1936-; Lib. Asst., 1936; Sec. to Hd. Libn., 1941; Asst. Libn., 1947; Hd. Libn., 1955-. Mbrships: Nat. Hon. Soc.; Va. Lib. Assn.; Southeastern Lib. Assn.; Assn. for Preservation of Va. Antiquities. Contbr. to Encyclopedia Americana. Address: 1807 Richmond Ave., Lynchburg, VA 24502, U.S.A. 5, 85.

WINK, Howard Lamar, Jr., b. 29 Dec. 1935. Mechanical Engineer. Educ: B.S., Mech. Engrng., Pa. State Univ., 1957; Mech. Engrng. in Engnrg. Mgmt., Speed Sci. Schl., Univ. of Louisville, 1973; Registered Profl. Engr., Ky., 1971 & Ga., 1974. Appts: 1st Lt., US Army Ordnance Corp., 1957-59; Mech. Engr., Ternstedt Div., Gen. Motors Corp., Warren, Mich., 1959-69; Project Engr.-Mgr., Quality

Improvement Design, Refrigerator Products Div., Gen. Elec. Co., Louisville, Ky., 1969-73; Mgr., Design Engrng., Lithonia Lighting, Div. of Nat. Servs. Ind., Conyers, Ga., 1973-. Mbrships: Soc. of Profl. Engrs.; Engrng. Soc. of Detroit; Soc. of Plastics Engrs.; Past Mbr., Appliance Engrng. Soc. (Sec., 1971-72). Thesis: Air Flow Control Damper Design Procedure, 1973. Holder of US & Can. Patents in Automotive field. Address: 4715 Holly Oak Place, Dunwoody, GA 30338, U.S.A. 7.

WINKLER, Joseph C., b. 20 May 1916. Financial Executive. Educ: B.S., N.Y. Univ., 1941. Appts: Gen. Mgr., Indl. Washing Machine Corp., 1941-48; Controller, Mojud Corp., N.Y.C., 1948-52; Controller & Asst. Treas., Barbizon Corp., N.Y.C., 1952-57; Controller, Ideal Toy Corp., N.Y.C., 1957-58; Dir., Finance & Admin., ibid, 1960-62, V.P., Finance, 1962-68, Sr. V.P., Finance, 1968-; Dir., Ideal Toy Co. Ltd., U.K.; Ideal Toy Corp., Australia; ITC Inds. Ltd., Hong Kong; Ideal Toy Corp. of Japan Ltd.; Ideal Toy Co., Canada. Mbrships: Financial Execs. Inst.; B'nai Brith; Troop Treas., Committeeman, Boy Scouts of Am., Tenafly, N.J. Address: 96 Buckingham Rd., Tenafly, NJ 07670, U.S.A.

WINKLER, Ulrich Edgar, b. 25 June 1925. Professor. Educ: Dr.sc.nat.; dipl. phys.ETH (Zurich, Switz.). Appts: Sci. collaborator, Inst. for solid state phys., Zurich, Switz., 1951-55; Phys., rsch. lab., CIBA, Basel, 1955-58; Prof., phys., HTL, Lucerne, 1958-71; chargé de cours, Univ. of Fribourg, 1958-; Prof., ibid, 1964-; Dir., Bauphys. Inst. AG Berne, 1971-. Mbrships: Schweiz. Lichttechn. Ges.; Pro Colore; Swiss Phys. Soc.; Kriegstechn. Ges.; Dpty. to gt. coun., Lucerne canton, 1969-71; Ges. fur Umweltschutz. Author of profl. publs. Address: Gurtenstrasse 55, CH-3122, Kehrsatz/BE, Switzerland. 43.

WINN, James Richard, b. 2 Aug. 1910. Retired Major-General, U.S. Army. Educ: Ky. Univ., U.S.A., 1928-30; B.S., U.S. Mil. Acad., 1934; M.A., Calif. Univ., L.A., 1941; Calif. Inst. Technol., 1941. Appts: Cmnd. 2nd Lt. U.S. Army, 1934; Var. assignments & schls., 1934-44; Exec. Off., HQ, 19th Corps Arty., Europe, 1944-45; Arty. Off., 1st U.S. Army, 1946-48; Advsr., Greek Army, Civil War, 1948-49; Assigned Nat. War Coll., 1950; Dept. Army Staff, 1950-53; Chief, Plans, European Cmnd., 1954-55; Field Arty. Grp. Cmndr., Europe, 1956; Fac. Army War Coll., 1956-59; Dpty. Chief of Staff, U.S. Army Continental Cmnd., 1959-61; Promoted Brig.-Gen., 1960; Cmndr., 1st Cav. Div. Arty., 1961-62; Promoted Major-Gen., 1962; Sr. Mbr., UN Armistice Commn., Korea, 1961; Cmndr., 2nd Region, U.S. Army Air Defense Cmnd., 1963-65; Chief, JUSMAG, Philippines, 1965-67; Cmndr., W. Region N. Am. Air Defense Cmnd. & Cmndr., 6th Region, U.S. Army Air Defense Cmnd., 1967-69; Retd. 1969. Mbr. Phi Sigma Kappa & Mil. Assns. Hons. incl: Legion of Merit (twice); French Croix de Guerre Medal w. palm. Address: 9024 El Dorado Dr., El Paso, TX 79925, U.S.A. 2.

WINN, William A., Jr., b. 3 Jan. 1920. Airline Captain. Appts: Pilot, Eastern Airlines, 1944; Capt., 1946; Line Pilot; Instr.; Check Pilot; Asst. Dir.-Flt., Mgr., Flt. Standards B-727; Mgr. Flying B-727; Pilot, 1st B-727 Jet into & out of Wash. Nat. & Houston Inter-continental Airports; Mil: USAAC Flt. Inst., Flt. Cmndr., 64th Trng. Detachment, Camden, SC. Mbrships: Org., Ansley Golf Club; Air Line Pilots Assn.; Am. Legion; Ata. Touchdown Club; Buckhead Lodge # Silver Wings Frat.; Soc. Appreciation Big Bands; Past

Pres., Ga. Southern Coll. Alumni Assn.; Bd. Dirs., Alumni Assn. & Fndn.; Advsry. Comm., Ata. Area Air Traffic Control; Advsry. Bd., Am. Security Coun. Recip. Alumnus of Yr. Award, Ga. Southern Coll., 1969, '73. Address: 39 Huntington Rd. N.E., Atlanta, GA 30309, U.S.A.

WINNBERG, Gösta Axel Fredrik, b. 2 Jan. 1910. Dentist. Educ: DDL. 1933; studied Oral Surg., The Rudolf-Virchow Hosp., Berlin, 1934 & at The Carolean Hosp. (Karolinska sjukhuset), Stockholm, 1944; studied Hypnosis, var. places, 1960. Appts: Pvte. Dental practitioner, Rimbo, 1933-43; Schl. Dentist, Rimbo, 1934-43; Asst. Supt., Dental Off., The Carolean Hosp., Stockholm, 1944; Pvte. Dental practitioner, Stockholm, 1945-; Asst. Prof. of Psychodonti, Univ. of Stockholm, Odontological Fac., 1964-; Gen. Sec., 2nd Scandinavian Congress for Hypnosis, 1972; Has given post-grad. courses in Psychodonti & Hypnosis in Sweden, Norway, Denmark & Gemany, 1965-. Mbrships: Swedish Dental Soc.; Scand Odontological Soc.; Féderation dentaire international, Swedish sect.; Soc. for Clin. & Expmtl. Hypnosis, Swedish sect.; Pres., Swedish Soc. for Psychodonti. Publs: Psychodonti; The Dentist isn't Dangerous; articles in profl. jrnls. Hons: Medal of The Royal Soc. for civilian air-raid precautions, 1942. Address: Norrmalmstörg 4, 111 46 Stockholm, Sweden. 43.

WINSETT, Marvin Davis, b. 13 Feb. 1902. Poet; Author; Editor; Lecturer. Appts. incl: Treas., 1955-61; Pres., 1962-66; Poetry Soc. of Tex.; Advsry. Bd., Am. Poetry League, 1962-64; V.P., 1963, 67, Pres., 1964-66; Nat. Fed. of State Poetry Socs.; Mbr., Nat. Poetry Day Comm., Tex., Co-Chmn., 1965-66; Chmn., Tex. Coun. for Promotion of Poetry; Staff Mbr., South & West Lit. Quarterly. Hon. Mbr., UPLI: Hon. Mbr., Avalon World Arts Acad.; Hon. Mbr., Poetry Soc. of Tex.; Acad. of Am. Poets (Fndr. Affiliate); Life Fellow, Int. Inst. Arts & Letters; Fellow, Royal Soc. of Arts, U.K.; Life, Sigma Delta Chi; Lambda Chi Alpha; Corresp., l'Etranger Acad. Francaise de la Poesie. Mbr., Advsry. Bd., Vachel Lindsay Assoc.; Mbr., Edit. Advsry. Bd., D.I.B.; Poet Laureate of Texas, 1962. Originator of Cyclus Verse Form. Publs. incl: contribs. to South & West, The Green World, Seydell Quarterly, American Bard, Kaleidograph, Frame, Manifold (London), Carovana (Italy), Poet Lore, Poet (India), Laurel Leaves (Philippines), Quicksilver; Sing Loud for Loveliness Anthol., 1962; Mitre Press Spring Anthologies, 1961-67; Southwester Anthol., 1937; Sea to Sea Anthols., 1957-67; Surf, Starts & Stone Anthol. of Tex. Poets, 1961; Avalon Anthol. of Texas Poets Golden Book Anthol.; Memorabilia Anthol., 1965; The Guild Anthol., 1966; The Hinds Create Anthol., 1961; Singing Muse; Anthol. of Am. Poetry, Book 3, etc.; (books) Winding Stairway; Basic Ad. Writing; April Always; Remembered Earth. Recip. many awards for poetry, inclng: Hon. Dr. Humane Letters, Free Univ. of Asia, 1968; FRSA; Citation for outstanding contribs. to poetry, South & West Inc., Instr. Literary Pub., 1968; Pres. Macapagal Gold Medal & Laurel Wreath as UPLY Hon. Poet Laureate Leader, 1965; Pres. Marcos Gold Medal and UPLI Decretum, 1968. Address: 3936 Colgate Street, Dallas, TX 75225, U.S.A. 3, 7, 11, 12, 16, 30, 113.

WINSLOW, Albert Foster, b. 12 May 1914. Chemical Botanist. Educ: Columbia Univ.; Grad., N.Y. Stock Exchange Schl. of Finance, 1937. Appts. incl: Treas., Arboreal Assocs., Inc., Harriman, N.Y., 1954-60; Pres., ibid, 1960-71; Chmn. of Bd., 1971-; Dir. & Treas.,

Chemtree Corp., Central Valley, N.Y., 1960-72; Dir. & Vice Chmn., Tuxedo Park Assn., N.Y., 1968-; Dir., Natural Disaster, Orange Co., 1971-73; Dpty. Dir., Civil Defense, ibid, 1973-. Mbrships. incl: AAAS; Int. Shade Tree Conf.; N.Y. State Arborists Assn., Veterans of For. Wars; Chmn., Civil Defense Comm., N.Y. State, Am. Legion, 1958-60; Am. Ordnance Assn.; Order of the Lafayette. Address: Cliff Rd., Tuxedo Park, NY 10987, U.S.A. 6, 16, 131.

WINSTON, Marian (Edith) Prince (Drachman), b. 2 Feb. 1924. Social Researcher; Writer; Editor. Educ: B.A., Hunter Coll., N.Y.C., 1943; M.L.S., UCLA, 1965; equivalent of M.A., CUNY, N.Y. Univ., Berkeley, UCLA. Appts: Staff Writer, Current Biography, H.W. Wilson Co., N.Y.C., 1943-47; Staff Writer, Pix Inc., ibid, 1947-50; Ed., UCLA, 1950-57, '65-66; Cons., Rand Corporation, Santa Monica. 1966-; Ed., free-lance Writer, Rschr., 1967-; Mbr., sev. govt. advsry. bodies. Mbrships. incl: Sr. Mbr., Tech. Communication Soc.; V.P., Santa Monica Women's Democratic Club; Mensa, Gtr. LA; Publs. incl: Co-author, The Distelfink in Pennsylvania Dutch Folk Art, Manual of Arm Amputee Checkout and Training; Manual of Lower Extremity Prosthetics; Nonsupport of Legitimate Children by Affluent Fathers as a Cause of Poverty and Welfare Dependence (w. Trude Forsher), 1971; about 300 mag. articles; newspaper & mag. articles on soc. problems of women & children; Contbr. Collier's Ency. Address: c/o Rand Corp., 1700 Main St., Santa Monica, CA 90406, U.S.A. 5, 9, 120, 138.

WINTERNITZ, Emanuel, b. 4 Aug. 1898. University Professor; Author; Lecturer; Curator. Educ: LL.D., Univ. of Vienna, 1922; Pvte. study of music, Vienna; Study of philos., Univ. of Hamburg. Appts: Corp. Lawyer, Vienna, 1929-38; Lectr., Fogg Mus., Cambridge, Mass. & other museums & univs., 1938-41; Curator, Musical Instruments, Metropol. Mus. of Art, N.Y.C., 1942-73; Curator Emeritus, 1974; Lectr., Columbia Univ., 1947-48; Vis. Lectr., Yale Univ. Schl. of Music & Rutgers Univ.; Mbr., Doctoral Fac., CUNY, 1968-. Mbrships. incl: Past Pres., Int. Comm. for Museums & Collects. of Musical Instruments, Int. Coun. of Museums; Past Coun. Mbr., Past Chmn., N.Y. Chapt., Am. Musicol. Soc. Publs: Books in U.S., U.K. & Germany, inclng: Musical Autographs from Monteverdi to Hindemith, 1965; Musical Instruments of the Western World, 1966,'67. Contbr. to num. jrnls., U.S. & Europe. Hons: Guggenheim Fellowship, 1946; Am. Coun. of Learned Socs. Fellowship, 1962; Bollingen Fndn. Fellowship, 1964. Address: Metropolitan Mus. of Art, 5th Ave. & 82nd St., N.Y., NY 10028, U.S.A. 2, 13, 21, 86.

WINTERS, Alice Graham (Mrs. Carl S. Winters), b. 5 July 1907. Writer; Minister; Civic Worker. Educ: Univ. of Rochester, N.Y.; Colgate-Rochester Divinity Schl. Appts: Min., Jr. Ch., Jackson, Mich., 1931-39, Oak Pk., Ill., 1939-59. Mbrships: Pres., Women's Bd., Salvation Army of Gtr. Chgo., Chgo. Drama League, Chgo. Mission Union; Chmn., P.R., Conf. of Club Pres. & Prog. Chmn., Chgo.; Chmn., Int. Rels., AAUW., Mich.; Prog. Dir., Chautauqua Woman's Club, N.Y.; Delta Zeta; Beta Sigma Phi; Kappa Delta Pi; Zonta. Contbr. of articles to theol. jrnls. Recip., citation for work w. youth, 1947. Address: 404 N. East Ave., Oak Park, IL 60302, U.S.A. 5, 8, 22, 130, 138.

WINTERS, Carl Sexson, b. 22 Feb. 1904. Minister-Lecturer. Educ: A.B., Franklin Coll., 1929; B.D., Colgate-Rochester Divinity Schl.,

1931; D.D., Lincoln Mem. Univ., 1941; H.H.D., Hillsdale Coll., 1958; D.D., Franklin Coll. Appts: Ordained to min., 1929; Pastor, Lincoln, N.Y., 1929, Jackson, Mich., 1931-39, & Oak Park, Ill., 1939-59; Lect. Staff, Gen. Motors Corp., 1958-. Mbrships: Kappa Delta Rho; Pi Kappa Delta; Chap., Ind. Soc. of Chgo.; Rotary; Shriner, 33rd degree, Masons; Oak Park Country Club; Grand Orator, Grand Lodge; V.P., Nat. Spkrs. Assn.; Spkrs. Assocs. Hons: Hon. Citizen, Dallas, New Orleans, Atlanta, State of Tex., Ky.; Ky. Col.; Man of the Yr., Dale Carnegie Inst., 1969. Address: 404 N. E. Ave., Oak Park, IL 60302, U.S.A. 2, 8, 22, 57, 130.

WINTHROP, John, b. 22 June 1936. Investment Company Executive. Educ: B.A., Harvard Univ., 1958; M.B.A., Grad. Schl. of Bus. Admin., Columbia Univ., 1962. Appts. incl: Ed., Atlantic Community Newsletter, Wash. D.C., 1962-63; Rsch. Trainee, Wood Struthers Winthrop, 1964-65; Investment Advsry. Trainee, ibid, 1965-66; Portfolio Mgr., ibid, 1967-68; Ptnr., ibid, 1968; V.P., Sec. & Mbr., Exec. Comm., ibid, 1969; Mgr., Financial Servs. Depts., ibid, 1971; Pres., de Vegh Mutual Fund, 1973. Mbrships. incl: Bond Club, N.Y.; N.Y. Soc. of Security Analysts; Harvard Club, N.Y.C.; Knickerbocker Club, N.Y. Publs: Book of Bad Verse, 1972; articles in financial jrnls. & Boston Globe. Hons: Seaton-Porter Prize, St. Mark's Schl., 1953. Address: c/o Wood Struthers Winthrop, 20 Exchange Pl., N.Y., NY 10005, U.S.A. 6.

WINTRINGHAM, W(illiam) T(ylee), b. 18 Jan. 1904. Television Researcher. Educ: B.S., Harvard Engrng. Schl., 1924. Appts: w. Am. Tel. & Tel. Co., 1924-34; Rschr., TV, Radio, Telephone, Bell Labs., 1934-65; Cons., TV, ibid, 1965-69; Indep. Cons., TV, 1969-. Fellowships: Inst. of Radio Engrs.; Soc. of Motion Picture & TV Engrs.; Hon., British Kinematograph, Sound & TV Soc. Mbrships. incl: Inst. Radio Engrs.; Chmn., IEEE, 1967-69; Engrng. V.P., Soc. of Motion Picture & TV Engrs., 1967-; Bd. Dirs., ISCC, 1972-73; Acoustical Soc. Am.; Optical Soc. Am. Author of tech. publs. Hons: Cert. for Contbns. to Color TV Standards, Radio-Electronics-TV Mfrs. Assn., 1954; Plaque, IRE-EIA, 1961; Cert., IEEE, 1970. Address: 56 Elmwood Ave., Chatham, NJ 07928, U.S.A. 6, 14, 26.

WIRSTA, Aristide, b. 22 Mar. 1922. Musicologist. Educ: Univs. in Vienna, Austria & Paris, France, 1947 & '55; Conservatoire Nat. Superiúr de Musique, Paris, France, 1948; Docteur de l'univ. de Paris, 1955; Docteur ès Lettres, 1974. Appts. incl: Stagiaire de recherce, Ctr. Nat. de la Recherche Scientifique, Paris, 1956-58; Attaché, C.N.R.S., 1958-62; Contractuel, ibid, 1965-; Lectr., Musicology, Free Ukrainian Univ., Munich, Germany, 1967-; Prof., ibid, 1974. Mbrships. incl: Pres., Assn. académique ukrainienne, Paris, France, 1960-; Gen. Sec., Acad. Int. libre des scis. et des lettres, Paris; Inst. d'Etudes Slaves; Sco. française de musicologie; Int. Musicological Soc.; V.P., Assn. Int. des Docteurs de l'Univ. de Paris. Publs. incl: Ecoles de violon au 18th siècle d'aprés les ouvrages didactiques, 1955; La filiation des violonistes selon leurs écoles respectives, 1955; l'Enseignement de Violon au 19th seècle, 1971. Address: 1 rue A. Camus, 92340 Bourg la Reine, France. 43.

WIRT, Sherwood Eliot, b. 12 Mar. 1911. Journalist. Educ: A.B., Univ. of Calif., U.S.A., 1932; B.D., Pacific Schl. of Religion, 1943; Ph.D., Univ. of Edinburgh, U.K., 1951; Postgrad. study, Hartford Theol. Sem.;

Princeton Theol. Sem.; Univ. of Zurich; Jung Psychol. Inst., Zurich, Switzerland. Appts: Reporter on newspapers in Martinez & San Fran., Calif. & Hilo, Hawaii, 1932-35; City Ed., Alaska Daily Press, Juneau, 1935-39; Pastor, 1st Congl. Ch., Collinsville, Conn., 1943-44; Chap. (Capt.), USAF, 1944-46; Min. to students, Univ. of Congl. Ch., Seattle, Wash., 1946-49; Pastor, Knox Presby. Ch., Berkeley, Calif., 1951-55; Hillside Presby., Oakland, ibid, 1955-59; Edit. Assoc., Christianity Today mag., Wash., D.C., 1960. Ed., Decision Mag., Mpls., Minn., 1960-. Mbrships: Theta Chi; Sigma Delta Chi; Evangelical Press Assn., U.S.-Canada (Pres., 1969-71). Publs. incl: Co-author, Living Quotations for Christmas, 1974; Enough and to Spare, 1973; Jesus Power, 1972; Love Song, translation of Augustine's Confessions, 1971; Passport to Life City, 1969; The Social Conscience of the Evangelical, 1968; Note Me, God, 1966. Address: 3734 48th Ave. S., Mpls., MN 55406, U.S.A. 8.

WISCHMANN, Adolf (Hermann Paul), b. 17 Oct. 1908. Evangelical Church Executive. Educ: Studied theol., Tübingen, Zurich, Berlin & Göttingen, 1928-32. Appts: Curate, Schaumburg-Lippe, 1923; Univ. Asst., Tübingen, 1934-35; Spiritual aid, Hanover, 1936; Student, area & town youth min., Göttingen, 1936-48; Dir., Evangelical Acad., Hermannsburg & dist., 1948-55; Area Supt., diocese of Osnabrück-Diepholz, 1955-56; Pres., Ch. external off., Evangelical Ch. in Germany, 1956-. Mbrships. incl: Deleg., nat. assembly of Luth. Int. Union, in Hanover, Mnpls., U.S.A., Helsinki, Finland & Evian; Deleg., nat. assembly, World Coun. of Churches, New Delhi, India, & Uppsala, Sweden; Central Comm., ibid 1968-; Advsry. Comm., Conf. European Churches. Author of religious books. Recip. of hons. Address: Kirchlichen Aussenamtes der Evangelischen Kirche in Deutschland, Bockenheimer Landstr. 109, 6 Frankfurt am Main, German Fed. Repub. 43, 92.

WISE, Betty Jean (Mrs. Eugene E. Wise), b. 27 Apr. 1932. Administrator; Social Worker; Educator. Educ: B.S. Elem. Educ., Crtl. State Univ., Ohio, 1954; M.S. Soc. Work, Univ. of Conn., 1956; Ohio State Univ., Columbus, 1973; Boston Univ., Mass., 1974. Appts: Dir., Soc. Serv., Booth Mat. Home & Hosp., Cinn., Ohio, 1958-59; Psych. Soc. Wkr., ibid, Spokane, Wash., 1959-60; Adult Educ. Inst., Fairchild AFB, Wash., 1962-64; Cons., Greenleigh Assoc. Inc., Spokane, ibid, 1964; Elem. Educ. Tchr., Hamilton Local Schl. Dist., 1965-69; Soc. Planner, City of Columbus, Ohio, 1969; Asst. Dean of Students, Wilmington Coll., Ohio, 1969-71; Incorporator, 1st Dir. of Attention to Neglected Diseases, Inc., 1971-72; Acting Dir., Counseling Ctr., Capital Univ., Columbus, Ohio, 1972-; Counselor & For. Student Advsr., 1973-. Mbrships. incl: Bd. Trustees & 2nd V.P., Children's Mental Hlth. Ctr., 1974; Royal Soc. Promotion Hlth., Ctr., Am. Assn. Higher Educ.; Alpha Kappa Alpha.; Inst. of African-Am. Studies, 1970. Recip. of AKA Achievement Award, Alpha Sigma Omega Chapt., 1969. Address: Counseling Ctr., Capital Univ., Columbus, OH 43209, U.S.A. 5, 8, 132.

WISE-CIOBOTARU, Gillian, b. 16 Feb. 1936. Artist. Educ: Central Schl., U.K., 1959; UNESCO Fellow, Prague, 1968; Postgrad. studies, Repin Inst., Leningrad, 1969-70. Appts. incl: Vis. tchr., Painting Schl., Chelsea Schl. of Art, London, 1971-73; Assoc. Lectr., ibid, 1973-74. Hon. Life mbr., Inst. of Contemporary Art, London. One-man shows: Exhibition of relief structures, Inst. of Contemporary Art (w. Anthony Hill), 1963; Axiom Gall., London, 1967. Major Exhibitions incl: 1st Nuremberg Biennale, Germany, & Open Air Sculpture Exhibition, Antwerp, 1969; Systems, Amos Anderson Mus., Helsinki & Whitechapel Gall., London, 1969-73. works in pub. collects. Commns. incl: Wall screen w. Anthony Hill for the Cunard Liner, Queen Elizabeth II, 1968; Mural for Med. Schl., Nottingham Hosp., Bldg. Design Ptnrship., 1974. Author of articles in jrnls. Address: 62 Courtfield Gdns., London, SW5 ONQ, U.K.

WISEMAN, Roy W., b. 27 June 1913. School Principal. Educ: B.S., Middle Tenn. State Univ., Murfreesboro, U.S.A., 1948; M.A., ibid, 1952. Appts: Elem. Schl. Prin., 18 yrs.; Prin., Navy H.S., Naples, Italy, 4 yrs.; H.S. Prin., 21 yrs. Mbrships. incl: Tenn. State Senator; Fndg. Pres., McMinnville Lions Club; Pres., Alumni Assn. Meddle Tenn. State Univ.; Nat. Congress, PTA; Exec. Comm., E. Tenn. Educ. Assn.; Pres., Warren Co & Bradley Co. Educ. Assn.; NEA; Veterans of For. Wars; Am. Legion; Sigma club. Publs: The School Administrator; Integration of Thirty-Four Retarded Adolescents into a Progressive High School Program; Curriculum Development; A Guide for the Secondary Teacher Counselor Program. Address: 102 Franklin St., McMinnville, TN 37110, U.S.A. 57, 125, 130.

WISHERT, Hazel Ferguson (Mrs. Tony B. Wishert). Purchasing Executive. Educ: Washburn Univ. Appts: Buyer Asst., Garlands, St. Louis, Mo., 1942-45; Girls' Wear Buyer, Palace Clothing Co., Topeka, Kan., 1945-51; Sportswear Buyer, ibid, 1947-51; Buyer, Women's Ready-to-Wear, 1965-71 & Dress Buyer, Plymouth Clothing Co., St. Joseph, Mo, 1971-73; Mgr., Palace Clothing Co., Prairie Village, Kan., 1973-. Mbrships: Am. Bus. Women's Assn.; Altrusa Int.; Pres., Presby. Women's Org.; Kappa Sigma Mothers Club; Woman's Div. Chmbr. of Comm.; Prairie Village Merchants Assn. Address: 1732 Amhurst Rd., Topeka, KS 66604, U.S.A. 5, 8, 16, 120, 132, 138.

WISNIEWSKI, Bernard Michael, b 29 July 1910. Advertising Artist; Portrait Artist. Educ: Ill. Inst: of Technol.; Pvte. Portraiture Study. Appts. incl: Prod. Designer, Hotpoint, 1945-46; ibid & Dev. Engr., Storkline Furniture Corp., 1946-47; Prod. Stylist, Sears Roebuck & Co., 1947-49; Adv. Illustrator, Waldie & Briggs, 1950-62; Adv. Artist DeVenny-Wood Studio, 1962-64; Adv. Mgr., G.C. Electronics, Rockford, Ill., 1964-65; Adv. Artist, Whitaker-Guernsey Studio, Chgo., 1965-66; Dir., Adv. & P.R., Dee Elec. Co., 1966-67; Chgo. Adv. Dir., Verve Adv., 1967-68; Adv. Prod., Vogue-Wright Studios, 1968-. Mbrships: Fndr. & 1st Pres., Ill. Chapt., Am. Artist Profl. League, 1963-65; Hon. Mbr., Regent Art League, Chgo. Former V.P. & Chmn. of Publicity, Pallet & Chisel Acad. of Fine Arts, 1963-65; Past Pres., Polish Arts Club of Chgo., 1962-63. Works in pvte. collects. Address: 4849 W. Addison St., Chicago, IL 60641, U.S.A. 8.

WISWALL, Frank Lawrence Jr., b. 21 Sept. 1939. International Maritime Lawyer. Educ: B.A., Colby Coll., 1962; J.D., Cornell Univ., N.Y., 1965; Ph.D. (juris), Cambridge Univ., U.K., 1967. Appts: Harbormaster, Charterboat Capt., Ferry Pilot; Tutorial Supvsr., Clare Coll., Cambridge Univ., U.K., 1966-67; Assoc., Burlingham Underwood Barron Wright & White, N.Y., 1967-73; Legal Advsr., Bur. Maritime Affairs, Repub. Liberia, 1968-; Lectr., Admiralty Law, Cornell Law Schl., U.S.A., 1969, '71 '73-74; Legal Comm., Inter-Govtl. Maritme Cons. Org., London, U.K., 1972; V.-Chmn., 1974-; Gen. Counsel-Pres., Liberian Servs., Inc., 1973-. Mbrships. incl: Fellow, Royal Histl. Soc., 1972; Bars of Maine, N.Y. & Supreme Ct. of U.S.A.; Am. Bar Assn.; Assn. Bar City of N.Y.; Admiralty Comm., 1971-74; Maritime Law Assn., U.S.; Fndn. Sec., Alpha Delta Phi; Phi Delta Phi; United Oxford & Cambridge Univ. Club, London; Castine Yacht Club, Maine. Publs: The Development of Admiralty Jurisdiction & Practice Since 1800, 1970; law review articles. Recip. Yorke Prize, 1968. Address: Meadow Farm, Castine, ME 04421, U.S.A. 6, 30, 128.

WITCHER, Nollie Averette, Jr., b. 17 Sept. 1931. Minister; Educator. Appts: Sci. Tchr., Robert E. Lee Jr. H.S., Danbille, Va.; Pastor, Cascade Bapt. Ch., Va.; Prin., Stonewall Jackson Elem. Schl. Mbrships: Nominating Comm., Danville Educ. Assn.; Deleg. to Conv., Va. Educ. Assn.; NEA. Hons: 10 yrs. Serv. as Pastor, Cascade Bapt. Ch., 1974; 8 yrs. Serv., Robert E. Lee Jr. H.S., 1970. Address: 1213 Greenwood Dr., Danville, VA 24541, U.S.A. 125.

WITH, Torben Kiorboe, b. 18 Aug. 1910. Physician; Specialist in Internal Medicine & Clinical Chemistry; Consultant Chemical Pathologist. Educ: M.D., Copenhagen Univ., 1941; Grad. in Pub. Hlth. ibid, 1946. Appts. incl: Dpty. Chief Physn., Rigshospitalet, Med. Dept. A, 1949-54; Physn. for Coll. Students, Copenhagen Univ., 1946-54; Cons. Chem. Pathol. (Chief, Ctrl. Lab. & Blood Bank), Svendborg Co. Hosp., 1954-. Mbrships. incl: Nutrition & Biochem. Socs., U.K.; Assn. of Clin. Pathols., U.K.; Canadian Soc. of Clin. Chems.; Deutsche Gesellschaft für Klinische Chemie; sev. Danish profl. orgs. Publs: Absorption, Metabolism & Storage of Vitamin A & Caroten, 1940; Biology of Bile Pigments, 1954; Biologie der Gallenfarbstoffe, 1960; Bile Pigments, 1968; On Porphyrin Esterification & Ester Hydrolysis, in Scand. Jrnl. Chem. Lab. Invest., Supp. 134, 1973. num. other papers in med. & popular jrnls. During past 10 yrs. specialized in work on porphyrins & porphyrias. Address: Centrallaboratoriet, Svendborg Sygehus, 5700 Svendborg, Denmark. 43, 50, 134.

WITHAM, W(illiam) Tasker, b. 20 May 1914. Educator. Educ: B.A., Drew Univ., 1936; M.A., Columbia Univ., 1940; Ph.D., Univ. of Ill., 1961. Appts: Tchr., Newton (N.J.) Schl. for Boys, 1936-38; Activities Sec., Bronx Union YMCA, N.Y.C., 1940-42; Prof. of Engl., Hiwassee Coll., Madisonville, Tenn., 1942-43, Hartwick Coll., Oneonta, N.Y., 1943-57, Ind. State Univ., Terre Haute, 1959-. Mbrships. incl: Mod. Humanities Rsch. Assn.; MLA of Am.; Midwest Mod. Lang. Assn.; Nat. Coun. of Tchrs. of Engl.; Phi Kappa Phi; Sigma Tau Delta; Hon. Mbr., Mark Twain & Eugene Field Socs. Publs: Americans as They Speak & Live, 1945; Panorama of American Literature, 1947; Living American Literature, 1947; The Adolescent in the American Novel, 1920-1960, 1964, rev. ed., 1974; conbr. to Annual Bibliog. of Engl. Lang. & Lit., 1964-. Address: Dept. of Engl. & Jrnlsm., Ind. State Univ., Terre Haute, IN 47809, U.S.A. 8, 13, 14, 15, 30, 82, 139.

WITHERS, (Hon.) William Robert, b. 8 Aug. 1931. Member of the Legislative Council of Western Australia. Educ: Schl. of Air Navigation, RAAF, 1951-52. Appts: Sr. Cloud Seeding Off., Radiophys. Div., Commonwealth Scientific & Indl Rsch. Org., 1957-64; Ord Irrigation Proj., 1964; Shire Cr., Wyndham-E. Kimberley, 1965; Dpty. Shire Pres., 1966-71; Justice of Peace, 1967; Consultative Cr., Kimberley, 1967-71; Mbr., Children's Ct., 1968; Mbr. Legislative Coun., N. Province, W.A., 1971-; Mbrships. incl: Chmn., Tourist

Proj. Comm.; Chmn., E. Kimberley Secondary Educ: Bd.; Northern Rep., State Reserves Advsry. Coun.; Pres., Kununurra Chmbr. of Comm.; W. Australian Club. Publs. incl: Remote Area Costs, 1962; Strangulation of Commerce & Industry by the Wan Provision of Education Facilities, 1969; Education of Aborigines, 1972; Community or Chaos, 1973. Paintings in Parliament House & Nat. Bank Coll. Address: Parliament House, Harvest Ter., Perth, W.A., Australia 6000. 23.

WITHERSPOON, Don Meade, b. 6 Mar. 1930. Veterinarian. Educ: D.V.M., Univ. of Ga., Athens, 1959; Ph.D., ibid, 1970; Dipl., Coll. of Theriogenol., 1973. Appts: Pvte. Prac. (gen.), for 5 yrs.; Asst. Prof.-Assoc. Prof., Large Animal Surg. & Med., Auburn Univ., 1964-66; Rsch. Assoc., Univ. of Ga., 1967-69; Prof., Large Animal Med. & Surg., ibid, 1969-; Chief, Food Producing Animal & Equine Sect., Coll. of Vet. Med., Dept. of Med. & Surg., 1969-73. Mbrships: Am. Assn. of Vet. Educators; AVMA; AAEP; AABP; ASSBS, Coll. of Theriogenol.; ASP & Pharmacol.; Ga. VMA; Phi Zeta. Publs: original rsch. reports, inclng., Development of Equine Peritoneal Fistula, Uses of Dyes to Trace Ovulation Process in Live Horse, Use of Fiber Optics to Study Activity of Equine Ovary, Recording of Nocturnal Tendency of Equine Ovary; Immunization Program for Feedlot Cattle (Steer Feeding Short Course sponsored by Ext. Animal Sci. Dept., Coop. Ext. Serv., Univ. of Ga.), 1970; many articles in profl. jrnls. Hons: Outstanding Tchr. in Clin. Med., Auburn Univ., 1967. Address: 355 Univ. Circle, Athens, GA 30601, U.S.A.

WITHOF, Hans Peter, b. 17 July 1930. Industrial Executive. Educ: Dipl. Degree for Engrng., Tech. Univ., Aachen, Germany. Appts: Georg. C.K. Withof GmbH., Kassel-Be, 1949, Mgr., 1954, V.P., 1961, Pres., 1962-; Chmn. of Bd., Withof Gerâtebau KG, Calden; Pres., Philips Elektronik Industrie GmbH, Hamburg. Mbrships: Rotary Club Int.; Dechema, Frankfurt; VDI, Dusseldorf; VDE, Frankfurt; ISA, Pitts., U.S.A.; Hon. Pres., Marketing-Club Nordhessen e.V., Kassel. Articles, incdl. control, marketing & mgmt. problems, newspapers. Address: Miramstr. 87, 35 Kassel-Be., German Fed. Repub. 43.

WITKIN, Erwin, b. 19 Aug. 1926. Physician; Consultant; Writer. Educ: B.A., Johns Hopkins Univ., Balt., Md., 1947; M.D., Univ. of Neb., 1951; Post Grad. Specialty Trng., Sinai of Balt., 1951-55. Appts: Pvte. Prac., Gyn., 1955-; Chief Med. Cons., Bur. of Hlth. Ins., Soc. Security Admin., 1966-69; Med. Cons., Block McGibony & Assocs., Inc., Silver Spring, Md., 1970-; Lectr., Columbia Univ. Schl. of Pub. Hlth. & Administrative Med. Prog. of Continuing Educ., 1967; Chmn., Sci. Prog. Comm., Interscientias, Inc., The Hague, The Netherlands. Mbrships. incl: Fellow, Am. Coll. of Ob. & Gyn.; AMA; Am. Soc. of Abdominal Surgs.; Assn. fo Pub. Hlth. Physns.; Am. Fertility Soc.; Royal Soc. of Hlth. Author of The Impact of Medicare,, 1971, & of articles in med. jrnls. Address: 6807 Maurleen Rd., Balt., MD 21209, U.S.A.

WITTER, Richard Earl, b. 6 Dec. 1926. Company Executive. Educ: A.B., Columbia Univ., 1950. Appts: Pres. & Gen. Mgr., F & S F Book Co. Inc., N.Y., Address: 78 Ravenhurst Ave., Staten Island, NY 10310, U.S.A. 6.

WITTHAUS, Karl, b. 26 Aug. 1892. Professor Emeritus. Educ: Coll. & Univ., Berlin, Germany. Univ. of Córdoba, Buenos Aires, Argentina. Appts: Vice Recor, Inst. Crespo;

Prof., Colegio Burmeister; Dir., Inst. Evangelico Am.; Prof. Philos., Lutheran Sem. of Theol. Publs: translations, inclng. Works of Luther in Spanish; Spanish-German Theological Dictionaires; contbr., articles to religious mags. Hons: 1st class Verdienstkreuz, Aug. 1962; Cross of Merit, W. Germany. Address: Ave. Independencia 28, 1° piso, dep. C. Santiago del Estero, Argentina.

WITTLIN, Joseph (Józef), b. 17 Aug. 1896. Writer. Educ: Univ. of Vienna, 1915-16; Univ. of Lvov, 1918. Appts. incl: Tchr., Polish Lang. & Lit., Gymnasium, Lvov, 1919-21; Lit. Dir., Municipal Theatre & Cofndr. & Lectr., Schi. of Drama, Lodz, 1921-24; Co-ed., Tyogonik Polski, Polish weekly, N.Y.C., 1941-43; w. Radio Free Europe, 1952. Mbrships. Incl: The Spring, Poznan, 1919-20; Corres. Mbr., German Acad. of Poetry & Lang., 1971-. Publs. incl: Hymny, 1920; Hymny, 1929; Powiesc o cierpliwym piechurze, 1954; Orfeusz w piekle XX wieku, 1963; poems in Najsybitniejsi poeci emigracji; transl. of approx. 20 novels & plays; contbr. num. articles to li†. mags. & jrnls. Hons. incl: Award, Polish PEN, 1935; Double Prize for The Salt of the Earth, Acad. of Independents, Wiadomosci Literackie, 1936; Golden Laurel, Polish Acad. of Lit., 1937; Prize for entire creative output, Jurzykowski Fndn., N.Y.C., 1969. Address: 5400 Fieldston Rd., New York, NY 10471, U.S.A.

WITTMANN, Stepher. J., b. 7 Jan. 1933. Anesthesiologist. Educ: B.S., Georgetown Univ., 1960; B.D.Med., Univ. of Md., 1966. Appts. incl: Res. Anesthesiologist, Univ. of Va., Charlottesville, 1967-69; Anesthesiologist, Fairfax Hosp., Va., & Wash. Sanitorium Hosp., Takoma Pk., Md., 1969-71; Asst. Chief Anesthesia., Tchr. Residency Prog., Wlater Reed Gen. Hosp., Wash. D.C., 1969-71; Anesthesiologist, & Med. Dir., Respiratory Therapy Dept., Manatee Mem. Hosp., Braderton, Fla., 1971-. Mbrships: Am. Soc. Anesthesiologists; Int. Rsch. Soc.; AMA. Contbr. profl. jrnl., Anesthesia & Analgesia. Recip., Meritorious Serv. Award, U.S. Army. Address: 5015 Manatee Ave. W., Bradenton, FL 33505, U.S.A.

WITTON-DAVIES, (The Ven.) Carlyle, b. 10 June 1913. Anglican Priest. Educ: Univ. Coll. of N. Wales, Bangor; Exeter & Cuddesdon Colls., Oxford; Hebrew Univ., Jerusalem. Appts: Asst. Curate, Buckley, Flints., 1937-40; Subwarden, St. Michael's Coll., Llandaff, 1940-44; Advsr. on Judaica to Anglican Bishop in Jerusalem, 1944-49; Canon Residentiary of Nazareth, St. George's Collegiate Ch., Jerusalem, 1947-49; Dean & Precentor, St. David's Cathedral, 1950-57; Archdeacon, Oxford & Canon of Christ Church, 1957-. Mbrships: Clergy Friendly Soc. (Chmn., 1961-63); Coun. of Christians & Jews: (Chmn., 1957-); Nikaean Club. Publs: Journey of a Lifetime, 1962; Translated Martin Buber's Hasidism, 1948 & The Prophetic Faith, 1949; Contbr. to Oxford Dictionary of Christian Church, 1957 & 1974, & The Mission of Israel, 1963. Hons; Hall-Houghton Septuagint Prizes at Oxford Univ., Jnr., 1938, Snr., 1939; Chap., Order of St. John of Jerusalem, 1954-. Address: Archdeacon's Lodging., Christ Church, Oxford, U.K. 1, 3.

WITTY, Robert Gee, b. 6 Oct. 1906. Educator; Clergyman. Educ: B.A., Willamette Univ., 1928; Kimball Schl. of Theol.; Princeton Theol. Sem.; B.D., Asbury Theol. Sem., 1932; Th.D., Burton Coll. & Sem., 1953; Ph.D., Univ. of Fla., 1959. Appts: Pastor, Ctrl. Bapt. Ch., 1943-70; Pres., Luther Rjce Sem., Jacksonville, Fla., 1967-. Mbrships: Am. Assn. of

Independent Coll. & Univ. Pres.; Tau Kappa Alpha; Pi Gamma Mu; Alpha Kappa Nu; Chmn., Comm., Promotion of Democracy 3 yrs.; Vice Chmn., Pastors' Conf., 1949, '70; Bd. of Missions, Fla. Bapt. Conv., 1969-72. Publs: Should a Christian Dance? ; The Rhetoric of Isaac Watts; Power for the Church; Help Yourself to Happiness; Signs of the Second Coming. Conbr. to profl. jrnls., periodicals. Address: Luther Rice Seminary, 1050 Hendricks Ave., Jacksonville, FL 32207, U.S.A. 7, 30.

WOETZEL, Robert Kurt, b. 5 Dec. 1930. Professor of International Politics & Law. Educ: B.A., Columbia Coll., S.C., U.S.A., 1952; Ph.D., Univ. of Oxford, 1954; J.D., Bonn Univ., Germany, 1959. Appts. incl: Asst. Prof. - Adjunct Assoc. Prof. of Pub. Law & Govt., Fordham Univ., Bronx, N.Y., 1959-63; Staff Mbr., Ctr. for Study of Democratic Insts., Santa Barbara, Calif., 1964-66; Prof. of Int. Pol. & Law, Boston Coll., Jesuit Univ., 1966-; Pres., Fndn. for Estab. of an Int. Criminal Ct., Newton, Mass., 1970-. Mbrships. incl: Chmn., Int. Criminal Ct. Comm., World Peace through Law Ctr., 1971-; Exec. Comm., U.S. Br., Int. Inst. of Space Law. 1970-; Sec. Gen., Int. Criminal Law Assn., 1965-; Int. Law Assn.; AIAA. Publs. incl: The Nuremberg Trials in International Law, 1960, revised edit., With a Postlude on the Eichmann Trial, 1962; The Philosophy of Freedom, 1966; Toward A Feasible International Criminal Court (w. J. Stone), 1970. Hons. incl: Curtis Gold Medal, 1952; Disting. Int. Criminal Lawyer Award, 1973. Address: P.O. Box 12, Newton, MA 02166, U.S.A. 3, 14, 15, 30.

WOFSEY, Marvin M. b. 1 June 1913. Professor. Educ: B.S., N.Y. Univ., 1935; M.A. Stats., 1942, Ph.D., Pub. Admin., 1967. Am. Univ. Appts: Budget Off., Acct., & Dir., Date Processing, Dept. of Navy, 1946-60; Hd., Computer Lab., Am. Univ., 1960-64; Hd., Systems Dept., Dept. of Defense Computer Inst., 1964-67; Prof., Mgmt., Geo. Wash. Univ., 1967-; Cons., 1967-; Guest Lectr., NATO, Paris. Mbrships: Int. Dir. & Mbr., Cert. Advsry. Comm., Data Processing Mgmt. Assn.; Sec., Digital Computer Trng., Assn. for Computer Machinery. Publs: Conversion to Automatic Data Processing: A Practival Primer, 1962; Management of Automatic Data Processing Systems, 1968; Management of ADP, 1973; Contbr. to num. jrnls. Hons: pres. Award, 1963, Life Mbrship., 1965, Data Processing Mgmt. Assn. Address: 200 Hall of Govt., Geo. Wash. Univ., Washington, DC 20006, U.S.A.

WOJATSEK, Charles, b. 29 Sept. 1916. Professor of History. Educ: Univ. of Brno, Czechoslovakia, 1935-36; B.A., Univ. of Bratislava, 1938; M.A., Univ. of Debrecen, 1938; Univ. of Fribourg, Switzerland, 1950-51; Ph.D., Univ. of Montreal, Canada, 1957. Appts: Asst. Prof., Univ. of Colo., U.S.A., 1960-65; Assoc. Prof., Bishop's Univ., Lennoxville, P.Q., Canada, 1966-. Mbrships: Canadian Histl. Assn.; Assn. of Canadian Slavists; Canadian World Univ. Comm.; Assn. Canadienne-Française pour l'Avancement des Scis. Publs: Hungarian Textbook & Grammar, 1962 & 1964; Intermediate Czech Reader, 1964; Articles in jrnls. Hons. incl: Rsch. Schlrship., Polish Min. of Higher Educ., Warsaw, 1973; Grant-in-Aid, British Coun., London, U.K., 1973. Address: Bishop's Univ., Lennoxville, P.Q. Canada. 13, 122.

WOLANIN, Alexander Stanley, b. 25 Sept. 1926. Electrical Engineer. Educ: B.E.E., Schl. of Engrng., Univ. of Pitts., 1952; Specialized courses Grad. Schl. of Engrng., ibid. Appts: Draftsman, Nat. Malleable & Steel Castings Co.,

1944-45, 1946-47; U.S. Army, 1945-46; Threading Machine Operator, Wheatland Tube Co., 1947-48, Sawhill Mfg. Co., 1948-49; Engr., Elec. Sect., Westinghouse Elec. Corp., E. Pitts., Pa., 1952-. Mbrships: Am. Inst. of Elec. Engrs. Responsible for elec. design of rotating rectifier elements in exciter rotor, Westinghouse Elec. Corp. Address: 405 George St., Sharon, PA 16146, U.S.A. 57.

WOLANIN, Anne Marie, b. 28 Mar. 1920. Business Lecturer & Secretary. Educ: Psychol., Westminster Coll., New Wilmington, Pa., 1947-48; (part-time 1948-65) Assoc. in Bus. Admin. degree, Youngstown Univ., Youngstown, Ohio, 1964; B.S. in Bus. Admin., ibid, 1965. Summa cum laude at following: Seminars for Secretaries & other Office Personnel, Pa. State Univ.; Cont. Educ., Shenango Valley Campus, Sharon, Pa., 1967-69; Understanding & Motivating Employees Seminar, Industrial Educ. Inst. of Boston, Mass., Pittsburgh, Pa., 1968; Bus. Letter Clinic, Shenango Valley Chamber of Comm., 1968. App. incl: (with Westinghouse Electric Corp., Sharon, pa.) Stenographer, Order Service, 1941-44; Special Duty Clerk & Clerical Asst., ibid, 1944-45; Sec. to Works Mgr., 1945-51; Sec. to Chmn., Transformer Mgmt. Unit, 1951-52; Sec. to Works Mgr., 1951-55; Sec. to Gen. Works Mgr., 1955-56; Sec. to Asst. Mgr., Transformer Div., 1956-58; Sec. to Mgr., New Plant Planning, 1958-59; (concurrently) Sec. to Plant Mgr., Muncie, Ind. Plant, 1959-61; Sec. to Mgr. of Mfrg., Ibid, 1960-61; Sec. to Engrng. & Marketing Mgr., ibid, 1960-61; Sec. to Engrng. Mgr., Distrib. Transformer Div., 1961-69; Sec. to Product Mgr., Underground Transformers & Equipment, Distrib. Transformer Div., 1969-; Part-time Instr., Guest Lectr. in Business, Pa. State Univ., Continuing Educ., Shenango Valley Campus, Sharon, Pa., 1968-. Mbrships. incl: Am. Heritage Soc.; Am. Forestry Ass.; Sharon Coll. Club; Youngstown State Univ. Alumni Ass.; Westinghouse Elec. Corp. Veterans' Assoc. Address: 2430 Smith-Stewart Road E., Girard, OH, 44420, U.S.A.

WOLANIN, Sophie Mae, b. 11 June 1915. Executive Secretary; Editor; Educator; Tutor; Scholar; Author; Civic Worker. Educ: Cert., Pa. State Coll., 1943-44; Cert., Sec. Sci., Univ. of S.C., Columbia, 1944-46; B.S., cum laude, Bus. Admin., ibid, 1946-48. Appts. incl: Clerk, Stenog., Sec., Mercer Co. Tax Collector's Off., Sharon, Pa., 1932-34; Receptionist, Soc. Sec., Stenog., Dr.'s Nurse-Assoc., Lab. Techn., Dr. A.I. Weisman, N.Y.C., 1934-37; Coil Winder & Assembler of Bushings & other components for transformers, Mfg. Dept., Westinghouse Elec. Corp., Sharon, 1937-39; Duplicator Op., Typist, Dictaphone Op., Stenog., Spec. Duty Clerk, Sec., Order Serv. Dept., ibid, 1939-44; Student Off. Sec. to Dean, Achl. of Commerce, & to Profs. in Acctng., Engl. & Pol. Sci. Depts., Univ. of S.C. Schl. of Comm. & Lib. Arts, 1944-46; Instr., Maths., Bus. Admin. & Sec. Scis., Univ. of S.C., 1946-48; Confidential Sec., Corp. Exec. HQ Treas. Dept., Westinghouse Elec. Corp., Pitts., Pa., 1949-54; Exec. Sec., Exec. HQ Westinghouse Credit Corp., Pitts., 1954-; Tutor, Engl. for For. Students, Univ. of Pitts. & Carnegie-Mellon Univ., 1959-; Charter Mbr., & Asst. Ed., Westinghouse Credit Corp. Publ., WCC News, 1959-; Charter Mbr. & Asst. Ed., Westinghouse Credit Corp. Publ., WCC News, 1968-71; Assoc. Ed., ibid, 1971-; Corres., Polish Radio, N. Am. serv., 1973-. Mbrships. incl: Vol. Servs., Pledge Auditor & Donation Solicitor, Community Chest Fnd. Drive, 1932-33, Am. Red Cross, WWII, 1939-44, Allegheny Co. Soc. for Crippled Children & Adults, 1964, Children's Hosp., Pitts., 1965, &

S. Oakland Rehab. Coun., 1967-69; Fndng. Assoc., Nat. Hist. Soc.; Am. Acad. Pol. & Soc. Sci.; AAUW; Int. Fed. Univ. Women; Allegheny Co. League of Women Voters; Bd. of Dirs., 1963-; Bulletin Ed., 1963-65; Reas., 1965-66; Histn., 1969-70; Pub. Rels., 1971-72, Bus. & Profl.; Life, Liturgical Conf. of N. Am., Cath. Univ., Wash., D.C.; Nat. Trust for Hist. Preservation; Westinghouse Vet. Employees Assn.; Hon., Coll. Club of Sharon 1965-; Charter, Jonathan Maxcy Club, Univ. of S.C., 1966-; Alumni Assn., & Educ., Fndn., ibid; Gen. Chmn., Tri-State Area, 1959 & Chmn., Pa. State Fund Dr., 1967-68; Sec. to Pres., Oakland Chmbr. of Comm., 1970-; Life, Allegheny Co. Schlrship. Assn;.; Am. Acad. of Pol. & Soc. Sci., Phila.; Am. Bible Soc.; Am. Judicature Soc.; Am. Mus. of Natural Hist. Assoc.; Life, Mercer Co. Hist. Soc.; Colonial Mbr., New England Hist. Geneal. Soc.; St. Paul's Cath. Altar Soc.; Smithsonian Assoc.; Soc. Commemorative de Femmes Celebres; Univ. Cath. Club of Pitts.; UN Assn. of U.S.A.; Repubn. Author of num. articles in var. publs.; Report. Asst., Oakland News, 1964-. Hons. incl: Ph.D., Colo. State Christian Coll., 1972; Sci., Columbia Univ., N.Y.C., for rsch. paper on German pol. philos., Francis Lieber, 1963, w. congratulatory letter from Sir Winston Churchill, Hon. Mbr. of the Acad., 1964; 1st Prizes, Needlework Exhibs., Allegheny Co. Fair, 1951; cited U.S. Congressional Record, 1969; designated TWA 'Girl Friday', 1970; elected to Nat. Register Prominent Ams., 1972-73; Life Fellow, Intercontinental Biographical Assn., U.K.; Hon. Mbr., Hypatian Lit. Soc., Univ. of S.C.; Women's Hall of Fame, Seneca, N.Y., 1971-72; Woman-of-the-yr. Plaque, Bus. & Profl. Women's Club of Pitts., 1972 & Woman-of-the-yr., Gold 'Nike' Pin, ibid, 1972. Recip. of Gold Lyre Music Award, Sharon H.S., 1933; Gold Plaque Award, Westinghouse Credit Corp., WCC News, 1968; Community Ldr. of Am. Award, 1971; Woman of the Yr., Bus. & Profl. Women's Club, Pitts., Pa., 1972; Gold Medal, Int. Who's Who in Community Serv.; Mbr., Nat. Voter Advsry Bd., Am. Security Coun., 1972. Address: Westinghouse Credit Corp., 3 Gateway Ctr. (23 S.), Pittsburgh, PA 15222, U.S.A.

WOLF, Adolph, b. 17 June 1913. Manufacturing Company Executive; Educ: Austin Jr. Coll., 1933-36; Lewis Inst., 1937-39; Northwestern Univ., 1940-41. Appts: Supt., Buick Motors, Melrose Park, Ill., 1940-44, & Poole Bros., Chgo., 1944-48; V.P., Mfg., Makatoy Co., Chgo., 1948-52; V.P., Mfg., Webcor Inc., Chgo., 1952-59; Administrative Asst. to Works Mgr., Zenith Radio, Chgo., 1959-61; V.P., Exec. V.P., Pres. & Chmn. of Bd., Electro Voice, Inc., Buchanan, Mich., 1961-73; V.P., Mfg., S. Bend Range Corp., S. Bend, Ind., 1973-. Mbrships: Republican Party; Luth. Ch. Address: 2709 Riverside Rd., Niles, MI 49120, U.S.A.

WOLF, Gotthard Karl August, b. 27 Dec. 1910. Scientific Film Institute Director. Educ: Dr. Ing., Tech. Univ., Breslau, Germany. Appts: Advsr., then Dept. Hd., Reichsanstalt für Film und Bild, Berlin, 1936; Dept. Dir., Inst. Für Film und Bild, 1945; Dir., Inst. für den Wissenschaftlichen Film, Göttingen, 1956-; Hon. Prof., Univ. of Göttingen, 1966; Hon. Prof., Tech. Univ., Hanover, 1966. Mbrships: Hon. Fellow, Royal Photographic Soc.; Rotary Club. Publs: Fndr. & Ed., Encylopaedia Cinematographica; Author, Der wissenschaftliche Dokumentationsfilm. Recip., Culture Prize, Deutsche Gesellschaft für Photographie, 1973. Address: Nonnenstieg 72, 34 Göttingen, German Fed. Repub. 43, 92.

WOLF, Hans-Heinrich, b. 12 May 1911. University Professor. Educ: Studied Sci. of Music & Theol., Univs. of Heidelberg, Tubingen, Bonn, Germany, Basel, Switzerland, Ch. Acad. of Bethel, U.S.A. & Yale Divinity Schl., New Haven, Conn. Married Brigitte Ruter, 1943; Four Children. Appts. incl: Co-Ldr. & Ldr., Pastoral-Kolleg der Evang. Kirche von Westfalen 1945-47; Prof. of Systemat. Theol., Ch. Acad., Bethel, Fed. Rep. of Germany, 1947-55; Dir., Ecumenical Inst. & Grad. Schl. of Ecumenical Studies of the World Coun. of Chs., Bossey Geneva, 1955-66; Prof. Ecumenics, Ruhr-Univ., Bochum, German Fed. Rep., 1966-. Mbrships. incl: Africa Soc., German Fed. Rep., Societas ethica. Publs. incl: Die Eingeit des Bundes, das Verhaltnis von Altem Testament und Neum Testament bei Calvin, 1959; Papers in profl. jrnls. Recip. D. Theol., Univ. of Heidelberg. Address: Haarkampstr. 19, 4630 Bochum, German Fed. Rep.

WOLFBEIN, Seymour Louis, b. 8 Nov. 1915. Economist. Educ: B.A., Brooklyn Coll., 1936; M.A., Columbia Univ., 1937; Ph.D., ibid, 1941. Appts: Econ., Div. of Rsch., Work Projs. AOM, 1939-42; Econ., Bur. of Labour Stats., 1942-46; Chief, Occupational Outlook Div., ibid, 1946-49; Manpower & productivity, 1949-50; Manpower & employment, 1950-59; Dpty. Asst. Sec. of Labour, U.S. Dept. of Labour, 1959-62; Dir., Off. of Manpower, Automation & Trng., 1962-65; Econ. Advsr. to Sec. of Labour, 1965-66; Dean, Schl. of Bus. Admin., Temple Univ., 1967-. Mbrships. incl: Fellow, Am. Statl. Assn., AAAS; Pres., Wash. Statl. Soc.; Trustee, Nat. Vocational Guidance Assn. Publs. incl: Work in American Society, 1972; Manpower Policy, 1973. Hons: Disting. Serv. Award, U.S. Dept. of Labour, 1954,'61; Eminent Career Award, Nat. Vocational Guidance Assn., 1970. Address: Schl. of Bus. Admin., Temple Univ., Phila., PA 19122, U.S.A. 2, 14.

WOLFE, Estemore A., b. 29 Dec. 1919. Educator; Insurance Director. Educ: Fla. Mem. Coll., U.S.A.; B.S., Jackson State Coll., Miss., 1947; M.Ed., Wayne State Univ., 1951; D.Ed., Boston Univ., Mass., 1958; Wayne State Univ., 1963-64; NY Univ., 1952-54; Univ. Hawaii, 1959. Appts: Writer, Miss. Enterprise weekly, Jackson, 1939-41; Served U.S. Army, WWII; Dir., Med. Labs., Detroit Metropol. Hosp., 1947-48; Tchr.-Counselor, Detroit Bd. Educ., 1948-55; Sec.-Treas.-2nd VP & Sec., Wright Mutual Ins. Co., Detroit, 1955-; Tchng., Lec.-Workshop Experience, var. univs. & colls. Mbrships. incl: Nat. Soc. Visual Educ.; Nat. Georgraphic Soc.; Am. Acad. Soc. & Pol. Sci.; Nat. Ins. Assng. Inc.; Detroit Coun. Ins. Execs.; Detroit Fedn. Tchrs. Nat. Fedn. Tchrs.; Detroit Assn. Radio & TV; Detroit Schoolmens Club; Detroit Metropol. Black Arts; Mich. Coun. Children & Youth, NAACP; Am. Mus. Natural Hist.; Nat. Assn. Intergrp. Rels. Officials; Am. Assn. Higher Educ.; Active civil rights movements. Recip. num. hons. Address: 10 W. Adams Ave., Suite 1401, Detroit, MI 48226, U.S.A. 131.

WOLFE, Gene Henry, b. 18 May 1936. Physicist. Educ: B.S., Univ. of Ill., 1958; M.S., ibid, 1959. Appts: Rsch. Assoc., Argonne Nat. Lab., Ill., 1958; Engr., McDonnel-Douglas Aircraft, St. Louis, Mo., 1959; Rsch. Physicist, IIT Rsch. Inst., Chgo., Ill., 1960-64; Rsch. Physicist, R.R. Donnelley & Sons, ibid, 1964-. Mbrships: Am. Optical Soc.; Knights of Columbus, Coronta Coun., 4th Degree, Calumet City; Our Lady of Knock, Schl. Bd., ibid; Am. Numismatic Assn.; Hammond Coin Club, Pres., Hammond, Ind.; Calumet City, Burnham

Republican Club, V.P.; Tau Beta Pi. Author of articles in profl. jrnls. inclng. "Gamma-Ray-Induced Expansion of Lithium Fluoride", Phys. Review, 1963. Address: 1309 Buffalo Ave., Calumet City, IL 60409, U.S.A. 8, 120.

WOLFE, Herbert Joseph, b. 8 Mar. 1925. Special Educator. Educ: B.S., Univ. of Pitts. Pa., 1948; M. Ed., ibid, 1952; Educl. Admin. Cert., ibid, 1963. Appts. incl: Tchr. & Wrestling & Track Coach-Administrative Prin., Schl. for Blind Children, Pitts. Pa., 1952-64; Asst. Supt.-Supt., The Md. Schl. for the Blind, 1964-; Publs. Comm., Am. Printing House for the Blind, 1966-70; Mbr., Gov. of Md.'s Commn. for Educ. of Handicapped, 1967; Chmn., Md. State Advsry. Comm. for Educ. of Deaf-Blind Children, 1972-; Mbr., Advsry. Comm., CEC Info. Ctr., 1972-75; Asst. Prof., Pediatrics (Educ.), Univ. of Md. Schl. of Med., 1973-. Mbrships: Fndr., first Kiwanis-sponsored blind Key Club in U.S., 1954; Eastern Athletic Assn. for Blind; Assn. for Educ. of Visually Handicapped; Baltimore Co. Coun. for Exceptional Children; Contbr. to profl. jrnl. Hons: Disting. Kiwanis Serv. Award, 1964. Address: 3501 Taylor Ave., Baltimore, MD 21236, U.S.A. 6.

WOLFE, Maurice Elizabeth Jackson (Mrs. Oscar Wolfe, Jr.), b. 2 Nov. 1907. Planter. Educ: Miss. State Coll. for Women, 1925-27; B.A., Univ. of Miss., 1930; M.A., Univ. of Ala., 1937. Appts: Tchr., Tippo Consolidated Schl., 1929-30; Tchr., Duncan Consolidated Schl., 1930-37; Tchr., Jackson City Schl. System, 1937-38; Ptnr., The Wolfe Co., 1961-. Mbrships: Colonial Dames of 17th Century; DAR; Treas., Duncan Meth. Ch.; Treas., Duncan Gdn. Club; Duncan Bridge Club; Shelby Wed. Bridge Club; Friday Bridge Luncheon Club; Chmn., Polio Dr., 1944-58; War Dr. Bond, 1942. Address: Box 155, Duncan, MS 38740, U.S.A. 5, 128.

WOLFE, Rolland Emerson, b. 25 Feb. 1902. University Professor. Educ: B.A., Manchester Coll., 1924; B.D., Oberlin Grad. Schl. of Theol., 1928; S.T.M., ibid, 1929; Ph.D., Harvard Univ., 1933. Appts: Lectr., Asst. Prof. & Acting Dean, Tufts Univ. Schl. of Relig., 1935-46; Harkness Prof., Biblical Lit., Case Western Reserve Univ., 1946-71; Adjunct Prof., Relig., Cleveland State Univ., 1971-. Mbrships: Pres., Am. Acad. of Relig.; Soc. of Biblical Lit.; Am. Oriental Soc.; Archaeological Inst. of Am; AAUP; Canadian Soc. of Biblical Studies; Chgo. Soc. of Biblical Rsch.; Comm. on Standard Med. Terminol. Publs. incl: Meet Amos & Hosea, 1945; Men of Prophetic Fire, 1951; What is the Bible?, 1962; Contbr. to Ency. of Relig. & The Interpreter's Bible. Hons: Monroe Award, Oberlin, 1928; D.D., Manchester Coll., 1952; Award "Best Prof. in the Humanities", Case Western Reserve Univ. 1967. Address: 3047 Edgehill Rd., Cleveland, OH 44118, U.S.A. 2, 13, 15, 51, 128, 131.

WOLFERS, Elsie Elizabeth (Mrs.), b. 7 Feb. 1906. Lecturer; Designer; Civic Leader. Educ: McDowell Schl. of Design & Illustration; N.Y. Schl. Radio & Drama; Carnegie Inst. Art; Univ. of Pitts. Activities incl: Org. & Dir., Dad's Club, grp. for needy children; Chmn., Community Cultural Prog., Long Beach, L.I.; Cultural Dir. under Eleanor Roosevelt for L.I.; Pres., Childrens Civic Theatre; Dir., Creative Arts Workshops, Univ. of Pitts.; Pres., Womens Club, Pitts.; Org. & Dir., Teach. tchng. prog. for the needs; Nat. 3rd V.P., Nat. League Am. Pen Women; Nat. Workshop Chmn., ibid. Works: Silver Fox Breeding in the United States: paintings in pvte. collect. tapes for the blind.

Hons: Sears Roebuck Award for Community Improvement; sev. small awards in crafts. Address: 1684 Hastings Mill Rd., Pitts., PA 15241, U.S.A. 5, 6, 138.

WOLFF, Kurt Heinrich, b. 20 May 1912. Professor. Educ: Univs. of Frankfurt & Munich, 1930-33; Univ. of Florence, 1934-35; Univ. of Chgo., 1943-44; Harvard Univ., 1955-56. Appts. incl: Rsch. Asst., Sociol., Southern Meth. Univ., 1939-43; Asst. & Assoc. Prof., Sociol., Ohio State Univ., 1945-59; Prof., sometime Chmn., Sociol., Brandeis Univ., 1959-69; Yellen Prof. of Soc. Rels., ibid, 1969-. Mbrships. incl: Bd. of Dirs., Sociol. Abstracts; Advsry. Ed. Bd., Praxis & Int. jrnl. of Contemp. Sociol.; Ed. Bd., Sociol. Focus. Publs: The Sociology of Georg Simmel (ed., trans.), 1950; George Simmel 1858-1918 (ed.), 1959; Emile Durkheim 1858-1917 (ed.), 1960; The Sociology of Knowledge (ed.), 1961; The Critical Spirit (co-ed., contbr.), 1967; Versuch Zu Einer Wissenssoziologie, 1968; Hungebung und Begriff, 1968; From Karl Mannheim (ed.), 1971; Von Einhorn Zu Einhorn, 1972; Trying Sociology, 1974. Recip. acad. hons. Address: c/o Dept. of Sociol., Brandeis Univ., Waltham, MA 02154, U.S.A. 2, 6, 8, 13, 14, 15, 28, 30, 50, 51, 55.

WOLFSON, Victor. Novelist; Playwright; TV Writer. Educ: Univ. of Wis. Mbrships: Exec. Bd., Dramatists Guild of Am.; PEN Club; Authors Guild; Dramatists Guild; Writers Guild. Plays: The Bitter Street, Excursion; Crime & Punishment; The Family; Pride's Crossing; American Gothic; Musical Version - Seventh Heaven; Love in the City; Boston Love Story. Novels: The Lonely Steeple; Eagle on the Plain; Midsummer Madness; My Prince My King!; Cabral. Biography: The Mayerling Murder; The Man Who Cared - Truman. TV: The Valiant Years - Churchill; Years of Decision - Truman; Roosevelt Story; Hitchcock's Invisible Man. Hons: Emmy Award for Churchill series; Edgar Allen Poe award for Midsummer Madness. Address: 549 E. 86th St., N.Y., NY 10028, U.S.A. 2.

WOLL, Robert H., b. 7 Sept. 1900. Merchant Banker. Appts: Mgr., N. Woll & Co., San Jose, Ill., 1929-38; Owner, ibid, 1938-69; Ptnr. w. son. 1969-; Organizer & Dir., San Jose Co. Bank, 1944-; V.P., ibid, 1944-; Mbrs., Advt. of Happy Hour Food Stores, 1947-53; Auditor, Allan Grove Twp., Mason Co., Ill., 1973-. Mbrships. incl: Am. Legion; United Meth. Ch. San Jose; Treas., Sunday Sch., 1924-49; Trustee of Ch., 1938-66; Pres. of Trustees, 1958-51; Hon. Trustee, 1966; Trustee of Sustaining Fund, 1951-; Chmn., Mason Co. Housing Bd., 1959-; Mason Co. Welfare Comm., 1945-71; Mason Co. Planning Comm., 1966-69; Treas., Green Hill Cemetery, 1938-56; Schl. Dir., San Jose, 1937-40; Boy Scout Comm., 1920-46; Local Salvation Army Comm., 1950-; Ill. Histl. Soc. Address: N. Woll & Co., San Jose, IL 62682, U.S.A. 8, 16, 120, 126, 131.

WOLLMAN, Harry, b. 26 Sept. 1932. University Professor. Educ: A.B., Harvard Coll., 1954; M.D., Harvard Med. Schl., 1958. Appts. incl: Cons., Anesthesiol., Valley Forge Army Hosp., 1965-66; Asst. Prof., Anesthesia, Univ. of Pa., 1965-68; Assoc. Prof., ibid, 1968-70; Prof., 1970-; Prof., Pharmacol., 1971-; Chmn., Comm. of Studies Involving Man, 1972-; Chmn., Dept. of Anesthesia & Robert Dunning Dripps Prof., 1972-. Mbrships. incl: Phi Beta Kappa; Sigma Xi; Dipl., Am. Bd. Anesthesiol.; Am. Physiol. Soc.; Assn. of Univ. Anesthetists; Pres., Pa. Soc. Anesthesiols., 1972-73; AMA; AAUP; Pa. Med. Soc.; Councilman, Assn. of Univ. Anesthetists, 1971-; Chmn., Comm. on

Fin. Resources, Soc. Acad. Anesthesia Chaimen, 1973-. Author of many sci. publs. Address: Dept. of Anesthesia, Hosp. of Univ. of Pa., 3400 Spruce St., Philadelphia, PA 19104, U.S.A.

WOLMA, Fred J., Jr., b. 10 Dec. 1916. Professor of Surgery. Educ: B.A., Univ. of Tex., Austin, 1940; Med. Coll. of Va., Richmond, 1943-44; St. Mary's Infirmary Galveston, Tex., 1946-47; Univ. of Tex. Med. Br., 1948-51. Appts: Instr., Gen. Surg., Univ. of Tex. Med. Br., Galveston, 1951-53; Asst. Prof., Surg., ibid, 1953-68; Assoc. Prof., 1968-69; Prof., 1969; Co-Dir., Emergency Room, 1963-66; Chief of Staff, 1968; Chief, Div. of Gen. Surg., 1968-70. Mbrships incl: Am. Coll. Surgs.; Am. Assn. for Surg. of Trauma; Southwestern Surg. Congress; Tex. Surg. Soc.; AMA; Pres., Galveston Co, Med. Soc., 1974; Singleton Surg. Soc.; Southern Med. Assn.; Royal Soc. Med.; Western Surg. Assn.; Southern Surg. Assn. Author of many publs. in field. Recip., Medallion, Am. Coll. of Surgs., 1970. Address: Univ. of Tex. Med. Br., Galveston, TX 77550, U.S.A.

WOLMAN, Benjamin B., b. 27 Oct. 1908. Psychoanalyst; Professor; Author. Educ: M.A., Univ. of Warsaw, Poland, 1932; Ph.D., ibid, 1935. Appts. incl: Vis. Assoc. Prof., Psychol., Yeshiva Univ., U.S.A., 1953-57; Clin. Lectr., Psych., & Supvsr., Psychotherapy, Post Doctoral Prog., Albert Einstein Coll. of Med., 1958-62; Clin. Prof., Psychoanalysis & Psychotherapy, Post Doctoral Prog., Adelphi Univ., 1963-65; Prof., Doctoral Prog. in Clin. Psychol., L.I. Univ. 1965-; Pvte Prac., psychoanalyis & psychotherapy, 1939-; Hon. Prof., Andres Bello Cath. Univ., Caracas, Venezuela. Mbrships: Pres., Int. Org. for the Study of Group Tensions; Fellow, Am. Psychological Assn.; Fellow, Assn. for the Advancement of Psychotherapy; Fellow, Am. Sociological Assn.; Assn. for Applied Psychoanalysis; Am. Acad. of Psychotherapy; Assn. for Group Psychotherapy. Author of 14 books & over 160 sci. papers in psychol. & related fields. Address: 10 W. 66 St. N.Y., NY 10023, U.S.A.

WOLTER, (Rev.) Allan Bernard, O.F.M., b. 24 Nov. 1913. Educator; Philosopher; Author. Educ: B.A., Our Lady of Angels Sem., 1937; M.A., Cath. Univ. of Am., 1942; Ph.D., ibid, 1947; Study of Theol., St. Joseph Sem., Teutopolis, Ill., 1937-41. Entered Franciscan Order, 1934; Ordained Roman Cath. Priest, 1940. Appts. incl: Asst. Prof., Chem., Bio. & Philos., Our Lady of Angels Sem., 1943-45; Assoc. Prof., Philos., Franciscan Inst. of St. Bonaventure Univ., 1946-52; Prof., 1952-62; Vis. Prof., Cath. Univ. of Am., 1962-63; Ordinary Prof., 1963-; Ed., Philos. Series, Franciscan Inst. Publs., 1946-62; Ed., Quincy Coll. Publs., 1964-; Vis. Prof., var. univs. Mbrships. incl: Am. Cath. Philosophical Assn.; Am. Philosophical Assn.; Mind Assn.; AAAS; Philos. of Sci. Assn.; Ed. Bd., Ency. of Philos., 1967, & Franciscan Studies, 1973-. Publs. incl: Articles in encys. & jrnls.; Book of Life, 1954; John Duns Scotus, A Treatise on God as First Principle, 1966. Recip., Sc.D., Quincy Coll., 1967. Address: Schl. of Philosophy, The Catholic Univ. of America, Wash. DC 20017, U.S.A. 2, 7, 13.

WOLTERINK, Lester Floyd, b. 28 July 1915. University Professor. Educ: B.A., Hope Coll., 1936; M.A. Univ. of Minn., 1940; Ph.D., ibid, 1943. Appts. incl: Tching. Asst., Zool., Univ. of Minn., 1936-41; Inst., Physiol. & Pharmacol., Mich. State Univ., 1941; Asst. Prof., ibid, 1945, Assoc. Prof., 1948, Prof., 1951, w. concurrent assignments at Mich. Agric

Exper. Stn.; var. appts. at Ames Rsch. Ctr. inclng. Proj. Sci., Biosatellite Proj., 1965-66; Nat. Rsch. Coun., 1974. Mbrships. incl: N.S.F. Cons., 1967-70; NASA Manned Space Comm., 1966; Pres., Mich. Nucleonic Soc., 1961-62; Cons., Am. Physiol. Soc., 1972-73; Sigma Xi; AAAS; AAUP; Am. Inst. of Biol. Scis.; Charter Mbr., Biophys. Soc.; N.Y. Acad. of Sci.; Ecol. Soc. Am.; Am. Soc. Zool.; Am. Astronaut. Soc.; Am. Ornithol. Union; sev. comms. of Mich. State Univ. Contbr. of num. articles to profl. jrnls. Address: Dept. of Physiol., Mich. State Univ., East Lansing, MI 48823, U.S.A. 8, 14, 28.

WOMER, (Rev.) Robert S., b. 27 Feb. 1908. Minister; Editor. Educ: LL.B., J.D., Detroit Coll. of Law; Special courses, Univ. of Chgo. Appts: Special preacher for Mich. Lords Day Alliance since age of 16 yrs.; Cons. Sec., ibid, 1928-32; Co. Gen. Sec., Sunday League Inc., 1933-56; Gen. Sec., ibid, 1956-; Ed., Sunday Guardian, 1956-. Mbr., Assocd. Ch. Press, 1952-. Author, The Depression & Some of its Causes; Ed., 6 courses on Sunday problem all over U.S. & Canada. Hons: D.D., Philathea Coll., London, Ont., Canada, 1952; Detroit Coll. of Law, 1968. Address: 279 Highland Ave., Newark, NJ 07104, U.S.A. 6.

WONG, Kenneth Yat Hoy, b. 23 Aug. 1932. Dentist. Educ: Univ. of Hawaii, 1950-53; D.D.S., Northwestern Univ., 1957. w. USAF Dental Corp., 1957-59. Mbrships: YMCA; Boy Scouts Am. United Fund; Am. Dental Assn.; Fed. Dentaire Int.; Honolulu Co. Dental Soc.; Int. Congress Gnathology; Chgo. Dental Soc.; Wiebrecht Fndn.; Omicron Kappa Upsilon; Delta Sigma Delta; Waialae Country Club; Century Club-U.S.C.; Chaminade Coll. Bd. of Govs., St. Louis; Hawaii State Dental Assn.; Am. Acad. Gnatholigic Orthopedics; Am. Acad. of Gen. Dentistry; Nat. Rifle Assn. Address: Kahala Office Tower, 4211 Waialae Ave., Suite 505, Honolulu, HI 96816, U.S.A. 9, 22, 57.

WOOD, Brian, b. 29 Sept. 1920. Company Director. Educ: Manchester Univ. & Royal Coll. of Technol., Salford, U.K. Appts: Sales Mgr., J. P. Stevens & Co. Inc., 1947-54; V.P. & Dir., Walker Bros. (N.Y.) Inc., 1954-62; Export Sales Mgr., Warner Bros. Corp., 1962-63; Exec. V.P. & Dir., Fenchurch Corp., 1964-, S. H. Lock (N.Y.) Inc., 1964-, Tozer Kemsley & Millbourn (Canada) Ltd., 1966-73, TKM (Pacific) Ltd., 1972-; Jt. Mng. Dir., Fenchurch (Curacao) N.V., 1968-. Mbrships: Trinidad & Tobago Chmbr. of Comm., N.Y. (1st V.P., Dir. & Fndng. Mbr.); Patterson Club, Fairfield, Conn.; Jamaica Club, Kingston; Union Club, Trinidad. Address: 109 Mill River Rd., Fairfield, CT, U.S.A. 6.

WOOD, Clara Rebecca Chaloupka, b. 10 Aug. 1917. Professor; Minister; Lecturer. Educ. incl: B.A., Manchester Coll., Ind., 1940; B.D., Yale Univ. Divinity Schl., 1945; M.A., Yale Univ. Grad. Schl. 1946; Th.D., Pacific Schl. of Relig., Calif., 1959; Ordained Min., Ch. of the Brethren & United Ch. of Christ. Appts. incl: Tchr., Prin., Libn., in Elem. & H. Schls., Iowa, Colo., Ind., 1935-49; Dir., Brethren Serv. Commn. in Poland, 1946-49; Prof. & Co.-Dir., Montana Schl. of Relig., Mont. State Univ., 1950-54; Pastor, Oakland Ch. of the Brethren, Calif., 1956-58; Tchr., Oakland H.S., 1959-60; Prof., Lewis & Clark Clark Coll. Portland, Ore., 1960-61; Tchr., Castlemont H.S., Oakland, Calif., 1962-64; Instr., Dept. of Humanities & Philos., Diablo Valley Coll., Calif., 1964-; Chmn., ibid, 3 yrs.; Interim Pastor, San Francisco Ch. of the Brethren, Calif., 1967. Mbrships. incl: Int. Assn. of Women Mins.; Nat. Assn. for Humanities Educ.; Calif. Humanities

& Tchrs.' Assns.; Fac. Assns. of Calif. Community & Diablo Valley Colls.; AAUW; Int. Assn. of Univ. Women. Publs. in field of humanities & relig. Address: 1011 Villa Nueva, El Cerrito, CA 94530, U.S.A. 5, 120.

WOOD, Harrell Ephraim, b. 23 Sept. 1925. Elementary School Principal. Educ: B.A., Bowling Green Coll. of Commerce, 1956; M.A., Geo. Peabody Coll., 1959; Admin. courses, Univ. of Ky., Eastern Univ. & Murray Univ. Appts: Bus. Educ. Tchr., Springfield Elem. Schl., 1967-73; Prin., Jefferson Elem. Schl., Henderson, Ky. Mbrships: Pres., Lions Club; Lincoln Trail Comprehensive Hlth. Planning Commn.; Ctrl. Ky. Community Action Coun., Cmdr., Am. Legion; Civil Defense; Past Master, Masonic Lodge; Elder, Christian Ch.; Delta Phi Epsilon. Address: 832 S. Adams St., Henderson, KY 42420, U.S.A. 125.

WOOD, Jeanne Clarke (Mrs. Helen Jeanne Wood), m. to Herman E. Jack Wood, b. 21 Dec. 1916. Welfare Executive. Educ: Dip., St. Margaret's Episc. Schl., Tappahannock, Va., 1931; Collegiate Schl. for Girls, Richmond, ibid, 1932-33. Appts: Asst. to Dr. & Mrs. J. Calvitt Clarke, Christian Chil,dren's Fund, Inc., Richmond, Va., 1938-64; Fndr., Pres. & Int. Dir. of Children, Inc., ibid, 1964-. Former Pres. & Mbr. of Philomathic Club, Augusta, Ga. Co-author w. Helen C. Clarke of: In Appreciation: A Story in Pictures of the World-Wide "Family" of Christian Children's Fund, Inc., 1958; Children's Christmastime Around The World, 1962; Children's Games Around The World, 1963; Children - Hope Of The World - Their Needs, 1965; Children — Hope Of The World - Their Friends, 1966. Hons. incl: commendation from Pres. of U.S., 1972; Citation from Gov. of Kanagwa Prefecture, Japan, 1972; Address: 1000 Westover Rd. (P.O. Box 5381), Richmond, VA 23220, U.S.A. 138.

WOOD, Kathleen Oliver (Mrs.), b. 17 Sept. 1921. Editor; Public Relations; Talk Show Hostess. Educ: Univ. of N.M., Albuquerque, 1949; Cleveland Coll., Western Reserve, Ohio, 1960-61. Appts: Tech. Sec., Gray Iron Fndrs. Soc., 1955-57; Tchr., Whiting Bus. Coll. 1957-62; Editl. Asst., Chem. Rubber Co., 1966; Ed., Writer, Jefferson Ency., World Publng. Co., 1967-68; Announcer, Disc Jockey, WCLV, Cleveland, Ohio, 1968-69; Talk Show Hostess, Radio Announcer, WERE, ibid, 1972-74; Asst. P.R. Dir., Ed., Univ. Circle "Highlights", 1971-. Mbrships. incl: Mensa, P.R., Cleveland; Women's Advt. Club, P.R.; Cleveland Advt. Club; Int. Assn. Bus. Communicators. Publs. incl: Greenwood (poetry), 1967; Ed./Publr., Smorgasbrain mag., 1968-. Address: P.O. Box 5612, Cleveland, OH 44101, U.S.A. 5, 138.

WOOD, Marylaird (Larry) (Mrs. Byron Wood), b. 18 Dec. 1928. Journalist; Free-lance Writer; Educator; Environmental Consultant. Educ: B.A., Univ. of Wash., Seattle; M.A., ibid; Stanford Univ.; Cert., Design & Photography, Univ. of Calif., Berkeley; Cert., Publs. Prod., Design, P.R., Univ. of Wis. Appts: Feature Writer, Seattle Wash. Times & San Fran. Chronicle; By-line Columnist, Oakland Tribune & P.R. Dir., Eastbay Regional Pk. Dist., Children's Home Soc. of N. Calif.; Free-lance Writer, var. nat. mags.; Staff Corres., Christian Sci. Monitor gen. reporting, Living Style, & Environmental coverage for Western Region; Spkr., civic & profl. grps. Mbrships. incl: P.R. Chmn., N. Calif., Phi Beta Kappa; Sigma Delta Chi, 1974; P.R. Soc. of Am., 1974; Nat. Assn. Educ. in Jrnlsm.; Past Pres., Theta Sigma Phi; Pres., N. Calif. Chapt., ibid; Int. Oceanog. Fndn., Miami, Fla.; San Fran. & Eastbay

Women's Press Clubs; Calif. Acad. of Environmental Newswriters, 1973; Int. & Nat. Environmental Communications Consultants. Publs. incl: English for Social Living; Over 700 articles & stories in nat. mags.; Pacific Coast Waterfront Series, Christian Sci. Monitor, 1974; Environmental series on Western Wildlife refuges, Women in Forestry. Address: 6161 Castle Dr., Oakland, CA 94611, U.S.A. 2, 5, 9, 22, 59, 120, 130.

WOOD, R. Edwin, b. 20 Nov. 1904. Estate Planning Executive. Educ: B.B.A., Univ. of Wash. Appts: Joined staff, Phoenix Mutual, 1929-; Home Off. Supvsr., ibid, 1936-40; Mgr., San Fran. Agcy., 1940-45, resigned to return to personal prod. Mbrships. Many Int. Comms., Million Dollar Round Table; Bd., Million Round Table Fndn.; Nat. Regional V.P., Am. Soc. of Chartered Life Underwriters; Var. comms., ibid; Nat. Co-Chmn., 25th anniversary class reunion, 1968; Past Pres., San Fran. Local Chapt., Life Underwriter's Assn.; Past Pres., Calif. State Chapt., ibid; Nat. Trustee, Nat. Assn. of Life Underwriters, Wash. D.C., 2 terms; Former Dir. & V.P., San Fran. Estate Planning Coun.; Former V.P., San Fran. Planning Corp; Masonic Order; U.S. Hospitality Comm., Olympic Games, Munich, German Fed. Repub., 1972. Hons. incl: Orr Trophy, for most outstanding contbn. to ind.; Kt. Cmdr., Court of Hon., Masonic Order. Address: Royal Towers, 1750 Taylor St., San Fran., CA 94133, U.S.A. 9, 27.

WOOD, Ruth Ridens, b. 24 June 1907. Teacher. Educ: B.A., Hardin-Simmons Univ., Abilene, Tex., 1937; M.Ed., Sul Ross State Univ., Alpine, Tex., 1957; Postgrad. work, var. univs.; Psychological Interne, Big Spring State Hosp., Tex., 1960-61. Appts. incl: Elem. work, Vancouver, Wash., 1942-46; 1st grad. McMinnville, Ore., 1946-48, Richland, Wash., 1948-49, Corpus Christi, Tex., 1949-50; 1st grade, Special Educ. & Psychological Testing, Odessa, Tex., 1950-72. Mbrships: Treas., Delta Iota Chapt., Delta Kappa Gamma, 1968-70; Treas., Beta Gamma Conclave, Kappa Kappa Iota, 1969-70; Nat. Coun. of Exceptional Children; Nat. & State Tchrs. Assn.; Tex. State Tchrs. Assn.; AAUW; Tex. Classroom Tchrs. Assn. Author of article in Rising Star Record; Chmn. for rsch., assembling & writing of Curric. Guide for Intermediate Level educable retarded children, 1970-71. Recip., Tchr. of the Yr. Award, Zavala Schl., Odessa, Tex., 1960. Address: 1503 Doran Dr., Odessa, TX 79761, U.S.A. 125.

WOOD, (William) Donald, b. 5 Apr. 1920. Professor; Economist. Educ: B.A., McMaster Univ., Canada; M.A., Queen's Univ.; Ph.D., A.M., Princeton Univ., U.S.A. Appts: Administrative Off., RCAF, 1940-45; Econs. Rsch. Advsr. & Mbr., many royal commns. & govt. bodies; Var. sr. positions in ind. & govt.; Hd., Employee Rels. Rsch. Div., Imperial Oil Ltd.; Prof. of Econs. & Dir., Indl. Rels. Ctr., Queen's Univ., Kingston, Ont., 1960-. Mbrships. incl: Int. & Am. Indl. Rels. Rsch. Assns.; Canadian Econs. & Pol. Sci. Assn. Publs. incl: Canadian Graduate Theses, 1919-1967: An Annotated Bibliography (w. L.A. Kelly & P. Kumar), 1970; Cost-Benefit Analysis & the Economics of Investment in Human Resources: An Annotated Bibliography (w. H. Campbell), 1970; An Empirical Analysis of Certified Bargaining Units, Ontario 1950-1970 (w. L.A. Kelly), 1973; The Current Industrial Relations Scene in Canada, 1973. Address: Indl. Rels. Ctr., Queen's Univ., Kingston, Ont., K7L 3N6, Canada. 6, 8, 30, 34, 88.

WOODALL, Stella, (Mrs.), b. 15 Jan. 1899. Writer & Poet. Educ: Univ. of Tex. Appts: Employed until retirement by U.S. Govt. as writer of Text Books, Training Manuals etc. for USAF; Free-lance profl. Writer & Poet. Mbrships. incl: Fndr. & Pres., Poetry Soc., San Antonio, Tex., 1969-; Chmn., S. Woodall Circle, Travis Pk. United Meth. Ch., San Antonio, 1965-; First V.P., Am. Poetry League; Nat. Advsry. Bd., ibid. Nat. Contest Chmn., ibid; Bd. of Dirs., Beautify San Antonio League; Past-Pres. & Bulletin Ed., Armed Forces Writers League. Publs. incl: Twelve Air Force Histories, inclng. a model Hist. for all Flying Training Air Force Bases; Air Force Text Books, Manuals; 3 books of Poems; Women of the Bible; Contbr. to num. anthols., & nat., State & local publs. Hons. incl: D.Litt., Andorra; Poet Laureate Int; Poet Laureate of Tex.; Churchmanship Award; Kbat Texas Star Award for Unselfish Pub. Serv.; Coun. of Pres. Award. Address: 3915 SW Military Drive, San Antonio, TX 78211, U.S.A. 5, 11, 57, 113, 138, 140.

WOODARD, Don Edwin, b. 4 Nov. 1931. Physician; University Professor. Educ: Undergrad. work, Univs. of Iowa & Mich., 1948-51; M.D., Med. Schl., Univ. of Iowa, 1955; Intern, Highland-Alemdia Co. Hosp., Oakland, Calif, 1955-56; Grad. Trng. Univ. of Colo. Med. Ctr., 1957-61. Currently, Assoc. Prof, Ob.-Gyn., Univ. of Colo. Med. Ctr. Mbrships. incl: Dipl., Am. Bd. of Ob.-Gyn.; Ctrl. Assn. of Ob.-Gyn.; Am. Coll. Ob.-Gyn.; Pres., Arapahoe Co. Cancer Soc.; 1968-70; State Bd., Am. Cancer Soc.; Am. & Colo. Ob. & Gyn. Socs.; AMA & State & Hosp. Bds.; YMCA; Elks; Rotarian; Young Republicans; Alpha Omega Alpha; Phi Rho Sigma; Pan Am. Surgn. Assn. Conbtr. of articles to med. jrnls. Recip. of hons. Address: 3601 S. Clarkson Englewood, CO 80110, U.S.A. 120.

WOODBRIDGE, Annie Emma Smith (Mrs. Hensley C. Woodbridge), b. 7 July 1915. College Teacher. Educ: B.A., Murray State Coll., 1935; M.A., Peabody Coll., 1936; Univs. of Wis. & Ky.; Univ. of Paris, Appts: Tchr., David Lipscomb Coll., 1937-44; Tchr., Bethel Coll., 1944-47; Tchr., Murray State Coll., 1948-54, '58-'64; Tchr., Southern Ill. Univ., 1966-. Mbr., AAUP. Address: 1804 W Freeman, Carbondale, IL 62901, U.S.A. 42.

WOODBRIDGE, Hensley Charles, b. 6 Feb. 1923. Librarian, Educ: A.B. Coll. William Mary, 1943; M.A., Harvard, 1946; Ph.D., Univ. of Ill., 1950; M.L.S., 1951; Student, Univ. Nacional de Mexico, 1941, '45. Appts: Corr. in Mexico for Worldover Press, 1945; Instr. French & Spanish, Univ. of Richmond, 1946-47; Tchng. Asst., Univ. of Ill., 1948-50; Ref. Libn., Ala. Poly Inst., 1951-53; Libn., Murray (Ky.) State Coll., 1953-65; Latin-Am. Bibliographer. Assoc. Prof. of Mod. Langs., S Ill. Univ., Carbondale, 1965-71; Prof., ibid, 1970-. Mbrships: Ky. Folklore Soc.; Medieval Soc. of Am.; Bibliog. Soc.; Am. Inst. de estudios madrilenos. Publs. incl: Tentative Bibliography of Ibero-Romance Linguistics (co-author), 1952; Jesse Stuart, a bibliography, 1960; Ruben Dario y el Cojo ilustrado (co-author), 1964. Ed., Ky. Lib. Assn. Bulletin, 1959-60, Ky. Folklore Record, 1963-64; Contbng. Ed., Am. Book Collector, 1965-; Co-Author, Jack London: A Biography, 1966; Assoc. Ed., Hispania, 1967-; Jesse & Jane Stuart, A Bibliography, 1969; Ed. & Publr., Jack London Newsletter, 1967-. Address: 1804, W. Freeman, Carbondale, IL 62901, U.S.A. 2, 30.

WOODGATE, Mildred Violet. Author. Appts: Worked in For. Off., London, .U.K.;

Libn. work; Worked at Wormwood Scrubbs Boys' Prison, London, 15 yrs. Mbr., Service Womens Club, London; Hon. mbr., Mark Twain Soc., 1946. Publs: Novels: The Silver Mirror; The Secret of the Sapphire Ring; The Two Houses on the Cliff; Pauline's Lady; Biographies: Père Lacordairs; Louis de Marillac; Jacqueline Pascal; Madame Swetchine; Charles de Condren; St. Vincent de Paul; Abbe Edgworth; Juniper Serra; Father Benson of Cowley; Father Congreve of Cowley; Sev. Children's books. Address: Hembury Fort House, Honiton, Devon, U.K. 3, 138.

WOODHURST, Robert Stanford, Jr., b. 12 July 1921. Architect. Educ: B.S., Clemson Univ., S.C., 1942. Appts: Capt., Pilot, USAF, 1942-46; Designer for Harold Woodward, Archt., Spartanburg, S.C., 1946-47; Assoc. Archt, F. Arthur Hazard, Archt., Augusta, Ga., & Gainesville, Fla., 1947-54; currently Ptnr., Woodhurst & O'Brien, Augusta, & V.P., Southeastern Archts. & Engrs., Augusta. Mbrships. incl: Va-. Offs., Ga. Assn. & Augusta Chapt., Am. Inst. of Archt.; Trustee, Historic Augusta Inc.; Soc. of Archtl. Histns. Many bldgs., Ga., inclng: Peabody Apts., 1st Bapt. Ch., Nat. Hills Shopping Ctr., Jeff Maxwell Lib., Augusta; Hephzibah H.S.; Women's Barracks & Dining Hall, Ft. Gordon. Hons. incl: Air Medal w. 7 Oak Leaf Clusters; French Croix de Guerre w. palms; Hon. mentions for design, 1966, 1968. Address: P.O. Box 899, Augusta, GA 30903, U.S.A. 7.

WOODING, (Sir) Hugh Olliviere Beresford, b. 14 Jan. 1904. Barrister at Law; Company Director. Educ: Queen's Royal Coll., Trinidad; Middle Temple, U.K. Appts: Barrister, 1927-62; Chief Justice, Trinidad & Tobago, 1962-68; currently, Co. Dir., Mbrships. incl: Coun., Bar. of Trinidad & Tobago, 1932-62; V.P., Trinidad & Tobago Bar Assn., 1956-62; Pres., Caribbean Bar Assn., 1960-62; Judicial Comm., Privy Coun., 1968; Hon. Master of the Bench, Inner Temple, 1968; Fndr. Mbr., & Sec., World Assn. of Judges, 1966-69; Coun. Univ. of W.I. 1967-; Chancellor, ibid, 1971-. Mayor, City of Port of Spain, 1943-44; Alderman, 1944-47. Author, A Collection of Addresses. 1968. Hons. incl: C.B.E., 1957; Kt. Bach., 1963. Privy Counsellor, 1966; LL.D., Univ. of W.I., 1967; Trinity Cross, Trinidad & Tobago, 1969. Address: P.O. Box 283, Port of Spain, Trinidad, W. Indies. 12.

WOODLAND, Everan Cornelius, Jr., b. 16 June 1929. Dentist. Educ: Georgetown Univ. Coll. of Arts & Scis., 1947-50; D.D.S., Georgetown Univ. Schl. of Dentistry, 1954; Grad. work, Naval Grad. Schl. & Georgetown Grad. Schl., 1964-65. Appts. incl: Pvte. prac. of dentistry, Kensington, Md., 1957-60; Commnd. Lieut., Dental Corps, USN, 1960, & promoted to Capt., 1971; Staff, Submarine Base, New London, Conn., 1960-62; Staff, USS Kitty Hawk, 1962-64; Sr. Dental Off., Naval Air Stn., Willow Grove, Pa., 1965-68; Sr. Dental Off., USS Grand Canyon, 1968-70; Hd., Endodontics Naval Dental Clin., Newport, R.I., 1970-73; Sr. Dental Off., Naval Stn., Mayport, Fla., 1973-. Mbrships. incl: Am. Dental Assn.; Delta Sigma Delta; Club Pres., Toastmasters Int., 1966-67; Assn. of Mil. Surgs. of U.S. Naval Inst. Hons: Nat. Defense Serv. Medal:` Viet Nam Serv. Medal; Viet Nam Campaign Medal. Address: 1300 Kings Rd., Neptune Beach, FL 32233, U.S.A. 6.

WOOD-LEGH, Kathleen Louise, b. 2 Sept. 1901. Historian. Educ: B.A., M.A., McGill Univ., Montreal, Canada; B.Litt., St. Hilda's Coll., Oxford, U.K.; Ph.D., Newnham Coll., Cambridge, 1932; Litt.D., ibid, 1967. Appts:

Supvsr. in Hist. for var. colls., Cambriage, 1965-; Birkbeck Lectr., Cambridge, 1954-55; Hulsean Lectr., 1971-73. Fellow, Royal Histl. Soc. Assoc., Newnham Coll., 1964-. Publs: Studies in Church Life in England in the Reign of Edward III; A Small Household of the XV Century; Perpetual Chantries in Britain; Articles in Review of English Studies, The English Historical Review, The Law Quarterly Review. Recip., Leverhulme Award, 1945-46 & 1951-52. Address: 49 Owlstone Road, Cambridge, U.K. 3.

WOODMAN, Grey Musgrave, b. 26 Jan. 1922. Psychiatrist. Educ: M.A., Oxford Univ., U.K., 1943; B.M.B.Ch., Guys' Hosp. 1945. Appts. incl: House Physn., Whipps Cross Hosp., London, 1949-50; Registrar, 1951-53; Registrar, Newcastle Gen. Hosp., 1953-54; Gen. Prac., Southall 1954-56; Contract Physn., USAF 7520th U.S. AF Hosp., London 1956-59; Res., Psych., Univ. of Okla, U.S.A., 1959-62; Staff Psych., Mental Hlth. Ctr., Kansas City, Mo., 1962-; Pvte. Prac., ibid, 1968-; Mbrships. incl: Am. Psych. Assn.; World Fed. for Mental Hlth.; Int. Assn. of Soc. Psych.; AMA; British Med. Assn.; Royal Soc. Med. Address: Exec. Bldg., Suite 120, 4121 W. 83rd St., Prairie Village, KS 66208, U.S.A.

WOODROOF, Horace Malcolm, b. 17 Nov. 1906. Public Relations Employee; Author. Educ: 4th Grade until age 14 yrs.; self-taught during 33 yrs. penal confinement; sev. courses, basic electronics, Nat. Schl., Calif. Appts: Tchr., practical electronics, radio-TV classes in penal instns.; Shipping Clerk, var. firms, 1962-67. Mbrships: Rivergate Ch. of Christ; 7th Step Fndn. Author, Stone Wall College, 1970. Contbr., newspaper articles. Recip., certs. in recognition of crime prevention & ch. work. Address: 108 Monticello Ave., Madison, TN 37115, U.S.A. 30.

WOODROOFE, Percy William, b. 16 Jan. 1916. Company Executive. Appts. incl: Joined W. Woodroofe Ltd. (Soft Drink Mfrs.), 1931; Dir., ibid, 1947; Mng. Dir., ibid, 1957-; Chmn., Dirs., ibid & subsidiaries, 1960-; Fellow, Brit. Bottlers' Inst.; Rep. of Soft Drink Ind. on Mgmt. Comm., S.A. Food Technol. Assn., 1958-60, 1963-65; Pres., S.A. Soft Drink Mfrs. Assn., 1962-63, 1971-73; Pres., S.A. Employers' Fedn., 1965-71, 1972-74; Rep., ibid, on S.A. Govt. Factories & Indl. Welfare Bd., 1967-74 & Exec. Mbr., Productivity Promotion Coun. of Australia (S.A. Div.), 1968-74; Chmn., Club Hotels Pty. Ltd., Norwood, 1972-74; former Pres., Australian Coun. of Soft Drink Mfrs. Mbrships: CTA Club; Norwood Footballers' Assn. Address: 138 Penfold Road, Wattles Park, S.A., Australia 5066. 23.

WOODRUFF, Edwin Townsend, b. 6 Aug. 1915. Television pioneer, producer & director; Business Consultant. Educ: Newark Schl. of Engrng., N.J. Appts: Pres., Cinetel Ltd., London & N.Y., 1950-64; Pres., Bahama Pub. Rels. Ltd., 1964-. Mbrships: Fndr. Pres., TV Prods. Assn.; Rotary Club of Nassau. Address: P.O. Box N 4859, Nassau, Bahamas. W. Indies. 109.

WOODRUFF, (Sir) Michael Francis Addison, b. 3 Apr. 1911. Surgeon; University Professor. Educ: Queen's Coll., Univ. of Melbourne. Appts: House Surg., Sr. House Surg. & Clin. Asst., Royal Melbourne Hosp., 1938-40; Capt., Australian Army Med. Corps, 1941-45; Tutor, Surg., Univ. of Sheffield, 1946-48; Sr. Lectr., Univ. of Aberdeen, 1948-52; Prof., Surg., Univ. of Otago, N.Z.,

1953-57; Prof., Surg. Sci., Univ. of Edinburgh, & Surg., Edinburgh Royal Infirmary, 1957-; Dir., Nuffield Transplantation Surg. Unit, Edinburgh, 1962. Mbrships: Fellow, Royal Soc.; Fellow, Royal Coll. of Surgs., England, Edinburgh & Australasia; Pres., Int. Transplantation Soc.; Fellow, Assn. of Surgs. of G.B. & Ireland; Brit. Med. Assn. Hons: Knighthood, 1969; Lister Medal, 1970. Address: Dept. of Surg., Univ. of Edinburgh Med. Schl., Teviot Place, Edinburgh EH8 9AG, U.K. 1, 23, 35, 43, 50.

WOODS, Theodore N. III, b. 1 Jan. 1948. Artist. Educ: A.A., Glendale Community Coll., 1968; B.F.A., M.F.A., Ariz. State Univ., 1969-72; Appts: Vis. Staff Instr., Phoenix Coll., 1973, Glendale Community Coll., 1973-. Exhibs: Southwest Fine Arts Biennal, N.M.; Fine Arts, Ariz., 1970, '71; 12th. Ariz. Annual; 1st. & 2nd. Four Corners Biennial, Phoenix Art Mus., Ariz.; 7th. & 8th. Southwestern Art Invitational, Yuma, ibid; 7th. Nat. Drawing & Small Sculpture Show, Tex., 1973; Dimensions '72, '73, '74, Ariz.; Ariz. Commn. of Arts & Humanities travelling show, 1972, '73, '74; rep. in pvte. collects. & collect., Ariz. State Univ. Artist-in-Res., Nat. Endowment for Arts & Humanities, Mesa, Ariz., 1972-73. Address: c/o Robert L. Dickson, 3338 W. Belmont Ave., Phoenix, AZ 85021, U.S.A. 37.

WOODWARD, Cleveland Landon, b. 25 June 1900. Artist; Illustrator. Educ: Wis. Univ.; Cinn. Art Acad., 1923-26; Charles Hawthorne's Cape Cod Schl. of Art, summer 1924; British Art Acad., Rome, Italy, 1928-29. Appts: Lectr., Biblical Art, schls., colls. & museums, many yrs.; Instr., Oil Painting, Eastern Shore Acad. Fine Arts, 1972-; Advsr., ibid, 1972-. Mbrships: Co-Fndr. & 1st Bd. of Dirs., Cape Cod Art Assn.; Bd. of Dirs., Eastern Shore Art Assn., 1971-74; Rotary Club, Fairhope, Ala.; Life mbr., Mobile Art Assn.; Fndr., Woodward Coffee Club, Fairhope, Ala., & Cape Cod, Mass. Works incl: Mural, Samuel & Eli, 7th Presby. Ch., Cinn., Ohio, 1949; Mural, Peter & John, W. End Bapt. Ch., Mobile, Ala., 1972. One-man shows incl. Mobile Art Gall., 1968 & 1971, & Percy Whiting Mus., Fairhope, Ala., 1969 & 1971; Many exhibitions & permanent collects. in U.S.A.; Illustrator of books. Recip., Annual purchase, Permanent Collect., Mobile Art Gall., Ala. Address: P.O. Box 466, Fairhope, AL 36532, U.S.A. 2, 37.

WOODWARD, Frederick Richard, b. 5 May 1939. Museum, Art Gallery Curator. Educ: B.Sc. Appts: Tech. Asst., Asst. Keeper, Natural Hist., City of Birmingham Mus. & Art Gall., U.K., 1960-65; Asst. Keeper, City of Liverpool Mus., 1965; Dpty. Dir., Mus., Art Galls. & Coats Observatory, 1965-69; Curator, Shipley Art Gall. & Saltwell Park Mus., Gateshead, 1969-. Mbrships: Malachol. Soc.; Soc. of Antiquities of Scotland; Conchol. Soc. of G.B. & Ireland. Author num. monographs on mollusks. Address: Shipley Art Gallery, Prince Consort Rd., Gateshead, NE8 4JB, Co. Durham, U.K.

WOODWARD, Grace Steele (Mrs. Guy H. Woodward). Historian; Biographer. Educ: Mo. Univ.; Univ. of Okla. Publs: The Man Who Conquered Pain, 1962; The Cherokees, 1963; Pocahontas, 1969. Mbrships: The Arts Club of Wash. DC; The Assn. for the Preservation of Va. Antiquities, Richmond, Va.; The Gilcrease Museum of History & Art, Tulsa, Okla.; Tuesday Writers of Tulsa, Okla.; Theta Sigma Phi. Co-author, Secret of Sherwood Forest—Oil Production in England during WWII, 1973-74; 2 other works, forthcoming. Hons: Okla. Hall of Fame, 1969; Awarded 1st Prize, Okla. Writers' Confederation, 1970;

Honored by Nat. Coun. of Cherokee Tribe of Indians, 1973. Address: 3618 S Atlanta Ave., Tulsa, OK 74105, U.S.A. 5, 30.

WOODWARD, John (William), b. 19 Sept. 1920. Author; Publisher; Editor; Poet; Playwright. Appts: Libn., Rolls-Royce, Ltd.; Personnel & Admin. Off., ibid; Employment & Welfare Off.; Chmn., 4 Names Publng. Co.; on Edit. & Advsry. Bds.: Royal Blue Book; International Who's Who in Poetry; Biography of Monaco; County Authors Today Series; Cecil Day-Lewis, The Poet Laureate, A Bibliography; Directory of Public Affairs, etc.; Advsr., Int. Poetry Soc. Int. Mbrships. incl: Life Fellow, Int. Inst. Arts & Letters; Life Pres., V.P., Int. Writers Guild & Soc. of New Authors; Life Pres., Derby Writers' Guild, Derby & Derbyshiry Dumas Assn., Derby Int. Writers Guild; Life Int. Coun. Ldrs. & Schols., Lancashire Authors Assn.; Arts Theatre Club; Life Fellow, Intercontinental Biog. Assn.; V.P., Int. Poetry Soc., Eastern Ctr., Poetry Soc. of London (N.Y.); Int. Acad. of Ldrship. & World Inst. of Drs., Publs. incl: Poems: Beyond the Dawn; Prelude; Fugue; Pebbles in the Pool; Though Roses Die; The Haunted Ballroom; Lucifer Reflects; Hold Back the Dawn; Not Bread Alone; The Agony & the Ecstacy; Four Names Anthology; Plays: Divorce by Death; A Woman's Place; Come Back, Peter; A Gift from the Gods; Winter Sunshine; The Perfect Man; The Assassin; Gallows Close; Beyond the Bridge; Tudor England; Cry with the Thunder; The Reluctant Dustman; Dilute with Water; Spare that Tree. Recip. of many hons. inclng: Kt. of Mark Twain, (U.S.A.), 1971, Kt. of Grace, Sovereign Order of St. John of Jerusalem (Malta), 1972; Elected Prominent American, 1970; Int. Award of Hon. Medallion & Dip. of Distinction, 1969. Address: Abbots Lodge, 2 Madeley St., Derby DE3 8EX, U.K. 3, 11, 30, 43, 128, 129, 131, 133.

WOODWARD, Katharine Burchell, b. 13 Jan. 1889. Educator. Educ: B.A., Vanderbilt Univ., Nashville, Tenn., 1919; Geo. Peabody's Coll. for Tchrs.; Dip. de Suficienco, Centro de Estudios Historicos, Madrid, 1924; Middlebury Coll. Spanish Schl., Middlebury, Vt.; Columbia Univ.; M.A., Stanford Univ., Calif., 1930. Appts. incl: Spanish & Latin Tchr.-Hd., Spanish Dept., Woodrow Wilson HS, Portsmouth, Va., 1919-56; Va. Chmn., Comm. for the Revision of Mod. For. Langs. Prog., 1932-34. Mbrships. incl: Organizer, V.P., Sec.-Treas., Life Mbr., Va. Chapt., Am. Assn. of Tchrs. of Spanish & Portuguese; 1st Corres. Sec., Iota State, Delta Kappa Gamma; Organizer & Pres., Gamma Chapt., ibid; Organizer 4 more chapts., Tidewater, Va., 1957-68; Fac. Advsr., Spanish Club (inclng. Pan Am. League), Woodrow Wilson HS, 1919-56; NEA; Va. Educ. Assn.; Mu Chapt., Sigma Delta Pi, Middleburg (Vt.) Spanish Schl., 1941; Assoc. Mbr., Pi Pi Int. Club in Christian Philos., 1942; Amigos de Espanas, 1964. Publs: Proverbs in Don Quijote by Cervantes (thesis). Hons. incl: Medal in Instrumental Music, 1906; Commodore Vanderbilt Statuette, Vanderbilt Alumni Campaign, 1962; The Katharine B. Woodward Prize in Spanish, Vanderbilt Univ., awarded 1943, endowed 1962. Address: Hotel Governor Dinwiddie, Portsmouth, VA 23704, U.S.A. 125.

WOODWORTH, David P., b. 5 Oct. 1932. Librarian; Lecturer. Educ: Schl. of Libnship., Leeds U.K. Appts: Asst., Dewsbury Pub. Lib., 1949-51; Sr. Asst., ibid, 1954-55; Sr. Asst., Northamptonshire Co. Lib., 1955-58; Dpty. Co. Libn., Tech., ibid, 1958-59; Libn.-Info. Off., Nat. Coal Bd., Cheltenham, 1960-62; Tech. Libn., Brit. Cast Iron Rsch. Assn., Birmingham,

1962-64; Libn., Brit. Inst. of Mgmt., London, 1964-65; Libn., Port of London Authority, 1965-66. Mbrships: Chmn., Round Table, 1972-73; Am. Lib. Assn.; 1956; Served on comms. of var. profl. bodies. Publs: Guide to Current British Journals, 1st. edit. 1970; 2nd edit. 1973; Directory of Publishers of British Journals, 2 vols. Also conthr. to profl. jrnls. Address: The Quintain, 12 Windmill Close, Ashby-de-la-Zouch, Leics. LE6 5EQ, U.K.

WOOTTON, Thelma Athel McCarty (Mrs. Ralph E. Wootton), b. 24 May 1905. Librarian. Educ: A.B., 1927, M.A. in Lib. Sci., 1959, Ind. Univ. Appts: Libn., Lafayette H.S., Ind., 1925-36; Asst. Libn., Wells Mem. Lib., Lafayette, 1938-55; Hd. Libn., ibid, 1955-. Mbrships: Reading Badge Counselor, Boy Scouts of Am.; White Shrine of Jerusalem; Past Pres., Delta Kappa Gamma; Past Mbr., Corp. Bd., Lafayette Alumni Chapt., Phi Mu; Order of Eastern Star; Past Pres., Altrusa Club; Past Mbr., Offl. Bd., Meth. Ch. Address: 2605 S. 9th St., Lafayette, IN 47905, U.S.A. 5, 8, 132.

WORKMAN, David Frank, b. 5 July 1901. School Administrator. Educ: Shippensburg Coll.; B.S., Franklin & Marshall Coll., 1925; M.A., Columbia Tchrs. Coll., 1929; Completed study for Ed.D., N.Y. Univ. Appts: Asst. Prin. & Sci. Tchr., Liberty Ctrl. H.S., 1922-23; Supervising Prin., Lemasters, 1925-27, Waldwick, 1927-61; Hd. Admnstr.; Retd., 1962. Mbrships. incl: Phi Delta Kappa; Masons: NEA; N.J. Educ. Assn.; Hd., Ch. of God of the Woods; N.J. State Schoolmasters Assn.; Past Civil Defence Chmn.; Past Pres., Past Chief, Waldwick (N.J.) Vol. Firemen; Dir., 1st Fed. Bank; Fndr., Waldwick Skating Club. Hons: Waldwick Vol. Firemen's Award, 1961; Citizen Award, WBA, 1972. Address: 21 Pennington Ave., Waldwick, NJ 07463, U.S.A. 15, 130.

WORNER, Ruby Kathryn, b. 22 Nov. 1900. Textile Scientist. Educ: B.S., 1921, M.S., 1922, Ph.D., Chem., 1925, Univ. of Chgo. Appts: Assoc. Prof., Chem. & Physics, Okla. Coll. for Women, 1925-27; Asst. Chem., Bur. of Econ. Standards, U.S. Dept. of Agric., 1927-29; Nat. Bur. of Standards, Wash., D.C., 1929-40; Southern Regional Rsch. Lab., USDA, New Orleans, 1940-62; Vis. Fulbright Prof. & Cons., Univ. of Alexandria, Egypt, 1960-61; Tech. Off., Textiles, UN/FAO, Cotton Rsch. Proj., Giza, Etypt, 1963-65; Bibliographer, Tech. Manual, Am. Assn. of Textile Chems. & Colorists, 1966-71; Vol. Textile Cons. Philippine Textile Rsch. Inst., Manila, 1970. Mbrships: Am. Assn. of Textile Chems. & Colorists; 2nd V.P., Am. Soc. for Testing & Mats.; Brit. Textile Inst.; Am. Chem. Soc.; Fellow, AAAS; Sigma Xi; Fellow, Am. Inst. of Chems. Publs: Var. articles; Chapts. in tech. books. Hons: Award of Merit, 1964, Hon. Mbr. Comm. D-13, 1967, Fellow, Am. Soc. for Testing & Mats.; Disting. Alumni Serv. Award, Shimer Coll., 1967. Address: 5021 N. University, Apt. P, Peoria, IL 61614, U.S.A. 5, 14, 132.

WORSHAM, Bertrand Ray, b. 14 Feb. 1926. Physician; Psychiatrist. Educ: B.A., Univ. of Ark., 1951; M.D., Schl. of Med., ibid, 1955; Fellowship in Psych., Menninger Schl. of Psych., 1958. Appts: Pvte. prac., psych., 1959-; Cons., Okla. City VA Hosp., State Hlth. Dept., & Soc. Security Admin., 1959-; Dir., Regional Guidance Ctr., Univ. of Okla., 1966-68; Cmdr., USNR. Mbrships: World Fedn. for Mental Hlth.; AMA; Am. Psych. Assn.; Fellow, Royal Soc. of Hlth.; Electorate, Am. Security Coun.; Electorate, Okla. Athletic Hall of Fame. Hons: Physn's Recognition Award. Address: 9915 N.

Kelley, Oklahoma City, OK 73112, U.S.A. 7, 112, 128, 129, 131.

WORTH, Reginald Stanley, b. 8 June 1901. Engineer. Educ: Pembroke Coll., Cambridge, U.K. Appts: Dir., The Nestle Co. Ltd., U.K., 1940-43; Mng. Dir., ibid, 1943-58; Chmn., 1958-73; Gen. Mgr., Nestle Alimentana S.A., Switzerland, 1958-66; Dir., ibid, 1966-; Chmn., Comm. of Enquiry into Bacon & Ham Curing Ind.; Hon. Chmn., The Nestle Co. Ltd., U.K., 1973. Mbrships: Exec. Comm., Creamery Proprietors' Assn., 1940-; Exec. Comm., Chocolate & Confectionery Alliance, 1940-; Chmn., Canners' War Time Assn., 1942-46; Pres., Coun. of Food Mfrs. Fedn. Inc.; Exec. Comm., Prog. of Co-operation in Ind., FAO, 1960; Chmn., Dev. Assn., Aiglon Coll., Switzerland, 1967; V.P., Nat. Liberal Club, London; Ulster Reform Club, Belfast; Royal Wimbledon Gold Club. Recip., C.B.E., 1946. Address: 108 Ave. de Sully, 1814, La Tour de Peilz, Vaud, Switzerland. 41, 43.

WORTLEY, Austin Miles, Jr., b. 29 Nov. 1921. Corporate Executive. Educ: Grad., Valley Forge Mil. Acad., 1940; Temple Univ. Appts: Sales Engr., Edgcomb Steel Co., 1946-60; Penguin Inds., Inc., 1960-, Pres. & Chmn. of Bd. Mbrships: Tredyffrin Township Bd. of Supvsrs. 1964-67; Chester Co. Airport Authority (Chmn., 1966-71); Ctrl. & Western Chester Co. Indl. Dev. Corp., (Pres. & Dir., 1970-71), Authority (Dir., 1970-71); Dir., Chester Co. Dev. Coun.; Fraternal Order of Police. Recip. of Purple Heart & Presl. Citation, WWII. Address: Hopewell Farm, R.D.1, Downingtown, PA 19335, U.S.A. 6.

WORTZ, Carl Haglin III, b. 9 May 1921. Business Consultant. Educ: B.S., Bus. Univ. of Ark.; Degree in Meterologyb, Spartan Schl. of Aerodynamics; AMA Mgmt. Courses for Presidents. Appts: Gen. Mgr., Wortz Co., 1946-56; Pres., Wortz Co. Crackers & Cookies, 1956-71; Bus. Analyst & Cons., Wortz Assocs., 1971-; Dir., In Mac, Live Oak Rsch., ibid. Mbrships: Past Pres., Biscuit Bakrs Inst.; Past Dir., Biscuit & Cracker Manufacture Assn.; Sigma Alpha Epsilon; Hon. Citizen, New Orleans, La.; Hon. Citizen, Ft. Worth, Tex. Painter of water colors. Address: P.O. Box 45565, Dallas, TX 75235, U.S.A. 7, 16, 130.

WOUK, Herman, b. 27 May 1915. Author. Educ: A.B., Columbia Univ., 1934. Appts. incl: Radio Writer, 1934-41; Deck Off., U.S. Naval Reserve, 1941-46; Novelist & Playwright, 1946-. Publs: Aurora Dawn, 1947; The City Boy, 1948; The Caine Mutiny, 1951; Marjorie Morningstar, 1955; Youngblood Hawke, 1962; Don't Stop the Carnival, 1965. Plays: The Traitor, 1949; The Caine Mutiny Court-Martial, 1954; Nature's Way, 1957; (non-fiction) This Is My God, 1959. Mbrships: Bd. Mbr., Wash. Nat. Symph.; Council Mbr., Authors' Guild; Authors' League; Dramastists Guild; Nat. Press Club. Hons: Pulitzer Prize for Fiction, 1952; Columbia Univ. Medal for Excellence, 1952; Hon. L.H.D., Yeshiva Univ., 1954; Hon. LL.D., Clark Univ., 1960. Address: c/o Harold Matson Co., Inc., 22 E. 40th St., New York, 10016, U.S.A. 2, 6, 34.

WRANGLÉN, Karl Gustaf (Gösta), b. 19 Mar. 1923. University Professor. Educ: Chem. Eng., Royal Inst. Technol., Stockholm, Sweden, 1947; Dr.Eng., 1950; Dr.Techn., 1955. Appts: Guest Wkr., Nat. Bur. of Standards, Wash. D.C., U.S.A., 1950; Rsch. Assoc., var. Swedish inds., 1951-57; Prof., Electrochem. & Corrosion Sci., Royal Inst. Technol., Stockholm, 1963. Mbrships: Pres. Elect., Int. Soc. Electrochem., 1973-74; Pres.,

1975-76; Tech. Expert, Stockholm Civic Ct. & Svea Ct. of Appeal; Hon. coun., Int. Corrosion Congresses. Author, An Introduction to Corrosion & Protection of Metals, 1967. Address: Royal Inst. of Technol., 100 44 Stockholm 70, Sweden. 43, 134.

WREN, Melvin C(larence), b. 18 June 1910. Historian. Educ: B.A., M.A., Ph.D., Univ. of Iowa, 1936-39; Post-Doctoral study, Univ. of Calif., 1945-46. Appts: Instr.-Prof. of Hist., Univ. of Mont., 1940-67; Chmn., Dept. Hist., ibid, 1958-67; Vis. Prof. Hist., Univ. of Wash., 1958; Lectr., Univ. of Md., Overseas, 1962-63; Prof. Hist., Univ. of Toledo, Ohio, 1967-; Chmn., Dept. Hist., ibid, 1967-69; Vis. Prof. Hist., Univ. of Neb., 1971. Mbrships. incl: Am. Hist. Assn.; Am. Pol. Assn.; Phi Kappa Phi; Phi Alpha Theta. Publs: The Course of Russian History, 1958, 3rd Edit. 1968; Ancient Russia, 1965; The Western Impact upon Tsarist Russia, 1970. Contbr. to var. histl. jrnls. Recip., Fellowship, Am. Coun. Learned Socs., 1948. Address: Univ. of Toledo, Toledo, OH 43606, U.S.A. 2, 8, 30.

WRETLIND, Karl Arvid Johannes, b. 28 Jan. 1919. Professor. Educ: M.D., Med. Fac., Karolinska Inst., Stockholm. Appts: Asst. Prof., Pharmacol., Karolinska Inst., 1949-62; Prof., Nutrition & Food Hygiene, Swedish Nat. Inst. of Hlth., 1962-70; Hd., Nutrition Unit, Karolinska Inst., 1970. Mbrships: Royal Swedish Acad. of Engrng. Scis.; Rotary Int. & Past Pres., Solna Rotary Club; European Grp. of Nutritionists; Swedish Nutrition Soc.; Swedish Soc. of Physns.; Chmn., Swedish Food Law Comm., 1963-70. Developer of new approaches to human, animal nutrition; Over 200 papers. Hons: Royal Order of Polar Star, 1965; Cmdr., Royal Order of Vasa, 1972. Address: Karlavägen 53, 114 49 Stockholm, Sweden.

WRIGHT, Abner Augustus. Medical Practitioner. Educ: Howard Univ., Wash., D.C.; Royal Coll. of Physns. & Surgs., Edinburgh & Glasgow, U.K. Appts: Med. Off., Kingston Pub. Hosp., Jamaica; Med. Off., Frankfield, ibid; Med. Off., May Pen, ibid. Mbrships. incl: Pres., Med. Assn., Jamaica; Chmn., Milk River Mineral Bath, Glenmuir High Schl., Vere Free Schls; Jamaica Nat. Reserve Coun.; Jamaica Agricl. Soc.; Past Master, Clarendon Dist. Grand Lodge (Scotland) in Jamaica. Address: May Pen, Jamaica, West Indies.

WRIGHT, Alma McIntyre (Mrs. Robert O. Wright), b. 31 July 1909. Publisher; Editor; Writer. Educ: B.S., Univ. of Tenn., Knoxville, 1932. Appts: Rec. Sec., African Violet Soc. Am., 1946-48; Ed., African Violet Mag., 1947-63; Pres., 1948-49; Mbrship. Sec., 1953-63; Exec. Dir., 1960-63; Ed., Master list of African Violets; Pres., Indoor Gardener Publng. co. Inc., Knoxville, Tenn., 1963; Ed., Gesneriad Saintpaulia News, Am. Gesneria Soc. & Saintpaulia Int., 1963; Rec. Sec., Saintpaulia Int., 1963. Mbrships: Am. Hort. Soc. Garden Writers Am. Address: 4752 Calumet Dr. S.W., Knoxville, TN 37919, U.S.A. 5, 7, 16, 22, 128.

WRIGHT, Bruce Stanley, b. 17 Sept. 1912. Wildlife Biologist. Educ: B.Sc., Univ. of N.B., Canada, 1936; M.Sc., Univ. of Wis., U.S.A., 1947. Appts: Rsch. Off., Dominion Forest Serv., 1937-45; Ducks Unlimited, Canada, 1945-46; Dir., Northeastern Wildlife Stn., Fredericton, N.B., 1947-. Mbrships: Fndg. Dir., Atlantic Region, Canadian Soc. of Wildlife & Fishery Biologists; Wildlife Soc.; Am. Soc. of Mammalogists; Am. Ornithologists Union; Fndg. Mbr., Fredericton Garrison Club; Fac. Club, Univ. of N.B. Publs. incl: High Tide & an

East Wind-the story of the Black Duck, 1954; The Ghost of North America-the story of the Eastern Panther, 1959; Wildlife Sketches Near & Far, 1962; The Monarch of Mularchy Mountain, 1963; Black Duck Spring, 1966; the Frogmen of Burma, 1968; The Astern Panther-a question of Survival, 1972. Recip., John Pearce Mem. Award, N.E. Sect., Wildlife Soc., 1971. Address: Northeastern Wildlife Stn., Univ. of N.B., Fredericton, N.B., Canada. 30, 131.

WRIGHT, C.T., b. 4 Oct. 1942. Professor of History & Political Science. Educ: B.S., Ft. Valley State Coll., Ga.; M.A., Atlanta Univ., Ga.; Ph.D., Boston Univ., Mass.; further studies, George Williams Coll., Downers Grove Ill., Carnegie-Mellon Univ., Pitts., Pa. Appts: Tchr., Walton Co. Bd. Educ., Monroe, Ga., 1965-67; Staff Mbr., Human Rels. Ctr., Boston Univ., 1971-72; Asst. Prof., Atlanta Univ., Summer 1971-73; Asst. Prof., Chmn. Dept. of Hist. & Pol. Sci., Dir. Human Rels. Prog., Morris Brown Coll., Atlanta, 1973-. Mbrships, incl: Am. & Southern Histl. Assns.; Org. Am. Histns.; Assn. Study of Afro-Am. Life & Hist.; Walton Co. Democratic Exec. Comm.; Pres., Madison Missionary Bapt. Sunday Schl. Cong.; Phi Beta Sigma. Recip., acad. fellowships & awards. Address: 806 Wildwood Dr., Social Circle, GA 30279, U.S.A. 125.

WRIGHT, Daniel Earl, b. 15 July 1951. Teacher. Educ: B.A., W. Va. Inst. of Technol., 1972; Grad. work on Mstrs. degree, Marshall Univ. Appts. incl: Substitute Tchr., Jan.-June, 1973; Tchr., Nuttall H.S., 1973-74. Mbrships. incl: W. Va. Democratic State Exec. Comm., 1974. W. Va. Young Democrats', State Treas., 1973 & mbr., State Exec. comm., ibid, 1972-; Fayette Co. Young Democrats', Sec., Pres., 1972; McGovern-Shriver Campaign Dir., Fayette Co., 1972; NEA; W. Va. Educ. Assn.; Assn. of Classroom Tchrs.; Classroom Educ. Assn.; Co. Educ. Assn.; W. Va. Technol. Alumni Assn.; Oak Hill 1st Presby. Ch., Presby. Witness Comm., Chmn., Presby. Youth, Presby. Serv. Comm.; Deleg., Educl. Workshops, 1971, 1974 from Oak Hill 1st Presby. Ch.; Elected Deacon, Oak Hill 1st Presby. Ch., 1974; Ch. Schl. Tchr., 1969-. Hons. incl: DAR Hist. Award, 1962, 1965. Am. current Events Award, 1968. Address: P.O. Box 303, Oak Hill, WV 25901, U.S.A. 117, 125.

WRIGHT, F. Vernon, b. 26 Dec. 1916. President, Federal Intermediate Credit Bank of New Orleans. Educ: Bus. Admin., Northeast Mo. State Tchrs. Coll., 1937; Personnel Mgmt., Washington & Jefferson Coll., 1943; Money & Banking & Personnel Admin., Am. Univ., Biarritz, France, 1946; Gen. Mgmt., Am. Mgmt. Assn.; 1962; Govt., Brookings Instn., 1965. Appts: incl: Mgr. & Sec.-Treas., Farmington Prod. Credit Assn., Mo., 1946-58; Illini Prod. Credit Assn., Carlinville, Ill., 1958-60; Asst. V.P., Fed. Intermediate Credit Bank of St. Louis, Mo., 1960-61; Dpty. Gov. & Dir. Prod. Credit Serv., Farm Credit Admin., Wash. D.C., 1961-70; Pres., Fed. Intermediate Credit Bank of New Orleans, La., 1970-. Mbrships. incl: Am. Mgmt. Assn.; Pres.'s Assn., ibid; Greater New Orleans Chamb. of Comm.; Dir., Agribusiness Comm., ibid; Planning Comm., Southern Farm Forum; Pi Omega Pi. Address: P.O. Box 50062, New Orleans, LA 70150, U.S.A. 2, 57, 125.

WRIGHT, Harold Lee, b. 6 May 1912. Department Store Executive. Educ: B.C.S., Drake Univ., 1934. Appts: Trainee, J.C. Penney Co., Okla. City, 1934; Dept. Mgr., Muskogee, Okla., 1935-36; Asst. Mgr., St. Joseph, Mo., 1938-42; Greenville, S.C., 1942-43; Lt., USNR, 1942-46; Mgr., Anniston, Ala., 1947-48; Dist. Mgr., Dallas, Tex., 1948-50, Atlanta, Ga.,

1950-54; Regional Mgr., Mpls., Minn., 1954-62, Chgo., Ill., 1962, V.P., 1969; Bus. Cons., Barrington, Ill., 1974. Mbrships: Jr. & Sr. Warden, Episc. Vestryman; Dir., Ill. Retail Merchants Assn.; Chi Delta, Drake Univ.; Elks Club Barrington Hills Country Club. Recip. Double 'D' Award for Disting. Achievement, Drake Univ., 1974. Address: 254 Donlea Rd., Barrington Hills, IL 60010, U.S.A.

WRIGHT, Helen John, b. 9 Apr. 1914. Home Economist. Educ: Pre-Med., Baylor Univ., 2 yrs.; B.S., Home Econ. & Sci., Queens Coll., N.C.; Grad. study, N.C. State Univ., Colo. State Univ., Withrop Coll., Univ. of Ariz. & Kan. State Univ.. Appts: Ext. Home. Econ., Mecklenburg Co., Univ. of N.C. Nutrition Cons., S & W Cafeterias; Dietician, Mem. Hosp., Charlotte, N.C.; Ext. Econ., Univ. of Nev., Univ. of Wyo. w. Indian tribes. Mbrships. icnl: Var. comms., Nat. & state Assns. of Ext. Home Econs. & Alternate Western Regional Dir., Nat. Assn.; Nat. & state Home Econs. Assns., inclng. Treas., N.C., Pres., Wyo. & N.C., Sec., Nev.; Epsilom Sigma Phi; Alpha Kappa Gamma; AAUW; Altrusa Club, Charlotte; Charlotte Woman's Club. Publs: 7 booklets for Indians on nutrition, grooming, sewing. Hons: Certs. of Merit, U.S. Dept. of Agric., 1965, '70, '72; Cert. of Merit, Epsilom Sigma Phi, Ph.D., Evergreen Coll. Address: 1395 Hillcrest Drive, Lander, WY 82520, U.S.A. 5.

WRIGHT, Melton Fisher, b. 9 Aug. 1922. Educator. Educ: A.B., Bob Jones Univ., 1945; M.Ed., Univ. of Va., 1951. Appts: Tchr., Prin., Boyce H.S., Va., 1947-51; Prin., Main St. Elem. Schl., 1951-55, W.H. Keister Schl., 1955-56 & Harrisonburg H.S., 1956-58, all in Harrisonburg, Va.; Dir., Instrn., Frederick Co. Pub. Schls., 1958-66; Asst. Supt., ibid, 1966-68; Div. Supvsr. of Schls., 1968-. Pres., Northern Va. Supts. Assn., State Supts. Advsry. Grp. Mbrships: Phi Delta Kappa; Kappa Delta Pi; Hon. Ky. Col.; Pres., Va. Educ. Assn., 1969; many state educ. comms. Publs: Giant for God, 1951; Into the Light, 1955; The Beloved Schoolmaster, 1958; Fortress of Faith, 1960; Thoughts on Education, 1968. Hons: LL.D., Bob Jones Univ., 1961; State Hon. FFA Award, Va., 1970; James Monroe Award, Monroe Coll., 1960; Recog. Medal, Lord Fairfax Coll., 1972; Pres.'s Award, Va. Educ. Assn., 1970. Address: P.O. Box 221, Winchester, VA 22601, U.S.A. 2, 7, 15, 126.

WRIGHT, R. Glenn, b. 15 Apr. 1932. Professor of Literature. Educ: B.S., Purdue Univ., 1954; M.A., Univ. of Iowa, 1955; Ph.D., Geo. Wash. Univ., 1968. Appts: Intelligence Analyst, Pentagon, U.S. Army, 1956-58; Admin. Asst. & Speech Writer, For. Affairs Div., Legislative Ref. Serv., Lib. of Cong., 1959-61; Tchng. Fellow, Geo. Wash. Univ., 1961-64; ssoc. Prof., & Dir., Studies in Lit., Justin Morrill Coll., Mich. State Univ., 1964-. Mbrships: MLA; Midwest Mod. Lang. Assn.; Mbr., Nat. Coun., Am. Studies Assn.; Past Chapt. Pres., Mich. Am. Studies Assn.; AAUP; Am. Popular Culture Assn. Publs: Ed., Compiler, Author Bibliography of English Language Fiction in Library of Congress through 1950, 8 vols., 1973; Ed., Chronological Bibliography of English Language Fiction in Library of Congress through 1950, 8 vols., 1974. Author, sci. fiction & popular culture articles. Address: Justin Morrill Coll., Snyder Hall, Mich. State Univ., E. Lansing, MI 48824, U.S.A.

WRIGHT, Rae Verne. Librarian. Educ: B.A., Ohio State Univ., 1947; M.S.L.S.,̍ Lib. Schl., Columbia Univ., N.Y.C., 1958. Appts: Ref. Asst., N.Y. Acad. of Med., 1955-59; Asst.

Libn., Univ. of Ghana, 1959-61; Acting Chief Libn., Inst. of Jamaica, 1964-71; Sr. Sub-Libn. (Med. Libn), Univ. of Benin, Nigeria, 1972-. Mbr., Phi Beta Kappa. Publs: Guide to Jamaican Reference Material in the West Indies Reference Library, 1965, reprint 1967; papers on Caribbean Library Resources (w. P. Dunn), published in Research Library Cooperation in the Caribbean, 1973; Ed. & contbr., Book Power on East Street, weekly column in Daily Gleaner, Kingston, Jamaica, 1969-70. Address: Benin University Library, PMB 1191, Benin City, Nigeria.

WRIGHT, Ralph Edwin, b. 23 Feb. 1922. High School Principal. Educ: A.B., Bradley Polytechnic Inst., 1943; M.A., Bradley Univ., 1950; Ph.D., ibid, 1955. Appts. incl: Civil Educ. Off., U.S. Civil Serv., CAF-11, Nilgate Mil. Govt. Team, Niigata, Japan, 1946-49; Grad. Asst. & Summer Schl. Instr., Placement Off., Bradley Univ., Peoria, Ill., 1950-52; Dir. of Guidance & Soc. Studies Tchr., Farmington, Community H.S., Farmington, Ill., 1952-54; Admin. Asst. & Guidance Dir., Lincoln-Way Community H.S., New Lennox, Ill., 1954-58; Guest Instr., Bradley Univ., Wionna State Coll. & Mankato State Coll., Minn., 1955-65; Prin., John Marshall Sr. H.S., Rochester, Minn., 1958-65; Prin., Mayo H.S., Rochester, Minn., 1965-. Mbrships. incl: REA; MEA; NEA; MASSP; SSP; Rotary Club; Bd. Dirs., Rochester Meth. Hosp. & YMCA, Camp Olson; Charter Mbr. & 1st Pres., Beta Psi Chapt., Phi Delta Kappa; Assoc.' CFK (Ltd.), 1973-, participant PASCL Proj., 1971-. Contbr. to profl. & acad. jrnls. & newspapers. Hons. incl: U.S. Govt. Commendation for work in Japan, 1946-49. Address: 726 6th St., Southwest Rochester, MN 55901, U.S.A. 15.

WRIGHT, (The Very Rev.) Ronald William Vernon Selby, b. 12 June 1908. Minister of the Church of Scotland. Educ: Edinburgh Acad., U.K., 1915-21; M.A., Edinburgh Univ., 1933; D.D., ibid, 1956; New Coll., Edinburgh, 1933-36. Appts. incl: Fndr. & Hon. Warden, Canongate Boys' Club, 1927-; Min., Canongate (Kirk of Holyrood House) & Edinburgh Castle, 1936-; Chap. to H.M. Forces, 1938-46; Sr. Chap., ibid, 1942-46; Hon. Sr. Chap., 1946-; Chap. to H.M. the Queen, 1961-; Moderator, Presbytery, Edinburgh, 1963-64; Moderator, Gen. Assembly of the Ch. of Scotland, 1972-73; Chap. to H.M. Bodyguard for Scotland (The Royal Company of Archers); Chap. to Merchant Co. of Edinburgh; J.P. Edinburgh. Mbrships: Fellow, Royal Soc. of Edinburgh; Fellow, Royal Soc. of Arts; Athenaeum Club, London; New Club, Edinburgh. Publs. incl: Asking them Questions, 6 vols.; Take Up God's Armour; Fathers of the Kirk; Radio Padre Talks. Hons: Cmdr., Royal Victorian Order; Territorial Decoration. Address: Manse of the Canongate, Edinburgh, EH8 8BR, U.K. 1, 3, 41.

WRIGHT, Russell Melvin, b. 9 June 1904. Osteopathic Physician and Surgeon. Educ: Grad., Slippery State Coll., 1923; Coll. of Osteopathic Physn. & Surgs., Des Moines, Iowa, 1929; B.S., Gt. Lakes Coll., 1944; Internship, Detroit Osteopathic Hosp., 1929-30. Appts. incl: Surg. Staff Mbr., Detroit Osteopathic Hosp., Mich., 1929-74; Past Chief of Staff, ibid; Instr., Denver Polyclin., Summers 1939-44; Team Physn., Detroit Tigers, Pro-Basketball Team, 1952-70, Detroit Pistons, 1967-74, U.S. Weight Lifting Team, 1966-74; Instr., P.E., Olivet Coll., 1971; Nat. Lectr. & Writer, Sports Med.; Held clins. on weightlifting for Int. Fedn. of Weight Lifting in many cities throughout the world. Mbrships. incl: Pres., Med. Comm., Int. Fedn. of Weight Lifting, 1964-74; Life Mbr.,

Amateur Athletic Union; Mich. Assn. of Phys. Fitness & Sports; Am. & Mich. Osteopathic Assns.; Am. Coll. of Osteopathic Surgs.; V.P., U.S. Weightlifting Med. Comm., 1973-. Hons. incl: Disting. Alumnus, Slippery Rock State Coll., 1973; Humanitarian Award, Mich. Sport Sages, 1973. Address: Wright By The Sea, Delray Beach, FL 33444, U.S.A.

WRIGLEY, Elizabeth Springer (Mrs. Oliver K. Wrigley), b. 4 Oct. 1915. Corporation Executive; Library Director. Educ: A.B., Univ. of Pitts., 1935; B.S., Carmegie Inst. of Technol., 1936. Appts: Procedure Analyst, U.S. Steel Corp., 1942-43; Trustee, Francis Bacon Fndn., Inc., 1950-; Pres., ibid, 1954-; Dir., Francis Bacon Lib., 1960-. Mbrships: Order of the Eastern Star; White Shrine; Alpha Delta Pi; Modern Humanities Rsch. Assn.; Renaissance Soc. of Am.; Hon. V.P., Am. Cryptogram Assn., 1972-73; ALA; Special Libs. Assn.; Calif. Lib. Assn. Publs: Ed., The Skeleton Text of the Shakespeare Folio, by W.C. Arensberg, 1952; STC Numbes in the Library of the Francis Bacon Foundation, 1958; Wing Numbers in the Francis Bacon Library, 1959; Supplement to STC & Wing Numbers in the Francis Bacon Library, 1967; The Lee-Bernard Collection in American Political Theory, 1972; Co-ed. w. D.W. Davies, A Concordance to the Essays of Francis Bacon, 1973. Address: The Francis Bacon Fndn., Inc., 655 N. Dartmouth Ave., Claremont, CA 91711, U.S.A. 5, 9, 59.

WROTTESLBY, Arthur John Francis, b. 18 June 1908. Barrister-at-Law; Writer. Educ: Univ. Coll., Oxford Univ., U.K., 1926-30; B.A., 1929; Law degree, 1930; M.A., 1933. Appts. incl: Called to Bar, Inner Temple, 1932; Part-time Lectr., City of London Coll., 1937-39, 1945-46; Part-time Legal Advsr., London Express Newspapers, 1946-53; WWII Serv., 1939-45, Capt., Royal Norfolk Regiment, France & Belgium, 1940, N. Africa, 1942-43, Norway, 1945 & Judge Advocate Gen.'s Dept., 1942-43, 1944-45; Special Asst., Off. of Chief Solicitor & Legal Adviser, British Transport Commn., 1953-62, British Railways Bd., 1962-73. Mbrships: United Univ. Club, 1932-50; Oxford Union Soc., 1926-; Railway Club, 1925-, Pres., 1973-. Publs. incl: A Magistrate's Handbook, 2nd edit. w. S.R.C. Bosanquet, Q.C., 1950; You & The Law, 1951; Famous Underground Railways Of The World, 1956; The Midland & Great Northern Joint Railways, 1970; various articles & reviews in transport & legal publs., Sunday Express & contbns. in other publs. on similar subjects. Address: 48 Warrington Crescent, London, W9 1EP, U.K. 3, 35.

WROUGHTON, John Presbury, b. 27 Oct. 1934. School Master. Educ: M.A., Hertford Coll., Oxford, U.K. Appts: Asst. Master, Dame Allan's Schl., Newcastle Upon Tyne, 1959; Asst. Master, Ashby-de-la-Zouch Boys' Grammar Schl., 1962; Hd., Hist. Dept., King Edward's Schl., Bath, 1965; 2nd Master, ibid, 1974; Vis. Fellow, Fitzwilliam Coll., Cambridge, 1971. Mbrships: Fellow, Royal Histl. Soc.; Nat. Club; PEN. Publs: Cromwell & the Roundheads, 1969; Plots, Traitors & Spies, 1653-85, 1970; Smuggling (w. John Paxton), 1971; Documents on British Political History, 3 vols., 1971-73; Bath in the Age of Reform, 1830-41, 1972; The Civil War in Bath & North Somerset, 1973. Address: 11 Powlett Court, Bath, BA2 6QJ, U.K. 3, 137.

WU, William Lung Shen, b. 1 Sept. 1921. Physician. Educ: A.B., Stanford Univ., 1943; M.D., ibid, 1946; Univ. of Neb. Grad. Schl., 1946-48; M.S., Tulane Univ., 1955; Naval Schl. of Aviation Med., Fla., 1956; Designated Naval

Flight Surg. No. 1115. Appts. incl: Res. in Pathol., Lincoln Gen. & Bryan Mem. Hosps., 1947-48; Fellowship & Instr., Tulane Univ., Asst. Vis. & Vis. Physn., Charity Hosp. & Hutchinson Mem. Diagnostic & Cancer Detection Clins., New Orleans, 1948-54; Asst. Chief., Internal Med. & i/c of Heart Stn., U.S. Naval Hosp., N.C., 1955; Wing/Squad. Flight Surg., Sr. Watch Officer, USNR, 1956-57; Aerospace Med. Specialist, Gen. Dynamics/Convair, 1958-61; & Gen. Dynamics/Astronautics, 1961-65; Aerospace Med. & Bioastronautics Specialist, Lovelace Fndn. for Med. Educ. & Rsch., 1965-; Phys. (Int. Med.), Laguna Honda Hosp. & Rehab. Ctr., San Fran., 1968-. Mbrships. incl: Sigma Xi; N.Y. Acad. of Scis.; AMA; Calif. & San Diego Co. Med. Assns.; Civil Aviation Med. Assn.; AIAA; V.Chmn., San Diego Chapt., PTGME, IEEE, 1962-; Fellow, San Diego Biomed. Rsch. Inst.; Bd. of Dirs., ibid, 1961-; Chmn. of Fellows, 1963; various positions Inst. of Environmental Scis. Author of num. reports, articles, papers in field. Address: 200 Coronado Ave., Daly City, CA 94015, U.S.A. 120, 129, 131.

WULFF, Louis Leopold Victor, b. 8 Nov. 1905. Journalist & Author. Appts: Reporter, Lobby & Diplomatic Corres., Press Assn., 1924-28; Court Corres., 1928-50; War Corres., 1940-45; Columnist & Feature Writer, London Evening News, 1953-67; Currently P.R. Cons. & Freelance. Mbrships: Chmn., London Press Club, 1954, 55, 72 & 73, V.P., 1965; Liveyman Carmens Co.; Fellow, Inst. Dirs.; Devonshire Club; Nat. Union Jrnlsts. Publs: Queen of Tomorrow; Queen Mary; Elizabeth & Philip; Royal Family in Wartime; Silver Wedding. Recip., M.V.O. (4th), 1944. Address: Crocknorth Cottage, E. Horsley, Leatherhead, Surrey, U.K. 41.

WUNDERLICH, Freidrich, b. 23 Jan. 1896. Methodist Bidhop. Educ: Philos. & Theol., Leipzig, Germany & Evanston, U.S.A. Appts: Sec., Christian Educ., Methodist Ch., Germany, 1924-41; Pastor, Hamburg, ibid, 1931-39; Prof., Theol.-Pres., Sem., Meth. Ch., Frankfurt, Mainz, 1939-53; Bishop, Meth. Ch., Germany, 1953-68; Retd., 1968; Appointed Bishop, Meth. Ch., Scandinavia, 1970. Mbrships: Past Pres., Free Ch. Coun., Germany; Co-Fndr., 'Bread for the World', 1959; Deleg., World Assembly Chs., Evanston, U.S.A., 1954 & New Delhi, India, 1961; Rep., World Meth. Coun., World coun. Chs., Geneva, Switzerland, 1971. Hons: D.D., dePauw Univ., U.S.A., 1952; D.D., Birmingham S. Coll., 1956; L.H.D., Baldwin Wallace Coll., 1967; Wichern Plakatte, 1968. Address: 34 Grillparzerstr., 6 Frankfurt/M., German Fed. Repub. 92

WUNDERMAN, Irwine, b. 24 Apr. 1931. Scientist-Engineer. Educ: B.S.E.E., CCNY, 1952; M.S.E.E., Univ. of S. Calif., 1956; Ph.D., Stanford Univ., 1964. Appts: Advanced Rsch. Engr., Lockheed Aircraft Corp., 1952-56; Engrng. Mgr., Hewlett Packard Co., 1956-67; Pres., Cintra Inc., 1967-; Bd. Mbr., Cintra Inc.; Photo Physics Inc.; Automated Control Technol.; Equity Sci. Inc. Mbrships: Chmn., San Francisco Subsect. on Instrumentation, IEEE; Am. Phys. Soc.; Optical Soc. of Am.; Illumination AAAS; N.Y. Acad. Scis.; Am. Inst. Physics; Am. Mgmt. Assn.; Sigma Xi. Publs: Radiometric & Photometric Measurements; Mind over Mexico; approx. 25 papers in Engrng. jrnls., e.g. Electronics, Applied Optics, etc. Hons: Outstanding Invited Paper Award, Internation Solid State Circuits Conf., Phila., Pa., 1965. Address: 655 Eunice Ave., Mountain View, CA 94040, U.S.A. 9, 14, 59.

WUNSCHHEIM REICHSTRITTER, Alfons Von, b. 28 June 1904. Industrialist. Educ: LL.D., Vienna Univ. Appts. incl: Mng. Dir., Sprecher & Schuh Ltd., Linz; Chmn., Bd. Dirs., AG Der Voslauer Kammgarnfabrik, Bad Vöslau. Mbrships: Bd. Mbr., Assn. of Austrian Industrialists, Vienna & Linz; Councillor, Upper Austrian Chmbr. of Comm.; Employer's Deleg. to Int. Labor Conf., Geneva; Hd., Delegn. to Int. Hunting Coun. (CIC), Paris, France; Rotary, Linz; Pres., Hunting Mus., Schloss Hohenbrunn, Upper Austria. Publs: The Basis Of Productivity In U.S.A. (Ich Und Uncle Sam), 1956. Hons: Kt. of Grace & Devotion of Sovereign Order of St. John of Malta; Groszes Ehrenzeichen Für Verdienste Um Die Republik Osttereich; Cross of Hon. 1st Class de Litteris & Artibus. Address: J. Genuiterweg 9, A 4020 Leonding, Austria. 12, 43, 86, 123.

WÜRDINGER, Hans, b. 18 May 1903. Emeritus Professor of Commercial Law, Company Law & Maritime Law. Educ: Law studies, Munich, Germany, 1922-26; Dr.jur., ibid, 1928; 2nd law exam., 1929; Inaugurated, Univ. of Munich, 1933. Appts: Prof. of Law, Göttingen, 1934, Breslau, 1935, Vienna, 1938, Hamburg, 1944; Emeritus Prof., 1969-. Mbrships: Co-Chmn., Komm. des Deutschen Juristentags für Konzernrecht, 1960-63; Special Advsr., Commn. of European Econ. Community, Brussels, for harmonising laws of trading cos.; Deutscher Juristentag; Gesellschaft für Rechtsvergleichung. Publs. incl: Schiffshypotheken und Schiffsgläubigerrechte, 1961; Kommentar zum Handelsrecht (co-author), 3rd edit. 1967; Grosskommentar zum Aktiengesetz (co-author), 3rd edit. 1970; Aktien- und Konzernrecht, 3rd edit. 1973; German Company Law, forthcoming 1974. Recip., disting. serv. medal, German Fed. Repub., 1973. Address: Tassilostr. 22, D-8035 Gauting, German Fed. Repub. 43, 92.

WURM, Stephen Adolphe, Linguist; Educator. Educ: Ph.D., Univ. of Vienna, Austria. Appts: Lectr., Altaic Linguistics, Vienna Univ., 1945-51; Linguistic Expert, Ctrl. Asian Rsch. Ctr., London, U.K., 1952-54; Rsch. Fellow, Linguistics, Australian Nat. Univ., 1957-63; Professorial Fellow, Linguistics, ibid, 1964-67; Prof., ibid, 1968-; Vis. Lectr., N.-Western Univ., Ill., U.S.A., 1962; Vis. Prof., Ind. Univ., Bloomington, 1964 & Univ. of Hawaii, 1968. Mbrships. incl: Pres., Linguistic Soc. of Australia, 1967-70; Australian Inst. of Aboriginal Studies, 1961-; Coun. & Exec. Coun., ibid, 1967-. Num. Publs. incl: Languages of Australia & Tasmania, 1971; Co-Ed., Current Trends in Linguistics, Vol. 8: Linguistics in Oceania, 1971. Address: Dept. of Linguistics, Schl. of Pacific Studies, Inst. of Adv. Studies, Australian Nat. Univ., Box 4, P.O. Canberra, A.C.T., Australia 2600.

WÜSTER, Eugen, b. 3 Oct. 1898. Professor. Educ: Univs. of Technol., Berlin-Charlottenburg & Stuttgart; Dipl.-Ing.; Dr.techn. Appts: Owner & Dir., Wüster & Co. (power-stn., cold rolling mills, small tool factory), Wieselburg, 1931-. Mbrships: Fndr. & Pres., Tech. Comm., "Terminol. (principles & coord.)", Int. Org. for Standardization; Pres., Terminol. Commn., Assn. Int. of Applied Linguistics (AILA); Permanent Austrian Deleg., Coun. of Int. Electrotech. Commn. Publs: Enzyklopädisches Wörterbuch Esperanto-Deutsch, 1923-29; Internationale Sprachnormung in der Technik, 1931, '66, '70, Russian ed., 1935; Herstellung der Sägeblätter für Holz, 1952; Bibliography of monolingual scientific & technical vocabularies, 1955, '59; The Machine Tool, 1968; The Road to Infoterm, 1974. Recip. num. distinctions from

Austrian State & Austrian & German orgs., also Diamond Jubilee Medal, Inst. of Linguists, U.K., 1973. Address: A 3250 Wieselburg, Austria. 43, 86.

WYATT, Hazel Frances, b. 28 Jan. 1919. Welfare Worker. Educ: B.S., Bethel Coll. Appts: Clerk in Variety Store; Mgr., one floor, 1942-60; w. Dept. of Pub. Welfare, 1960-; Welfare Wkr., ibid, 1967-. Mbrships: Bd. Dirs., Paris Mental Hlth. Ctr.; V.P., County Coun. of Home Demonstration Clubs; Past Pres. & V.P., Home Demonstration Clubs. Contbr. to the Progressive Farmer & Tennessee Republican. Hons: Woman of the Yr. from Home Demonstration Clubs, 1966. Address: Rte. 2, Box 141, Huntingdon, TN 38344, U.S.A. 125, 138.

WYATT, Joyce Eileen (Mrs. Derek G. Wraith), b. 18 Aug. 1924. Artist. Educ: Hornsey Coll. of Art. Mbrships: Coun. Mbr., Royal Soc. of Miniature Painters, Sculptors & Gravers; Artistes Francais; Soc. of Women Artists; United Soc. of Art; Royal Glasgow Inst.; Miniature Soc.; Int. Art Assn.; Hesketh Hubbard Art Soc. Hons: Prix Roland, 1964, Silver Medal, 1965, Gold Medal, 1969, Paris Salon, Artistes Français. Address: Arundel House, Northcliffe Drive, Totteridge, London N.20, U.K. 19, 43, 138.

WYATT, William Stanley, b. 20 Sept. 1921. Artist; Teacher. Educ: B.A., Columbia Coll., 1943; M.A., Columbia Univ., 1947; Studied at Chgo. Art Inst., 1946 & 1951, Brooklyn Mus. Schl., 1948. Appts: Assoc. Prof., & Chmn., Art Dept., Waynesburg Coll., Pa., 1950-52; Lectr., Schl. of Painting & Sculpture, Columbia Univ., N.Y.C., 1952-60; Asst. Prof. & Dept. Rep., Art Dept., Baruck Schl., N.Y.C., 1962-68; Assoc. Prof. & Asst. Chmn., Evening Div., CCNY, 1968-74. Mbrships: Royal Soc. of Arts, London, U.K.; Newcomen Soc., N. Am.; Salmagundy Club; AAUP. Over 50 one-man exhibitions & grp. shows, 1946-74; In over 75 pvte. collects.; Illustrator for var. jrnls. Hons: Presidential Unit Citation, USN, WWII, 1945; Award for Excellence in Illustration, Am. Alumni Mag. Assn., 1958. Address: 75 River Rd., Grand View-on-Hudson, NY 10960, U.S.A. 6, 37.

WYBLE, John Franklin, Jr., 15 Sept. 1936. Dentist. Educ: B.S., Univ. of Pitts., 1960; D.D.S., ibid, 1964. Appts: Capt., Dental Corps, U.S. Army, 1964-66; Pvte. Prac., Greensburg, Pa., 1966-72 & Monroeville, Pa., 1972-; Bd. Dirs., United Cerebral Palsy Treatment Ctr., Spring Ch., Pa., 1971-. Mbrships: Odontological Soc. Western Pa.; Pa. Dental Soc.; Am. Dental Assn. Address: Northern Pike Pavilion, Monroeville, PA 15146, U.S.A. 6.

WYCKOFF, Ralph Walter Graystone, b. 9 Aug. 1897. Scientist. Educ: B.S., Hobart Coll., 1916; Ph.D., Cornell Univ., 1919. Appts: incl: Assoc. Dir. i/c of virus rsch., Lederle Labs., 1937-43; Rsch. Dir. & Biophysicist, Nat. Insts. of Hlth., 1945-59; Prof. of Physics, Univ. of Ariz., 1959-; Dir. de Recherche, Ctr. Nat. de la Recherche Scientifique, 1959-62, 1969; Exchange Prof., Sorbonne, Paris, France, 1965; Sci. Attache, U.S. Embassy, London, U.K., 1952-54. Mbrships: incl: V.P. & Pres., Int. Union of Crystallography, 1951-57; Nat. Acad. of Sci.; Fellow, Am. Phys. Soc.; Am. Acad. of Arts & Scis.; Past Pres., Am. Crystallographic Assn.; Past Pres., Am. Soc. of Electron Microscopy; Fellow, AAAS; Hon. mbr., Royal Microscopical Soc.; For. mbr., Royal Netherlands Acad. of Sci., 1949, Royal Soc., London, 1951. Author of sev. books, & about 400 papers & lects. publd. in sci. jrnls. Recip. of

hons. Address: Dept. of Physics, Univ. of Ariz., Tucson, AZ 85721, U.S.A. 2, 14, 34.

WYETH, Harold E., b. 19 Sept. 1919. Licensed Master Mariner; Marine Operations Consultant. Appts: Merchant Marine Off., U.S. Army Transportation Corps, 1942-46; Submarine Cable Off. & Navigator, Commercial Pacific Cable Co., 1946-51; Staff Capt., U.S. Army Transportation Corps, 1951-58; Pvte. Prac., Deep Ocean Projs. Cons., 1959-61; Mgr., Sea Installations, & Cons., Marine Ops., Gen. Elec. Co., 1961-67 & 1970-; Mgr., Undersea Installations Dept., Ocean Systems, Inc., 1967-70. Mbrships: Marine Technol. Soc.; Nat. Acad. of Engrng.; Masonic Lodge. Address: 1640 S. Ivy Trail, Baldwinsville, NY 13027, U.S.A. 6, 7.

WYKES, Alan, b. 21 May 1914. Author; Journalist. Educ: Wallington Grammar Schl. Appts: Fiction Ed., Strand Mag., 1947-49; Fiction Exec., Hulton Press, 1950-61. Mbrships: Hon. Sec., Savage Club; Press Club. Num. publs. incl: Novels—The Music Sleeping; Happyland; Pursuit Till Morning; The Pen Friend; Non-fiction—The Brabazon Story; The Royal Hampshire Regiment; A Concise Survey of American Literature; A Sex by Themselves; The Nuremberg Rallies; Lucrezia Borgia; The Doctor & His Enemy; The Horse in History. Address: 382 Tilehurst Rd., Reading RG3 3NG, U.K. 3.

WYLDE, Hildegarde Howard (profl. name Howard) (Mrs. Henry Anson Wylde), b. 3 Apr. 1901. Avian Paleontologist. Educ: A.B., Univ. of Calif., Berkeley, 1924; A.M., ibid, 1926; Ph.D., 1928. Appts: incl: Tchng. Fellow, Paleontol., Univ. of Calif., Berkeley, 1925-26; Rsch. Fellow, Zool., ibid, 1927-28; Avian Paleontol., Mus. Natural Hist., L.A., 1928-38; Curator, Avian Paleontol., ibid, 1939-51; Chief Curator, Div. of Sci., 1951-61; Rsch. Assoc., Avian Paleontol., 1961- Mbrships. incl: Hon. Mbr., Southern Calif. Acad. Scis.; Cooper Ornithol. Soc., Soc. Vertebrate Paleontol.; Fellow, Geol. Soc. Am., Am. Ornithols. Union, AAAS, Calif. Acad. Scis.; Phi Beta Kappa; Sigma Xi; Soroptimists. Author of publs. in field. Recip., Brewster Award in Ornithol., Am. Ornithols. Union. Address: 2045-Q Via Mariposa E., Laguna Hills, CA 92653, U.S.A. 2, 5, 9, 14.

WYLER, Veit, b. 28 Aug. 1908. Solicitor. Educ: Law studies, Univs. in Zurich, Vienna, Hamburg, Leipzig & Paris. Appts. incl: Law Prac., Zurich, Switzerland, 1935-; Mbr., Legal Commn. & Assns. Active Mbr. sev. religious & civic assns. inclng. Chmn., Swiss Zionist Fedn., V.Chmn., Jewish Communities, Hebrew Univ., Keren Kajemet, Keren Hajessod—United Appeal, Hon. Chmn. many yrs., currently Bd. of Govs. & Mbr., Exec. Coun., Weizmann Inst. Fndr., Publr. & Ed., monthly publn., Das Neve Israel, Zürich (zionist pol., cultural & economical illustrated paper), 1948-. Main Co-Ed., Mrs. Anna Katherina Wyler-Salten (Culture & Illustrations), ibid. Address: Boecklinstreet 27, 8032 Zurich, Zürich, Switzerland. 94.

WYLER, Wilfred, b. 24 Feb. 1908. Certified Public Accountant. Educ: B.S., Harvard Coll., 1928; M.B.A., N.Y. Univ., 1934; post-grad. work, Columbia Univ., 1935-38. Appts: Sr. Ptnr., Wilfred Wyler & Co. Ltd., C.P.A.'s. Mbrships: N.Y. State Soc. of C.P.A.'s; Trustee, former Chmn. of Budget Comm. & Treas., Jewish Home & Hosp. for Aged.; Vice Chmn., former Chmn. & Treas., Jt. Retirement Bd.; Bd. of Overseers, Jewish Theol. Sem. of Am.; Pres., Fan & Sig Wyler Fndn.; Harmonie Club.

Address: c/o Wilfred Wyler & Co., 200 Park Ave., N.Y., NY 10017, U.S.A. 6, 55.

WYNDHAM, Norman Richard, b. 11 Aug. 1907. Surgeon. Educ: Sydney Univ., Australia; M.B., B.S., 1931; M.D., 1938; M.S., 1938; F.R.C.S., 1935; F.R.A.C.S., 1937. Former appts: Hon. Surg., Royal Prince Alfred Hosp.; Vis. Surg., Repatriation Gen. Hosp., Concord; Mbr., Ct. of Examiners, Royal Australian Coll. of Surgs.; Lectr., Clin. Surg., Univ. of Sydney; served WWII; Ldr., Surg. team, Viet Nam, 1968. Present Appts: Cons. Surg., Royal Prince Alfred Hosp., Masonic Hosp., Tyde Hosp., Hornsby Dist. Hosp., Gosford Hosp.; Lectr., pt.-time, Dept. of Embryol. & Histol., Sydney Univ. Mbrships: Union Club, Sydney; Royal Sydney Yacht Squadron. Hons: Clayton Mem. Prize in Med., 1931; O.B.E., 1970. Address: 100 Carillon Ave., Newtown, N.S.W., Australia, 2042. 128.

WYNN, Freda Walker (Mrs. Edward L. Wynn), b. 24 Dec. 1937. Educator. Educ: B.S., Miss. Coll., Clinton, 1958; Masters in Supvsn. & Admin., Fla. State Univ., Tallahassee, 1970. Appts: Tchr., grades 3-8; Dir., Summer Prog., Maclay Day Schl., 1969; Treas. & Co-Owner, Skipper's Corner, Inc. Mbrships: Leon Co. Pres., 1968-70, State Corres. Sec., 1971-73, Assn. for Childhood Educ.; Fla. Educ. Assn.; NEA; IRA; Pres., Epsilon Chapt., Alpha Delta Kappa, 1970-72; Bd. of Dir., Sec., Tallahassee Jr. Mus., 1968-70; Reviewer for Profl. Prac. Coun., State Dept. of Educ.; Tallahassee Jr. Woman's Club, 1966-68. Address: 4913, Buck Lake Rd., Tallahassee, FL 32301, U.S.A. 5, 125.

WYNNE, George B., b. 20 May 1902. Civil Engineer. Educ: B.S.C.E., Univ. of N.C., 1924; Alexander Hamilton Inst. Appts: Prof. Engr. in U.S., 1924-48; Cons. Engr., Am. & Mediterranean Area, 1948-65; Prof., Tech. Coll., 1967-. Fellow, Am. Soc. Civil Engrs. Mbrships: Nat. Soc. Profl. Engrs.; Am. Concrete Inst.; Raleigh Engrs. Club; Scottish & York Rite, Mason & Shriner; Tau Beta Pi. Author of Building Estimating (pending publ.). Address: 3042 Churchill Rd., Raleigh, NC 27607, U.S.A. 7, 83.

WYNSHAW, Frances. Art Gallery Owner & Director. Educ: Grad., Cooper Union, N.Y.C.; studied, Brooklyn Mus. of Art, N.Y., Pratt Inst. Graphic Ctr., N.Y., Sumi Painting w. Prof. Motoi Oi & Graphic Workshop, San Giorgio Maggiore, Venice, Italy. Appts. incl: Former Designer of Art Posters & related material & Art Dir., Advt. Art Agcy.; currently, Owner & Dir., Avanti Galls. specializing in contemporary Am. & European art. Mbrships: Metropolitan Mus. of Art, N.Y.C.; Marshall Chess Club, N.Y.C. Exhibd. L.A. Co. Mus., L.A. Art Assn., Manchester Art Assn., Conn. & Graphic Workshop, San Giorgio Maggiore, Venice, Italy. Address: 145 E. 72 St., N.Y.C., NY 10021, U.S.A. 37.

WYRICK, Charles Lloyd, Jr., b. 5 May 1939. Art Museum Director. Educ: B.A., Davidson Coll., N.C., U.S.A.; M.F.A., Univ. of N.C. Appts: Instr., Stephens Coll., Columbia, Mo.; Artmobile Coord., & Asst. Hd., Progs. Div., Va. Mus. of Fine Arts; Exec. Dir., Assn. for the Preservation of Va. Antiquities; Pres., Rsch. & Restoration Inc.; Dir., Del. Art Mus., Wilmington; Critic, Art & Arch., Richmond News Leader, 1971-73. Mbrships: Bd. of Visitors, Davidson Coll.; Assn. of Art Mus. Dirs.; Am. Assn. of Museums; Nat. Trust for Historic Preservation; Soc. of Archtl. Histns. Publs: The 17th Street Farmers Market; Contbns. to Arts in Va. mag. Recip., First Prize, Special Column Writing, Va. Press Assn., 1973. Address: Delaware Art Museum, 2301 Kentmere Parkway, Wilmington, DE 19806, U.S.A. 37.

WYSE, Alexander John, b. 8 Sept. 1938. Painter & Sculptor. Educ: Coll. of Art, Cheltenham, U.K.; Royal Coll. of Art, London. Appt: Engraving Instr. to Eskimos, Cape Dorset, N.W. Territory, Canada, 1962-63. Collaborator in publs: The Alphabet Book, 1968; The One to Fifty Book, 1973. One-man shows: Pennel Gall, Toronto, Ont., 1968 & 1970; Peale Gall., Phila, Pa., U.S.A.; Arwin Gall., Detroit, Mich. Num. paintings, mostly in pvte. collects., U.S.A. & Canada. 2 Sculptures, Canadian Art Bank. Hons: Num. grants & prizes. Address: 125 Noel St., Ottawa K1M 2A4, Ont., Canada. 37.

X

XEFLOUDAS, Stelios, b. 16 Oct. 1902. Writer. Educ: Grad., Fac. of Philos., Univ. of Sorbonne, Paris. Appts: Tchr. of H.S. Lit., 1924; Hd. of Sect., Letters, Libs. & Archives, Min. of Educ., 1945-64; Ret., 1964; Gen. Sec., Home of Arts & Letters, until 1967; Sec., Greek Nat. Commn. for UNESCO, until 1967. Mbrships: Nat. Soc. Greek Writers; Community of European Writers. Publs: (novels) The Note-Book of Pavlos Fotinos, 1930; Interior Symphony, 1930; EVA, 1934; At the Light of the White Angel, 1936; The Circle, 1944; The Men of Legend, 1946; Ullysses without Ithaka, 1957; You, Mr. X. & a Little Prince, 1961; Don Quixote, 1964; The Dictator, 1964; also essays, anthols. & articles in jrnls. Hons: Gold Cross, King Geo., 1945; 1st State Prize for Lit. (Kratikon Vraveion) for You, Mr. X. & A Little Prince, 1962. Address: 64, Aristotelousstr., Athens (103), Greece. 43.

XENAKIS, Jason. Professor of Philosophy. Educ: Ph.D., Harvard. Appts: Former Tchr., Univ. of N.C., Chapel Hill, La. State Univ., Baton Rouge, & Univ. of Alta., Canada. Former Mbrships. incl: Eastern Div., Am. Philosophical Assn.; Mind Assn.; Aristotelian Soc.; Sect. Chmn., Vienna World Philos. Congress, 1968. Publs: Epictetus: Philosopher—The Rapist, 1969; Over 40 Articles in most branches of philos. & on ancient philos. in Analysis, Mind, Revue Philosophique, Philosophical Studies, Jrnl. of Philos., Phronesis, Logique et Analyse, Theoria, Synthese, Kantstudien, New Scholasticism, Philosophy & Phenomenological Rsch., Jrnl. for the Sci. Study of Relig., Sophia ("Stoic Suicide Therapy", 1972), Inquiry ("Hippies & Cynics", 1973), & others; 15 book reviews in jrnls. inclng. Philos. & Phenomenological Rsch.; Rdr. of papers, Vienna World Philos. Congress, 1968, & Varna World Philos. Congress, 1973. Recip., Fellowships, Oberlin Coll., U.S.A., 1947-48, Harvard, 1949-50, & Am. Friends Serv. Comm., summers 1949, 1951. Address: Deree Coll., P.O. Box 472, Athens, Greece. 13.

XENOS, Alecos, b. 2 May 1912. Composer. Educ: dip. in counterpoint, advanced musical theory, orchestration & trombone, Athens Conservatory. Appts: 1st Trombone, Athens State Orch., 1937-52, Orch. of the Nat. State Opera, 1949-67; Composer, 1940-; occasional Tchr. Mbrships: Pres., Panhellenic Assn. of Musicians; Sec. Gen., Fedn. of Musical Orgs. of Greece; Coun., Greek Composers Union. Publs. incl: Overture to Liberty, 1941; The Deer (suite), 1944; Digenis (symphonic poem), 1948; Symphony for a Large Orchestra, 1948; Prometheus (ballet), 1960; Spartacus (symphonic poems & ballet), 1963; Cyprus (symphonic poems), 1964; Cycle of Songs for Orchestra & Voice, 1965; Elegy, 1967; Symphony No. 2, 1968; Cycle of Songs for Peace, 1969; incidental stage music. Hons. incl: Prize for Symphony for Large Orchestra, Int. Festival of Youth, 1948; Prize for Prometheus (ballet), Panhellenic Competition of Serious Music, Greek Nat. Broadcasting Inst., 1962; Prize of Athens for Cycle of Songs for Orch. & Voice. Address: 19 Athanassiou Diakou, Holargos, Athens, Greece. 43.

XIROTIRIS, Nicolaos John, b. 26 Feb. 1900. Professor of Sociology. Educ: Philos. degree, Univ. of Athens; Ph.D., Schl. of Philos., Univ. of Munich, German Fed. Repub. Appts. incl: Hdmaster., 1936; Dir., Expmtl. Schl. of Univ. of Thessaloniki, 1941; Prof. of Sociol., Superior Ind. Schl., Thessaloniki, 1958. Mbrships: Bd. of Dirs., Greek Sociol. Soc. & Nat. Ctr. of Soc. Rsch.; Soc. for Deviant Children. Publs. incl: Magna Civitas Magna Solitudo, 1970; Generations & Conflicts, 1970; Our Defects & Education, 1971; The Problems of Education & Professionalization, 1972; Man, Money & the Industrial Spirit of Our Age, 1972; Prejudice As an Anti-Social Phenomenon, 1972; The Process from "Me" to "You", 1973; The Difficulties of Communication, 1973; Economic Values & Humanist Values, 1973; Violence, Terrorism & Blackmail as Symptoms of an International Moral Crisis, 1974; articles in jrnls. & newspapers. Hons: Medal of Bravery; Medal of Merit, City of Messologi. Address: 41 Dimitriou Gounari St., Thessaloniki, Greece. 34.

Y

YAKSICH, Stella R. Nurse Educator. Educ: St. Luke's Hosp. Schl. of Nursing, Cleveland, Ohio, 1945; B.S., Nursing Educ., 1953; M. Pub. Hlth., Grad. Schl. of Pub. Hlth., Univ. of Pitts., Pa., 1958; Ph.D., Schl. of Educ., ibid, 1969. Appts. incl: Supvsr., Student Advsr., Staff Nurse, Vis. Nurse Assn., Allegheny Co., Pitts., Pa., 1949-56; Instr., Univ. of Pitts., 1956-57; Supvsr., Pub. Hlth. Nursing, Allegheny Co. Hlth. Dept., Pitts., Pa., 1958-59; Acting Chmn., Pub. Hlth. Nursing Sect., 1961-65; Coord., Pub. Hlth. Nursing, 1969-70; Assoc. Prof., ibid & Asst. Dean, Student Affairs, Schl. of Nursing, Univ. of Pitts., 1971; Assoc. Prof., Schl. of Educ., ibid, 1973-. Mbrships. incl: Am. Acad. of Pol. & Soc. Sci.; Am. Nurses Assn.; Nat. League for Nursing; Fellow, Am. Pub. Hlth. Assn.; Sigma Theta Tau; Pi Lambda Theta; Phi Delta Gamma. Publs. incl: Identifying the Needs of Patients Hospitalized for Diagnostic & Surgical Procedures: an Analytical Study, 1972. Hons. incl: Ten Yr. Serv. Award, Am. Red Cross; Latern Ceremony, Disting. Alumnae, Univ. of Pitts. Address: Univ. of Pitts. School of Nursing, 448B Scaife Hall, Pittsburgh, PA 15261, U.S.A. 5.

YAKUBIK, Anne Gavula, b. 28 Mar. 1921. Assistant Secretary. Appts: Secretarial duties, Butler Pa. YMCA, 1939-41; Secretarial duties, Butler Community Chest, 1941-43; Hot Mill Schedule Clerk, Armco Steel Corp., 1943-45; Teller & Asst. Mgr., Workingmens Bldg. & Loan Assn., 1953-61; Asst. Sec., Pitts. Home Savings & Loan Assn. (merger w. Workingmens Bldg. & Loan, 1961), 1961-. Mbrships: Corres. Sec., PTA; Ladies Guild, St. John's Byzantine Cath. Ch.; Attendance Comm., Soroptomist Club of Butler Co. Address: 210 Penn Ave., Lyndora, PA 16045, U.S.A. 5, 6, 132, 138.

YANAGIHARA, Hikaru, b. 13 Sept. 1918. Professor; Priest. Educ: B.A., Tokyo Imperial Univ., Japan, 1941; Grad. Schl., Kyoto Imperial Univ., 1945-48; M.Div., Episcopal Theological Schl., Cambridge, Mass., U.S.A., 1951; M.A., Tchrs. Coll., Columbia Univ., N.Y., 1953; Ph.D., ibid, 1958. Appts. incl: Lectr., Div. of Gen. Educ., Rikkyo (St. Paul's) Univ., Tokyo, 1961-68; Asst. Prof., Dept. of Christian Studies, Fac. of Arts, ibid, 1968-; Prof., ibid, 1972-; Staff mbr., Japan Inst. of Christian Educ., 1968-; Dir., ibid, 1970-72; Dean, Fac. of Arts, 1972-; Interdisciplinary Coord. for Fac. of Arts; Priest, Nippon Seikokai (Anglican Ch. of Japan). Mbrships: Japan Assn. for Religious Studies; Japan Soc. of Christian Studies. Author of var. articles & translations in educ., theol. & Ch. hist. Address: House 2, Rikkyo Univ., 3-34-1 Nishi-ikebukuro, Toshima-ku, Tokyo 171, Japan.

YANG, Winston, L.Y., b. 1 June 1935. University Professor. Educ: B.A., Nat. Taiwan Univ., 1957; Ph.D., Stanford Univ., U.S.A., 1970. Appts: Asst. Prof., Asian Studies, Winthrop Coll., 1967-68; Asst. Prof., Chinese Lit., Calif. State Univ., San Fran., 1968-69; Chmn., Dept. of Asian Studies, Winthrop Coll., 1969-70; Assoc. Prof., Asian Studies, Seton Hall Univ., 1970-71; Chmn., Dept. of Asian Studies, ibid, 1971-72; Prof. & Dir., Fellowship Prog. in Chinese & Japanese, 1972-. Mbrships: MLA of Am.; Assn. for Asian Studies; Chmn., Exec. Bd., Chinese Lang. Tchrs. Assn. Publs: Bibliography of the Chinese Language, 1966; The San-kuo chih yen-i: Studies in Its Courses, History, & Authorship, 1973. Contbr. to jrnls. Address: Dept. of Asian Studies, Seton Hall Univ., S. Orange, NJ 07079, U.S.A. 13.

YANNAS, Ioannis, V., b. 14 Apr. 1935. University Professor. Educ: A.B., Harvard Coll., 1953; M.S., MIT, 1969; M.A., Princeton Univ., 1965; Ph.D., ibid, 1966. Appts: Rsch. Chemist, W.R. Grace & Co., 1959-63; Asst. Prof., Fibers & Polymers Labs., Dept. of Mech. Engrng., MIT, 1966-68; Du Pont Asst. Prof., ibid, 1968-69; Assoc. Prof., 1969-. Mbrships: N.Y. Acad. of Scis.; Sigma Xi; Biomed. Engrng. Soc.; Am. Chem. Soc.; AAAS. Author of over 40 publs. in tech. jrnls. in areas of phys. chem., polymer physics & biophysics. Hons: Schlr., Harvard Coll., 1954; Fellow, Esso Standard Oil, MIT, 1958; Nat. Insts. of Hlth. Fellow, Princeton Univ., 1963-66; Du Pont Young Fac. Award, MIT, 1968. Address: Room 3-334, MIT, 77 Massachusetts Ave., Cambridge, MA 02139, U.S.A. 14, 130.

YANNOULIS, Georg, b. 27 Apr. 1908. University Professor. Educ: Vienna. Appts: Asst. Prof., Univ. of Graz, Austria, 1951; Prof., Aristotle Univ. of Greece, Salonika, 1951. Fellowships: Royal Soc. London; Int. Coll. Surg. Mbrships. incl: O.R.L. Soc. of Vienna; Coll. Int. of Brcnchio.; Corres., Austrian, German & Rumania O.R.L. Socs.; Hon., Balkan Soc. Publs: E.N.T. Book for Students & Doctors; E.N.T. Atlas; Atlas Adeno Sialography; Atlas Crystalography; (film) Homotransplantations of the Membrano-bone system in hard of hearing patients & especially in ear dysplasias. Hons: Greek war hons, 1940-41; Greek Phoenix, 1952; Greek Taxiarchon, 1962; Big Silver Cross of Austria, 1972. Address: Yannoulis Megistis 21 (Olimos), Kalamaki, Athens, Greece.

YANOFSKY, Daniel Abraham, b. 26 Mar. 1925. Barrister-at-Law. Educ: B.S., Univ. of Man., 1944; LL.B., ibid, 1951; Bachelor of Civil Law, Oxford Univ., U.K., 1953. Appts: Mbr., Man. & Man. & Canadian Bar Assns., Law Soc. of Man.; Chess Ed., Winnipeg Press, 1954-74; Ed., Canadian Chess Chats, 1955-63; Alderman, City of W. Kildonan, 1961-67, Dpty. Mayor, 1967-69; Mayor, 1969-71; Chmn., Comm. of Environment, City of Winnipeg Coun., 1971-74. Publs: Chess the Hard Way; Winning Chess Endings; 100 Years of Chess in Canada. Hons: Gold Medallist, Univ. of Man., 1951; Int. Chess Grand Master, World Int. Chess Fedn., 1964; Order of Canada, Gov.-Gen. of Canada, 1972. Address: 62 Ashbury Bay, Winnipeg, Manitoba R2V 2T4, Canada.

YAO, Mungo K.L., b. 4 Feb. 1912. Painter; Art Critic; Educator. Educ: Wu-hsi Chinese Coll. of Art, Shanghai Univ., China. Appts. incl: Prof., Cheng-Tze Coll.; Pres., Cheng-Kiang Art Coll.; Chief Rsch.-Chmn., Rsch. Comm., Nat. Mus. of Hist.; Dir., China Hall., World Fair N.Y., 1965 & Int. Expo, Montreal, 1968. 6 one man exhibs., 1931-55; Participant num. nat. & int. exhibs., 1956-73. Mbrships. incl: Nat. Art Assn., Taiwan; Exec. Bd., China Writers Soc.; Exec. Bd., Provincial Art Assn., Kiangsu. Publs. incl: On Chinese Painting, 1966; The Ancient Handcraft of China, 1973; The Ancient Pottery of China, 1973. Compositions incl: Paintings of Wu-Chang-seh & Chi Pai-Shih, 1967; The Style of Pu Yu's Painting, 1972; The Style of Chang Ta-chien's Painting, 1973. Collects. incl: Nat. Art Hall, Taiwan; Thailand Nat. Mus.; Nat. Mus., Chile. Recip., Award for Disting. Contribution to Fine Art of China, Min. of Educ., Repub. of China, 1968. Address: Nat. Mus. of Hist., 49 Nan Hai Rd., Taipai, Taiwan, Repub. of China.

YARBOROUGH, Betty Jane Hathaway, b. 17 Apr. 1927. Professor of Elementary Education. Educ: A.B., Duke Univ., Durham, N.C., U.S.A., 1948; M.A., Wm. & Mary Coll.,

Williamsburg, Va., 1955; Dip. of Adv. Grad. Study, Univ. of Va., 1959; Ed.D., ibid, 1964. Appts. incl: Hd., Engl. Dept., Cradock H.S., Portsmouth, Va., 1951-56; Supvsr. H.S.'s, & Dir., Developmental Reading Prog., Norfolk Co., Va., 1957-66; Dir., Lang. Arts, Pub. Schls., Chesapeake, Va., 1966-72; Prof., Elem. Educ., Old Dominion Univ., Norfolk, Va., 1972-; Diagnostician, Psychiatric Assocs. Ltd., Portsmouth, 1972-. Mbrships. incl: Am. Educl. Rsch. Assn.; Am. Psychological Assn.; Nat. Conf. on Rsch. in Engl.; Coun. for Exceptional Children; Past Pres., Va. Educl. Rsch. Assn., & Va. State Reading Assn.; Kappa Delta Pi; Theta Alpha Phi; Delta Kappa Gamma. Publs. incl: Teaching English to Slow Learners, 1962; Sound & Sense in Spelling, 96 vols., 1964-68; 5 other books; Contbns. to ency., yrbook., & jrnls. Hons. incl: Ullin W. Levell Award, Univ. of Va., 1967; All Am. Press Award for Excellence in Educl. Jrnlsm., 1971. Address: 3008 Ferguson Dr., Portsmouth, VA 23703, U.S.A. 5, 13, 22, 57, 125, 138.

YARBROUGH, Karen Marguerite, b. 4 Mar. 1938. Geneticist. Educ: Perkinston Jr. Coll., Miss., 1956-58; B.S., Miss. State Univ., State Coll., Miss., 1961; M.S., ibid, 1963; Ph.D., N.C. State Univ., Raleigh, 1967. Appts. incl: Rsch. Asst., Miss. State Univ., 1961-63; Rsch. Asst., Dept. of Genetics, N.C. State Univ., 1963-67; Asst. Prof., Bio., Univ. of Southern Miss., 1967-70; Assoc. Prof., Microbio. ibid, 1970-73, Assoc. Prof. & Dir., Inst. of Genetics, 1973-. Mbrships. incl: Am. Soc. of Human Genetics; Genetics Soc. of Am.; Soc. of Sigma Xi; Phi Sigma Soc.; N.Y. Acad. of Sci.; Miss. Acad. of Sci.; Delta Kappa Gamma Soc.; Pres., Zeta Tau Alpha Frat., 1959-61; Pres., Panhellenic Coun., 1960-61; Pres., Women's Student Govt. Assn., 1959-61. Num. papers in profl. jrnls. Hons. incl: Zeta Tau Alpha Fndn. Schlrship., 1959; John Rust Trust Fund Schol., 1958-60. Address: Rte. 10, Box 152A, Hattiesburg, MS 39401, U.S.A. 125.

YAREMKO, John, b. 10 Aug. 1918. Lawyer. Educ: Univ. of Toronto, Canada; B.A., Osgoode Hall Law Schl., 1941; called to Bar by proxy during WWII, personally 1946; Hon. LL.D., Waterloo Luth. Univ., 1968. Appts. incl: Asst. Examiner, Dean of Law Schl.; Special Lectr. to Veteran's Class in Law; Lectr. & Examiner in Law Prac.; apptd. Q.C., 1953; elected Ont. Provincial Plmnt., 1951, 1955, 1959, 1963, 1967 & 1971; apptd. Min. without Portfolio & Min. of Transport, 1958; Provincial Sec. & Registrar, 1960; 1st Provl. Sec. & Min. of Citizenship, 1961; Min. Pub. Welfare, 1966; Min. of Soc. & Family Servs., 1967; Provl. Sec. & Min. of Citizenship, 1971; 1st Solicitor Gen., 1972. Mbrships. incl: former Pres., Lawyers Club; Hon. Indian Chief "Bright Sky"; Hon. Mbr., Canadian Italian Bus. & Profl. Men's Assn.; Hon. Mbr., Hungarian Freedom Fighters; Hon. Mbr., Canadian Arcadian Assn., 1973; Canadian Bar Assn. Hons. incl: Qu. Elizabeth Coronation Medal; Canada Medal, Confederation; Children's Aid Soc. Metro Toronto Medal, 1968; Taras Shevchenki Medal, Ukrainian Canadian Comm. Address: 1 Connable Drive, Toronto, Ont., M5R 1Z7, Canada. 6, 12, 88, 128, 139.

YARKER, Mary Dickson, b. 19 Oct. 1894. Medical Practitioner. Educ: Grad., Univ. of Pitts., Pa., U.S.A., 1920; M.D., Womens Med. Coll. of Phila., 1925. Appts: Intern, Woman's Hosp. of Phila., 1925-26; Mbr., Bd. of Mgrs., ibid, 1934-70; Staff Mbr., 1940-65; Chief, Clin. Pediatrics, 1963-65. Mbrships: AMA; Pa. Med. Soc.; Phila. Co. Med. Soc.; Am. Acad. of Family Physns.; Pres., Pa. Med. Missionary Soc., 1968; Pres., Am. Med. Womens Assn., 1956-58;

Pres., Phila. Club of Med. Women, 1959-61; League of Women Voters. Address: 604 Sussex Rd., Wynnewood, PA 19096, U.S.A. 5.

YARMOLINSKY, Adam, b. 17 Nov. 1922. Professor of Law. Educ: A.B., Harvard Univ., 1943; LL.B., Yale Law Schl., 1948. Appts. incl: Law Clerk to Judge Charles E. Clark, U.S. 2nd Circuit Ct. of Appeals, 1948-49, Mr. Justice Reed, U.S. Supreme Ct., 1949-51; Law. Prac. w. firms in N.Y.C., 1949-50, Wash. D.C., 1951-55; Pub. Affairs Ed., Doubleday & Co., publrs., 1957-59; Special Asst. to U.S. Sec. of Defense, 1961-64; Prin. Dpty. Asst., 1965-66; Prof. of Law, Harvard Law Schl., 1966-72; Chief Exec. Off., Welfare Island Dev. Corp., N.Y.C., 1970-72; Ralph Waldo Emerson Prof., Univ. of Mass., 1972-. Mbr., Fellow, var. profl., community & learned orgs. Publs: Case Studies in Personnel Security (ed.), 1955; Recognition of Excellence, 1960; The Military Establishment, 1971. Articles, var. jrnls. Recip., Disting. Pub. Serv. Medal, U.S. Dept. of Defense, 1966. Address: Univ. of Massachusetts, 1 Washington Mall, Boston, MA 02108, U.S.A. 2, 30, 114, 128, 129.

YASSIN, Salim, b. 10 Oct. 1937. Professor of Economics & Planning. Educ: B.A., Univ. of Damascus, 1960; M.A., Univ. of Colo., 1963; Ph.D., ibid, 1965. Appts: Vice Dean, 1966, Vice Dean & Acting Dean, 1967-69, Fac. of Econ. Scis., Univ. of Aleppo; V.P. & Acting Pres., Univ. of Aleppo, 1969-71; Pres., Univ. of Lattakia, 1971-. Mbrships: Am. Econs. Assn.; Higher Bd. of Syrian Univs.; Bd., Inst. of Econs. & Soc. Planning, Syria. Publs: The Theory of Correlation; Principles of Economics Development & Planning; International Economics. Recip. I.I.E., 1961. Address: Univ. of Lattakia, Lattakia, Syria.

YATES, Helen Eva. World Public Relations Writer & Lecturer. Educ: Jrnlsm., Columbia, N.Y.; Design, Art Inst., Chgo. Appts: Woman's Ed., China Press, Shanghai; Ed.-Publr., New Orleans Life, mag.; Radio Prog. on Travel, KFRC, San Fran.; Free-lance writer for Colliers, C.S. Monitor, etc.; Lectr., San Diego State Univ., Calif. Western Univ., San Diego, etc. Mbrships: PEN Club; L.A. Press Club; For. Press Club, Hollywood. Publs: The World is Your Oyster; Bali, Enchanted Isle; How to Travel for Fun; Shopping in India; Shopping in Hong Kong; Shopping all over the World; World House, Her Magic Island (both forthcoming); Articles on art in jrnls. inclng. Today's Art, Country Life, House & Gardens, Sunset. Hons: Thos. Cook award, for the World Is Your Oyster, best travel book of the yr.; U.S. Govt. approbation & world reprint for Collier's mag. article. Address: c/o N.Y. agt., Bertha Klausner, 71 Park Ave., N.Y. 16, NY, U.S.A. 5, 138.

YATRON, Michael, b. 20 July 1921. Professor of English Literature. Educ: B.S., State Coll., Kutztown, Pa., 1942; Grad. Schl. of Arts & Scis., Harvard Univ., 1942-43; Univ. of Calif., Berkeley, 1943-44; M.A., Temple Univ., Phila., Pa., 1950; Ph.D., ibid, 1957. Appts: Tchng. Asst., Temple Univ., 1949-50; Instr. in Engl., Univ. of Puerto Rico, Mayaguez, 1953-55; Prof., Delaware State Coll., 1957-63; Prof., Kutztown State Coll., 1963-. Publs: America's Literary Revolt, 1959; Sappho's Island, a novel under pseudonym Byron Sorel, 1964; In Pink Balloons, a novel under pseudonym Bryon Sorel, 1967. Address: 1533 Garfield Ave., Wyomissing, PA 19610, U.S.A.

YEATMAN, Margaret, b. 10 Sept. 1913. Educator; Director of Guidance. Educ: B.S., West Chester State Coll., Pa., 1947; M.Ed., Univ. of Me., 1961. Appts: Tchr., Kennett Sq.,

Pa., 1935-42, Girard Coll., Phila., Pa., 1947-52; Guidance Counselor & Tchr., Swarthmore P.S. Pa., 1952-62; Guidance Counselor, Brookhaven Jr. H.S., Chester, Pa., 1962-64, Newark, Del. Pub. Schl., 1964-67; Asst. Dean of Women, Univ. of Me., 1967-69; Assoc. Dean, Res. Halls, ibid, 1969-70; Dir. of Guidance, Milford Schl., Me., 1971-73; Resource Tchr., (Spec. Educ.), Auburn, Me. Pub. Schl., 1973-. Mbrships: Am. Personnel & Guidance Assn.; Am. Schl. Counselors Assn.; Nat. Assn. of Women Dean & Counselors; Nat. Voc. Guidance Assn.; AAUW; Me. Tchrs. Assn.; New England Assn. for Measurement & Evaluation in Guidance. Address: 65 Fern St., Auburn, ME 04210, U.S.A. 5.

YEH CHI WEI, b. 16 Dec. 1913. Artist in oil painting. Educ: Shanghai Coll. of Fine Arts, China. Art Tchr., Sr. Tchr., Chung Cheng H.S., Singapore, 1938-63. Mbrships: Nat. Day Art Exhibition Working Comm., 1969-73; Vice-Chmn., Singapore Art Soc., 1968-71; Chmn., Soc. of Chinese Artists, 1968-70; Chmn., S.E. Asia Art Assn., 1969-74; Ldr., Ten-Men Art Tour. Paintings incl: Miaw Girl (Thailand), 1962; Floating Market (Thailand), 1964; It's A Long Wait for Mother's Return, 1966; Bali Horse Carriage (Indonesia), 1967; Dayak Fan Dance (E. Malaysia Sarawak), 1968; Life of the Mountain Tribe (Thailand), 1969; Finaer Dance (Thailand), 1969; Borobudur (Indonesia), 1969; Ajanta, 1973; Indian Dance, 1973; Harvest, 1973. Address: 24 Paya Lebar St., Singapore 19.

YELLOTT, Kathleen Lapsley Sightler, b. 24 Feb. 1905. Hospital Administrator; Legislative Representative of Health Legislation. Educ: Nursing & Special Trng., Pediatrics & Geriatrics; Hosp. sponsored Seminars, Pub. Hlth.; Special Studies, Pol. Sci. Appts: Admnstr., Palms Hosp., 1944-65; Tex. Legislative Rep., Nursing Homes, Wash. D.C., 1953-56. Mbrships: Pres., Tex. Nursing Homes Assn., 1952-56; Pres., S.E. Tex. Hosp. Coun., 1954-55; Pres., Pub. Affairs Forum, Lumberton, Tex.; Mbr., Nat. Assn. of Parliamentarians; Tex. Gerontological Soc.; Tex. Gulf Coast Histl. Soc.; Daughters of the Confederacy; Pres., ibid, 1962. Address: Rte. 3, Box 566, Silsbee, TX 77656, U.S.A. 5.

YEMM, Warren Joseph, b. 7 May 1940. Certified Public Accountant. Educ: Northwestern Univ., Evanston, Ill.; B.Sc., Spring Hill Coll., Mobile, Ala., 1963. Appts: 1st Lt., QMC, U.S. Army, 1963-65; Staff Acct., Morrison & Smith, Certified Pub. Accts., Mobile, Ala., 1959-63, 1965-68, Ptnr., 1968-. Mbrships: Am. Inst. Certified Pub. Accts.; Ala. Soc. Certified Pub. Accts.; Educ. Comm. Mbr., ibid, 1970-73, Treas., Mobile Chapt., 1969-70; Southern States Conf. Certified Pub. Accts.; Finance & Budget Chmn., 1970 Annual Convention; Mobile Chapt., Spring Hill Coll. Alumni; Off. & Bd. Mbr., ibid, 1968-73; Kiwanis Club, Mobile. Recip., Army Commendation Medal, 1965. Address: Morrison & Smith, Certified Public Accountants, P.O. Box 374, Mobile, AL 36601, U.S.A. 117, 125.

YEN, Chen-Hsing, b. 10 July 1912. University President. Educ: B.S., Nat. Tsinghua Univ., 1930; Ph.D., State Univ. of Iowa, 1937. Appts: Prof., Nat. Southwestern Assn. Univ., 1941-46; Chief Engr., Yellow River Engrng. Bur., 1946-47; Kaohsiung Harbour Bur., 1949-57; Dean, Coll. of Engrng., Nat. Honan Univ., 1947-48, Nat. Taiwan Univ., 1953-55; Dir., Engrng. Dept., Chinese Naval Gen. HW, 1948-49; Pres., Provincial Cheng Kung Univ., 1957-65; Commnr., Dept. of Educ., Taiwan Provincial Govt., 1962-63; Min. of Educ., Exec.

Yuan, 1965-69; Chmn., Nat. Youth Commn., 1966-70, Atomic Energy Coun., Repub. of China, 1966-72; Pres., Nat. Tsinghua Univ., 1969-70, Nat. Taiwan Univ., 1970-, Chung Shan Inst. of Sci. & Technol., 1969-. Mbrships: Coun., Acad. Sinica, 1960-; Nat. Sci. Coun., 1965-; Pres., Chinese Inst. of Engrs., 1966-67, Chinese Inst. of Civil Engrng., 1966-67, Phi Tao Phi, 1973-; Bds. of Dirs., US Educl. Fndn., Repub. of China & China Fndn. for Promotion of Educ. & Culture. Publs: The Tractive Force on Pebbles by Flowing Water; Soil Compaction & Its Application; Higher Education & Social Progress; Determination of the Best Proportion of Canal Bends. Twice Recip., Medal of the Order of the Brilliant Star. Address: Nat. Taiwan Univ., 1 Roosevelt Rd., Sec. 4, Taipei, Taiwan, Repub. of China.

YERGER, John Henry, b. 4 Jan. 1914. Community Organization Executive. Educ: B.A., Muhlenburg Coll., Allentown, Pa., 1935; M.S., Boston Univ., Mass., 1942. Appts. incl: Supvsr., Pa. Dept. Pub. Asst., 1935-40; Exec., Am. Red Cross, Boston, Cape Cod, Worcester, Hudson Co., NJ, 1942-50; Exec. Dir., Ottawa Community Chest, Canada, 1950-55; ibid, United Appeal for Metro. Toronto, 1955-71; V.P., Field Services, Fund Raising & Local United Way Services, United Way Am., Int. HQ for United Fund Movement, Wash.D.C., 1972-; also Cons. to nat. orgs. in USA & Canada, 1946-; raised over 300 million dollars for charity. Mbrships. incl: Fellow, Royal Soc. of Hlth.; Chmn. Int. Conven., United Community Funds & Councils, LA, Calif., 1972; Nat. Assn. of Soc. Wkrs., USA. Contbr. to profl. jrnls. Recip. of many civic awards inclng. Citations for Outstanding Community Serv., 1972, Canadian Red Cross Soc., Boy Scouts of Canada & City of Toronto; Order of St. John, for conspicuous serv. to charity & humanity', HM Queen Elizabeth II, 1960. Address: Skyline Towers, Apt. 1104 North, 5601 Seminary Rd., Falls Church, VA 22041, U.S.A. 7, 22, 57, 128, 131

YESKO, Elmer George, b. 23 Nov. 1918. Dentist. Educ. incl: B.A., Harvard Univ., 1940; D.D.S., Temple Univ., 1961; M.P.H., Univ. of Pitts., 1969. Appts: Ensign-Lt. Cmdr., USN, 1942-55; Admin. Off., Chief Naval Air Trng., 1945-46; Personal Pilot, Sec. of Navy, 1946-48; Personnel War Planning, Wash., 1948; Special Intelligence & Watch Comm., Wash., 1951-53; Retd. USN, 1955; w. State Hlth. Depts., Va., Mich., Pa., 1962-73; Pvte. Prac. Dentistry, Harrisburg, Pa., 1967-73; Cons., Special Patient Care, Commonwealth of Pa., Harrisburg, 1973-; Asst. Naval Attaché, Naval Attaché Air, U.S. Embassy, Baghdad, Iraq, & Tehran, Iran. Mbrships. incl: Fellow, Am. Pub. Hlth. Assn.; Royal Soc. Hlth.; Am. Dental Assn. Author papers var. aspects dental care. Recip., Air Medal w. 2 Oak Leaf Clusters. Address: R.D. 3, Harvest View Ln., Penn Farm Estates, Duncansville, PA 16635, U.S.A. 6.

YI, Ha-Yun, b. 9 Apr. 1906. Poet. Educ: B.A. Fac. of Lit., Hosei Univ., Tokyo, 1929. Appts: Prof., Dong-Kook Univ., 1945-49; Prof. of Coll. of Educ., Seoul Nat. Univ., 1949-72; Prof., Duk-Sung Women's Seoul, 1971-. Mbrships: Chmn., Comp. Lit. Soc. of Korea; Int. PEN, Korean Ctr. Publs: Poems from English & French, 1933, '48, '54; Anthologies, 1939, '46, '49, '55; Waterwheel, 1939; Irish Literary Renaissance. Recip., Nat. Merit Medal, 1970. Address: 50-20 Dongsoong-Dong, Chongno-Goo, Seoul, Korea.

YOAKUM, Anna Margaret, b. 13 Jan. 1933. Chemist. Educ: B.S., Maryville Coll., Tenn., 1954; M.S., Univ. of Fla., Gainesville, 1956;

Doct., ibid, 1960. Appts: Supvsr., Control Lab., Greenback Inds., Inc., 1956-59; Rsch. Chemist, Analytical & Basic Rsch. Divs., Chemstrand Rsch. Ctr., 1960-64; Sr. Rsch. Staff, Analytical Chem. Div., Oak Ridge Nat. Lab., 1964-69; V.P. & Dir., Rsch. & Dev., Stewart Labs., Inc., 1968-71; Exec. V.P., Lab. Dir., ibid, 1971-. Mbrships: Soc. for Applied Spectroscopy; Am. Chem. Soc.; Am. Soc. for Testing & Materials; N.Y. Acad. of Scis.; Am. Inst. of Chemists; Knoxville Execs. Club; Phi Beta Kappa, 1960; Phi Kappa Phi, 1956; Sigma Xi, 1958. Author of articles & papers in field. Address: c/o Stewart Labs., Inc., 820 Tulip Ave., Knoxville, TN 37921, U.S.A. 5, 14, 125.

YOKEN, Melvin Barton, b. 25 June 1939. Professor. Educ: B.A., Mass. Univ., U.S.A., 1960; M.A., Brown Univ., 1961; Ph.D., Mass. Univ. Appts: Instr.-Asst. Prof., Southeastern Mass. Univ., 1966-. Mbrships: MLA; Am. Assn. Tchrs. of French; Am. Coun. on Tchng. of For. Langs. Pres., Friends of Fall River Pub. Lib.; Pres., Bd. of Dirs., Amicale of Middlebury. Publs: Claude Tiller's Novelistic World; Recent articles: Paleneo, Mass. For. Lang. Bulletin, 1973; Wise Guy, Solomon, Outlook, 1974; Interview with Terry Dunnahoo, 1974; Contbr. to Le Travailleur (Worcester, Mass.); Book reviewer: Boston Herald-Am.; New Bedford Standard Times. Address: Mod. Lang. Dept., Southeastern Mass. Univ., No. Dartmouth, MA 02747, U.S.A. 13.

YOKOYAMA, Mitchel Mitsuo, b. 6 Mar. 1927. Doctor. Educ: M.D., Juntendo Med. Coll., Tokyo, Japan, 1950; D.M.S. (Ph.D.), Tokyo Med. & Dental Univ., 1958. Appts: Vis. Scientist, Nat. Inst. of Hlth., 1959-64; Dir. of Rsch., Kuakini Med. Rsch. Inst., 1965-73; Clin. Assoc. Prof., Dept. of Genetics & Med., Univ. of Hawaii, 1966-73; Cons. in Hematol., Tripler Army Med. Ctr., 1972-73; Dir. of Labs., Kallestad Labs., Inc., Chaska, Minn., 1973-; Pres., Fndn. of Molecular Med., 1973-. Mbrships: Am. Assn. of Immunologists; Int. Soc. of Transplantation; Int. Soc. of Hematol.; Int. Soc. of Blood Transfusion; Soc. of Sigma Xi; Am. Fedn. for Clin. Rsch.; Reticuloendothelial Soc. Author of articles in med. jrnls. Hons. incl: Dist. Sci. Award, State of Hawaii, 1973; Nat. Award, Mexican Nat. Soc. of Clin. Pathol., 1973. Address: Kallestad Labs., Inc., 1000 Lake Hazeltine Dr., Chaska, MN 55318, U.S.A.

YONDA, Alfred William, b. 10 Aug. 1919. Mathematician. Educ: B.S., Univ. of Ala., 1952; M.A., ibid, 1954. Appts: Mathn., U.S. Army Ballistic Rsch. Labs., Aberdeen, Md., 1954-56; Instr. in Maths., Univ. of Ala., 1954 & Temple Univ., 1956-57; Assoc. Sci., Avco Corp., Wilmington, Mass., 1957-59; Sr. Mbr., Tech. Staff, RCA, N.Y., 1959-66; Mgr., Software Systems Lab., Equipment Div., Raytheon Co., Sudbury, Mass., 1966-72; Prin. Engr., Missile Systems Div., ibid, Bedford, Mass., 1972-73; Mgr., Systems Analysis & Programming Dept., GTE Sylvania, Needham, Mass., 1973-. Mbrships: Treas., Medway Lib. Bd. of Trustees, 1973-; N.Y. Acad. of Scis.; Am. Math. Soc.; AAAS; Math. Assn. Am.; Assn. for Comp. Machinery; Past Pres., Ala. Chapt., Pi Mu Epsilon, 1953-54; Grafton Area Bd. of Mental Hlth., Sigma Xi; Pres., Milford Area Assn. for Retarded Children, 1970-72; Blackstone Valley Mental Hlth. & Retardation Area Bd. Address: 12 Sunset Dr., Medway, MA 02053, U.S.A. 6, 14, 28.

YONGE, (Sir) Charles Maurice, b. 9 Dec. 1899. Marine Biologist. Educ: Univ. of Edinburgh, 1919-24. Appts: Asst. Naturalist, Plymouth Lab., 1924-27; Balfour Student,

Univ. of Cambridge, 1927-29; Ldr., Gt. Barrier Reef Expedition, 1928-29; Physiol., Plymouth Lab., 1930-32; Prof. of Zool., Univ. of Bristol, 1933-44; Regius Prof. of Zool., Univ. of Glasgow, 1944-64; Rsch. Fellow, ibid, 1965-70; Hon. Fellow, Univ. of Edinburgh, 1970-. Mbrships. incl: Coun., Royal Soc., 1952-54 & 68-70; Pres., Royal Soc. of Edinburgh, 1970-73. Publs. incl: The Seas (w. F.S. Russell); The Sea Shore; Oysters; British Marine Life; Guide to the Sea Shore (w. John Barrett); Physiology of Mollusca (ed. w. K.M. Wilbur); num. sci. papers dealing primarily w. marine Mollusca, esp. the Bivalvia, 1923-. Hons. incl: Hon. D.Sc., Univ. of Bristol, 1959, Heriot-Watt Univ., 1971; Darwin Medal, Royal Soc. of London, 1968. Address: 13 Cumin Pl., Edinburgh EH9 2JX, U.K.

YORK, Albert W., b. 10 Apr. 1915. Consultant. Educ: Univ. of Ala. Appts. incl: Dir. & Fndr., York Mfg. Co., A.N.J. Co.; Marketing & Advt. Dir., Riviera Estates Inc., A.N.J. Corp., 1949; Dir. & Fndr., York Realty Co., Realtors, A.N.J. Co., 1957; Pres., Homeowners Mortgage Corp., A.N.J. Corp., 1959; Pres., Multiple Listing Inc., A.N.J. Corp., 1968; Housing Commnr., City of Plainfield, N.J., 1969. Mbrships: Nat. Assn. of Realtors; Pres., Plainfield Area Bd. of Realtors, 1960; Dir., N.J. Assn. of Real Estate Bds.; Investment, Commercial & Residential Divs., Nat. Inst. of Real Estate Brokers; Nat. Assn. of Housing & Redev. Officials. Author of papers in field. Assoc. Developer, "Case" Popcorn Machine, soon available to mfr. Address: 308 U.S. Highway 22, Green Brook, NJ 08812, U.S.A.

YORKE, Signa Leonie. Educator. Educ: Bethlehem Tchrs. Coll., Jamaica; Univ. of London Inst. of Educ, U.K., 1955-57; Appts. incl: 1st woman Educ. Off. i/c tchr. educ., Belize, British Honduras, 1959-61; Organiser, Intermediate Trng. Ctr. for Tchrs., 1961-63; Prin., St. George's Trng. Coll., 1964-65; Prin., Belize Tchrs. Coll., 1965-67; Dean, St. John's Coll. (Jr. Coll.), 1970-. Mbrships. incl: Nat. Lib. Bd., Belize; Assn. of Hds. of Secondary Schls, ibid; Advsry Bd., Belize Inst. of Soc. Rsch. & Action; Nat. Comm. for the Caribbean Examinations Coun.; Hons: Dip. Ed., Univ. of London Inst. of Educ., 1968; M.Ed., Newcastle Upon Tyne Univ., 1971; M.B.E., 1971. Address: St. John's Junior College, Landivar, Box 548, Belize City, Belize, British Honduras.

YOSEPIAN, Jane Marie. Educator. Educ: B.S., Univ. of Ill., 1956; M.S., Univ. of Utah, 1958; Postgrad. study, Colo. Coll., Conn. Coll., Art Inst. of Chgo., Ariz. State Univ. Appts: Instr., Phys. Educ. for Women, Univ. of R.I., 1958-60; Asst. Prof., ibid, 1960. Mbrships: Nat. Assn. for Armenian Studies & Resch.; Am., R.I. Assns. for Hlth., Phys. Educ. & Recreation; AAUP; Eastern Assn. of Phys. Educ. for Coll. Women; R.I. Div., Girls & Women's Sports; Amateur Fencer's League of Am. Prod. of film, Plastic Body—A Dance Demonstration for High Schools & Colleges. Hons: Names Specialist in Mod. Dance by U.S. State Dept., & sent as Tchr., Lectr. in S. Am., 1965; Cons. in Bolivarian Games, S. Am., 1965. Address: 811 W. Lawrence Ave., Chicago, IL 60640, U.S.A. 5, 6, 130.

YOST, (Rev.) Frank Donald, b. 23 June 1927. Clergyman; Archivist. Educ: Columbia Union Coll., Takoma Park, Md., 1944-46; B.A., Andrews Univ., Berrien Springs, Mich., 1949; M.A., The Am. Univ., Wash. D.C., 1961; Grad., Syracuse Univ., N.Y. Appts. incl: Mini. Intern, Battle Creek, Mich., 1949-50; Edit. Asst. & Asst. Ed., The Youth's Instr., Wash. D.C., 1950-56; Asst. Sec., Youth Dept., Gen. Conf.

of Seventh-day Adventists & Ed., MV Kit, 1957-61; Tchr., Newbury Park, Calif., 1961-64; Asst. Prof., Jrnlsm., Southern Missionary Coll., Collegedale, Tenn., 1964-67; Var. Edit. Positions, Review & Herald Publng. Assn., Wash. D.C., 1967-73; Archivist, Gen. Conf. of Seventh-day Adventists, ibid, 1973-. Mbrships. incl: Soc. of Am. Archivists; Assn. for Educ. in Jrnlsm.; Regional Archives Grps. Publs. incl: Writing for Adventist Magazines, 1968; Many articles & edits. in Seventh-day Adventists mags. Address: Gen. Conf. of Seventh-day Adventists, 6840 Eastern Ave. N.W., Washington, DC 20012, U.S.A.

YOST, Martha Emma Bradfield (Mrs.), b. 31 Jan. 1902. Missionary; Educator. Educ: B.A., Pepperdine Coll., LA, 1955; M.A., ibid, 1961; Calif. Univ. Ext., Long Beach; Univ. of Southern Calif., LA; UCLA; Seminar, Univ. of Rome, 1968. Appts: Tchr., Palomar Schl. for Boys, Perris, Pub. Schls., Lawndale, Bellflower, Gdn. Grove, Calif.; Asst. Night Cnslr., Compton Jr. Coll., 1954-55; Cons., Alumni Inst., Mito, Japan; Tchr. & Cnslr. (Missionary Educator), Jr. & Sr. Colls., Japan; currently Instr., Continuing Educ., Pepperdine Univ., Inglewood Ctr., LA. Mbrships. incl: Gdn. Grove Bus. & Profl. Women's Club & related state, nat. & int. instns.; Capt., US Communications Corps; Fellow, Am. Assn. Mental Deficiency; Life, NEA; Tchr., Co-Workers Sunday Schl., 1st Christian Ch., Long Beach, Calif.; Christian Women's Fellowship; Life, Nat. Retired Tchrs. Assn.; Coun. Exceptional Children. Recip., Dolores Award, Pepperdine Univ. Educl. Alumni Assn., 1967. Address: 2324 Cedar Ave., Apt. 3, Long Beach, CA 90806, U.S.A. 5, 9, 22, 57, 59, 128, 132, 138.

YOU, Richard Wonsang, b. 23 Dec. 1916. Physician & Surgeon. Educ: B.S., Hawaii Univ., U.S.A. 1939; M.D., Creighton Med. Schl., 1943; Postgrad. med. work in North Am., South Am., Asia, Europe & Africa, 1943-44. Appts: U.S. Med. Corps, 1944-46; Post & Compound Surg., P.O.W. Camp, Hawaii, 1945-46; 117th Station Hosp., 1946-47; Hawaii Nat. Guard, 1947-50; Physn. to 7 Football Teams & Hula Bowl Football Games, 1947-50; Active in all fields of sports org., promotion & coaching, 1951-. Mbr. num. assns., comms., couns. & fndns. in field; Creighton Univ. Alumni Assn. (Hawaii Chapt.). Author num. articles on sports for nat. & int. magazines. Hons: Asiatic-Pacific Serv. Medal, 1944-46; World War II Victory Medal, 1944-46; Hawaiian Wrestling Champion, 1935, 1939; Qualified for final U.S. Olympic Wrestling Tryouts, Philadelphia, Pa., 1936; U.S. Del. & Mbr., Int. Weightlifting Federation Congress, Olympic Games, Helsinki, Finland, 1952, Melbourne, Australia, 1956, & recip. of many other hons. for work in field. Address: 1270 Queen Emma St., Suite 106, Honolulu, HI 96813, U.S.A. 9, 114, 128, 130, 131.

YOUNG, Alexander Kenneth, b. 19 Dec. 1913. Physician; Medical Direcotr. Educ: Glasgow Royal Tech. Coll. U.K.; M.B., Ch.B., Univ. of Glasgow, ibid, 1939; var. postgrad. med. courses, U.S.A. & Canada; Licenciate Med. Coun. of Canada, 1948. Appts. incl: Pvte. Med. Prac., U.K., 1940-47; Med. Off., Ground Defence & Camouflage, Air Min., ibid, 1940-44; Admiralty Surg., ibid, 1944-46; pvte. med. prac., Vancouver, B.C., Canada, 1948-51; Dir., Univ. Hlth. Serv. Univ. of B.C., ibid, 1951-61; Dir., Student Hlth. Serv. & Prof., Phys. Educ., Univ. of N.M., U.S.A., 1961-69; Staff Physn. (Sr. grade), Dept. of Internal. Med., VA Hosp., Providence, R.I., 1969-70; Med. Dir., B.C. Hydro & Power Authority, Vancouver B.C., Canada, 1971-. Mbrships. incl: Fellow, Royal Soc. of Hlth., 1971, Am. Coll. Hlth. Assn.,

1968, Am. Coll. of Sports Med., 1962; Canadian, B.C. & Vancouver Med. Assns.; Occupational Hlth. Comm. of B.C.; past, many other couns. & comms. Winner of schol. awards. Address: B.C. Hydro & Power Authority, 970 Burrard St., Vancouver, 1, V6Z 1Y3, B.C., Canada. 9.

YOUNG, Allan, b. 21 June 1939. University Professor. Educ: B.A., Harpur Coll. SUNY, 1961; M.B.A., Columbia Univ., 1963; Ph.D., ibid, 1967. Appts: Lectr., City Coll., Baruch Schl. of Bus., 1965-66; Asst. Prof.-Assoc. Prof., Schl. of Bus., Syracuse Univ., 1966-. Mbrships: Financial Mgt. Assn.; Manuscript Reviewer, Manuscript Reviewer, Eastern Finance Assn.; Am. Econs. Assn.; Am. Inst. of Decision Scis.; Beta Gamma Sigma. Contbr. financial, acctcy. & bus. jrnls. Hons: Haskins & Sell Prize Fellowship, 1962; N.Y. State Soc. of Certified Pub. Accts. Prize, 1963; Profl. Acctng. Prize, 1963; Doctoral Study Award, Columbia Univ., 1965. Address: 27 Ely Dr., Fayetteville, NY 13066, U.S.A. 6.

YOUNG, Bernice Elizabeth, b. 7 Oct. 1931. Author; Publicist. Educ: Vassar Coll., Poughkeepsie, N.Y.; Western Reserve Univ., Cleveland, Oh. Appts: P.R. Advsr., Trinity Cathedral, Cleveland, Oh., 1957-68; Asst. to Dir. of Advt., Charles of the Ritz, 1961-64; Dir. Beatles (U.S.A.) Ltd., 1964-67; Protestant Media Advsr, Girl Scouts of the U.S.A., 1968; Publicity Chmn., St. Thomas Ch. Benefit, & Account Exec., Addison, Goldstein & Walsh, 1969-70; Author, 1970-. Mbrships: Bd. of Dirs., Sheltering Arsm Children's Servs.; Altar Guild, St. Thomas Ch., N.Y.C. Publs. incl: Harlem, the Story of a Changing Community, 1972; The Picture Story of Henry Aaron, & Great Tribes of Africa (in preparation); other books, reviews & radio programmes. Hons.: Nat. Hon. Soc., 1947; French Medal for Linguistic Proficiency. Address: 333 E. 34th St., Apt. 17H, N.Y., NY 10016, U.S.A. 30.

YOUNG, John C., b. 26 Mar. 1909. Artist. Appts. incl: Owner, John Young Gall., Kahala Hilton Hotel, Honolulu, Hawaii; Art Instr., Honolulu Acad. of Arts, Honolulu, Hawaii; Art Critic, Honolulu Star Bulletin, Honolulu, Hawaii. Mbrships: Chmn., Cultural Activities Comm., E.-W. Ctr., Honolulu; former Pres., Hawaii Painters & Sculptors League; Trustee, Tennent Art Fndn., Honolulu; Honolulu Acad. of Arts; Honolulu Symphony Soc. One Man Exhibs: Honolulu Acad. of Arts; DeYoung Mus., San Fran., Calif.; Gump's, San Fran.; Palace Legion of Honor, San Fran.; San Fran. Art Mus.; Santa Barbara Mus., Calif.; L.A. Co. Mus., Calif.; Woodside Gall., Seattle, Wash.; Dallas N. Gall., Dallas, Tex.; Corcoran Gall., Wash. DC. Exhibd. in Grp. shows in U.S.A., Germany & New Zealand inclng. Pacific Heritage Travelling Exhib. to Berlin & Art in Embassies Prof. Exhib., Smithsonian Instn., Wash. DC, 1970. Hons: 1st Prize in Oil Painting, Water Colour Painting & Wood Block Print, all Honolulu Acad. of Arts. Address: John Young Gall., 5000 Kahala Ave., Honolulu, HI 96816, U.S.A.

YOUNG, Jon Nathan, .b. 30 May 1938. Archaeologist. Educ: B.A., Univ. of Ariz., Tucson, 1960; Ph.D., ibid, 1967; M.A., Univ. of Ky., Lexington, 1962. Appts. incl: Tchng. Asst., Dept. of Anthropol., Univ. of Ariz., Tucson, 1966-67; Co-Fndr. & Archaeol. Field Dir., Summer-at-Taos Prog., Ft. Burgwin Rsch. Ctr., Ranchos de Taos, N.M., summers 1968-71; Rsch. Archaeol., U.S.D.I., Nat. Pk. Serv., S.W. Archaeol. Ctr., Gila Pueblo, Globe, Ariz., 1967-71; U.S.D.I., Nat. Pk. Serv. Ariz. Archaeol. Ctr., Univ. of Ariz., Tucson 1971-.

Sec., Interior's Exec. Order Cons., W. & S.W. US, Nat. Pk. Servs. Interagcy. Servs. Div., Tucson, 1972-. Mbrships: Fellow, Am. Anthropol. Assn. & AAAS; Fellow, Royal Anthropol. Inst. Gt. Britain & Ireland; Assoc., Current Anthropol. Soc. Calif. Archaeol.; Ariz. Archaeol. & Histl. Soc.; Coun. Abandoned Mil. Posts; Kit Carson Mem. Fndn.; Phi Beta Kappa; Sigma Xi; Phi Kappa; Sigma Xi; Phi Kappa Phi; Alpha Kappa Delta; White Rag Soc. of Nat. Coun. of YMCA; Gila Co. Archaeol. & Histl. Soc. (Incorporator, Bd. of Dirs., V.P.); Bd. of Dirs., Mus. of San Carlos Apache; Histl. Soc. of N.M. Author of The Salado Culture in Southwestern Prehistory.; Chapts., articles, reviews & comments var. learned publs. Address: 6970 Camino Namara, Tucson, AZ 85715, U.S.A. 9, 130, 139.

YOUNG, Kenneth Ray, b. 17 July 1943. Minister of the Gospel; Bible College Teacher. Educ: B.A., Stephen A. Austin State Univ., 1969; M.A., ibid, 1970; Southern Bible Coll., Houston, Tex. Appts: Pastor, Pentecostal Ch. of God, Kountze, Tex.; Sectional Youth Ldr., Beaumont Sect., Pentecostal Ch. of God; Pastor, Pentecostal Ch. of God, Lufkin, Tex.; Lufkin Sect. Dist. Presbtter, Pentecostal Ch. of God; Tchr., Scurry HS, Scurry, Tex.; Christian Serv. Dir. & Chmn. of the Soc. Sci. Dept., Southern Bible Coll., Houston, Tex.; Americanization Tchr., Houston Community Coll. Prog. Mbrships: Precinct Chmn., Repub. Party; Soc. for Pentecostal Studies. Contbr. articles to the Southern Bible Coll. Alumni Newsletter. Address: 5202 McCarty, Houston, TX 77029, U.S.A. 125, 130.

YOUNG, Marie Shipley (formerly Opal Marie Shipley) (Mrs. Harry M. Young, Jr.), b. 30 Oct. 1919. Guidance Counselor. Educ: B.S., John Brown Univ., Siloam Springs, Ark., 1940; M.S., Univ. of Ky., Lexington, 1946; Grad. studies, APSU, Murray State Univ. & Univ. of Ky. Appts: Nat. Youth Admin. Worker, Lake Ft. Smith, Ark., 1940; Farm Security Supvsr., Dyess, Ark., Lake Village, Ark. & Lake Providence, La., 1941-43; USNR Wave Ensign—Lt., 1943-45; 7th Gr. Tchr., 1955-56, HS Home Econs. Tchr., 1957-59, Guidance Cnslr., 1960-74, Christian Co. Bd. of Educ., Ky. Mbrships. incl: Local Advsr., 1968-74, State Exec. Sec., 1973-75, Ky. Assn. of Nat. Hon. Socs.; Sec., Ky. Personnel & Guidance Assn., 2 yrs.; Delta Kappa Gamma; Kappa Delta Pi; NEA; Mbr. & Pianist, McKenzie Kirk Presby. Ch., Herdon, Ky. Publs: History of Eighth Naval District, 1945; Nutrition Study, 1947. Hons. incl: Commendation, Comdt., Eighth Naval Dist., 1945; Selected for Cnslr. Trng. Workshop, Univ. of Ky., 1960. Address: Rte. 1, Melrose Farms Inc., Herndon, KY 42236, U.S.A. 5, 138.

YOUNG, Morris Nathan, b. 20 July 1909. Physician. Appts: Pvte. Prac., Ophthalmol., N.Y.C., 1945-; Assoc. Attng. & Assoc. Prof. Ophthalmol., N.Y. Polyclin. Hosp. & Med. Schl; Ophthalmologist, Wickersham Hosp., N.Y.C.; Currently Dir. Ophthalmol., Beekman Downtown Hosp., ibid. Mbrships: Harvard Club, N.Y.C.; Delaware & Hudson Canal Soc.; N.Y. Univ. Fac. Club; Hon., Chinatown N.Y. Lions Club. Publs: Hobby Magic, 1950; Houdini on Magic (w. Gibson), 1953; Bibliography of Memory, 1961; Houdini's Fabulous Magic (w. Gibson), 1961; How to Develop an Exceptional Memory (w. Gibson), 1962; How to Read Faster & Remember More (w. Young), 1965. Hons: Order of Lafayette; Grand Hospitaller, Kt. Comdr. Kts. of Malta, Order of St. John of Jerusalem. Address: 170 Broadway, N.Y., NY 10038, U.S.A. 14, 17, 22, 30.

YOUNG, Peter, b. 28 July 1915. Military Historian. Educ: M.A., Trinity Coll., Oxford Univ., U.K. Appts: British Army Regular Off., Lt. Col-Brigadier, 1938-46; Qaid., 9th Regiment, Arab Legion, 1953-56; Rdr., Mil. Hist., R.M.A., Sandhurst. Mbrships. incl: Fellow, Soc. of Antiquaries, London; Capt.-Gen., Sealed Knot Soc. of Cavaliers & Roundheads; Fellow, Royal Histl. Soc.; Fellow, Royal Geogl. Soc. Author num. mil. hist. publs., incl. The Arab Legion, 1972; Will Shakespeare: Top Military Expert, 1972; George Washington's Army, 1972; Blücher's Army, 1972; Ed., Cruso, Militarie Instructions for the Cavall'rie, 1972; Armies of the English Civil War, 1973; Napoleon and His Marshals, 1973; Wellington's Masterpiece (w. Lt. Col. James Lawford), 1973; Gen. Ed. & contbr. to The War Game, 1973; Ed., Atlas of the Second World War, 1973; The Machinery of War, 1973. Hons: M.C., 1941, 1st & 2nd Bars, 1943; D.S.O., 1942; Order of El Istiqlal of Jordan, 1954. Address: Bank House, Ripple, Tewkesbury, Gloucs., GL20 6EP, U.K. 1.

YOUNG, William Harvey, b. 30 Nov. 1899. Economist. Educ: B.B.A., Univ. of Tex., 1921; M.B.A., ibid, 1922; B.A., 1923; Ph.D., Brookings Instn., Wash. D.C., 1928. Appts. incl: Special Agent, U.S. Bur. of For. & Domestic Commerce, 1928-29; on staff, Brookings Instn., 1929-30; Econ., Coal Econs. Div., U.S. Bur. of Mines, 1930-37; Prin. Econ., Nat. Bituminous Coal Commn., 1937-43; Chief of Rsch. Sect., Solid Fuels Admin. for War, 1943-44; Chief, Bituminous Coal Sect., U.S. Bur. of Mines, 1944-69. Mbrships. incl: Am. Econ. Assn.; Am. Statl. Assn.; Sr. V.P., D.C. Chapt., Sons. of Am. Revolution; Alpha Kappa Psi; Pi Gamma Mu. Publs: Source of Coal Used by Electrical Power Plants, 1930; chapts. in books & articles in profl. jrnls. Address: 2817-31 St., N.W., Washington DC 20008, U.S.A. 6, 14

YOUNGER, Rachel King (Mrs. William Stuart Younger), b. 11 Feb. 1923. Clinical Chemist. Educ: Maryville Coll., Tenn., 1941-43; B.A., Vanderbilt Univ., Nashville, 1943-45; Grad. Schl., ibid, 1960; Registered Chem., Am. Soc. of Clin. Pathols.; Cert. Med. Asst., Clin., Assn. Am. Med. Assts., 1973; Lic. Clin. Chem., State of Tenn., Supvsr.; sev. other profl. certs. inclng. CDC Lipid Standardization Prog., 1972, 73. Appts: Techn., Blood Chem. Lab., Vanderbilt Univ. Hosp., Nashville, 1952-53; Asst. Chief., Lab. & X-ray, Maury Co. Hosp., Columbia, 1953-55; Chief Biochem. & Chief Supvsr., Surg. Biochem., S.R. Light Lab. for Surg. Rsch., Dept. of Surg., Vanderbilt Univ. Hosp., 1955-; Instr. in Surg. Rsch., ibid, 1963-69; Asst. Prof., Surg., Vanderbilt Univ. Schl. of Med., 1969-; Lectr., Univ. of Tenn., 1972, 73 & 74 & Meharry Med. Coll., 1973. Mbrships. incl: Am. Assn. Clin. Chems.; Am. Soc. Clin. Pathols.; Pres.-Elect, Nashville Chapt., 1974-75, House of Delegs., Tenn. Soc., 1973-74, on sev. comms., Am. Assn. Med. Assts.; Am. Oil Chems. Soc.; Sigma Xi; Alpha Omicron Pi; CLA Advsry. Bd., State Vocational-Tech. Schl., 1974. Contbr. num. artifles to profl. publs. Hons: Gold Medal Paper, Southeastern Surg. Congress, New Orleans, La., 1969. Address: 3800 Hobbs Rd., Nashville, TN 37215, U.S.A. 125.

YOUNG-JAMES, Douglas Alexander de Singleton, b. 10 July 1914. Squadron Leader, RAF (ret.'d); Author. Educ: Bristol Univ. appts. incl: perm. RAF Command, 1939-62; SESO no. 206 grp. RAF Canal Zone, 1952-54; Hd. of Br., Air Min., 1953-57; Contractors Liaison Off., Hartlebury, 1958-60; Air Min., 1960-62. Mbrships. incl: RAF Club; Royal Soc.

Lit.; Pres., Aspian Soc., 1946-; Fellow, Inst. of Dirs.; Dir., St. Hugh's Soc., 1958-; mbr. coun., United Servs. Cath. Assn., 1958-. Publs. incl: Memoirs of an ASP, 1965; Donald Campbell—An Informal Biography, 1968. Hons. incl: Kt., Grand Cross, 1973; H.E. Prior of London, 1972. Address: 21 Ilchester Mansions, Abingdon Rd., London W8 6AE, U.K. 3, 20, 32, 49, 68, 99.

YOUNGLOVE, Ruth Anne (Mrs. Benjamin Rhees Loxley), b. 14 Feb. 1909. Artist. Educ: B.E., UCLA, 1932; pvte. studies w. Orrin A. White & Marion Kavanaugh Wachtel. Appts. incl: Substitute Tchr., Pasadena City Schls., Calif.; Pvte. Tchr. of Art. Exhibs: num. grp. shows arranged by profl. orgs. in galls. & mus. of Southern Calif., 1931-. One-man Shows: Permanent Display, Bank of Am. Main Br., Pasadena, Calif.; Community Serv. Ctr., Pasadena, 1972-; Glendale Fed. Savings & Loan of Pasadena, 1973. Mbrships: Calif. Nat. Water Color Soc.; Assoc., Am. Watercolor Soc.; Life Mbr., Laguna Beach Art Assn.; Hospitality Chmn., 4 yrs., Patron Chmn., 10 yrs., Pasadena Soc. of Artists; Sec., Pasadena Artists Assocs., 2 yrs.; Artists League of Seal Beach. Hons: 1st Prize, Weaving, LA Co. Fair; 2nd Prize, Watercolor, Artists League of Seal Beach, 1968; Hon. Mention, ibid, 1967; 1st Prize, Watercolor, ibid, 1969. Address: 1180 Yocum St., Pasadena, CA 91103, U.S.A. 5, 37, 138.

YOUNIS, Adele Linda. Professor of History. Educ: B.Ed. Sci., R.I. Coll., 1933; M.A., Boston Univ., 1943; Brown Univ., 1948-49; Ph.D., Boston Univ., 1961; Am.-Middle East Inst., 1962. Appts. incl: Joseph Case H.S., Swansea, Mass., 1942-47; Bryant Coll., 1947-52; Asst. Prof., Salem Coll., 1956-61; Assoc. Prof., ibid, 1961-65; Prof., Hist., Dept. of Hist., 1965-; Lectr. on Immigration, Beirut, Lebanon, World Lebanese Union, 1968. Bicentennial Studies on Arabic-speaking Americans for State of Pa. Hist. works.; Chmn., Hist. Dept. on Non-Western Studies in World Civilization. Mbrships. incl: Fall River Coun., 1950's; Corres. Sec., Fall River Br., AAUW, 1950-52; 1st V.P., ibid, 1952-54; Pres., 1954-56; Chmn., Higher Educ., Mass. State Div., AAUW, 1958-61; N.Engl. Assn. Women Histns.; Advsry. Bd., Bicentennial Rsch. Assoc. Publ.; Marquis Biographical Lib. Soc.; Am., New Engl. & Mass. Hist. Assns.; Acad. Pol. Sci; Publs. incl: The Arab-Americans—A Study in Assimilation, 1969; Poetry: Tribute to James P. Khoury, Tribute in Courage; Translations var. Oriental poetry & prose works; "Know Your Neighbor" Series, Fall River Herald News, 1952; Prog., Fall River Proj: American Together, 1954; Values of History in Human Affairs; Place of History; contbr. of articles to other profl. publs. & jrnls. Recip. many hons. Address: Salem State Coll., Salem, MA 01970, U.S.A. 5, 6, 13, 15.

YOUTZ, Dorothy Jane (Keyser), b. 23 Mar. 1919. Medical Care Administration Consultant. Educ: A.B., Wellesley Coll., Mass.; Grad. work, State Univ. of Iowa, Iowa City; Int. Bus. Machines Schl.; Special courses in admin. & mgmt., U.S. Civil Serv. Commn. Appts. incl: Administrative Analyst, U.S. Pub. Hlth. Serv., 1945-49; Chief, records cons. unit, ibid, 1949-53; Prin. Advsr. for Jt. CB-PHS State Plan, 1953-54; Staff Asst., Div. of Indian Hlth., 1953-61; Off. of Hlth. Planning, D.C. Dept. of Hlth., 1961-69; Special Asst., Chief, Dept. of Human Resources, 1970-72; Free-lance cons. in med. care admin., 1972-. Mbrships. incl: 1st V.P., Group Hlth. Assn. of Wash.; Bd. of Dirs., ibid, 1969-75; Fellow, Am. Pub. Hlth. Assn.; Bus. & Profl. Women; AAUW; League of Women Voters; Zonta. Author of articles,

report & book review, & of book, History of the Capita City Schl. of Nursing, forthcoming. Recip. of hons. Address: Rural Route 1, Box 117, Elkins, WV 26241, U.S.A.

YRAN, Knut, b. 8 June 1920. Designer. Appts: Free-lance Designer; Owner, diary publishing co.; Chief Designer, Aschehoug Publrs.; Prod. Mgr., Norwegian film team; Hd., Indl. Design, Philips Concern, Eindhoven, Netherlands, 1966-. Mbrships: Tegnerforbundet; Norske Yrkestegnere; Norwegian Deleg., Nordiska Tegner; Chambre Belge des Graphistes; Pres., Int. Coun. of Graphic Design Assns., 1966-68. Works incl: Murals in factories & official bldgs; Indl. designs of all kinds from ships to watches; Posters; Drawings. Publs: Books on poetry & on book design; Articles in various jrnls. & annuals. Hons. incl: World Poster Trophy, 1953; Grand Prix St. Eloix (twice), World Watchmakers Fedn.; Num. other nat. & int. prizes for book design, indl. design, & arch. Address: Philips Concern Industrial Design Centre, Dela Building 5, Eindhoven, Netherlands.

YRJÖLÄ, Erkki Olavi, b. 24 Oct. 1922. Vice-Managing-Director. Educ: M.Sc., Helsinki Univ. Technol., Finland. Appts: Tchr., Elec. Engrng., Helsinki Inst. Technol., Finland, 1948-49; Testing Engr., Elec. Inspectorate, ibid, 1949-55; Hd., Dept.-V.-Mng. Dir., Elec. Inspte., 1955-. Mbrships: Pres., Finnish Electrotech. Standards Assn. & Comm. Testing Stns. Int. Commn. Rules Approval Elec. Equipment; Comm. Action Int. Electrotech. Commn. Author sev. articles on elec. safety & standardization questions in Finnish for. tech. periodicals. Hons: Finnish Medal of Freedom II Mil., 1942; Finnish Cross of Freedom IV Mil., 1944; Kt., 1st Class, Lion of Finland, 1973. Address: Elec. Inspectorate, SF-00210 Helsinki 21, Finland. 43, 134.

YRJÖNEN, (Kaarlo) Sakari, b. 21 Dec. 1923. Chamber of Commerce Director. Educ: LL.B., Hamina Univ., Helsinki, 1949. Appts: Mgr., Union of Finnish Lawyers, 1949-51; Notary, Pielisjärvi Judicial Dist., 1951; Asst. Sec., Helsinki Tax Off., 1951-52; Mgr., Oulu Chmbr. of Comm., 1952-55; Asst. Mgr., Ctrl. Chmbr. of Comm., Finland, 1955-64; Mng. Dir., ibid, 1965-. Mbrships. incl: Coun., Int. Chmbr. of Comm., 1965-; Bds., Finnish Sect., Int. Chmbr. of Comm., 1965-, Finnish Port Union, 1958-, Assn. of Finnish Businessmen, 1964-, Finnish Sect., Int. Law Assn., 1965-, Deutsche-Finnische Vereinigung, 1964-, Finnish-Am. Chmbr. of Comm., 1970-; Pres., Helsinki Rotary Club, 1970-71. Contbr. articles on econ. & commercial subjects to var. jrls., mags., etc. Hons: Finnish Cross of Liberty 4th Class, 1944; ibid, w. oak leaves, 1944; Order of Merit, German Fed. Repub., 1959; Kt. 1st Class, Finnish Order of the Lion, 1964; Cmdr., ibid, 1969; C.B.E., 1971; Hungarian Banner Order 2nd Class, 1971. Address: Ctrl. Chmbr. of Comm. of Finland, Fabianinkatu 14, 00100 Helsinki 10, Finland. 43.

YUN, Chongsun, b. 23 July 1934. Dentist. Educ: B.A., Univ. of Maine, U.S.A., 1958; D.D.S., Coll. of Dentistry, N.Y. Univ., 1962; Intern, L.I. Coll. Hosp., 1963. Appts: Instr. in Operative Dentistry, Coll. of Dentistry, N.Y. Univ., 1963-65; Attng. Staff, L.I. Coll. Hosp., 1963-68; Attng. Staff, Roosevelt Hosp., 1968-; Pvte. Prac., N.Y.C., 1963-. Mbrships: First Dist. Dental Soc., Am. Dental Assn.; Chmn., Korean Student Fund of N.Y., 1972-; Pres., Korean Golf Assn. of N.Y., 1972; Bd., Kyungki Alumni Assn. of N.Y.; Omicron Kappa Upsilon. Author, Illustrated Teaching Aids for Closed Circuit TV Instruction, 1961. Hons: Prosthetic

Award, Coll. of Dentistry, N.Y. Univ., 1962; Citation, Humanitarian Serv. Award, Korean Lang. Schl. of N.Y., 1973. Address: 400 Madison Ave., N.Y., NY 10017, U.S.A. 6.

YUZON, Amado M., b. 30 Aug. 1906. Lawyer; University Professor; Author. Educ: sev. degrees. Appts. incl: Mbr., First Congress of Philippines; Tech. Asst. under four RP Presidents, 1952-65; Cultural Envoy, 1965; Actng. Nat. Commnr. of Culture, 1965-66; Mbr., Interim Nat. Assembly, 1973. Active Mbr. many prof., lit. & cultural orgs. incl: Pres., Pampangan Fed.; Foreign Poetry Soc. of England; Royal Soc. of Lit.; Royal Asiatic Soc.; Canadian Authors Assoc.; Poetry Soc. Am.; Acad. Am. Poets; Am. Poetry League; Assoc. Int. de Poesia, Rome; Patron, World Poetry Soc. Intercontinental; Patron, Am. Jr. Poetry Soc.; Int. Acad. Poets; Centro Studie Scambi Int.; Dir., For. Mbrs. Dept., Fench Acad. of Poetry, Paris; Cath. Poetry Soc. of Am.; Poets of the Pacific; Am. Acad. of Pol. & Soc. Sci. Author of sev. pub. works in Filipino including Salitang Paka-Versus, 1933. English works incl: Dr. Rizal in Translations, 1933; The Life of Lam-ang, 1956; The Citizens Poems, 1960, Ed., Laurel Leaves. Contbr. to many Philippine & foreign newspapers & jrnls. Laureateships incl: (regional) Pampanga, 1930-; First Poet Laureate Far Eastern Univ., 1934-36; RP Nat. Poet Laureate, 1959-; (continental) of Asia, 1965; of S.Am., 1966; of Liberia, Pakistan, Austria, Rome, Ill., Tex., Colo., S. Dak., N.Y. Address: c/o UPLI-Yuzon, The Poets' Corner, Makyapo, Guagua, Pampanga, Philippines. 2, 3, 11..

Z

ZACHRISON, Sten J.G., b. 20 Aug. 1913. Agricultural Administration Official. Educ: Agronomist (Econ.), Agricultural Univ., Uppsala, 1942. Appts: Asst., Bd. of Agric., Stockholm, 1942-45; Asst., Agricultural Employers Assn., Stockholm, 1945-48; Dir., Agricultural Soc., Karlskrona, 1948-49; Dir., Assn. Agricultural Socs., Stockholm, 1949-67; Dir. of Agric., Skaraborg, Skara, 1967-. Mbr. & Chmn., Swedish Anglers Assn., Stockholm. Kt. Cmdr. of Order of N. Star, 1972. Address: Box 224, S-532 00 Skara, Sweden.

ZAGIER, Hélène Johanna De Boey (Mrs. David D. Zagier), b. 23 Feb. 1918. Psychiatrist; Educator; Educ: Barnard Coll., N.Y., 1936-38; N.Y. Univ., 1941-42; M.D., Geo. Wash. Univ., 1947. Appts: Mil. Surg., U.S. Armed Forces, Germany, 1948-52; Pediatrician, USAF, Tachikawa, Japan, 1952-54; Res., Eastern State Hosp., Williamsburg, Va., 1955-56; Medfield State Hosp., Mass., 1956-57; Jawaii State Hosp., 1957-58; Dir., Mental Hlth. Servs. Clin., Kingsport, Tenn., 1958-59; Chief, Outpatient Clin., San Joaquin Co. Hosp., Stockton, Calif., 1959-65; on Fac., Am. Coll. of Switzerland, Leysin, 1965-; Assoc. Dir., Cantonal Psych. Hosp., Valais, Switzerland, 1966-71; Supvsr. in Psychotherapy, ibid, 1971-. Mbrships: Am. & Swiss Psych. Assns.; Royal Coll. of Psychs., U.K. Address: Villa Quand Même, Aux Fontaines sur Monthey 1870, Switerland. 5.

ZAHAVY, Zev, b. 8 Sept. 1920. Educator; Author; Clergyman. Educ: B.A., Yeshiva Univ., 1939; M.H.L., ibid, 1948; Ordained, Isaac Elchanan Tehological Sem., 1942; Grad. Schl., Univ. of Ky., 1942-43; Columbia Univ., 1943-45; Ph.D., Yeshiva Univ., 1959. Appts. incl: Rabbi, Congregation Zichron Ephraim, 1952-61; Nat. Community Dir., Am. Assn. Educ., 1961-62; Instr., Grad. Schl., Yeshiva Univ., 1960-62; Bur. Dir., N.Y.C. Dept. of Investigation, 1962-65; Prof., CUNY, 1965-. Mbrships. incl: Pres., Limud Soc., 1962-; Cons., Mayor's Commn. on Human Rels., N.Y.C., 1961-62; Chmn., UN Appeal for Children; Assoc. Chief Chap., N.Y. Civil Defense; Chap., St. Vincent's Hosp. & Mem. Hosp., N.Y.C.; V.P., N.Y. Region, Rabbinical Coun. of Am.; V.P., Gimel Fndn.; Bd. of Educ., Manhattan Day Schl., N.Y.C. Publs. incl: Unraveling Dante's Gibberish, 1972; Earliest Recorded Theatre, 1973; Whitman as Guru, 1973; Ed., Lib. of Literary Classics, 1974, & The Classic Ency. of Judaic Philos., 1974. Hon: Ambassador, Yeshiva Univ., 1959. Address: 210 E. 68 St., N.Y., NY 10021, U.S.A. 6, 55.

ZAHEDI, (His Excellency) Ardeshir, b. 17 Oct. 1928. Iranian Government Official & Diplomat. Educ: Am. Coll. of Beirut, Lebanon; B.S., State Univ. of Utah, U.S.A. Appts. incl: Govt. Serv. in Iran, as Treas., Jt. Iran-Am. Commn., & Asst. to Dir. of Pt. IV Prog., 1950, Special Advsr. to Prime Min., 1953, Chamberlain to His Imperial Majesty, The Shahanshah of Iran, 1954-; For. Min. of Iran, 1967-71; Ambassador of Iran to U.S.A., 1960-62, 1973-, & to U.K., 1962-66; Hd. of Iranian Mission, 105th Anniversary Celebration, Argentina, 1960; Iranian Rep. at signing of Treaty banning Nuclear Tests, London, U.K., 1963, & at Independence Celebrations of Commonwealth of Bahamas, 1973; Hd. of Iranian Delegation at Inauguration of Pres. of Brazil, 1974. Recip., num. hons., nat. & African, Asian, European, Middle E. & S. Am. Address: Imperial Embassy of Iran, Washington, DC 20008, U.S.A.

ZAHLEN, Jean-Pierre, b. 31 Mar. 1922. Statistician. Educ: Maths., Univ. of Nancy, France, 1946-48; Stats. & Econs., Inst. of Stats., Univ. of Paris, 1948-50; Diploma of Statn., ibid, 1951. Appts: Attaché in Econs., Min. of Nat. Econ., Luxembourg, 1952; Hd., Dept. of Studies, Methods & Gen. Stats., Off. of Stats., High Auth. of ECCS, 1954; Dept. Hd., Differdange Works, HADIR, 1956; Proxy, 1960; Dpt. Hd. & Proxy, Dept. of Gen. Stats., ARBED, Hd. Off., Luxembourg, 1968; Chief Engr. & Proxy, 1969; Dpty. Mgr., Corp. Planning, 1974; Prof. of Math. Stats., Ctr. Européen de Formation des Statisticiens et Economistes des Pays en voie de développement, CESD, Paris, 1963-67; Rdr., Int. Univ. for Comp. Sci., Luxembourg, 1967-. Mbrships: Int. Statl. Inst.; Inst. Grand-Ducal, Sect. des sciences morales et politiques; Paris Statl. Soc.; Belgian Nat. Comm., l'Organisation Scientifique; Sci. Coun., CESD; Co-Ed., Statistiche Hefte; Lions Club, Luxembourg. Contbr. publs. on maths., stats., econs. & ops. rsch. to field. Address: Directeur adjoint d'ARBED, Service "Corporate Planning", 19, avenue de la Liberté, Luxembourg, Grand-Duchy of Luxembourg. 43.

ZAIM, Sabahaddin, b. 15 May 1926. Professor of Economics. Educ: Grad., Schl. of Pol. Sci., Univ. of Ankara, 1947; Grad., Schl. of Law, ibid, 1950; Ph.D., Schl. of Econs., Univ. of Istanbul, 1955; rsch. work, Cornell Univ., U.S.A., 1956-57, Munich Univ., German Fed. Repub., 1963-64. Appts: var. admin. posts, Istanbul, 1947-53; Asst. Prof., Univ. of Istanbul, 1953-57, Assoc. Prof., Fac. of Econs., 1957-65, Full Prof., 1965-; Hd., Comms. of Soc. Affairs & of Nat. Union, 1960-61; Mbr., Bd. of Dirs., Nat. Productivity Ctr., 1966-67; Mbr. Bd. of Dirs., Gumus Engine Indl. Corp.; Auditor of Anadolu Glass Ind. Grp. Mbrships. incl: Indl. Rels. Rsch. Assn., U.S.A.; Int. Indl. Rels. Assn., Geneva; Bd. Dirs., Fndn. Sci. Dev. Author, books, papers, reports, var. areas econs. & econ. rsch. Address: Băgdat Cad. 329, Erenköy-Istanbul, Turkey.

ZAINI, b. 17 Mar. 1924. Painter; Graphic Artist; Pastelist; Illustrator; Designer. Educ: Studied art w. Wakidj, Kayutanam Schl. of Mohammed Sjafei, Sumatra, Indonesia; Studied w. Basuki Abdullah & S. Soedjojono, Jakarta, 1940. Appts: Instr., Cultural Coun., Jakarta, 1959-65; Instr., Educl. Inst. of Art, Jakarta, 1972-. Mbrships: Young Indonesian Artists Assn., Jogjakarta, 1948; Union of Indonesian Painters, Jakarta, 1949; Consultative Org. for Nat. Culture, Jakarta, 1960-; Indonesian Fndn., Jakarta, 1970; Fndr., Fndn. of Art & Design, Jakarta, 1959. One-man exhibs: Chase Manhattan's art exhib., Jakarta, 1972; Jakarta Art Ctr., 1973. Exhibs. incl: India 2nd Triennial Exhib. of Contemporary World Art, New Delhi, 1971; Pertamina Exhib. of Art, Jakarta, 1971; Asian Art Exhibs., Jakarta, 1968, & Singapore, 1972; Six Collectors' Exhib., Jakarta, 1972; Cipta Art Gall., Jakarta, 1972, 1973. Recip. of hons. Address: Jalan Sumber Cipta IV/11, Jakarta, Indonesia.

ZAJCEW, Mykola, b. 5 Nov. 1894. Chemical Engineer. Educ: Chem. Ing.; Tech. Univ. of Prague, Czechoslovakia, 1924; D.Sc., Ukrainian Tech. Univ., Germany, 1957. Appts. incl: Asst. Assoc. Prof., Ukrainian Tech. Univ., Czechoslovakia, 1924-35; Chief Chem., Kosmos Factories, 1937-45; Prof. of Chem., Hd. of Dept., & Vice Rector, Ukrainian Tech. Univ., Regensburg & Munich, Germany, 1945-51; Rsch. Chem., Engelhard Inds., Newark, N.J., U.S.A., 1951-65; Cons., ibid, 1965-. Mbrships: Am. Oil Chems. Soc.; N.Y. Acad. of Scis.; Sectl.

Dir., Shevchenko Scientific Soc.; Sectl. Dir., Ukrainian Acad. of Arts & Scis. in the U.S.; German Soc. for Fat Rsch.; Ukrainian Engrs. Soc. of Am. Holder, many European & U.S. patents in chem. technol. Recip., Cert. of Recognition with Silver Badge for outstanding contbns. to chem. sci. & technol., Am. Chem. Soc., 1971. Address: 147 Norwood St., Newark, NJ 07106, U.S.A. 6, 14.

ZALAIT, Messim, b. 30 Jan. 1923. Painter. Educ: Acad. of Fine Art, Baghdad Painting Tchr.'s Sem.; AVMI Inst. of Arts. Appts: Painting Tchr., Tel-Aviv, Israel, 1955-69; Profl. Painter, 1969-. Has given sev. one-man shows, 1963-. Has participated in sev. grp. shows in Israel & abroad. Mbrships: Israel Painters & Sculptors Assn.; Country Club of Israel. Hons: Prize & works acquired, Min. of Educ. & Culture, 1964; Monaco Prize, Mod. Art Exhib., 1967; Grant, Jerusalem, 1968. Address: 55 B. Metudella, Tel-Aviv, Israel. 94.

ZALD, Mayer N., b. 17 June 1931. Professor of Sociology. Educ: B.A., Univ. of Mich., 1953; M.A., Univ. of Hawaii, 1955; Ph.D., Univ. of Mich., 1961. Appts: Assoc. Prof., Vanderbilt Univ., 1964-68; Prof., ibid, 1968-; Chmn., Dept., Sociol. & Anthropol., 1971-. Mbrships: Am. Sociol. Assn.; Soc. Sci. Study of Soc. Problems; Southern Sociol. Soc. Publs: Organizational Change: The Political Economy of the YMCA, 1970; Occupations & Organizations in American Life; Power in Organizations (Ed.), 1970. Address: Dept. Sociol. & Anthropol., Box 1811 Station B, Vanderbilt Univ., Nashville, TN 37235, U.S.A.

ZALDIVAR, Gladys B., b. 5 Nov. 1936. University Lecturer & Instructor. Educ: B.A., Inst. of Secondary Educ., Camaguey, Cuba, 1957; Ed.D., Univ. of Havana, 1973; M.A., Univ. of Md., Coll. Pk., U.S.A. Appts: Instr., Spanish & Spanish Am. Lang. & Lit., var. schls. & colls., Cuba, 1961-63; Jrnlst., Min. of Labor mags. & reviews, Cuba, 1964-67; Instr., Spanish Lang., Univ. of Md., Coll. Pk., U.S.A., 1968-; Lectr., Spanish, Spanish Am. Lang. & Lit., Western Md. Coll., Westminster, Md., 1968-. Mbrships. Am. Assn. Tchrs. Spanish & Portuguese; Circle of Panamerican Culture; Cuban Drs. in Educ. Nat. Assn. in Exile. Author, The Wanderer (poetry), 1971. Contbr., poetry, var. mags., Cuba, Argentina, Spain, Italy, Mexico, etc. Recip., 1st Prize for Poetry, State Coun. of Culture Award, Cuba, 1963. Address: Hannah More Campus, Route 140, Reisterstown, MD 21136, U.S.A. 125.

ZAMBETAKIS, Emmanuel, b. 15 Oct. 1919. School Inspector. Educ: Schl. of Philos. Univ. of Athens, Greece; Dr.Ph., Schl. of Philos., Sorbonne, Paris, France. Appts: Dir., Trng. Coll., 1959-72; Gen. Insp. of High & Elem. Schls., Crete, Greece, 1972-74. Publs: Educational Bibliography, 1956; Greek Educational Bibliography, 1966; Teaching Methods of the Subjects Taught in Our Schools, 1970. Author of eleven essays on the 19th Century Revolutions in Crete, based on official documents. Contbr. of articles to the Great Paedagogical Encyclopaedia & to sev. profl. jrnls. Address: 65, King George II Ave., Heraklion, Crete, Greece.

ZAMBROWSKY, Seymour M., 15 Apr. 1911. Rabbi. Educ: Colls. in U.S.A.; Postgrad. courses in philos., psychol. & lit.; Rabbinical Sem. Appts. incl: Exec. Dir., Mizrachi Zionist Youth Org. of Am.; Nat. V.P., ibid; Ed. of publs.; Rabbi, Cleveland Heights Jewish Ctr., Ohio; Mbr., praesedium, Rabbinical Coun. of Cleveland; Lectr., Jewish Tchrs.' Inst., Cleveland; Advsr., Cleveland Hts. City Coun. on

religious matters; Deleg., Am. Jewish Conf., N.Y.C. & Pittsburgh, Pa.; Nat. Exec. Sec., Mizrachi-Zionist Org. of Am.; Ldr., Zionist Emergency Coun. of Am.; Pres., Mizrachi Zionist Org. of Canada, Bd. of Dirs., World Jewish Nat. Fund. Mbrships. incl: Pres., Bd. of Jewish Mins. of Greater Montreal, Quebec, Canada; Nat. Family Conf.; Soc. Planning Comm., Jewish Fedn. for Community Servs.; Organizer, all-Canadian Conf. of Rabbis.; Chmn., Mizrachi Hapoel Hamizrachi World Org. Contbr. of articles to newspapers; radio broadcaster. Hons: Dr. Churgin Award of Educ.; Canadian Govt. Award. Address: 4984 Victoria Ave., Montreal, Canada. 55.

ZAN, (Rev.) Augustine Juraj, b. 1 June 1911. Author; Educator. Educ: Th.M., Theol. Fac. Nitra, Univ. of Bratislava, Czechoslovakia. Ordained, 1935. Appts: Asst. & Pastor, 1937-45; Papal Deleg. for Refugees, 1946-50; Tchr., Albany, N.Y., 1952-62; Chap., Prof. of Theol., Tchr. Trng. Coll., S. Heart, Danville, Pa., 1962-73. Mbrships: Assn. Int. Writers & Authors; Slovak League of Am.; Corres., Jednota; 3rd degree, Kt. of Columbus. Publs: The Light in The Darkness; Jehovah Witnesses; Cathechism of the Adults (2 eds.); From the Eternal Sources; Our Way; Return to the Father; Our Truth; Our Life; Our All; The Word of God; 900 articles of pastoral & theol. concern in religious jrnls. Recip. of Papal Citation, 1967 & '69. Address: Maria Joseph Manor, Danville, PA 17821, U.S.A. 49.

ZANDER, Josef, b. 19 June 1918. Medical Doctor. Educ: Studied med., Univs. of Marburg, Heidelberg & Tübingen, German Fed. Repub., 1941-46; Med. state exam. & M.D. 1946; Dept. of Pathol., Univ. of Tübingen, 1946; Kaiser-Wilhelm Inst. of Biochem., Tübingen, 1947-49; Dept. of Ob. & Gyn., Univs. of Marburg & Cologne, 1949-56. Appts: Rsch. Assoc., Dept. of Biochem., Univ. of Utah, Salt Lake City, U.S.A., 1956-57; Hd. Physn., Dept. of Ob. & Gyn., Univ. of Cologne, German Fed. Repub., 1958-64; Prof. & Chmn., Dept. of Ob. & Gyn., Univ. of Heidelberg, 1964-69; Prof. & Chmn., 1st Dept. of Ob. & Gyn., Univ. of Munich, 1970-. Mbrships: Fellow, Am. Coll. of Surgs.; Endocrine Soc.; Soc. of Pelvic Surgs.; Deutsche Gesellschaft für Gynäkologie & Geburtshilfe; Deutsche Gesellschaft für Endokrinologie. Author of about 200 publs. in var. int. & German jrnls. Hon: Deutsche Akad. der Naturforscher Leopoldina, Halle. Address: I. Frauenklinik & Hebammenschule der Univ. Munich, Maistrasse 11, 8000 Munich 2, German Fed. Repub. 92.

ZANDY, Hassan F., born 11 Mar. 1912. Professor of Physics. Educ: B.Sc., M.Sc., Univ. of Birmingham, U.K.; Ph.D., Univ. of Tehran, Iran. Appts: Instr., Phys., Coll. of Engrng., Univ. of Tehran, 1937-46; Asst. Prof., ibid, 1950-53; Assoc. Prof., Phys., Coll. of Arts & Sci., Univ. of Bridgeport, U.S.A., 1954-66; Prof., ibid, 1967-. Mbrships. incl: Am. Assn. Adv. of Sci.; Am. Assn. Univ. Profs.; Am. Inst. Phys. Contbr. of Sci. articles to Proc. Phys. Soc., U.K.; Nature; Phys. Rev.; Phys. Tchr. Hons. incl: Fac. Rsch. Grant, 1969-70; Gold Medal & Citations, 1949, '64, '69; Fulbright Fellowships, 1953-54. Address: Dept. of Phys., Univ. of Bridgeport, Bridgeport, Conn. 06602, U.S.A. 6, 14, 28.

ZANELLA, Silvio, b. 9 Oct. 1918. Painter. Educ: Studies at Acad. Fine Arts, Brera, Milan. Italy. Appts: Fndr., 1st Nat. City Art Gall., 1950; Registrar & Curator, Civil Gall. Mod. Art, Gallarate; Dir., Artistic, Archaeolog. & Histl. Studies Mus., ibid. Mbr. num. Italian, American & Swiss Acads.; Lions. Creative Works: 45

1-man exhibs., inclng: Cavallino Gall., Venice, Italy; Bussola Gall., Turin, ibid; Bergamini & Gianferrari Galls., Milan; Defacqz Gall., Brussels, Belgium; Kontakt Gall., Anversa & Likum Gall., Zagabria; Pntngs. exhib. in Mod. Art Mus. in Florence, Pisa, Undine, Jesi, Malerata, Saronno, Gallarate, Ancona & at for. Muss. in N.Y., U.S.A.; Paris, France; Moscow, U.S.S.R.; Madrid, Spain; Stockholm, Sweden, etc. Publd. 5 Monographs, 1966-72. Hons. incl: 1st Prizes at Trieste, 1953; Pavia, 1964; Terni, 1952, '54; Gallarate, 1950, '57; Capo d'Orlando, 1963; Saronno, 1964; Busto Arsizio, 1965; Int. European Art Prize, Ancona, 1965; Int. Prize, Auronzo, 1966; Ponzone Biellese, 1966; Sciacca, 1967. Address: Abitazione Estudio, Via R. Sanzio 20, Gallarate (VA) 21013, Italy.

ZANGANEH, Ahmed Ebrahimi, b. 1914. Company President. Educ: Dipl. Ing. (E.I.T., E.S.E., P.T.T., Paris); Ph.D.; Special course, London Univ., U.K. Appts: Pres., Bd. of Dirs., Kermanshah Sugar Co. & Lorestan Sugar Co.; Pres., Indl. Credit Bank, Iran & Now-Kar Co.; Bd. mbr., Investment & Dev. Bank, Fars-Khozestan Cement Co.; Dir., sugar factories; Gen. Dir., Labour & Arts Min.; Asst. Gen., ibid; Min. of Econ.; Min. of P.T.T.; Gen. Mgr., Plan Org.; Prof., Teheran Univ. Mbrships: Iran-France Club; Engrs.' Inst. Author of High Tension (Electricity). Recip., Medallion of Teheran Univ. Address: Kuyesahabgharanieh, Mina Ave., Teheran, Iran.

ZANGWILL, Estelle R., b. 8 Mar. 1929. Speech Pathologist. Educ: B.S., Univ. of Pitts., 1950; M.S., ibid, 1963. Speech Pathologist, Speech Clin. of Children's Hosp., Pitts., 1963-. Mbrships: Am. Speech & Hearing Assn.; Bd., local chapt., World Federalists; Chartiers Mental Hlth.-Mental Retardation Assn.; Aux., Allegheny Co. Med. Soc. Address: 109 Oak Park Pl., Pitts., PA 15243, U.S.A. 5, 138.

ZANGWILL, Willard Ira, b. 18 Mar. 1938. Professor; Management Consultant. Educ: A.B., Columbia Univ., 1959; M.S., Stanford Univ., 1963; Ph.D., ibid, 1965. Appts: (former) Assoc. Prof., Univ. of Calif., Berkeley & Am. Univ., Wash.D.C.; Special Asst. of Admin., Nat. Aeronautics & Space Admin., U.S. Govt.; Dir., Educl. Evaluation, Dept. of Hlth., Educ. & Welfare, U.S. Govt.; Pres., Sullivan Educl. Systems; currently Prof., Univ. of Ill., Urbana. Mbrships: Inst. of Mgmt. Scis.; Ops. Rsch. Soc.; Phi Beta Kappa; Dept. Ed., Management Sci., 1968. Publs: Nonlinear Programming—A Unified Approach, 1969; about 40 articles in profl. jrnls. Recip. Fellowships, Nat. Sci. Fndn., 1963 & Ford Fndn., 1967. Address: c/o University of Illinois, Urbana, IL, U.S.A.

ZAPHIRIS, Leonidas J., b. 30 Sept. 1893. Insurance Executive. Educ: Coll. of St. Jean Baptiste de la Salle, Rhodes; corres. studies, Oxford, U.K. Appts: Cotton Merchant, Egypt, 1912; Isn. Specialist, Greece, 1971; Gen. Agt. & Legal Rep. in Greece for La Prevoyance grp. of fire, marine & accident ins. cos., Paris, France, 1932; Gen. Agt. for Mannheimer Versicherungs-AG, Mannheim, Germany; Fndr., Pres. of Bd., & main share-holder, Lloyd-Hellenique Compagnie Ame. d'Assurances, Athens. Mbrships: Philos. Club; Parnassos Athens; Rotary Club, Athesn; Phenix Masonic Lodge, Athens; Deutscher Verein für Versicherungswissenschaft e.V. Berlin. Var. articles & papers, ins. subjects. Address: Lloyd-Hellenique, 59 University Ave., Athens 131, Greece. 43.

ZARA, Louis, b. 2 Aug. 1910. Author; Editor. Educ: Crane Jr. Coll., Chgo.; Univ. of Chgo. Appts: Dir., Book Div. & V.P., Ziff-Davis Publishing Co., 1946-53 & 1958-62; Ed.-in-Chief, Masterpieces, 1950; Pres., Publrs. Cons. Inc., 1954-56; Ed.-in-Chief, Trade Books, Follett Publishing Co., 1962-65; Ed.-in-Chief, Mineral Digest, 1969-. Mbrships. incl: Fellow, Royal Numismatic Soc.; Fellow, Am. Numismatic Soc.; Authors' Guild; Authors' League of Am.; Mineralogical Soc. of Am.; PEN; O'seas Press Club of Am. Publs. incl: Novels: Blessed is the Man, 1935; Give Us this Day, 1936; This Land is Ours, 1940; Against this Rock, 1943; Ruth Middleton, 1946; Rebel Run, 1951; In the House of the King, 1952; Blessed is the Land, 1954; Dark Rider, 1961; Non-fiction: Jade, 1969; Locks & Keys, 1969; short stories in mags., anthols. & textbooks. Hons: Fndn. for Lit. Award, 1940; Daroff Mem. Fiction Prize, 1955. Address: 35 E. 35th St., N.Y., NY 10016, U.S.A. 2, 6.

ZARISH, Joseph Frederick, b. 13 Mar. 1919. Furniture Manufacturing Executive. Educ: B.S., Univ. of Ill., 1940; Postgrad., Northwestern Havana Bus. Univ. Appts: Fndr., export co., Havana, Cuba, 1946; Salesman, 1946-48, Mgr., Chgo. Off., 1947, Asst. to Pres., 1948, Salmanson & Co., N.Y.C.; Nat. Sales & Merchandising Mgr., Sealy Inc., Chgo., 1948-53; V.P. Merchandising, Schnadig Corp. & Subs. Int., Karpen, 1956; V.P. Mktng., Schnadig Corp., 1958-60; Pres., Flagship Enterprises, 1950-65; Pres., Award Exhibs. Inc., 1956-62; V.P. Mktng. & Dir., Strokline Corp., 1961-62; Pres. & Dir., Chamberlin Metal Prod. Co., 1962-64; Dir., Sandymac Corp., 1961-63; Pres., Canterbury House, Peru, Ind., 1964-; Cons., Savings Bonds Div., U.S. Sec. Treas. Staff. Mbrships: Steering Comm., Nat. Conf. Christians & Jews; Mbrship. Chmn., Mississinewa Reservoir Dev. Assn.; Chmn., Miami Co. Heart Fund Ind. Gifts, 1971-72; Chmn., Ind. Div. Miami Co. Heart Fund, 1971-74; Bd. of Trustees, Delta Phi, 1970-; Treas., 1974, Bd. of Dirs., Chgo. Chapt., Am. Diabetic Assn.; Exec. Comm., Treas., 1974, United Fund, Peru, Ind.; Peru Circus, 1971-; Clarence Darrow Community Ctr., Hull House, 1969-; Peru Chmbr. of Comm., 1965-; Alpha Kappa Psi. Publs: promotional booklets; articles in sales jrnls. Recip., Kimberly Clark Promotional Award, 1953. Address: 1275 Warwick Ct., Deerfield, IL 60015, U.S.A. 139.

ZARRAS, John, b. 1 Dec. 1903. Lecturer; Civil Servant. Educ: Law degree, Fac. of Law, Athens Univ., Greece, 1922; LL.D., Schl. of Law, Paris, France, 1937; Rsch. Fellowship, Rockefeller Fndn., 1934-36; Fellowship, Acad. of Int. Law, The Hague, Netherlands, 1939; Rsch. work. Ph.D., Schl. of Econ., London Univ., U.K., 1942. Appts: Greek Govt. del. & U.N. rep., int. confs., 1934-65; w. Greek Min. of Labour, 27 yrs., Dir.-Gen., 1942-47; Soc. & Snr. Soc. Affairs Off., U.N., 1947-64; Lectr., Athens Univ., 1950-; Chief, Div. of Soc. Affairs, European Off., U.N., 1963-64; Cons., Soc. Policy, Greek Min. of Coord., 1965; Sec.-Gen., Min. of Labour, 1965-67. Mbrships: Exec. Comm. & Govng. Bd., YWCA Schl. of Soc. Work; V.P., Govng. Bd., Greek Assn. for U.N. & other socs.; Athen's Club. Author num. soc. & econ. publs.; & sev. articles on soc. policy, pub. in Greek & for. reviews. Hons: Greek & for. decorations; Prize for best dr.'s thesis of yr., Schl. of Law, Paris Univ., France, 1937. Address: 8 Pittakou St., Athens, 119, Greece. 43.

ZARZYCKI, Jerzy (George) Marian, b. 21 June 1925. Engineer. Educ: M.Sc.Eng., Warsaw Tech. Univ., Poland, 1948; D.Sc.Eng., Swiss Fed. Inst. of Technol., Zurich, 1952. Appts: Rsch. Engr., Instr. Photogrammetry, Swiss Fed.

Inst. Technol., Zurich, 1948-51; Rsch. Scientist, Wild Co., Heerbrugg, Switzerland, 1951-52; NRC Can. Fellow, 1952-53; Chief Engr., V.P., Canadian Aero Serv., Ltd., Ottawa, 1953-66; Pres., Terra Surveys, Ltd., Ottawa, 1966-; Dir., ibid & Terra Surveys Holdings, Ltd.; Guest Prof., Photogrammetry, Laval Univ., Quebec City, 1964-. Mbrships. incl: Bd. of Dirs., Treas., 12th Int. Cong. for Photogrammetry, Ottawa; Dir., Nat. Arts Ctr. Orch. Assn.; Bd. of Specialization, Assn. Profl. Engrs. Ont.; Pres., Canadian Inst. of Surveying, 1972-73. Author, num. scientific & tech. articles. Address: 23 Helene Boulay Dr., Lucerne, P.Q., T9H 5E2, Canada. 6.

ZASLOW, Jerry, b. 29 Mar. 1918. Surgeon; Attorney. Educ: M.D., Temple Univ. Med. Schl., Phila., Pa., 1940; M.S., Mayo Clin., Univ. of Minn., 1947; J.D., Temple Univ. Law Schl., Phila., Pa., 1971. Appts: Surg., Fellow, Mayo Clin., 1944-47; Assoc. Surg., Albert Einstein Med. Ctr., Phila., 1947-; Chmn., Dept. Surg., John F. Kennedy Mem. Hosp., ibid, 1963-, Rolling Hill Hosp., Elkins Pk., Pa., 1952-; Sr. Attng. Surg., Latter Two Hosp. Mbrships: Sigma Xi; Dir., Phila. Co. Med. Soc.; Fellow, Am. Coll. Surg., Int. Coll. Surg., Am. Assn. Abdominal Surgs., AMA, Pa. State Med. Soc., Am. Coll. Legal Med.; Am. Bar Assn.; Pa. Bar Assn.; Phila. Bar Assn.; Trial Lawyers Assn.; Lawyers' Club of Phila.; Phila. Acad. Surg. Contbr. of articles to profl. jrnls. Address: 1420 Academy Ln., Elkins Pk., PA 19117, U.S.A. 6.

ZAUNMÜLLER, Wolfram Bruno, b. 9 Apr. 1923. Owner of Translation Bureau. Educ: D.phil., Univ. of Graz, Austria, 1950; Tchr.'s exam., 1950. Appts: Judicial Interpreter, Engl. & Italian; Owner, Translation Bur., Linz, 1950-. Mbrships: Speech Soc. of Vienna; Dante Alighieri Soc., Linz; Austro-Scandinavian Soc., Linz; Austro-Ibero Club, Linz. Publs: Books on lang., inclng. Index Lexicorum, 1959; Exhibs. of paintings & drawings. Address: Translation Bur. Dr. W. Zaunmüller, Auerspergstr. 19, A-4020 Linze, Austria. 86.

ZAVALA, Albert, b. 10 Mar. 1930. Psychologist. Educ: B.A., Willamette Univ., 1959; M.A., Mich. State Univ., 1969; Ph.D., Kan. State Univ., 1966. Appts. incl: Asst. Dir., Skills Rsch. Prog., Am. Inst. for Rsch., Wash., 1964-67; Adjunct Prof., State Univ. Coll., Buffalo, 1968-; Prin. Psychologist, Hd. Life Scis., Calspan Corp., Buffalo, 1967-73; Exec. Dir., Mental Hlth. Servs., Erie Co. Corp. IV, Buffalo, 1973-. Mbrships. incl: Cons., U.S. Cabinet Assn.; AAAS; Human Factors Soc.; Interam. Soc. Psychol.; Int. Assn. Identificatio; Sigma Xi; Psi Chi; Exec. Comm., Buffalo State Hosp.; Exec. Comm., Erie Co. Dept. of Mental Hlth. Publs: Personal Appearance Identification (co-ed.), 1971; Determining the Hierarchical Structure of a Body of Information, 1971. Recip. of fellowships. Address: 3465 Broadway, Cheektowaga, NY 14227, U.S.A. 6, 14, 131.

ZAVITZIUNOS, George, b. 24 Dec. 1909. Physician; Psychoanalyst. Educ: Med. Schl., Univ. of Montpellier, France, 1928-33; Grad., Paris Psychoanalytic Soc., 1950. Appts: Tchng., Sprvsng. & Trng. Analyst, Canadian Psychoanalytic Soc., 1951-61; Tchng., Sprvsng. & Trng. Analyst, Canadian Psychoanalytic Inst., 1961-; Sr. Lectr., Dept. of Psych., Div. Psychoanalytic Educ., Downstate Med. Ctr., SUNY, 1962-66; Assoc. Prof. Psych., McGill Univ., Montreal, 1968-72; Clin. Assoc. Prof. Psych., Georgetown Univ., 1972-. Mbrships. incl: Fellow, Am. Psychiatric Assn.; Charter Fellow, Am. Coll. Psychoanalysts; Charter Mbr., Canadian Psychoanalytic Soc., & Inst.;

Int. Psychoanalytic Assn.; Am. Psychoanalytic Assn. Num. contbns. profl. jrnls. inclng. Int. Jrnl. Psycho-Analysis. Address: 10201 Grosvernor Pl., Apt. 410, N. Bethesda, MD 20852, U.S.A.

ZAWADZKI, Michal I(gnacy), b. 29 Sept. 1915. Economist. Educ: M.S. Warsaw, Poland, 1938; B.Litt., Oxford Univ., U.K., 1951; Ph.D., Univ. of Ill., U.S.A., 1955. Appts: Asst. Agric. Econ., Bristol Univ., U.K., 1950-51; Rsch. Assoc., Univ. of Chgo., U.S.A., 1955; Asst. Prof., Agric. Econs., R.I. Univ., 1955-59; Asst. Prof., Econs., Loyola Univ., L.A., Calif., 1959-61; Statn., State of Calif. Motor Vehicle Pollution Control Bd., 1961-65; Assoc. Resources Econ., Dept. of Water Resources, Calif., 1965-; Tchr., pt.-time, Calif. State Coll., 1964-. Mbrships: Am. Agric. Econ. Assn.; Western Agric. Econ. Assn.; var. Polish Am. Socs. Publs: Rhodesia, 1943; Co-author, Poland, 1955; Egg Supply & Marketing in the N.C. Region, 1954; Factors Affecting Consumption of Dry Skim & the Evaporated Milk in R.I., 1960. Address: 1911 Parnell Ave., L.A., CA 90025, U.S.A. 9, 14.

ZAWORSKI, Kathleen Mae, b. 1 Feb. 1944. Educator. Educ: B.A., San Diego Coll. for Women, 1965; M.A., Baylor Univ., 1966; Standard Secondary Tchng. Credential, Univ. of San Diego, 1971; Standard Community Coll. Tchng. Credential, ibid, 1972. Appts: Tchr., Cathedral Girls' H.S., San Diego, Calif., 1964-65; Chmn., Dept. of Theatre Arts, Univ. of San Diego, 1966-72; Tchr., Speech Arts & Hist., Miramar Coll., San Diego, Calif., 1972-. Mbrships: Sec., Univ. of San Diego Chapt., AAUP, 1967-68; Am. Educl. Theatre Assn.; Kappa Gamma Pi. Dir. of several prods., Univ. of San Diego: The Glass Menagerie, 1966; The Little Foxes, 1967; An Evening With Contemporary American Playwrights, 1968; The Member of the Wedding, 1969; The Absence of a Cello, 1970; The Firebugs, 1970; Lovers, 1971. Recip., Best Actress Award, Univ. of San Diego, 1963-64. Address: 2879 Freeborn Way, El Cajon, CA 92020, U.S.A. 5.

ZAYDON, Jemille Ann, b. 21 Feb. 1940. Educator. Educ: B.S., Marywood Coll., Scranton, Pa., 1963; Postgrad. work, var. colls., 1963-73. Appts. incl: Columbus Elem. Schl., Westfield, N.J. Schl. System, 1965-66; Remedial Reading Instr. & Acad. Coord. for dev. of progs. in educ. & trng., residential affairs, personnel & P.R., Keystone Job Corps Ctr. for Women, RCA Serv. Co., Drums, Pa., 1966-73; Curric. Cons. for the Mentally Retarded, Vienna, Austria, 1974. Mbrships. incl: Life mbr., Sigma Tau Delta Int.; Life mbr., Lambda Iota Tau; Charter Pres., Theta Chi Beta; Affiliated, Nat. Assn. for Retarded Children; NEA. Publs. incl: The Keystone Job Corps Description & Student Handbook, 1967; Ed., Lebonese Am. Jrnl., 1957-65. Hons. incl: Educator's Award, Dade Co., Fla., 1973; Ph.D., Colo. Christian Coll., Evergreen, 1973. Address: 608 N. Main Ave., Scranton, PA 18504, U.S.A. 5, 138.

ZDZISŁAW, Slinwiński, b. 20 July 1910. Musician. Appts: Hd., Sect., Dept. of Music, Min. of Art & Culture, 1945-46; Vice Dir., Polish Music Publ, Cracow, 1946-47; Gen. Dir., Poznan Philharmonic Orch., 1946-58; Nat. Philharmonic Orch., Warsaw, 1958-69; Gen. Dir., Grand Opera House, Teatr Wielki, Warsaw, 1965-; Mbr., Org. Comm., Inst. Chopin Competition, 1949-; Presidium, Autumn in Warsaw Int. Fests. of Contemp. Music, 1958-; Pres., Org. Comm., Int. Henryk Wieniawski Violin Competition, Pozana, 1952-57. Mbr., Assn. of Authors, Zaiks, Warsaw. Contbr. to newspapers & periodicals. Hons: Gold Cross of Merit, 1952; Kt., Order of Polonia Restituta, 1959; Officer, ibid, 1969; Gold Order of Merit, Warsaw City, 1972; Deserving Cultural Wkr., 1968. Address: Kredytowa 8, 1.44, Warsaw, Poland. 34.

ZEBDI, Kamel, b. 17 July 1927. Poet; Artist; Painter. Educ: Dip., Schl. of the Louvre, Paris, France. Appts: Mus. Curator; Cultural Attache, Moroccan Embassy, Paris; Cultural Attache, Moroccan Embassy, Copenhagen, Denmark. Author, 3 collects. of poems. Exhibs. of paintings, Morocco & other countries. Hons: Prize, French Acad., 1961; Prize of Morocco, 1973. Address: 2 Rue Zebdi, Rabat, Morocco.

ZECH, Walter, b. 12 Nov. 1918. Publisher. Educ: Bank trng., Poensgen, Marx & Co., Düsseldorf, Germany. Appts: Publishers' trng., Die Welt, 1947-49; Publ. Dir., Textil-Export-Jrnl. & Elegante Welt, Düsseldorf, 1950-52; Publ. Dir., VDI-Verlag GmbH, Düsseldorf, 1952-62; Publisher & Mag. Assoc., Mainzer Verlagsanstalt & Druckerei Will & Rothe KG, Mainz, & subsidiary cos., 1962-. Mbrships. incl: B:orsenverein für den deutschen Buchhandel; Ind. Club, Düsseldorf; Union Interalliée, Paris, France; Int. Gutenberggesellschaft, e.V., Mainz; Kulturkreis, Bundesverband der deutschen Ind.; Kuratorium Deutsche Sporthilfe, e.V., Frankfurt; Hon. mbr., Fachverband Zeitungsdruck; Hon. V.P., Fedn. Int. de la Presse Périodique, London, U.K. Hons: Ring of hon., Mainz, 1968;Disting. serv. medal, German Fed. Repub., 1968; Address: Pressehaus, Postfach 3120, D-6500 Mainz, German Fed. Repub.

ZECKENDORF, William, Jr., b. 31 Oct. 1929. Real Estate Executive. Educ: Univ. of Ariz., 1950. Appts: U.S. Army, 1952-54; Pres., Webb & Knapp, 1962-65; Chmn. Bd., Gen. Property Corp.; Dir., Chmn Bd., Soc. Hill Towers Inc., Phila.; Chmn. Bd., Domaine LaBelle Pl., Montreal, P.Q.; Pres., Mayfair House, N.Y.C.; Pres., Lincoln Towers; Dir., Gen. Leisure, Inc.; Chmn., Real Estate Comm.; Mbr. Exec. Bd. N.Y. Coun. Boy Scouts of Am.; Mbr., Bd. Trustees, L.I. Univ., Chmn. of Bd., Bldg. & Grounds Comm., Educ. Policies Comm. Mbrships: Officier Commandeur, Confrerie des Chevaliers du Tastevin; Ambassadeurs Club, London, U.K. Address: Croton Lake Rd., Mt. Kisco, NY, U.S.A.

ZELLER, Bernhard, b. 19 Sept. 1919. Museum & Archives Director. Educ: Studied hist., German & Latin, 1943, 1945-50; Grad., 1949; 1st & 2nd state exams., 1950, 1951. Appts: Asst., Kultusministerium, Stuttgart, German Fed. Repub. & positions as tchr., 1950-53; Archivist, 1953-; Dir., Schiller Nat. Mus. & Deutsche Literaturarchiv, 1955-. Mbrships: Akad. der Wissenschaften & Literatur, Mainz; Kommn. für geschichtliche Landeskunde, Baden-Württemberg; Germanistische Kommn., Deutsche Forschungsgemeinschaft; Acting Chmn., Württembergischer Geschicts- & Altertumsverein. Publs: Das Heilig-Geist-Spital in Lindau am Bodensee, 1952; Schiller, 1958; Hermann Hesse. Eine Chronik in Bildern, 1960; Hermann Hesse, 1963; Kurt Wolff Briefwechsel eines Verlegers (w. Ellin Otten); Co-ed., Yrbook. of Deutsche Schillergesellschaft & histl.-critical edit. of the works & letters of Eduard Mörike. Address: Postfach 57, 7142 Marbach a. N., German Fed. Repub.

ZELLMER, Kathleen O'Toole, b. 14 Sept. 1916. Educator. Educ: B.S., Miami Univ., Oxford, Ohio; M.A., Western Reserve Univ., Cleveland, Ohio, 1955; Grad. work, Univ. of Chgo., Ill., 1957-59; Newspaper Fund Fellow, Seton Hall, E. Orange, N.J., 1965; Ph.D., Am. Univ., Wash. D.C., 1972. Appts. incl: Tchr., gifted students, Highland Park, Ill., 1957-61; Dir., Reading Clin., Temple Sch., Wash. D.C., 1961-63; Prin., Rev. Thomas Daniels Greek Schl., Wash. D.C., 1963-64; Tchr., Eastern H.S., Wash. D.C., 1964-; Sr. Engl. Advsr., award winning Easterner, schl. newspaper; Dir., Urban Jrnlsm. Workshop, Am. Univ., 1968-71; Educl. Cons., civic grps., curric. & philos. Mbrships. incl: Publicity Chmn., Phi Delta Gamma; Schlrship. Chmn., Theta Sigma Phi; Alumni Pres., Kappa Delta Epsilon; Ohio State Dir., Status of Women, AAUW, 1950-52; Publicity Chmn., Nat. Coun. Tchrs. of Engl. conven., 1968. Author of educl. books & articles; Poetry publd. in newspapers & one anthol. Recip. of hons. Address: 5603 Ontario Circle, Sumner, MD 20016, U.S.A. 5.

ZENICH, Margrett Barton, b. 4 Dec. 1915. Librarian & Information Scientist. Educ: B.A., Southeastern State Coll., Okla., 1938; B.A. in Lib. Sci., Univ. of Okla., 1951; Special Cert. in Aircraft Engrng., Okla. Univ.; Special Student, Univ. of Tex. Appts: Tchr., 1938-39; Procurement Agt., U.S. Army Air Force; Libn., Okla. City Pub. Schls., 1947-51; Libn., White Sands Missile Range N.M., 1951-54; Tech. Libn., ibid, 1954-68; Chief, Sci. & Tech. Info. Div., Off. Chief of Engrs., Wash. D.C., 1968-. Mbrships. incl: ALA; Pres., Rio Grande Chapt., Chmn., Documentation Div., Special Lib. Assn.; Co-Sponsor, Fed. Interagency Field Libns.' Workshop. Chmn., Long Range Planning Comm. for Army Libs. Workshop; Am. Soc. for Testing & Masts.; Am. Soc. for Engrng. Educ. Publs: Co-author, Funding Library Research in the Federal Government; articles in Drexel Lib. Quarterly. Address: 4712 Poplar Dr., Alexandria, VA 22310, U.S.A. 5, 7, 22, 132, 138.

ZENNER, Hans O., b. 1 Mar. 1918. Librarian. Educ: Ph.D., Univ. of Cologne, Germany, 1954; M.A.L.S., Kent State Univ., U.S.A., 1958. Appts: Prof., For. Langs., Sioux Falls Coll., S.D., 1955-58; Libn., ibid, 1958-66; Libn., Thiel Coll., Greenville, Pa., 1966-. Mbrships: ALA; Delta Phi Alpha; Nat. Geog. Soc. Author of A History of the Library of Sioux Falls College. Named Citizen of the Week, Sioux Falls Argus Ldr., 1965. Address: 111 Clinton St., Greenville, PA 16125, U.S.A. 6, 15.

ZEPHIRIN, Clifford F., b. 23 June 1923. Bakery Proprietor. m. Dorothy Rosalind Dash, 2 s., Mark & Andre, 2 d., Diane & Yolande. Appts: Govng. Dir., C.F. Zephirin Ltd., Bakers & Mfrs. Reps. Mbrships: Vice Chmn., Barbados Dev. Bank; Fellowship, Inst. of British Bakers; Flour Milling & British Baking Rsch. Assn.; Coun., Jr. Cmbr. of Comm. Address: P.O. Box 7, Bridgetown, Barbados, W. Indies. 109.

ZEPOS, Panayotis, b. 1 Dec. 1908. University Professor. Educ: Dr. iur., Univ. of Athens, Greece, 1931; Berlin, Germany, 1931-33. Appts. incl: Prof., Fac. Law, Univ. of Thessaloniki, Greece, 1940; Dean, ibid, 1945; Prof., Fac. Law, Univ. of Athens, 1953; Dean, ibid, 1959; Dir., Hellenic Inst. of Int. & For. Law, 1960; Mbr., Athens Acad., 1970. Mbrships. incl: Pres., Govng. Coun., Hellenic Archaeol. Soc.; Soc. of Byzantine Studies; Int. Inst. for Unification of Pvte. Law, 1960-73. Publs. incl: Jus Graecorumanum, vols. I-VIII, 1931, 62; Greek Law, 1949; Law of Obligations, 2 vols., 1955-65; Nomiken Prochieron of M. Photeinopoulos 1875, 1959; num. articles in field. Hons. incl: Dr.iur., Univ. of Freiburg/Breisgau, 1957; Off., Order of the

Phoenix, 1952; Xenion (Festschrift for Pan J. Zepos), 1973. Address: Homer St. 18, Athens 135, Greece. 43.

ZERLENTIS, Constantin, b. 2 Apr. 1917. Professor. Educ: Dir., Sci., Agric. Coll., Athens, Greece; Saloniki Univ., ibid; Postgrad. study, U.K., U.S.A. & W. Germany. Currently, Prof., Systematic Bot., Agric. Coll., Athens, Greece. Publs: Contbr., Plant Geography of the Cyclades Islands, 1952 & Flora of Mount Hymettus, 1965; Author sci. jrnl. papers: Uber Wirkstoffe der Condurangin-Gruppe in Marsdenia erecta R.Br. (w. D. Frohne), 1962; Untersuchungen über die Wirkung des in Marsdenia erects R.Br., 1965; Synoecological and toxicological studies on Marsdenia erect R.Br., 1958; Marsdenia erecta R.Br., eine in den östlichen Mittelmeerländern heimische keimungshemmende Giftpflanze der Asclepiadaceen, 1962; Blutzuckersenkende Teegemische, 1964; Die Glykoside von Marsdenia erecta R.Br. 1. Mittlg.: Isolierungen. (w. A. Saner, W. Stöcklin, T. Reichstein), 1970; Books: The Plants of the Lycabettus Hill, 1959; Toxic Species of the Genus Mercurialis, 1960; Contbr., the amelioration of poor pastures in Greece, 1958; Remarks on the exam. of Cannabis sativa L. samples, 1965. Address: Agricl. Coll. Athens, Dept. Systematic Botany, Botanikos Kipos, Iera Odos 75, Athens 301, Greece.

ZETLIN, Lev, b. 14 July 1918. Consulting Engineer; College Professor. Appts. incl: Chief Structural Engr., Israeli Air Force, 1947-50; Rsch. Assoc., Struct. Engrng., Cornell Univ., 1951-53; Asst. Prof., Civil Engrng., 1953-55; Vis. Prof., Manhattan Coll., N.Y., 1956-59; Guest Lectr. & Seminars, leading U.S. Univs., 1959-; Prof., Civil Engrng., Pratt Inst., N.Y., 1961-67; Prin. Lev Zetlin & Assocs., Cons. Engrs., 1956-; Currently, Prof. Engrng. & Arch., Univ. of Va. Mbrships: Chmn., Consultor Comm., Manhattan Coll.; Fellow & Mbr., sev. socs., e.g. Am. Soc. of Civil Engrs. & Am. Soc. of Mil. Engrs. Publs. incl: Chapt. on 'Stadiums' in Ency. Britannica; Contbr. of articles to profl. publs. on concrete & concrete structures & suspension structures. Hons: Gold Medal, Soc. Arts, Scis., Lettres, French Acad., 1969; Kts. of Malta, Order of St. John of Jerusalem. Address: 95 Madison Ave., N.Y., NY 10016, U.S.A. 6, 14, 28, 128.

ZHUKOV, Georgi Alexandrovich, b. 23 Apr. 1908. Journalist. Educ: Lomonosov Int., Moscow. Appts: Jrnlst., Local Papers in Lugansk & Kharkov, 1927-32, Komsomolskaya Pravds, 1932-46, Pravda, 1946-47; Ed. Bd., Komsomolskaya Pravda, 1932-46; Paris Bur., Pravda, 1947-52; For. Ed., Pravda, 1952-57; Chmn., USSR Coun., Mins.' State Comm. for Cultural Rels. w. For. Countries, 1952-67; Pravda Pol. Commentator. Mbrships: Praesidium, World Peace Coun.; V.P., Soviet Comm. of Peace; Chmn., Soviet-French Parly. Grp.; For. Affairs Commn., Supreme Soviet of the USSR; Pres., USSR-France Soc. Publs. incl: Russians & Japan, 1945; Soldier's Life, 1946; The West After War, 1948; Three Months in Geneva, 1954; Japan, 1962; One MIG from a Thousand, 1963; These Seventeen Years, 1963; The People of the Thirties, 1964; Vietnam, 1965; America, 1967; The People of the Forties, 1968; Chilean Diary, 1970; The U.S.A. on the Threshold of the Seventies, 1970; People in the War, 1972; Thirty-three Visas, 1972; The Time of Great Changes, 1973. Hons: Orders of Lenin, Red Banner of Labour (2), & Red Star; Joliot-Curie Medal; Lenin Prize for Jrnlsm.; Vorovsky Prize; Union of Soviet Jrnlsts. Prize; Int. Org. of Jrnlsts. Prize. Address: 24 Pravda St., Moscow, USSR.

ZICKA FOOSE, Opal Lively, b. 19 Jan. 1919. Kindergarten Teacher. Educ: B.S., Concord Tchrs. Coll.; M.Ed., Univ. of Fla., postgrad. work in creative writing, sci. & early childhood educ. Appts: Tchr., elem. schls., W. Va., 19 yrs.; Tchr., 1st grade & kindergarten, Fla., 21 yrs.; currently w. Palma Sola Kindergarten, Bradenton, Fla. Mbrships: Past Pres., Trenton Womans Club, Gilchrist Educ. Assn., Concord Coll. Alumni Assn., Beta Tau Chapt., Alpha Delta Kappa, Nu Conclave of Kappa Kappa Iota; Past Worthy High Priestess, White Shrine of Jerusalem; Past Matron, Order of Eastern Star; Past Sec., PTA; AAUW; Democrat Womens Club; Jr. Sci. Mus. Bd. Author of book, China Cat Chan, & poems, Little Blue Eyes, Journey South. Address: 5724 22nd St. W., Bradenton, FL 33507, U.S.A. 125.

ZIEGLER, Hans Konrad, b. 1 Mar. 1911. Electronics Research & Development Executive. Educ: B.S., Tech. Univ. of Munich, Germany 1932, M.S., 1934, Ph.D., 1936. Appts: Chief Engr., later V.P. for Rsch. & Dev., Rosenthal Isolatoreu GmbH, Selb, Germany, 1936-47; Cons., Signal Corps Engrng. Labs., Ft. Monmouth, N.J., U.S.A., 1947-55; Asst., later Asst. Dir. for Rsch., 1955-58, Dir., Astro-Electronics Div., 1958-59, Chief Sci., U.S. Army Signal Rsch. & Dev. Labs., 1959-63, Chief. Sci. & Dpty. for Sci., U.S. Army Electronics Cmnd., 1963-71, Dir., U.S. Army Electronics Technol. & Devices Lab., 1971-. Mbr., Fellow & Off., profl. orgs. Some 40 publs., elec., electronical & space electronical fields. Holder, sev. patents. Hons. incl: Meritorious Serv. Awards, U.S. Govt., 1963, 1969; U.S. Antarctica Serv. Medal, 1964. Address: RD 1, E. Larchmont Dr., Colts Neck, NJ 07722, U.S.A. 2, 6, 14, 22, 68.

ZIEL, Ron, b. 17 July 1939. Artist; Writer; Photographer. Educ: B.F.A., Pratt Inst., Brooklyn, N.Y., 1961. Appts: Off., U.S. Army Signal corps; Asst. Art Dir. w. N.Y.C. advt. firm; w. Dan's Papers (L.I. publrs.) as Art Dir., Advt. Mgr., Exec. Ed., 1967-; Chmn. & Co-Chmn., var. Comms. & Local Govt. Commns. at Co. & town level to deal w. the Transportation & Energy Crisis. Extensive travel for purposes of photography & search for steam locomotives. Mbrships. incl: Steering Comm., Suffolk Co. Bicentennial Celebration Commn. Publs: The Twilight of Steam Locomotives, 1963; Story of Steamtown & Edaville, 1965; Steel Rails to the Sunrise (w. G.H. Foster), 1965; Steam in the Sixties (w. G.H. Foster), 1967; Steel Rails to Victory, 1970, German edit. 1973; Southern Steam Specials (w. M. Eagleson), 1970; Twilight of World Steam (w. M. Eagleson), 1973. Hons: Award for Steel Rails to Victory, N.Y. Book Publrs., 1970. Address: Box 433, Montauk Hwy., Bridgehampton, NY 11932, U.S.A.

ZIELONKA, (Rabbi) David M., b. 30 Apr. 1935. Ordained Rabbi; Lecturer. Educ: B.A., Univ. of Cinn., 1957; B. Hebrew Letters, Jewish Inst. of Religion, Cinn., 1959; M.A., ibid, 1962; Fellowship, 1962-64. Appts. incl: (Congl.) Valley Temple, Cinn., 1964-68; Temple B'nai Israel, Elmira, N.Y., 1968-73; Temple Covenant of Peace, Easton, Pa., 1973-; (Other) Chaplain, Veterans Admin. Ctr., N.Y., 1969-73; Lectr., Elmira Coll., 1969-70, Jewish Chautauqua Soc., 1968-; Pa. Federation of Temple Youth Ldrship. Inst., 1970-; Vis. Lectr., Bucknell Univ., 1974-. Publs: Manual of the Am. Jewish Archives (ed.), 1961; The Eager Immigrants (w. R.J. Wechman), 1972. Address: 2155 Gateway Ter., Easton, PA 18042, U.S.A. 6, 130.

ZIEMBA, Marifred Lebhart, b. 27 June 1928. Harpist. Educ: Mus.B., Univ. of Wyo.,

1951; grad. study, Univ. of Calif., L.A. Appts: Farmer Harpist, Colo. Symph., Denver, & Ariz. Symph., Phoenix; Instr. in harp, Univ. of S.C.; Harpist, Columbia Philharmonic Orch., S.C. Arts Commn. schl. concerts & Total Arts Proj. concerts; TV, radio & supper club appearances; pvte. tchng. Mbrships: Am. Harp Soc.; Sigma Alpha Iota; Organizer, Sumter (S.C.) Assn. for Retarded Children; Pres., ibid, 2 yrs.; Bd. of Dirs., S.C. Assn. for Retarded Children, 2 yrs. Address: 1024 Universal Dr., Columbia, SC 29209, U.S.A. 125.

ZILELI, Mehmet Seref, b. 11 July 1915. Medical Doctor. Educ: Grad., Istanbul Med. Schl., 1941; Res., Istanbul Univ. Hosp., 1949-53; Res., Binghamton City Hosp., N.Y., U.S.A., 1953-54; Fellow, Endocrinol., Colo. State Univ., 1954-55; Rsch. Fellow, Peter Bent Brigham Hosp., Harvard Univ., Boston, 1955-57. Appts: Pub. Hlth. Serv., Turkey, 1944-49; Assoc. Prof., Med., Med. Schl. Ankara, 1959; Prof., Chief in Med., Hacettepe Med. Schl., Ankara, 1964-73; Prof., Med., 1973-. Mbrships: Am. Endocrine Soc.; Turkish Physiol. soc. Publs: Sci. papers in Turkish, Am., Engl. & Swiss jrnls. Hons: A.E. Bennett Fndn. Award, San Fran., Calif., 1958. Address: Kocatepe Binektasi Sok. 31/8, Ankara, Turkey.

ZILLIACUS, (Johan) Henrik, b. 23 Jan. 1908. Professor of Greek Philology. Educ: Phil. magister, Helsinki Univ., 1930; Phil. dr. ibid, 1935. Appts: Lectr., Greek Philol., Helsinki Univ., 1938-44; Prof., Greek Lit., ibid, 1944-74; Dir., Inst. Romanum Finlandiae, Rome, 1956-59. Mbrships: Soc. Scientiarum Fennica, 1948-; Chmn., 1969-70; New Soc. of Letters, Lund, 1955-; Royal Danish Acad. of Scis. & Letters, 1972-; Ovidianum (Bucuresti), 1972-; Assn. Int. des Papyrologues; Assn. Int. di Archeol. Classica, Rome; Hellenic Soc., 1946. Author sev. publs. in field. Hons: Liberty Cross w. swords, 1942; Cmdr., White Rose of Finland, 1968; Cmdr., Order of Lion of Finland, 1952; Cmdr., Greek Phoenix Order, 1961; Cmdr., Stella della Solidarieta Italiana, 1960. Address: Parkgatan 9 B, 00140 Helsinki 14, Finland. 43.

ZILLIACUS, Ville V., b. 9 Apr. 1914. Broadcasting Executive. Educ: M.A., Helsinki Univ., Finland, 1936. Appts: Tchr., Colls., Finland, 1936-39; Prof., Finnish Lang. & Lit., Stockholm Univ., Sweden, 1941-50; Corres. for Scandinavia, Finnish Broadcasting Co., 1941-50; Asst. Dir., Radio, ibid, 1950-58; Hd., TV Progs., 1958-70; Dir., TV Progs., Channel 1; Hd., Int. Rels., 1970-. Hons: Lib. Cross, War Medal, 1939-40; Finn. Lion Ord.; Swedish Wasa Order. Address: Kauniainen, Finland. 90.

ZIMERING, Max, b. 4 Mar. 1907. Certified Public Accountant; Associate Professor of Accounting. Educ: B.B.A., CCNY, U.S.A., 1933; Cert. Pub. Acct., State of N.Y., 1936; M.B.A., N.Y. Univ., 1942. Appts. incl: Acct., Off. of Comptroller, Tax Dept., N.Y.C., 1935-38; Instr., Schl. of Bus., CCNY, 1938-48; Asst. Prof., Acctng., ibid, 1948-58; Assoc. Prof., 1958-68; Assoc. Prof., Acctng., Baruch Coll., 1968-. Mbrships. incl: Am. Inst. of Cert. Pub. Accts.; N.Y. State Soc. of Cert. Pub. Accts.; Am. Acctng. Assn.; Soc. of Municipal Accts.; Fed. Govt. Acctng. Assn.; Am. Profs. for Peace in the Middle East; Am. Jewish Comm.; Past Pres., Dist. 34, Zionist Org. of Am.; Pres., Alumni Assn. of CCNY Schl. of Bus., 1965-66. Publs. incl: Teaching Installment Sales; Notes on Consolidations; Advanced Accounting Problems, 2 vols.; Contbns. to profl. jrnls. Hons. incl: Outstanding Alumnus Award, 1962; Cert. of Honor, State of Israel, 1964; Maccabee Award Cert., Brooklyn Div.,

State of Israel Bonds, 1974. Address: 144 Pembroke St., Brooklyn, NY 11235, U.S.A. 6, 30, 55, 64.

ZIMMERMAN, Gordon G., 8 Mar. 1922. Educator; Minister. Educ: B.A., Sterling Coll., U.S.A.; M.A., Bowling Green State Univ.; Ph.D., Mich. Univ. Appts: Min., Sterling Mennonite Ch., Kan.; Evangelical Mennonite Ch., Wauseon, Ohio; Prof.-Dean, Univ. of the Pacific; Dir., Dev.-V.P., Acad. Affairs, Taylor Univ.; Chmn. & Prof. of Speech, Greenville Coll. Mbrships: Phi Kappa Phi; Pi Kappa Delta; Phi Eta Sigma; Speech Communication Assn.; Ctrl. States Speech Assn.; Club Pres., Rotary Int. Co-Author Public Speaking: Philosophy and Practice. Recip. Outstanding Tchr. of Yr. Award, 1960. Address: Dept. of Speech, Greenville Coll., Greenville, IL 62246, U.S.A. 15, 57, 108, 126, 141.

ZIMMERMAN, Naoma, (Mrs.) b. 2 Aug. 1914. Psychiatric Social Worker; Family Therapist; Communication Specialist; Lecturer; Consultant; Author. Educ: M.A., Univ. of Chgo., 1940. Appts: Case Wkr.-Therapist, Family Serv. of S. Lake Co., Ill., 1958; Cons., Family Therapy to H.S.s, Soc. Work Agcys. etc.; Pvte. Prac.; Lectr.-Tchr., Family Therapy, Summer Fac., Univ. of Chgo., 1967-71. Mbrships: Am. Ortho Psych. Assn.; Nat. Assn. of Soc. Wkrs. Publs: Sleepy Forest, 1943; Timothy Tic-Tock, 1943; Sleepy Village, 1944; The New Comer, 1944; Baby Animals, 1955; Little Deer, 1956; Farm Animals, 1966; Corky meets a Spaceman, 1960; Corky in ORBIT, 1962. Address: 465 Drexel Ave., Glencoe, IL 60022, U.S.A. 5, 30, 132

ZIMMERMAN, William Harold, b. 1 Oct. 1937. Artist. Educ: Cinn. Art Acad., Ohio. Asst. Mng. Art Dir., Gibson Greeting Card Co., Cinn., Ohio. Mbrships: Wilson Ornithological Soc.; Audubon Nat. Soc.; Soc. of Animal Artists. Co-author & Illustrator, Topflight, Speed Index to Waterfowl of North America, 1966; Author & Illustrator, Waterfowl of North America, 1974. Recip., Best Animal Painting Award, Cinn. Annual Zoo Animal Art Show, Cinn., Ohio, 1966. Subject of articles in jrnls. Address: R.R. 3 Box 64 A, Nashville, IN 47448, U.S.A. 37.

ZIMMERMANN, Wilhelm, b. 19 Aug. 1910. University Professor. Educ: Univs. of Bonn, Vienna, Hamburg & Breslau, 1929-39; Ph.D., M.D., Dipl. Chem. Appts: Assoc. Prof., Univ. of Breslau; Dir., State Medizinal-Untersucmungsamt at Trier; Prof. & Dir., Inst. for Hygiene & Microbiol., Univ. of Saarbrücken-Hamburg. Mbrships. incl: Deutsche Gesellschaft für Hygiene und Mikrobiology; Affiliate, Royal Soc. of Med.; N.Y. Acad. of Scis. Contbr., some 170 publs., var. jrnls. Address: BRD 665 Hamburg-Einoed (Saar), Gartenstr. 18, German Federal Republic. 43, 92.

ZINBERG, Dorothy Shore, b. 25 Feb. 1928. Sociologist. Educ: B.A., Boston Univ. 1949; M.A., ibid, 1958; Ph.D., Harvard Univ., 1966; Postdoctoral Fellow, Univ. Coll., London, U.K., 1968-69; Postdoctoral Fellow, Harvard Univ., 1969-70. Appts. incl: Rsch. Assoc., Ctr. for Rsch. in Careers, Grad. Schl. of Educ., Harvard Univ., 1966-67; Rsch. Sociologist, Dept. of Chem., Univ. Coll., London, U.K., 1968-69; Rsch. Sociologist to Univ. Hlth. Servs., Dept. of Chem., Harvard Univ., U.S.A. 1969-72; Lectr., Sociol., Rsch. Fellow, Prog. for Sci. & Int. Affairs, ibid, 1972-. Mbrships: Am. Sociological Assn.; Eastern Sociological Assn.; AAAS; Rsch. Comm. on Sociol. of Sci., Int. Sociological

Assn.; Fedn. of Am. Scientists. Author of publs. in field. Hons. incl: Nuffield Fndn. Grant, Univ. Coll., London, U.K., 1971-72; Sloan Fndn. Grant, 1972-73; Ford Fndn. Grant, 1973-. Address: Harvard Univ., Prog. for Sci. & Int. Affairs, 9 Divinity Ave., Cambridge, MA 02138, U.S.A. 5, 14.

ZINKE, Otto Paul, b. 25 Feb. 1908. University Professor. Educ: Dipl. Ing., Tech. Univ., Berlin, 1932; Dr. Ing., ibid, 1936. Appts: Asst., later Chief Engr., Tech. Univ., Berlin, 1932-40; Lectr., High Frequency Techniques, ibid, 1940; Prof. & Hd. of Dept., Heinrich-Hertz Inst., Berlin, 1942; Engr., Centre National d'Etudes des Télécommunications, Paris, France, 1948-50; Chief of Labs., Siemens & Halske, Munich, German Fed. Repub., 1951-55; Full Prof. for Elec. Communication Systems & Components, Tech. Univ. of Darmstadt, 1955-. Mbrships. incl: IEEE, U.S.A.; Deutsche Physikalische Gesellschaft, Frankfurt; European Phys. Soc., Genoa, Switzerland. Publs. incl: Hochfrequenz-Mestechik, 1938, 3rd edit., 1959; Widerstande, Kondensatoren, Spulen und ihre Werkstoffe, 1965; 60 papers, tech. jrnls. Address: Richard-Wagner-Weg 69, D61 Darmstadt, German Federal Republic. 43.

ZINSERLING, Heino, b. 24 Oct. 1891. Painter; Graphic Artist; Sculptor. Educ: Univs. of Leipzig & Munich; Acad. of Arts, Munich & Kassel. Appts: Tchr., H.S., Hamburg, Handwerkskammer, Hamburg, Arbeitslosenbildungswerk, Hamburg, Arbeitsamt, Hamburg, Angestellte-Gewerkschaft, Hamburg; Former Dir., pvte. schl., tchng. drawing, painting, graphics & perspective. Mbrships: Hon. mbr., Berufsverband der bildender Künstler Hamburgs, 1971; Hon. mbr., Int. Acad. for Poetry, Art & Sci., Rome, Italy (Accademia Int. Tommaso Campanella di Lettere, Arti, Science); Int. Arts Guild, Monte Carlo Monaca, 1969. Work in museums in German Fed. Repub.; Designer of int. medals & dips. Entered in golden book, Int. Acad. for Poetry, Art & Sci., Tomasco Campanella, Rome, 1970. Address: Neuenfelderstr. 4, 2102 Hamburg 93, German Fed. Repub. 19.

ZIPLANS, Emilija Emily Karklins, (Mrs. Erwin M. Ziplans), b. 17 June 1917. Librarian. Educ: Univ. of Latvia, 1941-44; B.A., Univ. of Toronto, Canada, 1960; B.L.S., ibid, 1961. Appts: Libn., Circulation Dept., Univ. of Toronto, 1961-64; Hd. Libn., New Coll., 1964-67; Hd. Libn. of var. sects., Book Selection Dept., Univ. of Toronto Lib., 1967-73; Hd. Libn., Book Selection Sect., Sigmund Samuel Lib., Univ. of Toronto, 1973-. Mbrships: Canadian Lib. Assn.; ALA; Bibliographical Soc. of Canada; Assn. Advancement Baltic Studies; Stratford (Ont.) Shakespearean Festival Fndn.; Art Gall., Ont.; Latvian Sororities Assn., Past Pres., Toronto Chapt.; Sorority Varoviksne. Compiler, Baltic Material in the University of Toronto Library, 1972. Address: 18 Waring Ct., Willowdale, Ont. M2N 4G7, Canada. 5, 132, 138.

ZIRKIND, Ralph. b. 20 Oct. 1918. Professor; Scientific Consultant. Educ: B.S., CCNY, 1940; M.S., Ill. Inst. of Technol., 1946; Ph.D., Univ. of Md., 1950; D.Sc., Univ. of R.I., 1968. Appts: Physicist, Navy Dept., 1941-50, Oakridge Nat. Lab., 1950-51; Chief Physicist, Navy Dept., 1951-60; Physicist, Advanced Rsch. Proj. Agcy., 1960-64; Prof., Polytech. Inst. of Bklyn., 1964-70, Univ. of R.I., 1970-; Proj. Sci., Gen. Rsch. Corp., 1974-. Mbrships: Am. Phys. Soc.; Int. Astronautics Fedn.; Ed. Bd., Infrared Jrnl. of Phys., 1964-; Sigma Pi

Sigma, 1948; Sigma Xi, 1965; Eta Kappa Nu, 1971. Publs. incl: Jet Propulsion Series Vol. XII; FarInfrared Properties of Solids: Electromagnetic Sensing of Earth from Satellites; Electronic Image Processing Techniques; PIB Lecture Notes on Radiation Processes; URI Lecture Notes on Remote Sensing; University of Michigan Notes on Infrared Astrophysics; contbr. articles to COSPAR, IUGG/WMO, Planetary Scis., APS, etc. Hons: Meritorious Civilian Serv. Award, USN, 1956, Sec. of Defense, 1970; SPIE Serv. Award. Address: 820 Hillsboro Dr., Silver Spring, MD 20902, U.S.A. 14.

ZISSIS, James, b. 10 Mar. 1934. Corporation President. Educ: Adv. Courses, Econs. & Acctng., Athens, Greece; Adv. Courses, Bus. Admin. & Mgmt., U.S.A. Appts: Mbr., Off. Greek Merchant Marine; Entered restaurant franchise, Dagwood Inc., Ohio; Fndr., Spears Construction & Dev. Co.; Pres., Owner, Pacific Coast Steamship Laundry, Inc., 1961; Owned San Rafael Assocs., (Smyth Smoother Movers) Calif., 1962; Fndr., Pres., Am. Plan Investment Corp., San Fran., 1964-; Owner, Trans World Capital Corp. inclng. subsidiaries Thrifty Int., Car Rental System-Athens Greece and Europe, Zodiac Maritime Corp., Trans World Capital S.A.-Geneva, Am. Plan Int.-Beirut. Address: 111 Pine St., Suite 1400, San Francisco, CA 94111, U.S.A.

ZIVKOVIC, Peter D., b. 10 July 1930. Associate Professor of Language & Literature. Educ: B.A., Univ. of Ill., 1957; M.A., ibid, 1959; M.F.A., Univ. of Iowa, 1960. Appts: Baseball & Football Coach, Slippery Rock State Coll., 1956; Asst. Instr., Univ. of Ill., 1957-59, Univ. of Iowa, 1960; Instr., Auburn Univ., Ala., 1960-63, Asst. Prof., 1963-66; Asst. Prof., Ga. Tech., 1967-69; Assoc. Prof., Fairmont State Coll., 1969-. Mbrships: W. Va. Poetry Soc.; Ga. Writers Assn.; MLA; Nat. Fedn. State Poetry Socs. Publs: Bezich (novella), 1969; Little Book, Little Book, Tell Me Your Name (poetry), 1974; over 200 poems, stories & reviews in jrnls. & mags. Hons: Many poetry & prose awards & prizes, inclng. Huntington, Charleston, Morgantown Awards, W. Va. Poetry Soc., 1973. Address: Route 4, Box 577, Fairmont, WV 26554, U.S.A. 11.

ZLOBEC, Sanjo, b. 16 Nov. 1940. Assistant Professor of Mathematics. Educ: Dip. Engrng., Zagreb, Yugoslavia, 1963; M.Sc., ibid, 1967; Ph.D., Northwestern Univ., Ill., U.S.A., 1970. Appts: Tchg. Asst., Univ. of Zagreb, 1965-68; Rsch. Engr., Northwestern Univ., 1968-69, Lectr., 1969-70; Asst. Prof., McGill Univ., Canada, 1970-. Mbrships: Am. Math. Soc.; Soc. for Ind. & Applied Maths.; Inst. of Maths., Univ. of Zagreb. Contbr. to profl. publs. incl: Glasnik Mat., 1967; SIAM Jrnl. Control 8, 1970; SIAM Review 12, 1970; Israel Jrnl. Maths. 7, 1970 (w. A. Ben-Israel); SIAM Jrnl. Applied Maths. 21, 1971. Hons. incl: Fulbright Travel Grant, 1968; Nat. Rsch. Coun. of Canada Grants, 1970- & 1971-72. Address: 1230 McGregor Ave., Montreal 109, P.Q., Canada.

ZOLOTAS, Xenophon, b. 26 Mar. 1904. Professor. Educ: Univs. of Athens, Leipzig & Paris. Appts: Prof., Econs., Univ. of Salonica, 1928 & Univ. of Athens, 1931-; Chmn., Bd. of Dirs., Agric. Bank of Greece, 1936-40; Jt. Gov., Bank of Greece (after liberation), 1944-45; Mbr., UNRRA Coun., 1946; Gov., Int. Monetary Fund for Greece, 1946-67; Mbr. Greek Delegation to UN Gen. Assembly, 1948-53; Deleg., Econ. Comm. for Europe, 1949-54; Gov. Bank of Greece, 1955-67; Mbr.,

"Group of Four" for remodelling of OEEC, 1960. Mbr., Acad. of Athens. Publs. incl: The Gold Trap and the Dollar, 1968; Speculocracy & the International Money System, 1969; The International Money Mess, 1973; From Anarchy to International Monetary Order, 1973. Hons. incl: Grand Cross, Royal Order of Phoenix. Address: 25, Dionyssiou Areopagitou St., Athens 402, Greece.

ZOPF, Paul Edward, Jr., b. 9 July 1931. Professor. Educ: B.S., Univ. of Conn., Storrs, 1953; M.S., Univ. of Fla., Gainesville, 1955; Ph.D., ibid, 1966; Further study, Tulane Univ., New Orleans, La., 1956-59. Appts. incl: Asst. Prof.-Assoc. Prof., Sociol., Guildford Coll., 1959-68; Prof., ibid, 1968-; Assoc. Acad. Dean, 1967-68; Chmn., Dept. of Sociol., 1969-; Dana Prof., Sociol. (endowed chair), 1970-; Cons. for law enforcement prog., Greensboro, 1969-. Mbrships. incl: Am. Sociological Assn.; Int. Union for Sci. Study of Population; AAAS; Rural Sociol. Soc. Publs. incl: North Carolina; A Demographic Profile, 1967; Demography: Principles & Methods (w. T. Lynn Smith), 1970, 2nd edit. 1974; 15 articles for profl. jrnls., monographs, etc. Address: 815 George White Rd., Greensboro, NC 27410, U.S.A. 7, 14, 15, 22, 30, 125.

ZORANOVITCH, Vladislav, b. 15 Nov. 1892. College Director; Writer. Educ: M.Agric., Vienna Univ., Austria; M.Nat.Sci., Toulouse Univ., France; Doct., ibid. Fndr. & Dir., Metaxa Nicolitch Coll., Kifissia, nr. Athens, Greece. Mbr., Greek Lit. Club. Publs: The Prosecutor; La Mobilisation Generale; Virgin Wife; The Confession of a Nun; Mister Voronesco; The Dirty Blood; Pericles from Mantzourana (Best Seller). Recip., Red Cross, Yugoslavia, 1915. Address: 93 Queen Sophia Ave., Athens 602, Greece. 43.

ZORBALAS, George, b. 1 Aug. 1907. Retired Army Officer; Ex-Minister of Public Order. Educ: Grad., Mil. Acad.; Signal Schl.; Higher War Coll.; Snr. Offs.' Tactics Schl. Appts: Regular Army serv., 1929-49: Cmndr., sev. cavalry-armour units; staff off.; instr., mil. schls.; tank co. cmndr., resistance work, 1940-45; fought against Communist guerillas, 1946-49; wounded 4 times in battle; Aide-de-Camp, King Paul, 1950-51; Became Min. of Pub. Order, 1964. Mbrships: Friends of Educ. Soc.; Hellenic Scout Bd. of Dirs.; Hellenic Gymnastics & Athletics socs. Bds. of Dirs.; Philippos Soc. Bd. of Dirs. Hons: Silver Cross of Order of King George A, without swords, 1946; Golden Cross, Phoenix, ibid, 1946; Golden Cross, w. swords, 1947; Knight Cmndr. Cross, Order of Phoenix w. swords, 1950; Knight Cmndr. Cross of Order of King George A, 1959; Knight Cmndr. High Cross, Order of Phoenix, 1962; Golden Order of Merit, Gallant Action, 1941, 1960; War Cross, B' Class, 1943, 1960; War Cross, C' Class, 1945, 1962; Medal for Outstanding Acts, 1942, 1948, 1949, 1950, & num. others. Address: 22 Korytsas St., Papagos, Athens, Greece.

ZUBCHEVICH, Emira D. (Mrs. Sead Zubchevich), b. 18 Sept. 1920. Physician. Educ: Med. Schl., Univ. of Vienna, Austria, 1943; Intern, Gen. Hosp., ibid, 1943-44; Internal Med., Univ. of Vienna, 1944-45; Pediatrics, Childrens Hosp., Glanzing, Vienna, 1945-48; Res. Trng. in Psych., Columbus State Hosp., Ohio, U.S.A., 1963-66. Appts. incl: Physn., Columbus State Inst., Ohio, 1960-62; Dir. of Admission & Receiving Ctr., ibid, 1966-68; Physn., Specialist, Centreville Med. Grp., Fredericktown, Pa., 1968-; Cons., local schls., Youth Dev. Ctr., ibid; Cons. Staff Mbr., Green Co. Gen. Hosp. Mbrships. incl: Dipl.,

Am. Bd. Psych. & Neurol.; AMA; Pa. Med. Soc.; Wash. Co. Med. Soc.; Am. Psych. Assn.; Pa. Psych. Assn.; Pan Am. Med. Assn.; Wash. Co. Mental Hlth. Assn.; Am. • Inst. Hypnosis. Address: P.O. Box 61, Beallsville, PA 15313, U.S.A. 5, 17.

ZUBERI, Masarrat Husain, b. 25 June 1911. Civil Servant. Educ: St. John's Coll., Agra Univ., India; St. Catherine's Coll., Cambridge Univ., U.K.; M.A. Appts. incl: w. Ctrl. Sect., Govt. of India, 1942-47, Sec., Min. of Communications, 1946-47; Controller, Civil Aviation, Posts & Telegraphs, Road Transport & Ports, Min. of Communications, Pakistan, 1947-51; Jt. Sec., Min. of Commerce, 1952-53; Sec. W. Pakistan Coun. of Admin. for Integration of Provinces, 1954-55; Commnr., Peshawar Div., 1955-58, Bhawalpur Div., 1958-60; Sec., Min. of Fuel, Power & Natural Resources, 1961-62, Min. of Communications, 1962-68; Sec. Gen. & Ambassador Regional Cooperation for Div. Iran, Pakistan & Turkey, 1968-71. Fndr., Pres., & Chmn., sev. learned orgs. Hons. incl: O.B.E., 1946; S.Q.A., Pakistan, 1959; S.P.K., Pakistan, 1964; H.Q.A., Pakistan, 1971. Address: c/o Monopoly Control Authority, Govt. of Pakistan, Islamabad, Pakistan. 34.

ZUCCARELLI, Frank Edward, b. 23 Oct. 1921. Painter; Illustrator; Educator. Educ: Newark Schl. of Indl. & Fine Art, N.J.; Art Students League, N.Y.; B.F.A., Kean Coll. of N.J. Appts: Serv. WWII, USMC, Pacific Theatre; Free-lance Artist & Illustrator (fiction & advt.); Fine Artist & Instr., Spectrum Inst. for Advt. Arts., Somerville, N.J. Mbrships: Salmagundi Club, N.Y.; Fellow, Am. Artists Profl. League, N.Y.; Am. Veterans' Soc. of Artists; Burr Artists; Navy Art Cooperation & Liaison Comm., USN; Combat Artist, Dept. of Navy, Wash., D.C.; Jury of Awards, 1971 Salmagundi Club. Major Commns.: for USN, Newport, R.I., 1971 Presidential Visit; Shipboard Cruise USS McDonnell, DE 1043; Dahlgren Weapons Lab., Va., 1971; Assignment; Civilian Sailors, w. U.S. 6th Fleet, Mediterranean, 1972. Works in Collects. of USN, Wash., D.C.; USMC, Barstow, Calif; Abraham Sharpe, NY; Malcolm Forbes, NY.; num. pvte. collects. Hons: sev. awards & prizes incl. Salmagundi Prize, 1969, '70; Best in Show, Metuchen Cultural Commn., 1970; 3rd Award, Am. Artists Profl. League, William Edwards Coll., 1970. Address: 61 Appleman Rd., Somerset, NJ 08873, U.S.A. 6, 37, 57.

ZUCKER, Moses, b. 14 Jan. 1904. Professor of Talmud & Biblical Exegesis. Educ: Grad., Univ. of Vienna, Austria; Grad., Jewish Theological Sem., Vienna; Ph.D., Dropsie Coll., Phila., Pa., U.S.A. Appt: Prof. of Talmud & Biblical Exegesis, Jewish Theological Sem. of Am. Fellowships: Am. Acad. of Jewish Rsch., Guggenheim Fndn. Publs. incl: On the History of Polemics between Judaism & Islam, 1937; The Meaning of the Title of Saadya's Philosophical Book, al Amanat wal Itikadat, 1942; A Critique Against the Writings of Saadya Gaon by Rabbi Mubasbir, 1954; Notes on the New Fragments of Saadya's Polemic against Hivi al Balkha, 1966; Fragments of Saadya's Kitab Tahsil Al-Sharai Al-Sama iyah, 1972. Hons. incl: JTS Ginzburg Prize for Talmud, Jewish Theological Sem. of Am., 1962-63. Address: 70 La Salle St., Apt. 16G N.Y., NY 10027, U.S.A.

ZUGRAVESCU, Ioan, b. 29 May 1910. Professor of Organic Chemistry. Educ: Master in Chem. Sci., Bucharest Univ., 1931; Dr. in Organic Chem., ibid, 1934; Dr. Docent of Scis., 1964. Appts: Asst., Organic Chem. Dept., Univ. of Bucharest, 1936-48; Prof. of Organic Chem.,

Inst. of Alimentar Ind., 1949-56, Jassy Univ. 1956-; Dir., Macromolecular Chem. Inst. 'P. Poni', 1963-71. Mbrships: Corres. Mbr., Romanian Acad., 1963-. Publs: Heterocycles polymeres, 1971; N-ylids chemistry, 1974; 140 works in diverse sci. jrnls. Recip. Dr. h.c., Nantes Univ., France, 1973. Address: Str. Dr. Obedenaru No. 21, Bucharest 6, Romania.

ZUK DE BATIZ, (Mrs.) Eva Maria, b. 6 Jan. 1946. Pianist. Educ: J.M. Olivares Schl. Music, Caracas, Venezuela; Dip. de Hon., 1959; Prof. Pianist, Venezuelan Min. Educ., 1959; Bach. Mus., Juilliard Schl. Music, N.Y, U.S.A, 1965; M.Sc., ibid, 1966; summer courses, Aspen, Colo., 1966 & Mozarteum, Salzburg, Austria, 1970; Postgrad. study u. Prof. Drzewiecki, Warsaw, Poland, 1967-68. Profl. experience incls: Soloist, Venezuelan Symph. Orch.; Venezuelan Ctrl. Univ. Chmbr. Orch.; Dominican Nat. Symph. Orch.; Nat. Symph. Orchs., Costa Rica, Guatemala & Mexico; Mexican Opera Orch.; Symph. Orch., Xalapa, Mexico; Polish Philharmonics, Lodz, Katowice, Rybnic, Wroclaw, Olsztyn; Polish & Belgian Radio & TV Symph. Orchs.; Mozarteum Symph. Orch., Salzburg, Austria; Recitals, radio & TV appearances incl: Carnegie Recital Hall, N.Y.C, U.S.A; Wash. DC; Mexico City; Caracas, Venezuela; San Juan, Puerto Rico; Vienna & Salzburg, Austria; Augsburg, Germany; Warsaw Philharmonic Recital Hall; TV & radio. Recip. num. hons. inclng. Order, Andrés Bello, Pres., Venezuela, Caracas, 1973. Address: c/o Maria Salazar, Consul, Embajada de Venezuela Londres 167. Zona Rosa, Mexico, D.F.

ZULETA-ALVAREZ, Enrique, b. 1 July 1923. Professor of Philosphy & Letters. Educ: Grad., Nat. Univ. of Cuyo, Mendoza, Argentina; Postgrad., Inst. of Hispanic Culture, Madrid Spain 1944-55; Grad., Librarianship, Nat. Univ. of Cuyo, 1961. Appts. incl: Provincial Dir. of Culture, Mendoza & Dir., Gen. San Martin Pub. Lib., 1958-61; Dir., Ctrl. Lib., Nat. Univ. of Cuyo, 1962-69; Titular Prof., ibid, 1964-; Vis. Prof., Nat. Univ. of Chile, Santiago, 1959; Vis. Prof., Univ. of N.M., Albuquerque, U.S.A., 1961-62; Vis. Prof., Univ. of Bordeaux, France, 1970. Mbrships. incl: Cuyo Inst. of Hispanic Culture; Hist. of Ideas Comm., Pan-Am. Union; Latin-Am. Studies Assn., U.S.A.; Am. Assn. of Tchrs. of Spanish & Portuguese. Publs. incl: América en el Pensamiento de Maeztu, 1965; La Literatura de Hispanoamérica, 1967; El Nacionalismo, 2 vols., 1974; 10 other books. Address: Rufino Ortega 217, Mendoza, Argentina.

ZUMAN, Petr, b. 13 Jan. 1926. Professor of Chemistry. Educ: R.N.Dr., Charles Univ., Prague, Czechoslovakia, 1950; Dr.Sc., Czechslovakia Acad. of Sci., Prague, 1960; D.Sc., Univ. of Birmingham, U.K., 1968. Appts: Hd., Organic Polarography Div., Polarographic Inst., Czechoslovakia Acad. of Sci., Prague, 1950-68; Sr. Vis. Fellow, Dept. of Chem., Univ. of Birmingham, U.K., 1966-70; Disting. Rsch. Prof., Dept. of Chem., Clarkson Coll. of Technol., Potsdam, N.Y., U.S.A. Mbrships: Past Sec., Int. Union of Pure & Applied Chem., Commn. on Electroanal. Chem.; Vice Chmn., Northern N.Y. Sect., Am. Chem. Soc.; Past Vice Chmn., Organic Div., Int. Soc. for Electrochem.; Fellow, Chem. Soc., London, U.K. Author of sci. books & papers. Recip., Heyrovsky Medal, Prague, 1960. Address: Dept. of Chem., Clarkson Coll. of Technol., Potsdam, NY 13676, U.S.A. 6, 14.

ZUMBRUN, Alvin John Thomas, b. 9 Aug. 1926. Criminologist. Educ: B.A., Univ. of Md., 1952; M.A., ibid, 1956; J.D., Univ. of Balt., 1970; Master Correctional Educ., Coppin State Coll., 1972. Appts. incl: Mng. Dir., Balt. Criminal Justice Commn., 1956-59; Exec. Dir., Md. Crime Investigating Commn., 1959-69; Currently a Dir., ibid; Prof. & Curric. Coord., Catonsville Community Coll.'s Police Admin. & Corrections Curric., 1969-73; Full Prof., ibid, 1973-. Mbrships. incl: -Pres., Md. Acad. of Criminal Profs., 1969-72; Nat. Dist. Att.'s Assn.; AAUP; Int. Soc. of Criminol.; Nat. Coun. on Crime & Delinquency; Am. Sociological Assn.; Am. Acad. of Pol. & Soc. Scis.; Criminol. Sect., AAAS; Int. Assn. of Chiefs of Police. Author of publs. in field. Hons. incl. Am. Fedn. of Police Honor Award, 1972. Address: P.O. Box 9349, Catonsville, MD 21228, U.S.A. 6, 28, 129.

ZUMTOBEL, Martin, b. 24 Jan. 1904. Merchant. Educ: Univ. of Cologne, Germany; Univ. of Innsbruck, Austria; Tradesman's Dip.; J.D. Appts: Joined firm F.M. Zumtobel, 1924; Procurator, 1930; Mng. Assoc., F.M. Zumtobel, 1937; Fndr., F.M. Zumtobel, Salzburg, 1939; Taking over of Mosterel Zumtobal, Dornbirn, 1940; Fndr., A & O, Zentralkontor GmbH, Vienna, 1956; Pres., Bd. of Dirs., ibid; Mng. Assoc., A & O, Handelshof, Frauscher & Zumtobel KG, Salzburg. Mbrships. incl: Chmn., Landesgremium Grosshandel mit Nahrungs- & Genussmitteln, Vorarlberg; Comm. mbr., Bundesgremium des Grosshandels mit Nahrungs- & Genussmitteln, Vienna; Comm. mbr., Landesinnung des Nahrungs- & Genussmittelgewerbes; Vereinigung Osterreichischer Kerzenzieher; Bd. of Dirs., Verband der Kaffee- & Tee-Importeure Osterreichs; Pres., Vereinigung Osterreichischer Zuckergrosshändler. Hon: Kommerzialrat, 1957. Address: Sägerstr. 1, A 6850 Dornbirn, Austria. 1.

ZUSS, Michael E. b. 24 Feb. 1917. Adjunct Professor of Philosophy. Educ: Grad., H.S., 1935; B.A. (Magna Cum Laude), M.A., Queens Coll., CUNY, 1972. Appts: Adjunct Prof., N.Y. Inst. of Technol., Old Westbury, L.I.; Assoc. Adminstr. & Registrar, Mt. Sinai Schl. of Med. Doctoral Prog. in Biomed. Scis. Mbrships: L.I. Philosophical Soc.; B'nal B'rith; Lodge Pres., ibid, 1965-66; Co. Chmn., Adult Educ., 1966-68; Phi Beta Kappa, 1972; Alpha Sigma Lambda, 1972. Publs: Fundamentals of the Relationship of the Philosophy of William of Ockham & David Hume; The Enigma of Jonathan Edwards Explored; The Philosophical Basis of the Concepts of Freedom & Liberty of Moses Maimonides & William of Ockham. Address: 143-23 Barclay Ave., Flushing, NY 11355, U.S.A.

ZWAENEPOEL, Paul Pil, b. 7 Jan. 1924. University President. Educ: A.B., Ph.B., Our Lady of Grace Coll., Brussels, Belgium, 1945; M.A., St. Joseph's Coll., Louvain, ibid, 1949; M.A. in Ed., St. Louis Univ., Baguio City, Philippines, 1964. Appts: Prof. of Philos., Baguio Colls., Philippines, 1949-51; Dir., St. Augustine's Schl., Tagudin, Ilocos Sur, 1951-52; Prof. of Philos., Tagudin Jr. Coll., ibid, 1951-52; Dean, St. Mary's Coll., Bayombong, Nueva Vizcaya, 1952-59; Regent, Coll. of Engrng. & Arch., St. Louis Univ., Baguio City, 1959-64; Sec. Gen., St. Louis Univ., ibid, 1962-63. Mbrships. incl: Coord. Comm., Sci. Educ. Proj. of Philippines; Sec. Gen., Assn. of Cath. Univ. of the Philippines; Rotary Club Int.; Manila-Philippine Chapt., Phi Delta Kappa; Alpha Phi Omega, Ohio, U.S.A. Contbr. of many articles to profl. jrnls. Hons. incl: Dr. of Pedagogy of Arts, Gt. China Arts Coll. (World Univ.), Hong Kong, 1972; Univ. Medal of Honor, Kyung Hee Univ., Seoul, Korea, 1972; LL.D., Kyung Hee Univ., Seoul,

Korea, 1973. Address: St. Louis Univ., P.O. Box 71, Baguio City B-202, Philippines. 131.

ZWANE, Ambrose Phesheya, b. 30 Apr. 1924. Physician. Educ: M.B., B.Ch., Med. Schl., Univ. of Witwatersrand, Johannesburg, 1951. Appts: Hd. Physn. & House Surg., Charles Johnson Mem. Hosp., Zululand, 1952; Med. Staff, Mbabane Govt. Hosp., Swaziland, 1953-59; Med. Off., Hlatikulu Govt. Hosp., Southern Swaziland, 1959; Pres. Gen., Ngwane Nat. Liberatory Congress, 1962, & active as ldr. & wkr. w. this pol. party since that date; currently gen. practitioner of med. Recip., Independence Medal. Address: Ilanga Centre, Manzini, P.O. Box 766, Swaziland.

ZWARTKRUIS, Theodorus Henricus Joannes, b. 22 Nov. 1909. Bishop of Haarlem. Educ: Univ. of Louvain, Belgium; Theologicum, Warmond, Netherlands; Ph.D., Nijmegen R.C. Univ. Appts: Ordination as Priest, 1934; Tchng. Staff, Hageveld Jr. Sem., 1939-61; Dean of Haarlem, 1961-66, Bishop of Haarlem, 1966-. Mbr., For. Press Assn. in The Netherlands. Publ., Book of English & American Literature. Hons: Canon of St. Bavo Chapt., Ghent, Belgium; Kt. of Netherlands Lion; Chap. of Westminster Cathedral, London, U.K. Address: 80 Nieuwe Gracht, Haarlem, Netherlands. 43.

ZWEERTS, Arnold, b. 29 Nov. 1918. Mosaic Artist. Educ: Schl. for Arts & Crafts, Amsterdam, Netherlands; Schl. for Art Tchr. Trng.; Royal Acad. of Art, Amsterdam; Royal Acad. of Art, Copenhagen, Denmark; Acad. Belli Arti, Ravenna, Italy; M.F.A., Inst. Allende, Univ. Guanajuato, Mexico. Appts. incl: Instr., Appreciation of Art, Stedelyk, Rijksmuseum, Amsterdam, 1954-57; Asst. Prof., Drawing & Painting, Art Inst. of Chgo., U.S.A., 1957-73; Lectr., Dept. of Fine Arts, Loyola Univ., Chgo., 1968-. Mbrships: Midwest Designer Craftsmen; Dutch Immigrant Soc.; Knickerbocker Soc. of Chgo. Exhibitions: One-man shows: Amsterdam, 1948; U.S.A., 1953; Lib., Downers Grove, 1968; Three-man show, Art Inst. of Chgo., 1966; Group Shows, U.K. & U.S.A.; Commns. for mosaics, oil paintings & a fresco; Work in pub. collects., Netherlands & Mexico; Work in pvte. collects., Denmark, U.K., Norway, Holland, U.S.A. Address: 4805 Forest Ave., Downers Grove, IL 60515, U.S.A. 37.

ZWICKER, Otto, b. 28 Mar. 1914. Director. Educ: Mech. Engrng.; Admin. Acad. Appts: Dir., Kongresshaus, Salzburg, Austria, cons. bur. for tourism; Dir., Kongresshaus, Innsbruck, 1972-. Mbrships: 1st Pres., Europäische Arbeitsgemeinschaft der Berufsverbände für Kur- & Fremdenverkehrsfachleute; Gen. Sec. & 1st Pres., Osterreichischer Kongressverband; Co-Fndr. & Exec. Pres., Int. Kongresspaläste; Fndr., Volkshochschule Salzburg; Co-Fndr. & Mng. V.P., Verband Osterreichischen Volkshochschulen; Fndr., Salzburger Bildungswerk; Co-Fndr., Osterreichisches Bildungswerk. Author of articles in newspapers & of var. brochures. Recip. of hons. in Austria & abroad, inclng. ring of hon., Salzburg. Address: Kongresshaus Innsbruck, Rennweg 3-5, 6020 Innsbruck, Austria.

ZYCHLINSKA, Rajzel, b. 27 July 1910. Poet. Educ: NY City Coll., U.S.A. Mbr. PEN Club, NY. Publs: Poetry: Poems, 1936; The Rain Sings, 1939; To Clear Shores, 1948; Silent Doors, 1962; Autumn Sfnares, 1969; Lexicon of Modern Yiddish Literature, 1960. Hons: Lit. Prize, In sich mag., NY 1935; Chaim Greenberg Prize, Pioneer Women, NY, 1963; Lit. Award for book, Autumn Sfnares, Melbourne, Australia, 1970. Address: Cathedral Stn., P.O. Box 204, 215 W. 104 St., N.Y., NY 10025, U.S.A. 55, 138.

ZYDANOWICZ, Maria. Graphic Artist; Painter. Educ: Acad. Fine Arts, Warsaw, Poland. Asst., Fac. of Graphic Arts, Acad. of Fine Arts, Warsaw, 1947-52. Mbrships: Polish Union Plastic Artists; Int. Arts Guild, Monte Carlo. Exhibs., Poland, Belgium, France, Denmark, Italy, Monaco. Hons: Dip. Officiel en Finale, Deauville, France, 1971; Dip. awarded to grp. of Polish Artists, Monte Carlo, Monaco; Dip. of Hon., Holstebro, Denmark, 1973. Address: 11a/3 Grottgera St., Warsaw, Poland.

ZYLINSKI, Doris M. (Mrs.), b. 27 May 1926. Nurse. Educ: R.N., Jennie Edmundson Mem. Hosp., Council Bluffs, Iowa; B.S., Univ. of Evansville, Ind.; M.S., Univ. of Calif., San Fran. Appts. incl: Nursing Educ. Dir., Osawatomie State Hosp., Kan., 1953-54, 55-57; Dir., Nurses, Evansville State Hosp., Ind., 1954-55; Psych. Nursing Educ. Dir., Mendocine State Hosp., Calif., 1958-60. Dir., Nurses, Napa State Hosp., 1960-63; Nursing Serv. Admnstr., State Dept. of Mental Hygiene, 1963-69; Cons., Nat. Inst. of Mental Hlth., Wash.; Dir., Hlth. Occupations, Napa Coll., 1969-. Mbrships incl: Spec. Cons., NIMH, Medicare Progs., Psych. Facilities, 1970-71; Hosp. Staff Dev. Sub-Comm., NIMH, 1964-68; Chmn., CLN Psych. Mental Hlth. Advsry. Comm., 1965-67; Chmn., WICHE, Psych. Mental Hlth. Advsry. Comm., 1968-69. Address: 4299 Lorac Court, Napa, CA 94558, U.S.A. 5, 9, 128.

ADDENDUM

K

KAIRYS, Anatole, b. 28 Aug. 1914. Educator; Writer; Editor. Educ: Kaunas Univ., USSR, 1938-40; Dip. Ped. (M.A.), Fac. Humanities, Dept. Philos., Vilnius Univ., 1940-42; Postgrad. work Innsbruck Univ., Austria, 1945; Tuebingen, Germany, 1946; Chgo., Ill., USA, 1951. Appts: Dir., Pupils Home, Vilnius, Lithuania, 1940-42; Prin., HS, Siauliai, ibid, 1942-44; V.P., Secondary School., in exile, Nuertingen, Germany, 1946; Ed., Tremtiniu Mokykla (The School in Exile), Educl. monthly, 1946; Ed., Naujoji Ausra (The New Dawn), monthly mag., Chgo., Ill., USA, 1947-50; Ed., I Laisve (Toward Freedom), 4-monthly mag., ibid, 1974. Mbr. & off. hldr. num. Lithuanian orgs. Publs. incl: Poems: Windswept Leaves, 1946; The Golden Seed, 1953; Plays: The Tree of Freedom, 1955; Diagnosis, 1956; 2nd ed., Latvian, '66; The Chicken Farm, 1965; Curriculum vitae, 1966; 2nd ed., Engl., '71; The Light Indeed, 1968; Eldorado, 1968; The Heritage, 1969; 2nd ed., Latvian, '70; The Faithful Grass, 1971 (novel); The Silver Day, 1972. Recip. sev. hons. Address: c/o Jesuit Fathers, 2345 W. 56th St., Chgo., IL, 60636, U.S.A.

KAPLAN, David L., b. 14 Feb. 1918. Statistician. Educ: B.A., N.Y. Univ., 1939; Postgrad. work, ibid, 1939-40, Am. Univ., 1940-45. Appts: Statn., U.S. Census Bur., Wash., 1940-49; Chief, Occupation & Ind. Stats., 1950-56; Census planner, 1957-62; Asst. Chief, Population Div., 1962-68; Coord., 1970 census of population & housing, 1966-73; Chief, demographic census staff, 1971-; U.S. Rep., working grp. on population censuses, Conf. of European Statns., 1963-. Mbrships: Fellow & Mbr. of Coun., Am. Statistical Assn.; Fellow, AAAS; Past Dir., Population Assn. of Am.; Past Pres., Wash. Statistical Soc. Contbr. to profl. jrnls. Hons: Silver Medal Award, U.S. Dept. of Comm., 1952; Gold Medal, ibid, 1971. Address: U.S. Bur. of the Census, Wash. DC 20233, U.S.A. 7, 14.

KEEFE, John Russell, b. 2 June 1946. Public Accountant. Educ: B.B.A., Stetson Univ., U.S.A., 1968. Appts: Maths. Tchr., Nova HS, Ft. Lauderdale, Fla., U.S.A.; Sr. Acct., Ringel, Heeb & Co., Cert. Pub. Accts.; Currently, Pres., Top Floor, Inc., Real Estate & Electronics Corp., Margate, Fla.; Treas., Don Jon Enterprises, Inc., Investment Corp., ibid; Ptnr., Keefe, McCullough, Carpenter & Sneider, Cert. Pub. Accts., ibid. Mbrships: Am. Inst. CPA's; Fla. Inst. CPA's; Broward Co. Chapt. CPA's; Treas., Margate Khoury League; Pres., Margate Optimist Club; NW Broward Rotary Club; Broward Dolphins Booster Club; Coral Springs Co. Club; Men's Golf Assn.; Sponsor Jr. Exchange Club Nova HS; Pres., Stetson Univ. Schl. Bus., 1967-68; V.P., Omicron Delta Kappa Ldrship.; Cmndr. (Pres.), Sigma Nu; Senator, Student Govt. Assn.; Inter-Frat. Coun.; Pres., Green Cir. Ldrship.; Sigma Nu Alumni Assn.; Active in Girls' Softball League & Men's League; St. Ambrose Episc. Ch. Coll. Nat Finalist, Sigma Nu Man of Yr. Award, 1968. Address: 6711 NW 1st Ct., Margate, FL 33063, U.S.A. 125.

M

MARVIN, John George, b. 8 May 1912. Clergyman & Church Executive. Educ: B.S., Davidson Coll., 1933; ThB., Princeton Theological Sem., 1936. Appts: Pastor, Windsor Presby. Ch., N.Y., 1936-37, 1st Presby. Ch., Montrose, Pa., 1937-44. The Presby. Ch., Lewistown, Pa., 1944-52 & St. Andrew Presby. Ch., Denton, Tex., 1952-61; Presby. Exec. for Gtr. Kan. City, 1961-65; Sr. Minister, 1st Presby. Ch., Bartlesville, Okla., 1965-69 & Chevy Chase Presby Ch., Wash. D.C., 1969-. Mbrships: Beta Theta Pi; Rotarian; Kenwood Club; Am. Philatelic Soc.; Wash. Clergy. Publs: Culture Comes to Chevy Chase; Early Admission of Baptized Children; The Essence of Barthian Theology; South of the Border. Contbr. to: Outreach; Forward; Today; etc. Hons: D.D., Coll. of Emporia, 1964; LL.D., Tarkio Coll., 1964; Disting. Citizen Award, 1955; Alaska Preaching Mission, 1958; Brit.-Am. Preaching Exchange, 1972. Address: 1 Chevy Chase Circle, Wash. DC 20015, U.S.A. 7.

MAXWELL, Michael Eric Christian, b. 6 Jan. 1936. Symphony Orchestra Manager. Educ: studied music & arch., Auckland Univ., New Zealand, 1954-56. Appts: Prog. Off., New Zealand Broadcasting Corp., 1955-59; Orchestra Mgr., Philharmonia Orch., London, 1960-63; Tour Mgr., Royal Philharmonic Orch. 1963; Mgr., Princeton Chamber Orch., N.J., U.S.A., 1964-65; Promotion Dir., N.Y. Philharmonic, 1965-66; Asst. Mgr., The Cleveland Orch. 1966-70; Gen. Mgr., ibid, 1970-. Mbrships: Bd. of Dirs., Univ. Circle Inc.; Advsry. Trustee, Cleveland Music Schl. Settlement; Circle Ctr. Community Progs. Comm.; Jr. Comm., Engl. Speaking Union, Cleveland; Past, Music Panel, Ohio Arts Coun.; Past, Bd. of Dirs., Am. Symphony Orch. League. Contbr. to Am. Record Guide, 1965-66. Address: Severance Hall, 11001 Euclid Ave., Cleveland, OH, U.S.A. 2, 4, 8, 22, 130, 139.

MOORE, Oscar Keeling, b. 5 May 1916. Economic Theorist; International Economist; Physiologist; Horticulturist. Educ: Rsch. Fellow, Univs. of Fla. & Md.; B.S., Univ. of Fla., 1938; M.S., Univ. of Md., 1940; Ph.D., Univ. of Fla., 1962. Appts: incl: Economist, For. Agric. Serv., Wash., D.C., 1945-47; w. For. Serv. of U.S., 1947-56; Econ. Advsr. & Ed., The Hearst Corp., N.Y.C., 1962-63; Prof., Econs., E. Carolina Univ., 1963-. Fellow, Smithsonian Inst. Mbrships. incl: Phi Kappa Phi; Beta Gamma Sigma; Alpha Zeta; Sigma Xi; Econometric Soc.; Am. Econ. Assn. Publs: Brazilian Coffee & World Coffee Trade, 1953; The Argentine Economy, 1953; The Brazilian Coffee Economy, 1962. Contbr. to sev. U.S. Govt. publs. Author of approx. 283 articles in nat. mags., N.Y. Times & learned jrnls. Address: Dept. of Economics, E. Carolina Univ., P.O. Box 2767, E. Carolina Stn., Greenville, NC 27834, U.S.A.

S

SKONBERG, Madelon Baenzier, b. 8 Sept. 1906. Educator; Musician. Educ. incls: Student, Bush Conservatory, 1927-28; Ill. State Normal Univ., 1932; Chgo. Music Coll., 1935-37; N. Park Coll., 1940-42; Tchrs. Coll., 1957-58; Mus. B. in Piano & Theory, Cosmopolitan Schl. Music; postgrad., Northwestern Schl. Music Grad Schl., 1963-. Appts. incl: Music Critic, Musical Ldr., 1950-67; Adjudicator, Nat. Guild of Piano Auditions, 1955; Instr., Piano & Organ, Cosmopolitan Schl. of Music, 1956-62, Grad. Schl., Northwestern Univ. Schl. Music, 1962-. Mbrships. incl: Art Inst. Chgo.; Soc. Am. Musicians; Nat. League Am. Pen Women; Nat., Ill. State Music Tchrs. Assns. Contbr. of articles to mags. & jrnls. Address: 2601 W. Sunnyside Ave., Chicago, IL 60625, U.S.A. 5, 8.

LIBRARIES

A large proportion of each edition of *Dictionary of International Biography* is distributed via library agents, wholesale and retail booksellers, and purchasing bodies of the calibre of Her Majesty's Stationery Office, British Council, etc., and it is, therefore, not possible to list all libraries in all countries housing *D.I.B.* unless the librarians themselves advise us directly of *D.I.B.* acquisition.

The following is as complete a list of libraries throughout the world stocking *D.I.B.* as we are able to prepare without further advices from other librarians:

NATIONAL AND STATE

AUSTRALIA:
Library Board of Western Australia, Perth.
National Gallery of Victoria, Melbourne.
National Library, Canberra.
State Library of Queensland, Brisbane.
Public Library of South Australia, Adelaide.
State Library of Victoria, Melbourne.

BERMUDA:
The Bermuda Library, Hamilton.

BOLIVIA:
National Library and Archives, Sucre.

BOTSWANA:
Botswana National Library, Gaberones.

CAMEROUN:
Bibliotheque National du Cameroun, Yaounde

CANADA:
Bibliotheque Nationale Montreal.
National Library of Canada, Ottawa.
National Science Library, National Research Council, Ontario.
Provincial Library of Manitoba, Winnipeg.
Provincial Library, Regina, Saskatchewan.
Provincial Library, Victoria, B.C.

DENMARK:
Staatsbiblioteket, Aarhus.

EL SALVADOR:
National Library, San Salvador.

ETHIOPIA:
National Library, Addis Ababa.

FRANCE:
Bibliotheque National, Paris.

GERMANY:
Staats und Universitats Bibliothek, Hamburg.

GHANA:
Library Board, Accra.

GREECE:
National Library, Athens.

HAITI:
Bibliotheque Nationale, Port-au-Prince.

INDIA:
National Archives of India, New Delhi.

IRAN:
National Library, Tehran.

IRELAND:
National Library, Dublin.

ITALY:
Biblioteca Nationale, Turin.
Biblioteca Nazionale, "Victorio Emanuele II", Rome.

IVORY COAST:
Bibliotheque Nationale, Abidjan.

KOREA:
National Library, Seoul.

LEBANON:
Bibliotheque National, Beirut.

LIECHTENSTEIN:
Landesbibliothek, Vaduz.,

LUXEMBOURG:
Bibliotheque Nationale, Luxembourg City.

MALAYSIA:
National Archives of Malaysia, Petaling Jaya.

MEXICO:
Biblioteca Nacional, Mexico City.

MONACO:
Bibliotheque de Monaco, Monte Carlo.

MOROCCO:
Bibliotheque Generale et Archives du Maroc, Rabat.

NAPAL:
National Library, Katmandu.

NETHERLANDS:
Provinciale Bibliotheek van Fresland, Leeuwarden.
The Royal Library, The Hague.

NEW ZEALAND:
National Library of New Zealand, Wellington.

NICARAGUA:
Biblioteca Nacional, Managua.

NIGERIA:
National Archives Library, Ibadan
Western State Library, Ibadan.

PANAMA:
Biblioteca Nacional, Panama City.

PARAGUAY:
Biblioteca Nacional, Asuncion.

PERU:
Biblioteca de la Escuela Nacional de Belas Artes, Lima.

PHILIPPINES:
Bureau of Public Libraries, Manila.

PORTUGAL:
Academia Nacional de Belas Artes Biblioteca, Lisbon.   Uniao Nacional Biblioteca, Lisbon.

RHODESIA:
National Archives, Salisbury.

SAN MARINO:
Biblioteca del Museo Nazionale, San Marino.

SINGAPORE:
National Library, Singapore.

SOUTH AFRICA:
  State Library, Pretoria.

SPAIN:
  Biblioteca de la Real Academia Espanola,
    Madrid.

SWEDEN:
  National Museum Library, Stockholm.

SWITZERLAND:
  Schweizerische Landesbibliothek, Bern.

TANZANIA:
  Library Service, Dar-es-Salaam.

TUNISIA:
  Bibliotheque Nationale, Tunis.

TURKEY:
  National Library, Ankara.

UNITED KINGDOM:
  Bodleian Library, Oxford.
  British Museum (Dept. of Printed Books),
    London.
  National Library of Scotland, Edinburgh.
  National Library of Wales, Aberystwyth.

UNITED STATES OF AMERICA:
  Arkansas Library Commission, Little Rock
  California State Library, Sacramento.
  Colorado State Library, Denver.
  Connecticut State Library, Hartford.

Illinois State Library, Springfield.
Library of Congress, Washington, D.C.
Library of Hawaii, Honolulu.
Louisiana State Dept. of Education, Baton
  Rouge.
Louisiana State Library, Baton Rouge.
Michigan State Library, Lansing.
Missouri State Library, Jefferson City.
National Archives, Washington, D.C.
Nebraska Public Library Commission,
  Lincoln.
New York State Library, Bureau of Academic
  and Research Libraries, Albany.
New York State Assembly, Albany, N.Y.
Pennsylvania State Library.
Smithsonian Institution, Washington, D.C.
State Archives, Salt Lake City, Utah.
State Library of Massachusetts, Boston.
Texas State Library, Austin.
Washington State Library, Olympia.
West Virginia Library Commission,
  Charleston.

VATICAN CITY STATE:
  Biblioteca Apostolica Vaticana, Vatican City.

VENEZUELA:
  Biblioteca Nacional, Caracas.

YUGOSLAVIA:
  Narodna Biblioteka, Beograd.

ZANZIBAR:
  Zanzibar Library, Zanzibar.

UNIVERSITY AND COLLEGE

ARGENTINA
  Academia Argentina de Letras, Buenos Aires

AUSTRIA:
  Innsbruck University.

AUSTRALIA:
  Adelaide University, S.A.
  Australian National University, Canberra,
    A.C.T.
  Latrobe University, Melbourne, Vic.
  Macquarie University, North Sydney, N.S.W.
  Monash University, Clayton, Vic.
  New England University, Armidale, N.S.W.
  Sydney Teachers' College, Sydney, N.S.W.
  University College of Townsville.
  University of Melbourne, Vic.
  University of Newcastle.
  University of Queensland, Brisbane.
  University of Sydney, Dept of Psychiatry,
    Camperdown, N.S.W. & Fisher Library.
  University of Tasmania, Hobart.

BAHAMAS:
  Bahamas Academy of S.D.A., Nassau.

BELGIUM:
  E Storia-Scienta, P.U.B.A., Ghent.
  Free University of Brussels.
  Ghent University.

CANADA:
  Alberta University, Edmonton.
  British Columbia University, Vancouver.
  Brock University, St. Catherines, Ont.
  Canadian Institute of International Affairs,
    Toronto, Ont.
  Carleton University, Ottawa, Ont.
  College Bibliocentre Don Mills, Ontario.
  College de L'Assomption, Joliette, Quebec.
  College de Montreal, Quebec.
  College Jesus-Marie, Montreal, P.Q.
  College Rigaud de Vaudreuil, Bibliotheque
    Bourget, P.Q.
  College St. Alexandre, Limbour, Quebec.

College St. Ignace, Montreal, P.Q.
Dalhousie University, Health Sciences
  Library, N.S.
Lakehead College of Arts, Sciences, etc., Port
  Arthur, Ont.
Lakehead University Library, Port Arthur, On
Laval University, Quebec.
Loyola of Montreal, Georges P. Vanier
  Library, P.Q.
McGill University, Quebec.
McMaster University, Mills Memorial
  Library, Hamilton, Ont.
Memorial University of Newfoundland, St. Joh
Mennonite Brethren Bible College, Winnipeg,
  Manitoba.
Mount Allison University, Sackville, N.B.
Newfoundland University, St. John's.
Notre Dame University, Nelson, B.C.
Ottawa University, Ottawa, Ont.
Queen's University, Kingston, Ont.
St. Francis Xavier University, Antigonish, N.S.
St. Lawrence College, Quebec.
St. Mary's University, Halifax, N.S.
Saskatchewan University, Regina.
Sir George Williams University, Montreal,
  Quebec.
Trent University, Ont.
Universite de Montreal, Quebec.
Universite de Sherbrooke, Quebec.
University of Calgary, Alta.
University of Guelph, Ontario.
University of Manitoba, Extension Library,
  Winnipeg.
University of New Brunswick, Fredericton.
University of Toronto, Ont.
University of Western Ontario, London.
University of Windsor, Ont.
Waterloo University, Ont.
York University, Toronto, Ont.

CENTRAL AFRICAN REPUBLIC:
  Librairie Universitaire de Rwanda.

COLOMBIA:
  Universidad del Valle, Cali.

COSTA RICA:
Universidad de Costa Rica.

DENMARK:
Botanical Institute, University of Aarhus.
Copenhagen University.

ETHIOPIA:
Haile Selassie I University, Addis Ababa.
Haile Selassie University College of
Agriculture, Dire Dawa.

FRANCE:
Bordeaux University.
Caen University.
Ecole Nationale Veterinaire D'Alfort,
Maisons-Alfort.
Libraire des Sciences & Techniques Francais
et Etrangeres, Paris.
Montpelier University.
Nancy University.
Paris Conservatoire de Musique.
Sorbonne University, Paris.
Rennes University.
Toulouse University.

GERMANY:
Universitats Bibliothek, Munich.

GUYANA:
University of Guyana, Georgetown.

HONDURAS:
University of Tegucigalpa.

HONG KONG:
Hong Kong Baptist College, London.
University of Hong Kong.

INDIA:
Andhra University, Dr. V.S. Krishna
Memorial Library.
Aligarh Muslim University, Maulana Azad
Library, U.P.
Bombay University.
Punjab Agricultural University, Hissar.
Rabindra Bharati University, Calcutta.

IRAQ:
Baghdad University.

IRELAND:
Trinity College, Dublin University.
University College, Dublin.

ISRAEL:
Hebrew University, Jerusalem.
Israel Academy of Science & Humanities,
Jerusalem.
Tel-Aviv University.

ITALY:
Accademia Nazionale dei Lincei, Rome.
American Academy in Rome.
Johns Hopkins University, Bologna.
Libreria University, Gregoriana, Rome.
Universitaira Alessandrina, Rome.

JAMAICA:
Mico College, Kingston.
University of the West Indies, Mona.

KENYA:
University College, Nairobi.

LEBANON:
American University of Beirut.
International College, Beirut.
Middle East College, Beirut.

LESOTHO:
University of Botswana, Lesotho &
Swaziland.

LIBERIA:
The University, Monrovia.

MALAWI:
University of Malawi, Limbe.

MALAYSIA:
Muslim College.
The University, Kuala Lumpur.

NEW ZEALAND:
University of Otago, Dundedin.

NIGERIA:
University of Lagos.
University of Zaria, Northern Nigeria.

NORWAY:
Royal University, Oslo.

PAKISTAN:
University of Karachi.

PANAMA:
Canal Zone College, Bilboa.

PHILIPPINES:
Central Philippine University Library, Iloila
City.
Philippine Women's Univeristy, Manila.
University of the Philippines at Quezon City
& Diliman Rizal.
University of San Carlos, Cebu City.
University of San Thomas, Manila.

POLAND:
Biblioteka Glowna, Medical Academy,
Krakow.

PUERTO RICO:
Catholic University of Puerto Rico, Valdes
Library, Ponce.
Inter-American University, San German.
University of Puerto Rico, Rio Piedras.

SENEGAL:
Bibliotheque de l'Universite, Dakar.

SOLOMON ISLANDS:
British Solonons Training College, Honiara.

SOUTH AFRICA:
University of Natal, Durban.

SUDAN:
Khartoum Technical Institute.
University of Khartoum.

SWEDEN:
Kunglige Vetenskapsakademiens Bibliotek,
Stockholm.
Uppsala University.

TONGA:
Tonga Teacher Training College.

TRINIDAD:
University of the West Indies, St. Augustine.

UGANDA:
Makere University, Kampala.
Uganda Technical College, Kampala.

UNITED KINGDOM:
Bath University of Technology, Bath,
Somerset.
Bridgwater Technical College, Somerset.
Bruford (Rose) Training College, Sidcup,
Kent.
Cambridge University.
City University, London.
Coventry College of Education, Warwickshire.
Dartford College of Education, Kent.
Durham University Library, County Durham.

Edge Hill College of Education, Ormskirk, Lancs.
Ewell Technical College, Surrey.
Glasgow University, Scotland.
Guildford Technical College, Surrey.
Hackney Technical College, London.
Hatfield College of Technology, Hertfordshire.
Kingston College of Art, Surrey.
London University.
Manchester University.
Mather College of Education, Manchester, Lancs.
Newcastle-upon-Tyne University, Dept. of Music.
North West Kent College of Technology, Kent.
Norwood Technical College, London.
Plymouth College of Technology, Devon.
Queen's University, Belfast, N. Ireland.
St. Andrew's University, Scotland.
St. Bartholomew's Hospital Medical College, London.
Sussex University, Brighton.
Trinity College of Music, London.
University of Bradford, Yorks.
University of Leicester.
University of Surrey, London.

UNITED STATES OF AMERICA:
Academy Immaculate Conception, Ferdinand, Ind.
Adams State College, Alamosa, Colo.
Adelphi Suffolk College, Oakdale, N.Y.
Adelphi University, Garden City, Long Island, N.Y.
Adrian College, Shipman Library, Mich.
Agnes Scott College, McCain Library, Decatur, Ga.
Agricultural & Tech. College of North Carolina, Greensboro.
Alabama University, Birmingham.
Alaska University College, Alaska.
Albany State College, Ga.
Albion College, Mich.
Albright College, Reading, Pa.
Alcorn A. & M. College, Lorman, Miss.
A.M. & N. College, Pine Bluff, Arkansas.
Amundsen-Mayfair Junior College, Chicago, III.
Anderson College, Ind.
Andrews University, James White Library, Berrien Springs, Mich.
Anglo State College, San Angelo, Tex.
Aquinas College, Grand Rapids, Mich.
Arizona State University, Tempe.
Arlington State College, Tex.
Army & Navy Academy, Carlsbad, Calif.
Ashbury College, Wilmore, Ky.
Atlanta University, School of Library Science, Ga.
Auburn University, Ala.
Augsburg College, George Sverdrup Library, Minneapolis, Minn.
Augusta College, Ga.
Austin College, Sherman, Tex.
Austin State College, Nacagdoches, Tex.
Babson Institute, Babson Park, Mass.
Baker University, Baldwin City, Kan.
Baldwin-Wallace Coll., Ritter Library, Berea, Ohio.
Baptist College at Charleston, S.C.
Baylor University, Armstrong Browning Library, Waco, Tex.
Baylor University Medical Centre, Dallas, Tex.
Belfer Graduate School of Science, Yeshiva Univ., N.Y.
Beliot College Libraries, Wis.
Berry Academy, Barstow Memorial Library, Mount Berry, Ga.
Bethel College, McKenzie, Tenn.
Bethune-Cookman College, Daytona Beach, Fla.
Biola Library, La Mirada, Calif.
Bloomfield College, N.J.
Bluefield College, Va.

Blue Mountain Community College, Pendleton, Ore.
Boone Junior College, Iowa.
Boston State College, Mass.
Boston University, Mass.
Bowling Green State University, Ohio.
Brandeis University, Waltham, Mass.
Bridgewater College, Va.
Brigham Young University, Provo, Utha.
Brooklyn College, N.Y.
Broome Community College, Binghamton, N.Y.
Brophy College Prep. Library, Phoenix, Ariz.
Bryn Mawr College, Pa.
Bucknell Univ., Lewisburg, Pa.
Butler University, Indianapolis, Ind.
Cabarrus Memorial Hospital School of Nursing, Concord, N.C.
Cabrini College, Radnor, Pa.
California College of Arts & Crafts, Meyer Library, Oakland, Calif.
California Institute of Technology, Jet Propulsion Laboratory Library, Pasadena, Calif.
California State College at Dominguez Hills, Gardena & Long Beach.
Calvary Bible College, Kansas Cith, Mo.
Camden Country College, Blackwood, N.J.
Cameron State College, Lawton, Okla.
Campbell College, Carrie Rich Memorial Library, Buies Creek, N.C.
Campbellsville College, Ky.
Capital University, Columbus, Ohio.
Carnegie Inst. of Tech., Pittsburg, Pa.
Carnegie—Mellon University, Pittsburg, Pa.
Centenary College of Louisiana, Shreveport, La.
Central Connectitut State College, New Britain, Conn.
Central Methodist College, Fayette.
Central Missouri State College, Warrensburg, Mo.
Central State University, Wilberforce, Ohio.
Central State College, Ellensburg, Wash.
Charlotte College, N.C.
Chicago City College, III.
Chicago State College, III.
Christian Theological Seminary, Indianapolis, Ind.
Cincinnati University, Ohio.
City College Library, Baruch School, N.Y.
City College of the City University of New York, Cohen Library.
Claremont Colleges, Hannold Library, Calif.
Clarion State College, Carlson Library, Pa.
Clarkson College of Technology, Potsdam, N.Y.
Clearly College, Ypsilanti, Mich.
Clover Park Community College, Tacoma, Wash.
Coalinga Junior College, Calif.
Colgate University, Hamilton, N.Y.
College Center of the Finger Lakes, Corning, N.Y.
College of Steubenville, Starvaggi Memorial Library, Ohio.
Colorado School of Mines, Arthur Lakes Library, Golden.
Colorado Women's College, Denver.
Columbia College, S.C.
Columbia State Community College, Tenn.
Columbia University, Butler Library, N.Y.
Columbus Dominican Education Centre, Ohio.
Community College of Baltimore, Md.
Concordia Teachers College, Link Library, Seward, Neb.
Concordia Theological Seminary, Springfield, III.
Connecticut College for Women, New London.
Conn. University, Wilbur Cross Library, Storrs.
Connecticut University Law School, West Hartford.
Coppin State College, Baltimore, Md.

Cornell College Library, Mt. Vernon, Iowa.
Cornell University, College of Home Ed., Medical College & Law Libraries, Ithaca, N.Y.
Corning Community College, Arthur A. Houghton Jr. Library, N.Y.
County College of Morris, Dover, N.J.
Covenant College, Lookout Mountain, Tenn.
Creighton University, Omaha, Neb.
Crozer Theological Seminary, Chester, Pa.
Dabney S. Lancaster Community College, Forge, Va.
Dallas Baptist College, Tex.
David Lipscomb College, Nashville, Tenn.
Davidson College, N.C.
Dayton University, Albert Emanuel Library, Ohio.
DeAndreis Seminary Library, Lemont, Ill.
Defiance College, The Anthony Wayne Library, Ohio.
Delta State College, Roberts Memorial Library, Cleveland, Miss.
Denver University, Mary Reed Library, Colo.
DePaul University, Chicago, Ill.
Dickinson College, Carlisle, Pa.
Doana College, Crete, Neb.
Dominican College, Washington, D.C.
Drake University, Des Moines, Iowa.
Drew University, Madison, N.J.
Drexel Institute of Tech., Philadelphia, Pa.
Duke University, School of Forestry, Durham, N.C.
Dutchess Community College, Poughkeepsie, N.Y.
Dyer Institute of Interdisciplinary Studies, New Hope, Pa.
D'Youville College, Buffalo, N.Y.
East Carolina College, Greenville, N.C.
East Carolina University Library, Greenville, N.C.
Eastern Kentucky State College, Richmond, Ky.
East Texas Baptist College, Marshall.
Edgewood College of the Sacred Heart, Madison, Wis.
Edinboro State College, Hamilton Library, Pa.
Emanuel College Library, Boston, Mass.
Emory & Henry College, Emory, Va.
Emory University, A.W. Calhoun Medical Library, Atlanta, Ga.
Fairfield University, Conn.
Fairleigh Dickinson University, Rutherford, Ga.
Ferris State College, Big Rapids, Mich.
Ferrum Junior College, Ferrum, Va.
Findlay College, Ohio.
Fisk University, Nashville, Tenn.
Florence State College, Ala.
Florida A & M Univ. Lib., Tallahassee, Fla.
Florida University, Gainesville, Fla.
Florida State University, Tallahassee, Fla.
Fordham University, Bronx, N.Y.
Fort Wayne Bible College, Lehman Memorial Library, Ind.
Fredonia State University College, N.Y.
Fresno City College, Calif.
Furman University, Greenville, S.C.
Gallaudet College, Washington, D.C.
George Peabody College for Teachers, Nashville, Tenn.
Georgetown University, Medical & Dental School, McNally Mem. Library, Washington, D.C.
Georgia Institute of Technology, Atlanta.
Georgia Southwestern College, Americus.
Georgia State College, Atlanta.
George Washington University, Washington, D.C.
Gettysburg College, Pa.
Glassboro State College, N.J.
Glendale Community College, Instructional Materials Center, Ariz.
Glenville State College, Robert F. Kidd Library, W. Va.
Golden West College Library, Huntington Beach, Calif.

Gonzaga University, Spokane, Wash.
Gordon College, Wenham, Mass.
Grace College, Winona Lake, Ind.
Grambling College, La.
Grand Canyon College, Phoenix, Ariz.
Grays Habor College, Aberdeen, Wash.
Great Falls College, Mont.
Green Mountain College, Burke Surdam Library, Poultney, Vt.
Greenville Tech. Education Center, S.C.
Grove City College, Henry Buhl Library, Pa.
Guilford Tech. Institute, Jamestown, N.C.
Gustavus Adolphus College, St. Peter, Minn.
Hampden-Sydney College, Va.
Hanover College, Indiana.
Harding College, Searcy, Ark.
Harvard University Library, Law School Library, Houghton Library, Eidener Library, & Channing Lab., Cambridge, Mass.
Hebrew Union College Library, Cincinnati, Ohio.
Hibbing State Junior College, Minn.
Highlands University, Las Vegas, N.M.
Hill Junior College, Hillsboro, Tex.
Hillsdale College, Mich.
Hobart College, Geneva, N.Y.
Hofstra University, Hempstead, Long Island, N.Y.
Howard College, Birmingham, Ala.
Howard Payne College, Dept. of Speech & Drama, Brownwood, Tex.
Howard University, Washington, D.C.
Huntingdon College, Montgomery, Ala.
Illinois Inst. of Technology, Chigago, Ill.
Illinois Teachers College, Chicago North, Ill.
Immaculate Heart College, Los Angeles, Calif.
Indiana Inst. of Tech., McMillen Library, Fort Wayne.
Indiana University, Bloomington, & at South Bend, Ind.
Ithaca College, Ithaca, N.Y.
Jackson State College, Miss.
Jacksonville State College, Ala.
John Carroll University, Grasselli Library, Cleveland, Ohio.
Judson College, Marion, Ala.
Kansas State College of Pittsburg, Porter Library, Kan.
Kansas State University, Manhattan, Kan.
Kansas Wesleyan University, Salina, Kan.
Kendall College, Evanston, Ill.
Kent State University, Ohio.
Kentucky State College, Blazer Library, Frankfort, Ky.
Kentucky University, Lexington, Ky.
Kentucky Western State College, Bowling Green, Ky.
Kings College, Briarcliff Manor, N.Y.
Lackawanna Junior College, Seeley Memorial Library, Scranton, Pa.
Lake City Junior College & Forest Ranger School, Fla.
Lake Erie College, Lincoln Library, Painsville, Ohio.
Lake Michigan College, Benton Harbor, Mich.
Lamar State College of Tech., Beaumont, Tex.
Langston University, C. Lamar Harrison Library, Langston, Okla.
Lee College, Baytown, Texas.
Lee College, Cleveland, Tenn.
Lehigh County Community College, Allentown, Pa.
Lehigh University, Bethlehem, Pa.
Le Journeau College, Longview, Tex.
Le Moyne College, Syracuse, N.Y.
Lewis College, Lockport, Ill.
Lexington Theological Seminary, Ky.
Limestone College, Kate Montgomery Library, Gaffney, S.C.
Lincoln College, Ill.
Lincoln University, Jefferson City, Mo.
Lincoln University, Nail Memorial Library, Philadelphia, Pa.

Linfield College, McMinnville, Ore.
Livingstone College, Carnegie Library & W. J.
  Walls Center Hood Theological Seminary
  Library, Salisbury, N.C.
Lock Haven State Coll., Pa.
Long Island University Library & Graduate
  Library School Library, Greenville, Long
  Island, N.Y.
Loras College, Dubuque, Iowa.
Loretto Heights College, Colo.
Louisiana State University Library & Law
  School Library, Baton Rouge, La.
Louisiana School of Social Welfare, La.
Layola University of Los Angeles, Calif.
Lutheran School of Theology at Chicago, Ill.
Lycoming College, Williamsport, Pa.
Lynchburg College, Va.
Macalester College, St. Paul, Minn.
MacCormack Junior College, Chicago, Ill.
MacMurray College, Henry Pfeiffer Library,
  Jacksonville, Ill.
Madison College Library, Harrisonburg, Va.
Manchester College, North Manchester, Ind.
Manhattan Bible College, Kan.
Mankato State College, Highland Campus
  Library, Minn.
Marian College, Indianapolis, Ind.
Marietta College, Ohio.
Mark Hopkins College, Brattleboro, Vt.
Marquette University School of Medicine,
  Milwaukee, Wis.
Marshall University, Huntingdon, W.Va.
Mary College, Bismark, N.D.
Marygrove College, Detroit, Mich.
Marywood College, Dept. of Librarianship,
  Scranton, Pa.
Massachusetts College of Art, Boston.
Massachusetts University, Dept. of Romance
  Languages, Amherst.
Medaille College, Scholastica Library,
  Buffalo, N.Y.
Memphis State University, Tenn.
Mercer University, Macon, Ga.
Merrimack College, North Andover, Mass.
Messiah College, Grantham, Pa.
Miami University, Middletown, Ohio.
Michigan College of Osteopathic Med., Mich.
Michigan State University, East Lansing, Mich.
Michigan Technological University,
  Houghton, Mich.
Middlebury College, Vt.
Middle Georgia College, Conran, Ga.
Middle Tennessee State University,
  Murfreesboro, Tenn.
Mid-South Bibe College, Memphis, Tenn.
Military College of South Carolina—The
  Citadel—Charleston, S.C.
Millikin University, Decatur, Ill.
Minnesota University, Minneapolis.
Mississippi State College for Women,
  Columbus, Miss.
Missouri University, Kansas City & Columbia,
  Mo.
Monmouth College, Ill.
Monmouth College, Guggenheim Memorial
  Library, N.J.
Montgomery Junior College, Takoma Park,
  Md.
Moore College of Art, Philadelphia, Pa.
Moorhead State College, Minn.
Moravian College, Bethlehem, Pa.
Morningside College, Sioux City, Iowa.
Mount St. Mary College, Los Angeles, Calif.
Nevada Southern University, Las Vegas.
Nevada University, Reno.
Newark State Coll., N.J.
Newberry College, Wessels Library, S.C.
New Haven College, West Haven, Conn.
New Mexico Inst. of Mining & Tech.,
  Socorro, N.M.
New Mexico University, Albuquerque.
New York Academy of Medicine.
New York City Community College, Namm
  Hall Library, Brooklyn, N.Y.

New York Military Academy, West Point,
  N.Y.
New York State College of Agriculture &
  Home Economics, Albert R. Mann
  Library, Ithaca, N.Y.
New York University, Education Library.
New York University, Washington Sq.
  College, N.Y.
New York University Libraries, Tech.
  Services Div.
New York University Medical Center, N.Y.
North American Baptist Seminary, Sioux
  Falls, Iowa.
North Carolina University at Charlotte &
  Chapel Hill.
North Carolina Women's College, Greensboro.
North Central College & Seminary,
  Napierville, Ill.
North Dakota State University, Fargo.
Northeast Louisiana State College, Monroe.
Northeast Missouri State Teachers College,
  Kirksville.
Northern Illinois University, Dekalb.
Northern State College, Aberdeen, S.D.
North Georgia College, Dahlonega, Ga.
North Florida Junior College, Madison.
North Shore Community College, Beverly,
  Mass.
Northwest Community College, Powell,
  Wyoming.
Northwest Nazarene College, Nampa, Idaho.
Northwestern College, Orange City, Iowa.
Northwestern Conn. Community College,
  Winsted.
Northwestern Lutheran
  Theological Seminary, St. Paul,
  Minn.
Northwestern State College, Russell Library,
  Natchitoches, La.
Northwestern University, Evanston, Ill.
Notre Dame College, Wilton, Conn.
Nyack Missionary College, N.Y.
Ohio Northern University, Ada.
Ohio State University Libraries, Columbus.
Oklahoma Christian College, Oklahoma City.
Olivet Nazarene College, Kankakee, Ill.
Oregon College of Education, Monmouth.
Otis Art Institute, Los Angeles, Calif.
Ottawa University, Kan.
Pacific School of Religion, Berkeley, Calif.
Pacific University, Forest Grove, Ore.
Pan American College, Edinburg, Tex.
Park College, Parkville, Mo.
Parkland College, Champaign, Ill.
Peterson State College, Wayne, N.J.
Pennsylvania State University, University
  Park.
Pensacola Junior College, Fla.
Pima College, Learning Resource Center,
  Tucson, Ariz.
Polytechnic Institute of Brooklyn.
Portland State College, Ore.
Portland State University, Ore.
Potomac State College, Keyser, W.Va.
Pratt Community College, Kan.
Pratt Institute, Brooklyn, N.Y.
Purdue University, Indianapolis Campus
  Library, Ind.
Radford College, Radford, Va.
Rend Lake College, Mt. Vernon, Ill.
Rensselaer Polytechnic Inst., Troy, N.Y.
Rhode Island College, James P. Adams
  Library, Providence.
Rhode Island University, Kingston.
Ricks College, Rexburg, Idaho.
Robert Morris Junior College, Corapolis, Pa.
Rochester Inst. of Technology, N.Y.
Rockford College, Ill.
Rockland Community Coll. Lib.,
  Suffern, N.Y.
Rollins College, Winter Park, Fla.
Sacramento City College, Calif.
Sacred Heart University Library,
  Bridgeport, Conn.

Saginaw Valley College, University Center, Mich.
San Gamon State Univ. Springfield, Ill.
St. Ambrose College, Davenport, Ohio.
St. Andrews Presbyterian College, De Tamble
  Library, Laurinburg, N.C.
St. Anselm's College, Manchester, N.H.
St. Bonaventure University, N.Y.
St. Catherine College, St. Paul, Minn.
St. Cloud State College, Minn.
St. Francis College, Loretto, Pa.
St. John's University, Jamaica, N.Y.
St. Lawrence Seminary, Mount Calvary, Wis.
St. Leonard College, Dayton, Ohio.
St. Louis University, Mo.
St. Mary's Seminary, Perryville, Mo.
St. Michael's College, Winooski, Vt.
St. Paul's College, Concordia, Miss.
St. Paul's College, Lawrenceville, Va.
St. Paul School of Theology, Dana Dawson
  Library, Kansas City, Mo.
St. Petersburg Junior College, Fla.
St. Thomas College, St. Paul, Minn.
St. Thomas Seminary, Louisville, Ky.
Salem College, Winston-Salem, N.C.
Samford University, Birmingham, Ala.
San Diego University, Calif.
San Fernando Valley State College, Social
  Sciences Reference Library, Northridge,
  Calif.
San Jose State College, Calif.
San Mateo Junior College, Calif.
Santa Clara University, Calif.
Savannah State College, Ga.
School of Advanced International Studies,
  Washington, D.C.
Seton Hall University, South Orange, N.J.
Shippensburg State College, Pa.
Siena College, Memphis, Tenn.
Simmons College, Boston, Mass.
Slippery Rock State College, Maltey Library,
  Pa.
Southern Colorado State College, Pueblo.
Southern Illinois University, Carbondale.
Southern Methodist University, Fondern
  Library, Dallas, Tex.
Southern Oregon College, Ashland, Ore.
South Florida University, Extension Library,
  Bay Campus, St. Petersburg.
Southwest Missouri State College, Springfield.
Southwest Texas State College, San Marcos.
Southwestern Association of God College,
  Nelson Memorial Library, Waxahachie,
  Tex.
Southwestern Community College, Creston,
  Iowa.
Southwestern University, Georgetown, Tex.
Stanford Research Institute, Menlo Park,
  Calif.
Stanford University, Hoover Institution
  Library, Jackson Library & Law Library,
  Calif.
State College for Women, Memorial Library,
  Columbus, Miss.
State University Colleges of New York at
  Binghamton, Brockport, Albany, Buffalo,
  Fredonia, Oswego, & Oyster Bay.
State University of New York, Medical
  Center, N.Y.
Stephen F. Austin State College, Nacagdoches,
  Tex.
Sterling College, Kan.
Sul Rosa College, Alpine, Tex.
Syracuse University, N.Y.
Takiro College, Mo.
Tarleton State College, Stephenville, Tex.
Taylor University, Upland, Ind.
Temple University, Health Sciences Center,
  Philadelphia, Pa.
Tennessee A. & J. State University, Nashville.
Texas A. & M. University, College Station.
Texas Christian University, Mary Coutts
  Burnett Library, Fort Worth.
Texas North State University, Denton.
Texas Tech. College, Lubbock.

Texas Women's University, Denton.
Toledo University, Ohio.
Trenton State College, Library Science
  Dept. Library, N.J.
Trinity College, Washington, D.C.
Trinity University, San Antonio, Texas.
Truett McConnell College, Cleveland, Ga.
Tulane University, Rudolph Matas Medical
  Library & University Library, New
  Orleans, La.
Tulsa University, Okla.
Tusculum College, Tenn.
Union College, Brabourville, Ky.
United Theological Seminary, New Brighton,
  Minn.
Unity School of Christianity, Lee's Summitt,
  Mo.
University of Albuquerque, N.M.
University of Arizona, Tucson.
University of Arkansas, Fayetteville.
University of Bridgeport, Conn.
University of California at Berkeley (General
  Ref. Library), Irving, Los Angeles,
  Riverside, San Diego (La Jolla) & Santa
  Barbara.
University of California, San Francisco
  Medical Center Library.
University of Chicago, Chicago, Ill.
University of Cincinnati, Cincinnati, Ohio.
University of Colorado, Denver Center &
  Medical Center Libraries, Denver.
University of Connecticut.
University of Georgia Libraries, Ga.
University of Hawaii at Hilo & Honolulu.
University of Houston, Tex.
University of Illinois at the Medical Center,
  Chicago, Ill.
University of Iowa, Iowa City.
University of Kansas Medical Center, Kansas
  City.
University of Louisville, Ky.
University of Maine, Portland.
University of Maryland at Baltimore & College
  Park (School of Lib. & Information
  Services).
University of Miami, Coral Gables, Fla.
University of Michigan, Ann Arbor, Mich.
University of Minnesota, St. Paul.
University of Mississippi, Miss.
University of N. Carolina at Asheville
University of Notre Dame, Ind.
University of Oklahoma, Medical Center
  Library, Norman.
University of Oregon, Eugene, Ore.
University of Pittsburgh, Pa.
University of the Pacific, School of
  Dentistry Library, San Francisco, Calif.
University of South Carolina, McKissick
  Memorial Library, Columbia.
University of South Dakota, Vermillion.
University of Southern Mississippi,
  Hattiesburg.
University of Tennessee, Knoxville.
University of Tennessee, College of
  Pharmacy, Memphis.
University of Texas, Dental Branch, Houston.
University of Texas, Institute of Latin
  American Studies, Austin.
University of Texas, The Humanities
  Research Center, Austin.
University of Texas Medical Branch,
  Galveston, Tex.
University of Utah, Middle East Center,
  Library, Salt Lake City.
University of Washington, College of Forest
  Resources, Seattle, Wash.
University of Wisconsin, Research &
  Development Center, Madison, Wis.
University of Wyoming, Laramie.
USACGSE, Fort Leavenworth, Kan.
U.S. International University, Elliot Campus
  Library, San Diego, Calif.
U.S. Merchant Marine Academy, Kings Point,
  Long Island, N.Y.

U.S. Military Acad. West Point, N.Y.
Utah State University, Logan, Utah.
Valparaiso University, Moellering Library, Ind.
Villanova University, Falver Memorial Library,
Pa.
Virginia C'wealth Univ., Richmond.
Virginia Military Institute, Lexington.
Virginia State College, Petersburg, Va.
Virginia Union University, Richmond.
Virginia University, Charlottesville.
Voohees College, Denmark, S.C.
Wabash College, Crawfordsville, Ind.
Washington & Lee University, Lexington, Va.
Wayland Academy, Beaver Dam, Wis.
Waynesburg College, Pa.
Webster College, St. Louis, Mo.
Wentworth Military Academy, Lexington, Mo.
Wesleyan College, Macon, Ga.
Western Kentucky University, Margie Helm
Library, Bowling Green.
Western Michigan University, Reference
Library, Kalamazoo.
Western New Mexico University, Silver City.
Westminster College, Reeves Library, Fulton,
Miss.
West Virginia University, Morgantown, W. Va.
West Virginia Wesleyan College, Buckhammon,
W. Va.

Wilberforce University, Ohio.
Wilkes College, Wilkes-Barre, Pa.
William Jewell College, Liberty, Mo.
Wilmington College, N.C.
Wilmington College, Wilmington, Ohio.
Winona State College, Maxwell Library, Minn.
Winthrop College, Rock Hill, S.C.
Wisconsin State College, Whitewater.
Wisconsin State University at Oshkosh,
Plattesville, Stevens Point, Superior (Jim
Dan Hall Library) & Whitewater.
Wittenburg University, Springfield, Ohio.
Wofford College, Spartanburg, S.C.
Woodward State Hospital-School, Iowa.
Wright State University, Dayton, Ohio.
Xavier University, Cincinnati, Ohio.
Xavier University, New Orleans, La.
Yale University, Economic Growth Center &
Medical Libraries, Newhaven, Conn.
Yeshive University, Belfer Graduate School
of Science, N.Y.
York Coll. Lib., Jamaica, N.Y.

U.S.S.R.:
Leningrad University, Gorki Scientific Library.

ZAMBIA:
University of Zambia, Lusaka.

PUBLIC

AUSTRALIA:
Ballarat Municipal Libraries, Victoria.
Bendigo Regional Library, Victoria.
Canberra Public Library Service, Kingston
City of Moorabbin Free Library, Bentleigh,
Vic.
City of Sydney Public Library, Sydney.
Edgeworth, David, Memorial Public Library,
Cessnock, N.S.W.
Geelong Regional Library, Victoria.
Greater Wallongong (City) Public Library,
N.S.W.
Launceston City Library, Tasmania.
Naomi Regional Library committee,
Tamworth.
Newcastle Public Library, N.S.W.
Public Library of New South Wales, Sydney.
Public Library of South Australia, Adelaide.
BRITISH HONDURAS:
British Honduras Library Service, Belize.
The Central Library, Belize City.

CANADA:
Atwater Library, Montreal, Quebec.
Bibliotheque de la Ville de Montreal, Quebec.
Brampton Public Library, Ontario.
Edmonton Public Library, Alberta.
Fraser-Hickson Library, Montreal, Quebec.
Fraser Valley Regional Library, Abbotsford,
B.C.
Kingston Public Library, Ontario.
Kirkland Lake Public Library, Ontario.
Lake Ontario Regional Library System,
Kingston, Ontario.
London Public Library & Art Museum,
Ontario.
Medicine Hat Public Library, Alberta.
Metropolitan Central Library, Toronto.
Montreal City Library.
Oakville Public Library, Ontario.
Port Colborne Library, Ontario.
Provincial Lib., Regina, Sask.
Sarnia Public Library, Ontario.
Toronto Public Library, Ontario.
Township of Toronto Public Library,
Cooksville, Ontario.
Victoria Public Library, B.C.
Western Manitoba Regional Library.
Winnipeg Public Library, Manitoba.

CEYLON:
Colombo Public Library.

COLOMBIA:
Bibioteca Luis Angel Arango, Bogota.

FALKLAND ISLANDS:
Stanley Public Library.

FRANCE:
Librairie Fueri-Lamy, Marseille.
Municipal Library, Antibes.
Municipal Library, Cannes, Grasse, Menton
& Nice.

GERMANY:
Ex Libris, Frankfurt-am-Main.

IRELAND:
City of Dublin Public Libraries.
Cork County Library, Cork.
County Galway Libraries.
Sligo County Library.
Wexford County Library.

ITALY:
Alla Biblioteca Civica, Cuneo.
Biblioteca Civica, Trieste.
Biblioteca Fardelliana, Trapani.
Libreria Internazionale di Stefano, Genova.

LIBERIA:
Central Public Library, Monrovia.

MALAYSIA:
Perak Library, Ipoh.

MALTA:
Gozo Public Library, Victoria, Gozo, Malta
G.C.

MAURITUS:
Institute Public Library, Port Louis.

MONACO:
Bibliotheque Caroline, Monte Carlo.
Bibliotheque Communale, Monte Carlo.

NEW ZEALAND:
Auckland Public Libraries.
Cambridge Public Library, Waikato.
Dargaville Municipal Library, North Auckland.
Dunedin Public Library.
Invercargill Public Library.

Napier Public Library.
Palmerston North Public Library.
Wanganui Public Library.
Wellington Public Libraries.

PHILIPPINES:
Manila City Library.

SOUTH AFRICA:
Boksburg Public Library.
Cape Town City Libraries.
Johannesburg Public Library.

SWITZERLAND:
Municipal Library, Geneva.

UNITED KINGDOM:
Aberdare Public Library, Wales.
Aberdeen Public Library, Scotland.
Accrington Public Library, Lancashire.
Andover Public Library, Hampshire.
Antrim County Library, Ballymena, Belfast.,
   N. Ireland.
Ayr Public Library, Scotland.
Bacup Public Library, Lancashire.
Barnes Borough Library, London.
Barnsley Public Library, Yorkshire.
Batley Public Libraries, Yorkshire.
Belfast Public Libraries, N. Ireland.
Bilston Public Library, Staffordshire.
Birkenhead Public Libraries, Cheshire.
Birmingham Public Libraries, Warwickshire.
Blackburn Public Library, Lancashire.
Blyth Central Public Library, Northumberland.
Bournemouth Public Library, Hampshire.
Bradford Public Library, Yorkshire.
Brierley Hill Public Library, Staffordshire.
Bristol Central Library, Gloucestershire.
British Library, Wetherby, Yorks.
Buckinghamshire County Library, Aylesbury.
Buxton Public Library & Museum, Derbyshire.
Caernarvon County Library, Wales.
Camborne Public Library, Cornwall.
Camden Central Library, London.
Cardiff Public Libraries, Wales.
Cardiganshire Joint Library, Public Library,
   Aberystwyth, Wales.
Castleford Public Library, Yorkshire.
Chatham Public Library, Kent.
Chelmsford Public Library, Essex.
Clayton-le-Moors Public Library, Lancashire.
Cumberland County Library, Carlisle.
Dagenham Public Library, Essex.
Darlington Public Library, Co. Durham.
Dartmouth Public Library, Devon.
Darwen Public Library, Lacnashire.
Deptford Public Libraries, New Cross, London.
Dorset County Libraries, Dorchester.
Dunbarton County Library, Scotland.
Dukinfield Public Library, Cheshire.
Ealing Public Library, London.
East Riding of Yorkshire County Council,
   Beverley, Yorkshire.
Eccles Corporation, Central Library,
   Manchester, Lancashire.
Edinburgh Public Library, Scotland.
Enfield Public Library, London.
Epsom & Ewell Public Libraries, Ewell,
   Surrey.
Erith Public Libraries, Kent.
Essex County Library, Chelmsford.
Fife County Library, Kirkcaldy, Scotland.
Fleetwood Public Library, Lancashire.
Flintshire County Library Service, Hawarden.
Folkestone Public Library, Kent.
Gateshead Public Libraries, Co. Durham.
Gillingham Central Libraries, Kent.
Glamorgan County Library, Bridgend.
Gosforth Public Library, Northumberland.
Gosport Public Library, Hampshire.
Grantham Public Library, Lincolnshire.
Gravesend Central Library, Kent.
Grimsby Public Library & Museum,
   Lincolnshire.
Hampshire County Library, Winchester.

Hanley Public Library, Stoke-on-Trent,
   Staffordshire.
Harlow Central Library, Essex.
Hereford City Library, Herefordshire.
Herefordshire County Libraries, Hereford.
Hertfordshire County Libaries, Hertford.
Heywood Public Library, Lancashire.
Holborn Public Library, London.
Horsforth Public Library, Yorkshire.
Hull Public Library, Yorkshire.
Hythe Public Library, Kent.
Ilkeston Public Library, Derbyshire.
Ilkley Public Library, Yorkshire.
Inverness Public Library & Museum,
   Inverness, Scotland.
Keighley Public Library, Yorkshire.
Kensington Central Library, London.
Kent County Library, Maidstone.
Kettering Public Library, Northamptonshire.
Kidderminster Public Library, Worcestershire.
Kingston-upon-Thames Central Library,
   Surrey.
Kirkcaldy Public Library, Scotland.
Lancaster Public Library, Lancashire.
Leeds Central Library, Yorkshire.
Lewisham Public Library, London.
Lichfield Public Library, Staffordshire.
Lincoln City Libraries, Lincolnshire.
Liverpool Public Libraries, Lancashire.
Llanelly Public Library, Wales.
Londonderry County Council, County
   Library Hq., Coleraine, N. Ireland.
Maidenhead Public Library, Berkshire.
Maidstone Public Library, Kent.
Manchester Public Libraries, Lancashire.
Merioneth County Library, Penariag,
   Dolgellau, Wales.
Middlesborough Public Library, Yorkshire.
Middleton Central Library, Manchester,
   Lancashire.
Mitcham Public Library, Surrey.
Monmouthshire County Library, Caerleon,
   Wales.
Montrose Public Library, Scotland.
Neath Public Libraries, Wales.
Newcastle-under-Lyme, Central Library,
   Staffordshire.
Newcastle-upon-Tyne Public Library,
   Northumberland.
Northampton Public Library,
   Northamptonshire.
Oadby Public Library, Leicestershire.
Oldbury Public Library, Worcestershire.
Oxford Public Libraries, Oxfordshire.
Paddington Public Library, London.
Paisley Public Library, Scotland.
Pembrokeshire County Library, Haverfordwest,
   Wales.
Penarth Urban District Libraries, Wales.
Perth & Kinross County Libraries, Perth,
   Scotland.
Plymouth Central Library, Devon.
Poole Public Library, Dorset.
Port Talbot Central Public Library, Wales.
Purley Central Library, Surrey.
Redditch Public Library, Worcestershire.
Rhyl Public Library, N. Wales.
Rochdale Public Library, Lancashire.
Rothwell Public Library, Yorkshire.
Rowley Regis Public Library, Staffordshire.
Royal Leamington Spa Public Library,
   Warwickshire.
Sale Public Library, Cheshire.
Salford Central Library, Lancashire.
Scunthorpe Public Library, Lincolnshire.
Sheffield City Libraries, Yorkshire.
Shoreditch Central Library, Hackney, London.
St. Albans Public Library, Hertfordshire.
South Shields Public Library, Co. Durham.
Southwark Central Library, London.
Sowerby Bridge, Public Library, Devon.
Staffordshire County Library, Stafford.
Stepney Public Library, London.
Stirling County Library, Scotland.

Stockport Central Library, Cheshire.
Stoke-on-Trent Central Library, Hanley,
    Staffordshire.
Stourbridge Public Library, Worcestershire.
Sunderland Public Library, Co. Durham.
Surbiton Public Library, Surrey.
Sussex County Library, Chichester.
Sutton Public Libraries, Surrey.
Tamworth Public Library, Staffordshire.
Taunton Public Library, Somerset.
Thurrock Central Library, Grays, Essex.
Walsall Central Library & Art Gallery,
    Staffordshire.
Walthamstow Central Library, London.
Wandsworth District Library, London.
Warwickshire County Library, Warwick.
Westminster Public (Reference) Library,
    London.
Weston-Super-Mare Public Library & Museum,
    Somerset.
West Sussex County Library, Sussex.
Whitehaven Public Library & Museum,
    Cumberland.
Wolverhampton Public Library, Staffordshire.
Worksop Public Library & Museum,
    Nottinghamshire.
Yeovil Public Library & Museum, Somerset.
York Public Library, Yorkshire.

UNITED STATES OF AMERICA:
Adas Shalom Library, Detroit, Mich.
Agawam Public Library, Mass.
A.K. Smiley Public Library, Redlands, Calif.
Aiken-Bamberg-Barnwell-Edgefield Regional
    Library, Aiken, S.C.
Akron Public Library, Ohio.
Alexandria Library, Va.
Anniston Public Library, Ala.
Asbury Park Free Public Library, N.J.
Austin Public Library, Tex.
Belmont Memorial Library, Mass.
Bemidji Library, Minn.
Bennett Martin Public Library, Lincoln, Neb.
Birmingham Public Library, Ala.
Bloomfield Free Public Library, Jarvie,
    Foundation, N.J.
Boston Public Library, Mass.
Bridgeport Public Library, Conn.
Brooklyn Public Library, N.Y.
Bucks County Free Library, Levittown, Pa.
Buena Park Library Distric, Calif.
Camas Public Library, Washington.
Cambria Public Library, Johnstown, Pa.
Camden Free Public Library, N.J.
Canton Public Library, Ohio.
Carnegie Library of Pittsburgh, Pa.
Center County Library, Bellefonte, Pa.
Charles H. Taylor Memorial Library,
    Hampton, Va.
Chicago Public Library, Ill.
Cincinnati & Hamilton County Public
    Library, Ohio.
City of Danville Public Library, Va.
City of Lakeland Public Library, Fla.
Colonial Williamsburg Research Library, Va.
Corona Public Library, Calif.
Country Club Hills Public Library, Ill.
Craven-Pamilco-Carteret Regional Library,
    New Bern, N.C.
Current River Regional Library, Van Buren,
    Mo.
Dallas Public Library, Tex.
Danville Public Library, Ill.
Davemport Public Library, Iowa.
Decatur Public Library, Ill.
DeKalb Public Library, Ill.
Donnell Library Center, New York, N.Y.
East Islip Public Library, N.Y.
East Moline Public Library, Ill.
El Dorado County Free Library, Placerville,
    Calif.
El Paso Public Library, Tex.
Elyria Public Library, Ohio.
Erie County Public Library, Pa.

Everett Public Lib., Wash.
Forbes Library, Northampton, Mass.
Fort Lauderdale Public Library, Fla.
Fort Wayne Public Library, Ind.
Fullerton Public Library, Calif.
Glendive Public Library, Mont.
Greensboro Public Library, N.C.
Grosse Pointe Public Library, Mich.
Hamden Library, Hamden, Conn.
Harlingen Public Library, Tex.
Herrick Public Library, Holland, Mich.
Hutchison County Library, Borger, Tex.
Idaho Falls Public Library, Idaho.
Indian River County Library, Vero Beach, Fla.
Island Trees Public Library, Levittown, N.Y.
Jennings County Public Library, North
    Vernon, Ind.
Kanawha County Public Library, Charleston,
    W. Va.
Kansas City Public Library, Mo.
Kearny Public Library, Kearny, N.Y.
Kern County Library, Bakersfield, Calif.
King County Library System, Seattle, Wash.
Kirkwood Public Library, Mo.
Kitsap Regional Library, Bremerton, Wash.
Lake Blackshear Regional Library, Americus,
    Ga.
Lakewood Public Library, N.J.
La Retama Public Library, Corpus Christi,
    Tex.
Leesburg Public Library, Fla.
Leon County Public Library, Tallahassee, Fla.
Lima Public Library, Ohio.
Los Angeles Public Library, Calif.
Madison Public Library, N.J.
Martin Memorial Library, York, Pa.
Mary H. Weir Public Library, Weirton, W. Va.
McKinley Memorial Library, Niles, Ohio.
Memphis Public Library, Tenn.
Mid-West Library Service, St. Louis, Mo.
Milwaukee Public Library, Wis.
Minot Public Library, N.D.
Mobile Public Library, Ala.
Moline Public Library, Ill.
Monessen Public Library, Pa.
Monterey County Library, Salinas, Calif.
Naples Public Library, Naples, N.Y.
National City Public Library, Calif.
Neenah Public Library, Wis.
Nevada State Library.
Newark Public Library, N.J.
New Bedford Free Public Library, Mass.
Newburgh Free Library, N.Y.
New Caanan Public Library, Conn.
New Castle Public Library, Ind.
Newton Public Library, Kan.
Niles Public Library, Ill.
Nioga Library System, Niagara Falls, N.Y.
Northbrook Public Library, Ill.
North Platte Public Library, Neb.
Oak Park Public Library, Ill.
Okefenokee Regional Library, Waycross, Ga.
Oklahoma County Libraries, Oklahoma City,
    Okla.
Ontario City Library, Calif.
Palatine Public Library, Ill.
Paramus Free Public Library, N.J.
Portage County District Library, Hiram, Ohio.
Port Angeles Public Library, Wash.
Portsmouth Public Library, Va.
Pottstown Public Library, Pa.
Prairie Hills Library System, Ottumwa, Iowa.
Prince George's Regional Library, Hyattsville,
    Md.
Public Library of Cincinnati & Hamilton Co.,
    Ohio.
Public Library of Groves, Tex.
Public Library of Knoxville & Knox County,
    Tenn.
Public Library of Pine Bluff & Jefferson
    County, Ark.
Queen's Borough Public Library, Jamaica, N.Y.
Rainier City Library, Ore.
Reading Public Library, Mass.

Richland County Public Library, Columbia, S.C.
Riverside Public Library, Calif.
Roanoke Public Library, Va.
Rolla Public Library, Mo.
Russell Library, Middletown, Conn.
Sacramento City Library, Sacramento, Calif.
St. Charles Parish Library, Hahnville, La.
St. Mary Parish Library, Franklin, La.
Salem Public Library, Mass.
Salinas Public Library, Calif.
San Bernardino County Free Library, Calif.
San Diego Public Library, Calif.
San Francisco Public Library, Calif.
San Jose Public Library, Calif.
Santa Barbara Public Library, Calif.
Shawnee Library System, Charterville, III.
Solano County Free Library, Fairfield, Calif.
Somerset Public Library, Mass.
South Bend Public Library, Ind.
Southwestern Missouri Library Service,
    Bolivar, Mo.
Stanford L. Warren Public Library, Durham,
N.C.
Suffolk Co-operative Library System,
    Patchogue, N.Y.
Swarthmore Public Library, Pa.
Toledo Public Library, Ohio.
Topeka Public Library, Kan.
Twinsburg Public Library, Ohio.
Tyrrell Public Library, Beaumont, Tex.
Umatilla County Library, Pendleton, Ore.
Wadsworth Public Library, Geneseo, N.Y.
Wallerstein County Library, Staten Island,
    N.Y.
Walpole Public Library, Walpole, Mass.
Walter Hampden Memorial Library, Gramercy
    Pk., New York, N.Y.
Watertown Free Public Library, Wis.
Wauwatosa Public Library, Wis.
Wichita City Library, Kan.
Wilson County Negro Public Library, N.C.
Woburn Public Library, Mass.
York County Library, Rock Hill, S.C.

SPECIAL

AUSTRIA:
International Atomic Energy Agency, Vienna.

AUSTRALIA:
"The Advertiser", Editorial Library, Adelaide,
    S.A.
"The Age", Melbourne, Vic.
Australian War Memorial, Canberra, A.C.T.
Botanic Garden, Adelaide, S.A.
Commonwealth Parliamentary Library,
    Canberra, A.C.T.
Dept. of Tech. Education, Sydney, N.S.W.
Ethiopian Consulate General, Sydney, N.S.W.
Herald & Weekly Times, Ltd., Melbourne,
    Vic.
Monaco Consulate, Melbourne, Vic.
National Gallery of Victoria, Melbourne, Vic.
Parliamentary Library, Brisbane, Qld.
Parliamentary Library, Perth, W.A.
Reserve Bank of Australia, Sydney, N.S.W.
Royal Botanic Gardens, South Yarra, Vic.
School of Nimes, Kalgoorlie, W.A.
Waite Agricultural Research Institute, Glen
    Osmond, S.A.
West Australian Newspapers Ltd., Perth, W.A.
Western Australian Museum, Perth, W.A.

BAHAMAS:
Nassau Cabinet Office.

CANADA:
Atomic Energy of Canada, Ltd., Chalk River,
    Ont.
Bibliotheque de la Legislature, Quebec, P.Q.
Canadian Broadcasting Corporation, Toronto,
    Ont.
Canadian O'Seas Telecommunications Corp.
CEGEP de Longuevil Library, Jaques-Cartier,
    Wuebec, P.Q.
City Clerk's Dept., Libraries Div., Montreal,
    P.Q.
Co-operative Book Center of Canada, Toronto.
    Ont.
Dept. of Forestry and Rural Dev., Ottawa,
    Ont.
Dominion Observatory Library, Dept. Energy,
    Mines & Resources, Ottawa, Ont.
Institutions Financieres Compagnies et
    Cooperatives, Gouvernement du Quebec,
    P.Q.
Legislative Library, Charlottetown, P.E.I.
Library of Parliament, Ottawa, Ont.
Merck Frosst Lab., Montreal, P.Q.
New Brunswick Museum, St. John, N.B.
Ontario Instute for Studies in Education,
    Toronto, Ont.
Quebec Ministry of Health, Dept. of
    Sanitation, Montreal, P.Q.

Science Council of Canada, Ottawa, Ont.
Smith Kline & French, Montreal, P.Q.

ETHIOPIA:
Imperial Library, Grand Palace, Addis Ababa.

FRANCE:
Bibliotheque des Etudes Poetiques, Paris.
Bibliotheque de l'Institut de France, Paris.
Bibliotheque du Conservatoire de Musique,
    Paris.
Bureau de Documentation, Paris.
Euro Finance, Paris.
Faculte de Medecine et de Pharmacie,
    Clermont-Ferrand.
Librairie Larousse, Paris.
Librairie des Meridiens, Paris.

FRENCH SOMALILAND:
American-African Finance Corp., Djibouti.

GERMANY:
German Soc. for Documentation,
    Frankfurt-am-Main.

INDIA:
Indian Airlines, New Delhi.
Parliamentary Library, New Delhi.

IRAQ:
Kandalla's Private Medical Library.

IRELAND:
Monaco Consulate, Dublin.
Royal Dublin Society.

ISRAEL:
Israel Atomic Energy Commission, Yavne.

ITALY:
Academie de la Valliere, Rome.
International Centre for Conservation, Rome.
Keats-Shelley Memorial Assoc. House, Rome.
Libreria Commissionaria Sansoni, Firenze
Libreria Ledi, Milan.

JAMAICA:
Institute of Jamaica, Kingston.

KENYA:
Kenya East African Railways & Harbours,
    Nairobi.

KUWAIT:
Kuwait Chamber of Commerce & Industry,
    Kuwait City.

LIBYA:
British Council, Tripoli.

MALTA:
Malta Drydocks Corporation, Malta G.C.

MONACO:
Bibliotheque du Palais, Monte Carlo.

NEW ZEALAND:
General Assembly Library, Parliament House, Wellington.

NORWAY:
Norsk Nobelinstittuts Bibliotek, Oslo.

PAKISTAN:
National Assembly Libraries, Karachi.

PANAMA:
Gorgas Memorial Laboratory Library, Balboa Heights, Canal Zone.

PHILIPPINES:
Pambansang Lupon Sa Pagpapaunlad NG Agham, (National Science Development Board) Rizal.
United Poets Laureate International, Quezon City.

POLAND:
Brazilian Embassy, Warsaw.

PORTUGAL:
Gulbenkian (Calouste) Foundation, Lisbon.

PUERTO RICO:
El Mundo, Inc., San Juan.
Instituto de Cultura Puertorriquena, San Juan.

SAUDI ARABIA:
Ministry of Information, Riyadh.

SOUTH AFRICA:
South Africa Foundation, Johannesburg.

SUDAN:
Ministry of Justice, Khartoum.

SWITZERLAND:
American African Finance Corp., Geneva.
DuPont de Nemours International, Geneva.
Geneva Arts Club.
Monsanto Research, S.A., Zurich.
Swiss Federal Institute of Technology, Zurich.

SYRIAN ARAB REPUBLIC:
Ministry of Petroleum, Electricity & Industrial Projects, Damascus.

UNITED KINGDOM:
American Embassy, London.
"Author's & Writer's Who's Who" offices, London.
Bishopsgate Institute, London.
Brewers Society, London.
British Council, London.
British Drama League, London.
British Records Assoc., Records Preservation Section, London.
"Burke's Peerage" office, London.
Central Office of Information, London.
Chartered Insurance Institute, London.
Chartered Institute of Secretaries, London.
"Daily Telegraph", London.
Dept. of Education & Science Library, London.
English-Speaking Union, Page Memorial Library.
Foreign Office, Printed Library, London.
Granada T.V. Library, Manchester.
Houses of Parliament Library, Belfast, Northern Ireland.
Imperial Chemical Industries, Blackley, Manchester.
India Office Library, Foreign & Commonwealth Office, London.
Intelligence Centre, The L.P.E., Ltd., London.
Institute of Contemporary Arts, London.
Institute of Mechanical Engineers, London.

Keats-Shelley Memorial Assoc., London.
Leicester Galleries, London.
Library Association, London.
London Library.
Lumley Cazalet Ltd., London.
Madden Galleries, London.
Manchester Public Libraries, Henry Watson Music Library.
Metropolitan Police Reference Library, New Scotland-Yard, London.
"Music Book" office, London.
National Liberal Club, London.
New South Wales Govt. Offices, London.
North Devon Athenaeum, Barnstaple.
"Oxford Mail" offices.
Pitman (Sir Isaac) & Sons, Ltd., Library, London.
Poetry Society, London.
Public Record Office, London.
Publishers & General Export Services, Ltd., London.
Reform Club, London.
Royal College of Surgeons of England, London.
Royal College of Surgeons, Edinburgh, Scotland.
Royal Commonwealth Society, London.
Royal Festival Hall, London.
Royal Geographical Society, London.
Royal Library, Windsor Castle, Berks.
Royal Military Academy, Sandhurst, Camberley, Surrey.
Royal Naval College, Greenwich.
Royal Scottish Academy of Music, Glasgow, Scotland. ·
Royal Society of Arts, London.
Royal United Service Institution, London.
Rylands (John) Library, Manchester.
Sark (Dame of) Library, Channel Islands.
Society for Theatre Research, London.
Society for Genealogists, London.
Spalding Gentlemen's Society, Lincs.
Stevens & Brown Ltd., Godalming, Surrey.
The Music Centre, City of Leeds.
Theosophical Society, London.
"Time & Tide" offices, London.
Ulster Museum, Belfast, N. Ireland.
United States Information Center, London.
Victoria & Albert Museum, Theatre Section, London.
Warwickshire Education Committee, Warwickshire.
"Who's Who" office, London.
"Who's Who in Theatre" office, London.

UNITED STATES OF AMERICA:
Addison-Wesley Publishing Co., Danvers, Mass.
Aerospace Corp., San Bernardino, Calif.
Air Training Command Library, Randolph AFB, Tex.
Albany City Hall, Ga.
American Antiquarian Society, Worcester, Mass.
American Art Archives, Detroit, Mich.
American Cancer Society, Medical Library, N.Y.
American Cartagemen Publishing Co., Detroit, Mich.
American Dental Assn., Chicago, JII.
American Geographical Society, N.Y.
American Hospital Assn., Chicago, III.
American Institute of Foreign Trade, Phoenix, Ariz.
American Library Assn., Chicago, III.
American Medical Assn., Chicago, III.
American Museum of Natural History, N.Y.
American Philosophical Society, Philadelphia, Pa.
Ames Library, Mass.
Anaconda Aluminium Co., Louisville, Ky.
Arco Chemical Company, Glenolden, Pa.
Avco-Everett Research Lab., Everett, Mass.
Bacon (Francis) Library, Claremont, Calif.
Baltimore Museum of Art, Md.

Bechtel Corporation Library, Gaithersburg, Md.
Bell Telephone Labs., N.J.
Bible Institute of Los Angeles, Biola Library,
La Mirada, Calif.
Board of Education of the City of New York,
Professional Library, N.Y.
Board of Parish Education, Lutheran Church
in America, Philadelphia, Pa.
Boston Symphony Orchestra, Mass.
Bresler Galleries, Inc., Milwaukee, Wis.
British Information Services, N.Y.
Brookley Air Force Base Library, Ala.
Broward County Board of Public Instruction,
Fort Lauderdale, Fla.
Bulletin Company, Philadelphia, Pa.
Bunker-Ramo Corporation, Canoga Park,
Calif.
Business & Professional Women's Fund,
Washington, D.C.
California State Fisheries Laboratory,
Terminal Island, Calif.
Car City Insurance Co., Detroit, Mich.
Carol M. Newman Library, Blacksburg, Va.
"Chicago Tribune", Ill.
Children's (The) Memorial Hospital, Chicago,
Ill.
Church of Christ, Costa Mesa, Calif.
The Clinton-Essex-Franklin Library, Plattsburgh,
N.Y.
Colorado Council of Churches, Denver.
Commission onon Human Rights, Research
Library, N.Y.C.
"Contemporary Authors" offices, Detroit, Mich.
Cortese Clinic, Indianapolis, Ind.
Cowles Magazine & Broadcasting Inc., N.Y.
Dayton Art Institute, Ohio.
Denver Post (The), Denver, Colo.
Dept. of Commerce Library,
Washington, D.C.
Dept. of Health, Education & Welfare, Food
& Drug, Administration, Washington, D.C.
Dept. of Housing & Rural Development,
Washington, D.C.
Des Moines Art Center, Iowa.
Detroit Free Press, Mich.
Dun & Bradstreet, Business Library, N.Y.
DuPont de Nemours & Co., Marshall Lab.,
Philadelphia, Pa.
Education & World Affairs, N.Y.
E.I. DuPont de Nemours & Co., Technical
Library, Wilmington, Del.
Eleutherian Mills Historical Library,
Greenville, Wilmington, Del.
Escambia County Board of Public Instruction,
Pensacola, Fla.
Esso Production Research Co. Library,
Houston, Tex.
Esso Research & Engineering Co. Library,
Linden, N.J.
Export-Import Bank of Washington,
Washington, D.C.
Filson Club, Louisville, Ky.
Florida Board of Conservation, Tallahassee.
Ford Foundation, N.Y.
Forest Products Labora ory, U.S. Dept. of
Agriculture, Madison, Wis.
Freedoms Foundation, Valley Forge, Pa.
Garden Center of Greater Cleveland, Ohio.
Geisinger Memorial Hospital, Danville, Pa.
Genealogical Soc. of the Church of Jesus
Christ of Latter Day Saints, Inc.,
Salt Lake City, Utah.
General Dynamics, Pomona Division, Calif.
Georgia Power Company Library, Atlanta, Ga.
Golden Gate Baptist Seminary Library, Mill
Valley, Calif.
Graduate Theological Union Bibliographical
Center, Berkeley, Calif.
Grand Lodge of Texas, Waco.
Guggenheim Foundation, N.Y.
Gulf Research & Development Co., Merriam,
Kan.
Hampden (Walter) Mem. Library, N.Y.
Hammond Museum, North Salem, N.Y.

Hawaii Dept. of Education, Honolulu.
Health Research, Inc., Buffalo, N.Y.
H.J. Heinz Company Library, Pittsburgh, Pa.
Houston Museum of Fine Arts, Tex.
Hughes Aircraft Co., Research Library,
Malibu, Calif.
Institute for Space Studies, N.Y.
Institute of Heraldry, U.S. Army, Washington,
D.C.
Institutum Divi Thomae Foundation,
Cincinnati, Ohio.
Instrucional Material Center, Birmingham,
Ala.
International Minerals & Chemical Corp.,
Skokie, Ill.
Jackson Laboratory, Bar Harbor, Me.
Joint Bank Fund Library, Washington, D.C.
Kennecott Copper Corporation, N.Y.C.
King County Hospital, Seattle, Wash.
Kingsville Publishing Co., Tex.
Lackland Air Force Base, Officer Training
School Library, Tex.
Lakeland Village, State of Washington, Dept.
of Institution's, Medical Lake, Washington.
Library Central Processing Office, School
Libraries, Lawrence L.I., N.Y.
Library of the Supreme Council, Washington,
D.C.
Lockheed California Co., Central Library,
Burbank, Calif.
Lone Star Gas Co., Dallas, Tex.
Long Island Jewish Hospital, N.Y.
Lutheran Council (National), N.Y.
Marion County Board of Public Instruction,
Ocala, Fla.
Maryland Historical Society Library,
Baltimore.
Mayo Foundation, Minn.
McGraw-Hill Publications, N.Y.
Medical Exams Building, Dept. of Forensic
Medicine Library, N.Y.
Memorial Sloane-Kettering Cancer Center, N.Y.
Menninger Foundation, Topeka, Kan.
Miles Laboratories, Inc., Elkhart, Ind.
Montefiore Hospital & Medical Center, Bronx,
N.Y.
Morristown Memorial Hospital, N.J.
Mount Sinai Hospital, N.Y.
Museum of Fine Arts, Houston, Tex.
Naha Air Base Library, Ryukyu Islands.
Natick Laboratories, Natick, Mass.
National Center for Atmospheric Research,
Boulder, Colo.
National Conference of Christians & Jews,
Inc.—Lazarus Library of Intergroup
Relations, N.Y.
National Federation of Settlements &
Neighborhood Centers (U.S.A.), N.Y.
National Park Service, Interior Dept.,
Washington, D.C.
Nelson-Atkins Gallery of Art, Kansas City,
Mo.
New School for Social Research, N.Y.
Newcomen Soeity of North America,
Downingtown, Pa.
New England Institute for Medical Research,
Ridgefield, Conn.
Newhouse Galleries, Inc., N.Y.
New York Stock Exchange, N.Y.
North Carolina Memorial Hospital, Div. of
Health Affairs Lib., Chapel Hill.
Ohio Historical Society Library, Columbus.
Ovaltine Food Products, Ill.
Puducah City Hall, Ky.
Pan American World Airways, N.Y.
Park Synagogue, Kravitz Memorial Library,
Cleveland, Ohio.
Phoenix Art Museum, Ariz.
"Police Digest", Chicago, Ill.
Port of New York Authority, N.Y.
Potash Co. of America, Carlsbad, N.M.
P.P.G. Industries, Glass Research Center
Library, Pittsburgh, Pa.
Product Safety Research Corp., Sherman

Oaks, Calif.
Radio Corp. of America, Princeton, N.J.
Rand Corporation, Santa Monica, Calif.
Reiss-Davis Clinic for Child Guidance, Los
Angeles, Calif.
Reserve Officers Assn. U.S.A., Mo.
Richardson (The) Company, Melrose Park, Ill.
Rockefeller Foundation, N.Y.
Rutherford B. Hayes Library, Freemont, Ohio.
"Saturday Review" Library, N.Y.
St. Luke's Presbyterian Hospital, Chicago, Ill.
St. Vincent Charity Hospital, Cleveland, Ohio.
School Library Services, Wichita, Kan.
Scott Paper Co., Research Library,
Philadelphia, Pa.
Sheppard Air Force Base Library, Tex.
South Carolina State Hospital, Horger Library,
Columbia.
Southern Baptist Theological Seminary,
Louisville, Ky.
Southwest Research Institute, San Antonio,
Tex.
Special Service Library Division, Fort Belvoir,
Va.
Spencer Kellogg, Research Center Library,
Buffalo, N.Y.
Sport Fishing Institute, Washington, D.C.
Standard & Poor's Corp., N.Y.
Standard Oil Company (New Jersey) Central
Library.
Starr Commonwealth for Boys, Albion, Mich.
State Department of Education, Sacramento,
Calif.
State Department of Mental Health, Lansing,
Mich.
State of Illinois—
Department of Public Instruction,
Springfield.
Div. of Vocational Rehabilitation,
Springfield.
State of New Jersey, Div. on Civil Rights,
Trenton, N.J.
Steuben Glass Reference Library, N.Y.
Supreme Court Law Library, Santa Fe, N.M.
Temple Israel of Greater Miami, Fla.

Texas Instruments, Dallas.
Theology Library, Claremont, Calif.
"Time", Inc., Library, N.Y.
Truman (Harry S.) Library, Independence,
Mo.
Union Electric Co., St. Louis, Mo.
Union League Club Library, New York, N.Y.
United Hospital Fund of New York, N.Y.
United Nations Library, N.Y.
United States Army Special Services Agency
Library Div.
United States Army, Terrestrial Sciences
Center, Hanover, N.H.
United States Atomic Energy Commission,
Washington, D.C.
United States Bureau of Mines, Amarillo,
Tex.
United States Dept. of Agriculture, Soil &
Water Conservation, Beltsville, Md.
United States Dept. of Health, Education &
Welfare, Washington, D.C.
United States Dept. of Treasury, Washington,
D.C.
United States Plywood—Champion Papers
Inc., Chicago, Ill.
United States Steel Corp., N.Y.
Upper Room Devotional Library & Museum,
Nashville, Tenn.
Veterans Administration Center, Main Library,
Dayton, Ohio.
Veterans Administration Hospital Library,
Tacoma, Wash.
Veterans Administration Hospital, Washington,
D.C.
Vocational Rehabilitation, Springfield, Ill.
Wool Bureau, Inc., New York, N.Y.
World Trade Center Libraries, San Francisco,
Calif.
Young & Rubicam, Inc., N.Y.

YUGOSLAVIA:
Medical Facility, Novi Saol.

U.S.S.R.:
Biblioteka Akademii Nauk—SSSR, Moscow.

SCHOOL

AUSTRALIA:
Geelong College, Vic.
Knox Grammar School, Wahroonga, N.S.W.
Launceston Church Grammar School,
Tasmania.
Presbyterian Girls' College, Warwick, Qld.

CANADA:
MacDonald High School, Quebec.
Rideau High School, Ottawa, Ont.

MALAYSIA:
High School, Serapak, Kuala Lumpur.

UNITED KINGDOM:
Aveley Secondary School, South Ockendon.
Beaufoy School, Kennington, London.
Bromley Grammar Girls' School, Kent.
Downside School, Bath, Somerset.
Eton College, Windsor.
Harrow School, Harrow.
Owen's Boys' School, London.
Radley College, Abingdon.
Rishworth School, Halifax.
Rugby School, Warwickshire.
Stockwell Manor School, London.
Wincheshter College, Winchester.

UNITED STATES OF AMERICA:
Academy of Immaculate Conception,
Ferdinand, Ind.
Albany Public Schools Library Services, N.Y.
Allen Park High School, Mich.
Ashland City School District, Ashland, Ohio.
Baptist Sunday School Board, Southern

Baptist Convention, Dargan-Carver Library,
Nashville, Tenn.
Belmont Public School, Belmont, Mass.
Bergen County Tech. High School,
Hackensack, N.J.
Beverly Hills Unified School District, Calif.
Booker T. Washington Junior High School,
Mobile, Ala.
Brittonkill Central Schools, Troy, N.Y.
Bucks County Public Schools, Doylestown,
Pa.
Buckeley Junior High School, New London,
Conn.
Central Junior High School, Norman, Okla.
Chopticon High School, Morganza, Md.
Clarksville Community School Corp., Ind.
Clayton, School District of Mo.
Delhart High School, Tex.
De La Warr School District, Dela.
Denton School District, Wash.
East Meadow Public Schools, N.Y.
Easton Area High School, Pa.
Fay School, Southboro, Mass.
Friends School, Baltimore, Md.
Fullerton High School, Calif.
Gallia Academy High School, Little Falls,
Minn.
Granite School District, Salt Lake City,
Utah.
Hauppauge Union Free School District No. 6,
N.Y.
Haverford Junior High School, Haverton, Pa.
Henry Hudson Regional High School,
Highlands, N.J.
Hobart High School, Akron, Ohio.

Howland Junior High School, Warren, Ohio.
Hutchison School for Girls, Memphis, Tenn.
Intermediate School 49, Library, Brooklyn,
  N.Y.
Leflore County High School, Itta Bena, Miss.
Lexington Public Schools, Mass.
Lincoln High School, Greenville County, S.C.
Lincoln High School, Wisconsin Rapids, Wis.
Lordstown Local School, Warren, Ohio.
Lutheran School of Theology, Chicago, Ill.
Medfield Junior High School, Mass.
Milford High School, Mass.
Monsey Elementary School, Monsey, N.Y.
Mooers Central School, N.Y.
Mr. Anthony Union High School District,
  No. 14, Bennington, Vt.
Myrtle Point High School, Ore.
North Hills Schools, Pittsburgh, Pa.
North Lawrence Community Schools, Bedford,
  Ind.
North Shore School, Chicago, Ill.
Northwood Junior High School, Fort Wayne,
  Ind.
Parsippany High School, N.J.
Pence School, Fort Leonard Wood, Mo.
Pittston Area School District, Pa.
Premontre High School, Green Bay, Wis.
Ramapo Central School District No. 2, Spring
  Valley, N.Y.
Rich County School District, Randolph, Utah.
Riverview Gardens School District, St. Louis,
  Mo.

Roby School, Shepherdsville, Ky.
St. Augustine High School, Chicago, Ill.
St. Clara Academy, Sinsinawa, Wis.
St. Francis Convent, Milwaukee, Wis.
St. Francis High School, Little Falls, Minn.
St. Gertrude's Convent, Cottonwood, Idaho.
St. John's High School, Toledo, Ohio.
School District of the City of Royal Oak,
  Mich.
South St. Paul Public Schools, S. St. Paul,
  Minn.
Statesville Senior High School, N.C.
Sweet Home School District, Ore.
Thomas Jefferson Senior High School, Port
  Arthur, Tex.
Todd County Central High School, Elkton,
  Ky.
Trenton High School, Ohio.
Union County Schools Library District,
  Monroe, N.C.
Wappingers Central School District,
  Multi-Media Library, Beacon, N.Y.
Wellwood Junior High School, Fayetteville,
  N.Y.
West Orange—Cove Consolidated Independent
  School District, Orange, Tex.
Woodburg High School, Conn.
Wilcox Public Schools, Ariz.
William Penn Charter School, Philadelphia,
  Pa.
Winona High School, Miss.
Yakima Public Schools Library Services, Wash.

Owners of the Royal Edition of Dictionary of International Biography

The following are owners of the Royal Edition of Dictionary of International Biography:

H.M. Queen Elizabeth II.

H.I.M. Haile Selassie I,
Emperor of Ethiopia.

H.I.M. The Shahanshah of Iran.

H.S.H. The Prince of Monaco,
Rainier III.

General Francisco Franco Baha-Monde,
Prime Minister and Chief of State, Spain.

President Sayed Ismail El—Azhari,
of the Sudan.

His Excellency Ferdinand E. Marcos,
President of the Republic of the Philippines.

General Anastasio Somoza Debayle,
President of the Republic of Nicaragua.

H.M. Hassan II,
King of Morocco.

H.R.H. Jean,
Grand Duke of Luxembourg.

H.M. Bhumibol Adulyadej,
King of Thailand.

Paul Morris Aaroe,
301 Hardwick St., Belvidere,
NJ 07823, U.S.A.

Albert M. Aboody, M.D.,
3 Bell Cove,
Kings Point, NY 11024, U.S.A.

Sylvia Cohen Ackerman,
89-15 Parsons Blvd., Apt. 1L.,
Jamaica, NY 11432, U.S.A.

Addie Frank Adams,
P.O. Box 550,
1707 Pecan St.,
Bastrop, TX 78602, U.S.A.

Robert Hayden Alcorn,
Suffield,
CT 06078, U.S.A.

Norman Allan,
Norman Allan & Company,
17540 Wyoming,
Detroit 21, MI U.S.A.

Baron Lanfranco Amato di Campolevrini,
108 Sandringham Dr.,
Downsview, Toronto,
Ont., Canada.

Marcus J. Andersen, D.D.S.,
Box 512,
Brigham City,
UT 84302, U.S.A.

Raphael Cleve Anno,
22103 So. Neptune Ave.,
Carson, CA 90745, U.S.A.

Dorothy Fry Arbuckle,
Lake Village,
IN 46349, U.S.A.

Alice Catt Armstrong,
'Cordell Views', 1331 Cordell Place,
Los Angeles, CA 90069, U.S.A.

Hillard J. Aronson,
52 Tecumseh Drive,
Longmeadow,
MA 01106, U.S.A.

Dr. Arthur Arnold,
40 S. Clay St., Hinsdale,
IL U.S.A.

Mrs. Pauline Porter Asbill,
1417 Barnwell St., Columbia,
SC 29201, U.S.A.

The Hon. Jose D. Aspiras,
Office of the President,
Malacanang Palace, Manila, Philippines.

Barton Baker,
801 Times Square Bldg.,
Rochester, NY 14614, U.S.A.

Dr. Sri Ram Bakshi,
Dept. of Theatre, State Univ. Coll.,
Brockport, NY 14420, U.S.A.

J. Wm. Baldwin,
P.O. Box 33,
Hyattsville,
MD 20781, U.S.A.

William Carroll Barrett,
Apt. 7, Coloma Apts., Box 218,
Coloma, MI 49038, U.S.A.

Mrs. H. Barrows,
500 East 77 St., New York,
NY 10021, U.S.A.

Dr. Frederick H. Barth,
4150 City Avenue, Philadelphia,
PA 19131, U.S.A.

Dr. James E. Bauerle,
112 Cas-Hills, San Antonio,
TX 78213, U.S.A.

Charles W. Beagle,
102 West Nassau Avenue,
South Plainfield,
NJ 07080, U.S.A.

George R. Bechtel, Jr.,
1417 Brooklyn Ave. S.W.,
Canton,
OH 44710, U.S.A.

James Milton Bell, M.D.,
Clinical Director,
Berkshire Farm for Boys,
Canaan, NY 12029, U.S.A.

Mrs. I.F. Belser,
3913 Kilbourne Rd., Columbia,
SC 29205, U.S.A.

Leon Bercovici,
127 Avenue Winston Churchill,
1180 Brussels, Belgium.

Lt.-Col. T.M. Beveridge, USA Ret.,
1617 Oakland Blvd., Fort Worth,
TX 76103, U.S.A.

Florence E. Sanford Bielemeier,
99-36 213th St., Queens Village L.I.,
NY 11429, U.S.A.

William F. Big Spring, Sr.,
Box 51, East Glacier Pk.,
MT 59434, U.S.A.

Mrs. Gene H. Binning,
3101 Rolling Stone Road,
Oklahoma City,
OK 73120, U.S.A.

Dr. Harold S. Black,
120 Winchip Rd., Countryside,
Summit, NJ 07901, U.S.A.

Arthur I. Bodkins,
77 Summer St., Boston,
MA U.S.A.

Richard R. Bogardus,
505 North Park Dr., Arlington,
VA 22203, U.S.A.

Sergei Bongart,
533 West Rustic Rd., Santa Monica,
CA 90402, U.S.A.

Mrs. M. Bordallo,
P.O. Box 1458,
Agana, GU 96910,
Guam U.S. Territory.

Mrs. Odecye E. Bostick,
3146 Cache Rd., Apt. 119,
Lawton, OK 73501, U.S.A.

John J. Bowater, F.H.G.,
12300 North Menny Drive, Granada Hills,
CA 91344, U.S.A.

H.E. The Rev. Dr. J.R. Bowering, OSL,
First Methodist Church,
115 Ocean Ave., Island Heights,
NJ 08732, U.S.A.

Jose M.J. Bravo y Herrera,
1600 Blue Jay Way, L.A.,
CA 90069, U.S.A.

Dick Briggs,
2169 Homedale Rd., Klamath Falls,
OR 97601, U.S.A.

Kenneth E. Britain,
P.O. Box 599,
17906 Rolling Creek Drive,
Houston, TX 77001, U.S.A.

George S. Brosky,
Regal Arms Apartments,
456 Keoniana St., Honolulu,
HI 96815, U.S.A.

Christian E. Burckel,
100 Rockledge Rd.,
Bronxville,
NY 10708, U.S.A.

Dr. William F. Burns,
21 Brooklawn Drive,
Pompton Plains, NJ, U.S.A.

Professor W.E. Caldwell,
Department of Psychology,
The George Washington University,
Washington, DC 20006, U.S.A.

Dr. Dorothy J. Campbell,
St. Francis Xavier Univ.,
Antigonish, N.S., Canada.

Dr. Louis J. Camuti,
P.O. Box 146,
Fleetwood Station,
Mount Vernon,
NY 10552, U.S.A.

Naomi L. Campbell,
333 Athol Ave., Oakland,
CA 94606, U.S.A.

Horace M. Cardwell,
P.O. Box 1447,
Lufkin, TX 75901, U.S.A.

Elsie Gossett Care,
1619 Towne House, Harrisburg,
PA 17102, U.S.A.

Joseph T. Carney,
240 East Palisade Ave.,
Englewood, NJ, U.S.A.

Professor Lloyd G.K. Carr,
Rio Grande College, Rio Grande,
OH 45674, U.S.A.

Mitchell B. Carroll,
20 East 74th St.,
New York,
NY 10021, U.S.A.

Michael R. Cashman,
138 Rue Théophile Vander Elst,
1170 Brussels, Belgium.

Mrs. Bryant T. Castellow,
Cuthbert, CA 31740, U.S.A.

Dr. Psyche Cattell,
314 N. West End Ave.,
Lancaster, PA 17602, U.S.A.

Mrs. D.J. Clark,
R.D. No. 3, Box 238,
Ligonier, PA 15658, U.S.A.

T.H. Coates,
8 Normanby Road,
Kew,
Victoria, Australia 3101.

Gifford A. Cochran,
227 Eden Road,
Palm Beach,
FL 33480, U.S.A.

Mr & Mrs. Henry Sutcliffe Coe,
P.O. Box 877, San Jose,
CA 95106, U.S.A.

Beatrice Helen Collins,
New Orleans, LA 70126, U.S.A.

F. Ethel Collins,
Box 536, 317 Presidential Way,
Guilderland, NY 12084, U.S.A.

Dr. Thomas Carroll Committe,
Gamma Coll., Univ. of West Fla.,
Pensacola, FL 32504, U.S.A.

Billy Ray Francis Cook,
1508 Crossroads of the World,
Hollywood, CA 90028, U.S.A.

Floyd Cook,
6322 Craigway Rd.,
Spring, TX 77373, U.S.A.

Robert T. Coolidge,
27 Rosemount Ave., Westmount 217,
Quebec, Canada.

W.F. Corman,
Southland Telephone Company,
P.O. Drawer N,
Atmore, AL 36502, U.S.A.

The Rev. Arthur G-T Courteau,
351 Mockingbird Valley Rd.,
Louisville, KY 40207, U.S.A.

Alberta Lee Cox,
8400 E. 85th St., Raytown,
MO 64138, U.S.A.

Henry Bartholomew Cox,
11305 Riverview Rd., Oxon Hill,
MD 20022, U.S.A.

Ansel Elbert Creamer,
410 Poplar St.,
Florence SC, U.S.A.

Mrs. Margaret Crume,
264 West 73rd St., New York,
NY 10023, U.S.A.

Marilyn A.E. Cunningham,
104 Brady Ln., Bloomfield Hills,
MI 48013, U.S.A.

William A. Curci,
4947 Fulton Drive, N.W., Canton,
OH 44718, U.S.A.

Harry Cooke Cushing, IV,
Via Sardegna 29, Rome, Italy.

Professor Bror Danielsson,
Skeppargatan 84,
11459, Stockholm, Sweden.

Reverend R.H. Dean, B.A., B.Ed., M.A.C.E.,
"Bramoura", Baker Road,
Harkaway, Victoria, Australia 3806.

Dr. Angell O. de la Sierra,
University of Puerto Rico,
Faculty of Natural Sciences,
Cayey Campus,
Cayey, Puerto Rico 00633.

Leonard DeLue,
6861 S. Clayton Way,
Littleton,
CO 80122, U.S.A.

Mrs. Aryola Marieanne Demos,
4985 Meadow Park Drive,
Pittsburgh,
PA 15236, U.S.A.

Raymond L. DeProy,
3110 West 43rd Ave., Vancouver 13,
British Columbia, Canada.

Mrs. Dorothy E. de Rivera,
509 Willow Avenue,
Deerfield, IL 60015, U.S.A.

Col. Homer Diman, U.S.A.F. (Ret.),
Sky Harbour—Apt. 3-B,
St. Petersburg,
FL 33711, U.S.A.

T.B. Donaldson, C.B.E.,
P.O. Box N 4868,
Nassau, Bahamas.

Leonore Gutierrez Doody,
4134 Falkirk Ln.,
Houston, TX 77025, U.S.A.

Marguerite Ruth Dow,
1231 Richmond St., Apt. 909,
London, Ont., Canada.

Leslie P. Dudley,
10354 Wilshire Boulevard No. 1,
Los Angeles, CA 90024, U.S.A.

Mary Elizabeth Dufner, M.D., J.D., F.C.A.P.,
F.C.L.M., F.R.S.H.,
9617 Leon Street,
Philadelphia, PA 19114, U.S.A.

Martha Verge duPont,
'Montmorency', Greenville,
DE 19807, U.S.A.

Dr. René A. Dupuis,
'La Châtelainie',
CH 2072 Saint-Blaise/Neuchâtel, Switzerland.

Hon. Romon M. Durano,
House of Representatives,
Manila, Philippines.

Professor Robert P. Eager,
Department of Anatomy, Yale University,
School of Medicine, 333 Cedar St.,
New Haven, CT 06510, U.S.A.

Professor Uno Ebrelius,
Kalkbrännerigatan 5,
S-216 11 Malmö,
Sweden.

Professor Joseph W. Ehrenreich,
535 N. Brand Blvd. Suite 402,
Glendale, CA 91203, U.S.A.

James E. Eller,
536 Caren Drive, Virginia Beach,
VA 23452, U.S.A.

Rev. Dr. John F. Elliott,
3980 Edgehill Rd., Fort Worth,
TX 76116, U.S.A.

Rev. Dr. Charles T. Epps,
521 Bramhall Avenue,
Jersey City,
NJ 07304, U.S.A.

Dr. Ismail Ersevim,
63 Beverly Rd., Arlington,
MA 02174, U.S.A.

Dr. Argelia Velez Esquivel,
838 Foxboro Lane,
Dallas, TX 75241, U.S.A.

Raymond Evans,
1453 Wabash St., Denver,
CO 80220, U.S.A.

Dr. Rafik S. Farag,
68 E. Third St., Peru,
IN 46970, U.S.A.

Anis Farah,
Schl. of Engrng., Laurentian Univ.,
Sudbury, Ont., Canada.

Nicholas E.N. Farmakis,
13 Voukourestiou St.,
Athens, Greece.

Ross Farrens,
2495 Skyline Blvd., Reno,
NV 89502, U.S.A.

Marie Formanek Fawcett,
North St. & Hawkwood Ln.,
Greenwich, CT 06830, U.S.A.

John Fejervary,
Varni-Lite Corp. of Am.,
3005 Copper Rd., Santa Clara,
CA 95051, U.S.A.

J.L. Felts,
P.O. Box 156, Tahlequah,
OK 74464, U.S.A.

Adam E. Feret. Jr., D.M.D.,
169 Mountain Avenue,
Westfield,
NJ 07090, U.S.A.

Dean S.M. Field,
The Real & Rare Gall. Ltd.,
1430—1436 Yonge St.,
Toronto, Canada.

Blanche Finch,
2479 Peachtree Road. N.E.,
Apt. 1305,
Atlanta, GA 30305, U.S.A.

Fisk University,
Nashville, TN, U.S.A.

Wayne A. Forester,
Executive Secretary,
The American Association of Criminology,
Box 3014, University Station,
Eugene, OR 97403, U.S.A.

John Lile Forsyth,
'Caloola', Peak Crossing,
Queensland Q4305, Australia.

W. Dean Frischknecht,
212 Withycombe Hall, Ore. State Univ.,
Corvallis, OR 97331, U.S.A.

Miss Grace E. Frysinger,
3133 Connecticut Ave., N.W.,
Wash. DC 20008, U.S.A.

Dr. Francis J. Funke,
14320 N.W. 16th Court, Miami,
FL 33167, U.S.A.

James William Gentry,
8659 Lookout Mountain Avenue, Los Angeles,
CA 90046, U.S.A.

Carl Gerdau,
c/o Mrs Sandra Blewer,
1035—5th Ave.,
N.Y., NY 10028, U.S.A.

Rochella Sue Gerger,
1608 Longworth House Office Bldg.,
Wash. DC 20515, U.S.A.

Herbert Gerisch,
c/o. Big Bau-Investitions-Gesellschaft mbH.,
Fleethörn 32/34,
23 Kiel,
German Fed. Repub.

Dr. Richard P. Germann,
Whispering Elms,
3940 Elm Lane, Waukegan,
IL 60085, U.S.A.

V. McDonald Gibson, F.A.I.M.,
11 Kinane Street,
Brighton,
Victoria, Australia 3192.

Dr. Richard Jay Goldberg,
4814 Brandenburg Place, Tarzana,
CA 91356, U.S.A.

Richard D. Goldner, M.D.,
1024 N. Michigan Ave., Saginaw,
MI 48602, U.S.A.

Dr. Joseph L. Goodman,
29 Broughton Street,
Charleston, SC 29407, U.S.A.

Dr. Thomas M. Goolsby, Jr.,
20 Glenn Forest Athens,
CA 30603, U.S.A.

Samuel H. Gorton,
7627 Westside Hwy., Castle Rock,
Wash. DC 98611, U.S.A.

James A. Grazier,
c/o USAID/TCSP,
APO 09676, NY, U.S.A.

Homer Henry Greenlee, D.V.M.,
c/o Animal Hospital,
618 S. Jennings Ave., Ft. Worth TX, U.S.A.

Warwick L. Greville,
1532 S. Arlington Heights Rd.,
Arlington Heights, IL 60005, U.S.A.

Mrs. Gratia Bailey Groves,
1212 Crystal Towers North,
1600 South Eads St., Arlington,
VA 22202, U.S.A.

Dr. Marion H. Groves,
2231 East 67th St., Chicago,
IL 60649, U.S.A.

John V. Grundamis,
185 N.E. Hartman Circle,
Fridley, MN 55432, U.S.A.

Dr. Farid S. Haddad,
Orient Hospital,
Beirut, Lebanon.

Theodosia Doris S. Haley,
375 Riverside Drive, (Apt. 11AA),
New York, NY 10025, U.S.A.

Mrs. Rebecca E. L. Hall,
P.O. Box 1677,
Wilmington, NC, U.S.A.

Dr. Daniel Kasberg Halvorsen,
111 W. Main St., Owatonna,
MN 55060, U.S.A.

William H. Hand,
Hand Laboratory,
Nyack, NY, U.S.A.

Jason A. Hannah, M.D.,
5 Douglas Drive,
Toronto,
Ontario, M4W 2B2, Canada.

Leslie B. Harmer,
P.O. Box 171,
Devonshire, 4, Bermuda.

Margwyn S. Harris,
3305 Sunbeam St., Houston,
TX 77051, U.S.A.

Lt.-Col. Leonard D. Hausner,
1925 West Evergreen Ave., Chicago,
IL 60622, U.S.A.

George Austin Hay,
1607 16th St. N.W.,
Washington, DC 20009, U.S.A.

Mrs. Gladys L. Heath,
113 N. Houston St.,
Fort Worth, TX 76102, U.S.A.

Dermont J. J. Hellier,
'The Algarve', Boundary Road,
Mount Eliza, Melbourne,
Victoria, Australia 3930.

Dr. Jasna P. Heurtley,
16 East 98 St., New York,
NY 10029, U.S.A.

Professor William H. Hewitt,
1218 South Pugh St., State College,
PA 16801, U.S.A.

R. Eugene Holley,
Commerce Bldg., 206 Seventh St.,
Augusta, GA 30902, U.S.A.

Dr. Lawrence M. Holloway,
10283 Corunna Rd., Swartz Creek,
MI 48473, U.S.A.

Steele Holman,
1050 N. Point, Apt. 1604,
Fontana Towers,
San Francisco, CA, U.S.A.

Dr. Charles A. Hopkins,
30 North Michigan Ave., Suite 1223,
Chicago, IL 60602, U.S.A.

Dr. Schuyler Dean Hoslett,
Schuyler Lane, South Twenty-First Pl.,
Sturgeon Bay, WI 54235, U.S.A.

Mr. Justice Samuel O. Ighodaro,
Midwest Boundary Settlement Commission,
Benin City, Nigeria.

Dr. Edgar Inselberg,
Biology Dept., Western Michigan University,
Kalamazoo, MI 49001, U.S.A.

Dr. Carol G. Jacob,
309 N. St. S.W.,
Wash. DC 20024, U.S.A.

Richard H. Janusz,
1270 Ala Moana Blvd.,
Honolulu, HI 96814, U.S.A.

Elmer K. Jeska,
419 East Church Street,
Swanton, OH 43558, U.S.A.

Victor Emmanuel Jesudoss,
No. 1, Road 5/13E,
Petaling Jaya, Malaysia.

Carl August Johnson,
920 House Ave., Cheyenne,
WY 82001, U.S.A.

Dr. Lynn Eric Johnson,
432 E. 400 South, Orem,
UT 84057, U.S.A.

Ollie Bernard Johnson,
P.O. Box 2145, Memphis,
TN 38101, U.S.A.

Mrs. Myrtis Barham Jones,
5608 Geyer Springs Road,
Little Rock,
AR 72209, U.S.A.

William A. Jones,
122 S. 39th St., Apt. 302,
Omaha, NB 68131, U.S.A.

J. Robert Jordan,
1221 San Vicente Blvd.,
Santa Monica,
CA 90402, U.S.A.

Harold Rowan Joseph,
P.O. Box 96, Northridge,
CA 91324, U.S.A.

Charles E. Kaempen,
3202 Larkstone Drive, Orange,
CA 92667, U.S.A.

H.E.A. to Gabremascal Kaflegzi,
Ambassador, Imperial Ethiopian Embassy,
London, S.W.7, England.

Earl S. Kalland,
3090 S. High Street, Denver,
CO 80210, U.S.A.

Rev. Ridell Archibald Kelsey,
9001 W. Lincoln Ave.,
Brookfield, IL 60513, U.S.A.

Rev. Gary W. Kendrick,
The Episcopal Diocesan Center, P.O. Box M,
Capitol Hill Station Denver,
CO 80218, U.S.A.

Rev. Dr. Thomas A. Kane,
120 Hill Street,
Whitinsville,
MA 01588, U.S.A.

David Anthony Keogh,
London, England.

Geraldine Young Kerlin,
59 Wain St., P.O. Box 112,
Wellsboro, PA 16901, U.S.A.

Rubie G. Kilchrist,
1207 Lafayette Street, Lafayette,
LA 70501, U.S.A.

Lyun Joon Kim,
Hanyang University,
8¬2 Hangdang-dong, Sungdong-ku,
Seoul, Korea.

John T. Kimball,
P.O. Box F-1192,
Freeport, Bahamas.

Mrs. Vesta Kimble,
701 West Hullum St., Breckenridge,
TX 76024, U.S.A.

Dr. Charles Ross King,
1415 Raible Ave., Anderson,
IN 46100, U.S.A.

George F. Kneller,
372 Hilgard Ave., Los Angeles,
GA 90024, U.S.A.

Walter O. Kraft,
925 Paseo El Merador,
Palm Springs,
CA 92262, U.S.A.

John H. Krenkel,
619 E. Erie Drive, Tempe,
AZ 85281, U.S.A.

Mrs. Peter B. Kuhl,
736 S. Windsor Blvd., Los Angeles,
CA 90005, U.S.A.

Wilhelm G.A. Kullberg,
P.O. Box 62,
1751 Halden, Norway.

Donald Jay Kurlander,
Edison Bldg., Clark & Adams Sts.,
Chicago, IL 60093, U.S.A.

William Houston Landers,
P.O. Box 22005, Denver,
CO 80222, U.S.A.

Margo Terzian Lang,
Marhaba Studio,
6127 Calle del Paisano,
Scottsdale, AZ 85251, U.S.A.

Mrs. Howard A. LaRose,
Mocking Bird Hill, Lake George,
NY 12845, U.S.A.

Mrs. Marian L. Larson,
4954 N. Kentucky Ave., Chicago,
IL 60630, U.S.A.

H.R.H. Marziano II F.G.M. Pio Lavaréllo
Obrénovitsch,
Via Piemonte 101,
00187 Rome, Italy.

Irwin H. & Silvia W. Leiferman,
Imperial House, 5255 Collins Ave.,
Miami Beach, FL, U.S.A.

Ralph F. LePore,
22 Hamilton Ave., Wheeling,
WV 26003, U.S.A.

Carl Mervin Lewis,
100 Pricefield Rd.,
Toronto 5, Ont., Canada.

(John) Aaron D. Lewis,
165 West End Ave., New York,
NY 10023, U.S.A.

Gregorio S. Licaros,
Central Bank of the Philippines,
Manila, Philippines.

Delmore Liggett,
Clearview Heights, Rising Sun,
IN 47040, U.S.A.

Dr. G. Logaras,
L. Kaftanzoglou 8,
Salonica 363,
Greece.

Antonios A. Loizos,
51 Posseidonos Ave.,
Pal. Phaliron,
Athens, Greece.

Noble Don Achille di Lorenzo,
113 Parco Margherita,
Villa di Lorenzo,
80121 Naples, Italy.

Edwin T. Lovelace, III,
P.O. Drawer E, Orange,
TX 77630, U.S.A.

James C. Lovelace, D.F.C., C.D.,
804 Cabot House,
500 King's Road, Sydney,
N.S., B1S 1B2, Canada.

Professor Arne J. Lundervold,
EEG-laboratoriet,
Rikshospitalet, Pilestredet 32,
Oslo 1, Norway.

Mrs. Ruby E.C.S. Lyells,
1116 Montgomery Street,
Jackson, MS 39203, U.S.A.

DeSoto B. McCabe,
12390 S.W. 8 St.,
Miami, 33144, U.S.A.

Angus M. MacFarlane,
McMaster Univ., Hamilton,
Ont., Canada.

Col. James G.W. MacLamroc,
Box 1588, Greensboro,
NC 27402, U.S.A.

Mrs. Miriam T. McVeigh,
8200—14th Street North, St. Petersburg,
FL 33702, U.S.A.

Prof. Stanley Bruce McWhorter,
Jamestown, KY 42629, U.S.A.

Doris G. Maddox,
1002 Munson Dr., College Station,
TX 77840, U.S.A.

Dr. Winston J. Mahabir,
5950 N.W. Marine Drive,
Vancouver 8, British Columbia,
Canada.

Professor Kathleen Mahaffey,
Box 5476, University of Puerto Rico,
Mayagüez, Puerto Rico 00708.

Dr. Boshra Halim Makar,
St. Peter's College, Math. Dept.,
Jersey City, NJ 07306, U.S.A.

Professor Charles Habib Malik,
American University of Beirut,
Beirut, Lebanon.

Professor Sylvia E. Mallery,
12 Washington Avenue,
Cobleskill, NY 12043, U.S.A.

Major General Clarence Churchill Mann,
Deer's Bush, R R 2 Newmarket,
Ontario, Canada.

Moissaye Marans,
200 Clinton Street, Brooklyn,
NY 11201, U.S.A.

Senora Josefa E. Marcos,
Malacanang Palace,
Manila, Philippines.

Dr. A.E. Maresch,
Dagsboro, DE 19939, U.S.A.

Anthony Markarian, M.D.,
1266 Aurora Dr., El Centro,
CA 92243, U.S.A.

Ronald V. Markham,
1850 One Bentall Ctr.,
Vancouver, B.C., Canada.

Dr. Helen Vasiliou Martin-Trigona,
Crystal House, No. 835,
1900 South Eads St.,
Arlington, VA 22202, U.S.A.

Harris Masterson,
1406 Kirby Drive, Houston,
TX 77019, U.S.A.

Carlo Maxia,
via Calabria 15, Cagliari,
Sardinia.

William L. May,
10022 East Coronado Drive, Baton Rouge,
LA 70815, U.S.A.

Raymond Henry Meckley,
4233 Webster Drive, York,
PA 17402, U.S.A.

Dr. Salvador J. Mejia,
130 San Leandro Way, San Francisco,
CA, U.S.A.

Adrian J. Merrett,
Minera Place, Hereford Terrace,
Leominster, Herefordshire, England.

Mrs. Andel W. Mickins,
5814 North West 18th Ave., Miami,
FL 33142, U.S.A.

Mary Frances Miller,
8354 Ruthby, Houston,
TX 77017, U.S.A.

Orval Henson Minney,
2008 Mulberry St., Harrisburg,
PA 17104, U.S.A.

Mrs. Wm. H. Mitchell,
1639 Pembroke Ave., Winston-Salem,
NC, U.S.A.

Abraham Mizrahi, M.D.,
7 Jason Lane, Mamaroneck,
NY 10543, U.S.A.

Leo Mol,
104 Claremont Avenue, Winnipeg,
Manitoba, R2H 1V9, Canada.

Mrs. Barbara H.H. Mook,
5222 Twenty-sixth Rd., N.,
Arlington, VA 22207, U.S.A.

R. Albert Moore, Jr.,
4011 Shelbyville Road,
Louisville, KY 40207, U.S.A.

Edward Cecil Music,
341 South Lake Drive,
Prestonburg, KY 41653, U.S.A.

Paul M. Muller,
4484 Dean Dr., Ventura,
CA 93003, U.S.A.

America E. Nelson,
505 N. Lake Shore Dr., Chicago,
IL 60611, U.S.A.

Miss Elizabeth Nelson,
Shape Elementary School,
A.P.O. 09055, Shape, Belgium.

H. Tracy Nelson,
3161 First National Bank Bldg.,
Dallas, TX 75202, U.S.A.

Dr. Hava Neumann,
Dept. of Biophysics,
Weizmann Inst. of Science,
Rehovot, Israel.

The Reverend Canon William H.P. Nevils,
1402 32nd Avenue South, Seattle,
Wash. DC 98144, U.S.A.

Beverly Nichols,
Ham Common, Surrey, England.

Robert Henry Noce, M.D.,
P.O. Drawer RR, Carmel,
CA 93921, U.S.A.

James Norbury, F.R.S.A.,
155 Southwood Lane, Highgate,
London, N.6, England.

Frances A. Norman,
2501 Olympus Dr., Salt Lake City,
UT 84117, U.S.A.

George Irving Norman, Jr.,
2501 Olympus Drive, Salt Lake City,
UT, U.S.A.

Roger Norman,
West Wickham, Bucks., England.

Chief Dr. C.M. Norman-Williams,
Motunde House,
6 Hagley Street,
Yaba, P.O. Box 34,
Lagos, Nigeria.

Gene Madelene S. Obert,
303 Tempa Dr., Victoria,
TX 77901, U.S.A.

James F. O'Dwyer, M.A., M. Div.,
2445 Country Club Blvd.,
Stockton, CA 95204, U.S.A.

Bernard A. O'Neill,
18570 Aspesi Dr., Saratoga,
CA 95070, U.S.A.

Judge Charles D. Onyeama,
International Court of Justice,
The Hague, The Netherlands.

Professor D.F. Orchard,
University of N.S.W.,
P.O. Box 1, Kensington,
New South Wales, Australia.

Dr. Alice M. Padawer-Singer,
130 E. 67th St., Apt. 6B,
New York, NY 10021, U.S.A.

Dr. Abraham D. Paler,
P.O. Box 2875,
University of Guam, Agana, Guam 96910.

Agnes Mae High Palmer,
5 Forest Rd., Davenport,
IA 52803, U.S.A.

Felix Papenheim,
Marktstr. 17,
7107 Neckarsulm (Wurtt.),
German Fed. Repub.

Prof. Antanas Paplauskas Ramunas,
Fac. of Educ., University of Ottawa,
Ottawa, Ont., Canada.

Peter J. Pappas,
30 Butternut Drive,
Norwich, CT 06360, U.S.A.

Dr. John T. Parente,
360 East 72 St., New York,
NY 10021, U.S.A.

Edith L. Parker,
4817 E. Speedway, Tucson,
AZ 85712, U.S.A.

John W. Payne,
2971 California St., San Francisco,
94115, U.S.A.

Dorothy DeL. Pearce,
6145 St. Charles Ave.,
New Orleans, 70118, U.S.A.

R.W. Pearse,
38 Richmond Drive,
Brampton, Ontario, Canada.

Dr. John C. Pearson,
Director, Wisconsin State University,
Stevens Point, WI 54481, U.S.A.

Norman Pearson,
P.O. Box 4362, Station C,
London, Ont., Canada.

Don Pendleton,
Route 3, Box 657,
Nashville, IN 47448, U.S.A.

Rev. Charles E. Pepper,
2513 Roger Ave., N.E., Odessa,
TX 79760, U.S.A.

Bruno R. Peraglie, M.D.,
495 Owens Road, Brownsville,
TX 78520, U.S.A.

Dr. Lindsey S. Perkins,
715 W. Harvard St., Orlando,
FL 32804, U.S.A.

Raam S. Pershadsingh,
63 Duke Street, Kingston,
Jamaica, West Indies.

John Peters, M.D.,
Box 10, Norwood,
CO 81423, U.S.A.

Joseph Petro,
460 West 2nd St., Lexington,
KY 40508, U.S.A.

Robert J. Philips,
President, Howe-Baker Engineers, Inc.,
P.O. Box 956, Tyler, TX 95701,
U.S.A.

Frederick P. Pittera,
300 E 40th St.,
N.Y., NY 10016, U.S.A.

Dr. Edwin Hemingway Pleasants,
Box 781, Lexington, VA, U.S.A.

Mrs. Mittie P.J. Polek,
6206 E. 149th Street,
Grandview,
MO 64030, U.S.A.

Louis F. Polk,
P.O. Box 967, Dayton,
OH 45401, U.S.A.

Joshua Roy Porter,
Queen's Bldg., Univ. of Exeter,
Exeter, Devon, U.K.

Bhairo Prasad, Q.C.,
3 King Street, New Amsterdam,
Berbice, Guyana, South America.

V.E. Prescott-Pickup,
Prescott-Pickup & Co. Ltd.,
Unit Seven,
Stanmore Industrial Estate,
Bridgnorth, Salop. WV15 5JD, U.K.

Frances J. Preston,
510 Elder Lane,
Winnetka, IL 60093, U.S.A.

Kendall Preston, Jr.,
Parsons Road, Dublin,
NH 03444, U.S.A.

Dr. Augusto Proano,
5422 MacArthur Blvd., Vancouver,
Washington DC 98661, U.S.A.

Dr. Nicholas Henry Pronko,
525 Longford Lane, Wichita,
KS 67206, U.S.A.

E. Allen Propst,
253 S.E. Scravel Hill Rd.,
Battle Ground Meadows, Albany,
OR, U.S.A.

Clifton Ernest Pugh,
"Dunmoochin", Cottlesbridge,
Victoria, Australia 3099.

L.E. Ravenscroft,
20 Barina Crescent, Croydon,
Victoria, Australia 3136.

Dr. John A. Ray,
5039 Central Ave.,
St. Petersburg, FL 33710, U.S.A.

Alma Burns Reitzel,
Rural Route 3, Box 750,
Newton, NC 28658, U.S.A.

Dr. Sam Rhem,
P.O. Box 1335, Pasadena,
TX 77501, U.S.A.

Dorothy Williams Rice,
Old Frontenac,
MN 55026, U.S.A.

Miss Virginia Richmond,
2054 Kenilworth, Los Angeles,
CA 90039, U.S.A.

Dr. W.E. Riley,
2040 Chase Street, Gary,
IN 46404, U.S.A.

Floyd & Marion Rinhart,
Box 340—Rte. 3,
Melbourne Beach,
FL 32951, U.S.A.

Florence & Mabel Rippel,
140 N. Sunset Pl., Monrovia,
CA 91016, U.S.A.

Bruce McNeil Robertson,
Route2—Box 208,
Gooding, ID 83330, U.S.A.

Raymond A. Robillard,
"Hillcreek",
1305 Milldam Road, Towson,
MD 21204, U.S.A.

Mrs. Ida Rice Rogers,
2409 W. 16th St. North, Little Rock,
AR 72114, U.S.A.

Dr. Alfred Victor Roman,
8 Camelot Court, Englishtown,
NJ 07726, U.S.A.

Menachem Z. Rosensaft,
30 East 71st St., New York,
NY 10021, U.S.A.

John Rossel,
5054 West Catalpa Ave., Chicago,
IL 60630, U.S.A.

Dr. Nathaniel H. Rowe,
University of Michigan Schl. of Dentistry,
Dept. of Pathology, 1011 North University,
Ann Arbor, MI 48104, U.S.A.

Grant R. Rubly,
P.O. Box 154, Malvern,
AR 72104, U.S.A.

Mrs. Shirley Rudd-Ottley,
President,
Leadership Development Institute,
76 Pembroke Street, Port-of-Spain,
Trinidad, West Indies.

Dr. Antoinette Schamoi,
4100 Cromwell Ave., L.A.,
CA 90027, U.S.A.

Dr. Sascha L. Stanislav Schnittmann,
915 Commercial St., Suite No. 3,
San Jose, CA 95112, U.S.A.

Helen E. Scott,
University Terrace Motel Apts.,
5242 Fowler Ave., Temple Terrace,
Tampa, FL 33610, U.S.A.

Michael Scriven,
1384 Queens Road, Berkeley,
CA 94708, U.S.A.

Robert M. Scriver,
P.O. Box 172, Browning,
MT 59417, U.S.A.

Edward P.G. Seaga,
Consulting Services Limited,
P.O. Box 573, Kingston 10,
Jamaica, West Indies.

L.E.G. Seagroatt,
Messrs. Seagroatt & Campbell,
P.O. Box 790, Kuala Lumpur, Malaysia.

Clara K. Searles,
5228 Cornell Ave., Downers Grove,
IL 60515, U.S.A.

LCDR. Arthur D. Seeland, C.H.C., U.S.N.,
187B Centre St., Barnegat, NJ 08005, U.S.A.

Dr. Florence R. Serlin,
171 W 71 South, N.Y., NY 10023, U.S.A

Evelyn Hicks Shannon,
3741 E. Fairway Dr., Mt. Brook Gardens,
Birmingham, AL, U.S.A.

Ruth Collier Sharpe,
El Morya, 956 West Point Rd.,
Lake Oswego, OR 97034, U.S.A.

Mrs. Virginia L. Sherman,
19212 Lanark St., Reseda, CA 91335, U.S.A.

Mrs. Samuel 'Lorena' Simon,
411 Fifth Ave., Port Arthur, TX 77640, U.S.A.

Kjell Müller Skyllstad,
Insitute of Musicology,
Slemdalsveien 7, Oslo 3, Norway.

Mrs. Paul Smart,
138 Good Wives River Rd., Darien,
CT 06820, U.S.A.

Dr. Helen C. Smith,
409 Lincoln St., Evansville, WI 53536, U.S.A.

Ray W. Smith,
P.O. Box 43, Dublin,
N.Y. 03444, U.S.A.

Joan Wellhouse Stein,
No. 1 Regency Square, 1901 Arlington Expressway,
Jacksonville, FL 32211, U.S.A.

C. Albert Stevenson,
730 Santiago Ave., Long Beach, CA 90804, U.S.A.

DeParx Stimson,
121 Idlewilde Drive, Winston-Salem,
NC 27106. U.S.A.

Rose Sowa,
Educ. Br. P.O. Box 546, Hq. USARBCO,
APO San Francisco, CA 96331, U.S.A.

Carole Jean Stoessel,
329 South Fulton Street,
Salisbury, NC 28144, U.S.A.

Mrs. Dorothy F.M. Stoplin,
140 East Carpenter Rd., Flint, MI 48505, U.S.A.

William Allin Storrer,
School of Communications,
Ithaca College, Ithaca,
NY 14850, U.S.A.

William C. Strasser,
President, Montgomery College,
Rockville, MD 20850, U.S.A.

Andreas N. Stratos,
10 Skoufa Street,
Athens, Greece.

Richard L. Strauss,
Liguanea Club Cottage,
Kingston 5,
Jamaica, West Indies.

Eugene G. Sukup,
Sukup Mfg. Co., Sheffield,
IA 50475, U.S.A.

Faruk A. Sunter,
Güven Sokak no. 26,
Kavaklidere, Ankara, Turkey.

Malcolm Graham Sutherland, Jr.,
92 Buskirk Addition, Logan,
WV 25601, U.S.A.

Jean-Jacques A. Symoens,
Rue Saint-Quentin 69,
B-1040 Brussels, Belgium.

Henry O. Tavitian, M.D.,
53-54 97th St., Rego Park, Queens,
NY 11368, U.S.A.

John King Taylor, M.R.S.H.,
110 Peacock Drive, San Rafael, CA 94901, U.S.A.

Dr. C.K. Teutsch,
1900 Avenue of the Stars, Suite 1785,
Century City, Los Angeles, CA 90067, U.S.A.

Charles H. Thom, M.D.,
100 Central Avenue, Staten Island,
NY 10301, U.S.A.

Evan W. Thomas, M.D.,
The Institutes for the Achievement of
Human Potential, 8801 Stenton Ave.,
Philadelphia, PA 19118, U.S.A.

Frances C. Tobin,
605 N. Rodeo Dr., Beverly Hills,
CA 90210, U.S.A.

John Triantaphyllopoulos,
22 Anagnostopoulos Street,
Athens 136, Greece.

Professor L.S. Trotter,
27 Birdseye Glen, Verona, NJ, U.S.A.

Robert Ingersoll Tupper,
P.O. Box 52, Main Street,
Hebron, CT 06248, U.S.A.

Justin Leroy Turner,
37 Whiting Farm Rd.,
Branford, CT 06514, U.S.A.

Roland W. Turner,
London, England.

H.E. Senor Don Marcel Ulvert,
Ambassador, Embassy of the Republic of
Nicaragua, London, S.W.1. England.

Michael J. Vaughn,
21 Carriage Sq. Waco,
TX 76708, U.S.A.

Antonio De Jesus Villegas,
Mayor of Manila, City Hall,
Manila, Philippines.

Robert C. Vincent,
Vincent Ranch, Boise City, OK 73933,
U.S.A.

Mrs. N.D. Wainwright, Jr.,
1519 Dewey Street, Hollywood,
FL 33020, U.S.A.

Arnoldo Wald,
Avenida Rio Branco, 123-18 Andar,
Rio de Janeiro, Brazil.

Hugh Gregory Wales,
1130 S. Michigan Ave., No. 1103,
Chicago, IL 60605, U.S.A.

John Alexander Walker,
104 Coffey Street,
North Wilkesboro,
NC 28659, U.S.A.

Cr. J.G. Walker, M.B.E.,
'Lambeth', Camden Park,
Longreach, Qld., Australia 4730.

William B. Warke,
Ste. 320, 355 Burrard Street,
Vancouver, B.C. V6C 2G8, Canada.

Dr. Max. E. Webber,
2261 W. 229th St., Torrance, CA 90501, U.S.A.

Eleanor Perlstein Weinbaum,
Beaumont, TX, U.S.A.

Dr. Hiram C. Weld,
364 North Ardmore Road,
Columbus, OH 43209, U.S.A.

Mark A. Wells,
P.O. Box 385, Raymondville, TX 78580, U.S.A.

Paul Terence Wertlake,
332 Lupine Way, Short Hills,
NJ 07078, U.S.A.

Harold H. White,
2831 E. 14th St., Joplin,
MO 64801, U.S.A.

John Jamieson White, Jr.,
4222 Leland St., Chevy Chase, MD 20015, U.S.A.

Walter E. White,
The Juliana, Apt. 704,
100 Bronson Ave., Ottawa 4, Canada.

Paxton Whitehead,
Shaw Festival, Box 774,
Niagara on the Lake,
Ontario, Canada.

Edward A. Whitescarver,
Route 2, Box 73, Grafton,
WV 26354, U.S.A.

Dr. Clifford Wilk,
30 N. Michigan Ave., Chicago, IL
60602, U.S.A.

Dr. Wm. G. Wilkerson,
428 Bergen Ave., Jersey City, NJ 07304, U.S.A.

Giula Williams,
1914-4th Avenue North, Birmingham,
AL 35203, U.S.A.

Marie S. Wilner,
1248 White Plains Rd., Bronx, NY 10473, U.S.A.

Homer M. Wilson,
H.M. Wilson Company,
11501 Chimney Rock, Houston,
TX 77035, U.S.A.

Miss Anne M. Wolanin,
2430 Smith-Stewart Rd. E.,
Girard, OH 44420, U.S.A.

Dr. Sophie Mae Wolanin,
Westinghouse Credit Corporation,
3 Gateway Centre (21 West),
Pittsburgh, PA 15222, U.S.A.

Chester L. Wolfe,
1316 Woodhill Rd.,
Columbia, MO 65201, U.S.A.

George B. Wood, O.B.E.,
Savage Club, London, W.C.2, England.
Zenon R. Wynnytsky, M.D.,
2600 Somia Drive, Cleveland, OH 44134, U.S.A.

Victor John Yannacone, Jr.,
39 Baker St., P.O. Drawer 109,
Patchogue, NY 11772, U.S.A.

L. Yarnold,
London, England.

York Public Library,
York, England.

Dr. Paul A. Young,
33 Hickory Dr., Oak Brook,
IL 60521, U.S.A.

Dr. The Hon. Amado M. Yuzon,
President, United Poets Laureate International,
124 Mayon, Quezon City, Philippines.

John Zenic,
P.O. Box 27, Incline Village, NV 89450, U.S.A.

Dr. Melvin E. Zichek,
1111-16th St., Central City NB 68826, U.S.A.

Mrs. Emilija E. Ziplans,
18 Waring Court, Willowdale, Ont., Canada.

Frank E. Zuccarelli,
61 Appleman Road, Somerset,
NJ 08873, U.S.A.

Dr. Nazih Zuhdi,
1211 N. Shartel, Okla. City,
OK 73103, U.S.A.